EUROPEAN RAIL TIMETABLE

SPRING 2023

GENERAL INFORMATION

EXTRA FEATURES

TIMETABLES

…Summer International Supplement
Selected advance timings from June 12.
See pages 670–674

CONTACT DETAILS

Director and Editor-in-chief John Potter

Editor Chris Woodcock

Editorial Team Graham Benbow, Andrea Collins, Richard Stirk, Reuben Turner, Peter Weller

Commercial Manager Gemma Donaldson

Subscriptions Manager Peter Weller

Cover created by Andrea Collins website: www.millstonecreative.co.uk
Printed and bound by CPI Group (UK) Ltd, Croydon, CR0 4YY
Front cover: 150 years of the European Rail Timetable.

ISBN 978-1-8384080-6-0

European Rail Timetable Limited (formerly *Thomas Cook European Rail Timetable*)
28 Monson Way
Oundle
Northamptonshire PE8 4QG, United Kingdom
website: www.europeanrailtimetable.eu
e-mail: editorial@europeanrailtimetable.eu
sales: sales@europeanrailtimetable.eu
telephone: +44 (0)1832 270198 Mondays to Fridays 1000 - 1600

Company Number 8590554

Every care has been taken to render the timetable correct in accordance with the latest advices, but changes are constantly being made by the administrations concerned and the publishers cannot hold themselves responsible for the consequences of either changes or inaccuracies.

CALENDAR

2023 CALENDRIER CALENDARIO KALENDER CALENDARIO **2023**

JANUARY

M	T	W	T	F	S	S
①	②	③	④	⑤	⑥	⑦
30	31	–	–	–	–	1
2	3	4	5	6	7	8
9	10	11	12	13	14	15
16	17	18	19	20	21	22
23	24	25	26	27	28	29

FEBRUARY

M	T	W	T	F	S	S
①	②	③	④	⑤	⑥	⑦
–	–	1	2	3	4	5
6	7	8	9	10	11	12
13	14	15	16	17	18	19
20	21	22	23	24	25	26
27	28	–	–	–	–	–

MARCH

M	T	W	T	F	S	S
①	②	③	④	⑤	⑥	⑦
–	–	1	2	3	4	5
6	7	8	9	10	11	12
13	14	15	16	17	18	19
20	21	22	23	24	25	26
27	28	29	30	31	–	–

APRIL

M	T	W	T	F	S	S
①	②	③	④	⑤	⑥	⑦
–	–	–	–	–	1	2
3	4	5	6	7	8	9
10	11	12	13	14	15	16
17	18	19	20	21	22	23
24	25	26	27	28	29	30

MAY

M	T	W	T	F	S	S
①	②	③	④	⑤	⑥	⑦
1	2	3	4	5	6	7
8	9	10	11	12	13	14
15	16	17	18	19	20	21
22	23	24	25	26	27	28
29	30	31	–	–	–	–

JUNE

M	T	W	T	F	S	S
①	②	③	④	⑤	⑥	[illegible]
–	–	–	1	2	3	[illegible]
5	6	7	8	9	10	[illegible]
12	13	14	15	16	17	[illegible]
19	20	21	22	23	24	[illegible]
26	27	28	29	30	[illegible]	[illegible]

JULY

M	T	W	T	F	S	S
①	②	③	④	⑤	⑥	⑦
31	–	–	–	–	1	2
3	4	5	6	7	8	9
10	11	12	13	14	15	16
17	18	19	20	21	22	23
24	25	26	27	28	29	30

AUGUST

M	T	W	T	F	S	S
①	②	③	④	⑤	⑥	⑦
–	1	2	3	4	5	6
7	8	9	10	11	12	13
14	15	16	17	18	19	20
21	22	23	24	25	26	27
28	29	30	31	–	–	–

SEPTEMBER

M	T	W	T	F	S	S
①	②	③	④	⑤	⑥	⑦
–	–	–	–	1	2	3
4	5	6	7	8	9	10
11	12	13	14	15	16	17
18	19	20	21	22	23	24
25	26	27	28	29	30	–

OCTOBER

M	T	W	T	F	S	S
①	②	③	④	⑤	⑥	⑦
30	31	–	–	–	–	1
2	3	4	5	6	7	8
9	10	11	12	13	14	15
16	17	18	19	20	21	22
23	24	25	26	27	28	29

NOVEMBER

M	T	W	T	F	S	S
①	②	③	④	⑤	⑥	⑦
–	–	1	2	3	4	5
6	7	8	9	10	11	12
13	14	15	16	17	18	19
20	21	22	23	24	25	26
27	28	29	30	–	–	–

DECEMBER

M	T	W	T	F	S	S
①	②	③	④	⑤	⑥	⑦
–	–	–	–	1	2	3
4	5	6	7	8	9	10
11	12	13	14	15	16	17
18	19	20	21	22	23	24
25	26	27	28	29	30	31

2024 **2024**

JANUARY

M	T	W	T	F	S	S
①	②	③	④	⑤	⑥	⑦
1	2	3	4	5	6	7
8	9	10	11	12	13	14
15	16	17	18	19	20	21
22	23	24	25	26	27	28
29	30	31	–	–	–	–

FEBRUARY

M	T	W	T	F	S	S
①	②	③	④	⑤	⑥	⑦
–	–	–	1	2	3	4
5	6	7	8	9	10	11
12	13	14	15	16	17	18
19	20	21	22	23	24	25
26	27	28	29	–	–	–

MARCH

M	T	W	T	F	S	S
①	②	③	④	⑤	⑥	⑦
–	–	–	–	1	2	3
4	5	6	7	8	9	10
11	12	13	14	15	16	17
18	19	20	21	22	23	24
25	26	27	28	29	30	31

APRIL

M	T	W	T	F	S	S
①	②	③	④	⑤	⑥	⑦
1	2	3	4	5	6	7
8	9	10	11	12	13	14
15	16	17	18	19	20	21
22	23	24	25	26	27	28
29	30	–	–	–	–	–

MAY

M	T	W	T	F	S	S
①	②	③	④	⑤	⑥	⑦
–	–	1	2	3	4	5
6	7	8	9	10	11	12
13	14	15	16	17	18	19
20	21	22	23	24	25	26
27	28	29	30	31	–	–

JUNE

M	T	W	T	F	S	S
①	②	③	④	⑤	⑥	⑦
–	–	–	–	–	1	2
3	4	5	6	7	8	9
10	11	12	13	14	15	16
17	18	19	20	21	22	23
24	25	26	27	28	29	30

PUBLIC HOLIDAYS 2023

JOURS FÉRIÉS GIORNI FESTIVI FEIERTAGE DÍAS FESTIVOS

The dates given below are those of national public holidays. They do not include regional, half-day or unofficial holidays. Passengers intending to travel on public holidays, or on days immediately preceding or following them, are strongly recommended to reserve seats and to confirm timings locally. Further information regarding special transport conditions applying on holiday dates may be found in the introduction to each country.

Austria: Jan. 1, 6, Apr. 10, May 1, 18, 29, June 8, Aug. 15, Oct. 26, Nov. 1, Dec. 8, 25, 26.

Belgium: Jan. 1, Apr. 9, 10, May 1, 18, 28, 29, July 21, Aug. 15, Nov. 1, 11, Dec. 25.

Bosnia-Herzegovina: Jan. 1, 2, Mar. 1, May 1, 2. *Other religious holidays are observed in certain areas.*

Bulgaria: Jan. 1, 2, Mar. 3, Apr. 14 – 17, May 1, 6, 8, 24, Sept. 6, 22, Dec. 24 – 27.

Croatia: Jan. 1, 6, Apr. 9, 10, May 1, 30, June 8, 22, Aug. 5, 15, Nov. 1, 18, Dec. 25, 26.

Czech Republic: Jan. 1, Apr. 7, 10, May 1, 8, July 5, 6, Sept. 28, Oct. 28, Nov. 17, Dec. 24, 25, 26.

Denmark: Jan. 1, Apr. 6, 7, 9, 10, May 1, 5, 18, 28, 29, June 5, Dec. 25, 26.

Estonia: Jan. 1, Feb. 24, Apr. 7, 9, May 1, 28, June 23, 24, Aug. 20, Dec. 24, 25, 26.

Finland: Jan. 1, 6, Apr. 7, 10, May 1, 18, June 23, 24, Nov. 4, Dec. 6, 24, 25, 26.

France: Jan. 1, Apr. 10, May 1, 8, 18, 29, July 14, Aug. 15, Nov. 1, 11, Dec. 25.

Germany: Jan. 1, 6*, Apr. 7, 10, May 1, 18, 29, June 8*, Aug. 15*, Sept. 20*, Oct. 3, 31*, Nov. 1*, 22*, Dec. 25, 26.
* *Observed in certain regions: see also page 366.*

Great Britain: *England & Wales*: Jan. 2, Apr. 7, 10, May 1, 8, 29, Aug. 28, Dec. 25, 26.
Scotland: Jan. 2, 3, Apr. 7, May 1, 8, 29, Aug. 7, Nov. 30, Dec. 25, 26.

Greece: Jan. 1, 6, Feb. 27, Mar. 25, Apr. 14, 17, May 1, June 5, Aug. 15, Oct. 28, Dec. 25, 26.

Hungary: Jan. 1, Mar. 15, Apr. 7, 10, May 1, 29, Aug. 20, Oct. 23, Nov. 1, Dec. 25, 26.

Iceland: Jan. 1, Apr. 6, 7, 9, 10, 20, May 1, 18, 28, 29, June 17, Aug. 7, Dec. 25, 26.

Ireland (Northern): Jan. 2, Mar. 17, Apr. 7, 10, May 1, 8, 29, July 12, Aug. 28, Dec. 25, 26.

Ireland (Republic): Feb. 6, Mar. 17, Apr. 10, May 1, June 5, Aug. 7, Oct. 30, Dec. 25, 26.

Italy: Jan. 1, 6, Apr. 9, 10, 25, May 1, June 2, Aug. 15, Nov. 1, Dec. 8, 25, 26.

Kosovo: Jan. 2, 9, Feb. 17, Apr. 9, 10, 16, 17, 22, May 1, 9, June 29, Dec. 25.

Latvia: Jan. 1, Apr. 7, 9, 10, May 1, 4, 14, 28, June 23, 24, July 8, 10, Nov. 18, 20, Dec. 24, 25, 26, 31.

Lithuania: Jan. 1, Feb. 16, Mar. 11, Apr. 9, 10, May 1, June 24, July 6, Aug. 15, Nov. 1, 2, Dec. 24, 25, 26.

Luxembourg: Jan. 1, Apr. 10, May 1, 9, 18, 29, June 23, Aug. 15, Nov. 1, Dec. 25, 26.

North Macedonia: Jan. 2, 7, Apr. 17, 22, May 1, 24, Aug. 2, Sept. 8, Oct. 11, 23, Dec. 8. *Other religious holidays are observed in certain areas.*

Moldova: Jan. 1, 7, 8, Mar. 8, Apr. 16, 17, 24, May 1, 9, June 1, Aug. 27, 31, Dec. 25.

Netherlands: Jan. 1, Apr. 7, 9, 10, 27, May 5, 18, 28, 29, Dec. 25, 26.

Norway: Jan. 1, Apr. 6, 7, 9, 10, May 1, 17, 18, 28, 29, Dec. 25, 26.

Poland: Jan. 1, 6, Apr. 9, 10, May 1, 3, 28, June 8, Aug. 15, Nov. 1, 11, Dec. 25, 26.

Portugal: Jan. 1, Apr. 7, 9, 25, May 1, June 8, 10, Aug. 15, Oct. 5, Nov. 1, Dec. 1, 8, 25.

Romania: Jan. 1, 2, 24, Apr. 14, 16, 17, May 1, June 1, 4, 5, Aug. 15, Nov. 30, Dec. 1, 25, 26.

Serbia: Jan. 1, 2, 3, 7, Feb. 15, 16, Apr. 14 – 17, May 1, 2, Nov. 11.

Slovakia: Jan. 1, 6, Apr. 7, 10, May 1, 8, July 5, Aug. 29, Sept. 1, 15, Nov. 1, 17, Dec. 24, 25, 26.

Slovenia: Jan. 1, 2, Feb. 8, Apr. 9, 10, 27, May 1, 2, 28, June 25, Aug. 15, Oct. 31, Nov. 1, Dec. 25, 26.

Spain: Jan. 1, 6, Apr. 7, May 1, Aug. 15, Oct. 12, Nov. 1, Dec. 6, 8, 25. *Also many regional and local holidays.*

Sweden: Jan. 1, 6, Apr. 7, 9, 10, May 1, 18, 28, June 6, 24, Nov. 4, Dec. 25, 26.

Switzerland: Jan. 1, 2*, 6*, Mar. 19*, Apr. 7*, 10*, May 1*, 18, 29*, June 8*, Aug. 1, 15*, Nov. 1*, Dec. 8*, 25, 26*. *Also some local holidays.*
* *Observed in certain regions.*

Turkey: Jan. 1, Apr. 23, May 1, 19, July 15, Aug. 30, Oct. 29 (also 2023 feast holiday periods Apr. 21 – 24, June 28 - July 2).

MOVABLE HOLIDAYS

Fêtes mobiles – Feste mobile
Bewegliche Feste – Fiestas movibles

	2023	2024
Good Friday	Apr. 7 •	Mar. 29 *
Easter Monday	Apr. 10 •	Apr. 1 *
Ascension Day	May 18 •	May 9 *
Whit Monday (Pentecost)	May 29 •	May 20 *
Corpus Christi	June 8	May 30

• *One week later in the Orthodox calendar*
* *Five weeks later in the Orthodox calendar*

TIME COMPARISON

COMPARAISON DES HEURES COMPARAZIONE DELLE ORE ZEITVERGLEICH COMPARACIÓN DE LAS HORAS

West European Time	*WINTER: UTC* *SUMMER: UTC +1*	Ireland, Portugal, United Kingdom; Iceland *(UTC all year)*
Central European *Time*	*WINTER: UTC +1* *SUMMER: UTC +2*	Albania, Austria, *Belgium*, Bosnia, Croatia, *Czech Rep.*, Denmark, France, *Germany*, Hungary, Italy, *Luxembourg*, North Macedonia, Malta, *Montenegro*, Netherlands, Norway, *Poland*, Serbia, Slovakia, *Slovenia*, Spain, Sweden, *Switzerland*
East European Time	*WINTER: UTC +2* *SUMMER: UTC +3*	*Bulgaria*, Estonia, *Finland*, *Greece*, *Latvia*, *Lithuania*, *Moldova*, Romania, *Ukraine*; Belarus and Western Russia *(UTC + 3 all year)*; Kaliningrad *(UTC + 2 all year)*; Turkey *(UTC + 3 all year)*

Daylight Saving Time ('Summer Time') applies in 2023 between 0100 GMT on March 26 and 0100 GMT on October 29 (*GMT = Greenwich Mean Time = UTC*)

NEWSLINES

EUROPEAN RAIL TIMETABLE - 150 YEARS

In March 1873, the very first edition of Cook's Continental Time Tables & Tourist's Hand Book was published and so this, the Spring 2023 edition, marks the 150th anniversary of this historic publication. On pages 666 to 669 we have reproduced the special feature that appeared in the March 2013 edition (marking the 140th anniversary) which outlines the history of the timetable, including key events during the 140 years of Thomas Cook ownership. We have, of course, added an additional section covering events of the subsequent ten years under the stewardship of the current timetable team. We are very pleased that we were able to continue production of this unique publication and, despite recent challenges, we hope to continue producing the timetable for years to come.

Most of our tables have now been fully checked and updated following the winter timetable change. The first version of our **Summer International Supplement** will be found on pages 670 to 674 with advance versions of a small selection of international tables valid from June 11. This seasonal Spring edition also includes the latest versions of all Beyond Europe tables together with an updated *Rail Extra* feature which contains useful transport information on a country by country basis. Please note that 2023 schedules for many tourist railways contained in the *Rail Extra* feature were still not confirmed as we closed for press, so 2022 timings are still shown where this is the case. We hope to have all timings updated in time for the Summer edition.

So that readers who only purchase the printed version of the timetable can keep fully up to date with the latest developments, we have included on pages 36 and 37 extracts of *Newslines* that appeared in the January and February digital editions.

We are aware of a number of quality issues that affected our printed Winter 2022/2023 edition for which we must apologise. Most notably, the content on certain pages was not aligned correctly meaning it was difficult to read content that was printed too close to the binding. A small number of timetables also contained some uncut pages. These issues were immediately raised with our printers whose subsequent investigations identified a problem with the use of a newly installed printing press. We have been assured that these issues will not occur in future editions.

We would like to thank readers who responded to our request for feedback on the new thinner paper we are now using. Comments were generally positive but we acknowledge there are some disadvantages of the new paper. The feedback has proved useful during our ongoing discussions with regards to future paper supply.

INTERNATIONAL

The overnight service between Zürich and Praha via Linz will be suspended from May 2 to May 29 due to engineering work (Table **52**).

FRANCE

We have decided to publish timings in Tables **301**, **307**, **310**, **319** and **325** valid from either late March or early April to make it easier for readers to plan future journeys on these routes. Please consult previous editions for timings valid before the published timetable comes into force. Note that services between Angoulême and Saintes (Table **301**) are operated by bus from March 25 to June 25. We have pieced together information from several sources to show what we believe is the correct timetable. However, we strongly advise readers to check timings locally if intending to travel on this route.

SPAIN

The fourth *Media Distancia* service between Granada and Almeria, which was suspended during the pandemic, was reinstated from February 20, meaning the overall service is back to the pre-pandemic level (Table **673**).

The line between Medinaceli and Soria, which has been closed since November 2022 for track replacement work, has now reopened meaning direct services between Madrid and Soria have been restored. (Table **651**).

The daily *AVE* service (trains **3982**/**3981**) between València Joaquín Sorolla and Sevilla Santa Justa will call additionally at Ciudad Real from March 5 (Tables **660** and **668**).

Alvia services between Cádiz and Madrid will be recast from March 5 (Table **673**).

Information received shortly before we closed for press indicates that the bus service run by Spanish Railways between Aranjuez and Utiel via Cuenca will be withdrawn from March 4 (Table **669**). We understand an alternative bus service is being arranged between Aranjuez and Cuenca which we hope to be able to show in the April edition.

NORWAY

The latest official information regarding the new 22-kilometre double-track *Follobanen* line between Oslo and Ski is that it will remain closed until further notice. Therefore, services in Table **770** will continue to operate with amended Oslo timings until the problem with the new infrastructure has been resolved.

GERMANY

Readers should note that timings in the German section of this edition are only valid until March 31. Major alterations affecting many long distance services will occur from April 1 when the key section of high-speed line between Kassel and Fulda is temporarily closed until December 9 to enable route upgrade work to take place. The most significant changes will be found in Tables **850**, **900** and **902** and so, to help readers plan future journeys on these routes, we have included advance versions of these particular tables (which will be found on pages 566 to 570). Services on most other routes will generally continue as normal until at least May 26, although changes to local services may occur on the various diversionary routes that will be used during the closure period. Readers should note that alterations on and around public holidays during April and May are not generally shown in this edition. The whole German section will be fully updated for the period from April 1 to May 26 in the April and May digital editions.

HUNGARY

As is usual during the spring and summer, an enhanced timetable operates to the Lake Balaton area. Special versions of Tables **1220** and **1225**, valid from May 15 to June 16, are included in this edition and will be found on pages 559 and 560. Further updated versions of these tables will be published in future editions covering the high-summer period from June 17.

TURKEY

Turkish railways has reported that the *Güney Ekspresí* from Ankara to Kurtalan, the *Vangölü Ekspresí* from Ankara to Tatvan and the *4 Eylül Mavi Tren* from Ankara to Malatya are once again running throughout following the devastating earthquake which struck the region recently (Table **1575**).

LITHUANIA

Work to electrify the railway between Kaisiadorys and Radviliskis will cause significant alterations to the service shown in Table **1805** until an as yet unspecified date in May. We have included what we believe to be the correct timetable, however, it should be regarded as subject to confirmation and we strongly advise readers check timings locally using the website www.ltglink.lt.

SUMMER INTERNATIONAL SUPPLEMENT

Table 88 (Summer): Austrian Railways' *nightjet* service between Wien and Roma (trains **40233**/**40294**) will convey additional through cars between Wien and Ancona during the summer.

BEYOND EUROPE

INDIA

All tables checked and updated to reflect the October 2022 timetable change.

THAILAND

Thursday January 19 saw the opening to long-distance passenger trains of the new Bangkok Krung Thep Aphiwat Central Terminal station, formerly known as Bang Sue Grand. All long-distance trains, except those on the Eastern line and with train numbers in the 200 and 300 series, use the new station. The station is also currently served by the SRT Dark Red, Light Red and Airport Link commuter rail routes as well as a large number of bus routes. In the future it will also be served by the Don Mueang – Suvarnabhumi – U-Tapao high-speed railway and planned high-speed routes to Nong Khai, Padang Besar and Chiang Mai. All tables have been updated with the latest timings.

CONTINUED ON PAGE 571

EXPLANATION OF STANDARD SYMBOLS

	EXPLANATION OF SYMBOLS	*EXPLICATION DES SIGNES*	*DELUCIDAZIONE DEI SEGNI*	*ZEICHENERKLÄRUNG*	*EXPLICACIÓN DE LOS SIGNOS*
	SERVICES	**SERVICES**	**SERVIZI**	**DIENSTE**	**SERVICIOS**
12	Through service (1st and 2nd class seats)	Relation directe (places assises 1re et 2e classe)	Relazione diretta (con posti di 1a e 2a classe)	Direkte Verbindung (Sitzplätze 1. und 2. Klasse)	Relación directa (con asientos de 1a y 2a clase)
	Sleeping car	Voiture-lits	Carrozza letti	Schlafwagen	Coche-camas
	Couchette car	Voiture-couchettes	Carrozza cuccette	Liegewagen	Coche-literas
✕	Restaurant car	Voiture-restaurant	Carrozza ristorante	Speisewagen	Coche-restaurante
Ÿ	Snacks and drinks available *(see page 10)*	Voiture-bar ou vente ambulante *(voir page 10)*	Carrozza bar o servizio di buffet *(vedere pagina 10)*	Imbiss und Getränke im Zug *(siehe Seite 10)*	Servicio de cafetería o bar móvil *(véase pág. 10)*
2	Second class only	Uniquement deuxième classe	Sola seconda classe	Nur zweite Klasse	Sólo segunda clase
	Bus or coach service	Service routier	Servizio automobilistico	Buslinie	Servicio de autobuses
	Ferry service	Service maritime	Servizio marittimo	Schifffahrtslinie	Servicio marítimo
	DAYS OF RUNNING	**JOURS DE CIRCULATION**	**GIORNI DI EFFETTUAZIONE**	**VERKEHRSTAGE**	**DÍAS DE CIRCULACIÓN**
⚒	Mondays to Saturdays except holidays*	Du lundi au samedi, sauf les fêtes*	Dal lunedì al sabato, salvo i giorni festivi*	Montag bis Samstag außer Feiertage*	De lunes a sábado, excepto festivos*
Ⓐ	Mondays to Fridays except holidays*	Du lundi au vendredi, sauf les fêtes*	Dal lunedì al venerdì, salvo i giorni festivi*	Montag bis Freitag außer Feiertage*	De lunes a viernes, excepto festivos*
Ⓑ	Daily except Saturdays	Tous les jours sauf les samedis	Giornalmente, salvo il sabato	Täglich außer Samstag	Diario excepto sábados
Ⓒ	Saturdays, Sundays and holidays*	Les samedis, dimanches et fêtes*	Sabato, domenica e giorni festivi*	Samstage, Sonn- und Feiertage*	Sábados, domingos y festivos*
†	Sundays and holidays*	Les dimanches et fêtes*	Domenica e giorni festivi*	Sonn- und Feiertage*	Domingos y festivos*
①②	Mondays, Tuesdays	Les lundis, mardis	Lunedì, martedì	Montag, Dienstag	Lunes, martes
③④	Wednesdays, Thurdays	Les mercredis, jeudis	Mercoledì, giovedì	Mittwoch, Donnerstag	Miércoles, jueves
⑤⑥	Fridays, Saturdays	Les vendredis, samedis	Venerdì, sabato	Freitag, Samstag	Viernes, sábados
⑦	Sundays	Les dimanches	Domenica	Sonntag	Domingos
①–④	Mondays to Thursdays	Des lundis aux jeudis	Dal lunedì al giovedì	Montag bis Donnerstag	De lunes a jueves
	OTHER SYMBOLS	**AUTRES SIGNES**	**ALTRI SIMBOLI**	**SONSTIGE SYMBOLE**	**OTROS SÍMBOLOS**
IC **29**	Train number (**bold figures** above train times)	Numéro du train (en **caractères gras** au-dessus de l'horaire du train)	Numero del treno (in **neretto** sopra gli orari del treno)	Zugnummer (über den Fahrplanzeiten in **fetter Schrift** gesetzt)	Número del tren (figura en **negrita** encima del horario del tren)
♦	See footnotes (listed by train number)	Renvoi aux notes données en bas de page (dans l'ordre numérique des trains)	Vedi in calce alla pagina l'annotazione corrispondente al numero del treno	Siehe die nach Zugnummern geordneten Fußnoten	Véase al pie de la página la nota correspondiente al número del tren
R	Reservation compulsory	Réservation obligatoire	Prenotazione obbligatoria	Reservierung erforderlich	Reserva obligatoria
	Frontier station	Gare frontalière	Stazione di frontiera	Grenzbahnhof	Estación fronteriza
✈	Airport	Aéroport	Aeroporto	Flughafen	Aeropuerto
|	Train does not stop	Sans arrêt	Il treno non ferma qui	Zug hält nicht	El tren no para aquí
━	Separates two trains in the same column between which no connection is possible	Sépare deux trains de la même colonne qui ne sont pas en correspondance	Separa due treni della stessa colonna che non sono in coincidenza	Trennt zwei in derselben Spalte angegebene Züge, zwischen denen kein Anschluß besteht	Separa dos trenes de la misma columna entre los cuales no hay enlace
→	Continued in later column	Suite dans une colonne à droite	Continuazione più avanti a destra	Fortsetzung weiter rechts	Continuación a la derecha
←	Continued from earlier column	Suite d'une colonne à gauche	Seguito di una colonna a sinistra	Fortsetzung von links	Continuación desde la izquierda
v.v.	Vice versa	Vice versa	Viceversa	Umgekehrt	A la inversa
	** Public holiday dates for each country are given on page 4.* *Other, special symbols are explained in table footnotes or in the introduction to each country.*	** Les dates des fêtes légales nationales sont données en page 4.* *D'autres signes particuliers sont expliqués dans les notes ou bien dans l'avant-propos relatif à chaque pays.*	** Per le date dei giorni festivi nei diversi paesi vedere pagina 4.* *Altri segni particolari vengono spiegati nelle note in calce ai quadri o nella introduzione attinente a ogni paese.*	** Gesetzlichen Feiertage der jeweiligen Länder finden Sie auf Seite 4.* *Besondere Symbole sind in den Fußnoten bzw. in der Einleitung zu den einzelnen Ländern erklärt.*	** Las fechas de los días festivos en cada país figuran en la página 4.* *La explicación de otros signos particulares se da en las notas o en el preámbulo correspondiente a cada país.*

ABOUT THE EUROPEAN RAIL TIMETABLE

What is the European Rail Timetable?

The European Rail Timetable is a concise guide to rail and ferry schedules throughout Europe, and also includes selected areas of the world outside Europe. Needless to say, it cannot be comprehensive (it would run into thousands of pages), but through our knowledge and experience, together with valuable feedback from our readers, we can select those services which we believe will satisfy the needs of most travellers.

When do the services change?

There is a major annual timetable change in mid-December affecting almost all European countries, with many countries having a second change in mid-June. There are, of course, exceptions. For example, the British summer timetable starts in late May, Sweden changes again in mid-August, whilst there are changes in Ukraine from late March (coinciding with the clock change). Many holiday areas also have separate timetables for the high-summer period, particularly areas of France, Italy and Hungary. In fact, changes can happen at any time of year, and railways issue amendments either on set dates or as and when necessary. Engineering work also causes frequent changes, and shipping schedules can change at any time.

How are the trains selected for inclusion?

People travel for many reasons, whether for leisure, business, sightseeing, visiting friends or relations, or just for the fun of it, and there are no hard and fast rules for selecting the services that we show. Naturally, major towns and inter-city services are shown as a matter of course, but the level of smaller places and local trains shown will depend on the country and even the area. It's surprising just how many minor lines we manage to squeeze in! Generally we will show a greater number of local trains in areas which are popular tourist destinations or where other services are sparse.

It is not possible to show suburban trains within cities or conurbations, or most outer-suburban routes to places close to large cities. However, where there are places of particular interest or importance in this category we do try to show brief details of frequency and journey time.

When should I use the International section?

The rail tables are divided into two sections - International (Tables **9** to **99**) and Country by Country (Tables **100** upwards). For some international services between adjacent countries (for example Stockholm - Oslo or Hamburg - Århus) it is necessary to use the relevant Country tables - the index or maps will guide you. Local trains which cross international frontiers will usually only be found in the Country sections.

Some international trains also carry passengers internally within each country and will therefore be found in the Country tables as well as the International section. Some services are primarily for international travel and will therefore only be found in the International section - this includes *Eurostar* trains (London - Paris / Brussels / Amsterdam) and *Thalys* services (Paris - Brussels - Amsterdam / Köln), as well as certain long-distance night trains.

What about places outside Europe?

The European Rail Timetable includes the whole of Turkey and Russia. Furthermore, our **Beyond Europe** section at the back of each edition features timetables from different areas of the world each month. Eight areas are featured, each appearing at least twice a year. The areas covered are **India, South East Asia, Australia, New Zealand, China, Japan, South America, North America, South Korea, Africa and the Middle East**. Details of when each region appears will be found in the introduction of the Beyond Europe section. Please note that we include **all** of the latest Beyond Europe sections in our expanded Winter and Summer editions.

What else does it contain?

A summary of international sleeper services will be found on page 35, listing types of accommodation, operators and facilities on board.

We also include a summary of European rail passes (see the list of contents on page 3 for its current location) with a more detailed version appearing in our expanded seasonal Summer and Winter editions. The seasonal editions also include a *Rail Extra* feature containing useful transport based information on a country by country basis (including details of many popular tourist railways).

Our timetables and other products may be purchased from our website **www.europeanrailtimetable.eu**.

HOW TO USE THE TIMETABLE

Using the index

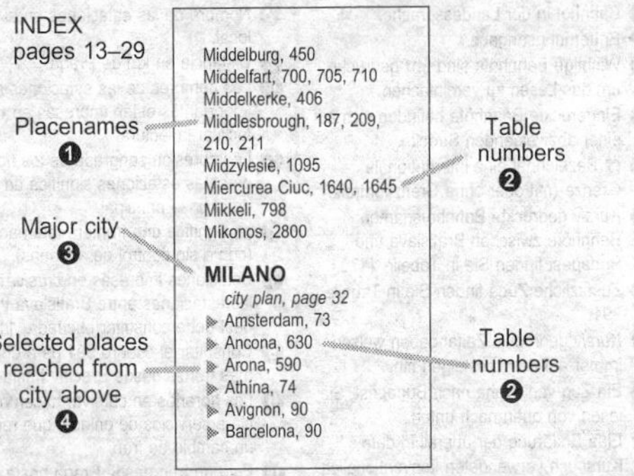

Look up the two places between which you are travelling. It can often be helpful to start your search from the *smaller* of the two locations. ❺

Using the maps

The maps can be the quickest way of finding the required table number, if you already know the geographical location of the places required. ❿

COMMENT TROUVER VOTRE TRAIN

❶ Localité.
❷ Numéros des tableaux.
❸ Grande ville.
❹ Localités sélectionnées à gagner de la grande ville en haut.
❺ Cherchez les deux bouts du parcours désiré sur la liste des villes. Commencer par la ville de moindre importance peut faciliter la recherche.
❻ Ligne principale.
❼ Ligne secondaire.
❽ Ligne à grande vitesse.
❾ Liaison en autocar.
❿ La consultation des cartes – si vous savez déjà la location géographique de vos points de départ et d'arrivée – est le moyen le plus rapide de repérer les numéros des tableaux relatifs à votre parcours.

COME TROVARE IL VOSTRO TRENO

❶ Località.
❷ Numeri dei quadri-orario.
❸ Grandi città.
❹ Principali destinazione raggiungibili dalla località in neretto sopra.
❺ Cercate le localita' tra le quali dovrete viaggiare; spesso può essere di aiuto iniziare la ricerca dalla località più piccola.
❻ Principale linea ferroviaria.
❼ Linea ferroviaria secondaria.
❽ Linea ad alta velocità.
❾ Autobus.
❿ Le mappe sono il metodo più rapido per trovare i numeri dei quadri-orario di cui avete bisogno, quando gia' siete a conoscenza della collocazione geografica delle localita' di partenza e arrivo del vostro viaggio.

WIE FINDE ICH MEINEN ZUG?

❶ Ortsname.
❷ Tabellennummer.
❸ Großstadt.
❹ Knotenpunkte erreichbar von der Großstadt oben.
❺ Suchen Sie Ihre Start- und Endbahnhof im Ortsverzeichnis. Dazu empfehlen wir, Ihre Suche aus der Richtung des *kleineren* Ortes aufzunehmen.
❻ Hauptstrecke.
❼ Nebenstrecke.
❽ Hochgeschwindigkeitsstrecke.
❾ Busverbindung.
❿ Kennen Sie die geographische Lage der Ausgangs- und Bestimmungsorte Ihrer Reise, dann empfehlen wir einen Blick in die im Kursbuch enthaltene Übersichtskarte.

COMO BUSCAR SU TREN

❶ Localidad.
❷ Números de los cuadros horarios.
❸ Gran ciudad.
❹ Principales destinos accesibles a través de esta localidad.
❺ Busque los dos lugares a través de los cuales viaja. Normalmente facilita la búsqueda empezar por la localidad más pequeña.
❻ Línea principal.
❼ Línea secundaria.
❽ Línea de alta velocidad.
❾ Línea de autobuses.
❿ Los mapas pueden ser la forma más rápida de encontrar los cuadros que debe consultar, si ya conoce el punto de inicio y conclusión de su viaje.

Reading the tables

Numbers in circles refer to translations below

Trains run daily unless otherwise shown by symbol or footnote (15)

Table number and route (1)

d. = depart, a. = arrive (the first time in a column is always a departure time, the last is an arrival). (14)

Train category (where shown) (13)

Station names in local language (2)

Train number (where shown) (12)

Distance from Praha in km (3)

Standard symbols (e.g. Ⓐ, Ⓡ, ✕) are explained on page 6.

Important stations are shown in **bold** for clarity (4)

Other symbols (e.g. ⊖) and letters (**E**, **r**) are explained below the table.

Indented station: shows a branch off the main route of the table (5)

♦ means footnotes are listed by train number. (11)

1150 PRAHA - BRNO - WIEN / BRATISLAVA

km	*Sample table*		271	EC 71	EC● 131	EC 345	SC* 15	EC 273	EC 73	475	EC 275	EC 103
				✕			🍷	✕	✕			✕
			Ⓐ		♦	♦	Ⓡ		⊖	♦	E	♦
	Praha Holešovice	d.	...	...	...	...	...	0730	0830	...	0930	...
0	**Praha** hlavni ▷	d.	...	...	...	0528	0557	|	|	0918	|	...
62	Kolín ▷	d.	...	...	...	0613	|	0813	|	1013	1013	...
154	**Pardubice** ▷	d.	...	...	...	0636	0659	0836	0936	1036	1036	...
164	Česká Třebová ▷	d.	...	*0551*	...	0711	|	0911	|	1111	1111	...
255	**Brno** hlavní	a.	...	*0711*	...	0814	0825	1014	1114	1214	1214	...
255	**Brno** hlavní **1162**	d.	...	0716	...	0816	0827	1016	1116	1216	1216	...
314	**Břeclav** **1162**	a.	...	0751	...	0851	0900	1051	1151	1251	1251	...
314	**Břeclav** **991**	d.	0553	0802	0755	0855	0902	1055	1202	1255	1255	1302
	Wien Süd **991**	a.	|	0902	|	|	1002	|	1302	|	|	1402
332	Kúty 🏛	d.	0610	...	0810	0910	...	1110	...	1310	1310	...
396	**Bratislava** Hlavná	a.	0653r	...	0853	0947	...	1147	...	1347	1347	...
	Budapest Keleti **1170**	a.	...	...	...	1232	...	1432	...	...	...	...

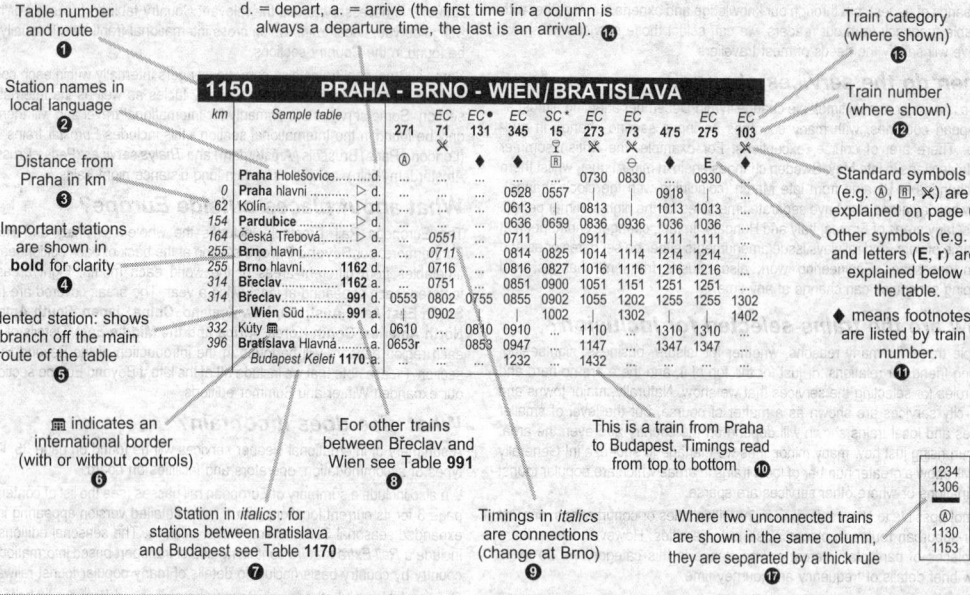

🏛 indicates an international border (with or without controls) (6)

For other trains between Břeclav and Wien see Table **991** (8)

This is a train from Praha to Budapest. Timings read from top to bottom (10)

1234
1306
▬
Ⓐ
1130
1153

Station in *italics*: for stations between Bratislava and Budapest see Table **1170** (7)

Timings in *italics* are connections (change at Brno) (9)

Where two unconnected trains are shown in the same column, they are separated by a thick rule (17)

CLASSES OF TRAVEL:
Trains have 1st and 2nd class seats unless otherwise shown. However, local trains may only have 2nd class seats. (15)

TIME ZONES:
Times are in local time (Russian times are in Moscow time). For time zones see page 4. Timings are given in 24 hour clock (see page 11). (16)

COMMENT LIRE LES TABLEAUX

1. Numéro et parcours du tableau.
2. Nom de la gare en langue locale.
3. La distance en km de Praha.
4. Les noms de gares importantes sont imprimés en **gras** pour faciliter la lecture.
5. La mise en retrait des noms de gares indique une ligne d'embranchement.
6. 🏛 indique une frontière internationale (avec ou sans le contrôle).
7. Les noms de gares imprimés en *italique:* vous trouverez des gares sur le trajet Bratislava - Budapest en consultant le tableau **1170**.
8. Consultez le tableau **991** pour trouver des trains supplémentaires de Břeclav à Wien.
9. Les heures en *italique* indiquent une *correspondance* et supposent dans tous les cas un changement de train.
10. Ici un train de Praha à Budapest. Lire de haut en bas.
11. Les signes conventionnels sont expliqués à la page 6. Les autres signes et lettres sont expliqués en bas du tableau. Le symbole ♦ à l'en-tête d'une colonne signifie qu'il faut consulter le note qui porte le numéro du train concerné.
12. Le numéro du train (en cas échéant).
13. Indication de catégorie (en cas échéant).
14. d. = départ, a. = arrivée. Pour chaque train la *première* mention est toujours une heure de *départ*, la *dernière* toujours une heure d'*arrivée*.
15. Sauf indication contraire, les trains circulent *tous les jours* et y compris des places assises de 1ère et 2ème classe.
16. Toutes les indications horaires sont données en heures locales (voir page 4). En Russie c'est à l'heure Moskva.
17. Deux trains de la même colonne qui ne sont pas en correspondance sont separés par une règle épaisse.

COME SI CONSULTA UN QUADRO ORARIO

1. Numero del quadro e percorso.
2. Nome della stazione nella lingua locale.
3. Distanze in km da Praha.
4. I nomi delle stazioni piu' importante sono stampati in **neretto** per renderne più facile la lettura.
5. I nomi delle stazioni rientrati rispetto alla colonna principale indicano una diramazione dal percorso principale del quadro-orario in questione.
6. 🏛 indica una stazione di confine (con o senza controllo).
7. Stazioni in *corsivo*: per gli orari tra le stazione di Bratislava e Budapest bisogna consultare il quadro **1170**.
8. Consultare il quadro **991** per ulteriori treni da Břeclav a Wien.
9. Gli orari *in corsivo* si riferiscono a servizi *in coincidenza* che implicano un cambio di treno.
10. Questo e' un treno da Praha a Budapest. La lettura viene fatta dall'alto verso il basso.
11. I simboli convenzionali sono spiegate a pagina 6. Altri simboli e lettere sono spiegati sotto il quadro-orario in questione. Il simbolo ♦ all'inizio di una colonna-orario significa che bisogna fare riferimento alla nota corrispondente al numero del treno in questione.
12. Numero del treno (quando indicato).
13. Classificazione del treno (quando indicato).
14. d. = partenza, a. = arrivo. Notare che l'orario che compare per *primo* nel quadro-orario è sempre un l'orario di *partenza*, mentre quello che compare per *ultimo* è sempre l'orario di *arrivo*.
15. Se non ci sono altre indicazioni i treni si intendono giornalieri, con prima e seconda classe di viaggio.
16. Gli orari sono sempre espressi in ora locale (in Russia e' utilizzati l'ora di Mosca). Per informazioni sui fusi orari vedere a pagina 4.
17. Quando nella colonna-orario ci sono due treni che non sono in coincidenza tra loro, questo e' indicato dalla linea in grassetto che li separa.

WIE LESE ICH DIE FAHRPLÄNE

1. Tabellennummer und Strecke.
2. Bahnhof in der Landessprache.
3. Entfernungsangabe.
4. Wichtige Bahnhöfe sind **fett** gedruckt um das Lesen zu vereinfachen.
5. Eingerückte Bahnhöfe befinden sich auf einer abzweigenden Strecke.
6. 🏛 Bezeichnet eine internationale Grenze (mit oder ohne Grenzkontrolle).
7. *Kursiv* gedruckte Bahnhofsnamen: Bahnhöfe zwischen Bratislava und Budapest finden Sie in Tabelle **1170**.
8. Zusätzliche Züge finden Sie in Tabelle **991**.
9. *Kursiv* gedruckte Zeitangaben weisen immer auf das Umsteigen hin.
10. Ein Zug von Praha nach Budapest. Sie lesen von oben nach unten.
11. Eine Erklärung der überall in dem Kursbuch verwendeten konventionellen Zeichen finden Sie auf Seite 6. Anderen Zeichen und Buchstaben finden Sie unter der Fahrplantabelle. Das Zeichen ♦ im Kopf der Zugspalte bedeutet: Sehen Sie bei der Fußnote des Zuges mit der betreffenden Zugnummer nach.
12. Zugnummer (wo zutreffend).
13. Zuggattung (wo zutreffend).
14. d. = Abfahrt, a. = Ankunft. Es handelt sich stets bei der ersten für einen Zug angegebenen Zeit um eine Abfahrtzeit, bei der letzten um eine Ankunftzeit.
15. Sofern nicht anders angemeldet, verkehren die Züge *täglich*. Im Allgemeinen führen die Züge die 1. und 2. Wagenklasse.
16. Fahrzeiten sind immer in der jeweiligen Landeszeit angegeben (Seite 4). Russische Fahrzeiten sind auf Moskauer Zeit.
17. Im Falle von zwei Züge in der gleichen Spalte ohne Anschlussmöglichkeit, liegt das Zeichen ▬ zwischen den Zügen.

COMO LEER LOS CUADROS

1. Número y línea del cuadro.
2. Nombre de las estaciones en el idioma local.
3. Distancia en km de Praga.
4. Los nombres de las estaciones más importantes están impresas en **negrita** facilitar la lectura.
5. La impresión sangrada de los nombres de estas estaciones significa un ramal de la línea principal.
6. 🏛 significa una frontera internacional (con o sin control de aduanas).
7. Estaciones impresas en *cursiva*: para las estaciones entre Bratislava y Budapest debe consultar el cuadro **1170**.
8. Consultar el cuadro **991** para encontrar más trenes desde Břeclav hasta Viena.
9. Los horarios en cursiva, hacen referencia a servicios de enlace, que requieren un cambio de tren.
10. Esto un tren desde Praga hasta Budapest. Leer de arriba a abajo.
11. La explicación de los signos convencionales se da en la página 6. Ostros símbolos y letras se explican al pie del cuadro. El símbolo ♦ en el encabezamiento de la columna quiere decir: consulte la nota que lleva el número del tren interesado.
12. Número de tren (si se indica).
13. Tipo de tren (si se indica).
14. d. = salida, a. = llegada. Nótese que el primer horario indicado en las columnas es siempre un horario de salida, y el último un horario de llegada.
15. Salvo indicación contraria, los trenes circulan *a diario* y llevan plazas sentadas de primera y segunda clases.
16. Todas las indicaciones horarias son en horario local (Para Rusia se utiliza la hora local de Moscú). Para comprobar las franjas horarias mirar la página 4. Los horarios utilizan el sistema horario de 24h (ver página 11).
17. Cuando dos trenes que no tienen conexión aparecen en la misma columna, estos se encuentran separados por el símbolo ▬.

Reading the footnotes

These footnotes relate to the sample table on page 8 ❶

In certain tables, footnotes are listed by train number, shown by ♦ on relevant trains ❷

♦ –	**NOTES** (LISTED BY TRAIN NUMBERS)
102/3 –	POLONIA – [12] ✕ Warszawa - Ostrava - Břeclav - Wien and v.v.
131 –	MORAVIA – [12] Bohumin - Ostrava - Břeclav - Bratislava.
345 –	AVALA – [12] ✕ Praha - Bratislava - Budapest - Beograd. Conveys on ⑤ June 12 - Sept. 18 ▬ 2 cl. Praha - Beograd (**335**) - Thessaloniki.
475 –	JADRAN – June 19 - Sept. 4. ▬ 1, 2 cl., ▬ 2 cl., [2] Praha - Bratislava - Zagreb - Split (Table **92**); [12] Praha - Bratislava.
E –	SLOVAN, not June 19 - Sept. 4.
r –	0659 on ©.
▷ –	See also Table **1160**.
⊖ –	Runs 10 mins later on Aug. 15.
• –	*Ex* in Slovakia.
* –	Pendolino tilting train. Classified *EC* in Austria.
	OTHER TRAIN NAMES :
71 –	GUSTAV MAHLER
73 –	FRANZ SCHUBERT

Letters and symbols may be found above the timings (e.g. **E**) or against individual times (e.g. **r**).

Symbols may also appear in the station column (e.g. ▷). ❻

Train names are sometimes listed separately. ❺

Train **345** is named 'AVALA' and runs daily from Praha to Beograd with 1st and 2nd class seats and a restaurant car. On Fridays June 12 to September 18, a through couchette car runs from Praha to Thessaloniki, attached to train **335** between Beograd and Thessaloniki. ❸

Train **475** is named 'JADRAN' and runs only from June 19 to September 4. It has a sleeper, couchettes and second class seats from Praha to Split via Bratislava and Zagreb, as well as first and second class seats only going as far as Bratislava. Further details will be found in Table **92**. ❹

Always read the footnotes; they may contain important information. Standard symbols are explained on page 6. ❼

Dates shown are where a train **starts** its journey (unless otherwise noted). Some notes show both directions of the train (e.g. **102/3**) with "and v.v." ❽

FURTHER HINTS ON READING THE TIMETABLE

- Refer to the introduction to each country for important information such as train types, supplements, compulsory reservation, and the dates of validity of the timings. Exceptions are noted in individual tables.
- For dates of public holidays see page 4.
- Please allow adequate time for changing trains, especially at large stations. Connections are not guaranteed, especially when late running occurs (connecting trains are sometimes held for late running trains).
- A Glossary of common terms appears on page 12.

LES NOTES EN BAS DU TABLEAU

❶ Ces notes se rapportent au example de tableau à la page 8.
❷ Dans certains tableaux, le symbole ♦ à l'en-tête d'une colonne signifie qu'il faut consulter le note qui porte le numéro du train concerné.
❸ Le train **345** s'appelle AVALA et circule tous les jours de Praha à Beograd avec des places assises de 1ère et 2ème classe et une voiture-restaurant. Tous les vendredis du 12 juin jusqu'au 18 sept il y a aussi une voiture-couchettes de Praha à Thessaloniki, qui se joint au train **335** entre Beograd et Thessaloniki.
❹ Le train **475** s'appelle JADRAN et circule seulement entre le 19 juin et le 4 septembre. Il compris des voitures-lits, couchettes et places assises de 2ème classe à Split via Zagreb, et des places assises de 1ère et 2ème classe jusqu'à Bratislava. Voir le tableau **92**.
❺ Les noms des trains sont parfois indiqués séparément.
❻ Les lettres et signes sont situés à l'en-tête d'une colonne ou à côté d'une heure dans la colonne. Une signe peut sortir également a côté d'un nom de gare.
❼ Les notes peuvent vous donner des informations importantes. Les signes conventionels sont expliqués à la page 6.
❽ Sauf indication contraire, les jours et dates de circulation mentionnés sont ceux applicables à la *gare d'origine* du train (mentionnée si elle ne figure pas sur le tableau même dans les notes). Les notes peuvent expliquer les deux sens d'un train (e.g. **102/3**) utilisant "and v.v." (et vice versa).

PLUS DE CONSEILS

- Il vous est fortement recommandé de consulter aussi l'introduction à chaque section nationale: vous y trouverez des précisions concernant la classification des trains, les prestations offertes à bord des trains, les suppléments, la réservation des places, etc.
- Jours fériés - voir page 4.
- Aucune correspondance n'est garantie pourtant. N'oubliez pas non plus que dans les grandes gares les changements peuvent entraîner une longue marche et l'emprunt d'escaliers.
- Lexique - voir page 12.

NOTE ALLA FINE DEL QUADRO-ORARIO

❶ Queste note si riferiscono all' esempio a pagina 8.
❷ In certi quadri-orario, il simbolo ♦ nelle note di testa significa che bisogna fare riferimento alla nota con il numero di treno corrispondente.
❸ Il treno **345** si chiama AVALA ed e' giornaliero tra Praha a Beograd con posti di 1ª e 2ª classe e carrozza ristorante. Il venerdì dal 12 giugno fino al 18 settembre e' aggiunta a Beograd una carrozza cuccette diretta a Thessaloniki, combinandosi con il treno **335** tra Beograd e Thessaloniki.
❹ Il treno **475** si chiama JADRAN ed e' operativo solo dal 19 giugno al 4 settembre. Il treno si compone di carrozze letti, carrozze cuccette, e posti di 2ª classe tra Praha e Split, via Bratislava e Zagrabria; inoltre ci sono anche posti di 1ª e 2ª classe fino a Bratislava. Consultare anche il quadro-orario **92** al riguardo
❺ I nomi dei treni sono talvolta indicati separatamente.
❻ Lettere e simboli possono essere sia alla testa di una colonna-orario, che accanto all'orario del treno stesso. Un simbolo potrebbe anche essere accanto al nome di una stazione.
❼ E' importante leggere sempre le note a le informazioni a fine quadro. I segni convenzionali sono elencati e spiegati a pagina 6.
❽ Salvo casi in cui sia diversamente indicato, le date di circolazione dei treni si riferiscono sempre alla stazione dove il treno inizia il suo viaggio (come viene riportato nelle note a fine quadro, e Inoltre nel quadro stesso).

ALTRI CONSIGLI UTILI

- Vi consigliamo vivamente di consultare anche l'introduzione dedicata ad ogni nazione. Troverete importanti informazioni riguardanti i servizi di trasporto di ciascun paese, così come le categorie dei treni, la ristorazione, il pagamento di supplementi, le necessità di prenotazione, ecc.
- I giorni festivi suddivisi per paese sono elencati a pagina 4.
- Le coincidenze indicate non sono garantite. Tenete presente che che nelle grandi stazioni il trasferimento tra due binari potrebbe significare un lungo tratto da percorrere a piedi e con l'uso di scale.
- Il glossario si trova a pagina 12.

FUSSNOTEN

❶ Fußnoten beziehen sich auf die Beispieltabelle auf Seite 8.
❷ ♦: Sehen Sie bei der Fußnote des Zuges mit der betreffenden Zugnummer nach.
❸ Zug **345** heißt AVALA und fährt täglich zwischen Praha und Beograd mit Sitzplätzen 1. und 2. Klasse. An Freitagen vom 12. Juni bis 18. September führt dieser Zug durchgehende Liegewagen von Praha nach Thessaloniki (mit Zug **335** vereinigt von Beograd nach Thessaloniki).
❹ Zug **475** heißt JADRAN und fährt nur von 19. Juni bis 4. September. Er führt Schlaf-, Liege und Sitzwagen 2. Klasse von Praha nach Split über Zagreb, auch Sitzwagen 1. und 2. Klasse, die nur bis Bratislava fahren. Auf Tabelle **92** finden Sie weitere Informationen.
❺ Zugnamen können besonders aufgeführt sein.
❻ Zeichen und Buchstaben finden sich im Kopf der Zugspalte oder neben einer bestimmten Zeitangabe. Zeichen sind auch in der Bahnhofsspalte möglich.
❼ In Fußnoten findet man wichtige Informationen. Standardzeichen sind auf Seite 6 erklärt.
❽ Die erwähnten Tage und Zeitabschnitte für Züge, die nicht täglich verkehren, gelten für den Ausgangsbahnhof des Zuges (wenn dieser nicht in der Tabelle steht, ist er in einer Fußnote erwähnt). Fußnoten dürfen beide Richtungen erklären (z.B. **102/3**), mit "and v.v." (und umgekehrt).

WEITERE HINWEISE

- Es ist zu empfehlen, die Einleitungen zu jedem einzelnen Land zu lesen. Darin werden Sie wichtige Informationen über die Besonderheiten jedes Landes finden: Zugcharakterisierung, Services an Bord der Züge, Zuschlagpflicht, Reservierungsbedingungen usw.
- Feiertage - siehe Seite 4.
- Anschlussversäumnisse durch Verspätung oder Ausfall von Zügen sind immer möglich. Bitte beachten Sie, dass auf Großstadtbahnhöfen häufig längere Fußwege zurückgelegt bzw. Treppen benutzen werden müssen.
- Glossar - siehe Seite 12.

LAS NOTAS AL PIE DEL CUADRO

❶ Estas notas hacen referencia al ejemplo de la página 8.
❷ El símbolo ♦ ciertas tablas horarias significa: que hay que consultar la nota a pie de página con el número correspondiente.
❸ El Tren **345** se llama AVALA y circula a diario entre Praga y Belgrado con plazas sentadas de 1ra y 2da clase, además de con coche-restaurante. Los Viernes del 12 de junio al 18 de septiembre el tren lleva coches litera desde Praga hasta Tesalónica que se combinan con el tren **335** entre Belgrado y Tesalónica.
❹ El Tren **475** se llama JADRAN y circula solamente del 19 de junio al 4 de septiembre. El Tren **475** se llama JADRAN y circula solamente del 19 de junio al 4 de sept. El tren dispone de lleva vagones de coches cama, litera, y plazas sentadas de 2da clase entre Praga y Split a través de Zagreb, también plazas sentadas de 1ra y 2da clase hasta Bratislava. Consulte el cuadro **92**.
❺ Los nombres de los Trenes a veces son enumerados por separado.
❻ Las letras y signos se encuentran en el encabezamiento de las distintas columnas horarias o adyacentes a horas de salida individuales. Los símbolos también pueden aparecer en la columna de la estación.
❼ Lea siempre las notas a pie de cuadro ya que pueden contener información importante. La explicación de los signos convencionales se da en la página 6.
❽ Salvo indicación contraria los días y fechas de circulación de los trenes son aquéllos mencionados en la estación de *origen* del tren. Algunas notas muestran ambas direcciones del tren mediante la nota "and v.v." (y viceversa).

INFORMACIÓN ADICIONAL

- Se recomienda vivamente que consulte también los preámbulos al comienzo de cada sección nacional: le proporcionarán datos importantes sobre las particularidades de cada país: tipos de trenes, restauración, pago de suplementos, y necesidades de reservación anticipada.
- Días festivos - cunsulte la página 4.
- Los trasbordos no se pueden garantizar, sobretodo en el caso de retrasos. Hay que ser consciente también que el trasbordo en las estaciones de grandes ciudades puede suponer un desplazamiento bastante largo a pie y el uso de escaleras.
- Glosario - cunsulte la página 12.

The following is designed to be an outline guide to travelling around Europe by train. For further details of types of accommodation available, catering, supplements etc., see the introduction to each country.

BUYING YOUR TICKET

Train tickets must be purchased before travelling, either from travel agents or at the station ticket office (or machine). Where a station has neither a ticket office nor a ticket machine, the ticket may usually be purchased on the train.

Tickets which are not dated when purchased (for example in France and Italy) must be validated before travel in one of the machines at the entrance to the platform.

In certain Eastern European countries foreign nationals may have to buy international rail tickets at the office of the state tourist board concerned and not at the railway station. The tickets can sometimes only be purchased in western currency and buying tickets can take a long time.

Most countries in Europe offer two classes of rail accommodation, usually 1st and 2nd class. 1st class is more comfortable and therefore more expensive than 2nd class. Local trains are often 2nd class only. In Southern and Eastern Europe, 1st class travel is advisable for visitors as fares are reasonable and 2nd class can be very overcrowded.

RESERVATIONS

Many express trains in Europe are restricted to passengers holding advance seat reservations, particularly in France, Italy, Sweden and Spain. This is indicated by the symbol ® in the tables, or by notes in the introduction to each country. All *TGV, Eurostar* and *Thalys* trains require advance reservation, as do all long-distance trains in Spain.

Reservations can usually be made up to two months in advance. A small fee is charged, but where a supplement is payable the reservation fee is often included. Reservations can often be made on other long-distance services and this is recommended at busy times.

SUPPLEMENTS

Many countries have faster train services for which an extra charge is made. This supplement is payable when the ticket is purchased and often includes the price of a seat reservation. The supplement can sometimes be paid on the train, but usually at extra cost. The introduction to each country gives further information. On certain high-speed services, the first class fare includes the provision of a meal.

RAIL PASSES

Passes are available which give unlimited travel on most trains in a given area. These range from Interrail and Eurail passes which cover most of Europe for up to one month, to local passes which cover limited areas for one day. Further details of Interrail and Eurail passes appear elsewhere in this edition, and a special feature on rail passes appears in the twice-yearly Independent Travellers Edition.

FINDING YOUR TRAIN

At most stations departures are listed on large paper sheets (often yellow), and / or on electronic departure indicators. These list trains by departure, giving principal stops, and indicate from which platform they leave.

On each platform of principal European stations, a display board can be found giving details of the main trains calling at that platform. This includes the location of individual coaches, together with their destinations and the type of accommodation provided.

A sign may be carried on the side of the carriage indicating the train name, principal stops and destination and a label or sign near the door will indicate the number allocated to the carriage, which is shown on reservation tickets. 1st class accommodation is usually indicated by a yellow band above the windows and doors and/or a figure '1' near the door or on the windows

A sign above the compartment door will indicate seat numbers and which seats are reserved. In non-compartment trains, reserved seats have labels on their headrests. In some countries reserved seats are not marked and occupants will be asked to move when the passenger who has reserved the seat boards the train.

LUGGAGE & BICYCLES

Luggage may be registered at many larger stations and sent separately by rail to your destination. In some countries, bicycles may also be registered in advance and certain local and some express trains will convey bicycles (there may be a charge). The relevant railways will advise exact details on request.

✕ CATERING 🍸

Many high-quality and long-distance trains in Europe have restaurant cars serving full meals, usually with waiter service. An at-seat service may also be provided to passengers in first class accommodation. Such trains are identified with the symbol ✕ in the tables. Full meals may only be available at set times, sometimes with separate sittings, and may only be available to passengers holding first class tickets. However, the restaurant car is often supplemented by a counter or trolley service offering light snacks and drinks.

Other types of catering are shown with the symbol 🍸. This varies from a self-service buffet car serving light meals (sometimes called bistro or café) to a trolley which is wheeled through the train, serving drinks and light refreshments. Where possible, the introduction to each country gives further information on the level of catering to be expected on particular types of train.

Please note that the catering shown may not be available throughout the journey and may be suspended or altered at weekends or on holidays.

SLEEPING CARS 🛏

Sleeping cars are indicated by the symobol 🛏 in the tables. Standard sleeping car types have bedroom style compartments with limited washing facilities and full bedding. Toilets are located at one or both ends of the coach. An attendant travels with each car or pair of cars and will serve drinks, snacks and breakfast at an extra charge. Traditionally, 1st class sleeping compartments have one or two berths (in Britain and Norway two berth compartments require only 2nd class tickets) and 2nd class compartments have three berths. Some trains convey special T2 cabins, shown as 🛏 (T2) in the tables, with one berth in 1st class and two berths in 2nd class. On certain routes it is now possible to reserve a single compartment with a 2nd class ticket.

Compartments are allocated for occupation exclusively by men or by women except when married couples or families occupy all berths. Children travelling alone, or who cannot be accommodated in the same compartment as their family, are placed in women's compartments. In Russia and other countries of the CIS, however, berths are allocated in strict order of booking and men and women often share the same compartments.

Some trains have communicating doors between sleeping compartments which can be opened to create a larger room if both compartments are occupied by the same family group. Berths can be reserved up to 2 months (3 months on certain trains) before the date of travel and early reservation is recommended as space is often limited. Berths should be claimed within 15 minutes of boarding the train or they may be resold.

HOTEL TRAINS

High quality overnight trains, often referred to as Hotel trains, run on a selection of national and international routes. The facilities are of a higher standard than those offered in conventional sleeping cars, and special fares are payable. The trains fall into the following categories:

ÖBB nightjet: Many night trains radiating from Germany and Austria, are operated by Austrian Railways and are branded *ÖBB nightjet*. They operate on 17 routes serving four countries and all convey sleeping-car, couchette and seating accommodation. Standard sleeping-car compartments can be configured with one, two or three berths and have a washbasin (with toiletries provided). *Deluxe* sleeping-car compartments can also be configured with one, two or three berths and have an en-suite washroom with WC, washbasin and shower (shower gel and towels are provided). The sleeping-car fare includes a welcome drink, a bottle of water, a newspaper and a full breakfast served in the morning (including free hot drink refills). Four and six berth couchettes are available, the price of which includes a bottle of water and a small breakfast. Women only, family and wheelchair couchette compartments are provided. 2nd class seating cars (with six seat compartments) are also conveyed. Reservation is compulsory in all categories of accommodation and special all-inclusive fares are available. Please note that Interrail and Eurail pass holders must pay a special pass holders fare.

Trenhotel (Spain). These *Talgo*-type trains run on the international routes from Madrid to Lisboa and from Irún / Hendaye to Lisboa. They also operate on internal routes within Spain, from Barcelona to A Coruña, Granada and Vigo, and from Madrid to A Coruña, Ferrol and Pontevedra. The highest class of accommodation is *Gran Clase*, which has shower and toilet facilities in each compartment and can be used for single or double occupancy.

Compartments with showers are also available on some domestic overnight services in Sweden and Italy, and on certain other international routes as indicated on our international overnight services summary on page 35.

COUCHETTES ▬

Couchettes (▬) are a more basic form of overnight accommodation consisting of simple bunk beds with a sheet, blanket and pillow. The couchettes are converted from ordinary seating cars for the night, and there are usually 4 berths per compartment in 1st class, 6 berths in 2nd class. On certain trains (e.g. in Austria and Italy), 4 berth compartments are available to 2nd class passengers, at a higher supplement. Washing and toilet facilities are provided at the ends of each coach. Men and women are booked into the same compartments and are expected to sleep in daytime clothes. A small number of trains in Germany, however, have women-only couchette compartments.

INTERNATIONAL OVERNIGHT SERVICES

A summary of international overnight services will be found on page 35 which specifies the various types of accommodation and catering provided on each individual service (including details of the operator).

CAR-SLEEPERS

Trains which convey motor cars operate throughout much of Europe and are shown in Table **1** for international services and Table **2** for other services. The motor cars are conveyed in special wagons while passengers travel in sleeping cars or couchettes, usually (but not always) in the same train.

WHEELCHAIR ACCESS ♿

Most main-line domestic and international trains, together with an increasing number of local trains, are specially equipped to accommodate passengers in wheelchairs. Access ramps are available at many stations and some trains are fitted with special lifts. These trains have at least one wheelchair space, and are equipped with accessible toilets.

Most railways publish guides to accessibility, and many countries provide dedicated staff to assist disabled travellers. Wheelchair users normally need to reserve in advance, stating their requirements.

HEALTH REQUIREMENTS

It is not mandatory for visitors to Europe to be vaccinated against infectious diseases unless they are travelling from areas where these are endemic. For travellers' peace of mind, however, protection against the following diseases should be considered:

COVID-19	Measles / Rubella
Hepatitis A / B	Polio
HIV	Tetanus
Influenza	Tuberculosis

Full information is available from the manual published by the World Health Organisation, and travellers should seek advice from their Travel Agent.

DRINKING WATER

Tap water is usually safe to drink in most parts of Europe. The water in washrooms or toilets on trains is, however, not suitable for drinking. Those who doubt the purity of the tap water are recommended to boil it, to use sterilisation tablets, or to drink bottled water.

CLIMATE

Most of Europe lies within the temperate zone but there can be considerable differences between North and South, East and West, as illustrated in the table below. Local temperatures are also affected by altitude and the difference between summer and winter temperatures tends to be less marked in coastal regions than in areas far removed from the sea.

	Bucuresti	Dublin	Madrid	Moskva
JANUARY				
Highest	3°	8°	10°	– 6°
Lowest	– 5°	2°	3°	– 12°
Rain days	9	13	8	11
APRIL				
Highest	18°	12°	18°	10°
Lowest	5°	5°	8°	2°
Rain days	10	11	10	9
JULY				
Highest	30°	20°	32°	23°
Lowest	15°	12°	19°	14°
Rain days	10	11	3	12
OCTOBER				
Highest	18°	14°	19°	8°
Lowest	5°	7°	11°	2°
Rain days	8	12	10	10

Highest = Average highest daily temperature in °C
Lowest = Average lowest daily temperature in °C
Rain days = Average number of days with recorded precipitation

Source: World Weather Information Service

FIND US ON FACEBOOK!

www.facebook.com/EuropeanRailTimetable
and on **Twitter** @EuropeanRailTT

CURRENCY CONVERSION

The information shown below is intended to be indicative only. Rates fluctuate from day to day and commercial exchange rates normally include a commission element.

Country	unit	code	1 GBP =	1 USD =	1 EUR =	100 JPY =
Euro zone (‡)	**euro**	**EUR**	**1.13**	**0.92**	**1.00**	**0.69**
Albania	lek	ALL	130.80	107.99	115.11	80.12
Belarus	rubl	BYN	3.02	2.50	2.66	1.85
Bosnia	marka	BAM	2.22	1.83	1.95	1.36
Bulgaria	lev	BGN	2.22	1.83	1.95	1.36
Czech Republic	koruna	CZK	26.96	22.25	23.72	16.51
Denmark	krone	DKK	8.46	6.98	7.44	5.18
Georgia	lari	GEL	3.19	2.63	2.80	7.95
Hungary	forint	HUF	435.55	359.59	383.30	266.78
Iceland	krona	ISK	175.33	144.75	154.30	107.39
Macedonia	denar	MKD	70.28	58.03	61.85	43.05
Moldova	leu	MDL	22.70	18.74	19.98	13.90
Norway	krone	NOK	12.47	10.30	10.98	7.64
Poland	złoty	PLN	5.39	4.45	4.74	3.30
Romania	leu	RON	5.59	4.61	4.92	3.42
Russia	ruble	RUB	90.01	75.06	80.01	55.68
Serbia	dinar	RSD	133.31	110.06	117.32	81.65
Sweden	krona	SEK	12.56	10.37	11.05	7.69
Switzerland	franc	CHF	1.12	0.92	00.98	0.68
Turkey	lira	TRY	22.85	18.87	20.11	14.00
Ukraine	hryvnya	UAH	44.73	36.93	39.36	27.39
United Kingdom	pound	GBP	1.00	0.82	0.88	0.61
United States	dollar	USD	1.21	1.00	1.06	0.74

‡ – Austria, Belgium, Croatia, Cyprus, Estonia, Finland, France, Germany, Greece, Ireland, Italy, Latvia, Lithuania, Luxembourg, Malta, the Netherlands, Portugal, Slovakia, Slovenia and Spain.

The euro is also legal tender in Andorra, Kosovo, Monaco, Montenegro, San Marino, and the Vatican City.

PASSPORTS AND VISAS

Nationals of one country intending to travel to or pass through another country normally require a valid passport and will also require a visa unless a special visa-abolition agreement has been made between the countries concerned. The limit of stay permitted in each country is usually 3 months.

Applications for visas should be made well in advance of the date of travel to the local consulate of the country concerned. Consuls usually make a charge for issuing a visa. Before issuing a transit visa, a consul normally requires to see the visa of the country of destination.

The possession of a valid passport or visa does not necessarily grant the holder automatic access to all areas of the country to be visited. Certain countries have zones which are restricted or prohibited to foreign nationals.

All border controls have been abolished, however, between those countries which have signed the **Schengen Agreement** (see list below), and a visa allowing entry to any of these countries is valid in all of them.

LIST OF SCHENGEN AREA COUNTRIES

Austria, Belgium, Czech Republic, Croatia, Denmark, Estonia, Finland, France, Germany, Greece, Hungary, Iceland, Italy, Latvia, Lithuania, Luxembourg, Malta, Netherlands, Norway, Poland, Portugal, Slovakia, Slovenia, Spain, Sweden, Switzerland.

METRIC CONVERSION TABLES

The Celsius system of temperature measurement, the metric system of distance measurement and the twenty-four hour clock are used throughout this book. The tables below give Fahrenheit, mile and twelve-hour clock equivalents.

TEMPERATURE

°C	°F
−20	−4
−15	5
−10	14
−5	23
0	32
5	41
10	50
15	59
20	68
25	77
30	86
35	95
40	104

Conversion formulae:
°C = (°F – 32) x 5 / 9
°F = (°C x 9 / 5) + 32

DISTANCE

km	miles	km	miles	km	miles
1	0.62	45	27.96	300	186.41
2	1.24	50	31.07	400	248.55
3	1.86	55	34.18	500	310.69
4	2.49	60	37.28	600	372.82
5	3.11	65	40.39	700	434.96
6	3.73	70	43.50	800	497.10
7	4.35	75	46.60	900	559.23
8	4.97	80	49.71	1000	621.37
9	5.59	85	52.82	1100	683.51
10	6.21	90	55.92	1200	745.65
15	9.32	95	59.03	1300	807.78
20	12.43	100	62.14	1400	869.92
25	15.53	125	77.67	1500	932.06
30	18.64	150	93.21	2000	1242.74
35	21.75	175	108.74	3000	1864.11
40	24.85	200	124.27	4000	2485.48

TIME

Midnight departure	= 0000
1 am	= 0100
5 am	= 0500
5.30 am	= 0530
11 am	= 1100
12 noon	= 1200
1 pm	= 1300
3.45 pm	= 1545
Midnight arrival	= 2400

GLOSSARY

🔑	FRANCAIS	ITALIANO	DEUTSCH	ESPAÑOL
additional trains	d'autres trains	ulteriori treni	weitere Züge	otros trenes
also	[circule] aussi	[si effettua] anche	[verkehrt] auch	[circula] también
alteration	modification	variazione	Änderung	modificación
approximately	environ	circa	ungefähr	aproximadamente
arrival, arrives (a.)	arrivée, arrive	arrivo, arriva	Ankunft, kommt an	llegada, llega
and at the same minutes past each hour until	puis toutes les heures aux mêmes minutes jusqu'à	poi ai stessi minuti di ogni ora fino a	und so weiter im Takt bis	luego a los mismos minutos de cada hora hasta
calls at	s'arrête à	ferma a	hält in	efectúa parada en
certain	déterminé	certo	bestimmt	determinado
change at	changer à	cambiare a	umsteigen in	cambiar en
composition	composition	composizione	Zugbildung	composición
confirmation	confirmation	conferma	Bestätigung	confirmación
connection	correspondance, relation	coincidenza, relazione	Anschluss, Verbindung	correspondencia, enlace
conveys	comporte, achemine	ha in composizione	befördert, führt	lleva
daily	tous les jours	giornalmente	täglich	diariamente
delay	retard	ritardo	Verspätung	retraso
departure, departs (d.)	départ, part	partenza, parte	Abfahrt, fährt ab	salida, sale
earlier	plus tôt	più presto	früher	más temprano
engineering work	travaux de voie	lavori sul binario	Bauarbeiten	obras de vía
even / uneven dates	jours pairs / impairs	giorni pari / dispari	gerade / ungerade Daten	fechas pares / impares
every 30 minutes	toutes les 30 minutes	ogni 30 minuti	alle 30 Minuten	cada 30 minutos
except	sauf	escluso	außer	excepto
fast(er)	(plus) rapide	(più) rapido	schnell(er)	(más) rápido
for	pour	per	für	para
from Rennes	(en provenance) de Rennes	(proviene) da Rennes	von Rennes	(procede) de Rennes
from Jan. 15	à partir du 15 janvier	dal 15 di gennaio	vom 15. Januar (an)	desde el 15 de enero
hourly	toutes les heures	ogni ora	stündlich	cada hora
hours (hrs)	heures	ore	Stunden	horas
journey	voyage, trajet	viaggio, percorso	Reise	viaje, trayecto
journey time	temps de parcours	tempo di tragitto	Reisezeit	duración del recorrido
later	plus tard	più tardi	später	más tarde
may	peut, peuvent	può, possono	kann, können	puede(n)
minutes (mins)	minutes	minuti	Minuten	minutos
not	ne [circule] pas	non [si effettua]	[verkehrt] nicht	no [circula]
not available	pas disponible	non disponibile	nicht erhältlich	no disponible
on the dates shown in Table **81**	les jours indiqués dans le tableau **81**	nei giorni indicati nel quadro **81**	an den in der Tabelle **81** angegebene Daten	los días indicados en el cuadro **81**
only	seulement	esclusivamente	nur	sólo
operator	entreprise de transports	azienda di trasporto	Verkehrsunternehmen	empresa de transportes
other	autre	altro	andere	otros
runs	circule	circola, si effettua	verkehrt	circula
sailing	traversée	traversata	Überfahrt	travesía
ship	bateau, navire	nave, battello	Schiff	barco
stopping trains	trains omnibus	treni regionali	Nahverkehrszüge	trenes regionales
stops	s'arrête	ferma	hält	efectúa parada
subject to	sous réserve de	soggetto a	vorbehaltlich	sujeto a
summer	été	estate	Sommer	verano
supplement payable	avec supplément	con pagamento di supplemento	zuschlagpflichtig	con pago de suplemento
then	puis	poi	dann	luego
through train	train direct	treno diretto	durchgehender Zug	tren directo
timings	horaires	orari	Zeitangaben	horarios
to York	vers, à destination de York	(diretto) a York	nach York	(continúa) a York
to / until July 23	jusqu'au 23 juillet	fino al 23 di luglio	bis zum 23. Juli	hasta el día 23 de julio
to pick up	pour laisser monter	per viaggiatori in partenza	zum Zusteigen	para recoger viajeros
to set down	pour laisser descendre	per viaggiatori in arrivo	zum Aussteigen	para dejar viajeros
unless otherwise shown	sauf indication contraire	salvo indicazione contraria	sofern nicht anders angezeigt	salvo indicación contraria
valid	valable	valido	gültig	válido
when train **44** runs	lors de la circulation du train **44**	quando circola il treno **44**	beim Verkehren des Zuges **44**	cuando circula el tren **44**
winter	hiver	inverno	Winter	invierno

INDEX OF PLACES by table number

The BEYOND EUROPE section is indexed separately - see the back of each edition

🚆 Connection by train from the nearest station shown in this timetable.
⛴ Connection by boat from the nearest station shown in this timetable.
🚌 Connection by bus from the nearest station shown in this timetable.
10/355 Consult both indicated tables to find the best connecting services.

D

DEN HAAG

DIJON

DORTMUND

DRESDEN

DUBLIN

DUISBURG

DÜSSELDORF

E

T

TALLINN

TORINO

TOULOUSE

U

UTRECHT

V

VENEZIA

city plan, page 34

CRUISE TRAINS

The services shown in the European Rail Timetable are the regular scheduled services of the railway companies concerned. However, a number of specialised operators also run luxurious cruise trains taking several days to complete their journey. Overnight accommodation is provided either on the train or in hotels. Cruise trains are bookable only through the operating company or its appointed agents and normal rail tickets are not valid on these trains. A selection of operators is shown below.

The Danube Express: Fully escorted holidays in central and eastern Europe by luxury private train based in Budapest. Operator: Danube Express, Offley Holes Farm, Charlton Road, Preston, Hitchin, SG4 7TD, UK; ✆ +44 (0)1462 441400. Website: www.danube-express.com

Belmond Royal Scotsman: Luxury tours of Scotland starting from Edinburgh. Operator: Belmond Royal Scotsman, Shackleton House, 4 Battle Bridge Lane, London, SE1 2HP, UK; ✆ 0845 217 0799 (UK only) or +44 (0) 20 3117 1300. Website: www.royalscotsman.com

El Transcantábrico and **El Expreso de La Robla**: Rail cruises along Spain's northern coast. Operator: Trenes Turísticos de Lujo, Plaza de los Ferroviarios s/n., 33012 Oviedo, Asturias, Spain; ✆ +34 902 555 902, fax +34 985 981 711. Website: www.trenesturisticosdelujo.com

Trans-Siberian Express: Tours by private hotel train along the Trans-Siberian Railway. Operator: Golden Eagle Luxury Trains, Denzell House, Denzell Gardens, Dunham Road, Altrincham, WA14 4QF, UK; ✆ +44 (0)16 1 928 9410, fax +44 (0)161 941 6101. Website: www.goldeneagleluxurytrains.com.

Venice Simplon-Orient-Express: This well-known luxury train runs once or twice weekly from late March to early November, mostly on its established London - Paris - Venezia route. Operator: Belmond VSOE, Shackleton House, 4 Battle Bridge Lane, London, SE1 2HP, UK; ✆ 0845 217 0799 (UK only) or +44 (0) 20 3117 1300. Website: www.vsoe.com

LIST OF ADVERTISERS

AERA	66, 79, 159, 292, 562
BAHNREISEN SUTTER	52, 66, 562
COOL CULINARIA	76, 322
ECONEX	inside front cover
EUROPE BY RAIL	652
EUROPEAN RAIL TIMETABLE	521, inside back cover
HIDDEN EUROPE	100, 313, inside back cover
LOCOMOTIVES INTERNATIONAL	58, 77, 105, 328
MIDDLETON PRESS	571
MILLSTONE CREATIVE	47, 80
RAILBOOKERS	65, 106, 282
ROVOS RAIL	57, 73

LIST OF RETAILERS

The European Rail Timetable is available for purchase direct from the retailers listed below. Some also stock the Rail Map Europe.

Great Britain	
Blackwell's Bookshop	Oxford
Daunt Books	Six stores in London
Foyles	London and Birmingham
Magazine Heaven	Rushden Lakes, Northamptonshire
Stanfords	London and Bristol
Tornado Books & Hobbies	Birmingham
Austria	
Buchhandlung und Antiquariat	Wien
Freytag & Berndt	Wien
Belgium	
Press Shop / Relay	Brugge railway station
France	
La Librairie du Voyage	Rennes
Smith&Son (formerly WHSmith)	Paris, 248 Rue de Rivoli
Germany	
FachBuchZentrum & Antiquariat Stiletto	München Neuhausen
Freytag & Berndt	Regensburg and Nürnberg
Gleisnost Reisebuero	Freiburg railway station
GVE-Verlag / BahnBuchShop	Berlin Lichtenberg railway station info@gve-verlag.de
Dussmann das Kulturkaufhaus	Berlin, Friedrichstraße 90
Schropp Maps	Berlin, Hardenbergstraße 9a
Dr.Götze Land & Karte	Hamburg
Italy	
Anglo-American Bookshop	Roma
Netherlands	
Stanley & Livingstone	Den Haag
The American Book Center	Amsterdam
Treinreiswinkel	Amsterdam and Leiden
Sweden	
Kartbutiken	Stockholm
Switzerland	
Rail Map Shop	Trogen

CITY STATION LOCATION PLANS

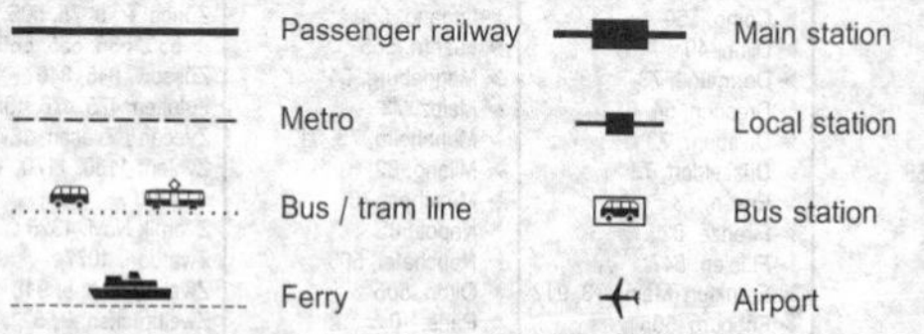

Only those metro, bus, and tram lines which provide inter-station links or connect outlying main stations to the city centre are shown.

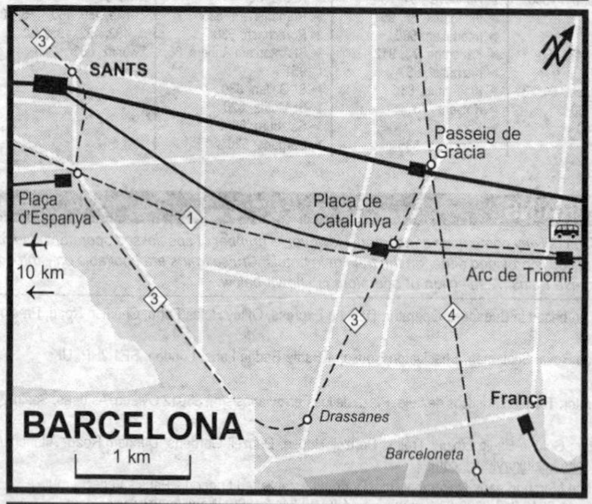

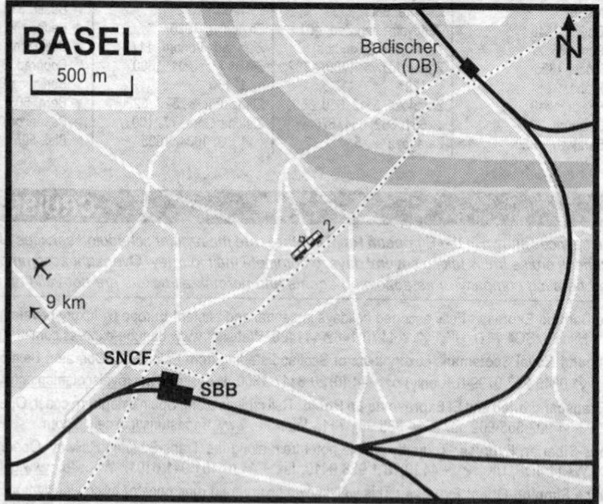

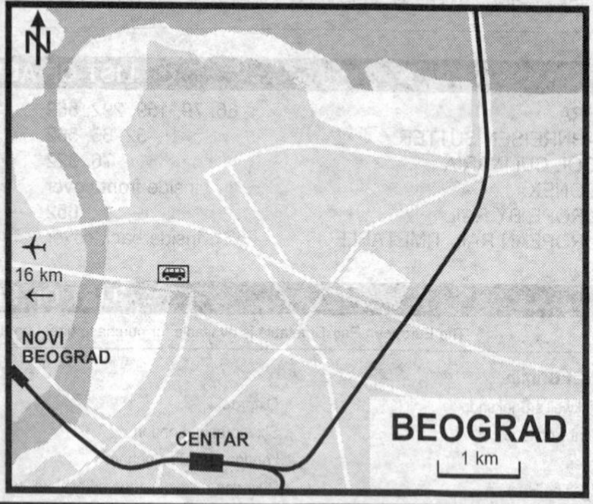

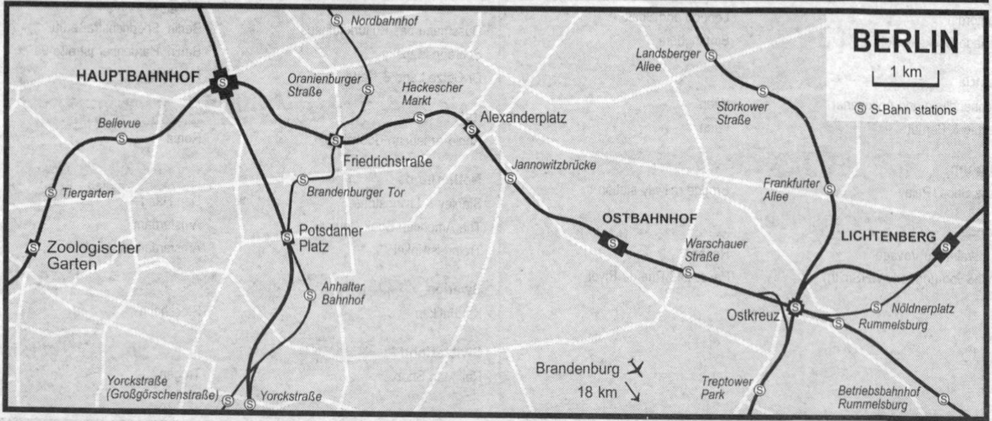

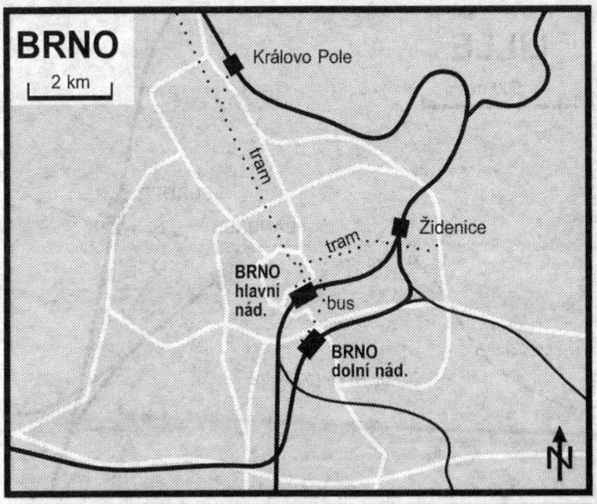
BRNO
2 km
Královo Pole
tram
Židenice
tram
BRNO
hlavní
nád.
bus
BRNO
dolní nád.

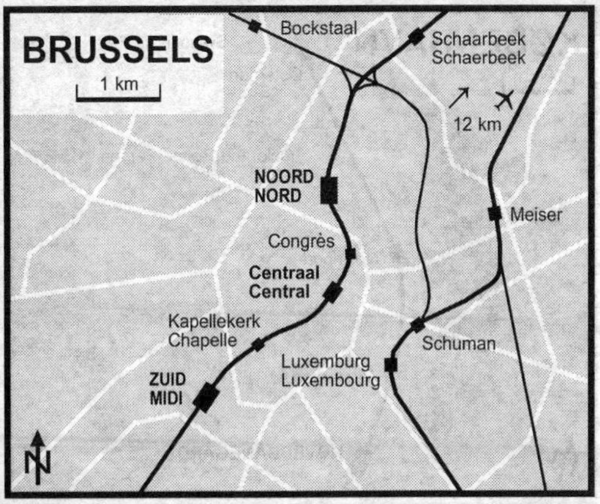
BRUSSELS
1 km
Bockstaal
Schaarbeek
Schaerbeek
12 km
NOORD
NORD
Meiser
Congrès
Centraal
Central
Kapellekerk
Chapelle
Schuman
Luxemburg
Luxembourg
ZUID
MIDI

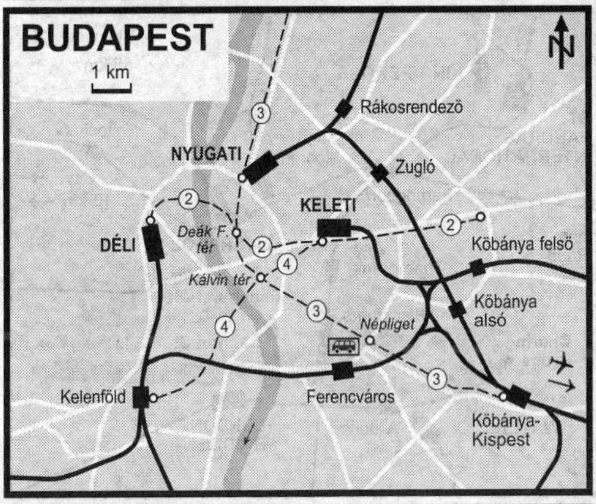
BUDAPEST
1 km
Rákosrendező
NYUGATI
Zugló
KELETI
DÉLI
Deák F. tér
Kőbánya felső
Kálvin tér
Kőbánya alsó
Népliget
Kelenföld
Ferencváros
Kőbánya-Kispest

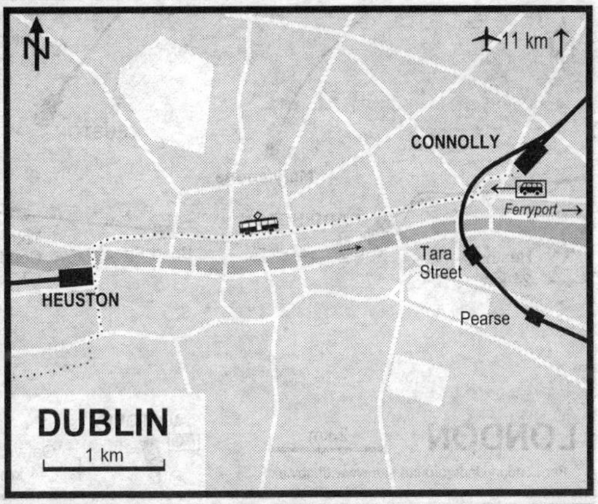
11 km
CONNOLLY
Ferryport
Tara
Street
HEUSTON
Pearse
DUBLIN
1 km

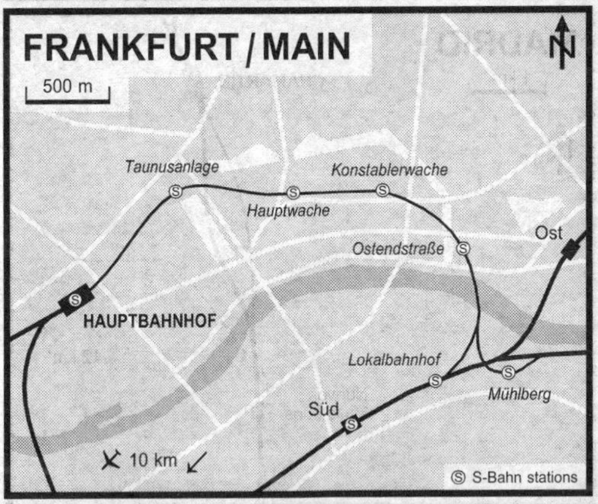
FRANKFURT / MAIN
500 m
Taunusanlage
Konstablerwache
Hauptwache
Ostendstraße
Ost
HAUPTBAHNHOF
Lokalbahnhof
Mühlberg
Süd
10 km
S-Bahn stations

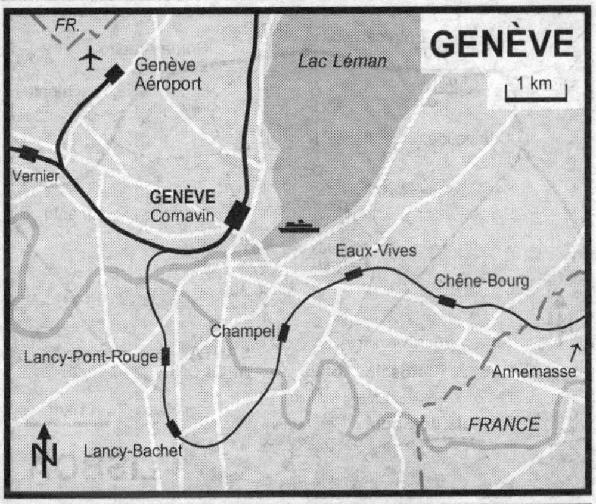
FR.
Genève
Aéroport
Lac Léman
GENÈVE
1 km
Vernier
GENÈVE
Cornavin
Eaux-Vives
Chêne-Bourg
Champel
Lancy-Pont-Rouge
Annemasse
FRANCE
Lancy-Bachet

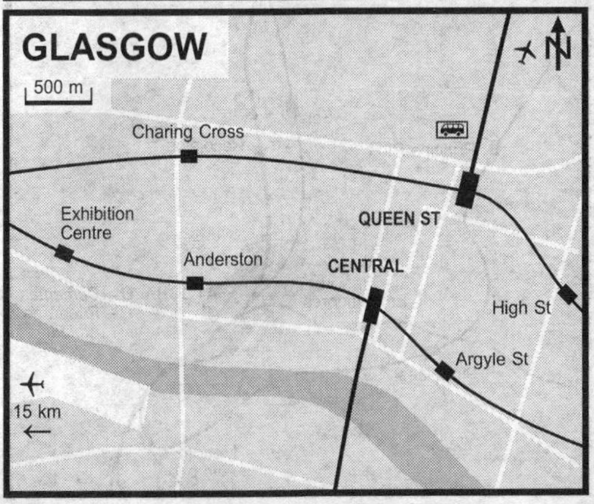
GLASGOW
500 m
Charing Cross
Exhibition
Centre
QUEEN ST
Anderston
CENTRAL
High St
Argyle St
15 km

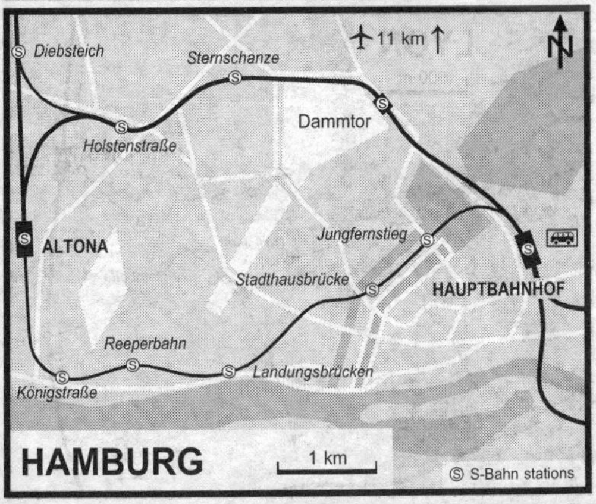
Diebsteich
11 km
Sternschanze
Dammtor
Holstenstraße
ALTONA
Jungfernstieg
Stadthausbrücke
HAUPTBAHNHOF
Reeperbahn
Landungsbrücken
Königstraße
HAMBURG
1 km
S-Bahn stations

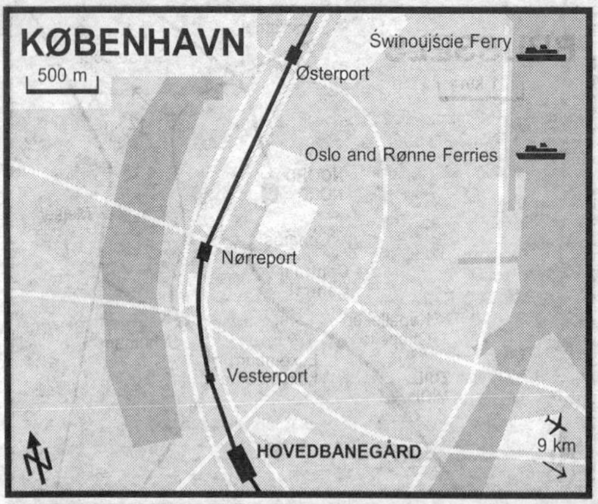
KØBENHAVN
500 m
Świnoujście Ferry
Østerport
Oslo and Rønne Ferries
Nørreport
Vesterport
HOVEDBANEGÅRD
9 km
N

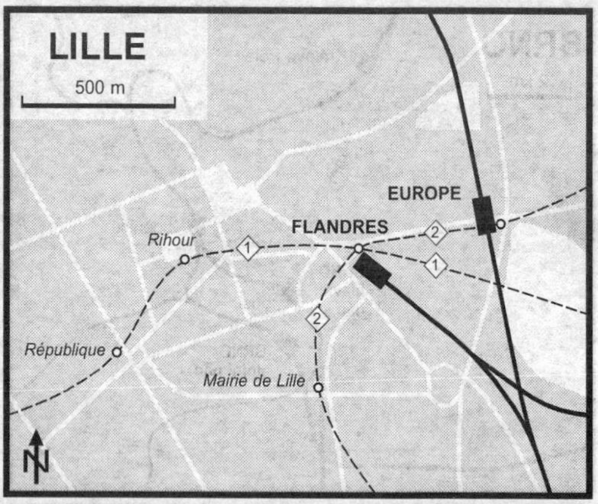
LILLE
500 m
EUROPE
FLANDRES
Rihour
1
2
République
Mairie de Lille
N

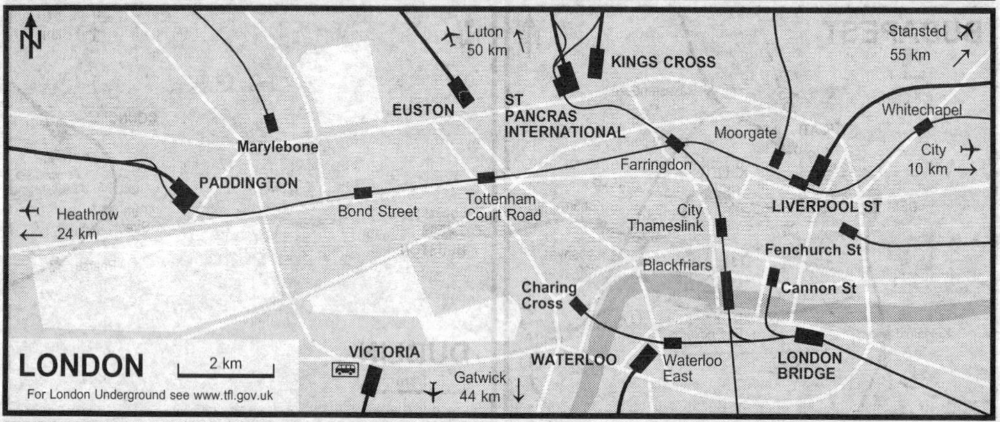
N
Luton
50 km
Stansted
55 km
KINGS CROSS
EUSTON
ST PANCRAS INTERNATIONAL
Whitechapel
Marylebone
Moorgate
City
10 km
Farringdon
PADDINGTON
Tottenham Court Road
Bond Street
LIVERPOOL ST
Heathrow
24 km
City Thameslink
Fenchurch St
Blackfriars
Charing Cross
Cannon St
VICTORIA
WATERLOO
Waterloo East
LONDON BRIDGE
Gatwick
44 km
LONDON
2 km
For London Underground see www.tfl.gov.uk

Entrecampos
Roma
Sete Rios
Roma-Areeiro
Sintra
Oriente
Areeiro
Campolide
Alameda
São Sebastião
Oriente
Marquês de Pombal
Rato
Restauradores
SANTA APOLÓNIA
Rossio
Baixa-Chiado
Rossio
Cascais
Cais do Sodré
Terreiro do Paço
1 km
Barreiro
LISBOA
N

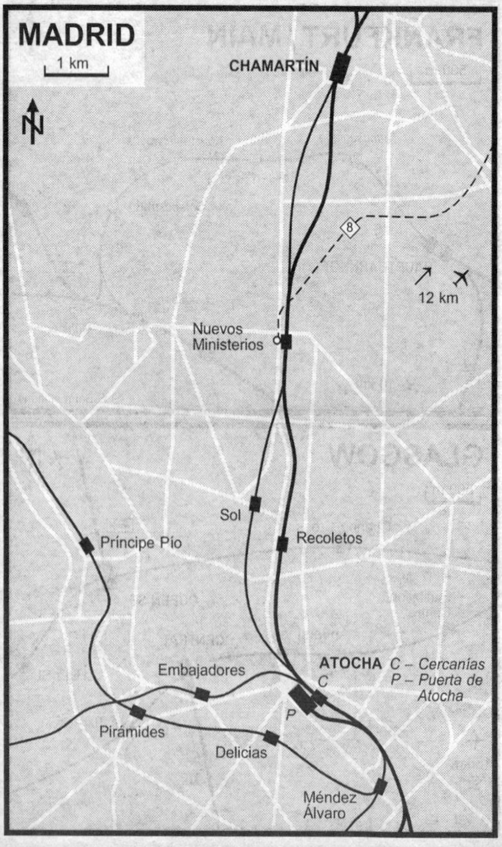
MADRID
1 km
CHAMARTÍN
N
8
12 km
Nuevos Ministerios
Sol
Recoletos
Príncipe Pío
Embajadores
ATOCHA
C – Cercanías
P – Puerta de Atocha
C
P
Pirámides
Delicias
Méndez Álvaro

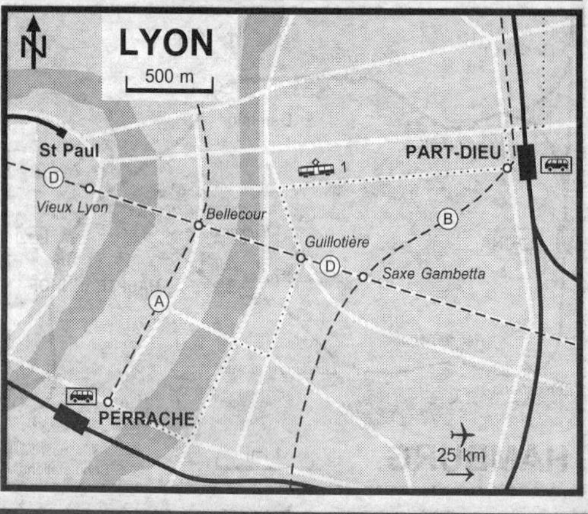
N
LYON
500 m
St Paul
PART-DIEU
1
D
Vieux Lyon
B
Bellecour
Guillotière
D
Saxe Gambetta
A
PERRACHE
25 km

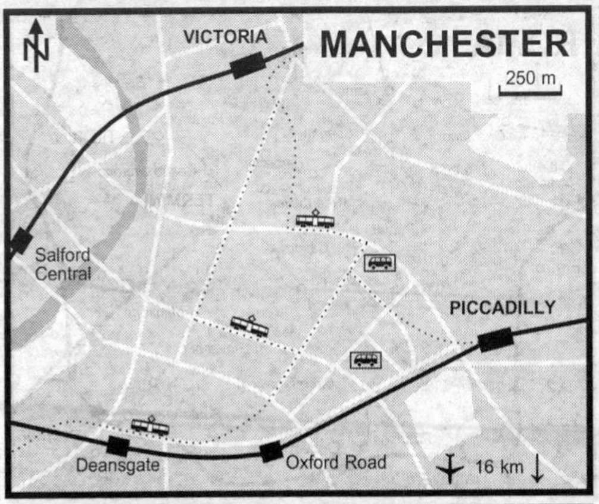
MANCHESTER
250 m
VICTORIA
Salford Central
PICCADILLY
Deansgate
Oxford Road
16 km

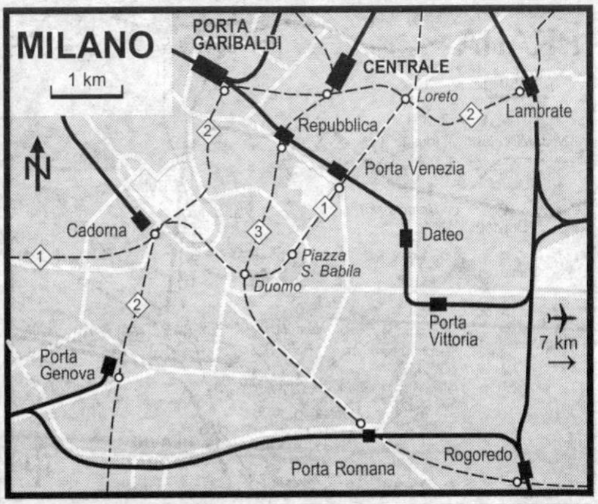
MILANO
1 km
PORTA GARIBALDI
CENTRALE
Loreto
Lambrate
Repubblica
Porta Venezia
Cadorna
Dateo
Piazza S. Babila
Duomo
Porta Vittoria
7 km
Porta Genova
Rogoredo
Porta Romana

27 km
Savyolovsky
Rizhskaya
Yaroslavskaya
BELORUSSKAYA
(Smolenskaya)
OKTYABRSKAYA
(Leningradski vokzal)
Komsomolskaya
Kazanskaya
Kurskaya
KIYEVSKAYA
Paveletskaya
MOSKVA
1 km

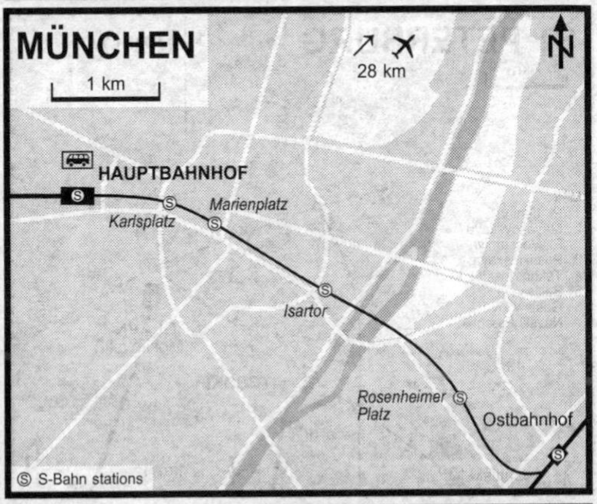
MÜNCHEN
1 km
28 km
HAUPTBAHNHOF
Marienplatz
Karlsplatz
Isartor
Rosenheimer Platz
Ostbahnhof
Ⓢ S-Bahn stations

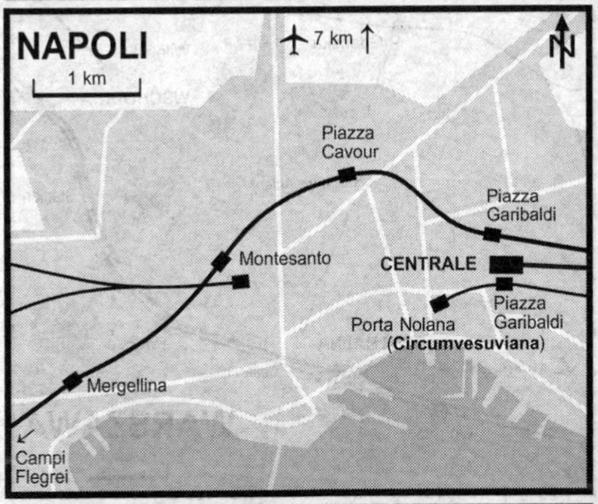
NAPOLI
1 km
7 km
Piazza Cavour
Piazza Garibaldi
Montesanto
CENTRALE
Piazza Garibaldi
Porta Nolana
(Circumvesuviana)
Mergellina
Campi Flegrei

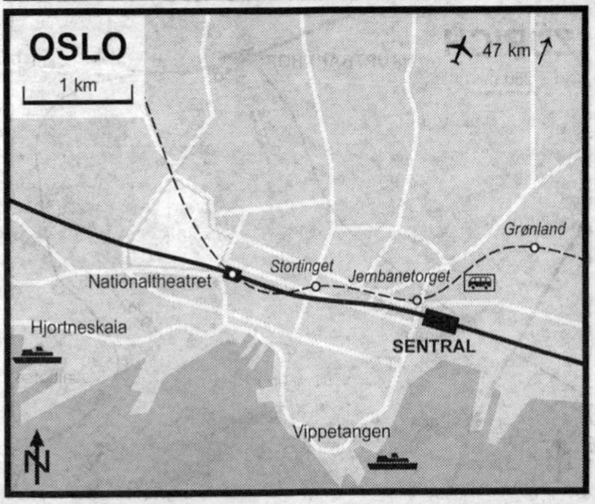
OSLO
1 km
47 km
Grønland
Nationaltheatret
Stortinget
Jernbanetorget
Hjortneskaia
SENTRAL
Vippetangen

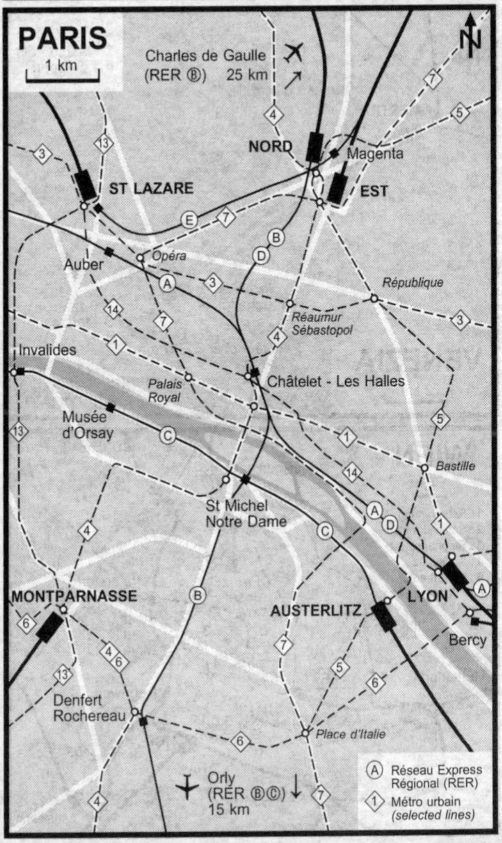
PARIS
1 km
Charles de Gaulle
(RER Ⓑ) 25 km
NORD
Magenta
ST LAZARE
EST
Auber
Opéra
République
Réaumur Sébastopol
Invalides
Châtelet - Les Halles
Palais Royal
Musée d'Orsay
Bastille
St Michel Notre Dame
MONTPARNASSE
AUSTERLITZ
LYON
Bercy
Denfert Rochereau
Place d'Italie
Orly
(RER ⒷⒸ)
15 km
Ⓐ Réseau Express Régional (RER)
◇ Métro urbain
(selected lines)

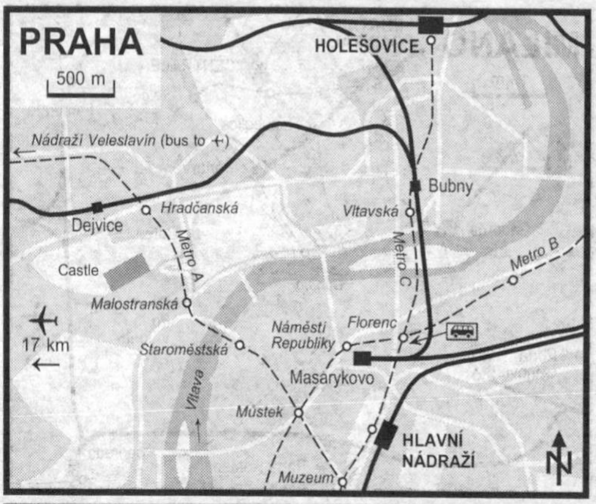
PRAHA
500 m
HOLEŠOVICE
Nádraží Veleslavín (bus to ✈)
Bubny
Dejvice
Hradčanská
Vltavská
Metro A
Metro C
Metro B
Castle
Malostranská
17 km
Staroměstská
Náměstí Republiky
Florenc
Masarykovo
Vltava
Můstek
HLAVNÍ NÁDRAŽÍ
Muzeum

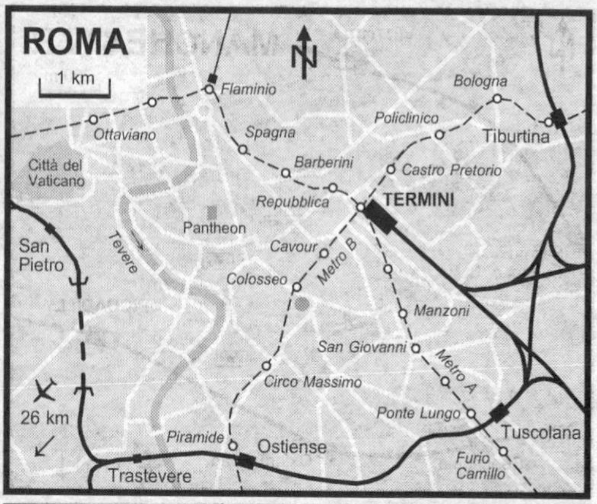
ROMA
1 km
Flaminio
Bologna
Ottaviano
Spagna
Policlinico
Tiburtina
Città del Vaticano
Barberini
Castro Pretorio
Repubblica
TERMINI
San Pietro
Pantheon
Tevere
Cavour
Metro B
Colosseo
Manzoni
San Giovanni
Metro A
Circo Massimo
26 km
Ponte Lungo
Piramide
Ostiense
Tuscolana
Trastevere
Furio Camillo

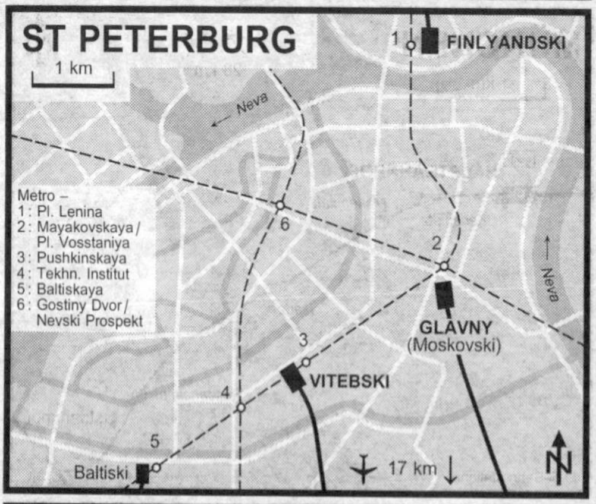
ST PETERBURG
1 km
1
FINLYANDSKI
Neva
Metro –
1 : Pl. Lenina
2 : Mayakovskaya / Pl. Vosstaniya
3 : Pushkinskaya
4 : Tekhn. Institut
5 : Baltiskaya
6 : Gostiny Dvor / Nevski Prospekt
6
2
Neva
GLAVNY (Moskovski)
3
VITEBSKI
4
5
Baltiski
17 km

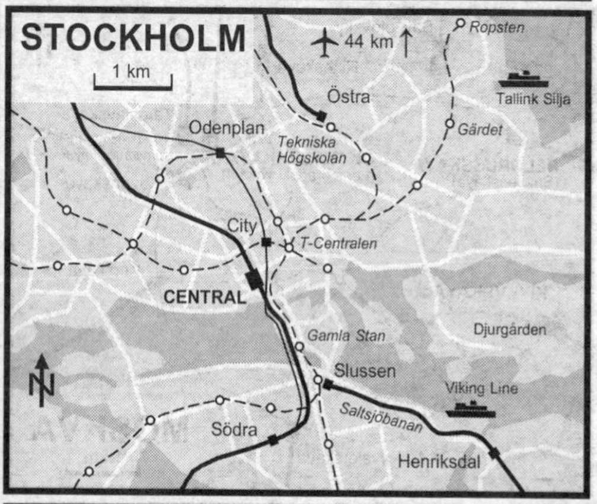
STOCKHOLM
1 km
44 km
Ropsten
Östra
Tallink Silja
Odenplan
Tekniska Högskolan
Gärdet
City
T-Centralen
CENTRAL
Gamla Stan
Djurgården
Slussen
Viking Line
Saltsjöbanan
Södra
Henriksdal

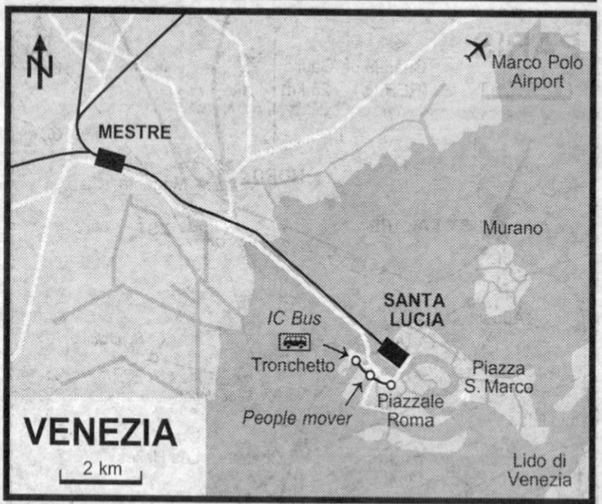
Marco Polo Airport
MESTRE
Murano
SANTA LUCIA
IC Bus
Tronchetto
Piazza S. Marco
Piazzale Roma
People mover
VENEZIA
2 km
Lido di Venezia

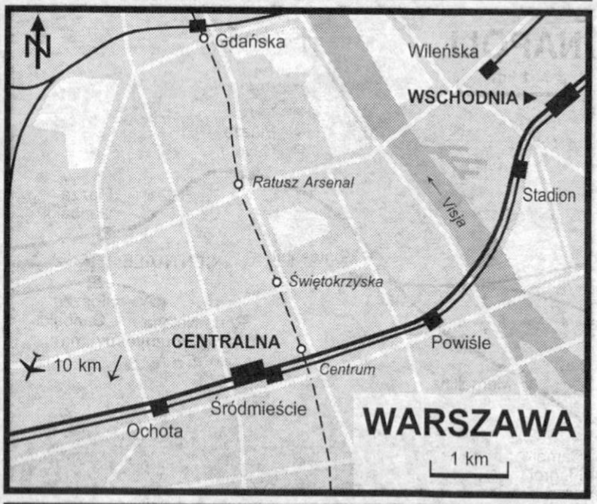
Gdańska
Wileńska
WSCHODNIA
Stadion
Ratusz Arsenal
Visla
Świętokrzyska
CENTRALNA
Powiśle
10 km
Centrum
Ochota
Śródmieście
WARSZAWA
1 km

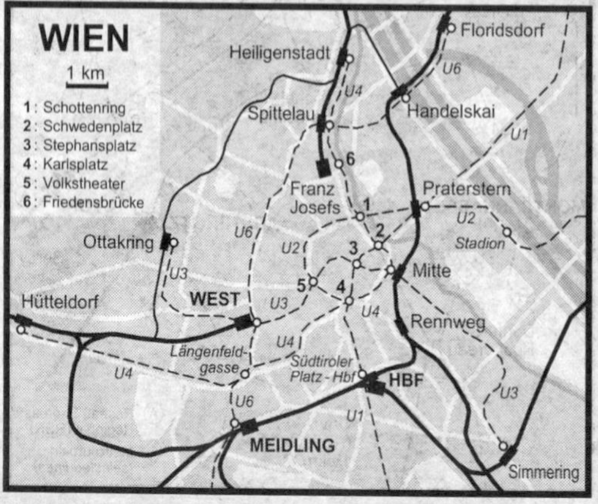
WIEN
1 km
1 : Schottenring
2 : Schwedenplatz
3 : Stephansplatz
4 : Karlsplatz
5 : Volkstheater
6 : Friedensbrücke
Floridsdorf
Heiligenstadt
U6
U4
Spittelau
Handelskai
U1
6
Franz Josefs
Praterstern
1
U2
Ottakring
U6
2
Stadion
U2
3
U3
Mitte
5
4
Hütteldorf
WEST
U3
U4
Rennweg
Längenfeld-gasse
U4
Südtiroler Platz - Hbf
HBF
U4
U6
U1
U3
MEIDLING
Simmering

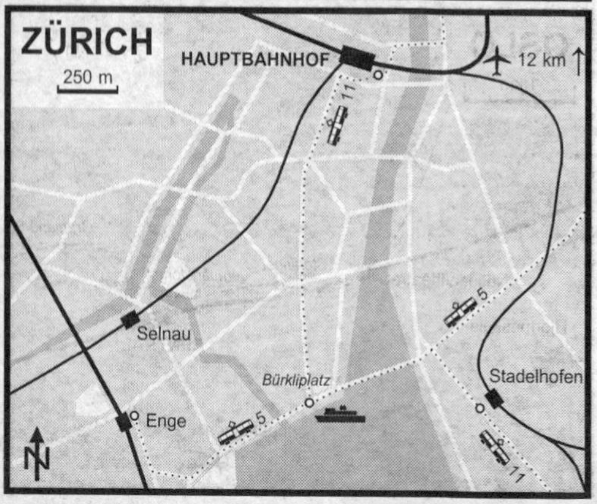
ZÜRICH
250 m
HAUPTBAHNHOF
12 km
11
5
Selnau
Bürkliplatz
Stadelhofen
Enge
5
11

SELECTED DAILY INTERNATIONAL SLEEPER SERVICES

From	To	Train no.	Brand	Facilities and owner	Train Name	International table no.
Amsterdam	Zürich	403/402	Nightjet	1, 2 cl.(öbb), 2 cl.(öbb)		73
Amsterdam	Wien	40421/40490	Nightjet	1, 2 cl. (öbb), 2 cl.(öbb)		73
Stuttgart	Budapest	50237/50462	Euro Night	1, 2 cl.(mav), 2 cl.(mav)	Kálmán Imre	32, 65
Wien	Bucureşti	347/346	Euro Night	1, 2 cl.(cfr), 2 cl.(cfr), (cfr)	Dacia	32, 61
Wien	Bucureşti	50347/349	Euro Night	1, 2 cl.(cfr)		61
Budapest	Bucureşti	473/472	Euro Night	1, 2 cl.(cfr), 1, 2 cl.(cfr)	Ister	32, 61
Zürich	Praha	50467/50466	Euro Night	1, 2 cl. (čd)		52
Zürich	Praha	458/459	Euro Night	1, 2 cl. (čd)	Canopus	52, 54
Berlin	Zürich	409/408	Nightjet	1, 2 cl. (öbb), 2 cl.(öbb)		54, 73
Berlin	Wien	457/456	Nightjet	1, 2 cl. (öbb), 2 cl.(öbb)	Metropol	77
Berlin	Budapest	40457 / 40476	Nightjet	1, 2 cl. (mav), 2 cl.(mav)	Metropol	77
Warszawa	Kyiv	68/67		1, 2 cl.(uz)	Kyiv Ekspres	56
Praha	Budapest	573-477/476-572	Euro Night	1, 2 cl. (čd), 2 cl.(čd)	Metropol	60
Budapest	Beograd	341/340		1, 2 cl.(žs), 2 cl.(žs)		61
Beograd	Thessaloníki	335/334		2 cl.(mz)	Hellas Express	61
Bucuresti	Istanbul	461/492		2 cl. 4-berth (tcdd)	Bosphor	61
Hamburg	Wien	491/490	Nightjet	1, 2 cl. (öbb), 2 cl.(öbb)		53, 64
Hamburg	Zürich	471/470	Nightjet	1, 2 cl. (öbb), 2 cl.(öbb)		54, 73
Hamburg	Innsbruck	40491/40420	Nightjet	1, 2 cl. (öbb), 2 cl.(öbb)		53, 64
München	Roma	295/294	Nightjet	1, 2 cl. (db), 2 cl.(db)		70
Stuttgart	Venezia	237/236	Nightjet	1, 2 cl. (db), 2 cl.(db)		70
München	La Spezia	40295/40235	Nightjet	1, 2 cl. (db), 2 cl.(db)		70
Stuttgart	Zagreb	50237/414	Euro Night	1, 2 cl.(hz), 2 cl.(hz)		62
Stuttgart	Rijeka	60237/480	Euro Night	1, 2 cl.(hz)		62
Zürich	Zagreb	40465/40414	Euro Night	1, 2 cl.(hz), 2 cl.(hz)		86
Zürich	Budapest	40467/40462	Euro Night	1, 2 cl.(mav), 2 cl.(mav)		86
Zürich	Graz	465/464	Nightjet	1, 2 cl. (öbb), 2 cl.(öbb)		86
Zürich	Wien	467/466	Nightjet	1, 2 cl. (öbb), 2 cl.(öbb)		86
Wien	Roma	40233/40294	Nightjet	1, 2 cl. (öbb), 2 cl.(öbb)		88
Wien	Venezia	237/236	Nightjet	1, 2 cl. (öbb), 2 cl.(öbb)		88
Wien	La Spezia	233/235	Nightjet	1, 2 cl.(ti), 2 cl.(ti)		88
Košice	Kyiv	8813-29/81-8812		1, 2 cl.(uz)		96
Wien	Kyiv	40147/40749		1, 2 cl.(uz)	Hortobágy	96
Warszawa	Budapest	407-457-477 / 476-456-406		1, 2 cl.(pkp), 2 cl.(pkp)		99
Warszawa	Wien	407/40456		1, 2 cl. (pkp)	Chopin	99
Warszawa	Praha	407-442 / 443-406		1, 2 cl.(pkp), 2 cl.(pkp)		99
Non daily sleepers (other seasonal services operate):						
Düsseldorf	Wien	40421/40490	Nightjet	1, 2 cl. (öbb), 2 cl.(öbb)		28, 53, 66
Düsseldorf	Innsbruck	421/420	Nightjet	1, 2 cl. (öbb), 2 cl.(öbb)		28, 53
Brussels	Wien	425/50490	Nightjet	1, 2 cl. (öbb), 2 cl.(öbb)		21, 53
Paris	Wien	469/468	Nightjet	1, 2 cl. (öbb), 2 cl.(öbb)		32
Amsterdam	Innsbruck	421/420	Nightjet	1, 2 cl. (öbb), 2 cl.(öbb)		28, 53
Berlin	Stockholm	301/300	Euro Night	2 cl.(bne)	Berlin Night Express	50

Note: This list excludes trains not shown in our International section (e.g. Czech Republic to Slovakia, Ukraine to Russia).

Shower.

Shaded services are suspended until further notice.

Key to ownership of sleeping cars:
bdz - Bulgarian; bc - Belarussian; bne - Berlin Night Express; cd - Czech; cfr - Romanian; db - German; hz - Croatian;
mav - Hungarian; mz - Macedonian; öbb - Austrian; pkp - Polish; renfe - Spanish; rzd - Russian; sbb - Swiss; ti - Italian;
uz - Ukrainian; zs - Serbian.

Steam trains in the European Rail Timetable

There are numerous tourist and heritage lines operating around Europe, most of which operate a seasonal service using steam or heritage diesel traction. Unfortunately, space limitations mean that we are unable to show timings for most of these lines. However, there are a number of routes that offer a daily service throughout the year and for these we do include timings, together with a few services hauled by steam traction on main-line rail routes. The panel below lists tourist railway **steam** train schedules that are included in our regular timetable pages.

Readers should note that our expanded seasonal editions (published in March, June, September and December) provide details of many other tourist railways in our special ***Rail Extra*** feature, including a brief description of selected routes and an overview of the service provided. The feature also includes other useful rail travel information on a country by country basis.

COUNTRY	RAILWAY	TABLE	NOTES
GREAT BRITAIN	The Shakespeare Express	**127**	Regular summer Sunday main-line steam excursions between Stratford upon Avon and Birmingham
	Ffestiniog / Welsh Highland Railways	**160**	Two narrow gauge railways linked at Porthmadog running through spectacular Welsh mountain landscapes
	North Yorkshire Moors Railway	**211**	Regular services run from spring to autumn, many steam-hauled through to Whitby via a link to the main line at Grosmont
	The Jacobite	**218**	A regular main-line steam excursion operating from spring to autumn over the spectacular West Highland line
FRANCE	Train des Pignes	**359**	A summer Sunday steam-hauled service running over part of the scenic Nice to Digne route
SWITZERLAND	Brienz Rothorn Bahn	**553**	A swiss mountain rack railway operating regular steam services from June to October
PORTUGAL	Comboio Historico	**694**	Enjoy a steam-hauled journey along the scenic Douro Valley between Régua and Tua at weekends from June to October
SWEDEN	Arvidsjaur Jämvägsförening	**766**	Operates twice a week from mid-July to early August over a section of the Inlandsbanan (Arvidsjaur - Slagnäs)
GERMANY	Rügensche Bäderbahn	**844a**	Daily steam services on the island of Rügen
	Lößnitzgrundbahn	**853**	Daily steam services between Radebeul Ost and Radeburg (near Dresden)
	Weißeritztalbahn	**853**	Daily steam services between Freital-Hainsberg and Kurort Kipsdorf (near Dresden)
	Zittauer Schmalspurbahn	**853**	Daily steam services between Zittau and Kurort Jonsdorf / Kurort Oybin
	Harzer Schmalspurbahnen	**867**	A famous narrow gauge network in central Germany with some services steam-hauled on a daily basis
	Fichtelbergbahn	**882**	Daily steam services between Cranzahl and Kurort Oberwiesenthal
AUSTRIA	Zillertalbahn	**955**	A single return steam service runs on selected days from May to October
	Achenseebahn	**956**	A narrow gauge steam rack railway with daily services running May to October
	Pinzgauer Lokalbahn	**957**	A single return steam service runs once or twice a week at certain times of the year
	Schneebergbahn	**984**	Most service are operated by modern diesel trains but a steam service also runs on Sundays during the summer
	Mariazellerbahn	**994**	An occasional steam service runs along this world famous mountain route (also a service hauled by heritage electric traction)
	Murtalbahn	**998**	Steam trains run between Murau and Tamsweg once or twice a week during the summer
POLAND	Koleje Wielkopolskie	**1099**	The popular scheduled steam services operating on the Wolsztyn to Poznań and Wolsztyn to Leszno routes
CZECH REPUBLIC	Jindřichohradecké Místní Dráhy	**1169**	A steam train runs on Saturdays from April to September (daily during July and August)

JANUARY NEWSLINES

INTERNATIONAL

We understand that RENFE (Spanish Railways) may reinstate its international high-speed services Madrid – Barcelona – Marseille (*AVE* **19725/19730**) and Barcelona – Lyon (*AVE* **10737/10742**) as early as Monday January 16 (Tables **13** and **657**). The Marseille train will initially run four days a week, departing Madrid at 1325, returning from Marseille at 0803. The Lyon service will run Mondays to Fridays, departing Barcelona at 0822, returning from Lyon at 1435. Both services are expected to run daily from May 24.

The *Kulturzug / Pociag do Kultury* service between Berlin and Wrocław was suspended from January 2. We await confirmation of the date when it will return, possibly during the spring (Tables **58** and **1086**).

European Sleeper Coöperatie U.A. has announced its overnight service will commence from May 25 between Brussels and Berlin via Amsterdam (Table **78**). The service is expected to be extended to Dresden and Praha from December 2023 (this is not currently possible due to ongoing engineering work in the Czech Republic limiting the number of trains that can use the route).

In a late timetable change, the overnight service Stuttgart – Venezia (*NJ* **237/236**), Zagreb (*EN* **40237/414**) and Budapest (*EN* **50237/50462**) does not now serve München Hbf. However, it continues to call at München Ost in both directions (Tables **62**, **65**, **70**, **890** and **930**).

GREAT BRITAIN

The opening of a new station at Inverness Airport did not take place on December 11, as reported in last month's Newslines (Table **225**). The revised opening date for the station is now January 21.

FRANCE

While rechecking TER schedules in the Hauts-de-France and Normandie regions (Tables **251**– **277**) we noticed a number of changes compared to information published in the Winter edition, most notably that some trains during the middle part of the day do not run and that certain evening peak trains only run on Fridays. In addition, services between Boulogne and Calais (Table **261**) are operated by bus until February 5 (please check locally for amended timings).

The validity of the current Corsican Railways timetable has been extended to February 26 (Table **369**).

NETHERLANDS

New schedules in the Netherlands saw a general reduction in the number of services operating on certain routes, particularly on Fridays to Sundays. Unfortunately we did not manage to include all of these changes in time for the Winter edition meaning a number of tables were not showing the correct timetable, for which we must apologise. However, all tables have now been fully checked and updated and, to better show the amended service patterns, we have made a number of structural changes to certain tables. Note that the service between Dordrecht and Lelystad via Amsterdam Zuid (which no longer runs at weekends), has been moved from Table **460** to a new Table **452**.

SPAIN

The Madrid – Orihuela high-speed line extension to Murcia was inaugurated on December 20 with the three existing high-speed *AVE* services between Madrid and Orihuela extended to Murcia, together with the addition of a fourth service between the cities (Table **668**). RENFE (Spanish Railways) has also introduced up to ten *Avant* local high-speed services in each direction between Alicant and Murcia which have been added to an expanded panel below Table **672**.

Intercity services between Barcelona and València have been retimed, including train **697/694** *Torre del Oro* Barcelona – València – Sevilla – Cádiz, timings for which will be found in Tables **661**, **668**, **671**, **672**, **672a** and **678**.

Early morning weekend services on the Plasencia – Mérida – Badajoz axis have been retimed (Tables **677** and **678**). The first *Alvia* service from Madrid to Salamanca has also been retimed on Saturdays and Sundays (Table **679**).

Rail services between Canfranc and Huesca have resumed following the completion of route upgrade work (Table **670**).

In order to include Murcia in Table **668**, we have had to make a number of table number changes. The Madrid – Cartagena table, previously **668a**, has been moved to page 325 and renumbered **672b**. The Granada – Málaga / Córdoba – Sevilla table, previously **673**, has been moved to page 327 and renumbered **678a** (the previous Table **678a**, Barcelona / Madrid – Granada, has been removed as these journeys are already shown in Table **660**).

PORTUGAL

For the first time in several years, CP (Portuguese Railways) issued a general timetable revision on December 11 alongside most of the rest of Europe. Unfortunately, the new schedules were received too late for inclusion in the Winter edition, but the Portuguese section has now been fully updated with the revised schedules.

NORWAY

A brand new 22-kilometre double-track line, mostly in tunnel, between Oslo and Ski was opened on December 11. With a maximum permitted speed of 200 km/h journey times on the Oslo – Halden – Göteborg route were initially reduced by around ten minutes. However, a serious technical issue arose, resulting in the line being closed a few days later. As a result, trains are currently being diverted via the original route with extended journey times. It is hoped the tunnel will reopen by February 1 when the faster journey times will be restored. We have added an appropriate warning to Table **770** with regards to amended timings at Oslo while the problem with the new infrastructure is being resolved.

GERMANY

A small number of long-distance trains on the Köln – Koblenz – Mainz – Mannheim – Stuttgart route have been temporarily withdrawn from early January, but are due to be reinstated from April (Tables **800** and **912**).

Services between Görlitz and Zittau are partially operated by bus (between Hagenwerda and Zittau) until June 10. Table **854** has been updated with amended timings.

POLAND

Many Szczecin – Rzepin – Poznań – Warszawa *InterCity* services in Table **1003** have been switched to the more direct route via Krzyż (Table **1010**).

CZECH REPUBLIC

In last month's Tables **60** and **1100**, *RJ* **258/9** *Vindobona* Graz – Wien – Praha was shown as running to and from Děčín, but this subsequently turned out not to be the case at this present time. However, the Děčín extension is expected to commence from July 1 when the service will be renumbered **256/7**.

SLOVAKIA

We have rechecked all of our Slovakian tables against recently updated information and there have been a number of minor timing and train number changes. In Table **1180**, most *Ex* trains between Bratislava and Košice have had calls at Margecany added (these calls were not shown in earlier versions of the timetables). Owing to a compiling error, we included some trains between Starý Smokovec and Tatranská Lomnica in Table **1182** which are not currently running, so we have removed them for the time being. We will reinstate them once a date for the start of these services has been announced.

TURKEY

TCDD (Turkish Railways) has once again recast its high-speed schedules (Table **1570**). Timings of some long-distance express trains have also been adjusted, along with most regional services.

A much reduced service is currently running on the busy Mersin to Adana route (Table **1585**). This is due to route upgrade work taking place which is part of the long-term Mersin – Adana – Osmaniye – Gaziantep – Şanlıurfa high-speed project.

FEBRUARY NEWSLINES

INTERNATIONAL

More details of the merger between Thalys and Eurostar were revealed recently. Trains from both companies will have new branding applied with the Thalys brand disappearing completely. The websites, apps and loyalty schemes will also be combined. Spare Eurostar trains will be used on existing Thalys services to increase capacity.

Berlin Night Express between Berlin and Stockholm (trains **301/300**) will run daily except Saturdays from March 30 to November 6. Swedish Railways' overnight service between Stockholm and Hamburg (*EN* **497/496**) will be extended to Berlin from April 11 (Table **50**).

Kulturzug / Pociag do Kultury Berlin – Wrocław was suspended from January 2 and we are still awaiting confirmation of when it will start running again, possibly from April (Tables **58** and **1086**).

GREAT BRITAIN

The service between Bedford and Bletchley is operated by bus until at least May 20 (Table **142a**). This is due to Vivarail, the maintainers of the rolling stock used on the route, going into administration.

Tables **115** (Bristol – Taunton) and **118** (Cardiff – Bristol) have been combined to form a revised Table **115**. Hopefully this will make it easier to plan journeys in the area with through journeys more clearly shown (with the use of footnotes greatly reduced).

SWITZERLAND

The Swiss *Rheintallinie* between Sargans and Rorschach will be partially operated by bus for eight months from February 27 to October 29. This is to allow major track upgrade work to take place between Buchs and Altstätten, including track doubling in certain locations. A special version of Table **534** will be found on page 561 with amended schedules during this period.

SPAIN

Having obtained the necessary documentation, Renfe (Spanish Railways) commenced driver training from January 16 on the international routes to Marseille and Lyon. Once driver training is complete, Renfe intend to start running *AVE* **19725/19730** Madrid – Marseille and *AVE* **10737/10742** Barcelona – Lyon as soon as possible in their previous train paths. The Marseille service will initially run four days per week departing Madrid at 1325 and returning from Marseille at 0803 the following day. The Lyon service will run Mondays to Fridays in both directions, departing Barcelona at 0822 and returning from Lyon at 1435. Both services may start running daily from late May (Tables **13** and **657**).

Antequera AV station opened on January 25 following the closure of the adjacent Antequera Ciudad station the previous day. *Avant* high-speed shuttle services between Granada and Sevilla / Málaga (Table **678a**), together with *AVE* services between Barcelona / Madrid and Granada (Table **660**) now make additional stops at Antequera AV which has resulted in some timing adjustments. On the same date, the fourth *Avant* service between Granada and Sevilla, which was suspended at the beginning of the pandemic, was reinstated.

Additional *AVE* services commenced between Madrid and Málaga on January 23 (Table **660**). The Sundays only 2030 departure from Madrid to Málaga (*AVE* **2202**) and 2000 from Málaga to Madrid (*AVE* **2203**) now run daily. The final *AVE* service on Fridays from Madrid to Málaga now departs later at 2130; the last Sunday departure from Málaga to Madrid has been retimed to depart 78 minutes later, at 2118.

As expected, *iryo* introduced two high-speed services in each direction between Madrid and València on December 16 with two further services to be added from February 10 (Table **668**). *iryo*'s Spanish network will expand further from March 31 with two services between Madrid and Sevilla and two between Madrid and Málaga with additional trains added from May 5 and May 19 (Table **660**). The Madrid to Alacant route will also gain an *iryo* service from June 2 (Table **668**).

NORWAY

Following on from last month's news item about problems with the operation of the new 22-kilometre double-track line between Oslo and Ski, the latest official information states that it will remain closed until further notice. However, some reports suggest that it may reopen by mid-February. We have updated the warning in Table **770** with regards to amended timings at Oslo which apply until the problem with the new infrastructure has been resolved.

GERMANY

The line between Dessau and Bitterfeld is partially closed until April 21 which affects regional services in the area. Rail replacement buses will run between Dessau and Wolfen and the amended schedules will be found in a special version of Table **848** on page 562.

A reduced service will operate on the route between Nürnberg and Bamberg from February 11 to March 31 to enable route upgrade work to take place. This will affect both long-distance and regional services with affected trains indicated in Tables **850** and **875**.

The 15-kilometre section of line between Rostock and Rövershagen will be closed from March 4 to April 14 affecting journeys between Rostock and Stralsund. Our previously published special version of Table **830**, which shows amended timings during the work, has been further updated with the addition of non-stop rail replacement buses between Rostock and Stralsund which connect with *IC* and *ICE* services. The amended table will be found on page 562.

POLAND

Services between Katowice and Bielsko Biała are subject to alteration from February 25 with buses replacing trains between the two stations (Table **1060**).

SLOVAKIA

Schedules of local services between Bratislava and Nové Zámky have been altered with some trains withdrawn and journey times increased by up to 30 minutes (Table **1175**).

HUNGARY

There are a number of minor changes from February 4 as follows:

An additional late evening service from Füzesabony (departing 2255) to Miskolc has been introduced (Table **1261**).

The 0612 from Hatvan now departs earlier, at 0608 (Table **1262**).

All of the hourly *IC* trains in Table **1270** once again call at Püspökladány (this station call had been reduced to one train every two hours at the December timetable change).

The frequency of the tram-train service between Szeged and Hódmezővásárhely increases to every 20 minutes at peak times on Mondays to Fridays (Table **1292**).

LITHUANIA

Work to electrify the railway between Kaišiadorys and Radviliškis will cause significant alteration to services in Table **1805** from February 6 until May. As we closed for press, revised schedules for the period were still to be confirmed but on Mondays to Saturdays there will be two return train pairs Vilnius – Klaipeda with no trains running between Kaunas and Šiauliai. Services between Klaipeda and Šiauliai will not be running all the way to Šiauliai. On Sundays, services Vilnius – Klaipeda and Kaunas – Šiauliai will run as normal. We strongly advise readers check timings locally using the website www.ltglink.lt. The next stage of electrification is planned from the autumn of 2023 when work will take place between Šiauliai and Klaipeda.

BEYOND EUROPE - CHINA

High-speed rail services between Guangzhou and Hong Kong resumed on January 15 (Table **7105**).

BEYOND EUROPE - THAILAND

Thursday January 19 saw the opening of the new Bangkok Krung Thep Aphiwat Central Terminal station (Bangkok Revolution Central Station, formerly known as Bang Sue Grand). All long-distance trains (except those on the Eastern line and with numbers in the 200 and 300 series) will use the new station. The station is also currently served by the SRT Dark Red, Light Red and Airport Link commuter rail routes as well as a large number of bus routes, and in the future will also be served by the Don Mueang–Suvarnabhumi–U-Tapao high-speed railway and planned high-speed routes to Nong Khai, Padang Besar and Chiang Mai. We plan to show updated timings for all services in the Beyond Europe section of the Spring edition.

BEYOND EUROPE - NORTH AMERICA

Works to restore and stabilise the railway between San Clemente and Oceanside in California (Table **9322**) have been delayed due to heavy rain, with passenger services now expected to resume in March rather than February. We have been informed that Amtrak plans to restore a second daily round trip on the Cascades route between Seattle and Vancouver from March 7 (Table **9315**).

AUTO-TRAIN, AUTOREISEZÜGE, MOTORAIL

Car-carrying trains are composed of special wagons or vans for the conveyance of motorcars usually with sleeping cars and couchettes enabling the driver and passengers to travel overnight in comfort in the same train. Some services convey vehicles separately allowing passengers a choice of trains for their own journey. Some shorter distance services run by day and convey seating coaches.

Cars are often loaded on the trains at separate stations from the passenger station and may be loaded some time before the passenger train departs. International car-carrying trains are shown in Table **1**, Domestic car-carrying trains in Table **2**. Some services also carry passengers without cars.

Details of Channel Tunnel shuttle services may be found on page 46. Details of domestic car-carrying shuttle trains may be found as follows: Austria (Table **969**), Germany (Table **821**), Italy (Table **590**), Slovenia (Table **1302**) and Switzerland (Tables **545** and **562**).

Readers should be careful to check that dates refer to current schedules, as old dates may be left in the table until such time as current information is received. Loading and train times may vary on some dates, but will be confirmed by the agent when booking.

Contact details:

BahnTouristikExpress: ✆ +49 (0)91 12 403 822. www.rdc-deutschland.de

ÖBB Nightjet: ✆ +43 (0) 5 1717. www.nightjet.com

Optima Tours: ✆ +49 (0)89 54 880 111. www.optimatours.de

Urlaubs-Express: ✆ +49 (0)22 18 002 0820. www.urlaubs-express.de

For the contact details of national operators please see the relevant country headings.

1 INTERNATIONAL CAR-CARRYING TRAINS

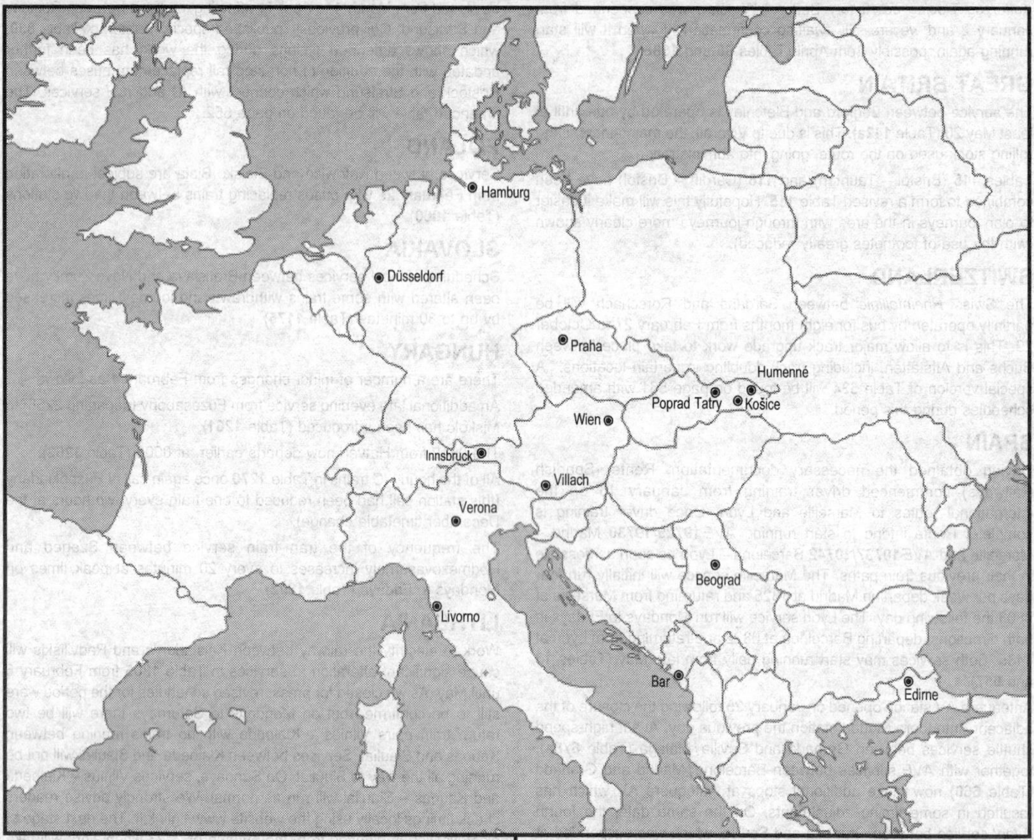

BAR

BEOGRAD:
Bar load time not advised, depart 1900, Beograd arrive 0615.
Train **432**: 🛏 1, 2 cl., ▬ 2 cl., 🚗.

BEOGRAD

BAR:
Beograd load time not advised, depart 2110, Bar arrive 0812.
Train **433**: 🛏 1, 2 cl., ▬ 2 cl., 🚗.

DÜSSELDORF

INNSBRUCK: *Urlaubs-Express*
July 4, Aug. 6, 25, Sept. 12, 22, Oct. 1.
Düsseldorf Hbf load time not advised, depart 2136, Innsbruck Hbf arrive 0829.
Train **1389**: 🛏, ▬ ✕.

VERONA: *Urlaubs-Express*
⑤ July 2 - Sept. 24 (not Aug. 6).
Düsseldorf Hbfload time not advised, depart 1844, Verona Porta Nuova arrive 0955.
Train **1385**: 🛏, ▬ ✕.

VILLACH: *Urlaubs-Express*
July 7, 21, Aug. 1, 15, 22, Sept. 5.
Düsseldorf Hbf load time not advised, depart 1934, Villach Autoverladung arrive 0846.
Train **1387**: 🛏, ▬ ✕.

WIEN: *Urlaubs-Express*
Sept. 19, Oct. 3, 8, 15.
Düsseldorf Hbf load time not advised, depart 2136, Wien Hbf ARZ arrive 0852.
Train **1851**: 🛏, ▬ ✕.

EDIRNE

VILLACH: *Optima Tours*
June 2, 6, 10, 16, 20, 24, 30, July 4, 8, 14, 18, 22, 28, Aug. 1, 5, 11, 15, 19, 25, 29, Sept. 2, 8, 15, 19, 23, 29, Oct. 3, 7, 13, 17, 21, 27, Nov. 2, 9.
Timings vary. ▬ ✕.

HAMBURG

INNSBRUCK: *ÖBB Nightjet*
Daily.
Hamburg Altona load 1900 - 1945, depart 2029, Innsbruck Hbf arrive 0914.
Train **40491**: 🛏 1, 2 cl., ▬ 2 cl. (4, 6 berth), 🚗.

VERONA: *Urlaubs-Express*
June 25, July 2, 9, 16, 23, 30, Aug. 13, 20, 27, Sept. 3, 10, 17, 24.
Hamburg Altona load time not advised, depart 1800, Verona Porta Nuova arrive 0955.
Train **1395**: 🛏, ▬ ✕.

VILLACH: *Urlaubs-Express*
June 23, July 7, 21, Aug. 1, 15, 22, Sept. 5.
Hamburg Altona load time not advised, depart 1851, Villach Autoverladung arrive 0846.
Train **1397**: 🛏, ▬ ✕.

WIEN: *Urlaubs-Express*
Sept. 19, Oct. 3, 8, 15.
Hamburg Altona load time not advised, depart 2035, Wien Hbf ARZ arrive 0852.
Train **1371**: 🛏, ▬ ✕.

HELSINKI

MOSKVA: *SERVICE SUSPENDED*
Helsinki load time not advised, depart 1844, Moskva Oktyabrskaya arrive 0919.
Train **31**: 🛏 1, 2 cl., ✕.

INTERNATIONAL CAR-CARRYING TRAINS

HUMENNÉ

PRAHA:
Daily (not Dec. 24, 31).
Humenné load 1835 - 1845, depart 1930, Praha hlavní nádraží arrive 0755.
Train *EN* **442**: 🛌 1, 2 cl., 🛏 2 cl. 🚗.

INNSBRUCK

DÜSSELDORF: *Urlaubs-Express*
July 15, Aug. 7, 26, Sept. 13, 23, Oct. 2.
Innsbruck Hbf load time not advised, depart 2012, Düsseldorf Hbf arrive 0708.
Train **1388**: 🛌, 🛏 ✕.

HAMBURG: *ÖBB Nightjet*
Daily.
Innsbruck Hbf load 1945 - 2005, depart 2044, Hamburg Altona arrive 0847.
Train **40420**: 🛌 1, 2 cl., 🛏 2 cl. (4, 6 berth), 🚗.

KOŠICE

PRAHA:
Daily.
Košice load 2005 - 2015, depart 2157, Praha hlavní nádraží arrive 0732.
Train *EN* **444**: 🛌 1, 2 cl., 🛏 2 cl. 🚗.

LIVORNO

WIEN: *ÖBB Nightjet*
④⑥ May 27 - Oct. 9.
Livorno Centrale load 1630 - 1800, depart 1920, Wien Hbf ARZ arrive 0842.
Train **1234**: 🛌 1, 2 cl., 🛏 2 cl. (4, 6 berth), 🚗 🍸.
Note: starts at Verona Porta Nuova Aug. 12 – 28 (load 1920 - 2020, d. 2153).

MOSKVA

HELSINKI: *SERVICE SUSPENDED*
Moskva Oktyabrskaya load time not advised, depart 2310, Helsinki arrive 1330.
Train **32**: 🛌 1, 2 cl., ✕.
Note: Helsinki arrival time is 1 hour earlier in Winter (see Table ***1910****).*

POPRAD TATRY

PRAHA:
⑥ until Oct. 30.
Poprad Tatry load 2205 - 2215, depart 2332, Praha hlavní nádraží arrive 0732.
Train *EN* **442**: 🛌 1, 2 cl., 🛏 2 cl. 🚗.

PRAHA

HUMENNÉ:
Daily (not Dec. 24, 31).
Praha hlavní nádraží load 1945 - 2000, depart 2205, Humenné arrive 1033.
Train *EN* **443**: 🛌 1, 2 cl., 🛏 2 cl. 🚗.

KOŠICE:
Daily.
Praha hlavní nádraží load 2000 - 1030, depart 2218, Košice arrive 0829.
Train *EN* **443**: 🛌 1, 2 cl., 🛏 2 cl. 🚗.

POPRAD TATRY:
⑤ until Oct. 29.
Praha hlavní nádraží load 2015 - 2045 (until Oct. 5), depart 2218, Poprad Tatry arrive 0641.
Train *EN* **443**: 🛌 1, 2 cl., 🛏 2 cl. 🚗.

SPLIT

WIEN: *ÖBB Nightjet*
③⑥ June 19 - Sept. 11.
Split load 1500 - 1545, depart 1648, Wien Hbf ARZ arrive 0858.
Train **1252**: 🛌, 🚗.

VERONA

DÜSSELDORF: *Urlaubs-Express*
⑥ June 26 - Sept. 25 (not Aug. 7).
Verona Porta Nuova load time not advised, depart 1805, Düsseldorf Hbf arrive 0843.
Train **1384**: 🛌, 🛏 ✕.

HAMBURG: *Urlaubs-Express*
June 26, July 3, 10, 17, 24, 31, Aug. 14, 21, 28, Sept. 4, 11, 18, 25.
Verona Porta Nuova load time not advised, depart 1805, Hamburg Altona arrive 0955.
Train **1394**: 🛌, 🛏 ✕.

VILLACH

DÜSSELDORF: *Urlaubs-Express*
July 8, 22, Aug. 2, 16, 23, Sept. 6.
Villach Autoverladung load time not advised, depart 1800, Düsseldorf Hbf arrive 0757.
Train **1386**: 🛌, 🛏 ✕.

EDIRNE: *Optima Tours*
June 4, 8, 12, 18, 22, 26, July 2, 6, 10, 16, 20, 24, 30, Aug. 3, 7, 13, 17, 21, 27, 31, Sept. 4, 11, 17, 21, 25, Oct. 1, 5, 9, 15, 19, 23, 29 Nov. 7.
Timings vary. 🛏 ✕.

HAMBURG: *Urlaubs-Express*
June 24, July 8, 22, Aug. 2, 16, 23, Sept. 6.
Villach Autoverladung load time not advised, depart 1800, Hamburg Altona arrive 0826.
Train **1396**: 🛌, 🛏 ✕.

WIEN

DÜSSELDORF: *Urlaubs-Express*
Sept. 20, Oct. 4, 9, 16.
Wien Hbf ARZ load time not advised, depart 1954, Düsseldorf arrive 0725.
Train **1850**: 🛌, 🛏 ✕.

HAMBURG: *Urlaubs-Express*
Sept. 20, Oct. 4, 9, 16.
Wien Hbf ARZ load time not advised, depart 1954, Hamburg Altona arrive 0852.
Train **1370**: 🛌, 🛏 ✕.

LIVORNO: *ÖBB Nightjet*
③⑤ May 26 - Oct. 8.
Wien Hbf ARZ load 1905 - 1930, depart 2001, Livorno Centrale arrive 0900.
Train **1237**: 🛌 1, 2 cl., 🛏 2 cl. (4, 6 berth), 🚗 🍸.
Note: terminates at Verona Porta Nuova Aug. 11 – 27 (a. 0638).

SPLIT: *ÖBB Nightjet*
②⑤ June 18 - Sept. 10.
Wien Hbf ARZ load 1600 - 1645, depart 1801, Split arive 0950.
Train **1253**: 🛌, 🚗.

DOMESTIC LONG-DISTANCE CAR-CARRYING TRAINS 2

AUSTRIA

Daily return services operate from Feldkirch to Graz, Villach and Wien Hbf ARZ.

CROATIA

Split - Zagreb and v.v.:
Split load times not advised, depart 2140, Zagreb a. 0547 (not July 28, 29, 31, Aug. 17, 21).
Zagreb load times not advised, depart 2305, Split a. 0705 (not July 28, 30, Aug. 16, 20, Sept. 4).
Summer only (until Sept. 4). Trains **820 / 821**: 🛌 1, 2 cl., 🛏 2 cl., 🚗.

FINLAND

Services operate on the following routes - contact operator for schedules:

Helsinki - Kemijärvi and v.v.
Helsinki - Oulu and v.v.
Kolari - Tampere and v.v.
Rovaniemi - Turku and v.v.
Helsinki - Kolari and v.v.
Helsinki - Rovaniemi and v.v.
Rovaniemi - Tampere and v.v.

Note: Helsinki trains load and unload at Pasila station (3 km north of Helsinki station)

GERMANY

Düsseldorf Hbf - **München** Ost and v.v. (operator: Urlaubs-Express):
From Düsseldorf July 4, 28, Aug. 11, Sept. 19, Oct. 3, 8, 15.
From München July 15, 29, Aug. 12, Sept. 20, Oct. 4, 9, 16.

Hamburg Altona - **Lörrach** and v.v. (operator: BahnTouristikExpress):
From Hamburg: June 4, 18, 23, 25, 27, July 1, 3, 6, 8, 10, 15 – 17, 21 – 24, 28 – 31, Aug. 1, 4 – 8, 11 – 15, 20, 27, Sept. 3, 5, 10, 12, 17, 19, 24, 26, Oct. 1, 3, 8, 15.
From Basel: June 5, 19, 24, 26, 28, July 2, 4, 7, 9, 11, 16 – 18, 22 – 25, 29 – 31, Aug. 1, 2, 12 – 16, 21, 28, Sept. 4, 6, 11, 13, 18, 20, 25, 27, Oct. 2, 4, 9, 16.

Hamburg Altona - **Lörrach** and v.v. (operator: Urlaubs-Express):
From Hamburg June 4, 18, 23, 25, 27, July 1, 3, 8, 10, 15 – 17, 21 – 24, 28 – 31, Aug. 1, 4 – 8, 11 – 15, 20, 27, Sept. 3, 5, 10, 12, 17, 19, 24, 26, Oct. 1, 3, 8, 15.
From Lörrach June 5, 19, 24, 26, 28, July 2, 4, 9, 11, 16 – 18, 22 – 25, 29 – 31, Aug. 1, 2, 5 – 9, 12 – 16, 21, 28, Sept. 4, 6, 11, 13, 18, 20, 25, 27, Oct. 2, 4, 9, 16.

GERMANY (continued)

Hamburg Altona - **München** Ost and v.v. (operator: Urlaubs-Express):
From Hamburg July 4, 14, 28, Aug. 6, 11, 25, Sept. 12, 19, 22, Oct. 1, 3, 8, 15.
From München July 5, 15, 29, Aug. 7, 12, 26, Sept. 13, 20, 23, Oct. 2, 4, 9, 16.

GREECE

Athína - Thessaloníki and v.v.: *SERVICE SUSPENDED*
Athína load by 2150, depart 2350, Thessaloníki arrive 0520.
Thessaloníki load by 2150, depart 2350, Athína arrive 0506.
Daily. Trains **600 / 601**.

RUSSIA

Services operate on the following routes - contact operator for schedules:

Kazan - Adler and v.v.
Moskva - Adler and v.v.
Moskva - Rostov na Donu and v.v.
St. Peterburg - Adler and v.v.
Kazan - Rostov na Donu and v.v.
Moskva - Kazan and v.v.
Moskva - St. Peterburg and v.v.
St. Peterburg - Vorkuta and v.v.

SLOVAKIA

Bratislava - Humenne and v.v.:
Bratislava load 2125 - 2135, depart 2253, Humenné arrive 0633.
Humenné load 2040 - 2050, depart 2145, Bratislava arrive 0549.
Daily (not Dec. 24, 31). Trains **615 / 614**: 🛌 1, 2 cl., 🛏 2 cl., 🚗.

Bratislava - Košice and v.v.:
Bratislava load 2110 - 2120, depart 2253, Košice arrive 0444.
Košice load 2210 - 2220, depart 2345, Bratislava arrive 0549.
Daily. Trains **615 / 614**: 🛌 1, 2 cl., 🛏 2 cl., 🚗.

Scenic Rail Routes of Europe

The following is a list of some of the most scenic rail routes of Europe, timings for most of which can be found within the timetable (the relevant table number has been specified in bold). Routes marked * are some of the editorial team's favourite journeys. Please note that this list does not include specialised mountain and tourist railways.

Types of scenery: C - Coastline, F - Forest, G - Gorge, L - Lake, M - Mountain, R - River

AUSTRIA

Bruck an der Mur - Villach	M R	**980**
Gmunden - Stainach Irdning*	ML	**961**
Innsbruck - Brennero	M	**595**
Innsbruck - Garmisch*	M	**895**
Innsbruck - Schwarzach-St Veit	M G	**960**
Krems - Emmersdorf	R	**991**
Landeck - Bludenz*	M	**951**
St Pölten - Mariazell*	M	**994**
Salzburg - Villach*	M G	**970**
Selzthal - Kleinreifling - Steyr	M G R	**976/977**
Wiener Neustadt - Graz	M	**980**

BELGIUM and LUXEMBOURG

Liège - Luxembourg*	R	**446**
Liège - Marloie	R	**447**
Namur - Dinant	R	**440**

BULGARIA

Septemvri - Dobrinishte	M	**1510**
Sofia - Burgas	M	**1500**
Tulovo - Gorna Orjahovica	M	**1525**

CROATIA and BOSNIA

Novi Grad - Sarajevo	M G R	**1350**
Ogulin - Split	M	**1330**
Rijeka - Ogulin	M	**1310**
Sarajevo - Ploče	M G R	**1355**

CZECH REPUBLIC

Karlovy Vary - Mariánské Lázně	R F	**1123**
Karlovy Vary - Chomutov	R	**1110**
Praha - Děčín	R	**1100**

DENMARK

Struer - Thisted	C	**716**

FINLAND

Kouvola - Joensuu	L F	**797**

FRANCE

Aurillac - Neussargues	M G	**331**
Bastia - Ajaccio	M	**369**
Bourg-en-Bresse - Bellegarde	M	**341**
Chambéry - Bourg St Maurice	M	**366**
Chambéry - Modane	ML	**367**
Chamonix - Martigny*	M G	**572**
Clermont Ferrand - Béziers	M G	**332**
Clermont Ferrand - Nîmes*	M G R	**333**
Dole - St Claude	M G	**376**
Gap - Briançon	ML	**358**
Genève - Aix les Bains	M R	**364**
Grenoble - Veynes - Marseille	M	**358**
Marseille - Ventimiglia	C	**360/361**
Mouchard - Montbéliard	R	**378**
Nice - Digne	M	**359**
Nice - Cuneo*	M G	**581**
Perpignan - Latour de Carol*	M G	**354**
Portbou - Perpignan	C	**355**
Sarlat - Bergerac	R	**318**
Toulouse - Latour de Carol	M	**312**
Valence - Veynes	M	**358**

GERMANY

Arnstadt - Meiningen	M	**870**
Dresden - Děčín	G R	**1100**
Freiburg - Donaueschingen	G F	**938**
Garmisch - Reutte - Kempten	M	**888**
Heidelberg - Neckarelz	R	**923/924**
Koblenz - Mainz*	G R	**911/914**
München - Lindau	M	**935**
Murnau - Oberammergau	ML	**897**
Naumburg - Saalfeld	R	**849**
Niebüll - Westerland	C	**821**

GERMANY - continued

Nürnberg - Pegnitz	G R	**880**
Offenburg - Konstanz	M F	**916**
Pforzheim - Nagold / Wildbad	F	**941**
Plattling - Bayerisch Eisenstein	F	**929**
Rosenheim - Berchtesgaden	ML	**890/891**
Rosenheim - Wörgl	M	**951**
Siegburg/Bonn - Siegen	R	**807**
Stuttgart - Singen	F	**940**
Titisee - Seebrugg	L F	**938**
Trier - Koblenz - Giessen	R	**906/915**
Ulm - Göppingen	M	**930**
Ulm - Tuttlingen	R	**938**

GREAT BRITAIN and IRELAND

Alnmouth - Dunbar	C	**180**
Barrow in Furness - Maryport	C	**159**
Coleraine - Londonderry	C	**231**
Dun Laoghaire - Wicklow	C	**237**
Edinburgh - Aberdeen	C	**222**
Exeter - Newton Abbot	C	**110/111**
Glasgow - Oban / Mallaig*	ML	**218**
Inverness - Kyle of Lochalsh*	M C	**226**
Lancaster - Carlisle - Carstairs	M G R	**154**
Liskeard - Looe	R	**113**
Llanelli - Craven Arms	M	**146**
Machynlleth - Pwllheli	M C	**148**
Perth - Inverness	M	**223**
Plymouth - Gunnislake	R	**113**
St Erth - St Ives	C	**113**
Sheffield - Chinley	M	**193/206**
Shrewsbury - Aberystwyth	M R	**147**
Skipton - Settle - Carlisle	M R	**173**

GREECE

Diakoftó - Kalávrita	M G	**1455**

HUNGARY

Budapest - Szob	R	**1255**
Eger - Szilvásvárad	M	**1299**
Székesfehérvár - Balatonszentgyörgy	L	**1220**
Székesfehérvár - Tapolca	L	**1225**

ITALY

Bologna - Pistoia	M	**583**
Bolzano - Merano	M	**595**
Brennero - Verona*	M	**595**
Brig - Arona	ML	**590**
Catania - Randazzo	M	**644**
Domodossola - Locarno*	M G	**551**
Firenze - Viareggio	M	**614**
Fortezza - San Candido	M	**597**
Genova - Pisa	C	**610**
Genova - Ventimiglia	C	**580**
Lecco - Tirano	ML	**593**
Napoli - Palermo	C	**641**
Napoli - Sorrento	C	**639**
Roma - Pescara	M	**624**
Salerno - Reggio Calabria	C	**640**
Taranto - Reggio Calabria	C	**637**
Torino - Aosta	M	**586**
Ventimiglia - Cuneo*	M G	**581**

NORWAY

Bergen - Oslo*	ML	**780/781**
Bodø - Trondheim	ML	**787**
Dombås - Åndalsnes	M	**785**
Drammen - Larvik	C	**783**
Myrdal - Flåm*	M C	**781**
Oslo - Kongsvinger	R	**750**
Oslo / Røros - Trondheim	ML	**784/785**
Stavanger - Kristiansand	M	**775**

POLAND

Jelenia Góra - Walbrzych	M	**1084**
Kraków - Zakopane	M	**1066**
Olsztyn - Elk	L	**1035**

POLAND (continued)

Tarnów - Krynica	M	**1078**

PORTUGAL

Covilhã - Entroncamento	M R	**691**
Pampilhosa - Guarda	M	**692**
Porto - Coimbra	C R	**690**
Porto - Pocinho*	R	**694**
Porto - Valença	M C	**696**

ROMANIA

Braşov - Ploeşti	M	**1600**
Caransebeş - Craiova	M G R	**1630**
Feteşti - Constanţa	R	**1680**
Oradea - Cluj Napoca	R	**1625**
Salva - Sighetu Marmaţiei	M R F	**1660**
Salva - Suceava	M F	**1660**

SERBIA and MONTENEGRO

Kraljevo - Mitrovica / Mitrovicë	M R	**1375**
Priboj - Bar	ML	**1370**

SLOVAKIA

Banská Bystrica - Brezno - Košice	M	**1188**
Žilina - Poprad Tatry	M	**1180**

SLOVENIA

Jesenice - Sežana	M G R	**1302**
Maribor - Zidani Most	M	**1315**
Maribor - Bleiburg	M G R	**1315**
Villa Opicina - Ljubljana - Zagreb	G R	**1305**

SPAIN

Algeciras - Ronda	M R	**673**
Barcelona - Latour de Carol	M	**656**
Bilbao - San Sebastián	M	**686**
Bilbao - Santander	M	**687**
Ferrol - Gijón*	C	**681**
Granada - Almería	M	**673**
Huesca - Canfranc	M G R	**670**
León - Monforte de Lemos	M	**682**
León - Oviedo	M	**685**
Lleida - La Pobla de Segur	ML	**653**
Málaga - Bobadilla	G	**673**
Santander - Oviedo	M C	**687**
Zaragoza - València	M R	**670**

SWEDEN

Bollnäs - Ånge - Sundsvall	ML	**761**
Borlänge - Mora	ML F	**758**
Borlänge - Ludvika - Frövi	ML F	**755**
Narvik - Kiruna	M F	**765**
Östersund - Storlien	L F	**761**

SWITZERLAND

Andermatt - Göschenen	G	**576**
Basel - Delémont - Moutier	M R	**505a**
Basel / Luzern / Zurich - Chiasso	ML	**547/548**
Chur - Arosa	M G	**545**
Chur - Brig - Zermatt*	M	**575/576**
Chur - St Moritz*	M G	**545**
Davos - Filisur	M G	**545**
Davos - Landquart	M	**545**
Interlaken Ost - Jungfraujoch*	M	**564**
Interlaken Ost - Luzern	ML	**561**
Interlaken West - Spiez	L	**560**
Lausanne - Brig	ML R	**570**
Lausanne - Neuchâtel - Biel	ML	**505**
Montreux - Zweisimmen - Lenk	ML G	**566**
Rorschach - Kreuzlingen	L	**538**
St Moritz - Scuol Tarasp	M	**545**
St Moritz - Tirano*	M	**545**
Spiez - Zweisimmen	G	**563**
Thun - Kandersteg - Brig*	ML	**562**
Zürich - Chur	ML	**520**

City Plans are on pages 30 – 34

AIRPORT → CITY CENTRE LINKS

Airport code and name	City	Distance	Journey	Transport ‡	City terminal	Table
AAR Aarhus	Aarhus	37 km	40 mins	🚌 flybus: connects with flights	Banegårdspladsen, Central rail station	
ABZ Aberdeen, Dyce	Aberdeen	11 km	40 mins	🚌 **727**: ①–⑤ ± 6 per hour; ⑥⑦ ± 3 per hour	Union Square bus station.	
ALC Alacant	Alacant	12 km	30 mins	🚌 **C6**: every 20 mins 0705 - 2000	Plaza Puerta del Mar	
AMS Amsterdam, Schiphol	Amsterdam	17 km	17 mins	Train: every 10 mins	Centraal rail station	**451, 460**
	Rotterdam	65 km	45 mins	Train: every 30 mins	Centraal rail station	**451, 460**
	Den Haag	43 km	35 mins	Train: every 30 mins	Centraal rail station	**460**
AOI Ancona (also known as Marche)	Ancona	16 km	30 mins	1) 🚌 *Aerobus* 2) Train: hourly at peak times: 17 mins	Main rail station	
ATH Athína, Elefthérios Venizélos	Athína	27 km	39 mins	Metro line **3**: 2 per hour	Syntagma	**1440**
	Piréas	41 km	90 mins	🚌 **X96**: 3 - 4 per hour	Platía Karaiskáki	
BCN Barcelona, Aeroport del Prat	Barcelona	14 km	19 mins	Train: 2 per hour	Sants. Also calls at Passeig de Gràcia rail station (26 mins)	**659**
BSL Basel - Mulhouse - Freiburg	Basel	9 km	20 mins	🚌 **50**: ①–⑤ 8 per hour; ⑥⑦ 6 per hour	SBB rail station / Kannenfeldplatz	
	Freiburg	60 km	55 mins	🚌: ①–⑤ every 1 - 2 hours; ⑥⑦ every 2 hours	Rail station	
BHD Belfast, City, George Best	Belfast	2 km	15 mins	🚌 *Airlink* **600**: ①–⑥ every 20 mins; ⑦ every 40 mins	Europa Buscentre. Also train from Sydenham rail station	
BFS Belfast, International	Belfast	26 km	40 mins	🚌 *Airbus* **300**: Ⓐ every 15 mins; ⑥ every 20; ⑦ every 30	Europa Buscentre (adjacent to Great Victoria St rail station)	
BEG Beograd, Nikola Tesla	Beograd	18 km	35 mins	🚌 **72**: every 30 minutes	Rail station	
BER Berlin, Brandenburg	Berlin	24 km	30 mins	Train *Regional* **RE7 / RB14 / FEX**: 4 per hour	Hbf, also Sudkreuz, Ostkreuz rail stations	**847a**
BER Berlin, Brandenburg T5	Berlin	24 km	28 mins	Train **S9**: 3 per hour	Hbf, also Ost, Alexanderplatz and Zoo rail stations	
BIQ Biarritz - Anglet - Bayonne	Biarritz	3 km	15 mins	🚌 *Chronoplus* **36**: every hour approx.	Town centre	
	Bayonne	7 km	23 mins	🚌 *Chronoplus* **4**: every hour approx.	Rail station	
BIO Bilbao, Sondika	Bilbao	10 km	45 mins	🚌 Bizkaibus **A-3247**: every 20 mins 0620 - 0000	Plaza Moyúa (Metro station Moyúa)	
BLL Billund	Vejle	25 km	34 mins	🚌 *Sydtrafik* **43**	Town centre	
BHX Birmingham, International	Birmingham	12 km	11 mins	Train: ①–⑥ ± 9 per hour, ⑦ 6 per hour	New Street rail station from International	**114, 141, 145, 150**
BLQ Bologna, Guglielmo Marconi	Bologna	8 km	7 mins	Train *Marconi Express*: daily every 7 mins 0540 - 1810	Centrale rail station	
BOD Bordeaux, Mérignac	Bordeaux	12 km	30 mins	🚌 *30'Direct*: every 45 mins 0825 - 2245	St Jean rail station	
	Bordeaux	12 km	45 mins	🚌 **1**: every 10 mins 0500 - 2400	St Jean rail station	
BOH Bournemouth, Hurn	Bournemouth	10 km	38 mins	🚌 **737** *Yellow Buses*: hourly 0600 - 1900	Rail station, Bus station (Travel Interchange)	
BTS Bratislava, Milan Rastislav Štefánika	Bratislava	10 km	25 mins	🚌 **61**: 3 - 4 per hour	Main rail station (Hlavná stanica)	
BRE Bremen	Bremen	3 km	20 mins	Tram **6**: ①–⑥ every 10 mins, ⑦ every 20 mins	Main rail station	
VBS Brescia, Montichiari, Verona	Verona	50 km	45 mins	🚌 connects with Ryanair flights	Main rail station	
	Brescia	18 km	20 mins	🚌 connects with Ryanair flights	Main rail station	
BRS Bristol, International	Bristol	13 km	30 mins	🚌 *Airport Flyer Exp*: ①–⑥ 3 - 6 per hour; ⑦ 2 - 6 per hour	Temple Meads rail station, also bus station	
BRQ Brno	Brno	8 km	20 mins	🚌 **76**: 2 per hour	Main rail station, also bus station	
BRU Brussels, Zaventem	Brussels	12 km	25 mins	Train: 6 per hour	Midi / Zuid rail station (also calls at Central and Nord)	**401**
	Antwerpen	38 km	34 mins	Train: Ⓐ 2 per hour, Ⓒ hourly.	Centraal	**420, 432**
OTP Bucuresti, Henri Coanda, Otopeni	Bucuresti	16 km	45 mins	🚌 **783**; ①–⑤ every 15 - 30 mins; ⑥⑦ every 30 mins	Piata Victoriei (800m from Nord station or 1 stop on subway)	
	Bucuresti	23 km	25 mins	Train: every 40 mins	Main rail station	
BUD Budapest, Ferihegy	Budapest	16 km	40 mins	🚌 **200E**: every 10 - 20 mins	Nagyvárad-tér metro station (metro connection to city centre)	
	Budapest	18 km	25 mins	Train: 2 - 6 per hour	🚌 **200E**, to Ferihegy station then train to Nyugati rail station.	
BZG Bydgoszcz	Bydgoszcz	4 km	30 mins	🚌 **80**: 2 per hour	Main rail station	
CCF Carcassonne, Salvaza	Carcassonne	5 km	10 mins	🚌: connects with Ryanair flights	Place Davilla and Carcassonne rail station	
CWL Cardiff	Cardiff	19 km	40 mins	🚌 *Airbus Xpress* **T9**: ①–⑥ hourly, ⑦ every 2 hours	Central rail station, city centre	
	Cardiff	19 km	50 mins	🚌 to Rhoose then train: ①–⑥ hourly, ⑦ every 2 hours	Central rail station	
CTA Catania Fontanarossa	Catania	5 km	9 mins	Train: hourly ± 2 per hour, 🚌 shuttle to station	Main rail station Catania Centrale, also Messina and Syracuse	
CRL Charleroi, Brussels South	Brussels	55 km	60 mins	🚌 *Brussels City Shuttle*: every 30 mins	Brussels Midi (corner of Rue de France / Rue de l'Instruction)	
	Charleroi	11 km	18 mins	🚌 *Line* **A**: ①–⑤ 2 per hour, ⑥⑦ hourly	Main rail station	
ORK Cork	Cork	8 km	25 mins	🚌 **226**: ①–⑥ 2 per hour, ⑦ hourly	Rail station, also Parnell Place bus station	
LDY Derry (Londonderry)	Londonderry	11 km	30 mins	🚌 connects with flights	Foyle Street bus station	
DNR Dinard - Pleurtuit - St-Malo	St Malo	14 km	20 mins	Taxis only. Dinard 6 km 10 mins		
DTM Dortmund, Wickede	Dortmund	10 km	25 mins;	🚌 AirportExpress: every hour	Main rail station (Hbf). Also 🚌 to Holzwickede rail station	
DRS Dresden	Dresden	15 km	21 mins	Train (S-Bahn **S2**): every 30 mins	Main rail stations (Hbf and Neustadt)	**857a**
DUB Dublin	Dublin	11 km	60 mins	🚌 **16**: every 10 mins (15 mins on ⑦)	Bus station (Busáras) 30min, O'Connell St.	
	Belfast	157 km	130 mins	🚌 **705X**: 15 per day (0155 - 2255)	Glengall Street (City Centre) also serves Dublin city centre.	
DBV Dubrovnik, Čilipi	Dubrovnik	21 km	30 mins	🚌 *Atlas Bus*: connects with flights	Bus station	
DUS Düsseldorf, International	Düsseldorf	7 km	12 mins	Train (S-Bahn **S11**): Ⓐ every 20 mins, Ⓒ every 30 mins	Main rail station (Hauptbahnhof)	**800, 802**
EMA East Midlands, Nottingham - - Leicester - Derby	East Midlands	10 km	10 mins	Taxi shuttle	East Midlands Parkway rail station	
	Nottingham	21 km	55 mins	🚌 *Skylink*: 24/7, every 20 mins peak times	Greyfriar Gate (pending re-opening of Broadmarsh bus station)	
	Derby	19 km	45 mins	🚌 *Skylink*: 24/7, every 20 mins peak times	Bus station	
	Loughborough	8 km	25 mins	🚌 *Skylink*: 24/7, every 20 mins peak times	Lemyngton Street / High Street	
	Leicester	23 km	55 mins	🚌 *Skylink*: 24/7, every 20 mins peak times	St Margaret's bus station	
EDI Edinburgh, Turnhouse	Edinburgh	11 km	25 mins	🚌 *Airlink* **100**: every 20 mins. 0430 - 0030.	Haymarket rail station; St Andrew Square (for Waverley station)	
	Edinburgh	11 km	35 mins	Tram: every 3 - 8 mins 0618 - 1853, every 10 mins until 2248	Haymarket rail station; St Andrew Square (for Waverley station)	
ERF Erfurt	Erfurt	6 km	25 mins	Tram Line 4: Ⓐ 3 - 6 per hour, Ⓒ 2 per hour	Main rail station (Hauptbahnhof)	
EBJ Esbjerg	Esbjerg	12 km	21 mins	🚌 **7c / 944X**: hourly	*Bybusterminal*	
EXT Exeter	Exeter	8 km	35 mins	🚌 **56**: 1 per hour	St Davids rail station	
FAO Faro	Faro	6 km	20 mins	🚌 *Proxima* **16**: hourly	Rail station, Bus station	
FLR Firenze, Amerigo Vespucci	Firenze	7 km	20 mins	🚌 BusItalia *Vola in bus* **62**: every 30 mins	Santa Maria Novella rail station	
HHN Frankfurt, Hahn	Frankfurt	120 km	105 mins	🚌 connects with Ryanair flights	Mannheimer Straße, adjacent to main rail station (Hauptbahnhof)	
Also 🚌 to; Bingen, 60 mins; Heidelberg hbf, 140 mins; Koblenz, 70 mins; Köln hbf, 135 mins; Luxembourg, 110 mins; Mainz, 70 mins; Mannheim, 110 mins						
FRA Frankfurt	Frankfurt	10 km	15 mins	Train (S-Bahn **S8** or **S9**): 4 - 6 times hourly	Main rail station (Hauptbahnhof)	**917a**
FDH Friedrichshafen	Friedrichshafen	4 km	7 mins	Train: 1 - 2 trains per hour	Main rail station (Stadt) or Harbour (Hafen)	
GDN Gdańsk, Lech Walesa	Gdańsk	10 km	22 mins	Train *PKM*: Port Lotniczy, 3 - 4 per hour	Wrzeszcz rail station, then 3 stops (every 15 mins) to Gjówny	
GVA Genève	Genève	6 km	6 mins	Train: 5 times hourly	Cornavin rail station	**505, 570**
GOA Genova, Cristoforo Colombo	Genova	7 km	30 mins	🚌 *Volabus*: 1 - 2 per hour	Principe rail station	

‡ – The frequencies shown apply during daytime on weekdays and are from the airport to the city centre. There may be fewer journeys in the evenings, at weekends and during the winter months. Extended 🚌 journey times could apply during peak hours.

5 AIRPORT → CITY CENTRE LINKS

City Plans are on pages 30 – 34

Airport code and name	City	Distance	Journey	Transport ‡	City terminal	Table
GRO Girona	Girona	12 km	25 mins	🚌: hourly	Rail / Bus station (Estación autobuses)	
	Barcelona	102 km	70 mins	🚌 connects with Ryanair flights	Estacio del Nord, corner of carrer Ali Bei 80 / Sicilia	
GLA Glasgow, International	Glasgow	15 km	25 mins	🚌 **500**: ①–⑥ every 10 mins, ⑦ every 15 mins.	Central rail station	
PIK Glasgow, Prestwick	Glasgow	61 km	50 mins	Train: ①–⑥ 4 per hour, ⑦ 2 per hour	Central rail station	**216**
GOT Göteborg, Landvetter	Göteborg	25 km	30 mins	🚌: ①–⑤ 3 per hour, ⑥⑦ 2 - 3 per hour	Nils Ericson Terminalen (bus station) / Central rail station	
GRZ Graz	Graz	9 km	9 mins	Train **S5**: ①–⑥ 1 - 2 per hour, ⑦ every hour ¶	Main rail station (Hauptbahnhof)	**980**
GNB Grenoble, St Geoirs	Grenoble	37 km	45 mins	🚌 connects with flights	Main rail station, also bus station	
HAM Hamburg, Fuhlsbüttel	Hamburg	11 km	25 mins	Train (S-Bahn **S1**): every 10 mins	Main rail station (Hauptbahnhof)	
HAJ Hannover, Langenhagen	Hannover	15 km	18 mins	Train (S-Bahn **S5**): every 30 mins	Main rail station (Hauptbahnhof)	**809**
HEL Helsinki, Vantaa	Helsinki	19 km	35 mins	Train: ①–⑥ 4 - 6 per hour, ⑦ 3 - 4 per hour	Main rail station	
NOC Ireland West Airport Knock	Ballyhaunis	22 km	30 mins	🚌 **64**: 0855, 1255. 🚌 **440**: 1058, 1758.	Rail station **64** Ballyhaunis, **440** Claremorris	**235**
IOM Isle of Man, Ronaldsway	Douglas	16 km	30 mins	🚌 **1**: hourly (every 30 mins during peak periods)	Lord street	
IST İstanbul, Havalimani	İstanbul	43 km	60 mins	🚌 *HAVAIST* **5** Airport Shuttle	Esenler Intercity Bus Terminal (city centre)	
SAW İstanbul, Sabiha Gökçen	İstanbul	32 km	60 mins	🚌: 1 – 2 per hour, 0540 - 2040	Bus station. Also Pendik rail station is 4km from airport	
XRY Jerez	Jerez	10 km	9 mins	Train: 11 trains per day	Jerez de la Frontera, then to Cadiz	**671**
FKB Karlsruhe - Baden-Baden	Baden-Baden	8 km	15 mins	🚌 **285** 1 an hour to Baden-Baden	Rail station; also **234, X34** to Rastatt rail station	
KTW Katowice, Pyrzowice	Katowice	34 km	50 mins	🚌 *ZTM*: **AP3** 1 per hour approx	Katowice Dworzec (main rail station)	
KUN Kaunas	Kaunas	13 km	40 mins	🚌 **29**	City centre	
	Vilnius	102 km	90 mins	🚌 connects with Ryanair flights	Hotel Panorama, close to bus and rail stations	
KLU Klagenfurt	Klagenfurt	5 km	25 mins	🚌 **45** (or walk to Annabichl rail station, then train or 🚌 **40**)	Main rail station and bus station	
CPH København, Kastrup	København	12 km	15 mins	Train: every 10 mins	Main rail station (Hovedbanegård)	**703**
	Malmö	36 km	22 mins	Train: every 20 mins	Central rail station	**703**
CGN Köln / Bonn, Konrad Adenauer	Bonn	25 km	32 mins	🚌 **SB60**: ①–⑤ 2 per hour; ⑥⑦ 1 - 2 per hour	Main rail station (Hauptbahnhof)	
	Köln	15 km	16 mins	Train **S13**: ①–⑤ every 20 mins, ⑥⑦ every 30 mins	Main rail station (Hbf). Also to Mönchengladbach, Koblenz	**802**
KRK Kraków John Paul II Airport (Balice)	Kraków	12 km	17 mins	Train: 2 per hour, from Lotnisko station	Kraków Główny	**1099**
KBP Kyiv, Boryspil	Kyiv	34 km	40 mins	Train: 1 - 2 per hour	Main rail station **Airport Temporarily Closed**	
LBA Leeds - Bradford	Leeds	16 km	45 mins	🚌 *Flyer* **A1**: 2 per hour	Main rail station and bus station	
	Bradford	11 km	40 mins	🚌 *Flyer* **A2, A3**: 2 per hour	Interchange rail station	
AOC Leipzig, Altenburg - Nobitz	Leipzig	75 km	70 mins	🚌 **250** *ThüSac*: connects with Ryanair flights	Main rail station. Also stops at Altenburg rail station after 15 mins	
LEJ Leipzig - Halle	Leipzig	20 km	14 mins	Train: 2 - 3 per hour	Main rail station (Hauptbahnhof)	**866, 881**
	Halle	18 km	12 mins	Train: 2 per hour	Main rail station (Hauptbahnhof)	**866, 881**
LNZ Linz, Blue Danube	Linz	12 km	19 mins	🚌 **601** connects with Ryanair flights	Main rail station. Also free 🚌 to Hörsching rail station, 3 mins	
LIS Lisboa, Portela	Lisboa	3 km	9 mins	Train, Red (Vermelho) line: every 5 - 9 mins	Oriente rail station. For Santa Apolónia change at São Sebastião	
LPL Liverpool, John Lennon	Liverpool	11 km	37 mins	🚌 **500**: every 30 mins 0400 - 2400	Lime Street rail station, Liverpool One bus station	
LJU Ljubljana, Jože Pučnik, Brnik	Ljubljana	26 km	45 mins	🚌: Ⓐ hourly 0500 - 2000, Ⓒ 0700, every 2 hours 1000 - 2000	Bus station (Avtobusna postaja)	
LCJ Łódź, Lublinek	Łódź	6 km	20 mins	🚌 **65A, 65B**	Kaliska rail station	
LCY London, City	London	12 km	25 mins	Train (Docklands Light Railway): every 8 - 10 mins	Bank underground (tube) station	**100**
LGW London, Gatwick	London	44 km	30 mins	Train *Gatwick Express*: every 15 minutes	Victoria rail station	**102, 100, 185**
LHR London, Heathrow	London	24 km	15 mins	Train *Heathrow Express*: every 15 minutes	Paddington rail station	**100**
	London	24 km	58 mins	Underground train (tube): every 6 - 12 mins	King's Cross St Pancras rail station	**100**
LTN London, Luton	London	50 km	35 mins	🚌 to Parkway rail station, then train: 6 - 7 per hour	St Pancras International rail station	**103, 100, 170**
SEN London, Southend	London	64 km	55 mins	Train: 3 per hour	Liverpool Street rail station	
STN London, Stansted	London	55 km	46 mins	Train *Stansted Express*: every 15 minutes	Liverpool Street rail station	**100**
LBC Lübeck, Blankensee	Lübeck	8 km	30 mins	🚌 **6**: 2 per hour.	Bus station (bus stop 5). Also train from Flughafen 300m walk	**827**
LUZ Lublin	Lublin	10 km	15 mins	Train: ①–⑥ 2 - 3 per day, ⑦ 1 per day, connects with flights	Main rail station	
LUX Luxembourg, Findel	Luxembourg	7 km	25 mins	🚌 **16**: ①–⑥ every 15 mins ⑦, every 30 mins	Central rail station	
LWO Lviv, Skniliv	Lvov	10 km	25 mins	Trolleybus **29**: every 9 - 16 minutes 0600 - 2215	City Centre	
LYS Lyon, St Exupéry	Lyon	23 km	30 mins	Tram *RhôneExpress*: 4 per hour	Part Dieu rail station	
	Chambéry	87 km	60 mins	🚌 Flixbus: 2 per day	Bus station (gare routière)	
	Grenoble	91 km	65 mins	🚌 Flixbus: hourly 0830 - 2000	Bus station (gare routière); Place de la Grenoble	
MAD Madrid, Barajas T4	Madrid	12 km	16 mins	Train Cercanías from T4: every 15/20 mins 0602 - 2225.	Chamartín, also Atocha 29 mins. 🚌 from T4 to T1, T2 and T3.	
AGP Málaga	Málaga	8 km	12 mins	Train: every 30 mins	María Zambrano (Renfe) and Centro-Alameda rail stations	**662**
MMX Malmö, Sturup	Malmö	30 km	40 mins	🚌 *flygbussarna*: 1 - 2 per hour	Central rail station	
MAN Manchester	Manchester	16 km	20 mins	Train: every 10 minutes 0419 - 0038	Piccadilly rail station	
MRS Marseille, Provence	Marseille	28 km	25 mins	🚌 L91: every 30 mins. See also rail / bus on Table **351**	St Charles rail station; also 🚌 to Aix TGV rail stn. every 30 mins	
FMM Memmingen	Memmingen	5 km	10 mins	🚌 **2, 810**	Bus station and rail station; also 🚌 to München, 80 mins	
LIN Milano, Linate	Milano	9 km	20 mins	1) 🚌 **73**: every 10 mins; 2) 🚌 *Starfly*: every 30 mins	1) Piazza S. Babila, Metro line 1; 2) Centrale rail station	
MXP Milano, Malpensa	Milano	45 km	40 mins	Train: 1) Malpensa Express: every 30 mins; 2) 1 - 2 per hour	1) Cadorna and Bovisa rail stations; 2) Centrale rail station	**606**
		45 km	50 mins	🚌 *Bus Express*: 2 per hour. 🚌 *Shuttle Air*: 3 per hour	Centrale rail station. Also 🚌 to Gallarate (Table **590**)	
BGY Milano, Orio al Serio, Bergamo	Milano	45 km	60 mins	🚌: 1 - 2 per hour	Centrale rail station (Air Terminal)	
	Bergamo	4 km	10 mins	🚌 **ATB 1**: 2 per hour	Rail station	
MSQ Minsk	Minsk	42 km	60 mins	🚌 **173, 300**	Vostochniy and Moskovskiy bus stations	
DME Moskva, Domodedovo	Moskva	35 km	47 mins	Train, *Aeroexpress*: 1 - 2 per hour approx	Paveletskaya rail station	**1901**
SVO Moskva, Sheremetyevo	Moskva	35 km	35 mins	Train, *Aeroexpress*: 1 - 2 per hour approx	Belorusskaya rail station	**1901**
VKO Moskva, Vnukovo	Moskva	28 km	40 mins	Train, *Aeroexpress*: 1 per hour approx	Kiyevskaya rail station	**1901**
MUC München, International	München	37 km	40 mins	Train: **S1**, **S8** for Hbf, every 10 mins; **S8** for Ost, every 20 mins	Main rail stations (Hauptbahnhof, Ostbahnhof)	**892**
	Freising	6 km	10 mins	Train: hourly 0828 - 0028	Rail station for Regensburg and connections to Passau	**892, 878**
RMU Murcia, Corvera	Murcia	25km	30 mins	🚌 connects with flights	City centre	
NTE Nantes, Atlantique	Nantes	9 km	20 mins	🚌 *Tan Air*: ⚒ 0615 - 2315, † 0700 - 2315; every 20/30 mins	Main rail station	
NAP Napoli, Capodichino	Napoli	7 km	15 mins	🚌 *Alibus*: 2 per hour	Piazza Garibaldi (Centrale rail station)	
NCL Newcastle, International	Newcastle	9 km	25 mins	Metro train: every 12 mins	Main rail station	

‡ – The frequencies shown apply during daytime on weekdays and are from the airport to the city centre. There may be fewer journeys in the evenings, at weekends and during the winter months. Extended 🚌 journey times could apply during peak hours.

¶ – Graz Airport - Feldkirchen rail station is located about 300 metres away from the airport.

City Plans are on pages 30 – 34

AIRPORT → CITY CENTRE LINKS 5

Airport code and name	City	Distance	Journey	Transport ‡	City terminal	Table
NCE Nice, Côte d'Azur	Nice	5 km	7 mins	Train from Nice St Augustin (see note ◧)	SNCF station	**361**
		7 km	24 mins	Tram **2**: ①–⑤ every 9 mins, ⑥ 6 per hour, ⑦ 5 per hour	Magnan (Central Nice), Durandy (Nice Ville)	
FNI Nîmes - Arles - Camargue	Nîmes	12 km	20 mins	🚌 connects with Ryanair flights	Rail station	
NWI Norwich	Norwich	8 km	24 mins	🚌 **501**: ①–⑥ 4 per hour 0805 - 1735	Bus station	
NUE Nürnberg	Nürnberg	6 km	12 mins	Train U-bahn **U2**: 4 - 6 per hour	Main rail station (Hauptbahnhof)	
ODS Odesa	Odesa	9 km	30 mins	🚌 **117**: Trolleybus **14**	Rail station	
OSL Oslo, Gardermoen	Oslo	49 km	19 mins	Train *Flytoget*: 3 - 6 per hour	Central rail station	**771**
TRF Oslo, Sandefjord Torp	Oslo	123 km	116 mins	🚌 to Torp rail station (4 mins), then train to Oslo	Also 🚌 to Oslo Bus terminal	**783**
RYG Oslo, Rygge	Oslo	69 km	51 mins	🚌 connects with Ryanair flights to Rygge rail station (4 km).	Sentral rail station (51 mins from Rygge to Oslo Sentral)	**770**
OSR Ostrava, Leoš Janáček	Ostrava	31km	31 mins	Train **S4**: 10 per day	Ostrava hlavní	
PMO Palermo, Falcone-Borsellino	Palermo	24 km	45 mins	Train *Trinacria express*: ①–⑥ 2 per hour, ⑦ hourly	Centrale rail station	
PMI Palma, Mallorca	Palma	11 km	30 mins	🚌 **A1**: every 30 mins	Paseo de Mallorca, Plaça d'Espanya (for rail stations), the Port	
BVA Paris, Beauvais	Paris	80 km	75 mins	🚌 connects with Ryanair and WizzAir flights	Porte Maillot, Metro (Line 1) for Châtelet Les Halles, Gare de Lyon	
CDG Paris, Charles de Gaulle	Paris	25 km	35 mins	RER train (Line B): every 7 - 15 mins	Nord, Châtelet Les Halles, and St Michel rail stations	**398**
	Disneyland	23 km	45 mins	🚌 **VEA** Magical Navette / Shuttle: every 20 minutes	Disneyland Resort, Disneyland hotels	
ORY Paris, Orly	Paris	15 km	35 mins	🚌 to Pont de Rungis, then RER train (Line C): 4 per hr.	Austerlitz, St Michel, Musée d'Orsay, and Invalides rail stns.	**398**
	Paris	15 km	35 mins	ORLYVAL shuttle to Antony then RER train, (Line B): 4 per hr.	Châlet-Les-Halles, Nord rail stations	**398**
PGF Perpignan, Rivesaltes	Perpignan	5 km	15 mins	🚌 connects with flights	Rail station, bus station (gare routière)	
PSA Pisa, Galileo Galilei	Pisa	2 km	5 mins	People Mover: every 5 - 8 minutes 0600 - 2400	Centrale rail station	
OPO Porto	Porto	17 km	35 mins	Metro Train: Line E, 3 per hour	Campanhã rail station	
POZ Poznań, Ławica	Poznań	6 km	21 mins	🚌 **159** *MPK*: 2 - 3 per hour	Rail station (Główny)	
PRG Praha, Václav Haveľ	Praha	24 km	25 mins	🚌 **AE** *Airport Express*: every 20 - 30 mins 0530 - 2100	Hlavní rail station	
	Praha	17 km	60 mins	🚌 **119**: every 10 mins	Nádraží Veleslavín metro station, then Metro line A to muzeum	
PUY Pula	Pula	6 km	15 mins	🚌 connects with flights	Main bus station	
REU Reus	Reus	6 km	11 mins	🚌 **50** *Hispano Igualadina*: hourly 0800, 0905 - 2005	Rail station	**652**
	Barcelona	90 km	90 mins	🚌 *Hispano Igualadina* connects with Ryanair flights	Sants rail station	
KEF Reykjavík, Keflavík	Reykjavík	50 km	45 mins	🚌 *flybus* connects with all flights	BSÍ bus terminal	
RIX Riga	Riga	13 km	30 mins	🚌 **22**: every 10 - 30 mins	Abrenes iela (street) next to rail station	
RJK Rijeka	Rijeka	30 km	45 mins	🚌 *Autotrans*: connects with flights	Bus station, Jelačić Square	
CIA Roma, Ciampino	Roma	15 km	35 mins	🚌 *Airlink*: 1 - 3 per hour, to Ciampino, then train	Termini rail station	**622**
FCO Roma, Fiumicino	Roma	26 km	42 mins	Train: ①–⑥ 4 per hour, ⑦ 2 per hour	Ostiense and Tiburtina rail stations	**622**
(also known as Leonardo da Vinci)		26 km	32 mins	Train *Leonardo Express*: every 30 mins	Termini rail station	**622**
RTM Rotterdam	Rotterdam	5 km	20 mins	*Airport Shuttle* **33**: ①–⑤ every 10 mins, ⑥⑦ every 15 mins	Groot Handelsgebouw (adjacent to Centraal rail station)	
RZE Rzeszów, Jasionka	Rzeszów	15 km	20 mins	🚌 **51**: connects with flights	Main rail station and bus station	
LED St Peterburg, Pulkovo II	St Peterburg	17 km	60 mins	🚌 **39, 39Ex, K39** (Minivan Taxi)	Moskovskaya Metro station, Line 2 for Nevski Pr. (see City Plans)	
SZG Salzburg, W. A. Mozart	Salzburg	5 km	22 mins	🚌 **2**: ①–⑥ every 10 - 20 mins, ⑦ every 20 mins	Main rail station	
SIP Simferopol	Simferopol	12 km	28 mins	🚌 **49a, 20** (trolleybus): every 10–15 mins	Main rail station	
SKP Skopje, Alexander the Great	Skopje	14 km	25 mins	🚌 Airport Shuttle Service: connects with flights	Bus station	
SOF Sofia, International	Sofia	10 km	26 mins	Train Line **1**: from Terminal 2, every 10 mins	City centre. Change at Serdika for Line **2**, for Central rail station	
SOU Southampton	Southampton	8 km	8 mins	Train: 50 metres from terminal, 4 - 5 trains per hour	Central rail station	**106, 114**
SPU Split, Kaštela	Split	16 km	50 mins	🚌: connects with flights	Bus station. Departs 200m from Airport terminal	
SVG Stavanger, Sola	Stavanger	14 km	30 mins	🚌: ①–⑤ every 20 mins, ⑥ 2 per hour, ⑦ hourly	Atlantic Hotel / Fiskepiren	
ARN Stockholm, Arlanda	Stockholm	44 km	20 mins	*Arlanda Express* train: every 15 mins	Central rail station	**747, 760**
NYO Stockholm, Skavsta	Stockholm	103 km	80 mins	🚌: connects with flights	Cityterminal (bus station), also 🚌 to Nyköping rail station	
VST Stockholm, Västerås	Stockholm	107 km	75 mins	🚌: connects with Ryanair flights	Cityterminal (bus station), also 🚌 **941** to Västerås rail station	
SXB Strasbourg, Entzheim	Strasbourg	10 km	8 mins	Train: from Entzheim Aéroport (300m walk) 1 - 5 per hour	Gare Centrale (Central rail station)	**382**
STR Stuttgart, Echterdingen	Stuttgart	20 km	27 mins	Train (S-Bahn **S2, S3**): 2 - 4 times hourly	Main rail station (Hauptbahnhof)	**936a**
SZZ Szczecin, Goleniów	Szczecin	35 km	40 mins	Train: 14 - 20 per day.	Szczecin Główny.	
TLL Tallinn, Ülemiste	Tallinn	5 km	27 mins	🚌: various frequent services 0600 - 0000	Balti jaam (rail station)	
TMP Tampere, Pirkkala	Tampere	18 km	25 mins	🚌 connects with Ryanair flights	Main rail station	
TBS Tbilisi	Tbilisi	19 km	35 mins	Train	Rail station	**1995**
TIA Tirana (Tiranë), Nënë Tereza	Tirana	12 km	45 mins	🚌 *1. Rinas Express, 2. LU-NA shpk*: every hour 0600 - 1800	1. National Museum city centre 2. National Theatre of Opera	
TRN Torino, Caselle	Torino	16 km	20 mins	*GTT* train: every 30 mins	Torino Porta Susa rail station. Change at Venaria for 🚌 **SF2**	
	Torino	16 km	30 mins	🚌: ①–⑤ half hourly, ⑥⑦ hourly	Torino Porta Nuova and Porta Susa rail stations	
TLS Toulouse, Blagnac	Toulouse	8 km	38 mins	Tram **T2**: every 15 minutes for Arènes then Metro line **A**	for Marengo-SNCF, then 300m to Matabiau rail station	
	Toulouse	8 km	20 mins	🚌 *Aero*: every 20 minutes	Place Jeanne d'Arc / Matabiau rail / bus station (gare routière)	
TRS Trieste, Ronchi dei Legionari	Trieste	33 km	29 mins	Train: hourly	Rail station	**601**
	Monfalcone	5 km	6 mins	Train: hourly	Rail station	**601**
TRD Trondheim, Værnes	Trondheim	33 km	37 mins	Train: ①–⑤ hourly, ⑥⑦ every two hours	Rail station. Værnes rail station is 220m from Airport terminal	**787**
VLC València	València	9 km	22 mins	Train Lines **3, 5**: Ⓐ every 15 mins; Ⓒ every 20 mins	Xátiva for Nord rail station	
VCE Venezia, Marco Polo	Venezia	12 km	25 mins	🚌 **5, 35**: 2 per hour	Piazzale Roma (see city plans p32)	
	Venezia		80 mins	Waterbus *Alilaguna*: ± every 30 mins	Lido 53 - 63 mins / Piazza S. Marco, 72 - 80 mins	
TSF Venezia, Treviso	Venezia	30 km	70 mins	🚌: connects with flights	Mestre rail station, Piazzale Roma (see city plans p32)	
VRN Verona, Villafranca	Verona	12 km	20 mins	🚌: every 20 mins 0635 - 2335	Rail station	
VNO Vilnius	Vilnius	4 km	7 mins	Train: every ± 40 minutes	Rail station	**1816**
WAW Warszawa, Frederic Chopin, Okęcie,	Warszawa	13 km	23 mins	SKM / KM train: 3 - 5 per hour	Śródmieście (2 - 3 per hr) or Centralna (1 - 2 per hr) rail stations	
WMI Warszawa, Modlin	Warszawa	40 km	59 mins	🚌 to Modlin rail stn, then train: approx 1 - 2 per hour	Centralna or Gdánska rail stations	**1099**
NRN Weeze, Niederhein	Düsseldorf	70 km	75 mins	🚌: connects with Ryanair flights	Main rail station (Hauptbahnhof) Worringer Street	
	Düsseldorf	74 km	82 mins	🚌 **SW1**: to Weeze rail station, then train	Main rail station (Hauptbahnhof)	**802**
VIE Wien, Schwechat	Wien	21 km	16 mins	*City Airport Train (CAT)*: every 30 mins (special fares)	Mitte rail station	**985**
	Wien	21 km	25 mins	S-bahn: every 30 mins	Mitte rail station	**985**
	Bratislava	54 km	60 mins	🚌 *ÖBB - Postbus / Slovak Lines*: hourly	AS Mlynské nivy (bus station) / Einsteinnova/Petrzalka	**985**
WRO Wrocław, Copernicus	Wrocław	10 km	40 mins	🚌 **106**: every 15 minutes	Rail station, bus station	
ZAG Zagreb	Zagreb	17 km	40 mins	🚌: 1 - 2 per hour connects with flights	Bus station (Autobusni kolodvor), Avenija Marina Drzica	
ZAZ Zaragoza	Zaragoza	10 km	30 mins	🚌: ①–⑥ 1 - 2 per hour 0615 - 2315, ⑦ hourly 0645 - 2245	Paseo María Agustin, 150m from Portillo rail station	
ZRH Zürich	Zürich	10 km	13 mins	Train: 7 - 8 per hour	Main rail station (HB)	**505, 510, 530, 535, 555, 560**
ZQW Zweibrücken	Zweibrucken	4 km	10 mins	Taxi	Rail station. Also 🚌 **199** to Saarbrücken	**918**

‡ – The frequencies shown apply during daytime on weekdays and are from the airport to the city centre. There may be fewer journeys in the evenings, at weekends and during the winter months. Extended 🚌 journey times could apply during peak hours.

◧ – Nice St Augustin station is approximately 800m from Terminal 1.

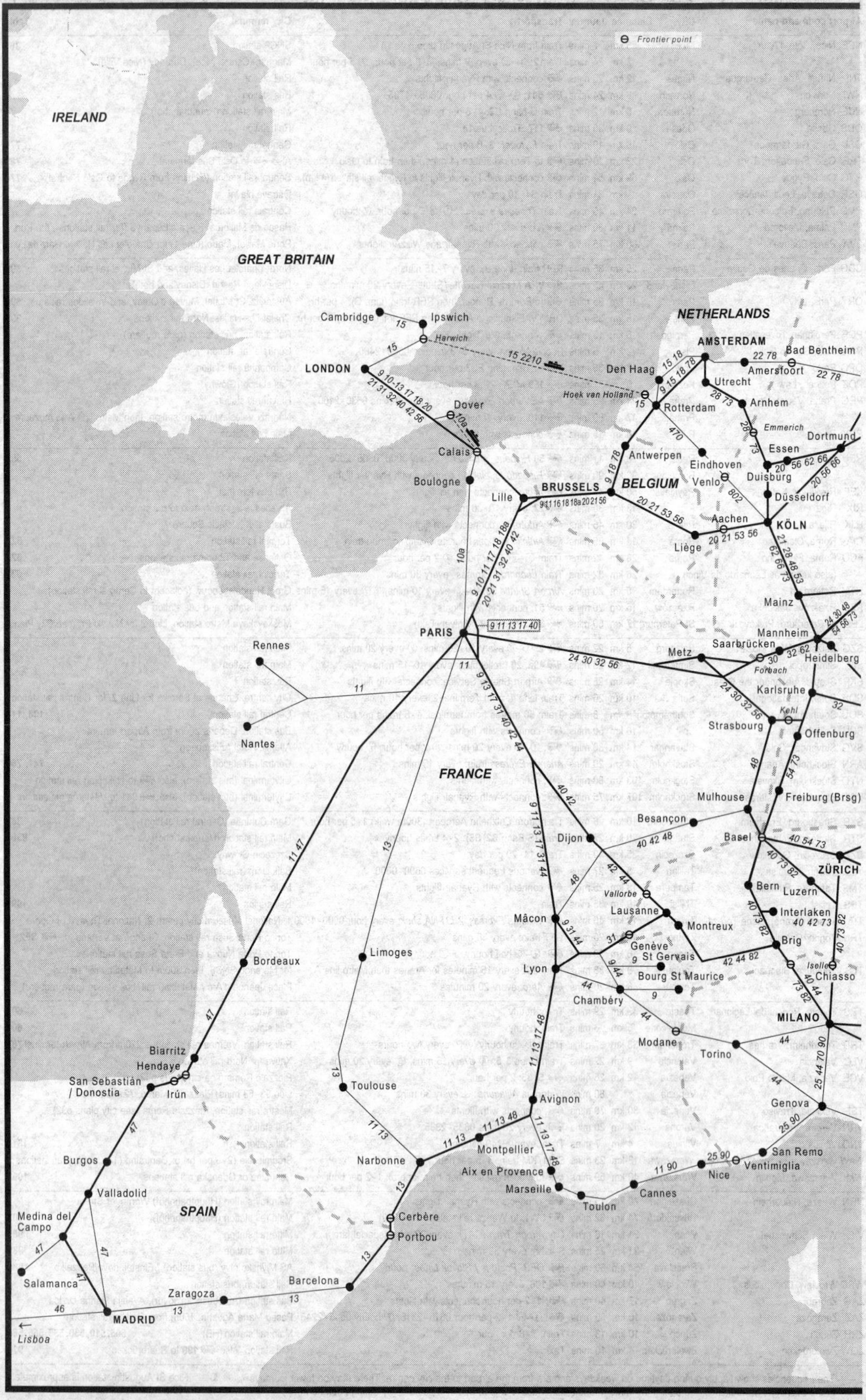

Frontier point
IRELAND
GREAT BRITAIN
NETHERLANDS
BELGIUM
FRANCE
SPAIN
Cambridge
Ipswich
Harwich
LONDON
Dover
Calais
Boulogne
Lille
BRUSSELS
Antwerpen
Rotterdam
Hoek van Holland
Den Haag
AMSTERDAM
Utrecht
Amersfoort
Bad Bentheim
Arnhem
Emmerich
Eindhoven
Venlo
Essen
Dortmund
Duisburg
Düsseldorf
Aachen
Liège
KÖLN
Mainz
Mannheim
Heidelberg
Saarbrücken
Forbach
Metz
Karlsruhe
Kehl
Strasbourg
Offenburg
Freiburg (Brsg)
Mulhouse
Basel
ZÜRICH
Bern
Luzern
Interlaken
Brig
Iselle
Chiasso
MILANO
Besançon
Dijon
Vallorbe
Lausanne
Montreux
Genève
St Gervais
Bourg St Maurice
Mâcon
Lyon
Chambéry
Modane
Torino
Genova
San Remo
Ventimiglia
Nice
Cannes
Toulon
Marseille
Aix en Provence
Avignon
Montpellier
Narbonne
Cerbère
Portbou
Barcelona
Toulouse
Limoges
Bordeaux
Biarritz
Hendaye
Irún
San Sebastián / Donostia
Burgos
Valladolid
Medina del Campo
Salamanca
Zaragoza
MADRID
Lisboa
PARIS
Rennes
Nantes
15 2210
9 10-13 17 18 20
21 31 32 40 42 56
10a
9 11 16 18 18a 20 21 56
9 10 11 17 18 18a
20 21 31 32 40 42
9 11 13 17 40
24 30 32 56
9 13 17 31 40 42 44
40 42
9 11 13 17 31 44
11 47
20 21 53 56
21 28 48 53
62 66 73
24 30 48
54 56 73
32 62
24 30 32 56
40 54 73
40 73 82
40 42 73
40 42 48
42 44 82
40 44
73 82
25 44 70 90
25 90
11 90
11 13 17 48
11 13 48
11 13 17 48
11 13
15 18
9 15 18 78
22 78
28 73
20 56 62 66
470
802

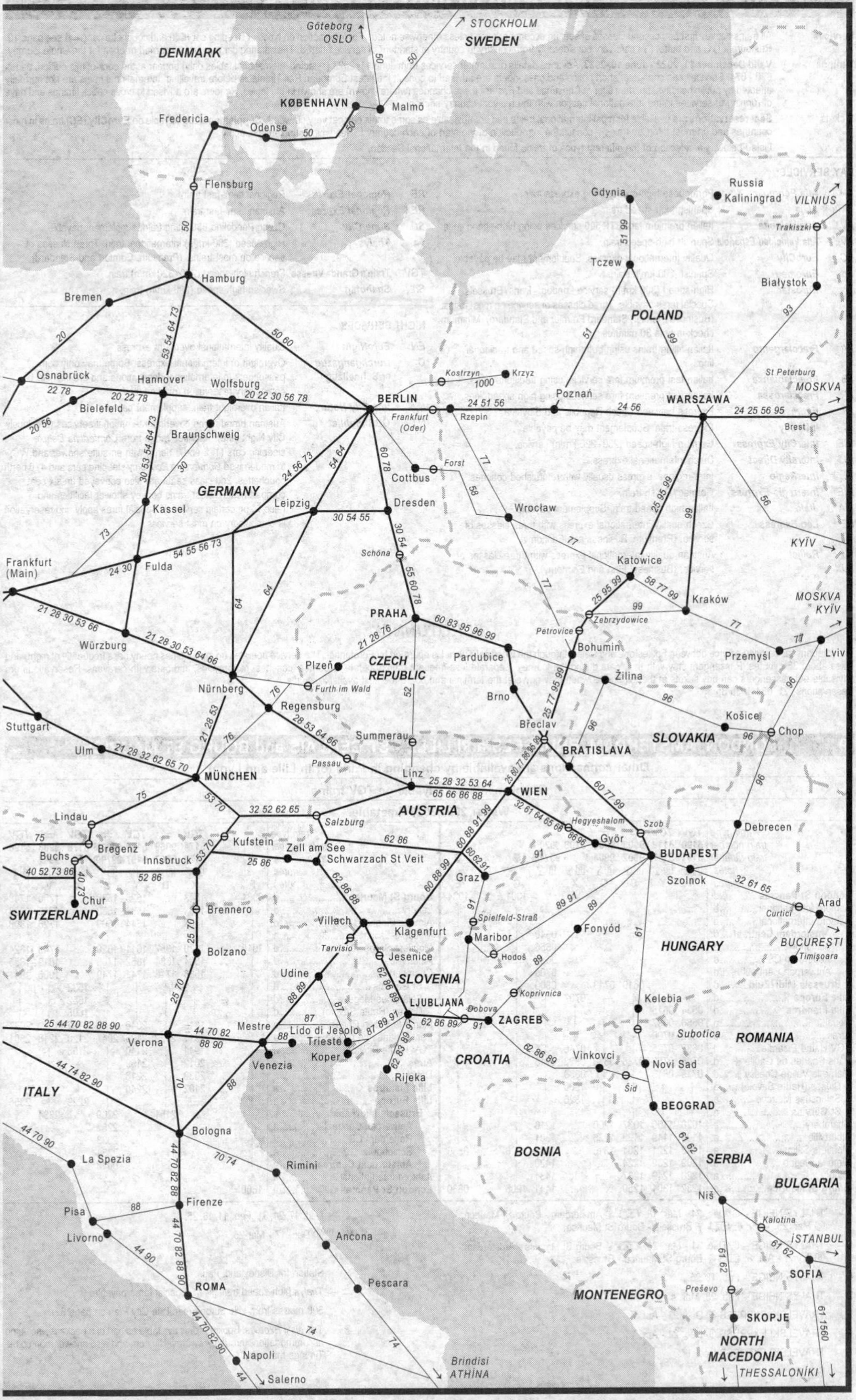
DENMARK
SWEDEN
Göteborg
OSLO
STOCKHOLM
KØBENHAVN
Malmö
Fredericia
Odense
Flensburg
Hamburg
Bremen
Osnabrück
Bielefeld
Hannover
Wolfsburg
Braunschweig
BERLIN
Frankfurt (Oder)
Rzepin
Kostrzyn
Krzyz
Cottbus
Forst
Leipzig
Dresden
Schöna
GERMANY
Kassel
Fulda
Frankfurt (Main)
Würzburg
Nürnberg
Regensburg
Stuttgart
Ulm
MÜNCHEN
Lindau
Bregenz
Buchs
Chur
SWITZERLAND
Innsbruck
Kufstein
Salzburg
Zell am See
Schwarzach St Veit
Passau
Summerau
Linz
AUSTRIA
WIEN
Hegyeshalom
Graz
Spielfeld-Straß
Maribor
Hodoš
Villach
Tarvisio
Klagenfurt
Jesenice
SLOVENIA
LJUBLJANA
Dobova
ZAGREB
Koprivnica
CROATIA
Rijeka
Koper
Trieste
Lido di Jesolo
Udine
Mestre
Venezia
Brennero
Bolzano
Verona
Bologna
ITALY
La Spezia
Pisa
Livorno
Firenze
Rimini
Ancona
Pescara
ROMA
Napoli
Salerno
Brindisi
ATHÍNA
PRAHA
Plzeň
Furth im Wald
CZECH REPUBLIC
Pardubice
Brno
Břeclav
Bohumín
Petrovice
Zebrzydowice
Žilina
BRATISLAVA
SLOVAKIA
Košice
Chop
POLAND
Gdynia
Tczew
Poznań
WARSZAWA
Wrocław
Katowice
Kraków
Przemyśl
Lviv
Russia
Kaliningrad
VILNIUS
Trakiszki
Białystok
St Peterburg
MOSKVA
Brest
KYÏV
Győr
Szob
BUDAPEST
Szolnok
Debrecen
HUNGARY
Fonyód
Kelebia
Subotica
Novi Sad
Vinkovci
Šid
BEOGRAD
SERBIA
BOSNIA
MONTENEGRO
Niš
Preševo
SKOPJE
NORTH MACEDONIA
THESSALONÍKI
Kalotina
SOFIA
BULGARIA
ÍSTANBUL
ROMANIA
Arad
Curtici
BUCUREŞTI
Timişoara

INTERNATIONAL SERVICES

Services All trains convey first and second classes of seating accommodation unless otherwise noted. For information on types of sleeping car (🛏) and couchette car (🛏) see page 10. Restaurant (✕) and buffet (🍷) cars vary considerably from country to country in standard of service offered. The catering car may not be carried or open for the whole journey.

Timings **Valid December 11, 2022 - June 10, 2023**. Advance details of summer services from June 11, 2023 (selected international tables only) appear at the back of this edition, pages 670 - 674. Services can change at short notice and passengers are advised to consult the latest European Rail Timetable before travelling. International trains are not normally affected by public holidays, but may alter at Christmas and Easter - these changes (where known) are shown in the tables. Readers are advised to cross-check timings and days of running of services in the International section with the relevant country section.

Tickets **Seat reservations** are available for most international trains and are advisable as some trains can get very crowded. **Supplements** are payable on **EuroCity** (*EC*) trains in most countries and on most InterCity trains – consult the introduction at the start of each country to see which supplements apply.

Listed below is a selection of the different types of trains found in the International Section.

DAY SERVICES:

AP	***Alfa Pendular***	Portuguese high-quality tilting express train.
Alvia	***Alvia***	Spanish high-speed train.
AV	***Alta Velocità***	Italian premium fare **ETR 500** services using high-speed lines.
AVE	***Alta Velocidad Española***	Spanish high-speed train.
EC	***EuroCity***	Quality international express. Supplement may be payable.
Em	***Euromed***	Spanish 200 km/h train.
☆	***Eurostar***	High-speed (300 km/h) service London - Paris / Brussels. Special fares payable. Three classes of service on most trains: (Business Premier, Standard Premier and Standard). Minimum check-in time 30 minutes.
FA	***Frecciargento***	Italian tilting trains using both high-speed and traditional lines.
FB	***Frecciabianca***	Italian fast premium fare services using traditional lines.
FR	***Frecciarossa***	Italian fast premium fare services using high-speed lines.
Ex	***Express***	Express between Czech Republic and Slovakia.
IC	***InterCity***	Express train. Supplement may be payable.
ICE	***InterCity Express***	German high-speed (230 - 320 km/h) service.
ICd	***Intercity Direct***	Dutch international express.
IR	***InterRegio***	Inter-regional express usually with refurbished coaches.
IRE	***Interregio-Express***	German / Polish train.
ITA	***.italo***	Italian high-speed train. Supplement payable.
LE	***Leo Express***	Czech quality international express with three classes of service: (Premium, Business and Economy).
RJ *RJX*	***Railjet***	Austrian quality international express with three classes of service: (Business, First and Economy).
RE	***Regional Express***	Regional semi-fast train.
REX	***Regional Express***	Austrian semi-fast train.
SC	***SuperCity***	Czech Pendolino **680** tilting train, supplement payable.
⇌	***Thalys***	High-speed (300 km/h) international train. Three classes of service on most trains: (Premium, Comfort and Standard).
TGV	**Train à Grande Vitesse**	French high-speed (270 - 320 km/h) train.
Sn	***Snabbtåg***	Swedish high-speed (200 km/h) train.

NIGHT SERVICES:

EN	***EuroNight***	Quality international overnight express.
D	***Durchgangszug*** or **Schnellzug**	Overnight or international express. Some may only convey passengers to international destinations and are likely to be compulsory reservation, marked [R].
ICN	***InterCity Notte***	Italian overnight train, supplement payable.
NJ	***ÖBB nightjet***	Austrian brand name covering international services (previously City Night Line). Facilities range from *Comfortline Deluxe* sleeping cars (1, 2 and 3 berth) with en-suite shower and WC, to modernised *Comfortline Economy* sleeping cars and 4 / 6 berth couchettes. 2nd class seats are also conveyed (in six seat compartments). Most trains convey shower facilities and 🍷 (also ✕ on certain services). Special fares apply and reservation is compulsory on most services.

EUROTUNNEL

The frequent car-carrying service between Folkestone and Calais through the **Channel Tunnel** is operated by Eurotunnel. The service operates up to four times hourly (less frequently at night) and takes about 35 minutes. Passengers stay with their cars during the journey. Separate less-frequent trains operate for lorries, coaches, motorcycles, and cars with caravans. Reservations are advisable but passengers can buy tickets at the toll booths when they arrive at the terminal and board the next available shuttle.
Reservations: ✆ 08443 35 35 35.

9 LONDON, AMSTERDAM, BRUSSELS and LILLE - ST GERVAIS and BOURG ST MAURICE

Other connections are available by changing in Paris (or in Lille and Lyon)

Supplements are payable on TGV trains

Winter 2022/2023 timetable.

train type		*TGV*	*TGV*	⇌	⇌	*TGV*	⇌			
train number		**5190**	**5116**	**9903**	**9906**	**5108**	**9920/1**			
train number		**5191**	**5117**	**9902**	**9904**		**9924/5**	❦		❦
notes		[R] 🍷	[R] 🍷	[R] 🍷	[R] 🍷	[R] 🍷	[R] 🍷			
notes		**X**	**Y**	**C**	**C**	**X**	**A**	**G**		**E**
London St Pancras	d.	...	...	...	...	...	...	1001	...	1934
Ashford International	a.	...	...	...	...	...	...	|	...	|
Ashford International	d.	...	...	...	...	...	...	|	...	|
Amsterdam Centraal	d.	...	...	...	...	...	0540	|	...	|
Schiphol	d.	...	...	...	...	...	0556	|	...	|
Rotterdam CS	d.	...	...	...	...	...	0625	|	...	|
Antwerpen Centraal	d.	...	...	...	...	...	0706	|	...	|
Brussels Midi / Zuid	d.	...	...	0610	0713	...	0800	|	...	|
Lille Europe	d.	...	...	|	|	0707	|	|	...	|
Lille Flandres ◇	d.	0534	0615	|	|	|	|	|	...	|
Douai	d.	0556	0637	|	|	|	|	|	...	|
Arras	d.	0612	0700	|	|	|	|	|	...	|
TGV Haute Picardie	d.	0632	0725	|	|	0746	|	|	...	|
Paris Charles de Gaulle ✈	d.	0705	0759	0738	0838	0822	0918	|	...	|
Marne la Valleé Chessy §	d.	0719	0813	|	|	0838	|	|	...	|
Cluses (Haute Savoie)	a.	|	|	|	|	1300	|	|	...	|
Salanches Megève	a.	|	|	|	|	1325	|	|	...	|
St Gervais	a.	|	|	|	|	1336	|	|	...	|
Chambéry	a.	1028	1106	1037	1200	...	1216	|	...	|
Albertville	a.	1108	1149	1123	1235	...	1301	|	...	|
Moûtiers-Salins	a.	1148	1221	1201	1316	...	1356	1826	...	0536
Aime la Plagne	a.	1209	1239	1224	...	...	1420	|	...	|
Landry	a.	1220	1249	1237	...	...	1431	|	...	|
Bourg St Maurice	a.	1232	1301	1250	...	...	1441	1905	...	0630

train type				*TGV*	⇌	*TGV*	⇌	*TGV*	⇌	*TGV*
train number				**5174**	**9969**	**5196**	**9987/6**	**5178**	**9983**	**5198**
train number		❦		**5175**	**9967**	**5197**	**9979/8**		**9982**	
notes				[R] 🍷	[R] 🍷	[R] 🍷	[R] 🍷	[R] 🍷	[R] 🍷	[R] 🍷
notes		**F**		**X**	**D**	**Y**	**B**	**X**	**V**	**Y**
Bourg St Maurice	d.	0931	...	1343	...	1525	1538	...	1700	1748
Landry	d.	|	...	1353	...	1534	1550	...	1715	1758
Aime la Plagne	d.	|	...	1403	...	1544	1609	...	1726	1808
Moûtiers-Salins	a.	|	...	|	...	|	|	...	|	|
Moûtiers-Salins	d.	1018	...	1420	1557	1611	1629	...	1743	1824
Albertville	d.	|	...	1504	1634	1652	1708	...	1819	1855
Chambéry	d.	|	...	1553	1716	1741	1749	...	1906	1941
St Gervais	d.	|	...	|	|	|	|	1532	|	|
Salanches Megève	d.	|	...	|	|	|	|	1552	|	|
Cluses (Haute Savoie)	d.	|	...	|	|	|	|	1608	|	|
Marne la Vallée Chessy §	a.	|	...	1845	|	2046	|	2102	|	2247
Paris Charles de Gaulle ✈	a.	|	...	1911	2022	2106	2047	2120	2218	2301
TGV Haute Picardie	a.	|	...	1944	|	2140	|	2158	|	|
Arras	a.	|	...	2012	|	2159	|	|	|	|
Douai	a.	|	...	2039	|	2216	|	|	|	|
Lille Flandres ◇	a.	|	...	2102	|	2240	|	|	|	|
Lille Europe	a.	|	...	...	|	...	|	2229	|	2356
Brussels Midi / Zuid	a.	|	...	...	2151	...	2209	...	2334	...
Antwerpen Centraal	a.	|	...	...	...	...	2257	...	...	...
Rotterdam CS	a.	|	...	...	...	...	2333	...	...	...
Schiphol	a.	|	...	...	...	...	2354	...	...	...
Amsterdam Centraal	a.	|	...	...	...	...	0013	...	...	...
Ashford International	a.	|	...	...	...	...	...	...	...	...
London St Pancras	a.	1600	...	...	...	...	...	...	...	...

A – THALYS NEIGE – ⑥ Dec. 24 - Mar. 18: (12) 🍷 Amsterdam - Bourg St Maurice; ⑥ Mar. 25. - Apr. 8: (12) 🍷 Brussels - Bourg St Maurice.

B – THALYS NEIGE – ⑥ Dec. 31 - Mar. 25: (12) 🍷 Bourg St Maurice - Amsterdam; ⑥ Apr. 1 - Apr. 8: (12) 🍷 Bourg St Maurice - Brussels.

C – THALYS NEIGE – Feb. 18, 25.

D – THALYS NEIGE – Feb. 25, Mar. 4.

E – TRAVELSKI EXPRESS ⑤ Dec. 23 - Apr. 7.

F – TRAVELSKI EXPRESS ⑥ Dec. 24 - Apr. 15.

G – TRAVELSKI EXPRESS Dec. 17.

V – Feb. 25.

X – Dec. 17, 24, 31, Feb. 11, 18, 25.

Y – ⑥ Dec. 17 - Mar 25.

§ – Station for Disneyland, Paris.

⇌ – *Thalys* high-speed train [R] 🍷. Special fares payable.

◇ – 500 metres from Lille Europe (see Lille City Plan on page 32).

❦ – *Travelski Express*. Bookings only available as part of a package, including accommodation, through www.travelski.com and also snowcarbon.co.uk. Timings may vary.

LONDON - LILLE - PARIS and BRUSSELS *by Eurostar* 10

Special fares payable that include three classes of service: business premier, standard premier and standard. All times shown are local times (France and Belgium are one hour ahead of Great Britain). All Eurostar services are [R], non-smoking and convey ✕ in Business Premier and Standard Premier, 🍸 in Standard.
See shaded panel in Table **10** on page 47 for information about recommended arrival times at departure station.

Service February 5 - March 25.
For service March 26 - May 20 see page 48. For service May 21 - July 29 see page 670.
From February 5 until March 6 services will arrive 10 minutes later / depart 10 minutes earlier at Paris Nord due to engineering work

km	km	*train number*	**9080**	**9106**	**9002**	**9004**	**9110**	**9008**	**9114**	**9010**	**9116**	**9014**	**9018**	**9022**	**9126**	**9024**	**9132**			
		notes	①–⑤	①–⑤	⑥	①–⑤	⑥			⑥				⑦						
		notes		**A**					**A**						**A**					
0	*0*	**London** St Pancras .... d.	0601	0616	0631	0701	0704	0801	0816	0831	0901	0931	1024	1131	1104	1231	1301	...	...	...
35	*35*	Ebbsfleet International .... d.	│	│	│	│	│	│	│	│	│	│	│	│	│	│	│	...	...	...
90	*90*	Ashford International .... d.	│	│	│	│	│	│	│	│	│	│	│	│	│	│	│	...	...	...
166	*166*	Calais Fréthun .... a.	│	│	│	│	│	│	│	│	│	│	│	│	│	│	│	...	...	...
267	*267*	Lille Europe .... a.	│	│	│	│	0926	│	│	│	1127	│	│	│	1326	│	1527	...	...	...
	373	**Brussels** Midi / Zuid .... a.	│	0912	│	│	1005	│	1112	│	1205	│	│	│	1405	│	1606	...	...	...
492		**Paris** Nord .... a.	0920	...	0947	1017	...	1120	...	1147	...	1247	1347	1447	...	1547	...	...	...	...

train number	**9032**	**9142**	**9036**	**9038**	**9040**	**9044**	**9046**	**9046**	**9152**	**9152**	**9050**	**9158**	**9054**							
notes				⑤⑦			①②③	⑤		⑤	Ⓑ									
notes							④⑥⑦		**A C**	**A**			❦							
London St Pancras .... d.	1431	1504	1531	1601	1631	1731	1756	1801	1801	1813	1901	1934	2001	...	...	...	...	...	...	...
Ebbsfleet International .... d.	│	│	│	│	│	│	│	│	│	│	│	│	│	...	...	...	...	...	...	...
Ashford International .... d.	│	│	│	│	│	│	│	│	│	│	│	│	│	...	...	...	...	...	...	...
Calais Fréthun .... a.	│	│	│	│	│	│	│	│	│	│	│	│	│	...	...	...	...	...	...	...
Lille Europe .... a.	│	1726	│	│	│	│	│	│	2026	│	│	2200	│	...	...	...	...	...	...	...
Brussels Midi / Zuid .... a.	│	1805	│	│	│	│	│	│	2113	2112	│	2238	│	...	...	...	...	...	...	...
Paris Nord .... a.	1747	...	1850	1920	1947	2047	2115	2117	...	...	2217	...	2322	...	...	...	...	...	...	...

train number	**9007**	**9009**	**9011**	**9117**	**9013**	**9015**	**9119**	**9019**	**9023**	**9135**	**9027**	**9031**	**9035**	**9141**	**9037**	**9039**	**9145**	**9043**	**9047**	
notes	①–⑥	①–⑤	⑥⑦		①–⑤		①–⑥	⑤⑦			⑦		⑥		⑦		Ⓑ			
notes							**A**										**A**			
Paris Nord .... d.	0713	0743	0813	...	0843	0913	...	1013	1113	...	1213	1313	1413	...	1443	1513	...	1613	1713	...
Brussels Midi / Zuid .... d.	│	│	│	0852	│	│	0951	│	│	1256	│	│	│	1452	│	│	1556	│	│	...
Lille Europe .... d.	│	│	│	0930	│	│	│	│	│	1335	│	│	│	1530	│	│	1635	│	│	...
Calais Fréthun .... d.	│	│	│	│	│	│	│	│	│	│	│	│	│	│	│	│	│	│	│	...
Ashford International .... a.	│	│	│	│	│	│	│	│	│	│	│	│	│	│	│	│	│	│	│	...
Ebbsfleet International .... a.	│	│	│	│	│	│	│	│	│	│	│	│	│	│	│	│	│	│	│	...
London St Pancras .... a.	0830	0900	0930	0957	1000	1030	1100	1130	1230	1357	1330	1430	1530	1557	1602	1630	1657	1730	1830	...

train number	**9153**	**9051**	**9157**	**9055**	**9059**	**9163**	**9167**	**9063**												
notes		Ⓑ				⑥	Ⓑ	Ⓑ												
notes			**A**				**A**													
Paris Nord .... d.	...	1813	...	1913	2013	...	...	2113	...	...	...	...	...	...	...	...	...	...	...	...
Brussels Midi / Zuid .... d.	1756	│	1851	│	│	2022	2056	│	...	...	...	...	...	...	...	...	...	...	...	...
Lille Europe .... d.	1835	│	│	│	│	2100	2133	│	...	...	...	...	...	...	...	...	...	...	...	...
Calais Fréthun .... d.	│	│	│	│	│	│	│	│	...	...	...	...	...	...	...	...	...	...	...	...
Ashford International .... a.	│	│	│	│	│	│	│	│	...	...	...	...	...	...	...	...	...	...	...	...
Ebbsfleet International .... a.	│	│	│	│	│	│	│	│	...	...	...	...	...	...	...	...	...	...	...	...
London St Pancras .... a.	1857	1930	2000	2036	2130	2127	2157	2230	...	...	...	...	...	...	...	...	...	...	...	...

A – To / from Amsterdam, see Table **18**. **C** – ①②③④⑦. ❦ – Depart 1931, 1946 on certain dates.

EUROSTAR – WHEN SHOULD I ARRIVE AT THE STATION?

Figures shown below are minutes before scheduled departure, the first being the recommended arrival time with the second indicating when gates close. Connections at Paris, Lille and Brussels, shown in our international section, have been set to allow time to reach the check-in area before the gate closes. **NOTE**: We have set the minimum connecting time at Brussels and Lille to 45 minutes (allowing up to 15 minutes to transfer to the check-in area). For cross-Paris connections we have allowed a minimum of 105 minutes (60 minutes to transfer between Paris stations and 15 minutes to check-in before the gate closes). In most cases longer connecting times are shown, but readers may still wish to consider booking earlier connecting services.

Station	*Recommended*	*Gates close*	*Station*	*Recommended*	*Gates close*
LONDON ST PANCRAS	90	30	**ROTTERDAM CENTRAAL**	60–90	30
PARIS NORD	90–120	30	**AMSTERDAM CENTRAAL**	60–90	30
BRUSSELS MIDI / ZUID	90–120	30	**MARNE LA VALLÉE**	90–120	30
LILLE EUROPE	90	30			

LONDON – PARIS *by rail–sea–rail* 10a

Other services are available by taking normal service trains between London and Dover (Tables **100**, **101**), sailings between Dover and Calais (Table **2110**) and normal service trains between Calais and Paris, by changing at Boulogne (Table **261**), passengers making their own way between stations and docks at Dover and Calais, allowing at least 1 hour for connections.

French train number			⛴					⚡			⛴					⚡		⛴						
sea crossing (see below)							⑦		Ⓐ	⑥		Ⓒ	Ⓐ											
notes																								
London St Pancras .... d.	...	...	...	...	...	...	...	0907	...	...	...	...	...	...	...	1307	...	...	...	...	...	...	...	...
London Charing Cross .... d.	...	...	...	...	...	...	0812v	│	0900	0859	...	...	...	...	...	│	1259	...	...	...	...	...	...	...
Dover Priory ❦ .... a.	...	...	...	...	...	...	1036	1012	1019	1049	...	...	...	...	...	1412	1449	...	...	...	...	...	...	...
Dover Eastern Docks ▦ ❦ . d.	...	...	0955	...	...	...	...	...	...	...	1340	...	...	...	...	...	...	1725	...	...	...	...	...	...
Calais Port ▦ ❖ .... a.	...	...	1225	...	...	...	...	...	...	...	1610	...	...	...	...	...	...	1955	...	...	...	...	...	...
Calais Ville ❖ .... d.	...	...	...	1436	...	...	...	...	...	...	...	1737	1738	...	...	...	...	...	...	...	...	...	...	...
Boulogne Ville .... d.	...	...	...	1504	...	...	...	...	...	...	...	1804	1804	...	...	...	...	...	...	...	...	...	...	...
Amiens .... a.	...	...	...	1620	...	...	...	...	...	...	...	1921	1920	...	...	...	...	...	...	...	...	...	...	...
Paris Nord .... a.	...	...	...	1729	...	...	...	...	...	...	...	2029	2056	...	...	...	...	...	...	...	...	...	...	...

French train number				⛴	⚡						⛴			⚡					⛴		⚡	⚡		
sea crossing (see below)		⑥	Ⓐ						Ⓒ	✕		Ⓐ	Ⓒ				Ⓐ	⑥		Ⓐ	⑥	Ⓑ		
notes										**A**														
Paris Nord .... d.	...	...	...	...	...	...	...	...	0931	1031	...	...	...	...	...	...	...	...	...	...	...	...	...	...
Amiens .... d.	...	0532	0547	...	...	...	...	...	1037	1140	...	...	...	...	...	...	1248	1332	...	...	...	...	...	...
Boulogne Ville .... d.	...	0658	0708	...	...	...	...	...	1155	1258	...	...	...	...	...	...	1408	1458	...	...	...	...	...	...
Calais Ville ❖ .... a.	...	0738	0742	...	...	...	...	...	1227	1326	...	...	...	...	...	...	1442	1538	...	...	...	...	...	...
Calais Port ▦ ❖ .... d.	...	...	...	1035	...	...	...	...	...	...	1550	...	...	...	...	...	...	...	1850	...	...	...	...	...
Dover Eastern Docks ▦ ❦ . a.	...	...	...	1105	...	...	...	...	...	...	1620	...	...	...	...	...	...	...	1920	...	...	...	...	...
Dover Priory ❦ .... d.	...	...	...	...	1248	1300	...	...	...	...	...	1754	1800	1848	...	...	...	...	...	2100	2145	2148	...	...
London Charing Cross .... a.	...	...	...	...	│	1449	...	...	...	...	...	1949	1949	│	...	...	...	...	...	2249	│	│	...	...
London St Pancras .... a.	...	...	...	...	1354	...	...	...	...	...	...	...	...	1957	...	...	...	...	...	...	2254	2254	...	...

A – Until Feb. 4 and from Apr. 3. **v** – London **Victoria**. ⚡ – Supplement payable.

⛴ – Ship service, operated by P & O Ferries. ✕ on Ship. Pre-book only. One class only on ship. Check-in will close 90 minutes before departure. 60 minutes allowed between rail station and port. Disembark 30 minutes after arrival in port.

❦ – Passengers make their own way between Dover Priory and Dover Eastern Docks.
❖ – 🚌 service between Calais Port and Calais Ville station and v.v.

10 LONDON - LILLE - PARIS and BRUSSELS *by Eurostar*

Special fares payable that include three classes of service: business premier, standard premier and standard. All times shown are local times (France and Belgium are one hour ahead of Great Britain). All Eurostar services are Ⓡ, non-smoking and convey ✕ in Business Premier and Standard Premier, 🍸 in Standard.
See shaded panel in Table **10** on page 47 for information about recommended arrival times at departure station.

Service March 26 - May 20.
For service February 5 - March 25 see page 47. For service May 21 - July 29 see page 670.

km	km	*train number*	**9080**	**9106**	**9002**	**9004**	**9110**	**9008**	**9114**	**9010**	**9116**	**9014**	**9018**	**9022**	**9126**	**9024**	**9132**	**9028**		
		notes	①–⑤	①–⑤	⑥	①–⑤	⑥			⑥				⑦				①–⑥		
		notes	**B**	**AD**		**B**			**A**					**E**	**A**			**D**		
0	*0*	**London** St Pancras........ d.	0601	0616	0631	0701	0704	0801	0816	0831	0855	0931	1026	1131	1104	1231	1301	1331	...	...
35	*35*	Ebbsfleet International........ d.																	...	...
90	*90*	Ashford International.......... d.																	...	...
166	*166*	Calais Fréthun.................... a.																	...	...
267	*267*	Lille Europe........................ a.					0926				1127				1326		1527		...	...
	373	**Brussels** Midi / Zuid........ a.		0912			1005		1112		1205				1405		1606		...	...
492		**Paris** Nord........................ a.	0920	...	0947	1017	...	1120	...	1147	...	1247	1357	1447	...	1547	...	1647	...	...

train number	**9032**	**9142**	**9036**	**9038**	**9040**	**9044**	**9046**	**9046**	**9152**	**9152**	**9050**	**9158**	**9054**							
notes				⑤⑦			①②③④⑥⑦	⑤		⑤	Ⓑ									
notes				**G**		**H**			**AC**	**A**										
London St Pancras............ d.	1431	1504	1531	1601	1631	1731	1756	1801	1804	1813	1901	1934	2001	...	...	...	...	...	...	...
Ebbsfleet International .... d.														...	...	...	...	...	...	...
Ashford International.......... d.														...	...	...	...	...	...	...
Calais Fréthun .... a.														...	...	...	...	...	...	...
Lille Europe .... a.		1726							2030			2200		...	...	...	...	...	...	...
Brussels Midi / Zuid.......... a.		1805							2112	2112		2238		...	...	...	...	...	...	...
Paris Nord.......................... a.	1747	...	1850	1920	1947	2047	2117	2117	...	...	2217	...	2317	...	...	...	...	...	...	...

train number	**9007**	**9009**	**9011**	**9117**	**9013**	**9015**	**9119**	**9019**	**9023**	**9135**	**9027**	**9031**	**9033**	**9035**	**9141**	**9037**	**9039**	**9145**	**9043**	**9047**
notes	①–⑥	①–⑤	⑥⑦		①–⑤		①–⑥				⑦		⑦	⑥		⑦		Ⓑ		
notes	**J**	**D**	**G**		**D**		**AD**				**K**		**K**			**G**		**A**		
Paris Nord.......................... d.	0713	0743	0813	...	0843	0913	...	1013	1113	...	1213	1313	1343	1413	...	1443	1503	...	1613	1703
Brussels Midi / Zuid.......... d.				0852			0951			1256					1452			1556		
Lille Europe .... d.				0930						1335					1530			1635		
Calais Fréthun .... d.																				
Ashford International.......... a.																				
Ebbsfleet International .... a.																				
London St Pancras............ a.	0830	0900	0930	0957	1000	1030	1100	1130	1230	1357	1330	1430	1500	1530	1600	1602	1639	1657	1730	1832

train number	**9153**	**9051**	**9157**	**9055**	**9059**	**9163**	**9167**	**9063**												
notes		Ⓑ				⑥	Ⓑ	Ⓑ												
notes			**A**				**A**													
Paris Nord.......................... d.	...	1813	...	1903	2013	...	...	2103	...	...	...	...	...	...	...	...	...	...	...	...
Brussels Midi / Zuid.......... d.	1756		1851			2020	2055		...	...	...	...	...	...	...	...	...	...	...	...
Lille Europe .... d.	1835					2058	2135		...	...	...	...	...	...	...	...	...	...	...	...
Calais Fréthun .... d.									...	...	...	...	...	...	...	...	...	...	...	...
Ashford International.......... a.									...	...	...	...	...	...	...	...	...	...	...	...
Ebbsfleet International .... a.									...	...	...	...	...	...	...	...	...	...	...	...
London St Pancras............ a.	1857	1930	2000	2039	2130	2127	2157	2239	...	...	...	...	...	...	...	...	...	...	...	...

A – To / from Amsterdam, see Table **18**.
B – Not Apr. 10, May 1.
C – ①②③④⑦.
D – Not Apr. 10, May 1.
E – Also Apr. 1, 8, 10, 15, May 1, 8.
G – Also Apr. 10, May 1.
H – Not Mar. 31, Apr. 7, 14.
J – Not Apr. 10, May 1, 8.
K – Also Apr. 10, May 1, 8.

LONDON / BRUSSELS - LILLE - CHARLES DE GAULLE ✈ - WESTERN / SOUTHERN FRANCE 11

DAY TRAINS (FOR NIGHT TRAINS SEE TABLE 13). Supplements are payable on *TGV* trains. Connections at Lille are not guaranteed. Other connections available via Paris.

km	train type	TGV	TGV	TGV	TGV	TGV	TGV	TGV	TGV	TGV	TGV	TGV	TGV	TGV
	train number	5102	7831	7669	5202	5010	9810	5210	7867	9870	9812	5113	6823	5224
	train number	5103	7830	7668	5203		9811	5211	7866	9871	9813		6822	5225
	notes	R ♀ A	R ⊠	R ⊠	R ♀	R ♀ ⚒	R ♀	R ♀	R ⊠	R ♀	R ♀	R ♀ ⑥	R ♀ Ⓐ	R ♀
	London St Pancras d.	...	...	...	...	...	...	...	...	...	...	...	...	...
	Brussels Midi / Zuid d.	...	...	...	...	...	0635	...	...	0717	0817	...	...	...
	Tourcoing d.	...	...	0602	...	...	|	...	0744	|	|	...	...	...
	Lille Europe a.	...	...	|	...	...	0712	...	|	0751	0852	...	...	...
0	**Lille** Europe d.	0550	...	|	...	0724	0724	0752	|	0802	0903	0903	...	...
	Lille Flandres ◇ d.	|	...	|	0615	|	|	|	|	|	|	|	...	0932
	Douai d.	|	...	|	0637	|	|	|	|	|	|	|	...	1001
	Arras d.	|	...	|	0700	|	|	|	|	|	|	|	...	1019
99	TGV Haute Picardie d.	|	...	0643	0725	0754	0754	|	|	|	|	|	...	1045
203	Paris Charles de Gaulle ✈ a.	0645	...	0712	0754	0823	0823	0842	0848	0853	0953	0953	...	1113
203	Paris Charles de Gaulle ✈ d.	0651	0655	0717	0810	0829	0829	0848	0854	0859	0958	0958	...	1119
227	Marne la Vallée § d.	0707	0712	0732	0835	0843	0843	0902	0910	|	1012	1012	...	1132
	Strasbourg a.	|	|	|	|	|	|	|	|	1105	|	|	...	|
289	Massy TGV d.	|	|	0812	0909	|	|	0942	|	...	|	|	...	1210
	Le Mans a.	|	|	|	|	|	|	1029	|	...	|	|	...	|
	Rennes a.	|	|	|	|	|	|	1120	|	...	|	|	...	|
	Angers St Laud a.	|	|	|	|	|	|	...	|	...	|	|	...	1402
	Nantes a.	|	|	|	|	|	|	...	|	...	|	|	...	1444
	St Pierre des Corps a.	|	|	0906	1006	|	|	...	|	...	|	|	...	...
	Poitiers a.	|	|	0940	1041	|	|	...	|	...	|	|	...	...
	Angoulême a.	|	|	1023	1123	|	|	...	|	...	|	|	...	...
	Bordeaux a.	|	|	1102	1202	|	|	...	|	...	|	|	...	...
	Le Creusot TGV a.	|	|	...	...	|	|	...	|	...	|	|	...	...
521	**Lyon** Part Dieu a.	0900	|	...	...	1030	1030	...	1100	...	1202	1202	1210	...
	Lyon St Exupéry ✈ a.	|	|	...	...	|	|	...	|	...	|	|	|	...
	Valence TGV a.	|	|	...	...	1115	1115	...	1145	...	1245	1245	1247	...
	Avignon TGV a.	1009	0947	...	...	1152	1152	...	|	...	|	1328	|	...
	Nîmes a.	|	|	...	...	|	|	...	|	...	1334	|	1335	...
	Nîmes Pont-du-Gard a.	|	|	...	...	|	|	...	1229	...	|	|	|	...
	Montpellier Sud de France a.	|	|	...	...	|	|	...	1253	...	|	|	|	...
	Montpellier Saint-Roch a.	|	|	...	...	|	|	...	...	...	1402	|	1405	...
	Béziers a.	|	|	...	...	|	|	...	...	...	...	|	1446	...
	Narbonne a.	|	|	...	...	|	|	...	...	...	...	|	1502	...
	Toulouse Matabiau a.	|	|	...	...	|	|	...	...	...	...	|	1619	...
	Perpignan a.	|	|	...	...	|	|	...	...	...	...	|	...	...
	Aix en Provence TGV a.	1031	1009	...	...	|	|	...	...	...	...	|	...	...
	Marseille St Charles a.	1046	1024	...	...	1224	1224	...	...	...	...	1401	...	...
	Toulon a.	...	...	...	...	...	...	...	...	...	...	...	...	...
	St Raphaël - Valescure a.	...	...	...	...	...	...	...	...	...	...	...	...	...
	Cannes a.	...	...	...	...	...	...	...	...	...	...	...	...	...
	Nice a.	...	...	...	...	...	...	...	...	...	...	...	...	...

train type	☆	TGV	TGV	TGV	TGV	☆	TGV	☆	☆	TGV	TGV	TGV	TGV	TGV
train number	9110	9826	5026	5026	7840	9116	7835	9074	9126	9830	9874	6825	7844	5120
train number		9827			7841		7834			9831	9875	6824	7845	5121
notes	R ✕ ⑥	R ♀	R ♀ Ⓑ	R ♀ ⑥ B	R ⊠	R ✕	R ⊠	R ✕ C	R ✕	R ♀	R ♀	R ♀	R ⊠	R D
London St Pancras d.	0704	...	...	...	...	0855	...	1031	1104	...	...	...	...	...
Brussels Midi / Zuid d.	|	1017	...	...	...	|	...	|	|	1317	1317	...	...	...
Tourcoing d.	|	|	...	...	...	|	...	|	|	|	|	...	...	...
Lille Europe a.	0926	1052	...	...	...	1127	...	1254	1326	1352	1352	...	...	...
Lille Europe d.	...	1103	1103	1103	...	...	...	|	...	1402	1402	...	...	1518
Lille Flandres ◇ d.	...	|	|	|	1132	...	1301	|	...	|	|	...	1520	|
Douai d.	...	|	|	|	|	...	|	|	...	|	|	...	|	|
Arras d.	...	|	|	|	|	...	|	|	...	|	|	...	|	|
TGV Haute Picardie d.	...	|	|	|	|	...	|	|	...	|	|	...	1607	|
Paris Charles de Gaulle ✈ a.	...	1153	1153	1153	1225	...	1353	|	...	1452	1452	...	1635	1610
Paris Charles de Gaulle ✈ d.	...	1159	1159	1159	1231	...	1358	|	...	1457	1457	...	1640	1627
Marne la Vallée § d.	...	1211	1211	1211	1246	...	1412	1355	...	1512	1523	...	1654	1642
Strasbourg a.	...	|	|	|	|	...	|	...	...	|	1737	...	|	|
Massy TGV d.	...	|	|	|	|	...	|	...	...	|	...	...	|	|
Le Mans a.	...	|	|	|	|	...	|	...	...	|	...	...	|	|
Rennes a.	...	|	|	|	|	...	|	...	...	|	...	...	|	|
Angers St Laud a.	...	|	|	|	|	...	|	...	...	|	...	...	|	|
Nantes a.	...	|	|	|	|	...	|	...	...	|	...	...	|	|
St Pierre des Corps a.	...	|	|	|	|	...	|	...	...	|	...	...	|	|
Poitiers a.	...	|	|	|	|	...	|	...	...	|	...	...	|	|
Angoulême a.	...	|	|	|	|	...	|	...	...	|	...	...	|	|
Bordeaux a.	...	|	|	|	|	...	|	...	...	|	...	...	|	|
Le Creusot TGV a.	...	|	|	|	|	...	|	...	...	|	...	...	|	|
Lyon Part Dieu a.	...	1404	1404	1404	|	...	1602	...	...	1700	...	1810	|	1834
Lyon St Exupéry ✈ a.	...	|	...	|	1433	...	|	...	...	|	...	|	1842	|
Valence TGV a.	...	1446	...	1446	|	...	|	...	...	|	...	1846	1929	1921
Avignon TGV a.	...	|	...	|	1527	...	1712	...	...	1807	...	|	2006	|
Nîmes a.	...	|	...	|	|	...	|	...	...	|	...	1935	|	2016
Nîmes Pont-du-Gard a.	...	1526	...	1526	|	...	|	...	...	|	...	|	|	|
Montpellier Sud de France a.	...	1550	...	1550	|	...	|	...	...	|	...	|	|	|
Montpellier Saint-Roch a.	...	...	...	...	|	...	|	...	...	|	...	2006	|	2054
Béziers a.	...	...	...	...	|	...	|	...	...	|	...	2050	|	...
Narbonne a.	...	...	...	...	|	...	|	...	...	|	...	2103	|	...
Toulouse Matabiau a.	...	...	...	...	|	...	|	...	...	|	...	2219	|	...
Perpignan a.	...	...	...	...	|	...	|	...	...	|	...	...	|	...
Aix en Provence TGV a.	...	...	...	...	1549	...	|	...	...	1829	...	...	2028	...
Marseille St Charles a.	...	...	...	...	1608	...	1743	...	...	1844	...	...	2043	...
Toulon a.	...	...	...	...	...	...	...	...	...	...	...	...	...	...
St Raphaël - Valescure a.	...	...	...	...	...	...	...	...	...	...	...	...	...	...
Cannes a.	...	...	...	...	...	...	...	...	...	...	...	...	...	...
Nice a.	...	...	...	...	...	...	...	...	...	...	...	...	...	...

A – Ⓐ Dec. 12 - Mar. 24.
⚒ Mar. 27 - Dec. 9.

B – ⑥ Mar. 11 - Nov. 4.

C – ①③⑤⑦ Feb. 5 - June 5. Depart London 1026, 1014 on certain dates. See Table **17**.

D – ⑤ (④⑤⑦ Mar. 9 - Nov. 5).

§ – Marne la Vallée - Chessy (station for Disneyland).

◇ – 500 metres from Lille Europe (see Lille City Plan on page 32).

△ – To / from Lorient or Quimper on dates in Table **285**.

☆ – Eurostar train. Special fares payable. ✕ in Business Premier and Standard Premier, ♀ in Standard. Business Premier not available to Marne la Vallée - Chessy. See shaded panel in Table **10** on page 47 for information about recommended arrival times at departure station. Valid Feb. 5 - May 20.

⊠ – OUIGO low-cost TGV service. Internet bookings only at www.ouigo.com. Timings may vary.

11 LONDON / BRUSSELS - LILLE - CHARLES DE GAULLE ✈ - WESTERN / SOUTHERN FRANCE

DAY TRAINS (FOR NIGHT TRAINS SEE TABLE 13). Supplements payable on all *TGV* services. Connections at Lille are not guaranteed. Other connections available via Paris.

train type		☆	*TGV*	*TGV*	*TGV*	*TGV*	*TGV*	*TGV*	*TGV*	*TGV*		☆	*TGV*	*TGV*	*TGV*	*TGV*	*TGV*		
train number		**9132**	**5120**	**9836**	**9836**	**9835**	**5036**	**5240**	**9838**	**9833**		**9142**	**5124**	**5130**	**9872**	**7814**	**9846**		
train number				**9837**	**9837**			**5241**	**9839**					**5131**	**9873**	**7815**			
notes		🅁 🍴	🅁 ④⑤⑦	🅁 🍷 ①② ③④	🅁 🍷 ⑤⑥⑦	🅁 🍷 ⑥	🅁 🍷 Ⓑ	🅁 🍷	🅁 🍷 △	🅁 🍷		🅁 🍴	🅁 🍷 Ⓑ	🅁 🍷 ▷	🅁 🍷	🅁 🍷 ⊠	🅁 🍷 Ⓑ		
London St Pancras d.	...	1301	...	...	...	...	...	...	...	...	...	1504	...	...	...	...	...	...	...
Brussels Midi / Zuid d.	...	│	...	1617	1617	1617	...	...	1655	1655	...	│	...	...	1817	...	1917	...	...
Tourcoing d.	...	│	...	│	│	│	...	...	│	│	...	│	...	...	│	...	│	...	...
Lille Europe a.	...	1527	...	1653	1653	1653	...	...	1727	1727	...	1726	...	...	1852	...	1951	...	...
Lille Europe d.	...	...	1602	1703	1703	1703	1703	...	1739	1739	...	...	1826	...	1903	...	2001	...	...
Lille Flandres ◇ d.	...	...	│	│	│	│	│	1716	│	│	...	...	│	1857	│	1938	│	...	...
Douai d.	...	...	│	│	│	│	│	│	│	│	...	...	│	│	│	│	│	...	...
Arras d.	...	...	│	│	│	│	│	│	│	│	...	...	│	│	│	│	2035	...	...
TGV Haute Picardie d.	...	...	│	│	│	│	│	│	1815	1815	...	...	1855	│	│	│	│	...	...
Paris Charles de Gaulle ✈ a.	...	...	1653	1753	1753	1753	1753	1810	1842	1842	...	...	1923	1949	1954	│	2016	...	...
Paris Charles de Gaulle ✈ d.	...	...	1658	1758	1758	1758	1758	1818	1847	1847	...	...	1928	1954	2002	│	2121	...	...
Marne la Vallée § d.	...	...	1713	1813	1813	1813	1813	1832	1900	1900	...	...	1954	2004	│	2052	2137	...	...
Strasbourg a.	...	...	│	│	│	│	│	│	│	│	...	...	│	...	2159	│	│	...	...
Massy TGV d.	...	...	│	│	│	│	│	1912	1942	1942	...	...	│	...	...	│	│	...	...
Le Mans a.	...	...	│	│	│	│	│	│	2029	2029	...	...	│	...	...	│	│	...	...
Rennes a.	...	...	│	│	│	│	│	│	2119	│	...	...	│	...	...	│	│	...	...
Angers St Laud a.	...	...	│	│	│	│	│	│	...	2110	...	...	│	...	...	│	│	...	...
Nantes a.	...	...	│	│	│	│	│	│	...	2151	...	...	│	...	...	│	│	...	...
St Pierre des Corps a.	...	...	│	│	│	│	│	2006	...	...	...	...	│	...	...	│	│	...	...
Poitiers a.	...	...	│	│	│	│	│	2040	...	...	...	...	│	...	...	│	│	...	...
Angoulême a.	...	...	│	│	│	│	│	2123	...	...	...	...	│	...	...	│	│	...	...
Bordeaux a.	...	...	│	│	│	│	│	2202	...	...	...	...	│	...	...	│	│	...	...
Le Creusot TGV a.	...	...	│	│	│	│	│	...	...	...	...	...	│	...	...	│	2249	...	...
Lyon Part Dieu a.	...	...	1900	2000	2000	2000	2000	...	...	...	...	...	2140	...	...	2248p	2329	...	...
Lyon St Exupéry ✈ a.	...	...	│	│	│	│	│	...	...	...	...	...	│	...	...	...	...	...	...
Valence TGV a.	...	...	1946	2047	2047	2047	2047	...	...	...	...	...	│	...	...	...	...	...	...
Avignon TGV a.	...	...	│	│	│	2128	│	...	...	...	...	...	2302	...	...	...	...	...	...
Nîmes a.	...	...	│	2134	2134	│	2134	...	...	...	...	...	│	...	...	...	...	...	...
Nîmes Pont-du-Gard a.	...	...	2029	│	│	│	│	...	...	...	...	...	│	...	...	...	...	...	...
Montpellier Sud de France a.	...	...	2053	│	│	│	│	...	...	...	...	...	│	...	...	...	...	...	...
Montpellier Saint-Roch a.	...	...	...	2205	2205	│	2205	...	...	...	...	...	│	...	...	...	...	...	...
Béziers a.	...	...	...	...	2256	│	...	...	...	...	...	...	│	...	...	...	...	...	...
Narbonne a.	...	...	...	...	2312	│	...	...	...	...	...	...	│	...	...	...	...	...	...
Toulouse Matabiau a.	...	...	...	...	│	│	...	...	...	...	...	...	│	...	...	...	...	...	...
Perpignan a.	...	...	...	...	2359	│	...	...	...	...	...	...	│	...	...	...	...	...	...
Aix en Provence TGV a.	...	...	...	...	...	2150	...	...	...	...	...	...	2326	...	...	...	...	...	...
Marseille St Charles a.	...	...	...	...	...	2207	...	...	...	...	...	...	2341	...	...	...	...	...	...
Toulon a.	...	...	...	...	...	...	...	...	...	...	...	...	...	...	...	...	...	...	...
St Raphaël - Valescure a.	...	...	...	...	...	...	...	...	...	...	...	...	...	...	...	...	...	...	...
Cannes a.	...	...	...	...	...	...	...	...	...	...	...	...	...	...	...	...	...	...	...
Nice a.	...	...	...	...	...	...	...	...	...	...	...	...	...	...	...	...	...	...	...

train type		*TGV*	*TGV*	*TGV*	*TGV*	*TGV*	*TGV*	*TGV*	*TGV*	*TGV*	*TGV*	*TGV*	*TGV*	*TGV*		*TGV*	☆		
train number		**9809**	**9852**	**9890**	**5420**	**5152**	**9886**	**9884**	**5260**	**5156**	**7838**	**9854**	**5054**	**5054**		**7818**	**9135**		
train number			**9853**	**9891**	**5421**	**5153**		**9885**	**5261**		**7839**	**9855**				**7819**			
notes		🅁 🍷 Ⓐ	🅁 🍷 ①–⑥	🅁 🍷 ⑦	🅁 🍷 ①–⑥	🅁 🍷 ▷	🅁 🍷	🅁 🍷	🅁 🍷	🅁 ①⑤	🅁 ⊠	🅁 🍷	🅁 🍷 ①②③ ④⑥	🅁 🍷 ⑤		🅁 ⊠	🅁 🍴		
Nice d.	...	...	...	...	...	...	...	...	...	...	...	...	...	...	...	...	...	...	...
Cannes d.	...	...	...	...	...	...	...	...	...	...	...	...	...	...	...	...	...	...	...
St Raphaël - Valescure d.	...	...	...	...	...	...	...	...	...	...	...	...	...	...	...	...	...	...	...
Toulon d.	...	...	...	...	...	...	...	...	...	...	...	...	...	...	...	...	...	...	...
Marseille St Charles d.	...	...	...	...	...	...	...	...	...	...	0613	0636	0636	0636	...	...	...	...	...
Aix en Provence TGV d.	...	...	...	...	...	...	...	...	...	...	0628	0651	0651	0651	...	...	...	...	...
Perpignan d.	...	...	...	...	...	...	...	...	...	...	│	│	│	│	...	...	...	...	...
Toulouse Matabiau d.	...	...	...	...	...	...	...	...	...	...	│	│	│	│	...	...	...	...	...
Narbonne d.	...	...	...	...	...	...	...	...	...	...	│	│	│	│	...	...	...	...	...
Béziers d.	...	...	...	...	...	...	...	...	...	...	│	│	│	│	...	...	...	...	...
Montpellier Saint-Roch d.	...	...	...	...	...	...	...	...	...	0524	│	│	│	│	...	...	...	...	...
Montpellier Sud de France d.	...	...	...	...	...	...	...	...	...	│	│	│	│	│	...	...	...	...	...
Nîmes Pont-du-Gard d.	...	...	...	...	...	...	...	...	...	│	│	│	│	│	...	...	...	...	...
Nîmes d.	...	...	...	...	...	...	...	...	...	0555	│	│	│	│	...	...	...	...	...
Avignon TGV d.	...	...	...	...	...	...	...	...	...	│	0650	0716	0717	0716	...	...	...	...	...
Valence TGV d.	...	...	...	...	...	...	...	...	...	0645	│	│	│	│	...	...	...	...	...
Lyon St Exupéry ✈ d.	...	...	...	...	...	...	...	...	...	│	0744	│	│	│	...	...	...	...	...
Lyon Part Dieu d.	...	...	0550	...	...	...	...	...	...	0730	│	0830	0830	0830	...	0904p	...	...	...
Le Creusot TGV d.	...	...	0632	...	...	...	...	...	...	│	│	│	│	│	...	│	...	...	...
Bordeaux d.	...	...	│	...	...	...	...	...	0558	│	│	│	│	│	...	│	...	...	...
Angoulême d.	...	...	│	...	...	...	...	...	0636	│	│	│	│	│	...	│	...	...	...
Poitiers d.	...	...	│	...	...	...	...	...	0719	│	│	│	│	│	...	│	...	...	...
St Pierre des Corps d.	...	...	│	...	...	...	...	...	0754	│	│	│	│	│	...	│	...	...	...
Nantes d.	...	...	│	...	...	...	0601	...	│	│	│	│	│	│	...	│	...	...	...
Angers St Laud d.	...	...	│	...	...	...	0640	...	│	│	│	│	│	│	...	│	...	...	...
Rennes d.	...	...	│	...	...	...	│	0625	│	│	│	│	│	│	...	│	...	...	...
Le Mans d.	...	...	│	...	...	...	0730	0730	│	│	│	│	│	│	...	│	...	...	...
Massy TGV d.	...	...	│	...	...	...	0826	0826	0855	│	│	│	│	│	...	│	...	...	...
Strasbourg d.	...	...	│	0607	0607	...	│	│	│	│	│	│	│	│	...	│	...	...	...
Marne la Vallée § d.	...	...	0752	│	│	0851	0901	0901	0930	0921	0946	1021	1021	1021	...	1112	...	...	...
Paris Charles de Gaulle ✈ a.	...	...	0802	0757	0758	0902	0911	0911	0941	0933	│	1032	1032	1032	...	1121	...	...	...
Paris Charles de Gaulle ✈ d.	...	...	0807	0806	0811	0907	0916	0916	0946	0946	│	1037	...	1037	...	1127	...	...	...
TGV Haute Picardie d.	...	...	│	│	0840	│	0950	0950	│	│	│	│	...	│	...	│	...	...	...
Arras a.	...	...	│	│	│	│	│	│	│	│	│	│	...	│	...	│	...	...	...
Douai a.	...	...	│	│	│	│	│	│	│	│	│	│	...	│	...	│	...	...	...
Lille Flandres ◇ a.	...	...	│	│	│	│	│	│	1040	1040	1044	│	...	│	...	1221	...	...	...
Lille Europe a.	...	...	0858	0858	0907	0957	1017	1017	...	...	...	1127	...	1127	...	...	...	...	...
Lille Europe d.	...	0720	0909	0908	...	...	1027	1027	...	...	...	1137	...	...	...	...	1335	...	...
Tourcoing a.	...	│	│	│	...	...	│	│	...	...	...	│	...	...	...	...	│	...	...
Brussels Midi / Zuid a.	...	0755	0943	0943	...	...	1101	1101	...	...	...	1217	...	...	...	...	│	...	...
London St Pancras a.	...	...	...	...	...	...	...	...	...	...	...	...	...	...	...	...	1357	...	...

p – Lyon **Perrache**.

▽ – To / from Le Croisic on dates in Table **288**.

△ – To / from Lorient or Quimper on dates in Table **285**.

▷ – To / from Dijon, Besancon and Mulhouse (Table **370**).

§ – Marne la Vallée - Chessy. Station for Disneyland Paris.

◇ – 500 metres from Lille Europe (see Lille City Plan on page 32).

☆ – Eurostar train. Special fares payable. 🍴 in Business Premier and Standard Premier, 🍷 in Standard. See shaded panel in Table **10** on page 47 for information about recommended arrival times at departure station. Valid Feb. 5 - May 20.

⊠ – OUIGO low-cost TGV service. Internet bookings only at www.ouigo.com. Timings may vary.

SOUTHERN / WESTERN FRANCE - CHARLES DE GAULLE ✈ - LILLE - BRUSSELS / LONDON 11

DAY TRAINS (FOR NIGHT TRAINS SEE TABLE 13). Supplements payable on all *TGV* services. Connections at Lille are not guaranteed. Other connections available via Paris.

train type	TGV	TGV	TGV	TGV	☆	TGV	TGV	☆	TGV	TGV	TGV	TGV	☆	TGV	TGV	TGV	TGV	☆
train number	5062	5062	9862	9862	9141	7842	5280	9145	6870	9866	5066	5158	9153	5284	9821	7860	5192	9057
train number			9863	9863		7843	5281		6871	9867				5285		7861	5193	
notes	R 🍸	R 🍸	R 🍸	R 🍸	R ✕	R	R 🍸	R ✕	R 🍸	R 🍸	R 🍸	R 🍸	R ✕	R 🍸	R 🍸	R	R 🍸	R ✕
						⊠						⑥				⊠		
	A	B	①-⑤	E				Ⓑ			C						H	J
Nice d.	...	...	...	...	...	...	...	...	...	...	...	...	...	...	...	...	...	...
Cannes d.	...	...	...	...	...	...	...	...	...	...	...	...	...	...	...	...	...	...
St Raphaël - Valescure d.	...	...	...	...	...	...	...	...	...	...	...	...	...	...	...	...	...	...
Toulon d.	...	...	...	...	...	...	...	...	...	...	...	...	...	...	...	...	...	...
Marseille St Charles d.	...	...	...	...	...	1002	...	...	...	1212	1212	...	...	...	...	...	1333	...
Aix en Provence TGV d.	...	...	...	...	...	1017	...	...	...	1226	1226	...	...	...	...	...	1351	...
Perpignan d.	...	...	...	0708	...	|	...	...	...	|	|	...	...	...	...	...	|	...
Toulouse Matabiau d.	...	...	...	|	...	|	...	...	0743	|	|	...	...	...	...	...	|	...
Narbonne d.	...	...	...	0749	...	|	...	...	0859	|	|	...	...	...	...	...	|	...
Béziers d.	...	...	...	0805	...	|	...	...	0915	|	|	...	...	...	...	...	|	...
Montpellier Saint-Roch d.	...	0859	...	0859	...	|	...	...	|	|	|	1157	...	...	...	...	|	...
Montpellier Sud de France d.	0912	|	0912	|	...	|	...	...	1007	|	|	|	...	...	...	1359	|	...
Nîmes Pont-du-Gard d.	0933	|	0933	|	...	|	...	...	1030	|	|	|	...	...	...	1421	|	...
Nîmes d.	|	0927	|	0927	...	|	...	...	|	|	|	1226	...	...	...	|	|	...
Avignon TGV d.	|	|	|	|	...	1039	...	...	|	1249	1249	|	...	...	...	|	1413	...
Valence TGV d.	1015	1015	1015	1015	...	|	...	...	1115	|	|	1313	...	...	...	|	|	...
Lyon St Exupéry ✈ d.	|	|	|	|	...	1133	...	...	|	|	|	|	...	...	...	1534	|	...
Lyon Part Dieu d.	1100	1100	1100	1100	...	|	...	...	1150	1356	1356	1356	...	...	...	|	1520	...
Le Creusot TGV d.	|	|	|	|	...	|	...	...	...	|	|	|	...	...	...	|	|	...
Bordeaux d.	|	|	|	|	...	|	...	...	...	|	|	|	...	1258	...	|	|	...
Angoulême d.	|	|	|	|	...	|	...	...	...	|	|	|	...	1336	...	|	|	...
Poitiers d.	|	|	|	|	...	|	...	...	...	|	|	|	...	1419	...	|	|	...
St Pierre des Corps d.	|	|	|	|	...	|	...	...	...	|	|	|	...	1454	...	|	|	...
Nantes d.	|	|	|	|	...	|	...	...	...	|	|	|	...	|	...	|	|	...
Angers St Laud d.	|	|	|	|	...	|	...	...	...	|	|	|	...	|	...	|	|	...
Rennes d.	|	|	|	|	...	|	1200	...	...	|	|	|	...	|	...	|	|	...
Le Mans d.	|	|	|	|	...	|	1302	...	...	|	|	|	...	|	...	|	|	...
Massy TGV d.	|	|	|	|	...	|	1355	...	...	|	|	|	...	1555	...	|	|	...
Strasbourg d.	|	|	|	|	...	|	|	...	...	|	|	|	...	|	...	|	|	...
Marne la Vallée § d.	1255	1255	1255	1255	...	1323	1431	...	...	1550	1550	1550	...	1631	...	1730	1712	1803
Paris Charles de Gaulle ✈ a.	1304	1304	1304	1304	...	1332	1441	...	...	1600	1600	1600	...	1641	...	1739	1721	|
Paris Charles de Gaulle ✈ d.	1309	1309	1309	1309	...	1337	1458	...	...	1607	1607	1607	...	1647	...	1744	1729	|
TGV Haute Picardie d.	1340	1339	1340	1339	...	|	|	...	...	|	|	|	...	1731	...	1814	1802	|
Arras a.	1358	1356	1358	1356	...	|	|	...	...	|	|	|	...	|	...	|	1820	|
Douai a.	|	|	|	|	...	|	|	...	...	|	|	|	...	|	...	|	1838	|
Lille Flandres ◇ a.	|	|	|	|	...	1430	|	...	...	|	|	|	...	|	...	1844	1900	|
Lille Europe a.	1424	1424	1424	1424	...	...	1549	...	...	1657	1657	1657	...	1757	...	...	...	|
Lille Europe d.	...	...	1451	1451	1530	...	...	1635	...	1708	...	...	1835	...	1808	...	...	|
Tourcoing a.	...	...	|	|	|	...	...	|	...	|	...	...	|	...	|	...	...	|
Brussels Midi / Zuid a.	...	...	1525	1525	|	...	...	|	...	1743	...	...	|	...	1843	...	...	|
London St Pancras a.	...	...	...	...	1557	...	...	1657	...	...	...	...	1857	...	...	...	...	1927

train type	TGV	TGV	TGV	TGV	TGV	TGV	☆	☆	TGV	TGV	TGV	TGV	TGV	TGV	TGV
train number	5192	5092	5288	9868	9864	9894	9163	9167	7832	7660	5182	9882	7836	6872	5186
train number	5193		5289		9865	9895			7833	7661		9883	7837	6873	5187
notes	R 🍸	R 🍸	R 🍸	R 🍸	R 🍸	R 🍸	R ✕	R ✕	R	R	R 🍸	R 🍸	R	R 🍸	R 🍸
	Ⓑ	⑦					⑥	Ⓑ	⊠	⊠			⊠		
															D
Nice d.	...	...	...	...	...	...	...	...	...	...	...	...	...	...	...
Cannes d.	...	...	...	...	...	...	...	...	...	...	...	...	...	...	...
St Raphaël - Valescure d.	...	...	...	...	...	...	...	...	...	...	...	...	...	...	...
Toulon d.	...	...	...	...	...	...	...	...	...	...	...	...	...	...	...
Marseille St Charles d.	...	...	...	1512	...	...	...	...	1648	...	...	1712	1825	...	...
Aix en Provence TGV d.	...	...	...	1526	...	...	...	...	|	...	...	1726	1840	...	...
Perpignan d.	...	...	...	|	...	...	...	...	|	...	...	|	|	...	...
Toulouse Matabiau d.	...	...	...	|	...	...	...	...	|	...	...	|	|	1543	...
Narbonne d.	...	...	...	|	...	...	...	...	|	...	...	|	|	1659	...
Béziers d.	...	...	...	|	...	...	...	...	|	...	...	|	|	1715	...
Montpellier Saint-Roch d.	...	...	...	|	1451	...	...	...	|	...	...	|	|	|	...
Montpellier Sud de France d.	...	...	...	|	|	...	...	...	|	...	1712	|	|	1807	...
Nîmes Pont-du-Gard d.	...	...	...	|	|	...	...	...	|	...	1733	|	|	1830	...
Nîmes d.	...	...	...	|	1519	...	...	...	|	...	|	|	|	|	...
Avignon TGV d.	...	...	...	1549	|	...	...	...	1719	...	|	1749	1902	|	...
Valence TGV d.	...	...	...	|	1615	...	...	...	|	...	1815	|	|	1915	...
Lyon St Exupéry ✈ d.	...	...	...	|	|	...	...	...	1815	...	|	|	1959	|	...
Lyon Part Dieu d.	1550	1550	...	1700	1700	...	...	...	|	...	1900	1900	|	1950	2030
Le Creusot TGV d.	|	|	...	|	|	...	...	...	|	...	|	|	|	...	|
Bordeaux d.	|	|	...	|	|	...	...	...	|	1658	|	|	|	...	|
Angoulême d.	|	|	...	|	|	...	...	...	|	1736	|	|	|	...	|
Poitiers d.	|	|	...	|	|	...	...	...	|	1820	|	|	|	...	|
St Pierre des Corps d.	|	|	...	|	|	...	...	...	|	1855	|	|	|	...	|
Nantes d.	|	|	1518	|	|	...	...	...	|	|	|	|	|	...	|
Angers St Laud d.	|	|	1602	|	|	...	...	...	|	|	|	|	|	...	|
Rennes d.	|	|	|	|	|	...	...	...	|	|	|	|	|	...	|
Le Mans d.	|	|	1657	|	|	...	...	...	|	|	|	|	|	...	|
Massy TGV d.	|	|	1754	|	|	...	...	...	|	1955	|	|	|	...	|
Strasbourg d.	|	|	|	|	|	1701	...	...	|	|	|	|	|	...	|
Marne la Vallée § d.	1751	1751	1828	1853	1853	|	...	...	2015	2032	2053	2053	2152	...	2221
Paris Charles de Gaulle ✈ a.	1801	1801	1837	1902	1902	1906	...	...	2024	2042	2102	2102	2202	...	2231
Paris Charles de Gaulle ✈ d.	1807	...	1843	1907	1907	1912	...	...	...	2057	2107	2107	2207	...	2237
TGV Haute Picardie d.	1839	...	|	|	|	1941	...	...	...	2134	|	|	|	...	|
Arras a.	1856	...	|	|	|	|	...	...	...	|	|	|	|	...	|
Douai a.	1914	...	|	|	|	|	...	...	...	|	|	|	|	...	|
Lille Flandres ◇ a.	1944	...	|	|	|	|	...	...	...	2204	|	|	|	...	|
Lille Europe a.	...	...	1935	1958	1958	2008	...	...	...	|	2157	2157	|	...	2326
Lille Europe d.	...	...	...	2009	2009	2027	2028	2133	...	|	...	2208	|	...	...
Tourcoing a.	...	...	...	|	|	|	|	|	...	2231	...	|	2309	...	...
Brussels Midi / Zuid a.	...	...	...	2043	2043	2101	|	|	...	...	...	2243	...	...	...
London St Pancras a.	...	...	...	...	...	...	2127	2157	...	...	...	...	...	...	...

A – ①⑤ Jan. 6 - Feb. 27. ①-⑤ Mar. 3 - May 12.
B – ⑥ Jan. 7 - Mar. 4. ⑥⑦ Mar. 11 - May 14.
C – ⑦ Jan. 8 - Mar. 5. ①⑤⑦ Mar. 10 - Nov. 6.
D – ⑦ May 14 - Sept. 10.
E – ⑥⑦ Mar. 11 - May 14.
H – ⑥ Apr. 1 - Dec. 9.
J – ①③⑤⑦ Feb. 5 - June 5. See Table **17**.

§ – Marne la Vallée - Chessy, station for Disneyland Paris.
◇ – 500 metres from Lille Europe (see Lille City Plan on page 32).
⊠ – OUIGO low-cost TGV service. Internet bookings only at www.ouigo.com. Timings may vary.

☆ – Eurostar train. Special fares payable. ✕ in Business Premier and Standard Premier, 🍸 in Standard. Business Premier not available from Marne la Vallée - Chessy. See shaded panel in Table **10** on page 47 for information about recommended arrival times at departure station. Valid Feb. 5 - May 20.

13 LONDON - PARIS - BARCELONA - MADRID

train type	AVE	TGV	AVE		TGV	AVE		AVE	☆	TGV		☆	3731	3731		3975	3975		AVE
train number	19730	9711	3142		9713	3172		10742	9031	9715		9040	[R]	[R]		[R]	[R]		3142
train number/notes						⑧							⑤	⑦		①–⑤	⑥⑦		
notes	B	A						D					G	G	2	F	F	2	
London St Pancras d.	...	...	...	...	...	...	...	...	0931	...	...	1631	...	...	...	...	...	...	...
Lille Europe d.	...	...	...	...	...	...	...	...	│	...	...	│	...	...	...	...	...	...	...
Paris Nord a.	...	...	...	...	...	...	...	...	1247	...	...	1947	...	...	...	...	...	...	...
Paris Gare de Lyon d.	...	0656	...	...	0938	...	...	...	...	1454	...	...	...	...	...	...	...	...	...
Paris Austerlitz d.	...	│	...	...	│	...	...	...	...	│	...	...	2114	2142	...	2114	2142	...	...
Les Aubrais-Orléans d.	...	│	...	...	│	...	...	...	...	│	...	...	2228	2256	...	2228	2256	...	...
Lyon Part Dieu d.	...	│	...	...	│	...	...	1435	...	│	...	...	│	│	...	│	│	...	...
Valence TGV d.	...	0909	...	...	1158	...	...	1511	...	1709	...	...	│	│	...	│	│	...	...
Marseille St Charles d.	0804	│	...	...	│	...	...	│	...	│	...	...	│	│	...	│	│	...	...
Aix en Provence TGV d.	0818	│	...	...	│	...	...	│	...	│	...	...	│	│	...	│	│	...	...
Avignon TGV d.	0840	│	...	...	│	...	...	│	...	│	...	...	│	│	...	│	│	...	...
Nîmes Pont-du-Gard d.	│	0948	...	...	│	...	...	│	...	1749	...	...	│	│	...	│	│	...	...
Nîmes Centre d.	0908	│	...	...	1246	...	...	1557	...	│	...	...	│	│	...	│	│	...	...
Montpellier Saint-Roch d.	0939	│	...	...	1318	...	...	1628	...	│	...	...	│	│	...	│	│	...	...
Montpellier Sud de France d.	│	1017	...	...	│	...	...	│	...	1817	...	...	│	│	...	│	│	...	...
Béziers d.	1017	1106	...	...	1410	...	...	1715	...	1906	...	...	│	│	...	│	│	...	...
Toulouse Matabiau d.	│	│	...	...	│	...	...	│	...	│	...	...	│	│	...	│	│	...	...
Carcassonne d.	│	│	...	...	│	...	...	│	...	│	...	...	0734a	0734a	...	│	│	...	...
Narbonne d.	1033	1123	...	...	1427	...	...	1731	...	1923	...	...	0813a	0813a	...	│	│	...	...
Perpignan d.	1112	1203	...	...	1504	...	...	1810	...	2003	...	...	0917a	0917a	...	│	│	...	...
Latour de Carol 🚌 a.	│	│	...	...	│	...	...	│	...	│	...	...	│	│	...	0906	0906	1025	...
Cerbère 🚌 a.	│	│	...	...	│	...	...	│	...	│	...	...	1003	1003	...	...	...	│	...
Portbou 🚌 a.	│	│	...	...	│	...	...	│	...	│	...	...	...	...	1035	...	...	│	...
Figueres Vilafant ◇ a.	1140	1227	...	...	1529	...	...	1834	...	2027	...	...	...	...	1058x	...	...	│	...
Girona a.	1157	1244	...	...	1546	...	...	1851	...	2044	...	...	...	...	1138	...	...	│	...
Barcelona Sants a.	1238	1325	...	...	1627	...	...	1932	...	2125	...	...	...	...	1310	...	...	1346	...
Barcelona Sants d.	1250	...	1400	...	...	1700	...	...	...	...	...	...	...	...	...	...	...	...	1400
Zaragoza Delicias a.	1422	...	1542	...	...	1822	...	...	...	...	...	...	...	...	...	...	...	...	1542
Madrid Puerta de Atocha a.	1545	...	1712	...	...	1945	...	...	...	...	...	...	...	...	...	...	...	...	1712

train type	AVE	AVE	TGV	☆	AVE	avlo	TGV	AVE	TGV	AVE		3974	3974		3730	3730	☆	☆
train number	10737	3071	9708	9059	3093	6303	9704	3123	9706	19725		[R]	[R]		[R]	[R]	9019	9023
train number/notes		①–④										①–⑤	⑥⑦		⑤	⑦	⑤⑦	
notes	D								A	C	2	F	F	2	G	G	H	
Madrid Puerta de Atocha d.	...	0700	...	...	0930	1030	...	1230	...	1325	...	...	...	...	...	...	...	...
Zaragoza Delicias d.	...	│	...	...	1046	1146	...	1346	...	1450	...	...	...	...	...	...	...	...
Barcelona Sants a.	...	0930	...	...	1237	1315	...	1540	...	1622	...	...	...	...	...	...	...	...
Barcelona Sants d.	0822	...	1033	...	...	...	1432	...	1610	1634	1431	...	...	1516	...	...	...	...
Girona d.	0903	...	1114	...	...	...	1513	...	1651	1715	│	...	...	1648	...	...	...	...
Figueres Vilafant ◇ d.	0919	...	1131	...	...	...	1530	...	1708	1732	│	...	...	1727x	...	...	...	...
Portbou 🚌 d.	│	...	│	...	...	...	│	...	│	│	│	...	...	1751	...	...	...	...
Cerbère 🚌 d.	│	...	│	...	...	...	│	...	│	│	│	...	...	1756	1832	1830	...	...
Latour de Carol 🚌 d.	│	...	│	...	...	...	│	...	│	│	1751	1842	1842	...	│	│	...	...
Perpignan a.	0937	...	1155	...	...	...	1554	...	1732	1758	...	│	│	...	1921d	1918d	...	...
Narbonne a.	1015	...	1239	...	...	...	1639	...	1840	1840	...	│	│	...	2043d	2028d	...	...
Carcassonne d.	│	...	│	...	...	...	│	...	│	│	...	│	│	...	2122d	2106d	...	...
Toulouse Matabiau d.	│	...	│	...	...	...	│	...	│	│	...	│	│	...	│	│	...	...
Béziers a.	│	...	1255	...	...	...	1655	...	1857	1856	...	│	│	...	│	│	...	...
Montpellier Sud de France a.	│	...	│	...	...	...	│	...	1947	│	...	│	│	...	│	│	...	...
Montpellier Saint-Roch a.	1121	...	1344	...	...	...	1743	...	│	1945	...	│	│	...	│	│	...	...
Nîmes Centre a.	1155	...	1415	...	...	...	│	...	│	2022	...	│	│	...	│	│	...	...
Nîmes Pont-du-Gard a.	│	...	│	...	...	...	1818	...	2010	│	...	│	│	...	│	│	...	...
Avignon TGV a.	│	...	│	...	...	...	│	...	│	2047	...	│	│	...	│	│	...	...
Aix en Provence TGV a.	│	...	│	...	...	...	│	...	│	2111	...	│	│	...	│	│	...	...
Marseille St Charles a.	│	...	│	...	...	...	│	...	│	2130	...	│	│	...	│	│	...	...
Valence TGV a.	1243	...	1502	...	...	...	1903	...	2051	...	...	│	│	...	│	│	...	...
Lyon Part Dieu a.	1320	...	│	...	...	...	│	...	│	...	...	│	│	...	│	│	...	...
Les Aubrais-Orléans a.	...	...	│	...	...	...	│	...	│	...	...	0523	0610	...	0523	0610	...	...
Paris Austerlitz a.	...	...	│	...	...	...	│	...	│	...	...	0650	0719	...	0650	0719	...	...
Paris Gare de Lyon a.	...	...	1721	...	...	...	2121	...	2305	...	...	...	...	...	...	...	...	...
Paris Nord d.	...	...	...	2013	...	...	...	...	...	...	...	...	...	...	...	...	1013	1113
Lille Europe a.	...	...	...	│	...	...	...	...	...	...	...	...	...	...	...	...	│	│
London St Pancras a.	...	...	...	2130	...	...	...	...	...	...	...	...	...	...	...	...	1130	1230

A – July 8 - Sept. 3.

B – ②③④⑤ until Apr. 23; daily Apr. 24 - Dec. 9. Start date subject to confirmation.

C – ①②③④ until Apr. 23; daily Apr. 24 - Dec. 9. Start date subject to confirmation.

D – ①–⑤ until Apr. 23; daily Apr. 24 - Dec. 9. Start date subject to confirmation.

F – INTERCITÉS DE NUIT 🛏 1, 2 cl., (2) Paris - Latour de Carol and v.v. Subject to alteration from Mar. 27.

G – INTERCITÉS DE NUIT 🛏 1, 2 cl., (2) Paris - Cerbère and v.v. Subject to alteration from Mar. 27.

H – ⑤⑦ (daily Mar. 26 - May 20).

a – Arrival time.

x – Figueres.

TGV – *Train à Grande Vitesse* [R] 🍸 ✗.

AVE – Alta Velocidad Española [R] 🍸 ✗.

avlo – Low-cost AVE.

✗ – Supplement payable.

◇ – 🚌 connections available to Figueres bus station. (Table **657**).

☆ – Eurostar train. [R], ✕ in Business Premier and Standard Premier, 🍸 in Standard. Special fares payable. See shaded panel in Table **10** on page 47 for information about recommended arrival times at departure station. Valid Feb. 5 - May 20.

LONDON - AMSTERDAM *by rail–sea–rail via Harwich - Hoek van Holland* 15

notes	①–⑥	①–⑤	⑥	①–⑥	①–⑥	①–⑥	①–⑥		⑦	⑦	⑦	⑦	⑦	⑦		①–⑤	⑥	①–⑥	①–⑥	⑥⑦	②–⑤	②–⑥	⑦	②–⑦		
				🚢	🚋						🚢	🚋							🚢	🚋	🚋					
London Liverpool Street d.	...	0616	0636	...	...	...	...	...	0644	...	...	...	...	...	...	1845	1936	...	...	...	...	...	...	...	...	...
Colchester d.	...	0714	0738	...	...	...	...	...	0748	...	...	...	...	...	...	1957	2032	...	...	...	...	...	...	...	...	...
Manningtree d.	...	0722	0746	...	...	...	...	...	0756	...	...	...	...	...	...	2005	2040	...	...	...	...	...	...	...	...	...
Cambridge d.	...	|	|	...	...	...	...	...	|	...	...	...	...	...	...	|	|	1947	...	...	...	...	...	...	...	...
Ipswich d.	0658	|	|	...	...	...	...	...	|	0752	...	...	...	...	...	|	|	2103	...	...	...	...	...	...	...	...
Harwich International d.	0725	0740	0805	0900	...	...	...	...	0811	0815	1000	...	...	...	...	2023	2055	2129	2300	...	...	...	...	...	...	...
Hoek van Holland Haven a.	...	...	...	1715	1751	...	...	...	...	...	1800	1847	...	...	...	...	...	...	0800	0847	0851	...	...	...	...	...
Schiedam Centrum a.	...	...	...	...	1816	1843	1846	...	...	...	...	1910	1928	1946	...	...	...	...	...	0910	0915	0928	0943	0946	...	...
Rotterdam Centraal a.	...	...	...	...	...	1848	|	...	...	...	...	...	1933	|	...	...	...	...	...	...	...	0933	0948	|	...	...
Den Haag HS a.	...	...	...	...	...	...	1901	...	...	...	...	...	...	2001	...	...	...	...	...	...	...	...	...	1001	...	...
Schiphol ✈ a.	...	...	...	...	...	...	|	...	...	...	...	...	...	|	...	...	...	...	...	...	...	...	...	|	...	...
Amsterdam Centraal a.	...	...	...	...	...	...	1955	...	...	...	...	...	...	2055	...	...	...	...	...	...	...	...	...	1055	...	...

notes	⑦	⑦	⑦	①	①	①		
			🚢	🚋				
London Liverpool Street d.	2000	...	...	...	...	...	...	...
Colchester d.	2055	...	...	...	...	...	...	...
Manningtree d.	2103	...	...	...	...	...	...	...
Cambridge d.	|	1945	...	...	...	...	...	...
Ipswich d.	|	2103	...	...	...	...	...	...
Harwich International d.	2119	2126	2300	...	...	...	...	...
Hoek van Holland Haven a.	...	...	0800	0851	...	...	...	...
Schiedam Centrum a.	...	...	...	0914	0928	0946	...	...
Rotterdam Centraal a.	...	...	...	...	0933	|	...	...
Den Haag HS a.	...	...	...	...	...	1001	...	...
Schiphol ✈ a.	...	...	...	...	...	|	...	...
Amsterdam Centraal a.	...	...	...	...	...	1055	...	...

notes	⑦	⑦	⑦	⑦	⑦	⑦						
			🚋	🚢								
Amsterdam Centraal d.	...	1104	...	...	...	...	...	...	...	...	...	...
Schiphol ✈ d.	...	|	...	...	...	...	...	...	...	...	...	...
Den Haag HS d.	...	1159	...	...	...	...	...	...	...	...	...	...
Rotterdam Centraal d.	1206	|	...	...	...	...	...	...	...	...	...	...
Schiedam Centrum d.	1211	1213	1219	...	...	...	...	...	...	...	...	...
Hoek van Holland Haven d.	...	...	1242	1345	...	...	...	...	...	...	...	...
Harwich International a.	...	...	...	1945	2030	2138	...	...	...	...	...	...
Ipswich a.	...	...	...	...	|	2204	...	...	...	...	...	...
Cambridge a.	...	...	...	...	|	...	...	...	...	...	...	...
Manningtree a.	...	...	...	...	2042	...	...	...	...	...	...	...
Colchester a.	...	...	...	...	2052	...	...	...	...	...	...	...
London Liverpool Street a.	...	...	...	...	2144	...	...	...	...	...	...	...

notes	①–⑥	①–⑥	①–⑥	①–⑥	①–⑥	⑥	①–⑤						⑥	⑦	①–⑤	⑥	①–⑤	⑦								
			🚋	🚢							🚋	🚢														
Amsterdam Centraal d.	1134	...	...	...	...	...	...	...	...	1904	...	...	...	...	...	...	...	...	...	...	...	...	...	...	...	...
Schiphol ✈ d.	|	...	...	...	...	...	...	...	...	|	...	...	...	...	...	...	...	...	...	...	...	...	...	...	...	...
Den Haag HS d.	1229	...	...	...	...	...	...	...	...	1959	...	...	...	...	...	...	...	...	...	...	...	...	...	...	...	...
Rotterdam Centraal d.	|	1227	...	...	...	...	...	...	2006	|	...	...	...	...	...	...	...	...	...	...	...	...	...	...	...	...
Schiedam Centrum d.	1243	1231	1256	...	...	...	...	...	2011	2013	2018	...	...	...	...	...	...	...	...	...	...	...	...	...	...	...
Hoek van Holland Haven d.	...	...	1320	1415	...	...	...	...	...	...	2042	2200	...	...	...	...	...	...	...	...	...	...	...	...	...	...
Harwich International a.	...	...	...	1945	2045	2138	2147	...	...	...	...	0630	0720	0720	0745	0750	0800	0850	...	...	...	...	...	...	...	...
Ipswich a.	...	...	...	...	|	2204	2213	...	...	...	...	...	|	|	0815	0817	|	0914	...	...	...	...	...	...	...	...
Cambridge a.	...	...	...	...	|	...	...	...	...	...	...	...	|	|	0941	0940	|	1039	...	...	...	...	...	...	...	...
Manningtree a.	...	...	...	...	2057	...	...	...	...	...	...	...	0732	0732	...	...	0816	...	...	...	...	...	...	...	...	...
Colchester a.	...	...	...	...	2107	...	...	...	...	...	...	...	0742	0742	...	...	0827	...	...	...	...	...	...	...	...	...
London Liverpool Street a.	...	...	...	...	2214	...	...	...	...	...	...	...	0846	0858	...	...	0938	...	...	...	...	...	...	...	...	...

🚋 – Tram, Rotterdam Metro line **B**.

SEA CROSSING (for rail / sea / rail journeys): 🚢 – Ship operated by Stena Line. [R]. Stena Plus lounge (supplement payable) and 🍴 on ship. A cabin must be booked on night sailings.

LILLE - BRUSSELS (Summary Table) 16

train type	*TGV*	*TGV*	☆	*TGV*	*TGV*	☆		☆	*TGV*	☆	*TGV*	☆	*TGV*		*TGV*	*TGV*	☆		☆	*TGV*	
train number	**9809**	**9852**	**9110**	**9886**	**9854**	**9116**		**9126**	**9862**	**9132**	**9866**	**9142**	**9821**		**9868**	**9894**	**9152**		**9158**	**9882**	
notes	Ⓐ	**9890**	⑥	**9884**	**9855**				**9863**		**9867**				**9864**	**9895**				**9883**	
notes								**A**									**AB**				
Lille Europe d.	0720	0909	0930	1027	1137	1130	...	1330	1451	1530	1708	1730	1808	...	2009	2027	2030	...	2203	2208	...
Brussels Midi / Zuid a.	0755	0943	1005	1101	1211	1205	...	1405	1525	1606	1743	1805	1843	...	2043	2101	2113	...	2238	2243	...

train type	*TGV*	*TGV*	*TGV*	☆		*TGV*		☆	*TGV*	☆	*TGV*	☆	*TGV*	*TGV*	☆	*TGV*	*TGV*	☆	☆		
train number	**9810**	**9870**	**9812**	**9117**		**9826**		**9135**	**9830**	**9141**	**9832**	**9145**	**9836**	**9838**	**9153**	**9844**	**9846**	**9163**	**9167**		
notes	**9811**	**9871**	**9813**			**9827**			**9874**		**9833**	Ⓑ	**9837**	**9839**		**9845**		⑥	Ⓑ		
notes												**A**							**A**		
Brussels Midi / Zuid d.	0635	0717	0817	0852	...	1017	...	1256	1317	1452	1503	1556	1617	1654	1756	1817	1917	2022	2056	...	...
Lille Europe a.	0712	0751	0852	0926	...	1052	...	1330	1352	1526	1538	1630	1653	1728	1830	1852	1951	2100	2130	...	...

A – To / from Amsterdam, see Table **18**. **B** – ①②③④⑦. *TGV*– High-speed train. [R] 🍸. ☆ – Eurostar train. [R], 🍴 in Business Premier and Standard Premier, 🍸 in Standard. Special fares payable. Gates close 45 minutes before departure from Brussels. Valid Feb. 5 - May 20.

LONDON - MARSEILLE and MARNE LA VALLÉE 17

train type		☆		☆		
train number		**9084**		**9074**		
train number		**9085**				
notes				**A**		
London St Pancras d.	...	0715	...	1031	...	...
Ebbsfleet International d.	...	|	...	|	...	...
Ashford International d.	...	|	...	|	...	...
Lille Europe a.	...	|	...	1254	...	...
Marne la Vallée § a.	...	|	...	1355	...	...
Lyon Part Dieu a.	...	1300	...	...	...	...
Avignon TGV a.	...	1408	...	...	...	...
Marseille St Charles a.	...	1447	...	...	...	...

train type		☆		☆	☆	
train number		**9057**		**9087**	**9087**	
train number				**9086**	**9086**	
notes		**A**				
Marseille St Charles d.	...	...	...	1522	...	...
Avignon TGV d.	...	...	...	1559	...	...
Lyon Part Dieu d.	...	...	...	1725	...	...
Marne la Vallée § d.	...	1803	...	|	...	...
Lille Europe d.	...	|	...	2021	2136	...
Ashford International a.	...	|	...	...	2134	...
Ebbsfleet International a.	...	|	...	...	|	...
London St Pancras a.	...	1927	...	...	2212	...

A – ①③⑤⑦ Feb. 5 - June 5. Depart London 1026, 1014 on certain dates.

§ – Marne la Vallée - Chessy (station for Disneyland).

☆ – Eurostar train. [R], 🍴 in Standard Premier, 🍸 in Standard. Special fares payable. See shaded panel in Table **10** on page 47 for information about recommended arrival times at departure station. Eurostar will not serve Ebbsfleet International or Ashford International in 2023.

☛ **Shaded services are suspended until further notice.**

18 LONDON / PARIS - BRUSSELS - AMSTERDAM

train type	ICd	⇌	IC	⇌	⇌	ICd	ICd	⇌	⇌	⇌	⇌	☆	⇌	ICd	⇌	☆	⇌	IC	⇌	
train number	**9211**	**9397**	**9691**	**9303**	**9303**	**9219**	**9223**	**9309**	**9309**	**9411**	**9411**	**9106**	**9315**	**9227**	**9315**	**9110**	**9317**	**9693**	**9321**	
notes		Ⓐ		⑥	Ⓐ			⑥	Ⓐ	⑥		①–⑤	⑦		⚒	⑥			Ⓐ	
notes								**A**		**F**	**G**	**C**					**H**			
London St Pancras d.	...	...	...	...	...	...	...	...	...	...	...	0616	...	...	...	0704	...	...	...	...
Marne la Vallée - Chessy § d.	...	...	...	...	...	...	...	...	...	...	...	|	...	...	...	|	...	...	...	...
Paris Charles de Gaulle ✈ d.	...	...	...	...	...	...	...	...	...	...	...	|	...	...	...	|	...	...	...	...
Paris Nord d.	...	...	...	...	0613	...	...	0710	0725	0743	0755	|	0807	...	0825	|	0855	...	0922	...
Lille Europe d.	...	...	...	...	|	...	...	|	|	|	|	|	|	...	|	0930	|	...	|	...
Brussels Midi / Zuid ◧ a.	...	...	...	...	0745	...	...	0845	0847	0917	0917	0912	0939	...	0947	1005	1017	...	1044	...
Brussels Midi / Zuid ◧ △ d.	0544	0652	0644	0752	0752	0744	0844	0852	0852	...	...	0922	0952	0944	0952	...	...	1044	1052	...
Brussels Airport ✈ d.	0611	|	0711	|	|	0811	0911	|	|	...	...	|	|	1011	|	...	...	1111	|	...
Mechelen d.	0624	|	0724	|	|	0824	0924	|	|	...	...	|	|	1024	|	...	...	1124	|	...
Antwerpen Centraal a.	0644	0727	0744	0827	0827	0844	0944	0927	0927	...	...	|	1027	1044	1027	...	...	1144	1127	...
Breda a.	0718	|	0818	|	|	0918	1018	|	|	...	...	|	|	1118	|	...	...	1218	|	...
Breda d.	0726	|	0826	|	|	0926	1026	|	|	...	...	|	|	1126	|	...	...	1226	|	...
Rotterdam Centraal a.	0749	0802	0849	0902	0902	0949	1049	1002	1002	...	...	1032	1102	1149	1102	...	...	1249	1202	...
Den Haag HS a.	|	|	0920	|	|	|	|	|	|	...	...	|	|	|	|	...	...	1320	|	...
Schiphol ✈ a.	0822	0825	...	0925	0925	1022	1122	1025	1025	...	...	|	1125	1222	1125	...	...	...	1225	...
Amsterdam Centraal a.	0838	0844	...	0944	0944	1038	1138	1044	1044	...	...	1113	1144	1238	1144	...	...	...	1244	...

train type	☆	⇌	ICd	⇌	☆	ICd	⇌	⇌	ICd	⇌	⇌	⇌	☆	⇌	IC	ICd	⇌			
train number	**9114**	**9423**	**9235**	**9327**	**9116**	**9239**	**9333**	**9435**	**9243**	**9337**	**9937**	**9339**	**9126**	**9341**	**9695**	**9251**	**9351**			
notes							⑤			②③④	①⑤⑦			Ⓐ						
notes														**A**						
London St Pancras d.	0816	...	...	...	0855	...	...	...	...	...	...	...	1104	...	...	...	...	...	...	...
Marne la Vallée - Chessy § d.	|	...	...	...	|	...	...	...	...	...	1143	...	|	...	...	...	...	...	...	...
Paris Charles de Gaulle ✈ d.	|	...	...	...	|	...	...	...	...	...	1158	...	|	...	...	...	...	...	...	...
Paris Nord d.	|	0955	...	1025	|	...	...	1155	...	...	|	1222	|	1255	...	...	1422	...	...	...
Lille Europe d.	|	|	...	|	1130	...	...	|	...	...	|	|	1330	|	...	...	|	...	...	...
Brussels Midi / Zuid ◧ a.	1112	1117	...	1147	1205	...	...	1317	...	...	1311	1344	1405	1417	...	...	1544	...	...	...
Brussels Midi / Zuid ◧ △ d.	1122	...	1144	1152	...	1244	1252	...	1344	1322	1322	1352	1422	...	1444	1544	1552	...	...	...
Brussels Airport ✈ d.	|	...	1211	|	...	1311	|	...	1411	|	|	|	|	...	1511	1611	|	...	...	...
Mechelen d.	|	...	1224	|	...	1324	|	...	1424	|	|	|	|	...	1524	1624	|	...	...	...
Antwerpen Centraal a.	|	...	1244	1227	...	1344	1327	...	1444	1357	1357	1427	|	...	1544	1644	1627	...	...	...
Breda a.	|	...	1318	|	...	1418	|	...	1518	|	|	|	|	...	1618	1718	|	...	...	...
Breda d.	|	...	1326	|	...	1426	|	...	1526	|	|	|	|	...	1626	1726	|	...	...	...
Rotterdam Centraal a.	1232	...	1349	1302	...	1449	1402	...	1549	1432	1432	1502	1532	...	1649	1749	1702	...	...	...
Den Haag HS a.	|	...	|	|	...	|	|	...	|	|	|	|	|	...	1722	|	|	...	...	...
Schiphol ✈ a.	|	...	1422	1325	...	1522	1425	...	1622	1455	1455	1525	|	...	...	1822	1725	...	...	...
Amsterdam Centraal a.	1313	...	1438	1344	...	1538	1444	...	1638	1514	1514	1544	1613	...	...	1838	1744	...	...	...

train type	☆	ICd	⇌	⇌	⇌	ICd	⇌	⇌	☆	IC	⇌	⇌	ICd	⇌	⇌	⇌	ICd	⇌		
train number	**9132**	**9255**	**9357**	**9357**	**9459**	**9259**	**9363**	**9365**	**9142**	**9697**	**9369**	**9471**	**9267**	**9375**	**9375**	**9977**	**9271**	**9381**		
notes			⑤⑦	①–④			Ⓑ	Ⓐ						Ⓐ	⑦	⑥⑦				
notes												**J**			**E**					
London St Pancras d.	1301	...	...	...	...	...	...	...	1504	...	...	...	...	...	...	...	...	...	...	...
Marne la Vallée - Chessy § d.	|	...	...	...	...	...	...	...	|	...	...	...	...	...	...	1833	...	...	...	...
Paris Charles de Gaulle ✈ d.	|	...	...	...	...	...	...	...	|	...	...	...	...	...	...	1848	...	...	...	...
Paris Nord d.	|	...	1522	...	1555	...	1625	1655	|	...	1725	1755	...	1825	1825	|	...	1925	...	...
Lille Europe d.	1530	...	|	...	|	...	|	|	1730	...	|	|	...	|	|	|	...	|	...	...
Brussels Midi / Zuid ◧ a.	1606	...	1644	...	1717	...	1747	1817	1805	...	1847	1917	...	1947	1947	2000	...	2047	...	...
Brussels Midi / Zuid ◧ △ d.	...	1644	1652	1652	...	1744	1752	...	...	1844	1852	...	1944	1952	...	2022	2044	2052	...	...
Brussels Airport ✈ d.	...	1711	|	|	...	1811	|	...	...	1911	|	...	2011	|	...	|	2111	|	...	...
Mechelen d.	...	1724	|	|	...	1824	|	...	...	1925	|	...	2024	|	...	|	2124	|	...	...
Antwerpen Centraal a.	...	1744	1727	1727	...	1844	1827	...	...	1944	1927	...	2044	2027	...	2057	2144	2127	...	...
Breda a.	...	1818	|	|	...	1918	|	...	...	2018	|	...	2118	|	...	|	2218	|	...	...
Breda d.	...	1826	|	|	...	1926	|	...	...	2026	|	...	2126	|	...	|	2226	|	...	...
Rotterdam Centraal a.	...	1849	1802	1802	...	1949	1902	...	...	2049	2002	...	2149	2102	...	2132	2249	2202	...	...
Den Haag HS a.	...	|	|	|	...	|	|	...	...	2122	|	...	|	|	...	|	|	|	...	...
Schiphol ✈ a.	...	1922	1825	1825	...	2022	1925	...	...	2149	2025	...	2222	2125	...	2155	2322	2225	...	...
Amsterdam Centraal a.	...	1938	1844	1844	...	2038	1944	...	...	2205	2044	...	2238	2144	...	2214	2338	2244	...	...

train type	☆	☆	⇌	⇌	⇌	☆	⇌	⇌												
train number	**9152**	**9152**	**9387**	**9387**	**9389**	**9158**	**9393**	**9395**												
notes notes		⑤	⑤⑦	①–④				⑦												
notes	**L**			**A**	**Q**		**K**	**E**												
London St Pancras d.	1804	1813	...	...	...	1934	...	...	...	...	...	...	...	...	...	...	...	...	...	...
Marne la Vallée - Chessy § d.	|	|	...	...	...	|	...	...	...	...	...	...	...	...	...	...	...	...	...	...
Paris Charles de Gaulle ✈ d.	|	|	...	...	...	|	...	...	...	...	...	...	...	...	...	...	...	...	...	...
Paris Nord d.	|	|	2022	2022	2055	|	2125	2155	...	...	...	...	...	...	...	...	...	...	...	...
Lille Europe d.	2033	|	|	|	|	2203	|	|	...	...	...	...	...	...	...	...	...	...	...	...
Brussels Midi / Zuid ◧ a.	2112	2112	2144	2144	2217	2238	2247	2317	...	...	...	...	...	...	...	...	...	...	...	...
Brussels Midi / Zuid ◧ △ d.	2122	2122	2152	...	...	...	...	...	...	...	...	...	...	...	...	...	...	...	...	...
Brussels Airport ✈ d.	|	|	|	...	...	...	...	...	...	...	...	...	...	...	...	...	...	...	...	...
Mechelen d.	|	|	|	...	...	...	...	...	...	...	...	...	...	...	...	...	...	...	...	...
Antwerpen Centraal a.	|	|	2227	...	...	...	...	...	...	...	...	...	...	...	...	...	...	...	...	...
Breda a.	|	|	|	...	...	...	...	...	...	...	...	...	...	...	...	...	...	...	...	...
Breda d.	|	|	|	...	...	...	...	...	...	...	...	...	...	...	...	...	...	...	...	...
Rotterdam Centraal a.	2232	2232	2302	...	...	...	...	...	...	...	...	...	...	...	...	...	...	...	...	...
Den Haag HS a.	|	|	|	...	...	...	...	...	...	...	...	...	...	...	...	...	...	...	...	...
Schiphol ✈ a.	|	|	2325	...	...	...	...	...	...	...	...	...	...	...	...	...	...	...	...	...
Amsterdam Centraal a.	2313	2313	2344	...	...	...	...	...	...	...	...	...	...	...	...	...	...	...	...	...

A – Mar. 19 - July 15.

C – Not Apr. 10, May 1.

E – Also Apr. 10, May 1, 28; not Apr. 9, May 1, 29.

F – Dec. 11 - Mar. 18.

G – Ⓐ Dec. 11 - Mar. 18. ⚒ Mar. 19 - July 15.

H – ① Dec. 11 - Mar. 18. ①⑥ Mar. 19 - July 15.

J – Ⓑ Dec. 11 - Mar. 18. Daily Mar. 19 - July 15.

K – ⑤ Dec. 11 - Mar. 18. Ⓐ Mar. 19 - July 15.

L – ①②③④⑦.

Q – ①②③④⑥ Dec. 11 - Mar. 18. ⑥ Mar. 19 - July 15.

§ – Station for Disneyland.

ICd – *Intercity direct* services.

◧ – Connections at Brussels are not guaranteed.

⇌ – *Thalys* high-speed train. 🅡🍸. Special fares payable. Three classes of service: (Premium, Comfort and Standard). Valid Dec. 11 - July 15.

△ – All *IC* and *ICd* services also call at Brussels Central and Brussels Nord, 5 and 12 minutes after Brussels Midi / Zuid respectively.

☆ – Eurostar train. 🅡, ✕ in Business Premier and Standard Premier, 🍸 in Standard. Special fares payable. See shaded panel in Table **10** on page 47 for information about recommended arrival times at departure station. Valid Feb. 5 - May 20.

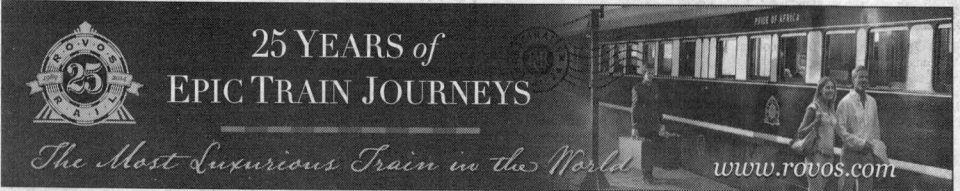

Brussels - Disneyland: see Table 11

AMSTERDAM - BRUSSELS - PARIS / LONDON 18

km	km	train type	⇌	⇌	⇌	☆		⇌	⇌	☆		⇌	⇌	IC	⇌	ICd	⇌			
		train number	**9302**	**9304**	**9308**	**9117**		**9310**	**9412** **9312**	**9119**		**9316**	**9916**	**9692**	**9322**	**9216**	**9424**			
		notes	Ⓐ	① U	⚒			Ⓐ		①–⑥ B		Ⓐ	①⑤⑥⑦							
0	0	**Amsterdam** Centraal d.	...	...	...	...	...	0615	...	0747	...	0715	0715	0555	0815	0725	...	...	...	...
17	17	Schiphol ✈ ⊕ d.	...	...	...	...	...	0634	...	|	...	0734	0734	0611	0834	0740	...	...	...	...
60		Den Haag HS d.	...	...	...	...	...	|	...	|	...	|	|	0640	|	|	...	...	...	...
82	70	**Rotterdam** Centraal d.	...	...	...	...	...	0658	...	0828	...	0758	0758	0710	0858	0810	...	...	...	...
140	117	Breda a.	...	...	...	...	...	|	...	|	...	|	|	0734	|	0834	...	...	...	...
140	117	Breda d.	...	...	...	...	...	|	...	|	...	|	|	0742	|	0842	...	...	...	...
181	•165	**Antwerpen** Centraal d.	...	...	...	...	...	0734	...	|	...	0833	0833	0816	0933	0916	...	...	...	...
		Mechelen d.	...	...	...	...	...	|	...	|	...	|	|	0837	|	0937	...	...	...	...
		Brussels Airport ✈ d.	...	...	...	...	...	|	...	|	...	|	|	0850	|	0950	...	...	...	...
229	212	**Brussels** Midi / Zuid ◧ △ a.	...	...	...	...	...	0808	...	0938	...	0908	0908	0917	1008	1017	...	...	...	...
229	212	**Brussels** Midi / Zuid ◧ d.	0643	0713	0743	0852	...	0813	0843	0951	...	0916	0920	...	1013	...	1043	...	...	...
		Lille Europe a.	|	|	|	0926	...	|	|	|	...	|	|	...	|	...	|	...	...	...
541	524	**Paris** Nord a.	0805	0835	0905	|	...	0935	1005	|	...	1038	|	...	1135	...	1205	...	...	...
		Paris Charles de Gaulle ✈ a.	...	...	...	|	...	...	...	|	...	...	1033	...	...	...	...	...	...	...
		Marne la Vallée - Chessy § a.	...	...	...	|	...	...	...	|	...	...	1048	...	...	...	...	...	...	...
		London St Pancras a.	...	...	...	0957	...	...	...	1100	...	...	...	...	...	...	...	...	...	...

train type	⇌	ICd		⇌	⇌	☆	ICd	⇌	⇌	IC	☆	ICd	⇌	⇌	⇌	☆	ICd	⇌		
train number	**9328**	**9220**		**9334**	**9334**	**9135**	**9224**	**9336**	**9340**	**9694**	**9141**	**9232**	**9346**	**9448**	**9352**	**9145**	**9236**	**9354**		
notes	⚒			Ⓐ	Ⓒ			Ⓐ					Ⓐ			Ⓑ		⑤		
Amsterdam Centraal d.	0915	0825	...	1015	1015	...	0925	...	1115	...	...	1125	1215	...	1315	1347	1225	...	...	...
Schiphol ✈ ⊕ d.	0934	0840	...	1034	1034	...	0940	...	1134	...	...	1140	1234	...	1334	|	1240	...	...	...
Den Haag HS d.	|	|	...	|	|	...	|	...	|	1040	...	|	|	...	|	|	|	...	...	...
Rotterdam Centraal d.	0958	0910	...	1058	1058	...	1010	...	1158	1110	...	1210	1258	...	1358	1428	1310	...	...	...
Breda a.	|	0934	...	|	|	...	1034	...	|	1134	...	1234	|	...	|	|	1334	...	...	...
Breda d.	|	0942	...	|	|	...	1042	...	|	1142	...	1242	|	...	|	|	1342	...	...	...
Antwerpen Centraal d.	1033	1016	...	1133	1133	...	1116	...	1233	1216	...	1316	1333	...	1433	|	1416	...	...	...
Mechelen d.	|	1037	...	|	|	...	1137	...	|	1237	...	1337	|	...	|	|	1437	...	...	...
Brussels Airport ✈ d.	|	1050	...	|	|	...	1150	...	|	1250	...	1350	|	...	|	|	1450	...	...	...
Brussels Midi / Zuid ◧ △ a.	1108	1117	...	1208	1208	...	1217	...	1308	1317	...	1417	1408	...	1508	1538	1517	...	...	...
Brussels Midi / Zuid ◧ d.	1113	...	...	...	1216	1256	...	1242	1321	...	1452	...	...	1443	1516	1556	...	1537	...	...
Lille Europe a.	|	...	...	...	|	1330	...	|	|	...	1526	...	...	|	|	1630	...	|	...	...
Paris Nord a.	1235	...	...	...	1338	|	...	1405	1444	...	|	...	...	1605	1638	|	...	1659	...	...
Paris Charles de Gaulle ✈ a.	...	...	...	...	...	|	...	...	...	...	|	...	...	...	...	|	...	...	...	...
Marne la Vallée - Chessy § a.	...	...	...	...	...	|	...	...	...	...	|	...	...	...	...	|	...	...	...	...
London St Pancras a.	...	...	...	...	...	1357	...	...	...	...	1600	...	...	...	...	1657	...	...	...	...

train type	⇌	⇌	ICd		⇌	☆	IC	⇌	☆		⇌	ICd	⇌		ICd	⇌	⇌	☆		
train number	**9358**	**9358**	**9240**		**9364**	**9153**	**9696**	**9366**	**9157**		**9370**	**9248**	**9472**		**9252**	**9376**	**9380**	**9163**		
notes	⑤	A						F			Ⓑ					Ⓑ	G	⑥		
Amsterdam Centraal d.	1415	...	1325	...	1515	...	...	...	1647	...	1615	1525	...	...	1625	1715	...	...	...	...
Schiphol ✈ ⊕ d.	1434	...	1340	...	1534	...	...	...	|	...	1634	1540	...	...	1640	1734	...	...	...	...
Den Haag HS d.	|	...	|	...	|	...	1440	...	|	...	|	|	...	...	|	|	...	...	...	...
Rotterdam Centraal d.	1458	...	1410	...	1558	...	1510	...	1728	...	1658	1610	...	...	1710	1758	...	...	...	...
Breda a.	|	...	1434	...	|	...	1534	...	|	...	|	1634	...	...	1734	|	...	...	...	...
Breda d.	|	...	1442	...	|	...	1542	...	|	...	|	1642	...	...	1742	|	...	...	...	...
Antwerpen Centraal d.	1533	...	1516	...	1633	...	1616	...	|	...	1733	1716	...	...	1816	1833	...	...	...	...
Mechelen d.	|	...	1537	...	|	...	1637	...	|	...	|	1737	...	...	1837	|	...	...	...	...
Brussels Airport ✈ d.	|	...	1550	...	|	...	1650	...	|	...	|	1750	...	...	1850	|	...	...	...	...
Brussels Midi / Zuid ◧ △ a.	1608	...	1617	...	1708	...	1717	...	1838	...	1808	1817	...	...	1917	1908	...	...	...	...
Brussels Midi / Zuid ◧ d.	1621	1621	...	...	1713	1756	...	1743	1851	...	1813	...	1842	...	...	1913	1941	2020	...	...
Lille Europe a.	|	|	...	...	|	1830	...	|	|	...	|	...	|	...	...	|	|	2058	...	...
Paris Nord a.	1744	1744	...	...	1835	|	...	1905	|	...	1935	...	2005	...	...	2035	2105	|	...	...
Paris Charles de Gaulle ✈ a.	...	...	...	...	...	|	...	...	|	...	...	...	...	...	...	...	...	|	...	...
Marne la Vallée - Chessy § a.	...	...	...	...	...	|	...	...	|	...	...	...	...	...	...	...	...	|	...	...
London St Pancras a.	...	...	...	...	...	1857	...	...	2000	...	...	...	...	...	...	...	...	2127	...	...

train type	⇌	☆	ICd	⇌	⇌		IC	⇌	⇌		ICd		ICd	⇌	ICd					
train number	**9382**	**9167**	**9256**	**9484**	**9388**		**9698**	**9394**	**9394**		**9264**		**9268**	**9398**	**9272**					
notes		Ⓑ		H	Ⓑ			Ⓐ	⑦					⑦						
Amsterdam Centraal d.	1815	1847	1725	...	1915	...	...	2015	2015	...	1925	...	2025	2115	2125	...	...	...	...	...
Schiphol ✈ ⊕ d.	1834	|	1740	...	1934	...	...	2034	2034	...	1940	...	2040	2134	2140	...	...	...	...	...
Den Haag HS d.	|	|	|	...	|	...	1840	|	|	...	|	...	|	|	|	...	...	...	...	...
Rotterdam Centraal d.	1858	1928	1810	...	1958	...	1910	2058	2058	...	2010	...	2110	2158	2210	...	...	...	...	...
Breda a.	|	|	1834	...	|	...	1934	|	|	...	2034	...	2134	|	2234	...	...	...	...	...
Breda d.	|	|	1842	...	|	...	1942	|	|	...	2042	...	2142	|	2242	...	...	...	...	...
Antwerpen Centraal d.	1933	|	1916	...	2033	...	2016	2133	2133	...	2116	...	2216	2233	2316	...	...	...	...	...
Mechelen d.	|	|	1937	...	|	...	2037	|	|	...	2137	...	2237	|	2337	...	...	...	...	...
Brussels Airport ✈ d.	|	|	1950	...	|	...	2050	|	|	...	2150	...	2250	|	2350	...	...	...	...	...
Brussels Midi / Zuid ◧ △ a.	2008	2038	2017	...	2108	...	2117	2208	2208	...	2217	...	2317	2308	0017	...	...	...	...	...
Brussels Midi / Zuid ◧ d.	2016	2055	...	2043	2116	...	...	...	2216	...	...	...	...	...	...	...	...	...	...	...
Lille Europe a.	|	2130	...	|	|	...	...	...	|	...	...	...	...	...	...	...	...	...	...	...
Paris Nord a.	2138	|	...	2205	2238	...	...	...	2338	...	...	...	...	...	...	...	...	...	...	...
Paris Charles de Gaulle ✈ a.	...	|	...	...	...	...	...	...	...	...	...	...	...	...	...	...	...	...	...	...
Marne la Vallée - Chessy § a.	...	|	...	...	...	...	...	...	...	...	...	...	...	...	...	...	...	...	...	...
London St Pancras a.	...	2157	...	...	...	...	...	...	...	...	...	...	...	...	...	...	...	...	...	...

A – ①②③④⑦ (not Apr. 4, 30, May 8, 28).

B – Not Apr. 10, May 1.

F – Ⓐ Jan. 8 - July 15 (not Mar. 16).

G – ⑤ Dec. 11 - Mar. 18 (not Mar. 3).
Ⓐ Mar. 19 - July 15.

H – Ⓑ Dec. 11 - Mar. 18.
Daily Mar. 19 - July 15.

U – Not May 8, June 12.

§ – Station for Disneyland.

• – Distance via Breda is 174km.

◧ – Connections at Brussels are not guaranteed.

△ – All *IC* and *ICd* services also call at Brussels Nord and Brussels Central, 12 and 5 minutes before Brussels Midi / Zuid respectively.

⇌ – *Thalys* high-speed train. 🅁 🍸. Special fares payable. Three classes of service: (Premium, Comfort and Standard). Valid Dec. 11 - July 15.

☆ – Eurostar train. 🅁, ✕ in Business Premier and Standard Premier, 🍸 in Standard. Special fares payable. See shaded panel in Table **10** on page 47 for information about recommended arrival times at departure station. Valid Feb. 5 - May 20.

20 LONDON, PARIS and BRUSSELS - KÖLN, HAMBURG and BERLIN

For the full service London - Brussels see Table **10**. For Paris - Brussels see Table **18**. Connections at Brussels are not guaranteed.

train type	*ICE*	*ICE*	*ICE*	⇌	*ICE*	*ICE*	*ICE*	*ICE*	⇌	*ICE*	*ICE*		☆	⇌	⇌	☆	*ICE*	*ICE*	*ICE*		⇌	*ICE*	*ICE*	
train number	**11**	**555**	**206**	**9303**	**13**	**13**	**557**	**202**	**9411**	**859**	**612**		**9106**	**9315**	**9315**	**9110**	**15**	**559**	**200**		**9423**	**951**	**610**	
notes				①–⑤	Ⓐ	Ⓒ			①–⑥				①–⑤	⑦	①–⑥	⑥								
													B											
London St Pancras d.	...	...	...	...	...	...	...	...	...	...	...	...	0616	...	...	0704	...	...	...	...	...	...	...	...
Paris Nord d.	...	...	...	0613	...	...	...	...	0755p	...	...	...	|	0807	0825	|	...	...	...	...	0955	...	...	...
Brussels Midi/Zuid a.	...	...	...	0745	...	...	...	...	0917	...	...	...	0912	0939	0947	1005	...	...	...	...	1118	...	...	...
Brussels Midi/Zuid d.	0623	...	...	...	0823	0825	...	...	0925	...	...	...	...	...	...	...	1025	...	...	...	1125	...	...	...
Brussels Nord d.	0631	...	...	...	0832	0834	...	...	|	...	...	...	...	...	...	...	1034	...	...	...	|	...	...	...
Liège Guillemins d.	0712	...	...	...	0914	0914	...	...	1013	...	...	...	...	...	...	...	1114	...	...	...	1213	...	...	...
Aachen 🏛 a.	0736	...	...	...	0936	0936	...	...	1034	...	...	...	...	...	...	...	1136	...	...	...	1235	...	...	...
Köln Hbf a.	0816	...	...	...	1015	1015	...	...	1115	...	...	...	...	...	...	...	1215	...	...	...	1315	...	...	...
Köln Hbf d.	...	0848	0910	...	...	...	1045	1111	...	1148	1211	...	...	...	...	...	...	1248	1311	...	1325	1348	1411	...
Wuppertal Hbf a.	...	0914	0941	...	...	...	1114	|	...	1214	1241	...	...	...	...	...	...	1314	|	...	|	1414	1441	...
Hagen Hbf a.	...	0932	0959	...	...	...	1132	|	...	1232	1259	...	...	...	...	...	...	1332	|	...	|	1432	1459	...
Düsseldorf Hbf a.	...	|	|	...	...	...	|	1132	...	|	|	...	...	...	...	...	...	|	1332	...	1347	|	|	...
Duisburg Hbf a.	...	|	|	...	...	...	|	1145	...	|	|	...	...	...	...	...	...	|	1345	...	1401	|	|	...
Essen Hbf a.	...	|	|	...	...	...	|	1158	...	|	|	...	...	...	...	...	...	|	1358	...	1416	|	|	...
Bochum Hbf a.	...	|	|	...	...	...	|	1209	...	|	|	...	...	...	...	...	...	|	1409	...	...	|	|	...
Dortmund Hbf a.	...	|	1021	...	...	...	|	1222	...	|	1321	...	...	...	...	...	...	|	1422	...	...	|	1521	...
Hamm (Westf) a.	...	1002	|	...	...	...	1202	|	...	1302	|	...	...	...	...	...	...	1402	|	...	...	1502	|	...
Bielefeld Hbf a.	...	1036	|	...	...	...	1236	|	...	1336	|	...	...	...	...	...	...	1436	|	...	...	1536	|	...
Münster a.	...	|	1055	...	...	...	|	1255	...	|	1354	...	...	...	...	...	...	|	1455	...	...	|	1554	...
Osnabrück Hbf a.	...	|	1121	...	...	...	|	1321	...	|	1421	...	...	...	...	...	...	|	1521	...	...	|	1621	...
Bremen Hbf a.	...	|	1215	...	...	...	|	1415	...	|	1515	...	...	...	...	...	...	|	1615	...	...	|	1715	...
Hannover Hbf a.	...	1128	|	...	...	...	1328	|	...	1428	|	...	...	...	...	...	...	1528	|	...	...	1628	|	...
Hamburg Hbf a.	...	|	1314	...	...	...	|	1514	...	|	1614	...	...	...	...	...	...	|	1714	...	...	|	1814	...
Berlin Hbf a.	...	1315	...	...	...	...	1515	...	...	1615	...	...	...	...	...	...	...	1715	...	...	...	1815	...	...

train type	⇌	☆	*ICE*	*ICE*	*ICE*		⇌	*ICE*	*ICE*		⇌	☆	*ICE*	*ICE*	*EC*		⇌	*ICE*	☆	*ICE*	*ICE*	*EC*		
train number	**9327**	**9116**	**315**	**651**	**108**		**9435**	**953**	**518**		**9339**	**9126**	**17**	**653**	**8**		**9351**	**317**	**9132**	**317**	**655**	**6**		
notes																		Ⓐ		Ⓒ				
London St Pancras d.	...	0855	...	...	...	...	...	...	...	...	...	1104	...	...	...	...	...	...	1301	...	...	...	...	...
Paris Nord d.	1025	|	...	...	...	...	1155	...	...	...	1222	|	...	...	...	...	1422	...	|	...	...	...	...	...
Brussels Midi/Zuid a.	1147	1205	...	...	...	...	1317	...	...	...	1344	1405	...	...	...	...	1544	...	1607	...	...	...	...	...
Brussels Midi/Zuid d.	...	...	1225	...	...	...	1325	...	...	...	...	...	1425	...	...	...	...	1622	...	1625	...	...	...	...
Brussels Nord d.	...	...	1234	...	...	...	|	...	...	...	...	...	1434	...	...	...	...	1632	...	1634	...	...	...	...
Liège Guillemins d.	...	...	1314	...	...	...	1413	...	...	...	...	...	1514	...	...	...	...	1714	...	1714	...	...	...	...
Aachen 🏛 a.	...	...	1336	...	...	...	1435	...	...	...	...	...	1536	...	...	...	...	1736	...	1736	...	...	...	...
Köln Hbf a.	...	...	1415	...	...	...	1515	...	...	...	...	...	1615	...	...	...	...	1815	...	1815	...	...	...	...
Köln Hbf d.	...	...	...	1448	1510	...	1525	1548	1611	...	...	...	...	1648	1709	...	...	...	...	...	1848	1909	...	...
Wuppertal Hbf a.	...	...	...	1514	|	...	|	1614	|	...	...	...	...	1714	|	...	...	...	...	...	1914	|	...	...
Hagen a.	...	...	...	1532	|	...	|	1632	|	...	...	...	...	1732	|	...	...	...	...	...	1932	|	...	...
Düsseldorf Hbf a.	...	...	...	|	1532	...	1552	|	1632	...	...	...	...	|	1731	...	...	...	...	...	|	1931	...	...
Duisburg Hbf a.	...	...	...	|	1545	...	...	|	1645	...	...	...	...	|	1745	...	...	...	...	...	|	1945	...	...
Essen Hbf a.	...	...	...	|	1558	...	...	|	1658	...	...	...	...	|	1758	...	...	...	...	...	|	1958	...	...
Bochum Hbf a.	...	...	...	|	1609	...	...	|	1708	...	...	...	...	|	1808	...	...	...	...	...	|	2008	...	...
Dortmund Hbf a.	...	...	...	|	1622	...	...	|	1722	...	...	...	...	|	1821	...	...	...	...	...	|	2021	...	...
Hamm (Westf) a.	...	...	...	1602	|	...	...	1702	|	...	...	...	...	1802	|	...	...	...	...	...	2002	|	...	...
Bielefeld a.	...	...	...	1636	|	...	...	1736	|	...	...	...	...	1836	|	...	...	...	...	...	2036	|	...	...
Münster a.	...	...	...	|	1655	...	...	|	1755	...	...	...	...	|	1854	...	...	...	...	...	|	2054	...	...
Osnabrück a.	...	...	...	|	1721	...	...	|	1821	...	...	...	...	|	1921	...	...	...	...	...	|	2121	...	...
Bremen Hbf a.	...	...	...	|	1815	...	...	|	1915	...	...	...	...	|	2015	...	...	...	...	...	|	2217	...	...
Hannover Hbf a.	...	...	...	1728	|	...	...	1828	|	...	...	...	...	1928	|	...	...	...	...	...	2128	|	...	...
Hamburg Hbf a.	...	...	...	|	1914	...	...	|	2014	...	...	...	...	|	2114	...	...	...	...	...	|	2316	...	...
Berlin Hbf a.	...	...	...	1915	...	...	...	2015	...	...	...	...	...	2115	...	...	...	...	...	...	2311	...	...	...

train type	☆	⇌	*ICE*	*ICE*	*ICE*		⇌	☆	*ICE*	*ICE*	*IC*	*EN*		⇌	*ICE*		⇌	*ICE*						
train number	**9132**	**9459**	**947**	**957**	**514**		**9363**	**9142**	**19**	**657**	**2341**	**xxxx**		**9471**	**512**		**9375**	**319**						
notes				⑤⑦			Ⓑ			⑤⑦	**1941**	①③⑤		Ⓑ			Ⓑ	⑦						
			T	**h**						**y**		**Z**		**G**				**t**						
London St Pancras d.	1301	...	...	...	...	...	...	1504	...	...	...	...	...	...	...	...	...	...	...	...	...	...	...	...
Paris Nord d.	|	1555	...	...	...	...	1625	|	...	...	...	...	...	1755	...	...	1825	...	...	...	...	...	...	...
Brussels Midi/Zuid a.	1606	1717	...	...	...	...	1747	1805	...	...	...	...	...	1917	...	...	1947	...	...	...	...	...	...	...
Brussels Midi/Zuid d.	...	1725	...	...	...	...	...	...	1825	...	...	1922	...	1925	...	...	...	2025	...	...	...	...	...	...
Brussels Nord d.	...	|	...	...	...	...	...	...	1834	...	...	|	...	|	...	...	...	2034	...	...	...	...	...	...
Liège Guillemins d.	...	1813	...	...	...	...	...	...	1914	...	...	|	...	2013	...	...	...	2114	...	...	...	...	...	...
Aachen 🏛 a.	...	1834	...	...	...	...	...	...	1936	1959	...	|	...	2034	...	...	...	2136	...	...	...	...	...	...
Köln Hbf a.	...	1915	...	...	...	...	...	...	2015	2045	...	|	...	2115	...	...	...	2213	...	...	...	...	...	...
Köln Hbf d.	...	1918	1928	1948	2011	...	...	...	...	2048	2113	|	...	2118	2212	...	...	...	...	...	...	...	...	...
Wuppertal Hbf a.	...	|	|	2014	2041	...	...	...	...	2114	2142	|	...	|	|	...	...	...	...	...	...	...	...	...
Hagen Hbf a.	...	|	|	2032	2059	...	...	...	...	2132	2200	|	...	|	|	...	...	...	...	...	...	...	...	...
Düsseldorf Hbf a.	...	1940	1950	|	|	...	...	...	...	|	|	|	...	2140	2233	...	...	...	...	...	...	...	...	...
Duisburg Hbf a.	...	1953	2008	|	|	...	...	...	...	|	|	|	...	2202	2247	...	...	...	...	...	...	...	...	...
Essen Hbf a.	...	2007	2021	|	|	...	...	...	...	|	|	|	...	2215	2300	...	...	...	...	...	...	...	...	...
Bochum Hbf a.	...	|	2033	|	|	...	...	...	...	|	|	|	...	|	|	...	...	...	...	...	...	...	...	...
Dortmund Hbf a.	...	2038	2045	|	2121	...	...	...	...	|	2221	|	...	2243	|	...	...	...	...	...	...	...	...	...
Hamm (Westf) a.	...	...	2107	2102	|	...	...	...	...	2202	2243	|	...	...	|	...	...	...	...	...	...	...	...	...
Bielefeld Hbf a.	...	...	2136	2136	|	...	...	...	...	2236	2318	|	...	...	|	...	...	...	...	...	...	...	...	...
Münster a.	...	...	|	|	2154	...	...	...	...	|	|	|	...	...	0002	...	...	...	...	...	...	...	...	...
Osnabrück Hbf a.	...	...	|	|	2221	...	...	...	...	|	|	|	...	...	...	...	...	...	...	...	...	...	...	...
Bremen Hbf a.	...	...	|	|	2315	...	...	...	...	|	|	|	...	...	...	...	...	...	...	...	...	...	...	...
Hannover Hbf a.	...	...	2228	2228	|	...	...	...	...	2328	0018	|	...	...	...	...	...	...	...	...	...	...	...	...
Hamburg Hbf a.	...	...	|	|	0015	...	...	...	...	|	...	|	...	...	...	...	...	...	...	...	...	...	...	...
Berlin Hbf a.	...	...	0014	0014	...	...	...	...	...	0114	...	0648	...	...	...	...	...	...	...	...	...	...	...	...

B – Not Apr. 10, May 1.

G – Calls at Düsseldorf Flughafen ✈ arrives 2149.

T – ①②③④⑥ (also Apr. 9, 30; not Apr. 6, 10, May 1, 17, 29).

Z – From May 25, European Sleeper: 🛏 1, 2 cl. (1, 2, 3 berth) 🛏 2 cl. (4, 6 berth), Brussels - Amsterdam - Berlin (Table **78**).

h – Also Apr. 6, 10, May 1, 17, 29; not Apr. 9, 30.

p – 0743 on ⑥.

t – Not Apr. 9, 30, May 28.

y – Also Apr. 6, 10, May 1, 17, 29; not Apr. 7, 9, 30.

⇌ – *Thalys* high-speed train. 🅁 🍸. Special fares payable. Three classes of service: Premium, Comfort and Standard. Valid Dec. 11 - Mar. 18.

☆ – Eurostar train. 🅁, ✕ in Business Premier and Standard Premier, 🍸 in Standard. Special fares payable. See shaded panel in Table **10** on page 47 for information about recommended arrival times at departure station. Valid Feb. 5 - May 20.

BERLIN, HAMBURG and KÖLN - BRUSSELS, PARIS and LONDON 20

For the full service Brussels - London see Table **10**. For Brussels - Paris see Table **18**. Connections at Brussels are not guaranteed.

train type	⇌	☆	*EN*	*ICE*	*IC*	*ICE*	⇌	*ICE*	*EC*	⇌	*EC*	*ICE*	*ICE*	⇌	⇌	☆	*EC*	*ICE*	*ICE*	☆
train number	**9412**	**9119**	**xxxx**	**101**	**2319**	**18**	**9322**	**513**	**115**	**9424**	**7**	**656**	**316**	**9334**	**9336**	**9135**	**9**	**654**	**16**	**9141**
notes	①–⑥ J	①–⑥ D	②④⑦ Z	⚒	⚒							⚒		⑥⑦	①–⑤					
Berlin Hbf ... d.	...	...	2256	...	...	...	...	...	...	...	...	0425	...	...	...	...	...	0646	...	...
Hamburg Hbf ... d.	...	...	|	...	...	...	...	...	...	...	0437	|	...	...	...	...	0646	|	...	...
Hannover Hbf ... d.	...	...	|	...	...	...	...	...	...	...	|	0621	...	...	...	...	|	0831	...	...
Bremen Hbf ... d.	...	...	|	...	...	...	...	...	...	...	0540	|	...	...	...	...	0744	|	...	...
Osnabrück Hbf ... d.	...	...	|	...	...	...	...	...	...	...	0636	|	...	...	...	...	0836	|	...	...
Münster ... d.	...	...	|	...	0503	...	...	0603	0630	...	0702	|	...	...	...	...	0903	|	...	...
Bielefeld Hbf ... d.	...	...	|	...	|	...	...	|	|	...	|	0721	...	...	...	...	|	0922	...	...
Hamm (Westf) ... d.	...	...	|	...	|	...	...	|	|	...	|	0754	...	...	...	...	|	0954	...	...
Dortmund Hbf ... d.	0458	...	|	0528	0536	...	...	0636	|	0651	|	|	...	...	...	...	|	|	...	...
Bochum Hbf ... d.	|	...	|	|	0548	...	...	0648	|	|	|	|	...	...	...	...	|	|	...	...
Essen Hbf ... d.	0539	...	|	|	0600	...	...	0700	|	0739	0757	|	...	...	...	...	0957	|	...	...
Duisburg Hbf ... d.	0553	...	|	|	0613	...	...	|	0734	|	0810	|	...	...	...	...	1010	|	...	...
Düsseldorf Hbf ... d.	0614	...	|	|	0627	...	...	0724	0749	0809	0824	|	...	...	...	...	1024	|	...	...
Hagen Hbf ... d.	|	...	|	0557	|	...	...	|	|	|	|	0823	...	...	...	...	|	1023	...	...
Wuppertal Hbf ... d.	|	...	|	0615	|	...	...	|	|	|	|	0840	...	...	...	...	|	1040	...	...
Köln Hbf ... a.	0641	...	|	0646	0650	...	...	0749	0815	0836	0850	0909	...	...	...	...	1050	1109	...	...
Köln Hbf ... d.	0645	...	|	...	...	0742	...	...	...	0845	...	...	0942	...	...	...	...	...	1142	...
Aachen 🏛 ... d.	0723	...	|	...	...	0821	...	...	...	0924	...	...	1021	...	...	...	...	...	1221	...
Liège Guillemins ... d.	0753	...	|	...	...	0846	...	...	...	0951	...	...	1046	...	...	...	...	...	1246	...
Brussels Nord ... a.	|	...	|	...	...	0926	...	...	...	|	...	...	1126	...	...	...	...	...	1326	...
Brussels Midi/Zuid ... a.	0836	...	0927	...	...	0935	...	...	...	1035	...	...	1135	...	...	...	...	...	1335	...
Brussels Midi/Zuid ... d.	0843	0951	...	...	...	...	1013	...	...	1043	...	...	...	1216	1242	1256	...	...	...	1452
Paris Nord ... a.	1005	|	...	...	...	...	1135	...	...	1205	...	...	...	1338	1405	|	...	...	...	|
London St Pancras ... a.	...	1100	...	...	...	...	...	...	...	...	...	...	...	...	...	1357	...	...	...	1600

train type	*ICE*	*ICE*	⇌	⇌	☆	*ICE*	*ICE*	*ICE*	⇌	⇌	☆	*ICE*	*ICE*	*ICE*	⇌	☆	*ICE*	*ICE*	⇌
train number	**517**	**954**	**9448**	**9448**	**9145**	**107**	**652**	**314**	**9358**	**9364**	**9153**	**109**	**650**	**14**	**9370**	**9157**	**611**	**950**	**9472**
notes			⑦	①–⑥	Ⓑ				Ⓑ						Ⓑ				
Berlin Hauptbahnhof ... d.	...	0746	...	...	...	...	0846	...	...	...	...	...	1046	...	...	...	...	1146	...
Hamburg Hbf ... d.	0745	|	...	...	...	0845	|	...	...	...	...	1045	|	...	...	...	1145	|	...
Hannover Hbf ... d.	|	0931	...	...	...	|	1031	...	...	...	...	|	1231	...	...	...	|	1331	...
Bremen Hbf ... d.	0844	|	...	...	...	0944	|	...	...	...	...	1144	|	...	...	...	1244	|	...
Osnabrück Hbf ... d.	0937	|	...	...	...	1037	|	...	...	...	...	1236	|	...	...	...	1337	|	...
Münster ... d.	1002	|	...	...	...	1102	|	...	...	...	...	1302	|	...	...	...	1402	|	...
Bielefeld Hbf ... d.	|	1022	...	...	...	|	1122	...	...	...	...	|	1322	...	...	...	|	1422	...
Hamm (Westf) ... d.	|	1054	...	...	...	|	1154	...	...	...	...	|	1354	...	...	...	|	1454	...
Dortmund Hbf ... d.	1035	|	1051	...	...	|	|	...	...	...	...	|	|	...	...	...	1435	|	...
Bochum Hbf ... d.	|	|	|	...	...	|	|	...	...	...	...	|	|	...	...	...	|	|	...
Essen Hbf ... d.	|	|	1126	...	...	1157	|	...	...	...	...	1357	|	...	...	...	|	|	1543
Duisburg Hbf ... d.	|	|	|	...	...	1209	|	...	...	...	...	1410	|	...	...	...	|	|	1557
Düsseldorf Hbf ... d.	|	|	1154	...	...	1223	|	...	...	...	...	1423	|	...	...	...	|	|	1613
Hagen Hbf ... d.	1057	1123	|	...	...	|	1223	...	...	...	...	|	1423	...	...	...	1457	1523	|
Wuppertal Hbf ... d.	1114	1140	|	...	...	|	1240	...	...	...	...	|	1440	...	...	...	1514	1540	|
Köln Hbf ... a.	1146	1209	1226	...	...	1249	1309	...	...	...	...	1449	1509	...	...	...	1546	1609	1641
Köln Hbf ... d.	...	...	1243	1243	...	...	...	1342	...	...	...	...	...	1540	...	...	...	...	1645
Aachen 🏛 ... d.	...	...	1324	1324	...	...	...	1421	...	...	...	...	...	1621	...	...	...	...	1724
Liège Guillemins ... d.	...	...	1351	1351	...	...	...	1446	...	...	...	...	...	1646	...	...	...	...	1751
Brussels Nord ... a.	...	...	|	|	...	...	...	1526	...	...	...	...	...	1726	...	...	...	...	|
Brussels Midi/Zuid ... a.	...	...	1435	1435	...	...	...	1535	...	...	...	...	...	1735	...	...	...	...	1835
Brussels Midi/Zuid ... d.	...	...	1443	1443	1556	...	...	...	1613	1713	1756	...	...	...	1813	1851	...	...	1842
Paris Nord ... a.	...	...	1605	1605	|	...	...	...	1735	1835	|	...	...	...	1935	|	...	...	2005
London St Pancras ... a.	...	...	...	...	1657	...	...	...	...	...	1857	...	...	...	...	2000	...	...	...

train type	*ICE*	*ICE*	*ICE*	⇌	☆	☆	*ICE*	*ICE*	⇌	*IC*	*ICE*	*ICE*	⇌	*ICE*	*ICE*	*ICE*
train number	**201**	**558**	**12**	**9382**	**9163**	**9167**	**613**	**1050**	**9484**	**2213**	**556**	**10**	**9394**	**205**	**554**	**318**
notes					⑥	Ⓑ			Ⓑ				⑦			⑦t
Berlin Hauptbahnhof ... d.	...	1246	...	...	...	...	...	1306	...	...	1446	...	...	...	1646	...
Hamburg Hbf ... d.	1245	|	...	...	...	...	1345	|	...	1444	|	...	...	1645	|	...
Hannover Hbf ... d.	|	1431	...	...	...	...	|	1456	...	|	1631	...	...	|	1831	...
Bremen Hbf ... d.	1344	|	...	...	...	...	1444	|	...	1544	|	...	...	1744	|	...
Osnabrück Hbf ... d.	1437	|	...	...	...	...	1537	|	...	1636	|	...	...	1837	|	...
Münster ... d.	1502	|	...	...	...	...	1602	|	...	1703	|	...	...	1902	|	...
Bielefeld Hbf ... d.	|	1522	...	...	...	...	|	1553	...	|	1722	...	...	|	1922	...
Hamm (Westf) ... d.	|	1554	...	...	...	...	|	1626	...	|	1754	...	...	|	1954	...
Dortmund Hbf ... d.	|	|	...	...	...	...	1635	1651	...	|	|	...	...	|	|	...
Bochum Hbf ... d.	|	|	...	...	...	...	|	1704	...	|	|	...	...	|	|	...
Essen Hbf ... d.	1556	|	...	...	...	...	|	1715	...	1757	|	...	...	1955	|	...
Duisburg Hbf ... d.	1609	|	...	...	...	...	|	1731	...	1810	|	...	...	2008	|	...
Düsseldorf Hbf ... d.	1623	|	...	...	...	...	|	1745	1810	1824	|	...	...	2022	|	...
Hagen Hbf ... d.	|	1623	...	...	...	...	1657	|	|	|	1823	...	...	|	2023	...
Wuppertal Hbf ... d.	|	1640	...	...	...	...	1714	|	|	|	1840	...	...	|	2040	...
Köln Hbf ... a.	1649	1709	...	...	...	...	1746	1817	1841	1850	1909	...	...	2049	2111	...
Köln Hbf ... d.	...	...	1741	...	...	...	...	...	1844	...	...	1940	...	...	...	2142
Aachen 🏛 ... d.	...	...	1821	...	...	...	...	...	1924	...	...	2021	...	...	...	2221
Liège Guillemins ... d.	...	...	1846	...	...	...	...	...	1951	...	...	2046	...	...	...	2246
Brussels Nord ... a.	...	...	1926	...	...	...	...	...	|	...	...	2126	...	...	...	2326
Brussels Midi/Zuid ... a.	...	...	1935	...	...	...	...	...	2035	...	...	2135	...	...	...	2335
Brussels Midi/Zuid ... d.	...	...	...	2016	2020	2055	...	...	2043	...	...	...	2216	...	...	...
Paris Nord ... a.	...	...	...	2138	|	|	...	...	2205	...	...	...	2338	...	...	...
London St Pancras ... a.	...	...	...	...	2127	2157	...	...	...	...	...	...	...	...	...	...

D – Not Apr. 10, May 1.

J – Calls at Düsseldorf Flughafen ✈ departs 0604.

Z – From May 25, European Sleeper: 🛏 1, 2 cl. (1, 2, 3 berth) 🛏 2 cl. (4, 6 berth), Berlin - Amsterdam - Brussels (Table **78**).

t – Also Apr. 10, May 1, 29; not Apr. 9, 30, May 28.

☆ – Eurostar train. 🅁, ✕ in Business Premier and Standard Premier, 🍸 in Standard. Special fares payable. See shaded panel in Table **10** on page 47 for information about recommended arrival times at departure station. Valid Feb. 5 - May 20.

⇌ – *Thalys* high-speed train. 🅁 🍸. Special fares payable. Three classes of service: (Premium, Comfort and Standard). Valid Dec. 11 - Mar. 18.

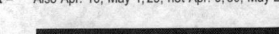

INTERNATIONAL

21 LONDON, PARIS and BRUSSELS - FRANKFURT - MÜNCHEN

For the full service London - Brussels see Table **10**. For Paris - Brussels see Table **18**. Connections at Brussels are not guaranteed.

Services between Frankfurt and München subject to alteration from April 1

train type	*ICE*	*ICE*	*ICE*	*ICE*	*EC*	⇌	*ICE*	*ICE*	*EC*	*ICE*	*ICE*	*ICE*	⇌	*ICE*	*ICE*	*ICE*	☆	⇌	⇌	☆	*ICE*	*ICE*	*ICE*	*ICE*	*ICE*
train number	**11**	**571**	**593**	**529**	**7**	**9303**	**13**	**13**	**9**	**573**	**595**	**27**	**9411**	**625**	**517**	**29**	**9106**	**9315**	**9315**	**9110**	**15**	**575**	**597**	**627**	**29**
notes						①–⑤	Ⓐ	Ⓒ					①–⑥				①–⑤ **M**	⑦	①–⑥	⑥					
London St Pancras.....d.	...	...	...	...	...	...	...	...	...	...	...	...	...	...	...	...	0616	...	...	0704	...	...	...	...	...
Paris Nord ....d.	...	...	...	...	...	0613	...	...	...	...	...	...	0755**p**	...	...	...	|	0807	0825	|	...	...	...	...	...
Brussels Midi / Zuid .....a.	...	...	...	...	...	0745	...	...	...	...	...	...	0917	...	...	...	0912	0939	0947	1005	...	...	...	...	...
Brussels Midi / Zuid .....d.	0623	...	...	...	...	...	0823	0825	...	...	...	...	0925	...	...	...	...	...	...	...	1025	...	...	...	...
Brussels Nord..............d.	0631	...	...	...	...	...	0832	0834	...	...	...	...	|	...	...	...	...	...	...	...	1034	...	...	...	...
Liège Guillemins ....d.	0712	...	...	...	...	...	0914	0914	...	...	...	...	1013	...	...	...	...	...	...	...	1114	...	...	...	...
Aachen Hbf 🏛 ....a.	0736	...	...	...	...	...	0936	0936	...	...	...	...	1034	...	...	...	...	...	...	...	1136	...	...	...	...
Köln Hbf ....a.	0816	...	...	...	...	...	1015	1015	...	...	...	...	1115	...	...	...	...	...	...	...	1215	...	...	...	...
Köln Hbf ....d.	0825	...	...	...	0853	...	1018	1018	1053	...	...	...	...	1145**x**	1155	1153	...	...	...	...	1218	...	...	...	...
Bonn Hbf ....a.	|	...	...	...	0912	...	|	|	1112	...	...	...	...	|	|	1212	...	...	...	...	|	...	...	...	...
Koblenz Hbf................a.	|	...	...	...	0946	...	|	|	1146	...	...	...	...	|	|	1246	...	...	...	...	|	...	...	...	←
Mainz Hbf...................a.	|	...	...	...	1039	...	|	|	1239	...	...	...	...	|	|	1339	...	...	...	...	|	...	...	...	1342
Frankfurt Flughafen ✈ .a.	0917	0924	...	...	...	...	1117	1117	...	1124	...	...	...	1233	1250	→	...	...	...	...	1317	1324	...	...	1359
Frankfurt (Main) Hbf..a.	0931	|	0950	0953	...	...	1131	1131	...	|	1150	1222	...	1248	|	...	...	...	...	...	1331	|	1350	1353	1413
Würzburg Hbf..........a.	...	|	|	1101	...	...	...	...	...	|	|	1332	...	1401	|	...	...	...	...	...	...	|	|	1501	1532
Nürnberg Hbf ....a.	...	|	|	1158	...	...	...	...	...	|	|	1427	...	1500	|	...	...	...	...	...	...	|	|	1559	1627
Wien Hbf..................a.	...	|	|	|	...	...	...	...	...	|	|	1847	...	|	|	...	...	...	...	...	...	|	|	|	2047
Mannheim Hbf ....a.	...	0956	1027	|	...	...	...	...	...	1156	1227	...	...	|	1323	...	...	...	...	...	...	1356	1427	|	...
Stuttgart Hbf.............a.	...	1038	1108	|	...	...	...	...	...	1238	1308	...	...	|	1408	...	...	...	...	...	...	1438	1508	|	...
Ulm Hbf......................a.	...	...	1158	|	...	...	...	...	...	...	1358	...	...	|	1510	...	...	...	...	...	...	...	1558	|	...
Augsburg Hbf..............a.	...	...	1241	|	...	...	...	...	...	...	1441	...	...	|	1553	...	...	...	...	...	...	...	1641	|	...
München Hbf.............a.	...	...	1313	1306	...	...	...	...	...	...	1513	...	...	1606	1626	...	...	...	...	...	...	...	1716	1706	...

train type / number	⇌	*ICE*	*ICE*	*ICE*	⇌	☆	*ICE*	*ICE*	*ICE*	*ICE*	*ICE*	⇌	*ICE*	*ICE*	*ICE*		⇌	☆	*ICE*	*ICE*	*ICE*	*ICE*	*ICE*	*EN*	
train number	**9423**	**629**	**229**	**519**	**9327**	**9116**	**315**	**577**	**1219**	**721**	**229**	**9435**	**723**	**611**	**927**		**9339**	**9126**	**17**	**579**	**17**	**691**	**725**	**50237**	
notes																			⑥ **J**		Ⓑ **K**			**E**	
London St Pancras.....d.	...	...	...	...	...	0855	...	...	...	...	...	...	...	...	...	...	...	1104	...	...	...	...	...	...	...
Paris Nord ....d.	0955	...	...	...	1025	|	...	...	...	...	...	1155	...	...	...	...	1222	|	...	...	...	...	...	...	...
Brussels Midi / Zuid .....a.	1118	...	...	...	1147	1205	...	...	...	...	...	1317	...	...	...	...	1344	1405	...	...	...	...	...	...	...
Brussels Midi / Zuid .....d.	1125	...	...	...	...	...	1225	...	...	...	...	1325	...	...	...	...	...	...	1425	...	1425	...	...	...	...
Brussels Nord..............d.	|	...	...	...	...	...	1234	...	...	...	...	|	...	...	...	...	...	...	1434	...	1434	...	...	...	...
Liège Guillemins ....d.	1213	...	...	...	...	...	1314	...	...	...	...	1413	...	...	...	...	...	...	1514	...	1514	...	...	...	...
Aachen Hbf 🏛 ....a.	1235	...	...	...	...	...	1336	...	...	...	...	1435	...	...	...	...	...	...	1536	...	1536	...	...	...	...
Köln Hbf ....a.	1315	...	...	...	...	...	1415	...	...	...	...	1515	...	...	...	...	...	...	1615	...	1615	...	...	...	...
Köln Hbf ....d.	...	1344**x**	1353	1355	...	...	1427	...	...	...	...	...	1545**x**	1555	1553	...	...	...	1620	...	1620	...	...	...	...
Bonn Hbf ....a.	...	|	1412	|	...	...	|	...	...	...	...	...	|	|	1612	...	...	...	|	...	|	...	...	...	...
Koblenz Hbf................a.	...	|	1446	|	...	...	|	...	...	...	←	...	|	|	1646	...	...	...	|	...	|	...	...	...	...
Mainz Hbf...................a.	...	|	1539	|	...	...	|	...	...	...	1542	...	|	|	1739	...	...	...	|	...	|	...	...	...	...
Frankfurt Flughafen ✈ .a.	...	1433	→	1450	...	...	1517	1524	...	...	1559	...	1633	1650	1759	...	...	...	1717	1724	1725	...	...	...	...
Frankfurt (Main) Hbf..a.	...	1448	...	|	...	...	1531	|	1550	1554	1613	...	1648	|	1813	...	...	...	1731	|	1740	1750	1753	...	...
Würzburg Hbf..........a.	...	1601	...	|	...	...	...	|	|	1701	1732	...	1801	|	1932	...	...	...	...	|	...	|	1901	...	...
Nürnberg Hbf ....a.	...	1658	...	|	...	...	...	|	|	1759	1827	...	1859	|	2028	...	...	...	...	|	...	|	1959	...	...
Wien Hbf..................a.	...	|	...	|	...	...	...	|	|	|	2305	...	|	|	...	...	...	...	...	|	...	|	|	...	...
Mannheim Hbf ....a.	...	|	...	1523	...	...	...	1556	1627	|	...	...	|	1723	...	...	...	...	...	1755	...	1827	|	...	...
Stuttgart Hbf.............a.	...	|	...	1608	...	...	...	1638	1708	|	...	...	|	1808	...	...	...	...	...	1838	...	1908	|	2029	...
Ulm Hbf......................a.	...	|	...	1710	...	...	...	...	1758	|	...	...	|	1910	...	...	...	...	...	...	...	1958	|	2151	...
Augsburg Hbf..............a.	...	|	...	1753	...	...	...	...	1841	|	...	...	|	1953	...	...	...	...	...	...	...	2041	|	2248	...
München Hbf.............a.	...	1807	...	1826	...	...	...	...	1913	1911	...	...	2007	2026	...	...	...	...	...	...	...	2113	2111	2354**o**	...

train type	⇌	*ICE*	☆	*ICE*	*ICE*	*ICE*	*ICE*	⇌	*ICE*	*ICE*	⇌	☆	*ICE*	*ICE*	*ICE*	*ICE*	*IC*	⇌	*ICE*	*ICE*	*NJ*	*NJ*	⇌	*ICE*	*ICE*
train number	**9351**	**317**	**9132**	**317**	**771**	**693**	**729**	**9459**	**1021**	**615**	**9363**	**9142**	**19**	**773**	**695**	**1021**	**2215**	**9473**	**617**	**2027**	**421**	**425**	**9375**	**319**	**619**
notes		Ⓐ		Ⓒ							Ⓑ										♣ **A**	①③⑤ **B**♣	Ⓑ	⑦ **h**	
London St Pancras.....d.	...	...	1301	...	...	...	...	...	...	...	...	1504	...	...	...	...	...	...	...	...	...	...	...	...	...
Paris Nord ....d.	1422	...	|	...	...	...	...	1555	...	...	1625	|	...	...	...	...	...	1755	...	...	...	...	1825	...	...
Brussels Midi / Zuid .....a.	1544	...	1606	...	...	...	...	1717	...	...	1747	1805	...	...	...	...	...	1917	...	...	...	...	1947	...	...
Brussels Midi / Zuid .....d.	...	1622	...	1625	...	...	...	1725	...	...	...	...	1825	...	...	...	...	1925	...	...	...	1932	...	2025	...
Brussels Nord..............d.	...	1632	...	1634	...	...	...	|	...	...	...	...	1834	...	...	...	...	|	...	...	...	1943	...	2034	...
Liège Guillemins ....d.	...	1714	...	1714	...	...	...	1813	...	...	...	...	1914	...	...	...	...	2013	...	...	...	2033	...	2114	...
Aachen Hbf 🏛 ....a.	...	1736	...	1736	...	...	...	1834	...	...	...	...	1936	...	...	...	...	2034	...	...	...	2119	...	2136	...
Köln Hbf ....a.	...	1815	...	1815	...	...	...	1915	...	...	...	...	2015	...	...	...	...	2115	...	...	...	|	...	2213	...
Köln Hbf ....d.	...	1818	...	1818	...	...	...	...	1953**z**	1955	...	...	2017	...	...	...	2053	...	2155	2153**z**	2226	|	...	...	2355
Bonn Hbf ....a.	...	|	...	|	...	...	...	...	2012	|	...	...	|	...	...	...	2112	...	|	2212	2309	2309	...	...	|
Koblenz Hbf................a.	...	|	...	|	...	...	...	...	2046	|	...	...	|	...	...	...	2146	...	|	2246	2344	2344	...	...	|
Mainz Hbf...................a.	...	|	...	|	...	...	...	...	2142	|	...	...	|	...	...	...	2239	...	|	2339	0054	0054	...	...	|
Frankfurt Flughafen ✈ .a.	...	1917	...	1917	1924	...	...	...	2159	2050	...	...	2117	2124	...	←	2259	...	2254	2359	0115	0115	...	...	0054
Frankfurt (Main) Hbf..a.	...	1931	...	1931	|	1950	1953	...	2213	|	...	...	2131	|	2150	2222	2312	...	|	0013	0129**f**	0129**f**	...	...	0110
Würzburg Hbf..........a.	...	...	...	...	|	|	2101	...	→	|	...	...	...	|	|	2344	...	...	|	...	0240	0240	...	...	|
Nürnberg Hbf ....a.	...	...	...	...	|	|	2159	...	...	|	...	...	...	|	|	0042	...	...	|	...	0336	0336	...	...	|
Wien Hbf..................a.	...	...	...	...	|	|	|	...	...	|	...	...	...	|	|	...	...	...	|	...	|	0919	...	...	|
Mannheim Hbf ....a.	...	...	...	...	1955	2027	|	...	...	2124	...	...	...	2155	2227	...	...	...	2327	...	|	...	...	...	0202
Stuttgart Hbf.............a.	...	...	...	...	2038	2108	|	...	...	2208	...	...	...	2255	2308	...	...	...	0008	...	|	...	...	...	0333
Ulm Hbf......................a.	...	...	...	...	...	2158**t**	|	...	...	2310	...	...	...	...	2358**j**	...	...	...	...	...	|	...	...	...	0438
Augsburg Hbf..............a.	...	...	...	...	...	2241**t**	|	...	...	2353	...	...	...	...	0046**j**	...	...	...	...	...	0623	...	...	...	0530
München Hbf.............a.	...	...	...	...	...	2313**t**	2311	...	...	0028	...	...	...	...	0118**j**	...	...	...	...	...	0711	...	...	...	0603

A – *ÖBB nightjet* 🛏 1, 2 cl., ▬ 2 cl. (4, 6 berth), (2) Amsterdam - Köln - München - Innsbruck ♣ (Table **53**).

B – ①③⑤: *ÖBB nightjet* 🛏 1, 2 cl., ▬ 2 cl. (4, 6 berth), (2) Brussels - Wien ♣ (Table **53**).

E – KÁLMÁN IMRE – 🛏 1, 2 cl., ▬ 2 cl. (4, 6 berth), (2) Stuttgart - München - Budapest. Also conveys cars to Venezia (Table **70**), Zagreb and Rijeka (Table **62**).

J – ⑥ (also Apr. 9, 30; daily May 27 - Sept 10; also Sept. 11).

K – Ⓑ Dec. 11 - May 26, Sept. 12 - Dec. 8 (not Apr. 9, 30).

M – Not Apr. 10, May 1.

♣ – Special fares apply.

⇌ – *Thalys* high-speed train. 🅁 🍸. Special fares payable. Three classes of service: (Premium, Comfort and Standard). Valid Dec. 11 - Mar. 18.

☆ – Eurostar train. 🅁, ✕ in Business Premier and Standard Premier, 🍸 in Standard. Special fares payable. See shaded panel in Table **10** on page 47 for information about recommended arrival times at departure station. Valid Feb. 5 - May 20.

f – Frankfurt (Main) **Süd**.

h – Not Apr. 9, 30, May 28.

j – ⑥⑦.

o – München **Ost**.

p – 0743 on ⑥.

t – Not ⑥.

x – Köln **Messe / Deutz** (Table **910**). Connections from Köln Hbf depart every 2 - 5 minutes, journey time 2 - 3 minutes.

z – Departs from Köln **Messe / Deutz** on certain dates.

MÜNCHEN - FRANKFURT - BRUSSELS, PARIS and LONDON 21

For the full service London - Brussels see Table **10**. For Paris - Brussels see Table **18**. Connections at Brussels are not guaranteed.

train type	*ICE*	*ICE*	⇌	☆	*NJ*	*IC*	*ICE*	*ICE*	*NJ*	⇌	*ICE*	*ICE*	⇌	*ICE*	*ICE*	*IC*	*ICE*	⇌	⇌	☆
train number	**618**	**222**	**9412**	**9119**	**420**	**2212**	**774**	**18**	**50490**	**9322**	**2026**	**616**	**9424**	**822**	**694**	**2441**	**316**	**9334**	**9336**	**9135**
notes		Ⓐ		①–⑥	♣				②④⑦					①–⑥				⑥⑦	①–⑤	
notes				**D**	**B**				**C**♣					**p**						
München Hbf ... d.	0001	...	...	...	2250	...	...	...	...	...	...	0332	...	0449	...	...	...	...	...	...
Augsburg Hbf ... d.	0032	...	...	...	2323	...	...	...	...	...	...	0404	...	|	...	...	...	...	...	...
Ulm Hbf ... d.	0117	...	...	...	|	...	...	...	...	...	...	0447	...	|	...	...	...	...	...	...
Stuttgart Hbf ... d.	0222	...	...	...	|	...	0502	...	...	...	...	0551	...	|	0650	...	...	...	...	...
Mannheim Hbf ... d.	0401	...	...	...	|	...	0604	...	...	...	...	0636	...	|	0732	...	...	...	...	...
Wien Hbf ... d.	|	...	...	...	|	...	|	...	2013	...	...	|	...	|	|	...	...	...	...	...
Nürnberg Hbf ... d.	|	...	...	...	0141	...	|	...	0141	...	...	|	...	0600	|	...	...	...	...	...
Würzburg Hbf ... d.	|	...	...	...	|	...	|	...	|	...	...	|	...	0655	|	...	...	...	...	...
Frankfurt (Main) Hbf ... d.	0446	0526	...	...	0347**f**	...	|	0628	0347**f**	...	...	|	...	0804	0808	...	0816	...	...	...
Frankfurt Flughafen ✈ ... d.	0500	0539	...	...	0359	...	0635	0642	0359	...	...	0706	...	...	...	...	0831	...	...	...
Mainz Hbf ... d.	|	|	...	...	0418	...	...	|	0418	...	0617	|	...	...	...	0717	|	...	...	...
Koblenz Hbf ... d.	|	|	...	...	0513	0605	...	|	0513	...	0713	|	...	...	...	0813	|	...	...	...
Bonn Hbf ... d.	|	|	...	...	0601	0645	...	|	0601	...	0745	|	...	...	...	0846	|	...	...	...
Köln Hbf ... a.	0603	0632	...	...	0651	0705	...	0733	|	...	0805	0804	...	...	...	0905	0932	...	...	...
Köln Hbf ... d.	...	...	0645	...	...	...	...	0742	|	...	...	...	0845	...	...	...	0942	...	...	...
Aachen Hbf 🏛 ... d.	...	...	0723	...	...	...	...	0821	0747	...	...	...	0924	...	...	...	1021	...	...	...
Liège Guillemins ... d.	...	...	0753	...	...	...	...	0846	0850	...	...	...	0951	...	...	...	1046	...	...	...
Brussels Nord ... a.	...	...	|	...	...	...	...	0926	0942	...	...	...	|	...	...	...	1126	...	...	...
Brussels Midi / Zuid ... a.	...	...	0836	...	...	...	...	0935	0952	...	...	...	1035	...	...	...	1135	...	...	...
Brussels Midi / Zuid ... d.	...	...	0843	0951	...	...	...	...	...	1013	...	...	1043	...	...	...	...	1216	1242	1256
Paris Nord ... d.	...	...	1005	|	...	...	...	...	...	1135	...	...	1205	...	...	...	...	1338	1405	|
London St Pancras ... a.	...	...	...	1100	...	...	...	...	...	...	...	...	...	...	...	...	...	...	...	1357

train type	*EN*	*ICE*	*ICE*	*ICE*	*ICE*	☆	*ICE*	*ICE*	*ICE*	⇌	*IC*	*ICE*	*ICE*	*ICE*	*ICE*	⇌	⇌	*IC*	*ICE*	*ICE*	*ICE*	*ICE*	*ICE*	⇌	☆
train number	**50462**	**728**	**692**	**770**	**16**	**9141**	**1020**	**612**	**726**	**9448**	**2047**	**724**	**690**	**578**	**314**	**9358**	**9364**	**2045**	**228**	**1218**	**720**	**576**	**14**	**9370**	**9157**
notes																Ⓑ								Ⓑ	
notes	**A**																								
München Hbf ... d.	0550**o**	0648	0642	...	...	...	...	0728	0747	...	...	0848	0846	...	...	...	...	...	...	1047	1051	...	...	...	...
Augsburg Hbf ... d.	0648	|	0713	...	...	...	...	0801	|	...	...	|	0918	...	...	...	...	...	...	1118	|	...	...	...	...
Ulm Hbf ... d.	0738	|	0758	...	...	...	...	0847	|	...	...	|	1001	...	...	...	...	...	...	1201	|	...	...	...	...
Stuttgart Hbf ... d.	0837	|	0851	0923	...	...	...	0951	|	...	...	|	1051	1123	...	...	...	...	...	1251	|	1323	...	...	...
Mannheim Hbf ... d.	▬	|	0932	1004	...	...	...	1036	|	...	...	|	1132	1204	...	...	...	...	...	1332	|	1404	...	...	...
Wien Hbf ... d.	...	|	|	|	...	...	...	|	|	...	...	|	|	|	...	...	...	...	0651	|	|	|	...	...	...
Nürnberg Hbf ... d.	...	0800	|	|	...	...	...	|	0859	...	...	1000	|	|	...	...	...	...	1130	|	1159	|	...	...	...
Würzburg Hbf ... d.	...	0855	|	|	...	...	...	|	0955	...	...	1055	|	|	...	...	...	...	1224	|	1255	|	...	...	...
Frankfurt (Main) Hbf ... d.	*IC*	1004	1008	|	1026	...	...	|	1109	...	...	1204	1208	|	1226	...	...	...	1336	1408	1404	|	1426	...	...
Frankfurt Flughafen ✈ ... d.	**2049**	...	...	1035	1042	...	...	1107	1121	...	...	...	...	1235	1242	...	...	...	...	...	...	1435	1442	...	...
Mainz Hbf ... d.	0920	...	...	...	|	...	1020	|	|	...	1120	...	...	...	|	...	...	1320	...	...	...	...	|	...	...
Koblenz Hbf ... d.	1013	...	...	...	|	...	1113	|	|	...	1213	...	...	...	|	...	...	1413	...	...	...	...	|	...	...
Bonn Hbf ... d.	1045	...	...	...	|	...	1145	|	|	...	1246	...	...	...	|	...	...	1446	...	...	...	...	|	...	...
Köln Hbf ... a.	1106	...	...	...	1132	...	1205	1205	1215**z**	...	1305	...	...	...	1333	...	...	1505	...	...	...	...	1533	...	...
Köln Hbf ... d.	...	...	...	...	1142	...	...	...	...	1243	▬	...	...	...	1342	...	...	▬	...	...	...	...	1540	...	...
Aachen Hbf 🏛 ... d.	...	...	...	...	1221	...	...	...	...	1324	...	...	...	...	1421	...	...	...	...	...	...	...	1621	...	...
Liège Guillemins ... d.	...	...	...	...	1246	...	...	...	...	1351	☆	...	...	...	1446	...	...	...	...	...	...	...	1646	...	...
Brussels Nord ... a.	...	...	...	...	1326	...	...	...	...	|	**9145**	...	...	...	1526	...	...	☆	...	...	...	...	1726	...	...
Brussels Midi / Zuid ... a.	...	...	...	...	1335	...	...	...	...	1435	Ⓑ	...	...	...	1535	...	...	**9153**	...	...	...	...	1735	...	...
Brussels Midi / Zuid ... d.	...	...	...	...	...	1452	...	...	...	1443	1556	...	...	...	...	1613	1713	1756	...	...	...	...	...	1813	1851
Paris Nord ... a.	...	...	...	...	...	|	...	...	...	1605	|	...	...	...	...	1735	1835	|	...	...	...	...	...	1935	|
London St Pancras ... a.	...	...	...	...	...	1600	...	...	...	...	1657	...	...	...	...	...	...	1857	...	...	...	...	...	...	2000

train type	*ICE*	*ICE*	*ICE*	⇌	*EC*	*ICE*	*ICE*	*ICE*	*ICE*	*ICE*	⇌	☆	☆	*ICE*	*ICE*	*ICE*	⇌	*ICE*	*ICE*	*ICE*	*ICE*	*EC*	*ICE*	⇌	*ICE*
train number	**228**	**518**	**628**	**9472**	**8**	**28**	**596**	**626**	**574**	**12**	**9382**	**9163**	**9167**	**28**	**516**	**624**	**9484**	**26**	**594**	**622**	**572**	**6**	**10**	**9394**	**318**
notes									**1094**	**122**		⑥	Ⓑ				Ⓑ							⑦	⑦**t**
notes																									
München Hbf ... d.	...	1128	1151	...	...	...	1245	1250	...	...	...	...	...	...	1328	1351	...	...	1447	1451	...	...	...	...	...
Augsburg Hbf ... d.	...	1201	|	...	...	...	1318	|	...	...	...	...	...	...	1401	|	...	...	1518	|	...	...	...	...	...
Ulm Hbf ... d.	...	1247	|	...	...	...	1401	|	...	...	...	...	...	...	1447	|	...	...	1601	|	...	...	...	...	...
Stuttgart Hbf ... d.	...	1351	|	...	...	...	1451	|	1523	...	...	...	...	...	1551	|	...	...	1651	|	1723	...	...	...	...
Mannheim Hbf ... d.	...	1436	|	...	...	...	1532	|	1604	...	...	...	...	...	1636	|	...	...	1732	|	1804	...	...	...	...
Wien Hbf ... d.	0651	|	|	...	...	0913	|	|	|	...	...	...	...	...	|	|	...	1113	|	|	|	...	...	...	...
Nürnberg Hbf ... d.	1130	|	1257	...	...	1330	|	1400	|	...	...	...	...	...	|	1500	...	1531	|	1600	|	...	...	...	...
Würzburg Hbf ... d.	1224	|	1355	...	...	1424	|	1455	|	...	...	...	...	...	|	1555	...	1624	|	1655	|	...	...	...	...
Frankfurt (Main) Hbf ... d.	1342	|	1509	...	...	1542	1608	1604	|	1628	...	...	...	...	|	1709	...	1736	1808	1804	|	...	1828	...	2016
Frankfurt Flughafen ✈ ... d.	1358	1507	1522	...	...	1557	...	...	1635	1642	...	...	...	←	1707	1721	...	...	...	...	1835	...	1842	...	2029
Mainz Hbf ... d.	1420	|	|	...	1520	1618	...	...	...	|	...	...	...	1620	|	|	...	...	...	...	...	1720	|	...	|
Koblenz Hbf ... d.	1513	|	|	...	1613	→	...	...	...	|	...	...	...	1713	|	|	...	...	...	...	...	1813	|	...	|
Bonn Hbf ... d.	1545	|	|	...	1645	...	...	...	...	|	...	...	...	1745	|	|	...	...	...	...	...	1845	|	...	|
Köln Hbf ... a.	1605	1605	1614**z**	...	1705	...	...	...	...	1733	...	...	...	1805	1804	1814**z**	...	...	...	...	...	1905	1931	...	2140
Köln Hbf ... d.	...	...	...	1645	...	...	...	...	...	1741	...	...	...	...	...	...	1844	...	...	...	...	...	1940	...	2142
Aachen Hbf 🏛 ... d.	...	...	...	1724	...	...	...	...	...	1821	...	...	...	...	...	...	1924	...	...	...	...	...	2021	...	2221
Liège Guillemins ... d.	...	...	...	1751	...	...	...	...	...	1846	...	...	...	...	...	...	1951	...	...	...	...	...	2046	...	2246
Brussels Nord ... a.	...	...	...	|	...	...	...	...	...	1926	...	...	...	...	...	...	|	...	...	...	...	...	2126	...	2326
Brussels Midi / Zuid ... a.	...	...	...	1835	...	...	...	...	...	1935	...	...	...	...	...	...	2035	...	...	...	...	...	2135	...	2335
Brussels Midi / Zuid ... d.	...	...	...	1842	...	...	...	...	...	...	2016	2020	2055	...	...	...	2043	...	...	...	...	...	...	2216	...
Paris Nord ... d.	...	...	...	2005	...	...	...	...	...	...	2138	|	|	...	...	...	2205	...	...	...	...	...	...	2338	...
London St Pancras ... a.	...	...	...	...	...	...	...	...	...	...	...	2127	2157	...	...	...	...	...	...	...	...	...	...	...	...

A – KÁLMÁN IMRE – 🛏 1, 2 cl., ▬ 2 cl. (4, 6 berth), (2.) Budapest - München - Stuttgart. Also conveys cars from Venezia (Table **70**), Zagreb and Rijeka (Table **62**).

B – *ÖBB nightjet* 🛏 1, 2 cl., ▬ 2 cl. (4, 6 berth), (2.) Innsbruck - München - Köln - Amsterdam ♣ (Table **53**).

C – ②④⑦: *ÖBB nightjet* 🛏 1, 2 cl., ▬ 2 cl. (4, 6 berth), (2.) Wien - Brussels ♣ (Table **53**).

D – Not Apr. 10, May 1.

f – Frankfurt (Main) **Süd**.

o – München **Ost**.

p – Not Apr. 10, May 1, 29.

t – Also Apr. 10, May 1, 29; not Apr. 9, 30, May 28.

z – Köln **Messe / Deutz** (Table **910**). Connections to Köln Hbf depart every 2 - 5 minutes, journey time 2 – 3 minutes.

⇌ – *Thalys* high-speed train. Ⓡ 🍸. Special fares payable. Three classes of service: (Premium, Comfort and Standard). Valid Dec. 11 - Mar. 18.

☆ – Eurostar train. Ⓡ, ✕ in Business Premier and Standard Premier, 🍸 in Standard. Special fares payable. See shaded panel in Table **10** on page 47 for information about recommended arrival times at departure station. Valid Feb. 5 - May 20.

♣ – Special fares apply.

22 AMSTERDAM - BERLIN

train type	IC	IC	IC	IC		IC		IC	IC		IC		IC	IC	IC	ICE		RE	IC	IC		EN	
train number	245	245	245	141		143		145	147		149		241	241	241	655			243	243		xxxx	
notes	⑦	①–⑥	①–⑥										⑥	⑧	⑦		⑥	⑥	⑦	①–⑤	①–⑤	①③⑤	
		C	K											H						E		Z	
Amsterdam Centraal d.	...	...	0502	0700	...	0910	...	1100	1300	...	1500	...	1710	1710	1710	...	...	...	1900	1900	...	2234	...
Hilversum d.	...	...	0525	0722	...	0932	...	1122	1322	...	1522	...	1732	1732	1732	...	...	...	1922	1922	...	|	...
Amersfoort d.	...	...	0540	0736	...	0945	...	1136	1336	...	1536	...	1745	1745	1745	...	...	...	1936	1936	...	2313	...
Apeldoorn d.	...	...	0605	0809	...	1010	...	1201	1401	...	1601	...	1810	1810	1810	...	...	...	2001	2001	...	|	...
Deventer d.	...	...	0617	0821	...	1022	...	1218	1418	...	1618	...	1822	1822	1822	...	...	...	2018	2018	...	2349	...
Almelo d.	...	...	0642	0846	...	1047	...	1246	1446	...	1646	...	1847	1847	1847	...	...	...	2046	2046	...	|	...
Hengelo ▲ d.	...	...	0655	0858	...	1059	...	1258	1458	...	1658	...	1859	1859	1859	...	1934	...	2058	2058	2134	|	...
Bad Bentheim 🛃 ▲ a.	...	0721	0711	0916	...	1116	...	1316	1516	...	1716	...	1916	1916	1916	...	1952	...	2116	2116	2152	0109	...
Rheine ▲ a.	...	0733	0733	0940	...	1140	...	1340	1540	...	1740	...	...	1940	1940	...	2012	2038	2140	...	2212	|	...
Osnabrück Hbf ▲ a.	0803	0803	0803	1006	...	1206	...	1406	1606	...	1806	...	...	2006	2006	...	2045	2113	2206	...	2245	|	...
Minden a.	0847	0847	0847	1046	...	1246	...	1446	1646	...	1846	...	...	2046	2046	...	...	2207	2246	...	...	|	...
Hannover Hbf a.	0918	0918	0918	1118	...	1318	...	1518	1718	...	1918	...	...	2118	2118	2131	...	2250	2318	...	...	|	...
Wolfsburg a.	0953	0953	0953	1153	...	1353	...	1553	1753	...	1953	...	...	...	2153	|	...	...	...	...	...	|	...
Stendal a.	1025	1025	1025	1225	...	1425	...	1625	1825	...	2025	...	...	...	2225	|	...	...	...	...	...	|	...
Berlin Hauptbahnhof a.	1125	1125	1125	1325	...	1525	...	1725	1925	...	2125	...	...	...	2325	2311	...	...	...	...	...	0648	...
Berlin Ostbahnhof a.	1136	1136	1136	1336	...	1536	...	1736	1936	...	2136	...	...	...	2336	2322	...	...	...	...	...	...	...

train type		IC		ICE	IC	RE		IC	IC	IC		IC		IC		IC		IC		IC		EN	
train number		244		646	242			240	240	240		148		146		144		142		140		zzzz	
notes	①	①		①–⑥	①–⑥	⑦	⑦	⑦	①–⑥													②④⑦	
		J		A	A					B												Z	
Berlin Ostbahnhof d.	...	...	...	0413	...	...	...	...	0621	...	...	0821	...	1021	...	1221	...	1421	...	1621	...	...	...
Berlin Hauptbahnhof d.	...	...	...	0425	...	...	...	...	0633	...	...	0833	...	1033	...	1233	...	1433	...	1633	...	2256	...
Stendal d.	...	...	...	0515	...	...	...	...	0732	...	...	0932	...	1132	...	1332	...	1532	...	1732	...	|	...
Wolfsburg d.	...	...	...	0547	...	...	...	...	0801	...	...	1001	...	1201	...	1401	...	1601	...	1801	...	|	...
Hannover Hbf d.	...	...	...	0618	0640	0709	...	...	0840	0840	...	1040	...	1240	...	1440	...	1640	...	1840	...	|	...
Minden d.	...	...	...	...	0712	0752	...	...	0911	0911	...	1111	...	1311	...	1511	...	1711	...	1911	...	|	...
Osnabrück Hbf ▲ d.	0614	...	...	...	0753	0841	0914	...	0953	0953	...	1153	...	1353	...	1553	...	1753	...	1953	...	|	...
Rheine ▲ d.	0648	...	...	...	0820	0921	0948	...	1020	1020	...	1220	...	1420	...	1620	...	1820	...	2020	...	|	...
Bad Bentheim 🛃 ▲ d.	0709	0744	...	...	0844	...	1009	1044	1044	1044	...	1244	...	1444	...	1644	...	1844	...	2044	...	0409	...
Hengelo ▲ a.	0726	0801	...	...	0901	...	1026	1101	1101	1101	...	1301	...	1501	...	1701	...	1901	...	2101	...	|	...
Almelo a.	...	0813	...	...	0913	...	...	1113	1113	1113	...	1313	...	1512	...	1713	...	1913	...	2113	...	|	...
Deventer a.	...	0841	...	...	0941	...	...	1141	1141	1141	...	1341	...	1537	...	1741	...	1941	...	2141	...	0516	...
Apeldoorn a.	...	0858	...	...	0958	...	...	1158	1158	1158	...	1358	...	|	...	1758	...	1958	...	2158	...	|	...
Amersfoort a.	...	0924	...	...	1024	...	...	1224	1224	1224	...	1424	...	1613	...	1824	...	2024	...	2224	...	|	...
Hilversum a.	...	0938	...	...	1038	...	...	1238	1238	1238	...	1438	...	1627	...	1838	...	2038	...	2238	...	|	...
Amsterdam Centraal a.	...	1000	...	...	1100	...	...	1300	1300	1300	...	1500	...	1649	...	1900	...	2100	...	2300	...	0631	...

A – ①–⑥ (not Apr. 10, May 1, 29).
B – Daily Apr. 3 - June 22.
C – ①–⑥ Dec. 12 - Apr. 1.
E – ①–⑤ Dec. 12 - Mar. 31.
H – ⑧ (daily Apr. 3 - June 22).

J – ① Apr. 3 - Aug. 28 (also Apr. 11, May 2, 30; not Apr. 10, May 1, 29).
K – ①–⑥ Apr. 3 - June 22 (not Apr. 10, May 1, 29).
Z – From May 25, European Sleeper: 🛏 1, 2 cl. (1, 2, 3 berth) 🛏 2 cl. (4, 6 berth), Brussels - Amsterdam - Berlin and v.v. (Table **78**).

▲ – For other regional trains Hengelo – Osnabrück and v.v. see Table **811** on page 381.

24 PARIS - MOSKVA

Paris Est d.	...	...	**Moskva** Belorusskaya d.	...	...
Saarbrücken d.	...	...	Vyazma d.	...	...
Frankfurt (Main) Süd d.	...	...	Smolensk Tsentralny § d.	...	...
Ertfurt Hbf d.	...	...	Orsha Tsentralnaya § d.	...	...
Berlin Hbf a.	...	...	**Minsk** d.	...	...
Berlin Hbf d.	...	...	Baranavichy d.	...	...
Berlin Lichtenberg a.	...	...	Brest Tsentralny a.	...	...
Berlin Lichtenberg d.	...	...	Brest Tsentralny 🛃 d.	...	...
Frankfurt (Oder) 🛃 d.	...	...	Terespol 🛃 a.	...	...
Rzepin d.	...	...	Terespol d.	...	...
Poznań Gł. d.	...	...	**Warszawa** Wschodnia a.	...	...
Warszawa Centralna d.	...	...	**Warszawa** Wschodnia d.	...	...
Warszawa Wschodnia a.	...	...	**Warszawa** Centralna d.	...	...
Warszawa Wschodnia d.	...	...	Poznań Gł. d.	...	...
Terespol a.	...	...	Rzepin d.	...	...
Terespol 🛃 d.	...	...	Frankfurt (Oder) 🛃 a.	...	...
Brest Tsentralny 🛃 a.	...	...	**Berlin** Lichtenberg a.	...	...
Brest Tsentralny d.	...	...	**Berlin** Lichtenberg d.	...	...
Baranavichy a.	...	...	**Berlin** Hbf a.	...	...
Minsk a.	...	...	**Berlin** Hbf d.	...	...
Orsha Tsentralnaya § a.	...	...	Ertfurt Hbf d.	...	...
Smolensk Tsentralny § a.	...	...	**Frankfurt** (Main) Süd a.	...	...
Vyazma a.	...	...	Saarbrücken a.	...	...
Moskva Belorusskaya a.	...	...	**Paris** Est a.	...	...

Notes for tables 24 and 25

§ – 🛃: Osinovka (BY) / Krasnoye (RU).

25 NICE - MOSKVA

Nice d.	...	...	**Moskva** Belorusskaya d.	...	...
Monaco-Monte Carlo d.	...	...	Vyazma d.	...	...
Menton d.	...	...	Smolensk Tsentralny § d.	...	...
Ventimiglia 🛃 d.	...	...	Orsha Tsentralnaya § d.	...	...
Bordighera d.	...	...	**Minsk** d.	...	...
San Remo d.	...	...	Baranavichy d.	...	...
Genova Piazza Principe d.	...	...	Brest Tsentralny a.	...	...
Milano Rogoredo d.	...	...	Brest Tsentralny 🛃 d.	...	...
Verona d.	...	...	Terespol 🛃 a.	...	...
Bolzano / Bozen d.	...	...	Terespol d.	...	...
Brennero / Brenner 🛃 d.	...	...	**Warszawa** Wschodnia a.	...	...
Innsbruck Hbf d.	...	...	**Warszawa** Wschodnia d.	...	...
Jenbach d.	...	...	**Warszawa** Centralna d.	...	...
Kirchberg in Tirol d.	...	...	Katowice d.	...	...
Zell am See d.	...	...	Chałupki 🛃 d.	...	...
Bischofshofen d.	...	...	Bohumín 🛃 d.	...	...
Linz Hbf d.	...	...	Břeclav 🛃 d.	...	...
Wien Hbf d.	...	...	**Wien** Hbf d.	...	...
Břeclav 🛃 d.	...	...	Linz Hbf d.	...	...
Bohumín 🛃 d.	...	...	Bischofshofen d.	...	...
Chałupki 🛃 d.	...	...	Zell am See d.	...	...
Katowice d.	...	...	Kirchberg in Tirol d.	...	...
Warszawa Centralna d.	...	...	Jenbach d.	...	...
Warszawa Wschodnia a.	...	...	Innsbruck Hbf d.	...	...
Warszawa Wschodnia d.	...	...	Brennero / Brenner 🛃 d.	...	...
Terespol a.	...	...	Bolzano / Bozen d.	...	...
Terespol 🛃 d.	...	...	Verona d.	...	...
Brest Tsentralny 🛃 a.	...	...	Milano Rogoredo d.	...	...
Brest Tsentralny d.	...	...	Genova Piazza Principe d.	...	...
Baranavichy a.	...	...	San Remo d.	...	...
Minsk a.	...	...	Bordighera d.	...	...
Orsha Tsentralnaya § a.	...	...	Ventimiglia 🛃 d.	...	...
Smolensk Tsentralny § a.	...	...	Menton a.	...	...
Vyazma a.	...	...	Monaco-Monte Carlo a.	...	...
Moskva Belorusskaya a.	...	...	**Nice** a.	...	...

AMSTERDAM - FRANKFURT, WIEN and MÜNCHEN 28

train type		ICE	ICE	ICE			ICE	ICE	ICE			ICE	ICE	ICE	ICE		ICE	ICE	ICE			ICE	ICE	ICE		
train number		121	621	515			105	595	27			123	629	519	229		125	723	611			127	727	613		
notes	Ⓐ						C																			
Amsterdam Centraal d.	...	0638	...	...	...	...	0808	...	...	...	...	1038	...	...	...	...	1238	...	...	...	...	1438	...	...	...	...
Rotterdam Centraal d.	0605	|	...	...	...	0735	|	...	...	...	1005	|	...	...	...	1205	|	...	...	...	1405	|	...	...	...	...
Utrecht Centraal d.	0642	0706	...	...	...	0812	0834	...	...	...	1042	1104	...	...	...	1242	1304	...	...	...	1442	1504	...	...	...	...
Arnhem ◐ ▲ d.	...	0737	...	...	...	...	0907	...	...	...	...	1137	...	...	...	...	1337	...	...	...	...	1537	...	...	...	...
Oberhausen Hbf ◐ ▲ d.	...	0826	...	...	...	...	0958	...	...	...	...	1226	...	...	...	...	1426	...	...	...	...	1626	...	...	...	...
Duisburg Hbf ▲ d.	...	0834	...	...	...	...	|	...	...	...	...	1234	...	...	...	...	1434	...	...	...	...	1634	...	...	...	...
Düsseldorf Hbf ▲ d.	...	0851	...	...	...	...	1019	...	...	...	...	1248	...	...	...	...	1450	...	...	...	...	1650	...	...	...	...
Köln Messe / Deutz d.	...	|	...	...	...	...	|	...	...	...	...	|	...	...	...	...	|	...	...	...	...	|	...	...	...	...
Köln Hbf a.	...	0919	...	...	...	...	1045	...	...	...	...	1315	...	...	...	...	1519	...	...	...	...	1716	...	...	...	...
Köln Hbf d.	...	0928	...	...	...	...	1055	...	...	...	...	1321	...	...	1353	...	1528	...	...	...	...	1728	...	...	...	...
Frankfurt Flughafen ✈ a.	...	1017	...	1051	...	...	1120	...	1201	...	...	1417	...	1451	1559	...	1617	...	1651	...	...	1817	...	1851	...	...
Frankfurt (Main) Hbf a.	...	1031	1053	|	...	...	|	...	1212	...	...	1431	1453	|	1613	...	1631	1653	|	...	...	1832	1853	|	...	...
Würzburg a.	...	...	1201	|	...	...	|	...	1332	...	...	...	1601	|	1732	...	...	1801	|	...	...	...	2001	|	...	...
Nürnberg a.	...	...	1259	|	...	...	|	...	1427	...	...	...	1658	|	1827	...	...	1859	|	...	...	...	2100	|	...	...
Regensburg a.	...	...	|	|	...	...	|	...	1524	...	...	...	|	|	1924	...	...	|	|	...	...	...	|	|	...	...
Praha hl. n. ¶ a.	...	...	|	|	...	...	|	...	|	...	...	...	|	|	|	...	...	|	|	...	...	...	|	|	...	...
Mannheim a.	...	...	|	1123	...	...	1223	1230	|	...	...	...	|	1523	|	...	...	|	1723	...	...	...	|	1923	...	...
Stuttgart a.	...	...	|	1208	...	...	...	1308	|	...	...	...	|	1608	|	...	...	|	1808	...	...	...	|	2008	...	...
Ulm a.	...	...	|	1310	...	...	...	1358	|	...	...	...	|	1710	|	...	...	|	1910	...	...	...	|	2110	...	...
Augsburg a.	...	...	|	1353	...	...	...	1441	|	...	...	...	|	1753	|	...	...	|	1953	...	...	...	|	2153	...	...
München Hbf a.	...	...	1406	1426	...	...	...	1513	|	...	...	...	1807	1826	|	...	...	2007	2026	...	...	...	2206	2226	...	...
Passau 🚌 a.	...	...	...	...	...	...	...	...	1625	...	...	...	...	...	2026	...	...	...	...	...	...	...	...	...	...	...
Linz Hbf a.	...	...	...	...	...	...	...	...	1726	...	...	...	...	...	2134	...	...	...	...	...	...	...	...	...	...	...
Wien Hbf a.	...	...	...	...	...	...	...	...	1847	...	...	...	...	...	2305	...	...	...	...	...	...	...	...	...	...	...

train type		ICE	ICE	ICE		ICE	ICE	NJ	NJ
train number		129	615	821		221	617	40421	421
notes								A	B
Amsterdam Centraal d.	...	1638	...	...	...	1838	...	1930	1930
Rotterdam Centraal d.	1605	|	...	...	1805	|	...	|	|
Utrecht Centraal d.	1642	1704	...	...	1842	1904	...	2002	2002
Arnhem ◐ ▲ d.	...	1737	...	...	...	1937	...	2037	2037
Oberhausen Hbf ◐ ▲ d.	...	1826	...	...	...	2026	...	|	|
Duisburg Hbf ▲ d.	...	1834	...	...	...	2034	...	|	|
Düsseldorf Hbf ▲ d.	...	1849	...	...	...	2048	...	2144	2144
Köln Messe / Deutz d.	...	|	...	...	...	|	...	|	|
Köln Hbf a.	...	1915	...	...	...	2115	...	2214	2214
Köln Hbf d.	...	1921	...	...	...	2128	...	2216	2216
Bonn Hbf d.	...	|	...	...	...	|	...	2311	2311
Koblenz d.	...	|	...	...	...	|	...	2346	2346
Mainz d.	...	|	...	...	...	|	...	0041	0041
Frankfurt Flughafen ✈ a.	...	2017	2051	...	...	2217	2255	0103**d**	0103**d**
Frankfurt (Main) Hbf a.	...	2031	|	2053	...	2231	|	|	|
Frankfurt (Main) Süd a.	...	...	|	|	...	...	|	0117**d**	0117**d**
Würzburg a.	...	...	|	2201	...	...	|	0239	0239
Nürnberg a.	...	...	|	2259	...	...	|	0336	0336
Regensburg a.	...	...	|	|	...	...	|	0511	|
Praha hl. n. ¶ a.	...	...	|	|	...	...	|	|	|
Mannheim a.	...	...	2124	|	...	...	2327	|	|
Stuttgart a.	...	...	2208	|	...	...	0008	|	|
Ulm a.	...	...	2310	|	...	...	...	|	|
Augsburg a.	...	...	2353	|	...	...	...	|	0624
München Hbf a.	...	...	0028	0019	...	...	...	|	0711
Innsbruck Hbf a.	...	...	...	...	...	...	...	|	0914
Passau 🚌 a.	...	...	...	...	...	...	...	0616	...
Linz Hbf a.	...	...	...	...	...	...	...	0747	...
Wien Hbf a.	...	...	...	...	...	...	...	0919	...

train type	ICE	ICE		NJ	NJ	ICE	ICE		ICE	ICE	ICE	
train number	222	222		420	40490	616	220		614	820	128	
notes	Ⓐ	Ⓒ		B	A					①–⑥		
Wien Hbf d.	...	...	...	...	2013	...	...	...	...	...	...	...
Linz Hbf d.	...	...	...	...	2136	...	...	...	...	...	...	...
Passau 🚌 d.	...	...	...	...	2253	...	...	...	...	...	...	...
Innsbruck Hbf d.	...	...	...	2044	|	...	...	...	...	...	...	...
München Hbf d.	...	...	...	2250	|	0332	...	...	0533	0553	...	...
Augsburg d.	...	...	...	2324	|	0404	...	...	0604	|	...	...
Ulm d.	...	...	...	|	|	0447	...	...	0647	|	...	...
Stuttgart d.	...	...	...	|	|	0551	...	...	0751	|	...	...
Mannheim d.	...	...	...	|	|	0636	...	...	0836	|	...	...
Praha hl. n. ¶ d.	...	...	...	|	|	|	...	...	|	|	...	...
Regensburg d.	...	...	...	|	2356	|	...	...	|	|	...	...
Nürnberg d.	...	...	...	0141	0141	|	...	...	|	0702	...	...
Würzburg d.	...	...	...	|	|	|	...	...	|	0755	...	...
Frankfurt (Main) Süd d.	...	...	...	0345**a**	0345**a**	|	...	...	|	|	...	...
Frankfurt (Main) Hbf d.	0526	...	...	|	|	|	0728	...	|	0904	0926	...
Frankfurt Flughafen ✈ d.	0539	...	...	0356**a**	0356**a**	0706	0742	...	0906	...	0942	...
Mainz a.	|	...	...	0416	0416	...	|	...	...	...	|	...
Koblenz a.	|	...	...	0511	0511	...	|	...	...	...	|	...
Bonn Hbf a.	|	...	...	0559	0559	...	|	...	...	...	|	...
Köln Hbf a.	0632	...	...	0651	0651	...	0833	...	...	...	1033	...
Köln Hbf d.	0640	0640	...	0658	0658	...	0841	...	...	...	1041	...
Köln Messe / Deutz a.	|	|	...	|	|	...	|	...	...	...	|	...
Düsseldorf Hbf ▲ a.	0705	0705	...	0725	0725	...	0905	...	...	...	1105	...
Duisburg Hbf ▲ a.	0724	0724	...	0740	0740	...	0923	...	...	...	1122	...
Oberhausen Hbf ◐ ▲ a.	0732	0732	...	|	|	...	0932	...	...	...	1132	...
Arnhem ◐ ▲ a.	0827	0827	...	0844	0844	...	1027	...	...	...	1227	...
Utrecht Centraal a.	0859	0859	0918	0952	0925	...	1059	1118	...	...	1259	1318
Rotterdam Centraal a.	|	|	0955	|	|	...	|	1155	...	...	|	1355
Amsterdam Centraal a.	0929	0929	...	0958	0958	...	1129	...	...	...	1329	...

train type	ICE	ICE	ICE			ICE	ICE	ICE			ICE	ICE	ICE	ICE			ICE	ICE	ICE			ICE	ICE	ICE		
train number	612	726	126			610	722	124			28	596	626	122 12			26	594	104			514	620	120		
notes																			C					Ⓑ		
Wien Hbf d.	...	...	...	...	...	...	...	...	...	...	0913	...	...	...	...	...	1113	...	...	...	...	...	...	...	...	...
Linz Hbf d.	...	...	...	...	...	...	...	...	...	...	1034	...	...	...	...	...	1234	...	...	...	...	...	...	...	...	...
Passau 🚌 d.	...	...	...	...	...	...	...	...	...	...	1134	...	...	...	...	...	1337	...	...	...	...	...	...	...	...	...
München Hbf d.	0728	0747	...	...	...	0928	0951	...	...	...	|	1245	1250	...	...	...	|	1447	...	...	...	1528	1551	...	...	...
Augsburg d.	0801	|	...	...	...	1001	|	...	...	...	|	1318	|	...	...	...	|	1518	...	...	...	1601	|	...	...	...
Ulm d.	0847	|	...	...	...	1047	|	...	...	...	|	1401	|	...	...	...	|	1601	...	...	...	1647	|	...	...	...
Stuttgart d.	0951	|	...	...	...	1151	|	...	...	...	|	1451	|	...	...	...	|	1651	...	...	...	1751	|	...	...	...
Mannheim d.	1036	|	...	...	...	1236	|	...	...	...	|	1532	|	...	...	...	|	1729	1736	...	...	1836	|	...	...	...
Praha hl. n. ¶ d.	|	|	...	...	...	|	|	...	...	...	|	|	|	...	...	...	|	...	|	...	...	|	|	...	...	...
Regensburg d.	|	|	...	...	...	|	|	...	...	...	1235	|	|	...	...	...	1435	...	|	...	...	|	|	...	...	...
Nürnberg d.	|	0859	...	...	...	|	1100	...	...	...	1330	|	1400	...	...	...	1531	...	|	...	...	|	1657	...	...	...
Würzburg d.	|	0955	...	...	...	|	1155	...	...	...	1424	|	1455	...	...	...	1624	...	|	...	...	|	1755	...	...	...
Frankfurt (Main) Hbf d.	|	1104	1126	...	...	|	1304	1326	...	...	1536	1608	1604	1628	...	...	1742	...	|	...	...	|	1904	1928	...	...
Frankfurt Flughafen ✈ d.	1106	...	1142	...	...	1306	...	1342	...	...	...	...	...	1642	...	...	1755	...	1809	...	...	1906	...	1942	...	...
Köln Hbf a.	...	...	1233	...	...	...	...	1432	...	...	...	...	...	1733	...	...	...	...	1904	...	...	...	...	2033	...	...
Köln Hbf d.	...	...	1241	...	...	...	...	1441	...	...	...	...	...	1746	...	...	...	...	1914	...	...	...	...	2041	...	...
Köln Messe / Deutz a.	...	...	|	...	...	...	...	|	...	...	...	...	...	|	...	...	...	...	|	...	...	...	...	|	...	...
Düsseldorf Hbf ▲ a.	...	...	1305	...	...	...	...	1509	...	...	...	...	...	1809	...	...	...	...	1935	...	...	...	...	2105	...	...
Duisburg Hbf ▲ a.	...	...	1323	...	...	...	...	1525	...	...	...	...	...	1823	...	...	...	...	1949	...	...	...	...	2123	...	...
Oberhausen Hbf ◐ ▲ a.	...	...	1332	...	...	...	...	1533	...	...	...	...	...	1832	...	...	...	...	1957	...	...	...	...	2132	...	...
Arnhem ◐ ▲ a.	...	...	1427	...	...	...	...	1627	...	...	...	...	...	1927	...	...	...	...	2057	...	...	...	...	2227	...	...
Utrecht Centraal a.	...	...	1459	1518	...	...	...	1659	1718	...	...	...	...	1959	2018	...	...	...	2129	2148	...	...	...	2258	2318	...
Rotterdam Centraal a.	...	...	|	1555	...	...	...	|	1755	...	...	...	...	|	2055	...	...	...	|	2225	...	...	...	|	2355	...
Amsterdam Centraal a.	...	...	1529	...	...	...	...	1729	...	...	...	...	...	2028	...	...	...	...	2159	...	...	...	...	2329	...	...

A – *ÖBB nightjet* 🛏 1, 2 cl., 🛏 2 cl. (4, 6 berth), (2) Amsterdam - Wien and v.v. ♣ (Table **53**).

B – *ÖBB nightjet* 🛏 1, 2 cl., 🛏 2 cl. (4, 6 berth), (2) Amsterdam - Innsbruck and v.v. ♣ (Table **53**).

C – (12) 🍸 Amsterdam - Mannheim - Basel and v.v. (Table **73**).

a – Arrival time.

d – Departure time.

◐ – 🚌 between Arnhem and Oberhausen is Emmerich.

⊖ – Via Köln - Frankfurt high speed line.

♣ – Special fares apply.

¶ – For connections to / from Praha via Schwandorf see Table **76**.

▲ – For other regional trains Düsseldorf – Arnhem and v.v. See Table **802** on page 374 (service *RE19*).

🚌 – **DB / ČD** *ExpressBus*. 🅁 🍸. Rail tickets valid. 2nd class only. See Table **76**.

☛ – Köln **Messe / Deutz** (Table **910**). Connections from Köln Hbf depart every 2 – 5 mins., journey time 2 – 3 mins.

30 PARIS - FRANKFURT - BERLIN, LEIPZIG, DRESDEN and PRAHA

Alternative services Paris - Frankfurt are available via Brussels (Table **21**). Alternative services Paris - Berlin are available via Brussels (Table **20**).

train type	TGV	ICE	ICE	EC	ICE	TGV	ICE	ICE	EC	ICE	ICE	ICE	ICE	ICE	ICE	ICE	ICE	ICE	ICE	ICE	ICE	ICE	TGV	NJ
train number	**9561**	**372**	**1559**	**177**	**623**	**9551**	**370**	**1651**	**179**	**627**	**9553**	**276**	**1655**	**725**	**9563**	**274**	**1657**	**729**	**9555**	**1659**	**1021**	**9557**	**9559**	**409**
notes	🅁★					🅁★					🅁★				🅁★				🅁★			🅁★	🅁★	
notes	⚒																		Ⓑ	Ⓑ		Ⓑ	⑥	
		Z					Z												f	b		f	t	A
Paris Est ... d.	0720	...	...	...	...	0907	...	...	...	...	1310	...	...	...	1521	...	...	...	1710	...	...	1907	1907	...
Strasbourg ... d.	0912	...	...	...	...	|	...	...	...	...	|	...	...	...	1713	...	...	...	|	...	...	|	|	...
Forbach 🏛 ... d.	◧	...	...	...	...	1047	...	...	...	...	|	...	...	...	◧	...	...	...	|	...	...	2049	2049	...
Saarbrücken ... d.	|	...	...	...	...	1058	...	...	...	...	1459	...	...	...	|	...	...	...	1859	...	...	2059	2059	...
Kaiserlautern ... d.	|	...	...	...	...	1136	...	...	...	...	1537	...	...	...	|	...	...	...	1937	...	...	2137	2136	...
Karlsruhe Hbf ... d.	0955	...	...	...	...	|	...	...	...	...	|	...	...	...	1755	...	...	...	|	...	...	|	|	...
Mannheim ... d.	1021	...	...	...	...	1219	...	...	...	...	1619	...	...	...	1821	...	...	...	2019	...	...	2219	2219	2342
Frankfurt (Main) Hbf ... d.	1059	1114	1119	...	1153	1259	1314	1319	...	1353	1659	1714	1719	1753	1859	1914	1919	1953	2059	2119	2222	2259	2259	0052
Würzburg ... a.	...	|	|	...	1301	...	|	|	...	1501	...	|	|	1901	...	|	|	2101	...	|	2344	...	...	|
Nürnberg ... a.	...	|	|	...	1359	...	|	|	...	1559	...	|	|	1959	...	|	|	2159	...	|	0042	...	...	|
Fulda ... a.	...	1210	1213	...	...	...	1410	1414	...	...	...	1810	1813	...	...	2010	2013	...	...	2213	...	...	...	0148
Erfurt ... a.	...	|	1338	...	...	...	|	1538	...	...	...	|	1938	...	...	|	2138	...	...	2338	...	...	...	0314
Leipzig Hbf ... a.	...	|	1424	...	...	...	|	1624	...	...	...	|	2024	...	...	|	2224	...	...	0028j	...	...	...	0448
Dresden Hbf ... a.	...	|	1538	1710	...	...	|	1738	1910	...	...	|	2138	...	...	|	2338	...	...	...	...	...	...	|
Děčín (🏛 = Schöna) ... a.	...	|	...	1757	...	...	|	...	1957	...	...	|	...	...	...	|	...	...	...	...	...	...	...	|
Praha Holešovice ... a.	...	|	...	1925	...	...	|	...	2125	...	...	|	...	...	...	|	...	...	...	...	...	...	...	|
Praha hl. n. ... a.	...	|	...	1935	...	...	|	...	2135	...	...	|	...	...	...	|	...	...	...	...	...	...	...	|
Kassel Wilhelmshöhe ... a.	...	1243	...	...	...	...	1443	...	...	...	...	1843	...	...	...	2043	...	...	...	...	...	...	...	|
Göttingen ... a.	...	1303	...	...	...	...	1503	...	...	...	...	1903	...	...	...	2103	...	...	...	...	...	...	...	|
Braunschweig ... a.	...	1359	...	...	...	...	1559	...	...	...	...	1959	...	...	...	2159	...	...	...	...	...	...	...	|
Wolfsburg ... a.	...	1418	...	...	...	...	1618	...	...	...	...	2018	...	...	...	2218	...	...	...	...	...	...	...	|
Berlin Hauptbahnhof ... a.	...	1529	...	...	...	...	1729	...	...	...	...	2129	...	...	...	2329	...	...	...	...	...	...	...	0720

train type	NJ	ICE	ICE	ICE	ICE	ICE	ICE	ICE	ICE	ICE	ICE	ICE	ICE	ICE	ICE	ICE	TGV	ICE	ICE	EC	ICE	TGV	EC	ICE	ICE	ICE	ICE
train number	**408**	**9558**	**9568**	**9586**	**822**	**1656**	**275**	**9556**	**9566**	**728**	**1654**	**277**	**9554**	**724**	**1652**	**279**	**9552**	**626**	**373**	**176**	**1558**	**9560**	**174**	**622**	**1556**	**375**	**9550**
notes		🅁★	🅁★	🅁★				🅁★	🅁★				🅁★				🅁★					🅁★					🅁★
notes		①–⑤	Ⓑ	⑥	①–⑥	①–⑥	①–⑤	①–⑤	⑥				⑥⑦														Ⓑ
	A	h	f		p	p	Z	h	t			Z	k						Z							Z	f
Berlin Hauptbahnhof ... d.	2051	...	...	...	...	...	0429	...	...	...	...	0629	...	...	...	0829	...	...	1229	...	...	...	...	...	...	1429	...
Wolfsburg ... d.	|	...	...	...	...	...	0538	...	...	...	...	0738	...	...	...	0938	...	...	1338	...	...	...	...	...	...	1538	...
Braunschweig ... d.	|	...	...	...	...	...	0557	...	...	...	...	0757	...	...	...	0957	...	...	1357	...	...	...	...	...	...	1557	...
Göttingen ... d.	|	...	...	...	...	...	0652	...	...	...	...	0852	...	...	...	1052	...	...	1452	...	...	...	...	...	...	1652	...
Kassel Wilhelmshöhe ... d.	|	...	...	...	...	...	0714	...	...	...	...	0914	...	...	...	1114	...	...	1514	...	...	...	...	...	...	1714	...
Praha hl. n. ... d.	|	...	...	...	...	...	|	...	...	...	...	|	...	...	...	|	...	...	|	0825	...	...	1025	...	...	|	...
Praha Holešovice ... d.	|	...	...	...	...	...	|	...	...	...	...	|	...	...	...	|	...	...	|	0834	...	...	1034	...	...	|	...
Děčín (🏛 = Schöna) ... d.	|	...	...	...	...	...	|	...	...	...	...	|	...	...	...	|	...	...	|	1001	...	...	1201	...	...	|	...
Dresden Hbf ... d.	|	...	...	...	...	...	|	...	...	...	0610	|	...	...	0810	|	...	...	|	1052	1210	...	1252	...	1410	|	...
Leipzig Hbf ... d.	2346	...	...	...	...	0533	|	...	...	...	0733	|	...	...	0933	|	...	...	|	...	1333	...	...	...	1533	|	...
Erfurt ... d.	0124	...	...	...	...	0618	|	...	...	...	0818	|	...	...	1018	|	...	...	|	...	1418	...	...	...	1618	|	...
Fulda ... d.	0247	...	...	...	...	0743	0747	...	...	...	0943	0947	...	...	1143	1147	...	...	1547	...	1543	...	...	...	1743	1747	...
Nürnberg ... d.	|	...	...	...	0600	|	|	...	...	0800	|	|	...	1000	|	|	...	1400	|	...	|	...	...	1600	|	|	...
Würzburg ... d.	|	...	...	...	0655	|	|	...	...	0855	|	|	...	1055	|	|	...	1455	|	...	|	...	...	1655	|	|	...
Frankfurt (Main) Hbf ... d.	0400	0556	0656	0656	0804	0836	0844	0856	0856	1004	1036	1044	1056	1204	1236	1244	1256	1604	1644	...	1636	1656	...	1804	1836	1844	1856
Mannheim ... d.	0439	0640	0738	0740	...	...	...	0940	0939	...	...	...	1140	...	...	...	1342	...	...	...	...	1738	...	...	...	...	1940
Karlsruhe Hbf ... d.	...	|	0806	|	...	...	...	|	1006	...	...	...	|	...	...	...	|	...	...	...	...	1805	...	...	...	...	|
Kaiserlautern ... d.	...	0722	|	0822	...	...	...	1022	|	...	...	...	1224	...	...	...	1424	...	...	...	...	|	...	...	...	...	2022
Saarbrücken ... d.	...	0801	|	0901	...	...	...	1101	|	...	...	...	1302	...	...	...	1503	...	...	...	...	|	...	...	...	...	2101
Forbach 🏛 ... a.	...	0810	◧	0912	...	...	...	|	◧	...	...	...	1311	...	...	...	|	...	...	...	...	◧	...	...	...	...	2110
Strasbourg ... a.	...	|	0847	|	...	...	...	|	1047	...	...	...	|	...	...	...	|	...	...	...	...	1848	...	...	...	...	|
Paris Est ... a.	...	0951	1038	1054	...	...	...	1252	1238	...	...	...	1452	...	...	...	1654	...	...	...	...	2041	...	...	...	...	2252

A – *ÖBB nightjet* – 🛏 1, 2 cl., 🛏 2 cl. (4, 6 berth), (2.) Zürich - Mannheim - Berlin and v.v. Special fares apply.

Z – Subject to alteration from Apr. 1.

b – Not Apr. 7, 9, 30, May 28.

f – Not Apr. 9, 30, May 28.

h – Not Apr. 10, May 1, 29.

j – ①⑥ (also Apr. 6, 10, May 1, 17, 29; not Apr. 30, May 19, 28).

k – Also Apr. 10, May 1, 29.

p – Not Apr. 10, May 1, 29.

t – Also Apr. 9, 30, May 28.

◧ – 🏛 is at Kehl.

★ – *Alleo* ICE / TGV service. A DB / SNCF joint enterprise.

31 LONDON - GENÈVE

For the full service Paris - Genève, see Table **341**. See shaded panel in Table **10** on page 47 for information about recommended arrival times at departure station. Additional Eurostar services are available, see Table **10**.

train type	☆	TGV	☆	TGV	☆	TGV	☆	TGV	☆	TGV	☆	TGV
train number	**9080**	**9765**	**9008**	**9773**	**9014**	**9775**	**9018**	**9777**	**9024**	**9791**	**9036**	**9789**
notes	①–⑤					L		L		**9781**		Ⓑ
notes	B	♥		♥		♥		♥		♥		♥
London St Pancras **10** ... d.	0601	...	0801	...	0931	...	1014	...	1231	...	1531	...
Lille Europe ... d.	|	...	|	...	|	...	|	...	|	...	|	...
Paris Nord **10** ... a.	0920	...	1120	...	1247	...	1357	...	1547	...	1850	...
Paris Gare de Lyon ... d.	...	1015	...	1214	...	1410	...	1614	...	1814	...	2016
Lyon Part Dieu ... a.	...	|	...	|	...	|	...	|	...	|	...	|
Bellegarde ... a.	...	1300	...	1500	...	1700	...	1900	...	2101	...	2300
Genève ... a.	...	1330	...	1530	...	1730	...	1930	...	2130	...	2330

train type	TGV	☆	☆	TGV	☆	☆	TGV	☆	TGV	☆	☆		TGV	☆	☆	TGV	☆
train number	**9760**	**9027**	**9031**	**9764**	**9035**	**9039**	**9768**	**9043**	**9770**	**9051**	**9055**	**96566**	**5192**	**9163**	**9167**	**9774**	**9059**
notes	①–⑥	⑦			⑥		L			Ⓑ				⑥	Ⓑ	L	
notes	♥	C		♥			♥		♥							♥	
Genève ... d.	0629	...	...	0824	...	...	1029	...	1229	...	...	1330	...	...	...	1429	...
Bellegarde ... d.	0702	...	...	0900	...	...	1102	...	1302	...	...	1400	...	...	...	1502	...
Lyon Part Dieu ... d.	|	...	...	|	...	...	|	...	|	...	...	1525	1600	...	...	|	...
Paris Gare de Lyon ... a.	0942	...	...	1142	...	...	1350	...	1542	...	...	...	|	...	...	1749	...
Paris Nord **10** ... d.	...	1213	1313	...	1413	1513	...	1613	...	1813	1903	...	|	...	...	...	2013
Lille Europe ... d.	...	|	|	...	|	|	...	|	...	|	|	...	1944f	2100	2135	...	|
London St Pancras **10** ... a.	...	1330	1430	...	1530	1630	...	1730	...	1930	2039	...	...	2133	2157	...	2130

B – Not Apr. 10, May 1.

C – Also Apr. 10, May 1, 8.

L – To / from Lausanne (Table **42**).

f – Lille **Flandres** (◇).

◇ – 500 metres from Lille Europe (see Lille City Plan on page 30).

♥ – *TGV Lyria* service. 🅁 🍸. Special fares payable, three classes of service: Business 1ère, Standard 1ère and Standard. At-seat meal service in Business 1ère. Valid Dec. 11 - May 14.

☆ – Eurostar train. 🅁, ✕ in Business Premier and Standard Premier, 🍸 in Standard. Special fares payable. See shaded panel in Table **10** on page 47 for information about recommended arrival times at departure station. Connections across Paris between *TGV* and Eurostar services are not guaranteed. Valid Feb. 5 - May 20.

LONDON - PARIS - MÜNCHEN - WIEN - BUDAPEST - BUCURESTI 32

Alternative London - München services are available via Brussels (Table **21**)

	RJX 61	IC 79 ❖	ICE 511	RJX 65	IC 473 ❖	EC 113	RJX 563	ICE 9571 ★	ICE 513	RJX 67	EN 347 ❖	TGV 9551 ★	ICE 595	RJX 69	☆ 9080	ICE 9573 ★	☆ 9002	TGV 9593 ★	ICE 517	RJX 261	☆ 9014	TGV 9575 ★	ICE 1011	NJ 295 Ⓡ	RJX 367
															①–⑤	Ⓑ	⑥	⑥							
		J			B						M				k	f		j							
London St Pancras **10** d.	...	...	...	...	...	...	...	...	...	...	...	...	...	...	0601	...	0631	...	...	...	0931	...	...	...	...
Paris Nord **10** a.	...	...	...	...	...	...	...	...	...	...	...	...	...	...	0920	...	0947	...	...	...	1247	...	...	...	...
Paris Est d.	...	...	...	...	...	...	...	0655	...	...	...	0907	...	...	...	1055	...	1055	...	...	...	1354	...	...	...
Strasbourg d.	...	...	...	...	...	...	...	0846	...	...	...	|	...	...	...	1246	...	1246	...	...	...	1546	...	...	...
Kehl 🏛 d.	...	...	...	...	...	...	...	|	...	...	...	◧	...	...	...	|	...	|	...	...	...	|	...	...	...
Karlsruhe Hbf d.	...	...	...	...	...	...	...	0928	...	...	...	|	...	...	...	1328	...	1328	...	...	...	1628	...	...	...
Mannheim Hbf d.	...	...	0731	...	...	...	...	|	...	...	...	1217	1230	...	...	|	...	|	...	...	...	|	...	...	...
Stuttgart Hbf d.	...	...	0814	...	...	0958	...	1005	1014	...	...	...	1315	...	...	1405	...	1405	1414	...	...	1704	1728	...	...
Ulm Hbf d.	...	...	0912	...	...	1056	...	▬	1112	...	...	...	1400	...	...	...	...	...	1512	...	...	...	1812	...	...
Augsburg Hbf d.	...	...	0955	...	...	1141	...	...	1155	...	...	...	1443	...	...	...	...	...	1555	...	...	...	1855	...	...
München Pasing a.	...	...	1017	...	...	|	...	...	1217	...	...	...	1504	...	...	...	...	...	1617	...	...	...	1918	...	...
München Hbf a.	...	...	1026	...	...	1210	...	...	1226	...	...	...	1513	...	...	...	...	...	1626	...	...	...	1927	...	...
München Hbf d.	0723	...	...	1128	...	1217	...	...	...	1329	...	...	...	1529	...	...	...	...	...	1730	...	...	...	2009	...
Salzburg Hbf 🏛 a.	0858	...	...	1258	...	1359	1408	EC	...	1458	...	...	...	1658	...	...	...	...	...	1858	...	...	...	2152	2208
Linz Hbf a.	1015	...	...	1415	...	...	1514	**149**	...	1615	...	...	...	1815	...	...	...	...	...	2015	...	...	...	...	2317
St Pölten Hbf a.	1101	...	...	1501	...	...	1600	**A**	...	1701	...	...	...	1901	...	...	...	...	...	2101	...	...	...	...	0003
Wien Hbf a.	1132	...	...	1532	...	...	1630	1642	...	1732	1942	...	...	1932	...	...	...	...	...	2132	...	...	...	...	0033
Hegyeshalom 🏛 a.	1225	...	...	1625	...	...	...	1725	...	1825	2025	...	...	...	...	...	...	...	...	2225	...	...	...	...	...
Györ a.	1253	...	...	1653	...	...	...	1753	...	1853	2053	...	...	...	...	...	...	...	...	2253	...	...	...	...	...
Budapest Keleti a.	1419	1510	...	1819	1910	...	...	1919	...	2019	2220	...	...	...	...	...	...	...	...	0019	...	...	...	...	...
Bucuresti Nord a.	...	0830	...	...	1233	...	...	...	...	...	1600	...	...	...	...	...	...	...	...	...	...	...	...	...	...

	☆ 9018	TGV 9577 ★	☆ 9024	TGV 9591	TGV 9579 ★	TGV 9579 ★	ICE 693	☆ 9032	ICE 9557 ★	TGV 9559 ★	☆ 9036	NJ 469
		Ⓑ			⑥	Ⓑ	Ⓑ		Ⓑ	⑥		②⑤⑦
		f			j				f	j		E
London St Pancras **10** d.	1024	...	1231	...	...	...	...	1431	...	...	1531	...
Paris Nord **10** a.	1357	...	1547	...	...	...	...	1747	...	...	1850	...
Paris Est d.	...	1555	▬	1725	1755	1755	...	...	1907	1907	▬	1958
Strasbourg d.	...	1746	...	1918	1946	1946	...	...	|	|	...	0036
Kehl 🏛 d.	...	|	...	|	|	|	...	...	◧	◧	...	|
Offenburg a.	...	|	...	1939	|	|	...	...	|	|	...	|
Freiburg (Brsg) Hbf a.	...	|	EN	2026	|	|	...	...	|	|	ICE	|
Karlsruhe Hbf d.	...	1827	**50237**	...	2028	2028	...	...	|	|	**695**	0215
Mannheim Hbf d.	...	|	**K**	...	|	|	...	...	2217	2217	2230	|
Stuttgart Hbf d.	...	1920	2029	...	2114	2104	2115	...	...	...	2308	|
Ulm Hbf d.	...	2023	2153	...	2212	...	2200	...	...	...	...	|
Augsburg Hbf d.	...	2107	2302	...	2258	...	2243	...	...	...	...	|
München Pasing a.	...	|	|	...	|	...	2304	...	...	...	...	|
München Hbf a.	...	2136	|	...	2326	...	2313	...	...	...	...	0543o
München Hbf d.	...	...	2354o	...	...	...	...	...	...	...	...	|
Salzburg Hbf 🏛 a.	...	...	0128	...	...	...	...	...	...	...	...	0726
Linz Hbf a.	...	...	0452	...	...	...	...	...	...	...	...	0844
St Pölten Hbf a.	...	...	0600	...	...	...	...	...	...	...	...	0936
Wien Hbf a.	...	...	0634	...	...	...	...	...	...	...	...	1012
Hegyeshalom 🏛 a.	...	...	0723	...	...	...	...	...	...	...	...	...
Györ a.	...	...	0753	...	...	...	...	...	...	...	...	...
Budapest Keleti a.	...	...	0919	...	...	...	...	...	...	...	...	...
Bucuresti Nord a.	...	...	...	...	...	...	...	...	...	...	...	...

	TGV 9590	ICE 616	ICE 9558 ★	TGV 9578 ★	TGV 9588	☆ 9031			
	①–⑤		①–⑤	①–⑥	⑥⑦				
			h	h					
Bucuresti Nord d.	...	...	...	...	...	...	...	...	...
Budapest Keleti d.	...	...	...	...	...	...	...	...	...
Györ d.	...	...	...	...	...	...	...	...	...
Hegyeshalom 🏛 d.	...	...	...	...	...	...	...	...	...
Wien Hbf d.	...	...	...	...	...	...	...	...	...
St Pölten Hbf d.	...	...	...	...	...	...	...	...	...
Linz Hbf d.	...	...	...	...	...	...	...	...	...
Salzburg Hbf 🏛 d.	...	...	...	...	...	...	...	...	...
München Hbf a.	...	...	...	...	...	...	...	...	...
München Hbf d.	...	0332	...	...	...	...	...	...	...
München Pasing d.	...	0340	...	...	...	...	...	...	...
Augsburg Hbf d.	...	0404	...	...	...	...	...	...	...
Ulm Hbf d.	...	0447	...	...	...	...	...	...	...
Stuttgart Hbf d.	...	0551	...	0652	...	...	...	...	...
Mannheim Hbf d.	...	0628	0640	|	...	...	...	...	...
Karlsruhe Hbf d.	...	...	|	0732	...	...	...	...	...
Freiburg (Brsg) Hbf d.	0634	...	|	|	0708	...	...	...	...
Offenburg d.	0713	...	|	|	0746	...	...	...	...
Kehl 🏛 d.	|	...	◧	|	|	...	...	...	...
Strasbourg a.	0740	...	|	0813	0813	...	...	...	...
Paris Est a.	0935	...	0952	1005	1005	...	...	...	...
Paris Nord **10** d.	...	...	...	...	...	1313	...	...	...
London St Pancras **10** a.	...	...	...	...	...	1430	...	...	...

	EN 50462	TGV 9576 ★	☆ 9039	IC 1296	ICE 690	ICE 9574 ★	☆ 9047	RJX 260	ICE 518	RJX 262	ICE 596	ICE 9572 ★	TGV 9592 ★	☆ 9063	EN 346 ❖	RJX 60	ICE 594	TGV 9560 ★	IC 472 ❖	RJX 62	IC 266		NJ 468	☆ 9031
				①–⑥								Ⓑ	⑥	Ⓑ									①④⑥	
	K											f	j		M				B				D	
Bucuresti Nord d.	...	...	...	...	...	...	...	...	...	...	...	...	...	...	1400	...	...	...	1745	...	...	...	...	...
Budapest Keleti d.	2040	...	...	...	...	...	...	...	...	...	...	...	...	...	0540	0740	...	...	0850	0940	...	...	...	...
Györ d.	2202	...	...	...	...	...	...	...	...	...	...	...	...	...	0702	0902	...	...	...	1102	...	...	...	...
Hegyeshalom 🏛 d.	2232	...	...	...	...	...	...	...	...	...	...	...	...	...	0732	0932	...	...	...	1132	...	...	...	...
Wien Hbf d.	2327	...	...	...	...	...	...	0628	...	0828	...	...	...	...	0821	1028	...	...	...	1228	...	...	1940	...
St Pölten Hbf d.	0001	...	...	...	...	...	...	0659	...	0859	...	...	...	...	...	1059	...	...	...	1259	...	...	2015	...
Linz Hbf d.	0059	...	...	...	...	...	...	0745	...	0945	...	...	...	...	...	1145	...	...	...	1345	...	...	2102	...
Salzburg Hbf 🏛 d.	0405	...	...	0543	...	...	...	0900	...	1100	...	...	...	...	...	1300	...	...	...	1500	...	...	2218	...
München Hbf a.	0550o	...	...	0730	...	...	...	1033	...	1232	...	...	...	...	...	1432	...	...	...	1632	...	...	|	...
München Hbf d.	|	0651	...	...	0846	...	...	...	1128	...	1245	...	...	...	...	...	1447	...	...	...	1658	...	0003o	...
München Pasing d.	|	|	...	...	0855	...	...	...	1136	...	1254	...	...	...	...	...	1456	...	...	...	1706	...	|	...
Augsburg Hbf d.	0648	0721	...	...	0918	...	...	...	1201	...	1318	...	...	...	...	...	1518	...	...	...	1733	...	|	...
Ulm Hbf d.	0738	0804	...	...	1001	...	...	...	1247	...	1401	...	...	...	...	...	1601	...	...	...	1818	...	|	...
Stuttgart Hbf d.	0837	0911	...	...	1043	1052	...	...	1351	...	1443	1452	1452	...	...	...	1651	...	...	...	1912	...	|	...
Mannheim Hbf d.	...	|	...	...	...	|	...	...	1428	...	...	|	|	...	...	...	1729	1738	...	...	|	...	|	...
Karlsruhe Hbf d.	...	0953	...	...	...	1131	...	...	...	...	...	1532	1532	...	...	...	...	1805	...	...	1952	...	0412	...
Kehl 🏛 d.	...	|	...	...	...	|	...	...	...	...	...	|	|	...	...	...	...	◧	...	...	...	...	|	...
Strasbourg a.	...	1037	...	...	...	1213	...	...	...	...	...	1613	1613	...	...	...	...	1848	...	...	...	...	0506	...
Paris Est a.	...	1231	...	...	...	1405	...	...	...	...	...	1805	1805	...	...	...	...	2041	...	...	...	...	0942	...
Paris Nord **10** d.	...	...	1503	...	...	...	1703	...	...	...	...	...	...	2103	...	...	...	...	...	...	...	...	...	1313
London St Pancras **10** a.	...	...	1630	...	...	...	1832	...	...	...	...	...	...	2239	...	...	...	...	...	...	...	...	...	1430

A – 🚃 12 HORTOBÁGY – Wien - Budapest - Szolnok (arrive 2102) - Debrecen (2235) - Zahony (0010). Conveys 🛏 1, 2 cl. Wien - Zahony - Lviv - Kyïv (Table **96**).

B – *EuroNight* ISTER – 🛏 1, 2 cl., 🛌 1, 2 cl., 🚃 2 Budapest - Bucuresti and v.v.

D – ①④⑥: *ÖBB nightjet* – 🛏 1, 2 cl., 🛌 2 cl. (4, 6 berth), 🚃 2 Wien - Salzburg - Paris. Special fares apply.

E – ②⑤⑦: *ÖBB nightjet* – 🛏 1, 2 cl., 🛌 2 cl. (4, 6 berth), 🚃 2 Paris - Salzburg - Wien. Special fares apply.

J – MUNTENIA – 🚃 2 Budapest - Timişoara - Bucureşti and v.v.

K – KÁLMÁN IMRE – 🛏 1, 2 cl., 🛌 2 cl. (4, 6 berth) 🚃 2 Stuttgart - Budapest and v.v. Also conveys cars to and from Venezia (Table **70**), Zagreb and Rijeka (Table **62**).

M – DACIA – 🛏 1, 2 cl., 🛌 2 cl., 🚃 2 Wien - Budapest - Bucuresti and v.v.

f – Not Apr. 9, 30, May 28.

h – Not Apr. 10, May 1, 29.

j – Also Apr. 9, 30, May 28.

o – München **Ost**.

◧ – 🏛 is at Forbach.

RJ – ÖBB *Railjet* service. ✕, 🚃 1 (business class), 🚃 1 (first class), 🚃 2 (economy class).

★ – *Alleo* ICE / TGV service. A DB / SNCF joint enterprise.

TGV – Ⓡ, supplement payable, 🍸.

WB – *WESTbahn* service. Special fares payable.

❖ – Compulsory reservation for international journeys between Hungary and Romania.

☆ – Eurostar train. Ⓡ, ✕ in Business Premier and Standard Premier, 🍸 in Standard. Special fares payable. See shaded panel in Table **10** on page 47 for information about recommended arrival times at departure station. Valid Feb. 20 - May 20.

‡ – Train number **9596** on ⑦.

40 LONDON - PARIS - BASEL - ZÜRICH, INTERLAKEN, BRIG and MILANO

train type/number		TGV	IC	IC	EC	IC	☆	TGV	EC	IC	IR	IC	EC		☆	TGV	IC	IC	IR	IC	EC	
train number		9203	967	814	151	567	9082	9211	7	820	2327	573	321		9008	9213	977	824	2331	577	323	
notes		♥			Ⓡ 🍷 ⊗		①–⑤ j	♥					Ⓡ 🍷 ⊗			♥					Ⓡ 🍷 ⊗	
London St Pancras d.	...	...	...	...	...	...	0601	...	...	...	...	...	...	...	0801	...	...	...	...	...	...	...
Paris Nord a.	...	...	...	...	...	...	0920	...	...	...	...	...	...	...	1120	...	...	...	...	...	...	...
Paris Gare de Lyon d.	...	0715	...	...	...	...	...	1020	...	...	...	...	...	...	...	1219	...	...	...	...	...	...
Dijon d.	...	|	...	...	...	...	...	1201	...	...	...	...	...	...	...	1401	...	...	...	...	...	...
Besançon TGV ⊖ d.	...	|	...	...	...	...	...	|	...	...	...	...	...	...	...	|	...	...	...	...	...	...
Belfort TGV ⊡ d.	...	0941	...	...	...	...	...	|	...	...	...	...	...	...	...	|	...	...	...	...	...	...
Mulhouse d.	...	1006	...	...	...	...	...	1306	...	...	...	...	...	...	...	1506	...	...	...	...	...	...
Basel SBB a.	...	1026	...	...	...	...	...	1326	...	...	...	...	...	...	...	1526	...	...	...	...	...	...
Basel SBB d.	...	1033	1056	...	1103	...	...	1333	1356	...	1403	...	...	...	...	1533	1556	...	1603	...	...	...
Zürich HB a.	...	1126	|	...	|	1138	...	1426	|	...	|	1438	1533	...	...	1626	|	...	|	1638	1733	...
Landquart a.	...	...	|	...	|	1242	...	...	|	...	|	1542	|	...	...	...	|	...	|	1742	|	...
Chur a.	...	...	|	...	|	1252	...	...	|	...	|	1552	|	...	...	...	|	...	|	1752	|	...
Luzern a.	...	...	|	...	1205	...	...	...	|	...	1505	...	|	...	...	...	|	...	1705	...	|	...
Arth Goldau a.	...	...	|	...	1245	...	...	...	|	...	1545	...	1616	...	...	...	|	...	1745	...	1816	...
Arth Goldau d.	...	...	|	...	1249	...	...	...	|	...	...	...	1618	...	...	...	|	...	...	...	1818	...
Bellinzona a.	...	...	|	...	1342	...	...	...	|	...	...	...	1712	...	...	...	|	...	...	...	1912	...
Lugano a.	...	...	|	...	1358	...	...	...	|	...	...	...	1732	...	...	...	|	...	...	...	1932	...
Chiasso 🏛 a.	...	...	|	...	1456	...	...	...	|	...	...	...	1802	...	...	...	|	...	...	...	2002	...
Bern a.	...	...	1156	1207	|	...	...	...	1456	1507	...	...	|	...	...	...	1656	1707	...	...	|	...
Thun a.	...	...	1223	1225	|	...	...	...	1523	1525	...	...	|	...	...	...	1723	1725	...	...	|	...
Spiez a.	...	...	1233	1236	|	...	...	...	1533	1536	...	...	|	...	...	...	1733	1736	...	...	|	...
Interlaken West a.	...	...	1251	|	|	...	...	...	1551	|	...	...	|	...	...	...	1751	|	...	...	|	...
Interlaken Ost a.	...	...	1258	|	|	...	...	...	1558	|	...	...	|	...	...	...	1758	|	...	...	|	...
Brig a.	...	...	...	1311	|	...	...	...	...	1611	...	...	|	...	...	...	...	1811	...	...	|	...
Como San Giovanni a.	...	...	...	...	1501	...	...	...	...	...	...	...	1810	...	...	...	...	...	...	...	2010	...
Milano Centrale a.	...	...	...	...	1550	...	...	...	...	...	...	...	1850	...	...	...	...	...	...	...	2050	...

train type/number	☆	TGV	ICE	IC	IR	IC	EC	☆	TGV	ICE	IR	IC	IC	IC	IR	IC	☆	TGV	IR	IC	IC	
train number	9014	9215	371	828	2335	583	325	9018	9219	373	2339	1087 1089	585	889	2441	691	9024	9223	2343	989	589	4293
notes		♥	Ⓡ 🍷 ⊗				Ⓡ 🍷 ⊗		♥					①–⑤				♥				
London St Pancras d.	0931	...	...	...	...	...	...	1024	...	...	...	...	...	...	...	...	1231	...	...	...	...	...
Paris Nord a.	1247	...	...	...	...	...	...	1357	...	...	...	...	...	...	...	...	1547	...	...	...	...	...
Paris Gare de Lyon d.	...	1415	...	...	...	...	...	...	1619	...	...	...	...	...	...	...	...	1819	...	...	...	...
Dijon d.	...	|	...	...	...	...	...	...	|	...	...	...	...	...	...	...	...	2001	...	...	...	...
Besançon TGV ⊖ d.	...	|	...	...	...	...	...	...	|	...	...	...	...	...	...	...	...	|	...	...	...	...
Belfort TGV ⊡ d.	...	1640	...	...	...	...	...	...	1841	...	...	...	...	...	...	...	...	|	...	...	...	...
Mulhouse d.	...	1706	...	...	...	...	...	...	1906	...	...	...	...	...	...	...	...	2106	...	...	...	...
Basel SBB a.	...	1726	...	...	...	...	...	...	1926	...	...	...	...	...	...	...	...	2126	...	...	...	...
Basel SBB d.	...	1733z	1756	...	1803	1833	...	...	1933	1956	2003	2028	...	...	...	2103	...	2133	2203	2156	...	...
Zürich HB a.	...	1826z	|	...	|	1926	1933	...	2026	|	|	|	2038	2105	2205	|	...	2226	|	|	2238	...
Landquart a.	...	...	|	...	|	2042	|	...	...	|	|	|	2142	|	|	|	...	...	|	|	2349	...
Chur a.	...	...	|	...	|	2052	|	...	...	|	|	|	2152	|	|	|	...	...	|	|	2357	...
Luzern a.	...	...	|	...	1905	...	|	...	...	|	2105	|	...	|	|	2205	...	...	2305	|	...	...
Arth Goldau a.	...	...	|	...	1945	...	2016	...	...	|	2145	|	...	2145	2245	2245	...	...	2338	|	...	...
Arth Goldau d.	...	...	|	...	...	...	2018	...	...	|	...	|	...	2149	...	2249	...	...	...	|	...	...
Bellinzona a.	...	...	|	...	...	...	2112	...	...	|	...	|	...	2242	...	2342	...	...	...	|	...	...
Lugano a.	...	...	|	...	...	...	2132	...	...	|	...	|	...	2302	...	0002	...	...	...	|	...	...
Chiasso 🏛 a.	...	...	|	...	...	...	2202	...	...	|	...	|	...	2330	...	0030	...	...	...	|	...	...
Bern a.	...	...	1856	1907	...	...	|	...	...	2056	...	2126	...	...	...	...	...	...	...	2256	...	...
Thun a.	...	...	1923	1925	...	...	|	...	...	2125	...	2152	...	...	...	...	...	...	...	2226	...	...
Spiez a.	...	...	1933	1936	...	...	|	...	...	2136	...	2202	...	...	...	...	...	...	...	2337	...	0013
Interlaken West a.	...	...	1952	|	...	...	|	...	...	2154	...	|	...	...	...	...	...	...	...	2355	...	|
Interlaken Ost a.	...	...	1958	|	...	...	|	...	...	2159	...	|	...	...	...	...	...	...	...	2400	...	|
Brig a.	...	...	...	2011	...	...	|	...	...	...	...	2241f	...	...	...	...	...	...	...	...	...	0123
Como San Giovanni a.	...	...	...	...	...	...	2210	...	...	...	...	...	...	...	...	...	...	...	...	...	...	...
Milano Centrale a.	...	...	...	...	...	...	2250	...	...	...	...	...	...	...	...	...	...	...	...	...	...	...

train type	IC	IC	IR	ICE	TGV	☆	IC	IC	IC	IR	IC	TGV	☆	EC	IC	EC	IR	ICE	TGV	☆	☆	
train number	862	558	2308	372	9206	9039	866	562	1060	2312	962	9210	9043	312	566	50	2316	278	9218	9051	9055	
notes					♥							♥		Ⓡ 🍷 ⊗		Ⓡ 🍷 ⊗			♥	Ⓑ		
Milano Centrale d.	...	...	...	...	...	...	...	...	...	...	...	...	...	0710	...	0720	...	...	...	...	...	...
Como San Giovanni d.	...	...	...	...	...	...	...	...	...	...	...	...	...	0754	...	◧	...	...	...	...	...	...
Brig d.	...	...	...	...	...	...	...	...	0718	...	...	...	...	|	...	0918	...	...	...	...	...	...
Interlaken Ost d.	...	...	...	0558	...	...	...	...	|	...	0800	...	...	|	...	|	...	1000	...	...	...	...
Interlaken West d.	...	...	...	0603	...	...	...	...	|	...	0805	...	...	|	...	|	...	1005	...	...	...	...
Spiez d.	...	...	...	0622	...	...	...	...	0754	...	0822	...	...	|	...	0954	...	1022	...	...	...	...
Thun d.	...	...	...	0633	...	...	...	...	0804	...	0833	...	...	|	...	1004	...	1033	...	...	...	...
Bern d.	...	...	...	0704	...	...	...	...	0836	...	0904	...	...	|	...	1036	...	1104	...	...	...	...
Chiasso 🏛 d.	...	...	...	|	...	...	...	...	|	...	|	...	...	0805	...	|	...	|	...	...	...	...
Lugano d.	...	...	...	|	...	...	0701	...	|	...	|	...	...	0830	...	|	...	|	...	...	...	...
Bellinzona d.	0507	...	...	|	...	...	0718	...	|	...	|	...	...	0847	...	|	...	|	...	...	...	...
Arth Goldau a.	0611	...	...	|	...	...	0811	...	|	...	|	...	...	0942	...	|	...	|	...	...	...	...
Arth Goldau d.	0615	...	0603	|	...	...	0815	...	|	0803	|	...	...	0945	...	|	1003	|	...	...	...	...
Luzern d.	|	...	0654	|	...	...	|	...	|	0854	|	...	...	|	...	|	1054	|	...	...	...	...
Chur d.	|	0608	|	|	...	...	|	0808	|	|	|	...	...	|	1008	|	|	|	...	...	...	...
Landquart d.	|	0618	|	|	...	...	|	0818	|	|	|	...	...	|	1018	|	|	|	...	...	...	...
Zürich HB d.	0655	0722	|	|	0734	...	0855	0922	|	|	|	0934	...	1027	1122	|	|	|	1134	...	...	...
Basel SBB a.	...	...	0756	0801	0828	...	...	...	0932	0956	1001	1028	...	...	...	1132	1156	1201	1228	...	...	...
Basel SBB d.	...	...	...	...	0834	...	...	...	...	...	...	1034	...	...	...	...	...	...	1234	...	...	...
Mulhouse a.	...	...	...	...	0853	...	...	...	...	...	...	1053	...	...	...	...	...	...	1253	...	...	...
Belfort TGV ⊡ a.	...	...	...	...	0917	...	...	...	...	...	...	|	...	...	...	...	...	...	1317	...	...	...
Besançon TGV ⊖ a.	...	...	...	...	|	...	...	...	...	...	...	|	...	...	...	...	...	...	|	...	...	...
Dijon a.	...	...	...	...	|	...	...	...	...	...	...	1158	...	...	...	...	...	...	|	...	...	...
Paris Gare de Lyon a.	...	...	...	...	1141	...	...	...	...	...	...	1340	...	...	...	...	...	...	1540	...	...	...
Paris Nord d.	...	...	...	...	...	1503	...	...	...	...	...	...	1613	...	...	...	...	...	...	1813	1903	...
London St Pancras a.	...	...	...	...	...	1639	...	...	...	...	...	...	1730	...	...	...	...	...	...	1930	2039	...

f – 2303 on ⑦.

j – Not Apr. 10, May 1.

z – © (also May 19).

⊡ – Full name: Belfort Montbéliard TGV.

⊖ – Full name: Besancon Franche-Comté TGV.

◧ – 🏛 between Brig and Milano is Domodossola. Ticket point is **Iselle**.

♥ – *TGV Lyria* service. Ⓡ ✕. Special fares payable, three classes of service: Business 1ère, Standard 1ère and Standard. At-seat meal service in Business 1ère. Compulsory reservation for international journeys. Supplement payable for international journeys and for internal journeys within Italy. Valid Dec. 11 - May 14.

☆ – Eurostar train. Ⓡ, ✕ in Business Premier and Standard Premier, 🍷 in Standard. Special fares payable. See shaded panel in Table **10** on page 47 for information about recommended arrival times at departure station. Valid Feb. 5 - May 20.

MILANO, BRIG, INTERLAKEN and ZÜRICH - BASEL - PARIS - LONDON 40

train type	EC	IC	IC	IR	EC	TGV	☆	EC	IC	EC	IR	IC	TGV	EC	IC	IC	IC	TGV
train number	314	570	1068	2320	6	9222	9059	316	574	52	2324	974	9226	318	684	980	580	9234
notes	Ⓡ🍷 ⊗					♥		Ⓡ🍷 ⊗		Ⓡ🍷 ⊗			♥	Ⓡ🍷 ⊗				♥
Milano Centrale d.	0910	...	...	...	...	...	...	1110	...	1120	...	...	...	1310	...	...	...	...
Como San Giovanni d.	0950	...	...	...	...	...	...	1150	...	◧	...	...	...	1350	...	...	...	...
Brig d.	|	...	1118	...	...	...	...	|	...	1318	...	...	...	|	...	...	...	...
Interlaken Ost d.	|	...	|	...	1200	...	...	|	...	|	...	1400	...	|	...	1700	...	...
Interlaken West d.	|	...	|	...	1205	...	...	|	...	|	...	1405	...	|	...	1705	...	...
Spiez d.	|	...	1154	...	1222	...	...	|	...	1354	...	1422	...	|	...	1722	...	...
Thun d.	|	...	1204	...	1233	...	...	|	...	1404	...	1433	...	|	...	1733	...	...
Bern d.	|	...	1236	...	1304	...	...	|	...	1436	...	1504	...	|	...	1804	...	...
Chiasso 🛃 d.	1005	...	|	...	|	...	...	1205	...	|	...	|	...	1405	...	|	...	...
Lugano d.	1030	...	|	...	|	...	...	1230	...	|	...	|	...	1430	1602	|	...	...
Bellinzona d.	1047	...	|	...	|	...	...	1247	...	|	...	|	...	1447	1617	|	...	...
Arth Goldau a.	1142	...	|	...	|	...	...	1342	...	|	...	|	...	1542	1711	|	...	...
Arth Goldau d.	1145	...	|	1203	|	...	...	1345	...	|	1403	|	...	1545	1715	|	...	...
Luzern d.	|	...	|	1254	|	...	...	|	...	|	1454	|	...	|	1754	|	...	...
Chur d.	|	1208	|	|	|	...	...	|	1408	|	|	|	...	|	|	|	1708	...
Landquart d.	|	1218	|	|	|	...	...	|	1418	|	|	|	...	|	|	|	1718	...
Zürich HB d.	1227	1322	|	|	|	1334	...	1427	1522	|	|	|	1534	1627	|	|	1822	1834
Basel SBB a.	...	...	1332	1356	1401	1428	...	...	...	1532	1556	1601	1628	...	1856	1901	...	1928
Basel SBB d.	...	...	...	...	...	1434	...	...	...	...	...	...	1634	...	...	...	...	1934
Mulhouse a.	...	...	...	...	...	1453	...	...	...	...	...	...	1653	...	...	...	...	1953
Belfort TGV ⊡ a.	...	...	...	...	...	|	...	...	...	...	...	...	|	...	...	...	...	2018
Besançon TGV ⊖ a.	...	...	...	...	...	|	...	...	...	...	...	...	|	...	...	...	...	|
Dijon a.	...	...	...	...	...	1558	...	...	...	...	...	...	1758	...	...	...	...	|
Paris Gare de Lyon a.	...	...	...	...	...	1741	...	...	...	...	...	...	1942	...	...	...	...	2251
Paris Nord d.	...	...	...	...	...	...	2013	...	...	...	...	...	...	...	...	...	...	...
London St Pancras a.	...	...	...	...	...	...	2130	...	...	...	...	...	...	...	...	...	...	...

⊖ – Full name: Besancon Franche-Comté TGV.

⊡ – Full name: Belfort Montbéliard TGV.

◧ – 🛃 between Brig and Milano is Domodossola. Ticket point is **Iselle**.

☆ – Eurostar train. Ⓡ, ✕ in Business Premier and Standard Premier, 🍷 in Standard. Special fares payable. See shaded panel in Table **10** on page 47 for information about recommended arrival times at departure station. Valid Feb. 5 - May 20.

♥ – *TGV Lyria* service. Ⓡ 🍷. Special fares payable, three classes of service: Business 1ère, Standard 1ère and Standard. At-seat meal service in Business 1ère. Valid Dec. 11 - May 14.

⊗ – Compulsory reservation for international journeys. Supplement payable for international journeys and for internal journeys within Italy.

LONDON - PARIS - LAUSANNE - BRIG 42

train type	TGV	IR	TGV	IR	☆	☆	TGV	IR	☆	TGV	IR	☆	TGV	IR	☆	TGV	IR
train number	9761	1715	9261		9002	9004	9269	1825	9014	9775	1731	9018	9777	1735	9024	9277	1837
notes	♥ ①–⑥		♥		⑥	①–⑤ k	♥			♥			♥			♥	
London St Pancras **10** d.	...	...	...	...	0631	0701	...	...	0931	...	...	1024	...	...	1231	...	...
Paris Nord **10** a.	...	...	...	...	0947	1017	...	...	1247	...	...	1357	...	...	1547	...	...
Paris Gare de Lyon d.	0616	...	0753	...	...	...	1154	...	...	1410	...	...	1614	...	...	1747	...
Dijon d.	|	...	0935	...	...	...	1335	...	...	|	...	...	|	...	...	1933	...
Frasne a.	◧	...	1042	...	...	...	1442	...	...	◧	...	...	◧	...	...	2042	...
Vallorbe 🛃 a.	|	...	1057	...	...	...	1457	...	...	|	...	...	|	...	...	2057	...
Lausanne a.	1014	...	1152	...	...	...	1537	...	...	1814	...	...	2014	...	...	2137	...
Lausanne d.	...	1021	...	1221	...	...	...	1550	...	...	1821	...	...	2021	...	...	2150
Montreux a.	...	1043	...	1243	...	...	...	1611	...	...	1843	...	...	2043	...	...	2211
Aigle a.	...	1053	...	1253	...	...	...	1622	...	...	1853	...	...	2053	...	...	2222
Martigny a.	...	1111	...	1311	...	...	...	1643	...	...	1911	...	...	2111	...	...	2243
Sion a.	...	1125	...	1325	...	...	...	1657	...	...	1925	...	...	2125	...	...	2257
Sierre a.	...	1135	...	1335	...	...	...	1708	...	...	1935	...	...	2135	...	...	2308
Visp a.	...	1153	...	1353	...	...	...	1723	...	...	1953	...	...	2153	...	...	2326
Brig a.	...	1202	...	1402	...	...	...	1732	...	...	2002	...	...	2202	...	...	2332

train type	IR	TGV	☆	IR	TGV	☆	EC	IR	TGV	☆	IR	TGV	☆	IR	TGV	IR	TGV
train number	1806	9264	9039	1810	9768	9043	32	1816	9268	9055	1818	9774	9059	1824	9270	1828	9784
notes		♥			♥		Ⓡ🍷 ⊗		♥			♥			♥		♥ Ⓑ
Brig d.	0524	...	...	0726	...	...	1016	1026	...	...	1126	...	...	1426	...	1626	...
Visp d.	0532	...	...	0735	...	...	|	1035	...	...	1135	...	...	1435	...	1635	...
Sierre d.	0550	...	...	0750	...	...	|	1050	...	...	1150	...	...	1450	...	1650	...
Sion d.	0601	...	...	0801	...	...	1047	1101	...	...	1201	...	...	1501	...	1701	...
Martigny d.	0616	...	...	0816	...	...	|	1116	...	...	1216	...	...	1516	...	1716	...
Aigle d.	0638	...	...	0837	...	...	|	1137	...	...	1237	...	...	1537	...	1737	...
Montreux d.	0648	...	...	0848	...	...	1123	1148	...	...	1248	...	...	1548	...	1748	...
Lausanne a.	0710	...	...	0910	...	...	1142	1210	...	...	1310	...	...	1610	...	1810	...
Lausanne d.	...	0723	...	...	0945	...	...	...	1223	...	...	1345	...	...	1623	...	1945
Vallorbe 🛃 d.	...	0800	...	...	|	...	...	...	1300	...	...	|	...	...	1700	...	|
Frasne a.	...	0813	...	...	◧	...	...	...	1313	...	...	◧	...	...	1713	...	◧
Dijon a.	...	0926	...	...	|	...	...	...	1424	...	...	|	...	...	1824	...	|
Paris Gare de Lyon a.	...	1112	...	...	1350	...	...	...	1614	...	...	1749	...	...	2009	...	2345
Paris Nord **10** d.	...	...	1503	...	...	1613	...	...	...	1903	...	...	2013	...	...	...	...
London St Pancras **10** a.	...	...	1630	...	...	1730	...	...	...	2039	...	...	2130	...	...	...	...

k – Not Apr. 10, May 1.

◧ – Via Genève.

◇ – Stopping train. 2nd class only.

♥ – *TGV Lyria* service. Ⓡ 🍷. Special fares payable, three classes of service: business 1ère, standard 1ère and standard. At-seat meal service in first class. Valid Dec. 11 - May 14.

⊗ – Compulsory reservation for international journeys. Supplement payable for international journeys and for internal journeys within Italy.

☆ – Eurostar train. Ⓡ, ✕ in Business Premier and Standard Premier, 🍷 in Standard. Special fares payable. See shaded panel in Table **10** on page 47 for information about recommended arrival times at departure station. Valid Feb. 5 - May 20.

44 PARIS - TORINO - MILANO - VENEZIA and ROMA

train type	TGV	FR	ITA		FR	ITA	FR	FR	FR	TGV	FR		TGV	FR	FR	FR	ITA	TGV	ICN		FR	
train number	**9241**	**9543**	**8153**		**9281**	**8987**	**9735**	**9641**	**9547**	**9245**	**9325**		**9251**	**9759**	**9567**	**9559**	**9963**	**9249**	**797**		**9287**	
train number						R																
notes	R ✕	R	R		R	⚡	R	R	R	R ✕	R		R ✕	R	R	R	R	R ✕	R		R	
notes	♣	⚡	⚡		A	①④⑤⑥⑦	⚡	⚡ ⑧	⚡	♣ B	⚡		♣ C	⚡	⚡ ①–⑤	⚡ ⑥⑦	⚡	♣	H ⚡		A	
Paris Gare de Lyon d.	0639	...	...	...	0725	...	...	...	...	0943	...	...	1238 x	...	...	...	...	1445	...	...	1512	...
Lyon Part Dieu d.	|	...	...	...	0930	...	...	...	...	|	...	...	|	...	...	...	...	|	...	...	1720	...
Lyon St Exupéry TGV ✈ d.	|	...	...	...	|	...	...	...	...	|	...	...	|	...	...	...	...	|	...	...	|	...
Chambéry d.	0944	...	...	...	1054	...	...	...	...	1244	...	...	1544	...	...	...	...	1744	...	...	1849	...
Modane 🏛 d.	1058	...	...	...	1210	...	...	...	...	1355	...	...	1655	...	...	...	...	1855	...	...	2010	...
Oulx ▲ a.	1123	...	...	...	|	...	...	...	...	1423	...	...	1726	...	...	...	...	1923	...	...	|	...
Torino Porta Susa a.	1223	1310	1330	...	1318	...	...	1400	...	1521	1550	...	1815	1850	1910	1910	1935	2022	2040	...	2120	...
Novara a.	|	|	|	...	|	...	...	|	...	|	|	...	|	|	|	|	|	|	2137	...	|	...
Milano Porta Garibaldi ✣ a.	1349	|	|	...	|	...	...	|	...	1650	1645	...	1949	|	|	|	|	2149	2213	...	|	...
Milano Centrale a.	...	1402	1430	...	1407	...	...	1450	...	...	|	...	...	|	2002	2002	2030	...	|	...	2207	...
Milano Centrale d.	...	1410	1440	...	...	1435	1445	1500	1510	...	|	...	...	|	2010	2010	2040	...	|	...	...	...
Verona Porta Nuova a.	...	|	|	...	...	1547	1558	|	|	...	|	...	...	2053	|	|	|	...	|	...	...	...
Venezia Mestre a.	...	|	|	...	...	1652	1700	|	|	...	|	...	...	2155	|	|	|	...	|	...	...	...
Venezia Santa Lucia a.	...	|	|	...	...	1703	1712	|	|	...	|	...	...	...	|	|	|	...	|	...	...	...
Reggio Emilia AV a.	...	1456	1528	...	...	...	...	|	1556	...	1740	...	...	...	2056	2056	2128	...	|	...	...	...
Bologna Centrale a.	...	1524	1554	...	...	...	...	1604	1624	...	1809	...	...	...	2124	2124	2154	...	|	...	...	...
Firenze SMN a.	...	1604	1635	...	...	...	...	|	1704	...	1850	...	...	...	2204	2204	2235	...	|	...	...	...
Roma Termini a.	...	1749	1819	...	...	...	...	1810	1849	...	2035	...	...	...	2349	0025	0019	...	0553t	...	...	...
Napoli Centrale a.	...	1913	1928f	...	...	...	...	...	2010	...	2203	...	...	...	...	...	...	...	0846	...	...	...
Salerno a.	...	2005	2011	...	...	...	...	...	2057	...	...	...	...	...	...	...	...	...	0945	...	...	...

train type		FR	TGV	FR		ICN		FR	ITA	TGV		ITA	FR	TGV		FA	FR	ITA	FR	FR	TGV	
train number		**9292**	**9240**	**9292**		**798**		**9516**	**9916**	**9244**		**9920**	**9310**	**9252**		**9728**	**9415**	**9928**	**9296**	**9532**	**9248**	
train number																						
notes		R	R ✕	R		R		R	R	R ✕		R	R	R ✕		R	R	R	R	R	R ✕	
notes		A	♣	A		H ⚡		⚡	⚡	♣ B		⚡	⚡	♣ C		⚡	⚡	⚡	A	⚡	♣	
Salerno d.	...	...	...	...	...	2038	...	0550	0620	...	...	0720	...	...	...	...	0846	...	...	...	...	...
Napoli Centrale d.	...	...	...	...	...	2135	...	0640	0720	...	...	0820	0855	...	...	...	0940	...	...	1040	...	...
Roma Termini d.	...	...	...	...	...	2355t	...	0810	0840	...	...	0940	1025	...	...	...	1110	1140	...	1210	...	...
Firenze SMN d.	...	...	...	...	...	|	...	0955	1025	...	...	1125	1210	...	...	...	1255	1325	...	1355	...	...
Bologna Centrale d.	...	...	...	...	...	|	...	1036	1106	...	...	1206	1251	...	...	...	1336	1406	...	1436	...	...
Reggio Emilia AV d.	...	...	...	...	...	|	...	1100	1130	...	...	1230	1313	...	...	...	1400	1435	...	1500	...	...
Venezia Santa Lucia d.	...	...	...	...	...	|	...	|	|	...	...	|	|	...	...	1148	|	|	...	|	...	...
Venezia Mestre d.	...	...	...	...	...	|	...	|	|	...	...	|	|	...	...	1200	|	|	...	|	...	...
Verona Porta Nuova d.	...	...	...	...	...	|	...	|	|	...	...	|	|	...	...	1302	|	|	...	|	...	...
Milano Centrale a.	...	...	...	...	...	|	...	1150	1220	...	...	1320	1358	...	...	1415	1450	1520	...	1550	...	...
Milano Centrale d.	...	0625	...	...	...	|	...	1202	1230	...	...	1330	1410	...	...	...	1502	1530	1553	1602	...	...
Milano Porta Garibaldi d.	...	|	0600	...	...	0655a	...	|	|	1210	...	|	|	1410	...	...	|	|	|	|	1610	...
Novara d.	...	|	|	...	...	0802a	...	|	|	|	...	|	|	|	...	...	|	|	|	|	|	...
Torino Porta Susa d.	...	0711	0736	...	...	0905	...	1249	1318	1336	...	1418	1459	1539	...	...	1549	1629	1640	1649	1738	...
Oulx ▲ d.	...	|	0836	...	...	...	...	...	...	1436	...	...	...	1636	...	...	...	...	|	...	1836	...
Modane 🏛 a.	...	0833	0903	...	...	...	...	...	...	1503	...	...	...	1703	...	...	...	...	1750	...	1906	...
Chambéry a.	...	0951	1015	...	...	...	...	...	...	1615	...	...	...	1815	...	...	...	...	1906	...	2014	...
Lyon St Exupéry TGV ✈ a.	...	|	|	←	...	...	...	...	...	|	...	...	...	|	...	...	...	...	|	...	|	...
Lyon Part Dieu a.	...	1110	|	1126	...	...	...	...	...	|	...	...	...	|	...	...	...	...	2023	...	|	...
Paris Gare de Lyon a.	...	→	1316	1322	...	...	...	...	...	1916	...	...	...	2116	...	...	...	...	2239	...	2330	...

A – *Frecciarossa* ETR1000 high-speed service.
B – ⑥⑦ (daily Feb. 11 - Mar. 12, Apr. 15 - May 1, also Apr. 10, May 12, 18, 19; not May 6, 7).
C – ①–⑤ Mar. 13 - Apr. 14, (also Mar. 4, Apr. 8; not Apr. 10), Apr. 22, 29, May 2 - 5, 15 - 17, 22 - 27.
H – 🛋 1, 2 cl., 🛏 2 cl. (4 berth) Torino - Milano - Salerno and v.v.

a – Arrival time.
d – Departure time.
f – Napoli **Afragola**.

t – Roma **Tiburtina**.
x – Also 1241, 1242, 1243, 1246 on certain dates.
y – Calls at Aix les Bains at 1303, Mâcon Loché TGV 1433.

⚡ – Supplement payable.
♣ – *TGV* France-Italy service. R ✕ Special fares payable.
▲ – Station for the resorts of Cesana, Claviere and Sestriere.
✣ – Change at Torino Porta Susa for stations beyond Milano.

MADRID - BADAJOZ - LISBOA / PORTO 46

		IC		*IC*	*IC*		🚌		*MD*				*IC*	*IC*		🚌		🚌	
		190	**5500**	**512**	**523**		**B**		**17902**			**5502**	**528**	**529**		**A**		**B**	
		2	2	[R]	[R]				2	2	2	2	[R]	[R]		⑤⑦			
		⚒									Ⓑ								
Madrid Chamartín ‡	d.	...	0830	...	...	...	...	...	...	...	...	...	...	...	...	...	...	...	...
Madrid Atocha Cercanías	d.	...	0850	...	...	...	...	...	...	1055	...	...	...	...	...	...	...	...	...
Madrid Estación Sur ✣	d.	...	|	...	...	...	...	0930	...	|	...	...	...	...	...	...	1430	...	2230	...
Talavera de la Reina	d.	...	1015	...	...	...	...	|	...	1222	...	...	...	...	...	...	|	...	|	...
Navalmoral de La Mata	d.	...	1053	...	...	...	...	|	...	1257	...	...	...	...	...	...	|	...	|	...
Monfragüe–Plasencia	d.	...	1123	...	...	...	...	|	...	1325	...	...	...	...	...	...	|	...	|	...
Cáceres	d.	...	1201	...	...	...	...	|	...	1425	...	...	...	...	...	...	1845	...	0200	...
Mérida	a.	...	1237	...	...	...	...	|	...	1505	...	...	...	...	...	...	|	...	|	...
Mérida	d.	...	1247	...	...	...	...	|	...	...	1531	1814	...	...	...	...	|	...	|	...
Badajoz 🏢 ⊠	ES a.	...	1324	1409	...	...	...	1445	...	...	1611	1900	1941	...	...	...	2000	...	0400	...
Elvas 🏢	PT a.	...	...	1325	...	...	...	|	...	...	...	...	1857	...	...	...	|	...	|	...
Abrantes	a.	...	...	1520	...	...	...	|	...	...	...	...	2053	...	...	...	|	...	|	...
Entroncamento	a.	...	...	1552	1600	1630	...	|	...	...	...	...	2137	2201	2300	...	|	...	|	...
Lisboa Oriente	a.	...	...	...	1652	|	...	1630	...	...	...	...	...	2252	|	...	2200	...	0545	...
Lisboa S Apolónia	a.	...	...	...	1700	|	...	...	...	...	...	...	...	2300	|	...	...	...	...	...
Coimbra B	a.	...	...	...	...	1730	...	...	...	...	...	...	...	...	2359	...	...	...	...	...
Aveiro	a.	...	...	...	...	1802	...	...	...	...	...	...	...	...	0030	...	...	...	...	...
Porto Campanhã	a.	...	...	...	...	1852	...	...	...	...	...	...	...	...	0123	...	...	...	...	...

		IC		*IC*			*MD*		🚌	🚌		*IC*	*IC*		*IC*		🚌		🚌
		520	**4407**	**541**	**5501**		**17907**		**A**	**B**		**720**	**513**	**5503**	**193**		**A**		**B**
		[R]	2	[R]	2	2	2					[R]	[R]	2	2		⑤⑦		
		⚒													Ⓑ				
Porto Campanhã	d.	...	0637	...	...	...	...	...	...	...	...	...	1038	...	...	...	...	...	...	...
Aveiro	d.	...	0732	...	...	...	...	...	...	...	...	...	1131	...	...	...	...	...	...	...
Coimbra B	d.	...	0804	...	...	...	...	...	...	...	...	...	1202	...	...	...	...	...	...	...
Lisboa S Apolónia	d.	...	|	0745	0815	...	...	...	...	...	...	...	|	1230	...	...	...	...	...	...
Lisboa Oriente	d.	...	|	0753	0823	...	...	...	...	0915	1000	...	|	1239	...	...	...	1245	...	2145
Entroncamento	d.	...	0900	0919	0923	0928	...	...	...	|	|	...	1300	1329	1336	...	...	|	...	|
Abrantes	d.	...	...	...	...	0959	...	...	...	|	|	...	...	...	1407	...	...	|	...	|
Elvas 🏢	PT d.	...	...	...	...	1159	...	...	...	|	|	...	...	...	1612	...	...	|	...	|
Badajoz 🏢 ⊠	ES d.	...	...	...	...	1313	1430	...	...	|	1345	...	...	...	1726	1736	...	1700	...	0125
Mérida	a.	...	...	...	...	...	1516	...	...	|	|	...	...	...	...	1810	...	|	...	|
Mérida	d.	...	...	...	...	...	...	1531	...	|	|	...	...	...	...	1820	...	|	...	|
Cáceres	d.	...	...	...	...	...	...	1613	...	|	|	...	...	...	...	1901	...	1830	...	|
Monfragüe–Plasencia	d.	...	...	...	...	...	...	1709	...	|	|	...	...	...	...	1938	...	|	...	|
Navalmoral de La Mata	d.	...	...	...	...	...	...	1736	...	|	|	...	...	...	...	2005	...	|	...	|
Talavera de la Reina	d.	...	...	...	...	...	...	1818	...	|	|	...	...	...	...	2041	...	|	...	|
Madrid Estación Sur ✣	a.	...	...	...	...	...	...	|	...	1900	1910	...	...	...	...	|	...	2220	...	0640
Madrid Atocha Cercanías	a.	...	...	...	...	...	...	1938	...	...	...	...	...	...	...	2204	...	...	...	...
Madrid Chamartín ‡	a.	...	...	...	...	...	...	...	...	...	...	...	...	...	...	2218	...	...	...	...

A – 🚌 operated by Avanza, rail tickets not valid; www.avanzabus.com
B – 🚌 operated by Alsa, rail tickets not valid; www.alsa.es

‡ – Full name is Madrid-Chamartín-Clara Campoamor.

✣ – Madrid south bus station close to Méndez Álvaro metro (see Madrid city plan on page 32).
⊠ – Badajoz railway station is 1 km north of Badajoz city centre and Badajoz bus station is 2.5 km south of Badajoz city centre.

ES – Spain (Central European Time).
PT – Portugal (West European Time).

PARIS - HENDAYE / IRÚN - MADRID 47

train type / number			*TGV*	*MD*	*RE*		*IC*	*Alvia*	
train number			**8531**	**18014**	**18318**		**4276**	**4176**	
notes			[R] ⚡	2	2				
			①–⑥				⑦	①–⑥	
			m						
Paris Montparnasse	d.	...	0708	...	...	...	...	...	...
Paris Austerlitz	d.	...	|	...	...	...	...	...	...
Les Aubrais-Orléans	d.	...	|	...	...	...	...	...	...
Bordeaux St Jean	d.	...	0920	...	...	...	...	...	...
Biarritz	d.	...	1105	...	...	...	...	...	...
Hendaye	a.	...	1147	...	...	...	...	...	...
Irún 🏢	a.	...	...	1317	...	1437	...	...	...
San Sebastián / Donostia	a.	...	...	1342	...	1502	1517	1517	...
Vitoria / Gasteiz	a.	...	...	1555	...	...	1657	1657	...
Miranda de Ebro	a.	...	...	1616	...	...	1718	1718	...
Burgos Rosa Manzano	a.	...	...	1715	...	...	1815	1815	...
Valladolid Campo Grande	a.	...	...	1844	1856	...	1903	1903	...
Medina del Campo	a.	...	...	1915	1933	...	|	|	...
Salamanca	a.	...	...	|	2027	...	|	|	...
Ávila	a.	...	...	2001	...	...	|	|	...
Madrid Chamartín	d.	...	...	2142p	...	...	2010	2010	...

train type / number			*RE*	*Alvia*		*TGV*			
train number			**18302**	**4087**		**8544**			
notes			2			[R] ⚡			
Madrid Chamartín	d.	...	...	0843	...	...	...	...	...
Ávila	d.	...	...	|	...	...	...	...	...
Salamanca	d.	...	0715	|	...	...	...	...	...
Medina del Campo	d.	...	0802	|	...	...	...	...	...
Valladolid Campo Grande	d.	...	0828	0949	...	...	...	...	...
Burgos Rosa Manzano	d.	...	...	1037	...	...	...	...	...
Miranda de Ebro	d.	...	...	1137	...	...	...	...	...
Vitoria / Gasteiz	d.	...	...	1158	...	...	...	...	...
San Sebastián / Donostia	d.	...	...	1337	1406	...	...	...	...
Irún	a.	...	...	...	1433	...	...	...	...
Hendaye 🏢	a.	...	...	...	...	1612	...	...	...
Biarritz	a.	...	...	...	...	1639	...	...	...
Bordeaux St Jean	a.	...	...	...	...	1840	...	...	...
Les Aubrais-Orléans	a.	...	...	...	...	|	...	...	...
Paris Austerlitz	a.	...	...	...	...	|	...	...	...
Paris Montparnasse	a.	...	...	...	...	2058	...	...	...

m – Not Apr. 10, May 1, 8, 29, Aug. 15.
p – Madrid **Principe Pio**.
⚡ – Supplement payable.
Alvia – [R] 🍷 ⚡.

FRANKFURT - STRASBOURG - LYON - MARSEILLE 48

train type		*ICE*	*ICE*	*TGV*	*TGV*		*ICE*	*TGV*	*TGV*	
train number		**511**	**9568**	**9877**	**9826**		**107**	**9580**	**9836**	
notes			[R] ★	[R]	[R]			**9581**	[R]	
			Ⓑ h					[R] ★	⚠	
Köln Hbf	d.	0549	...	...	...	...	1255	...	...	...
Frankfurt (Main) Hbf	d.	|	0656	...	...	...	|	1356	...	...
Mannheim	d.	0723	0738	...	...	...	1423	1439	...	...
Karlsruhe	d.	...	0806	...	...	...	...	1512	...	...
Baden-Baden	d.	...	|	...	...	...	...	1535	...	...
Strasbourg	a.	...	0847	...	...	...	...	1602	...	...
Strasbourg	d.	...	...	0904	...	...	...	1615	...	...
Mulhouse	a.	...	...	0956	...	...	...	1705	...	...
Belfort Montbéliard TGV	a.	...	...	1020	...	...	...	1731	...	...
Besançon TGV ⊖	a.	...	...	1043	...	...	...	1755	...	...
Chalon sur Saône	a.	...	...	|	...	...	...	1853	...	...
Lyon Part Dieu	a.	...	...	1300	1410	...	...	1956	2010	...
Avignon TGV	a.	...	...	1425	|	...	...	2109	|	...
Aix en Provence TGV	a.	...	...	1449	|	...	...	2133	|	...
Marseille St Charles	a.	...	...	1506	|	...	...	2148	|	...
Nîmes Centre	a.	...	...	...	|	...	...	...	2135	...
Nîmes Pont-du-Gard	a.	...	...	...	1527	...	...	...	|	...
Montpellier Sud de France	a.	...	...	...	1550	...	...	...	|	...
Montpellier Saint-Roch	a.	...	...	...	...	...	...	...	2202	...

train type		*TGV*	*TGV*	*ICE*	*TGV*	*TGV*	*TGV*	*ICE*	*ICE*	
train number		**9898**	**9583**	**106**	**9862**	**9862**	**5516**	**9563**	**514**	
notes		[R]	**9582**		[R]	[R]	[R]			
			[R] ★		①–⑤	⑥⑦				
Montpellier Saint-Roch	d.	0629	...	...	...	0859	...	...	...	...
Montpellier Sud de France	d.	|	...	...	0912	|	...	...	...	...
Nîmes Pont-du-Gard	d.	|	...	...	0933	|	...	...	...	...
Nîmes Centre	d.	0700	...	...	|	0927	...	...	...	...
Marseille St Charles	d.	|	0812	...	|	|	0946	...	...	...
Aix en Provence TGV	d.	|	0826	...	|	|	1000	...	...	...
Avignon TGV	d.	|	0848	...	|	|	1023	...	...	...
Lyon Part Dieu	d.	0824	1004	...	1050	1050	1132	...	...	...
Chalon sur Saône	d.	...	1106	...	...	...	1244	...	...	...
Besançon TGV ⊖	d.	...	1203	...	...	...	1409	...	...	...
Belfort Montbéliard TGV	d.	...	1227	...	...	...	1433	...	...	...
Mulhouse	d.	...	1254	...	...	...	1459	...	...	...
Strasbourg	a.	...	1343	...	...	...	1554	...	...	...
Strasbourg	d.	...	1355	...	...	...	...	1713	...	...
Baden-Baden	a.	...	1422	...	...	...	...	|	...	...
Karlsruhe	a.	...	1446	...	...	...	...	1753	...	...
Mannheim	a.	...	1518	1536	...	...	...	1818	1836	...
Frankfurt (Main) Hbf	a.	...	1559	|	...	...	...	1859	|	...
Köln Hbf	a.	...	...	1704	...	...	...	...	2004	...

h – Not Apr. 9, 30, May 28.
★ – *Alleo* TGV service. A DB / SNCF joint enterprise.
⚠ – See Table **355** for alterations to service.
⊖ – Full name: Besançon Franche-Comté TGV.

50 OSLO, STOCKHOLM and KØBENHAVN - HAMBURG and BERLIN

train type / train number				*IC*	*ICE*			*1/3*			*Sn*		*IC*	*ICE*									
train number				**393**	**1601**			[R]		**1047**	**519**		**395**	**1605**									
notes				[R]				Ⓑ			①-⑤		[R]										
notes				**Q**				**A**															
Oslo Sentral d.	...	...	...	...	...	...	...	...	...	...	...	...	...	...	...	...	...	...	...	...	...	...	...
Stockholm Central d.	...	...	...	...	...	...	...	2309	...	...	0519	...	...	...	...	...	...	...	...	...	...	...	...
Göteborg d.	...	...	...	...	...	...	...	|	...	0640	|	...	...	...	...	...	...	...	...	...	...	...	...
Malmö C ⊡ d.	...	...	0613	...	...	...	...	0602f	0633	0953	0948	1013	...	...	...	...	...	...	...	...	...	...	...
København H. ⊡ d.	...	...	0649	0726	...	...	...	...	0709	1029	...	1049	1126	...	...	...	...	...	...	...	...	...	...
Odense d.	...	...	...	0840	...	...	...	...	...	...	...	...	1240	...	...	...	...	...	...	...	...	...	...
Kolding d.	...	...	...	0918	...	...	...	...	...	...	...	...	1318	...	...	...	...	...	...	...	...	...	...
Padborg 🏛 d.	...	...	...	1002	...	...	...	...	...	...	...	...	1402	...	...	...	...	...	...	...	...	...	...
Hamburg Hbf a.	...	...	...	1205	1234	...	...	...	...	...	...	...	1602	1634	...	...	...	...	...	...	...	...	...
Berlin Hbf a.	...	...	...	...	1420	...	...	...	...	...	...	...	...	1820	...	...	...	...	...	...	...	...	...

train type / train number		*Sn*	**103**		*Sn*		*IC*	*ICE*	*ICE*		**107**	**111**					**119**			*IC*	*EN*	*EN*	
train number		**525**	**391**	**1079**	**527**		**397**	**609**	**905**		**393**	**395**	**1111**	**1135**	**301**		**397**	**1143**		**399**	**497**	**497**	
notes			①-⑤		**10527**		[R]	Ⓑ			⑥	Ⓑ								[R]			
notes							**Q**	**m**							**D**					**R**	**GP**	**GS**	
Oslo Sentral d.	...	...	0608	...	...	...	...	...	...	...	0808	1010	...	...	...	...	1410	...	...	...	...	...	...
Stockholm Central d.	...	0821	|	...	0922	...	...	...	...	...	|	|	...	...	1623	...	|	...	...	...	1734	1734	...
Göteborg d.	...	|	0945	1040	|	...	...	...	...	...	1145	1345	1440	1740	|	...	1740	1840	...	...	|	|	...
København H. ⊡ d.	...	|	...	|	|	...	...	...	...	...	...	...	|	|	|	...	...	|	...	...	|	|	...
Malmö C ⊡ d.	...	1250	...	1353	1357	1413	...	...	...	...	...	...	1751	2053	2225z	...	...	2153	2233	...	2333	2333	...
København H. ⊡ d.	...	1325	...	1429	...	1449	1526	...	...	...	...	...	...	...	2307h	...	...	2229	2309	0001	0004k	0004k	...
Odense d.	...	...	...	...	...	...	1640	...	...	...	...	...	...	...	|	...	...	...	...	0137	0202	0202	...
Kolding d.	...	...	...	...	...	...	1718	...	...	...	...	...	...	...	|	...	...	...	...	|	|	|	...
Padborg 🏛 d.	...	...	...	...	...	...	1802	...	...	...	...	...	...	...	|	...	...	...	...	0328	|	|	...
Hamburg Hbf a.	...	...	...	...	...	...	2002	2034	2151	...	...	...	...	...	0531	...	...	...	...	0626	0635j	0638	...
Berlin Hbf a.	...	...	...	...	...	...	...	2223	2353	...	...	...	...	...	0847	...	...	...	...	...	...	0900	...

train type		*ICE*	*IC*		*Sn*				*ICE*	*IC*		*Sn*		**2**									
train number		**808**	**396**		**542**	**1082**			**804**	**394**		**542**	**1114**	[R]									
notes		①-⑥	[R]							[R]		Ⓑ		Ⓑ									
notes		**w**	**Q**											**F**									
Berlin Hbf d.	...	0638	...	...	...	...	...	...	1038	...	...	...	...	...	...	...	...	...	...	...	...	...	...
Hamburg Hbf d.	...	0825	0856	...	...	...	...	...	1221	1253	...	...	...	...	...	...	...	...	...	...	...	...	...
Padborg 🏛 a.	...	...	1053	...	...	...	...	...	...	1453	...	...	...	...	...	...	...	...	...	...	...	...	...
Kolding a.	...	...	1140	...	...	...	...	...	...	1540	...	...	...	...	...	...	...	...	...	...	...	...	...
Odense a.	...	...	1218	...	...	...	...	...	...	1618	...	...	...	...	...	...	...	...	...	...	...	...	...
København H. ⊡ d.	...	...	1334	1347	1419	1427	...	...	...	1734	1747	1819	1827	...	...	...	...	...	...	...	...	...	...
Malmö C ⊡ d.	...	...	...	1426	1504	1508	...	...	...	...	1826	1904	1908	2232	...	...	...	...	...	...	...	...	...
København H. ⊡ d.	...	...	...	...	|	|	...	...	...	...	...	|	|	|	...	...	...	...	...	...	...	...	...
Göteborg a.	...	...	...	...	|	1820	...	...	...	...	...	|	2220	|	...	...	...	...	...	...	...	...	...
Stockholm Central a.	...	...	...	...	1937	...	...	...	...	...	...	2341	...	0555	...	...	...	...	...	...	...	...	...
Oslo Sentral a.	...	...	...	...	...	...	...	...	...	...	...	...	...	...	...	...	...	...	...	...	...	...	...

train type / train number			*ICE*	*IC*		*EN*	*EN*		*ICE*	*IC*					**396**								
train number			**800**	**392**		**496**	**496**		**502**	**390**		**300**	**1026**	**300**	**126**								
notes				[R]						**398**													
notes				**Q**		**GP**	**GS**			**T** [R]		**C**		**C**									
Berlin Hbf d.	...	...	1438	...	...	...	1837	...	2138	...	...	2057	...	...	...	...	...	...	...	...	...	...	...
Hamburg Hbf d.	...	...	1621	1654	...	2155j	2150	...	2334	2356	...	2359	...	...	...	...	...	...	...	...	...	...	...
Padborg 🏛 a.	...	...	...	1854	...	|	|	...	...	0302	...	|	...	...	...	...	...	...	...	...	...	...	...
Kolding a.	...	...	...	1940	...	|	|	...	...	|	...	|	...	...	...	...	...	...	...	...	...	...	...
Odense a.	...	...	...	2018	...	0154	0154	...	...	0516	...	|	...	...	...	...	...	...	...	...	...	...	...
København H. ⊡ d.	...	...	...	2134	2147	0347k	0347k	...	...	0700	0707	0647h	...	←	...	...	...	...	...	...	...	...	...
Malmö C ⊡ d.	...	...	...	...	2226	0424	0424	...	...	...	0746	0735	0808	0919	...	...	...	...	...	...	...	...	...
Göteborg a.	...	...	...	...	...	|	|	...	...	...	...	→	1120	|	1415	...	...	...	...	...	...	...	...
Stockholm Central a.	...	...	...	...	...	0955	0955	...	...	...	...	...	...	1410	|	...	...	...	...	...	...	...	...
Oslo Sentral a.	...	...	...	...	...	...	...	...	...	...	...	...	...	...	1743	...	...	...	...	...	...	...	...

A – Ⓑ: 🛏 1,2 cl., ▬ 2 cl., [2] 🍷 [R] Stockholm - Malmö.
C – BERLIN NIGHT EXPRESS Ⓑ Mar. 31 - Nov. 6 (not Apr. 6–9, 30, July 22–31): ▬ 2 cl., 🍷 [R] Berlin - Stockholm. ✕ Malmö - Stockholm. Special fares apply.
D – BERLIN NIGHT EXPRESS Ⓑ Mar. 30 - Nov. 4 (not Apr. 6–9, 30, July 22–31): ▬ 2 cl., 🍷 [R] Stockholm - Berlin. ✕ Stockholm - Malmö. Special fares apply.
F – Ⓑ: 🛏 1,2 cl., ▬ 2 cl., [2] 🍷 [R] Malmö - Stockholm.
G – 🛏 1,2 cl., ▬ 2 cl. (6 berth), [2] 🍷 [R] Stockholm - Hamburg and v.v.
H – HUNGARIA – [12] ✕ Hamburg - Berlin - Praha.
P – Dec. 11 - Apr. 10.
Q – Not June 17 - Aug. 20.
R – Dec. 17 - Jan. 2 (not Dec. 25, Jan. 1).
T – Dec. 16 - Jan. 1 (not Dec. 24, 31).
S – Apr. 11 - Dec. 9.

f – On certain dates arrive 0538. Connection to København depart Malmö C 0613, arrive København 0649.

h – Ørestad (5 km from København).
j – Hamburg **Altona**.
k – København Lufthavn ✈.
m – Not Apr. 7, 9, 30, May 28.
w – Not Apr. 10, May 1, 29.
x – Arrive 0725.
z – Arrive 2115.

Sn – *Snabbtåg* high speed train. [R] ✕.
⊡ – Additional services Malmö - København and v.v. are available, see Table **703**.

52 PRAHA - LINZ - ZÜRICH

	EC	*RJX*	*EC*	*RJX*	*EC*	*RJX*		*EN*	*EN*	
	331	**162**	**333**	**166**	**335**	**760**		**337**	**458**	
	🍷	✕	🍷	✕	🍷	✕		**50466**		
								B	**C**	
Praha hl. n. d.	0621	...	1021	...	1421	...	...	1821	1825	...
Tábor d.	0721	...	1121	...	1521	...	...	1921	|	...
Veselí nad Lužnicí d.	|	...	|	...	|	...	...	|	|	...
České Budějovice d.	0806	...	1206	...	1606	...	...	2006	|	...
Summerau 🏛 d.	0908	...	1308	...	1708	...	...	2108	|	...
Linz Hbf a.	1006	...	1406	...	1806	...	...	2206	|	...
Linz Hbf d.	...	1045	...	1445	...	1845	...	0059	|	...
Salzburg a.	...	1153	...	1553	...	1953	...	0212	|	...
Innsbruck Hbf a.	...	1344	...	1744	...	2144	...	0423	|	...
Zürich HB a.	...	1720	...	2120	...	...	...	0820	0905	...

	RJX	*EC*	*EC*	*RJX*	*EC*	*RJX*	*RJX*	*EC*	*EN*	*EN*
	765	**332**	**163**	**563**	**334**	**165**	**869**	**336**	**459**	**50467**
	✕	🍷	✕	✕	🍷	✕	✕	🍷		**330**
									C	**A**
Zürich HB d.	...	...	0840	...	...	1040	...	...	1959	2140
Innsbruck Hbf d.	0817	...	1211	1217	...	1411	1514	...	|	0128
Salzburg d.	1007	...	...	1407	...	...	1707	...	|	0345
Linz Hbf a.	1115	...	...	1515	...	...	1815	...	|	0452
Linz Hbf d.	...	1154	...	...	1554	...	...	1854	|	0652
Summerau 🏛 a.	...	1250	...	...	1652	...	...	1952	|	0750
České Budějovice a.	...	1352	...	...	1752	...	...	2052	|	0852
Veselí nad Lužnicí a.	...	|	...	...	|	...	...	2120	|	|
Tábor a.	...	1437	...	...	1837	...	...	2137	|	0937
Praha hl. n. a.	...	1539	...	...	1939	...	...	2240	0935	1039

A – *EuroNight* 🛏 1,2 cl. Zürich (*EN* **50467**) - Linz (**330**) - Praha (not May 3–29). [12] 🍷 Linz - Praha.
B – *EuroNight* 🛏 1,2 cl. Praha (**337** / *EN* **50466**) - Linz - Zürich (not May 2–28). [12] 🍷 Praha - Linz.
C – *EuroNight* 🛏 1,2 cl., ▬ 2 cl. (4, 6 berth), [2] Zürich - Dresden - Praha and v.v. (Table **54**).

f – ⚒.

RJX – ÖBB *Railjet* service. [1] (premium class), [1] (first class), [2] (economy class), ✕.

HAMBURG / DÜSSELDORF / BRUSSELS - NÜRNBERG - INNSBRUCK / WIEN 53

		NJ 491	NJ 40491	NJ 425 ①③⑤	NJ 40421	NJ 421	
		C	D	G	A	B	
Hamburg Altona	d.	2011	2011	...	...	...	...
Hamburg Hbf	d.	2029	2029	...	...	...	...
Hannover Hbf	d.	2157	2157	...	...	...	...
Göttingen	d.	2259	2259	...	...	...	...
Amsterdam Centraal	d.	|	|	...	1930	1930	...
Utrecht Centraal	d.	|	|	...	2003	2003	...
Arnhem	d.	|	|	...	2037	2037	...
Duisburg Hbf	d.	|	|	...	|	|	...
Düsseldorf Hbf	d.	|	|	...	2143	2143	...
Brussels Midi/Zuid	d.	|	|	1932	|	|	...
Liège Guillemins	d.	|	|	2033	|	|	...
Aachen 🏛	d.	|	|	2139	|	|	...
Köln Hbf	d.	|	|	|	2216	2216	...
Bonn Hbf	d.	|	|	2311	2311	2311	...
Koblenz Hbf	d.	|	|	2346	2346	2346	...
Mainz Hbf	d.	|	|	0056	0056	0056	...
Frankfurt Flughafen ✈	d.	|	|	0120	0120	0120	...
Frankfurt (Main) Süd	d.	|	|	0131	0131	0131	...
Würzburg Hbf	d.	0135	0135	0242	0242	0242	...
Nürnberg Hbf	a.	0253	0253	0336	0336	0336	...
Nürnberg Hbf	d.	0408	0435	0408	0408	0435	...
Regensburg Hbf	a.	0505	|	0505	0505	|	...
Augsburg Hbf	a.	|	0623	|	|	0623	...
München Hbf	a.	|	0711	|	|	0711	...
Kufstein 🏛	a.	|	0826	|	|	0826	...
Wörgl Hbf	a.	|	0837	|	|	0837	...
Jenbach	a.	|	0853	|	|	0853	...
Innsbruck Hbf	a.	|	0914	|	|	0914	...
Passau 🏛	a.	0613	...	0613	0613	...	...
Wels Hbf	a.	0714	...	0714	0714	...	...
Linz Hbf	a.	0746	...	0746	0746	...	...
St Pölten Hbf	a.	0842	...	0842	0842	...	...
Wien Meidling	a.	0911	...	0911	0911	...	...
Wien Hbf	a.	0919	...	0919	0919	...	...

		NJ 40490	NJ 490	NJ 50490 ②④⑦	NJ 420	NJ 40420
		Q	C	K	P	D
Wien Hbf	d.	2013	2013	2013	...	...
Wien Meidling	d.	2021	2021	2021	...	...
St Pölten Hbf	d.	2047	2047	2047	...	...
Linz Hbf	d.	2136	2136	2136	...	...
Wels Hbf	d.	2150	2150	2150	...	...
Passau 🏛	d.	2253	2253	2253	...	...
Innsbruck Hbf	d.	|	|	|	2044	2044
Jenbach	d.	|	|	|	2106	2106
Wörgl Hbf	d.	|	|	|	2123	2123
Kufstein 🏛	d.	|	|	|	2135	2135
München Hbf	d.	|	|	|	2250	2250
Augsburg Hbf	d.	|	|	|	2323	2323
Regensburg Hbf	d.	2356	2356	2356	|	|
Nürnberg Hbf	a.	0056	0056	0056	0052	0052
Nürnberg Hbf	d.	0141	0151	0141	0141	0151
Würzburg Hbf	a.	|	0247	|	|	0247
Frankfurt (Main) Süd	a.	0345	|	0345	0345	|
Frankfurt Flughafen ✈	a.	0356	|	0356	0356	|
Mainz Hbf	a.	0416	|	0416	0416	|
Koblenz Hbf	a.	0511	|	0511	0511	|
Bonn Hbf	a.	0558	|	0558	0558	|
Köln Hbf	a.	0651	|	|	0651	|
Aachen 🏛	a.	|	|	0722	|	|
Liège Guillemins	a.	|	|	0848	|	|
Brussels Midi/Zuid	a.	|	|	0952	|	|
Düsseldorf Hbf	a.	0723	|	...	0723	|
Duisburg Hbf	a.	0740	|	...	0740	|
Arnhem	a.	0851	|	...	0851	...
Utrecht Centraal	a.	0929	|	...	0929	...
Amsterdam Centraal	a.	0959	|	...	0959	...
Göttingen	a.	...	0551	...	...	0551
Hannover Hbf	a.	...	0649	...	...	0649
Hamburg Hbf	a.	...	0847	...	...	0847
Hamburg Altona	a.	...	0904	...	...	0904

NOTES FOR TABLES 53 AND 54

A – ÖBB nightjet 🛏 1,2 cl., ▬ 2 cl. (4,6 berth), [2] Amsterdam - Wien. ♣.
B – ÖBB nightjet 🛏 1,2 cl., ▬ 2 cl. (4,6 berth), [2] Amsterdam - Innsbruck. ♣.
C – ÖBB nightjet 🛏 1,2 cl., ▬ 2 cl. (4,6 berth), [2] Hamburg - Wien and v.v. ♣.
D – ÖBB nightjet 🛏 1,2 cl., ▬ 2 cl. (4,6 berth), [2] Hamburg - Innsbruck and v.v. ♣.
G – ①③⑤: ÖBB nightjet 🛏 1,2 cl., ▬ 2 cl. (4,6 berth), [2] Brussels - Wien. ♣.
H – CANOPUS 🛏 1,2 cl., ▬ 2 cl. (4,6 berth), [2] Zürich - Praha and v.v.
Also conveys [1] ✕ Leipzig - Praha and v.v.
K – ②④⑦: ÖBB nightjet 🛏 1,2 cl., ▬ 2 cl. (4,6 berth), [2] Wien - Brussels. ♣.
P – ÖBB nightjet 🛏 1,2 cl., ▬ 2 cl. (4,6 berth), [2] Innsbruck - Amsterdam. ♣.
Q – ÖBB nightjet 🛏 1,2 cl., ▬ 2 cl. (4,6 berth), [2] Wien - Amsterdam. ♣.
R – ÖBB nightjet 🛏 1,2 cl., ▬ 2 cl. (4,6 berth), [2] Hamburg - Zürich and v.v. ♣.
S – ÖBB nightjet 🛏 1,2 cl., ▬ 2 cl. (4,6 berth), [2] Berlin - Zürich and v.v. ♣.

♣ – Special fares apply.

ZÜRICH - BASEL - HAMBURG / BERLIN / PRAHA 54

		EN 458 40458	NJ 408	NJ 471
		H	S	R
Praha hl. n.	d.	1826	...	...
Dresden Hbf	d.	2110	...	...
Hamburg Altona	d.	|	...	2152
Hamburg Hbf	d.	|	...	2207
Berlin Hbf	d.	|	2051	|
Berlin Südkreuz	d.	|	2101	|
Halle (Salle) Hbf	d.	|	2228	|
Leipzig Hbf	d.	2346	2346	|
Hannover Hbf	d.	|	|	0030
Fulda	d.	0247	0247	|
Frankfurt (Main) Süd	a.	|	|	0432
Frankfurt (Main) Hbf	a.	0346	0346	|
Mannheim Hbf	a.	0439	0439	|
Karlsruhe Hbf	a.	0507	0507	0602
Baden-Baden	a.	0526	0526	|
Offenburg	a.	0545	0545	0637
Freiburg (Brsg) Hbf	a.	0617	0617	0721
Basel Bad Bf 🏛	a.	0656	0656	0759
Basel SBB	a.	0720	0720	0810
Zürich HB	a.	0905	0905	1005

		NJ 409	EN 459 40459	NJ 470
		S	H	R
Zürich HB	d.	1959	1959	2059
Basel SBB	d.	2113	2113	2213
Basel Bad Bf 🏛	d.	2122	2122	2222
Freiburg (Brsg) Hbf	d.	2158	2158	2258
Offenburg	d.	2231	2231	2333
Baden-Baden	d.	|	|	2354
Karlsruhe Hbf	d.	2307	2307	0019
Mannheim Hbf	d.	2342	2342	|
Frankfurt (Main) Hbf	d.	0052	0052	|
Frankfurt (Main) Süd	d.	|	|	0214
Fulda	a.	0148	0148	|
Hannover Hbf	a.	|	|	0529
Leipzig Hbf	a.	0448	0448	|
Halle (Salle) Hbf	a.	0537	|	|
Berlin Südkreuz	a.	0713	|	|
Berlin Hbf	a.	0720	|	|
Hamburg Hbf	a.	...	|	0754
Hamburg Altona	a.	...	|	0810
Dresden Hbf	a.	...	0705	...
Praha hl. n.	a.	...	0938	...

FRANKFURT - LEIPZIG - DRESDEN - PRAHA 55

train type			EC				EC	ICE		EC	ICE		EC	ICE		EC	ICE		EC		EN	
train number			171				253	1555		379	1557		175	1559		177	1651		179		459	
notes			✕ D				✕ H	✕		✕ D	✕		✕ F	✕		✕ D	✕		✕		P	
Frankfurt (Main) Hbf	d.	...	...	...	...	...	...	0716	...	...	0919	...	...	1119	...	...	1319	...	...	...	0052	...
Fulda	d.	...	...	...	...	...	...	0814	...	...	1015	...	...	1215	...	...	1416	...	...	...	0150	...
Erfurt Hbf	d.	...	...	...	...	...	...	0940	...	...	1140	...	...	1340	...	...	1540	...	...	...	0316	...
Leipzig Hbf	d.	...	0700	...	...	0900	...	1031	1100	...	1231	1300	...	1431	1500	...	1631	1700	...	...	0545	...
Dresden Hbf	d.	...	0841	0910	...	1041	1110	1138	1241	1310	1338	1441	1510	1538	1641	1710	1738	1841	1910	...	0708	...
Bad Schandau 🏛 ◧	d.	...	...	0936	...	...	1136	...	...	1336	...	...	1536	...	...	1736	...	...	1936	...	0733	...
Děčín 🏛 ◧	d.	...	...	1002	...	...	1202	...	...	1402	...	...	1602	...	...	1802	...	...	2002	...	0802	...
Praha Holešovice	a.	...	...	1125	...	...	1322	...	...	1525	...	...	1725	...	...	1925	...	...	2125	...	0925	...
Praha hl. n.	a.	...	...	1135	...	...	...	...	...	1535	...	...	1735	...	...	1935	...	...	2135	...	0935	...

train type		EC		ICE	EC		ICE	EC		ICE	EC		ICE	EC		ICE	EC		ICE		EN	
train number		178		1650	176		1558	174		1556	378		1554	172		1552	170		1550		458	
notes		✕		✕	✕ D		✕	✕ F		✕	✕ D		✕	✕ H		✕	✕ D		✕ Ⓑf		P	
Praha hl. n.	d.	0625	...	...	0825	...	...	1025	...	...	1225	...	...	1425	...	...	1625	...	...	...	1825	...
Praha Holešovice	d.	0634	...	...	0834	...	...	1034	...	...	1234	...	...	1434	...	...	1634	...	...	...	1834	...
Děčín 🏛 ◧	d.	0801	...	...	1001	...	...	1201	...	...	1401	...	...	1601	...	...	1801	...	...	...	2001	...
Bad Schandau 🏛 ◧	d.	0822	...	...	1022	...	...	1222	...	...	1422	...	...	1622	...	...	1822	...	...	...	2021	...
Dresden Hbf	d.	0852	0906	1010	1052	1106	1210	1252	1306	1410	1452	1506	1610	1652	1706	1810	1852	1906	...	...	2110	...
Leipzig Hbf	d.	...	1050	1133	...	1250	1333	...	1450	1533	...	1650	1733	...	1850	1933	...	2050	2133	...	2346	...
Erfurt Hbf	d.	...	...	1218	...	...	1418	...	...	1618	...	...	1818	...	...	2018	...	...	2218	...	0124	...
Fulda	d.	...	...	1343	...	...	1543	...	...	1743	...	...	1943	...	...	2143	...	...	2343	...	0247	...
Frankfurt (Main) Hbf	a.	...	...	1436	...	...	1636	...	...	1836	...	...	2036	...	...	2236	...	...	0040	...	0346	...

D – [12] ✕ Berlin - Dresden - Praha and v.v.
F – [12] ✕ Flensburg - Dresden - Praha and v.v.
H – HUNGARIA – [12] ✕ Hamburg - Dresden - Praha - Budapest and v.v.
P – 🛏 1,2 cl., ▬ 2 cl. (4,6 berth), [2] Praha - Frankfurt - Zürich and v.v. See Table **54**.
f – Not Apr. 7, 9, 30, May 28.
◧ – Ticketing point is Schöna.

56 LONDON / PARIS - KÖLN - BERLIN - WARSZAWA - KYIV / MOSKVA

train type	*EC*	*ICE*	*EC*		*ICE*	*EC*	*ICE*	*EC*	*ICE*	*EC*	*IE*	*ICE*	*EC*	*ICE*	*ICE*	*EC*	☆	⇌	*ICE*	*ICE*	*EC*	⇌	☆	*ICE*	*ICE*
train number	**41**	**541**	**45**	**68*LJ***	**843**	**57**	**553**	**47**	**855**	**59**	**11**	**555**	**49**	**13**	**557**	**247**	**9106**	**9315**	**15**	**559**	**249**	**9423**	**9116**	**315**	**651**
notes	①–⑥	①–⑥	**T**	**12011**		**W**		**B T**		**N**			**T**			**T**	①–⑤				Ⓑ				
	T f w	**f**		**C**													**k**				**T g**				
London St Pancras d.	...	...	...	...	...	...	...	...	...	...	...	...	...	...	...	...	0616	...	...	...	...	...	0855	...	...
Paris Nord d.	...	...	...	...	...	...	...	...	...	...	...	...	...	...	...	...	|	0825j	...	...	...	0955	|	...	...
Paris Est d.	...	...	...	...	...	...	...	...	...	...	...	...	...	...	...	...	|	|	...	...	...	|	|	...	...
Brussels Midi/Zuid d.	...	...	...	...	...	...	...	...	...	...	0623	...	...	0823	...	...	0912	0947	1025	...	...	1117	1205	1225	...
Liège Guillemins d.	...	...	...	...	...	...	...	...	...	...	0712	...	...	0914	...	...	...	...	1114	...	...	...	...	1314	...
Aachen ⊞ d.	...	...	...	...	...	...	...	...	...	...	0739	...	...	0939	...	...	...	...	1139	...	...	...	...	1339	...
Köln Hbf a.	...	...	...	...	...	...	...	...	...	...	0816	...	...	1015	...	...	...	...	1215	...	...	...	...	1415	...
Köln Hbf d.	...	0426	...	...	0542	...	0648	...	0748	...	...	0848	...	...	1045	...	...	...	...	1248	...	...	...	...	1448
Bielefeld Hbf d.	...	0640	...	...	0738	...	0838	...	0938	...	...	1038	...	...	1238	...	...	...	...	1438	...	...	...	...	1638
Hannover Hbf d.	...	0731	...	...	0831	...	0931	...	1031	...	...	1131	...	...	1331	...	...	...	...	1531	...	...	...	...	1731
Berlin Hbf a.	...	0915	...	...	1015	...	1115	...	1215	...	...	1315	...	...	1515	...	...	...	...	1715	...	...	...	...	1915
Berlin Hbf d.	0552	...	0951	...	...	1052	...	1152	...	1252	...	...	1351	...	...	1552	...	...	...	...	1752	...	...	...	...
Berlin Ostbahnhof d.	0601	...	1003	...	...	1103	...	1203	...	1303	...	...	1403	...	...	1603	...	...	...	...	1803	...	...	...	...
Frankfurt (Oder) ⊞ d.	0649	...	1049	...	...	1149	...	1249	...	1349	...	...	1449	...	...	1649	...	...	...	...	1849	...	...	...	...
Rzepin d.	0710	...	1110	...	...	1208	...	1310	...	1410	...	...	1510	...	...	1710	...	...	...	...	1910	...	...	...	...
Poznań Gł. d.	0837	...	1236	...	...	...	...	1440	...	1532	...	...	1642	...	...	1837	...	...	...	...	2037	...	...	...	...
Warszawa Centralna a.	1139t	...	1533t	...	...	...	...	1722	...	...	...	...	1942t	...	...	2129t	...	...	...	...	|	...	...	...	...
Warszawa Wschodnia d.	1201t	...	1551t	1754	...	...	...	1746	...	...	...	...	1956t	...	...	2138t	...	...	...	...	2342t	...	...	...	...
Terespol a.	...	...	...	|	...	...	...	...	...	...	...	...	...	...	...	...	...	...	...	...	...	...	...	...	...
Brest Tsentralny ⊞ a.	...	...	...	|	...	...	...	...	...	...	...	...	...	...	...	...	...	...	...	...	...	...	...	...	...
Lublin a.	...	...	...	1949	...	...	...	...	...	...	...	...	...	...	...	...	...	...	...	...	...	...	...	...	...
Kyiv a.	...	...	...	1307	...	...	...	...	...	...	...	...	...	...	...	...	...	...	...	...	...	...	...	...	...
Minsk a.	...	...	...	...	...	...	...	...	...	...	...	...	...	...	...	...	...	...	...	...	...	...	...	...	...
Orsha Tsentralnaya § a.	...	...	...	...	...	...	...	...	...	...	...	...	...	...	...	...	...	...	...	...	...	...	...	...	...
Smolensk Tsentralny ⊞ § a.	...	...	...	...	...	...	...	...	...	...	...	...	...	...	...	...	...	...	...	...	...	...	...	...	...
Moskva Belorusskaya ‡ a.	...	...	...	...	...	...	...	...	...	...	...	...	...	...	...	...	...	...	...	...	...	...	...	...	...

train type/number	*ICE*	⇌	*EC*	*ICE*	*ICE*	⇌	*EC*	*ICE*	*ICE*	⇌	☆	*EC*	*ICE*	*ICE*	*EC*	*ICE*	*EC*	*ICE*	*ICE*	*EC*	*ICE*		*EC*	*ICE*	*EC*
train number	**954**	**9448**	**248**	**650**	**14**	**9370**	**246**	**558**	**12**	**9382**	**9167**	**48**	**556**	**10**	**58**	**856**	**46**	**554**	**318**	**56**	**844**	**67*KJ***	**44**	**552**	**40**
notes			①–⑥			Ⓑ					Ⓑ								⑦**q**			**21010**			Ⓑ
			T f				**T**					**T**			**N**		**B T**			**W**		**C**	**T**		**T g m**
Moskva Belorusskaya ‡ d.	...	...	...	...	...	...	...	...	...	...	...	...	...	...	...	...	...	...	...	...	...	...	...	...	...
Smolensk Tsentralny ⊞ § d.	...	...	...	...	...	...	...	...	...	...	...	...	...	...	...	...	...	...	...	...	...	...	...	...	...
Orsha Tsentralnaya § d.	...	...	...	...	...	...	...	...	...	...	...	...	...	...	...	...	...	...	...	...	...	...	...	...	...
Minsk d.	...	...	...	...	...	...	...	...	...	...	...	...	...	...	...	...	...	...	...	...	...	...	...	...	...
Kyiv d.	...	...	...	...	...	...	...	...	...	...	...	...	...	...	...	...	...	...	...	...	...	1814z	...	...	...
Lublin d.	...	...	...	...	...	...	...	...	...	...	...	...	...	...	...	...	...	...	...	...	...	0823	...	...	...
Brest Tsentralny ⊞ d.	...	...	...	...	...	...	...	...	...	...	...	...	...	...	...	...	...	...	...	...	...	|	...	...	...
Terespol d.	...	...	...	...	...	...	...	...	...	...	...	...	...	...	...	...	...	...	...	...	...	|	...	...	...
Warszawa Wschodnia a.	...	...	0404	...	...	...	0539	...	...	...	...	0809t	...	...	...	...	1014	...	...	...	...	1012	1214t	...	1549t
Warszawa Centralna d.	...	...	0415	...	...	...	0556	...	...	...	...	0827t	...	...	...	...	1025	...	...	...	...	...	1225t	...	1604t
Poznań Gł. d.	...	...	0726	...	...	...	0922	...	...	...	...	1126	...	...	1226	...	1325	...	...	...	...	...	1526	...	1926
Rzepin d.	...	...	0850	...	...	...	1050	...	...	...	...	1250	...	...	1350	...	1450	...	...	1547	...	...	1650	...	2050
Frankfurt (Oder) ⊞ a.	...	...	0909	...	...	...	1109	...	...	...	...	1309	...	...	1409	...	1509	...	...	1609	...	...	1709	...	2109
Berlin Ostbahnhof a.	...	...	0955	...	...	...	1155	...	...	...	...	1355	...	...	1455	...	1555	...	...	1655	...	...	1755	...	2157
Berlin Hbf a.	...	...	1005	...	...	...	1207	...	...	...	...	1405	...	...	1505	...	1605	...	...	1705	...	...	1807	...	2205
Berlin Hbf d.	0746	...	▬	1046	...	...	▬	1246	...	...	...	...	1446	...	...	1546	...	1646	...	...	1746	...	...	1846	...
Hannover Hbf a.	0928	...	...	1228	...	...	...	1428	...	...	...	...	1628	...	...	1728	...	1828	...	...	1928	...	...	2028	...
Bielefeld Hbf a.	1020	...	...	1320	...	...	...	1520	...	...	...	...	1720	...	...	1820	...	1920	...	...	2020	...	...	2120	...
Köln Hbf a.	1209	...	...	1509	...	...	...	1709	...	...	...	...	1909	...	...	2009	...	2111	...	...	2209	...	...	2313	...
Köln Hbf d.	...	1243	☆	...	1540	...	...	...	1741	...	...	...	...	1940	...	...	...	...	2142	...	...	...	...	...	...
Aachen ⊞ a.	...	1316	**9145**	...	1616	...	☆	...	1816	...	...	...	...	2016	...	...	...	...	2215	...	...	...	...	...	...
Liège Guillemins a.	...	1344	Ⓑ	...	1644	...	**9157**	...	1844	...	...	...	...	2044	...	...	...	...	2244	...	...	...	...	...	...
Brussels Midi/Zuid a.	...	1435	1556	...	1735	1813	1851	...	1935	2016	2056	...	...	2135	...	...	...	...	2335	...	...	...	...	...	...
Paris Est a.	...	|	|	...	...	|	|	...	...	|	|	...	...	...	...	...	...	...	...	...	...	...	...	...	...
Paris Nord a.	...	1605	|	...	...	1935	|	...	...	2138	|	...	...	...	...	...	...	...	...	...	...	...	...	...	...
London St Pancras a.	...	...	1657	...	...	...	2000	...	...	...	2157	...	...	...	...	...	...	...	...	...	...	...	...	...	...

A – From Mar. 12.

B – From June 11.

C – KYIV EKSPRES / KIEV EXPRESS – 🛏 1, 2 cl. Warszawa - Kyiv and v.v.

N – BERLIN GDANSK EXPRESS / GEDANIA (12) ✕ Ⓡ Berlin - Poznań - Gdynia and v.v.

T – BERLIN WARSZAWA EXPRESS – (12) ✕ Ⓡ Berlin - Warszawa and v.v.

W – WAWEL – (12) ✕ Ⓡ Berlin - Wrocław - Krakow - Przemyśl and v.v.

f – Not Apr. 10.

g – Not Apr. 9.

j – 0807 on ⑦.

k – Not Apr. 10, May 1.

m – Also calls at Berlin Ostkreuz 2151.

q – Also Apr. 10, May 1, 29; not Apr. 9, 30, May 28.

t – From Mar. 10 does not call at Warszawa Centralna and Warszawa Wschodnia. From Mar. 10 calls at Warszawa Gdańska. See Table **1001** for timings.

w – Also calls at Berlin Ostkreuz 0606.

z – Passengers may be required to board the train earlier for customs and passport control.

§ – ⊞: Osinovka (BY) / Krasnoye (RU).

‡ – Also known as Moskva **Smolenskaya** station.

☆ – Eurostar train. Special fares payable. ✕ in Business Premier and Standard Premier, 🍸 in Standard. Additional services are shown on Table **10**. See shaded panel in Table **10** on page 47 for information about recommended arrival times at departure station. Valid Feb. 5 - May 20.

⇌ – *Thalys* high-speed train. Ⓡ 🍸. Three classes of service: Premium, Comfort and Standard. Special fares payable. Valid Dec. 11 - Mar. 18.

57 BERLIN - GDYNIA

	EC/IC			*IC/EC*	
	59			**58**	
	75000			**57000**	
	Ⓡ			Ⓡ	
	G			**G**	
Berlin Hbf d.	1252	...	**Gdynia** Gł. d.	0906	...
Berlin Ost d.	1303	...	Sopot d.	0915	...
Frankfurt (Oder) ⊞ d.	1349	...	**Gdańsk** Gł. d.	0932	...
Rzepin a.	1407	...	Tczew d.	0949	...
Poznań Gł. a.	1532	...	Bydgoszcz Gł. d.	1055	...
Gniezno a.	1605	...	Inowrocław d.	1121	...
Inowrocław a.	1634	...	Gniezno d.	1151	...
Bydgoszcz Gł. a.	1700	...	**Poznań** Gł. d.	1226	...
Tczew a.	1808	...	Rzepin d.	1350	...
Gdańsk Gł. a.	1824	...	Frankfurt (Oder) ⊞ a.	1409	...
Sopot a.	1841	...	**Berlin** Ost a.	1455	...
Gdynia Gł. a.	1852	...	**Berlin** Hbf a.	1505	...

G – GEDANIA (12) ✕ Ⓡ Berlin - Poznań - Gdynia and v.v.

58 BERLIN - WROCŁAW

	IRE	*EC/IC*	*IRE*	*NJ*		*IC/EC*	*IRE*	*IRE*	*NJ*
	5837	**57**	**5839**	**457**		**56**	**5836**	**5838**	**456**
	69020	**73000**	**69022**	**14010**		**37000**	**69005**	**69007**	**47010**
	K B	**W**	**K A**	**M**		**W**	**K C**	**K A**	**M**
Berlin Hbf. d.	...	1052	...	1843	**Wrocław** Gł. d.	1309	1733	2019	0538
Berlin Lichtenberg d.	0743	|	1443	|	Legnica d.	1344	1815	2103	0616
Berlin Ostkreuz d.	0748	|	1448	|	Zagań d.	|	|	|	|
Cottbus d.	0932	|	1632	|	Záry d.	|	|	|	|
Forst ⊞ a.	|	|	|	|	Tuplice d.	|	|	|	|
Forst ⊞ d.	|	|	|	|	Forst ⊞ a.	|	|	|	|
Tuplice d.	|	|	|	|	Forst ⊞ d.	|	|	|	|
Záry a.	|	|	|	|	**Cottbus** a.	|	2026	2303	|
Zagań a.	|	|	|	|	**Berlin** Ostkreuz a.	|	2152	0050	|
Legnica a.	1141	1416	1843	2208	**Berlin** Lichtenberg a.	|	2158	0055	|
Wrocław Gł. a.	1229	1450	1937	2243	**Berlin** Hbf. a.	1705	...	...	0951

A – Dec. 16, 23, 30.

B – Dec. 17, 24, 31.

C – Dec. 11, 18, 26, Jan. 1.

K – KULTURZUG / POCIAG DO KULTURY - (2) Berlin - Wrocław and v.v. For International journeys only. Special fares apply. Service suspended temporarily but may resume from April.

M – *ÖBB nightjet* METROPOL – 🛏 1, 2 cl., ▬ 2 cl., (2) Berlin - Wrocław - Wien and v.v. (Table **77**).

W – WAWEL – (12) ✕ Ⓡ Berlin - Wrocław - Krakow - Przemyśl and v.v.

HAMBURG - BERLIN - PRAHA - WIEN / BUDAPEST 60

train type	EC	RJ	EC		RJ	EC	RJ	EC	EC	RJ	EC	EC	RJ	EC		EC	RJ	EC	EC	RJ	EC	EC	RJ
train number	271	71	273	1031	73	275	75	277	459	259	279	171	79	131	1035	173	371	281	379	373	283	175	375
notes	✕	✕ ⚒	✕	🍷 ♥	✕	✕	✕	✕	✕ M	✕	✕	✕	✕	✕ V	🍷 ♥	✕ L	✕	✕	✕ H	✕	✕	✕ J	✕
Hamburg Altona d.	...	...	...	...	...	...	...	...	...	...	...	...	...	...	...	0635	...	...	...	...	...	...	...
Hamburg Hbf d.	...	...	...	...	...	...	...	...	...	...	...	...	...	...	...	0648	...	...	0851	...	...	1051	...
Berlin Hbf d.	...	...	...	...	...	...	...	...	...	...	...	0716	...	...	...	0901	...	...	1116	...	...	1316	...
Berlin Südkreuz d.	...	...	...	...	...	...	...	...	...	...	...	0723	...	...	...	0908	...	...	1123	...	...	1323	...
Dresden Hbf d.	...	...	...	...	...	...	...	...	0708	...	...	0910	...	...	...	1110	...	...	1310	...	...	1510	...
Bad Schandau 🏛 ⊖ d.	...	...	...	...	...	...	...	...	0733	...	...	0936	...	...	...	1136	...	...	1336	...	...	1536	...
Děčín d.	...	...	...	...	...	...	...	...	0802	...	...	1002	...	...	...	1202	...	...	1402	...	...	1602	...
Ústí nad Labem hl. n. d.	...	...	...	...	...	...	...	...	0819	...	...	1019	...	...	...	1219	...	...	1419	...	...	1619	...
Praha Holešovice a.	...	...	...	...	...	...	...	...	0925	...	...	1125	...	...	...	1325	...	...	1525	...	...	1725	...
Praha hl. n. a.	...	...	...	...	...	...	...	...	0938	...	...	1135	...	...	...	1335	...	...	1535	...	...	1735	...
Praha hl. n. d.	...	0412	0512	0538	0612	0712	0812	0912	...	1024	1112	...	1212	...	1238	1345	1412	1512	...	1612	1712	...	1812
Pardubice d.	...	|	|	|	|	|	|	|	...	|	|	...	|	...	|	1446	|	|	...	|	|	...	|
Brno hl. n. d.	0622	0722	0822	0848	0922	1022	1122	1222	...	1322	1422	...	1522	...	1548	1622	1722	1822	...	1922	2022	...	2122
Břeclav a.	0652	0752	0852	0918	0952	1052	1152	1252	...	1352	1452	...	1552	...	1618	1652	1752	1852	...	1952	2052	...	2152
Břeclav d.	0655	0755	0855	0920	0955	1055	1155	1255	...	1355	1455	...	1555	1555	1620	1655	1755	1855	...	1955	2055	...	2155
Wien Hbf a.	|	0849	|	1021	1049	|	1249	|	...	1449	|	...	1649	|	1721	|	1849	|	...	2049	|	...	2249
Wien Meidling a.	|	0903	|	1032	1103	|	1303	|	...	1503	|	...	1703	|	1732	|	1903	|	...	2103	|	...	...
Wiener Neustadt Hbf a.	|	0928	|	|	1128	|	1328	|	...	1530	|	...	1728	|	|	|	1928	|	...	2128	|	...	...
Graz Hbf a.	|	1133	|	|	1333	|	1533	|	...	1734	|	...	1933	|	|	|	2133	|	...	2333	|	...	...
Kúty 🏛 a.	0711	...	0911	|	...	1111	...	1311	...	...	1511	...	...	1611	|	1711	...	1911	...	...	2111	...	...
Bratislava hl. st. a.	0754	...	0954	|	...	1154	...	1354	...	...	1554	...	...	1701	|	1754	...	1954	...	...	2154	...	...
Štúrovo 🏛 △ a.	0924	...	1124	◐	...	1324	...	1524	...	...	1724	...	...	1836	◐	1924	...	2124	...	...	...	...	...
Budapest Nyugati a.	1028	...	1228	|	...	1428	...	1628	...	...	1828	...	...	1949	|	2028	...	2228	...	...	...	...	...
Budapest Déli a.	...	...	...	1314	...	...	...	...	...	...	...	...	...	...	2014	...	...	...	...	...	...	...	...

train type	EC	EC	EN	NJ	NJ			
train number	177	179	575	40457	457			
notes	✕	✕	477 B	477 S	R			
Hamburg Altona d.	...	...	...	...	...	...	...	...
Hamburg Hbf d.	...	...	...	...	...	...	...	...
Berlin Hbf d.	1516	1716	...	1843	1843	...	...	...
Berlin Südkreuz d.	1523	1723	...	|	|	...	...	...
Dresden Hbf d.	1710	1910	...	|	|	...	...	...
Bad Schandau 🏛 ⊖ d.	1736	1936	...	|	|	...	...	...
Děčín d.	1802	2002	...	◧	◧	...	...	...
Ústí nad Labem hl. n. d.	1819	2019	...	|	|	...	...	...
Praha Holešovice a.	1925	2125	...	|	|	...	...	...
Praha hl. n. a.	1935	2135	...	|	|	...	...	...
Praha hl. n. d.	...	...	2234	|	|	...	...	...
Pardubice d.	...	...	|	|	|	...	...	...
Brno hl. n. d.	...	...	0141	|	|	...	...	...
Břeclav a.	...	...	0211	0410	0410	...	...	...
Břeclav d.	...	...	0502	0502	0549	...	...	...
Wien Hbf a.	...	...	|	|	0700	...	...	...
Wien Meidling a.	...	...	|	|	|	...	...	...
Wiener Neustadt Hbf a.	...	...	|	|	0751	...	...	...
Graz Hbf a.	...	...	|	|	1002	...	...	...
Kúty 🏛 a.	...	...	0511	0511	...	...	...	...
Bratislava hl. st. a.	...	...	0554	0554	...	...	...	...
Štúrovo 🏛 △ a.	...	...	0724	0724	...	...	...	...
Budapest Nyugati a.	...	...	0829	0829	...	...	...	...

train type/number	EC	EC	EC	EC	RJ	EC	EC	EC	
train number	178	176	174	282	70	104	378	280	
notes	✕	✕	✕ K	✕	✕	✕	✕ G	✕	
Budapest Nyugati d.	...	...	...	...	...	...	...	0529	...
Štúrovo 🏛 △ d.	...	...	...	...	...	...	...	0634	...
Bratislava hl. st. d.	...	...	...	0606	...	...	...	0806	...
Kúty 🏛 d.	...	...	...	0649	...	...	...	0849	...
Graz Hbf d.	...	...	...	|	...	0528	...	|	...
Wiener Neustadt Hbf d.	...	...	...	|	...	0730	...	|	...
Wien Meidling d.	...	...	...	|	...	0757	...	|	...
Wien Hbf d.	...	...	...	|	0710	0810	...	|	...
Břeclav a.	...	...	...	0704	0804	0904	...	0904	...
Břeclav d.	...	...	...	0707	0807	...	...	0907	...
Brno hl. n. d.	...	...	...	0738	0838	...	...	0938	...
Pardubice d.	...	...	...	|	|	...	...	|	...
Praha hl. n. a.	...	...	...	1042	1142	...	...	1242	...
Praha hl. n. d.	0625	0825	1025	...	...	...	1225	...	...
Praha Holešovice d.	0634	0834	1034	...	...	...	1234	...	...
Ústí nad Labem hl. n. d.	0739	0939	1139	...	...	...	1339	...	...
Děčín d.	0801	1001	1201	...	...	...	1401	...	...
Bad Schandau 🏛 ⊖ a.	0820	1020	1220	...	...	...	1420	...	...
Dresden Hbf a.	0852	1052	1252	...	...	...	1452	...	...
Berlin Südkreuz a.	1036	1236	1436	...	...	...	1636	...	...
Berlin Hbf a.	1043	1243	1443	...	...	...	1644	...	...
Hamburg Hbf a.	...	...	1711	...	...	...	1912	...	...
Hamburg Altona a.	...	...	...	...	...	...	...	...	...

train type/number	RJ	EC		EC	RJ	EC	EC	RJ	EC	EC	RJ	EC	RJ		EC	RJ	EC	RJ		EN	NJ	NJ	
train number	72	172	1032	130	74	170	278	258	458	276	78	274	370	1036	272	372	270	374		476 574	40476 456	456	
notes	✕	✕ L	🍷 ♥	✕ V	✕	✕	✕	✕	✕ M	✕	✕	✕	✕	🍷 ♥	✕	✕	✕	✕		C	T	R	
Budapest Déli d.	...	...	0745	...	...	...	...	...	...	...	...	...	...	1445	...	...	...	...	...	...	...	...	...
Budapest Nyugati d.	...	0729	|	0812	...	...	0929	...	...	1129	...	1329	...	|	1529	...	1729	...	...	1929	1929	...	...
Štúrovo 🏛 △ d.	...	0834	◐	0924	...	...	1034	...	...	1234	...	1434	...	◐	1634	...	1834	...	...	2034	2034	...	...
Bratislava hl. st. d.	...	1006	|	1057	...	...	1206	...	...	1406	...	1606	...	|	1806	...	2006	...	...	2206	2206	...	...
Kúty 🏛 d.	...	1049	|	1148	...	...	1249	...	...	1449	...	1649	...	|	1849	...	2049	...	...	2249	2249	...	...
Graz Hbf d.	0626	|	|	|	0826	...	|	1025	...	|	1226	|	1426	|	|	1626	|	1826	...	|	|	1921	...
Wiener Neustadt Hbf d.	0832	|	|	|	1032	...	|	1232	...	|	1432	|	1632	|	|	1832	|	2032	...	|	|	2135	...
Wien Meidling d.	0857	|	1027	|	1057	...	|	1257	...	|	1457	|	1657	1727	|	1857	|	2057	...	|	|	|	...
Wien Hbf d.	0910	|	1039	|	1110	...	|	1310	...	|	1510	|	1710	1736	|	1910	|	2110	...	|	|	2210	...
Břeclav a.	1004	1104	1136	1204	1204	...	1304	1404	...	1504	1604	1704	1804	1836	1904	2004	2104	2204	...	2304	2304	2307	...
Břeclav d.	1007	1107	1138	...	1207	...	1307	1407	...	1507	1607	1707	1807	1838	1907	2007	2107	2207	...	0507	2350	2350	...
Brno hl. n. d.	1038	1138	1209	...	1238	...	1338	1438	...	1538	1638	1738	1838	1909	1938	2038	2136	2236	...	0538	|	|	...
Pardubice d.	|	1318	|	...	|	...	|	|	...	|	|	|	|	|	|	|	...	...	...	|	|	|	...
Praha hl. n. a.	1342	1413	1519	...	1542	...	1642	1735	...	1842	1942	2042	2141	2214	2241	2343	...	...	...	0842	|	|	...
Praha hl. n. d.	...	1425	...	...	...	1625	...	...	1826	...	...	...	...	...	...	...	...	...	...	...	|	|	...
Praha Holešovice d.	...	1434	...	...	...	1634	...	...	1835	...	...	...	...	...	...	...	...	...	...	...	|	|	...
Ústí nad Labem hl. n. d.	...	1539	...	...	...	1739	...	...	1939	...	...	...	...	...	...	...	...	...	...	...	|	|	...
Děčín d.	...	1601	...	...	...	1801	...	...	2001	...	...	...	...	...	...	...	...	...	...	...	◧	◧	...
Bad Schandau 🏛 ⊖ a.	...	1620	...	...	...	1820	...	...	2019	...	...	...	...	...	...	...	...	...	...	...	|	|	...
Dresden Hbf a.	...	1652	...	...	...	1852	...	...	2054	...	...	...	...	...	...	...	...	...	...	...	|	|	...
Berlin Südkreuz a.	...	1855	...	...	...	2036	...	...	...	...	...	...	...	...	...	...	...	...	...	...	|	|	...
Berlin Hbf a.	...	1902	...	...	...	2043	...	...	...	...	...	...	...	...	...	...	...	...	...	...	0951	0951	...
Hamburg Hbf a.	...	2117	...	...	...	...	...	...	...	...	...	...	...	...	...	...	...	...	...	...	...	...	...
Hamburg Altona a.	...	2134	...	...	...	...	...	...	...	...	...	...	...	...	...	...	...	...	...	...	...	...	...

B – METROPOL – 🛏 1, 2 cl., ▬ 2 cl. Praha (**575**) - Břeclav (**477**) - Budapest. [12] ✕ Praha - Břeclav. [12] Břeclav - Budapest.

C – METROPOL – 🛏 1, 2 cl., ▬ 2 cl. Budapest (**476**) - Břeclav (**574**) - Praha. [12] Budapest - Břeclav. [12] ✕ Břeclav - Praha.

G – [12] ✕ Praha - Dresden - Berlin - Hamburg - Kiel (arrive 2022). On certain Mondays runs Dresden - Berlin - Hamburg - Kiel.

H – [12] ✕ Kiel (depart 0742) - Hamburg - Berlin - Dresden - Praha. On certain Mondays runs Kiel - Hamburg - Berlin - Dresden.

J – [12] ✕ Flensburg (depart 0833) - Hamburg - Praha.

K – [12] ✕ Praha - Hamburg - Flensburg (arrive 1907).

L – HUNGARIA – [12] ✕ Hamburg - Budapest and v.v.

M – [12] ✕ Leipzig - Dresden - Praha and v.v. Also conveys CANOPUS 🛏 1, 2 cl., ▬ 2 cl. (4, 6 berth), [2] Zürich - Dresden - Praha and v.v.

R – *ÖBB nightjet* METROPOL – 🛏 1, 2 cl., ▬ 2 cl., [2] Berlin - Wrocław - Bohumín - Břeclav - Wien - Graz and v.v.

S – *ÖBB nightjet* METROPOL – 🛏 1, 2 cl., ▬ 2 cl., [2] Berlin (**40457**) - Wrocław - Bohumín - Břeclav (**477**) - Budapest.

T – *ÖBB nightjet* METROPOL – 🛏 1, 2 cl., ▬ 2 cl., [2] Budapest (**40476**) - Břeclav (**456**) - Bohumín - Wrocław - Berlin.

V – BATHORY – [12] ✕ Terespol - Warszawa - Katowice - Břeclav - Budapest and v.v. (Table **99**).

♥ – Operated by REGIOJET. Separate fare tariff applies.

△ – Routeing point for international tickets : Szob.

⊖ – Routeing point for international tickets : Schöna.

RJ – ÖBB *Railjet* service. [1] (business class), [1] (first class), [2] (economy class), ✕.

◐ – 🏛 at Hegyeshalom.

◧ – Via Wrocław and Bohumín (Table **77**).

☛ – Additional services Praha - Wien and Praha - Bratislava are operated by REGIOJET. For timings see Table **1150**.

61 WIEN - BUDAPEST - BEOGRAD / BUCUREŞTI and İSTANBUL / THESSALONÍKI

train type	*IC*		*IC*			*IC*	*IC*						*IC*				463		*EN*	*EN*	*EN*	
train number	73	1335	712	600		551	75		🚌	7991	493	493	79	1095	463	465	465	463	473	347	50347	
notes	R		R	🚌	🚌	R	R		①–⑥	2			R	463	2	2	493	R	R	R	348	
	H	K		✣	✣		P		❦		A	C	G	J	J	J	R U	W T	R	S	R E	
Wien Hbf d.	...	...	...	...	...	...	...	...	...	...	...	...	...	...	...	...	...	...	...	1942	1942	...
Budapest Keleti d.	0710	...	0753n	...	...	...	0910	...	...	...	...	...	1510	...	...	...	...	...	1910	2245	2245	...
Lökösháza a.	1010	...	|	...	...	...	1210	...	...	...	...	...	1810	...	...	...	...	...	2210	0159	0159	...
Curtici 🏛 a.	1155	...	|	...	...	...	1355	...	...	...	...	...	1955	...	...	...	...	...	2355	0349	0349	...
Arad a.	1237	...	|	...	...	...	1543	...	...	...	...	...	2046	...	...	...	...	...	0038	0428	0428	...
Timişoara a.	1327	...	|	...	...	...	|	...	...	...	...	...	2139	...	...	...	...	...	|	|	0552	...
Braşov a.	|	...	|	...	...	...	0055	...	...	...	...	...	|	...	...	...	...	...	0954	1326	|	...
Bucureşti Nord d.	2359	...	|	...	...	...	...	...	...	...	...	...	0830	1055	...	...	1055	1055	1233	1547	1600	...
Videle a.	...	...	|	...	...	...	...	...	...	...	...	...	...	1150	...	...	1150	1150	...	...	...	...
Giurgiu Nord 🏛 a.	...	...	|	...	...	...	...	...	...	...	...	...	...	1301	...	...	1301	1301	...	...	...	...
Giurgiu Nord 🏛 d.	...	...	|	...	...	...	...	...	...	...	...	...	...	1320	...	...	1320	1320	...	...	...	...
Ruse 🏛 a.	...	...	|	...	...	...	...	...	...	...	...	...	...	1345	...	...	1345	1345	...	...	...	...
Ruse 🏛 d.	...	...	|	...	...	...	...	...	...	...	...	...	...	1420	...	...	1420	1420	...	...	...	...
Gorna Orjahovica d.	...	...	|	...	...	...	...	...	...	...	...	...	...	1610	1615	1725	1730	1615	...	...	...	...
Szeged d.	...	...	1015	1025	...	...	...	...	...	...	...	...	...	...	|	|	|	|	...	...	...	...
Kelebia 🏛 d.	...	...	...	1145x	...	...	...	...	...	...	...	...	...	...	|	|	|	|	...	...	...	...
Subotica 🏛 a.	...	...	...	1205	1500	...	...	...	...	...	...	...	...	...	|	|	|	|	...	...	...	...
Novi Sad a.	...	...	...	...	1650	1745	...	...	...	...	...	...	...	...	|	|	|	|	...	...	...	...
Beograd Centar a.	...	1825	...	...	...	1821	...	...	...	...	...	...	...	...	|	|	|	|	...	...	...	...
Niš a.	...	2308	...	...	...	...	...	...	0620	...	...	...	...	...	|	|	|	|	...	...	...	...
Tabanovci 🏛 a.	...	0320	...	...	...	...	...	...	|	...	...	...	...	...	|	|	|	|	...	...	...	...
Skopje a.	...	0425	...	...	...	...	...	...	|	...	...	...	...	...	|	|	|	|	...	...	...	...
Gevgelija 🏛 a.	...	0650	...	...	...	...	...	...	|	...	...	...	...	...	|	|	|	|	...	...	...	...
Dimitrovgrad (Serbia) 🏛 a.	...	|	...	...	...	...	...	...	0802	...	...	...	...	...	|	|	|	|	...	...	...	...
Dragoman 🏛 a.	...	|	...	...	...	...	...	...	...	1400	...	...	...	...	|	|	|	|	...	...	...	...
Pleven a.	...	|	...	...	...	...	...	...	...	|	...	...	...	...	1725	|	|	1725	...	...	...	...
Mezdra a.	...	|	...	...	...	...	...	...	...	|	...	...	...	...	1840	|	|	1840	...	...	...	...
Vidin 🏛 a.	...	|	...	...	...	...	...	...	...	|	...	...	...	...	|	|	|	|	...	...	...	...
Sofia a.	...	|	...	...	...	...	...	...	...	1500	...	...	...	...	2010	|	|	2010	...	...	...	...
Sofia d.	...	|	...	...	...	...	...	...	...	...	1830	1830	...	...	...	|	|	...	...	...	...	...
Dimitrovgrad (Bulgaria) a.	...	|	...	...	...	...	...	...	...	...	2228	2224	...	...	...	2216	2147	...	...	...	...	...
Svilengrad a.	...	|	...	...	...	...	...	...	...	...	2332	2337	...	...	...	...	2332	...	...	...	...	...
Kapikule 🏛 a.	...	|	...	...	...	...	...	...	...	...	0037	0137	...	...	...	...	0037	...	...	...	...	...
Çerkezköy a.	...	|	...	...	...	...	...	...	...	...	0359	0453	...	...	...	...	0359	...	...	...	...	...
Halkalı ◇ a.	...	|	...	...	...	...	...	...	...	...	0534	0600	...	...	...	...	0534	...	...	...	...	...
İstanbul Sirkeci ◇ a.	...	|	...	...	...	...	...	...	...	...	◇	◇	...	...	...	...	◇	...	...	...	...	...
İstanbul Söğütlüçesme ◇ a.	...	|	...	...	...	...	...	...	...	...	◇	◇	...	...	...	...	◇	...	...	...	...	...
Ankara a.	...	|	...	...	...	...	...	...	...	...	...	...	...	...	...	...	...	...	...	...	...	...
Kulata 🏛 a.	...	|	...	...	...	...	...	...	...	...	...	...	...	...	...	...	...	...	...	...	...	...
Thessaloníki a.	...	1033	...	...	...	...	...	...	...	...	...	...	...	...	...	...	...	...	...	...	...	...

train type/number		*EN*	*EN*	*EN*	492										*IC*	*IC*	*RJX*	*IC*			*IC*	*IC*
train number	1334	349	346	472	464	462	492	492	7990		2906	464	462	1094	78	74	264	570		600	723	72
notes		2 R	R	R	462	R			2	🚌	2	2	2		R	R		R	🚌	🚌	R	R
	L	E	S	R	R F	W T	B	D		❦		J	J	J	G	P			✣	✣		H
Thessaloníki d.	1851	...	...	...	...	...	...	...	...	...	...	...	...	...	...	...	...	...	...	...	...	...
Kulata 🏛 d.	|	...	...	...	...	...	...	...	...	...	...	...	...	...	...	...	...	...	...	...	...	...
Ankara d.	|	...	...	...	...	...	...	...	...	...	...	...	...	...	...	...	...	...	...	...	...	...
İstanbul Söğütlüçesme ◇ d.	|	...	...	...	◇	...	◇	◇	...	...	...	...	...	...	...	...	...	...	...	...	...	...
İstanbul Sirkeci ◇ d.	|	...	...	...	◇	...	◇	◇	...	...	...	...	...	...	...	...	...	...	...	...	...	...
Halkalı ◇ d.	|	...	...	...	2045	...	2045	2240	...	...	...	...	...	...	...	...	...	...	...	...	...	...
Çerkezköy d.	|	...	...	...	2237	...	2237	0007	...	...	...	...	...	...	...	...	...	...	...	...	...	...
Kapikule 🏛 d.	|	...	...	...	0220	...	0220	0320	...	...	...	...	...	...	...	...	...	...	...	...	...	...
Svilengrad d.	|	...	...	...	0325	...	0325	0325	...	...	...	...	...	...	...	...	...	...	...	...	...	...
Dimitrovgrad (Bulgaria) d.	|	...	...	...	0600	...	0424	0442	...	...	...	0600	...	...	...	...	...	...	...	...	...	...
Sofia a.	|	...	...	...	|	...	0935	0935	...	...	...	|	...	...	...	...	...	...	...	...	...	...
Sofia d.	|	...	...	...	|	0715	...	...	0920	...	...	|	0715	...	...	...	...	...	...	...	...	...
Vidin 🏛 d.	|	...	...	...	|	|	...	...	|	...	...	|	|	...	...	...	...	...	...	...	...	...
Mezdra d.	|	...	...	...	|	0844	...	...	|	...	...	|	0844	...	...	...	...	...	...	...	...	...
Pleven d.	|	...	...	...	|	1001	...	...	|	...	...	|	1001	...	...	...	...	...	...	...	...	...
Dragoman 🏛 d.	|	...	...	...	|	|	...	...	1019	...	...	|	|	...	...	...	...	...	...	...	...	...
Dimitrovgrad (Serbia) 🏛 d.	|	...	...	...	|	|	...	...	...	1200	...	|	|	...	...	...	...	...	...	...	...	...
Gevgelija 🏛 d.	1948	...	...	...	|	|	...	...	...	|	...	|	|	...	...	...	...	...	...	...	...	...
Skopje d.	2219	...	...	...	|	|	...	...	...	|	...	|	|	...	...	...	...	...	...	...	...	...
Tabanovci 🏛 d.	2329	...	...	...	|	|	...	...	...	|	...	|	|	...	...	...	...	...	...	...	...	...
Niš d.	0337	...	...	...	|	|	...	...	...	1400	1552	|	|	...	...	...	...	...	...	...	...	...
Beograd Centar d.	0813	...	...	...	|	|	...	...	...	...	2110	|	|	...	...	...	...	0935	...	...	...	...
Novi Sad d.	...	...	...	...	|	|	...	...	...	...	...	|	|	...	...	...	...	1011	1040	...	...	...
Subotica 🏛 d.	...	...	...	...	|	|	...	...	...	...	...	|	|	...	...	...	...	...	1230	1445	...	...
Kelebia 🏛 d.	...	...	...	...	|	|	...	...	...	...	...	|	|	...	...	...	...	...	...	1505x	...	...
Szeged d.	...	...	...	...	|	|	...	...	...	...	...	|	|	...	...	...	...	...	...	1630	1645	...
Gorna Orjahovica d.	...	...	...	...	1125	1125	...	...	...	...	...	1036	1130	...	...	...	...	...	...	...	|	...
Ruse 🏛 a.	...	...	...	...	1320	1320	...	...	...	...	...	...	1324	...	...	...	...	...	...	...	|	...
Ruse 🏛 d.	...	...	...	...	1410	1410	...	...	...	...	...	...	...	1410	...	...	...	...	...	...	|	...
Giurgiu Nord 🏛 a.	...	...	...	...	1440	1440	...	...	...	...	...	...	...	1440	...	...	...	...	...	...	|	...
Giurgiu Nord 🏛 d.	...	...	...	...	1500	1500	...	...	...	...	...	...	...	1500	...	...	...	...	...	...	|	...
Videle d.	...	...	...	...	1608	1608	...	...	...	...	...	...	...	1608	...	...	...	...	...	...	|	...
Bucureşti Nord d.	...	1345	1400	1745	1708	1708	...	...	...	...	...	...	...	1708	2205	...	...	...	...	...	|	0546
Braşov d.	...	|	1621	2022	...	...	...	...	...	...	...	...	...	...	|	0523	...	...	...	...	|	|
Timişoara d.	...	2356	|	|	...	...	...	...	...	...	...	...	...	...	0826	|	...	...	...	...	|	1538
Arad d.	...	0120	0120	0452	...	...	...	...	...	...	...	...	...	...	0921	1417	...	...	...	...	|	1629
Curtici 🏛 d.	...	0210	0210	0534	...	...	...	...	...	...	...	...	...	...	0934	1534	...	...	...	...	|	1734
Lököshaza d.	...	0200	0200	0540	...	...	...	...	...	...	...	...	...	...	0940	1540	...	...	...	...	|	1740
Budapest Keleti a.	...	0520	0520	0850	...	...	...	...	...	...	...	...	...	...	1250	1850	1940	...	...	...	1907n	2050
Wien Hbf a.	...	0821	0821	...	...	...	...	...	...	...	...	...	...	...	...	...	2221	...	...	...	...	...

A – Apr. 26 - Oct. 30: SOFIA EXPRESS – 🛏 1, 2 cl., 🛌 2 cl. (4-berth) Sofia - Halkalı.
B – Apr. 25 - Oct. 29: SOFIA EXPRESS – 🛏 1, 2 cl., 🛌 2 cl. (4-berth) Halkalı - Sofia.
C – Oct. 31 - Dec. 10: SOFIA EXPRESS – 🛏 1, 2 cl., 🛌 2 cl. (4-berth) Sofia - Halkalı.
D – Oct. 30 - Dec. 10: SOFIA EXPRESS – 🛏 1, 2 cl., 🛌 2 cl. (4-berth) Halkalı - Sofia.
E – 🛏 1, 2 cl. Wien - Timişoara - Bucureşti and v.v.
F – June 2 - Oct. 1: BOSPHOR EXPRESS – 🛌 2 cl. (4-berth) İstanbul (**12502/492/1622**) - Dimitrovgrad (**464**) - Gorna Orjahovica (**462/1094**) - Ruse - Bucureşti.
G – MUNTENIA – (2) Budapest - Timişoara - Bucureşti and v.v.
H – TRAIANUS – (2) Budapest - Timişoara - Bucureşti and v.v.
J – Oct. 4 - Dec. 10.
K – June 3 - Sept. 20: HELLAS – 🛌 2 cl., (2) Beograd - Thessaloníki.
L – June 2 - Sept. 19: HELLAS – 🛌 2 cl., (2) Thessaloníki - Beograd.
P – FOGARAS – (12) Budapest - Braşov and v.v.
R – *EuroNight* ISTER – 🛏 1, 2 cl., 🛌 1, 2 cl., (2) Budapest - Bucureşti and v.v.
S – DACIA - 🛏 1, 2 cl., 🛌 2 cl., (2) Wien - Braşov - Bucureşti and v.v.

T – June 3 - Oct. 3.
U – June 4 - Oct. 3: BOSPHOR EXPRESS – 🛌 2 cl. (4-berth) Bucureşti (**463/1095**) - Ruse - Gorna Orjahovica (**465**) - Dimitrovgrad (**493/12501**) - İstanbul.
W – (2) ROMANIA – Bucureşti - Ruse - Sofia and v.v.

n – Budapest **Nyugati**.
x – Kelebia **Drž. Granica**.

✣ – Engineering work is affecting services between Budapest and Kelebia until 2024. For through journeys between Budapest and Subotica see Tables **1290** & **1295**. Rail tickets are not valid on bus services Szeged - Kelebia - Subotica or Subotica - Novi Sad.
❦ Rail tickets are not valid on bus services Dimitrovgrad (Serbia) - Niš.
◇ – Frequent surburban services operate from Halkalı to İstanbul Sirkeci (journey time 38 mins.) and İstanbul Söğütlüçesme (51 mins). See Table **1570**.
☛ **Shaded services are suspended until further notice.**

FRANKFURT - MÜNCHEN - LJUBLJANA - ZAGREB - BEOGRAD - THESSALONÍKI 62

train type/number	RJ	D	EC	EC	EC	EC	D	D	EC	EC	EN	EN	EN	D	🚌	
train number	111	211	217	113	113 213	115	315	315 411	219	117	60237	40237	40465	413 2	①-⑥	7991 2
notes		T			◧	W		P			R	L	B		⚞	
Dortmund Hbf d.	...	...	...	...	...	...	...	...	...	...	...	...	...	...	...	...
Münster Hbf d.	...	...	...	...	...	0630	...	...	...	...	...	...	...	...	...	...
Köln Hbf d.	...	...	...	...	...	0817	...	...	...	...	...	...	...	...	...	...
Frankfurt (Main) Hbf d.	...	...	...	0822	0822	|	...	...	1220	1420	...	...	...	...	...	...
Saarbrücken d.	...	...	0537	|	|	|	...	...	|	|	...	...	...	...	...	...
Mannheim d.	...	...	0711	|	|	1102	...	...	|	|	...	...	...	...	...	...
Heidelberg d.	...	...	|	0914	0914	|	...	...	1313	1513	...	...	...	...	...	...
Stuttgart Hbf d.	...	...	0758	0958	0958	1158	...	...	1358	1559	2029	2029	...	...	...	...
Ulm d.	...	...	0855	1055	1055	1256	...	...	1456	1656	2153	2153	...	...	...	...
Augsburg d.	...	...	0941	1142	1142	1341	...	...	1541	1741	2302	2302	...	...	...	...
München Hbf d.	0816	...	1016	1218	1218	1416	...	...	1616	1817	2354o	2354o	...	...	...	...
Salzburg Hbf 🏛 d.	1012	...	1216	1412	1412	1612	...	...	1816	2012	0210	0210	...	...	...	...
Bischofshofen d.	1054	...	1312	1454	1454	1654	...	...	1912	2054	|	|	...	...	...	...
Selzthal a.	|	...	1439	|	|	|	...	...	2039	|	|	|	...	...	...	...
Graz a.	|	...	1614	|	|	|	...	...	2214	|	|	|	...	...	...	...
Schwarzach St Veit d.	1111	...	...	1511	1511	1711	...	...	...	2111	0428	0428	0425	...	...	...
Bad Gastein d.	1142	...	...	1542	1542	1742	...	...	...	2142	0459	0459	0458	...	...	...
Villach Hbf a.	1243	1253	...	1643	1643	1843	1853	...	...	2243	0604	0604	0604	...	...	...
Klagenfurt a.	1316	|	...	1717	|	1916	|	...	...	2316	|	|	|	...	...	...
Jesenice 🏛 a.	...	1329	...	...	1729	...	1929	...	...	...	0659	0659	0659	...	...	...
Ljubljana a.	...	1431	...	...	1832	...	2033	2105	...	...	0809	0809	0809	...	...	...
Rijeka a.	...	|	...	...	|	...	|	|	...	...	1125	|	|	...	...	...
Dobova 🏛 a.	...	1623	...	...	2006	...	2241	2241	...	...	...	1000	1000	...	...	...
Zagreb a.	...	1710	...	...	2045	...	...	2337	...	...	...	1039	1039	...	...	...
Zagreb d.	...	1735	...	...	...	...	...	2341	...	...	...	...	...	1057	...	...
Vinkovci a.	...	2142	...	...	...	...	...	0303	...	...	...	...	...	1503	...	...
Tovarnik 🏛 a.	...	...	...	...	...	...	...	|	...	...	...	...	...	...	...	...
Šid 🏛 a.	...	...	...	...	...	...	...	0341	...	...	...	...	...	...	...	...
Beograd Centar a.	...	...	...	...	...	...	...	0605	...	...	...	...	...	...	...	...
Beograd Topčider d.	...	...	...	...	...	...	...	...	...	...	...	...	...	...	...	...
Niš a.	...	...	...	...	...	...	...	...	...	...	...	...	...	...	0620	...
Dimitrovgrad (Serbia) 🏛 a.	...	...	...	...	...	...	...	...	...	...	...	...	...	...	0802	1400
Dragoman 🏛 a.	...	...	...	...	...	...	...	...	...	...	...	...	...	...	...	1500
Sofia a.	...	...	...	...	...	...	...	...	...	...	...	...	...	...	...	...
Tabanovci 🏛 a.	...	...	...	...	...	...	...	...	...	...	...	...	...	...	...	...
Skopje a.	...	...	...	...	...	...	...	...	...	...	...	...	...	...	...	...
Gevgelija 🏛 a.	...	...	...	...	...	...	...	...	...	...	...	...	...	...	...	...
Thessaloníki a.	...	...	...	...	...	...	...	...	...	...	...	...	...	...	...	...

train type		🚌		D	EN	EN	EN	EC	D	D	EC	EC	EC	EC	D	RJ
train number	7990		2906	412	40414	414	480	218	410 314	314	114	112	212 112	216	210	110
notes	2	⚞	2	2	B	L	S		Q		W		◧		T	
Thessaloníki d.	...	...	...	...	...	...	...	...	...	...	...	...	...	...	...	...
Gevgelija 🏛 d.	...	...	...	...	...	...	...	...	...	...	...	...	...	...	...	...
Skopje d.	...	...	...	...	...	...	...	...	...	...	...	...	...	...	...	...
Tabanovci 🏛 d.	...	...	...	...	...	...	...	...	...	...	...	...	...	...	...	...
Sofia d.	0920	...	...	...	...	...	...	...	...	...	...	...	...	...	...	...
Dragoman 🏛 d.	1019	...	...	...	...	...	...	...	...	...	...	...	...	...	...	...
Dimitrovgrad (Serbia) 🏛 d.	...	1200	...	...	...	...	...	...	...	...	...	...	...	...	...	...
Niš d.	...	1400	1552	...	...	...	...	...	...	...	...	...	...	...	...	...
Beograd Topčider a.	...	...	|	...	...	...	...	...	...	...	...	...	...	...	...	...
Beograd Centar d.	...	...	2110	...	...	...	...	...	2058	...	...	...	...	...	...	...
Šid 🏛 d.	...	...	...	...	...	...	...	...	0022	...	...	...	...	...	...	...
Tovarnik 🏛 d.	...	...	...	...	...	...	...	...	|	...	...	...	...	...	...	...
Vinkovci d.	...	...	...	1416	...	...	...	...	0103	...	...	...	...	...	0839	...
Zagreb a.	...	...	...	1820	...	...	...	...	0428	...	...	...	...	...	1240	...
Zagreb d.	...	...	...	...	1938	1938	...	...	0440	...	...	...	0705	...	1250	...
Dobova 🏛 d.	...	...	...	...	2019	2019	...	...	0540	0540	...	...	0745	...	1334	...
Rijeka d.	...	...	...	...	|	|	1847	...	|	|	...	...	|	...	|	...
Ljubljana d.	...	...	...	...	2208	2208	2208	...	0717	0726	...	...	0923	...	1527	...
Jesenice 🏛 d.	...	...	...	...	2315	2315	2315	...	...	0832	...	...	1022	...	1632	...
Klagenfurt d.	...	...	...	...	|	|	|	...	...	|	0842	1027	|	...	|	1642
Villach Hbf d.	...	...	...	...	0013	0013	0013	...	...	0908	0916	1116	1116	...	1708	1716
Bad Gastein a.	...	...	...	...	0114	0114	0114	...	...	...	1016	1216	1216	...	...	1816
Schwarzach St Veit a.	...	...	...	...	0145	0145	0145	...	...	...	1048	1248	1248	...	...	1848
Graz d.	...	...	...	...	...	|	|	0545	...	...	|	|	|	1145	...	|
Selzthal d.	...	...	...	...	...	|	|	0719	...	...	|	|	|	1319	...	|
Bischofshofen a.	...	...	...	...	...	|	|	0848	...	...	1105	1305	1305	1448	...	1905
Salzburg Hbf 🏛 a.	...	...	...	...	...	0245	0245	0944	...	...	1148	1348	1348	1544	...	1948
München Hbf a.	...	...	...	...	...	0550o	0550o	1141	...	...	1341	1541	1541	1741	...	2141
Augsburg a.	...	...	...	...	...	0645	0645	1214	...	...	1414	1615	1615	1814	...	...
Ulm a.	...	...	...	...	...	0736	0736	1301	...	...	1501	1702	1702	1901	...	...
Stuttgart Hbf a.	...	...	...	...	...	0837	0837	1359	...	...	1559	1801	1801	1959	...	...
Heidelberg a.	...	...	...	...	...	...	...	1444	...	...	|	1844	1844	|	...	...
Mannheim a.	...	...	...	...	...	...	...	|	...	...	1655	|	|	2047	...	...
Saarbrücken a.	...	...	...	...	...	...	...	|	...	...	|	|	|	2216	...	...
Frankfurt (Main) Hbf a.	...	...	...	...	...	...	...	1540	...	...	|	1940	1940	...	...	...
Köln Hbf a.	...	...	...	...	...	...	...	...	...	...	1943	...	...	...	...	...
Münster Hbf a.	...	...	...	...	...	...	...	...	...	...	|	...	...	...	...	...
Dortmund Hbf a.	...	...	...	...	...	...	...	...	...	...	2104	...	...	...	...	...

B – 1, 2 cl., 2 cl. (4, 6 berth) Zürich - Schwarzach St Veit - Zagreb and v.v. (Table **86**).
C – MIMARA – 12 Frankfurt (**112**) - Villach (**212**) - Jesenice 🏛 - Zagreb.
D – MIMARA – 12 Zagreb (**213**) - Jesenice 🏛 - Villach (**113**) - Frankfurt.
L – LISINSKI – 1, 2 cl., 2 cl. (4, 6 berth), 2 Stuttgart - Zagreb and v.v.
P – June 20 - Sept. 13: 2 cl., 12 Ljubljana - Zagreb - Beograd.
Q – June 21 - Sept. 14: 2 cl., 12 Beograd - Zagreb - Ljubljana.
R – Mar. 31 - Apr. 17, May 12 - Sept. 3: 1, 2 cl., 2 cl. Stuttgart - Rijeka.
S – Mar. 30 - Apr. 16, May 11 - Sept. 2: 1, 2 cl., 2 cl. Rijeka - Stuttgart.

T – SAVA – 12 Villach - Jesenice 🏛 - Ljubljana - Zagreb - Vinkovci and v.v.
W – WÖRTHERSEE – 12 ✕ Münster - Klagenfurt and Klagenfurt - Dortmund.

o – München **Ost**.

⚞ – Rail tickets are not valid on bus services Dimitrovgrad (Serbia) - Niš.
◧ – Supplement payable: Jesenice 🏛 - Zagreb and v.v.
☛ **Shaded services are suspended until further notice.**

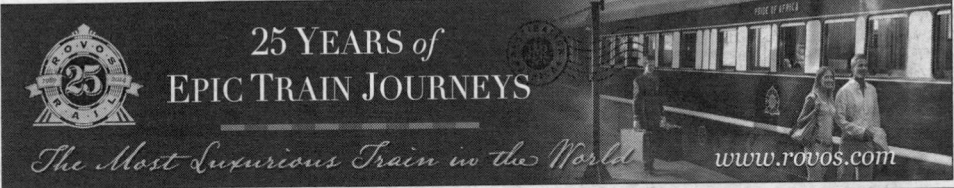

64 HAMBURG and BERLIN - WIEN - BUDAPEST

For alternative services via Břeclav see Table 60

train type	ICE	ICE	ICE	ICE	ICE	RJX	ICE	ICE	RJX	ICE	ICE	RJX	ICE	ICE	ICE	EN	ICE	ICE	ICE	ICE	ICE	ICE	NJ	IC	
train number	501	21	503	783	23	65	505	91	67	585	93	165	507	787	27	347	509	789	29	1601 1711	881	229	491	95	
notes	①–⑥ m			✣		C		✣	C	✣				✣		Ⓡ D		✣			✣		A		
Hamburg Hbf d.		...	...	0554	...	...	...	0801	...	0901	...	...	...	1001	...	...	...	1201	...	...	1401	...	2029	...	...
Hannover Hbf d.	...	...	...	0726	...	...	...	0926	...	1022	...	...	...	1126	...	...	...	1326	...	...	1526	...	2157	...	...
Berlin Hbf d.	0428	...	0629	|	...	...	0829	|	...	|	1004	...	1029	|	...	...	1229	|	...	1429	|	...	|	...	...
Leipzig Hbf d.	0548	...	0748	|	...	...	0948	|	...	|	|	...	1148	|	...	...	1348	|	...	1548	|	...	|	0035	...
Nürnberg Hbf d.	0808	0831	0953	1024	1031	...	1153	1231	...	1325	1332	...	1353	1424	1431	...	1552	1624	1631	1753	1824	1831	0408	0600	...
Passau 🛃 d.	...	1026	...	...	1229	...	...	1429	...	...	1529	...	...	...	1629	...	...	...	1829	...	...	2031	0615	0824	...
Linz Hbf a.	...	1126	...	...	1326	...	...	1526	...	...	1626	...	...	...	1726	...	...	...	1929	...	...	2134	0746	0925	...
Wien Hbf a.	...	1247	...	...	1447	1542	...	1647	1740	...	1747	1842	...	...	1847	1942	...	...	2047	...	...	2305	0919	1047	...
Budapest Keleti § a.	...	...	...	...	...	1819	...	...	2019	...	...	2119	...	...	...	2220	...	...	...	...	...	...	...	...	...

train type	ICE	ICE	ICE	EN	ICE	ICE	ICE	RJX	ICE	ICE	RJX	ICE	ICE	ICE	RJX	ICE	ICE	ICE	RJX	ICE	ICE	ICE	IC	EC	NJ
train number	228	538	508	346	28	586	506	162	92	586	60	26	504	584	62	90	502	582	64	22	580	500	94	148	490
notes				Ⓡ D						✣	C			✣	C	✣		✣	C		✣ ⑦			J	A
Budapest Keleti § d.	...	...	...	0540	...	...	...	0640	...	...	0740	...	...	...	0940	...	...	...	1140	...	...	...	...	1640	...
Wien Hbf d.	0651	...	...	0821	0913	...	...	0921	1013	...	1021	1113	...	...	1221	1313	...	...	1421	1513	...	...	1913	1921	2013
Linz Hbf d.	0817	...	...	...	1034	...	...	...	1134	...	...	1234	...	...	...	1434	...	...	...	1634	...	...	2034	...	2136
Passau 🛃 a.	0922	...	...	...	1131	...	...	...	1231	...	...	1331	...	...	...	1531	...	...	...	1731	...	...	2137	...	2235
Nürnberg Hbf a.	1127	1133	1204	...	1327	1333	1404	...	1428	1434	...	1528	1604	1633	...	1729	1804	1833	...	1928	2032	2004	2400	...	0056
Leipzig Hbf a.	...	|	1410	...	...	|	1610	...	|	|	...	...	1810	|	...	|	2010	|	...	...	|	2210	0453	...	|
Berlin Hbf a.	...	|	1529	...	...	|	1731	...	1753	|	...	...	1931	|	...	|	2129	|	...	...	|	2336	0632	...	|
Hannover Hbf a.	...	1532	...	...	...	1732	...	...	...	1732	...	...	...	1932	...	2033	...	2132	...	...	2341	...	...	...	0649
Hamburg Hbf a.	...	1729	...	...	...	1929	...	...	...	1855	...	...	...	2059	...	2155	...	2255	...	...	0116	...	...	...	0847

A – *ÖBB nightjet* – 🛏 1, 2 cl., ▬ 2 cl. (4, 6 berth), [2] Hamburg - Wien and v.v. Special fares apply. See Table **53**.

C – ÖBB *Railjet* service: München - Wien - Budapest and v.v.

D – DACIA – 🛏 1, 2 cl., ▬ 2 cl., [2] Wien - Budapest - Bucuresti and v.v.

J – SEMMELWEIS – [12] Budapest - Wien.

m – Not Apr. 10, May 1, 29.

§ – 🛃 is at Hegyeshalom.

RJ | *RJX* – ÖBB *Railjet* service, ✕, [1] (business class), [1] (first class), [2] (economy class).

✣ – Subject to alteration from Apr. 1.

65 STUTTGART - MÜNCHEN - SALZBURG - WIEN - BUDAPEST - BUCUREŞTI

train type	RJX	EN	RJX	EC	RJX	RJX	EC	RJX	RJ	RJX	EC	RJX	EC	RJX	EC	RJX	EC	RJX	EC	RJX	RJX	EN	EC	RJX	RJX	EC
train number	41	467	761	141	269	265	143	61	111	765	145	63	217	161	147	65	113	563	149	67	165	347	115	165	69	219
notes		B					L												G			Ⓡ D				
Stuttgart Hbf d.	...	...	...	...	...	...	...	...	...	...	...	...	0758	...	...	...	0958	...	...	...	...	...	1158	...	...	1358
München Hbf d.	...	...	...	...	...	0623	...	0723	0816	...	...	0929	1016	...	...	1128	1217	...	...	1329	...	...	1416	...	1529	1616
Salzburg Hbf 🛃 a.	...	...	...	...	0708	0758	...	0858	0959	...	...	1058	1159	...	...	1258	1359	...	...	1458	...	...	1559	...	1658	1759
Salzburg Hbf 🛃 d.	...	0436	0605	...	0816	0807	...	0907	...	1008	...	1107	...	1208	...	1307	▬	1408	...	1507	...	...	...	1608	1707	...
Linz Hbf d.	...	0558	0716	...	0902	0917	...	1017	...	1116	...	1217	...	1316	...	1417	...	1516	...	1617	...	...	...	1716	1817	...
St Pölten Hbf d.	...	0710	0802	...	0925	1003	...	1103	...	1202	...	1303	...	1402	...	1503	...	1602	...	1703	...	...	...	1802	1903	...
Wien Meidling d.	...	0744	0825	...	0940	1027	...	1127	...	1225	...	1327	...	1425	...	1527	*EN*	1625	...	1727	...	...	...	1825	1925	...
Wien Hbf d.	0740	0755	0830	0840	1025	1032	1040	1140	...	1230	1240	1340	...	1430	1437	1542	**473**	1630	1642	1740	1842	1942	...	1830	1932	...
Hegyeshalom 🛃 a.	0825	...	...	0925	1053	...	1125	1225	...	...	1325	1425	...	...	1521	1625	Ⓡ	...	1725	1825	1925	2025	...	...	...	...
Győr a.	0853	...	...	0953	1219	...	1153	1253	...	...	1353	1453	...	...	1553	1653	C	...	1753	1853	1953	2053	...	...	...	...
Budapest Keleti a.	1019	...	...	1119	...	...	1319	1419	...	...	1519	1619	...	...	1719	1819	1910	...	1919	2019	2119	2220	...	...	...	...
Bucureşti Nord a.	...	...	...	...		...	...	...	...	...	...	...	...	...	...	...	1233	...	...	...	...	1600	...	...	...	...

train type	RJX	EC	RJX	EC	RJX	RJ	RJX	IC	RJ	EN	
train number	167	341	261	117	169	1299	663	1291	367	50237	
notes	Q					Ⓑ		Ⓑ		A	
Stuttgart Hbf d.	...	...	...	1559	...	...	...	1758	...	2029	...
München Hbf d.	...	...	1730	1817	...	1917	...	2017	...	2354o	...
Salzburg Hbf 🛃 a.	...	...	1858	1959	...	2100	...	2202	...	0128	...
Salzburg Hbf 🛃 d.	1808	...	1907	...	2008	...	2108	...	2208	0343	...
Linz Hbf d.	1916	...	2017	...	2116	...	2216	...	2319	0510	...
St Pölten Hbf d.	2002	...	2103	...	2202	...	2302	...	0005	0602	...
Wien Meidling d.	2025	...	2127	...	2225	...	2325	...	0026	0629	...
Wien Hbf d.	2030	2042	2140	...	2230	...	2330	...	0033	0640	...
Hegyeshalom 🛃 a.	...	2125	2225	...	...	...	...	...	...	0723	...
Győr a.	...	2153	2253	...	...	...	...	...	...	0753	...
Budapest Keleti a.	...	2319	0019	...	...	...	...	...	...	0919	...
Bucureşti Nord a.	...	...	...	...	...	...	...	...	...	...	...

train type	RJX	IC	RJX	RJX	EC	RJX	EN	RJX	EC	RJX
train number	368	1290	260	160	218	262	346	162	114	60
notes				P			Ⓡ D			
Bucureşti Nord d.	...	...	...	...	...	...	1400	...	...	...
Budapest Keleti d.	...	...	...	...	...	...	0540	0640	...	0740
Győr d.	...	...	...	...	...	...	0702	0802	...	0902
Hegyeshalom 🛃 d.	...	...	...	...	...	...	0732	0832	...	0932
Wien Hbf d.	0530	...	0628	0730	...	0828	0821	0930	...	1028
Wien Meidling d.	0537	...	0635	0737	...	0835	...	0937	...	1035
St Pölten Hbf d.	0600	...	0659	0800	...	0859	...	1000	...	1059
Linz Hbf d.	0646	...	0745	0846	...	0945	...	1046	...	1145
Salzburg Hbf 🛃 a.	0754	...	0853	0952	...	1053	...	1152	...	1253
Salzburg Hbf 🛃 d.	...	0800	0900	...	1000	1100	...	...	1200	1300
München Hbf a.	...	0941	1033	...	1141	1232	...	...	1341	1432
Stuttgart Hbf a.	...	1159	...	...	1359	...	...	...	1559	...

train type	EC	RJX	EC	EN	RJX	EC	RJX	EC	RJX	EC	RJX		RJX	EC	RJX	RJ	RJX	EC	RJX	RJX		EC	NJ	RJX	EN	
train number	140	564	112	472	62	142	166	216	64	144	168		66	146	760	110	68	148	762	42		340	466	264	50462	
notes	J			Ⓡ C								2		N							2		B		A	
Bucureşti Nord d.	...	...	...	1745	...	...	...	...	...	...	...	...	...	...	...	...	...	...	...	...	...	...	...	...	...	...
Budapest Keleti d.	0840	...	...	0850	0940	1040	...	...	1140	1240	...	...	1340	1440	...	...	1540	1640	...	1740	...	1840	...	1940	2040	...
Győr d.	1002	...	...	...	1102	1202	...	...	1302	1402	...	...	1502	1602	...	...	1702	1802	...	1902	...	2002	...	2102	2202	...
Hegyeshalom 🛃 d.	1032	...	...	...	1132	1232	...	...	1332	1432	...	...	1532	1632	...	...	1732	1832	...	1932	...	2032	...	2132	2232	...
Wien Hbf d.	1121	1130	...	...	1228	1321	1330	...	1428	1521	1530	...	1628	1721	1730	...	1828	1921	1930	2030	...	2118	2127	2221	2327	...
Wien Meidling d.	...	1137	...	...	1235	...	1337	...	1435	...	1537	...	1635	...	1737	...	1835	...	1937	2037	...	...	2135	...	2335	...
St Pölten Hbf d.	...	1200	...	...	1259	...	1400	...	1459	...	1600	...	1659	...	1800	...	1859	...	2000	2100	...	...	2202	...	0001	...
Linz Hbf d.	...	1246	...	...	1345	...	1446	...	1545	...	1646	...	1745	...	1846	...	1945	...	2046	2146	...	...	2258	...	0059	...
Salzburg Hbf 🛃 a.	...	1352	...	...	1453	...	1552	...	1653	...	1752	...	1853	...	1952	...	2053	...	2152	2251	...	...	0024	...	0212	...
Salzburg Hbf 🛃 d.	...	...	1400	...	1500	...	...	1600	1700	...	...	1815	1900	...	...	2000	2100	...	...	...	2300	...	...	...	0403	...
München Hbf a.	...	...	1541	...	1632	...	...	1741	1831	...	...	2006	2031	...	...	2141	2231	...	...	...	0058	...	...	...	0550o	...
Stuttgart Hbf a.	...	...	1759	...	...	...	...	1959	...	...	...	...	...	...	...	...	...	...	...	...	...	...	...	...	0837	...

A – KÁLMÁN IMRE – 🛏 1, 2 cl., ▬ 2 cl. (4, 6 berth) [2] Stuttgart - Budapest and v.v. Also conveys cars to and from Venezia (Table **70**), Zagreb and Rijeka (Table **62**).

B – *ÖBB nightjet*. WIENER WALZER - 🛏 1, 2 cl., ▬ 2 cl. (4, 6 berth), [2] Wien - Salzburg - Zürich and v.v.

C – *EuroNight* ISTER – 🛏 1, 2 cl., ▬ 1, 2 cl., [2] Budapest - Bucureşti and v.v.

D – DACIA – 🛏 1, 2 cl., ▬ 2 cl., [2] ✕ Wien - Budapest - Bucureşti and v.v.

G – [12] Wien - Budapest - Szolnok (arrive 2102) - Debrecen (2235) - Zahony (0010). Conveys 🛏 1, 2 cl. Wien - Zahony - Lviv - Kyïv; see Table **96**.

J – [12] Zahony (depart 0405) - Debrecen (0531) - Szolnok (0657) - Budapest - Wien. Conveys 🛏 1, 2 cl. Kyïv - Lviv - Zahony - Wien; see Table **96**.

L – TRANSILVANIA – [12] ✕ Wien - Budapest - Szolnok (arrive 1502) - Cluj Napoca (2225).

N – TRANSILVANIA – [12] ✕ Cluj Napoca (depart 0740) - Szolnok (1257) - Budapest - Wien.

P – From Bratislava, depart 0608.

Q – To Bratislava, arrive 2152.

o – München **Ost**.

r – ①–⑥.

RJ | *RJX* – ÖBB *Railjet* service, ✕, [1] (business class), [1] (first class), [2] (economy class).

♥ – Operated by REGIOJET. Separate fare tariff applies.

DORTMUND - KÖLN - FRANKFURT - WIEN - BUDAPEST 66

train type	*ICE*	*ICE*	*ICE*	*ICE*	*ICE*	*EN*	*ICE*	*ICE*	*NJ*	*RJX*
train number	**21**	**23**	**91**	**91**	**27**	**347**	**29**	**229**	**40421**	**269**
notes			**P**	**Q**		**D** 🅁			**A**	
Dortmund Hbf..........d.	...	0431	...	0629	0829	...	1029	1229	...	...
Düsseldorf Hbf..........d.	...	0524	...	⊙	0924	...	1124	⊙	2143	...
Köln Hbf..........d.	...	0553	...	0753	0953	...	1153	1353	2216	...
Bonn Hbf..........d.	...	0614	...	0814	1014	...	1214	1414	2311	...
Koblenz Hbf..........d.	...	0648	...	0848	1048	...	1248	1448	2346	...
Mainz Hbf..........d.	...	0740	...	0942	1142	...	1342	1542	0056	...
Frankfurt Flug. ✈..........d.	...	0801	...	1001	1201	...	1401	1601	0120	...
Frankfurt (M) Hbf..........d.	0621	0822	...	1022	1222	...	1421	1621	0131f	...
Würzburg Hbf..........d.	0735	0934	1134	1134	1335	...	1535	1735	0242	...
Nürnberg Hbf..........d.	0831	1031	1231	1231	1431	...	1631	1831	0408	...
Regensburg Hbf..........d.	0926	1126	1326	1326	1526	...	1726	1926	0505	...
Passau Hbf 🏛..........d.	1026	1229	1429	1429	1629	...	1829	2031	0613	...
Linz..........a.	1126	1326	1526	1526	1726	...	1926	2134	0746	...
Wien Hbf..........a.	1247	1447	1647	1647	1847	...	2047	2305	0919	...
	RJX	*RJX*		*RJX*			*RJX*			
	63	**65**		**67**			**261**			
Wien Hbf..........d.	1340	1542	...	1740	...	1942	2140	...	...	0942
Hegyeshalom 🏛..........a.	1425	1625	...	1825	...	2025	2225	...	...	1025
Budapest Keleti..........a.	1619	1819	...	2019	...	2220	0019	...	...	1219

train type	*ICE*	*EN*	*RJX*	*RJX*	*ICE*	*RJX*	*RJX*	*EC*	*NJ*	
train number	**228**	**346**	**60**	**62**	**90**	**64**	**66**	**148**	**40490**	
notes		**D** 🅁			**Q**			**S**	**A**	
Budapest Keleti..........d.	...	0540	0740	0940	...	1140	1340	1640	...	...
Hegyeshalom 🏛..........d.	...	0732	0932	1132	...	1332	1532	1832	...	...
Wien Hbf..........a.	...	0821	1021	1221	...	1421	1621	1921	...	...
		ICE	*ICE*	*ICE*		*ICE*	*ICE*			
		28	**26**	**90**		**22**	**20**			
				P						
Wien Hbf..........d.	0651	0913	1113	1313	1313	1513	1713	...	2013	...
Linz..........d.	0817	1034	1234	1434	1434	1634	1834	...	2136	...
Passau Hbf 🏛..........a.	0922	1131	1331	1531	1531	1731	1934	...	2235	...
Regensburg Hbf..........a.	1030	1233	1433	1633	1633	1833	2033	...	2354	...
Nürnberg Hbf..........a.	1127	1327	1528	1729	1729	1928	2128	...	0056	...
Würzburg Hbf..........a.	1222	1422	1622	1823	1823	2022	2222	...	|	...
Frankfurt (M) Hbf..........a.	1336	1536	1736	...	1936	2136	2337	...	0345f	...
Frankfurt Flug. ✈..........a.	1355	1555	1755	...	1955	2156	...	...	0356	...
Mainz Hbf..........a.	1418	1618	1818	...	2018	2218	...	...	0416	...
Koblenz Hbf..........a.	1511	1711	1911	...	2111	2311	...	...	0511	...
Bonn Hbf..........a.	1543	1743	1943	...	2143	2343	...	...	0558	...
Köln Hbf..........a.	1605	1805	2005	...	2205	0005	...	...	0651	...
Düsseldorf Hbf..........a.	⊙	1832	2031	...	⊙	0034	...	...	0723	...
Dortmund Hbf..........a.	1721	1922	2121	...	2321	0125	...	...	...	...

A – *ÖBB nightjet* 🛏 1, 2 cl., 🛏 2 cl. (4, 6 berth), [2] Amsterdam - Düsseldorf - Wien and v.v. ♣ (Table **53**).

D – DACIA – 🛏 1, 2 cl., 🛏 2 cl., [2] ✕ Wien - Budapest - Bucureşti and v.v.

P – Dec. 11 - Mar. 31.

Q – Apr. 1 - Dec. 9.

S – SEMMELWEIS – [12] Budapest - Wien.

f – Frankfurt (Main) **Süd**.

⊙ – Via Hagen, Wuppertal (Table **800**).

♣ – Special fares apply.

RJ – ÖBB *Railjet* service. [1] (business class), [1] (first class), [2] (economy class), ✕.

MÜNCHEN - INNSBRUCK - VENEZIA and MILANO 70

	EC	*EC*	*EC*	*FR*	*EC*		*FR*	*FR*	*EC*	*EC*	*FA*	*EC*	*FR*	*FR*	*EC*	*FR*	*EC*	*EC*		*NJ*	*NJ*		*NJ*		
	1281	**81**	**37**	**9732**	**83**		**9738**	**9439**	**85**	**42**	**8525**	**87**	**9751**	**9756**	**89**	**9759**	**287**	**289**		**295**	**40295**		**237**		
	♥	♥	🅁	🅁	♥		🅁	**9441**	♥	🅁	🅁	♥	🅁	🅁	♥	🅁	♥	♥							
	⑥⑦	①–⑤	⊗	⚡	**P**	2	⚡	🅁⚡		⊗	⚡		⚡	⚡		⚡				**B**	**D**		**C**		
			🍷	🍷			🍷	🍷		🍷	🍷		🍷	🍷		🍷				🍷	🍷		🍷		
Stuttgart Hbf..........d.	...	...	...	...	...	...	...	...	...	...	...	...	...	...	...	...	...	...	...	...	...	...	2029	...	...
München Hbf..........d.	0734	0734	...	...	0934	...	...	...	1132	...	...	1334	...	...	1534	...	1734	1934	...	2009	2009	...	|	...	...
München Ost..........d.	0744	0744	...	...	0944	...	...	...	1144	...	...	1344	...	...	1544	...	1744	1944	...	2020	2020	...	2354	...	...
Kufstein 🏛..........a.	0834	0834	...	...	1034	...	...	...	1234	...	...	1434	...	...	1634	...	1834	2034	...	|	|	...	|	...	...
Wörgl..........a.	0844	0844	...	...	1044	...	...	...	1244	...	...	1444	...	...	1644	...	1844	2044	...	|	|	...	|	...	...
Jenbach..........a.	0858	0858	...	...	1058	...	...	...	1258	...	...	1458	...	...	1658	...	1858	2059	...	|	|	...	|	...	...
Innsbruck Hbf..........a.	0918	0918	...	...	1118	...	...	...	1318	...	...	1518	...	...	1718	...	1918	2118	...	|	|	...	|	...	...
Innsbruck Hbf..........d.	0924	0924	...	...	1124	...	...	...	1324	...	...	1524	...	...	1724	...	...	...	...	|	|	...	|	...	...
Brennero / Brenner 🏛..........a.	1000	1000	...	...	1200	...	...	...	1400	...	...	1600	...	...	1800	...	...	...	...	◧	◧	...	◧	...	...
Bolzano / Bozen..........a.	1127	1127	...	...	1327	...	...	...	1527	...	...	1727	...	...	1927	...	...	...	...	|	|	...	|	...	...
Trento..........a.	1202	1202	...	...	1402	...	...	...	1602	...	...	1802	...	...	2002	...	...	...	...	|	|	...	|	...	...
Padova..........a.	|	|	...	...	|	...	...	...	|	...	...	|	...	...	|	...	...	...	...	|	0457	...	|	...	...
Verona..........a.	1256	1256	1330	1402	1458	1521	1532	...	1658	1732	1752	1858	1930	1932	2056	2130	...	...	...	|	0551	...	|	...	...
Padova..........a.	1358	|	1412	|	|	1619	|	...	1756	|	|	|	2012	|	...	2212	...	...	...	|	|	...	|	...	...
Venezia Mestre..........a.	1414	|	1428	|	|	1636	|	...	1812	|	|	|	2028	|	...	2228	...	...	...	|	|	...	0822	...	...
Venezia Santa Lucia..........a.	1428	|	1440	|	|	1648	|	...	1825	|	|	|	2040	|	...	2240	...	...	...	|	|	...	0834	...	...
Milano Centrale..........a.	...	|	...	1515	|	...	1645	...	...	1855	|	|	...	2045	...	...	...	...	...	|	0742j	...	...	...	...
Genova Piazza Principe a.	...	|	...	...	|	...	...	...	...	...	|	|	...	...	...	...	...	...	...	|	0938	...	...	...	...
La Spezia Centrale..........d.	...	|	...	...	|	...	...	...	...	...	|	|	...	...	...	...	...	...	...	|	1110	...	...	...	...
Bologna Centrale..........a.	...	1410	...	...	1619	...	...	1655	...	...	1842	2016	...	...	...	...	...	...	...	0515	...	...	...	...	...
Rimini..........a.	...	...	...	...	1733t	...	...	|	...	...	|	...	...	...	...	...	...	...	...	|	...	...	...	...	...
Firenze SMN..........a.	...	...	...	...	...	...	...	1730	...	...	1925¶	...	...	...	...	...	...	...	...	0618	...	...	...	...	...
Roma Termini..........a.	...	...	...	...	...	...	...	1910	...	...	2045	...	...	...	...	...	...	...	...	0910	...	...	...	...	...

	EC	*EC*	*FR*	*FR*	*EC*	*FR*	*FR*	*FR*	*EC*	*FB*	*FR*	*FR*	*FR*	*EC*	*FA*	*EC*		*FR*	*EC*	*EC*	*EC*		*NJ*	*NJ*	*NJ*
	288	**286**	**9708**	**9705**	**88**	**8504**	**9716**	**8709**	**86**	**9715**	**9717**	**9724**	**9518**	**84**	**8512**	**82**		**9737**	**10**	**80**	**1280**		**236**	**294**	**40235**
	♥	♥	🅁	🅁	♥	🅁	🅁	🅁	♥	🅁	🅁⚡	🅁	🅁	♥	🅁	♥		🅁	🅁	♥	♥				
			⚡	⚡		⚡	⚡	⚡		⚡	⑥⑦	⚡	⚡	**R**	⚡			⚡	⊗	①–⑤	⑥⑦		**F**	**B**	**G**
			🍷	🍷		🍷	🍷	🍷		🍷	🍷	🍷	🍷		🍷			🍷	🍷				🍷	🍷	🍷
Roma Termini..........d.	...	...	...	...	...	0645	...	...	...	...	...	...	0920	...	1045	...	...	...	...	...	...	...	...	2017	...
Firenze SMN..........d.	...	...	...	...	...	0803¶	...	...	...	...	...	...	1100	...	1203¶	...	...	...	...	...	...	...	...	2231	...
Rimini..........d.	...	...	...	...	...	|	...	...	...	...	...	...	|	1034f	|	...	...	...	...	...	...	...	...	|	...
Bologna Centrale..........d.	...	...	...	...	0745	0845	...	...	...	...	...	...	1135	1152	1245	...	1410	...	...	1550	...	...	...	2345	...
La Spezia Centrale..........d.	...	...	...	...	|	|	...	...	...	...	...	...	...	|	|	...	|	...	...	|	...	...	...	|	1710
Genova Piazza Principe d.	...	...	...	...	|	|	...	...	...	...	...	...	...	|	|	...	|	...	...	|	...	...	...	|	1950
Milano Centrale..........d.	...	...	...	0715	|	|	...	0915	...	0945	1015	...	...	|	1305	...	|	1515	...	|	...	...	...	|	2126j
Venezia Santa Lucia..........d.	...	...	0720	|	|	|	...	|	...	|	|	1050	...	|	|	1335	|	|	1520	|	1535	...	2105	|	|
Venezia Mestre..........d.	...	...	0732	|	|	|	0902	|	...	|	|	1102	...	|	|	1347	|	|	1532	|	1547	...	2117	|	|
Padova..........d.	...	...	0748	|	|	|	0918	|	...	|	|	1118	...	|	|	1403	|	|	1548	|	1603	...	|	|	|
Verona..........d.	...	...	0830	0828	0901	0937	1000	1028	1101	1058	1128	1200	...	1301	1428	1501	1540	1628	1630	1701	1701	...	|	|	2258
Padova..........d.	...	...	...	...	|	...	...	...	|	...	...	...	...	|	...	|	...	...	...	|	|	...	|	|	2343
Trento..........d.	...	...	...	...	0959	...	...	...	1159	...	...	...	...	1359	...	1559	...	...	...	1759	1759	...	|	|	|
Bolzano / Bozen..........d.	...	...	...	...	1034	...	...	...	1234	...	...	...	...	1434	...	1634	...	...	...	1834	1834	...	|	|	|
Brennero / Brenner 🏛..........d.	...	...	...	...	1200	...	...	...	1400	...	...	...	...	1600	...	1800	...	...	...	2000	2000	...	◧	◧	◧
Innsbruck Hbf..........a.	...	...	...	...	1236	...	...	...	1436	...	...	...	...	1636	...	1836	...	...	...	2036	2036	...	|	|	|
Innsbruck Hbf..........d.	0717	1040	...	...	1240	...	...	...	1440	...	...	...	...	1640	...	1840	...	...	...	2040	2040	...	|	|	|
Jenbach..........d.	0735	1102	...	...	1302	...	...	...	1502	...	...	...	...	1702	...	1902	...	...	...	2102	2102	...	|	|	|
Wörgl..........d.	0749	1116	...	...	1316	...	...	...	1516	...	...	...	...	1716	...	1916	...	...	...	2116	2116	...	|	|	|
Kufstein 🏛..........a.	0757	1124	...	...	1324	...	...	...	1524	...	...	...	...	1724	...	1924	...	...	...	2124	2124	...	|	|	|
München Ost..........a.	0849	1217	...	...	1416	...	...	...	1616	...	...	...	...	1816	...	2014	...	...	...	2216	2216	...	0550	|	|
München Hbf..........a.	0902	1227	...	...	1427	...	...	...	1627	...	...	...	...	1827	...	2026	...	...	...	2227	2227	...	|	0922	0922
Stuttgart Hbf..........a.	...	...	...	...	...	...	...	...	...	...	...	...	...	...	...	...	...	...	...	...	...	...	0837	...	...

B – *ÖBB nightjet* – 🛏 1, 2 cl., 🛏 2 cl. (4, 6 berth), [2] München - Villach - Tarvisio 🏛 - Roma and v.v. Special fares apply.

C – *ÖBB nightjet* – 🛏 1, 2 cl., 🛏 2 cl. (4, 6 berth), [2] Stuttgart (**237**) - Tarvisio 🏛 - Venezia. Special fares apply.

D – *ÖBB nightjet* – 🛏 1, 2 cl., 🛏 2 cl. (4, 6 berth), [2] München (**295**) - Villach (**233**) - Tarvisio 🏛 - Milano - Genova - La Spezia. Special fares apply.

F – *ÖBB nightjet* – 🛏 1, 2 cl., 🛏 2 cl. (4, 6 berth), [2] Venezia (**236**) - Tarvisio 🏛 - Stuttgart. Special fares apply.

G – *ÖBB nightjet* – 🛏 1, 2 cl., 🛏 2 cl. (4, 6 berth), [2] La Spezia (**235**) - Genova - Milano - Tarvisio 🏛 - Villach (**294**) - München. Special fares apply.

P – [12] München - Bologna - (Rimini May 25 - Sept. 9).

R – [12] (Rimini May 26 - Sept. 10) - Bologna - München.

f – May 26 - Sept. 10.

j – Milano **Rogoredo**.

t – May 25 - Sept. 9.

⊗ – Compulsory reservation for international journeys. Supplement payable for international journeys and for internal journeys within Italy.

◧ – 🏛 is Tarvisio (Table **88**).

⚡ – Supplement payable.

♥ – DB-ÖBB EuroCity service.

¶ – Firenze **Campo di Marte**.

73 AMSTERDAM, BERLIN, DORTMUND and KÖLN - BASEL - ZÜRICH and MILANO

train type	ICE	EC	ICE	ICE	EC	ICE	EC	ICE	EC	ICE	EC	ICE	ICE	IR	EC	ICE	ICE	EC	ICE	EC	EC
train number	3	315	271	5	327	101	151	275	57	71	7	121	277	2327	321	105	73	9	279	9	323
notes	Ⓐ	R ⊗	1271 M	⚒	R ⊗		R ⊗	❖	R ⊗	❖					R ⊗		❖				R ⊗
Hamburg Hbf d.	...	...	0045e	...	...	...	...	...	...	0618	0437	...	...	...	...	...	0824	0645	...	...	...
Bremen Hbf d.	...	...	|	...	...	...	...	...	...	|	0540	...	...	...	...	...	|	0744	...	...	...
Berlin Hbf d.	...	...	|	...	...	...	...	0429p	...	|	|	...	0629	...	...	...	|	|	0829	...	...
Hannover Hbf d.	...	...	0210e	...	...	...	...	|	...	0741	|	...	|	...	...	...	0941	|	|	...	...
Dortmund Hbf d.	...	...	|	...	...	0528v	...	|	...	|	|	...	|	...	...	...	|	|	|	...	...
Essen Hbf d.	...	...	|	...	...	|	...	|	...	|	0757	...	|	...	...	...	|	0957	|	...	...
Amsterdam Centraal d.	...	...	|	...	...	|	...	|	...	|	|	0638	|	...	...	0808	|	|	|	...	...
Utrecht Centraal d.	...	...	|	...	...	|	...	|	...	|	|	0706	|	...	...	0834	|	|	|	...	...
Arnhem ⊙ d.	...	...	|	...	...	|	...	|	...	|	|	0737	|	...	...	0907	|	|	|	...	...
Duisburg Hbf d.	...	...	|	...	...	h	...	|	...	|	0810	0834	|	...	...	|	|	1010	|	...	...
Düsseldorf Hbf d.	...	...	|	...	...	|	...	|	...	|	0824	0851	|	...	...	1019	|	1024	|	...	...
Köln Hbf d.	...	...	|	...	...	0655	...	|	...	|	0853	0928	|	...	...	1055	|	1053	|	...	...
Bonn Hbf d.	...	...	|	...	...	|	...	|	...	|	0914	|	|	...	...	|	|	1114	|	...	...
Koblenz Hbf d.	...	...	|	...	...	⊖	...	|	...	|	0948	⊖	|	...	...	⊖	|	1148	|	...	...
Mainz Hbf d.	...	...	|	...	...	|	...	|	...	|	1042	|	|	...	...	|	|	1242	|	...	...
Frankfurt Flughafen ✈ d.	...	...	|	...	...	0751	...	|	...	|	|	1018	|	...	...	1151	|	|	|	...	...
Frankfurt (Main) Hbf d.	...	...	0550	0648	...	|	0806	0850	...	1006	|	1031	1050	...	...	|	1206	|	1250	...	...
Mannheim Hbf d.	...	...	0633	0735	...	0835	0847	0935	...	1046	1123	...	1135	...	...	1235	1246	1323	1335	...	...
Karlsruhe Hbf d.	0556	...	0658	0800	...	0900	0911	1000	...	1111	1149	...	1200	...	...	1300	1311	1349	1400	...	...
Freiburg (Brsg) Hbf d.	0702	...	0804	0902	...	1005	1014	1102	...	1214	1250	...	1303	...	...	1402	1414	1455	1501	...	...
Basel Bad Bf 🏛 a.	0736	...	0837	0936	...	1038	1045	1136	...	1246	1322	...	1337	...	...	1436	1446	1528	1536	←	...
Basel SBB a.	0747	...	0847	0947	...	1047	1054	1147	...	1255	1333	...	1347	...	...	1447	1455	1536	1547	1536	...
Basel SBB ★ d.	0806	...	0906	...	...	...	1103	1156	1228	1306	1356	...	...	1403	...	...	1506	1606	...	1606	...
Bern a.	|	...	|	...	...	...	|	1256	1326	|	1456	...	...	|	...	...	|	→	...	|	...
Interlaken Ost a.	|	...	|	...	...	...	|	1358	|	|	1558	...	...	|	...	...	|	...	...	|	...
Zürich HB a.	0900	0933	1000	...	1033	...	|	...	|	1400	...	...	...	|	1533	...	1600	...	...	1700	1733
Chur a.	...	|	1123	...	|	...	|	...	|	1523	...	...	...	|	|	...	1723q	...	...	...	|
Arth-Goldau a.	...	1016	...	...	1116	...	1245	...	|	...	...	...	...	1545	1616	...	...	...	...	...	1816
Bellinzona a.	...	1112	...	...	1212	...	1342	...	|	...	...	...	...	...	1712	...	...	...	...	...	1912
Lugano a.	...	1132	...	...	1230	...	1358	...	|	...	...	...	...	...	1732	...	...	...	...	...	1932
Chiasso 🏛 a.	...	1202	...	...	1255	...	1446	...	◧	...	...	...	...	...	1802	...	...	...	...	...	2002
Como San Giovanni a.	...	1210	...	...	1308	...	1501	...	|	...	...	...	...	...	1810	...	...	...	...	...	2038
Milano Centrale a.	...	1250	...	...	1409f	...	1550	...	1640	...	...	...	...	...	1850	...	...	...	...	...	2050

train type	ICE	ICE	EC	EC	ICE	ICE	ICE	ICE	ICE	ICE	ICE		NJ	EC		NJ	EC		NJ	EC
train number	107	75	59	325	123	371	109	77	125	373	79		403	311		408	315		471	327
notes		❖	R ⊗	R ⊗		❖		❖			❖		E	R ⊗		B	R ⊗		A	R ⊗
Hamburg Hbf d.	0845	1024	...	...	...	...	1045	1224	...	...	1424	...	...	...	...	...	...	...	2207	...
Bremen Hbf d.	0944	|	...	...	...	...	1144	|	...	...	|	...	...	...	...	...	...	...	2311	...
Berlin Hbf d.	|	|	...	...	...	1029	|	|	...	1229	|	...	...	...	...	2051	...	...	|	...
Hannover Hbf d.	|	1141	...	...	...	|	|	1341	...	|	1541	...	...	...	...	|	...	...	0030	...
Dortmund Hbf d.	|	|	...	...	...	|	|	|	...	|	|	...	...	...	...	|	...	...	|	...
Essen Hbf d.	1157	|	...	...	...	|	1347	|	...	|	|	...	...	...	...	|	...	...	|	...
Amsterdam Centraal d.	|	|	...	...	1038	|	|	|	1238	|	|	...	2045	...	...	|	...	...	|	...
Utrecht Centraal d.	|	|	...	...	1104	|	|	|	1304	|	|	...	2126	...	...	|	...	...	|	...
Arnhem ⊙ d.	|	|	...	...	1137	|	|	|	1337	|	|	...	|	...	...	|	...	...	|	...
Duisburg Hbf d.	1209	|	...	...	1234	|	1410	|	1434	|	|	...	2301	...	...	|	...	...	|	...
Düsseldorf Hbf d.	1223	|	...	...	1248	|	1423	|	1450	|	|	...	2316	...	...	|	...	...	|	...
Köln Hbf d.	1255	|	...	...	1321	|	1455	|	1528	|	|	...	2353	...	...	|	...	...	|	...
Bonn Hbf d.	|	|	...	...	|	|	|	|	|	|	|	...	0014	...	...	|	...	...	|	...
Koblenz Hbf d.	⊖	|	...	...	⊖	|	⊖	|	⊖	|	|	...	0049	...	...	|	...	...	|	...
Mainz Hbf d.	|	|	...	...	|	|	|	|	|	|	|	...	0142	...	...	|	...	...	|	...
Frankfurt Flughafen ✈ d.	1351	|	...	...	1418	|	1551	|	1618	|	|	...	0211	...	...	|	...	...	|	...
Frankfurt (Main) Hbf d.	|	1406	...	...	1431	1450	|	1606	1631	1650	1806	...	0245	...	...	0400	...	...	0432x	...
Mannheim Hbf d.	1435	1446	...	...	...	1535	1635	1646	...	1735	1846	...	0333	...	...	0441	...	...	|	...
Karlsruhe Hbf d.	1500	1511	...	...	...	1600	1700	1711	...	1800	1911	...	0403	...	...	0509	...	...	0604	...
Freiburg (Brsg) Hbf d.	1602	1614	...	...	...	1702	1802	1814	...	1901	2014	...	0529	...	...	0619	...	...	0723	...
Basel Bad Bf 🏛 a.	1636	1646	...	...	...	1736	1836	1846	...	1936	2046	...	0611	...	...	0656	...	...	0759	...
Basel SBB a.	1647	1655	...	...	...	1747	1847	1855	...	1947	2055	...	0620	...	...	0720	...	...	0810	...
Basel SBB ★ d.	...	1706	1728	...	...	1756	...	1906	...	1956	2106	...	|	...	...	|	...	...	|	...
Bern a.	...	|	1826	...	...	1856	...	|	...	2056	|	...	|	...	...	|	...	...	|	...
Interlaken Ost a.	...	|	|	...	...	1958	...	|	...	2159	|	...	|	...	...	|	...	...	|	...
Zürich HB a.	...	1800	|	1933	...	...	...	2000	...	...	2200	...	0805	0833	...	0905	0933	...	1005	1033
Chur a.	...	1923	|	|	...	...	...	...	...	...	...	...	...	|	...	...	|	...	...	|
Arth-Goldau a.	...	...	|	2016	...	...	...	...	...	...	...	...	...	0916	...	...	1016	...	...	1116
Bellinzona a.	...	...	|	2112	...	...	...	...	...	...	...	...	...	1012	...	...	1112	...	...	1212
Lugano a.	...	...	|	2132	...	...	...	...	...	...	...	...	...	1032	...	...	1132	...	...	1230
Chiasso 🏛 a.	...	...	◧	2202	...	...	...	...	...	...	...	...	...	1102	...	...	1202	...	...	1255
Como San Giovanni a.	...	...	|	2210	...	...	...	...	...	...	...	...	...	1110	...	...	1210	...	...	1308
Milano Centrale a.	...	...	2140	2250	...	...	...	...	...	...	...	...	...	1150	...	...	1250	...	...	1409f

A – *ÖBB nightjet* – 🛏 1, 2 cl., ▬ 2 cl. (4, 6 berth), [2] Hamburg - Frankfurt - Zürich. Special fares apply. (Table **53**).
B – *ÖBB nightjet* – 🛏 1, 2 cl., ▬ 2 cl. (4, 6 berth), [2] Berlin - Frankfurt - Zürich. Special fares apply. (Table **53**).
E – *ÖBB nightjet* – 🛏 1, 2 cl., ▬ 2 cl. (4, 6 berth), [2] Amsterdam - Frankfurt - Zürich. Special fares apply.
M – [12] 🍸 (Hamburg ① also Apr. 11, May 2, 30, Oct. 4; not Apr. 10, May 1, 29, Oct. 2) - Frankfurt - Basel - Chur.

e – ① (also Apr. 11, May 2, 30, Oct. 4; not Apr. 10, May 1, 29, Oct. 2).
f – Milano **Lambrate**.
h – Via Hagen and Wuppertal.
p – Ⓐ.
q – Ⓒ.

v – ⚒.
x – Frankfurt (Main) **Süd**.

⊙ – 🏛 is at Emmerich.
◧ – Via Brig. 🏛 is at Domodossola; ticket point is **Iselle**.
⊖ – Via Köln - Frankfurt high speed line.
★ – Connections at Basel are not guaranteed.
⊗ – Compulsory reservation for international journeys. Supplement payable for international journeys and for internal journeys within Italy.
❖ – Subject to alteration from Apr. 1.

CONNECTING SERVICES

Basel - Luzern - Chiasso: Table **550**, Basel - Bern - Interlaken and Brig: Table **560**.
Zürich - Landquart - Chur: Table **520**, Chur - St Moritz: Table **540**, Zürich - Bellinzona - Chiasso: Table **550**.

MILANO and ZÜRICH - KÖLN, DORTMUND, BERLIN and AMSTERDAM 73

train type		*ICE*	*ICE*	*ICE*	*ICE*	*ICE*	*ICE*	*ICE*	*EC*	*EC*	*EC*	*ICE*	*EC*	*ICE*	*ICE*	*EC*	*ICE*	*EC*	*EC*	*ICE*	*EC*	*ICE*
train number		**78**	**372**	**126**	**76**	**370**	**124**	**74**	**312**	**8**	**50**	**278**	**8**	**72**	**12** **122**	**6**	**276**	**6**	**314**	**70**	**158**	**104**
notes		✤	✤		✤			✤	[R] ⊗		[R] ⊗			✤					[R] ⊗	✤	[R] ⊗	
Milano Centrale	d.	...	...	...	...	...	...	...	0710	...	0720	...	...	...	...	...	...	...	0910	...	1010	...
Como San Giovanni	d.	...	...	...	...	...	...	...	0754	...	|	...	...	...	...	...	...	...	0950	...	1059	...
Chiasso 🏛	d.	...	...	...	...	...	...	...	0805	...	◧	...	...	...	...	...	...	...	1005	...	1130	...
Lugano	d.	...	...	...	...	...	...	...	0830	...	|	...	...	...	...	...	...	...	1030	...	1201	...
Bellinzona	d.	...	...	...	...	...	...	...	0847	...	|	...	...	...	...	...	...	...	1047	...	1218	...
Arth-Goldau	d.	...	...	...	...	...	...	...	0945	...	|	...	...	...	...	...	...	...	1145	...	1315	...
Chur	d.	...	...	...	...	...	...	...	|	...	|	...	...	1037	...	...	...	...	|	1237	|	...
Zürich HB	d.	0559	...	...	0759	...	...	0959	1027	1059	|	...	...	1159	...	...	...	...	1227	1359	|	...
Interlaken Ost	d.	|	0558	...	|	...	...	|	...	|	|	1000	...	|	...	1200	...	...	...	|	|	...
Bern	d.	|	0704	...	|	...	...	|	...	|	1036	1104	←	|	...	1304	...	←	...	|	|	...
Basel SBB ★	a.	0653	0801	...	0853	...	...	1053	...	1153	1132	1201	1153	1253	...	1401	...	1401	...	1453	1456	...
Basel SBB	d.	0706	0813	...	0906	1013	...	1106	...	1220	...	1213	1220	1306	...	1427	1413	1427	...	1506	...	1513
Basel Bad Bf 🏛	d.	0714	0822	...	0914	1022	...	1114	...	→	...	1222	1228	1314	...	→	1422	1435	...	1514	...	1522
Freiburg (Brsg) Hbf	d.	0748	0855	...	0948	1055	...	1148	...	...	...	1255	1304	1348	...	...	1455	1507	...	1548	...	1555
Karlsruhe Hbf	d.	0851	1000	...	1051	1200	...	1251	...	...	...	1400	1412	1451	...	...	1600	1613	...	1651	...	1700
Mannheim Hbf	a.	0914	1024	...	1114	1224	...	1314	...	...	...	1424	1437	1514	...	...	1624	1637	...	1714	...	1724
Frankfurt (Main) Hbf	a.	0952	1108	1126	1152	1308	1326	1352	...	...	...	1508	|	1552	1628	...	1708	|	...	1752	...	|
Frankfurt Flughafen ✈	a.	|	|	1139	|	|	1339	|	...	...	...	|	|	|	1639	...	|	|	...	|	...	1806
Mainz Hbf	a.	|	|	|	|	|	|	|	...	...	...	|	1518	|	|	...	|	1718	...	|	...	|
Koblenz Hbf	a.	|	|	⊖	|	|	⊖	|	...	...	...	|	1611	|	⊖	...	|	1811	...	|	...	⊖
Bonn Hbf	a.	|	|	|	|	|	|	|	...	...	...	|	1643	|	|	...	|	1843	...	|	...	|
Köln Hbf	a.	|	|	1233	|	|	1432	|	...	...	...	|	1705	|	1733	...	|	1905	...	|	...	1904
Düsseldorf Hbf	a.	|	|	1305	|	|	1509	|	...	...	...	|	1731	|	1809	...	|	1931	...	|	...	1935
Duisburg Hbf	a.	|	|	1323	|	|	15 25	|	...	...	...	|	1745	|	1823	...	|	1945	...	|	...	1949
Arnhem ⊙	a.	|	|	1427	|	|	1627	|	...	...	...	|	|	|	1927	...	|	|	...	|	...	2057
Utrecht Centraal	a.	|	|	1459	|	|	1659	|	...	...	...	|	|	|	1959	...	|	|	...	|	...	2129
Amsterdam Centraal	a.	|	|	1529	|	|	1729	|	...	...	...	|	|	|	2028	...	|	|	...	|	...	2159
Essen Hbf	a.	|	|	...	|	|	...	|	...	...	...	|	1758	|	...	...	|	1958	...	|	...	...
Dortmund Hbf	a.	|	|	...	|	|	...	|	...	...	...	|	1821	|	...	...	|	2022	...	|	...	...
Hannover Hbf	a.	1217	|	...	1417	|	...	1617	...	...	...	|	|	1817	...	...	|	|	...	2017	...	...
Berlin Hbf	a.	|	1529	...	|	1729	...	|	...	...	...	1929	|	|	...	...	2129	|	...	|	...	...
Bremen Hbf	a.	|	...	...	|	...	...	|	...	...	...	...	2015	|	...	...	...	2217	...	|	...	...
Hamburg Hbf	a.	1336	...	...	1536	...	...	1736	...	...	...	...	2114	1936	...	...	...	2316	...	2139	...	...

train type		*EC*	*EC*	*IC*	*ICE*	*ICE*	*ICE*	*ICE*	*EC*	*ICE*	*ICE*	*EC*	*ICE*	*EC*	*NJ*	*NJ*	*EC*	*NJ*
train number		**52**	**316**	**776**	**274**	**120**	**376**	**102**	**318**	**272** **292**	**100**	**320**	**4**	**308**	**409**	**470**	**310**	**402**
notes		[R] ⊗	[R] ⊗		✤		✤		[R] ⊗			[R] ⊗		[R] ⊗	**A**	**B**	[R] ⊗	**C**
Milano Centrale	d.	1120	1110	...	...	...	...	...	1310	...	...	1510	...	1551j	...	...	1810	...
Como San Giovanni	d.	|	1150	...	...	...	...	...	1350	...	...	1550	...	1650	...	...	1850	...
Chiasso 🏛	d.	◧	1205	...	...	...	...	...	1405	...	...	1605	...	1705	...	...	1905	...
Lugano	d.	|	1230	...	...	...	...	...	1430	...	...	1630	...	1730	...	...	1930	...
Bellinzona	d.	|	1247	...	...	...	...	...	1447	...	...	1647	...	1747	...	...	1947	...
Arth-Goldau	d.	|	1345	...	...	...	...	...	1545	...	...	1745	...	1845	...	...	2045	...
Chur	d.	|	|	...	...	...	...	...	|	1537t	...	|	1737t	|	...	...	|	...
Zürich HB	d.	|	1427	1459	...	...	...	...	1627	1659	...	1827	1859	1927	1959	2059	2127	2159
Interlaken Ost	d.	|	...	|	...	...	1500	...	...	|	...	...	|	...	|	|	...	|
Bern	d.	1436	...	|	...	...	1604	...	...	|	...	...	|	...	|	|	...	|
Basel SBB ★	a.	1532	...	1553	...	...	1701	...	...	1753	...	...	1953	...	2053	2153	...	|
Basel SBB	d.	1538	...	...	1613	...	1707	1713	...	1813	1913	...	2013	...	2113	2213	...	2313
Basel Bad Bf 🏛	d.	1552	...	...	1622	...	1715	1721	...	1822	1921	...	2022	...	2122	2222	...	2323
Freiburg (Brsg) Hbf	d.	1624	...	...	1655	...	1748	1753	...	1855	1954	...	2054	...	2158	2258	...	0005
Karlsruhe Hbf	d.	1729	...	...	1800	...	1851	1900	...	2000	2100	...	2202	...	2307	0019	...	0120
Mannheim Hbf	a.	1758	...	...	1824	...	1914	1924	...	2024	2124	...	2224	...	2340	|	...	0149
Frankfurt (Main) Hbf	a.	1844	...	...	1908	1928	1952	|	...	2108	|	...	2308	...	0027	0210x	...	0245
Frankfurt Flughafen ✈	a.	...	...	...	|	1939	|	2006	...	...	2206	...	|	...	|	|	...	0326
Mainz Hbf	a.	...	...	...	|	|	|	|	...	...	|	...	|	...	|	|	...	0346
Koblenz Hbf	a.	...	...	...	|	⊖	|	⊖	...	...	⊖	...	|	...	|	|	...	0441
Bonn Hbf	a.	...	...	...	|	|	|	|	...	...	|	...	|	...	|	|	...	0524
Köln Hbf	a.	...	...	...	|	2033	|	2104	...	...	2307	...	|	...	|	|	...	0553
Düsseldorf Hbf	a.	...	...	...	|	2105	|	...	...	...	|	...	|	...	|	|	...	0623
Duisburg Hbf	a.	...	...	...	|	2123	|	...	...	...	|	...	|	...	|	|	...	0640
Arnhem ⊙	a.	...	...	...	|	2227	|	...	...	...	|	...	|	...	|	|	...	|
Utrecht Centraal	a.	...	...	...	|	2258	|	...	...	...	|	...	|	...	|	|	...	0833
Amsterdam Centraal	a.	...	...	...	|	2329	|	...	...	...	|	...	|	...	|	|	...	0914
Essen Hbf	a.	...	...	...	|	...	|	...	...	...	|	...	|	...	|	|	...	...
Dortmund Hbf	a.	...	...	...	|	...	|	...	...	...	0024	...	|	...	|	|	...	...
Hannover Hbf	a.	...	...	...	|	...	2217f	...	...	...	...	...	|	...	|	0529	...	...
Berlin Hbf	a.	...	...	...	2329	...	|	...	...	...	...	...	0347z	...	0720	|	...	...
Bremen Hbf	a.	...	...	...	...	...	|	...	...	...	...	...	|	...	...	|	...	...
Hamburg Hbf	a.	...	...	...	...	...	2342f	...	...	...	...	...	0537z	...	...	0754	...	...

A – *ÖBB nightjet* – 🛏 1,2 cl., ▬ 2 cl. (4, 6 berth), [2] Zürich - Frankfurt - Berlin. Special fares apply. (Table **53**).
B – *ÖBB nightjet* – 🛏 1,2 cl., ▬ 2 cl. (4, 6 berth), [2] Zürich - Frankfurt - Hamburg. Special fares apply. (Table **53**).
C – *ÖBB nightjet* – 🛏 1,2 cl., [12] Zürich - Frankfurt - Amsterdam. Special fares apply.
f – Not ⑥.
j – Milano **Lambrate**.
t – ©.
x – Frankfurt (Main) **Süd**.
z – ⑦.

⊙ – 🏛 is at Emmerich.
◧ – Via Brig. 🏛 is at Domodossola; ticket point is **Iselle**.
★ – Connections at Basel are not guaranteed.
⊖ – Via Köln - Frankfurt high speed line.
⊗ – Compulsory reservation for international journeys. Supplement payable for international journeys and for internal journeys within Italy.
✤ – Subject to alteration from Apr. 1.

CONNECTING SERVICES

Basel - Luzern - Chiasso: Table **550**. Basel - Bern - Interlaken and Brig: Table **560**.

Zürich - Landquart - Chur: Table **520**, Chur - St Moritz: Table **540**, Zürich - Bellinzona - Chiasso: Table **550**.

74 MILANO - PÁTRA - ATHÍNAI

train type	FB			IC	FB			
train number	8803			605	8809			
notes	🅁 ✕	⛴		🅁 ✕	🅁 ✕	⛴	⛴	
	✓	SF		✓	✓	SF	SF	
Milano Centrale d.	0735	...	...	0705	1035	...	...	...
Bologna d.	0945	...	...	0958	1245	...	...	...
Ancona d.	1130	...	...	1228	1436	...	...	...
Ancona Marittima d.	...	1330	...	|	|	1630	...	...
Pescara Centrale d.	...	|	...	1401	1547	|	...	...
Foggia d.	...	|	...	1551	1722	|	...	...
Bari Centrale a.	...	|	...	1705	1825	|	...	...
Bari Marittima d.	...	|	...	...	...	|	1930	...
Pátra a.	...	1430	...	...	...	1500	1300	...
Athína Lárisa a.	...	❖	...	...	...	❖	❖	...

train type			FB				FB	IC		
train number			8820				8820	612		
notes		⛴	🅁 ✕	⛴		⛴	🅁 ✕	🅁 ✕		
		SF	✓	SF		SF	✓	✓		
Athína Lárisa d.	...	❖	...	❖	...	❖	...	...	...	...
Pátra d.	...	1730	...	1730	...	1800	...	...	...	...
Bari Marittima a.	...	|	...	|	...	0930	...	...	...	...
Bari Centrale d.	...	|	...	|	...	...	1132	1155	...	...
Foggia d.	...	|	...	|	...	...	1239	1313	...	...
Pescara Centrale d.	...	|	...	|	...	...	1414	1502	...	...
Ancona Marittima a.	...	1400	...	1630	...	...	|	|	...	...
Ancona d.	...	...	1525	...	...	...	1525	1638	...	...
Bologna a.	...	...	1715	...	...	...	1718	1901	...	...
Milano Centrale a.	...	...	1925	...	...	...	1925	2145	...	...

✓ – Supplement payable.

❖ – For 🚌/rail connections Pátra - Athína and v.v. see Tables **1440**, **1450**.

SF – **Superfast Ferries**, for days of running see Tables **2715**, **2755**.

75 MÜNCHEN - ZÜRICH

train type		EC	EC	EC	EC	EC	EC	EC		
train number		198	196	194	192	190	98	96		
notes		✕	✕	✕	✕	✕	✕	✕		
				A						
München Hbf d.	...	0655	0855	1055	1255	1455	1652	1852	...	...
Buchloe d.	...	0736	0936	1136	1336	1536	1736	1936	...	...
Memmingen d.	...	0801	1001	1201	1401	1601	1801	2001	...	...
Lindau Reutin ⊞ d.	...	0852	1052	1252	1452	1652	1852	2052	...	...
Bregenz ⊞ d.	...	0900	1100	1300	1500	1700	1900	2100	...	...
St Margrethen ⊞ a.	...	0909	1109	1309	1509	1709	1909	2109	...	...
St Gallen a.	...	0928	1128	1328	1528	1728	1928	2128	...	...
Winterthur a.	...	1001	1201	1401	1601	1801	2001	2201	...	...
Zürich Flughafen ✈ a.	...	1016	1216	1416	1616	1816	2016	2216	...	...
Zürich HB a.	...	1027	1227	1427	1627	1827	2027	2227	...	...

train type		EC	EC	EC	EC	EC	EC	EC		
train number		97	99	191	193	195	197	199		
notes		✕	✕	✕	✕	✕	✕	✕		
						B				
Zürich HB d.	...	0733	0933	1133	1333	1533	1733	1933	...	...
Zürich Flughafen ✈ d.	...	0743	0943	1143	1343	1543	1743	1943	...	...
Winterthur d.	...	0758	0958	1158	1358	1558	1758	1958	...	...
St Gallen d.	...	0832	1032	1232	1432	1632	1832	2032	...	...
St Margrethen ⊞ d.	...	0851	1051	1251	1451	1651	1849	2051	...	...
Bregenz ⊞ d.	...	0902	1102	1302	1502	1702	1902	2102	...	...
Lindau Reutin ⊞ d.	...	0910	1110	1310	1510	1710	1910	2110	...	...
Memmingen a.	...	0959	1159	1359	1558	1759	1959	2159	...	...
Buchloe a.	...	1023	1223	1423	1622	1823	2022	2223	...	...
München Hbf a.	...	1104	1304	1504	1704	1904	2104	2304	...	...

A – ⑦ Apr. 2 - Oct. 22 (also Sept. 16; not Apr. 9, 30, May 21, 28, Sept. 17, 24, Oct. 1).

B – ⑤ Mar. 31 - Oct. 20 (not Apr. 28, May 19, 26, Sept. 22, 29).

76 MÜNCHEN and NÜRNBERG - PRAHA

train type	RE	RE	ALX	ALX		RE	ALX	ALX	ALX		RE	ALX		RE	ALX		RE	ALX		RE	ALX		RE	ALX	
train number			365	365			79853	353	353			355			357			359			361			363	
notes	①–⑥	⑥⑦	⚒	†			†	⚒	†			¶			¶			¶			¶			¶	
notes			¶	¶				¶	¶																
München Hbf d.	...	...	0444	...	...	...	0644	0644	...	...	...	0843	...	...	1043	...	...	1243	...	...	1443	...	...	1643	...
Nürnberg Hbf d.	0434	0535	|	...	...	0738	|	|	...	...	0943	|	...	1143	|	...	1343	|	...	1543	|	...	1743	|	...
Regensburg d.	|	|	0615	0615	...	|	0815	0815	...	...	|	1014	...	|	1214	...	|	1414	...	|	1615	...	|	1814	...
Schwandorf d.	0542	0643	0654	0654	...	0846	0842	0852	0852	...	1046	1052	...	1246	1252	...	1446	1452	...	1647	1652	...	1846	1852	...
Furth im Wald ⊞ d.	...	...	0740	0740	...	...	...	0940	0940	...	...	1140	...	...	1340	...	...	1540	...	...	1740	...	...	1940	...
Plzeň hl. n. a.	...	...	0847	0847	...	...	...	1047	1047	...	...	1247	...	...	1447	...	...	1647	...	...	1847	...	...	2047	...
Praha hl. n. a.	...	...	1021	1021	...	...	...	1221	1221	...	...	1421	...	...	1621	...	...	1821	...	...	2021	...	...	2221	...

train type	ALX	RE		ALX	RE		ALX	RE		ALX	RE		ALX	RE		ALX	RE		ALX	ALX	RE				
train number	362			360			358			356			354			352			350	350					
notes	¶			¶			¶			¶			¶			¶			¶	¶					
notes																			⑥	Ⓑ					
Praha hl. n. d.	0538	...	...	0738	...	...	0938	...	...	1138	...	...	1338	...	...	1538	...	...	1738	1738	...	...	...	...	...
Plzeň hl. n. d.	0711	...	...	0911	...	...	1111	...	...	1311	...	...	1511	...	...	1711	...	...	1911	1911	...	...	...	...	...
Furth im Wald ⊞ a.	0820	...	...	1020	...	...	1220	...	...	1420	...	...	1620	...	...	1820	...	...	2020	2020	...	...	...	...	...
Schwandorf a.	0904	0907	...	1104	1107	...	1304	1307	...	1504	1507	...	1704	1707	...	1904	1908	...	2105	2105	2110	...	...	...	...
Regensburg a.	0945	|	...	1145	|	...	1345	|	...	1545	|	...	1745	|	...	1945	|	...	...	2149	|	...	...	...	...
Nürnberg Hbf a.	|	1014	...	|	1214	...	|	1414	...	|	1615	...	|	1814	...	|	2014	...	...	|	2222	...	...	...	...
München Hbf a.	1118	...	...	1318	...	...	1518	...	...	1718	...	...	1918	...	...	2118	...	...	...	2321	...	...	...	...	...

¶ – *Ex* in the Czech Republic.

ALX – Arriva Länderbahn Express.

77 BERLIN - WROCŁAW - WIEN / BUDAPEST / PRZEMYŚL

train type / number	EC/IC	NJ	NJ
train number	57	457	457
notes	73000		477
	W	A	S
Berlin Hbf d.	1052	1843	1843
Berlin Ost d.	1103	1853	1853
Frankfurt / Oder d.	1149	1949	1949
Rzepin d.	1211	2012	2012
Zielona Góra d.	1256	2057	2057
Glogów d.	1334	2135	2135
Wrocław Gł a.	1454	2257	2257
Wrocław Gł d.	1500	2307	2307
Opole Gł. d.	1542	2359	2359
Kedzierzyn-Koźle d.	|	0039	0039
Racibórz d.	|	0107	0107
Bohumín d.	|	0215	0215
Ostrava hlavní d.	|	0224	0224
Břeclav a.	|	0410	0410
Wien Hbf a.	|	0700	|
Graz Hbf a.	|	1002	|
Bratislava hl. st. a.	|	...	0554
Budapest Nyugati a.	|	...	0820
Gliwice a.	1631	...	...
Katowice a.	1702	...	...
Kraków Gł. a.	1759	...	...
Rzeszów a.	1942	...	...
Przemyśl a.	2058	...	...

train type / number	IC/EC	NJ	NJ
train number	37000	476	456
notes	56	456	
	W	T	A
Przemyśl d.	0708	...	...
Rzeszów d.	0814	...	...
Kraków Gł. d.	0952	...	...
Katowice d.	1048	...	...
Gliwice d.	1130	...	...
Budapest Nyugati d.	|	1940	...
Bratislava hl. st. d.	|	2206	...
Graz Hbf d.	|	|	1921
Wien Hbf d.	|	|	2210
Břeclav d.	|	2350	2350
Ostrava hlavní a.	|	0131	0131
Bohumín a.	|	0140	0140
Racibórz a.	|	0300	0300
Kedzierzyn-Koźle a.	|	0328	0328
Opole Gł. a.	1216	0409	0409
Wrocław Gł a.	1245	0505	0505
Wrocław Gł d.	1255	0520	0520
Glogów a.	1419	0649	0649
Zielona Góra a.	1455	0726	0726
Rzepin a.	1544	0819	0819
Frankfurt / Oder a.	1609	0844	0844
Berlin Ost a.	1655	0940	0940
Berlin Hbf a.	1705	0951	0951

A – *ÖBB nightjet* METROPOL – 🛏 1, 2 cl., ▬ 2 cl., (2) Berlin - Graz and v.v.

S – *ÖBB nightjet* METROPOL – 🛏 1, 2 cl., ▬ 2 cl., (2) Berlin (**457**) - Břeclav (**477**) - Budapest.

T – *ÖBB nightjet* METROPOL – 🛏 1, 2 cl., ▬ 2 cl., (2) Budapest (**476**) - Břeclav (**456**) - Berlin.

W – WAWEL – (12) ✕ Berlin - Przemyśl and v.v.

⊖ – ⊞ = Medyka / Mostiska II.

PL – Poland (UTC + 1 winter, UTC + 2 summer).

UA – Ukraine (UTC + 2 winter, UTC + 3 summer).

78 BRUSSELS - AMSTERDAM - BERLIN - (PRAHA)

train type	EN	
train number	xxxx	
notes	①③⑤	
	Z	X
Brussels Midi / Zuid d.	1922	1922
Antwerpen Centraal d.	2001	2001
Roosendaal d.	2044	2044
Rotterdam Centraal d.	2121	2121
Den Haag HS d.	2142	2142
Amsterdam Centraal d.	2234	2234
Deventer d.	2349	2349
Bad Bentheim ⊞ d.	0109	0109
Hannover Hbf d.	|	|
Berlin Hbf a.	0648	0552
Dresden Neustadt a.	...	0743
Dresden Hbf a.	...	0749
Bad Schandau ⊞ a.	...	0816
Děčín a.	...	0841
Ústí nad Labem hl. n. a.	...	0900
Praha Holešovice a.	...	1014
Praha hl. n. a.	...	1024

train type	EN	
train number	zzzz	
notes	②④⑦	
	Z	X
Praha hl. n. d.	...	1831
Praha Holešovice d.	...	1841
Ústí nad Labem hl. n. d.	...	1945
Děčín d.	...	2011
Bad Schandau ⊞ d.	...	2029
Dresden Hbf d.	...	2102
Dresden Neustadt d.	...	2108
Berlin Hbf d.	2256	2305
Hannover Hbf a.	|	|
Bad Bentheim ⊞ a.	0409	0422
Deventer a.	0516	0517
Amsterdam Centraal a.	0631	0631
Den Haag HS a.	|	|
Rotterdam Centraal a.	0732	0732
Roosendaal a.	0816	0816
Antwerpen Centraal a.	0843	0847
Brussels Midi / Zuid a.	0927	0927

X – Provisional timings from Dec. 2023.

Z – From May 25, European Sleeper: 🛏 1, 2 cl. (1, 2, 3 berth) ▬ 2 cl. (4, 6 berth), Brussels - Berlin and v.v.

GENÈVE, BASEL and ZÜRICH - MILANO, VENEZIA and ROMA 82

train type	IC	EC	IC	EC	IR	EC	IR	EC	FR	IC	EC	IC	EC	FR	IR	EC	IC	EC	FR	IR	IR	EC	EC	FR	
train number	802	35	659	307	2311	313	1807	51	9531	663	311	806	37 47	9529	2315	315	667	327	9543	1815	2319	53	317	9541	
notes		🅁 🍸 ⊗		🅁 🍸 ⊗		🅁 🍸 ⊗		🅁 🍸 ⊗	🅁 🍴 ⚡		🅁 🍸 ⊗		🅁 🍸 ⊗	🅁 🍴 ⚡		🅁 🍸 ⊗		🅁 🍸 ⊗	🅁 🍴 ⚡			🅁 🍸 ⊗	🅁 🍸 ⊗	🅁 🍴 ⚡	
Genève Aéroport ✈ d.	...	...	...	...	...	...	...	...	...	...	...	...	...	...	...	...	...	...	...	1001	...	...	...	...	...
Genève d.	...	0539	...	...	...	...	0609	...	...	...	...	...	0739	...	...	...	...	...	...	1011	...	...	...	...	...
Lausanne d.	...	0618	...	...	...	...	0650	...	...	...	...	...	0818	...	...	...	...	...	...	1050	...	...	...	...	...
Montreux d.	...	0637	...	...	...	...	0711	...	...	...	...	...	0837	...	...	...	...	...	...	1111	...	...	...	...	...
Aigle d.	...	|	...	...	...	...	0722	...	...	...	...	...	|	...	...	...	...	...	...	1122	...	...	...	...	...
Martigny d.	...	|	...	...	...	...	0743	...	...	...	...	...	|	...	...	...	...	...	...	1143	...	...	...	...	...
Sion d.	...	0712	...	...	...	...	0757	...	...	...	...	...	0912	...	...	...	...	...	...	1157	...	...	...	...	...
Zürich HB d.	...	|	...	0633	...	0733	|	...	...	...	0833	...	|	...	...	0933	...	1033	...	|	...	...	1133		
Basel SBB d.	...	|	0503	|	0603	|	|	0628	...	0703	|	...	|	...	0803	|	0903	|	...	|	1003	1028	|	...	...
Olten d.	...	|	0530	|	0630	|	|	0658	...	0830	|	...	|	...	0830	|	0930	|	...	|	1030	1058	|	...	...
Bern d.	0607	|	|	|	|	|	|	0734	...	|	|	0807	|	...	|	|	|	|	...	|	|	1134	|	...	...
Spiez d.	0636	|	|	|	|	|	|	0805	...	|	|	0836	|	...	|	|	|	|	...	|	|	1205	|	...	...
Luzern d.	|	|	0618	|	0718	|	|	|	...	0818	|	|	|	...	0918	|	1018	|	...	|	1118	|	|	...	...
Arth-Goldau d.	|	|	0645	0718	0745	0818	|	|	...	0845	0918	|	|	...	0945	1018	1045	1118	...	|	1145	|	1218	...	...
Bellinzona d.	|	|	...	0814	▬	0914	|	|	...	▬	1014	|	|	...	...	1114	...	1214	...	|	...	|	1314	...	...
Lugano d.	|	|	...	0832	...	0932	|	|	...	...	1032	|	|	...	...	1132	...	1232	...	|	...	|	1332	...	...
Chiasso 🏛 d.	|	|	...	0902	...	1002	|	|	...	...	1102	|	|	...	...	1202	...	1302	...	|	...	|	1402	...	...
Como San Giovanni a.	|	|	...	0910	...	1010	|	|	...	...	1110	|	|	...	...	1210	...	1310	...	|	...	|	1410	...	...
Visp d.	0703	|	...	|	...	|	0825	0833	...	...	|	0903	|	...	...	|	...	|	...	1225	...	1233	|	...	...
Brig d.	0711	0744	...	|	...	|	0832	0844	...	...	|	0911	0944	...	...	|	...	|	...	1232	...	1244	|	...	...
Domodossola 🏛 ¶ a.	...	0812	...	|	...	|	...	0912	...	...	|	...	1012	...	...	|	...	|	...	...	...	1312	|	...	...
Stresa a.	...	0838	...	|	...	|	...	0938	...	...	|	...	|	...	...	|	...	|	...	...	...	1338	|	...	...
Gallarate a.	...	|	...	|	...	|	...	|	...	...	|	...	1105	...	...	|	...	|	...	...	...	|	|	...	...
Milano Centrale a.	...	0940	...	1009f	...	1050	...	1040	...	...	1150	...	1140	...	...	1250	...	1409f	...	...	...	1440	1450	...	...
		|		|	*ITA* **9927** 🅁 🍴 ⚡					*FR* **9723** 🅁 🍴 ⚡	|					*FR* **9533** 🅁 🍴 ⚡		|					*FR* **9737** 🅁 🍴 ⚡		
Milano Centrale d.	...	1005	...	1011f	1040	...	...	...	1110	1145	1205	...	...	1220	...	1320	...	1411f	1410	...	...	...	1515	1520	...
Verona Porta Nuova a.	...	1128	...	|	|	...	...	...	|	1258	1328	...	...	|	...	|	...	|	|	...	...	...	1628	|	...
Venezia Mestre a.	...	1228	...	|	|	...	...	...	|	1358	1428	...	...	|	...	|	...	|	|	...	...	...	1728	|	...
Venezia Santa Lucia a.	...	1240	...	|	|	...	...	...	|	1410	1440	...	...	|	...	|	...	|	|	...	...	...	...	|	...
Genova a.	...	...	...	|	|	...	...	...	|	...	...	...	...	|	...	|	...	1549	|	...	...	...	...	|	...
Bologna Centrale a.	...	...	...	1122	1152	...	...	...	1222	...	...	...	...	1322	...	1422	...	...	1522	...	...	...	...	1622	...
Firenze SMN a.	...	...	...	...	1235	...	...	...	1259	...	...	...	...	1359	...	1459	...	...	1604	...	...	...	...	1659	...
Roma Termini a.	...	...	...	...	1419	...	...	...	1440	...	...	...	...	1540	...	1640	...	...	1749	...	...	...	...	1840	...
Napoli Centrale a.	...	...	...	...	1543	...	...	...	1602	...	...	...	...	1700	...	1800	...	...	1912	...	...	...	...	2000	...

train type	IR	EC	FR	IR	EC	IR	EC	FR	IC	IC	EC	FR	IR	EC	FR	EC	IR	EC	IR	EC	ICN	IC	EC	IR	EC
train number	2421	151	9545	2323	319 329	1819	57	9549	971	818	39	9553	2327	321	9557	153	2331	323	1829	59	797	828	41	2335	325
notes		🅁 🍸 ⊗ F	🅁 🍴 ⚡		🅁 🍸 ⊗		🅁 🍸 ⊗	🅁 🍴 ⚡			🅁 🍸 ⊗	🅁 🍴 ⚡		🅁 🍸 ⊗	🅁 🍴 ⚡	🅁 🍸 ⊗		🅁 🍸 ⊗		🅁 🍸 ⊗	🅁 ⚡ A		🅁 🍸 ⊗		🅁 🍸 ⊗
Genève Aéroport ✈ d.	...	...	...	...	...	1201	...	...	...	...	...	...	...	...	...	...	...	...	1701	...	...	...	...	...	...
Genève d.	...	...	...	...	...	1211	...	...	...	...	1339	...	...	...	...	...	...	...	1711	...	...	...	1839	...	...
Lausanne d.	...	...	...	...	...	1250	...	...	...	...	1418	...	...	...	...	...	...	...	1750	...	...	...	1918	...	...
Montreux d.	...	...	...	...	...	1311	...	...	...	...	1437	...	...	...	...	...	...	...	1811	...	...	...	1937	...	...
Aigle d.	...	...	...	...	...	1322	...	...	...	...	|	...	...	...	...	...	...	...	1822	...	...	...	|	...	...
Martigny d.	...	...	...	...	...	1343	...	...	...	...	|	...	...	...	...	...	...	...	1843	...	...	...	|	...	...
Sion d.	...	...	...	...	...	1357	...	...	...	...	1512	...	...	...	...	...	...	...	1857	...	...	...	2012	...	...
Zürich HB d.	1205	...	...	...	1333	|	...	...	...	...	|	...	...	1533	...	...	...	1733	|	...	...	...	|	...	1933
Basel SBB d.	|	1103	...	1203	|	|	1228	...	1256	...	|	...	1403	|	...	1503	1603	|	|	1728	...	...	|	1803	|
Oltern d.	|	1130	...	1230	|	|	1258	...	1329	...	|	...	1430	|	...	1530	1630	|	|	1758	...	...	|	1830	|
Bern d.	|	|	...	|	|	|	1334	...	1356	1407	|	...	|	|	...	|	|	|	|	1834	...	1907	|	|	|
Spiez d.	|	|	...	|	|	|	1405	...	...	1436	|	...	|	|	...	|	|	|	|	1905	...	1936	|	|	|
Luzern d.	|	1218	...	1318	|	|	|	...	...	|	|	...	1518	|	...	1618	1718	|	|	|	...	|	|	1918	|
Arth-Goldau d.	1245	1249	...	1345	1418	|	|	...	...	|	|	...	1545	1618	...	1649	1745	1818	|	|	...	|	|	1945	2018
Bellinzona d.	...	1344	...	...	1514	|	|	...	...	|	|	...	...	1714	...	1744	...	1914	|	|	...	|	|	...	2114
Lugano d.	...	1410	...	...	1532	|	|	...	...	|	|	...	...	1732	...	1810	...	1932	|	|	...	|	|	...	2132
Chiasso 🏛 d.	...	1455	...	...	1602	|	|	...	...	|	|	...	...	1802	...	1855	...	2002	|	|	...	|	|	...	2202
Como San Giovanni a.	...	1501	...	...	1610	|	|	...	...	|	|	...	...	1810	...	1903	...	2010	|	|	...	|	|	...	2210
Visp d.	...	|	...	...	|	1425	1433	...	...	1503	|	...	...	|	...	|	...	|	1925	1933	...	2003	|	...	|
Brig d.	...	|	...	...	|	1432	1444	...	...	1511	1544	...	...	|	...	|	...	|	1932	1944	...	2011	2044	...	|
Domodossola 🏛 ¶ a.	...	|	...	...	|	...	1512	...	...	...	1612	...	...	|	...	|	...	|	...	2012	...	...	2112	...	|
Stresa a.	...	|	...	...	|	...	1539	...	...	...	1639	...	...	|	...	|	...	|	...	|	...	...	2138	...	|
Gallarate a.	...	|	...	...	|	...	|	...	...	...	|	...	...	|	...	|	...	|	...	2103	...	...	|	...	|
Milano Centrale a.	...	1550	...	...	1650	...	1640	...	...	...	1740	...	...	1850	...	1950	...	2050	...	2140	...	...	2240	...	2250
		FR **9743** 🅁 🍴 ⚡					*FR* **9747** 🅁 🍴 ⚡				*FR* **9751** 🅁 🍴 ⚡			*FR* **9755** 🅁 🍴 ⚡				**2085** 2		**2087** 2					**2051** 2
Milano Centrale d.	...	1615	1615	...	...	...	1715	1720	...	...	1815	1820	...	1915	1920	...	...	2125	...	2225	2317g	...	...	...	0015
Verona Porta Nuova a.	...	1728	|	...	...	...	1828	|	...	...	1928	|	...	2028	|	...	...	2315	...	0015	|	...	...	...	0215
Venezia Mestre a.	...	1828	|	...	...	...	1928	|	...	...	2028	|	...	2128	|	...	...	...	...	...	|	...	...	...	...
Venezia Santa Lucia a.	...	1840	|	...	...	...	...	|	...	...	2040	|	...	2140	|	...	...	...	...	...	|	...	...	...	...
Genova a.	...	...	|	...	...	...	...	|	...	...	...	|	...	...	|	...	...	...	...	...	|	...	...	...	...
Bologna Centrale a.	...	...	1722	...	...	...	...	1822	...	...	...	1922	...	...	2022	...	...	...	...	...	0215	...	...	...	...
Firenze SMN a.	...	...	1759	...	...	...	...	1859	...	...	...	1959	...	...	2059	...	...	...	...	...	0407y	...	...	...	...
Roma Termini a.	...	...	1940	...	...	...	...	2040	...	...	...	2140	...	...	2240	...	...	...	...	...	0717t	...	...	...	...
Napoli Centrale a.	...	...	2100	...	..	...	...	2200	...	...	...	2300	...	...	...	...	...	...	...	...	0938	...	...	...	...

A – 🛏 1, 2 cl., 🛏 2 cl. (4 berth), 🚃(2) Milano - Napoli - Salerno.

F – From Frankfurt (depart 0806). Table **73**.

f – Milano **Lambrate**.

g – Milano **Porta Garibaldi**.

t – Roma **Tiburtina**.

y – Firenze **Campo di Marte**.

⚡ – Supplement payable.

¶ – Ticketing point is **Iselle**.

⊗ – Compulsory reservation for international journeys. Supplement payable for international journeys and for internal journeys within Italy.

82 ROMA, VENEZIA and MILANO - ZÜRICH, BASEL and GENÈVE

train type	EC	IR	EC	IR	ICN			IC	IC	FR⚡	FR	FR⚡	IR	FR	FR	FR	FR	IR	EC	IR	FR	IR	EC	IC	IR
train number	312	2316	50	1814	798	2051	2122	817	968	9500 9582	9702	9600	2320	9504	9708	9508	9714	1822	316	2324	9518	2328	34	1076	1826
notes	Ⓡ🍷 ⊗		Ⓡ🍷 ⊗		A	2				Ⓡ✕ ①–⑥	Ⓡ✕ ⚡	Ⓡ✕ ①–⑥		Ⓡ✕ ⚡	Ⓡ✕ ⚡	Ⓡ✕ ⚡	Ⓡ✕ ⚡		Ⓡ🍷 ⊗		Ⓡ✕ ⚡		Ⓡ🍷 ⊗		
Napoli Centrale d.	...	...	...	...	2131	...	...	...	...	...	...	...	...	...	...	...	...	...	...	...	0800	...	...	...	...
Roma Termini d.	...	...	...	...	2353t	...	...	...	...	...	...	0600	...	0620	...	0720	...	...	...	...	0920	...	...	...	...
Firenze SMN d.	...	...	...	...	0315y	...	...	...	...	0643	...	|	...	0800	...	0900	...	...	...	...	1100	...	...	...	...
Bologna Centrale d.	...	...	...	...	|	...	0528	...	...	0721	...	|	...	0838	...	0938	...	...	...	...	1138	...	...	...	...
Genova d.	...	...	...	...	|	...	|	...	...	|	...	|	...	|	...	|	...	...	...	...	|	...	...	...	...
Venezia Santa Lucia d.	...	...	...	...	|	...	|	...	...	|	0620	|	...	|	0720	|	0820	...	...	...	|	...	...	...	...
Venezia Mestre d.	...	...	...	...	|	...	|	...	...	|	0632	|	...	|	0732	|	0832	...	...	...	|	...	...	...	...
Verona Porta Nuova d.	...	...	...	...	|	0545	|	...	...	|	0732	|	...	|	0832	|	0932	...	...	...	|	...	...	...	...
Milano Centrale a.	...	...	...	...	0711g	0735	0800	...	...	0830	0845	0855	...	0943	0945	1040	1045	...	...	...	1240	...	...	...	...
						EC	EC					EC			EC		EC				EC				
						156	32					314			158		52				318				
						Ⓡ🍷 ⊗	Ⓡ🍷 ⊗					Ⓡ🍷 ⊗			Ⓡ🍷 ⊗		Ⓡ🍷 F ⊗				Ⓡ🍷 ⊗				
Milano Centrale d.	0710	...	0720	...	...	0810	0820	...	...	...	...	0910	...	...	1010	...	1120	...	1110	...	1310	...	1320	...	...
Gallarate d.	|	...	0754	...	...	|	|	...	...	...	...	|	...	...	|	...	|	...	|	...	|	...	|	...	...
Stresa d.	|	...	|	...	...	|	0921	...	...	...	...	|	...	...	|	...	1220	...	|	...	|	...	1412	...	...
Domodossola 🏛 ¶ d.	|	...	0848	...	...	|	0948	...	...	...	...	|	...	...	|	...	1248	...	|	...	|	...	1448	...	...
Brig a.	|	...	0916	0926	...	|	1014	1048	...	...	...	|	...	...	|	...	1316	1326	|	...	|	...	1514	1518	1526
Visp a.	|	...	0925	0932	...	|	|	1055	...	...	...	|	...	...	|	...	1325	1332	|	...	|	...	|	1525	1532
Como San Giovanni d.	0754	...	|	|	...	0904	|	|	...	...	...	0950	...	...	1059	...	|	|	1150	...	1350	...	|	|	|
Chiasso 🏛 a.	0758	...	|	|	...	0924	|	|	...	...	...	1005	...	...	1124	...	|	|	1205	...	1405	...	|	|	|
Lugano a.	0830	...	|	|	...	1002	|	|	...	...	...	1030	...	...	1202	...	|	|	1230	...	1430	...	|	|	|
Bellinzona a.	0845	...	|	|	...	1016	|	|	...	...	...	1045	...	...	1216	...	|	|	1245	...	1445	...	|	|	|
Arth-Goldau a.	0942	1015	|	|	...	1111	|	|	...	...	...	1142	1215	...	1311	...	|	|	1342	1415	1542	1615	|	|	|
Luzern a.	|	1041	|	|	...	1141	|	|	...	...	...	|	1241	...	1341	...	|	|	|	1441	|	1641	|	|	|
Spiez a.	|	|	0953	|	...	|	|	1123	...	...	...	|	|	...	|	...	1353	|	|	|	|	|	|	1553	|
Bern a.	|	|	1024	|	...	|	|	1154	1204	...	...	|	|	...	|	...	1424	|	|	|	|	|	|	1624	|
Olten a.	|	1128	1103	|	...	1228	|	...	1230	...	...	|	1328	...	1428	...	1503	|	|	1528	|	1728	|	1703	|
Basel SBB a.	|	1156	1132	|	...	1256	|	...	1301	...	...	|	1356	...	1456	...	1532	|	|	1556	|	1756	|	1732	|
Zürich HB a.	1027	...	...	|	...	...	|	...	...	...	...	1227	...	...	...	...	...	|	1427	...	1627	...	|	...	|
Sion a.	...	...	...	1001	...	...	1047	...	...	...	...	...	...	...	...	...	...	1401	...	...	...	...	1547	...	1601
Martigny a.	...	...	...	1016	...	...	|	...	...	...	...	...	...	...	...	...	...	1416	...	...	...	...	|	...	1616
Aigle a.	...	...	...	1037	...	...	|	...	...	...	...	...	...	...	...	...	...	1437	...	...	...	...	|	...	1637
Montreux a.	...	...	...	1048	...	...	1123	...	...	...	...	...	...	...	...	...	...	1448	...	...	...	...	1623	...	1648
Lausanne a.	...	...	...	1110	...	...	1142	...	...	...	...	...	...	...	...	...	...	1510	...	...	...	...	1642	...	1710
Genève a.	...	...	...	1152	...	...	1221	...	...	...	...	...	...	...	...	...	...	1552	...	...	...	...	1721	...	1752
Genève Aéroport ✈ a.	...	...	...	1159	...	...	...	...	...	...	...	...	...	...	...	...	...	1559	...	...	...	...	...	...	1759

train type/number	FR	FR	EC	EC	IR	EC	FR	EC	IR	EC	IC	FR	EC	IR	EC	IC	FR	EC	EC	IC	IC	EC	IR	EC	
train number	9728	9526	320	54 60	1830	308	9532	322 332	2336	36 46	1084	9536	56 58	1836	310	692	9540	42	44	1088	338	324	2340	326	
notes	Ⓡ✕ ⚡	Ⓡ✕ ⚡	Ⓡ🍷 ⊗	Ⓡ🍷 ⊗		Ⓡ🍷 ⊗	Ⓡ✕ ⚡	Ⓡ🍷 ⊗		Ⓡ🍷 ⊗		Ⓡ✕ ⚡	Ⓡ🍷 ⊗		Ⓡ🍷 ⊗		Ⓡ✕ ⚡	Ⓡ🍷 ⊗ ⑤⑥	Ⓡ🍷 ⊗ ⑦–④			Ⓡ✕ ⊗		Ⓡ🍷 ⊗	
Napoli Centrale d.	...	1000	...	...	...	...	1200	...	...	...	...	1300	...	...	...	...	1400	...	...	...	...	...	...	...	...
Roma Termini d.	...	1120	...	...	...	...	1320	...	...	...	...	1420	...	...	...	...	1522	...	...	...	...	...	...	...	...
Firenze SMN d.	...	1300	...	...	...	...	1500	...	...	...	...	1600	...	...	...	...	1700	...	...	...	...	...	...	...	...
Bologna Centrale d.	...	1338	...	...	...	1447	1538	...	...	...	...	1638	...	...	...	...	1738	...	...	...	...	...	...	...	...
Genova d.	...	|	...	...	...	|	|	...	...	...	...	|	...	...	...	...	|	...	...	...	...	...	...	1813	...
Venezia Santa Lucia d.	1150	|	...	...	...	|	|	...	...	...	...	|	...	...	1520	...	|	1618	1618	...	...	...	...	|	...
Venezia Mestre d.	1202	|	...	...	...	|	|	...	...	...	...	|	...	...	1532	...	|	1630	1630	...	...	...	...	|	...
Verona Porta Nuova d.	1302	|	...	...	...	|	|	...	...	...	...	|	...	...	1632	...	|	1732	1732	...	...	...	...	|	...
Milano Centrale a.	1415	1440	...	...	...	1550f	1645	...	...	...	...	1742	...	...	1755	...	1842	1855	1855	...	...	...	...	1950f	...
Milano Centrale d.	...	...	1510	1520	...	1552f	...	1710	...	1720	...	...	1820	...	1810	...	...	1920	1920	...	...	1910	...	1952f	...
Gallarate d.	...	...	|	|	...	|	...	|	...	|	...	...	|	...	|	...	...	1954	1954	...	...	|	...	|	...
Stresa d.	...	...	|	1620	...	|	...	|	...	1821	...	...	1920	...	|	...	...	|	|	...	...	|	...	|	...
Domodossola 🏛 ¶ d.	...	...	|	1648	...	|	...	|	...	1848	...	...	1948	...	|	...	...	2048	2048	...	...	|	...	|	...
Brig a.	...	...	|	1716	1726	|	...	|	...	1914	1918	...	2016	2026	|	...	...	2114	2114	2118	...	|	...	|	...
Visp a.	...	...	|	1725	1732	|	...	|	...	|	1925	...	2026	2032	|	...	...	|	2132	2125	...	|	...	|	...
Como San Giovanni d.	...	...	1550	|	|	1650	...	1750	...	|	|	...	|	|	1850	...	...	|	|	|	...	1950	...	2050	...
Chiasso 🏛 a.	...	...	1605	|	|	1705	IC	1805	...	|	|	...	|	|	1905	...	...	|	|	|	...	2005	...	2105	...
Lugano a.	...	...	1630	|	|	1730	688	1830	...	|	|	...	|	|	1930	...	...	|	|	|	...	2030	...	2130	...
Bellinzona a.	...	...	1645	|	|	1745		1845	...	|	|	...	|	|	1945	...	...	|	|	|	...	2045	...	2145	...
Arth-Goldau a.	...	...	1742	|	|	1842	1915	1942	2015	|	|	...	|	|	2042	2115	...	|	|	|	...	2142	2215	2242	...
Luzern a.	...	...	|	|	|	|	1941	|	2041	|	|	...	|	|	|	2141	...	|	|	|	...	|	2241	|	...
Spiez a.	...	...	|	1753	|	|	|	|	|	|	1953	...	2053	|	|	|	...	|	|	2153	...	|	|	|	...
Bern a.	...	...	|	1824	|	|	|	|	|	|	2024	...	2124	|	|	|	...	|	|	2224	2236	|	|	|	...
Olten a.	...	...	|	1903	|	|	2028	|	2128	|	2103	...	2203	|	|	2228	...	|	|	...	2303	|	2328	|	...
Basel SBB a.	...	...	|	1932	|	|	2056	|	2156	|	2132	...	2232	|	|	2300	...	|	|	...	2337	|	2400	|	...
Zürich HB a.	...	...	1827	...	|	1927	...	2027	...	|	...	...	...	|	2127	...	...	|	|	...	...	2227	...	2327	...
Sion a.	...	...	...	...	1801	...	...	...	...	1947	...	...	...	2101	...	...	...	2147	2159	...	...	...	...	...	...
Martigny a.	...	...	...	...	1816	...	...	...	...	|	...	...	...	2116	...	...	...	|	2215	...	...	...	...	...	...
Aigle a.	...	...	...	...	1837	...	...	...	...	|	...	...	...	2137	...	...	...	|	2237	...	...	...	...	...	...
Montreux a.	...	...	...	...	1848	...	...	...	...	2023	...	...	...	2148	...	...	...	2223	2248	...	...	...	...	...	...
Lausanne a.	...	...	...	...	1910	...	...	...	...	2042	...	...	...	2210	...	...	...	2242	2310	...	...	...	...	...	...
Genève a.	...	...	...	...	1952	...	...	...	...	2121	...	...	...	2252	...	...	...	2321	2355	...	...	...	...	...	...
Genève Aéroport ✈ a.	...	...	...	...	1959	...	...	...	...	...	...	...	...	2259	...	...	...	...	0003	...	...	...	...	...	...

A – 🛏 1, 2 cl., 🛏 2 cl. (4 berth), 🚃 Salerno - Milano.

F – To Frankfurt (arrive 1844).

f – Milano **Lambrate**.

g – Milano **Porta Garibaldi**.

t – Roma **Tiburtina**.

y – Firenze **Campo di Marte**.

⚡ – Supplement payable.

¶ – Ticketing point is **Iselle**.

⊗ – Compulsory reservation for international journeys. Supplement payable for international journeys and for internal journeys within Italy.

For Summer service from June 11 see page 672

ZÜRICH - INNSBRUCK - WIEN, GRAZ, ZAGREB and BUDAPEST 86

train type / number	*RJX*	*RJX*	*IC*	*RJ*	*D*	*RJX*	*RJ*	*EC*	*EC*	*RJX*	*EC*	*RJX*	*EC*	*D*	*IC*	*RJX*	*EC*	*RJX*	*EC*	*RJX*	*RJX*	*NJ*	*EN*	*D*	*EN*	*NJ*	
train number	**669**	**765**	**515**	**111**	**211**	**161**	**596**	**217**	**163**	**563**	**113**	**165**	**115**	**315**	**611**	**167**	**219**	**169**	**117**	**367**	**369**	**465**	**40465**	**413**	**40467**	**467**	
notes	✖	✖	🍷	✖		✖	✖	🍷	✖	✖	**213**	✖	🍷		🍷	✖	🍷	✖	**1217**	✖	✖						
					T	**G**			**B**		**H**								🍷			**Z**	**A**	2	**C**	**W**	
Zürich HB ... d.	...	...	...	...	...	0640	...	...	0840	...	...	1040	...	...	...	1240	...	1440	...	1640	1840	2040	2040	...	2140	2140	...
Sargans ... d.	...	...	...	...	...	0736	...	...	0936	...	...	1136	...	...	...	1336	...	1536	...	1736	1936	2137	2137	...	2236	2236	...
Buchs 🏛 ... d.	...	...	...	...	...	0754	...	...	1000	...	...	1154	...	...	...	1354	...	1554	...	1800	1954	2205	2205	...	2305	2305	...
Feldkirch ... d.	...	0613	...	...	...	0817	...	...	1017	...	...	1217	...	...	...	1417	...	1617	...	1817	2017	2245	2245	...	2324	2324	...
Bludenz ... d.	...	0626	...	...	...	0830	...	...	1030	...	...	1230	...	...	...	1430	...	1630	...	1830	2030	2301	2301	...	2340	2340	...
St Anton am Arlberg . d.	...	0703	...	...	...	0903	...	...	1103	...	...	1303	...	...	...	1503	...	1703	...	1903	2103	2345	2345	...	|	|	...
Landeck - Zams ... d.	...	0727	...	...	...	0927	...	...	1127	...	...	1327	...	...	...	1527	...	1727	...	1927	2127	0009	0009	...	0036	0036	...
Ötztal ... d.	...	0751	...	...	...	0948	...	...	1148	...	...	1348	...	...	...	1548	...	1748	...	1951	2151	|	|	...	|	|	...
Innsbruck Hbf ... d.	0510	0817	0821	...	...	1017	...	...	1221e	1217	...	1417	...	...	...	1617	...	1817	...	2017	2217	0056	0056	...	0128	0128	...
Jenbach ... d.	0527	|	0844	...	...	|	...	...	1244	|	...	|	...	...	...	|	...	|	...	|	|	|	|	...	|	|	...
Wörgl ... d.	0541	0843	0859	...	...	1043	...	...	1259	1243	...	1443	...	...	...	1643	...	1843	...	2043	2243	|	|	...	|	|	...
Kitzbühel ... d.	|	|	0929	...	...	|	...	...	1329	|	...	|	...	...	...	|	...	|	...	|	|	|	|	...	|	|	...
St Johann in Tirol ... d.	|	|	0937	...	...	|	...	...	1337	|	...	|	...	...	...	|	...	|	...	|	|	|	|	...	|	|	...
Saalfelden ... d.	|	|	1005	...	...	|	...	...	1405	|	...	|	...	...	...	|	...	|	...	|	|	|	|	...	|	|	...
Zell am See ... d.	|	|	1015	...	...	|	...	...	1416	|	...	|	...	...	...	|	...	|	...	|	|	|	|	...	|	|	...
Schwarzach St Veit ... a.	|	|	|	...	...	|	...	...	|	|	...	|	...	...	...	|	...	|	...	|	|	0317	0317	...	|	|	...
Salzburg Hbf ... d.	0707	1007	|	1012	...	1207	1212	1215	|	1407	...	1607	1612	...	1615	1807	1815	2007	2012	2206	0012	|	|	...	0350	0436	...
Bischofshofen ... a.	|	|	|	1052	...	|	1252	1302	|	|	...	|	1652	...	1702	|	1902	|	2052	...	...	0336	|	...	|	|	...
Schwarzach St Veit ... a.	|	|	1046	1109	...	|	1309	|	1446	|	1511	|	1709	...	|	|	|	|	2109	...	...	|	|	...	|	|	...
Selzthal ... a.	|	|	1239	|	...	|	|	1439	1639	|	|	|	|	...	1839	|	2039	|	|	...	...	0504	|	...	|	|	...
Graz Hbf ... a.	|	|	1414	|	...	|	|	1614	1814	|	|	|	|	...	2014	|	2214	|	|	...	...	0700	|	...	|	|	...
Villach Hbf ... a.	|	|	▬	1243	1253	|	1443	...	...	|	1643	|	1843	1853	▬	|	...	|	2243	...	...	...	0604	...	|	|	...
Klagenfurt ... a.	|	|	...	1316	|	|	1513	...	...	|	1718	|	1916	|	**411**	|	...	|	2316	...	...	...	|	...	|	|	...
Jesenice 🏛 ... a.	|	|	...	...	1329	|	▬	...	...	|	1729	|	▬	1926	**P**	|	...	|	...	...	...	...	0659	...	|	|	...
Ljubljana ⊙ ... a.	|	|	...	...	1431	|	...	...	...	|	1832	|	...	2033	2105	|	...	|	...	...	...	...	0809	...	|	|	...
Zagreb ⊙ ... a.	|	|	...	...	1710	|	...	...	...	|	2045	|	...	...	2337	|	...	|	...	...	...	...	1039	1057	|	|	...
Vinkovci ⊕ ... a.	|	|	...	...	2142	|	...	...	...	|	▬	|	...	...	0303	|	...	|	...	...	...	...	...	1503	|	|	...
Beograd Centar ⊕ . a.	|	|	...	...	...	|	...	...	...	|	...	|	...	...	0610	|	...	|	...	...	...	...	...	...	|	|	...
Linz Hbf ... a.	0815	1115	...	...	...	1315	...	...	...	1515	...	1715	...	...	...	1915	...	2115	...	...	...	...	...	...	0452	0558	...
St Pölten ... a.	0900	1200	...	...	...	1400	...	...	...	1600	*EC*	1800	*EN*	...	...	2000	...	2200	...	...	...	...	...	...	0600	0710	...
Wien Meidling ... a.	0925	1225	*EC*	...	...	1425	*EC*	...	...	1625	**149**	1825	**347**	...	...	2025	...	2225	...	...	...	...	...	...	0626	0744	...
Wien Hbf. ... a.	0932	1232	**145**	...	...	1432	**147**	...	...	1632	**D**	1832	**K**	...	...	2032	...	2232	...	...	...	...	...	...	0634	0755	...
Wien Hbf. ... d.	0940	...	1240	...	...	...	1437	...	...	...	1642	1842	1942	...	...	2042	...	...	...	...	...	...	...	...	0658	...	...
Bratislava hl. st. a.	|	...	|	...	...	...	|	...	...	...	|	|	|	...	...	2151	...	...	...	...	...	...	...	...	|	...	...
Hegyeshalom 🏛 ... a.	1025	...	1325	...	...	...	1521	...	...	...	1725	1925	2025	...	...	...	...	...	...	...	...	...	...	...	0723	...	...
Györ ... a.	1053	...	1353	...	...	...	1553	...	...	...	1753	1953	2053	...	...	...	...	...	...	...	...	...	...	...	0753	...	...
Budapest Keleti ... a.	1219	...	1519	...	...	...	1719	...	...	...	1919	2119	2220	...	...	...	...	...	...	...	...	...	...	...	0919	...	...

train type / number	*RJX*	*RJX*	*EC*	*RJ*	*RJX*	*D*	*D*	*EC*	*RJX*	*RJX*	*RJX*	*EC*	*EC*	*EC*	*RJX*	*RJX*	*RJX*	*RJX*	*IC*	*D*	*RJX*	*RJX*	*NJ*	*EN*	*NJ*	*D*	*EN*
train number	**366**	**368**	**218**	**691**	**160**	**410**	**314**	**114**	**162**	**60**	**766**	**212**	**164**	**216**	**62**	**166**	**64**	**168**	**610**	**210**	**66**	**760**	**466**	**40462**	**464**	**412**	**40414**
notes	✖	✖	🍷	✖	✖			🍷	✖	✖	✖	**112**	🍷	🍷	✖	✖	✖	✖	🍷		✖	✖					
						Q						**H**	**B**					**G**		**T**			**W**	**E**	**Z**	2	**A**
Budapest Keleti ... d.	...	...	...	...	...	...	...	...	0640	0740	...	...	...	...	0940	...	1140	...	...	...	1340	...	...	2040	...	...	...
Györ ... d.	...	...	...	...	...	...	...	...	0802	0902	...	...	...	...	1102	...	1302	...	...	...	1502	...	...	2202	...	...	...
Hegyeshalom 🏛 ... d.	...	...	...	...	...	...	...	...	0832	0932	...	...	...	...	1132	...	1332	...	...	...	1532	...	...	2232	...	...	...
Bratislava hl. st. d.	...	...	...	...	0610	...	...	...	|	|	...	...	...	...	|	...	|	...	...	...	|	...	...	|	...	...	...
Wien Hbf ... a.	...	...	...	...	0718	...	...	...	0918	1021	...	...	...	...	1221	...	1421	...	...	...	1621	...	...	2321	...	...	...
Wien Hbf ... d.	...	...	...	...	0728	...	...	...	0928	1028	1128	...	...	...	▬	1328	▬	1528	...	...	▬	1728	2127	2327	...	...	...
Wien Meidling ... d.	...	...	...	...	0735	...	...	...	0935	1035	1135	...	...	...	...	1335	...	1535	...	...	...	1735	2135	2335	...	...	...
St Pölten ... d.	...	...	...	...	0759	...	...	...	0959	1059	1159	...	...	...	...	1359	...	1559	...	...	...	1759	2201	0001	...	...	...
Linz Hbf ... d.	...	...	...	...	0845	...	...	...	1045	1145	1245	...	...	...	...	1445	...	1645	...	...	...	1845	2256	0059	...	...	...
Beograd Centar ⊕ . d.	...	...	...	...	|	2100	...	...	|	|	|	...	...	...	...	|	...	|	...	...	...	|	|	|	...	...	...
Vinkovci ⊕ ... d.	...	...	...	...	|	0104	...	...	|	|	|	...	...	...	...	|	...	|	...	0839	...	|	|	|	...	1416	...
Zagreb ⊙ ... d.	...	...	...	...	|	0440	...	...	|	|	|	0705	...	...	...	|	...	|	...	1250	*RJ*	|	|	|	...	1820	1938
Ljubljana ⊙ ... d.	...	...	...	...	|	0718	0726	...	|	|	|	0923	...	...	*IC*	|	...	|	...	1527	**110**	|	|	|	...	...	2208
Jesenice 🏛 ... d.	...	...	...	...	|	▬	0832	...	|	|	|	1017	...	...	**793**	|	*IC*	|	...	1632	✖	|	|	|	...	...	2315
Klagenfurt ... d.	...	...	...	0645	|	*IC*	|	0842	|	|	|	1027	...	...	1245	|	**518**	|	...	|	1642	|	|	|	...	...	|
Villach Hbf ... d.	...	...	...	0716	|	**512**	0908	0916	|	|	|	1116	...	...	1316	|	🍷	|	...	1708	1716	|	|	|	...	...	0013
Graz Hbf ... d.	...	...	0545	|	|	0745	...	|	|	|	|	|	0945	1145	|	|	1345	|	1545	...	|	|	|	|	2226	...	|
Selzthal ... d.	...	...	0719	|	|	0919	...	|	|	|	|	|	1119	1319	|	|	1519	|	1719	...	|	|	|	|	0028	...	|
Schwarzach St Veit ... d.	...	...	|	0852	|	|	...	1052	|	|	|	1248	1313	|	1452	|	|	|	|	...	1852	|	|	|	|	...	|
Bischofshofen ... d.	...	...	0857	0907	|	1057	...	1107	|	|	|	...	|	1457	1507	|	1650	|	1857	...	1907	|	|	|	0158	...	|
Salzburg Hbf ... d.	0554	0756	0944	0948	0956	1144	...	1148	1156	1253	1356	...	|	1544	1548	1556	|	1756	1944	...	1948	1956	0230	0230	|	...	|
Schwarzach St Veit ... d.	|	|	...	...	|	...	...	...	|	...	|	...	|	...	...	|	1713	|	...	...	...	|	|	|	0232	...	0232
Zell am See ... d.	|	|	...	...	|	...	...	...	|	...	|	...	1344	...	...	|	1744	|	...	...	...	|	|	|	|	...	|
Saalfelden ... d.	|	|	...	...	|	...	...	...	|	...	|	...	1354	...	...	|	1754	|	...	...	...	|	|	|	|	...	|
St Johann in Tirol ... d.	|	|	...	...	|	...	...	...	|	...	|	...	1422	...	...	|	1822	|	...	...	...	|	|	|	|	...	|
Kitzbühel ... d.	|	|	...	...	|	...	...	...	|	...	|	...	1430	...	...	|	1830	|	...	...	...	|	|	|	|	...	|
Wörgl ... d.	0719	0919	...	...	1119	...	...	...	1319	...	1519	...	1502	...	...	1719	1902	1919	...	...	...	2119	|	|	|	...	|
Jenbach ... d.	|	|	...	...	|	...	...	...	|	...	|	...	1518	...	...	|	1918	|	...	...	...	|	|	|	|	...	|
Innsbruck Hbf ... d.	0748	0948	...	...	1148	...	...	...	1347	...	1544	...	1548	...	...	1747	1940	1948	...	...	...	2148	0431	0431	0453	...	0453
Ötztal ... d.	0812	1012	...	...	1212	...	...	...	1412	...	...	...	1612	...	...	1812	...	2012	...	...	...	2212	|	|	|	...	|
Landeck - Zams ... d.	0833	1033	...	...	1233	...	...	...	1433	...	...	...	1633	...	...	1833	...	2036	...	...	...	2236	0520	0520	0545	...	0545
St Anton am Arlberg . d.	0857	1057	...	...	1257	...	...	...	1457	...	...	...	1657	...	...	1857	...	2100	...	...	...	2300	|	|	0616	...	0616
Bludenz ... d.	0931	1131	...	...	1331	...	...	...	1531	...	...	...	1731	...	...	1931	...	2134	...	...	...	2337	0625	0625	0706	...	0706
Feldkirch ... d.	0944	1148	...	...	1348	...	...	...	1548	...	...	...	1744	...	...	1948	...	2148	...	...	...	2348	0640	0640	0739	...	0739
Buchs 🏛 ... a.	0959	1206	...	...	1406	...	...	...	1606	...	...	...	1759	...	...	2006	...	2203	...	...	...	...	0656	0656	0754	...	0754
Sargans ... a.	1023	1223	...	...	1423	...	...	...	1623	...	...	...	1823	...	...	2023	...	2223	...	...	...	...	0723	0723	0823	...	0823
Zürich HB ... a.	1120	1320	...	...	1520	...	...	...	1720	...	...	...	1920	...	...	2120	...	2320	...	...	...	...	0820	0820	0920	...	0920

A – *ÖBB nightjet* – 🛏 1, 2 cl., 🛌 2 cl. (4, 6 berth), (2) Zürich - Zagreb and v.v.

B – TRANSALPIN (1) (observation car), (12) 🍷 Zürich - Innsbruck - Graz and v.v.

C – 🛏 1, 2 cl., 🛌 2 cl., (2) Zürich - Wien - Budapest. Conveys 🛏 1, 2 cl. (**50467**) Zürich - Linz - Praha (Table **52**). Special fares payable.

D – HORTOBÁGY (12) Wien - Budapest - Szolnok (arrive 2102) - Debrecen (2235) - Záhony (0010). Conveys 🛏 1, 2 cl. Wien (**40147**) - Budapest - Záhony - Lviv - Kyïv (Table **96**).

E – 🛏 1, 2 cl., 🛌 2 cl., (2) Budapest - Wien - Zürich. Conveys 🛏 1, 2 cl. (**50466**) Praha - Linz - Zürich (Table **52**). Special fares payable.

G – (12) 🍷 Zürich - Innsbruck - Wien and v.v. Conveys (12) 🍷 Bolzano (depart 0745; arrive 2220, *RJX* **185/184**) - Innsbruck - Wien and v.v.

H – (12) Schwarzach St Veit - Villach - Klagenfurt and Schwarzach St Veit - Villach - Ljubljana - Zagreb and v.v.

K – DACIA – 🛏 1, 2 cl., 🛌 2 cl., (2) ✖ Wien - Budapest - Bucureşti.

P – June 20 - Sept. 13: 🛌 2 cl., (12) Ljubljana - Zagreb - Beograd.

Q – June 21 - Sept. 14: 🛌 2 cl., (12) Beograd - Zagreb - Ljubljana.

T – SAVA – (12) Villach - Jesenice 🏛 - Ljubljana - Zagreb - Vinkovci and v.v.

W – *ÖBB nightjet* WIENER WALZER – 🛏 1, 2 cl., 🛌 2 cl. (4, 6 berth), (2) Zürich - Wien and v.v. Special fares payable.

Z – Zürich - Graz: *ÖBB nightjet* ZÜRICHSEE – 🛏 1, 2 cl., 🛌 2 cl. (4, 6 berth), (2) Zürich - Graz and v.v.

e – Arrive 1211.

j – Change at Villach.

RJ – ÖBB *Railjet* service. ✖, (1) (business class), (1) (first class), (2) (economy class).

⊙ – 🏛 between Ljubljana and Zagreb is Dobova.

⊕ – 🏛 between Vinkovci and Beograd is Šid.

☛ **Shaded services are suspended until further notice.**

For Summer service from June 11 see page 672

87 LJUBLJANA - TRIESTE - UDINE / VENEZIA

	1824			*EC* 134		1810	1896		1896
	2			E		Ⓑ 2	2		2
Ljubljana d.	0547	...	...	1421	...	1613	...	...	1850
Postojna d.	0657	...	...	1531	...	1726	...	...	2003
Pivka d.	0709	...	...	1544	...	1741	...	...	2016
Divača d.	0729	...	...	1605	...	1804	...	...	2037
Sežana 🏛 d.	0738	...	...	1615	...	1815	...	...	2048
Villa Opicina 🏛 a.	0749	...	...	1626	...	1826	...	...	2059
Villa Opicina 🏛 d.	0803	...	...	1645	...	...	1823	...	2104
Trieste Centrale a.	0833	...	...	1716	...	...	1853	...	2132
Trieste Centrale d.	0852	0916	...	...	1816	...	...	1858	...
Monfalcone d.	0916	0940	...	...	1840	...	...	1922	...
Trieste Airport d.	0921	0945	...	...	1845	...	...	|	...
Cervignano-Aquileia-Grado d.	0929	0953	...	...	1853	...	...	|	...
Udine a.	0954	|	...	...	|	...	...	2006	...
Venezia Mestre a.	...	1109	...	...	2011	...	...	2146	...
Venezia Santa Lucia a.	...	1121	...	...	2021	...	...	2159	...
Milano Centrale a.	...	...	...	...	...	...	...	...	...

		1825		*FR* 9707		*EC* 135			1897
		2				F			2
Milano Centrale d.	...	...	...	0745	...	...	...	...	...
Venezia Santa Lucia d.	0639	...	...	|	1039	...	...	1639	...
Venezia Mestre d.	0651	...	...	1011	1051	...	...	1651	...
Udine d.	|	...	...	|	|	...	...	|	1755
Cervignano-Aquileia-Grado d.	0807	...	...	1126	1207	...	...	1807	1822
Trieste Airport d.	0815	...	...	1135	1215	...	...	1815	1829
Monfalcone d.	0821	...	...	1142	1221	...	...	1821	1834
Trieste Centrale a.	0844	...	...	1205	1244	...	...	1844	1857
Trieste Centrale d.	...	0903	...	...	...	1252	...	...	1907
Villa Opicina 🏛 a.	...	0928	...	...	...	1320	...	...	1937
Villa Opicina 🏛 d.	...	0943	...	...	...	1338	...	...	1945
Sežana 🏛 d.	...	0955	...	...	...	1350	...	...	2016
Divača d.	...	1005	...	...	...	1400	...	...	2026
Pivka d.	...	1026	...	...	...	1421	...	...	2047
Postojna d.	...	1038	...	...	...	1434	...	...	2059
Ljubljana a.	...	1146	...	...	...	1540	...	...	2210

E – [12] Wien (**151**) - Ljubljana (**134**) - Trieste.

F – [12] Trieste (**135**) - Ljubljana (**150**) - Wien.

88 WIEN - KLAGENFURT - VENEZIA, MILANO and ROMA

train type / number		*REX*			*IC*		*RJ*	*RJ*	*EC*	*RJ*	*RJ*	*REX*		*NJ*	*NJ*		*NJ*	*NJ*		*NJ*		
train number		1821	131		533		535	73	140	133	539	1823		40233	233		1237	1237		237		
notes		1817 2	✕		✕		✕	✕	J	✕	✕	1819 2		A	B		G	H		C		
Praha hlavní d.	...	...	...	...	...	...	...	0612	...	...	...	...	...	...	...	...	...	...	...	...	...	...
Břeclav d.	...	...	...	...	...	...	...	0955	...	...	...	...	...	...	...	...	...	...	...	...	...	...
Budapest Keleti d.	...	...	...	...	...	...	...	|	0840	...	...	...	...	...	...	...	...	...	...	...	...	...
Györ d.	...	...	...	...	...	...	...	|	1002	...	...	...	...	...	...	...	...	...	...	...	...	...
Wien Hbf d.	...	...	0625	...	0825	...	1025	1049	1121	1225	1425	...	...	1918	1918	...	2001	2001	...	2127	...	...
Wien Meidling d.	...	...	0632	...	0832	...	1032	...	...	1232	1432	...	...	1925	1925	...	2008	2008	...	2135	...	...
Bruck an der Mur d.	...	...	0815	...	1015	...	1215	...	...	1415	1615	...	...	2121	2121	...	2222	2222	...	|	...	...
Klagenfurt Hbf d.	...	...	1022	...	1222	...	1422	...	...	1622	1822	...	...	2336	2336	...	0021	0021	...	|	...	...
Linz Hbf d.	...	...	|	...	|	...	|	...	...	|	|	...	...	|	|	...	|	|	...	2258	...	...
Salzburg Hbf d.	...	...	|	...	|	...	|	...	...	|	|	...	...	|	|	...	|	|	...	0140	...	...
Villach Hbf d.	...	0945	1050	...	1246	...	1446	...	...	1649	1846	1929	...	0055	0134	...	0045	0045	...	0445	...	...
Tarvisio 🏛 a.	...	1013	1112	...	...	...	...	...	...	1712	...	1957	...	0119	0157	...	0108	0108	...	0508	...	...
Udine a.	...	1130	1216	...	...	...	...	...	...	1816	...	2113	...	|	|	...	|	|	...	0623	...	...
Trieste Centrale a.	...	1259x	|	...	...	...	...	...	...	|	...	2239x	...	|	|	...	|	|	...	|	...	...
Venezia Mestre a.	...	...	1402	...	...	...	...	...	...	1952	...	...	...	|	|	...	|	|	...	0823	...	...
Venezia Tronchetto ★ a.	...	...	|	...	...	...	...	...	...	|	...	...	...	|	|	...	|	|	...	|	...	...
Venezia Santa Lucia a.	...	...	1414	...	...	...	...	...	...	2004	...	...	...	|	|	...	|	|	...	0834	...	...
Padova a.	...	...	...	...	...	...	...	...	...	...	...	...	...	|	0457	...	0415	0423	...	...	...	...
Verona Porta Nuova a.	...	...	...								...	...	...	|	0551	...	|	|	...	...	...	...
Milano Rogoredo a.	...	...	...								...	...	...	|	0742	...	|	|	...	...	...	...
Genova Piazza Principe a.	...	...	...								...	...	...	|	0938	...	|	|	...	...	...	...
La Spezia Centrale a.	...	...	...								...	...	...	|	1110	...	|	|	...	...	...	...
Bologna Centrale a.	...	...	...								...	...	...	0515	...	...	0541	0541	...	...	...	...
Firenze SMN a.	...	...	...								...	...	...	0618	...	...	0653	0713	...	...	...	...
Pisa Centrale a.	...	...	...								...	...	...	|	...	...	0831	0840	...	...	...	...
Livorno Centrale a.	...	...	...								...	...	...	|	...	...	0850	0900	...	...	...	...
Roma Termini a.	...	...	...	...	...	...	...	...	...	...	...	...	...	0910	...	...	...	...	...	...	...	...

OTHER CONNECTING SERVICES

Praha - Wien : Table **1150**
Budapest - Wien : Table **1250**
Venezia - Roma : Table **600**
Venezia - Milano : Table **605**

train type / number	*REX*	*RJ*		*RJ*		*RJ*	*EC*	*EC*	*RJX*	*RJ*	*IC*		*REX*	*RJ*		*NJ*	*NJ*	*NJ*	*NJ*	*NJ*	*NJ*	
train number	1816	534		536		132	100	272	165	372	632		1818	130		236	1234	1234	1234	235	40294	
notes	1820 2	✕		✕		✕		✕		✕	🍷		1822 2	✕		C	K	E	D	B	A	
Roma Termini d.	...	...	...	...	...	...	...	...	...	...	...	...	...	...	...	...	...	...	...	...	2017	...
Livorno Centrale d.	...	...	...	...	...	...	...	...	...	...	...	...	...	...	...	...	1532	1920	1920	...	|	...
Pisa Centrale d.	...	...	...	...	...	...	...	...	...	...	...	...	...	...	...	...	1550	1945	1946	...	|	...
Firenze SMN d.	...	...	...	...	...	...	...	...	...	...	...	...	...	...	...	...	|	2105	2105	...	2231	...
Bologna Centrale d.	...	...	...	...	...	...	...	...	...	...	...	...	...	...	...	...	|	2223	2223	...	2345	...
La Spezia Centrale d.	...	...	...	...	...	...	...	...	...	...	...	...	...	...	...	...	|	|	|	1710	|	...
Genova Piazza Principe d.	...	...	...	...	...	...	...	...	...	...	...	...	...	...	...	...	|	|	|	1950	|	...
Milano Rogoredo d.	...	...	...	...	...	...	...	...	...	...	...	...	...	...	...	...	|	|	|	2126	|	...
Verona Porta Nuova d.	...	...	...	...	...	...	...	...	...	...	...	...	...	...	...	...	|	|	|	2258	|	...
Padova d.	...	...	...	...	...	...	...	...	...	...	...	...	...	...	...	...	2336	2349	2349	2343	|	...
Venezia Santa Lucia d.	...	...	...	...	...	0956	...	...	...	...	...	...	...	1552	...	2105	|	|	|	|	|	...
Venezia Tronchetto ★ d.	...	...	...	...	...	|	...	...	...	...	...	...	...	|	...	|	|	|	|	|	|	...
Venezia Mestre d.	...	...	...	...	...	1008	...	...	...	...	...	...	...	1604	...	2117	0017	|	|	|	|	...
Trieste Centrale d.	0545x	...	...	...	...	|	...	...	...	...	...	...	1550x	|	...	|	|	|	|	|	|	...
Udine d.	0714	...	...	...	...	1146	...	...	...	...	...	...	1722	1746	...	2301	|	|	|	|	|	...
Tarvisio 🏛 d.	0827	...	...	...	...	1249	...	...	...	...	...	...	1840	1849	...	|	0319	0319	0319	0245	0325	...
Villach Hbf a.	0854	0914	...	1114	...	1311	...	...	...	...	1714	...	1907	1911	...	0042	0341	0341	0341	0307	0347	...
Salzburg Hbf a.	...	|	...	|	...	|	...	...	...	...	|	...	...	|	...	0404	|	|	|	|	|	...
Linz Hbf a.	...	|	...	|	...	|	...	...	...	...	|	...	...	|	...	0558	|	|	|	|	|	...
Klagenfurt Hbf a.	...	0937	...	1137	...	1337	...	...	...	...	1737	...	...	1937	...	|	0407	0407	0407	0438	0438	...
Bruck an der Mur a.	...	1144	...	1344	...	1544	...	...	...	...	1944	...	...	2144	...	|	0620	0620	0620	0639	0639	...
Wien Meidling a.	...	1328	...	1528	...	1728	...	...	...	...	2128	...	...	2328	...	0744	0836	0836	0836	0845	0845	...
Wien Hbf a.	...	1335	...	1535	...	1735	1810	...	1842	1910	2135	...	...	2335	...	0755	0842	0842	0842	0852	0852	...
Györ a.	...	...	...	...	...	...	|	...	1953	|	...	...	...	...	...	...	...	...	...	...	...	...
Budapest Keleti a.	...	...	...	...	...	...	|	...	2119	|	...	...	...	...	...	...	...	...	...	...	...	...
Břeclav a.	...	...	...	...	...	...	1904	1907	...	2004	...	...	...	...	...	...	...	...	...	...	...	...
Praha hlavní a.	...	...	...	...	...	...	...	2241	...	2343	...	...	...	...	...	...	...	...	...	...	...	...

A – *ÖBB nightjet* 🛏 1, 2 cl., ▬ 2 cl. (4, 6 berth), [2] 🍷 Wien - Roma and v.v.

B – *ÖBB nightjet* 🛏 1, 2 cl., ▬ 2 cl. (4, 6 berth), [2] 🍷 Wien - Milano - Genova - La Spezia and v.v.

C – *ÖBB nightjet* 🛏 1, 2 cl., ▬ 2 cl. (4, 6 berth), [2] Wien - Venezia and v.v.

D – ④⑥ May 27 - June 10: *ÖBB nightjet* 🛏 1, 2 cl., ▬ 2 cl. (4, 6 berth), [2] 🍷 Livorno - Firenze - Wien.

E – ④⑥ July 1 - Sept. 30: *ÖBB nightjet* 🛏 1, 2 cl., ▬ 2 cl. (4, 6 berth), [2] 🍷 Livorno - Firenze - Wien.

G – ③⑤ May 26 - June 11, Sept. 8 - Oct. 8: *ÖBB nightjet* 🛏 1, 2 cl., ▬ 2 cl. (4, 6 berth), [2] 🍷 Wien - Firenze - Livorno.

H – ③⑤ June 16 - Sept. 3: *ÖBB nightjet* 🛏 1, 2 cl., ▬ 2 cl. (4, 6 berth), [2] 🍷 Wien - Firenze - Livorno.

J – [12] Zahony (depart 0405) - Debrecen (0531) - Szolnok (0657) - Budapest - Wien. Conveys 🛏 1, 2 cl. Kyïv - Lviv - Zahony - Wien; see Table **96**.

K – July 10, 17, 24, Aug. 7, Sept. 25, Oct. 2, 9: *ÖBB nightjet* 🛏 1, 2 cl., ▬ 2 cl. (4, 6 berth), [2] 🍷 Livorno - Wien.

x – Ⓒ.

⚡ – Supplement payable.

★ – See Venezia City Plan on page 32.

RJ – ÖBB *Railjet* service. [1] (business class), [1] (first class), [2] (economy class), ✕.

🚌 – **ÖBB** *IC Bus*. Rail tickets valid. Ⓡ. Supplement payable. 2nd class only. Connections to / from Wien are made at Villach.

VILLACH - LJUBLJANA - ZAGREB - BUDAPEST and BEOGRAD 89

train type	*D*	*D*	*D*	*D*	*EC*	*D*	*D*	1604	480	*D*
train number	**415**	**247**	**581**	**211**	**213**	**315**	**315**	**1247**	**1247**	**1205**
notes	**413**		**201**				**411**	**959**	**959**	
notes		**H**	**R**				**P**	**K**	**E**	**C**
Villach Hbf ... d.	0625	...	...	1253	1653	1853	...	...	...	...
Koper ... a.	|	...	...	|	|	|	...	2015	...	...
Rijeka ... d.	|	...	...	|	|	|	...	|	1847	...
Ljubljana ... d.	0830	0935	...	1445	1837	2105	2105	0030	0030	...
Dobova 🏛 ... d.	1015	|	...	1646	2021	2241	2306	|	|	...
Split ... d.	|	|	...	|	|	...	|	|	|	1828
Zagreb ... a.	1039	|	...	1710	2045	...	2337	|	|	0243
Zagreb ... d.	*1057*	|	1635	1735	...	...	2341	|	|	0317
Vinkovci ... a.	*1442*	|	|	2142	...	...	0303	|	|	|
Šid 🏛 ... a.	...	|	|	...	...	...	0341	|	|	|
Beograd Centar ... a.	...	|	|	...	...	...	0605	|	|	|
Koprivnica 🏛 ... d.	...	|	1801	...	...	...	...	|	|	0449
Gyékényes 🏛 ... a.	...	|	1812	...	...	...	...	|	|	0549
Nagykanizsa ... a.	...	|	1902	...	...	...	...	|	|	0616
Hodoš 🏛 ... a.	...	1248	|	...	...	...	...	0338	0338	|
Zalaegerszeg ... a.	...	1337	|	...	...	...	...	0431	0431	|
Fonyód ... a.	...	|	2022	...	...	...	...	|	|	0718
Siófok ... a.	...	|	2101	...	...	...	...	|	|	0749
Székesfehérvár ... a.	...	1611	2136	...	...	...	...	0811	0811	0825
Budapest Déli ... a.	...	1659	2224	...	...	...	...	0859	0859	|
Budapest Keleti ... a.	...	...	...	...	...	...	...	...	...	0935

train type	*D*	*D*	*EC*	*D*	*D*	*D*	*D*	*D*	9008	1281
train number	**410**	**314**	**212**	**210**	**412**	**246**	**204**	**1204**	**1246**	**1246**
notes	**314**				**414**		**2214**		**1605**	**1605**
notes	**Q**					**H**	**R**	**D**	**J**	**G**
Budapest Keleti ... d.	...	...	...			...	...	1845	...	...
Budapest Déli ... d.	...	...	...	...	...	0900	1535	|	2035	2100
Székesfehérvár ... d.	...	...	...	...	...	0946	1621	1943	2116	2146
Siófok ... d.	...	...	...	...	...	|	1657	2027	|	|
Fonyód ... d.	...	...	...	...	...	|	1737	2100	|	|
Zalaegerszeg ... d.	...	...	...	...	...	1222	|	|	0012	0020
Hodoš 🏛 ... d.	...	...	...	...	...	1315	|	|	0103	0112
Nagykanizsa ... d.	...	...	...	...	...	|	1908	2159	|	|
Gyékényes 🏛 ... d.	...	...	...	...	...	|	1958	2255	|	|
Koprivnica 🏛 ... a.	...	...	...	...	...	|	2009	2306	|	|
Beograd Centar ... d.	2058	...	...	...	...	|	|	|	|	|
Šid 🏛 ... d.	0022	...	...	...	...	|	|	|	|	|
Vinkovci ... d.	0103	...	...	0839	*1416*	|	|	|	|	|
Zagreb ... a.	0428	...	...	1240	*1820*	|	2210	0022	|	|
Zagreb ... d.	0440	...	0705	1250	1938	|	...	0038	|	|
Split ... a.	|	...	|	|	|	|	...	0846	|	|
Dobova 🏛 ... d.	0540	0540	0745	1334	2019	|	...	...	|	|
Ljubljana ... d.	0717	0726	0923	1527	2208	1635	...	...	0603	0634
Rijeka ... a.	...	|	|	|	|	...	...	...	|	0934
Koper ... a.	...	|	|	|	|	...	...	...	0833	...
Villach Hbf ... a.	...	0908	1058	1708	2348	...	...	...	...	...

C – ADRIA ①③⑥ June 19 - Aug. 29; : 🛏 1, 2 cl., ▬ 2 cl., [2] Split - Zagreb - Budapest.

D – ADRIA ②⑤⑦ June 18 - Aug. 28: 🛏 1, 2 cl., ▬ 2 cl., [2] Budapest - Zagreb - Split.

E – ISTRA June 24 - Aug. 27: 🛏 1, 2 cl., ▬ 2 cl., [2] Rijeka - Hodoš 🏛 - Budapest (Table **91**).

G – ISTRA June 23 - Aug. 26: 🛏 1, 2 cl., ▬ 2 cl., [2] Budapest - Hodoš 🏛 - Rijeka (Table **91**).

H – CITADELLA [2] Budapest - Hodoš - Ljubljana and v.v. (Table **91**).

J – ISTRA June 17 - Aug. 29: ▬ 2 cl. [2] Budapest - Hodoš 🏛 - Koper (Table **91**).

K – ISTRA June 18 - Aug. 30: ▬ 2 cl. [2] Koper - Hodoš 🏛 - Budapest (Table **91**).

P – June 20 - Sept. 13: ▬ 2 cl., [12] Ljubljana - Zagreb - Beograd.

Q – June 21 - Sept. 14: ▬ 2 cl., [12] Beograd - Zagreb - Ljubljana.

R – AGRAM-TOPART [2] Zagreb - Budapest and v.v.

RJ – ÖBB *Railjet* service. [1] (business class), [1] (first class), [2] (economy class), ✕.

☛ **Shaded services are suspended until further notice.**

MARSEILLE - NICE - MILANO, ROMA and VENEZIA 90

train type		*IC*	*FB*			*IC*	*IC*	*FB*	*FR*	*FA*			*IC*	*IC*	*ITA*	*FR*			*IC*	*IC*		*IC*	*ICN*	*ICN*	*ICN*
train number		**631**	**8613**			**745**	**665**	**8619**	**9547**	**9741**			**635**	**673**	**8997**	**9663**			**681**	**679**		**639**	**1963**	**799**	**799**
train number																									
notes		Ⓡ	Ⓡ 🍷		2	Ⓡ	Ⓡ	Ⓡ 🍷	Ⓡ 🍷	Ⓡ 🍷			Ⓡ 🍷	Ⓡ	Ⓡ 🍷	Ⓡ 🍷			Ⓡ	Ⓡ		Ⓡ 🍷	Ⓡ	Ⓡ	Ⓡ
notes		⚡	⚡			⚡	⚡	⚡	⚡	⚡			⚡	⚡	⚡	⚡			⚡	⚡		⚡	⚡	⚡	⚡
notes																Ⓑ							C	AP	AQ
Marseille St Charles ... d.	...	...	...	0548	...	...	...	...	...	...	0957	...	...	...	...	...	1157	...	...	...	...	...	...	...	...
Toulon ... d.	...	...	...	0644	...	...	...	...	...	...	1044	...	...	...	...	...	1244	...	...	...	...	...	...	...	...
Cannes ... d.	0521x	...	...	0812	0822	...	...	...	...	...	1211	1222	...	...	...	...	1411	...	...	...	1752	...	...	...	...
Nice ... d.	0604	...	...	0848	0906	...	...	...	...	...	1241	1309	...	...	...	...	1441	1543	...	...	1836	...	...	...	...
Monaco - Monte Carlo ... d.	0629	...	...	▬	0932	...	...	...	...	...	...	1334	...	...	...	...	▬	1609	...	...	1902	...	...	...	...
Ventimiglia 🏛 ... d.	0701	0910	...	*IC* **511**	1001	1103	...	...	...	...	...	1401	1510	...	...	...	*FR*	1635	1703	...	1931	1943	...	...	...
San Remo ... d.	...	0923	...	Ⓡ ⚡	...	1120	...	...	...	...	...	...	1523	...	...	...	**9567**	...	1720	...	...	1956	...	...	...
Genova Piazza Principe ... a.	...	1105	1210	1224	...	1305	1347	1502	...	...	...	...	1705	1747	...	...	Ⓡ ⚡	...	1908	1947	...	2142	2156	2207	2353
Milano Centrale ... a.	...	1255	|	|	...	1455	|	|	1510	1545	...	...	1855	|	1935	1925	2010	...	2057	|	...	2340	|	|	|
Verona ... a.	...	...	|	|	...	...	|	|	|	1658	...	...	...	|	2047	|	|	...	...	|	...	...	|	|	|
Venezia Santa Lucia ... a.	...	...	|	|	...	...	|	|	|	1812	...	...	...	|	2203	|	|	...	...	|	...	...	|	|	|
La Spezia Centrale ... a.	...	...	1315	1350	...	...	1521	1615	|	...	...	...	...	1921	...	|	|	...	...	2121	...	...	2306	2352	0125
Pisa Centrale ... a.	...	...	1404	1447	...	...	...	1704	|	...	...	...	...	2017	...	|	|	...	...	2217	...	...	2356	0048	0216
Firenze SMN ... a.	...	...	|	|	...	...	...	|	1704	...	...	...	...	...	...	|	2204	...	...	...	...	...	...	|	|
Roma Termini ... a.	...	...	1703	1803	...	...	...	2003	1849	...	...	...	...	...	...	2240	2349	...	...	...	...	...	...	0543o	0543o
Napoli Centrale ... a.	...	...	...	2029	...	...	...	...	2010	...	...	...	...	...	...	0005	...	...	...	...	...	...	...	0817	0817

train type	*ICN*			*ICN*	*IC*	*ICN*	*IC*		*IC*	*ICN*		*IC*			*IC*	*IC*	*IC*	*FR*	*FR*	*IC*		*ITA*	*FR*	*IC*	*IC*
train number	**796**			**796**	**658**	**1962**	**633**		**662**	**1962**		**659**			**637**	**510**	**674**	**9728**	**9415**	**641**		**8984**	**9584**	**680**	**675**
train number																									
notes	Ⓡ ⚡	2		Ⓡ ⚡	Ⓡ	Ⓡ ⚡	Ⓡ 🍷		Ⓡ	Ⓡ ⚡	2	Ⓡ			Ⓡ 🍷	Ⓡ	Ⓡ	Ⓡ 🍷	Ⓡ 🍷	Ⓡ 🍷		Ⓡ 🍷	Ⓡ 🍷	Ⓡ	Ⓡ
notes	A			A	⚡	C	⚡		⚡	C		⚡			⚡	⚡	⚡	⚡	⚡	⚡		⚡	⚡	⚡	⚡
notes	⑥⑦	⚒		①–⑤		⑥⑦				①–⑤	Ⓐ										⑤⑥⑦				
Napoli Centrale ... d.	2146	...	...	2146	...	...	...	...	...	...	...	...	...	...	...	0731	...	...	0940	...	...	...	1140	...	...
Roma Termini ... d.	0011o	...	...	0011o	...	...	...	...	...	...	...	...	...	...	...	0957	...	...	1110	...	...	...	1310	...	...
Firenze SMN ... d.	|	...	...	|	...	...	...	...	...	...	...	...	...	...	...	|	...	...	1255	...	...	...	1455	...	...
Pisa Centrale ... d.	0326	...	...	0500	0542	0557	...	...	0642	0647	...	...	...	...	...	1302	1342	...	|	...	...	...	|	...	...
La Spezia Centrale ... d.	0425	...	...	0552	0638	0654	...	...	0738	0758	...	...	...	...	...	1405	1438	...	|	...	...	...	|	1638	...
Venezia Santa Lucia ... d.	|	...	...	|	|	|	...	...	|	|	...	...	...	...	...	|	|	1148	|	...	...	1357	|	|	...
Verona ... d.	|	...	...	|	|	|	...	...	|	|	...	...	...	...	...	|	|	1302	|	...	...	1512	|	|	...
Milano Centrale ... d.	|	...	...	|	|	|	0710	...	|	|	...	0910	...	...	1110	|	|	1415	1450	1510	...	1625	1650	|	1705
Genova Piazza Principe ... d.	0601	0646	...	0757	0816	0839	0858	...	0915	0936	0943	1058	...	...	1258	1535	1614	...	...	1658	...	...	...	1815	1858
San Remo ... d.	...	0906	...	...	...	...	1042	...	▬	...	1145	1241f	...	...	1442	...	...	...	...	1842	...	...	...	...	2041
Ventimiglia 🏛 ... a.	...	0922	1022	...	...	...	1054	1206	...	...	1203	1258f	1315	...	1454	...	...	...	...	1854	1952	...	...	...	2058
Monaco - Monte Carlo ... a.	...	...	1057	...	...	...	...	1241	...	...	...	...	1350	...	...	...	...	...	...	...	2027	...	...	...	...
Nice ... a.	...	...	1123	...	...	...	...	1305	1320	...	...	...	1415	1420	...	...	...	...	...	...	2051	...	...	...	...
Cannes ... a.	...	...	1210	...	...	...	...	1410	1353	...	...	...	1508	1453	...	...	...	...	...	...	2138	...	...	...	...
Toulon ... a.	...	...	...	...	...	...	...	...	1515	...	...	...	...	1615	...	...	...	...	...	...	...	...	...	...	...
Marseille St Charles ... a.	...	...	...	...	...	...	...	...	1602	...	...	...	...	1703	...	...	...	...	...	...	...	...	...	...	...

A – 🛏 1, 2 cl., ▬ 2 cl. (4 berth), [2] Torino - Genova - Napoli - Salerno and v.v.

C – 🛏 1, 2 cl., ▬ 2 cl. (4 berth) Milano - Genova - Pisa - Siracusa and v.v.
🛏 1, 2 cl., ▬ 2 cl. (4 berth) Milano - Genova - Pisa - Palermo and v.v.

P – ①–⑤ Dec. 12 - Mar. 15.

Q – ⑥⑦ (daily Mar. 16 - Dec. 10).

f – On © depart San Remo 1257, arrive Ventimiglia 1312.

o – Roma **Ostiense**.

x – Not ⑥.

⚡ – Supplement payable.

For Summer service from June 11 see page 674

91 WIEN - LJUBLJANA and ZAGREB

train type	*EC*			*D*	*EC*	*IC*	*IC*	
train number	**151**	**483**	**2752**	**246**	**159**¶	**523**	**310**	
notes	**134**		2		✕✓	2	🍷	
	✕E		🚌	G	C			
Wien Hbf.......d.	0758	...	...	...	1558	...	...	...
Wien Meidling.......d.	0805	...	...	...	1605	...	...	...
Wiener Neustadt Hbf.......d.	0832	...	...	...	1632	...	...	...
Budapest Keleti.......d.	|	...	...	...	|	...	1615	...
Budapest Déli.......d.	|	...	...	0900	|	...	|	...
Szombathely.......d.	|	...	...	|	|	...	1906	...
Hodoš 🏛.......d.	|	...	...	1315	|	...	|	...
Graz Hbf.......d.	1037	...	...	|	1839	...	2137	...
Spielfeld-Straß 🏛.......d.	1125	...	...	|	1926	...	2225	...
Maribor.......a.	1140	...	...	|	1941	2005	2240	...
Pragersko.......a.	1145	...	...	1432	2004	2018	2259	...
Zidani Most.......a.	1303	...	...	1536	|	2118	0002	...
Dobova 🏛.......a.	|	...	...	|	2146	|	|	...
Zagreb.......a.	|	...	...	|	2225	|	|	...
Ljubljana.......a.	1400	1520	1550	1635	...	2208	0056	...
Koper.......a.	|	|	1817	...	...	...	...	...
Rijeka.......a.	|	1827	...	...	...	...	...	...
Villa Opicina 🏛.......a.	1626	...	...	...	...	...	...	...
Trieste.......a.	1652	...	...	...	...	...	...	...

train type/number	*IC*	*IC*	*ICS*	*EC*	*D*			*EC*
train number	**311**	**508**	**14**	**158**	**247**	**2751**	**482**	**135**
notes	🍷		2	✕✓		2		**150**
				C	H	🚌		✕F
Trieste.......d.	...	...	...	...	...	...	...	1252
Villa Opicina 🏛.......d.	...	...	...	...	...	...	...	1336
Rijeka.......d.	...	...	...	...	...	...	1150	|
Koper.......d.	...	0525	...	...	...	1004	|	|
Ljubljana.......d.	0505	0753	0805	...	0935	1245	1457	1555
Zagreb.......d.	|	...	|	0705	|	...	...	|
Dobova 🏛.......d.	|	...	|	0803	|	...	...	|
Zidani Most.......d.	0559	...	0850	|	1030	...	...	1701
Pragersko.......d.	0700	...	0943	0944	1133	...	...	1800
Maribor.......d.	0719	...	0955	1019	|	...	...	1821
Spielfeld-Straß 🏛.......a.	0734	...	...	1034	|	...	...	1836
Graz Hbf.......a.	0823	...	...	1122	|	...	...	1922
Hodoš 🏛.......a.	|	...	...	|	1248	...	...	|
Szombathely.......a.	1053	...	...	|	|	...	...	|
Budapest Déli.......a.	|	...	...	|	1659	...	...	|
Budapest Keleti.......a.	1344	...	...	|	...	...	...	|
Wiener Neustadt Hbf.......a.	...	...	...	1328	...	...	...	2128
Wien Meidling.......a.	...	...	...	1355	...	...	...	2155
Wien Hbf.......a.	...	...	...	1402	...	...	...	2202

C – CROATIA 12 ✕ Wien - Zagreb and v.v.
E – EMONA 12 ✕ Wien - Ljubljana. Conveys 12 Wien (**151**) - Ljubljana (**134**) - Trieste.
F – EMONA 12 ✕ Ljubljana - Wien. Conveys 12 Trieste (**135**) - Ljubljana (**150**) - Wien.
G – CITADELLA 2 Budapest - Hodoš - Ljubljana and v.v. (Table **89**).

✓ – Supplement payable.
◇ – Stopping train.
¶ – Train number **1259** on ⓒ.

92 PRAHA - BRATISLAVA - ZAGREB - RIJEKA / SPLIT — 2022 service

		EN		*RJ*	*RJ*	
		1153		**1221**	**1221**	
		C		A	A	
Praha hl. n.......d.	...	...	...	1638	1638	...
Kolín.......d.	...	...	...	1722	1722	...
Brno hl. n.......d.	...	...	...	1948	1948	...
Břeclav.......d.	...	...	...	2020	2020	...
Bratislava hl. st.......d.	...	1551	...	2132	2132	...
Györ.......d.	...	|	...	|	|	...
Budapest Kelenföld.......d.	...	|	...	|	|	...
Wien Hbf.......d.	...	1801	...	|	|	...
Wien Meidling.......d.	...	1808	...	|	|	...
Wiener Neustadt Hbf.......d.	...	1850	...	|	|	...
Graz Hbf.......d.	...	2102	...	|	|	...
Spielfeld-Straß 🏛.......d.	...	2148	...	|	|	...
Maribor.......d.	...	2205	...	|	|	...
Dobova 🏛.......d.	...	0023	...	|	|	...
Zagreb.......a.	...	0048	...	0517	0517	...
Ogulin.......a.	...	0248	...	0751	0751	...
Rijeka.......a.	...	|	...	1013	|	...
Gračac.......a.	...	|	...	...	1030	...
Knin.......a.	...	0709	...	...	|	...
Perković.......a.	...	0818	...	...	|	...
Split.......a.	...	0950	...	...	1344	...

		RJ	*RJ*		*EN*	
		1046	**1046**		**1152**	
		B	B		D	
Split.......d.	...	1551	...	...	1728	...
Perković.......d.	...	|	...	...	1844	...
Knin.......d.	...	|	...	...	1949	...
Gračac.......d.	...	1900	...	...	|	...
Rijeka.......d.	...	|	1955	...	|	...
Ogulin.......d.	...	2222	2222	...	2340	...
Zagreb.......d.	...	0113	0113	...	0200	...
Dobova 🏛.......a.	...	|	|	...	0225	...
Maribor.......a.	...	|	|	...	0436	...
Spielfeld-Straß 🏛.......a.	...	|	|	...	0502	...
Graz Hbf.......a.	...	|	|	...	0553	...
Wiener Neustadt Hbf.......a.	...	|	|	...	0808	...
Wien Meidling.......a.	...	|	|	...	0851	...
Wien Hbf.......a.	...	|	|	...	0858	...
Budapest Kelenföld.......a.	...	|	|	...	|	...
Györ.......a.	...	|	|	...	|	...
Bratislava hl. st.......a.	...	0828	0828	...	1049	...
Břeclav.......a.	...	0936	0936	...	...	...
Brno hl. n.......a.	...	1007	1007	...	...	...
Kolín.......a.	...	1230	1230	...	...	...
Praha hl. n.......a.	...	1314	1314	...	...	...

A – ①③⑥ May 28 - Sept. 26 (daily July 1 - Aug. 31): 2 cl. (4 berth), 2 Praha - Rijeka / Split.
B – ②④⑦ May 29 - Sept. 27 (daily July 2 - Sept. 1): 2 cl. (4 berth), 2 Rijeka / Split - Praha.
C – ②⑤ June 3 - Sept. 23: 1, 2 cl., 2 Bratislava - Split.
D – ③⑥ June 4 - Sept. 24: 1, 2 cl., 2 Split - Bratislava.

93 WARSZAWA - VILNIUS

train type			*IC*					
train number			**31100**	**24**				
notes			**144**					
			V					
Warszawa Centralna.......d.	...	...	0735	...	...	...	...	...
Warszawa Wschodnia.......d.	...	...	0745	...	...	...	...	...
Białystok.......d.	...	...	1045	...	...	...	...	...
Suwałki.......d.	...	...	1256	...	...	...	...	...
Mockava 🏛 ◐.......§ a.	...	...	1441	1505	...	...	...	...
Šeštokai.......§ a.	...	...	...	|	...	...	...	...
Kaunas.......§ a.	...	...	...	1626	...	...	...	...
Vilnius.......§ a.	...	...	...	1734	...	...	...	...

train type				*IC*				
train number			**23**	**143**				
notes				**13000**				
				V				
Vilnius.......§ d.	...	...	1210	...	...	...	...	...
Kaunas.......§ d.	...	...	1320	...	...	...	...	...
Šeštokai.......§ d.	...	...	|	...	...	...	...	...
Mockava 🏛 ◐.......§ d.	...	...	1441	1514	...	...	...	...
Suwałki.......d.	...	...	...	1527	...	...	...	...
Białystok.......d.	...	...	...	1741	...	...	...	...
Warszawa Wschodnia.......a.	...	...	...	2003	...	...	...	...
Warszawa Centralna.......a.	...	...	...	2013	...	...	...	...

V – HAŃCZA – 12 Kraków - Warszawa - Białystok - Mockava and v.v. (Table **1042**).
§ – Lithuanian time.
◐ – 🏛 = Trakiszki (Poland) / Mockava (Lithuania); ticketing point is Mockava.

95 MOSKVA - WARSZAWA - PRAHA and WIEN

Moskva Belorusskaya.......d.	...	...	...	...	...	...	...	...	...
Smolensk Tsentralny 🏛.......§ d.	...	...	...	...	...	...	...	...	...
Orsha Tsentralnaya.......§ d.	...	...	...	...	...	...	...	...	...
Minsk.......d.	...	...	...	...	...	...	...	...	...
Brest Tsentralny 🏛.......a.	...	...	...	...	...	...	...	...	...
Brest Tsentralny 🏛.......d.	...	...	...	...	...	...	...	...	...
Terespol 🏛.......a.	...	...	...	...	...	...	...	...	...
Terespol 🏛.......d.	...	...	...	...	...	...	...	...	...
Warszawa Wschodnia.......a.	...	...	...	...	...	...	...	...	...
Warszawa Centralna.......a.	...	...	...	...	...	...	...	...	...
Katowice.......a.	...	...	...	...	...	...	...	...	...
Bohumín 🏛.......a.	...	...	...	...	...	...	...	...	...
Ostrava hlavní.......a.	...	...	...	...	...	...	...	...	...
Břeclav.......a.	...	...	...	...	...	...	...	...	...
Wien Hbf.......a.	...	...	...	...	...	...	...	...	...
Olomouc.......a.	...	...	...	...	...	...	...	...	...
Pardubice.......a.	...	...	...	...	...	...	...	...	...
Praha hlavní.......a.	...	...	...	...	...	...	...	...	...

Praha hlavní.......d.	...	...	...	...	...	...	...	...	...
Pardubice.......d.	...	...	...	...	...	...	...	...	...
Olomouc.......d.	...	...	...	...	...	...	...	...	...
Wien Hbf.......d.	...	...	...	...	...	...	...	...	...
Břeclav.......d.	...	...	...	...	...	...	...	...	...
Ostrava hlavní.......d.	...	...	...	...	...	...	...	...	...
Bohumín 🏛.......d.	...	...	...	...	...	...	...	...	...
Katowice.......d.	...	...	...	...	...	...	...	...	...
Warszawa Centralna.......d.	...	...	...	...	...	...	...	...	...
Warszawa Wschodnia.......d.	...	...	...	...	...	...	...	...	...
Terespol 🏛.......a.	...	...	...	...	...	...	...	...	...
Terespol 🏛.......d.	...	...	...	...	...	...	...	...	...
Brest Tsentralny 🏛.......a.	...	...	...	...	...	...	...	...	...
Brest Tsentralny 🏛.......d.	...	...	...	...	...	...	...	...	...
Minsk.......a.	...	...	...	...	...	...	...	...	...
Orsha Tsentralnaya.......§ a.	...	...	...	...	...	...	...	...	...
Smolensk Tsentralny 🏛.......§ a.	...	...	...	...	...	...	...	...	...
Moskva Belorusskaya.......a.	...	...	...	...	...	...	...	...	...

§ – 🏛: Osinovka (BY) / Krasnoye (RU).

WIEN / BUDAPEST / PRAHA / BRATISLAVA - LVIV - KYIV 96

train number	IC		SC	8862	40149
train number	34	603	241	29	EC 149
notes	🅁	✕	🍷🅁		749
notes	C			P	B
Wien Hbf ..... d.	...	...	...	...	1642
Budapest Nyugati ..... d.	0723	...	...	...	|
Budapest Keleti ..... d.	|	...	...	...	1940
Szolnok ..... d.	0838	...	...	...	2104
Debrecen ..... d.	0953	...	...	...	2237
Záhony 🏛 ..... d.	1223	...	...	...	0110
Praha hl. n. ..... d.	|	...	0625	...	|
Bratislava hl. st. ..... d.	|	0813	|	...	|
Žilina ..... d.	|	1042	1119	...	|
Košice ..... a.	|	1403	1418	1513	|
Čierna nad Tisou 🏛 ..... a.	|	...	...	1651	|
Chop 🏛 ..... a.	1340	...	...	1847	0228
Mukachevo ..... a.	1530	...	...	2155	0622
Lviv ..... a.	...	...	...	0220	1014
Khmelnytsky ..... a.	...	...	...	|	|
Vinnytsya ..... a.	...	...	...	|	|
Kyiv ..... a.	...	...	...	1011	1722

train number	749	81	SC		IC
train number	40749	8861	240	612	33
notes	EC 140		🍷🅁	✕	🅁
notes	A	Q			C
Kyiv ..... d.	1407	1830	...	...	...
Vinnytsya ..... d.	|	2149	...	...	...
Khmelnytsky ..... d.	|	2356	...	...	...
Lviv ..... d.	2100	0409	...	...	...
Mukachevo ..... d.	0054	0852	...	...	1230
Chop 🏛 ..... d.	0328	1135	...	...	1410
Čierna nad Tisou 🏛 ..... d.	|	1204	...	...	|
Košice ..... d.	|	1349	1459	1557	|
Žilina ..... a.	|	...	1751	1918	|
Bratislava hl. st. ..... a.	|	...	|	2147	|
Praha hl. n. ..... a.	|	...	2233	...	|
Záhony 🏛 ..... a.	0246	...	...	...	1327
Debrecen ..... a.	0529	...	...	...	1605
Szolnok ..... a.	0652	...	...	...	1720
Budapest Keleti ..... a.	0820	...	...	...	|
Budapest Nyugati ..... a.	|	...	...	...	1837
Wien Hbf ..... a.	1121	...	...	...	...

A – HORTOBÁGY – 🛏 1, 2 cl. Kyiv (**749**) - Lviv (**145**) - Chop (**140**) - Záhony - Budapest - Wien. [12] Záhony - Wien.

B – HORTOBÁGY – 🛏 1, 2 cl. Wien (**149**) - Budapest - Záhony - Chop (**146**) - Lviv (**749**) - Kyiv. [12] Wien - Záhony.

C – LATORCA – [12] Budapest - Záhony - Chop - Mukachevo and v.v.

P – 🛏 1, 2 cl. Košice (**8862**) - Čierna nad Tisou - Chop (**29**) - Lviv - Kyiv.

Q – 🛏 1, 2 cl. Kyiv (**81**) - Lviv - Chop (**8861**) - Čierna nad Tisou (**8802**) - Košice.

☛ **Shaded services are suspended until further notice.**

WARSZAWA and KRAKÓW - PRAHA, WIEN and BUDAPEST 99

train type/train number	IC¶	EC	LE	IC¶	EC	EC	IC¶	IC	IC¶	RJ	IC¶	IC¶	EC	IC	EC¶	EC	EC	IC	TLK	EN	EN	EN	RJ
train number	101	273	412	116	103	277	114	114	131	79	114	105	281	212	112	107	283	110	310	407	407	407	1022
notes/train number	✕	✕	🍷	✕	✕	✕	🍷	131	✕	✕	🍷	✕	🍷		🍷	✕	🍷	🍷		457	457	442	
notes			①⑥	⊡	⊡		⊡	⊡	⊡		⊡	⊡		⊡	⊡	⊡		⊡	🅁	477			
notes	H		N	Z	X		L	2	V		L	E		J	Z	W			R	B	C	P	G
Gdynia Główny ..... d.	...	...	...	...	...	...	...	...	...	...	...	...	...	...	...	1021	...	...	...	...	...	...	...
Gdańsk Główny ..... d.	...	...	...	...	...	...	...	...	...	...	...	...	...	...	...	1048	...	...	...	...	...	...	...
Warszawa Wschodnia ..... d.	...	...	...	0456	0532	...	...	...	...	...	...	...	...	...	1251	|	...	1649	...	1922	1922	1922	...
Warszawa Centralna ..... d.	...	...	...	0507	0543	...	...	...	0827j	...	...	...	...	...	1302	1413j	...	1659	...	1938j	1938j	1938j	...
Przemyśl ..... d.	...	...	...	|	|	...	0746	0746	|	...	...	1101	...	...	|	|	...	|	...	|	|	|	2125
Rzeszów ..... d.	...	...	...	|	|	...	0852	0852	|	...	...	1208	...	...	|	|	...	|	1723	|	|	|	2218
Kraków Główny ..... d.	...	...	0559	|	|	...	1043	1043	|	...	...	1406	...	1437	|	|	...	|	1935	2245	2245	2245	0002
Katowice ..... d.	0451	...	0706	0814	0909	...	1141	1141	1122	...	...	1502	...	1542	1622	1704	...	2022	2046	2348	2348	2348	0100
Chałupki 🏛 ..... d.	0624	...	|	0937	1025	...	1307	1307	1259	...	←	1624	...	1729	1742	1824	...	2143	2218	0122	0122	0122	|
Bohumín 🏛 ..... a.	0630	...	0833	0943	1030	...	1313	1313	1305	...	1313	1630	...	1735	1748	1830	...	|	2224	0128	0128	0128	0225
Bohumín 🏛 ..... d.	0642	...	0849	1005	1042	...	1405	1342	1342	...	1405	1642	...	1805	1805	1842	...	|	...	0215	0215	0336	0245
Ostrava hl. n. ..... a.	0649	...	0855	1012	1049	...	→	1349	1349	...	1412	1649	...	1812	1812	1849	...	2156	...	0222	0222	0344	0252
Přerov ..... a.	0744	...	0953	|	1140	...	...	1444	1444	...	|	1744	...	|	|	1944	...	...	...	|	|	|	|
Olomouc ..... a.	|	...	1008	1117	|	...	...	|	|	...	1517	|	...	1917	1917	|	...	...	...	|	|	0450	0355
Pardubice ..... a.	|	...	1127	1244	|	...	...	|	|	...	1644	|	...	2044	2044	|	...	...	...	|	|	0622	0527
Praha hl. n. ..... a.	|	...	1224	1355	|	...	...	|	|	...	1748	|	...	2155	2155	|	...	...	...	|	|	0738	0629
Břeclav ..... a.	0845	0855	...	...	1245	1255	...	1545	1545	1555	...	1845	1855	...	...	2045	2055	...	...	0410	0410	...	...
Wien Hbf ..... a.	0949	|	...	...	1349	|	...	|	|	1649	...	1949	|	...	...	2149	|	...	...	|	0700	...	...
Graz ..... a.	...	|	...	...	...	|	...	|	|	...	...	2222	|	...	...	...	|	...	...	|	1002	...	...
Kúty 🏛 ..... a.	...	0911	...	...	...	1311	...	1611	1611	...	...	...	1911	...	...	...	2111	...	...	0511	...	...	...
Bratislava hl. st. ..... a.	...	0954	...	...	...	1354	...	1701	1701	...	...	...	1954	...	...	...	2154	...	...	0554	...	...	...
Štúrovo 🏛 △ ..... a.	...	1124	...	...	...	1524	...	1836	1836	...	...	...	2124	...	...	...	...	...	...	0724	...	...	...
Budapest Nyugati ..... a.	...	1228	...	...	...	1628	...	1949	1949	...	...	...	2228	...	...	...	...	...	...	0829	...	...	...

train type/train number	TLK	IC	EC	EC	IC¶	IC	EC	EC	IC¶	RJ	EC	IC¶	EC	EC	EC	IC¶	LE	EC	IC¶	RJ	EN	EN	EN
train number	311	111	282	106	113	213	280	104	115	74	130	115	130	276	102	117	413	272	100	1023	456	476	443
notes/train number		🍷	🍷	✕	🍷	2	🍷	✕	🍷	✕	115	🍷	✕	✕	✕	🍷	🍷	✕	✕		406	456	406
notes	🅁	⊡		⊡	⊡	⊡		⊡	⊡		⊡	⊡	⊡		⊡	⊡	⑤⑦					406	
notes	R			W	Z	J		E	L		2	L	V		X	Z	M		H	G	D	A	Q
Budapest Nyugati ..... d.	...	...	...	...	...	...	0529	...	...	...	0812	...	0812	1129	...	...	...	1529	...	...	...	1929	...
Štúrovo 🏛 △ ..... d.	...	...	...	...	...	...	0634	...	...	...	0924	...	0924	1234	...	...	...	1634	...	...	...	2034	...
Bratislava hl. st. ..... d.	...	...	0606	...	...	...	0806	...	...	...	1057	...	1057	1406	...	...	...	1806	...	...	...	2206	...
Kúty 🏛 ..... d.	...	...	0649	...	...	...	0849	...	...	...	1148	...	1148	1449	...	...	...	1849	...	...	...	2249	...
Graz ..... d.	...	...	|	...	...	...	|	0526	...	...	|	...	|	|	...	...	...	|	...	...	1921	|	...
Wien Hbf ..... d.	...	...	|	0610	...	...	|	0810	...	1110	|	...	|	|	1410	...	...	|	1810	...	2210	|	...
Břeclav ..... d.	...	...	0704	0710	...	...	0904	0910	...	1204	1210	...	1210	1504	1510	...	...	1904	1910	...	2350	2350	...
Praha hl. n. ..... d.	...	...	...	|	0615	0615	...	|	1015	...	|	...	|	...	|	1415	1500	...	|	2200	|	|	2213
Pardubice ..... d.	...	...	...	|	0718	0718	...	|	1118	...	|	...	|	...	|	1518	1602	...	|	2253	|	|	2325
Olomouc ..... d.	...	...	...	|	0845	0845	...	|	1245	...	|	...	|	...	|	1645	1722	...	|	0015	|	|	0101
Přerov ..... d.	...	...	...	0813	|	|	...	1013	|	...	1313	...	1313	...	1613	|	1738	...	2013	|	|	|	|
Ostrava hl. n. ..... d.	...	0604	...	0908	0950	0950	...	1108	1350	...	1408	←	1408	...	1708	1747	1836	...	2108	0118	0133	0133	0216
Bohumín 🏛 ..... a.	...	|	...	0915	0957	0957	...	1115	1357	...	1415	1357	1415	...	1715	1754	1842	...	2115	0126	0140	0140	0224
Bohumín 🏛 ..... d.	0402	|	...	0927	1009	1017	...	1127	1446	...	1446	1446	1454	...	1727	1809	1914	...	2127	0248	0318	0318	0318
Chałupki 🏛 ..... a.	0408	0618	...	0933	1015	1023	...	1133	→	...	1452	1452	1500	...	1733	1815	|	...	2133	|	0324	0324	0324
Katowice ..... a.	0543	0740	...	1054	1132	1205	...	1248	...	...	1610	1610	1632	...	1848	1943	2036	...	2259	0410	0440	0440	0440
Kraków Główny ..... a.	0649	|	...	|	|	1311	...	1349	...	...	1707	1707	|	...	|	|	2138	...	...	0509	0549	0549	0549
Rzeszów ..... a.	0852	|	...	|	|	...	...	1546	...	...	1859	1859	|	...	|	|	...	...	...	0657	|	|	|
Przemyśl ..... a.	...	|	...	|	|	...	...	1712	...	...	2018	2018	|	...	|	|	...	...	...	0817	|	|	|
Warszawa Centralna ..... a.	...	1038j	...	1334j	1429	...	...	...	...	...	...	...	1951	...	2147	2243j	...	...	...	...	|	|	|
Warszawa Wschodnia ..... a.	...	...	...	|	1441	...	...	...	...	...	...	...	2001	...	2156	2259	...	...	...	...	0934	0934	0934
Gdańsk Główny ..... a.	...	...	...	1630	...	...	...	...	...	...	...	...	...	...	...	...	...	...	...	...	...	...	...
Gdynia Główny ..... a.	...	...	...	1658	...	...	...	...	...	...	...	...	...	...	...	...	...	...	...	...	...	...	...

A – 🛏 1, 2 cl., ▬ 2 cl., [2] Budapest (**476**) - Břeclav (**456**) - Bohumín (**406**) - Kraków - Warszawa. Conveys 🛏 1, 2 cl., ▬ 2 cl., [2] Budapest (**476**) - Břeclav (**456**) - Bohumín - Wrocław - Berlin.

B – 🛏 1, 2 cl., ▬ 2 cl., [2] Warszawa (**407**) - Kraków - Bohumín (**457**) - Břeclav (**477**) - Budapest. Conveys 🛏 1, 2 cl., ▬ 2 cl., [2] Berlin (**457**) - Wrocław - Břeclav (**477**) - Budapest.

C – CHOPIN – 🛏 1, 2 cl., ▬ 2 cl. [2] Warszawa (**407**) - Kraków - Bohumín (**457**) - Wien - Graz. Conveys 🛏 1, 2 cl., ▬ 2 cl., [2] Berlin (**457**) - Wrocław - Bohumín - Wien - Graz.

D – CHOPIN – 🛏 1, 2 cl., ▬ 2 cl. [2] Graz (**456**) - Wien - Bohumín (**406**) - Kraków - Warszawa. Conveys 🛏 1, 2 cl., ▬ 2 cl., [2] Graz (**456**) - Wien (**456**) - Bohumín - Wrocław - Berlin.

E – PORTA MORAVIA / PORTA MORAVICA – [12] Przemyśl - Bohumín - Graz and v.v. ✕ Bohumín - Graz and v.v.

G – *RegioJet* 🛏 (3, 4 berth), [2] Praha - Przemyśl and v.v.

H – MORAVIA – [12] ✕ Katowice - Wien and v.v.

J – GALICJA – [2] Kraków - Katowice - Ostrava - Praha and v.v.

L – CRACOVIA – [12] 🍷 Przemyśl - Praha and v.v.

M – ⑤⑦: LEO EXPRESS – [12] 🍷 Praha - Kraków.

N – ①⑥: LEO EXPRESS – [12] 🍷 Kraków - Praha.

P – 🛏 1, 2 cl., ▬ 2 cl., [2] Warszawa (**407**) - Bohumín (**442**) - Praha.

Q – 🛏 1, 2 cl., ▬ 2 cl., [2] Praha (**443**) - Bohumín (**406**) - Warszawa.

R – ROZTOCZE – [12] Lublin (depart 1430; arrive 1148) - Rzeszów - Bohumín and v.v.

V – BÁTHORY – [12] ✕ Terespol (depart 0617; arrive 2206) - Warszawa - Budapest and v.v.

W – SOBIESKI – [12] ✕ Gdynia - Wien and v.v.

X – POLONIA – [12] ✕ Warszawa - Wien and v.v.

Z – SILESIA – [12] ✕ Warszawa - Praha and v.v.

j – Warszawa **Gdańska**.

△ – Routeing point for international tickets: Szob.

⊡ – Supplement payable in Poland; Reservation compulsory in Poland.

* – Classified *Ex* in Czech Republic.

¶ – Classified *EC* in Czech Republic.

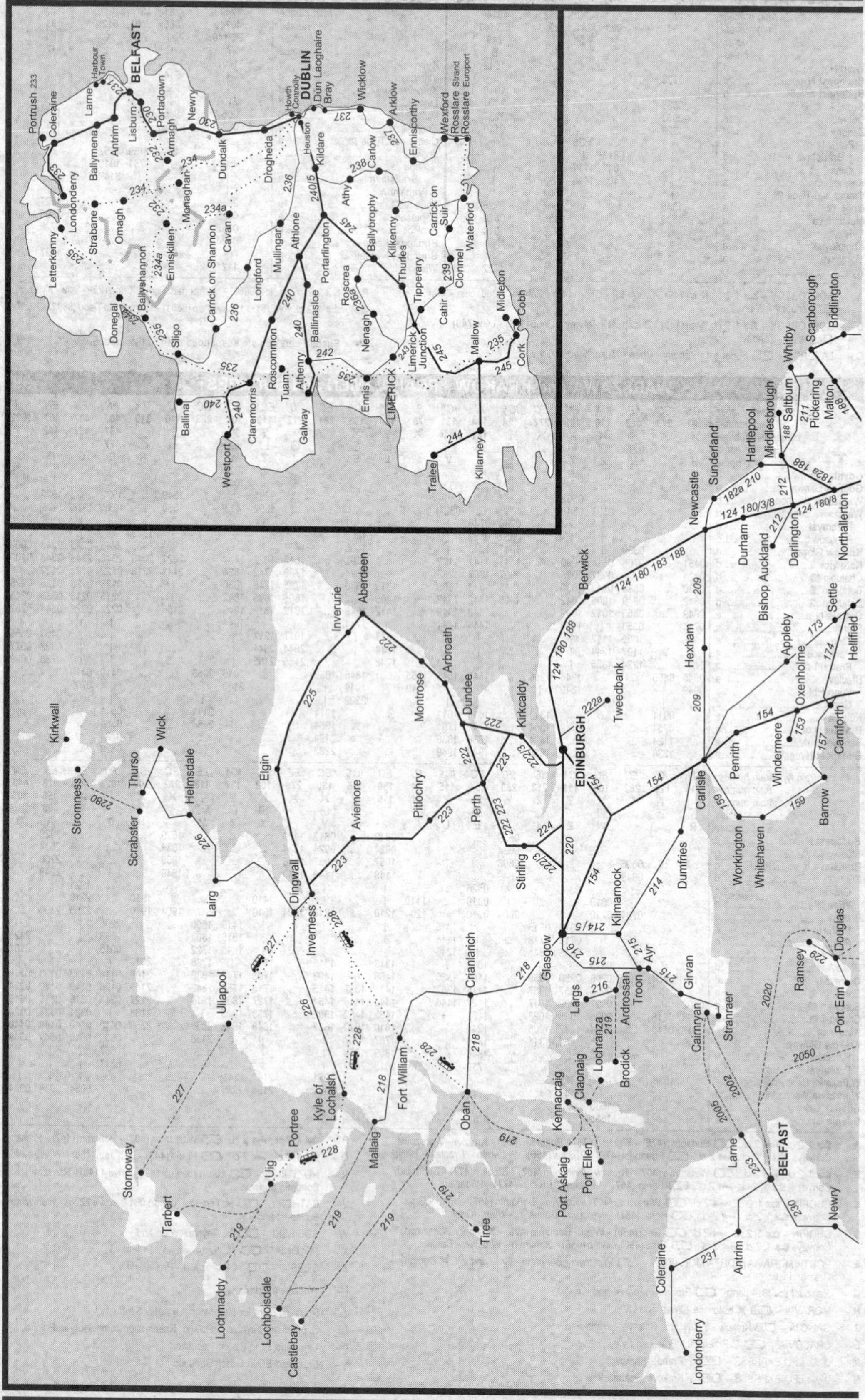
BELFAST
DUBLIN
LIMERICK
Portrush
Coleraine
Larne
Harbour
Town
Ballymena
Antrim
Lisburn
Portadown
Armagh
Newry
Dundalk
Drogheda
Howth
Connolly
Dún Laoghaire
Bray
Heuston
Kildare
Wicklow
Arklow
Enniscorthy
Wexford
Rosslare Strand
Rosslare Europort
Londonderry
Strabane
Omagh
Monaghan
Enniskillen
Cavan
Letterkenny
Donegal
Ballyshannon
Sligo
Carrick on Shannon
Longford
Mullingar
Athlone
Portarlington
Athy
Carlow
Kilkenny
Ballybrophy
Thurles
Roscrea
Nenagh
Tipperary
Limerick Junction
Carrick on Suir
Waterford
Clonmel
Cahir
Midleton
Cobh
Cork
Mallow
Ballinasloe
Athenry
Galway
Ennis
Roscommon
Tuam
Claremorris
Ballina
Westport
Killarney
Tralee
Kirkwall
Stromness
Thurso
Wick
Scrabster
Helmsdale
Lairg
Dingwall
Inverness
Elgin
Inverurie
Aberdeen
Aviemore
Pitlochry
Perth
Dundee
Arbroath
Montrose
Kirkcaldy
EDINBURGH
Tweedbank
Stirling
Glasgow
Crianlarich
Fort William
Mallaig
Kyle of Lochalsh
Oban
Ullapool
Stornoway
Tarbert
Uig
Portree
Lochmaddy
Lochboisdale
Castlebay
Tiree
Port Askaig
Port Ellen
Kennacraig
Claonaig
Lochranza
Brodick
Largs
Ardrossan
Troon
Ayr
Kilmarnock
Girvan
Stranraer
Cairnryan
Dumfries
Carlisle
Berwick
Newcastle
Hexham
Sunderland
Hartlepool
Middlesbrough
Saltburn
Whitby
Scarborough
Bridlington
Pickering
Malton
Durham
Bishop Auckland
Darlington
Northallerton
Penrith
Appleby
Settle
Hellifield
Oxenholme
Windermere
Carnforth
Barrow
Workington
Whitehaven
Douglas
Ramsey
Port Erin
Larne
Antrim
Coleraine
Londonderry
Newry

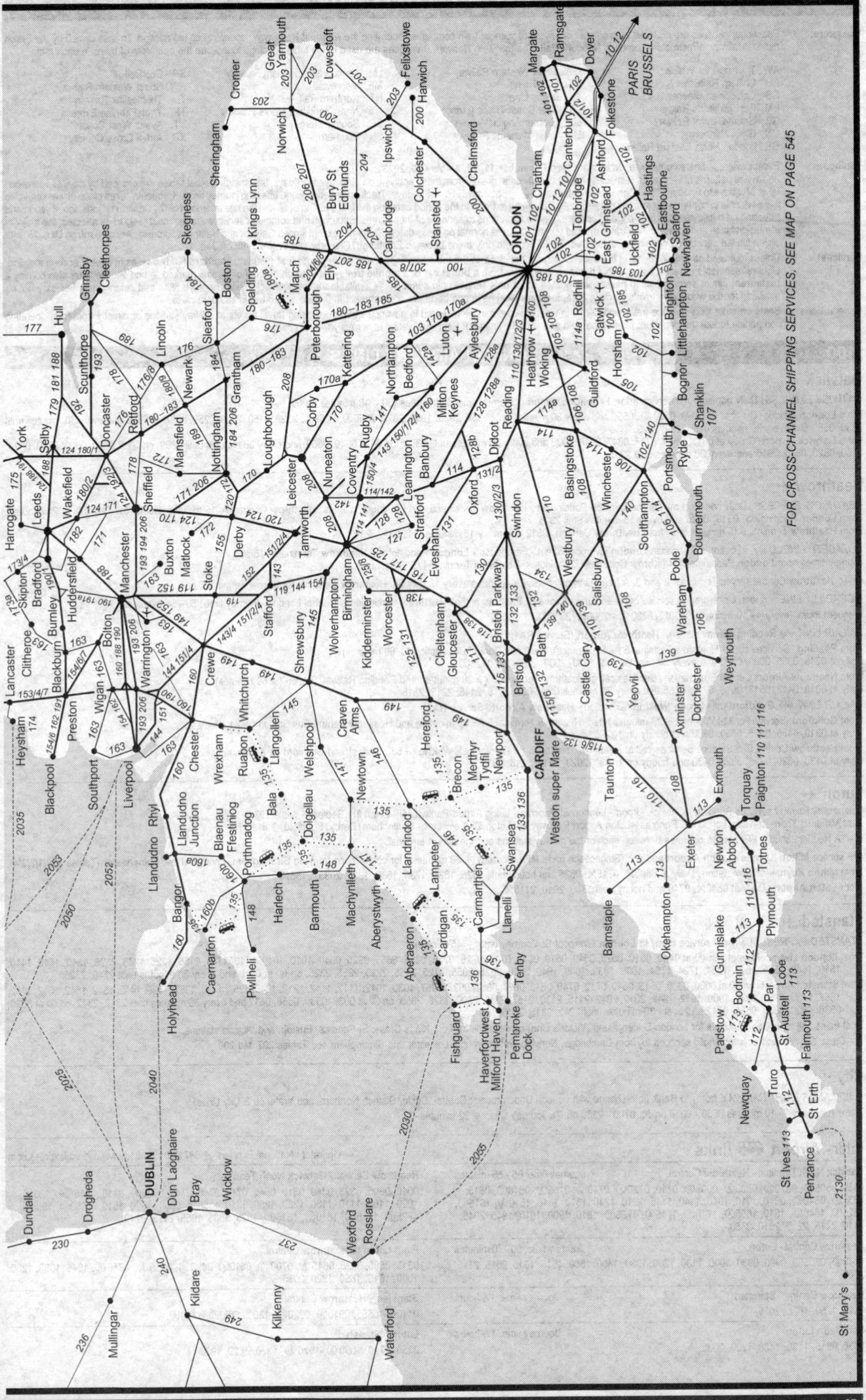
FOR CROSS-CHANNEL SHIPPING SERVICES, SEE MAP ON PAGE 545
LONDON
CARDIFF
DUBLIN
PARIS
BRUSSELS
Margate
Ramsgate
Dover
Folkestone
Ashford
Canterbury
Chatham
Hastings
Eastbourne
Seaford
Newhaven
Brighton
Littlehampton
Bognor
Uckfield
East Grinstead
Tonbridge
Redhill
Gatwick
Horsham
Guildford
Woking
Heathrow
Reading
Aylesbury
Luton
Stansted
Chelmsford
Colchester
Harwich
Felixstowe
Ipswich
Bury St Edmunds
Cambridge
Ely
March
Peterborough
Kings Lynn
Norwich
Great Yarmouth
Lowestoft
Cromer
Sheringham
Skegness
Boston
Spalding
Sleaford
Grantham
Lincoln
Newark
Grimsby
Cleethorpes
Scunthorpe
Hull
York
Selby
Doncaster
Retford
Harrogate
Leeds
Wakefield
Sheffield
Mansfield
Nottingham
Loughborough
Leicester
Kettering
Corby
Northampton
Bedford
Milton Keynes
Rugby
Coventry
Nuneaton
Tamworth
Leamington
Banbury
Oxford
Didcot
Swindon
Stratford
Evesham
Birmingham
Wolverhampton
Kidderminster
Worcester
Cheltenham
Gloucester
Bristol Parkway
Bristol
Bath
Westbury
Salisbury
Basingstoke
Winchester
Southampton
Portsmouth
Ryde
Shanklin
Bournemouth
Poole
Wareham
Dorchester
Weymouth
Castle Cary
Yeovil
Axminster
Taunton
Weston super Mare
Exeter
Exmouth
Barnstaple
Okehampton
Newton Abbot
Torquay
Paignton
Totnes
Plymouth
Gunnislake
Looe
Bodmin
Par
Padstow
St Austell
Newquay
Truro
Falmouth
St Erth
St Ives
Penzance
St Mary's
Newport
Swansea
Llanelli
Carmarthen
Tenby
Pembroke Dock
Haverfordwest
Milford Haven
Fishguard
Cardigan
Aberaeron
Lampeter
Aberystwyth
Machynlleth
Barmouth
Harlech
Pwllheli
Porthmadog
Caernarfon
Bangor
Holyhead
Llandudno
Llandudno Junction
Rhyl
Blaenau Ffestiniog
Bala
Dolgellau
Llandrindod
Newtown
Welshpool
Brecon
Merthyr Tydfil
Hereford
Craven Arms
Shrewsbury
Llangollen
Ruabon
Wrexham
Chester
Whitchurch
Crewe
Stafford
Stoke
Derby
Matlock
Buxton
Manchester
Warrington
Liverpool
Wigan
Bolton
Southport
Preston
Blackpool
Blackburn
Burnley
Huddersfield
Bradford
Skipton
Clitheroe
Lancaster
Heysham
Dundalk
Drogheda
Dún Laoghaire
Bray
Wicklow
Wexford
Rosslare
Waterford
Kilkenny
Kildare
Mullingar

GREAT BRITAIN

Operators: Passenger services are provided by a number of private passenger train companies operating the **National Rail** (www.nationalrail.co.uk) network on lines owned by the British national railway infrastructure company **Network Rail**. The following Network Rail codes are used in the table headings to indicate the operators of trains in each table:

AW Transport for Wales	GW Great Western Railway	LM London Northwestern Railway	SR ScotRail
CH Chiltern Railways	HT Hull Trains	ME Merseyrail	SW South Western Railway
CS Caledonian Sleeper	IL Island Line	NT Northern Rail	TL Thameslink Railway
EM East Midlands Railway	LD East Coast Trains (Lumo)	NY North Yorkshire Moors Railway	TP TransPennine Express
GC Grand Central Railway	LE Greater Anglia	SE Southeastern	VT Avanti West Coast
GN Great Northern	LM West Midlands Railway	SN Southern	XC Arriva Cross Country
GR London North Eastern Railway			

Timings: Except where indicated otherwise, timings are valid **December 11, 2022 - May 20, 2023**
As service patterns at weekends (especially on ⑦) usually differ greatly from those applying on Mondays to Fridays, the timings in most tables are grouped by days of operation: Ⓐ = Mondays to Fridays; ⚒ = Mondays to Saturdays; ⑥ = Saturdays; ⑦ = Sundays. Track engineering work, affecting journey times, frequently takes place at weekends, so it is advisable to confirm your journey details locally if planning to travel in the period between the late evening of ⑥ and the late afternoon of ⑦. Confirm timings, too, if you intend travelling on public holidays (see page 4) as there may be alterations to services at these times. Suburban and commuter services are the most likely to be affected; the majority of long-distance and cross-country trains marked Ⓐ and ⚒ run as normal on these dates. No trains (except limited Gatwick and Heathrow Express services) run on **Dec. 25**, with only a limited service on certain routes on **Dec. 26**. In Scotland only trains between Edinburgh / Glasgow and England run on **Jan. 1**.

Services: Unless indicated otherwise (by '2' in the train column or '2nd class' in the table heading), trains convey both **first** (1st) and **standard** (2nd) classes of seated accommodation. Light refreshments (snacks, hot and cold drinks) are available from a **buffet car** or a **mobile trolley service** on board those trains marked 🍸 and ✕: the latter also convey a **restaurant car** or serve meals to passengers at their seats (this service is in some cases available to first-class ticket holders only). Note that catering facilities may not be available for the whole of a train's journey. **Sleeping-cars** (🛏) have one berth per compartment in first class and two in standard class.

Reservations: Seats on most long-distance trains and berths in sleeping-cars can be reserved in advance when purchasing travel tickets at railway stations or directly from train operating companies (quote the departure time of the train and your destination). Seat reservation is normally free of charge.

100 LONDON AIRPORT LINKS

Gatwick ✈

GATWICK EXPRESS: Daily non-stop rail service from / to **London Victoria**. Journey time: 30 minutes (30 – 40 minutes on ⑦).

From **London** Victoria: On ⚒ at 0514 Ⓐ, 0529 ⑥, 0559 and every 30 minutes until 1859, 1928, 1958, 2029, 2056Ⓐ, 2059⑥, 2129, 2159, 2229, 2259; on ⑦ at 0500 and every 30 minutes until 0830, 0859 and every 30 minutes until 2159, 2229.
From **Gatwick Airport**: On Ⓐ at 0611, 0643, 0717, 0847, 0918, 0939 and every 30 minutes until 2309; On ⑥ at 0540, 0609 and every 30 minutes until 2309; on ⑦ at 0550, 0620, 0650, 0720, 0750, 0820, 0845, 0915 and every 30 minutes until 2315.

Heathrow ✈

HEATHROW EXPRESS: Daily non-stop rail service **London** Paddington - **Heathrow** Terminal 5 and v.v. Journey times: **Heathrow** Central ♣, 15 minutes, **Heathrow** Terminal 5, 21 minutes.
From **London** Paddington: 0510, 0525 and every 15 minutes until 2325.
From **Heathrow** Terminal 5 (5 minutes later from **Heathrow** Central): 0512 and every 15 minutes until 2342, 2357.

ELIZABETH LINE: Daily, frequent, rail services **London** Liverpool Street - Farringdon - **London** Paddington - **Heathrow** Terminals 4 / 5 and v.v.
Journey times from **London** Paddington: **Heathrow** Central ♣, 24 minutes, **Heathrow** Terminal 4 / 5, 30 minutes.

♣ – **Heathrow** Central serves Terminals 2 and 3. A free rail transfer service operates every 15 minutes **Heathrow** Central - **Heathrow** Terminal 5 and v.v.

PICCADILLY LINE: London Underground service between **Kings Cross St Pancras** and all **Heathrow** terminals via Central London. Journey time: 50 – 58 minutes.
Frequent trains (every 4 – 10 minutes) 0530⚒ / 0730⑦ - 2300⚒ / 2330⑦.

RAILAIR LINK 🚌 **Reading** railway station - **Heathrow Airport** (Service **RA1**).
From **Reading**: Services call at Heathrow Terminal 5 (± 51 minutes), Heathrow Central Bus Station (± 69 minutes):
Daily at 0246, 0355, 0500, 0530 and every 30 minutes until 1930, 2000, 2100, 2200, 2300.
From **Heathrow Airport** Central Bus Station: Services call at Heathrow Terminal 5 (± 20 minutes) and Reading Railway Station (± 69 minutes).
Daily at 0018, 0413, 0513, 0618, 0718, 0755 and every 30 minutes until 2025, 2118, 2148, 2218, 2318.

RAILAIR LINK 🚌 **Guildford** rail station - **Woking** rail station - **Heathrow Airport** (Service **RA2**).
From **Guildford**: Services call at Woking (± 29 minutes later), Heathrow Terminal 5 (± 55 minutes) and Heathrow Central Bus Station (± 81 minutes).
Daily at 0310, 0455, 0555, 0650, 0800 and hourly until 2200.
From **Heathrow** Central Bus Station: Services call at Heathrow Terminal 5 (± 17 minutes), Woking (± 53 minutes), and Guildford (± 81 minutes).
Daily at 0430, 0620, 0720, 0820, 0930 and hourly until 1930, 2020, 2115, 2215, 2315.

Luton ✈

Thameslink Railway services Brighton - Gatwick Airport - London St Pancras - Luton Airport Parkway ◧ - Luton ◧ - Bedford: Table **103**.
East Midlands Trains services London St Pancras - Luton Airport Parkway ◧ - Luton ◧ - Leicester - Nottingham / Derby / Sheffield: Table **170**.

◧ – A frequent shuttle 🚌 service operates between each of the railway stations and the airport terminal.

🚌 service **Milton Keynes - Luton Airport** and v.v. (Stagecoach route **MK1**. Journey ± 60 minutes); for connections from / to **Birmingham**, **Liverpool** and **Manchester** (Tables **150/1/2/3/4**).
From **Milton Keynes** railway station: Daily at 0600⚒, 0715⚒, 0825 and hourly until 1525, 1635, 1735, 1835, 1935, 2035, 2155⚒.
From **Luton Airport**: Daily at 0640⚒, 0740 and hourly until 1840, 2010, 2110⚒.

Stansted ✈

STANSTED EXPRESS: Daily rail service from / to **London** Liverpool St. Journey time ± 45 minutes.
From **London** Liverpool Street: on Ⓐ at 0440, 0510, 0525, 0540, 0610, 0640, 0710, 0725, 0755, 0825, 0855, 0925, 0940, 1010, 1040, 1110, 1140, 1155, 1225, 1255, 1325, 1340, 1410, 1440, 1510, 1540, 1555, 1625, 1654, 1724, 1754, 1809, 1839, 1909, 1940, 2010, 2025, 2055, 2125, 2155, 2225, 2255, 2325; on Ⓒ at 0410 and every 30 minutes until 2240, 2325.
From **Stansted Airport**: on Ⓐ at 0030, 0600, 0615, 0640, 0712, 0740, 0813, 0827, 0857, 0927, 0957, 1030, 1042, 1112, 1142, 1212, 1243, 1257, 1330, 1357, 1430, 1442, 1512, 1542, 1612, 1642, 1657, 1730, 1757, 1827, 1900, 1912, 1942, 2012, 2042, 2115, 2130, 2157, 2230, 2300, 2328, 2359; on ⑥ at 0030, 0530, 0558, 0612 and every 30 minutes until 2312, 2342; on ⑦ at 0030, 0530, 0600, 0630, 0655, 0712 and every 30 minutes until 2242, 2315, 2345.
Most trains call at **Tottenham Hale** for London Underground (Victoria Line) connections to / from Kings Cross, St Pancras, Euston, and Victoria stations.
For *Cross Country* and *Greater Anglia* services to / from Cambridge, Norwich, Peterborough, Leicester and Birmingham see Tables **207** and **208**.

City ✈

DOCKLANDS LIGHT RAILWAY from / to **Bank** (interchange with London Underground: Central, Circle, District, Northern, and Waterloo & City Lines).
Trains run every 7 - 10 minutes 0530 - 0030 on ⚒, 0700 - 2330 on ⑦. Journey time: ± 22 minutes.

Inter - Airport 🚌 links

Operator: National Express ✆ 08717 81 81 81. www.nationalexpress.com

Gatwick North Terminal - **Heathrow** Central. Journey time: 65 - 85 minutes
0350, 0505Ⓐ, 0520Ⓒ, 0535Ⓐ, 0605Ⓒ, 0710, 0720Ⓐ, 0740Ⓒ, 0755Ⓐ, 0810Ⓒ, 0815, 0835Ⓐ, 0840Ⓒ, 0940, 1010, 1040, 1140, 1145, 1210, 1240, 1310, 1410, 1510Ⓐ, 1515Ⓒ, 1525Ⓐ, 1540Ⓒ, 1610, 1655Ⓐ, 1710Ⓒ, 1745Ⓐ, 1755Ⓒ, 1810, 1900, 1910, 1945, 2045, 2110, 2215, 2230, 2310, 2350.

Heathrow Central - **Gatwick** North Terminal.
0040, 0305, 0325, 0340, 0510, 0545, 0710, 0740, 0745, 0800Ⓐ, 0910, 0915Ⓒ, 0920Ⓐ, 1020, 1100, 1110, 1150, 1230, 1250, 1310, 1355, 1450Ⓒ, 1500, 1510, 1550Ⓒ, 1605Ⓐ, 1725Ⓒ, 1745Ⓐ, 1810Ⓒ, 1815Ⓒ, 1825, 1835, 1955, 2115, 2240.

Heathrow Central - **Luton**. Journey time: 50 - 70 minutes
0640Ⓐ, 0655Ⓒ, 0900, 0930, 1000, 1130, 1200, 1330, 1400, 1600, 1615, 1815, 2015, 2115, 2300.

From **Luton** to **Heathrow** Central.
0315, 0505, 0625, 0645 Ⓐ, 0700 Ⓒ, 0810Ⓐ, 0825 Ⓒ, 0835 Ⓐ, 0845 Ⓒ, 1045, 1050, 1250, 1300, 1515, 1650, 1820, 2035.

Heathrow Central - **Stansted**. Journey time: 1½ hours
0920, 1250, 1635, 2035.

Stansted - **Heathrow** Central.
0410Ⓒ, 0555, 0910Ⓐ, 0920Ⓒ, 1300, 1700Ⓒ, 1710Ⓐ.

Stansted - **Luton**. Journey time: 1½ hours
0030, 0915, 1130, 1400, 1700, 2000.

Luton - **Stansted**.
0250, 0720, 1000 Ⓐ, 1020 Ⓒ, 1320, 1620, 1920.

Via Faversham

km				Ⓐ	Ⓐ	Ⓐ	Ⓐ	Ⓐ		Ⓐ	Ⓐ	Ⓐ		Ⓐ	Ⓐ	Ⓐ	Ⓐ		Ⓐ	Ⓐ	Ⓐ	Ⓐ		Ⓐ	Ⓐ	Ⓐ	Ⓐ	Ⓐ
0	**London** St Pancras	d.	Ⓐ	...	0620	0720	0748	0820	...	0920	1020	1120	...	1220	1320	1420	1520	...	1620	1650	1716	1746	...	1816	1850	1920	2020	2120
9	Stratford International	d.		...	0627	0727	0755	0827	...	0927	1027	1127	...	1227	1327	1427	1527	...	1627	1657	1723	1753	...	1823	1857	1927	2027	2127
35	Ebbsfleet International	d.		...	0639	0739	0809	0839	...	0939	1039	1139	...	1239	1339	1439	1539	...	1639	1709	1735	1805	...	1835	1909	1939	2039	2139
52	Rochester	d.		...	0657	0758	0830	0858	...	0958	1058	1158	...	1258	1358	1458	1558	...	1658	1729	1755	1826	...	1855	1927	1958	2058	2158
54	Chatham	d.		...	0700	0801	0833	0901	...	1001	1101	1201	...	1301	1401	1501	1601	...	1701	1732	1758	1830	...	1858	1930	2001	2101	2201
70	Sittingbourne	d.		*0606*	0718	0819	0850	0919	...	1019	1119	1219	...	1319	1419	1519	1619	...	1719	1751	1816	1847	...	1916	1948	2019	2119	2219
83	Faversham	d.		0622	0728	0831	0859	0931	...	1031	1131	1231	...	1331	1431	1531	1630	...	1730	1801	1827	1858	...	1927	1957	2031	2131	2231
100	Herne Bay	d.		0637	...	0845	...	0945	...	1045	1145	1245	...	1345	1445	1545	*1650*	...	*1750*	...	1841	1913	...	1941	...	2045	2145	2245
118	**Margate**	d.		0654	...	0859	...	0959	...	1059	1159	1259	...	1359	1459	1559	*1707*	...	*1807*	...	1856	1929	...	1956	...	2059	2159	2259
126	**Ramsgate**	a.		0706	...	0910	...	1010	...	1110	1210	1310	...	1410	1510	1611	*1720*	...	*1819*	...	1907	...	...	2010	...	2110	2210	2310

		Ⓐ A	Ⓐ	Ⓐ B		⑥	⑥		⑥	⑥	⑥		⑥	⑥	⑥		⑦	⑦	⑦		⑦	⑦		⑦	⑦	⑦
London St Pancras	d.	2220	2320	2350	⑥	...	...	...	...	0720	0820		2220	2320	2350	⑦	...	...	0820	...	0920	1020		2120	2220	2320
Stratford International	d.	2227	2327	2357		...	...	...	...	0727	0827		2227	2327	2357		...	...	0827	...	0927	1027		2127	2227	2327
Ebbsfleet International	d.	2239	2339	0009		...	...	...	...	0739	0839	and at	2239	2339	0009		...	...	0839	...	0939	1039	and at	2139	2239	2339
Rochester	d.	2258	2358	0028		...	*0641*	...	0721	0758	0858	the same	2258	2358	0028		...	0821	0858	...	0958	1058	the same	2158	2258	2358
Chatham	d.	2301	0002	0031		...	*0645*	...	0724	0801	0901	minutes	2301	0001	0031		...	0824	0901	...	1001	1101	minutes	2201	2301	0002
Sittingbourne	d.	2319	0019	0048s		*0615*	*0715*	...	0741	0819	0919	past each	2319	0019	0049		0739	0843	0918	...	1018	1118	past each	2218	2318	0019
Faversham	d.	2329	0029	0059		0630	0730	...	0751	0831	0931	hour until	2331	0030	0058		0752	0854	0928	...	1028	1128	hour until	2228	2327	0028
Herne Bay	d.	*0006*	...	*0120*s		0645	0745	...	0806	0845	0945		2345	*0108*	*0139*s		0807	0909	0942	...	1042	1142		2242	*0009*	...
Margate	d.	*0023*	...	*0136*s		0702	0802	...	0823	0859	0959		2359	*0125*	*0155*s		0824	0926	0956	...	1056	1156		2256	*0026*	...
Ramsgate	a.	*0035*	...	*0150*		0714	0814	...	0835	0910	1010		0010	*0137*	*0208*		0838	0938	1010	...	1110	1208		2308	*0038*	...

			Ⓐ	Ⓐ	Ⓐ	Ⓐ	Ⓐ	Ⓐ	Ⓐ		Ⓐ	Ⓐ	Ⓐ	Ⓐ	Ⓐ		Ⓐ	Ⓐ	Ⓐ	Ⓐ		Ⓐ	Ⓐ	Ⓐ	Ⓐ		⑥
Ramsgate	d.	Ⓐ	...	*0425*	...	*0518*	*0556*	*0618*	*0712*	...	*0740*	*0812*	*0842*	0920	1020		1620	*1650*	*1750*	1920	...	2020	2120	2152	2252	⑥	*0442*
Margate	d.		...	*0436*	0521	*0529*	0619	0651	*0723*	...	*0752*	*0823*	*0853*	0930	1030	and at	1630	*1701*	*1801*	1930	...	2030	2130	2204	2304		*0453*
Herne Bay	d.		...	*0453*	0535	*0546*	0633	0705	*0739*	...	*0808*	*0839*	*0910*	0945	1045	the same	1645	*1718*	*1817*	1945	...	2045	2145	2221	2321		*0510*
Faversham	d.		0500	0528	0549	0619	0647	0719	0800	...	0829	0900	0932	1000	1100	minutes	1700	1802	1902	2000	...	2100	2200	2248t	2339		0530
Sittingbourne	d.		0508	0536	0557	0627	0655	0727	0810	...	0840	0910	0940	1010	1110	past each	1710	1810	1910	2010	...	2110	2210	2259	2349		0540
Chatham	d.		0525	0553	0614	0644	0712	0744	0828	...	0859	0928	0958	1028	1128	hour	1728	1828	1928	2028	...	2128	2228	2322	...		0558
Rochester	d.		0529	0557	0618	0648	0716	0747	0832	...	0902	0932	1002	1032	1132	until	1732	1832	1932	2032	...	2132	2232	2325	...		0602
Ebbsfleet International	a.		0547	0614	0635	0706	0734	0805	0849	...	0919	0949	1019	1049	1149		1749	1849	1949	2049	...	2149	2249	...	...		0619
Stratford International	a.		0558	0625	0646	0718	0746	0817	0900	...	0930	1000	1030	1100	1200		1800	1900	2000	2100	...	2200	2300	...	...		0630
London St Pancras	a.		0606	0633	0654	0727	0754	0826	0908	...	0940	1008	1038	1110	1208		1808	1908	2008	2108	...	2208	2310	...	...		0638

		⑥	⑥		⑥	⑥		⑥	⑥		⑥	⑥	⑥		⑦	⑦	⑦		⑦	⑦		⑦	⑦	⑦
Ramsgate	d.	...	0620		1220	1320		1920	2020	...	2120	2152	2320	⑦	...	*0652*	0820		1420	1520		2120	*2152*	2252
Margate	d.	...	0630	and at	1230	1330	and at	1930	2030	...	2130	2204	2332		...	*0705*	0830	and at	1430	1530	and at	2130	*2204*	2304
Herne Bay	d.	...	0645	the same	1245	1345	the same	1945	2045	...	2145	2221	2348		...	*0721*	0845	the same	1445	1545	the same	2145	*2221*	2321
Faversham	d.	0600	0700	minutes	1300	1400	minutes	2000	2100	...	2200	2237	0007		0700	0800	0900	minutes	1500	1600	minutes	2200	2244	2337
Sittingbourne	d.	0610	0710	past each	1310	1410	past each	2010	2110	...	2210	2245	0017		0710	0810	0910	past each	1510	1610	past each	2210	2255	2347
Chatham	d.	0628	0728	hour	1328	1428	hour	2028	2128	...	2228	2302	...		0728	0828	0928	hour	1528	1628	hour	2228	2314	...
Rochester	d.	0632	0732	until	1323	1423	until	2032	2132	...	2232	2305	...		0732	0832	0932	until	1532	1632	until	2232	2317	...
Ebbsfleet International	a.	0649	0749		1349	1449		2049	2149	...	2249	...	...		0749	0849	0949		1549	1649		2249	...	...
Stratford International	a.	0700	0800		1400	1500		2100	2200	...	2300	...	...		0800	0900	1000		1600	1700		2300	...	...
London St Pancras	a.	0708	0808		1410	1508		2108	2210	...	2308	...	...		0808	0908	1008		1610	1708		2308	...	...

Via Ashford and Dover

km				②–⑤	Ⓐ	Ⓐ	Ⓐ	Ⓐ	Ⓐ	Ⓐ	Ⓐ	Ⓐ	Ⓐ	Ⓐ	Ⓐ	Ⓐ	Ⓐ		Ⓐ	Ⓐ	Ⓐ	Ⓐ	Ⓐ	Ⓐ	Ⓐ	Ⓐ	Ⓐ
0	**London** St Pancras	d.	Ⓐ	0012	...	...	...	...	0637	0707	0737	0804	0837	0907	0934	1007	1037		1407	1437	1507	1537	1605	1637	1707	1720	1734
9	Stratford International	d.		0019	...	...	...	...	0644	0714	0744	0811	0844	0914	0941	1014	1044		1414	1444	1514	1544	1612	1644	1714	1727	1741
35	Ebbsfleet International	d.		0030	...	...	...	...	0655	0725	0755	0822	0855	0925	0955	1025	1055	and at	1425	1455	1525	1555	1623	1655	1725	|	1752
90	Ashford International	d.		0050	0521	0601	0630	0700	0716	0748	0816	0846	0916	0946	1016	1046	1116	the same	1446	1516	1546	1619	1646	1718	1748	1757	1815
112	**Folkestone** Central	d.		...	0537	0620	|	0720	|	0803	|	0901	|	1001	|	1101	|	minutes	1501	|	1601	|	1701	|	1804	|	1830
124	**Dover** Priory	a.		...	0548	0631	|	0731	|	0814	|	0912	|	1012	|	1112	|	past each	1512	|	1612	|	1712	|	1815	|	1841
112	Canterbury West	d.		...	...	|	0653	|	0740	...	0833	|	0933	|	1033	|	1133	hour until	...	1533	...	1634	...	1733	|	1813	...
140	Ramsgate	a.		...	...	0711	0717	0815	0804	...	0854	0950	0957	1050	1056	1150	1156		...	1556	...	1655	...	1755	1855	1833	...
149	**Margate**	a.		...	...	...	0728	...	0815	...	0908	...	1007	...	1107	...	1207		...	1606	...	1706	...	1806	...	1845	...

		Ⓐ	Ⓐ	Ⓐ	Ⓐ		Ⓐ	Ⓐ	①	②	③–⑤		⑥	⑥	⑥	⑥	⑥	⑥	⑥	⑥		⑥	⑥		⑦	⑦
London St Pancras	d.	1750	1804	1837	1907		2237	2307	2337	2337	2337	⑥	0012	...	...	...	0637	...	0737	0804	❖	2304	2337	⑦	0012	...
Stratford International	d.	1757	1811	1844	1914		2244	2314	2344	2344	2344		0019	...	...	...	0644	...	0744	0811		2311	2344		0019	...
Ebbsfleet International	d.	|	1822	1855	1925	and at	2255	2325	2355	2355	2355		0030	...	...	...	0655	...	0755	0822	and at	2322	2355		0030	...
Ashford International	d.	1827	1845	1916	1946	the same	2316	2346	0016	0016	0016		0050	0600	0635	0646	0716	0746	0816	0846	the same	2346	0016		0050	0746
Folkestone Central	d.	|	1900	|	2001	minutes	|	0001	|	|	|		...	0615	|	0701	|	0801	|	0901	minutes	0001	|		...	0801
Dover Priory	a.	|	1911	|	2013	past each	|	0012	|	|	|		...	0626	|	0712	|	0812	|	0913	past each	0012	|		...	0812
Canterbury West	d.	1843	|	1933	|	hour until	2331	|	*0037*j	0033	0033		...	|	0658	|	0733	|	0833	|	hour until	|	0033		...	|
Ramsgate	a.	1903	1949	1956	2051		2355	0050	0110	0055	0056		...	0704	0723	0750	0756	0850	0856	0950		0050	0056		...	0850
Margate	a.	1915	...	2007	...		0007v	...	0121	*0121*r	0106		...	...	0735	...	0807	...	0907	...		...	0107		...	...

		⑦	⑦	⑦	⑦		⑦	⑦	⑦
London St Pancras	d.	...	...	0837	0904	❖	2237	2307	2337
Stratford International	d.	...	...	0844	0911		2244	2314	2344
Ebbsfleet International	d.	...	...	0855	0922	and at	2255	2325	2355
Ashford International	d.	0816	0846	0916	0946	the same	2316	2346	0014
Folkestone Central	d.	|	0901	|	1001	minutes	|	0001	...
Dover Priory	d.	|	0912	|	1013	past each	|	0012	...
Canterbury West	d.	0833	|	0933	|	hour until	2333	...	...
Ramsgate	a.	0856	0950	0956	1050		2356	...	...
Margate	a.	0907	...	1007	...		0007	...	...

			Ⓐ	Ⓐ	Ⓐ	Ⓐ	Ⓐ	Ⓐ	Ⓐ	Ⓐ	Ⓐ	Ⓐ	Ⓐ	Ⓐ	Ⓐ
Margate	d.	Ⓐ	...	...	...	0540	...	0615	...	0644	...	0715	...	0748	...
Ramsgate	d.		...	0455	...	0552	...	0628	0602	0656	...	0728	0708	0800	...
Canterbury West	d.		...	0518	...	0613	...	0649	|	0717	...	0749	|	0823	...
Dover Priory	d.		*0430*	|	0538	|	0616	|	0645	|	0716	|	0748	|	0848
Folkestone Cent	d.		*0441*	|	0548	|	0626	|	0655	|	0726	|	0758	|	0858
Ashford Int'l	d.		0510	0542	0606	0630	0644	0706	0713	0734	0744	0806	0816	0840	0916
Ebbsfleet Int'l	a.		0528	0600	0624	0648	0702	|	0731	0754	0802	|	0834	0858	0934
Stratford Int'l	a.		0540	0614	0636	0700	0714	0734	0742	0805	0814	0834	0846	0910	0946
London St Pancras	a.		0548	0622	0644	0708	0722	0742	0751	0814	0823	0843	0854	0918	0954

		Ⓐ	Ⓐ	Ⓐ	Ⓐ		Ⓐ	Ⓐ	Ⓐ	Ⓐ	Ⓐ	Ⓐ	Ⓐ	Ⓐ	Ⓐ		Ⓐ	Ⓐ	Ⓐ	Ⓐ	Ⓐ	Ⓐ		⑥	⑥	⑥
Margate	d.	0848	...	0950	...		...	1548	...	1648	...	1748	...	1850	...		2150	...	...	...	2250	...	⑥	...	0550	...
Ramsgate	d.	0900	0907	1002	1007		...	1600	...	1700	...	1800	...	1902	1907		2202	2207	2240	...	2302	2307		0502	0602	0607
Canterbury West	d.	0921	|	1023	|	and at	...	1621	...	1721	...	1823	...	1923	|	and at	2223	|	2304	...	2323	|		0523	0623	|
Dover Priory	d.	|	0945	|	1048	the same	1544	|	1646	|	1748	|	1848	|	1948	the same	|	2248	|	2300	|	2348		|	|	0648
Folkestone Central	d.	|	0955	|	1058	minutes	1554	|	1656	|	1758	|	1858	|	1958	minutes	|	2258	|	2311	|	2358		|	|	0658
Ashford International	d.	0940	1016	1040	1116	past each	1616	1640	1716	1740	1816	1842	1917	1940	2016	past each	2240	2316	2326	2330	2338	0019		0540	0640	0716
Ebbsfleet International	a.	0958	1036	1058	1136	hour until	1634	1700	1734	1758	1834	1900	1937	1958	2034	hour until	2258	2334	...	...	...	...		0558	0658	0734
Stratford International	a.	1010	1048	1110	1148		1646	1711	1746	1810	1846	1911	1948	2010	2046		2310	2346	...	...	...	...		0610	0710	0746
London St Pancras	a.	1018	1056	1118	1156		1654	1719	1754	1818	1854	1919	1957	2018	2054		2318	2354	...	...	...	...		0618	0718	0754

		⑥	⑥	⑥	⑥		⑥	⑥	⑥	⑥		⑦	⑦	⑦	⑦		⑦	⑦	⑦	⑦	⑦	⑦	⑦	⑦	⑦	⑦
Margate	d.	0650	...	0750	...	⊠	2150	...	2250	...	⑦	...	...	0750	...		...	1850	...	1950	...	2050	...	2150	...	2250
Ramsgate	d.	0702	0707	0802	0807		2202	2207	2302	2307		0705	0710	0802	0807		1807	1902	1907	2022	2007	2102	2107	2202	2207	2302
Canterbury West	d.	0723	|	0823	|	and at	2223	|	2323	|		0726	|	0823	|	and at	|	1923	|	2023	|	2123	|	2223	|	2323
Dover Priory	d.	|	0748	|	0845	the same	|	2248	|	2348		|	0748	|	0848	the same	1848	|	1948	|	2048	|	2189	|	2248	|
Folkestone Central	d.	|	0758	|	0855	minutes	|	2258	|	2358		|	0758	|	0858	minutes	1858	|	1958	|	2058	|	2158	|	2258	|
Ashford International	d.	0740	0816	0840	0916	past each	2240	2316	2338	0018		0743	0816	0840	0916	past each	1918	1940	2016	2040	2116	2140	2216	2240	2315	2338
Ebbsfleet International	a.	0758	0834	0858	0934	hour until	2258	2334	...	...		0801	0834	0858	0934	hour until	1937	1958	2034	2058	2134	2158	2234	2258	...	...
Stratford International	a.	0810	0846	0910	0946		2310	2346	...	...		0813	0846	0910	0946		1948	2010	2046	2110	2146	2210	2246	2310	...	...
London St Pancras	a.	0818	0854	0918	0954		2318	2354	...	...		0821	0854	0918	0954		1957	2018	2054	2118	2154	2218	2254	2318	...	...

A – On ② service is operated by 🚌 from Faversham (Faversham d. 2356, Herne Bay a. 0033**s**, Margate a. 0041, Ramsgate a. 0102).

B – On ③ mornings service is operated by 🚌 from Faversham (Faversham d. 0106, Herne Bay a. 0143**s**, Margate a. 0151**s**, Ramsgate a. 0212).

f – *2355* on ② (by 🚌 from Ramsgate).

j – Arrival time. Connection by 🚌 from Ashford.

r – Connection by 🚌.

s – Calls to set down only.

t – Arrives 2236.

v – Not ③ mornings.

❖ – xx04 departures may be up to 3 minutes later from London St Pancras, Stratford International and Ebbsfleet International.

⊠ – Timings of xx45 from Dover may be up to 3 minutes later.

102 LONDON - THE SOUTH and SOUTH EAST SE, SN

Typical off-peak journey time in hours and minutes
READ DOWN ↓ READ UP ↑

During peak hours on Ⓐ (0600 - 0900 and 1600 - 1900) services generally run more frequently (particularly to and from London) and journey times may vary.

LONDON VICTORIA - RAMSGATE SE

km					
0	0h00	↓	d. **London** Victoria ....a.	↑	1h57
18	0h17	↓	d. Bromley South.......d.	↑	1h40
53	0h47	↓	d. Rochester..............d.	↑	1h12
72	1h09	↓	d. Sittingbourne ....d.	↑	0h50
84	1h21	↓	d. Faversham.............d.	↑	0h42
101	1h36	↓	d. Herne Bay..............d.	↑	0h26
119	1h49	↓	d. Margate.................d.	↑	0h10
128	1h59	↓	a. **Ramsgate**.............d.	↑	0h00

Frequency: Hourly.
Usual departures:
From London Victoria at xx40 (not 1440, 1540 on Ⓐ).
From Ramsgate at xx52 (not 1552, 1652 on Ⓐ).

LONDON VICTORIA - DOVER SE

km					
0	0h00	↓	d. **London** Victoria ....a.	↑	2h02
18	0h17	↓	d. Bromley South.......d.	↑	1h43
53	0h47	↓	d. Rochester..............d.	↑	1h17
72	1h09	↓	d. Sittingbourne ....d.	↑	0h58
84	1h21	↓	d. Faversham ....d.	↑	0h47
99	1h37	↓	d. Canterbury East ....d.	↑	0h27
124	1h58	↓	a. **Dover** Priory ....d.	↑	0h00

Frequency: Hourly.
Usual off-peak departures:
From London Victoria at xx10 on ⚒; xx12 on ⑦.
From Dover Priory at xx18 on ⚒; xx50 on ⑦.

LONDON CHARING CROSS - CANTERBURY WEST SE

km					
0	0h00	↓	d. **London** Ch Cross ..a.	↑	1h46
1	0h03	↓	d. **London** W'loo (E)..a.	↑	1h42
3	0h08	↓	d. **London** Bridge......a.	↑	1h36
36	0h32	↓	d. Sevenoaks ....d.	↑	1h13
48	0h40	↓	d. Tonbridge...............d.	↑	1h04
90	1h20	↓	a. Ashford Int'l...........d.	↑	0h27
113	1h38	↓	a. **Canterbury** West ..d.	↑	0h00

Frequency: Hourly.
Usual off-peak departures:
From London Charing Cross at xx29.
From Canterbury West at xx37.

LONDON CHARING CROSS - DOVER SE

km					
0	0h00	↓	d. **London** Ch Cross .a.	↑	1h58
1	0h03	↓	d. **London** W'loo (E)..a.	↑	1h53
3	0h08	↓	d. **London** Bridge......a.	↑	1h42
36	0h32	↓	d. Sevenoaks ....d.	↑	1h18
48	0h40	↓	d. Tonbridge...............d.	↑	1h06
90	1h20	↓	d. Ashford Int'l...........d.	↑	0h29
113	1h40	↓	d. Folkstone Central ..d.	↑	0h12
124	1h52	↓	a. **Dover** Priory ....d.	↑	0h00

Frequency: Hourly.
Usual off-peak departures:
From London Charing Cross at xx59.
From Dover at xx00. (Timings vary after 1400 departure on Ⓐ.)

LONDON VICTORIA - ASHFORD INTERNATIONAL SE

km					
0	0h00	↓	d. **London** Victoria ....a.	↑	1h29
18	0h17	↓	d. Bromley South.......d.	↑	1h14
28	0h28	↓	d. Swanley ....d.	↑	1h03
56	0h52	↓	d. West Malling ....d.	↑	0h42
64	1h03	↓	d. Maidstone East .....d.	↑	0h30
68	1h09	↓	d. Bearsted ....d.	↑	0h25
95	1h31	↓	a. **Ashford** Int'l..........d.	↑	0h00

Frequency: Hourly.
Usual off-peak departures:
From London Victoria at xx55.
From Ashford International at xx55.

LONDON CHARING CROSS - HASTINGS SE

km					
0	0h00	↓	d. **London** Ch Cross ..a.	↑	1h43
1	0h03	↓	d. **London** W'loo (E)..a.	↑	1h39
3	0h08	↓	d. **London** Bridge ....a.	↑	1h35
36	0h34	↓	d. Sevenoaks ....d.	↑	1h09
43	0h43	↓	d. Tonbridge...............d.	↑	1h00
55	0h55	↓	d. Tunbridge Wells △ d.	↑	0h49
89	1h33	↓	d. Battle ....d.	↑	0h16
100	1h45	↓	a. **Hastings**...............d.	↑	0h00

Frequency: Twice an hour.
Usual off-peak departures:
From London Charing Cross at xx08, xx38 on ⚒; xx16, xx46 on ⑦.
From Hastings at xx21, xx46 on ⚒; xx32, xx50 on ⑦.

LONDON VICTORIA - EASTBOURNE SN

km					
0	0h00	↓	d. **London** Victoria ....a.	↑	1h26
17	0h16	↓	d. East Croydon ....d.	↑	1h09
43	0h33	↓	d. Gatwick Airport......d.	↑	0h53
61	0h50	↓	d. Haywards Heath.....d.	↑	0h34
81	1h06	↓	d. Lewes ....d.	↑	0h19
106	1h27	↓	a. **Eastbourne** ....d.	↑	0h00

Frequency: Every 30 minutes on ⚒; hourly on ⑦.
Usual off-peak departures:
From London Victoria at xx24, xx54‡ on ⚒; xx46 on ⑦.
From Eastbourne at xx05, xx33¶ on ⚒; xx00 on ⑦.

ASHFORD - HASTINGS - EASTBOURNE - (BRIGHTON) SN

km					
0	0h00	↓	d. **Ashford** Int'l...........a.	↑	1h20
14	0h12	↓	d. Appledore...............d.	↑	1h07
25	0h23	↓	d. Rye ....d.	↑	0h56
41	0h42	↓	d. Ore ....d.	↑	0h40
42	0h45	↓	d. **Hastings**...............d.	↑	0h36
50	0h57	↓	d. Bexhill ....d.	↑	0h25
67	1h14	↓	a. **Eastbourne** ....d.	↑	0h00

Frequency: Hourly.
Usual off-peak departures:
From Ashford at xx25.
From Eastbourne at xx49 on ⚒; xx56 on ⑦.
☛ Local services are available Brighton / Lewes - Eastbourne - Hastings v.v.

LONDON BRIDGE - UCKFIELD SN

km					
0	0h00	↓	d. **London** Bridge......a.	↑	1h15
16	0h16	↓	d. East Croydon ....d.	↑	0h59
32	0h29	↓	d. Oxted....................d.	↑	0h44
57	0h55	↓	d. Eridge △...............d.	↑	0h17
70	1h01	↓	d. Crowborough.........d.	↑	0h12
74	1h15	↓	a. **Uckfield**................d.	↑	0h00

Frequency: Hourly.
Usual off-peak departures:
From London Bridge at xx07 on ⚒.
From Uckfield at xx33 on ⚒.
On ⑦ use East Grinstead services from / to London Victoria and change trains at Oxted (Uckfield d. xx34).

LONDON VICTORIA - EAST GRINSTEAD SN

km					
0	0h00	↓	d. **London** Victoria ....a.	↑	0h56
17	0h17	↓	d. East Croydon ....d.	↑	0h37
33	0h37	↓	d. Oxted....................d.	↑	0h16
42	0h43	↓	d. Lingfield ....d.	↑	0h12
48	0h54	↓	a. **East Grinstead** ▽ d.	↑	0h00

Frequency: Every 30 minutes.
Usual off-peak departures:
From London Victoria at xx20, xx50 on ⚒⊠; xx21, xx51 on ⑦.
From East Grinstead at xx06, xx36 on ⚒⊠; xx12, xx42 on ⑦.

LONDON VICTORIA - LITTLEHAMPTON SN

km					
0	0h00	↓	d. **London** Victoria ....a.	↑	1h42
17	0h16	↓	d. East Croydon ....a.	↑	1h25
43	0h33	↓	d. Gatwick Airport......a.	↑	1h09
61	0h50	↓	d. Haywards Heath....a.	↑	0h54
82	1h06	↓	d. Hove ....a.	↑	0h35
96	1h21	↓	d. Worthing ....d.	↑	0h21
114	1h41	↓	a. **Littlehampton** ......d.	↑	0h00

Frequency: Every 30 minutes on ⚒; hourly on ⑦.
Usual off-peak departures:
From London Victoria at xx16, xx46 on ⚒✥; xx16 on ⑦.
From Littlehampton at xx13, xx43 on ⚒✥; xx13 on ⑦.

LONDON VICTORIA - BOGNOR REGIS SN

km					
0	0h00	↓	d. **London** Victoria ....a.	↑	1h50
17	0h16	↓	d. East Croydon ....d.	↑	1h30
43	0h37	↓	d. Gatwick Airport......d.	↑	1h08
61	1h03	↓	d. Horsham ....d.	↑	0h50
94	1h30	↓	d. Arundel ....d.	↑	0h16
110	1h40	↓	d. Barnham ....d.	↑	0h07
116	1h46	↓	a. **Bognor Regis** .....d.	↑	0h00

Frequency: Every 30 minutes on ⚒; hourly on ⑦.
Usual off-peak departures:
From London Victoria at xx05, xx35 on ⚒; xx35 on ⑦.
From Bognor Regis at xx29, xx56 on ⚒; xx31 on ⑦.

BRIGHTON - PORTSMOUTH HARBOUR SN

km	◧				◧
0	0h00	↓	d. **Brighton** ....d.	↑	1h19
2	0h04	↓	d. Hove ....d.	↑	1h15
16	0h22	↓	d. Worthing ....d.	↑	0h57
35	0h42	↓	d. Barnham ....d.	↑	0h39
45	0h49	↓	d. Chichester.............d.	↑	0h31
59	1h04	↓	d. Havant ....d.	↑	0h17
71	1h16	↓	a. **Portsmouth** & SS.d.	↑	0h04
72	1h20		a. **Portsmouth** Hbr ...d.		0h00

Frequency: Hourly.
Usual off-peak departures:
From Brighton at xx00 on ⚒; xx30 on ⑦.
From Portsmouth & Southsea at xx33 on ⚒; xx17 on ⑦.
See note ◧.

BRIGHTON - SOUTHAMPTON CENTRAL SN

km	◐				◐
0	0h00	↓	d. **Brighton**...............d.	↑	1h45
2	0h04	↓	d. Hove ....d.	↑	1h41
16	0h23	↓	d. Worthing ....d.	↑	1h23
35	0h46	↓	d. Barnham ....d.	↑	1h00
45	0h54	↓	d. Chichester.............d.	↑	0h52
59	1h06	↓	d. Havant ....d.	↑	0h38
75	1h22	↓	d. Fareham ....d.	↑	0h23
98	1h48	↓	a. **Southampton** C ...d.	↑	0h00

Frequency: Hourly.
Usual off-peak departures:
From Brighton at xx30 on Ⓐ; xx32 on ⑥; xx00 on ⑦.
From Southampton at xx26 on ⚒; xx30 on ⑦.
See note ◐.

LONDON WATERLOO - READING SW

km					
0	0h00	↓	d. **London** Waterloo . a.	↑	1h22
16	0h16	↓	d. Richmond............ d.	↑	1h03
18	0h20	↓	d. Twickenham .... d.	↑	0h58
30	0h33	↓	d. Staines................. d.	↑	0h36
46	0h53	↓	d. Ascot.................... d.	↑	0h28
70	1h20		a. **Reading** .... d.	↑	0h00

Frequency: Every 30 minutes.
Usual off-peak departures:
From London Waterloo at xx20, xx50 on ⚒; xx09, xx39 on ⑦.
From Reading at xx12, xx42 on ⚒; xx24, xx54 on ⑦.

LONDON WATERLOO - WINDSOR SW

km					
0	0h00	↓	d. **London** Waterloo . a.	↑	0h56
16	0h20	↓	d. Richmond .... d.	↑	0h34
18	0h24	↓	d. Twickenham .... d.	↑	0h30
30	0h39	↓	d. Staines.................. d.	↑	0h15
41	0h53	↓	a. **Windsor** ▷ .... d.	↑	0h00

Frequency: Every 30 minutes.
Usual off-peak departures:
From London Waterloo at xx03, xx33 on ⚒; xx25, xx44 on ⑦.
From Windsor at xx23, xx53 on ⚒; xx01, xx34 on ⑦.

SEAFORD - BRIGHTON SN

km					
0	0h00	↓	d. **Seaford** ....a.	↑	0h36
4	0h05	↓	d. Newhaven Harbour .d.	↑	0h30
5	0h07	↓	d. Newhaven Town.....d.	↑	0h28
15	0h19	↓	d. Lewes ....d.	↑	0h18
22	0h26	↓	d. Falmer ....d.	↑	0h09
28	0h35	↓	a. **Brighton**...............d.	↑	0h00

Frequency: Every 30 minutes.
Usual off-peak departures:
From Seaford at xx25, xx53 on ⚒; xx29, xx59 on ⑦. Not 1253 on Ⓐ.
From Brighton at xx11, xx41 on ⚒; xx17, xx47 on ⑦. Not 1211 on Ⓐ.

TONBRIDGE - REDHILL SN

km					
0	0h00	↓	d. **Tonbridge** ....a.	↑	0h31
7	0h08	↓	d. Penshurst..............d.	↑	0h22
15	0h15	↓	d. Edenbridge............d.	↑	0h16
22	0h21	↓	d. Godstone ....d.	↑	0h10
32	0h35	↓	a. **Redhill**...................d.	↑	0h00

Frequency: Hourly.
Usual off-peak departures:
From Tonbridge at xx01 on ⚒§; xx26 on ⑦.
From Redhill at xx00 on ⚒; xx09 on ⑦.

◧ – Journey time on ⑦ extended by up to 17 minutes.
◐ – Journey time on ⑦ extended by up to 10 minutes.
▷ – Windsor and Eton Riverside.
§ – Timings vary after 1501 departure on Ⓐ.
‡ – Not 1054, 1354 on ⑥.

✥ – On Ⓐ not 1146, 1246 from London Victoria; not 0943, 1043, 1443 from Littlehampton.
⊠ – On Ⓐ: hourly at xx50 from 0850 until 1350 from London Victoria; hourly at xx06 from 1006 until 1506 from East Grinstead.

¶ – Not 0833, 1833 on ⑥.
△ – **Spa Valley Railway** (🚂 Eridge - Tunbridge Wells West: *8 km*). ✆ 01892 537715. www.spavalleyrailway.co.uk
▽ – **Bluebell Railway** (🚂 East Grinstead - Sheffield Park: *18 km*). ✆ 01825 720800. www.bluebell-railway.com

SN, TL BEDFORD - LONDON - GATWICK ✈ - BRIGHTON 103

km			⚒	⚒	⚒	Ⓐ	⑥	⚒	⚒	⚒	⚒	⚒	⚒	⚒		⚒	⚒	⚒	⚒	⚒	⑥	Ⓐ		⑦	⑦
0	**Bedford** 170 d.	⚒	0015	0115	0215	0253	0253	0315	0343	0413	0443	0515	0548	0618		2118	2148	2216	2243	2307	2337	2343	⑦	0553	0623
31	Luton 170 d.		0040	0140	0240	0318	0318	0340	0408	0438	0508	0540	0613	0643		2143	2213	2241	2308	2332	0002	0010		0619	0649
33	Luton Airport P ✈ ◇ 170 d.		0043	0143	0243	0321	0321	0343	0411	0441	0511	0543	0616	0646	and	2146	2216	2244	2311	2335	0005	0013		0622	0652
48	St. Albans d.		0055	0155	0255	0333	0333	0355	0423	0453	0523	0555	0627	0657	at the	2157	2227	2255	2323	2347	0017	0025		0634	0704
80	**London** St Pancras 170 d.		0132	0232	0332	0402	0402	0432	0452	0520	0550	0620	0650	0720	same	2220	2250	2322	2352	0022	0052	0054		0710	0741
82	Farringdon 185 d.		|	|	|	|	|	|	0456	0524	0554	0624	0654	0724	minutes	2224	2254	2327	2356	0027	|	|		—	—
83	**London** Blackfriars 185 d.		0140	0240	0340	0410	0410	0440	0501	0529	0559	0629	0659	0729	past	2229	2259	2331	0002	0031	0102	0102		⑦	⑦
84	**London** Bridge 185 d.		|	|	|	|	|	|	|	0535	0605	0635	0705	0735	each	2235	2305	2337	|	|	|	|		0709	0739
99	East Croydon 185 d.		0207	0307	0407	0437	0437	0507	0528	0549	0619	0649	0719	0749	hour	2249	2319	2351	0028	0058	0128	0128		0723	0753
124	Gatwick Airport ✈ 185 d.		0230	0330	0430	0458	0505	0532	0548	0605	0635	0705	0735	0805	until	2305	2335	0022	0049	0120	0158	0158		0743	0815
142	Haywards Heath 185 d.		...	...	...	0514	0520	0550	0603	0622	0652	0722	0751	0821		2322	2352	0040	0104	...	0214	0214		0758	0832
163	**Brighton** 185 a.		...	...	...	0532	0538	0610	0624	0643	0713	0743	0814	0844		2343	0013	0100	0124	...	0228	0228		0818	0852

	⑦	⑦	⑦	⑦	⑦		⑦	⑦	⑦	⑦	⑦	⑦
Bedford 170 d.	0653	0731	0803	0817	0847	♠	2118	2148	2208	2243	2307	2343
Luton 170 d.	0719	0757	0829	0842	0912		2143	2213	2233	2308	2332	0008
Luton Airport P ✈ ◇ 170 d.	0722	0800	0832	0845	0915	and	2146	2216	2236	2311	2335	0011
St. Albans d.	0734	0812	0844	0857	0927	at the	2157	2227	2248	2323	2347	0023
London St Pancras 170 d.	0811	0841	0910	0924	0954	same	2224	2254	2324	2352	0023	0052
Farringdon 185 d.	—	—	—	0928	0958	minutes	2228	2258	2328	2356	0028	|
London Blackfriars 185 d.	⑦	⑦	⑦	0933	1003	past	2233	2303	2333	0002	0031	0102
London Bridge 185 d.	0809	0839	0909	0939	1009	each	2239	2309	2339	|	|	|
East Croydon 185 d.	0823	0853	0923	0953	1023	hour	2253	2323	2353	0028	0058	0128
Gatwick Airport ✈ 185 d.	0843	0909	0939	1009	1039	until	2309	2339	0017	0049	0120	0158
Haywards Heath 185 d.	0858	0926	0954	1024	1054		2326	2358	0034	0104	...	0214
Brighton 185 a.	0918	0946	1014	1044	1114		2346	0018	0054	0124	...	0228

		⚒	⚒	⚒	⚒	⚒	⑥	Ⓐ
Brighton 185 d.	⚒	0002	...	...	...	...	0412	0412
Haywards Heath 185 d.		0023	...	...	...	...	0426	0426
Gatwick Airport ✈ 185 d.		0042	0146	0246	0346	0421	0441	0441
East Croydon 185 d.		0110	0210	0310	0410	0440	0510	0510
London Bridge 185 d.		|	|	|	|	|	0525	0525
London Blackfriars 185 d.		0136	0236	0336	0436	0506	0531	0531
Farringdon 185 d.		|	|	|	|	0511	0536	0536
London St Pancras 170 d.		0144	0244	0344	0444	0516	0540	0540
St Albans City d.		0218	0317	0417	0517	0541	0601	0605
Luton Airport P ◇ 170 d.		0230	0330	0430	0530	0553	0613	0618
Luton 170 d.		0234	0334	0434	0534	0557	0617	0622
Bedford 170 a.		0259	0359	0459	0559	0622	0642	0647

	⚒	⚒	Ⓐ	⑥	Ⓐ	⑥	Ⓐ	⑥	⚒	⚒	⚒	⚒		⚒	⚒	Ⓐ	⑥	⚒	⚒		⚒	⚒	⚒	⚒
Brighton 185 d.	0526	0556	0626	0628	0656	0658	0726	0728	0756	0826	0858	0928		1528	1558	1628	1628	1658	1728		2128	2158	2228	2256
Haywards Heath 185 d.	0549	0619	0649	0649	0719	0719	0749	0749	0819	0849	0919	0949		1549	1619	1649	1649	1719	1749		2149	2219	2249	2317
Gatwick Airport ✈ 185 d.	0606	0636	0706	0706	0736	0736	0806	0806	0836	0906	0936	1006	and	1606	1636	1706	1706	1736	1806	and	2206	2236	2306	2334
East Croydon 185 d.	0621	0651	0721	0721	0751	0751	0821	0821	0851	0921	0951	1021	at the	1621	1651	1721	1721	1751	1821	at the	2221	2251	2321	2353
London Bridge 185 d.	0635	0706	0736	0736	0806	0806	0836	0836	0906	0936	1006	1036	same	1636	1706	1736	1736	1806	1836	same	2236	2306	2336	|
London Blackfriars 185 d.	0642	0712	0742	0742	0812	0812	0842	0842	0912	0942	1012	1042	minutes	1642	1712	1742	1742	1812	1842	minutes	2242	2312	2342	0022
Farringdon 185 d.	0646	0716	0746	0746	0816	0816	0846	0846	0916	0946	1016	1046	past	1646	1716	1746	1746	1816	1846	past	2246	2316	2346	0026
London St Pancras 170 d.	0651	0721	0751	0751	0821	0821	0851	0851	0921	0951	1021	1051	each	1651	1721	1751	1751	1821	1851	each	2251	2321	2351	0031
St Albans City d.	0711	0739	|	0811	|	0841	0909	0911	0941	1011	1041	1111	hour	1711	1741	1809	1811	1841	1911	hour	2316	2346	0016	0058
Luton Airport P ✈ ◇ 170 d.	0723	0752	0815	0823	0845	0853	|	0937	0954	1023	1053	1123	until	1723	1753	|	1823	1853	1923	until	2328	2358	0028	0109
Luton 170 d.	0727	0755	0819	0827	0849	0857	0921	0941	0957	1027	1057	1127		1727	1757	1822	1827	1857	1927		2332	0002	0032	0114
Bedford 170 a.	0752	0822	0840	0852	0910	0922	0944	1007	1022	1052	1122	1152		1752	1822	1843	1852	1922	1952		2357	0027	0057	0139

	⚒		⑦	⑦	⑦	⑦	⑦	⑦	⑦	⑦	⑦	⑦	⑦	⑦	⑦	⑦	⑦		⑦	⑦	⑦	⑦	⑦	⑦	⑦
Brighton 185 d.	2323	⑦	0002	0542	0557	0628	0657	0728	0757	...	0829	0859	0929	0959	1029	1059	1129		2059	2129	2157	2229	2242	2318	2342
Haywards Heath 185 d.	2344		0023	0604	0618	0649	0718	0749	0818	...	0851	0921	0951	1021	1051	1121	1151	and	2121	2151	2218	2251	2304	2334	0003
Gatwick Airport ✈ 185 d.	0001		0042	0619	0635	0704	0735	0804	0835	0830	0906	0936	1006	1036	1106	1136	1216	at the	2136	2206	2236	2306	2321	2351	0021
East Croydon 185 d.	0024		0110	0640	0654	0725	0754	0825	0853	0903	0921	0951	1021	1051	1121	1151	1221	same	2151	2221	2251	2321	2340	0012	0040
London Bridge 185 d.	|		|	0656	0712	0742	0812	0842	0908	0919	0936	1006	1036	1106	1136	1206	1236	minutes	2206	2236	2306	2336	|	|	|
London Blackfriars 185 d.	0050		0136	—	—	—	—	—	—	0926	0942	1012	1042	1112	1142	1212	1242	past	2212	2242	2312	2347	0006	0038	0106
Farringdon 185 d.	|		|	⑦	⑦	⑦	⑦	⑦	⑦	0930	0946	1016	1046	1116	1146	1216	1246	each	2216	2246	2316	2351	0011	|	|
London St Pancras 170 d.	0058		0144	0633	0733	0803	0833	0851	0921	0935	0951	1021	1051	1121	1151	1221	1251	hour	2221	2251	2321	2356	0016	0046	0114
St Albans City d.	0133		0219	0708	0808	0838	0908	0915	0945	0959	1016	1046	1116	1146	1216	1241	1311	until	2241	2313	2347	0024	0050	0120	0142
Luton Airport P ✈ ◇ 170 d.	0144		0230	0719	0819	0849	0919	0928	0956	1011	1029	1059	1128	1159	1229	1252	1322		2252	2324	2359	0036	0101	0131	0153
Luton 170 d.	0149		0235	0724	0824	0854	0924	0931	1001	1015	1032	1102	1132	1202	1232	1257	1327		2257	2329	0003	0040	0106	0136	0158
Bedford 170 a.	0214		0259	0749	0849	0919	0949	0956	1026	1040	1057	1127	1157	1227	1257	1322	1352		2322	2354	0028	0105	0131	0201	0223

◇ – Luton Airport Parkway.
♠ – The 2017 departure from Bedford arrives Brighton 2246.

☛ Additional trains run Bedford - Gatwick Airport and v.v. Frequent services (operated by SN/GX) also run **London Victoria** - **Gatwick** ✈ - **Brighton** and v.v. (4 trains per hour on ⚒, 2 trains per hour on †).
For other services London Victoria - Gatwick Airport and v.v. see Table **100**.

SW 🍸 on most trains LONDON - GUILDFORD - PORTSMOUTH 105

km			Ⓐ	Ⓐ	Ⓐ	Ⓐ	Ⓐ	Ⓐ	Ⓐ	Ⓐ	Ⓐ	Ⓐ		Ⓐ	Ⓐ	Ⓐ	Ⓐ	Ⓐ	Ⓐ	Ⓐ	Ⓐ	Ⓐ	Ⓐ	Ⓐ	Ⓐ
0	**London** Waterloo 108 d.	Ⓐ	...	0508	0545	0615	0700	0730	0800	0830	0900	0930		1430	1500	1530	1600	1630	1700	1730	1800	1830	1900	1930	2000
39	Woking 108 d.		...	0552	0617	0643	0725	0755	0826	0855	0925	0955	and at	1455	1525	1554	1625	1655	1725	1755	1824	1855	1924	1955	2025
49	Guildford d.		0509	0603	0630	0655	0733	0804	0833	0903	0933	1003	the same	1503	1533	1604	1634	1703	1734	1810	1834	1906	1934	2004	2034
69	Haslemere d.		0524	0628	0655	0720	0753	0824	0854	0924	0956	1021	minutes	1521	1553	1628	1653	1724	1754	1828	1852	1925	1952	2024	2055
88	Petersfield d.		0545	0645	0711	0736	0805	0835	0905	0935	1013	1032	past each	1532	1604	1645	1704	1736	1806	1840	1904	1937	2004	2036	2112
107	Havant a.		0600	0659	0726	0753	0819	0851	0918	0951	1027	1045	hour until	1545	1617	1659	1717	1749	1818	1852	1917	1953	2017	2051	2126
118	**Portsmouth** & Southsea a.		0616	0716	0747	0809	0831	0904	0931	1003	1044	1057		1557	1629	1719	1730	1803	1831	1905	1929	2006	2030	2104	2148
120	**Portsmouth** Harbour a.		0620	0721	0751	0813	0836	0908	0936	1008	1049	1102		1602	1636	1725	1736	1809	1838	1911	1938	2012	2034	2108	...

	Ⓐ	Ⓐ	Ⓐ	Ⓐ	Ⓐ	Ⓐ	Ⓐ		⑥	⑥	⑥	⑥	⑥		⑥	⑥	⑥	⑥	⑥	⑥	⑥		⑦	⑦	⑦
London Waterloo 108 d.	2030	2100	2130	2200	2230	2300	2332	⑥	...	0520	0645	0730	0800		2100	2130	2200	2230	2300	2315	2345	⑦	...	0800	0830
Woking 108 d.	2055	2125	2155	2225	2255	2327	2359		...	0613	0713	0755	0825	and at	2125	2155	2225	2255	2327	2344	0014		0732	0833	0902
Guildford d.	2104	2134	2204	2234	2304	2340	0009		0515	0625	0725	0803	0833	the same	2133	2203	2233	2304	2336	2353	0026		0742	0842	0912
Haslemere d.	2122	2155	2223	2255	2323	0005	0034		0530	0650	0749	0821	0853	minutes	2154	2221	2254	2324	2354	0013	0051		0807	0907	0930
Petersfield d.	2133	2212	2234	2312	2334	0021	0050		0546	0706	0806	0832	0904	past each	2205	2232	2305	2335	0005	0024	0107		0823	0923	0941
Havant a.	2146	2231	2246	2326	2349	0036	0105		0601	0722	0824	0845	0917	hour until	2218	2245	2318	2348	0018	0036	0122		0838	0940	0954
Portsmouth & Southsea a.	2158	2247	2303	2343	0002	0052	0120		0617	0738	0848	0857	0930		2230	2257	2330	0001	0030	0049	0138		0853	0955	1007
Portsmouth Harbour a.	2203	2252	2307	2348	0006	...	0124		0622	0743	0852	0902	0936		2236	2302	2336	0005	0035	0054	...		0857	1000	1011

	⑦	⑦	⑦	⑦		⑦	⑦	⑦	⑦	⑦
London Waterloo 108 d.	0900	0930	1000	1030		2130	2200	2230	2300	2330
Woking 108 d.	0933	1002	1033	1102	and at	2202	2232	2302	2332	0002
Guildford d.	0942	1012	1042	1112	the same	2212	2242	2312	2342	0012
Haslemere d.	1007	1030	1107	1130	minutes	2230	2307	2330	0007	0029
Petersfield d.	1023	1041	1123	1141	past each	2241	2323	2341	0023	0040
Havant a.	1040	1053	1140	1153	hour until	2253	2342	2353	0038	0053
Portsmouth & Southsea a.	1055	1106	1156	1207		2307	2357	0006	0053	0105
Portsmouth Harbour a.	1100	1111	1200	1213		2311	0001	0010	0058	0109

		Ⓐ	Ⓐ	Ⓐ		Ⓐ	Ⓐ	Ⓐ	Ⓐ
Portsmouth Harbour d.	Ⓐ	0425	0512	0545	...	0615	0642	0713	0745
Portsmouth & Southsea d.		0430	0517	0550	...	0620	0647	0718	0750
Havant d.		0446	0530	0604	...	0634	0700	0732	0804
Petersfield d.		0503	0544	0618	...	0648	0715	0747	0818
Haslemere d.		0521	0558	0637	...	0702	0734	0801	0832
Guildford d.		0550	0624	0701	...	0719	0753	0819	0853
Woking 108 a.		0600	0635	0711	...	0727	|	0826	|
London Waterloo 108 a.		0630	0709	0743	...	0754	0830	0855	0930

	Ⓐ	Ⓐ	Ⓐ	Ⓐ		Ⓐ	Ⓐ	Ⓐ	Ⓐ		Ⓐ	Ⓐ	Ⓐ	Ⓐ	Ⓐ	Ⓐ	Ⓐ	Ⓐ	Ⓐ	Ⓐ	Ⓐ	Ⓐ		⑥	⑥
Portsmouth Harbour d.	0815	0845	0903	0945	❖	1403	1445	1515	1545	...	1615	1645	1715	1745	1815	1845	1915	1945	2019	2119	2219	2319	⑥	0441	0515
Portsmouth & Southsea d.	0820	0850	0908	0950		1408	1450	1520	1550	...	1619	1650	1719	1750	1820	1849	1919	1950	2024	2124	2224	2324		0445	0520
Havant d.	0834	0904	0924	1004	and at	1424	1504	1533	1604	...	1634	1704	1734	1804	1835	1903	1934	2004	2040	2140	2240	2340		0501	0536
Petersfield d.	0848	0918	0940	1018	the same	1440	1518	1547	1618	...	1648	1718	1748	1818	1849	1917	1948	2018	2057	2157	2257	2357		0518	0553
Haslemere d.	0902	0932	1000	1032	minutes	1500	1536	1600	1637	...	1702	1737	1802	1831	1902	1930	2002	2032	2115	2215	2315	0015		0539	0611
Guildford d.	0919	0951	1019	1049	past each	1519	1552	1621	1701	...	1719	1801	1822	1855	1923t	1949	2018	2049	2140	2239	2339	0038		0604	0634
Woking 108 a.	0927	0959	1026	1057	hour until	1526	1600	1629	1711	...	1726	1811	1833	1904	|	1956	2026	2058	2157	2251	2351	...		0612	0644
London Waterloo 108 a.	0955	1031	1052	1124		1551	1629	1701	1745	...	1754	1843	1859	1929	2000	2027	2051	2129	2228	2320	0034	...		0641	0713

	⑥	⑥	⑥		⑥	⑥	⑥	⑥	⑥		⑦	⑦	⑦	⑦	⑦		⑦	⑦	⑦	⑦		⑦	⑦	⑦
Portsmouth Harbour d.	0615	0645	0715	⊠	2015	2045	2119	2219	2319	⑦	0648	0732	0748	0832	0848	...	0932	0948	1032	1048	⊠	2148	2232	2248
Portsmouth & Southsea d.	0620	0650	0720		2020	2050	2124	2224	2324		0653	0737	0752	0837	0852	...	0937	0952	1037	1052		2152	2237	2252
Havant d.	0634	0703	0734	and at	2034	2103	2140	2240	2340		0707	0750	0807	0850	0907	...	0950	1007	1050	1107	and at	2207	2250	2307
Petersfield d.	0648	0717	0748	the same	2048	2117	2156	2257	2357		0729	0804	0824	0904	0924	...	1004	1024	1104	1124	the same	2224	2304	2324
Haslemere d.	0702	0730	0802	minutes	2102	2130	2214	2315	0015		0742	0817	0842	0917	0942	...	1017	1042	1117	1142	minutes	2242	2317	2342
Guildford d.	0719	0749	0819	past each	2119	2149	2237	2340	0037		0805	0835	0905	0935	1005	...	1035	1105	1135	1205	past each	2305	2335	0008
Woking 108 a.	|	0756	0826	hour until	2126	2158	2247	2351	...		0813	0842	0915	0942	1015	...	1042	1114	1144	1214	hour until	2314	2342	0017
London Waterloo 108 a.	0804	0824	0852		2152	2225	2316	0030	...		0851	0923	0953	1019	1050	...	1122	1150	1217	1244		2344	0015	...

t – Arrives 1918.
❖ – The 1303 from Portsmouth Harbour arrives London Waterloo at 1457.
⊠ – Arrivals at London Waterloo may vary ± 4 minutes.

106 LONDON - SOUTHAMPTON - BOURNEMOUTH - WEYMOUTH

🍷 on most trains. SW

km			①	Ⓐ	Ⓐ	Ⓐ	Ⓐ	Ⓐ	Ⓐ	Ⓐ	Ⓐ	Ⓐ	Ⓐ	Ⓐ	Ⓐ	Ⓐ		Ⓐ	Ⓐ	Ⓐ	Ⓐ	Ⓐ	Ⓐ	Ⓐ	Ⓐ	Ⓐ
0	**London** Waterloo 108 d.	Ⓐ	0010	...	...	...	0530	...	...	0630	...	0703	0735	0805	0835	0905		1505	1535	1605	1635	1705	1735	1805	1835	1905
39	Woking 108 d.		0042	...	...	...	0601	...	...	0657	...	0730	0800	|	0900	|	and	|	1600	|	1659u	|	|	|	|	|
77	Basingstoke 108 114 d.		0101	...	...	...	0621	...	...	0718	...	0750	0819	0849	|	0949	at	1549	|	1648	1719	1746	1817	1846	1917	1948
107	Winchester 114 d.		0118	...	...	...	0638	...	...	0735	...	0807	0836	0906	0933	1005	the	1605	1633	1706	1735	1803	1833	1903	1934	2005
120	**Southampton** ✈ 114 d.		0132	...	...	...	0653	...	...	0750	...	0818	0850	0914	0942	1014	same	1614	1642	1715	1744	1811	1842	1911	1943	2014
128	**Southampton** Cen 114 d.		0140	...	...	0622	0702	...	0730	0759	...	0827	0859	0925	0951	1025	minutes	1626f	1653	1725	1755f	1822f	1853f	1922f	1954f	2025f
149	Brockenhurst 114 d.		...	...	0615	0641	0718	...	0757	0820	...	0844	0913	0939	1005	1039	past	1640	1709	1740	1810	|	|	|	|	2041
174	**Bournemouth** 114 d.		...	0611	0644	0712	0746	0804	0817	0847	0904	0912	0932f	1004	1024f	1104	each	1702	1725	1757	1826	1851	1923	1950	2022	2101f
183	Poole d.		...	0624	0657	0725	0758	0817	0830	0900	0917	0923	0944	1014	1037	1114	hour	1717	1738	1809	1838	1903	1935	2003	2038	2113
193	Wareham d.		...	0638	0711	0739	0812	0831	...	0912	0931	...	0956	1028	1049	1128	until	1730	1750	1823	1850	1917	1947	2017	2049	2126
219	Dorchester South d.		...	0658	0731	0759	0833	0851	...	0933	0951	...	1013	1054f	1105	1149		1751	1809	1849	1907	1937	2005	2037	2107	2147
230	**Weymouth** a.		...	0709	0742	0810	0844	0902	...	0944	1002	...	1023	1106	1116	1202		1802	1818	1902	1918	1950	2015	2050	2117	2159

	Ⓐ	Ⓐ	Ⓐ	Ⓐ	Ⓐ	Ⓐ	Ⓐ		⑥	⑥	⑥	⑥	⑥	⑥	⑥	⑥	⑥	⑥	⑥	⑥		⑥	⑥	⑥	⑥	⑥
London Waterloo 108 d.	1935	2005	2035	2105	2135	2235	2335	⑥	0105	...	...	...	0530	...	0630	...	0735	0805	0835	0905		1835	1905	1935	2005	2035
Woking 108 d.	2000	|	2100	|	2200	2300	0004		0142	...	...	...	0603	...	0657	...	0800	|	0900	|	and	1900	|	2000	|	2101
Basingstoke 108 114 d.	|	2049	|	2149	|	|	0035		0209s	...	...	...	0624	...	0718	...	0821	0849	|	0948	at	|	1949	|	2049	|
Winchester 114 d.	2032	2105	2133	2205	2234	2333	0051		0226s	...	...	...	0643	...	0734	...	0838	0905	0933	1005	the	1933	2006	2033	2105	2133
Southampton ✈ 114 d.	2041	2114	2142	2217	2243	2342	0105		0239s	...	...	...	0656	...	0748	...	0851	0914	0942	1014	same	1942	2014	2042	2114	2142
Southampton Cen 114 d.	2051	2125	2151	2227	2251	2353	0113		0249	...	...	0620	0705	0721	0800f	0817	0900	0924	0951	1024	minutes	1951	2024	2051	2124	2151
Brockenhurst 114 d.	2105	2142	2205	2247	2306	0007	0129s		...	...	0615	0639	0722	0740	0817	0838	0914	0938	1005	1038	past	2005	2038	2105	2143	2205
Bournemouth 114 d.	2124f	2208	2224f	2313	2324f	0024	0152		...	0611	0644	0711f	0749	0811f	0844	0909f	0933f	1004f	1024f	1104f	each	2024f	2104f	2124f	2212	2224f
Poole d.	2137	...	2237	...	2337	0036	...		...	0624	0657	0724	0802	0824	0857	0922	0946	1014	1037	1114	hour	2037	2114	2137	2226	2237
Wareham d.	2149	...	2249	...	2349	...	...		...	0638	0711	0738	0813	0838	0909	0935	0958	1028	1049	1128	until	2049	2126	2149	...	2249
Dorchester South d.	2209	...	2309	...	0010	...	...		...	0658	0731	0758	0834	0858	0929	0956	1014	1051	1105	1149		2105	2151	2209	...	2309
Weymouth a.	2220	...	2320	...	0022	...	...		...	0709	0742	0809	0845	0909	0940	1007	1023	1102	1115	1201		2113	2202	2220	...	2320

	⑥	⑥	⑥	⑥	⑥		⑦	⑦	⑦	⑦	⑦	⑦	⑦	⑦		⑦	⑦	⑦	⑦		⑦	⑦	⑦	⑦	⑦
London Waterloo 108 d.	2105	2135	2205	2235	2305	⑦	0010	0105	...	...	...	0753	0835	0853		1435	1454	1535	1605		2035	2105	2135	2205	2305
Woking 108 d.	|	2200	|	2300	2332		0040	0149	...	...	...	0828	0907	0928	and	1507	1528	1607	1637	and	2107	2137	2207	2237	2337
Basingstoke 108 114 d.	2148	|	2248	|	2352		0100	0216s	...	0748	...	0848	0927	0947	at	1527	1547	1627	1657	at	2127	2157	2227	2257	2357
Winchester 114 d.	2205	2233	2305	2333	0011		0116	0233s	...	0807	...	0908	0944	1007	the	1544	1607	1644	1714	the	2144	2214	2244	2314	0014
Southampton ✈ 114 d.	2217	2242	2314	2342	0026		0129	0246s	...	0825	...	0927	0953	1025	same	1553	1625	1653	1727	same	2153	2227	2253	2327	0028
Southampton Cen 114 d.	2229	2251	2324	2351	0037		0138	0256	...	0834	0903	0935	1003	1033	minutes	1603	1634	1703	1736	minutes	2203	2236	2303	2336	0040
Brockenhurst 114 d.	2248	2305	2343	0005	0053s		0154s	...	...	0855	0917	0957	1017	1055	past	1617	1655	1717	1757	past	2217	2257	2317	2355	0056s
Bournemouth 114 d.	2317	2327	0010	0029	0117		0219	...	0839	0924	0939f	1024	1039f	1122	each	1639f	1723	1739f	1824	each	2239f	2324	2339f	0022	0120
Poole d.	2330	2340	0023	0041	0128		...	...	0851	0933	0951	1033	1051	1133	hour	1651	1732	1751	1833	hour	2251	2333	2351	0034	0132
Wareham d.	...	2351	...	...	...		...	...	0903	...	1003	...	1103	...	until	1703	...	1803	...	until	2303	...	0003	...	...
Dorchester South d.	...	0012	...	...	...		...	...	0924	...	1024	...	1124	...		1724	...	1824	...		2324	...	0024	...	...
Weymouth a.	...	0023	...	...	...		...	...	0935	...	1035	...	1135	...		1735	...	1837	...		2336	...	0035	...	...

		Ⓐ	Ⓐ	Ⓐ	Ⓐ	Ⓐ	Ⓐ	Ⓐ	Ⓐ	Ⓐ	Ⓐ	Ⓐ	Ⓐ	Ⓐ	♠	Ⓐ	Ⓐ	Ⓐ	Ⓐ	Ⓐ	Ⓐ	Ⓐ	Ⓐ	Ⓐ	Ⓐ	Ⓐ
Weymouth a.	Ⓐ	...	...	...	0555	0625	0655	...	0725	0755	0820	0903	0920	1003		1503	1520	1603	1620	1703	1720	1803	1820	1903	1920	1959
Dorchester South d.		...	...	...	0607	0637	0707	...	0737	0807	0833	0913	0933	1013	and	1513	1533	1613	1633	1713	1733	1813	1833	1913	1937f	2011
Wareham d.		...	...	...	0627	0657	0727	...	0757	0827	0853	0928	0953	1028	at	1528	1553	1628	1653	1728	1753	1828	1853	1928	1957	2028
Poole d.		0500	0540	0555	0641	0711	0741	0805	0811	0841	0907	0940	1007	1040	the	1540	1607	1640	1707	1740	1807	1840	1907	1940	2009	2040
Bournemouth 114 d.		0515	0555	0611	0656	0726	0756	0822f	0827	0856	0922f	0959f	1022f	1059f	same	1559f	1622f	1659f	1722f	1759f	1822f	1859f	1922f	1959f	2022	2059f
Brockenhurst 114 d.		0537	0611	0640	|	|	0811	0844	0855	0911	0944	1014	1044	1114	minutes	1614	1644	1714	1744	1814	1844	1914	1944	2014	2044	2114
Southampton Cen 114 d.		0555	0630	0700	0730f	0800f	0830f	0900	0918	0930f	1000	1030	1100	1130	past	1630	1700	1730	1800	1830	1900	1930	2000	2030	2100	2130
Southampton ✈ 114 d.		0603	0638	0708	0738	0808	0838	0908	...	0938	1008	1038	1108	1138	each	1638	1708	1738	1808	1838	1908	1938	2008	2038	2108	2138
Winchester 114 d.		0618	0648	0718	0748	0818	0848	0918	...	0948	1018	1048	1118	1148	hour	1648	1718	1748	1818	1848	1918	1948	2018	2048	2118	2148
Basingstoke 108 114 a.		0635	0704	0734	|	0834	|	0936	...	|	1034	|	1135	|	until	|	1734	|	1834	|	1934	|	2034	|	2134	|
Woking 108 a.		0655	|	|	|	0853	0922	0955	...	1021	|	1120	|	1220		1720	|	1820	|	1925	|	2021	|	2122	2153	2223
London Waterloo 108 a.		0727	0749	0817	0848	0926	0953	1024	...	1049	1120	1149	1221	1249		1751	1820	1849	1920	1951	2020	2049	2127	2151	2222	2249

	Ⓐ	Ⓐ	Ⓐ	Ⓐ		⑥	⑥	⑥	⑥	⑥	⑥	⑥	⑥	⑥	⑥	♠	⑥	⑥	⑥	⑥	⑥	⑥	⑥	⑥	⑥	⑥
Weymouth a.	2007	2100	2210	2310	⑥	...	...	...	...	0542	0617	0655	0720	0803	0820		1803	1820	1903	1920	...	2010	2058	...	2210	2310
Dorchester South d.	2021	2112	2223	2322		...	...	...	...	0552	0629	0707	0733	0813	0833	and	1813	1833	1913	1933	...	2022	2110	...	2222	2322
Wareham d.	2042	2132	2242	2342		...	...	...	...	0610	0649	0727	0753	0828	0853	at	1828	1853	1928	1953	...	2042	2130	...	2242	2342
Poole d.	2054	2144	2354	2354		...	...	...	0526	0624	0703	0741	0807	0840	0907	the	1840	1907	1940	2007	2040	2054	2142	2154	2254	2354
Bournemouth 114 d.	2112f	2212c	2312f	0003		...	...	...	0542	0642f	0722f	0759f	0822f	0858f	0922f	same	1859f	1922f	1959f	2022f	2059f	2112f	2159f	2212f	2312f	0003
Brockenhurst 114 d.	2139	2239	2339	...		...	...	...	0610	0710	0744	0814	0844	0914	0944	minutes	1914	1944	2014	2044	2114	2139	2214	2239	2339	...
Southampton Cen 114 d.	2200	2300	2358	...		0512	0530	0600	0630	0730	0800	0830	0900	0929	1000	past	1930	2000	2030	2100	2130	2200	2230	2300	2359	...
Southampton ✈ 114 d.	2208	2308	...	...		0520	0541	0608	0638	0738	0808	0838	0908	0938	1008	each	1938	2008	2038	2108	2138	2208	2238	2308	0010	...
Winchester 114 d.	2224	2324	...	...		0534	0600	0623	0648	0748	0818	0848	0918	0948	1018	hour	1948	2018	2048	2118	2148	2223	2256	2325	...	...
Basingstoke 108 114 a.	2240	2324	...	...		0550	0618	0639	0704	|	0834	|	0935	|	1034	until	|	2034	|	2134	|	2239	2312	2343	...	...
Woking 108 a.	2259	0018	...	...		0628	0658	0659	0723	0821	|	0920	|	1020	|		2020	|	2120	2154	2219	2259	2332	0018	...	...
London Waterloo 108 a.	2331	...	...	...		0657	0734	0729	0752	0849	0920	0949	1020	1049	1121		2051	2120	2149	2223	2249	2331	0012	0104	...	...

		⑦	⑦	⑦	⑦	⑦		⑦	⑦	⑦	⑦		⑦	⑦	⑦	⑦		⑦	⑦	⑦	⑦	⑦	⑦	⑦	⑦
Weymouth a.	⑦	...	...	...	...	0748	...	...	0848	...	0948		...	1248	...	1348		1745	...	1848	...	1958	2058	2158	2258
Dorchester South d.		...	...	...	...	0800	...	...	0900	...	1000	and	...	1300	...	1400	and	1800f	...	1900	...	2010	2110	2210	2310
Wareham d.		...	...	...	...	0820	...	...	0920	...	1020	at	...	1320	...	1420	at	1820	...	1920	...	2030	2130	2230	2330
Poole d.		...	...	0720	0750	0832	...	0855	0932	0955	1032	the	1355	1332	1355	1432	the	1832	1855	1932	1955	2050j	2150j	2250j	2350j
Bournemouth 114 d.		...	...	0736f	0806f	0850f	...	0906	0951f	1006	1050	same	1306	1350	1406	1450	same	1850	1906	1950	2006	2106	2208f	2308f	0003
Brockenhurst 114 d.		...	...	0803	0833	0909	...	0933	1009	1033	1109	minutes	1333	1409	1433	1509	minutes	1909	1933	2009	2033	2133	2235	2336	...
Southampton Cen 114 d.		0655	0755	0826	0855	0925	...	0955	1025	1055	1125	past	1355	1425	1455	1525	past	1925	1955	2025	2055	2155	2255	2355	...
Southampton ✈ 114 d.		0703	0803	0834	0903	0933	...	1003	1033	1103	1133	each	1403	1433	1503	1533	each	1933	2003	2033	2103	2203	2303	...	...
Winchester 114 d.		0723	0823	0843	0923	0942	...	1023	1042	1123	1142	hour	1423	1442	1517	1542	hour	1942	2017	2042	2117	2217	2323	...	...
Basingstoke 108 114 a.		0742	0844	0901	0942	0958	...	1042	1058	1142	1158	until	1443	1458	1533	1558	until	1958	2033	2058	2133	2234	2342	...	...
Woking 108 a.		0802	0903	0928	1002	1019	...	1102	1118	1203	1218		1502	1518	1553	1618		2018	2053	2118	2153	2254	0002	...	...
London Waterloo 108 a.		0846	0943	1011	1043	1053	...	1141	1154	1237	1249		1537	1549	1625	1649		2049	2124	2149	2224	2324	0033	...	...

Brockenhurst - Lymington Pier (for ⛴ to Isle of Wight).
Journey 11 minutes. Trains call at Lymington Town 6 minutes later:
Ⓐ: 0559 and every 30 minutes until 0929, 1012 and every 30 minutes until 1612, 1644, 1714, 1744, 1814, 1848 and every 30 minutes until 2218.
⑥: 0612, 0642 and every 30 minutes until 2112, 2148, 2218.
⑦: 0859, 0929 and every 30 minutes until 2059, 2129, 2159.

Lymington Pier - Brockenhurst.
Journey 11 minutes. Trains call at Lymington Town 2 minutes later:
Ⓐ: 0614 and every 30 minutes until 0944, 1027 and every 30 minutes until 1627, 1659, 1729, 1759, 1829, 1903 and every 30 minutes until 2203, 2236.
⑥: 0627, 0657 and every 30 minutes until 2127, 2203, 2236.
⑦: 0914, 0944 and every 30 minutes until 2114, 2144, 2214.

c – Arrives 2157.
f – Arrives 4–6 minutes earlier.
j – Arrives 8 minutes earlier.
s – Calls to set down only.
u – Calls to pick up only.
♠ – The 0920⑥, 1003⑥, 1420Ⓐ from Weymouth arrive London Waterloo 3 minutes later than shown.
☛ For ⛴ services Portsmouth / Poole – Jersey / Guernsey / St Malo and v.v., see Table **2100**.

107 PORTSMOUTH - RYDE - SHANKLIN

2nd class IL

Through fares including ferry are available. Allow 10 minutes for connections between trains and ferries. Operator: Wightlink ✆ 0333 999 7333. www.wightlink.co.uk

⛴

Portsmouth Harbour - Ryde Pierhead:
0515Ⓐ, 0615Ⓐ, 0715 and hourly until 1815, 1920, 2020 (not 1115 and 1415 on Ⓐ).

Ryde Pierhead - Portsmouth Harbour: Journey: ± 22 minutes
0545Ⓐ, 0645Ⓐ, 0745 and hourly until 1845, 1947, 2052 (not 1145 and 1445 on Ⓐ).

Additional services may operate on Ⓐ and on public holidays.

Service shown valid until April 2. Ryde Pier is closed for re-construction - a minibus service operates between Ryde Pierhead and Ryde Esplanade and v.v. Journey: ± 23 minutes

Ryde Esplanade - Shanklin (trains call at Sandown ± 17 minutes later): *14 km*
0612Ⓐ, 0616⑥, 0644Ⓐ, 0716, 0744Ⓐ, 0816, 0916, 0945⑥, 1016*, 1045⑥, 1116*, 1145⑥, 1216*, 1316*, 1416*, 1516*, 1545Ⓐ, 1616, 1645⚒, 1716, 1745⚒, 1816, 1916, 2016, 2116, 2216.

Shanklin - Ryde Esplanade (trains call at Sandown ± 5 minutes later):
0558Ⓐ, 0646⚒, 0718Ⓐ, 0746, 0846, 0946*, 1019⑥, 1046*, 1119⑥, 1146*, 1246*, 1346*, 1446*, 1518Ⓐ*, 1546*, 1618⚒*, 1646, 1718⚒, 1746, 1818⚒, 1846, 1946, 2046, 2146, 2245.

* – Also calls at Smallbrook Junction on request (connection with **Isle of Wight Steam Railway**, see note △) 7 minutes from Ryde / 16 minutes from Shanklin, when Steam Railway is operating.

△ – **Isle of Wight Steam Railway** (🚂 Smallbrook Junction - Haven Street - Wootton: *9 km*). ✆ 01983 882204. www.iwsteamrailway.co.uk

SW LONDON - SALISBURY - EXETER 108

km			⚒	Ⓐ	⑥	Ⓐ	⑥	Ⓐ	⑥	⑥	Ⓐ	⑥	Ⓐ	Ⓐ	⚒	⑥F	⚒	Ⓐ	⚒	⑥	Ⓐ	⚒	⚒	⚒	⚒	⚒
0	**London** Waterloo **106** d.	⚒	...	...	...	...	...	...	...	0635	0635	0710	0710	0750	0820	0850	0920	...	1020	1050	...	1120	1150j	1220	1250j	1320
39	Woking **106** d.		...	...	...	...	...	...	...	0702	0702	0736	0736	0817	0846	0916	0946	...	1046	1116	...	1146	1216j	1246	1316j	1346
77	Basingstoke **106** d.		...	...	...	...	...	...	...	0723	0724	0759	0800	0838	0906	0938	1008	1038	1108	1138	1137	1208	1238	1308	1338	1407
107	Andover d.		...	...	...	...	...	...	...	0745	0747	0822	0822	0900	0924	1000	1026	1100	1126	1200	1159	1226	1300	1325	1400	1424
134	**Salisbury** a.		...	...	...	...	...	...	...	0805	0806	0842	0843	0920	0943	1020	1043	1119	1144	1220	1218	1243	1320	1344	1420	1443
134	**Salisbury** **140** d.		...	...	...	0610	0615	0738	0747	0813	0808	0847	0847	0924	0947	...	1047	1124	1147	▬	1222	1247	...	1347	▬	1447
169	Gillingham d.		...	0551	...	0642	0642	0811	0814	0900b	0837	0917	0917	|	1017	...	1117	|	1217	...	|	1317	...	1417	...	1517
190	Sherborne d.		...	0606	...	0657	0657	0826	0829	0915	...	0932	0932	◧	1032	...	1132	◧	1232	...	◧	1332	...	1432	...	1532
197	**Yeovil** Junction a.		...	0612	...	0703	0703	0832	0835	0920	...	0938	0938	|	1038	...	1138	1300g	1238	Ⓐ	1400g	1338	...	1438	Ⓐ	1538
197	**Yeovil** Junction **139** d.		...	0615	0615	0707	0707	0839	0839	...	...	0939	0942	|	1039	...	1139	|	1239	1317	|	1339	...	1439	1451	1539
200	**Yeovil** Pen Mill **139** a.		...	|	|	|	|	|	|	...	...	|	|	1038	|	...	|	1253	|	1322	1352	|	...	|	1456	|
211	Crewkerne d.		...	0625	0624	0716	0716	0849	0849	...	...	0949	0951	...	1049	...	1149	...	1249	...	...	1349	...	1449	...	1549
233	Axminster d.		0550	0657a	0657a	0737	0738	0903	0903	...	...	1003	1006	...	1103	...	1203	...	1303	...	...	1403	...	1503	...	1603
249	Honiton d.		0604	0712	0712	0752	0754t	0916	0916	...	...	1016	1018	...	1116	...	1216	...	1316	...	...	1416	...	1515	...	1616
277	**Exeter** St Davids △ a.		0632	0745	0743	0822	0823	0945	0943	...	...	1042	1043	...	1143	...	1242	...	1342	...	...	1442	...	1543	...	1643

	Ⓐ	⚒	⚒	Ⓐ	⑥	Ⓐ	⑥	Ⓐ	Ⓐ W	Ⓐ	⑥	Ⓐ	⑥	⑥	Ⓐ	Ⓐ	⑥	Ⓐ	⑥	Ⓐ	Ⓐ	⑥	Ⓐ	Ⓐ	⑥	⑥
London Waterloo **106** d.	...	1420	1450j	1520	1520	...	1620	1620	1650	1723	1720	1753	1750	1820	1823	...	1920	1920	2020	2020	2120	2120	...	2220	2220	2339
Woking **106** d.	...	1446	1516j	1546	1546	...	1646	1646u	|	|	1746	|	1816	1846	|	...	1946	1946u	2046	2046	2146	2146	...	2246	2247	0008
Basingstoke **106** d.	1438	1508	1537	1608	1608	1638	1708	1707	1738	1807	1808	1838	1838	1908	1907	1939	2008	2007	2108	2107	2207	2208	2237	2307	2308	0029
Andover d.	1500	1526	1600	1627	1626	1700	1726	1730	1800	1830	1826	1900	1900	1926	1930	2001	2026	2030	2126	2129	2229	2230	2300	2329	2330	0051
Salisbury a.	1520	1545	1620	1644	1642	1721	1742	1750	1821	1850	1843	1920	1920	1943	1950	2021	2045	2050	2144	2149	2249	2249	2322	2349	2350	0111
Salisbury **140** d.	1525	1547	...	1647	1647	1723	1747	1754	1823	1854	1847	1924	1927	1947	1954	2024	2047	2054	2148	2151	...	2255	...	2351	...	...
Gillingham d.	1548	1617	...	1717	1717	1752t	1817	1819	1852t	1920	1919	1954t	|	2017	2020	2051	2117	2119	2217	2218	...	2319s	...	0015s	...	...
Sherborne d.	...	1632	...	1732	1732	1807	1832	1834	1907	1935	1934	2009	◧	2032	2035	2106	2132	2134	2232	2233	...	2334s	...	0030s	...	...
Yeovil Junction a.	...	1638	...	1738	1738	1813	1838	1840	1912	1940	1939	2014	2045g	2038	2040	2112	2138	2139	2238	2239	...	2340	...	0036	...	...
Yeovil Junction **139** d.	...	1639	...	1739	1739	...	1839	1841	1917	1941	1941	2019	|	2039	2041	2117	2139	2142	2239	2240	...	...	...	...	...	...
Yeovil Pen Mill **139** a.	...	|	...	|	|	...	|	|	1924	|	|	2026	2037	|	|	2124	|	|	|	|	...	...	...	...	...	...
Crewkerne d.	...	1649	...	1749	1749	...	1849	1850	...	1951	1950	...	...	2049	2051	...	2149	2152	2249	2250	...	...	...	...	...	...
Axminster d.	...	1703	...	1804	1803	...	1903	1905	...	2005	2005	...	...	2103	2105	...	2203	2206	2303	2305	...	...	...	...	...	...
Honiton d.	...	1716	...	1816	1816	...	1916	1918	...	2017	2016	...	...	2117	2117	...	2217	2218	2315	2338r	...	...	...	...	...	...
Exeter St Davids △ a.	...	1744	...	1849	1841	...	1942	1944	...	2042	2042	...	...	2142	2143	...	2245	2244	...	0005	...	...	...	...	...	...

	①–④	⑤		⑦	⑦	⑦	⑦	⑦	⑦	⑦	⑦	⑦	⑦	⑦	⑦	⑦	⑦	⑦	⑦	⑦	⑦	⑦	⑦	⑦e	⑦	⑦
London Waterloo **106** d.	2340	2340	⑦	...	...	...	0815	0915	1015	1115	1215	...	1315	1415	...	1520	1620	1720	1745	1820	1845	1920	2020	2120	2220	2335
Woking **106** d.	0009	0009		...	...	...	0846	0946	1046	1146	1246	...	1345	1446	...	1546	1646	1746	1813	1846	1913	1946	2046	2146	2246	0008
Basingstoke **106** d.	0029	0029		...	0804	...	0907	1007	1107	1207	1307	1331	1407	1507	1531	1607	1707	1807	1834	1907	1934	2007	2107	2207	2307	0040
Andover d.	0051	0051		...	0826	...	0924	1026	1125	1224	1325	1354	1424	1524	1553	1625	1724	1825	1856	1925	1956	2025	2126	2224	2329	0103
Salisbury a.	0111	0111		...	0846	...	0941	1043	1142	1242	1343	1414	1442	1540	1613	1646	1742	1842	1917	1943	2017	2042	2143	2242	2348	0122
Salisbury **140** d.	...	0114		0654	0847	...	0947	1047	1147	1247	1347	1419	1447	1547	1614	1647	1747	1847	...	1947	...	2047	2147	2247	...	...
Gillingham d.	...	0137s		0717	0917	...	1018	1117	1217	1317	1417	1451c	1517	1617	1643	1717	1817	1917	...	2017	...	2117	2218	2318	...	...
Sherborne d.	...	0153s		0732	0932	...	1033	1132	1232	1332	1432	1506	1532	1632	...	1732	1832	1932	...	2032	...	2132	2233	2333	...	...
Yeovil Junction a.	...	0159		0738	0938	...	1038	1138	1238	1338	1438	1511	1538	1638	...	1738	1838	1938	...	2038	...	2138	2238	2338	...	...
Yeovil Junction **139** d.	...	...		0739	0939	0946	1039	1139	1239	1339	1439	1516	1539	1639	...	1739	1839	1940	...	2039	...	2139	...	2339	...	...
Yeovil Pen Mill **139** a.	...	...		|	|	0951	|	|	|	|	|	1521	|	|	...	|	|	|	...	|	...	|	...	|	...	...
Crewkerne d.	...	...		0749	0949	...	1049	1149	1249	1349	1449	...	1549	1649	...	1749	1849	1950	...	2049	...	2149	...	2349	...	...
Axminster d.	...	...		0804	1003	...	1103	1203	1303	1403	1503	...	1603	1703	...	1803	1903	2004	...	2103	...	2204	...	0009	...	...
Honiton d.	...	...		0817	1016	...	1116	1216	1316	1416	1516	...	1616	1716	...	1816	1916	2017	...	2117	...	2217	...	0020s	...	...
Exeter St Davids △ a.	...	...		0847	1044	...	1142	1243	1343	1442	1542	...	1642	1746	...	1842	1942	2043	...	2143	...	2244	...	0047	...	...

		Ⓐ	Ⓐ	Ⓐ	⑥	⑥	Ⓐ	Ⓐ	Ⓐ	⑥	Ⓐ	⑥C	Ⓐ	⑥	Ⓐ	⚒	⑥	⚒	⚒	Ⓐ	⚒E	⚒	⚒	Ⓐ	⚒	Ⓐ
Exeter St Davids ▽ d.	⚒	...	...	0510	0510	...	...	...	...	...	0640	0640	0725	0725	...	0823	...	0925	...	...	1025	...	1125	...	1225	...
Honiton d.		...	...	0541	0541	0620	0620	...	...	...	0712	0713	0752	0755	...	0855	...	0955	...	...	1055	...	1155	...	1255	...
Axminster d.		...	...	0553	0552	0631	0631	...	...	...	0724	0724	0804	0806	...	0906	...	1006	...	...	1106	...	1206	...	1306	...
Crewkerne d.		...	...	0606	0605	0644	0644	...	...	...	0737	0737	0817	0819	...	0919	...	1019	...	...	1119	...	1219	...	1319	...
Yeovil Pen Mill **139** d.		...	0541	|	|	|	|	0655	0711	...	|	|	|	|	...	|	...	|	...	1044	|	...	|	1255	|	1324
Yeovil Junction **139** a.		..	0546	0615	0614	0653	0653	|	0716	...	0745	0746	0825	0828	...	0929	...	1028	...	|	1128	...	1228	1300	1328	|
Yeovil Junction d.		0514	0550	0620	0620	0654	0654	|	0720	...	0750	0753	0829	0829	...	0929	0953	1029	...	|	1129	...	1229	▬	1329	1317f
Sherborne d.		0520	0556	0626	0626	0700	0700	◧	0726	...	0756	0759	0835	0835	...	0935	0959	1035	...	◧	1135	...	1235	...	1335	◧
Gillingham d.		0536	0612	0642	0642	0717	0716	|	0742	...	0812	0817	0851	0851	0918	0951	1017	1051	...	|	1151	...	1251	...	1351	|
Salisbury **140** a.		0601	0639	0707	0707	0742	0741	0812	0808	...	0838	0842	0917	0916	0943	1017	1042	1116	...	1209	1217	...	1317	⚒	1417	1443
Salisbury d.		0606	0645	0715	0721	0746	0745	0815	0815	0821	0846	0847	0921	0921	0947	1021	1047	1121	1147	1221	1221	1247	1321	1347	1421	1447
Andover d.		0626	0705	0735	0738	0806	0805	0835	0835	0838	0906	0906	0938	0938	1006	1038	1106	1138	1206	1238	1238	1306	1338	1406	1438	1506
Basingstoke **106** d.		0651	0730	0759	0758	0830	0828	0859	0859	0857	0928	0930	0957	0957	1029	1057	1130	1157	1230	1257	1257	1330	1357	1430	1457	1530
Woking **106** d.		|	|	|	0818	0850	...	0919	0919	0916	...	0950	1017	1016	...	1116	1150	1216	1250j	1316	1316	1350j	1416	1450j	1516	1551
London Waterloo **106** a.		0736	0814	0844	0849	0919	...	0951	0951	0949	...	1019	1049	1049	...	1149	1219	1249	1319j	1349	1349	1419j	1449	1519j	1549	1618

	Ⓐ	⚒	⚒	Ⓐ	⚒	⑥	Ⓐ	⚒	⚒	⑥	Ⓐ	⚒	⑥	Ⓐ	Ⓐ	Ⓐ	⑥	Ⓐ	⑥	Ⓐ	⑥	Ⓐ	⑥	Ⓐ	⑥	Ⓐ
Exeter St Davids ▽ d.	...	1325	...	...	1425	...	...	1525	...	1625	1625	...	1725	1725	1748	1825	1825	...	...	1925	1925	...	...	2025	2025	...
Honiton d.	...	1355	...	...	1455	...	...	1555	...	1655	1656	...	1756	1756	1818	1856	1855	...	...	1955	1955	...	...	2055	2056	...
Axminster d.	...	1406	...	...	1506	...	...	1606	...	1706	1707	...	1808	1808	1828	1908	1906	...	...	2006	2006	...	...	2106	2108	...
Crewkerne d.	...	1419	...	...	1519	...	...	1619	...	1719	1720	...	1821	1821	▬	1921	1919	...	...	2019	2019	...	...	2119	2121	...
Yeovil Pen Mill **139** d.	1354	|	...	1500	|	...	...	|	...	|	|	...	|	|	...	|	|	...	...	|	|	2030	2039	|	|	2130
Yeovil Junction **139** a.	1400	1428	...	|	1528	...	...	1628	...	1728	1729	...	1829	1829	...	1929	1928	...	...	2028	2028	2035	2045	2128	2129	2135
Yeovil Junction d.	▬	1429	...	1451f	1529	...	...	1629	...	1729	1730	...	1830	1830	...	1930	1929	...	...	2029	2029	▬	...	2129	2130	...
Sherborne d.	...	1435	...	◧	1535	...	...	1635	...	1735	1736	...	1837	1837	...	1937	1935	...	...	2035	2035	...	...	2135	2137	...
Gillingham d.	...	1451	...	|	1551	...	1618	1651	...	1751	1752	...	1852	1852	...	1952	1951	...	...	2051	2051	...	...	2151	2152	...
Salisbury **140** a.	⑥	1516	...	1612	1616	...	1643	1716	...	1816	1822	...	1918	1922	Ⓐ	2022	2016	...	...	2121	2116	Ⓐ	...	2221	2218	...
Salisbury d.	1447	1521	1547	1621	1621	1647	1647	1720	1747	1821	1826	1847	1921	1924	1947	2023	2026	2047	2052	2125	2126	2150	...	2225	2226	...
Andover d.	1506	1538	1606	1638	1638	1706	1706	1737	1806	1838	1843	1906	1942	1947c	2006	2041	2045	2106	2112	2142	2145	2209	...	2244	2245	...
Basingstoke **106** d.	1530	1557	1630	1657	1657	1730	1728	1757	1828	1857	1901	1929	2010	2011	2029	2059	2111	2129	2130	2200	2209	2233	...	2308	2309	...
Woking **106** d.	1551	1616	1650	1716	1716	1750	...	1816	1850j	1916	1921	1950j	2036t	2032	...	2118	2136t	...	2150	2219	2228	...	...	2327	2329	...
London Waterloo **106** a.	1619	1649	1719	1751	1751	1819	...	1849	1919j	1949	1949	2019j	2104	2104	...	2149	2204	...	2219	2249	2258	...	...	2356	2359	...

	Ⓐ	Ⓐ	⑥	Ⓐ	⑥	Ⓐ		⑦	⑦	⑦	⑦	⑦		⑦	⑦	⑦	⑦	⑦	⑦	⑦	⑦	⑦	⑦	⑦	⑦
Exeter St Davids ▽ d.	...	2125	2125	2225	2300	2306	⑦	...	...	0824	...	0925		1425	...	1525	...	1625	1725	1825	1925	2025	2125	2225	2313
Honiton d.	...	2156	2156	2257	2332	2337		...	...	0856	...	0955	and	1455	...	1555	...	1655	1755	1855	1955	2056	2156	2258	2340s
Axminster d.	...	2208	2208	2308	2343	2348		...	...	0907	...	1006	at	1506	...	1606	...	1706	1806	1906	2006	2108	2208	2309	2352s
Crewkerne d.	...	2221	2221	2321	2356	0001		...	...	0920	...	1019	the	1519	...	1619	...	1719	1819	1919	2019	2121	2221	2322	0008s
Yeovil Pen Mill **139** d.	2152	|	|	|	|	|		...	...	|	0953	|	same	|	1543	|	...	|	|	|	|	|	|	|	|
Yeovil Junction **139** a.	|	2229	2229	2330	0005	0009		...	...	0929	|	1028	minutes	1528	1548	1628	...	1728	1828	1928	2028	2129	2229	2331	0017
Yeovil Junction d.	2145f	2230	2230	2331	0006	...		0729	0829	0930	0945f	1029	past	1529	1553	1629	...	1729	1829	1929	2029	2130	2230	2333	...
Sherborne d.	◧	2236	2237	|	|	...		0735	0835	0936	◧	1035	each	1535	1559	1635	...	1735	1835	1935	2035	2137	2237	|	...
Gillingham d.	|	2252	2252	|	|	...		0751	0851	0952	|	1051	hour	1551	1618	1651	1717	1751	1851	1951	2051	2152	2252	|	...
Salisbury **140** a.	2342	2319	2323	0017	0041	...		0816	0916	1016	1112	1116	until	1616	1643	1716	1742	1816	1916	2016	2116	2217	2317	0020	...
Salisbury d.	...	...	...	...	...	...		0827	0927	1027	1127	1127		1627	1644	1727	1744	1827	1927	2021	2121	2227	...	...	...
Andover d.	...	...	...	...	...	...		0845	0945	1045	1145	1145		1645	1704	1745	1803	1845	1945	2040	2140	2246	...	...	...
Basingstoke **106** d.	...	...	...	...	...	...		0904	1004	1104	1204	1204		1704	1728	1804	1827	1904	2004	2104	2204	2310	...	...	...
Woking **106** d.	...	...	...	...	...	...		0924	1025	1124	1224	1224		1724	|	1824	|	1924	2024	2124	2224	2330	...	...	...
London Waterloo **106** a.	...	...	...	...	...	...		1000	1057	1157	1254	1254		1754	1819	1854	1917	1954	2054	2154	2254	2358	...	...	...

☛ Additional services **London** Waterloo - **Salisbury** and v.v.:
From **London** Waterloo: on Ⓐ at 0850; on ⑥ at 0750, 0950, 1350, 1550, 1650, 1850, 1950, 2050, 2250; on ⑦ at 1945, 2045.
From **Salisbury**: on Ⓐ at 0510, 0543; on ⑥ at 0515, 0547, 0620, 0646, 0947; on ⑦ at 0647, 0727, 1844.

C – Conveys 🚂 Castle Cary - London (Tables **139**/**140**).
E – On ⑥ conveys 🚂 Frome - Salisbury - London (Tables **139** and **140**).
F – To Frome (Tables **139** and **140**).
W – To Westbury (Table **139**).

a – Arrives 13 minutes earlier.
b – Arrives 0842.
c – Arrives 7–8 minutes earlier.
e – Does not call at Exeter Central.
f – Calls at Yeovil Junction before Yeovil Pen Mill.
g – Calls at Yeovil Pen Mill before Yeovil Junction.
j – ⑥ only.
r – Arrives 2316.
s – Calls to set down only.

t – Arrives 5 minutes earlier.
u – Calls to pick up only.
◧ – Via Westbury (Tables **139** and **140**).
△ – Trains to Exeter St Davids also call at **Exeter Central** 5–6 minutes earlier.
▽ – Trains from Exeter St Davids also call at **Exeter Central** 4–5 minutes later.

110 LONDON - EXETER - PAIGNTON and PLYMOUTH GW

km		Ⓐ 2★	Ⓐ 2★	Ⓐ 🍷★	Ⓐ 2	Ⓐ 🍷	Ⓐ2 ★B	Ⓐ 2★	Ⓐ 🍷★	Ⓐ 🍷	Ⓐ 🍷D	Ⓐ 🍷	Ⓐ2 ★D	Ⓐ 🍷★	Ⓐ 🍷	Ⓐ 🍷	Ⓐ 🍷	Ⓐ ★D	Ⓐ 🍷★	Ⓐ 🍷	Ⓐ 🍴	Ⓐ 2D	Ⓐ 🍷	Ⓐ2 ★D	Ⓐ 🍷★	Ⓐ 🍷	Ⓐ 🍷
0	**London** Padd 130/1/2/3/4 d.	...	...	...	...	0637	...	...	0704	0804	★	0904	...	0937	1004	1035	1104	...	1204	1233	1304	...	1404	...	1436	1504	1604
58	**Reading** 130/1/2/3/4 d.	...	...	...	...	0703	...	...	0730	0829	...	0929	...	1002	1029t	1101	1129	...	1229t	1301	1329t	...	1429t	...	1502	1529t	1629t
85	Newbury d.	...	...	...	...	|	...	...	0745	|	...	|	...	1017	|	1116	|	...	|	1316	|	...	|	...	1517	|	|
154	Westbury 140 d.	...	...	...	...	|	...	...	0822	|	...	|	...	1055	|	1156	|	...	|	1356	|	...	|	...	1554	|	|
186	Castle Cary 140 d.	...	...	...	...	|	...	...	0842	|	...	|	...	1115	|	1217	|	...	|	1416	|	...	|	...	1614	|	1728
	Bristol T M 115/6 132 d.	...	0540	...	0650	|	0749	0752	|	|	0856	|	0956	|	|	|	|	1155	|	|	|	1355	|	1455	|	|	|
230	Taunton 115 116 d.	...	0622	...	0737	0818	0826	0857	0903	0945	0957	1048	1056	1137	1146	1239	1247	1255	1346	1438	1445	1456	1547	1555	1635	1649	1749
253	Tiverton Parkway 116 d.	...	0635	...	0749	|	0838	|	0916	|	1009	1100	1108	1149	1158	|	1259	1307	|	|	1458	1508	1559	1606	|	1702	1802
279	**Exeter** St Davids 116 a.	...	0650	...	0804	0841	0852	0924	0929	1007	1023	1114	1123	1204	1211	1307	1313	1322	1409	1507	1512	1523	1612	1621	1659	1715	1815
279	**Exeter** St Davids 111 116 d.	0625	0655	0727	0809	0845	0855	0925	0931	1012	1025	1116	1125	1207	1214	...	1315	1325	1412	...	1513	1525	1615	1628	1701	1717	1820
311	Newton Abbot 111 116 d.	0651	0724	0751	0829	|	0921	0951	0958	1032	1051	1136	1151	1232	1236	...	1335	1351	1432	...	1534	1546	1635	1653	1726	1738	1841
321	Torquay 111 116 d.	|	|	|	|	|	|	|	1011	|	|	|	|	1245	|	...	|	|	|	...	|	|	|	|	1739	|	|
324	**Paignton** 111 116 a.	|	|	|	|	|	|	|	1016	|	|	|	|	1250	|	...	|	|	|	...	|	|	|	|	1744	|	|
325	Totnes 116 d.	0704	0736	0802	0841	|	0934	1004	...	1044	1104	1148	1204	...	1248	...	1347	1403	1444	...	1545	1559	1647	1707	...	1749	1852
363	**Plymouth** 116 a.	0736	0805	0831	0910	0936	1002	1033	...	1109	1133	1214	1232	...	1313	...	1413	1432	1509	...	1612	1629	1712	1735	...	1817	1920
	Newquay 112 a.	|	|	...	|	|	|	|	...	|	|	...	|	...	|	...	...	|	|	...	...	|	|	|	...	|	|
	Penzance 112 a.	0940	1010	...	1110	1140	1212	1240	...	1307	1340	...	1440	...	1507	...	...	1642	1708	...	...	1841	1923	1940	...	2010	2120

	Ⓐ 🍷	Ⓐ 🍷	Ⓐ 🍷★	Ⓐ 🍷	Ⓐ 2D	Ⓐ 🍷	①–④ 🍴	⑤ 🍴	Ⓐ2 ★D	Ⓐ 🍷★	Ⓐ 🍷	Ⓐ 2	Ⓐ 2	Ⓐ 🍷	Ⓐ A	⑥ 2★	⑥ 2	⑥ ★	⑥ 2★	⑥ 2★	⑥ 🍷	⑥ 2★	⑥ 🍷	⑥2 ★D	⑥ 🍷	⑥ 🍷	⑥ ★D
London Padd 130/1/2/3/4 d.	1636	1704	1736	1804	...	1836	1904	1904	...	2003	2104	...	...	2202	2345	...	...	...	...	...	...	...	0804	...	0835	0904	...
Reading 130/1/2/3/4 d.	1702	1729t	1803	1829t	...	1901	1929	1929t	...	2029	2129	...	...	2227	0049u	...	...	...	...	...	...	...	0829	...	0902	0930	...
Newbury d.	1717	|	1819	1844	...	1916	|	|	...	2044	2144	...	...	|	|	...	...	...	...	...	...	...	|	...	0917	|	...
Westbury 140 d.	1757	|	1856	|	...	1959	|	|	...	2121	2222	...	...	|	|	...	...	...	...	...	...	...	|	...	0957	|	...
Castle Cary 140 d.	1817	|	1916	|	...	2019	|	|	...	2141	2242	...	...	|	|	...	...	...	...	...	...	...	|	...	1017	1027	...
Bristol T M 115/6 132 d.	|	|	|	|	1857	|	|	|	1953	|	|	2200	2305	2348	|	...	0520	0537	...	0640	0742	0755	|	0855	|	|	0955
Taunton 115 116 d.	1838	1848	1938	1949	2001	2041	2049	2049	2058	2202	2303	2314	0009s	0044s	0237	...	0615	0627	...	0730	0814	0859	0945	0952	1039	1048	1055
Tiverton Parkway 116 d.	|	1901	1950	|	2013	2053	2101	2101	2110	2214	2316	2329	0024s	0057s	|	...	|	0639	...	0742	|	|	|	1004	1052	|	1107
Exeter St Davids 116 a.	1902	1915	2004	2012	2029	2109	2115	2115	2124	2228	2330	2347	0040	0112s	0307	...	0645	0653	...	0756	0837	0924	1009	1018	1107	1110	1122
Exeter St Davids 111 116 d.	1911	1920	2006	2014	2041	2111	2118	2118	2138	2230	2335	...	...	|	0411	0628	...	0655	0722	0800	0845	0926	1011	1025	...	1114	1125
Newton Abbot 111 116 d.	1933	1943	2044	2034	2101	2131	2139	2139	2204	2255	2355	...	...	0133s	0433	0654	...	0724	0749	0826	0905	0952	1032	1051	...	1135	1151
Torquay 111 116 d.	|	|	2111	|	|	|	|	|	|	|	|	...	...	|	|	|	...	|	|	|	|	|	|	|	...	|	|
Paignton 111 116 a.	|	|	2125	|	|	|	|	|	|	|	|	...	...	|	|	|	...	|	|	|	|	|	|	|	...	|	|
Totnes 116 d.	1944	1954	...	2046	2113	2143	2151	2151	2217	2307	0006	...	...	|	|	0707	...	0736	0801	0838	0917	1005	1044	1104	...	1147	1203
Plymouth 116 a.	2013	2020	...	2112	2143	2209	2217	2217	2246	2336	0033	...	...	0210	0511	0737	...	0804	0831	0907	0943	1034	1110	1132	...	1213	1232
Newquay 112 a.	...	|	...	|	|	...	|	|	...	...	...	...	...	...	|	|	...	|	|	|	|	|	|	|	...	...	|
Penzance 112 a.	...	2224	...	2259	2340	...	*0035*	0035	...	...	...	...	...	...	0754	0935	...	1012	1040	1114	1141	1240	1308	1340	...	...	1440

	⑥ 🍷	⑥ 🍷★	⑥ 🍷	⑥2 ★D	⑥ 🍷	⑥ 🍷	⑥ 🍷	⑥ ★D	⑥ 🍷	⑥2 ★D	⑥ 🍷★	⑥ 🍷	⑥2 ★D	⑥ 🍷	⑥ 🍷★	⑥ 🍷	⑥ 🍷	⑥2 ★D	⑥ 🍷★	⑥ 🍷★	⑥ 2D	⑥ 🍷	⑦ 2★	⑦ 2★	⑦ 🍷	⑦ 🍷	⑦ 🍷
London Padd 130/1/2/3/4 d.	1004	1035	1104	...	1204	1235	1304	...	1404	...	1435	1504	...	1604	1636	1704	1804	...	1904	2004	...	2032	...	...	0751	0813	0851
Reading 130/1/2/3/4 d.	1030	1101	1130	...	1230	1301	1330	...	1429	...	1501	1529	...	1629	1701	1730	1829	...	1929	2029	...	2057	...	...	0821	0838	0918
Newbury d.	|	1116	|	...	|	1316	|	...	|	...	1516	|	...	|	1716	|	|	...	1944	2044	...	|	...	...	0839	|	|
Westbury 140 d.	|	1153	|	...	|	1356	|	...	|	...	1553	|	...	|	1753	|	|	...	2024	2121	...	|	...	...	0917	|	1003
Castle Cary 140 d.	|	1213	|	...	|	1419	|	...	|	...	1613	|	...	1728	1813	|	|	...	2044	2141	...	|	...	...	0937	|	1023
Bristol T M 115/6 132 d.	|	|	|	1155	|	|	|	1354	|	1455	|	|	1555	|	|	|	|	1853	|	|	2152	2208	...	0800	|	0949	|
Taunton 115 116 d.	1147	1235	1245	1300	1347	1441	1449	1456	1547	1555	1635	1647	1655	1750	1834	1847	1945	1953	2106	2203	2257	2307	...	0856	0958	1026	1044
Tiverton Parkway 116 d.	1159	|	1257	1313	|	|	1501	1508	1559	1607	|	1659	1707	1802	1847	1859	1957	2005	2118	2215	2311	2320	...	0909	1010	1039	|
Exeter St Davids 116 a.	1213	1258	1311	1330	1410	1506	1514	1523	1613	1623	1657	1713	1723	1816	1900	1914	2010	2019	2132	2229	2326	2335	...	0923	1024	1056	1108
Exeter St Davids 111 116 d.	1216	1301	1314	1332	1413	...	1517	1526	1615	1625	1700	1715	1725	1820	1902	1917	2013	2027	2136	2232	...	...	0838	0924	1026	...	1110
Newton Abbot 111 116 d.	1236	1331	1334	1400	1433	...	1537	1552	1635	1651	1726	1736	1753	1841	1928	1938	2034	2054	2201	2257	...	...	0903	0950	1046	...	1130
Torquay 111 116 d.	|	1342	|	|	|	...	|	|	|	|	|	|	|	|	1941	|	|	|	|	|	...	...	|	|	|	...	|
Paignton 111 116 a.	|	1347	|	|	|	...	|	|	|	|	|	|	|	|	1946	|	|	|	|	|	...	...	|	|	|	...	|
Totnes 116 d.	1248	...	1346	1412	1445	...	1549	1605	1647	1704	|	1748	1806	1853	...	1949	2046	2107	2213	2309	...	...	0915	1001	1058	...	1142
Plymouth 116 a.	1315	...	1412	1440	1511	...	1615	1633	1713	1732	1801	1814	1834	1922	...	2016	2112	2135	2239	2338	...	...	0945	1030	1124	...	1210
Newquay 112 a.	|	...	...	|	|	...	|	|	|	|	...	|	|	...	...	|	|	...	...	...	...	...	|	|	|	...	|
Penzance 112 a.	1509	...	...	1640	1709	...	1811	1841	1909	1940	...	2010	2041	...	...	2217	2315	...	...	...	...	...	1141	1231	1332	...	1406

	⑦ 2	⑦ 🍷	⑦ 🍷★	⑦ 🍷	⑦2 ★D	⑦ 🍷	⑦ 2D	⑦ 🍷★	⑦ 🍷	⑦2 ★D	⑦ 🍷	⑦2 ★D	⑦ 🍷	⑦ 🍷	⑦2 ★D	⑦ 🍷	⑦ 2★	⑦ 🍷	⑦ 🍷	⑦ 🍷★	⑦ 2	⑦ 🍷	⑦ 🍷	⑦ 🍷★	⑦ 🍷	⑦ 🍷★	⑦ 🍷	⑦ A
London Padd 130/1/2/3/4 d.	...	1003	1036	1103	...	1203	...	1236	1303	...	1403	...	1436	1503	...	1603	...	1637	1703	1630	...	1803	1800	1836	1903	2003	2103	2350
Reading 130/1/2/3/4 d.	...	1028	1101	1128	...	1228	...	1301	1328	...	1428	...	1501	1528	...	1628	...	1701	1728	1655	...	1828	1825	1901	1928	2028	2128	0051
Newbury d.	...	|	1116	|	...	|	...	1316	|	...	|	...	1516	|	...	|	...	1717	|	|	...	|	|	1916	|	2044	|	|
Westbury 140 d.	...	|	1156	|	...	|	...	1355	|	...	|	...	1556	|	...	|	...	1757	|	|	...	|	|	1955	|	2122	|	|
Castle Cary 140 d.	...	|	1216	|	...	|	...	1415	|	...	|	...	1616	|	...	|	...	1817	|	|	...	|	|	2015	|	2142	|	|
Bristol T M 115/6 132 d.	0955	|	|	|	1146	|	1254	|	|	1354	|	1454	|	|	1554	|	...	|	|	1810	1825	|	1937	|	|	|	|	|
Taunton 115 116 d.	1050	1144	1237	1245	1251	1343	1354	1436	1444	1453	1544	1552	1637	1645	1657	1743	...	1838	1846	1906	1932	1944	2009	2036	2045	2203	2242s	|
Tiverton Parkway 116 d.	1101	1156	|	1257	1304	1356	|	|	1457	1505	1556	|	|	1658	1708	1755	...	|	1858	|	|	1957	|	|	2058	2216	2255s	|
Exeter St Davids 116 a.	1116	1209	1300	1309	1318	1409	1423	1459	1509	1519	1609	1616	1701	1711	1723	1808	...	1901	1912	1929	1958	2011	2032	2100	2112	2230	2311	0323
Exeter St Davids 111 116 d.	1120	1213	1302	1313	1321	1412	...	1501	1516	1524	1613	1619	...	1714	1724	1811	1820	1903	1914	1931	...	2013	2034	2101	2114	2232	...	0436
Newton Abbot 111 116 d.	1139	1234	1327	1333	1347	1432	...	1530	1537	1550	1633	1647	...	1735	1753	1831	1846	1923	1934	1956	...	2033	2054	2127	2135	2257	...	0457
Torquay 111 116 a.	|	|	1338	|	|	|	...	1543	|	|	|	|	...	|	|	|	|	|	|	|	...	|	|	|	|	|	...	|
Paignton 111 116 a.	|	|	1344	|	|	|	...	1549	|	|	|	|	...	|	|	|	|	|	|	|	...	|	|	|	|	|	...	|
Totnes 116 a.	1151	1245	...	1345	1359	1444	...	...	1549	1602	1645	1659	...	1746	1805	1843	1858	1935	1946	2008	...	2045	2106	2138	2147	2309	...	|
Plymouth 116 a.	1220	1312	...	1412	1428	1510	...	...	1615	1630	1711	1727	...	1813	1833	1909	1926	2004	2012	2034	...	2111	2132	2207	2214	2335	...	0536
Newquay 112 a.	|	|	...	...	|	|	...	...	...	|	|	|	...	...	|	|	|	...	|	...	...	|	...	...	...	...	...	|
Penzance 112 a.	1429	1506	...	...	1628	1705	...	...	...	1832	1905	1934	...	...	2031	2103	2137	...	2206	...	...	2312	...	...	...	...	...	0754

A – THE NIGHT RIVIERA – Conveys 🛏 1, 2. cl and 💺2. See also note ‡ on next page.
B – From Gloucester (Table **138**).
D – From Cardiff (Table **115**).
f – Arrives 1046.
s – Stops to set down only.
t – Stops to pick up only on ⑤.
u – Stops to pick up only.
★ – Also calls at Dawlish (10–15 minutes after Exeter) and Teignmouth (15–18 minutes after Exeter).

111 *See also Tables 110 and 116* EXETER - PAIGNTON 2nd class GW

km		Ⓐ	⑥	⑥	Ⓐ	⑥	Ⓐ	Ⓐ	⑥	Ⓐ	⑥	⚒	Ⓐ	⑥	⚒	⚒	⑥	Ⓐ	Ⓐ	⑥	⚒	Ⓐ	⑥	⚒	⑥	Ⓐ
0	**Exeter** St Davids d.	0458	0500	0530	0534	0555	0558	0630	0635	0659	0659	0730	0800	0808	0832	0900	0930	0934	0959	1005	1028	1100	1100	1129	1201	1202
20	Dawlish d.	0519	0521	0546	0550	0618	0621	0653	0658	0722	0722	0758	0825	0829	0900	0913	1004	1004	1014	1027	1052	1113	1116	1152	1217	1230
24	Teignmouth d.	0524	0526	0551	0555	0623	0626	0658	0703	0727	0727	0803	0830	0834	0905	0918	1009	1009	1019	1032	1057	1118	1121	1157	1222	1235
32	Newton Abbot d.	0533	0534	0559	0603	0632	0635	0706	0712	0737	0735	0812	0838	0843	0913	0925	1017	1017	1035c	1042	1106	1126	1138r	1205	1230	1243
42	Torquay d.	0544	0545	0610	0614	0643	0646	0719	0723	0748	0747	0823	0849	0854	0924	0937	1029	1028	1046	1054	1118	1137	1150	1218	1243	1254
45	**Paignton** 🚂 a.	0550	0552	0616	0620	0650	0652	0726	0729	0754	0755	0830	0855	0900	0931	0945	1035	1034	1052	1100	1125	1143	1158	1225	1250	1300

	⑥	Ⓐ	Ⓐ	⑥	Ⓐ	⑥	Ⓐ	⑥	⚒	Ⓐ		⑥	Ⓐ	⑥	Ⓐ	⑥	Ⓐ	⑥	⚒	⚒	Ⓐ	⑥	Ⓐ	⑥	Ⓐ	⑥	Ⓐ
Exeter St Davids d.	1229	1231	1300	1306	1329	1336	1400	1406	1429	1500	...	1505	1529	1530	1558	1605	1631	1631	1703	1732	1800	1801	1831	1835	1901	1906	1930
Dawlish d.	1252	1254	1313	1329	1352	1403	1413	1428	1452	1513	...	1521	1552	1553	1619	1629	1702	1703	1730	1803	1835	1835	1851	1902	1935	1932	1950
Teignmouth d.	1257	1259	1318	1335	1357	1408	1418	1434	1457	1518	...	1526	1557	1558	1624	1635	1707	1708	1736	1808	1840	1840	1856	1907	1940	1937	1955
Newton Abbot d.	1306	1312t	1326	1343	1405	1417	1426	1443	1505	1526	...	1541j	1609t	1606	1631	1644	1715	1716	1744	1816	1848	1848	1904	1915	1948	1945	2010j
Torquay a.	1318	1323	1337	1355	1417	1428	1437	1454	1517	1537	...	1552	1620	1618	1644	1655	1726	1728	1756	1827	1900	1900	1917	1928	1959	1956	2021
Paignton 🚂 a.	1325	1329	1343	1402	1424	1435	1443	1500	1525	1543	...	1558	1626	1625	1650	1702	1731	1735	1802	1835	1909	1906	1924	1934	2005	2003	2027

	Ⓐ	⑥	Ⓐ	Ⓐ	⑥	Ⓐ	⑥	Ⓐ		⑦	⑦	⑦	⑦	⑦	⑦	⑦	⑦	⑦	⑦	⑦	⑦	⑦	⑦	⑦	⑦	⑦
Exeter St Davids d.	2002	2016	2031	2059	2136	2201	2232	2302	...	0827	0930	1030	1126	1230	1305	1329	1427	1505	1530	1628	1700	1729	1828	1935	2039	2132
Dawlish d.	2015	2046	2105	2133	2148	2224	2244	2325	...	0855	0958	1053	1153	1253	1329	1352	1450	1532	1553	1651	1715	1752	1851	1958	2106	2155
Teignmouth d.	2020	2051	2110	2138	2153	2229	2249	2330	...	0900	1003	1058	1158	1258	1334	1357	1455	1537	1558	1656	1720	1757	1856	2003	2111	2200
Newton Abbot d.	2027	2100	2117	2146	2200	2237	2256	2337	...	0907	1011	1105	1205	1305	1342	1404	1503	1544	1605	1703	1728	1804	1904	2011	2119	2207
Torquay a.	2040	2111	2129	2158	...	2249	...	2349	...	0919	1023	1117	1217	1317	1353	1416	1514	1556	1618	1715	1739	1816	1915	2022	2130	2219
Paignton 🚂 a.	2046	2117	2135	2204	...	2255	...	2355	...	0925	1029	1123	1223	1323	1400	1422	1520	1602	1624	1721	1745	1822	1921	2028	2136	2225

c – Arrives 1026.
j – Arrives 8 minutes earlier.
r – Arrives 1128.
t – Arrives 5–6 minutes earlier.
🚂 – Dartmouth Steam Railway (Paignton - Kingswear). ✆ 01803 555 872. www.dartmouthrailriver.co.uk

GW PLYMOUTH and PAIGNTON - EXETER - LONDON 110

km	Ⓐ	Ⓐ 🍷v	Ⓐ 🍷	Ⓐ D	Ⓐ 🍷	Ⓐ 🍷☆	Ⓐ 🍷	Ⓐ 🍷☆	Ⓐ2 D☆	Ⓐ 🍷	Ⓐ 🍷☆	Ⓐ2 D☆	Ⓐ 🍷	Ⓐ 2D	Ⓐ 🍷	Ⓐ 🍷☆	Ⓐ D	Ⓐ 🍷	Ⓐ 🍷	Ⓐ 🍷	Ⓐ 2D	Ⓐ 🍴	Ⓐ 🍷☆	Ⓐ 🍷	Ⓐ 🍷	Ⓐ2 D☆	Ⓐ 🍷
	Penzance 112 d.	...	...	...	...	...	0503	...	0540	0605	...	0640	0710	0740	0815	...	0850	0910	1020	...	1050	...	...	1215	...	1250	...
	Newquay 112 d.	...	...	...	...	...	|	...	|	|	...	|	|	|	|	...	|	|	|	...	|	...	...	|	...	|	...
0	**Plymouth** 116 d.	...	0454	...	0549	0534	0655	0640	0746	0815	0835	0850	0915	0937	1015	...	1051	1112	1215	...	1250	1316	...	1414	...	1448	1515
38	Totnes 116 d.	...	|	...	|	0602	|	0709	0814	0842	0903	0916	0942	1005	1042	...	1120	1139	1242	...	1319	1343	...	1441	...	1516	1542
	Paignton 111 116 d.	...	|	...	|	|	|	|	|	|	|	|	|	|	|	1055	|	|	|	...	|	|	1410	|	...	|	|
	Torquay 111 116 d.	...	|	...	|	|	|	|	|	|	|	|	|	|	|	1101	|	|	|	...	|	|	1416	|	...	|	|
52	Newton Abbot 111 116 d.	...	0530	...	0625	0615	0731	0721	0826	0854	0916	0929	0954	1018	1054	1113	1133	1151	1255	...	1331	1355	1427	1454	...	1528	1554
84	**Exeter** St Davids 111 116 a.	...	0548	...	0643	0639	0750	0746	0851	0913	0939	0953	1012	1038	1113	1136	1152	1212	1313	...	1351	1413	1450	1512	...	1552	1612
84	**Exeter** St Davids 116 d.	...	0552	0636	0646	0652	0752	0758	0852	0915	0943	0955	1015	1044	1115	1142	1154	1215	1315	1343	1353	1416	1454	1514	1542	1553	1615
110	Tiverton Parkway 116 d.	...	0606	0650	|	0706	|	0812	0906	0929	|	|	1029	1058	1129	|	|	1229	1330	1358	|	1430	|	1529	|	|	1629
133	Taunton 115 116 d.	...	0620	0704	0709	0719	0815	0825	0920	0942	1006	1019	1042	1111	1142	1205	1218	1242	1343	1411	1419	1443	1517	1541	1605	1617	1642
205	**Bristol** T M. 115/6 132 a.	0510	|	0816	|	|	|	|	1020	|	|	1117	|	1217	|	|	1316	|	|	|	1516	|	|	|	|	1719	|
	Castle Cary 140 a.	|	0639	...	|	0738	|	0844	...	|	1026	...	|	...	|	1225	...	|	|	1430	...	|	|	|	1624	...	|
	Westbury 140 a.	0549y	0700	...	|	0759	|	0909	...	|	1046	...	|	...	|	1247	...	|	|	1450	...	|	1553	|	1644	...	|
	Newbury a.	0644	0744	...	0813	0841	|	|	...	|	1123	...	|	...	|	1330	...	|	|	1531	...	|	|	|	1724	...	|
337	**Reading** 130/1/2/3/4 a.	0708	0802	...	0830	0857	0930	1002	...	1057	1138	...	1202	...	1258	1347	...	1402	1458	1547	...	1557	1643	1701	1742	...	1757
395	**London** Padd 130/1/2/3/4 a.	0736	0835	...	0901	0924	0955	1029	...	1129	1204	...	1227	...	1329	1416	...	1427	1529	1614	...	1629	1711	1729	1808	...	1824

	Ⓐ 🍷	Ⓐ 🍷	Ⓐ2 G☆	Ⓐ 🍴	Ⓐ 🍷	Ⓐ 2D	Ⓐ 🍷☆	Ⓐ 🍷	Ⓐ 2D	Ⓐ 2☆	Ⓐ 2☆	Ⓐ 2☆	Ⓐ 2☆	Ⓐ 2	Ⓐ A	⑥	⑥ D	⑥ 🍷	⑥ 🍷	⑥ 🍷	⑥ 🍷☆	⑥2 D☆	⑥ 🍷	⑥ 🍷☆	⑥2 D☆	⑥ 🍷	⑥ 2D	⑥ 🍷
Penzance 112 d.	1415	...	1550	1615	...	1650	...	1750	...	1815	...	1915	...	...	2145		...	...	...	...	...	0540	0612	...	0640	0710	...	0815
Newquay 112 d.	|	...	|	|	...	|	...	|	...	|	...	|	...	...	|		...	...	...	...	...	|	|	...	|	|	...	|
Plymouth 116 d.	1615	1650	1750	1816	...	1848	...	1950	...	2024	...	2125	2225	2315	2354		...	0558	...	0655	0640	0747	0814	...	0848	0914	...	1014
Totnes 116 d.	1642	1718	1819	1843	...	1917	...	2017	...	2052	...	2155	2255	2344	0022		...	0625	...	|	0710	0815	0841	...	0917	0941	...	1041
Paignton 111 116 d.	|	|	|	|	...	|	1905	|	...	|	2108	|	|	|	|		...	|	...	|	|	|	|	0855	|	|	...	|
Torquay 111 116 d.	|	|	|	|	...	|	1911	|	...	|	2113	|	|	|	|		...	|	...	|	|	|	|	0901	|	|	...	|
Newton Abbot 111 116 d.	1654	1731	1832	1855	...	1929	1921	2029	...	2106	2125	2208	2308	2357	0036		...	0637	...	0732	0723	0828	0854	0914	0929	0954	...	1054
Exeter St Davids 111 116 a.	1712	1749	1900	1915	...	1948	1953	2048	...	2133	2159	2237	2333	0020	0100		...	0656	...	0751	0756	0852	0913	0943	0953	1013	...	1113
Exeter St Davids 116 d.	1715	1751	1903	1917	1935	1950	1955	2050	2106	...	2200	2242	...	...	0107		0549	0700	0733	0752	0758	0855	0916	0945	0955	1016	1043	1116
Tiverton Parkway 116 d.	1729	1806	|	1932	1950	|	2010	2104	|	...	2217	2256	...	...	|		0604	0715	|	|	0812	|	0931	|	|	1031	|	1131
Taunton 115 116 d.	1742	1818	1927	1944	2003	2016	2023	2117	2132	...	2233	2310	...	...	0140		0616	0728	0758	0815	0825	0919	0944	1009	1019	1044	1108	1144
Bristol T M. 115/6 132 a.	|	|	2002	|	2057	2118	|	2150	2230	...	2316	0004	...	...	|		0719	|	0855	|	|	1015	|	|	1116	|	1218	|
Castle Cary 140 a.	|	1838	...	|	|	...	2042	|	...	...	...	...	...	...	|		...	0747	|	|	0844	...	|	1028	...	|	...	|
Westbury 140 a.	|	1858	...	|	|	...	2101	|	...	...	...	...	...	...	|		...	0808	|	|	0909	...	|	1048	...	|	...	|
Newbury a.	|	1935	...	|	|	...	2139	|	...	...	...	...	...	...	|		...	0847	|	0925	|	...	|	1127	...	|	...	|
Reading 130/1/2/3/4 a.	1857	1954	...	2100	2208	...	2200	2309	...	...	...	...	...	...	0400s		...	0903	1010	0943	1004	...	1101	1143	...	1159	...	1259
London Padd 130/1/2/3/4 a.	1924	2019	...	2129	2236	...	2229	2356	...	...	...	...	...	...	0507		...	0929	1036	1009	1029	...	1129	1209	...	1229	...	1329

	⑥ 🍷☆	⑥2 D☆	⑥ 🍷	⑥ 🍷	⑥ 🍷☆	⑥ D☆	⑥ 🍷	⑥ 🍷	⑥ 🍷☆	⑥2 D☆	⑥ 🍷	⑥2 D☆	⑥ 🍷	⑥ 🍷	⑥ 2☆	⑥ 🍷	⑥ D☆	⑥ 🍷	⑥ 2	⑥ 2☆	⑥ 2☆	⑦	⑦ 2	⑦ 🍷	⑦ 🍷☆	⑦ 2D	⑦ 🍷	⑦2 D☆
Penzance 112 d.	...	0852	0912	1015	...	1050	...	1218	...	1250	...	1350	1420	...	1550	1620	1650	1750	...	1815	...		...	...	...	...	...	...
Newquay 112 d.	...	|	|	|	...	|	...	|	...	|	...	|	|	...	|	|	|	|	...	|	...		...	...	...	...	...	...
Plymouth 116 d.	...	1049	1114	1214	...	1250	1314	1415	...	1448	1514	1548	1615	1650	1748	1816	1849	1950	...	2020	2150		...	...	0827	...	0912	0947
Totnes 116 d.	...	1118	1141	1241	...	1318	1341	1442	...	1517	1541	1615	1642	1719	1817	1843	1917	2017	...	2048	2219		...	...	0854	...	0939	1015
Paignton 111 116 d.	...	|	|	|	...	|	|	|	1456	|	|	|	|	|	|	|	|	|	...	|	|		...	...	|	...	|	|
Torquay 111 116 d.	...	|	|	|	...	|	|	|	1502	|	|	|	|	|	|	|	|	|	...	|	|		...	...	|	...	|	|
Newton Abbot 111 116 d.	...	1130	1154	1254	...	1331	1353	1454	1513	1530	1554	1628	1655	1731	1830	1856	1930	2029	...	2102	2232		...	...	0907	...	0952	1027
Exeter St Davids 111 116 a.	...	1154	1214	1313	...	1351	1412	1513	1541	1554	1613	1653	1715	1751	1854	1916	1954	2048	...	2130	2307		...	...	0931	...	1011	1051
Exeter St Davids 116 d.	1143	1155	1216	1316	1343	1352	1416	1516	1543	1556	1615	1655	1717	1755	1904	1918	1955	2051	2119	...	...		0759	0830	0933	0946	1012	1052
Tiverton Parkway 116 d.	|	|	1231	1331	|	1406	1431	1530	|	|	1630	|	1731	1811	1918	1932	2010	2105	2134	...	...		0814	0845	0947	1000	|	1106
Taunton 115 116 d.	1207	1220	1244	1344	1406	1420	1444	1543	1607	1620	1643	1720	1744	1825	1932	1945	2023	2119	2150	...	...		0827	0857	1000	1013	1034	1119
Bristol T M. 115/6 132 a.	|	1316	|	|	|	1516	|	|	|	1720	|	1816	|	|	2016	|	2125	2149	2247	...	...		0932	|	|	1108	|	1212
Castle Cary 140 a.	1226	...	|	|	1426	...	|	|	1626	...	|	...	|	1844	...	2004	...	|	...	...	...		...	0917	1019	...	|	...
Westbury 140 a.	1248	...	|	|	1446	...	|	|	1646	...	|	...	|	1907	...	2024	...	|	...	...	...		...	0936	1038	...	1111	...
Newbury a.	1329	...	|	|	1528	...	|	|	1728	...	|	...	|	1945	...	|	...	|	...	...	...		...	1018	1118	...	|	...
Reading 130/1/2/3/4 a.	1346	...	1359	1500	1546	...	1600	1658	1744	...	1758	...	1859	2002	...	2115	...	2311	...	...	...		...	1035	1134	...	1158	...
London Padd 130/1/2/3/4 a.	1410	...	1429	1529	1611	...	1629	1729	1809	...	1829	...	1929	2026	...	2139	...	2342	...	...	...		...	1059	1159	...	1224	...

	⑦ 🍷	⑦ 🍷☆	⑦2 D☆	⑦ 🍷	⑦ 🍷	⑦ 🍷	⑦2 D☆	⑦ 🍷	⑦ D☆	⑦ 🍷	⑦ 🍷☆	⑦ 2D	⑦ 🍷	⑦ 🍷	⑦ D☆	⑦ 🍷	⑦ 🍷	⑦ 🍷☆	⑦ 2☆	⑦ 🍷	⑦ 🍷☆	⑦ 🍷	⑦ 🍷☆	⑦ 2	⑦ 🍷	⑦ 🍷	⑦ 2☆	⑦ A
Penzance 112 d.	0815	...	0849	0918	1018	...	1050	...	1148	1218	...	...	...	...	1349	1418	...	...	1450	1518	...	1618	...	...	1750	...	...	2115
Newquay 112 d.	|	...	|	|	|	...	|	...	|	|	...	...	...	...	|	|	...	...	|	|	...	|	...	...	|	...	...	|
Plymouth 116 d.	1010	...	1047	1115	1215	...	1245	...	1345	1415	...	...	1456	1515	1545	1615	...	...	1645	1715	1745	1815	1915	...	1945	2015	2145	2320
Totnes 116 d.	1037	...	1115	1141	1241	...	1313	...	1414	1441	...	...	|	1541	1615	1641	...	...	1713	1741	1814	1841	1943	...	2012	2042	2213	2348
Paignton 111 116 d.	|	1036	|	|	|	...	|	...	|	|	1453	...	|	|	|	|	...	1652	|	|	|	|	|	...	|	|	|	|
Torquay 111 116 d.	|	1042	|	|	|	...	|	...	|	|	1459	...	|	|	|	|	...	1658	|	|	|	|	|	...	|	|	|	|
Newton Abbot 111 116 d.	1050	1055	1127	1154	1254	...	1325	...	1427	1454	1509	...	1532	1554	1627	1654	...	1710	1726	1754	1826	1854	1956	...	2025	2054	2225	0001
Exeter St Davids 111 116 a.	1109	1119	1155	1213	1313	...	1352	...	1452	1511	1533	...	1551	1613	1652	1711	...	1735	1758	1813	1850	1913	2020	...	2043	2113	2250	0023
Exeter St Davids 116 d.	1111	1121	1157	1215	1315	1333	1353	1413	1453	1515	1534	1543	1555	1615	1653	1715	1732	1737	...	1815	1852	1915	2021	2030	2048	2115	...	0058
Tiverton Parkway 116 d.	1125	|	|	1229	1329	|	|	1429	|	1529	|	1559	|	1629	1707	1730	|	|	...	1830	|	1929	2036	2045	2103	2129	...	|
Taunton 115 116 d.	1138	1149f	1220	1243	1342	1356	1417	1442	1516	1542	1558	1612	1620	1642	1720	1743	1757	1802	...	1842	1915	1942	2048	2106r	2116	2142	...	|
Bristol T M. 115/6 132 a.	|	|	1314	|	|	|	1511	|	1612	|	|	1711	1658	|	1815	|	1854	|	...	|	|	|	|	2210	|	2222	...	|
Castle Cary 140 a.	|	1208	...	|	|	1416	...	|	...	|	1619	...	|	|	...	|	|	1821	...	|	|	|	|	...	2135	|	...	|
Westbury 140 a.	|	1229	...	|	|	1435	...	|	...	|	1635	...	|	|	...	|	|	1841	...	|	1954	|	|	...	2155	|	...	|
Newbury a.	|	1310	...	|	|	1517	...	|	...	|	1720	...	|	|	...	|	|	1923	...	|	|	|	|	...	2234	|	...	|
Reading 130/1/2/3/4 a.	1253	1327	...	1358	1457	1535	...	1558	...	1658	1736	...	1806	1757	...	1858	2010	1939	...	1957	2041	2058	2204	...	2250	2339	...	0405s
London Padd 130/1/2/3/4 a.	1320	1353	...	1424	1524	1559	...	1624	...	1724	1805	...	1836	1824	...	1924	2039	2005	...	2024	2105	2123	2229	...	2333	0013	...	0503

A – THE NIGHT RIVIERA – Conveys 🛏 1, 2. cl and (2). See also note ‡.
D – To Cardiff (Table **115**).
G – To Gloucester (Table **138**).
f – Arrives 1144.
r – Arrives 2058.
s – Calls to set down only.
v – Via Trowbridge (Table **140**).
y – Departs 0559.
☆ – Also calls at Teignmouth (7 – 10 minutes after Newton Abbot) and Dawlish (12 – 15 minutes after Newton Abbot).
‡ – Passengers may occupy cabins at London Paddington from 2230 and at Penzance from 2045⑦/2115Ⓐ.

GW 2nd class PAIGNTON - EXETER 111

*See also Tables **110** and **116***

	⚒	②-⑥	Ⓐ	⑥	⑥	Ⓐ	⑥	Ⓐ	Ⓐ	⑥	⚒	⑥	Ⓐ	⑥	Ⓐ	⑥	Ⓐ	⑥	⑥	Ⓐ	Ⓐ	⑥	⑥	Ⓐ	⚒	⑥	Ⓐ
Paignton 🚂 d.		0001	0604	0610	0637	0639	0710	0719	0739	0750	0815	0840	0853	0855	0916	0916	0945	0948	1017	1024	1042	1055	1118	1120	1153	1218	1221
Torquay d.		0006	0609	0615	0642	0644	0715	0724	0744	0755	0820	0846	0858	0901	0921	0922	0950	0956	1023	1029	1047	1100	1124	1125	1559	1224	1226
Newton Abbot d.		0018	0634a	0628	0655	0656	0735c	0736	0756	0807	0832	0900	0910	0914	0933	0934	1009t	1011	1036	1041	1105t	1113	1137	1138	1212	1236	1238
Teignmouth d.		0025	0641	0635	0702	0703	0742	0743	0803	0814	0839	0907	0917	0922	0940	0942	1016	1018	1044	1048	1112	1120	1144	1145	1219	1244	1245
Dawlish d.		0030	0646	0640	0707	0708	0747	0748	0808	0819	0844	0912	0922	0927	0945	0947	1021	1024	1049	1053	1117	1125	1150	1150	1224	1249	1250
Exeter St Davids a.		0047	0711	0710	0736	0742	0812	0814	0841	0841	0910	0934	0950	0943	1010	1009	1047	1047	1110	1110	1147	1147	1210	1210	1248	1309	1310

	⑥	Ⓐ	⚒	⑥	Ⓐ	⚒	⑥	Ⓐ	⑥	Ⓐ	⑥	Ⓐ	Ⓐ	⑥	Ⓐ	⑥	⑥	Ⓐ	⑥	Ⓐ	⑥	Ⓐ	⚒	⑥	Ⓐ	⑥	Ⓐ
Paignton 🚂 d.	1253	1255	1318	1353	1355	1418	1441	1452	1518	1522	1539	1551	1616	1615	1640	1652	1714	1719	1739	1748	1818	1818	1850	1918	1920	1938	1944
Torquay d.	1259	1300	1324	1358	1400	1424	1446	1458	1524	1527	1544	1556	1621	1621	1645	1657	1720	1724	1744	1753	1824	1824	1855	1923	1925	1943	1949
Newton Abbot d.	1312	1312	1337	1411	1412	1437	1458	1512	1537	1539	1557	1611	1633	1634	1657	1710	1734	1736	1757	1805	1837	1840	1909	1936	1937	1955	2001
Teignmouth d.	1319	1319	1344	1418	1419	1444	1505	1519	1544	1546	1604	1618	1640	1641	1704	1717	1741	1743	1804	1812	1844	1847	1916	1943	1944	2002	2008
Dawlish d.	1324	1324	1349	1424	1424	1449	1510	1524	1550	1551	1609	1623	1645	1647	1709	1723	1746	1748	1809	1817	1849	1852	1921	1948	1949	2007	2013
Exeter St Davids a.	1346	1347	1409	1447	1447	1510	1537	1547	1609	1609	1640	1646	1710	1711	1735	1748	1813	1814	1838	1842	1909	1909	1944	2012	2009	2029	2038

	Ⓐ	⑥	Ⓐ	⑥	Ⓐ	Ⓐ	Ⓐ	Ⓐ	⑦	⑦	⑦	⑦	⑦	⑦	⑦	⑦	⑦	⑦	⑦	⑦	⑦	⑦	⑦	⑦	⑦	⑦	⑦
Paignton 🚂 d.	2028	2016	2055	2121	2108	2139	2220	2320		0930	1036	1057	1154	1253	1353	1415	1440	1551	1614	1640	1730	1751	1853	1943	2054	2145	2235
Torquay d.	2033	2022	2100	2126	2113	2144	2225	2325		0936	1042	1102	1159	1259	1358	1420	1445	1557	1620	1645	1736	1757	1859	1948	2100	2150	2240
Newton Abbot d.	2045	2035	2112	2139	2125	2156	2237	2337		0956f	1055	1114	1211	1311	1410	1432	1457	1610	1633	1657	1748	1809	1912	2000	2112	2202	2253
Teignmouth d.	2052	2042	2119	2146	2132	2203	2244	2344		1003	1102	1121	1218	1318	1417	1439	1504	1617	1640	1704	...	1816	1919	2007	2119	2209	2300
Dawlish d.	2057	2047	2124	2151	2137	2208	2249	2349		1008	1107	1126	1223	1323	1422	1444	1509	1622	1645	1709	...	1821	1924	2012	2124	2214	2305
Exeter St Davids a.	2114	2113	2149	2213	2159	2233	2314	0014		1038	1119	1151	1249	1348	1447	1509	1547	1648	1711	1749	...	1846	1949	2037	2148	2240	2320

a – Arrives 0620.
c – Arrives 0726.
f – Arrives 0945.
t – Arrives 5 – 6 minutes earlier.
🚂 – Dartmouth Steam Railway (Paignton - Kingswear). ✆ 01803 555 872. www.dartmouthrailriver.co.uk

112 PLYMOUTH - NEWQUAY and PENZANCE GW, XC

km			Ⓐ	Ⓐ	Ⓐ	Ⓐ	Ⓐ	Ⓐ	Ⓐ	Ⓐ	Ⓐ	Ⓐ	Ⓐ	Ⓐ	Ⓐ	Ⓐ	Ⓐ	Ⓐ	Ⓐ	Ⓐ	Ⓐ	Ⓐ	Ⓐ	Ⓐ	Ⓐ	Ⓐ	Ⓐ
			2		A	🍷	2	🍷	2	2E	2	2	2	2	🍷	2G	2	🍷	2	B	2	2B	🍷	2	2	2	B
	London Padd **110**	d.	Ⓐ	...	...	2345p	...	...	...	...	...	...	...	...	...	0637	...	...	0804	...	...	...	...	1004	...	...	...	...
	Bristol T M **110 116**	d.		...	...	|	...	...	...	...	...	0540	...	0650	...	|	0749	0752	|	...	0856	...	0956	|	...	...	...	1155
0	**Plymouth**	d.		...	0535	|	0618	0639	0712	...	0743	0808	0847	0912	...	0945	1015	1044	1120	...	1142	1219	1246	1317	...	1343	1418	1446
7	Saltash	d.		...	0544	|	|	0648	0723	...	0752	0825	0856	0923	...	0954	1026	1055	|	...	1151	1228	1255	|	...	1356	1427	1455
29	Liskeard	d.		...	0604	0612	0641	0707	0745	...	0811	0843	0917	0944	...	1014	1045	1114	1144	...	1212	1246	1314	1341	...	1415	1445	1513
43	Bodmin Parkway 🚌	d.		...	0616	0626	0654	0719	0758	...	0823	0855	0929	0956	...	1026	1057	1125	1156	...	1224	1257	1326	1354	...	1427	1457	1525
49	Lostwithiel	d.		...	0621	0633	|	0724	0804	...	0829	0900	0934	1001	...	1031	1102	1130	|	...	1229	1302	1331	|	...	1432	1502	1531
56	Par ❖♡	d.		0600	0629	0641	0707	0731	0811	0818	0836	0907	0941	1008	1013	|	1109	1138	1206	1213	1236	1309	1337	1404	1413	1438	1509	1537
89	**Newquay** ❖♡	a.		0652	|	|	|	|	|	0910	|	|	|	|	1105	|	|	|	|	1305	|	|	|	|	1505	|	|	|
63	St Austell	d.		...	0636	0649	0714	0739	0819	...	0843	0914	0948	1014	...	1043	1116	1145	1213	...	1244	1317	1345	1411	...	1446	1517	1545
86	Truro	d.		...	0659	0707	0731	0756	0836	...	0901	0931	1004	1031	...	1100	1133	1202	1230	...	1301	1334	1401	1429	...	1502	1533	1602
101	Redruth	d.		...	0710	0720	0743	0807	0848	...	0914	0943	1016	1043	...	1112	1145	1214	1242	...	1312	1346	1413	1441	...	1514	1545	1614
107	Camborne	d.		...	0717	0728	|	0814	0855	...	0920	0949	1023	1049	...	1119	1151	1220	1248	...	1319	1352	1419	1448	...	1520	1551	1620
119	St Erth	d.		...	0729	0742	0803	0826	0908	...	0931	1001	1034	1101	...	1131	1203	1231	1258	...	1331	1403	1431	1458	...	1531	1603	1633
128	**Penzance**	a.		...	0738	0754	0812	0835	0919	...	0940	1010	1043	1110	...	1140	1212	1240	1307	...	1340	1412	1440	1507	...	1540	1612	1642

		Ⓐ	Ⓐ	Ⓐ	Ⓐ	Ⓐ	Ⓐ	Ⓐ	Ⓐ	Ⓐ	Ⓐ	Ⓐ	Ⓐ	Ⓐ	Ⓐ	Ⓐ	Ⓐ	Ⓐ		⑥	⑥	⑥	⑥	⑥	⑥	⑥ 2	⑥	⑥
		🍷	2	2	2	2B	🍷	2	2B	🍷	2	C	🍷	2	🍷	🍷	2B	2N		2	A	2	2E	2	2	E		🍷
London Padd **110**	d.	1204	...	...	...	...	1404	...	...	1504	...	...	1604	...	1704	1804	...	1904c	⑥	...	2345p	...	...	...	...	...	...	...
Bristol T M **110 116**	d.	|	...	...	...	1355	|	...	1455	|	...	1645	|	...	|	|	1857	|		...	|	...	...	0537	...	...	0640	0742
Plymouth	d.	1515	...	1547	1555	1647	1720	...	1746	1821	1830	1851	1925	...	2029	2117	2146	2238		0517	|	...	0740	0807	...	0845	0911	0946
Saltash	d.	|	...	1556	1616	1656	1730	...	1755	|	1848	|	1934	...	2038	|	2155	2247		|	|	...	0749	0825	...	0854	0922	0955
Liskeard	d.	1539	...	1614	1639	1714	1749	...	1814	1845	1910	1919	1954	...	2058	2141	2214	2306		0540	0605	...	0809	0844	...	0913	0945	1012
Bodmin Parkway 🚌	d.	1552	...	1626	1651	1725	1802	...	1826	1857	1922	1931	2006	...	2110	2153	2226	2318		0552	0619	...	0821	0856	...	0925	0957	1025
Lostwithiel	d.	|	...	1631	1656	1730	1808	...	1831	|	1927	|	|	...	2115	|	2231	2323		0557	0626	...	0826	0901	...	0930	1003	|
Par ❖♡	d.	1602	1613	1638	1704	1738	1815	1823	1838	1908	1933	|	2016	2029	2122	2204	2238	2330		0605	0634	0652	0833	0908	0925	0937	1010	1035
Newquay ❖♡	a.	|	1705	|	|	|	|	1915	|	|	|	|	|	2121	|	|	|	|		|	|	0743	|	|	1016	|	|	|
St Austell	d.	1609	...	1645	1712	1746	1822	...	1845	1915	1940	1949	2023	...	2129	2211	2245	2338		0611	0643	...	0840	0915	...	0944	1017	1043
Truro	d.	1627	...	1702	1731	1802	1839	...	1901	1932	1956	2009	2040	...	2147	2228	2302	2355		0627	0703	...	0856	0932	...	1000	1034	1100
Redruth	d.	1639	...	1714	1742	1814	1851	...	1913	1944	2009	2021	2052	...	2159	2239	2313	0007		0640	0717	...	0908	0944	...	1012	1045	1112
Camborne	d.	1646	...	1720	1749	1820	1858	...	1919	1951	2015	|	2059	...	2205	|	2319	0013		0646	0724	...	0914	0950	...	1018	1052	1119
St Erth	d.	1659	...	1731	1801	1832	1913	...	1931	2001	2026	2037	2111	...	2215	|	2331	0026		0658	0739	...	0926	1003	...	1031	1105	1132
Penzance	a.	1708	...	1740	1810	1841	1923	...	1940	2010	2035	2047	2120	...	2224	2259	2340	0035		0707	0750	...	0935	1012	...	1040	1114	1141

		⑥	⑥	⑥	⑥	⑥	⑥	⑥	⑥	⑥	⑥	⑥		⑥	⑥	⑥	⑥	⑥	⑥	⑥	⑥	⑥	⑥	⑥	⑥	⑥	⑥	⑥
		2	2	🍷	2	2B	2	B	🍷	2	2			2B	🍷	2	2	🍷	2B	🍷	2	2B	🍷	2B	C	2	2	D
London Padd **110**	d.	...	...	0804	...	...	...	...	1004	...	...	...	...	...	1204	...	...	1304	...	1404	...	...	1504	...	...	...	...	...
Bristol T M **110 116**	d.	...	0755	|	...	0855	...	0955	|	...	...	...	...	1155	|	...	...	|	1354	|	...	1455	|	1555	1645	...	...	1745
Plymouth	d.	1015	1043	1115	...	1142	1220	1243	1318	...	1343	1417	...	1443	1518	...	1542	1618	1644	1718	...	1744	1820	1836	1902	1927	...	1953
Saltash	d.	1024	1055	|	...	1151	1229	1252	|	...	1352	1426	...	1452	|	...	1552	|	1653	|	...	1753	|	1854	|	1936	...	|
Liskeard	d.	1043	1114	1140	...	1212	1244	1312	1343	...	1413	1445	...	1512	1543	...	1614	1643	1714	1743	...	1813	1845	1914	1925	1955	...	2016
Bodmin Parkway 🚌	d.	1055	1126	1152	...	1224	1256	1324	1355	...	1425	1457	...	1524	1555	...	1625	1655	1726	1755	...	1825	1857	1926	1938	2007	...	2028
Lostwithiel	d.	1100	1131	|	...	1229	1301	1329	|	...	1430	1503	...	1529	|	...	1630	|	1731	|	...	1830	|	1931	|	2012	...	|
Par ♡	d.	1108	1138	1203	1212	1236	1308	1336	1406	1412	1438	1510	...	1536	1606	1612	1638	1706	1738	1806	1813	1837	1908	1939	|	2019	2025	|
Newquay ♡	a.	|	|	|	1303	|	|	|	|	1503	|	|	...	|	|	1703	|	|	|	|	1904	|	|	|	|	|	2116	|
St Austell	d.	1115	1145	1211	...	1243	1315	1343	1414	...	1444	1517	...	1543	1614	...	1645	1714	1745	1813	...	1844	1915	1945	1956	2026	...	2046
Truro	d.	1131	1202	1229	...	1300	1332	1400	1431	...	1501	1534	...	1600	1631	...	1702	1730	1802	1830	...	1900	1932	2002	2015	2043	...	2102
Redruth	d.	1143	1214	1241	...	1312	1344	1412	1443	...	1513	1543	...	1612	1643	...	1714	1742	1814	1842	...	1912	1944	2014	2027	2055	...	2113
Camborne	d.	1150	1220	1248	...	1318	1350	1418	1450	...	1519	1552	...	1618	1650	...	1720	1749	1820	1849	...	1918	1950	2020	|	2101	...	|
St Erth	d.	1203	1231	1259	...	1331	1401	1431	1500	...	1531	1605	...	1631	1700	...	1731	1802	1832	1900	...	1931	2001	2032	2043	2113	...	2132
Penzance	a.	1212	1240	1308	...	1340	1410	1440	1509	...	1540	1614	...	1640	1709	...	1740	1811	1841	1909	...	1940	2010	2041	2053	2122	...	2140

		⑥	⑥		⑦	⑦	⑦	⑦	⑦	⑦	⑦	⑦	⑦	⑦	⑦	⑦	⑦	⑦	⑦	⑦	⑦	⑦		⑦	⑦	⑦	⑦	⑦
		🍷	🍷		2	🍷	2	2E		🍷	🍷	2	2	🍷	2	2B	🍷		2	B	🍷	2B		2B	🍷	2E	🍷	🍷
London Padd **110**	d.	1704	1804	⑦	...	...	...	...	...	0751	0851	...	...	1003	...	...	1203	...	...	...	1403	...	...	...	1603	...	1703	1803
Bristol T M **110 116**	d.	|	|		...	...	...	...	0800	|	|	...	0955	|	...	1146	|	...	...	1354	|	1454	...	1554	|	...	|	|
Plymouth	d.	2023	2123		0845	0914	...	0947	1032	1130	1215	...	1234	1315	1340	1430	1515	1540	...	1635	1715	1740	...	1835	1915	1940	2015	2115
Saltash	d.	2033	|		0901	|	...	0955	1045	1140	|	...	1243	|	1349	1439	|	1549	...	1644	|	1749	...	1845	|	1949	|	2124
Liskeard	d.	2053	2147		0919	0938	...	1016	1104	1159	1239	...	1301	1339	1409	1458	1539	1607	...	1702	1739	1809	...	1902	1939	2008	2039	2144
Bodmin Parkway 🚌	d.	2105	2159		0931	0950	...	1027	1116	1212	1252	...	1314	1352	1421	1510	1552	1618	...	1714	1751	1821	...	1914	1951	2020	2052	2156
Lostwithiel	d.	|	2205		0937	|	...	1031	1121	1217	|	...	1319	|	1426	1515	|	1623	...	1720	|	1826	...	1919	|	2025	|	2201
Par ♡	d.	2115	2212		0944	1000	1004	1040	1128	1225	1303	1315	1327	1403	1433	1522	1602	1631	1635	1727	1802	1833	...	1926	2002	2033	2103	2208
Newquay ♡	a.	|	|		|	|	1056	|	|	|	|	1407	|	|	|	|	|	|	1727	|	|	|	...	|	|	|	|	|
St Austell	d.	2122	2219		0951	1008	...	1047	1135	1233	1310	...	1334	1410	1440	1529	1610	1638	...	1734	1810	1840	...	1932	2009	2039	2110	2216
Truro	d.	2139	2236		1018	1025	...	1103	1152	1251	1327	...	1351	1427	1456	1546	1627	1655	...	1753	1827	1856	...	1953f	2026	2056	2127	2233
Redruth	d.	2151	2247		1019	1036	...	1115	1203	1303	1339	...	1402	1439	1508	1558	1639	1707	...	1804	1839	1907	...	2004	2038	2107	2139	2244
Camborne	d.	2157	2254		1026	1043	...	1121	1210	1310	1346	...	1408	1446	1514	1604	1646	1714	...	1811	1846	1914	...	2010	2044	2114	2146	2251
St Erth	d.	2208	2306		1038	1053	...	1132	1222	1323	1357	...	1420	1457	1526	1619f	1656	1726	...	1823	1856	1925	...	2022	2054	2128	2157	2303
Penzance	a.	2217	2315		1047	1102	...	1141	1231	1332	1406	...	1429	1506	1535	1628	1705	1735	...	1832	1905	1934	...	2031	2103	2137	2206	2312

A – THE NIGHT RIVIERA – Conveys 🛏 1, 2. cl and [2]. See also note ‡ on page 95. **For overnight journeys only.**
B – From Cardiff Central (Tables **110** and **115**).
C – From Edinburgh (Table **116**).
D – From Aberdeen (Tables **222** and **116**).
E – From Exeter St Davids (Table **110**).
G – From Gloucester (Tables **138** and **110**).
N – On ⑤ conveys [12] and 🍷.
c – ⑤ only.
f – Arrives 5–6 minutes earlier.
p – Previous night.

113 BRANCH LINES and BUS CONNECTIONS IN DEVON and CORNWALL 2nd class GW

EXETER - EXMOUTH *'The Avocet Line'* *18 km*

From Exeter St Davids: on Ⓐ at 0520, 0544, 0607, 0648, 0716, 0745, 0817, 0846, 0916, 0953, 1015, 1051, 1115, 1151, 1215, 1250, 1313, 1351, 1415, 1451, 1515, 1550, 1616, 1649, 1715, 1739, 1818, 1846, 1913, 1948, 2015, 2042, 2118, 2152, 2240, 2340; on ⑥ at 0608, 0648, 0717, 0746, 0817, 0845, 0915, 0945, 1017, 1052, 1116, 1152, 1217, 1252, 1317, 1352, 1417, 1453, 1516, 1545, 1617, 1646, 1716, 1751 1816, 1846, 1916, 2017, 2117, 2217, 2313; on ⑦ at 0817, 0915, 0950, 1012, 1041, 1115, 1155, 1216, 1252, 1315, 1350, 1415, 1451, 1516, 1551, 1616, 1651, 1717, 1752, 1816, 1850, 1953, 2049, 2153, 2258.

From Exmouth: on Ⓐ at 0019 ②–⑤, 0551, 0615, 0655, 0724, 0754, 0824, 0854, 0923, 0957 and at the same minutes past each hour until 1523, 1555, 1623, 1657, 1726, 1756, 1826, 1856, 1924, 1956, 2024, 2054, 2126, 2156, 2225, 2320; on ⑥ at 0019, 0655, 0725, 0755, 0825, 0855, 0925, 0955, 1024, 1057 and at the same minutes past each hour until 1457, 1525, 1555, 1626, 1656, 1726, 1756, 1828, 1857, 1925, 1958, 2058, 2154, 2254, 2349; on ⑦ at 0855, 0955, 1021, 1054, 1123, 1157, 1226, 1257, 1324, 1357, 1424, 1457, 1524, 1555, 1624, 1656, 1723, 1757, 1824, 1856, 1959, 2056, 2127, 2230, 2335.

Journey: 37–40 minutes. Trains call at Exeter Central 3–4 minutes from Exeter St Davids.

EXETER - BARNSTAPLE *'The Tarka Line'* *63 km*

From Exeter St Davids: on Ⓐ at 0522, 0612, 0708, 0810, 0919 and hourly until 1519, 1618, 1719, 1821, 1922, 2023, 2127, 2255⑤; on ⑥ at 0524, 0616, 0710, 0818, 0920, 1019 and hourly until 1419, 1520, 1619, 1720, 1822, 1922, 2025, 2125; on ⑦ at 0836, 0918, 1020, 1117, 1219, 1319, 1419, 1520, 1618, 1719, 1819, 1919, 2017.

From Barnstaple: on Ⓐ at 0625, 0722, 0835 and hourly until 1535, 1631, 1733, 1838, 1942, 2041, 2141, 2241①–④, 2311⑤; on ⑥ at 0007, 0631, 0726, 0834, 0935, 1035, 1135, 1232, 1335, 1435, 1535, 1639, 1736, 1843, 1942, 2040, 2140, 2240; on ⑦ at 0937, 1037, 1132, 1236, 1336, 1431, 1532, 1630, 1737, 1832, 1935, 2036, 2136.

*Journey: 65 minutes. Trains call at **Crediton** (11 minutes from Exeter / 54 minutes from Barnstaple) and **Eggesford** (40 minutes from Exeter / 25 minutes from Barnstaple).*

PLYMOUTH - GUNNISLAKE *'The Tamar Valley Line'* *24 km*

From Plymouth:
on Ⓐ at 0457, 0630, 0824, 1028, 1228, 1428, 1638, 1838, 2130; on ⑥ at 0627, 0822, 1024, 1224, 1424, 1636, 1826, 2130; on ⑦ at 0903, 1110, 1320, 1520, 1744.

From Gunnislake:
on Ⓐ at 0542, 0725, 0919, 1119, 1319, 1519, 1733, 1933, 2222; on ⑥ at 0716, 0914, 1114, 1314, 1514, 1734, 1918, 2220; on ⑦ at 1011, 1211, 1411, 1611, 1835.

Journey: 45–60 minutes.

LISKEARD - LOOE *'The Looe Valley Line'* *14 km*

From Liskeard:
on Ⓐ at 0557, 0713, 0830, 0936, 1036, 1136, 1236, 1346, 1446, 1550, 1654, 1757, 1900, 2005, 2105; on ⑥ at 0600, 0722, 0827, 0936, 1036, 1136, 1236, 1350, 1450, 1554, 1656, 1758, 1858, 2000, 2102; on ⑦ from Apr. 2 at 0931, 1035, 1210, 1350, 1511, 1630, 1755, 2015.

From Looe:
on Ⓐ at 0630, 0754, 0905, 1008, 1106, 1208, 1306, 1418, 1516, 1625, 1725, 1830, 1930, 2037, 2137; on ⑥ at 0632, 0755, 0902, 1008, 1105, 1208, 1305, 1422, 1519, 1629, 1726, 1830, 1928, 2032, 2136; on ⑦ from Apr. 2 at 1004, 1112, 1242, 1434, 1542, 1705, 1845, 2050.

Journey: 28–33 minutes.

EXETER - OKEHAMPTON *'The Dartmoor Line'* *40 km*

From Exeter St. Davids:
0630⚒, 0738⚒, 0839⚒, 0843⑦, 0937⑦, 0939⚒, 1037⚒, 1040⑦, 1136, 1237, 1337, 1437, 1537, 1637, 1738⑥, 1740Ⓐ, 1742⑦, 1845, 1933⑥, 1942Ⓑ, 2110⑥, 2115Ⓐ, 2118⑦.

From Okehampton:
0725⚒, 0825⚒, 0925, 1025⚒, 1030⑦, 1125⑦, 1127⚒, 1225⑦, 1227⚒, 1325, 1425, 1525, 1623⑦, 1625⚒, 1725, 1830⚒, 1833⑦, 1929, 2027⑦, 2030⚒, 2201⑦, 2219Ⓐ, 2224⑥.

*Journey: 40–42 minutes. Trains call at **Crediton** (approx. 10 minutes from Exeter).*

GW, XC — PENZANCE and NEWQUAY - PLYMOUTH — 112

	Ⓐ 🍷	Ⓐ 2	Ⓐ 2B	Ⓐ 🍷	Ⓐ 2B	Ⓐ 2	Ⓐ 🍷	Ⓐ 2B	Ⓐ 🍷	Ⓐ B	Ⓐ 2	Ⓐ 🍷	Ⓐ 🍷C	Ⓐ 2	Ⓐ 🍷	Ⓐ 2B	Ⓐ 2	Ⓐ 2	Ⓐ 2	Ⓐ 🍷	Ⓐ 2B	Ⓐ 2	Ⓐ 2	Ⓐ 2	Ⓐ 🍷	Ⓐ 2
Penzance d.	0503	0520	0540	0605	0640	...	0710	0740	0815	0850	...	0910	0925	0950	1020	1050	...	1115	1150	1215	1250	...	1315	1350	1415	1450
St Erth d.	|	|	0548	|	0648	...	0719	0748	0824	0857	...	0920	0934	0958	1029	1058	...	1123	1158	1224	1258	...	1323	1357	1424	1458
Camborne d.	|	0540	0600	0622	0701	...	0730	0801	0835	0911	...	0934	|	1011	1040	1111	...	1136	1211	1235	1311	...	1336	1411	1435	1511
Redruth d.	0524	|	0606	0629	0707	...	0737	0807	0842	0918	...	0941	0954	1017	1046	1117	...	1142	1217	1242	1317	...	1342	1417	1442	1517
Truro d.	0536	0555	0618	0641	0720	...	0749	0820	0854	0930	...	0955	1007	1030	1058	1130	...	1155	1229	1255	1330	...	1354	1429	1454	1529
St Austell d.	0553	...	0633	0658	0736	...	0805	0835	0910	0946	...	1011	1023	1046	1115	1146	...	1211	1246	1311	1346	...	1410	1445	1511	1545
Newquay ♡ d.	|	...	|	|	|	0712	|	|	|	|	0915	|	|	|	|	|	1109	|	|	|	|	1310	|	|	|	|
Par ♡ d.	|	...	0639	0705	0743	0801	0812	0842	0919	0953	1004	1019	|	1053	1124	1153	1157	1217	1253	1319	1353	1358	1417	1452	1519	1553
Lostwithiel d.	|	...	0647	0712	0750	...	0819	0849	|	1000	...	|	|	1102	|	1159	...	1224	1259	|	1359	...	1424	1459	|	1600
Bodmin Parkway 🚂 d.	0609	...	0652	0719	0755	...	0826	0855	0931	1007	...	1031	1041	1108	1136	1205	...	1229	1305	1331	1405	...	1429	1506	1531	1605
Liskeard d.	0622	...	0705	0732	0808	...	0839	0908	0944	1019	...	1044	1053	1122	1149	1217	...	1242	1317	1344	1417	...	1442	1518	1544	1618
Saltash d.	0637	...	0726	0753	0828	...	0857	0925	|	1038	...	|	|	1140	|	1236	...	1300	1338	|	1435	...	1500	1535	|	1636
Plymouth a.	0648	...	0743	0805	0846	...	0908	0934	1008	1048	...	1107	1116	1150	1212	1245	...	1310	1352	1409	1445	...	1509	1545	1608	1645
Bristol T M **110 116** a.	|	...	1020	|	1117	...	|	1217	|	1316	...	|	1326	...	|	1516	...	...	...	|	1719	...	...	...	|	...
London Padd **110** a.	0955	...	...	1129	...	...	1227	...	1329	...	...	1427	...	...	1529	...	...	...	...	1729	...	...	...	...	1924	...

	Ⓐ 2	Ⓐ 2	Ⓐ 2G	Ⓐ 🍷	Ⓐ 2B	Ⓐ 2	Ⓐ 2	Ⓐ 🍷	Ⓐ 2E	Ⓐ	Ⓐ 2	Ⓐ 2	Ⓐ	Ⓐ	Ⓐ 2	Ⓐ A	Ⓐ	⑥ 2	⑥ 2B	⑥ 🍷	⑥ 2B	⑥ 🍷	⑥ 2	⑥ 2	⑥ 🍷	⑥ 2B
Penzance d.	...	1515	1550	1615	1650	...	1715	1750	1815	1850	...	1915	2015	2100	...	2145	2208	0515	0540	0612	0640	0710	...	0740	0815	0852
St Erth d.	...	1523	1558	1624	1658	...	1722	1759	1823	1857	...	1923	2023	2109	...	2155	2217	|	0549	|	0649	0719	...	0749	0825	0900
Camborne d.	...	1536	1611	1635	1711	...	1736	1812	1836	1911	...	1936	2036	2122	...	2208	2231	0532	0602	0629	0702	0733	...	0802	0836	0913
Redruth d.	...	1542	1617	1642	1717	...	1743	1818	1842	1918	...	1942	2043	2129	...	2216	2237	0538	0608	0636	0708	0740	...	0808	0843	0919
Truro d.	...	1554	1630	1655	1730	...	1755	1830	1854	1930	...	1955	2055	2141	...	2229	2250	0550	0620	0648	0720	0752	...	0820	0856	0931
St Austell d.	...	1610	1646	1711	1746	...	1811	1846	1910	1946	...	2011	2111	2157	...	2247	2306	...	0636	0705	0736	0808	...	0836	0913	0947
Newquay ♡ d.	1510	|	|	|	|	1719	|	|	|	|	1922	|	|	|	2126	|	|	...	|	|	|	|	0748	|	|	|
Par ♡ d.	1559	1617	1653	1719	1753	1807	1817	1853	1917	1953	2011	2018	2118	2205	2215	2256	2313	...	0643	0712	0743	0815	0838	0843	0920	0954
Lostwithiel d.	...	1624	1700	|	1759	...	1825	1900	1924	2000	...	2025	2125	2212	...	|	2320	...	0649	|	0749	|	...	0850	|	1000
Bodmin Parkway 🚂 d.	...	1629	1705	1731	1805	...	1832	1907	1929	2007	...	2031	2131	2218	...	2308	2326	...	0655	0724	0755	0827	...	0856	0932	1006
Liskeard d.	...	1641	1718	1744	1817	...	1844	1921	1942	2019	...	2044	2144	2231	...	2324	2338	...	0708	0737	0808	0840	...	0910	0946	1018
Saltash d.	...	1704	1735	|	1835	...	1903	|	2000	2041r	...	2104	2201	2249	...	|	|	...	0727	0755	0828	0858	...	0928	|	1038
Plymouth a.	...	1720	1744	1807	1844	...	1915	1946	2009	2051	...	2121	2213	2259	...	|	0002	...	0745	0806	0846	0909	...	0937	1009	1048
Bristol T M **110 116** a.	...	...	2002	|	2118	...	...	2150	...	...	...	0004	...	...	...	|	...	...	1015	|	1116	|	...	...	|	1316
London Padd **110** a.	...	...	...	2129	...	...	...	2356	...	...	...	...	...	...	...	0507	...	...	...	1129	...	1229	...	...	1329	...

	⑥ 🍷	⑥ 2	⑥ 2	⑥ 🍷	⑥ B	⑥ 2	⑥	⑥ 🍷	⑥ 2B	⑥ 2	⑥ 2	⑥ 2B	⑥ 🍷	⑥ 2	⑥ 2	⑥	⑥ 2	⑥ 🍷	⑥ B	⑥ 2	⑥ 2	⑥ 🍷	⑥ 2E	⑥ 2	⑥ 2	⑥	⑥ 2
Penzance d.	0912	0950	...	1015	1050	1115	1150	1218	1250	...	1315	1350	1420	1450	...	1515	1550	1620	1650	...	1715	1750	1815	...	1930	2043	...
St Erth d.	0922	0958	...	1025	1059	1123	1159	1228	1259	...	1323	1359	1429	1458	...	1524	1559	1629	1659	...	1724	1759	1823	...	1939	2051	...
Camborne d.	0936	1011	...	1036	1112	1136	1212	1239	1312	...	1336	1412	1440	1511	...	1537	1612	1640	1712	...	1737	1813	1836	...	1952	2104	...
Redruth d.	0943	1017	...	1043	1119	1142	1219	1246	1318	...	1342	1418	1447	1517	...	1544	1618	1647	1719	...	1743	1820	1843	...	1958	2111	...
Truro d.	0956	1030	...	1056	1131	1154	1231	1259	1330	...	1354	1430	1500	1530	...	1556	1630	1700	1731	...	1755	1832	1855	...	2010	2123	...
St Austell d.	1013	1046	...	1113	1147	1210	1247	1315	1346	...	1410	1446	1516	1546	...	1612	1646	1716	1747	...	1811	1848	1911	...	2026	2139	...
Newquay ♡ d.	|	|	1020	|	|	|	|	|	|	1310	|	|	|	|	1510	|	|	|	|	1710	|	|	|	1908	|	|	2120
Par ♡ d.	1020	1053	1110	1120	1154	1217	1254	1323	1353	1400	1417	1453	1523	1553	1600	1619	1653	1723	1754	1800	1818	1855	1918	1958	2033	2146	2212
Lostwithiel d.	|	1059	...	|	1201	1223	1301	|	1359	...	1423	1459	|	1559	...	1626	1659	|	1801	...	1824	1902	1925	...	2039	2153	2219
Bodmin Parkway 🚂 d.	1032	1105	...	1132	1207	1229	1307	1335	1405	...	1429	1505	1535	1605	...	1632	1705	1735	1807	...	1830	1909	1931	...	2045	2159	2225
Liskeard d.	1046	1118	...	1146	1220	1241	1320	1348	1418	...	1442	1518	1548	1618	...	1645	1718	1748	1820	...	1843	1923	1945	...	2102r	2212	2238
Saltash d.	|	1136	...	|	1237	1259	1339	|	1435	...	1500	1536	|	1636	...	1704	1736	|	1837	...	1901	|	2003	...	2122	2230	2258
Plymouth a.	1109	1145	...	1209	1247	1309	1353	1411	1445	...	1509	1546	1611	1645	...	1722	1745	1811	1847	...	1910	1947	2012	...	2140	2240	2314
Bristol T M **110 116** a.	|	...	...	|	1516	...	...	|	1720	...	...	1816	|	...	...	...	2016	|	2125	...	...	2149	...	...	...	...	...
London Padd **110** a.	1429	...	...	1529	...	...	...	1729	...	...	...	...	1929	...	...	...	...	2139	...	...	...	2342	...	...	...	...	...

	⑥	⑦ 🍷	⑦ 2B	⑦ 🍷	⑦ C	⑦ 🍷	⑦ 2	⑦ 2B	⑦ B	⑦ 🍷	⑦ 2	⑦ B	⑦ 2	⑦ 🍷	⑦ 2E	⑦ 🍷	⑦ 2	⑦ 🍷	⑦ 2	⑦ 2	⑦ 🍷	⑦ 2	⑦	⑦ 2	⑦ A	⑦
Penzance d.	2130	0815	0849	0918	0930	1018	...	1050	1148	1218	1250	1349	...	1418	1450	1518	1548	1618	1645	...	1750	1815	1915	2040	2115	2128
St Erth d.	2139	0823	0857	0927	0938	1028	...	1059	1156	1227	1258	1357	...	1427	1458	1527	1556	1627	1653	...	1758	1823	1924	2048	2125	2137
Camborne d.	|	0834	0909	0938	|	1039	...	1112	1209	1238	1311	1410	...	1438	1510	1540	1608	1638	1706	...	1812	1836	1937	2101	2137	2151
Redruth d.	2156	0840	0915	0945	0955	1046	...	1118	1216	1245	1317	1417	...	1445	1516	1547	1613	1645	1713	...	1819	1842	1943	2108	2146	2158
Truro d.	2208	0852	0927	0957	1008	1058	...	1129	1228	1257	1329	1429	...	1457	1527	1559	1625	1657	1725	...	1831	1854	1956	2120	2201	2211
St Austell d.	2225	0909	0943	1013	1024	1114	...	1145	1244	1313	1345	1445	...	1513	1543	1616	1640	1713	1741	...	1847	1910	2012	2136	2219	2227
Newquay ♡ d.	|	|	|	|	|	|	1058	|	|	|	|	|	1425	|	|	|	|	|	|	1755	|	|	|	|	|	|
Par ♡ d.	|	0916	0949	1021	|	1122	1147	1152	1251	1321	1352	1452	1515	1521	1550	1623	1646	1721	1747	1845	1854	1917	2019	2143	|	2234
Lostwithiel d.	|	|	0955	|	|	|	...	1158	1258	|	1359	1459	...	|	1557	|	1653	|	1754	...	|	1924	2026	2150	|	2241
Bodmin Parkway 🚂 d.	2242	0927	1001	1033	1041	1134	...	1203	1304	1333	1404	1505	...	1533	1602	1635	1658	1733	1800	...	1906	1929	2032	2156	2235	2248
Liskeard d.	2254	0940	1013	1046	1055	1147	...	1215	1317	1346	1419	1518	...	1546	1615	1648	1710	1746	1814	...	1919	1942	2045	2209	2250	2301
Saltash d.	|	0958	1033	|	|	|	...	1233	1334	|	1440	1535	...	|	1632	|	1728	|	1833	...	|	2000	2104	2226	|	2318
Plymouth a.	2318	1008	1042	1109	1120	1210	...	1242	1344	1409	1450	1543	...	1609	1642	1711	1737	1809	1846	...	1943	2009	2120	2238	|	2328
Bristol T M **110 116** a.	...	|	1314	|	1324	|	...	1511	1612	|	...	1815	...	|	...	|	...	|	...	...	|	...	...	...	|	...
London Padd **110** a.	...	1320	...	1424	...	1524	...	...	...	1724	...	...	...	1924	...	2024	...	2123	...	...	2333	...	...	...	0503	...

A – THE NIGHT RIVIERA – Conveys 🛏 1, 2. cl and (2). See also note ‡ on page 95. **For overnight journeys only.**
B – To Cardiff Central (Tables **110** and **115**).
C – To Edinburgh (Table **116**).
E – To Exeter St Davids (Table **110**).
G – To Gloucester (Tables **138** and **110**).
r – Arrives 5–6 minutes earlier.
♡ – Par - Newquay: *'The Atlantic Coast Line'*.
🚂 – Bodmin & Wenford Railway (Bodmin Parkway - Bodmin General - Boscarne Junction *10 km*). ✆ 01208 73555. www.bodminrailway.co.uk

GW 2nd class — BRANCH LINES and BUS CONNECTIONS IN DEVON and CORNWALL — 113

Rail tickets are generally not valid on 🚌 services shown in this table.

BODMIN PARKWAY - PADSTOW — *Go Cornwall Bus 🚌 service 11*

From Bodmin Parkway station:
on ⚒ at 0643, 0813, 0913 and hourly until 1613, 1715, 1815, 1923, 2023, 2123;
on ⑦ at 0955, 1155, 1355, 1555, 1755.

From Padstow Station Road:
on ⚒ at 0635, 0735, 0755**n**, 0800**p**, 0935 and hourly until 1435, 1530**n**, 1535**p** 1635, 1735**p**, 1745**n**, 1830, 1930, 2030, 2130;
on ⑦ at 0930, 1130, 1330, 1530, 1730.

Journey: 68 minutes. Buses also make calls in Bodmin town centre and at Bodmin General station, and call at ***Wadebridge*** *(35 minutes after Bodmin / 25 minutes after Padstow).*

TRURO - FALMOUTH DOCKS — *'The Maritime Line'* — *20 km*

From Truro:
on Ⓐ at 0600, 0627, 0713, 0743, 0815 and every 30 minutes until 1615, 1646, 1718, 1749, 1820, 1906, 1941, 2050, 2156, 2256;
on ⑥ at 0604, 0631, 0715 and every 30 minutes until 1645, 1718, 1748, 1838, 1912, 1942, 2047, 2148, 2244;
on ⑦ at 0850, 0950, 1050, 1155, 1255, 1355, 1500 1600, 1700, 1758, 1900, 2000, 2100, 2205.

From Falmouth Docks:
on Ⓐ at 0627, 0713, 0743, 0815 and every 30 minutes until 1615, 1646, 1718, 1749, 1820, 1906, 1941, 2017, 2122, 2226, 2322;
on ⑥ at 0631, 0715, 0745, 0815 and every 30 minutes untill 1645, 1718, 1748, 1838, 1912, 1942, 2008, 2120, 2215, 2310;
on ⑦ at 0921, 1021, 1121, 1221, 1321, 1421, 1526, 1626, 1726, 1824, 1926, 2026, 2127, 2233.

Trains call at ***Falmouth Town*** *22 minutes after Truro and 3 minutes after Falmouth Docks.*
Journey: 25 minutes.

ST AUSTELL - EDEN PROJECT — *First Kernow 🚌 service 27*

From St Austell bus station:
On Ⓐ at 0905, 0935 and hourly until 1635.
On ⑥ at 0835 and hourly until 1635.

From Eden Project:
⚒ at 0947 and hourly until 1647, 1717.

Journey: 20 minutes.

ST ERTH - ST IVES — *'The St Ives Bay Line'* — *7 km*

From St Erth:
on Ⓐ at 0706, 0750, 0838, 0938, 1018 and every 30 minutes until 1848, 1920, 1950, 2020, 2050, 2120, 2221;
on ⑥ at 0701, 0750, 0850, 0924, 0952, 1022, 1051, 1122 and every 30 minutes until 1652, 1726, 1808, 1907, 2005, 2036, 2117, 2147;
on ⑦ at 0918, 0959, 1048, 1148 and every 30 minutes until 1748, 1833, 1933.

From St Ives:
on Ⓐ at 0732, 0807, 0902, 1003 and every 30 minutes until 1703, 1732, 1803, 1833, 1905, 1934, 2005, 2034, 2105, 2137, 2248;
on ⑥ at 0730, 0806, 0904, 0937, 1006, 1036, 1105, 1136 and every 30 minutes until 1706, 1740, 1828, 1922, 2020, 2052, 2131, 2205;
on ⑦ at 0941, 1012, 1103 and every 30 minutes until 1803, 1903, 1948.

Journey: 15 minutes.

n – Schooldays - check locally for details.
p – School holidays (check locally for details) and ⑥.

114 BIRMINGHAM - READING - SOUTHAMPTON - BOURNEMOUTH

Most services convey 🍸 XC

km			Ⓐ	⑥	⑥	Ⓐ	⚒A	⚒	⚒	Ⓐ	⑥	Ⓐ	⚒	Ⓐ	⑥	Ⓐ	⚒	⑥	Ⓐ	⑥	Ⓐ	⑥	Ⓐ	⑥
	Manchester Piccadilly **119** d.		...	...	0511	0511	...	0725	0825	0925	0924	...	1025	1125	1125	...	1225	1325	1325	1425	1425	1525	1525	1625
	Newcastle **124** d.	⚒	...	...	|	|	...	|	|	|	|	0835	|	|	|	1035	|	|	|	|	|	|	|	|
	York **124** d.		...	...	|	|	...	|	|	|	|	0937	|	|	|	1137	|	|	|	|	|	|	|	|
0	**Birmingham** New Street... **142 150** d.		0604	0604	0703	0703	0803	0903	1003	1103	1103	1133	1203	1303	1303	1333	1403	1503	1503	1603	1603	1703	1703	1803
13	Birmingham Int'l ✈ **142 150** d.		0614	0614	0713	0713	0813	0913	1013	1113	1113	|	1213	1313	1313	|	1413	1513	1513	1613	1613	1713	1713	1813
30	Coventry **141 142 150** d.		0625	0625	0726	0725	0826	0926	1026	1126	1126	|	1226	1325	1326	|	1426	1526	1526	1626	1626	1726	1726	1826
45	Leamington Spa **128 141** d.		0637	0637	0739	0738	0838	0941	1038	1138	1138	1202	1238	1337	1338	1403	1438	1538	1538	1638	1638	1738	1738	1838
77	Banbury **128** d.		0655	0655	0756	0755	0855	0958	1055	1155	1155	1218	1255	1355	1354	1419	1455	1555	1555	1656	1656	1755	1756	1855
114	Oxford a.		0714	0714	0814	0814	0914	1016	1114	1214	1213	...	1314	1413	1413	...	1515	1614	1614	1714	1714	1814	1814	1914
114	Oxford **131** d.		0716	0716	0818	0816	0916	1018	1116	1215	1216	...	1316	1416	1416	...	1515	1617	1616	1716	1716	1817	1816	1917
158	**Reading** **131** a.		0745	0742	0840	0846	0940	1044	1141	1241	1239	...	1341	1439	1439	...	1539	1641	1639	1741	1740	1841	1840	1940
158	**Reading** d.		0752	...	0852	0852	...	1052	...	1252	1252	...	...	1452	1452	...	...	1652	1652	...	1752	1852	...	...
183	Basingstoke **106** a.		0809	...	0909	0910	...	1109	...	1309	1309	...	...	1509	1509	...	...	1709	1709	...	1809	1909	...	...
213	Winchester **106** a.		0826	...	0926	0926	...	1126	...	1326	1326	...	...	1526	1526	...	...	1726	1726	...	1826	1926	...	...
226	**Southampton** Airport ✈ **106** a.		0834	...	0935	0935	...	1135	...	1335	1334	...	...	1535	1534	...	...	1734	1735	...	1834	1934	...	...
234	**Southampton** Central **106** a.		0842	...	0943	0943	...	1143	...	1343	1342	...	...	1543	1542	...	...	1742	1743	...	1842	1942	...	...
255	Brockenhurst **106** a.		|	...	0958	0958	...	|	...	|	|	...	...	|	|	...	...	|	|	...	1858	1958	...	...
280	**Bournemouth** **106** a.		0913	...	1013	1013	...	1213	...	1413	1413	...	...	1613	1613	...	...	1813	1817	...	1913	2013	...	...

	Ⓐ	⑥	Ⓐ	Ⓐ	⑥		Ⓐ	⑥	Ⓐ	⑦	⑦	⑦	⑦	⑦	⑦	⑦	⑦	⑦	⑦	⑦	⑦	⑦	⑦	⑦
Manchester Piccadilly **119** d.	1625	1725	1725	1825	1825	...	1925	1925	2025		...	...	0827	0927	1026	1123	1225	1325	1425	1525	1625	1725	1825	1925
Newcastle **124** d.	|	|	|	|	|	...	|	|	|	⑦	...	...	|	|	|	|	|	|	|	|	|	|	|	|
York **124** d.	|	|	|	|	|	...	|	|	|		...	...	|	|	|	|	|	|	|	|	|	|	|	|
Birmingham New Street.. **142 150** d.	1803	1903	1903	2003	2003	...	2103	2103	2203		...	0904	1003	1103	1203	1303	1403	1503	1603	1703	1803	1903	2003	2103
Birmingham Int'l ✈ **142 150** d.	1813	1913	1913	2013	2013	...	2112	2113	2213		...	0914	1013	1113	1213	1313	1413	1513	1613	1713	1813	1913	2013	2113
Coventry **141 142 150** d.	1826	1926	1926	2026	2026	...	2125	2126	2225		...	0925	1026	1126	1226	1326	1426	1526	1626	1726	1826	1926	2026	2127
Leamington Spa **128 141** d.	1838	1938	1939	2039	2038	...	2137	2138	2237		...	0937	1038	1138	1238	1338	1438	1538	1638	1738	1838	1938	2038	2139
Banbury **128** d.	1856	1955	1956	2056	2054	...	2155	2155	2255		...	0955	1055	1155	1255	1355	1455	1555	1655	1755	1855	1955	2055	2156
Oxford a.	1914	2013	2014	2114	2114	...	2213	2213	2313		...	1013	1113	1213	1313	1413	1513	1613	1713	1813	1913	2013	2113	2214
Oxford **131** d.	1916	2016	2018	2116	2116	...	2216	2216	2316		...	1016	1116	1216	1316	1416	1516	1616	1716	1816	1916	2016	2116	2216
Reading **131** a.	1941	2039	2042	2141	2140	...	2239	2239	2349		...	1039	1139	1239	1339	1439	1539	1639	1739	1839	1939	2039	2139	2239
Reading d.	1950	2052	...	2152	2152	...	2249	2252	...		0952	...	1152	...	1352	...	1552	...	1752	...	1952	2052	2152	...
Basingstoke **106** a.	2010	2109	...	2209	2209	...	2307	2309	...		1011	...	1210	...	1410	...	1609	...	1810	...	2010	2110	2209	...
Winchester **106** a.	2026	2126	...	2226	2226	...	2327	2326	...		1027	...	1226	...	1426	...	1626	...	1826	...	2026	2126	2224	...
Southampton Airport ✈ **106** a.	2035	2134	...	2234	2234	...	2335	2334	...		1035	...	1234	...	1434	...	1634	...	1834	...	2034	2134	2233	...
Southampton Central **106** a.	2043	2144	...	2244	2242	...	2344	2342	...		1042b	...	1242b	...	1442b	...	1642b	...	1842b	...	2045c	2142b	2242	...
Brockenhurst **106** a.	|	|	...	|	|	...	...	...	...		1103c	...	|	...	|	...	|	...	1903c	...	|	|	...	...
Bournemouth **106** a.	2115	2215	...	2317	2319	...	...	...	...		1126	...	1326	...	1525	...	1725	...	1926	...	2126	2226	...	...

		⑥	Ⓐ	Ⓐ	⑥	Ⓐ	⑥		Ⓐ	⑥	⑥	Ⓐ	⚒		Ⓐ	Ⓐ	⑥	⚒		Ⓐ	⚒	⚒	⚒	⚒
Bournemouth **106** d.		...	...	...	...	0630	...	...	0730	0745	...	...	0945	...	...	...	...	1145	...	...	...	1345	...	1545
Brockenhurst **106** d.		...	...	...	...	|	...	...	|	|	...	...	1000	...	...	...	...	|	...	...	...	|	...	|
Southampton Central **106** d.	⚒	...	0515	...	0615	0715j	...	...	0815j	0815	...	...	1015	...	...	...	...	1215	...	...	...	1415	...	1615
Southampton Airport ✈ **106** d.		...	0523	...	0623	0723	...	...	0823	0823	...	...	1023	...	...	...	...	1223	...	...	...	1423	...	1623
Winchester **106** d.		...	0531	...	0631	0731	...	...	0831	0831	...	...	1031	...	...	...	...	1231	...	...	...	1431	...	1631
Basingstoke **106** d.		...	0548	...	0649	0749	...	...	0849	0849	...	...	1048	...	...	...	...	1248	...	...	...	1448	...	1649
Reading a.		...	0605	...	0706	0809	...	...	0907	0907	...	...	1106	...	...	...	...	1306	...	...	...	1506	...	1706
Reading **131** d.		0615	0615	0715	0715	0815	0815	...	0916	0915	1015	1016	1115	...	...	1216	1215	1315	...	...	1415	1515	1615	1715
Oxford **131** a.		0638	0637	0738	0738	0838	0838	...	0937	0938	1038	1039	1138	...	...	1237	1238	1338	...	...	1438	1538	1638	1738
Oxford d.		0639	0639	0739	0739	0839	0839	...	0939	0939	1039	1040	1139	...	...	1239	1239	1339	...	...	1439	1539	1639	1739
Banbury **128** d.		0658	0658	0758	0758	0858	0858	...	0957	0958	1058	1058	1158	...	1228	1258	1258	1358	...	1430	1458	1558	1658	1758
Leamington Spa **128 141** d.		0715	0716	0816	0816	0916	0915	...	1015	1016	1115	1116	1216	...	1249	1316	1316	1416	...	1449	1515	1616	1716	1816
Coventry **141 142 150** d.		0730	0730	0830	0830	0930	0930	...	1030	1030	1130	1130	1230	...	|	1330	1330	1430	...	|	1530	1630	1730	1830
Birmingham Int'l ✈ **142 150** d.		0741	0741	0841	0841	0941	0941	...	1041	1041	1141	1141	1241	...	|	1341	1341	1441	...	|	1541	1641	1741	1841
Birmingham New Street.. **142 150** a.		0751	0751	0851	0851	0951	0951	...	1051	1051	1151	1151	1251	...	1448	1351	1351	1451	...	1518	1551	1651	1751	1851
York **124** a.		|	|	|	|	|	|	...	|	|	|	|	|	...	1540	|	|	|	...	...	|	|	|	|
Newcastle **124** a.		|	|	|	|	|	|	...	|	|	|	|	|	...	1644	|	|	|	...	...	|	|	|	|
Manchester Piccadilly **119** a.		0929	0929	1029	1029	1129	1129	...	1229	1229	1329	1329	1429	...	...	1529	1529	1629	...	...	1729	1829	1929	2029

	Ⓐ	⑥	Ⓐ	⑥		Ⓐ	⑥	Ⓐ	⑥		⑦	⑦	⑦	⑦	⑦		⑦	⑦	⑦	⑦	⑦	⑦	⑦	⑦
Bournemouth **106** d.	1645	...	...	1745	...	1845	...	1945	1945	⑦	...	...	0940	...	1140	...	...	1340	...	1540	...	1740	...	1940
Brockenhurst **106** d.	|	...	...	|	...	1900	...	|	2000		...	...	0955	...	|	...	...	|	...	|	...	1755	...	|
Southampton Central **106** d.	1715	...	...	1815	...	1915	...	2015	2015		...	0915	1015r	...	1215r	...	...	1415r	...	1615r	...	1815r	...	2015r
Southampton Airport ✈ **106** d.	1723	...	...	1823	...	1923	...	2023	2023		...	0923	1023	...	1223	...	...	1423	...	1623	...	1823	...	2023
Winchester **106** d.	1731	...	...	1831	...	1931	...	2033	2032		...	0931	1031	...	1231	...	...	1431	...	1631	...	1831	...	2031
Basingstoke **106** d.	1749	...	...	1849	...	1949	...	2049	2049		...	0949	1049	...	1249	...	...	1449	...	1649	...	1849	...	2049
Reading a.	1808	...	...	1906	...	2007	...	2107	2106		...	1006	1106	...	1306	...	...	1506	...	1706	...	1906	...	2106
Reading **131** d.	1815	1815	1915	1915	...	2015	2015	2114	2115		0915	1015	1115	1215	1315	...	1415	1515	1615	1715	1815	1915	2015	2112
Oxford **131** a.	1838	1838	1938	1938	...	2037	2038	2137	2138		0938	1038	1138	1238	1338	...	1438	1538	1638	1738	1838	1938	2038	2133
Oxford d.	1839	1839	1939	1939	...	2039	2039	2139	2139		0939	1039	1139	1239	1339	...	1439	1539	1639	1739	1839	1939	2039	2135
Banbury **128** d.	1858	1858	1958	1958	...	2058	2058	2157	2158		0958	1058	1158	1258	1358	...	1458	1558	1658	1758	1858	1958	2058	2153
Leamington Spa **128 141** d.	1916	1916	2016	2016	...	2116	2116	2216	2216		1016	1116	1216	1316	1416	...	1516	1616	1716	1816	1916	2016	2116	2214
Coventry **141 142 150** d.	1930	1930	2030	2030	...	2130	2130	2228	2230		1030	1130	1230	1330	1430	...	1530	1630	1730	1830	1930	2030	2130	2226
Birmingham Int'l ✈ **142 150** d.	1941	1941	2041	2041	...	2141	2141	2238	2240		1041	1141	1241	1341	1441	...	1541	1641	1741	1841	1941	2041	2141	2236
Birmingham New Street.. **142 150** a.	1951	1951	2051	2051	...	2151	2151	2248	2250		1051	1151	1251	1351	1451	...	1551	1651	1751	1851	1951	2051	2151	2247
York **124** a.	|	|	|	|	...	|	|	...	...		|	|	|	|	|	...	|	|	|	|	|	|	|	...
Newcastle **124** a.	|	|	|	|	...	|	|	...	...		|	|	|	|	|	...	|	|	|	|	|	|	|	...
Manchester Piccadilly **119** a.	2129	2129	2230	2230	...	2331	2329	...	...		1230	1329	1429	1529	1629	...	1729	1829	1929	2029	2129	2229	2328	...

A – From Nottingham (Table **120**).

b – Departs 8–10 minutes later.
c – Departs 5–7 minutes later.

j – Arrives 13 minutes earlier.
r – Arrives 5–9 minutes earlier.

114a GATWICK AIRPORT ✈ - READING

GW

km			Ⓐ	Ⓐ	Ⓐ	Ⓐ	Ⓐ	Ⓐ	Ⓐ	Ⓐ	Ⓐ	Ⓐ	Ⓐ	Ⓐ	Ⓐ	Ⓐ	Ⓐ	Ⓐ	Ⓐ	Ⓐ	Ⓐ	Ⓐ	Ⓐ
0	**Gatwick Airport** ✈ **185** d.	Ⓐ	0510	0600	...	0702	0759	0900	0929	1029	1129	1229	1329	1429	1529	1630	1729	1829	1929	2029	2129	2229	2320
10	Redhill **185** ⊡ d.		0530	0615	0642	0716	0816	0914	0943	1043	1143	1243	1343	1443	1543	1645	1745	1845	1945	2043	2144	2243	2334
43	Guildford ⊡ d.		0603	0649	0728	0750	0848	0947	1014	1114	1214	1314	1414	1514	1618	1716	1819	1916	2016	2114	2228	2326	0006
84	**Reading** ⊡ a.		0651	0734	0816	0834	0925	1018	1053	1151	1251	1351	1451	1551	1703	1802	1909	2004	2053	2156	2320	0017	0044

		⑥	⑥	⑥		⑥	⑥	⑥	⑥	⑥		⑦	⑦	⑦		⑦	⑦	⑦	⑦
Gatwick Airport ✈ **185** d.	⑥	0524	0629	0729	and at the same	1929	2029	2059	2217	2320	⑦	0611	0815	0915	and at the same	2015	2103	2218	2304
Redhill **185** ⊡ d.		0542	0643	0743	minutes past	1943	2043	2113	2231	2334		0623	0828	0928	minutes past	2028	2115	2231	2316
Guildford ⊡ d.		0615	0714	0814	each hour until	2016	2114	2146	2313	0006		0656	0901	1001	each hour until	2101	2158	2304	0001
Reading ⊡ a.		0704	0751	0851		2058	2158	2226	0003	0044		0741	0941	1038		2140	2245	2345	0049

		Ⓐ	Ⓐ	Ⓐ	Ⓐ	Ⓐ	Ⓐ	Ⓐ	Ⓐ		Ⓐ	Ⓐ	Ⓐ	Ⓐ	Ⓐ	Ⓐ	Ⓐ	Ⓐ		⑥	⑥
Reading ⊡ d.	Ⓐ	0432	0531	0626	0651	0750	0901	1004	1101	and at the same	1601	1650	1750	1901	2001	2101	2134	2333	⑥	0426	0600
Guildford ⊡ d.		0512	0612	0705	0748f	0837	0940	1042	1140	minutes past	1640	1739	1837	1940	2040	2139	2221	0023		0510	0640
Redhill **185** ⊡ a.		0544	0646	0738	0839	0908	1012	1114	1212	each hour until	1713	1812	1909	2012	2112	2213	2303	0055		0541	0711
Gatwick Airport ✈ **185** a.		0555	0658	0753	0854	0925	1025	1125	1226		1725	1824	1920	2025	2125	2225	2315	0107		0554	0724

	⑥	⑥	⊙	⑥	⑥	⑥	⑥	⑥	⑥		⑦	⑦	⑦	⑦		⑦	⑦	⑦	⑦
Reading ⊡ d.	0701	0801	and at the same	1801	1901	1920	2032	2133	2334	⑦	0603	0657	0821	0921	and at the same	1921	2012	2113	2303
Guildford ⊡ d.	0741	0840	minutes past	1840	1940	2007	2112	2220	0022		0641	0735	0900	1000	minutes past	2000	2058	2200	2349
Redhill **185** ⊡ a.	0812	0911	each hour until	1911	2013	2043	2143	2303	0053		0713	0807	0934	1034	each hour until	2034	2141	2234	0030
Gatwick Airport ✈ **185** a.	0824	0924		1924	2024	2054	2154	2316	0104		0726	0823	0944	1045		2046	2154	2247	0041

f – Arrives 5 minutes earlier.

⊙ – Additional train: Reading d. 1320, Guildford d. 1407, Redhill a. 1442, Gatwick a. 1454. The 1401 from Reading does not run.
⊡ – Additional trains run Redhill - Reading and v.v.

GW 2nd class — CARDIFF - BRISTOL - TAUTON — 115

km		Ⓐ	Ⓐ§	Ⓐ	Ⓐ	Ⓐ	Ⓐ§	Ⓐ	ⒶA§	Ⓐ	Ⓐ	Ⓐ	Ⓐ§	Ⓐ	Ⓐ	Ⓐ	Ⓐ§	Ⓐ	Ⓐ§	Ⓐ	Ⓐ	Ⓐ	Ⓐ	Ⓐ	Ⓐ	Ⓐ	Ⓐ§
0	**Cardiff** Central ‡ d.		...	...	...	...	...	0628	...	...	0657	0728	0800	0828	0900	0928	1000	1030	1100	1130	1200	1230	1300	1330	1400	1430	1500
19	Newport ‡ d.		...	...	...	...	...	0642	...	...	0710	0742	0814	0842	0914	0942	1014	1044	1114	1144	1214	1244	1314	1344	1415	1444	1513
61	**Bristol** Temple Meads a.		...	...	...	...	...	0718	...	...	0750	0816	0852	0920	0953	1016	1050	1117	1150	1216	1250	1319	1350	1417	1450	1517	1549
	Bristol Temple M **116 132** d.		0500	0525	0540	0650	0703	0722	0749	0752	...	0820	0856	0923	0956	1021	1055	1122	1155	1222	1256	1322	1355	1422	1455	1522	1551
	Portsmouth Hbr **140** a.		|	|	|	|	|	0953	|	|	...	1052	|	1052	|	1252	|	1352	|	1452	|	1552	|	1652	|	1752	|
92	Weston-super-Mare ... **132** d.		0534	0545	|	0709	0737	...	|	0827	...	...	0928	...	1026	...	1126	...	1225	...	1325	...	1428r	...	1525	...	1627
104	Highbridge and Burnham .. d.		0544	0556	|	0719	0748	...	|	0838	...	...	0939	...	1036	...	1137	...	1235	...	1335	...	1438	...	1535	...	1638
114	Bridgwater d.		0551	0604	0611	0726	0755	...	0815	0845	...	...	0946	...	1043	...	1144	...	1242	...	1342	...	1445	...	1542	...	1645
133	**Taunton** **116 132** a.		0604	0616	0620	0735	0806	...	0824	0856	...	...	0956	...	1055	...	1155	...	1252	...	1352	...	1455	...	1552	...	1656
	Exeter St Davids **110/6** . a.		...	0644	0650	0804	...	...	0852	0924	...	...	1023	...	1123	...	...	...	1322	...	...	...	1523	...	1621	...	...
	Penzance **112** a.		...	...	1010	1110	...	...	1212	1240	...	...	1340	...	1440	...	...	...	1642	...	...	...	1841	...	1940	...	...

	Ⓐ	Ⓐ§	Ⓐ	Ⓐ	ⒶF	Ⓐ	Ⓐ	ⒶF	Ⓐ	ⒶP	Ⓐ	Ⓐ§	Ⓐ	Ⓐ	Ⓐ	ⒶC	Ⓐ	Ⓐ	⑤	①–④	ⒶB	⑤	①–④	⑥	⑥	⑥§	⑥
Cardiff Central ‡ d.	1530	1600	1627	1700	...	1727	1800	...	1830	1900	1930	2000	2030	2100	...	2130	...	2200	2230	2230	...	2330	2330		...	...	...
Newport ‡ d.	1545	1615	1641	1714	...	1741	1815	...	1844	1914	1944	2013	2044	2113	...	2144	...	2216	2244	2248	...	2344	2350		...	...	...
Bristol Temple Meads a.	1617	1650	1715	1749	...	1815	1850	...	1919	1951	2016	2055	2121	2150	...	2221	...	2303	2320	2336	...	0025	0040		...	...	...
Bristol Temple M **116 132** d.	1622	1652	1722	1753	1815	1824	1857	1910	1924	1953	2024	2058	2125	...	2200	...	2305	...	...	...	2348	...	...		0520	0537	0619
Portsmouth Hbr **140** a.	1854	|	1952	|	|	2052	|	|	2149	|	2304	|	2353	...	|	...	|	...	...	...	|	...	...		|	|	|
Weston-super-Mare ... **132** d.	...	1730	...	1829	1843	...	1932	1945r	...	2029	...	2138r	...	...	2239r	...	2340	...	...	...	0015s	...	...		0543	0557	0649
Highbridge and Burnham .. d.	...	1741	...	1839	1854	...	1942	1956	...	2039	...	2149	...	...	2250	...	2351	...	...	...	0026s	...	...		0554	0608	0659
Bridgwater d.	...	1748	...	1846	1901	...	1950	2003	...	2046	...	2156	...	...	2257	...	2358	...	...	...	0033s	...	...		0602	0616	0706
Taunton **116 132** a.	...	1759	...	1856	1912	...	1959	2014	...	2056	...	2207	...	...	2314	...	0009	...	...	...	0044s	...	...		0614	0626	0717
Exeter St Davids **110/6** .. a.	...	...	...	...	...	...	2029	...	...	2124	...	...	...	...	2347	...	0040	...	...	...	0112	...	...		0645	0653	...
Penzance **112** a.	...	...	...	...	...	...	2340	...	...	...	...	...	...	...	...	...	...	...	...	...	...	...	...		...	1012	...

	⑥§	⑥	⑥	⑥	⑥	⑥	⑥	⑥	⑥§	⑥F	⑥	⑥§		⑥	⑥	⑥	⑥	⑥	⑥	⑥	⑥	⑥	⑥	⑥	⑥§	⑥	⑥§
Cardiff Central ‡ d.	...	0630	...	...	...	0727	0800	0827	0900	...	0927	1000	...	1030	1100	1130	1200	1227	1300	1330	1400	1430	1500	1530	1600	1627	1700
Newport ‡ d.	...	0644	...	...	...	0741	0814	0841	0913	...	0941	1013	...	1044	1114	1144	1214	1241	1314	1344	1414	1444	1514	1544	1613	1641	1713
Bristol Temple Meads a.	...	0719	...	...	...	0817	0852	0917	0950	...	1018	1050	...	1117	1149	1216	1249	1313	1349	1417	1450	1517	1550	1617	1647	1717	1750
Bristol Temple M **116 132** d.	0640	0723	0725	0742	0755	0822	0855	0922	0955	1010	1023	1055	...	1122	1155	1222	1255	1322	1354	1422	1455	1522	1555	1622	1655	1722	1755
Portsmouth Hbr **140** a.	|	0951	|	|	|	1051	|	1151	|	|	1251	|	...	1351	|	1452	|	1551	|	1651	|	1751	|	1851	|	1951	|
Weston-super-Mare ... **132** d.	0700	...	0759	|	0827r	...	0924	...	1024	1035	...	1124	...	...	1225	...	1325	...	1426	...	1525	...	1625	...	1724	...	1823
Highbridge and Burnham .. d.	0711	...	0809	|	0838	...	0934	...	1035	1046	...	1135	...	...	1235	...	1335	...	1436	...	1535	...	1636	...	1735	...	1834
Bridgwater d.	0718	...	0816	|	0846	...	0941	...	1042	1054	...	1142	...	...	1242	...	1342	...	1443	...	1542	...	1643	...	1742	...	1842
Taunton **116 132** a.	0728	...	0826	0813	0857	...	0950	...	1052	1105	...	1153	...	...	1252	...	1352	...	1453	...	1551	...	1653	...	1753	...	1853
Exeter St Davids **110/6** .. a.	0756	...	...	0837	0924	...	1018	...	1122	...	...	...	...	...	1330	...	...	...	1523	...	1623	...	1723	...	...	...	...
Penzance **112** a.	1114	...	...	1141	1240	...	1340	...	1440	...	...	...	...	...	1640	...	...	...	1841	...	1940	...	2041	...	...	...	...

	⑥	⑥	⑥F	⑥	⑥P	⑥	⑥	⑥F		⑥	⑥	⑥F	⑥	⑥	⑥J	⑥	⑥	⑦	⑦§	⑦J	⑦	⑦	⑦	⑦	⑦	⑦	⑦
Cardiff Central ‡ d.	1627	1700	...	1727	1800	1827	1900	...	...	1930	1954	...	2030	2100	...	2200	2247		...	...	...	0918	1000	...	1025	1055	1125
Newport ‡ d.	1641	1713	...	1741	1814	1841	1914	...	...	1943	2008	...	2043	2114	...	2214	2302		...	...	...	0936	1013	...	1039	1109	1139
Bristol Temple Meads a.	1717	1750	...	1817	1850	1917	1950	...	...	2016	2047	...	2115	2150	...	2250	2341		...	...	...	1015	1052	...	1112	1143	1210
Bristol Temple M **116 132** d.	1722	1755	1808	1822	1853	1922	1955	2011	...	2022	...	2108	2121	2152	2208	...	...		0800	0949	0955	1020	...	1102	1115	1146	1215
Portsmouth Hbr **140** a.	1951	|	|	2051	|	2151	|	|	...	2250	...	|	2350	|	|	...	...		|	|	|	1151	...	|	1351	|	1451
Weston-super-Mare ... **132** d.	...	1823	1836	...	1926	...	2028	2040	...	...	...	2139	...	2226	2235s	...	...		0828	|	1024	...	...	1129	...	1223	...
Highbridge and Burnham .. d.	...	1834	1847	...	1935	...	2038	2052	...	...	...	2150	...	2237	2247s	...	...		0838	|	1033	...	...	1138	...	1233	...
Bridgwater d.	...	1842	1855	...	1942	...	2045	2100	...	...	...	2157	...	2244	2254s	...	...		0845	1015	1040	...	...	1145	...	1240	...
Taunton **116 132** a.	...	1853	1906	...	1951	...	2055	2112	...	...	...	2208	...	2255	2306	...	...		0855	1025	1049	...	...	1155	...	1250	...
Exeter St Davids **110/6** .. a.	...	...	...	...	2019	...	...	...	...	...	...	...	...	2326	2335	...	...		0923	1056	1116	...	...	...	...	1318	...
Penzance **112** a.	...	...	...	...	...	...	...	...	...	...	...	...	...	...	...	...	...		1231	...	1429	...	...	...	...	1628	...

	⑦	⑦	⑦§	⑦	⑦	⑦	⑦	⑦	⑦	⑦F	⑦	⑦	⑦B	⑦	⑦	⑦		⑦§	⑦	⑦B	⑦	⑦	⑦§	⑦	⑦W	⑦Z	⑦
Cardiff Central ‡ d.	1200	1225	1300	1325	1400	1425	1500	1525	1555	...	1625	1700	...	1725	...	1740	...	1800	1825	...	1900	1925	2000	2030	2130	2230	2311
Newport ‡ d.	1214	1239	1313	1339	1414	1439	1516	1540	1610	...	1639	1714	...	1739	...	1754	...	1815	1839	...	1914	1940	2013	2044	2144	2244	2325
Bristol Temple Meads a.	1249	1310	1349	1410	1449	1510	1550	1611	1644	...	1710	1749	...	1810	...	1831	...	1849	1911	...	1950	2011	2049	2121	2220	2320	2359
Bristol Temple M **116 132** d.	1254	1315	1354	1415	1454	1515	1554	1620	1653	1705	1715	1754	1810	1815	1825	1840	...	1851	1915	1937	1954	2015	2053	2128	...	...	...
Portsmouth Hbr **140** a.	|	1551	|	1651	|	1751	|	1852	|	|	1952	|	|	2050	|	2123	...	|	2149	|	|	2249	|	2356	...	...	...
Weston-super-Mare ... **132** d.	1323	...	1423	...	1524	...	1628r	...	1720	1734	...	1825	1839	...	1900	...	...	1927	...	|	2028	...	2126	...	...	...	...
Highbridge and Burnham .. d.	1334	...	1433	...	1534	...	1637	...	1730	1745	...	1835	|	...	1912	...	...	1937	...	|	2039	...	2136	...	...	...	...
Bridgwater d.	1341	...	1440	...	1541	...	1644	...	1737	1752	...	1842	1854	...	1920	...	...	1944	...	|	2046	...	2143	...	...	...	...
Taunton **116 132** a.	1352	...	1450	...	1551	...	1656	...	1747	1803	...	1853	1904	...	1931	...	...	1955	...	2008	2058	...	2154	...	...	...	...
Exeter St Davids **110/6** .. a.	1423	...	1519	...	1623	...	1723	...	...	...	...	...	1929	...	1958	...	...	...	...	2032	...	...	...	...	...	...	...
Penzance **112** a.	...	...	1832	...	1940	...	2031	...	...	...	...	...	...	...	...	...	...	...	...	...	...	...	...	...	...	...	...

	Ⓐ	①	②–⑥	Ⓐ	Ⓐ	Ⓐ	ⒶW	ⒶR	Ⓐ	Ⓐ	ⒶC	ⒶF	Ⓐ§		Ⓐ	Ⓐ§	Ⓐ	Ⓐ	Ⓐ	Ⓐ	Ⓐ	Ⓐ	Ⓐ	Ⓐ§	Ⓐ	Ⓐ§	Ⓐ
Penzance **112** a.		...	...	...	...	...	...	...	...	...	...	...	...	...	...	...	...	0540	...	0640	...	0740	...	0850	...	...	...
Exeter St Davids **110/6** .. a.		...	...	...	...	...	...	...	...	...	...	...	0636	...	...	...	...	0852	...	0955	...	1044	...	1154	...	...	...
Taunton **116 132** d.		...	...	...	0514	...	...	...	0611	0637	...	0655	0704	...	...	0819	...	0920	...	1019	...	1111	...	1218	...	1308	...
Bridgwater d.		...	...	...	0525	...	...	...	0621	0648	...	0706	0715	...	...	0829	...	0930	...	1029	...	1121	...	1228	...	1318	...
Highbridge and Burnham .. d.		...	...	...	0532	...	...	...	0629	0655	...	0713	0722	...	...	0836	...	0937	...	1036	...	1128	...	1235	...	1325	...
Weston-super-Mare ... **132** d.		...	...	...	0545	...	...	...	0640	0710r	...	0724	0739r	...	...	0847	...	0948	...	1047	...	1147f	...	1247	...	1347f	...
Portsmouth Hbr **140** d.		...	...	...	|	...	...	...	|	|	...	|	|	...	0601	|	0721	|	0823	|	0923	|	1023	|	1123	|	1223
Bristol Temple M **116 132** a.		...	...	...	0618	...	...	...	0716	0744	...	0752	0816	...	0847	0920	0952	1020	1050	1117	1150	1217	1251	1316	1350	1415	1450
Bristol Temple Meads d.		0520	0520	0553	...	0628	0653	0706	0724	...	0755	...	0821	...	0858	0927	0959	1027	1058	1127	1157	1227	1259	1327	1357	1427	1458
Newport ‡ a.		0600	0606	0628	...	0704	0736	0749	0807	...	0833	...	0903	...	0932	1002	1038	1105	1131	1203	1231	1306	1332	1403	1434	1506	1533
Cardiff Central ‡ a.		0621	0621	0642	...	0718	0750	0803	0822	...	0847	...	0920	...	0946	1019	1052	1121	1146	1221	1245	1326	1349	1420	1448	1520	1550

	Ⓐ	Ⓐ	Ⓐ	Ⓐ	Ⓐ	Ⓐ		Ⓐ§	Ⓐ	Ⓐ§	Ⓐ	ⒶA	Ⓐ	Ⓐ	ⒶJ	Ⓐ	ⒶE	⑤	①–④		⑤	①–④	⑤	①–④	ⒶQ	Ⓐ§	Ⓐ
Penzance **112** a.	1050	...	...	...	1250	...	...	...	...	...	...	1550	...	...	...	1650	1750	...	...	...	...	...	...	...	...	...	1915
Exeter St Davids **110/6** .. a.	1353	...	...	...	1553	...	...	...	...	...	...	1903	...	...	1935	1950	2050	...	...	...	2106	2106	...	...	2200	...	2242
Taunton **116 132** d.	1419	...	1520	...	1617	...	...	1711	...	1810	...	1927	1914	...	2003	2016	2117	...	...	...	2132	2132	...	...	2233	2244	2310
Bridgwater d.	1429	...	1530	...	1627	...	...	1722	...	1821	...	1937	1924	...	2014	2026	|	...	...	...	2143	2143	...	...	|	2254	2320
Highbridge and Burnham .. d.	1436	...	1537	...	1634	...	...	1729	...	1828	...	|	1932	...	|	2034	|	...	...	...	2150	2150	...	...	|	2301	2327
Weston-super-Mare ... **132** d.	1447	...	1547	...	1645	...	...	1745r	...	1845r	...	|	1947r	...	2029	2047	|	...	...	...	2201	2201	...	...	|	2313	2341
Portsmouth Hbr **140** d.	|	1323	|	1423	|	1523	...	|	1623	|	1723	|	|	1824	|	|	|	1923	1923	...	|	|	2023	2023	|	|	|
Bristol Temple M **116 132** a.	1516	1551	1616	1651	1719	1752	...	1819	1850	1920	1952	2002	2016	2050	2057	2118	2150	2151	2151	...	2230	2230	2251	2251	2316	2347	0004
Bristol Temple Meads d.	1527	1557	1627	1657	1724	1757	...	1824	1858	1922	1957	...	2020	2057	...	2131	...	2157	2157	...	2234	2234	2258	2258	...	...	...
Newport ‡ a.	1604	1631	1704	1733	1756	1832	...	1910	1935	2007	2032	...	2101	2133	...	2204	...	2232	2238	...	2306	2313	2332	2338	...	...	...
Cardiff Central ‡ a.	1622	1645	1720	1750	1821	1846	...	1927	1949	2023	2046	...	2124	2147	...	2218	...	2246	2258	...	2320	2333	2346	2358	...	...	...

	⑥	⑥	⑥	⑥	⑥S	⑥§	⑥	⑥	⑥	⑥	⑥		⑥	⑥	⑥	⑥	⑥	⑥	⑥	⑥	⑥§	⑥	⑥§	⑥	⑥	⑥	⑥
Penzance **112** a.		...	...	...	...	...	...	...	...	...	...	...	0540	...	0640	...	...	...	0852	...	...	...	1050	...	...	...	1250
Exeter St Davids **110/6** .. a.		...	...	...	...	0549	...	...	...	...	...	...	0855	...	0955	...	1043	...	1155	...	...	...	1352	...	...	...	1556
Taunton **116 132** d.		0513	...	...	...	0616	...	...	...	0820	...	...	0919	...	1019	...	1108	...	1220	...	1318	...	1420	...	1520	...	1620
Bridgwater d.		0524	...	...	...	0626	...	...	...	0830	...	...	0929	...	1029	...	1118	...	1230	...	1329	...	1430	...	1530	...	1630
Highbridge and Burnham .. d.		0531	...	...	...	0633	...	...	...	0837	...	...	0937	...	1037	...	1125	...	1237	...	1336	...	1437	...	1537	...	1637
Weston-super-Mare ... **132** d.		0542	...	...	...	0646	...	...	...	0848	...	...	0947	...	1047	...	1147f	...	1248	...	1348	...	1448	...	1547	...	1648
Portsmouth Hbr **140** d.		|	...	...	...	|	...	...	0608	|	0723	...	|	0823	|	0923	|	1023	|	1123	|	1223	|	1323	|	1423	|
Bristol Temple M **116 132** a.		0618	...	...	...	0719	...	...	0847	0916	0953	...	1015	1050	1116	1151	1218	1252	1316	1352	1415	1451	1516	1550	1616	1650	1720
Bristol Temple Meads d.		...	0628	0654	0703	0723	0757	0825	0857	0929	0957	...	1030	1057	1132	1157	1232	1257	1323	1357	1432	1457	1532	1557	1622	1657	1732
Newport ‡ a.		...	0701	0729	0744	0756	0830	0857	0931	1006	1031	...	1106	1131	1207	1231	1307	1330	1356	1430	1508	1531	1607	1631	1700	1732	1806
Cardiff Central ‡ a.		...	0715	0746	0759	0810	0845	0913	0945	1021	1045	...	1122	1145	1222	1245	1321	1345	1412	1445	1527	1545	1620	1645	1720	1746	1821

A – To/from Gloucester (Table **138**).
B – (12) and 🍸 London Paddington - Plymouth and v.v. (Table **110**).
C – To/from Frome (Table **139**).
E – (12) and 🍸 Penzance - London Paddington (Table **110**).
F – (12) and 🍸 London Paddington - Taunton and v.v. (Table **132**).
J – (12) and 🍸 London Paddington - Exeter St Davids and v.v. (Table **110**).
K – From Apr. 2 from Weymouth; until Mar. 26 from Frome (Table **139**).
P – To/from Plymouth (Table **110**).
Q – From Paignton (Table **110**).
R – (12) and 🍸 London Paddington - Cardiff (Table **134**).
S – (12) and 🍸 London Paddington - Swansea (Table **134**).
W – To/from Westbury (Table **140**).
Z – To Warminster (Table **140**).
f – Arrives 9–10 minutes earlier.
r – Arrives 5–8 minutes earlier.
t – Portsmouth and Southsea.
‡ – For additional services see Tables **117**, **133** and **149**.
§ – Conveys (12).

115 TAUNTON - BRISTOL - CARDIFF

2nd class GW

	⑥	⑥	⑥	⑥§	⑥	⑥A§	⑥	⑥		⑥F	⑥§	⑥E	⑥	⑥	⑥F	⑥	⑥	⑦	⑦	⑦	⑦W	⑦	⑦K	⑦§	⑦	⑦P	⑦
Penzance 112 a.	...	1350	...	...	...	...	1550	...	...	...	1650	1750	...	...	...	...	...		...	...	...	...	...	...	...	...	...
Exeter St Davids 110/6 a.	...	1655	...	...	...	...	1904	...	...	...	1955	2051	...	...	...	2119	...		...	0759	...	...	...	0946	...	1052	...
Taunton 116 132 d.	...	1720	...	1819	...	1909	1932	...	...	1958	2023	2119	...	2128	2140	2150	...		...	0827	...	...	...	1013	...	1119	...
Bridgwater d.	...	1730	...	1830	...	1920	1942	...	...	2009	2033	|	...	2138	2151	2201	...		...	0838	...	...	...	1023	...	1128	...
Highbridge and Burnham d.	...	1737	...	1837	...	1927	|	...	...	2016	2040	|	...	2145	2158	2208	...		...	0846	...	...	...	1030	...	1135	...
Weston-super-Mare 132 d.	...	1747	...	1848	...	1940	1956	...	...	2029	2052	|	...	2155	2210	2225r	...		...	0857	...	...	...	1041	...	1146	...
Portsmouth Hbr 140 d.	1523	|	1623	|	1723	|	|	1823	...	|	|	|	1923	|	|	|	2023		...	|	...	...	...	|	0908	|	1013t
Bristol Temple M 116 132 a.	1751	1816	1851	1916	1951	2007	2016	2052	...	2056	2125	2149	2151	2229	2237	2247	2252		...	0932	...	...	...	1108	1147	1212	1246
Bristol Temple Meads d.	1757	1832	1857	1927	1957	...	...	2057	...	...	2128	...	2200	...	...	...	2256		0905	...	0940	1010	1040	1111	1156	1214	1256
Newport ‡a.	1832	1906	1932	2013	2031	...	...	2131	...	...	2202	...	2237	...	...	...	2337		0948	...	1010	1043	1109	1144	1227	1243	1326
Cardiff Central ‡a.	1846	1921	1947	2027	2045	...	...	2145	...	...	2215	...	2257	...	...	...	2357		1008	...	1024	1102	1124	1158	1241	1259	1340

	⑦	⑦	⑦	⑦	⑦		⑦	⑦§	⑦	⑦B	⑦	⑦	⑦F	⑦§		⑦	⑦J	⑦	⑦	⑦F	⑦	⑦	⑦§	⑦	⑦	⑦	⑦§
Penzance 112 a.	0849	...	...	...	1050	...	...	1148	...	...	...	...	...	1350	...	...	...	...	...	...	...	...	...	...	...	...	...
Exeter St Davids 110/6 a.	1157	...	...	...	1353	...	...	1453	...	1555	1543	...	...	1655	...	...	1732	...	...	...	...	...	...	...	2030	...	...
Taunton 116 132 d.	1220	...	1318	...	1417	...	...	1516	...	1620	1612	...	1703	1720	...	...	1757	1811	...	1858	1926	...	2017	...	2106	...	2210
Bridgwater d.	1230	...	1328	...	1427	...	...	1526	...	1631	1623	...	1713	1730	...	...	1808	1821	...	1909	1936	...	2027	...	2117	...	2220
Highbridge and Burnham d.	1237	...	1335	...	1434	...	...	1533	...	|	1631	...	1720	1737	...	...	1815	1828	...	1916	1943	...	2034	...	2125	...	2227
Weston-super-Mare 132 d.	1247	...	1346	...	1444	...	...	1544	...	|	1642	...	1730	1748	...	...	1826	1840	...	1927	1953	...	2045	...	2135	...	2239
Portsmouth Hbr 140 d.	|	1108	|	1208	|	...	1308	|	1408	|	|	1508	|	|	...	1608	|	|	1708	|	|	1808	|	1908	|	2008	|
Bristol Temple M 116 132 a.	1314	1346	1413	1448	1511	...	1546	1612	1640	1658	1711	1746	1759	1815	...	1845	1854	1913	1940	1955	2026	2040	2118	2140	2210	2240	2312
Bristol Temple Meads d.	1316	1356	1415	1456	1513	...	1556	1614	1656	...	1713	1756	...	1818	...	1855	...	...	1945	...	...	2045	...	2145	...	2247	...
Newport ‡a.	1348	1425	1447	1530	1543	...	1627	1646	1730	...	1747	1826	...	1849	...	1930	...	...	2016	...	...	2118	...	2219	...	2319	...
Cardiff Central ‡a.	1403	1440	1502	1545	1558	...	1641	1700	1744	...	1801	1841	...	1903	...	1944	...	...	2030	...	...	2131	...	2233	...	2333	...

← ← ← FOR NOTES SEE PREVIOUS PAGE.

116 BIRMINGHAM - BRISTOL - PAIGNTON and PLYMOUTH

Most services convey 🍸 XC

km		Ⓐ	Ⓐ	Ⓐ D	Ⓐ	Ⓐ	Ⓐ	Ⓐ	Ⓐ	Ⓐ	Ⓐ	Ⓐ	Ⓐ	Ⓐ	Ⓐ	Ⓐ ★	Ⓐ B	Ⓐ	Ⓐ ⊠	Ⓐ b	Ⓐ
	Glasgow Central 124 220 d.	...	...	...	...	...	...	...	...	...	...	...	...	0748	...	...	...	...	...	...	...
	Edinburgh Waverley 124 220 d.	...	...	...	...	...	...	...	...	0606	0701	0806	...	0905	1003	...	1106	...	1203	1305	...
	Newcastle 124 d.	...	...	...	...	...	...	0640	...	0740	0840	0939	...	1041	1139	...	1241	...	1337	1440	...
	York 124 d.	...	...	...	...	...	0645	0744	...	0845	0944	1044	...	1144	1244	...	1344	...	1444	1544	...
	Leeds 124 d.	...	...	...	0611	...	0710	0811	...	0911	1011	1111	...	1211	1311	...	1411	...	1511	1611	...
	Sheffield 124 d.	...	...	...	0653	...	0753	0856	...	0956	1056	1155	...	1256	1355	...	1456	...	1556	1656	...
	Manchester Picc 119 d.	...	...	...	|	0703	|	|	0903	|	|	|	...	|	|	...	|	...	|	|	1703
0	**Birmingham** New Street 117 d.	...	...	0712	0812	0842	0912	1012	1042	1112	1212	1312	1342	1412	1512	1542	1612	1642	1712	1812	1842
73	Cheltenham Spa 117 138 d.	...	...	0752	0852	0932	0952	1052	1129	1152	1252	1352	1430	1452	1552	1630	1652	1730	1752	1852	1929
135	**Bristol** Parkway 138 d.	...	...	0827	0929g	1002	1022	1121	1210	1222	1321	1423	1501	1521	1622	1701	1722	1759	1824	1937	1958
145	**Bristol** Temple Meads 138 a.	...	...	0839	0938	1012	1032	1131	1220	1233	1333	1433	1514	1534	1632	1710	1732	1808	1833	1946	2007
145	**Bristol** Temple Meads 115 110 d.	0640	0812	0845	0945	...	1045	...	...	1245	1345	1445	...	1545	1645	1712	1745	1845	...	1949	...
217	Taunton 115 110 d.	0711	0843	0917	1017	...	1117	...	...	1317	1417	1517	...	1617	1717	1743	1817	1924	...	2021	...
240	Tiverton Parkway 110 d.	0723	0855	0930	1030	...	1130	...	...	1330	1430	1530	...	1630	1730	1755	1830	1936	...	2033	...
266	**Exeter** St Davids 110 111 a.	0737	0909	0945	1044	...	1144	...	...	1344	1444	1544	...	1644	1746	1809	1844	1950	...	2048	...
	Exeter St Davids 110 111 d.	0743	0912	0947	1049	...	1149	...	...	1349	1449	1549	...	1648	1749	1811	1849	1952	...	2049	...
298	Newton Abbot 110 111 d.	0803	0937f	1009	1110	...	1211	...	...	1409	1509	1609	...	1709	1809	1836	1909	2011	...	2109	...
308	Torquay 110 111 a.	|	0946	|	|	...	|	...	...	|	|	|	...	|	|	1845	|	|	...	|	...
311	**Paignton** 110 111 a.	|	0954	|	|	...	|	...	...	|	|	|	...	|	|	1852	|	|	...	|	...
312	Totnes 110 d.	0815	...	1021	1122	...	1223	...	...	1421	1521	1621	...	1721	1821	...	1921	2023	...	2121	...
350	**Plymouth** 110 a.	0841	...	1047	1149	...	1250	...	...	1448	1547	1648	...	1747	1848	...	1947	2049	...	2150	...
	Newquay 112 a.	...	...	...	...	...	...	...	...	...	...	...	...	...	|	...	...	...	...	...	...
	Penzance 112 a.	...	...	...	...	...	...	...	...	...	...	...	...	...	2047	...	...	...	...	...	...

	Ⓐ	Ⓐ	Ⓐ c	Ⓐ	⑥	⑥	⑥	⑥ D	⑥	⑥	⑥	⑥	⑥	⑥	⑥	⑥	⑥	⑥	⑥	⑥ ★	⑥ B	⑥
Glasgow Central 124 220 d.	...	...	...	...		...	...	...	...	...	...	...	...	...	...	...	...	0748	...	...	...	...
Edinburgh Waverley 124 220 d.	1405	1508	1607	1707		...	...	...	...	...	...	...	...	0606	0658	0807	...	0908	1005	...	1108	1205
Newcastle 124 d.	1539	1639	1738	1840		...	...	...	...	...	...	...	...	0739	0839	0940	...	1043	1139	...	1242	1339
York 124 d.	1644	1744	1845	1944		...	...	...	...	...	0611	0744	...	0845	0944	1044	...	1145	1244	...	1345	1445
Leeds 124 d.	1711	1811	1911	2011		...	...	...	0609	...	0711	0811	...	0911	1011	1111	...	1211	1311	...	1411	1511
Sheffield 124 d.	1756	1856	1956	2056		...	...	...	0653	...	0756	0856	...	0956	1055	1155	...	1256	1356	...	1456	1556
Manchester Picc 119 d.	|	|	|	|		...	...	...	|	0703	|	|	0903	|	|	|	...	|	|	...	|	|
Birmingham New Street 117 d.	1912	2012	2110	2212		...	...	0712	0812	0842	0912	1012	1042	1112	1212	1312	1342	1412	1512	...	1612	1712
Cheltenham Spa 117 138 d.	1952	2053	2152	2252		...	...	0752	0852	0929	0952	1052	1129	1152	1252	1352	1429	1452	1552	...	1652	1752
Bristol Parkway 138 d.	2022	2127f	2234	2321		...	...	0825f	0925	0959	1025f	1125	1158	1227	1325	1425	1458	1525	1625	...	1725	1825f
Bristol Temple Meads 138 a.	2032	2137	2244	2331		...	...	0836	0934	1008	1036	1135	1207	1238	1336	1434	1507	1536	1634	...	1735	1834
Bristol Temple Meads 115 110 d.	...	2145	...	...		0607	0810	0845	0945	...	1045	...	...	1245	1345	...	...	1545	1645	1710	1745	...
Taunton 115 110 d.	...	2216	...	...		0714	0842	0917	1017	...	1117	...	...	1317	1417	...	...	1617	1717	1741	1817	...
Tiverton Parkway 110 d.	...	2228	...	...		0726	0854	0930	1030	...	1130	...	...	1330	1430	...	...	1630	1730	1753	1830	...
Exeter St Davids 110 111 a.	...	2242	...	...		0740	0908	0945	1044	...	1145	...	...	1344	1444	...	...	1646	1745	1807	1844	...
Exeter St Davids 110 111 d.	...	2244	...	...		0743	0912	0949	1049	...	1149	...	...	1349	1449	...	...	1649	1749	1810	1847	...
Newton Abbot 110 111 d.	...	2303	...	...		0802	0934	1009	1109	...	1209	...	...	1409	1509	...	...	1709	1809	1838	1909	...
Torquay 110 111 a.	...	|	...	...		|	0945	|	|	...	|	...	...	|	|	...	...	|	|	1847	|	...
Paignton 110 111 a.	...	|	...	...		|	0952	|	|	...	|	...	...	|	|	...	...	|	|	1854	|	...
Totnes 110 d.	...	2315	...	...		0814	...	1021	1121	...	1221	...	...	1421	1521	...	...	1721	1822	...	1921	...
Plymouth 110 a.	...	2344	...	...		0840	...	1047	1148	...	1247	...	...	1448	1548	...	...	1747	1848	...	1947	...
Newquay 112 a.	...	...	...	...		...	...	...	...	...	...	...	...	...	...	...	...	...	|	...	|	...
Penzance 112 a.	...	...	...	...		...	...	...	...	...	...	...	...	...	...	...	...	...	2053	...	2140	...

	⑥	⑥	⑥	⑥	⑥ d	⑦	⑦	⑦	⑦	⑦	⑦	⑦	⑦	⑦ ★	⑦	⑦	⑦	⑦	⑦ B	⑦	⑦ d	⑦
Glasgow Central 124 220 d.	...	...	...	...	...		...	...	...	...	...	...	...	...	...	...	...	...	...	...	...	...
Edinburgh Waverley 124 220 d.	1309	...	1404	1505	1606		...	...	...	...	...	...	0908	...	1005	1105	1205	1309	1408	1508	1608	1708
Newcastle 124 d.	1443	...	1539	1638	1739		...	...	...	...	...	0933	1039	...	1140	1240	1339	1441	1540	1640	1739	1839
York 124 d.	1544	...	1644	1744	1845		...	...	...	...	0935	1032	1145	...	1244	1343	1439	1544	1642	1744	1842	1938
Leeds 124 d.	1611	...	1711	1811	1911		...	...	0811	0900	1000	1101	1211	...	1311	1411	1511	1611	1711	1811	1911	2011
Sheffield 124 d.	1656	...	1756	1856	1956		...	...	0856	0958	1056	1156	1256	...	1356	1456	1556	1656	1756	1856	1956	2056
Manchester Picc 119 d.	|	1703	|	|	|		...	...	|	|	|	|	|	...	|	|	|	|	|	|	|	|
Birmingham New Street 117 d.	1812	1842	1912	2012	2112		...	0930	1030	1130	1212	1312	1412	1442	1512	1612	1712	1812	1912	2012	2112	2212
Cheltenham Spa 117 138 d.	1852	1929	1952	2052	2152		...	1010	1110	1210	1252	1352	1452	1526	1552	1652	1752	1852	1952	2052	2152	2252
Bristol Parkway 138 d.	1925	1958	2025	2125f	2231		...	1040	1142	1243	1324	1425	1524	1557	1625f	1725f	1825	1925	2025f	2125f	2231	2321
Bristol Temple Meads 138 a.	1936	2007	2036	2134	2240		...	1049	1151	1253	1333	1436	1536	1608	1636	1734	1836	1936	2035	2135	2240	2330
Bristol Temple Meads 115 110 d.	1945	...	...	2145	...		0844	1055	1156	...	1345	...	1545	1614	...	1745	...	1945	...	2145	...	...
Taunton 115 110 d.	2017	...	...	2217	...		0915	1126	1228	...	1417	...	1617	1652	...	1817	...	2017	...	2217	...	...
Tiverton Parkway 110 d.	2030	...	...	2230	...		0927	1138	1240	...	1430	...	1630	1704	...	1830	...	2030	...	2230	...	...
Exeter St Davids 110 111 a.	2044	...	...	2244	...		0941	1152	1256	...	1444	...	1644	1718	...	1844	...	2043	...	2244	...	...
Exeter St Davids 110 111 d.	2049	...	...	2249	...		0942	1153	1258	...	1449	...	1649	1719	...	1849	...	2049	...	2246	...	...
Newton Abbot 110 111 d.	2109	...	...	2309	...		1002	1213	1318	...	1509	...	1709	1743	...	1909	...	2110	...	2306	...	...
Torquay 110 111 a.	|	...	...	|	...		|	|	|	...	|	...	|	1753	...	|	...	|	...	|	...	...
Paignton 110 111 a.	|	...	...	|	...		|	|	|	...	|	...	|	1800	...	|	...	|	...	|	...	...
Totnes 110 d.	2121	...	...	2321	...		1014	1225	1331	...	1521	...	1722	...	...	1921	...	2122	...	2318	...	...
Plymouth 110 a.	2147	...	...	2347	...		1040	1251	1357	...	1551	...	1748	...	...	1947	...	2148	...	2344	...	...
Newquay 112 a.	...	...	...	...	...		...	...	...	...	...	...	...	...	...	...	...	...	...	...	...	...
Penzance 112 a.	...	...	...	...	...		...	...	...	...	...	...	...	...	...	...	...	...	...	...	...	...

B – From Aberdeen (Table **222**).
D – From Derby (Table **124**).
b – Also calls at Gloucester (a. 1902 / d. 1908).
c – Also calls at Gloucester (a. 2200 / d. 2205).
f – Arrives 5 – 7 minutes earlier.
g – Arrives 0921.
★ – Also calls at Dawlish (10 – 15 minutes after Exeter) and Teignmouth (15 – 18 minutes after Exeter).
⊠ – Connects at Bristol Temple Meads with train in previous column.

XC Most services convey 🍷 PLYMOUTH and PAIGNTON - BRISTOL - BIRMINGHAM 116

		Ⓐ Sc	Ⓐ	Ⓐ	Ⓐ	Ⓐ	Ⓐ	Ⓐ C	Ⓐ ☆	Ⓐ	Ⓐ		Ⓐ	Ⓐ	Ⓐ	Ⓐ	Ⓐ	Ⓐ	Ⓐ	Ⓐ
Penzance **112** d.	Ⓐ	...	...	...	...	...	...	...	...	...	...	...	0925	...	...	...	...	...	...	...
Newquay **112** d.		...	...	...	...	...	...	...	...	...	...	...	...	...	...	...	...	...	...	...
Plymouth 110 d.		...	...	0525	0627	0725	...	0927	...	...	...	...	1127	1153	1227	...	1327	...	1427	1527
Totnes 110 d.		...	...	0551	0653	0751	...	0953	...	...	...	...	1153	1219	1253	...	1353	...	1453	1553
Paignton 110 d.		...	...	|	|	|	...	|	1014	...	...	...	|	|	|	...	|	...	|	|
Torquay 110 d.		...	...	|	|	|	...	|	1020	...	...	...	|	|	|	...	|	...	|	|
Newton Abbot 110 d.		...	...	0603	0706	0804	...	1005	1030	...	...	...	1206	1231	1306	...	1406	...	1506	1606
Exeter St Davids 110 a.		...	...	0622	0725	0823	...	1024	1053	...	...	...	1225	1250	1325	...	1425	...	1525	1625
Exeter St Davids 110 d.		...	...	0625	0727	0827	...	1027	1055	...	...	...	1227	1252	1327	...	1427	...	1527	1627
Tiverton Parkway 110 d.		...	...	0638	0741	0841	...	1041	1109	...	...	...	1241	1306	1341	...	1441	...	1541	1641
Taunton 115 110 d.		...	...	0651	0753	0853	...	1053	1122	...	...	...	1253	1318	1353	...	1453	...	1553	1653
Bristol Temple Meads 115 110 a.		...	...	0725	0827	0924	...	1124	1154	...	...	...	1326	1356	1426	...	1525	...	1624	1727
Bristol Temple Meads 138 d.		0624	0634	0735	0835	0932	1036	1134	1200	1235	1300	...	1335	1400	1435	1500	1535	1600	1635	1735
Bristol Parkway 138 d.		0634	0643	0744	0844	0944	1045	1144	1209	1244	1309	...	1344	1409	1444	1509	1544	1609	1644	1744
Cheltenham Spa 117 138 d.		0718	0713	0815	0915	1015	1115	1215	1240	1315	1340	...	1415	1440	1515	1540	1615	1640	1715	1815
Birmingham New Street 117 a.		0816	0755	0855	0958	1055	1158	1255	1321	1355	1421	...	1455	1525	1555	1626	1655	1726	1755	1855
Manchester Piccadilly **119** a.		...	|	|	|	|	|	|	...	|	|	...	|	1659	|	...	|	1859	|	|
Sheffield **124** a.		...	0918	1017	1119	1218	1317	1417	...	1519	1548	...	1618	...	1718	...	1819	...	1918	2018
Leeds **124** a.		...	1001	1101	1201	1301	1401	1501	...	1601	|	...	1702	...	1802	...	1904	...	2002	2102
York **124** a.		...	1030	1130	1230	1330	1430	1530	...	1630	1639	...	1730	...	1831	...	1931	...	2030	...
Newcastle **124** a.		...	1129	1229	1329	1432	1529	1632	...	1729	1744	...	1831	...	1932	...	2032	...	2128	...
Edinburgh Waverley **124 220** a.		...	1300	1406	1501	1606	1706	1807	...	1904	...	...	2011	...	2108	...	2213	...	2305	...
Glasgow Central **124 220** a.		...	...	...	...	...	1813	...	...	2013	...	...	...	...	...	...	...	...	...	...

	Ⓐ	Ⓐ	Ⓐ	Ⓐ		⑥ c	⑥	⑥	⑥	⑥	⑥ B	⑥ ☆	⑥	⑥	⑥	⑥	⑥	⑥	⑥	⑥
Penzance **112** d.	...	...	...	...	⑥	...	...	...	...	...	...	...	...	...	...	...	...	...	...	...
Newquay **112** d.	...	...	...	...		...	...	...	...	...	...	...	...	...	...	...	...	...	...	...
Plymouth 110 d.	1627	...	1827	...		...	0527	0624	0725	...	0927	...	...	1127	...	1227	...	...	1427	1527
Totnes 110 d.	1653	...	1853	...		...	0553	0650	0751	...	0953	...	...	1153	...	1253	...	...	1453	1553
Paignton 110 d.	|	...	|	2019		...	|	|	|	...	|	1010	...	|	...	|	...	...	|	|
Torquay 110 d.	|	...	|	2025		...	|	|	|	...	|	1016	...	|	...	|	...	...	|	|
Newton Abbot 110 d.	1706	...	1906	2035		...	0606	0703	0803	...	1006	1026	...	1206	...	1306	...	...	1506	1606
Exeter St Davids 110 a.	1725	...	1925	2054		...	0625	0722	0822	...	1025	1050	...	1225	...	1325	...	...	1525	1625
Exeter St Davids 110 d.	1727	...	1927	2056		...	0627	0727	0827	...	1027	1055	...	1227	...	1327	...	...	1527	1627
Tiverton Parkway 110 d.	1741	...	1941	2109		...	0641	0741	0841	...	1041	1109	...	1241	...	1341	...	...	1541	1641
Taunton 115 110 d.	1753	...	1953	2122		...	0653	0753	0853	...	1053	1122	...	1253	...	1353	...	...	1553	1653
Bristol Temple Meads 115 110 a.	1824	...	2024	2156		...	0724	0824	0924	...	1124	1153	...	1324	...	1426	...	...	1624	1726
Bristol Temple Meads 138 d.	1835	1935	2035	2200		0615	0735	0835	0935	1035	1135	1200	1235	1335	1400	1435	1535	1600	1635	1735
Bristol Parkway 138 d.	1844	1944	2044	2209		0624	0744	0844	0944	1044	1144	1209	1244	1344	1409	1444	1544	1609	1644	1744
Cheltenham Spa 117 138 d.	1915	2015	2115	2242		0710	0815	0915	1015	1115	1215	1240	1315	1415	1440	1515	1615	1640	1715	1815
Birmingham New Street 117 a.	1955	2055	2201	2341		0755	0855	0955	1055	1155	1255	1321	1355	1455	1518	1555	1655	1718	1755	1855
Manchester Piccadilly **119** a.	|	|	...	...		|	|	|	|	|	|	...	|	|	1659	|	|	1859	|	|
Sheffield **124** a.	2119	2224	...	...		0919	1019	1119	1218	1317	1419	...	1519	1617	...	1718	1819	...	1919	2019
Leeds **124** a.	2202	2334	...	...		1001	1101	1201	1301	1401	1501	...	1601	1701	...	1802	1903	...	2004	2102
York **124** a.	...	...	...	...		1030	1130	1230	1330	1430	1530	...	1630	1730	...	1831	1930	...	2030	2146
Newcastle **124** a.	...	...	...	...		1129	1230	1329	1432	1529	1629	...	1730	1833	...	1932	2035	...	2129	...
Edinburgh Waverley **124 220** a.	...	...	...	...		1305	1402	1502	1606	1704	1805	...	1903	2008	...	2108	2212	...	2301	...
Glasgow Central **124 220** a.	...	...	...	...		...	...	...	...	1813	...	...	2013	...	...	...	...	...	...	...

	⑥	⑥	⑥ D		⑦ c	⑦	⑦ A	⑦	⑦ ☆	⑦	⑦		⑦	⑦	⑦	⑦	⑦	⑦	⑦	⑦
Penzance **112** d.	...	...	...	⑦	...	...	...	...	...	0930	...	...	...	...	...	...	...	...	...	...
Newquay **112** d.	...	...	...		...	...	...	...	...	|	...	...	...	...	...	...	...	...	...	...
Plymouth 110 d.	1627	...	1827		...	...	0927	1027	...	1127	1225	...	...	1427	...	1627	...	...	1827	...
Totnes 110 d.	1653	...	1853		...	...	0953	1053	...	1153	1251	...	...	1453	...	1653	...	...	1853	...
Paignton 110 d.	|	...	|		...	...	|	|	1049	|	|	...	...	|	...	|	...	1820	|	...
Torquay 110 d.	|	...	|		...	...	|	|	1055	|	|	...	...	|	...	|	...	1826	|	...
Newton Abbot 110 d.	1706	...	1906		...	...	1005	1106	1109	1206	1304	...	...	1506	...	1706	...	1836	1906	...
Exeter St Davids 110 a.	1725	...	1925		...	...	1024	1125	1133	1225	1323	...	...	1525	...	1725	...	1855	1925	...
Exeter St Davids 110 d.	1727	...	1927		...	...	1027	1127	1135	1227	1325	...	...	1527	...	1727	...	1857	1927	...
Tiverton Parkway 110 d.	1741	...	1941		...	...	1041	1141	1148	1241	1339	...	...	1541	...	1741	...	1910	1941	...
Taunton 115 110 d.	1753	...	1953		...	...	1053	1153	1201	1253	1351	...	...	1553	...	1753	...	1923	1953	...
Bristol Temple Meads 115 110 a.	1826	...	2024		...	...	1124	1224	1245	1324	1424	...	...	1626	...	1826	...	1957	2026	...
Bristol Temple Meads 138 d.	1835	1931	2031		0915	1031	1131	1231	1300	1331	1429	...	1531	1631	1731	1831	1931	...	2031	2210
Bristol Parkway 138 d.	1844	1940	2040		0924	1040	1140	1240	1309	1340	1438	...	1540	1640	1740	1840	1940	...	2040	2219
Cheltenham Spa 117 138 d.	1915	2011	2111		1011	1111	1211	1311	1340	1411	1509	...	1611	1711	1811	1911	2011	...	2111	2250
Birmingham New Street 117 a.	1955	2053	2154		1049	1149	1249	1349	1418	1450	1548	...	1649	1750	1850	1950	2049	...	2150	2330
Manchester Piccadilly **119** a.	|	|	...		|	|	|	|	...	|	|	...	|	|	|	|	|	...	|	...
Sheffield **124** a.	2119	2221	...		1217	1318	1419	1518	...	1617	1718	...	1820	1919	2020	2119	2217	...	2318	...
Leeds **124** a.	2202	2323	...		1301	1401	1501	1601	...	1701	1802	...	1901	2002	2104	2202	2303	...	0013	...
York **124** a.	...	...	...		1329	1429	1529	1629	...	1729	1830	...	1930	2030	2130	...	...	...	...	...
Newcastle **124** a.	...	...	...		1427	1528	1628	1728	...	1830	1931	...	2028	2131	...	...	...	...	...	...
Edinburgh Waverley **124 220** a.	...	...	...		1600	1705	1759	1901	...	2007	2105	...	2208	2306	...	...	...	...	...	...
Glasgow Central **124 220** a.	...	...	...		...	1813	...	2015	...	...	...	...	...	...	...	...	...	...	...	...

A – To Dundee (Table **222**).
B – To Aberdeen (Table **222**).
C – To Aberdeen on ⑤ (Table **222**).
D – To Derby (Table **124**).

S – To Stansted Airport (Tables **117** and **208**).
c – Also calls at Gloucester (a. 0704 / d. 0708 on Ⓐ, a. 0650 / d. 0659 on ⑥, a. 0950 / d. 1002 on ⑦).
☆ – Also calls at Teignmouth (7 – 10 minutes after Newton Abbot) and Dawlish (12 – 15 minutes after Newton Abbot).

117 BIRMINGHAM - CARDIFF

AW, XC

km		Ⓐ	Ⓐ2	Ⓐ	Ⓐ2	Ⓐ	Ⓐ2	Ⓐ	Ⓐ	Ⓐ2	Ⓐ	Ⓐ2	Ⓐ	Ⓐ2	Ⓐ🍸	Ⓐ2	Ⓐ🍸	Ⓐ2	Ⓐ🍸	Ⓐ2	Ⓐ🍸	Ⓐ2	Ⓐ🍸	Ⓐ2	Ⓐ🍸
	Nottingham **120** d.		...	...	b	...	...	...	0600	...	0704	b	0808	...	0907	...	1007	b	1107	...	1207	...	1307	b	1407
	Derby **116 120** d.		...	...	...	...	...	0610	0638	...	0738	...	0841	...	0940	...	1041	...	1140	...	1238	...	1338	...	1438
0	**Birmingham** New Street ... **116** d.		...	0500	...	0537	...	0712	0730	...	0830	...	0930	...	1030	...	1130	...	1230	...	1330	...	1430	...	1530
43	Worcestershire Parkway d.		...	|	...	|	...	|	0758	...	0858	...	0958	...	1058	...	1158	...	1258	...	1358	...	1458	...	1558
73	Cheltenham Spa **116 135 138** d.		0537	0606	0632	0640	0746	0750	0815	0846	0915	0945	1015	1045	1115	1145	1215	1245	1315	1345	1415	...	1515	...	1615
83	**Gloucester** **135 138** d.		0548	0616	0643	0651	0758	...	0827	0858	0927	0958	1027	1100	1127	1159	1227	1307**g**	1328	1359**c**	1427	1457	1527	1555	1627
115	Lydney 🚂 d.		0607	0635	0703	0710	0817	...	|	0917	|	1017	1046	1119	|	1218	|	1326	1347	1418	|	1516	|	1614	1646
127	Chepstow d.		0617	0645	0713	0720	0826	...	0853	0926	0953	1026	|	1129	1153	1227	1253	1336	|	1427	1453	1525	1553	1623	1655
138	Caldicot d.		0625	0653	0723	0728	0835	...	|	0935	|	1035	|	1137	|	1236	|	1344	|	1436	|	1534	|	1632	|
155	Newport **118 134 149** a.		0642	0709	0742	0746	0850	...	0911	0950	1011	1050	1111	1152	1211	1251	1311	1359	1412	1451	1511	1549	1611	1649	1713
174	**Cardiff** Central **118 134 149** a.		0656	0722	0755	0800	0908	...	0925	1007	1025	1107	1125	1207	1225	1304	1325	1413	1425	1505	1525	1604	1625	1707	1726

	Ⓐ2	Ⓐ	Ⓐ2	Ⓐ	Ⓐ2	Ⓐ🍸	Ⓐ	Ⓐ2	Ⓐ	Ⓐ2	Ⓐ	Ⓐ2	Ⓐ	ⒶL	Ⓐ	⑤2	①–④ 2	⑥	⑥2	⑥	⑥2	⑥	⑥2	⑥	⑥
Nottingham **120** d.	...	1507	...	1607	...	...	1707	...	1805	b	1908	b	*1935*	...	*2041*	...			...	...	n	...	...	...	0600
Derby **116 120** d.	...	1538	...	1638	...	1731	1738	...	1838	...	1941	...	2031	...	2131	...	...		...	...	...	...	...	0610	0637
Birmingham New Street ... **116** d.	...	1630	...	1730	...	1812	1830	...	1930	...	2030	...	2110	2130	2212	...	...		...	0500	...	0542	...	0712	0730
Worcestershire Parkway d.	...	1658	...	1758	...	|	1858	...	1958	...	2058	...	|	2158	...	...	...		...	|	...	|	...	|	0758
Cheltenham Spa .. **116 135 138** d.	1646	1719	1745	1819	1846	1852	1915	1946	2015	...	2115	...	2152	2221	2250	2258	2258		0533	0604	0630	0644	0746	0750	0815
Gloucester **135 138** d.	1700	1730	1800	1830	1857	1902	1927	2000**c**	2027	2056	2125	2151	2200	2230	...	2310	2310		0548**c**	0615	0642	0657	0757	...	0827
Lydney 🚂 d.	1719	1749	1819	|	1918	...	|	2019	|	2115	2144	2211	...	...	...	2330	2330		0607	0635	0701	0716	0816	...	|
Chepstow d.	1729	|	1829	|	1927	...	|	2028	|	2125	2153	2221	...	...	...	2339	2339		0617	0644	0710	0726	0825	...	0853
Caldicot d.	1737	|	1837	|	1936	...	|	2037	|	2133	2202	2229	...	...	...	2348	2348		0625	0653	0719	0734	0834	...	|
Newport **118 134 149** a.	1753	1815	1853	1915	1954	...	2012	2052	2109	2148	2216	2250	...	...	...	0007	0014		0640	0707	0737	0750	0851	...	0912
Cardiff Central .... **118 134 149** a.	1813	1828	1909	1928	2009	...	2026	2107	2124	2204	2236**f**	2314**h**	...	...	...	0022	0037		0653	0720	0759	0805	0908	...	0926

	⑥2	⑥	⑥2	⑥	⑥2	⑥🍸	⑥2	⑥🍸	⑥2	⑥🍸	⑥2	⑥🍸	⑥2	⑥🍸	⑥2	⑥🍸	⑥2	⑥	⑥2	⑥	⑥2	⑥	⑥2	⑥	Ⓐ2
Nottingham **120** d.	...	0703	n	0807	...	0907	...	1007	n	1107	...	1207	...	1307	n	1407	...	1507	...	1607	...	1707	...	1807	n
Derby **116 120** d.	...	0736	...	0842	...	0938	...	1038	...	1138	...	1238	...	1338	...	1438	...	1539	...	1638	...	1739	...	1838	...
Birmingham New Street ... **116** d.	...	0830	...	0930	...	1030	...	1130	...	1230	...	1330	...	1430	...	1530	...	1630	...	1730	...	1830	...	1930	...
Worcestershire Parkway d.	...	0858	...	0958	...	1058	...	1158	...	1258	...	1358	...	1458	...	1558	...	1658	...	1758	...	1858	...	1958	...
Cheltenham Spa .. **116 135 138** d.	0846	0915	0945	1015	1041	1115	1146	1215	1246	1315	1346	1415	1446	1515	1546	1615	1646	1715	1745	1819	1846	1915	1946	2015	2045
Gloucester **135 138** d.	0901**c**	0927	1001**d**	1027	1052	1127	1158	1227	1257	1327	1358	1427	1500**c**	1527	1557	1627	1658	1727	1756	1830	1858	1927	1958	2027	2059**c**
Lydney 🚂 d.	0920	|	1020	1046	1111	|	1217	|	1316	1346	1417	|	1519	|	1616	1646	1717	1746	1815	|	1917	|	2017	|	2118
Chepstow d.	0929	0953	1029	|	1120	1153	1226	1253	1325	|	1426	1453	1528	1553	1625	1656	1726	|	1825	|	1927	|	2027	|	2128
Caldicot d.	0938	|	1038	|	1129	|	1235	|	1334	|	1435	|	1537	|	1634	|	1735	|	1833	|	1935	|	2035	|	2136
Newport **118 134 149** a.	0953	1012	1054	1111	1145	1212	1250	1312	1349	1411	1450	1511	1552	1611	1649	1713	1750	1811	1848	1912	1950	2009	2050	2109	2151
Cardiff Central .... **118 134 149** a.	1008	1027	1109	1125	1200	1226	1306	1325	1407	1425	1507	1525	1606	1625	1703	1727	1807	1827	1906	1925	2007	2022	2108	2122	2211

	⑥	⑥2	⑥🍸	⑥2	⑦	⑦2	⑦2	⑦🍸	⑦	⑦2	⑦	⑦	⑦2	⑦🍸	⑦🍸	⑦2	⑦🍸	⑦🍸	⑦2	⑦🍸	⑦🍸	⑦2	⑦🍸	⑦🍸	⑦2
Nottingham **120** d.	1907	n	*1932*	...		...	...	...	0955	...	1116	1216	...	1316	1416	...	1512	1616	...	1716	1816	...	*1825*	*1923*	...
Derby **116 120** d.	1938	...	2031	...		...	...	...	1020	...	1140	1240	...	1340	1440	...	1537	1640	...	1742	1840	...	1931	2031	...
Birmingham New Street ... **116** d.	2030	...	2112	...		...	*0930*	1012	1112	...	1230	1330	...	1430	1530	...	1630	1730	...	1830	1930	...	2012	2112	...
Worcestershire Parkway d.	2058	...	|	...		...	|	1040	1140	...	1258	1358	...	1458	1558	...	1658	1758	...	1858	1958	...	|	|	...
Cheltenham Spa .. **116 135 138** d.	2115	2145	2152	2258		...	1038	1100	1200	1235	1318	1415	1409	1515	1615	1610	1715	1815	1835	1915	2015	2010	2050	2152	...
Gloucester **135 138** d.	2127	2156	2200	2309		0845	1048	1111	1211	1246	1330	1425	1429**a**	1530**c**	1625	1629**d**	1725	1828	1848	1925	2025	2033**e**	...	2200	2240
Lydney 🚂 d.	2146	2215	...	2328		0904	1107	|	|	1305	|	|	1448	|	|	1648	|	|	1907	|	|	2052	...	...	2259
Chepstow d.	2156	2225	...	2338		0914	1116	|	|	1314	|	|	1458	|	|	1658	|	|	1916	|	|	2102	...	...	2308
Caldicot d.	2204	2233	...	2346		0922	1125	|	|	1323	|	|	1506	|	|	1706	|	|	1925	|	|	2111	...	...	2317
Newport **118 134 149** a.	2219	2254	...	0008		0944	1140	1153	1253	1338	1412	1507	1521	1612	1708	1721	1807	1911	1941	2007	2107	2133	...	...	2332
Cardiff Central .... **118 134 149** a.	2244	2314	...	0030		1004	1155	1207	1306	1353	1425	1525	1536	1625	172	1735	1821	1925	1956	2020	2120	2148	...	...	2347

	Ⓐ	Ⓐb2	Ⓐ	ⒶC	Ⓐ2	Ⓐ	Ⓐ2	Ⓐ	Ⓐb2	Ⓐ	Ⓐ2	Ⓐ🍸	Ⓐ2	Ⓐ	Ⓐb2	Ⓐ🍸	Ⓐ2	Ⓐ🍸	Ⓐ2	Ⓐ🍸	Ⓐb2	Ⓐ🍸	Ⓐ2	Ⓐ🍸	Ⓐ2
Cardiff Central .... **118 134 149** d.		0422	...	...	0610	0640	0705	0745	0806	0845	0906	0945	1008	1045	1107	1145	1210	1245	1307	1345	1408	1445	1508	1545	1608
Newport **118 134 149** d.		0440	...	...	0624	0654	0720	0801	0824	0900	0921	0959	1023	1101	1122	1159	1225	1259	1322	1359	1423	1459	1523	1559	1623
Caldicot d.		0500	...	...	0637	0707	0733	|	0837	|	0934	|	1036	|	1135	|	1238	|	1336	|	1439	|	1537	|	1636
Chepstow d.		0508	...	...	0645	0715	0741	|	0845	0919	0942	1016	1044	|	1143	1216	1247	1316	1344	|	1447	1519	1545	1616	1645
Lydney 🚂 d.		0517	...	...	0654	0724	0750	0827	0854	|	0951	|	1053	1125	1152	|	1255	|	1353	1423	1456	|	1554	|	1653
Gloucester **135 138** d.		0538	...	0708	0717	0745	0811	0849	0915	0949	1017**c**	1049**c**	1117	1149	1217**c**	1245	1317	1349**c**	1413	1449**c**	1516	1549	1616	1645	1717
Cheltenham Spa .. **116 135 138** d.		0548	0713	0718	0727	0755	0821	0859	0924	0959	1027	1059	1127	1159	1226	1255	1327	1359	...	1459	...	1559	1626	1655	1724
Worcestershire Parkway d.		...	|	0736	...	0814	...	0914	...	1014	...	1114	...	1214	...	1314	...	1414	...	1514	...	1614	...	1714	...
Birmingham New Street ... **116** a.		...	0755	0816	...	0845	...	0945	...	1045	...	1145	...	1245	...	1345	...	1445	...	1545	...	1645	...	1745	...
Derby **116 120** a.		...	0840	...	...	0932	...	1033	...	1132	...	1232	...	1332	...	1432	...	1536	...	1632	...	1731	...	1837	...
Nottingham **120** a.		...	*0922*	...	...	1003	...	1103	...	1204	...	1303	...	1403	...	1503	...	1603	...	1705	...	1805	...	1906	...

	Ⓐ🍸	Ⓐ2	Ⓐ🍸	Ⓐ2	Ⓐ	Ⓐb2	Ⓐ	Ⓐb2	Ⓐ	Ⓐ2	Ⓐ	Ab2	⑤b2	⑤2	A2	⑥	⑥n2	⑥🍸	⑥E	⑥2	⑥	⑥2	⑥	⑥n2	⑥
Cardiff Central .... **118 134 149** d.	1645	1708	1745	1807	1845	1910	1950	2009	2106	2110	2145	2206	2212	2320	2312		0440	...	...	0610	0640	0707	0745	0805	0845
Newport **118 134 149** d.	1659	1723	1759	1823	1859	1925	2004	2025	2120	2125	2159	2224	2227	2334	2330		0457	...	...	0626	0654	0722	0800	0820	0859
Caldicot d.	|	1736	|	1838	|	1938	2017	2038	|	2138	|	2245	2240	2348	2351		0510	...	...	0640	0707	0736	|	0833	|
Chepstow d.	|	1745	1816	1847	1918	1946	2025	2046	|	2146	|	2254	2249	2357	0001		0518	...	...	0649	0715	0745	|	0841	0916
Lydney 🚂 d.	1725	1753	|	1857	|	1958	2034	2056	|	2155	|	2302	2257	0005	0009		0527	...	...	0657	0724	0754	0825	0850	|
Gloucester **135 138** d.	1749	1818**c**	1845	1919	1949	2024	2056	2120	2203	2218	2249	2333	2334**p**	0026	0033		0548	0659	0705	0718	0745	0818	0849	0912	0949**c**
Cheltenham Spa .. **116 135 138** d.	1759	1826	1855	1928	1959	...	2106	...	2213	2228	2259	2348	2349	*0043*	...		0558	0710	0714	0729	0755	0828	0859	0922	0959
Worcestershire Parkway d.	1814	...	1914	...	2014	...	2120	...	2232	...	|	...	...	...	...		...	|	0733	...	0814	...	0914	...	1014
Birmingham New Street ... **116** a.	1845	...	1945	...	2045	...	2154	...	2305	...	2358	...	...	...	...		...	0755	0806	...	0845	...	0945	...	1045
Derby **116 120** a.	1932	...	2031	...	2138	...	2250	...	...	...	...	...	...	...	...		...	0840	...	...	0931	...	1032	...	1131
Nottingham **120** a.	2004	...	2105	...	2217	...	2326	...	...	...	...	...	...	...	...		...	*0922*	...	...	1003	...	1103	...	1204

	⑥2	⑥🍸	⑥2	⑥	⑥n2	⑥🍸	⑥2	⑥🍸	⑥2	⑥🍸	⑥n2	⑥🍸	⑥2	⑥🍸	⑥2	⑥🍸	⑥2	⑥🍸	⑥2	⑥	⑥n2	⑥	⑥n2	⑥	⑥2
Cardiff Central .... **118 134 149** d.	0904	0945	1008	1045	1107	1145	1208	1245	1307	1345	1407	1445	1507	1545	1607	1645	1707	1745	1809	1845	1907	2000	2009	2048	2110
Newport **118 134 149** d.	0920	0959	1023	1100	1122	1159	1222	1259	1322	1359	1422	1459	1522	1559	1622	1659	1722	1759	1824	1859	1922	2014	2025	2102	2125
Caldicot d.	0935	|	1036	|	1135	|	1235	|	1335	|	1435	|	1535	|	1635	|	1735	|	1838	|	1935	2027	2038	|	2138
Chepstow d.	0944	1016	1044	|	1143	1217	1244	1316	1343	|	1443	1518	1543	1616	1643	|	1743	1817	1846	1916	1943	2036	2046	|	2147
Lydney 🚂 d.	0952	|	1053	1124	1152	|	1252	|	1352	1423	1452	|	1552	|	1652	1724	1752	|	1855	|	1952	2044	2055	|	2155
Gloucester **135 138** d.	1013	1049**c**	1114	1149**c**	1213	1245	1314	1349**c**	1413	1449**c**	1513	1549**c**	1613	1645	1713	1749**c**	1813	1845	1916	1949**c**	2013	2107	2116	2149**c**	2216
Cheltenham Spa .. **116 135 138** d.	1024	1059	1124	1159	1223	1255	1324	1359	1424	1459	1523	1559	1623	1655	1722	1759	1823	1855	1926	1959	2023	2118	2126	2159	2225
Worcestershire Parkway d.	...	1114	...	1214	...	1314	...	1414	...	1514	...	1614	...	1714	...	1814	...	1914	...	2014	...	|	...	2214	...
Birmingham New Street ... **116** a.	...	1145	...	1245	...	1345	...	1445	...	1545	...	1645	...	1745	...	1845	...	1945	...	2045	...	2207	...	2245	...
Derby **116 120** a.	...	1232	...	1331	...	1431	...	1536	...	1631	...	1731	...	1836	...	1931	...	2031	...	2131	...	2255	...	2331	...
Nottingham **120** a.	...	1303	...	1403	...	1503	...	1603	...	1703	...	1803	...	1903	...	2003	...	2103	...	2215	...	2327	...	...	...

	⑥n2	⑥2	⑦	⑦2	⑦	⑦2	⑦	⑦	⑦2	⑦🍸	⑦🍸	⑦2	⑦🍸	⑦🍸	⑦2	⑦🍸	⑦🍸	⑦2		⑦🍸	⑦🍸	⑦D	⑦🍸	⑦2	⑦
Cardiff Central .... **118 134 149** d.	2207	2315		0823	...	1030	1048	1145	1229	1245	1345	1429	1445	1545	1629	1645	1745	1829	...	1845	...	1945	...	2024	2045
Newport **118 134 149** d.	2221	2334		0841	...	1044	1102	1159	1243	1258	1401	1443	1459	1559	1643	1659	1759	1843	...	1859	...	1959	...	2038	2059
Caldicot d.	2235	2356		0905	...	1059	|	|	1256	|	|	1457	|	|	1657	|	|	1857	...	|	...	|	...	2051	|
Chepstow d.	2244	0005		0914	...	1107	|	|	1305	|	|	1505	|	|	1706	|	|	1906	...	|	...	|	...	2100	|
Lydney 🚂 d.	2252	0014		0922	...	1116	|	|	1313	|	|	1514	|	|	1714	|	|	1914	...	|	...	|	...	2108	|
Gloucester **135 138** d.	2314	0036		0944	1002	1138	1149	1249**d**	1335	1349**d**	1449	1535	1549**d**	1649**d**	1736	1749**d**	1849**d**	1935	...	1949**d**	...	2049	...	2131	2149**d**
Cheltenham Spa .. **116 135 138** d.	...	...		0956	1011	1148	1159	1259	1345	1359	1459	1545	1559	1659	1746	1759	1859	1945	...	1959	2011	2059	2111	...	2159
Worcestershire Parkway d.	...	...		...	|	...	1214	1314	...	1414	1514	...	1614	1714	...	1814	1914	...	...	2014	|	2114	|	...	2214
Birmingham New Street ... **116** a.	...	...		...	1049	...	1245	1345	...	1445	1545	...	1645	1745	...	1845	1945	...	...	2045	2049	2145	2150	...	2245
Derby **116 120** a.	...	...		...	1136	...	1329	1429	...	1531	1629	...	1729	1829	...	1931	2029	...	...	2129	2140	...	2239	...	...
Nottingham **120** a.	...	...		...	*1253*	...	1353	1453	...	1555	1653	...	1754	1854	...	1957	2054	...	...	2154	*2245*	...	...	...	...

A – ①–④.
C – 🚃12 and 🍸 Bristol Temple Meads - Stansted Airport (Tables **116** and **208**).
D – 🚃12 Cardiff - Leicester (Table **208**).
E – 🚃12 to Stansted Airport (Table **208**).
L – 🚃12 Leicester - Gloucester (Table **208**).

a – Arrives 1419.
b – From Mar. 27.
c – Arrives 5–6 minutes earlier.
d – Arrives 7–8 minutes earlier.
e – Arrives 2022.
f – 2229 on ⑤.
g – Arrives 1255.

h – Arrives 2259 on ⑤.
n – From Apr. 1.
p – Arrives 2318.

🚂 – DEAN FOREST RAILWAY (Lydney Junction - Parkend. *7 km*).
✆ 01594 845840. www.deanforestrailway.co.uk
Lydney Junction station is 10 minutes walk from the National Rail station.

XC Most services convey 🍷 BIRMINGHAM - MANCHESTER 119

km			Ⓐ	Ⓐ	Ⓐ	ⒶS	Ⓐ	Ⓐ	Ⓐ	Ⓐ	Ⓐ	Ⓐ	Ⓐ	Ⓐ	Ⓐ	Ⓐ	Ⓐ	Ⓐ	Ⓐ	Ⓐ	Ⓐ	Ⓐ
	Bournemouth **114** d.		...	...	...	...	...	0630	0730	...	0945	...	1145	...	...	1345	...	...	1545	1645	...	1845
	Reading **114** d.	Ⓐ	...	...	...	0615	0715	0815	0916	1016	1115	1216	1315	...	1415	1515	...	1615	1715	1815	1915	2015
	Plymouth **116** d.		...	...	...	|	|	|	|	|	|	|	|	1153	|	|	...	|	|	|	|	|
	Exeter St Davids **116** d.		...	...	...	|	|	|	|	|	|	|	|	1252	|	|	...	|	|	|	|	|
	Bristol Temple Meads **116** d.		...	...	...	|	|	|	|	|	|	|	|	1400	|	|	1600	|	|	|	|	|
0	**Birmingham** New St **144 150** d.		0601	0701	0726	0801	0901	1001	1101	1201	1301	1401	1501	1531	1601	1701	1731	1801	1901	2001	2101	2201
20	Wolverhampton **144 150** d.		0619	0719	0745	0819	0919	1019	1119	1219	1319	1419	1519	1549	1619	1719	1749	1819	1919	2019	2119	2219
46	Stafford **144** d.		0633	0733	0800	0833	0933	1033	1133	1233	1333	1433	1533	1604	1633	1733	1803	1833	1933	2033	2133	2233
72	Stoke on Trent **144 152** d.		0649	0750	|	0849	0949	1049	1149	1249	1349	1449	1549	1621	1649	1749	1821	1849	1949	2049	2149	2249
104	Macclesfield **152** d.		0706	0806	|	0906	1006	1106	1206	1306	1406	1506	1606	1637	1706	1806	1837	1906	2006	2106	2206	2307
123	Stockport **152** d.		0720	0820	0851	0918	1019	1119	1219	1319	1418	1519	1619	1651	1719	1819	1851	1919	2019	2119	2219	2321
132	**Manchester** Piccadilly **152** a.		0729	0829	0859	0929	1029	1129	1229	1329	1429	1529	1629	1659	1729	1829	1859	1929	2029	2129	2230	2331

		⑥	⑥	⑥	⑥	⑥S	⑥	⑥	⑥	⑥	⑥		⑥	⑥	⑥	⑥	⑥	⑥	⑥	⑥	⑥	⑥
Bournemouth **114** d.		...	...	...	...	...	...	0745	...	0945	...	...	1145	...	...	1345	...	...	1545	...	1745	...
Reading **114** d.	⑥	...	...	...	0615	0715	0815	0915	1015	1115	1215	...	1315	...	1415	1515	...	1615	1715	1815	1915	2015
Plymouth **116** d.		...	...	...	|	|	|	|	|	|	|	...	|	...	|	|	...	|	|	|	|	|
Exeter St Davids **116** d.		...	...	...	|	|	|	|	|	|	|	...	|	...	|	|	...	|	|	|	|	|
Bristol Temple Meads **116** d.		...	...	...	|	|	|	|	|	|	|	...	|	1400	|	|	1600	|	|	|	|	|
Birmingham New St **144 150** d.		0601	0701	0726	0801	0901	1001	1101	1201	1301	1401	...	1501	1531	1601	1701	1731	1801	1901	2001	2101	2201
Wolverhampton **144 150** d.		0619	0719	0745	0818	0919	1018	1119	1219	1319	1419	...	1519	1548	1619	1719	1748	1819	1919	2019	2119	2218
Stafford **144** d.		0633	0733	0800	0832	0933	1033	1133	1233	1333	1433	...	1533	1602	1633	1733	1802	1833	1933	2033	2133	2232
Stoke on Trent **144 152** d.		0649	0749	|	0849	0949	1049	1149	1249	1349	1449	...	1549	1621	1649	1750	1821	1849	1949	2049	2149	2248
Macclesfield **152** d.		0706	0806	|	0906	1006	1106	1206	1306	1406	1506	...	1606	1637	1706	1806	1837	1906	2006	2106	2206	2305
Stockport **152** d.		0718	0820	0851	0920	1019	1119	1219	1319	1419	1519	...	1619	1651	1720	1820	1951	1919	2019	2120	2219	2318
Manchester Piccadilly **152** a.		0729	0829	0859	0929	1029	1129	1229	1329	1429	1529	...	1629	1659	1729	1829	1859	1929	2029	2129	2230	2329

		⑦		⑦	⑦		⑦S	⑦		⑦	⑦		⑦	⑦	⑦		⑦	⑦		⑦		⑦
Bournemouth **114** d.		...	...	...	...	...	...	0940	...	...	1140	...	...	1340	...	...	1540	...	...	1740	...	...
Reading **114** d.	⑦	...	...	...	0915	...	1015	1115	...	1215	1315	...	1415	1515	1615	...	1715	1815	...	1915	...	2015
Plymouth **116** d.		...	...	...	|	...	|	|	...	|	|	...	|	|	|	...	|	|	...	|	...	|
Exeter St Davids **116** d.		...	...	...	|	...	|	|	...	|	|	...	|	|	|	...	|	|	...	|	...	|
Bristol Temple Meads **116** d.		...	...	...	|	...	|	|	...	|	|	...	|	|	|	...	|	|	...	|	...	|
Birmingham New St **144 150** d.		0901	...	1001	1101	...	1201	1301	...	1401	1501	...	1601	1701	1801	...	1901	2001	...	2101	...	2201
Wolverhampton **144 150** d.		0918	...	1018	1118	...	1219	1319	...	1419	1519	...	1619	1719	1819	...	1919	2019	...	2119	...	2219
Stafford **144** d.		0932	...	1032	1132	...	1233	1333	...	1433	1533	...	1633	1733	1833	...	1933	2033	...	2133	...	2233
Stoke on Trent **144 152** d.		0954	...	1052f	1152	...	1249	1349	...	1449	1549	...	1649	1749	1849	...	1949	2049	...	2149	...	2249
Macclesfield **152** d.		1011	...	1109	1208	...	1306	1406	...	1506	1606	...	1706	1806	1906	...	2006	2106	...	2206	...	2305
Stockport **152** d.		1026	...	1124	1222	...	1319	1419	...	1519	1619	...	1719	1819	1919	...	2019	2120	...	2221	...	2320
Manchester Piccadilly **152** a.		1037	...	1132	1230	...	1329	1429	...	1529	1629	...	1729	1829	1929	...	2029	2129	...	2229	...	2328

		Ⓐ	Ⓐ	Ⓐ	Ⓐ	Ⓐ	Ⓐ	Ⓐ	Ⓐ	Ⓐ	Ⓐ	Ⓐ		Ⓐ	Ⓐ	Ⓐ	Ⓐ	Ⓐ	Ⓐ	Ⓐ	ⒶS	Ⓐ
Manchester Piccadilly **152** d.		0511	0624	0703	0725	0825	0903	0925	1025	1125	1225	1325	...	1425	1525	1625	1703	1725	1825	1903	1925	2025
Stockport **152** d.	Ⓐ	|	0633	0713	0734	0833	0913	0933	1033	1134	1233	1333	...	1433	1533	1633	1713	1734	1833	1913	1933	2033
Macclesfield **152** d.		|	0647	0726	0747	0846	0926	0946	1046	1147	1246	1346	...	1446	1546	1646	1726	|	1846	1926	1946	2046
Stoke on Trent **144 152** d.		0605	0704	0744	0804	0904	0944	1004	1104	1205	1304	1404	...	1504	1604	1704	1744	|	1904	1944	2004	2104
Stafford **144** d.		0622	0724	0800	0821	0922	1000	1021	1121	1222	1321	1421	...	1521	1622	1721	1800	1821	1921	2000	2021	2121
Wolverhampton **144 150** d.		0639	0741	0815	0839	0939	1015	1039	1139	1239	1339	1439	...	1539	1639	1739	1815	1839	1939	2015	2039	2139
Birmingham New St **144 150** a.		0657	0804	0833	0856	0957	1033	1056	1156	1256	1356	1456	...	1556	1656	1756	1833	1855	1956	2033	2056	2156
Bristol Temple Meads **116** a.		|	...	1012	|	|	1220	|	|	|	|	|	...	|	|	|	2007	|	|	...	|	|
Exeter St Davids **116** a.		|	...	...	|	|	...	|	|	|	|	|	...	|	|	|	...	|	|	...	|	|
Plymouth **116** a.		|	...	...	|	|	...	|	|	|	|	|	...	|	|	|	...	|	|	...	|	|
Reading **114** a.		0846	...	...	1044	1141	...	1241	1340	1439	1539	1639	...	1740	1840	1941	...	2042	2141	...	2239	2349
Bournemouth **114** a.		1013	...	...	1213	...	...	1413	...	1613	...	1817	...	1913	...	2115	...	...	2317	...	...	...

	Ⓐ	Ⓐ		⑥	⑥	⑥	⑥	⑥	⑥		⑥	⑥	⑥		⑥	⑥	⑥	⑥	⑥	⑥	⑥	⑥S
Manchester Piccadilly **152** d.	2125	2203		0511	0703	0725	0825	0903	0924	...	1025	1125	1225	...	1325	1425	1525	1625	1703	1725	1825	1925
Stockport **152** d.	2133	2213	⑥	|	0711	0734	0834	0912	0932	...	1033	1133	1233	...	1333	1433	1533	1633	1711	1734	1833	1933
Macclesfield **152** d.	2146	2226		|	0724	0747	0846	0925	0946	...	1046	1146	1246	...	1346	1446	1546	1646	1725	1747	1846	1946
Stoke on Trent **144 152** d.	2204	2244		0606	0744	0804	0904	0944	1004	...	1104	1204	1304	...	1404	1504	1604	1704	1744	1805	1905	2004
Stafford **144** d.	2221	2300		0623	0801	0821	0921	1001	1021	...	1121	1221	1321	...	1421	1521	1621	1721	1801	1828r	1922	2021
Wolverhampton **144 150** d.	2241	2316		0640	0815	0839	0939	1015	1039	...	1138	1239	1338	...	1439	1539	1639	1739	1815	1842	1939	2039
Birmingham New St **144 150** a.	2257	2333		0657	0833	0856	0956	1033	1056	...	1156	1256	1357	...	1456	1556	1657	1756	1833	1858	1956	2056
Bristol Temple Meads **116** a.	...	...		|	1008	|	|	1207	|	...	|	|	|	...	|	|	|	|	2007	|	|	|
Exeter St Davids **116** a.	...	...		|	...	|	|	...	|	...	|	|	|	...	|	|	|	|	...	|	|	|
Plymouth **116** a.	...	...		|	...	|	|	...	|	...	|	|	|	...	|	|	|	|	...	|	|	|
Reading **114** a.	...	...		0840	...	1042	1141	...	1239	...	1341	1439	1539	...	1641	1741	1841	1940	...	2039	2140	2239
Bournemouth **114** a.	...	...		1013	...	1213	...	...	1413	...	...	1613	...	...	1813	...	2013	...	...	2215	2319	...

	⑥	⑥		⑦	⑦	⑦	⑦		⑦	⑦	⑦		⑦	⑦		⑦	⑦S		⑦	⑦		⑦
Manchester Piccadilly **152** d.	2025	2125		0827	0927	1026	1123	...	1225	1325	1425	...	1525	1625	...	1725	1825	...	1925	2108	...	2204
Stockport **152** d.	2033	2133	⑦	0835	0935	1036	1133	...	1233	1333	1433	...	1533	1633	...	1733	1833	...	1933	2118	...	2212
Macclesfield **152** d.	2046	2146		|	0948	1049	1146	...	1246	1346	1446	...	1546	1646	...	1746	1846	...	1946	2131	...	2225
Stoke on Trent **144 152** d.	2104	2204		|	1008	1106	1204	...	1305	1404	1504	...	1604	1704	...	1804	1904	...	2004	2154	...	2246
Stafford **144** d.	2124	2221		0925	1025	1124	1221	...	1321	1421	1521	...	1621	1721	...	1821	1921	...	2021	2210	...	2303
Wolverhampton **144 150** d.	2141	2240		0940	1039	1139	1239	...	1339	1439	1539	...	1639	1739	...	1839	1939	...	2040	2228	...	2318
Birmingham New St **144 150** a.	2200	2257		0957	1056	1157	1256	...	1356	1456	1556	...	1656	1756	...	1856	1956	...	2057	2248	...	2334
Bristol Temple Meads **116** a.	...	...		|	|	|	|	...	|	|	|	...	|	|	...	|	|	...	|	...	...	...
Exeter St Davids **116** a.	...	...		|	|	|	|	...	|	|	|	...	|	|	...	|	|	...	|	...	...	...
Plymouth **116** a.	...	...		|	|	|	|	...	|	|	|	...	|	|	...	|	|	...	|	...	...	...
Reading **114** a.	...	...		1139	1239	1339	1439	...	1539	1639	1739	...	1839	1939	...	2039	2139	...	2239	...	...	...
Bournemouth **114** a.	...	...		1326	...	1525	...	...	1725	...	1926	...	...	2126	...	2226	...	...	...	...	...	...

S – From / to Southampton Central (Table **114**). f – Arrives 1047. r – Arrives 1820.

120 BIRMINGHAM - NOTTINGHAM — XC

km		Ⓐ	Ⓐ	Ⓐ🍷	Ⓐ	Ⓐ🍷	Ⓐ	Ⓐ🍷	Ⓐ	Ⓐ🍷	Ⓐ	Ⓐ🍷	Ⓐ🍷	Ⓐ🍷	Ⓐ	Ⓐ	Ⓐ🍷	Ⓐ	Ⓐ🍷	Ⓐ	Ⓐ🍷	Ⓐ	Ⓐ🍷	Ⓐ	Ⓐ🍷
	Cardiff Central **117** d.	...	...	...	...	...	0640	...	0745	...	0845	...	0945	...	1045	...	1145	...	1245	...	1345	...	1445	...	1545
0	**Birmingham** New Street **124** d.	0619	0649	0719	0749	0818	0849	0912	0949	1012	1049	1118	1149	1219	1249	1318	1349	1418	1449	1512	1549	1618	1649	1712	1749
28	Tamworth **124** d.	0638	0706	0738	0806	0835	0908	0929	1006	1029	1109	1135	1206	1239	1308	1335	1408	1435	1508	1529	1608	1635	1708	1730	1812
48	Burton-on-Trent **124** d.	0650	0718	0750	0818	0846	0920	0941	1018	1041	1120	1147	1218	1253	1320	1346	1420	1446	1520	1542	1620	1646	1720	1742	1823
67	**Derby** **124** a.	0702	0733	0804	0833	0900	0932	0953	1033	1052	1132	1200	1232	1305	1332	1359	1432	1458	1536	1553	1632	1658	1731	1755	1837
67	**Derby** **155 172** d.	0708	0742	0809	0840	0912	0940	0959	1039	1059	1140	1213	1240	1313	1340	1412	1440	1513	1540	1600	1640	1712	1740	1759	1843
93	**Nottingham** **155 172** a.	0736	0807	0834	0906	0933	1003	1023	1103	1122	1204	1235	1303	1336	1403	1435	1503	1535	1603	1623	1705	1736	1805	1825	1906

	Ⓐ	Ⓐ🍷	Ⓐ	Ⓐ🍷	Ⓐ	Ⓐ	Ⓐ	⑥	⑥	⑥🍷	⑥	⑥🍷	⑥	⑥🍷	⑥	⑥🍷	⑥	⑥🍷	⑥🍷	⑥🍷	⑥	⑥	⑥🍷	⑥	⑥🍷
Cardiff Central **117** d.	...	1645	...	1745	1845	1950	...	...	...	...	...	...	0640	...	0745	...	0845	...	0945	...	1045	...	1145	...	1245
Birmingham New Street **124** d.	1818	1849	1912	1949	2049	2203	2309	0619	0649	0719	0749	0812	0849	0918	0949	1012	1049	1112	1149	1212	1249	1312	1349	1412	1449
Tamworth **124** d.	1835	1908	1929	2008	2108	2227	2328	0638	0706	0738	0806	0829	0908	0935	1006	1029	1108	1129	1206	1229	1308	1329	1408	1429	1508
Burton-on-Trent **124** d.	1847	1920	1941	2020	2120	2239	2340	0650	0718	0750	0818	0841	0920	0946	1018	1041	1120	1141	1218	1241	1320	1341	1420	1441	1520
Derby **124** a.	1901	1932	1952	2031	2138	2250	2354	0701	0734	0804	0835	0852	0931	0959	1032	1053	1131	1155	1232	1252	1331	1353	1431	1453	1536
Derby **155 172** d.	1913	1940	1957	2040	2146	2258	2358	0710	0742	0808	0840	0859	0940	1008	1040	1101	1140	1201	1240	1301	1340	1401	1440	1501	1540
Nottingham **155 172** a.	1936	2004	2018	2105	2217	2326	0018	0738	0806	0831	0905	0922	1003	1029	1103	1122	1204	1223	1303	1324	1403	1424	1503	1523	1603

	⑥	⑥🍷	⑥	⑥🍷	⑥	⑥🍷	⑥	⑥🍷	⑥	⑥🍷	⑥	⑥	⑥	⑦🍷	⑦🍷	⑦	⑦	⑦🍷	⑦🍷	⑦🍷	⑦🍷	⑦🍷	⑦🍷	⑦🍷	⑦🍷
Cardiff Central **117** d.	...	1345	...	1445	...	1545	...	1645	...	1745	1845	2000	2048	...	...	1048	1145	1245	1345	1445	1545	1645	1745	1845	*1945*
Birmingham New Street **124** d.	1512	1549	1612	1649	1712	1749	1812	1849	1912	1949	2049	2210	2249	1003	1149	1249	1349	1449	1549	1649	1749	1849	1949	2049	2203
Tamworth **124** d.	1529	1608	1629	1708	1730	1808	1829	1908	1929	2008	2108	2228	2308	1019	1206	1306	1406	1508	1606	1706	1806	1908	2006	2106	2220
Burton-on-Trent **124** d.	1541	1620	1641	1720	1744	1820	1841	1920	1941	2020	2120	2240	2320	1030	1218	1318	1418	1520	1618	1718	1818	1920	2017	2117	|
Derby **124** a.	1553	1631	1653	1731	1755	1836	1852	1931	1952	2031	2131	2255	2331	1040	1229	1329	1429	1531	1629	1729	1829	1931	2029	2129	2239
Derby **155 172** d.	1601	1640	1701	1740	1759	1840	1856	1940	1959	2040	2146	2259	*2347*	...	1233	1333	1433	1535	1633	1733	1833	1937	2034	2134	...
Nottingham **155 172** a.	1624	1703	1724	1803	1824	1903	1924	2003	2019	2103	2215	2327	*0014*	...	1253	1353	1453	1555	1653	1754	1854	1957	2054	2154	...

	Ⓐ	Ⓐ A	Ⓐ	Ⓐ	Ⓐ	Ⓐ	Ⓐ🍷	Ⓐ	Ⓐ🍷	Ⓐ	Ⓐ🍷	Ⓐ	Ⓐ🍷	Ⓐ	Ⓐ🍷	Ⓐ🍷	Ⓐ🍷	Ⓐ	Ⓐ	Ⓐ🍷	Ⓐ	Ⓐ🍷	Ⓐ	Ⓐ🍷	Ⓐ
Nottingham **155 172** d.	0600	0639	0704	0737	0808	0839	0907	0941	1007	1041	1107	1141	1207	1241	1307	1341	1407	1441	1507	1541	1607	1641	1707	1741	1805
Derby **155 172** a.	0633	0701	0734	0802	0838	0907	0937	1001	1038	1101	1136	1202	1235	1301	1335	1402	1435	1501	1535	1601	1635	1702	1734	1806	1831
Derby **124** d.	0638	0713	0738	0806	0841	0910	0940	1010	1041	1110	1140	1210	1238	1310	1338	1410	1438	1510	1538	1610	1638	1710	1738	1810	1838
Burton-on-Trent **124** d.	0650	0723	0752	0818	0852	0921	0954	1021	1052	1121	1151	1221	1250	1324	1350	1421	1450	1524	1550	1621	1650	1724	1750	1824	1850
Tamworth **124** d.	0703	0734	0803	0830	0903	0933	1006	1033	1103	1133	1203	1233	1303	1336	1403	1433	1503	1536	1603	1632	1703	1736	1803	1836	1903
Birmingham New Street **124** a.	0724	0755	0825	0855	0924	0955	1024	1055	1124	1155	1224	1255	1325	1355	1424	1456	1526	1555	1624	1655	1723	1755	1824	1855	1924
Cardiff Central **117** a.	0925	...	1025	...	1125	...	1225	...	1325	...	1425	...	1525	...	1625	...	1726	...	1828	...	1928	...	2026	...	2124

	Ⓐ	Ⓐ	Ⓐ	Ⓐ	Ⓐ	Ⓐ🍷	⑥	⑥ A	⑥	⑥	⑥	⑥	⑥🍷	⑥	⑥🍷	⑥	⑥🍷	⑥	⑥🍷	⑥	⑥🍷	⑥🍷	⑥🍷	⑥	⑥
Nottingham **155 172** d.	1845	1908	1935	2041	2136	...	0600	0642	0703	0737	0807	0841	0907	0941	1007	1041	1107	1141	1207	1241	1307	1341	1407	1441	1507
Derby **155 172** a.	1907	1938	2004	2106	2206	...	0631	0704	0731	0802	0837	0904	0935	1001	1034	1101	1135	1201	1235	1301	1335	1401	1435	1501	1535
Derby **124** d.	1912	1941	2010	2110	2210	2250	0637	0713	0736	0806	0842	0910	0938	1010	1038	1110	1138	1210	1238	1310	1338	1410	1438	1510	1539
Burton-on-Trent **124** d.	1923	1953	2021	2124	2221	2300	0649	0723	0750	0818	0853	0921	0952	1021	1050	1121	1150	1221	1250	1324	1350	1421	1450	1524	1550
Tamworth **124** d.	1935	2005	2033	2136	2232	2310	0702	0734	0803	0830	0904	0933	1003	1033	1103	1133	1203	1233	1303	1336	1403	1433	1503	1536	1603
Birmingham New Street **124** a.	1956	2024	2055	2158	2301	2327	0724	0755	0824	0855	0924	0955	1024	1055	1124	1155	1224	1255	1324	1355	1425	1456	1524	1555	1624
Cardiff Central **117** a.	...	2236**a**	...	...	...	...	0926	...	1027	...	1125	...	1226	...	1325	...	1425	...	1525	...	1625	...	1727	...	1827

	⑥🍷	⑥	⑥🍷	⑥	⑥🍷	⑥	⑥	⑥	⑥	⑥	⑥	⑥🍷	⑦	⑦	⑦	⑦🍷	⑦🍷	⑦🍷	⑦🍷	⑦🍷	⑦🍷	⑦	⑦	⑦	⑦🍷
Nottingham **155 172** d.	1541	1607	1641	1707	1741	1807	1845	1907	1932	2039	2137	...	0955	1116	1216	1316	1416	1512	1616	1716	1816	1915	2016	2117	...
Derby **155 172** a.	1601	1635	1701	1735	1801	1834	1905	1935	2003	2104	2207	...	1015	1136	1236	1337	1436	1533	1636	1738	1836	1937	2036	2139	...
Derby **124** d.	1610	1638	1710	1739	1810	1838	1910	1938	2010	2110	2213	2229	1020	1140	1240	1340	1440	1537	1640	1742	1840	1941	2040	2142	2231
Burton-on-Trent **124** d.	1621	1650	1724	1750	1824	1850	1921	1950	2021	2124	2224	2239	1031	1151	1251	1351	1451	1548	1651	1753	1851	1952	2051	2153	2241
Tamworth **124** d.	1633	1703	1736	1803	1836	1903	1933	2003	2033	2136	2235	2249	1043	1203	1303	1403	1503	1600	1703	1804	1903	2003	2103	2205	2251
Birmingham New Street **124** a.	1655	1724	1755	1824	1855	1924	1955	2024	2055	2158	2306	2308	1101	1221	1321	1421	1521	1621	1721	1823	1921	2025	2121	2226	2309
Cardiff Central **117** a.	...	1925	...	2022	...	2122	...	2244	...	...	...	...	1306	1425	1525	1625	1721	1821	1925	2020	2120	...	...	...	...

A – To Reading (Table **114**).

a – Arrives 2229 on ⑤.

XC BIRMINGHAM - SHEFFIELD - LEEDS - YORK - NEWCASTLE - EDINBURGH 124

km	Ⓐ		Ⓐ	Ⓐ	Ⓐ	Ⓐ	Ⓐ	Ⓐ	Ⓐ	Ⓐ	Ⓐ		ⒶD	ⒶH	Ⓐ	Ⓐ	ⒶB	Ⓐ	Ⓐ	Ⓐ	Ⓐ	Ⓐ	Ⓐ
	Plymouth **116**	d.	...	...	...	...	...	0525	0627	0725	...	...	0927	...	...	...	1127	1227	1327	1427	1527	1627	...
	Bristol Temple Meads **116**	d.	...	...	...	...	0634	0735	0835	0932	1036	...	1134	...	1235	1300	1335	1435	1535	1635	1735	1835	1935
	Southampton Central **114**	d.	...	...	...	...	|	|	|	|	|	...	|	...	|	|	|	|	|	|	|	|	|
	Reading **114**	d.	...	...	...	...	|	|	|	|	|	...	|	...	|	|	|	|	|	|	|	|	|
0	**Birmingham** New Street **120**	d.	...	0603	0630	0703	0803	0903	1003	1103	1203	...	1303	1330	1403	1430	1503	1603	1703	1803	1903	2003	2103
28	Tamworth **120**	d.	...	|	|	0719	0819	|	1019	|	1219	...	|	|	1419	|	|	1620	|	1819	|	2019	2129
48	Burton on Trent **120**	d.	...	|	|	0730	0830	0926	|	1126	|	...	1326	|	|	|	1526	|	1727	|	1926	|	2140
67	**Derby** **120**	a.	...	0635	0706	0740	0840	0936	1038	1136	1237	...	1336	1405	1438	1504	1538	1640	1737	1842	1937	2037	2150
	Derby **170**	d.	...	0645	0717	0750	0845	0945	1045	1145	1245	...	1345	1417	1445	1517	1545	1645	1745	1845	1945	2045	2152
105	Chesterfield **170**	d.	...	0703	|	0808	0905	|	1105	|	1305	...	|	|	1505	|	1605	1705	1805	|	|	2105	|
125	**Sheffield** **170**	d.	...	0721**b**	0749	0822	0922	1021	1121	1221	1321	...	1421	1452	1521	1552	1621	1721	1821	1921	2021	2121	2228
154	Doncaster **180**	d.	...	|	0819**b**	|	|	|	|	|	|	...	|	1519	|	1617	|	|	|	|	|	|	2301
171	Wakefield Westgate **180**	d.	...	0747	|	0847	0947	1047	1147	1247	1347	...	1447	|	1547	|	1647	1747	1850	1947	2047	2147	2319
187	**Leeds** **180**	a.	...	0803	|	0902	1001	1101	1201	1301	1401	...	1501	|	1601	|	1702	1802	1904	2002	2102	2202	2334
	Leeds **188 191**	d.	0543	0808	|	0908	1008	1108	1208	1308	1408	...	1508	|	1608	|	1707	1808	1908	2008	...	...	...
199	**York** **180 188 191**	a.	0605	0830	0842	0930	1030	1130	1230	1330	1430	...	1530	1540	1630	1639	1730	1831	1931	2030	...	...	...
	York **180 188**	d.	0627	0832	0844	0932	1032	1132	1232	1332	1432	...	1532	1546	1632	1645	1731	1832	1934	2032	...	...	...
270	Darlington **180 188**	d.	0655	0900	0915	1000	1100	1200	1300	1403	1500	...	1600	1614	1700	1713	1800	1901	2002	2059	...	...	...
305	Durham **180 188**	d.	0713	0917	0932	1017	1117	1217	1317	1420	1517	...	1617	1631	1717	1730	1818	1919	2020	2116	...	...	...
328	**Newcastle** **180 188**	a.	0729	0929	0945	1029	1129	1229	1329	1432	1529	...	1632	1644	1729	1744	1831	1932	2033	2128	...	...	...
	Newcastle **180 188**	d.	0735	0933	...	1035	1132	1236	1332	1435	1537	...	1635	...	1736	...	1837	1935	2039	2135	...	...	...
384	Alnmouth **180**	a.	|	0957	...	|	|	|	1358	|	1601	...	1702	...	1800	...	|	2000	|	2200	...	...	...
436	Berwick upon Tweed **180**	a.	0820	1019	...	|	1217	|	1419	|	1623	...	|	...	1822	...	1924	2023	2124	|	...	...	...
528	**Edinburgh** Waverley **180 188**	a.	0903	1107	...	1204	1300	1406	1501	1606	1706	...	1807	...	1904	...	2011	2108	2213	2305	...	...	...
620	*Glasgow Central* **220**	a.	...	...	...	...	...	...	...	...	1813	...	...	...	2013	...	...	...	...	...	...	...	...

⑥		⑥	⑥	⑥	⑥	⑥	⑥	⑥		⑥	⑥	⑥C	⑥	⑥	⑥		⑥	⑥	⑥	⑥	⑥	⑥	⑥
Plymouth **116**	d.	...	...	...	...	...	0527	0624	...	0725	...	0927	...	...	1127	...	1227	...	1427	1527	1627	...	1827
Bristol Temple Meads **116**	d.	...	...	...	...	0615	0735	0835	...	0935	1035	1135	1235	...	1335	...	1435	1535	1635	1735	1835	1931	2031
Southampton Central **114**	d.	...	...	...	...	|	|	|	...	|	|	|	|	...	|	...	|	|	|	|	|	|	|
Reading **114**	d.	...	...	...	...	|	|	|	...	|	|	|	|	...	|	...	|	|	|	|	|	|	|
Birmingham New Street **120**	d.	...	0603	0630	0703	0803	0903	1003	...	1103	1203	1303	1403	1428	1503	...	1603	1703	1803	1903	2003	2103	2203
Tamworth **120**	d.	...	0619	0646	0719	0819	|	1019	...	|	1219	|	1419	|	|	...	1620	|	1819	|	2020	2120	2220
Burton on Trent **120**	d.	...	0630	0657	0730	0830	0926	|	...	1126	|	1326	|	|	1526	...	|	1726	|	1926	|	2131	2231
Derby **120**	a.	...	0640	0707	0740	0840	0936	1037	...	1136	1237	1336	1437	1458	1538	...	1639	1736	1837	1937	2039	2142	2242
Derby **170**	d.	...	0645	0717	0750	0845	0945	1045	...	1145	1245	1345	1445	1500	1545	...	1645	1745	1845	1945	2045	2145	...
Chesterfield **170**	d.	...	0703	|	0808	0905	|	1105	...	1205	|	1405	|	|	1605	...	1705	1805	|	2005	|	2205	...
Sheffield **170**	d.	...	0721	0750	0822	0921	1021	1121	...	1221	1321	1422	1521	1529	1621	...	1721	1821	1921	2021	2121	2225	...
Doncaster **180**	d.	...	|	0819**b**	|	|	|	|	...	|	|	|	|	1558	|	...	|	|	|	|	|	2250	...
Wakefield Westgate **180**	d.	...	0747	|	0847	0947	1047	1147	...	1247	1347	1447	1547	|	1647	...	1747	1847	1950	2047	2147	2308	...
Leeds **180**	a.	...	0803	|	0902	1001	1101	1201	...	1301	1401	1501	1601	|	1701	...	1802	1903	2004	2102	2202	2323	...
Leeds **188 191**	d.	...	0808	|	0908	1008	1108	1208	...	1308	1408	1508	1608	|	1708	...	1808	1908	2008	2108	...	...	...
York **180 188 191**	a.	...	0830	0840	0930	1030	1130	1230	...	1330	1430	1530	1630	1618	1730	...	1831	1930	2030	2146	...	...	...
York **180 188**	d.	...	0832	0844	0932	1032	1132	1232	...	1332	1432	1532	1632	1620	1732	...	1832	1934	2031	...	...	...	...
Darlington **180 188**	d.	...	0900	0916	1000	1100	1201	1300	...	1403	1500	1600	1700	1648	1800	...	1901	2005	2100	...	...	...	...
Durham **180 188**	d.	...	0917	0933	1017	1117	1217	1317	...	1420	1517	1617	1717	1705	1817	...	1919	2022	2116	...	...	...	...
Newcastle **180 188**	a.	...	0929	0946	1030	1129	1230	1329	...	1432	1529	1629	1730	1718	1833	...	1932	2035	2129	...	...	...	...
Newcastle **180 188**	d.	0738	0933	...	1035	1133	1234	1334	...	1435	1535	1633	1734	...	1839	...	1936	2042	2135	...	...	...	...
Alnmouth **180**	a.	|	0957	...	|	|	|	1358	...	|	1559	1700	1759	...	|	...	2001	|	2200	...	...	...	...
Berwick upon Tweed **180**	a.	0823	1019	...	|	1218	|	1420	...	|	1621	|	1821	...	1922	...	2024	2127	|	...	...	...	...
Edinburgh Waverley **180 188**	a.	0908	1103	...	1201	1305	1402	1502	...	1606	1704	1805	1903	...	2008	...	2108	2212	2301	...	...	...	...
Glasgow Central **220**	a.	...	...	...	...	...	...	...	...	...	1813	...	2013	...	...	...	...	...	...	...	...	...	...

⑦		⑦	⑦	⑦	⑦		⑦	⑦	⑦		⑦A	⑦		⑦B	⑦		⑦	⑦	⑦		⑦	⑦	⑦
Plymouth **116**	d.	...	...	...	...	...	...	...	...	...	0927	1027	...	1127	1225	...	...	1427	...	...	1627	...	1827
Bristol Temple Meads **116**	d.	...	...	...	...	...	...	0915	1031	...	1131	1231	...	1331	1429	...	1531	1631	1731	...	1831	1931	2031
Southampton Central **114**	d.	...	...	...	...	...	...	|	|	...	|	|	...	|	|	...	|	|	|	...	|	|	|
Reading **114**	d.	...	...	...	...	...	...	|	|	...	|	|	...	|	|	...	|	|	|	...	|	|	|
Birmingham New Street **120**	d.	...	...	...	0903	...	1003	1103	1203	...	1303	1403	...	1503	1603	...	1703	1803	1903	...	2003	2103	2203
Tamworth **120**	d.	...	...	...	0919	...	1019	|	1219	...	|	1419	...	|	1620	...	|	1820	|	...	2020	2119	2220
Burton on Trent **120**	d.	...	...	...	0930	...	1030	1126	|	...	1326	|	...	1526	|	...	1726	|	1926	...	|	2130	|
Derby **120**	a.	...	...	...	0940	...	1040	1136	1237	...	1336	1437	...	1536	1639	...	1736	1839	1937	...	2039	2140	2239
Derby **170**	d.	...	...	...	0945	...	1045	1145	1245	...	1345	1445	...	1545	1645	...	1745	1845	1945	...	2045	2145	2245
Chesterfield **170**	d.	...	...	...	1005	...	1105	1205	|	...	1405	|	...	1605	1705	...	1805	1905	|	...	|	|	2305
Sheffield **170**	d.	...	...	0921	1021	...	1121	1221	1321	...	1421	1521	...	1621	1721	...	1821	1921	2023	...	2121	2221	2321
Doncaster **180**	d.	...	...	|	|	...	|	|	|	...	|	|	...	|	|	...	|	|	|	...	|	|	|
Wakefield Westgate **180**	d.	...	...	0947	1047	...	1147	1247	1347	...	1447	1547	...	1647	1747	...	1847	1947	2049	...	2147	2249	|
Leeds **180**	a.	...	...	1001	1102	...	1201	1301	1401	...	1501	1601	...	1701	1802	...	1901	2002	2104	...	2202	2303	0013
Leeds **188 191**	d.	...	0916	1006	1106	...	1206	1307	1405	...	1507	1606	...	1706	1806	...	1907	2005	2107	...	...	...	...
York **180 188 191**	a.	...	0940	1029	1129	...	1229	1329	1429	...	1529	1629	...	1729	1830	...	1930	2030	2130	...	...	...	...
York **180 188**	d.	...	0943	1031	1131	...	1231	1331	1431	...	1531	1631	...	1731	1831	...	1931	2031	...	...	...	...	...
Darlington **180 188**	d.	...	1011	1059	1159	...	1259	1358	1459	...	1559	1659	...	1758	1900	...	1959	2100	...	...	...	...	...
Durham **180 188**	d.	...	1028	1116	1216	...	1316	1415	1516	...	1616	1716	...	1815	1918	...	2016	2118	...	...	...	...	...
Newcastle **180 188**	a.	...	1040	1128	1228	...	1328	1427	1528	...	1628	1728	...	1830	1931	...	2028	2131	...	...	...	...	...
Newcastle **180 188**	d.	0945	1042	1131	1230	...	1331	1431	1530	...	1631	1730	...	1836	1932	...	2036	2134	...	...	...	...	...
Alnmouth **180**	a.	1013	|	|	|	...	1355	|	1554	...	1655	1757	...	|	1958	...	|	2159	...	...	...	...	...
Berwick upon Tweed **180**	a.	|	1124	1216	|	...	1416	|	1615	...	|	1818	...	1919	2020	...	2123	|	...	...	...	...	...
Edinburgh Waverley **180 188**	a.	1112	1210	1259	1358	...	1505	1600	1705	...	1759	1901	...	2007	2105	...	2208	2306	...	...	...	...	...
Glasgow Central **220**	a.	...	...	...	...	...	...	...	1813	...	...	2015	...	...	...	...	...	...	...	...	...	...	...

A – To Dundee (Table **222**).
B – From Penzance (Tables **112**/**116**).
C – To Aberdeen (Table **222**).
D – To Aberdeen on ⑤ (Table **222**).
H – From Banbury (Table **114**).

b – Arrives 5–6 minutes earlier.

124 EDINBURGH - NEWCASTLE - YORK - LEEDS - SHEFFIELD - BIRMINGHAM XC

Ⓐ	Ⓐ	Ⓐ	Ⓐ	Ⓐ	Ⓐ	Ⓐ H	Ⓐ	Ⓐ	Ⓐ H	Ⓐ	Ⓐ B	Ⓐ C	Ⓐ	Ⓐ	Ⓐ	Ⓐ	Ⓐ	Ⓐ	Ⓐ	Ⓐ	Ⓐ
Glasgow Central **220** d.	...	...	...	...	...	...	...	...	...	0748	...	...	...	...	...	...	...	...	...	...	1900
Edinburgh Waverley 180 188 d.	...	...	...	...	0606	...	0701	0806	...	0905	1003	1106	1203	1305	1405	1508	1607	...	1707	1808	2003
Berwick upon Tweed 180 d.	...	...	...	...	0648	...	0746	0848	...	0948	1047	1150	1245	|	1446	|	|	...	1751	1852	2047
Alnmouth 180 d.	...	...	...	...	0710	...	0807	|	...	1009	|	1211	|	1410	|	|	1705	...	|	1915	2108
Newcastle 180 188 a.	...	...	...	...	0737	...	0836	0938	...	1036	1136	1237	1334	1437	1535	1633	1734	...	1837	1941	2135
Newcastle 180 188 d.	...	...	...	0640	0740	0835	0840	0939	1035	1041	1139	1241	1337	1440	1539	1639	1738	1835	1840	1942	2137
Durham 180 188 d.	...	...	...	0653	0753	0848	0854	0955	1048	1053	1153	1254	1351	1453	1552	1653	1752	1849	1854	1955	2150
Darlington 180 188 d.	...	...	...	0711	0811	0906	0912	1012	1106	1111	1212	1311	1411	1512	1610	1711	1810	1907	1912	2013	2208
York 180 188 a.	...	...	...	0738	0839	0934	0939	1039	1134	1138	1239	1338	1438	1539	1636	1738	1838	1933	1938	2041	2235
York 180 188 191 d.	...	...	0645	0744	0845	0937	0944	1044	1137	1144	1244	1344	1444	1544	1644	1744	1845	1936	1944	2044	...
Leeds 188 191 a.	...	...	0708	0808	0908	|	1008	1108	|	1208	1308	1408	1508	1608	1708	1808	1908	|	2008	2107	...
Leeds 180 d.	...	0611	0710	0811	0911	|	1011	1111	|	1211	1311	1411	1511	1611	1711	1811	1911	|	2011	2111	...
Wakefield Westgate 180 d.	...	0623	0723	0823	0923	|	1023	1123	|	1223	1323	1423	1523	1623	1723	1823	1923	|	2023	2123	...
Doncaster 180 d.	...	|	|	|	|	1000	|	|	1159	|	|	|	|	|	|	|	|	1959	|	|	...
Sheffield 170 d.	...	0653	0753	0856	0956	1024	1056	1155	1224	1256	1355	1456	1556	1656	1756	1856	1956	2024	2056	2202b	...
Chesterfield 170 d.	...	0706	0806	0908	|	|	1108	|	|	1308	|	|	1608	1708	1808	|	2008	|	|	2225	...
Derby 170 a.	...	0724	0824	0926	1027	1051	1126	1226	1251	1326	1426	1526	1626	1727	1826	1926	2026	2051	2126	2243	...
Derby 120 d.	0610	0727	0827	0931	1031	1053	1131	1231	1253	1331	1431	1528	1631	1731	1831	1931	2031	2053	2131	2250	...
Burton on Trent 120 d.	0620	0738	0838	0941	|	|	|	|	|	1341	|	1539	|	1742	|	1941	|	|	2141	2300	...
Tamworth 120 d.	0631	0750	0850	|	1050	|	|	1250	|	|	1450	|	1649	|	1849	|	2049	|	2151	2310	...
Birmingham New Street 120 a.	0653	0808	0908	1004	1108	1127	1204	1308	1327	1404	1508	1604	1706	1806	1906	2005	2106	2130	2208	2327	...
Reading **114** a.	|	|	|	|	|	...	|	|	...	|	|	|	|	|	|	|	|	...	|	...	...
Southampton Central **114** a.	|	|	|	|	|	...	|	|	...	|	|	|	|	|	|	|	|	...	|	...	...
Bristol Temple Meads **116** a.	0839	0938	1032	1131	1233	...	1333	1433	...	1534	1632	1732	1833	1946	2032	2137	2244	...	2331	...	...
Plymouth **116** a.	1047	1149	1250	...	1448	...	1547	1648	...	1747	1848	1947	...	2150	...	2344	...	...	...	...	...
⑥	⑥	⑥	⑥	⑥	⑥		⑥	⑥	⑥	⑥	⑥ B	⑥	⑥	⑥	⑥		⑥	⑥	⑥	⑥	⑥
Glasgow Central **220** d.	...	...	...	...	...	...	...	...	...	0748	...	C B	...	...	...	...	...	...	...	...	...
Edinburgh Waverley 180 188 d.	...	...	...	...	0606	...	0658	0807	...	0908	1005	1108	1205	1309	1404	...	1505	1606	...	1709	1807
Berwick upon Tweed 180 d.	...	...	...	...	0648	...	0745	0849	...	0948	1047	1152	1245	|	1445	...	|	|	...	1753	1851
Alnmouth 180 d.	...	...	...	...	0710	...	0807	0911	...	|	|	1213	|	1411	|	...	|	1704	...	|	1912
Newcastle 180 188 a.	...	...	...	...	0737	...	0837	0938	...	1036	1136	1240	1334	1438	1533	...	1630	1733	...	1837	1938
Newcastle 180 188 d.	...	...	...	...	0739	...	0839	0940	1035	1043	1139	1242	1339	1443	1539	...	1638	1739	1835	1839	1943
Durham 180 188 d.	...	...	...	...	0752	...	0853	0954	1048	1055	1154	1255	1352	1455	1552	...	1651	1753	1848	1853	1955
Darlington 180 188 d.	...	...	...	...	0811	...	0911	1012	1106	1113	1212	1312	1412	1513	1610	...	1711	1811	1906	1912	2013
York 180 188 a.	...	...	...	...	0839	...	0938	1039	1134	1139	1239	1340	1441	1539	1636	...	1738	1838	1933	1938	2039
York 180 188 191 d.	...	...	0611	0744	0845	...	0944	1044	1137	1145	1244	1345	1445	1544	1644	...	1744	1845	1936	1944	2045
Leeds 188 191 a.	...	...	0658	0808	0908	...	1008	1108	|	1208	1308	1408	1508	1608	1708	...	1808	1908	|	2008	2108
Leeds 180 d.	...	0609	0711	0811	0911	...	1011	1111	|	1211	1311	1411	1511	1611	1711	...	1811	1911	|	2011	2111
Wakefield Westgate 180 d.	...	0623	0723	0823	0923	...	1023	1123	|	1223	1323	1423	1523	1623	1723	...	1823	1923	|	2023	2123
Doncaster 180 d.	...	|	|	|	|	...	|	|	1159	|	|	|	|	|	|	...	|	|	1959	|	|
Sheffield 170 d.	...	0653	0756f	0856	0956	...	1055	1155	1224	1256	1356	1456	1556	1656	1756	...	1856	1956	2024	2056	2156
Chesterfield 170 d.	...	0706	0808	0908	|	...	1108	|	|	1308	|	1508	1608	1708	1808	...	|	2008	|	2108	2208
Derby 170 a.	...	0724	0826	0926	1027	...	1126	1226	1251	1326	1427	1526	1626	1726	1826	...	1926	2026	2051	2126	2227
Derby 120 d.	0610	0727	0828	0931	1031	...	1131	1231	1253	1331	1431	1528	1631	1731	1828	...	1931	2031	2053	2131	2229
Burton on Trent 120 d.	0620	0738	0838	0941	|	...	1142	|	|	1341	|	1539	|	1741	|	...	1941	|	|	2141	2239
Tamworth 120 d.	0631	0750	0849	|	1050	...	|	1250	|	|	1450	|	1649	|	1847	...	|	2049	|	2151	2249
Birmingham New Street 120 a.	0648	0808	0906	1004	1108	...	1206	1308	1328	1404	1508	1603	1706	1804	1904	...	2004	2107	2124	2208	2308
Reading **114** a.	|	|	|	|	|	...	|	|	...	|	|	|	|	|	|	...	|	|	...	...	...
Southampton Central **114** a.	|	|	|	|	|	...	|	|	...	|	|	|	|	|	|	...	|	|	...	...	...
Bristol Temple Meads **116** a.	0836	0934	1036	1135	1238	...	1336	1434	...	1536	1634	1735	1834	1936	2036	...	2134	2240	...	...	...
Plymouth **116** a.	1047	1148	1247	...	1448	...	1548	...	...	1747	1848	1947	...	2147	...	...	2347	...	...	...	...
⑦	⑦	⑦	⑦		⑦	⑦		⑦	⑦		⑦	⑦		⑦ C	⑦	⑦		⑦	⑦		⑦
Glasgow Central **220** d.	...	...	...	...	...	...	...	...	...	...	...	...	...	...	...	...	...	...	...	...	1900
Edinburgh Waverley 180 188 d.	...	...	...	...	...	0908	...	1005	1105	...	1205	1309	...	1408	1508	1608	...	1708	1806	...	2018
Berwick upon Tweed 180 d.	...	...	...	...	...	0950	...	|	1149	...	1245	|	...	1448	|	|	...	1750	1850	...	2102
Alnmouth 180 d.	...	...	...	...	...	|	...	1106	1210	...	|	1411	...	|	|	1706	...	|	|	...	|
Newcastle 180 188 a.	...	...	...	...	...	1035	...	1136	1236	...	1331	1438	...	1534	1636	1735	...	1834	1936	...	2148
Newcastle 180 188 d.	...	...	...	...	0933	1039	...	1140	1240	...	1339	1441	...	1540	1640	1739	...	1839	1941	...	...
Durham 180 188 d.	...	...	...	...	0946	1052	...	1153	1252	...	1353	1454	...	1553	1652	1753	...	1851	1953	...	...
Darlington 180 188 d.	...	...	...	...	1004	1110	...	1211	1310	...	1411	1512	...	1611	1710	1811	...	1908	2011	...	...
York 180 188 a.	...	...	...	...	1030	1138	...	1237	1336	...	1437	1538	...	1637	1740	1840	...	1936	2037	...	...
York 180 188 191 d.	...	...	0935	...	1032	1145	...	1244	1343	...	1439	1544	...	1642	1744	1842	...	1938	2044	...	...
Leeds 188 191 a.	...	...	0958	...	1100	1209	...	1308	1408	...	1506	1609	...	1709	1808	1908	...	2007	2108	...	...
Leeds 180 d.	0811	0900	1000	...	1101	1211	...	1311	1411	...	1511	1611	...	1711	1811	1911	...	2011	2111	...	...
Wakefield Westgate 180 d.	0823	0912	1012	...	1113	1223	...	1323	1423	...	1523	1623	...	1723	1823	1923	...	2023	2123	...	...
Doncaster 180 d.	|	0931	1031	...	1132	|	...	|	|	...	|	|	...	|	|	|	...	|	|	...	...
Sheffield 170 d.	0856	0958	1056	...	1156	1256	...	1356	1456	...	1556	1656	...	1756	1856	1956	...	2056	2156	...	...
Chesterfield 170 d.	0908	1011	1108	...	|	1308	...	|	1508	...	1608	1708	...	1808	|	|	...	|	2208	...	...
Derby 170 a.	0927	1029	1128	...	1226	1327	...	1426	1526	...	1626	1726	...	1826	1926	2026	...	2126	2226	...	...
Derby 120 d.	0931	1031	1131	...	1231	1331	...	1431	1531	...	1631	1731	...	1831	1931	2031	...	2130	2231	...	...
Burton on Trent 120 d.	|	|	1142	...	|	1342	...	|	1541	...	|	1741	...	|	1941	|	...	2140	2241	...	...
Tamworth 120 d.	|	1053	|	...	1249	|	...	1449	|	...	1649	|	...	1849	|	2049	...	2150	2251	...	...
Birmingham New Street 120 a.	1020	1119	1206	...	1306	1406	...	1506	1606	...	1706	1806	...	1906	2004	2105	...	2207	2309	...	...
Reading **114** a.	|	|	|	...	|	|	...	|	|	...	|	|	...	|	|	|	...	|	...	...	...
Southampton Central **114** a.	|	|	|	...	|	|	...	|	|	...	|	|	...	|	|	|	...	|	...	...	...
Bristol Temple Meads **116** a.	1151	1253	1333	...	1436	1536	...	1636	1734	...	1836	1936	...	2035	2135	2240	...	2330	...	...	...
Plymouth **116** a.	1357	...	1551	...	...	1748	...	...	1947	...	...	2148	...	...	2344	...	...	...	...	...	...

B – To Penzance (Tables **112**/**116**).
C – From Aberdeen (Table **222**).
H – To Banbury (Table **114**).

b – Arrives 2155.
f – Arrives 0751.

LM 2nd class — BIRMINGHAM - WORCESTER - HEREFORD — 125

km			Ⓐ	Ⓐ	Ⓐ	Ⓐ	Ⓐ	Ⓐ		Ⓐ	Ⓐ	Ⓐ	Ⓐ	Ⓐ	Ⓐ	Ⓐ	Ⓐ	Ⓐ	Ⓐ	Ⓐ		⑥	⑥	⑥	⑥
0	**Birmingham** New Street .... ★ d.		...	...	0659	0720	0800	0850	✣	1550	1650	1720	1750	1820	1920	2000	2100	2200	2300	2259		...	0650	0750	0850
21	Bromsgrove .... d.	Ⓐ	...	...	0721	0744	0822	0912		1611	1712	1744	1812	1842	1942	2021	2121	2223	2321	|	⑥	...	0712	0810	0912
32	Droitwich Spa .... ★ d.		...	...	0731	0756	0832	0922	and	1620	1722	1756	1822	1852	1953	2031	2131	2233	2331	2336		...	0722	0820	0922
40	**Worcester** Shrub Hill .... ★ a.		...	...	|	0803	0839	|		|	1729	|	1833	|	2007	2039	|	2241	2338	|		...	|	|	|
	Worcester Shrub Hill **138 130** d.		0556	0625	|	0808	0844	|	hourly	|	1733	|	...	|	2016	2106	|	2257	...	|		0630	|	|	|
41	**Worcester** Foregate St **130** ★ d.		0559	0631	0742	0811	0847	0932		1630	1736	1806	...	1901	2019	2109	2141	2300	...	2347		0632	0732	0831	0931
54	Great Malvern .... **130 138** d.		0611	0643	0800f	0822	0904f	0945	until	1643	1748	1819	...	1914	2031	2124	2200f	2311	...	...		0645	0745	0846	0945
65	Ledbury .... **130** d.		0624	0658	0814	...	0917	0959		1657	1801	1831	...	1927	2045	2147r	2219f	...	...	...		0659	0759	0859	0959
87	**Hereford** .... **130** a.		0644	0713	0829	...	0932	1014		1713	1817	1846	...	1942	2101	2204	2234	...	...	...		0717	0817	0914	1014

		⑥	⑥	⑥	⑥	⑥	⑥	⑥	⑥		⑦	⑦	⑦	⑦	⑦	⑦	⑦	⑦	⑦	⑦	⑦	⑦	⑦	⑦	⑦
Birmingham New Street ..... ★ d.		1650	1720	1750	1850	1950	2050	2120	2221		...	1000	1100	1200	1300	1400	1500	1600	1700	1800	1900	2000	2100	2200	2230
Bromsgrove .... d.		1712	1744	1812	1912	2012	2111	2142	2241	⑦	...	1020	1120	1220	1320	1420	1520	1621	1721	1820	1920	2020	2120	2220	2250
Droitwich Spa .... ★ d.	and	1722	1756	1822	1922	2022	2121	2152	2251		...	1030	1129	1232	1329	1430	1531	1631	1731	1832	1931	2030	2130	2237	2300
Worcester Shrub Hill .... ★ a.		|	|	1829	|	|	|	|	|		...	1038	|	1240	|	|	1537	1638	|	1841	1939	2044	2138	2246	2307
Worcester Shrub Hill .. **138 130** d.	hourly	|	|	1833	|	|	|	|	|		0859	1042	|	1247	|	|	1552	1648	|	1848	1946	2059	2142	2251	...
Worcester Foregate St. **130** ★ d.		1731	1805	1836	1931	2034	2135f	2201	2301		0902	1045	1139	1250	1339	1442	1555	1651	1739	1851	1951	2101	2145	2254	...
Great Malvern .... **130 138** d.	until	1745	1817	1848	1944	2048	2147	2214	2315		0914	1101	...	1302	...	1454	1607	1703	...	1903	2003	2125	2157	2305	...
Ledbury .... **130** d.		1759	...	1901	1959	2101	...	2228	...		0926	1113	...	1315	...	1506	1619	1716	...	1915	2015	2139	2210	...	...
Hereford .... **130** a.		1814	...	1916	2014	2117	...	2243	...		0944	1129	...	1332	...	1522	1635	1734	...	1932	2031	2155	2229	...	...

		Ⓐ	Ⓐ	Ⓐ	Ⓐ	Ⓐ	Ⓐ	Ⓐ	Ⓐ		Ⓐ	Ⓐ	Ⓐ	Ⓐ	Ⓐ	Ⓐ	Ⓐ	Ⓐ		⑥	⑥	⑥	⑥	⑥	⑥
Hereford .... **130** d.		0449	0523	...	0710	0732	...	0837	0939	✣	1739	...	1848	1951	2058	2128	2200	2259		...	...	0618	0639	0737	0839
Ledbury .... **130** d.	Ⓐ	0506	0540	...	0726	0750	...	0855	0958		1759	...	1904	2007	2114	2145	2217	2315	⑥	...	...	0635	0659	0759t	0858
Great Malvern .... **130 138** d.		0543	0553	0646	0737	0807f	0836	0908	1010	and	1811	...	1915	2019	2126	2156	2229	2326		...	0617	0654f	0711	0810	0910
Worcester Foregate St. **130** ★ d.		0602f	0606	0658	0750	0824f	0849	0924	1024		1825	...	1928	2032	2138	2208	2242	2339		...	0628	0708	0723	0823	0923
Worcester Shrub Hill .. **138 130** a.		|	0609	0700	0752	|	|	|	|	hourly	|	...	|	|	2140	|	2245	2348		...	|	0712	0725	|	|
Worcester Shrub Hill .... ★ d.		|	0625	0705	0758	|	|	|	|		|	1850	|	|	2150	|	...	...		0607	|	...	0731	|	|
Droitwich Spa .... ★ d.		0611	0633	0713	0806	0833	0858	0932	1033	until	1834	1858	1937	2041	2158	2217	...	...		0615	0637	...	0739	0833	0933
Bromsgrove .... d.		0621	0643	0723	|	0842	0908	0943	1043		1843	1908	1947	2051	|	2225	...	...		|	0647	...	0747	0843	0943
Birmingham New Street ..... ★ a.		0649	0709	0746	0839	0909	0937	1008	1109		1910	1937	2019	2120	2236	2252	...	...		0646	0719	...	0816	0909	1009

	⑥	⑥		⑥	⑥	⑥	⑥	⑥	⑥		⑦	⑦	⑦	⑦	⑦	⑦	⑦	⑦	⑦	⑦	⑦	⑦	⑦	⑦	⑦
Hereford .... **130** d.	...	0938	✣	1739	1842	1940	2035	2131	2250		...	...	1005	...	1202	1227	1402	1427	1558	1656	1803	...	1956	2100	2241
Ledbury .... **130** d.	...	0958		1758	1901	1959	2101r	2155f	2306	⑦	...	...	1022	...	1218	1246	1419	1445	1619t	1717	1819	...	2017	2117	2259
Great Malvern .... **130 138** d.	...	1010	and	1810	1911	2010	2113	2207	2317		...	0858	1034	1050	1230	1300	1431	1458	1631	1731	1831	1857	2029	2128	2311
Worcester Foregate St. **130** ★ d.	...	1023		1823	1924	2023	2125	2218	2329		0854	0911	1051	1155	1242	1349	1443	1511	1643	1743	1843	1911	2041	2140	2323
Worcester Shrub Hill .. **138 130** a.	...	|	hourly	|	|	|	2127	2222	2336		0856	0914	1054	|	1244	|	1445	1514	1645	1745	1845	1914	2043	|	2327
Worcester Shrub Hill .... ★ d.	0949	|		|	|	|	2131	...	...		0905	1005	1058	|	1250	|	1450	1539	1651	1750	1850	1958	2050	|	...
Droitwich Spa .... ★ d.	0957	1033	until	1833	1933	2033	2139	...	...		0913	1013	1106	1204	1258	1358	1458	1547	1659	1758	1858	2007	2058	2149	...
Bromsgrove .... d.	1007	1043		1843	1943	2043	2149	...	...		0922	1023	1116	1214	1308	1408	1508	1557	1709	1808	1908	2016	2108	2158	...
Birmingham New Street ..... ★ a.	1038	1109		1909	2009	2110	2218	...	...		0945	1046	1139	1237	1337	1437	1537	1620	1737	1837	1937	2039	2137	2221	...

f – Arrives 6–7 minutes earlier.
r – Arrives 9 minutes earlier.
t – Arrives 5 minutes earlier.
✣ – Timings may vary ± 3 minutes.

★ – Regular trains also operate Birmingham **Moor Street** - Birmingham **Snow Hill** - Kidderminster - Droitwich Spa - Worcester Shrub Hill / Worcester Foregate St (2 trains per hour on ⚒, hourly on ⑦). Journey times from Birmingham Moor Street: to Kidderminster ± 40 minutes, Droitwich Spa ± 50 minutes, Worcester Shrub Hill or Foregate St ± 65 minutes.
Kidderminster is the station for the **Severn Valley Railway** (🚂 Kidderminster - Bridgnorth: *26 km*). ✆ 01299 403816. www.svr.co.uk

LM 2nd class — STRATFORD UPON AVON - BIRMINGHAM — 127

km			Ⓐ	Ⓐ	Ⓐ	Ⓐ		Ⓐ	Ⓐ	Ⓐ	Ⓐ	Ⓐ	and at	Ⓐ	Ⓐ	Ⓐ	Ⓐ		Ⓐ	Ⓐ	Ⓐ	Ⓐ	Ⓐ	Ⓐ
0	**Stratford upon Avon** .. d.	Ⓐ	0623	0700	0723	0826	...	0852	0926	1001	1026	1103	the same	1703	1726	1803	1827	...	1903	1927	2027	2127	2230	2330
13	Henley in Arden .... d.		0637	0712	0739	0841	...	|	0941	|	1041	|	minutes	|	1741	|	1842	...	|	1942	2042	2142	2243	|
40	**Birmingham** Moor St .. a.		0720	0745	0821	0920	...	0934	1021	1051	1121	1152	past each	1751	1821	1850	1922	...	1952	2023	2122	2225	2319	0006
41	**Birmingham** Snow Hill a.		...	0747	0824	0922	...	0936	1023	1053	1123	1154	hour until	1753	1823	1852	1924	...	1954	2025	2124	2227	2321	0012

		⑥	⑥	⑥	⑥	and at	⑥	⑥	⑥	⑥	⑥	⑥	⑥	⑥	⑥		⑦	⑦	⑦	⑦		⑦	⑦	⑦
Stratford upon Avon .. d.	⑥	0700	0726	0826	0902	the same	1726	1802	1826	1908	1926	2026	2126	2231	2330	⑦	0927	1027	1126	1226	and	1727	1827	1927
Henley in Arden .... d.		0716	0741	0841	|	minutes	1741	|	1841	|	1941	2041	2140	2245	|		0942	1042	1141	1241	hourly	1743	1843	1943
Birmingham Moor St .. a.		0754	0821	0921	0951	past each	1821	1850	1921	1950	2021	2118	2217	2319	0007		1016	1117	1216	1317	until	1815	1915	2015
Birmingham Snow Hill a.		0802	0823	0923	0953	hour until	1823	1852	1923	1953	2023	2120	2223	2321	0010		1019	1119	1218	1319		1817	1917	2017

		Ⓐ	Ⓐ	Ⓐ	Ⓐ	Ⓐ	Ⓐ	Ⓐ	Ⓐ	and at	Ⓐ	Ⓐ	Ⓐ	Ⓐ	Ⓐ	Ⓐ	Ⓐ	Ⓐ	Ⓐ	Ⓐ		⑥	⑥	⑥
Birmingham Snow Hill d.	Ⓐ	0611	0622	0725	0757	0828	0859	0928	0958	the same	1559	1628	1658	1728	1758	1828	1926	2028	2128	2228	⑥	0625	0725	0758
Birmingham Moor St .. d.		0614	0625	0728	0800	0831	0902	0931	1001	minutes	1602	1631	1701	1731	1801	1831	1929	2031	2131	2231		0628	0728	0801
Henley in Arden .... d.		|	0703	0806	|	0906	|	1006	|	past each	|	1706	|	1806	|	1906	2007	2107	2209	2307		0706	0806	|
Stratford upon Avon .. a.		0655	0720	0823	0848	0921	0943	1023	1046	hour until	1650	1723	1751	1823	1859	1923	2024	2123	2226	2323		0721	0823	0841

	⑥	⑥	⑥	⑥	⑥	⑥	and at	⑥	⑥	⑥	⑥	⑥	⑥	⑥	⑥	⑥	⑥		⑦	⑦	⑦	⑦		⑦
Birmingham Snow Hill d.	0827	0857	0928	0958	1027	1058	the same	1558	1627	1658	1728	1758	1827	1927	2027	2128	2227	⑦	0836	0927	1027	1127	and	1827
Birmingham Moor St .. d.	0830	0902	0931	1001	1030	1101	minutes	1601	1630	1701	1731	1801	1830	1930	2030	2131	2230		0839	0930	1030	1130	hourly	1830
Henley in Arden .... d.	0905	|	1005	|	1105	|	past each	|	1705	|	1806	|	1905	2006	2106	2208	2306		|	1003	1103	1201	until	1901
Stratford upon Avon .. a.	0923	0944	1023	1043	1123	1141	hour until	1644	1723	1744	1821	1848	1923	2023	2123	2225	2326		0911	1017	1121	1218		1915

🚂 – **THE SHAKESPEARE EXPRESS** – 🚃12, ✕ (1st class only) and 🍷 Birmingham Snow Hill - Stratford upon Avon and v.v. on ⑦ Feb. 12, Apr. 16, May 28, July 16 - Sept. 3, Nov. 5 2023.
National Rail tickets NOT valid.
From Birmingham Snow Hill 1000 and 1356 (Birmingham Moor Street 5 minutes later); from Stratford upon Avon at 1236 and 1613. Journey time: 59–68 minutes.
To book and confirm timings contact **Vintage Trains Ltd**. ✆ 0121 708 4960. www.vintagetrains.co.uk/the-shakespeare-express

CH 2nd class — LONDON - BANBURY - BIRMINGHAM and STRATFORD UPON AVON — 128

km			②-⑤	①	Ⓐ	Ⓐ	Ⓐ	Ⓐ	Ⓐ	Ⓐ	Ⓐ	Ⓐ	Ⓐ	Ⓐ	Ⓐ	Ⓐ		Ⓐ	Ⓐ	Ⓐ	Ⓐ	Ⓐ	Ⓐ	Ⓐ	Ⓐ
0	**London** Marylebone . **128a** ◇ d.		0005	0005	...	...	0604	0617	0710	0735	0811	...	0841	0910	...	1010	...	...	1037	1110	...	1137	1210	...	1234
45	High Wycombe .... **128a** ◇ d.	Ⓐ	0036	0039	...	...	0628	0702	|	0805	|	...	0917	0936	...	1036	...	...	1101	1135	...	1201	1235	...	1258
88	Bicester North .... ◇ d.		0106	0110	0548	...	0655	0733	0754	0834	0855	...	0946	|	...	|	...	...	1128	|	...	1228	|	...	1324
111	Banbury .... **114** ◇ d.		0124	0128	0604	...	0708	0749	0807	0848	0908	...	1004	1009	...	1107	...	...	1142	1208	...	1241	1308	...	1340
143	Leamington Spa .... **114** d.		...	...	0625	0654	0725	0808	0825	0906	0926	0940	...	1026	1032	1126	...	1132	1200	1227	1232	1259	1326	1332	1358
146	Warwick .... d.		...	...	0630	0659	0729	0814	0829	0911	0930	0945	...	|	1038	|	...	1137	1204	|	1238	1303	|	1337	1402
147	Warwick Parkway .... d.		...	...	0633	|	0733	|	0833	0914	0934	|	...	1033	|	1133	...	|	1208	1233	|	1306	1333	|	1406
168	**Stratford-upon-Avon** .... a.		...	...	|	0728	|	0843	|	|	|	1014	...	|	|	|	...	1204	|	|	|	|	|	1404	|
169	Solihull .... a.		...	...	0649	...	0752	...	0844	0930	0945	...	...	1044	1100	1144	...	...	1223	1245	1300	1323	1344	...	1422
180	**Birmingham** Moor Street .... a.		...	...	0700	...	0803	...	0853	0944	0954	...	...	1056	1114	1156	...	...	1234	1256	1314	1334	1356	...	1434
181	**Birmingham** Snow Hill .... a.		...	...	0705	...	0809	...	0859	...	0959	...	...	...	...	...	...	...	1240	...	...	1340	...	...	1440

	Ⓐ	Ⓐ	Ⓐ	Ⓐ	Ⓐ	Ⓐ	Ⓐ	Ⓐ	Ⓐ		Ⓐ	Ⓐ	Ⓐ	Ⓐ	Ⓐ	Ⓐ	Ⓐ	Ⓐ	Ⓐ	Ⓐ	Ⓐ	Ⓐ	Ⓐ	Ⓐ	Ⓐ
London Marylebone ... **128a** ◇ d.	...	1337	1410	...	1437	1510	...	1537	1618	...	1647	...	1714	1721	1747	...	1815	1821	1847	1915	1946	2010	2036	...	2110
High Wycombe .... **128a** ◇ d.	...	1401	1434	...	1501	1535	...	1601	1646	...	|	...	|	1756	|	...	|	1854	|	|	|	2035	|	...	2134
Bicester North .... ◇ d.	...	1427	|	...	1528	|	...	1628	1711	...	1734	...	|	1828	1835	...	|	1926	1933	2002	2033	2059	2125	...	2156
Banbury .... **114** ◇ d.	...	1440	1507	...	1544	1608	...	1641	1724	...	1747	...	1809	1844	1848	...	1909	1942	1951	2016	2047	2112	2139	...	2213
Leamington Spa .... **114** d.	1432	1458	1525	1532	1601	1625	1635	1659	1741	...	1804	1811	1827	...	1905	1932	1928	...	2009	2034	2105	2130	2157	2226	2231
Warwick .... d.	1438	1502	|	1537	1605	1630	1640	1703	|	...	1808	1816	|	...	1909	1937	|	...	2013	|	2109	|	2201	2231	2235
Warwick Parkway .... d.	|	1506	1530	|	1609	1633	|	1707	1747	...	1812	|	1834	...	1913	|	1935	...	2017	2040	2112	2136	2205	|	2239
Stratford-upon-Avon .... a.	|	|	|	1608	|	|	1711f	|	|	...	|	1852	|	...	|	2005	|	...	|	|	|	|	|	2258	|
Solihull .... d.	1500	1521	1544	...	1624	1645	1702	1723	1802	...	1826	...	1849	...	1928	...	1950	...	2032	2055	2133	2148	2220	...	2301
Birmingham Moor Street .... a.	1514	1534	1556	...	1635	1655	1714	1736	1812	...	1838	...	1859	...	1938	...	2000	...	2042	2107	2143	2200	2232	...	2309
Birmingham Snow Hill .... a.	...	1540	...	...	1641	1700	...	1741	1818	...	...	...	1902	...	1945	...	2004	...	2047	...	2148	...	2238	...	2312
Kidderminster .... ▲ a.	...	...	...	...	...	...	...	...	...	...	...	...	1940	...	...	...	2045	...	...	...	...	...	...	...	2349r

f – Change at Hatton (a. 1646 / d. 1650).
r – Stourbridge Junction.

◇ – Additional services operate between these stations.
▲ – Only through services are shown to Kidderminster.
Regular local trains also operate Birmingham **Moor Street** - Birmingham **Snow Hill** - Kidderminster (2 trains per hour on ⚒, hourly on ⑦).
Kidderminster is the station for the **Severn Valley Railway** (🚂 Kidderminster - Bridgnorth: *26 km*). ✆ 01299 403816. www.svr.co.uk

128 LONDON - BANBURY - BIRMINGHAM and STRATFORD UPON AVON

2nd class CH

	Ⓐ	Ⓐ	Ⓐ	Ⓐ	⑥	⑥	⑥	⑥	⑥	⑥	⑥		⑥	⑥	⑥	⑥	⑥	⑥	⑥	⑥		⑥	⑥	⑥	⑥
London Marylebone 128a ◇ d.	2208	2233	2307	2311		0005	...	...	0700	...	0800	...	0900	1000	...	1100	1200	...	1237	1300	...	1400	...	1500	1600
High Wycombe 128a ◇ d.	2234	2303	|	2346		0036	...	0615	0725	...	0825	...	0926	1024	...	1126	1224	...	|	1326	...	1425	...	1526	1624
Bicester North ◇ d.	2259	2330	2350	b		0106	...	0646	0754	...	0856	...	0957	1051	...	1155	1251	...	1326	1357	...	1452	...	1557	1651
Banbury 114 ◇ d.	2313	2343	0004	0111		0124	0600	0703	0807	...	0913	...	1012	1109	...	1209	1309	...	1339	1410	...	1509	...	1612	1709
Leamington Spa 114 d.	2331	0002	0024	...		...	0621	0721	0825	0840	0932	...	1031	1127	1132	1229	1327	1332	1357	1431	...	1527	1532	1631	1727
Warwick d.	|	0007	0028	...		...	0625	0725	0829	0844	0936	...	1037	1131	1137	1234	1331	1337	1402	1437	...	1531	1537	1637	1731
Warwick Parkway d.	2337	0011	0031	...		...	0629	0729	0833	|	0940	...	1043	1135	|	1238	1335	|	1406	1443	...	1535	|	1643	1735
Stratford-upon-Avon a.	|	|	|	...		...	|	|	|	0914	|	...	|	|	1208	|	|	1408	|	|	...	|	1608	|	|
Solihull a.	2349	0026	0043	...		...	0646	0750	0848	...	1001	...	1059	1157	...	1253	1357	...	1421	1459	...	1557	...	1659	1757
Birmingham Moor Street a.	0001	0039	0055	...		...	0658	0802	0900	...	1012	...	1112	1209	...	1306	1409	...	1436	1512	...	1609	...	1712	1809
Birmingham Snow Hill a.	...	...	...	...		...	...	...	...	...	...	...	...	...	...	...	...	...	...	...	...	...	...	...	...

	⑥	⑥	⑥	⑥	⑥	⑥		⑥	⑥	⑥	⑥		⑥	⑥	⑥	⑥	⑥	⑦	⑦	⑦	⑦	⑦		⑦	⑦
London Marylebone 128a ◇ d.	...	1700	1800	...	1837	1900	...	1937	2000	...	2037	...	2100	2208	2240	2315	2345		0800	0900	...	1000	...	1100	1200
High Wycombe 128a ◇ d.	...	1724	1824	...	|	1925	...	|	2024	...	|	...	2126	2232	2315	2350	0021		0825	0925	...	1025	...	1125	1225
Bicester North ◇ d.	...	1753	1852	...	1926	1953	...	2023	2052	...	2126	...	2157	2257	2346	0021	0052		0853	0954	...	1052	...	1157t	1252
Banbury 114 ◇ d.	...	1807	1905	...	1943	2007	...	2037	2109	...	2139	...	2212	2310	0003	0037	0111		0910	1012t	...	1109	...	1212	1309
Leamington Spa 114 d.	1732	1825	1925	1932	2001	2025	...	2055	2127	2132	2157	...	2231	2328	...	...	...		0928	1031	1044	1127	...	1231	1327
Warwick d.	1737	1830	1929	1937	2006	2030	...	2059	2131	2137	2202	...	2237	2332	...	...	...		0933	1037	1049	1131	...	1237	1331
Warwick Parkway d.	|	1835	1932	|	2010	2033	...	2103	2135	|	2206	...	2243	2337	...	...	...		0938	1043	|	1135	...	1243	1335
Stratford-upon-Avon a.	1808	|	|	2008	|	|	...	|	|	2208	|	...	|	|	...	...	...		|	|	1115	|	...	|	|
Solihull a.	...	1850	1947	...	2032	2048	...	2118	2159	...	2220	...	2259	2352	...	...	...		1000	1059	...	1157	...	1259	1357
Birmingham Moor Street a.	...	1858	2000	...	2045	2102	...	2127	2212	...	2232	...	2312	0004	...	...	...		1012	1112	...	1209	...	1312	1409
Birmingham Snow Hill a.	...	1902	...	...	...	...	...	2131	...	...	...	...	...	...	...	...	...		...	...	...	...	...	...	...
Kidderminster ▲ a.	...	1941	...	...	...	...	...	2209	...	...	...	...	...	...	...	...	...		...	...	...	...	...	...	...

	⑦	⑦	⑦		⑦	⑦	⑦		⑦	⑦	⑦		⑦		⑦		⑦	⑦		⑦	⑦	⑦		⑦	⑦
London Marylebone 128a ◇ d.	...	1237	1300	...	1400	...	1500	...	1600	...	1700	...	1800	...	1837	...	1900	1937	...	2000	2100	2208	...	2240	2315
High Wycombe 128a ◇ d.	...	|	1326	...	1425	...	1525	...	1625	...	1725	...	1825	...	|	...	1925	|	...	2025	2125	2232	...	2315	2350
Bicester North ◇ d.	...	1326	1357	...	1452	...	1557t	...	1652	...	1754	...	1852	...	1926	...	1954	2026	...	2055	2153	2257	...	2346	0021
Banbury 114 ◇ d.	...	1339	1412	...	1509	...	1612	...	1709	...	1808	...	1909	...	1940	...	2009	2040	...	2113	2207	2310	...	0003	0037
Leamington Spa 114 d.	1340	1357	1431	...	1527	1540	1631	...	1727	1740	1827	...	1927	1940	1958	...	2028	2058	...	2132	2225	2328	...	...	...
Warwick d.	1345	1401	1437	...	1531	1545	1637	...	1731	1745	1832	...	1931	1945	2003	...	2034	2103	...	2136	2231	2333	...	...	...
Warwick Parkway d.	|	1405	1443	...	1535	|	1643	...	1735	|	1838	...	1935	|	2007	...	2040	2107	...	2140	2237	2337	...	...	...
Stratford-upon-Avon a.	1411	|	|	...	|	1611	|	...	|	1811	|	...	|	2011	|	...	|	|	...	|	|	|	...	...	...
Solihull a.	...	1420	1459	...	1557	...	1659	...	1757	...	1855	...	1957	...	2022	...	2056	2122	...	2202	2254	2352	...	...	...
Birmingham Moor Street a.	...	1432	1512	...	1609	...	1712	...	1809	...	1904	...	2009	...	2034	...	2109	2131	...	2214	2306	0004	...	...	...
Birmingham Snow Hill a.	...	...	...	...	...	...	...	...	...	...	1908	...	...	...	...	...	...	2135	...	...	...	...	...	...	...
Kidderminster ▲ a.	...	...	...	...	...	...	...	...	...	...	1945	...	...	...	...	...	...	2210	...	...	...	...	...	...	...

	Ⓐ	Ⓐ	Ⓐ	Ⓐ	Ⓐ		Ⓐ	Ⓐ	Ⓐ	Ⓐ	Ⓐ		Ⓐ	Ⓐ	Ⓐ	Ⓐ		Ⓐ	Ⓐ	Ⓐ	Ⓐ		Ⓐ	Ⓐ	Ⓐ
Kidderminster ▲ d.		...	...	...	...	...	...	...	...	0624r	0641r	...	...	0715r	...	0807	...	...	...	...	...	...	...	...	...
Birmingham Snow Hill d.		...	...	...	...	...	...	...	...	0656	0707	...	0719	0746	0822	0851	...	...	0912	...	...	...	1012	...	...
Birmingham Moor Street d.		...	0515	...	0542	...	0610	...	0630	0700	0711	...	0722	0750	0825	0855	...	...	0915	0926	0955	...	1015	...	1055
Solihull d.		...	0523	...	0551	...	0619	...	0639	0714	0722	...	0736	0759	0833	0907	...	...	0925	0935	1004	...	1024	...	1104
Stratford upon Avon d.		...	|	...	|	...	|	0606	|	|	|	...	*0733*c	|	|	|	...	0858	|	|	|	...	|	1034	|
Warwick Parkway d.		...	0535	...	0605	...	0634	|	0654	0734	0740	...	|	0811	0848	0919	...	|	0940	|	1016	...	1039	|	1117
Warwick d.		...	|	...	0608	...	|	0640	0658	0737	|	...	0803	0815	0852	|	...	|	0943	0955	|	...	1043	1101	|
Leamington Spa 114 d.		...	0541	...	0613	...	0641	0647	0705	0743	0748	...	0809	0821	0857	0925	...	0930	0947	1003	1023	...	1048	1107	1123
Banbury 114 ◇ d.		0517	0559	...	0631	...	0659	...	0725	...	0806	...	0829	0841	0916	0942	...	...	1005	...	1041	...	1106	...	1141
Bicester North ◇ d.		0533	0611	0622	0647	...	0712	...	0739	...	0819	...	0845	0855	0930	|	...	...	1018	...	|	...	1119	...	|
High Wycombe 128a ◇ d.		0559	0636	0653	|	...	|	...	|	...	0841	...	0913	0920	|	|	...	...	|	...	1115	...	|	...	1214
London Marylebone 128a ◇ a.		0633	0703	0732	0736	...	0803	...	0836	...	0910	...	0957	0947	1022	1042	...	...	1112	...	1145	...	1210	...	1245

	Ⓐ	Ⓐ	Ⓐ	Ⓐ		Ⓐ	Ⓐ	Ⓐ		Ⓐ	Ⓐ	Ⓐ	Ⓐ		Ⓐ	Ⓐ	Ⓐ	Ⓐ		Ⓐ	Ⓐ	Ⓐ		Ⓐ	Ⓐ
Birmingham Snow Hill d.	...	...	...	...	...	...	1312	...	...	...	1412	...	...	...	1512	...	1612	1651	...	1707	...	...	...	1752	1832
Birmingham Moor Street d.	1115	1122	1155	...	...	1255	1315	1322	...	1355	1415	...	1455	...	1515	1522	1615	1654	...	1710	1721	...	...	1755	1835
Solihull d.	1124	1131	1203	...	...	1304	1324	1331	...	1404	1424	...	1504	...	1524	1531	1624	1703	...	1719	1731	...	...	1804	1849
Stratford upon Avon d.	|	|	|	1234	...	|	|	|	...	|	|	1434	|	...	|	|	*1618*f	|	...	|	|	1739	...	|	|
Warwick Parkway d.	1139	|	1215	|	...	1316	1340	|	...	1415	1439	|	1516	...	1541	|	1642	1714	...	1736	|	|	...	1824	1907
Warwick d.	1142	1152	1218	1259	...	|	1343	1352	...	|	1442	1502	|	...	1544	1554	1645	1717	...	1739	1752	1806	...	1827	|
Leamington Spa 114 d.	1146	1200	1222	1305	...	1323	1348	1358	...	1422	1446	1508	1522	...	1550	1602	1649	1722	...	1743	1759	1812	...	1831	1912
Banbury 114 ◇ d.	1204	...	1243	...	...	1341	1406	...	...	1440	1504	...	1541	...	1608	...	1707	1740	...	1804	...	1831	...	1849	1931
Bicester North ◇ d.	1217	...	1257	...	...	1354	1422	...	...	1453	1517	...	|	...	1621	...	1721	1753	...	1820	...	...	...	1905	1944
High Wycombe 128a ◇ d.	|	...	1325	...	...	1424	|	...	...	1515	1544	...	1614	...	1648	...	1747	1814	...	1845	...	...	...	1935	2010
London Marylebone 128a ◇ a.	1311	...	1405		......	1453	1511	...	...	1545	1611	...	1643	...	1715	...	1820	1841	...	1914	...	...	...	2008	2037

	Ⓐ	Ⓐ	Ⓐ	Ⓐ	Ⓐ	Ⓐ	Ⓐ	Ⓐ	Ⓐ	Ⓐ	⑥	⑥	⑥	⑥	⑥	⑥	⑥		⑥	⑥	⑥	⑥	⑥	⑥	⑥
Kidderminster ▲ d.	1804	...	...	...	...	...	...	...	...	...		...	...	...	...	0637	0712	...	...	...	...	...	...	...	...
Birmingham Snow Hill d.	1846	...	...	2015	2110	...	...	2211	...	2330		...	...	...	...	0712	0748	...	...	...	...	...	...	...	...
Birmingham Moor Street d.	1849	...	1917	2018	2118	...	...	2214	...	2333		...	...	0615	0637	0716	0752	...	...	0815	0835	0914	0937	...	1037
Solihull d.	1902	...	1929	2028	2127	...	...	2229	...	2348		...	...	0624	0646	0725	0801	...	...	0823	0846	0924	0947	...	1046
Stratford upon Avon d.	|	1912	|	|	|	2135	...	|	2314	|		...	...	|	|	|	|	...	0753	|	|	|	|	1034	|
Warwick Parkway d.	1922	|	1949	2043	2146	|	...	2251	|	0010		...	...	0639	0710	0740	0816	...	|	0838	0910	0938	1004	|	1110
Warwick d.	1925	1943	1953	2046	2149	2201	...	2254	2333	0013		...	...	0642	0714	0744	|	...	0823	0841	0914	0942	1008	1102	1114
Leamington Spa 114 d.	1929	...	1958	2055	2155	2205	2217	2300	2337	0018		...	...	0649	0719	0750	0823	...	0829	0846	0919	0947	1015	1108	1119
Banbury 114 ◇ d.	...	...	2017	2114	2212	...	2237	2325	2358	0039		0604	0621	0709	0737	0809	0842	...	...	0906	0937	1005	1035	...	1137
Bicester North ◇ d.	...	...	2032	2127	2225	...	2254	...	...	...		0620	0635	0723	0754	0822	0855	...	...	0921	0954	1020	1049	...	1154
High Wycombe 128a ◇ d.	...	...	2102	2148	2250	...	2319	...	...	...		0650	0706	|	0823	|	0926	...	...	|	1023	|	1122	...	1223
London Marylebone 128a ◇ a.	...	...	2138	2217	2317	...	2358	...	...	...		0723	0737	0812	0849	0912	0953	...	...	1012	1049	1112	1149	...	1250

	⑥	⑥	⑥	⑥	⑥	⑥	⑥	⑥	⑥	⑥	⑥		⑥	⑥	⑥	⑥	⑥	⑥	⑥	⑥	⑥	⑥	⑦	⑦	⑦
Birmingham Snow Hill d.	...	...	...	...	...	...	...	...	...	...	...	...	...	...	...	...	...	...	...	...	2257	2337		...	...
Birmingham Moor Street d.	1114	1137	...	1237	1337	...	1437	1514	1537	...	1637	...	1735	...	1835	2015	...	2118	...	2218	2300	2340		...	...
Solihull d.	1123	1148	...	1246	1347	...	1446	1523	1547	...	1647	...	1746	...	1845	2024	...	2127	...	2233	2317	2356		...	...
Stratford upon Avon d.	|	|	1234	|	|	1434	|	|	|	1634	|	...	|	1834	|	|	2034	|	2215	|	|	|		...	...
Warwick Parkway d.	1138	1204	|	1310	1404	|	1510	1538	1604	|	1710	...	1804	|	1910	2039	|	2148	|	2255	2336	0015		...	...
Warwick d.	1142	1208	1302	1315	1408	1502	1514	1542	1608	1702	1715	...	1809	1902	1915	2042	2102	2151	2235	2258	2338	0018		...	...
Leamington Spa 114 d.	1147	1215	1308	1320	1415	1508	1519	1547	1615	1708	1720	...	1815	1908	1920	2048	2108	2158	2241	2305	2345	0025		...	...
Banbury 114 ◇ d.	1207	1235	...	1337	1435	...	1538	1607	1635	...	1737	...	1835	...	1937	2106	...	2218	2302	2327	...	...		0750	0834
Bicester North ◇ d.	1221	1249	...	1354	1449	...	1554	1621	1649	...	1754	...	1849	...	1954	2119	...	2235	...	...	...	...		0804	0850
High Wycombe 128a ◇ d.	|	1322	...	1423	1522	...	1623	|	1722	...	1823	...	1922	...	2023	2145	...	2304	...	...	...	...		0835	0921
London Marylebone 128a ◇ a.	1312	1349	...	1450	1549	...	1650	1712	1749	...	1849	...	1949	...	2050	2213	...	2354	...	...	...	...		0911	0953

	⑦	⑦	⑦	⑦	⑦	⑦		⑦	⑦	⑦	⑦	⑦	⑦	⑦		⑦	⑦	⑦	⑦	⑦	⑦	⑦	⑦	⑦	⑦
Kidderminster ▲ d.	...	...	...	...	...	1000	...	1030	...	...	...	...	...	...	...	...	...	...	...	...	...	...	...	...	...
Birmingham Snow Hill d.	...	...	...	...	...	1033	...	1108	...	...	...	...	...	...	...	...	...	...	...	...	...	...	...	...	...
Birmingham Moor Street d.	0828	0847	0912	...	0937	1037	...	1112	1137	...	1237	1337	...	1437	...	1512	1537	...	1637	1737	...	1837	2017	...	2118
Solihull d.	0837	0855	0924	...	0946	1047	...	1121	1147	...	1246	1347	...	1446	...	1522	1547	...	1646	1747	...	1846	2026	...	2126
Stratford upon Avon d.	|	|	|	0936	|	|	...	|	|	1236	|	|	1436	|	...	|	|	1636	|	|	1836	|	|	2036	|
Warwick Parkway d.	0852	0915	0938	|	1009	1104	...	1137	1204	|	1310	1404	|	1510	...	1537	1604	|	1710	1804	|	1910	2043	|	2146
Warwick d.	0855	0918	0941	1001	1015	1109	...	1141	1209	1301	1315	1409	1501	1515	...	1541	1609	1701	1715	1809	1901	1915	2046	2101	2149
Leamington Spa 114 d.	0901	0923	0947	1008	1020	1115	...	1147	1215	1308	1320	1415	1508	1520	...	1547	1615	1708	1720	1815	1908	1920	2052	2109	2155
Banbury 114 ◇ d.	0918	0941	1007	...	1038	1134	...	1207	1235	...	1337	1435	...	1537	...	1609t	1635	...	1737	1835	...	1937	2110	2132	2218
Bicester North ◇ d.	|	0957	1021	...	1055	1148	...	1221	1249	...	1354	1449	...	1554	...	1623	1649	...	1754	1849	...	1954	2122	...	2235
High Wycombe 128a ◇ d.	|	1025	|	...	|	1221	...	|	1322	...	1423	1522	...	1623	...	|	1722	...	1823	1922	...	2023	|	...	2304
London Marylebone 128a ◇ a.	1017	1053	1112	...	1148	1247	...	1312	1350	...	1449	1549	...	1649	...	1717	1749	...	1850	1949	...	2049	2213	...	2354

b – Via Oxford (Table 128a).
c – Change at Hatton (a. 0751 / d. 0756).
f – Change at Hatton (a. 1632 / d. 1637).
r – Stourbridge Junction.
t – Arrives 5 – 6 minutes earlier.
◇ – Additional services operate between these stations.
▲ – Only through services are shown to / from Kidderminster. Regular local trains available. See note ▲ on page 107.

CH 2nd class LONDON - HIGH WYCOMBE - OXFORD and LONDON - AYLESBURY 128a

km			②-⑤	Ⓐ	Ⓐ	Ⓐ	Ⓐ	Ⓐ	Ⓐ	Ⓐ	Ⓐ	Ⓐ	Ⓐ	Ⓐ	Ⓐ	Ⓐ	Ⓐ	Ⓐ	Ⓐ	Ⓐ	Ⓐ	Ⓐ	Ⓐ	Ⓐ
0	**London** Marylebone ...... 128 d.	Ⓐ	0001	...	...	0609	0657	0714	0744	0814	0837	0901	0935	1003	1040	1107	1140	1205	1240	1306	1340	1404	1440	1505
45	High Wycombe .... 128 d.		0029	...	...	0640	0721	0738	0812	|	0906	|	0959	|	1112	|	1212	|	1310	|	1410	|	1513	|
90	Bicester Village .... d.		0056	0554	0625	0710	0747	0806	0838	0902	0934	0956	1023	1054	1142	1155	1239	1257	1334	1355	1434	1454	1540	1555
103	**Oxford** Parkway .... d.		0105	0605	0634	0722	0755	0817	0846	0911	0944	1007	1032	1103	1151	1206	1248	1306	1342	1404	1443	1504	1549	1604
108	**Oxford** .... a.		0115	0611	0643	0730	0803	0825	0855	0919	0952	1015	1040	1111	1159	1214	1256	1314	1351	1412	1451	1513	1557	1612

	Ⓐ	Ⓐ	Ⓐ	Ⓐ	Ⓐ	Ⓐ	Ⓐ	Ⓐ	Ⓐ	Ⓐ	Ⓐ	Ⓐ	Ⓐ	Ⓐ	ⒶA		⑥	⑥	⑥	⑥	⑥	⑥	⑥	⑥
London Marylebone .... 128 d.	1540	1615	1650	1717	1750	1818	1850	1918	1950	2040	2106	2132	2201	2237	2311	⑥	0001	0556	0612	0642	0712	0742	0812	0842
High Wycombe .... 128 d.	1613	|	1714	|	1815	|	1916	1950	2022	2110	2145	2204	2228	2318	2346		0029	0626	0700	0716	0752	0815	0852	0915
Bicester Village .... d.	1639	1703	1740	1810	1840	1905	1943	2024	2047	2133	2216	2235	2256	2345	0017		0056	0655	0735	0750	0823	0847	0923	0950
Oxford Parkway .... d.	1648	1712	1750	1822	1849	1915	1953	2034	2057	2142	2225	2244	2307	2354	0025		0105	0704	0747	0800	0833	0858	0933	1000
Oxford .... a.	1656	1721	1758	1830	1857	1923	2001	2043	2105	2150	2233	2252	2315	0004	0032		0115	0712	0755	0808	0841	0906	0941	1008

	♣	⑥	⑥	⑥	⑥	⑥	⑥	⑥		⑦	⑦	⑦	⑦	⑦	♣	⑥	⑥	⑦	⑦	⑦	⑦	⑦
London Marylebone .... 128 d.	and at	1942	2012	2042	2112	2142	2212	2310	⑦	...	0742	0812	0842	0912	and at	1942	2012	2042	2112	2142	2212	2310
High Wycombe .... 128 d.	the same	2016	2052	2116	2152	2216	2252	2339		...	0816	0852	0916	0952	the same	2016	2052	2116	2152	2216	2252	2340
Bicester Village .... d.	minutes	2050	2123	2150	2223	2250	2323	0010		0749	0850	0923	0950	1023	minutes	2050	2123	2150	2223	2250	2323	0010
Oxford Parkway .... d.	past each	2103	2133	2200	2232	2303	2333	0020		0758	0903	0933	1000	1033	past each	2103	2133	2200	2233	2303	2333	0020
Oxford .... a.	hour until	2111	2141	2208	2240	2311	2341	0031		0806	0911	0941	1008	1041	hour until	2111	2141	2208	2241	2311	2341	0028

		Ⓐ	Ⓐ	Ⓐ	Ⓐ	Ⓐ	Ⓐ	Ⓐ	Ⓐ	Ⓐ	Ⓐ	Ⓐ	Ⓐ	Ⓐ	Ⓐ	Ⓐ	Ⓐ	Ⓐ	Ⓐ	Ⓐ	Ⓐ	Ⓐ	Ⓐ	Ⓐ
Oxford .... d.	Ⓐ	0535	0558	0634	0700	0743	0802	0824	0840	0906	0938	1005	1039	1111	1142	1204	1235	1304	1340	1411	1441	1513	1543	1611
Oxford Parkway .... d.		0541	0605	0648	0706	0749	0811	0830	0849	0912	0945	1012	1045	1118	1148	1210	1241	1311	1348	1417	1447	1519	1549	1617
Bicester Village .... d.		0551	0616	0658	0717	0800	0824	0839	0859	0922	0957	1023	1056	1128	1157	1220	1250	1323	1401	1426	1457	1528	1558	1626
High Wycombe .... 128 d.		0624	0645	0729	0743	0834	0857	0902	0929	|	|	1051	1122	1159	1219	1251	1315	1351	1428	1451	1522	1550	|	1653
London Marylebone .... 128 a.		0701	0729	0800	0825	0906	0936	0940	0959	1017	1047	1124	1157	1236	1258	1323	1343	1423	1508	1525	1601	1626	1647	1723

	Ⓐ	Ⓐ	Ⓐ	Ⓐ	Ⓐ	Ⓐ	Ⓐ	Ⓐ	Ⓐ	Ⓐ	Ⓐ	Ⓐ	Ⓐ		⑥	⑥	⑥	⑥	⑥	⑥	⑥	⑥	
Oxford .... d.	1638	1722	1757	1820	1856	1931	1951	2026	2048	2131	2215	2242	2315	⑥	0611	0641	0711	0741	0811	0841	0911	0941	and at
Oxford Parkway .... d.	1644	1728	1803	1827	1902	1938	1958	2032	2054	2137	2221	2248	2321		0617	0647	0717	0749	0817	0847	0917	0947	the same
Bicester Village .... d.	1657	1738	1815	1838	1914	1949	2011f	2042	2107	2146	2230	2300	2331		0628	0700	0728	0800	0828	0900	0928	1000	minutes
High Wycombe .... 128 d.	|	1809	1838	1910	|	2018	2043	2110	2140	2214	2300	2333	0004		0656	0733	0757	0833	0857	0933	0957	1033	past each
London Marylebone .... 128 a.	1754	1837	1911	1937	2011	2045	2111	2141	2211	2245	2337	0019	...		0734	0809	0839	0909	0941	1009	1039	1109	hour until

	⑥	⑥	⑥	⑥	⑥	⑥		⑦	⑦	⑦		⑦	⑦	⑦	⑦		⑦	⑦	⑦	⑦	⑦	⑦	⑦
Oxford .... d.	2011	2041	2111	2141	2211	2327	⑦	0741	0811	0841	...	0911	0941	1011	1041	and at	1941	2011	2041	2111	2141	2211	2327
Oxford Parkway .... d.	2017	2047	2117	2148	2217	2333		0747	0817	0848	...	0919	0948	1017	1047	the same	1948	2017	2047	2117	2148	2217	2333
Bicester Village .... d.	2028	2059	2128	2200	2227	2346		0757	0828	0900	...	0932	1000	1028	1100	minutes	2000	2028	2100	2128	2200	2227	2346
High Wycombe .... 128 d.	2057	2130	2157	2233	2255	...		|	0857	0933	...	0959	1033	1057	1133	past each	2033	2057	2133	2157	2233	2255	...
London Marylebone .... 128 a.	2139	2204	2239	2309	2337	...		0852	0939	1009	...	1042	1109	1139	1209	hour until	2109	2139	2209	2239	2309	2337	...

LONDON - AYLESBURY (60 km, journey ± 60 minutes)

From London Marylebone: on Ⓐ at 0010**a**, 0633*, 0652*, 0727*, 0757*, 0817, 0827, 0857*, 0913, 0927, 0956*, 1013, 1057*, 1113, 1127, 1157*, 1213, 1227, 1257*, 1310, 1357*, 1413, 1456*, 1513, 1527, 1556, 1611*, 1642*, 1653, 1710, 1730*, 1742, 1758*, 1811, 1831*, 1843, 1900*, 1932, 1956*, 2013, 2023, 2057*, 2113, 2157*, 2211, 2257*, 2322, 2357*; on ⑥ at 0010, 0653, 0727*, 0757*, 0827, 0857*, 0927, 0957*, 1027, 1057*, 1127, 1157*, 1227, 1257*, 1357*, 1457*, 1557*, 1627, 1657* and at the same minutes past each hour until 2027, 2057*, 2157*, 2217, 2257*, 2320, 2357; on ⑦ at 0010, 0757* and hourly until 1557*, 1627, 1657* and at the same minutes past each hour until 2027, 2057*, 2157*, 2227, 2257*, 2327, 2345.

From Aylesbury: on Ⓐ at 0521*, 0549*, 0607, 0625*, 0638, 0710*, 0730*, 0741, 0802*, 0818*, 0845*, 0923*, 0950, 1020*, 1028, 1050, 1120*, 1150, 1220*, 1231, 1250 and at the same minutes past each hour until 1620*, 1629, 1714, 1750*, 1820, 1847*, 1920, 1948*, 2020, 2120*, 2124, 2150, 2250; on ⑥ at 0515, 0556, 0620*, 0650, 0720*, 0750, 0820*, 0850*, 0920*, 0950, 1020*, 1050, 1120*, 1150, 1220*, 1233, 1320*, 1333, 1420*, 1433, 1520*, 1550 and at the same minutes past each hour until 1920*, 1933, 2020*, 2033, 2120*, 2133, 2220*; on ⑦ at 0720*, 0730, 0820*, 0850*, 0920, 0950*, 1020*, 1033 and at the same minutes past each hour until 1520*, 1550 and at the same minutes past each hour until 1920*, 1933, 2020*, 2033, 2120*, 2150, 2250*.

A – To Banbury (Table 128). Departs 0040.
a – ②-⑤.
f – Arrives 2006.
* – Continues to / starts from Aylesbury Vale Parkway (arrives 9–11 minutes after and departs 5 minutes before Aylesbury).
♣ – The 0942, 1142, 1342, 1542 and 1742 departures from London Marylebone depart Oxford Parkway xx03 and arrive Oxford xx11.

GW Most London trains convey 🍸 LONDON - CHELTENHAM 130

km			Ⓐ	Ⓐ	Ⓐ2	Ⓐ	Ⓐ	Ⓐ	Ⓐ	Ⓐ	Ⓐ	Ⓐ	Ⓐ	Ⓐ	Ⓐ	Ⓐ	Ⓐ	Ⓐ	Ⓐ2	Ⓐ	Ⓐ	Ⓐ2		⑥	⑥	⑥	⑥
0	**London** Pad....... 132 133 d.	Ⓐ	0535	0628	A	0727	0828	0928	1028	1128	1228	1328	1428	1528	1630	1730	1830	1928	C	2028	2128	...	⑥	...	0728	0828	0928
58	Reading............... 132 133 d.		0600	0653	...	0753	0853	0954	1053	1153	1253	1353	1453	1553	|	|	1855	|	...	2053	2153	...		...	0753	0854	0953
85	Didcot Parkway.§ 132 133 d.		0614	0707	...	|	0906	1007	1107	1207	1307	1406	1506	1606	1706	1806	1908	2004	...	2107	2206	...		...	0806	0908	1007
124	**Swindon** .... 132 133 a.		0630	0724	...	0820	0922	1023	1122	1223	1322	1423	1522	1625	1723	1821	1924	2019	...	2122	2222	...		...	0823	0924	1024
	Swindon .... d.		0633	0730	0754	0822	0929	1028	1128	1228	1328	1428	1528	1628	1730	1825	1926	2025	2054	2127	2229	2342		0729	0828	0928	1028
164	Stroud .... d.		0701	0758	0822	0850	0956	1057	1156	1256	1357	1457	1557	1657	1758	1854	1955	2054	2122	2156	2257	0010		0756	0857	0956	1056
183	Gloucester .... a.		0718	0817	0847	0908	1014	1115	1214	1314	1414	1514	1617	1715	1816	1921	2015	2116	2142	2215	2315	0029		0813	0914	1014	1114
	Gloucester .... 138 d.		0725	0823	0854	0920	1021	1121	1220	1322	1420	1521	1624	1722	1823	1928	2023	2123	2157	2226	2321	0034		0820	0919	1019	1119
194	**Cheltenham** Spa...... 138 a.		0733	0832	0903	0930	1031	1131	1231	1331	1428	1530	1632	1730	1831	1937	2032	2132	2205	2234	2331	0043		0833	0929	1029	1129
223	**Worcester** Shrub Hill 138 a.		0758	...	...	...	...	...	...	...	...	...	...	...	...	...	...	2208	...	...	...	...		...	...	...	...

	⑥	⑥	⑥	⑥	⑥	⑥	⑥	⑥	⑥	⑥	⑥2	⑥2		⑦	⑦	⑦2	⑦	⑦	⑦2	⑦	⑦2	⑦2	⑦	⑦2	⑦2	⑦	⑦2
London Pad....... 132 133 d.	1028	1128	1228	1328	1428	...	1628	1728	1828	1928	...	...	⑦	...	...	...	...	...	...	...	...	...	1733	...	...	...	...
Reading.............. 132 133 d.	1053	1153	1253	1353	1453	...	1653	1754	1853	1953	...	...		...	...	...	...	...	...	...	...	...	1758	...	...	...	...
Didcot Parkway..§ 132 133 d.	1106	1206	1306	1406	1506	...	1706	1809	1906	2006	...	...		...	...	...	...	...	...	...	...	...	1811	...	...	...	...
Swindon .... 132 133 a.	1123	1224	1323	1423	1523	...	1723	1826	1923	2023	...	...		...	...	...	...	...	...	...	...	...	1828	...	...	...	...
Swindon .... d.	1128	1228	1328	1428	1528	1628	1728	1828	1928	2027	2125	2241		0935	1032	1130	1232	1331	1430	1530	1629	1730	1829	1929	2031	2130	2313
Stroud .... d.	1156	1257	1356	1457	1556	1657	1757	1857	1956	2055	2153	2309		1001	1059	1157	1259	1358	1457	1557	1656	1757	1857	1956	2058	2158	2340
Gloucester .... a.	1214	1314	1414	1514	1614	1714	1815	1915	2013	2112	2213	2329		1019	1116	1219	1318	1417	1522	1617	1718	1818	1916	2018	2121	2218	0001
Gloucester .... d.	1219	1319	1419	1519	1619	1719	1820	1921	2019	2120	2220	...		1027	1122	1223	1322	1422	1525	1622	1723	1822	1923	2024	2124	2224	0004
Cheltenham Spa....... 138 a.	1228	1329	1429	1529	1629	1728	1829	1931	2028	2131	2230	...		1036	1130	1231	1332	1432	1533	1631	1732	1830	1932	2032	2132	2232	0013
Worcester Shrub Hill. 138 a.	...	...	...	...	...	...	...	...	...	...	...	...		...	...	...	...	...	...	...	...	...	...	...	...	...	...

		Ⓐ	Ⓐ	Ⓐ	Ⓐ	Ⓐ	Ⓐ	Ⓐ	Ⓐ	Ⓐ	Ⓐ	Ⓐ	Ⓐ	Ⓐ	Ⓐ2	Ⓐ	Ⓐ	Ⓐ	Ⓐ	Ⓐ2		⑥2	⑥	⑥	⑥	⑥	⑥
Worcester Shrub Hill. 138 d.	Ⓐ	...	...	...	0724	...	...	...	...	...	...	...	...	...	A	...	...	...	...	...	⑥	...	...	...	...	...	...
Cheltenham Spa....... 138 d.		0456	0553	0648	0758	0859	0959	1059	1159	1259	1359	1459	1559	1659	...	1759	1859	1959	2059	2216		0548	0649	0758	0859	0959	1059
Gloucester .... 138 a.		0505	0602	0657	0807	0907	1008	1108	1209	1308	1408	1508	1608	1708	...	1808	1909	2009	2109	2225		0557	0659	0808	0909	1009	1109
Gloucester .... d.		0511	0610	0705	0813	0913	1015	1113	1214	1315	1414	1513	1613	1714	1750	1814	1916	2017	2117	2228		0605	0711	0814	0916	1016	1116
Stroud .... d.		0526	0627	0724	0830	0928	1030	1130	1231	1330	1431	1531	1630	1731	1807	1831	1932	2034	2133	2244		0621	0731	0833	0933	1034	1134
Swindon .... a.		0555	0655	0753	0859	0956	1058	1158	1259	1359	1459	1559	1658	1759	1834	1859	2001	2103	2201	2312		0649	0759	0902	1001	1103	1203
Swindon .... 132 133 d.		0556	0658	0757	0902	0958	1100	1159	1301	1400	1500	1600	1700	1801	...	1902	2003	2104	2203	...		...	0801	0903	1003	1104	1204
Didcot Parkway..§ 132 133 d.		0613	0715	0814	0919	1016	1117	1217	1317	1417	1517	1617	1717	1818	...	1919	2020	2121	2220	...		...	0817	0919	1019	1121	1221
Reading.............. 132 133 a.		0625	0728	0826	0932	1028	1130	1229	1330	1429	1530	1629	1729	1830	...	1931	2032	2133	2232	...		...	0830	0933	1032	1134	1234
London Pad....... 132 133 a.		0654	0759	0854	1000	1059	1159	1259	1359	1459	1557	1659	1759	1901	...	1959	2100	2207	2304	...		...	0859	0959	1059	1159	1259

	⑥	⑥	⑥	⑥	⑥	⑥	⑥	⑥	⑥	⑥	⑥2		⑦2	⑦2	⑦	⑦	⑦2	⑦		⑦	⑦2	⑦	⑦2	⑦2	⑦	⑦2	⑦
Worcester Shrub Hill. 138 d.	...	...	...	...	...	...	...	...	...	...	...	⑦	...	...	...	...	...	...	...	...	...	...	...	...	...	...	...
Cheltenham Spa....... 138 d.	1159	1259	1359	1459	1559	1659	1759	1859	2002	2105	2132		...	0934	1054	1155	1301	1401	...	1501	1601	1701	1801	1900	2000	2100	2200
Gloucester .... 138 a.	1209	1309	1409	1509	1609	1709	1809	1907	2011	2114	2142		...	0943	1106	1205	1311	1410	...	1513	1611	1714	1811	1911	2009	2111	2210
Gloucester .... d.	1215	1316	1416	1516	1616	1717	1816	1916	2016	2119	2145		0910	0946	1115	1217	1317	1419	...	1516	1617	1717	1818	1917	2017	2117	2213
Stroud .... d.	1234	1334	1434	1534	1634	1734	1834	1933	2034	2136	2202		0927	1003	1132	1235	1335	1436	...	1534	1636	1734	1835	1934	2034	2134	2232
Swindon .... a.	1302	1402	1502	1602	1702	1802	1902	2002	2102	2205	2230		0955	1030	1201	1303	1403	1504	...	1602	1704	1803	1902	2001	2102	2202	2259
Swindon .... 132 133 d.	1304	1404	1504	...	1704	1804	...	2004	2104	2206	...		...	...	1201	...	...	...	...	1602	...	1804	...	...	...	...	...
Didcot Parkway..§ 132 133 d.	1320	1420	1520	...	1720	1820	...	2020	2120	2223	...		...	...	1219	...	...	...	...	1620	...	1821	...	...	...	...	...
Reading.............. 132 133 a.	1333	1433	1533	...	1733	1833	...	2033	2133	2236	...		...	...	1231	...	...	...	...	1632	...	1833	...	...	...	...	...
London Pad....... 132 133 a.	1359	1459	1559	...	1759	1859	...	2059	2200	2305	...		...	...	1259	...	...	...	...	1659	...	1859	...	...	...	...	...

A – From / to Salisbury (Tables 134 and 140).
C – From Westbury (Table 134).
§ – See Table 132 for connecting services to / from Oxford and Banbury.

131 LONDON - OXFORD - WORCESTER - HEREFORD

Most trains convey 🍸 GW

km		Ⓐ	Ⓐ	Ⓐ	Ⓐ	Ⓐ	Ⓐ	Ⓐ	Ⓐ	Ⓐ	Ⓐ	Ⓐ	Ⓐ	Ⓐ	Ⓐ	Ⓐ	Ⓐ	Ⓐ	Ⓐ	Ⓐ	Ⓐ	Ⓐ	Ⓐ	Ⓐ
0	**London** Paddington ▷ d.	...	0505	0550	0650	0750	0850	0950	1050	1150	1250	1350	1450	1520	1550	1658	1734	1757	1858	1950	2050	2150	2250	2318
30	Slough ▷ d.	...	0522	0604	0704	0804	0904	1005	1104	1204	1305	1404	1504	1534	1604u	|	|	|	|	2004	2104	2204	2307	2335
58	Reading ▷ d.	...	0539	0618	0718	0819	0919	1019	1119	1219	1319	1418	1518	1548	1619u	|	1800	|	|	2019	2118	2218	2328	0008b
103	**Oxford** ▷ d.	0510	0607	0653	0744	0844	0945	1045	1145	1246	1344	1445	1545	1615	1645	1746	1824	1848	1945	2045	2143	2245	2359a	0035
148	Moreton in Marsh d.	0535	...	0727	0822	0918	1019	1119	1223	1319	1418	1519	1619	1656	1719	1824	1858	1926	2020	2119	2217	2322	0036	...
172	Evesham d.	0553	...	0756f	0841	0936	1038	1134	1241	1334	1436	1537	1638	1714	1748f	1843	1913	1944	2038	2138	2235	2340	0055	...
187	Worcestershire Parkway d.	0607	...	0809	0854	0949	1051	1146	1254	1347	1449	1550	1651	1727	1801	1856	1923	1956	2051	2151	2248	2353	0106	...
194	**Worcester** Shrub Hill 125 138 a.	0615	...	0817	0904j	0957	1059	1154	1301	1354	1457	1558	1705k	1735	1810	1903	1931	2004	2059k	2159	2255	0002	...	...
195	**Worcester** Foregate St 125 a.	...	...	0820	0917	1000	1102	1158	...	1357	1500	1601	1712	1741	1813	1906	1934	2007	2108	2202	2259	...	...	...
208	Great Malvern 125 138 a.	...	...	0835	0929	1013	1114	1213	...	1410	...	1613	...	...	1830	1924	1947	...	2120	2214t	2311	...	...	...
219	Ledbury 125 a.	...	...	...	...	...	...	1226	...	1424	...	...	...	...	...	...	2001k	...	2138j	2241	...	...	...	...
241	**Hereford** 125 a.	...	...	...	...	...	...	1244	...	1441	...	...	...	...	...	...	2026	...	2204	2258	...	...	...	...

	⑥	⑥	⑥	⑥	⑥	⑥	⑥	⑥	⑥	⑥	⑥	⑥	⑥	⑥	⑥	⑥	⑥	⑦	⑦	⑦	⑦	⑦	⑦
London Paddington ▷ d.	0550	0650	0750	0850	0950	1050	1150	1250	1350	1450	1550	1650	1750	1850	1950	2050	2150	...	0843	0921	0946	1046	1146
Slough ▷ d.	0605	0705	0805	0905	1005	1105	1205	1305	1405	1505	1605	1705	1805	1905	2005	2105	2205	...	0857	0935	1000	1100	1200
Reading ▷ d.	0619	0720	0820	0920	1019	1119	1219	1319	1419	1519	1619	1719	1819	1919	2019	2119	2219	...	0912	0948	1013	1114	1218a
Oxford ▷ d.	0648	0745	0845	0945	1045	1148a	1245	1345	1448a	1545	1645	1745	1845	1945	2045	2143	2250	0858	0950a	1020	1044	1144	1244
Moreton in Marsh d.	0722	0819	0919	1019	1119	1222	1318	1421	1522	1619	1719	1819	1921	2019	2121	...	2326	0932	1024	...	1118	1218	1318
Evesham d.	0741	0849f	0938	1038	1137	1241	1336	1440	1540	1638	1738	1838	1940	2037	2140	...	2345	0951	1043	...	1137	1237	1337
Worcestershire Parkway d.	0755	0903	0952	1052	1151	1255	1350	1454	1553	1652	1753	1852	1955	2051	2154	...	2359	1004	1056	...	1149	1249	1349
Worcester Shrub Hill 125 138 a.	0802	0910	0959	1059j	1158	1302j	1357	1501j	1600	1659	1802j	1859	2005	2058	2201	...	0006	1011	1103k	...	1158	1257	1358t
Worcester Foregate St 125 a.	0805	0913	1002	1112	1201	1312	1400	1511	1603	1702	1812	1902	2008	2101	2204j	...	...	1016	1111	...	1201	1300	1417
Great Malvern 125 138 a.	0818	0925	1015	1124	1213	1325	1412	...	1615	1714	1829	1914	...	2113k	2224	...	...	1028	1123	...	1213t	1312	1429
Ledbury 125 a.	...	...	...	...	1226	...	1425	...	...	...	...	1928	...	2131r	...	...	...	...	...	...	1242	...	1442
Hereford 125 a	...	...	...	...	1244	...	1443	...	...	...	...	1945	...	2205	...	...	...	...	...	...	1300	...	1500

	⑦	⑦	⑦	⑦	⑦	⑦	⑦	⑦	⑦	⑦
London Paddington ▷ d.	1246	1346	1446	1546	1646	1746	1846	1946	2046	2146
Slough ▷ d.	1300	1400	1500	1600	1700	1800	1900	2000	2100	2159
Reading ▷ d.	1314	1414	1514	1614	1714	1814	1914	2014	2115	2213
Oxford ▷ d.	1344	1444	1544	1644	1744	1844	1944	2044	2144	2242
Moreton in Marsh d.	1418	1518	1618	1718	1818	1918	2018	2118	2218	2316
Evesham d.	1437	1537	1637	1737	1837	1937	2037	2137	2237	2334
Worcestershire Parkway d.	1449	1549	1649	1749	1849	1949	2049	2149	2249	2347
Worcester Shrub Hill 125 138 a.	1458	1558	1658	1800	1858	1958	2103	2202	2258	2356
Worcester Foregate St 125 a.	1501	1601	1700	1805	1901	2000	2109	2205	...	...
Great Malvern 125 138 a.	1513	1617j	1713	1817n	1913	2012	2121	2217	...	...
Ledbury 125 a.	...	1641	...	1842	...	...	2138	...	...	...
Hereford 125 a.	...	1659	...	1859	...	...	2155	...	...	...

	Ⓐ	Ⓐ	Ⓐ	Ⓐ	Ⓐ	Ⓐ	Ⓐ	Ⓐ	Ⓐ
Hereford 125 d.	...	...	...	0449	0523	...	...	0640	...
Ledbury 125 d.	...	...	...	0506	0540	...	...	0700	...
Great Malvern 125 138 d.	...	...	...	0519	0553	...	...	0713	...
Worcester Foreg'te St 125 d.	...	...	...	0532	0606	...	...	0726	...
Worcester S Hill 125 138 d.	...	...	0514	0537	0610	0643	0701	0731	0813
Worcestershire Parkway d.	...	...	0521	0543	0616	0649	|	0738	0819
Evesham d.	...	...	0535	0553	0635a	0700	0721	0751	0834
Moreton in Marsh d.	...	...	0554	0609	0654	0715	0740	0810	0853
Oxford ▷ d.	0520	0600	0632	0648	0732	0753	0826	0849	0932
Reading ▷ a.	0546	0628j	0653	0709	0754	0814	...	0912	0955
Slough ▷ a.	0606	0651	|	|	|	|	...	|	1009
London Paddington ▷ a.	0622	0706	0724	0738	0824	0842	...	0938	1024

	Ⓐ	Ⓐ	Ⓐ	Ⓐ	Ⓐ	Ⓐ	Ⓐ	Ⓐ	Ⓐ	Ⓐ	Ⓐ	Ⓐ	Ⓐ	Ⓐ	Ⓐ	Ⓐ	⑥	⑥	⑥	⑥	⑥	⑥	⑥	⑥
Hereford 125 d.	...	...	...	...	...	1318	...	1518	...	...	...	...	...	...	...	2200	...	0618	0713	...	...	...	...	...
Ledbury 125 d.	...	...	...	...	...	1335	...	1535	...	...	...	...	...	...	...	2217	...	0635	0730	...	...	...	...	...
Great Malvern 125 138 d.	0856	0954	1059	1155	...	1352a	...	1555b	1631	...	...	1905	1945	...	...	2229	0554	0654b	0743	...	0850	0958	1050	1155
Worcester Foregate St 125 d.	0909	1008	1112	1209	...	1405	1516	1609	1644	1726	1758	1918	1958	2100	...	2242	0608	0708	0756	0825	0904	1012	1104	1209
Worcester Shrub Hill 125 138 d.	0915	1016a	1116	1217a	1316	1414a	1520	1613	1653a	1730	1803	1924	2003	2104	...	2251a	0612	0712	0810f	0830	0913a	1017	1115b	1215
Worcestershire Parkway d.	0921	1022	1122	1223	1322	1420	1526	1619	1659	1736	1809	|	2009	2110	...	2258	0619	0718	0818	0837	0919	1023	1121	1221
Evesham d.	0935	1035	1136	1236	1336	1433	1536	1633	1714	1751	1824	1941	2024	2125	...	2311	0635	0732	0833	0851	0933	1037	1135	1235
Moreton in Marsh d.	0953	1054	1154	1255	1354	1452	1552	1653	1748p	1819b	1847a	1956	2045	2146	...	2330	0654	0751	0852	0910	0951	1056	1154	1254
Oxford ▷ d.	1032	1132	1232	1332	1432	1532a	1630	1732	1832a	1901	1932	2032	2132	2232	2305	0011	0732	0832	0932a	0948	1032	1132	1232	1332
Reading ▷ a.	1054	1155	1254	1355	1455	1553	1653	1756	1857	1923	1954	2053	2153	2259	2335	0041	0754	0854	0954	1014	1054	1154	1254	1354
Slough ▷ a.	1108	1209	1308	1409	1509	1607	1708	1811	1911	1939	2009	2109	2207	2325	2357	0057	0807	0908	1007	|	1107	1208	1308	1407
London Paddington ▷ a.	1124	1224	1324	1424	1524	1624	1724	1829	1927	1954	2024	2125	2224	2350	0020	0120	0824	0924	1024	1039	1124	1224	1324	1424

	⑥	⑥	⑥	⑥	⑥	⑥	⑥	⑥	⑥	⑥	⑦	⑦	⑦	⑦	⑦	⑦	⑦	⑦	⑦	⑦	⑦	⑦	⑦	⑦
Hereford 125 d.	...	1318	...	1513	...	...	...	...	2020	...	...	...	...	...	...	1227	...	1427	1531	...	1730	...	...	...
Ledbury 125 d.	...	1335	...	1530	...	...	...	...	2038	...	...	...	...	...	...	1246	...	1445	1548	...	1748	...	...	...
Great Malvern 125 138 d.	...	1355b	1450	1542	1700	1743	1900	...	2055a	2242	...	0858	0955	1050	1155	1300	1356	1458	1600	1658	1801	1857	1956	2040
Worcester Foregate St 125 d.	1305	1409	1504	1555	1714	1804b	1914	2000	2109	2255	0815	0911	1009	1104	1211	1313	1409	1511	1613	1711	1815	1911	2009	2053
Worcester Shrub Hill 125 138 d.	1312	1415	1515b	1613f	1718	1815b	1918	2015f	2120b	2302	0820	0915	1015	1108	1213	1317	1414	1515	1617	1715	1819	1915	2013	2059
Worcestershire Parkway d.	1319	1421	1521	1619	1724	1821	1924	2021	2142	2308	0826	0921	1021	1114	1221	1323	1420	1521	1623	1721	1824	1921	2019	2106
Evesham d.	1333	1435	1535	1633	1737	1835	1937	2035	2201	2322	0839	0934	1034	1129	1234	1336	1433	1535	1636	1735	1838	1935	2032	2123
Moreton in Marsh d.	1351	1454	1554	1651	1756	1854	1956	2054	2154	...	0857	0953	1053	1147	1250	1354	1451	1553	1654	1753	1856	1953	2051	2143
Oxford ▷ d.	1431	1531	1632	1732	1832	1932	2032	2132	2238	...	0930	1030	1130	1230b	1330a	1430	1530	1630	1730	1830	1930	2030	2127	2223
Reading ▷ a.	1453	1553	1654	1754	1854	1954	2054	2154	2304	...	0957	1056	1156	1256	1355	1458	1557k	1657	1757	1856	1955k	2058	2153	2252
Slough ▷ a.	1507	1609	1707	1807	1907	2007	2107	2207	2321	...	1012	1109	1213	1311	1413	1513	1613	1713	1812	1912	2013	2112	2206	2311
London Paddington ▷ a.	1522	1624	1722	1824	1924	2024	2124	2224	2340	...	1029	1124	1229	1329	1429	1528	1629	1729	1828	1929	2028	2129	2221	2339

OTHER SERVICES LONDON - OXFORD

	②–⑤	Ⓐ	Ⓐ	Ⓐ	Ⓐ	and at	Ⓐ	Ⓐ	Ⓐ	Ⓐ		Ⓐ	Ⓐ	Ⓐ	⑥	⑥	⑥	⑥	⑥	and at	⑥	⑥	⑥
London Paddington d.	0032	0505	0720	0820	0920	the same	1420	1620	1828	1930	...	2020	2120	2220	0032	0520	0620	0720	0820	the same	1920	2020	2119
Slough d.	0050	0522	0734	|	0934	minutes	1434	1634	|	|	...	2035	2134	|	0050	0536	0635	0735	0835	minutes	1936	2035	2135
Reading d.	0115	0839	0749	0846	0948	past each	1449	1648	|	1955	...	2049	2148	2245	0115	0550	0649	0750	0849	past each	1951	2049	2153
Oxford a.	0146	0607	0812	0918	1015	hour until	1513	1713	1913	2018	...	2113	2213	2308	0146	0619	0722	0814	0913	hour until	2016	2112	2223

	⑦	⑦	⑦	⑦	⑦	⑦	and at	⑦	⑦	⑦	⑦
London Paddington d.	0921	1021	1120	1220	1321	1420	the same	1920	2119	2300	2333
Slough d.	0935	1035	1135	1235	1335	1435	minutes	1935	|	|	0001
Reading d.	0948	1048	1148	1248	1348	1448	past each	1948	2146	2337	0019
Oxford a.	1020	1120	1220	1323	1418	1519	hour until	2019	2216	*0029**	*0125**

	①	Ⓐ	Ⓐ	Ⓐ	Ⓐ	Ⓐ	and at	Ⓐ
Oxford d.	*0005**	0707	0742	0902	0959	1102	the same	1701
Reading a.	0050	0733	0809	0924	1023	1126	minutes	1724
Slough a.	0116	|	|	|	1038	1140	past each	1738
London Paddington a.	0143	0805	0837	0952	1054	1155	hour until	1757

	Ⓐ	Ⓐ	Ⓐ	Ⓐ	⑥	⑥	⑥	and at	⑥	⑥	⑦	⑦	⑦	⑦		⑦	⑦	⑦	⑦		⑦	⑦	⑦	⑦
Oxford d.	1802	2006	2102	2202	0549	0632	0701	the same	2102	2200	0859	1055	1155	1255	...	1355	1455	1555	1655	...	1755	1855	1955	*2305**
Reading a.	1826	2028	2124	2225	0616	0655	0726	minutes	2125	2229	0929	1125	1225	1326	...	1425	1525	1625	1725	...	1823	1925	2024	0023
Slough a.	1842	2042	2138	2238	0631	0709	0739	past each	2138	2254	0943	1138	1238	1342	...	1436	1538	1638	1738	...	1838	1938	2038	0045
London Paddington a.	1859	2057	2154	2254	0649	0724	0754	hour until	2153	2314	0959	1154	1253	1357	...	1453	1553	1653	1753	...	1853	1954	2053	0115

a – Arrives 5 – 7 minutes earlier.
b – Arrives 8 – 10 minutes earlier.
f – Arrives 11 – 15 minutes earlier.
j – Departs 8 – 11 minutes later.
k – Departs 5 – 7 minutes later.
n – Departs 1829.
p – Arrives 1732.
r – Departs 2149.
t – Departs 13 – 16 minutes later.
u – Calls to pick up only.
* – By 🚌 from / to Didcot Parkway.
▷ – See panel below main table for additional services London - Oxford and v.v. See Tables **130**, **132** and **133** for other services London - Reading and v.v.

131a SLOUGH - WINDSOR

Journey time: 6 minutes 2nd class GW

From Slough:
Ⓐ: 0530, 0549, 0607, 0626, 0650, 0710, 0730, 0750, 0809, 0830, 0856 and every 20 minutes until 2316, 2340.
⑥: 0556, 0616, 0646, 0716, 0746, 0816 and every 20 minutes until 2016, 2046, 2116, 2146, 2214, 2246, 2322, 2352.
⑦: 0822, 0852, 0912 and every 20 minutes until 1852, 1922 and every 30 minutes until 2252, 2315.

From Windsor & Eton Central:
Ⓐ: 0539, 0558, 0616, 0640, 0659, 0719, 0739, 0759, 0818, 0839, 0905, 0925 and every 20 minutes until 2325, 2354.
⑥: 0606, 0626, 0656, 0726, 0756, 0826 and every 20 minutes until 2026, 2056, 2126, 2156, 2224, 2256, 2332.
⑦: 0002, 0832, 0902 and every 20 minutes until 1902, 1932 and every 30 minutes until 2302, 2325.

GW Most trains convey 🍸

LONDON - BRISTOL - TAUNTON

132

km			ⒶQ	Ⓐ	Ⓐ	Ⓐ	Ⓐ	Ⓐ	Ⓐ	Ⓐ	Ⓐ	Ⓐ	Ⓐ	Ⓐ	Ⓐ	Ⓐ	Ⓐ	Ⓐ	Ⓐ	Ⓐ	Ⓐ	Ⓐ	Ⓐ	Ⓐ
0	**London** Paddington 130 133 d.	Ⓐ	0523	0545	0632	0702	0732	0802	0832	0902	0932	1002	1032	1102	1132	1202	1231	1302	1332	1402	1432	1502	1532	1602
58	Reading 130 133 d.		0549	0610	0657	0727	0800	0827	0857	0927	0958	1027	1058	1127	1157	1227	1258	1327	1358	1427	1457	1527	1558	1627
85	Didcot Parkway ♥ 130 133 d.		0603	|	0712	0741	0814	0841	0912	0941	1013	1040	1112	1140	1212	1240	1312	1340	1412	1440	1512	1540	1612	1641
124	Swindon 121 130 133 d.		0621	0637	0730	0758	0831	0858	0929	0958	1030	1057	1129	1157	1230	1301	1329	1357	1429	1458	1529	1557	1630	1658
151	Chippenham 121 d.		0633	0649	0742	0810	0843	0910	0940	1014	1041	1109	1141	1209	1242	1313	1341	1409	1441	1511	1541	1609	1642	1710
172	Bath 140 d.		0646	0705	0757	0823	0856	0923	0953	1027	1054	1122	1154	1223	1256	1326	1354	1423	1454	1524	1554	1623	1655	1723
190	**Bristol** Temple Meads 140 110/5/6 a.		0657	0717	0813	0836	0910	0935	1005	1039	1106	1135	1206	1236	1309	1339	1406	1435	1508	1536	1606	1635	1707	1735
221	Weston-super-Mare 115 116 a.		...	...	...	...	...	...	...	...	...	...	...	...	...	...	...	...	...	...	1640	...	1742	...
262	**Taunton** 110 115 116 a.		...	...	...	...	...	...	...	...	...	...	...	...	...	...	...	...	...	...	...	...	...	...

	Ⓐ	Ⓐ	Ⓐ	Ⓐ	Ⓐ	Ⓐ	Ⓐ	Ⓐ	Ⓐ	Ⓐ	ⒶE	Ⓐ	Ⓐ		⑥	⑥	⑥	⑥	⑥	⑥	⑥	⑥	⑥	⑥
London Paddington 130 133 d.	1633	1702	1732	1801	1834	1902	1932	2001	2032	2102	2202	2232	2332	⑥	0630	0702	0732	0802	0832	0902	0932	1002	1032	1102
Reading 130 133 d.	1658	1727	1757	1827	1900u	1927	1958	2027	2057	2127	2227	2259	0005		0655	0727	0757	0827	0859	0927	0958	1027	1057	1127
Didcot Parkway ♥ 130 133 d.	1712	1741	1811	1841	1913	1941	2011	2040	2112	2140	2241	2313	0020		0709	0740	0812	0840	0913	0940	1013	1040	1112	1140
Swindon 121 130 133 d.	1730	1758	1828	1859	1930	1958	2028	2057	2129	2157	2258	2332	0038		0726	0757	0828	0858	0930	0957	1030	1057	1129	1157
Chippenham 121 d.	1741	1810	1840	1913	1942	2010	2040	2109	2141	2209	2311	2344	0050		0738	0809	0841	0910	0942	1009	1042	1109	1141	1210
Bath 140 d.	1754	1825	1853	1926	1956	2025	2053	2122	2154	2224	2324	2357	0103		0751	0823	0854	0923	0955	1023	1055	1123	1155	1223
Bristol Temple Meads 140 110/5/6 a.	1805	1840	1905	1939	2007	2040	2108	2134	2206	2239	2335	0009	0115		0803	0835	0906	0935	1007	1035	1107	1135	1209	1235
Weston-super-Mare 115 116 a.	1842	...	1939	...	2042	...	2150	...	2249	...	0015s	...	...		...	...	...	...	1033	...	...	...	1232	...
Taunton 110 115 116 a.	1912	...	2014	...	...	...	...	...	...	...	0044	...	...		...	...	...	...	1105	...	...	...	...	...

	⑥	⑥	⑥	⑥	⑥	⑥	⑥	⑥	⑥	⑥		⑥	⑥	⑥	⑥	⑥	⑥	⑥	⑥	⑥	⑥B	⑥	⑥	⑥
London Paddington 130 133 d.	1132	1202	1232	1302	1332	1402	1432	1502	1532	1602	...	1631	1702	1732	1802	1832	1902	1932	2002	2013	2032	2132	2230	2330
Reading 130 133 d.	1157	1227	1257	1327	1357	1427	1457	1527	1557	1627	...	1657	1727	1800	1827	1857	1927	1958	2027	2044	2057	2157	2256	0005
Didcot Parkway ♥ 130 133 d.	1212	1240	1312	1340	1412	1440	1512	1540	1612	1640	...	1712	1740	1815	1840	1912	1940	2012	2040	2059	2112	2210	2309	0020
Swindon 121 130 133 d.	1230	1257	1329	1357	1429	1458	1529	1557	1629	1657	...	1729	1757	1832	1857	1929	1957	2028	2057	2118	2129	2227	2326	0038
Chippenham 121 d.	1241	1310	1341	1409	1441	1510	1541	1609	1641	1709	...	1740	1809	1844	1909	1941	2009	2040	2109	...	2140	2239	2338	0050
Bath 140 d.	1254	1323	1354	1423	1455	1523	1554	1623	1654	1723	...	1753	1823	1857	1923	1956	2022	2053	2122	...	2153	2253	2351	0103
Bristol Temple Meads 140 110/5/6 a.	1306	1335	1406	1435	1509	1535	1606	1635	1706	1735	...	1805	1835	1909	1935	2008	2037	2105	2134	...	2205	2305	0003	0115
Weston-super-Mare 115 116 a.	1333	...	1434	...	1540	...	1630	...	1742	...	...	1834	...	1939	...	2039	...	2137	...	...	2235s	...	...	...
Taunton 110 115 116 a.	...	...	...	...	...	...	...	...	...	...	...	1906	...	...	...	2112	...	2208	...	...	2306	...	...	...

		⑦B	⑦	⑦	⑦	⑦	⑦	⑦	⑦	⑦	⑦	⑦E	⑦	⑦	⑦E		⑦	⑦	⑦	⑦	⑦	⑦	⑦	⑦
London Paddington 130 133 d.	⑦	0813	0900	1030	1130	1230	1330	1430	1500	1530	1600	1630	1700	1730	1800	...	1830	1900	1930	2030	2130	2215	2300	2333
Reading 130 133 d.		0838	0929	1055	1155	1255	1355	1455	1525	1555	1625	1655	1725	1755	1825	...	1855	1925	1955	2055	2155	2239	2337	0019
Didcot Parkway ♥ 130 133 d.		0854	0949	1108	1208	1308	1408	1508	1538	1608	1638	1708	1738	|	1838	...	|	1938	|	|	2208	2253	2351s	0034s
Swindon 121 130 133 d.		0911	1006	1125	1225	1325	1425	1525	1554	1625	1654	1725	1754	1822	1854	...	1922	1954	2022	2122	2225	2310	0010s	0052s
Chippenham 121 d.		0922	1018	1137	1237	1337	1437	1537	1607	1637	1707	1737	1807	1833	1907	...	1933	2007	2033	2133	2237	2321	0023s	0104s
Bath 140 d.		0934	1031	1150	1250	1350	1450	1550	1620	1650	1720	1750	1820	1846	1919	...	1946	2020	2046	2146	2250	2334	0034s	0116s
Bristol Temple Meads 140 110/5/6 a.		0945	1043	1202	1303	1402	1502	1602	1634	1702	1736	1804	1833	1859	1932	...	1958	2032	2102	2159	2302	2346	0049	0130
Weston-super-Mare 115 116 a.		|	1108	1236	...	1433	...	|	...	1731	...	1837	...	1940	|	...	2039	...	...	2235	...	...	...	...
Taunton 110 115 116 a.		1025	...	...	...	...	...	1641	...	1803	...	1904	...	...	2008	...	...	...	...	...	...	...	...	...

		Ⓐ	Ⓐ	Ⓐ	Ⓐ	Ⓐ	Ⓐ	Ⓐ	Ⓐ	Ⓐ	Ⓐ	Ⓐ	Ⓐ	Ⓐ	Ⓐ	Ⓐ	Ⓐ	Ⓐ		Ⓐ	Ⓐ	Ⓐ	Ⓐ	Ⓐ
Taunton 110 115 116 d.	Ⓐ	...	...	...	...	...	...	...	...	0655	0723	...	...	...	...	...	...	...	...	...	...	...	...	...
Weston-super-Mare 115 116 d.		...	...	...	...	...	0620	0652	...	0724	0754	...	...	...	...	...	...	...	...	...	...	...	...	...
Bristol Temple Meads 140 110/5/6 d.		0453	0510	0525	0547	0630	0700	0730	0750	0800	0830	0900	0930	1000	1030	1100	1130	1200	...	1230	1300	1330	1400	1430
Bristol Parkway 133 d.		0503	|	|	|	|	|	|	|	|	|	|	|	|	|	|	|	|	...	|	|	|	|	|
Bath 140 d.		|	|	0538	0602	0643	0713	0743	0804	0813	0843	0913	0943	1013	1043	1113	1143	1213	...	1243	1313	1343	1413	1443
Chippenham 121 d.		|	a	0552	0615	0656	0726	0756	0816	0826	0856	0928	0956	1026	1056	1126	1156	1226	...	1256	1326	1356	1426	1456
Swindon 121 130 133 d.		0528	|	0606	0630	0710	0740	0809	0831	|	0910	0945	1010	1040	1111	1140	1211	1240	...	1310	1340	1410	1441	1510
Didcot Parkway ♠ 130 133 d.		0546	|	|	0647	0726	|	0827	0848	|	0927	1002	1029	1057	1128	1157	1228	1257	...	1327	1357	1428	1457	1527
Reading 130 133 a.		0558	0708	0631	0659	0738	|	0839	0900	|	0939	1014	1041	1109	1140	1209	1240	1309	...	1339	1409	1440	1509	1539
London Paddington 130 133 a.		0626	0736	0659	0729	0808	0829	0905	0929	0926	1006	1042	1108	1136	1206	1238	1306	1337	...	1405	1436	1506	1536	1607

	Ⓐ	Ⓐ	Ⓐ	Ⓐ	Ⓐ	Ⓐ	Ⓐ	Ⓐ	Ⓐ	Ⓐ	ⒶB	ⒶD	⑤		⑥	⑥	⑥	⑥	⑥	⑥	⑥	⑥	⑥B	⑥
Taunton 110 115 116 d.	...	...	...	...	...	...	...	...	...	...	2003	2117	...	⑥	...	...	...	...	...	...	0657	...	0758	...
Weston-super-Mare 115 116 d.	...	...	...	...	...	...	1728	...	1829	...	2029	|	...		...	...	...	...	0620	...	0727	...	0827	...
Bristol Temple Meads 140 110/5/6 d.	1500	1530	1600	1630	1700	1729	1800	1830	1900	2000	2100	2200	2240		0530	0600	...	0630	0700	0730	0800	0830	0900	0930
Bath 140 d.	1513	1543	1614	1643	1713	1745	1813	1843	1913	2013	2113	2213	2253		0543	0613	...	0643	0713	0744	0813	0843	0913	0945
Chippenham 121 d.	1526	1556	1626	1657	1726	1757	1826	1856	1926	2026	2125	2227	2306		0556	0626	...	0656	0726	0757	0826	0856	0926	0958
Swindon 121 130 133 d.	1540	1610	1640	1714	1741	1811	1840	1910	1940	2040	2139	2242	2320		0611	0641	0700	0711	0741	0811	0841	0912	0941	1012
Didcot Parkway ♠ 130 133 d.	1557	1627	1657	|	1757	1828	1858	1927	1958	2057	2156	2258	2337		0628	0658	0719	0727	0756	0827	0857	0927	0956	1027
Reading 130 133 a.	1609	1639	1709	1738	1809	1840	1910	1939	2010	2109	2208	2309	2351		0641	0711	0733	0740	0810	0841	0910	0941	1010	1041
London Paddington 130 133 a.	1639	1706	1740	1805	1838	1907	1939	2006	2036	2134	2236	2356	0030		0707	0737	0758	0806	0839	0905	0937	1006	1036	1108

	⑥	⑥	⑥	⑥	⑥	⑥	⑥	⑥	⑥	⑥		⑥	⑥	⑥	⑥	⑥	⑥	⑥	⑥	⑥	⑥	⑥	⑥D	⑥
Taunton 110 115 116 d.	...	...	...	...	...	1132	...	...	...	...	...	...	...	...	...	...	...	...	...	...	...	1958	2119	2140
Weston-super-Mare 115 116 d.	...	...	...	...	...	1202	...	1302	...	1402	...	...	1501	...	1602	...	1702	...	1802	...	...	2029	|	2210
Bristol Temple Meads 140 110/5/6 d.	1000	1030	1100	1130	1200	1230	1300	1330	1400	1430	...	1500	1530	1600	1630	1700	1730	1800	1830	1900	2000	2100	2200	2240
Bath 140 d.	1014	1043	1113	1143	1213	1243	1313	1344	1413	1443	...	1513	1543	1613	1643	1713	1743	1813	1843	1913	2013	2113	2213	2254
Chippenham 121 d.	1027	1056	1126	1156	1226	1256	1326	1357	1426	1456	...	1526	1556	1626	1656	1726	1756	1826	1856	1926	2026	2126	2227	2308
Swindon 121 130 133 d.	1041	1111	1141	1211	1241	1311	1341	1411	1441	1511	...	1541	1611	1641	1711	1741	1811	1841	1911	1941	2041	2140	2241	2322
Didcot Parkway ♠ 130 133 d.	1056	1126	1156	1226	1256	1326	1356	1426	1456	1526	...	1556	1626	1656	1726	1756	1826	1856	1926	1956	2056	2156	2257	2339
Reading 130 133 a.	1110	1140	1210	1240	1310	1340	1410	1440	1510	1540	...	1610	1640	1710	1740	1810	1840	1910	1940	2010	2110	2209	2311	2352
London Paddington 130 133 a.	1137	1207	1237	1306	1337	1408	1437	1507	1537	1608	...	1635	1707	1737	1807	1837	1906	1937	2007	2035	2137	2239	2342	0033

		⑦	⑦	⑦	⑦	⑦		⑦	⑦	⑦	⑦		⑦	⑦	⑦	⑦	⑦E	⑦	⑦	⑦B		⑦	⑦	⑦E
Taunton 110 115 116 d.	⑦	...	...	...	...	...	...	...	...	...	...	...	...	...	...	...	1620	...	1703	1757	...	1858	...	2142
Weston-super-Mare 115 116 d.		...	0829	...	...	1131	...	...	...	1328	...	...	...	...	1528	...	|	...	1730	1826	...	1927	2028	2204
Bristol Temple Meads 140 110/5/6 d.		0745	0900	1000	1100	1200	...	1230	1300	1400	1430	...	1500	1530	1600	1630	1700	1730	1800	1900	...	2000	2100	2230
Bath 140 d.		0758	0913	1013	1113	1213	...	1243	1313	1413	1444	...	1513	1543	1613	1643	1713	1743	1813	1913	...	2013	2113	2243
Chippenham 121 d.		0810	0926	1026	1126	1226	...	1256	1326	1426	1457	...	1526	1556	1626	1656	1726	1755	1826	1926	...	2026	2126	2255
Swindon 121 130 133 d.		0824	0940	1040	1140	1240	...	1310	1340	1440	1514	...	1540	1611	1640	1710	1740	1810	1840	1940	...	2040	2140	2309
Didcot Parkway ♠ 130 133 d.		0841	0956	1056	1156	1256	...	1326	1356	1456	...	...	1556	1627	1656	1726	|	1826	1858	1958	...	2058	2157	2326
Reading 130 133 a.		0854	1009	1109	1209	1309	...	1340	1409	1509	...	...	1609	1640	1709	1740	1806	1840	1910	2010	...	2111	2210	2339
London Paddington 130 133 a.		0921	1036	1136	1235	1336	...	1406	1435	1536	...	...	1636	1706	1735	1808	1836	1907	1938	2039	...	2136	2237	0013

B – To/from Exeter St Davids (Table **110**).
D – From Penzance (Tables **110**/**112**).
E – To/from Plymouth (Table **110**).
Q – To Swansea via Bristol Parkway arr. 0716 (Table **133**).

a – Via Westbury (Table **110**).
b – ②–⑤ only.
c – ① only. By 🚌. Arrives Oxford 0125.
d – ① only. By 🚌. Arrives Didcot Parkway 25 minutes later.
f – Departs 1814.
g – By 🚌. Arrives Oxford 2340.
h – By 🚌. Arrives Oxford 0029.
k – To Banbury (additional journey time ± 28 minutes).
n – From Banbury (departs ± 28 minutes earlier).
r – Arrives 5 minutes earlier.
s – Calls to set down only.
t – By 🚌. Arrives Didcot Parkway 2345.

♥ – Connecting services **Didcot Parkway - Oxford (- Banbury)**. Journey time ± 13–20 minutes.

On Ⓐ at 0011 **b**, 0045 **c**, 0057 **b**, 0133 **b**, 0520, 0553, 0629 **k**, 0649, 0734 **k**, 0807, 0834, 0905, 0910 **k**, 0940, 1006, 1035, 1104, 1136, 1204 **k**, 1234, 1304, 1336, 1404 **k**, 1436, 1504, 1536, 1603 **k**, 1620, 1637, 1703, 1734 **k**, 1800, 1848, 1905 **k**, 1936, 2010, 2037 **k**, 2106, 2135 **k**, 2205, 2241, 2319, 2345.

On ⑥ at 0011, 0057, 0133, 0604, 0609 **k**, 0634, 0639, 0702, 0708, 0736, 0807 **k**, 0836, 0907, 0936, 1007 **k**, 1036, 1106, 1134, 1206 **k**, 1235, 1306, 1336, 1406 **k**, 1434, 1506, 1536, 1606 **k**, 1636, 1706, 1736, 1806 **k**, 1836, 1906, 1936 **k**, 2006, 2036, 2104 **k**, 2135, 2202, 2209, 2234, 2240.

On ⑦ at 0930, 1005, 1030, 1105, 1130, 1205, 1230, 1305, 1330, 1403, 1430, 1503, 1530, 1603, 1630, 1703, 1731, 1803, 1830, 1903, 1931, 2003, 2030, 2103, 2130, 2201, 2228, 2300 **g**, 2359 **h**.

♠ – Connecting services **(Banbury -) Oxford - Didcot Parkway**. Journey time ± 12–19 minutes.

On Ⓐ at 0005 **d**, 0011 **b**, 0045 **b**, 0335 **d**, 0355 **b**, 0500, 0520, 0540, 0600, 0604, 0637 **n**, 0707, 0721, 0742, 0758 **n**, 0827, 0836, 0906 **n**, 0921, 0936, 1005, 1037 **n**, 1106, 1137, 1207, 1238, 1306, 1337 **n**, 1406, 1437, 1507, 1536 **n**, 1606, 1636, 1707, 1736, 1807, 1836, 1906 **n**, 1936, 2010, 2037 **n**, 2108, 2127, 2207 **n**, 2232, 2245, 2305.

On ⑥ at 0011, 0045, 0515, 0549, 0607, 0640, 0708, 0736 **n**, 0807, 0837, 0907, 0937 **n**, 1007, 1037, 1105, 1137 **n**, 1206, 1237, 1306, 1337 **n**, 1407, 1437, 1506, 1537 **n**, 1607, 1637, 1707, 1737 **n**, 1807, 1837, 1907, 1937 **n**, 2007, 2037, 2107 **n**, 2137, 2200, 2204, 2238.

On ⑦ at 0859, 0930, 1030, 1055, 1130, 1155, 1230, 1255, 1330, 1355, 1430, 1455, 1530, 1555, 1630, 1655, 1730, 1755, 1830, 1855, 1930, 1955, 2030, 2127, 2223, 2305 **t**.

133 LONDON - BRISTOL PARKWAY - CARDIFF - SWANSEA

Most trains convey 🍸 GW

km			Ⓐ◇	Ⓐ	Ⓐ	Ⓐ	Ⓐ	Ⓐ	Ⓐ	Ⓐ	Ⓐ	Ⓐ	Ⓐ	Ⓐ	Ⓐ	Ⓐ	Ⓐ	Ⓐ	Ⓐ	Ⓐ	Ⓐ	Ⓐ	Ⓐ	Ⓐ	Ⓐ	ⒶG
0	**London** Paddington 130 132 d.		0523	0648	0712	0748	0818	0848	0918	0948	1018	1048	1118	1148	1218	1248	1318	1348	1418	1448	1518	1548	1618	1648	1718	1748
58	Reading 130 132 d.	Ⓐ	0549	0713	0739	0813	0843	0913	0943	1013	1043	1113	1143	1213	1243	1313	1343	1413	1443	1513	1543	1613	1643	1713	1743	1813
85	Didcot Parkway § 130 132 d.		0603	|	0754	|	|	|	|	|	|	|	|	|	|	|	|	|	|	|	|	|	1658	|	1756	|
124	Swindon 130 132 d.		0621	0741	0812	0841	0910	0941	1011	1041	1111	1140	1210	1240	1310	1340	1410	1440	1510	1540	1610	1640	1715	1742f	1813	1841
180	**Bristol** Parkway 132 d.		0728r	0804	0835	0905	0934	1005	1035	1105	1134	1204	1235	1303	1334	1405	1435	1504	1533	1604	1633	1704	1740	1805	1838	1904
215	Newport ‡ a.		0749	0824	0853	0923	0955	1023	1053	1123	1156	1225	1302	1321	1352	1423	1500	1522	1552	1623	1655	1722	1759	1823	1859	1922
234	**Cardiff** Central ‡ a.		0803	0839	0909	0938	1010	1037	1111	1137	1213	1239	1317	1335	1407	1437	1516	1536	1607	1637	1709	1737	1814	1837	1915	1938
	Cardiff Central 136 d.		0807	0842	...	0942	...	1040	...	1140	...	1242	...	1338	...	1440	...	1539	...	1639	...	1742	1824	1840	1918	1941
266	Bridgend 136 a.		0826	0901	...	1001	...	1059	...	1159	...	1301	...	1357	...	1459	...	1558	...	1658	...	1801	1849	1859	1946	2000
286	Port Talbot 136 a.		0838	0913	...	1013	...	1111	...	1211	...	1313	...	1409	...	1511	...	1610	...	1710	...	1813	1901	1912	1959	2012
295	Neath 136 a.		0845	0920	...	1020	...	1119	...	1219	...	1320	...	1416	...	1519	...	1617	...	1718	...	1820	1908	1919	2006	2019
307	**Swansea** 136 a.		0858	0933	...	1034	...	1131	...	1231	...	1333	...	1429	...	1531	...	1630	...	1730	...	1833	1921	1932	2019	2032

	Ⓐ	Ⓐ	Ⓐ	Ⓐ	⑤	①–④	⑤	①–④	⑤	①–④		⑥F	⑥	⑥	⑥	⑥	⑥	⑥	⑥	⑥	⑥	⑥	⑥	⑥	⑥	⑥H
London Paddington 130 132 d.	1818	1848	1918	1948	2048	2048	2148	2148	2248	2248		...	0648	0748	0848	0948	1048	1148	1213	1248	1348	1448	1548	1618	1648	1718
Reading 130 132 d.	1843	1913	1943	2013	2113	2113	2213	2213	2319	2318	⑥	...	0713	0814	0913	1013	1113	1213	1240	1313	1413	1513	1613	1643	1713	1743
Didcot Parkway § 130 132 d.	1858	|	|	|	|	|	|	|	2335	2335		...	|	|	|	|	|	|	1256	|	|	|	|	1657	|	1757
Swindon 130 132 d.	1915	1940	2010	2040	2140	2140	2240	2240	2352	2352		...	0740	0841	0940	1040	1140	1240	1319	1340	1440	1540	1640	1715	1740	1814
Bristol Parkway 132 d.	1940	2004	2038f	2105	2203	2203	2304	2304	0015	0015		0724	0804	0905	1005	1104	1204	1304	1343	1404	1504	1604	1704	1739	1804	1838
Newport ‡ a.	1958	2025	2057	2123	2223	2232	2322	2329	0034	0040		0744	0825	0924	1024	1124	1224	1323	1403	1423	1526	1624	1723	1758	1823	1900
Cardiff Central ‡ a.	2013	2039	2115	2140	2241	2250	2337	2347	0047	0058		0759	0838	0939	1038	1137	1237	1338	1417	1437	1541	1637	1738	1812	1837	1914
Cardiff Central 136 d.	2020	2042	2124	2143	2252	2252	2351	2351	0050	0103		0803	0842	0942	1040	1139	1239	1341	...	1441	1544	1641	1739	...	1840	1919
Bridgend 136 a.	2047	2101	2145	2202	2311	2311	0012	0012	0111	0122		0822	0901	1001	1059	1158	1258	1400	...	1500	1603	1700	1758	...	1859	1938
Port Talbot 136 a.	2059	2113	2157	2214	2323	2323	0024	0024	0135	0143		0835	0914	1013	1111	1210	1310	1412	...	1512	1618	1712	1810	...	1911	1950
Neath 136 a.	2106	2120	2204	2221	2330	2330	0031	0031	0143	0151		0843	0922	1021	1118	1218	1318	1419	...	1520	1626	1719	1818	...	1919	1958
Swansea 136 a.	2119	2133	2217	2234	2343	2343	0044	0044	0155	0203		0855	0934	1033	1132	1230	1330	1432	...	1532	1638	1732	1830	...	1932	2012

	⑥	⑥	⑥	⑥	⑥	⑥	⑥		⑦	⑦	⑦H	⑦	⑦	⑦H	⑦	⑦H	⑦	⑦	⑦	⑦	⑦	⑦	⑦	⑦	⑦	⑦
London Paddington 130 132 d.	1748	1818	1848	1915	1948	2048	2202		...	0833	0933	1016	1043	1143	1243	1343	1413	1443	1543	1643	1743	1843	1943	2043	2143	2237
Reading 130 132 d.	1813	1843	1913	1941	2013	2113	2227	⑦	...	0859	0958	1043	1109	1209	1309	1409	1440	1509	1609	1709	1809	1909	2009	2109	2209	2315
Didcot Parkway § 130 132 d.	|	1857	|	1955	|	|	2240		...	0914	1011	1058	|	|	|	|	1455	|	|	|	|	|	2022	2122	2222	2329s
Swindon 130 132 d.	1840	1915	1940	2014	2040	2140	2257		...	0931	1032f	1117	1136	1236	1336	1436	1515	1536	1636	1736	1836	1936	2039	2139	2239	2346s
Bristol Parkway 132 d.	1904	1940	2004	2039	2104	2205	2319		0858	0954	1055	1146	1201	1300	1400	1500	1539	1600	1700	1800	1900	2000	2103	2203	2303	0009
Newport ‡ a.	1923	1959	2023	2058	2123	2224	...		0924	1016	1114	...	1221	1321	1419	1525	1558	1620	1725	1820	1921	2021	2122	2224	2321	...
Cardiff Central ‡ a.	1940	2013	2039	2111	2138	2247	...		0943	1031	1128	...	1235	1335	1433	1540	1613	1634	1739	1834	1935	2035	2136	2238	2336	...
Cardiff Central 136 d.	1942	2015	2040	2113	2140	2251	...		0945	1035	1130	...	1236	1337	1437	1540	...	1637	1740	1837	1936	2036	2136	2239	2339	...
Bridgend 136 a.	2001	2034	2059	2132	2159	2310	...		1004	1056	1150	...	1255	1356	1456	1600	...	1659	1759	1857	1955	2055	2156	2258	2359	...
Port Talbot 136 a.	2013	2046	2111	2144	2211	2322	...		1016	1108	1202	...	1307	1411	1508	1612	...	1714	1811	1909	2007	2107	2208	2310	0011	...
Neath 136 a.	2020	2053	2119	2152	2219	2330	...		1024	1115	1209	...	1315	1419	1516	1620	...	1722	1819	1916	2015	2115	2215	2318	0019	...
Swansea 136 a.	2033	2106	2131	2204	2231	2343	...		1036	1129	1222	...	1329	1431	1529	1632	...	1734	1831	1929	2027	2127	2228	2330	0032	...

		ⒶC	Ⓐ	Ⓐ	Ⓐ	Ⓐ	Ⓐ		Ⓐ	Ⓐ	Ⓐ	ⒶH	Ⓐ	Ⓐ	Ⓐ	Ⓐ	Ⓐ	Ⓐ	Ⓐ	Ⓐ✕	Ⓐ	Ⓐ	Ⓐ	Ⓐ	Ⓐ	Ⓐ
Swansea 136 d.		...	0346	0459	0528	0558	0628	...	0657	0720	0743	0823	...	0923	...	1023	...	1123	...	1223	...	1323	...	1423	...	1523
Neath 136 d.	Ⓐ	...	0358	0511	0540	0610	0640	...	0710	0732	0755	0835	...	0935	...	1035	...	1135	...	1235	...	1335	...	1435	...	1535
Port Talbot 136 d.		...	0405	0518	0547	0617	0647	...	0717	0739	0802	0842	...	0942	...	1042	...	1142	...	1242	...	1342	...	1442	...	1542
Bridgend 136 d.		...	0427	0531	0600	0630	0700	...	0730	0752	0815	0855	...	0955	...	1055	...	1155	...	1255	...	1355	...	1455	...	1555
Cardiff Central 136 a.		...	0504	0551	0620	0650	0720	...	0750	0812	0835	0915	...	1015	...	1115	...	1215	...	1315	...	1415	...	1515	...	1615
Cardiff Central ‡ d.		...	0507	0554	0623	0653	0723	...	0755	0817	0841	0918	0950	1018	1041	1118	1150	1218	1254	1318	1353	1418	1454	1518	1554	1618
Newport ‡ d.		...	0525	0607	0637	0706	0737	...	0808	0830	0854	0931	1004	1033	1055	1131	1203	1231	1307	1331	1406	1431	1507	1531	1607	1630
Bristol Parkway 132 d.		0503	0554	0628	0659	0729	0802	...	0829	0856	0916	0956	1024	1056	1124t	1156	1225	1255	1328	1356	1427	1451	1527	1556	1627	1653
Swindon 130 132 d.		0528	0618	0653	0723	0753	0826	...	0853	0920	0940	1021	1048	1121	1149	1220	1249	1320	1352	1420	1451	1517	1551	1620	1651	1719
Didcot Parkway § 130 132 d.		0546	0636	|	|	|	|	...	|	|	|	|	1105	|	|	|	|	|	|	|	|	|	|	|	|	1735
Reading 130 132 a.		0558	0648	0718	0749	0818	|	...	0919	0945	1006	1045	1118	1146	1214	1245	1314	1345	1416	1445	1515	1544	1616	1645	1717	1747
London Paddington 130 132 a.		0626	0716	0744	0816	0844	0914	...	0944	1011	1034	1111	1144	1211	1240	1312	1341	1414	1444	1512	1541	1609	1641	1714	1744	1814

	Ⓐ	Ⓐ	Ⓐ	Ⓐ	Ⓐ	Ⓐ		Ⓐ	⑤	①–④		⑥	⑥	⑥	⑥	⑥	⑥		⑥	⑥H	⑥	⑥	⑥	⑥	⑥	⑥
Swansea 136 d.	...	1623	...	1723	1823	1923	...	2023	2123	2123		0356	0525	0552	0623	0644	0723	...	0741	0822	0923	1022	1124	1222	1324	
Neath 136 d.	...	1635	...	1735	1835	1935	...	2035	2135	2135	⑥	0408	0537	0604	0635	0655	0735	...	0753	0834	0935	1034	1136	1234	1336	
Port Talbot 136 d.	...	1642	...	1742	1842	1942	...	2042	2142	2142		0415	0544	0611	0642	0703	0745	...	0801	0841	0943	1042	1144	1242	1344	
Bridgend 136 d.	...	1655	...	1756	1855	1955	...	2055	2155	2155		0428	0557	0624	0655	0716	0759	...	0815	0854	0956	1055	1158	1255	1356	
Cardiff Central 136 a.	...	1715	...	1816	1915	2017	...	2115	2215	2215		0449	0618	0645	0716	0737	0820	...	0838	0915	1017	1116	1219	1316	1417	...
Cardiff Central ‡ d.	1654	1720	1754	1818	1918	2021	...	2120	2218	2218		0514	0619	0647	0718	0741	0822	...	0841	0918	1018	1118	1221	1318	1421	1441
Newport ‡ d.	1707	1735	1807	1831	1931	2034	...	2133	2233	2233		0526	0633	0700	0732	0755	0835	...	0855	0934	1032	1133	1234	1332	1434	1455
Bristol Parkway 132 d.	1729	1756	1828	1853	1955	2055	...	2155	2255	2302		0555	0656	0721	0757	0821	0856	...	0919f	0957	1057	1157	1257	1357	1457	1518
Swindon 130 132 d.	1753	1820	1851	1917	2020	2119	...	2219	...	...		0619	0720	0747	0821	0846	0921	...	0946	1021	1121	1221	1321	1421	1521	1546
Didcot Parkway § 130 132 d.	|	|	|	1934	|	|	...	|	...	...		0635	|	0803	|	0903	|	...	1004	|	|	|	|	|	|	1605
Reading 130 132 a.	1817	1847	1916	1946	2044	2144	...	2243	...	...		0648	0745	0816	0846	0916	0946	...	1017	1046	1146	1246	1346	1446	1547	1619
London Paddington 130 132 a.	1845	1914	1944	2015	2110	2209	...	2309	...	...		0714	0812	0844	0912	0942	1012	...	1041	1112	1211	1311	1414	1512	1613	1644

	⑥	⑥	⑥	⑥	⑥	⑥	⑥		⑦	⑦	⑦	⑦	⑦	⑦	⑦	⑦H		⑦	⑦	⑦H	⑦	⑦	⑦H	⑦	⑦	⑦H
Swansea 136 d.	1423	1526	1622	1726	1822	1926	2022		...	0755	...	0835	0923	1022	1123	1223	...	1323	1422	1523	...	1624	1724	1824	1924	2019
Neath 136 d.	1435	1538	1634	1738	1834	1938	2034	⑦	...	0807	...	0847	0935	1035	1135	1235	...	1335	1434	1535	...	1636	1736	1836	1936	2031
Port Talbot 136 d.	1443	1546	1642	1747	1842	1946	2042		...	0814	...	0854	0942	1042	1142	1243	...	1342	1441	1542	...	1643	1743	1842	1942	2037
Bridgend 136 d.	1455	1558	1655	1800	1855	1959	2055		...	0827	...	0907	0955	1055	1155	1255	...	1357	1454	1555	...	1656	1756	1856	1956	2051
Cardiff Central 136 a.	1517	1619	1716	1821	1917	2020	2116		...	0848	...	0928	1016	1116	1216	1316	...	1418	1515	1616	...	1717	1817	1917	2017	2112
Cardiff Central ‡ d.	1518	1623	1718	1822	1919	2022	2118		...	0850	...	0930	1020	1120	1220	1320	...	1420	1516	1620	1650	1720	1820	1920	2020	2120
Newport ‡ d.	1532	1636	1731	1835	1932	2035	2131		...	0908	...	0948	1033	1133	1233	1334	...	1433	1529	1633	1705	1733	1835	1934	2033	2133
Bristol Parkway 132 d.	1557	1657	1757	1857	1957	2056	2152		0845	0934	1003	1025	1055	1155	1255	1355	...	1455	1555	1655	1727	1755	1858	1955	2055	2155
Swindon 130 132 d.	1621	1721	1821	1921	2021	2120	2214		0909	1000	1027	1049	1118	1219	1319	1419	...	1520	1619	1719	1751	1819	1923	2019	2119	2219
Didcot Parkway § 130 132 d.	|	|	|	|	|	2136	...		0925	|	|	|	|	|	|	|	...	|	|	|	1809	|	|	2036	2135	2236
Reading 130 132 a.	1646	1747	1846	1946	2046	2149	...		0937	1025	1053	1115	1144	1244	1344	1444	...	1545	1645	1744	1823	1844	1948	2049	2148	2249
London Paddington 130 132 a.	1712	1811	1913	2011	2111	2216	...		1005	1052	1120	1139	1209	1309	1409	1509	...	1610	1709	1810	1850	1909	2014	2113	2214	2324

C – From Bristol Temple Meads (dep. 0453).
F – From Bristol Temple Meads (dep. 0703).
G – (12) and ✕ London - Carmarthen (Table **136**).
H – To / from Carmarthen (Table **136**).

f – Arrives 5–7 minutes earlier.
r – Arrives 0717.
s – Calls to set down only.
t – Arrives 1115.

◇ – Via Bristol Temple Meads (see Table **132**).
‡ – For additional services see Tables **115**, **117** and **149**.
§ – See Table **132** for connecting services to / from Oxford and Banbury.

GW 2nd class — SWINDON - WESTBURY — 134

km		Ⓐ A	Ⓐ	Ⓐ		Ⓐ	Ⓐ	Ⓐ	Ⓐ T	Ⓐ		⑥	⑥		⑥	⑥	⑥		⑥	⑥		⑥	⑥
0	**Swindon** 132 d.	0611	0845	1105	...	1315	1514	1736	1852	2045	⑥	0835	0935	...	1105	1305	1510	...	1605	1735	...	1935	2107
27	Chippenham 132 d.	0627	0900	1121	...	1330	1530	1752	1907	2100		0857f	0950	...	1121	1321	1530f	...	1620	1750	...	1950	2122
37	Melksham d.	0636	0910	1131	...	1340	1539	1803	1917	2110		0906	1000	...	1130	1330	1539	...	1630	1800	...	2000	2132
46	Trowbridge 140 d.	0646	0919	1140	...	1349	1549	1812	1927	2119		0916	1009	...	1140	1340	1549	...	1639	1809	...	2009	2141
52	**Westbury** 140 a.	0653	0926	1147	...	1356	1558	1820	1934	2126		0923	1016	...	1148	1348	1556	...	1646	1817	...	2016	2149

	⑦	⑦E	⑦G	⑦C	⑦H		⑦	⑦
Swindon 132 d.	0914	1141	1341	1544	1744	...	1929	2125
Chippenham 132 d.	0930	1156	1356	1559	1759	...	1945	2140
Melksham d.	0940	1205	1405	1609	1809	...	1954	2150
Trowbridge 140 d.	0949	1214	1414	1618	1818	...	2004	2159
Westbury 140 a.	0956	1223	1421	1625	1825	...	2011	2206

	Ⓐ	Ⓐ D		Ⓐ	Ⓐ		Ⓐ	Ⓐ
Westbury 140 d.	0517	0705	...	0737	0946	...	1217	1416
Trowbridge 140 d.	0523	0711	...	0743	0952	...	1223	1422
Melksham d.	0533	0721	...	0753	1002	...	1233	1432
Chippenham 132 d.	0543	0731	...	0803	1014	...	1243	1442
Swindon 132 a.	0559	0747	...	0819	1034	...	1259	1501

	Ⓐ	Ⓐ	Ⓐ B		⑥	⑥	⑥		⑥	⑥	⑥		⑥	⑥		⑦ W	⑦		⑦ G	⑦ C		⑦ C	⑦ C	⑦
Westbury 140 d.	1625	1834	2006	⑥	0744	0834	1007	...	1205	1405	1506	...	1636	1835	⑦	0820	1044	...	1245	1440	...	1652	1835	2024
Trowbridge 140 d.	1631	1840	2012		0750	0840	1013	...	1211	1411	1512	...	1642	1841		0827	1049	...	1252	1446	...	1658	1841	2030
Melksham d.	1641	1850	2022		0800	0850	1023	...	1221	1423	1522	...	1652	1851		0837	1100	...	1301	1456	...	1708	1851	2040
Chippenham 132 d.	1651	1904	2032		0810	0905f	1038f	...	1237f	1438	1532	...	1708f	1905f		0847	1111	...	1311	1506	...	1718	1901	2050
Swindon 132 a.	1708	1921	2050		0826	0923	1054	...	1255	1454	1548	...	1725	1924		0903	1128	...	1328	1523	...	1734	1917	2106

A – To Southampton Central (Table **140**).
B – To Cheltenham Spa (Table **130**).
C – To / from Frome (Table **139**).
D – From Salisbury to Cheltenham Spa (Tables **140** and **130**).
E – From Apr. 2 conveys (2) to Weymouth (Table **139**).
G – To / from Weymouth (Table **139**).
H – To Salisbury (Table **140**).
T – From Gloucester to Salisbury (Tables **140** and **130**).
W – From Warminster (Table **140**).
f – Arrives 5 – 7 minutes earlier.

WELSH LONG DISTANCE BUS SERVICES — 135

Traws Cymru operate several long distance bus services through Wales linking a number of main towns not served by rail services. The principal routes are shown below with the number of through journeys each way each day. For full timings and fares: ✆ +44 (0) 300 200 22 33; www.trawscymru.info

Service T1: Aberystwyth - Aberaeron - Lampeter/Llanbedr - Carmarthen and v.v.: on ⚒ 10 journeys; ⑦ 4 journeys.

Service T2: Aberystwyth - Machynlleth - Dolgellau - Minfford (for Portmeirion) - Porthmadog - Caernarfon - Bangor and v.v.: on ⚒ 7 journeys; ⑦ 2 journeys.

Service T3: Wrexham - Ruabon - Llangollen 🚂 - Corwen 🚂 - Bala 🚂 - Dolgellau - Barmouth and v.v.: on ⚒ 7 journeys; ⑦ 4 journeys.

Service T4: Newtown - Llandrindod Wells - Builth Wells - Brecon - Merthyr Tydfil * (- Cardiff *) and v.v.: on ⚒ 7 journeys; ⑦ 4 journeys.

Service T5: Aberystwyth - Aberaeron - New Quay - Cardigan - Fishguard - Haverfordwest and v.v.: on ⚒ 5 journeys; ⑦ No service.

Service T6: Brecon - Ystradgynlais - Neath - Swansea and v.v.: on ⚒ 10 journeys; ⑦ 5 journeys.

Service T10: Bangor - Betws y Coed - Corwen and v.v.: on ⚒ 5 journeys; ⑦ 3 journeys.

Service T11: Haverfordwest - St Davids - Fishguard and v.v.: on ⚒ 6 journeys; ⑦ No service.

Service T12: Machynlleth - Newtown - Welshpool - Oswestry (- Ruabon - Wrexham) and v.v.: on ⚒ 5 journeys; ⑦ No service.

Service T14: Brecon - Hay-on-Wye - Hereford and v.v.: on ⚒ 4 journeys; ⑦ No service.

Other short workings also operate on most services.

* – Frequent local trains also operate Merthyr Tydfil - Cardiff and v.v.

🚂 – Heritage and Tourist Railways: **Llangollen Railway**: Llangollen - Corwen and v.v. (16km): ✆ +44 (0) 1978 860 979; www.llangollen-railway.co.uk
Bala Lake Railway: (narrow gauge) Bala - Llanuwchllyn and v.v. (7km): ✆ +44 (0) 1678 540 666; www.bala-lake-railway.co.uk

AW 2nd class — CARDIFF - SWANSEA - SOUTH WEST WALES — 136

km			Ⓐ	Ⓐ	Ⓐ	Ⓐ	Ⓐ	Ⓐ	Ⓐ	Ⓐ	Ⓐ	Ⓐ 🍷	Ⓐ	Ⓐ K🍷	Ⓐ 🍷	Ⓐ 🍷	Ⓐ 🍷	Ⓐ 🍷	Ⓐ 🍷	Ⓐ 🍷	Ⓐ 🍷	Ⓐ	Ⓐ 🍷	Ⓐ 🍷	Ⓐ 🍷	Ⓐ C🍷	Ⓐ 🍷
	Manchester Picc 149 d.	Ⓐ	...	...	...	...	...	...	...	...	...	...	...	...	...	...	...	0730	...	...	0930	...	...	1130	...	...	...
0	**Cardiff** Central 134 d.		...	...	...	...	...	...	0535	0631	...	0745	...	0900	...	1007	...	1049	1147	...	1256	1312	1346	1445	...	1513	1544
32	Bridgend 134 d.		...	...	...	...	...	...	0606	0658	...	0805	...	0920	...	1027	...	1109	1207	...	1316	1331	1406	1505	...	1533	1605
52	Port Talbot 134 d.		...	...	...	...	...	...	0622	0715	...	0820	...	0935	...	1039	...	1125	1219	...	1331	1346	1419	1517	...	1549	1617
61	Neath 134 d.		...	...	...	...	...	...	0633	0728	...	0832	...	0946	...	1046	...	1137	1226	...	1338	1358	1427	1525	...	|	1624
73	**Swansea** 134 a.		...	...	...	...	...	...	0650	0749	...	0850	...	1003	...	1100	...	1157	1240	...	1353	1416	1440	1538	...	|	1638
73	**Swansea** 146 d.		...	...	...	...	...	0541	0654	0753	0817	0903	...	1004	1058	1108	1149	1200	1252	1341	1357	...	1457	1545	1557	|	1644
91	Llanelli 146 d.		...	...	...	...	...	0600	0713	0812	0834	0922	...	1023	1115	1127	1209	1220	1311	1358	1416	...	1516	1604	1620	1626	1703
124	**Carmarthen** a.		...	...	...	...	...	0637	0744	0844	|	0953	...	1055	|	1154	1238	1249c	1337	1429	1446c	...	1542	1636	1648	...	1734
124	**Carmarthen** d.		0450	0530	0550	0600	...	0641	0746	0848	|	1003	1055	...	|	1158	1255	...	1345	1452	...	...	1546	...	1652	...	1738
147	Whitland d.		0506	0547	0606	0615	...	0659	0803	0904	0912	1018	1112	...	1150	1215	1312	...	1400	1508	...	...	1601	...	1709	...	1753
172	Tenby d.		|	0624a	|	|	...	0732t	|	0943a	|	|	1143	...	|	|	1345	...	|	1545a	...	...	|	...	1746a	...	|
191	**Pembroke Dock** a.		|	0656	|	|	...	0807	|	1013	|	|	1215	...	|	|	1415	...	|	1618	...	...	|	...	1819	...	|
166	Clarbeston Road ⊗ d.		0520	...	0620	0630	0720	...	0818	...	0927	1033	...	...	1203	1229	...	...	1415	...	...	...	1616	...	...	...	1808
174	Haverfordwest d.		0532	...	|	0638	|	...	0826	...	|	1041	...	...	|	1238	...	...	1423	...	...	...	1625	...	...	...	1816
189	**Milford Haven** a.		0552	...	|	0658	|	...	0843	...	|	1103	...	...	|	1300	...	...	1445	...	...	...	1643	...	...	...	1838
191	**Fishguard** Harbour a.		...	...	0645	...	0744	...	...	...	0951	...	...	...	1226	...	...	...	...	...	...	...	...	...	...	...	...

	Ⓐ 🍷	Ⓐ 🍷	Ⓐ 🍷	Ⓐ 🍷	Ⓐ	Ⓐ 🍷	Ⓐ	Ⓐ A	Ⓐ M	Ⓐ	Ⓐ A	Ⓐ	⑤	①–④	Ⓐ		⑥	⑥	⑥	⑥	⑥	⑥	⑥	⑥	⑥	⑥ 🍷	⑥
Manchester Picc 149 d.	...	...	1330	...	...	1530	...	...	1630	...	...	...	...	...	...	⑥	...	...	...	...	...	...	...	...	...	...	...
Cardiff Central 134 d.	1602	...	1704	1747	1808	1904	...	1941	1947	...	...	2108	2218	2218	2315		...	...	...	...	...	...	0535	0643	0643	0756	...
Bridgend 134 d.	1622	...	1728	1807	1833	1924	...	2001	2007	...	...	2128	2244	2246	2347		...	...	...	...	...	...	0608	0703	0703	0816	...
Port Talbot 134 d.	1638	...	1743	1822	1849	1939	...	2013	2019	...	...	2145	2256	2259	0003		...	...	...	...	...	...	0623	0718	0718	0830	...
Neath 134 d.	1650	...	1754	1829	1901	1951	...	2020	2027	...	←	2153	2303	|	0016		...	...	...	...	...	...	0635	0729	0729	0838	...
Swansea 134 a.	1707	...	1811	1842	1917	2009	...	2032	2042	...	2032	2208	2316	|	0034		...	...	...	...	...	...	0653	0747	0747	0851	...
Swansea 146 d.	1710	1752	1814	1853	*1928*	2013	...	→	...	2048	2104	2225	2319	|	0051		...	...	...	...	...	0543	0655	0752	0752	0902	...
Llanelli 146 d.	1730	1812	1832	1913	*1948*	2032	...	▬	...	2108	2119	2246	2338	2330	0109s		...	...	...	...	...	0602	0714	0812	0812	0921	...
Carmarthen 146 a.	1802	1847	1903	1938	*2023*	2059	...	Ⓐ	...	2140	2152	2319	0012	0001	0142		...	...	...	...	...	0636	0746	0844	0844	0952	...
Carmarthen d.	1805	...	1909	1941	...	...	2103	2110	...	2142	...	2321f	...	...	...		0449	0530	0550	0600	...	0641	0749	0848	0848	0956	1055
Whitland d.	1821	...	1924	1956	...	...	2119	2126	...	2158	...	2336f	...	...	...		0505	0547	0606	0615	...	0700	0804	0907	0908	1014	1111
Tenby a.	|	...	1953	|	...	...	|	2154	...	|	...	|	...	...	...		|	0624a	|	|	...	0733t	|	0942t	|	|	1145t
Pembroke Dock a.	|	...	...	|	...	...	|	2225	...	|	...	|	...	...	...		|	0656	|	|	...	0805	|	1013	|	|	1219
Clarbeston Road ⊗ d.	1836	...	...	2011	...	...	2134	...	...	2213	...	2352f	...	...	...		0519	...	0621	0630	0720	...	0819	...	0923	1029	...
Haverfordwest d.	|	...	...	2019	...	...	|	...	...	2224	...	2359f	...	...	...		0531	...	|	0638	|	...	0827	...	|	1037	...
Milford Haven a.	|	...	...	2041	...	...	|	...	...	2246	...	0021f	...	...	...		0552	...	|	0658	|	...	0846	...	|	1059	...
Fishguard Harbour a.	1900	...	...	...	...	...	2159	...	...	...	...	...	...	...	...		...	...	0646	...	0744	...	...	...	0947	...	...

	⑥ K🍷	⑥ 🍷	⑥ 🍷	⑥ 🍷	⑥ 🍷	⑥ 🍷	⑥ 🍷	⑥ 🍷	⑥ 🍷	⑥ 🍷	⑥ 🍷	⑥	⑥ 🍷	⑥ 🍷	⑥ 🍷	⑥	⑥ 🍷	⑥	⑥ 🍷	⑥ A	⑥	⑥ M🍷	⑥ 🍷	⑥	⑥	⑥	⑥
Manchester Picc 149 d.	...	...	...	...	0730	...	...	0930	...	...	1130	...	...	...	1330	...	...	...	1530	...	...	1630	...	...	...	...	...
Cardiff Central 134 d.	0859	...	1005	...	1059	1207	...	1258	1400	...	1505	1512	1535	1604	1702	1744	1805	...	1903	1919	...	2001	...	2104	2208	2227	*2251*
Bridgend 134 d.	0919	...	1025	...	1119	1227	...	1318	1421	...	1525	1532	1558	1623	1725	1804	1825	...	1924	1939	...	2021	...	2124	2235	2255	*2311*
Port Talbot 134 d.	0934	...	1038	...	1134	1238	...	1333	1433	...	1537	1548	1611	1638	1740	1820	1840	...	1939	1952	...	2033	...	2139	2247	2311	*2323*
Neath 134 d.	0945	...	1046	...	1145	1245	...	1345	1440	...	1544	1600	1618	1646	1751	1832	1848	...	1951	2000	...	2041	...	2147	2254	2322	*2331*
Swansea 134 a.	1003	...	1101	...	1203	1259	...	1403	1453	...	1558	1618	1632	1659	1808	1850	1901	...	2010	2012	...	2054	...	2159	2307	2340	*2343*
Swansea 146 d.	1005	1058	1105	1154	1207	1308	1353	1405	1501	1552	1604	...	1639	1704	1811	...	1905	1940	2013	2025	...	...	2105	2226	2311	2343	0012
Llanelli 146 d.	1024	1115	1125	1214	1226	1327	1410	1425	1520	1609	1623	...	1658	1722	1830	...	1924	2000	2032	2041	...	...	2122	2246	2330	0003	0031s
Carmarthen 146 a.	1056	|	1151	1244	1256c	1356	1441	1454c	1546	1641	1655c	...	1729	1753	1901	...	1950	2034	2058	2109	...	...	2155	2318	0004	0036	0103
Carmarthen d.	...	|	1157	1258	...	1401	1458	...	1550	1700	...	...	1733	1802	1905	...	1957	...	2100	...	2114	...	2203	...	...	...	...
Whitland d.	...	1150	1216	1314	...	1418	1514	...	1605	1716	...	...	1748	1817	1921	...	2013	...	2115	...	2129	...	2218	...	...	...	...
Tenby a.	...	|	|	1345	...	|	1545	...	|	1747	...	...	|	|	1953	...	|	...	2143	...	|	...	|	...	...	...	...
Pembroke Dock a.	...	|	|	1418	...	|	1618	...	|	1820	...	...	|	|	2024	...	|	...	2216	...	|	...	|	...	...	...	...
Clarbeston Road ⊗ d.	...	1203	1231	...	...	1433	...	...	1620	...	...	...	1803	1832	...	...	2028	...	...	...	2143	...	2237	...	...	...	...
Haverfordwest d.	...	|	1239	...	...	1441	...	...	1628	...	...	...	1811	|	...	...	2036	...	...	...	|	...	2245	...	...	...	...
Milford Haven a.	...	|	1301	...	...	1503	...	...	1650	...	...	...	1833	|	...	...	2059	...	...	...	|	...	2307	...	...	...	...
Fishguard Harbour a.	...	1226	...	...	...	...	...	...	...	...	...	...	...	1856	...	...	...	...	...	...	2208	...	...	...	...	...	...

FOR NOTES SEE NEXT PAGE ▶ ▶ ▶

136 CARDIFF - SWANSEA - SOUTH WEST WALES

2nd class AW

⑦																										
	⑦	⑦	⑦	⑦	⑦	⑦	⑦	⑦	⑦	⑦	⑦	⑦	⑦	⑦	⑦	⑦	⑦	⑦	⑦	⑦	⑦	⑦	⑦	⑦	⑦	⑦
				🍷	F🍷	A			🍷	A	🍷	🍷	A		🍷	🍷		🍷	🍷	🍷	🍷		🍷			
Manchester Picc 149 d.	...	...	...	...	...	...	...	...	0930	...	1030	1129	...	...	1231	1330	...	1430	1430	1530	1630	...	1730	1830	...	1930
Cardiff Central 134 d.	...	0804	...	0953	1114	1130	1204	...	1320	1337	1410	1451	1540	...	1605	1707	...	1810	1810	1902	1956	2019	2050	2149	2230	2300
Bridgend 134 d.	...	0827	...	1023	1134	1151	1234	...	1340	1357	1430	1512	1601	...	1625	1728	...	1832	1832	1923	2015	2040	2111	2209	2250	2320
Port Talbot 134 d.	...	0840	...	1039	1147	1203	1248	...	1355	1412	1445	1527	1613	...	1640	1744	...	1848	1848	1938	2030	2055	2126	2224	2303	2336
Neath 134 d.	...	0848	...	1047	1155	1210	|	...	1402	1420	1452	1534	1621	...	1648	1753	...	1857	1857	1945	2038	2103	2134	2231	2312	2345
Swansea 134 a.	...	0901	...	1100	1208	1222	|	...	1421	1431	1507	1549	1632	...	1701	1807	...	1911	1911	2001	2052	2117	2149	2246	2325	2359
Swansea 146 d.	...	▬	1043	1104	1212	1229	|	1401	...	1439	1525	...	1640	1647	1705	...	1837	1916	1916	...	*2058*	2120	...	2250	2336	...
Llanelli 146 d.	...	...	1100	1124	1232	1245	1320	1421	...	1454	1546	...	1655	1707	1725	...	1857	1936	1936	...	*2118*	2140	...	2309	2356	...
Carmarthen a.	...	⑦	1125	1159	1304	1318	1348	1454	...	1528	1611	...	1723	1741	1750	...	1931	2006	2006	...	*2150*	2207	...	2342	0032	...
Carmarthen d.	0955	1019	1129	1202	1308	...	1357	1459	...	...	1615	...	...	1744	1806	...	1935	2012	2012	...	*2155*	2214	...	...	...	...
Whitland d.	1012	1036	1144	1219	1323	...	1413	1516	...	...	1631	...	...	1800	1822	...	1952	2032r	2037r	...	*2211*	2229	...	...	...	...
Tenby d.	|	1106	|	|	|	...	|	1545	...	...	|	...	...	1829	|	...	|	|	2106	...	|	|	...	...	...	...
Pembroke Dock a.	|	1137	|	|	|	...	|	1619	...	...	|	...	...	1902	|	...	|	|	2137	...	|	|	...	...	...	...
Clarbeston Road ⊗ d.	1028	...	1157	1236	1337	...	1428	...	...	...	1646	...	...	...	1837	...	2008	2049	...	...	*2224*	2245	...	...	...	...
Haverfordwest d.	1036	...	|	1244	|	...	1436	...	...	...	1654	...	...	...	1847	...	2017	2057	...	...	|	2253	...	...	...	...
Milford Haven a.	1055	...	|	1303	|	...	1459	...	...	...	1711	...	...	...	1907	...	...	2120	...	...	|	2310	...	...	...	...
Fishguard Harbour a.	...	...	1223	...	1401	...	...	...	...	...	...	...	...	...	...	...	...	...	...	...	*2249*	...	...	...	...	...

Ⓐ																										
	Ⓐ	Ⓐ	Ⓐ	Ⓐ	Ⓐ	Ⓐ	Ⓐ	Ⓐ	Ⓐ	Ⓐ	Ⓐ	Ⓐ	Ⓐ	Ⓐ	Ⓐ	Ⓐ	Ⓐ	Ⓐ	Ⓐ	Ⓐ	Ⓐ	Ⓐ	Ⓐ	Ⓐ	Ⓐ	Ⓐ
		M	🍷		🍷		🍷		🍷	🍷	🍷		🍷	🍷	🍷	🍷	🍷	🍷		🍷	🍷	🍷	P🍷	🍷	🍷	
Fishguard Harbour d.	...	...	...	...	...	0650	...	...	0751	...	...	0954	...	...	...	...	1250	...	...	...	...	...	...	...	...	...
Milford Haven d.	...	...	...	...	0554	|	0701	...	|	0901	...	|	...	1103	...	...	|	1300	...	...	...	1507	...	...	...	1710
Haverfordwest d.	...	...	...	...	0609	|	0716	...	|	0916	...	|	...	1118	...	...	|	1315	...	...	...	1522	...	...	...	1725
Clarbeston Road ⊗ d.	...	...	...	...	0617	0714	0724	...	0813	0924	...	1016	...	1126	...	...	1312	1323	...	...	...	1530	...	...	...	1733
Pembroke Dock d.	...	...	...	...	|	▬	|	0659	|	|	0909	|	...	|	1109	...	|	|	...	1309	...	|	...	1506	...	|
Tenby d.	...	...	...	...	|	...	|	0729	|	|	0940	|	...	|	1142t	...	|	|	...	1342t	...	|	...	1538	...	|
Whitland d.	...	...	...	...	0632	Ⓐ	0737	0756	0828	0938	1009	1029	...	1141	1210	...	1326	1337	...	1411	...	1545	...	1607	...	1748
Carmarthen a.	...	...	...	...	0647	A	0753	0813	0843	0954	1027	1046	...	1157	1228	...	1342	1353	...	1429	...	1601	...	1624	...	1804
Carmarthen d.	0438	...	0545	0603	0652	0725	0756	0815	0853	1000	1030	...	1058	1201	1231	1301	1347	1357	...	1432	1501	1606	...	1627	1655	1808
Llanelli 146 d.	0501	...	0615	0633	0722	0758	0826	0845	0923	1025	1056	...	1128	1226	1259	1331	1411	1422	...	1459	1531	1631	1645	1653	1725	1838
Swansea 146 a.	0520	...	0635	0654	0741	0814	0845	0903	0945	1042	1117	...	1148	1245	1318	1350	|	1443	...	1516	1553	1651	1703	1718	1744	1901
Swansea 134 d.	...	0536	0638	0704	0749	0823	0848	...	0951	1045	...	...	1152	1249	...	1400	|	1448	1505	...	1601	1655	1705	...	1747	1904
Neath 134 d.	...	0548	0653	0715	0800	0835	0903	...	1002	1101	...	...	1203	1305	...	1411	|	1500	1521	...	1612	1706	1720	...	1803	1920
Port Talbot 134 d.	...	0555	0705	0722	0807	0842	0915	...	1011	1113	...	...	1212	1317	...	1419	1447	1508	1533	...	1620	1713	1731	...	1815	1933
Bridgend 134 d.	...	0612	0719	0737	0822	0855	0930	...	1025	1128	...	...	1226	1332	...	1434	1504	1523	1550	...	1634	1725	1746	...	1830	1949
Cardiff Central 134 a.	...	0632	0747	0808	0847	0915	0951	...	1047	1150	...	...	1248	1354	...	1458	1527	1545	1612	...	1658	1746	1808	...	1851	2016
Manchester Picc 149 a.	...	1015	1115	...	...	...	1315	...	...	1515	...	...	...	1715	...	...	...	1915	...	...	...	2115	...	...	...	...

	Ⓐ	Ⓐ	Ⓐ	Ⓐ	Ⓐ	Ⓐ	Ⓐ	Ⓐ	Ⓐ	Ⓐ	Ⓐ	⑥	⑥	⑥	⑥	⑥	⑥	⑥	⑥	⑥	⑥	⑥	⑥	⑥	⑥	⑥
														T	🍷		🍷		A	🍷	🍷	🍷	🍷	🍷		🍷
Fishguard Harbour d.	...	...	1905	...	...	...	...	...	2215	...	...	...	...	...	...	...	...	0650	...	...	...	0751	...	...	0954	...
Milford Haven d.	...	...	|	1915	...	2041	...	...	|	...	2325	0021	...	...	...	...	0554	|	...	0700	...	|	0857	...	|	...
Haverfordwest d.	...	...	|	1930	...	2056	...	...	|	...	2340	0036	...	...	...	...	0609	|	...	0716	...	|	0912	...	|	...
Clarbeston Road ⊗ d.	...	...	1927	1938	...	2104	...	...	2237	...	2348	0044	...	...	...	...	0617	0714	...	0723	...	0813	0920	...	1016	...
Pembroke Dock d.	1709	...	|	|	...	|	...	2109	|	2227	|	|	...	...	...	...	|	...	...	|	0659	|	|	0909	|	...
Tenby d.	1740	...	|	|	2010	|	...	2155g	|	2257	|	|	...	...	...	...	|	...	...	|	0729	|	|	0939	|	...
Whitland d.	1809	...	1940	1952	2037	2118	...	2224	2251	2325	0003	0057	...	...	...	...	0631	...	...	0737	0756	0827	0935	1007	1029	...
Carmarthen a.	1827	...	1957	2008	2053	2135	...	2243	2308	2343	0021	0116	...	...	...	...	0647	...	...	0753	0813	0842	0951	1025	1046	...
Carmarthen d.	1830	1850	2000	2012	2100	...	...	...	2311	...	...	...	0434	...	0554	0615	0651	...	0724	0755	0816	0855	0959	1029	...	1101
Llanelli 146 d.	1857	1922	2025	2037	2130	...	...	...	2341	...	...	...	0459	...	0624	0645	0721	...	0757	0825	0844	0925	1024	1056	...	1131
Swansea 146 a.	1918	1945	2042	2057	2150	...	...	...	0002	...	...	...	0517	...	0644	0705	0740	...	0814	0845	0900	0946	1041	1117	...	1150
Swansea 134 d.	...	1949	...	2101	2153	...	2230	...	...	...	...	...	...	0530	0649	0710	0747	...	0822	0848	...	0953	1045	...	...	1159
Neath 134 d.	...	2000	...	2112	2208	...	2245	...	...	...	...	...	...	0542	0700	0726	0759	...	0834	0903	...	1006	1101	...	...	1210
Port Talbot 134 d.	...	2007	...	2119	2220	...	2257	...	...	...	...	...	...	0549	0708	0737	0806	...	0841	0915	...	1014	1113	...	...	1218
Bridgend 134 d.	...	2021	...	2131	2235	...	2314	...	...	...	...	...	...	0606	0722	0753	0821	...	0854	0930	...	1028	1128	...	...	1231
Cardiff Central 134 a.	...	2046	...	2211	2302	...	2339	...	...	...	...	...	...	0630	0746	0835	0849	...	0915	0951	...	1049	1150	...	...	1252
Manchester Picc 149 a.	...	...	...	...	...	...	...	...	...	...	...	...	...	1015	1115	...	...	...	...	1315	...	1515	...	...	...	...

	⑥	⑥	⑥	⑥	⑥	⑥	⑥	⑥	⑥	⑥	⑥	⑥	⑥	⑥	⑥	⑥	⑥	⑥	⑥	⑥	⑥	⑥	⑥	⑦	⑦	⑦
	🍷	🍷	🍷	🍷	🍷	🍷	🍷	🍷		🍷	🍷														🍷	
Fishguard Harbour d.	...	...	...	1241	...	...	...	...	...	...	...	...	...	...	...	1900	...	...	...	...	2215	...	...	...	...	...
Milford Haven d.	1101	...	...	|	1300	...	...	1509	...	...	...	1706	...	...	...	|	1912	...	2116	...	|	...	2308	...	...	...
Haverfordwest d.	1116	...	...	|	1315	...	...	1524	...	...	...	1721	...	...	...	|	1927	...	2131	...	|	...	2323	...	...	...
Clarbeston Road ⊗ d.	1124	...	...	1303	1323	...	...	1532	...	...	...	1729	...	...	...	1922	1935	...	2139	...	2237	...	2331	...	...	...
Pembroke Dock d.	|	1109	...	|	|	1309	...	|	...	1509	...	|	...	1712	...	|	|	1913	|	2109	|	2218	|	...	...	...
Tenby d.	|	1142t	...	|	|	1344t	...	|	...	1544t	...	|	...	1746t	...	|	|	1956v	|	2144t	|	2247	|	...	...	...
Whitland d.	1139	1211	...	1316	1337	1413	...	1546	...	1612	...	1744	...	1814	...	1935	1949	2023	2154	2213	2251	2315	2346	...	...	...
Carmarthen a.	1155	1228	...	1332	1353	1430	...	1602	...	1631	...	1800	...	1832	...	1952	2005	2039	2211	2232	2307	2333	0004	...	...	...
Carmarthen d.	1159	1233	1302	1336	1357	1434	1501	1606	...	1634	1701	1807	...	1836	1853	...	2009	2049	▬	...	2316	...	...	...	...	0934
Llanelli 146 d.	1224	1300	1332	1406	1422	1501	1531	1631	...	1700	1731	1836	...	1902	1925	...	2034	2119	...	...	2346	...	...	...	...	0959
Swansea 146 a.	1243	1317	1352	|	1442	1518	1550	1651	...	1721	1750	1855	...	1923	1947	...	2053	2141	⑥	...	0008	...	...	...	...	1016
Swansea 134 d.	1246	...	1357	|	1445	...	1555	1658	1712	*1726*	1754	1900	1910	...	1952	...	2057	2144	2237	...	...	...	...	0825	0935	...
Neath 134 d.	1302	...	1408	|	1501	...	1606	1709	1727	*1738*	1805	1911	1925	...	2003	...	2108	2159	2252	...	...	...	...	0836	0946	...
Port Talbot 134 d.	1314	...	1416	1434	1513	...	1614	1717	1739	*1747*	1812	1919	1937	...	2011	...	2115	2211	2304	...	...	...	...	0845	0954	...
Bridgend 134 d.	1329	...	1432	1449	1526	...	1629	1732	1755	*1800*	1827	1933	1953	...	2025	...	2127	2227	2320	...	...	...	...	0902	1009	...
Cardiff Central 134 a.	1351	...	1458	1521	1547	...	1650	1753	1819	*1821*	1848	1956	2017	...	2048	...	2149	2252	2342	...	...	...	...	0924	1031	...
Manchester Picc 149 a.	1715	...	...	...	1915	...	...	2115	...	...	...	...	...	...	...	...	...	...	...	...	...	...	...	1312	1416	...

	⑦	⑦	⑦	⑦	⑦	⑦	⑦	⑦	⑦	⑦	⑦	⑦	⑦	⑦	⑦	⑦	⑦	⑦	⑦	⑦	⑦	⑦	⑦	⑦	⑦	⑦	⑦
	🍷	🍷		A	🍷	🍷			🍷	A	🍷		🍷	A	🍷	H🍷			A	S			F				
Fishguard Harbour d.	...	...	...	...	...	...	...	1240	...	...	...	1420	...	...	...	...	...	...	...	...	...	...	...	...	...	2303	...
Milford Haven d.	...	...	...	...	...	1124	...	|	...	...	1330	|	...	...	1531	...	...	1730	...	...	...	1940	...	2135	...	|	2323
Haverfordwest d.	...	...	...	...	...	1139	...	|	...	...	1345	|	...	...	1546	...	...	1745	...	...	...	1955	...	2151	...	|	2338
Clarbeston Road ⊗ d.	...	...	...	...	...	1147	...	1302	...	...	1353	1442	...	...	1554	...	...	1753	...	...	...	2003	...	2159	...	2325	2347
Pembroke Dock d.	...	...	...	...	...	|	1158	|	...	...	|	|	...	...	|	...	1624	|	...	...	1904	|	...	|	2201	|	|
Tenby d.	...	...	...	...	...	|	1228	|	...	...	|	|	...	...	|	...	1654	|	...	...	1934	|	...	|	2231	|	|
Whitland d.	...	...	...	...	...	1202	1258	1315	...	...	1409	1455	...	...	1610	...	1724	1808	...	...	2003	2019	...	2213	2300	2338	0003
Carmarthen a.	...	...	...	...	...	1217	1315	1332	...	...	1426	1512	...	...	1627	...	1742	1825	...	...	2020	2035	...	2230	2320	2355	0023
Carmarthen d.	...	1030	1053	1127	...	1229	1320	1338	...	1417	1434	1517	...	1623	1639	...	1751	...	1920	...	2032	...	2116	2234	...	...	...
Llanelli 146 d.	...	1055	1125	1154	...	1254	1352	1403	...	1451	1459	1549	...	1657	1709	...	1824	...	1954	2005	2104	...	2143	2304	...	...	...
Swansea 146 a.	...	1117	1148	1210	...	1313	1413	|	...	1509	1518c	1614	...	1712	1733	...	1849	...	2012	2026	2131	...	2206	2324	...	...	...
Swansea 134 d.	1032	1130	...	1223	1251	1343	...	|	1457	1523	1531	...	1652	1724	1737	1834	*1924*	...	2019	2040	...	...	2210	2329	...	...	...
Neath 134 d.	1043	1141	...	1235	1303	1354	...	1427	1508	1535	1542	...	1703	1736	1748	1846	*1936*	...	2031	2051	...	...	2221	2341	...	...	...
Port Talbot 134 d.	1051	1149	...	1243	1310	1402	...	1434	1515	1542	1549	...	1711	1743	1755	1854	*1942*	...	2037	2059	...	...	2229	2349	...	...	...
Bridgend 134 d.	1107	1204	...	1255	1326	1417	...	1447	1530	1555	1604	...	1726	1756	1810	1911	*1956*	...	2051	2114	...	...	2245	0005	...	...	...
Cardiff Central 134 a.	1130	1227	...	1316	1347	1440	...	1510	1552	1616	1633	...	1749	1817	1833	1933	*2017*	...	2112	2137	...	...	2307	0031	...	...	...
Manchester Picc 149 a.	1515	1614	...	...	1717	1816	...	...	1915	...	2015	...	2115	...	2218	...	...	...	...	...	...	...	...	...	...	...	...

A – To/from London (operated by GW, see Table **134**). Conveys [12] and 🍷.
C – From Holyhead (Tables **149** and **160**).
F – To Hereford (Table **149**).
H – To Shrewsbury (Table **149**).
K – From Crewe (Table **149**).
M – [12] and ✕ Manchester Piccadilly - Swansea and v.v.
P – To Chester (Table **149**).
S – From Shrewsbury (Table **146**).
T – [12] and 🍷 Swansea - Manchester Piccadilly.

a – Arrives 8–11 minutes earlier.
c – Connects with train in previous column.
e – Arrives 0928.
f – ⑤ only.
g – Arrives 2138.

r – Arrives 2029.
s – Calls to set down only.
t – Arrives 4–7 minutes earlier.
v – Arrives 1942.

⊗ – Trains call at Clarbeston Road on request (except trains starting or terminating there).

GW 2nd class — WORCESTER - GLOUCESTER - BRISTOL — 138

km			Ⓐ	Ⓐ	ⒶA	Ⓐ	ⒶE	ⒶE	ⒶB	ⒶE	ⒶB	ⒶK	ⒶE	ⒶB	ⒶE	ⒶE	ⒶB	ⒶK	Ⓐ	Ⓐ	Ⓐ	Ⓐ	Ⓐ		⑥	⑥
0	**Great Malvern** ....125 130 d.	Ⓐ	...	...	...	...	...	...	0845	...	1041	...	1242	...	...	...	1643	...	...	...	...	2116	...	⑥	...	...
13	**Worcester** Foregate St 125 130 d.		...	...	...	...	...	...	0857	...	1053	...	1254	...	1451	...	1655	...	1853	...	...	2129	...		...	...
14	**Worcester** Shrub Hill... 125 130 d.		0520	...	...	...	0707	*0724*	0900	...	1056	...	1257	...	1456	...	1658	...	1857	...	...	2133	2236		...	...
39	Ashchurch for Tewkesbury........ d.		0537	...	*0631*	...	0724	|	0917	...	1113	...	1314	...	1514	...	1715	*1809*	1913	...	...	2150	2253		...	*0634*
48	Cheltenham Spa............ ◧ 116 d.		0547	0614	*0640*	...	0734	*0758*	0926	...	1123	...	1324	...	1524	...	1724	*1819*	1923	...	...	2200	2303		*0604*	0655
61	**Gloucester**............................ ◧ a.		0556	0623	*0649*	...	0743	*0807*	0935	...	1133	...	1333	...	1535	...	1736	*1827*	1934	...	...	2210	2313		*0612*	0705
	Gloucester.............................. d.		0604	0626	0700	0731	0748	0842	0941	1040	1141	1242	1338	1440	1540	1641	1741	*1842*	1942	2041	2111	2212	2317		0617	0708
115	**Bristol** Parkway ....116 a.		0640	0701	0732	0808	0823	0917	1016	1114	1217	1317	1415	1515	1615	1716	1816	*1917*	2016	2116	2145	2246	2346		0652	0742
124	**Bristol** Temple Meads........116 a.		0653	0716	0747	0828	0835	0932	1028	1126	1229	1329	1428	1528	1627	1728	1829	*1932*	2029	2129	2205	2258	2358		0708	0754

	⑥	⑥E	⑥B	⑥E	⑥B	⑥B	⑥E	⑥B	⑥B	⑥E	⑥B	⑥K	⑥	⑥	⑥	⑥K		⑦	⑦	⑦	⑦	⑦	⑦	⑦	⑦	⑦
Great Malvern.............125 130 d.	0636	...	...	...	...	...	...	...	...	...	...	...	...	...	...	2124	⑦	...	...	...	...	...	...	...	...	...
Worcester Foregate St. 125 130 d.	0649	...	0853	...	1053	...	1253	...	1453	...	1653	...	1853	...	...	2137		...	...	...	1344	1547	1737	1941	...	2158
Worcester Shrub Hill.... 125 130 d.	0652	...	0856	...	1057	...	1257	...	1457	...	1657	...	1857	...	...	2140		...	0957	1154	1357f	1554r	1758j	1952f	...	2218j
Ashchurch for Tewkesbury......... d.	0708	...	0913	...	1113	...	1313	...	1513	...	1713	...	1913	...	...	2156		...	1014	1211	1414	1614	1814	2014	...	2235
Cheltenham Spa............. ◧ 116 d.	0718	...	0923	...	1123	...	1323	...	1523	...	1723	...	1923	...	2152	2206		0925	1023	1222	1423	1623	1824	2025	2152	2245
Gloucester............................ ◧ a.	0727	...	0932	...	1132	...	1333	...	1532	...	1732	...	1932	...	2200	2216		0935	1033	1232	1434	1634	1834	2036	2200	2255
Gloucester.............................. d.	0735	0840	0941	1041	1145	1241	1341	1441	1541	1641	1741	1841	1940	2107	2205	2218		0938	1040	1238	1441	1641	1841	2042	2205	2305
Bristol Parkway .... 116 a.	0810	0915	1016	1116	1221	1316	1416	1516	1616	1716	1816	1916	2015	2141	2230	2253		1015	1116	1312	1516	1714	1916	2113	2230	2341
Bristol Temple Meads........ 116 a.	0830	0928	1029	1128	1233	1328	1428	1528	1628	1728	1828	1928	2027	2154	2240	2306		1028	1128	1324	1528	1727	1928	2126	2240	2353

		Ⓐ	Ⓐ	ⒶS	ⒶF	ⒶB	ⒶB	ⒶF	ⒶE	ⒶF	ⒶE	ⒶB	ⒶE	ⒶB	ⒶE	ⒶB	Ⓐ	ⒶA	Ⓐ	Ⓐ	Ⓐ		⑥	⑥	⑥S	⑥
Bristol Temple Meads........ 116 d.	Ⓐ	...	0610	0624	0742	0837	0939	1041	1137	1238	1339	1439	1538	1639	1738	1842	1938	2008	2057	2144	2246	⑥	...	0615	...	0638
Bristol Parkway .... 116 d.		...	0622	0634	0755	0850	0951	1052	1149	1250	1351	1455	1551	1656	1751	1856	1950	2020	2111	2158	2302		...	0624	...	0650
Gloucester.............................. a.		...	0700	0704	0832	0927	1028	1130	1226	1329	1430	1532	1629	1733	1829	1932	2030	2055	2148	2236	2339		...	0650	...	0730
Gloucester............................ ◧ d.		0604	0712	0708	...	0934	...	1138	*1245*	1337	...	1536	*1645*	1738	*1845*	1939	...	*2123*	2151	*2249*	...		0521	0659	0705	0739
Cheltenham Spa............. ◧ 116 d.		0615	0723	0718	...	0945	...	1148	*1255*	1348	...	1547	*1655*	1750	*1855*	1950	...	*2132*	2201	*2258*	...		0531	0707	0714	0749
Ashchurch for Tewkesbury......... d.		0623	0732	0725	...	0953	...	1156	*1303*	1356	...	1555	*1703*	1758	*1903*	1958	...	*2141*	2209	...	...		0539	...	0722	0757
Worcester Shrub Hill.... 125 130 a.		0640	0750	...	...	1010	...	1212	...	1413	...	1613	...	1817	...	2015t	...	*2208*	2227	...	...		0556	...	...	0814c
Worcester Foregate St. 125 130 a.		0643	0758	...	...	1016	...	1217	...	1416	...	1617	...	1823	...	2026	...	...	...	...	...		0559	...	...	0833
Great Malvern.............125 130 a.		...	0810	...	...	1028	...	1229	...	...	...	1629	...	...	...	2040	...	...	...	...	...		0616	...	...	...

	⑥F	⑥F	⑥B	⑥B	⑥E	⑥F	⑥E	⑥B	⑥E	⑥B	⑥E	⑥B	⑥B	⑥T	⑥	⑥		⑦	⑦	⑦	⑦	⑦	⑦	⑦	⑦	⑦
Bristol Temple Meads........ 116 d.	0739	0838	0938	1039	1139	1239	1339	1439	1539	1639	1738	1839	1939	2010	2108	2211	⑦	0915	0938	1138	1338	1538	1738	1937	2138	2242
Bristol Parkway .... 116 d.	0751	0851	0951	1051	1151	1251	1351	1451	1551	1650	1751	1850	1951	2022	2119	2223		0924	0950	1149	1349	1549	1749	1949	2149	2254
Gloucester.............................. a.	0830	0929	1028	1129	1230	1329	1430	1529	1630	1728	1829	1928	2029	2058	2157	2259		0950	1026	1228	1429	1629	1829	2030	2229	2330
Gloucester............................ ◧ d.	*0849*	0937	...	1138	*1245*	1338	...	1538	*1645*	1738	...	1940	2036	*2107*	*2216*	...		1002	1038	1234	1435	1634	1839	2036	...	*0004*
Cheltenham Spa............. ◧ 116 d.	*0858*	0948	...	1148	*1255*	1348	...	1548	*1655*	1748	...	1950	2045	*2118*	*2225*	...		1010	1048	1244	1444	1644	1848	2045	...	*0013*
Ashchurch for Tewkesbury......... d.	...	0956	...	1156	*1303*	1356	...	1556	*1703*	1756	...	1958	...	*2125*	...	...		...	1056	1252	1453	1653	1857	2054	...	...
Worcester Shrub Hill.... 125 130 a.	...	1012t	...	1212	...	1412	...	1612	...	1813	...	2014	...	...	...	...		...	1114	1308a	1508a	1709t	1913	2110	...	...
Worcester Foregate St. 125 130 a.	...	1020	...	1217	...	1417	...	1616	...	1819	...	2020	...	...	...	...		...	...	1321	1519	1719	1919	...	...	...
Great Malvern.............125 130 a.	...	...	...	...	...	...	...	...	...	...	...	2032	...	...	...	...		...	...	...	...	...	...	...	...	...

A – To/from Penzance (Tables **115** and **110**).
B – To/from Westbury or Warminster (see Table **140**).
E – To/from Weymouth (Table **139**).
F – From Fareham, Southampton Central, Salisbury or Portsmouth & Southsea (Table **140**).
K – To Frome (Table **139**).

S – To Stansted Airport (Tables **117** and **208**).
T – From Taunton (Table **115**).
a – Departs 9–10 minutes later.
c – Departs 0830.
d – Departs 5 minutes later.

f – Arrives 10–11 minutes earlier.
j – Arrives 18 minutes earlier.
r – Arrives 1549.
t – Departs 6–8 minutes later.
◧ – See also Tables **117** and **130**.

GW, SW — BRISTOL - WESTBURY - WEYMOUTH — 139

km			Ⓐ	ⒶE	ⒶG	ⒶC		ⒶV	ⒶC	ⒶV	ⒶC	ⒶA		ⒶE	ⒶC	ⒶC	Ⓐ	ⒶT	Ⓐ		⑥	⑥	⑥C	⑥G	⑥C	⑥E		⑥C	⑥G
0	**Bristol** Temple M 140 d.	Ⓐ	...	0842	...	0945	...	...	1145	...	1346	1445	...	1645	1745	1947	2049	2225	2345	⑥	...	0840	0935	...	1142	1442	...	1743	...
19	Bath....................140 d.		...	0901	...	1003	...	...	1203	...	1404	1503	...	1703	1803	2006	2107	2241	0004		...	0858	0954	...	1200	1500	...	1801	...
34	Bradford on Avon 140 d.		...	0916	...	1019	...	...	1219	...	1419	1518	...	1719	1818	2023	2123	2253	0019		...	0914	1010	...	1216	1516	...	1817	...
39	Trowbridge..........140 d.		...	0923	...	1025	...	...	1225	...	1426	1525	...	1725	1825	2029	2130	2259	0026		...	0921	1016	...	1222	1522	...	1823	...
45	**Westbury** ....140 a.		...	0930	...	1032	...	...	1232	...	1433	1532	...	1732	1832	2036	2137	2306	0033		...	0928	1022	...	1229	1529	...	1830	...
	Westbury ....110 d.		0652	0932	0956	1033	...	1205	1234	1257	1436	1534	...	1734	1833	2039	2140	2311	0034		0645	0929	1031	1057	1231	1531	...	1832	1958
54	Frome...................... d.		0701	0942	1005	1043	...	1221t	1243	1318t	1447	1545	...	1743	1843	2049	2149	2320	0043		0654	0938	1040	1106	1240	1540	...	1841	2007
77	Castle Cary.........110 d.		0719	0959	1022	1059	...	1238	1300	1339	...	1605	...	1801	1901	...	2207	...	...		0711	0955	1057	...	1257	1557	...	1859	2024
96	Yeovil Pen Mill ....108 d.		0735	1013	1038	1113	...	1255	1314	1354	...	1619	...	1820t	1917	...	2223	...	...		0730t	1009	1111	...	1311	1611	...	1920f	2039
	Yeovil Junction 108 a.		|	|	...	|	...	1300	|	1400	...	|	...	|	|	...	|	...	...		|	|	|	...	|	|	...	|	2045
116	Maiden Newton......... d.		0758	1037	...	1137	...	...	1337	...	...	1643	...	1843	1940	...	2246	...	...		0753	1032	1136	...	1336	1637	...	1943	...
128	Dorchester West....... d.		0810	1047	...	1153t	...	...	1353t	...	...	1653	...	1854	1951	...	2257	...	...		0804	1043	1153t	...	1354f	1653t	...	1954	...
140	**Weymouth** .... a.		0823	1100	...	1207	...	...	1406	...	...	1706	...	1906	2003	...	2309	...	...		0818	1056	1208	...	1408	1708	...	2009	...

	⑥C	⑥	⑥A		⑦	⑦	⑦Sc	⑦S	⑦S	⑦	⑦	⑦
Bristol Temple M 140 d.	1945	2046	2312	⑦	...	0934	...	...	...	1648	1748	2048
Bath ....140 d.	2003	2104	2330		...	0951	...	...	...	1706	1806	2107
Bradford on Avon. 140 d.	2019	2119	2346		...	1007	...	...	...	1722	1822	2123
Trowbridge ....140 d.	2025	2126	2352		...	1013	1215	1414	1618	1729	1829	2130
Westbury............140 a.	2032	2133	2359		...	1020	1223	1421	1625	1736	1836	2137
Westbury............110 d.	2033	2134	0001		0905	1021	1228	1422	1628	1737	1837	2138
Frome.........................d.	2043	2147	0010		0914	1031	1240	1432	1638	1746	1846	2147
Castle Cary..........110 d.	...	2203	...		0931	1047	1257	1448	...	...	1903	2204
Yeovil Pen Mill.....108 d.	...	2219	...		0947	1103	1313	1502	...	...	1917	2220
Yeovil Junction . 108 a.	...	|	...		|	|	|	|	...	...	|	|
Maiden Newton...........d.	...	2243	...		1016t	1130t	1336	1526	...	...	1940	2243
Dorchester West.........d.	...	2253	...		1029	1141	1347	1537	...	...	1951	2254
Weymouth..................a.	...	2307	...		1042	1154	1359	1551	...	...	2003	2306

		ⒶT	Ⓐ	ⒶG	Ⓐ	ⒶC	ⒶG	ⒶC	ⒶG	ⒶC	ⒶG	ⒶC
Weymouth ....d.	Ⓐ	...	0526	...	0642	0850	...	1111	...	1311	...	1455
Dorchester West ....d.		...	0539	...	0655	0903	...	1125	...	1325	...	1508
Maiden Newton ....d.		...	0551	...	0707	0915	...	1139	...	1339	...	1527f
Yeovil Junction . 108 d.		...	|	...	|	|	...	|	1317	|	1451	|
Yeovil Pen Mill ..... 108 d.		...	0618	0655	0735t	0944f	1044	1201	1324	1402	1500	1550
Castle Cary.......... 110 d.		...	0632	0710	0750	1006f	1106f	1216	1339	1416	1514	1607
Frome..........................d.		0642	0654t	0727	0808	1023	1124	1233	1356	1434	1531	1624
Westbury .... 110 a.		0650	0713	0736	0817	1032	1133	1242	1405	1443	1540	1633
Westbury .... 140 d.		0659	0720	...	0818	1037	...	1246	...	1444	...	1640
Trowbridge........... 140 d.		0705	0726	...	0824	1043	...	1252	...	1451	...	1646
Bradford on Avon . 140 d.		0711	0732	...	0830	1049	...	1258	...	1457	...	1652
Bath Spa.............. 140 d.		0730	0750	...	0848	1107	...	1316	...	1514	...	1710
Bristol T Meads .. 140 a.		0748	0808	...	0906	1127	...	1335	...	1532	...	1728

	Ⓐ	ⒶD	Ⓐ	ⒶF		⑥G	⑥	⑥C		⑥G	⑥C	⑥C	⑥C		⑥	⑥		⑦Tb	⑦Tc	⑦G	⑦	⑦S	⑦S	⑦	⑦S	⑦	⑦S	⑦	⑦
Weymouth.................d.	1730	...	2015	...	⑥	...	0638	0846	...	...	1110	1310	1455	...	1728	2020	⑦	...	0801	...	...	1101	...	1410	...	1610	...	1753	2010
Dorchester West.........d.	1743	...	2028	...		...	0651	0859	...	...	1124	1323	1508	...	1741	2033		...	0814	...	...	1115	...	1423	...	1623	...	1806	2023
Maiden Newton...........d.	1755	...	2040	...		...	0704	0912	...	...	1137	1336	1521	...	1754	2046		...	0827	...	...	1129	...	1436	...	1635	...	1818	2035
Yeovil Junction . 108 d.	|	1917	|	2145		...	|	|	...	...	|	|	|	...	|	|		...	|	0946	...	|	...	|	...	|	...	|	|
Yeovil Pen Mill..... 108 d.	1820	1926	2103	2152		...	0729	0936	...	...	1200	1400	1544	...	1819	2110		...	0851	0953	...	1152	...	1501	...	1658	...	1846f	2058
Castle Cary.......... 110 d.	1844j	1940	2117	2220r		0736	0754j	0950	...	...	1214	1414	1606f	...	1834	2124		...	0905	1007	...	1215f	...	1515	...	1712	...	1907t	2112
Frome..........................d.	1902	1957	2134	2245t		0754	0811	1012t	...	1130	1232	1431	1624	...	1851	2142		0922	0922	1024	1125	1232	1421	1533	1643	1730	1824	1924	2129
Westbury............ 110 a.	1911	2006	2144	2255		0803	0820	1023	...	1139	1241	1440	1634	...	1901	2151		0931	0931	1033	1134	1241	1430	1542	1651	1739	1833	1934	2138
Westbury............ 140 d.	1918	...	2145	...		...	0825	1040	...	...	1242	1441	1640	...	1902	2157		0941	0941	...	1136	1245	1440	1543	1652	1740	1835	1940	2140
Trowbridge .... 140 d.	1924	...	2152	...		...	0831	1046	...	...	1248	1448	1647	...	1908	2203		0947	0947	...	1142	1252	1446	1549	1658	1746	1841	1946	2146
Bradford on Avon. 140 d.	1930	...	2158	...		...	0838	1052	...	...	1254	1454	1653	...	1914	2209		0953	0953	...	1148	...	...	1555	...	1752	...	1952	2152
Bath Spa.............. 140 d.	1943	...	2216	...		...	0901	1110	...	...	1311	1511	1710	...	1928	2227		1011	1011	...	1207	...	...	1612	...	1811	...	2010	2210
Bristol Temple M 140 a.	2001	...	2235	...		...	0920	1128	...	...	1329	1529	1728	...	1947	2246		1047	1047	...	1225	...	...	1630	...	1829	...	2029	2228

A – From/to Great Malvern (Table **138**).
C – From/to Gloucester (Table **138**).
D – From London Waterloo (Table **108**).
E – From Worcester (Table **138**).
F – To Salisbury (Table **140**).

G – From/to London Waterloo (Tables **108** and **140**).
S – From/to Swindon (Table **134**).
T – To/from Cardiff Central (Table **118**).
V – From Basingstoke (Tables **108** and **140**).
b – Until Mar. 26.

c – From Apr. 2.
f – Arrives 8–10 minutes earlier.
j – Arrives 11–13 minutes earlier.
r – Arrives 2205.
t – Arrives 5–7 minutes earlier.

140 BRISTOL - WESTBURY - SOUTHAMPTON - PORTSMOUTH

2nd class GW, SW

km		⚒	⚒	Ⓐ	ⒶP	⑥	Ⓐ	⑥	ⒶR	⚒	ⒶG	⑥	Ⓐ🍷	⑥F	⚒d	⑥	Ⓐ	Ⓐ	⚒	⚒	Ⓐ	⑥	⚒A	ⒶG	⑥L	⚒	⚒
	Cardiff Central **118** d.		...	...	...	...	...	...	...	...	...	0630	0628	...	...	0727	0728	...	0827	...	0928	0927	...	...	...	1030	1130
0	**Bristol** Temple Meads **139** d.		...	0500	0510	...	0551	0546	...	0639	...	0723	0722	...	0735	0822	0820	0904	0922	...	1021	1023	1043	...	...	1122	1222
19	Bath Spa **139** d.		...	0513	|	...	0609	0604	...	0658	...	0736	0735	...	0754	0835	0837	0921	0935	...	1035	1037	1101	...	...	1135	1235
34	Bradford on Avon **139** d.		...	0525	0535	...	0626	0620	...	0714	...	0748	0747	...	0810	0847	0849	0933	0947	...	1047	1049	1117	...	...	1147	1247
39	Trowbridge **132a 139** d.		...	0532	0541	...	0632	0626	0646	0720	...	0754	0753	...	0817	0853	0856	0940	0954	...	1053	1055	1123	...	...	1154	1253
45	**Westbury** **132a 139** a.		...	0539	0549	...	0639	0633	0653	0727	...	0801	0800	...	0824	0900	0903	0949	1002	...	1100	1102	1132	...	...	1201	1301
	Westbury d.		0523	0548	...	0601	0641	0648	0655	...	0740	0802	0803	0810	...	0901	0904	0952	1003	1037	1101	1103	...	1139	1143	1202	1301
53	Warminster d.		0531	0556	...	0609	0649	0658	0704	...	0748	0811	0811	0818	...	0911	0912	1001	1011	1045	1111	1113	...	1148	1150	1210	1311
85	**Salisbury** d.		0554	0618	...	0632	0711	0724	0737f	...	0812	0833	0833	0838	...	0933	0934	...	1033	1106	1133	1135	...	1209	1211	1233	1333
112	Romsey d.		...	0637	...	0650	0730	0743	0756	...	...	0852	0853	...	...	0951	0952	...	1051	...	1152	1153	...	...	...	1251	1351
123	**Southampton** Central a.		...	0647	...	0702	0740	0755g	0807	...	...	0902	0903	...	...	1003	1003	...	1103	...	1202	1204	...	...	...	1303	1404
147	Fareham a.		...	0710	...	0727	0803	0824	...	...	...	0926	0927	...	...	1027	1027	...	1127	...	1228	1227	...	...	...	1327	1427
164	**Portsmouth** & Southsea a.		...	0731	...	0747	0822	0844	...	...	...	0946	0947	...	...	1046	1047	...	1147	...	1247	1246	...	...	...	1347	1447
165	**Portsmouth** Harbour a.		...	0738	...	0752	0827	0849	...	...	...	0951	0953	...	...	1051	1052	...	1152	...	1252	1251	...	...	...	1352	1452

	ⒶA	⚒	ⒶT	⑥A	⚒	ⒶT	⚒	⑥A	ⒶA	⑥	Ⓐ	Ⓐ	⚒	Ⓐ	⑥	Ⓐ	ⒶA	⑥A	ⒶC	⑥	Ⓐ	⑥	Ⓐ	⑥	Ⓐ	⑥	Ⓐ
Cardiff Central **118** d.	...	1227	...	...	1330	...	1430	...	...	1530	1530	...	1627	...	1727	1727	...	...	...	1827	1830	1930	1930	2030	2030	...	...
Bristol Temple Meads **139** d.	1242	1322	...	1345	1422	...	1522	1542	1545	1622	1622	1706	1722	1810	1822	1824	1843	1845	...	1922	1924	2022	2024	2121	2125	2140	2145
Bath Spa **139** d.	1300	1335	...	1403	1435	...	1535	1600	1603	1635	1635	1724	1735	1827	1835	1837	1901	1903	...	1935	1937	2035	2037	2134	2138	2158	2203
Bradford on Avon **139** d.	1316	1347	...	1419	1447	...	1547	1616	1618	1647	1647	1738	1747	1843	1847	1850	1916	1919	...	1947	1949	2047	2049	2146	2150	2210	2219
Trowbridge **132a 139** d.	1322	1354	...	1425	1453	...	1554	1622	1625	1653	1654	1744	1754	1850	1854	1857	1923	1925	1927	1954	1957	2054	2055	2152	2157	2216	2226
Westbury **132a 139** a.	1329	1401	...	1432	1501	...	1601	1629	1632	1700	1701	1751	1801	1857	1901	1904	1930	1932	1934	2001	2004	2101	2102	2159	2204	2223	2233
Westbury d.	1331	1402	1413	...	1501	1544	1602	...	...	1701	1703	1752	1802	...	1902	1905	...	...	1935	2002	2005	2103	2106	2203	2205	...	2234
Warminster d.	1340	1410	1423	...	1511	1552	1610	...	...	1710	1711	1802	1810	...	1910	1913	...	...	1945	2011	2013	2111	2114	2213	2214	...	2242
Salisbury d.	...	1433	1443	...	1533	1612	1633	...	...	1733	1733	...	1833	...	1933	1933	...	...	2006	2033	2035	2133	2137	2235	2237	...	2302
Romsey d.	...	1451	...	...	1551	...	1651	...	...	1751	1752	...	1851	...	1951	1952	...	...	...	2052	2053	2152	2155	2254	2255	...	2321
Southampton Central a.	...	1503	...	...	1603	...	1703	...	...	1803	1802	...	1903	...	2003	2002	...	...	...	2103	2104	2202	2206	2304	2306	...	2331
Fareham a.	...	1527	...	...	1627	...	1727	...	...	1827	1827	...	1927	...	2027	2027	...	...	...	2127	2126	2226	2241	2327	2330	...	2354
Portsmouth & Southsea a.	...	1547	...	...	1648	...	1747	...	...	1846	1849	...	1947	...	2046	2047	...	...	...	2146	2144	2245	2259	2345	2348	...	0015
Portsmouth Harbour a.	...	1552	...	...	1652	...	1752	...	...	1851	1854	...	1952	...	2051	2052	...	...	...	2151	2149	2250	2304	2350	2353	...	...

	⑥	ⒶE	⚒K	ⒶA	⑥A	⑦	⑦	⑦T	⑦	⑦	⑦	⑦	⑦	⑦	⑦	⑦	⑦	⑦	⑦	⑦R	⑦	⑦	⑦	⑦	⑦	⑦	⑦
Cardiff Central **118** d.	...	2130	...	...	...		...	...	0918	...	1025	1125	1225	...	1325	1425	...	1525	1625	...	1725	1740	1825	1925	2030	2130	2230
Bristol Temple Meads **139** d.	2215	2225	...	2304	2312		0920	...	1020	1034	1115	1215	1315	1334	1415	1515	1541	1620	1715	...	1815	1840	1915	2015	2128	2235	2330
Bath Spa **139** d.	2233	2241	...	2322	2330		0933	...	1035	1151	1135	1233	1333	1352	1433	1533	1600	1638	1735	...	1830	1858	1928	2033	2146	2254	2343
Bradford on Avon **139** d.	2249	2253	...	2338	2346		0945	...	1047	1107	1147	1249	1345	1404	1449	1545	1616	1650	1747	...	1842	1914	1940	2049	2158	2310	2355
Trowbridge **132a 139** d.	2255	2259	...	2344	2352		0953	...	1054	1113	1153	1255	1352	1410	1455	1552	1623	1656	1753	1818	1850	1920	1947	2055	2204	2316	0002
Westbury **132a 139** a.	2302	2306	...	2351	2359		0959	...	1101	1120	1200	1302	1359	1416	1502	1559	1630	1703	1800	1825	1857	1927	1954	2102	2211	2323	0009
Westbury d.	...	...	2314	...	...		1001	1043	1102	...	1202	1303	1402	1418	1504	1602	...	1705	1802	1826	1901	1929	2000	2103	2212	...	0010
Warminster d.	...	...	2322	...	...		1011	1051	1110	...	1211	1311	1411	1426	1512	1611	...	1714	1810	1834	1909	1937	2009	2111	2220	...	0019
Salisbury d.	...	...	2342	...	...		1033	1112	1133	...	1235	1334	1435	1447	1536	1634	...	1737	1833	1855	1932	2000	2032	2134	2243	...	...
Romsey d.	...	...	...	...	...		1052	...	1151	...	1254	1352	1454	1505	1554	1653	...	1755	1851	...	1950	2018	2051	2152	2301	...	...
Southampton Central a.	...	...	...	...	...		1102	...	1202	...	1304	1403	1504	1516	1605	1703	...	1806	1902	...	2001	2029	2101	2203	2312	...	...
Fareham a.	...	...	...	...	...		1126	...	1226	...	1326	1426	1527	1538	1627	1727	...	1828	1927	...	2026	2057	2126	2226	2334	...	...
Portsmouth & Southsea a.	...	...	...	...	...		1146	...	1246	...	1346	1446	1546	...	1647	1746	...	1848	1947	...	2044	2117	2144	2244	2352	...	...
Portsmouth Harbour a.	...	...	...	...	...		1151	...	1251	...	1351	1451	1551	...	1651	1751	...	1852	1952	...	2050	2123	2149	2249	2356	...	...

	⚒	Ⓐ	⑥A	ⒶA	ⒶE	ⒶJ	ⒶA	⑥A	Ⓐ	⑥	⑥A	ⒶA	Ⓐ	⑥	ⒶA	⑥A	ⒶG	⚒	⑥L	⚒	ⒶA	⑥A	ⒶQ	Ⓐ	⑥	ⒶQ	⑥
Portsmouth Harbour d.		...	...	...	...	...	...	...	0601	0608	...	...	0721	0723	...	...	...	0823	...	0923	...	...	...	1023	1023	...	1123
Portsmouth & Sou'sea d.		...	...	...	...	...	...	0539	0605	0612	...	...	0726	0727	...	...	...	0827	...	0927	...	...	...	1027	1027	...	1127
Fareham d.		...	...	0510	...	...	...	0600	0625	0632	...	...	0746	0747	...	...	...	0847	...	0947	...	...	...	1047	1047	...	1147
Southampton Central d.		...	...	0533	...	...	...	0626	0647	0657	...	...	0810	0810	0823	...	...	0910	...	1010	...	...	...	1110	1110	...	1210
Romsey d.		...	...	0545	...	...	...	0638	0659	0711	...	...	0821	0821	0835	...	...	0921	...	1021	...	...	...	1122	1121	...	1221
Salisbury d.		...	0605	0606	...	0635	...	0705f	0719	0730	...	...	0840	0842	0902f	...	0924	0942	1026	1040	1112	1113	1124	1142	1141	1222	1240
Warminster d.		...	0626	0627	...	0656	0730	0726	0740	0751	...	...	0901	0903	0925	...	0944	1002	1046	1101	1133	1134	1144	1203	1202	1243	1303
Westbury a.		...	0636	0638	...	0704	0739	0735	0751	0800	...	...	0912	0913	0935	...	0952	1011	1054	1111	1142	1142	1152	1211	1210	1251	1312
Westbury **132a 139** d.		0558	0638	0640	0659	0705	0741	0738	0800	0805	0840	0842	0913	0915	0940	0940	...	1012	...	1112	1143	1143	...	1212	1212	...	1313
Trowbridge **132a 139** d.		0604	0644	0646	0705	0711	0748	0744	0806	0812	0846	0848	0920	0921	0946	0946	...	1018	...	1118	1149	1150	...	1218	1218	...	1320
Bradford on Avon **139** d.		0610	0650	0652	0711	...	0754	0750	0812	0818	0852	0854	0926	0927	0952	0952	...	1024	...	1124	1155	1156	...	1224	1224	...	1326
Bath Spa **139** d.		0628	0708	0710	0730	...	0812	0808	0829	0834	0910	0912	0939	0941	1010	1010	...	1038	...	1138	1212	1213	...	1238	1240	...	1339
Bristol Temple M **139** a.		0647	0728	0728	0748	...	0831	0827	0847	0847	0928	0930	0952	0953	1028	1028	...	1050	...	1151	1230	1231	...	1251	1252	...	1352
Cardiff Central **118** a.		0750	...	...	0847	...	...	...	0946	0945	...	...	1052	1045	...	...	...	1146	...	1245	...	...	...	1349	1345	...	1445

	Ⓐ	⚒A	⚒	Ⓐ	⚒	⑥A	ⒶA	⑥	Ⓐ		⚒	⑥A	ⒶA	⑥	Ⓐ	⑥A	Ⓐ	⑥	Ⓐ	⑥	Ⓐ	⑥T	⑥	Ⓐ	⚒	Ⓐ	⑥
Portsmouth Harbour d.	1123	...	1223	...	1323	...	...	1423	1423	...	1523	...	...	1623	1623	...	...	1723	1723	...	...	...	1823	1824	...	1923	1923
Portsmouth & Sou'sea d.	1127	...	1227	...	1327	...	...	1427	1427	...	1527	...	...	1627	1627	...	...	1727	1727	...	...	...	1827	1829	...	1927	1927
Fareham d.	1147	...	1247	...	1347	...	...	1447	1447	...	1547	...	...	1647	1647	...	...	1747	1747	...	...	...	1847	1849	...	1947	1947
Southampton Central d.	1211	...	1310	...	1410	...	...	1510	1511	...	1609	...	...	1710	1711	...	...	1810	1810	...	...	...	1910	1911	...	2011	2010
Romsey d.	1222	...	1321	...	1421	...	...	1522	1522	...	1621	...	...	1721	1722	...	...	1821	1822	...	...	...	1921	1923	...	2023	2021
Salisbury d.	1242	...	1342	...	1440	...	...	1541	1543	...	1642	...	...	1742	1742	...	...	1841	1842	...	...	1927	1942	1942	2011c	2042	2041
Warminster d.	1303	1325c	1403	...	1501	...	1530	1602	1604	...	1703	1730	1730	1803	1803	...	1830	1902	1903	...	...	1946	2003	2003	2032c	2103	2102
Westbury a.	1311	1336c	1411	...	1511	...	1539	1610	1612	...	1711	1739	1739	1811	1811	...	1839	1911	1911	...	...	1954	2011	2011	2041c	2111	2110
Westbury **132a 139** d.	1312	1340	1412	1426	1512	1540	1542	1612	1612	...	1712	1741	1745	1812	1812	1840	1845	1912	1912	1942	1945	...	2012	2012	2042	2112	2112
Trowbridge **132a 139** d.	1318	1346	1418	1432	1518	1546	1548	1618	1619	...	1718	1747	1751	1818	1818	1846	1851	1919	1918	1948	1951	...	2018	2019	2048	2119	2118
Bradford on Avon **139** d.	1324	1352	1424	1439	1524	1552	1554	1624	1625	...	1724	1753	1757	1824	1824	1852	1857	1925	1924	1954	1957	...	2024	2025	2054	2125	2124
Bath Spa **139** d.	1338	1410	1438	1502	1538	1610	1612	1638	1638	...	1738	1811	1818	1838	1838	1910	1917	1939	1938	2012	2018	...	2040	2038	2112	2138	2138
Bristol Temple Meads **139** a.	1350	1428	1451	1520	1551	1628	1630	1650	1651	...	1752	1829	1836	1851	1850	1928	1935	1951	1952	2032	2036	...	2052	2050	2132	2151	2151
Cardiff Central **118** a.	1448	...	1550a	...	1645	...	...	1746	1750	...	1846	...	...	1947	1949	...	...	2045	2046	...	...	...	2145	2147	...	2258h	2257

	⑥	Ⓐ	Ⓐ	⑥	Ⓐ	⑥	⑦	⑦R	⑦	⑦H	⑦	⑦E	⑦	⑦	⑦	⑦	⑦	⑦	⑦	⑦	⑦	⑦	⑦	⑦	⑦	⑦	⑦
Portsmouth Harbour d.	2023	2023	...	...	2123	2123		...	...	...	0908	...	...	1108	1208	1308	1408	...	1508	1608	1708	1808	...	1908	2008	2108	2204
Portsmouth & Sou'sea d.	2027	2027	...	...	2127	2127		...	...	...	0913	...	1013	1113	1213	1313	1413	...	1513	1613	1713	1813	...	1913	2013	2113	2212
Fareham d.	2047	2045	...	...	2147	2146		...	...	...	0933	...	1033	1133	1233	1333	1433	...	1533	1633	1733	1833	...	1933	2033	2133	2232
Southampton Central d.	2112	2111	...	...	2222	2224		...	...	...	0957	...	1057	1157	1257	1357	1457	...	1557	1657	1757	1857	...	1957	2058	2157	2257
Romsey d.	2123	2122	...	...	2235	2236		...	...	...	1008	...	1108	1208	1308	1408	1508	...	1608	1708	1808	1908	...	2008	2111	2208	2308
Salisbury d.	2142	2142	...	...	2300t	2258		...	...	...	1027	...	1127	1227	1327	1427	1527	...	1627	1727	1828	1927	1959	2027	2130	2228	2327
Warminster d.	2203	2203	2228	...	2321	2319		0811	...	...	1048	...	1148	1248	1348	1448	1548	...	1648	1749	1849	1949	2020	2048	2151	2249	2348
Westbury a.	2213	2211	2238	...	2330	2331		0819	...	...	1058	...	1157	1258	1356	1458	1558	...	1658	1757	1857	2000	2029	2057	2201	2257	2358
Westbury **132a 139** d.	2214	2212	2242	2241	2336	...		0820	0845	0941	1102	1136	1202	1302	1401	1502	1602	1640	1702	1805	1902	2002	2030	2102	2202	2258	...
Trowbridge **132a 139** d.	2220	2218	2248	2247	2342	...		0827	0851	0947	1108	1142	1208	1308	1407	1508	1608	1646	1708	1811	1908	2008	2037	2108	2208	2304	...
Bradford on Avon **139** d.	2226	2224	2254	2253	2348	...		...	0857	0953	1114	1148	1214	1314	1413	1514	1614	1652	1714	1817	1914	2014	2043	2114	2214	2310	...
Bath Spa **139** d.	2240	2238	2312	2311	0002	...		...	0916	1011	1128	1207	1228	1328	1430	1528	1627	1710	1728	1832	1928	2028	2100	2128	2228	2323	...
Bristol Temple Meads **139** a.	2252	2251	2331	2330	0015	...		...	0934	1031	1147	1225	1246	1346	1448	1546	1640	1728	1746	1845	1940	2040	2118	2140	2240	2339	...
Cardiff Central **118** a.	2357	2358r	...	...	...	...		...	1024	1124	1241	...	1340	1440	1545	1641	1744	...	1841	1944	2030	2131	...	2233	2333	...	...

A – From/to Gloucester, Cheltenham Spa, Worcester or Great Malvern (see Table **138**).
C – From Gloucester (Tables **130** and **134**).
E – From/to Frome (Table **139**).
F – Castle Cary - London Waterloo (Tables **108** and **139**).
G – Yeovil Pen Mill - London Waterloo and v.v. (Tables **108** and **139**).
H – From Apr. 2 from Weymouth; until Mar. 26 from Frome (Table **139**).
J – To Cheltenham Spa (Tables **130** and **134**).
K – From Yeovil Junction on Ⓐ (Table **139**).
L – London Waterloo - Frome and v.v. (Tables **108** and **139**).
P – To London Paddington (Table **110**).
Q – Basingstoke - Yeovil Junction (Tables **108** and **139**).
R – To/from Swindon (Table **134**).
T – Yeovil Junction - London Waterloo and v.v. (Tables **108** and **139**).

a – Arrives 1545 on ⑥.
c – Ⓐ only.
d – Runs 4 minutes later on Ⓐ.
f – Arrives 9–11 minutes earlier.
g – Departs 0803.
h – Arrives 2246 on ⑤.
r – Arrives 2346 on ⑤.
t – Arrives 5–7 minutes earlier.

LM LONDON - NORTHAMPTON - BIRMINGHAM 141

Only selected services are shown. See Table **150** for faster services London - Watford / Milton Keynes / Rugby - Coventry - Birmingham and v.v.

km			Ⓐ	Ⓐ	Ⓐ	Ⓐ	Ⓐ	Ⓐ	Ⓐ	Ⓐ	Ⓐ	Ⓐ	Ⓐ	Ⓐ		Ⓐ	Ⓐ	Ⓐ	Ⓐ	Ⓐ	Ⓐ	Ⓐ	Ⓐ	Ⓐ	Ⓐ
0	**London** Euston 143 d.	Ⓐ	...	...	0535	0621	...	0723	0756	0823	0856	0923	0956	1023		1556	1626	1656	1726	1756	1826	1856	1923	1956	2023
28	Watford Junction d.		...	...	0555	0636	...	0738	|	0838	|	0938	|	1038	and	|	|	|	|	|	|	|	1938	|	2038
64	Leighton Buzzard d.		...	...	0626	0654	...	0755	0825	0855	0925	0955	1025	1055	at	1625	1655	1725	1755	1824	1854	1924	1955	2025	2054
75	Bletchley d.		...	...	0633	0701	...	0802	0832	0902	0932	1002	1032	1102	the	1632	1702	1732	1802	1831	1901	1931	2002	2032	2101
80	Milton Keynes 143 d.		...	...	0638	0707	0738	0808	0838	0908	0938	1008	1038	1108	same	1638	1710	1738	1808	1839	1907	1337	2008	2038	2107
106	**Northampton** 143 a.		...	...	0655	0724	0754	0825	0855	0925	0955	1025	1055	1125	minutes	1655	1727	1755	1825	1855	1924	1954	2025	0254	2123
106	**Northampton** 143 d.		0542	0642	0711	0737	0810	0840	0910	0940	1010	1040	1110	1140	past	1706	1741	1806	1840	1906	1940	2010	2040	2107	2132
136	Rugby 143 d.		0605	0705	0734	0801	0835	0904	0934	1004	1034	1104	1134	1204	each	1734r	1804	1834	1904	1934r	2004	2034	2104	2134	2159
154	Coventry 114 d.		0615	0715	0745	0812	0846	0915	0945	1015	1045	1115	1145	1215	hour	1745	1815	1845	1915	1945	2015	2045	2115	2145	2215
171	**Birmingham** Int ✈ 114 d.		0634	0734	0803	0830	0905	0934	1004	1034	1104	1134	1204	1234	until	1804	1834	1904	1934	2004	2034	2104	2134	2204	2234
185	**Birmingham** New St 114 a.		0646	0744	0814	0844	0914	0945	1014	1044	1114	1145	1214	1244		1814	1844	1914	1945	2013	2045	2114	2145	2214	2243

	Ⓐ	Ⓐ	Ⓐ	Ⓐ	Ⓐ	Ⓐ	Ⓐ		⑥	⑥	⑥	⑥	⑥	⑥	⑥		⑥	⑥	⑥	⑥	⑥	⑥	⑥	⑥	⑥
London Euston 143 d.	2056	2123	2150	2209	2239	2309	2342	⑥	...	...	0539	0621	...	0723	0756		1556	1626	1656	1726	1756	1826	1856	1920	1946
Watford Junction d.	|	2139	2205	2229	2300	2329	0007		...	...	0558	0636	...	0738	|	and	|	|	|	|	|	|	|	1935	|
Leighton Buzzard d.	2125	2156	2222	2301	2334	0003	0035		...	...	0629	0652	...	0755	0825	at	1625	1655	1725	1755	1825	1855	1925	1952	2018
Bletchley d.	2132	2203	2229	2308	2341	0010	0042		...	...	0636	0659	...	0802	0832	the	1632	1702	1732	1802	1832	1902	1932	1959	2025
Milton Keynes 143 d.	2138	2208	2235	2317	2348	0019	0050		...	...	0641	0705	0738	0808	0838	same	1638	1708	1738	1808	1838	1908	1938	2008	2031
Northampton 143 a.	2154	2225	2255	2334	0007	0036	0108		...	...	0658	0722	0755	0825	0855	minutes	1655	1725	1755	1825	1855	1925	1955	2025	2049
Northampton 143 d.	2216	...	2312	...	...	...	...		0542	0642	0710	0740	0810	0840	0910	past	1710	1740	1810	1840	1910	1940	2010	2040	2103
Rugby 143 d.	2241	...	2334	...	...	...	...		0604	0704	0734	0804	0834	0904	0934	each	1734	1804	1834	1904	1934	2004	2034	2104	2125
Coventry 114 d.	2254	...	2345	...	...	...	...		0615	0715	0745	0815	0845	0915	0945	hour	1745	1815	1845	1915	1945	2015	2045	2115	2135
Birmingham Int ✈ 114 d.	2313	...	0004	...	...	...	...		0634	0734	0804	0834	0904	0934	1004	until	1804	1834	1904	1934	2004	2034	2104	2134	2154
Birmingham New St 114 a.	2324	...	0023	...	...	...	...		0645	0744	0815	0846	0914	0945	1014		1814	1844	1914	1944	2014	2044	2114	2147	2202

	⑥	⑥	⑥	⑥	⑥	⑥	⑥	⑥	⑥		⑦	⑦	⑦	⑦B	⑦	⑦B	⑦	⑦	⑦B	⑦	⑦	⑦B	⑦	⑦	⑦	⑦
London Euston 143 d.	2003	2021	2039	2109	2127	2149	2210	2237	2330	⑦	0655	...	0724	0751	0824	0856	...	0925	0956	...	1024	1052	...	1124	1222	1256
Watford Junction d.	2020	2037	2054	2128	2143	2208	2229	2257	2350		0715	...	0744	0807	0844	0911	...	0945	1012	...	1044	1114	...	1144	1237	|
Leighton Buzzard d.	|	|	2128	2158	2211	2242	2259	2331	0024		0749	...	0814	0837	0914	0941	...	1015	1042	...	1114	1144	...	1214	1253	1324
Bletchley d.	2047	|	2135	2205	2218	2253	2310	2338	0031		0756	...	0820	0843	0920	0948	...	1021	1049	...	1120	1151	...	1220	1300	1331
Milton Keynes 143 d.	2052	2108	2140	2213	2227	2257	2314	2347	0040		0804	...	0829	0852	0929	0956	...	1030	1057	...	1129	1159	...	1226	1306	1338
Northampton 143 a.	2110	2125	2156	2230	2243	2314	2332	0005	0058		0823	...	0847	0910	0947	1015	...	1047	1115	...	1146	1217	...	1244	1324	1354
Northampton 143 d.	...	2140	2205	2231	2254	...	...	...	...		...	...	0906	0927	0959	1028	1037	1100	1129	1140	1159	1221	1240	1309	1340	1409
Rugby 143 d.	...	2204	2228	2253	2316	...	...	...	...		...	0857	0928	0949	1022	1050	1114	1123	1151	1203	1222	1242	1303	1331	1404	1432
Coventry 114 d.	...	2215	2240	2303	2327	...	...	...	...		...	0908	0938	...	1033	...	1115	1134	...	1215	1233	...	1315	1343	1415	1443
Birmingham Int ✈ 114 d.	...	2234	2258	2313	2345	...	...	...	...		...	0921	0957	...	1052	...	1133	1153	...	1234	1252	...	1334	1402	1434	1502
Birmingham New St 114 a.	...	2243	2311	2322	0003	...	...	...	...		...	0939	1008	...	1103	...	1144	1204	...	1244	1303	...	1344	1413	1445	1514

		⑦	⑦	⑦	⑦	⑦	⑦	⑦	⑦	⑦	⑦	⑦
London Euston 143 d.		1856	1922	1956	2020	...	2107	2131	2203	2242	2300	2340
Watford Junction d.	and	|	1937	|	2035	...	2123	2146	2222	2303	2320	0001
Leighton Buzzard d.	at	1924	1953	2024	2052	...	2153	2217	2251	2333	2353	0034
Bletchley d.	the	1931	2000	2031	2100	...	2200	2224	2258	2340	2359	0041
Milton Keynes 143 d.	same	1938	2006	2038	2106	...	2208	2233	2307	2349	0008	0050
Northampton 143 a.	minutes	1954	2024	2054	2123	...	2226	2248	2325	0005	0026	0107
Northampton 143 d.	past	2009	2040	2059	2130	2159	2239	2312	2333	...	...	...
Rugby 143 d.	each	2032	2103	2121	2153	2221	2301	2334	2355	...	...	...
Coventry 114 d.	hour	2043	2114	2135	2204	2235	2312	2346	0005	...	...	...
Birmingham Int ✈ 114 d.	until	2102	2133	2153	2222	2253	2321	0004	...	...	...	...
Birmingham New St 114 a.		2114	2142	2205	2234	2305	2340	0016	...	...	...	...

		Ⓐ	Ⓐ	Ⓐ	Ⓐ	Ⓐ	Ⓐ	Ⓐ
Birmingham N St 114 d.	Ⓐ	...	...	...	0535	...	0613	0634
Birmingham Int ✈ 114 d.		...	...	...	0545	...	0625	0644
Coventry 114 d.		...	...	0539	0604	...	0644	0704
Rugby 143 d.		...	...	0552	0615	...	0656	0715
Northampton 143 a.		...	...	0613	0637	...	0721	0737
Northampton 143 d.		0414	0503	0617	0639	0650	0730	0749
Milton Keynes 143 d.		0432	0520	0632	0656	0707	0745	0806
Bletchley d.		0437	0524	|	0701	0712	|	0811
Leighton Buzzard d.		0444	0531	|	0708	0719	|	0818
Watford Junction d.		0514	0601	0654	|	|	|	|
London Euston 143 a.		0538	0622	0710	0738	0751	0820	0848

	Ⓐ	Ⓐ	Ⓐ	Ⓐ	Ⓐ	Ⓐ		Ⓐ	Ⓐ	Ⓐ	Ⓐ		Ⓐ	Ⓐ	Ⓐ	Ⓐ	Ⓐ	Ⓐ		⑥	⑥	⑥	⑥	⑥	⑥
Birmingham New St 114 d.	0706	0736	0806	0836	0906	0936		1906	1936	2006	2036	...	...	2114	2136	2206	2250	2311	⑥	...	...	...	0535	0613	0636
Birmingham Int ✈ 114 d.	0716	0746	0816	0846	0916	0946	and	1916	1946	2016	2046	...	...	2125	2146	2216	2308	2322		...	...	...	0546	0624	0646
Coventry 114 d.	0735	0804	0835	0905	0935	1005	at	1935	2005	2035	2105	...	...	2144	2205	2235	2327	2334		...	...	...	0605	0643	0705
Rugby 143 d.	0745	0815	0845	0916	0946	1016	the	1946	2016	2046	2117	...	...	2154	2216	2246	2338	2345		...	...	...	0616	0654	0716
Northampton 143 a.	0808	0839	0907	0938	1007	1038	same	2008	2038	2107	2138	...	...	2217	2237	2310	0001	0008s		...	...	...	0638	0716	0739
Northampton 143 d.	0818	0848	0918	0948	1018	1048	minutes	2016	2048	2116	2141	...	2214	...	2251	2328	...	|		0405	0448	0535	0641	0718	0748
Milton Keynes 143 d.	0835	0904	0935	1005	1035	1105	past	2034	2105	2132	2158	...	2231	...	2308	2345	...	0027		0423	0504	0551	0658	0735	0805
Bletchley d.	0840	0909	0940	1010	1040	1110	each	2039	2110	|	2203	...	2237	...	2313	2350	...	|		0429	0509	0556	0703	0740	0810
Leighton Buzzard d.	0847	0916	0947	1017	1047	1117	hour	2046	2117	|	2210	...	2244	...	2320	2357	...	|		0436	0519	0603	0710	0747	0817
Watford Junction d.	|	0933	|	1033	|	1133	until	|	2133	|	2232	...	2313	...	2351	0027	...	0056s		0511	0552	0629	|	|	0833
London Euston 143 a.	0917	0948	1017	1050	1117	1150		2116	2149	*2224*	2252	...	2337	...	0012	0048	...	0117		0534	0616	0649	0741	0817	0849

	⑥	⑥		⑥	⑥	⑥	⑥	⑥		⑥	⑥	⑥	⑥	⑥	⑥	⑥		⑦	⑦	⑦	⑦	⑦	⑦	⑦	⑦
Birmingham New St 114 d.	0706	0736		1736	1806	1836	1906	1936	...	2006	2036	2106	...	2136	2206	2250	⑦	...	...	...	...	...	0832	0907	0934
Birmingham Int ✈ 114 d.	0716	0746	and	1746	1816	1746	1916	1946	...	2016	2046	2116	...	2146	2217	2302		...	...	...	...	...	0849	0925	0951
Coventry 114 d.	0735	0805	at	1805	1835	1905	1935	2005	...	2035	2105	2135	...	2205	2237	2321		...	...	...	...	...	0909	0944	1010
Rugby 143 d.	0746	0816	the	1816	1846	1916	1946	2016	...	1046	2116	2146	...	2216	2248	2331		...	...	...	...	...	0919	0955	1020
Northampton 143 a.	0809	0839	same	1838	1909	1938	2008	2039	...	2108	2138	2208	...	2238	2309	2354		...	...	...	...	...	0942	1018	1041
Northampton 143 d.	0918	0848	minutes	1849	1918	1946	2018	2050	...	2118	2148	2209	2231	2248	2323	...		*0615*t	0750	0824	0850	0925	...	1031	1042
Milton Keynes 143 d.	0835	0904	past	1905	1935	2003	2036	2106	...	2136	2208	2225	2248	2307	2340	...		0710	0806	0841	0906	0942	...	1049	1059
Bletchley d.	0840	0909	each	1910	1940	2008	2040	2111	...	2141	|	2230	2253	2312	2345	...		0715	0811	0846	0911	0947	...	1054	1103
Leighton Buzzard d.	0847	0916	hour	1917	1947	2015	2047	|	...	2148	2217	2237	2300	2319	2352	...		0722	0818	0853	0918	0954	...	1101	1110
Watford Junction d.	|	0933	until	1934	|	2035	2111	2143	...	2218	2244	2312	2330	2353	0015	...		0751	0848	0924	0948	1023	...	1125	1139
London Euston 143 a.	0918	0950		1949	2032	2054	2130	2203	...	2240	2304	2333	2356	0015	0033	...		0814	0910	0950	1010	1044	...	1146	1203

	⑦	⑦B	⑦	⑦	⑦		⑦	⑦	⑦	⑦	⑦	⑦	⑦		⑦	⑦	⑦	⑦B	⑦	⑦	⑦B	⑦	⑦	⑦	⑦
Birmingham New St 114 d.	1006	...	1034	1106	1134		1506	1532	1606	1633	1706	1733	1806	...	1833	1906	1933	...	2006	2034	...	2106	2136	2210	2256
Birmingham Int ✈ 114 d.	1023	...	1046	1116	1146	and	1516	1544	1616	1645	1715	1745	1816	...	1845	1915	1944	...	2016	2046	...	2125	2148	2228	2308
Coventry 114 d.	1037	...	1108	1136	1204	at	1535	1603	1635	1704	1734	1804	1835	...	1904	1934	2003	...	2035	2105	...	2138	2208	2247	2320
Rugby 143 d.	1047	1116	1121	1147	1216	the	1546	1614	1646	1715	1745	1816	1846	...	1916	1945	2015	2027	2046	2116	2129	2148	2220	2257	2332
Northampton 143 a.	1107	1138	1145	1209	1237	same	1607	1635	1707	1736	1807	1839	1907	...	1937	2008	2037	2047	2108	2137	2152	2211	2241	2318	2352s
Northampton 143 d.	1116	1142	1147	1215	1248	minutes	1615	1646	1715	1747	1815	1848	1915	...	1948	2016	...	2048	2126	...	2154	2218	...	2327	|
Milton Keynes 143 d.	1130	1157	1204	1232	1305	past	1632	1703	1732	1804	1832	1905	1932	...	2005	2033	...	2103	2142	...	2211	2235	...	2343	0012s
Bletchley d.	1135	1202	1209	1237	1310	each	1637	1708	1737	1809	1837	1910	1937	...	2010	2038	...	|	2147	...	2216	2240	...	2348	|
Leighton Buzzard d.	1142	1209	1216	1244	1317	hour	1644	1715	1744	1816	1844	1917	1944	...	2017	2045	...	|	2154	...	2223	2247	...	2355	|
Watford Junction d.	1210	1227	1235	|	1334	until	|	1733	|	1834	|	1934	|	...	2034	|	...	|	2225	...	2254	2318	...	0027	0042s
London Euston 143 a.	1228	1242	1251	1315	1350		1715	1749	1815	1849	1915	1950	2015	...	2050	2124	...	2153	2246	...	2316	2339	...	0047	0100

B – To / from Crewe via Nuneaton (Table **143**).
r – Arrives 6 minutes earlier.
s – Stops to set down only.
t – Connection by 🚌.

LM 2nd class only NUNEATON - COVENTRY - LEAMINGTON SPA 142

km		⚒	⚒	⚒	⚒		♣		⑥	Ⓑ	Ⓐ
0	**Nuneaton** d.	0637	0737	0837	0937	1037	and	2137	2224	2237	2327
16	Coventry 114 d.	0700	0800	0900	1000	1100	hourly	2200	2246	2301	2349
24	Kenilworth d.	0708	0808	0908	1008	1108	until	2208	2253	2309	2356
32	**Leamington Spa** 114 a.	0715	0815	0915	1015	1116		2215	2300	2316	0003

	⑥	Ⓐ	⚒	⚒	⚒	⚒					Ⓐ
Leamington Spa 114 d.	0540	0542	0640	0740	0840	0940	1040	and	2040	2138	2240
Kenilworth d.	0547	0549	0647	0747	0846	0946	1047	hourly	2047	2145	2247
Coventry 114 d.	0556	0557	0656	0756	0856	0956	1056	until	2056	2156	2300
Nuneaton a.	0618	0619	0718	0818	0918	1018	1118		2118	2218	2322

♣ – On Ⓐ Nuneaton d. 1335 (not 1337), Coventry d. 1356 (not 1400).

142a BEDFORD - BLETCHLEY LM

All services Bedford - Bletchley and v.v. are by 🚌 until further notice (connecting services Bletchley - Milton Keynes and v.v. are by train).

km		Ⓐ	⑥		⑥	Ⓐ	⑥	Ⓐ	Ⓐ		⑥	Ⓐ	⑥		⚒	⚒	⑥	Ⓐ		⚒	⚒	⚒	Ⓐ
0	**Bedford** d.	0603	0604	...	0704	0714	0747	0819	0848	...	0848	0955	1004	...	1104	1155	1255	1258	...	1355	1455	1555	1648
20	Woburn Sands d.	0650	0651	...	0751	0801	0834	0906	0935	...	0935	1042	1051	...	1151	1242	1342	1345	...	1442	1542	1642	1735
27	**Bletchley** ‡ a.	0705	0706	...	0806	0816	0849	0921	0950	...	0950	1057	1106	...	1207	1257	1357	1400	...	1457	1557	1657	1750
	Milton Keynes **142** ‡ a.	*0716*	*0742*	...	*0837*	*0837*	*0908*	*0937*	*1007*	...	*1008*	*1107*	*1137*	...	*1237*	*1308*	*1408*	*1415*	...	*1508*	*1608*	*1707*	*1807*

	⑥	Ⓐ	⑥	⚒		⑥	Ⓐ	Ⓐ	⑥	⑥	Ⓐ
Bedford d.	1655	1755	1755	1855	...	1956	1955	2112	2112	2219	2228
Woburn Sands d.	1742	1842	1842	1942	...	2043	2042	2159	2159	2306	2315
Bletchley ‡ a.	1757	1857	1857	1957	...	2058	2057	2214	2214	2321	2330
Milton Keynes **142** ‡ a.	*1807*	*1919*	*1907*	*2007*	...	*2140*	*2117*	*2227*	*2257*	*2346*	*2347*

	⑥	Ⓐ	⑥	Ⓐ	⑥	Ⓐ
Milton Keynes **142** ‡ d.	*0504*	*0432*	*0551*	*0550*	*0630*	*0707*
Bletchley ‡ d.	0516	0517	0616	0624	0700	0732
Woburn Sands d.	0533	0536	0633	0641	0717	0749
Bedford a.	0620	0642	0720	0728	0804	0836

	⑥	Ⓐ	Ⓐ	Ⓐ	Ⓐ		⑥	⚒	⚒		⚒	⚒	⚒	⚒		⚒	Ⓐ	⑥		⚒	⑥	Ⓐ	⚒
Milton Keynes **142** d.	*0735*	*0735*	*0835*	*0905*	*1005*	...	*1005*	*1035*	*1135*	...	*1235*	*1335*	*1435*	*1535*	...	*1635*	*1727*	*1735*	...	*1835*	*2003*	*2005*	*2105*
Bletchley d.	0800	0801	0906	0917	1018	...	1017	1101	1201	...	1301	1401	1501	1601	...	1701	1738	1806	...	1901	2025	2025	2132
Woburn Sands ‡ d.	0817	0818	0923	0934	1035	...	1034	1118	1218	...	1318	1418	1518	1618	...	1718	1755	1823	...	1918	2042	2042	2149
Bedford ‡ a.	0904	0905	1010	1021	1122	...	1021	1205	1305	...	1405	1505	1605	1705	...	1805	1842	1910	...	2005	2129	2129	2236

143 LONDON - CREWE via Trent Valley LM

See Tables **151** and **154** for other fast services London - Milton Keynes - Stafford - Crewe.

km			Ⓐ	⑥	Ⓐ	⑥	⑥‡	Ⓐ	⑥	⚒		⚒	⑥	Ⓐ	⚒	⚒‡	⚒	⚒‡	⑥	Ⓐ	⑥	Ⓐ	Ⓐ‡	⑥‡	Ⓐ‡	⑥
0	**London** Euston **141 150/2** d.	⚒	...	...	...	...	0633	0643	0643	0746		1446	1546	1546	1646	1702	1746	1802	1846	1846	1940	1946	2016	2031	2033	2035
28	Watford Junction **141 150** d.		...	...	...	...	|	|	|	|	and	|	|	|	|	|	|	|	|	|	|	|	2031u	2046u	|	2050
78	Milton Keynes **141 150/2** d.		...	...	...	...	0700	0716	0706	0819	at the	1519	1619	1619	1719	|	1819	|	1919	1919	2024	2019	2052	|	|	2122
104	Northampton **141** d.		0520	0515	0601	0602	|	|	|	|	same	|	|	|	|	|	|	|	|	|	|	|	|	|	|	|
135	Rugby **141 150/2** d.		0543	0543f	0624	0625	|	0739	0739	0842	minutes	1542	1642	1642	1742	|	1842	|	1942	1942	2048	2042	|	|	|	2146
158	Nuneaton **152** d.		0555	0555	0637	0637	|	0754	0754	0857	past	1557	1657	1657	1757	|	1857	|	1957	1957	2100	2057	2125	|	|	2157
178	Tamworth (Low Level) d.		0610	0610	0653	0653	0744	0808	0808	0911	each	1611	1711	1713	1813	1809	1913	1909	2011	2013	2114	2111	|	2155	2139	2211
188	Lichfield Trent Valley d.		0616	0616	0659	0659	0750	0814	0814	0918	hour	1618	1718	1720	1820	1816	1920	1916	2018	2020	2120	2118	|	2202	2146	2217
217	Stafford **152** d.		0633	0633	0717	0720	0806	0832	0835	0935	until	1635	1735	1737	1837	1832	1937	1932	2035	2037	2139	2135	2150	|	2200	2241
268	**Crewe** **152** a.		0654	0654	0740	0739	0824	0851	0854	0954		1654	1754	1757	1858	1850	1957	1950	2054	2057	2159	2154	2208	2229	2217	2302

	Ⓐ	Ⓐ‡	Ⓐ	Ⓐ‡	Ⓐ‡		⑦	⑦‡	⑦	⑦‡	⑦	⑦	⑦		⑦	⑦‡
London Euston **141 150/2** d.	2046	2110	2146	2200	2203	⑦	0751	0820	0856	0919	0956	1052	1245		1945	2039
Watford Junction **141 150** d.	|	2125u	|	|	|		0807	0836u	0911	0936u	1012	1114	|	and	|	|
Milton Keynes **141 150/2** d.	2119	|	2219	2240	2245u		0852	0908	0956	1008	1057	1159	1319	at the	2019	2124
Northampton **141** d.	|	|	|	|	|		0927t	|	1028t	|	1129t	1221	|	same	|	|
Rugby **141 150/2** d.	2142	2204	2242	|	2310		0951	|	1051	|	1152	1244	1342	minutes	2042	|
Nuneaton **152** d.	2157	2215	2254	|	2322		1005	|	1104	|	1205	1256	1357	past	2057	|
Tamworth (Low Level) d.	2211	|	2308	2320s	...		1019	1001	1118	1101	1219	1310	1411	each	2111	2203
Lichfield Trent Valley d.	2218	|	2314	2327s	...		1025	1008	1124	1108	1225	1317	1418	hour	2118	2210
Stafford **152** d.	2235	2240	2338f	2341s	...		1046	1024	1146	1124	1244	1333	1435	until	2135	2225
Crewe **152** a.	2258	2259	0007	0011	...		1105	1042	1205	1142	1303	1352	1457		2154	2243

		Ⓐ	⑥	Ⓐ	⚒‡
Crewe **152** d.	⚒	0510	0525	0545	...
Stafford **152** d.		0533	0544	0609	...
Lichfield Trent Valley d.		0549	0602	0620	0642
Tamworth (Low Level) d.		0556	0608	0628	0649
Nuneaton **152** d.		0612	0624	0650	|
Rugby **141 150/2** d.		0625	0640	0706	|
Northampton **141** a.		|	|	|	|
Milton Keynes **141 150/2** a.		0648	0702	0730	0725
Watford Junction **141 150** a.		|	|	|	|
London Euston **141 150/2** a.		0724	0738	0806	0800

	Ⓐ‡	⑥‡	⑥	Ⓐ	⚒		⚒	Ⓐ	⑥	⑥	Ⓐ	Ⓐ	⑥	⑥‡	Ⓐ	Ⓐ
Crewe **152** d.	...	...	0713	0713	0813		1713	1813	1813	1913	1913	2013	2013	...	2113	2213
Stafford **152** d.	0654	0655	0732	0732	0832	and	1732	1832	1832	1932	1932	2032	2032	...	2132	2232
Lichfield Trent Valley d.	0710	0710	0749	0751	0849	at the	1749	1849	1849	1949	1949	2049	2049	2117	2149	2249
Tamworth (Low Level) d.	0718	0717	0756	0757	0856	same	1756	1856	1856	1956	1956	2056	2056	2123	2156	2256
Nuneaton **152** d.	|	|	0811	0812	0911	minutes	1811	1911	1911	2011	2011	2111	2111	|	2211	2311
Rugby **141 150/2** d.	0737	0736	0826	0827	0926	past	1826	1926	1926	2026	2028	2126	2126	|	2226	2328
Northampton **141** a.	|	|	|	|	|	each	|	|	|	2048	|	|	|	|	2249	...
Milton Keynes **141 150/2** a.	|	|	0848	0849	0948	hour	1848	1948	1948	...	2052	2148	2150	2201	...	...
Watford Junction **141 150** a.	|	|	|	|	|	until	|	|	2019	...	|	|	2224	2236s	...	...
London Euston **141 150/2** a.	0827	0831	0924	0925	1024		1924	2024	2039	...	2128	2224	2244	2258	...	...

		⑦	⑦		⑦	⑦	⑦	⑦	⑦‡
Crewe **152** d.	⑦	0952	1113		1813	1913	2013	2113	2123
Stafford **152** d.		1017f	1132	and	1832	1932	2034	2131	2142
Lichfield Trent Valley d.		1036	1149	at the	1849	1949	2051	2148	2200
Tamworth (Low Level) d.		1043	1156	same	1856	1956	2058	2155	2207
Nuneaton **152** d.		1058	1211	minutes	1911	2011	2114	2210	2219
Rugby **141 150/2** d.		1116	1227	past	1927	2027	2129	2225	2232
Northampton **141** a.		1138	|	each	|	2047	2152	2347	|
Milton Keynes **141 150/2** a.		1156	1248	hour	1948	2102	2210	...	2305
Watford Junction **141 150** a.		1227	|	until	|	|	2253	...	2336s
London Euston **141 150/2** a.		1242	1325		2025	2153	2316	...	2353

f – Arrives 5–7 minutes earlier.
t – Arrives 13–17 minutes earlier.
s – Calls to set down only.
u – Calls to pick up only.
‡ – Fast service operated by VT (see Tables **152**–**154** for further details).

144 BIRMINGHAM - CREWE - LIVERPOOL LM

km			⑥	Ⓐ	Ⓐ	⚒		⚒	⑥	Ⓐ	⑥	Ⓐ	⑥	Ⓐ	Ⓐ		⑦	⑦	⑦	⑦	⑦		⑦	⑦
0	**Birmingham** New Street **119** ▷ d.	⚒	...	...	0533	0634		1934	2034	2034	2134	2134	2233	2234	2322	⑦	...	0932	1034	1134	1234		2134	2152
19	Wolverhampton **119** ▷ d.		...	...	0553	0653	and at	1953	2053	2053	2153	2153	2252	2253	2342		...	0951	1053	1153	1253	and at	2153	2210
43	Stafford **119 143 153** d.		...	...	0611	0711	the same	2011	2111	2111	2211	2211	2310	2314	2359		...	1009	1109	1209	1311	the same	2211	2227
82	**Crewe** **143 153** d.		0532	0534	0632	0732	minutes	2032	2132	2132	2231	2232	2329	2343	0024		0920	1030	1130	1230	1332	minutes	2232	2306
118	Runcorn **153** d.		0600	0602	0658	0758	past each	2058	2153	2158	...	2258	...	...	...		0946	1056	1156	1256	1359	past each	2258	...
131	**Liverpool** South Parkway ‡ a.		0610	0611	0706	0807	hour until	2106	2202	2206	...	2307	...	...	...		0955	1105	1205	1305	1407	hour until	2308	...
140	**Liverpool** Lime Street **153** a.		0624	0622	0718	0818		2118	2212	2217	...	2317	...	...	...		1005	1115	1215	1315	1418		2320	...

		⚒		⑥	Ⓐ		⚒	⚒		⚒	⚒		Ⓐ	Ⓐ		⑦		⑦	⑦		⑦		⑦	⑦
Liverpool Lime Street **153** d.	⚒	...	...	0607	0610	...	0633	0733		2033	2132	...	2233	2333	⑦	...	...	...	1033		2133	...	2233	2340
Liverpool South Parkway ‡ d.		...	...	0617	0620	...	0643	0743	and at	2043	2142	...	2243	2343		...	...	...	1043	and at	2143	...	2243	2350
Runcorn **153** d.		...	...	0625	0628	...	0651	0751	the same	2051	2350	...	2251	2351		...	...	...	1051	the same	2151	...	2251	0002
Crewe **143 153** d.		0617	...	0650	0651	...	0719	0819	minutes	2119	2219	...	2320	0020		0905	...	0959	1119	minutes	2219	...	2321	0031
Stafford **119 143 153** d.		0639	...	0709	0709	...	0739	0839	past each	2139	2239	...	...	...		0951	...	1043	1139	past each	2239	...	...	...
Wolverhampton **119** ▷ a.		0656	...	0726	0727	...	0756	0857	hour until	2156	2258	...	...	...		1008	...	1059	1156	hour until	2256	...	...	...
Birmingham New Street **119** ▷ a.		0718	...	0748	0748	...	0818	0919		2219	2318	...	...	...		1038	...	1136	1218		2318	...	...	...

f – Arrives 5–6 minutes earlier. t – Arrives 8–9 minutes earlier. ‡ – 🚌 connections available to / from Liverpool John Lennon Airport ✈. ▷ – See also Tables **145** and **150**.

145 BIRMINGHAM - SHREWSBURY - CHESTER 2nd class AW

km			⑥	Ⓐ	⚒ A	Ⓐ	⚒ B	Ⓐ	⚒	⚒ 🍷	⑥	Ⓐ	⚒ 🍷	Ⓐ C	⚒ F 🍷	⑥ 🍷	⚒ 🍷	⚒ F 🍷	⑥ 🍷	Ⓐ 🍷	Ⓐ 🍷	⑥ 🍷	⚒ F 🍷	⑥ 🍷	Ⓐ C	⑥ 🍷	Ⓐ 🍷
0	**Birmingham** Int ✈ d.	⚒	...	...	...	...	...	...	...	...	...	...	0708	...	0808	...	0908	1008	...	...	1108	1108	1208	...	...	1308	1308
13	**Birmingham** New St d.		...	...	0530	...	...	...	0556	0622	...	...	0722	...	0822	...	0922	1022	...	...	1122	1122	1222	...	...	1322	1322
34	Wolverhampton d.		...	...	0549	...	...	...	0615	0642	...	...	0741	...	0841	...	0941	1041	...	...	1141	1141	1241	...	...	1341	1341
59	Telford Central d.		...	...	|	...	...	...	0641	0659	...	...	0758	...	0858	...	0958	1058	...	...	1158	1158	1259	...	...	1358	1358
65	Wellington d.		...	...	|	...	...	...	0650	0707	...	...	0806	...	0905	...	1005	1106	...	...	1206	1206	1307	...	...	1406	1406
81	**Shrewsbury** a.		...	...	|	...	...	...	0703	0722	...	...	0821	...	0920j	...	1020	1120	...	...	1220	1220	1322	...	...	1420	1422
	Aberystwyth **147** a.		...	...	|	...	...	...	...	0921	...	...	|	...	1121	...	|	1322	...	...	|	|	1522	...	...	|	|
	Cardiff Central **149** d.		...	...	|	...	...	...	...	...	0520	0512	|	0648	...	0722	|	...	0922	0923	|	|	...	1123	1125	|	|
81	**Shrewsbury** d.		0519	0533	|	0557	...	0700	...	...	0726	0728	0825	0850	...	0927	1024	...	1128	1130	1225	1225	...	1327	1330	1423	1426
110	Gobowen d.		0540	0551	|	0614	...	0719	...	...	0743	0745	0843	0908	...	0944	1042	...	1145	1147	1243	1243	...	1345	1348	1441	1444
122	Ruabon d.		0553	0603	|	0625	...	0731	...	...	0755	0757	0855	0921	...	0956	1054	...	1157	1159	1255	1255	...	1357	1401	1453	1456
129	Wrexham General d.		0605f	0610	|	0635	0703	0741	...	...	0802	0804	0902	0929	...	1003	1101	...	1204	1209	1302	1302	...	1406	1409	1500	1502
149	**Chester** **160** a.		0622	0630	0645	0657	0720	...	...	...	0820	0821	0920	0947	...	1020	1121	...	1223	1226	1319	1320	...	1424	1426	1517	1521
	Holyhead **160** a.		...	...	0823	...	...	...	...	...	1019	1009	1112b	1118	...	1212	1324k	...	1418	1418	1520	1510	...	1621	1619	1717	1718

A – 🚃12 and 🍷 Birmingham New Street - Crewe - Holyhead (Table **160**).
B – 🚃12 and 🍷 Wrexham - London Euston (Table **160**).
C – 🚃12 and ✕ Cardiff - Holyhead.
F – Conveys 🚃2 Birmingham - Pwllheli (Table **148**).
b – ⑥ only.
f – Arrives 0601.
j – Arrives 0922 on ⑥.
k – Arrives 1314 on ⑥.

AW 2nd class — BIRMINGHAM - SHREWSBURY - CHESTER — 145

	⚒ F🍷	⚒ 🍷	⑥ 🍷	Ⓐ 🍷	⚒ F🍷	⑥ 🍷	Ⓐ 🍷	Ⓐ L	⑥	Ⓐ	⚒	Ⓐ C	⚒	⑥ 🍷	Ⓐ	⚒	Ⓐ R🍷	Ⓐ	⑥	⚒ E🍷	⚒	⑥ J	Ⓐ	⚒ M	⑥	①–④	⑤
Birmingham Int ✈ d.	1408	...	1508	1508	1608	...	...	1708	1708	...	...	...	1808	...	...	...	...	1908	1908	1938	2008	...	...	2108	...	...	...
Birmingham New St d.	1422	...	1522	1522	1622	...	...	1722	1722	...	1756	...	1822	...	...	1856	...	1922	1922	1956	2022	...	...	2122	...	...	...
Wolverhampton d.	1441	...	1541	1541	1641	...	...	1741	1741	...	1815	...	1841	...	...	1915	...	1941	1941	2015	2041	...	...	2141	...	...	...
Telford Central d.	1459	...	1558	1558	1659	...	...	1758	1758	...	1841	...	1859	...	...	1941	...	1959	1959	2033	2059	...	...	2159	...	...	...
Wellington d.	1507	...	1606	1606	1707	...	...	1806	1806	...	1850	...	1907	...	...	1950	...	2007	2007	2040	2107	...	...	2207	...	...	...
Shrewsbury a.	1521	...	1620	1620	1722	...	...	1821	1821	...	1903	...	1922	...	...	2003	...	2023	2021	2057	2122	...	...	2223	...	...	...
Aberystwyth 147 a.	1721	...	|	|	1921	...	...	|	|	...	▬	...	2125	...	...	...	...	|	|	...	2336	...	...	|	...	...	...
Cardiff Central 149 d.	...	1322	|	|	...	1522	1523	|	|	...	...	1714	▬	1723	...	...	1825	|	|	...	...	1941	1941	|	2055	2115	2115
Shrewsbury d.	...	1528	1625	1625	...	1729	1728	1826	1827	...	...	1909	...	1928	1932	...	2027	2028	2026	...	...	2143	2146	2226	2306	2317	2317
Gobowen d.	...	1545	1643	1643	...	1746	1746	1844	1845	...	...	|	...	1945	1950	...	|	2046	2044	...	...	2200	2204	2244	|	|	|
Ruabon d.	...	1557	1655	1655	...	1758	1758	1856	1856	...	⑥	|	⑥	1957	2002	...	⊕	2058	2056	...	...	2212	2216	2256	⊕	⊕	⊕
Wrexham General d.	...	1604	1702	1702	...	1805	1805	1903	1903	1916	1922	1940	1950	2004	2008	...	|	2105	2103	...	...	2219	2222	2303	|	|	|
Chester 160 a.	...	1622	1719	1722	...	1823	1822	1921	1921	1937	1944	1957	2008	2024	2028	...	2126	2123	2124	...	...	2236	2241	2322	0023	0027	0027
Holyhead 160 a.	...	1821	1915	1918	...	2025	2020	...	2125	...	...	2141	...	2224	2231	...	...	...	...	...	...	...	0048t	...	...	*0212*	*0224*

	⑥ T	Ⓐ	⑥	Ⓐ	⑦	⑦	⑦ F🍷	⑦ 🍷	⑦ F🍷	⑦ 🍷	⑦	⑦ F🍷	⑦ 🍷	⑦ 🍷	⑦ F🍷	⑦ 🍷	⑦ 🍷	⑦	⑦	⑦ E🍷	⑦	⑦	⑦	⑦	⑦	⑦	⑦
Birmingham Int ✈ d.	...	...	...	2306		...	0951	1108	1208	1308	...	1408	...	1508	1608	...	1708	1808	1908	1938	2008	2108	...	...	2211	2240	2306
Birmingham New St d.	2236	...	2335	2334		0825	1004	1122	1222	1322	1356	1422	...	1522	1622	...	1722	1822	1922	1957	2022	2122	2156	...	2224	2255	2325
Wolverhampton d.	2255	...	2355	0004		0844	1023	1141	1241	1341	1414	1443	...	1543	1643	...	1742	1842	1941	2015	2042	2141	2214	...	2243	2316	2350
Telford Central d.	2312	...	0022	0032		0911	1048	1159	1258	1358	1441	1500	...	1600	1700	...	1759	1859	1958	2034	2100	2158	2241	...	2303	|	0017
Wellington d.	2318	...	0030	0040		0920	1057	1207	1306	1405	1450	1508	...	1608	1708	...	1807	1907	2006	2041	2107	2206	2250	...	2311	|	0024
Shrewsbury a.	2332	...	0045	0055		0932	1112	1222	1320	1419	1503	1522	...	1625	1723	...	1821	1921	2020	2054	2121	2220	2303	...	2327	2348	0039
Aberystwyth 147 a.	▬	...	...	...		▬	1321	|	1521	|	...	1723	...	|	1920	...	|	2122	|	...	2315	|	▬	...	...	|	...
Cardiff Central 149 d.	⑥	...	...	...		⑦	▬	|	...	|	...	...	1329	|	...	1522	|	...	|	...	▬	|	...	2107	...	|	...
Shrewsbury d.	2336	2340	...	...		1016	...	1223	...	1422	...	...	1533	1630	...	1732	1827	...	2026	...	...	2235	...	2319	...	2348	...
Gobowen d.	2354	2358	...	...		1034	...	1241	...	1440	...	...	1551	1648	...	1749	1845	...	2044	...	...	|	...	|	...	|	...
Ruabon d.	0006	0010	...	...		1046	⑦B	1253	...	1452	...	...	1603	1700	...	1801	1857	...	2056	...	⑦	⊕	⑦	⊕	...	⊕	...
Wrexham General d.	0012	0016	...	...		1053	1206	1301	...	1459	...	...	1610	1707	...	1809	1906	...	2103	...	2235	|	2337	|	...	|	...
Chester 160 a.	0030	0035	...	...		1112	1223	1319	...	1519	...	...	1629	1727	...	1826	1925	...	2123	...	2254	2333	2357	0034	...	0044	...
Holyhead 160 a.	...	...	...	...		...	...	...	...	...	...	...	1838	...	...	2019	2129	...	...	...	...	...	...	*0213*	...	...	...

	⚒	Ⓐ	⑥	Ⓐ	⚒	⚒ E🍷	⑥	Ⓐ	Ⓐ	⑥	Ⓐ C	⑥ Q	Ⓐ Q	Ⓐ	⑥	⚒ G🍷	⑥	Ⓐ 🍷	Ⓐ 🍷	⑥ 🍷	Ⓐ F🍷	⑥ F🍷	⚒ 🍷	⑥ 🍷	Ⓐ R🍷	Ⓐ F🍷	⑥ F🍷
Holyhead 160 d.		...	...	...	...	...	0425	0425	...	...	0533	0519	...	0624	0631	...	0715	0731	0805	0819	...	...	0927	1030	1040	...	...
Chester 160 d.		...	...	0532	0545	...	0612	0620	...	...	0716	0730	...	0820	0820	...	0930	0930	1020	1020	...	...	1136	1221	1221	...	...
Wrexham General d.		...	...	0547	0605	...	0632	0635	...	...	0732	0745	0750	0834	0835	...	0946	0945	1034	1035	...	...	1151	1235	1236	...	...
Ruabon d.		...	...	0555	▬	...	0639	0642	...	...	|	0752	0758	0841	0842	...	0952	0952	1041	1042	...	...	1158	1242	1243	...	...
Gobowen d.		...	...	0608	...	...	0651	0654	...	...	|	0804	0810	0853	0854	...	1004	1004	1053	1054	...	...	1210	1254	1255	...	...
Shrewsbury a.		...	...	0628	...	...	0710	0714	...	...	0802	0824	0828	0912	0913	...	1031	1024	1112	1113	...	...	1231	1313	1314	...	...
Cardiff Central 149 a.		...	...	|	...	...	0921	0917	...	...	0959	|	|	1118	1116	...	|	|	1314	1315	...	...	|	1521	1511	...	...
Aberystwyth 147 d.		...	...	|	⑥	...	...	...	0523	0526	...	|	|	...	...	0728	|	|	...	...	0929	0929	|	...	...	1128	1129
Shrewsbury d.		0518	0522	0630	0630	0704	...	...	0730	0730	...	0830	0833	...	...	0930	1034	1030	...	...	1130	1133	1234	...	...	1330	1332
Wellington d.		0532	0536	0644	0644	0718	...	...	0744	0744	...	0844	0847	...	...	0944	1048	1044	...	...	1144	1146	1248	...	...	1344	1346
Telford Central d.		0538	0543	0651	0651	0725	...	...	0751	0751	...	0851	0854	...	...	0951	1055	1051	...	...	1151	1153	1255	...	...	1351	1353
Wolverhampton a.		0555	0602	0710	0710	0743	...	...	0810	0810	...	0911	0912	...	...	1010	1113	1110	...	...	1210	1211	1313	...	...	1410	1411
Birmingham New St a.		0616	0622	0732	0731	0808	...	...	0832	0832	...	0932	0932	...	...	1032	1133	1132	...	...	1232	1232	1333	...	...	1432	1432
Birmingham Int ✈ a.		0648	0650	0753	0753	0831	...	...	0853	0853	...	0953	0954	...	...	1053	1153	1153	...	...	1253	1253	1353	...	...	1453	1453

	⑥ 🍷	Ⓐ C	Ⓐ 🍷	⑥ 🍷	⚒ F🍷	⚒ 🍷		⑥ 🍷	Ⓐ 🍷	⚒ F🍷	⑥ 🍷	Ⓐ 🍷	Ⓐ	Ⓐ C	⑥ 🍷	Ⓐ	⑥	Ⓐ	⑥	Ⓐ B	⑥	Ⓐ P	Ⓐ F	⑥	Ⓐ	⑥ B	Ⓐ
Holyhead 160 d.	1128	1133	1148	1232	...	1327	...	1425	1433	...	1525	1538	...	1634	1648	...	...	1728	1728	...	...	...	...	...	...	...	1922
Chester 160 d.	1335	1316	1338	1415	...	1536	...	1614	1623	...	1730	1735	...	1821	1833	1833	1839	1917	1931	2020	2023	2032	...	...	...	2111	2118
Wrexham General d.	1351	1331	1353	1429	...	1551	...	1629	1637	...	1745	1751	...	1838	1848	1850	1856	1932	1946	2034	2039	|	...	...	2046	2126	2137
Ruabon d.	1358	1338	1400	1436	...	1558	...	1636	1644	...	1752	1758	...	1845	1855	▬	...	1939	1953	...	2046	|	...	...	2053	▬	2144
Gobowen d.	1410	1352	1412	1448	...	1610	...	1648	1656	...	1804	1810	...	1859	1907	...	...	1951	2005	...	2059	|	...	...	2106	...	2157
Shrewsbury a.	1429	1413	1431	1507	...	1630	...	1707	1715	...	1823	1829	...	1919	1926	⚒	...	2013	2026	...	2119	|	...	...	2127	...	2217
Cardiff Central 149 a.	|	1618	|	1710	...	|	...	1912	1925	...	|	|	...	2128	2130	🍷	...	...	▬	...	...	|	...	...	...	...	|
Aberystwyth 147 d.	|	...	|	...	1329	|	...	...	...	1529	|	|	...	...	...	1727	...	...	⚒	...	...	|	1929	1929	...	Ⓐ	|
Shrewsbury d.	1430	...	1432	...	1530	1634	...	...	...	1730	1830	1830	1840	...	...	1930	...	...	2040	...	...	|	2130	2130	...	2140	2218
Wellington d.	1444	...	1446	...	1544	1648	...	...	...	1744	1844	1844	1854	...	...	1944	...	...	2054	...	...	|	2144	2144	...	2154	2231
Telford Central d.	1451	...	1453	...	1551	1655	...	...	...	1751	1851	1851	1902	...	...	1951	...	...	2102	...	...	|	2151	2151	...	2202	2237
Wolverhampton a.	1510	...	1511	...	1612	1712	...	...	...	1811	1911	1910	1931	...	...	2010	...	...	2131	...	...	2139	2210	2210	...	2231	2255
Birmingham New St a.	1532	...	1532	...	1632	1733	...	...	...	1832	1932	1932	1951	...	...	2032	...	...	2151	...	...	2200	2235	2232	...	2251	2328
Birmingham Int ✈ a.	1553	...	1553	...	1653	1753	...	...	...	1852	1953	1952	...	...	...	2053	...	...	...	...	...	...	2252	...	...	...	...

	⑥	Ⓐ A	⚒	⚒	⑦	⑦	⑦ 🍷	⑦ 🍷	⑦ E🍷	⑦ 🍷	⑦ 🍷	⑦ 🍷	⑦ F🍷		⑦ 🍷	⑦ F🍷	⑦	⑦ F🍷	⑦	⑦ 🍷	⑦ B🍷	⑦	⑦ 🍷	⑦ F	⑦	⑦	⑦
Holyhead 160 d.	1921	1949	...	...		...	...	...	...	...	...	1020	...	...	...	...	...	...	...	1625	...	...	1826	...	...	...	...
Chester 160 d.	2130	2134	...	2232		0813	...	0920	...	...	1132	1229	...	...	1334	...	1535	...	1731	1826	1910	1939	2027	...	2127	2205	2302
Wrexham General d.	2145	|	...	2247		0829	...	0935	...	...	1148	1244	...	...	1349	...	1551	...	1748	1841	1925	1954	|	...	2142	2222	|
Ruabon d.	2152	|	...	2254		▬	...	0942	...	...	1155	1251	...	...	1356	...	1558	...	1756	1848	▬	2001	⊕	...	2149	...	⊕
Gobowen d.	2204	|	...	2306		...	...	0954	...	...	1207	1303	...	...	1408	...	1610	...	1808	1900	...	2013	|	...	2201	...	|
Shrewsbury a.	2224	|	...	2327		...	...	1013	...	...	1226	1322	...	...	1427	...	1629	...	1828	1920	⑦	2033	2120	...	2221	...	0017
Cardiff Central 149 a.	|	|	...	...		...	...	|	...	...	|	1528	...	...	|	...	|	...	|	2130	F🍷	|	|	...	|	...	...
Aberystwyth 147 d.	|	|	...	...		⑦	...	|	...	0929	|	...	1129	...	|	1329	|	1527	|	...	1727	|	|	1929	|	...	...
Shrewsbury d.	2227	|	2240	...		0810	0917	1016	1112	1133	1233	...	1330	...	1430	1531	1631	1731	1831	...	1930	2033	2120	2133	2224	...	...
Wellington d.	2241	|	2254	...		0824	0931	1030	1127	1147	1247	...	1343	...	1444	1545	1645	1745	1845	...	1944	2047	|	2147	2238	...	...
Telford Central d.	2248	|	2302	...		0830	0938	1036	1133	1154	1254	...	1349	...	1451	1552	1652	1751	1852	...	1950	2054	|	2154	2246	...	...
Wolverhampton a.	2308	2234	2332	...		0848	0957	1053	1150	1212	1312	...	1407	...	1508	1609	1709	1809	1910	...	2007	2112	2152	2212	2314	...	...
Birmingham New St a.	2329	2254	2351	...		0910	1017	1115	1210	1232	1333	...	1432	...	1531	1631	1730	1830	1931	...	2030	2132	2212	2232	...	...	...
Birmingham Int ✈ a.	...	...	...	...		0930	1034	1130	1231	1255	1352	...	1454	...	1552	1655	1752	1850	1952	...	2052	2151	2233	2249	...	...	...

A – ⟨12⟩ and 🍷 Birmingham New Street - Crewe - Holyhead and v.v. (Table **160**).
B – ⟨12⟩ and 🍷 London Euston - Wrexham (Table **160**).
C – ⟨12⟩ and ✕ Holyhead - Cardiff and v.v.
E – From/London Euston (Table **150**).
F – Conveys ⟨2⟩ Pwllheli - Birmingham and v.v. (Table **148**).
G – On ⑥ conveys ⟨2⟩ Barmouth - Birmingham (Table **148**).
J – To Llandudno Junction (Table **160**).
L – To Llandudno (Table **160**).
M – To Manchester Piccadilly (Table **160**).
P – ⟨12⟩ and 🍷 Chester - Crewe - Birmingham New Street (Table **160**).
Q – Also conveys ⟨2⟩ Crewe - Birmingham International (Table **149**).
R – From/to Llanelli (Table **136**).
T – To Crewe (Table **149**).
t – Arrives 0043 on ⑥ mornings.
⊕ – Via Crewe (Table **149**).

AW 2nd class — SHREWSBURY - SWANSEA — 146

km		Ⓐ	⚒	⚒	Ⓐ	⑥	⑦	Ⓐ	⑥	⑦A	⚒	Ⓐ
0	**Shrewsbury** 149 d.	0419	0522	0855	1121	1126	1204	1517	1524	1620	1807	2129
20	Church Stretton 149 d.	0437	0540	0913	1142	1144	1222	1535	1542	1639	1825	2147
32	Craven Arms 149 d.	0448	0550	0923	1152	1154	1232	1545	1552	1649	1836	2157
52	Knighton d.	0510	0625t	0947	1217	1219	1256	1609	1616	1713	1900	2221
84	**Llandrindod** a.	0545	0706	1027	1257	1259	1335	1649	1656	1750	1939	2300
84	**Llandrindod** d.	▬	0706	1028	1257	1259	1340	1701	1702	1805	1941	...
110	Llanwrtyd a.	...	0736	1057	1326	1328	1409	1729	1730	1835	2009	...
110	Llanwrtyd d.	Ⓐ	0740	1103	1341	1341	1411	1735	1733	1836	2015	...
128	Llandovery d.	0626	0805	1128	1407	1407	1436	1800	1758	1902	2040	...
146	Llandeilo d.	0650	0827	1150	1428	1428	1458	1822	1820	1923	2102	...
159	Pantyffynnon d.	0708	0844	1207	1446	1446	1515	1839	1837	1941	2119	...
178	Llanelli 136 a.	0729	0909	1237	1506	1508	1536	1904	1857j	2002	2141	...
196	**Swansea** 136 a.	0805	0934	1303	1534	1539	1602	1937	1939	2026	2212c	...
211	**Carmarthen** 136 a.	...	...	...	...	...	...	...	...	...	...	...

	Ⓐ	⚒	⚒	⑦	⚒	Ⓐ	⑥	⑦	Ⓐ	⑥	Ⓐ
Carmarthen 136 d.	0447	...	...	...	...	...	...	...	...	...	...
Swansea 136 d.	|	0547	0908	1110	1140	1418	1430	1535	1816	1818	...
Llanelli 136 d.	0513	0608	0931	1133	1203k	1446v	1454	1558	1842	1842	...
Pantyffynnon d.	0534	0629	0952	1154	1231	1509	1507	1618	1901	1904	...
Llandeilo d.	0554	0649	1012	1214	1251	1529	1535	1638	1921	1924	...
Llandovery d.	0615	0711	1034	1236	1313	1551	1557	1700	1942	1946	...
Llanwrtyd a.	▬	0736	1057	1259	1336	1614	1620	1724	2005	2009	...
Llanwrtyd d.	...	0740	1103	1301	1342	1617	1622	1725	2009	2015	...
Llandrindod a.	Ⓐ	0813	1135	1331	1414	1649	1654	1756	2039	2047	...
Llandrindod d.	0550	0813	1136	1344	1415	1701	1702	1759	2041	2048	2310
Knighton d.	0643n	0851	1217r	1422	1454	1740	1740	1838	2128	2127	2345
Craven Arms 149 d.	0706	0914	1241	1444	1516	1802	1803	1900	2151	2152	0007
Church Stretton 149 d.	0719	0927	1254	1457	1529	1815	1816	1913	2204	2205	0020
Shrewsbury 149 a.	0738	0946	1314	1513	1546	1832	1833	1935	2221	2226	0037

A – To Cardiff Central (Table **136**).
c – On Ⓐ arrives 2208.
f – Arrives 0648.
j – Departs 1909.
k – On ⑥ departs 1208.
n – Arrives 0624.
r – Arrives 1212.
t – Arrives 0614.
v – Arrives 1437.

147 SHREWSBURY - ABERYSTWYTH 2nd class AW

km			⚒	⚒🍷	⑥🍷	Ⓐ🍷	⚒🍷	Ⓐ🍷	⑥🍷	Ⓐ🍷	⑥🍷	⚒🍷	⚒🍷	⚒	⑥🍷	Ⓐ🍷	⑥🍷	Ⓐ🍷	Ⓐ	⑥	⚒	⑥	Ⓐ		⑦
	Birmingham New St **145** .. d.	⚒	...	...	0622	0622	0822	...	...	1022	1022	1222	1422	...	1622	1622	...	...	1822	1822	...	2022	2022	⑦	🚌
0	**Shrewsbury** d.		...	0624	0727	0727	0930	1029	1029	1127	1129	1328	1527	...	1727	1730	1827	1833	1930	1930	2032	2143	2150		0830
32	Welshpool d.		...	0646	0752	0749	0952	1051	1051	1149	1151	1351	1552	...	1749	1752	1850	1855	1952	1952	2054	2205	2212		0905
54	Newtown d.		...	0701	0807	0804	1007	1106	1106	1204	1206	1406	1607	...	1804	1807	1905	1910	2007	2007	2109	2220	2227		0930
63	Caersws d.		...	0708	0814	0811	1014	1113	1113	1211	1213	1413	1614	...	1811	1814	1912	1917	2014	2014	2116	2227	2234		0945
98	**Machynlleth** a.		...	0742	0845	0843	1045	1141	1142	1242	1244	1444	1645	...	1842	1843	1945	1946	2048	2048	2143	2257	2302		1025
98	**Machynlleth** **148** ▷ d.		0647	0746	0849	0848	1050	1142	1146	1247	1249	1449	1650	1801	1848	1849	1946	1947	2049	2053	2150	2303	2306		1025
104	Dovey Junction **148** ▷ d.		0655	0755	0856	0855	1056	1154	1155	1255	1257	1455	1656	|	1856	1857	1955	1955	2057	2101	2158	2309	2312		1035
118	Borth ▷ d.		0705	0805	0906	0905	1106	1204	1205	1305	1307	1505	1706	|	1906	1907	2005	2005	2107	2111	2208	2319	2322		1055
131	**Aberystwyth** ▷ a.		0721	0822	0921	0921	1121	1220	1221	1322	1322	1522	1721	1829	1921	1921	2022	2020	2122	2125	2222	2335	2336		1120

	⑦	⑦🍷	⑦🍷	⑦🍷	⑦🍷	⑦🍷	⑦🍷	⑦🍷	⑦	⑦
Birmingham New St **145** d.	...	1004	1222	...	1422	...	1622	...	1822	2022
Shrewsbury d.	1027	1128	1330	1429	1528	1629	1727	1828	1927	2128
Welshpool d.	1051	1150	1352	1451	1551	1651	1749	1850	1949	2150
Newtown d.	1106	1205	1407	1506	1606	1706	1804	1905	2004	2205
Caersws d.	1113	1212	1414	1514	1613	1713	1812	1912	2011	2212
Machynlleth a.	1143	1243	1445	1545	1642	1742	1843	1941	2042	2240
Machynlleth **148** ▷ d.	1143	1248	1449	1546	1647	1743	1847	1942	2047	2245
Dovey Junction **148** ▷ d.	1155	1256	1457	1555	1655	1755	1855	1956	2055	2251
Borth ▷ d.	1205	1306	1507	1605	1706	1805	1905	2006	2105	2301
Aberystwyth ▷ a.	1221	1321	1521	1620	1723	1821	1920	2021	2122	2315

		Ⓐ	⑥	⑥🍷	Ⓐ🍷	Ⓐ🍷	⑥🍷	Ⓐ🍷	⑥🍷
Aberystwyth ▷ d.	⚒	0523	0526	0629	0629	0728	0729	0829	0829
Borth ▷ d.		0538	0541	0644	0644	0743	0744	0844	0844
Dovey Junction **148** ▷ d.		0548	0551	0654	0654	0753	0754	0858f	0859f
Machynlleth **148** ▷ a.		0556	0559	0702	0702	0801	0804	0906	0907
Machynlleth d.		0558	0602	0703	0705	0805	0808	0906	0908
Caersws d.		0624	0629	0730	0732	0832	0835	0933	0935
Newtown d.		0631	0636	0737	0739	0839	0842	0940	0942
Welshpool d.		0645	0650	0752	0754	0854	0856	0955	0956
Shrewsbury a.		0708	0713	0814	0819	0918	0920	1020	1019
Birmingham New St **145** a.		0832	0832	...	...	1032	1032	...	...

	⚒🍷	Ⓐ🍷	⑥🍷	⚒🍷	Ⓐ🍷	⑥🍷	⚒🍷	Ⓐ🍷	⑥	Ⓐ🍷	⑥🍷	⚒		⑦	⑦	⑦	⑦🍷	⑦🍷	⑦🍷	⑦🍷	⑦🍷	⑦🍷	⑦🍷	⑦🍷	⑦
Aberystwyth ▷ d.	0929	1128	1129	1229	1329	1329	1529	1727	1728	1831	1831	1929	⑦	0829	0929	1029	1129	1229	1329	1429	1527	1629	1727	1929	2319
Borth ▷ d.	0944	1143	1144	1244	1344	1344	1544	1742	1742	1846	1846	1944		0844	0944	1044	1144	1244	1344	1444	1543	1644	1743	1944	2334
Dovey Junction **148** ▷ d.	0954	1153	1155	1257r	1354	1354	1554	1752	1752	1856	1856	1959t		0858f	0954	1056	1154	1257r	1357	1459t	1555	1656	1753	1954	2344
Machynlleth **148** ▷ a.	1002	1202	1203	1306	1402	1402	1602	1800	1800	1905	1904	2007		0906	1002	1103	1202	1305	1404	1507	1602	1703	1801	2002	2353
Machynlleth d.	1008	1205	1207	1306	1407	1407	1608	1805	1805	1909	1906	2011		0907	1008	1104	1206	1306	1407	1508	1606	1703	1805	2006	...
Caersws d.	1035	1232	1234	1333	1434	1434	1635	1835	1832	1936	1933	2038		0934	1035	1132	1233	1333	1434	1535	1635	1734	1832	2033	...
Newtown d.	1042	1239	1241	1340	1441	1441	1642	1842	1839	1943	1940	2045		0941	1042	1139	1240	1340	1441	1542	1642	1741	1839	2040	...
Welshpool d.	1056	1254	1255	1354	1455	1455	1656	1857	1855	1957	1957	2100		0956	1057	1154	1254	1354	1456	1556	1656	1755	1854	2054	...
Shrewsbury a.	1119	1317	1319	1419	1518	1521	1720	1921	1919	2020	2025	2125		1019	1121	1219	1318	1419	1519	1618	1720	1819	1917	2118	...
Birmingham New St **145** a.	1232	1432	1432	...	1632	1632	1832	2032	2032	...	...	2235		...	1232	...	1432	...	1631	...	1830	...	2030	2232	...

▷ – Additional journeys Machynlleth - Aberystwyth and v.v.:
From Machynlleth at 0450Ⓐ, 0452⑥, 0541 Ⓐ, 0547⑥, 0750⑦, 0849⑦, 0947⑦, 1049⑦, 1350⑦.
From Aberystwyth at 1829⑦, 2029Ⓒ, 2035⑥, 2129Ⓒ, 2132⑥, 2229⚒, 2338⑥, 2339Ⓐ.

f – Arrives 0854.
r – Arrives 1254.
t – Arrives 5 minutes earlier.

148 MACHYNLLETH - PWLLHELI 2nd class AW

km			Ⓐ	⑥	⚒	Ⓐ	⑥	Ⓐ	⑥	Ⓐ	⑥	Ⓐ	⑥	⚒	⑥	Ⓐ	⑥	Ⓐ		⑦	⑦	⑦		⑦	⑦
	Birmingham New St **145** .. d.	⚒	...	...	...	*0622*	*0622*	0822	0822	1022	1022	1222	1222	1422	1622	1622	*1922**	*1922**	⑦	...	1004	1222	...	1422	1622
	Shrewsbury **147** d.		...	...	...	*0727*	*0727*	0930	0930	1127	1129	1328	1329	1527	1727	1730	*2032*	*2032*		...	1128	1330	...	1528	1727
0	**Machynlleth** **147** d.		0507	0509	0643	0852	0853	1055	1055	1251	1252	1456	1456	1655	1904	1904	2147	2147		1004	1251	1453	...	1650	1855
6	Dovey Junction **147** d.		0513	0515	0649	0858	0859	1101	1101	1257	1258	1502	1502	1701	1910	1910	2153	2153		1010	1300	1459	...	1656	1901
16	Aberdovey d.		0526	0528	0702	0911	0912	1114	1114	1310	1311	1515	1515	1714	1923	1923	2206	2206		1023	1313	1512	...	1709	1914
22	Tywyn 🚂 a.		0534	0536	0712	0921	0921	1124	1124	1320	1320	1525	1525	1725	1933	1933	2216	2216		1029	1320	1519	...	1718	1921
22	Tywyn 🚂 d.		0534	0536	0714	0929	0929	1130	1130	1325	1324	1526	1525	1729	1933	1933	2217	2217		1030	1324	1531	...	1729	1924
37	Fairbourne d.		0553	0555	0732	0948	0948	1149	1148	1344	1343	1545	1544	1747	1951	1951	2235	2236		1049	1343	1549	...	1747	1943
41	**Barmouth** d.		0606	0608	0747	1001	1001	1201	1201	1357	1356	1558	1557	1800	2004	2004	2248	2248		1058	1356	1559	...	1759	1953
58	Harlech a.		...	...	0813	1026	1026	1226	1227	1422	1421	1623	1622	1825	2028	2030	2313	2314		1124	1422	1624	...	1825	2018
58	Harlech d.		...	...	0825	1026	1026	1226	1227	1431	1431	1628	1629	1833	2029	2030	2314	2314		1125	1431	1624	...	1830	2022
67	Penrhyndeudraeth d.		...	...	0838	1039	1039	1239	1240	1444	1444	1640	1641	1845	2041	2043	2327	2327		1138	1444	1637	...	1843	2035
69	Minffordd **160** d.		...	...	0841	1042	1042	1242	1243	1447	1447	1644	1645	1849	2045	2047	2330	2331		1142	1448	1641	...	1847	2038
72	**Porthmadog** **160** d.		...	...	0850	1051	1051	1251	1252	1456	1456	1652	1653	1857	2053	2055	2337	2339		1154f	1456	1647	...	1855	2044
80	Criccieth d.		...	...	0857	1058	1058	1258	1259	1503	1503	1700	1700	1904	2101	2103	2345	2347		1201	1503	1654	...	1902	2052
93	**Pwllheli** a.		...	...	0912	1113	1113	1313	1314	1519	1520	1717	1715	1920	2116	2118	2359	0001		1217	1519	1710	...	1918	2107

		⑥	Ⓐ	⚒	⚒		Ⓐ	⑥	Ⓐ	⑥		⑥	Ⓐ	⚒	Ⓐ	⑥	⑥	Ⓐ		⑦	⑦		⑦	⑦	⑦
Pwllheli d.	⚒	...	...	0629	0724	...	0934	0934	1137	1137	...	1338	1338	1537	1742	1742	2026	2026	⑦	0934	1128	...	1340	1533	1736
Criccieth d.		...	...	0643	0738	...	0948	0948	1151	1151	...	1352	1352	1551	1756	1756	2040	2040		0948	1142	...	1354	1547	1750
Porthmadog **160** d.		...	...	0653	0747	...	0957	0958	1201	1201	...	1402	1402	1601	1806	1806	2056f	2056f		0958	1157f	...	1406	1557	1800
Minffordd **160** d.		...	...	0657	0752	...	1001	1002	1205	1205	...	1406	1406	1605	1810	1810	2101	2100		1002	1201	...	1410	1601	1805
Penrhyndeudraeth d.		...	...	0701	0756	...	1005	1006	1209	1209	...	1410	1410	1609	1814	1814	2104	2104		1006	1205	...	1414	1605	1809
Harlech a.		...	...	0717	0811	...	1022	1023	1226	1224	...	1427	1427	1626	1830	1830	2120	2119		1023	1219	...	1428	1622	1823
Harlech d.		...	...	0717	0821	...	1029	1028	1228	1228	...	1428	1428	1629	1830	1830	2120	2119		1028	1221	...	1434	1629	1827
Barmouth d.		0645	0645	0749	0852f	...	1059	1059	1255	1255	...	1455	1455	1656	1857	1857	2147	2146		1101f	1250	...	1501	1656	1854
Fairbourne d.		0653	0653	0757	0900	...	1107	1107	1303	1303	...	1503	1503	1704	1905	1905	2155	2154		1109	1258	...	1509	1704	1903
Tywyn 🚂 a.		0714	0714	0817	0922	...	1129	1129	1325	1325	...	1526	1526	1726	1927	1927	2217	2216		1130	1319	...	1528	1726	1923
Tywyn 🚂 d.		0714	0714	0817	0927	...	1130	1130	1325	1325	...	1526	1526	1727	1934	1935	2217	2217		1130	1320	...	1528	1727	1924
Aberdovey d.		0720	0720	0823	0933	...	1136	1136	1331	1331	...	1532	1532	1733	1940	1941	2223	2223		1136	1326	...	1536	1733	1930
Dovey Junction **147** d.		0736	0736	0838	0948	...	1150	1152	1346	1346	...	1547	1547	1748	1956	1956	2238	2238		1151	1341	...	1552	1749	1948
Machynlleth **147** a.		0743	0743	0848	0955	...	1158	1158	1352	1353	...	1553	1555	1756	2004	2004	2245	2245		1158	1349	...	1600	1757	1955
Shrewsbury **147** a.		0920	*0918*	*1020*	1119	...	1317	1319	1518	1521	...	1719	1720	*1921*	2125	*2125*	...	...		1318	1519	...	1720	1917	2118
Birmingham New St **145** a.		1032	*1032*	*1133**	1232	...	1432	1432	1632	1632	...	1832	1832	*2032*	2235	*2232*	...	...		1432	1631	...	1830	2030	2232

f – Arrives 5–7 minutes earlier.

* – Change at Shrewsbury and Machynlleth.

🚂 – Talyllyn Railway (Tywyn Wharf - Abergynolwyn - Nant Gwernol: *12 km*). ✆ 01654 710472. www.talyllyn.co.uk

149 CARDIFF - HEREFORD - CREWE - MANCHESTER AW

km			②–⑤ 2	Ⓐ 2🍷	Ⓐ 2	Ⓐ 2	Ⓐ ✕S	Ⓐ ✕	Ⓐ2 🍷C	Ⓐ ⚒	Ⓐ 2🍷	Ⓐ2 🍷M		Ⓐ ✕	Ⓐ ✕	Ⓐ2 🍷M	Ⓐ ✕	Ⓐ 2🍷	Ⓐ2 🍷M	Ⓐ ✕	Ⓐ 2🍷	Ⓐ 🍷M	Ⓐ ✕	Ⓐ ✕	Ⓐ2 🍷M
0	**Cardiff** Central **134** § d.	Ⓐ	0030	0435	0512	0538	0635	0648	0750	0849	0923	0954	...	1052	1125	1154	1249	1322	1357	1449	1523	1549	1649	1714	1749
19	Newport **134** § d.		0049	0454	0531	0556	0649	0702	0804	0903	0936	1008	...	1106	1139	1208	1303	1337	1411	1503	1537	1602	1703	1728	1803
30	Cwmbrân d.		0100	0505	0542	0606	0659	0713	0814	0914	0947	1018	...	1116	1149	1218	1313	1347	1421	1513	1547	1613	1713	1738	1813
35	Pontypool & New Inn d.		0106	0511	0548	0612	|	0720	0820	|	0952	|	...	|	1155	|	|	1353	|	|	1553	1618	|	1744	1818
50	Abergavenny d.		0118	0521	0557	0621	0713	0730	0829	0927	1002	1031	...	1130	1205	1231	1327	1402	1435	1527	1602	1627	1727	1754	1828
89	**Hereford** d.		0151	0547	0625	0650	0739	0756	0856	0953	1027	1057	...	1156	1231	1257	1353	1429	1500	1553	1628	1653	1753	1820	1853
109	Leominster d.		...	0600	0638	0703	0752	|	0909	1006	|	1110	...	1209	|	1310	1406	|	1513	1607	1641	1706	1806	|	1906
127	Ludlow d.		...	0612	0649	0714	0803	0818	0920	1018	1048	1121	...	1220	1253	1321	1417	1451	1524	1619	1652	1717	1817	|	1917
138	Craven Arms **146** d.		...	0620	0657	0722	0812	|	0929	1026	1057	1129	...	|	|	1329	|	1500	1533	|	1701	1725	|	|	1926
150	Church Stretton **146** d.		...	0630	0706	0731	0821	|	0939	1036	1106	1138	...	|	|	1338	|	1509	1542	|	1710	1734	|	|	1935
170	**Shrewsbury** **146** a.		...	0647	0721	0746	0838	0847	0954	1052	1124	1153	...	1250	1323	1353	1447	1524	1557	1648	1724	1749	1846	1909	1950
170	**Shrewsbury** ¶ d.		...	0647	0728	0749	0844	0850	0954	1053	1130	1154	...	1251	1330	1354	1447	1528	1557	1652	1728	1750	1848	1909	1950
200	Whitchurch ¶ d.		...	0710	|	0809	0906	|	|	|	|	|	...	|	|	|	1506	|	|	|	|	1809	1907	|	|
223	**Crewe** ¶ a.		...	0730	|	0828	0928	|	1028	1129	|	1228	...	1328	|	1427	1528	|	1628	1729	|	1828	1928	|	2028
	Chester **145 160** a.		...	|	0821	|	|	0947	|	|	1226	|	...	|	1426	|	|	1623	|	|	1822	|	|	1957	|
	Holyhead **145 160** a.		...	|	1009	|	|	1118	|	|	1418	|	...	|	1619	|	|	1822	|	|	2020	|	|	2141	|
263	Stockport a.		...	0800	...	0901	1001	...	1101	1201	...	1301	...	1401	...	1501	1601	...	1701	1801	...	1901	2001	...	2101
273	**Manchester** Piccadilly a.		...	0813	...	0915	1015	...	1115	1215	...	1315	...	1415	...	1515	1615	...	1715	1814	...	1915	2015	...	2115

C – From Carmarthen (Table **136**).
M – From Milford Haven (Table **136**).
S – From Swansea (Table **136**).
V – To Birmingham International (Table **145**).

§ – See also Tables **115** and **117**.
¶ – Additional journeys Shrewsbury - Whitchurch - Crewe and v.v. (all 2nd class only):
From Shrewsbury at 0530⚒, 0819⚒, 0825⑦, 1019⚒, 1024⑦, 1219⚒, 1424⑦, 1419⚒, 1614Ⓐ, 1619⑥, 1624⑦, 1824⑦, 1825Ⓐ, 1830⑥, 2024⑦, 2032⚒.
From Crewe at 0519⚒, 0640Ⓐ**V**, 0719⑥**V**, 0734Ⓐ**V**, 0919, 1119⚒, 1125⑦, 1319, 1519, 1719, 1919⑦, 1931⚒, 2128⚒, 2145⑦.

AW CARDIFF - HEREFORD - CREWE - MANCHESTER 149

	Ⓐ2 🍷L	Ⓐ ✕	Ⓐ 2	Ⓐ 2	Ⓐ 2	Ⓐ 2
Cardiff Central . **134** § d.	1825	1855	1941	2005	2115	2155
Newport .... **134** § d.	1838	1909	1955	2020	2129	2213
Cwmbrân .... d.	1849	1920	2005	2030	2140	2224
Pontypool & New Inn . d.	1854	|	2010	2035	|	2230
Abergavenny .... d.	1904	1933	2020	2045	2153	2240
Hereford .... d.	1929	1959	2046	2111	2220	2308
Leominster................. d.	|	2012	2059	2124	2233	2321
Ludlow........................ d.	1950	2024	2110	2135	2244	2332
Craven Arms ....**146** d.	1959	|	2118	2143	2253	2342
Church Stretton ...**146** d.	2008	|	2127	2152	2302	2351
Shrewsbury........**146** a.	2026	2053	2142	2207	2317	0008
Shrewsbury..... **145** ¶ d.	2027	2058	2146	2208	2317	0013
Whitchurch .... ¶ d.	|	|	|	2234	2343	0039
Crewe .... ¶ a.	2100	2136	|	2256	0005	0104
Chester **145 160**..... a.	2126	|	2241	|	0027	...
Holyhead **145 160** .. a.	...	|	0048r	|	...	...
Stockport .... a.	...	2208	...	2324	...	...
Manchester Piccadilly a.	...	2227	...	2341	...	...

⑥

	⑥ 🍷	⑥ 2	⑥ 2	⑥ 🍷S	⑥ 🍷2	⑥2 🍷C	⑥ ✕	⑥ 🍷2	⑥2 🍷M	⑥ 🍷	⑥ 🍷2	⑥2 🍷M	⑥ ✕	⑥ 🍷2	⑥2 🍷M	⑥ ✕	⑥ 🍷2	⑥2 🍷M	⑥ ✕
Cardiff Central . **134** § d.	0435	0520	0537	0635	0722	0752	0849	0922	0953	1052	1123	1154	1252	1322	1355	1453	1522	1549	1650
Newport .... **134** § d.	0449	0533	0552	0649	0737	0806	0904	0937	1007	1106	1137	1207	1306	1336	1409	1507	1536	1603	1704
Cwmbrân .... d.	0459	0544	0602	0701	0747	0816	0914	0947	1017	1116	1147	1218	1317	1346	1419	1517	1546	1613	1715
Pontypool & New Inn . d.	0505	0544	0608	|	0753	0821	|	0952	|	|	1153	|	|	1352	|	|	1552	1618	1721
Abergavenny .... d.	0515	0559	0617	0716	0802	0831	0928	1002	1030	1130	1202	1231	1330	1401	1432	1531	1601	1628	1731
Hereford .... d.	0542	0624	0647d	0742	0830	0856	0954	1027	1056	1156	1228	1256	1356	1427	1458	1557	1627	1653	1757
Leominster................. d.	0555	0637	0700	0755	|	0909	1007	1041	1109	1209	|	1309	1409	|	1511	1610	1640	1716	1810
Ludlow........................ d.	0607	0648	0711	0807	0851	0920	1018	1052	1120	1220	1249	1320	1421	1448	1522	1621	1651	1717	1821
Craven Arms ....**146** d.	0616	0657	0721	0816	0859	0929	1027	1100	1129	|	1257	1329	|	1456	1531	|	1659	1726	|
Church Stretton ...**146** d.	0626	0706	0730	0826	0908	0939	1036	1109	1138	|	1307	1338	|	1505	1541	|	1708	1735	|
Shrewsbury........**146** a.	0642	0721	0748	0843	0924	0953	1053	1124	1153	1250	1322	1353	1450	1525	1556	1650	1722	1750	1850
Shrewsbury..... **145** ¶ d.	0645	0726	0749	0846	0927	0954	1054	1128	1153	1251	1327	1353	1452	1528	1557	1652	1729	1750	1852
Whitchurch .... ¶ d.	0708	|	0809	0905	|	|	|	|	1210	|	|	1410	|	|	|	|	|	1809	|
Crewe .... ¶ a.	0729	|	0828	0928	|	1028	1130	|	1228	1328	|	1428	1529	|	1628	1729	|	1828	1929
Chester **145 160**..... a.	|	0820	|	|	1020	|	|	1223	|	|	1424	|	|	1622	|	|	1822	|	|
Holyhead **145 160** .. a.	|	1019	|	|	1212	|	|	1418	|	|	1621	|	|	1821	|	|	2024	|	|
Stockport .... a.	0800	...	0901	1000	...	1101	1201	...	1301	1401	...	1501	1601	...	1701	1801	...	1901	2001
Manchester Piccadilly a.	0815	...	0915	1015	...	1115	1215	...	1315	1415	...	1515	1615	...	1715	1815	...	1915	2016

	⑥ 🍷2	⑥2 🍷M	⑥ 🍷	⑥ 2J	⑥ 2	⑥ 2	⑥ 2M
Cardiff Central . **134** § d.	1723	1756	1855	1941	2005	2055	2152
Newport .... **134** § d.	1736	1809	1909	1955	2020	2109	2206
Cwmbrân .... d.	1747	1820	1920	2005	2031	2121	2216
Pontypool & New Inn . d.	1752	1825	|	2011	2036	|	2222
Abergavenny .... d.	1802	1835	1934	2020	2046	2134	2231
Hereford .... d.	1827	1900	2000	2046	2112	2200	2257
Leominster................. d.	|	1913	2013	2059	2125	2214	▬
Ludlow........................ d.	1848	1924	2025	2110	2136	2225	...
Craven Arms ....**146** d.	1857	|	|	2118	2144	2233	...
Church Stretton ...**146** d.	1906	|	|	2127	2153	2242	⑥
Shrewsbury........**146** a.	1921	1951	2056	2143	2208	2257	N
Shrewsbury..... **145** ¶ d.	1928	1952	2058	2143	2209	2306	2335
Whitchurch .... ¶ d.	|	2009	|	|	2235	2332	2359
Crewe .... ¶ a.	|	2028	2135	|	2257	2354	0020
Chester **145 160**..... a.	2024	|	|	2236	|	0023	...
Holyhead **145 160** .. a.	2224	|	|	...	|	...	...
Stockport .... a.	...	2101	2208	...	2326	...	...
Manchester Piccadilly a.	...	2115	2223	...	2340	...	...

⑦

	⑦ 2	⑦ 2	⑦ 2S	⑦2 🍷S	⑦2 🍷S	⑦2 🍷C	⑦ 🍷2	⑦2 🍷S	⑦2 🍷M	⑦ 🍷2	⑦2 🍷S	⑦2 🍷M	⑦2 🍷S	⑦2 🍷M	⑦ 🍷S	⑦ 2K	⑦ 2	⑦ 2C
Cardiff Central . **134** § d.	...	0830	0935	1034	1140	1236	1329	1351	1454	1522	1600	1640	1755	1840	1940	...	2107	2319
Newport .... **134** § d.	...	0852	0953	1049	1154	1250	1343	1405	1510	1535	1614	1655	1810	1855	1956	...	2124	2337
Cwmbrân .... d.	...	0903	1004	1103	1206	1306	1353	1415	1524	1546	1628	1709	1824	1909	2010	...	2134	2348
Pontypool & New Inn . d.	...	0909	1010	1109	1212	1311	1359	|	|	1551	|	1715	1830	|	2016	...	2140	2354
Abergavenny .... d.	...	0918	1021	1119	1223	1321	1408	1428	1537	1601	1641	1725	1839	1922	2026	...	2149	0004
Hereford .... d.	...	0947	1048	1149	1250	1349	1435	1454	1604	1626	1707	1753	1906	1950	2054	...	2219	0035
Leominster................. d.	...	1001	1102	1202	1304	1403	1448	1507	|	1639	|	1806	1919	2004	2108	...	2232	▬
Ludlow........................ d.	...	1012	1113	1213	1316	1414	1459	1518	1626	1650	1729	1817	1931	2015	2119	...	2243	...
Craven Arms ....**146** d.	...	1020	|	1223	|	1423	1508	|	|	1659	|	1826	|	2023	2129	...	2252	...
Church Stretton ...**146** d.	...	1029	|	1232	|	1433	|	|	|	1708	|	1835	|	2032	2138	...	2301	⑦
Shrewsbury........**146** a.	...	1046	1145	1249	1343	1449	1529	1553	1654	1722	1755	1850	1959	2047	2155	...	2317	2K
Shrewsbury..... **145** ¶ d.	0955	1048	1147	1252	1347	1455	1533	1554	1656	1732	1756	1854	2003	2051	...	2235	2319	2348
Whitchurch .... ¶ d.	|	|	|	|	|	|	|	|	|	|	|	|	|	|	...	|	2345	|
Crewe .... ¶ a.	1026	1123	1224	1328	1419	1530	|	1627	1728	|	1829	1926	2035	2127	...	2306	0007	0020
Chester **145 160**..... a.	|	|	*1319*t	|	*1519*t	|	1629	*1727*t	|	1826	*1925*t	|	*2122*t	|	...	2333	0034	0044
Holyhead **145 160** .. a.	|	|	|	|	|	|	1838	|	|	2019	*2129*t	|	|	|	...	...	...	...
Stockport .... a.	1100	|	1300	1400	1503	1602	...	1701	1802	...	1901	2001	2102	2204	...	...	...	...
Manchester Piccadilly a.	1117	1218	1312	1416	1515	1614	...	1717	1816	...	1915	2015	2115	2218	...	...	...	...

Ⓐ

	Ⓐ 2	Ⓐ 🍷	Ⓐ 2	Ⓐ2 🍷C	Ⓐ 2	Ⓐ ✕	Ⓐ ✕	Ⓐ2 🍷C	Ⓐ 2	Ⓐ ✕	Ⓐ2 🍷C	Ⓐ ✕	Ⓐ ✕	Ⓐ2 🍷C	Ⓐ2 🍷L	Ⓐ ✕	Ⓐ ✕	Ⓐ2 🍷T	Ⓐ ✕	Ⓐ2 🍷C	Ⓐ 🍷2	Ⓐ2 🍷S	Ⓐ 🍷2	Ⓐ ✕	Ⓐ ✕
Manchester Piccadilly d.	...	...	...	...	...	0628	...	0730	...	0830	0930	...	1030	1130	...	1230	...	1330	1430	1530	...	1630	1731	...	1830
Stockport .... d.	...	...	...	...	...	0637	...	0739	...	0839	0939	...	1040	1139	...	1240	...	1339	1440	1539	...	1640	1739	...	1840
Holyhead **145 160** .. d.	...	...	...	...	0425	|	0533	|	0625	|	|	0805	|	|	1040	|	1133	|	|	|	1433	|	|	1634	|
Chester **145 160**..... d.	...	...	...	...	0620	|	0716	|	0820	|	|	1020	|	|	1221	|	1316	|	|	|	1623	|	|	1821	|
Crewe .... ¶ d.	...	0454	...	0557	|	0709	|	0810	|	0910	1010	|	1110	1210	|	1310	|	1410	1510	1610	|	1710	1810	|	1910
Whitchurch .... ¶ d.	...	|	...	0618	|	|	|	|	|	|	|	|	|	|	|	|	|	1429	|	1629	|	|	1829	|	|
Shrewsbury..... **145** ¶ a.	...	0528	...	0645	0713	0746	0802	0841	0912	0943	1040	1112	1143	1241	1314	1343	1413	1450	1543	1650	1715	1743	1849	1919	1943
Shrewsbury........**146** d.	...	0537	0610	0647	0713	0746	0805	0844	0913	0944	1040	1113	1144	1242	1314	1346	1418	1451	1544	1651	1716	1744	1853	1925	1944
Church Stretton ...**146** d.	...	0552	0626	0703	0728	0802	|	0859	0928	|	1055	1128	|	1257	1329	|	|	1506	|	1706	1731	|	1908	1941	1959
Craven Arms ....**146** d.	...	0601	0634	0711	0736	0812	|	0907	0936	|	|	1136	|	|	1337	|	|	1514	|	1714	1739	|	1916	1950	2009
Ludlow........................ d.	...	0610	0643	0720	0744	0821	0837	0914	0943	1012	1109	1143	1212	1311	1345	1414	|	1521	1612	1721	1746	1813	1923	1959	2019
Leominster................. d.	...	0621	0654	0731	0754	0832	|	0925	0954	1023	1120	1154	|	1321	1355	|	|	1532	1623	1732	1757	1824	1934	|	2030
Hereford .... d.	0529	0642d	0710	0747	0811	0849	0902	0945	1011	1039	1145a	1211	1239	1338	1413	1442d	1512d	1551	1639	1751	1816	1840	1951	2024	2047
Abergavenny .... d.	0553	0704	0734	0812	0834	0911	|	1008	1034	1102	1208	1234	1302	1401	1436	1505	1534	1614	1702	1814	1840	1903	2014	2047	2110
Pontypool & New Inn . d.	0604	0714	0745	0823	0844	0921	|	1017	1044	|	1219	|	|	1411	|	|	|	1624	1712	1824	|	1913	2024	|	2120
Cwmbrân .... d.	0609	0720	0750	0828	0849	0926	|	1022	1049	1115	1225	1247	1316	1416	|	1518	1547	1629	1717	1829	1853	1919	2029	2101	2126
Newport .... **134** § a.	0621	0732	0801	0840	0900	0938	0943	1033	1101	1128	1236	1258	1328	1430	1457	1529	1558	1640	1729	1840	1906	1931	2041	2114	2138
Cardiff Central . **134** § a.	0635	0747	0818	0858	0917	0956	0959	1048	1116	1153	1252	1314	1342	1445	1511	1544	1618	1703	1743	1857	1925	1945	2101	2128	2155

	Ⓐ 2	Ⓐ 2	Ⓐ 2	Ⓐ 2	Ⓐ 2
Manchester Piccadilly d.	1930	2030	2130	...	2232j
Stockport .... d.	1939	2039	2319	...	2241j
Holyhead **145 160** .. d.	|	|	|	...	|
Chester **145 160**..... d.	|	|	|	...	|
Crewe .... ¶ d.	2010	2120	2210	...	2314
Whitchurch .... ¶ d.	2029	|	2231	...	2335
Shrewsbury..... **145** ¶ a.	2049	2155	2258	...	0001
Shrewsbury........**146** d.	2052	2156	...	2309	...
Church Stretton ...**146** d.	2107	2211	...	2325	...
Craven Arms ....**146** d.	2115	2219	...	2333	...
Ludlow........................ d.	2122	2226	...	2342	...
Leominster................. d.	2133	2237	...	2353	...
Hereford .... d.	2154d	2311c	...	0010	...
Abergavenny .... d.	2217	2334	...	0034	...
Pontypool & New Inn . d.	|	2344	...	0044	...
Cwmbrân .... d.	2229	2349	...	0049	...
Newport .... **134** § a.	2244	0002	...	0102	...
Cardiff Central . **134** § a.	2306f	0022b	...	0123	...

⑥

	⑥ 2	⑥ 2	⑥ 🍷	⑥2 🍷C	⑥ 2	⑥ 🍷	⑥2 🍷C	⑥ 2	⑥ ✕	⑥2 🍷C	⑥ 🍷2	⑥ 🍷	⑥2 🍷C	⑥ 🍷2	⑥ ✕	⑥2 🍷P	⑥ 🍷2	⑥ ✕	⑥2 🍷P	⑥ 🍷2
Manchester Piccadilly d.	...	...	...	...	...	0627	0730	...	0830	0930	...	1030	1130	...	1230	1330	...	1430	1530	...
Stockport .... d.	...	...	...	...	...	0637	0739	...	0839	0939	...	1039	1139	...	1240	1339	...	1440	1539	...
Holyhead **145 160** .. d.	...	...	...	...	0425	|	|	0631	|	|	0819	|	|	1030	|	|	1232	|	|	1425
Chester **145 160**..... d.	...	...	...	...	0612	|	|	0820	|	|	1020	|	|	1221	|	|	1415	|	|	1614
Crewe .... ¶ d.	...	...	0454	0555	|	0709	0810	|	0910	1010	|	1110	1210	|	1310	1410	|	1510	1610	|
Whitchurch .... ¶ d.	...	...	|	0616	|	|	|	|	|	|	|	|	|	|	|	1429	|	|	1629	|
Shrewsbury..... **145** ¶ a.	...	...	0528	0643	0710	0747	0840	0913	0944	1040	1113	1143	1241	1313	1342	1448	1507	1544	1650	1707
Shrewsbury........**146** d.	...	...	0536	0645	0716	0749	0844	0914	0945	1040	1116	1146	1244	1316	1344	1452	1515	1546	1652	1711
Church Stretton ...**146** d.	...	...	0554	0700	0731	|	0859	0929	|	1055	|	|	1259	1331	|	1507	|	|	1707	1726
Craven Arms ....**146** d.	...	...	0603	0708	0739	|	0907	0937	|	1103	|	|	1307	1339	|	1515	|	|	1715	1734
Ludlow........................ d.	...	...	0612	0715	0747	0818	0915	0944	1013	1111	1142	1214	1314	1346	1412	1523	1541	1614	1722	1742
Leominster................. d.	...	...	0623	0726	0758	0829	0927	0955	|	1121	1153	|	1325	1357	|	1533	|	1625	1733	1752
Hereford .... d.	0010	0519	0648z	0744	0815	0848	0946	1012	1037	1139	1210	1238	1342	1416	1435	1549	1606	1646	1750	1809
Abergavenny .... d.	0034	0543	0710	0807	0838	0911	1010	1035	1100	1204	1233	1302	1405	1439	1457	1612	1629	1709	1813	1832
Pontypool & New Inn . d.	0044	0554	0720	0817	0848	0922	1021	1044	|	|	1243	|	1415	|	|	|	1639	|	1823	|
Cwmbrân .... d.	0049	0559	0725	0823	0853	0929	1027	1049	1113	1216	1248	1315	1421	1453	1510	1625	1644	1723	1828	1845
Newport .... **134** § a.	0102	0610	0737	0836	0905	0941	1039	1100	1129	1229	1259	1329	1436	1505	1521	1637	1655	1739	1841	1856
Cardiff Central . **134** § a.	0123	0626	0751	0858	0921	0959	1053	1116	1150	1255	1315	1349	1452	1521	1537	1657	1710	1755	1858	1912

	⑥2 🍷S	⑥ 🍷2	⑥ 🍷2	⑥ 🍷	⑥ 2	⑥ 2	⑥ 2	⑥ 2
Manchester Piccadilly d.	1630	1730	...	1830	1930	2030	2130	2233
Stockport .... d.	1640	1739	...	1840	1939	2039	2139	2242
Holyhead **145 160** .. d.	|	|	1648	|	|	|	|	|
Chester **145 160**..... d.	|	|	1833	|	|	|	|	|
Crewe .... ¶ d.	1710	1810	|	1910	2010	2110	2210	2314
Whitchurch .... ¶ d.	|	1829	|	|	2029	2131	2231	2335
Shrewsbury..... **145** ¶ a.	1743	1849	1926	1947	2050	2159	2258	0005
Shrewsbury........**146** d.	1744	1854	1927	1950	2053	2201	...	▬
Church Stretton ...**146** d.	|	1909	1942	2005	2108	2218	...	...
Craven Arms ....**146** d.	|	1917	1950	2014	2116	2226	...	...
Ludlow........................ d.	1812	1924	1957	2023	2123	2233	...	⑥
Leominster................. d.	1823	1935	|	2034	2134	2244	...	2
Hereford .... d.	1839	1952	2027	2050	2153	2301	...	2315
Abergavenny .... d.	1902	2015	2050	2113	2217	2324	...	2338
Pontypool & New Inn . d.	1912	2025	|	2122	|	2334	...	|
Cwmbrân .... d.	1917	2030	2102	2128	2230	2339	...	2350
Newport .... **134** § a.	1929	2041	2114	2139	2244	2350	...	0002
Cardiff Central . **134** § a.	1957	2100	2130	2153	2310	0014	...	0026

⑦

	⑦ 🚌	⑦ 🍷F	⑦2 🍷S	⑦2 🍷M	⑦2 🍷S	⑦ 🍷2	⑦2 🍷M	⑦2 🍷S	⑦2 🍷M	⑦2 🍷S	⑦2 🍷S	⑦2 🍷S	⑦ 🍷2	⑦ 2C	⑦ 2S	⑦ 2	⑦ 2
Manchester Piccadilly d.	...	...	0930	1030	1129	...	1231	1330	1430	1530	1630	1730	...	1830	1930	2030	...
Stockport .... d.	...	...	0941	1039	1139	...	1241	1340	1440	1540	1640	1740	...	1840	1940	2040	...
Holyhead **145 160** .. d.	...	...	|	|	|	1020	|	|	|	|	|	|	1625	|	|	|	...
Chester **145 160**..... d.	...	...	*0920*t	|	*1132*t	1229	|	*1334*t	|	*1535*t	|	*1731*t	1826	|	*1939*t	|	2302
Crewe .... ¶ d.	...	...	1014	1110	1210	|	1310	1410	1510	1610	1713	1810	|	1913	2010	2110	2330
Whitchurch .... ¶ d.	...	...	1033	|	|	|	|	|	|	|	|	|	|	|	|	2130	2351
Shrewsbury..... **145** ¶ a.	...	...	1054	1141	1240	1322	1341	1445	1546	1643	1743	1839	1920	1946	2045	2156	0017
Shrewsbury........**146** d.	0750	...	1105	1146	1244	1325	1344	1448	1548	1645	1746	1843	1922	1946	2049	2204	...
Church Stretton ...**146** d.	0815	...	1121	|	|	1340	|	1504	|	1700	|	1858	1938	|	2105	2220	...
Craven Arms ....**146** d.	0835	...	1129	|	|	1348	|	1512	|	1708	|	1906	1946	|	2113	2228	...
Ludlow........................ d.	0855	...	1138	1214	1311	1356	1411	1521	1618	1716	1814	1914	1954	2014	2122	2236	...
Leominster................. d.	0920	...	1149	1224	1323	1407	1423	1532	1629	1727	1824	|	2004	2024	2133	2246	...
Hereford .... d.	0950	1006	1208	1242	1342	1423	1447	1548	1647	1743	1843	1940	2022	2041	2149	2305	...
Abergavenny .... d.	...	1030	1231	1306	1405	1446	1510	1612	1711	1806	1906	2004	2045	2104	2213	2328	...
Pontypool & New Inn . d.	...	1040	1241	1316	1415	1456	|	1623	|	1816	1916	|	2056	|	2224	2338	...
Cwmbrân .... d.	...	1045	1247	1322	1420	1501	1523	1628	1725	1821	1922	2016	2101	2117	2229	2343	...
Newport .... **134** § a.	...	1057	1258	1333	1432	1512	1537	1639	1739	1835	1936	2028	2113	2127	2239	2356	...
Cardiff Central . **134** § a.	...	1111	1315	1351	1448	1528	1555	1657	1755	1853	1951	2046	2130	2144	2257	0017	...

C – To/from Carmarthen (Table **136**).
F – To Fishguard Harbour (Table **136**).
J – To Llandudno Junction (Table **160**).
K – From/to Birmingham International (Table **145**).
L – To/from Llanelli (Table **136**).
M – To/from Milford Haven (Table **136**).

N – From Birmingham New St (Table **145**).
P – To Pembroke Dock (Table **136**).
S – From Swansea (Table **136**).
T – To Tenby (Table **136**).

a – Arrives 1136.
b – Arrives 0015 on ⑥ mornings.
c – Arrives 2253.
d – Arrives 5–7 minutes earlier.
f – Arrives 2255 on ⑤.
j – ① only.

r – Arrives 0043 on ⑥.
t – Change at Shrewsbury.
z – Arrives 0637.

§ – See also Tables **115** and **117**.
¶ – See note ¶ on page 120 for additional journeys Shrewsbury - Whitchurch - Crewe and v.v.

150 LONDON - BIRMINGHAM - WOLVERHAMPTON

Most trains convey 🍷 VT

Certain services continue to / from destinations in Table **154**. For slower trains via Northampton see Table **141**.

km			⚒	⚒	⚒	⚒	⚒	⚒	⚒	⚒	⚒		⚒	⚒	Ⓐ	⑥	Ⓐ	⑥	⚒	⚒	⑥	⚒	⚒	Ⓐ	⑥
0	**London** Euston **143 152/3 160** d.	⚒	0616	0710	0716	0810	0816	0840	0910	0916	0940	and	1416	1440	1516	1516	1536	1540	1616	1640	1710	1716	1740	1810	1810
28	Watford Junction △ d.		0631	|	0731	|	0831	|	|	0931	|	at the	1431	|	|	1531	1551	|	1631	|	|	1731	|	|	|
80	Milton Keynes **143 152/3 160** d.		0652	|	0752	|	0852	|	|	0952	|	same	1452	|	1548	1552	|	|	1652	|	|	1752	|	|	|
133	Rugby d.		0715	|	0815	|	0915	|	|	1015	|	minutes	1515	|	1612	1615	|	|	1715	|	|	1815	|	|	|
151	Coventry **114** a.		0725	0804	0825	0904	0925	0934	1004	1025	1034	past	1525	1534	1621	1625	1634	1634	1725	1734	1804	1825	1834	1904	1904
168	Birmingham Int ✈ **114** a.		0736	0815	0836	0915	0936	0945	1015	1036	1045	each	1536	1545	1636	1636	1645	1645	1736	1745	1815	1836	1845	1915	1915
182	**Birmingham** New St. **114 119** a.		0748t	0827	0848t	0927	0948	0956r	1027	1048t	1056	hour	1548t	1556	1647t	1648	1657	1656	1748t	1757	1827	1848	1856r	1927	1926r
190	Sandwell & Dudley a.		0815	...	0915	...	...	1015	...	1115	...	until	1615	...	1715	1715	...	...	1815	...	...	...	1915	...	1946
202	**Wolverhampton** **119** a.		0829	...	0929	...	...	1029	...	1129	...		1629	...	1729	1729	...	...	1829	...	...	...	1929	...	1959

	⚒S	⚒	⚒	⚒	⑥	Ⓐ	Ⓐ	⑥		Ⓐ	⑥	Ⓐ	⑥	Ⓐ	⑥	Ⓐ	①–④	⑤	①–④	⑤		⑦	⑦	⑦	⑦	⑦
London Euston **143 152/3 160** d.	1816	1840	1910	1916	1934	1940	2006	2025	...	2040	2104	2106	2122	2136	2142	2230	2300	2300	2330	2330	⑦	0748	0850	0952	1049	1152
Watford Junction △ d.	1831	|	|	1931	|	|	|	2041	...	|	|	|	2139	2151	2158	2246	2318	2318	|	|		0803	0906	1007	1107	1207
Milton Keynes **143 152/3 160** d.	1852	|	|	1952	|	|	2037	2114	...	|	2151	2137	2218	2211u	2232	2329	2358	2358	0029	0026		0845	0939	1040	1139	1231
Rugby d.	1915	|	|	2015	|	|	|	2135	...	|	2215	|	2241	2233	2258	2359	0031	0052	0059	0109		0923	1014	1115	1215	1254
Coventry **114** a.	1925	1934	2004	2025	2032	2034	2104	2146	...	2134	2225	2204	2251	2242	2307	0009	0040	0101	0109	0119		0933	1024	1125	1225	1303
Birmingham Int ✈ **114** a.	1936	1945	2015	2036	2045	2045	2115	2156	...	2145	2236	2215	2301	2253	2318	0020	0050	0111	0120	0129		0943	1034	1136	1236	1314
Birmingham New St **114 119** a.	1948f	1956r	2027r	2048	2056r	2056r	2127r	2209r	...	2156r	2247	2227r	2315	2305	2329c	0033	0102	0123	0132	0142		0955r	1046t	1147t	1247t	1325
Sandwell & Dudley a.	|	2016	2046	...	2115	2116	2146	2227	...	2215	2258	2246	2328	2316	2255	|	|	|	|	|		1015	1116	1215	1315	...
Wolverhampton **119** a.	2013	2029	2059	...	2129	2129	2159	2240	...	2229	2311	2258	2341	2328	0009	0103	0130	0153	0202	0211		1029	1130	1229	1329	...

	⑦	⑦	⑦	⑦	⑦	⑦	⑦	⑦	⑦	⑦	⑦		⑦	⑦	⑦	⑦	⑦S	⑦	⑦	⑦	⑦	⑦	⑦	⑦	⑦	⑦
London Euston **143 152/3 160** d.	1239	1309	1315	1339	1415	1439	1509	1515	1539	1609	1615	...	1639	1715	1739	1809	1815	1839	1909	1915	2009	2036	2057	2153	2225	2324
Watford Junction △ d.	|	|	1330	|	1430	|	|	1530	|	|	1630	...	|	1730	|	|	1830	|	|	1930	|	|	2112	2212	2241	2339
Milton Keynes **143 152/3 160** d.	|	|	1352	|	1452	|	|	1552	|	|	1652	...	|	1752	|	|	1852	|	|	1952	|	2114	2144	2247	2314	0013
Rugby d.	|	|	1415	|	1515	|	|	1615	|	|	1715	...	|	1815	|	|	1915	|	|	2015	|	2138	|	2323	2348	0048s
Coventry **114** a.	1334	1404	1425	1434	1525	1534	1604	1625	1634	1704	1725	...	1734	1825	1834	1904	1925	1934	2004	2025	2104	2147	2215	2333	2358	0059s
Birmingham Int ✈ **114** a.	1345	1415	1436	1445	1536	1545	1615	1636	1645	1715	1736	...	1745	1836	1845	1915	1936	1945	2015	2036	2115	2158	2226	2343	0008	0112s
Birmingham New St **114 119** a.	1356r	1427	1448t	1456	1548	1556r	1627	1648	1656r	1727	1748t	...	1756	1848	1856r	1927	1948f	1956r	2027r	2047	2128f	2209f	2238	2355	0022	0123s
Sandwell & Dudley a.	1415	...	1515	...	...	1615	...	...	1715	...	1815	...	...	...	1915	...	|	2015	2046	...	2146	2226	2249	|	|	|
Wolverhampton **119** a.	1429	...	1529	...	...	1629	...	...	1729	...	1829	...	...	...	1929	...	2013	2028	2059	...	2158	2240	2302	0016	0042	0143

		Ⓐ	Ⓐ	⑥	Ⓐ	⑥	⚒	⚒	⚒	Ⓐ	⑥	⚒M	⚒T	⚒S	⚒	⑥	Ⓐ	⑥	Ⓐ	⚒	⚒	⚒	⚒	⚒	
Wolverhampton **119** d.	⚒	0500	...	...	0543	0543	0605	0615	0645	...	...	0715	0741	0745	...	0845	0845	...	...	0945	...	...	1045	...	and
Sandwell & Dudley d.		|	...	...	0554	0554	0616	0626	0656	...	...	0725	0752	0758	...	0856	0856	...	...	0956	...	...	1056	...	at the
Birmingham New St **114 119** d.		0530a	0552	0552	0607	0607	0629	0647j	0717a	0721	0721	0747j	0817j	0821j	0847	0917h	0920j	0921	0947	1017b	1021	1047	1120j	1147	same
Birmingham Int ✈ **114** d.		0541	0603	0603	0618	0618	0640	0658	0728	0733	0733	0758	0828	0833	0858	0928	0933	0933	0958	1028	1033	1058	1133	1158	minutes
Coventry **114** d.		0552	0615	0615	0629	0629	0651	0710	0740	0745	0745	0810	0840	0845	0910	0940	0945	0945	1010	1040	1045	1110	1145	1210	past
Rugby d.		0604	|	0627	|	|	0702	|	|	0756	0756	|	|	0856	|	|	0956	0956	|	|	1056	|	1156	|	each
Milton Keynes **143 152/3 160** a.		0623	0642	0646	0656	0656	|	|	|	0815	0816	|	|	0916	|	|	1015	1016	|	|	1116	|	1215	|	hour
Watford Junction ▽ a.		0647	|	|	|	0718	0741	|	|	|	0838	|	|	0938	|	|	1038	1038	|	|	1138	|	1238	|	until
London Euston **143 152/3 160** a.		0703	0717	0721	0731	0735	0757	0809	0839	0851	0854	0906	0938	0954	1006	1038	1054	1054	1106	1138	1154	1207	1254	1306	

	⚒	⚒	Ⓐ	⑥	Ⓐ	⚒	⚒	⚒	⑥	Ⓐ	⚒	Ⓐ	⑥	Ⓐ	Ⓐ	⑥	Ⓐ	⑥	⑥	Ⓐ	Ⓐ		⑦	⑦	⑦	⑦
Wolverhampton **119** d.	1445	...	1545	1545	...	...	1645	...	1745	1745	...	1845	1845	...	1945	1945	2045	2045	2137	2145	2245	⑦	0803	0833	0903	1003
Sandwell & Dudley d.	1456	...	1556	1556	...	...	1656	...	1756	1756	...	1856	1856	...	1956	1956	2056	2056	2148	2156	2256		0814	0844	0914	1014
Birmingham New St **114 119** d.	1521j	1547	1617h	1621j	1621	1647	1720j	1747	1817h	1820j	1847	1920j	1921j	1947	2021j	2021j	2111	2117j	2203	2217h	2311		0826	0856	0930a	1030a
Birmingham Int ✈ **114** d.	1533	1558	1628	1633	1633	1658	1733	1758	1828	1833	1858	1933	1933	1958	2032	2033	2122	2128	2214	2228	2322		0837	0907	0941	1041
Coventry **114** d.	1545	1610	1640	1645	1645	1710	1745	1810	1840	1845	1910	1945	1945	2010	2045	2045	2134	2141	2226	2240	2334		0849	0919	0953	1053
Rugby d.	1556	|	|	1656	1656	|	1756	|	|	1856	|	1956	1956	|	2056	2056	|	2152	2237	2251	2345		0900	|	1004	1105
Milton Keynes **143 152/3 160** a.	1615	|	|	1715	1716	|	1815	|	|	1915	|	2015	2017	|	2115	2117	2201	2214	2259	2323	0026		0934	1002	1038	1138
Watford Junction ▽ a.	1638	|	|	1738	1738	|	1838	|	|	1938	|	2037	2050	|	2137	2150	2227	2248	2334	2355	0056		1003	1031	1110	1206
London Euston **143 152/3 160** a.	1654	1706	1738	1754	1754	1806	1854	1906	1936	1954	2006	2055	2113	2106	2153	2214	2245	2310	0001	0018	0117		1028	1056	1134	1223

	⑦	⑦	⑦	⑦S	⑦	⑦	⑦	⑦	⑦	⑦		⑦	⑦	⑦	⑦	⑦	⑦	⑦	⑦	⑦	⑦	⑦	⑦	⑦	⑦	⑦
Wolverhampton **119** d.	1103	1115	1145	1153	1215	1245	...	1345	...	1445	...	...	1545	...	...	1645	...	...	1745	...	1845	...	1945	2045	2203	2231
Sandwell & Dudley d.	1114	1126	1156	|	1226	1256	...	1356	...	1456	...	...	1556	...	...	1656	...	...	1756	...	1856	...	1956	2056	2214	2242
Birmingham New St **114 119** d.	1126	1147a	1217h	1221	1247a	1321j	1347	1421j	1447	1521j	...	1547	1617h	1621	1647	1717h	1721	1747	1821j	1847	1921j	1947	2021j	2121j	2230a	2256
Birmingham Int ✈ **114** d.	1137	1158	1228	1233	1258	1333	1358	1433	1458	1533	...	1558	1628	1633	1658	1728	1733	1758	1833	1858	1933	1958	2033	2133	2241	2308
Coventry **114** d.	1149	1210	1240	1245	1310	1345	1410	1445	1510	1545	...	1610	1640	1645	1710	1740	1745	1810	1845	1910	1945	2010	2045	2145	2253	2320
Rugby d.	1200	|	|	1256	|	1356	|	1456	|	1556	...	|	|	1656	|	|	1756	|	1856	|	1956	|	2056	2156	2304	2332
Milton Keynes **143 152/3 160** a.	1220	|	|	1316	|	1415	|	1515	|	1615	...	|	|	1716	|	|	1816	|	1915	|	2015	|	2117	2229	2336	0012s
Watford Junction ▽ a.	|	|	|	1339	|	1439	|	1539	|	1639	...	|	|	1739	|	|	1839	|	1939	|	2039	|	2148	2301	0006	0042
London Euston **143 152/3 160** a.	1257	1309	1339	1355	1407	1455	1507	1555	1607	1655	...	1707	1739	1755	1807	1839	1855	1907	1955	2007	2055	2108	2211	2322	0028	0100

M – From Manchester Piccadilly (Table **152**).
S – To / from Shrewsbury (Table **145**).
T – From Manchester Picadilly on Ⓐ (Table **152**).

a – Arrives 7–9 minutes earlier.
b – Arrives 1006.
c – Departs 2343.
f – Departs 8–9 minutes later.
h – Arrives 10–11 minutes earlier.
j – Arrives 12–14 minutes earlier.
r – Departs 10–12 minutes later.
s – Calls to set down only.
t – Departs 19–21 minutes later.
△ – Trains call here to pick up only.
▽ – Trains call here to set down only.

151 LONDON - LIVERPOOL

Most trains convey 🍷 VT

km			Ⓐ	⑥	⚒		⚒	⚒	Ⓐ	⑥	Ⓐ	⑥	Ⓐ		⑦	⑦	⑦	⑦	⑦		⑦	⑦	⑦
0	**London** Euston **142/3 150/2/4 160** d.	⚒	0636	0633	0743		1743	1843	1907	1937	1943	2012	2200	⑦	0820	0919	1019	1116	1242		1942	2039	2121
80	Milton Keynes **142/3 150/2/4 160** d.		0712	0705	0815	and	1815u	1915u	|	2015	2015	|	2240		0908	1008	1109	1210	1315	and	2015	2124	|
135	Rugby **142/3 150** d.		|	|	|		|	|	|	|	|	2120	|		|	|	1145	1233	|		|	|	|
155	Nuneaton **143** d.		|	|	|	hourly	|	|	|	|	|	|	|		|	|	|	|	|	hourly	|	|	2259
215	Stafford **143 144** d.		0805	0806	|		|	|	|	|	|	2152	2341s		1024	1124	1221	1306	|		|	2225	2325
254	Crewe **143 144 152 154 160** d.		0826	0826	0926	until	1926	2026	2045	2126	2126	2211	0011s		1043	1143	1243	1325	1326	until	2126	2245	2348
290	Runcorn **144** a.		0843	0843	0943		1943	2043	2103	2143	2143	2228	0032s		1100	1200	1300	1342	1443		2143	2302	0006
312	**Liverpool** Lime Street **144** a.		0904	0904	1004		2004	2105	2122	2204	2204	2245	0049		1118	1218	1318	1404	1504		2204	2328	0029

		⚒	⚒	Ⓐ	⑥	⚒	⚒		⚒	⚒	Ⓐ	⑥	Ⓐ		⑦	⑦	⑦	⑦	⑦		⑦	⑦	⑦
Liverpool Lime Street **144** d.	⚒	0525	0604	0643	0643	0740	0843		1743	1843	1943	1943	2051	⑦	0810	0835	0935	1043	1143		1843	1943	2043
Runcorn **144** d.		0542	0620	0702	0703	0759	0902	and	1802	1902	2002	2002	2112		0827	0854	0954	1102	1202	and	1902	2002	2102
Crewe **143 144 152 154 160** d.		0603	|	|	0723	0823	0923		1823	1923	2023	2023	2135		0849	0915	1015	1123	1223		1923	2023	2123
Stafford **143 144** d.		0622	0654	|	|	|	|	hourly	|	|	|	|	2155		|	0934	1034	|	|	hourly	|	2043	2142
Nuneaton **143** d.		|	|	|	|	|	|		|	|	|	|	2221		0929	|	|	|	|		|	|	2219
Rugby **142 143 150** d.		0653	0738	|	|	|	|	until	|	|	|	|	2234		|	|	|	|	|	until	|	|	2233
Milton Keynes **142/3 150/2/4 160** d.		0715	|	|	0827	0927	1027		1927	2027t	2127	2131	2257		|	1044	1148	1231	1327		2027	2137	2306
London Euston **142/3 150/2/4 160** a.		0753	0831f	0856	0903	1003	1104		2003	2126r	2205	2225	2356		1104	1140	1227	1306	1404		2105	2237	2355

f – Arrives 0827 on Ⓐ.
r – Arrives 2103 on Ⓐ.
s – Calls to set down only.
t – Departs 2031 on ⑥.
u – Calls to pick up only on Ⓐ.

VT Most trains convey 🍷 LONDON - MANCHESTER 152

km			Ⓐ	⑥	Ⓐ	⚒	⚒	⚒	⚒	⚒	⚒	⚒	⚒		⚒	⚒	⚒	⚒	⚒	⚒	⚒	⚒	⚒	⚒	⚒	⚒
0	**London** Euston 143/50/1/3/4 d.	⚒	...	...	0610	0629	0646	0713	0733	0753	0813	0833	0853		1513	1533	1553	1613	1633	1653	1713	1733	1753	1813	1833	1853
80	Milton Keynes 143 150/1/4 d.		...	...	0642	0700	0721			0824			0924	and at			1624			1724			1824			1924v
	Rugby 143 d.		...	...			0744v			0847v			0947				1647			1745t			1845t			1947
	Nuneaton 143 d.		...	...	0711			0810			0910			the same	1610			1710			1810			1910		
235	Stoke on Trent 119 d.		...	...	0746		0827	0844		0927	0944		1027		1644		1727	1744		1827	1844		1927	1944		2027
267	Macclesfield 119 d.		...	...	0802		0843			0943			1043	minutes			1743			1843			1943			2043
	Stafford 143 d.		...	...		0750			0850			0950				1650			1750t			1850t			1950	
	Crewe 154 143 d.		0610	0710		0810			0910			1010		past each		1710			1810			1910			2010	
	Wilmslow d.		0626	0726		0826			0926			1026				1726			1826			1926			2026	
287	Stockport 119 a.		0634	0735	0817	0835	0856	0909	0935	0956	1009	1035	1056	hour until	1709	1735	1756	1809	1835	1856	1909	1935	1956	2009	2035	2056
296	**Manchester** Piccadilly 119 a.		0643	0743	0825	0845	0905	0919	0944	1005	1019	1044	1105		1723f	1744	1805	1819	1844	1905	1919	1944	2005	2019	2044	2105

	⚒	⚒	Ⓐ	Ⓐ	⑥	Ⓐ	⑥	Ⓐ	Ⓐ		⑦	⑦	⑦	⑦	⑦	⑦	⑦	⑦	⑦		⑦	⑦	⑦	⑦	⑦	⑦
London Euston 143/50/1/3/4 d.	1913	1931	1953	2016	2018	2053	2101	2133	2203	⑦	0807	0816	0916	1016	1116	1208	1232	1252	1312		1932	1952	2012	2031	2125	2149
Milton Keynes 143 150/1/4 d.			2024	2052	2104	2124	2146	2205	2245u		0857	0901	1002	1104	1203	1240		1324		and at		2024			2218	2242
Rugby 143 d.			2047	2114		2147			2310									1347		the same		2047				2319
Nuneaton 143 d.	2010			2125	2136				2324			0946	1048	1149	1233	1310			1410	minutes			2110			2330
Stoke on Trent 119 d.	2044		2127		2210	2227		2308	2355s			1022	1125	1224	1311	1344		1427	1445	past each		2127	2144		2335	
Macclesfield 119 d.			2143		2225	2244		2324	0011s			1037	1140	1240	1327			1443		until		2143			2352	
Stafford 143 d.		2050		2150			2236										1350				2050			2150		2353s
Crewe 154 143 d.		2110		2210			2304				1020						1410				2110			2210		0016s
Wilmslow d.		2126		2226			2321				1035						1426				2126			2226		
Stockport 119 a.	2109	2135	2156	2235	2238	2258	2330	2338	0027s		1043	1050	1153	1253	1340	1410	1435	1456	1510		2134	2156	2209	2235	0004	0039s
Manchester Piccadilly 119 a.	2119	2144	2205	2245	2250	2307	2342	2348	0039		1055	1101	1204	1302	1350	1419	1444	1506	1519		2143	2205	2220	2244	0014	0048

		⚒	⚒	⚒	⑥	Ⓐ	Ⓐ	⚒	⚒	⚒	⚒	⚒	⚒	⚒	⚒	⚒		⚒	⚒	⚒	⑥	Ⓐ	⑥	Ⓐ	⑥	Ⓐ
Manchester Piccadilly 119 d.	⚒	0505	0555	0603	0611	0615	0624	0631	0655	0715	0735	0755	0815	0835	0855	0915		1655	1715	1735	1755	1815	1815	1835	1835	1855
Stockport 119 d.		0514	0604		0620	0624	0633	0641	0704	0724	0744	0804	0824	0844	0904	0924		1704	1724	1744	1804	1824	1824	1844	1844	1904
Wilmslow d.			0613	0620					0713			0813			0913		and at	1713			1813					1913
Crewe 143 154 d.		0537	0632	0640					0732			0832			0932		the same	1732			1832					1932
Stafford 143 d.		0556		0659			0724r		0752			0852			0952		minutes	1752			1852					1952
Macclesfield 119 d.					0633	0637	0647	0654		0737			0837			0937	past each		1737			1837	1837			
Stoke on Trent 119 d.					0649	0653	0704	0710		0753	0810		0853	0910		0953	until		1753	1810		1853	1853	1910	1910	
Nuneaton 143 d.		0620	0711	❖				0743			0843			0943						1843				1943	1943	
Rugby 143 d.		0633					❖			0834v			0934v			1034			1834			1934	1934			
Milton Keynes 143 150/1/4 d.		0654			0746	0746s				0855			0955			1055			1855			1955	1955			
London Euston 143/50/1/3/4 a.		0727	0813	0906	0820	0823	0938	0844	0909	0928	0941	1009	1027	1042	1110	1128		1909	1927	1941	2025	2027	2043	2041	2058	2113

	⑥	Ⓐ	⑥	Ⓐ	Ⓐ	⑥	Ⓐ		⑦	⑦	⑦	⑦	⑦	⑦	⑦	⑦	⑦	⑦		⑦	⑦	⑦	⑦	⑦	⑦	⑦
Manchester Piccadilly 119 d.	1855	1915	1915	1955	2015	2015	2115	⑦	0805	0820	0920	1020	1035	1115	1135	1155	1215	1235		1815	1835	1855	1915	1935	2021	2055
Stockport 119 d.	1904	1924	1924	2004	2024	2024	2124		0814	0829	0930	1029	1046	1126	1146	1206	1224	1244	and at	1824	1844	1904	1924	1944	2030	2104
Wilmslow d.	1913			2013					0822			1037				1213			the same			1913				
Crewe 143 154 d.	1932			2032					0841			1056				1232			minutes			1932				
Stafford 143 d.	1952			2052					0900							1252			past each			1952				
Macclesfield 119 d.		1937	1937		2037	2037	2137			0843	0943		1059	1139	1159		1237		until	1837			1937		2043	2117
Stoke on Trent 119 d.		1953	1953		2053	2053	2153			0900	0959		1117	1155	1215		1253	1310		1853	1910		1953	2010	2059	2134
Nuneaton 143 d.		2027	2026		2129								1149					1343			1943			2043		
Rugby 143 d.		2040	2039										1204				1334			1934			2034			2215
Milton Keynes 143 150/1/4 d.	2042	2101	2102		2158	2202	2303		1009		1117	1216	1226	1254			1355			1955			2055		2200	2251
London Euston 143/50/1/3/4 a.	2133	2133	2152	2214	2231	2258	2359		1059	1110	1212	1254	1300	1328	1343	1410	1428	1442		2028	2042	2114	2147	2201	2257	2342

f – Arrives 1719 on ⑥.
r – Calls after Stoke-on-Trent.
s – Calls to set down only.
t – Calls to set down only on Ⓐ.
u – Calls to pick up only.
v – Calls to pickup only on Ⓐ.
❖ – Via Birmingham New Street (Table **150**).

NT 2nd Class PRESTON - OXENHOLME - WINDERMERE 153

km			⚒	⚒	⚒		⚒	Ⓐ	⑥	⚒	⚒	⚒		⚒	⚒	⚒		⚒	⚒	⚒	⚒	⑥g 🚌	⑥h
	Manchester Airport ✈ 157 d.	⚒	...	...	...	...	...	0829	0829	...	...	1129	...	...	...	1429	...	...	...	1729	...	...	...
	Manchester Piccadilly 157 d.		...	...	...	...	...	0850	0850	...	...	1150	...	...	...	1450	...	...	...	1750	...	...	...
	Preston 154 157 d.		...	...	...	...	...	0945	0945	...	...	1245	...	...	...	1533	...	...	...	1844	...	...	...
	Lancaster 154 157 d.		0600	...	...	...	...	1002	1003	...	...	1303	...	...	...	1551	...	...	...	1902	...	...	...
0	**Oxenholme** 154 d.		0617	0730	0829	...	0930	1021	1033	1121	1239	1333	...	1439	1537	1632	...	1742	1830	1922	2018	2115	2117
4	Kendal d.		0621	0734	0833	...	0934	1025	1037	1125	1243	1338	...	1443	1541	1637	...	1746	1834	1926	2022	2125	2121
16	**Windermere** a.		0636	0749	0848	...	0949	1041	1053	1140	1258	1353	...	1455	1556	1652	...	1801	1849	1942	2037	2155	2136

	Ⓐ	⑥g 🚌	⑥h	Ⓐ		⑦c 🚌	⑦d		⑦c	⑦d	⑦	⑦	⑦		⑦	⑦	⑦	⑦		⑦	⑦	⑦	⑦
Manchester Airport ✈ 157 d.	...	...	...	...	⑦	...	...	...	...	...	...	...	...	...	...	...	1430	...	...	...	1730	...	...
Manchester Piccadilly 157 d.	...	...	...	...		...	0853	...	...	...	...	...	1154j	...	...	...	1448	...	...	...	1748	...	...
Preston 154 157 d.	...	...	...	...		...	0948	...	1030	...	...	...	1246	...	...	...	1558	...	...	...	1834	...	...
Lancaster 154 157 d.	...	...	...	...		...	1006	...	1047	...	...	...	1304	...	...	...	1616	...	...	...	1852	...	...
Oxenholme 154 d.	2120	2200	2206	2222		0945	1030t	...	1104	1117	1202	1245	1333	...	1422	1529	1632	1730	...	1833	1928	2022	2121
Kendal d.	2124	2210	2210	2226		0955	1034	...	1109	1121	1206	1249	1337	...	1426	1533	1636	1734	...	1837	1933	2026	2125
Windermere a.	2139	2240	2225	2241		1025	1049	...	1123	1135	1219	1304	1353	...	1441	1548	1652	1749	...	1852	1948	2041	2140

		⚒	⚒	⚒	Ⓐ	⑥	⚒	⚒	⚒		⚒	⚒	⚒	⚒		⚒	⚒	⚒	Ⓐ	⑥h	⑥g	⑥h	⑥g 🚌
Windermere d.	⚒	0642	0756	0852	0955	1008	1057	1147	1307	...	1358	1459	1600	1708	...	1805	1856	1948	2042	2042	2042	2140	2140
Kendal d.		0656	0810	0903	1009	1022	1111	1201	1321	...	1412	1513	1614	1722	...	1819	1910	2002	2056	2056	2056	2154	2210
Oxenholme 154 d.		0701	0815	0908	1016	1029	1116	1206	1328	...	1417	1518	1627v	1727	...	1824	1917	2007	2101	2101	2101	2159	2225
Lancaster 154 157 a.		...	...	...	1033q	1047	...	...	1344k	...	...	...	1643k	...	...	...	1934	...	...	...	2121	...	...
Preston 154 157 a.		...	...	...	1108	1105k	...	...	1407	...	...	...	1708	...	...	...	1953a	...	...	...	...	...	...
Manchester Piccadilly 157 a.		...	...	...	1158	1158	...	...	1458	...	...	...	1758	...	...	...	2058	...	...	...	...	...	...
Manchester Airport ✈ 157 a.		...	...	...	1215	1215	...	...	1515	...	...	...	1815	...	...	...	2115	...	...	...	...	...	...

	Ⓐ	⑥h		⑥g 🚌	Ⓐ		⑦c 🚌	⑦d	⑦	⑦		⑦	⑦	⑦	⑦	⑦		⑦	⑦	⑦		⑦	⑦
Windermere d.	2147	2229	...	2225	2247	⑦	1030	1053	1139	1224	...	1308	1359	1446	1555	1659	...	1800	1901	1957	...	2047	2147
Kendal d.	2201	2243	...	2255	2301		1100	1107	1153	1236	...	1322	1413	1500	1609	1713	...	1814	1916	2011	...	2101	2201
Oxenholme 154 d.	2206	2250	...	2310	2308		1115	1112	1158	1241	...	1329	1418	1505	1616	1718	...	1819	1923	2016	...	2106	2218p
Lancaster 154 157 a.	...	2305	...	2355	2324		...	...	...	...	...	1345	...	...	1633n	...	...	...	1937	...	...	...	2233
Preston 154 157 a.	...	2324	...	0035	2345		...	...	...	...	...	1407	...	...	1706	...	...	...	1958b	...	...	...	2252
Manchester Piccadilly 157 a.	...	...	...	...	...		...	...	...	...	...	1456	...	...	1756	...	...	...	2056	...	...	...	...
Manchester Airport ✈ 157 a.	...	...	...	...	...		...	...	...	...	...	1514	...	...	1818	...	...	...	2114	...	...	...	...

a – Departs 2010.
b – Departs 2013.
c – From Apr. 2.
d – Until Mar. 26.
g – From Apr. 1.
h – Until Mar. 25.
j – Manchester **Oxford Road**.
k – Departs 5–7 minutes later.
n – Departs 1648.
p – Arrives 2206.
q – Departs 1050.
t – Arrives 1022.
v – Arrives 1619.

154 LONDON, BIRMINGHAM and MANCHESTER - PRESTON - EDINBURGH and GLASGOW

TP, VT

km			Ⓐ	⑥	Ⓐ	⑥	⚒	⚒	Ⓐ	⑥g	Ⓐ	⑥		⚒	⚒	⚒	⚒	⚒	Ⓐ	⑥	Ⓐ	⑥	⚒	⚒	⚒
0	**London Euston** ... 143 150/2/3 160 d.		...	...	...	...	...	...	...	...	0531	0603	...	...	...	...	0730	0616	...	...	0830	0830	0716	...	0930
80	Milton Keynes ... 143 150/2/3 160 d.	⚒	...	...	...	...	...	...	...	...	0615	0638	...	...	...	...	|	0652	...	...	|	|	0752	...	|
	Birmingham New St ... 144 150 d.		...	...	...	...	...	0605	...	...	|	|	...	0707	...	...	|	0807	...	...	|	|	0907	...	|
	Wolverhampton ... 144 150 d.		...	...	0520	0523	...	0632	...	...	|	|	...	0732	...	...	|	0832	...	...	|	|	0932	...	|
253	Crewe ... 143 144 152 153 160 d.		...	...	0600	0559	...	0708	...	...	0727	0754	...	0808	...	...	|	0908	...	...	|	|	1008	...	|
291	Warrington Bank Quay ... d.		...	...	0618	0617	...	0727	...	...	0745	0812	...	0826	...	...	0915	0927	...	...	1015	1015	1027	...	1115
	Manchester Airport ✈ ... 156 157 d.		...	...	|	|	0603	|	0704	0704	|	|	...	|	...	0804	|	|	0904	0904	|	|	|	1004	|
	Manchester Piccadilly ... 156 157 d.		0457	0457	|	|	0622	|	0721	0721	|	|	...	|	...	0821	|	|	0921	0921	|	|	|	1021	|
	Liverpool Lime Street ... 162 d.		|	|	|	|	|	|	|	|	|	|	...	|	0812	|	|	|	|	|	|	|	|	|	|
310	Wigan North Western ... 157 162 d.		|	|	0629	0628	|	0738	|	|	0757	0823	...	0837	0842	|	0926	0938	|	|	1026	1026	1038	|	1126
334	**Preston** ... 156 157 158 162 d.		0536	0536	0644	0644	0704	0755	0800	0801	0814r	0838	...	0854	0858	0903	0941	0953	1006r	1003	1041	1041	1054	1059	1141
	Blackpool North ... 156 162 a.		|	|	|	|	|	|	|	|	|	|	...	|	|	|	|	|	|	|	|	|	1114	|	|
368	Lancaster ... 157 158 d.		0552	0552	0700	0700	0720	0810	0816	0818	0830	0853	...	0909	0914	0919	0957	1009	1022	1023	1057	1056	...	1114	1157
398	Oxenholme ... 158 d.		0606	0606	0714	0714	0734	0824	0830	0832	0844	0907	...	|	0928	0933	|	1023	1036	1037	1112	1112	...	1128	|
450	Penrith ... d.		0631	0631	0739	0739	0759	|	0856	0858	|	0933	...	0945	0953	0958	1032	|	1101	1102	|	1137	...	1153	1232
478	Carlisle ... 214 d.		0651	0648	0756	0756	0816	0903	0913	0915	0922	0949	...	1002	1010	1015	1048	1102	1118	1118	1150	1154	...	1210	1249
519	Lockerbie ... d.		0711	0707	0814	0814	0835	|	0932	0935	|	|	...	|	1029	1035	|	|	1138	1138	|	|	...	1229	|
641	**Edinburgh** Waverley ... △ a.		|	|	|	|	0938	1018	|	|	|	|	...	|	|	1137	|	1218	|	|	|	|	...	1332	|
643	**Glasgow** Central ... 214 a.		0819	0822	0916	0926	...	...	1033	1039	1039	1059	...	1116	1131	...	1201	...	1239	1241	1304	1308	...	...	1402

	⚒	Ⓐ	⑥	⚒	⚒	⚒	⑥g	Ⓐd	⚒	⚒	⚒	Ⓐ	⑥	⚒	⑥	Ⓐ	⚒	Ⓐ	⑥	⚒g	Ⓐ	⑥	⑥	Ⓐ	⚒
London Euston ... 143 150/2/3 160 d.	0840	...	...	1030	0916	...	...	...	1130	1016	...	1230	1230	1116	...	...	1330	1216	1216	...	1430	1430	1316	1316	...
Milton Keynes ... 143 150/2/3 160 d.	|	...	...	|	0952	...	...	...	|	1052	...	|	|	1152	...	...	|	1352	1352	...	|	|	1352	1352	...
Birmingham New St ... 144 150 d.	1007	...	...	|	1107	...	...	...	|	1207	...	|	|	1307	...	...	|	1407	1407	...	|	|	1507	1507	...
Wolverhampton ... 144 150 d.	1032	...	...	|	1132	...	...	...	|	1232	...	|	|	1332	...	...	|	1432	1432	...	|	|	1532	1532	...
Crewe ... 143 144 152 153 160 d.	1108	...	...	|	1208	...	...	...	|	1308	...	|	|	1408	...	...	|	1508	1508	...	|	|	1608	1608	...
Warrington Bank Quay ... d.	1127	...	...	1215	1227	...	...	...	1315	1327	...	1415	1415	1427	...	...	1515	1527	1527	...	1615	1614	1627	1627	...
Manchester Airport ✈ ... 156 157 d.	|	1104d	1104g	|	|	1204	...	...	|	|	1304	|	|	|	1404	1404	|	|	|	1504	|	|	|	|	...
Manchester Piccadilly ... 156 157 d.	|	1121d	1121g	|	|	1222	...	...	|	|	1321	|	|	|	1421	1421	|	|	|	1521	|	|	|	|	...
Liverpool Lime Street ... 162 d.	|	|	|	|	|	|	1212	1212	|	|	|	|	|	|	|	|	|	|	|	|	|	|	|	|	1612
Wigan North Western ... 157 162 d.	1138	|	|	1226	1238	|	1245	1250	1326	1338	|	1426	1426	1438	|	|	1526	1538	1538	|	1626	1626	1638	1638	1643
Preston ... 156 157 158 162 d.	1153	1203	1204g	1241	1253	1259	1308	1309	1341	1354	1405	1441	1441	1454	1503	1503	1541	1554	1554	1601	1641	1642	1654	1653	1701
Blackpool North ... 156 162 a.	|	|	|	|	|	|	|	|	|	|	|	|	|	1514	|	|	|	|	|	|	|	|	|	|	|
Lancaster ... 157 158 d.	1208	1219	1220	1257	1309	1315	1324	1326	1357	1410	1421	1457	1457	...	1519	1519	1557	1610	1610	1619	1657	1658	1710	1709	1717
Oxenholme ... 158 d.	1222	1233	1234	|	1323	1329	1340	1341	1411	|	1435	|	1511	...	1533	1533	1611	1624	1624	1633	1712	1712	1724	1723	1731
Penrith ... d.	|	1258	1259	1332	|	1355	1406	1406	|	1446	1500	1532	|	...	1558	1559	|	|	1649	1658	1738	1737	1749	1749	1756
Carlisle ... 214 d.	1301	1315	1315	1349	1402	1415	1423	1424	1449	1502	1517	1549	1549	...	1615	1616	1649	1703	1706	1715	1755	1754	1806	1806	1813
Lockerbie ... d.	|	1334	1335	|	|	1434	1441	1443	|	|	1537	|	|	...	1634	1635	|	|	|	1734	1814	|	|	|	1831
Edinburgh Waverley ... △ a.	1418	|	|	|	|	1537	|	|	|	1618	|	|	|	...	1737	1741	|	1821	1821	|	|	|	|	|	|
Glasgow Central ... 214 a.	...	1439	1439	1500	1517	...	1544	1546	1603	...	1642	1701	1700	...	...	...	1800	...	...	1839	1917	1909	1917	1923	1949e

	⚒	⚒	⚒	Ⓐ	⑥	⚒	⑥	Ⓐ		⚒	Ⓐ	⚒	Ⓐ	⑥	⚒g	⚒	Ⓐ	⑥	Ⓐd	⑥g	Ⓐ	Ⓐ	⑥	⑥	⑥
London Euston ... 143 150/2/3 160 d.	...	1530	1416	...	...	1630	1516	1516	...	...	1707	1730	1616	1616	...	1830	1740	1740	...	...	...	1930	1928	1840	...
Milton Keynes ... 143 150/2/3 160 d.	...	|	1452	...	...	|	1548	1548	...	...	|	|	1652	1652	...	|	|	|	...	...	...	|	|	|	...
Birmingham New St ... 144 150 d.	...	|	1607	...	...	|	1707	1707	...	...	|	|	1807	1807	...	|	1907	1907	...	...	...	|	|	2007	...
Wolverhampton ... 144 150 d.	...	|	1632	...	...	|	1732	1732	...	...	|	|	1832	1832	...	|	1932	1932	...	...	...	|	|	2032	...
Crewe ... 143 144 152 153 160 d.	...	|	1708	...	...	|	1808	1808	...	...	1845	|	1908	1908	...	|	2008	2008	...	...	...	|	2104	2109	...
Warrington Bank Quay ... d.	...	1715	1727	...	...	1815	1827	1827	...	...	1904	1915	1927	1927	...	2015	2027	2027	...	...	...	2116	2126	...	...
Manchester Airport ✈ ... 156 157 d.	1604	|	|	1704	1704	|	|	|	...	1804	|	|	|	|	1904	|	|	|	...	...	2004	|	|	...	2104
Manchester Piccadilly ... 156 157 d.	1621	|	|	1721	1721	|	|	|	...	1821	|	|	|	|	1921	|	|	|	...	...	2022	|	|	...	2119
Liverpool Lime Street ... 162 d.	|	|	|	|	|	|	|	|	...	|	|	|	|	|	|	|	|	|	2013	2013	|	|	|	...	|
Wigan North Western ... 157 162 d.	|	1726	1738	|	|	1826	1838	1838	...	|	1918	1926	1938	1938	|	2026	2038	2038	2044	2044	|	2128	2137	...	|
Preston ... 156 157 158 162 d.	1704	1741	1754	1803	1803	1841	1853	1853	...	1905r	1939	1941	1955	1955	2005	2041	2055	2052	2100	2058	2105	2143	2155	...	2158
Blackpool North ... 156 162 a.	|	|	|	|	|	|	|	|	...	|	2000	|	|	|	|	|	|	...	|	...	|	|	...	...	...
Lancaster ... 157 158 d.	1722	1757	1810	1819	1819	1857	1908	1909	...	1921	...	1957	2011	2011	2021	2057	2110	...	2116	...	2121	2158	...	...	...
Oxenholme ... 158 d.	1735	1812	1824	1833	1833	1911	1923	|	...	1935	...	2012	2027	2025	2035	2111	2124	...	2130	...	2135	2212	...	...	...
Penrith ... d.	1800	|	1849	1859	1859	1936	1948	1944	...	2001	...	2037	|	2050	2101	2136	|	...	...	...	2201	2238	...	...	...
Carlisle ... 214 d.	1817	1850	1905	1916	1915	1952	2005	2001	...	2018	...	2054	2105	2107	2118	2153	2203	...	...	...	2218	2254	...	...	...
Lockerbie ... d.	1837	|	|	1935d	1935	|	|	|	...	2037	...	|	|	|	2137	2211	|	...	...	...	2237	|	...	...	...
Edinburgh Waverley ... △ a.	1940	|	2024	|	|	|	|	|	...	2141	...	|	2221	2222	|	|	|	...	...	...	2341	|	...	...	...
Glasgow Central ... 214 a.	...	2001	...	2039d	2040	2104	2121	2112	...	...	...	2208	...	...	2240	2312	2317	...	...	...	...	0009	...	...	...

	Ⓐ	Ⓐ	⑥	Ⓐ	Ⓐ		⑦	⑦	⑦	⑦	⑦	⑦	⑦	⑦	⑦	⑦	⑦	⑦	⑦	⑦	⑦	⑦	⑦j	⑦	⑦
London Euston ... 143 150/2/3 160 d.	...	2033	2031	1940	2110		...	...	...	...	...	0847	0748	...	0946	0850	...	1046	0952	...	1229	1049	...	...	1329
Milton Keynes ... 143 150/2/3 160 d.	...	|	|	|	|	⑦	...	...	...	...	...	0934	0845	...	1035	0939	...	1134	1040	...	|	1139	...	...	|
Birmingham New St ... 144 150 d.	...	|	|	2107	|		...	0845	0907	...	...	|	1007	...	|	1107	...	|	1207	...	|	1307	...	...	|
Wolverhampton ... 144 150 d.	...	|	|	2137	|		...	0904	0932	...	...	|	1032	...	|	1132	...	|	1232	...	|	1332	...	...	|
Crewe ... 143 144 152 153 160 d.	...	2219	2232	2238	2302		...	0939	1008	...	...	1058	1110	...	1158	1210	...	1257	1308	...	|	1408	...	...	|
Warrington Bank Quay ... d.	...	2237	2250	...	2320		...	0956	1027	...	...	1116	1128	...	1217	1228	...	1315	1327	...	1415	1427	...	...	1515
Manchester Airport ✈ ... 156 157 d.	2104	|	|	...	|		0905j	|	|	...	1010	|	|	1110	|	|	1212j	|	|	1313	|	|	...	1410	|
Manchester Piccadilly ... 156 157 d.	2119	|	|	...	|		0924j	|	|	...	1026	|	|	1125	|	|	1226j	|	|	1327	|	|	...	1426	|
Liverpool Lime Street ... 162 d.	|	|	|	...	|		|	|	|	1012	|	|	|	|	|	|	|	|	|	|	|	|	1412	|	|
Wigan North Western ... 157 162 d.	|	2248	2304	...	2332		|	1008	1038	1044	|	1127	1139	|	1228	1239	|	1326	1338	|	1426	1438	1443	|	1526
Preston ... 156 157 158 162 d.	2208f	2300	2318	...	2346		1017a	1022	1054	1100	1108	1142	1156	1205	1243	1254	1305	1341	1354	1404	1442	1454	1459	1505	1541
Blackpool North ... 156 162 a.	|	...	...	...	...		|	...	|	|	|	|	|	|	|	|	|	|	|	|	|	|	|	|	|
Lancaster ... 157 158 d.	2226	...	...	...	...		1037	...	1110	1116	1125	1158	1211	1221	1258	1310	1321	1357	1411	1422	1458	1510	1515	1521	1558
Oxenholme ... 158 d.	...	...	...	...	...		1051	...	1125	1132	1139	1212	1226	1235	1312	1324	1335	1411	|	1436	1512	1524	1529	1535	|
Penrith ... d.	...	...	...	...	...		1117	...	1151	1158	|	1237	|	1301	1338	|	1401	1436	1446	1501	|	|	1555	1600	1635
Carlisle ... 214 d.	...	...	...	...	...		1134	...	1208	1215	1221	1254	1305	1318	1354	1403	1418	1453	1503	1517	1550	1603	1612	1617	1652
Lockerbie ... d.	...	...	...	...	...		1152	...	|	1234	1240	|	|	1337	|	|	1437	|	|	1537	|	|	1631	1637	|
Edinburgh Waverley ... △ a.	...	...	...	...	...		|	...	|	|	1343	|	1422	|	|	|	1540	|	1620	|	|	|	|	1743	|
Glasgow Central ... 214 a.	...	...	...	...	...		1255	...	1325	1336	...	1410	...	1444	1507	1518	...	1606	...	1643	1707	1717	1733	...	1806

	⑦	⑦j	⑦	⑦	⑦	⑦	⑦	⑦	⑦	⑦	⑦	⑦	⑦	⑦	⑦j	⑦	⑦	⑦	⑦	⑦	⑦	⑦	⑦	⑦	⑦
London Euston ... 143 150/2/3 160 d.	1239	...	1429	1315	...	1529	1439	...	1629	1539	...	...	1729	1615	...	1801	1829	1739	...	1901	1929	1839	2028	1939	2053
Milton Keynes ... 143 150/2/3 160 d.	|	...	|	1352	...	|	|	...	|	|	...	...	|	1652	...	|	|	|	...	|	|	|	|	|	2139
Birmingham New St ... 144 150 d.	1407	...	|	1507	...	|	1607	...	|	1707	...	...	|	1807	...	|	|	1907	...	|	|	2007	|	2107	|
Wolverhampton ... 144 150 d.	1432	...	|	1532	...	|	1632	...	|	1732	...	...	|	1832	...	|	|	1932	...	|	|	2032	|	2132	|
Crewe ... 143 144 152 153 160 d.	1508	...	|	1608	...	|	1708	...	|	1808	...	...	|	1908	...	1950f	|	2008	...	2042	|	2107	2203	2207	2250
Warrington Bank Quay ... d.	1527	...	1615	1627	...	1715	1727	...	1815	1827	...	...	1915	1927	...	2010	2015	2027	...	...	2115	...	2221	...	2308
Manchester Airport ✈ ... 156 157 d.	|	1510	|	|	1610	|	|	1710	|	|	...	1810	|	|	1910	|	|	|	2010	...	|	...	|	...	|
Manchester Piccadilly ... 156 157 d.	|	1527	|	|	1626	|	|	1726	|	|	...	1826	|	|	1926	|	|	|	2026	...	|	...	|	...	|
Liverpool Lime Street ... 162 d.	|	|	|	|	|	|	|	|	|	|	1812	|	|	|	|	|	|	|	|	...	|	...	|	...	|
Wigan North Western ... 156 162 d.	1538	|	1626	1638	|	1726	1738	|	1827	1838	1843	|	1926	1938	|	2021	2026	2038	|	...	2126	...	2232	...	2319
Preston ... 156 157 158 162 d.	1555	1606	1642	1655	1705	1742	1754	1807	1842	1854	1859	1904	1942	1954	2007	2042	2041	2052	2103	...	2141	...	2245	...	2335
Blackpool North ... 156 162 a.	|	|	|	|	|	|	|	|	|	|	|	|	|	|	|	2101	|	...	|	...	|	...	...	...	...
Lancaster ... 157 158 d.	1611	1622	1658	1711	1721	1758	1810	1823	1857	1909	1915	1920	1958	2010	2023	...	2057	...	2119	...	2157	...	...	...	...
Oxenholme ... 158 d.	|	1636	1713	1726	1735	1813	1824	1837	1911	|	1929	1934	2012	2025	2039	...	2111	...	2133	...	2211	...	...	...	...
Penrith ... d.	1646	1702	1738	1752	1801	|	1849	1902	1937	1945	1954	2000	2037	2050	2105	...	2136	...	2159	...	2236	...	...	...	...
Carlisle ... 214 d.	1703	1719	1755	1809	1818	1851	1906	1919	1953	2003	2011	2017	2053	2107	2122	...	2153	...	2216	...	2253	...	...	...	...
Lockerbie ... d.	|	1738	|	1827	1837	|	|	1938j	|	|	2030	2036	|	|	2141	...	|	...	2235	...	|	...	...	...	...
Edinburgh Waverley ... △ a.	1820	|	|	|	1940	|	2025	|	|	|	|	2139	|	2226	|	...	|	...	|	...	|	...	...	...	...
Glasgow Central ... 214 a.	...	1841	1911	1928	...	2005	...	2040j	2104	2118	2133	...	2205	...	2247	...	2308	...	2347	...	0005	...	...	...	...

a – Arrives 1004.
d – From Mar. 6.
e – Arrives 1946 on ⑥.
f – Arrives 8–10 minutes earlier.
g – From Mar. 4.
j – From Mar. 5.
r – Arrives 5–7 minutes earlier.

△ – All trains to **Edinburgh** Waverley call at Haymarket 5–9 minutes earlier.

TP, VT GLASGOW and EDINBURGH - PRESTON - MANCHESTER, BIRMINGHAM and LONDON 154

km		⚒	Ⓐ	⑥	⚒	⑥	Ⓐ	⚒	Ⓐ	⑥	①	②–⑤	⑥	⚒	⚒	Ⓐ	⑥	⚒	⑥	Ⓐ	⚒a	⑥	Ⓐ	⚒
	Glasgow Central 214 d.	...	...	...	...	0426	0428	...	...	...	0422	0452	0452	0533	0548	...	...	0630	...	...	0709	0735	0736	0800
	Edinburgh Waverley ▽ d.	...	...	...	...	|	|	...	...	...	|	|	|	|	|	0612	0613	|	0652	0652	|	|	|	|
	Lockerbie d.	...	...	...	...	|	|	...	...	...	0550d	0608k	0553	|	|	0712	0712	0726	|	|	0810	|	|	|
	Carlisle 214 d.	...	...	...	...	0545	0543	...	...	...	0622f	0630	0623r	0647	0703	0734	0734	0746	0804	0807	0833	0850	0849	0910
	Penrith d.	...	...	...	...	0600	0559	...	...	...	0645f	0645	0644r	0702	0719	0749	0749	0802	0819	0823	0848	|	|	|
	Oxenholme 158 d.	...	...	...	...	0624	0623	0626a	...	...	0709	0709	0708	0726	0743	0813	0813	0826	0843	|	0913	0926	0925	|
	Lancaster 157 158 d.	0513	...	...	0628	0640	0638	0643	0700	0658	0724	0724	0723	0741	0758	0831	0828	0841	0858	0859	0928	0941	0940	0958
	Blackpool North 156 162 d.	|	0530	...	|	|	|	|	|	|	|	|	|	|	|	|	|	|	|	|	|	|	|	|
0	**Preston** 156 157 158 162 d.	0533	0600	0618	0647	0700	0659	0703	0718	0718	0749r	0749r	0747r	0801	0818	0850	0847	0901	0918	0918	0948	1001	1001	1018
24	Wigan North Western 157 162 d.	0546	0612	0631	|	0713	0712	0717	0731	0731	|	|	|	0814	0831	|	|	0914	0931	0931	|	1014	1014	1031
	Liverpool Lime Street 162 a.	|	|	|	|	|	|	0759	|	|	|	|	|	|	|	|	|	|	|	|	|	|	|	|
59	**Manchester** Piccadilly 156 157 a.	|	|	|	0726	|	|	...	|	|	0827	0827	0827	|	|	0926	0926	|	|	|	1026	|	|	|
77	**Manchester** Airport ✈ 156 157 a.	|	|	|	0745	|	|	...	|	|	0844	0844	0844	|	|	0946	0946	|	|	|	1044	|	|	|
—	Warrington Bank Quay d.	0557	0624	0642	...	0723	0723	...	0742	0742	...	...	...	0825	0842	...	...	0925	0942	0942	...	1025	1025	1042
0	Crewe 143 144 152 153 160 a.	|	0646j	0700	...	|	|	...	0800	0800	...	...	...	|	0900	...	...	|	1000	1000	...	|	|	1100
63	Wolverhampton 144 150 a.	|	|	0738	...	|	|	...	0839	0839	...	...	...	|	0939	...	...	|	1039	1039	...	|	|	1139
82	**Birmingham** New St 144 150 a.	|	|	0804	...	|	|	...	0906	0906	...	...	...	|	1006	...	...	|	1106	1107	...	|	|	1206
	Milton Keynes 150/2/3 160 a.	0727	|	|	...	|	|	...	1017	|	...	...	...	|	|	...	...	|	1217	1217	...	|	|	1317
	London Euston 143 150/2/3 160 a.	0800	0835	0938	...	0912	0914	...	1054	1038	...	...	...	1012	1138	...	...	1112	1254	1254	...	1212	1213	1354

	Ⓐ	⚒	⑥	⚒	⚒	Ⓐ	⑥	⚒	⚒	⚒	⚒	⚒		⚒a	⑥	Ⓐ	Ⓐ	⑥	⚒	⚒	⚒	⚒	⚒	⚒	⑥
Glasgow Central 214 d.	0745	...	0810	0838	...	0906	0909	0936	...	...	1040	...	...	1107	1133	1136	1156	1156	1204h	...	1240	...	1309	1335	...
Edinburgh Waverley ▽ d.	|	0812	|	|	0852	|	|	|	...	1012	|	1052	...	|	|	|	|	|	|	1212	|	1252	|	|	...
Lockerbie d.	0902	0911	0916	|	|	1010	1009	|	...	1111	|	|	...	1209	|	|	|	|	1306	1311	|	|	1409	|	...
Carlisle 214 d.	0927r	0933	0938	0948	1006	1035	1033	1049	...	1133	1149	1205	...	1233	1248	1249	1312	1311	1328	1334	1349	1407	1433	1449	...
Penrith d.	0942	0948	0953	1003	|	1050	1048	|	...	1148	|	1221	...	1248	1304	1305	|	|	1343	1349	|	1422	1448	|	...
Oxenholme 158 d.	1006	1012	1017	|	1042	1114	1112	1125	...	1212	1225	|	...	1312	|	|	|	|	1407	1413	1425	|	1512	1525	...
Lancaster 157 158 d.	1022	1027	1032	1039	1057	1131	1130	1140	...	1227	1240	1256	...	1327	1339	1340	1359	1359	1423	1428	1440	1458	1528	1540	...
Blackpool North 156 162 d.	|	|	|	|	|	|	|	|	1151	|	|	|	...	|	|	|	|	|	|	|	|	|	|	|	1551
Preston 156 157 158 162 d.	1051f	1047	1052	1100	1118	1150	1149	1201	1218	1246	1301	1318	...	1347	1400	1401	1418	1418	1453g	1447	1501	1518	1547	1601	1618
Wigan North Western 157 162 d.	1104c	|	1105a	1113	1131	|	|	1214	1231	|	1314	1331	...	|	1413	1414	1431	1431	1505	|	1514	1531	|	1614	1631
Liverpool Lime Street 162 d.	1149c	|	1149a	|	|	|	|	|	|	|	|	|	...	|	|	|	|	|	1550	|	|	|	|	|	|
Manchester Piccadilly 156 157 a.	...	1126	...	|	|	1226	1226	|	|	1326	|	|	...	1426	|	|	|	|	...	1526	|	|	1626	|	|
Manchester Airport ✈ 156 157 a.	...	1144	...	|	|	1244	1244	|	|	1344	|	|	...	1444	|	|	|	|	...	1544	|	|	1644	|	|
Warrington Bank Quay d.	...	...	...	1125	1142	...	...	1225	1242	...	1325	1342	...	...	1423	1425	1442	1442	...	...	1525	1542	...	1625	1642
Crewe 143 144 152 153 160 a.	...	...	...	|	1200	...	...	|	1300	...	|	1400	...	...	|	|	1500	1500	...	...	|	1600	...	|	1700
Wolverhampton 144 150 a.	...	...	...	|	1241	...	...	|	1339	...	|	1439	...	...	|	|	1539	1539	...	...	|	1639	...	|	1739
Birmingham New St 144 150 a.	...	...	...	|	1306	...	...	|	1406	...	|	1506	...	...	|	|	1606	1606	...	...	|	1706	...	|	1806
Milton Keynes 150/2/3 160 a.	...	...	...	|	1417	...	...	|	1517	...	|	1617	...	...	|	|	|	1717	...	...	|	1817	...	|	|
London Euston 143 150/2/3 160 a.	...	...	...	1312	1454	...	...	1412	1554	...	1512	1654	...	...	1612	1612	1738	1754	...	...	1712	1854	...	1813	1936

	Ⓐ	⑥	Ⓐ	⚒	Ⓐ	⑥	Ⓐ	⑥	Ⓐ	⑥	Ⓐ	⑥	⑥	Ⓐ	⚒a	Ⓐ	⑥		Ⓐ	⑥	Ⓐ	⑥	Ⓐ	⑥	⚒
Glasgow Central 214 d.	...	...	...	1434	...	...	1508	1508	1538	1538	1557	1557	...	...	1612	1640	1640	...	...	...	1707	1709	1730	1730	...
Edinburgh Waverley ▽ d.	...	1410	1412	|	1452	1452	|	|	|	|	|	|	1611	1612	|	|	|	...	1652	1652	|	|	|	|	1811
Lockerbie d.	...	1509	1513	|	|	|	1609	1610	|	|	|	|	1710	1711	1716	|	|	...	|	|	1810	1810	1827	1826	1911
Carlisle 214 d.	...	1534	1535	1548	1608	1604	1631	1633	1648	1648	1711	1710	1733	1734	1741	1753	1752	...	1808	1807	1834	1833	1847	1846	1934
Penrith d.	...	1549	1550	|	1623	1620	1646	1648	1703	1703	|	|	1748	1749	1757	1808	1808	...	|	|	1849	1848	1902	1901	1949
Oxenholme 158 d.	...	1613	1614	1624	|	1644	1712	1712	|	|	1747	1746	1812	1813	1821	1832	1832	...	1844	1843	1913	1912	1926	1925	2013
Lancaster 157 158 d.	...	1628	1629	1639	1659	1659	1728	1727	1739	1739	|	|	1827	1828	1837	1847	1847	...	1859	1858	1929	1928	1941	1940	2028
Blackpool North 156 162 d.	1551	|	|	|	|	|	|	|	|	|	|	|	|	|	|	|	|	...	|	|	|	|	|	|	|
Preston 156 157 158 162 d.	1618	1648	1648	1659	1718	1718	1748	1745	1801	1801	1818	1818	1847	1847	1857	1907	1906	...	1918	1918	1948	1948	2001	2000	2047
Wigan North Western 157 162 d.	1631	|	|	1712	1731	1731	|	|	1814	1814	1831	1831	|	|	1909	1919	1919	...	1931	1931	|	|	2014	2013	|
Liverpool Lime Street 162 d.	|	|	|	|	|	|	|	|	|	|	|	|	|	|	1946	|	|	...	|	|	|	|	|	|	|
Manchester Piccadilly 156 157 a.	|	1726	1726	|	|	|	1826c	1826a	|	|	|	|	1926	1926	...	|	|	...	|	|	2026	2026	|	|	2126
Manchester Airport ✈ 156 157 a.	|	1744	1744	|	|	|	1844c	1844a	|	|	|	|	1946	1946	...	|	|	...	|	|	2046	2046	|	|	2146
Warrington Bank Quay d.	1642	...	...	1725	1742	1742	...	...	1825	1825	1842	1842	...	...	...	1930	1930	...	1942	1942	...	...	2025	2024	...
Crewe 143 144 152 153 160 a.	1700	...	...	|	1800	1800	...	...	|	|	1900	1900	...	...	...	|	|	...	2000	2000	...	...	2044	2042	...
Wolverhampton 144 150 a.	1739	...	...	|	1839	1837	...	...	|	|	1941	1941	...	...	...	|	|	...	2041	2041	...	...	|	|	...
Birmingham New St 144 150 a.	1806	...	...	|	1906	1906	...	...	|	|	2006	2006	...	...	...	|	|	...	2105	2105	...	...	|	|	...
Milton Keynes 150/2/3 160 a.	1917	...	...	|	2017	2019	...	...	|	1944	2116	2120	...	...	...	2047	2050	...	2202	2218	...	...	2153	2157	...
London Euston 143 150/2/3 160 a.	1954	...	...	1912	2055	2113	...	...	2012	2029	2153	2214	...	...	...	2119	2140	...	2245	2310	...	...	2227	2255	...

	Ⓐ	⑥	Ⓐ	⑥	⑥a	Ⓐ	Ⓐ	Ⓐ	⑦	⑦	⑦	⑦	⑦	⑦	⑦	⑦	⑦	⑦	⑦	⑦	⑦	⑦	⑦	⑦	⑦
Glasgow Central 214 d.	1840	1840	...	...	1846	1908c	2006	...	...	...	...	...	...	...	0916	0934	0946	...	1013	1034	...	1107	1135	1155
Edinburgh Waverley ▽ d.	|	|	1852	1852	|	|	|	2011	...	...	...	...	...	...	|	|	|	1013	|	|	1051	|	|	|
Lockerbie d.	|	|	|	|	1955	2008c	2103	2111	...	...	...	...	...	...	1022	|	|	1112	1117	|	|	1210	|	|
Carlisle 214 d.	1949	1949	2007	2004	2017	2030	2125	2133	...	...	...	...	...	...	1044	1050	1102	1134	1139	1147	1207	1233	1250	1306
Penrith d.	|	2004	|	2020	2032	2045	2141	2148	...	...	...	...	...	...	1059	1105	1118	1149	1154	1203	|	1248	1305	|
Oxenholme 158 d.	2025	2028	2043	2044	2056	2109	2205	2212	...	...	...	...	...	...	1123	1129	1142	1213	1218	1227	1243	1312	|	1342
Lancaster 157 158 d.	2040	2043	2058	2059	2113	2125	2220	2227	...	...	...	...	...	...	1138	1144	1157	1228	1235	1242	1258	1327	1341	1358
Blackpool North 156 162 d.	|	|	|	|	|	|	|	|	...	...	...	...	...	...	|	|	|	|	|	|	|	|	|	|
Preston 156 157 158 162 d.	2059	2105	2118	2118	2134	2146	2239	2246	0854	0859	1001	1017	1057	1118	1157	1203	1218	1247	1355	1301	1318	1347	1401	1418
Wigan North Western 157 162 d.	2112	2118	2131	2131	|	|	2252	|	0906	0912	1014	1030	1110	1131	|	1216	1231	|	1306b	1314	1331	|	1414	1431
Liverpool Lime Street 162 d.	|	|	|	|	|	|	|	|	0944	|	|	|	|	|	|	|	|	|	1343b	|	|	|	|	|
Manchester Piccadilly 156 157 a.	|	|	|	|	2221	2224	|	2325	...	|	|	|	|	|	1242	|	|	1326	...	|	|	1426	|	|
Manchester Airport ✈ 156 157 a.	|	|	|	|	2241	2241	|	2346	...	|	|	|	|	|	1258	|	|	1344	...	|	|	1442	|	|
Warrington Bank Quay d.	2123	2129	2142	2142	...	...	2304	...	...	0923	1025	1041	1121	1142	...	1227	1242	...	...	1325	1342	...	1425	1442
Crewe 143 144 152 153 160 a.	|	2148	2200	2200	...	...	2328	...	...	0941	1043	1102	1140	1200	...	|	1300	...	...	|	1400	...	|	1500
Wolverhampton 144 150 a.	|	2223	2241	2240	...	...	...	...	...	|	|	1134	|	1239	...	|	1339	...	...	|	1439	...	|	1539
Birmingham New St 144 150 a.	|	2248	2305	2305	...	...	...	...	...	|	|	1203	|	1306	...	|	1406	...	...	|	1506	...	|	1606
Milton Keynes 150/2/3 160 a.	2246s	...	0027	...	...	...	...	...	...	1108	1210	...	|	1417	...	|	1517	...	...	|	1617	...	|	|
London Euston 143 150/2/3 160 a.	2340	...	0117	...	...	...	...	...	...	1209	1246	...	1319	1455	...	1418	1555	...	...	1518	1655	...	1618	1739

	⑦	⑦	⑦	⑦	⑦	⑦	⑦	⑦	⑦	⑦	⑦	⑦	⑦	⑦	⑦	⑦	⑦	⑦	⑦	⑦	⑦	⑦b	⑦	⑦	⑦b
Glasgow Central 214 d.	...	1235	...	1312	1335	1355	1401	...	1434	...	1505	1535	1555	...	1638	...	1703	1734	...	1834	...	1847	1915b	2008	...
Edinburgh Waverley ▽ d.	1212	|	1251	|	|	|	|	1412	|	1451	|	|	|	1614	|	1651	|	|	1813	|	1851	|	|	|	2014
Lockerbie d.	1311	|	|	1414	|	|	1502	1511	|	|	1613	|	|	1713	|	|	1805	1831	1913	|	|	1954	2016b	2104	2113
Carlisle 214 d.	1333	1350	1406	1436	1449	1507	1524	1533	1548	1603	1635	1649	1710	1735	1751	1807	1828	1851	1935	1948	2007	2016	2038	2025	2135
Penrith d.	1348	|	1421	1451	|	1523	1539	1548	1603	1619	1650	|	1726	1750	1806	|	1843	1906	1950	|	2022	2031	2053	2141	2150
Oxenholme 158 d.	1412	1426	|	1515	1525	|	1603	1612	1627	1643	1714	1725	|	1814	1830	1843	1907	1930	2014	2024	|	2055	2117	2205	2214
Lancaster 157 158 d.	1427	1441	1458	1530	1540	1558	1618	1627	1642	1658	1729	1740	|	1829	1845	1858	1923	1945	2029	2039	2058	2112	2132	2220	2229
Blackpool North 156 162 d.	|	|	|	|	|	|	|	|	|	|	|	|	|	|	|	|	|	|	|	|	|	|	|	|	|
Preston 156 157 158 162 d.	1446	1501	1518	1549	1601	1618	1638	1647	1701	1718	1748	1801	1817	1848	1904	1918	1945r	2004	2048	2058	2118	2131	2151	2241	2248
Wigan North Western 157 162 d.	|	1514	1531	|	1614	1631	1651	|	1714	1731	|	1814	1831	|	1917	1931	|	2017	|	2113	2131	2145	|	2254	|
Liverpool Lime Street 162 d.	|	|	|	|	|	|	1728	|	|	|	|	|	|	|	|	|	|	|	|	|	|	2220	|	|	|
Manchester Piccadilly 156 157 a.	1524	|	|	1624	|	|	...	1724	|	|	1824b	|	|	1925	|	|	2019b	|	2124	|	|	...	2225	|	2322
Manchester Airport ✈ 156 157 a.	1542	|	|	1642	|	|	...	1742	|	|	1842b	|	|	1942	|	|	2039b	|	2142	|	|	...	2246	|	2342
Warrington Bank Quay d.	...	1525	1542	...	1625	1642	...	...	1725	1742	...	1825	1842	...	1928	1942	...	2028	...	2124	2142	...	...	2305	...
Crewe 143 144 152 153 160 a.	...	|	1600	...	|	1700	...	...	|	1800	...	|	1900	...	|	2000	...	2047	...	2147r	2200	...	...	2325	...
Wolverhampton 144 150 a.	...	|	1639	...	|	1741	...	...	|	1839	...	|	1941	...	|	2041	...	|	...	2229	2236	...	...	...	...
Birmingham New St 144 150 a.	...	|	1706	...	|	1806	...	...	|	1906	...	|	2006	...	|	2106	...	|	...	2251	2259	...	...	...	...
Milton Keynes 150/2/3 160 a.	...	|	|	...	|	1917	...	...	1844	2017	...	|	2119	...	2045	2230	...	2154	...	0012s	...	...	...	...	...
London Euston 143 150/2/3 160 a.	...	1718	1839	...	1818	1955	...	...	1918	2055	...	2018	2211	...	2131	2322	...	2252	...	0100	...	...	...	...	...

a – From Mar. 4.
b – From Mar. 5.
c – From Mar. 6.
d – Arrives 0537.
f – Arrives 8–10 minutes earlier.
g – Arrives 1441.
h – Departs 1208 on ⑥.
j – Departs 0655.
k – Arrives 0552.
r – Arrives 5–7 minutes earlier.
s – Calls to set down only.
▽ – All trains from **Edinburgh** Waverley call at Haymarket 4–6 minutes later.

155 CREWE - STOKE - DERBY - NOTTINGHAM

2nd class only EM

km		⚒	Ⓐ	⑥	⚒	⚒	⚒	⚒	⚒	⚒	⚒	⚒	⚒	⚒	Ⓐ	⑥	⑦	⑦	⑦	⑦	⑦	⑦	⑦	⑦
0	**Crewe** d.	0608	0705	0709	0908	1008	1108	1210	1410	1510	1610	1708	1910	2010	2121	2127	1410	1510	1610	1710	1810	1910	2010	2122
24	Stoke on Trent d.	0633	0728	0735r	0933	1033	1133	1233	1433	1533	1632	1733	1934	2034	2147	2151	1432	1532	1634	1735r	1836r	1935r	2039r	2144
33	Blythe Bridge d.	0645	0740	0747	0945	1045	1145	1245	1445	1545	1644	1745	1946	2046	2159	2203	1444	1543	1645	1746	1847	1946	2046	2156
51	Uttoxeter d.	0657	0752	0759	0957	1057	1157	1257	1457	1557	1656	1757	1958	2058	2211	2215	1456	1555	1657	1758	1859	1958	2058	2208
82	**Derby** 120 172 a.	0720n	0816c	0822n	1019n	1119	1219	1319f	1519n	1619	1719n	1819	2021f	2120t	2233a	2238	1518	1617	1720	1820	1921	2021	2120	2230
108	**Nottingham** 120 172 a.	0756	0849	0859	1056	1154	1253	1355	1554	1654	1754j	1853j	2053j	2146t	2302	...	*1555*	*1653*	*1754*	*1854*	*1957*	*2054*	*2154*	*2359*

	⚒	⚒		⚒	Ⓐ	⑥	⚒	⚒	⚒	⚒	Ⓐ	⚒	⚒	⚒	⚒	⑥	Ⓐ	⑦	⑦	⑦	⑦	⑦	⑦	⑦
Nottingham 120 172 d.	0716	0817	...	0916	1016	1016	1216	1316	1416	1516	🚐	1716	1816	1916	2016	2116	2119	*1416*	*1512*	*1616*	*1716*	*1816*	*1915*	*2016*
Derby 120 172 d.	0745	0848r	...	0948r	1047r	1048r	1248r	1348r	1448r	1548j	1645	1746r	1848r	1948r	2047r	2145r	2148r	1445	1544	1645	1746	1845	1945	2044
Uttoxeter d.	0809	0910	...	1010	1109	1110	1310	1410	1510	1610	|	1810	1910	2010	2110	2207	2210	1506	1606	1706	1807	1906	2006	2105
Blythe Bridge d.	0822	0924	...	1024	1123	1124	1324	1424	1524	1624	|	1824	1924	2024	2123	2221	2224	1519	1618	1719	1819	1919	2019	2118
Stoke on Trent d.	0835	0937	...	1037	1137	1137	1337	1437	1537	1637	1817	1837	1937	2037	2136	2234	2237	1533	1633	1733	1833	1933	2033	2131
Crewe a.	0858	0958	...	1058	1158	1158	1358	1458	1558	1658	...	1858	1958	2058	2158	2255	2258	1554	1654	1754	1854	1954	2054	2152

a – Departs 2239.
c – Departs 0823.
f – Departs 4–6 minutes later on Ⓐ.
j – Arrives 5–7 minutes earlier on Ⓐ.
n – Departs 4–5 minutes later.
r – Arrives 4–6 minutes earlier.
t – On ⑥ departs Derby 2130 and arrives Nottingham 2155.
v – Departs 3 minutes later on Ⓐ.

156 MANCHESTER - PRESTON - BLACKPOOL

2nd Class only NT

For other trains Manchester - Preston and v.v. see Tables **154** and **157**.

km		⚒	⚒	⚒	⚒	⚒	⚒	⚒	⚒	⚒	♣	⚒	⚒	⚒	⚒		⚒	⚒	⚒	⚒	Ⓐ	⑦b	⑦d	⑦
0	**Manchester** Airport ✈ d.	0448	0548	0617	0648	0717	0748	0817	0848	0917	and at	1948	2017	2048	2117	...	2148	2217	2248	2317	2346	0736	...	0841
17	**Manchester** Piccadilly d.	0504	0602	0633	0702	0733	0802	0833	0902	0933	the same	2002	2033	2102	2133	...	2202	2235	2302	2332	0009	0800	0800	0902
35	Bolton d.	0523	0622	0652	0723	0753	0822	0853	0922	0953	minutes	2022	2053	2122	2153	...	2222	2254	2322	2351	0024	0819	0819	0923
67	**Preston** 173a 191 d.	0553	0700	0730	0801	0830	0900	0930p	1000	1028	past each	2100	2130	2154	2230	...	2302	2330	0004	0026	0058	0857	0857	0959
96	**Blackpool** N 191 a.	0618	0726	0753	0827	0854	0925	0953	1025	1052	hour until	2126	2153	2221	2253	...	2318	2353	0021	0049	0124	0922	0922	1025

	⑦	⑦	⑦	⑦	⑦	⑦	⑦	⑦		⑦	⑦	⑦	⑦
Manchester Airport ✈ d.	...	1033	...	1110	...	1242	...	1345	and at	1945	2045	2145	2246
Manchester Piccadilly d.	1002t	1055	1103t	1125	1203t	1304	1302t	1401	the same	2001	2101	2201	2302
Bolton d.	1020	1113	1120	|	1219	|	1318	1420	minutes	2020	2120	2221	2321
Preston 173a 191 d.	1059	1136	1151	1204	1255	1355	1357	1458	past each	2056	2159	2300	2357
Blackpool North 191 a.	1126	...	1215	...	1319	...	1424	1525	hour until	2122	2225	2329	0023

	⚒	⚒	⚒	⚒	⚒	⚒	⚒	⚒
Blackpool N 191 d.	0500	0522	0556	0622	0654	0722	0754	0823
Preston 173a 191 d.	0524	0549	0620	0649	0722	0749	0821	0851
Bolton d.	0554	0621	0654	0722	0753	0822	0854	0921
Manchester Picc a.	0615	0645	0715	0745	0816	0845	0915	0945
Manchester Apt ✈ a.	0631	0700	0736	0800	0836	0900	0936	1000

	⚒	♣	⚒	⚒	⚒		⚒	⑥	Ⓐ	⑦	⑦	⑦	⑦	⑦	⑦	⑦	⑦	⑦	⑦		⑦	⑦	⑦	⑦
Blackpool North 191 d.	0855	and at	2022	2059	2122	...	2222	2307	2322	0752	...	0900	1000	...	1100	...	1151	1250	1351	and at	1948	2050	2151	2222
Preston 173a 191 d.	0920	the same	2050	2124	2149	...	2249	2334	2338	0818	0912	0926	1026	1112	1126	1157	1221	1318	1419	the same	2015	2119	2219	2251
Bolton d.	0954	minutes	2121	2154	2221	...	2321	0008	0022	0847	|	0958	1058	|	1158	|	1254	1353	1454	minutes	2054	2153	2252	2325
Manchester Piccadilly a.	1016	past each	2145	2215	2247	...	2345	0026	0043	0908t	0955t	1017t	1117t	1156	1215t	1242	1320	1420	1520	past each	2120	2220	2318	2346
Manchester Airport ✈ a.	1036	hour until	2201	2236	2302	...	0001	0044	0102	...	1025	...	...	1220	...	1258	1336	1437	1536	hour until	2136	2236	2334	...

b – From Apr. 2.
d – Until Mar. 26.
p – Arrives 0924.
t – Manchester **Oxford Road**.
v – Manchester **Victoria**.
♣ – Timings at Preston and Blackpool may vary ± 2 minutes.

157 MANCHESTER - PRESTON - BARROW IN FURNESS

2nd Class only NT

For other trains Manchester - Preston/Lancaster and v.v. see Tables **154** and **156**.

km		⚒	⚒	⚒	⚒	Ⓐ	⑥	⚒D	⚒A	⚒	⚒	⚒D	⚒A	⚒	⚒	⚒D	⚒A	⚒	⚒	⚒	⚒	⚒D	ⒶA	⑥B	⚒
0	**Manchester** Airport ✈ d.	...	0529	...	...	0729	0729	0829	...	0929	1029	1129	...	1229	1329	1429	...	1529	...	1629	...	1729	...	...	1829
17	**Manchester** Piccadilly d.	...	0549	...	...	0750	0750	0850	...	0950	1050	1150	...	1250	1350	1450	...	1550	...	1650	...	1750	...	...	1850
35	Bolton d.	...	0608	...	...	0808	0808	0909	...	1008	1108	1208a	...	1309a	1408	1508	...	1609	...	1709	...	1809	...	...	1909
67	**Preston** a.	...	0632	...	...	0833	0832	0933	...	1032	1132	1236	...	1345c	1433	1532	...	1632	...	1732	...	1835	...	...	1932
	Preston d.	0518	0633	...	...	0833	0842	0945	...	1033	1145	1245	...	1346	1445	1533	...	1633	...	1734	...	1844	...	...	1934
101	Lancaster 174 d.	0538	0653	0733	0822	0851	0859	1002	1013	1051	1202	1303	1318	1405	1502	1550	1602	1652	1727	1751	1836	1902	1913	1913	1951
111	Carnforth 174 d.	0549	0703	0744	0832	0900	0909	...	1023	1101	1212	...	1329	1414	1512	...	1612	1701	1737	1801	1845	...	1923	1923	2001
121	Arnside d.	0559	0712	0754	0842	0910	0919	...	1033	1110	1221	...	1339	1424	1522	...	1623	1711	1747	1811	1855	...	1933	1933	2010
126	Grange over Sands d.	0605	0718	0800	0848	0916	0924	...	1039	1116	1227	...	1345	1429	1527	...	1629	1716	1753	1817	1901	...	1939	1939	2016
141	Ulverston d.	0621	0733	0816	0902	0931	0940	...	1055	1131	1242	...	1401	1444	1543	...	1646	1732	1808	1832	1917	...	1955	1955	2031
157	**Barrow in Furness** a.	0642	0755	0838	0922	0953	1001	...	1117	1154	1302	...	1422	1505	1605	...	1709	1753	1830	1853	1939	...	2017	2017	2053

	⚒	Ⓐ	⑥g	⑥h	⑥g	d	⑦A	⑦An	⑦D	⑦Ap	⑦	⑦	⑦D	⑦A	⑦	⑦	⑦A	⑦D	⑦	⑦	⑦D	⑦	⑦	⑦	⑦
Manchester Airport ✈ d.	1929	...	...	...	...	2159	...	...	...	...	0936	1033	...	...	1242	1330	*1410*	1430	1530	1630	1730	...	1830	1930	...
Manchester Piccadilly d.	1950	...	...	...	...	2220	...	...	0853	...	0955	1055	1154j	...	1304	1348	*1426*	1448	1548	1648	1748	...	1848	1948	...
Bolton d.	2008	...	...	...	...	2239	...	...	0910	...	1011	1113	1208	...	1322	1409	*1444*	1509	1609	1709	1809	...	1909	2010	...
Preston a.	2032	...	...	...	...	2307	...	...	0936	...	1035	1136	1232	...	1355	1437	*1503*	1536	1637	1736	1833	...	1937	2036	...
Preston d.	2033	...	*2125z*	2211	*2230z*	2310	...	...	0948	...	1039	1147	1246	...	1358	1446	*1505*	1558	1648	1747	1834	...	1947	2046	...
Lancaster 174 d.	2051	2209	2226	2231	2330	2330	...	*0945z*	1005	1011	1059	1204	1303	1314	1415	1504	1603	1615	1706	1804	1851	1902	2004	2104	2220
Carnforth 174 d.	2100	2218	2235	2241	2339	2341	0855	1021	...	1021	1109	1214	...	1324	1425	1513	1613	...	1715	1814	...	1914	2014	2114	2230
Arnside d.	2110	2228	2245	2251	2349	2351	0905	1031	...	1031	1118	1223	...	1334	1434	1523	1623	...	1725	1823	...	1925	2023	2123	2240
Grange over Sands d.	2116	2234	2251	2257	2355	2357	0911	1037	...	1037	1123	1229	...	1340	1440	1528	1629	...	1730	1828	...	1931	2028	2128	2246
Ulverston d.	2131	2250	2307	2313	0010	0012	0927	1053	...	1053	1138	1244	...	1356	1455	1543	1645	...	1745	1843	...	1947	2043	2143	2301
Barrow in Furness a.	2153	2312	2329	2335	0032	0034	0948	1115	...	1115	1159	1304	...	1418	1516	1604	1707	...	1806	1904	...	2008	2105	2204	2323

	⚒	⚒	⚒	⚒	⚒	⚒	⚒	⚒D	⚒A	⚒	⚒	⚒D	⚒A	⚒	Ⓐ	⑥	ⒶD	⚒A	⚒	⚒	⚒	⚒D	Ⓐ	⑥	⚒
Barrow in Furness d.	0458	0550	0612	0650	0712	0748	0848	...	0958	1051	1151	...	1250	1352	1447	1447	...	1550	1651	1719	1802	...	1856	1903	1945
Ulverston d.	0516	0609	0631	0709	0730	0807	0907	...	1017	1110	1210	...	1308	1411	1506	1506	...	1608	1710	1737	1821	...	1915	1922	2004
Grange over Sands d.	0528	0624	0647	0724	0744	0822	0922	...	1032	1125	1225	...	1324	1426	1521	1521	...	1624	1725	1752	1836	...	1931	1938	2019
Arnside d.	0534	0630	0653	0729	0750	0828	0928	...	1039	1130	1231	...	1330	1432	1527	1527	...	1630	1731	1758	1842	...	1936	1943	2024
Carnforth 174 d.	0543	0642	0706	0743	0802	0839	0940	...	1055t	1142	1243	...	1343	1443	1538	1538	...	1643	1743	1810	1854	...	1952	1955	2043y
Lancaster 174 d.	0550	0649	0716	0751	0812	0848	0950	1047	1105	1149	1250	1349	1353	1452	1548	1550t	1650	1653	1750	1820	1905	1935	2000	2003	2050
Preston a.	0608	0710	...	0809	...	0906	1008	1108	...	1208	1308	1407	...	1510	1606	1608	1708	...	1808	...	...	1953	2019	2022	2108
Preston d.	0610	0711	...	0810	...	0909	1010	1110	...	1210	1310	1410	...	1511	1607	1610	1710	...	1810	...	...	2010	...	...	2110
Bolton d.	0634	0737	...	0836	...	0934	1034	1134	...	1234	1334	1434	...	1534	|	1634	1734	...	1834	...	...	2034	...	...	2134
Manchester Piccadilly a.	0658	0758	...	0858	...	0958	1058	1158	...	1258	1358	1458	...	1558	1658	1658	1758	...	1858	...	...	2058	...	...	2158
Manchester Airport ✈ a.	0715	0815	...	0915	...	1015	1115	1215	...	1315	1415	1515	...	1615	1715	1715	1815	...	1915	...	...	2115	...	...	2215

	Ⓐ	⑥g	⑥h	Cd	⑥g	⑦	⑦p	⑦p	⑦n	⑦	⑦	⑦	⑦D	⑦Ap	⑦An	⑦	⑦	⑦D	⑦A	⑦	⑦A	⑦D	⑦	⑦	⑦
Barrow in Furness d.	2045	2042	2042	2145	2146	0753	0841	0905	0905	0952	1052	1147	...	1253	1317	1349	1447	...	1550	1646	1746	...	1851	1952	2046
Ulverston d.	2104	2101	2101	2204	2204	0812	0859	0922	0924	1010	1111	1206	...	1311	1335	1407	1505	...	1608	1705	1805	...	1909	2011	2105
Grange over Sands d.	2119	2116	2116	2219	2220	0827	0914	0934	0939	1025	1126	1221	...	1324	1354	1422	1520	...	1624	1720	1820	...	1925	2026	2020
Arnside d.	2125	2122	2122	2226	2226	0833	0920	0940	0945	1031	1131	1227	...	1330	1359	1428	1526	...	1630	1725	1827	...	1931	2031	2126
Carnforth 174 d.	2138	2134	2134	2238	2238	0845	0931	0951	0957	1043	1143	1239	...	1342	1406	1439	1537	...	1642	1736	1842	...	1943	2043	2138
Lancaster 174 d.	2148	2143	2143	2246	2248	...	0945t	1001	*1025*	1051	1151	1247	1349	1352	1420	1449	1546	1648	1652	1749t	1851	1939	1951	2050	2148
Preston a.	...	...	2205	2310	*2335z*	...	1004	...	...	1110	1209	1306	1407	...	...	1507	1605	1706	...	1807	...	1958	2014	2108	...
Preston d.	...	...	...	...	...	...	1009	...	...	1112	1211	1312	1411	...	...	1511	1612	1710	...	1810	...	2013	...	2112	...
Bolton d.	...	...	...	...	...	...	1032	...	...	1135	1234	1335	1436	...	...	1534	1635	1734	...	1833	...	2036	...	2136	...
Manchester Piccadilly a.	...	...	...	...	...	...	1047j	...	...	1156	1256	1354	1456	...	...	1555	1655	1756	...	1855	...	2056	...	2155	...
Manchester Airport ✈ a.	...	...	...	...	...	...	...	...	...	1220	1316	1416	1514	...	...	1613	1713	1818	...	1914	...	2114	...	2213	...

A – From/to Carlisle (Table **159**).
B – To Millom (Table **159**).
C – From Carlisle on Ⓐ (Table **159**).
D – To/from Windermere (Table **153**).
a – ⑥ only.
c – Arrives 1335 on ⑥.
d – Ⓐ (also ⑥ until Mar. 25).
g – From Apr. 1.
h – Until Mar 25.
j – Manchester **Oxford Road**.
n – From Apr. 2.
p – Until Mar. 26.
t – Arrives 5–7 minutes earlier.
y – Arrives 2035.
z – Connection by 🚐.

NT 2nd class — BARROW - WHITEHAVEN - CARLISLE — 159

km			⚒	⚒	⚒	⚒	⚒	⚒	⚒	⚒	⚒	⚒	⚒	⚒	⚒	⑥	Ⓐ	Ⓐ	⚒	⚒	⑥	Ⓐ	⑥	Ⓐ
	Lancaster 157 d.	⚒	...	...	...	...	...	...	...	1013	...	...	1318	...	...	...	...	...	1602	...	...	...	...	...
0	**Barrow in Furness** d.		...	...	0558	0651	0750	0927	1022	1119	1206	1316	1424	1449	1544	1611	1615	...	1716	1807	1857	1912	1944	1944
26	Millom d.		...	...	0627	0719	0818	0955	1050	1147	1234	1344	1451	1517	1612	1639	1644	...	1744	1834	1925	1940	2011	2012
47	Ravenglass for Eskdale 🚂 d.		...	...	0645	0737	0835	1012	1107	1204	1251	1401	1508	1534	1629	1656	1701	...	1802	1849	1942	1957	2028	...
56	Sellafield d.		...	...	0700	0753	0849	1032t	1122	1217	1303	1413	1520	1547	1641	1708	1712	...	1814	1900	1953	2012	2041	...
74	**Whitehaven** d.		...	0630	0723	0816	0909	1051	1145	1236	1338	1438	1540	1612	1701	1729	...	1749	1838	1921	2013	2037	2102	...
85	Workington d.		0549	0648	0742	0834	0928	1109	1203	1253	1356	1456	1559	1633r	1719	1747	...	1807	1856	1943r	2035r	2055	2120	...
92	Maryport d.		0557	0656	0750	0843	0936	1117	1211	1301	1404	1505	1608	1643	1728	1756	...	1816	1904	1953	2044	2104	2128	...
119	Wigton d.		0619	0718	0812	0904	0957	1138	1233	1323	1426	1526	1629	1705	1749	1817	...	1837	1925	2014	2106	2125	...	...
138	**Carlisle** a.		0639	0738	0832	0925	1017	1158	1253	1341	1450	1546	1651	1725	1810	1841	...	1857	1945	2034	2126	2145	...	...

	⑥	Ⓐ	⚒	Ⓐ	⚒		⑦	⑦a	⑦b	⑦	⑦	⑦C	⑦a	⑦b	⑦	⑦	⑦	⑦	⑦	⑦	⑦	⑦	⑦	⑦
Lancaster 157 d.	1913	1913	...	...	...	⑦	...	...	...	...	...	...	1011	C	...	...	1314	...	...	1603	...	...	...	...
Barrow in Furness d.	2018	2018	2110	...	2211		...	...	...	0905	...	0950	1116	1116	1218	1309	1419	1455	1558	1718	...	1825	...	1909
Millom d.	2046	2046	2138	...	2239		...	...	...	0933	...	1017	1144	1144	1245	1336	1444	1523	1625	1747	...	1853	...	1937
Ravenglass for Eskdale 🚂 d.	...	2103	▬	...	...		...	...	...	...	...	1034	1201	1201	1302	1353	1459	1541	1642	1804	...	...	...	...
Sellafield d.	...	2115	⑥	...	...		...	...	...	...	...	1046	1213	1213	1315	1405	1507	1551	1654	1816	...	...	...	...
Whitehaven d.	...	2134	2209	2209	...		...	...	...	...	1016	1111	1234	1234	1338	1426	1529	1611	1716	1840	1938	...	2030	...
Workington d.	...	2152	2227	2227	...		0855	0940	0957	...	1034	1129	1252	1252	1358	1444	1547	1629	1734	1858	1956	...	2048	...
Maryport d.	...	2200	2236	2236	...		0904	0949	1006	...	1043	1137	1301	1301	1408	1453	1556	1637	1743	1907	2005	...	2057	...
Wigton d.	...	2221	...	2257	...		0925	1010	1027	...	1104	1159	1322	1322	1430	1514	1617	1659	1804	1928	2026	...	2118	...
Carlisle a.	...	2241	...	2317	...		0945	1030	1047	...	1124	1219	1342	1342	1450	1534	1637	1719	1824	1948	2046	...	2138	...

		⚒	⚒	⚒	⚒	⚒	⚒	⚒	⚒	⚒	⚒	⚒	⚒	⚒	⚒	Ⓐ	Ⓐ	⑥	⚒	⚒	Ⓐ	⑥	⑥	⑥
Carlisle d.	⚒	...	...	0553	0619	0710	0808	0902	1013	1107	1210	1307	1408	1441	1512	...	1559	1626	1707	1751	...	1846	...	1909
Wigton d.		...	...	0611	0636	0731	0826	0920	1031	1125	1227	1325	1426	1458	1530	...	1617	1644	1725	1809	...	1904	...	1927
Maryport d.		...	0548	0633	0700	0755	0848	0941	1053	1146	1249	1346	1447	1520	1551	...	1638	1705	1746	1830	...	1925	...	1948
Workington d.		...	0558	0644	0711	0806	0858	0952	1103	1157	1259	1357	1458	1530	1602	...	1648	1715	1757	1841	...	1936	...	1959
Whitehaven d.		...	0618	0704	0730	0825	0918	1012	1123	1216	1319	1416	1517	1550	1621	...	1708	1736	1818	1900	...	1956	...	2020
Sellafield d.		...	0639	0724	0750	0844	0939	1031	1147	1239	1340	1441	1542	1611	1641	1725	...	1755	1840	1927	...	...	...	2040
Ravenglass for Eskdale 🚂 d.		...	0650	0734	0801	0854	0949	1042	1157	1249	1350	1451	1552	1622	1651	1735	...	1805	1849	1939	...	...	...	2050
Millom d.		0610	0709	0753	0820	0914	1008	1101	1216	1307	1409	1511	1611	1642	1712	1754	...	1825	1905	2001	2029	...	2059	2109
Barrow in Furness a.		0641	0741	0826	0853	0947	1040	1136	1248	1339	1441	1543	1644	1714	1745	1826	...	1857	1937	2036	2101	...	2129	2141
Lancaster 157 a.		...	...	...	...	1105	...	...	1353	...	...	1653	...	...	...	...	...	...	...	...	...	...	...	...

	ⒶB	⚒	Ⓐ	⑥	⑥	Ⓐ		⑦	⑦	⑦a	⑦b	⑦a	⑦b	⑦	⑦	⑦	⑦	⑦	⑦	⑦	⑦	⑦	⑦	⑦
Carlisle d.	1909	2000	2055	2106	2149	2201	⑦	...	...	0945	...	1023	1041	1106	1207	1324	1401	1510	1616	1710	1810	1910	2010	2110
Wigton d.	1927	2018	2113	2124	2206	2219		...	...	1002	...	1041	1058	1124	1225	1342	1419	1528	1634	1728	1828	1928	2028	2128
Maryport d.	1948	2039	2134	2145	2227	2241		...	0917	1024	1024	1103	1120	1145	1246	1403	1440	1549	1655	1749	1849	1949	2049	2149
Workington d.	1958	2050	2145	2156	2238	2251		...	0927	1033	1033	1113	1130	1156	1258	1414	1451	1600	1706	1800	1900	2000	2100	2200
Whitehaven d.	2017	2109	2204	2215	2257	2310		...	0947	1051	1051	1133	1150	1216	1318	1433	1510	1619	1725	1819	1919	2019	2119	2219
Sellafield d.	2040	▬	...	...	...	...		...	1007	1109	1109	1151	1208	1239	1337	1451	1529	1642	1744	1841	▬	...	...	...
Ravenglass for Eskdale 🚂 d.	2050	⚒	...	...	...	...		...	1017	1119	1119	1201	1218	1249	1347	1501	1539	1652	1754	1851	⑦	...	...	...
Millom d.	2109	2200	...	...	...	...		0950	1036	1137	1137	1219	1236	1308	1406	1517	1557	1711	1814	1910	1925	...	...	...
Barrow in Furness a.	2142	2231	...	...	...	...		1021	1108	1209	1209	1251	1308	1340	1438	1548	1629	1743	1846	1942	1957	...	...	...
Lancaster 157 a.	2246	...	...	...	...	...		...	...	...	...	...	1352	1420	...	1652	...	1851	...	...	...	...	...	...

B – To Preston (Table 157).
C – From Carnforth (Table 157).
a – Until Mar. 26.
b – From Apr. 2.
r – Arrives 5–6 minutes earlier.
t – Arrives 1025.
🚂 – Ravenglass and Eskdale Railway. ✆ 01229 717171. www.ravenglass-railway.co.uk

AW, VT — HOLYHEAD - CHESTER - LONDON/MANCHESTER — 160

km			②–⑤ 2	Ⓐ 2	Ⓐ 2	Ⓐ 2	Ⓐ 2	Ⓐ ✕	Ⓐ 2	Ⓐ 2	Ⓐ ✕	Ⓐ ✕W	Ⓐ 2	Ⓐ 2	Ⓐ ✕	Ⓐ 2	Ⓐ ✕	Ⓐ2 🍷B	Ⓐ 2🍷	Ⓐ 2🍷	Ⓐ ✕	Ⓐ 2🍷	Ⓐ2 🍷B	Ⓐ 2🍷	Ⓐ 🍷L	Ⓐ ✕	Ⓐ 2🍷
0	**Holyhead** ▽ d.	Ⓐ	...	...	...	...	0425	0448	0501	...	0533	0549	...	0624	0649	...	...	0731	...	0805	0853	...	0927	...	1040	...	...
40	Bangor d.		...	...	...	...	0457	0514	0532	...	0601	0615	...	0703	0715	...	...	0811	...	0855r	0919	...	1006	...	1109	...	...
	Llandudno ‡ d.		...	...	...	...	│	│	│	0553	│	│	0643	│	│	0743	...	│	0843	│	│	0943	│	1043	│	...	1143
64	Llandudno Junction ‡ d.		...	...	0438	...	0515	0532	0555	0607	0621	0633	0653	0723	0733	0753	...	0835	0853	0923f	0937	0953	1029	1053	1127	...	1153
71	Colwyn Bay d.		...	...	0444	...	0521	0539	0601	0613	0628	0640	0659	0729	0740	0759	...	0841	0859	0930	0944	0959	1036	1059	1133	...	1159
88	Rhyl d.		...	...	0456	...	0531	0550	0612	0625	0639	0651	0712	0739	0751	0812	...	0851	0912	0940	0955	1012	1046	1112	1143	...	1212
94	Prestatyn d.		...	...	0502	...	0537	│	0618	0631	│	0657	0718	0745	0757	0818	...	0857	0918	0947	1001	1018	1053	1118	1149	...	1218
136	**Chester** a.		...	...	0534	...	0609	0617	0649	0705	0712	0724	0749	0815	0824	0849	...	0927	0951	1016	1027	1049	1125	1149	1217	...	1249
136	**Chester** 190 ♥ d.		0351	0455t	0537	0552	0620	0620	0653	...	0716	0732	0753	0820	0832	0852	0920	0930	0952	1020	1032	1052	1136	1152	1221	1232	1252
170	**Crewe** ♥ § d.		│	│	0559	│	│	0655	│	...	│	0755	│	│	0852	│	0943	│	│	│	1055	│	│	│	│	1255	│
	Stafford § a.		│	│	...	│	│	│	│	...	│	│	│	│	...	│	│	│	│	│	1113	│	│	│	│	1313	│
	London Euston § a.		│	│	...	│	│	0835	│	...	│	0935	│	│	...	│	1131	│	│	│	1235	│	│	│	│	1435	│
	Shrewsbury 145 a.		│	│	...	│	0713	...	│	...	0802	...	│	0912	...	│	...	1024	│	1112	...	│	1231	│	1314	...	│
	Cardiff Central 149 a.		│	│	...	│	0917	...	│	...	0959	...	│	1116	...	│	...	│	│	1314	...	│	│	│	1511	...	│
	Birmingham N St 145 a.		│	│	...	│	...	...	│	...	...	...	│	...	...	│	...	1132	│	...	...	│	1333	│	...	...	│
165	Warrington Bank Quay 190 d.		│	│	...	0620	...	...	0721	...	...	...	0821	...	...	0921	...	...	1021	...	...	1121	...	1221	...	...	1321
201	**Manchester** Piccadilly a.		0452	0557	...	0654	...	...	0754	...	...	...	0854	...	...	0954	...	...	1054	...	...	1154	...	1254	...	...	1354
217	**Manchester** Airport a.		0513	0618	...	0715	...	...	0815	...	...	...	0914	...	...	1015	...	...	1115	...	...	1215	...	1315	...	...	1415

	Ⓐ ✕	Ⓐ2 🍷B	Ⓐ 2🍷	Ⓐ ✕	Ⓐ 2🍷	Ⓐ2 🍷B	Ⓐ ✕	Ⓐ 2🍷	Ⓐ 2🍷	Ⓐ ✕	Ⓐ 2🍷	Ⓐ 2	Ⓐ ✕	Ⓐ2 🍷B	Ⓐ 2	Ⓐ ✕	Ⓐ 2	Ⓐ 2	Ⓐ 2	Ⓐ 2	Ⓐ 2	Ⓐ ✕	Ⓐ 2	Ⓐ 2	Ⓐ 2	Ⓐ ✕	Ⓐ ...
Holyhead ▽ d.	1133	1148	...	1246	1306	1327	...	...	1433	1449	...	...	...	1538	...	1634	...	1728	...	...	1826	...	...	...	1922	1949	...
Bangor d.	1201	1220	...	1312	1340	1406	...	...	1500	1515	...	...	...	1616	...	1702	...	1807	...	...	1905	...	...	...	2000	2018	...
Llandudno ‡ d.	│	│	...	│	│	│	...	1441	│	│	1543	...	...	│	1643	│	1743	│	...	1843	│	...	1936	...	│	│	...
Llandudno Junction ‡ d.	1219	1245	1253	1330	1358	1431	...	1451	1526	1533	1553	1623	...	1639	1653	1720	1753	1833	1839	1853	1931	...	1946	...	2023	2036	...
Colwyn Bay d.	1226	1251	1259	1337	1404	1437	...	1457	1532	1540	1559	1629	...	1645	1659	1727	1759	│	1845	1859	1937	...	1952	...	2029	2043	...
Rhyl d.	1237	1300	1312	1348	1417	1447	...	1510	1543	1551	1612	1640	...	1656	1712	1742	1812	│	1855	1912	1947	...	2004	...	2038	2054	...
Prestatyn d.	1243	1306	1318	1354	1423	1452	...	1516	1549	1557	1618	1646	...	1702	1718	1748	1818	│	1901	1918	1953	...	2010	...	2044	2100	...
Chester a.	1312	1334	1349	1421	1451	1525	...	1547	1619	1625	1649	1717	...	1731	1749	1817	1849	1913	1931	1949	2022	...	2039	...	2114	2127	...
Chester 190 ♥ d.	1316	1338	1352	1432	1452	1536	1532	1552	1623	1632	1652	...	1732	1735	1752	1821	1852	1917	...	1952	2023	2032	2040	2052	2119	2134	2152
Crewe ♥ § d.	│	│	│	1455	│	│	1555	│	│	1655	│	...	1755	│	│	│	│	│	...	│	2044	2104j	2102	│	│	2157	│
Stafford § a.	│	│	│	1513	│	│	1613	│	│	1713	│	...	1813	│	│	│	│	│	...	│	...	2123	...	│	│	2215	│
London Euston § a.	│	│	│	1635	│	│	1735	│	│	1835	│	...	1935	│	│	│	│	│	...	│	...	│	...	│	│	│	│
Shrewsbury 145 a.	1413	1431	│	...	│	1630	...	│	1715	...	│	...	...	1829	│	1919	│	2013	...	│	...	a	...	│	2217	a	│
Cardiff Central 149 a.	1618	│	│	...	│	│	...	│	1925	...	│	...	...	│	│	2128	│	...	...	│	...	│	...	│	│	│	│
Birmingham N St 145 a.	...	1532	│	...	│	1733	...	│	...	...	│	...	...	1932	│	...	│	...	...	│	...	2328	...	│	2328	2254	│
Warrington Bank Quay 190 d.	...	...	1421	...	1521	...	...	1621	...	...	1720	...	...	...	1821	...	1920	...	...	2021	...	...	...	2121	...	...	2221
Manchester Piccadilly a.	...	...	1454	...	1554	...	...	1654	...	...	1754	...	...	...	1854	...	1954	...	...	2054	...	...	...	2154	...	...	2255
Manchester Airport a.	...	...	1515	...	1615	...	...	1715	...	...	1815	...	...	...	1915	...	2015	...	...	2115	...	...	...	2215	...	...	2314

‡ – Additional trains **Llandudno - Llandudno Junction**. Journey time ± 10 minutes.
On Ⓐ at 0708, 0802, 1020, 1252, 1319, 1414, 1617, 1808, 1905, 2016, 2111.
On ⑥ at 0708, 0805, 0907, 1010, 1019, 1108, 1208, 1250, 1317, 1408, 1508, 1607, 1620, 1708, 1808, 1902, 1913, 2008.
On ⑦ at 1022, 1139, 1218, 1328, 1353, 1547, 1617, 1720.

‡ – Additional trains **Llandudno Junction - Llandudno**. Journey time ± 10 minutes.
On Ⓐ at 0540, 0613, 0651, 0731, 0824, 0940, 1240, 1305, 1427, 1604, 1826, 1837, 1959, 2058.
On ⑥ at 0651, 0731, 0824, 0925, 1006, 1030, 1123, 1225, 1237, 1303, 1425, 1528, 1605, 1625, 1725, 1825, 1841, 1928.
On ⑦ at 1126, 1244, 1340, 1406, 1534, 1604, 1631, 1705.

♥ – Additional trains **Chester - Crewe**. Journey time ± 23 minutes.
On ⚒ at 0446, 0551, 0646 Ⓐ, 0754, 0853, 0954, 1054, 1154, 1254, 1354, 1454, 1554, 1654, 1752, 1854, 1954, 2032 ⑥, 2054, 2128 Ⓐ.
On ⑦ at 0805, 0838, 0857, 0939, 0957, 1057, 1157, 1222, 1259, 1322, 1422, 1557, 1622, 1657, 1754, 1901, 1955, 2053, 2152.

♥ – Additional trains **Crewe - Chester**. Journey time ± 23 minutes.
On ⚒ at 0722, 0823, 0924, 1025, 1048 ⑥, 1124, 1224, 1324, 1424, 1524, 1624, 1724, 1824, 1924, 2024, 2137 ⑥, 2224, 2321 ⑥, 2330 Ⓐ.
On ⑦ at 1007, 1104, 1155, 1254, 1357, 1500, 1557, 1929, 2027, 2203, 2339.

FOR OTHER NOTES SEE NEXT PAGE → → →

160 HOLYHEAD - CHESTER - LONDON / MANCHESTER

AW, VT

	Ⓐ 2	Ⓐ 2	Ⓐ 2	Ⓐ 2B	⑥ 2	⑥ 2	⑥ 2	⑥ 2	⑥ 2	⑥ ✕	⑥ 2	⑥ 2	⑥ 2B	⑥ ✕	⑥ 2	⑥ 2	⑥ 2	⑥ 2B	⑥ ✕	⑥ 2♀	⑥ 2♀	⑥ ✕	⑥ 2♀	⑥2 ♀B	⑥ 2♀	⑥ 2♀
Holyhead ▽ d.	...	2031	...	...	...	...	...	...	0425	...	...	...	0519	0549	...	0631	...	0715	0753	...	0819	0849	...	0928	...	1030
Bangor d.	...	2100	...	...	...	...	...	...	0457	...	...	...	0558	0615	...	0703	...	0754	0819	...	0858	0915	...	1007	...	1102
Llandudno ‡ d.	2043	|	2145	...	...	...	...	...	|	...	...	...	|	|	...	|	0743	|	|	0843	|	|	0943	|	1043	|
Llandudno Junction ‡ d.	2053	2129f	2157	...	...	...	0440	...	0517	...	0532	...	0624	0633	0653	0723	0753	0821	0837	0853	0922	0933	0953	1034	1053	1123
Colwyn Bay d.	2059	2135	2203	...	...	...	0446	...	0523	...	0538	...	0630	0640	0659	0729	0759	0827	0844	0859	0928	0940	0959	1041	1059	1130
Rhyl d.	2112	2147	2218	...	...	...	0458	...	0533	...	0553	...	0641	0651	0712	0740	0812	0838	0855	0912	0939	0951	1012	1051	1112	1140
Prestatyn d.	2118	2153	2224	...	...	...	0504	...	0539	...	0559	...	0647	0657	0718	0746	0818	0844	0901	0918	0945	0957	1018	1058	1118	1147
Chester a.	2150	2225	2259	...	...	...	0535	...	0608	...	0633	...	0718	0724	0749	0816	0849	0915	0924	0949	1016	1024	1049	1130	1149	1217
Chester 190 ♥ d.	...	2230	2301	2322	0352	0455	0535	0552	0612	0628	0639	0653	0730	0732	0752	0820	0852	0930	0932	0952	1020	1032	1052	1136	1152	1221
Crewe ♥ § d.	...	2252	2325	|	|	|	0558	|	|	0655r	0705	|	|	0755	|	|	|	|	0955	|	|	1055	|	|	|	|
Stafford § a.	...	...	...	|	|	|	...	|	|	0713	...	|	|	0813	|	|	|	|	1013	|	|	1113	|	|	|	|
London Euston § a.	...	...	...	|	|	|	...	|	|	0835	...	|	|	0935	|	|	|	|	1135	|	|	1235	|	|	|	|
Shrewsbury 145 a.	...	...	...	|	|	|	...	|	0710	...	...	|	0824	...	|	0913	|	1031	...	|	1113	...	|	1231	|	1313
Cardiff Central 149 a.	...	...	...	|	|	|	...	|	0921	...	...	|	|	...	|	1116	|	|	...	|	1315	...	|	|	|	1521
Birmingham N St 145 a.	...	...	...	|	|	|	...	|	...	...	...	|	0932	...	|	...	|	1133	...	|	...	...	|	1333	|	
Warrington Bank Quay 190 d.	...	...	...	2350	|	|	...	0620	...	...	...	0721	...	...	0821	...	0921	...	...	1021	...	...	1121	...	1221	...
Manchester Piccadilly a.	...	...	...	0022	0452	0554	...	0654	...	...	...	0754	...	...	0854	...	0954	...	...	1054	...	...	1154	...	1254	...
Manchester Airport a.	...	...	...	...	0513	0615	...	0715	...	...	...	0815	...	...	0915	...	1015	...	...	1115	...	...	1215	...	1315	...

	⑥ ✕	⑥ 2♀	⑥2 ♀B	⑥ 2♀	⑥ 2♀	⑥ ✕	⑥ 2♀	⑥2 ♀B	⑥ ✕	⑥ 2♀	⑥ 2♀	⑥ ✕	⑥ 2♀	⑥2 ♀B	⑥ 2♀	⑥ 2♀	⑥ 2♀	⑥ 2	⑥ 2	⑥ 2	⑥ 2	⑥ 2	⑥ 2	⑥ 2	⑥ 2	⑥ 2	⑥ 2B
Holyhead ▽ d.	...	...	1128	...	1232	...	...	1327	1353	...	1425	1449	...	1525	...	1648	...	1728	...	1825	...	1921	...	...	2035	...	...
Bangor d.	...	...	1208	...	1259	...	1332	1406	1420	...	1452	1515	...	1604	...	1715	...	1807	...	1904	...	2000	...	...	2102	...	...
Llandudno ‡ d.	...	1143	|	1240	|	...	|	|	|	1443	|	|	1543	|	1643	|	1743	|	1843	|	1943	|	...	2043	|	2144	...
Llandudno Junction ‡ d.	...	1153	1233	1253	1317	...	1356	1427	1438	1453	1517	1533	1553	1630	1653	1735	1753	1833	1855	1929	1953	2026	...	2053	2133r	2156	...
Colwyn Bay d.	...	1159	1240	1259	1323	...	1402	1433	1444	1459	1524	1540	1559	1636	1659	1741	1759	1839	1901	1935	1959	2032	...	2059	2139	2202	...
Rhyl d.	...	1212	1251	1312	1334	...	1415	1444	1455	1512	1534	1551	1612	1647	1712	1752	1812	1850	1914	1945	2012	2043	...	2112	2151	2217	...
Prestatyn d.	...	1218	1257	1318	1340	...	1421	1450	1501	1518	1541	1557	1618	1653	1718	1758	1818	1856	1920	1950	1018	2049	...	2118	2157	2223	...
Chester a.	...	1249	1329	1349	1410	...	1452	1524	1525	1549	1611	1625	1649	1725	1749	1829	1849	1927	1951	2018	2049	2120	...	2149	2227	2256	...
Chester 190 ♥ d.	1232	1252	1335	1352	1415	1432	1453	1536	1532	1552	1614	1632	1652	1730	1752	1833	1852	1931	1952	2019	2052	2130	2152	...	2231	2301	2323
Crewe ♥ § d.	1255	|	|	|	|	1455	|	|	1555	|	|	1655	|	|	|	|	|	|	|	2041	|	|	|	...	2253	2327	|
Stafford § a.	1313	|	|	|	|	1513	|	|	1613	|	|	1713	|	|	|	|	|	|	|	...	|	|	|	...	...	...	|
London Euston § a.	1435	|	|	|	|	1635	|	|	1735	|	|	1835	|	|	|	|	|	|	|	...	|	|	|	...	...	...	|
Shrewsbury 145 a.	...	|	1429	|	1507	...	|	1630	...	|	1707	...	|	1823	|	1926	|	2026	|	...	|	2224	|	...	...	...	|
Cardiff Central 149 a.	...	|	|	|	1710	...	|	|	...	|	1912	...	|	|	|	2130	|	...	|	...	|	|	|	...	...	...	|
Birmingham N St 145 a.	...	|	1532	|	...	...	|	1733	...	|	...	...	|	1932	|	...	|	...	|	...	|	2329	|	...	...	...	|
Warrington Bank Quay 190 d.	...	1321	...	1421	...	...	1521	...	...	1621	...	...	1721	...	1821	...	1921	...	2021	...	2121	...	2219	...	...	...	2350
Manchester Piccadilly a.	...	1354	...	1454	...	...	1554	...	...	1654	...	...	1754	...	1854	...	1954	...	2054	...	2153	...	2254	...	...	...	0023
Manchester Airport a.	...	1415	...	1515	...	...	1615	...	...	1715	...	...	1815	...	1915	...	2015	...	2115	...	2215	...	...	...	...	...	...

	⑦ 2	⑦ 2	⑦ ♀	⑦ 2	⑦ 2♀	⑦ ♀	⑦ 2♀	⑦ 2	⑦ 2♀	⑦ ♀W	⑦ 2♀	⑦ ♀	⑦ 2	⑦ ♀	⑦ 2	⑦ ♀	⑦ 2	⑦ ♀	⑦ 2♀	⑦ 2	⑦ 2	⑦ 2♀	⑦ 2	⑦ 2	⑦ ♀	⑦ 2
Holyhead ▽ d.	...	0750	...	0849	...	0938	...	...	1020	...	...	...	...	1253	...	1349	...	...	1430	1530	...	1625	...	1729	1753	...
Bangor d.	...	0829	...	0917	...	1005	...	...	1059	...	...	...	...	1319	...	1415	...	...	1509	1557	...	1704	...	1756	1819	...
Llandudno ‡ d.	...	|	...	|	...	|	...	1107	|	...	...	...	1317	|	1420	|	1519	...	|	|	1644	|	1803	|	|	1859
Llandudno Junction ‡ d.	...	0853	...	0937	...	1026	1035	1117	1123	...	...	...	1327	1337	1430	1433	1529	...	1534f	1623	1654	1725	1813	1822	1838	1908
Colwyn Bay d.	...	0859	...	0943	...	1032	1042	...	1129	...	...	...	▬	1344	▬	1440	▬	...	1540	1629	▬	1731	▬	1828	1844	▬
Rhyl d.	...	0908	...	0956	...	1043	1054	...	1142	...	...	...	...	1355	...	1451	...	...	1554	1642	...	1744	...	1840	1855	...
Prestatyn d.	...	|	...	1001	...	1049	1100	...	1147	...	...	...	⑦	1401	⑦	1457	⑦	...	1559	1648	⑦	1749	⑦	1845	1901	⑦
Chester a.	...	0939	...	1033	...	1119	1133	...	1221	...	...	...	2	1425	2♀	1524	2♀	...	1634	1721	2♀	1822	2	1917	1927	2
Chester 190 ♥ d.	0841	0942	1014	1039	1038	1128	1135	...	1229	1232	1236	1332	1336	1432	1436	1532	1536	1632	1636	1722	1736	1826	1836	1922	1931	1936
Crewe ♥ § d.	|	|	1037	1102	|	1151	|	...	|	1255	|	1355	|	1455	|	1555	|	1655	|	1743	|	|	|	1944	1951	|
Stafford § a.	|	|	1055	...	|	1209	|	...	|	1313	|	1413	|	1513	|	1613	|	1713	|	...	|	|	|	...	...	|
London Euston § a.	|	|	1237	...	|	1336	|	...	|	1436	|	1536	|	1636	|	1736	|	1836	|	...	|	|	|	...	...	|
Shrewsbury 145 a.	|	|	...	...	|	...	|	...	1322	...	|	...	|	...	|	...	|	...	|	...	|	1920	|	...	...	|
Cardiff Central 149 a.	|	|	...	...	|	...	|	...	1528	...	|	...	|	...	|	...	|	...	|	...	|	2130	|	...	...	|
Birmingham N St 145 a.	|	|	...	...	|	...	|	...	...	...	|	...	|	...	|	...	|	...	|	...	|	...	|	...	...	|
Warrington Bank Quay 190 d.	0908	1010	...	...	1105	...	1203	...	...	...	1303	...	1403	...	1503	...	1603	...	1703	...	1803	...	1903	...	...	2003
Manchester Piccadilly a.	0943	1045	...	...	1139	...	1238	...	...	...	1336	...	1438	...	1538	...	1638	...	1738	...	1838	...	1938	...	...	2038
Manchester Airport a.	...	...	...	...	...	...	...	...	...	...	1357	...	1457	...	1556	...	1656	...	1756	...	1856	...	1956	...	...	2056

	⑦2 ♀B	⑦ 2	⑦ 2♀	⑦ 2	⑦ 2	⑦ 2	⑦ 2	⑦ 2
Holyhead ▽ d.	1826	...	1931	...	2033	...	...	2140
Bangor d.	1905	...	2010	...	2112	...	...	2209
Llandudno ‡ d.	|	...	|	...	|	...	2138	|
Llandudno Junction ‡ d.	1923	...	2035	...	2139	...	2148	2229
Colwyn Bay d.	1929	...	2041	...	2145	...	▬	2235
Rhyl d.	1943	...	2055	...	2156	...	...	2245
Prestatyn d.	1949	...	2101	...	2202	...	⑦	2251
Chester a.	2022	...	2135	...	2233	...	2	2319
Chester 190 ♥ d.	2027	2036	2135	2143	2237	2242	2303	...
Crewe ♥ § d.	2050	|	2200	|	2301	|	2327	...
Stafford § a.	|	|	...	|	...	|	|	...
London Euston § a.	|	|	...	|	...	|	|	...
Shrewsbury 145 a.	2120	|	...	|	...	|	0017	...
Cardiff Central 149 a.	|	|	...	|	...	|	...	...
Birmingham N St 145 a.	2212	|	...	|	...	|	...	...
Warrington Bank Quay 190 d.	...	2104	...	2210	...	2309	...	...
Manchester Piccadilly a.	...	2139	...	2245	...	2343	...	...
Manchester Airport a.	...	2155	...	2259	...	2359	...	...

	②–⑤ 2	① 2	① 2	②–⑤ 2	① 2B	②–⑤ 2	Ⓐ ✕	Ⓐ 2	Ⓐ 2	Ⓐ 2	Ⓐ 2	Ⓐ 2
Manchester Airport d.	...	...	2307p	2320p	...	...	...	0525	...	0625	...	0725
Manchester Piccadilly d.	...	...	2325p	2337p	...	0026	...	0542	...	0644	...	0744
Warrington Bank Quay 190 d.	...	...	2358p	|	...	|	...	0619	...	0717	...	0817
Birmingham New St 145 d.	...	...	|	|	2255p	|	0530	|	...	|	...	|
Cardiff Central 149 d.	2115p	2107p	|	|	|	|	|	|	...	|	0512	|
Shrewsbury 145 d.	2317p	2319p	|	|	2348p	|	a	|	...	|	0728	|
London Euston § d.	|	|	|	|	|	|	|	|	...	|	|	|
Stafford § d.	|	|	|	|	|	|	0604	|	...	|	|	|
Crewe ♥ § d.	0008	0012f	|	|	0021	|	0626	|	0656	|	|	|
Chester 190 ♥ a.	0027	0034	0028	0037	0044	0119	0645	0651	0719	0750	0821	0850
Chester d.	...	...	0039	0038	...	...	0647	0652	0721	0751	0825	0855
Prestatyn d.	...	...	0104	0104	...	...	0714	0721	0749	0819	0852	0923
Rhyl d.	...	...	0110	0110	...	...	0720	0727	0755	0825	0858	0929
Colwyn Bay d.	...	...	0121	0121	...	...	0731	0741	0809	0839	0912	0943
Llandudno Junction ‡ d.	...	...	0128	0131	...	...	0738	0748	0818	0847	0918	0953
Llandudno ‡ a.	...	...	|	|	...	...	|	0758	|	0857	|	1001
Bangor d.	...	...	0145	0148	...	...	0756	...	0840	...	0941	...
Holyhead ▽ a.	...	...	0212	0224	...	...	0822	...	0922	...	1009	...

	Ⓐ ✕	Ⓐ 2♀	Ⓐ ✕	Ⓐ 2	Ⓐ 2♀	Ⓐ ✕	Ⓐ2 ♀B	Ⓐ 2♀	Ⓐ ✕	Ⓐ 2♀	Ⓐ 2♀	Ⓐ2 ♀B	Ⓐ 2♀	Ⓐ ✕	Ⓐ 2♀	Ⓐ ✕	Ⓐ2 ♀B	Ⓐ 2♀	Ⓐ 2♀	Ⓐ 2♀	Ⓐ ✕	Ⓐ2 ♀B	Ⓐ 2♀	Ⓐ 2♀	Ⓐ 2♀	Ⓐ ✕	Ⓐ2 ♀B
Manchester Airport d.	...	0825	...	...	0925	...	...	1025	...	...	1125	...	1225	...	1325	...	...	1425	...	1525	...	...	1625	...	1725	...	...
Manchester Piccadilly d.	...	0844	...	...	0944	...	...	1044	...	...	1144	...	1244	...	1344	...	...	1444	...	1544	...	...	1644	...	1744	...	...
Warrington Bank Quay 190 d.	...	0920	...	...	1017	...	...	1120	...	...	1217	...	1317	...	1417	...	...	1517	...	1617	...	...	1717	...	1816	...	...
Birmingham N St 145 d.	...	|	...	...	|	...	0922	|	...	...	|	1122	|	...	|	...	1322	|	...	|	...	1522	|	...	|	...	1722
Cardiff Central 149 d.	0648	|	...	...	|	...	|	|	...	0923	|	|	|	1125	|	...	|	|	1322	|	...	|	|	1523	|	...	|
Shrewsbury 145 d.	0850	|	...	...	|	...	1025	|	...	1130	|	1225	|	1330	|	...	1426	|	1528	|	...	1625	|	1728	|	...	1826
London Euston § d.	|	|	...	...	|	0902	|	|	1002	|	|	|	|	|	|	1302	|	|	|	|	1502	|	|	|	|	1702	|
Stafford § d.	|	|	...	...	|	1024	|	|	1124	|	|	|	|	|	|	1424	|	|	|	|	1624	|	|	|	|	1832	|
Crewe ♥ § d.	|	|	0945	1005	|	1045	|	|	1145	|	|	|	|	|	|	1445	|	|	|	|	1645	|	|	|	|	1853	|
Chester 190 ♥ a.	0947	0956	1005	1028	1050	1105	1121	1151	1206	|	1250	1319	1350	1426	1450	1505	1521	1550	1623	1650	1705	1722	1755	1822	1850	1913	1921
Chester d.	0951	0959	1013	1028	1055	1113	1124	1152	...	1231	1251	1325	1351	1432	1451	...	1525	1551	1629	1651	1711	1726	1751	1826	1851	1921	1932
Prestatyn d.	|	1026	1040	1055	1118	1139	1150	1219	...	1257	1319	1352	1419	1500	1519	...	1551	1619	1654	1719	1738	1753	1819	1853	1918	1948	2000
Rhyl d.	|	1032	1046	1101	1125	1145	1157	1225	...	1304	1325	1358	1425	1507	1525	...	1558	1626	1701	1726	1744	1759	1826	1859	1924	1954	2007
Colwyn Bay d.	|	1042	1057	1115	1135	1156	1211	1239	...	1315	1339	1408	1439	1518	1539	...	1607	1640	1711	1740	1755	1813	1840	1913	1934	2005	2021
Llandudno Junction ‡ d.	1031	1050	1105	1122	1143	1203	1221	1246	...	1323	1347	1418	1447	1534r	1547	...	1620f	1647	1719	1747	1803	1825f	1847	1919	1945	2012	2029
Llandudno ‡ a.	|	|	|	1132	|	|	|	...	...	|	1358	|	1458	|	1558	...	|	1658	|	1757	|	|	1858	|	|	|	2039
Bangor d.	1048	1107	1129r	...	1200	1223	1244	...	...	1340	...	1442	...	1551	...	...	1644	...	1742	...	1820	1848	...	1937	2010	2030	...
Holyhead ▽ a.	1118	1145	1158	...	1228	1250	1324	...	...	1418	...	1520	...	1619	...	...	1718	...	1822	...	1847	1918	...	2020	2039	2056	...

B – To / from Birmingham International (Table **145**).
L – To / from Llanelli (Tables **136** and **149**).
M – To Milford Haven (Tables **149** and **136**).
W – Conveys 🛏12 and ✕ London - Chester - Wrexham and v.v. (Table **145**).

a – Via Wolverhampton (see Table **145**).
c – Arrives 2042.
f – Arrives 5 – 6 minutes earlier.
j – Arrives 2052.
p – Previous night.
r – Arrives 7 – 8 minutes earlier.

t – Departs 0502 on ①.
▽ – For ⛴ connections to/from **Dublin** see Table **2040**.
§ – See also Tables **143**, **150**, **151**, **152**, **154**.
‡ – For additional services Llandudno - Llandudno Junction and v.v. see previous page.
♥ – For additional services Chester - Crewe and v.v. see previous page.

AW, VT — MANCHESTER / LONDON - CHESTER - HOLYHEAD — 160

	Ⓐ 2	Ⓐ ✕	Ⓐ ✕W	Ⓐ 2	Ⓐ 2	Ⓐ 2L	Ⓐ ✕	Ⓐ 2	Ⓐ ✕	Ⓐ 2	Ⓐ 2	①–④ 2	⑤ 2	Ⓐ 2🍷	⑤ 2	①–④ 2	⑥	⑥ 2	⑥ 2	⑥ 2	⑥ ✕		⑥ 2	⑥ 2	⑥ 2	⑥ 2	⑥ 2
Manchester Airport d.	1825	...	...	...	1925	...	...	2025	...	...	2125	...	...	2225	2320	2320		...	2320p	...	...	...	0525	...	0625	...	0725
Manchester Piccadilly d.	1844	...	...	...	1945	...	...	2044	...	...	2144	...	...	2244	2337	2337		...	2337p	0026	...	...	0542	...	0644	...	0744
Warrington Bank Quay **190** d.	1917	...	...	...	2017	...	...	2117	...	...	2217	...	...	2323	|	|		...	|	|	...	...	0619	...	0717	...	0817
Birmingham N St **145** d.	|	...	...	...	|	...	...	|	...	...	|	...	...	|	|	|		...	|	|	0530	...	|	...	|	...	|
Cardiff Central **149** d.	|	1714	...	...	|	1825	...	|	...	...	|	1941	1941	|	|	|		2115p	|	|	|	...	|	...	|	0520	|
Shrewsbury **145** d.	|	1909	...	1932	|	2027	...	|	...	...	|	2146	2146	|	|	|		2317p	|	|	a	...	|	...	|	0726	|
London Euston § d.	|	|	1802	|	|	|	1902	|	2002	...	|	|	|	|	|	|		|	|	|	|	...	|	...	|	|	|
Stafford § d.	|	|	1932	|	|	|	2032	|	2124	...	|	|	|	|	|	|		|	|	|	0604	...	|	...	|	|	|
Crewe ♥ § d.	|	|	1953	|	|	2103	2053	|	2145	2136	|	|	|	|	|	|		0008	|	|	0626	...	|	0701	|	|	|
Chester **190** ♥ a.	1950	1957	2013	2028	2050	2126	2113	2150	2204	2158	2250	2241	2241	2353	0037	0037		0027	0037	0121	0645	...	0651	0723	0750	0820	0850
Chester d.	...	2001	...	2031	▬	...	2122	...	2206	2212	...	2257	2257	...	0038	0038		...	0038	...	0647	...	0652	0725	0751	0824	0851
Prestatyn d.	...	|	...	2059	...	...	2149	...	2230	2240	...	2325	2325	...	0104	0104		...	0104	...	0714	...	0720	0751	0819	0851	0919
Rhyl d.	...	2031	...	2106	Ⓐ	...	2155	...	2236	2246	...	2331	2331	...	0110	0110		...	0110	...	0720	...	0727	0759	0826	0858	0925
Colwyn Bay d.	...	2042	...	2120	2	...	2206	...	2247	2300	...	2345	2345	...	0121	0121		...	0121	...	0731	...	0741	0808	0840	0909	0939
Llandudno Junction ‡ d.	...	2054f	...	2129	2132	...	2213	...	2255	2308	...	2353	2359	...	0128	0131		...	0128	...	0738	...	0749	0817	0847	0922r	0947
Llandudno ‡ a.	...	|	...	|	2143	...	|	...	|	|	...	|	|	...	|	|		...	|	...	|	...	0758	|	0856	|	0956
Bangor d.	...	2111	...	2151	...	...	2231	...	2312	2332	...	0015	0021	...	0145	0148		...	0145	...	0756	...	...	0840	...	0945	...
Holyhead ▽ a.	...	2141	...	2231	...	...	2257	...	2339	0014	...	0043	0048	...	0212	0224		...	0212	...	0823	...	...	0921	...	1019	...

	⑥2 🍷B	⑥ 2🍷	⑥ 2🍷	⑥ 2🍷	⑥ ✕	⑥2 🍷B	⑥ 2🍷	⑥ ✕	⑥ 2🍷		⑥ 2🍷	⑥2 🍷B	⑥ 2🍷	⑥ ✕	⑥ 2🍷	⑥ 2🍷	⑥ ✕	⑥2 🍷B	⑥ 2🍷	⑥ 2🍷	⑥ 2🍷	⑥2 🍷B	⑥ 2🍷	⑥ ✕	⑥ 2🍷	⑥ 2🍷	⑥ ✕
Manchester Airport d.	...	0825	...	0925	...	...	1025	...	...	...	1125	...	1225	...	...	1325	...	...	1425	...	1525	...	1625	...	...	1725	...
Manchester Piccadilly d.	...	0844	...	0944	...	...	1044	...	...	...	1144	...	1244	...	...	1344	...	...	1444	...	1544	...	1644	...	...	1744	...
Warrington Bank Quay **190** d.	...	0917	...	1017	...	...	1117	...	...	...	1218	...	1317	...	...	1417	...	...	1517	...	1620	...	1717	...	...	1817	...
Birmingham N St **145** d.	0722	|	...	|	...	0922	|	...	...	...	|	1122	|	...	...	|	...	1322	|	...	|	1522	|	...	...	|	...
Cardiff Central **149** d.	|	|	0722	|	...	|	|	...	0922	...	|	|	|	...	1123	|	...	|	|	1322	|	|	|	...	1522	|	...
Shrewsbury **145** d.	0825	|	0927	|	...	1024	|	...	1128	...	|	1225	|	...	1327	|	...	1423	|	1528	|	1625	|	...	1729	|	...
London Euston § d.	|	|	|	|	0902	|	|	1002	|	...	|	|	|	1202	|	|	1302	|	|	|	|	|	|	1602	|	|	1702
Stafford § d.	|	|	|	|	1024	|	|	1124	|	...	|	|	|	1324	|	|	1424	|	|	|	|	|	|	1724	|	|	1832
Crewe ♥ § d.	|	|	|	|	1045	|	|	1145	|	...	|	|	|	1345	|	|	1445	|	|	|	|	|	|	1745	|	|	1853
Chester **190** ♥ a.	0919	0950	1020	1050	1105	1119	1150	1205	1223	...	1250	1320	1350	1406	1424	1450	1504	1517	1550	1622	1650	1719	1750	1805	1822	1850	1913
Chester d.	0924	0951	1024	1051	1114	1124	1151	1211	1227	...	1251	1324	1351	...	1428	1451	1511	1525	1551	1630	1651	1724	1751	1811	1825	1851	...
Prestatyn d.	0951	1019	1050	1119	1138	1151	1218	1238	1254	...	1319	1350	1419	...	1455	1519	1539	1553	1619	1655	1719	1752	1819	1838	1854	1919	...
Rhyl d.	0958	1026	1056	1126	1144	1158	1224	1244	1301	...	1326	1357	1426	...	1502	1526	1545	1600	1626	1701	1726	1758	1826	1844	1900	1926	...
Colwyn Bay d.	1008	1040	1107	1140	1155	1208	1238	1255	1312	...	1340	1406	1440	...	1513	1540	1556	1609	1640	1711	1740	1812	1841	1855	1915	1940	...
Llandudno Junction ‡ d.	1021r	1047	1117	1147	1203	1218	1245	1303	1322	...	1347	1416	1447	...	1525f	1547	1604	1622f	1647	1719	1747	1822	1848	1903	1925	1947	...
Llandudno ‡ a.	|	1056	|	1157	|	|	|	|	|	...	1357	|	1457	...	|	1557	|	|	1657	|	1757	|	1859	|	|	1957	...
Bangor d.	1038	...	1141	...	1220	1235	1308	1320	1339	...	...	1439	...	...	1542	...	1621	1645	...	1742	...	1846	...	1920	1942	...	...
Holyhead ▽ a.	1112	...	1212	...	1247	1314	...	1347	1418	...	...	1510	...	...	1621	...	1652	1717	...	1821	...	1915	...	1947	2024	...	...

	⑥ 2B	⑥ 2	⑥ ✕	⑥ 2🍷	⑥ 2	⑥ ✕W	⑥ 2	⑥ 2	⑥ 2	⑥ 2	⑥ 2	⑥ 2	⑥ 2	⑦	⑦ 2	⑦ 🚌	⑦ 2	⑦ 2	⑦ 🍷	⑦ 2🍷	⑦ 2	⑦ 2🍷	⑦ 2	⑦ 2🍷	⑦ 2🍷	⑦ 2🍷	⑦ 2🍷
Manchester Airport d.	...	1825	...	...	1925	...	...	2025	...	2125	2225	...	...		...	...	...	...	...	...	...	...	...	...	...	...	...
Manchester Piccadilly d.	...	1844	...	...	1945	...	...	2044	...	2144	2244	2314	...		...	0718	...	0948	...	1052	...	1156	...	1256	...	1357	...
Warrington Bank Quay **190** d.	...	1917	...	...	2017	...	...	2117	...	2217	2317	2348	...		...	0828	...	1020	...	1126	...	1230	...	1332	...	1429	...
Birmingham N St **145** d.	1722	|	...	...	|	...	...	|	...	|	|	|	...		...	|	...	|	...	|	...	|	...	|	...	|	...
Cardiff Central **149** d.	|	|	...	1723	|	...	...	|	1941	|	|	|	2055		...	|	...	|	...	|	...	|	...	|	...	|	...
Shrewsbury **145** d.	1827	|	...	1928	|	...	...	|	2143	|	|	|	2306		...	|	...	|	...	|	...	|	...	|	...	|	...
London Euston § d.	|	|	1802	|	|	1902	...	|	|	|	|	|	|		...	|	...	|	...	|	...	|	...	|	...	|	...
Stafford § d.	|	|	1932	|	|	2024	...	|	|	|	|	|	|		...	|	...	|	...	|	...	|	...	|	...	|	...
Crewe ♥ § d.	|	|	1953	|	|	2045	2100	|	|	|	|	|	2358		0835	|	0925	|	1036	|	1127	|	1227	|	1327	|	1429
Chester **190** ♥ a.	1921	1950	2013	2024	2050	2105	2122	2150	2236	2250	2347	0016	0023		0856	0928	0944	1049	1155	1155	1147	1258	1252	1359	1347	1456	1449
Chester d.	1926	▬	2019	2032	▬	...	2126	...	2240	▬	...	...	...		0900	▬	0951	▬	1057	▬	1201	▬	1303	...	1404	▬	1450
Prestatyn d.	1954	...	2046	2101	...	...	2154	...	2308	...	...	...	...		0926	...	1020	...	1124	...	1230	...	1336	...	1433	...	1518
Rhyl d.	2000	⑥	2052	2107	⑥	...	2201	...	2314	⑥	...	...	...		0932	⑦	1026	⑦	1130	⑦	1237	⑦	1343	...	1440	⑦	1524
Colwyn Bay d.	2014	2	2103	2118	2	...	2215	...	2328	🚌	...	...	...		0941	2	1040	2	1141	2	1247	2	1358	...	1454	2	1538
Llandudno Junction ‡ d.	2022	2030	2111	2128	2131	...	2223	...	2334	2348	...	...	...		0949	1003	1050	1053	1148	1200	1257	1300	1409	...	1503	1506	1548
Llandudno ‡ a.	|	2040	|	|	2142	...	|	...	...	|	...	...	...		|	1013	|	1103	|	1210	|	1310	|	...	|	1516	|
Bangor d.	2044	...	2128	2145	...	...	2247	...	...	0013	...	...	...		1006	...	1116	...	1207	...	1314	...	1433	...	1520	...	1611
Holyhead ▽ a.	2125	...	2155	2224	...	...	2317	...	...	0048	...	...	...		1037	...	1158	...	1233	...	1342	...	1505	...	1559	...	1643

	⑦ 🍷	⑦ 2🍷	⑦ 2	⑦ 🍷	⑦ 2🍷	⑦ 2🍷	⑦ 2	⑦ 2🍷	⑦ 2	⑦ 🍷	⑦ 2🍷		⑦ 2	⑦ 2🍷	⑦ 🍷W	⑦2 🍷B	⑦ 2	⑦ 🍷	⑦ 2	⑦ 🍷	⑦ 2	⑦ 2	⑦ 2	⑦ 2	⑦ 2B	⑦ 2	⑦ 🍷
Manchester Airport d.	...	1441	...	...	...	1541	...	1641	...	...	...	...	...	1741	...	...	1841	...	1941	...	2041	...	2141	...	...	2240	2307
Manchester Piccadilly d.	...	1457	...	...	...	1557	...	1657	...	...	...	...	...	1757	...	...	1857	...	1957	...	2057	...	2157	...	...	2258	2325
Warrington Bank Quay **190** d.	...	1529	...	...	...	1629	...	1729	...	...	...	...	...	1829	...	...	1931	...	2031	...	2129	...	2232	...	...	2330	2358
Birmingham N St **145** d.	...	|	...	...	...	|	...	|	...	...	...	...	...	|	...	1722	|	...	|	...	|	...	|	...	2122	|	|
Cardiff Central **149** d.	...	|	...	...	1329	|	...	|	...	...	1522	...	...	|	...	|	|	...	|	...	|	...	|	...	|	|	|
Shrewsbury **145** d.	...	|	...	...	1533	|	...	|	...	...	1732	...	...	|	...	1827	|	...	|	...	|	...	|	...	2235	|	|
London Euston § d.	1302	|	...	1401	|	|	...	|	...	1601	|	...	...	|	1701	|	|	1801	|	1901	|	...	|	...	|	|	|
Stafford § d.	1424	|	...	1524	|	|	...	|	...	1724	|	...	...	|	1824	|	|	1924	|	2024	|	...	|	...	|	|	|
Crewe ♥ § d.	1445	|	1529	1545	|	|	1629	|	1735	1745	|	...	1829	|	1845	|	|	1955	|	2052c	|	2129	|	2229	2309	|	|
Chester **190** ♥ a.	1505	1557	1550	1605	1629	1657	1653	1758	1755	1805	1826	...	1848	1858	1904	1925	2001	2015	2100	2112	2157	2149	2300	2251	2333	2358	0028
Chester d.	1517	...	1602	...	1636	▬	1702	▬	1802	...	1830	...	1852	...	1917	1935	...	2020	▬	2117	...	2201	...	2302	...	...	0039
Prestatyn d.	1544	...	1630	...	1704	...	1735	...	1830	...	1858	...	1921	...	1944	2003	...	2047	...	2144	...	2229	...	2330	...	...	0104
Rhyl d.	1550	...	1637	...	1711	⑦	1741	⑦	1837	...	1905	...	1927	...	1950	2010	...	2053	⑦	2150	...	2236	...	2337	...	...	0110
Colwyn Bay d.	1601	...	1651	...	1725	2	1756	2	1851	...	1919	...	1941	...	2001	2024	...	2104	2	2201	...	2250	...	2346	...	...	0121
Llandudno Junction ‡ d.	1609	...	1701	...	1734	1740	1806	1833	1901	...	1928	...	1951	...	2009	2033	...	2112	2125	2209	...	2257	...	2354	...	...	0128
Llandudno ‡ a.	|	...	|	...	|	1750	|	1843	|	...	|	...	|	...	|	|	...	|	2135	|	...	|	...	|	...	...	|
Bangor d.	1626	...	1718	...	1757	...	1830	...	1918	...	1951	...	2014	...	2029	2056	...	2129	...	2226	...	2314	...	0017	...	...	0145
Holyhead ▽ a.	1653	...	1759	...	1838	...	1903	...	1959	...	2019	...	2044	...	2056	2129	...	2156	...	2253	...	2356	...	0051	...	...	0213

← ← ← FOR NOTES SEE PREVIOUS PAGE

AW 2nd class only — LLANDUDNO - BLAENAU FFESTINIOG — 160a

km		⚒	⚒	⚒	⑦	⑥	Ⓐ	⑦	Ⓐ	⑥	⑦	⑦	⑥	Ⓐ
0	**Llandudno** d.	...	*0708*	1019	1022	1317	1319	1328	1617	1620	*1547*	1859	1902	1905
5	**Llandudno** Junction a.	...	*0718*	1028	1030	1326	1328	1337	1626	1630	*1557*	1908	1910	1914
5	**Llandudno** Junction d.	0530	0728	1032	1034	1329	1337	1340	1629	1633	1615	1915	1914	1923
18	Llanrwst d.	0548	0752	1055	1057	1352	1401	1403	1653	1656	1638	1938	1938	1947
24	Betws y Coed d.	0554	0758	1101	1103	1358	1407	1409	1659	1702	1644	1944	1944	1953
44	**Blaenau Ffestiniog** d.	0624	0832	1134	1136	1432	1440	1441	1732	1735	1716	2016	2020	2027

	⚒	Ⓐ	⑥	⚒Z	⑦	⚒	⑦	⑦	⚒W	⑦	⚒
Blaenau Ffestiniog d.	0624	0835	0846	1135	1142	1456	1459	1728	1735	2020	2022t
Betws y Coed d.	0650	0902	0913	1202	1208	1523	1525	1755	1802	2047	2049t
Llanrwst d.	0656	0908	0919	1208	1214	1529	1531	1801	1808	2053	2055t
Llandudno Junction a.	0722	0937	0949	1234	1241	1559	1559	1830	1836	2122	2125
Llandudno Junction d.	*0731*	0940	1006	1237	1244	1604	*1604*	1833	1837	2125	2131
Llandudno a.	*0741*	0950	1015	1247	1254	1615	*1614*	1843	1847	2135	2143

W – On ⑥ Llandudno Junction a. 1840, d. 1841, Llandudno a. 1851. **Z** – On Ⓐ Llandudno Junction a. 1238, d. 1240, Llandudno a. 1250. **t** – 5 minutes later on Ⓐ.

CAERNARVON - PORTHMADOG - BLAENAU FFESTINIOG — 160b

△ A special service is currently operating - see note ❦

km	All services are 🚂							
0	**Blaenau Ffestiniog** d.	...	...	...	...	...	...	...
19	Minffordd d.	...	...	...	...	...	...	...
22	**Porthmadog** Hbr d.	...	...	...	...	...	...	...
35	Beddgelert d.	...	...	...	...	...	...	...
42	Rhyd Ddu d.	...	...	...	...	...	...	...
50	Waunfawr d.	...	...	...	...	...	...	...
61	**Caernarfon** a.	...	...	...	...	...	...	...

Caernarfon d.	...	...	...	...	...	...	...
Waunfawr d.	...	...	...	...	...	...	...
Rhyd Ddu d.	...	...	...	...	...	...	...
Beddgelert d.	...	...	...	...	...	...	...
Porthmadog Hbr d.	...	...	...	...	...	...	...
Minffordd d.	...	...	...	...	...	...	...
Blaenau Ffestiniog d.	...	...	...	...	...	...	...

△ – Operators: Ffestiniog Railway and Welsh Highland Railway. ✆ 01766 516024. www.festrail.co.uk

❦ – A special service is currently operating.
Trains can be boarded at Porthmadog for return journeys to Tan-y-Bwlch, Blaenau Ffestiniog, Beddgelert or Caernarfon and all tickets have to be pre-booked online. A similar offering is available between Caernarfon and Porthmadog. Please see the website above for full details.

161 Caledonian Sleeper LONDON - SCOTLAND CS

Service shown is valid until March 3, 2023

All trains in this table convey 🛏 (Classic, Club or Double) and (2). Only available for overnight journeys. **Reservation compulsory**. Conveys ✕ and 🍸. All-inclusive fares are available (www.sleeper.scot/tickets). Holders of regular tickets and rail passes may travel in seated accommodation free of charge (Ⓡ); travel in sleeping accommodation is also possible on payment of the appropriate supplement (a first-class ticket is required for Club or Double rooms). Early booking is recommended.

*See Table **154** for day trains*		⑦	⑦	⑦	Ⓐ	Ⓐ	Ⓐ	⑦	⑦	Ⓐ	Ⓐ
		◐	◐	◐	◐	◐	◐	⊕	⊕	⊕	⊕
London Euston	d.	2059	2059	2059	2115	2115	2115	2330	2330	2350	2350
Watford Junction	d.	|	|	|	|	|	|	2349	2349	0013	0013
Crewe	d.	2335	2335	2335	2345	2345	2345	|	|	|	|
Preston	d.	0020	0020	0020	0030	0030	0030	|	|	|	|
Carlisle	a.	|	|	|	|	|	|	0440	0440	0507	0507
Motherwell	a.	|	|	|	|	|	|	|	0656	|	0656
Glasgow Central ⊠	a.	|	|	|	|	|	|	|	0722	|	0722
Edinburgh Waverley ⊠	a.	|	|	|	|	|	|	0730	...	0730	...
Dundee **222**	a.	0613	|	|	0613	|	|	...	...	...	...
Aberdeen **222**	a.	0750	|	|	0750	|	|	...	...	...	...
Perth **223**	a.	...	0543	|	...	0543	|	...	...	...	...
Inverness **223**	a.	...	0842	|	...	0842	|	...	...	...	...
Fort William **218**	a.	...	...	0957	...	...	0957	...	...	...	...

*See Table **154** for day trains*		⑦	⑦	Ⓐ	Ⓐ	Ⓐ	Ⓐ	Ⓐ	⑦	⑦	⑦
		⊕	⊕	◧	⊕						
Fort William **218**	d.	...	...	...	...	1950	...	...	1900	...	...
Inverness **223**	d.	...	...	...	...	|	2045	...	|	2026	...
Perth **223**	d.	...	...	...	...	|	2326	...	|	2306	...
Aberdeen **222**	d.	...	...	...	...	|	|	2026‡	|	|	2034
Dundee **222**	d.	...	...	...	...	|	|	2148‡	|	|	2156
Edinburgh Waverley	d.	2315	...	2340	...	|	|	|	|	|	|
Glasgow Central	d.	|	2315	|	2340	|	|	|	|	|	|
Motherwell	d.	|	2330	|	2357	|	|	|	|	|	|
Carlisle	d.	0144	0144	0145	0145	|	|	|	|	|	|
Preston	a.	|	|	|	|	0435	0435	0435	0430	0430	0430
Crewe	a.	|	|	|	|	0525	0525	0525	0528	0528	0528
Watford Junction	a.	0638	0638	0638	0638	|	|	|	|	|	|
London Euston ⊡	a.	0707	0707	0707	0707	0749	0749	0749	0749	0749	0749

◐ – Sleeping-car passengers may occupy their cabins from 2030.
⊕ – Sleeping-car passengers may occupy their cabins from 2230.
◧ – Sleeping-car passengers may occupy their cabins from 2300.
⊡ – Sleeping-car passengers from Edinburgh and Glasgow may occupy their cabins until 0730.
⊠ – Sleeping-car passengers may occupy their cabins until 0800 following arrival at these stations.
‡ – On ⑤ departs Aberdeen 2143, Dundee 2309.

162 BLACKPOOL - PRESTON - LIVERPOOL

*See also Table **154*** 2nd class NT

km		⚒	⚒	⚒	⚒	⚒	⚒		⚒	⚒	⚒	⚒	⚒	⚒	⑦	⑦	⑦	⑦	⑦	⑦		⑦	⑦
0	**Blackpool** North d.	⚒	0604	0704	0803	0905	1004		1706	1804	1905	2004	2105	2217	⑦	0755	0836	0937	1037	1137		2037	2203
28	**Preston** d.		0629	0729	0828	0930	1029	and	1731	1829	1930	2029	2130	2242		0823	0903	1004	1104	1204	and	2104	2229
52	Wigan North Western d.		0648	0748	0848	0949	1048	hourly	1750	1848	1949	2048	2151	2304		0842	0922	1023	1123	1223	hourly	2123	2248
70	St Helens Central d.		0700	0804	0907	1001	1101	until	1802	1900	2001	2101	2204	2321		0858	0939	1040	1140	1239	until	2139	2305
89	**Liverpool** Lime Street a.		0720	0829	0943	1021	1121		1824	1920	2021	2120	2230	2352		0920	1008	1109	1209	1309		2208	2334

		⚒	⚒	⚒	⚒		⚒	⚒	Ⓐ	⑥	Ⓐ		⑦	⑦	⑦	⑦		⑦	⑦	⑦	⑦	⑦	⑦
Liverpool Lime Street d.	⚒	0637	0739	0812	0839		2039	2115	2215	2315	2315	⑦	0829	0913	1017	1115		1815	1912	2012	2112	2215	2315
St Helens Central d.		0655	0756	0828	0856	and	2056	2143	2243	2344	2344		0856	0939	1044	1141	and	1842	1939	2039	2138	2242	2342
Wigan North Western d.		0709	0809	0842	0909	hourly	2109	2159	2259	0002	0004		0912	0955	1100	1157	hourly	1858	1955	2055	2154	2259	2358
Preston a.		0734	0834	0857	0933	until	2134	2220	2321	0023	0027		0933	1016	1121	1219	until	1919	2016	2116	2215	2320	0019
Blackpool North a.		0757	0857	...	0958		2158	2246	2347	...	*0124*		0959	1041	1146	1244		1944	2041	2143	2240	2345	0044

163 MANCHESTER and LIVERPOOL local services

2nd class ME, NT

MANCHESTER - CLITHEROE

Journey time: ± 76–80 minutes *57 km* NT

From Manchester Victoria:
Trains call at Bolton ± 19 and Blackburn ± 50 minutes later.
⚒: 0543, 0743, 0844, 0943 and hourly until 2043, 2143, 2215.
⑦: 0755, 0839, 0945, 1048, 1144 and hourly until 1645, 1756, 1845, 1945, 2112, 2207.

From Clitheroe:
Trains call at Blackburn ± 23 and Bolton ± 54 minutes later:
⚒: 0620, 0652, 0722 and hourly until 1523, 1625, 1721, 1823, 1916, 2023, 2123, 2239.
⑦: 0923, 1023 and hourly until 1623, 1719, 1823, 1947, 2023, 2123, 2243.

MANCHESTER - BUXTON

Journey time: ± 56–63 minutes *41 km* NT

From Manchester Piccadilly:
Trains call at Stockport ± 10, Hazel Grove ± 19 and New Mills Newtown ± 33 minutes later.
⚒: 0620, 0650, 0721, 0750, 0820, 0851, 0920, 0951 and hourly until 1551, 1620, 1651, 1721, 1751, 1820, 1851, 1920, 2020, 2120, 2219, 2310Ⓐ.
⑦: 0850, 0945, 1047, 1149, 1250, 1351, 1449 and hourly until 2049, 2150, 2248.

From Buxton:
Trains call at New Mills Newtown ± 21, Hazel Grove ± 34 and at Stockport ± 46 minutes later.
⚒: 0550, 0613, 0643, 0716, 0745, 0816, 0845, 0916, 0946 and hourly until 1546, 1615, 1646, 1716, 1745, 1816, 1846, 1916, 2013, 2114, 2159Ⓐ, 2213⑥, 2258.
⑦: 0813, 0855, 1001, 1058, 1157, 1300, 1356 and hourly until 1956, 2059, 2203, 2257.

CREWE - MANCHESTER AIRPORT ✈

Journey time: ± 42 minutes *37 km* NT

From Crewe:
Trains call at Wilmslow ± 26 minutes
⚒: 0616, 0716, 0815, 0916 and hourly until 1816, 1916.

From Manchester Airport:
Trains call at Wilmslow ± 14 minutes later.
⚒: 0551, 0701, 0801 and hourly until 1701, 1801, 1901.

MANCHESTER - WIGAN - SOUTHPORT

Journey time: ± 75 minutes *62 km* NT

From Manchester Victoria:
Trains call at Wigan Wallgate ± 35 minutes later.
⚒: 0607, 0632, 0708, 0727**p**, 0806, 0827**p**, 0908, 0927**p**, 1009, 1027**p** and at the same minutes past each hour until 1527**p**, 1606, 1627**p**, 1707, 1727**p**, 1807, 1827**p**, 1909, 1927**p**, 2027**p**, 2130**p**, 2232①–④, 2240⑤⑥.
⑦: 0825, 0926, 1025 and hourly until 2025, 2132.

From Southport:
Trains call at Wigan Wallgate ± 30 minutes later.
⚒: 0605**p**, 0626, 0705**p**, 0726, 0805**p**, 0832, 0905**p**, 0926, 1005**p**, 1032, 1103**p**, 1126, 1203**p**, 1232, 1305**p**, 1326, 1405**p**, 1432, 1505**p**, 1526, 1605**p**, 1632, 1705**p**, 1726, 1805**p**, 1832, 1902**p**, 1929, 1958**p**, 2105**p**, 2226.
⑦: 0842, 0938 and hourly until 2138, 2254.

MANCHESTER - NORTHWICH - CHESTER

Journey time: ± 92 minutes *73 km* NT

From Manchester Piccadilly:
Trains call at Stockport ± 10, Altrincham ± 26 and Northwich ± 55 minutes later.
⚒: 0606⑥, 0610Ⓐ, 0709, 0810 and hourly until 1910, 2009, 2110, 2210, 2313Ⓐ, 2321⑥.
⑦: 0906, 1103, 1310, 1509, 1709, 1909, 2104.

From Chester:
Trains call at Northwich ± 32, Altrincham ± 62 and Stockport ± 75 minutes later.
⚒: 0556, 0649, 0756 and hourly until 2156, 2252.
⑦: 0904, 1056, 1259, 1503, 1703, 1906, 2059.

LIVERPOOL - BIRKENHEAD - CHESTER

Journey time: ± 42 minutes *29 km* ME

From Liverpool Lime Street (Low Level):
Trains call at Liverpool Central ± 2 minutes and Birkenhead Central ± 9 minutes later.
⚒: 0538, 0608, 0643, 0713, 0743, 0755Ⓐ, 0813, 0820Ⓐ, 0843, 0858⑥, 0913, 0928, 0943, 0958 and every 15 minutes until 1858, 1913 and every 30 minutes until 2343.
⑦: 0813, 0843 and every 30 minutes until 2313, 2343.

From Chester:
Trains call at Birkenhead Central ± 33 minutes and Liverpool Central ± 44* minutes later.
⚒: 0555, 0630, 0700, 0722Ⓐ, 0730⑥, 0737Ⓐ, 0752Ⓐ, 0800⑥, 0807Ⓐ, 0815⑥, 0831, 0845 and every 15 minutes until 1830, 1900 and every 30 minutes until 2300.
⑦: 0800, 0830 and every 30 minutes until 2300.

LIVERPOOL - RUNCORN - CHESTER

Journey time: ± 50 minutes *43 km* AW

From Liverpool Lime Street:
Trains call at Liverpool South Parkway ± 9 minutes and Runcorn ± 19 minutes later.
⚒: 0744, 0947, 1147, 1347, 1546, 1747, 2047, 2201⑥, 2322Ⓐ.
⑦: 0945, 1156, 1356, 1557, 1756, 1957, 2137, 2321.

From Chester:
Trains call at Runcorn ± 26 minutes and Liverpool South Parkway ± 35 minutes later.
⚒: 0638Ⓐ, 0645⑥, 0843, 1043, 1243, 1443, 1642, 1945, 2143⑥, 2202Ⓐ.
⑦: 0831, 1047, 1247, 1447, 1647, 1847, 2047, 2228.

LIVERPOOL - SOUTHPORT

Journey time: ± 44 minutes *30 km* ME

From Liverpool Central:
⚒: 0608, 0623, 0638, 0653, 0708 and every 15 minutes until 2308, 2323, 2338.
⑦: 0808, 0823, 0853, 0923, 0953, 1023, 1053 and every 30 minutes until 2323, 2338.

From Southport:
⚒: 0537, 0552, 0607, 0622, 0642 and every 15 minutes until 2257, 2318.
⑦: 0758, 0828, 0858, 0928, 0958, 1028 and every 30 minutes until 2228, 2258.

p – Starts/terminates at Manchester **Oxford Road**, not Victoria.
* – Trains FROM Chester call at Liverpool Lime Street, then Liverpool Central.

EM Most trains convey 🍷 LONDON - LEICESTER - NOTTINGHAM, DERBY and SHEFFIELD 170

km			②–⑥	Ⓐ	⑥	Ⓐ	Ⓐ	⑥	⑥	Ⓐ	⑥	⚒	⑥	Ⓐ	⑥	Ⓐ	⑥	Ⓐ	⑥	Ⓐ	Ⓐ	⑥	⑥	Ⓐ	⑥	Ⓐ
0	**London** St Pancras 170a d.	⚒	0015	...	...	...	0527	...	0530	0559	0600	0605	0630	0632	0633	0635	0702	0702	0705	0705	0730	0732	0735	0735	0802	0803
116	Kettering 170a d.		0141	...	...	0606	|	0610	|	|	|	0653	|	|	0721	0727	|	|	0757	0758	|	|	0822	0826	|	|
133	Market Harborough d.		|	...	...	0616	|	0620	|	|	|	0704	|	|	0731	0737	|	|	0807	0808	|	|	0832	0836	|	|
159	**Leicester** 189 d.		0236j	0548	0551	0641a	0636	0646a	0639	0706	0707	0719	0734	0742	0745	0750	0807	0809	0821	0825	0840	0837	0846	0849	0906	0909
180	Loughborough 189 d.		|	0558	0601	0652	0646	0656	0649	|	0717	0729	0744	0752	0755	|	|	|	0831	0835	0850	0847	|	|	|	|
191	East Midlands Parkway d.		|	0606	0608	0659	0653	0704	0657	|	0724	0737	0753	0800	|	|	|	|	0838	0842	0857	0854	|	|	|	|
204	**Nottingham** 189 ‡ a.		|	|	|	0712	|	0719	|	|	|	0751	|	|	0811	0821	|	|	0853	0900	|	|	0911	0911	|	|
207	**Derby** 124 a.		0256	0619f	0622f	...	0707	...	0709	0728	0735	...	0806f	0814	...	...	0827	0830	...	...	0911	0908f	...	...	0927	0930
246	Chesterfield 124 ‡ a.		...	0642	0644	...	0725	...	0728	0746	0753	...	0828	0832	...	...	0846	0851	...	...	0929	0930	...	...	0945	0948
265	**Sheffield** 124 ‡ a.		...	0708	0708	...	0743	...	0743	0801	0806	...	0844	0845	...	...	0900	0906	...	...	0942	0945	...	...	1000	1001

	⑥	Ⓐ	⑥	Ⓐ	⑥	Ⓐ	⑥	Ⓐ	⑥	Ⓐ	⚒	⚒	⑥	Ⓐ	⚒	⚒	⚒	⚒	⚒	⚒	⚒	⚒	⚒	⚒	⚒	⚒
London St Pancras 170a d.	0805	0806	0832	0832	0835	0835	0902	0902	0905	0905	0932	0935	1002	1002	1005	1032	1035	1102	1105	1132	1135	1202	1205	1232	1235	1302
Kettering 170a d.	0854	0855	|	|	0922	0926	|	|	0953	0956	|	1022	|	|	1054	|	1122	|	1153	|	1221	|	1253	|	1322	|
Market Harborough d.	0904	0905	|	|	0932	0936	|	|	1003	1006	|	1032	|	|	1104	|	1132	|	1203	|	1231	|	1304	|	1332	|
Leicester 189 d.	0917	0920	0937	0940	0946	0950	1006	1010	1018	1020	1037	1046	1106	1108	1117	1137	1147	1207	1217	1235	1246	1306	1318	1336	1346	1406
Loughborough 189 d.	0927	0930	0947	0950	|	|	|	|	1028	1030	1047	|	|	|	1127	1147	|	|	1227	1247	|	|	1328	1346	|	|
East Midlands Parkway d.	0935	0938	0954	0958	|	|	|	|	1035	1038	1054	|	|	|	1135	1154	|	|	1235	1254	|	|	1335	1354	|	|
Nottingham 189 ‡ a.	0948	0949	|	|	1009	1011	|	|	1049	1050	|	1109	|	|	1150	|	1211r	|	1248	|	1309	|	1350	|	1408	|
Derby 124 a.	...	...	1008	1011	...	...	1027	1030	...	...	1108	...	1127	1129	...	1208	...	1227	...	1308	...	1327	...	1408	...	1428
Chesterfield 124 ‡ a.	...	...	1028	1029	...	...	1045	1049	...	...	1129r	...	1145	1147	...	1228	...	1246	...	1328	...	1346	...	1428	...	1446
Sheffield 124 ‡ a.	...	...	1041	1042	...	...	1058	1105	...	...	1142	...	1158	1201	...	1244	...	1300	...	1343	...	1400	...	1444	...	1505n

	⚒	⚒	⚒	⚒	⚒	⚒	⚒	⚒	⚒	⚒	⚒	⑥	Ⓐ	⑥	Ⓐ	⑥	Ⓐ	⑥	Ⓐ	⑥	Ⓐ	⑥	Ⓐ	⑥	Ⓐ	⑥
London St Pancras 170a d.	1305	1332	1335	1402	1405	1432	1435	1502	1505	1532	1535	1602	1602	1605	1605	1632	1632	1635	1635	1702	1702	1705	1705	1732	1732	1735
Kettering 170a d.	1353	|	1422	|	1453	|	1522	|	1552	|	1622	|	|	1652	1652	|	|	1722	1726	|	|	1752	1758	|	|	1822
Market Harborough d.	1403	|	1432	|	1503	|	1532	|	1602	|	1632	|	|	1704	1703	|	|	1732	1737	|	|	1803	1808	|	|	1832
Leicester 189 d.	1418	1436	1446	1506	1517	1537	1546	1606	1617	1636	1646	1706	1706	1718	1718	1736	1741	1745	1751	1806	1811	1818	1823	1836	1841	1846
Loughborough 189 d.	1428	1446	|	|	1528	1547	|	|	1627	1646	|	|	|	1728	1728	1746	1751	|	|	|	|	1828	1834	1846	1851	|
East Midlands Parkway d.	1435	1454	|	|	1535	1554	|	|	1634	1654	|	|	|	1735	1737	1753	1758	|	1804	|	|	1835	1841	1854	1859	|
Nottingham 189 ‡ a.	1448	|	1508	|	1549	|	1609	|	1650	|	1709	|	|	1749	1751	|	|	1807	1821	|	|	1848	1855	|	|	1909
Derby 124 a.	...	1508	...	1528	...	1609	...	1628	...	1708	...	1726	1728	...	...	1807	1813f	...	...	1827	1834	...	...	1909	1912	...
Chesterfield 124 ‡ a.	...	1527	...	1547	...	1628	...	1646	...	1730	...	1745	1747	...	...	1828	1835	...	...	1845	1852	...	...	1928	1931	...
Sheffield 124 ‡ a.	...	1542	...	1600	...	1642	...	1700	...	1745	...	1758	1805	...	...	1843	1848	...	...	1900	1916	...	...	1942	1948	...

	Ⓐ	⑥	Ⓐ	⑥	Ⓐ	⑥	Ⓐ	⑥	Ⓐ	⑥	Ⓐ	⑥	Ⓐ	⑥	Ⓐ	⑥	Ⓐ	⚒	⑥	Ⓐ	Ⓐ T	⚒	⚒ C	⚒	⚒	⑥
London St Pancras 170a d.	1735	1802	1802	1805	1805	1832	1832	1835	1835	1902	1902	1905	1905	1932	1932	1935	1935	2002	2005	2005	...	2031	2034	2102	2105	2132
Kettering 170a d.	1826	|	|	1852	1857	|	|	1922	1933j	|	|	1954	1956	|	|	2022	2026	|	2053	2057	...	|	2121	|	2153	|
Market Harborough d.	1836	|	|	1903	1907	|	|	1932	1943	|	|	2004	2006	|	|	2032	2036	|	2103	2107	...	|	2131	|	2203	|
Leicester 189 d.	1850	1906	1910	1918	1921	1936	1941	1946	1957	2006	2010	2018	2020	2037	2041	2046	2050	2106e	2117	2123	2130	2136	2146	2206	2218	2236
Loughborough 189 d.	|	|	|	1928	1931	1946	1951	|	2007	|	|	2028	2031	2047	2051	|	|	|	2128	2133	2152	2146	|	|	2228	2246
East Midlands Parkway d.	1903	|	|	1935	1938	1954	1959	|	|	|	|	2035	2038	2054	2058	2100	2104	|	2136	2141	2207j	2154	|	|	2235	2254
Nottingham 189 ‡ a.	1913	|	|	1951	1956	|	|	2009	2025	|	|	2048	2053	|	|	2110	2114	|	2148	2155	2230	|	2207	|	2248	|
Derby 124 a.	...	1927	1931	...	...	2007	2012	...	...	2028	2031	...	...	2108	2112	...	...	2131	...	...	...	2211	...	2228	...	2304
Chesterfield 124 ‡ a.	...	1945	1949	...	...	2026	2031	...	...	2047	2051	...	...	2127	2131	...	...	2150	...	...	...	2230	...	2246	...	2322
Sheffield 124 ‡ a.	...	2000	2002	...	...	2040	2049	...	...	2101	2116	...	...	2141	2145	...	...	2204	...	...	...	2243	...	2301	...	2334

	Ⓐ	Ⓐ	⑥	⑥	Ⓐ	⑥	Ⓐ	Ⓐ	Ⓐ		⑦	⑦	⑦	⑦	⑦	⑦	⑦	⑦	⑦	⑦	⑦	⑦	⑦	⑦	⑦	⑦
London St Pancras 170a d.	2132	2135	2135	2215	2232	2232	2235	2305	2335	⑦	...	0900	0930	1000	1030	1100	1130	1202	1234	1302	1334	1402	1434	1502	1532	1535
Kettering 170a d.	|	2222	2225	2304	|	2319	2322	0037	0055		...	1019	1049	1119	1149	1219	1242	|	1330	|	1433	|	1521	|	1618	1624
Market Harborough d.	|	2232	2235	2314	|	2329	2332	|	|		...	1029	1059	1129	1159	1229	1252	1257	1340	1355	1443	1455	1531	1555	|	1634
Leicester 189 d.	2238	2246	2249	2328	2337	2345	2346	0130j	0149j		1015	1044	1114	1144	1218	1244	1308	1313	1356	1411	1502	1511	1547	1611	1642	1653
Loughborough 189 d.	2248	|	2259	2338	2347	2355	2356	0140	0159		1025	1054	1124	1154	1228	1254	|	1323	1406	1421	1512	1521	1557	1621	1652	1703
East Midlands Parkway d.	2256	2300	2306	2345	2354	0002	0004	0148	0207		1032	1102	1132	1202	1235	1302	|	1330	1414	1428	1519	1529	1605	1629	1659	1711
Nottingham 189 ‡ a.	|	2310	2316	|	|	0018	0022	|	0219		|	1115	|	1214	|	1315	1329	|	1427	|	1533	|	1623	|	|	1723
Derby 124 a.	2309	...	...	2355	0008	0046	...	0201	...		1048	...	1145f	...	1250	...	...	1344v	...	1442v	...	1542f	...	1642v	1713	...
Chesterfield 124 ‡ a.	2328	...	...	...	0026	...	...	...	...		1111	...	1209	...	1310	...	...	1409	...	1510	...	1609	...	1710	1733	...
Sheffield 124 ‡ a.	2341	...	...	...	0039	...	...	...	...		1126	...	1224	...	1327	...	...	1429	...	1527	...	1627	...	1727	1749	...

	⑦	⑦	⑦	⑦	⑦	⑦	⑦	⑦	⑦	⑦	⑦	⑦	⑦	⑦	⑦	⑦	⑦	⑦	⑦	⑦	⑦	⑦	⑦	⑦	⑦	⑦
London St Pancras 170a d.	1602	1605	1632	1635	1702	1705	1732	1735	1802	1805	1832	1835	1902	1905	1932	1935	2002	2005	2032	2035	2102	...	2135	2202	2232	2300
Kettering 170a d.	|	1651	|	1722	|	1751	|	1821	|	1851	|	1921	|	1951	|	2021	|	2051	|	2121	|	...	2230	|	2334	0018
Market Harborough d.	1655	1701	|	1732	|	1801	|	1831	|	1901	|	1931	|	2001	|	2031	|	2101	|	2131	|	...	2240	2256	2344	0028
Leicester 189 d.	1709	1719	1738	1748	1806	1819	1838	1849	1907	1918	1938	1947	2007	2019	2038	2048	2106	2117	2138	2147	2208	2230	2256	2312	2359	0044
Loughborough 189 d.	|	1729	1748	|	|	1829	1848	|	|	1928	1948	|	|	2029	2048	2058	2116	2127	2148	|	2218	2240	2306	|	0009	0054
East Midlands Parkway d.	1723	1736	1755	1802	1820	1836	1855	1902	1920	1935	1955	2001	2020	2036	2055	2105	2124	2135	2155	|	2225	2247	2313	2325	0017	0101
Nottingham 189 ‡ a.	|	1750	|	1815	|	1850	|	1912	|	1950	|	2011	|	2050	|	2115	|	2147	|	2212	|	|	2326	|	0029	|
Derby 124 a.	1733	...	1809f	...	1830	...	1909	...	1930	...	2009	...	2030	...	2109	...	2134	...	2209	...	2239	2257	2350	2339	...	0111
Chesterfield 124 ‡ a.	1751	...	1831	...	1848	...	1928	...	1950	...	2030	...	2049	...	2127	...	2152	...	2227	...	2257	...	...	2357	...	...
Sheffield 124 ‡ a.	1805	...	1846	...	1905	...	1947	...	2005	...	2046	...	2106	...	2141	...	2208	...	2242	...	2316	...	...	0013	...	...

		②–⑤	①	②–⑤	①	⑥	Ⓐ	⑥	Ⓐ	Ⓐ	⑥	Ⓐ	⚒	⚒	⚒	⑥	Ⓐ	⑥	Ⓐ B	⑥	Ⓐ	⑥	Ⓐ B	⑥	Ⓐ	⑥
Sheffield 124 ‡ d.	⚒	...	...	...	...	...	...	...	0458	...	0530	0530	...	0556	...	0633	0630	...	...	0700	0700	...	...	0731	0733	...
Chesterfield 124 ‡ d.		...	...	...	...	...	...	...	0510	...	0542	0542	...	0608	...	0645	0644	...	...	0712	0713	...	...	0743	0745	...
Derby 124 d.		0357	0420	0412	0440	0447	0447	0459	0530	...	0602	0602	...	0628	...	0705	0705	...	...	0732	0733	...	...	0804	0805	...
Nottingham 189 ‡ d.		|	|	|	|	|	0514	0526	|	0549	|	|	0612	|	0649	|	|	0712	0712	|	|	0746	0749	|	|	0812
East Midlands Parkway d.		0410	0433	0422	0453	0500	0527	0536	0543	|	|	0615	0624	0641	0659	|	|	0724	0726	0745	|	|	0759	|	|	0824
Loughborough 189 d.		0417	0441	0430	0500	0508	0534	0543	0550	|	|	|	0632	0648	|	0719	0719	0732	|	0752	0750	|	|	|	0819	0832
Leicester 189 d.		0434j	0452	0446j	0512	0519	0547	0554	0602	0610	0623	0630	0643	0700	0713	0731	0732	0743	0743	0803	0801	0813	0814	0827	0830	0843
Market Harborough d.		|	0505	|	0525	0533	0600	0608	|	0624	0637	|	0656	|	0727	|	|	0757	0757	|	|	0826	0828	|	|	0857
Kettering 170a d.		0522	|	0535	0535	|	0611	0618	|	0636	0647	|	0706	|	0737	|	|	0807	0808	|	|	0836	0838	|	|	0907
London St Pancras 170a a.		0610	0610	0636	0636	0626	0701	0704	0709	0733	0736	0739	0757	0809	0827	0836	0836	0855	0856	0907	0909	0927	0927	0934	0937	0954

	Ⓐ	Ⓐ	⑥	⚒	⚒	⚒	⚒	⚒	⑥	Ⓐ	⚒	⚒	⚒	⑥	Ⓐ	⚒	⚒	⚒	⑥	Ⓐ	⚒	⚒	⚒	⑥	Ⓐ	⚒
Sheffield 124 ‡ d.	...	0752	0800	...	0835	...	0900	...	0929	0937	...	1000	...	1036	1036	...	1100	...	1130	1137	...	1200	...	1236	1237	...
Chesterfield 124 ‡ d.	...	0812	0812	...	0848	...	0912	...	0941	0949	...	1013	...	1048	1049	...	1112	...	1142	1149	...	1212	...	1249	1249	...
Derby 124 d.	...	0832	0832	...	0909	...	0932	...	1005j	1009	...	1033	...	1108	1110	...	1132	...	1208t	1209	...	1232	...	1309	1309	...
Nottingham 189 ‡ d.	0813	|	|	0850	|	0912	|	0950	|	|	1012	|	1050	|	|	1112	|	1150	|	|	1212	|	1250	|	|	1312
East Midlands Parkway d.	0825	0845	0845	|	|	0924	0945	|	|	|	1024	1046	|	|	|	1124	1145	|	|	|	1225	1245	|	|	|	1325
Loughborough 189 d.	|	0853	0852	|	|	0932	0953	|	|	|	1032	1053	|	|	|	1132	1152	|	|	|	1232	1252	|	|	|	1332
Leicester 189 d.	0840	0904	0904	0912	0931	0943	1004	1013	1027	1032	1043	1104	1112	1130	1133	1143	1204	1213	1231	1232	1243	1303	1313	1332	1332	1343
Market Harborough d.	0852	|	|	0926	|	0956	|	1026	|	|	1056	|	1125	|	|	1157	|	1226	|	|	1257	|	1326	|	|	1357
Kettering 170a d.	0911j	|	|	0936	|	1006	|	1036	|	|	1106	|	1136	|	|	1207	|	1236	|	|	1307	|	1336	|	|	1407
London St Pancras 170a a.	1006	1009	1007	1027	1039	1055	1109	1127	1139	1138	1155	1210	1227	1239	1237	1254	1309	1327	1336	1339	1354	1409	1427	1436	1442	1454

	⚒	⚒	⑥	Ⓐ	⚒	⚒	⚒	⑥	Ⓐ	⑥	Ⓐ	⚒	⚒	⑥	Ⓐ	⑥	Ⓐ	⚒	⑥	Ⓐ	⑥	Ⓐ	⑥	Ⓐ	⑥	Ⓐ
Sheffield 124 ‡ d.	1300	...	1336	1337	...	1400	...	1436	1437	...	...	1500	...	1537	1537	...	...	1600	...	...	1637	1637	...	...	1700	1701
Chesterfield 124 ‡ d.	1312	...	1349	1349	...	1412	...	1448	1449	...	...	1512	...	1549	1549	...	...	1613	...	...	1649	1649	...	...	1712	1714
Derby 124 d.	1332	...	1409	1409	...	1432	...	1510	1509	...	...	1532	...	1611	1609	...	...	1633	...	...	1711	1709	...	...	1732	1734
Nottingham 189 ‡ d.	|	1350	|	|	1412	|	1449	|	|	1512	1512	|	1550	|	|	1612	1612	|	1650	1650	|	|	1712	1712	|	|
East Midlands Parkway d.	1345	|	|	|	1424	1445	|	|	|	1524	1525	1545	|	|	|	1624	1625	1646	|	|	|	|	1724	1725	1745	1748
Loughborough 189 d.	1352	|	|	|	1432	1452	|	|	|	1532	1532	1552	|	|	|	1632	1632	1653	|	|	|	|	1732	1732	1752	1755
Leicester 189 d.	1404	1413	1431	1432	1443	1504	1512	1532	1532	1543	1543	1603	1612	1632	1630	1643	1643	1704	1713	1715	1733	1730	1743	1745	1804	1806
Market Harborough d.	|	1426	|	|	1456	|	1526	|	|	1556	1557	|	1625	|	|	1656	1657	|	1726	1728	|	|	1756	1758	|	|
Kettering 170a d.	|	1436	|	|	1506	|	1536	|	|	1606	1607	|	1636	|	|	1706	1707	|	1736	1739	|	|	1806	1808	|	|
London St Pancras 170a a.	1509	1527	1536	1539	1554	1608	1627	1636	1639	1654	1656	1710	1727	1739	1740	1754	1806	1809	1827	1826	1836	1840	1854	1904	1909	1910

B – From Lincoln (Table **184**).
C – To Lincoln on Ⓐ (Table **184**).
T – From Peterborough (Table **208**).

a – Arrives 11–12 minutes earlier.
e – Departs 2111 on Ⓐ.
f – Departs 5–6 minutes later.
j – Arrives 5–7 minutes earlier.
n – Arrives 1500 on ⑥.
r – Arrives 3 minutes earlier on Ⓐ.
t – Arrives 1200.
v – Departs 7–9 minutes later.

‡ – For trains Nottingham - Sheffield and v.v. see Tables **171** and **206**.

170 SHEFFIELD, DERBY and NOTTINGHAM - LEICESTER - LONDON

Most trains convey 🍸 EM

	Ⓐ	⑥	Ⓐ	⑥	Ⓐ	⑥	⚒	⚒	Ⓐ	⑥	⚒	⚒	⑥	Ⓐ	⚒	Ⓐ	⑥	⚒	⑥	Ⓐ	⑥	Ⓐ	⑥	⑥	Ⓐ
Sheffield 124 ‡ d.	...	...	1732	1731	...	...	1800	...	1837	1837	...	1900	...	...	1937	...	...	2000	...	...	2030	2037	...	2100	2101
Chesterfield 124 ‡ d.	...	...	1745	1749	...	...	1812	...	1849	1849	...	1912	...	...	1949	...	...	2012	...	...	2042	2049	...	2114	2113
Derby 124 d.	...	...	1808	1811	...	...	1832	...	1909	1909	...	1932	...	...	2010	...	...	2032	...	...	2102	2107	...	2134	2134
Nottingham 189 ‡ d.	1750	1750	|	|	1810	1812	|	1850	|	|	1912	|	1950	1949	|	2011	2012	|	2050	2048	|	...	2125	|	|
East Midlands Parkway d.	|	|	|	|	1823	1824	1845	|	|	|	1924	1945	|	|	|	2023	2024	2045	|	2102	2112	...	2137	2149	2147
Loughborough 189 d.	|	|	|	|	1830	1832	1852	|	|	|	1932	1952	|	2004	|	2031	2032	2052	|	2110	2119	...	2145	2157	2154
Leicester 189 d.	1811	1813	1830	1833	1841	1843	1903	1911	1930	1932	1943	2003	2013	2015	2032	2042	2043	2104	2114	2123	2129	...	2156	2207	2206
Market Harborough d.	1824	1826	|	|	1857	1856	|	1925	|	|	1956	|	2026	2028	|	2056	2056	|	2127	2137	...	...	2209	...	|
Kettering 170a d.	1834	1836	|	|	1907	1906	|	1935	|	|	2006	|	2036	2038	|	2106	2106	|	2137	2147	...	...	2219	...	|
London St Pancras 170a a.	1926	1927	1938	1936	1954	1954	2007	2027	2036	2039	2054	2109	2126	2134	2139	2156	2154	2208	2234	2239	...	...	2322	...	2316

	Ⓐ	Ⓐ	Ⓐ	⑥	Ⓐ	⚒	⑥	Ⓐ		⑦	⑦	⑦	⑦	⑦	⑦	⑦	⑦	⑦	⑦	⑦	⑦	⑦	⑦	⑦	⑦
Sheffield 124 ‡ d.	...	2145	2156	2201	2229	...	2320	2330	⑦	...	...	...	...	0823	...	0926	...	...	1052	...	1152	...	1252	1331	...
Chesterfield 124 ‡ d.	...	2201	2210	2213	2245	...	2332	2354		...	...	...	...	0835	...	0938	...	...	1105	...	1204	...	1304	1344	...
Derby 124 d.	...	2220	2234	2231	2308	...	0006	0015		0700	...	0751	...	0855	...	0958	...	...	1126	...	1225	...	1325	1406	...
Nottingham 189 ‡ d.	2140	|	...	...	...	2318	...	...		|	0724	|	0821	|	0926	|	1016	1110	|	1209	|	1310	|	|	1410
East Midlands Parkway d.	2156	2233	...	...	...	2332	...	...		0711	0734	0804	0833	0908	0936	1011	1026	1122	1140	1221	1239	1323	1339	1416	1423
Loughborough 189 d.	|	2241	...	...	...	2340	...	...		|	0741	0811	0841	0915	0943	1019	1033	1130	1147	1229	1247	1330	1347	|	1430
Leicester 189 d.	2215j	2252	...	...	...	2353	...	...		0726	0753	0823	0853	0927	0956	1031	1046	1144	1200	1242	1259	1343	1359	1432	1443
Market Harborough d.	2228	2305	...	...	...	...	...	...		0743	0810	0840	0910	0944	1013	1044	1059	1158	1213	1256	1312	1356	1412	|	1456
Kettering 170a d.	2240	2315	...	...	...	...	...	...		0753	0820	0850	0920	0954	1023	1054	1109	1208	|	1306	|	1406	|	|	1506
London St Pancras 170a a.	2352	0023	...	...	...	...	...	...		0916	0943	1012	1041	1111	1142	1211	1219	1256	1308	1353	1408	1455	1508	1539	1556

	⑦	⑦	⑦	⑦	⑦	⑦	⑦	⑦	⑦	⑦	⑦	⑦	⑦	⑦	⑦	⑦	⑦	⑦	⑦	⑦	⑦	⑦	⑦	⑦	⑦
Sheffield 124 ‡ d.	1351	1432	...	1451	...	1531	...	1551	...	1628	...	1651	...	1728	...	1751	...	...	1851	...	1951	2029	...	...	2236
Chesterfield 124 ‡ d.	1404	1446	...	1504	...	1544	...	1604	...	1640	...	1703	...	1741	...	1803	...	...	1903	...	2003	2042	...	...	2249
Derby 124 d.	1425	1506	...	1528j	...	1606	...	1628j	...	1701	...	1725	...	1802	...	1826	...	...	1923	...	2025	2103	...	...	2322
Nottingham 189 ‡ d.	|	|	1506	|	1547	|	1610	|	1647	|	1710	|	1745	|	1810	|	1845	1906	|	1959	|	|	2109	2150	...
East Midlands Parkway d.	1439	1516	1520	1542	1557	1616	1623	1642	1657	1712	1723	1739	1757	1813	1823	1839	1857	1919	1937	2012	2039	2117	2121	2202	...
Loughborough 189 d.	1446	|	1528	1550		|	1630	1649	|	1719	1730	1746	|	|	1830	1846	|	1926	1944	2019	2046	2124	2129	2210	...
Leicester 189 d.	1459	1532	1543	1602	1613	1632	1643	1702	1713	1732	1743	1802j	1813	1829	1843	1902j	1913	1943t	1959	2032	2059	2136	2141	2221	...
Market Harborough d.	1512	|	1556	|	1626	|	1656	|	1726	|	1756	|	1826	1842	1856	|	1926	1956	|	2045	2112	2150	2154	...	...
Kettering 170a d.	|	|	1606	|	1636	|	1706	|	1736	|	1806	|	1836	|	1906	|	1936	2006	|	2055	|	2200	2205	...	...
London St Pancras 170a a.	1609	1639	1655	1709	1727	1739	1755	1809	1827	1839	1855	1909	1927	1939	1955	2009	2027	2055	2108	2155	2208	2303	2309	...	...

j – Arrives 5 minutes earlier. t – Arrives 1937. ‡ – For trains Sheffield - Nottingham see Tables **171** and **206**.

170a LONDON - KETTERING - CORBY

Most trains convey 🍸 EM

See Table **170** for other services London - Kettering and v.v.

km			dE	Ⓐ	ⒶF	ⒶG	Ⓐ	ⒶG	Ⓐ	ⒶG	Ⓐ	Ⓐ	Ⓐ	Ⓐ	Ⓐ	ⒶA	Ⓐ	Ⓐ	⊠	Ⓐ	Ⓐ	Ⓐ	Ⓐ	Ⓐ
0	**London** St Pancras d.	Ⓐ	0015	0545	0559	0605	0617	0635	0647	0705	0718	0749	0818	0847	0915	0945	1015	1045		1616	1647	1717	1747	1817
47	Luton ✈ Parkway d.		0055	0607	|	|	0643	|	0709	|	0742	0811	0841	0912	0937	1007	1037	1107	and at	1639	1709	1741	1812	1842
49	Luton d.		0059	0610	|	|	0646	|	0712	|	0745	0814	0845	0915	0940	1011	1040	1110	the same	1642	1712	1744	1815	1845
80	Bedford d.		0122	0626	|	0639	0701	0711	0728	|	0800	0830	0901	0930	0956	1025	1056	1126	minutes	1658	1728	1800	1830	1901
105	Wellingborough d.		0132	0637	0642	|	0713	|	0739	0751	0811	0841	0912	0942	1007	1036	1107	1137	past each	1709	1739	1811	1842	1912
116	Kettering d.		0141	0646	...	0653	0722	0726	0748	0757	0820	0849	0921	0951	1016	1045	1117	1146	hour until	1718	1748	1820	1851	1920
128	**Corby** a.		...	0654	...	...	0730	...	0756	...	0828	0857	0929	0959	1024	1055	1125	1154		1726	1756	1828	1859	1928

	ⒶA	Ⓐ	Ⓐ	Ⓐ		Ⓐ	Ⓐ	ⒶF	Ⓐ		⑥E	⑥	⑥F	⑥G	⑥	⑥G	⑥	⑥G	⑥	⑥		⑥	⑥
London St Pancras d.	1835	1847	1915	1945		2215	2247	2305	2354	⑥	0015	0533	0600	0605	0608	0633	0646	0705	0715	0745		2115	2145
Luton ✈ Parkway d.	|	1909	1937	2007	and at	2238	2316	2346	0033		0054	0601	|	|	0630	|	0708	|	0737	0807	and at	2137	2207
Luton d.	|	1912	1940	2010	the same	2241	2319	|	0036		0059	0604	|	|	0633	|	0711	|	0740	0810	the same	2140	2210
Bedford d.	|	1928	1956	2026	minutes	2256	2340	|	0100		0122	0619	|	0638	0649	0706	0727	0739	0756	0826	minutes	2156	2228
Wellingborough d.	|	1939	2007	2037	past each	2308	2352	0021	0111		0132	0630	0642	|	0701	|	0738	0750	0808	0838	past each	2208	2240
Kettering d.	1938f	1948	2016	2047	hour until	2317	0001	0036	0120		0141	0639	...	0652	0710	0720	0748	0756	0816	0846	hour until	2216	2248
Corby a.	1946	1956	2025	2056		2325	0009	...	0128		...	0649	...	...	0718	...	0757	...	0824	0854		2224	2256

	⑥	⑥		⑦G	⑦F	⑦G	⑦F	⑦G	⑦G	⑦	⑦G	⑦	⑦G	⑦	⑦		⑦	⑦	⑦	⑦	⑦E	⑦	⑦G	⑦E
London St Pancras d.	2218	2235	⑦	0900	0930	1000	1030	1100	1130	1214	1234	1314	1334	1414	1444		1944	2014	2044	2114	2135	2212	2232	2300
Luton ✈ Parkway d.	2240	|		0932	1002	1033	1103	1133	1203	1236	1257	1336	1357	1436	1506	and at	2006	2036	2106	2136	2157	2236	2254	2330
Luton d.	2243	|		0936	|	1037	|	1137	|	1239	|	1339	1400	1439	1509	the same	2009	2039	2109	2139	|	2239	|	|
Bedford d.	2259	2316	★	1000	1030	1100	1130	1200	1224	1255	1311	1355	1414	1455	1525	minutes	2025	2055	2125	2155	2211	2255	2313	2359
Wellingborough d.	2310	2335		1012	1042	1112	1142	1212	1235	1307	1323	1407	1426	1507	1537	past each	2037	2107	2137	2207	2223	2307	2326	0011
Kettering d.	2319	|		1018	1048	1118	1148	1218	1241	1316	1329	1416	1432	1516	1547	hour until	2045	2117	2145	2217	2229	2316	2332	0017
Corby a.	_2349*_	_0030*_		...	_1108_	...	_1210_	_1238_	...	1324	_1356_	1424	_1454_	1525	1555		...	2125	...	2225	...	2324	...	...

		Ⓐ	ⒶE	Ⓐ	Ⓐ	Ⓐ	Ⓐ	Ⓐ	Ⓐ	Ⓐ	ⒶA	Ⓐ	Ⓐ		Ⓐ	Ⓐ	Ⓐ	Ⓐ	Ⓐ	Ⓐ	ⒶA	Ⓐ	Ⓐ	Ⓐ
Corby d.	Ⓐ	0432	...	0539	0610	0638	0709	0739	0808	0839	0848	0910	0938		1203	1239	1309	1339	1409	1439	1508	1540	1610	1640
Kettering d.		0440	0535	0547	0618	0647	0717	0747	0816	0847	0911t	0919	0947	and at	1211	1247	1318	1347	1418	1447	1518	1548	1618	1648
Wellingborough d.		0448	|	0555	0626	0655	0725	0755	0825	0855	|	0927	0955	the same	1219	1255	1327	1355	1426	1455	1528	1556	1627	1656
Bedford d.		0507	|	0609	0640	0710	0740	0810	0839	0911	|	0940	1010	minutes	1238r	1310	1340	1410	1440	1510	1540	1610	1641	1712
Luton d.		0529	|	0625	0656	0726	0755	0825	0855	0926	|	0956	1025	past each	1255	1325	1356	1425	1456	1525	1555	1626	1657	1727
Luton ✈ Parkway d.		0532	0613	0628	0659	0729	0758	0828	0858	0929	|	0959	1029	hour until	1258	1328	1359	1428	1459	1528	1558	1629	1700	1730
London St Pancras a.		0602	0636	0651	0724	0754	0824	0851	0921	0953	1006	1023	1052		1321	1351	1422	1451	1522	1551	1623	1653	1724	1753

	Ⓐ	ⒶF	Ⓐ	ⒶG	Ⓐ	ⒶG	Ⓐ	Ⓐ	Ⓐ	Ⓐ	Ⓐ	Ⓐ	ⒶG	Ⓐ		⑥	⑥	⊠	⑥	⑥	⑥G	⑥	⑥G	⑥
Corby d.	1711	...	1739	...	1806	...	1838	1909	1939	2010	2039	2142	...	2233	⑥	0510	0540		2040	2110	...	2140	_2201_	2240
Kettering d.	1719	...	1748	1808	1815	1834	1846	1918	1948	2018	2048	2151	2240	2242		0519	0549	and at	2048	2119	2137	2148	2219	2248
Wellingborough d.	1727	1754	1756	1815	1823	1841	1854	1927	1956	2027	2056	2159	|	2250		0527	0557	the same	2056	2127	|	2156	2227	...
Bedford d.	1741	|	1810	|	1840r	|	1909	1940	2010	2041	2110	2213	|	2304		0540	0610	minutes	2110	2140	2155	2210	|	...
Luton d.	1756	|	1826	|	1855	|	1924	1956	2025	2056	2126	2229	|	2322		0556	0626	past each	2125	2156	|	2225	|	...
Luton ✈ Parkway d.	1759	|	1829	|	1858	|	1927	1959	2028	2059	2129	2232	2316	2325		0559	0629	hour until	2128	2159	|	2228	|	...
London St Pancras a.	1822	1840	1852	1904	1921	1926	1950	2022	2051	2122	2152	2255	2352	2356		0623	0652		2151	2222	2234	2251	2322	...

		⑦E	⑦G	⑦E	⑦G	⑦F	⑦G	⑦F	⑦G	⑦	⑦	⑦	⑦	⑦	⑦		⑦	⑦	⑦F	⑦	⑦G	⑦	⑦F	⑦G
Corby d.	⑦	...	...	...	...	...	_1000_	_1038_	...	1141	1227	1310	1341	1410	1440		1910	1940	...	2005	...	2110	_2140_	...
Kettering d.		0753	0820	0850	0920	0954	1023	1054	1109	1149	1235	1318	1349	1418	1448	and at	1918	1948	...	2018r	2055	2118	2200	2205
Wellingborough d.		0800	0827	0857	0927	1001	1031	1101	1116	1158	1244	1326	1357	1426	1456	the same	1926	1956	...	2026	2102	2126	2207	2213
Bedford d.		0812	0844	0914	0944	1014	1044	1114	1130	1210	1256	1339	1410	1439	1509	minutes	1940	2009	...	2039	2115	2139	2220	2227
Luton d.		0834	|	|	1004	|	1103	|	|	1225	1312	1355	1425	1455	1525	past each	1956	2025	2044	2055	|	2155	2235	2242
Luton ✈ Parkway d.		0838	0907	0937	1008	1039	1107	1136	1154	1228	1315	1358	1428	1458	1528	hour until	1959	2028	|	2058	2131	2158	2238	2246
London St Pancras a.		0916	0943	1012	1041	1111	1142	1211	1219	1252	1339	1422	1452	1522	1552		2023	2052	2108	2122	2155	2223	2303	2309

A – Conveys [12] London St Pancras - Melton Mowbray and v.v. (see panel).
E – To/from Derby (Table **170**).
F – To/from Sheffield (Table **170**).
G – To/from Nottingham (Table **170**).

d – ②–⑤ only.

f – Arrives 1927.
r – Arrives 4–5 minutes earlier.
t – Arrives 0857.
★ – On ⑦ additional trains run from Kettering to Corby at 0945 and 1015.
⊠ – Timings may vary ± 2 minutes.
* – Connection by 🚌.

(LONDON -) CORBY - MELTON MOWBRAY

km		Ⓐ	Ⓐ		Ⓐ	Ⓐ
	London St Pancras d.	0945	1835	**Melton Mowbray** d.	0815	1435
	Kettering d.	1045	1938	Oakham d.	0827	1447
0	**Corby** d.	1055	1947	**Corby** d.	0848	1508
23	Oakham a.	|	2006	Kettering a.	0857	1517
43	**Melton Mowbray** a.	1123	2017	**London** St Pancras a.	1006	1623

NT 2nd class — NOTTINGHAM - SHEFFIELD - HUDDERSFIELD and LEEDS — 171

NOTTINGHAM - SHEFFIELD - LEEDS

km		⚒	⚒	⚒	⚒	⚒	⚒	⚒	⚒R	⚒	⚒L	⚒	⚒L	⚒	♥	⚒L	⚒	⑥L	ⒶL	⚒	ⒶL	⑥L	⚒
0	**Nottingham** ...... 170 206 d.	...	...	...	0520	...	...	0616	...	0718	...	0817	...	0917		...	1717	...	...	1817	...	...	1917
18	Langley Mill .... d.	...	...	...	|	...	...	0635	...	0737	...	0836	...	0936	and	...	1736	...	...	1836	...	...	1936
29	Alfreton .... 206 d.	...	...	...	|	...	...	0643	...	0745	...	0844	...	0944	at the	...	1744	...	...	1846	...	...	1945
45	Chesterfield ...... 170 206 d.	...	...	...	0551	0625	...	0653	...	0758	...	0856	...	0955	same	...	1755	...	...	1856	...	...	1956
64	**Sheffield** .... 170 206 a.	...	...	...	0615	0642	...	0712	...	0816	...	0914	...	1013	minutes	...	1814	...	...	1914	...	...	2013
64	**Sheffield** .... 192 193 d.	0528	0602	0619	...	0644	0704	0718	0745	0819	0845	0918	0945	1018	past	1744	1818	1846	1848	1918	1945	1947	2018
70	Meadowhall ...... 192 193 d.	0534	0608	0625	...	0650	0710	0724	0752	0825	0852	0924	0952	1024	each	1750	1824	1852	1854	1924	1951	1953	2024
90	Barnsley .... d.	0558	0630	0640	...	0706	0732	0741	0806	0840	0909	0940	1011	1040	hour	1808	1838	1910	1910	1940	2011	2011	2040
107	Wakefield Kirkgate .... d.	0616	0649	0655	...	0723	0750	0757	0821	0856	0925	0955	1026	1055	until	1825	1855	1925	1926	1955	2026	2026	2055
130	**Leeds** .... a.	0644	0724	0714	...	0744	0823	0815	0844	0914	0943	1014	1044	1114		1844	1916	1944	1945	2014	2044	2044	2114

	⚒L	⚒	Ⓐ	⑥	⚒	⚒	⑦	⑦	⑦B	⑦	⑦	⑦	⑦	⑦	⑦	⑦	⑦	⑦	⑦	⑦	⑦	⑦	⑦	⑦
Nottingham ...... 170 206 d.	...	2017	2115	2112	...	2318	...	...	0918	...	1017	1118	1218	1318	1418	1520	1619	1719	1819	1919	...	2015	2133	2233
Langley Mill .... d.	...	2036	2139	2136	...	2336	...	...	0938	...	1036	1137	1237	1337	1437	1538	1637	1737	1837	1938	...	2034	2157	2257
Alfreton .... 206 d.	...	2044	2147	2144	...	2344	...	...	0946	...	1044	1145	1245	1345	1445	1546	1645	1745	1845	1946	...	2042	2205	2305
Chesterfield ...... 170 206 d.	...	2055	2157	2155	...	2354	...	...	0956	...	1055	1156	1256	1356	1456	1557	1656	1757	1856	1957	...	2055	2216	2316
Sheffield .... 170 206 a.	...	2114	2216	2214	...	0013	...	...	1015	...	1114	1214	1315	1414	1515	1614	1714	1816	1914	2016	...	2115	2234	2335
Sheffield .... 192 193 d.	2045	2118	2218	2218	2231	...	0839	0917	1017	1051	1117	1216	1317	1417	1517	1617	1717	1817	1917	2017	2047	2116	2244	...
Meadowhall ...... 192 193 d.	2051	2124	2224	2224	2237	...	0845	0923	1023	1057	1123	1223	1323	1423	1523	1623	1724	1823	1923	2023	2053	2122	2249	...
Barnsley .... d.	2111	2140	2240	2240	2259	...	0907	0938	1038	1112	1137	1237	1337	1437	1537	1637	1738	1837	1937	2037	2115	2136	2312	...
Wakefield Kirkgate .... d.	2126	2155	2255	2255	2319	...	0925	0958	1053	1130	1153	1257	1355	1455	1555	1654	1755	1853	1953	2053	2133	2152	2332	...
Leeds .... a.	2144	2213	2316	2314	2356	...	0958	1018	1113	1205	1214	1316	1414	1514	1614	1714	1814	1914	2016	2114	2206	2214	0006	...

	⚒	⚒	⚒	Ⓐ	⑥	⚒R	⚒L	⚒	⚒L	⚒	⚒L	⚒	♥	⚒	⚒L	⚒	⚒L	⚒	⚒L	⚒	⚒	⚒	⚒
Leeds .... d.	...	...	...	...	...	...	0638	0709	0738	0804	0837	0909		1609	1638	1709	1738	1803	1838	1905	1932	2004	2032
Wakefield Kirkgate .... d.	...	...	...	...	...	...	0655	0727	0756	0821	0855	0925	and	1625	1655	1728	1756	1821	1858	1921	2003	2021	2103
Barnsley .... d.	...	*0523*	0552	...	...	...	0712	0743	0812	0837	0911	0941	at the	1641	1711	1744	1812	1837	1914	1937	2022	2037	2122
Meadowhall ...... 192 193 d.	...	*0543*	0613	...	...	...	0726	0802f	0828	0856	0927	0957	same	1657	1727	1758	1828	1856f	1929	1957f	2043	2051	2144
Sheffield .... 192 193 a.	...	*0551*	0621	...	...	...	0733	0809	0836	0904	0934	1004	minutes	1704	1734	1805	1835	1904	1936	2004	2051	2100	2152
Sheffield .... 170 206 d.	0515	0603	...	0642	0645	0703	...	0811	...	0906	...	1007	past	1706	...	1807	...	1906	...	2006	...	2104	...
Chesterfield ...... 170 206 d.	0530	0619	...	0659	0701	0718	...	0827	...	0922	...	1023	each	1722	...	1823	...	1922	...	2022	...	2120	...
Alfreton .... 206 d.	0543	0629	...	0710	0712	0729	...	0837	...	0933	...	1033	hour	1733	...	1834	...	1933	...	2033	...	|	...
Langley Mill .... d.	0551	0636	...	0718	|	0736	...	0844	...	0940	...	1040	until	1740	...	1841	...	1940	...	2040	...	|	...
Nottingham ...... 170 206 a.	0611	0700	...	0736	0739	0800t	...	0903	...	0959	...	1058		1758	...	1859	...	1959	...	2059	...	2200	...

	⚒	Ⓐ	⚒	⑥	Ⓐ	⑥	⚒	Ⓐ	⑦	⑦	⑦	⑦		⑦	⑦	⑦	⑦B	⑦	⑦	⑦	⑦	⑦	⑦
Leeds .... d.	2104	...	2137	...	...	...	2232	2302	...	0832	0910	1009		1509	1609	1709	1809	1909	2009	2017	2109	2209	2220
Wakefield Kirkgate .... d.	2122	...	2154	...	...	...	2303	2333	...	0903	0927	1026	and	1526	1626	1726	1826	1926	2026	2048	2130	2226	2251
Barnsley .... d.	2138	...	2211	...	...	...	2322	2352	...	0921	0943	1042	at the	1542	1642	1742	1842	1942	2042	2106	2146	2241	2309
Meadowhall ...... 192 193 d.	2155	...	2230	...	...	...	2343	0015	...	0942	0957	1056	same	1557	1657	1757	1857	1956	2056	2132f	2159	2257	2331
Sheffield .... 192 193 a.	2203	...	2240	...	...	...	2351	0024	...	0949	1004	1104	minutes	1604	1706	1804	1904	2003	2103	2139	2206	2304	2338
Sheffield .... 170 206 d.	2205	2238	...	2256	2338	2342	...	...	0905	...	1007	1106	past	1606	1706	1806	1906	2006	2107	...	2209	*2330*	...
Chesterfield ...... 170 206 d.	2221	2253	...	2311	0002	2356	...	...	0921	...	1023	1122	each	1622	1722	1822	1922	2022	2122	...	2224	*2344*	...
Alfreton .... 206 d.	2231	2304	...	2322	|	|	...	...	0932	...	1034	1133	hour	1633	1733	1833	1933	2033	2133	...	2235	*2355*	...
Langley Mill .... d.	2238	|	...	|	|	|	...	...	0940	...	1041	1140	until	1640	1740	1840	1940	2040	2141	...	2243	*0002*	...
Nottingham ...... 170 206 a.	2257	2327	...	2347	0038	0030	...	...	1001	...	1101	1201		1700	1800	1900	2000	2100	2201	...	2306	*0023*	...

SHEFFIELD - HUDDERSFIELD *'The Penistone Line'*

km		⚒	⚒	⚒		⚒	⚒	⚒		⚒	⚒	⚒	⑦	⑦	⑦L	⑦L	⑦L	⑦L		⑦L	⑦	⑦	⑦	⑦
0	**Sheffield** ...... 192 193 d.	0537	0630	0735	and	1635	1734	1834	...	1935	2035	2238	0938	1038	1138	1237	1338	1438	...	1536	1639	1741	1839	1939
6	Meadowhall .. 192 193 d.	0543	0636	0741		1641	1740	1840	...	1941	2041	2244	0944	1044	1144	1243	1344	1444	...	1542	1645	1747	1845	1945
26	Barnsley .... d.	0605	0702	0803	hourly	1703	1802	1902	...	2003	2103	2307	1006	1106	1206	1305	1406	1502	...	1604	1702	1809	1905f	2007
38	Penistone .... d.	0620	0719	0819		1720	1821	1918	...	2019	2119	2324	1023	1123	1223	1322	1423	1519	...	1621	1719	1825	1922	2024
59	**Huddersfield** .... a.	0652	0750	0851	until	1751	1852	1950	...	2050	2150	2355	1054	1154	1254	1353	1454	1550	...	1652	1751	1856	1953	2055

	⚒	⚒	⚒	⚒	⚒		⚒	⚒	⚒	⚒	⚒	⚒	⚒	⑦	⑦	⑦L	⑦L	⑦L	⑦L	⑦L	⑦L	⑦	⑦	⑦
Huddersfield .... d.	0613	0712	0810	0912	1012	and	1712	1751	1813	1912	2012	2112	2250	0910	1015	1119	1215	1319	1415	1515	1615	1715	1815	1915
Penistone .... d.	0644	0743	0842	0943	1043		1743	1826f	1846	1943	2043	2143	2324	0941	1046	1150	1246	1350	1446	1546	1646	1746	1849	1946
Barnsley .... d.	0701	0800	0859	1000	1100	hourly	1800	1845	1902	2000	2100	2200	2340	0958	1102	1207	1303	1407	1503	1603	1703	1803	1906	2003
Meadowhall . 192 193 d.	0722	0823	0922	1022	1121		1822	1910	1924	2022	2121	2221	0002	1019	1117	1228	1319	1428	1521	1626	1721	1827	1920	2024
Sheffield ..... 192 193 a.	0729	0830	0929	1029	1128	until	1829	1919	1933	2029	2129	2229	0009	1028	1125	1236	1328	1437	1529	1634	1729	1834	1929	2032

A – From London St. Pancras (Table 170).
B – To/from Carlisle (Table 173).
D – To Derby (Table 170).
G – To Gainsborough Central (Table 178).
L – To/from Lincoln (Table 178).
R – From Retford (Table 178).
f – Arrives 5 minutes earlier.
r – Arrives 2318 on ⑥.
t – Arrives 0755 on Ⓐ.
v – Ⓐ only.
♥ – Timings may vary ± 3 minutes.

EM 2nd class — NOTTINGHAM - WORKSOP and MATLOCK — 172

NOTTINGHAM - WORKSOP *'The Robin Hood Line'*

km		⚒	⚒	⚒	⚒		⚒	Ⓐ	⚒	Ⓐ	⚒	⚒	⚒	⚒	⑥	Ⓐ	⑥	⑦	⑦	⑦	⑦	⑦	⑦	⑦	⑦	⑦
0	**Nottingham** .... d.	0517	0625	0725	0825	and	1625	1700	1725	1800	1825	1925	2025	2125	2209	2225	2258	0812	0912	1112	1312	1512	1614	1812	1912	2022
28	Mansfield .... d.	0551	0701	0802	0902	hourly	1702	1730	1802	1830	1902	2002	2102	2202	2248	2302	2332	0845	0948	1145	1345	1545	1647	1845	1949	2055
50	**Worksop** .... a.	0625	0733	0833	0934	until	1733	...	1833	...	1934	2033	2133	2236	2325	2336	...	...	...	...	...	...	...	...	...	...

	⚒	⚒	Ⓐ	⚒		⚒	Ⓐ	⚒	Ⓐ	⚒	⚒	⚒	Ⓐ	⑥	Ⓐ	⑥	Ⓐ	⑦	⑦	⑦	⑦	⑦	⑦	⑦	⑦
Worksop .... d.	0535	0636	...	0739	and	1639	...	1739	...	1839	1939	2039	2139	2139	2239	2239	2343	...	...	...	...	...	...	...	...
Mansfield .... d.	0611	0712	0745	0812	hourly	1712	1745	1812	1847	1912	2012	2112	2212	2214	2314	2314	0010	0900	1002	1200	1400	1557	1701	1900	2108
Nottingham .... a.	0650	0750	0824	0854	until	1751	1815	1850	1923	1950	2050	2150	2250	2253	2348	2353	0049	0938	1035	1233	1434	1630	1739	1939	2141

NOTTINGHAM - DERBY - MATLOCK

km		⚒	⑥	Ⓐ	⑥	Ⓐ	⚒	§	⚒	Ⓐ	⑥	⚒	Ⓐ	⑥	⚒	⚒	⑦	⑦	⑦	⑦		⑦	⑦	⑦	⑦	⑦
0	**Nottingham** .... ‡ d.	...	0542	...	...	0653	0753t	★	1654t	1754	...	...	...	...	...	...	...	0930	1127	1330	★	1729	1825	1923	2024	2122
26	**Derby** .... ‡ a.	...	0611	...	...	0722	0822t		1722t	1822	...	...	...	...	...	...	...	0957	1154	1358		1756	1852	1950	2052	2149
26	**Derby** .... d.	0540	0630	0633	0724	0735	0833	and	1734	1824	1833	1934	2023	2033	2136	2233	0756	0959	1156	1359	and	1758	1854	1951	2053	2153
34	Duffield .... ◧ d.	0547	0637	0640	0731	0742	0840		1741	1831	1840	1941	2030	2040	2143	2240	0803	1006	1203	1406		1805	1901	1958	2100	2200
46	Whatstandwell . ◧ d.	0601	0651	0654	0745	0756	0854	hourly	1755	1845	1854	1955	2044	2054	2157	2254	0817	1020	1217	1420	hourly	1819	1915	2012	2114	2214
50	Cromford .... d.	0606	0657	0659	0750	0801	0859		1800	1850	1859	2000	2049	2100	2202	2259	0822	1025	1222	1426		1824	1920	2018	2120	2220
52	Matlock Bath ... ◧ d.	0609	0959	0702	0753	0804	0902	until	1803	1853	1902	2003	2052	2103	2205	2302	0825	1028	1225	1429	until	1827	1923	2021	2123	2223
53	**Matlock** .... ◧ a.	0614	0702	0705	0756	0807	0908		1806	1856	1905	2007	2055	2106	2209	2306	0828	1031	1228	1432		1830	1926	2024	2126	2226

	Ⓐ	⑥	⚒	⑥	Ⓐ	⚒		⚒	⚒	⚒	⚒	⚒	⚒	⚒	⑥	Ⓐ	⚒	⑦	⑦	⑦	⑦	⑦		⑦	⑦	⑦
Matlock .... ◧ d.	0617	0619	0710	0810	0813	0913	★	1513	1613	1713	1813	1913	2013	2115	2213	2219	2312	0839	1038	1237	1442	1540	★	2042	2144	2256
Matlock Bath .... ◧ d.	0619	0622	0712	0812	0815	0915		1515	1615	1715	1815	1915	2015	2118	2215	2221	2314	0841	1040	1239	1444	1542		2044	2146	2258
Cromford .... d.	0622	0625	0715	0815	0818	0918	and	1518	1618	1718	1818	1918	2018	2121	2218	2224	2317	0844	1043	1242	1447	1545	and	2047	2149	2301
Whatstandwell . ◧ d.	0627	0630	0720	0820	0823	0923		1523	1623	1723	1823	1923	2023	2126	2223	2229	2320	0849	1048	1247	1452	1550		2052	2154	2306
Duffield .... ◧ d.	0642	0645	0735	0835	0838	0938	hourly	1538	1638	1738	1839	1938	2038	2142	2238	2245	2337	0904	1103	1302	1508	1606	hourly	2107	2209	2323
Derby .... a.	0649	0653	0745	0842	0845	0946		1547	1647	1745	1846	1947	2045	2149	2246	2253	2345	0911	1110	1309	1515	1613		2114	2216	2330
Derby .... ‡ d.	0650	...	0746t	...	0848	...	until	1548t	1651t	1747t	...	...	...	...	...	...	2346	0914	1112	1312	1516	1615	until	2116	2219	2332
Nottingham .... ‡ a.	0722	...	0815t	...	0922	...		1618t	1723t	1817t	...	...	...	...	...	...	0014	0941	1139	1339	1544	1641		2143	2245	2359

f – Arrives 5–7 minutes earlier on ⑥.
r – Arrives 4–6 minutes earlier on Ⓐ.
★ – Timings may vary ± 4 minutes.
‡ – See Tables 120 and 155 for trains Nottingham - Derby and v.v.
§ – No departures from Nottingham 0953 - 1453 (these trains start from Derby).
g – Arrives 0653 on ⑥.
t – Ⓐ only.

◧ – Visitor attractions near these stations:
Duffield: Ecclesbourne Valley Railway (shares National Rail station). ✆ 01629 823076. www.e-v-r.com
Whatstandwell: Crich National Tramway Museum (1.6 km walk). ✆ 01773 854321. www.tramway.co.uk
Matlock Bath: Heights of Abraham (short walk to cable car). ✆ 01629 582365. www.heightsofabraham.com
Matlock: Peak Rail (shares National Rail station). ✆ 01629 580381. www.peakrail.co.uk

173 LEEDS - SETTLE - CARLISLE

All ⚒ trains convey 🍷 2nd class NT

km		Ⓐ	⑥	⚒	⚒	⚒	⚒		⚒	⚒	⚒	⚒	⚒A	⑦		⑦D	⑦	⑦	⑦	⑦	⑦A
	London Kings Cross **180** d.	...	...	...	...	...	...	...	...	...	...	...	1803	...	...	...	...	...	...	...	1835
0	**Leeds** 174 ▷ d.	0515	0620	0748	0919	1049	1318	...	1518	1648	1819	1949	2039	0859	...	1116	1232	1423	1623	1852	2100
27	Keighley 🚂 174 ▷ d.	0542	0648	0812	0942	1113	1343	...	1543	1713	1842	2012	2101s	0927	...	1139	1255	1447	1647	1916	2119s
42	**Skipton** 174 ▷ d.	0559	0706	0826	0959	1127	1357	...	1559	1727	1856	2027	2119	0945	...	1152	1309	1503	1701	1933	2135
58	Hellifield 174 d.	0615	0720	0840	1013	1141	1409	...	1613	1741	1910	2042	...	0959	...	1205	1323	1517	1713	1945	...
66	**Settle** d.	0623	0728	0850	1022	1151	1417	...	1620	1749	1919	2050	...	1007	...	1213	1333	1526	1721	1953	...
76	Horton in Ribblesdale d.	0632	0737	0858	1031	1159	1425	...	1629	1758	1927	2059	...	1016	...	|	1342	1535	1730	2002	...
84	Ribblehead d.	0640	0745	0906	1039	1207	1433	...	1637	1806	1935	2108	...	1024	...	|	1351	1543	1738	2010	...
93	Dent d.	0649	0754	0916	1048	1217	1443	...	1646	1815	1944	...	...	1034	...	|	1401	1553	1748	2020	...
99	Garsdale d.	0655	0800	0921	1054	1222	1448	...	1652	1821	1950	...	...	1040	...	|	1407	1559	1753	2025	...
115	Kirkby Stephen d.	0707	0812	0934	1106	1235	1501	...	1704	1833	2002	...	...	1053	...	1252	1420	1612	1806	2038	...
132	Appleby d.	0720	0825	0948	1119	1248	1514	...	1717	1846	2015	...	...	1106	...	1305	1432	1624	1819	2051	...
149	Langwathby d.	0734	0839	1001	1132	1302	1528	...	1731	1900	2028	...	...	1120	...	|	1446	1638	1833	2105	...
166	Armathwaite d.	0747	0852	1015	1146	1316	1541	...	1744	1913	2042	...	...	1134	...	|	1500	1652	1847	2119	...
182	**Carlisle** a.	0802	0907	1030	1201	1331	1602	...	1800	1928	2057	...	...	1152	...	1342	1515	1708	1903	2139	...

	⚒A	Ⓐ	⑥	⑥	Ⓐ	⑥	⚒	⚒	⚒	⚒		⚒	Ⓐ	⑥	⚒	⑦	⑦	⑦D	⑦	⑦	⑦
Carlisle d.	...	0549	...	0753	0824	0927	1058	1340	1450	1618	...	1824	2013	2015	...	0925	1223	1520	1607	1725	1911
Armathwaite d.	...	0603	...	0808	0838	0941	1112	|	1504	1632	...	1838	2027	2029	...	0939	1237	1534	|	1739	1925
Langwathby d.	...	0617	...	0822	0852	0955	1126	|	1518	1646	...	1852	2041	2043	...	0953	1251	1548	|	1753	1939
Appleby d.	...	0631	...	0836	0906	1009	1141	1416	1532	1700	...	1906	2055	2057	...	1007	1305	1602	1644	1808	1953
Kirkby Stephen d.	...	0644	...	0849	0920	1023	1154	1429	1546	1714	...	1920	2108	2111	...	1021	1319	1615	1657	1822	2007
Garsdale d.	...	0658	...	0903	0933	1036	1208	|	1559	1727	...	1933	2121	2124	...	1034	1332	1628	|	1835	2020
Dent d.	...	0703	...	0908	0938	1041	1213	|	1604	1732	...	1938	|	|	...	1040	1338	1633	|	1841	2026
Ribblehead d.	...	0713	0713	0918	0948	1051	1222	|	1614	1742	...	1948	|	|	2145	1049	1347	1643	|	1850	2035
Horton in Ribblesdale d.	...	0719	0719	0925	0954	1057	1229	|	1620	1748	...	1954	|	|	2151	1056	1354	1650	|	1857	2042
Settle d.	...	0727	0727	0933	1002	1105	1237	1506	1628	1756	...	2002	2146	2148	2159	1104	1402	1658	1734	1906	2051
Hellifield 174 d.	...	0736	0736	0941	1011	1113	1244	1514	1637	1805	...	2011	|	|	2208	1113	1411	1707	1742	1913	2059
Skipton 174 ▷ a.	0656	0752	0752	0957	1026	1127	1259	1528	1654a	1821a	...	2027	2206a	2209	2225	1130	1430	1720	1757	1928	2116
Keighley 🚂 174 ▷ a.	0708u	0805	0807	1009	1038	1138	1310	1541	1709	1839	...	2039	2221	2221	2241	1140	1440	1733	1808	1940	2127
Leeds 174 ▷ a.	0733	0834	0835	1034	1108	1204	1338	1605	1738	1908	...	2106	2248	2248	2311	1206	1508	1805	1834	2007	2155
London Kings Cross **180** a.	1000r	...	...	...	...	...	...	...	...	...	...	...	...	...	...	...	...	...	...	...	...

Local trains **Bradford Forster Square** - **Skipton** and v.v. *30 km*. Journey: ± 38 minutes. Trains call at **Keighley** (± 22 minutes later from Bradford, ± 14 minutes from Skipton).
From Bradford Forster Square: On ⚒ at 0603, 0641, 0711, 0741, 0810, 0836, 0908, 0941, 1011 and every half hour until 2011, 2048, 2120, 2211, 2311; on ⑦ at 0948 and hourly until 2248.
From Skipton: On ⚒ at 0604, 0634, 0709, 0737, 0820, 0834, 0904 and every half hourly until 1803, 1841, 1904, 1934, 2004, 2034, 2133, 2234; on ⑦ at 0842 and hourly until 2042, 2139.

Other local trains **Leeds** - **Skipton** and v.v. Journey ± 45 minutes. Trains call at **Keighley** (± 25 minutes later from Leeds, ± 14 minutes from Skipton).
From Leeds: On ⚒ at 0515Ⓐ, 0626, 0656, 0723, 0752, 0825, 0854, 0926 and every 30 minutes until 1656, 1719, 1742, 1755, 1826 and every 30 minutes until 2256, 2320; on ⑦ at 1016, 1126, 1157, 1216, 1316, 1416, 1516, 1611, 1716 and hourly until 2116, 2220, 2323.
From Skipton: On ⚒ at 0545, 0618, 0640, 0701, 0716, 0730, 0744, 0809, 0845, 0917 and every 30 minutes until 1617, 1645, 1717, and every 30 minutes until 2117, 2149, 2247; on ⑦ at 0834, 0912 and hourly until 1612, 1714, 1812, 1912, 2012, 2122, 2212, 2315.

A – [12] and 🍷 London Kings Cross - Skipton and v.v. (Table **180**).
D – From/to Nottingham (Table **171**).
a – Departs 5–7 minutes later.
r – Arrives 0950 on ⑥.
s – Calls to set down only.
u – Calls to pick up only.
▷ – See panels below main table for other local services (also for services Skipton - Bradford and v.v.).
🚂 – Keighley and Worth Valley Railway (Keighley - Haworth - Oakworth - Oxenhope, *8 km*). ✆ 01535 645214. www.kwvr.co.uk

174 LEEDS - LANCASTER - MORCAMBE - HEYSHAM

2nd class NT

km	km		⑥	Ⓐ	⚒A	⚒	⚒	⚒	Ⓐ	⑥	⚒	⑥	Ⓐ	Ⓐ	⑥	⑦	⑦	⑦	⑦D	⑦		⑦
0	0	**Leeds** 173 d.	...	...	*0626*	0819	1018	...	1218	1218	1418	1726	1726	1918	1918	0831	1033	...	1329	1532	...	1731
27	27	Keighley 🚂 173 d.	...	...	0704	0842	1043	...	1243	1243	1443	1752	1752	1943	1943	0859	1056	...	1352	1555	...	1754
42	42	Skipton 173 d.	0519	0522	0725	0856	1057	...	1258	1258	1458	1809	1810	2000	2000	0917	1110	...	1406	1609	...	1808
58	58	Hellifield 173 d.	0534	0537	0740	0910	1111	...	1312	1312	1513	1823	1824	2014	2014	0931	1124	...	1420	1623	...	1822
66	66	Giggleswick d.	0545	0548	0750	0921	1122	...	1323	1323	1523	1834	1834	2025	2025	0941	1134	...	1431	1634	...	1833
82	82	Bentham d.	0601	0603	0805	0935	1136	...	1337	1337	1538	1849	1849	2040	2040	0956	1148	...	1445	1648	...	1847
103	103	Carnforth 157 d.	0621	0622	0826	0957	1201	...	1401	1403	1603	1914	1915	2106	2109g	1016	1210	...	1507	1710	...	1909
113		**Lancaster** ✣ 157 a.	0630	0631	*0848*	1006b	1211	1244	1409	1411	1611f	1923a	1924a	2115	2117	1025	1220	1230	1518h	1721	...	1919
120	112	Morecambe ✣ a.	*0725*	*0725*	...	1028	1226	1255	1424	1427	1634	1951	1953	*2145*	*2145*k	1041	...	1241	1534	1735	...	1933
127	119	**Heysham** Port a.	...	...	...	...	...	1313	...	...	...	...	...	...	...	...	...	1300	...	...	...	...

	⚒	⚒		⚒	⚒		⚒	⚒		⚒	Ⓐ	⑥		⚒	⑦	⑦	⑦	⑦		⑦	⑦
Heysham Port d.	...	...	...	...	...	...	1321	...	...	...	...	...	...	...	...	1304	...	...	...	...	...
Morecambe ✣ d.	*0558*	*0901*	...	1032	1233	...	1339	1433	...	1731	2005	2010	...	*2056*	1049	1322	...	1538	...	1738	2004
Lancaster ✣ 157 d.	0648	0941	...	1046	1248g	...	1349	1447	...	1745	2030d	2030c	...	2131	1103	1333	1344	1552	...	1752	2017
Carnforth 157 d.	0658	0951	...	1056	1258	...	...	1457	...	1756	2040	2040	...	2143	1114	...	1354	1603	...	1802	2029
Bentham d.	0718	1011	...	1116	1318	...	...	1517	...	1815	2100	2100	...	2202	1135	...	1414	1622	...	1822	2048
Giggleswick d.	0734	1027	...	1132	1333	...	...	1533	...	1831	2116	2116	...	2218	1150	...	1429	1637	...	1837	2103
Hellifield 173 d.	0745	1039	...	1142	1343	...	...	1543	...	1842	2126	2126	...	2228	1202	...	1440	1648	...	1848	2115
Skipton 173 a.	0802	1056h	...	1157	1358	...	...	1558	...	1858	2141	2141	...	2244	1219	...	1456	1704	...	1904	2132
Keighley 🚂 173 a.	0817	1110	...	1208	1409	...	...	1609	...	1909	2155	2155	...	...	1232	...	1508	1717	...	1915	2143
Leeds 173 a.	0841	1138	...	1238	1438	...	...	1638	...	1939	2222	2222	...	...	1304	...	1537	1746	...	1945	2209

A – From Bradford Forster Square (d. 0641).
a – Departs 1940.
b – Departs 1016.
c – Arrives 2015.
d – Arrives 2020.
f – Departs 1623.
g – Arrives 5–7 minutes earlier.
h – Departs 5 minutes later.
k – Until Dec. 31 and Feb. 18 - Mar. 25.
n – Jan. 7 - Feb. 11 and from Apr. 1.

🚂 – Keighley and Worth Valley Railway (Keighley - Haworth - Oakworth - Oxenhope, *8 km*). ✆ 01535 645214. www.kwvr.co.uk
✣ – Full service Lancaster - Morecambe and v.v.: **From Lancaster**: On ⚒ at 0519, 0618, 0714, 0755, 0841, 0922, 1016Ⓐ, 1017⑥, 1059, 1128, 1214, 1244, 1359, 1413Ⓐ, 1415⑥, 1438, 1525, 1623, 1644, 1713, 1804, 1828, 1917, 1940, 2034**k**, 2135, 2204Ⓐ, 2204⑥**k**, 2237Ⓐ; on ⑦ at 1027, 1130, 1230, 1339, 1427, 1523, 1627, 1724, 1814, 1922, 2030, 2132.
From Morecambe: On ⚒ at 0558, 0659, 0735, 0822, 0901, 0941, 1032, 1115, 1141, 1233, 1339, 1421, 1433, 1501, 1540, 1638, 1702, 1731, 1822, 1842, 1934, 2005Ⓐ, 2010⑥, 2056Ⓐ, 2056⑥**n**, 2058⑥**k**, 2148Ⓐ, 2148⑥**k**, 2220Ⓐ, 2221⑥**k**, 2252Ⓐ; on ⑦ at 1049, 1203, 1322, 1356, 1442, 1538, 1651, 1738, 1829, 2004, 2105, 2200.

175 LEEDS - HARROGATE - YORK

2nd class NT

See Table **180** for through services London - Harrogate and v.v. See Tables **124** and **188** for direct services Leeds - York and v.v.

km		⚒	⚒	⚒	⚒	⚒	⚒	⚒	⚒	⚒	and at	⚒	⚒	⚒	⚒	⚒	⚒	⚒	⚒	⚒	⚒	⚒	⚒	⚒	⚒	⚒
0	**Leeds** d.	0605	0623	0633	0659	0715	0732	0801	0829	0859	the same	1529	1559	1629	1659	1709	1729	1739	1749	1809	1829	1859	1929	2006	2029	2129
29	**Harrogate** d.	0641	0651	0709	0735	0752	0808	0837	0905	0935	minutes	1605	1635	1705	1735	1746	1805	1815	1825	1846	1905	1935	2005	2042	2105	2205
36	Knaresborough d.	0651	...	0717	0743	...	0817	0846	0915	0944	past each	1615	1644	1714	1744	1757	1814	1826	1841f	1855	1915	1944	2014	2051	2114	2214
62	**York** a.	0720	...	0746	0811	...	0846	0915	0944	1011*	hour until	1642	1711	1742	1812	...	1844	...	1915	...	1944	2011	2048r	2120	2144	2241

	⚒	⚒	⑦	⑦	⑦	⑦	⑦	⑦	⑦	⑦	⑦	⑦	⑦	and at	⑦	⑦	⑦	⑦	⑦	⑦	⑦	⑦	⑦	⑦	⑦	⑦
Leeds d.	2239	2339	0906	0936	1006	1036	1106	1136	1206	1236	1306	1336	1406	the same	1706	1736	1806	1836	1906	1936	2006	2036	2105	2136	2227	2331
Harrogate d.	2316	0018	0942	1012	1042	1112	1142	1212	1242	1312	1342	1412	1442	minutes	1742	1812	1842	1912	1942	2012	2042	2112	2142	2212	2303	0007
Knaresborough d.	...	...	0951	1021	1051	1121	1151	1221	1251	1321	1351	1421	1451	past each	1751	1821	1851	1921	1951	2021	2051	2122	2152	2221	...	...
York a.	...	...	1019	1059	1126	1152	1223	1251	1326	1355	1425	1453	1523	hour until	1825	1857	1922	1953	2022	2049	2121	...	2222	...	...	...

	⚒	⚒	⚒	⚒	⚒	⚒	⚒	⚒	⚒	⚒	⚒	⚒	⚒	⚒	⚒	⚒	Ⓐ	⑥	⚒	⚒	and at	⚒	⚒	⚒	⚒	⚒
York d.	...	...	...	...	...	0648	0707	...	0742	0812	...	0847	0910	0942	1012	1043	1110	1112	1142	1211	the same	1642	1712	...	1743	1813
Knaresborough d.	...	...	...	0654	...	0714	0736	...	0807	0837	0905	0912	0936	1007	1037	1108	1136	1137	1207	1237	minutes	1707	1737	...	1809	1838
Harrogate d.	0607	0633	0656	0704	0714	0724	0745	0805	0816	0846	0913	0921	0945	1017	1046	1117	1146	1146	1216	1246	past each	1716	1746	1811	1819	1847
Leeds a.	0644	0710	0728	0741	0749	0802	0822	0841	0853	0922	0950	0956	1022	1052	1122	1153	1221	1222	1253	1323	hour until	1752	1823	1848	1855	1923

	⚒	⚒	⚒	⚒	Ⓐ	⑥	⚒	⚒	⑦	⑦	⑦	⑦	⑦	⑦	⑦		⑦	⑦	⑦	⑦	⑦	and at	⑦	⑦	⑦	⑦
York d.	1842	1911	1944	2011	2110	2110	2211	2243	...	...	0946	...	1046	1116	1145	...	1215	1245	1310	1345	1415	the same	2015	2045	2145	...
Knaresborough d.	1907	1937	2009	2036	2135	2136	2236	2309	...	...	1011	1041	1111	1141	1211	...	1241	1311	1341	1411	1441	minutes	2041	2111	2211	...
Harrogate d.	1917	1946	2019	2046	2144	2147	2245	2318	0922	0952	1022	1052	1122	1152	1222	...	1252	1322	1352	1422	1452	past each	2052	2122	2222	2312
Leeds a.	1953	2022	2055	2122	2221	2224	2322	2355	0958	1028	1058	1128	1158	1228	1258	...	1328	1358	1428	1458	1528	hour until	2128	2158	2258	2351

f – Arrives 1834.
r – Arrives 2044 on ⑥.
* – Arrivals in York may vary ± 3 minutes.

EM 2nd class PETERBOROUGH - LINCOLN - DONCASTER 176

km			Ⓐ	Ⓐ	ⒶR	Ⓐ		Ⓐ	Ⓐ	Ⓐ	Ⓐ	Ⓐ	Ⓐ	Ⓐ	Ⓐ		ⒶR	Ⓐ		⑥	⑥	⑥	⑥
0	**Peterborough** 180 d.	Ⓐ	0632	0731	0832	1028	...	1226	1321	1416	1511	1626	1710	1818	1926	...	2104	2311	⑥	0634	0734	0836	0936
27	Spalding d.		0652	0751	0852	1048	...	1246	1341	1440f	1532	1646	1729	1838	1946	...	2124	2333		0656	0756	0856	0956
57	Sleaford d.		0714	0813	0918	1117	...	1316	1406	1506f	1553	1708	1750	1906f	2008	...	2146	|		0718	0819	0918	1018
91	**Lincoln** 178 180 d.		0743	0845	0948	1148	...	1349	1435	1536	1622	1742	1820	1938	2037	...	2215	0017		0747	0851	0947	1049
117	Gainsborough Lea Road 178 d.		...	0907	...	1209	...	1414f	...	...	...	1803	...	1959	...	...	...	...		...	0912	...	1110
151	**Doncaster** a.		...	0934	...	1241	...	1442	...	...	...	1828	...	2025	...	...	...	...		...	0937	...	1136

	⑥	⑥	⑥		⑥	⑥		⑥	⑥
Peterborough 180 d.	1202	1356	1528	...	1642	1829	...	2050	...
Spalding d.	1222	1416	1548	...	1702	1849	...	2110	...
Sleaford d.	1244	1438	1610	...	1724	1911	...	2132	2218
Lincoln 178 180 d.	1315	1512	1642	...	1754	1944f	...	2202	2247
Gainsborough Lea Road 178 d.	1336	1533	...	...	...	2006	...	...	...
Doncaster a.	1403	1600	...	...	...	2032	...	...	...

		Ⓐ	ⒶR	Ⓐ		Ⓐ	Ⓐ	Ⓐ	Ⓐ
Doncaster d.	Ⓐ	...	...	...	...	0947	...	...	1250
Gainsborough Lea Road 178 d.		...	...	...	...	1011	...	...	1314
Lincoln 178 180 d.		0612	0709	0810	...	1035	1142	1234	1337
Sleaford d.		0641	0739	0839	...	1104	1211	1303	1407
Spalding d.		0701	0759	0900	...	1124	1231	1323	1427
Peterborough 180 a.		0721	0819	0921	...	1145	1254	1343	1447

	Ⓐ	Ⓐ	Ⓐ		Ⓐ	Ⓐ	Ⓐ		Ⓐ		⑥	⑥R	⑥	⑥	⑥		⑥	⑥	⑥		⑥	⑥	⑥
Doncaster d.	...	1455	...	...	...	...	1847	...	2049	⑥	...	...	...	0945	...	...	1146	...	1415	...	1615	...	2046
Gainsborough Lea Road 178 d.	...	1519	...	...	...	...	1911	...	2113		...	...	...	1009	...	...	1210	...	1439	...	1639	...	2110
Lincoln 178 180 d.	1434	1543	1633	...	1750	1835	1936	...	2137		0610	0718	0807	1031	1033	...	1235	1404	1502	...	1704	1934	2134
Sleaford d.	1503	1614	1708f	...	1820	1905	2009	...	2207		0639	0748	0837	...	1103	...	1304	1434	1532	...	1736	2003	2203
Spalding d.	1523	1635	1728	...	1839	1925	2029	...	2227		0659	0808	0857	...	1123	...	1324	1454	1552	...	1756	2023	...
Peterborough 180 a.	1546	1653	1748	...	1859	1945	2051	...	2248		0719	0827	0917	...	1143	...	1344	1514	1611	...	1816	2045	...

R – To/from Newark North Gate (Table **189**).

f – Arrives 4–5 minutes earlier.

NT 2nd class HULL - BRIDLINGTON - SCARBOROUGH 177

km			⚒	⚒	⚒A	⚒A	⚒A		⚒A	⚒C	⚒		⑦	⑦A	⑦A	⑦A	⑦A	⑦A	⑦A	⑦A	⑦A	⑦A	⑦A	⑦A
0	**Hull** △ d.	⚒	0533	0639	0725	0821	0921	★	1821	1923	2216	⑦	0835	1000	1048	1157	1305	1349	1446	1600	1650	1759	1906	2047
13	Beverley △ d.		|	0653	0739	0835	0935		1835	1937	2230		0849	1015	1102	1213	1320	1405	1502	1616	1707	1815	1920	2101
31	Driffield △ d.		|	0707	0753	0848	0947	and	1847	1949	2244		0905	1030	1117	1228	1334	1420	1517	1631	1722	1830	1935	2116
50	**Bridlington** △ a.		0608	0725	0810	0903	1003	hourly	1903	2004	2301		0921	1048	1134	1246	1349	1436	1533	1647	1738	1846	1950	2132
50	**Bridlington** d.		0609	0730	0812	0904	1003	until	1903	2005	...		0922	1052	1134	1253	1352	1442	1540	1653	1744	1852	1952	...
71	Filey d.		0629	0752	0833	0925	1024		1925	2026	...		0944	1116	1156	1317	1416	1516f	1619r	1718	1816f	1916	2016	...
87	**Scarborough** a.		0646	0810	0850	0942	1043		1942	2043	...		1003	1132	1214	1333	1432	1532	1635	1736	1832	1932	2032	...

		⚒A	⚒B	⚒A	⚒B	⚒A		⚒A	ⒶA	⑥A	⚒A	⚒		ⒶA	⑦	⑦	⑦A		⑦A	⑦A	⑦	⑦	⑦
Scarborough d.	⚒	0653	...	...	0815	0900		1801	1900	1900	2000	2118	⑦	...	1013	1056	1201		1901	2000	...	...	2126
Filey d.		0708	...	...	0830	0916	and	1817	1915	1915	2017	2133		...	1028	1111	1216	and	1916	2015	...	...	2141
Bridlington a.		0730	...	...	0852	0940	hourly	1839	1938	1939	2040	2156		...	1051	1133	1239	hourly	1939	2038	...	...	2204
Bridlington △ d.		0734	0755	0839	0853	0940	until	1839	1938	1940	2040	2156		0941	1052	1134	1240	until	1940	2039	2124	2144	2204
Driffield △ d.		0750	0810	0852	0909	0953		1855	1951	1953	2054	2211		0956	1108	1149	1255		1955	2054	2139	2157	2220
Beverley △ d.		0805	0827	0905	0923	1006		1907	2004	2005	2106	2226		1013	1123	1204	1310		2010	2109	2154	2209	2234
Hull △ a.		0820	0842	0920	0939	1022		1922	2019	2020	2121	2240		1029	1139	1220	1326		2027	2123	2210	2225	2250

A – From/to Sheffield (Table **192**).
B – To/from York (Table **179**).
C – From Sheffield on ⑥ (Table **192**).

f – Arrives 8–10 minutes earlier.
r – Arrives 1559.
★ – Timings may vary ± 2 minutes.

△ – Additional trains Hull - Bridlington and v.v.:
From Hull on ⚒ at 0558, 0613, 0744, 0801, 0900, 1003, 1100 **B**, 1159 **B**, 1300 **B**, 1400 **B**, 1500 **B**, 1600 **B**, 1702 **B**, 1734, 1801 **B**, 1900 **B**, 1958 **B**, 2021, 2100 Ⓐ **B**, 2116 ⑥: on ⑦ at 1718, 1944 **A**.
From Bridlington at 0645, 0705, 0911, 0956 **B** and hourly until 1756 **B**, 1825, 1856 **B**, 2000, 2058 **B**, 2137, 2233, 2306; on ⑦ at 1823.

NT 2nd class LINCOLN and CLEETHORPES - SHEFFIELD 178

km			⚒N	⚒L	⚒	⚒L	⚒	⚒L	⚒	⚒L	⚒L	⚒L	⑥C	⚒L	⚒L	⚒L	⚒L	⑥C	⚒L	⑥L	ⒶL	Ⓐ	⚒L	⚒
0	**Lincoln** 176 d.	⚒	...	...	0643	0723	...	0826	...	0915	1018	1122		1215	1328	1415	1521	...	1617	1723	1723	...	1823	...
	Gainsborough Central d.		...	...	|	|	0816	|	0916	|	|	|	1214	|	|	|	|	1615	|	|	|	1816	|	1901
26	Gainsborough Lea Road 176 d.		...	...	0704	0744	|	0847	|	0936	1039	1142	|	1236	1349	1436	1542	|	1638	1744	1747	|	1844	|
40	Retford d.		0613	0656	0717	0757	0832	0900	0932	0951	1054	1158	1231	1251	1403	1451	1556	1631	1653	1757	1800	1832	1857	1920
52	Worksop d.		0625	0708	0729	0807	0843	0910	0944	1002	1106	1209	1243	1302	1414	1502	1607	1643	1704	1808	1811	1846	1907	1933
78	**Sheffield** a.		0702v	0743	0804	0843	0917	0942	1017	1042	1141	1241	1317	1340	1446	1543	1642	1717	1742	1843	1845	1925	1944	2012

	⚒L	⑥C	⑥	Ⓐ	⚒	⚒	⚒	⚒		⑦	⑦H	⑦H	⑦H	⑦H	⑦	⑦H	⑦	⑦	⑦	⑦	⑦	⑦	⑦	⑦
Lincoln 176 d.	1929	...	2019	2019	2129	...	...	2244	⑦	...	1014	1114	1215	1314	...	1412	1511	1612	1715	1815	1919	2017	2120	2151
Gainsborough Central d.	|	2015	|	|	|	...	...	|		...	|	|	|	|	...	|	|	|	|	|	|	|	|	|
Gainsborough Lea Road 176 d.	1951	|	2040	2040	2150	...	...	2305		...	1035	1135	1236	1335	...	1433	1532	1633	1736	1836	1940	2038	2141	2212
Retford d.	2003	2031	2053	2053	2204	2251	...	2318		0912	1050	1150	1251	1350	1416	1448	1547	1648	1751	1851	1955	2053	2156	2227
Worksop d.	2013	2043	2104	2108	2215	2303	2321	2329		0925	1102	1201	1302	1401	1428	1459	1557	1659	1802	1902	2006	2105	2207	2238
Sheffield a.	2042	2117	2138	2145	2248	2336	2358	0005		0959	1134	1233	1334	1435	1500	1532	1630	1732	1836	1934	2039	2135	2241	2312

km			⚒	Ⓐ	⑥	⚒	⚒B	⚒L	⑥C	Ⓐ	⚒L	⚒L	⚒L	⚒L	⑥C	⚒L	⚒L	⚒L		⚒L	⑥C	⚒L	⚒	⚒L
0	**Sheffield** d.	⚒	0545	0610	0613	0635	0658	0737	0753	0755	0838	0937	1038	1138	1154	1237	1339	1437	...	1537	1554	1638	1654	1737
25	Worksop d.		0615	0633	0636	0707	0729	0759	0824	0827	0911	1010	1111	1211	1225	1306	1408	1506	...	1606	1625	1709	1725	1809
38	Retford d.		0625	0646	0649	0717	0739	0809	0834	0837	0921	1020	1121	1222	1239r	1316	1418	1516	...	1616	1635	1719	1735	1819
	Gainsborough Lea Road 176 d.		0640	...	...	0731	|	0824	|	|	0937	1035	1137	1237	|	1331	1433	1531	...	1631	|	1734	|	1834
54	**Gainsborough Central** a.		|	...	...	|	0755	|	0851	0852	|	|	|	|	1255	|	|	|	...	|	1651	|	1750	|
	Lincoln 176 a.		0703	...	...	0755	...	0846	...	...	1001	1058	1202	1300	...	1354	1456	1554	...	1654	...	1758	...	1857

	⚒	⚒L	⚒L	Ⓐ	⑥	⚒	⚒		⑦	⑦	⑦	⑦		⑦H	⑦	⑦H	⑦H	⑦H	⑦H	⑦H	⑦	⑦	⑦	⑦
Sheffield d.	1754	1838	1939	2053	2053	2143	2243	⑦	0845	0941	1041	1141	...	1241	1314	1336	1441	1542	1637	1738	1842	1934	2020	2123
Worksop d.	1825	1914	2009	2123	2124	2214	2314		0906	1012	1105	1212	...	1309	1345	1405	1507	1608	1709	1804	1914	2000	2051	2154
Retford d.	1835	1924	2019	2133	2134	2227	...		0916	1022	1115	1222	...	1319	1356	1415	1517	1618	1719	1814	1924	2010	2100	2204
Gainsborough Lea Road 176 d.	|	1939	2034	2148	2149	...	...		0931	1037	1130	1237	...	1334	...	1430	1532	1633	1734	1829	1939	2025	2115	2219
Gainsborough Central a.	1850	|	|	|	|	...	...		|	|	|	|	...	|	...	|	|	|	|	|	|	|	|	|
Lincoln 176 a.	...	2005	2057	2211	2212	...	...		0954	1100	1154	1300	...	1357	...	1453	1555	1656	1757	1852	2002	2048	2138	2242

B – From Barnsley (Table **171**).
C – To/from Cleethorpes (See panel below main table).
H – To/from Huddersfield (Table **171**).
L – To/from Leeds (Table **171**).
N – To Nottingham (Table **171**).

r – Arrives 1234.
t – Arrives 1218.
v – Arrives 0657 on ⑥.

CLEETHORPES - GAINSBOROUGH - SHEFFIELD

km		⑥	⑥	⑥
0	**Cleethorpes** 193 d.	1114	1511	1917
5	Grimsby Town 189 193 d.	1121	1518	1924
28	Barnetby 189 193 d.	1141	1537	1942
34	Brigg d.	1147	1543	1948
61	**Gainsborough Central** a.	1214	1609	2015
114	*Sheffield 178* a.	1317	1717	2117

	⑥	⑥	⑥
Sheffield 178 d.	0753	1154	1554
Gainsborough Central d.	0851	1305	1651
Brigg d.	0912	1327	1713
Barnetby 189 193 d.	0924	1338	1723
Grimsby Town 189 193 a.	0947	1359	1747
Cleethorpes 193 a.	0957	1409	1757

NT 2nd class HULL - YORK 179

km			⚒	Ⓐ	⑥	⚒	⚒B	⚒S	⚒B	⚒B	⚒B	⚒B	⚒B	⚒B	⚒B	⚒B	⚒B	⚒B	⚒	ⒶB	⑥B	Ⓐ		⑦	⑦
0	**Hull** 181 189 d.	⚒	0545	0619	0622	0746	0846	0947	1047	1147	1247	1346	1447	1547	1647	1750	1847	1944	2050	2148	2148	...	⑦	0839	1040
50	Selby 181 189 d.		0627	0657	0659	0827	0926	1024	1126	1224	1327	1423	1524	1624	1727	1827	1927	2022	2127	2230	2230	2345		0917	1115
84	**York** a.		0658	0732	0732	0858	0957	1058	1157	1249	1359	1444	1558	1650	1759	1859	1958	2055	2200	2253	2301	0008		0947	1145

	⑦	⑦	⑦	⑦	⑦		⑦	⑦	⑦	⑦	⑦	⑦
Hull 181 189 d.	1146	1234	1346	1421	1539	...	1639	1725	1841	1935	2023	...
Selby 181 189 d.	1223	1311	1421	1456	1614	...	1714	1800	1916	2010	2101	2244
York a.	1243	1345	1442	1526	1645	...	1747	1823	1946	2042	2124	2316

		⚒	⚒	⚒	⚒	⚒B	⚒B	⚒B	⚒B
York d.	⚒	0536	0615	0730	0845	0945	1045	1145	1244
Selby 181 189 d.		0559	0649	0803	0915	1015	1114	1215	1315
Hull 181 189 a.		0630	0738	0854	0954	1053	1154	1254	1354

	⚒B	⚒B	⚒B	⚒B	⚒B	⚒B	ⒶB	⑥	⚒	⚒		⑦	⑦	⑦	⑦	⑦	⑦	⑦	⑦	⑦	⑦	⑦	⑦	⑦	⑦
York d.	1345	1443	1546	1644	1745	1845	1943	1943	2144	2247	⑦	0851	1001	1041	1152	1250	1356	1454	1552	1651	1754	1845	1955	2053	2151
Selby 181 189 d.	1415	1515g	1618	1715	1816	1915	2013	2013	2215	2318		0922	1021	1113	1213	1321	1425	1515	1623	1721	1828	1914	2017	2115	2224
Hull 181 189 a.	1455	1554	1657	1756	1855	1954	2054	2054	2253	0002		0959	1057	1150	1247	1358	1500	1551	1700	1757	1902	1949	2051	2201	...

B – To/from Bridlington (Table **177**).
S – From Scarborough (Table **177**).
g – Arrives 1510.

180 LONDON - LEEDS, YORK, NEWCASTLE and EDINBURGH

Most services convey 🍷 GR

km			⚒	⚒	⑥	Ⓐ	⚒A	⚒	⑥	Ⓐ	⚒	⑥	Ⓐ	⚒	⚒	⚒	⚒	⚒	Ⓐ	⑥	⚒	⚒	⚒	⚒	⚒	⚒
0	**London** Kings Cross 181/2/3/5 d.		...	...	...	...	...	0555	...	...	0615	0633	0633	0700	0703	0706	0730	0733	0800	0800	0803	0806	0830	0833	0900	0903
44	Stevenage 185 d.	⚒	...	...	...	...	...	0617	...	...	0638	0654	0656	|	|	0728	|	0756	|	|	|	|	|	0855	|	|
123	**Peterborough** 185 176 d.		...	...	...	...	...	0648	...	...	0709	0724	0726	0748	0752	0759	0818	|	|	|	0851	0854	0918	|	0948	0952
170	Grantham 181 d.		...	...	...	...	...	0707	...	...	0728	0743	0746	|	|	0819	|	0842	|	|	|	0916	|	0941	|	|
193	Newark North Gate 189 d.		...	...	...	...	...	0719	...	...	0742	|	|	|	|	0832	0847	|	|	|	|	0929	0946	|	|	|
219	**Lincoln** 189 176 a.		...	...	...	...	...	|	...	...	|	|	|	|	|	|	|	|	|	|	|	0956	|	|	|	|
223	Retford 181 d.		...	...	...	...	...	0734	...	...	0757	|	|	|	|	0847	|	|	|	|	|	...	|	|	|	|
251	**Doncaster** 181 182 d.		...	...	0608	0610	...	0749	...	...	0812	0819	0819	|	0842	0903	0911	0915	|	|	0943	...	1011	1014	|	1042
283	Wakefield Westgate 124 a.		...	...	|	|	...	0806	...	...	|	0834	0834	|	0859	|	|	0931	|	|	1001	...	|	1031	|	1059
299	**Leeds** 124 175 188 a.		...	...	|	|	0708	0823	...	...	|	0852	0852	|	0916	|	|	0945	|	|	1017	...	|	1047	|	1116
328	Harrogate 175 a.		...	...	|	|	|	—	...	...	|	...	...	|	...	|	|	1024	|	|	...	...	|	...	|	...
303	**York** 124 183 188 d.		...	...	0635f	0635f	0735	...	...	...	0835	...	...	0855	...	0929	0935	...	0955f	0956	...	...	1035	...	1054	...
351	Northallerton 183 188 d.		...	...	0655	0655	|	...	...	...	0855	...	...	|	...	...	|	...	|	|	...	...	1055	...	|	...
374	Darlington 124 188 d.		...	...	0709	0708	0803	...	...	...	0910	...	...	0924	...	...	1006	...	1023	1024	...	...	1109	...	1124	...
409	Durham 124 188 d.		...	...	0727	0727	0821	...	...	...	0927	...	...	|	...	...	1025	...	|	|	...	...	1127	...	|	...
432	**Newcastle** 124 188 a.		...	...	0741	0740	0834	Ⓐ	...	...	0940	...	...	0951	...	...	1039	...	1050	1051	...	...	1140	...	1151	...
	Newcastle 124 188 d.		0622	0707	0744	0742	0847	0856	0911	0919	0946	...	...	0953	...	...	1041	...	1053	1054	...	...	1144	...	1153	...
488	Alnmouth 124 a.		0650	0739	0809	0808	|	|	0942	0950	|	...	...	|	...	...	1107	...	|	|	...	...	|	...	|	...
540	Berwick upon Tweed 124 a.		0715	0800	0832	0831	0937	0940	1003	1011	|	...	...	1036	...	...	|	...	1135	1137	...	...	|	...	1236	...
632	**Edinburgh** Waverley 124 188 a.		0807	0855	0920	0924	1023	1029	1058	1103	1114b	...	...	1128c	...	...	1212	...	1222	1226	...	...	1312	...	1327c	...

	Ⓐ	⑥	⚒	⚒	⚒A	⚒	⚒	⚒	⚒	⑥	Ⓐ	⚒	⚒	⚒	⚒	⚒B	⚒	⚒	⚒	⚒	Ⓐ	⑥	⚒	⑥	Ⓐ	⚒
London Kings Cross 181/2/3/5 d.	0906	0906	0930	0933	1000	1003	1006	1030	1033	1100	1100	1103	1106	1130	1133	1200	1203	1206	1230	1233	1300	1300	1303	1306	1306	1330
Stevenage 185 d.	0928	0928	|	0956	|	|	1028	|	1056	|	|	|	1129	|	1156	|	|	1228	|	1256	|	|	|	1328	1328	|
Peterborough 185 176 d.	0959	1001	1018	|	|	1052	1100	1118	|	|	|	1152	1159	1218	|	|	1252	1300	1318	|	1348	1348	1352	1358	1401	1418
Grantham 181 d.	1020	1021	|	1041	|	|	1120	|	1141	|	|	|	1219	|	1242	|	|	1322	|	1342	|	|	|	1416	1422	|
Newark North Gate 189 d.	1033	1035	1046	|	|	|	1135	1146	|	|	|	|	1233	1246	|	|	|	1337	1347	|	|	|	|	1428	1435	1446
Lincoln 189 176 a.	|	|	|	|	|	|	1200	|	|	|	|	|	|	|	|	|	|	1402	|	|	|	|	|	|	|	|
Retford 181 d.	1049	1050	|	|	|	|	...	|	|	|	|	|	1251f	|	|	|	|	...	|	|	|	|	|	1447f	1451	|
Doncaster 181 182 d.	1105	1106	1110	1115	|	1143	...	1211	1214	|	|	1243	1306	1311	1315	|	1343	...	1411	1415	|	|	1443	1505	1506	1511
Wakefield Westgate 124 a.	|	|	|	1131	|	1159	...	|	1230	|	|	1259	|	|	1330	|	1359	...	|	1430	|	|	1459	|	|	|
Leeds 124 175 188 a.	|	|	|	1146	|	1216	...	|	1247	|	|	1316	|	|	1345	|	1416	...	|	1448	|	|	1516	|	|	|
Harrogate 175 a.	|	|	|	1224	|	...	...	|	...	|	|	...	|	|	1424	|	...	...	|	...	|	|	—	|	|	|
York 124 183 188 d.	1130	1130	1135	...	1155	...	...	1235	...	1254	1255	...	1330	1335	...	1355f	...	...	1435	...	1455	1455	...	1529	1530	1535
Northallerton 183 188 d.	—	...	|	...	|	...	...	1255	...	|	|	...	...	|	...	|	...	...	1455	...	|	|	...	—	...	1555
Darlington 124 188 d.	...	...	1206	...	1224	...	...	1309	...	1323	1324	...	...	1408	...	1423	...	...	1509	...	1523	1523	...	...	...	1609
Durham 124 188 d.	...	...	1223	...	|	...	...	1327	...	|	|	...	...	1426	...	|	...	...	1527	...	|	|	...	...	...	1626
Newcastle 124 188 a.	⚒	...	1237	...	1252	...	...	1339	...	1349	1352	...	...	1440	...	1450	...	...	1540	...	1549	1549	⑥	Ⓐ	...	1639
Newcastle 124 188 d.	1206	...	1240	...	1254	...	...	1343	...	1352	1355	...	...	1442	...	1455	...	...	1545	...	1552	1559	1614	1614	...	1641
Alnmouth 124 a.	1238	...	1307	...	|	...	...	|	...	|	|	...	...	1508	...	|	...	...	|	...	|	|	1644	1645	...	1710
Berwick upon Tweed 124 a.	1259	...	|	...	1337	...	...	|	...	1434	1437	...	...	|	...	1538	...	...	|	...	1634	1641	1705	1706	...	|
Edinburgh Waverley 124 188 a.	1352	...	1415b	...	1427d	...	...	1509	...	1527	1523	...	...	1616	...	1626d	...	...	1714b	...	1723	1726	1800	1804	...	1816

	⚒	⚒A	⚒	⚒	⚒	⚒	ⒶK	⑥	Ⓐ	⑥	Ⓐ	⑥	ⒶQ	⚒C	⚒	⑥	ⒶA	⚒	⚒	⚒	⚒G	⑥	Ⓐ	⚒	ⒶH	⑥H
London Kings Cross 181/2/3/5 d.	1333	1400	1403	1406	1430	1433	1500	1500	1503	1503	1506	1506	1525	1530	1533	1600	1600	1603	1606	1630	1633	1700	1700	1703	1718	1718
Stevenage 185 d.	1355	|	|	1428	|	1456	|	|	|	|	1528	1528	|	|	1556	|	|	|	1628	|	1655	|	|	|	|	|
Peterborough 185 176 d.	|	|	1451	1459	1518	|	|	|	1551	1554	1558	1559	|	1618	|	|	|	1652	1700	1718	|	|	|	1751	1810	1810
Grantham 181 d.	1442	|	|	1520	|	1542	|	|	|	|	1617	1618	|	|	1642	|	|	|	1721	|	1741	|	|	|	1829	1829
Newark North Gate 189 d.	|	|	|	1534	1546	|	|	|	|	|	1630	1632	|	1646	|	|	|	|	1737	1746	|	|	|	|	1841	1841
Lincoln 189 176 a.	|	|	|	1601	|	|	|	|	|	|	|	|	|	|	|	|	|	|	1802	|	|	|	|	|	|	|
Retford 181 d.	|	|	|	...	|	|	|	|	|	|	1645	1651f	|	|	|	|	|	|	...	|	1804	|	|	|	|	|
Doncaster 181 182 d.	1515	|	1543	...	1610	1616	|	|	1643	1644	1705f	1707	|	1710	1716	|	|	1741	...	1811	1821	|	|	1843	1908	1904
Wakefield Westgate 124 a.	1531	|	1559	...	|	1632	|	|	1659	1700	|	|	|	|	1734	|	|	1759	...	|	1836	|	|	1900	...	...
Leeds 124 175 188 a.	1545	|	1616	...	|	1651	|	|	1716	1716	|	|	|	|	1749	|	|	1816	...	|	1851	|	|	1917	...	...
Harrogate 175 a.	1625	|	...	...	|	...	|	|	...	...	|	|	|	|	1831	|	|	...	...	|	...	|	|	...	...	...
York 124 183 188 d.	...	1555	...	...	1635	...	1656	1654	...	...	1728	1730	1726f	1735	...	1756f	1756	...	...	1835	...	1855	1857g	...	...	...
Northallerton 183 188 d.	...	|	...	...	1655	...	|	|	...	...	...	...	...	1756	...	|	|	...	...	1856	...	|	|	...	...	...
Darlington 124 188 d.	...	1624	...	...	1708	...	1726	1724	...	...	...	...	...	1809	...	1825	1824	...	...	1910	...	1927	1926	...	...	...
Durham 124 188 d.	...	|	...	...	1725	...	|	|	...	...	...	...	...	1827	...	|	|	...	...	1928	...	|	|	...	...	...
Newcastle 124 188 a.	...	1651	...	...	1740	...	1752	1750	...	...	...	...	...	1841	...	1854	1850	...	...	1941	...	1953	1952	...	...	...
Newcastle 124 188 d.	...	1658	...	...	1743	...	1755	1753	...	...	...	...	...	1843	...	1857	1854	...	...	1945	...	1956	1958	...	...	...
Alnmouth 124 a.	...	|	...	...	|	...	|	|	...	...	...	...	...	1909	...	|	|	...	...	|	...	|	|	...	...	...
Berwick upon Tweed 124 a.	...	1743	...	...	|	...	1838	1836	...	...	...	...	...	|	...	1940	1936	...	...	|	...	2038	2040	...	...	...
Edinburgh Waverley 124 188 a.	...	1830	...	...	1911	...	1922	1929	...	...	...	...	...	2015	...	2025	2020	...	...	2114	...	2123	2124	...	...	...

	Ⓐ	⑥	Ⓐ	⑥	Ⓐ	Ⓐ	⑥	⑥F	ⒶF	⑥	Ⓐ	Ⓐ	⑥	ⒶG	⑥	Ⓐ	⑥	⚒	⚒	①–④	⑤	⑥	⚒P	ⒶD	⑥	Ⓐ
London Kings Cross 181/2/3/5 d.	1730	1730	1733	1733	1748	1800	1800	1803	1803	1818	1818	1830	1830	1833	1833	1900	1900	1903	1906	1930	1930	1930	1933	2000	2000	2003
Stevenage 185 d.	|	|	1755	1756	|	|	|	|	|	|	|	|	|	1856	1856	|	|	|	1928	|	|	|	1955	|	|	|
Peterborough 185 176 d.	1819	1818	|	|	1838	|	|	1851	1855f	1906	1910	1918	1918	|	|	|	|	1951	2000	2018	2018	2018	|	|	2048	2052
Grantham 181 d.	|	|	1842	1841	1906	|	|	|	|	1926	1929	|	|	1943	1943	|	|	|	2021	|	|	|	2041	|	|	|
Newark North Gate 189 d.	1847	1848	|	|	|	|	|	1922	1925	|	|	1947	1948	|	|	|	|	|	2037	2047	2047	2047	|	|	2117	2121
Lincoln 189 176 a.	|	|	|	|	|	|	|	|	|	|	|	|	|	|	|	|	|	|	2103	|	|	|	|	|	|	|
Retford 181 d.	|	|	|	|	1929	|	|	|	|	1949	|	|	|	2007	2007	|	|	|	...	|	|	|	|	|	|	|
Doncaster 181 182 d.	|	|	1916	1917	1945	|	|	1950	1950	2008	|	2011	2012	2022	2022	|	|	2042	...	2111	2111	2112	2114	|	2141	2145
Wakefield Westgate 124 a.	|	|	1935	1932	2000	|	|	2006	2006	2024	|	|	|	2038	2037	|	|	2059	...	|	|	|	2130	|	|	2201
Leeds 124 175 188 a.	|	|	1950	1950	2017	|	|	2021	2021	2041	|	|	|	2053	2052	|	|	2116	...	|	|	|	2147	|	|	2221
Harrogate 175 a.	|	|	2030	...	...	|	|	—	—	...	|	|	|	...	2130	|	|	...	...	|	|	|	...	|	|	...
York 124 183 188 d.	1929	1931	...	...	...	1952f	1954	...	...	...	2019	2036	2036	...	...	2058	2054f	...	...	2134	2134	2136	...	2153f	2205	...
Northallerton 183 188 d.	|	|	...	...	...	|	|	...	...	...	2039	|	2055	...	...	|	|	...	...	2154	2154	2156	...	|	|	...
Darlington 124 188 d.	1957	2000	...	...	...	2022	2024	...	...	...	2053	2106	2109	...	...	2126	2125	...	...	2208	2208	2209	...	2222	2234	...
Durham 124 188 d.	2015	2017	...	...	...	|	|	...	...	...	2111	2125	2127	...	...	|	|	...	...	2226	2226	2227	...	2240	2252	...
Newcastle 124 188 a.	2028	2030	...	...	...	2048	2050	⑥	Ⓐ	...	2125	2139	2141	...	...	2153	2153	...	...	2240	2240	2241	...	2254	2306	...
Newcastle 124 188 d.	2035	2034	...	...	...	2051	2055	2059	2101	...	...	2142	...	...	...	2156	...	...	...	...	2242	...	...	...	...	...
Alnmouth 124 a.	2059	|	...	...	...	|	2123	2129	2129	...	...	2210	...	...	...	|	...	...	...	...	2310	...	...	...	...	...
Berwick upon Tweed 124 a.	|	|	...	...	...	2134	2145	2151	2150	...	...	|	...	...	...	2238	...	...	...	...	2333	...	...	...	...	...
Edinburgh Waverley 124 188 a.	2208	2159	...	...	...	2220	2238	2241	2248	...	...	2316	...	...	...	2324	...	...	...	...	0020	...	...	...	...	...

	⑥	⑥	Ⓐ	⑥	Ⓐ	Ⓐ	⑥	Ⓐ	Ⓐ	Ⓐ		⑦	⑦	⑦	⑦	⑦	⑦	⑦	⑦	⑦	⑦	⑦	⑦	⑦A	⑦	⑦
London Kings Cross 181/2/3/5 d.	2003	2030	2033	2100	2100	2133	2200	2200	2300	2333		...	...	...	...	...	...	0848	0900	0903	0922	0930	0933	1000	1003	1007
Stevenage 185 d.	|	|	2055	|	2123	2156	|	|	|	|		...	...	...	...	...	...	|	|	0925	|	|	0956	|	|	|
Peterborough 185 176 d.	2052	2119	2126	2148	2153	2228	2248	2248	2344s	0017s	⑦	...	...	...	...	...	...	|	|	0955	1012	1018	1027	|	1052	1057
Grantham 181 d.	2112	2139	2146	|	|	2248	2307	2308	0012s	0045s		...	...	...	...	...	...	|	|	1014	|	|	1047	|	|	1117
Newark North Gate 189 d.	|	2152	2159	|	2222	2302	2320	2322	0025s	0058s		...	...	...	...	...	...	|	|	1027	|	|	1104f	|	|	1130
Lincoln 189 176 a.	|	|	|	|	|	|	|	|	|	|		...	...	...	...	...	...	|	|	|	|	|	1129	|	|	|
Retford 181 d.	|	2208	|	|	|	2317	2335	|	|	|		...	...	...	...	...	...	|	|	|	|	1057	...	|	|	|
Doncaster 181 182 d.	2145	2224	2224	|	2249f	2337	2350	2354f	0053s	0125s		...	...	...	...	...	0936	|	|	1052	1059	1112	...	|	1143f	1156
Wakefield Westgate 124 a.	2204	2240	2240	|	|	2353	0006	|	|	|		...	...	...	...	...	|	|	|	1108	|	|	...	|	|	1211
Leeds 124 175 188 a.	2221	2257	2257	|	|	0010	0023	|	|	0220		...	...	...	...	0830	|	|	|	1122	|	|	...	|	|	1228
Harrogate 175 a.	...	...	...	|	|	...	...	|	|	...		...	...	...	...	|	|	|	|	1200	|	|	...	|	|	...
York 124 183 188 d.	...	...	...	2258	2312	...	...	0022f	0129	...		...	...	...	...	0900f	1000	1036	1051	—	1121	1135	...	1155a	1208f	...
Northallerton 183 188 d.	...	...	...	2319	2344	...	...	0043s	...	...		...	...	...	...	0921	|	|	|	...	|	|	...	|	|	...
Darlington 124 188 d.	...	...	...	2333	2357	...	...	0057s	...	...		...	...	...	...	0935	1029	1105	1119	...	1151	1204	...	1224	1238	...
Durham 124 188 d.	...	...	...	2351	0015	...	...	0121s	...	...		...	...	...	...	0954	1047	1123	|	...	1210	1222	...	|	1256	...
Newcastle 124 188 a.	...	...	...	0005	0043	...	...	0153	...	...		...	...	...	...	1007	1059	1136	1147	⑦	1226	1235	...	1251	1308	...
Newcastle 124 188 d.	...	...	...	...	...	...	...	...	...	...		0845	0915	0919	0945	1010	1102	1139	1152	1156	...	1239	...	1253	1311	...
Alnmouth 124 a.	...	...	...	...	...	...	...	...	...	...		0913	|	0949	1012	1039	|	|	|	1226	...	1303	...	|	|	...
Berwick upon Tweed 124 a.	...	...	...	...	...	...	...	...	...	...		0935	0957	1010	|	1103	1145	|	1234	1247	...	|	...	1337	|	...
Edinburgh Waverley 124 188 a.	...	...	...	...	...	...	...	...	...	...		1027	1048	1104	1112	1158	1231	1309	1318	1347	...	1418	...	1420	1435	...

FOR NOTES SEE PAGE 138 ▶ ▶ ▶ ▶

GR Most services convey 🍷 — LONDON - LEEDS, YORK, NEWCASTLE and EDINBURGH — 180

	⑦	⑦	⑦	⑦	⑦	⑦	⑦B	⑦	⑦	⑦	⑦	⑦	⑦	⑦	⑦	⑦A	⑦	⑦	⑦	⑦	⑦	⑦	⑦	⑦	⑦	⑦M
London Kings Cross 181/2/3/5 d.	1030	1100	1103	1122	1130	1133	1200	1203	1222	1230	1233	1300	1303	1330	1333	1400	1403	1430	1436	1500	1503	1530	1533	1600	1605	1630
Stevenage 185 d.	|	|	1125	|	|	1155	|	|	|	|	1256	|	1325	|	1356	|	|	|	1457	|	1525	|	1556	|	|	|
Peterborough 185 176 d.	1118	|	1155	|	1218	1225	|	1251	1311	1318	|	|	1356	1418	1427	|	1451	1519	|	|	1555	1619	1627	|	1653	1719
Grantham 181 d.	|	|	1214	1225	|	1244	|	1311	|	|	1343	|	1415	|	1452f	|	1511	|	|	|	1615	1639	1651f	|	1713	|
Newark North Gate 189 d.	1147	|	1228	|	|	1259	|	1324	|	1347	|	|	1429	|	|	|	1524	1547	1555f	|	1628	|	1707	|	1726	1747
Lincoln 189 176 a.	|	|	|	|	|	1325	|	|	|	|	|	|	|	|	|	|	|	|	1622	|	|	|	1732	|	|	|
Retford 181 d.	|	|	|	|	1257	...	|	|	|	|	|	|	|	1457	1520f	|	|	|	...	|	1643	|	...	|	|	|
Doncaster 181 182 d.	1211	|	1252	|	1312	...	|	1350	1359	1411	1420	|	1454	1512	1536	|	1550	1611	...	|	1658	1711	...	|	1752	1811
Wakefield Westgate 124 a.	|	|	1308	|	|	...	|	1406	|	|	1437	|	1510	|	1559	|	1606	|	...	|	1714	|	...	|	1808	|
Leeds 124 175 188 a.	|	|	1324	|	|	...	|	1423	|	|	1454	|	1524	|	1619	|	1623	|	...	|	1728	|	...	|	1826	|
Harrogate 175 a.	|	|	1402	|	|	...	|	...	|	|	...	|	1559	|	...	|	—	|	...	|	1807	|	...	|	...	|
York 124 183 188 d.	1235	1252f	...	1318f	1335	...	1351	...	1421	1434	...	1455	...	1535	...	1553f	...	1635	...	1652f	...	1736f	...	1753	...	1835
Northallerton 183 188 d.	1255	|	...	1337	|	...	|	...	|	1454	...	|	...	|	...	|	...	1654	...	|	...	|	...	|	...	1855
Darlington 124 188 d.	1309	1320	...	1349	1404	...	1420	...	1450	1508	...	1524	...	1604	...	1622	...	1707	...	1721	...	1805	...	1821	...	1909
Durham 124 188 d.	1327	|	...	1408	1422	...	|	...	1509	1526	...	|	...	1622	...	|	...	1725	...	|	...	1824	...	|	...	1927
Newcastle 124 188 a.	1340	1346	...	1420	1435	...	1447	...	1523	1540	...	1550	...	1635	...	1648	⑦	1739	...	1747	...	1836	...	1847	...	1940
Newcastle 124 188 d.	1342	1349	...	1423	1438	...	1450	...	...	1545	...	1553	...	1638	...	1652	1711	1743	...	1752	...	1842	...	1850	...	1942
Alnmouth 124 a.	|	|	...	|	1502	...	|	...	...	|	...	|	...	1703	...	|	1741	|	...	|	...	1906	...	|	...	|
Berwick upon Tweed 124 a.	|	1431	...	|	|	...	1535	...	...	|	...	1635	...	|	...	1735	1802	|	...	1834	...	|	...	1932	...	|
Edinburgh Waverley 124 188 a.	1510	1517	...	1558	1609	...	1618	...	...	1710	...	1720	...	1808	...	1819	1859	1909	...	1918	...	2012	...	2017	...	2113

	⑦	⑦	⑦	⑦H	⑦	⑦	⑦	⑦	⑦	⑦	⑦F	⑦		⑦	⑦	⑦	⑦G	⑦	⑦	⑦	⑦	⑦	⑦	⑦	⑦	⑦
London Kings Cross 181/2/3/5 d.	1635	1700	1705	1722	1730	1735	1800	1803	1827	1830	1835	1900	...	1903	1906	1930	1935	2000	2005	2035	2100	2105	2135	2200	2205	2235
Stevenage 185 d.	1658	|	|	|	|	1758	|	|	|	|	1857	|	...	|	1928	|	1958	|	|	2057	|	|	2156	|	|	|
Peterborough 185 176 d.	|	|	1753	|	1818	|	1848	1853	|	|	|	|	...	1951	1959	2019	2028	2048	2054	2128	2149	2153	2228	2249	2253	2326s
Grantham 181 d.	1742	|	|	1827	1838	1843	|	|	|	|	1941	|	...	|	2018	|	2047	|	|	2147	|	|	2247	|	2312	2346s
Newark North Gate 189 d.	|	|	1821	1840	|	|	|	1922	|	1947	|	|	...	2020	2034	2048	|	|	|	2201	|	2222	2259	|	2326	2358s
Lincoln 189 176 a.	|	|	|	|	|	|	|	|	|	|	|	|	...	|	2059	|	|	|	|	|	|	|	|	|	|	|
Retford 181 d.	1805	|	|	|	|	|	|	|	|	|	2005	|	...	|	...	|	|	|	2134	|	|	|	2314	|	|	|
Doncaster 181 182 d.	1821	|	1848	1903	1910	1916	|	1949	|	2011	2020	|	...	2044	...	2116f	2122	|	2149	2225	|	2250	2335	2343	2355	0029s
Wakefield Westgate 124 a.	1837	|	1903	...	|	1932	|	2006	|	|	2038	|	...	2102	...	|	2137	|	2205	2241	|	2308	2351	|	|	|
Leeds 124 175 188 a.	1855	|	1919	...	|	1949	|	2021	|	|	2053	|	...	2119	...	|	2152	|	2222	2258	|	2326	0008	|	|	0111
Harrogate 175 a.	...	|	1956	...	|	...	|	2100	|	|	...	|	...	...	...	|	...	|	...	...	|	...	...	|	|	...
York 124 183 188 d.	...	1850	...	...	1937	...	2000	—	2025f	2036	...	2053f	...	...	...	2139	...	2156	...	...	2300	...	...	0012	0020	...
Northallerton 183 188 d.	...	|	...	...	|	...	|	...	|	2056	...	|	...	...	...	|	...	2230	...	...	2335	...	...	0046s	...	...
Darlington 124 188 d.	...	1920	...	...	2007	...	2029	...	2055	2111	...	2122	...	...	...	2222	...	2243	...	...	2350f	...	...	0059s	...	...
Durham 124 188 d.	...	|	...	...	2025	...	|	...	2113	2129	...	|	...	...	...	2240	...	2302	...	...	0008	...	...	0117s	...	...
Newcastle 124 188 a.	...	1946	...	...	2038	...	2055	⑦	2127	2141	...	2149	...	...	...	2309	...	2332	...	...	0038	...	...	0149	...	...
Newcastle 124 188 d.	...	1951	...	...	2041	...	2100	2114	...	2145	...	2153	...	...	...	...	...	...	...	...	...	...	...	...	...	...
Alnmouth 124 d.	...	|	...	...	2110	...	|	2144	...	|	...	2221	...	...	...	...	...	...	...	...	...	...	...	...	...	...
Berwick upon Tweed 124 d.	...	2034	...	...	|	...	2142	2205	...	2227	...	2242	...	...	...	...	...	...	...	...	...	...	...	...	...	...
Edinburgh Waverley 124 188 a.	...	2119	...	...	2215	...	2227	2259	...	2312	...	2333	...	...	...	...	...	...	...	...	...	...	...	...	...	...

⚒	⚒	⚒	Ⓐ	⑥	⚒	⚒	⚒	⚒	⚒	ⒶJ	⑥	Ⓐ	⑥	⚒	Ⓐ	⑥	Ⓐ	Ⓐ	⑥H	⑥F	ⒶH	ⒶF	⑥	Ⓐ	⑥
Edinburgh Waverley 124 188 d.	...	...	...	...	...	...	...	...	G	...	...	...	...	...	...	...	...	0540	...	...	...	...	...	...	0526
Berwick upon Tweed 124 d.	...	...	...	...	...	...	...	...	...	...	...	...	...	...	...	...	0600	|	...	...	...	...	...	...	0625
Alnmouth 124 d.	...	...	...	...	...	...	...	...	...	...	...	...	...	...	...	...	0622	|	...	...	...	...	...	...	0645
Newcastle 124 188 a.	...	...	...	...	...	...	...	...	...	...	...	...	...	...	...	...	0652	0702	...	...	...	...	...	←	0716
Newcastle 124 188 d.	...	...	...	...	0445	...	0526	...	...	0559	0600	...	...	...	0630	0630	0655	0704	...	...	...	...	0655	0655	—
Durham 124 188 d.	...	...	...	...	0500	...	0539	...	...	0612	0613	...	...	...	0644	0643	→	|	...	...	...	...	0708	0708	...
Darlington 124 188 d.	...	...	...	...	0517	...	0558	...	...	0631	0632	...	...	...	0703	0702	...	|	...	...	...	...	0727	0732j	...
Northallerton 183 188 d.	...	...	...	...	0528	...	0610	...	...	|	|	...	...	...	0715	0714	...	|	...	...	...	...	|	|	ⒶR
York 124 183 185 d.	0440	...	...	...	0600	...	0632	...	...	0702f	0702	...	...	...	0737	0737	...	|	...	...	...	...	0757	0802	0813f
Harrogate 175 d.	|	...	...	...	|	...	|	...	...	|	|	...	...	...	|	|	...	|	...	...	...	...	|	|	|
Leeds 124 175 188 d.	|	0505	0530	0530	|	0605	|	0640	0700	|	|	...	...	0715	|	|	...	|	...	0740	...	0741	|	|	|
Wakefield Westgate 124 d.	|	0518	0543	0543	|	0618	|	0653	0713	|	|	...	...	0728	|	|	...	|	...	|	...	0754	|	|	|
Doncaster 181 182 d.	0506	0536	0602	0603	0623	0637	0655	0714	|	|	|	...	...	0747	|	|	...	|	0758	0810	0757	0814	0828	|	|
Retford 181 d.	|	0550	|	|	|	0651	|	|	|	|	|	...	...	|	|	|	...	|	|	|	|	|	|	0835	|
Lincoln 189 176 d.	|	|	|	|	|	|	|	|	|	|	|	0730	0730	|	|	|	...	|	|	|	|	|	|	|	|
Newark North Gate 189 d.	0536	0606	0626	0627	0646	0706	|	0738	|	|	|	0758	0759	|	|	|	...	|	0823	0833	0822	0839	|	|	|
Grantham 181 d.	0548	0617	0638	0640	0658	0719	0727	|	|	|	|	|	|	0819	|	|	...	|	0835	|	0833	|	|	|	|
Peterborough 185 176 d.	0610	0640	0700	0702	0720	0740	0749	|	|	0813f	0820	0829	0829	|	0846	0850	...	|	0858	0901	|	0908	|	|	|
Stevenage 185 d.	|	|	|	|	|	|	|	|	|	|	|	0858	0900	0905	|	|	...	|	|	|	|	|	|	|	|
London Kings Cross 181/2/3/5 a.	0701	0731	0750	0753	0810	0831	0840	0853	0901	0909	0910	0923	0923	0931	0935	0939	...	0940	0947	0950	0954	1000	0954	1003	1022

	Ⓐ	⚒	⑥	ⒶK	⚒	⑥G	ⒶG	⚒	⚒	⚒	Ⓐ	⑥	⚒	ⒶM	⑥M	⚒	⚒	⑥	Ⓐ	⚒	⚒	⑥	Ⓐ	⚒	⚒	⚒
Edinburgh Waverley 124 188 d.	0530	0548	0624	0626	...	...	...	0655	0730	...	...	...	...	0800	0800	0830	...	...	...	...	0900	0930	0930	0933	...	...
Berwick upon Tweed 124 d.	0630	0634	0708	0713	...	...	...	|	0812	...	...	...	...	|	|	0913	...	...	...	...	|	1012	1012	1026	...	...
Alnmouth 124 d.	0650	0656	|	|	...	...	...	|	|	...	...	...	...	0901	0901	|	...	...	...	...	|	|	|	1047	...	...
Newcastle 124 188 a.	0721	0727	0752	0755	...	...	...	0824	0855	...	...	...	...	0927	0928	0956	...	...	...	...	1024	1056	1055	1121	...	...
Newcastle 124 188 d.	—	0730	0759	0801	...	...	...	0828	0858	...	...	...	...	0930	0930	0959	...	...	...	...	1026	1059	1058	—	...	...
Durham 124 188 d.	...	0743	|	|	...	...	...	0841	|	...	...	...	...	0943	0944	|	...	...	...	...	1040	|	|	...	...	...
Darlington 124 188 d.	...	0802	0828	0831	...	...	...	0900	0927	...	...	...	...	1002	1003	1028	...	...	...	...	1100	1127	1128	...	...	...
Northallerton 183 188 d.	...	|	|	|	...	...	...	0911	|	...	...	...	...	|	|	|	...	...	...	...	1111	|	|	...	...	...
York 124 183 185 d.	⚒	0832	0858	0901	...	...	...	0933	0957	...	1002	1002	...	1032	1032	1058	...	...	...	...	1133	1158	1158	...	1202	...
Harrogate 175 d.	0737	|	|	|	...	...	...	|	|	...	|	|	0936	|	|	|	...	...	...	...	|	|	|	⚒	|	1136
Leeds 124 175 188 d.	0815	|	|	|	0846	0915	0915	|	|	0945	|	|	1015	|	|	|	1045	...	...	1115	|	|	|	1145	|	1215
Wakefield Westgate 124 d.	0830	|	|	|	0858	0928	0929	|	|	0957	|	|	1028	|	|	|	1058	...	...	1128	|	|	|	1158	|	1228
Doncaster 181 182 d.	0849	0856	|	|	0919	0947	0949	0956	|	1017	1025	1029	1047	1057	1058	|	1120	...	...	1147	1155	|	|	1218	1225	1247
Retford 181 d.	|	|	|	|	|	|	|	|	|	|	1040	1045	|	|	|	|	|	...	...	|	|	|	|	|	1239	|
Lincoln 189 176 d.	|	|	|	|	|	|	|	|	|	|	|	|	|	|	|	|	|	1127	1127	|	|	|	|	|	|	|
Newark North Gate 189 d.	|	0920	|	|	|	|	|	1021	|	|	1055	1059	|	1121	1121	|	|	1159f	1156f	|	1219	|	|	|	1255	|
Grantham 181 d.	0923	|	|	|	|	1018	1020	|	|	|	1107	1110	1118	|	|	|	|	1210	1209	1219	|	|	|	|	1307	1318
Peterborough 185 176 d.	|	0950	|	|	1010	|	|	1050	|	1109	1129	1131	|	1150	1151	|	1211	1231	1230	|	1247	|	|	1309	1329	|
Stevenage 185 d.	1007	|	|	|	|	1105	1105	|	|	|	1158	1200	1203	|	|	|	|	1300	1259	1305	|	|	|	|	1359	1405
London Kings Cross 181/2/3/5 a.	1031	1041	1049	1052	1101	1131	1131	1139	1150	1204d	1222	1223	1231	1240	1248	1249	1301	1323	1326	1331	1339	1349	1352	1401	1424	1431

	⚒	⚒A	⚒	⚒	⚒	⚒	⚒B	⚒	Ⓐ	⑥	⚒	Ⓐ	⑥	⚒A	⚒	⚒	⚒	⚒	⚒	⚒	⑥	Ⓐ	⚒	Ⓐ	⑥	⚒
Edinburgh Waverley 124 188 d.	1000	1030	...	...	...	1100	1130	...	...	...	...	1200	1200	1230	...	...	...	1300	1330	...	...	...	...	1400	1400	1408
Berwick upon Tweed 124 d.	|	1112	...	...	...	|	|	...	...	...	...	|	|	1313	...	...	...	|	1413	...	...	...	...	|	|	1500
Alnmouth 124 d.	1100	|	...	...	...	|	|	...	...	...	...	1301	1301	|	...	...	...	|	|	...	...	...	...	1500	1459	1521
Newcastle 124 188 a.	1127	1156	...	...	...	1224	1254	...	...	...	...	1327	1327	1356	...	...	...	1423	1456	...	...	...	...	1528	1527	1554
Newcastle 124 188 d.	1129	1158	...	...	...	1226	1257	...	...	...	...	1330	1330	1359	...	...	...	1426	1459	...	...	...	...	1532	1530	...
Durham 124 188 d.	1143	|	...	...	...	1240	|	...	...	...	...	1343	1344	|	...	...	...	1440	|	...	...	...	...	1546	1543	...
Darlington 124 188 d.	1202	1228	...	...	...	1300	1325	...	...	...	...	1402	1402	1428	...	...	...	1459	1527	...	...	...	...	1605	1603	...
Northallerton 183 188 d.	|	|	...	...	...	1311	|	...	...	...	...	|	|	|	...	...	...	1511	|	...	...	...	...	|	|	...
York 124 183 185 d.	1232	1258	...	...	...	1333	1359	...	1402	1405	...	1432	1432	1458	...	...	...	1533	1558	...	1603	1603	...	1634	1633	...
Harrogate 175 d.	|	|	...	...	...	|	|	...	|	|	1336	|	|	|	...	...	...	|	|	...	|	|	1536	|	|	...
Leeds 124 175 188 d.	|	|	1245	...	1315	|	|	1345	|	|	1415	|	|	|	1445	...	1515	|	|	1545	|	|	1615	|	|	...
Wakefield Westgate 124 d.	|	|	1258	...	1328	|	|	1358	|	|	1428	|	|	|	1458	...	1528	|	|	1558	|	|	1628	|	|	...
Doncaster 181 182 d.	1255	|	1318	...	1347	1356	|	1419	1427	1430	1447	1456	1455	|	1519	...	1547	1556	|	1617	1630	1626	1648	1657	1658	...
Retford 181 d.	|	|	|	...	|	|	|	|	1443	1445	|	|	|	|	|	...	|	|	|	|	1644	1641	|	|	|	...
Lincoln 189 176 d.	|	|	|	1324	|	|	|	|	|	|	|	|	|	|	|	1527	|	|	|	|	|	|	|	|	|	...
Newark North Gate 189 d.	1319	|	|	1354f	|	1420	|	|	1457	1500	|	1520	1519	|	|	1554r	|	1620	|	|	1659	1656	|	1720	1721	...
Grantham 181 d.	|	|	|	1407	1418	|	|	|	1508	1511	1518	|	|	|	|	1606	1618	|	|	|	1710	1708	1719	|	|	...
Peterborough 185 176 d.	1350	|	1410	1430	|	1448	|	1510	1530	1532	|	1550	1551f	|	1610	1630	|	1650	|	1710	1731	1730	|	1750	1749	...
Stevenage 185 d.	|	|	|	1459	1505	|	|	|	1559	1600	1605	|	|	|	|	1659	1705	|	|	|	1800	1759	1805	|	|	...
London Kings Cross 181/2/3/5 a.	1439	1451	1501	1523	1531	1540	1550	1601	1622	1624	1633	1641	1646	1649	1703	1722	1731	1740	1751	1801	1823	1823	1831	1841	1846	...

FOR NOTES SEE NEXT PAGE ▶ ▶ ▶ ▶

180 EDINBURGH - NEWCASTLE - YORK and LEEDS - LONDON

Most services convey 🍸 GR

	Ⓐ	⑥	⚒	⚒	Ⓐ	⑥	⚒	⚒	⚒	Ⓐ	⑥	Ⓐ	⑥	Ⓐ	⑥	⚒	Ⓐ	⑥	⚒	Ⓐ	⑥	⑥	Ⓐ	Ⓐ A	⑥ A
Edinburgh Waverley .. **124 188** d.	1430	1430	...	...	...	...	1500	1530	...	...	...	...	...	1600	1600	1630	...	...	...	1700	1700	...	...	1730	1730
Berwick upon Tweed .... **124** d.	1513	1512	...	...	...	...	|	1614	...	...	...	...	...	|	|	1712	...	...	...	|	|	...	...	1816	1816
Alnmouth .... **124** d.	|	|	...	...	...	...	|	|	...	...	...	...	...	|	|	|	...	...	...	1800	1801	...	...	|	|
Newcastle .... **124 188** a.	1558	1556	...	...	...	...	1624	1657	...	...	...	...	...	1724	1723	1757	...	...	...	1826	1827	...	...	1900	1900
Newcastle .... **124 188** d.	1600	1558	...	...	...	...	1626	1659	...	...	...	...	...	1727	1726	1759	...	...	...	1829	1829	...	...	1902	1902
Durham .... **124 188** d.	|	|	...	...	...	...	1640	|	...	...	...	...	...	1740	1740	|	...	...	...	1842	1843	...	...	|	|
Darlington .... **124 188** d.	1629	1627	...	...	...	...	1659	1728	...	...	...	...	...	1759	1758	1828	...	...	...	1900	1902	...	...	1932	1932
Northallerton .... **183 188** d.	|	|	...	...	...	...	1711	|	...	...	...	...	...	1810	1811	|	...	...	...	|	|	...	...	|	|
York .... **124 183 185** d.	1658	1658	...	...	...	...	1733	1758	...	1802	1802	...	...	1833	1832	1859	...	...	...	1931	1931	...	...	2001	2001
Harrogate .... **175** d.	|	|	...	...	...	...	|	|	...	|	|	1736	1736	|	|	|	...	...	...	|	|	...	...	|	|
Leeds .... **124 175 188** d.	|	|	1645	...	1715	1715	|	|	1745	|	|	1815	1815	|	|	|	1845	1845	1916	|	|	1945	1945	|	|
Wakefield Westgate .... **124** d.	|	|	1658	...	1728	1728	|	|	1758	|	|	1828	1829	|	|	|	1858	1859	1929	|	|	1958	1958	|	|
Doncaster .... **181 182** d.	|	|	1718	...	1746	1747	1756	|	1818	1827	1825	1848	1847	1855	1856	|	1919	1923f	1948	1953	1955	2017	2017	2027	2025
Retford .... **181** d.	|	|	|	...	1800	1801	|	|	|	1842	1839	|	|	|	|	|	|	|	|	|	|	|	|	|	|
Lincoln .... **189 176** d.	|	|	|	1726	|	|	|	|	|	|	|	|	|	|	|	|	|	|	|	|	|	|	|	|	|
Newark North Gate .... **189** d.	|	|	|	1754	|	|	1820	|	|	1857	1855	|	|	1918	1920	|	|	|	|	2016	2019	|	|	|	|
Grantham .... **181** d.	|	|	|	1806	1821	1824	|	|	|	1909	1907	1919	1919	|	|	|	|	|	2019	|	|	|	|	|	|
Peterborough .... **185 176** d.	|	|	1809	1830f	|	|	1849	|	1910	1930	1930	|	|	1946	1950	|	2010	2015	|	2045	2051f	2104	2107	2116	2118
Stevenage .... **185** d.	|	|	|	1859	1906	1909	|	|	|	1959	1959	2005	2004	2015	2020	2030	|	|	2105	2116	2121	|	|	2145	2148
London Kings Cross **181/2/3/5** a.	1849	1852	1901	1922	1931	1933	1946c	1953	2001	2022	2023	2028	2031	2039	2046	2055	2059	2109	2131	2139	2146	2154	2200	2209	2216

	⚒	⑥	⑥	Ⓐ	⑥		Ⓐ	⑥	Ⓐ A	⑤	⑦	⑦	⑦	⑦	⑦	⑦	⑦	⑦	⑦	⑦	⑦	⑦	⑦	⑦	⑦ G
Edinburgh Waverley .. **124 188** d.	1734	...	1831	1830	1900	...	1936	2000	2100	2200		...	...	...	...	...	...	...	...	...	...	...	...	...	...
Berwick upon Tweed .... **124** d.	1827	...	1913	1920	1947	...	2019	2052	2153	2247		...	...	...	...	...	...	...	...	...	...	...	...	...	...
Alnmouth .... **124** d.	1847	...	|	1943	2008	...	2040	2114	2214	2307		...	...	...	...	...	...	...	...	...	...	...	...	...	...
Newcastle .... **124 188** a.	1920	...	1957	2014	2041	...	2109	2146	2242	2349		...	...	...	...	...	...	...	...	...	...	...	...	...	...
Newcastle .... **124 188** d.	—	...	—	2017	2043	...	2115	...	2245	...		...	...	0755	...	...	0825	0855	...	...	0925	...	1000	...	...
Durham .... **124 188** d.	...	...	...	2030	2058	...	2129	...	2259	...		...	...	0809	...	...	0838	0908	...	...	0938	...	|	...	...
Darlington .... **124 188** d.	...	...	...	2049	2118	...	2148	...	2320	...		...	...	0827	...	...	0856	0927	...	...	0956	...	1029	...	...
Northallerton .... **183 188** d.	...	...	...	|	2131	...	2200	...	2345s	...		...	...	|	...	...	|	|	...	...	1007	...	|	...	...
York .... **124 183 185** d.	...	...	...	2119	2157	...	2223	...	0011	...		0800	...	0858	...	...	0926	0958	...	...	1029	...	1058	...	...
Harrogate .... **175** d.	...	...	Ⓐ	|	|	...	|	...	|	...		|	...	|	...	...	|	|	...	0915	|	...	|	...	...
Leeds .... **124 175 188** d.	...	2015	2045	|	|	...	|	...	0042	...		|	0805	|	0840	0905	|	|	0940	1005	|	...	|	1045	1105
Wakefield Westgate .... **124** d.	...	2028	2058	|	|	...	|	...	...	...		|	0818	|	0855	0918	|	|	0953	1018	|	...	|	1059	1118
Doncaster .... **181 182** d.	...	2048	2117	2142	2220	...	2248	...	...	...		0823	0838	|	0920f	0939	|	|	|	1038	1055	...	|	1118	1139
Retford .... **181** d.	⚒	2102	2132	|	...	...	2304	...	...	...		|	0852	|	|	|	|	|	1021	1052	|	...	|	1136	|
Lincoln .... **189 176** d.	2025	|	|	|	...	...	|	...	...	...		|	|	|	|	|	|	|	|	|	|	1055	|	|	|
Newark North Gate .... **189** d.	2051	2118	|	2206	...	...	2318	...	...	...		|	0908	|	|	1002	1009	|	1040f	1107	1119	1123	|	|	1203
Grantham .... **181** d.	2104	2130	2155	2218	...	...	2330	...	...	...		|	0920	|	|	1015	1021	|	|	1118	|	1134	|	|	1216
Peterborough .... **185 176** d.	2128	2150	2217	2239	...	...	2358	...	...	...		0911	0942	1004	1007	1036	1041	1105	1109	1139	1151	1158f	1206	|	1239
Stevenage .... **185** d.	2159	|	2246	2308	...	...	0039s	...	...	...		0941	|	|	|	1107	1112	|	|	|	|	1227	|	|	1309
London Kings Cross **181/2/3/5** a.	2224	2239	2309	2331	...	...	0115	...	...	...		1006	1037	1052	1057	1135	1138	1156	1159	1227	1239	1250	1255	1258	1335

	⑦	⑦	⑦	⑦	⑦	⑦	⑦	⑦	⑦	⑦	⑦	⑦	⑦	⑦	⑦	⑦ A	⑦	⑦	⑦	⑦	⑦ B	⑦	⑦	⑦ A	⑦
Edinburgh Waverley .. **124 188** d.	0900	0930	...	0933	1000	1030	...	1100	1120	1130	...	...	...	1200	1220	1230	...	...	1300	1320	1330	...	1400	1430	1421
Berwick upon Tweed .... **124** d.	|	1013	...	1027	|	1113	...	|	|	1213	...	...	...	|	|	1313	...	...	1343	|	1413	...	|	|	1519
Alnmouth .... **124** d.	|	|	...	1047	1101	|	...	|	|	|	...	...	...	1301	|	|	...	...	|	|	|	...	1501	|	1539
Newcastle .... **124 188** a.	1023	1056	...	1119	1127	1156	...	1223	1246	1256	...	...	...	1327	1347	1356	...	...	1426	1445	1456	...	1528	1553	1613
Newcastle .... **124 188** d.	1027	1100	...	—	1130	1158	...	1226	1252	1300	...	...	1315	1330	1350	1359	...	1416	1432	1451	1459	...	1531	1555	—
Durham .... **124 188** d.	1041	|	...	...	1144	|	...	1239	1306	|	...	...	1329	1344	1404	|	...	1429	|	1505	|	...	1545	|	...
Darlington .... **124 188** d.	1100	1129	...	...	1203	1227	...	1259	1324	1330	...	...	1348	1403	|	1430	...	1449	1501	1524	1528	...	1604	1625	...
Northallerton .... **183 188** d.	1112	|	...	...	|	|	...	1311	|	|	...	...	1400	|	|	|	...	1502	|	|	|	...	|	|	...
York .... **124 183 185** d.	1133	1158	...	⑦	1232	1256	...	1332	1355	1401	...	...	1423	1432	1449	1500	...	1524	1530	1555	1601	...	1633	1658	...
Harrogate .... **175** d.	|	|	...	1115	|	|	...	|	|	|	...	1315	|	|	|	|	...	|	|	|	|	1536	|	|	...
Leeds .... **124 175 188** d.	|	|	...	1205	|	|	1305	|	|	|	...	1405	|	|	|	|	1505	|	|	|	|	1616	|	|	...
Wakefield Westgate .... **124** d.	|	|	...	1218	|	|	1318	|	|	|	...	1418	|	|	|	|	1518	|	|	|	|	1629	|	|	...
Doncaster .... **181 182** d.	1157	|	...	1237	1255	|	1338	1356	|	|	...	1437	1448	1455	|	|	1537	1547	1554	|	|	1648	1657	|	...
Retford .... **181** d.	1212	|	...	|	|	|	|	1411	|	|	...	|	|	|	|	|	|	|	1609	|	|	|	|	|	⑦
Lincoln .... **189 176** d.	|	|	1223	|	|	|	|	|	|	|	1420	|	|	|	|	|	|	|	|	|	|	|	|	|	1650
Newark North Gate .... **189** d.	|	|	1249	1300	1319	|	1401	|	|	|	1446	1500	|	1519	|	|	1601	1611	|	|	|	|	1720	|	1724e
Grantham .... **181** d.	|	|	1302	1313	|	|	1413	|	|	|	1459	1512	|	|	1539	|	1613	|	|	|	|	1719	|	|	1735
Peterborough .... **185 176** d.	1253	|	1324	1333	1351f	|	1434	1451	|	|	1523	1534	1538	1551f	|	|	1634	1642	1650	|	|	|	1751	|	1805
Stevenage .... **185** d.	|	|	1354	|	|	|	1503	|	|	|	1554	|	|	|	|	|	1704	|	|	|	|	1804	|	|	1834
London Kings Cross **181/2/3/5** a.	1341	1348	1417	1421	1440	1445	1527	1540	1547	1550	1620	1623	1627	1640	1643	1651	1729	1736	1739	1747	1753	1827	1842	1849	1857

	⑦	⑦	⑦	⑦	⑦	⑦	⑦	⑦	⑦	⑦	⑦	⑦ A	⑦	⑦	⑦	⑦	⑦	⑦	⑦	⑦	⑦	⑦	⑦	⑦ M	⑦
Edinburgh Waverley .. **124 188** d.	...	...	1450	...	1500	1530	...	...	...	1600	1620	1630	...	...	1700	1730	1733	1800	...	1830	1900	1916	2000	2018	2100
Berwick upon Tweed .... **124** d.	...	...	1533	...	|	1612	...	...	...	|	|	1713	...	...	|	1817	1828	|	...	1913	1947	2008	2048	2102	2149
Alnmouth .... **124** d.	...	...	|	...	|	|	...	...	...	1701	|	|	...	...	|	|	1849	1901	...	|	|	2028	2110	|	2210
Newcastle .... **124 188** a.	...	...	1616	...	1623	1656	...	...	...	1727	1747	1756	...	...	1823	1859	1920	1928	...	1956	2030	2057	2141	2148	2237
Newcastle .... **124 188** d.	...	1606	1618	...	1626	1701	...	...	...	1730	1752	1800	...	...	1828	1903	—	1930	...	2000	2033	2101	2144	...	...
Durham .... **124 188** d.	...	1620	1631	...	1641	|	...	...	...	1744	|	|	...	...	1842	|	...	1944	...	|	2047	2117	2157	...	...
Darlington .... **124 188** d.	...	1639	1650	...	1701	1729	...	...	...	1803	1822	1830	...	...	1901	1930	...	2003	...	2030	2106	2135	2215	...	...
Northallerton .... **183 188** d.	...	1651	|	...	|	|	...	...	...	|	1834	|	...	...	1913	|	...	|	...	|	|	|	2227	...	...
York .... **124 183 185** d.	...	1713	1723	...	1731	1759	...	...	...	1832	1855	1902	...	...	1935	2001	...	2032	...	2100	2135	2213	2301	...	...
Harrogate .... **175** d.	...	|	|	...	|	|	...	1705	...	|	|	|	1800	...	|	|	⑦	|	...	|	|	|	|	...	...
Leeds .... **124 175 188** d.	1645	|	|	1716	|	|	...	1747	1815	|	|	|	1845	1916	|	|	1946	|	2045	|	|	2243	|	...	...
Wakefield Westgate .... **124** d.	1658	|	|	1729	|	|	...	1800	1828	|	|	|	1859	1930	|	|	1959	|	2058	|	|	...	|	...	...
Doncaster .... **181 182** d.	1721f	1736	|	1748	1758f	|	...	1818	1847	1855	|	|	1922	1948	1959	|	2021	2056	2117	2126f	2158	...	2324	...	...
Retford .... **181** d.	|	|	|	1802	|	|	...	|	|	|	|	|	|	2003	|	|	|	|	2131	|	|	...	...	...	...
Lincoln .... **189 176** d.	|	|	|	|	|	|	1800	|	|	|	|	|	|	|	|	|	|	|	|	|	|	...	...	...	...
Newark North Gate .... **189** d.	1746	|	1804	|	|	|	1826	1845	|	1919	|	|	1947	|	2022	|	2046	2120	|	2150	2222	...	...	...	...
Grantham .... **181** d.	|	1808	|	1825	1831	|	1839	|	1919	|	1945	|	|	2026	|	2049	|	|	2154	2203	2234	...	...	...	...
Peterborough .... **185 176** d.	1814	|	1833	|	1852	|	1903f	1913	|	1952	|	|	2016	|	2051	2109	2115	2150	2216	2225	2256	...	...	...	...
Stevenage .... **185** d.	|	|	|	1910	|	|	1932	|	2004	|	|	|	|	2111	|	|	|	|	2245	2255	2334s	...	...	...	...
London Kings Cross **181/2/3/5** a.	1905	1917	1922	1935	1942	1947	1959	2006	2028	2042	2049	2053	2106	2135	2140	2158	2205	2239	2310	2318	2359	...	...	...	...

NOTES for pages 136 – 138.

- **A** – To/from Aberdeen (Table **222**).
- **B** – To/from Inverness (Table **224**).
- **C** – To Glasgow Central on Ⓐ (Table **220**).
- **D** – To Sunderland (a. 2322).
- **F** – To/from Skipton (Table **173**).
- **G** – To/from Bradford Forster Square (Table **182**).
- **H** – To/from Hull (Table **181**).
- **J** – From Sunderland (d. 0539).
- **K** – To/from Stirling (Table **222**).
- **M** – To/from Glasgow Central (Table **220**).
- **P** – To Bradford Forster Square on ⑥ (Table **182**).
- **Q** – To Middlesbrough (a. 1818).
- **R** – From Middlesbrough (d. 0708).
- **a** – Arrives 1147.
- **b** – Arrives 4 – 5 minutes earlier on ⑥.
- **c** – Arrives 6 – 8 minutes earlier on Ⓐ.
- **d** – Arrives 4 – 5 minutes earlier on Ⓐ.
- **e** – Arrives 8 minutes earlier.
- **f** – Arrives 5 – 7 minutes earlier.
- **g** – Arrives 1849.
- **j** – Arrives 0726.
- **r** – Arrives 1548 on ⑥.
- **s** – Calls to set down only.
- **t** – 8 minutes later on Ⓐ.

180a 🚌 PETERBOROUGH - KINGS LYNN 🚌

First Excel service **XL**

From **Peterborough** railway station to **Kings Lynn** bus station: Journey 81 minutes. Buses call at **Wisbech** bus station ± 43 minutes later.

⚒: 0704 Ⓐ, 0734, 0809, 0844 and every 30 minutes until 1844, 1944, 2044, 2249: ⑦: 0944, 1044 and hourly until 1944.

From **Kings Lynn** railway station to **Peterborough** bus station: Journey 80 minutes. Buses call at **Wisbech** bus station ± 32 minutes later.

⚒: 0532 Ⓐ, 0602, 0632, 0702, 0732, 0802, 0832, 0902, 0932, 1007 and every 30 minutes until 1707, 1807, 1907, 2127: ⑦: 0807 and hourly until 1807.

HT All trains convey 🍸 LONDON - HULL 181

km		Ⓐ	Ⓐ	Ⓐ	Ⓐ	Ⓐ	Ⓐ△	Ⓐ	Ⓐ
0	**London** Kings Cross 180 d.	0727	0948	1148	1348	1548	1718	1848	2030
170	Grantham 180 d.	0828	1050	1250	1449	1650	1829	1952	2131
223	Retford 180 d.	0852	1111	1311	1512	1712	|	2014	2153
251	**Doncaster** 180 192 a.	0905	1126	1326b	1526	1726	1908	2027	2206
280	Selby a.	0923	1143	1346	1543	1743	1926	2046	2223
313	Brough 192 a.	0945	1204	1408	1607	1807	1947	2108	2245
330	**Hull** 177 192 a.	0959	1218	1426	1626	1824	2004	2123	2259
343	Beverley 177 a.	...	...	...	...	1842	...	2148	...

km		⑥	⑥	⑥	⑥	⑥△	⑥	⑥
0	**London** Kings Cross 180 d.	0727	0948	1148	1448	1718	1748	1948
170	Grantham 180 d.	0828	1049	1249	1550	1829	1850	2051
223	Retford 180 d.	0853	1111	1311	1611	|	1912	2114
251	**Doncaster** 180 192 a.	0906	1124	1326b	1626	1904c	1925	2127
280	Selby a.	0923	1143	1346	1644	1927	1942	2145
313	Brough 192 a.	0945	1204	1408	1706	1948	2004	2206
330	**Hull** 177 192 a.	0959	1218	1425	1725	2005	2017	2220
343	Beverley 177 a.	...	...	...	...	...	2042	...

km		⑦	⑦	⑦	⑦	⑦△	⑦	⑦
0	**London** Kings Cross 180 d.	1049	1250	1448	1627	1722	1749	1952
170	Grantham 180 d.	1149	1350	1550	1729	1827	1854	2052
223	Retford 180 d.	1211	1412	1611	1750	|	1915	2114
251	**Doncaster** 180 192 a.	1227	1426	1627b	1804	1903	1929	2127
280	Selby a.	1244	1443	1646	1821	1922	1945	2144
313	Brough 192 a.	1307	1505	1708	1843	1945	2007	2207
330	**Hull** 177 192 a.	1320	1520	1722	1857	2002	2021	2220
343	Beverley 177 a.	...	...	...	...	...	2041	...

	Ⓐ	Ⓐ△	Ⓐ	Ⓐ	Ⓐ	Ⓐ	Ⓐ	Ⓐ
everley 177 d.	0605	...	0753	...	...	...	...	...
ull 177 d.	0626	0700	0824	1034	1233	1508	1708	1909
rough d.	0638	0713	0836	1046	1245	1520	1721	1921
elby d.	0702	0736	0901	1109	1308	1543	1745	1945
oncaster 180 d.	0721	0757	0924f	1126	1325	1605	1804	2004
etford 180 d.	0741a	|	0939	1141	1339	1619	1818	2018
rantham 180 d.	0803	0833	1001	1202	1400	1640	1839	2040
ondon Kings Cross 180 a.	0914	0954	1106	1306	1506	1746	1945	2146

	⑥	⑥△	⑥		⑥	⑥	⑥	⑥
everley 177 d.	0557	...	...	...	...	...	...	...
ull 177 d.	0617	0700	0824	...	1033	1330	1531	1836
rough d.	0629	0713	0837	...	1045	1343	1543	1848
elby d.	0652	0736	0901	...	1108	1408	1606	1911
oncaster 180 d.	0710	0758f	0925	...	1125	1426	1625	1928
etford 180 d.	|	|	0939	...	1139	1440	1639	1942
rantham 180 d.	0740	0835	1001	...	1200	1501	1701	2004
ondon Kings Cross 180 a.	0847	0947	1106	...	1307	1608	1808	2114

	⑦	⑦	⑦	⑦		⑦	⑦
everley 177 d.	...	1051	...	...	...	...	...
ull 177 d.	0905	1111	1250	1436	...	1621	1847
rough d.	0917	1123	1302	1448	...	1634	1859
elby d.	0940	1146	1325	1511	...	1704	1922
oncaster 180 d.	0959	1204	1343	1529	...	1726	1940
etford 180 d.	1013	1218	1357	1543	...	1740	1954
rantham 180 d.	1035	1239	1418	1606	...	1802	2015
ondon Kings Cross 180 a.	1141	1343	1536	1716	...	1908	2119

– Arrives 0736. b – Departs 5 minutes later. c – Departs 1912. f – Arrives 5 minutes earlier. △ – Operated by GR (Table **180**).

GC All trains convey 🍸 LONDON - BRADFORD 182

km		Ⓐ	Ⓐ	Ⓐ	Ⓐ△	Ⓐ△		Ⓐ
0	**London** Kings Cross 180 d.	1057	1456	1627	1633	1833	...	1948
251	**Doncaster** 180 d.	1235a	1631	1759	1821	2022	...	2119
278	Pontefract Monkhill d.	1259	1655	|	|	|	...	|
292	Wakefield Kirkgate d.	1315	1714	1833j	1838e	2040e	...	2141
322	Halifax 190 d.	1346	1746	1909	|	|	...	2226
335	**Bradford** Interchange 190 a.	1400	1800	1923	1929f	2129f	...	2242

km		⑥	⑥	⑥	⑥△	⑥△	⑥
0	**London** Kings Cross 180 d.	1048	1525	1627	1633	1933	1957
251	**Doncaster** 180 d.	1222	1702	1802	1821	2114	2134
278	Pontefract Monkhill d.	|	|	|	|	|	2158
292	Wakefield Kirkgate d.	1251	1724	1833j	1838e	2132e	2215
322	Halifax 190 d.	1321	1757	1909	|	|	2246
335	**Bradford** Interchange 190 a.	1335	1812	1923	1929f	2218f	2300

km		⑦		⑦	⑦	⑦	⑦△
0	**London** Kings Cross 180 d.	1150	...	1550	1853	1927	1935
251	**Doncaster** 180 d.	1321	...	1721	2039b	2102	2122
278	Pontefract Monkhill d.	|	...	|	|	|	|
292	Wakefield Kirkgate d.	1346	...	1750	2100	2124	2139e
322	Halifax 190 d.	1420	...	1821	2133	2158	|
335	**Bradford** Interchange 190 a.	1434	...	1835	2147	2213	2222f

	Ⓐ△	Ⓐ	Ⓐ		Ⓐ△	Ⓐ	Ⓐ
radford Interchange 190 d.	0630f	0655	0758	...	0843f	1023	1450
alifax 190 d.	|	0710	0811	...	|	1040	1503
Vakefield Kirkgate d.	0713e	0745a	0856	...	0929e	1118	1539
ontefract Monkhill d.	|	0759	|	...	|	1133	1554
oncaster 180 d.	|	0831	0934	...	0949	1203	1622a
ondon Kings Cross 180 a.	0859	1008	1114	...	1131	1344	1808

	⑥△	⑥		⑥	⑥△	⑥	⑥
radford Interchange 190 d.	0630f	0656	...	0846	0843f	1022	1523
alifax 190 d.	|	0710	...	0859	|	1036	1536
Vakefield Kirkgate d.	0713e	0745	...	0941	0928e	1117	1618
ontefract Monkhill d.	|	0759	...	0956	|	1133	1633
oncaster 180 d.	|	0833r	...	1024	0947	1204	1708
ondon Kings Cross 180 a.	0901	1007	...	1159	1131	1344	1847

	⑦	⑦△		⑦	⑦	⑦
radford Interchange 190 d.	0804	1025f	...	1211	1512	1559
alifax 190 d.	0817t	|	...	1224	1525	1612
Vakefield Kirkgate d.	0849	1118f	...	1258	1602	1644
ontefract Monkhill d.	|	|	...	|	|	|
oncaster 180 d.	0911	1139	...	1321	1625	1711
ondon Kings Cross 180 a.	1040	1335	...	1453	1756	1842

a – Arrives 6–8 minutes earlier. b – Arrives 2026. e – Wakefield Westgate. f – Bradford Forster Square. j – Arrives 1824. r – Arrives 0824. t – Not Feb. 19 - Mar. 26. △ – Operated by GR (Table **180**).

GC All trains convey 🍸 LONDON - YORK - SUNDERLAND 182a

km		①	Ⓐ	Ⓐ	Ⓐ	Ⓐ	Ⓐ	Ⓐ△
0	**London** Kings Cross 180 d.	0827	1127	1256	1427	1648	1927	2000
303	**York** 180 188 d.	1025a	1323	1451	1620	1846a	2123	2153a
339	Thirsk 188 d.	1043	1339	1514	1637	1902	2139	|
351	Northallerton 180 188 d.	1059	1349	1522	1646	1910	2148	|
375	Eaglescliffe d.	1117	1404	1544	1703	1929	2204	|
399	Hartlepool a.	1135	1422	1605	1722	1947c	2222	|
428	**Sunderland** a.	1204	1449	1637	1752	2021	2252	2322

km		⑥	⑥	⑥		⑥	⑥	⑥
0	**London** Kings Cross 180 d.	0748	1127	1318	...	1427	1648	1927
303	**York** 180 188 d.	0946	1324	1517	...	1623b	1845	2124
339	Thirsk 188 d.	1003	1340	1534	...	1640	1901	2140
351	Northallerton 180 188 d.	1016	1348	1543	...	1700	1910	2149
375	Eaglescliffe d.	1033	1404	1603	...	1717	1929	2206
399	Hartlepool a.	1052	1423	1622	...	1735	1947c	2225
428	**Sunderland** a.	1126	1451	1651	...	1806	2021	2252

km		⑦	⑦	⑦	⑦	⑦
0	**London** Kings Cross 180 d.	0950	1348	1523	1653	1822
303	**York** 180 188 d.	1142	1538	1724	1842	2012
339	Thirsk 188 d.	1158	1555	1740	1900	2028
351	Northallerton 180 188 d.	1207	1605	1757	1912	2046
375	Eaglescliffe d.	1224	1622	1814	1930	2103
399	Hartlepool a.	1243	1640	1833	1949	2123
428	**Sunderland** a.	1308	1706	1908	2021	2150

	Ⓐ△	Ⓐ	Ⓐ	Ⓐ	Ⓐ		Ⓐ	Ⓐ
Sunderland d.	0539	0646	0853	0954	1230	...	1530	1730
Hartlepool d.	|	0715	0917	1019	1254	...	1554	1756
Eaglescliffe d.	|	0735	0940	1042	1315	...	1615	1820
Northallerton 180 188 d.	|	0755	0959	1059	1340	...	1633	1842
Thirsk 188 d.	|	0804	1008	1109	1349	...	1643	1853
York 180 188 d.	0702	0822	1026	1141d	1408	...	1710	1912
London Kings Cross 180 a.	0909	1014	1231	1354	1607	...	1907	2107

	⑥	⑥	⑥	⑥	⑥	⑥
Sunderland d.	0644	0829	0955	1218	1530	1730
Hartlepool d.	0714	0854	1020	1242	1554	1754
Eaglescliffe d.	0734	0922	1042	1301	1620a	1814
Northallerton 180 188 d.	0755	0940	1104	1319	1640	1833
Thirsk 188 d.	0804	0950	1121a	1330	1650	1843
York 180 188 d.	0822	1009	1150a	1353	1712	1902
London Kings Cross 180 a.	1014	1214	1350	1544	1906	2100

	⑦	⑦	⑦		⑦	⑦
Sunderland d.	0923	1028	1212	...	1414	1815
Hartlepool d.	0947	1052	1236	...	1439	1839
Eaglescliffe d.	1008	1112	1257	...	1458	1900
Northallerton 180 188 d.	1026	1134	1315	...	1516	1921
Thirsk 188 d.	1035	1143	1325	...	1525	1929
York 180 188 d.	1054	1208	1346a	...	1547	1949
London Kings Cross 180 a.	1241	1355	1542	...	1742	2142

a – Arrives 5–7 minutes earlier. b – Arrives 1614. c – Departs 1952. d – Arrives 1126. △ – Operated by GR (Table **180**).

LD All trains convey 🍸 2nd class only LONDON - NEWCASTLE - EDINBURGH 183

km		Ⓐ	Ⓐ		Ⓐ	Ⓐ		Ⓐ
0	**London** Kings Cross 180 d.	0545	1045	...	1218	1448	...	2027
44	Stevenage 180 d.	0610u	|	...	1241u	|	...	|
432	**Newcastle** 180 d.	0842	1347	...	1517	1750	...	2308
632	**Edinburgh** Waverley 180 a.	1008	1513	...	1641	1913	...	0047

km		⑥	⑥	⑥		⑥	⑥
0	**London** Kings Cross 180 d.	0545	1025	1218	...	1548	1827
44	Stevenage 180 d.	0610u	|	1241u	...	|	|
432	**Newcastle** 180 d.	0841	1318	1517	...	1850	2124c
632	**Edinburgh** Waverley 180 a.	1007	1442	1641	...	2015	2258

km		⑦	⑦		⑦	⑦	⑦
0	**London** Kings Cross 180 d.	0852	1023	...	1209	1624	1924
44	Stevenage 180 d.	0913u	1045u	...	1235u	|	|
432	**Newcastle** 180 d.	1146c	1316c	...	1510	1920	2209
632	**Edinburgh** Waverley 180 a.	1310	1442	...	1637	2047	2334

	Ⓐ	Ⓐ		Ⓐ	Ⓐ	Ⓐ
dinburgh Waverley 180 d.	0623	0924	...	1119	1613	1958
lewcastle 180 d.	0757c	1055	...	1250	1747c	2133
tevenage 180 a.	|	|	...	1518s	2019s	0024s
ondon Kings Cross 180 a.	1051	1347	...	1545	2045	0105

	⑥	⑥	⑥		⑥	⑥	⑥
dinburgh Waverley 180 d.	0536	0856	1256	...	1525	1756	2056
lewcastle 180 d.	0713a	1022	1422	...	1655	1934a	2220
tevenage 180 a.	|	1248s	1648s	...	|	2202s	...
ondon Kings Cross 180 a.	1004	1314	1714	...	1947	2226	...

	⑦	⑦		⑦		⑦	⑦
dinburgh Waverley 180 d.		1053	...	1355	...	1549	1853
lewcastle 180 d.	0820	1220	...	1522	...	1716	2021
tevenage 180 a.	1039s	|	...	1739s	...	1944s	2258s
ondon Kings Cross 180 a.	1103	1456	...	1809	...	2009	2320

a – Arrives 9–11 minutes earlier. c – Arrives 5–7 minutes earlier. s – Calls to set down only. u – Calls to pick up down only.

EM 2nd class SKEGNESS - NOTTINGHAM 184

km		⚒	⑥	Ⓐ	Ⓐ	⑥	⚒	⑥	Ⓐ	⚒	Ⓐ	⑥	⚒	⚒
0	**Skegness** d.	...	...	...	0706	0709	0818	0917	0920	1015	1114	1115	1215	1315
8	Wainfleet d.	...	...	...	0716	0719	0827	0926	0929	1024	1123	1124	1224	1324
38	Boston d.	...	0615	0613	0743	0746	0852	0951	0954	1049	1149	1154	1249	1351
66	Sleaford d.	...	0637	0635	0810	0812	0915	1016	1017	1113	1218	1217	1313	1415
89	Grantham a.	...	0707	0704	0840	0841	0940	1041	1042	1139	1243	1242	1339	1441
89	Grantham 206 d.	0542	0711	0711	0843	0844	0944	1045	1045	1146	1247	1245	1342	1443
126	**Nottingham** 206 a.	0625	0750	0751	0923	0920	1019	1120	1120	1219	1322	1321	1417	1522

km		⚒	⚒	Ⓐ	⑥	⚒	⑥	Ⓐ	⑥	Ⓐ	Ⓐ	⑥	⑥	Ⓐ
0	**Skegness** d.	1416	1514	1614	1615	1722	1815	1815	1915	1920	2016	2022	2115	2120
8	Wainfleet d.	1425	1523	1624	1625	1731	1824	1824	1924	1929	2025	2031	2124	2129
38	Boston d.	1450	1548	1652	1652	1758	1851	1855f	1949	1954	2050	2056	2151	2154
66	Sleaford d.	1514	1614	1716	1714	1821	1915	1920	2016	2017	2116	2121	2213	2217
89	Grantham a.	1540	1641	1741	1739	1847	1942	1947	2043	2044	2141	2146	2240	|
89	Grantham 206 d.	1543	1645	1745	1743	1849	1946	1950	2047	2047	2145	2150	2244	|
126	**Nottingham** 206 a.	1621	1719	1822	1819	1923	2025	2030	2121	2121	2221	2227	2316	2305

	⑦	⑦	⑦	⑦	⑦	⑦	⑦	⑦	⑦	⑦	⑦	⑦
Skegness d.	...	1015	1115	1215	1415	1515	1615	1715	1815	1907	2022	2045
Wainfleet d.	...	1024	1124	1224	1424	1524	1624	1724	1824	1916	2031	2054
Boston d.	0915	1052	1151	1252	1453	1552	1653	1754f	1853	1943	2056	2121
Sleaford d.	0938	1115	1213	1315	1515	1614	1715	1816	1916	2007	...	2143
Grantham a.	1005	1142	1240	1342	1542	1641	1742	1843	1943	2034	...	2210
Grantham 206 d.	1010	1147	1245	1347	1547	1645	1747	1849	1947	2038	...	2215
Nottingham 206 a.	1045	1221	1321	1422	1624	1724	1821	1926	2021	2111	...	2252

	⚒	Ⓐ	⑥	Ⓐ	⑥	⚒	⚒	⑥	Ⓐ	⚒
Nottingham 206 d.	0509v	0547	0549	0642	0645	0746	0845	0955	0955	1045
Grantham 206 a.	0552	|	|	0720	0722	0824	0928	|	|	1125
Grantham d.	▬	|	|	0725	0726	0827	0931	|	|	1128
Sleaford d.	⚒	0638	0645	0752	0753	0856	0956	1042	1042	1154
Boston d.	0620	0719c	0720r	0820	0819	0921	1020	1106	1111f	1218
Wainfleet d.	0644	0746	0747	0845	0843	0945	1044	1131	1140	1242
Skegness a.	0655	0758	0758	0855	0853	0956	1056	1141	1151	1253

	⚒	⚒	⚒	⚒	⚒	⑥	Ⓐ	⑥	Ⓐ	⚒	⑥	Ⓐ	⑥	Ⓐ	⑥
Nottingham 206 d.	1145	1245	1345	1445	1545	1645	1645	1745	1748	1846	1946	1948	2045	2048	2141
Grantham 206 a.	1221	1325	1422	1525	1627	1728	1730	1825	1830	1924	2024	2029	2125	2129	2214
Grantham d.	1224	1327	1427	1527	1629	1732	1733	1829	1834	1927	2028	2033	2129	2132	2217
Sleaford d.	1250	1354	1453	1553	1655	1800	1803	1854	1901	1956	2056	2058	2154	2158	2243
Boston d.	1316	1418	1517	1621	1718	1824	1827	1918	1925	2020	2120	2123	2218	2222	...
Wainfleet d.	1340	1442	1541	1645	1745	1849	1851	1942	1950	2044	...	...	...	...	...
Skegness a.	1350	1454	1552	1657	1757	1859	1902	1952	2000	2055	...	...	...	...	...

	⑦	⑦	⑦	⑦	⑦	⑦	⑦	⑦	⑦	⑦	⑦	⑦
Nottingham 206 d.	0830	0850	0950	1150	1250	1350	1450	1550	1650	1747	1830	1945
Grantham 206 a.	0916	0923	1027	1228	1327	1428	1527	1628	1729	1828	1905	2024
Grantham d.	▬	0927	1030	1231	1330	1432	1530	1631	1732	1832	1909	2028
Sleaford d.	⑦	0952	1057	1257	1356	1457	1556	1657	1758	1857	1934	2053
Boston d.	0920	1017	1120	1321	1420	1524	1620	1721	1822	1922	1959	2116
Wainfleet d.	0945	1042	1145	1346	1445	1548	1645	1746	1847	1946	2023	...
Skegness a.	0955	1052	1155	1356	1455	1559	1655	1756	1857	1957	2034	...

c – Arrives 0701. f – Arrives 5–6 minutes earlier. r – Arrives 0708. v – Departs 0513 on Ⓐ.

185 KINGS LYNN, CAMBRIDGE and PETERBOROUGH - LONDON - GATWICK ✈ - BRIGHTON GN, TL

KINGS LYNN - CAMBRIDGE - LONDON

km			Ⓐ	⑥	⑥	Ⓐ	Ⓐ	⑥	Ⓐ	⑥	Ⓐ	Ⓐ	⑥	Ⓐ	⑥	Ⓐ	Ⓐ	⑥	Ⓐ	⑥	Ⓐ	Ⓐ	⑥	Ⓐ
0	**Kings Lynn** d.	⚒	0443	...	...	...	0539	0544	0610	...	0618	0641	0644	...	...	0710	...	0744	0748	...	...	0844	0844	...
14	Downham Market d.		0457	...	...	...	0553	0558	0625	...	0635	0655	0658	...	...	0725	...	0758	0802	...	...	0858	0858	...
42	Ely **207 208** d.		0516	0517	0553	...	0613	0617	0642	0653	0653	0714	0717	0729	0747	0744	0800	0817	0825	0853	0845	0917	0917	0947
66	**Cambridge** **207 208** a.		0535	0536	0612	...	0634	0637	0702	0712	0712	0734	0737	0747	0806	0804	0820	0837	0845	0912	0905	0936	0937	1007
66	**Cambridge** d.		0539	0537	0614	0609	0640	0644	0709	0714	0717	0739	0744	0750	0814	0809	0821	0844	0850	0914	0909	0942	0944	1014
159	**London** Kings Cross a.		0633	0633	0703	0703	0733	0734	0803	0803	0825d	0833	0833	0920d	0903	0903	0950d	0933	0948	1004	1004	1033	1034	1105

	⑥	⑥	Ⓐ	Ⓐ	⑥	⚒	⚒		⚒	⚒	Ⓐ	⑥	⚒	Ⓐ	⑥	Ⓐ	⑥	⚒	⚒	Ⓐ	⑥	Ⓐ	⑥
Kings Lynn d.	0919	0944	0946	...	1012	1044	...	and at	...	1544	...	...	1644	1716	...	1741	1744	...	1844	...	...	1940	1940
Downham Market d.	0933	0958	1000	...	1028	1058	...	the same	...	1558	...	...	1658	1728	...	1755	1758	...	1858	...	...	1954	1958
Ely **207 208** d.	0954	1017	1018	1053	1053	1117	1153	minutes	1553	1617	1642	1653	1718	1746	1753	1815	1817	1853	1917	1945	1953	2017j	2018
Cambridge **207 208** a.	1013	1037	1038	1112	1112	1138	1213	past each	1613	1637	1702	1712	1737	1805	1812	1836	1837	1913	1937	2006	2012	2038	2037
Cambridge d.	1014	1044	1044	1114	1114	1144	1214	hour until	1614	1644	1708	1714	1742	1808	1814	1844	1844	1914	1944	2014	2014	2044	2044
London Kings Cross a.	1103	1133	1132	1203	1205	1234	1303		1705	1733	1803	1803	1833	1903	1903	1933	1936	2003	2033	2103	2103	2133	2133

	⚒	⚒	⚒	⚒	Ⓐ	⑥	⚒	Ⓐ	⑥	⚒	⑦	⑦	⑦	⑦	⑦		⑦	⑦	⑦	⑦	⑦	⑦	⑦
Kings Lynn d.	...	2040n	...	2140n	...	...	...	2244	2258	...		...	...	...	0825	and	1725	1754	1825	1925	2025	2125	2225
Downham Market d.	...	2058	...	2158	...	...	...	2258	2312	...		...	...	...	0839		1739	1808	1839	1939	2039	2139	2239
Ely **207 208** d.	2053	2117	2153	2217	2246	2253	...	2316	2329	...		...	...	...	0857	hourly	1757	1825	1857	1957	2057	2157	2257
Cambridge **207 208** a.	2113	2137	2212	2237	2306	2312	...	2336	2348	...		...	...	...	0916		1816	1843	1916	2016	2116	2216	2316
Cambridge d.	2114	2144	2214	2244	2314	2314	2335	...	...	2354		0640	0728	0822	0922	until	1822	1844	1922	2022	2122	2222	2320
London Kings Cross a.	2203	2233	2303	2334	0008	0004	0058	...	...	0110		0750	0832	0911	1011		1912	1936	2011	2111	2211	2312	0050

		①	②–⑥	Ⓐ	⚒	⑥	Ⓐ	⚒	⑥	Ⓐ	⑥	Ⓐ	⑥	Ⓐ	⑥	Ⓐ	Ⓐ	⑥	Ⓐ	⑥	⚒	⑥	Ⓐ	⑥
London Kings Cross d.	⚒	0003	0033	...	0503	0542	0542	0603	0642	0642	0712	0712	0742	0740	0812	0810	0842	0842	0910	0912	0942	1012	1012	1042
Cambridge a.		0133	0144	...	0614	0630	0630	0713	0730	0733	0800	0804	0830	0830	0900	0901	0930	0930	1003	1000	1030	1100	1101	1130
Cambridge **207 208** d.		...	...	0550	...	0632	0634	...	0735	0739	0803	0809	0835	0835	0903	0906	0935	0935	1005	1003	1035	1103	1105	1135
Ely **207 208** d.		...	...	0608	...	0655	0653	...	0755	0802j	0823	0830	0855	0856	0923	0926	0956	0955	1025	1023	1055	1123	1125	1155
Downham Market d.		...	...	0624	...	0717	0719	...	0817	0821	...	...	0917	0919	...	...	1019	1017	...	...	1117	...	...	1217
Kings Lynn a.		...	...	0638	...	0731	0733	...	0831	0835	...	...	0935	0934	...	...	1033	1035	...	...	1131	...	...	1231

	Ⓐ	⚒	⚒		⚒	⚒	⑥	Ⓐ	Ⓐ	⑥	Ⓐ	⑥	Ⓐ	⑥	Ⓐ	⑥	Ⓐ	⑥	⑥	Ⓐ	Ⓐ	⑥	Ⓐ
London Kings Cross d.	1042	1112	1142	and at	1512	1542	1612	1612	1639	1642	1709	1712	1739	1742	1809	1812	1839	1842	1912	1912	1907d	1942	1939
Cambridge a.	1133	1201	1230	the same	1600	1630	1700	1704	1732	1730	1805	1800	1832	1830	1903	1900	1932	1930	2000	2005	2015	2030	2033
Cambridge **207 208** d.	1137	1203	1235	minutes	1603	1635	1703	1705	1737	1735	1810	1803	1837	1835	1908	1905	1937	1935	2003	2007	2016	2035	2038
Ely **207 208** d.	1157	1224	1255	past each	1626	1655	1723	1724	1756	1755	1829	1823	1856	1855	1926	1926	1956	1955	2024	2026	2032	2054	2056
Downham Market d.	1217	...	1317	hour until	...	1717	...	...	1814	1817	...	...	1917	1917	1943	1942	2013	2017	2042	...	2049	2117	2117
Kings Lynn a.	1231	...	1331		...	1732	...	...	1828	1831	...	...	1931	1931	1957	1956	2027	2031	2056	...	2107	2131	2131

	⑥	Ⓐ	⚒	⑥	Ⓐ	⑥	Ⓐ	⚒	⑥	Ⓐ	⚒	⚒	⑦	⑦	⑦	⑦	⑦		⑦	⑦	⑦	⑦	⑦
London Kings Cross d.	2012	2009	2039r	2112	2109	2142	2139	2209r	2242	2239	2309r	2342		0033	0633	0754	0912	and	1912	2012	2112	2212	2312
Cambridge a.	2104	2103	2133	2204	2203	2230	2233	2303	2330	2333	0004	0036		0144	0746	0858	0959		2001	2059	2159	2259	0003
Cambridge **207 208** d.	2106	2108	2135	2205	2205	2235	2236	2305	2335	2338	0007	...		...	...	0904	1004	hourly	2004	2104	2204	2304	0006
Ely **207 208** d.	2125	2128	2155	2225	2227	2255	2256	2325	2355	2358	0027	...		...	...	0922	1022		2022	2122	2223	2322	0024
Downham Market d.	2142	...	2217	...	...	2311	2317	...	0011	0014	0043	...		...	...	0939	1039	until	2039	2139	2239	2339	0041
Kings Lynn a.	2156	...	2231	...	...	2325	2331	...	0025	0028	0057	...		...	...	0953	1053		2053	2153	2253	2353	0055

PETERBOROUGH and CAMBRIDGE - STEVENAGE - LONDON - GATWICK AIRPORT - HORSHAM and BRIGHTON ❖

km			⚒	⚒	⚒	⚒	⚒	⚒	⚒	⚒	⚒		⚒	⚒	⚒	⚒	⚒	⚒	⚒	⚒	⚒	⚒	⚒	⚒	⚒	⚒
0	**Peterborough** d.	⚒	0324	0419	...	0454	...	...	0554	...	0624		...	1824	...	1852	1924	...	1954	2024	...	2054	2124	...	2154	2224
28	Huntingdon d.		0338	0433	...	0510	...	...	0610	...	0640		...	1840	...	1910	1940	...	2010	2040	...	2110	2140	...	2210	2240
	Cambridge d.		|	|	0454	|	0524	0554	|	0623	|		1823	|	1853	|	|	1954	|	|	2054	|	|	2154	|	|
79	Stevenage d.		0417	0513	0532	0547	0602	0632	0647	0701	0717	and at	1902	1917	1932	1947	2017	2032	2047	2117	2130	2147	2217	2232	2247	2317
119	Finsbury Park d.		0445	0537	0552	0607	0622	0652	0708	0722	0738		1922	1938	1952	2008	2038	2052	2108	2137	2152	2208	2237	2252	2308	2338
	London Kings Cross a.		0451	|	|	|	|	|	|	|	|	the same	|	|	|	|	|	|	|	|	|	|	|	|	|	2344
122	**London** St Pancras **103** d.		...	0545	0600	0615	0630	0700	0715	0730	0745		1930	1945	2000	2015	2045	2100	2115	2145	2200	2215	2245	2300	2315	...
124	Farringdon **103** d.		...	0549	0604	0619	0634	0704	0719	0734	0749	minutes	1934	1949	2004	2019	2049	2104	2119	2149	2204	2219	2249	2304	2319	...
126	**London** Blackfriars **103** d.		...	0554	0609	0624	0639	0709	0724	0739	0754		1939	1954	2009	2024	2054	2109	2124	2154	2209	2224	2254	2309	2324	...
127	**London** Bridge **103** d.		...	0600	0615	0630	0645	0715	0730	0745	0800	past each	1945	2000	2015	2030	2100	2115	2130	2200	2215	2230	2300	2315	2330	...
143	East Croydon **102 103** d.		...	0617	0629	0647	0659	0729	0747	0759	0817		1959	2017	2029	2047	2117	2129	2147	2217	2229	2247	2316	2329	2347	...
	Redhill **102** d.		...	0637	|	0707	|	|	0807	|	0837	hour until	|	2037	|	2107	2137	|	2207	2237	|	2309	2335	|	0002	...
153	Gatwick Airport ✈ **102 103** d.		...	0650	0645	0720	0715	0745	0817	0815	0847		2015	2047	2045	2116	2149	2145	2217	2247	2245	2319	2345	2349	0017	...
165	**Horsham** **102** a.		...	0712	|	0744	|	|	0842	|	0912		|	2110	|	...	2212	|	2240	2310	|	2342	0008	|	0040	...
	Haywards Heath **103** d.		...	...	0700	...	0730	0800	...	0830	...		2030	...	2100	...	...	2200	...	...	2300	...	...	0006	...	...
	Brighton **103** a.		...	...	0718	...	0748	0818	...	0848	...		2048	...	2118	...	...	2218	...	...	2318	...	...	0022	...	...

	⚒	⚒	⚒	⚒	⑦	⑦△	⑦△	⑦	⑦	⑦		⑦	⑦	⑦	⑦	⑦
Peterborough d.	...	2254	2320	...		0545	0645	0745	...	0845		...	2045	...	2145	2245
Huntingdon d.	...	2310	2334	...		0601	0659	0759	...	0859		...	2059	...	2159	2259
Cambridge d.	2253	|	|	2354		|	|	|	0828	|		2028	|	2128	|	|
Stevenage d.	2332	2350	0013	0034		0640	0740	0836	0906	0936	and at	2106	2136	2206	2236	2339
Finsbury Park d.	2352	0010	0040	0100		0714	0802	0856	0926	0956		2126	2156	2226	2256	2359
London Kings Cross a.	2359	0018	0046	0110		0722	0810	0902	|	1002	the same	|	2202	|	2302	0005
London St Pancras **103** d.	...	...	...	...		▬	▬	▬	0934	▬		2135	▬	2235	▬	...
Farringdon **103** d.	...	...	...	...		...	...	...	0938	...	minutes	2139	...	2239	...	...
London Blackfriars **103** d.	...	...	...	...		⑦	⑦	⑦	0943	⑦		2144	⑦	2244	...	...
London Bridge **103** d.	...	...	...	...		0719	0819	0921	0951	1021	past each	2151	2221	2251	⑦	...
East Croydon **102 103** d.	...	...	...	...		0735	0835	0935	1006	1035		2206	2235	2306	2323	...
Redhill **102** d.	...	...	...	...		0755	0855	0948	|	1048	hour until	|	2248	|	2342	...
Gatwick Airport ✈ **102 103** d.	...	...	...	...		0809	0909	1003	1021	1103		2221	2303	2321	2351	...
Horsham **102** a.	...	...	...	...		0831	0931	1025	|	1125		|	2325	|	0014	...
Haywards Heath **103** d.	...	...	...	...		...	...	...	1038	...		2238	...	2338	...	...
Brighton **103** a.	...	...	...	...		...	...	...	1054	...		2254	...	2354	...	...

		①	①	②–⑥	⚒
Brighton **103** d.	⚒	...	...	...	...
Haywards Heath **103** d.		...	...	...	...
Horsham **102** d.		...	...	...	...
Gatwick ✈ **102 103** d.		...	...	...	...
Redhill **102** d.		...	...	...	...
East Croydon **102 103** d.		...	...	...	...
London Bridge **103** d.		...	...	...	...
London Blackfriars **103** d.		...	...	...	...
Farringdon **103** d.		...	...	...	...
London St Pancras **103** d.		...	...	...	...
London Kings Cross d.		0032	0132	0136	0518
Finsbury Park d.		0039	0139	0143	0524
Stevenage d.		0113	0221	0210	0545
Cambridge d.		|	|	|	|
Huntingdon d.		0153s	0257s	0247	0624
Peterborough a.		0211	0315	0306	0643

km		⚒	⚒	⚒	⚒	⚒	⚒	⚒	⚒	⚒	⚒	⚒	⚒	⚒	⚒	⚒	⚒	⚒	♣	⚒	⚒	⚒	⚒	⚒	⚒	⚒
0	**Brighton** **103** d.	...	...	...	0506	...	0544c	...	0614	...	0644	...	0714	...	0744	...	0814	...		...	1714	...	1744	...	1814	...
21	Haywards Heath **103** d.	...	...	...	0529	...	0601c	...	0631	...	0701	...	0731	...	0801	...	0831	...		...	1731	...	1801	...	1831	...
	Horsham **102** d.	...	...	...	|	0525	|	0554	|	0624	|	0654	|	0724	|	0755	|	0824		1654	|	1724	|	1754	|	1824
55	Gatwick Airport ✈ **102 103** d.	...	...	...	0546	0549	0616	0619	0646	0649	0716	0719	0746	0749	0816	0818	0846	0849	and at	1719	1746	1749	1816	1819	1846	1849
	Redhill **102** d.	...	...	...	|	0559	|	0629	|	0659	|	0729	|	0759	|	0829	|	0859		1729	|	1759	|	1829	|	1859
65	East Croydon **102 103** d.	...	...	...	0601	0615	0631	0645	0701	0715	0731	0745	0801	0815	0831	0845	0901	0915	the same	1745	1801	1815	1831	1845	1901	1915
81	**London** Bridge **103** d.	...	...	...	0616	0631	0646	0701	0716	0731	0746	0801	0816	0831	0846	0901	0916	0931		1801	1816	1831	1846	1901	1916	1931
82	**London** Blackfriars **103** d.	...	...	...	0622	0637	0652	0707	0822	0737	0752	0807	0822	0837	0852	0907	0922	0937	minutes	1807	1822	1837	1852	1907	1922	1937
84	Farringdon **103** d.	...	...	...	0626	0641	0656	0711	0726	0741	0756	0811	0826	0841	0856	0911	0926	0941		1811	1826	1841	1856	1911	1926	1941
86	**London** St Pancras **103** d.	...	...	...	0631	0646	0701	0716	0731	0746	0801	0816	0831	0846	0901	0916	0931	0946	past each	1816	1831	1846	1901	1916	1931	1946
	London Kings Cross d.	0548	0533	0618	|	|	|	|	|	|	|	|	|	|	|	|	|	|		|	|	|	|	|	|	|
90	Finsbury Park d.	0554	0541	0624	0639	0654	0712j	0723	0742j	0754	0812j	0824	0842j	0854	0912j	0924	0942j	0954	hour until	1824	1839	1854	1912j	1924	1939	1954
130	Stevenage d.	0614	0602	0644	0702	0714	0733	0743	0803	0814	0833	0844	0903	0914	0933	0944	1003	1014		1844	1900	1914	1933	1944	2000	2014
179	**Cambridge** d.	|	0644	|	0744	|	0813	|	0842	|	0912	|	0942	|	1012	|	1042	|		|	1943	|	2011	|	2043	|
	Huntingdon d.	0650	...	0720	...	0750	...	0818	...	0850	...	0920	...	0950	...	1020	...	1050		1920	...	1950	...	2020	...	2050
	Peterborough a.	0710t	...	0737	...	0806	...	0840k	...	0908	...	0936	...	1007	...	1039	...	1105		1939	...	2005	...	2040	...	2105

c – Ⓐ only.
d – London **Liverpool Street**.
f – On ⑥ departs Brighton 5–8 minutes later.
j – Arrives 5 minutes earlier.
k – Arrives 6 minutes earlier on Ⓐ.
n – Departs 4 minutes later on Ⓐ.
r – Departs 3 minutes later on ⑥.
s – Calls to set down only.
t – Arrives 0705 on ⑥.
♣ – Arrivals at Peterborough may vary by up to 4 minutes.
△ – Subject to alteration from Feb. 19 to Mar. 26 with partial 🚌 replacement (earlier departures from Peterborough and Huntingdon).
❖ – See Table **180** for fast trains Peterborough - London Kings Cross (operated by GR). See upper panel for other fast trains Cambridge - London Kings Cross and v.v.

GN, TL KINGS LYNN, CAMBRIDGE and PETERBOROUGH - LONDON - GATWICK - BRIGHTON 185

	⚒	⚒	⚒	⚒	⚒	⚒	⚒	⚒	⚒	⚒	⚒	⚒	⚒	⚒	⑦	⑦	⑦	⑦	⑦	⑦	⑦		⑦	⑦	⑦
righton .... 103 d.	1844	...	1914	...	...	2014	...	...	2114	...	...	2214	...	...		...	...	...	*0757*	...	0919		...	2119	...
laywards Heath .... 103 d.	1901	...	1931	...	...	2031	...	...	2131	...	...	2231	...	...		...	...	...	*0818*	...	0935		...	2135	...
Horsham .... 102 d.	|	1855	|	1925	1955	|	2025	2055	|	2125	...	|	2225	2311		...	0645	0745	|	0845	|		2045	|	2145
atwick Airport ✈. 102 103 d.	1916	1919	1946	1949	2019	2046	2049	2119	2146	2150	2219	2246	2249	2335		...	0707	0807	0853	0908	0953	and at	2108	2153	2208
edhill .... 102 d.	|	1929	|	1959	2029	|	2059	2129	|	2204	2234	|	2304	2349		...	0722	0822	|	0926	|		2126	|	2226
ast Croydon .... 102 103 d.	1931	1945	2001	2015	2045	2101	2115	2145	2201	2216	2245	2301	2315	0010		...	0739	0839	0909	0939	1009	the same	2139	2209	2239
ondon Bridge .... 103 d.	1946	2001	2016	2031	2101	2116	2131	2201	2216	2231	2301	2316	2331	|		...	0758	0857	0925	0957	1025		2155	2225	2255
ondon Blackfriars .... 103 d.	1952	2007	2022	2037	2107	2122	2137	2207	2222	2237	2307	2322	2337	0037		...	▬	▬	0932	▬	1032	minutes	▬	2232	▬
arringdon .... 103 d.	1956	2011	2026	2041	2111	2126	2141	2211	2226	2241	2311	2326	2341	0041		...	...	...	0936	...	1036		...	2236	...
ondon St Pancras .... 103 d.	2001	2016	2031	2046	2116	2131	2146	2216	2231	2246	2316	2331	2346	0046		...	⑦	⑦	0941	⑦	1041	past each	⑦	2241	⑦
London Kings Cross .... d.	|	|	|	|	|	|	|	|	|	|	|	|	|	|		0732	0812	0912	|	1012	|		2212	|	2322
insbury Park .... d.	2009	2024	2038	2054	2124	2138	2154	2224	2238	2254	2324	2338	2354	0054		0738	0818	0918	0948	1018	1048	hour until	2218	2248	2328
tevenage .... d.	2030	2044	2108	2114	2144	2208	2214	2244	2308	2314	2344	0009	0014	0122		0804	0838	0938	1008	1039	1108		2239	2308	2348
Cambridge .... d.	2112	|	2148	|	|	2248	|	|	2347	|	|	0055	|	|		|	|	|	1047	|	1148		|	2347	|
untingdon .... d.	...	2120	...	2150	2220	...	2250	2320	...	2350	0020	...	0051	0201v		0842	0913	1013	...	1113	...		2313	...	0022
eterborough .... a.	...	2135	...	2205	2235	...	2307	2339	...	0009	0039	...	0109	0219v		0858	0929	1029	...	1129	...		2331	...	0041

– 🚐 connection ⑦ mornings Feb. 19 - Mar. 26; Huntingdon a. 0323, Peterborough a. 0408.

TP Most trains convey 🍷 THE NORTH EAST and YORKSHIRE - MANCHESTER and LIVERPOOL 188

km	km		⚒	①	⑥	②–⑤	②–⑤	⑥	①	Ⓐ	⚒	⚒	⚒	⑥	②–⑤	①	⚒	⚒	⚒	⚒	⚒	⚒	⚒	⚒	⑥	Ⓐ	⚒
0		**Edinburgh** .... 124 180 d.		...	...	...	...	...	...	...	...	...	...	...	...	...	...	...	...	...	...	...	...	...	...	...	...
199		**Newcastle** .... 124 180 d.		...	...	...	...	...	...	...	...	...	...	0426	0426	0451	...	...	...	0535	0606	...	...	...	0705	0709	...
222		Durham .... 124 180 d.		...	...	...	...	...	...	...	...	...	...	0738	0439	0519	...	...	...	0551	0618	...	...	...	0717	0721	...
257		Darlington .... 124 180 d.		...	...	...	...	...	...	...	...	...	...	0456	0456	0537	...	...	...	0610	0636	...	...	...	|	|	...
	0	**Saltburn** .... 212 d.		...	...	...	...	...	...	...	...	...	...	|	|	|	...	...	...	|	|	0554	...	...	|	|	0651
	8	Redcar Central .... 212 d.		...	...	...	...	...	...	...	...	...	...	|	|	|	...	...	...	|	|	0603	...	...	|	|	0706
	20	**Middlesbrough** .... 212 d.		...	...	...	...	...	...	...	...	...	...	|	|	|	...	...	...	|	|	0620	...	...	|	|	0719
279	45	Northallerton .... 124 180 d.		...	...	...	...	...	...	...	...	...	...	|	|	|	...	...	...	0620	|	0650	...	...	|	|	0750
292	▬	Thirsk .... d.		...	...	...	...	...	...	...	...	...	...	|	|	|	...	...	...	0630	|	0659	...	...	|	|	0759
	0	**Scarborough** .... d.		...	...	...	...	...	...	...	...	...	...	|	|	|	...	...	0546	|	|	|	...	0648	|	|	|
	34	Malton .... d.		...	...	...	...	...	...	...	...	...	...	|	|	|	...	...	0610	|	|	|	...	0712	|	|	|
327	67	**York** .... 124 180 a.		...	...	...	...	...	...	...	...	...	...	0537	0542	0603	...	...	0636	0647	0703	0717	...	0738	0757	0803	0817
▬	▬	**York** .... 124 d.		0134	0138	0138	0235	0252	0252	...	0503	...	0537	0540	0544	0606	0617	...	...	0649	0705	0719	...	0740	0804	0805	0819
	0	**Hull** .... d.		|	|	|	|	|	|	...	|	0459	|	|	|	|	|	0601	...	|	|	|	0653	|	|	|	|
	50	Selby .... d.		|	|	|	|	|	|	...	|	0535	|	|	|	|	|	0633	...	|	|	|	0725	|	|	|	|
368	83	**Leeds** .... 124 a.		0200	0218	0216	0313	0318	0318	...	0540	0557	0603	0622	0623	0628	0642	0658	...	0713	0728	0742	0756	0804	0827	0828	0842
		Leeds .... d.		0201	0218	0220	0317	0320	0319	...	0545	0559	0605	0630	0630	0631	0645	0700	...	0715	0730	0745	0800	0807	0830	0830	0845
383		Dewsbury .... d.		|	|	|	|	|	|	...	0556	|	0616	|	|	|	0657	|	...	0726	|	0757	|	|	0841	0841	0857
396		Huddersfield .... d.		0240**y**	0256	0258	0356	0356	0356	...	0607	0618	0625	0650	0650	0651	0707	0718	...	0736	0748	0807	0818	0825	0851	0851	0907
425		Stalybridge .... d.		|	|	|	|	|	|	...	|	0637	0655	|	|	|	|	0737	...	0803	|	|	0837	0855	|	|	|
436		**Manchester** Victoria .... a.		|	|	|	|	|	|	0554	0637	0650	|	0722	0722	0722	0737	0750	...	|	0822	0838	0850	|	0922	0922	0937
440		**Manchester** Piccadilly .... a.		0333	0329	0350	0456	0428	0456	|	0649	|	0711	|	|	|	0749	|	...	0821	|	0849	|	0910	|	|	0949
456		**Manchester** Airport ✈ .... a.		0351	0352	0407	0515	0454	0514	|	0711	|	...	|	|	|	0810	|	...	...	|	0910	|	...	|	|	1010
487		**Liverpool** Lime Street .... a.		...	...	...	...	...	...	0634	...	0732	...	0800	0801	0801	...	0834	...	...	0905f	...	0933	...	0959	0959	...

	⑥	Ⓐ	⚒	⑥	Ⓐ	⑤⑥	⚒	⚒	⚒	⚒	⑤⑥	⚒	⚒	⚒	⚒	⚒	⑤⑥	⚒	⚒	Ⓐ	⑥	⚒	⚒	⚒	⚒	⚒	⚒
dinburgh .... 124 180 d.	0526	0530	...	...	...	a	...	...	...	...	a	...	...	...	...	...	a	...	...	...	...	...	...	0933	...	...	...
ewcastle .... 124 180 d.	0716	0721	0743	0801	0801	...	...	...	...	0902j	...	...	...	...	0943	1006	...	...	...	...	...	1101j	...	1121	...	1142	1202r
urham .... 124 180 d.	▬	▬	0800	0815	0818	...	...	...	...	0918	...	...	...	...	0959	1018	...	...	...	...	...	1117	...	▬	...	1200	1218
arlington .... 124 180 d.	...	...	0818	0833	0836	...	...	...	...	0936	...	...	...	...	1017	1036	...	...	...	...	...	1134	...	...	...	1218	1236
Saltburn .... 212 d.	...	...	|	|	|	...	0748	...	...	|	...	0845	...	...	|	|	...	0951	...	...	...	|	1051	...	...	|	|
Redcar Central .... 212 d.	...	...	|	|	|	...	0807	...	...	|	...	0907	...	...	|	|	...	1007	...	...	...	|	1107	...	...	|	|
Middlesbrough .... 212 d.	...	...	|	|	|	...	0820	...	...	|	...	0920	...	...	|	|	...	1020	...	...	...	|	1120	...	...	|	|
orthallerton .... 124 180 d.	...	...	0829	|	|	...	0850	...	...	|	...	0950	...	...	1028	|	...	1050	...	...	...	|	1150	...	...	1229	|
hirsk .... d.	...	⚒	|	|	|	...	0859	...	...	|	...	0959	...	...	|	|	...	1059	...	...	...	|	1159	...	...	|	|
Scarborough .... d.	...	0748	|	|	|	0819	|	...	0845	|	0918	|	...	0948	|	|	1018	|	...	1035	1048	|	|	...	1148	|	|
Malton .... d.	...	0812	|	|	|	0844	|	...	0909	|	1942	|	...	1012	|	|	1042	|	...	1059	1112	|	|	...	1212	|	|
ork .... 124 180 a.	...	0838	0848	0859	0902	0910	0917	...	0938	1003	1008	1017	...	1038	1047	1102	1109	1117	...	1126	1138	1201	1217	...	1238	1248	1302
ork .... 124 d.	⚒	...	0850	0905	0904	...	0919	...	0940	1005	...	1020	...	...	1049	1105	...	1120	...	1128	1140	1204	1220	⚒	...	1249	1304
Hull .... d.	0755	...	|	|	|	...	|	0903	|	|	...	|	1000	...	|	|	...	|	1103	|	|	|	|	1203	...	|	|
Selby .... d.	0833	...	|	|	|	...	|	0935	|	|	...	|	1032	...	|	|	...	|	1135	|	|	|	|	1235	...	|	|
eeds .... 124 a.	0857	...	0913	0927	0928	...	0943	0957	1003	1027	...	1042	1056	...	1112	1127	...	1142	1157	1203	1203	1227	1242	1257	...	1312	1327
eeds .... d.	0900	...	0915	0930	0930	...	0945	1000	1007	1030	...	1045	1100	...	1115	1130	...	1145	1200	1207	1207	1230	1245	1300	...	1315	1330
ewsbury .... d.	|	...	0927	|	|	...	0957	|	1018	|	...	1057	|	...	1127	|	...	1157	|	1218	1218	|	1257	|	...	1326	|
uddersfield .... d.	0918	...	0936	0948	0948	...	1007	1018	1028	1048	...	1107	1118	...	1136	1148	...	1207	1218	1228	1228	1248	1307	1318	...	1338	1348
talybridge .... d.	0937	...	0955	|	|	...	|	1036	1047	|	...	|	1137	...	1200	|	...	|	1237	1247	1247	|	|	1337	...	1401	|
anchester Victoria .... a.	0950	...	|	1022	1022	...	1037	1050	|	1122	...	1137	1150	...	|	1222	...	1238	1250	|	|	1322	1337	1350	...	|	1422
Manchester Piccadilly .... a.	|	...	1013	|	|	...	1049	|	1104	|	...	1149	|	...	1218	|	...	1249	|	1304	1304	|	1349	|	...	1418	|
Manchester Airport ✈ .... a.	|	...	...	|	|	...	1109	|	...	|	...	1210	|	...	...	|	...	1309	|	...	...	|	1410	|	...	...	|
iverpool Lime Street .... a.	1031	...	...	1059	1100	...	...	1131	...	1159	...	...	1231	...	...	1259	...	...	1331	...	...	1404f	...	1431	...	...	1459

	⚒	⚒	⚒	⚒	⚒	⚒	⚒	⚒	⚒	⚒	⚒	⚒	⚒	⑤⑥	⚒	⚒	⚒	⚒	⚒	⚒	⑤⑥	⚒	⚒	⚒	⑥	Ⓐ	⑤⑥
dinburgh .... 124 180 d.	...	...	...	...	...	...	...	...	...	...	...	...	...	a	...	...	...	...	1408	...	a	...	...	...	...	...	a
ewcastle .... 124 180 d.	...	...	...	1304	...	...	...	1343	1402	...	...	...	1503	...	...	...	...	1543	1554	1602	...	...	...	...	1703	1706	...
urham .... 124 180 d.	...	...	...	1317	...	...	...	1359	1418	...	...	...	1515	...	...	...	...	1559	...	1617	...	...	...	...	1718	1719	...
arlington .... 124 180 d.	...	...	...	1335	...	...	...	1417	1436	...	...	...	1533	...	...	...	...	1617	...	1635	...	...	...	...	1736	1737	...
Saltburn .... 212 d.	1151	...	...	|	1251	...	...	|	|	1351	...	...	|	...	1451	...	...	|	...	|	...	1551	...	...	|	|	...
Redcar Central .... 212 d.	1207	...	...	|	1307	...	...	|	|	1407	...	...	|	...	1507	...	...	|	...	|	...	1607	...	...	|	|	...
Middlesbrough .... 212 d.	1220	...	...	|	1320	...	...	|	|	1420	...	...	|	...	1520	...	...	|	...	|	...	1620	...	...	|	|	...
orthallerton .... 124 180 d.	1250	...	...	|	1350	...	...	1428	|	1450	...	...	|	...	1550	...	...	1628	...	|	...	1650	...	...	|	|	...
hirsk .... d.	1259	...	...	|	1359	...	...	|	|	1459	...	...	|	...	1559	...	...	|	...	|	...	1659	...	...	|	|	...
Scarborough .... d.	|	...	1248	|	|	...	1348	|	|	|	...	1448	|	1518	|	...	1548	|	...	|	1618	|	...	1648	|	|	1718
Malton .... d.	|	...	1312	|	|	...	1412	|	|	|	...	1512	|	1542	|	...	1612	|	...	|	1642	|	...	1712	|	|	1742
ork .... 124 180 a.	1317	...	1338	1402	1417	...	1438	1448	1503	1518	...	1538	1600	1609	1617	...	1638	1647	...	1702	1709	1717	...	1738	1802	1803	1808
ork .... 124 d.	1320	...	1340	1405	1420	...	...	1449	1504	1520	...	1540	1601	...	1620	...	...	1649	...	1704	...	1720	...	1740	1805	1805	...
Hull .... d.	|	1303	|	|	|	1403	...	|	|	|	1503	|	|	...	|	1603	...	|	...	|	...	|	1703	|	|	|	...
Selby .... d.	|	1335	|	|	|	1435	...	|	|	|	1535	|	|	...	|	1635	...	|	...	|	...	|	1735	|	|	|	...
eeds .... 124 a.	1343	1357	1403	1427	1442	1457	...	1512	1527	1542	1557	1603	1627	...	1642	1657	...	1712	...	1727	...	1742	1757	1804	1827	1828	...
eeds .... d.	1345	1400	1407	1430	1445	1500	...	1515	1530	1545	1600	1606	1630	...	1645	1700	...	1715	...	1730	...	1745	1800	1807	1829	1830	...
ewsbury .... d.	1357	|	1418	|	1457	|	...	1526	|	1557	|	1617	|	...	1657	|	...	1727	...	|	...	1757	|	1818	|	|	...
uddersfield .... d.	1407	1418	1428	1448	1507	1518	...	1536	1548	1607	1618	1627	1648	...	1707	1718	...	1737	...	1748	...	1807	1818	1828	1848	1849	...
talybridge .... d.	|	1437	1447	|	|	1537	...	1555	|	|	1637	1654	|	...	|	1738	...	1801	...	|	...	|	1837	1857	|	|	...
anchester Victoria .... a.	1438	1450	|	1522	1537	1550	...	|	1622	1637	1605	|	1722	...	1737	1751	...	|	...	1822	...	1838	1850	|	1920	1922	...
Manchester Piccadilly .... a.	1449	|	1504	|	1549	|	...	1611	|	1649	|	1712	|	...	1749	|	...	1818	...	|	...	1849	|	1914	|	|	...
Manchester Airport ✈ .... a.	1509	|	...	|	1610	|	...	...	|	1710	|	...	|	...	1810	|	...	...	...	|	...	1910	|	...	|	|	...
iverpool Lime Street .... a.	...	1531	...	1559	...	1631	...	...	1704t	...	1731	...	1759	...	...	1835	...	...	...	1904	...	...	1931	...	2006	2004	...

a – From Mar. 31.
– Arrives 5–6 minutes earlier on ⑥.
j – Departs 4 minutes later on ⑥.
r – Departs 1206 on Ⓐ.
t – Arrives 1659 on Ⓐ.

188 THE NORTH EAST and YORKSHIRE - MANCHESTER and LIVERPOOL

Most trains convey 🍷 TP

	⚒	⚒	⚒	⚒	⚒	⚒	⚒	⚒	⚒	⚒	⚒	⚒	⚒	⚒	⚒	⚒	⑥	Ⓐ	⑥	Ⓐ	⚒	Ⓐ	⑥	⚒	⑥	Ⓐ	⑥	Ⓐ
Edinburgh 124 180 d.	...	...	...	...	...	...	...	...	...	...	1734	...	...	...	...	...	...	...	1906	1911	...	...	...	...	...	...	...	...
Newcastle 124 180 d.	...	...	...	1743	1804	...	...	...	1906	...	1920	...	2002	...	...	...	...	...	2057	2058	...	...	...	...	2149	2201	...	...
Durham 124 180 d.	...	...	...	1759	1819	...	...	...	1922	...	▬	...	2014	...	...	...	...	...	2114	2115	...	...	...	...	2205	2214	...	...
Darlington 124 180 d.	...	...	...	1817	1837	...	...	...	|	...	...	...	2032	...	...	...	...	...	2132	2133	...	...	...	...	2223	2232	...	...
Saltburn 212 d.	1651	...	...	|	|	1751	...	...	|	1851	...	...	|	...	...	2008	...	...	|	|	2051	...	...	...	|	|	2151	2151
Redcar Central 212 d.	1707	...	...	|	|	1807	...	...	|	1907	...	...	|	...	...	2019	...	...	|	|	2107	...	...	...	|	|	2204	2207
Middlesbrough 212 d.	1720	...	...	|	|	1820	...	...	|	1920	...	...	|	...	...	2036	...	...	|	|	2120	...	...	...	|	|	2217	2220
Northallerton 124 180 d.	1750	...	...	1828	|	1850	...	...	|	1950	...	...	2043	...	...	2105	...	...	2142	2143	2150	...	...	...	2234	2243	2248	2250
Thirsk d.	1759	...	...	|	|	1859	...	...	|	1959	...	...	|	...	...	2113	...	...	|	|	2159	...	...	...	|	|	2256	2259
Scarborough d.	|	...	1748	|	|	|	...	1848	|	|	...	1948	|	...	...	|	2048	2058	|	|	|	...	...	2148	|	|	|	|
Malton d.	|	...	1812	|	|	|	...	1912	|	|	...	2012	|	...	...	|	2112	2122	|	|	|	...	...	2212	|	|	|	|
York 124 180 a.	1817	...	1838	1848	1903	1918	...	1938	2002	2017	...	2038	2102	...	...	2133	2138	2148	2201	2202	2220	...	...	2238	2253	2302	2317	2317
York 124 d.	1818	...	1841	1850	1906	1919	...	1940	2005	2020	...	2040	2105	...	...	...	...	...	2205	2205	▬	...	...	▬	...	...	...	2319
Hull d.	|	1804	|	|	|	|	1903	|	|	|	2003	|	|	...	2103	...	...	...	|	|	...	2204	2204	...	...	...	...	|
Selby d.	|	1836	|	|	|	|	1935	|	|	|	2035	|	|	...	2135	...	...	...	|	|	...	2236	2236	Ⓐ	...	...	...	|
Leeds 124 a.	1842	1858	1927	1912	1928	1943	1957	2004	2027	2043	2059	2103	2127	...	2210	...	...	...	2226	2226	⑥	2259	2258	🚌	...	...	...	2345
Leeds d.	1845	1900	...	1915	1930	1945	2000	...	2030	2045	...	2115	2130	2147	...	...	...	...	2230	2230	2247	...	2300	2315	...	...	...	2347
Dewsbury d.	1857	|	...	1927	|	1957	|	...	|	2057	...	2126	2142	2204	...	...	...	...	2241	2241	2304	...	|	2340	...	...	...	|
Huddersfield d.	1907	1918	...	1938	1948	2007	2018	...	2048	2107	...	2136	2151	2228f	...	...	...	...	2251	2252	2326j	...	2318	0005s	...	...	...	0031
Stalybridge d.	|	1937	...	2009	|	|	2039	...	|	|	...	2157	|	2256	...	...	...	...	|	|	2355	...	2337	|	...	...	...	|
Manchester Victoria a.	1937	1950	...	|	2022	2037	|	...	2122	2138	...	|	2222	|	...	...	...	...	2323	2323	|	...	2350	|	...	...	...	0116
Manchester Piccadilly a.	1949	|	...	2027	|	2049	2056	...	|	2149	...	2212	|	2312	...	...	...	...	|	|	0011	...	...	0105	...	...	...	...
Manchester Airport ✈ a.	2010	|	...	...	|	2110	...	...	|	2210	...	...	|	...	...	...	...	...	|	|	...	...	...	...	...	...	...	...
Liverpool Lime Street a.	...	2032	...	...	2056	...	...	...	2205	...	...	...	2313	...	...	...	...	...	0005	0005	...	...	...	...	...	...	...	...

	⚒	⚒	⚒		⑦	⑦	⑦	⑦	⑦	⑦	⑦	⑦d	⑦	⑦	⑦d	⑦	⑦	⑦	⑦	⑦	⑦d	⑦	⑦	⑦	⑦	⑦	⑦	⑦
Edinburgh 124 180 d.	...	...	...		...	...	...	...	...	...	...	...	...	...	...	...	...	...	...	...	...	...	...	...	...	...	...	0933
Newcastle 124 180 d.	...	...	...	⑦	...	...	...	0749	0759	...	...	...	...	0903	...	...	...	...	0939	1006	...	...	...	...	1106	...	...	1119
Durham 124 180 d.	...	...	...		...	...	...	0801	0815	...	...	...	...	0915	...	...	...	...	0954	1018	...	...	...	...	1118	...	...	▬
Darlington 124 180 d.	...	...	...		...	...	...	0819	0833	...	...	...	...	0933	...	...	...	...	1010	1036	...	...	...	...	1136	...	...	...
Saltburn 212 d.	...	...	2310		...	...	...	|	|	...	...	...	...	|	...	...	...	...	|	|	...	0951	...	...	|	1048	...	...
Redcar Central 212 d.	...	...	2318		...	...	...	|	|	...	...	...	...	|	...	...	...	...	|	|	...	1004	...	...	|	1104	...	...
Middlesbrough 212 d.	...	...	2331		...	...	...	|	|	...	...	...	...	|	...	0927	...	...	|	|	...	1018	...	...	|	1117	...	...
Northallerton 124 180 d.	...	...	2359		...	...	...	|	0844	...	...	...	...	|	...	|	...	...	1021	|	...	1050	...	...	|	1149	...	...
Thirsk d.	...	...	0008		...	...	...	|	|	...	...	...	...	|	...	|	...	...	|	|	...	1058	...	...	|	1157	...	...
Scarborough d.	...	2245	|		...	...	...	|	|	...	...	0835	0848	|	0918	|	...	0948	|	|	1018	|	...	1044	|	|	...	1148
Malton d.	...	2311	|		...	...	...	|	|	...	...	|	0912	|	0942	|	...	1014	|	|	1042	|	...	1108	|	|	...	1212
York 124 180 a.	...	2335	0034		...	...	...	0846	0903	...	...	0920	0937	0959	1009	1015	...	1039	1043	1102	1110	1115	...	1134	1202	1215	...	1238
York 124 d.	...	2239v	...		0818	...	0840	0848	0905	0916	...	...	0939	1004	...	1019	...	...	1049	1104	...	1117	...	1136	1203	1217	...	...
Hull d.	2308	|	...		|	0803	|	|	|	|	0855	...	|	|	...	|	1003	...	|	|	...	|	1105	|	|	|	1203	...
Selby d.	2340	|	...		|	0835	|	|	|	|	0930	...	|	|	...	|	1035	...	|	|	...	|	1137	|	|	|	1235	...
Leeds 124 a.	0006	0005v	...		0841	0857	0904	0912	0928	0944	0955	...	1003	1029	...	1043	1056	...	1112	1127	...	1143	1158	1202	1228	1243	1257	...
Leeds d.	...	0010v	...		...	0900	0907	0915	0930	0945	1000	...	1012	1030	...	1045	1100	...	1115	1130	...	1145	1200	1215	1230	1245	1300	...
Dewsbury d.	...	|	...		...	|	|	0927	|	0958	|	...	1026	|	...	1057	|	...	1127	|	...	1157	|	1226	|	1256	|	...
Huddersfield d.	...	|	...		...	0918	0925	0937	0948	1008	1018	...	1036	1048	...	1108	1118	...	1136	1148	...	1208	1218	1236	1248	1308	1318	...
Stalybridge d.	...	|	...		...	0937	0954	|	|	|	1036	...	|	|	...	|	1137	...	|	|	...	|	1237	|	|	|	1337	...
Manchester Victoria a.	...	|	...		...	0950	|	|	1022	1040	1050	...	|	1122	...	1138	1150	...	|	1222	...	1238	1250	|	1321	1338	1350	...
Manchester Piccadilly a.	...	0125v	...		...	|	1014	1019	|	1056	|	...	1112	|	...	1149	|	...	1212	|	...	1250	|	1312	|	1350	|	...
Manchester Airport ✈ a.	...	...	...		...	|	...	...	|	1118	|	...	...	|	...	1213	|	...	...	|	...	1312	|	...	|	1412	|	...
Liverpool Lime Street a.	...	...	...		...	1034	...	...	1059	...	1127	...	...	1159	...	...	1228	...	...	1259	...	...	1329	...	1358	...	1429	...

	⑦	⑦	⑦	⑦	⑦	⑦	⑦	⑦	⑦	⑦	⑦	⑦	⑦	⑦	⑦d	⑦	⑦	⑦	⑦	⑦	⑦	⑦d	⑦	⑦	⑦	⑦	⑦d	⑦
Edinburgh 124 180 d.	...	...	...	...	...	...	...	...	...	...	...	...	...	...	...	...	...	...	...	...	...	...	...	1421	...	...	...	...
Newcastle 124 180 d.	1143	1203	...	...	...	1303	...	...	...	1343	1402	...	...	...	...	1505	...	...	...	1543	1600	...	...	1613	...	1705	...	...
Durham 124 180 d.	1200	1215	...	...	...	1318	...	...	...	1359	1417	...	...	...	...	1518	...	...	...	1600	1614	...	...	▬	...	1717	...	...
Darlington 124 180 d.	1218	1233	...	...	...	1336	...	...	...	1416	1435	...	...	...	...	1536	...	...	...	1618	1632	...	...	...	...	1735	...	...
Saltburn 212 d.	|	|	1150	...	...	|	1249	...	...	|	|	1350	...	...	...	|	1449	...	...	|	|	...	1549	...	...	|	...	1649
Redcar Central 212 d.	|	|	1205	...	...	|	1304	...	...	|	|	1402	...	...	...	|	1504	...	...	|	|	...	1604	...	...	|	...	1704
Middlesbrough 212 d.	|	|	1218	...	...	|	1317	...	...	|	|	1415	...	...	...	|	1517	...	...	|	|	...	1617	...	...	|	...	1717
Northallerton 124 180 d.	1229	|	1249	...	...	|	1349	...	...	|	|	1447	...	...	...	|	1549	...	...	1629	|	...	|	...	...	|	...	1750
Thirsk d.	|	|	1257	...	...	|	1357	...	...	|	|	1455	...	...	...	|	1559	...	...	|	|	...	1653	...	...	|	...	1759
Scarborough d.	|	|	|	...	1243	|	|	...	1348	|	|	|	...	1448	1518	|	|	...	1548	|	|	1618	|	...	1643	|	1718	|
Malton d.	|	|	|	...	1307	|	|	...	1412	|	|	|	...	1512	1542	|	|	...	1612	|	|	1642	|	...	1707	|	1724	|
York 124 180 a.	1248	1300	1314	...	1333	1403	1414	...	1438	1442	1502	1513	...	1538	1609	1602	1616	...	1638	1647	1659	1708	1714	...	1733	1803	1808	1816
York 124 d.	1249	1302	1316	...	1334	1404	1416	...	...	1446	1504	1515	...	1540	...	1605	1618	...	...	1648	1703	...	1716	...	1735	1803	...	1818
Hull d.	|	|	|	1303	|	|	|	1403	...	|	|	|	1503	|	...	|	|	1603	...	|	|	...	|	1703	|	|	...	|
Selby d.	|	|	|	1335	|	|	|	1436	...	|	|	|	1535	|	...	|	|	1635	...	|	|	...	|	1735	|	|	...	|
Leeds 124 a.	1313	1328	1343	1357	1403	1428	1443	1457	...	1513	1528	1543	1556	1604	...	1628	1643	1657	...	1713	1729	...	1744	1757	1803	1827	...	1843
Leeds d.	1315	1330	1345	1400	1415	1430	1445	1500	...	1515	1530	1545	1600	1615	...	1630	1645	1700	...	1715	1730	...	1745	1800	1816	1830	...	1845
Dewsbury d.	1326	|	1356	|	1426	|	1457	|	...	1526	|	1557	|	1626	...	|	1657	|	...	1726	|	...	1757	|	1827	|	...	1858
Huddersfield d.	1336	1348	1408	1418	1436	1448	1508	1518	...	1536	1548	1608	1618	1636	...	1648	1708	1718	...	1736	1749	...	1808	1818	1837	1848	...	1908
Stalybridge d.	|	|	|	1437	|	|	|	1537	...	|	|	|	1637	|	...	|	|	1737	...	|	|	...	|	1837	|	|	...	|
Manchester Victoria a.	|	1422	1438	1450	|	1521	1538	1550	...	|	1621	1638	1650	|	...	1721	1738	1750	...	|	1821	...	1838	1850	|	1921	...	1938
Manchester Piccadilly a.	1412	|	1450	|	1512	|	1550	|	...	1612	|	1650	|	1712	...	|	1750	|	...	1812	|	...	1850	|	1912	|	...	1950
Manchester Airport ✈ a.	...	|	1512	|	...	|	1612	|	...	...	|	1712	|	...	...	|	1812	|	...	...	|	...	1912	|	...	|	...	2012
Liverpool Lime Street a.	...	1459	...	1529	...x	1558	...	1629	...	...	1658	...	1729	...	...	1758	...	1829	...	...	1901	...	...	1928	...	2000	...	...

	⑦	⑦	⑦	⑦	⑦	⑦	⑦		⑦	⑦	⑦	⑦	⑦		⑦	⑦	⑦	⑦	⑦	⑦	⑦	⑦	⑦	⑦	⑦	⑦	⑦	⑦
Edinburgh 124 180 d.	...	...	...	...	...	...	...	...	...	...	...	1733	...	...	...	...	...	...	...	1916	...	...	...	...	...	...	...	...
Newcastle 124 180 d.	...	...	1740	1804	...	...	...	...	1906	...	...	1920	...	...	2006	...	...	...	...	2101	...	...	...	...	...	2157	...	...
Durham 124 180 d.	...	...	1759	1817	...	...	...	...	1922	...	...	▬	...	...	2018	...	...	...	...	2117	...	...	...	...	...	2210	...	...
Darlington 124 180 d.	...	...	1817	1835	...	...	...	...	|	...	...	...	...	...	2036	...	...	...	...	2135	...	...	...	...	...	2228	...	...
Saltburn 212 d.	...	...	|	|	1742	...	...	...	|	1849	...	...	...	...	|	...	...	1949	...	|	...	2048	...	2149	...	|	...	2311
Redcar Central 212 d.	...	...	|	|	1801	...	...	...	|	1904	...	...	...	...	|	...	...	2005	...	|	...	2104	...	2159	...	|	...	2319
Middlesbrough 212 d.	...	...	|	|	1814	...	...	...	|	1918	...	...	...	...	|	...	...	2018	...	|	...	2118	...	2212	...	|	...	2333
Northallerton 124 180 d.	...	...	1828	|	1844	...	...	...	|	1950	...	...	...	...	|	...	...	2050	...	|	...	2148	...	2242	...	|	...	|
Thirsk d.	...	...	|	|	1853	...	...	...	|	1958	...	...	...	...	|	...	...	2058	...	|	...	2157	...	2251	...	|	...	|
Scarborough d.	...	1742	|	|	|	...	1836	...	|	|	...	...	1943	...	|	...	...	|	2048	|	...	|	2148	|	...	|	2245	|
Malton d.	...	1806	|	|	|	...	1900	...	|	|	...	...	2007	...	|	...	...	|	2112	|	...	|	2212	|	...	|	2311	|
York 124 180 a.	...	1832	1849	1902	1911	...	1926	...	2002	2016	...	...	2033	...	2102	...	...	2119	2138	2213	...	2225	2238	2317	...	2321	2335	0033
York 124 d.	...	1835	1849	1904	1916	...	1929	...	2005	2018	...	⑦	2035	...	2104	...	...	...	...	2216	...	...	...	2318	...	...	2339	...
Hull d.	1803	|	|	|	|	1903	|	...	|	|	...	2003	|	...	|	...	2103	...	...	|	2203	...	...	|	2301	...	|	...
Selby d.	1835	|	|	|	|	1935	|	...	|	|	...	2036	|	...	|	...	2135	...	...	|	2236	...	...	|	2334	...	|	...
Leeds 124 a.	1857	1916	1914	1927	1943	1957	2004	...	2028	2043	...	2100	2104	...	2127	...	2158	...	...	2243	2258	...	...	2344	2358	...	0005	...
Leeds d.	1900	...	1915	1930	1945	2000	...	...	2030	2045	2047	...	2107	...	2130	2147	...	...	...	2245	2300	...	...	2347	...	...	0007	...
Dewsbury d.	|	...	1927	|	1957	|	...	...	|	2057	2104	...	2118	...	2142	2204	...	...	...	2256	|	...	...	|	...	...	|	...
Huddersfield d.	1918	...	1936	1948	2008	2018	...	...	2048	2108	2122	...	2132j	...	2151	2222	...	...	...	2306	2318	...	...	0027j	...	...	|	...
Stalybridge d.	1937	...	|	|	|	2045	...	...	|	|	2150	...	2155	...	|	2249	...	...	...	|	2337	...	...	|	...	...	|	...
Manchester Victoria a.	1950	...	|	2021	2038	|	...	...	2122	2138	|	...	|	...	2221	|	...	...	...	2335	2350	...	...	0112	...	...	|	...
Manchester Piccadilly a.	|	...	2012	|	2049	2102	...	...	|	2150	2205	...	2212	...	|	2304	...	...	...	|	...	...	...	...	...	...	0123	...
Manchester Airport ✈ a.	|	...	...	|	2108	...	...	...	|	2212	...	...	...	...	|	...	...	...	...	|	...	...	...	...	...	...	...	...
Liverpool Lime Street a.	2034	...	...	2100	...	...	...	...	2202	...	...	...	...	...	2302	...	...	...	...	0017	...	...	...	...	...	...	...	...

d – From Apr. 2. f – Arrives 2221. j – Arrives 5 minutes earlier. r – Arrives 0058 on ⑥ mornings. v – Ⓐ only.

TP Most trains convey 🍷 MANCHESTER and LIVERPOOL - THE NORTH EAST and YORKSHIRE 188

		①	⑥	②–⑤	①	⑥	⚒	②–⑤	⚒	Ⓐ	⑥	Ⓐ	⑥	⚒	⚒	Ⓐ	⑥	⚒	⚒	⚒	Ⓐ	Ⓐ	⑥	⚒	⚒	⚒	⚒	⚒
verpool Lime Street .....d.		...	...	...	...	...	...	...	...	...	...	...	...	...	...	0520	0520	...	...	...	...	...	...	0624	...	0654	...	0724
Manchester Airport ✈..d.	⚒	0038	0038	0038	...	...	...	...	...	0359	0422	...	...	...	...	|	|	0540	...	...	...	...	...	|	0644	|	...	|
Manchester Piccadilly..d.		0053	0103	0053	0242	0242	...	0242	...	0413	0437	...	...	...	0535	|	|	0558	...	...	0627	...	0627	|	0658	|	0729	|
anchester Victoria........d.		|	|	|	|	|	...	|	...	|	|	0500	0500	0530	|	0558	0558	0615	...	0630	|	...	|	0700	0715	0730	|	0800
talybridge ....d.		|	|	|	|	|	...	|	...	|	|	|	|	0541	0550	|	|	|	...	0641	0643	...	0643	|	|	0741	0743	|
uddersfield ....d.		|	0133	|	0349a	0351c	...	0346a	...	0515f	0531	|	|	0601	0614	0626	0630r	0646	...	0701	0717r	...	0717r	0730	0746	0800	0812	0828
ewsbury ....d.		|	|	|	|	|	...	|	...	|	|	|	|	|	|	|	|	0657	...	|	0727	...	0727	|	0757	|	|	0837
eeds...............................a.		0206	0208	0223	0408	0430	...	0421	...	0550	0550	0612	0612	0622	0634	0647	0649	0710	...	0722	0740	...	0740	0749	0810	0822	083	0850
eeds......................124 d.		0211	0219	0225	0420	0432	...	0430	0535	0552	0552	0614	0615	0631	0637	0649	0651	0713	...	0727	0743	...	0743	0751	0813	0827	0845	0851
Selby..............................d.		|	|	|	|	|	...	|	0554	|	|	|	|	0658	|	|	|	|	...	0752	|	...	|	|	|	0848	|	|
Hull..................................a.		|	|	|	|	|	...	|	0626	|	|	|	|	0739	|	|	|	|	...	0828	|	...	|	|	|	0925	|	|
ork.........................124 a.		0239	0258	0314	0446	0457	...	0511	▬	0616	0615	0637	0637	...	0701	0712	0714	0736	...	▬	0805	...	0806	0818	0836	...	0902	0914
ork................. 124 180 d.		...	...	...	...	...	0505	...	...	0618	0616	0639	0642	...	0704	0714	0719	0739	0803	...	0807	...	0808	0821	0839	...	0903	0921
Malton............................d.		...	...	...	...	...	|	...	...	0642	0641	|	|	...	0729	|	|	|	0828	...	|	...	|	|	|	...	0928	|
Scarborough..............a.		...	...	...	...	...	|	...	...	0708	0707	|	|	...	0753	|	|	|	0855	...	|	...	|	|	|	...	0954	|
hirsk ....d.		...	...	...	...	...	0528	...	...	...	...	0656	0659	...	...	|	|	0756	...	...	|	...	|	|	0856	...	...	|
orthallerton...... 124 180 d.		...	...	...	...	...	0536	...	...	...	...	0705	0708	...	...	|	0738	0807	...	...	0826	...	0827	|	0906	...	...	|
Middlesbrough.....212 a.		...	...	...	...	...	0632	...	...	...	...	0736	0738	...	...	|	|	0838	...	...	|	...	|	|	0936	...	...	|
Redcar Central......212 a.		...	...	...	...	...	0646	...	...	...	...	0749	0755	...	...	|	|	0850	...	...	|	...	|	|	0948	...	...	|
Saltburn ....212 a.		...	...	...	...	...	0658	...	...	...	...	0806	0806	...	...	|	|	0906	...	...	|	...	|	|	0958	...	...	|
arlington.......... 124 180 d.		...	...	...	...	...	0557‡	...	...	...	...	...	...	...	...	0742	0751	...	...	...	0839	...	0840	0849	...	...	...	0949
urham .... 124 180 d.		...	...	...	...	...	...	...	⚒	...	...	...	...	...	...	0758	0807	...	...	⑥	0855	...	0856	0905	...	...	...	1006
ewcastle......... 124 180 a.		...	...	...	...	...	...	...	0707	...	...	...	...	...	...	0816	0823	...	...	0911	0911	0919	0913	0918	...	...	...	1022
dinburgh .... 124 180 a.		...	...	...	...	...	...	...	0855	...	...	...	...	...	...	...	...	...	...	1058	...	1103	...	...	...	...	...	...

	⑤⑥	⚒	Ⓐ	⑥	⚒	⚒	Ⓐ	⑥	⑤⑥	⚒	⚒	⚒	⑤b	⚒	⑥d	⚒	⚒	⚒	⚒	⚒	⚒	Ⓐ	⑥	⚒	⚒	⚒	⚒	⚒
iverpool Lime Street .....d.	b	...	0754	0754	...	...	0824	0824	b	...	0854	...	...	0924	...	...	...	0954	...	1022	...	1054	1054	...	1124	...	...	1154
Manchester Airport ✈..d.	...	0744	|	|	...	...	|	|	...	0844	|	...	...	|	...	0940	...	|	...	|	1044	|	|	...	|	1144	...	|
Manchester Piccadilly....d.	...	0758	|	|	...	0830	|	|	...	0858	|	0935	...	|	...	0958	...	|	1035	|	1058	|	|	1135	|	1158	...	|
lanchester Victoria........d.	...	0815	0830	0830	...	|	0900	0900	...	0915	0930	|	...	1000	...	1015	...	1030	|	1100	1115	1130	1130	|	1159	1215	...	1230
talybridge ....d.	...	|	0842	0842	...	0844	|	|	...	|	0941	0951	...	|	...	|	...	1041	1051	|	|	1141	1141	1151	|	|	...	1241
luddersfield ....d.	...	0846	0901	0901	...	0917r	0930	0930	...	0946	1001	1009	...	1030	...	1045	...	1101	1117f	1128	1146	1201	1201	1209	1230	1246	...	1301
ewsbury ....d.	...	0857	|	|	...	0927	|	|	...	0957	|	1018	...	|	...	1057	...	|	1127	|	1157	|	|	1218	|	1257	...	|
eeds...............................a.	...	0910	0922	0922	...	0941	0949	0949	...	1010	1021	1031	...	1049	...	1110	...	1121	1140	1149	1210	1221	1221	1231	1249	1310	...	1321
eeds......................124 d.	...	0913	0927	0927	...	0942	0951	0951	...	1013	1027	1034	...	1051	...	1113	...	1127	1142	1151	1213	1227	1227	1234	1251	1313	...	1327
Selby..............................a.	...	|	0947	0950	...	|	|	|	...	|	1047	|	...	|	...	|	...	1153	|	|	|	1248	1252	|	|	|	...	1354
Hull..................................a.	...	|	1025	1037	...	|	|	|	...	|	1125	|	...	|	...	|	...	1225	|	|	|	1325	1329	|	|	|	...	1429
ork.........................124 a.	...	0936	...	...	...	1004	1014	1014	...	1036	▬	1101	...	1115	...	1136	...	...	1205	1214	1236	...	...	1300	1314	1336	...	...
ork................. 124 180 d.	0932	0939	...	...	1003	1007	1018	1021	1032	1039	...	1103	1120	1121	1132	1139	1203	...	1207	1222	1239	...	...	1303	1320	1339	1403	...
Malton............................d.	0957	|	...	...	1028	|	|	|	1059	|	...	1129	1145	|	1157	|	1229	...	|	|	|	...	...	1329	|	|	1429	...
Scarborough..............a.	1021	|	...	...	1053	|	|	|	1125	|	...	1153	1209	|	1221	|	1253	...	|	|	|	...	...	1353	|	|	1453	...
hirsk ....d.	...	0956	...	...	...	|	|	|	...	1056	...	...	...	|	...	1156	...	...	|	|	1256	...	...	...	|	1356	...	...
lorthallerton...... 124 180 d.	...	1007	...	...	...	1026	|	|	...	1107	...	...	...	|	...	1205	...	...	1226	|	1305	...	...	...	|	1407	...	...
Middlesbrough.....212 a.	...	1038	...	...	...	|	|	|	...	1138	...	...	...	|	...	1238	...	...	|	|	1336	...	...	...	|	1438	...	...
Redcar Central......212 a.	...	1049	...	...	...	|	|	|	...	1149	...	...	...	|	...	1249	...	...	|	|	1347	...	...	...	|	1449	...	...
Saltburn ....212 a.	...	1058	...	...	...	|	|	|	...	1158	...	...	...	|	...	1258	...	...	|	|	1358	...	...	...	|	1458	...	...
arlington.......... 124 180 d.	...	...	...	...	...	1039	1046	1049	...	...	...	...	...	1149	...	...	...	...	1239	1250	...	...	...	...	1348	...	...	...
urham .... 124 180 d.	...	...	...	...	...	1055	1103	1105	...	...	⚒	...	...	1205	...	...	...	...	1255	1306	...	...	...	...	1404	...	...	...
ewcastle......... 124 180 a.	...	...	...	...	...	1113	1115	1119	...	...	1206	...	...	1219	...	...	...	...	1313	1322	...	...	...	...	1419	...	...	...
dinburgh .... 124 180 a.	...	...	...	...	...	...	...	...	...	...	1356	...	...	...	...	...	...	...	...	...	...	...	...	...	...	...	...	...

	⚒	⚒	⚒	⚒	⚒	⚒	⚒	⚒	⚒	⑥	Ⓐ	⑥	Ⓐ	⑤⑥	⚒	⚒	⚒	⚒	⑤⑥	⚒	⚒	⑥	Ⓐ	⚒	⚒	⑤⑥	⚒	⚒
iverpool Lime Street .....d.	...	1224	...	1254	...	1324	...	...	1354	...	...	1424	1424	b	...	1454	...	1524	b	...	...	1554	1554	...	1624	b	...	1654
Manchester Airport ✈..d.	...	|	1244	|	...	|	1344	...	|	...	...	|	|	...	1444	|	...	|	...	1544	...	|	|	...	|	...	1644	|
Manchester Piccadilly..d.	1235	|	1258	|	1335	|	1358	...	|	1435	1435	|	|	...	1458	|	1535	|	...	1558	...	|	|	1630	|	...	1658	|
lanchester Victoria........d.	|	1300	1315	1330	|	1400	1415	...	1430	|	|	1500	1500	...	1515	1530	|	1600	...	1615	...	1630	1630	|	1700	...	1715	1730
talybridge ....d.	1251	|	|	1341	1350	|	|	...	1442	1451	1451	|	|	...	|	1541	1550	|	...	|	...	1641	1641	1644	|	...	|	1741
luddersfield ....d.	1317f	1329	1346	1401	1409	1430	1446	...	1501	1517f	1517f	1529	1529	...	1546	1601	1612	1630	...	1646	...	1701	1701	1717r	1730	...	1747	1801
ewsbury ....d.	1327	|	1357	|	1418	|	1457	...	|	1527	1527	|	|	...	1557	|	|	|	...	1657	...	|	|	1726	|	...	1757	|
eeds...............................a.	1340	1349	1410	1421	1431	1449	1510	...	1521	1541	1541	1549	1549	...	1610	1621	1631	1649	...	1710	...	1721	1721	1739	1749	...	1810	1821
eeds......................124 d.	1342	1351	1413	1427	1434	1451	1513	...	1527	1542	1542	1551	1551	...	1613	1627	1634	1651	...	1713	...	1726	1727	1742	1751	...	1813	1827
Selby..............................a.	|	|	|	1447	|	|	|	...	1551	|	|	|	|	...	|	1653	|	|	...	|	...	1749	1753	|	|	...	|	1847
Hull..................................a.	|	|	|	1525	|	|	|	...	1630	|	|	|	|	...	|	1728	|	|	...	|	...	1829	1835	|	|	...	|	1927
ork.........................124 a.	1405	1414	1436	▬	1501	1515	1536	...	...	1605	1605	1614	1614	...	1637	...	1700	1717	...	1737	...	...	...	1804	1819	...	1837	▬
ork................. 124 180 d.	1407	1420	1439	...	1504	1519	1539	1604	...	1607	1607	1616	1617	1632	1639	...	1702	1721	1732	1739	1803	...	...	1806	1822	1832	1839	...
Malton............................d.	|	|	|	...	1529	|	|	1630	...	|	|	|	|	1657	|	...	1729	|	1757	|	1829	...	...	|	|	1857	|	...
Scarborough..............a.	|	|	|	...	1553	|	|	1654	...	|	|	|	|	1723	|	...	1754	|	1821	|	1853	...	...	|	|	1923	|	...
hirsk ....d.	|	|	1456	...	...	|	1556	...	...	|	|	|	|	...	1656	...	...	|	...	1756	...	...	...	1822	|	...	1856	...
lorthallerton...... 124 180 d.	1426	|	1505	...	...	|	1605	...	...	1626	1626	|	|	...	1707	...	...	|	...	1805	...	...	...	1830	|	...	1905	...
Middlesbrough.....212 a.	|	|	1538	...	...	|	1638	...	...	|	|	|	|	...	1738	...	...	|	...	1835	...	...	...	|	|	...	1936	...
Redcar Central......212 a.	|	|	1549	...	...	|	1649	...	...	|	|	|	|	...	1749	...	...	|	...	1848	...	...	...	|	|	...	1953	...
Saltburn ....212 a.	|	|	1558	...	...	|	1658	...	...	|	|	|	|	...	1758	...	...	|	...	1906h	...	...	...	|	|	...	2004	...
arlington.......... 124 180 d.	1439	1448	...	...	...	1550	...	...	...	1639	1639	1644	1647	...	...	...	...	1749	...	...	...	...	...	1843	1850	...	...	...
urham .... 124 180 d.	1456	1505	...	⚒	...	1606	...	...	...	1655	1659	1700	1705	...	...	...	...	1805	...	...	...	...	...	1900	1906	...	...	⑥
ewcastle......... 124 180 a.	1513	1522	...	1614	...	1620	...	...	...	1713	1717	1716	1721	...	...	...	...	1818	...	...	...	...	...	1919	1920	...	...	2059
dinburgh .... 124 180 a.	...	...	...	1804	...	...	...	...	...	...	...	...	...	...	...	...	...	...	...	...	...	...	...	...	...	...	...	2241

	⚒	Ⓐ	⑥	⚒	⚒	⚒	⚒	⚒	⚒	⚒	⑥	Ⓐ	⑥	Ⓐ	Ⓐ	⑥	⚒	⚒	⚒	⚒	⚒	⚒	⚒	⑥	Ⓐ	⑥	Ⓐ	⑥
iverpool Lime Street .....d.	...	1724	1725	...	1754	...	...	1824	...	...	1854	1854	1924	1924	...	...	...	...	...	2024	...	...	...	2106	2106	...	...	...
Manchester Airport ✈..d.	...	|	|	1744	|	...	...	|	1844	...	|	|	|	|	1940	1940	...	...	...	|	2040	...	...	|	|	2140	2140	...
Manchester Piccadilly..d.	1730	|	|	1758	|	...	1830	|	1858	...	|	|	|	|	1958	1958	...	1958	2042	|	2058	...	2058	|	|	2158	2158	2158
lanchester Victoria........d.	|	1800	1800	1815	1830	...	|	1900	1915	...	1930	1930	2000	2000	2015	2015	...	|	|	2100	2115	...	|	2145	2145	2215	2215	|
talybridge ....d.	1743	|	|	|	1841	...	1844	|	|	...	1941	1941	|	|	|	|	...	2013	|	|	|	...	2113	2158	2158	|	|	2213
luddersfield ....d.	1812	1830	1830	1846	1901	...	1917	1930	1946	...	2001	2001	2030	2030	2046	2046	...	2049t	2112	2130	2146	...	2151f	2217	2217	2246	2244	2252f
ewsbury ....d.	|	|	|	1857	|	...	1926	|	1956	...	|	|	|	|	2057	2057	...	2109	|	|	2157	...	2208	2227	2227	2257	|	2307
eeds...............................a.	1831	1849	1849	1910	1921	...	1939	1949	2009	...	2023	2023	2049	2049	2110	2110	...	2129	2131	2149	2211	...	2230	2240	2240	2310	2324	2326
eeds......................124 d.	1834	1851	1851	1913	1925	1934	1942	1951	2013	2020	2027	2027	2051	2052	2113	2113	2127	▬	2144	2152	2214	2223	▬	2242	2241	2313	2326	2328
Selby..............................a.	|	|	|	|	1951	|	|	|	|	|	2051	2055	|	|	|	|	2153	...	|	|	|	2257	...	|	|	|	|	|
Hull..................................a.	|	|	|	|	2025	|	|	|	|	|	2127	2131	|	|	|	|	2226	...	|	|	|	2329	...	|	|	|	|	|
ork.........................124 a.	1901	1914	1914	1937	...	2001	2006	2015	2036	2102	...	...	2114	2114	2136	2136	...	⚒	|	2217	2240	...	⚒	2305	2307	2340	2355	2354
ork................. 124 180 d.	1904	1917	1922	1939	...	2004	2007	2016	2039	2104	...	...	2120	2120	2139	2139	...	2203	2221	2221	...	...	2303	2307	2308	...	...	...
Malton............................d.	1929	|	|	|	...	2029	|	|	|	2129	...	...	|	|	|	|	...	2229	...	|	...	...	2328	|	|	...	...	...
Scarborough..............a.	1953	|	|	|	...	2053	|	|	|	2153	...	...	|	|	|	|	...	2253	...	|	...	...	2353	|	|	...	...	...
hirsk ....d.	▬	|	|	1958	...	...	|	|	2056	...	...	...	|	|	2156	2156	...	...	...	|	...	...	...	|	2330	...	...	...
lorthallerton...... 124 180 d.	...	|	|	2006	...	...	2026	|	2106	...	...	...	|	2139	2205	2207	...	...	...	2240	...	...	...	2326	2339	...	...	...
Middlesbrough.....212 a.	...	|	|	2039	...	...	|	|	2138	...	...	...	|	|	2235	2239	...	...	...	|	...	...	...	|	|	...	...	...
Redcar Central......212 a.	...	|	|	2050	...	...	|	|	2149	...	...	...	|	|	2247	...	...	...	...	|	...	...	...	|	|	...	...	...
Saltburn ....212 a.	...	|	|	2106	...	...	|	|	2158	...	...	...	|	|	2257	...	...	...	...	|	...	...	...	|	|	...	...	...
arlington.......... 124 180 d.	...	1946	1950	...	...	...	2039	2045	...	...	...	...	2148	2152	...	...	...	...	...	2253	...	...	...	2339	0009	...	...	...
urham .... 124 180 d.	Ⓐ	2002	2006	...	...	...	2055	2101	...	...	...	...	2204	2208	...	...	...	...	...	2309	...	...	...	2355	0023	...	...	...
ewcastle......... 124 180 a.	2101	2014	2021	...	...	...	2113	2117	...	...	...	...	2219	2221	...	...	...	...	...	2328	...	...	...	0012	0040	...	...	...
dinburgh .... 124 180 a.	2248	...	...	...	...	...	...	...	...	...	...	...	...	...	...	...	...	...	...	...	...	...	...	...	...	...	...	...

– Arrives 0334.
– From Mar. 31.
– Arrives 0315.

d – From Apr. 1.
f – Arrives 9 – 11 minutes earlier.
h – Arrives 1858 on ⑥.

r – Arrives 5 – 6 minutes earlier.
t – Arrives 2041.
‡ – Arrival time. Departs 0606. Calls before Middlesbrough.

TP Most trains convey 🍸 MANCHESTER and LIVERPOOL - THE NORTH EAST and YORKSHIRE 188

	Ⓐ	⑥	Ⓐ	Ⓐ	Ⓐ	⑥	Ⓐ	Ⓐ	⚒	⑤	①–④	⑦	⑦	⑦	⑦	⑦	⑦	⑦a	⑦	⑦		⑦	⑦	⑦	⑦a	⑦	⑦	⑦
Liverpool Lime Street d.		2154	🚌	2154	🚌			🚌	2254															0812				
Manchester Airport ✈ d.		│		│		2240	2240		│	2340	2340													│				
Manchester Piccadilly d.		│		│		2254	2258		│	2356	2356											0831		│				0927
Manchester Victoria d.		2230		2230		2305	2315		2330	0006	0006									0830		│		0857		0918	0930	│
Stalybridge d.		2243		2243		│	│		2343	│	│									0841		0844		│		│	0941	0943
Huddersfield d.		2311	2255	2310	2325	2332	2352	2355	0012	0034	0101									0901		0912		0930		0945	1001	1012
Dewsbury d.		│	2327		2350	2341	│	0027		│	│									0915		│		│		0957	│	│
Leeds a.		2331	0012		0015s	2354	0032	0112		0111	0136									0928		0933		0949		1010	1021	1031
Leeds 124 d.	2333	2333			│		0035			0113	0140				0836	0846				0930		0935		0950		1013	1027	1034
Selby a.	2352	2351			│		│			│	│				0900	│				0952		│		│		│	1047	│
Hull a.	0024	0024			│		│			│	│				0932	│				1024		│		│		│	1120	│
York 124 a.					0105		0114			0139	0218				▬	0911						1000		1016		1039	▬	1102
York 124 180 d.													0842	0904			0919	0932	0937			1003	1007	1020	1034	1039		1105
Malton d.													│	0929			│	0957	│			1028	│	│	1059	│		1130
Scarborough a.													│	0953			│	1023	│			1053	│	│	1123	│		1154
Thirsk d.													0859				│		0954				│	│		1100		
Northallerton 124 180 d.													0907				│		1008				1026	│		1111		
Middlesbrough 212 a.													0938				│		1039				│	│		1142		
Redcar Central 212 a.													0952				│		1052				│	│		1153		
Saltburn 212 a.													1004				│		1104				│	│		1204		
Darlington 124 180 d.																	0947						1039	1048				
Durham 124 180 d.															⑦		1003						1055	│			⑦	
Newcastle 124 180 a.															0919		1019						1113	1114			1156	
Edinburgh 124 180 a.															1104												1347	

	⑦	⑦a	⑦	⑦		⑦		⑦	⑦		⑦	⑦	⑦	⑦	⑦	⑦	⑦	⑦	⑦		⑦	⑦	⑦	⑦	⑦	⑦		⑦
Liverpool Lime Street d.	0921					0954			1025				1053		1120			1152			1224			1252		1325		
Manchester Airport ✈ d.	│					│			│				│		│	1137		│			│	1233		│		│		1336
Manchester Piccadilly d.	│			1008		│		1030	│			1100	│	1139	│	1201	1200	│	1239		│	1251	1300	│	1339	│		1353
Manchester Victoria d.	1000		1015	│		1029		│	1100		1115	│	1129	│	1200	1215	│	1229	│		1300	1315	│	1329	│	1400		1415
Stalybridge d.	│		│	1022		1041		1044	│		│	1112	1141	│	│	│	1212	1241	│		│	│	1312	1341	│	│		│
Huddersfield d.	1030		1046	1049f		1101		1117r	1130		1146	1149f	1201	1209	1230	1246	1249f	1301	1309		1330	1346	1349f	1401	1409	1430		1446
Dewsbury d.	│		1055	1109		│		1126	│		1157	1209	│	1218	│	1257	1309	│	1319		│	1357	1409	│	1418	│		1457
Leeds a.	1049		1108	1129		1121		1139	1149		1210	1229	1221	1231	1249	1310	1329	1321	1332		1349	1410	1429	1421	1431	1449		1510
Leeds 124 d.	1050		1112	▬		1127		1141	1151		1213		1227	1234	1250	1313	▬	1327	1334		1350	1413		1427	1434	1451		1513
Selby a.	│		│			1159		│	│		│		1252	│	│	│		1353	│		│	│		1451	│	│		│
Hull a.	│		│			1233		│	│		│		1328	│	│	│		1428	│		│	│		1523	│	│		│
York 124 a.	1115		1137	⑦				1207	1214		1236			1300	1315	1336	⑦		1400		1415	1437			1500	1514		1541
York 124 180 d.	1118	1128	1139	1203				1210	1223		1239			1303	1322	1339	1403		1402		1418	1437			1503	1522		1542
Malton d.	│	1153	│	1229				│	│		│			1329	│	│	1429		│		│	│			1529	│		
Scarborough a.	│	1221	│	1253				│	│		│			1354	│	│	1453		│		│	│			1553	│		
Thirsk d.	│		│					│	│		1256				│	1356			│		│	1455				│		1605
Northallerton 124 180 d.	│		1200					│	│		1305				│	1405			│		│	1504				│		│
Middlesbrough 212 a.	│		1231					│	│		1335				│	1435			│		│	1535				│		1643
Redcar Central 212 a.	│		1242					│	│		1348				│	1447			│		│	1547				│		1654
Saltburn 212 a.	│		1255					│	│		1356				│	1456			│		│	1556				│		1705
Darlington 124 180 d.	│							1238	1251						1409				1436t		1445					│		
Durham 124 180 d.	1159							1302r	1307						1426				│		1501					1605		
Newcastle 124 180 a.	1214							1319	1324						1440				1504		1516					1618		
Edinburgh 124 180 a.																												

	⑦	⑦	⑦	⑦	⑦a		⑦	⑦	⑦	⑦	⑦	⑦a		⑦	⑦	⑦		⑦	⑦	⑦a	⑦	⑦	⑦	⑦	⑦	⑦	⑦	⑦
Liverpool Lime Street d.		1352		1425					1452		1525					1552			1625				1652		1725			1752
Manchester Airport ✈ d.		│		│			1436		│		│			1536		│			│		1636		│		│	1736		│
Manchester Piccadilly d.	1400	│	1443	│			1453	1500	│	1539	│			1553	1600	│		1643	│		1653	1700	│	1739	│	1753	1800	│
Manchester Victoria d.	│	1429	│	1500			1515	│	1529	│	1600			1615	│	1629		│	1700		1715	│	1729	│	1800	1815	│	1829
Stalybridge d.	1412	1441	│	│			│	1512	1541	│	│			│	1612	1641		│	│		│	1712	1741	│	│	│	1813	1841
Huddersfield d.	1449f	1501	1517r	1530			1546	1549f	1601	1609	1630			1646	1649f	1701		1717r	1730		1746	1794f	1801	1809	1830	1846	1949f	1901
Dewsbury d.	1509	│	1527	│			1557	1609	│	1618	│			1657	1709	│		1727	│		1757	1809	│	1819	│	1857	1909	│
Leeds a.	1529	1521	1540	1549			1610	1629	1621	1631	1650			1710	1729	1721		1740	1749		1810	1829	1822	1832	1849	1910	1929	1921
Leeds 124 d.	▬	1527	1542	1551			1612		1627	1634	1652			1713	▬	1727		1742	1751		1813		1827	1834	1852	1913	▬	1927
Selby a.		1549	│	│			│		1654	│	│			│		1747		│	│		│		1847	│	│	│		1953
Hull a.		1621	│	│			│		1728	│	│			│		1820		│	│		│		1920	│	│	│		2024
York 124 a.	⑦	▬	1607	1614			1636			1701	1715			1738	⑦			1806	1815		1836			1902	1914	1938		
York 124 180 d.	1603		1607	1618	1632		1639			1703	1719	1727		1740	1803			1807	1821	1826	1839			1903	1917	1941		
Malton d.	1628		│	│	1657		│			1729	│	1752		│	1829			│	│	1851	│			1929	│	│		
Scarborough a.	1653		│	│	1723		│			1753	│	1816		│	1853			│	│	1918	│			1953	│	│		
Thirsk d.			│	│			1656				│			1757				│	│		1856				│	1958		
Northallerton 124 180 d.			1626	│			1705				│			1806				1828	│		1905				│	2007		
Middlesbrough 212 a.			│	│			1735				│			1836				│	│		1935				│	2038		
Redcar Central 212 a.			│	│			1746				│			1848				│	│		1947				│	2052		
Saltburn 212 a.			│	│			1756				│			1857				│	│		1956				│	2104		
Darlington 124 180 d.			1639	1648							1747							1841	1851						1946			
Durham 124 180 d.		⑦	1655	1705							1803							1857	1907						2003		⑦	
Newcastle 124 180 a.		1711	1718	1717							1816							1916	1921						2020		2114	
Edinburgh 124 180 a.		1859																									2259	

	⑦		⑦		⑦	⑦	⑦	⑦	⑦	⑦	⑦		⑦	⑦	⑦	⑦	⑦	⑦	⑦	⑦	⑦	⑦	⑦		⑦	⑦		⑦
Liverpool Lime Street d.					1825			1852		1925						2025				2109			2152			2254		
Manchester Airport ✈ d.					│	1836		│		│	1936					│	2036			│	2136		│		2237	│		2336
Manchester Piccadilly d.			1843		│	1853	1900	│		│	1953			2000	2043	│	2053		2058	│	2153	2200	│		2251	│		2350
Manchester Victoria d.			│		1900	1915	│	1929		2000	2015			│	│	2101	2115		│	2145	2216	│	2229		2315	2332		0001
Stalybridge d.			│		│	│	1912	1941		│	│			2012	│	│	│		2112	2159	│	2213	2241		2326	2344		│
Huddersfield d.			1917r		1930	1946	1949f	2001		2030	2046			2049f	2117r	2129	2146		2149f	2218	2246	2249f	2301		2346	0015		0031
Dewsbury d.			1927		│	1957	2009	│		│	2057			2109	2127	│	2157		2209	2227	2257	2304	│		2356			│
Leeds a.			1940		1949	2010	2029	2021		2049	2110			2129	2140	2149	2210		2229	2240	2310	2323	2320		0010			0107
Leeds 124 d.	1934		1944		1950	2013		2027	2027	2052	2112		2127	▬	2143	2152	2213	2227	▬	2243	2313	2327	2327		0014			0110
Selby a.	│		│		│	│		2047	│	│	│		2153		│	│	│	2256		│	│	2347	2347		│			│
Hull a.	│		│		│	│		2120	│	│	│		2229		│	│	│	2328		│	│	0019	0019		│			│
York 124 a.	2004		2008		2020	2037			2104	2114	2135			⑦	2210	2214	2236		⑦	2309	2341				0045			0139
York 124 180 d.	2006		2009		2021	2040			2106	2119	2136			2203		2216			2305	2310								
Malton d.	2031		│		│	│			2131	│	│			2229		│			2329	│								
Scarborough a.	2055		│		│	│			2155	│	│			2253		│			2353	│								
Thirsk d.			│		│	2057				│	2159					│				2332								
Northallerton 124 180 d.			2028		│	2105				│	2207					2245				2341								
Middlesbrough 212 a.			│		│	2135				│	2238					│												
Redcar Central 212 a.			│		│	2147				│	2249					│												
Saltburn 212 a.			│		│	2156				│	2259					│												
Darlington 124 180 d.			2041		2049					2154						2258				2355								
Durham 124 180 d.			2058		2106					2211						2314				0013								
Newcastle 124 180 a.			2114		2118					2225						2346				0044								
Edinburgh 124 180 a.																												

a – From Apr. 2. f – Arrives 8–9 minutes earlier. r – Arrives 5–6 minutes earlier. t – Arrives 1429.

EM 2nd class CLEETHORPES - GRIMSBY - LINCOLN - NEWARK - NOTTINGHAM - LEICESTER 189

km		Ⓐ	Ⓐ	ⒶL	ⒶL	Ⓐ	Ⓐ	Ⓐ	Ⓐ	Ⓐ	Ⓐ	Ⓐ	Ⓐ	Ⓐ	Ⓐ	Ⓐ	Ⓐ	Ⓐ	Ⓐ	Ⓐ	⑥	⑥	⑥	⑥	⑥
0	**Cleethorpes** 193 d.	...	0500	...	...	0550	...	...	...	...	...	...	...	...	🚌	...	...	...	...	2158	...	*0500*	0634	...	...
5	**Grimsby** Town 178 193 d.	...	0508	...	...	0558	...	0741	0839	...	1041	1241	...	1438	...	1641	...	1838	...	2206	...	*0508*	0642	...	0838
27	Barnetby 178 193 d.	...	0527	...	...	0616	...	0801	0858	...	1100	1300	...	1457	...	1700	...	1857	...	2225	...	*0526*	0702	...	0857
51	Market Rasen d.	...	0544	...	...	0632	...	0819	0914	...	1115	1315	...	1512	...	1715	...	1913	...	2242	...	*0543*	0717	...	0912
75	**Lincoln** 180 d.	0516	...	0614	0640	0652	0747	0838	0935	1035	1135	1336	1437	1532	1634	1737	1835	1932	2048	2306f	0518	0629	0739	0839	0933
01	Newark Castle ♧ d.	0558	...	0642	0714f	0721n	0814	0906	1003	1104	1203	1404	1504	1558	1729	1808	1903	2001	2114	2332	0600	0658	0806	0907	1003
29	**Nottingham** ♧ a.	0634	...	0706	0739	...	0839	0927	1025	1125	1225	1426	1526	1626	...	1835	1925	2022	2141	0003	0636	0725	0828	0928	1027

	⑥	⑥	⑥	⑥	⑥	⑥	⑥	⑥	⑥	⑥	⑥	⑦	⑦	⑦	⑦	⑦	⑦	⑦	⑦	⑦	⑦	⑦	⑦	⑦	⑦	⑦
leethorpes 193 d.	...	1030	...	...	...	...	...	...	...	1953	...	...	...	...	...	...	1330	...	...	...	...	1823	...	...	2050	...
rimsby Town 178 193 d.	...	1038	1240	...	1438	1638	...	1839	...	2001	...	...	...	...	...	...	1338	...	...	...	...	1831	...	...	2058	...
arnetby 178 193 d.	...	1057	1259	...	1457	1657	...	1859	...	2020	...	...	...	...	...	...	1358	...	...	...	...	1850	...	...	2117	...
arket Rasen d.	...	1112	1314	...	1512	1712	...	1914	...	2035	...	...	...	...	...	...	1413	...	...	...	...	1906	...	...	2133	...
incoln d.	1036	1133	1335	1437	1533	1731	1830	1934	2042	2054	2142	0900	1032	1124	1238	1338	1438f	1524	1635	1738	1852	1932c	2027	2103	2151	2251
ewark Castle ♧ d.	1104	1202	1403	1506	1605	1759	1858	2003	2110	...	2210	0929	1059	1153	1306	1405	1507	1553	1705	1808	1921	2001	2056	2132	...	2320
ottingham ♧ a.	1127	1226	1425	1527	1630	1825	1925	2029	2140	...	2240	1005	1124	1230	1332	1430	1544	1617	1740	1836	1957	2026	2121	2200	...	2356

	Ⓐ	Ⓐ	Ⓐ	Ⓐ	Ⓐ	Ⓐ	Ⓐ	Ⓐ	Ⓐ	Ⓐ	Ⓐ	Ⓐ	Ⓐ		Ⓐ	Ⓐ	ⒶL	Ⓐ	⑥	⑥	⑥	⑥	⑥	⑥	⑥
ottingham ♧ d.	...	0539	0637	0737	0835	1035	1133	1235	1334	1435	1634	1735	1835	...	2032	2132	2215	2237	...	0513	0555	...	0736	...	0934
ewark Castle ♧ d.	...	0606	0659	0803	0903	1101	1157	1301	1356	1500	1701	1804	1902	...	2100	2204	2243	2310	...	0535	0630	...	0800	0817n	0957
incoln d.	0458	0636	0736r	0836	0933	1131	1227	1332	1425	1532	1732	1834	1932	...	2130	2234	2313	2339	0520	0559	0659	0731	0830	0841	1026
arket Rasen d.	0514	0653	0752	...	0949	1147	...	1348	...	1548	1748	...	1948	...	2146	...	...	...	0536	...	...	0746	...	0857	...
arnetby 178 193 a.	0530	0708	0808	...	1005	1202	...	1403	...	1604	1804	...	2004	...	2201	...	...	...	0552	...	...	0802	...	0912	...
rimsby Town 178 193 a.	0549	0730	0829	...	1026	1223	...	1424	...	1625	1826	...	2026t	...	2223	...	...	...	0613	...	...	0822	...	0936	...
leethorpes 193 a.	0601	...	...	...	...	...	...	...	...	...	...	...	2043	...	2231	...	...	...	0621	...	...	...	...	0946	...

	⑥	⑥	⑥	⑥	⑥		⑥	⑥	⑥	⑥	⑥	⑦	⑦	⑦	⑦		⑦	⑦	⑦	⑦		⑦	⑦	⑦	⑦	⑦
ottingham ♧ d.	1038	1138	1238	1338	1440	...	1633	1738	1834	2031	2132	0933	1024	1125	1227	...	1337	1427	1536	1628	...	1727	1853	1930	2027	2230
lewark Castle ♧ d.	1101	1201	1301	1400	1503	...	1700	1803	1902	2057	2206	1009	1048	1201	1251	...	1401	1503	1601	1652	...	1803	1917	1955	2051	2306
incoln d.	1131	1230	1333	1429	1534	...	1731	1834	1931	2127	2232	1040	1115	1232	1317	...	1427	1534	1638r	1723	...	1836	1947	2025	2123	2336
larket Rasen d.	1147	...	1349	...	1549	...	1746	1850	...	...	...	...	1131	...	...	...	...	...	1654	...	...	1852	...	...	...	...
arnetby 178 193 a.	1202	...	1404	...	1605	...	1802	1906	...	...	...	...	1146	...	...	...	...	...	1710	...	...	1907	...	...	...	...
rimsby Town 178 193 a.	1225	...	1428	...	1627	...	1825	1930	...	...	...	...	1209	...	...	...	...	...	1733	...	...	1930	...	...	...	...
leethorpes 193 a.	...	...	...	...	...	...	...	1940	...	...	...	...	1219	...	...	...	...	...	1742	...	...	1942	...	...	...	...

LINCOLN - NEWARK NORTH GATE

See Table **180** for additional services (London Kings Cross -) Newark - Lincoln and v.v. Journey time ± 30 minutes.

rom Lincoln: On Ⓐ at 0516 **N**, 0600, 0652 **G**, 0911, 1002 **P**, 2233 **P**; on ⑥ at 0518 **N**, 0608, 0744, 1004, 1204, 1411, 1605, 1655, 1801, 1912, 2135; on ⑦ at 0835, 1106, 1248, 1427, 1545, 1710, 915, 1958, 2126, 2230.

rom Newark Northgate: On Ⓐ at 0637 **P**, 0730, 0948, 1039, 2315; on ⑥ at 0646 **P**, 0817 **G**, 1040, 1235, 1452, 1642, 1727, 1839, 1944, 2211; on ⑦ at 0915, 1140, 1335, 1455, 1644, 1755, 1945, 028, 2210, 2321.

G – From/to Cleethorpes (see table above).
L – To/from London St Pancras (Table **170**).
N – To Nottingham (Table **184**).
P – To/from Peterborough (Table **176**).

c – Arrives 1925.
f – Arrives 4–6 minutes earlier.
n – Newark North Gate.
r – Arrives 8–11 minutes earlier.
t – Departs 2036.

♧ – Additional journeys Newark Castle - Nottingham and v.v. Journey time: 28–36 minutes. **From Newark Castle on** Ⓐ at: 0627, 0736, 0841, 0936, 1136, 1243, 1343, 1436, 1639, 1736, 1843, 1945. On ⑥ at: 0736, 0841, 0940, 1136, 1243, 1343, 1438, 1636, 1736, 1835, 1941. **From Nottingham** on Ⓐ at: 0543, 0650, 0757, 0851, 1058, 1157, 1255, 1358, 1556, 1656, 1754, 1851. On ⑥ at: 0650, 0758, 0901, 1059, 1155, 1256, 1355, 1556, 1656, 1758, 1854.

NT 2nd class LEEDS - BRADFORD - HALIFAX - MANCHESTER - CHESTER 190

Additional trains run Leeds - Bradford - Manchester Victoria and v.v. on ⚒.

km		⚒	⚒	⚒	⚒	⚒	⚒	⚒	⚒	⚒	⚒		⚒	⚒	⚒	⚒	⚒	⚒	⚒	⚒	⑦	⑦		⑦
0	**Leeds** 191 d.	0542	0642	0743	0841	0942	1042	1142	1242	1342	1442	...	1542	1642	1742	1842	1942	2042	2142	2242	0819	0918	♣	2319
15	**Bradford** Interchange. 191 d.	0604	0704	0804	0904	1004	1104	1204	1306	1404	1504	...	1604	1704	1804	1904	2004	2104	2204	2303	0839	0939		2339
28	Halifax 191 d.	0616	0716	0816	0916	1016	1116	1216	1317	1416	1516	...	1616	1716	1816	1916	2016	2116	2216	2316	0850	0950	and	2350
42	Hebden Bridge 191 d.	0631	0731	0831	0931	1031	1131	1231	1331	1431	1531	...	1631	1731	1831	1931	2031	2131	2232	2330	0902	1002		0002
49	Todmorden 191a d.	0637	0737	0837	0937	1037	1137	1237	1337	1437	1537	...	1637	1737	1837	1937	2037	2137	2238	2336	0908	1008	hourly	0008
63	Rochdale 191a d.	0647	0747	0847	0947	1047	1147	1247	1347	1447	1547	...	1648	1747	1847	1947	2047	2147	2248	2351	0921	1021		0020
80	**Manchester** Victoria. 191a a.	0701	0801	0901	1001	1101	1201	1303	1401	1502	1601	...	1702	1802	1901	2001	2101	2204	2302	0005	0937	1035	until	0034
113	Warrington Bank Quay 160 d.	0740	0839	0938	1038	1139	1238	1339	1438	1538	1638	...	1738	1838	1938	2038	2138	...	...	...	...	...		...
142	**Chester** 160 a.	0809	0901	1001	1101	1203	1301	1401	1501	1601	1709	...	1809	1909	2001	2109	2201	...	...	...	...	...		...

	⚒	⚒	⚒	⚒	⚒	⚒	⚒	⚒	⚒	⚒	⚒	⚒	⚒	⚒	⚒	⚒	⚒	Ⓐ	⑥	Ⓐ	⑦		⑦	⑦
hester 160 d.	...	...	0623	0723	0821	0929	1027	1128	1229	1327	1429	1529	1629	1725	1825	1926	2029	...	...	2229	...	♥	...	...
Varrington Bank Quay. 160 d.	...	...	0650	0750	0848	0951	1050	1150	1250	1350	1450	1550	1650	1750	1850	1950	2050	...	...	2250	...		...	...
lanchester Victoria 191a d.	0551	0630	0721	0820	0921	1021	1120	1221	1321	1421	1521	1621	1721	1821	1922	2021	2121	2230	2257	2323	0854	and	2154	2254
Rochdale 191a d.	0610	0643	0734	0835	0934	1034	1134	1234	1334	1434	1534	1634	1734	1834	1935	2034	2134	2243	2310	2336	0907		2207	2307
odmorden 191a d.	0625	0658	0744	0845	0943	1043	1143	1243	1343	1443	1543	1643	1743	1843	1944	2043	2143	2254	2319	2351	0918	hourly	2218	2318
lebden Bridge 191 d.	0631	0704	0750	0851	0950	1050	1150	1250	1350	1450	1550	1650	1749	1850	1950	2050	2150	2301	2326	2357	0925		2225	2325
lalifax 191 d.	0645	0720	0805	0906	1005	1105	1205	1305	1405	1505	1605	1705	1804	1905	2005	2105	2205	2313	2337	0012	0938	until	2238	2338
radford Interchange 191 d.	0702	0737	0821	0922	1021	1121	1221	1321	1421	1521	1621	1721	1821	1921	2021	2121	2221	2329	2353	0026	0954		2254	2354
eeds 191 a.	0723	0759	0842	0942	1042	1142	1242	1342	1442	1542	1642	1742	1842	1942	2042	2142	2242	2347	0014	0043	1015		2316	0014

♥ – The 1154 from Manchester Victoria departs Todmorden 1222, Hebden Bridge 1229, Halifax 1244, Bradford Interchange 1300 and arrives Leeds 1320.
♣ – The 1919 from Leeds departs Bradford Interchange 1942, Halifax 1954, Hebden Bridge 2007, Todmorden 2014, Rochdale 2028 and arrives Manchester Victoria 2044.

NT 2nd class YORK - LEEDS - BLACKBURN - BLACKPOOL 191

km		⚒	⚒	⚒	⚒	⚒		⚒	⚒	⚒	⚒	⑦	⑦	⑦	⑦	⑦	⑦	⑦	⑦	⑦	⑦	⑦	⑦	⑦
0	**York** 124 188 d.	0519	0612	0713	0822	0922		1923	2023	2123	2219	0922	1021	1119	1223	1319	1419	1519	1624	1719	1826	1920	2023	2123
41	**Leeds** 124 188 190 d.	0557	0658	0755	0857	0957		1957	2058	2157	2257	0957	1057	1157	1257	1357	1457	1557	1657	1757	1906	1957	2058	2157
56	**Bradford** Interchange. 190 d.	0616	0717	0816	0917	1017	and	2017	2119	2216	2317	1016	1116	1216	1316	1416	1518	1616	1716	1816	1925	2016	2119	2216
69	Halifax 190 d.	0627	0728	0827	0928	1028		2028	2130	2227	2328	1027	1127	1227	1327	1427	1529	1627	1727	1827	1936	2027	2130	2227
83	Hebden Bridge 190 d.	0638	0741	0838	0941	1041	hourly	2041	2142	2238	2340	1042	1143	1244	1348	1449t	1548	1647f	1745	1846	1952	2045	2145f	2249t
103	Burnley Manchester Road . d.	0657	0803	0902	1002	1102		2102	2202	2302f	2359	1103	1204	1304	1407	1507	1607	1705	1804	1905	2011	2104	2204	2308
113	Accrington d.	0711	0813	0912	1012	1112	until	2112	2212	2312	0008	1113	1213	1314	1416	1516	1616	1714	1813	1914	2020	2113	2214	2317
123	**Blackburn** d.	0721	0821	0921	1021	1121		2121	2221	2321	0017	1124	1224	1325	1425	1525	1625	1723	1823	1924	2028	2124	2224	2326
142	**Preston** 156 a.	0745	0844	0938	1038	1138		2139	2239	2339	...	1142	1241	1342	1442	1543	1643	1741	1841	1941	2045	2141	2242	2343
171	**Blackpool North** 156 a.	0809	0909	1004	1108	1204		2206	2306	0004	...	1206	1305	1406	1506	1606	1706	1805	1905	2005	2109	2205	2309	0008

	⚒	⚒	⚒		⚒	⚒	⚒	⚒	⚒	⑦	⑦	⑦	⑦	⑦	⑦	⑦	⑦	⑦	⑦	⑦	⑦	⑦	⑦	⑦
Blackpool North 156 d.	0519	0619	0718		1819	1919	2019	2118	2202	...	...	0918	1023	1117	1217	1318	1418	1518	1615	1718	1818	1918	2020	2119
Preston 156 d.	0544	0644	0744		1844	1944	2044	2143	2226	...	...	0947	1047	1143	1241	1342	1442	1542	1641	1742	1842	1942	2044	2143
Blackburn d.	0604	0704	0804	and	1904	2004	2104	2202	2242	...	0904	1004	1104	1200	1257	1358	1459	1559	1659	1758	1858	1959	2102	2200
Accrington d.	0613	0712	0813		1912	2013	2112	2211	2250	...	0912	1012	1112	1208	1305	1406	1507	1607	1707	1806	1906	2007	2109	2208
Burnley Manchester Road d.	0622	0721	0822	hourly	1921	2022	2121	2220	2259	...	0921	1021	1121	1217	1314	1415	1516	1616	1716	1815	1915	2016	2118	2217
Hebden Bridge 190 d.	0642	0742	0843		1942	2043	2142	2241	2320	...	0941	1042	1141	1238	1336	1437	1537	1637	1737	1837	1937	2037	2140	2238
Halifax 190 d.	0653	0753	0854	until	1953	2054	2153	2252	2331	0858	0955	1056	1156	1252	1350	1452	1552	1652	1752	1852	1952	2051	2155	2253
Bradford Interchange 190 d.	0707	0807	0908		2007	2108	2207	2306	2348	0914	1010	1111	1210	1307	1405	1506	1607	1707	1808	1906	2007	2106	2209	2308
Leeds 124 188 190 a.	0729r	0826	0928		2026	2129	2227	2326c	0003	0935	1028	1128	1228	1327	1426	1526	1627	1726	1827	1926	2026	2125a	2227	2327
York 124 188 a.	0802	0857	0958		2057	2158	2302	0009	...	1013	1057	1158	1257	1357	1458	1557	1658	1758	1857	2001	2100	2200	2300	2357

a – Departs 2130.
c – Departs 2336.
f – Arrives 5–6 minutes earlier.
r – Departs 0737.
t – Arrives 7–8 minutes earlier.

191a MANCHESTER - BURNLEY - BLACKBURN

2nd class NT

km			⚒	⚒	⚒	⚒		⚒	⚒	⚒	⚒	⚒	⚒	⚒	⚒		⑦	⑦	⑦	⑦	⑦		⑦	⑦	⑦
0	Manchester Victoria d.	⚒	0604	0703	0804	0904		1604	1704	1804	1905	2004	2104	2204	2303	⑦	0833	0858	1000	1059	1200		2000	2100	2202
17	Rochdale d.		0617	0717	0817	0917	and	1617	1717	1817	1918	2017	2118	2217	2317		0854	0919	1021	1120	1221	and	2021	2121	2222
31	Todmorden d.		0633	0735	0835	0933	hourly	1635	1733	1835	1934	2033	2133	2233	2333		0909	0937	1038	1138	1238	hourly	2038	2138	2239
45	Burnley Manchester Road d.		0649	0751	0851	0949		1651	1749	1851	1950	2049	2149	2249	2349		0925	0953	1054	1154	1254		2054	2154	2255
54	Accrington d.		0659	0801	0901	0959	until	1701	1759	1901	2000	2059	2200	2259	2359		0936	1004	1104	1204	1304	until	2104	2204	2305
63	**Blackburn** a.		0710	0812	0912	1010		1712	1810	1912	2011	2110	2211	2314	0010		0952	1019	1119	1219	1320		2119	2219	2320

		⚒	⚒	⚒	⚒	⚒	⚒	⚒		⚒	⚒	⚒	⚒	⚒	⚒		⑦	⑦	⑦		⑦	⑦	⑦	⑦	⑦
Blackburn d.	⚒	0620	0718	0820	0920	1020	1119	1219		1820	1920	2020	2120	2220	2320	⑦	0748	0809	0909		1909	2013	2111	2210	2300
Accrington d.		0628	0726	0828	0928	1028	1127	1227	and	1828	1928	2028	2128	2228	2328		0756	0818	0918	and	1918	2022	2120	2219	2308
Burnley Manchester Road d.		0639	0737	0839	0939	1039	1138	1238	hourly	1839	1939	2039	2139	2239	2339		0807	0829	0929	hourly	1929	2033	2131	2230	2319
Todmorden d.		0656	0754	0856	0956	1056	1154	1255		1857	1956	2056	2156	2258	2356		0824	0846	0946		1946	2052	2148	2247	2335
Rochdale d.		0710	0810	0910	1010	1110	1208	1309	until	1911	2010	2110	2210	2312	0009		0838	0903	1003	until	2003	2109	2205	2304	2351
Manchester Victoria a.		0725	0825	0925	1025	1125	1225	1325		1926	2025	2125	2225	2327	0025		0900	0924	1024		2024	2130	2226	2325	0013

192 HULL - DONCASTER - SHEFFIELD

2nd class NT

km			⚒	⚒	⚒	⚒B	⚒A	⚒B	⚒B		⚒B	ⒶB	⑥B	⑥B	ⒶB	⚒		⑦	⑦	⑦A	⑦	⑦	⑦B		⑦B	⑦	⑦
0	**Hull** 181 d.	⚒	0519	0631	0721	0829	0926	1023	1125		1926	2021	2026	2125	2126	2245	⑦	0845	0927	1032	1125	1229	1329		2129	2153	2251
17	Brough 181 d.		0531	0643	0733	0841	0938	1035	1137	and	1938	2033	2038	2137	2138	2257		0902	0939	1044	1137	1241	1341	and	2141	2210	2308
38	Goole d.		0550	0658	0749	0856	0954	1050	1154	hourly	1954	|	|	2152	2153	2313		0918	0954	1058	1155	1256	1355	hourly	2155	2226	2324
66	**Doncaster** 181 a.		0613	0718	0818	0919	1018	1112	1219		2019	2113	2118	2214	2215	2339		0943	1019	1120	1217	1320	1419		2219	2254	2356
66	**Doncaster** 193 d.		0614	0720	0822	0920	1020	1115	1219	until	2021	2117	2121	2215	2216	2343		...	1021	1122	1219	1323	1421	until	2221	...	...
90	Meadowhall 193 d.		0633	0739	0840	0941	1038	1137	1238		2039	2135	2139	2233	2237	0008		...	1039	1143	1237	1341	1439		2243	...	...
96	**Sheffield** 193 a.		0642	0748	0848	0949	1048	1148	1249		2048	2143	2149	2241	2245	0017		...	1049	1151	1248	1350	1449		2250	...	...

		⚒B	⚒B	▽⊙	⚒	Ⓐ	⑥	⚒	⚒	⚒		⑦	⑦B	⑦B	⑦B	⑦B	⑦B	⑦B	⑦B	⑦B	⑦B	⑦B	⑦A	⑦A	⑦	⑦	⑦
Sheffield 193 d.	⚒	0542	0655		1856	1957	1957	2056	2157	2300	⑦	0804	0836	0925	1025	1134	1225	1324	1425	1525	1625	1725	1825	1925	2026	2126	2225
Meadowhall 193 d.		0548	0703	and	1902	2003	2003	2102	2203	2306		0810	0843	0931	1031	1141	1231	1331	1432	1531	1632	1731	1831	1931	2032	2132	2231
Doncaster 193 a.		0611	0724	hourly	1922	2022	2022	2122	2222	2325		0840	0902	0950	1050	1200	1251	1350	1453	1550	1654	1750	1850	1950	2051	2151	2250
Doncaster 181 d.		0614	0726		1924	2024	2029	2123	2225	2328		0842	0905	0952	1054	1203	1254	1352	1500	1552	1655	1802	1852	1952	2052	2152	2251
Goole d.		0639	0746	until	1942	|	|	2142	2244	2348		0908	0924	1017f	1114	1223	1317	1412	1519	1612	1718	1824	1911	2011	2116	2212	2316f
Brough 181 d.		0702	0801		1959	2101	2105	2157	2302	0003		0926	0939	1031	1129	1240	1332	1426	1534	1627	1735	1839	1926	2026	2135	2227	2336
Hull 181 a.		0722	0817		2012	2117	2124	2212	2315	0015		0946	0952	1044	1142	1254	1345	1440	1547	1640	1748	1852	1939	2041	2148	2240	2354

A – From / to Bridlington (Table 177).
B – From / to Scarborough (Table 177).
f – Arrives 6 minutes earlier.
▽ – Timings may vary by ± 3 minutes.
⊙ – On ⑥ the 0957 from Sheffield departs Doncaster 1030, Goole 1050, Brough 1104. and arrives Hull 1117

193 CLEETHORPES - DONCASTER - SHEFFIELD - MANCHESTER - LIVERPOOL

TP

km			⚒	⚒	⚒	⚒	⚒	⚒	⚒		⚒	⚒	⚒	Ⓐ		⑦	⑦	⑦	⑦	⑦		⑦	⑦	⑦	⑦
0	Cleethorpes 178 d.	⚒	...	...	...	0504	0624	0727	0824	◧	1924	2024	2124	2236	⑦	...	...	...	0926	1024		1827	1924	2024	2114
5	Grimsby Town 178 189 d.		...	...	...	0512	0632	0735	0832		1932	2032	2132	2244		...	...	...	0934	1032		1835	1932	2032	2122
29	Barnetby 178 189 d.		...	...	...	0532	0652	0755	0852		1952	2052	2152	2303		...	...	...	0953	1052		1855	1952	2052	2142
48	Scunthorpe d.		...	...	...	0547	0708	0811	0908		2008	2108	2208	2320		...	...	...	1010	1108		1908	2008	2108	2158
85	**Doncaster** a.		...	...	...	0625	0738	0841	0941	and	2038	2138	2238	2358		...	...	...	1039	1140	and	1941	2038	2142	2228
85	**Doncaster** 192 d.		...	...	0536	0626	0742	0843	0942		2042	2143	2244t	...		...	0842	0945	1043	1143		1942	2043	2144	2229
109	Meadowhall 192 d.		...	...	0559	0654	0759	0902	1002	hourly	2104	2202	2311t	...		...	0902	1005	1102	1200	hourly	2001	2103	2203	2300
115	**Sheffield** 192 a.		...	...	0607	0705	0806	0909	1009		2109	2209	2319t	...		...	0909	1012	1110	1209		2009	2109	2210	2307
115	**Sheffield** 206 d.		0319j	0508	0609	0708	0808	0911	1011	until	2111	2211	...	...		0751	0911	1014	1111	1211	until	2011	2111	2213	...
175	Stockport 206 a.		|	|	0653	0753	0853	0953	1053		2153	2255	...	...		0835	0952	1055	1155	1255		2058	2158	2302	...
184	**Manchester** Piccadilly 206 a.		0452j	0605	0705	0805	0906	1005	1105		2205	2307	...	...		0845	1003	1107	1207	1307		2107	2207	2319	...
	Manchester Airport ✈ a.		0527	|	|	|	|	|	|		|	2324t	...	...		|	|	|	|	|		|	|	...	...
210	Warrington Central 206 a.		...	0634	0734	0829	0929	1034	1134‡		2234	...	...	...		0916	1033	1131	1230	1331		2130	2230	...	...
231	**Liverpool** South P'way 206 a.		...	0649	0749	0849	0948	1049	1149		2249	...	...	...		0944	1051	1150	1249	1349		2148	2248	...	...
240	**Liverpool** Lime Street 206 a.		...	0701	0800	0900	1000	1100	1200		2300	...	...	...		0956	1102	1200	1302	1401		2159	2303	...	...

		⚒	⚒	⚒	⚒	⚒		⚒	⚒	⚒	⑥	Ⓐ	⑥	Ⓐ	Ⓐ		⑦	⑦	⑦	⑦		⑦	⑦	⑦	⑦
Liverpool Lime Street 206 d.	⚒	...	...	0614	0719	0819	♥	1819	1919	2019	2119	2119	...	2219	...	⑦	...	...	0920	1020		1920	2020	2120	2220
Liverpool South P'way 206 d.		...	...	0624	0729	0830		1830	1930	2030	2130	2129	...	2230	...		...	...	0931	1031		1931	2031	2131	2231
Warrington Central 206 d.		...	...	0642	0745	0842‡		1843	1743	2043	2142	2142	...	2243	...		...	...	0947	1047		1947	2046	2148	2247
Manchester Airport ✈ d.		...	0543	|	|	|		|	|	|	|	|	...	|	2331		...	...	|	|		|	|	|	|
Manchester Piccadilly 206 d.		...	0612	0712	0813	0913	and	1913	2013	2113	2213	2213	2313	2320	2352		0812	0909	1014	1120	and	2018	2118	2218	2313
Stockport 206 d.		...	0624	0724	0825	0923		1923	2022	2125	2223	2223	|	|	|		0822	0919	1023	1128		2028	2128	2227	2327
Sheffield 206 a.		...	0707	0809	0909	1009	hourly	2009	2108	2209	2303	2309	0031	0020	0126		0908	1009	1107	1208	hourly	2109	2211	2309	0010
Sheffield 192 d.		0554	0709	0811	0911	1011		2011	2111	2211	2304	2321	...	...	...		0910	1010	1110	1210		2111	2212	2311	...
Meadowhall 192 d.		0600	0715	0817	0917	1017	until	2017	2117	2217	|	|	...	...	...		0916	1016	1116	1216	until	2117	2218	|	...
Doncaster 192 a.		0632	0732	0836	0937	1036		2035	2140	2235	2328	2354	...	...	...		0936	1036	1136	1235		2135	2236	2338	...
Doncaster d.		0636	0734	0838	0939	1037		2037	2147	2238	...	...	...	...	...		0938	1038	1139	1237		2137	2239	...	...
Scunthorpe d.		0702	0801	0904	1005	1103		2103	2213	2313	...	...	...	...	...		1004	1104	1205	1303		2204	2305	...	...
Barnetby 178 189 d.		0718	0817	0919	1020	1118		2118	2229	2328	...	...	...	...	...		1019	1120	1220	1317		2219	2320	...	...
Grimsby Town 178 189 a.		0742	0844	0940	1041	1142		2140	2253	2350	...	...	...	...	...		1041	1144	1242	1343		2241	2344	...	...
Cleethorpes 178 a.		0751	0853	0951	1052	1152		2150	2304	0001	...	...	...	...	...		1051	1152	1252	1352		2251	2352	...	...

j – On ① departs Sheffield 0345, arrives Manchester Piccadilly 0437.
t – Ⓐ only.
♥ – The 1319 from Liverpool to Cleethorpes does not run.
◧ – The 0924 from Cleethorpes to Liverpool does not run.
‡ – Timings at Warrington may vary ± 5 minutes.

194 SHEFFIELD - MANCHESTER (Hope Valley service)

2nd class only NT

km			Ⓐ	Ⓐ	⑥	Ⓐ	⑥	⚒	⚒		⚒	⚒	⑥	Ⓐ	Ⓐ		⑦	⑦	⑦		⑦	⑦	⑦		⑦	⑦
0	**Sheffield** 193 d.	⚒	...	0618	0620	0711	0713	0728j	0814		2014	2114	2224	2246	2328	⑦	0914	1017	1115	...	1214	1314	1414		2014	2216
16	Grindleford d.		...	0633	0635	0726	0728	|	0828	and	2029	2129	2238	2301	2344		0928	1031	1129	...	1230	1329	1428	and	2028	2231
18	Hathersage d.		...	0638	0639	0729	0731	|	0832		2032	2132	2242	2304	2347		0932	1034	1133	...	1233	1332	1432		2032	2234
24	Hope d.		...	0646	0647	0736	0739	|	0839	hourly	2036	2140	2249	2312	2354		0939	1041	1140	...	1241	1340	1439	hourly	2039	2242
32	Edale d.		...	0653	0654	0745	0746	|	0846		2046	2147	2256	2319	0001		0947	1048	1147	...	1248	1347	1446		2046	2249
41	Chinley d.		0627	0701	0702	0754	0754	0804	0854	until	2054	2154	2304	2327	0008		0955	1055	1156	...	1256	1256	1455	until	2055	2258
67	**Manchester** Picc. 193 a.		0709	0736	0736	0834	0832	0835	0932		2132	2233	2341	0012	0036		1032	1133	1237	...	1333	1434	1534		2134	2337

		⚒	⚒	⚒		⚒	Ⓐ	⑥	⚒	Ⓐ	Ⓐ	⑥		⑦	⑦a	⑦b	⑦	⑦	⑦	⑦	⑦	⑦		⑦	⑦	⑦
Manchester Picc. 193 d.	⚒	0546	0640	0748		1849	1946	1948	2048	2148	2230	2230	⑦	0743	0829	0845	0931	1045	1145	1252	1345	1445		1945	2045	2213
Chinley d.		0615	0718	0823	and	1924	2019	2023	2124	2223	2254	2258		0821	0905	0921	1008	1121	1222	1322	1418	1520	and	2021	2118	2246
Edale d.		0623	0726	0831		1933	2027	2031	2132	2231	2302	2306		0830	0913	0929	1017	1130	1230	1331	1426	1529		2029	2126	2254
Hope d.		0630	0732	0837	hourly	1939	2032	2037	2138	2237	2308	2312		0837	0920	0936	1023	1136	1240	1337	1431	1535	hourly	2036	2131	2300
Hathersage d.		0637	0738	0844		1946	2038	2044	2145	2244	2316	2319		0844	0927	0943	1030	1143	1244	1344	1437	1542		2043	2137	2305
Grindleford d.		0641	0741	0848	until	1949	2042	2048	2149	2248	2320	2322		0848	0931	0947	1034	1147	1248	1348	1441	1546	until	2047	2141	2310
Sheffield 193 a.		0658	0805	0906		2006	2057	2105	2210f	2306	2336	2338		0905	0948	1004	1051	1205	1305	1405	1501	1605		2102	2202	2326

a – From Apr. 2.
b – Until Mar. 26.
c – Arrives 1836 on ⑥.
f – Arrives 2206 on ⑥.
j – Departs 0734 on ⑥.

LE — Most Norwich trains convey 🍸 — LONDON - HARWICH, IPSWICH and NORWICH — 200

	⚒	⚒ P	Ⓐ	⑥ 2	Ⓐ	⑥ 2	⑥	⚒	⚒ C	⑥ 2	⑥	Ⓐ	⑥	Ⓐ	⚒	⑥	Ⓐ	⑥ 2	Ⓐ 2	⚒	⚒	⑥ 2	Ⓐ 2	⚒	⚒	⚒
London Liverpool Street d.		...	...	0534	0600	0602	...	0625r	...	0636	0700	0700	0730	0730	0755r	0830	0830	0900	0900	0930	1000	1030	1030	1100	1130	1200
Chelmsford d.		...	...	0610	0630	0634	...	0656r	...	0710	|	|	0801	0802	|	0901	0902	|	|	1001	|	1101	1104	|	1201	|
Colchester d.		0540	0615	0643	0649	0704	...	0719	...	0738	0747	0748	0820	0822	0847	0920	0923	0947	0947	1020	1046	1120	1123	1147	1220	1247
Manningtree ★ d.		0548	0623	0651	0657	0712	...	0727	...	0746	0755	0756	0828	0830	0855	0928	0931	0955	0955	1028	1054	1128	1131	1155	1228	1255
Harwich Int'l ★ d.		|	|	|	|	|	...	|	0745r	0805	|	|	|	|	|	|	|	|	|	|	|	|	|	|	|	|
Harwich Town ★ a.		|	|	|	|	|	...	|	|	...	|	|	|	|	|	|	|	|	|	|	|	|	|	|	|	|
Ipswich 205 d.		0600	0639c	0702	0710	0725	0710	0739	0819f	...	0806	0811c	0839	0843	0906	0939	0943	1006	1008	1039a	1106	1139	1143	1207	1239	1306
Stowmarket 205 d.		0612	0650	...	0721	...	0721	0750	0835	...	|	0822	0851	0855	|	0951	0953	|	|	1051	|	1151	1154	|	1251	|
Diss d.		...	0702	...	0733	...	0733	0802	...	...	0826	0834	0903	0907	0927	1003	1005	1026	1028	1103	1126	1203	1206	1227	1303	1326
Norwich a.		...	0722	...	0752	...	0752	0820	...	...	0843	0852	0920	0924	0945	1020	1022	1043	1048	1122	1144	1220	1225	1247	1322	1346

	⚒	⚒	⚒	⚒ 2	⚒	⚒	⚒ 2	⚒	Ⓐ	⑥	Ⓐ	⑥	Ⓐ 2	Ⓐ	⑥	Ⓐ	⑥	Ⓐ 2	⑥	Ⓐ	Ⓐ 2	Ⓐ 2	⑥ 2	Ⓐ 2	⑥	Ⓐ
London Liverpool Street d.	1230	1300	1330	1400	1430	1500	1530	1600	1630	1630	1700	1700	1702	1730	1730	1750	1800	1802	1830	1830	1908	1845	1902	1902	1930	1930
Chelmsford d.	1301	|	1401	|	1501	|	1559	|	|	1701	|	|	1733	|	1801	|	|	1833	1901	|	1941	1919	|	|	2001	|
Colchester d.	1320	1347	1420	1447	1520	1547	1620	1646	1718	1720	|	1747	1759	1821	1820	1843	1847	1901	1920	1920	2011	1956	1947	1948	2020	2020
Manningtree ★ d.	1328	1355	1428	1455	1528	1555	1628	1654	1726	1728	1749	1755	1806	1829	1828	1851	1855	1909	1928	1928	2019	2005	1955	1956	2028	2029
Harwich Int'l ★ d.	|	|	|	|	|	|	|	|	|	|	|	|	|	|	|	|	|	|	|	|	|	2023	|	|	|	|
Harwich Town ★ a.	|	|	|	|	|	|	|	|	|	|	|	|	|	|	|	|	|	|	|	|	|	...	|	|	|	|
Ipswich 205 d.	1339	1407	1439	1506	1539	1606	1639	1706	1737	1739	1800	1806	1819	1840	1839	1903	1906	1923	1939	1940	2030	...	2008	2009	2039	2041
Stowmarket 205 d.	1351	|	1450	|	1551	|	1651	1717	1748	1751	1811	|	...	1851	1851	1914	|	...	1951	1951	...	...	|	2020	2051	2052
Diss d.	1403	1427	1502	1526	1603	1626	1703	1729	1800	1803	1823	1826	...	1903	1903	1927	1926	...	2003	2003	...	...	2028	2032	2103	2104
Norwich a.	1420	1447	1520	1546	1620	1647	1720	1750	1819	1820	1841	1843	...	1923	1920	1946	1943	...	2020	2023	...	...	2046	2050	2120	2121

	⑥ 2	⑥ 2	Ⓐ 2	⚒ 2	⑥ 2L	Ⓐ 2L	⑥ 2	Ⓐ	⚒ 2	⑥	Ⓐ	⚒ 2	⑥	Ⓐ	⚒ 2	⑥	Ⓐ	⑦	⑦ 2	⑦ 2	⑦	⑦ 2	⑦ 2C	⑦	⑦ 2P	⑦ 2
London Liverpool Street d.	1936	2000	2000	2030	...	...	2100	2100	2102	2130	2130	2200	2230	2230	2302	2330	2330		0644	...	...	...	...	0810	...	0907
Chelmsford d.	2009	|	|	2100	...	...	|	|	2134	2201	2200	2228	2301	2303	2334	2359	0001		0725	...	...	...	...	|	...	0942
Colchester d.	2032	2047	2050	2120	...	...	2148	2147	2204	2220	2220	2247	2320	2322	0004	0021	0021		0748	0813	...	0818	...	0916	0925	1011
Manningtree ★ d.	2040	2055	2058	2128	...	...	2156	2155	2212	2228	2229	2255	2328	2330	0012	0029	0029		0756	0821	...	0827	...	0924	0933	1019
Harwich Int'l ★ d.	2055	|	|	|	2138	2147	|	|	2227	|	|	|	|	|	|	|	|		0811	|	...	0844	0850	|	|	|
Harwich Town ★ a.	...	|	|	|	|	|	|	|	...	|	|	|	|	|	|	|	|		...	|	...	0849	|	|	|	|
Ipswich 205 d.	...	2106	2109	2139	2204	2213	2207	2207	...	2239	2243	2307	2339	2342	0030v	0041	0045c		...	0832	0842	...	0920c	0936	0955t	1030
Stowmarket 205 d.	...	|	2120	2151	...	...	...	2218	...	2251	2255	...	2351	2353	...	0052	0057		...	...	0853	...	0934	0947	1006	...
Diss d.	...	2126	2132	2203	...	...	...	2230	...	2303	2307	...	0003	0009	...	0105	0110		...	...	0905	...	...	0959	...	...
Norwich a.	...	2143	2149	2221	...	...	...	2248	...	2320	2326	...	0020	0027	...	0122	0133		...	...	0924	...	...	1017	...	...

	⑦	⑦ 2	⑦	⑦ 2	⑦ 2	⑦		⑦ 2	⑦	⑦ 2	⑦ 2	⑦	⑦	⑦ 2	⑦	⑦ 2	⑦ 2	⑦	⑦ 2	⑦ 2	⑦	⑦ 2	⑦	⑦ 2	⑦
London Liverpool Street d.	0930	1007	1030	1100	1107	1130	and	1707	1730	1800	1807	1830	1900	1907	1930	2000	2007	2030	...	2107	2130	2207	2230	2307	2330
Chelmsford d.	|	1042	|	|	1142	|	at	1742	|	|	1842	|	|	1942	|	2032	2042	|	...	2142	|	2242	|	2342	|
Colchester d.	1017	1111	1117	1144	1211	1217	the	1811	1817	1844	1911	1917	1944	2011	2017	2055	2111	2117	...	2211	2217	2311	2317	0011	0017
Manningtree ★ d.	1025	1119	1125	|	1219	1225	same	1819	1825	|	1919	1925	1952	2019	2025	2103	2119	2125	...	2219	2225	2319	2326	0019	0026
Harwich Int'l ★ d.	|	|	|	|	|	|	minutes	|	|	|	|	|	|	|	|	2119	|	|	2138	|	|	|	|	|	|
Harwich Town ★ a.	|	|	|	|	|	|	past	|	|	|	|	|	|	|	|	...	|	|	|	|	|	|	|	|	|
Ipswich 205 d.	1036	1133	1137	1201	1230	1236	each	1830	1836	1901	1930	1936	2003	2030	2036	...	2130	2136	2204	2231	2236	2331	2338	0031	0038
Stowmarket 205 d.	1048	...	1148	1213	...	1248	hour	...	1848	1912	...	1948	2014	...	2048	...	...	2148	...	...	2248	...	2349	...	0050
Diss d.	1100	...	1200	1225	...	1300	until	...	1900	1924	...	2000	2026	...	2100	...	...	2200	...	...	2300	...	0001	...	0103
Norwich a.	1117	...	1218	1243	...	1317		...	1917	1941	...	2017	2044	...	2117	...	...	2217	...	...	2318	...	0019	...	0120

	⚒	Ⓐ 2	⑥ 2	Ⓐ 2	Ⓐ	⑥	⑥	Ⓐ	⚒ 2	⚒ M	⑥ 2	Ⓐ 2	⑥ 2	⑥	Ⓐ		Ⓐ 2	Ⓐ	⑥	⑥ 2	Ⓐ 2	⑥	Ⓐ	⚒	⚒	⚒
Norwich d.		...	0500	0505	0530	0532	0600	0604	...	...	0632	0628	...	0700	0705	...	...	0726	0732	0800	0803	0832	0830	0903	0932	1000
Diss d.		...	0517	0522	0547	0549	0617	0621	...	...	0649	0645	...	0717	0722	...	...	0744	0749	0817	0820	0849	0847	0920	0949	1017
Stowmarket 205 d.		...	0529	0534	0559	|	0629	0633	...	...	|	0657	...	0729	0734	...	...	0756	|	0829	0832	|	|	0932	|	1029
Ipswich 205 d.		0512	0541	0546	0611	0610	0641	0645	0652	0658	0710	0709	...	0741	0748	...	...	0813	0810	0841	0844	0910	0910	0944	1010	1041
Harwich Town ★ d.		|	|	|	|	|	|	|	|	|	|	|	...	|	|	...	0755	|	|	|	|	|	|	|	|	|
Harwich Int'l ★ d.		|	|	|	|	|	|	|	|	0727	|	|	0720	|	|	...	0800	|	|	|	|	|	|	|	|	|
Manningtree ★ d.		0523	0550	0556	0620	0619	0650	0655	0702	...	0720	0719	0733	0751	0757	...	0817	0822	0820	0851	0853	0920	0919	0954	1019	1051
Colchester d.		0533	0559	0606	0630	0628	0659	0705	0712	...	0730	0730	0743	0801	0808	...	0835t	0832	0830	0901	0903	0930	0930	1003	1030	1101
Chelmsford d.		0556	0618	|	|	|	0718	|	0739	...	|	|	0809	0819	|	...	0857	|	|	0919	0921	|	|	1021	|	1118
London Liverpool Street a.		0632	0651	0654	0722	0715	0751	0758	0817	...	0815	0824	0846	0851	0859	...	0938	0925	0915	0951	1000	1015	1019	1055	1118	1151

	⚒	⚒	⚒ 2	⚒	⚒	⚒ 2	⚒	⚒		⚒	⑥	Ⓐ	⚒	⑥	Ⓐ	⚒ 2	⑥	Ⓐ	⚒	⑥ 2	Ⓐ 2	⚒	⑥	Ⓐ	⑥ 2	Ⓐ 2
Norwich d.	1030	1100	1132	1200	1232	1300	1330	1400	...	1430	1500	1500	1530	1600	1600	1630	1703	1703	1730	1800	1800	1832	1900	1900	...	1932
Diss d.	1047	1117	1149	1217	1249	1317	1348	1417	...	1447	1517	1517	1548	1617	1617	1648	1720	1720	1747	1817	1817	1849	1917	1917	...	1949
Stowmarket 205 d.	|	1129	|	1229	|	1329	|	1429	...	|	1529	1529	|	1629	1629	|	1732	1733	1759	1829	1829	|	1929	1929	...	|
Ipswich 205 d.	1110	1141	1210	1241	1310	1341	1410	1441	...	1509	1541	1543	1610	1641	1642	1710	1744	1749	1811	1841	1842	1910	1941	1942	2009	2010
Harwich Town ★ d.	|	|	|	|	|	|	|	|	...	|	|	|	|	|	|	|	|	|	|	|	|	|	|	|	|	|
Harwich Int'l ★ d.	|	|	|	|	|	|	|	|	...	|	|	|	|	|	|	|	|	|	|	|	|	|	|	|	|	|
Manningtree ★ d.	1119	1151	1219	1251	1319	1350	1419	1451	...	1519	1551	1553	1619	1651	1652	1719	1754	|	1820	1851	1852	1919	1951	1953	2019	2020
Colchester d.	1130	1201	1230	1301	1330	1401	1430	1501	...	1530	1601	1603	1630	1701	1704	1730	1803	1806	1830	1901	1903	1930	2001	2002	2029	2030
Chelmsford d.	|	1218	|	1319	|	1419	|	1519	...	|	1619	1621	|	1719	1721	|	1821	1823	|	1919	1921	|	2019	2020	|	|
London Liverpool Street a.	1215	1251	1315	1351	1416	1451	1517	1551	...	1615	1651	1657	1718	1751	1758	1820b	1853	1858	1916	1951	1953	2020b	2051	2054	2115	2119

	⑥	Ⓐ	⚒ 2	⚒ C	⑥ 2	Ⓐ	⚒ 2P	⑥	Ⓐ	⚒ 2	⑥	Ⓐ		⚒ 2P	⑥ 2	Ⓐ 2	⚒ 2	⑦	⑦ 2	⑦	⑦ 2	⑦ 2	⑦	⑦ 2	⑦ 2	⑦
Norwich d.	2000	2000	...	...	...	2032	...	2100	2102	...	2200	2202	...	...	...	...	2305		...	0657	...	...	0800	0825	...	0900
Diss d.	2017	2017	...	...	...	2049	...	2117	2119	...	2217	2219	...	...	...	...	2323		...	0714	...	...	0817	0842	...	0917
Stowmarket 205 d.	2029	2029	...	2046	...	|	2115	2129	2131	...	2229	2231	...	2310	...	...	2335		...	0725	...	...	0829	0854	...	0929
Ipswich 205 d.	2041	2045c	...	2101	2109	2110	2128	2141	2144	2223	2241	2243	...	2322	...	...	2349		...	0737	0752	0811	0841	0906	0911	0941
Harwich Town ★ d.	|	|	...	|	|	|	|	|	|	|	|	|	...	|	2326	2328	...		...	|	|	|	|	|	|	|
Harwich Int'l ★ d.	|	|	2045	2129	|	|	|	|	|	|	|	|	...	|	2331	2333	...		0720	|	0815	|	|	|	|	|
Manningtree ★ d.	2051	2054	2058	...	2119	2120	2137	2151	2153	2233	2251	2253	...	2331	2348	2350	...		0733	0746	...	0821	0851	|	0921	0951
Colchester d.	2101	2103	2112c	...	2129	2130	2150	2301	2203	2243	2301	2303	...	2342	2357	2359	...		0742	0756	...	0830	0900	0922	0930	1000
Chelmsford d.	2119	2121	2140	...	|	|	...	2324	2221	2309	2324	2325	...	...	...	...	...		0804	|	...	0859	|	|	0959	|
London Liverpool Street a.	2151	2155	2214	...	2215	2218	...	2358	2255	2348	2358	0003	...	...	...	...	...		0858	0900	...	0935	0947	1007	1035	1047

		⑦ 2	⑦	⑦ 2	⑦ 2	⑦	⑦	⑦ 2	⑦	⑦ 2	⑦	⑦ 2	⑦ 2P	⑦	⑦ 2	⑦ 2	⑦	⑦ 2C	⑦ 2	⑦ 2P	⑦	⑦ 2	⑦	⑦ 2	⑦ 2
Norwich d.	and	...	1500	1523	...	1600	1623	...	1700	...	1800	...	...	1900	...	...	2000	...	...	...	2100	...	2205	...	2305
Diss d.	at	...	1517	1540	...	1617	1640	...	1717	...	1817	...	...	1917	...	...	2017	...	...	...	2117	...	2222	...	2322
Stowmarket 205 d.	the	...	1529	1552	...	1629	1652	...	1729	...	1829	...	1912	1929	...	...	2029	2046	...	2111	2129	...	2234	...	2334
Ipswich 205 d.	same	1511	1541	1605	1611	1641	1705	1711	1741	1811	1841	1911	1925	1941	2011	...	2041	2103	2111	2123	2141	2211	2246	...	2346
Harwich Town ★ d.	minutes	|	|	|	|	|	|	|	|	|	|	|	|	|	|	...	|	|	|	|	|	|	|	2254	...
Harwich Int'l ★ d.	past	|	|	|	|	|	|	|	|	|	|	|	|	|	|	2030	|	2126	|	|	|	|	|	2259	...
Manningtree ★ d.	each	1521	1551	|	1621	1651	|	1721	1751	1821	1851	1921	1934	1951	2021	2043	2051	...	2120	2132	2151	2221	2255	2315	...
Colchester d.	hour	1530	1600	1621	1630	1700	1721	1730	1800	1830	1900	1930	1943	2000	2030	2052	2100	...	2130	2142	2200	2230	2304	2325	...
Chelmsford d.	until	1559	|	|	1659	|	|	1759	|	1859	|	1959	...	|	2059	2110	|	...	2159	...	|	2259	2325	...	...
London Liverpool Street a.		1635	1647	1709	1735	1747	1809	1835	1847	1935	1947	2035	...	2047	2135	2144	2147	...	2235	...	2247	2335	2359	...	...

C – To/from Cambridge (Table **205**).
P – To/from Peterborough (Table **205**).
L – To Lowestoft (Table **201**).
M – From Lowestoft on Ⓐ (Table **201**).

a – Departs 3 minutes later on Ⓐ.

b – Arrives 5 minutes earlier on ⑥.
c – Arrives 5–6 minutes earlier.
f – Arrives 0815 on ⑥.
r – Departs 5 minutes later on ⑥.
t – Arrives 8–11 minutes earlier.
v – Arrives 0024 on ⑥.

★ – All trains Manningtree - Harwich International - Harwich Town and v.v.

Manningtree - Harwich Town: on Ⓐ at 0553, 0701, 0722, 0801, 0859 and hourly until 1859, 2000, 2101, 2200, 2300, 2335; on ⑥ at 0556, 0659 and hourly until 2259, 2335; on ⑦ at 0827 and hourly until 2227.

Harwich Town - Manningtree on Ⓐ at 0524, 0626, 0728, 0755, 0828, 0926 and hourly until 1826, 1928, 2028, 2128, 2228, 2328; on ⑥ at 0626 and hourly until 2326; on ⑦ at 0854 and hourly until 2254.

201 IPSWICH - LOWESTOFT — 2nd class only — LE

km			Ⓐ	Ⓐ	Ⓐ		Ⓐ	Ⓐ	Ⓐ	Ⓐ	Ⓐ		Ⓐ H		⑥	◧	⑥ H		⑦	⑦	⑦	⑦	and in	⑦	⑦	⑦
0	**Ipswich** d.	Ⓐ	0620	0734	0916		1516	1554	1717	1813	1917		2216	⑥	0716		2215	⑦	1008	1110	1208	1310	the same	2010	2108	2202
17	Woodbridge d.		0637	0751	0931	and	1531	1617f	1732	1830	1932	and	2231		0731	and	2230		1025	1125	1225	1325	pattern	2025	2125	2219
36	Saxmundham d.		0744r	0813	0953	hourly	1553	1639	1754	1851	1954	hourly	2253		0753	hourly	2252		1047	1147	1247	1347	every	2047	2147	2240
65	Beccles d.		0815	0844	1024	until	1624	1718f	1825	1925	2025	until	2324		0824	until	2323		1118	1218	1318	1418	**two** hours	2118	2218	2311
79	**Lowestoft** a.		0833	0903	1042		1642	1736	1843	1943	2043		2342		0844		2341		1136	1236	1336	1436	until	2136	2236	2330

		Ⓐ H	Ⓐ	Ⓐ	Ⓐ	Ⓐ	Ⓐ	Ⓐ		Ⓐ	Ⓐ	Ⓐ	Ⓐ	Ⓐ	Ⓐ	Ⓐ		⑥		⑥		⑦	⑦	⑦	⑦		⑦
Lowestoft d.	Ⓐ	0524	0614	0640	0728	0907	1007	1106		1506	1606	1702	1807	1907	2007	2107	⑥	0606		2106	⑦	0805	0905	1005	1100		2000
Beccles d.		0540	0630	0656	0744	0925	1025	1124	and	1524	1627f	1725f	1825	1925	2025	2125		0624	and	2124		0821	0921	1021	1121f	and	2021f
Saxmundham d.		0611	0702	0727	0815	0956	1056	1155	hourly	1555	1705f	1756	1856	1956	2056	2156		0655	hourly	2155		0852	0952	1052	1152	hourly	2052
Woodbridge d.		0634	0725	0750	0838	1018	1118	1217	until	1617	1726	1818	1918	2018	2118	2218		0717	until	2217		0914	1014	1114	1214	until	2114
Ipswich a.		0652	0743	0808	0856	1035	1136	1235		1636	1743	1836	1936	2036	2136	2235		0735		2235		0931	1031	1131	1231		2131

H – To/from Harwich International (Table **200**). f – Arrives 6–8 minutes earlier. r – Arrives 0658. ◧ – The 1616 departure from Ipswich arrives Lowestoft at 1750.

203 NORWICH and IPSWICH local services — 2nd class — LE

NORWICH - GREAT YARMOUTH — Journey time ± 32 minutes — *30 km (33 km via Reedham)*

From Norwich: Trains noted '**r**' call at **Reedham** 18–21 minutes later.

Ⓐ: 0508, 0611, 0652, 0736r, 0836, 0936, 1035, 1134r, 1234, 1334, 1440, 1536, 1640, 1706, 1736, 1840, 1940, 2040, 2140, 2300.

⑥: 0530r, 0636, 0706, 0736r, 0809, 0836, 0936, 1034, 1134r, 1234, 1334, 1434, 1534, 1640, 1706, 1734, 1806, 1840, 1940, 2040, 2140, 2300.

⑦: 0736r, 0845 and the service repeats at the same times **every 2 hours** until 2136r, 2236.

From Great Yarmouth: Trains noted '**r**' call at **Reedham** 12–14 minutes later.

Ⓐ: 0543, 0624, 0658, 0732, 0817, 0917, 1017, 1117, 1217, 1317, 1417, 1517r, 1617, 1717, 1747r, 1817, 1917, 2017, 2117, 2217, 2334r.

⑥: 0615, 0717, 0745, 0817, 0847, 0917, 1017, 1117, 1217, 1317, 1417, 1512r, 1617, 1717, 1747r, 1817, 1847r, 1917, 2017, 2117, 2217, 2334r.

⑦: 0817r, 0922 and the service repeats at the same times **every 2 hours** until 2217r, 2317r.

NORWICH - LOWESTOFT — Journey time ± 43 minutes — *38 km*

From Norwich: Trains noted '**r**' call at **Reedham** 18–21 minutes later.

Ⓐ: 0536r, 0623r, 0645r, 0755r, 0855, 1005r, 1058, 1205r, 1255, 1405r, 1455r, 1550r, 1658r, 1750r, 1902r, 2005r, 2105r, 2205r, 2240r.

⑥: 0540r, 0650r, 0750r, 0855, 1005r, 1058, 1205r, 1258, 1405r, 1458r, 1555r, 1656r, 1750r, 1905r, 2005r, 2105r, 2205r, 2240r.

⑦: 0725, 0805r, 0907, 1005r, 1107, 1205r, 1307, 1405r, 1507, 1605r, 1707, 1805r, 1907, 2005r, 2058r.

From Lowestoft: Trains noted '**r**' call at **Reedham** 20–23 minutes later.

Ⓐ: 0537r, 0635r, 0733r, 0750r, 0850r, 0948r, 1057, 1148r, 1257, 1348r, 1457, 1548r, 1648r, 1748r, 1848r, 1955r, 2057, 2148r, 2248r, 2330r.

⑥: 0639r, 0740r, 0848r, 0948r, 1057, 1148r, 1257, 1348r, 1457, 1548r, 1648r, 1748r, 1848r, 1955r, 2057, 2148r, 2248r, 2330r.

⑦: 0859r, 0946r, 1105, 1146r, 1305, 1346r, 1505, 1546r, 1705, 1746r, 1905, 1946r, 2105, 2146r, 2335r.

NORWICH - SHERINGHAM (🚂) — Journey time ± 57 minutes — *49 km*

From Norwich:
Trains call at **Hoveton and Wroxham** 🚂 ± 15 minutes, and **Cromer** ± 45 minutes later.

⚒: 0511 Ⓐ, 0520 ⑥, 0540 Ⓐ, 0545 ⑥, 0715, 0821, 0945 and hourly until 1745, 1855, 2000, 2115, 2245 ①–④, 2305 ⑤⑥.

⑦: 0839, 0945, 1039, 1145, 1239, 1345, 1439, 1545, 1639, 1745, 1839, 1945, 2039.

From Sheringham:
Trains call at **Cromer** ± 11 minutes, and **Hoveton and Wroxham** 🚂 ± 39 minutes later.

⚒: 0007 ⑥, 0622 ⑥, 0618 Ⓐ, 0714Ⓐ, 0717⑥, 0822, 0943, 1046, 1143, 1246, 1343, 1446, 1545, 1648, 1748, 1851, 1954, 2109, 2217, 2347 ①–④ (also 0551 Ⓐ from Cromer).

⑦: 0007, 0942, 1043, 1142, 1243, 1342, 1443, 1542, 1643, 1742, 1843, 1942, 2043, 2143.

IPSWICH - FELIXSTOWE — Journey time ± 25 minutes — *25 km*

From Ipswich:

Ⓐ: 0504, 0604, 0714, 0825, 0857, 0958 and hourly until 2058, 2228.

⑥: 0558, 0658, 0758 and hourly until 2058, 2228.

⑦: 0955, 1055 and hourly until 1955.

From Felixstowe:

Ⓐ: 0534, 0636, 0747, 0854, 0928 and hourly until 2128, 2301.

⑥: 0628, 0728, 0828 and hourly until 2128, 2258.

⑦: 1025, 1125 and hourly until 2025.

r – Via Reedham.

🚂 – Heritage and Tourist railways:
NORTH NORFOLK RAILWAY: Sheringham - Holt and v.v. *8 km.* ✆ 01263 820800. www.nnrailway.co.uk
BURE VALLEY STEAM RAILWAY: Wroxham - Aylsham and v.v. ✆ 01263 733858. www.bvrw.co.uk

204 IPSWICH - CAMBRIDGE and PETERBOROUGH — 2nd class only — LE

km			Ⓐ	⑥	⚒C	Ⓐ	⑥	Ⓐ	⑥	⑥	Ⓐ	Ⓐ H	⑥ H	⚒	⑥	Ⓐ	⚒	⚒	Ⓐ	⑥	⚒	⚒	Ⓐ	⑥	⚒	⚒	⑥
0	**Ipswich** 200 d.	⚒	0510	0511	0600	0617	0619	0656	0720	0758	0801	0819	0821	0921	0958	1001	1021	1121	1156	1200	1221	1321	1358	1402	1420	1521	1558
19	Stowmarket 200 d.		0522	0525	0611	0631	0633	0710	0735	0809	0812	0834	0835	0936	1009	1012	1035	1135	1207	1211	1235	1335	1409	1412	1435	1535	1609
42	Bury St Edmunds d.		0543	0548	0629	0653	0654	0732	0758	0829	0830	0857	0859	0959	1029	1030	1059	1159	1228	1229	1259	1359	1429	1429	1459	1559	1629r
65	Newmarket d.		0602	0607	|	0713	0718r	0751	0818	|	|	0918	0918	1019	|	|	1118	1219	|	|	1318	1419	|	|	1518	1619	|
88	**Cambridge** 208 a.		0627	0630	|	0737	0740	0818	0841	|	|	0941	0940	1041	|	|	1141	1240	|	|	1341	1440	|	|	1541	1640	|
73	Soham d.		...	...	0649	...	...	...	...	0849	0850	...	...	...	1050	1049	...	...	1251	1249	...	...	1449	1449	...	...	1650
82	Ely 208 a.		...	...	0657	...	...	...	...	0858	0859	...	...	...	1059	1058	...	...	1259	1258	...	...	1458	1458	...	...	1659
108	March 208 a.		...	...	0716	...	...	...	...	0918	0918	...	...	...	1118	1117	...	...	1319	1318	...	...	1518	1518	...	...	1718
132	**Peterborough** 208 a.		...	...	0738	...	...	...	...	0939	0940	...	...	...	1140	1139	...	...	1340	1339	...	...	1540	1539	...	...	1740

	Ⓐ	⚒	⚒	Ⓐ	⑥	⚒	Ⓐ	⑥	⑥	Ⓐ	⚒	⚒	⚒		⑦	⑦	⑦ H	⑦ C	⑦	⑦	⑦		⑦	⑦	⑦	⑦
Ipswich 200 d.	1600	1621	1721	1742	1758	1821	1914	1921	2000	2001	2021	2120	2221	⑦	0736	0820	0920	0955	1020	1120	1155		1755	1820	1920	2105
Stowmarket 200 d.	1612	1635	1736	1755	1809	1835	1927	1935	2011	2013	2035	2135	2235		0750	0834	0934	1006	1034	1134	1207	and in	1807	1834	1934	2119
Bury St Edmunds d.	1629	1658	1758	1825f	1829r	1859	1959t	1959	2029	2030	2059	2159	2256		0811	0857	0957	1023	1057	1157	1225	the same	1825	1857	1957	2140
Newmarket d.	|	1718	1818	|	|	1918	2019	2019	|	|	2118	2219	...		0830	0914	1017	|	1116	1217	|	pattern	|	1916	2017	2159
Cambridge 208 a.	|	1741	1840	|	|	1940	2041	2041	|	|	2140	2242	...		0854	0937	1039	|	1138	1239	|	every	|	1938	2039	2224
Soham d.	1650	...	...	1846	1849	...	...	...	2049	2051	...	...	...		...	...	...	1042	...	...	1244	**two** hours	1844	...	...	...
Ely 208 a.	1659	...	...	1857	1858	...	...	...	2058	2059	...	...	...		...	...	...	1051	...	...	1253	until	1853	...	...	...
March 208 a.	1718	...	...	1918	1918	...	...	...	2118	2118	...	...	...		...	...	...	1112	...	...	1312		1912	...	...	...
Peterborough 208 a.	1741	...	...	1940	1939	...	...	...	2139	2139	...	...	...		...	...	...	1133	...	...	1334		1934	...	...	...

		Ⓐ	⑥	Ⓐ	Ⓐ	⑥	Ⓐ	⑥	⚒	⑥	Ⓐ	⚒	⑥	Ⓐ	⚒	⚒	⚒	⚒	⚒	⚒	⚒	⚒	⑥	Ⓐ	⑥	Ⓐ	⚒
Peterborough 208 d.	⚒	...	...	...	...	...	...	...	0750	...	...	...	0950	0950	...	...	1150	...	...	1350	...	...	1551	1550	...	...	...
March 208 d.		...	...	...	...	...	...	...	0810	...	...	...	1010	1010	...	...	1210	...	...	1410	...	...	1611	1610	...	...	...
Ely 208 d.		...	...	...	...	...	...	...	0831	...	...	...	1031	1032	...	...	1232	...	...	1431	...	...	1631	1631	...	...	...
Soham d.		...	...	...	...	...	...	...	0838	...	...	...	1039	1039	...	...	1239	...	...	1438	...	...	1639	1639	...	...	...
Cambridge 208 d.		...	...	...	0641	0642	0743	0746	|	0847	0847	0947	|	|	1047	1147	|	1247	1347	|	1447	1547	|	|	1646	1646	1746
Newmarket d.		...	...	...	0702	0703	0804	0807	|	0907	0907	1008	|	|	1107	1208	|	1307	1408	|	1507	1608	|	|	1707	1707	1807
Bury St Edmunds d.		0530	0625	0626	0726r	0726r	0826	0826	0859	0926	0926	1026	1100	1101	1126	1226	1300	1326	1426	1459	1526	1626	1700	1659	1727	1727	1827
Stowmarket 200 d.		0550	0645	0646	0746	0747	0847	0847	0914	0947	0947	1047	1115	1116	1147	1247	1315	1347	1447	1514	1547	1647	1715	1714	1747	1748	1847
Ipswich 200 a.		0605	0659	0701	0801	0802	0902	0902	0927	1002	1005	1102	1127	1128	1202	1302	1328	1402	1502	1527	1602	1702	1727	1727	1802	1804	1902

	⑥	Ⓐ	⑥	Ⓐ	⚒H	Ⓐ C	⑥ C	⚒		⚒	Ⓐ C	⑥ C	⚒		⑦	⑦	⑦	⑦	⑦		⑦ C	⑦	⑦ H	⑦ C	⑦	⑦
Peterborough 208 d.	1751	1750	...	...	...	1950	1952	...	...	...	2146	2147	...	⑦	...	...	...	...	1144	★	1741	...	...	1945	...	...
March 208 d.	1811	1810	...	...	...	2010	2012	...	...	...	2206	2207	...		...	...	...	...	1204		1801	...	...	2005	...	...
Ely 208 d.	1831	1831	...	...	...	2032	2033	...	...	...	2227	2227	...		...	...	...	...	1228	and in	1829	...	...	2027	...	...
Soham d.	1839	1839	...	...	...	2039	2040	...	...	...	2234	2235	...		...	...	...	...	1236	the same	1836	...	...	2035	...	...
Cambridge 208 d.	|	|	1847	1847	1947	|	|	2047	...	2147	|	|	2247		0900	0945	1045	1145	|	pattern	|	1845	1945	|	2045	2250
Newmarket d.	|	|	1907	1907	2008	|	|	2107	...	2208	|	|	2308		0926	1006	1105	1206	|	every	|	1905	2006	|	2106	2311
Bury St Edmunds d.	1900	1859	1926	1926	2026	2100	2101	2126	...	2226	2255	2255	2328		0946	1024	1124	1224	1257	**two** hours	1857	1924	2024	2056	2126	2331
Stowmarket 200 d.	1915	1915	1947	1947	2046	2115	2116	2147	...	2247	2310	2310	2348		1006	1045	1145	1245	1312	until	1912	1945	2046	2111	2145	2350
Ipswich 200 a.	1927	1927	2002	2004	2102	2128	2127	2202	...	2302	2321	2321	0002		1023	1100	1200	1300	1325		1924	2000	2103	2123	2200	0005

C – To/from Colchester (Table **200**).
H – To/from Harwich International (Table **200**).
f – Arrives 1817.
r – Arrives 4–5 minutes earlier.
t – Arrives 1948.
★ – Peterborough d. 1350 (not 1344), then March d. 1410, Ely d. 1432, Soham d. 1439, Bury St Edmunds d. 1500, Stowmarket d. 1515, Ipswich a. 1527.

EM 2nd class NORWICH - NOTTINGHAM - SHEFFIELD - MANCHESTER - LIVERPOOL 206

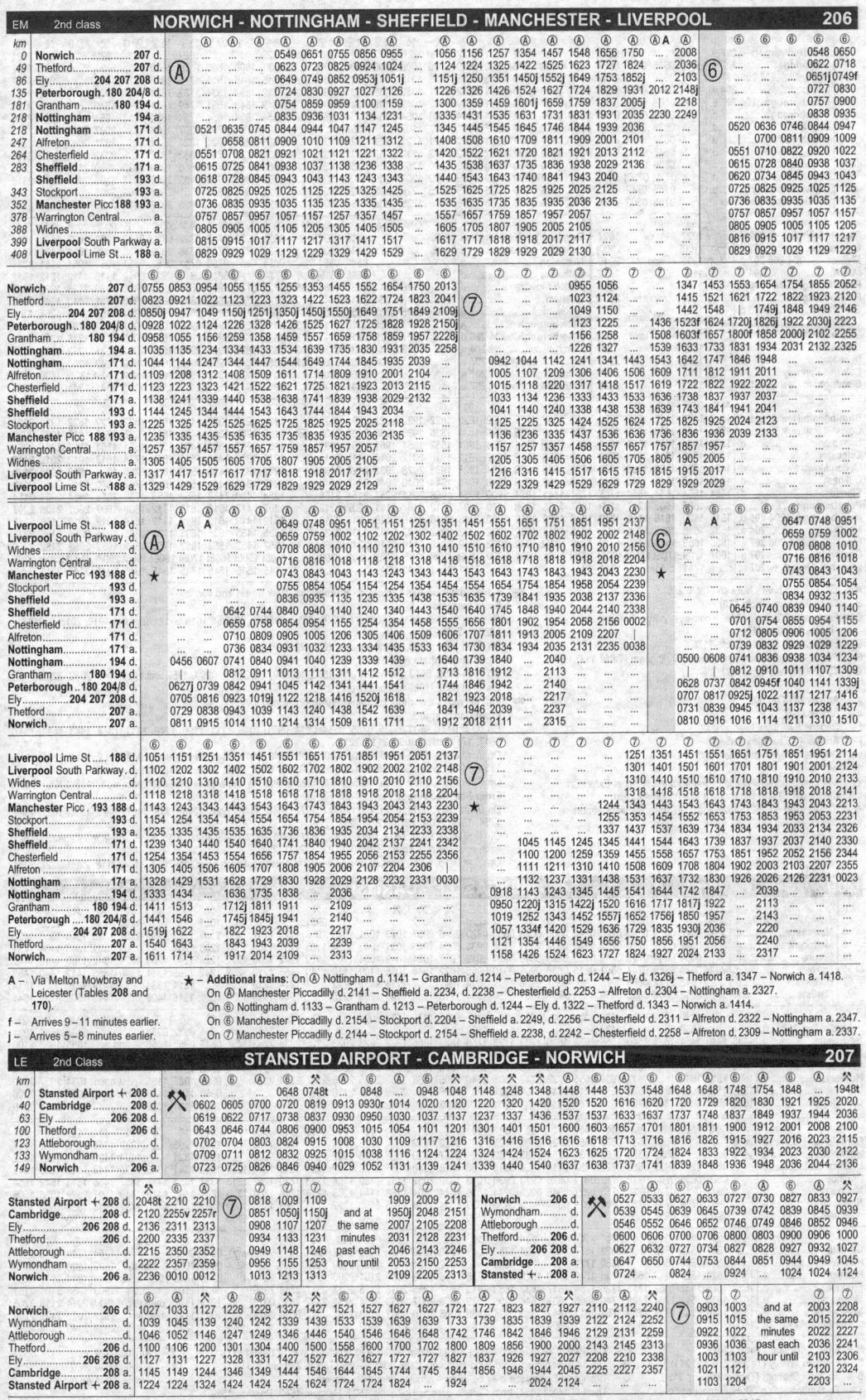

km			Ⓐ	Ⓐ	Ⓐ	Ⓐ	Ⓐ	Ⓐ	Ⓐ	Ⓐ		Ⓐ	Ⓐ	Ⓐ	Ⓐ	Ⓐ	Ⓐ	Ⓐ	Ⓐ	Ⓐ A	Ⓐ		⑥	⑥	⑥	⑥	⑥
0	**Norwich** 207 d.		...	...	...	0549	0651	0755	0856	0955	...	1056	1156	1257	1354	1457	1548	1656	1750	...	2008		...	...	...	0548	0650
49	Thetford 207 d.		...	...	...	0623	0723	0825	0924	1024	...	1124	1224	1325	1422	1525	1623	1727	1824	...	2036	⑥	...	...	...	0622	0718
86	Ely 204 207 208 d.	Ⓐ	...	...	...	0649	0749	0852	0953j	1051j	...	1151j	1250	1351	1450j	1552j	1649	1753	1852j	...	2103		...	...	...	0651j	0749f
135	**Peterborough** 180 204/8 d.		...	...	...	0724	0830	0927	1027	1126	...	1226	1326	1426	1524	1627	1724	1829	1931	2012	2148j		...	...	...	0727	0830
181	Grantham 180 194 d.		...	...	...	0754	0859	0959	1100	1159	...	1300	1359	1459	1601j	1659	1759	1837	2005j	|	2218		...	...	...	0757	0900
218	**Nottingham** 194 a.		...	...	...	0835	0936	1031	1134	1231	...	1335	1431	1535	1631	1731	1831	1931	2035	2230	2249		...	...	...	0838	0935
218	**Nottingham** 171 d.		0521	0635	0745	0844	0944	1047	1147	1245	...	1345	1445	1545	1645	1746	1844	1939	2036	...	...		0520	0636	0746	0844	0947
247	Alfreton 171 d.		|	0658	0811	0909	1010	1109	1211	1312	...	1408	1508	1610	1709	1811	1909	2001	2101	...	...		|	0700	0811	0909	1009
264	Chesterfield 171 d.		0551	0708	0821	0921	1021	1121	1221	1322	...	1420	1522	1621	1720	1821	1921	2013	2112	...	...		0551	0710	0822	0920	1022
283	**Sheffield** 171 a.		0615	0725	0841	0938	1037	1138	1236	1338	...	1435	1538	1637	1735	1836	1938	2029	2136	...	...		0615	0728	0840	0938	1037
	Sheffield 193 d.		0618	0728	0845	0943	1043	1143	1243	1343	...	1440	1543	1643	1740	1841	1943	2040	...	...	...		0620	0734	0845	0943	1043
343	Stockport 193 a.		0725	0825	0925	1025	1125	1225	1325	1425	...	1525	1625	1725	1825	1925	2025	2125	...	...	...		0725	0825	0925	1025	1125
352	**Manchester** Picc 188 193 a.		0736	0835	0935	1035	1135	1235	1335	1435	...	1535	1635	1735	1835	1935	2036	2135	...	...	...		0736	0835	0935	1035	1135
378	Warrington Central a.		0757	0857	0957	1057	1157	1257	1357	1457	...	1557	1657	1759	1857	1957	2057	...	...	...	...		0757	0857	0957	1057	1157
388	Widnes a.		0805	0905	1005	1105	1205	1305	1405	1505	...	1605	1705	1807	1905	2005	2105	...	...	...	...		0805	0905	1005	1105	1205
399	**Liverpool** South Parkway a.		0815	0915	1017	1117	1217	1317	1417	1517	...	1617	1717	1818	1918	2017	2117	...	...	...	...		0816	0915	1017	1117	1217
408	**Liverpool** Lime St 188 a.		0829	0929	1029	1129	1229	1329	1429	1529	...	1629	1729	1829	1929	2029	2130	...	...	...	...		0829	0929	1029	1129	1229

	⑥	⑥	⑥	⑥	⑥	⑥	⑥	⑥	⑥	⑥	⑥	⑥		⑦	⑦	⑦	⑦	⑦	⑦	⑦	⑦	⑦	⑦	⑦	⑦	⑦	⑦
Norwich 207 d.	0755	0853	0954	1055	1155	1255	1353	1455	1552	1654	1750	2013		...	...	...	0955	1056	...	...	1347	1453	1553	1654	1754	1855	2052
Thetford 207 d.	0823	0921	1022	1123	1223	1323	1422	1523	1622	1724	1823	2041		...	...	...	1023	1124	...	...	1415	1521	1621	1722	1822	1923	2120
Ely 204 207 208 d.	0850j	0947	1049	1150j	1251j	1350j	1450j	1550j	1649	1751	1849	2109j	⑦	...	...	...	1049	1150	...	...	1442	1548	|	1749j	1848	1949	2146
Peterborough 180 204/8 d.	0928	1022	1124	1226	1328	1426	1525	1627	1725	1828	1928	2150j		...	...	...	1123	1225	...	1436	1523f	1624	1720j	1826j	1922	2030j	2223
Grantham 180 194 d.	0958	1055	1156	1259	1358	1459	1557	1659	1758	1859	1957	2228j		...	...	...	1156	1258	...	1508	1603f	1657	1800f	1858	2000j	2102	2255
Nottingham 194 a.	1035	1135	1234	1334	1433	1534	1639	1735	1830	1931	2035	2258		...	...	...	1226	1327	...	1539	1633	1733	1831	1934	2031	2132	2325
Nottingham 171 d.	1044	1144	1247	1344	1447	1544	1649	1744	1845	1935	2039	...		0942	1044	1142	1241	1341	1443	1543	1642	1747	1846	1948	...	...	...
Alfreton 171 d.	1109	1208	1312	1408	1509	1611	1714	1809	1910	2001	2104	...		1005	1107	1209	1306	1406	1506	1609	1711	1812	1911	2011	...	...	...
Chesterfield 171 d.	1123	1223	1323	1421	1522	1621	1725	1821	1923	2013	2115	...		1015	1118	1220	1317	1418	1517	1619	1722	1822	1922	2022	...	...	...
Sheffield 171 a.	1138	1241	1339	1440	1538	1638	1741	1839	1938	2029	2132	...		1033	1134	1236	1333	1433	1533	1636	1738	1837	1937	2037	...	...	...
Sheffield 193 d.	1144	1245	1344	1444	1543	1643	1744	1844	1943	2034	...	...		1041	1140	1240	1338	1438	1538	1639	1743	1841	1941	2041	...	...	...
Stockport 193 a.	1225	1325	1425	1525	1625	1725	1825	1925	2025	2118	...	...		1125	1225	1325	1424	1525	1624	1725	1825	1925	2024	2123	...	...	...
Manchester Picc 188 193 a.	1235	1335	1435	1535	1635	1735	1835	1935	2036	2135	...	...		1136	1236	1335	1437	1536	1636	1736	1836	1936	2039	2133	...	...	...
Warrington Central a.	1257	1357	1457	1557	1657	1759	1857	1957	2057	...	...	...		1157	1257	1357	1458	1557	1657	1757	1857	1957	...	...	...	...	...
Widnes a.	1305	1405	1505	1605	1705	1807	1905	2005	2105	...	...	...		1205	1305	1405	1506	1605	1705	1805	1905	2005	...	...	...	...	...
Liverpool South Parkway a.	1317	1417	1517	1617	1717	1818	1918	2017	2117	...	...	...		1216	1316	1415	1517	1615	1715	1815	1915	2017	...	...	...	...	...
Liverpool Lime St 188 a.	1329	1429	1529	1629	1729	1829	1929	2029	2129	...	...	...		1229	1329	1429	1529	1629	1729	1829	1929	2029	...	...	...	...	...

		Ⓐ	Ⓐ	Ⓐ	Ⓐ	Ⓐ	Ⓐ	Ⓐ	Ⓐ	Ⓐ	Ⓐ	Ⓐ	Ⓐ	Ⓐ	Ⓐ	Ⓐ	Ⓐ	Ⓐ	Ⓐ		⑥	⑥	⑥	⑥	⑥	⑥	⑥
Liverpool Lime St 188 d.		A	A	...	...	0649	0748	0951	1051	1151	1251	1351	1451	1551	1651	1751	1851	1951	2137		A	A	...	...	0647	0748	0951
Liverpool South Parkway d.	Ⓐ	...	...	...	...	0659	0759	1002	1102	1202	1302	1402	1502	1602	1702	1802	1902	2002	2148	⑥	...	...	...	...	0659	0759	1002
Widnes d.		...	...	...	...	0708	0808	1010	1110	1210	1310	1410	1510	1610	1710	1810	1910	2010	2156		...	...	...	...	0708	0808	1010
Warrington Central d.		...	...	...	...	0716	0816	1018	1118	1218	1318	1418	1518	1618	1718	1818	1918	2018	2204		...	...	...	...	0716	0816	1018
Manchester Picc 193 188 d.	★	...	...	...	...	0743	0843	1043	1143	1243	1343	1443	1543	1643	1743	1843	1943	2043	2230	★	...	...	...	...	0743	0843	1043
Stockport 193 d.		...	...	...	...	0755	0854	1054	1154	1254	1354	1454	1554	1654	1754	1854	1958	2054	2239		...	...	...	...	0755	0854	1054
Sheffield 193 a.		...	...	...	...	0836	0935	1135	1235	1335	1438	1535	1635	1739	1841	1935	2038	2137	2336		...	...	...	...	0834	0932	1135
Sheffield 171 d.		...	...	0642	0744	0840	0940	1140	1240	1340	1443	1540	1640	1745	1848	1940	2044	2140	2338		...	...	0645	0740	0839	0940	1140
Chesterfield 171 d.		...	...	0659	0758	0854	0954	1155	1254	1354	1458	1555	1656	1801	1902	1954	2058	2156	0002		...	...	0701	0754	0855	0954	1155
Alfreton 171 d.		...	...	0710	0809	0905	1005	1206	1305	1406	1509	1606	1707	1811	1913	2005	2109	2207	|		...	...	0712	0805	0906	1005	1206
Nottingham 171 a.		...	...	0736	0834	0931	1032	1233	1334	1435	1533	1634	1730	1834	1934	2035	2131	2235	0038		...	...	0739	0832	0929	1029	1229
Nottingham 194 d.		0456	0607	0741	0840	0941	1040	1239	1339	1439	...	1640	1739	1840	...	2040	...	...	...		0500	0608	0741	0836	0938	1034	1234
Grantham 180 194 d.		|	|	0812	0911	1013	1111	1311	1412	1512	...	1713	1816	1912	...	2113	...	...	...		|	|	0812	0910	1011	1107	1309
Peterborough 180 204/8 d.		0627j	0739	0842	0941	1045	1142	1341	1441	1541	...	1744	1846	1942	...	2140	...	...	...		0628	0737	0842	0945f	1040	1141	1339j
Ely 204 207 208 d.		0705	0816	0923	1019j	1122	1218	1416	1520j	1618	...	1821	1923	2018	...	2217	...	...	...		0707	0817	0925j	1022	1117	1217	1416
Thetford 207 a.		0729	0838	0943	1039	1143	1240	1438	1542	1639	...	1841	1946	2039	...	2237	...	...	...		0731	0839	0945	1043	1137	1238	1437
Norwich 207 a.		0811	0915	1014	1110	1214	1314	1509	1611	1711	...	1912	2018	2111	...	2315	...	...	...		0810	0916	1016	1114	1211	1310	1510

	⑥	⑥	⑥	⑥	⑥	⑥	⑥	⑥	⑥	⑥	⑥	⑥		⑦	⑦	⑦	⑦	⑦	⑦	⑦	⑦	⑦	⑦	⑦	⑦	⑦	⑦
Liverpool Lime St 188 d.	1051	1151	1251	1351	1451	1551	1651	1751	1851	1951	2051	2137		...	...	...	...	...	1251	1351	1451	1551	1651	1751	1851	1951	2114
Liverpool South Parkway d.	1102	1202	1302	1402	1502	1602	1702	1802	1902	2002	2102	2148		...	...	...	...	...	1301	1401	1501	1601	1701	1801	1901	2001	2124
Widnes d.	1110	1210	1310	1410	1510	1610	1710	1810	1910	2010	2110	2156	⑦	...	...	...	...	...	1310	1410	1510	1610	1710	1810	1910	2010	2133
Warrington Central d.	1118	1218	1318	1418	1518	1618	1718	1818	1918	2018	2118	2204		...	...	...	...	...	1318	1418	1518	1618	1718	1818	1918	2018	2141
Manchester Picc 193 188 d.	1143	1243	1343	1443	1543	1643	1743	1843	1943	2043	2143	2230	★	...	...	...	...	1244	1343	1443	1543	1643	1743	1843	1943	2043	2213
Stockport 193 d.	1154	1254	1354	1454	1554	1654	1754	1854	1954	2054	2153	2239		...	...	...	...	1255	1353	1454	1552	1653	1753	1853	1953	2053	2231
Sheffield 193 a.	1235	1335	1435	1535	1635	1736	1836	1935	2034	2134	2233	2338		...	...	...	...	1337	1437	1537	1639	1734	1834	1934	2033	2134	2326
Sheffield 171 d.	1239	1340	1440	1540	1640	1741	1840	1940	2042	2137	2241	2342		...	1045	1145	1245	1345	1441	1544	1643	1739	1837	1937	2037	2140	2330
Chesterfield 171 d.	1254	1354	1453	1554	1656	1757	1854	1955	2056	2153	2255	2356		...	1100	1200	1259	1359	1455	1558	1657	1753	1851	1952	2052	2156	2344
Alfreton 171 d.	1305	1405	1506	1605	1707	1808	1905	2006	2107	2204	2306	|		...	1111	1211	1310	1410	1508	1609	1708	1804	1902	2003	2103	2207	2355
Nottingham 171 a.	1328	1429	1531	1628	1729	1830	1928	2029	2128	2232	2331	0030		...	1132	1237	1331	1438	1531	1637	1732	1830	1926	2026	2126	2231	0023
Nottingham 194 d.	1333	1434	...	1636	1735	1838	...	2036	...	...	...	...		0918	1143	1243	1345	1445	1541	1644	1742	1847	...	2039	...	...	...
Grantham 180 194 d.	1411	1513	...	1712j	1811	1911	...	2109	...	...	...	...		0950	1220j	1315	1422j	1520	1616	1717	1817j	1922	...	2113	...	...	...
Peterborough 180 204/8 d.	1441	1546	...	1745j	1845j	1941	...	2140	...	...	...	...		1019	1252	1343	1452	1557j	1652	1756j	1850	1957	...	2143	...	...	...
Ely 204 207 208 d.	1519j	1622	...	1822	1923	2018	...	2217	...	...	...	...		1057	1334f	1420	1529	1636	1729	1835	1930j	2036	...	2220	...	...	...
Thetford 207 a.	1540	1643	...	1843	1943	2039	...	2239	...	...	...	...		1121	1354	1446	1549	1656	1750	1856	1951	2056	...	2240	...	...	...
Norwich 207 a.	1611	1714	...	1917	2014	2109	...	2313	...	...	...	...		1158	1426	1524	1623	1727	1824	1927	2024	2133	...	2317	...	...	...

A – Via Melton Mowbray and Leicester (Tables **208** and **170**).

f – Arrives 9–11 minutes earlier.

j – Arrives 5–8 minutes earlier.

★ – **Additional trains**: On Ⓐ Nottingham d. 1141 – Grantham d. 1214 – Peterborough d. 1244 – Ely d. 1326**j** – Thetford a. 1347 – Norwich a. 1418.
On Ⓐ Manchester Piccadilly d. 2141 – Sheffield a. 2234, d. 2238 – Chesterfield d. 2253 – Alfreton d. 2304 – Nottingham a. 2327.
On ⑥ Nottingham d. 1133 – Grantham d. 1213 – Peterborough d. 1244 – Ely d. 1322 – Thetford d. 1343 – Norwich a. 1414.
On ⑥ Manchester Piccadilly d. 2154 – Stockport d. 2204 – Sheffield a. 2249, d. 2256 – Chesterfield d. 2311 – Alfreton d. 2322 – Nottingham a. 2347.
On ⑦ Manchester Piccadilly d. 2144 – Stockport d. 2154 – Sheffield a. 2238, d. 2242 – Chesterfield d. 2258 – Alfreton d. 2309 – Nottingham a. 2337.

LE 2nd Class STANSTED AIRPORT - CAMBRIDGE - NORWICH 207

km			Ⓐ	⑥	Ⓐ	⑥	⚒	Ⓐ	⑥	Ⓐ	⑥	⚒	⚒	⚒	⚒	Ⓐ	⑥	Ⓐ	⑥	⑥	Ⓐ	⑥	Ⓐ	⑥	Ⓐ	⚒
0	**Stansted Airport** ✈ 208 d.	⚒	...	...	...	0648	0748t	...	0848	...	0948	1048	1148	1248	1348	1448	1448	1537	1548	1648	1648	1748	1754	1848	...	1948t
40	**Cambridge** 208 d.		0602	0605	0700	0720	0819	0913	0930r	1014	1020	1120	1220	1320	1420	1520	1520	1616	1620	1720	1729	1820	1830	1921	1925	2020
63	Ely 206 208 d.		0619	0622	0717	0738	0837	0930	0950	1030	1037	1137	1237	1337	1436	1537	1537	1633	1637	1737	1748	1837	1849	1937	1944	2036
100	Thetford 206 d.		0643	0646	0744	0806	0900	0953	1015	1054	1101	1201	1301	1401	1501	1600	1603	1657	1701	1801	1811	1900	1912	2001	2008	2100
123	Attleborough d.		0702	0704	0803	0824	0915	1008	1030	1109	1117	1216	1316	1416	1516	1616	1618	1713	1716	1816	1826	1915	1927	2016	2023	2115
133	Wymondham d.		0709	0711	0812	0832	0925	1015	1038	1116	1124	1224	1324	1424	1524	1623	1625	1720	1724	1824	1833	1922	1934	2023	2030	2122
149	**Norwich** 206 a.		0723	0725	0826	0846	0940	1029	1052	1131	1139	1241	1339	1440	1540	1637	1638	1737	1741	1839	1848	1936	1948	2036	2044	2136

	⚒	⑥	Ⓐ		⑦	⑦	⑦		⑦	⑦	⑦
Stansted Airport ✈ 208 d.	2048t	2210	2210	⑦	0818	1009	1109		1909	2009	2118
Cambridge 208 d.	2120	2255v	2257r		0851	1050j	1150j	and at	1950j	2048	2151
Ely 206 208 d.	2136	2311	2313		0908	1107	1207	the same	2007	2105	2208
Thetford 206 d.	2200	2335	2337		0934	1133	1231	minutes	2031	2128	2231
Attleborough d.	2215	2350	2352		0949	1148	1246	past each	2046	2143	2246
Wymondham d.	2222	2357	2359		0956	1155	1253	hour until	2053	2150	2253
Norwich 206 a.	2236	0010	0012		1013	1213	1313		2109	2205	2313

		⑥	Ⓐ	⑥	Ⓐ	⑥	Ⓐ	⑥	Ⓐ	⚒
Norwich 206 d.	⚒	0527	0533	0627	0633	0727	0730	0827	0833	0927
Wymondham d.		0539	0545	0639	0645	0739	0742	0839	0845	0939
Attleborough d.		0546	0552	0646	0652	0746	0749	0846	0852	0946
Thetford 206 d.		0600	0606	0700	0706	0800	0803	0900	0906	1000
Ely 206 208 d.		0627	0632	0727	0734	0827	0828	0927	0932	1027
Cambridge 208 a.		0647	0650	0744	0753	0844	0851	0944	0949	1045
Stansted ✈ 208 a.		0724	...	0824	...	0924	...	1024	1024	1124

	⑥	Ⓐ	⚒	Ⓐ	⑥	⚒	⚒	⑥	Ⓐ	⑥	Ⓐ	⑥	Ⓐ	Ⓐ	⑥	⚒	⑥	Ⓐ	⚒		⑦	⑦		⑦	⑦
Norwich 206 d.	1027	1033	1127	1228	1229	1327	1427	1521	1527	1627	1627	1721	1727	1823	1827	1927	2110	2112	2240	⑦	0903	1003	and at	2003	2208
Wymondham d.	1039	1045	1139	1240	1242	1339	1439	1533	1539	1639	1639	1733	1739	1835	1839	1939	2122	2124	2252		0915	1015	the same	2015	2220
Attleborough d.	1046	1052	1146	1247	1249	1346	1446	1540	1546	1646	1648	1742	1746	1842	1846	1946	2129	2131	2259		0922	1022	minutes	2022	2227
Thetford 206 d.	1100	1106	1200	1301	1304	1400	1500	1558	1600	1700	1702	1800	1809	1856	1900	2000	2143	2145	2313		0936	1036	past each	2036	2241
Ely 206 208 d.	1127	1131	1227	1328	1331	1427	1527	1627	1627	1727	1727	1827	1837	1926	1927	2027	2208	2210	2338		1003	1103	hour until	2103	2306
Cambridge 208 a.	1145	1149	1244	1346	1349	1444	1546	1644	1645	1744	1745	1844	1856	1946	1944	2045	2225	2227	2357		1021	1121		2120	2324
Stansted Airport ✈ 208 a.	1224	1224	1324	1424	1424	1524	1624	1724	1724	1824	...	1924	...	...	2024	2124	...	...	...		1103	1204		2203	...

j – Arrives 6 minutes earlier. r – Arrives 11–12 minutes earlier. t – ⑥ only. v – Arrives 2245.

208 STANSTED AIRPORT ✈ - CAMBRIDGE - PETERBOROUGH - LEICESTER - BIRMINGHAM XC

km			Ⓐ	⑥	⑥	Ⓐ	Ⓐ	⑥	Ⓐ	⑥	⚒	⚒	⚒🍷	⚒🍷	⚒🍷		⚒🍷	⑥🍷	Ⓐ🍷	⚒🍷	⚒🍷	ⒶG	⚒	ⒶB	⚒	Ⓐ
0	**Stansted Airport** ✈ **207** d.		...	...	0527	0527	0612	0627	0721	0727	0821f	0921f	1027	...	1227	...	1427	...	...	1627	...	...	1821f	...	...	2021
40	**Cambridge** .... **207** d.	⚒	0515	0515	0557	0557	0657c	0658	0800	0800	0900	1000	1100	1200	1300j	...	1500j	1600	1600	1700j	1800	...	1900j	...	1958	2102
64	Ely .... **204 206 207** d.		0530	0530	0612	0612	0712	0713	0815	0815	0915	1015	1115	1215	1315	...	1515	1615	1615	1715	1815	...	1915	...	2015	2117
89	March .... **204** d.		0547	0547	0631	0631	0729	0730	0834	0832	0932	1032	1132	1232	1332	...	1532	1632	1634	1732	1834	...	1932	...	2032	2134
113	**Peterborough** .. **204 206** a.		0608	0608	0652	0652	0750	0751	0851	0849	0949	1049	1149	1249	1349	...	1549	1649	1651	1749	1851	...	1949	...	2049	2151
	Peterborough .... d.		0610	0610	0654	0654	0754	0754	0854	0854	0954	1054	1154	1254	1354	...	1554	1654	1654	1754	1854	...	1954	2012	2054	2200
131	Stamford .... d.		0623	0623	0707	0707	0807	0807	0907	0907	1007	1107	1207	1307	1407	...	1607	1707	1707	1807	1907	...	2007	2028	2107	2213
154	Oakham .... d.		0637	0637	0721	0721	0821	0821	0921	0921	1021	1121	1221	1321	1421	...	1621	1721	1721	1821	1921	...	2021	2043	2121	2227
174	Melton Mowbray .... d.		0648	0648	0732	0732	0832	0832	0932	0932	1032	1132	1232	1332	1432	...	1632	1732	1732	1832	1932	...	2032	2056	2132	2238
197	**Leicester** .... d.		0706	0708	0750	0750	0850	0850	0950	0950	1050	1150	1250	1350	1450	...	1650	1750	1750	1850	1950	2020	2050	2117	2150	2256
227	Nuneaton .... d.		0729j	0730j	0809	0816	0909	0909	1009	1009	1109	1209	1309	1409	1509	...	1709	1809	1816	1909	2009	2047	2109	...	2209	2315
244	Coleshill Parkway ...... △ d.		0745	0747	0825	0831	0925	0925	1025	1025	1125	1225	1325	1425	1525	...	1725	1825	1831	1925	2025	2102	2125	...	2225	2331
259	**Birmingham** New Street a.		0758	0803	0838	0845	0938	0938	1038	1038	1138	1238	1338	1438	1538	...	1738	1838	1845	1938	2038	2116	2139	...	2238	2344

		⑦		⑦
Stansted Airport ✈ **207** d.	⑦	1027	⊖	1927
Cambridge .... **207** d.		1100j		2000j
Ely .... **204 206 207** d.		1115	and at	2015
March .... **204** d.		1132	the same	2032
Peterborough ... **204 206** a.		1149		2049
Peterborough .... d.		1154	minutes	2054
Stamford .... d.		1207	past each	2107
Oakham .... d.		1221		2121
Melton Mowbray .... d.		1232	hour until	2132
Leicester .... d.		1250		2150
Nuneaton .... d.		1309		2209
Coleshill Parkway .... △ d.		1325		2225
Birmingham New Street a.		1339		2238

		ⒶA	⑥A	Ⓐ	⑥	⚒A	Ⓐ🍷	⑥🍷	Ⓐ🍷	⑥🍷	ⒶC	⑥E	Ⓐ🍷	⑥🍷	⚒🍷	⚒🍷
Birmingham New Street d.	⚒	...	...	0519	0522	...	0622	0622	0722	0722	0822	0822	1022	1022	1122	1222
Coleshill Parkway .... △ d.		...	...	0533	0536	...	0636	0636	0735	0736	0836	0836	1036	1036	1136	1236
Nuneaton .... d.		...	...	0549	0551	...	0651	0651	0750	0751	0853	0851	1051	1051	1151	1251
Leicester .... d.		...	...	0615	0615j	...	0714j	0714j	0818	0813	0914	0912	1113	1112	1212	1312
Melton Mowbray .... d.		0536	0542	0631	0631	0654	0732	0730	0837	0829	0931	0928	1130	1128	1228	1328
Oakham .... d.		0549	0554	0643	0643	0706	0743	0742	0849	0841	0942	0940	1141	1140	1240	1340
Stamford .... d.		0605	0607	0657	0657	0719	0757	0756	0903	0855	0956	0954	1155	1154	1254	1354
Peterborough .... a.		0621	0625	0710	0710	0736	0811	0809	0916	0909	1010	1007	1209	1207	1307	1407
Peterborough ... **204 206** d.		0627	0628	0713	0713	0737	0819	0816	0919	0916	1013	1015	1215	1216	1316	1416
March .... **204** a.		0643	0643	0732	0732	0754	0835	0832	0935	0932	1029	1031	1231	1232	1332	1432
Ely .... **204 206 207** a.		0701	0704	0753	0753	0814	0852	0849	0952	0950	1049	1048	1249	1250	1350	1449
Cambridge .... **207** a.		...	...	0808	0809	...	0913	0905t	1012	1006	1105t	1104t	1305t	1305t	1406	1505t
Stansted Airport ✈ **207** a.		...	...	0841	0841	...	0944	0941	...	...	1141	1141	1341	1341	...	1541

	⚒🍷	Ⓐ🍷	⑥🍷	⚒	Ⓐ	⑥	Ⓐ	⑥	Ⓐ	⑥	Ⓐ	⑥	Ⓐ	⑥	Ⓐ
Birmingham New Street d.	1322	1422	1422	1522	1622	1622	1652	1722	1722	1822	1822	1922	1922	2022	2022
Coleshill Parkway .... △ d.	1336	1436	1436	1536	1636	1636	1706	1736	1736	1836	1836	1936	1936	2036	2036
Nuneaton .... d.	1351	1451	1451	1551	1651	1651	1725j	1751	1751	1851	1852	1951	1951	2051	2051
Leicester .... d.	1412	1512	1512	1612	1713	1712	1756	1812	1817	1912	1916	2012	2015	2112	2116
Melton Mowbray .... d.	1428	1528	1528	1628	1730	1728	1816	1828	1834	1928	1933	2028	2032	2128	2132
Oakham .... d.	1440	1540	1540	1640	1741	1740	1827	1840	1846	1940	1944	2040	2043	2140	2144
Stamford .... d.	1454	1554	1554	1654	1755	1754	1841	1854	1900	1954	1958	2054	2057	2154	2158
Peterborough .... a.	1507	1607	1607	1707	1809	1807	1855	1908	1913	2007	2012	2107	2111	2207	2212
Peterborough ... **204 206** d.	1516	1620	1616	1716	1813	1816	1900	1916	1916	2016	2016	2116	2116	2216	2219
March .... **204** a.	1532	1636	1632	1735	1829	1832	1916	1932	1932	2032	2032	2132	2132	2232	2235
Ely .... **204 206 207** a.	1550	1653	1649	1756	1849	1849	1935t	1949	1952	2049	2049	2149	2149	2249	2252
Cambridge .... **207** a.	1607	1709	1705t	1816a	1905t	1905t	2001	2005	2009	2105t	2106t	2205t	2206t	2305	2309
Stansted Airport ✈ **207** a.	...	1741	1741	...	1941	1941	...	...	...	2141	2141	2241	2241	...	...

		⑦🍷	⑦🍷	⑦🍷	⑦	⑦	⑦	⑦	⑦	⑦	⑦
Birmingham New Street d.	⑦	1122	1222	1322	1422	1522	1622	1722	1822	1922	2022
Coleshill Parkway .... △ d.		1136	1236	1336	1436	1536	1636	1736	1836	1936	2036
Nuneaton .... d.		1151	1251	1351	1451	1551	1651	1751	1851	1951	2051
Leicester .... d.		1212	1318	1416	1516	1616	1714	1812	1912	2012	2112
Melton Mowbray .... d.		1228	1334	1433	1533	1633	1730	1828	1928	2028	2128
Oakham .... d.		1240	1346	1444	1544	1644	1742	1840	1940	2040	2140
Stamford .... d.		1254	1400	1458	1558	1658	1756	1854	1954	2054	2154
Peterborough .... a.		1307	1413	1512	1613	1712	1809	1907	2007	2108	2207
Peterborough ... **204 206** d.		1319	1419	1519	1619	1719	1819	1919	2019	2119	2217
March .... **204** a.		1335	1435	1535	1635	1735	1835	1935	2035	2135	2233
Ely .... **204 206 207** a.		1352	1452	1552	1652	1752	1852	1952	2052	2152	2250
Cambridge .... **207** a.		1408t	1508t	1608t	1709t	1808t	1908t	2008t	2108t	2208t	2306
Stansted Airport ✈ **207** a.		1445	1545	1645	1745	1845	1945	2045	2145	2245	...

A – 🚃2 Nottingham - Norwich (Table **206**).
B – To Nottingham (Table **170**).
C – From Bristol Temple Meads; conveys 🍷 from Birmingham (Tables **116** and **117**).
D – From Cardiff Central (Table **117**).
E – From Gloucester; conveys 🍷 from Birmingham (Table **117**).
G – To Gloucester (Table **117**).

a – Arrives 1813 on Ⓐ.
c – Arrives 0647.
f – Departs 6 minutes later on ⑥.
j – Arrives 4–5 minutes earlier.
t – Departs 5–6 minutes later.

△ – 🚌 connections available to and from the National Exhibition Centre (NEC) and Birmingham International Airport.
⊖ – 🍷 conveyed on 1527, 1627 and 1727 from Stansted Airport.

☛ **Additional journeys Leicester - Birmingham New Street and v.v.**
From Leicester:
On ⚒ at 0548⑥, 0618Ⓐ, 0648, 0722Ⓐ, 0817, 0915Ⓐ, 0918⑥, 1018 and hourly until 1918, 2018⑥, 2118, 2220⑥, 2226Ⓐ.
On ⑦ at 1020, 1120 and hourly until 2020, 2220.
From Birmingham New Street;
On ⚒ at 0552, 0652 and hourly until 1552, 1609Ⓐ, 1652⑥, 1709Ⓐ, 1752 and hourly until 2052, 2222.
On ⑦ at 0952, 1052 and hourly until 2152.

☛ **Full service Cambridge to Stansted Airport** ✈ and v.v.
From Cambridge:
On Ⓐ at 0444, 0517, 0635, 0735, 0814, 0914, 0951, 1048, 1111, 1150, 1248, 1311, 1348, 1448, 1511, 1547, 1647, 1711, 1911, 2050, 2111, 2211.
On ⑥ at 0451, 0540, 0610, 0640, 0649, 0736, 0748, 0811, 0848, 0911, 0948, 1048, 1111, 1148, 1248, 1311, 1350, 1448, 1511, 1548, 1648, 1711, 1748, 1848, 1911, 1948, 2048, 2111, 2211
On ⑦ at 0739, 0825, 0915, 0925, 1015, 1025 and at the same times past each hour until 2115, 2125, 2215.
From Stansted Airport:
On Ⓐ at 0527, 0612, 0721, 0821, 0921, 1027, 1048, 1148, 1227, 1248, 1348, 1427, 1448, 1537, 1627, 1648, 1754, 1821, 2021, 2210, 2227, 2257.
On ⑥ at 0527, 0627, 0648, 0727, 0748, 0827, 0848, 0927, 0948, 1027, 1048, 1148, and at the same times past each hour **every 2 hours** until 2048, 2210, 2227, 2327.
On ⑦ at 0818, 0909, 1009, 1027 and the same times past each hour until 2027, 2104, 2118, 2209, 2227, 2304.

209 NEWCASTLE - CARLISLE 2nd class NT

km			⚒	⚒	⚒	⚒	⚒H	⚒S	⚒	⚒	⚒	⚒	⚒	⚒	⑥	Ⓐ	⚒	⚒	⑥	Ⓐ	⚒	⚒	⚒	⚒	⚒	⚒	⚒	⚒
	Middlesbro' 210 ... d.	⚒	...	...	0548	...	...	0649	...	0731	...	...	0832	...	...	...	0931	...	...	...	1031	...	...	1132	...	...	1232	...
0	**Newcastle** .... d.		0542	0620	0702	0725	0740	0805	0823	0856	0923	0946	0957	1023	1031	1046	1056	1123	1147	1150	1159	1223	1239	1257	1323	1340	1355	1423
6	Metrocentre .... d.		0549	0629	0710	0734	0748	0814	0831	0906	0931	0954	1006	1031	1043	1054	1105	1131	1155	1201	1208	1231	1247	1306	1331	1348	1404	1431
19	Prudhoe .... d.		0604	0644	0725	0749	0758	0825	0846	0921	0942	1007	1021	1042	1054	1105	1120	1142	1206	1212	1223	1242	1259	1321	1342	1359	1419	1442
36	Hexham .... d.		0624	0659	0744	0802	0818	0838	0905	0940	0955	1022	1040	1055	1109	1118	1140	1155	1219	1232	1242	1255	1311	1340	1355	1412	1440	1455
62	Haltwhistle .... d.		0643	0722	0803	0825	...	0857	0928	...	1014	1042	...	1114	1132	1142	...	1214	1239	1253	...	1314	1334	...	1414	1435	...	1514
99	**Carlisle** .... a.		0712	0800	0835	0859	...	0934f	1001	...	1044	1116	...	1146	1205	1215	...	1244	1313	1327	...	1346	1406	...	1445	1508	...	1544

	Ⓐ	⑥	⚒K	⚒	⚒	⚒	⚒	⚒	⚒	⚒	⚒	⚒	⚒K	⚒	Ⓐ	⑥	⚒	⑥	Ⓐ
Middlesbro' 210 ... d.	...	...	1330	...	...	1432	...	...	...	...	1632	...	1731	...	...	...	...	...	2130
Newcastle .... d.	1433	1440	1454	1523	1540	1556	1623	1640	1703	1723	1756	1823	1855	1923	2023	2033	2125	2238	2253
Metrocentre .... d.	1441	1448	1503	1531	1548	1605	1631	1648	1713	1731	1805	1831	1904	1931	2031	2041	2133	2247	2302
Prudhoe .... d.	1452	1459	1518	1542	1559	1620	1642	1703	1728	1746	1821	1846	1919	1946	2046	2056	2148	2302	2317
Hexham .... d.	1505	1512	1537	1555	1612	1639	1655	1722	1747	1805	1840	1905	1938	2005	2105	2115	2207	2321	2336
Haltwhistle .... d.	1528	1535	...	1614	1632	...	1714	1745	...	1828	...	1928	...	2028	2126	2136	2230	...	...
Carlisle .... a.	1559	1607	...	1643	1707	...	1744	1817	...	1901	...	2002	...	2102	2156	2211	2305	...	...

		⑦	⑦	⑦	✥W	⑦K	⑦	⑦
Middlesbro' 210 ... d.	⑦	...	0832	0931		1730	1831	1931
Newcastle .... d.		0845	0955	1055	and at	1855	1955	2100
Metrocentre .... d.		0853	1003	1103	the same	1903	2003	2109
Prudhoe .... d.		0908	1017	1116	minutes	1915	2018	2124
Hexham .... d.		0927	1037	1135	past each	1934	2037	2143
Haltwhistle .... d.		0950	1100	1158	hour until	1957	2100	2206
Carlisle .... a.		1024	1134	1232		2028	2134	2240

		⚒S	⚒	⑥	Ⓐ	⚒	⚒	⚒	⚒	⚒	⚒	⚒	⚒	⚒	⚒	⚒	⚒K	⚒	⚒	⚒	⚒	⚒	⚒	⚒	⚒	⚒	⚒	⚒
Carlisle .... d.	⚒	...	...	0557	0557	0632	0659	0725	0802	0820	...	0922	0952	...	1023	1054	...	1125	1152	...	1225	1253	...	1332	1355	...	1437	1454
Haltwhistle .... d.		...	...	0629	0629	0703	0731	0754	0832	0852	...	0957	1020	...	1053	1122	...	1157	1220	...	1255	1321	...	1404	1423	...	1507	1522
Hexham .... d.		0609	0637	0652	0652	0725	0754	0814	0856	0918	0956	1018	1040	1055	1118	1142	1156	1218	1240	1256	1319	1341	1356	1425	1443	1456	1530	1542
Prudhoe .... d.		0626	0655	0704	0710	0742	0811	0826	0913	0930	1013	1030	1052	1112	1130	1154	1213	1230	1252	1313	1331	1353	1413	1437	1455	1513	1542	1554
Metrocentre .... d.		0641	0710	0720	0726	0758	0827	0846	0929	0944	1029	1044	1104	1128	1144	1208	1228	1244	1304	1329	1344	1405	1429	1449	1507	1529	1555	1606
Newcastle .... a.		0651	0720	0733	0736	0809	0839	0854	0945v	0955	1039	1054	1114	1138	1153	1222	1238	1255	1313	1339	1352	1413	1439	1457	1516	1539	1603	1615
Middlesbro' 210 ... a.		0818t	...	0858	0859	...	...	...	...	...	1200	...	...	1259	...	...	1400	...	...	1500	...	...	1559	...	...	1700	...	..

	⚒K	Ⓐ	⑥	⚒	⚒	⚒	⚒	⚒	⚒	⚒	⚒	Ⓐ	⑥	⚒	⚒	⚒T	⚒	⑥	Ⓐ
Carlisle .... d.	...	1521	1527	1552	...	1622	1654	...	1724	1753	...	1839	1849	...	2009	2107	2204	...	...
Haltwhistle .... d.	...	1553	1559	1620	...	1652	1722	...	1756	1821	...	1912	1921	...	2037	2139	2236	...	...
Hexham .... d.	1556	1614	1620	1640	1656	1716	1742	1759	1820	1841	1856	1935	1943	2000	2101	2200	2259	2327	2341
Prudhoe .... d.	1613	1626	1632	1652	1713	1728	1754	1817	1832	1853	1913	1947	1955	2018	2118	2217	2317	2345	2359
Metrocentre .... d.	1629	1638	1644	1704	1729	1740	1806	1832	1844	1905	1929	1959	2007	2033	2134	2233	2332	2357	0013
Newcastle .... a.	1639	1646	1652	1714	1739	1751	1815	1842	1853	1914	1939	2008	2016	2042	2143	2242	2342	0006	0024
Middlesbro' 210 ... a.	1800	...	...	...	1859	...	...	2004	...	...	2105	...	...	2204	2303	...	...	...	...

		⑦	⑦	U Z	⑦	⑦	⑦	⑦
Carlisle .... d.	⑦	0844	0952		1754	1848	1948	2038
Haltwhistle .... d.		0916	1022	and at	1822	1920	2020	2110
Hexham .... d.		0940	1045	the same	1846	1941	2043	2133
Prudhoe .... d.		0957	1103	minutes	1903	1958	2101	2151
Metrocentre .... d.		1013	1117	past each	1917	2014	2116	2206
Newcastle .... a.		1023	1127	hour until	1926	2023	2125	2216
Middlesbro' 210 ... a.		...	1249		2049	2149	2248	...

H – From Hartlepool (Table **210**).
K – From/to Whitby (Tables **210** and **211**).
S – To/from Saltburn (Tables **210** and **212**).
T – To Sunderland on Ⓐ; Hartlepool on ⚒ (Table **210**).

U – The 1054 and 1354 departures from Carlisle continue to Whitby (Tables **210** and **211**).
W – The 1430 departure from Middlesbrough starts from Whitby (Tables **210** and **211**).
Z – Timings at Haltwhistle may be up to 4 minutes later than shown.
The 1449 (not 1454) from Carlisle departs Haltwhistle 1521, Hexham 1542, Prudhoe 1559, Metrocentre 1615 and arrives Newcastle 1624.

f – Arrives 0929 on Ⓐ.
t – Arrives 0810 on Ⓐ.
v – Arrives 0941 on ⑥.

NT 2nd class MIDDLESBROUGH - NEWCASTLE 210

km			⚒	⚒S	⚒	⚒	⚒S	⚒	✣	⚒A	⚒	⚒	⚒	⚒A	⚒	⚒	⚒	Ⓐ	⑥		⑦	⑦	✣U	⑦	⑦	⑦	⑦
0	**Middlesbrough** .. d.	⚒	...	0649	0656	0731	0749	0831		1330	1431	1531	1632	1731	1831	1931	2030	2130	2130	⑦	0832	0930		1831	1931	2031	2131
9	Stockton .... d.		...	|	0707	0742	|	0841	and at	1341	1442	1542	1642	1742	1842	1941	2041	2141	2141		0843	0941	and at	1842	1942	2042	2142
28	Hartlepool ... **183** d.		0639v	b	0726	0801	b	0900	the same	1400	1501	1601	1701	1801	1901	2000	2100	2200	2200		0903	1000	the same	1901	2001	2101	2201
57	Sunderland . **183** d.		0708v	|	0756	0830	|	0931	minutes	1429	1530	1630	1730	1830	1930	2029	2129	2229	2229		0932	1029	minutes	1930	2030	2131	2231
76	**Newcastle** .... a.		0732	0800	0819	0855	0901	0955	past each	1452	1554	1655	1755	1852	1949	2051	2153	2250	2250		0951	1050	past each	1950	2050	2151	2251
	Hexham **209** ... a.		0818	0838	...	0940	...	1040	hour until	1537	1639	...	1840	1938	...	...	...	2336	...		1036	1134	hour until	2037	2143	...	...
	Carlisle **209** .... a.		...	0934f	...	...	...	...		...	...	...	...	...	...	...	...	...	...		1134	1232		2134	2240	...	...

		⚒S	ⒶS	⑥S	⑥	Ⓐ	⑥	Ⓐ	⚒	⚒	V	⚒	⚒	⚒	⚒	⚒	⑥	⚒		⑦	⑦A	⑦	⑦	✣W	⑦	⑦S	⑦
Carlisle **209** ..... d.	⚒	...	...	...	0557	0557	...	...	...	...		...	...	...	...	2009	...	2107	⑦	...	...	...	0953		1848	...	1948
Hexham **209** .... d.		...	0609	0609	0652	0652	...	...	...	0955	and at	1656	1759	1856	2000	2101	...	2200		...	...	...	1046	and at	1941	...	2043
Newcastle .... d.		0600	0653	0654	0734	0740	0833	0840	0942	1040	the same	1740	1845	1945	2045	2146	2233	2248		0831	0932	1031	1130	the same	2031	2114	2130
Sunderland .. **183** d.		0625	0712	0720	0758t	0801	0853	0901	1002	1101	minutes	1801	1906	2006	2106	2205	2308	2307		0851	0952	1051	1150	minutes	2051	|	2150
Hartlepool .... **183** d.		0657	0739	0747	0825	0828	0926	0928	1029	1128	past each	1828	1933	2033	2133	2232	2319	2334r		0918	1019	1118	1217	past each	2118	b	2217
Stockton .... d.		0716	0758	0806	0844	0847	0945	0947	1048	1147	hour until	1847	1952	2052	2152	2251	...	...		0937	1038	1137	1236	hour until	2137	|	2236
Middlesbrough .. a.		0728	0810	0818	0858	0859	0957	0959	1100	1200		1859	2004	2105	2204	2303	...	...		0949	1050	1149	1250		2149	2222	2248

A – To / from Whitby (Table **211**).
S – To / from Saltburn (Table **212**).
U – The 1430 and 1730 departures from Middlesbrough start from Whitby (Table **211**).
V – The 1156 and 1556 departures from Hexham continue to Whitby (Table **211**).
W – The 1054 and 1354 departures from Carlisle continue to Whitby (Table **211**).

b – Via Darlington (Table **212**).
f – 0929 on Ⓐ.
r – Ⓐ only.
t – Arrives 0752.
v – 4 minutes later on ⑥.
✣ – Timings between Carlisle and Newcastle and v.v. may vary by ± 4 minutes.

NT 2nd class MIDDLESBROUGH and PICKERING - WHITBY 211

km		⚒	⚒	⑦D	⚒	⑦B	⑦C	⚒H	⑦C	⚒H	⚒
0	**Middlesbrough** .... d.	0456	0654	0841	1019	1050	1351	1404	1652	1801	2042
18	Battersby .... d.	0525	0736r	0912	1050	1131r	1426	1438	1726	1832	2117
41	Glaisdale .... d.	0553	0810	0946	1124	1205	1500	1512	1800	1906	2149
46	Grosmont .... d.	|	0818	0954	1132	1213	1508	1520	1808	1914	2157
56	**Whitby** .... a.	0616	0838	1012	1151	1231	1526	1538	1826	1932	2216

	⚒	⚒	⑦D	⚒H	⑦C	⑦C	⚒H	⑦D	⚒	⚒
Whitby .... d.	0630	0845	1022	1159	1249	1550	1558	1834	1942	2223
Grosmont .... d.	0646	0902	1039	1216	1306	1608	1616	1851	1959	2239
Glaisdale .... d.	0656	0913	1050	1227	1317	1618	1627	1902	2010	2249
Battersby .... d.	0731	0948	1126	1303	1353	1655	1703	1938	2046	2324
Middlesbrough .... a.	0757	1015	1152	1330	1429	1728	1730	2004	2113	2351

km		🚂		🚂		🚂			🚂		
0	**Pickering** .... d.	...	...	0920	...	1200	...	...	1500	...	...
29	Grosmont .... a.	...	...	1025	...	1305	...	...	1605	...	...
29	Grosmont .... d.	0915	...	1040	...	1315	...	...	1630	...	...
39	**Whitby** .... a.	0945	...	1110	...	1345	...	...	1655	...	...

	🚂		🚂	🚂		🚂			🚂	
Whitby .... d.	1000	...	1235	...	...	1400	...	...	1710	...
Grosmont .... a.	1025	...	1300	...	...	1425	...	...	1735	...
Grosmont .... d.	1035	...	...	1330	...	1430	...	...	1740	...
Pickering .... a.	1140	...	...	1440	...	1540	...	...	1840	...

B – From Newcastle (Table **210**).
C – To / from Carlisle (Tables **209** and **210**).
D – To / from Darlington (Table **212**).
H – To / from Hexham (Table **210**).
r – Arrives 14 – 15 minutes earlier.
🚂 – Daily services April 4 - October 30 2022. The service for 2023 has not yet been announced. National Rail tickets **not** valid. An amended service operates on most ⑦ and on certain other dates - please confirm with operator. The North Yorkshire Moors Railway. ✆ 01751 472508. www.nymr.co.uk

NT 2nd class BISHOP AUCKLAND - DARLINGTON - MIDDLESBROUGH - SALTBURN 212

km			⑥	Ⓐ	⚒	⚒N	ⒶB	⑥B	⚒	⚒		⚒		⑦A	⑦	⑦	⑦	♥	⑦	⑦	⑦	⑦N	⑦
0	**Bishop Auckland** .... d.	⚒	...	...	...	...	...	...	0726	0826		2126	⑦	...	...	0814	0924		1924	2024	...	...	...
4	Shildon .... d.		...	...	...	...	...	...	0732	0832	and at	2132		...	...	0820	0930		1930	2030	...	...	...
8	Newton Aycliffe .... d.		...	...	...	...	...	...	0736	0836	the same	2136		...	...	0824	0934	and at	1934	2034	...	...	...
19	**Darlington** .... a.		...	...	...	...	...	...	0753	0853	minutes	2153		...	...	0841	0951	the same	1951	2051	...	...	...
19	**Darlington** .... ▶ d.		0614	0614	0628	...	...	...	0755	0855	past each	2155		0809	...	0842	0952	minutes	1952	2053	2127	2154	2252
43	**Middlesbrough** ... **188** ▶ d.		0647	0650t	0709v	0729	0811	0818	0824	0923	hour until	2224		0837	0845	0911	1021	past each	2021	2121	2157	2223	2320
55	Redcar Central ..... **188** ▶ d.		0657	0701	0721	0741	0824	0831	0836	0935		2236		...	0857	0923	1033	hour until	2033	2133	...	2235	...
63	**Saltburn** .... **188** ▶ a.		0711	0715	0735	0755	0838	0845	0853	0950		2250		...	0911	0937	1050		2047	2148	...	2249	...

		⚒	⚒C	⚒	⚒N	⚒		⚒	⚒	⚒	⚒		⑦	⑦	⑦	⑦	⑦	⑦A	⑦	♥	⑦	⑦A	⑦
Saltburn .... **188** ▷ d.	⚒	...	0622	0659	0722	0759		1957	2059	2159	2259	⑦	...	...	...	0957	1057	...	1157		1857	...	1957
Redcar Central ..... **188** ▷ d.		...	0635	0712	0735	0812	and at	2010	2112	2212	2312		...	...	...	1010	1110	...	1210		1910	...	2010
Middlesbrough .... **188** ▷ d.		...	0649	0726	0749	0825	the same	2024	2126	2226	2326		...	0823	0922	1024	1124	1153	1224	and at	1924	2005	2024
Darlington .... ▷ a.		...	0717	0755	0818	0853	minutes	2054	2154	2255	2354		...	0851	0950	1052	1153	1223	1252	the same	1952	2033	2052
Darlington .... d.		0644	...	0756	...	0855	past each	2055	...	...	...		0740	0852	0952	1053	1154	...	1253	minutes	1953	...	...
Newton Aycliffe .... d.		0659	...	0811	...	0910	hour until	2110	...	...	...		0755	0907	1007	1108	1209	...	1308	past each	2008	...	...
Shildon .... d.		0704	...	0816	...	0915		2115	...	...	...		0800	0912	1012	1113	1214	...	1313	hour until	2013	...	...
Bishop Auckland .... a.		0710	...	0822	...	0922		2122	...	...	...		0806	0918	1019	1120	1221	...	1320		2020	...	...

A – To / from Whitby (Table **211**).
B – From Hexham (Table **210**).
C – To Carlisle (Table **210**).
N – To / from Newcastle (Table **210**).
t – Arrives 0643.
v – Arrives 0659.
♥ – Timings may vary by ± 3 minutes.
▶ – Additional trains Darlington - Middlesbrough - Saltburn. From Darlington on ⚒ at 0822 and hourly until 2022.
▷ – Additional trains Saltburn - Middlesbrough - Darlington. From Saltburn on ⚒ at 0822 and hourly until 2122; on ⑦ at 2057, 2157, 2257.

SR 2nd class CARLISLE - DUMFRIES - GLASGOW 214

km			⚒	⚒	⚒	⚒	⚒	⑥		Ⓐ	Ⓐ	⑥	⚒	⚒	⚒	⚒	⚒	⚒	⚒	⚒	⚒	Ⓐ	⑥
	Newcastle **210** .... d.	⚒	...	...	...	...	...	...	...	...	...	...	...	...	...	...	...	...	...	...	...	...	...
0	**Carlisle** .... **154** d.		...	...	0608	0700	0809	0909	...	0917	0958	0957	1112	1215	1305	1408	1508	1608	1725	1759	1920	...	...
16	Gretna Green .... d.		...	...	0620	0712	0821	0921	...	0929	1010	1009	1124	1227	1318	1420	1521	1621	1741	1811	1932	...	...
28	Annan .... d.		...	...	0628	0728b	0829	0929	...	0937	1021	1021	1132	1235	1326	1429	1529	1630	1753	1820	1940	...	...
53	**Dumfries** .... d.		...	...	0647	0744	0848	0946	...	0954	1041	1046g	1149	1353	1344	1453t	1546	1653b	1810	1838	1957	2049	2049
124	Auchinleck .... d.		...	...	0735	...	0936	...	...	...	1130	1137	...	1342	...	1541	...	1741	...	1927	...	2139	2139
146	**Kilmarnock** .... ▽ d.		0620	0652	0755	...	0955	...	...	...	1156f	1157	...	1359	...	1559	...	1759	...	1957r	...	2157	2157
185	**Glasgow** Central .... **154** ▽ a.		0711	0734	0836	...	1037	...	...	...	1234	1234	...	1437	...	1636	...	1839	...	2037	...	2237	2234

	⚒	⑥	Ⓐ		⑦	⑦	⑦	⑦	⑦
Newcastle **210** .... d.	...	...	...	⑦	...	...	...	...	...
Carlisle .... **154** d.	2111	2310	2310		1311	1511	1711	1911	2126
Gretna Green .... d.	2123	2322	2322		1323	1523	1723	1923	2138
Annan .... d.	2131	2330	2330		1331	1531	1731	1931	2146
Dumfries .... d.	2148	2347	2350		1350	1548	1748	1950	2203
Auchinleck .... d.	...	...	...		1438	...	...	2038	...
Kilmarnock .... ▽ d.	...	...	...		1456	...	...	2057	...
Glasgow Central .... **154** ▽ a.	...	...	...		1543	...	...	2135	...

		⚒	⚒	⚒	⑥		⚒	⑥	⚒
Glasgow Central ...... **154** ▽ d.	⚒	...	...	...	...	...	0707	...	0913
Kilmarnock .... ▽ d.		...	...	...	...	...	0755a	...	0953
Auchinleck .... d.		...	...	...	...	...	0811	...	1009
Dumfries .... d.		0457	0604	0715	0758	...	0901	1002	1100
Annan .... d.		0512	0619	0730	0813	...	0916	1017	1115
Gretna Green .... d.		0521	0628	0739	0822	...	0927	1026	1124
Carlisle .... **154** a.		0534	0641	0755	0837	...	0943	1039	1140
Newcastle **210** .... a.		...	...	...	...	...	...	...	...

	⚒	⚒	⚒	⚒	⚒	⚒	Ⓐ	⑥	⚒	⚒	⚒	Ⓐ	Ⓐ	Ⓐ	Ⓐ	⑥	⚒		⑦	⑦	⑦	⑦	⑦
Glasgow Central .... **154** ▽ d.	...	1113	...	1313	...	1513	1611	1613	...	1728	1913	2017	2113	...	2213	2213	2313	⑦	...	...	1503	...	2206
Kilmarnock .... ▽ d.	...	1154	...	1355	...	1553	1654	1654	...	1825	1953	2054	2157	...	2253	2253	0001		...	...	1552	...	2243
Auchinleck .... d.	...	1210	...	1412	...	1609	1711	1711	...	1842	2010	...	2214	...	2309	2309	...		...	...	1608	...	2300
Dumfries .... d.	1159	1304b	1358	1501	1602	1707c	1800	1800	1905	1930	2100	...	2302	2307	2357	2359	...		1301	1501	1701	1902	2350
Annan .... d.	1214	1320	1413	1517	1617	1722	1816	1816	1920	...	2116	...	...	2322	...	0014	...		1316	1516	1716	1917	0005
Gretna Green .... d.	1223	1328	1422	1525	1626	1731	1824	1824	1929	...	2124	...	...	2331	...	0023	...		1325	1525	1727	1926	0014
Carlisle .... **154** a.	1238	1342	1439	1539	1639	1744	1838	1838	1943	...	2139	...	...	2343	...	0036	...		1338	1538	1739	1939	0027
Newcastle **210** .... a.	...	...	...	...	...	...	...	...	...	...	...	...	...	...	...	...	...		...	...	...	...	...

a – Arrives 0749.
b – Arrives 5 – 6 minutes earlier.
c – Arrives 1658.
f – Arrives 1146.
g – Arrives 1037.
r – Arrives 1943.
t – Arrives 1446.
▽ – Additional hourly services are available.

215 GLASGOW and KILMARNOCK - STRANRAER

2nd class SR

km		⚒	⑥	Ⓐ	Ⓐ	⑥	⚒	⑦	Ⓐ	⑥	⚒	⑦	Ⓐ	⑥	Ⓐ	⑥	⑦	⚒	⚒	⑦	Ⓐ	⑥	Ⓐ	⑥	⑦	⚒	⚒
0	**Glasgow** Central **216** d.	...	...	...	...	...	...	...	...	...	...	...	...	...	...	...	...	...	...	...	1712	1713	...	...	...	...	...
39	**Kilmarnock 214** a.	...	...	...	...	...	...	...	...	...	...	...	...	...	...	...	...	...	...	...	1752	1751	...	...	...	...	...
39	**Kilmarnock** d.	...	...	...	0801	0801	...	...	...	...	1202	...	...	...	...	...	...	...	1701	...	1803	1803	...	...	...	2108	...
56	Troon **216** d.	...	...	...	0814	0814	...	...	...	...	1215	...	...	...	...	...	...	...	1713	...	1816	1816	...	...	...	2120	...
64	**Ayr** 🚌 ⛴ **216** a.	...	...	...	0830	0827	...	...	...	...	1224	...	...	...	...	...	...	...	1730	...	1828	1830	...	...	...	2131	...
64	**Ayr** d.	0615	0725	0729	0832	0829	1029	1106	1129	1134	1226	1306	1424	1429	1531	1534	1506	1625	1732	1805	1830	1832	2027	2032	1927	2133	2230
97	Girvan d.	0641	0756f	0759f	0858	0855	1056	1136f	1156	1201	1252	1336f	1450	1455	1558	1601	1536f	1651	1804f	1835f	1856	1858	2053	2058	1953	2202	2256
121	Barrhill d.	...	0815	0818	...	...	...	1156	1215	1220	...	1356	...	...	1617	1620	1555	...	1824	1854	...	...	...	...	2017f	2221	...
162	**Stranraer** a.	...	0850	0853	...	...	...	1231	1250	1255	...	1431	...	...	1652	1655	1631	...	1858	1930	...	...	...	...	2053	2256	...

	Ⓐ	⑥	⑥	Ⓐ	⑥	Ⓐ	⚒	⚒	⑦	⚒	⑦	⚒		⑥	Ⓐ	⑦	⚒	Ⓐ	⑥	⑦	⑥	Ⓐ	⑥	Ⓐ	⑦	⚒	⚒
Stranraer d.	...	...	0700	0703	...	...	0901	...	1041	...	1241	1302	...	...	...	1441	...	1709	1709	1740	...	...	1908	1908	1940	...	...
Barrhill d.	...	...	0734	0737	...	...	0935	...	1116	...	1316	1336	...	...	...	1515	...	1744	1744	1814	...	...	1942	1942	2015	...	...
Girvan d.	0646	0652	0754	0757	0900	0903	0953	1100	1134	1300	1334	1354	...	1500	1501	1534	1656	1802	1802	1833	1912	1912	2001	2001	2033	2111	2305
Ayr a.	0713	0719	0821	0824	0928	0930	1023	1128	1202	1327	1402	1422	...	1527	1529	1601	1723	1833	1835	1901	1939	1944	2029	2031	2101	2138	2332
Ayr 🚌 ⛴ **216** d.	0714	0721	0823	0826	...	...	...	...	...	...	...	...	...	...	...	...	1725	...	...	...	...	...	2030	2032	...	...	...
Troon **216** d.	0725	0731	0835	0836	...	...	...	...	...	...	...	...	...	...	...	...	1735	...	...	...	...	...	2041	2043	...	...	...
Kilmarnock a.	0747	0747	0852	0852	...	...	...	...	...	...	...	...	...	...	...	...	1755	...	...	...	...	...	2055	2057	...	...	...
Kilmarnock 214 d.	...	...	0856	0856	...	...	...	...	...	...	...	...	...	...	...	...	...	...	...	...	...	...	...	...	...	...	...
Glasgow Central **216** a.	...	...	0936	0939	...	...	...	...	...	...	...	...	...	...	...	...	...	...	...	...	...	...	...	...	...	...	...

f – Arrives 4–5 minutes earlier.

⛴ – 🚌 connections operate between Ayr station and Cairnryan ferry port for pre-booked Rail & Sail ticket holders (see www.stenaline.co.uk/rail). For ⛴ Cairnryan - Belfast timings, see Table **2002**.

216 GLASGOW - AYR, ARDROSSAN and LARGS

SR

Typical off-peak journey time in hours and minutes
READ DOWN ↓ READ UP ↑

Journey times may be extended during peak hours on Ⓐ (0600 - 0900 and 1600 - 1900) and also at weekends.
The longest journey time by any train is noted in the table heading.

GLASGOW CENTRAL - AYR

Longest journey: 1 hour 04 minutes SR

km	△				△
0	0h00	↓	**Glasgow** Central d.	↑	0h49
43	0h25	↓	Kilwinning d.	↑	0h22
48	0h29	↓	Irvine d.	↑	0h18
56	0h37	↓	Troon d.	↑	0h11
61	0h41	↓	Prestwick Airport ✈ d.	↑	0h07
67	0h52	↓	**Ayr** a.	↑	0h00

From Glasgow Central: On ⚒ at 0015 ②–⑥, 0602, 0630, 0700, 0730, 0800, 0830, 0900, 0932, 1000, 1030Ⓐ, 1104, 1134, 1200Ⓐ, 1204⑥, 1304, 1403, 1434, 1531Ⓐ, 1534⑥, 1600⑥, 1628, 1730⑥, 1734Ⓐ, 1747Ⓐ, 1804, 1900, 1930, 2000⑥, 2030, 2130, 2230, 2300⑥, 2330. On ⑦ at 0900 and every 30 minutes until 1900, 2000, 2100, 2200, 2300, 2330.

From Ayr: On ⚒ at 0607⑥, 0615Ⓐ, 0650, 0715⑥, 0718Ⓐ, 0734 Ⓐ, 0741, 0805, 0829, 0853, 0936, 1007, 1036, 1108, 1134Ⓐ, 1140⑥, 1206, 1236, 1306, 1336, 1406, 1452, 1523, 1548, 1622, 1714, 1747, 1824, 1912, 1941Ⓐ, 1945⑥, 2045, 2145, 2300. On ⑦ at 0845 and every 30 minutes until 1945, 2045, 2145, 2300.

△ – Trains at 0015⚒ - 0800⚒ and 1834⚒ - 2330⚒ and all day on ⑦ call additionally at Paisley Gilmour Street. Additional slower trains also run.

GLASGOW CENTRAL - ARDROSSAN - LARGS

Longest journey: 1 hour 10 minutes SR

km					
0	0h00	↓	**Glasgow** Central d.	↑	0h59
12	0h10	↓	Paisley Gilmour St d.	↑	0h46
43	0h29	↓	Kilwinning d.	↑	0h25
50	0h38	↓	**Ardrossan** Sth Beach d.	↑	0h17
64	0h49	↓	Fairlie d.	↑	0h05
69	0h56		**Largs** a.		0h00

From Glasgow Central:
On ⚒ at 0614, 0715, 0848, 0948, 1048, 1148, 1248, 1349⑥, 1353Ⓐ, 1448, 1548, 1630, 1715 ⑥, 1725 Ⓐ, 1749, 1850Ⓐ, 1852⑥, 1945, 2045, 2145, 2245, 2315 ①–④⑥, 2345 ⑤. On ⑦ at 0940 and hourly until 2140, 2242.

From Largs:
On ⚒ at 0642, 0722 Ⓐ, 0742, 0833 Ⓐ, 0853 ⑥, 0953 and hourly until 1553, 1648, 1733, 1852, 1954Ⓐ, 2001⑥, 2054, 2152, 2253. On ⑦ at 0854 and hourly until 2154, 2300.

218 GLASGOW - OBAN, FORT WILLIAM and MALLAIG

2nd class; most trains convey 🍷 SR

km		⚒	⚒	⚒A	Ba	⚒	⚒		⑦	⑦	Bc	⚒	Bb	⑦	⑦	⚒	⚒	Ⓐ	⚒	⑦	⑦	⚒	①–④	⑤	⑥
	Edinburgh **220** d.	...	...	0450	...	...	...	...	...	...	...	...	...	...	...	...	...	...	...	...	...	...	...	...	...
0	**Glasgow** Queen Street d.	...	0520	|	...	0821	0821	...	...	0956	...	1036	...	1220	1220	1222	1222	...	1634	1821	1821	1823	1823	1823	1823
16	Dalmuir d.	...	0538	0605	...	0841	0841	...	...	1016	...	1059	...	1234	1234	1243	1243	...	1658	1836	1836	1842	1842	1842	1842
26	Dumbarton Central d.	...	0547	0616	...	0852	0852	...	...	1026	...	1108	...	1247	1247	1253	1253	...	1707	1845	1845	1851	1851	1851	1851
40	Helensburgh Upper d.	...	0603	0631	...	0907	0907	...	...	1041	...	1127	...	1306f	1306f	1308	1308	...	1722	1905f	1905f	1906	1906	1906	1906
51	Garelochhead d.	...	0614	0646	...	0918	0918	...	...	1052	...	1140	...	1318	1318	1320	1320	...	1733	1916	1916	1917	1917	1917	1917
68	Arrochar & Tarbet d.	...	0634	0708	...	0938	0938	...	...	1112	...	1200	...	1338	1338	1340	1340	...	1757f	1936	1936	1937	1937	1937	1937
81	Ardlui d.	...	0652f	0724x	...	0951	0951	...	...	1128	...	1214	...	1356f	1356f	1356	1356	...	1810	1951	1951	1951	1951	1951	1951
95	**Crianlarich** a.	...	0708	0745	...	1007	1007	...	...	1145	...	1230	...	1412	1412	1412	1412	...	1826	2007	2007	2007	2007	2007	2007
95	**Crianlarich** d.	...	0718	0747	...	1015	1021	...	...	1147	...	1233	...	1418	1424	1418	1424	...	1829	2014	2020	2014	2020	2020	2020
	Dalmally d.	...	0751f	|	...	1042	|	...	...	1215	...	1259	...	1444	|	1444	|	1705	1855	2040	|	2040	|	|	|
	Taynuilt d.	...	0811	|	...	1103	|	...	...	1239f	...	1320	...	1504	|	1505	|	1724	1919	2100	|	2102	|	|	|
162	**Oban** a.	...	0835	|	...	1127	|	...	...	1304	...	1343	...	1527	|	1528	|	1747	1942	2124	|	2126	|	|	|
115	Bridge of Orchy d.	...	...	0817	...	...	1048	...	...	...	...	...	...	...	1449	...	1449	...	...	...	2047	...	2045	2045	2045
140	Rannoch d.	...	...	0844	...	...	1109	...	...	...	...	...	...	...	1512	...	1512	...	...	...	2108	...	2108	2108	2108
177	Roy Bridge d.	...	...	0931x	...	...	1148	...	...	...	...	...	...	...	1550	...	1550	...	...	...	2146	...	2146	2146	2146
183	Spean Bridge d.	...	...	0938	...	...	1155	...	...	...	...	...	...	...	1556	...	1556	...	...	...	2153	...	2153	2156	2153
197	**Fort William** a.	...	...	0957	...	...	1208	...	...	...	...	...	...	...	1609	...	1609	...	...	...	2206	...	2206	2209	2206
197	**Fort William** d.	0830	...	...	1015	...	1212	...	1212	...	1250	...	1440	...	1619	...	1619	...	...	...	2214	...	2211	2214	2212
223	Glenfinnan d.	0905	...	...	|	...	1246	...	1246	...	|	...	|	...	1655	...	1655	...	...	...	2247	...	2247	2247	2246
251	Arisaig d.	0938	...	...	|	...	1319	...	1319	...	|	...	|	...	1728	...	1728	...	...	...	2320	...	2320	2320	2319
259	Morar d.	0946	...	...	|	...	1327	...	1327	...	|	...	|	...	1736	...	1736	...	...	...	2328	...	2328	2328	2327
264	**Mallaig** a.	0953	...	...	1226	...	1338	...	1338	...	1506	...	1642	...	1743	...	1743	...	...	...	2339	...	2339	2339	2338

	⚒	⚒	⚒		⚒	⚒	⑦	⑦	Ⓐ	Ba	⑦	⑥	Ⓐ		⚒	⚒	⑦	⑦	Bc	⑦A	⑦	⚒	Bb	⚒	ⒶA
Mallaig d.	...	0603	...	...	1010	...	...	1006	...	1410	...	...	...	...	1605	...	1601	...	1700	...	1815	1815	1840	...	...
Morar d.	...	0614	...	...	1017	...	...	1017	...	|	...	...	...	...	1612	...	1612	...	|	...	1822	1822	|	...	...
Arisaig d.	...	0623	...	...	1027	...	...	1026	...	|	...	...	...	...	1621	...	1621	...	|	...	1831	1831	|	...	...
Glenfinnan d.	...	0655	...	...	1101	...	...	1059	...	|	...	...	...	...	1654	...	1654	...	|	...	1904	1904	|	...	...
Fort William a.	...	0727	...	...	1134	...	...	1132	...	1603	...	...	...	...	1728	...	1728	...	1852	...	1937	1937	2032	...	...
Fort William d.	...	0744	...	...	1140	...	...	1140	...	...	...	...	...	...	1737	...	1737	...	...	1900	...	...	▬	...	1950
Spean Bridge d.	...	0757	...	...	1156	...	...	1156	...	...	...	...	...	...	1751	...	1751	...	...	1918	...	...	...	...	2009
Roy Bridge d.	...	0804	...	...	1202	...	...	1202	...	...	...	...	...	...	1757	...	1757	...	...	1926x	...	...	...	...	2017x
Rannoch d.	...	0847f	...	...	1242	...	...	1242	...	...	...	...	...	...	1838	...	1838	...	...	2015	...	...	...	...	2108
Bridge of Orchy d.	...	0907	...	...	1303	...	...	1303	...	...	...	...	...	...	1858	...	1858	...	...	2046	...	...	...	...	2137
Oban d.	0521	|	0857	...	|	1211	1211	|	1441	...	1611	1611	1611	...	|	1811	|	1811	...	|	...	...	...	2039	|
Taynuilt d.	0544	|	0920	...	|	1235	1238	|	1506	...	1638	1634	1634	...	|	1833	|	1833	...	|	...	...	...	2101	|
Dalmally d.	0603	|	0940	...	|	1300f	1259	|	1526	...	1658	1654	1654	...	|	1856	|	1856	...	|	...	...	...	2120	|
Crianlarich a.	0631	0931	1008	...	1327	1332	1326	1332	1554	...	1726	1722	...	...	1922	1927	1922	1927	...	2116	...	...	...	2148	2207
Crianlarich d.	0633	0933	1014	...	1337	1337	1337	1337	1556	...	1727	1724	...	...	1932	1932	1932	1932	...	2117	...	...	...	2148	2209
Ardlui d.	0651	0952f	1029	...	1355	1355	1355	1355	1611	...	1743	1742	...	...	1952	1952	1952	1952	...	2138x	...	...	...	2204	2228x
Arrochar & Tarbet d.	0710f	1006	1043	...	1409	1409	1409	1409	1627	...	1757	1756	...	...	2006	2006	2006	2006	...	2156	...	...	...	2218	2245
Garelochhead d.	0730	1032f	1104	...	1431	1431	1429	1429	1649	...	1819	1819	...	...	2026	2026	2026	2026	...	2222	...	...	...	2238	2311
Helensburgh Upper d.	0742	1044	1117	...	1444	1444	1440	1440	1700	...	1831	1831	...	...	2039	2039	2040	2040	...	2238	...	...	...	2250	2324
Dumbarton Central d.	0759	1059	1130	...	1459	1502	1456	1456	1713	...	1847	1844	...	...	2053	2053	2054	2054	...	2254	...	...	...	2303	2339
Dalmuir d.	|	1109	1139	...	1512	1512	1507	1507	1724	...	1858	1854	...	...	2106	2106	2104	2104	...	2305	...	...	...	2313	2351
Glasgow Queen Street a.	0842	1133	1156	...	1534	1534	1526	1526	1744	...	1920	1919	...	...	2125	2125	2120	2120	...	2328¶	...	...	...	2332	0015¶
Edinburgh **220** a.	...	...	...	...	...	...	...	...	...	...	...	...	...	...	...	...	...	...	...	0024	...	...	...	...	0111

A – Ⓡ. 🛏 (limited accommodation), 🛏 1, 2 cl. and ✕ London Euston - Fort William and v.v. (Table **161**).
B – THE JACOBITE – 🚂. Ⓡ. National Rail tickets **not** valid. To book ✆ 0333 996 6720 or visit www.westcoastrailways.co.uk

a – Apr. 3 - Oct. 27.
b – ⑥ May 6 - Sept. 23.
c – Ⓑ May 1 - Sept. 29.
f – Arrives 5–7 minutes earlier.
r – 0844 on ⑥.

s – Calls to set down only.
u – Calls to pick-up only.
x – Calls on request.
¶ – Low-level platforms. Calls to set down only.

SCOTTISH ISLAND FERRIES 219

Caledonian MacBrayne Ltd operates numerous ferry services linking the Western Isles of Scotland to the mainland and to each other. Principal routes – some of which are seasonal – are listed below (see also the map on page **90**). Service frequencies, sailing-times and reservations: ✆ +44 (0)800 066 5000; fax +44 (0)1475 635 235; www.calmac.co.uk

Ardrossan – Brodick (Arran)
Ardrossan – Campbeltown (Kintyre)
Barra – Eriskay
Tarbert – Lochranza (Arran)
Colintraive – Rhubodach (Bute)
Fionnphort – Iona (Iona)
Gallanach - Kerrera (Kerrera)
Gourock - Kilcreggan
Gourock - Dunoon
Kennacraig – Port Ellen (Islay)
Largs – Cumbrae (Cumbrae)
Leverburgh (Harris) – Berneray (North Uist)
Lochaline – Fishnish (Mull)
Mallaig – Armadale (Skye)
Mallaig – Eigg, Muck, Rum and Canna
Mallaig – Lochboisdale (South Uist)
Oban – Castlebay (Barra)
Oban – Coll and Tiree
Oban – Colonsay, Port Askaig (Islay) and Kennacraig
Oban – Craignure (Mull)
Oban – Lismore
Portavadie (Cowal & Kintyre) – Tarbert (Loch Fyne)
Sconser (Skye) – Raasay
Tayinloan – Gigha
Tobermory (Mull) – Kilchoan
*Uig (Skye) – Lochmaddy (North Uist)
*Uig (Skye) – Tarbert (Harris)
Ullapool – Stornoway (Lewis)
Wemyss Bay – Rothesay (Bute)

* – Uig pier will close for maintenance from Jan. 16 - Mar. 13 when the service will be diverted to Ullapool.

EDINBURGH - GLASGOW 220

GR, SR, XC

EDINBURGH - FALKIRK - GLASGOW QUEEN STREET

km		⚒	⚒	⚒	Ⓐ	⚒	Ⓐ	⚒	Ⓐ	⚒	Ⓐ	⚒	Ⓐ	⚒	⚒	☆	⚒	⚒	Ⓐ	⚒	Ⓐ	⚒	Ⓐ	⚒	Ⓐ
0	**Edinburgh** Waverley ... d.	0600	0645	0715	0730	0745	0759	0815	0830	0845	0900	0915	0930	0945	1015	and at	1545	1615	1630	1645	1700	1715	1730	1745	1800
2	Haymarket ... d.	0604	0651	0719	0735	0750	0805	0820	0836	0850	0905	0921	0935	0950	1021	the same	1549	1621	1634	1650	1705	1720	1734	1749	1805
28	Linlithgow ... d.	0618	0704	0732	|	0804	|	0835	|	0907	|	0936	|	1003	1036	minutes	1605	1634	|	1707	|	1734	|	1807	|
41	Falkirk High ... d.	0628	0714	0742	0756	0814	0829	0845	0854	0917	0923	0946	0955	1013	1046	past each	1614	1644	1652	1717	1724	1744	1755	1817	1825
76	**Glasgow** Queen Street a.	0648	0737	0807	0821	0838	0853	0908	0916	0938	0948	1007	1021	1035	1107	hour until	1637	1707	1714	1739	1748	1808	1818	1838	1848

	⚒	Ⓐ	⚒	⚒	⚒	⚒	⚒	⚒	⚒	⚒	⚒	⚒	⚒	⑦	⑦	⑦	⑦	⑦	⑦	⑦	☆⊡	⑦	⑦	⑦	⑦
Edinburgh Waverley .... d.	1815	1830	1845	1915	1945	2015	2045	2115	2145	2215	2245	2315	2345	0800	0830	0900	0930	1000	1030	1100	and at	2200	2230	2300	2330
Haymarket ... d.	1820	1835	1850	1920	1949	2020	2049	2122	2149	2219	2250	2321	2350	0804	0834	0904	0936	1004	1034	1104	the same	2204	2235	2304	2334
Linlithgow ... d.	1834	|	1905	1937	2004	2033	2102	2137	2205	2232	2307	2335	0004	0824	0854	0924	0954	1022	1047	1117	minutes	2217	2248	2317	2347
Falkirk High ... d.	1843	1855	1915	1946	2014	2043	2112	2146	2214	2242	2317	2345	0013	0834	0902	0934	1004	1032	1055	1127	past each	2227	2256	2327	2357
Glasgow Queen Street. a.	1906	1918	1936	2006	2034	2105	2136	2206	2236	2304	2338	0012	0037	0856	0924	0954	1024	1053	1115	1149	hour until	2247	2316	2348	0019

	⚒	⚒	⚒	Ⓐ	⚒	Ⓐ	⚒	Ⓐ	⚒	Ⓐ	⚒	Ⓐ	⚒	⚒	⚒	☆❖	⚒	⚒	Ⓐ	⚒	Ⓐ	⚒	Ⓐ	⚒	Ⓐ
Glasgow Queen Street. d.	0600	0645	0715	0730	0745	0800	0815	0830	0845	0900	0915	0930	0945	1015	1045	and at	1545	1615	1630	1645	1700	1715	1730	1745	1800
Falkirk High ... d.	0619	0704	0737	0756	0804	0822	0836	0855	0907	0922	0936	0954	1006	1035	1105	the same	1604	1634	1652	1706	1722	1736	1752	1806	1822
Linlithgow ... d.	0629	0714	0747	|	0814	|	0845	|	0916	|	0945	|	1016	1045	1115	minutes	1614	1645	|	1715	|	1745	|	1816	|
Haymarket ... ▽ a.	0642	0732	0800	0816	0832	0846	0859	0918	0929	0940	1003	1021	1032	1059	1128	past each	1631	1701	1719	1729	1749	1801	1818	1831	1850
Edinburgh Waverley .... a.	0649	0738	0806	0822	0838	0852	0904	0924	0934	0945	1008	1026	1039	1104	1133	hour until	1636	1706	1724	1734	1754	1808	1824	1839	1855

	⚒	Ⓐ	⚒	⚒	⚒	⚒	⚒	⚒	⚒	⚒	⚒	⚒	⚒	⑦	⑦	⑦	⑦	⑦	⑦	⑦	★⊙	⑦	⑦	⑦	⑦
Glasgow Queen Street. d.	1815	1830	1845	1915	1945	2015	2045	2115	2145	2215	2245	2315	2345	0756	0830	0900	0930	1000	1030	1100	and at	2200	2230	2300	2330
Falkirk High ... d.	1834	1853	1904	1934	2005	2036	2105	2135	2206	2236	2305	2334	0005	0816	0849	0919	0950	1020	1050	1120	the same	2220	2250	2320	2350
Linlithgow ... d.	1844	|	1916	1946	2015	2046	2114	2144	2216	2245	2314	2344	0014	0826	0859	0927	0959	1030	1059	1127	minutes	2227	2259	2327	2359
Haymarket ... ▽ a.	1858	1917	1929	2001	2028	2059	2128	2159	2231	2301	2330	2357	0028	0848	0919	0946	1017	1048	1112	1145	past each	2240	2312	2340	0012
Edinburgh Waverley .... a.	1903	1922	1935	2008	2033	2104	2133	2204	2236	2309	2338	0003	0036f	0853	0924	0952	1022	1053	1117	1150	hour until	2246	2318	2345	0017

EDINBURGH - MOTHERWELL - GLASGOW CENTRAL

km		⑥	Ⓐ	⚒2	⚒2	⑥2	Ⓐ2	⚒2		⚒2	⚒A	Ⓐ2	⑥2	Ⓐ2	⑥2	⚒A	ⒶB	⑥2	Ⓐ2	⑦A	⑦A	⑦B
0	**Edinburgh** Waverley ... d.	0624	0626	0742	1020	1150	1156	1349	...	1550	1712	1748	1748	1825	1829	1912	2019	2313	2313	1712	1914	2120
2	Haymarket ... d.	0629	|	0746	1024	1154	1200	1355	...	1554	1717	1753	1753	1830	1833	1917	2024	2317	2317	1717	1918	2125
71	Motherwell ... a.	0705	0705	0834	1103	1303	1303	1440	...	1639	1756	1848	1905	1933	1934	1955	2101	0013	0022	1753	1956	2203
92	**Glasgow** Central ... a.	0724	0725	0856	1127	1323	1326	1503	...	1658	1813	1912	1931	1955	1953	2013	2126	...	...	1813	2015	2224

	⚒2	⚒B	⚒2	⚒A	⑥2		Ⓐ2	Ⓐ2	⑥2	⑥2	Ⓐ2	⑥2	Ⓐ2	ⒶA	⑥		⚒2	⑥	Ⓐ	⑦A		⑦
Glasgow Central ... d.	...	0648	0705	0748	0940	...	0943	1145	1146	1340	1342	1534	1533	1900	1900	...	1947	2105	2105	1900	...	2058
Motherwell ... d.	0559	0704	0721	0807	1000	...	1005	1202	1202	1400	1403	1558	1558	1915	1915	...	2009	|	2123	1915	...	2118
Haymarket ... a.	0711	0747	0821	0850	1054	...	1055	1254	1255	1454	1502	1654	1704	1954	1953	...	2056	2155	|	1958	...	2203
Edinburgh Waverley ... a.	0716	0753	0827	0855	1059	...	1100	1259	1300	1459	1507	1700	1711	1959	2000	...	2101	2201	2221	2004	...	2208

☛ Trains also run **Edinburgh Waverley - Bathgate - Airdrie - Glasgow Queen Street Low Level** (up to four trains per hour on Ⓐ; two per hour on ⑥⑦).
☛ Trains also run **Edinburgh Waverley - Shotts - Glasgow Central** (one train per hour on ⚒; every two hours on ⑦).

A – To/from destinations on Tables **116** and **124**.
B – To/from London Kings Cross (Table **180**).
f – Arrives 0032 on Ⓐ.

⊙ – The 1230, 1530 and 1730 from Glasgow arrive Haymarket 1319, 1618 and 1817 and Edinburgh 1324, 1623 and 1823 respectively.
⊡ – The 1530 and 1730 from Edinburgh arrive Glasgow 1620 and 1820 respectively.
❖ – The 1315 from Glasgow arrives Haymarket 1404 and Edinburgh 1408⑥, 1410Ⓐ.

☆ – Timings may vary by ± 4 minutes.
★ – Timings may vary by ± 5 minutes.
▽ – Trains call to set down only.

GLASGOW and EDINBURGH - DUNDEE - ABERDEEN 222

GR, SR, XC

🍷 conveyed on most trains with first class seating.

km		⚒ 2G	⚒ A	⚒ 2E	⚒	⚒	⚒	⚒	⚒ 2	⚒	⚒	⚒ 2	⚒	⚒	⚒ 2	⚒ 2	⑦	⚒ 2	⚒	⚒	⚒ 2	⚒ 2	⑦	⚒	⚒ 2	⑦	⑦	⚒
0	**Edinburgh** Waverley 223/4 d.	...	...	...	...	0530	...	...	0600	0630	...	0700	0730	...	...	0801	0804	...	0830	...	...	0901	0910	0930	...	0915	...	...
2	Haymarket ... 223/4 d.	...	...	...	...	0535	...	...	0604	0635	...	0706	0735	...	...	0807	0809	...	0835	...	...	0905	0915	0935	...	0920	...	...
42	Kirkcaldy ... 223 d.	...	0516s	...	...	0604	...	...	0645	0703	...	0747	|	...	...	0848	|	...	|	...	...	0946	0950	|	...	1005	...	...
54	Markinch ... 223 d.	...	|	...	...	0613	...	...	0654	|	...	0756	|	...	...	0857	|	...	|	...	...	0955	|	|	...	1014	...	...
82	Leuchars ... △ d.	...	0544s	...	...	0634	...	...	0714	0726	...	0816	0827	...	...	0920	|	...	0932	...	...	1015	1015	1026	...	1035	...	...
	Glasgow Queen St. 223 d.	...	|	...	...	|	...	0551	|	|	...	|	|	0741	...	|	|	0810	|	0841	...	|	|	|	0908	|	0933	0941
	Stirling ... 223/4 d.	...	|	...	...	|	...	0621	|	|	...	|	|	0809	...	|	|	0838	|	0909	...	|	|	|	0944	|	1011	1011
	Perth ... 223 d.	...	|	0600	...	|	0638	0658	|	|	0755t	|	|	0847f	...	|	|	0914	|	0950	...	|	|	|	1021	|	1048	1046f
95	**Dundee** ... d.	0539	0605s	0625	0642	0649	0706f	0725	0728	0743	0824f	0830	0843	0909	0929	0934	0920	0939	0947	1012	1025	1029	1030	1041	1046	1051	1111	1114f
112	Carnoustie ... d.	0556	0622s	0640	|	0703	0722	0736	...	|	0841	...	|	|	0946	...	|	...	|	|	1039	...	|	|	...	|	1126	|
123	Arbroath ... d.	0603	0631s	0647	|	0712	0731	0744	...	0800	0849	...	0900	0925	0954	...	|	...	1007	1028	1047	...	1047	1058	...	1107	1134	1130
145	Montrose ... d.	0619	0648s	0702	|	0727	...	0758	...	0814	...	...	0914	0939	...	...	|	...	1021	1044	...	...	1103	1112	...	1122	1148	1148
184	Stonehaven ... d.	0645	0715s	0726	|	0751	...	0819	...	0835	...	...	0935	|	...	...	|	...	1042	|	...	...	1127	1133	...	1144	1212	|
210	**Aberdeen** ... a.	0706	0740	0746	0756	0812	...	0842	...	0852	...	...	0956	1015	...	...	1029	...	1105	1122	...	...	1147	1150	...	1206	1234	1239

	⚒ 2	⚒ 2	⚒ C	⚒	⑦	⑦	⚒ 2	⚒ 2	⚒	⑦ 2	⚒	⑦	⚒ 2	⚒ 2	⑦	⚒	⑦	⚒ 2	⚒ 2	⚒	⑦ 2	⚒	⑦	⚒ 2	⚒ 2	⚒ C	⚒ 2	⑦ C
Edinburgh Waverley 223/4 d.	...	1000	1027	...	...	1050	...	1100	1130	1132	...	...	...	1201	1241	...	...	...	1300	1330	1336	...	...	...	1400	1430	...	1433
Haymarket ... 223/4 d.	...	1005	1033	...	...	1054	...	1104	1135	1136	...	...	...	1205	1246	...	...	...	1304	1335	1340	...	...	...	1405	1435	...	1439
Kirkcaldy ... 223 d.	...	1046	1105	...	...	1123	...	1145	|	1208	...	...	...	1246	1315	...	...	...	1345	|	1412	...	...	...	1447	1507	...	1511
Markinch ... 223 d.	...	1055	|	...	...	|	...	1154	|	1217	...	...	...	1255	|	...	...	...	1354	|	1421	...	...	...	1457	|	...	|
Leuchars ... △ d.	...	1115	1130	...	...	1147	...	1214	1225	1239	...	...	...	1315	1338	...	...	...	1414	1428	1443	...	...	...	1518	1531	...	1536
Glasgow Queen St. 223 d.	...	|	|	1041	1045	|	...	|	|	|	1141	1145	...	|	|	1240	1243	...	|	|	|	1340	1345	...	|	|	1412	|
Stirling ... 223/4 d.	...	|	|	1109	1112	|	...	|	|	|	1210	1212	...	|	|	1313	1310	...	|	|	|	1408	1412	...	|	|	1448	|
Perth ... 223 d.	...	|	|	1140	1145	|	...	|	|	|	1244	1247	...	|	|	1344	1344	...	|	|	|	1445c	1450	...	|	|	1528	|
Dundee ... d.	1124	1129	1146	1203	1211	1211r	1224	1228	1240	1255	1307	1310	1324	1330	1353	1407	1408	1424	1431	1443	1457	1514f	1512	1527	1532	1550	1553	1552
Carnoustie ... d.	1141	...	|	|	|	|	1240	...	|	...	|	|	1338	...	|	|	|	1440	...	|	...	|	1524	1541	...	|	...	|
Arbroath ... d.	1149	...	1203	1220	1227	1227	1249	...	1259	...	1324	1326	1346	...	1409	1424	1425	1449	...	1500	...	1534	1531	1549	...	1607	...	1609
Montrose ... d.	...	...	1219	1234	1242	1242	...	...	|	...	1338	1341	...	...	1423	1438	1439	...	...	|	...	1548	1545	...	...	1623	...	1625
Stonehaven ... d.	...	...	1243	|	1304	1304	...	...	1331	...	|	1403	...	...	1447	|	1500	...	...	1534	...	|	1606	...	...	1646	...	1649
Aberdeen ... a.	...	...	1302	1313	1323	1323	...	...	1350	...	1414	1422	...	...	1505	1517	1517	...	...	1553	...	1629	1627	...	...	1706	...	1710

A – Ⓡ. 🛏 1, 2 class and (2) London Euston - Aberdeen. Departs London previous day. Train stops to set down only. See also Table **161**.
C – From destinations on Table **180**.
E – To Inverurie (Table **225**).
G – To Inverness (Table **225**).
c – Arrives 1437.
f – Arrives 5 minutes earlier.
r – Arrives 1200.
t – Ⓐ only.
s – Stops to set down only.
△ – Frequent 🚌 connections available to/from **St Andrews.** Journey 10 minutes. Operator: Stagecoach (routes 42, 94, 99).

222 GLASGOW and EDINBURGH - DUNDEE - ABERDEEN

GR, SR, XC

🍷 conveyed on most trains with first class seating.

	⚒ G	⚒ 2	⑦	⚒ 2	⚒	⚒ 2	⑦ 2	⚒	⑦	⚒ 2	⚒ 2	⑦	⚒	⚒ 2	⑦	⚒	⚒ 2	⚒ 2	⑦	⚒	⑦ 2	⚒ 2	⚒	⑦	⚒ 2	⑤⑥ D	⑦ D
Edinburgh Waverley **223/4** d.	...	...	...	1500	1530	...	1534	...	...	...	1600	1607	1630	...	...	...	...	1700	1705	1730	1734	...	...	...	1750	1813	1813
Haymarket **223/4** d.	...	...	...	1504	1535	...	1538	...	...	...	1604	1611	1635u	...	...	...	...	1704	1710	1738	1739	...	...	...	1757	1817	1817
Kirkcaldy **223** d.	...	...	...	1545	|	...	1610	...	...	...	1645	1642	|	...	...	...	...	1745	1740	|	1811	...	...	...	1840	|	|
Markinch **223** d.	...	...	...	1554	|	...	1623	...	...	...	1654	1651	|	...	...	...	...	1754	|	|	1820	...	...	...	1848	|	|
Leuchars △ d.	...	...	...	1614	1626	...	1645	...	...	...	1714	1710	1726	...	...	...	...	1817	1803	1832	1842	...	...	...	1909	|	|
Glasgow Queen St. **223** d.	1439	...	1450	|	|	1511	|	1539	1545	...	|	|	|	1610	1645	1638	...	|	|	|	|	1710	1741	1745	|	|	|
Stirling **223/4** d.	1509	...	1519	|	|	1542	|	1609	1612	...	|	|	|	1640	1712	1705	...	|	|	|	|	1745u	1814	1814	|	|	|
Perth **223** d.	1541	...	1555	|	|	1630	|	1643	1648	...	|	|	|	1720	1742	1746f	...	|	|	|	|	1830f	1850f	1847	|	|	|
Dundee d.	1604	1618	1617	1628	1641	1655	1659	1704	1710	1725	1729	1725	1742	1754f	1805	1809	1831	1833	1818	1856f	1856	1900	1913	1910	1923	1936	1929
Carnoustie d.	|	1634	|	...	|	...	...	|	|	1741	...	1740	|	1816	|	|	1853	...	|	|	...	...	1924	1922	...	|	...
Arbroath d.	1621	1643	1634	...	1659	...	...	1722	1726	1750	...	1747	1807f	1824	1821	1834	1902	...	1835	1913	...	...	1932	1929	...	|	...
Montrose d.	1635	...	1649	...	1713	...	...	1736	1741	...	...	1801	1822	...	1835	1851	...	...	1849	1927	...	...	1947	1944	...	|	...
Stonehaven d.	|	...	1712	...	1737	...	...	1757	1806	...	...	1824	1845	...	1856	|	...	...	1910	1948	...	...	2011	2010	...	|	...
Aberdeen a.	1713	...	1730	...	1755	...	...	1815	1825	...	...	1842	1904	...	1918	1931	...	...	1927	2005	...	...	2029	2029	...	2046	...

	⚒ 2	⑦ C	⚒ C	⚒	⚒ 2	⚒ 2	⑦ 2	Ⓐ C	⚒	⚒ 2	⚒	⑦	⚒ 2	Ⓐ C	⚒	⑦	⚒ 2	⚒ 2	⚒	⚒	⑦	⚒ 2	⑦ 2	⚒ 2	Ⓐ 2	⚒ 2	⑦ 2
Edinburgh Waverley **223/4** d.	...	1835	1835	...	...	1900	1915	1927	1931	...	...	...	2000	2034	...	2100	2100	...	2130	...	...	2200	2228	2300	...	...	...
Haymarket **223/4** d.	...	1841	1840	...	...	1905	1919	1933	1937	...	...	...	2004	2039	...	2105	2104	...	2136	...	...	2204	2232	2304	...	...	...
Kirkcaldy **223** d.	...	1913	1913	...	...	1946	2002	|	|	...	...	...	2047	2111	...	2134	2147	...	2204	...	...	2247	2315	2347	...	...	...
Markinch **223** d.	...	|	|	...	...	1954	2011	|	|	...	...	...	2055	|	...	2143	2155	...	|	...	...	2258	2324	2356	...	...	...
Leuchars △ d.	...	1937	1940	...	...	2015	2032	|	2027	...	...	...	2116	2139	...	2204	2216	...	2227	...	...	2322	2345	0016	...	...	...
Glasgow Queen St. **223** d.	1810	|	|	1841	...	|	|	|	|	1909	1937	1944	|	|	2040	|	|	...	|	2140	2145	|	|	|	2310	2335	2344
Stirling **223/4** d.	1843	|	|	1909	...	|	|	2012	|	1946	2005	2011	|	|	2108	|	|	...	|	2209	2212	|	|	|	2339	0004	0021
Perth **223** d.	1926	|	|	1944	...	|	|	...	|	2026	2043v	2049	|	|	2145	|	|	...	|	2246	2249	|	|	|	0018	0042	0100
Dundee d.	1950	1953	1957	2008	2015	2029	2048	...	2045	2052	2111f	2112	2133	2154	2212	2219	2230	2236	2255	2308	2312	2338	2359	0032	0044	...	...
Carnoustie d.	...	|	|	|	2032	...	...	...	|	...	2123	|	...	|	2224	|	...	2253	|	2325	2323	...	...	...	...	...	...
Arbroath d.	...	2010	2015	2025	2040	...	...	...	2102	...	2131	2128	...	2212	2231	2239	...	2301	2311	2332	2330	...	...	...	...	...	...
Montrose d.	...	2026	2030	2039	...	...	...	...	2116	...	2150	2142	...	2228	2246	2253	...	...	2325	2347	2345	...	...	...	...	...	...
Stonehaven d.	...	2050	2053	|	...	...	...	...	|	...	2214	2206	...	2252	|	2314	...	...	2347	0012	0006	...	...	...	...	...	...
Aberdeen a.	...	2110	2113	2121	...	...	...	...	2153	...	2234	2224	...	2311	2324	2335	...	...	0009	0032	0023	...	...	...	...	...	...

km																											
		⚒ 2	⚒ 2	⚒	⚒ 2	⚒ 2	⚒	⚒	⑦ 2	⚒ 2	⚒ 2	⚒	⚒ 2	⚒ G	⚒ 2	⑦	⚒	⚒ C	⚒ 2	⚒ D	⑦ 2	⚒ 2	⚒ 2	⚒	⚒	⚒ 2	Ⓐ 2
0	**Aberdeen** d.	0507	...	...	...	...	0534	0557	...	...	...	0639	...	0708	...	...	0738	0752	...	0820	...	...	...	0854	0904	...	...
26	Stonehaven d.	0526	...	...	...	...	|	0613	...	...	...	0655	...	0727	...	...	0754	0811	...	0837	...	...	...	|	0920	...	...
65	Montrose d.	0552	...	...	...	...	0609	0635	...	...	...	0715	...	0747	...	...	0814	0833	...	0859	...	...	...	0927	0940	...	...
87	Arbroath d.	▬	...	...	...	0606	0624	0649	...	0711	...	0730	0743	0801	...	...	0829	0850	...	0914	...	...	0922	0941	0955	...	*1006*
97	Carnoustie d.	⚒	...	...	...	0613	|	0656	...	0718	...	|	0750	|	...	...	|	|	...	|	...	...	0929	|	|	...	*1013*
115	**Dundee** d.	2	0540	0548	0635	0638	0648	0715f	0724	0735	0740	0752	0815	0826f	0840	0845	0850	0908	0915	0933	0925	0942	0943	0959	1013	1018	1040
149	**Perth** **223** d.	0516	|	0613	|	...	0711	|	|	...	|	0814	0842k	|	|	0907	0912	|	0941	|	|	|	...	1021	|	1043	|
202	Stirling **223/4** d.	0554	|	0652	|	...	0754	|	|	...	|	0844	0920k	|	|	0941	0946	|	1019	|	|	|	...	1051	|	1122	|
249	**Glasgow** Queen St. **223** a.	0639	|	0724	|	...	0832	|	|	...	|	0921	0956	|	|	1015	1015	|	1053	|	|	|	...	1120	|	1153	|
	Leuchars △ d.	...	0553	...	0651	...	...	0727	0737	...	0753	...	...	0838	0853	...	...	0922	...	|	0938	0956	...	...	1026	...	1053
	Markinch **223** d.	...	0615	...	0716	...	...	|	0759	...	0815	...	...	|	0914	...	...	|	...	|	1000	1018	...	...	|	...	1114
	Kirkcaldy **223** d.	...	0631	...	0727	...	...	|	0810	...	0826	...	...	|	0925	...	...	0947	...	|	1011	1028	...	...	|	...	1125
	Haymarket **223/4** a.	...	0713	...	0809	...	...	0828j	0858	...	0908	...	...	0930	1007	...	...	1019	...	1047	1055	1111	...	...	1114	...	1209a
	Edinburgh Waverley **223/4** a.	...	0721	...	0814	...	...	0833j	0903	...	0913	...	...	0937	1012	...	...	1026	...	1054	1100	1117	...	...	1122	...	1214a

	⑦	⚒	⑦ C	⚒ C	⑦ 2	⚒ 2	⑦ 2	⚒ 2	⑦	⚒	⚒	⚒ 2	⑦ D	⚒ 2	⑦ E	⚒	⑦ C	⚒ 2	⚒	⑦ 2	⚒ 2	⑦	⑦	⚒	⚒ 2	⚒	⚒ 2
Aberdeen d.	0930	0944	0947	0952	...	...	...	...	1033	1047	1101	...	1110	...	1132	1145	1147	...	1207	...	...	1230	1244	1254	...	1309	...
Stonehaven d.	0946	|	1006	1011	...	...	...	...	1049	|	1117	...	1127	...	1149	|	1206	...	1223	...	...	1247	1304	|	...	|	...
Montrose d.	1009	1021f	1028	1033	...	...	...	...	1109	1123	1137	...	1149	...	1211	1221	1228	...	1245	...	...	1308	1329	1327	...	1346	...
Arbroath d.	1024	1036	1045	1050	...	...	...	*1102*	1124	1138	1152	...	1204	*1210*	1225	1235	1245	...	1259	...	*1308*	1323	1343	1341	...	1401	*1409*
Carnoustie d.	1031	|	|	|	...	...	...	*1109*	|	|	|	...	|	*1217*	|	|	|	...	|	...	*1315*	|	1350	|	...	|	*1416*
Dundee d.	1050	1055	1104	1109	...	1115	1120	1140	1142	1156	1210	1215	1222	1240	1243	1253	1304	1310	1317	1320	1340	1343	1406	1359	1414	1419	1440
Perth **223** d.	1111	1120	|	|	...	1141	|	|	1215r	1218	|	1240	|	|	1309	1315	|	1345y	|	|	|	1407	|	1421	1440	|	|
Stirling **223/4** d.	1146	1152	|	|	1152	1227	|	|	1248	1248	|	1317	|	|	1344	1345	|	1423	|	|	|	1442	|	1451	1521	|	|
Glasgow Queen St. **223** a.	1214	1221	|	|	|	1301	|	|	1315	1321	|	1353	|	|	1412	1415	|	1454	|	|	|	1510	|	1521	1554	|	|
Leuchars △ d.	...	...	1118	1123	|	...	1133	1153	...	...	1223	...	|	1253	...	...	1318	...	1329	1333	1353	...	1419	...	...	1431	1453
Markinch **223** d.	...	...	|	|	|	...	1155	1214	...	...	|	...	|	1314	...	...	|	...	|	1356	1414	...	|	...	...	|	1514
Kirkcaldy **223** d.	...	...	1143	1148	|	...	1206	1225	...	...	|	...	|	1325	...	...	1344	...	|	1406	1425	...	1446	...	...	|	1525
Haymarket **223/4** a.	...	...	1216	1219	1235	...	1240	1307	...	...	1314	...	1336	1408	...	...	1420	...	1418	1440	1507	...	1517	...	...	1520	1607
Edinburgh Waverley **223/4** a.	...	...	1222	1225	1240	...	1245	1312	...	...	1320	...	1343	1413	...	...	1426	...	1426c	1445	1512	...	1523	...	...	1526	1612

	⑦	⚒	⑦ C	⚒	⚒ 2	⑦ 2	⚒ 2	⚒ 2	⑦	⚒	⚒ C	⚒ 2	⑦	⑦	⚒ 2	⚒	⚒	⚒ 2	⚒	⑦ 2	⚒ 2	⚒ 2	⚒ 2	⑦	⑦	⚒ 2	⚒
Aberdeen d.	1334	1346	1347	1356	...	...	...	...	1433	1444	1452	...	1508	1531	...	...	1535	...	1604	...	...	...	1630	1631	1704	...	1741
Stonehaven d.	1350	|	1406	1413	...	...	...	...	1450	|	1511	...	1528	1548	...	...	|	...	1620	...	...	...	|	1647	1720	...	1757
Montrose d.	1410	1423	1428	1437f	...	...	...	...	1511	1517	1533	...	1549	1612	...	...	1612	...	1648	...	...	...	1713f	1707	1743	...	1822
Arbroath d.	1425	1437	1445	1452	...	...	1504	...	1526	1531	1550	...	1603	1626	1559	...	1627	...	1703	...	...	1712	1728	1722	1758	*1817*	1836
Carnoustie d.	|	|	|	|	...	...	1511	...	|	|	|	...	1610	|	1606	...	|	...	1710	...	...	1719	|	|	|	*1824*	|
Dundee d.	1443	1456	1503	1510	1515	1515	1528	1542	1545	1554f	1609	1616	1624	1644	1624	1638	1647	1707	1724	1721	1740	1736	1750	1740	1817	1847	1854
Perth **223** d.	1504	1519	|	|	1541	|	...	|	1609	1615	|	1646f	|	1706	...	|	1713	1738f	|	|	|	...	1811	1801	|	|	1918
Stirling **223/4** d.	1544	1548	|	|	1621	|	...	|	1643	1644s	|	1726	|	1740	...	|	1747	1817	|	|	|	...	1843	1834	|	|	1949
Glasgow Queen St. **223** a.	1612	1619	|	|	1656	|	...	|	1712	1718	|	1758	|	1809	...	|	1822	1852	|	|	|	...	1914	1909	|	|	2022
Leuchars △ d.	...	...	1517	1522	...	1528	...	1555	...	...	1624	...	1637	...	...	1651	...	...	1736	1734	1753	...	...	...	1829	1900	...
Markinch **223** d.	...	...	|	|	...	1551	...	1616	...	...	|	...	|	...	...	1713	...	...	|	1757	1816	...	...	...	|	1921	...
Kirkcaldy **223** d.	...	...	1543	|	...	1601	...	1627	...	...	1649	...	1704	...	...	1724	...	...	|	1807	1827	...	...	...	1852	1932	...
Haymarket **223/4** a.	...	...	1618	1611e	...	1635	...	1710	...	...	1719	...	1734	...	...	1807	...	...	1824	1841	1906	...	...	...	1921	2015	...
Edinburgh Waverley **223/4** a.	...	...	1624	1618e	...	1640	...	1715	...	...	1725	...	1740	...	...	1813	...	...	1829	1846	1913	...	...	...	1926	2023	...

	⚒ 2	⚒ 2	⑦	Ⓐ C	⑦ 2	⚒	⚒ 2	⚒ 2	⑦	⚒	⚒ 2	⑦	⚒	⚒ 2	⑦	⚒	⑤ 2	①–④ B	⑦ B	⚒	⚒	⚒ 2	⚒ 2	⑤⑥	⑤ B	⚒	⑦ 2
Aberdeen d.	...	...	1745	1818	...	1840	...	...	1904	1915	...	1946	1947	...	2008	2010	...	2026	2034	2044	2106	...	...	2135	2143	2228	2226
Stonehaven d.	...	...	1801	1837	...	|	...	...	1921	1931	...	2006	|	...	2024	2026	...	2043u	2053u	2103	|	...	...	2152	2201u	2247	2246
Montrose d.	...	...	1824	1859	...	1916	...	...	1945	1956	...	2027	2020	...	2047	2048	...	2106u	2117u	2128	2139	...	...	2213	2226u	2311	2310
Arbroath d.	...	1846	1839	1916	...	1930	...	1938	1959	2010	...	2041	2037	2051	2102	2103	...	2123u	2133u	2142	2154	...	2205	2228	2244u	2325	2324
Carnoustie d.	...	1853	|	|	...	|	...	1944	2007	2016	...	|	|	2058	|	|	...	2131u	2141u	|	|	...	2211	|	2253u	2332	2331
Dundee d.	1914	1911	1858	1934	1916	1948	1953	2002	2023	2030	2044	2103	2101	2113	2120	2121	2149	2148u	2156u	2201	2212	2231	2229	2248	2309u	2349	2348
Perth **223** d.	1946y	...	1920	|	|	2014	|	...	|	|	|	2128f	2122	...	|	|	|	|	|	2223	|	|	...	|	|	0012t	0011
Stirling **223/4** d.	2027	...	1953	|	|	2046	|	...	|	|	|	2203	2152	...	|	|	|	|	|	2253	|	|	...	|	|	...	|
Glasgow Queen St. **223** a.	2056	...	2021	|	|	2115	|	...	|	|	|	2238	2222	...	|	|	|	|	|	2321	|	|	...	|	|	...	|
Leuchars △ d.	...	...	...	1948	1929	...	2005	...	2036	2043	2057	...	...	...	2132	2135	2202	2206u	2214u	...	2224	2244	...	|	2328u	...	|
Markinch **223** d.	...	...	...	|	1951	...	2027	...	|	|	2118	...	...	...	2154	2157	2224	|	|	...	|	2305	...	|	|	...	|
Kirkcaldy **223** d.	...	...	...	2013	2002	...	2037	...	2102	|	2129	...	...	...	2203	2206	2234	2233u	2242u	...	|	2316	...	|	2359u	...	|
Haymarket **223/4** a.	...	...	...	2043	2047	...	2124	...	2133	2143	2213	...	...	...	2231	2241	2318	...	...	...	2322	0034d	...	0005	...	...	*0125*
Edinburgh Waverley **223/4** a.	...	...	...	2049	2052	...	2129	...	2138	2149	2221	...	...	...	2238	2246	2324	...	...	...	2329	0039d	...	0013	...	...	*0135*

B – Ⓡ. 🛏 1, 2 class and (2) Aberdeen - London Euston. Train stops to pick up only. See also Table **161**.
C – From / to destinations on Table **180**.
D – From / to destinations on Table **124**.
E – From Inverurie (Table **225**).
G – To / from Inverness (Table **225**).

a – 4 minutes earlier on Ⓐ.
b – Arrives 1359 on ⑥.
c – Arrives 1422 on ⑥.
d – Arrives 33 minutes earlier on ⑥⑦ mornings.
e – 4–5 minutes later on ⑥.
f – Arrives 5–7 minutes earlier.

g – Arrives 1624.
h – Arrives 2103.
j – 9 minutes earlier on ⑥.
k – 4–6 minutes later on Ⓐ.
r – Arrives 1202.
s – Stops to set down only.
t – Ⓐ only.

u – Stops to pick up only.
v – Arrives 2034.
y – Arrives 8 minutes earlier.
z – 🚌 connection from Dundee d. 2355.

△ – Frequent 🚌 connections available to / from **St Andrews.** Journey 10 minutes. Operator: Stagecoach (routes 42, 94, 99).

SR 2nd class EDINBURGH - TWEEDBANK 222a

km		⚒	⚒	⚒	⚒	⚒	⚒	⚒	⚒	⚒	⚒	Ⓐ	⑥	⚒	⚒	⚒	⑥	Ⓐ	⚒	⚒	⚒	⚒	⚒	Ⓐ	⑥	⑥
0	**Edinburgh** Waverley .... d.		0610	0640	0714	0740	0811	0843	0915	0942	1011	1043	1043	1111	1143	1212	1243	1245	1310	1343	1413	1442	1511	1540	1543	1613
13	Eskbank .... d.		0632	0703	0733	0802	0832	0902	0934	1004	1034	1103	1105	1132	1203	1233	1302	1304	1332	1403	1433	1502	1532	1603	1602	1634
15	Newtongrange .... d.		0635	0706	0736	0805	0835	0905	0937	1007	1037	1106	1108	1135	1206	1236	1305	1307	1335	1406	1436	1505	1535	1606	1605	1637
53	Galashiels .... d.		0706	0737	0808	0836	0906	0937	1008	1038	1108	1137	1139	1206	1237	1307	1336	1338	1406	1437	1507	1536	1607	1638	1636	1708
57	**Tweedbank** .... a.		0710	0741	0812	0840	0910	0941	1013	1043	1114	1141	1143	1211	1242	1311	1340	1342	1410	1443	1512	1540	1611	1642	1640	1712

	Ⓐ	⑥	Ⓐ	⚒	Ⓐ	⑥	⑥	Ⓐ	⚒	⚒	⚒	⚒	⚒	⚒	⑦	⑦	⑦	⑦	⑦	⑦	⑦	⑦	⑦		⑦	⑦
Edinburgh Waverley ......d.	1619	1643	1645	1715	1741	1744	1816	1816	1842	1943	2043	2143	2242	2343		0912	1011	1113	1212	1312	1411	1515	1611	and hourly until	2212	2311
Eskbank ....d.	1638	1704	1706	1735	1805	1804	1835	1838	1904	2004	2102	2202	2302	0003		0931	1031	1132	1231	1331	1432	1534	1631		2232	2330
Newtongrange ....d.	1641	1707	1709	1738	1808	1807	1838	1841	1907	2007	2105	2205	2305	0006		0934	1034	1135	1234	1334	1435	1537	1634		2235	2333
Galashiels..........d.	1712	1738	1740	1809	1839	1838	1909	1912	1938	2037	2136	2236	2336	0037		1005	1105	1206	1305	1405	1507	1608	1705		2306	0004
Tweedbank..........a.	1716	1742	1744	1814	1843	1842	1913	1916	1943	2043	2140	2243	2341	0043		1009	1109	1210	1309	1409	1512	1612	1710		2310	0009

	⚒	⚒	⚒	⚒	⚒	⚒	⚒	⚒	⑥	Ⓐ	⚒	Ⓐ	⑥	⚒	⑥	Ⓐ	⚒	Ⓐ	⑥	⚒	⚒	⚒	⚒	Ⓐ	⑥	⚒
Tweedbank..........d.		0549	0620	0650	0719	0749	0819	0850	0921	0921	0951	1020	1020	1049	1119	1121	1149	1218	1219	1249	1319	1350	1419	1447	1450	1519
Galashiels..........d.		0553	0624	0654	0723	0753	0823	0854	0925	0925	0955	1024	1024	1053	1123	1125	1153	1222	1223	1253	1323	1354	1423	1451	1454	1523
Newtongrange ....d.		0622	0653	0723	0752	0822	0852	0923	0954	0954	1024	1053	1053	1122	1152	1154	1222	1251	1252	1322	1352	1423	1452	1520	1523	1552
Eskbank ....d.		0625	0656	0726	0755	0825	0855	0926	0957	0957	1027	1056	1056	1125	1155	1157	1225	1254	1255	1325	1355	1426	1455	1523	1526	1555
Edinburgh Waverley ......a.		0647	0720	0746	0817	0848	0915	0948	1019	1023	1048	1115	1118	1148	1218	1216	1250	1315	1321	1349	1419	1448	1518	1545	1549	1618

	⑥	Ⓐ	⑥	Ⓐ	⚒	⑥	Ⓐ	⑥	Ⓐ	⚒	⚒	⑥	Ⓐ	⚒	Ⓐ	⑥	⚒	⚒	⑦	⑦	⑦	⑦	⑦		⑦	⑦
Tweedbank..........d.	1549	1549	1619	1621	1650	1719	1722	1749	1751	1819	1849	1921	1923	2019	2114	2119	2219	2319		0848	0947	1047	1147	and hourly until	2143	2247
Galashiels..........d.	1553	1553	1623	1625	1654	1723	1726	1753	1755	1823	1853	1925	1927	2023	2118	2123	2223	2323		0852	0951	1051	1151		2147	2251
Newtongrange ....d.	1622	1622	1652	1655	1723	1752	1755	1822	1824	1852	1922	1954	1956	2052	2147	2152	2252	2352		0921	1020	1120	1220		2216	2320
Eskbank ....d.	1625	1625	1655	1658	1726	1755	1758	1825	1827	1855	1925	1957	1959	2055	2150	2155	2255	2355		0924	1023	1123	1223		2219	2323
Edinburgh Waverley ......a.	1648	1651	1715	1724	1752	1819	1819	1848	1850	1918	1948	2019	2023	2118	2210	2217	2319	0021		0943	1042	1143	1245		2243	2343

SR EDINBURGH and GLASGOW - PERTH - INVERNESS 223

Most Inverness trains convey 🍸.

km		⚒	⚒A	⚒2	⚒	⚒2	⚒	⑥	⚒2	⑦	⑦	⚒2	⚒	⚒	⚒	⑦2	⑦	⚒2	⚒2	⚒	⚒2	⚒	⑦	⚒2	⑦	⑦P	⑥
0	**Edinburgh** Waverley 222/4 d.	...	...	0635	...	0735	...	0837	0834	...	0925	0933	...	...	1033	1035	...	1038	1135	...	1235	1330	...	1334	1354	...	1435
2	Haymarket.......... 222/4 d.	...	...	0639	...	0739	...	0842	0840	...	0930	0939	...	...	1037	1039	...	1042	1139	...	1239	1335	...	1339	1358	...	1440
42	Kirkcaldy .... 222 d.	...	...	0723	...	0822	...	|	0924	...	|	1023	...	...	|	|	...	1125	1222	...	1322	|	...	1422	|	...	1524
54	Markinch .... 222 d.	...	...	0732	...	0831	...	|	0933	...	|	1032	...	...	|	|	...	1135	1231	...	1331	|	...	1431	|	...	1533
	Glasgow Queen St..222 d.	...	...	|	0707	|	0841	|	|	0933	|	|	1007	1041	|	|	1111	|	|	1207	|	|	1345	|	|	1438	|
	Stirling .... 222/4 d.	...	0459	|	0734	|	0909	0931	|	1011	1022	|	1036	1109	1117	1123	1141	|	|	1236	|	1416	1412	|	1438	1508	|
91	**Perth**.......... 222 d.	...	0543	0805	0811	0907	0948	1002	1010	1046	1056	1104	1116f	1137	1156	...	1221	1209	1303	1312	1410	1450	1448	1513	1512f	1546	1612
116	Dunkeld & Birnam .... d.	...	0603	...	0834f	...	...	1019	...	...	1112	...	1140r	...	1213	...	1239	...	...	1329	...	1507	...	...	1530	|	...
137	Pitlochry .... d.	...	0617	...	0847	...	...	1033	...	...	1130f	...	1154	...	1228	...	1253	...	...	1342	...	1521	...	...	1544	1614	...
148	Blair Atholl .... d.	...	0629	...	0856	...	...	|	...	...	1140	...	|	...	1238	...	|	...	...	|	...	1531	...	...	1553	|	...
186	Dalwhinnie.......... d.	...	0700	...	0921	...	...	|	...	...	1205	...	|	...	1303	...	|	...	...	|	...	1556	...	...	1622f	|	...
202	Newtonmore.......... d.	...	0712	...	0931	...	...	|	...	...	1216	...	|	...	1314	...	|	...	...	|	...	1607	...	...	1632	|	...
207	Kingussie.......... d.	0647	0718	...	0940	...	...	1115	...	...	1221	...	1236	...	1319	...	1337	...	...	1427	...	1615	...	...	1637	1656	...
226	Aviemore.......... 🚂 d.	0700	0743	...	0952	...	...	1129	...	...	1233	...	1249	...	1333	...	1349	...	...	1439	...	1629	...	...	1649	1709	...
237	Carrbridge.......... d.	0715c	0754	...	1002	...	...	|	...	...	1242	...	|	...	1342	...	1401f	...	...	|	...	1638	...	...	1658	|	...
282	**Inverness**.......... a.	0748	0842	...	1029	...	...	1201	...	...	1319	...	1325	...	1415	...	1429	...	...	1529	...	1706	...	...	1725	1745	...

	Ⓐ2	⚒	⑦	⚒2	⑦	⚒	⑥K	ⒶK	⚒2	⑦	⑦K	⚒	⚒	⚒2	⑦2	⑦P	⑦2	⚒2	⑦2	⚒	⚒	⚒	⚒	⚒2	⚒2	⑦2	⚒2
Edinburgh Waverley 222/4 d.	1440	...	...	1535	1552	...	1633	1633	1635	...	1632	...	1733	1736	1750	...	1806	1840	1855	...	...	1938	1942	2045	2145	2235	2245n
Haymarket..........222/4 d.	1444	...	...	1539	1557	...	1638	1638	1639	...	1637	...	1738	1741	1754	...	1810	1844	1859	...	...	1943	1946	2049	2149	2240	2249n
Kirkcaldy..........222 d.	1525	...	...	1622	|	...	|	|	1722	...	|	...	|	1826	1826	...	|	1927	|	...	...	|	2029	2125	2222	|	2326
Markinch..........222 d.	1534	...	...	1631	|	...	|	|	1731	...	|	...	|	1835	1836	...	|	1936	2003	...	...	|	2038	2134	2232	|	2335
Glasgow Queen St..222 d.	|	1507	1545	|	|	1638	|	|	|	1645	|	1741	|	|	|	1803	|	|	|	1906	1937	|	|	|	|	|	|
Stirling..........222/4 d.	|	1534	1612	|	1637	1705	1719	1719	|	1712	1722	1814	1823	|	|	1834	1910	|	|	1937	2005	2020	|	|	|	2333	|
Perth..........222 d.	1612	1617a	1646	1709	1711f	1741	1754	1757f	1809	1741	1801f	1845	1903	1910	1906	1912	1945	2008	2034	2028b	2034	2057f	2109	2208	2308	0011	0006
Dunkeld & Birnam.......... d.	...	1636	...	...	1727	...	|	|	...	...	...	...	1920	...	...	1929	...	...	...	2046	...	2116	...	...	...	...	...
Pitlochry.......... d.	...	1650	...	...	1741	...	1824	1827	...	...	1831	...	1934	...	...	1942	...	...	...	2100	...	2130	...	...	...	...	...
Blair Atholl.......... d.	...	1700	...	...	|	...	|	|	...	...	|	...	|	...	...	1952	...	...	...	|	...	2140	...	...	...	...	...
Dalwhinnie.......... d.	...	|	...	...	|	...	|	|	...	...	|	...	|	...	...	2017	...	...	...	2137f	...	2211r	...	...	...	...	...
Newtonmore.......... d.	...	|	...	...	|	...	|	|	...	...	|	...	|	...	...	2028	...	...	...	|	...	2222	...	...	...	...	...
Kingussie.......... d.	...	1738	...	...	1824	...	1910	1914	...	...	1916	...	2017	...	...	2033	...	...	...	2153	...	2227	...	...	...	...	...
Aviemore.......... 🚂 d.	...	1750	...	...	1837	...	1926	1930	...	...	1932	...	2032	...	...	2046	...	...	...	2205	...	2240	...	...	...	...	...
Carrbridge.......... d.	...	1758	...	...	|	...	|	|	...	...	|	...	|	...	...	2056	...	...	...	|	...	2249	...	...	...	...	...
Inverness.......... a.	...	1826	...	...	1910	...	2004	2007	...	...	2009	...	2124t	...	...	2126	...	...	...	2241	...	2318	...	...	...	...	...

	⚒2	⚒2	⚒2	⚒2	⚒2	⚒	⑦2	⚒	⑦2	⑦2	⚒K	⚒2	⑦2	⚒	⚒2	⚒	⑦K	⚒	⑦	⑦	⑦	⚒	⚒	Ⓐ2	⑥2	⑦	⚒2
Inverness.......... d.	...	...	...	0536	...	0644	...	...	...	...	0755	...	...	0842	...	0942	0940	...	...	1053	...	1050	...	...	...	1237	...
Carrbridge.......... d.	...	...	...	0603	...	|	...	...	...	...	|	...	...	0917	...	|	1011	...	...	|	...	|	...	...	...	1310	...
Aviemore.......... 🚂 d.	...	...	...	0612	...	0722	...	...	...	...	0832	...	...	0926	...	1031	1022	...	...	1128	...	1130	...	...	...	1319	...
Kingussie.......... d.	...	...	...	0624	...	0736	...	...	...	...	0847	...	...	0940	...	1043	1035	...	...	1139	...	1143	...	...	...	1338f	...
Newtonmore.......... d.	...	...	...	0629	...	|	...	...	...	...	|	...	...	0945	...	|	1040	...	...	|	...	|	...	...	...	1342	...
Dalwhinnie.......... d.	...	...	...	0640	...	|	...	...	...	...	|	...	...	0957	...	|	|	...	...	1152	...	|	...	...	...	|	...
Blair Atholl.......... d.	...	...	...	0704	...	0809	...	...	...	...	|	...	...	|	...	|	1117f	...	...	|	...	1216	...	...	...	1414	...
Pitlochry.......... d.	...	...	...	0716	...	0819	...	...	...	...	0929	...	...	1032r	...	1126	1127	...	...	1223	...	1230	...	...	...	1425	...
Dunkeld & Birnam.......... d.	...	...	...	0730	...	0834	...	...	...	...	|	...	...	1046	...	|	1141	...	...	1238	...	1242	...	...	...	1437	...
Perth..........222/4 d.	0600	0619	0716	0750	0806	0855	0850	0917	0917	0936	0959	1014	1010	1106	1115	1157	1201	1211	1215	1257	1309	1305f	1315	1324	1324	1456	1427
Stirling..........222 d.	|	|	|	0824	|	0934	|	|	0954	|	1034	|	1047	1145	|	1235	1238	|	1248	1328	1344	1337	1345	|	|	1534	|
Glasgow Queen St..222 a.	|	|	|	0856	|	|	|	|	|	|	|	|	|	1214	|	1311	|	|	1315	|	1412	|	1415	|	|	1607	|
Markinch..........222 d.	0631	0646	0753	...	0837	|	0919	0946	|	1007	|	1051	|	...	1148	...	|	1250	...	|	...	|	...	1353	1353	...	1456
Kirkcaldy..........222 d.	|	0657	0804	...	0849	|	0930	0958	|	|	|	1103	|	...	1159	...	|	1301	...	|	...	|	...	1405	1405	...	1508
Haymarket..........222/4 a.	0733	0742	0850	...	0947	1009	1018	1042	1045	1113	1108	1147	1138	...	1244	...	1314	1346	...	1405	...	1421	...	1446	1449	...	1553
Edinburgh Waverley 222/4 a.	0738	0747	0855	...	0953	1015	1023	1047	1050	1118	1114	1154	1143	...	1249	...	1320	1353	...	1410	...	1429	...	1451	1454	...	1558

	⚒	⚒	⚒	⑦	⑦	⚒2	⚒	⚒2	⑦	⑦	⚒	⚒	⑦	⑦2	⚒2	⚒	⚒2	⚒	⚒2	⚒	⑦	⑦	⚒2	Ⓐ	⑥	⑦B	ⒶB
Inverness.......... d.	1248	...	...	1326	...	...	1450	...	1522	...	...	1544	1626	...	...	1726	...	1853	...	...	1852	...	...	2023	2023	2026	2045
Carrbridge.......... d.	1324	...	...	|	...	...	|	...	|	...	...	1616	1658f	...	...	1759f	...	|	...	...	1925	...	...	2058	2058	|	|
Aviemore.......... 🚂 d.	1334	...	...	1407	...	...	1525	...	1557	...	...	1634r	1708	...	...	1808	...	1933r	...	...	1934	...	...	2107	2107	2119	2132
Kingussie.......... d.	1346	...	...	1418	...	...	1536	...	1608	...	...	1646	1720	...	...	1820	...	1945	...	...	1946	...	...	2119	2119	2133	2148
Newtonmore.......... d.	1351	...	...	|	...	...	|	...	|	...	...	1651	|	...	...	|	...	|	...	...	1951	...	...	2123	2123	2139	2154
Dalwhinnie.......... d.	1402	...	...	|	...	...	|	...	|	...	...	1703	|	...	...	|	...	|	...	...	2002	...	...	2137	2135	2154	2209
Blair Atholl.......... d.	|	...	...	|	...	...	|	...	|	...	...	1725	1753	...	...	|	...	|	...	...	2025	...	...	2201	2157	2220	2235
Pitlochry.......... d.	1433	...	...	1459	...	...	1617	...	1650	...	...	1735	1803	...	...	1905	...	2030	...	...	2035	...	...	2215	2208	2232	2247
Dunkeld & Birnam.......... d.	1446	...	...	|	...	...	1635f	...	1704	...	...	1750	1820	...	...	1920	...	2047	...	...	2049	...	...	2227	2220	2246	2303
Perth..........222/4 d.	1507	1519	1525	1529	1609	1621	1705d	1721	1722	1801	1804	1820d	1839	...	1913	1939	2004	2105	2110	2122	2119d	2128	2218	2246	2239	2306	2326
Stirling..........222 a.	1541	1548	|	1558	1643	|	1741	|	1752	1834	|	1853	1910	1919	|	2016	|	2136	|	2152	2151	2203	|	2319	2319	2351	2351
Glasgow Queen St..222 a.	|	1619	|	|	1712	|	1814	|	|	1909	|	1922	1942	|	|	2044	|	|	|	2222	|	2238	|	2359	2359	...	...
Markinch..........222 a.	|	...	1555	|	...	1652	...	1801	|	...	1833	...	...	|	1943	...	2039	|	2140	...	|	...	2246	...	...	...	...
Kirkcaldy..........222 a.	|	...	1606	|	...	1703	...	1812	|	...	1845	...	...	|	1954	...	2050	|	2150	...	|	...	2257	...	...	...	...
Haymarket..........222/4 a.	1627	...	1652	1638	...	1749	...	1848	1831	...	1929	...	...	2002	2042	...	2127	2221	2224	...	2234	...	2333	...	...	...	...
Edinburgh Waverley 222/4 a.	1633	...	1657	1647	...	1754	...	1858k	1837	...	1934	...	...	2007	2048	...	2133	2226	2229	...	2241	...	2342	...	...	...	...

A – R. 🛏 1, 2 class and 2 London Euston - Inverness (departs London previous day). Station calls are to set down only. See also Table **161**.
B – R. 🛏 1, 2 class and 2 Inverness - London Euston. Train stops to pick up only. See Table **161**.
K – From / to London Kings Cross (Table **180**)
P – To Elgin (Table **225**).

a – Arrives 1604.
b – Arrives 2018.
c – Arrives 0709.
d – Arrives 12 minutes earlier.
f – Arrives 4 – 6 minutes earlier.
h – 0942 on ⑥.

j – Arrives 0800 on Ⓐ.
k – Arrives 1853 on ⑥.
n – Departs 5 minutes later on Ⓐ.
r – Arrives 7 – 9 minutes earlier.
t – Arrives 2114 on ⑥.

🚂 – Strathspey Railway (Aviemore - Boat of Garten - Broomhill, *14 km*). ✆ 01479 810725. www.strathspeyrailway.co.uk

224 EDINBURGH - STIRLING — 2nd class only — SR

km		⚒	⚒	⚒	⚒	⚒	⚒	⚒	⚒	⚒	⚒	⚒	⚒	⚒	⚒	⚒	⚒	⚒	⚒	⚒	⚒	⚒	⚒	⚒
0	**Edinburgh** Waverley d.	0518	0533	0604	0632	0703	0734	0804	0834	0905	0935	1003	1036	1103	1133	1203	1233	1304	1337	1403	1433	1505	1535	1603
2	Haymarket d.	0523	0537	0608	0636	0707	0739	0809	0838	0910	0939	1007	1041	1108	1138	1207	1238	1308	1341	1407	1437	1509	1539	1607
28	Linlithgow d.	0542	0557	0628	0657	0727	0758	0830	0858	0929	0959	1027	1100	1127	1157	1226	1257	1327	1400	1427	1452	1528	1558	1628
41	Falkirk Grahamston d.	0553	0612r	0638	0707	0738	0812	0841	0908	0940	1012	1038	1111	1140	1208	1240	1312r	1341	1411	1438	1510	1540	1611	1638
58	**Stirling** a.	0606	0628	0656	0721	0757	0828	0858	0922	0957	1029	1056	1126	1156	1222	1258	1328	1356	1426	1501	1526	1558	1626	1652

	⚒	⚒	⚒	⚒	⚒	⚒	⚒	⚒	⚒	⚒	⑥	Ⓐ	⑦	⑦	⑦	⑦	⑦	⑦	⑦	⑦	⑦	⑦	⑦	⑦
Edinburgh Waverley d.	1638	1705	1736	1803	1835	1904	2003	2103	2204	2303	2332	2334	0935	1035	1112	1134	1205	1234	1305	1336	1406	1437	1507	1536
Haymarket d.	1642	1709	1742	1808	1839	1908	2007	2107	2208	2307	2336	2339	0939	1039	1116	1138	1211	1239	1309	1341	1410	1441	1511	1540
Linlithgow d.	1701	1730	1801	1829	1901	1928	2027	2126	2227	2326	2356	2359	1004	1058	1135	1159	1231	1258	1329	1402	1431	1502	1531	1601
Falkirk Grahamston d.	1714	1742	1814	1841	1914	1939	2037	2137	2241	2337	0006	0009	1015	1109	1146	1210	1244	1311	1339	1413	1441	1515	1542	1611
Stirling a.	1728	1800	1828	1859	1929	1954	2051	2150	2257	2350	0021	0023	1029	1123	1200	1224	1259	1325	1355	1427	1456	1530	1556	1625

	⑦	⑦	⑦	⑦	⑦	⑦	⑦	⑦	⑦	⑦
Edinburgh Waverley d.	1606	1636	1705	1734	1806	1835	1936	2035	2135	2235
Haymarket d.	1610	1641	1709	1738	1810	1839	1940	2039	2139	2240
Linlithgow d.	1631	1702	1731	1757	1832	1901	2001	2058	2158	2301
Falkirk Grahamston d.	1641	1712	1741	1808	1844	1912	2011	2109	2213r	2314
Stirling a.	1656	1727	1757	1822	1901	1926	2025	2123	2227	2331

	⚒	⚒	⚒	⚒	⚒	⚒	⚒	⚒	⚒
Stirling 222/3 d.	0538	0608	0635	0704	0729	0809	0834	0908	0940
Falkirk Grahamston d.	0552	0622	0650	0718	0743	0824	0848	0922	0955
Linlithgow d.	0603	0633	0701	0729	0754	0835	0858	0933	1006
Haymarket 222/3 a.	0622	0651	0720	0751	0813	0854	0915	0952	1025
Edinburgh Waverley 222/3 a.	0627	0656	0725	0756	0818	0859	0920	0957	1031

	⚒	⚒	⚒	⚒	Ⓐ	⑥	⚒	⚒	⚒	⚒	⚒	⚒	⚒	⚒	⚒	⚒	⚒	⚒	⚒	⚒	⚒	⚒	⚒	⑥	Ⓐ
Stirling d.	1003	1038	1104	1134	1204	1204	1240	1304	1331	1403	1438	1503	1534	1603	1633	1700	1734	1803	1828	1902	1940	2001	2038	2143	2144
Falkirk Grahamston d.	1017	1053	1118	1148	1221	1218	1254	1319	1347	1418	1452	1518	1548	1617	1647	1713	1752	1817	1844	1917	1954	2015	2052	2157	2159
Linlithgow d.	1028	1103	1130	1200	1231	1230	1304	1329	1358	1429	1503	1529	1559	1628	1657	1724	1804	1827	1855	1927	2004	2026	2103	2208	2209
Haymarket d.	1046	1121	1151	1220	1251	1251	1323	1348	1417	1451	1521	1550	1620	1646	1716	1742	1823	1846	1913	1949	2023	2044	2122	2227	2229
Edinburgh Waverley a.	1052	1126	1158	1225	1256	1256	1328	1354	1423	1456	1528	1556	1627	1652	1721	1748	1829	1852	1918	1954	2028	2049	2127	2232	2234

	⚒	⚒	⑦	⑦	⑦	⑦	⑦	⑦	⑦	⑦	⑦	⑦	⑦	⑦		⑦	⑦	⑦	⑦	⑦	⑦	⑦	⑦	⑦
Stirling 222/3 d.	2236	2325	0910	0954	1047	1109	1152	1208	1254	1308	1350	1418	1450	1518	...	1550	1618	1650	1718	1818	1919	2018	2108	2218
Falkirk Grahamston d.	2250	2342	0924	1011	1104	1123	1206	1222	1311	1322	1404	1432	1507	1532	...	1604	1632	1704	1732	1832	1933	2032	2123	2233
Linlithgow d.	2301	2352	0935	1023	1116	1134	1217	1233	1321	1333	1415	1443	1518	1543	...	1615	1643	1715	1742	1843	1944	2043	2133	2243
Haymarket 222/3 a.	2319	0011	1000	1045	1138	1152	1235	1251	1342	1353	1433	1501	1538	1601	...	1633	1701	1733	1801	1901	2002	2103	2152	2302
Edinburgh Waverley 222/3 a.	2324	0016	1005	1050	1143	1158	1240	1256	1347	1358	1438	1506	1546	1606	...	1639	1706	1739	1806	1906	2007	2108	2158	2307

r – Arrives 5 minutes earlier.

225 ABERDEEN - ELGIN - INVERNESS — 2nd class only — SR

km		⚒	⚒	⚒H	⚒D	⚒	⚒H	⚒	⚒🍷	⚒	⚒🍷	⚒	⚒G	⚒🍷	⚒	⚒B	⚒🍷	⚒🍷	⚒H	⚒	⑦G	⑦G	⑦G	⑦G	⑦🍷
0	**Aberdeen** ¶ d.	...	...	0617	0718	0730	0823	0841	1010	...	1156	...	1341	1525	...	1725	1818	2018	2200	2249	1003	1300	1524	1800	2128
10	Dyce ✈ ¶ d.	...	...	0625	0727	0739	0831	0850	1018	...	1205	...	1349	1534	...	1734	1827	2027	2208	2258	1012	1309	1532	1809	2137
22	Kintore ¶ d.	...	...	0635	0735	0747	0840	—	1027	...	1213	...	1359	1542	...	│	1835	2035	2218	2306	1020	1317	1542	1817	2146
27	**Inverurie** ¶ d.	...	...	0641	0742	0753	0846	...	1033	...	1219	...	1405	1549	...	1746	1842	2041	2224	2313	1026	1323	1547	1823	2151
44	Insch d.	...	...	0654	0755	...	0859	...	1047	...	1233	...	1419	1606	...	1759	1855	2054	2237	...	1039	1335	1600	1836	2203
65	Huntly d.	...	...	0711	0811	...	0915	...	1104	...	1250	...	1438	1623	...	1815	1911	2111	2254	...	1055	1352	1616	1852	2224
85	Keith d.	...	...	0726	0826	...	0930	⚒	1119	...	1304	...	1453	1647	...	1830	1926	2126	2309	...	1110	1407	1637	1907	2239
114	**Elgin** d.	0659	0721	0747	0849	...	0950	1051	1140	1236	1325	1425	1514	1709f	1800	1853	1946	2149	2329	...	1130	1427	1659	1928	2258
137	Forres d.	0712	0733	0800	0902	...	1003	1104	1153	1249	1338	1438	1527	1722	1813	1906	1959	2204	2342	...	1143	1440	1712	1941	2311
149	Nairn d.	0723	0746	0810	0915	...	1015	1117	1205	1300	1351	1449	1537	1734	1826	1918	2010	2215	2352	...	1154	1451	1726f	1952	2321
160	Inverness Airport ✈ ‡ d.	0732	0755	0819	0924	...	1024	1126	1214	1309	1400	1458	1546	1743	1835	1927	2019	2224	0002		1203	1500	1735	2001	2331
173	**Inverness** a.	0743	0807	0830	0935	...	1035	1137	1226	1320	1411	1510	1558	1755	1846	1939	2030	2237	0013	...	1214	1511	1749	2014	2342

	⚒A	⚒G	⚒	⚒	⚒🍷	⚒	⚒G	⚒	⚒🍷	⚒	⚒🍷	⚒🍷	⚒	⚒G	⚒H	⚒	⚒	⚒	⑦G	⑦G	⑦G	⑦G	⑦C	⑦🍷	⑦C
Inverness d.	0456	0552	...	0701	0855	0946	1056	1145	1238	1330	1428	1535	1622	1713	1805	1858	2037	2132	0959	1231	1529	1703	1800	2104	2143
Inverness Airport ✈ ‡ d.	0506	0602	...	0711	0905	1001f	1106	1155	1248	1340	1438	1546	1632	1723	1815	1908	2047	2142	1009	1241	1539	1713	1810	2114	2153
Nairn d.	0516	0612	...	0723	0916	1013	1116	1206	1300	1351	1449	1556	1642	1734	1827	1919	2057	2152	1019	1251	1548	1723	1820	2123	2203
Forres d.	0527	0622	...	0734	0930	1024	1126	1217	1311	1402	1500	1607	1653	1744	1838	1930	2108	2203	1030	1301	1558	1734	1830	2133	2214
Elgin d.	0539	0635	...	0757j	0953j	1038	1139	1231	1325	1415	1514	1620	1706	1801f	1855	1943	2122	2216	1043	1314	1611	1747	1843	2146	2227
Keith d.	0559	0654	...	0818	1013	...	1200	...	1346	...	1535	1640	...	1820	1915	...	...	2236	1103	1334	1632	1808	...	2207	...
Huntly d.	0613	0712	0747	0839	1028	...	1214	...	1400	...	1549	1655	...	1843	1938	...	...	2253	1123	1352f	1647	1822	...	2222	...
Insch d.	0628	0728	0803	0859	1048	...	1234	...	1419	...	1609	1711	...	1858	1954	...	...	2309	1139	1408	1703	1838	...	2238	...
Inverurie ¶ d.	0641	0740	0815	0911	1100	...	1246	...	1431	...	1621	1723	...	1911	2006	...	...	2321	1151	1420	1715	1850	...	2250	...
Kintore ¶ d.	0647	0746	0820	0917	1106	...	1251	...	1437	...	1627	1728	...	1917	2012	...	...	2327	1156	1426	1720	1856	...	2256	...
Dyce ✈ ¶ d.	0656	0756	0830	0926	1115	...	1300	...	1447	...	1636	1738	...	1926	2021	...	...	2336	1205	1435	1729	1904	...	2304	...
Aberdeen ¶ a.	0706	0805	0839	0936	1125	...	1309	...	1456	...	1645	1749	...	1937	2036	...	...	2346	1214	1444	1738	1914	...	2314	...

A – [12] Inverness - Edinburgh (Table **222**).
B – [12] and 🍷 from Glasgow Queen St (Table **222**).
C – [12] and 🍷 Glasgow Queen Street - Inverness - Elgin (Table **223**).
D – From Dundee (Table **222**).
E – [12] to Glasgow Queen Street (Table **222**).
G – Conveys [12] and 🍷.

H – Conveys [12].
P – From Perth (Table **222**).
f – Arrives 5 minutes earlier.
j – Arrives 10 minutes earlier.
‡ – Opens on Jan. 21.

¶ – Additional trains Aberdeen - Dyce - Kintore - Inverurie and v.v.:
From Aberdeen on ⚒ at 0749 **P**, 0858, 0950, 1042, 1109, 1141, 1226, 1252, 1311, 1400, 1436, 1504, 1542, 1600, 1625, 1657, 1739, 1757, 1900, 1927, 1957, 2058, 2141, 2249; on ⑦ at 1033, 1225, 1428, 1550, 1649, 2034.
From Inverurie on ⚒ at 0651, 0718, 0758, 0845, 0956, 1031, 1129, 1200, 1217, 1258, 1328, 1356, 1451, 1517, 1546, 1625, 1644, 1702, 1746, 1820, 1845, 1929, 2025, 2049, 2129, 2218; on ⑦ at 1104 **E**, 1255, 1458, 1619, 1730, 2102.

226 INVERNESS - THURSO, WICK and KYLE OF LOCHALSH — 2nd class — SR

km		⚒	⚒	⚒🍷	⚒	⚒		⚒	⚒🍷	⚒	⚒	Ⓐ	⑥	⚒🍷	⚒
0	**Inverness** d.	0700	0855	1041	1056	1143	...	1335	1400	1450	1712	1754	1754	1831	2129
16	Beauly d.	0715	0910	│	1113	1200	...	1350	1415	1505	1727	1809	1809	1846	2144
21	Muir of Ord d.	0723	0916	1101	1119	1209	...	1356	1423	1511	1733	1815	1815	1855	2150
30	Dingwall d.	0739	0929	1112	1132	1221	...	1411	1437	1524	1747	1829	1829	1908	2203
49	Garve d.	│	0952	│	1155	...	...	1434	│	│	│	1855f	1855f	│	│
75	Achnasheen d.	│	1019	│	1221	...	...	1504f	│	│	│	1922	1922	│	│
104	Strathcarron d.	│	1048	│	1253	...	...	1533	│	│	│	1958r	2007r	│	│
116	Stromeferry d.	│	1106	│	1310	...	...	1551	│	│	│	2015	2024	│	│
124	Plockton d.	│	1118	│	1322	...	...	1603	│	│	│	2027	2036	│	│
133	**Kyle of Lochalsh** a.	│	1131	│	1335	...	...	1616	│	│	│	2040	2049	│	│
51	Invergordon d.	0758	...	1130	...	...	...	...	1454	1541	1804	...	...	1927	2220
71	Tain d.	0817	...	1149	...	...	...	...	1513	...	1824	...	...	1946	2239
93	Ardgay d.	0833	...	1205	...	...	...	...	1529	...	1839	...	...	2002	...
108	Lairg d.	0853	...	1221	...	...	...	...	1545	...	...	...	...	2018	...
136	Golspie d.	0918	...	1246	...	...	...	...	1610	...	...	...	...	2043	...
146	Brora d.	0929	...	1257	...	...	...	...	1621	...	...	...	...	2053	...
163	Helmsdale d.	0947	...	1312	...	...	...	...	1636	...	...	...	...	2108	...
201	Forsinard d.	1021	...	1346	...	...	...	...	1712	...	...	...	...	2142	...
237	Georgemas Jcn a.	1045	...	1410	...	...	...	...	1736	...	...	...	...	2206	...
248	**Thurso** a.	1059	...	1424	...	...	...	...	1750	...	...	...	...	2220	...
248	**Thurso** d.	1102	...	1427	...	...	...	...	1753	...	...	...	...	2223	...
237	Georgemas Jcn d.	1114	...	1439	...	...	...	...	1805	...	...	...	...	2235	...
260	**Wick** a.	1131	...	1456	...	...	...	...	1822	...	...	...	...	2252	...

	⑦	⑦	⑦		⑦	⑦🍷	⑦	⑦
Inverness d.	0940	1059	1253	...	1533	1754	1754	2108
Beauly d.	0955	1115	1308	...	1548	1809	1809	2123
Muir of Ord d.	1001	1121	1314	...	1556	1815	1815	2129
Dingwall d.	1014	1134	1327	...	1609	1831	1833	2142
Garve d.	│	1158	│	...	│	│	1856	│
Achnasheen d.	│	1225	│	...	│	│	1922	│
Strathcarron d.	│	1255	│	...	│	│	1952	│
Stromeferry d.	│	1312	│	...	│	│	2009	│
Plockton d.	│	1324	│	...	│	│	2021	│
Kyle of Lochalsh a.	│	1347	│	...	│	│	2034	│
Invergordon d.	1032	...	1345	...	1626	1848	...	2200
Tain d.	1050	...	1403	...	...	1907	...	2218
Ardgay d.	...	...	...	...	...	1923	...	...
Lairg d.	...	...	...	...	...	1942	...	...
Golspie d.	...	...	...	...	...	2007	...	...
Brora d.	...	...	...	...	...	2018	...	...
Helmsdale d.	...	...	...	...	...	2033	...	...
Forsinard d.	...	...	...	...	...	2107	...	...
Georgemas Jcn a.	...	...	...	...	...	2131	...	...
Thurso a.	...	...	...	...	...	2145	...	...
Thurso d.	...	...	...	...	...	2148	...	...
Georgemas Jcn d.	...	...	...	...	...	2200	...	...
Wick a.	...	...	...	...	...	2217	...	...

f – Arrives 4 minutes earlier.

r – Arrives 1950.

SR 2nd class — THURSO, WICK and KYLE OF LOCHALSH - INVERNESS — 226

	⚒	⚒	⚒		⚒	⚒🍷	⚒	⚒	⚒	⚒	⚒🍷	⚒	⚒🍷	⚒	⚒	⑦	⑦	⑦		⑦🍷	⑦	⑦	⑦
Wick d.	...	...	...	...	0618	0802	...	...	...	...	1234	...	1600	...	...	...	...	...	...	1158	...	...	...
Georgemas Jcn. d.	...	...	...	...	0636	0820	...	...	...	...	1252	...	1618	...	...	...	...	...	...	1216	...	...	...
Thurso a.	...	...	...	...	0646	0830	...	...	...	...	1302	...	1628	...	...	...	...	...	...	1226	...	...	...
Thurso d.	...	...	...	...	0650	0834	...	...	...	...	1306	...	1632	...	...	...	...	...	...	1230	...	...	...
Georgemas Jcn. d.	...	...	...	...	0703	0847	...	...	...	...	1319	...	1645	...	...	...	...	...	...	1243	...	...	...
Forsinard d.	...	...	...	...	0727	0913	...	...	...	...	1347	...	1711	...	...	...	...	...	...	1309	...	...	...
Helmsdale d.	...	...	...	...	0800	0946	...	...	...	...	1421	...	1744	...	...	...	...	...	...	1342	...	...	...
Brora d.	...	...	...	...	0816	1002	...	...	...	...	1436	...	1800	...	...	...	...	...	...	1358	...	...	...
Golspie d.	...	...	...	...	0825	1012	...	...	...	...	1447	...	1810	...	...	...	...	...	...	1408	...	...	...
Lairg d.	...	0626	...	...	0852	1038	...	...	...	...	1512	...	1835	...	...	...	...	...	...	1433	...	...	...
Ardgay d.	0614	0643	...	...	0907	1054	...	...	...	...	1530	...	1851	1929	...	...	...	...	...	1449	...	...	...
Tain d.	0630	0659	...	...	0923	1110	...	...	...	...	1546	...	1907	1947	2244	1055	...	1408	...	1505	...	...	2223
Invergordon d.	0649	0719	...	...	0942	1131	...	...	...	1551	1610t	...	1925	2006	2303	1114	...	1427	...	1524	1631	...	2242
Kyle of Lochalsh d.	|	|	0611	...	|	|	...	1208	1346	|	|	1713	|	|	|	|	1020	|	...	|	|	1509	|
Plockton d.	|	|	0626	...	|	|	...	1221	1359	|	|	1726	|	|	|	|	1033	|	...	|	|	1525	|
Stromeferry d.	|	|	0638	...	|	|	...	1233	1411	|	|	1738	|	|	|	|	1045	|	...	|	|	1537	|
Strathcarron d.	|	|	0657	...	|	|	...	1252	1434t	|	|	1757	|	|	|	|	1103	|	...	|	|	1556	|
Achnasheen d.	|	|	0726	...	|	|	...	1320	1503	|	|	1826	|	|	|	|	1131	|	...	|	|	1624	|
Garve d.	|	|	0753	...	|	|	...	1347	1529	|	|	1852	|	|	|	|	1157	|	...	|	|	1651	|
Dingwall d.	0708	0738	0816	...	1001	1153	1245	1410	1552	1611	1630	1918	1942	2025	2321	1135	1220	1445	...	1542	1649	1714	2300
Muir of Ord d.	0722	0751	0830	...	1014	1207	1258	1422	1604	1624	1644	1931	1954	2038	2334	1148	1232	1457	...	1555	1702	1726	2313
Beauly d.	0728	0757	0835	...	1020	1212	1304	1427	1609	1629	1649	1936	|	2043	2339	1153	1237	1502	...	1600	1707	1732	2318
Inverness a.	0743	0812	0850	...	1038	1227	1321	1442	1627	1646	1706	1951	2012	2058	2354	1208	1252	1517	...	1615	1722	1747	2333

t – Arrives 5–6 minutes earlier.

Service until March 30 — 🚌 INVERNESS - ULLAPOOL - STORNOWAY — 227

	c ①–⑥ 🚌	c ①–⑥ ⛴	a ①–⑤ 🚌	a ①–⑤ ⛴	a ⑦ 🚌	a ⑦ ⛴	b ①–⑤ 🚌	b ①–⑤ ⛴	a ⑥ 🚌	a ⑥ ⛴	b ⑥⑦ 🚌	b ⑥⑦ ⛴
Inverness d.	0710	...	1410	...	1440	...	1500	...	1530	...	1530	...
Garve d.	0744	...	1444	...	1714	...	1534	...	1604	...	1604	...
Ullapool a.	0830	...	1530	...	1600	...	1620	...	1650	...	1650	...
Ullapool d.	...	0930	...	1630	...	1700	...	1730	...	1800	...	1830
Stornoway a.	...	1200	...	1900	...	1930	...	2000	...	2030	...	2100

	a ①–⑥ ⛴	a ①–⑥ 🚌	b ①–⑥ ⛴	b ①–⑥ 🚌	a ⑦ ⛴	a ⑦ 🚌	b ①–⑤ ⛴	b ①–⑤ 🚌	a ⑥ ⛴	a ⑥ 🚌	b ⑥⑦ ⛴	b ⑥⑦ 🚌
Stornoway d.	0600	...	0700	...	0930	...	1400	...	1400	...	1430	...
Ullapool a.	0830	...	0930	...	1200	...	1630	...	1630	...	1700	...
Ullapool d.	...	1020	...	0950	...	1220	...	1650	...	1705	...	1720
Garve d.	...	1102	...	1032	...	1302	...	1732	...	1747	...	1802
Inverness a.	...	1140	...	1110	...	1340	...	1810	...	1825	...	1840

☛ Latest passenger check-in for ⛴ is 30 minutes before departure.

a – Until Mar. 13. b – From Mar. 14. c – Runs 1 hour later from Mar. 14.

Operators: 🚌 Scottish Citylink (service **961**). www.citylink.co.uk ✆ +44 (0) 871 266 3333.
⛴ Caledonian MacBrayne. www.calmac.co.uk ✆ +44 (0) 800 066 5000.

Service until March 30 — 🚌 INVERNESS - ISLE OF SKYE / FORT WILLIAM - OBAN — 228

Service number	915	917	919 ①–⑥		918 ①–⑥	919		915 ①–⑥	915 ⑦	919/5 ①–⑥	919 ①–⑥		919 ①–⑥		918 ①–⑥		916	919	917		916		
Inverness bus station d.	...	0840	0900	...	...	1100	...	...	...	*1300*v	1300	...	1500	...	...	...	...	1715	1745	...	...	...	...
Invermoriston Public Hall d.	...	0933r	0953	...	...	1153	...	...	...	|	1353	...	1553	...	...	...	...	1808	1838r	...	...	...	...
Kyle of Lochalsh Old Slipway d.	...	1052	|	...	...	|	...	...	...	1552	|	...	|	...	...	...	...	|	1957	...	...	...	...
Portree Square a.	...	1154	|	...	...	|	...	...	...	1715	|	...	|	...	...	...	...	|	2056	...	...	...	...
Uig Pier a.	...	*1340*	|	...	...	|	...	...	...	1745	|	...	|	...	...	...	...	|	...	...	...	...	...
Fort Augustus bus stance d.	...	...	1004	...	...	1204	...	...	...	...	1404	...	1604	...	...	...	...	1819	...	...	...	...	...
Uig Pier d.	...	...	|	...	...	|	...	0930	...	...	|	...	|	...	...	...	1440	|	...	...	1815	...	...
Portree Square d.	0730	...	|	...	...	|	...	1035j	1035	...	|	...	|	...	...	...	1540p	|	...	...	1845	...	...
Kyle of Lochalsh Old Slipway d.	0833	...	|	...	...	|	...	1138	1138	...	|	...	|	...	...	...	1643	|	...	...	...	...	...
Invergarry Jct. bus bay A82 d.	0948f	...	1018	...	...	1218	...	1253f	1253f	...	1418	...	1618	...	...	...	1758f	1833	...	...	...	...	...
Fort William bus station a.	1035	...	1105	...	...	1305	...	1340	1340	...	1505	...	1705	...	...	...	1842	1917	...	...	...	...	...
Fort William bus station d.	...	...	...	...	1230	...	...	...	...	...	...	...	...	...	1750	...	...	...	...	...	...	...	...
Ballachulish Tourist Office d.	...	...	...	...	1300	...	...	...	...	...	...	...	...	...	1820	...	...	...	...	...	...	...	...
Oban Station Road a.	...	...	...	...	1403	...	...	...	...	...	...	...	...	...	1923	...	...	...	...	...	...	...	...

Service number	919 ①–⑥		919 ①–⑥	917		916		918 ①–⑥	915/9	915/9 ①–⑥	919		915			919 ①–⑥		918 ①–⑥	919		915		917
Oban Station Road d.	...	...	...	...	...	...	...	0930	...	...	...	...	...	...	...	...	...	1557	...	...	...	...	...
Ballachulish Tourist Office d.	...	...	...	...	...	...	...	1034	...	...	...	...	...	...	...	...	...	1701	...	...	...	...	...
Fort William bus station a.	...	...	...	...	...	...	...	1105	...	...	...	...	...	...	...	...	...	1732	...	...	...	...	...
Fort William bus station d.	0730	...	0930	...	...	1000	...	...	...	...	1230	...	1350	...	...	1430	...	...	1740	...	1850	...	...
Invergarry Jct. bus bay A82 d.	0814	...	1014	...	...	1044f	...	...	...	...	1314	...	1434f	...	...	1514	...	...	1824	...	1934f	...	...
Kyle of Lochalsh Old Slipway d.	|	...	|	...	...	1202	...	...	...	...	|	...	1552	...	...	|	...	...	|	...	2055c	...	...
Portree Square d.	|	...	|	...	...	1310	...	...	...	...	|	...	1715n	...	...	|	...	...	|	...	2154	...	...
Uig Pier a.	|	...	|	...	...	1340	...	...	...	...	|	...	1745	...	...	|	...	...	|	...	...	...	...
Fort Augustus bus stance d.	0828	...	1028	...	...	...	...	...	...	...	1328	...	...	...	...	1528	...	...	1838	...	...	...	...
Uig Pier d.	|	...	|	...	...	...	...	...	...	0930	|	...	...	...	...	|	...	...	|	...	...	...	*1440*
Portree Square d.	|	...	|	0900	...	...	...	...	1035	1035j	|	...	...	...	...	|	...	...	|	...	...	...	1745
Kyle of Lochalsh Old Slipway d.	|	...	|	1009	...	...	...	...	1136	1136	|	...	...	...	...	|	...	...	|	...	...	...	1849
Invermoriston opposite Public Hall d.	0839	...	1039	1124r	...	...	...	...	|	|	1339	...	...	...	...	1539	...	...	1849	...	...	...	2004r
Inverness bus station a.	0935	...	1135	1220	...	...	...	...	*1435*z	*1435*z	1435	...	...	...	...	1635	...	...	1942	...	...	...	2057

c – Arrives 2049.
f – On A87 at Invergarry Hotel.
j – Arrives 1000.
n – Arrives 1654.
p – Arrives 1510.
r – At Glenmoriston Arms.
v – Change at Invergarry, a. 1417 (Jct. bus bay on A82), d. 1434 (Invergarry Hotel on A87).
z – Change at Invergarry, a. 1253 (Invergarry Hotel on A87), d. 1314 (Jct. bus bay on A82).

Operator: Scottish Citylink. www.citylink.co.uk ✆ +44 (0) 871 266 3333.

✆ +44 (0) 1624 662525 — ISLE OF MAN RAILWAYS — 229

km	*Manx Electric Railway*	A	A	A	A	A	Af	A	A	Af
0	**Douglas** Derby Castle ‡ d.	0940	1010	1040	1140	1240	1340	1410	1510	1610
4	Groudle d.	0950	1020	1050	1150	1250	1350	1420	1520	1620
11	Laxey d.	1010	1040	1110	1210	1310	1410	1440	1540	1640
29	**Ramsey** a.	1055	1125f	1155	1255	1355	1455	1525	1625	...

	A	Af	Ag		A	A	Af	A	Af	A
Ramsey d.	1110	1140	1240	...	1340	1440	1510	1540	...	1640
Laxey d.	1155	1225	1325	...	1425	1525	1555	1625	1655	1725
Groudle d.	1213	1243	1343	...	1443	1543	1613	1643	1713	1743
Douglas Derby Castle ‡ a.	1225	1255	1355	...	1455	1555	1625	1655	1725	1755

km	*Snaefell Mountain Railway*	B	B	Br		B	Br	B
0	**Laxey** d.	1015	1045	1115	and at the same minutes past each hour until	1445	1515	1545
8	**Summit** a.	1045	1115	1145		1515	1545	1615

	Bp	Br	Br	Bn		Bn	B	B
Summit d.	1100	1120	1150	1220	and at the same minutes past each hour until	1520	1550	1640
Laxey a.	1130	1150	1220	1250		1540	1625	1710

km	*Isle of Man Steam Railway*	C	Ch	F	H	F	Ck	F	D✕	E
0	**Douglas** Railway Station ‡ d.	0950	1150	1250	1350	1430	1550	1730	1745	1900
9	Santon d.	1011x	1211x	1311x	1411x	1451	1611x	1751x	1806x	|
13	Ballasalla d.	1020	1220	1320	1420	1500	1620	1800	1815	1940
16	Castletown d.	1027	1227	1327	1427	1507	1627	1807	1822	1947
25	**Port Erin** a.	1050	1250	1350	1450	1530	1650	1830	1845	2015

	D✕	C	Ch	F	H	F	Ck	F	D✕	E
Port Erin d.	0745	1000	1200	1300	1400	1445	1600	1745	1915	2115
Castletown d.	0807	1027	1227	1327	1427	1507	1627	1807	1942	2142
Ballasalla d.	0815	1035	1235	1335	1435	1515	1635	1815	1949	2149
Santon d.	|	1047x	1247x	1347x	1447x	1527x	1647x	1827x	|	|
Douglas Railway Station ‡ a.	0845	1105	1305	1405	1505	1545	1705	1845	2030	2230

A – ②③④⑥⑦ Mar. 14 - Apr. 2; daily Apr. 4 - Sept. 17 (not Apr. 24, May 15, 22); ②–⑦ Sept. 19 - Oct. 29. An enhanced service runs on many dates April - September (check locally for details).
B – ②③④⑥⑦ Mar. 18 - Apr. 2; daily Apr. 4 - Sept. 17 (not Apr. 24, May 15, 22); ②–⑦ Sept. 19 - Oct. 29. An enhanced service operates May 29 - June 8.
C – ⑤–⑦ Mar. 10–19; ①④⑤⑥⑦ Mar. 23 - Apr. 3; daily Apr. 6 - Oct. 2 (not Apr. 25, 26, May 2, 9, 16, 23); ①④⑤⑥⑦ Oct. 5–29.
D – June 5–8. Reservation essential.
E – Apr. 13, May 11, June 15, July 6 - Aug. 31, Sept. 14, Oct. 12. Reservation essential.
F – May 27–31, June 1–4, 10, 11, July 8, 15, 22, 28, 29, ⑤⑥ Aug. 4–26.
H – ⑤–⑦ Mar. 10–19; ①④⑤⑥⑦ Mar. 23 - Apr. 3; daily Apr. 6–24; ①③④⑤⑥⑦ Apr. 27 - May 26 (also June 5–9); daily June 12–30; ⑧ July 2–27; ⑦–④ July 31 - Aug. 24; daily Aug. 27 - Oct. 2; ①④⑤⑥⑦ Oct. 5–29.

f – Not Mar. 14–30.
g – Runs 30 minutes earlier Mar. 14–30.
h – Runs 30 minutes earlier on dates in note **F**.
k – Runs 10 minutes later on dates in note **F**.
n – Runs 10 minutes earlier Mar. 18–30.
p – Runs 10 minutes later Mar. 18–30.
r – Not Mar. 18–30.
x – Calls on request.
‡ – 🚌 services **1**, **1H**, **2**, **2A**, **10**, **11**, **12**, **12A**, **13** connect Derby Castle and Lord Street Bus Station which is near the Steam Railway Station.

IRELAND

SEE MAP PAGE 86

Operators: Iarnród Éireann (**IÉ**), www.irishrail.ie Northern Ireland Railways (**NIR**), www.translink.co.uk Bus Éireann, www.buseireann.ie Ulsterbus, www.translink.co.uk and Dublin Area Rapid Transit (**DART**), www.irishrail.ie Most cross-border services are jointly operated.

Timings: Rail: **NIR** services are valid from June 14, 2021 until further notice. **IÉ** services are valid from December 11, 2022 until further notice. **DART** services are valid until further notice.
Bus: **Ulsterbus** services are valid until further notice. **Bus Éireann** services are valid until further notice.

Rail services: Except for *Enterprise* cross-border expresses (for details, see Table **230** below), **all trains** convey *Standard* (2nd) class seating. Most express trains in the Republic of Ireland, as noted in the tables, also have first class accommodation.
On public holiday dates in the **Republic of Ireland**, DART trains run as on Sundays; outer-suburban services to or from Drogheda and Dundalk do not run. Other services may be amended, though most main-line trains run normally. All services are subject to alteration during the Christmas, New Year and Easter holiday periods.

Bus services: **Bus Éireann** and **Ulsterbus**: services are shown in detail where there is no comparable rail service; only basic information is given for other routes. Buses do not always call at the rail station, but usually stop nearby. Where possible the stop details are given in the station bank or as a footnote. On longer routes, a change of bus may be required – please check with the driver. At holiday times bus travellers should consult detailed leaflets or seek further information from the operator. **Bus Éireann**: ✆ +353 1 836 6111 (Dublin) or + 353 21 450 8188 (Cork); **Ulsterbus**: ✆ + 028 9033 3000 (Translink, Belfast). **Dublin Busáras** (bus station) is a 5 minute walk from Dublin Connolly station.

The Dublin Tram service (Luas) connects Dublin Connolly and Heuston stations at frequent intervals. Journey time is 14 minutes, depending on traffic conditions.
See Dublin City Plan on page 31.

230 BELFAST - DUNDALK - DUBLIN — NIR, IÉ

Enterprise express trains (*E*) convey Standard (2nd) class and Plus (1st) class seating. 🍸 (Café Bar and trolley service) and ✕ (at-seat meal service in Plus) currently not available.

km		⚒	Ⓐ	Ⓐ	Ⓐ	⑥	Ⓐ	Ⓐ	⚒ 2	⑥	⚒	⚒ (*E*)	⑥	⚒ ♥	Ⓐ	⑥	⚒ (*E*)	⚒	Ⓐ	⑥	⚒ 2	⑥	Ⓐ	⑥	⚒ (*E*)	Ⓐ	⑥
0	**Belfast** LP ♣ § d.		...	...	...	...	...	0600	0650	...	0736j	0800	...	...	0959	1031t	1035	...	1159	1231t	1235	...	1329	1401t	1405	...	...
13	Lisburn § d.		...	...	...	...	...	0629	|	...	0803	|	...	...	1034	1041	|	...	1234	1241	|	...	1404	1411	|	...	...
42	Portadown § d.	⚒	...	...	...	...	...	0652	0721	...	0826	0831	...	...	1057	1105	1108	...	1257	1305	1306	...	1427	1435	1436	...	...
71	Newry d.		...	...	...	...	...	*0724*	0742	...	...	0853	...	...	...	...	1127	...	...	...	1327	...	▬	...	1458	...	...
95	**Dundalk** d.		0530	0630	0705	0705	...	...	0800	0810	...	0912	1015	1050	...	...	1146	1245	...	...	1346	...	Ⓐ	...	1518	...	...
131	Drogheda d.		0554	0655	0730	0730	0758	...	0822	0835	...	|	1040	1114	...	...	1207	1310	...	...	1407	1420	1450	...	1540	1550	1610
148	Balbriggan d.		0609	0712	0746	0746	0814	...	|	0851	...	|	1055	1128	...	...	|	1326	...	...	|	1436	1506	...	|	1605	1626
154	Skerries d.		0615	0718	0752	0752	0820	...	|	0857	...	|	1101	1134	...	...	|	1332	...	...	|	1442	1512	...	|	1611	1632
168	Malahide d.		0631	0736	0807	0807	0835	...	|	0913	...	|	1116	1149	...	...	|	1347	...	...	|	1457	1527	...	|	1627	1647
183	**Dublin** Connolly a.		0647	0759	0830	0830	0858	...	0900	0934	...	1005	1139	1209	...	...	1240	1411	...	...	1440	1518	1548	...	1620	1648	1707

	Ⓐ	⑥	⚒ (*E*)	⚒	Ⓐ	⑥	⑥	⚒ 2	⑥	⚒	Ⓐ	⚒ (*E*)	Ⓐ	⑥	Ⓐ	⑥	⑦		⑦	⑦ (*E*)	⑦ (*E*)	⑦ (*E*)	⑦ (*E*)		⑦ (*E*)		
Belfast LP ♣ § d.	1541	1601t	1605	...	1709	1731t	...	1805	...	1929	...	2005	2159	2222	2259	2322		...	...	0900	1105	1305	1605	...	1905	...	...
Lisburn § d.	1611	1611	|	...	1731	1741	...	|	...	2004	...	|	2234	2245	2334	2345		...	...	0913	|	|	|	...	|	...	...
Portadown § d.	1635	1635	1639	...	1759	1806	...	1839	...	2027	...	2039	2258	2310	2357	0009		...	...	0940	1136	1336	1636	...	1936	...	...
Newry d.	...	...	1701	...	1824	1830	...	1901	...	...	...	2101	2322	2334	...	...		...	...	1001	1158	1358	1658	...	1958	...	...
Dundalk d.	...	...	1720	...	...	...	...	1920	...	...	2040	2120	...	...	...	...		...	0930	1019	1217	1417	1717	...	2017	...	...
Drogheda d.	...	...	1741	1802	...	...	1850	1941	2010	...	2105	2141	...	...	...	...		...	0955	1040	1239	1439	1740	...	2040	...	...
Balbriggan d.	...	...	|	1818	...	...	1906	|	2026	...	2121	|	...	...	...	...		...	1010	|	|	|	|	...	|	...	...
Skerries d.	...	...	|	1824	...	...	1912	|	2032	...	2127	|	...	...	...	...		...	1016	|	|	|	|	...	|	...	...
Malahide d.	...	...	|	1839	...	...	1927	|	2047	...	2142	|	...	...	...	...		...	1031	|	|	|	|	...	|	...	...
Dublin Connolly a.	...	...	1817	1902	...	...	1949	2015	2105	...	2201	2215	...	...	...	...		...	1053	1120	1315	1515	1815	...	2115	...	...

	⚒	Ⓐ	⑥	Ⓐ	Ⓐ	⚒ (*E*)	⚒	⚒ w	⚒ 2	⚒	⑥	⚒	⚒ (*E*)	⚒	⚒	⚒ (*E*)	⑥	⚒	⚒ 2	⚒	Ⓐ	⑥	Ⓐ	⚒ (*E*)	⚒	⚒	⑥
Dublin Connolly d.		...	...	...	0715	0735	...	0850	0930	...	1000	1105	1120	...	1250	1320	1350	1445	1520	1544	1609	...	1628	1650	...	...	1715
Malahide d.		...	...	...	0729	|	...	0910	|	...	1024	1124	|	...	1305	|	1406	1504	|	1604	1625	...	1646	|	...	...	1738
Skerries d.	⚒	...	...	...	0744	|	...	0924	|	...	1038	1140	|	...	1320	|	1420	1518	|	1618	1640	...	1701	|	...	...	1754
Balbriggan d.		...	...	...	0749	|	...	0930	|	...	1044	1150	|	...	1325	|	1426	1524	|	1623	1645	...	1706	|	...	...	1800
Drogheda d.		...	...	...	0805	0807	...	0948	1006	...	1101	1210	1156	...	1344	1356	1444	1543	1553	1642	1703	...	1724	|	...	...	1817
Dundalk d.		...	...	...	...	0830	...	1018	1028	...	...	1235	1218	...	...	1418	▬	...	1615	...	▬	...	...	1748	...	...	1841
Newry d.		0635	0708	*0730*	...	0848	...	...	1046	...	...	...	1239	...	...	1436	...	...	1632	...	Ⓐ	...	...	1806	...	1850	...
Portadown § d.		0700	0733	0800	...	0909	0915	...	1108	1115	...	...	1304	1315	...	1458	1515	...	1655	...	1705	1715	...	1828	1845	1915	...
Lisburn § a.		0724	0755	0824	...	|	0937	...	|	1137	...	...	|	1337	...	|	1537	...	|	...	1729	1738	...	|	1907	1937	...
Belfast LP ♣ § a.		0745	0805t	0846	...	0945	1010	...	1145	1210f	...	...	1335	1410f	...	1535	1613f	...	1726	...	1738t	1748t	...	1905	1940	2010	...

	Ⓐ	Ⓐ	⑥	Ⓐ	⑥	⚒ (*E*)	⚒	⚒ ▲	⑥	⚒ 2	⚒	①–④	⑤	⚒	⚒		⑦		⑦ (*E*)	⑦ (*E*)	⑦ (*E*)	⑦ (*E*)		⑦ (*E*)		⑦	
Dublin Connolly d.	1721	...	...	1809	1840	1900	...	1920	2020	2050	...	2146	2146	2246	2347	...		...	1000	1200	1400	1600	...	1900	...	2135	...
Malahide d.	|	...	...	1830	1855	|	...	1940	2040	|	...	2209	2209	2304	0008	...		...	|	|	|	|	...	|	...	2157	...
Skerries d.	1758	...	...	1844	1909	|	...	1954	2054	|	...	2223	2223	2319	0022	...		...	|	|	|	|	...	|	...	2211	...
Balbriggan d.	1804	...	...	1850	1915	|	...	2000	2100	|	...	2229	2229	2324	0028	...		...	|	|	|	|	...	|	...	2217	...
Drogheda d.	1821	...	...	1908	1930	1934	...	2018	2118	2128	...	2247	2247	2321	0049	...		...	1032	1232	1432	1632	...	1933	...	2237	...
Dundalk d.	1846	...	...	1932	...	1955	...	...	...	2150	...	...	2312	0009	0115	...		...	1054	1254	1454	1654	...	1955	...	2301	...
Newry d.	1912	1950	...	...	...	2013	...	...	...	2207	...	...	...	...	...	...		...	1112	1312	1512	1712	...	2013	...	...	...
Portadown § d.	...	2015	2015	...	...	2033	2045	...	...	2228	2245	...	...	...	...	...		...	1133	1333	1533	1733	...	2033	...	...	...
Lisburn § a.	...	2037	2037	...	...	|	2107	...	...	|	2307	...	...	...	...	...		...	|	|	|	|	...	|	...	...	...
Belfast LP ♣ § a.	...	2110	2110	...	...	2105	2140	...	...	2300	2340	...	...	...	...	...		...	1208	1408	1608	1808	...	2108	...	...	...

f – On ⑥ terminates at Belfast Great Victoria Street 22–25 mins. earlier.
j – 7 minutes earlier on ⑥.
t – Belfast **Great Victoria Street**.
w – From Rosslare on Ⓐ, from Gorey on ⑥; see Table **237**.
▲ – 7–10 minutes later on Ⓐ.
♥ – 15–21 minutes later on ⑥.
§ – Other local trains run Belfast - Lisburn - Portadown and v.v.
♣ – Belfast Lanyon Place (formerly Central Station).

231 BELFAST - LARNE and BANGOR — NIR

From Belfast LP ♣ –
Ⓐ: 0655 **H**, 0750 **H**, 0855 **H** and hourly until 1355 **H**, 1455, 1555 **H**, 1643 **H**, 1744, 1825 **H**, 2025 **H**, 2225 **H**, 2325 **H**.
⑥: 0725 **H**, and every **two** hours until 2125 **H**, 2225 **H**, 2325 **H**.
⑦: 0955 **H**, and every **two** hours until 2155 **H**.

From Larne Town –
Ⓐ: 0608 **S**, 0648 **S**, 0758 **S** and hourly until 1458 **S**, 1556, 1623, 1738 **S**, 1828, 1928 **S**, 2128 **S**.
⑥: 0628 **S**, 0728 **S**, 0828 **S**, and every **two** hours until 2228 **S**.
⑦: 0858 **S**, and every **two** hours until 2058 **S**.

Trains call at: Carrickfergus 27 - 29 minutes from Belfast and 28 - 31 minutes from Larne and Whitehead 38 - 40 minutes from Belfast, 18 - 21 minutes from Larne.

Trains marked **H** arrive Larne **Harbour** 4 minutes after Larne **Town**. Trains marked **S** depart Larne **Harbour** 3 minutes before Larne **Town**. Journey time Belfast Central - Larne Harbour 57 - 65 mins.

A frequent train service operates between Belfast Lanyon Place ♣ and Bangor. Journey time 30–31 minutes. 20 km. Approximate timings from Belfast ①–⑥: 2 per hour at xx12 and xx42 minutes past each hour, ⑦: xx42. Approximate timings from Bangor ①–⑥: 2 per hour at xx25 and xx55 minutes past each hour, ⑦: xx25.

♣ – Belfast Lanyon Place (formerly Central Station).

232 🚌 BELFAST - ENNISKILLEN and ARMAGH — Ulsterbus 251, 261

From Belfast ★ to Enniskillen (Bus Stn) (journey time 2 hours 15 mins)
Ⓐ: 0805, 0905 and hourly until 1905, 2005.
⑥: 1005, 1205, 1405, 1505, 1605, 1805, 2005.
⑦: 1605, 2005.

From Enniskillen (Bus Stn) to Belfast ★
Ⓐ: 0725, 0825, and hourly until 1625, 1725, 1825 ◧.
⑥: 0725, 0925, 1125, 1225, 1325, 1525, 1725.
⑦: 1225, 1525, 1725.

From Belfast ★ to Armagh (Bus Stn) (journey time 1 hour 25 mins)
Ⓐ: 0800, 0945, 1045, 1145, 1245, 1345, 1445, 1645, 1715, 1745, 1845, 1945, 2115.
⑥: 1045, 1245, 1445, 1745, 1845, 2005.
⑦: 1335, 1735, 2015, 2200.

From Armagh (Bus Stn) to Belfast ★
Ⓐ: 0630, 0715, 0805, 0905, 1005, 1105, 1205, 1305, 1505, 1605, 1705, 1805.
⑥: 0730, 0905, 1105, 1305, 1605, 1705.
⑦: 1210, 1410, 1610, 1830, 2015.

Buses call at Portadown (Market Street) 40 - 75 minutes from Belfast and Portadown (Northern Bank) 20–30 minutes from Armagh (Bus Stn).

◧ – Change at Dungannon; arrive Europa Buscentre 2140.
★ – Europa Buscentre / Great Victoria St. Rail Station.

NIR BELFAST - LONDONDERRY and PORTRUSH 233

km		Ⓐ	⚒	⚒	⚒	⚒	⚒	✤	⚒	⚒	⚒		⑦	⑦	⑦	⑦	⑦		⑦	⑦	⑦	⑦		
	Belfast GVSt. ★ d.	0605	...	0710	...	0810	...	and at the	2110	...	2240	...	...	...	0910	...	1010	and at the	1910	...	2010	2110	...	...
0	**Belfast** LP ♣ d.	0615	...	0720	...	0820	...	same	2120	...	2250	...	...	...	0920	...	1020	same	1920	...	2020	2120	...	...
33	Antrim d.	0643	...	0747	...	0847	...	minutes	2247	...	2317	...	...	...	0947	...	1047	minutes	1947	...	2047	2147	...	...
52	Ballymena d.	0657	...	0803	...	0903	...	past every	2203	...	2330	...	...	...	1003	...	1103	past every	2003	...	2103	2200	...	...
97	**Coleraine** d.	0743	0745	0843	0845	0943	0945	hour	2243	2245	0005	...	0845	0945	1043	1045	1143	**two** hours	2043	2045	2143	2235	...	...
107	Portrush a.	|	0757	|	0857	|	0957	until	|	2257	...	...	0857	0957	|	1057	1157	until	|	2057	2157	...	...	...
151	**Londonderry** a.	0822	...	0922	...	1022	...		2322	...	...	...	...	...	1122	...	...		2122	...	...	...	...	...

	Ⓐ	⚒	Ⓐ	Ⓐ	⑥	⑥	⚒	⚒	✤	⚒	⚒	⚒	Ⓐ	⑥	⚒	⑦	⑦	⑦		⑦	⑦	⑦	⑦	⑦
Londonderry d.	...	...	0612	...	...	0642	...	0738	and at the	...	2038	...	2138	2138	...	...	...	0938	and at the	...	...	1938	...	...
Portrush d.	...	0605	|	0705	0700	|	0803	|	same	2103	|	2203	|	|	2303	0905	1003	|	same	1905	2003	|	2103	2203
Coleraine d.	0550	0621	0652	0719	0712	0721	0815	0819	minutes	2115	2119	2215	2219	2216	2315	0920	1015	1019	minutes	1919	2015	2019	2119	2215
Ballymena d.	0626	0700	0730	0800	...	0800	...	0900	past every	...	2200	...	2300	...	...	1000	...	1100	past every	2000	...	2100	2200	...
Antrim d.	0642	0714	0747	0814	...	0814	...	0914	hour	...	2214	...	2316	...	...	1014	...	1114	**two** hours	2014	...	2114	2214	...
Belfast LP ♣ a.	0710	0742	0816	0839	...	0841	...	0939	until	...	2239	...	2339	...	...	1039	...	1139	until	2039	...	2139	2239	...
Belfast GVSt. ★ a.	...	0752	0826	0851	...	0850	...	0950		...	2250	...	...	...	...	1050	...	1150		2050	...	2150	...	...

★ – Belfast GVSt. (Belfast Great Victoria St.) is the nearest station to Belfast City Centre and the Europa Buscentre is adjacent. ♣ – Belfast Lanyon Place (formerly Central Station).
✤ – 1010 depart from Belfast GVSt. runs to Portrush, arrives 1155. 1238 Ⓐ dep. Londonderry: change at Coleraine for Belfast.

Ulsterbus 212 express 🚌 service, Belfast - Londonderry. Journey time: 1 hour 40 minutes.
Ⓐ: 0630, 0700 and every 30 minutes until 1900, 1930 then 2030, 2130, 2300.
⑥: 0645, 0900, 1000, 1030 and every 30 minutes until 1900, 1930 then 2030, 2130, 2300.
⑦: 0830, 1030, 1100 and every 30 minutes until 1930 then 2030, 2130, 2215, 2300.

Ulsterbus 212 express 🚌 service, Londonderry - Belfast. Journey time: 1 hour 45 minutes.
Ⓐ: 0415, 0530, 0600, and every 30 minutes until 1700 then 1800, 1930, 2100, 2200, 2300.
⑥: 0645, 0730, 0800 and every 30 minutes until 1630, 1700 then 1800, 1930, 2100, 2200, 2300.
⑦: 0700, 0800, 0900, 0930 and every 30 minutes to 1730, 1800, 1900, 2100.

Ulsterbus X3, X4 🚌 DUBLIN - LONDONDERRY 234

	X4	X3	X4	X3	X4	X4	X3	X4	
Dublin Busáras d.	0630	1000	1100	1215	1515	1800	2015	2230	...
Dublin Airport ✈ △ d.	0650	1020	1120	1235	1535	1820	2035	2250	...
Monaghan d.	|	1205	|	1420	|	|	2220	|	...
Omagh ▽ a.	|	1300	|	1515	|	|	2315	|	...
Strabane ▽ a.	|	1330	|	1545	|	|	2345	|	...
Londonderry a.	1035	1400	1505	1615	1920	2155	0015	0155	...

	X4	X4	X4	X3	X4	X3	X3	X4	
Londonderry d.	0130	0415	0550	0700	0950	1200	1500	1730	...
Strabane △ d.	|	|	|	0730	|	1230	1530	|	...
Omagh △ d.	|	|	|	0800	|	1300	1600	|	...
Monaghan d.	|	|	|	0905	|	1405	1705	|	...
Dublin Airport ✈ ▽ a.	0500	0800	0935	1040	1335	1540	1840	2115	...
Dublin Busáras a.	0520	0820	0955	1100	1355	1600	1900	2135	...

△ – Buses call here to pick up only. ▽ – Buses call here to set down only. ☛ The calling point in each town is the bus station unless otherwise indicated.

Bus Éireann 30, X30 🚌 DUBLIN - DONEGAL 234a

Dublin Busáras d.	0630	0800	0930	1100	1230	1400	1530	1700	1830	2000	2300	0030
Dublin Airport ✈ △ d.	0650	0820	0950	1120	1250	1420	1550	1720	1850	2020	2320	0050
Virginia d.	0755	0925	1055	1225	1355	1525	1655	1825	1955	2125	0025	0155
Cavan d.	0835	0955	1135	1255	1435	1555	1735	1855	2035	2155	0055	0235
Enniskillen d.	0925	1040	1225	1340	1525	1640	1825	1940	2125	2240	0140	0325
Ballyshannon d.	1010	1120	1310	1420	1610	1720	1910	2020	2210	2320	0220	0410
Donegal ⊡ a.	1030	1135	1330	1435	1630	1735	1930	2035	2230	2335	0235	0430

Donegal ⊡ d.	0100	0400	0530	0700	0830	1000	1130	1300	1430	1600	1730	1900
Ballyshannon d.	0120	0420	0550	0720	0850	1020	1150	1320	1450	1620	1750	1920
Enniskillen d.	0200	0500	0635	0800	0935	1100	1235	1400	1535	1700	1835	2000
Cavan d.	0240	0540	0735	0840	1035	1140	1335	1440	1635	1740	1935	2040
Virginia d.	0310	0610	0805	0910	1105	1210	1405	1510	1705	1810	2005	2110
Dublin Airport ✈ ▽ a.	0415	0715	0910	1015	1210	1315	1510	1615	1810	1915	2110	2215
Dublin Busáras a.	0435	0735	0930	1035	1230	1335	1530	1635	1830	1935	2130	2235

△ – Buses call here to pick up only. ▽ – Buses call here to set down only. ⊡ – Donegal **Abbey Hotel**.

Bus Éireann 51, 64, 480 🚌 LONDONDERRY - GALWAY and GALWAY - CORK 235

	⚒									⑤⑦
Londonderry d.	...	...	...	0715	0915	1110	...	1530	1830	...
Letterkenny d.	...	...	...	0755	0957	1150	...	1610	1910	...
Donegal (Abbey Hotel) d.	...	0635	...	0840	1040	1240	...	1655	1955	...
Ballyshannon d.	...	0655	...	0900	1100	1300	...	1715	2015	...
Sligo d.	0600	0740	0800	1000	1200	1400	1600	1815	2105	2115
Ireland West Airport Knock d.	|	...	0905	1105	1305	1500	1705	|	...	|
Knock d.	0724	...	0924	1125	1324	1520	1725	1920	...	2230
Claremorris (Dalton St.) d.	|	...	|	1135	|	1530	1735	|	...	2240
Galway (Bus Station) ✤ a.	0900	...	1045	1240	1445	1635	1840	2040	...	2345

Galway (Bus Station) ✤ d.	...	...	0705	0805		1705	1805	1905	2005
Ennis d.	...	...	0820	0920		1820	1920	2020	2120
Shannon Airport ✈ d.	...	...	0850	0950	and	1850	1950	2050	2150
Limerick (Colbert Rail Station) a.	...	...	0920	1020	hourly	1920	2020	2120	2220
Limerick (Colbert Rail Station) d.	0725	0835	0935	1035	until	1935	2035	...	...
Mallow (Town Park) d.	0830	0940	1040	1140		2040	2140	...	...
Cork a.	0915	1025	1125	1225		2125	2225	...	...

Cork d.	...	...	0725	0825		1725	1825	1925	2055
Mallow (Town Park) d.	...	...	0800	0900		1800	1900	2000	2130
Limerick (Colbert Rail Station) a.	...	...	0910	1010	and	1910	2010	2110	2240
Limerick (Colbert Rail Station) d.	0725	0825	0925	1025	hourly	1925	2025	...	...
Shannon Airport ✈ d.	0755	0855	0955	1055	until	1955	2055	...	...
Ennis d.	0825	0925	1025	1125		2025	2125	...	...
Galway (Bus Station) ✤ a.	0945	1045	1145	1245		2145	2245	...	...

	⚒	⚒		⚒						⑤
Galway (Bus Station) ✤ d.	0600	...	0845	1030	...	1200	*1410*	1600	1810	...
Claremorris (Dalton St.) d.	0700	...	|	1135	...	1305	|	|	1911	...
Knock d.	0710	...	1005	1145	...	1315	*1530*	1725	1921	...
Ireland West Airport Knock d.	0730	...	1025	1205	...	1335	*1550*	1745	|	...
Sligo d.	0845	0855	1145	1310	1330	1500	1710	1905	2040	2100
Ballyshannon d.	...	0945	1232	...	1417	1547	1757	1952	...	2147
Donegal (Abbey Hotel) d.	...	1015	1252	...	1437	1607	1817	2012	...	2207
Letterkenny d.	...	1110	1340	...	1525	1655	1905	2100	...	2250
Londonderry a.	...	1145	1420	...	1605	1735	1945	2140	...	2330

✤ – Change buses at Galway. Minimum connection time 45 minutes. ☛ The calling point in each town is the bus station unless otherwise indicated.

IRELAND

236 DUBLIN - SLIGO IÉ

km		Ⓐ 🍷	⚒ 🍷	⚒ 🍷	⚒ 🍷	⚒ 🍷	A 🍷	⚒ 🍷	Ⓐ	Ⓐ	⚒ 🍷	Ⓐ		⑦ 🍷		⑦ 🍷		⑦ 🍷	B 🍷	⑦ 🍷		⑦ 🍷	
0	**Dublin** Connolly d.	0655	0905	1100	1300	1500	1600	1710	1717	1815	1915	2047	...	0905	...	1300	...	1500	1600	1710	...	1905	...
26	Maynooth d.	0731	0937	1136	1336	1536	1639	1744	1802	1858	1954	2129	...	0938	...	1336	...	1536	1637	1745	...	1944	...
83	Mullingar d.	0813	1018	1217	1418	1617	1720	1825	1851	1941	2034	2215	...	1019	...	1418	...	1617	1718	1825	...	2025	...
125	**Longford** d.	0853	1048	1249	1450	1647	1750	1855	1924	2012	2112	...	...	1050	...	1450	...	1648	1747	1858	...	2055	...
143	Dromod d.	0906	1101	1303	1504	1700	1804	1908	...	...	2124	...	...	1104	...	1504	...	1701	1804	1914	...	2106	...
159	Carrick on Shannon d.	0919	1114	1316	1517	1712	1816	1920	...	...	2136	...	...	1117	...	1517	...	1713	1818	1928	...	2118	...
173	Boyle d.	0933	1128	1329	1529	1724	1828	1931	...	...	2148	...	...	1139	...	1539	...	1732	1832	1941	...	2130	...
219	**Sligo** a.	1017	1216	1416	1616	1807	1905	2016	...	...	2225	...	...	1215	...	1615	...	1808	1907	2016	...	2207	...

	Ⓐ	Ⓐ	Ⓐ 🍷	⚒ 🍷	⚒ 🍷	⚒ 🍷	⚒ 🍷	⚒ 🍷	C 🍷	Ⓐ 🍷	⚒ 🍷		⑦ 🍷		⑦ 🍷		⑦ 🍷		⑦ 🍷		B 🍷		⑦ 🍷
Sligo d.	...	...	0540	0640	0905	1105	1305	1505	1655	1650	1900	...	0905	...	1105	...	1305	...	1505	...	1630	...	1905
Boyle d.	...	...	0612	0712	0937	1137	1337	1537	1729	1729	1937	...	0939	...	1138	...	1338	...	1538	...	1705	...	1942
Carrick on Shannon d.	...	...	0624	0726	0951	1151	1350	1550	1742	1742	1950	...	0951	...	1151	...	1350	...	1550	...	1719	...	1953
Dromod d.	...	...	0635	0738	1003	1203	1402	1602	1806	1806	2002	...	1003	...	1203	...	1402	...	1602	...	1731	...	2005
Longford d.	0538	0615	0649	0751	1016	1216	1415	1615	1825	1825	2015	...	1016	...	1216	...	1415	...	1615	...	1748	...	2018
Mullingar d.	0612	0649	0719	0821	1055	1254	1454	1654	1903	1905	2044	...	1055	...	1245	...	1454	...	1654	...	1826	...	2051
Maynooth d.	0655	0730	0810	0904	1136	1334	1535	1743	1944	1950	2125	...	1136	...	1326	...	1535	...	1742	...	1906	...	2132
Dublin Connolly a.	0740	0818	0849	0940	1209	1409	1608	1822	2015	2030	2159	...	1209	...	1358	...	1610	...	1814	...	1940	...	2205

A – ⚒ (Ⓐ June 6 - Aug. 30). B – ⑦ (not June 7 - Aug. 30). C – ⑥ (not June 6 - Aug. 30). ☛ **Shaded services are temporarily suspended.**

236a BALLYBROPHY - ROSCREA - LIMERICK IÉ

km		Ⓐ	⚒ 🍷	⚒		⚒h ◇🍴	⚒	⑦	⑦		
0	**Dublin** Heuston d.	...	0800	...	...	1800	...	1825	...	...	...
107	Ballybrophy d.	...	0856	0905	...	1857	1905	1936	1942	...	...
123	Roscrea d.	...	...	0922	...	...	1922	|	1959	...	...
154	Nenagh d.	0747	...	0955	...	...	1955	|	2032	...	...
199	**Limerick** Colbert a.	0840	...	1048	...	...	2048	2043	2125	...	...

	⚒	⚒		⚒	⚒ ◇🍷	⑦	⑦			
Limerick Colbert d.	0645	0740	...	1710	...	1735	1820	...	...	...
Nenagh d.	0750	|	...	1803	...	1828	|	...	...	...
Roscrea d.	0823	|	...	1836	...	1902	|	...	...	...
Ballybrophy d.	0843	0844	...	1855	1859	1921	1925	...	...	...
Dublin Heuston a.	...	0957	...	...	2004	...	2036	...	...	...

h – 🍴 on Ⓐ, 🍷 on ⑥. ◇ – Also conveys 1st class.

237 DUBLIN - ROSSLARE IÉ

km		⚒		⑥	Ⓐ		Ⓐ	⑥		Ⓐ	Ⓐ	Ⓐ	⑥		⑦	⑦		⑦		⑦			
0	**Dublin Connolly** ▲ d.		...	0805	0933	...	1333	1336	...	1633	1733	1835	1838	...		1025	...	1345	...	1845	...	...	...
11	Dún Laoghaire ▲ d.		...	0825	0957	...	1358	1357	...	1658	1758	1859	1856	...		1043	...	1406	...	1906	...	...	...
21	Bray ▲ d.		...	0845	1020	...	1422	1417	...	1722	1822	1920	1917	...		1103	...	1427	...	1927	...	...	...
47	Wicklow d.		...	0913	1045	...	1447	1445	...	1749	1849	1947	1946	...		1132	...	1452	...	1955	...	...	...
80	Arklow d.		...	0940	1114	...	1515	1511	...	1818	1921	2014	2013	...		1159	...	1519	...	2022	...	...	...
97	Gorey d.		...	0953	1127	...	1528	1525	...	1831	1935	2027	2026	...		1212	...	1535	...	2035	...	...	...
126	Enniscorthy d.		...	1013	1147	...	1547	1545	...	1856	1956	2047	2046	...		1233	...	1556	...	2056	...	...	...
150	**Wexford** d.		...	1034	1207	...	1608	1606	...	1917	2016	2110	2107	...		1254	...	1618	...	2117	...	...	...
160	Rosslare Strand d.		...	1052	1225	...	1625	1624	...	1933	2034	...	2124	...		1311	...	1637	...	2134	...	...	...
166	**Rosslare** Europort a.		...	1059	1231	...	1633	1632	...	1941	2042	...	2133	...		1319	...	1643	...	2142	...	...	...

	⚒	Ⓐ	Ⓐ y	⑥	Ⓐ	⑥		Ⓐ	⑥	Ⓐ	⑥		⑦		⑦		⑦		⑦				
Rosslare Europort d.		...	0535	...	0720	0720	...	1255	1255	1730	1755	...		...	0940	...	1420	...	1805	...	...	...	...
Rosslare Strand d.		...	0540	...	0726	0726	...	1301	1301	1736	1801	...		...	0946	...	1426	...	1811	...	...	...	...
Wexford d.		...	0557	...	0745	0745	...	1320	1320	1753	1819	...		...	1005	...	1447	...	1831	...	...	...	...
Enniscorthy d.		...	0620	...	0805	0807	...	1340	1342	1813	1841	...		...	1027	...	1509	...	1853	...	...	...	...
Gorey d.		0550	0643	0645	0825	0828	...	1400	1403	1836	1902	...		...	1047	...	1532	...	1913	...	...	...	...
Arklow d.		0602	0657	0701	0838	0840	...	1413	1415	1849	1914	...		...	1059	...	1546	...	1925	...	...	...	...
Wicklow d.		0632	0730	0735	0905	0915	...	1446	1445	1916	1945	...		...	1130	...	1612	...	1955	...	...	...	...
Bray ▲ d.		0659	0759	0805	0932	0943	...	1510	1513	1943	2011	...		...	1158	...	1640	...	2019	...	...	...	...
Dún Laoghaire ▲ d.		0720	0819	0825	0949	0959	...	1530	1531	2000	2027	...		...	1213	...	1654	...	2034	...	...	...	...
Dublin Connolly ▲ a.		0748	0847	0847	1018	1019	...	1556	1556	2028	2050	...		...	1232	...	1714	...	2051	...	...	...	...

y – To Dundalk; see Table **230**. ▲ – Additional surburban trains (*DART*) run Howth - Dublin Connolly - Dún Laoghaire - Bray. Trains run every 10 - 15 mins. on ⚒, every 20 - 30 mins. on ⑦.

238 DUBLIN - KILKENNY - WATERFORD IÉ

km		⚒	⚒ 🍷	Ⓐ	⚒ 🍷		⚒ 🍷	⚒ 🍷	⑤ 🍷	⚒ 🍷	⚒ 🍷	⚒ 🍷	Ⓐ	⑦		⑦ 🍷		⑦ 🍷		⑦ 🍷		⑦ 🍷	
0	**Dublin Heuston** △ d.		0720	0826	1015	...	1315	1510	1615	1640	1735	1835	2015		...	0910	...	1410	...	1745	...	1840	...
48	Kildare △ d.		0751	0847	1040	...	|	1538	|	1715	1805	1903	2100		...	0939	...	1438	...	1813	...	1904	...
72	Athy d.		0807	0913	1100	...	1356	1555	1656	1735	1825	1922	2114		...	0957	...	1457	...	1832	...	1927	...
90	Carlow d.		0822	0928	1112	...	1409	1606	1725	1747	1837	1938	2127		...	1010	...	1509	...	1844	...	1939	...
106	Muine Bheag d.		0835	...	1123	...	1421	1618	|	1759	1848	1949	...		...	1024	...	1521	...	1858	...	1951	...
130	**Kilkenny** a.		0900	...	1140	...	1438	1635	|	1817	1905	2007	...		...	1042	...	1541	...	1917	...	2009	...
130	**Kilkenny** d.		0903	...	1144	...	1443	1640	|	1821	1910	2012	...		...	1047	...	1545	...	1921	...	2014	...
147	Thomastown d.		0919	...	1155	...	1459	1656	|	1831	1920	2022	...		...	1057	...	1556	...	1932	...	2024	...
179	**Waterford** a.		0944	...	1223	...	1530	1721	1813	1904	1948	2054	...		...	1126	...	1624	...	2001	...	2054	...

	⚒	Ⓐ	⚒ 🍷	⚒ 🍷	⚒ 🍷	Ⓐ	⚒ 🍷	⚒ 🍷	⚒ 🍷	⑤⑥	⚒ 🍷	Ⓐ	⑦		⑦ 🍷		⑦ 🍷		⑦ 🍷		⑦ 🍷		
Waterford d.		...	0555	0650	0750	...	1100	1305	1450	1605	1825	...		...	0905	...	1240	...	1510	...	1805	...	...
Thomastown d.		...	0619	|	0809	...	1119	1324	1511	|	1846	...		...	0924	...	1259	...	1530	...	1824	...	...
Kilkenny a.		...	0634	0724	0824	...	1134	1339	1525	|	1900	...		...	0939	...	1314	...	1544	...	1839	...	...
Kilkenny d.		...	0637	0728	0828	...	1141	1343	1530	|	1911	...		...	0943	...	1318	...	1548	...	1843	...	...
Muine Bheag d.		...	0651	0743	0844	...	1155	1357	1545	|	1931	...		...	0957	...	1332	...	1603	...	1859	...	...
Carlow d.		0630	0703	0756	0856	1010	1207	1411	1557	1700	1943	2136		...	1010	...	1343	...	1615	...	1910	...	...
Athy d.		0641	0715	0810	0908	1021	1219	1423	1622	1713	1956	2147		...	1024	...	1355	...	1627	...	1926	...	...
Kildare △ d.		0659	0734	|	0927	1041	1239	1441	1642	1730	2015	2206		...	1043	...	1414	...	1646	...	1946	...	...
Dublin Heuston △ a.		0743	0807	0900	1000	1114	1316	1521	1712	1806	2046	2252		...	1122	...	1454	...	1724	...	2024	...	...

△ – For additional trains Dublin - Kildare and v.v, see Tables **240**, **245**.

239 LIMERICK - WATERFORD IÉ

km			⚒ 🍷	⚒			⚒	⚒	s	
0	**Limerick Colbert** d.	...	0855	...	...	...	1750	...	...	...
35	**Limerick Junction** d.	...	0921	0940	...	...	1822	1840	...	...
40	Tipperary d.	...	...	0954	...	...	...	1854	...	...
62	Cahir d.	...	...	1019	...	...	...	1919	...	...
79	Clonmel d.	...	...	1038	...	...	...	1938	...	...
101	Carrick on Suir d.	...	...	1103	...	...	...	2003	...	...
124	**Waterford** a.	...	...	1125	...	...	...	2025	...	...

		⚒	⚒			⚒	⚒		
Waterford d.	...	0720	...	...	...	1625	...	...	...
Carrick on Suir d.	...	0745	...	...	...	1650	...	...	...
Clonmel d.	...	0807	...	...	...	1712	...	...	...
Cahir d.	...	0826	...	...	...	1731	...	...	...
Tipperary d.	...	0848	...	...	...	1753	...	...	...
Limerick Junction a.	...	0903	0935	...	...	1808	1830	...	...
Limerick Colbert a.	...	...	1002	...	...	...	1855	...	...

IÉ DUBLIN - GALWAY, BALLINA and WESTPORT 240

km		⚒	⚒ 🍷	⚒ 🍷	⚒ 🍷	⚒ 🍷	⚒ 🍷	⚒ 🍷	⚒ 🍷	⚒ 🍷	⚒ 🍷	⚒	⚒ 🍷	⚒ 🍷	⚒ 🍷	⚒ 🍷	⑦ 🍷	⑦	⑦ 🍷	⑦ 🍷	⑦ 🍷	⑦ 🍷	⑦ 🍷	⑦ 🍷	⑦ 🍷	⑦
0	**Dublin Heuston 245** d.	...	0735	...	0925	1125	1245	1325	1445	1535	1630	1710	1730	1815	1830	1935	0800	...	1140	1340	1440	1540	1635	1830	1845	2030
48	Kildare **245** d.	...	0800	...	|	|	|	|	|	|	1658	1738	|	|	|	|	0825	...	1205	1409	|	|	|	1901	1914	|
67	Portarlington **245** d.	...	0814	...	1001	1200	1321	1403	1522	1613	|	1755	1812	|	1913	2009	0839	...	1219	1423	1516	|	1713	1915	1928	2107
93	Tullamore d.	0650t	0830	...	1018	1217	1338	1422	1541	1631	1726	1812	1829	1907	|	2031	0856	...	1244	1447	1540	1633	1731	1932	1953	2123
129	**Athlone** d.	0730	0905	0915	1050	1241	1404	1447	1605	1659	1749	1845	1858	1929	1952	2102	0922	0940	1309	1512	1605	1658	1802	2000	2022	2149
152	Ballinasloe d.	0744	0920k	|	1105	1258	|	1503	|	1714	1808	...	1914	|	2008	2118	0938	|	1324	|	1622	|	1819	|	2037	2204
187	Athenry **242** d.	0814	0948k	|	1127	1322	|	1524	|	1738	1832	...	1936	|	2029	2141	1004	|	1346	|	1645	|	1848	|	2059	2224
208	**Galway 242** a.	0835	1006k	|	1152	1344	|	1545	|	1759	1852	...	2001	|	2053	2204	1024	|	1405	|	1708	|	1908	|	2119	2244
160	Roscommon d.	▬	▬	0938	▬	...	1429	▬	1629	▬	▬	...	...	1958	▬	...	▬	1002	▬	1537	...	1732	▬	2023	▬	...
186	Castlerea d.	...	...	0957	...	...	1448	...	1648	...	...	...	...	2017	...	...	...	1021	...	1556	...	1751	...	2042	...	...
204	Ballyhaunis d.	...	...	1010	...	...	1501	...	1702	...	...	...	...	2030	...	...	...	1034	...	1610	...	1804	...	2055	...	...
222	Claremorris d.	Ⓐ	⚒	1024	⚒	...	1515	⚒	1716	⚒	⚒	...	...	2044	⚒	...	⑦	1048	⑦	1626	...	1820	⑦	2109	⑦	...
240	Manulla Junction § d.	0538	0840	1036	1039	...	1528	1532	1729	1732	1838	...	...	2057	2100	...	0813	1102	1105	1640	...	1834	1837	2122	2125	...
273	**Ballina** a.	0605	0907	|	1106	...	|	1600	|	1800	1906	...	...	|	2128	...	0841	|	1133	|	...	|	1905	|	2153	...
246	Castlebar d.	...	...	1043	...	...	1535	...	1736	...	...	...	...	2109	...	...	...	1109	...	1647	...	1841	...	2129	...	...
264	**Westport** a.	...	...	1056	...	...	1557	...	1756	...	...	...	...	2126	...	...	...	1127	...	1708	...	1906	...	2149	...	...

	Ⓐ	Ⓐ	Ⓐ	⚒ 🍷	⚒	⚒ 🍷	⚒	⚒ 🍷	⚒ 🍷	⚒	⚒ 🍷	⚒	⚒	⚒ 🍷	⚒ 🍷	⚒	⑦	⑦ 🍷	⑦	⑦	⑦ 🍷	⑦ 🍷	⑦ 🍷	⑦ 🍷	⑦	⑦ 🍷
Westport d.	...	...	0515	...	...	0715	...	0945	...	...	1310	...	...	1820	...	...	...	0750	...	...	1330	...	1550	...	...	1750
Castlebar d.	...	...	0528	...	...	0728	...	0957	...	...	1323	...	...	1833	...	...	...	0803	...	...	1343	...	1603	...	...	1803
Ballina d.	...	0505	|	...	0705	|	0935	|	...	1300	|	1455	1805	|	...	2027	0740	|	1030	1310	|	...	|	...	1735	|
Manulla Junction § d.	...	0532	0535	...	0733	0736	1003	1005	...	1328	1330	1525	1833	1839	...	2055	0808	0811	1058	1338	1349	...	1610	...	1803	1809
Claremorris d.	...	▬	0547	...	▬	0750	▬	1020	...	▬	1344	▬	▬	1852	...	▬	▬	0825	▬	▬	1402	...	1624	...	▬	1822
Ballyhaunis d.	...	...	0559	...	...	0804	...	1033	...	...	1357	...	...	1905	...	...	...	0839	...	...	1416	...	1643	...	...	1840
Castlerea d.	...	...	0612	...	⚒	0818	⚒	1046	...	Ⓐ	1410	⚒	⚒	1919	...	...	⑦	0853	⑦	⑦	1430	...	1658	...	⑦	1853
Roscommon d.	...	Ⓐ	0632	...	🍷	0838	🍷	1105	...	🍷	1432	🍷	🍷	1939	...	Ⓐ	🍷	0913	🍷	🍷	1451	...	1718	...	🍷	1913
Galway 242 d.	...	0525	|	0625	0730	|	0930	|	1105	1305	|	1505	1720	|	1920	2215	0805	|	1100	1300	|	1505	|	1700	1800	|
Athenry **242** d.	...	0543	|	0640	0748	|	0948	|	1128	1320	|	1520	1738	|	1937	2234	0821	|	1118	1317	|	1523	|	1718	1818	|
Ballinasloe d.	...	0606	|	|	0808	|	1012	|	1149	1345	|	1547	1805	|	2006	2300	0845	|	1141	1346	|	1546	|	1743	1845	|
Athlone d.	0520	0624	0700	0716	0826	0903	1028	1131	1208	1407	1458	1605	1828	2011	2031	2315	0902	0938	1159	1403	1516	1606	1747	1804	1903	1937
Tullamore d.	0544	0648	0722	0738	0849	0930	1056	1156	1237	1440	1524	1634	1850	2035	2056	...	0933	1002	1223	1429	1541	1633	1811	1830	1930	2014
Portarlington **245** d.	0602	0707	0741	|	0907	0949	1114	1224	1256	1508	1548	1652	1915	2053	2114	...	0951	1022	1243	1447	1601	1652	1829	1851	1957	2032
Kildare **245** d.	0614	0723	0757	0811	|	|	|	|	|	|	|	1706	1928	|	|	...	1001	|	1255	|	|	1706	1844	1906	|	|
Dublin Heuston 245 a.	0659	0759	0831	0843	0950	1027	1154	1304	1339	1548	1629	1740	2001	2136	2154	...	1037	1104	1328	1528	1642	1737	1915	1941	2041	2111

f – ⑤ only. **j** – Also runs on ⑥. **k** – Change at Athlone on ⑤. **t** – Ⓐ only. § – Passenger transfer point only. ☛ **Shaded services are temporarily suspended.**

✣ – Additional service on Ⓐ depart Athlone 0708, Roscommon 0729, Castlerea 0747, Ballyhaunis 0803, Claremorris 0818, Manulla Jct. 0832, Castlebar 0838, Westport arrive 0855.

IÉ LIMERICK JUNCTION - LIMERICK - GALWAY 242

km		⚒	⚒	⚒	⚒	⚒	⚒		⑦	⑦	⑦	⑦
0	**Limerick Jct** **243** d.	...	...	...	...	...	...	...	...	1137	...	...
35	**Limerick** ¶ **245** d.	0555	0920	1420	1630	1805	1950	...	0900	1203	1555	1815
74	Ennis **245** d.	0649x	1000	1501	1710	1844	2029	...	0942	1307	1636	1856
103	Gort d.	0713	1022	1523	...	1931	2051	...	1004	1331	1702	1923
132	Athenry **240** d.	0743	1054	1554	...	2009	2119	...	1035	1400	1733	1954
152	**Galway** **240** a.	0809	1113	1615	...	2032	2142	...	1055	1423	1751	2012

	⚒	⚒	⚒	⚒	⚒	⚒	⚒	⑦	⑦	⑦	⑦
Galway **240** d.	...	0615	1025	1345	...	1750	...	0825	1155	1610	1830
Athenry **240** d.	...	0633	1044	1408	...	1817	...	0843	1214	1633	1853
Gort d.	...	0704	1117	1435	...	1844	...	0912	1244	1703	1924
Ennis **245** d.	0650	0735	1141	1503	1720	1908	2035	0936	1307	1726	1947
Limerick ¶ **245** a.	0730	0820	1222	1542	1800	1949	2115	1020	1345	1805	2027
Limerick Jct **243** a.	...	...	...	...	...	...	...	...	1422	...	...

x – Arrive 0635. ¶ – Limerick Colbert. ☛ **Shaded services are temporarily suspended.**

IÉ LIMERICK JUNCTION - LIMERICK 243

Shuttle service connecting with main-line trains. *35 km.* Journey time: 25-40 minutes. For through services to or from Dublin Heuston see Table **245**.

From Limerick Junction ⚒: 0806, 0836, 0935, 1040, 1250, 1438, 1636, 1839, 2040, 2243.
⑦: 1136, 1333, 1547, 1732, 1844, 2030, 2300.

From Limerick Colbert ⚒: 0530, 0615, 0725, 0900, 0950, 1055, 1250, 1455, 1650, 1750, 1850, 2055.
⑦: 1050, 1250, 1505, 1645, 1750, 1950, 2220.

IÉ (DUBLIN -) CORK - MALLOW - TRALEE 244

km			⚒	⚒	⚒	⚒	⚒	⚒	Ⓐ ◇🍴	⑥ 🍷	⚒			⑦	⑦ ◇🍷	⑦	⑦	⑦	⑦	⑦	
0	**Cork** **245** d.	...	0625	0900	...	*1225*	*1425*	*1625*	...	...	2100	...	...	0855	*1010*	1215	1450	*1625*	1850	...	...
	Dublin **245** d.	...	|	*0700*	*0900*	*1100*	*1300*	*1500*	1705	1705	*1900*	...	...	|	0830	*1000*	*1300*	*1400*	*1700*	1905	...
34	**Mallow** **245** d.	...	0651	0920	1120	1320	1520	1725	1916	1916	2120	...	...	0921	1035	1251	1529	1724	1930	2112	...
66	Millstreet d.	...	0716	0948	1143	1348	1543	1747	1940	1940	2148	...	...	0944	1101	1316	1553	1748	1953	2137	...
100	Killarney d.	...	0747	1019	1220	1420	1620	1820	2020	2020	2216	...	...	1014	1134	1347	1625	1826	2031	2208	...
134	**Tralee** a.	...	0826	1058	1258	1458	1658	1858	2058	2058	2255	...	...	1050	1221	1423	1704	1901	2109	2247	...

		①	②–⑤	⚒	⚒	⚒	⚒	⚒	⚒	⚒			⑦		⑦ 🍷	⑦ 🍷	⑦	⑦	⑦ 🍷	⑦	
Tralee d.	...	0440	0550	0705	0905	1105	1305	1505	1705	1905	...	...	0710	...	1150	1350	1510	1710	1750	1915	...
Killarney d.	...	0515	0627	0744	0939	1139	1339	1539	1739	1939	...	...	0740	...	1224	1430	1543	1744	1828	1949	...
Millstreet d.	...	0542	0653	0814	1010	1210	1410	1610	1810	2010	...	...	0814	...	1253	1459	1614	1810	1857	2020	...
Mallow **245** d.	...	0608	0729z	0842	1038	1238	1438	1638	1843	2043	...	...	0841	...	1321	1527	1643	1836	1927	2046	...
Dublin **245** a.	...	*0820*	*0931*	1047	*1258*	*1458*	*1659*	*1904*	*2104*	*2259*	...	...	*1053*	...	1530	1739	*1854*	*2057*	2133	|	...
Cork **245** a.	...	*0720*	0754	*0915*	*1145*	*1344*	*1537*	*1737*	1905	2104	...	...	0914	...	*1352*	*1632*	*1727*	1907	*2037*	2115	...

z – Arrive 0718. ◇ – Also conveys 🛏 1.

CORK - COBH Journey time: 24 minutes *19 km.*

Ⓐ 0530, 0630, 0700, 0730, then half hourly until 1830, 1900, 2000, 2100, 2200, 2300.
⑥ 0600, 0700, 0800, 0900, then hourly until 1700, 1800, 2000, 2100, 2200, 2300.
† 0800, 0900, 1100, 1200, 1300, 1430, 1600, 1700, 1800, 1940, 2100, 2200.

COBH - CORK

Ⓐ 0600, 0700, 0730, 0800, then half hourly until 1900, 1930, 2030, 2130, 2230, 2330.
⑥ 0630, 0730, 0830, 0930, then hourly until 1730, 1830, 2030, 2130, 2230, 2330.
† 0830, 0930, 1130, 1230, 1330, 1500, 1630, 1730, 1830, 2030, 2130, 2230.

CORK - MIDLETON Journey time: 24 mins. *19 km.*

Ⓐ 0545, 0615, 0645, 0715, then half hourly until 1845, 1915, 2015, 2115, 2245.
⑥ 0615, 0715, 0815, 0915, 1015, then hourly until 2015, 2115, 2245.
† 0815, 0915, 1115, 1215, 1415, 1615, 1715, 1815, 2015.

MIDLETON - CORK

Ⓐ 0615, 0645, 0715, 0745, then half hourly until 1915, 1945, 2045, 2145, 2315.
⑥ 0645, 0745, 0845, 0945, 1045, then hourly until 2045, 2145, 2315.
† 0845, 0945, 1145, 1245, 1445, 1645, 1745, 1845, 2045.

245 DUBLIN - LIMERICK, TRALEE and CORK IÉ

All catering services are temporarily suspended. First class is reduced on many services.

km			⚒h ◇✕	⚒	⚒ ◇🍷	⚒	⚒ ◇🍷	⚒	⚒ ◇🍷	⚒	⚒ ◇🍷	⚒	⚒ ◇🍷	⚒	⚒ ◇🍷	⚒	⚒ ◇🍷	⚒	⚒ ◇🍷	⚒ 🍷	⚒ 🍷	⚒	⚒ ◇🍷	⚒
0	**Dublin Heuston** 240 d.		0700	...	0800	...	0900	...	1000	...	1100	...	1200	...	1300	...	1400	...	1500	1525	1530	...	1600	...
48	Kildare 240 d.		|	...	|	...	|	...	|	...	|	...	|	...	|	...	|	...	|	1612	1559	...	|	...
67	Portarlington 240 d.		|	...	|	...	|	...	|	...	|	...	|	...	|	...	|	...	|	1626	1610	...	|	...
82	Portlaoise d.	⚒	0746	...	|	...	0944	...	1044	...	1144	...	1244	...	1344	...	1444	...	|	1637	1620	...	|	...
107	Ballybrophy d.		|	...	|	...	1000	...	|	...	|	...	|	...	|	...	1500	...	|	...	1635	...	|	...
127	Templemore d.		|	...	0904	...	|	...	|	...	1208	...	|	...	|	...	|	...	|	...	1648	...	|	...
139	Thurles d.		0815	...	0914	...	1017	...	1113	...	1217	...	1314	...	1414	...	1518	...	1610	...	1656	...	1711	...
172	**Limerick Junction** § d.		0835	0836	0932	0935	1035	1040	1131	1136	1235	1250	1332	1336	1432	1436	1536	1540	1629	...	|	...	1730	1735
208	**Limerick Colbert** § 242 a.		|	0904	|	1003	|	1107	|	1204	|	1324	|	1404	|	1504	|	1608	|	...	1741	1805	|	1803
**	Ennis 242 a.		|	*0959*	|	...	|	...	|	1310	|	...	|	1455	|	...	|	1710	|	...	...	1843	|	...
208	Charleville d.		|	...	|	...	1059	...	|	...	1258	...	|	...	|	...	|	...	1651	...	...	...	|	...
232	**Mallow** 244 d.		0909	...	1007	...	1114	...	1205	...	1314	...	1407	...	1506	...	1610	...	1707	...	...	...	1804	...
	Tralee 246 a.		*1058*	...	|	...	|	...	|	...	*1458*	...	|	...	|	...	|	...	*1858*	...	...	...	|	...
266	**Cork** 244 a.		0937	...	1037	...	1145	...	1237	...	1344	...	1437	...	1537	...	1642	...	1737	...	...	...	1837	...

	⚒ 🍷	Ⓐ ◇✕	⑥ ◇🍷	Ⓐ ◇✕	⑥ 🍷	⚒	⚒ 🍷	Ⓐ ◇✕	⑥ ◇🍷	⚒	⚒ ◇🍷	⚒	⚒	⚒		⑦ ◇🍷	⑦	⑦	⑦ ◇🍷	⑦	⑦	⑦ 🍷	
Dublin Heuston 240 d.	1625	1700	1700	1705	1705	...	1725	1800	1800	...	1900	...	2100	...		0830	...	...	1000	...	...	1125	...
Kildare 240 d.	|	|	|	|	|	...	1754	|	|	...	|	...	|	...		|	...	...	|	...	...	1153	...
Portarlington 240 d.	1700	|	|	|	|	...	1805	|	|	...	|	...	|	...		|	...	...	|	...	...	1205	...
Portlaoise d.	1712	|	|	|	|	...	1815	|	|	...	1946	...	2144	...	⑦	0913	...	...	1044	...	...	1215	...
Ballybrophy d.	1729	|	|	1800	1800	...	1829	1857	1857	...	2001	...	|	...		|	...	...	|	...	...	1230	...
Templemore d.	1740	|	|	1812	1812	...	1842	|	|	...	2014	...	|	...		|	...	...	|	...	...	1244	...
Thurles d.	1750	|	|	1820	1820	...	1851	1915	1915	...	2022	...	2214	...		0941	...	...	1114	...	...	1253	...
Limerick Junction § d.	1813	1827	1827	|	|	1836	|	1933	1933	1937	2040	2040	2235	2243		1003	1008	...	1132	...	1136	|	...
Limerick Colbert § 242 a.	1840	|	|	|	|	1902	1940	|	|	2005	|	2107	|	2311		|	1035	...	|	...	1204	1340	...
Ennis 242 a.	...	|	|	|	|	...	*2031*	|	|	2110	|	...	|	...		|	1125	...	|	...	*1306*	...	...
Charleville d.	...	|	|	1858	1858	...	...	|	|	...	2104	...	|	...		1022	...	...	|	...	...	...	...
Mallow 244 d.	...	1859	1859	1916	1916	...	...	2008	2008	...	2119	...	2307	...		1037	...	1045	1206	1251	...	...	...
Tralee 246 a.	...	|	|	2058	2058	...	...	|	|	...	*2251*	...	|	...		1221	...	|	|	1423	...	...	...
Cork 244 a.	...	1932	1932			...	...	2037	2037	...	2148	...	2337	...		...	...	1106	1237	...	...	...	...

	⑦ ◇🍷	⑦	⑦ ◇🍷	⑦ 🍷	⑦ ◇🍷	⑦ ◇🍷	⑦ 🍷	⑦ ◇🍷	⑦		⑦ ◇🍷	⑦ 🍷	⑦ 🍷	⑦	⑦ ◇🍷	⑦	⑦	⑦	⑦ 🍷		⑦	⑦		
Dublin Heuston 240 d.	1200	...	1300	1325	1400	1500	1525	1600	...	...	1700	1800	1825	...	1900	1905	...	...	1925	...	2100	2110	...	...
Kildare 240 d.	|	...	|	1353	|	|	1553	|	...	...	|	|	1857	...	|	|	...	...	1950	...	|	2142	...	...
Portarlington 240 d.	|	...	|	1405	|	|	1605	|	...	...	|	|	1911	...	|	1942	...	...	2015	...	2136	2153	...	...
Portlaoise d.	|	...	|	1415	|	|	1615	|	...	...	|	|	1921	...	|	|	...	...	2026	...	|	2204	...	...
Ballybrophy d.	|	...	|	1430	|	|	1630	|	...	...	|	|	1936	...	|	|	...	...	2040	...	|	|	...	...
Templemore d.	|	...	|	1443	|	|	1643	|	...	...	|	|	1947	...	|	|	...	...	2052	...	|	|	...	...
Thurles d.	1309	...	1409	1452	1509	1609	1652	1709	...	...	1809	1908	1955	...	2009	2018	...	...	2101	...	2213	2233	...	...
Limerick Junction § d.	1329	1333	|	|	1529	|	|	1729	1732	...	|	1929	|	...	|	2040	2047	...	|	...	2235	|	...	...
Limerick Colbert § 242 a.	|	1401	|	1540	*1614*	|	1740	|	1759	1815	|	*2004*	2043	2050	|	|	2114	...	2149	...	*2328*	2320	...	...
Ennis 242 a.	|	...	|	*1636*	|	|	...	|	...	1855	|	|	...	2129	|	|	...	...	...	...	|	...	...	...
Charleville d.	|	...	1450	...	|	|	...	1751	...	...	|	|	...	...	|	2059	...	...	...	...	|	...	...	...
Mallow 244 d.	1402	...	1505	...	1600	1702	...	1806	...	...	1900	2000	...	...	2101	2115	...	2125	...	...	2307	...	...	...
Tralee 246 a.	|	...	|	...	*1901*	|	...	|	...	...	|	|	...	...	|	2248	...	|	...	...	|	...	...	...
Cork 244 a.	1434	...	1532	...	1632	1728	...	1837	...	...	1927	2034	...	...	2127	...	...	2150	...	...	2337	...	...	...

		⚒	⑥ 🍷	Ⓐ 🍷	Ⓐ 🍷	⚒ 🍷	⚒	Ⓐ ◇✕	⑥ ◇🍷	⚒	⚒ 🍷	⚒	⚒	⚒	Ⓐ ✕	⑥ 🍷	⚒	⚒ ◇🍷	⚒	⚒ ◇🍷	⚒	⚒ ◇🍷	⚒	⚒ ◇🍷
Cork 244 d.		...	0545	0545	0615	...	...	0700	0700	...	...	...	...	...	...	...	...	0925	...	1025	...	1125	...	1225
Tralee 246 d.		...	|	|	|	...	...	|	|	...	...	0705	...	...	0705	0705	...	|	...	|	...	|	...	*1105*
Mallow 244 d.	⚒	...	0609	0609	|	...	...	0722	0722	...	...	0844	...	...	0843	0843	...	0946	...	1046	...	1146	...	1246
Charleville d.		...	0623	0623	|	...	...	|	|	...	...	...	...	...	0858	0858	...	|	...	1102	...	|	...	|
Ennis 242 d.		...	|	|	|	...	...	|	|	0650	...	...	0745	...	|	|	...	|	...	|	...	|	*1147*	|
Limerick Colbert § 242 d.		0530	|	*0615*	|	0640	0725	|	|	0730	0740	...	0826	0900	|	|	0950	|	1055	|	1150	|	1250	|
Limerick Junction § d.		0558	0644	0644	|	|	0753	0755	0755	...	|	...	...	0926	0918	0918	1019	1022	1123	1125	1220	1222	1321	1324
Thurles d.		0615	0701	0701	|	0722	...	0814	0814	...	0823	...	...	...	|	|	...	1041	...	|	...	1241	...	|
Templemore d.		0624	|	|	|	0731	...	|	|	...	0832	...	...	...	|	|	...	|	...	1148	...	|	...	1346
Ballybrophy d.		0636	|	|	|	0742	...	|	|	...	0844	...	...	...	|	|	...	|	...	|	...	1259	...	|
Portlaoise d.		0654	|	|	|	0800	...	|	|	...	0902	...	...	...	|	|	...	1113	...	|	...	1317	...	1413
Portarlington 240 d.		|	|	|	|	0810	...	|	|	...	|	...	...	...	|	|	...	|	...	|	...	|	...	|
Kildare 240 d.		0718	|	|	|	0824	...	|	|	...	|	...	...	...	|	|	...	|	...	|	...	|	...	|
Dublin Heuston 240 a.		0750	0820	0820	0830	0857	...	0931	0931	...	0957	...	...	...	1047	1047	...	1200	...	1258	...	1406	...	1500

	⚒	⚒ ◇🍷	⚒	⚒	⚒ ◇🍷	⚒	⚒ ◇🍷	⚒	⚒ ◇🍷	⚒	⚒ ◇🍷	⚒	⚒	⚒ ◇🍷	Ⓐ ◇🍷	⚒	⚒ ◇🍷			⑦ 🍷	⑦ 🍷	⑦	⑦ 🍷	
Cork 244 d.	...	1325	...	...	1425	...	1525	...	1625	...	1725	...	...	1825	1925	...	2025	...		...	0825	...	...	...
Tralee 246 d.	...	|	...	...	|	...	|	...	*1505*	...	|	...	...	|	|	...	*1905*	...		...	*0710*	...	...	...
Mallow 244 d.	...	1345	...	...	1446	...	1546	...	1646	...	1746	...	...	1846	1947	...	2047	...	⑦	...	0846	...	...	...
Charleville d.	...	|	...	...	1502	...	|	...	1702	...	|	...	...	1902	|	...	|	...		...	0902	...	...	...
Ennis 242 d.	...	|	1325	...	|	1503	|	...	|	...	|	1720	...	|	|	1908	|	...		...	|	0942	...	...
Limerick Colbert § 242 d.	1350	|	1407	1455	|	1550	|	1650	|	1750	|	1800	1850	|	|	1948	*2055*	...		0825	|	1022	1025	...
Limerick Junction § d.	1420	1422	...	1524	1524	1622	1624	1718	1724	1822	1823	...	1918	1924	2024	...	2128	...		|	0924	...	|	...
Thurles d.	...	1440	...	...	1543	...	1641	...	1742	...	1841	...	...	1943	2042	...	2145	...		0908	|	...	1108	...
Templemore d.	...	|	...	...	|	...	|	...	1752	...	|	...	...	1952	|	...	|	...		0917	|	...	1117	...
Ballybrophy d.	...	|	...	...	|	...	|	...	|	...	1859	...	...	|	|	...	|	...		0929	|	...	1129	...
Portlaoise d.	...	1513	...	...	|	...	1713	...	1818	...	1917	...	...	2019	2114	...	2217	...		0946	|	...	1146	...
Portarlington 240 d.	...	|	...	...	|	...	|	...	|	...	|	...	...	|	|	...	|	...		0956	|	...	1155	...
Kildare 240 d.	...	|	...	...	|	...	|	...	|	...	|	...	...	|	|	...	|	...		1014	|	...	1211	...
Dublin Heuston 240 a.	...	1559	...	...	1659	...	1801	...	1906	...	2004	...	...	2106	2200	...	2303	...		1043	1053	...	1240	...

	⑦ ◇🍷	⑦ 🍷	⑦ ◇🍷	⑦ 🍷	⑦	⑦ ◇🍷	⑦ 🍷	⑦ ◇🍷	⑦ 🍷	⑦	⑦ ◇🍷	⑦ 🍷	⑦ ◇🍷	⑦	⑦ ◇🍷	⑦ 🍷	⑦	⑦ ◇🍷	⑦ 🍷	⑦	⑦ ◇🍷			
Cork 244 d.	1025	...	1225	...	...	1325	...	1425	...	...	1525	...	1625	...	1725	...	...	1825	...	...	1925	...	...	...
Tralee 246 d.	|	...	|	1150	...	*1150*	...	|	1345	...	|	...	*1510*	...	|	...	...	|	1750	...	|	...	...	...
Mallow 244 d.	1046	...	1246	1321	...	1346	...	1445	1528	...	1546	...	1646	...	1746	...	...	1846	1926	...	1946	...	...	...
Charleville d.	1102	...	1302	1337	...	|	...	1501	1543	...	|	...	1702	...	|	...	...	1902	|	...	|	...	...	...
Ennis 242 d.	|	...	|	|	1308	|	...	|	|	...	|	...	|	...	|	*1726*	...	|	|	*1900*	|	...	...	...
Limerick Colbert § 242 d.	*1050*	1225	*1250*	|	1354	|	1420	|	|	1550	|	1620	|	1750	|	1820	1845	|	|	1950	|	...	...	...
Limerick Junction § d.	1124	|	1323	1356	1422	1423	|	|	|	1618	1620	|	|	1819	1820	|	1914	1923	1958	2018	2020	...	...	...
Thurles d.	1143	1308	1342	1414	...	1441	1504	1538	1618	...	1639	1703	1740	...	1839	1902	...	1942	2017	...	2039	...	...	...
Templemore d.	|	1317	|	|	...	|	1513	|	|	...	|	1712	|	...	|	1911	...	|	|	...	|	...	...	...
Ballybrophy d.	|	1329	|	|	...	|	1526	|	|	...	|	1725	|	...	|	1924	...	|	|	...	|	...	...	...
Portlaoise d.	|	1346	|	|	...	|	1542	|	|	...	|	1743	|	...	|	1940	...	2014	|	...	2111	...	...	...
Portarlington 240 d.	|	1355	|	|	...	|	1551	|	1657	...	|	1752	|	...	|	1949	...	|	|	...	|	...	...	...
Kildare 240 d.	|	1411	|	|	...	|	1601	|	1711	...	|	1807	|	...	|	1959	...	|	|	...	|	...	...	...
Dublin Heuston 240 a.	1257	1440	1458	1533	...	1558	1632	1655	1742	...	1756	1837	1854	...	1955	2031	...	2059	2132	...	2158	...	...	...

◇ – Also conveys [1st class]. § – Also Table 243. ** – Limerick - Ennis: *39 km*. ☛ **Shaded services are temporarily suspended.**

FRANCE

SEE MAP PAGES 164 and 165

Operator: Société Nationale des Chemins de Fer Français (SNCF), unless otherwise shown.

Services: Most long distance trains convey first and second class accommodation; many regional services are now second class only (travel classes are not usually indicated in our tables). *TGV* (*Train à Grande Vitesse*) high-speed trains have a bar car selling drinks, light meals and refreshments (some short-distance services have only vending machines). Selected international *TGV* trains have an at-seat meal service in first class. Certain other long-distance trains, branded *Intercités*, also offer a refreshment service, often from a trolley wheeled through the train. Regional and local trains (outside Paris) are classified *TER* (*Transport Express Régional*). Domestic overnight trains convey modern couchettes (four-berth in first class, six-berth in second class) and reclining seats (second class only). Couchette compartments for the exclusive use of women are available on request. Note that all luggage placed on luggage racks must be labelled. The regular *TGV* network is branded ***inOui***. SNCF subsidiary ***Ouigo*** operate an extensive network of low-cost high-speed services, together with some traditional loco-hauled services (branded ***Ouigo Classique***). Tickets for Ouigo services are only available via its website.

Timings: **Valid December 11, 2022 - June 30, 2023** except where shown (services in northern and western France are valid until December 9, 2023). Amended services operate on and around public holidays; whilst we try to show holiday variations, passengers are advised to confirm train times locally before travelling during these periods. For Public holiday dates see page 4. Engineering work can often affect schedules; major changes are shown in the tables where possible but other changes may occur at short notice.

Tickets: Seat reservation is compulsory for travel by *TGV* and overnight trains (also other trains shown with [R]), and is also available for a small fee on many other long-distance trains. Advance reservation is recommended for travel to ski resorts during the winter sports season. **Special fares** (which include a seat reservation) are payable for travel by *TGV* trains, night trains and other services with compulsory reservation (pass holders must pay a special supplement to use these services). In north-eastern France regional tickets are valid on *TGV* services for many local journeys (without prior reservation) on payment of a €3 TER-GV supplement (this is indicated in the relevant tables where applicable). All rail tickets (except passes) must be date-stamped before boarding the train using the self-service validating machines (composteurs) at the platform entrances. Note that where two *TGV* units are coupled together, they will often carry different train numbers for reservation purposes.

Note: *TGV* services **Lille Europe - Charles de Gaulle ✈ - Marne-la-Vallée - Lyon / Bordeaux / Rennes / Nantes** are shown in the International section (Table **11**).

TGV NORD — 250

HIGH-SPEED TRAINS. For Paris Charles de Gaulle ✈ - Lille services see Table **11**. For Paris - Calais, Boulogne and Rang du Fliers services see page 166. Journeys to / from Paris are [R] with supplement. For other journeys, *TGV* and ♣ trains are classified *TER-GV* and require a Grande Vitesse supplement, €3 valid all day, [R] not required.

PARIS - LILLE FLANDRES

km		TGV	TGV	TGV	TGV	TGV	TGV	TGV	TGV	TGV	TGV	TGV	TGV	TGV	TGV	TGV	TGV	TGV	TGV	TGV	TGV	TGV	TGV	TGV	TGV	TGV	TGV
		7001	**7007**	**7011**	**7015**	**7023**	**7025**	**7027**	**7031**	**7035**	**7037**	**7043**	**7045**	**7047**	**7049**	**7053**	**7057**	**7061**	**7065**	**7069**	**7073**	**7077**	**7081**	**7085**	**7087**	**7297**	**7093**
		Ⓐ	①-⑥	①-④		⑥	Ⓑ	⑥	⑤-⑦	Ⓒ	Ⓐ	①-⑥	⑦	Ⓐ	⑤		Ⓐ		Ⓐ		⑤⑦	Ⓐ	⑦	⑥	⑤⑦	①-⑥	⑦
			d	e	f	g	h	g	j			d	k ▮		m	n		A			p		k ▮	g	p	d ⊖	q ⊡
0	**Paris** Nord d.	0643	0743	0813	0853	0943	1013	1043	1142	1243	1313	1443	1513	1543	1613	1643	1713	1743	1816	1843	1913	1943	2010	2043	2113	2225	2243
227	**Lille** Flandres a.	0748	0849	0918	0954	1048	1119	1148	1248	1348	1419	1548	1620	1648	1718	1748	1819	1848	1923	1950	2020	2048	2118	2148	2221	2348	2348

	TGV	TGV	TGV	TGV	TGV	TGV	TGV	TGV	TGV	TGV	TGV	TGV	TGV		TGV	TGV	TGV	TGV	TGV	TGV	TGV	TGV	TGV	TGV	TGV	TGV
	7200	**7200**	**7002**	**7006**	**7010**	**7014**	**7020**	**7026**	**7028**	**7030**	**7032**	**7038**	**7040**		**7044**	**7046**	**7052**	**7060**	**7064**	**7068**	**7072**	**7076**	**7078**	**7082**	**7084**	**7086**
			①-④	①-⑥	Ⓐ		①-⑥	①-⑥	⑦	⑥	Ⓐ	②-⑥	⑦		Ⓐ	Ⓒ	Ⓑ		⑤⑦	Ⓑ	Ⓐ	⑤-⑦	⑤		⑤	⑦
	⊙	●	e	d		f	d	d	k	g		r	k				s		p	t		j	m	B	m	q
Lille Flandres d.	0542	0552	0642	0712	0742	0812	0912	1012	1042	1112	1142	1312	1339	...	1442	1512	1612	1712	1742	1812	1842	1912	1942	2012	2042	2112
Paris Nord a.	0708	0708	0744	0814	0844	0914	1014	1114	1144	1214	1244	1414	1441	...	1544	1614	1714	1814	1844	1914	1944	2014	2044	2114	2144	2214

PARIS - VALENCIENNES, LILLE EUROPE and DUNKERQUE

Valenciennes services are subject to alteration Apr. 10, 22, 23, July 16, Aug. 5, 6, 12 – 15, 20. Dunkerque services are subject to alteration ⑥⑦ Apr. 29 - May 14.

km		♣	TGV	TGV	TGV	TGV	TGV	TGV	TGV	TGV	TGV	TGV	TGV		TGV	TGV	TGV	TGV	♣	TGV	TGV	TGV	TGV	TGV	TGV	TGV
			7251	**7155**	**7355**	**7159**	**7359**	**7163**	**7363**	**7165**	**7265**	**7365**	**7369**		**7171**	**7371**	**7173**	**7273**		**7375**	**7177**	**7277**	**7377**	**7181**	**7183**	**7283**
		Ⓐ	Ⓐ	Ⓐ	Ⓐ	⑥	⑥	⑦	⑦	Ⓐ	Ⓐ	⑥	Ⓐ		⑥	⑦	Ⓐ	⑤	Ⓐ	⑥	⑦	⑦	Ⓐ	Ⓐ	⑥	⑥
		▲				g	g	k	k			g			g	k		m		g	k	k			g	g
0	**Paris** Nord d.	...	0652	0752	0752	0852	0852	0952	0952	1048	1048	1052	1225	...	1352	1352	1428	1428	...	1552	1649	1649	1652	1752	1752	1752
179	Arras a.	...	0741	0840	0840	0940	0940	1040	1040	1141	1141	1140	1313	...	1440	1440	1517	1517	...	1641	1740	1740	1740	1840	1840	1840
179	Arras d.	0718	0745	0844	0851	0944	0951	1044	1051	1141	1144	1151	1317	...	1444	1450	1521	1534	...	1651	1742	1746	1751	1844	1844	1848
199	Lens a.	|	|	|	0902	|	1002	|	1102	|	|	1205	1329	...	|	1503	1532	|	...	1703	|	|	1802	|	|	|
204	Douai a.	|	|	0858	|	0958	|	1058	|	1159	|	|	|	...	1458	|	1603	|	...	|	1759	|	|	1858	1858	|
240	**Valenciennes** a.	|	|	0935	|	1035	|	1135	|	1235	|	|	|	...	1535	|	1631	|	...	|	1835	|	|	1935	1935	|
218	Béthune a.	|	|	...	0916	...	1016	...	1116	...	|	1218	1342	...	...	1516	...	|	...	1716	...	|	1816	...	...	|
	Lille Europe a.	0737	0809	...	|	...	|	...	|	...	1207	|	|	...	...	|	...	1558	...	|	...	1813	|	...	...	1912
	Lille Europe d.	...	0817	...	|	...	|	...	|	...	1213	|	|	...	...	|	...	...	1646	|	...	1818	|	...	...	1920
252	Hazebrouck a.	...	|	...	0939	...	1039	...	1139	...	|	1241	1405	...	...	1539	...	...	|	1739	...	|	1839	...	...	|
292	**Dunkerque** a.	...	0852	...	1004	...	1104	...	1204	...	1251	1306	1430	...	...	1604	...	...	1720	1804	...	1853	1904	...	...	1951

	TGV	TGV	TGV	TGV	TGV		TGV	TGV	TGV	TGV
	7185	**7385**	**7289**	**7289**	**7189**		**7389**	**7391**	**7295**	**7195**
	Ⓐ	Ⓑ	⑥	⑤	⑦		Ⓒ	Ⓐ	⑦	⑦
		s	g	m	k				k	k
Paris Nord d.	1852	1852	1952	1952	1952	...	1952	2025	2152	2152
Arras a.	1940	1940	2040	2041	2041	...	2041	2114	2240	2240
Arras d.	1944	1951	2044	2057	2044	...	2051	2124	2244	2248
Lens a.	|	2002	|	|	|	...	2102	2137	|	|
Douai a.	1958	|	|	|	2058	...	|	|	|	2302
Valenciennes a.	2035	|	|	|	2135	...	|	|	|	2338
Béthune a.	...	2016	|	|	...	...	2116	2151	|	...
Lille Europe a.	...	|	2108	2120	...	...	|	|	2308	...
Lille Europe d.	...	|	...	...	...	...	|	|	...	...
Hazebrouck a.	...	2039	...	...	...	...	2139	2214	...	...
Dunkerque a.	...	2104	...	...	...	...	2204	2242	...	...

	TGV	TGV	TGV	TGV	TGV	TGV	TGV	TGV	TGV	TGV
	7104	**7304**	**7106**	**7208**	**7112**	**7312**	**7212**	**7116**	**7516**	**7218**
	Ⓐ	Ⓐ	Ⓐ	Ⓐ	Ⓒ	⑥	⑦	①-⑥	①-⑥	⑦
						g	k	d	d	k
Dunkerque d.	...	0556	...	0653	...	0756	...	...	...	1125
Hazebrouck d.	...	0620	...	|	...	0820	...	...	...	|
Lille Europe a.	...	|	...	0729	...	|	...	...	...	1200
Lille Europe d.	...	|	...	0740	...	|	0851	...	1051	1205
Béthune d.	...	0643	...	|	...	0843	|	...	|	|
Valenciennes d.	0615	|	0656	|	0815	|	|	1015	|	|
Douai d.	0651	|	0735	|	0851	|	|	1051	|	|
Lens d.	|	0657	|	|	|	0857	|	|	|	|
Arras a.	0706	0710	0752	0801	0906	0910	0913	1106	1113	1225
Arras d.	0718	0718	0756	0808	0918	0918	0918	1118	1118	1232
Paris Nord a.	0808	0808	0847	0859	1008	1008	1008	1208	1208	1322

	TGV	TGV	TGV	TGV	TGV	TGV	TGV	TGV	TGV	TGV	TGV	TGV	TGV	TGV	TGV	♣	TGV	TGV	TGV	TGV	TGV	TGV	TGV	TGV	TGV
	7320	**7520**	**7322**	**7522**	**7124**	**7324**	**7326**	**7226**	**7130**	**7330**	**7230**	**7134**	**7534**	**7334**	**7238**		**7142**	**7342**	**7242**	**7144**	**7344**	**7544**	**7546**	**7346**	**7546**
	Ⓐ	Ⓐ	⑥	⑥	⑦	⑦	⑥	⑥	Ⓑ	Ⓐ	⑦	Ⓐ	①-⑥	⑦	Ⓐ	Ⓐ	Ⓒ	⑦	⑥	⑦	⑥	Ⓒ	Ⓐ	Ⓐ	⑦
			g	g	k	k	g	g	s		q		d	k		⊖		k	v	k	g	v			k
Dunkerque d.	1211	...	1256	...	...	1356	1501	...	...	1556	...	...	...	1656	1808	1834	...	1856	1858	...	1956	...	...	2028	...
Hazebrouck d.	1234	...	1320	...	...	1420	1525	...	...	1620	...	...	...	1720	|	|	...	1920	|	...	2020	...	...	2054	...
Lille Europe a.	|	...	|	...	...	|	|	...	...	|	...	...	...	|	1842	1910	...	|	1932	...	|	...	...	|	...
Lille Europe d.	|	1303	|	1351	...	|	|	1557	...	|	1651	...	1751	|	1851	1922	...	|	1936	...	|	2051	2102	|	2151
Béthune d.	1257	|	1343	|	...	1443	1548	|	...	1643	|	...	|	1743	|	|	...	1943	|	...	2043	|	|	2120	|
Valenciennes d.	|	|	|	|	1415	|	|	|	1615	|	|	1715	|	|	|	|	1916	|	|	2015	|	|	|	|	|
Douai d.	|	1323	|	|	1451	|	|	|	1651	|	|	1751	|	|	|	|	1953	|	|	2051	|	|	2134	|	|
Lens d.	1313	|	1357	|	|	1457	1602	|	|	1657	|	|	|	1757	|	|	|	1957	|	|	2057	|	|	2137	|
Arras a.	1330	1337	1409	1413	1508	1510	1615	1618	1706	1710	1713	1806	1813	1810	1913	1941	2008	2010	2000	2106	2113	2113	2148	2152	2213
Arras d.	1341	1341	1418	1418	1518	1518	1623	1623	1718	1718	1718	1818	1818	1818	1918	...	2018	2018	2018	2118	2118	2118	2158	2158	2218
Paris Nord a.	1432	1432	1508	1508	1608	1608	1714	1714	1808	1808	1808	1908	1908	1908	2008	...	2108	2108	2108	2214	2214	2214	2247	2247	2308

Other TER-GV trains	♣	♣	♣	♣	♣	♣	♣	♣	♣	♣
	Ⓐ	Ⓐ	Ⓐ	⑦	⑥	Ⓐ	Ⓐ	Ⓐ	Ⓐ	⑦
Lille Europe d.	0655	0846	1046	1116	1216	1317	1546	1746	1846	1920
Dunkerque a.	0733	0920	1120	1151	1251	1352	1620	1820	1920	1951

Other TER-GV trains	♣	♣	♣	♣	♣		♣	♣	♣	♣
	Ⓐ	Ⓐ	Ⓐ	①-⑥	Ⓐ		Ⓐ ◇	Ⓐ	⑦	⑦
Dunkerque d.	0756	0904	0956	1300	1446	...	1542	1700	1930	2027
Lille Europe a.	0833	0938	1033	1334	1520	...	1620	1734	2004	2101

A – ②③④⑤⑦ (also Apr. 10, May 1, 8, 29, July 15; not Apr. 11, May 2, 9, 18, 30, July 15, Aug. 15, 16, Nov. 1).
B – ①②③④⑦ (also May 19; not May 17, 18, July 13, Nov. 1).
C – Ⓐ until June 2, June 12 – 16, July 17 – 21, Sept. 4 – 8, Sept. 25 - Oct. 27, Nov. 6 – 17.
D – Ⓐ June 5 – 9, 19 – 30, July 3 – 13, 24 – 31, Aug. 1 - Sept. 1, Sept. 11 – 22, Oct. 30 - Nov. 3, Nov. 20 - Dec. 8.

d – Not Apr. 10, May 1, 8, 29, Aug. 15.
e – Also May 19; not Apr. 10, May 1, 8, 17, 18, 29, July 13, Aug. 15, Nov. 1.
f – Not Aug. 20.
g – Also May 18, July 14, Nov. 1.
h – Not May 18, July 14, Aug. 20, Nov. 1.
j – Also Apr. 10, May 1, 8, 17, 18, 29, July 13, Aug. 15, Nov. 1.
k – Also Apr. 10, May 1, 8, 29, Aug. 15.
m – Also May 17, July 13; not May 19, July 14.
n – Not Apr. 9, 30, May 7, 28.
p – Also Apr. 10, May 1, 8, 17, 29, July 13, Aug. 15; not Apr. 9, 30, May 7, 19, 28, July 14.
q – Also Apr. 10, May 1, 8, 29, Aug. 15; not Apr. 9, 30, May 7, 28.
r – Also Aug. 14; not Apr. 11, May 2, 9, 30, Aug. 15, 16.
s – Not May 18, July 14, Nov. 1.
t – Not Apr. 9, 30, May 7, 18, 28, July 14, Nov. 1.
v – Subject to alteration May 18, July 14, Nov. 1.

FOR OTHER FOOTNOTES AND TGV NORD SERVICES SEE PAGE 166.

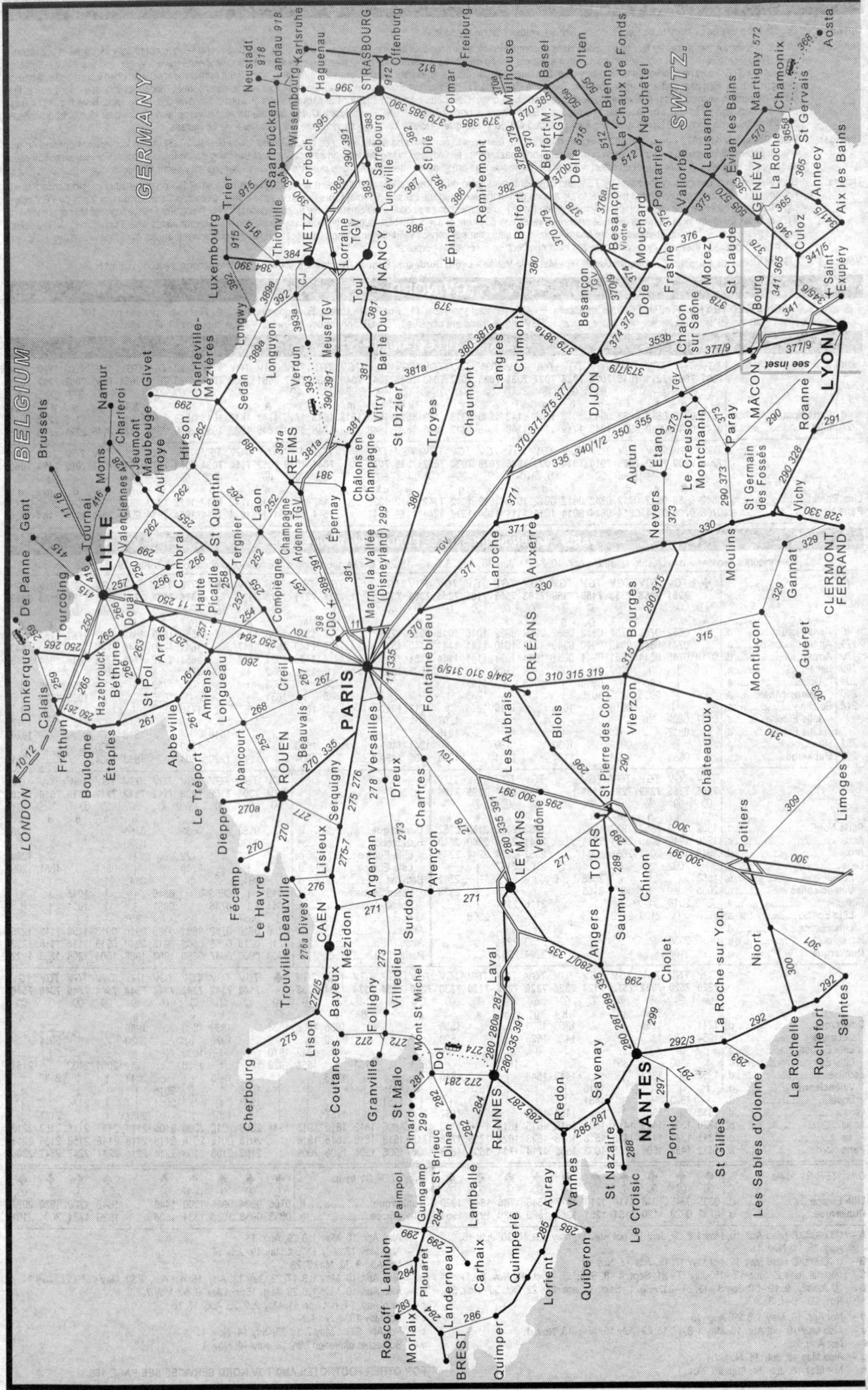
BELGIUM
GERMANY
SWITZ.
LONDON
Dunkerque
Calais
Fréthun
Boulogne
Étaples
De Panne
Gent
Brussels
Tourcoing
Tournai
Mons
Namur
Charleroi
LILLE
Valenciennes
Jeumont
Maubeuge
Aulnoye
Givet
Hazebrouck
Béthune
Douai
Arras
St Pol
Cambrai
Abbeville
Le Tréport
Amiens
Longueau
Haute Picardie
St Quentin
Hirson
Charleville-Mézières
Sedan
Tergnier
Laon
Compiègne
Creil
Beauvais
Abancourt
ROUEN
Dieppe
Fécamp
Le Havre
Serquigny
Lisieux
Trouville-Deauville
Dives
CAEN
Mézidon
Bayeux
Lison
Cherbourg
Coutances
Granville
Folligny
Villedieu
Mont St Michel
Argentan
Surdon
Alençon
Dreux
Chartres
Versailles
PARIS
CDG +
Marne la Vallée (Disneyland)
Champagne Ardenne TGV
REIMS
Épernay
Châlons en Champagne
Vitry
St Dizier
Bar le Duc
Verdun
Meuse TGV
Longuyon
Longwy
Luxembourg
Trier
Thionville
METZ
Saarbrücken
Forbach
Wissembourg
Neustadt
Landau
Karlsruhe
Haguenau
STRASBOURG
Offenburg
Freiburg
Colmar
Mulhouse
Basel
Olten
Sarrebourg
Lunéville
Lorraine TGV
NANCY
Toul
St Dié
Épinal
Remiremont
Belfort
Belfort-M. TGV
Delle
Biel
Bienne
La Chaux de Fonds
Neuchâtel
Pontarlier
Frasne
Vallorbe
Lausanne
Évian les Bains
Martigny
Chamonix
St Gervais
Aosta
Besançon
Viotte
Besançon TGV
Mouchard
Dole
DIJON
Culmont
Langres
Chaumont
Troyes
Laroche
Auxerre
Fontainebleau
Autun
Étang
Le Creusot
Montchanin
Chalon sur Saône
Morez
St Claude
Bourg
GENÈVE
La Roche
Annecy
Culoz
Aix les Bains
Saint Exupéry
LYON
see inset
MÂCON
Paray
Roanne
Nevers
Moulins
St Germain des Fossés
Vichy
Gannat
CLERMONT FERRAND
Montluçon
Guéret
Limoges
Bourges
Vierzon
ORLÉANS
Les Aubrais
Blois
St Pierre des Corps
TOURS
Vendôme
LE MANS
Chinon
Saumur
Angers
Cholet
Châteauroux
Poitiers
Niort
La Rochelle
Rochefort
Saintes
La Roche sur Yon
Les Sables d'Olonne
St Gilles
NANTES
Pornic
Savenay
St Nazaire
Le Croisic
Redon
Laval
RENNES
Dol
St Malo
Dinard
Dinan
St Brieuc
Lamballe
Guingamp
Paimpol
Lannion
Plouaret
Morlaix
Roscoff
Landerneau
BREST
Carhaix
Quimper
Quimperlé
Lorient
Auray
Vannes
Quiberon

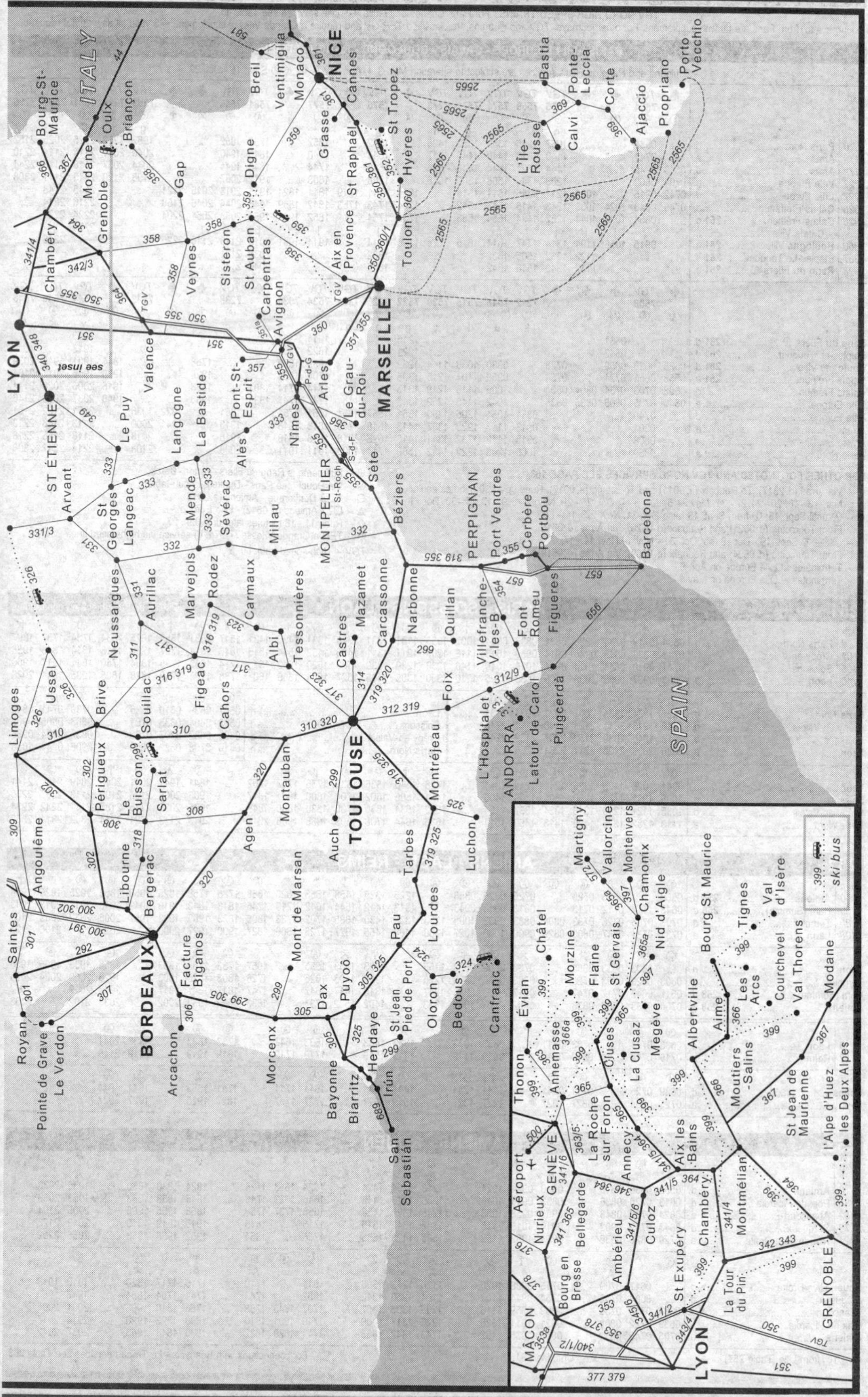
ITALY
SPAIN
ANDORRA
LYON
ST ÉTIENNE
MARSEILLE
NICE
TOULOUSE
BORDEAUX
MONTPELLIER
PERPIGNAN
Bourg-St-Maurice
Modane
Oulx
Briançon
Grenoble
Chambéry
Gap
Breil
Ventimiglia
Monaco
Cannes
Grasse
St Raphaël
St Tropez
Hyères
Toulon
Digne
Sisteron
St Auban
Veynes
Carpentras
Avignon
Aix en Provence
Valence
Arles
Le Grau-du-Roi
Nîmes
Sète
Pont-St-Esprit
Alès
La Bastide
Langogne
Le Puy
Arvant
St Georges
Langeac
Mende
Sévérac
Millau
Marvejols
Rodez
Carmaux
Albi
Tessonnières
Neussargues
Aurillac
Figeac
Cahors
Souillac
Brive
Ussel
Limoges
Périgueux
Le Buisson
Sarlat
Agen
Montauban
Castres
Mazamet
Carcassonne
Narbonne
Béziers
Quillan
Foix
L'Hospitalet
Latour de Carol
Puigcerdà
Villefranche-V-les-B
Font Romeu
Port Vendres
Cerbère
Portbou
Figueres
Barcelona
Bastia
Ponte-Leccia
Corte
Calvi
L'Île-Rousse
Ajaccio
Propriano
Porto Vecchio
Saintes
Angoulême
Royan
Pointe de Grave
Le Verdon
Libourne
Bergerac
Arcachon
Facture Biganos
Morcenx
Mont de Marsan
Dax
Puyoô
Pau
Auch
Tarbes
Lourdes
Montréjeau
Luchon
Oloron
Bedous
Canfranc
Bayonne
Biarritz
Hendaye
Irún
San Sebastián
St Jean Pied de Port
see inset
TGV
Thonon
Évian
Châtel
Martigny
Vallorcine
Montenvers
Chamonix
Nid d'Aigle
St Gervais
Flaine
Morzine
Annemasse
Cluses
La Clusaz
Megève
Aéroport
GENÈVE
La Roche sur Foron
Annecy
Aix les Bains
Albertville
Bourg St Maurice
Tignes
Val d'Isère
Les Arcs
Aime
Courchevel
Val Thorens
Moutiers-Salins
St Jean de Maurienne
Nurieux
Bellegarde
Culoz
Montmélian
l'Alpe d'Huez
les Deux Alpes
Bourg en Bresse
Ambérieu
St Exupéry
Chambéry
La Tour du Pin
GRENOBLE
MÂCON
LYON
399 ski bus

250 TGV NORD

TGV NORD HIGH-SPEED TRAINS. For Paris Charles de Gaulle ✈ - Lille services see Table **11**.

Journeys to / from Paris are 🅁 with supplement. For other journeys, *TGV* and ♣ trains are classified *TER-GV* and require a Grande Vitesse supplement, €3 valid all day, 🅁 not required.

PARIS - LILLE EUROPE - CALAIS - BOULOGNE - RANG DU FLIERS

Boulogne and Rang du Fliers services are subject to alteration Mar. 3, 4, Apr. 1, 2, 9, 16, ⑥⑦ Sept. 16 - Oct. 29.

km		♣	*TGV* 7551	♣	♣	*TGV* 7565	*TGV* 7569	*TGV* 7571	*TGV* 7571	*TGV* 7273	♣	*TGV* 7575	♣	*TGV* 7577	♣	*TGV* 7581	*TGV* 7585	♣	♣	*TGV* 7289	*TGV* 7289	*TGV* 7591	*TGV* 7591	*TGV* 7295
		Ⓐ	Ⓐ	Ⓐ	Ⓒ	⑥ g	Ⓐ	⑦ k	⑥ g	⑤ m	Ⓐ	⑥ g	Ⓐ	Ⓐ	†	Ⓐ	⑦ k	⚒	†	⑥ g	⑤ m	Ⓐ C	Ⓐ D	⑦ k
0	**Paris** Nord d.	...	0652	...	...	1052	1225	1352	1352	1428	...	1552	...	1652	...	1752	1852	...	...	1952	1952	2025	2025	2152
179	Arras a.	...	0741	...	...	1140	1313	1440	1440	1517	...	1641	...	1740	...	1840	1940	...	...	2040	2041	2114	2114	2240
179	Arras d.	0643	0745	...	...	1144	1321	1444	1448	1534	...	1645	...	1744	...	1848	1944	...	...	2044	2057	2118	2118	2244
227	**Lille** Europe a.	0704	0809	...	...	1208	1344	1508	1509	1558	...	1708	...	1808	...	1912	2007	...	...	2108	2120	2143	2141	2308
227	**Lille** Europe d.	0712	0815	0952	1002	1211	1345	1511	1515	...	1654	1711	1719	1811	1824	1915	2013	2015	2121	...	...	2145	2143	...
326	**Calais** Fréthun a.	0746	0843	1024	1033	1243	1416	1543	1542	...	1724	1743	1753	1842	1859	1946	2044	2046	2153	...	...	2216	2214	...
326	**Calais** Fréthun 261 d.	...	0854	1035	1044	1252	1424	1554	1553	...	1735	1754	...	1852	1904	1954	2053	2054	2204	...	...	2224	2224	...
	Calais Ville a.	...	|	|	|	|	|	|	|	...	|	|	...	|	|	|	|	|	|	...	...	2234	|	...
360	**Boulogne** Ville 261 a.	...	0915	1056	1104	1314	1447	1614	1615	...	1756	1814	...	1914	1931	2018	2113	2118	2225	...	...	...	2246	...
387	Étaples-Le Touquet 261 a.	...	...	...	1122	1332	1505	1632	...	...	...	1832	...	...	...	2036	2131	...	...	...	...	...	...	...
398	**Rang du Fliers** ⊕ 261 a.	...	...	...	1132	1342	1516	1642	...	...	...	1842	...	...	...	2046	2141	...	...	...	...	...	...	...

	♣	*TGV* 7508	♣	♣	♣	*TGV* 7212	*TGV* 7516	*TGV* 7518	*TGV* 7520	*TGV* 7522	*TGV* 7226	*TGV* 7230	*TGV* 7534	*TGV* 7534	♣	*TGV* 7238	♣	♣	*TGV* 7242	♣	*TGV* 7544	*TGV* 7546	*TGV* 7546
	Ⓐ	Ⓐ	Ⓐ	Ⓐ	⑥	⑦ k	①–⑥ d	⑦ k	Ⓐ ⊗	⑥ g	⑥ g	⑦ q	Ⓐ	⑥	Ⓐ	Ⓐ	†	Ⓐ ⊖	⑥ v	Ⓐ	Ⓒ v	Ⓐ ⊗	⑦ k
Rang du Fliers ⊕ 261 d.	...	...	0631	...	...	...	...	...	...	1215	...	...	1611	...	...	...	...	...	...	...	1903	...	...
Étaples-Le Touquet 261 d.	...	...	0642	...	...	...	...	...	...	1221	...	...	1622	...	...	...	...	...	...	...	1913	...	...
Boulogne Ville 261 d.	0528	0628	0659	...	0728	...	0930	1038	1144	1239	...	...	1639	1639	...	...	1758	...	...	1841	1931	1945	2039
Calais Fréthun 261 a.	0553	0655	0724	...	0754	...	0959	1104	1215	1305	...	...	1704	1704	...	...	1825	...	...	1908	1955	2017	2104
Calais Fréthun d.	0603	0703	0734	0804	0804	...	1005	1113	1219	1313	...	...	1714	1714	1801	...	1833	...	...	1915	2006	2020	2114
Lille Europe a.	0640	0735	0805	0835	0835	...	1042	1145	1259	1345	...	...	1747	1747	1835	...	1906	...	...	1946	2037	2056	2146
Lille Europe d.	...	0740	...	...	...	0851	1051	1205	1303	1351	1557	1651	1751	1751	...	1851	...	1922	1936	...	2051	2102	2151
Arras a.	...	0801	...	...	...	0913	1113	1225	1337	1413	1618	1713	1813	1813	...	1913	...	1941	2000	...	2113	2148	2213
Arras d.	...	0808	...	...	...	0918	1118	1232	1341	1418	1623	1718	1818	1818	...	1918	...	...	2018	...	2118	2158	2218
Paris Nord a.	...	0859	...	...	...	1008	1208	1322	1432	1508	1714	1808	1911	1911	...	2008	...	...	2108	...	2214	2247	2308

FOR OTHER FOOTNOTES AND TGV NORD SERVICES SEE PAGE 163.

⊖ – Via Arras (d. 2317). To Roubaix (a. 0011) and Tourcoing (a. 0017). Runs up to 30 minutes earlier Mar. 13 – 16, 20 – 24, 27 – 31, May 2 – 5, July 3 – 7, Oct. 25 – 29, Nov. 2 – 6, 9 – 13, 27 – 30, Dec. 1.

● – Ⓐ until Sept. 15; ① from Sept. 18 (also Oct. 31, Nov. 2, 3, 14 – 17). From Tourcoing (d. 0521) and Roubaix (d. 0526). Via Arras (d. 0618).

⊙ – ②③④⑤ Sept. 19 - Dec. 8 (not Oct. 31 - Nov. 3, Nov. 14 – 17). From Tourcoing (d. 0504) and Roubaix (d. 0509). Via Arras (d. 0619).

◧ – Terminates at Lille Europe on Apr. 9.

⊡ – Terminates at Lille Europe on May 1.

⊕ – Full name is Rang du Fliers - Verton - Berck.

⊗ – Via Douai (see Paris - Dunkerque sub-table).

⊖ – 🚌12 Dunkerque - Amiens (a. 2018).

▲ – 🚌12 Amiens (d. 0642) - Lille Europe.

◇ – Runs 11 – 18 minutes later until Jan. 27.

♣ – TER à Grande Vitesse (*TER-GV*) service via high-speed line.

TGV – High-speed train. 🅁. 🍸.

251 PARIS - SOISSONS - LAON

Service on Ⓒ subject to confirmation

km		Ⓐ	⑥	Ⓐ	†	Ⓐ	⑥	Ⓐ	†	⑥	Ⓐ	Ⓐ	†	⑥	†	Ⓐ	⑥	Ⓐ	†	⑥	Ⓐ	Ⓐ	⑥	†
0	**Paris** Nord d.	0634	0719	0734	0828	0834	0837	0934	1007	1055	1131	1231	1326	1331	1405	1431	1517	1531	1558	1625	1634	1734	1737	1807
61	Crépy-en-Valois d.	0713	0839	0813	0944	0914	0959	1013	1118	1209	1211	1311	1435	1453	1514	1516	1646	1611	1707	1736	1713	1814	1849	1928
105	Soissons d.	0741	0910	0841	1014	0941	1029	1040	1146	1236	1239	1339	1503	1520	1542	1543	1714	1639	1735	1804	1740	1841	1917	1956
140	**Laon** a.	0805	0937	0905	1038	1005	1053	1105	1210	1300	1305	1405	1527	1544	1606	1607	1738	1705	1759	1828	1805	1905	1941	2020

	⑥	Ⓐ	Ⓐ	†	⑥	Ⓐ	Ⓐ	
Paris Nord d.	1825	1834	1934	2007	2021	2031	2131	...
Crépy-en-Valois d.	1946	1913	2011	2124	2138	2111	2216	...
Soissons d.	2013	1940	2039	2153	2207	2139	2243	...
Laon a.	2038	2005	2105	2217	2231	2205	2307	...

	Ⓐ	Ⓐ	⑥	Ⓐ		Ⓐ	Ⓒ	†
Laon d.	0507	0539	0610	0636	...	0739	0741	0844
Soissons d.	0532	0604	0635	0701	...	0803	0805	0908
Crépy-en-Valois d.	0600	0632	0707	0729	...	0832	0834	0936
Paris Nord a.	0640	0708	0829	0808	...	0908	0944	1056

	Ⓐ	Ⓒ	⑥	†	Ⓐ	⑥	Ⓐ		⑥	†	Ⓐ	Ⓐ	†	Ⓐ	⑥		Ⓐ	Ⓐ	Ⓐ	†	⑥	⑤	⑥
Laon d.	0941	1028	1125	1226	1241	1244	1341	...	1428	1440	1536	1637	1735	1737	1752	...	1841	1941	2041	2045	2049	2139	2141
Soissons d.	1005	1052	1150	1250	1305	1309	1405	...	1454	1505	1602	1701	1800	1801	1817	...	1905	2005	2105	2109	2113	2203	2205
Crépy-en-Valois d.	1035	1121	1219	1318	1334	1337	1434	...	1522	1534	1630	1730	1830	1830	1848	...	1935	2035	2135	2137	2141	2232	2234
Paris Nord a.	1113	1232	1326	1429	1413	1453	1514	...	1633	1644	1708	1808	1938	1908	2011	...	2013	2113	2221	2244	2309	2311	2352

252 AMIENS - LAON - REIMS

km		①	Ⓐ	⑥	Ⓐ	Ⓐ	Ⓐ	Ⓐ	Ⓒ	Ⓐ	Ⓑ	⑥	Ⓐ	†	⚒	Ⓐ	Ⓐ	⚒	Ⓑ	Ⓐ	⑥	Ⓐ	⑤	†
0	**Amiens** 258 d.	0558	...	0625	0625	...	0725	0825	0858	...	1225	1325	1458	1558	1625	1658	1725	1758	1825	1858	1858	1925	1925	1958
59	Ham (Somme) 258 d.	0643	...	0712	0713	...	0813	0913	0943	...	1313	1412	1544	1642	1713	1745	1813	1843	1913	1943	1943	2013	2013	2043
80	Tergnier d.	0705	0705	0726	0733	0808	0833	0933	1005	1233	1332	1430	1605	1702	1733	1805	1833	1905	1933	1957	2005	2032	2033	2105
108	**Laon** a.	0731	0731	0747	0800	0829	0900	1000	1027	1300	1400	1455	1627	1723	1800	1827	1900	1927	2000	...	2027	...	2100	2127

	Ⓐ	⚒	Ⓐ	⚒		⚒	Ⓐ	†	Ⓐ		†	⚒	Ⓐ			Ⓐ	⑤	Ⓐ		Ⓐ	Ⓒ	Ⓐ	⑤
Laon d.	...	0603	0633	0655	...	0733	0809	0833	1155	...	1233	1333	1555	...	1657	1733	1755	1833	...	1855	1933	1955	1955
Tergnier d.	0603	0629	0703	0726	...	0803	0836	0903	1226	...	1303	1403	1626	...	1726	1803	1826	1903	...	1926	2003	2024	2026
Ham (Somme) 258 d.	0617	0647	0717	0747	...	0817	...	0919	1247	...	1316	1417	1647	...	1747	1817	1847	1917	...	1947	2019	...	2047
Amiens 258 a.	0700	0733	0802	0833	...	0902	...	1002	1333	...	1402	1502	1733	...	1833	1902	1933	2002	...	2033	2102	...	2133

km		Ⓐ	Ⓐ		Ⓐ	Ⓐ		Ⓒ	Ⓒ		⚒	†		⑥	Ⓐ		Ⓑ	Ⓐ		Ⓒ	Ⓐ			
0	**Laon** d.	0633	0711	...	0733	0811	...	0833	1033	...	1333	1433	...	1633	1641	...	1733	1833	...	1933	2041	...	...	...
52	**Reims** a.	0719	0749	...	0819	0849	...	0919	1119	...	1419	1519	...	1719	1719	...	1819	1919	...	2019	2119	...	...	...

	Ⓐ	Ⓐ		⑥	Ⓒ		†	⚒		Ⓐ	Ⓒ		Ⓐ	Ⓐ		Ⓐ	⑥		Ⓑ	Ⓐ			
Reims d.	0639	0725	...	0741	0941	...	1141	1241	...	1441	1541	...	1641	1711	...	1741	1833	...	1841	1941	...	...	...
Laon a.	0725	0804	...	0827	1027	...	1227	1327	...	1519	1627	...	1727	1757	...	1827	1920	...	1927	2027	...	...	...

253 AMIENS - ROUEN

km		Ⓐ	Ⓐ	Ⓐ A		⑥ A	†	Ⓐ		Ⓐ A	⑥	†		†	Ⓐ	Ⓐ		Ⓐ	⑥ A	† A		Ⓐ A	Ⓐ	
0	**Amiens** d.	0552	0658	0813	...	0830	0924	1024	...	1213	1254	1424	...	1624	1658	1724	...	1824	1830	1830	...	1930	2032	...
31	Poix de Picardie d.	0613	0720	0836	...	0853	0946	1046	...	1236	1316	1446	...	1646	1723	1746	...	1846	1853	1853	...	1953	2053	...
52	Abancourt ¶ d.	0624	0732	0848	...	0905	0958	1058	...	1248	1328	1458	...	1658	1737	1758	...	1858	1905	1905	...	2005	2104	...
73	Serqueux d.	0643	0749	0902	...	0919	1015	1115	...	1302	1345	1515	...	1715	...	1815	...	1915	1919	1919	...	2019	2123	...
121	**Rouen** Rive-Droite a.	0720	0826	0936	...	0953	1052	1152	...	1336	1423	1555	...	1755	...	1854	...	1952	1956	1953	...	2055	2202	...

	Ⓐ	Ⓐ	⑥ A		Ⓐ A	†	Ⓐ		Ⓐ A	Ⓐ x	⑥		Ⓐ	Ⓐ	⑥ A		† A	Ⓐ	Ⓐ A		Ⓒ	Ⓐ	
Rouen Rive-Droite d.	...	0617	0709	...	0715	0908	1025	...	1120	1213	1306	...	1611	...	1710	...	1710	1717	1820	...	1910	1913	...
Serqueux d.	...	0654	0742	...	0754	0944	1101	...	1154	1250	1342	...	1652	...	1743	...	1741	1754	1854	...	1947	1950	...
Abancourt ¶ d.	0624	0710	0756	...	0809	0959	1116	...	1208	1305	1357	...	1707	1746	1758	...	1756	1810	1908	...	2001	2005	...
Poix de Picardie d.	0639	0722	0808	...	0821	1011	1128	...	1220	1317	1409	...	1719	1801	1810	...	1808	1822	1920	...	2014	2017	...
Amiens a.	0705	0745	0832	...	0843	1035	1152	...	1243	1342	1433	...	1744	1829	1832	...	1830	1844	1943	...	2037	2042	...

A – To / from Lille (Table **257**).

x – Until Mar. 31.

¶ – For connections with Beauvais - Le Tréport services see Table **268**.

AMIENS - COMPIÈGNE 254

km		Ⓐ	Ⓐ	⑥	†	Ⓐ		⑥	†	Ⓐ	†	⑥		Ⓐ	⑥	†	Ⓐ	⑤		Ⓒ	Ⓐ	Ⓐ	Ⓒ	Ⓐ
0	**Amiens** 260 d.	0547	0617	0700	0734	0734	...	0914	0932	1054	1118	1127	...	1229	1247	1330	1443	1610	...	1618	1639	1702	1733	1752
5	Longueau 260 d.	|	|	|	|	0740	...	0920	0938	|	|	|	...	1235	1253	1336	|	|	...	|	|	1708	1739	|
36	Montdidier d.	0618	0652	0730	0805	0814	...	0954	1009	1125	1148	1157	...	1307	1324	1407	1513	1639	...	1648	1710	1742	1811	1827
76	**Compiègne** a.	0647	0728	0759	0833	0851	...	1030	1042	1151	1217	1226	...	1342	1359	1440	1540	1708	...	1717	1737	1820	1844	1904

	Ⓐ	†	⑥		Ⓐ	†	⑥	
Amiens 260 d.	1819	1910	1927	...	1930	2019	2037	...
Longueau 260 d.	1825	1916	|	...	|	2025	2043	...
Montdidier d.	1903	1941	1956	...	2003	2056	2115	...
Compiègne a.	1939	2009	2025	...	2029	2129	2148	...

	①	Ⓐ	Ⓐ		⑥	†	Ⓐ	
Compiègne d.	0544	0620	0659	...	0704	0739	0744	...
Montdidier d.	0619	0653	0739	...	0731	0806	0814	...
Longueau 260 d.	0652	|	0822	...	|	0829	|	...
Amiens 260 a.	0658	0726	0828	...	0759	0834	0845	...

	Ⓐ	Ⓐ	⑥	†	⑥		†	Ⓐ	⑥	†	Ⓐ		Ⓒ	Ⓐ	Ⓒ	Ⓐ	Ⓐ		⑥	Ⓐ	†	†	⑥
Compiègne d.	0823	0903	0918	0936	1106	...	1120	1232	1247	1333	1444	...	1621	1644	1736	1751	1831	...	1906	1913	1915	2022	2041
Montdidier d.	0856	0928	0953	1010	1131	...	1147	1307	1323	1408	1513	...	1648	1711	1811	1827	1904	...	1931	1939	1940	2056	2116
Longueau 260 d.	|	|	1022	1039	|	...	|	1338	1353	1438	|	...	|	|	1841	1859	|	...	|	|	|	2125	2146
Amiens 260 a.	0930	1000	1028	1044	1159	...	1213	1343	1359	1443	1544	...	1716	1746	1847	1905	1934	...	1959	2007	2007	2130	2151

PARIS - COMPIÈGNE - ST QUENTIN - CAMBRIAI and MAUBEUGE 255

km		⑥	Ⓐ 🚌	Ⓐ	Ⓐ	Ⓐ	⚒	Ⓑ		⑥	Ⓐ	Ⓒ	⑥	Ⓐ	Ⓐ	†	⑥	⑥	Ⓑ ⊡	Ⓐ	†	⑥	Ⓐ	⑥	Ⓐ ⊡
0	**Paris** Nord ◧ d.	...	...	...	0637	0719	...	0734	0834	...	0919	1019	...	...	...	...	1219	...	1234	1307	1319	...	...	1419	1434
51	Creil ◧ d.	...	...	...	0706	|	...	0804	0904	...	|	|	...	...	1148	...	|	...	1304	|	|	...	...	|	1504
84	**Compiègne** ◧ d.	...	...	0628	0728	0800	0804	0827	0927	...	1000	1100	...	...	1228	1235	1300	1304	1327	1400	1400	1404	...	1500	1527
108	Noyon d.	...	...	0649	0741	|	0829	0841	0941	...	|	|	...	...	1253	1258	|	1328	1341	|	|	1428	...	|	1541
124	Chauny d.	...	...	0701	0752	|	0840	0852	0952	...	|	|	...	...	1307	1310	|	1340	1352	|	|	1440	...	|	1552
131	Tergnier d.	...	...	0710	0800	|	0850	0900	1000	...	|	|	...	...	1313	1316	|	1347	1400	|	|	1447	...	|	1600
154	**St Quentin** 256 d.	0624	0723	0729	0813	0835	0908	0913	1013	1024	1033	1135	1224	1225	1332	1334	1333	1405	1413	1435	1433	1505	1529	1534	1613
181	Busigny 256 d.	0645	0823	...	...	|	...	...	...	1045	...	|	1245	1246	...	...	...	...	...	|	...	...	1550	|	...
207	**Cambrai** Ville 256 a.	|	|	...	...	|	...	...	...	|	...	|	|	|	...	...	...	...	...	|	...	...	...	|	...
217	Aulnoye Aymeries 262 d.	0709	0928	...	...	0906	...	...	...	1109	...	1210	1309	1316	...	...	...	...	...	1506	...	...	...	1606	...
229	**Maubeuge** 262 a.	...	...	...	...	0918	...	...	...	...	...	1220	...	...	...	...	...	...	...	1518	...	...	...	1615	...

	Ⓒ	Ⓐ	Ⓐ	Ⓐ	⑥	Ⓑ		Ⓒ	⚒	Ⓐ	Ⓐ		Ⓐ	†	Ⓐ			Ⓐ	†	Ⓐ	Ⓑ	Ⓐ	Ⓒ	Ⓐ 🚌
Paris Nord ◧ d.	...	...	...	...	1634	1634	1719	...	...	1734	1819	...	1834	1834	...	1919	...	1934	2019	2034	2134	2234	2237	...
Creil ◧ d.	...	...	...	...	1700	1704	|	...	...	1804	|	...	1905	1905	...	|	...	2004	|	2105	2208	2306	2303	...
Compiègne ◧ d.	...	...	1628	1704	1723	1727	1800	...	1804	1827	1900	1904	1928	1928	...	2000	2007	2027	2059	2127	2229	2327	2323	2337
Noyon d.	...	...	1653	1729	1737	1741	|	...	1828	1841	|	1928	1941	1942	...	|	2030	2041	|	2141	2243	...	2335	0007
Chauny d.	...	...	1706	1742	1749	1752	|	...	1841	1852	|	1941	1952	1954	...	|	2043	2052	|	2152	2253	...	2345	0032
Tergnier d.	...	...	1713	1749	1757	1800	|	...	1850	1900	|	1950	2000	2002	2005	|	2049	2059	|	2200	2300	...	2351	0049
St Quentin 256 d.	1624	1732	1732	1808	1810	1813	1835	1844	1908	1913	1936	2008	2013	2015	2019	2035	2108	2113	2133	2213	2313	...	0004	0117
Busigny 256 d.	1645	1754	...	...	1826	...	|	1906	...	...	1953	...	...	2031	2039	|	...	...	|	...	...	...	...	...
Cambrai Ville 256 a.	|	|	...	...	1850	...	|	|	...	...	2015	...	...	2054	|	|	...	...	|	...	...	...	...	...
Aulnoye Aymeries 262 d.	1709	1824	...	...	...	...	1906	1931	...	...	...	...	...	2100	2106	...	...	...	2205	...	...	...	...	...
Maubeuge 262 a.	...	...	...	...	...	...	1918	...	...	...	...	...	...	...	2118	...	...	...	2214	...	...	...	...	...

	Ⓐ	Ⓐ 🚌	⚒	Ⓐ	Ⓐ	Ⓐ	Ⓑ	⑥	Ⓐ	Ⓐ	Ⓑ	⚒	⑥	Ⓐ	⚒	†	Ⓐ	⑥	Ⓐ	⑥	Ⓐ	⑥	⚒ ⊙	†
Maubeuge 262 d.	...	...	...	...	0517	...	...	...	...	0642	...	...	...	...	0742	0842	...	...	...	1042	...	...	...	...
Aulnoye Aymeries 262 d.	...	...	...	...	0529	...	...	...	...	0654	...	...	0729	0729	0754	0854	...	...	...	1054	...	1129	...	...
Cambrai Ville 256 d.	...	...	...	...	|	0546	...	0606	...	|	...	...	|	|	|	|	...	...	...	|	...	|	...	1209
Busigny 256 d.	...	0451	...	...	0554	0610	...	0632	...	|	...	...	0754	0758	|	|	...	...	...	|	...	1153	...	1233
St Quentin 256 d.	0446	0536	0546	0552	...	0626	0646	0648	0652	0725	0746	0752	0814	0818	0825	0925	0946	1005	1046	1125	1151	1214	1246	1249
Tergnier d.	0501	...	0601	0611	...	|	0702	0701	0710	|	0802	0810	...	...	|	|	1001	1020	1101	|	1210	...	1301	1303
Chauny d.	0508	...	0609	0617	...	|	0709	0708	0716	|	0809	0817	...	...	|	|	1009	1026	1108	|	1217	...	1308	1310
Noyon d.	0520	...	0620	0630	...	|	0721	0719	0729	|	0820	0829	...	...	|	|	1020	1037	1118	|	1229	...	1319	1321
Compiègne ◧ d.	0534	...	0634	0654	...	0701	0735	0734	0754	0800	0835	0854	...	...	0900	0959	1034	1051	1132	1200	1254	...	1333	1336
Creil ◧ d.	0600	...	0700	...	...	|	0759	0759	...	|	0859	...	...	...	|	|	1059	1113	1159	|	...	...	1358	1359
Paris Nord ◧ a.	0626	...	0726	...	...	0741	0826	0826	...	0841	0926	...	...	...	0941	1041	1126	1138	1226	1241	...	...	1426	1426

	Ⓐ	⑥	⑥	⑥	Ⓐ	†	†	Ⓐ	Ⓐ		Ⓐ	†		Ⓐ	Ⓑ	Ⓒ	Ⓐ	Ⓒ		Ⓐ	⚒	†	†	†
Maubeuge 262 d.	...	...	...	...	...	...	1442	1542	...	...	...	1642	...	...	...	...	1742	1742	...	...	...	...	1952	...
Aulnoye Aymeries 262 d.	1219	...	1329	...	...	...	1454	1554	...	...	...	1653	...	...	...	1729	1754	1753	...	1846	...	1943	2003	...
Cambrai Ville 256 d.	|	...	|	...	...	...	|	|	...	...	...	|	...	...	...	|	|	|	...	|	...	|	|	...
Busigny 256 d.	1249	...	1353	...	...	...	|	|	1619	...	...	|	...	...	...	1753	|	|	...	1915	...	2008	|	...
St Quentin 256 d.	1309	1352	1414	1425	1446	1452	1525	1625	1640	1646	1652	1728	...	1746	1752	1815	1825	1827	1852	1936	1946	2028	2034	2047
Tergnier d.	...	1411	...	|	1501	1511	|	|	...	1701	1711	|	...	1801	1811	...	|	|	1911	1949	2001	...	|	2102
Chauny d.	...	1417	...	|	1508	1518	|	|	...	1709	1720	|	...	1809	1817	...	|	|	1920	...	2009	...	|	2108
Noyon d.	...	1430	...	|	1520	1531	|	|	...	1720	1733	|	...	1820	1829	...	|	|	1933	...	2020	...	|	2118
Compiègne ◧ d.	...	1454	...	1500	1534	1554	1600	1700	...	1734	1754	1801	...	1834	1854	...	1900	1901	1954	...	2034	...	2109	2133
Creil ◧ d.	...	...	...	|	1559	...	|	|	...	1759	...	|	...	1859	...	...	|	|	...	...	2059	...	|	2154
Paris Nord ◧ a.	...	...	...	1541	1626	...	1641	1741	...	1826	...	1841	...	1926	...	...	1941	1941	...	...	2126	...	2153	2224

⊡ – Runs 10 – 13 minutes later Creil - St Quentin on ②.
⊙ – Runs 6 – 16 minutes earlier on ②.

◧ – Other trains Paris - Compiègne at 0640 ⚒, 0737 Ⓐ, 0837 †, 0849 ⑥, 1037 Ⓐ, 1249 ⑥, 1337 Ⓐ, 1537 Ⓐ, 1637 ⚒, 1737 †, 1749 ⚒, 1822 Ⓐ, 1837 ⚒, 1937, 2037 †, 2149 ⑥; Compiègne - Paris at 0510 Ⓐ, 0610 ⚒, 0638 Ⓐ, 0639 †, 0706 Ⓐ, 0713 ⑥, 0718 Ⓐ, 0810, 1106 Ⓑ, 1115 ⑥, 1206, 1514 ⑥, 1610 Ⓑ, 1710, 1810 Ⓑ, 1906 Ⓐ, 1914 ⑥, 2011 Ⓐ.

LILLE - DOUAI - CAMBRAI - ST QUENTIN 256

km		Ⓐ ⊖	⑥ ⊖	Ⓐ	Ⓐ	Ⓐ	⑥	Ⓐ	Ⓐ	Ⓒ	† ⊖	Ⓒ	Ⓐ		⑤	Ⓒ	Ⓒ	Ⓐ	Ⓐ	Ⓐ	Ⓒ	Ⓐ	Ⓐ	Ⓒ	Ⓐ
0	**Lille** Flandres 257 d.	...	...	...	0623	0723	0805	0823	0923	1005	...	1205	1223	...	1323	1405	1605	1623	*1653*	1723	1805	1823	1923	2005	2023
34	Douai 257 d.	...	...	...	0647	0747	0826	0847	0947	1029	...	1229	1247	...	1347	1429	1629	1647	1725	1747	1829	1847	1947	2029	2047
66	Cambrai Ville ● d.	0546	0606	0631	0732	0832	0905	0932	1032	1055	1209	1255	1332	...	1432	1455	1655	1732	1807	1832	1855	1932	2032	2109	2132
82	Caudry d.	0600	0620	0645	0745	0845	0917	0945	1045	1108	1223	1308	1345	...	1445	1508	1708	1745	1824	1845	1908	1945	2045	2122	2145
92	Busigny 255 d.	0610	0632	0654	0754	0854	0926	0954	1054	1116	1233	1316	1354	...	1454	1516	1716	1753	1836	1854	1916	1954	2054	2131	2154
119	**St Quentin** 255 a.	0624	0646	0714	0812	0914	0946	1010	1110	1141	1247	1337	1410	...	1510	1540	1737	1810	1856	1910	1937	2010	2110	2150	2210

	Ⓐ	Ⓐ	Ⓐ	Ⓐ	Ⓒ	Ⓐ	Ⓒ		Ⓐ	Ⓒ	Ⓐ	Ⓒ	Ⓐ	Ⓒ	⑤	Ⓒ		Ⓐ	⑥ ⊖	Ⓐ	Ⓒ	Ⓐ ⊖	Ⓐ	† ⊖
St Quentin 255 d.	0450	0550	0650	0704	0711	0750	0924	...	0950	1110	1150	1324	1450	1524	1650	1724	...	1746	1810	1850	1911	1936	1949	2015
Busigny 255 d.	0506	0607	0706	0724	0732	0806	0946	...	1006	1131	1206	1346	1506	1546	1706	1746	...	1808	1826	1906	1932	1953	2007	2031
Caudry d.	0516	0616	0716	0736	0741	0816	0954	...	1016	1140	1216	1354	1516	1554	1716	1754	...	1816	1837	1916	1941	2003	2016	2041
Cambrai Ville ● d.	0538	0639	0738	0805	0803	0838	1009	...	1038	1202	1238	1409	1538	1609	1738	1809	...	1838	1850	1938	2003	2015	2038	2054
Douai 257 a.	0616	0716	0816	0834	0836	0916	1034	...	1116	1235	1316	1434	1616	1634	1816	1834	...	1916	...	2016	2035	...	2116	...
Lille Flandres 257 a.	0637	0737	0837	*0907*	0855	0937	1055	...	1137	1255	1337	1455	1637	1655	1837	1855	...	1937	...	2037	2055	...	2137	...

● – Other trains Douai - Cambrai Ville at 0625 Ⓐ, 0727 Ⓐ, 0731 ⑥, 0827 Ⓐ, 0927 Ⓐ, 0931 Ⓒ, 1127 Ⓐ, 1131 Ⓒ, 1327 Ⓐ, 1331 Ⓒ, 1531 Ⓒ, 1627 Ⓐ, 1731 Ⓒ, 1751 Ⓐ, 1827 Ⓐ, 1851 Ⓐ, 1922 †, 1927 Ⓐ, 1931 ⑥; Cambrai Ville - Douai at 0603 Ⓐ, 0633 Ⓐ, 0658 ⑥, 0703 Ⓐ, 0735 Ⓐ, 0856 Ⓒ, 0903 Ⓐ, 1003 Ⓐ, 1058 Ⓒ, 1258 Ⓒ, 1303 Ⓐ, 1403 Ⓐ, 1458 Ⓒ, 1658 Ⓒ, 1702 Ⓐ, 1858 ⑥, 1903 Ⓐ, 1958 †, 2003 Ⓐ.

⊖ – 🚌2 Cambrai - St Quentin - Paris and v.v. (Table **255**).

257 LILLE - DOUAI - ARRAS - AMIENS and PARIS

For *TGV* and *TER-GV* trains Lille Europe / Douai - Arras and v.v. via the high-speed line see Table **250**.

km		Ⓐ	Ⓐ A	⑥ A	Ⓐ	Ⓐ	Ⓒ	⑤	Ⓐ A	Ⓒ	Ⓐ	Ⓐ	Ⓒ	Ⓐ	Ⓒ	Ⓐ	Ⓐ	Ⓒ A	Ⓐ A	⑤	Ⓒ	Ⓐ	Ⓐ	Ⓒ
0	**Lille** Flandres **256** d.	0553	0653	0705	0753	0853	0905	0953	1053	1105	1153	1253	1305	1353	1505	1553	1653	1705	1753	1853	1905	1953	2058	2105
34	Douai **256** d.	0616	0716	0728	0816	0917	0926	1016	1116	1126	1216	1316	1326	1416	1526	1616	1716	1726	1816	1916	1926	2017	2120	2126
59	Arras d.	0632	0732	0742	0832	0932	0942	1032	1132	1142	1232	1332	1342	1432	1541	1632	1732	1742	1832	1932	1942	2032	2136	2142
96	Albert d.	0653	0750	0802	0851	0951	1003	1051	1150	1203	1251	1354	1403	1451	1603	1653	1752	1802	1850	1953	2003	2053	2156	2203
127	**Amiens** a.	0710	0813	0823	0910	1010	1023	1110	1213	1225	1310	1412	1423	1510	1623	1710	1812	1823	1910	2010	2023	2110	2214	2223

	Ⓐ	⑥	Ⓐ	Ⓐ	†	⑥ A	Ⓐ A	Ⓒ	Ⓐ	⑤	Ⓒ	Ⓐ A	Ⓒ	Ⓐ	Ⓐ	Ⓒ	Ⓐ	Ⓐ	Ⓒ A	Ⓐ	Ⓐ A	Ⓒ	Ⓐ
Amiens d.	0550	0636	0650	0750	0837	0837	0849	1037	1050	1150	1237	1250	1434	1450	1550	1637	1650	1750	1837	1850	1950	2043	2101
Albert d.	0607	0656	0707	0810	0856	0857	0909	1057	1108	1207	1257	1310	1454	1508	1608	1657	1708	1808	1857	1908	2010	2103	2121
Arras d.	0629	0717	0729	0829	0919	0919	0929	1119	1129	1229	1319	1330	1516	1529	1629	1719	1729	1829	1919	1929	2030	2126	2140
Douai **256** d.	0645	0732	0745	0845	0934	0934	0945	1134	1145	1245	1334	1345	1532	1545	1645	1734	1745	1845	1934	1945	2045	2141	2155
Lille Flandres **256** a.	0707	0755	0807	0907	0955	0955	1007	1155	1207	1307	1355	1407	1553	1607	1707	1755	1807	1907	1955	2007	2107	2202	2217

WEEKEND TER SERVICE LILLE - ARRAS - PARIS

	Ⓒ	Ⓒ		Ⓒ	Ⓒ
Lille Flandres **256** d.	0914	1914	**Paris** Nord d.	1022	1828
Douai **256** d.	0934	1935	Creil d.	1048	1856
Arras d.	0950	1951	Longueau d.	1124	1934
Longueau d.	1026	2026	Arras d.	1157	2010
Creil d.	1101	2106	Douai **256** d.	1211	2029
Paris Nord a.	1126	2129	**Lille** Flandres **256** a.	1232	2051

🚌 AMIENS - TGV HAUTE-PICARDIE 🚌

SNCF 🚌 service Ⓡ. Journey 45 minutes.
From **Amiens** at 0620, 0940, 1710.
From **TGV Haute-Picardie** at 1035, 1354, 1805, 1958.
For *TGV* departures and arrivals at TGV Haute-Picardie see Table **11**.

A – To / from Rouen (Table **253**).

258 AMIENS - ST QUENTIN

km		Ⓐ 🚌	⚒	†	⚒		Ⓐ	Ⓐ		Ⓐ
0	**Amiens** **252** d.	...	0746	1046	1246	...	1646	1746	1846	1946
59	Ham (Somme) **252** d.	0722	0822	1122	1322	...	1722	1822	1922	2022
76	**St Quentin** a.	0752	0842	1142	1342	...	1742	1842	1942	2042

	Ⓐ	⚒	Ⓐ 🚌	†		⚒	Ⓐ	⚒	†
St Quentin d.	0616	0716	0816	0916	...	1216	1716	1816	2016
Ham (Somme) **252** d.	0638	0738	0846	0938	...	1238	1738	1838	2038
Amiens **252** a.	0714	0814	0949	1014	...	1314	1816	1914	2114

259 CALAIS - DUNKERQUE - DE PANNE

km		Ⓐ	⑥	Ⓐ 🚌	Ⓐ	⑥	Ⓐ	Ⓐ	Ⓐ	Ⓐ
0	**Calais** Ville d.	0602	0702	0724	0900	1202	1302	1547	1735	1835
23	Gravelines d.	0624	0724	0800	0919	1224	1324	1605	1756	1856
46	**Dunkerque** a.	0647	0747	0845	0938	1247	1347	1625	1819	1919

	⑥	Ⓐ	Ⓐ 🚌	⚒		Ⓐ	Ⓐ	Ⓐ	Ⓐ
Dunkerque d.	0700	0703	0805	1300	...	1639	1730	1830	1930
Gravelines d.	0724	0724	0850	1324	...	1657	1754	1854	1954
Calais Ville a.	0743	0746	0926	1343	...	1713	1814	1914	2013

🚌 **DUNKERQUE - LEFFRINCKOUCKE - ADINKERKE (DE PANNE STATION)** Operator: DK'BUS (www.dkbus.com).
Route C1: Dunkerque Gare - Leffrinckoucke (Fort Des Dunes). Every 10 mins. (every 30 mins. on ⑦). Journey 20 mins.
Route 20: Leffrinckoucke (Fort Des Dunes) - Bray Dunes - Gare d'Adinkerke - De Panne. Every 30 mins. (hourly on ⑦). Journey 33 mins. Connects at De Panne with coastal tram (Table **406**).

260 PARIS - AMIENS

km		Ⓐ	⑥	Ⓐ	Ⓑ	⑥	⑥	Ⓐ		Ⓒ	Ⓒ	⚒ e	†	Ⓐ	⑥	†		⑥	③	B	①–③	④⑤	⑥	⑤
0	**Paris** Nord **255** d.	0604	0704	0731	0804	0807	0831	0907	...	0907	0931	1031	1107	1131	1150	1204	...	1307	1323	1329	1354	1410	1431	1504
51	Creil **255** d.	0631	0731	0758	0831	0843	|	0944	...	0943	|	|	1141	|	1217	1232	...	1341	|	|	1435	1439	|	1531
66	Clermont-de-l'Oise d.	0641	0742	|	0842	0857	|	0959	...	0957	|	|	1155	|	|	1241	...	1356	|	|	1445	1449	|	1541
81	St Just en Chaussée d.	0652	0752	|	0853	0913	|	1008	...	1013	|	|	1203	|	|	1251	...	1408	|	|	1455	1459	|	1551
126	Longueau **254** d.	0716	0817	0834	0917	0945	0933	1036	...	1045	1030	1131	1231	1233	1254	1316	...	1437	1438	1431	1519	1523	1534	1614
131	**Amiens** **254** a.	0723	0822	0838	0922	0951	0937	1042	...	1051	1034	1137	1237	1238	1300	1322	...	1443	1442	1439	1528	1528	1538	1620
	Boulogne Ville **261** a.	...	...	0957	...	...	1056	...	...	...	1153	1256	...	...	...	...	...	...	1603	1559	...	...	1656	...
	Calais Ville **261** a.	...	...	...	...	...	1130	...	...	...	1227	1329	...	...	...	...	...	...	...	...	...	...	1726	...

	†	⚒	†	Ⓐ	Ⓐ		Ⓒ	Ⓐ	⑥	Ⓐ	†			Ⓐ	Ⓐ				⑥	Ⓐ	†		f
Paris Nord **255** d.	1531	1604	1607	1631	1704	...	1707	1707	1731	1731	1749	...	1804	1831	1904	1907	1931	...	2004	2004	2031	2107	2228
Creil **255** d.	|	1631	1641	1658	1731	...	1739	1741	|	|	|	...	1831	|	1932	1941	|	...	2031	2034	|	2142	2300
Clermont-de-l'Oise d.	|	1642	1656	|	1742	...	1755	1758	|	|	|	...	1842	|	1943	1958	|	...	2041	2044	|	2158	2312
St Just en Chaussée d.	|	1653	1705	|	1753	...	1813	1813	|	|	|	...	1853	|	1953	2013	|	...	2052	2053	|	2207	2321
Longueau **254** d.	1633	1717	1734	1733	1817	...	1846	1845	1833	1833	1853	...	1917	1932	2017	2045	2033	...	2116	2117	2131	2236	2344
Amiens **254** a.	1637	1722	1738	1737	1822	...	1851	1851	1837	1838	1856	...	1922	1938	2022	2051	2037	...	2122	2122	2136	2241	2350
Boulogne Ville **261** a.	1808	...	...	1859	...	...	...	...	1956	...	2015	...	...	...	...	...	2156	...	...	...	...	...	...
Calais Ville **261** a.	1839	...	...	1931	...	...	...	...	2029	...	2047	...	...	...	...	...	2228	...	...	...	...	...	...

	Ⓐ g	Ⓐ	⑥		Ⓐ	Ⓐ	Ⓒ		Ⓐ	⚒	Ⓐ		Ⓐ		⚒		Ⓑ	†	⑥		Ⓐ	⑥	Ⓒ
Calais Ville **261** d.	...	...	...	...	...	...	...	...	...	...	...	...	...	...	0636	...	...	...	...	...	...	...	0935
Boulogne Ville **261** d.	...	...	...	...	...	...	...	...	...	...	...	...	...	...	0704	...	...	...	...	...	...	...	1004
Amiens **254** d.	0417	0506	0519	...	0538	0604	0621	...	0622	0638	0706	...	0722	0738	0823	...	0838	0917	0918	...	1008	1038	1123
Longueau **254** d.	0422	0512	0525	...	0545	0611	0627	...	0629	0645	0713	...	0730	0745	0829	...	0844	0923	0925	...	1015	1045	1130
St Just en Chaussée d.	0449	0542	0554	...	0609	0640	0654	...	|	0709	0742	...	|	0808	|	...	0908	0953	0955	...	1039	1109	|
Clermont-de-l'Oise d.	0501	0551	0603	...	0619	0659	0703	...	|	0719	0759	...	|	0818	|	...	0919	1002	1004	...	1050	1119	|
Creil **255** d.	0520	0611	0620	...	0631	0719	0720	...	|	0731	0819	...	|	0831	|	...	0931	1020	1021	...	1103	1130	|
Paris Nord **255** a.	0553	0644	0653	...	0656	0753	0753	...	0729	0756	0853	...	0829	0856	0929	...	0956	1053	1053	...	1129	1156	1229

	Ⓐ	⑥	⚒		†				†		Ⓑ		†	⑥	†		Ⓒ	Ⓐ	†		Ⓐ	†	Ⓐ
Calais Ville **261** d.	...	1137	...	...	...	...	1436	...	1536	...	...	...	...	...	...	...	1737	1738	...	...	...	1937	...
Boulogne Ville **261** d.	1100	1204	...	...	...	...	1504	...	1604	...	1700	...	...	...	...	...	1804	1804	...	...	...	2004	...
Amiens **254** d.	1223	1323	1438	...	1542	1606	1623	...	1723	1738	1823	...	1837	1902	1902	...	1923	1935	2038	...	2038	2124	2138
Longueau **254** d.	1230	1330	1445	...	1548	1612	1630	...	1730	1744	1830	...	1842	1910	1910	...	1930	1945	2044	...	2044	2132	2144
St Just en Chaussée d.	|	|	1509	...	1611	1642	|	...	|	1808	|	...	1905	1952	1953	...	|	2008	2107	...	2108	|	2208
Clermont-de-l'Oise d.	|	|	1520	...	1619	1700	|	...	|	1819	|	...	1914	2003	2003	...	|	2018	2117	...	2117	|	2218
Creil **255** d.	|	|	1531	...	1631	1720	|	...	|	1831	|	...	1925	2023	2022	...	|	2028	2131	...	2131	|	2231
Paris Nord **255** a.	1335	1429	1556	...	1656	1753	1729	...	1829	1856	1929	...	1953	2056	2056	...	2029	2056	2156	...	2157	2229	2256

B – ①②④⑤⑦. e – From Apr. 3. f – Not on Ⓐ Mar. 6 – 31. g – Not ②–⑤ Mar. 7 – 31.

(PARIS -) AMIENS - BOULOGNE - CALAIS 261

For *TGV* services see Table **250**. Other connections Paris - Calais are available by changing at Lille or Hazebrouck (Tables **250** / **265**). Additional trains are available Amiens - Abbeville and v.v.

km																								
		Ⓐ	⑥	Ⓐ		Ⓐ	Ⓐ	Ⓒ		Ⓐ	⑥	Ⓐ		Ⓐ	⑥	Ⓒ		Ⓐ	†	⚒ d		Ⓐ	Ⓐ	⑥
	Paris Nord **260** d.	...	...	...	...	...	...	...	...	...	...	0731	...	...	0831	0931	...	...	...	1031	...	...	...	...
0	**Amiens** d.	...	0532	0547	...	...	0647	0732	...	0743	0837	0840	...	...	0940	1037	...	1047	1128	1138	...	...	1248	1332
45	Abbeville d.	...	0600	0615	...	...	0715	0801	...	0811	0905	0906	...	...	1006	1103	...	1115	1157	1204	...	...	1316	1400
58	Noyelles sur Mer d.	...	0610	0624	...	...	0725	0810	...	0820	0914	0915	...	...	1015	1112	...	1124	1207	1213	...	...	1325	1410
85	Rang du Fliers-Verton-Berck d.	0545	0629	0643	...	0649	0743	0829	...	0839	0933	0933	...	1021	1033	1130	...	1143	1226	1231	...	...	1343	1429
96	Étaples-Le Touquet d.	0553	0637	0651	...	0657	0751	0837	...	0847	0941	0941	...	1029	1041	1138	...	1151	1235	1239	...	1253	1351	1437
123	**Boulogne** Ville d.	0614	0658	0708	...	0722	0808	0858	...	0904	1001	0957	...	1052	1058	1155	...	1208	1257	1256	...	1315	1408	1458
130	Wimille-Wimereux d.	0622	0706	|	...	0729	|	0906	...	|	1010	...	...	1100	|	|	...	|	1305	|	...	1323	|	1506
140	Marquise-Rinxent d.	0631	0715	0723	...	0738	0822	0915	...	0918	1018	...	...	1109	1108	1207	...	1222	1314	|	...	1332	1422	1515
157	**Calais** Fréthun d.	0645	0729	|	...	0759	|	0929	...	|	1031	...	...	1123	|	|	...	|	1329	|	...	1346	|	1529
165	**Calais** Ville a.	0655	0738	0742	...	0808	0841	0939	...	0938	1043	...	...	1132	1130	1227	...	1242	1338	1329	...	1355	1442	1538

	B	③	Ⓐ		†	⑥	Ⓐ		Ⓐ	†	②–⑤		Ⓐ	Ⓒ	Ⓐ		Ⓐ	⑥	Ⓐ		†	Ⓐ d	
Paris Nord **260** d.	1329	1323	...	...	...	1431	...	...	...	1531	...	...	...	...	1631	...	...	1731	...	...	1749	...	1931
Amiens d.	1440	1445	...	...	1532	1540	1548	...	...	1640	1645	...	...	1732	1740	...	...	1840	1848	...	1858	1948	2040
Abbeville d.	1506	1511	...	...	1601	1606	1616	...	...	1710	1713	...	...	1801	1806	...	...	1906	1916	...	1924	2016	2106
Noyelles sur Mer d.	1515	1520	...	...	1610	1615	1625	...	...	1721	1723	...	...	1810	1816	...	...	1915	1926	...	1933	2025	2115
Rang du Fliers-Verton-Berck d.	1533	1539	...	...	1629	1633	1644	...	1648	1742	1742	...	1747	1829	1835	...	1844	1933	1944	...	1952	2044	2133
Étaples-Le Touquet d.	1541	1547	1551	...	1637	1641	1652	...	1656	1750	1749	...	1755	1837	1843	...	1852	1941	1952	...	1959	2052	2141
Boulogne Ville d.	1559	1603	1615	...	1658	1657	1709	...	1721	1810	1806	...	1817	1858	1901	...	1915	1958	2009	...	2016	2109	2158
Wimille-Wimereux d.	...	...	1622	...	1706	|	|	...	1729	|	|	...	1825	1906	|	...	1923	|	|	...	|	|	|
Marquise-Rinxent d.	...	...	1632	...	1715	|	1723	...	1738	|	1821	...	1834	1915	|	...	1932	|	2024	...	|	2123	|
Calais Fréthun d.	...	...	1646	...	1729	|	|	...	1759	|	|	...	1848	1929	|	...	1946	|	|	...	|	|	|
Calais Ville a.	...	...	1655	...	1738	1726	1743	...	1808	1839	1840	...	1857	1938	1931	...	1955	2028	2044	...	2047	2143	2228

	①	Ⓐ	⚒		Ⓐ	⑥	Ⓐ		Ⓐ	Ⓒ	Ⓐ		Ⓒ	Ⓒ	Ⓐ		⑥	Ⓐ	⑥		Ⓐ	Ⓐ	†
Calais Ville d.	0418	0520	0636	...	0705	0711	0718	...	0757	0809	0920	...	0935	1009	...	...	1137	1144	1209	...	1218	1305	1317
Calais Fréthun d.	|	|	|	...	0714	0720	|	...	0806	0818	|	...	|	1019	...	...	|	1154	1219	...	|	1314	1327
Marquise-Rinxent d.	0435	0537	|	...	0725	0731	0736	...	0825	0830	0937	...	|	1031	...	...	|	1205	1230	...	1235	1325	1340
Wimille-Wimereux d.	|	|	|	...	0732	0738	|	...	0832	0838	|	...	|	1038	...	...	|	1212	1238	...	|	1333	1347
Boulogne Ville d.	0450	0550	0704	...	0739	0747	0751	...	0840	0847	0949	...	1004	1047	1100	...	1204	1220	1247	...	1250	1340	1356
Étaples-Le Touquet d.	0509	0608	0719	...	0800	0807	0809	...	0905	0907	1008	...	1019	1107	1119	...	1219	1241	1307	...	1307	1404	1416
Rang du Fliers-Verton-Berck d.	0518	0617	0727	...	0810	0816	0818	...	0914	0916	1018	...	1028	1116	1127	...	1228	...	1316	...	1317	...	1425
Noyelles sur Mer d.	0535	0635	0745	...	...	0834	0835	...	...	0934	1035	...	1045	1134	1145	...	1245	...	1334	...	1335	...	1443
Abbeville d.	0545	0644	0754	...	...	0843	0845	...	...	0943	1045	...	1054	1143	1154	...	1254	...	1343	...	1344	...	1452
Amiens a.	0612	0712	0820	...	...	0910	0912	...	...	1010	1112	...	1120	1210	1220	...	1320	...	1410	...	1412	...	1519
Paris Nord **260** a.	...	...	0929	...	...	...	...	...	...	...	...	...	1229	...	1335	...	1429	...	...	...	...	...	...

		Ⓐ		†	Ⓐ		⑥	Ⓑ		Ⓐ	Ⓒ		Ⓐ	Ⓐ		Ⓐ	②–⑤		⑥	Ⓐ		†	
Calais Ville d.	1436	1518	...	1536	1605	...	1614	...	...	1705	1737	...	1738	1805	...	1818	1907	...	1909	1920	...	1937	...
Calais Fréthun d.	|	|	...	|	1614	...	1623	...	...	1714	|	...	|	1814	...	|	1917	...	1918	|	...	|	...
Marquise-Rinxent d.	|	1535	...	|	1625	...	1635	...	...	1732	|	...	|	1825	...	1834	1928	...	1930	1937	...	|	...
Wimille-Wimereux d.	|	|	...	|	1632	...	1642	...	...	1740	|	...	|	1833	...	|	1935	...	1938	|	...	|	...
Boulogne Ville d.	1504	1550	...	1604	1640	...	1650	1700	...	1747	1804	...	1804	1840	...	1850	1953	...	1947	1950	...	2004	...
Étaples-Le Touquet d.	1519	1609	...	1619	1703	...	1710	1719	...	1812	1820	...	1819	1903	...	1908	2019	...	2007	2009	...	2020	...
Rang du Fliers-Verton-Berck d.	1527	1617	...	1628	1711	...	1719	1727	...	1819	1828	...	1827	1910	...	1916	2026	...	2016	2018	...	2028	...
Noyelles sur Mer d.	1545	1635	...	1645	...	...	1737	1745	...	...	1846	...	1845	...	...	1934	...	...	2034	2035	...	2046	...
Abbeville d.	1554	1644	...	1654	...	...	1746	1754	...	...	1855	...	1854	...	...	1943	...	...	2043	2045	...	2055	...
Amiens a.	1620	1712	...	1720	...	...	1815	1820	...	...	1921	...	1920	...	...	2010	...	...	2110	2112	...	2121	...
Paris Nord **260** a.	1729	...	...	1829	...	...	...	1929	...	...	2029	...	2056	...	...	...	...	...	...	...	...	2229	...

🚌 ABBEVILLE - LE TRÉPORT 🚌

🚌 number **732**. Subject to alteration during school holiday periods. *37 km*. Journey 70 minutes (* – 50 minutes):
From **Abbeville** at 0641 Ⓐ, 0820 ⑥, 0830 Ⓐ, 1125 Ⓒ *, 1220 ⚒, 1411 ⚒, 1520 Ⓑ, 1620 ⑥, 1735 Ⓐ, 1825 ⑥ *, 1825 Ⓐ, 1920 ⑥, 1930 Ⓐ, 1937 †, 2030 ⑤.
From **Le Tréport** at 0436 ① *, 0608 Ⓐ, 0624 ⑥, 0714 Ⓐ, 0819 ⑥, 0914 Ⓐ, 0929 Ⓒ, 1219 ⚒, 1619 ⑥, 1624 Ⓐ, 1655 † *, 1715 Ⓐ, 1729 Ⓒ, 1800 Ⓐ, 1919 ⑥.

B – ①②④⑤⑦.
d – From Apr. 3.

– *Chemin de fer de la Baie de Somme.* www.chemindefer-baiedesomme.fr.
Cayeux sur Mer - Saint Valery sur Somme - Noyelles sur Mer - Le Crotoy.
Noyelles sur Mer station is adjacent to the SNCF station.

LILLE - MAUBEUGE, JEUMONT, LAON and CHARLEVILLE MÉZIÈRES 262

km																								
		Ⓐ	Ⓐ	Ⓐ	Ⓐ	Ⓐ 🚌	Ⓐ	Ⓐ	Ⓐ	Ⓐ d	Ⓐ	⑥ e	⑥	⑥ 🚌	Ⓐ	Ⓐ d	Ⓐ	Ⓐ	⑥	Ⓐ d	Ⓐ 🚌	†	Ⓐ	Ⓐ
0	**Lille** Flandres d.	...	...	0535	0605	...	...	0635	...	0705	...	0705	...	...	0735	0805	...	0835	0835	0905	...	0905	...	...
48	Valenciennes d.	...	0551	0612	0642	...	...	0712	...	0742	0751	0753	...	...	0812	0842	0851	0912	0914	0942	...	0951	0951	1051
82	Aulnoye Aymeries **255** d.	...	0621	0637	0718	...	0721	0737	0745	0817	0821	0822	0830	...	0837	0917	0921	0937	0939	1017	...	1020	1021	1121
94	**Maubeuge** **255** a.	...	0631	0647	|	...	0731	0747	|	|	0831	0833	|	...	0847	|	0931	0947	0949	|	...	1032	1031	1131
104	**Jeumont** a.	...	0639	...	|	...	0739	...	|	|	0839	0842	|	...	...	|	0939	...	0958	|	...	1042	1039	1139
94	Avesnes d.	...	...	...	0729	...	...	...	0801	0829	...	...	0839	...	...	0929	...	...	...	1029	...	...	...	...
123	Hirson d.	0530	...	...	0754	0803	...	...	0831	0853	...	...	0904	0914	...	0954	...	...	...	1054	1103	...	...	...
179	**Laon** a.	0622	...	...	...	|	...	...	...	...	...	...	...	|	...	...	...	...	...	...	|	...	...	...
184	**Charleville-Mézières** a.	...	...	...	...	0903	...	...	...	...	...	...	...	1014	...	...	...	...	...	...	1203	...	...	...

	Ⓒ	Ⓒ	⑥	Ⓐ d	Ⓒ	Ⓐ	Ⓒ	Ⓒ	Ⓐ d	Ⓐ 🚌	Ⓐ	Ⓐ	Ⓒ	Ⓒ	Ⓐ d	Ⓐ	Ⓐ	Ⓐ	Ⓐ	Ⓒ	Ⓐ	Ⓒ	†
Lille Flandres d.	1035	...	...	1205	1205	1235	...	1235	1305	...	...	1335	1435	...	...	1535	1605	...	1635	1635	...	...	...
Valenciennes d.	1114	...	...	1242	1253	1312	...	1314	1342	...	1351	1412	1514	...	...	1612	1642	...	1712	1714	...	...	...
Aulnoye Aymeries **255** d.	1139	1146	...	1318	1322	1337	1347	1348	1417	...	1421	1437	1539	1602	1634	1637	1718	1721	1737	1739	1745	1746	...
Maubeuge **255** a.	1150	|	...	|	1333	1347	1357	|	|	...	1431	1447	1551	|	|	1647	|	1731	1747	1749	|	|	...
Jeumont a.	1158	|	...	|	1342	...	1406	|	|	...	1439	...	1559	|	|	...	|	1739	...	1758	|	|	...
Avesnes d.	...	1155	...	1329	...	...	...	1358	1429	...	...	...	...	1611	1649	...	1729	...	...	...	1801	1755	...
Hirson d.	...	1222	1246	1355	...	...	...	1422	1453	1503	...	...	...	1639	1719	...	1755	...	...	...	1830	1822	1828
Laon a.	...	...	1340	...	...	...	...	|	...	|	...	...	...	...	1824	...	...	...	...	...	...	...	1923
Charleville-Mézières a.	...	...	...	...	...	...	...	1502	...	1603	...	...	...	...	...	...	...	...	...	...	...	...	...

	⑥ 🚌	Ⓐ	Ⓐ	Ⓒ	Ⓐ	Ⓐ	Ⓐ 🚌	Ⓐ	⑥	Ⓒ	† 🚌		Ⓐ	Ⓒ	Ⓐ	Ⓐ	†	Ⓐ	Ⓐ	⑤	Ⓒ	Ⓐ	Ⓐ
Lille Flandres d.	...	1705	...	1705	1735	1805	...	...	1805	...	...	...	1835	1835	1905	...	1905	1935	2005	2035	2035	2105	2135
Valenciennes d.	...	1742	1751	1753	1812	1842	...	1851	1853	...	...	...	1912	1914	1942	1951	1951	2012	2042	2112	2114	2142	2212
Aulnoye Aymeries **255** d.	...	1818	1821	1823	1837	|	...	1920	1922	1946	...	...	1937	1939	2017	2021	2021	2037	2117	2137	2139	2218	2237
Maubeuge **255** a.	...	|	1835	1833	1845	|	...	1931	1933	|	...	...	1945	1950	|	2031	2031	2045	|	2147	2150	|	2245
Jeumont a.	...	|	1847	1842	1854	|	...	1939	1942	|	...	...	1954	1958	|	2039	2040	2054	|	...	2158	|	2254
Avesnes d.	...	1829	...	...	...	1910	...	...	...	1955	...	...	...	...	2029	...	...	...	2129	...	...	2229	...
Hirson d.	1829	1853	...	...	...	1932	1939	...	...	2022	2032	...	...	...	2054	...	...	...	2154	...	...	2255	...
Laon a.	|	|	...	...	...	...	|	...	...	...	|	...	...	...	...	...	...	...	...	...	...	...	...
Charleville-Mézières a.	1929	1935	...	...	...	...	2039	...	...	...	2132	...	...	...	...	...	...	...	...	...	...	...	...

FOR RETURN SERVICE AND FOOTNOTES SEE NEXT PAGE →

262 CHARLEVILLE MÉZIÈRES, LAON, JEUMONT and MAUBEUGE - LILLE

	Ⓐ	Ⓐ □	Ⓐ	Ⓐ	⑥	Ⓐ	Ⓐ	Ⓐ	Ⓐ	⑥	⚒	⑥	Ⓐ	Ⓐ	Ⓐ	Ⓐ	Ⓐ 🚌	Ⓐ	⑥	⑥ 🚌	Ⓒ	Ⓒ	Ⓐ	Ⓐ d
Charleville-Mézières d.	...	...	...	...	...	...	...	...	...	...	...	...	0631	...	...	...	0657	...	...	0731	...	...	...	...
Laon ◧ d.	...	...	...	...	...	...	...	...	...	...	...	...	|	0635	...	...	|	...	0738	|	...	...	...	...
Hirson ◧ d.	...	...	0507	...	...	...	0633	...	0616	0641	...	...	0709	0737	...	...	0757	0807	0829	0831	0841	...	...	0907
Avesnes d.	...	...	0532	...	...	...	0653	...	0644	0705	...	...	0733	0808	...	...	...	0832	...	...	0905	...	...	0932
Jeumont d.	...	0521	|	0606	0620	0621	|	0639	|	|	...	0720	|	|	...	0821	...	|	...	...	|	0904	0921	|
Maubeuge 255 d.	0513	0528	|	0614	0628	0628	|	0651	|	|	0713	0727	|	|	0813	0828	...	|	...	...	|	0911	0928	|
Aulnoye Aymeries 255 d.	0525	0540	0552	0625	0641	0642	|	0709	0715	0715	0724	0740	0752	0824	0825	0842	...	0852	...	...	0915	0924	0942	0952
Valenciennes d.	0550	...	0620	0650	0710	0709	0720	0739	0742	...	0748	0810	0820	...	0850	0909	...	0920	...	...	...	0948	1009	1020
Lille Flandres a.	0625	...	0655	0725	0755	...	0755	...	...	...	0825	0855	0855	...	0925	...	...	0955	...	...	...	1025	...	1055

	Ⓐ	Ⓐ	Ⓐ d	Ⓒ	†	⑥	Ⓐ 🚌	Ⓐ d	Ⓐ	Ⓐ	⑥ 🚌	Ⓒ	Ⓒ	Ⓐ 🚌	Ⓐ	⑥	Ⓒ	Ⓒ	Ⓐ	Ⓐ 🚌	Ⓐ d	Ⓐ	⑥	Ⓐ
Charleville-Mézières d.	...	...	...	...	...	...	0957	...	...	...	1131	...	...	...	...	...	...	...	...	1357	...	...	...	...
Laon ◧ d.	...	...	...	...	...	...	|	...	...	...	|	...	...	...	...	1245	...	...	...	|	...	...	...	...
Hirson ◧ d.	...	...	1007	1041	...	...	1057	1107	...	...	1231	1241	...	1248	...	1352	1443	...	...	1457	1507	...	...	...
Avesnes d.	...	...	1032	1105	...	...	...	1132	...	...	...	1305	...	1359	...	...	1507	...	...	...	1532	...	...	...
Jeumont d.	...	1021	|	|	1104	1120	...	|	...	1221	...	|	1304	|	...	...	|	1504	1521	...	|	...	1620	1621
Maubeuge 255 d.	1013	1028	|	|	1111	1128	...	|	1213	1228	...	|	1311	|	1413	...	|	1511	1528	...	|	1613	1628	1628
Aulnoye Aymeries 255 d.	1025	1042	1052	1115	1124	1141	...	1152	1225	1242	...	1315	1324	1415	1425	...	1517	1524	1540	...	1552	1625	1641	1642
Valenciennes d.	1050	1109	1120	...	1148	1210	...	1220	1250	1309	...	...	1348	...	1450	...	...	1548	...	...	1620	1650	1710	1709
Lille Flandres a.	1125	...	1155	...	1225	1255	...	1255	1325	...	...	...	1425	...	1525	...	...	1625	...	...	1655	1725	1755	...

	Ⓐ d	† 🚌	Ⓒ	⑥	Ⓐ	Ⓐ	†	Ⓐ	Ⓐ	Ⓐ	Ⓒ	Ⓐ	Ⓒ	Ⓒ	Ⓐ f	Ⓐ	Ⓐ 🚌	Ⓐ	Ⓐ	†	Ⓐ	⑤	Ⓐ	Ⓐ
Charleville-Mézières d.	...	1536	...	...	...	...	...	...	...	...	...	...	...	1803	...	...	1757	...	...	...	...	...	...	...
Laon ◧ d.	...	|	...	...	...	...	...	...	...	...	...	...	...	|	...	...	|	...	...	...	1845	...	...	...
Hirson ◧ d.	1622	1636	1649	...	...	...	...	1707	...	...	...	1807	...	1841	...	...	1857	1907	...	...	1952	2007	...	2107
Avesnes d.	1650	...	1714	...	...	...	...	1732	...	...	...	1832	...	1905	...	...	...	1932	...	...	...	2032	...	2132
Jeumont d.	|	...	|	1704	...	1714	1720	|	...	1821	1824	|	1856	|	1906	1921	...	|	2006	2020	...	|	2106	|
Maubeuge 255 d.	|	...	|	1711	1713	1722	1728	|	1813	1828	1832	|	1903	|	1914	1928	...	|	2014	2028	...	|	2114	|
Aulnoye Aymeries 255 d.	1705	...	1723	1724	1725	1735	1741	1752	1825	1842	1845	1852	1914	1924	1925	1942	...	1953	2025	2041	...	2052	2125	2152
Valenciennes d.	...	...	...	1748	1750	1803	1810	1820	1850	1909	1913	1920	...	1948	1950	2009	...	2020	2050	2110	...	2120	2150	2220
Lille Flandres a.	...	...	...	1825	1825	...	1855	1855	1925	...	1958	1955	...	2023	2025	...	...	2055	2125	2155	...	2155	2225	2255

◧ – Other trains Hirson - Laon and v.v. (* journey 90 minutes): from Hirson at 0625 ⑥, 0627 Ⓐ, 0710 Ⓐ 🚌 *, 0840 ⑥, 0923 †, 1041 ⑥, 1112 Ⓐ 🚌, 1236 Ⓐ 🚌 *, 1547 †, 1551 ⑤ 🚌, 1638 ⑥, 1754 ⑥ 🚌 *, 2022 Ⓐ 🚌; from Laon at 0819 Ⓐ, 0920 Ⓐ 🚌, 1021 † 🚌, 1047 ⑥, 1244 Ⓐ 🚌 *, 1444 †, 1515 ⑥, 1722 Ⓐ 🚌 *, 1726 †, 1815 ⑥, 1941 ⑥, 2006 †.

d – From Apr. 12.
e – Not Apr. 8 - May 27.
f – Not Apr. 3 - May 25.

FOR RETURN SERVICE SEE PREVIOUS PAGE.

263 ÉTAPLES - ARRAS

km																								
		Ⓐ	Ⓐ	⑥	①	⑥	Ⓐ	⑥	†	⑥	Ⓐ	†	Ⓐ	⑥	†	Ⓐ	Ⓐ	†	⑥	Ⓐ	Ⓒ	†	⑥	Ⓐ
0	**Étaples Le Touquet** d.	...	0515	0539	0626	0737	0830	0831	0831	1107	...	1152	1330	1349	1454	1526	1626	1637	1647	1737	1754	...	...	1900
12	Montreuil sur Mer d.	...	0525	0549	0635	0747	0840	0840	0840	1116	...	1201	1339	1359	1504	1535	1636	1647	1657	1746	1804	...	...	1910
33	Hesdin d.	...	0549	0615	0706	0813	0900	0911	0911	1147	...	1232	1410	1425	1530	1556	1700	1711	1717	1817	1830	...	...	1940
61	St Pol sur Ternoise a.	...	0614	0642	0732	0840	0924	0938	0938	1214	...	1259	1436	1452	1557	1620	1724	1736	1742	1844	1857	...	...	2007
61	St Pol sur Ternoise d.	0558	0629	0644	0734	0842	0926	0947	0954	1216	1243	1301	1438	1454	1600	1624	1731	1738	1744	1849	...	1922	1938	...
101	**Arras** a.	0635	0707	0721	0811	0919	1003	1024	1035	1253	1320	1338	1515	1531	1637	1701	1808	1815	1821	1926	...	2003	2019	...

	①	Ⓐ	Ⓐ	Ⓒ	⑥	Ⓐ	†	⑥	†	Ⓐ	⑥	Ⓐ	†	Ⓐ	⑥	Ⓐ	Ⓒ	Ⓐ	Ⓐ	†	⑥	⑤	†
Arras d.	...	...	0645	...	0857	0941	0955	1040	1124	1258	1450	1543	1556	1639	1700	1746	1753	...	1845	1922	1938	1939	...
St Pol sur Ternoise a.	...	...	0726	...	0938	1022	1031	1116	1201	1339	1531	1620	1637	1720	1737	1827	1840	...	1926	1959	2015	2015	...
St Pol sur Ternoise d.	0522	0636	...	0844	...	1032	1033	1118	1203	1341	1533	1632	1641	1747	...	...	...	1912	...	...	2017	...	2023
Hesdin d.	0547	0704	...	0909	...	1057	1100	1145	1230	1408	1600	1658	1709	1815	...	...	...	1938	...	...	2044	...	2051
Montreuil sur Mer d.	0606	0730	...	0932	...	1116	1125	1210	1255	1433	1625	1717	1734	1840	...	...	...	1957	...	...	2109	...	2116
Étaples Le Touquet a.	0615	0739	...	0941	...	1125	1134	1219	1304	1442	1634	1726	1743	1849	...	...	...	2006	...	...	2118	...	2125

265 ARRAS and LILLE - HAZEBROUCK - DUNKERQUE and CALAIS

See Table **250** for *TGV* and *TER-GV* services.

km																								
		Ⓐ	Ⓐ	⑤	⑥	Ⓐ		Ⓐ	⑥	Ⓐ	Ⓐ	⑥		Ⓐ	Ⓐ	⑥	Ⓐ	Ⓐ		Ⓐ	Ⓒ	Ⓒ	Ⓒ	Ⓐ
	Arras d.	...	...	...	...	...	...	0550	...	...	0615	...	...	...	0653	0705	...	0715	...	...	...	0805	...	...
	Lens d.	...	...	...	...	...	...	0608	...	...	0633	...	...	...	0709	0723	...	0733	...	...	...	0823	...	...
	Béthune d.	...	...	...	...	...	...	0626	...	...	0655	...	...	...	0726	0741	...	0755	...	...	...	0841	...	...
	Lillers d.	...	...	...	...	...	...	0635	...	...	0704	...	...	...	0735	0750	...	0804	...	...	...	0850	...	...
0	**Lille** Flandres d.	...	0540	...	...	0613	...	|	0639	0640	|	0705	...	0713	|	|	0740	|	...	0813	0813	|	0839	0840
22	Armentières d.	...	0554	...	...	0628	...	|	0653	0654	|	0721	...	0728	|	|	0754	|	...	0828	0829	|	0853	0854
47	Hazebrouck a.	...	0614	...	...	0646	...	0652	0710	0714	0721	0745	...	0746	0751	0806	0814	0821	...	0846	0852	0906	0910	0914
47	Hazebrouck d.	0523	0616	0623	0637	0648	...	0654	0712	0716	0723	0747	...	0748	0759	...	0816	0823	...	0848	0854	...	0912	0916
87	**Dunkerque** a.	|	0649	|	|	|	...	0728	|	0748	|	0819	...	|	0838	...	0848	|	...	|	0926	...	|	0948
68	St Omer d.	0541	...	0641	0656	0701	...	...	0724	...	0741	...	...	0801	...	...	...	0841	...	0901	...	...	0924	...
109	**Calais** Ville a.	0618	...	0718	0731	0728	...	...	0754	...	0818	...	...	0828	...	...	...	0918	...	0928	...	...	0954	...

	Ⓐ	⑤	Ⓐ	Ⓒ	Ⓐ		Ⓐ	Ⓐ	Ⓒ	Ⓒ	Ⓒ		⑤	Ⓐ	Ⓒ	⑥	Ⓐ		†	Ⓐ	Ⓐ	Ⓒ	Ⓒ
Arras d.	0815	...	0855	...	...	...	0915	...	1005	...	...	...	...	1155	1205	...	...	...	...	1215	1255	...	1305
Lens d.	0833	...	0909	...	...	...	0933	...	1023	...	...	...	...	1209	1223	...	...	...	...	1233	1309	...	1323
Béthune d.	0855	...	0926	...	...	...	0955	...	1041	...	...	...	...	1226	1241	...	...	...	...	1255	1326	...	1341
Lillers d.	0904	...	0935	...	...	...	1004	...	1050	...	...	...	...	1235	1250	...	...	...	...	1304	1335	...	1350
Lille Flandres d.	|	0913	|	0939	0940	...	|	1013	|	1039	1139	...	1213	|	|	1239	1240	...	1241	|	|	1313	|
Armentières d.	|	0928	|	0953	0954	...	|	1028	|	1053	1153	...	1228	|	|	1253	1254	...	1254	|	|	1329	|
Hazebrouck a.	0921	0946	0953	1010	1014	...	1022	1046	1106	1110	1210	...	1246	1251	1306	1310	1314	...	1311	1321	1350	1352	1406
Hazebrouck d.	0923	0948	...	1012	1016	...	...	1048	...	1112	1212	...	1248	1259	...	1311	1316	...	1313	1323	1352	1354	...
Dunkerque a.	|	|	...	1043	1048	...	...	|	...	|	1243	...	|	1338	...	|	1348	...	|	|	1426	1426	...
St Omer d.	0941	1001	...	...	...	...	...	1101	...	1124	...	...	1301	...	...	1325	...	...	1325	1341	...	...	...
Calais Ville a.	1018	1028	...	...	...	...	...	1128	...	1154	...	...	1330	...	...	1353	...	...	1354	1418	...	...	...

	⑥	Ⓐ	Ⓐ	Ⓐ	Ⓐ	Ⓒ		Ⓒ	Ⓒ	Ⓐ	Ⓐ	Ⓐ	Ⓒ	Ⓐ	Ⓐ	Ⓐ	Ⓐ		Ⓒ	Ⓐ	⑥	Ⓐ	Ⓐ
Arras d.	...	...	1321	...	...	...	...	1506	...	...	...	...	...	...	1615	...	1655	...	1706	...	...	...	...
Lens d.	...	...	1339	...	...	...	...	1523	...	...	...	...	...	...	1633	...	1709	...	1724	...	...	...	...
Béthune d.	...	...	1358	...	...	...	...	1540	...	...	...	...	...	...	1655	...	1726	...	1741	...	...	...	...
Lillers d.	...	...	1407	...	...	...	...	1549	...	...	...	...	...	...	1704	...	1735	...	1750	...	...	...	...
Lille Flandres d.	1339	1340	|	1413	...	1439	...	|	1539	1540	...	1613	1639	1640	|	1713	|	...	|	1732	1739	1740	...
Armentières d.	1353	1354	|	1428	...	1453	...	|	1553	1554	...	1628	1653	1654	|	1728	|	...	|	1747	1753	1754	...
Hazebrouck a.	1410	1414	1425	1446	...	1510	...	1606	1610	1614	...	1646	1710	1714	1721	1746	1752	...	1806	1807	1810	1814	...
Hazebrouck d.	1412	1416	1427	1448	1459	1512	...	...	1612	1616	1623	1648	1712	1716	1723	1748	1759	...	...	1809	1812	1816	1823
Dunkerque a.	1443	1450	|	|	1538	|	...	...	1645	1648	|	|	|	1748	|	|	1838	...	...	|	1843	1848	|
St Omer d.	...	...	1444	1501	...	1524	...	...	...	...	1641	1701	1724	...	1741	1801	...	...	...	1824	...	...	1841
Calais Ville a.	...	...	1520	1528	...	1554	...	...	...	...	1718	1728	1754	...	1818	1828	...	...	...	...	...	...	1919

FOR ADDITIONAL TRAINS AND FOOTNOTES SEE NEXT PAGE →

ARRAS and LILLE - HAZEBROUCK - DUNKERQUE and CALAIS 265

See Table **250** for *TGV* and *TER-GV* services.

	Ⓐ	Ⓐ	Ⓒ	Ⓐ	Ⓐ	Ⓒ	Ⓐ		Ⓐ	Ⓐ	Ⓐ	Ⓒ	Ⓒ	Ⓐ	Ⓐ		Ⓐ	Ⓒ	Ⓐ	Ⓐ	Ⓐ	Ⓐ	Ⓒ
Arras d.	1712	...	...	1755	...	...	...	...	1815	...	1855	1905	...	...	1915	...	...	...	...	...	...	2055	...
Lens d.	1735	...	...	1811	...	...	...	...	1833	...	1909	1923	...	...	1933	...	...	...	...	...	...	2109	...
Béthune d.	1759	...	...	1829	...	...	...	...	1855	...	1926	1941	...	...	1955	...	...	...	...	...	...	2126	...
Lillers d.	1812	...	...	1838	...	...	...	...	1904	...	1935	1950	...	...	2004	...	...	...	...	...	...	2135	...
Lille Flandres d.	|	1813	1813	|	1832	1839	1840	...	|	1913	|	|	1939	1940	|	...	2013	2039	2040	...	2113	|	2139
Armentières d.	|	1828	1829	|	1847	1853	1854	...	|	1928	|	|	1953	1954	|	...	2028	2053	2054	...	2128	|	2153
Hazebrouck a.	1835	1846	1852	1854	1907	1910	1914	...	1921	1946	1953	2006	2010	2014	2021	...	2046	2110	2114	...	2146	2151	2210
Hazebrouck d.	...	1848	1854	1859	1909	1912	1916	...	1923	1948	1959	...	2012	2016	2023	...	2048	2112	2116	2123	2148	2159	2212
Dunkerque a.	...	|	1926	1938	|	|	1948	...	|	|	2038	...	2043	2048	|	...	|	|	2148	|	|	2238	2243
St Omer d.	...	1901	...	...	1924	1924	...	...	1941	2001	...	...	...	...	2041	...	2101	2124	...	2141	2201	...	...
Calais Ville a.	...	1928	...	...	...	1954	...	...	2018	2028	...	...	...	...	2118	...	2128	2154	...	2218	2230	...	...
	Ⓐ	Ⓐ	Ⓐ	⑥	Ⓐ	Ⓐ	Ⓐ	Ⓐ	⑥	Ⓐ	⑥		Ⓐ	⑥	Ⓐ	Ⓐ	Ⓐ	⑥	Ⓐ	Ⓒ	Ⓐ	Ⓒ	⑤
Calais Ville d.	...	...	...	...	0531	...	0542	...	0606	...	...	...	...	...	0631	0642	...	...	...	...	...	...	0731
St Omer d.	...	...	...	...	0559	...	0619	...	0636	0638	...	...	...	...	0659	0719	...	...	0738	...	...	...	0759
Dunkerque d.	...	...	0512	0533	|	...	|	0612	|	|	...	...	0627	0633	|	|	0712	0717	|	...	0732	0733	|
Hazebrouck a.	...	...	0544	0605	0613	...	0636	0644	0648	0651	...	...	0700	0705	0713	0736	0744	0748	0751	...	0806	0805	0813
Hazebrouck d.	0508	0538	0546	0607	0615	0623	...	0646	0650	0653	0654	...	0702	0707	0715	0738	0746	0750	0753	0754	0808	0807	0815
Armentières d.	|	|	0606	0631	0633	|	...	0706	0707	0713	|	...	|	0731	0733	|	0806	0807	0813	|	|	0831	0833
Lille Flandres a.	|	|	0620	0647	0647	|	...	0720	0721	0728	|	...	|	0747	0747	|	0820	0821	0828	|	|	0847	0847
Lillers d.	0524	0557	...	...	...	0645	...	...	...	...	0711	...	0718	...	...	0757	...	...	...	0811	0824	...	...
Béthune d.	0534	0607	...	...	...	0700	...	...	...	...	0721	...	0728	...	...	0807	...	...	...	0822	0834	...	...
Lens d.	0552	0628	...	...	...	0726	...	...	...	...	0738	...	0746	...	...	0828	...	...	...	0839	0852	...	...
Arras a.	0607	0645	...	...	...	0747	...	...	...	...	0755	...	0800	...	...	0845	...	...	...	0856	0905	...	...
	Ⓐ	Ⓐ	Ⓒ	Ⓐ	Ⓐ	Ⓐ	Ⓐ		Ⓒ	Ⓒ	Ⓐ	Ⓐ	Ⓒ	Ⓐ	†		Ⓐ	⑥	†	⑥	Ⓐ	Ⓐ	Ⓒ
Calais Ville d.	0742	...	0806	...	0831	0842	...	...	...	...	...	0942	1006	...	...	...	...	...	...	...	1131	...	1206
St Omer d.	0819	...	0836	...	0859	0919	...	...	...	...	...	1019	1036	...	...	...	...	...	...	...	1159	...	1237
Dunkerque d.	|	0812	|	0832	|	|	0912	...	0917	...	...	|	|	...	1112	...	1112	1117	...	...	|	...	|
Hazebrouck a.	0836	0844	0848	0906	0913	0936	0944	...	0948	...	...	1036	1048	...	1144	...	1144	1148	...	...	1213	...	1249
Hazebrouck d.	...	0846	0850	0908	0915	0938	0946	...	0950	0954	1008	...	1050	1108	1146	...	1146	1150	1154	1154	1215	1238	1251
Armentières d.	...	0906	0907	|	0933	|	1006	...	1007	|	|	...	1107	|	1204	...	1206	1207	|	|	1233	|	1308
Lille Flandres a.	...	0920	0921	|	0947	|	1020	...	1021	|	|	...	1121	|	1219	...	1220	1221	|	|	1247	|	1322
Lillers d.	...	...	...	0924	...	0957	...	...	...	1010	1024	...	...	1124	...	...	...	...	1211	1211	...	1257	...
Béthune d.	...	...	...	0934	...	1007	...	...	...	1020	1034	...	...	1134	...	...	...	...	1221	1221	...	1307	...
Lens d.	...	...	...	0952	...	1028	...	...	...	1038	1052	...	...	1152	...	...	...	...	1238	1239	...	1328	...
Arras a.	...	...	...	1005	...	1045	...	...	...	1056	1105	...	...	1205	...	...	...	...	1255	1255	...	1345	...
	Ⓐ	Ⓒ	⑥	Ⓐ	⑥	Ⓒ	Ⓒ	Ⓐ	Ⓐ	Ⓐ	⑥		†	⑥	†	⑤	Ⓐ	Ⓐ	Ⓒ	Ⓐ	Ⓐ	Ⓐ	Ⓐ
Calais Ville d.	...	...	1242	1242	...	...	1406	...	1431	...	...	...	...	...	...	1531	1542	...	1606	...	1631	1642	...
St Omer d.	...	...	1318	1319	...	...	1436	...	1459	...	...	...	...	...	...	1559	1619	...	1636	...	1659	1719	...
Dunkerque d.	1232	1233	|	|	1317	...	|	1432	|	1512	1517	...	1517	...	...	|	|	1612	|	1632	|	|	1712
Hazebrouck a.	1307	1305	1336	1336	1348	...	1448	1506	1513	1544	1547	...	1548	...	...	1613	1636	1644	1648	1706	1713	1736	1744
Hazebrouck d.	...	1307	...	...	1350	1354	1450	1508	1515	1546	1549	...	1550	1554	1559	1615	1638	1646	1650	1708	1715	1738	1746
Armentières d.	...	1331	...	...	1407	|	1507	|	1533	1606	1607	...	1607	|	|	1633	|	1706	1707	|	1733	|	1806
Lille Flandres a.	...	1347	...	...	1421	|	1521	|	1547	1620	1621	...	1621	|	|	1647	|	1720	1721	|	1747	|	1820
Lillers d.	...	...	...	...	...	1411	...	1524	...	...	...	...	...	1610	1615	...	1657	...	...	1724	...	1757	...
Béthune d.	...	...	...	...	...	1421	...	1534	...	...	...	...	...	1619	1625	...	1707	...	...	1734	...	1807	...
Lens d.	...	...	...	...	...	1438	...	1552	...	...	...	...	...	1636	1641	...	1728	...	...	1752	...	1828	...
Arras a.	...	...	...	...	...	1456	...	1606	...	...	...	...	...	1651	1656	...	1745	...	...	1806	...	1845	...
	⑥	Ⓒ	Ⓒ	Ⓐ	Ⓐ	Ⓐ	⑥		†	Ⓐ	Ⓐ	Ⓐ	Ⓐ	Ⓒ	Ⓒ		Ⓐ	Ⓐ	Ⓐ	Ⓐ	Ⓒ	Ⓐ	Ⓐ
Calais Ville d.	...	...	...	1731	1742	...	1806	...	1806	...	1831	1842	...	...	...	...	...	1931	1942	...	2006	...	2031
St Omer d.	...	...	...	1759	1819	...	1835	...	1836	...	1859	1919	...	...	...	...	...	1959	2019	...	2036	...	2059
Dunkerque d.	1717	...	1733	|	|	1812	|	...	|	1838	|	|	1912	1917	...	...	1932	|	|	2012	|	2032	|
Hazebrouck a.	1748	...	1805	1813	1836	1844	1847	...	1849	1906	1913	1936	1944	1948	...	...	2006	2013	2036	2044	2048	2107	2113
Hazebrouck d.	1750	1754	1807	1815	1838	1846	1849	...	1851	1908	1915	...	1946	1950	1954	...	2008	2015	...	2046	2050	...	2115
Armentières d.	1807	|	1831	1833	|	1906	1907	...	1907	|	1933	...	2006	2007	|	...	|	2033	...	2106	2107	...	2133
Lille Flandres a.	1821	|	1847	1847	|	1920	1921	...	1921	|	1947	...	2020	2021	|	...	|	2047	...	2120	2121	...	2147
Lillers d.	...	1811	...	...	1857	...	...	...	...	1924	...	...	...	...	2011	...	2024	...	...	...	...	...	...
Béthune d.	...	1821	...	...	1907	...	...	...	...	1934	...	...	...	...	2021	...	2034	...	...	...	...	...	...
Lens d.	...	1838	...	...	1928	...	...	...	...	1952	...	...	...	...	2038	...	2052	...	...	...	...	...	...
Arras a.	...	1855	...	...	1945	...	...	...	...	2005	...	...	...	...	2056	...	2105	...	...	...	...	...	...

FOR ADDITIONAL SERVICES SEE PREVIOUS PAGE.

ST POL SUR TERNOISE - BÉTHUNE - LILLE 266

km																								
		Ⓐ	Ⓐ	⑥		Ⓐ	Ⓐ	Ⓐ		Ⓐ	⑥	Ⓐ		Ⓐ	Ⓐ	Ⓐ		†	⑥	Ⓐ		Ⓐ 🚌	Ⓐ	
0	**St Pol sur Ternoise** d.	...	0544	...	...	...	...	0639	...	...	0702	...	...	...	0739	...	...	...	...	...	...	0801	...	...
32	Béthune d.	0549	0618	0638	...	0645	0649	0711	...	0718	0736	0745	...	0749	0811	0818	...	0836	0839	0849	...	0908	0918	...
74	**Lille** Flandres a.	0644	0654	0730	...	0724	0744	...	...	0754	0829	0824	...	0844	...	0854	...	0929	0917	0944	...	...	0954	...
		⑥	⑥	Ⓐ 🚌		†	Ⓐ	Ⓐ		Ⓐ	⑥	†		Ⓐ	⑥	†		Ⓐ	⑥	Ⓐ		Ⓐ	†	
	St Pol sur Ternoise d.	0904	0959	1001	...	1005	...	...	...	...	1202	...	...	1215	...	...	...	1444	1503	...	...	...	1602	...
	Béthune d.	0938	1033	1108	...	1039	1118	1149	...	1218	1236	1236	...	1249	1337	1439	...	1518	1536	1549	...	1618	1636	...
	Lille Flandres a.	1018	1116	...	...	1117	1154	1244	...	1254	1329	1329	...	1344	1415	1517	...	1554	1617	1644	...	1654	1717	...
		Ⓐ	⑥	Ⓐ 🚌		Ⓐ	Ⓐ	Ⓐ		Ⓒ	Ⓐ	Ⓐ		Ⓒ	Ⓐ 🚌	Ⓒ		Ⓐ	Ⓐ	Ⓐ		Ⓐ		
	St Pol sur Ternoise d.	...	...	1628	...	...	...	1744	...	1802	...	...	...	...	1828	1859	...	...	...	...	...	...	...	...
	Béthune d.	1649	1739	1735	...	1745	1749	1818	...	1836	1845	1849	...	1939	1935	1931	...	1945	1949	2018	...	2045	...	...
	Lille Flandres a.	1744	1817	...	...	1824	1844	1854	...	1929	1924	1944	...	2017	...	...	...	2024	2044	2054	...	2124	...	...
		Ⓐ 🚌	Ⓐ	Ⓐ	Ⓐ 🚌		⑥	Ⓐ	Ⓐ 🚌	Ⓒ		Ⓐ	⑥	Ⓐ	Ⓐ		Ⓐ	Ⓐ	†	⑥		Ⓐ	⑥	†
	Lille Flandres d.	...	0615	0636	...	...	0642	0706	...	...	...	0715	0731	0736	0806	...	0815	...	0831	0842	...	0906	0954	1042
	Béthune d.	0700	0712	0715	0725	...	0722	0742	0752	0810	...	0812	0823	0815	0842	...	0912	0922	0924	0922	...	0942	1035	1124
	St Pol sur Ternoise a.	0807	...	...	0832	...	...	...	0859	0842	...	...	...	...	...	...	...	0954	...	...	...	...	1106	1156
		Ⓐ 🚌	⑥	Ⓐ	Ⓐ		†	⑥	Ⓐ	Ⓐ		⑥	Ⓐ	†	Ⓐ		⑥	Ⓐ	Ⓐ	⑥		Ⓐ	†	Ⓐ 🚌
	Lille Flandres d.	...	1141	1206	1215	...	1231	1231	1306	1315	...	1350	1406	1442	1515	...	1542	1606	1615	1631	...	1636	1642	...
	Béthune d.	1222	1220	1242	1312	...	1324	1325	1349	1412	...	1430	1442	1522	1612	...	1628	1644	1712	1724	...	1715	1724	1725
	St Pol sur Ternoise a.	1329	...	...	...	...	...	1356	1421	...	...	...	...	...	...	...	1659	1715	...	...	...	...	1756	1832
		Ⓐ	Ⓐ	Ⓐ	⑥		Ⓐ	Ⓐ	†	⑥		Ⓐ	Ⓐ	†	Ⓐ		Ⓐ	⑥	Ⓐ	Ⓐ		Ⓒ	Ⓐ	
	Lille Flandres d.	1706	1715	1736	1742	...	...	1815	1831	1831	...	1836	1906	...	1915	...	1936	1942	2015	2036	...	2042	2106	...
	Béthune d.	1742	1812	1815	1822	...	1832	1912	1924	1935	...	1915	1944	1950	2012	...	2024	2028	2112	2117	...	2112	2145	...
	St Pol sur Ternoise a.	...	...	...	...	...	1904	...	...	2007	...	...	2016	2021	...	...	...	2059	...	...	...	...	...	...

267 PARIS - BEAUVAIS - CREIL

km			Ⓐ	⑥	Ⓐ	Ⓐ	Ⓒ	Ⓐ	Ⓒ	Ⓐ			⚒	Ⓒ	⑥	Ⓐ		⑥	Ⓐ	Ⓐ	†	⑥	Ⓐ	⚒	Ⓑ	Ⓒ
0	**Paris** Nord	d.	0607	0631	0637	0737	0801	0850	0901	1001	1101	1201	1301	1401	1601	1607	1701	1801	1807	1837	1844	1901	1907	2001	2101	2201
	Persan-Beaumont	d.	0638	0712	0709	0809	0834	0924	0936	1036	1136	1236	1336	1436	1634	1638	1738	1835	1838	|	1928	1934	1937	2034	2136	2236
80	**Beauvais**	a.	0720	0752	0751	0851	0918	1005	1019	1118	1218	1318	1418	1518	1720	1720	1820	1920	1920	1947	2010	2020	2020	2118	2218	2319

		Ⓐ	⚒	Ⓐ	Ⓒ	Ⓐ	Ⓐ		⚒	†		⑥		⚒		⚒	Ⓐ		Ⓐ		⑥	†	Ⓐ	Ⓒ	†
Beauvais	d.	0513	0540	0613	0627	0640	0710	0740	0840	0940	1040	1140	1240	1340	1440	1640	1710	1740	1810	1843	1940	1951	2010	2040	2140
Persan-Beaumont	d.	|	0623	|	0710	0723	|	0823	0923	1022	1122	1222	1322	1422	1522	1723	1754	1823	1854	1923	2021	2032	2053	2123	2223
Paris Nord	a.	0625	0657	0725	0742	0755	0825	0857	0957	1057	1157	1257	1357	1457	1557	1757	1825	1857	1925	1957	2057	2109	2128	2159	2257

km			Ⓐ	Ⓐ	⑥	Ⓐ	Ⓐ	Ⓐ	⑥		†	Ⓐ	⑥	Ⓐ	†	Ⓐ	⑥	⚒		Ⓐ	Ⓐ	Ⓒ	Ⓐ	Ⓐ	†	⑥
0	**Beauvais**	d.	0529	0609	0636	0657	0753	0822	0920	...	0930	0947	1045	1144	1255	1300	1305	1609	...	1651	1736	1736	1804	1850	2025	2044
37	**Creil**	a.	0616	0644	0714	0749	0833	0906	1008	...	1007	1023	1121	1223	1334	1350	1352	1645	...	1743	1819	1826	1856	1934	2112	2132

		Ⓐ	Ⓐ	⑥	†	Ⓐ	⑥	Ⓐ	Ⓐ	†	⑥	Ⓐ	Ⓐ		⑥	Ⓒ	Ⓐ	⑥	⑥	Ⓐ	Ⓐ	Ⓐ	Ⓒ	Ⓐ	Ⓐ🚌
Creil	d.	0642	0721	0726	0830	0900	0927	1034	1133	1200	1212	1310	1359	...	1403	1646	1656	1716	1745	1753	1829	1906	1915	1948	2044
Beauvais	a.	0734	0811	0814	0909	0937	1007	1110	1211	1238	1249	1349	1449	...	1451	1724	1739	1802	1824	1841	1916	1956	2004	2024	2207

268 BEAUVAIS - LE TRÉPORT

km			Ⓐ	⑥		Ⓐ🚌	†		⑥	Ⓐ		⑥	Ⓐ		†	Ⓐ		⑥	⑥		⑤					
0	**Beauvais**	d.	...	...	...	0730	0938	...	0938	1235	...	1238	1528	...	1838	1839	...	1849	2038	...	2039	...	...	...	...	...
49	Abancourt ⊖	d.	0648	0742	...	0842	1025	...	1031	1325	...	1331	1621	...	1931	1926	...	1935	2124	...	2125	...	...	...	...	...
103	Eu	d.	0732	0826	...	0950	1109	...	1115	1409	...	1415	1705	...	2016	2011	...	2019	2208	...	2210	...	...	...	...	...
106	**Le Tréport**	a.	0736	0831	...	1005	1114	...	1120	1413	...	1420	1709	...	2020	2015	...	2024	2213	...	2214	...	...	...	...	...

		Ⓐ	Ⓐ🚌		Ⓐ	⑥		†	⑥		Ⓐ	Ⓐ		Ⓒ	Ⓐ		⑥	Ⓐ		†					
Le Tréport	d.	...	0535	...	...	0647	...	0735	0935	...	0954	1229	...	1235	1525	...	1736	1751	...	1835	...	...	...	...	...
Eu	d.	...	0550	...	...	0652	...	0740	0940	...	0959	1234	...	1240	1530	...	1741	1756	...	1840	...	...	...	...	...
Abancourt ⊖	d.	0610	0658	...	0708	0737	...	0826	1026	...	1044	1323	...	1326	1616	...	1827	1856	...	1926	...	...	...	...	...
Beauvais	a.	0655	...	...	0753	0822	...	0911	1111	...	1128	1408	...	1411	1700	...	1912	1946	...	2011	...	...	...	...	...

⊖ – For connections to / from Rouen see Table **253**.

270 PARIS - ROUEN - LE HAVRE

km			Ⓐ	⑥	Ⓐ	Ⓐ	Ⓐ	Ⓐ	⑥	Ⓐ ◧	⑥	⚒	Ⓒ ◧	Ⓐ ◧	Ⓒ	Ⓐ	Ⓐ ◧	Ⓒ ◧	⑥ A◧	† ◧	⑥ ◧	Ⓒ	Ⓐ	Ⓒ	◧	Ⓒ
0	**Paris** St Lazare	d.	...	...	...	0546	...	0609	0612	0640	...	0712	0740	0740	0812	0814	0840	0840	0912	0940	0940	...	1011	1012	1040	1112
57	Mantes la Jolie	d.	...	...	...	|	...	0649	0652	|	...	|	|	|	0852	0849	|	|	|	|	|	...	1050	1052	|	|
79	Vernon-Giverny	d.	...	...	...	0636	...	0705	0711	|	...	0804	|	|	0911	0905	|	|	|	|	|	...	1104	1111	|	1205
111	Val de Reuil	d.	...	...	...	0654	...	0723	0729	|	...	0823	|	|	0930	0925	|	|	|	|	|	...	1125	1130	|	1225
126	Oissel	d.	...	...	...	0703	...	0734	0739	|	...	0834	|	|	0939	0934	|	|	|	|	|	...	1134	1139	|	1234
140	**Rouen** Rive-Droite	a.	0600	0606	0640	0713	0722	0746	0748	0759	0807	0845	0859	0901	0948	0944	0957	1000	1032	1104	1104	1110	1144	1148	1159	1244
178	Yvetot	a.	0625	0631	0705	...	0747	...	...	0820	0834	...	0919	0922	...	...	1018	1021	...	1125	1127	1135	...	...	1220	...
203	Bréauté-Beuzeville	a.	0640	0644	0719	...	0802	...	...	0833	0847	...	0932	0935	...	...	1032	1034	...	1138	1142	1148	...	...	1234	...
228	**Le Havre**	a.	0657	0700	0735	...	0818	...	...	0850	0903	...	0946	0949	...	...	1046	1049	...	1152	1201	1205	...	...	1250	...

		⑥ ◧	Ⓐ	⑥	Ⓐ	Ⓒ	Ⓐ ◧	Ⓒ ◧	Ⓐ ◧	Ⓒ ◧	⑥	Ⓐ	Ⓒ	Ⓐ ◧	Ⓒ ◧	⑥ ◧	Ⓐ ◧	⑥	Ⓐ	Ⓐ	Ⓒ	Ⓐ ◧	Ⓒ ◧	Ⓐ	Ⓐ
Paris St Lazare	d.	1140	...	...	1212	1212	1240	1240	1340	1340	...	1412	1412	1440	1440	1540	1540	...	...	1611	1612	1640	1640	1650	...
Mantes la Jolie	d.	|	...	...	1250	1252	|	|	|	|	...	1451	1452	|	|	|	|	...	...	1650	1652	|	|	1728	...
Vernon-Giverny	d.	|	...	...	1305	1311	|	|	|	|	...	1506	1511	|	|	|	|	...	...	1706	1711	|	|	1749	...
Val de Reuil	d.	|	...	...	1325	1330	|	|	|	|	...	1525	1530	|	|	|	|	...	...	1726	1731	|	|	1808	...
Oissel	d.	|	...	...	1334	1339	|	|	|	|	...	1534	1539	|	|	|	|	...	...	1736	1741	|	|	1817	...
Rouen Rive-Droite	a.	1259	1305	1307	1344	1348	1359	1402	1459	1501	1510	1544	1548	1559	1603	1659	1659	1712	1735	1746	1750	1759	1803	1826	1835
Yvetot	a.	|	1332	1334	...	...	1420	1423	1520	1521	1535	...	...	1620	1623	|	1720	1736	1800	...	...	1820	1823	...	1900
Bréauté-Beuzeville	a.	|	1346	1347	...	...	1433	1436	1533	1535	1548	...	...	1633	1637	|	1733	1749	1815	...	...	1833	1837	...	1915
Le Havre	a.	1341	1403	1403	...	...	1448	1450	1548	1549	1604	...	...	1648	1650	1741	1748	1805	1831	...	...	1848	1851	...	1931

		Ⓑ	⑥	Ⓒ ◧	Ⓐ ◧	Ⓒ	Ⓐ	Ⓐ	Ⓒ	Ⓒ ◧	Ⓐ ◧	Ⓐ		Ⓒ ◧	Ⓐ ◧	Ⓐ	Ⓒ	Ⓐ ◧	Ⓒ ◧	†	Ⓐ	Ⓒ ◧	⑤ ◧	Ⓐ	Ⓒ
Paris St Lazare	d.	1712	1712	1740	1740	...	1749	1811	1812	1840	1840	1850	1911	1940	1940	2012	2012	2040	2040	2112	2112	2140	2140	2209	2212
Mantes la Jolie	d.	|	1752	|	|	...	|	1852	1852	|	|	|	|	|	|	2051	2051	|	|	|	2150	|	|	2247	2252
Vernon-Giverny	d.	1805	1807	|	|	...	1843	1910	1911	|	|	1942	2005	|	|	2107	2111	|	|	2205	2205	|	|	2335*	2307
Val de Reuil	d.	1825	1826	|	|	...	1903	1928	1930	|	|	2002	2025	|	|	2127	2130	|	|	2224	2225	|	|	0025*	2326
Oissel	d.	1834	1834	|	|	...	1913	1937	1939	|	|	2013	2034	|	|	2137	2139	|	|	2234	2234	|	|	0045*	2335
Rouen Rive-Droite	a.	1844	1844	1902	1903	1907	1923	1947	1948	2003	2004	2023	2044	2101	2106	2147	2148	2159	2203	2244	2245	2301	2303	0110*	2344
Yvetot	a.	...	...	|	1924	1932	...	...	...	2023	2025	...	...	|	|	...	...	2220	2223	...	...	|	|	...	...
Bréauté-Beuzeville	a.	...	...	|	1938	1945	...	...	...	2037	2038	...	...	|	|	...	...	2233	2237	...	...	|	|	...	...
Le Havre	a.	...	...	1944	1952	2001	...	...	...	2050	2053	...	...	2143	2148	...	...	2248	2250	...	...	2343	2345	...	...

		Ⓐ	Ⓐ	⑥	Ⓐ	Ⓐ ◧	Ⓐ	Ⓐ	Ⓐ	⑥	†	Ⓐ ◧	Ⓐ		⑥	Ⓒ ◧	Ⓐ ◧	Ⓒ	Ⓐ	Ⓐ	Ⓐ ◧	Ⓒ ◧	Ⓐ	Ⓒ	Ⓒ
Le Havre	d.	...	...	...	...	0520	...	...	0602	...	...	0630	...	...	0633	0706	0708	...	...	0733	0806	0806	...	...	0844
Bréauté-Beuzeville	d.	...	...	...	...	0535	...	...	0619	...	...	0645	...	...	0650	0721	0723	...	...	0750	0820	0921	...	...	0905
Yvetot	d.	...	...	...	...	0549	...	...	0635	...	...	0659	...	...	0704	0735	0737	...	...	0806	0834	0835	...	...	0918
Rouen Rive-Droite	d.	0517	0544	0604	0606	0613	0639	0700	0700	0717	0717	0724	0739	...	0729	0800	0801	0810	0816	0831	0859	0900	0915	0917	0943
Oissel	d.	0526	0553	0614	0616	|	0649	0711	...	0727	0726	|	0749	...	...	|	|	0820	0826	...	|	|	0925	0927	...
Val de Reuil	d.	0535	0603	0623	0632	|	0658	0719	...	0736	0735	|	0758	...	...	|	|	0829	0835	...	|	|	0934	0936	...
Vernon-Giverny	d.	0557	0625	0645	0655	|	0720	0741	...	0758	0755	|	0820	...	...	|	|	0849	0857	...	|	|	0956	0956	...
Mantes la Jolie	a.	0612	0642	0706	0710	|	|	0757	...	|	0810	|	|	...	...	|	|	0910	0913	...	|	|	1012	1012	...
Paris St Lazare	a.	0654	0718	0748	0750	0739	0816	0836	...	0848	0848	0839	0917	...	...	0923	0920	0948	0949	...	1023	1023	1048	1048	...

		Ⓒ	Ⓒ	Ⓐ	Ⓐ ◧	Ⓒ ◧	⑥	Ⓐ	Ⓒ	† ◧	Ⓒ	Ⓐ	Ⓒ ◧	Ⓐ ◧	Ⓐ	Ⓒ	⚒	Ⓐ ◧	⑥ ◧	Ⓒ	Ⓐ ◧	Ⓒ ◧	Ⓐ	◧	Ⓒ
Le Havre	d.	0906	...	...	1006	1006	...	1027	1029	1114	...	...	1206	1208	...	...	1233	1313	1314	...	1407	1408	1433	1508	...
Bréauté-Beuzeville	d.	0921	...	...	1020	1021	...	1047	1047	|	...	...	1221	1222	...	...	1250	|	|	...	1421	1422	1450	1522	...
Yvetot	d.	0935	...	...	1034	1035	...	1102	1102	|	...	...	1235	1236	...	...	1304	|	|	...	1435	1436	1504	1536	...
Rouen Rive-Droite	d.	1000	1011	1015	1059	1100	1116	1128	1128	1200	1211	1216	1300	1301	1315	1317	1329	1359	1400	1411	1500	1500	1529	1600	1611
Oissel	d.	|	1021	1024	|	|	1126	...	...	|	1221	1225	|	|	1325	1327	...	|	|	1421	|	|	...	|	1621
Val de Reuil	d.	|	1030	1033	|	|	1135	...	...	|	1230	1234	|	|	1333	1336	...	|	|	1430	|	|	...	|	1630
Vernon-Giverny	d.	|	1050	1055	|	|	1155	...	...	|	1250	1255	|	|	1355	1357	...	|	|	1450	|	|	...	|	1650
Mantes la Jolie	a.	|	1110	1110	|	|	1210	...	...	|	1310	|	|	|	1410	|	...	|	|	1510	|	|	...	|	1710
Paris St Lazare	a.	1122	1148	1148	1223	1223	1248	...	...	1323	1348	1348	1423	1423	1448	1448	...	1523	1523	1548	1623	1623	...	1723	1748

		Ⓐ	Ⓒ ◧	Ⓐ	Ⓐ	Ⓒ	Ⓒ ◧	Ⓐ ◧	Ⓒ	Ⓐ	Ⓐ ◧	Ⓒ ◧	† A◧		Ⓐ	Ⓒ ◧	Ⓐ ◧	Ⓒ	Ⓐ	Ⓐ	Ⓒ	Ⓐ ◧	Ⓒ ◧	Ⓒ	Ⓒ ◧
Le Havre	d.	...	1606	1607	...	...	1706	1708	...	...	1806	1806	...	...	...	1908	1908	...	...	1931	1933	2006	2014	...	2107
Bréauté-Beuzeville	d.	...	1620	1623	...	...	1721	1722	...	...	1820	1821	...	...	...	1922	1922	...	...	1948	1950	2020	|	...	2121
Yvetot	d.	...	1634	1637	...	...	1735	1736	...	...	1834	1835	...	...	...	1936	1936	...	...	2004	2004	2034	|	...	2135
Rouen Rive-Droite	d.	1615	1658	1658	1713	1717	1800	1801	1811	1814	1859	1900	1915	...	1917	2000	2001	2011	2017	2028	2029	2059	2100	2117	2200
Oissel	d.	1625	|	...	1723	1727	|	|	1821	1824	|	|	|	...	1927	|	|	2021	2026	...	...	|	|	2127	|
Val de Reuil	d.	1634	|	...	1734	1736	|	|	1830	1836	|	|	|	...	1936	|	|	2030	2035	...	...	|	|	2136	|
Vernon-Giverny	d.	1656	|	...	1757	1756	|	|	1852	1858	|	|	|	...	1956	|	|	2050	2056	...	...	|	|	2155	|
Mantes la Jolie	a.	|	|	...	|	|	|	|	1912	1914	|	|	|	...	2014	|	|	2110	|	...	...	|	|	2210	|
Paris St Lazare	a.	1748	1823	...	1849	1849	1923	1923	1948	1949	2023	2025	2048	...	2048	2123	2123	2148	2150	...	...	2223	2223	2248	2323

A – To / from Dieppe (Table **270a**). ◧ – 🅁 for journeys to / from Paris. * – Connection by 🚌.

FÉCAMP - LE HAVRE 270

For other trains Bréauté-Beuzeville - Le Havre and v.v. see previous page.

km		Ⓐ 🚌	Ⓐ	Ⓐ 🚌	†	⚒	†	⚒	† 🚌	†	⑥	Ⓐ 🚌	†		⚒	⑥	†	†	Ⓐ 🚌	⑥	Ⓑ		Ⓐ 🚌	⑥ 🚌	Ⓑ
0	**Fécamp** d.	0600	0645	0709	0733	0752	0933	0933	0953	1133	1134	1153	1333	...	1333	1532	1533	1633	1641	1733	1733	1833	1857	1905	1933
20	Bréauté-Beuzeville d.	0630	0707	0739	0754	0814	0954	0955	1023	1154	1156	1223	1354	...	1355	1552	1554	1655	1711	1754	1755	1853	1927	1935	1954
45	**Le Havre** a.	...	0729	...	...	0836	...	1017	...	...	1218	...	...	...	1417	1615	...	1717	...	...	1817	1917	...	...	...

	Ⓐ 🚌	Ⓐ 🚌	⚒	⑥ 🚌	†	Ⓐ 🚌	†	⑥		Ⓒ	Ⓐ 🚌	Ⓐ	Ⓒ	Ⓐ 🚌		Ⓐ 🚌	†	⚒	⑥ 🚌	Ⓐ	†	⑥ 🚌	Ⓑ	⑤ 🚌
Le Havre d.	...	...	0830	...	...	...	...	1037	1237	1437	...	1637	...	...	1736	...	...	1837	...	1937	...	...	...	...
Bréauté-Beuzeville d.	0730	0759	0855	0930	1001	1055	1101	1101	1301	1501	1458	1701	1701	1731	1801	1830	1901	1902	1958	2001	2001	2045	2101	2242
Fécamp a.	0800	0829	0915	1000	1021	1125	1121	1121	1321	1521	1528	1721	1721	1801	1821	1900	1921	1921	2028	2021	2021	2115	2121	2312

ROUEN - DIEPPE 270a

km		⑥	Ⓐ	Ⓐ	Ⓐ	⚒	Ⓐ	⑥ A	†		⑥	Ⓐ	Ⓒ		⚒	Ⓐ	Ⓐ	†	⚒		Ⓑ	Ⓐ	⑥	Ⓐ	
0	**Rouen** Rive-Droite d.	0646	0646	0718	0746	0910	1011	1032	1046	1210	1246	1346	1410	...	1610	1646	1709	1710	1746	1810	1846	1910	1912	2009	2124
63	**Dieppe** a.	0743	0747	0803	0847	0959	1059	1117	1147	1259	1349	1449	1459	...	1659	1747	1800	1759	1847	1859	1947	2000	1959	2059	2210

	Ⓐ	Ⓐ	⑥	⚒	Ⓐ	Ⓒ	Ⓐ	Ⓐ	⚒	†		Ⓐ	⑥	Ⓐ	Ⓐ	Ⓒ	†	Ⓐ	⑥	Ⓐ	† A	Ⓐ	Ⓒ	Ⓑ
Dieppe d.	0521	0615	0615	0700	0715	0744	0804	0815	1002	1017	1202	1315	1318	1402	1602	1604	1704	1715	1801	1815	1823	1902	1916	2002
Rouen Rive-Droite a.	0605	0716	0718	0751	0820	0831	0853	0916	1051	1116	1251	1416	1416	1451	1651	1650	1750	1816	1850	1916	1915	1949	2016	2050

A – To / from Paris (Table **270**).

CAEN - ALENÇON - LE MANS - TOURS 271

km		Ⓐ	Ⓐ	⑥	Ⓐ	Ⓐ 🚌	Ⓒ	Ⓐ 🚌		Ⓒ 🚌	⑥	Ⓒ	Ⓐ	Ⓐ	Ⓒ 🚌	†	Ⓐ		⑥	Ⓐ	†	Ⓐ	Ⓐ	†	🚌
0	**Caen** 275 277 d.	0611	0703	0716	0745	...	0914	0930	...	...	1045	1252	1254	1445	...	1646	1648	...	1745	1750	1750	1902	2009	2026	...
23	Mézidon 275 277 d.	0626	0718	0731	0800	...	0929	|	...	...	1058	1307	1309	1500	...	1701	1703	...	1800	1804	1807	1918	2024	2041	...
67	Argentan 273 d.	0653	0748	0758	0828	...	0953	1030	...	...	1126	1335	1336	1527	...	1729	1731	...	1827	1831	1834	1945	2051	2105	...
82	Surdon 273 d.	0702	0757	0807	0836	0924	|	|	...	1045	1136	1345	1345	1536	1543	|	1740	...	1836	1840	1844	1954	2100	|	2148
91	Sées d.	0710	0805	0814	0843	0934	|	|	...	1055	1143	1352	1352	1542	1553	1742	1747	...	1843	1847	1851	2001	2107	2118	2158
111	Alençon ◇ d.	0724	0824	0828	0859	0957	1018	1115	...	1118	1156	1408	1408	1557	1616	1757	1802	...	1856	1901	1908	2014	2120	2132	2221
166	**Le Mans** ◇ a.	0816	0916	0916	0946	...	1054	1230	...	...	1234	1451	1451	1634	...	1834	1833	...	1934	1934	1951	...	...	2208	...
	Tours (below) a.	...	...	...	1045	...	1204	...	...	...	...	1550	1550	...	...	...	...	...	...	...	2052	...	...	...	...

	①	Ⓐ	①	Ⓐ	⑥ 🚌	⑥	Ⓐ	Ⓐ	⑥ 🚌	Ⓐ 🚌	⑥	†	Ⓐ	⑥	† 🚌	⑤ 🚌	Ⓐ	Ⓐ	Ⓒ	⑥	Ⓐ	† 🚌	†	†
Tours (below) d.	...	...	...	...	...	...	...	...	...	...	0901	0915	1109	...	...	...	...	1628	1633	...	...	...	...	1914
Le Mans ◇ d.	...	...	0613	...	...	0725	0726	0826	...	0915	1026	1018	1226	1326	...	1350	1634	1733	1742	1831	1835	...	1943	2019
Alençon ◇ d.	0552	...	0653	0653	0710	0815	0758	0900	0942	1030	1102	1102	1305	1414	1445	1505	1722	1816	1822	1909	1915	1934	2018	2053
Sées d.	0604	...	0705	0705	0733	0827	0810	0913	1005	|	1115	1115	1318	1427	1508	|	1734	1828	1835	1921	1929	1957	2031	2105
Surdon 273 d.	0611	...	0712	0712	0743	0836	0817	0921	1015	|	1122	1122	1325	1434	1518	|	1742	1835	1842	1928	1936	2007	2039	|
Argentan 273 d.	0620	0620	0722	0722	...	0846	0827	0932	...	1115	1132	1132	1335	1444	...	1550	1751	1846	1852	1938	1947	...	2049	2120
Mézidon 275 277 d.	0646	0646	0747	0747	...	0912	0853	0957	...	|	1156	1157	1404	1509	...	|	1817	1914	1918	2004	2014	...	2115	2143
Caen 275 277 a.	0700	0700	0901	0801	...	0925	0907	1011	...	1215	1210	1211	1418	1523	...	1650	1831	1928	1932	2017	2029	...	2129	2156

km		⚒	Ⓐ	Ⓐ	Ⓐ	Ⓒ		Ⓐ	†	⚒	⑥	Ⓒ	Ⓐ			Ⓐ	†	Ⓐ	Ⓑ		⚒	Ⓐ	†	⑥ 🚌	† 🚌
	Caen (above) d.	...	...	...	0745	0914	...	...	...	...	...	1252	1254	...	...	...	...	...	...	...	...	...	1750	...	...
0	**Le Mans** d.	0620	0648	0736	0946	1054	...	1220	1239	1244	1320	1451	1451	...	1644	1720	1751	1819	1844	...	1919	1946	1951	...	...
49	Château du Loir d.	0651	0735	0806	1017	1121	...	1306	1325	1315	1404	1521	1521	...	1715	1806	1833	1906	1915	...	2007	2018	2021	2015	2025
96	St Pierre des Corps a.	|	...	|	|	1159	...	...	|	|	...	|	|	...	|	...	|	...	|	...	...	|	|	|	|
99	**Tours** a.	0732	...	0835	1045	1204	...	...	1353	1344	...	1550	1550	...	1744	...	1909	...	1945	...	...	2055	2052	2105	2130

	①	①	Ⓐ	Ⓐ	Ⓐ	⑥	Ⓐ	⑥	†	†	Ⓐ	Ⓐ	⑥	Ⓐ	⑤	Ⓐ	⑥	Ⓐ	Ⓒ	†	Ⓐ		†	⑤†
Tours d.	0522	0555	...	0609	...	0737	0752	0901	0915	1013	1109	1226	1229	...	1405	1510	...	1628	1633	...	1728	1825	1914	2125
St Pierre des Corps d.	|	|	...	|	...	|	|	0915	|	|	|	|	|	...	|	|	...	|	|	...	|	|	|	|
Château du Loir d.	0554	0629	0629	0647	0752	0809	0824	0952	0945	1045	1145	1259	1311	1328	1437	1545	1552	1700	1705	1752	1808	1859	1946	2158
Le Mans a.	0638	0718	0718	0732	0838	0853	0856	1022	1014	1131	1216	1331	1359	1415	1507	1616	1638	1730	1736	1838	1853	1931	2015	2233
Caen (above) a.	...	...	...	...	...	...	...	1210	1211	...	1418	...	...	...	...	...	...	1928	1932	...	...	...	2156	...

◇ – Other trains Alençon - Le Mans at 0541 ①, 0624 Ⓐ, 0641 Ⓐ, 0747 Ⓐ, 1241, 1514 †, 1624 Ⓐ, 1641 †, 1724 Ⓐ, 1824 ⚒, 2024 †; Le Mans - Alençon at 0643 Ⓐ, 0743 Ⓐ, 1243 Ⓐ, 1353 †, 1535 †, 1643 ⑥, 1653 Ⓐ, 1755 Ⓐ, 1843 †, 1902 Ⓐ, 1950 ⚒.

☛ At Le Mans 🚌 services use the Gare Routière (bus station) adjacent to the railway station.

CAEN - COUTANCES - GRANVILLE - RENNES 272

At Caen and Rennes 🚌 services use the bus station (gare routière) adjacent to the railway station.

km		Ⓐ	Ⓐ 🚌	Ⓐ	⑥	Ⓐ	†	Ⓒ	Ⓐ	Ⓐ	Ⓐ	Ⓒ	Ⓒ	⑥ 🚌	Ⓐ	Ⓐ 🚌	Ⓐ	Ⓒ	† 🚌	Ⓑ 🚌	Ⓐ	Ⓒ	Ⓐ	†
0	**Caen** 275 ◧ d.	0601	0730	0801	0811	0910	0910	1010	1110	1210	1308	1410	1512	...	1611	1615	1709	1712	1715	...	1810	1911	1915	2012
30	Bayeux 275 ◧ d.	0623	|	0823	0828	0927	0927	1027	1127	1227	1332	1427	1534	...	1633	|	1731	1734	|	...	1832	1932	1937	2034
57	Lison 275 ◧ d.	0640	|	0841	0842	0941	0941	1041	1141	1241	1349	1441	1552	...	1650	|	1748	1752	|	...	1849	1949	1953	2051
75	Saint Lô ◧ d.	0655	|	0856	0856	0956	0956	1056	1156	1256	1403	1456	1605	...	1705	|	1803	1804	|	...	1904	2003	2006	2104
105	Coutances ◧ d.	0722	|	0917	0917	1017	1022	1118	1218	1317	1425	1517	1627	...	1726	|	1831	1826	|	...	1925	2025	2027	2125
143	**Granville** a.	0749	|	*1005**	0942	1043	1048	1144	1244	...	*1515**	1543	1653	...	*1817**	|	1858	1852	|	...	1951	2051	*2118**	...
143	**Granville** 273 d.	0759	|	...	0955	...	1058	...	1258	...	...	...	...	1703	...	|	...	...	|	1903	...	...	...	...
157	Folligny 273 d.	0810	|	...	1007	...	1109	...	1309	...	...	...	...	|	...	|	...	...	|	|	...	...	...	...
176	Avranches d.	0824	0900	...	1023	...	1123	...	1323	...	...	...	...	1733	...	1745	...	...	1845	1933	...	...	...	...
198	Pontorson ⊡ d.	0842	|	...	1041	...	1141	...	1341	...	...	...	...	|	...	|	...	...	|	|	...	...	...	...
219	Dol de Bretagne 281 d.	0900	|	...	1058	...	1158	...	1358	...	...	...	...	|	...	|	...	...	|	|	...	...	...	...
277	**Rennes** 281 a.	0933	1020	...	1133	...	1233	...	1431	...	...	...	...	1853	...	1905	...	...	2005	2053	...	...	...	...

	Ⓐ	⑥	Ⓐ	Ⓐ	⑥	Ⓐ 🚌	†	†	Ⓐ	⑥	Ⓐ	† 🚌	Ⓒ	Ⓐ	Ⓐ	Ⓒ	Ⓐ	Ⓐ 🚌	Ⓒ	Ⓐ	Ⓒ	Ⓐ	†
Rennes 281 d.	...	...	...	...	...	0730	...	...	...	*0805**	...	1004	...	1126	...	...	*1513**	1615	...	...	1729	1757	...
Dol de Bretagne 281 d.	...	...	...	...	...	|	...	...	...	|	...	|	...	1159	...	...	|	|	...	...	1802	1830	...
Pontorson ⊡ d.	...	...	...	...	...	|	...	...	...	|	...	|	...	1215	...	...	|	|	...	...	1819	1848	...
Avranches d.	...	...	...	...	...	0851	...	...	...	*0925**	...	1124	...	1231	...	...	*1633**	1735	...	...	1835	1905	...
Folligny 273 d.	...	...	...	...	...	|	...	...	...	|	...	|	...	1246	...	...	|	|	...	...	1850	1924	...
Granville 273 a.	...	...	...	...	...	|	...	...	...	*0955**	...	1154	...	1256	...	...	*1703**	|	...	...	1901	1936	...
Granville d.	*0515**	...	0604	0655	0806	|	0905	0955	*0939**	1005	*1139**	...	1205	1307	...	1600	1712	|	1800	...	1912	1953	...
Coutances ◧ d.	0603	0627	0631	0732	0832	|	0932	1031	1031	1032	1231	...	1232	1337	1533	1628	1739	|	1827	1840	1939	2028	...
Saint Lô ◧ d.	0625	0649	0653	0755	0855	|	0954	1055	1055	1057	1255	...	1255	1402	1554	1650	1802	|	1850	1903	2002	2050	...
Lison 275 ◧ d.	0638	0702	0706	0808	0908	|	1008	1108	1108	1110	1308	...	1308	1415	1608	1703	1815	|	1903	1916	2015	2103	2118
Bayeux 275 ◧ d.	0655	0719	0723	0825	0925	|	1025	1125	1125	1126	1325	...	1325	1429	1625	1720	1829	|	1920	1934	2029	2117	2132
Caen 275 ◧ a.	0718	0742	0744	0846	0947	1020	1047	1147	1147	1148	1347	...	1347	1446	1647	1742	1845	1905	1942	1956	2045	2133	2151

◧ – Other trains Caen - Coutances at 0701 Ⓐ, 1010 Ⓐ; Coutances - Caen at 0627 ⑥, 0831 Ⓐ, 1641 Ⓐ. Additional trains are available Caen - Lison and v.v., some of which have 🚌 connections to / from Coutances.

⊡ – Full name is Pontorson - Mont St Michel (*10 km* from Mont St Michel).

* – Connection by 🚌.

273 PARIS - DREUX - GRANVILLE

🅁 required for journeys to / from Paris. Suburban trains run Paris - Dreux and v.v. approximately hourly. For connections Surdon - Alençon and v.v. see Table **271**.

km		①	Ⓐ g◧	Ⓐ e	Ⓐ e◧	Ⓒ f◧	Ⓒ d	Ⓒ d◧		†	②–⑤	①			⑥	⑤		⑤	Ⓒ	Ⓐ	①–④	⑤	Ⓐ	Ⓒ
0	**Paris** Montparnasse ...... **278** d.	...	0732	0732	0732	0854	0854	0854	...	0927	0945	0945	1054	1354	1527	1528	...	1613	1654	1713*	1813	1813	1943	1953
17	Versailles Chantiers .... **278** d.	...	|	|	|	0907	0907	0907	...	|	|	|	|	|	|	|	...	|	|	|	1827	1826	|	2007
82	**Dreux** .... d.	0529	0820	0820	0820	0941	0941	0941	...	1013	1033	1033	|	1440	1614	|	...	|	|	|	1914	1914	2044	2044
118	Verneuil sur Avre .... d.	0552	0840	0840	0840	1001	1001	1001	...	1036	1056	1056	1157	1459	1637	|	...	1731	1757	1831	1936	1936	2103	2104
142	L'Aigle .... d.	0605	0854	0853	0853	1014	1014	1014	...	1050	1109	1109	1211	1513	1650	1642	...	1745	1810	1845	1950	1950	2117	2117
183	Surdon .... **271** d.	0626	0915	0915	0915	1035	1036	1036	...	1114	1131	1134	|	1534	1715	|	...	1806	1831	1906	2014	2015	2138	2139
198	Argentan .... **271** d.	0635	0926	0926	0926	1046	1046	1046	...	1124	1140	1140	1241	1545	1724	1711	...	1816	1844	1917	2024	2024	2149	2149
226	Briouze .... d.	0652	0942	0942	0942	1102	1102	1102	...	1141	...	...	|	1601	...	|	...	|	|	1934	...	...	2205	2205
243	Flers .... d.	0702	0954	0953	0953	1113	1113	1113	...	1151	...	...	1305	1612	...	1734	...	1839	1908	1947	...	...	2216	2216
272	Vire .... d.	0719	1013	1010	1010	1129	1129	1129	...	1207	...	...	1321	1628	...	1750	...	1856	1927	2003	...	...	2232	2232
298	Villedieu les Poêles .... d.	0735	1029	1025	1025	1145	1144	1144	...	1223	...	...	1336	1643	...	1806	...	1911	1944	2019	...	...	2247	2247
313	Folligny .... **272** d.	0745	1039	1043	1049	1154	1202	1208	...	1233	...	...	|	|	...	|	...	|	|	2029	...	...	|	|
	Pontorson - Mont St Michel a.	|	|	|	1121	|	|	1240	...	|	...	...	|	|	...	|	...	|	|	|	...	...	|	|
328	**Granville** .... **272** a.	0755	1050	1053	...	1204	1212	...	...	1243	...	...	1354	1701	...	1825	...	1930	2002	2039	...	...	2305	2305

	①	②–⑤	⑥	†	Ⓐ	⑥	†		⑥	Ⓐ	⚒	†		†	†	⑤	Ⓒ d◧	Ⓒ d	Ⓐ e◧	Ⓐ e	Ⓒ f◧	Ⓐ g◧	†
Granville .... **272** d.	0450	...	...	...	0555	0625	0655	0900	...	...	1155	1400	1553	1703	...	1743	...	1830	...	1838	1843	1850	1953
Pontorson - Mont St Michel .... d.	|	...	...	...	|	|	|	|	...	...	|	|	|	|	...	|	1806	|	1814	|	|	|	|
Folligny .... **272** d.	|	...	...	...	|	|	|	|	...	...	|	|	|	|	...	1754	1853	1853	1901	1901	1854	1901	2004
Villedieu les Poêles .... d.	0508	...	...	...	0613	0643	0713	0918	...	...	1213	1418	1611	1721	...	1805	1904	1904	1911	1911	1903	1911	2014
Vire .... d.	0524	...	...	...	0628	0658	0728	0933	...	...	1228	1433	1627	1737	...	1821	1921	1921	1927	1927	1919	1927	2029
Flers .... d.	0541	...	...	...	0645	0715	0745	0950	...	...	1245	1450	1645	1754	...	1838	1939	1939	1944	1944	1937	1944	2047
Briouze .... d.	0552	...	...	...	0656	0726	0756	|	...	...	1256	1501	|	1804	...	1849	1950	1950	1955	1955	1949	1955	2058
Argentan .... **271** d.	0609	0612	0615	0634	0714	0744	0814	1016	1209	1213	1314	1519	1713	1822	1934	1906	2008	2008	2013	2013	2008	2013	2116
Surdon .... **271** d.	0618	0621	0624	0643	0723	0753	0823	1025	1218	1222	1323	1528	|	|	1943	...	2018	2018	2022	2022	2018	2022	|
L'Aigle .... d.	0642	0642	0649	0708	0745	0815	0845	1047	1243	1243	1345	1549	1743	1850	2007	...	2040	2040	2044	2044	2040	2044	2144
Verneuil sur Avre .... d.	0656	0656	0703	0721	0758	0828	0858	1101	1256	1257	1358	1603	1758	|	2020	...	2054	2054	2057	2057	2054	2057	2158
Dreux .... d.	0718	0718	0726	0743	0818	0848	0918	|	1318	1319	1418	|	|	|	2042	...	2115	2115	2117	2117	2115	2117	2217
Versailles Chantiers .... **278** d.	0805	0804	|	|	|	|	|	|	|	|	|	|	|	|	2120	...	|	|	|	|	|	|	2255
Paris Montparnasse .... **278** a.	0817*	0816*	0816	0830	0917	0940	1006	1206	1406	1415*	1506	1712	1915	2006	2132	...	2206	2206	2206	2206	2206	2206	2307

d – From June 3.
e – From June 2.
f – Until May. 29.
g – Until June 1.

◧ – Until June 1 a connecting 🚌 is available Villedieu les Poêles - Mont St Michel and v.v. (Mont St Michel Le Verger arrive 1123 Ⓐ / 1239 Ⓒ, depart 1803 Ⓒ / 1811 Ⓐ). From June 2 a connecting 🚌 is available Pontorson-Mont St Michel - Mont St Michel and v.v. (Mont St Michel Le Verger arrive 1201 Ⓐ / 1320 Ⓒ, depart 1724 Ⓒ / 1734 Ⓐ).
* – Paris **Vaugirard** (5 – 10 minute walk from Montparnasse main concourse).

274 🚌 RENNES - MONT ST MICHEL 🚌

Keolis Armor

km			●							
0	**Rennes** gare routière .... d.	0845	1045	1245	...	...	...	...	...	...
68	**Mont St Michel** Le Verger .... a.	0955	1155	1355	...	...	...	...	...	...

			●						
Mont St Michel Le Verger . d.	1000	1700	1800	...	...	...	...	...	...
Rennes gare routière .... a.	1110	1810	1910	...	...	...	...	...	...

Service until September 30, 2023. Services with note ● operate from April 1. Operator: Keolis Armor (www.keolis-armor.com). Rail tickets and passes not valid. The gare routière at Rennes is adjacent to the railway station. At Mont St Michel the coach terminates at Le Verger close to the tourist information office. A free *Passeur* motorised shuttle service operates along the causeway to Mont St Michel itself taking 25 minutes (or 45 minutes walk, *2.4 km*). Horse-drawn shuttles (*Maringotes*) taking 35 minutes are also available, fee payable.

275 PARIS - CAEN - CHERBOURG

🅁 required for journeys to / from Paris. Other services: Paris - Lisieux Table **276**; Lisieux - Caen Table **277**; Mézidon - Caen Table **271**, Caen - Lison Table **272**.

km		Ⓐ	Ⓐ	⑥	Ⓐ	†	⑤	†	⑥	⑥	Ⓐ	①–④	⑤Ⓒ	†	Ⓒ	Ⓐ	Ⓐ	⑤⑥		⑤Ⓒ			Ⓐ	Ⓐ	Ⓒ	⑤Ⓒ
0	**Paris** St Lazare .... d.	...	...	...	0612	...	0727	0759	0759	0828	0829	...	0859	0928	0959	0959	...	1027	1059	1159	1228	1259	1356	...	1428	1459
108	Evreux .... d.	...	...	...	0722	...	0838	|	|	0936	0940	...	|	1038	|	1105	...	1135	|	|	1334	|	1501	...	1535	|
160	Bernay .... d.	...	...	...	0747	...	0905	|	|	1001	1006	...	|	1103	|	1130	...	1200	|	|	1359	|	1526	...	1601	|
191	Lisieux .... ⊡ d.	...	...	...	0802	...	0922	|	|	1016	1022	...	|	1120	|	1145	...	1217	|	|	1416	|	1541	...	1616	|
216	Mézidon .... ⊡ d.	...	...	...	|	...	...	|	|	...	|	...	|	...	|	|	...	...	|	|	...	|	|	...	|	|
239	**Caen** .... ⊡ d.	0555	0653	0824	0827	0924	...	0959	1001	...	1046	1056	1101	...	1158	1207	1224	...	1301	1401	...	1501	1603	1626	1639	1701
269	Bayeux .... d.	0611	0709	0840	0843	0940	...	...	1017	...	...	1112	1118	...	...	...	1240	...	1318	...	...	1518	...	1642	...	1718
296	Lison .... d.	0625	0723	0854	0857	0954	...	...	1031	...	...	1126	1132	...	...	...	1254	...	1332	...	...	1532	...	1656	...	1732
314	Carentan .... d.	0636	0734	0905	0908	1005	...	...	1042	...	...	1134	1142	...	...	...	1305	...	1342	...	...	1543	...	1707	...	1742
343	Valognes .... d.	0651	0749	0920	0923	1020	...	...	1057	...	...	1149	1158	...	...	...	1320	...	1357	...	...	1558	...	1722	...	1757
371	**Cherbourg** .... a.	0706	0804	0935	0939	1035	...	...	1113	...	...	1204	1213	...	...	...	1335	...	1413	...	...	1613	...	1737	...	1813

	①–④	†	Ⓐ	Ⓐ	Ⓒ		Ⓐ	Ⓒ	⑥	Ⓑ	①–④	⑤	Ⓒ		Ⓐ	†	†	⑤	⊖	⑤	†	⑤⑥	①–④	⑤	Ⓒ
Paris St Lazare .... d.	...	1558	1558	1608	1628	1659	1709	1728	1759	1759	1808	1808	1828	1859	1908	1928	1959	1959	1959	2008	2028	2059	2059	2108	2230
Evreux .... d.	...	|	|	1714	1735	|	1817	1837	|	|	1920	1918	1935	|	2021	2037	|	|	2106	2113	2136	|	2206	2215	2335
Bernay .... d.	...	|	|	1740	1801	|	1843	1903	|	|	1946	1944	2001	|	2047	2103	|	|	2132	2138	2203	|	2231	2241	0001
Lisieux .... ⊡ d.	...	|	|	1755	1817	|	1858	1918	|	|	2000	2000	2017	|	2103	2118	|	|	2146	2154	2219	|	2246	2256	0016
Mézidon .... ⊡ d.	...	|	|	...	...	|	|	|	|	|	|	...	...	|	...	|	|	|	|	...	...	|	|	...	|
Caen .... ⊡ d.	1702	1759	1801	...	...	1905	1922	1940	2001	2004	2022	...	...	2101	...	2141	2202	2202	2209	...	...	2301	2310	...	0039
Bayeux .... d.	1718	...	1817	...	...	1922	...	...	...	2020	...	...	...	2118	...	...	...	2218	...	...	...	2318	2326	...	...
Lison .... d.	1732	...	1831	...	...	1936	...	...	...	2034	...	...	...	2132	...	...	...	2232	...	...	...	2332	2340	...	...
Carentan .... d.	1743	...	1842	...	...	1946	...	...	...	2045	...	...	...	2142	...	...	...	2243	...	...	...	2342	2350	...	...
Valognes .... d.	1758	...	1857	...	...	2001	...	...	...	2100	...	...	...	2157	...	...	...	2258	...	...	...	2357	0005	...	...
Cherbourg .... a.	1813	...	1912	...	...	2019	...	...	...	2119	...	...	...	2219	...	...	...	2313	...	...	...	0015	0020	...	...

	Ⓐ	Ⓐ	⑥	Ⓐ	Ⓐ	Ⓐ	Ⓐ	Ⓒ	Ⓒ	Ⓐ	Ⓐ	Ⓐ	Ⓒ	Ⓒ	Ⓐ	Ⓒ	Ⓐ	Ⓐ	Ⓒ	⑤	Ⓒ	⑤	Ⓒ	Ⓒ	Ⓐ
Cherbourg .... d.	...	...	...	0547	...	0618	0642	0645	...	...	0720	...	...	0844	0846	...	...	1045	1046	...	...	1132	...	1244	1247
Valognes .... d.	...	...	...	0602	...	0634	0658	0702	...	...	0735	...	...	0901	0902	...	...	1101	1102	...	...	1149	...	1300	1303
Carentan .... d.	...	...	...	0616	...	0648	0711	0715	...	...	0750	...	...	0915	0916	...	...	1115	1116	...	...	1203	...	1315	1317
Lison .... d.	...	...	...	0627	...	0659	0722	0727	...	...	0801	...	...	0926	0926	...	...	1125	1126	...	...	1215	...	1326	1327
Bayeux .... d.	...	...	...	0641	...	0713	0737	0740	...	...	0815	...	...	0940	0940	...	...	1139	1140	...	...	1229	...	1340	1341
Caen .... ⊡ d.	0458	0603	0652	0659	...	0729	0756	0759	0818	0820	0831	0854	0858	0959	0959	...	...	1158	1159	...	...	1248	1259	1359	1359
Mézidon .... ⊡ d.	|	|	|	|	...	...	|	|	|	|	...	|	|	|	|	...	...	|	|	...	...	|	|	|	|
Lisieux .... ⊡ d.	0521	0626	0715	|	0748	...	|	|	0841	0843	...	|	|	|	|	1041	1042	|	|	1240	1241	1311	|	|	|
Bernay .... d.	0536	0642	0730	|	0803	...	|	|	0856	0858	...	|	|	|	|	1057	1100	|	|	1256	1257	1326	|	|	|
Evreux .... d.	0603	0711	0757	|	0830	...	|	|	0923	0925	...	|	|	|	|	1126	1127	|	|	1323	1324	1353	|	|	|
Paris St Lazare .... a.	0715	0819	0903	0858	0938	...	0957	1002	1030	1031	...	1104	1102	1202	1202	1230	1231	1402	1402	1431	1429	1504	1502	1602	1602

	Ⓒ	⑥	⑤	Ⓒ	Ⓐ	Ⓒ	⑤				Ⓒ	Ⓐ	†	†	⑤	Ⓐ	Ⓒ	⑥	⑤†	①–④	⑤	⑥	†	†	†
Cherbourg .... d.	...	1341	1442	1442	1520	...	...	...	...	1645	...	1739	...	...	...	1818	1843	...	...	1916	1923	...	1941	...	2037
Valognes .... d.	...	1357	1458	1459	1536	...	...	...	...	1701	...	1756	...	...	...	1833	1859	...	...	1932	1939	...	1957	...	2053
Carentan .... d.	...	1411	1513	1513	1551	...	...	...	...	1714	...	1809	...	...	...	1848	1915	...	...	1946	1953	...	2010	...	2107
Lison .... d.	...	1422	1524	1524	1601	...	...	...	...	1725	...	1820	...	...	...	1859	1926	...	...	1957	2004	...	2021	...	2118
Bayeux .... d.	...	1436	1538	1538	1615	...	...	...	...	1739	...	1834	...	...	...	1913	1940	...	...	2011	2018	...	2035	...	2132
Caen .... ⊡ d.	1420	1455	1557	1557	1632	...	...	1657	...	1758	...	1853	1856	...	1920	1929	1959	2018	...	2030	2037	2055	2054	...	2151
Mézidon .... ⊡ d.	|	|	|	|	...	...	...	|	...	|	...	|	|	...	|	...	|	|	...	|	|	|	|	...	|
Lisieux .... ⊡ d.	1443	|	|	|	...	1634	1640	|	1741	|	1842	1914	|	1940	1943	...	|	2041	2042	2052	|	|	2117	2136	|
Bernay .... d.	1458	|	|	|	...	1650	1656	|	1757	|	1858	1929	|	1956	1958	...	|	2056	2058	2107	|	|	|	2153	|
Evreux .... d.	1525	|	|	|	...	1718	1723	|	1823	|	1924	1953	|	2023	2027	...	|	2123	2124	2134	|	|	|	2222	|
Paris St Lazare .... a.	1631	1702	1801	1802	...	1829	1829	1904	1930	2002	2031	2103	2101	2129	2136	...	2202	2229	2232	2251	2251	2301	2302	2330	2358

⊡ – **Lisieux - Mézidon - Caen** and v.v.: from Lisieux at 0604 Ⓐ, 0648 Ⓐ, 0703 Ⓐ, 0715 Ⓐ, 0743 ⑥, 0746 Ⓐ, 0812 ⚒, 0912 Ⓐ, 1104 Ⓐ, 1111 Ⓒ, 1204 ⚒, 1318 Ⓒ, 1323 Ⓐ, 1404 ⚒, 1700 Ⓐ, 1711 †, 1714 Ⓐ, 1751 ⚒, 1824 Ⓐ, 1831 Ⓒ, 1906 Ⓐ, 1924 Ⓐ, 1930 Ⓒ, 2011 ⚒; from Caen at 0551 Ⓐ, 0635 Ⓐ, 0709 Ⓐ, 0711 ⑥, 0737 Ⓐ, 0804 Ⓐ, 1005 Ⓒ, 1020 Ⓐ, 1120 ⚒, 1206, 1320 ⚒, 1604 Ⓐ, 1611 †, 1620 Ⓐ, 1635 ⑥, 1704, 1740 Ⓐ, 1805, 1823 Ⓐ, 1835 Ⓐ, 1906 ⚒, 1937 ⚒, 2004 †.

⊖ – ①②③④⑥.

PARIS - LISIEUX - TROUVILLE DEAUVILLE 276

🅁 required for journeys to / from Paris.

km		Ⓐ	⑥	Ⓐ	†	⑤	⑥	Ⓐ	†	⑥	⑤	Ⓒ	Ⓐ	Ⓐ	Ⓐ	Ⓒ	Ⓐ	⑤	①–④	Ⓒ	Ⓐ	†	⑤	†	⑤
0	**Paris** St Lazare 275 d.	...	...	...	...	0727	0828	...	0928	1027	1030	1228	1230	...	1608	1628	...	1808	...	1828	1908	...	2008	2028	2108
108	Evreux 275 d.	...	...	...	...	0838	0936	...	1038	1136	1135	1334	1334	...	1714	1735	...	1918	...	1935	2021	...	2113	2136	2215
160	Bernay 275 d.	...	...	...	...	0905	1001	...	1103	1201	1200	1400	1359	...	1740	1801	...	1944	...	2001	2047	...	2138	2203	2241
191	**Lisieux** 275 d.	0720	0735	0830	0844	0922	1016	1050	1120	1217	1216	1416	1415	1713	1755	1817	1841	2000	2011	2017	2103	2139	2154	2219	2256
209	Pont l'Évêque d.	0736	0749	0843	0858	0934	1029	1103	1133	1229	1228	1428	1427	1730	1808	1829	1854	2012	2025	2029	2115	2153	2205	2231	2308
221	**Trouville-Deauville** a.	0746	0758	0852	0908	0943	1038	1112	1142	1238	1237	1438	1437	1739	1818	1840	1905	2022	2034	2040	2127	2203	2215	2241	2318

	Ⓐ	Ⓐ	Ⓐ	Ⓐ	Ⓒ	Ⓒ	Ⓐ	⑤Ⓒ		Ⓒ	⑤	Ⓐ	Ⓒ	Ⓐ	Ⓐ	Ⓒ	Ⓐ	†	⑥	①–④	†	⑤	†	†
Trouville-Deauville d.	0558	0648	0726	0758	0808	1018	1020	1217	1346	1612	1619	1643	1718	1720	1756	1819	1912	1916	1950	2015	2018	2024	2046	2113
Pont l'Évêque d.	0606	0657	0735	0807	0817	1030	1029	1228	1356	1621	1628	1652	1728	1729	1808	1830	1921	1926	1959	2024	2030	2033	2055	2123
Lisieux 275 d.	0619	0712	0748	0822	0832	1043	1042	1240	1411	1634	1640	1707	1741	1742	1825	1842	1935	1940	2013	2038	2042	2045	2108	2136
Bernay 275 d.	...	...	0803	...	...	1059	1100	1256	...	1650	1656	...	1757	1757	...	1858	...	1956	...	...	2058	2101	...	2153
Evreux 275 d.	...	...	0830	...	...	1126	1127	1323	...	1718	1723	...	1823	1824	...	1924	...	2023	...	...	2124	2128	...	2222
Paris St Lazare 275 a.	...	...	0938	...	...	1230	1231	1431	...	1829	1829	...	1930	1930	...	2031	...	2129	...	...	2232	2232	...	2330

TROUVILLE DEAUVILLE - DIVES CABOURG 276a

Journey 30 minutes (45 minutes by 🚌).

From **Trouville-Deauville** at 1050 🚌 ⑥ **D**, 1053 ⑥ **E**, 1153 † **F**, 1253 ⑥ **E**, 1449 🚌 Ⓒ **G**, 1451 Ⓒ **E**, 1642 ⑥ **E**, 1738 † **F**, 1829 🚌 ⑤ **A**, 1853 ⑥ **E**, 1858 † **F**, 2044 ④ **B**, 2034 ⑤ **C**, 2044 🚌 ④⑤ **A**, 2053 ⑥ **E**.

From **Dives-Cabourg** at 0500 🚌 ① **H**, 0516 ① **J**, 1123 🚌 Ⓒ **G**, 1137 ⑥ **E**, 1241 † **F**, 1338 ⑥ **E**, 1517 🚌 † **G**, 1532 Ⓒ **E**, 1657 † **F**, 1724 🚌 Ⓒ **G**, 1738 ⑥ **E**, 1818 † **F**, 1942 ⑥ **E**

Also *NOMAD* 🚌 route **20** Deauville gare routière - Dives-sur-Mer - Cabourg and v.v. approximately hourly on Ⓐ, less frequently on Ⓒ. See www.nomadcar14.fr for details.

A – Until Mar. 31.
B – Apr. 6 - June 29.
C – From Mar. 31.
D – Until Mar. 25.
E – From Apr. 1.
F – From Apr. 2.
G – Until Mar. 26.
H – Until Mar. 27.
J – From Apr. 3.

ROUEN - LISIEUX - CAEN 277

At Caen 🚌 services use the bus station (gare routière) adjacent to the railway station.

km		Ⓐ	⑥	Ⓐ		Ⓐ	Ⓒ	Ⓐ 🚌		Ⓒ	Ⓐ	Ⓐ 🚌		†	Ⓐ	Ⓒ		Ⓐ	Ⓐ	Ⓒ		Ⓒ	Ⓐ	
0	**Rouen** Rive Droite d.	0601	0705	0707	...	0807	1006	1007	...	1206	1206	1407	...	1606	1607	1706	...	1709	1809	1816	...	1906	1907	...
23	Elbeuf-St Aubin d.	0617	0721	0722	...	0822	1021	|	...	1221	1224	|	...	1621	1622	1731	...	1724	1824	1831	...	1922	1922	...
73	Serquigny d.	0651	|	|	...	|	|	|	...	1254	1257	|	...	|	1650	1807	...	1758	1858	1906	...	|	|	...
83	Bernay 275 d.	0658	0755	0756	...	0855	1054	|	...	1302	1304	|	...	1654	1658	1815	...	1807	1907	1914	...	1954	1955	...
114	Lisieux 275 d.	0715	0812	0812	...	0912	1111	|	...	1318	1323	|	...	1711	1714	1831	...	1824	1924	1930	...	2011	2012	...
139	Mézidon 271 275 d.	0730	0826	0826	...	0926	1125	|	...	1333	1338	|	...	1725	1728	1845	...	1838	1938	1945	...	2026	2026	...
162	**Caen** 271 275 a.	0743	0840	0840	...	0940	1139	1147	...	1347	1353	1547	...	1739	1742	1858	...	1852	1952	1958	...	2040	2040	...

	Ⓐ	Ⓐ	⑥	Ⓐ		Ⓒ	Ⓐ 🚌	Ⓐ	Ⓒ		Ⓐ 🚌	Ⓐ	†	Ⓐ		Ⓒ	Ⓒ	Ⓐ	⑥		Ⓐ	†	
Caen 271 275 d.	0551	0709	0711	0804	...	1005	1006	1206	1206	...	1406	1604	1611	1704	...	1705	1804	1805	1906	...	1907	2004	...
Mézidon 271 275 d.	0605	0724	0725	0818	...	1019	|	1220	1220	...	|	1618	1626	1718	...	1719	1818	1819	1920	...	1920	2018	...
Lisieux 275 d.	0619	0739	0739	0832	...	1033	|	1234	1234	...	|	1632	1641	1732	...	1734	1832	1833	1934	...	1934	2032	...
Bernay 275 d.	0636	0756	0756	0849	...	1050	|	1250	1251	...	|	1648	1658	1748	...	1751	1849	1850	1950	...	1949	2048	...
Serquigny d.	0643	0804	0804	|	...	1058	|	1257	1259	...	|	1656	|	|	...	1759	|	|	|	...	|	|	...
Elbeuf-St Aubin d.	0716	0836	0836	0922	...	1136	|	1336	1336	...	|	1734	1730	1822	...	1835	1922	1922	2023	...	2022	2121	...
Rouen Rive Droite a.	0733	0852	0852	0940	...	1152	1146	1352	1353	...	1546	1750	1745	1838	...	1851	1937	1937	2039	...	2037	2137	...

PARIS - CHARTRES - LE MANS 278

For *TGV* trains Paris - Le Mans via the high-speed line see Table **280**. Additional trains run Nogent le Rotrou - Le Mans and v.v.

km		①†	Ⓐ	Ⓐ K	Ⓐ	Ⓐ	⑥	⚒	⚒	Ⓐ	⑥	⑥	Ⓐ			†			Ⓐ		⑥		⚒	†		
0	**Paris** Montparnasse d.	0002	...	...	0533	...	...	0609	0636	0709	...	...	0739	0809	0906	...	1009	1106	...	...	...	1209	1306	1306	1409	1506
17	Versailles Chantiers d.	0023	...	...	0546	...	...	0623	0652	0725	...	...	0753	0823	0922	...	1025	1122	...	...	...	1225	1322	1322	1425	1522
48	Rambouillet d.	0044	...	...	0605	...	...	0644	0712	0745	...	...	0815	0845	0942	...	1045	1142	...	...	...	1245	1342	1342	1445	1541
88	**Chartres** d.	0124	...	0616	0642	0645	...	0724	0739	0829	0829	...	0856	0924	1009	...	1124	1209	...	1229	...	1324	1409	1409	1524	1610
149	Nogent le Rotrou d.	...	0606	0657	...	0733	0734	...	0814	0922	0922	0927	...	...	1045	1124	...	1245	1306	1322	1335	...	1445	1444	...	1648
211	**Le Mans** a.	...	0655	0747	...	0822	0822	...	0850	...	...	1015	...	...	1122	1214	...	1322	1355	...	1423	...	1522	...	...	1727

	Ⓐ	Ⓐ	†	Ⓐ	Ⓐ	Ⓒ	Ⓐ	Ⓐ	L	Ⓑ	Ⓐ	Ⓐ	Ⓑ L		Ⓒ	Ⓐ	Ⓐ	Ⓐ		Ⓐ		①–④	⑤†		Ⓐ
Paris Montparnasse d.	...	...	...	...	1609	1609	1624	1639	1705	1709	1724	1739	1805	1809	...	1824	1839	1854	1906	1939	2009	2106	2106	2209	2302
Versailles Chantiers d.	...	...	...	...	1625	1625	1640	1655	1722	1725	1738	1755	1822	1825	...	1840	1855	1910	1922	1955	2025	2123	2123	2225	2321
Rambouillet d.	...	...	...	...	1645	1645	1700	1715	|	1745	1800	1815	|	1845	...	1900	1915	1929	1941	2015	2045	2140	2140	2245	2346
Chartres d.	...	1629	...	...	1724	1729	1729	1754	1807	1824	1829	1857	1907	1924	1932	1929	1954	1958	2009	2057	2124	2207	2210	2324	0022
Nogent le Rotrou d.	1706	1723	1735	1805	...	1825	1825	...	1845	...	1923	...	1945	...	2023	2023	...	...	2048	...	...	...	2246	...	...
Le Mans a.	1756	...	1825	1854	...	1917	1915	...	1925	...	...	...	2024	...	...	...	...	...	2129	...	...	...	2322	...	...

	Ⓐ	①	⚒	Ⓐ	⚒	Ⓐ		Ⓐ L	Ⓐ	⚒	Ⓐ	Ⓒ			Ⓐ	⚒	Ⓐ	Ⓐ	⚒	†		Ⓐ	⑥		
Le Mans d.	...	0338	...	...	...	...	...	0538	...	...	...	...	...	...	0630	...	0638	0707	0734	...	...	0807	0837	...	0938
Nogent le Rotrou d.	...	0414	...	...	...	0534	...	0616	...	...	0636	0636	...	...	0708	...	0730	0756	0812	0815	0837	0856	0925	...	1014
Chartres d.	0405	0452	0452	0535	0605	0630	0635	0656	0701	0705	0731	0730	...	0735	0751	0805	0834	...	0852	0852	0930	...	...	0935	1052
Rambouillet d.	0446	0521	0521	0616	0646	0701	0716	|	0731	0746	0801	...	...	0816	0819	0846	0903	...	0919	0919	...	...	...	1016	1119
Versailles Chantiers d.	0509	0541	0541	0638	0708	0722	0738	0741	0755	0808	0823	...	...	0838	0841	0908	0925	...	0939	0941	...	...	...	1038	1141
Paris Montparnasse a.	0520	0553	0553	0650	0720	0735	0750	0753	0806	0820	0835	...	...	0850	0853	0920	0936	...	0953	0952	...	...	...	1050	1153

					⚒	†			Ⓐ		Ⓐ	Ⓒ	Ⓐ	†	Ⓐ	Ⓐ	Ⓐ				Ⓐ			Ⓑ	†
Le Mans d.	...	1134	...	1238	1338	...	...	...	...	1534	...	...	...	1637	1638	...	1707	...	1738	...	1807	1907	1938	...	2138
Nogent le Rotrou d.	...	1212	...	1334	1414	1415	...	...	...	1612	1637	...	...	1725	1734	...	1756	...	1814	1843	1856	1956	2014	...	2215
Chartres d.	1135	1252	1335	1423	1452	1452	1535	...	1639	1652	1735	1735	1805	...	1824	1835	...	...	1852	1938	...	...	2052	2129	2252
Rambouillet d.	1216	1319	1416	...	1519	1519	1616	...	|	1719	1816	1816	1846	...	...	|	...	...	1919	2019	...	...	2119	2209	2319
Versailles Chantiers d.	1238	1341	1438	...	1541	1541	1638	...	|	1741	1838	1838	1908	...	...	|	...	...	1941	2041	...	...	2141	2229	2340
Paris Montparnasse a.	1250	1335	1450	...	1553	1553	1650	...	1737	1753	1850	1850	1920	...	...	1944	...	...	1953	2053	...	...	2153	2241	2353

OUIGO TRAINS PARIS - LE MANS - NANTES ★

Paris Austerlitz d.	1229	...	**Nantes** d.	1248	...
Juvisy d.	|	...	Angers St-Laud d.	1331	...
Massy-Palaiseau d.	1304	...	Le Mans d.	1422	...
Versailles Chantiers d.	1326	...	Chartres d.	1524	...
Chartres d.	1416	...	Versailles Chantiers d.	1606	...
Le Mans d.	1527	...	Massy-Palaiseau d.	1631	...
Angers St-Laud d.	1619	...	Juvisy d.	1652	...
Nantes a.	1711	...	**Paris** Austerlitz a.	1707	...

SUBURBAN TRAINS PARIS - VERSAILLES

- **RER Line C**: Paris Austerlitz - - Versailles Château Rive Gauche. Journey 40 minutes.
- **RER Line L**: Paris St Lazare - Versailles Rive Droite. Journey 35–40 minutes.
- **RER Line N**: Paris Montparnasse - Versailles Chantiers. Journey 13–27 minutes.

Trains run every 15–30 mins. 0600 - 2400 (2100 Line **C**). Line **C** serves St Michel Notre Dame. Detailed schedules can be found at www.transilien.com.

The Château is approx 600 metres from Château Rive Gauche station, approx 1400 metres from Rive Droite station and approx 1600 metres from Chantiers station.

K – To / from Angers St Laud (Table **280a**).
L – Not available for journeys Paris - Versailles and v.v. on Ⓐ.

★ – *Ouigo Classique*. Low-cost loco-hauled train. Internet booking only at www.ouigo.com. Outline timings – services may not run on all days shown (please confirm timings when booking). For other *Ouigo* trains Paris - Nantes via St Pierre des Corps, see Table **296**.

280 TGV BRETAGNE - PAYS DE LA LOIRE

Subject to alteration Mar. 13–24, Apr. 8–10, May 18–21, Sept. 23, 24, Oct. 7–20, 28, 29. *TGV* timings may vary by a few minutes - please check your reservation.
Many trains continue to destinations on Tables **281**, **284**, **285**, **288** and **293**. See Table **280a** for TER regional services Le Mans - Nantes/Rennes.

km		*TGV* 8601	*TGV* 8863	*TGV* 8911	*TGV* 7611	*TGV* 8701	*TGV* 8081	*TGV* 8901	*TGV* 8603	*TGV* 8703	*TGV* 7621	*TGV* 8803	*TGV* 8057	*TGV* 8605	*TGV* 8707	*TGV* 8913 8973	*TGV* 8691	*TGV* 8083	*TGV* 8609	*TGV* 8917	*TGV* 8871	*TGV* 8615 8715	*TGV* 8717	*TGV* 8807	*TGV* 8975
		①–⑤		①–⑥			①–⑥			①–⑤		①–⑥	⑥							⑥	⑧		⑥⑦		①–④
		A	B	e	⊠	B	f	C	D	g	⊠	f	h	E			k	E	B	m	n		p	F	q
0	**Paris** Montparnasse ... d.	0621	0626	0628	0643	0656	0704	0717	0730	0730	0741	0745	0825	0840	0840	0930	0954	0954	0955	1036	1034	1053	1153	1212	1220
	Le Mans ... d.	|	0732	0735	|	|	|	|	0837	0837	0841	|	|	|	|	1031	|	|	|	1136	1136	|	|	|	|
	Laval ... d.	|	|	|	|	|	0822	|	|	|	|	|	|	0958	0958	|	|	|	|	|	|	|	|	|	|
	Vitré ... d.	|	|	|	|	|	0842	|	|	|	|	|	|	|	|	|	|	|	|	|	|	|	|	|	|
364	**Rennes** ... a.	0756	|	|	0816	0825	0903	|	0925	0925	|	|	0954	1025	1025	|	1125	1125	1125	|	|	1225	1325	|	|
254	Sablé ... d.	...	|	|	...	...	...	|	...	...	|	0854	...	...	...	|	...	...	...	|	|	...	...	|	|
302	Angers St Laud ... d.	...	0816	0817	...	...	...	|	...	...	0922	0916	...	...	...	1116	...	...	...	1216	1216	...	...	|	|
390	**Nantes** ... a.	...	0854	0854	...	...	...	0919	...	...	1003	0959	...	...	...	1154	...	...	...	1258	1257	...	...	1419	1420

	TGV 8921	*TGV* 7615	*TGV* 8619	*TGV* 8085	*TGV* 8875	*TGV* 8977	*TGV* 8087	*TGV* 8623	*TGV* 8723	*TGV* 8923	*TGV* 8811	*TGV* 8879	*TGV* 7623	*TGV* 8813	*TGV* 8881	*TGV* 8629 8729	*TGV* 8631	*TGV* 8067	*TGV* 8817	*TGV* 8905	*TGV* 8927	*TGV* 8637	*TGV* 8639	*TGV* 8731
						⑤–⑦	⑧					①–⑤		⑤			⑤		①–⑤		⑤	①–④		
		⊠◧	G	H	J	p	K		L	k	M	N	⊠	t		P	t		Q	R	t	S	T	R
Paris Montparnasse ... d.	1236	1244	1256	1256	1321	1332	1353	1441	1441	1445	1445	1532	1536	1616	1633	1652	1653	1712	1717	1748	1748	1756	1756	1756
Le Mans ... d.	|	1346	|	|	1424	1432	|	|	|	|	|	1632	|	|	1733	|	|	1813	|	|	|	|	|	|
Laval ... d.	|	1416	|	|	|	|	|	1600	1600	|	|	|	|	|	|	|	|	1845	|	|	|	|	|	|
Vitré ... d.	|	|	|	|	|	|	|	|	|	|	|	|	|	|	|	|	|	|	|	|	|	|	|	|
Rennes ... a.	|	1443	1425	1425	|	|	1525	1625	1625	|	|	|	|	|	|	1825	1825	1911	|	|	|	1925	1925	1925
Sablé ... d.	|	...	...	...	1446	1454	...	...	...	|	|	|	|	|	|	...	...	...	|	|	|	...	...	...
Angers St Laud ... d.	1416	...	...	...	1509	1518	...	...	...	1613	1612	1716	1712	|	1816	...	...	...	|	1916	1916	...	...	...
Nantes ... a.	1454	...	...	...	1554	1555	...	...	...	1651	1653	1754	1750	1820	1854	...	...	...	1920	1957	1957	...	...	...

	TGV 8735	*TGV* 8093	*TGV* 8095	*TGV* 8821	*TGV* 8641 8739	*TGV* 8075	*TGV* 8931 8985	*TGV* 8823	*TGV* 8935	*TGV* 8887	*TGV* 8651	*TGV* 8649	*TGV* 8751	*TGV* 8097	*TGV* 8073	*TGV* 8937	*TGV* 8825	*TGV* 8655	*TGV* 8755	*TGV* 8063	*TGV* 8791	*TGV* 8939	*TGV* 8827	*TGV* 8791
	⑤		⑤	①–⑤		⑤		⑤	⑤		①–④	⑤	⑧	⑤	⑦	⑤	⑦	⑤	⑤		⑤	⑤		⑤
	t	R	t	U	P	t		t	t	P	S	t	n	t	v	t	v	t	t	P	w	x	V	y
Paris Montparnasse ... d.	1757	1811	1812	1818	1840	1839	1844	1920	1936	1936	1954	1954	1954	2011	2013	2046	2046	2053	2053	2112	2116	2149	2149	2212
Le Mans ... d.	|	|	|	|	|	1944	|	|	2033	2036	|	|	|	2113	2113	|	|	|	|	2213	2214	|	|	2313
Laval ... d.	|	1929	|	|	1958	2016	|	|	|	|	|	|	|	2143	2144	|	|	|	|	2244	2247	|	|	2344
Vitré ... d.	|	1949	|	|	|	2036	|	|	|	|	|	|	|	|	2205	|	|	|	|	|	2307	|	|	0004
Rennes ... a.	1927	2010	1942	|	2025	2056	|	|	|	|	2125	2125	2125	2211	2226	|	|	2225	2225	2311	2328	|	|	0027
Sablé ... d.	...	...	...	|	...	...	1952	|	|	|	...	...	...	...	...	|	|	...	...	...	...	|	|	...
Angers St Laud ... d.	...	...	...	|	...	...	2019	|	2116	2116	...	...	...	...	...	2217	2217	...	...	...	...	2316	2316	...
Nantes ... a.	...	...	...	2021	...	...	2059	2124	2201	2156	...	...	...	...	...	2254	2254	...	...	...	...	2357	2357	...

km		*TGV* 8860	*TGV* 8072	*TGV* 8900	*TGV* 8680	*TGV* 8802	*TGV* 8082	*TGV* 8790	*TGV* 8080	*TGV* 8602	*TGV* 8702	*TGV* 8910	*TGV* 8970	*TGV* 8804	*TGV* 8052	*TGV* 8604	*TGV* 8704	*TGV* 8808	*TGV* 8864	*TGV* 8606	*TGV* 8706	*TGV* 8054	*TGV* 8912	*TGV* 8056	*TGV* 7622
		①–⑤	①–⑤	①–⑤		①–⑤	⑥		①–⑤	①–⑥	①–⑥	①			⑧			①–⑥	①–⑥	①–⑥	①–⑥	⑦		⑥	
		W	X	W	Y	Z	m	B	X	f	f	★	B	⊖	n	Y	B	e	⊡	f	f	v		h	⊠
393	**Nantes** ... d.	0506	...	0605	...	0640	...	...	...	...	...	0704	0704	0705	...	...	...	0808	0805	...	...	...	0905	...	1039
305	Angers St Laud ... d.	0545	...	0646	...	|	...	...	...	...	...	0744	0744	0744	...	...	...	0848	0844	...	...	...	0944	...	1119
257	Sablé ... d.	0610	...	|	...	|	...	...	...	...	...	|	|	|	...	...	...	|	|	...	...	...	|	...	|
371	**Rennes** ... d.	|	0532	|	0635	|	0644	0700	0700	0735	0735	|	|	|	0747	0835	0835	|	|	0935	0935	0935	|	1028	|
	Vitré ... d.	|	0555	|	|	|	|	|	|	|	|	|	|	|	|	|	|	|	|	|	|	|	|	|	|
	Laval ... d.	|	0612	|	0705	|	0712	|	|	|	|	|	|	|	0815	|	|	|	|	1004	1004	1004	|	|	|
202	**Le Mans** ... d.	0634	0648	|	|	|	0745	0749	0749	|	|	|	|	|	0848	|	|	|	0926	|	|	|	1026	|	|
0	**Paris** Montparnasse ... a.	0733	0749	0815	0820	0841	0845	0850	0850	0908	0908	0912	0912	0914	0946	1005	1005	1014	1032	1119	1119	1120	1138	1203	1303

	TGV 8610	*TGV* 8710	*TGV* 8972	*TGV* 8868	*TGV* 8904	*TGV* 8916	*TGV* 8720	*TGV* 8084	*TGV* 7612	*TGV* 8874	*TGV* 8814	*TGV* 8622	*TGV* 8722	*TGV* 8922	*TGV* 8630	*TGV* 8086	*TGV* 8880	*TGV* 8074	*TGV* 8634	*TGV* 8690	*TGV* 8730	*TGV* 8984	*TGV* 8816	*TGV* 8636
				⑧		⑦	⑧				⑧	⑧						⑧			⑧			①–⑥
			H	●	⊕	⊗	⊖		⊠		n	n				E	▲	n	B	k	⊖		▶	f
Nantes ... d.	...	...	1103	1104	1205	1206	...	...	...	1302	1405	...	...	1505	...	...	1605	...	...	...	...	1709	1740	...
Angers St Laud ... d.	...	...	1143	1144	|	|	...	...	...	1342	1445	...	...	1544	...	...	1644	...	...	...	...	1748	|	...
Sablé ... d.	...	...	|	|	|	|	...	...	...	|	|	...	...	|	...	...	|	...	...	...	...	|	|	...
Rennes ... d.	1135	1135	|	|	|	|	1335	1335	1339	|	|	1535	1535	|	1635	1635	|	1631	1735	1735	1735	|	|	1835
Vitré ... d.	|	|	|	|	|	|	|	|	|	|	|	|	|	|	|	|	|	1658	|	|	|	|	|	|
Laval ... d.	1204	1204	|	|	|	|	|	|	|	|	|	|	|	|	|	|	|	1718	|	|	|	|	|	1904
Le Mans ... d.	|	|	1226	1225	|	|	|	|	|	1426	|	|	|	1626	|	|	1726	1749	|	|	|	|	|	|
Paris Montparnasse ... a.	1319	1319	1325	1325	1409	1409	1506	1506	1510	1525	1620	1708	1708	1728	1809	1809	1828	1849	1906	1906	1906	1917	1945	2020

	TGV 8088	*TGV* 8926	*TGV* 7624	*TGV* 8642	*TGV* 8928	*TGV* 8824	*TGV* 8986	*TGV* 8818	*TGV* 7616	*TGV* 8692	*TGV* 8092	*TGV* 8932	*TGV* 8930	*TGV* 8886	*TGV* 8096	*TGV* 8646	*TGV* 8746	*TGV* 8988	*TGV* 8826	*TGV* 8066	*TGV* 8652	*TGV* 8752	*TGV* 8934	*TGV* 8936
	⑧			⑧	⑦	⑦	①–⑥			⑦	⑦	①–⑥	⑦	①–⑥	⑦	⑧	①–⑥	⑦	⑤	⑦	⑦	⑦	⑦	⑦
	⊖		⊠	n	◀	☆	e	B	⊠	v	v	e	v	⊡	◀	⊖	f	v	t	v	v	v	v	◀
Nantes ... d.	...	1805	1836	...	1854	1857	1905	1905	...	...	...	2005	2005	2005	...	...	...	2103	2107	...	...	...	2204	2253
Angers St Laud ... d.	...	1844	|	...	1945	1944	1945	1944	...	...	...	2046	2044	2044	...	...	...	2143	2147	...	...	...	2244	|
Sablé ... d.	...	1907	|	...	|	|	|	|	...	...	...	|	|	|	...	...	...	|	|	...	...	...	|	|
Rennes ... d.	1835	|	|	1935	|	|	|	|	1948	2035	2035	|	|	|	2135	2135	2135	|	|	2150	2235	2235	|	|
Vitré ... d.	|	|	|	|	|	|	|	|	|	|	|	|	|	|	|	|	|	|	|	|	|	|	|	|
Laval ... d.	1904	|	|	|	|	|	|	|	2016	|	|	|	|	|	|	|	|	|	|	2219	|	|	|	|
Le Mans ... d.	|	1930	|	|	|	|	|	|	2049	|	|	2127	2126	2126	|	|	|	|	|	2252	|	|	|	|
Paris Montparnasse ... a.	2020	2031	2044	2108	2112	2112	2112	2112	2148	2208	2208	2226	2228	2235	2308	2311	2311	2316	2318	2349	0008	0008	0012	0055

A – Mar. 13–24, Oct. 9–20.
B – ①–⑤ **d** until July 7; ①–⑤ from Sept. 4.
C – ① until Mar. 20; ①–⑤ **d** Mar. 27 - July 7; ①–⑤ from Sept. 4.
D – ①–⑤ **d** until June 30; ①–⑥ July 3 - Sept. 2 (not Aug. 15); ①–⑤ from Sept. 4.
E – ⑥⑦ **j** until July 9; daily July 10 - Sept. 3; ⑥⑦ from Sept. 9.
F – ①–⑥ until July 9; ⑤⑥ July 14 - Sept. 2 (also July 13, Aug. 14); ①–⑥ from Sept. 4.
G – ①–⑥ **r** until July 1; daily July 3 - Sept. 3; ①–⑥ from Sept. 4.
H – ⑥ until July 1 (also May 18, 19); daily July 8 - Sept. 3; ⑥ from Sept. 9.
J – Daily until July 7; ①–④ July 10 - Aug. 31 (not July 13, Aug. 14, 15); daily from Sept. 4.
K – Until July 7 (not May 18, 19) and from Sept. 4.
L – ①②③④⑥ until July 6 (also May 19; not Apr. 10, May 1, 8, 17, 29); ①②③④⑦ July 9 - Sept. 3 (not July 13, Aug. 14); ①②③④⑥ from Sept. 4.
M – Daily until July 7 and from Sept. 4.
N – Not Apr. 10, May 1, 8, 18, 19, 29, July 14, 24–31, Aug. 1–15.
P – ①②③④⑥⑦ (also May 19, July 14; not May 17, July 13).
Q – Not Apr. 10, May 1, 8, 18, 19, 29, July 14, 24–27, 31, Aug. 1–3, 7–10, 14, 15.
R – ①②③④⑦ (not May 17, 18, July 13, Aug. 14).
S – ①–④ **u** until July 6; ①–④ from Sept. 4.
T – ⑦ until July 9 (also Apr. 10, May 1, 8, 29); ①②③④⑦ July 10 - Aug. 27 (not July 13, Aug. 14); ⑦ from Sept. 3.
U – Not Apr. 10, May 1, 8, 18, 19, 29, July 10–12, ①–④ July 17 - Aug. 31.
V – Not July 13, 21, 28, Aug. 4, 11, 18, 25, Sept. 1.
W – Not Apr. 10, May 1, 8, 18, 19, 29, July 14, Aug. 14, 15.
X – Not Apr. 10, May 1, 8, 18, 19, 29, July 14, Aug. 14, 15, Nov. 1.
Y – ①–⑤ **d** until July 7; ① July 10 - Aug. 28 (also Aug. 16; not Aug. 14); ①–⑤ from Sept. 4.
Z – Not Apr. 10, May 1, 8, 18, 19, 29, July 13, 14, 21, 24–31, Aug. 1–15, 18, 25, Sept. 1.

d – Not Apr. 10, May 1, 8, 18, 19, 29.
e – July 8 - Sept. 2 (not Aug. 15).
f – Not Apr. 10, May 1, 8, 29, Aug 15.
g – July 10 - Sept. 1 (not July 14, Aug. 14, 15).
h – Until Mar. 25.
j – Also Apr. 10, May 1, 8, 18, 19, 29.
k – July 8 - Sept. 3.
m – Also May 18, 19, July 14, Aug. 14.
n – Not May 18, 19, July 14, Aug. 14.

p – July 8 - Sept. 3 (also July 14, Aug. 14, 15).
q – July 10 - Aug. 31 (not July 13, Aug. 14, 15).
r – Not Apr. 10, May 1, 8, 29.
t – Also May 17, July 13; not May 19, July 14.
u – Not Apr. 10, May 1, 8, 17, 18, 29.
v – Also Apr. 10, May 1, 8, 29, Aug. 15.
w – Jan. 13 - Mar. 10.
x – July 21 - Sept. 1 (also July 13).
y – Not Jan. 13 - Mar. 10.

◧ – Does not call at Le Mans Apr. 3–7, 11–14, Oct. 2–6, 9–13, 28.
⊡ – ①–⑥ **r** until July 7; ①–⑥ from Sept. 4.
⊖ – ⑥⑦ **j** until July 9; ②–⑦ July 11 - Sept. 3 (also Aug. 14; not Aug. 16); ⑥⑦ from Sept. 9.
● – Until July 7 and from Sept. 4.
⊕ – ① until Mar. 20; ①–⑥ **r** Mar. 25 - July 7; ①–⑥ from Sept. 4.
⊗ – ⑦ until July 2; daily July 8 - Sept. 3; ⑦ from Sept. 10.
⊖ – ⑧ until July 2 (not May 18, 19); daily July 3 - Sept. 3; ⑧ from Sept. 4.
▲ – ⑧ until July 9; ⑦ July 16 - Sept. 3 (also Aug. 15); ⑧ from Sept. 4.
▶ – ①–⑤ **d** until June 30; ⑧ July 3 - Sept. 3 (not July 14, Aug. 14); ①–⑤ from Sept. 4.
◀ – July 9 - Sept. 3 (also Aug. 15).
★ – July 10 - Aug. 28 (also Aug. 16; not Aug. 14).
☆ – ⑦ until July 2 (also Apr. 10, May 1, 8, 29); ⑦ from Sept. 10.
⊠ – OUIGO low-cost TGV service. Internet booking only (www.ouigo.com).

TGV – High-speed train. 🅁. 🍷.

LE MANS - NANTES and RENNES 280a

TER regional services. For *TGV* services see Table **280**.

km		Ⓐ	Ⓐ	Ⓐ	⑥ A	Ⓐ	† A	Ⓐ	Ⓐ B	⑥	Ⓐ	⑥	Ⓒ	Ⓒ	Ⓐ	Ⓐ	Ⓐ	⑤	Ⓒ	†	⚒	Ⓐ	Ⓐ C	Ⓒ
0	**Le Mans** d.	0543	0617	0638	0700	0705	0718	0738	0749	0914	1040	1057	1121	1227	1230	1309	1505	1541	1552	1621	1636	1656	1738	1747
49	Sablé sur Sarthe **287** d.	0605	0643	0708	0726	0730	0739	0808	0825	0946	1103	1128	1144	1259	1301	1332	1531	1611	1623	1642	1701	1729	1808	1818
97	Angers St Laud **287** d.	0632	0722	0734	0804	0809	0805	0836	0905	*1034*	1130	1207	*1233*	1336	1339	1358	1607	1637	1701	*1729*	1729	1808	1836	1858
185	**Nantes** **287** a.	0713	...	0815	0846	...	0846	0915	...	*1115*	1213	...	*1315*	...	...	1440	...	1717	...	*1815*	1812	...	1916	...

	Ⓐ	⑥	Ⓐ	†	Ⓐ	Ⓐ	†	†
Le Mans d.	1756	1814	1838	1857	1910	1941	1943	2048
Sablé sur Sarthe **287** d.	1828	1847	1900	1918	1935	2012	2026	2110
Angers St Laud **287** d.	1905	*1927*	1936	1944	2013	2037	2106	2147
Nantes **287** a.	...	*2012*	2017	2027	...	2118	...	2227

	Ⓐ	Ⓐ	Ⓐ	Ⓐ	⚒	Ⓐ	Ⓐ	⑥
Nantes **287** d.	...	*0544*	0609	0644	...	0739	...	*0844*
Angers St Laud **287** d.	0552	*0628*	0706	0726	0752	0823	0855	*0927*
Sablé sur Sarthe **287** d.	0629	0716	0727	0750	0826	0853	0931	0954
Le Mans a.	0655	0748	0755	0820	0901	0915	0957	1016

	Ⓐ	⑥	Ⓒ		⑥	Ⓐ	†	Ⓐ	⚒	†	⑥	†	Ⓐ	Ⓑ	Ⓐ	Ⓐ	Ⓑ	⑥	Ⓑ	Ⓐ	⑥	Ⓐ	† A
Nantes **287** d.	*0941*	...	*1043*	1144	...	...	...	...	1542	*1544*	...	...	...	1644	...	1744	...	*1744*	1844	...	1915	*1941*	2108
Angers St Laud **287** d.	*1025*	1052	*1125*	1228	1252	1252	1349	1352	1625	*1627*	1654	1659	1703	1728	1753	1828	1850	1852	1930	1952	2004	*2025*	2152
Sablé sur Sarthe **287** d.	1054	1131	1154	1253	1330	1330	1427	1429	1654	1654	1733	1738	1739	1754	1829	1857	1927	1930	1953	2029	2026	2054	2217
Le Mans a.	1116	1203	1216	1319	1402	1405	1501	1455	1720	1716	1804	1811	1811	1817	1900	1919	1955	2002	2020	2055	2047	2116	2239

km		Ⓐ	Ⓐ	⑥	Ⓐ	Ⓐ		⑥	†	⚒	†	⑥		⑤	†	Ⓐ	Ⓐ	Ⓐ		Ⓐ		Ⓐ	†	Ⓐ
0	**Le Mans** d.	0627	0650	0701	0717	0820	...	0918	1120	1220	1439	1520	...	1534	1618	1620	1640	1720	...	1749	1824	1918	2024	2026
90	Laval **287** d.	0724	0754	0752	0811	0911	...	1012	1210	1332	1530	1610	...	1621	1711	1713	1731	1814	...	1853	1916	2025	2115	2117
125	Vitré **287** d.	0748	...	...	...	...	...	...	...	...	...	...	...	1641	...	...	1758	...	...	...	...	...	...	...
163	**Rennes** **287** a.	0820	...	...	...	...	...	...	...	...	...	...	...	1712	...	...	1830	...	...	...	...	...	...	...

	Ⓐ	Ⓐ	Ⓐ	Ⓐ	Ⓐ	⑥	⑥	†	Ⓐ	Ⓐ	Ⓒ		⑤	⑥	Ⓐ	†	Ⓐ	Ⓐ	⑥	Ⓐ	†	Ⓐ	†
Rennes **287** d.	...	...	...	0627	...	...	...	...	...	...	...	...	...	...	...	...	...	1742	...	...	...	...	...
Vitré **287** d.	...	...	...	0652	...	...	...	...	...	...	...	...	...	...	...	...	...	1814	...	...	...	...	...
Laval **287** d.	0604	0645	0659	0719	0804	0804	0922	0925	0944	1245	1247	...	1547	1622	1645	1647	1747	1832	1854	1908	1909	1947	2008
Le Mans a.	0706	0741	0804	0810	0855	0855	1012	1015	1038	1354	1341	...	1638	1713	1736	1739	1851	1924	1945	2016	2000	2039	2100

A – To / from Le Croisic (Table **288**). B – To / from Chartres (Table **278**). C – To / from Le Croisic on ⑤ (Table **288**).

PARIS - RENNES - ST MALO 281

TGV services are subject to alteration Apr. 8 – 10, Sept. 23, 24, Oct. 28. *TGV* timings may vary by a few minutes - please check your reservation.

km		*TGV* **8081** ①–⑥ f	*TGV* **8083** ⑥⑦ D	*TGV* **8085** E	*TGV* **8087** Ⓑ F	*TGV* **8095** ⑤ j	*TGV* **8093** G	*TGV* **8097** ⑤ j		
	Paris Montparnasse **280** d.	0704	0954	1256	1353	1812	1814	2011	...	...
0	**Rennes** **272** d.	0907	1130	1433	1532	1953	2014	2213	...	...
58	Dol **272** d.	0940	1204	|	|	2029	2047	2245	...	...
81	**St Malo** a.	0954	1222	1515	1627	2043	2101	2300	...	...

	TGV **8082** ⑥ k	*TGV* **8080** ①–⑤ m	*TGV* **8084**	*TGV* **8086** ⑥⑦ D	*TGV* **8088** Ⓑ H	*TGV* **8092** ⑦ p	*TGV* **8096** ⑦ q		
St Malo d.	0552	0607	1238	1539	1742	1937	2042	...	...
Dol **272** d.	0607	0624	|	1555	1758	1952	|	...	...
Rennes **272** a.	0640	0654	1329	1625	1829	2025	2125	...	...
Paris Montparnasse **280** a.	0845	0850	1506	1809	2020	2208	2308	...	...

	Ⓐ	⚒	Ⓐ	†	Ⓐ	⑥		⚒	†	Ⓐ	⑥	①–④	⑤	Ⓐ		Ⓐ	†	Ⓐ	⑥	Ⓐ	†	Ⓐ	⑥	Ⓐ		Ⓐ
Rennes **272** d.	0635	0735	0835	0935	0935	1040	1135	1235	1335	1335	1335	1435	1435	1600	1635	1704	1735	1735	1735	1804	1835	1835	1835	1935	2042	2139
Dol **272** d.	0714	0813	0914	1011	1013	1116	1214	1319	1411	1413	1421	1514	1519	1639	1713	1746	1811	1813	1816	1846	1914	1917	1921	2014	2121	2218
St Malo a.	0730	0829	0930	1025	1029	1130	1230	1335	1425	1429	1435	1530	1527	1655	1729	1804	1825	1829	1832	1904	1928	1933	1935	2030	2137	2234

	Ⓐ	Ⓐ	Ⓐ	⑥	Ⓐ	Ⓐ	⑥	†	Ⓐ		⚒	⑥		Ⓑ	Ⓐ	†	Ⓐ	⑥	Ⓐ		Ⓐ	Ⓐ	Ⓒ	Ⓐ	Ⓐ	Ⓒ
St Malo d.	0530	0627	0658	0723	0727	0758	0827	0834	0837	1030	1219	1323	...	1330	1430	1436	1600	1629	1703	1730	1803	1830	1832	1930	2030	2032
Dol **272** d.	0546	0643	0716	0739	0743	0817	0844	0848	0851	1046	1235	1339	...	1346	1446	1449	1616	1643	1719	1746	1819	1846	1846	1946	2046	2046
Rennes **272** a.	0625	0725	0756	0825	0825	0856	0925	0925	0925	1125	1317	1425	...	1425	1525	1525	1655	1720	1756	1825	1856	1925	1925	2025	2125	2125

D – ⑥⑦ **g** until July 9; daily July 10 - Sept. 3; ⑥⑦ from Sept. 9.
E – ⑥ until July 1 (also May 18, 19); daily July 8 - Sept. 3; ⑥ Sept. 9 - Dec. 9.
F – Ⓑ until July 7 and from Sept. 4 (not May 18, 19).
G – ①②③④⑦ (not May 17, 18, July 13, Aug. 14).
H – Ⓑ until until July 2 (not May 18, 19); daily July 3 - Sept. 3; Ⓑ from Sept. 4.
f – Not Apr. 10, May 1, 8, 29, July 15.
g – Also Apr. 10, May 1, 8, 18, 19, 29.
j – Also May 17, July 13; not May 19, July 14.
k – Also May 18, 19, July 14, Aug. 14.
m – Not Apr. 10, May 1, 8, 18, 19, 29, July 14, Aug. 14, 15, Nov. 1.
p – Also Apr. 10, May 1, 8, 29, Aug. 15.
q – July 9 - Sept. 3 (also Aug. 15).
TGV – High-speed train. 🅁. 🍷.

DOL - DINAN - ST BRIEUC 282

km		Ⓐ 🚌	Ⓐ 🚌	⚒	Ⓐ	⑥	⚒	†		⚒	Ⓐ	Ⓐ		Ⓒ	Ⓒ	Ⓐ	Ⓐ 🚌	Ⓐ 🚌	Ⓐ	⑥	⑤	①–④	†	⑤
0	**Dol** d.	...	...	...	0821	0847	0944	1110	...	1324	...	1655	...	...	1724	1736	...	...	1850	1928	2035	2052	2052	2249
32	**Dinan** a.	...	...	...	0844	0906	1004	1130	...	1344	...	1723	...	...	1752	1756	...	...	1913	1948	2055	2112	2112	2309
32	**Dinan** d.	0605	0620	0714	...	...	...	...	1205	...	1621	...	...	1743	...	...	1810	1820	...	...	...	...	...	...
73	Lamballe **284** d.	0718	|	0804	...	...	...	...	1256	...	1711	...	...	1833	...	...	1917	|	...	...	...	...	...	...
94	**St Brieuc** **284** a.	...	0720	0820	...	...	...	...	1311	...	1727	...	...	1849	...	...	...	1920	...	...	...	...	...	...

	Ⓐ	Ⓐ	Ⓐ	Ⓐ 🚌	Ⓐ 🚌	⑥	Ⓐ	⚒	Ⓒ	⚒	Ⓐ	Ⓒ	Ⓐ	Ⓒ	Ⓐ	Ⓐ 🚌	⑥	†	Ⓐ	Ⓐ	Ⓐ 🚌	Ⓐ 🚌	Ⓒ
St Brieuc **284** d.	...	...	...	0640	...	...	...	0846	...	...	1325	...	...	1620	...	1715	...	...	1751	...	1840	...	1859
Lamballe **284** d.	...	...	...	|	0635	...	...	0902	...	...	1341	...	...	1636	...	|	...	...	1807	...	|	1835	1915
Dinan a.	...	...	...	0740	0742	...	...	0951	...	...	1430	...	...	1725	...	1815	...	...	1856	...	1940	1948	2004
Dinan d.	0557	0701	0740	...	...	0807	0906	...	1013	1210	...	1527	1627	...	1811	...	1818	1846	...	1922	...	...	...
Dol a.	0617	0728	0808	...	...	0835	0934	...	1041	1230	...	1547	1647	...	1833	...	1838	1906	...	1941	...	...	...

🚌 MORLAIX - ROSCOFF 🚌 283

	⚒	Ⓐ	⑥	⚒	Ⓐ	⑥	③ m		③ n	Ⓒ	Ⓐ		†	⚒	Ⓐ n	⚒	Ⓐ	†	⚒	Ⓑ	⑤		
Morlaix, Gare SNCF d.	0655	0755	0800	0950	1110	1115	1215	...	1215	1425	1430	...	1540	1540	1625	1655	1745	1820	1820	2015	2055	...	...
St Pol de Léon, Ti Kastelliz ⊡ d.	0720	0825	0825	1010	1130	1135	1240	...	1247	1445	1450	...	1600	1605	1700	1720	1810	1840	1847	2035	2115	...	...
Roscoff, Ferry d.	0735	0840	0840	1025	1145	1150	|	...	|	|	1505	...	|	|	|	|	|	1855	1902	2050	2130	...	...
Roscoff, Quai d'Auxerre ⊙ a.	0740	0845	0845	1030	1150	1155	1255	...	1300	1500	1510	...	1615	1620	1715	1735	1825	1900	1907	2055	2135	...	...

	⚒	⚒	⚒		Ⓐ	†	⑥		†	Ⓐ	⑤		Ⓐ n	Ⓐ m	†		⑥	Ⓐ	Ⓒ		Ⓐ		
Roscoff, Quai d'Auxerre ⊙ d.	0655	0745	0845	...	1155	1200	1200	...	1345	1350	1555	...	1600	1650	1650	...	1705	1720	1900	...	1900	...	...
Roscoff, Ferry d.	|	|	0850	...	|	|	|	...	|	|	|	...	|	|	|	...	1710	1725	|	...	1905	...	...
St Pol de Léon, Ti Kastelliz ⊡ d.	0710	0800	0905	...	1210	1215	1215	...	1400	1405	1610	...	1615	1705	1705	...	1725	1740	1915	...	1920	...	...
Morlaix, Gare SNCF a.	0735	0825	0925	...	1237	1235	1240	...	1420	1425	1630	...	1635	1725	1725	...	1750	1805	1935	...	1940	...	...

m – School holidays only (check locally for dates).
n – Not during School holidays (check locally for dates).
⊡ – 300 metres from railway station.
⊙ – 400 metres from railway station.

284 (PARIS -) RENNES - LANNION and BREST

TGV services are subject to alteration Mar. 13 – 24, Apr. 8 – 10, Sept. 23, Oct. 7, 9 – 20. *TGV* timings may vary by a few minutes - please check your reservation.
For services Guingamp - Carhaix / Paimpol and v.v. see Table **299**.

km		Ⓐ	Ⓐ ◧	⑥	Ⓐ	Ⓐ	Ⓐ	Ⓐ	Ⓐ	⚒	⚒	*TGV* **8601** ①–⑤ d	*TGV* **7611** ⊠	Ⓐ	Ⓐ	*TGV* **8603** A	⚒	*TGV* **8605** B	Ⓐ	†	⑥	†	*TGV* **8609** ①–⑤ C	⑥	*TGV* **8691** g	† ◧
	Paris Montparnasse **280** d.	...	...	...	...	...	...	...	...	...	...	0621	0643	...	...	0730	...	0840	...	...	...	...	0955	...	0954	...
0	**Rennes** d.	...	...	...	...	0600	...	...	0700	...	0736	0800	0822	...	0836	0932	...	1032	...	...	1040	1040	1130	...	1134	...
80	Lamballe **282** d.	...	...	...	...	0637	...	...	0737	...	0828	|	|	...	0928	1011	...	1111	...	...	1119	1131	|	...	|	...
101	St Brieuc **282** d.	...	...	...	...	0650	...	0728	0750	0836	0844	0851	0909	0934	0943	1024	...	1124	...	...	1132	1142	1217	...	1223	...
132	Guingamp d.	...	...	...	0639	0706	...	0747	0806	0854	...	0907	0927	0952	...	1040	1048	1141	...	1146	1148	...	|	...	1240	...
158	Plouaret-Trégor d.	...	0627	...	0654	0719	...	0801	0820	0909	...	|	|	1007	...	|	1103	|	...	1201	1202	...	|	...	|	1255
175	**Lannion** a.	...	|	...	0710	|	...	0818	|	0926	...	|	|	1024	...	|	1119	|	...	1217	|	...	|	...	1310	|
189	Morlaix d.	0606	0650	0710	...	0737	0800	...	0838	...	...	0937	0958	...	...	1110	...	1210	1212	...	1220	...	|	1308	...	1312
	Landivisiau d.	0621	0707	0725	...	0752	0822	...	0854	...	...	|	|	...	...	|	...	|	1227	...	1236	...	|	1323	...	1327
230	Landerneau **286** d.	0633	0719	0737	...	0803	0834	...	0904	...	...	|	|	...	...	|	...	|	1239	...	1246	...	|	1336	...	1337
248	**Brest** **286** a.	0650	0735	0751	...	0815	0850	...	0916	...	...	1010	1032	...	...	1142	...	1243	1256	...	1258	...	1327	1350	...	1349

	Ⓐ	⑥	Ⓐ	⑤	*TGV* **8615**		⚒	†	*TGV* **8619** D	Ⓐ	Ⓒ	Ⓒ	⑤	⑤†	E	⑤	Ⓐ	*TGV* **8623**	Ⓐ	†	⚒		Ⓐ	† ◧	Ⓐ ◧
Paris Montparnasse **280** d.	...	...	...	...	1053	...	...	...	1256	...	...	...	...	...	...	...	...	1441	...	...	...	...	...	...	...
Rennes d.	...	...	...	1200	1232	...	1236	1335	1429	...	1435	...	...	1439	...	1539	...	1632	...	...	...	1636	1700	...	...
Lamballe **282** d.	...	...	...	1237	1310	...	1334	1413	|	...	1513	...	...	1527	...	1616	...	|	...	...	...	1726	1738	...	...
St Brieuc **282** d.	...	...	1237	1250	1323	...	1351	1426	1516	...	1526	...	...	1541	...	1628	1635	1719	...	...	1730	1741	1750	...	...
Guingamp d.	...	1242	1255	1306	1340	...	...	1442	|	...	1543	...	...	...	...	1645	1653	1735	...	1743	1750	...	1807	...	...
Plouaret-Trégor d.	...	1257	1310	|	1356	1408	...	|	|	...	1557	1605	...	...	...	|	1708	|	...	1758	1805	...	1821	1830	1846
Lannion a.	...	1313	1326	|	|	1425	...	|	|	...	|	1622	...	...	...	|	1724	|	...	1814	1826	...	|	1847	1903
Morlaix d.	1312	...	...	1336	1414	...	...	1511	|	1612	1616	...	1657	...	1712	1716	...	1804	1812	...	...	...	1840	...	...
Landivisiau d.	1327	...	...	1352	|	...	...	1527	|	1626	1632	...	1711	...	1727	1732	...	|	1827	...	...	...	1856	...	...
Landerneau **286** d.	1339	...	...	1402	|	...	...	1537	|	1638	1643	...	1724	...	1739	1743	...	|	1839	...	...	...	1906	...	...
Brest **286** a.	1356	...	...	1414	1447	...	...	1550	1625	1656	1655	...	1741	...	1756	1755	...	1837	1851	...	...	...	1918	...	...

	Ⓐ	Ⓒ	*TGV* **8629** F	*TGV* **8631** ⑤ t		⚒	*TGV* **8635** ⑤ t	*TGV* **8695** ⑤ t	*TGV* **8637** ①–④ G	*TGV* **8639** H	⑦–④ u	⑦–④	⑤⑥	⑤	*TGV* **8645** ⑤ t	*TGV* **8641** F	⑥–④	⑤	Ⓐ	*TGV* **8651** ①–④ G	*TGV* **8649** ⑤ t	⑤	†	*TGV* **8655** ⑤ t	*TGV* **8657** ⑦ m
Paris Montparnasse **280** d.	...	...	1652	1653	...	...	1744	1744	1756	1756	...	...	...	...	1856	1840	...	...	...	1954	1954	...	...	2053	2359
Rennes d.	1735	1735	1832	1832	...	1836	|	|	1932	1932	...	1936	1937	...	|	2032	...	2042	2046	2132	2132	...	2139	2232	|
Lamballe **282** d.	1813	1813	|	1911	...	1926	|	|	|	|	...	2026	2016	...	|	2111	...	2119	2136	|	2211	...	2218	|	|
St Brieuc **282** d.	1825	1826	1919	1924	...	1943	2004	2009	2019	2019	...	2038	2028	...	2108	2124	...	2132	2148	2219	2224	...	2230	2319	0423
Guingamp d.	1842	1842	1936	1941	1945	...	|	2027	|	2036	2043	...	2044	2054	|	2140	...	2149	...	2235	2241	...	2246	2335	0440
Plouaret-Trégor d.	|	1856	|	|	2000	...	|	2056	|	|	2057	...	2058	2109	|	2155	2158	2203	...	|	2256	2259	2300	|	|
Lannion a.	|	|	|	|	2016	...	|	...	|	|	2115	...	|	2125	|	|	2215	|	...	|	|	2316	|	|	|
Morlaix d.	1911	1915	2005	2010	...	...	2045	...	|	2105	...	...	2117	...	|	2214	...	2221	...	2305	2315	...	2319	0005	0511
Landivisiau d.	1927	1931	|	|	...	...	|	...	|	|	...	...	2132	...	|	|	...	2237	...	|	|	...	2334	|	|
Landerneau **286** d.	1938	1941	|	|	...	...	|	...	|	|	...	...	2143	...	|	2239	...	2247	...	|	2340	...	2344	|	0538
Brest **286** a.	1950	1953	2038	2043	...	...	2118	...	2129	2138	...	...	2155	...	2215	2251	...	2259	...	2338	2352	...	2357	0038	0552

	TGV **8680** J	⚒	Ⓐ	*TGV* **8602** ①–⑥ p	Ⓐ ◧	Ⓐ	⚒	Ⓐ	*TGV* **8604** J	Ⓐ	Ⓐ	Ⓐ	⑥	Ⓐ	*TGV* **8606** ①–⑥ p	†	Ⓐ	⚒		*TGV* **8610** K	⑥	⑥	Ⓐ	†	⚒
Brest **286** d.	...	...	...	0523	...	0539	...	...	0631	...	...	...	...	0701	0722	...	...	0801	...	0909	0944	...	...	1035	...
Landerneau **286** d.	...	...	...	|	...	0550	...	...	|	...	...	...	...	0717	|	...	...	0815	...	0922	0955	...	...	1046	...
Landivisiau d.	...	...	...	|	...	0600	...	...	|	...	...	...	...	0729	|	...	...	0827	...	|	1005	...	...	1056	...
Morlaix d.	...	...	...	0555	...	0616	...	...	|	...	...	...	...	0744	0754	...	...	0844	...	0945	1021	...	...	1112	...
Lannion d.	...	...	0545	|	0604	|	...	0625	|	...	0717	...	0740	...	|	...	0841	...	0936	|	|	1131	1140	|	...
Plouaret-Trégor d.	...	...	0600	|	0620	0632	...	0640	|	...	0733	...	0756	...	|	...	0857	...	0952	1003	1038	1147	1155	1129	...
Guingamp d.	...	...	0615	0624	...	0647	...	0657	|	...	0747	...	0809	...	0822	...	0911	...	...	1018	1052	1202	1209	1144	...
St Brieuc **282** d.	0538	0614	...	0641	...	0704	0714	0720	0741	0747	0805	0818	0828	...	0840	0919	0926	...	...	1036	1108	...	1225	1201	1202
Lamballe **282** d.	0551	0625	...	|	...	0715	0726	...	|	0758	...	0829	...	...	|	0930	...	...	...	1048	1120	...	...	1212	1216
Rennes a.	0629	0721	...	0729	...	0757	0821	...	0829	0852	...	0921	...	...	0929	1021	...	...	...	1129	1201	...	...	1253	1317
Paris Montparnasse **280** a.	0820	...	...	0908	...	...	...	...	1005	...	...	...	...	...	1119	...	...	...	...	1319	...	...	...	...	...

	TGV **7612** ⊠	†	† ◧	Ⓐ	Ⓐ		Ⓑ	*TGV* **8622** Ⓑ q	⑥	*TGV* **8630**	Ⓐ	Ⓒ	Ⓒ	⑤	*TGV* **8634** ①–⑤ C	*TGV* **8690** g	Ⓑ	⚒	†	Ⓐ	⑥	*TGV* **8636** B	†	⑤	Ⓒ
Brest **286** d.	1119	...	...	...	1250	...	1306	1331	1400	1414	...	...	1501	1509	1532	...	...	...	...	1601	1602	1614	1639	1648	...
Landerneau **286** d.	|	...	...	...	1306	...	1317	|	1413	|	...	...	1512	1520	|	...	...	...	...	1617	1613	|	1650	1704	...
Landivisiau d.	|	...	...	...	1318	...	1327	|	1425	|	...	...	1522	1530	|	...	...	...	...	1629	1623	|	1700	1717	...
Morlaix d.	1152	...	...	...	1333	...	1343	|	1439	1446	...	...	1538	1546	|	...	...	...	...	1644	1639	1647	1716	1734	...
Lannion d.	|	...	1231	1238	▬	1334	|	|	...	|	...	1534	|	|	|	1600	...	1630	1635	...	|	|	|	▬	1734
Plouaret-Trégor d.	|	...	1247	1254	⑥	1350	1400	|	...	1504	...	1550	1555	|	|	|	...	1646	1651	...	|	|	1732	⚒	1750
Guingamp d.	1222	...	...	1308		...	1414	|	...	1519	...	...	1610	1615	|	|	...	1659	1706	...	1709	1716	1747		1805
St Brieuc **282** d.	1240	1318	...	1326	1416	...	1431	1440	...	1536	1613	...	1627	1632	1641	1642	1712	1718	...	...	1726	1734	1804	1812	...
Lamballe **282** d.	|	1330	...	...	1427	...	1442	|	...	1548	1627	...	1638	1643	|	|	1727	...	...	...	1737	1747	1815	1826	...
Rennes a.	1333	1421	...	...	1521	...	1525	1529	...	1629	1720	...	1720	1725	1729	1729	1821	...	...	...	1817	1825	1857	1921	...
Paris Montparnasse **280** a.	1510	...	...	...	...	...	...	1708	...	1809	...	...	...	...	1906	1906	...	...	...	...	...	2020	...	...	...

	Ⓐ	①–④	⑤	*TGV* **8642** Ⓑ q	† ◧	Ⓐ ◧	*TGV* **8644** ⑦ r	Ⓐ	*TGV* **8692** ⑦ r	①–④	⑥	†	⑤	⑤	†	①–④	⑥	†	Ⓐ	⑥	*TGV* **8646** L	†	†	Ⓐ	*TGV* **8652** ⑦ r
Brest **286** d.	...	1701	1705	1722	1730	1740	1759	...	...	1806	1808	1809	1810	...	...	...	...	...	1901	1906	1922	1939	...	2009	2019
Landerneau **286** d.	...	1717	1716	|	1741	1754	|	...	...	1818	1821	1820	1822	...	...	...	...	...	1917	1917	|	1950	...	2020	|
Landivisiau d.	...	1730	1726	|	1751	1804	|	...	...	1828	1834	1830	1832	...	...	...	...	...	1929	1927	|	2000	...	2030	|
Morlaix d.	...	1747	1742	1755	1806	1818	|	...	...	1843	1948	1846	1847	...	...	...	...	...	1944	1942	1955	2016	...	2046	2051
Lannion d.	1735	...	|	|	|	|	|	...	1855	|	...	|	|	1932	...	1934	1936	1937	...	|	|	|	2037	|	|
Plouaret-Trégor d.	1751	...	1800	|	1823	1839	|	...	|	1859	...	|	1903	1948	...	1949	1952	1953	...	1959	|	2033	2053	|	|
Guingamp d.	1804	...	1816	1824	...	...	|	...	1925	1914	...	1915	1918	2003	...	2003	...	2008	...	2014	2024	2048	2107	2115	2121
St Brieuc **282** d.	1823	...	1832	1841	...	...	1910	1912	1943	1931	...	1932	1935	...	2018	2019	...	...	...	2031	2041	2105	...	2132	2138
Lamballe **282** d.	...	...	1843	|	...	...	|	1928	|	1942	...	1943	1946	...	2030	...	...	...	...	2042	|	2117	...	2143	2151
Rennes a.	...	...	1925	1929	...	...	|	2021	2029	2025	...	2025	2029	...	2121	...	...	...	...	2125	2129	2157	...	2225	2229
Paris Montparnasse **280** a.	...	...	...	2108	...	...	2124	...	2208	...	...	...	...	...	...	...	...	...	...	...	2311	...	...	...	0008

A – ①–⑤ **e** until June 30; ①–⑥ July 3 - Sept. 2 (not Aug. 15); ①–⑤ from Sept. 4.
B – ⑥⑦ **f** until July 9; daily July 10 - Sept. 3; ⑥⑦ from Sept. 9.
C – ①–⑤ **e** until July 7 and from Sept. 4.
D – ①–⑥ **h** until July 1; daily July 3 - Sept. 3; ①–⑥ from Sept. 4.
E – ①②③④⑥.
F – ①②③④⑥⑦ (also May 19, July 14; not May 17, July 13).
G – ①–④ until July 6 and from Sept. 4 (not Apr. 10, May 1, 8, 17, 18, 29).
H – ⑦ until July 9; ①②③④⑦ July 10 - Aug. 27 (not July 13, Aug. 14); ⑦ from Sept. 3.
J – ①–⑤ **e** until July 7; ① July 10 - Aug. 28 (also Aug. 16; not Aug. 14); ①–⑤ from Sept. 4.
K – Not Mar. 1 – 3, 6 – 10, Oct. 23, 24, 26, 27, 30, 31, Nov. 2, 3.
L – Ⓑ until July 2 (not May 18, 19); daily July 3 - Sept. 3; Ⓑ from Sept. 4.

d – Mar. 13 – 24, Oct. 9 – 20.
e – Not Apr. 10, May 1, 8, 18, 19, 29.
f – Also Apr. 10, May 1, 8, 18, 19, 29.
g – July 8 - Sept. 3.
h – Not Apr. 10, May 1, 8, 29.
m – Not Apr. 9, 30, May 7, 28.

◧ – 2 Lannion - Brest and v.v. (see both directions of Table).
⊠ – OUIGO low-cost TGV service. Internet booking only (www.ouigo.com).
TGV – High-speed train. Ⓡ. 🍸.

p – Not Apr. 10, May 1, 8, 29, July 15.
q – Not Apr. 9, May 18, 19, July 14, Aug. 14.
r – Also Apr. 10, May 1, 8, 29, Aug. 15.
t – Also May 17, July 13; not May 19, July 14.
u – From St Brieuc on ①–④ (d. 2027).

RENNES and NANTES - QUIMPER 285

TGV services are subject to alteration Apr. 8 – 10, May 18 – 21, Sept. 23, Oct. 7 – 10. *TGV* timings may vary by a few minutes - please check your reservation.

km		Ⓐ	Ⓐ	Ⓐ	Ⓐ	Ⓐ	⚒	*TGV* 8701 ①–⑤ A	Ⓐ	*TGV* 8703 ①–⑤ e	*TGV* 8705 ⑥ f	†	⑥	⑥	*TGV* 8707 B	†	Ⓐ	Ⓐ	⑥	*TGV* 8715	†	⑥	†	Ⓐ	Ⓒ
0	*Paris Montparnasse* **280** .. d.	...	...	...	...	...	...	0656	...	0730	0753	...	...	...	0840	...	...	...	...	1053	...	...	...	...	...
365	**Rennes** d.	0607	0621		0705	...	0740	0829	0840	0929	|	...	0943	...	1029	1135	1135	...	...	1229	...	...	...	1240	1240
	Nantes 288 d.	|	|	0614	|	0643	|	|	|	|	|	0919	|	0925	|	|	|	1118	1119	|	1215	1226	1242	|	|
	Savenay 288 d.	|	|	0639	|	0710	|	|	|	|	|	0951	|	0946	|	|	|	1140	1142	|	1246	1248		|	|
437	Redon d.	0643	0706	0711	0747	0747	0822	|	0924	|	|	1023	1023	1023	1106	1212	1217	1217	1215	|	1316	1320	1326	1324	1330
492	Vannes d.	0712	0737	...	0815	0815	0855	0928	0958	1029	1027	...	1052	1052	1132	1240	1246	1246	...	1328	...	...	1352	1355	1401
511	Auray ⊡ d.	0724	...	...	0828	0828	...	|	...	1042	1041	...	1104	1104	1145	1252	1258	1258	...	1341	...	...	|	...	...
545	Lorient d.	0746	...	...	0848	0848	...	0954	...	1101	1100	...	1124	1124	1203	1313	1318	1318	...	1400	...	...	1419	...	...
565	Quimperlé d.	0759	...	...	0901	0901	...	|	...	|	1113	...	1137	1137	|	1325	1331	1331	...	|	...	...	|	...	...
612	**Quimper** a.	0828	...	...	0929	0929	...	1028	...	1137	1153	...	1204	1204	1238	1353	1359	1359	...	1434	...	...	1455	...	...

	①⑤	*TGV* 8717 ⑥⑦ g	Ⓐ	†	⑥	⑥	⑤	⑤	*TGV* 7615 ⊠	†	⑤	*TGV* 8723 C	*TGV* 8723 D	Ⓐ	*TGV* 8725 E	†	⚒	Ⓒ F	Ⓐ	Ⓐ		Ⓐ	Ⓐ	†
Paris Montparnasse **280** d.	...	1153	...	...	...	...	...	...	1244	...	...	1441	1441	...	1459	...	...	...	...	...	...	...	...	...
Rennes d.	...	1329	...	1335	1335	...	1340	1435	1445	1453	1605	1629	1629	...	|	1635	1640	...	1705	...	1735	...	1740	...
Nantes 288 d.	1250	|	1314	|	|	1317	|	|	|	|	|	|	|	1614	|	|	|	1655	|	1646	|	1714	|	1719
Savenay 288 d.	|	|	1337	|	|	1340	|	|	|	|	|	|	|	1637	|	|	|	|	|	1709	|	1738	|	1753
Redon d.	1341	|	1411	1412	1418	1418	1424	1512	|	1542	1644	1705	1705	1711	|	1712	1724	1740	1747	1747	1812	1814	1824	1827
Vannes d.	1410	1428	...	1440	1447	1447	1455	1540	1547	1613	1714	1731	1731	...	1727	1741	1800	1809	1816	1816	1838	...	1855	
Auray ⊡ d.	1422	1441	...	1452	1459	1459	...	1551	1601	...	1726	|	1741	...	1740	1753	...	|	1828	1828	1850	...	...	...
Lorient d.	1443	1500	...	1513	1520	1520	...	1612	1620	...	1748	1758	1802	...	1758	1814	...	1838	1848	1848	1909	...	...	...
Quimperlé d.	1456	|	...	1525	1532	1532	...	1623	|	...	1759	1811	1815	...	1811	1826	...	|	1901	1901	1921	...	...	...
Quimper a.	1523	1534	...	1553	1559	1559	...	1651	1656	...	1826	1840	1844	...	1840	1853	...	1915	1929	1929	1950	...	...	...

	Ⓐ F	*TGV* 8727 ⑤ k	*TGV* 8729 G	⚒	⑤	†	⑥–④	*TGV* 8731 H	*TGV* 8735 ⑤ k	Ⓐ	⑥	⑥	Ⓐ	†	*TGV* 8739 G	*TGV* 8747 ⑤ k	Ⓐ	†	⑤	*TGV* 8751 J	*TGV* 8753 ⑤ N	*TGV* 8755 ⑤ k	*TGV* 8791 ⑤ m	*TGV* 8791 ⑤ n
Paris Montparnasse **280** d.	...	1641	1652	...	...	...	...	1756	1757	...	...	...	...	...	1840	1912	...	...	...	1954	2016	2053	2116	2212
Rennes d.	...	|	1829	...	1840	...	1840	1925	1931	...	1941	...	1940	1940	2029	|	...	...	2044	2129	|	2229	2332	0029
Nantes 288 d.	1757	|	|	1814	|	1827	|	|	|	1914	|	1926	|	|	|	|	2014	2016	|	|	|	|	|	|
Savenay 288 d.	|	|	|	1838	|	1848	|	|	|	1939	|	1947	|	|	|	|	2037	2050	|	|	|	|	|	|
Redon d.	1842	1849	|	1911	1917	1913	1924	|	|	2011	2024	2024	2024	2029	2105	|	2111	2123	2129	2205	2224	|	|	|
Vannes d.	1909	1916	1927	...	1945	1942	2003	2027	2029	...	2053	2053	2055	2100	2131	2136	...	...	2200	2231	2251	2327	0031	0128
Auray ⊡ d.	1921	1929	1940	...	1959	1955	...	|	2042	...	2105	2105	...	...	2144	|	...	...	...	2244	2304	2340	0044	0141
Lorient d.	1940	1948	1959	...	2016	2016	...	2054	2101	...	2126	2126	...	...	2202	2202	...	...	...	2302	2325	2358	0100	0159
Quimperlé d.	|	2002	|	...	2027	2029	...	|	|	...	2138	2138	...	...	2216	|	...	...	...	2316	2339	|	...	...
Quimper a.	2015	2031	2033	...	2053	2057	...	2128	2135	...	2206	2206	...	...	2245	2234	...	...	...	2345	0008	0032	...	...

	TGV 8790 ①–⑤ A	⑥	Ⓐ	*TGV* 8702 K	*TGV* 8702 ①–⑤ A	Ⓐ	Ⓐ	⑥	Ⓐ	⚒	*TGV* 8704 ①–⑤ A	Ⓐ F	Ⓐ	Ⓐ	*TGV* 8706 ①–⑥ p	†	†	①⑤	Ⓒ F	*TGV* 8710 L	⑥	Ⓐ	†	⚒
Quimper d.	...	...	...	0509	0513	0533	0533	...	...	...	0626	0650	...	...	0721	...	...	0836	0853	0909	1038	...	1058	...
Quimperlé d.	...	...	...	0538	0543	0600	0600	...	...	...	|	|	...	...	|	...	...	0903	|	0938	1104	...	1124	...
Lorient d.	0524	...	...	0552	0557	0614	0614	...	...	...	0701	0725	...	...	0756	...	...	0916	0927	0952	1117	...	1137	...
Auray ⊡ d.	|	...	...	0610	0615	0634	0634	...	...	...	|	0743	...	...	0814	...	...	0937	|	1010	1137	...	1159	...
Vannes d.	0550	0601	0602	0623	0628	0646	0646	0701	0702	...	0727	0755	0802	...	0827	0857	...	0949	0953	1023	1149	1159	1211	...
Redon d.	0616	0632	0632	0651	|	0720	0726	0732	0733	0747	|	0825	0832	0847	|	0928	0932	1021	1023	1051	1221	1230	1241	1247
Savenay 288 d.	|	|	|	|	|	|	0752	|	|	0820	|	|	|	0920	|	|	1005	|	|	|	|	|	|	1320
Nantes 288 a.	|	|	|	|	|	|	0816	|	|	0843	|	0908	|	0943	|	|	1039	1104	1105	|	|	|	|	1344
Rennes a.	0650	0721	0721	0725	0725	0756	...	0821	0817	...	0825	...	0917	...	0925	1017	...	...	...	1125	1256	1317	1317	...
Paris Montparnasse **280** a.	0850	...	...	0908	0908	...	...	...	...	...	1005	...	...	...	1119	...	...	...	...	1319	...	...	...	...

	TGV 8720 M	⑥	Ⓐ	Ⓐ	†	⑥	*TGV* 8722		†	⑥	Ⓒ	†	⑤	*TGV* 8724 q	†	Ⓐ		Ⓐ	†	*TGV* 8730 M	Ⓐ	†	Ⓐ	Ⓐ
Quimper d.	1127	...	1202	1202	1206	1236	1314	...	1339	...	1407	...	1407	1411	...	...	...	...	1505	1512	...	...	1557	...
Quimperlé d.	|	...	1229	1229	1233	1303	|	...	1405	...	1434	...	1434	|	...	...	...	...	1532	1542	...	...	1624	...
Lorient d.	1202	...	1242	1242	1246	1316	1350	...	1418	...	1447	...	1447	1446	...	...	...	...	1544	1556	...	...	1637	...
Auray ⊡ d.	|	...	1303	1303	1306	1336	1409	...	1439	...	1505	...	1507	1504	...	...	...	...	1605	1614	...	...	1658	...
Vannes d.	1228	1301	1315	1315	1318	1349	1422	...	1452	1503	1517	...	1519	1517	1556	1603	...	...	1617	1627	1657	1657	1710	...
Redon d.	|	1332	1350	1357	1350	1421	1450	...	1525	1534	1545	1550	1550	|	1627	1634	...	1647	1648	|	1728	1728	1741	1748
Savenay 288 d.	|	|	|	1423	|	|	|	...	|	|	|	1619	|	|	|	|	...	1720	1713	|	|	|	|	1820
Nantes 288 a.	|	|	|	1446	|	1504	|	...	1607	|	|	1644	|	|	|	|	...	1744	1736	|	|	|	|	1844
Rennes a.	1325	1421	1425	...	1425	...	1525	...	...	1617	1621	...	1625	|	1717	1717	...	...	...	1725	1813	1817	1817	...
Paris Montparnasse **280** a.	1506	...	...	...	...	...	1708	...	...	...	...	...	...	1747	...	...	...	...	...	1906	...	...	...	...

	Ⓒ	†	⑥	*TGV* 8732 ⑦ r	Ⓐ	†	⑥	Ⓑ	⑤	*TGV* 7616 ⊠	⑥	Ⓐ	Ⓐ	*TGV* 8742 ⑦ r	Ⓐ	†	Ⓐ	†	*TGV* 8744 ⑦ r	*TGV* 8746 ①–⑥ p	†	*TGV* 8794 ⑦ s	Ⓐ	*TGV* 8752 ⑦ r
Quimper d.	1613	...	...	1655	...	...	...	...	1716	1737	1754	...	...	1808	1835	1835	1835	1835	1909	1916	1944	...	2006	2020
Quimperlé d.	1639	...	...	|	...	...	...	...	1744	|	1821	...	...	1836	1901	1902	1901	1902	|	|	2010	...	2032	|
Lorient d.	1652	...	...	1730	...	...	...	...	1757	1812	1833	...	...	1850	1914	1915	1914	1915	1945	1951	2023	2028	2045	2055
Auray ⊡ d.	1710	...	...	|	...	...	...	...	1814	1831	1854	...	...	1908	1934	1936	1934	1936	2003	2009	2043	2047	2102	2113
Vannes d.	1722	...	...	1756	1803	1805	1811	...	1826	1844	1906	1904	...	1921	1946	1947	1946	1947	2016	2022	2055	2100	2114	2126
Redon d.	1750	1800	1801	|	1833	1836	1842	1847	1854	|	1940	1934	1947	1948	2021	2022	2027	2034	|	2049	2128	|	2142	|
Savenay 288 d.	|	1833	1833	|	|	|	|	1920	|	|	|	|	2020	|	|	|	2053	2106	|	|	|	|	|	|
Nantes 288 a.	|	1855	1907	|	|	|	|	1943	|	|	|	|	2043	|	|	|	2116	2140	|	|	|	|	|	|
Rennes a.	1825	...	...	|	1917	1920	1925	...	1929	1944	2016	2017	...	|	2057	2057	...	...	|	2125	2203	|	2217	2225
Paris Montparnasse **280** a.	...	...	...	2024	...	...	...	...	...	2148	...	...	...	2156	...	...	...	...	2245	2311	...	2329	...	0008

A – ①–⑤ **d** until July 7 and from Sept. 4.
B – Not Sept. 11 – 15, 18 – 22.
C – ①②③④⑥ **j** until July 6 and from Sept. 4.
D – ①②③④⑦ July 9 - Sept. 3 (not July 13, Aug. 14).
E – ⑤⑦ until July 2 (also Apr. 10, May 1, 8, 17, 29); ⑤⑥ July 7 - Sept. 2 (also July 13, Aug. 14); ⑤⑦ Sept. 8 - Dec. 8.
F – To / from Brest (Table **286**).
G – ①②③④⑥⑦ (also May 19, July 14; not May 17, July 13).
H – ①②③④⑦ (not May 17, 18, July 13, Aug. 14).
J – ⑤⑦ until May 7 (also May 1); Ⓑ May 8 - Dec. 8 (not May 18, 19, July 14, Aug. 14). Also to Lorient ①–④ until Mar. 23.
K – ⑥ until July 8; ①–⑥ July 10 - Sept. 2 (not Aug. 15); ⑥ from Sept. 9.
L – Not Sept. 25 – 29, Oct. 2 – 6.
M – Ⓑ until July 2 (not May 18, 19); daily July 3 - Sept. 3; Ⓑ from Sept. 4.
N – Runs to a different schedule Apr. 3 – 7, 11 – 14, Oct. 2 – 6, 9 – 13, 28.

d – Not Apr. 10, May 1, 8, 18, 19, 29.
e – July 10 - Sept. 1 (not July 14, Aug. 14, 15).
f – July 8 - Sept. 2 (also July 14, Aug. 14).
g – July 8 - Sept. 3 (also July 14, Aug. 14, 15).
j – Not Apr. 10, May 1, 8, 17, 18, 29.
k – Also May 17, July 13; not May 19, July 14.

m – Until Mar. 10.
n – Not Jan. 13 - Mar. 10.
p – Not Apr. 10, May 1, 8, 29, July 15.
q – July 8 - Sept. 3.
r – Also Apr. 10, May 1, 8, 29, Aug. 15.
s – July 9 - Sept. 3 (also Aug. 15).

⊡ – 🚌 **Auray - Quiberon** and v.v. (Breizhgo en Morbihan route **1**). Journey 75 minutes: From Auray at 0725 ⚒, 0755 ⚒, 0920 †, 0930 ⚒, 1055 Ⓐ, 1200 ⚒, 1205 †, 1355 †, 1405 ⚒, 1550 ⚒, 1605 †, 1620 ⚒, 1755 ⑤, 1825 ⚒, 1900 ⚒; from Quiberon at 0610 Ⓐ, 0658 Ⓐ, 0905 ⚒, 1055, 1250 ⚒, 1335 †, 1510 ⚒, 1630 †, 1705 ⚒, 1805 †, 1830 ⚒.

⊠ – OUIGO low-cost TGV service. Internet booking only (www.ouigo.com).

TGV – High-speed train. Ⓡ. 🍸.

286 BREST - QUIMPER

km																								
		Ⓐ H	Ⓐ	Ⓐ	Ⓒ H	Ⓐ		⑥	†	Ⓐ	†	⑥		⑥	†	Ⓐ	⑥	Ⓐ		†	⑥	Ⓐ	Ⓐ	†
0	**Brest** 284 d.	0546	0636	0741	0750	0837	...	1056	1156	1237	1335	1340	...	1432	1527	1625	1626	1735	...	1752	1757	1839	1942	2002
18	Landerneau 284 d.	|	0648	0753	|	0849	...	1108	1208	1248	1347	1352	...	1444	1539	1641	1637	1747	...	1804	1809	1851	1954	2014
72	Châteaulin d.	|	0734	0839	|	0933	...	1148	1248	1334	1431	1432	...	1528	1623	1724	1724	1832	...	1843	1849	1937	2044	2054
102	**Quimper** a.	0646	0755	0900	0851	0954	...	1209	1309	1356	1452	1453	...	1549	1644	1745	1745	1853	...	1904	1910	1958	2105	2115

	Ⓐ	Ⓐ	⑥	Ⓐ	⑥		†	Ⓐ	⑥	Ⓐ	†		⑥	†	†	⑥	Ⓐ		Ⓐ	Ⓐ	Ⓒ H	Ⓐ H	†
Quimper d.	0601	0711	0805	0910	1000	...	1030	1209	1219	1311	1408	...	1505	1600	1701	1701	1701	...	1809	1914	1917	2022	2144
Châteaulin d.	0631	0736	0835	0931	1021	...	1051	1230	1240	1336	1429	...	1526	1621	1722	1722	1722	...	1830	1935	|	|	2205
Landerneau 284 d.	0711	0816	0914	1006	1100	...	1130	1310	1319	1415	1507	...	1605	1700	1801	1801	1809	...	1915	2017	|	|	2244
Brest 284 a.	0724	0829	0926	1019	1112	...	1142	1322	1331	1427	1519	...	1617	1712	1813	1813	1821	...	1928	2030	2018	2123	2256

H – To/from Nantes (Table **285**).

287 RENNES - NANTES

Other journeys Rennes - Nantes and v.v. are possible by changing trains at Redon (see both directions of Table **285**).

km																								
		Ⓐ	Ⓐ		⚒	Ⓒ		Ⓐ	⚒		Ⓐ	†		⑤	⚒		Ⓐ	†					†	
0	**Rennes** d.	0636	0736	...	0836	1036	...	1131	1236	...	1336	1436	...	1536	1636	...	1731	1745	...	1836	1936	...	2036	...
145	**Nantes** a.	0752	0852	...	0952	1152	...	1252	1352	...	1452	1552	...	1652	1752	...	1852	1900	...	1953	2052	...	2152	...

	Ⓐ	Ⓐ		⚒	Ⓒ		⚒	†		Ⓐ	⑥		Ⓐ			Ⓑ	⚒		Ⓑ				
Nantes d.	0605	0705	...	0805	1005	...	1205	1305	...	1405	1509	...	1604	1705	...	1809	1905	...	2005	...	...	...	...
Rennes a.	0721	0821	...	0921	1121	...	1321	1421	...	1521	1625	...	1721	1821	...	1925	2021	...	2121	...	...	...	...

SLOWER TRAINS VIA SABLÉ SUR SARTHE

km																								
		Ⓐ	Ⓐ	Ⓐ	⚒	Ⓐ	⑥	Ⓐ		Ⓒ	Ⓐ		Ⓐ	Ⓐ	†	Ⓐ J		Ⓐ	Ⓐ	Ⓒ	Ⓐ	Ⓐ	†	⑤
0	**Rennes** 280a d.	0556	0627	0652	0656	0743	0856	0906	...	1056	1056	1155	1256	1456	1556	1656	...	1700	1742	1756	1800	1855	1920	2009
38	Vitré 280a d.	0617	0652	0716	0727	0814	0917	0927	...	1117	1117	1226	1317	1517	1617	1717	...	1730	1814	1817	1831	1916	1941	2040
73	Laval 280a d.	0636	0718	0735	0752	0839	0937	0947	...	1136	1136	1251	1336	1536	1636	1736	...	1755	1831	1837	1856	1935	2000	2106
126	Sablé sur Sarthe a.	0700	...	0759	...	...	1000	1010	...	1200	1200	...	1402	1600	1700	1800	...	...	...	1859	...	2000	2020	...
126	Sablé sur Sarthe 280a d.	0711	...	0811	...	...	1006	1011	...	1206	1209	...	1406	1611	1705	1811	...	...	...	1901	...	2012	2022	...
174	Angers St Laud 280a d.	0734	...	0836	...	...	1034	1034	...	1233	1233	...	1430	1637	1729	1836	...	...	...	1927	...	2034	2048	...
262	**Nantes** 280a a.	0815	...	0915	...	...	1115	1115	...	1315	1315	...	1515	1717	1815	1916	...	...	...	2012	...	2116	2134	...

	Ⓐ	Ⓐ	Ⓐ	⚒	Ⓐ		⑥	Ⓐ	Ⓒ		Ⓐ		Ⓐ	⑤	Ⓐ	†	Ⓐ			Ⓐ	Ⓒ	Ⓐ	Ⓑ
Nantes 280a d.	...	0544	...	...	0744	...	0844	0941	1046	...	1144	...	1344	...	1542	1544	...	...	...	...	1744	1744	1941
Angers St Laud 280a d.	...	0628	...	...	0828	...	0927	1025	1128	...	1228	...	1428	...	1625	1627	...	...	...	...	1827	1828	2025
Sablé sur Sarthe 280a a.	...	0652	...	...	0852	...	0951	1049	1149	...	1252	...	1452	...	1649	1649	...	...	...	...	1849	1852	2049
Sablé sur Sarthe d.	...	0655	...	...	0900	...	0957	1057	1157	...	1305	...	1457	...	1657	1657	...	...	...	...	1857	1900	2057
Laval 280a d.	0636	0719	0724	0801	0923	...	1020	1120	1221	1301	1327	...	1520	1621	1720	1720	1731	...	1805	1905	1920	1922	2120
Vitré 280a d.	0701	0740	0748	0826	0943	...	1040	1140	1240	1326	1345	...	1540	1641	1740	1740	1758	...	1830	1930	1940	1942	2140
Rennes 280a a.	0731	0801	0820	0857	1004	...	1101	1201	1301	1357	1408	...	1601	1712	1801	1801	1830	...	1901	2001	2005	2005	2201

J – To/from Le Croisic on ⑤ (Table **288**).

288 NANTES - ST NAZAIRE - LE CROISIC

TGV services are subject to alteration Oct. 28–31, Nov. 1–10. *TGV* timings may vary by a few minutes - please check your reservation.

km																								
								TGV 8911		*TGV* 8901					*TGV* 8913		*TGV* 8917					*TGV* 8921		
		Ⓐ	Ⓐ	Ⓐ	⑥	Ⓐ	Ⓐ	①–⑥ d	Ⓒ A	B	Ⓐ	Ⓒ E		Ⓐ		Ⓐ	⑥ f	Ⓐ	⑥	Ⓐ	Ⓐ		⚒	Ⓐ
	Paris Montparnasse 280 d.	...	...	...	...	...	...	0628	...	0717	...	...	...	...	0930	...	1036	...	...	...	...	1236	...	...
0	**Nantes** 285 d.	0638	0710	0738	0746	0810	0838	0900	0904	0924	1010	1011	1110	1134	1200	1238	1300	1310	1322	1338	1438	1500	1610	1638
39	Savenay 285 d.	0702	0731	0802	0819	0831	0902	|	0926	|	1032	1034	1131	1202	|	1302	|	1332	1357	1402	1502	|	1631	1702
64	**St Nazaire** d.	0724	0747	0824	0843	0847	0924	0937	0946	0958	1048	1050	1147	1224	1236	1324	1338	1347	1421	1424	1524	1536	1647	1724
79	Pornichet d.	...	0759	...	0856	0858	...	0949	1003	...	1100	1109	1159	...	|	...	1350	1359	1432	...	...	|	1659	...
83	La Baule Escoublac d.	...	0808	...	0906	0908	...	0957	1011	...	1108	1117	1208	...	1254	...	1359	1408	1440	...	...	1554	1708	...
90	**Le Croisic** a.	...	0821	...	0919	0921	...	1009	1024	...	1121	1129	1221	...	1303	...	1413	1421	1452	...	...	1603	1721	...

	TGV 8923												*TGV* 8905	*TGV* 8927				*TGV* 8931		*TGV* 8935		*TGV* 8937	*TGV* 8939
	g	Ⓐ	Ⓐ	† H	⑥ H	Ⓐ	Ⓐ	Ⓒ	Ⓐ	⑤ C	Ⓐ		D	⑤ h	†	⑥ E	⑤ E		⑤	⑤ h	⑥–④	⑤ h	⑤ j
Paris Montparnasse 280 d.	1445	...	...	...	...	...	...	...	...	...	...	...	1748	1748	...	...	...	1844	...	1936	...	2046	2149
Nantes 285 d.	1659	1710	1738	1747	1753	1804	1838	1846	1910	1918	1939	...	2000	2000	2010	2010	2010	2105	2134	2202	2213	2300	2359
Savenay 285 d.	|	1732	1802	1809	1815	1827	1902	1919	1931	1945	2003	...	|	|	2031	2032	2032	|	2202	|	2240	|	|
St Nazaire d.	1737	1748	1824	1825	1830	1847	1924	1944	1947	2010	2025	...	2036	2037	2046	2047	2049	2142	2219	2239	2255	2337	0037
Pornichet d.	1750	1800	...	1837	1842	1859	...	1957	1959	2021	...	...	...	2049	2057	2100	2104	|	2230	2251	2306	|	|
La Baule Escoublac d.	1757	1808	...	1905	1850	1908	...	2006	2008	2028	...	...	...	2056	2104	2108	2111	2159	2237	2259	2313	2354	0054
Le Croisic a.	1809	1821	...	1916	1902	1921	...	2019	2021	2041	...	...	...	2108	2121	2121	2124	2208	2249	2314	2325	0003	0103

		TGV 8900		*TGV* 8910							*TGV* 8912						*TGV* 8916	*TGV* 8904					
	①	①–⑤ k	⚒	① m	Ⓐ	⑥	Ⓐ	Ⓐ	Ⓐ	Ⓒ E		Ⓐ	Ⓐ	Ⓐ	Ⓒ	Ⓐ	F	G	Ⓐ	Ⓒ	Ⓐ	Ⓐ	Ⓐ
Le Croisic d.	0442	...	0539	0555	...	...	0638	...	0738	0739	0755	...	0838	...	0939	1039	1048	...	1139	1154	...	1239	...
La Baule Escoublac d.	0454	...	0551	0607	...	...	0651	...	0751	0752	0807	...	0850	...	0955	1052	1104	...	1151	1209	...	1252	...
Pornichet d.	0501	...	0558	|	...	...	0658	...	0758	0758	|	...	0859	...	1002	1059	1110	...	1158	1216	...	1259	...
St Nazaire d.	0513	0524	0610	0623	0634	0648	0710	0734	0810	0810	0824	0834	0910	1015	1014	1111	1124	1124	1210	1230	1234	1311	1334
Savenay 285 d.	0527	|	0625	|	0656	0709	0724	0757	0824	0825	|	0856	0925	1030	1031	1125	|	|	1225	1255	1256	1325	1356
Nantes 285 a.	0555	0559	0648	0658	0721	0742	0748	0821	0848	0847	0859	0921	0948	1052	1053	1148	1202	1159	1248	1328	1321	1348	1421
Paris Montparnasse 280 a.	...	0815	...	0912	...	...	...	...	...	...	1138	...	...	...	...	...	1409	1409	...	...	...	...	...

	TGV 8922						*TGV* 8926						*TGV* 8928				*TGV* 8930	*TGV* 8932				*TGV* 8934	*TGV* 8936
		Ⓐ	Ⓐ	Ⓒ	Ⓐ	Ⓐ		Ⓐ	†	⑥	Ⓐ		⑦ n	Ⓐ	Ⓒ E	Ⓐ	⑦ p	①–⑥ d	Ⓐ	† A	⑤	⑦ p	⑦ n
Le Croisic d.	1349	1438	...	1539	...	1638	1655	...	1719	1730	1739	...	1739	...	1834	1838	1848	1855	1938	1951	...	2049	2144
La Baule Escoublac d.	1402	1451	...	1552	...	1651	1707	...	1731	1743	1752	...	1755	...	1847	1850	1904	1909	1951	2007	...	2105	2157
Pornichet d.	|	1459	...	1559	...	1658	|	...	1738	1750	1759	...	|	...	1853	1858	1911	|	1958	2015	...	2111	|
St Nazaire d.	1419	1510	1534	1611	1634	1710	1724	1734	1748	1803	1811	...	1811	1834	1907	1910	1924	1925	2010	2027	2109	2124	2213
Savenay 285 d.	|	1525	1556	1625	1656	1725	|	1756	1812	1827	1825	...	|	1856	1922	1924	|	|	2025	2043	2124	|	|
Nantes 285 a.	1459	1548	1621	1648	1721	1748	1759	1821	1845	1849	1848	...	1848	1921	1948	1948	1959	1959	2048	2105	2158	2201	2247
Paris Montparnasse 280 a.	1728	...	...	...	...	...	2031	...	...	...	...	...	2112	...	...	...	2228	2226	...	...	...	0012	0055

A – To/from Le Mans (Table **280a**).
B – ① until Mar. 20; ①–⑤ **e** Mar. 27 - July 7; ①–⑤ Sept. 4 - Dec. 8.
C – 2 Le Mans - Le Croisic; 2 Rennes - Le Croisic.
D – ①②③④⑦ (not May 17, 18, July 13, Aug. 14).
E – To/from Orléans (Tables **289** and **296**).
F – ⑦ until July 2; daily July 8 - Sept. 3; ⑦ from Sept. 10.
G – ① until Mar. 20; ①–⑥ Mar. 25 - July 7 (not Apr. 10, May 1, 8, 29); ①–⑥ Sept. 4 - Dec. 9.
H – To/from Tours (Table **289**).
d – July 8 - Sept. 2 (not Aug. 15).
e – Not Apr. 10, May 1, 8, 18, 19, 29.
f – Also May 18, 19, July 14, Aug. 14.
g – July 8 - Sept. 3.
h – Also May 17, July 13; not May 19, July 14.
j – July 21 - Sept. 1 (also July 13).
k – Not Apr. 10, May 1, 8, 18, 19, 29, July 14, Aug. 14, 15.
m – July 10 - Aug. 28 (also Aug. 16; not Aug. 14).
n – July 9 - Sept. 3 (also Aug. 15).
p – Also Apr. 10, May 1, 8, 29, Aug. 15.
TGV – High-speed train. 🅁. 🍸.

NANTES - ANGERS - TOURS 289

TGV and *INTERCITÉS* services are subject to alteration Apr. 8–10, 22, 23, May 6–8, 18–21, 27–29, Sept. 24, Oct. 1, 14, Nov. 25, 26 and on other dates indicated in footnotes.
TGV and *INTERCITÉS* timings may vary by a few minutes - please check your reservation. See Table **335** for *TGV* trains Nantes - Lyon via Le Mans.
Additional local trains are available Angers - Saumur and v.v., and Saumur - Tours and v.v. Frequent connecting services operate St Pierre des Corps - Tours and v.v. (journey 5 minutes).

km		*TGV* 5300	★ 4402	★ 4404	*TGV* 5306	*TGV* 5306 ⑤ A	★ 4406			
0	**Nantes** 280 d.	0448	0626	1140	1244	1244	1447	...	...	...
88	Angers St Laud 280 d.	0527	0710	1222	1327	1327	1528	...	...	...
132	Saumur Rive Droit d.	0550	0732	1247	1350	1350	1553	...	...	...
202	**St Pierre des Corps** a.	0624	0805	1323	1424	1424	1631	...	...	...
	Massy TGV a.	0725	|	|	1520	1520	|	...	...	...
	Lyon Part Dieu **290** a.	0930	1312	1826	1730	1730	2124	...	...	...
	Marseille St Charles **355** a.	|	...	...	...	1927	...	...	...	...
	Montpellier ⊡ **355** a.	1120	...	...	...	...	...	...	...	...

	TGV 5351 C	★ 4502	★ 4504 D	★ 4506	*TGV* 5358					
Montpellier ⊡ **355** d.	...	...	...	...	1641	...	...	...	...	...
Marseille St Charles **355** d.	...	...	...	...	|	...	...	...	...	...
Lyon Part Dieu **290** d.	0630	0934	1200	1544	1826	...	...	...	...	...
Massy TGV d.	0843	|	|	|	2035	...	...	...	...	...
St Pierre des Corps d.	0946	1428	1658	2029	2132	...	...	...	...	...
Saumur Rive Droit d.	|	1500	1731	2101	2206	...	...	...	...	...
Angers St Laud 280 d.	1042	1523	1754	2124	2224	...	...	...	...	...
Nantes 280 a.	1119	1604	1846	2208	2309	...	...	...	...	...

TER REGIONAL TRAINS NANTES - TOURS

km		Ⓐ	Ⓐ	Ⓐ	Ⓒ	Ⓐ	Ⓐ	Ⓐ			†	⑤	①–④	Ⓐ	⑥	†		Ⓐ	Ⓐ	Ⓐ	†	†	⑥	†
	Le Croisic **288** d.	...	...	...	0739	...	...	...	...	...	...	...	...	...	...	...	...	...	...	...	...	1834	1834	...
0	**Nantes** 280a 287 d.	*0544*	0713	*0739*	0912	0913	*0941*	1113	...	*1144*	...	*1417*	*1417*	1611	*1542*	*1644*	...	1713	1814	*1844*	1913	2013	2014	2213
88	Angers St Laud 280a 287 d.	0635	0756	0835	0956	0957	1035	1156	...	1239	1358	1537	1537	1656	1735	1735	...	1757	1856	1935	1958	2057	2102	2256
132	Saumur Rive Droit d.	0710	0817	0910	1017	1021	1111	1217	...	1312	1434	1611	1611	1722	1819	1819	...	1821	1918	2010	2019	2118	2124	2316
199	**Tours** a.	0749	0859	...	1102	1054	1201	1259	...	1402	*1719*	1700	*1706*	1801	1859	1859	...	1901	2000	...	2101	2206	2209	2351
	Orléans **296** a.	...	1030	...	1219	...	...	1423	...	...	...	...	...	...	...	...	...	...	2124	...	...	2325	2328	...

	Ⓐ	Ⓐ	Ⓐ	Ⓐ	Ⓒ	Ⓐ	Ⓐ		Ⓐ	⑤	Ⓒ	⑥	†	Ⓐ	Ⓐ		Ⓐ	⑤	⑥	⑤	①–④	Ⓐ	†
Orléans **296** d.	...	...	...	0638	0638	...	1106	...	...	...	...	...	...	...	...	...	...	...	1638	1638	1638	...	1738
Tours d.	...	0656	...	0810	0810	0855	1237	...	1242	1440	1456	1552	1552	...	1600	...	...	...	1807	1807	1810	1839	1910
Saumur Rive Droit d.	0622	0738	0748	0841	0843	0937	1310	...	1349	1535	1539	1634	1634	1648	1639	...	1748	1748	1840	1840	1841	1948	1942
Angers St Laud 280a 287 d.	0702	0804	0824	0904	0906	1012	1333	...	1425	1602	1602	1657	1657	1723	1703	...	1824	1824	1904	1904	1904	2024	2006
Nantes 280a 287 a.	0746	0846	*0915*	0946	0947	*1115*	1415	...	*1515*	1646	1649	1742	1742	*1839*	1746	...	*1916*	*1916*	1946	1946	1946	*2118*	2047
Le Croisic **288** a.	...	...	...	...	1129	...	...	...	...	...	...	1902	1916	...	...	...	...	2041	2121	2124	...	...	...

A – Also May 17, July 13, Oct. 14; not May 19, July 14.
C – Not Mar. 1–3, 6–10, May 19–21, Sept. 11–15, 18–22, 25–29, Oct. 4–6, 14, 28, 29, Nov. 20–24, 27–30, Dec. 1.
D – Subject to alteration on ①–⑤ Nov. 6–24.
⊡ – Montpellier Sud-de-France.
★ – *INTERCITÉS.*
TGV – High-speed train. Ⓡ. 🍸.

TOURS - BOURGES - NEVERS - MOULINS - LYON 290

INTERCITÉS services are subject to alteration Apr. 8–10, 22, 23, May 6–8, 18–21, 27–29, Sept. 24, Oct. 1, 14, Nov. 25, 26 and on other dates indicated in footnotes.
INTERCITÉS timings may vary by a few minutes. See Table **335** for *TGV* trains Nantes / Tours - Massy - Lyon and v.v.

km		⚒	Ⓐ	Ⓐ		⚒	★ 4402			†	Ⓐ	★ 4404		★ 4406	Ⓑ	†		⑥	①–④	†	⑤		†	⚒
	Nantes **289** d.	...	...	...	...	...	0626	...	...	...	...	1140	...	1447	...	...	...	...	...	...	...	...	...	...
0	**Tours** d.	...	...	0628	...	0650	|	0928	...	...	1203	|	1404	|	1729	...	...	1757	1829	1829	1829	1929	2050	2051
3	St Pierre des Corps d.	...	...	0635	...	0658	0808	0935	...	...	1210	1326	1412	1634	1736	...	...	1804	1836	1836	1836	1936	2058	2058
32	Chenonceaux d.	...	...	0656	...	0719	|	0956	...	...	1230	|	1436	|	1756	...	...	1823	1855	1855	1855	1956	2125	2124
58	St Aignan Noyers d.	...	...	0713	...	0738	|	1013	...	...	1248	|	1452	|	1813	...	...	1840	1913	1913	1913	2013	2142	2141
113	Vierzon Ville 315 d.	...	...	0751	...	0819	0919	1052	...	...	1329	1437	1531	1740	1851	...	...	1919	1954	1954	1954	2054	2222	2220
145	**Bourges** 315 a.	...	...	...	...	0839	0941	1113	...	...	1349	1456	1549	1757	...	...	...	1942	2014	2014	2014	2114	2242	...
145	**Bourges** 315 d.	...	...	...	...	0841	0941	...	...	...	1351	1457	1551	1759	...	...	...	1944	2016	2016	2037	2116	...	...
214	**Nevers** 315 a.	...	...	...	...	0923	1023	...	...	...	1428	1539	1629	1835	...	...	...	2019	2103	2103	2128	2156	...	...
214	**Nevers** 330 d.	...	0532	...	0836	...	1032	...	...	1232	1439	1546	...	1842	...	...	...	...	...	...	...	...	...	...
274	**Moulins-sur-Allier** . 330 373 d.	...	0607	...	0911	...	1102	...	...	1310	1509	1616	...	1911	...	...	...	...	...	...	...	...	...	...
	Digoin 373 d.	...	0648	...	0953	...	|	...	...	1351	1551	|	...	|	...	...	...	...	...	...	...	...	...	...
	Paray le Monial 373 d.	0535	0701	...	1021	...	|	...	...	1403	1605	|	...	|	...	2009	...	...	...	...	...	...	...	...
315	St Germain des Fossés d.	|	|	...	|	...	1127	...	...	...	|	1642	...	1936	...	|	...	...	...	...	...	...	...	...
381	Roanne 328 d.	|	|	...	|	...	1206	...	...	...	|	1721	...	2014	...	|	...	...	...	...	...	...	...	...
474	**Lyon** Part Dieu 328 a.	0725	|	...	1210	...	1312	...	...	...	1752	1826	...	2124	...	2206	...	...	...	...	...	...	...	...
479	**Lyon** Perrache 328 a.	0733	0850	...	1218	...	1322	...	...	...	1803	1839	...	2137	...	2214	...	...	...	...	...	...	...	...

km		②–⑤	①	Ⓐ	Ⓐ	Ⓒ	①Ⓒ	②–⑤	⚒	Ⓒ	★ 4502	⑤		★ 4504 D	Ⓐ	Ⓐ	†	Ⓒ	★ 4506	Ⓐ	Ⓐ	†		Ⓐ
0	**Lyon** Perrache 328 d.	...	...	...	...	...	...	...	...	0825	0920	...	...	1147	...	1325	...	...	1532	1658	...	...	1808	1916
5	**Lyon** Part Dieu 328 d.	...	...	...	...	...	...	...	...	0838	0934	...	...	1200	...	1338	1413	...	1544	|	...	...	1822	1928
	Roanne 328 d.	...	...	...	...	...	...	...	...	|	1040	...	...	1306	...	|	|	...	1648	|	...	...	|	|
	St Germain des Fossés d.	...	...	...	...	...	...	...	...	|	1119	...	...	1345	...	|	|	...	1728	|	...	...	|	|
129	Paray le Monial 373 d.	...	...	...	...	...	...	...	...	1017	|	...	...	|	...	1517	1552	...	|	1849	...	...	2007	2111
140	Digoin 373 d.	...	...	...	...	...	...	...	...	1031	|	...	...	|	...	1531	...	...	|	...	...	...	2021	2124
196	**Moulins-sur-Allier** . 330 373 d.	...	...	...	...	...	...	...	...	1122	1141	...	...	1407	...	1622	...	...	1751	...	...	...	2111	2213
256	**Nevers** 330 a.	...	...	...	...	...	...	...	...	1201	1218	...	...	1439	...	1654	...	...	1822	...	...	...	2145	2246
256	**Nevers** 315 d.	...	...	0523	0609	0709	0933	0933	...	1201	1225	...	...	1447	1609	1704	...	1709	1829	...	...	1923	...	...
325	**Bourges** 315 a.	...	...	0601	0647	0749	1011	1012	...	1238	1301	...	...	1529	1646	1741	...	1748	1906	...	...	2003	...	...
325	**Bourges** 315 d.	...	0521	0603	0649	0751	1013	1014	1147	1240	1303	1448	...	1530	1648	1743	...	1750	1907	...	...	2005	...	...
357	Vierzon Ville 315 d.	0536	0540	0624	0709	0811	1033	1034	1208	1301	1323	1507	...	1550	1709	1803	...	1810	1927	...	2013	2025	...	...
412	St Aignan Noyers d.	0614	0619	0704	0749	0851	1111	1116	1249	1342	|	1549	...	|	1748	1843	...	1848	|	...	2052	2106	...	...
438	Chenonceaux d.	0636	0642	0723	0807	0908	1129	1134	1307	1400	|	1608	...	|	1806	1901	...	1905	|	...	2109	2124	...	...
467	St Pierre des Corps a.	0701	0707	0742	0826	0928	1148	1201	1327	1420	1425	1629	...	1655	1826	1920	...	1926	2026	...	2128	2144	...	...
470	**Tours** a.	0708	0714	0749	0835	0935	1155	1208	1334	1427	|	1636	...	|	1833	1927	...	1933	|	...	2135	2151	...	...
	Nantes **289** a.	...	...	...	...	...	...	...	...	...	1604	...	...	1846	...	...	...	...	2208	...	...	...	...	...

ADDITIONAL TRAINS TOURS - CHENONCEAUX - ST AIGNAN NOYERS

km		Ⓒ	Ⓐ ⊡	Ⓐ						
0	**Tours** d.	1451	1650	1751	1851	...	...	...	...	...
3	St Pierre des Corps d.	1458	1657	1758	1858	...	...	...	...	...
32	Chenonceaux d.	1525	1725	1824	1924	...	...	...	...	...
58	**St Aignan Noyers** a.	1546	1748	1846	1946	...	...	...	...	...

	Ⓐ ⊡	⑥	Ⓒ	Ⓐ ⊡	Ⓐ				
St Aignan Noyers d.	0632	0646	1630	1814	1916	2009	...	...	...
Chenonceaux d.	0655	0708	1652	1837	1938	2031	...	...	...
St Pierre des Corps a.	0721	0734	1717	1904	2004	2057	...	...	...
Tours a.	0728	0741	1723	1912	2011	2104	...	...	...

D – Subject to alteration ①–⑤ Nov. 6–24.
⊡ – Does not run during school holidays - please enquire locally for dates.
★ – *INTERCITÉS.*

291 ROANNE - ST ÉTIENNE

km		Ⓐ	Ⓐ	⚒		Ⓐ	⚒	Ⓐ		Ⓒ	Ⓐ		Ⓐ		Ⓐ		Ⓒ		Ⓐ				†
0	**Roanne** d.	0523	0556	0618	...	0656	0726	0826	...	0856	0956	1051	1226	1356	1456	...	1556	1656	1726	...	1826	1926	2026
80	**St Étienne** Châteaucreux a.	0633	0710	0733	...	0807	0837	0937	...	1007	1107	1203	1337	1407	1607	...	1707	1807	1837	...	1937	2037	2137

	Ⓐ	⚒	⚒			Ⓐ	⚒		Ⓐ				Ⓐ			Ⓐ	⚒			Ⓐ		
St Étienne Châteaucreux d.	0553	0623	0723	...	0823	0853	0953	...	1123	1223	1453	...	1555	1653	...	1723	1753	1823	...	1853	1955	2053
Roanne a.	0704	0734	0834	...	0934	1004	1104	...	1234	1334	1604	...	1704	1804	...	1834	1904	1934	...	2004	2104	2204

292 NANTES - LA ROCHELLE - BORDEAUX

INTERCITÉS services are subject to alteration Apr. 8 – 12, Oct. 7, 8, 14, 15, 21, 22, 28, 29.

km		Ⓐ	Ⓐ	⚒	Ⓐ	Ⓐ	Ⓐ	Ⓒ	Ⓐ	⚒	Ⓐ	3831 ★		Ⓒ	Ⓐ	3833 ★	⑥	Ⓒ	Ⓐ	Ⓐ	†	Ⓐ	†	Ⓐ	†
0	**Nantes** 293 d.	...	...	...	...	...	...	...	...	...	...	0755	...	...	...	1155	...	...	...	...	...	...	...	...	...
77	La Roche sur Yon 293 d.	...	...	...	...	...	...	...	...	...	...	0836	...	...	...	1236	...	...	...	...	...	...	...	...	...
113	Luçon d.	...	...	...	...	...	...	...	...	...	...	0900	...	...	...	1300	...	...	...	...	...	...	...	...	...
	La Rochelle P Dauphine d.	...	...	...	0540	...	0651	...	0729	0759	0831	|	...	1222	1228	|	1410	...	...	1512	1600	...	...	1640	...
180	**La Rochelle** Ville d.	...	0502	0527	0550	0610	0658	0728	0739	0806	0838	0943	1128	1229	1235	1343	1417	1526	...	1519	1607	1628	...	1650	1705
209	Rochefort d.	...	0531	0550	0620	0639	0730	0751	0803	0837	0909	1005	1151	1259	1306	1405	1448	1550	...	1548	1638	1651	...	1722	1730
253	Saintes d.	0540	...	0620	0711	...	...	0820	0837	...	0942	1034	1220	...	1340	1434	...	1619	1620	...	1712	1720	1720	1759	1802
	Angoulême **301** a.	|	...	|	...	...	...	|	|	...	...	|	|	...	...	|	...	|	|	...	...	|	|	...	|
	Jonzac d.	0620	...	0658	...	...	...	0859	0918	...	...	1111	1258	...	...	1511	...	1659	1658	...	...	1801	1800	...	1843
376	**Bordeaux** St Jean a.	0726	...	0805	...	...	...	1004	1024	...	...	1207	1404	...	...	1607	...	1803	1804	...	...	1906	1905	...	1952

	Ⓐ	3835 ★	Ⓐ	⚒	†	3837 ★	Ⓐ	Ⓑ	Ⓐ
Nantes 293 d.	...	1555	...	...	...	1755	...	...	1935
La Roche sur Yon 293 d.	...	1636	...	...	...	1836	...	...	2031
Luçon d.	...	1700	...	...	...	1900	...	...	2100
La Rochelle Porte Dauphine d.	1710	|	1805	1843	1843	|	2021	2128	|
La Rochelle Ville d.	1717	1743	1812	1850	1850	1943	2028	2135	2140
Rochefort d.	1747	1805	1843	1923	1920	2005	2059	2207	...
Saintes d.	...	1834	1918	1957	...	2034	2134	2241	...
Angoulême **301** a.	...	|	...	...	...	|	...	...	...
Jonzac d.	...	1911	...	...	...	2111	...	...	...
Bordeaux St Jean a.	...	2011	...	...	...	2207	...	...	...

	Ⓐ	Ⓐ	Ⓐ	Ⓐ	⚒	Ⓐ	Ⓐ	Ⓐ	3852 ★
Bordeaux St Jean d.	...	...	...	...	...	...	0556	0656	0753
Jonzac d.	...	...	...	...	...	...	0654	0754	0841
Angoulême **301** a.	...	...	...	...	...	...	|	|	|
Saintes d.	...	...	0549	...	0631	0725	0738	0840	0925
Rochefort d.	0542	...	0625	0645	0706	0800	...	0909	0956
La Rochelle Ville d.	0613	0619	0654	0716	0738	0843	...	0932	1019
La Rochelle Porte Dauphine a.	0619	|	...	0722	0743	0848	...	...	|
Luçon d.	...	0700	...	...	...	...	...	...	1100
La Roche sur Yon 293 d.	...	0724	...	...	...	...	...	...	1124
Nantes 293 a.	...	0805	...	...	...	...	...	...	1205

	⑥	Ⓐ	⑥	3854 ★	Ⓐ	Ⓐ	Ⓒ		3856 ★	Ⓐ	⑥	⑤	Ⓐ			Ⓐ	†	Ⓐ	3858 ★	†	Ⓐ		Ⓐ	†
Bordeaux St Jean d.	...	...	0842	0953	...	...	...	1256	1353	...	...	1456	...	1547	...	...	...	1656	1753	...	...	1855	1956	2002
Jonzac d.	...	...	0940	1041	...	...	...	1354	1441	...	...	1551	...	1645	...	...	...	1757	1841	...	...	1956	2054	2100
Angoulême **301** a.	...	...	|	|	...	...	...	|	|	...	...	|	...	|	...	...	...	|	|	...	...	|	|	|
Saintes d.	...	1004	1027	1125	1204	...	...	1440	1525	...	...	1635	1643	1731	1805	...	1847	1842	1925	...	1959	2042	2140	2146
Rochefort d.	1021	1039	1055	1156	1239	1306	1310	1509	1556	1613	1706	...	1719	1800	1839	1902	1922	...	1956	2022	2034	2111	2209	2215
La Rochelle Ville d.	1057	1110	1118	1219	1310	1337	1346	1532	1619	1648	1736	...	1750	1825	1909	1932	1954	...	2019	2056	2105	2134	2232	2238
La Rochelle Porte Dauphine a.	1102	1116	...	|	1316	1343	1350	...	|	1654	1742	...	1755	1832	1915	...	1959	...	|	2102	2111	...	...	...
Luçon d.	...	...	...	1300	...	...	...	...	1700	...	...	...	...	...	...	...	...	...	2100	...	...	...	...	...
La Roche sur Yon 293 d.	...	...	...	1324	...	...	...	...	1724	...	...	...	...	...	...	...	...	...	2124	...	...	...	...	...
Nantes 293 a.	...	...	...	1405	...	...	...	...	1805	...	...	...	...	...	...	...	...	...	2205	...	...	...	...	...

★ – *INTERCITÉS.*

293 NANTES - LES SABLES D'OLONNE

TGV services are subject to alteration Mar. 6 – 17, May 19, Oct. 23 - Nov. 3. *TGV* timings may vary by a few minutes - please check your reservation.

km		Ⓐ	Ⓐ	Ⓑ	⑥	Ⓒ h	⑥ j	† k	⑥	Ⓐ	*TGV* 8973	Ⓐ	†	⑥	*TGV* 8975 ①–④ d	Ⓐ	*TGV* 8977 ⑤–⑦ e	Ⓒ	Ⓐ	Ⓐ	Ⓐ	Ⓑ	⑥	⑤		*TGV* 8985	⑤†
	Paris M'parnasse **280** d.	...	...	...	...	...	...	...	...	...	0930	...	...	...	1220	...	1332	...	...	...	...	...	...	...	...	1844	...
0	**Nantes** 292 d.	0601	0708	0908	0935	1008	1009	1035	1108	1109	1205	1235	1308	1408	1431	1535	1606	1608	1635	1708	1735	1808	1835	1908	2008	2110	2213
77	La Roche sur Yon 292 a.	0651	0800	0959	1026	1103	1100	1125	1200	1202	1246	1325	1400	1500	1512	1625	1646	1700	1725	1759	1825	1900	1926	2000	2100	2150	2304
77	La Roche sur Yon d.	0653	0804	1000	1028	1105	*1124*	1127	1202	1214	1248	1327	1402	1502	1514	1627	1648	1702	1727	1801	1829	1904	1928	2002	2102	2153	2306
114	**Les Sables d'Olonne** a.	0722	0833	1030	1101	1132	*1151*	1153	1232	1244	1314	1400	1434	1532	1540	1659	1714	1734	1800	1828	1903	1936	2000	2031	2132	2219	2335

	Ⓐ	*TGV* 8970 ①–⑤ A	Ⓐ	Ⓐ	⑥	†	Ⓐ	Ⓐ	*TGV* 8972 B	⑥	Ⓑ	Ⓒ	Ⓐ	Ⓐ	⑥	Ⓐ	*TGV* 8984		†	Ⓐ	*TGV* 8986 ①–⑥ f	⑥ m	†	Ⓐ	*TGV* 8988 ⑦ g	†
Les Sables d'Olonne d.	0526	0544	0620	0651	0719	0728	0731	0928	0944	1030	1036	1201	1213	1328	1423	1428	1544	1628	1701	1728	1744	1828	1828	1832	1944	2028
La Roche sur Yon a.	0552	0608	0649	0725	0748	0757	0800	0957	1008	1100	1102	1233	1245	1357	1453	1457	1608	1657	1734	1757	1808	1857	1857	1901	2008	2057
La Roche sur Yon 292 d.	0554	0610	0659	0735	0750	0759	0802	0959	1010	1102	1104	1235	1259	1359	1455	1459	1610	1659	1736	1759	1810	1858	1859	1902	2011	2059
Nantes 292 a.	0650	0654	0754	0826	0846	0854	0854	1054	1054	1154	1157	1325	1354	1454	1550	1554	1656	1754	1828	1854	1854	1954	1954	1954	2052	2154
Paris Montparnasse **280** a.	...	0912	...	...	...	...	...	...	1325	...	...	...	...	...	...	...	1917	...	...	...	2112	...	...	...	2316	...

A – ①–⑤ until July 7 and from Sept. 4 (not Apr. 10, May 1, 8, 18, 19, 29).
B – ⑥ Dec. 17 - July 1 (also May 18, 19); daily July 8 - Sept. 3; ⑥ Sept. 9 - Dec. 9.
d – July 10 - Aug. 31 (not July 13, Aug. 14, 15).
e – July 8 - Sept. 3 (also July 13, 14, Aug. 14, 15).
f – July 8 - Sept. 2 (not Aug. 15).
g – Also Apr. 10, May 1, 8, 29, Aug. 15.
h – Until Apr. 30.
j – From May 6.
k – From May 1.
m – Until Apr. 29.
TGV – High-speed train. 🅁. 🍷.

294 PARIS - LES AUBRAIS - ORLÉANS

km		Ⓐ	Ⓐ	⚒	Ⓐ	②	C	†		⚒		Ⓑ	⑥	⚒	⑤	Ⓐ	Ⓒ	Ⓐ		Ⓐ	Ⓒ	Ⓐ		Ⓑ	Ⓒ	①–④
0	**Paris** Austerlitz 296 315 d.	0538	0623	0641	0823	0905	0919	1030	1123	1226	1323	1506	1523	1623	1627	1723	1726	1753	1823	1826	1920	1923	1926	2021	2133	2313
119	Les Aubrais-Orléans 296 315 a.	0707	0721	0816	0921	1020	1020	1159	1218	1401	1422	1621	1621	1719	1730	1818	1857	1851	1918	1956	2022	2021	2057	2121	2228	0017
121	**Orléans** a.	0713	0728	0822	0928	1027	1027	1204	1225	1407	1428	1627	1627	1725	1737	1825	1904	1858	1926	2002	2029	2029	2102	2128	2235	0024

	⚒	Ⓐ	Ⓐ	Ⓐ	Ⓐ	⑥	⚒	⑥	†	Ⓐ	†	⚒	⚒	Ⓐ	⑥		⑤†	Ⓐ	⚒		⑤†		Ⓐ	†	⚒
Orléans d.	0504	0603	0634	0703	0730	0744	0844	0934	0943	1004	1042	1132	1228	1334	1334	1534	1627	1704	1732	1827	1836	1931	1937	2034	2134
Les Aubrais-Orléans 296 315 d.	0511	0611	0640	0711	0747	0749	0851	0940	0951	1011	1048	1139	1235	1341	1341	1541	1634	1711	1739	1834	1843	1938	1944	2040	2141
Paris Austerlitz 296 315 a.	0608	0706	0738	0806	0833	0916	1008	1045	1047	1110	1218	1238	1406	1436	1440	1636	1737	1806	1837	2015	1956	2036	2117	2141	2236

C – ①③④⑤†.

PARIS - TOURS 295

TGV services via high-speed line. Timings may vary by a few minutes - please check your reservation for confirmed timings.
See Table **300** for *TGV* services Paris - Vendôme-Villiers - St Pierre des Corps and v.v. See Table **296** for TER regional services Paris Austerlitz - Blois - Tours and v.v.

km		*TGV* 8301	*TGV* 8303	*TGV* 8311	*TGV* 8313	*TGV* 8315	*TGV* 8317	*TGV* 8319	*TGV* 8321	*TGV* 8323
				⑤		①–⑤	①–⑤	Ⓑ	①–⑥	⑦
		A	B	e		f	f	g	h	j
0	**Paris** Montparnasse ....d.	0728	1225	1528	1628	1728	1752	1828	1928	2057
162	Vendôme-Villiers TGV......d.	0816	1315	1616	1716	1815	1843	1915	2016	2145
221	St Pierre des Corps ....a.	0835	1335	1635	1735	1835	1907	1935	2035	2205
224	**Tours** ....a.	0845	1345	1644	1743	1845	1915	1945	2045	2219

	TGV 8300	*TGV* 8306	*TGV* 8308	*TGV* 8310	*TGV* 8314	*TGV* 8316	*TGV* 8318	*TGV* 8320	*TGV* 8322	*TGV* 8324
	①–⑤	①–⑤	①–⑤	①–⑥		⑤			⑤	⑦
	f	f	k	h	m	e	C		n	j
Tours ....d.	0606	0642	0755	0813	1213	1617	1714	1856	1914	2116
St Pierre des Corps ......d.	0614	0654	0803	0825	1225	1625	1725	1904	1921	2124
Vendôme-Villiers TGV...d.	0635	0715	|	0846	1246	1646	1746	1925	1945	2151
Paris Montparnasse......a.	0723	0802	0904	0933	1333	1733	1833	2012	2035	2239

A – ①–⑥ **d** until July 8; ⑥ July 15 - Sept. 2 (also July 14, Aug. 14); ①–⑥ from Sept. 4.
B – Daily until July 9; ⑤⑥⑦ July 14 - Sept. 3 (also July 13, Aug. 14, 15); daily from Sept. 4.
C – Ⓑ until July 9; ⑤⑦ July 16 - Sept. 3 (also July 13); Ⓑ from Sept. 4.
Runs 20 minutes earlier Sept. 10, Oct. 22, 29.
d – Not Apr. 10, May 1, 8, 29.
e – Also May 17, July 13; not May 19, July 14.
f – Not Apr. 10, May 1, 8, 18, 19, 29, July 14, Aug. 14, 15.
g – Not May 18, 19, July 14, 24 – 27, 31, Aug. 1 – 3, 7 – 10, 14.
h – Not Apr. 10, May 1, 8, 29, Aug. 15.
j – Also Apr. 10, May 1, 8, 29, Aug. 15.
k – Not Apr. 10, May 1, 8, 18, 19, 29, July 13, 14, 24 – 28, 31, Aug. 1 – 4, 7 – 11, 14, 15.
m – Runs 15 minutes later Mar. 20, 21, ①–④ Sept. 4 – 20, Sept. 21, 22, ①–⑤ Oct. 2 - Nov. 24.
n – Until July 7 and from Sept. 8 (also May 17; not May 19).

ORLÉANS and PARIS - BLOIS - TOURS 296

See Table **295** for direct *TGV* services Paris Montparnasse - Tours and v.v. See Table **300** for other *TGV* services Paris Montparnasse - St Pierre des Corps and v.v.
Frequent trains run St Pierre des Corps - Tours and v.v. (journey time 5 minutes) and Les Aubrais-Orléans - Orléans and v.v. (journey time 4 minutes).

km																									
		Ⓐ	Ⓒ	Ⓐ	Ⓐ	Ⓐ	⚒	Ⓐ		⚒	†	⑥	⑥	Ⓐ	†	Ⓐ	⑥	Ⓒ	Ⓐ	⑥	Ⓐ	⑥	Ⓐ	Ⓐ	Ⓒ
			B	A												A									
0	**Orléans** ....d.	0558	0638	0638	0707	...	0738	0742	...	0839	0909	0938	...	1042	1046	1106	1142	1238	1253	...	...	...	...	1438	1438
	Paris Austerlitz .... ◧ d.	|	|	|	|	...	|	|	0737	|	|	|	0929	|	|	|	|	|	|	...	...	1238	1238	|	|
	Les Aubrais-Orléans .... ◧ d.	|	|	|	|	...	|	|	0836	|	|	|	1028	|	|	|	|	|	|	...	...	1335	1345	|	|
27	Beaugency.........................d.	0616	0657	0658	|	...	0756	0812	|	0857	0928	0957	|	1100	1103	1129	1212	1257	1312	...	...	|	|	1457	1457
59	Blois ....d.	0635	0717	0719	0732	0748	0815	0839	0902	0919	0947	1019	1054	1122	1122	1152	1230	1319	1333	1334	1351	1401	1413	1519	1519
91	Amboise.............................d.	0657	0736	0738	|	0808	0836	...	0921	0938	1006	1038	1114	1143	1140	1207	...	1339	1353	1357	1415	1420	1433	1538	1538
112	St Pierre des Corps ....a.	0715	0753	0753	0757	0825	0853	...	0934	0952	1020	1052	1126	1157	1154	1219	...	1353	1408	1414	1437	1434	1454	1552	1552
115	**Tours** ....a.	0722	0800	0801	0804	0830	0900	...	0941	1000	1027	1100	1133	1204	1201	1227	...	1400	1416	1422	1444	1440	1501	1559	1600

	Ⓐ	⑥	⑤	①–④	†	Ⓐ	Ⓐ	Ⓐ	⑥	†		Ⓐ	Ⓐ	†		⚒	Ⓐ ⊡	†	Ⓐ			Ⓑ	⑤Ⓒ	①–④
		B	B	A						A														
Orléans..d.	1538	1638	1638	1638	1638	1642	1700	1738	1738	1738	1742	1802	...	...	...	1840	1846	1859	...	1941	2041	2138	...	...
Paris Austerlitz.......................◧ d.	|	|	|	|	|	|	|	|	|	|	|	|	...	...	1738	|	|	|	1838	|	|	|	2308	2313
Les Aubrais-Orléans...............◧ d.	|	|	|	|	|	|	|	|	|	|	|	|	...	...	1835	|	|	|	1937	|	|	|	0035	0017
Beaugency ....d.	1556	1656	1657	1658	1657	1711	1720	1756	1757	1757	1811	|	...	...	|	1859	1915	1918	|	2000	2100	2157	|	|
Blois ....d.	1619	1714	1716	1719	1717	1730	1739	1816	1816	1817	1830	1834	1836	1836	1902	1919	1934	1939	2002	2019	2122	2219	0101	*0131**
Amboise ....d.	1638	1733	1735	1737	1737	...	1759	1835	1836	1837	...	|	1901	1901	1922	1938	...	1957	2022	2038	2141	2238	0120	|
St Pierre des Corps ....a.	1652	1747	1749	1752	1752	...	1815	1850	1851	1853	...	1857	1916	1919	1935	1952	...	2013	2035	2052	2155	2253	0134	|
Tours...a.	1659	1754	1757	1800	1800	...	1822	1857	1858	1900	...	1904	1923	1926	1941	2000	...	2020	2041	2059	2203	2300	0141	*0236**

km																									
		Ⓐ	Ⓐ	Ⓐ	⚒	Ⓐ	Ⓐ	Ⓐ	①	⑥	②–⑤	Ⓐ	Ⓐ	Ⓒ	Ⓐ	Ⓒ	Ⓐ	Ⓒ	Ⓒ	Ⓐ	Ⓒ	⑥	Ⓐ	⑥	Ⓐ
															A				B						A
0	**Tours** ....d.	0501	...	0601	0612	...	0636	...	0700	0701	0701	0732	0738	0739	0859	0905	0939	0939	1102	1106	1112	1200	1224	...	1259
3	St Pierre des Corps ....d.	0508	...	0608	0620	...	0643	...	0708	0709	0710	0739	0745	0746	0908	0912	0946	0946	1110	1114	1121	1207	1231	...	1307
24	Amboise.............................d.	0522	...	0622	0634	...	0658	...	0724	0726	0727	|	0759	0800	0922	0925	0959	1000	1124	1127	1133	1221	1245	...	1322
56	Blois ....d.	0543	0606	0643	0656	0704	0723	0727	0745	0747	0748	0806	0819	0820	0943	0949	1023	1021	1143	1148	1154	1242	1305	1325	1343
88	Beaugency.........................d.	0601	0625	0701	|	0722	...	0745	0806	0807	0809	|	0838	0839	1003	|	1044	1040	1201	|	|	1301	1324	1352	1403
115	Les Aubrais-Orléans .... ◧ a.	|	|	|	0723	|	...	|	|	|	|	|	|	|	|	1018	|	|	|	1221	1223	|	|	|	|
234	**Paris** Austerlitz .... ◧ a.	|	|	|	0822	|	...	|	|	|	|	|	|	|	|	1123	|	|	|	1322	1322	|	|	|	|
	Orléans ....a.	0620	0654	0722	...	0751	...	0814	0826	0827	0829	0835	0856	0858	1024	...	1103	1103	1219	...	...	1321	1347	1421	1423

	Ⓒ	Ⓐ	†	⑤	Ⓐ	⚒	†	Ⓐ	Ⓐ ⊡	Ⓑ		Ⓐ	Ⓐ ⊡	⑥	⚒		Ⓐ		Ⓐ	Ⓐ	†	Ⓐ	†	⑥
																			A				B	B
Tours...d.	1401	1435	1500	1500	1513	1601	1613	...	1643	1701	1713	1733	...	...	1742	1801	1843	1906	2000	2101	2130	2201	2206	2209
St Pierre des Corps ....d.	1408	1442	1507	1507	1521	1608	1620	...	1650	1708	1721	1740	...	...	1749	1808	1850	1913	2008	2108	2138	2208	2214	2217
Amboise ....d.	1422	1456	1521	1521	1534	1622	1632	...	1708	1722	1734	|	...	...	1807	1822	1908	1928	2022	2122	2152	2222	2229	2232
Blois ....d.	1443	1519	1541	1542	1556	1643	1653	1718	1731	1743	1756	1807	1812	1812	1830	1843	1930	1948	2043	2143	2213	2243	2249	2252
Beaugency ....d.	1502	1537	1559	1600	|	1702	|	1745	...	1802	|	|	1838	1838	...	1902	...	2006	2103	2201	2232	2301	2307	2310
Les Aubrais-Orléans..............◧ a.	|	|	|	|	1623	|	1717	|	...	|	1823	|	|	|	...	|	...	|	|	|	|	|	|	|
Paris Austerlitz.....................◧ a.	|	|	|	|	1722	|	1816	|	...	|	1922	|	|	|	...	|	...	|	|	|	|	|	|	|
Orléans...a.	1521	1555	1617	1619	...	1721	...	1815	...	1820	...	1834	1908	1908	...	1922	...	2025	2124	2222	2251	2322	2325	2328

OUIGO TRAINS PARIS - BLOIS - NANTES ★

Paris Austerlitz ....d.	0718	1810
Juvisy ....d.	0735	|
Les Aubrais-Orléans ....d.	0826	1925
Blois ....d.	0855	1954
St Pierre des Corps ....d.	0924	2035
Saumur....................................d.	|	2108
Angers St-Laud.....................d.	1018	2133
Nantes ....a.	1104	2215

Nantes ....d.	0735	1840
Angers St-Laud...........................d.	0821	1924
Saumur...d.	0844	1949
St Pierre des Corps ....d.	0922	2030
Blois ....d.	0956	2102
Les Aubrais-Orléans....................d.	1033	2133
Juvisy ....a.	1133	2233
Paris Austerlitz ....a.	1148	2248

A – To / from Nantes (Table **289**).
B – To / from Le Croisic (Tables **289** and **288**).
◧ – See also Tables **294** and **315**.
⊡ – Does not run during school holidays - please enquire locally for dates.
* – Connection by 🚌.
★ – *Ouigo Classique*. Low-cost train. Outline timings – services may not run on all days shown. Internet booking only at www.ouigo.com. See also Table **278**.

NANTES - PORNIC and ST GILLES CROIX DE VIE 297

km																							
		Ⓐ	Ⓐ	Ⓒ	Ⓒ	⑥		⚒ 🚌	⑥	†	Ⓐ	Ⓒ		† 🚌	Ⓐ		Ⓐ		Ⓐ	Ⓒ	Ⓒ	Ⓐ 🚌	Ⓐ
0	**Nantes** ....d.	0707	0707	0909	0909	1009	...	1025	1109	1109	1113	1209	...	1215	1229	1309	1429	...	1504	1509	1609	1615	1632
24	Ste Pazanne...............................d.	0747	0750	0945	0948	1042	...	|	1142	1142	1146	1240	...	|	1302	1342	1502	...	1535	1542	1642	|	1708
54	**Pornic** ....a.	0815	|	1013	|	|	...	|	1210	|	|	1308	...	|	1330	|	1530	...	|	1610	|	|	|
63	Challans ....d.	...	0814	...	1011	1106	...	1132	...	1206	1210	...	...	1320	...	1405	...	...	1557	...	1705	1715	1731
84	**St Gilles Croix de Vie** ....a.	...	0831	...	1028	1122	...	...	...	1223	1227	...	...	...	...	1422	...	...	1614	...	1722	...	1748

	Ⓐ	†	⑥ 🚌	Ⓐ		Ⓐ	†	Ⓐ	⑤ 🚌		Ⓐ	⑥		⑥	Ⓐ	Ⓐ	† 🚌		Ⓐ	†	⑥ 🚌	Ⓐ 🚌
Nantes ....d.	1632	1709	1715	1725	...	1748	1805	1818	1840	...	1841	1909	...	1909	1935	2015	2015	...	2035	2109	2110	2220
Ste Pazanne...d.	1712	1743	|	1758	...	1824	1838	1851	|	...	1916	1947	...	1950	2006	2046	|	...	2106	2142	|	2250r
Pornic ....a.	1740	1810	|	|	...	1852	|	|	|	...	1944	2015	...	|	|	2114	|	...	|	2210	|	|
Challans ....d.	...	...	1822	1823	...	...	1901	1913	1953	...	...	...	...	2013	2029	...	2120	...	2128	...	2215	2328
St Gilles Croix de Vie ....a.	...	...	...	1840	...	...	1918	1930	...	...	...	...	...	2030	2046	...	...	...	2145	...	2247	2359

r – Ste Pazanne **Rue du Vigneau**. s – From June 17.

FOR RETURN SERVICE SEE NEXT PAGE →

297 ST GILLES CROIX DE VIE and PORNIC - NANTES

	Ⓐ	Ⓐ 🚌	Ⓐ	Ⓐ	Ⓐ	Ⓐ	⑥	⑥	Ⓐ	⑥ 🚌	†	†		⑥	Ⓐ	† 🚌	⑥	Ⓐ	Ⓐ	⚒	⚒ 🚌	⚒
St Gilles Croix de Vie d.	0539	...	...	0639	...	0733	...	0733	...	...	...	0903	...	0907	0939	...	...	1042	...	1239	...	...
Challans d.	0556	0610	...	0656	...	0749	...	0750	...	0905	...	0919	...	0924	0956	1035	...	1059	...	1256	1333	...
Pornic d.	|	|	0628	|	0716	|	0740	|	0825	|	0909	|	...	|	|	|	1050	|	1150	|	|	1350
Ste Pazanne d.	0618	|	0657	0718	0745	0812	0818	0818	0853	|	0949	0949	...	0947	1018	|	1118	1121	1219	1318	|	1418
Nantes a.	0650	0720	0729	0750	0816	0844	0850	0850	0924	1010	1020	1020	...	1020	1050	1140	1150	1153	1250	1350	1440	1450

	Ⓐ	† 🚌	†	Ⓒ	Ⓐ	Ⓐ		†	⑤ 🚌	⑥	⑥	†	Ⓐ	Ⓐ	† 🚌		⑥	⑥	†	†	⑥ s	⑥ s
St Gilles Croix de Vie d.	1432	1350	...	1539	...	1626	...	...	1700	...	1733	1736	...	1804	...	...	...	1833	...	1933	...	2135
Challans d.	1449	1422	...	1556	...	1643	...	...	1732	...	1749	1752	...	1825	1840	...	...	1849	...	1949	...	2152
Pornic d.	|	|	1450	|	1609	|	...	1650	|	1740	|	|	1754	|	|	...	1840	|	1940	|	2130	|
Ste Pazanne d.	1511	1502r	1519	1618	1638	1707	...	1718	|	1818	1818	1815	1825	1852	|	...	1918	1918	2018	2018	2155	|
Nantes a.	1544	1542	1550	1650	1715	1745	...	1750	1842	1850	1850	1846	1904	1924	1940	...	1950	1950	2050	2050	2220	2235

FOR RETURN SERVICE AND FOOTNOTES SEE PREVIOUS PAGE.

299 OTHER LOCAL SERVICES

ANGERS ST LAUD - CHOLET — Journey 41 – 50 minutes *60 km*

From Angers St Laud at 0619 Ⓐ, 0723 Ⓐ, 0823 Ⓐ, 0930 ⑥, 1025 Ⓐ, 1123, 1254 ⚒, 1623, 1723 Ⓐ, 1758 Ⓐ, 1822 ⚒, 1926 Ⓐ, 1954 †, 2026 †, 2028 ⚒, 2123 Ⓐ, 2238 ⑤†.

From Cholet at 0550 Ⓐ, 0610 Ⓐ, 0645 Ⓐ, 0649 ⑥, 0711 Ⓐ, 0749 Ⓐ, 0849, 1049 Ⓐ, 1149 ⑥, 1234 Ⓐ, 1355, 1649 Ⓑ, 1749, 1845 †, 1849 Ⓐ, 1918 Ⓐ, 1924 Ⓒ, 2154 †.

BAYONNE - ST JEAN PIED DE PORT — *50 km*

	Ⓐ	Ⓒ	Ⓐ	Ⓒ	Ⓐ	Ⓒ	Ⓐ	⑥	Ⓐ	† d	⑤
Bayonne d.	0641	0816	0852	1124	1235	1419	1713	1819	1836	1929	2013
Cambo les Bains d.	0710	0841	0921	1149	1304	1444	1742	1844	1907	1954	2038
St Jean P de Port a.	0746	0917	0957	1225	1340	1520	1818	1920	1943	2030	2114

	⚒	Ⓐ	Ⓐ	Ⓒ	Ⓐ	Ⓐ	Ⓒ	⑥	Ⓐ	† d	Ⓐ
St Jean P de Port d.	0629	...	0840	0938	...	1223	1238	1638	1701	1718	1826
Cambo les Bains d.	0709	0815	0920	1015	1200	1303	1315	1715	1741	1755	1906
Bayonne a.	0735	0840	0947	1040	1225	1329	1340	1740	1805	1820	1931

BORDEAUX - MONT DE MARSAN — *147 km*

	Ⓐ	Ⓐ	Ⓒ	⚒		Ⓐ	Ⓒ	Ⓐ	Ⓐ	Ⓒ
Bordeaux St Jean **305** d.	0553	0745	0836	1045	1245	1445	1545	1653	1745	1745
Facture Biganos **305** d.	0619	0809	0859	1109	1309	1509	1609	1716	1809	1808
Morcenx **305** d.	0657	0847	0938	1147	1347	1547	1650	1756	1847	1846
Mont de Marsan a.	0727	0914	1007	1214	1416	1614	1715	1829	1913	1917

	⚒	†	Ⓐ
Bordeaux St Jean **305** d.	1945	2029	2031
Facture Biganos **305** d.	2009	2053	|
Morcenx **305** d.	2047	2134	2126
Mont de Marsan a.	2114	2159	2146

	Ⓐ	Ⓐ	⑥
Mont de Marsan d.	0524	0741	0840
Morcenx **305** d.	0545	0814	0908
Facture Biganos **305** d.	|	0851	0952
Bordeaux St J.. **305** a.	0652	0916	1017

			Ⓐ		⑥	†	Ⓐ	Ⓐ	Ⓒ	Ⓐ
Mont de Marsan d.	1046	1241	1446	1546	1741	1742	1755	1842	1942	2046
Morcenx **305** d.	1114	1314	1514	1614	1812	1806	1825	1914	2008	2113
Facture Biganos **305** d.	1152	1352	1554	1651	1853	1850	1905	1952	2051	2152
Bordeaux St Jean **305** a.	1217	1417	1617	1716	1917	1917	1930	2017	2117	2216

CARCASSONNE - LIMOUX - QUILLAN

km		Ⓐ 🚌	⚒	⑥ 🚌	Ⓐ 🚌	Ⓒ 🚌	⚒	⚒ 🚌	⚒	⚒ 🚌	† 🚌
0	**Carcassonne** d.	0635	0719	0800	0800	0915	1025	...	1230	...	1230
26	Limoux d.	0725	0748	0845	0847	0955	1054	1117	1258	1303	1310
54	**Quillan** a.	0813	...	0927	0938	1035	...	1205	...	1347	1400

	🚌	⚒	⚒ 🚌	Ⓐ 🚌	⚒	⚒ 🚌	Ⓐ 🚌	† 🚌	⚒	⚒ 🚌
Carcassonne d.	1415	1603	...	1715	1740	...	1820	1905	1909	...
Limoux d.	1450	1631	1635	1810	1807	1810	1915	1945	1937	1942
Quillan a.	1535	...	1725	1900	...	1900	2005	2035	...	2026

	⚒ 🚌	⚒	Ⓐ 🚌	Ⓐ 🚌	⚒	Ⓒ 🚌	Ⓐ 🚌	⚒ 🚌	⚒	† 🚌
Quillan d.	0542	...	0620	0705	...	0745	0820	1026	...	1100
Limoux d.	0625	0635	0655	0750	0800	0819	0903	1110	1132	1135
Carcassonne a.	...	0704	0750	...	0829	0910	0950	...	1201	1220

	🚌	⚒ 🚌	⚒	⚒ 🚌	⚒	⑤ 🚌	Ⓑ 🚌	⑥ 🚌	⚒	⚒ 🚌
Quillan d.	1245	1356	...	1545	...	1616	1710	1725	...	1820
Limoux d.	1326	1440	1445	1620	1644	1650	1745	1800	1820	1854
Carcassonne a.	1420	...	1515	...	1718	1740	1840	...	1849	1950

CHARLEVILLE MÉZIÈRES - GIVET — Journey 60 – 65 minutes *64 km*

From Charleville Mézières at 0635 Ⓐ, 0705 ⑥, 0735 Ⓐ, 0834 Ⓐ, 0835 ⑥, 0935 Ⓑ, 1035 ⚒, 1135 Ⓑ, 1235 ⚒, 1335 Ⓑ, 1435 ⚒, 1535 Ⓑ, 1635, 1705 Ⓐ, 1735 Ⓐ, 1805 Ⓐ, 1835, 1935 Ⓐ, 2035.

From Givet at 0517 Ⓐ, 0550 ⑥, 0620 Ⓐ, 0650 Ⓐ, 0720 ⑥, 0727 Ⓐ, 0820 †, 0827 Ⓐ, 0920 ⚒, 1020 †, 1027 Ⓐ, 1120 ⑥, 1150 Ⓐ, 1220 †, 1227 Ⓐ, 1320 ⚒, 1420 †, 1427 Ⓐ, 1520, 1620 Ⓐ, 1650 †, 1720 ⚒, 1820 Ⓐ, 1920.

DINARD - ST MALO

🚌 : Approximately hourly on Ⓐ (fewer on Ⓒ). Journey 21 – 26 minutes. *11 km.* Operator: Breizgo (en Ille-et-Vilaine). Route **16**.

⛴ : *Le Bus de Mer* passenger ferry operates a frequent daily service. Journey 10 minutes. Operator: Compagnie Corsaire (compagniecorsaire.com).

GUINGAMP - CARHAIX — Journey 65 – 70 minutes *56 km*

From Guingamp at 0751 Ⓐ, 0944 ⑥, 1043 Ⓐ, 1246 Ⓐ, 1343 Ⓒ, 1648 ⑤, 1745 ①②③④⑥, 1830 ⑤, 1940 ①②③④†, 2030 ⑤, 2207 ⑤.

From Carhaix at 0627 Ⓐ, 0829 ⑥, 0907 Ⓐ, 1102 Ⓒ, 1257 ①–④, 1406 Ⓐ, 1531 ⑤, 1606 Ⓒ, 1706 ⑤, 1758 ①–④, 1803 †, 1842 ⑤.

GUINGAMP - PAIMPOL — Journey: 47 – 53 minutes *47 km*

From **Guingamp** at 0644 Ⓐ, 0956 ⚒, 1153 †, 1343 Ⓐ, 1348 ⑥, 1501 †, 1537 Ⓐ, 1655 ⑤, 1738 ⑥–④, 1802 ⑤, 1950 ①②③④†, 2035 ⑤, 2202 ⑤.

From **Paimpol** at 0652 Ⓐ, 0852 ⚒, 0921 †, 1110 ⚒, 1404 †, 1440 Ⓐ, 1613 Ⓒ, 1634 ①–④, 1704 ⑤, 1806 ⑤, 1834 ①②③④†, 1911 ⑤⑥.

LILLE - LENS — Journey 42 – 46 minutes *39 km*

From Lille Flandres on Ⓐ at 0626, 0639, 0709, 0726, 0739, 0809, 0826, 0909, 0939, 1109, 1126, 1209, 1226, 1326, 1339, 1509, 1539, 1609, 1626, 1639, 1709, 1726, 1739, 1809, 1826, 1839, 1909, 1926, 1939, 2026, 2039, 2139; on ⑥ at 0647, 0748, 0806, 0816, 0948, 1148, 1206, 1219, 1319, 1357, 1548, 1606, 1719 1748, 1819, 1948, 2006, 2057; on † at 0816, 0948, 1148, 1206, 1319, 1449, 1606, 1648, 1819, 1948, 2006, 2057.

From Lens on Ⓐ at 0540, 0552, 0610, 0640, 0652, 0710, 0740, 0752, 0810, 0840, 0852, 0910, 0952, 1110, 1140, 1152, 1210, 1252, 1310, 1440, 1510, 1610, 1640, 1652, 1710, 1740, 1752, 1810, 1840, 1852, 1910, 1940, 1952, 2010; on ⑥ at 0638, 0702, 0711, 0737, 0753, 0836, 1036, 1110, 1202, 1236, 1301, 1436, 1511, 1636, 1702, 1836, 1910, 2036; on † at 0753, 1036, 1110, 1202, 1436, 1511, 1636, 1802, 1910, 1936.

NANTES - CHOLET — Journey 52 – 70 minutes *65 km*

From Nantes at 0629 Ⓐ, 0729 ⚒, 0829 Ⓑ, 0910 † 🚌, 0925 ⑥ 🚌, 1100 ⑥ 🚌, 1133 Ⓐ, 1259 ⚒, 1330 † 🚌, 1535 ⑥ 🚌, 1547 Ⓐ, 1620 Ⓐ 🚌, 1715 Ⓐ 🚌, 1729 Ⓐ, 1730 Ⓒ 🚌, 1829 Ⓑ, 1931 ⚒, 2035 †.

From Cholet at 0605 Ⓐ, 0640 Ⓐ, 0744 ⚒, 1010 Ⓑ, 1035 Ⓒ 🚌, 1240 ⚒, 1420 ⑥ 🚌, 1444 Ⓐ, 1603 † 🚌, 1609 Ⓐ, 1655 ⑥ 🚌, 1711 Ⓑ, 1745 Ⓐ 🚌, 1854 ⚒, 1935 †, 2023 ⑥ 🚌, 2028 Ⓑ 🚌.

PARIS - DISNEYLAND (Marne la Vallée - Chessy) — *32 km*

Trains run approximately every 15 – 30 minutes 0500 - 2400 on RER Line A: Châtelet les Halles - Gare de Lyon - Marne la Vallée Chessy (for Disneyland).

Operator: RATP. For *TGV* services serving Marne la Vallée see Tables **11** and **391**.

Journey: 39 minutes.

SOUILLAC - SARLAT 🚌 — *30 km*

From Souillac Gare SNCF at 0650 ①–⑤, 0840 †, 0940 ⑥, 1340, 1945 ①–⑤.

From Sarlat Gare SNCF at 0612 ①–⑤, 1222 ①–⑤, 1232 Ⓒ, 1310 ③, 1643 ①②④⑤, 1737 Ⓒ, 1815 ①–⑤.

🚌 (Nouvelle Aquitaine Cars Régionaux Ligne 6). Journey 40 – 45 minutes.

Warning! *Service is amended during school holiday periods.*

TOULOUSE - AUCH — Journey 85 – 95 minutes *88 km*

From Toulouse Matabiau at 0624 ⚒, 0724 Ⓐ, 0824, 1024, 1224, 1424, 1524 Ⓐ, 1624, 1722 Ⓐ, 1824, 2024.

From Auch at 0603 ⚒, 0705 Ⓐ, 0805, 0906 Ⓐ, 1005, 1205, 1406, 1605, 1705 Ⓐ, 1805, 2005.

TOURS - CHINON — Journey 46 – 54 minutes *49 km*

From Tours at 0640 ⚒ 🚌, 0729 Ⓐ, 0820 † 🚌, 0931 ⚒, 1220 † 🚌, 1232, 1505 ⊡, 1626 Ⓐ, 1732 Ⓐ, 1805 ⚒ 🚌, 1902, 2002 Ⓑ.

From Chinon at 0624 Ⓐ, 0657 ⚒, 0739 Ⓐ ⊡, 0839 Ⓐ, 0935 ⚒ 🚌, 1003 † 🚌, 1109 ⚒, 1339, 1600 Ⓐ ⊡, 1604 † 🚌, 1739 ⚒, 1838 Ⓑ, 2007 †, 2022 ⚒ 🚌.

VALENCIENNES - CAMBRAI — Journey 50 minutes *40 km*

From Valenciennes at 0650 ⑥, 0653 Ⓐ, 0753 Ⓐ 🚌, 0823 ⑥, 0953 Ⓐ, 1223 ⑥, 1249 Ⓐ, 1651 Ⓐ, 1723 Ⓒ, 1753 Ⓐ, 1853 Ⓐ 🚌, 1934 Ⓒ.

From Cambrai Ville at 0549 Ⓐ, 0653 ⑥, 0749 ⑥, 0753 Ⓐ, 1153 Ⓐ, 1249 ⑥, 1649 Ⓒ, 1653 Ⓐ, 1849 Ⓒ, 1853 Ⓐ.

d – Until May 28.

⊡ – Does not run on Ⓐ during school holidays - please enquire locally for dates.

PARIS - POITIERS - LA ROCHELLE and BORDEAUX 300

WARNING! Subject to alteration May 6–8, 17–20, July 13, Aug. 14, Sept. 8–17 Oct. 21–29. Certain trains will not call at Poitiers, Angoulême and Libourne.

TGV timings may vary by a few minutes - please check your reservation. Many *TGV* services continue to destinations on Tables **305**, **306** and **320**.
Frequent connecting services operate St Pierre des Corps - Tours and v.v. Journey time 5 minutes. For TER services Angoulême - Bordeaux see Table **302**.

PARIS - BORDEAUX NON-STOP SERVICES

km		*TGV* 8501	*TGV* 8571	*TGV* 8531	*TGV* 8503	*TGV* 7671	*TGV* 8537	*TGV* 8572		*TGV* 8473	*TGV* 8505	*TGV* 8541	*TGV* 8574	*TGV* 8547	*TGV* 8475	*TGV* 8509	*TGV* 8549	*TGV* 8590		*TGV* 8517	*TGV* 8551	*TGV* 8592	*TGV* 8477	*TGV* 8519	*TGV* 8553	*TGV* 8523
			①–⑥	①–⑥											⑦		Ⓑ	⑤					①–⑤		⑤	⑤
		A	d	d	B	⊠				C				D	f		g	h		E			j		h	h
0	**Paris** Montparnasse .... d.	0606	0634	0708	0708	0907	1008	1008	....	1108	1108	1208	1401	1401	1508	1508	1608	1608	...	1706	1807	1807	1844	1908	2002	2002
537	**Bordeaux** St Jean .... a.	0814	0848	0915	0915	1114	1214	1214	....	1314	1314	1415	1615	1615	1715	1715	1814	1814	....	1914	2014	2014	2051	2114	2214	2214

PARIS - POITIERS - LA ROCHELLE and BORDEAUX

km		*TGV* 8431	*TGV* 8371	*TGV* 8483	*TGV* 8331	*TGV* 8435	*TGV* 8533	*TGV* 8471	*TGV* 7669	*TGV* 8373	*TGV* 5202	*TGV* 5450	*TGV* 8375		*TGV* 8437	*TGV* 8437	*TGV* 9594	*TGV* 8379	*TGV* 8379	*TGV* 8377	*TGV* 8333	*TGV* 8335	*TGV* 7673	*TGV* 8361	*TGV* 7653	*TGV* 8485
		①–⑥				①–⑥	Ⓑ	⑥		⑥							⑥	⑤	⑦			①–④				
		d				F	k	m	G ⊠	m	H	J n			K	L	M p	h	f	N	P ◧	r	⊠	Q	⊠	
0	**Paris** Montparnasse ... **295** d.	0558	0647	0647	0726	0758	0758	0758	...	0824	...	...	0912	...	1003	1003	...	1212	1212	1216	1225	1226	1231	1337	1337	1415
	Vendôme-Villiers TGV **295** d.	|	|	|	0815	|	|	|	...	|	...	...	|	...	|	|	...	|	|	|	1315	1315	|	|	|	|
	St Pierre des Corps.... **295** a.	0706	|	|	0835	|	|	|	...	|	...	...	1012	...	1107	1107	...	|	1317	1317	1335	1335	|	|	|	1517
	St Pierre des Corps........... d.	0710	|	|	0841	|	|	|	0910	|	1010	1010	1016	...	1111	1110	1241	|	1320	1320	1342	1339	|	|	|	1521
	Tours .... d.	|	|	|	|	|	|	|	|	|	|	|	|	...	|	|	|	|	|	|	|	1354	|	|	|	|
	Châtellerault .... d.	|	|	|	0909	|	|	|	|	|	|	|	|	...	|	|	|	|	|	|	1414	1426	|	|	|	|
	Futuroscope .... d.	|	|	|	0925	|	|	|	|	|	|	|	|	...	|	|	|	|	|	|	1431	1441	|	|	|	|
318	**Poitiers**............................ a.	0740	0810	0810	0935	0917	0917	0918	0941	0946	1041	1041	1050	...	1141	1141	1317	1332	1352	1352	1449	1449	|	|	1457	1554
318	**Poitiers**............................ d.	0743	0814	0823	...	0920	0920	0921	0943	0949	1044	1044	1053	...	1144	1144	1320	1335	1355	1355	...	...	|	|	1459	1557
398	Niort .... d.	|	0903	|	...	|	|	|	|	1037	|	|	1141	...	|	|	|	1422	1441	1440	...	...	|	1538	|	|
465	**La Rochelle** Ville.......... a.	|	0944	|	...	|	|	|	|	1114	|	|	1225	...	|	|	|	1459	1518	1521	...	...	|	1631	|	|
	Angoulême .... d.	0826	...	0906	...	|	|	|	1025	...	1126	1126	...	...	|	1226	1400	...	...	...	...	...	1435	...	|	1637
	Libourne .... d.	|	...	0948	...	|	|	|	|	...	|	|	...	...	|	|	|	...	...	...	...	...	|	...	|	1718
540	**Bordeaux** St Jean .... a.	0902	...	1015	...	1018	1019	1019	1102	...	1202	1202	...	...	1246	1302	1435	...	...	...	...	...	1512	...	1609	1739

km		*TGV* 7653	*TGV* 8363	*TGV* 8447	*TGV* 8343	*TGV* 8389	*TGV* 8449	*TGV* 9404	*TGV* 5454	*TGV* 8365	*TGV* 8367	*TGV* 8355	*TGV* 8451		*TGV* 8391	*TGV* 8397	*TGV* 8491	*TGV* 8345	*TGV* 5240	*TGV* 8393	*TGV* 7659	*TGV* 8395	*TGV* 8495	*TGV* 8455	*TGV* 8347	*TGV* 8461
			②–④			⑦	①–④	⑥	Ⓑ	②–④						⑤						⑤⑦	⑤⑦		Ⓑ	⑤⑦
		R ⊠	S		T	f	r	U	J u	S	V	W	T		X	h		P	H		⊠	v	v	X	g ⊡	v
0	**Paris** Montparnasse ... **295** d.	1524	1540	1603	1657	1657	1657	...	...	1724	1728	1728	1740	...	1824	1824	1824	1828	...	1916	1941	2024	2024	2036	2057	2145
	Vendôme-Villiers TGV **295** d.	|	|	|	|	|	|	...	...	|	1815	1815	|	...	|	|	|	1915	...	|	|	|	|	|	2145	|
	St Pierre des Corps.... **295** a.	|	|	|	|	|	|	...	...	|	1835	1835	|	...	|	|	|	1935	...	2019	|	|	|	|	2205	2245
	St Pierre des Corps........... d.	|	|	|	|	|	|	1810	1810	|	1842	1842	|	...	|	|	|	1944	2010	2023	|	|	|	|	2209	2249
	Châtellerault .... d.	|	|	|	1816	1816	1817	|	|	|	|	|	|	...	|	|	|	2013	|	|	|	|	|	|	2236	|
	Futuroscope .... d.	|	|	|	|	|	|	|	|	|	|	|	|	...	|	|	|	|	|	|	|	|	|	|	|	|
	Poitiers............................ a.	1645	|	1724	1834	1831	1833	1840	1840	|	|	1917	|	...	1945	1945	1945	2032	2040	2055	|	2145	2145	|	2255	2321
	Poitiers............................ d.	1648	|	1727	...	1834	1837	1843	1843	|	|	...	|	...	1949	1949	1954	...	2043	2058	|	2149	2154	|	...	2323
394	Niort .... d.	1738	1738	|	...	1921	|	|	|	1921	1948	...	|	...	2040	2040	|	...	|	2144	|	2250	|	|	...	|
461	**La Rochelle** Ville.......... a.	1823	1823	|	...	1957	|	|	|	1959	2037	...	|	...	2121	2117	|	...	|	2225	|	2331	|	|	...	|
	Angoulême .... d.	...	...	1808	...	...	1928	1925	1925	...	...	...	1930	...	...	...	2036	...	2124	...	2131	...	2335	2229	...	0004
	Libourne .... d.	...	...	|	...	...	|	|	|	...	...	...	|	...	...	...	2119	...	|	...	|	...	2318	|	...	|
	Bordeaux St Jean .... a.	...	...	1844	...	...	2006	2002	2002	...	...	...	2006	...	...	...	2146	...	2202	...	2207	...	2343	2311	...	0042

TER REGIONAL SERVICES TOURS - POITIERS - ANGOULÊME and LA ROCHELLE

km		Ⓐ	Ⓐ	Ⓐ		Ⓐ	⚒	⚒		Ⓐ	Ⓐ	†		Ⓐ	⑥	†		Ⓒ	①	⑥		Ⓐ		⑥		†
0	**Tours**.............................. d.	...	...	...	...	...	0615	...	...	...	0735	...	...	...	...	...	...	...	...	...	...	...	...	...	...	1211
68	Châtellerault .... d.	...	...	...	...	0637	0709	...	...	0739	0828	...	...	0832	0839	0855	...	...	0916	1044	...	...	...	...	...	1306
90	Futuroscope .... d.	...	...	...	...	0701	0721	...	...	0804	0841	...	...	0856	0903	0907	...	...	0940	1108	...	...	...	...	...	1330
101	**Poitiers**............................ a.	...	...	...	...	0711	0729	...	...	0814	0848	...	...	0906	0911	0915	...	...	0950	1118	...	...	...	...	...	1339
101	**Poitiers**............................ d.	0601	0617	0637	...	0714	...	0752	...	0819	...	0908	...	...	0913	...	...	1001	...	...	...	1216	1223	1315	...	...
166	Ruffec .... d.	|	0653	|	...	0752	...	|	...	0857	...	0945	...	...	0949	...	...	|	...	...	...	1303	|	1358	...	...
213	**Angoulême** .... a.	|	0722	|	...	0820	...	|	...	0924	...	1014	...	...	1016	...	...	|	...	...	...	1332	|	1426	...	...
181	Niort .... d.	0653	...	0739	...	...	...	0852	...	...	...	...	...	...	...	...	...	1050	...	...	...	...	1320	...	...	...
248	**La Rochelle** Ville .... a.	0739	...	0824	...	...	...	0938	...	...	...	...	...	...	...	...	...	1137	...	...	...	...	1406	...	...	...

		⚒	Ⓐ	Ⓐ		Ⓐ		⑥		Ⓐ	Ⓒ	Ⓐ			†	Ⓐ		Ⓐ	Ⓐ	Ⓑ			Ⓐ	⑥		†
	Tours .... d.	1214	...	...	...	...	...	...	...	...	...	1623	...	...	...	...	...	1722	...	...	...	1822	...	...	...	2026
	Châtellerault .... d.	1306	...	...	...	...	...	1630	...	1639	...	1711	...	...	...	1739	...	1809	1838	...	...	1909	1939	2017	...	2113
	Futuroscope .... d.	1327	...	...	...	...	...	1654	...	1704	...	1723	...	...	...	1803	...	1822	1903	...	...	1922	2003	2041	...	2126
	Poitiers............................ a.	1339	...	...	...	...	...	1703	...	1713	...	1731	...	...	...	1812	...	1830	1912	...	...	1931	2013	2050	...	2133
	Poitiers............................ d.	...	1523	1618	...	1612	1710	...	...	1718	1718	...	...	1800	1818	1817	...	...	1917	1931	...	...	...	...	...	...
	Ruffec .... d.	...	|	1701	...	|	|	...	...	1801	1801	...	...	|	1904	1904	...	...	2002	|	...	...	...	...	...	...
	Angoulême .... a.	...	|	1729	...	|	|	...	...	1828	1829	...	...	|	1931	1931	...	...	2029	|	...	...	...	...	...	...
	Niort .... d.	...	1615	...	...	1720	1813	...	...	...	...	...	...	1859	...	...	...	...	...	2025	...	...	...	...	...	...
	La Rochelle Ville .... a.	...	1659	...	...	1806	1900	...	...	...	...	...	...	1944	...	...	...	...	...	2108	...	...	...	...	...	...

A – ①–⑤ until July 7 and from Sept. 4 (not Apr. 10, May 1, 8, 18, 19, 29).
B – ⑥ until July 8 (also May 18, 19); ①–⑥ July 10 - Sept. 2 (not Aug. 15); ⑥ from Sept. 9.
C – ⑥⑦ **e** until July 9; daily July 10 - Sept. 3; ⑥⑦ from Sept. 9.
D – ⑤⑦ until July 2 (also May 17, 18); daily July 7 - Sept. 3; ⑤⑦ from Sept. 8.
E – Ⓑ until July 2 (not May 18, 19); daily July 3 - Sept. 3; Ⓑ from Sept. 4.
F – ①–⑥ until July 7 and from Sept. 4 (not Apr. 10, May 1, 8, 29).
G – From Tourcoing (Table **11**).
H – From Lille (Table **11**).
J – From Strasbourg (Table **391**).
K – Mar. 1–3, 6–10, 13–17, 20–24, 27–31, May 15–17, 19, 22–26, June 12–16, 19–23, July 19, 21, 24, 25.
L – Not on dates in note **K**.
M – From Frankfurt (Table **11**).
N – ①②③④⑥ (also May 19, July 14; not Apr. 10, May 1, 8, 17, 29, July 13, Aug. 15).
P – ①–⑥ **q** until July 8; ⑤⑥ July 14 - Sept. 2 (also July 13, Aug. 14); ①–⑥ from Sept. 4.
Q – ⑤⑦ **s** until July 2; ⑤⑥⑦ July 7 - Sept. 3 (also July 13, Aug. 14, 15); ⑤⑦ from Sept. 8.
R – ①⑤⑥⑦ until July 9; daily July 10 - Sept. 3; ①⑤⑥⑦ from Sept. 4.
S – ②③④ until July 6 and from Sept. 5 (not Apr. 11, May 2, 9, 17, 18, 30).
T – ①–⑤ **u** until July 7; ⑤ July 21 - Sept. 1 (also July 13); ①–⑤ from Sept. 4.
U – From Freiburg (Table **11**). Also May 18, July 14, Aug. 14.
V – ⑤⑥ until July 8 (also May 17, 18); ①–⑥ July 10 - Sept. 2 (not Aug. 15); ⑤⑥ from Sept. 8.
W – ①–④ until July 6 and from Sept. 4 (not Apr. 10, May 1, 8, 17, 18, 29).
X – ①②③④⑦ (not May 17, 18, July 13, Aug. 14).

d – Not Apr. 10, May 1, 8, 29, Aug. 15.
e – Also Apr. 10, May 1, 8, 18, 19, 29.
f – Also Apr. 10, May 1, 8, 29, Aug. 15.
g – Not May 18, 19, July 14, Aug. 14.
h – Also May 17, July 13; not May 19, July 14.
j – Not Apr. 10, May 1, 8, 18, 19, 29, July 14, Aug. 14, 15.
k – July 9 - Sept. 3 (not July 14, Aug. 14).
m – July 8 - Sept. 2 (also July 14, Aug. 14).
n – July 8 - Sept. 3.
p – July 8 - Aug. 26.
q – Not Apr. 10, May 1, 8, 29.
r – July 10 - Aug. 31 (not July 13, Aug. 14, 15).
s – Also Apr. 10, May 1, 8, 17, 29; not May 19.
u – Not May 18, July 14, Aug. 14.
v – Also Apr. 10, May 1, 8, 17, 29, July 13, Aug. 15; not May 19, July 14.
◧ – Does not call at Châtellerault and Futuroscope Mar. 20, 21, ①–⑤ Oct. 2 - Nov. 24.
⊡ – Does not call at Châtellerault ⑦ Sept. 10 - Oct. 29.
⊠ – OUIGO low-cost TGV service. Internet booking only at www.ouigo.com.

TGV – High-speed train. Ⓡ. 🍷.

FOR RETURN SERVICES SEE NEXT PAGE →

300 BORDEAUX and LA ROCHELLE - POITIERS - PARIS

WARNING! Subject to alteration May 6–8, 17–20, July 13, Aug. 14, Sept. 8–17 Oct. 21–29. Certain trains will not call at Libourne, Angoulême and Poitiers.

TGV timings may vary by a few minutes - please check your reservation. Many *TGV* services continue to destinations on Tables **305**, **306** and **320**.
Frequent connecting services operate St Pierre des Corps - Tours and v.v. Journey time 5 minutes. For TER services Angoulême - Bordeaux see Table **302**.

BORDEAUX - PARIS NON-STOP SERVICES

	TGV 8478	*TGV* 8402	*TGV* 8404	*TGV* 8502	*TGV* 8530	*TGV* 8560	*TGV* 8504	*TGV* 8534	*TGV* 8562	*TGV* 8508	*TGV* 8581	*TGV* 8536	*TGV* 8540 8583	*TGV* 7672	*TGV* 8472	*TGV* 8418	*TGV* 8542	*TGV* 8420	*TGV* 8544	*TGV* 8514	*TGV* 8585	*TGV* 8516	*TGV* 8550	*TGV* 8587	*TGV* 8522 8589
	①–⑥	Ⓐ		①–⑥		①–⑥			⑦	Ⓑ	①–⑥					①–⑤		①–⑤		⑤–⑦	⑥⑦	Ⓑ		①–⑤	⑦
	d	e		d		d			f	g	d	A		⊠	A	B	C	B		k	m	g	D	n	f
Bordeaux St Jean ..... d.	0646	0712	0744	0846	0946	0946	1046	1212	1212	1246	1346	1346	1546	1646	1708	1708	1745	1746	1846	1846	1937	1945	2050	2050	2219
Paris Montparnasse ..... a.	0854	0919	0957	1052	1153	1153	1252	1420	1420	1452	1552	1552	1752	1852	1926	1926	1952	1952	2058	2058	2152	2152	2259	2259	0027

BORDEAUX and LA ROCHELLE - POITIERS - PARIS

km		*TGV* 8350	*TGV* 8352	*TGV* 8430	*TGV* 8330	*TGV* 8480		*TGV* 8370	*TGV* 5260	*TGV* 8332	*TGV* 8360	*TGV* 8432	*TGV* 7652		*TGV* 8362	*TGV* 5440	*TGV* 9406	*TGV* 8338	*TGV* 8340	*TGV* 8486		*TGV* 8374	*TGV* 7656	*TGV* 7656	*TGV* 5284	*TGV* 8378
		①	②–⑤					①–⑥		①–⑤	①–④					①–⑥	⑦	①–⑤	①–⑤							
		p	E	F		G		d	H	n	J		⊠			Kd	Lf	r ◧	B ⊡				⊠ ⊖	⊠ ●	H	
0	**Bordeaux** St Jean ..... d.	...	...	0540	...	0517	...	...	0558	...	...	0658	0850	...	...	0854	0854	...	...	1013	...	...	1158	1220	1258	...
	Libourne ..... d.	...	...	|	...	0541	...	...	|	...	...	|	|	...	...	|	|	...	...	1042	...	...	|	|	|	...
114	Angoulême ..... d.	...	...	0618	...	0624	...	...	0636	...	...	0736	0927	...	...	0935	0935	...	...	1124	...	...	1236	|	1336	...
	La Rochelle Ville ..... d.	...	...	|	...	|	...	0539	|	...	0706	|	|	...	0847	|	|	...	...	|	...	1044	|	|	|	1347
	Niort ..... d.	...	...	|	...	|	...	0621	|	...	0743	|	|	...	0929	|	|	...	...	|	...	1126	|	|	|	1429
	Poitiers ..... a.	...	...	|	...	0704	...	0708	0716	...	|	0816	1010	...	|	1016	1016	...	...	1204	...	1209	|	|	1416	1516
	Poitiers ..... d.	0518	0612	|	0632	0713	...	0713	0719	0727	|	0819	1012	...	|	1019	1019	1112	1119	1215	...	1215	|	|	1419	1519
	Futuroscope ..... d.	|	|	|	|	|	...	|	|	|	|	|	|	...	|	|	|	1122	1130	|	...	|	|	|	|	|
	Châtellerault ..... d.	|	|	|	0652	|	...	|	|	0746	|	|	|	...	|	|	|	1136	1144	|	...	|	|	|	|	|
	Tours ..... d.	|	|	|	|	|	...	|	|	|	|	|	|	...	|	|	|	1213	|	|	...	|	|	|	|	|
	St Pierre-des-Corps ..... a.	0550	0644	|	0722	|	...	|	0750	0815	|	0854	|	...	1035	1050	1050	1220	1215	|	...	|	1338	1338	1450	1551
	St Pierre des Corps .... **295** d.	0554	0654	|	0725	|	...	|	...	0825	|	0854	|	...	1039	...	...	1224	1225	|	...	|	1342	1342	...	1554
	Vendôme-Villiers TGV **295** d.	|	0715	|	0746	|	...	|	...	0846	|	|	|	...	|	...	...	1245	1246	|	...	|	|	|	...	|
542	**Paris** Montparnasse ... **295** a.	0701	0802	0808	0833	0838	...	0838	...	0933	0937	1006	1134	...	1142	...	...	1332	1333	1341	...	1341	1441	1441	...	1657

	TGV 8470	*TGV* 8512	*TGV* 8342	*TGV* 8380	*TGV* 8344		*TGV* 5444	*TGV* 9598	*TGV* 8488	*TGV* 8488	*TGV* 7660	*TGV* 8364		*TGV* 8442	*TGV* 8346	*TGV* 8450	*TGV* 8388	*TGV* 8394	*TGV* 7642		*TGV* 8476	*TGV* 7674	*TGV* 8454	*TGV* 8392	*TGV* 8396
	⑥				①–④			⑥		①–④				⑦			⑦	②–④			⑦		⑤⑦	⑤⑦	⑦
	s		M	N	J		Kv	P	M	J	Q ⊠			f			f	R	S ⊠		f	⊠	w	w	x
Bordeaux St Jean ..... d.	1446	1446	...	...	...	...	1558	1558	1619	1619	1658	...	...	1758	...	1838	...	...	...	...	1950	2045	2109	...	...
Libourne ..... d.	|	|	...	...	...	...	|	|	1642	1642	|	...	...	|	...	|	...	...	...	...	|	|	|	...	...
Angoulême ..... d.	1523	1523	...	...	...	...	1636	1636	1726	1726	1736	...	...	1836	...	1916	...	...	...	...	2027	2123	2152	...	...
La Rochelle Ville ..... d.	|	|	...	1547	...	...	|	|	|	|	|	1658	...	|	...	|	1837	1925	1925	...	|	|	|	2101	2148
Niort ..... d.	|	|	...	1624	...	...	|	|	|	|	|	1740	...	|	...	|	1915	2007	2007	...	|	|	|	2143	2226
Poitiers ..... a.	|	|	...	1711	...	...	1717	1717	1807	1807	1817	|	...	|	...	1955	1959	2050	2050	...	|	|	2231	2235	2314
Poitiers ..... d.	|	|	1619	1714	1718	...	1720	1720	1809	1809	1820	|	...	|	1923	2004	2004	2053	2053	...	|	|	2241	2241	2314
Futuroscope ..... d.	|	|	1630	|	|	...	|	|	|	|	|	|	...	|	1933	|	|	|	|	...	|	|	|	|	|
Châtellerault ..... d.	|	|	1644	|	|	...	|	|	|	1828	|	|	...	|	1947	|	|	|	|	...	|	|	|	|	|
St Pierre-des-Corps ..... a.	|	|	1715	|	1750	...	1751	1751	|	|	1851	|	...	1937	2016	2036	2036	|	|	...	2128	|	2312	2312	|
St Pierre des Corps ..... **295** d.	|	|	1725	|	1754	...	...	...	|	|	...	|	...	1939	2019	2039	2039	|	|	...	2132	|	2315	2315	|
Vendôme-Villiers TGV ..... **295** d.	|	|	1746	|	|	...	...	...	|	|	...	|	...	|	|	|	|	|	|	...	|	|	|	|	|
Paris Montparnasse ..... **295** a.	1713	1713	1833	1837	1857	...	...	...	1933	1948	...	1941	...	2049	2120	2141	2141	2215	2115	...	2233	2315	0017	0017	0039

TER REGIONAL SERVICES LA ROCHELLLE and ANGOULÊME - POITIERS - TOURS

	Ⓐ	Ⓐ	Ⓐ	⚒		Ⓐ	⑥	①	②–⑤		Ⓐ	⑥	†	①		②–⑤	Ⓐ		⚒		⑥	†		Ⓐ	
La Rochelle Ville ..... d.	...	...	...	...	...	...	...	0603	...	...	0625	0634	...	...	...	...	0716	0750	...	...	...	...	...	...	1224
Niort ..... d.	...	...	...	...	...	...	...	0648	0648	...	0713	0715	...	...	...	...	0757	0835	...	...	...	...	...	...	1309
Angoulême ..... d.	...	...	...	...	...	0631	...	|	|	...	|	|	...	0720	...	0731	|	|	0831	...	...	1032	...	1231	|
Ruffec ..... d.	...	...	...	...	...	0656	...	|	|	...	|	|	...	0746	...	0758	|	|	0858	...	...	1058	...	1304	|
Poitiers ..... a.	...	...	...	...	...	0746	...	0751	0751	...	0807	0801	...	0828	...	0843	0857	0924	0944	...	...	1142	...	1352	1402
Poitiers ..... d.	0548	0608	0655	0736	...	0747	0748	...	...	...	...	...	0825	0831	...	...	...	...	...	...	0959	...	1228	...	...
Futuroscope ..... d.	0558	0615	0705	0744	...	0756	0758	...	...	...	...	...	0833	0840	...	...	...	...	...	...	1009	...	1238	...	...
Châtellerault ..... d.	0622	0627	0729	0756	...	0821	0822	...	...	...	...	...	0845	0906	...	...	...	...	...	...	1033	...	1302	...	...
Tours ..... a.	...	0717	...	0844	...	...	...	...	...	...	...	...	...	...	...	...	...	...	...	...	...	...	1402	...	...
	⑥	Ⓐ	⑥	Ⓐ		Ⓐ	Ⓒ	Ⓐ	†		Ⓐ	Ⓐ	Ⓐ			Ⓑ	⑥		Ⓐ		⚒	†	Ⓐ	Ⓑ 🚌	⑤†
La Rochelle Ville ..... d.	...	...	...	...	...	...	...	...	...	...	...	1556	...	1714	...	1738	...	...	...	...	1836	...	...	...	1935
Niort ..... d.	...	...	...	...	...	...	...	...	...	...	...	1642	...	1802	...	1823	...	...	...	...	1921	...	...	...	2020
Angoulême ..... d.	1343	...	...	...	...	...	...	...	1631	...	1632	|	1731	|	...	|	...	1842	...	...	|	...	1932	...	|
Ruffec ..... d.	1409	...	...	...	...	...	...	...	1701	...	1659	|	1759	|	...	|	...	1909	...	...	|	...	2000	...	|
Poitiers ..... a.	1456	...	...	...	...	...	...	...	1740	...	1741	1744	1840	1900	...	1928	...	1946	...	...	2016	...	2039	...	2111
Poitiers ..... d.	...	1504	1546	1548	...	1644	1732	1732	...	...	1749	...	1850	...	...	...	1931	...	2008	...	...	2023	...	2055	...
Futuroscope ..... d.	...	1512	1556	1559	...	1654	1740	1740	...	...	1758	...	1900	...	...	...	1941	...	2018	...	...	2033	...	2113	...
Châtellerault ..... d.	...	1524	1622	1625	...	1718	1753	1753	...	...	1822	...	1925	...	...	...	2005	...	2039	...	...	2054	...	2142	...
Tours ..... a.	...	1613	...	...	...	...	1846	1849	...	...	...	...	...	...	...	...	...	...	2119	...	...	2136	...	...	...

A – ⑥⑦ **h** until July 9; daily July 10 - Sept. 3; ⑥⑦ from Sept. 9.
B – ①–⑤ until July 7 and from Sept. 4 (not Apr. 10, May 1, 8, 18, 19, 29).
C – ⑦ **j** until July 2; daily July 8 - Sept. 8; ⑦ from Sept. 10.
D – Ⓑ until July 2 (not May 18, 19); daily July 3 - Sept. 3; Ⓑ from Sept. 4.
E – ②–⑤ until July 7 and from Sept. 5 (not Apr. 11, May 2, 9, 18, 19, 30).
F – ①–⑤ **q** until July 7; ① July 10 - Aug. 28 (also July 16; not July 14); ①–⑤ from Sept. 4.
G – ①–⑥ **j** until July 1; ①–⑤ July 3 - Sept. 1 (not July 14, Aug. 14, 15); ①–⑥ from Sept. 4.
H – To Lille (Table **11**).
J – ①–④ until July 6 and from Sept. 4 (not Apr. 10, May 1, 8, 17, 18, 29).
K – To Strasbourg (Table **391**).
L – To Freiburg (Table **391**).
M – ⑤⑥⑦ **t** until July 9; daily July 10 - Sept. 3; ⑤⑥⑦ from Sept. 8.
N – ⑤⑦ **u** until July 2 (also May 17); daily July 7 - Sept. 3; ⑤⑦ from Sept. 8.
P – July 8 - Aug. 26. To Frankfurt (Table **11**).
Q – To Tourcoing (Table **11**).
R – ②③④ until July 6 and from Sept. 5 (not Apr. 11, May 2, 9, 17, 18, 30).
S – ①⑤⑥⑦ until July 9; daily July 10 - Sept. 3; ①⑤⑥⑦ from Sept. 4.

d – Not Apr. 10, May 1, 8, 29, Aug. 15.
e – July 3–21 and Aug. 16 - Sept. 1.
f – Also Apr. 10, May 1, 8, 29, Aug. 15.
g – Not May 18, 19, July 14, Aug. 14.
h – Also Apr. 10, May 1, 8, 18, 19, 29.
j – Not Apr. 10, May 1, 8, 29.
k – Also Apr. 10, May 1, 8, 17, 18, 29, Aug. 14, 15.
m – Also Apr. 10, May 1, 8, 18, 19, 29, July 14, Aug. 14, 15.
n – Not Apr. 10, May 1, 8, 18, 19, 29, July 14, Aug. 14, 15.
p – Also Apr. 11, May 2, 9, 30, Aug. 16; not Apr. 10, May, 1, 8, 29, Aug. 14.
q – Not Apr. 10, May 1, 8, 18, 19, 29.
r – July 10 - Sept. 1 (not July 14, Aug. 14, 15).
s – July 8 - Sept. 2 (also July 14, Aug. 14).
t – Also Apr. 10, May 1, 8, 17, 18, 29.
u – Also Apr. 10, May 1, 8, 17, 29; not May 19.
v – July 8 - Sept. 3.
w – Also Apr. 10, May 1, 8, 17, 29, July 13, Aug. 15; not May 19, July 14.
x – July 9 - Sept. 3 (also Aug. 15).

◧ – Does not call at Futuroscope and Châtellerault Aug. 28 - Sept. 1.
⊡ – Does not call at Futuroscope and Châtellerault Mar. 20, 21, ①–③ Sept. 4–20, ①–⑤ Oct. 2 - Nov. 24.
⊖ – Mar. 2, 7, 8, Apr. 3–7, 11–14, 17–21, 24–28, May 2–5, 9–12, 30, 31, June 1, 2, 5–9, 19–23, 26–30, July 3–7, 26, 28, 31, Aug. 1, 11, Oct. 16–20, Nov. 20–Dec. 8.
● – Not on dates in note ☆. Runs 10–15 minutes earlier Sept. 11–15, Oct. 9–13.
⊠ – OUIGO low-cost TGV service. Internet booking only at www.ouigo.com.
TGV – High-speed train. 🅁. 🍸.

FOR RETURN SERVICE SEE PREVIOUS PAGE.

ANGOULÊME and NIORT - SAINTES - ROYAN 301

SERVICE MARCH 25 - JUNE 25. SUBJECT TO CONFIRMATION.

km		Ⓐ 🚌	Ⓐ	Ⓐ	Ⓐ 🚌	Ⓐ	†	⑥	🚌	⑥	Ⓑ	🚌	⚒	†	Ⓐ	Ⓐ 🚌		🚌	⑥	†	Ⓐ 🚌	Ⓐ	Ⓒ 🚌		🚌
0	**Angoulême** d.	0530	...	...	0645	...	...	...	0920	...	...	1103	...	...	...	1240	...	1445	...	...	1600	...	1600	...	1710
49	Cognac d.	0639	...	...	0754	...	...	...	1029	...	...	1158	...	...	...	1349	...	1540	...	...	1709	...	1709	...	1819
	Niort d.	|	...	0638	|	...	0914	...	|	0959	...	|	1145	...	1244	|	1450	|	...	...	|	...	|	1749	|
75	**Saintes** a.	0715	...	0747	0830	...	1020	...	1105	1107	...	1234	1249	...	1351	1425	1555	1616	...	...	1745	...	1745	1907	1855
75	**Saintes** d.	...	0744	...	...	0850	1023	1046	...	1119	1122	...	1252	1254	1354	...	...	...	1630	1636	...	1821	...	1915	...
	La Rochelle Ville **292** a.	...	|	...	...	|	|	|	...	|	|	...	|	|	|	...	...	...	|	|	...	|	...	|	...
111	**Royan** a.	...	0812	...	...	0916	1050	1113	...	1145	1148	...	1319	1320	1420	...	...	...	1658	1702	...	1850	...	1946	...

	Ⓐ 🚌	Ⓐ		🚌	⚒	†	⑤	†	🚌
Angoulême d.	1835	...	...	1940	...	...	...	...	2140
Cognac d.	1944	...	...	2035	...	...	...	...	2249
Niort d.	|	1840	...	|	...	1955	2051	...	|
Saintes a.	2020	2022	...	2111	...	2103	2202	...	2325
Saintes d.	...	...	2052	...	2125	2125	2205	2250	2325
La Rochelle Ville **292** a.	...	...	|	...	|	|	|	|	|
Royan a.	...	...	2119	...	2151	2152	2232	2317	0009

	Ⓐ 🚌	⚒ 🚌	Ⓐ 🚌	Ⓐ	Ⓐ	Ⓐ	⚒ 🚌	Ⓐ	⑥
Royan d.	...	...	0510	...	0541	0616	...	0715	0744
La Rochelle Ville **292** d.	...	...	|	...	|	|	...	|	|
Saintes a.	...	...	0555	...	0607	0643	...	0741	0810
Saintes d.	0440	0535	0555	0558	...	0646	0730	0752	0813
Niort a.	|	|	|	0716	...	0805	|	0857	0919
Cognac d.	0515	0610	|	...	...	...	0805	...	...
Angoulême a.	0610	0719	0720	...	...	...	0914	...	...

km			🚌	⚒	Ⓐ	⚒ 🚌	Ⓐ	Ⓒ	Ⓑ 🚌		🚌	†	†	Ⓑ 🚌	Ⓐ	Ⓐ 🚌	⚒	†	Ⓐ	Ⓑ 🚌	†	🚌		†	⑤
0	**Royan** d.	0859	...	...	1049	...	1221	1221	...	1449	...	...	1604	...	1641	...	...	1736	1749	...	1844	...	1928	...	...
	La Rochelle Ville **292** d.	|	...	...	|	...	|	|	...	|	...	...	|	...	|	...	...	|	|	...	|	...	|	...	...
36	**Saintes** a.	0927	...	...	1115	...	1248	1249	...	1515	...	...	1631	...	1706	...	...	1804	1815	...	1911	...	1954	...	...
36	**Saintes** d.	...	0935	1008	...	1130	1251	1252	1300	...	1525	1620	...	1640	...	1730	1807	1807	...	1825	...	1925	...	2006	2017
116	**Niort** a.	...	|	1115	...	|	1400	1403	|	...	|	1725	...	|	...	|	1915	1917	...	|	...	|	...	2111	2122
	Cognac d.	...	1010	...	...	1205	...	...	1335	...	1600	...	...	1715	...	1805	...	...	...	1900	...	2000	...	...	...
	Angoulême a.	...	1105	...	...	1314	...	...	1430	...	1709	...	...	1824	...	1900	...	...	...	2009	...	2109	...	...	...

BORDEAUX - ANGOULÊME, PÉRIGUEUX, BRIVE and LIMOGES 302

For *TGV* services Bordeaux - Angoulême see Table **300**.

km		Ⓐ	Ⓐ	⑥	Ⓐ	Ⓐ	Ⓐ	Ⓐ A	⚒	†	⚒	Ⓐ	⑥ A	†	Ⓐ	Ⓒ	Ⓒ	Ⓐ	Ⓐ	Ⓐ A	Ⓒ	Ⓐ	Ⓐ	Ⓐ
0	**Bordeaux** St Jean **306** d.	...	...	...	...	0550	0604	0625	0650	0715	0724	0827	0827	0950	1026	1027	...	1127	...	1227	1229	1251	1301	...
37	Libourne **306** d.	...	...	...	...	0612	0626	0652	0712	0738	0747	0852	0852	1011	1053	1052	...	1152	...	1252	1252	1312	1325	...
53	Coutras **306** d.	...	...	...	...	0625	0636	0702	0725	|	0758	0903	0903	1024	|	1103	...	1203	...	1302	1302	1325	|	...
135	**Angoulême** a.	...	...	...	...	0716	|	|	0815	|	|	|	|	1114	|	|	...	|	...	|	|	1414	|	...
93	Mussidan d.	...	...	...	...	...	0706	0730	...	|	0820	0932	0932	...	|	1131	...	1231	...	1332	1332	...	|	...
129	**Périgueux** a.	...	...	...	...	...	0730	0758	...	0823	0838	0953	0953	...	1138	1153	...	1253	...	1353	1353	...	1412	...
129	**Périgueux** ◧ d.	0430	0603	0631	0709	...	0738	0801	...	0830	0845	...	0956	...	1144	...	1224	...	1318	1356	1400	...	1419	1526
203	**Brive la Gaillarde** ◧ a.	|	|	|	|	...	|	0855	...	|	|	...	1049	...	|	...	|	...	|	1448	|	...	|	|
166	Thiviers d.	0458	0634	0703	0738	...	0804	...	...	0853	0910	...	...	...	1206	...	1255	...	1353	...	1422	...	1442	1554
228	**Limoges** Benedictins a.	0544	0725	0749	0825	...	0845	...	...	0934	0951	...	...	...	1249	...	1341	...	1439	...	1505	...	1523	1649

		Ⓒ	Ⓐ	†	Ⓐ		Ⓐ	Ⓒ	Ⓐ	Ⓐ	Ⓐ	†	Ⓐ	Ⓒ	Ⓐ		Ⓐ	Ⓐ	†	†	Ⓑ	⑥	
Bordeaux St Jean **306** d.	1426	...	1527	...	...	1627	...	...	1650	1701	1725	1733	1800	1828	1827	1850	1902	1927	1927	...	2027	2027	2127
Libourne **306** d.	1452	...	1552	...	...	1650	...	...	1712	1725	1750	1758	1825	1849	1852	1912	1925	1953	1952	...	2052	2052	2152
Coutras **306** d.	1503	...	1603	1625	...	1700	...	...	1725	1734	1803	1808	1835	|	1903	1924	|	2003	2002	...	2103	2103	2203
Angoulême a.	|	...	|	1716	...	|	...	...	1815	|	|	|	|	|	|	2012	|	|	|	...	|	|	|
Mussidan d.	1532	...	1631	...	...	1729	...	...	...	1804	1832	1837	1904	|	1931	...	|	2032	2031	...	2132	2132	2232
Périgueux a.	1553	...	1653	...	...	1753	...	...	...	1832	1854	1858	1926	1934	1956	...	2011	2053	2053	...	2153	2153	2253
Périgueux ◧ d.	...	1609	...	...	1711	...	1811	1824	...	...	1908	...	1929	1941	...	...	2023	...	2056	2129	...	2156	...
Brive la Gaillarde ◧ a.	...	|	...	...	|	...	|	|	...	...	|	...	2024	|	...	...	|	...	2149	|	...	2249	...
Thiviers d.	...	1637	...	...	1741	...	1850	1855	...	...	1931	...	...	2003	...	...	2045	...	...	2157	...	...	...
Limoges Benedictins a.	...	1725	...	...	1827	...	1940	1941	...	...	2015	...	...	2046	...	...	2131	...	...	2245	...	...	...

	Ⓐ	⚒	Ⓐ	⑥	Ⓐ	Ⓐ	Ⓐ	Ⓐ	Ⓐ	Ⓐ	⑥	Ⓑ	⑥ A	⑥	Ⓐ	⚒	†	⚒	†	Ⓐ	Ⓒ	Ⓐ A	Ⓐ
Limoges Benedictins d.	...	...	...	...	...	...	0550	...	...	0610	0614	...	...	...	0712	0830	...	...	0936	1012	1056	...	...
Thiviers d.	...	...	...	...	...	...	0635	...	...	0701	0701	...	...	...	0802	0908	...	...	1014	1050	1135	...	...
Brive la Gaillarde ◧ d.	...	...	...	...	0534	...	|	...	...	|	|	...	0737	...	|	|	...	...	|	|	|	1116	...
Périgueux ◧ a.	...	...	...	...	0625	...	0657	...	...	0735	0731	...	0827	...	0830	0928	...	...	1035	1111	1158	1207	...
Périgueux d.	0450	0531	0559	0605	0627	...	0704	0731	...	...	...	0806	0830	...	...	0936	...	1005	1042	1118	1205	1210	...
Mussidan d.	0511	0553	0624	0627	0652	...	0726	0753	...	...	...	0827	0852	...	...	|	...	1027	|	1137	1227	1232	...
Angoulême d.	|	|	|	|	|	0645	|	|	0745	...	...	|	|	0839	...	|	0943	|	|	|	|	|	1230
Coutras **306** d.	0539	0622	0653	0656	0721	0735	0756	0822	0835	...	...	0856	0921	0927	...	|	1034	1056	|	|	1256	1301	1321
Libourne **306** d.	0550	0634	0705	0708	0731	0749	0807	0834	0849	...	...	0908	0933	0941	...	1022	1046	1108	1132	1207	1306	1311	1336
Bordeaux St Jean **306** a.	0618	0659	0732	0732	0758	0810	0832	0859	0910	...	...	0932	0958	1004	...	1047	1109	1132	1157	1232	1329	1335	1405

	Ⓐ	Ⓐ	Ⓒ	Ⓒ	Ⓐ		†	Ⓐ	Ⓐ	Ⓒ	Ⓐ		Ⓐ		Ⓒ	Ⓐ		†	Ⓐ	⑥	†	Ⓐ	†
Limoges Benedictins d.	1139	...	1208	...	1256	...	...	1546	...	1627	1637	...	1733	...	1815	1838	...	1913	2024	2028	2109	2210	2310
Thiviers d.	1231	...	1253	...	1335	...	...	1631	...	1716	1722	...	1817	...	1853	1932	...	2004	2110	2115	2158	2256	2355
Brive la Gaillarde ◧ d.	|	...	|	...	|	...	...	|	...	|	|	1712	|	...	|	|	...	|	|	|	|	|	|
Périgueux ◧ a.	1300	...	1319	...	1359	...	...	1657	...	1743	1757	1804	1841	...	1916	2000	...	2031	2136	2141	2225	2321	0021
Périgueux d.	...	1322	...	1405	1405	1605	1700	1705	...	...	...	1807	1848	...	1923	...	2010	...	...	...	...	...	...
Mussidan d.	...	1343	...	1427	1427	1627	1727	1727	...	...	...	1835	|	...	|	...	2031	...	...	...	...	...	...
Angoulême d.	...	|	...	|	|	|	|	|	1745	...	...	|	|	1845	|	...	|	...	...	...	...	...	...
Coutras **306** d.	...	1411	...	1456	1456	1656	1756	1757	1836	...	...	1904	|	1933	|	...	2059	...	...	...	...	...	...
Libourne **306** d.	...	1422	...	1508	1506	1708	1808	1807	1848	...	...	1914	1934	1946	2010	...	2110	...	...	...	...	...	...
Bordeaux St Jean **306** a.	...	1444	...	1532	1531	1732	1832	1832	1910	...	...	1937	1958	2011	2032	...	2133	...	...	...	...	...	...

PÉRIGUEUX - BRIVE - TULLE

	Ⓐ	⑥	Ⓐ		Ⓐ	⑥	†			Ⓐ	⑥		† B	Ⓐ	Ⓒ		⑤	①-④	Ⓐ		†	Ⓐ	⑥
Bordeaux St Jean (above) d.	...	...	...	...	0625	0827	...	...	...	1227	...	...	...	...	...	...	...	...	1800	...	1927	...	2027
Périgueux d.	0626	0626	0734	...	0801	0956	0956	...	1237	1356	1600	...	1610	1653	1756	...	1800	1801	1929	...	2056	2106	2156
Brive la Gaillarde a.	0727	0734	0836	...	0855	1049	1056	...	1338	1448	1701	...	1709	1756	1903	...	1903	1901	2024	...	2149	2207	2249
Brive la Gaillarde **326** d.	...	0737	...	...	0902	1052	1059	...	...	1451	...	...	1712	...	...	...	...	1911	...	...	...	...	...
Tulle **326** a.	...	0802	...	...	0928	1117	1124	...	...	1516	...	...	1738	...	...	...	...	1938	...	...	...	...	...

	Ⓐ	⚒	⑥		Ⓐ	Ⓒ	Ⓐ		†	⑥	Ⓐ		†	Ⓐ				⑤ B	† B		†	Ⓐ	⑤
Tulle **326** d.	...	...	0707	...	...	0819	1048	...	...	1217	...	...	...	...	...	...	...	1740	1743	...	...	...	1907
Brive la Gaillarde **326** a.	...	...	0734	...	...	0843	1113	...	...	1241	...	...	...	...	...	...	...	1809	1810	...	...	...	1935
Brive la Gaillarde d.	0534	0622	0737	...	0746	0846	1116	...	1127	1244	1249	...	1414	1647	1712	...	1813	1813	1813	...	1936	1938	1938
Périgueux a.	0625	0724	0827	...	0853	0946	1207	...	1227	1354	1355	...	1514	1751	1804	...	1918	1918	1918	...	2039	2040	2040
Bordeaux St Jean (above) a.	0758	...	0958	...	...	...	1335	...	...	...	...	...	...	...	1937	...	...	...	...	...	...	...	...

A – To / from Tulle (see lower part of Table).

B – To / from Ussel (Table **326**).

◧ – See lower part of Table for additional services.

303 LIMOGES - MONTLUÇON

SERVICE UNTIL APRIL 30.

km																									
			Ⓐ	Ⓐ	Ⓐ 🚌		Ⓐ	Ⓐ	Ⓐ 🚌		Ⓐ	Ⓐ	Ⓐ	Ⓐ			⑥	⑥ 🚌	†	† 🚌	⑥	Ⓒ	†	Ⓒ	
0	**Limoges** Benedictins d.		0648	0729	0900	...	...	1306	...	...	1548	1706	1806	2027	...		0805	...	0911	...	1219	1507	1706	1907	...
78	Guéret d.	Ⓐ	0758	0838	1051	...	1109	1418	1425	...	1658	1824	1916	2135	...	Ⓒ	0914	0930	1021	1030	1328	1616	1824	2015	...
156	**Montluçon** Ville a.		...	...	...	...	1209	...	1533	...	...	...	2016	...	...		...	1038	...	1138	...	1716	...	...	...

		Ⓐ	Ⓐ 🚌	Ⓐ		Ⓐ	Ⓐ	Ⓐ 🚌		Ⓐ	Ⓐ		Ⓐ			⑥	Ⓒ	⑥	† 🚌	†	⑥ 🚌	⑥	†	
Montluçon Ville d.		...	0554	...	...	0738	...	...	...	1516	...	...	...	...		...	0838	...	1530	...	1610	...	...	...
Guéret d.	Ⓐ	0621	0700	0716	...	0840	1120	1335	...	1617	1739	...	1834	...	Ⓒ	0755	0939	1203	1630	1640	1716	1728	1826	...
Limoges Benedictins a.		0730	...	0828	...	0949	1230	1526	...	1726	1849	...	1945	...		0904	1049	1312	...	1749	...	1837	1935	...

305 BORDEAUX - TARBES and HENDAYE

TGV services are subject to alteration Ⓐ Mar. 20 - Apr. 28, May 28, ①–⑤ June 19–30, ①–⑤ July 3–13, ①–⑤ Sept. 18–29, Oct. 9–20, Nov. 4, 5, 25.
TGV timings may vary by a few minutes - please check your reservation. For overnight trains Paris - Lourdes - Hendaye see Table **319**. For connections Hendaye - Irún see Table **689**.

km																										
															TGV		*TGV*		*TGV*	*TGV*					*TGV*	*TGV*
															8571		**8531**		**8533**	**8535**					**8537**	**8572**
		Ⓐ	①	Ⓐ	Ⓐ	⑥	Ⓐ	Ⓐ	①	⑥	⑥	†	Ⓐ	Ⓑ	①–⑥	†	①–⑥	Ⓐ	Ⓑ	⑥	Ⓒ	Ⓒ	Ⓐ	Ⓐ		
														E	**d**		**d**		**e**	**f**		**E**				
	Paris Montparnasse **300** d.	...	...	...	...	...	...	...	...	...	...	...	...	...	0634	...	0708	...	0758	0916	...	...	...	...	1008	1008
0	**Bordeaux** St Jean **299 306** d.	...	0449	...	...	...	0614	0614	0614	0744	0744	0819	0819	0819	0854	0919	0920	1019	1025	|	1116	1116	...	...	1220	1220
40	Facture Biganos **299 306** d.	...	0513	...	...	...	0638	0638	0638	0810	0810	0841	0841	0841	|	0940	|	1041	|	|	1139	1139	...	...	|	|
109	Morcenx **299** d.	...	0555	...	...	...	0714	0714	0714	0853	0853	0919	0919	0919	|	1012	|	1112	|	|	1211	1211	...	...	|	|
148	Dax a.	...	0621	...	...	...	0733	0733	0733	0914	0914	0938	0945	0945	1005	1030	1030	1131	1132	1230	1230	1230	...	...	1328	1328
148	Dax ◨ d.	0547	0631	0641	0703	0720	0740	0744	0744	0921	0927	0941	0945	0949	1006	1033	1032	1138	1136	1234	1237	1244	1242	1244	1332	1336
179	Puyoô **325** d.	|	|	0659	|	|	|	0802	0802	|	0945	|	|	1007	|	1051	|	|	|	|	|	1302	1300	|	|	|
193	Orthez **325** d.	|	|	0710	|	|	|	0813	0813	|	0955	|	|	1018	|	1101	|	|	|	|	|	1312	1310	|	|	1404
233	Pau **325** d.	|	|	0734	|	|	|	0836	0837	|	1019	|	|	1041	1055	1124	|	|	|	|	|	1337	1336	|	|	1427
272	Lourdes **325** d.	|	|	0805	|	|	|	...	0906	|	...	|	|	...	1131	1155	|	|	|	|	|	...	1406	|	|	1503
293	**Tarbes** **325** a.	|	|	0821	|	|	|	...	...	|	...	|	|	...	1147	1210	|	|	|	|	|	...	1421	|	|	1519
199	**Bayonne** ◨ d.	0631	0717	...	0747	0804	0828	...	...	0954	...	1017	1017	...	...	...	1105	1210	1208	1305	1308	...	...	1328	1406	...
209	Biarritz ◨ d.	0640	0726	...	0756	0813	0837	...	...	1004	...	1026	1026	...	...	...	1118	1220	1221	1317	1317	...	...	1337	1419	...
222	St Jean de Luz ◨ d.	0656	0742	...	0812	0829	0852	...	...	1022	...	1041	1041	...	...	...	1134	1235	1238	1333	1332	...	...	1353	1435	...
235	**Hendaye** ◨ a.	0709	0755	...	0826	0842	0906	...	...	1035	...	1056	1055	...	...	...	1147	1249	1251	1347	1349	...	...	1407	1447	...

				TGV					*TGV*	*TGV*							*TGV*	*TGV*					*TGV*	*TGV*	*TGV*
				8541					**8547**	**8574**							**8549**	**8590**					**8551**	**8592**	**8553**
	Ⓐ	Ⓐ	Ⓒ		†		⑥	Ⓐ			Ⓐ	⑥	Ⓑ	⑥	†	Ⓐ	Ⓑ	⑤		①–④	⑤	⑤			⑤
								F	**A**								**g**	**h**							**hj**
Paris Montparnasse **300** d.	...	...	...	1208	...	...	...	...	1401	1401	...	...	...	...	...	...	1608	1608	...	...	...	...	1807	1807	2002
Bordeaux St Jean **299 306** d.	1318	1318	...	1421	...	1518	1518	1518	1616	1616	...	1719	1719	...	1719	1719	1820	1820	1846	1919	1919	1919	2020	2020	2218
Facture Biganos **299 306** d.	1341	1341	...	|	...	1541	1541	1541	|	|	...	1740	1741	...	1741	1741	|	|	1908	1941	1941	1941	|	|	|
Morcenx **299** d.	1412	1412	...	|	...	1612	1612	1612	|	|	...	1817	1818	...	1818	1818	|	|	1945	2017	2017	2017	|	|	|
Dax a.	1431	1431	...	1529	...	1635	1631	1635	1728	1728	...	1836	1841	...	1841	1841	1928	1928	2008	2036	2038	2038	2128	2128	2327
Dax ◨ d.	1438	1442	1438	1532	1542	1637	1642	1642	1728	1732	1744	1839	1847	1847	1851	1852	1932	1936	2011	2039	2045	2052	2131	2136	2330
Puyoô **325** d.	|	1500	|	|	1600	|	1700	1700	|	|	|	1857	|	|	1909	1910	|	|	|	2057	|	2110	|	|	|
Orthez **325** d.	|	1510	|	|	1610	|	1710	1711	|	1801	|	1907	|	|	1920	1920	|	|	|	2108	|	2120	|	2204	|
Pau **325** d.	|	1534	|	|	1634	|	1734	1734	|	1826	|	1931	|	|	1943	1944	|	2024	|	2131	|	2144	|	2227	|
Lourdes **325** d.	|	...	|	|	1705	|	1805	...	|	1902	|	...	|	|	...	2018	|	2100	|	...	|	2215	|	2303	|
Tarbes **325** a.	|	...	|	|	1720	|	1820	...	|	1920	|	...	|	|	...	2033	|	2115	|	...	|	2230	|	2319	|
Bayonne ◨ d.	1510	...	1522	1606	...	1723	...	...	1759	...	1828	...	1920	1931	...	...	2006	...	2043	...	2116	...	2206	...	0004
Biarritz ◨ d.	1519	...	1531	1619	...	1732	...	...	1812	...	1837	...	1929	1940	...	...	2018	...	2052	...	2126	...	2218	...	0015
St Jean de Luz ◨ d.	1534	...	1546	1635	...	1747	...	...	1828	...	1853	...	1944	1956	...	...	2034	...	2107	...	2141	...	2235	...	0031
Hendaye ◨ a.	1548	...	1600	1647	...	1801	...	...	1851	...	1907	...	1958	2009	...	...	2047	...	2121	...	2155	...	2247	...	0045

						TGV	*TGV*				*TGV*	*TGV*					*TGV*	*TGV*						*TGV*	*TGV*
						8560	**8530**				**8534**	**8562**					**8581**	**8536**						**8583**	**8540**
	Ⓐ	Ⓐ	①	Ⓐ	⚒	①–⑥		⚒	Ⓐ	Ⓒ		⑦	①	Ⓐ	Ⓐ	⑥	①–⑥		⑥	†	Ⓐ	Ⓐ	†		
						d						**k**					**d**	**B**							
Hendaye ◨ d.	...	0451	...	...	0555	...	0712	0727	0810	...	0932	...	...	...	1010	1042	...	1112	1156	1210	...	1232	1253	...	1312
St Jean de Luz ◨ d.	...	0503	...	...	0608	...	0726	0739	0822	...	0944	...	...	...	1022	1054	...	1125	1208	1223	...	1244	1305	...	1325
Biarritz ◨ d.	...	0515	...	...	0620	...	0739	0751	0834	...	0957	...	...	...	1034	1106	...	1137	1220	1235	...	1256	1317	...	1338
Bayonne ◨ d.	...	0529	...	...	0633	...	0754	0805	0848	...	1011	...	...	...	1048	1120	...	1152	1234	1249	...	1310	1331	...	1353
Tarbes **325** d.	...	|	0514	...	|	0646	|	|	|	0748	|	0859	...	...	|	|	1036	|	|	|	1200	|	|	1238	|
Lourdes **325** d.	...	|	0528	...	|	0704	|	|	|	0802	|	0923	0955	...	|	|	1100	|	|	|	1214	|	|	1302	|
Pau **325** d.	0505	|	0559	0559	|	0731	|	|	|	0832	|	0951	1023	1023	|	|	1127	|	|	|	1244	|	|	1329	|
Orthez **325** d.	0529	|	0622	0622	|	0754	|	|	|	0856	|	|	1048	1048	|	|	|	|	|	|	1307	|	|	1352	|
Puyoô **325** d.	0540	|	0633	0633	|	|	|	|	|	0907	|	|	1058	1058	|	|	|	|	|	|	1318	|	|	|	|
Dax ◨ a.	0558	0602	0652	0652	0717	0822	0826	0849	0920	0925	1046	1038	1116	1116	1120	1154	1219	1226	1317	1320	1337	1342	1415	1420	1424
Dax d.	0610	0610	0654	0654	0720	0831	0831	...	0923	0928	1048	1048	1128	1128	1128	1157	1228	1228	...	1323	1350	1350	...	1429	1429
Morcenx **299** d.	0629	0629	0714	0714	0739	|	|	...	0944	0947	|	|	1147	1147	1147	1216	|	|	...	1344	1409	1409	...	|	|
Facture Biganos **299 306** d.	0706	0706	0751	0751	0816	|	|	...	1018	1019	|	|	1219	1219	1219	1248	|	|	...	1418	1441	1441	...	|	|
Bordeaux St Jean **299 306** a.	0731	0731	0816	0816	0839	0940	0940	...	1041	1041	1206	1206	1241	1241	1241	1310	1340	1340	...	1441	1503	1503	...	1540	1540
Paris Montparnasse **300** a.	...	...	...	...	...	1153	1153	...	...	...	1420	1420	...	...	...	...	1552	1552	...	...	...	...	...	1752	1752

					TGV						*TGV*		*TGV*						*TGV*	*TGV*					*TGV*
					8542						**8544**		**8585**						**8587**	**8550**					**8589**
	Ⓐ	†	†	⑤		Ⓐ	⑥	⑥	†	†		Ⓒ	⑥⑦	Ⓐ	Ⓐ	†	†	Ⓐ	①–⑤		①–④	⑥	⑤†	⑤Ⓒ	⑦
					C								**p**						**q**	**D**					**k**
Hendaye ◨ d.	1353	...	1410	...	1512	1504	...	1504	...	1549	1612	1653	...	...	1657	...	1750	1755	...	1812	1857	...	...	1857	...
St Jean de Luz ◨ d.	1405	...	1422	...	1525	1516	...	1516	...	1601	1626	1705	...	...	1709	...	1802	1807	...	1825	1910	...	...	1909	...
Biarritz ◨ d.	1417	...	1434	...	1538	1528	...	1528	...	1613	1639	1717	...	...	1721	...	1814	1819	...	1837	1923	...	...	1921	...
Bayonne ◨ d.	1431	...	1447	...	1553	1542	...	1542	...	1626	1654	1731	...	...	1735	...	1828	1833	...	1853	1937	...	...	1935	...
Tarbes **325** d.	|	1338	|	1432	|	|	...	|	...	|	|	|	1636	1639	|	...	|	|	1738	|	|	1838	...	|	1926
Lourdes **325** d.	|	1352	|	1446	|	|	...	|	...	|	|	|	1700	1653	|	...	|	|	1802	|	|	1852	...	|	1943
Pau **325** d.	|	1422	|	1516	|	|	1517	|	1601	|	|	|	1728	1723	|	1803	|	|	1829	|	|	1923	1923	|	2011
Orthez **325** d.	|	1446	|	1540	|	|	1541	|	1626	|	|	|	1751	1746	|	1828	|	|	1852	|	|	1947	1948	|	|
Puyoô **325** d.	|	1457	|	1551	|	|	1552	|	1637	|	|	|	|	1757	|	1838	|	|	|	|	|	1958	1958	|	|
Dax ◨ a.	1515	1515	1519	1610	1625	1614	1610	1614	1654	1658	1726	1815	1819	1816	1820	1856	1900	1917	1920	1924	2020	2015	2016	2021	2058
Dax d.	...	1527	1527	...	1625	1617	1622	1622	1706	1706	1731	...	1823	1828	1828	1908	1908	...	1929	1929	...	2028	2028	2028	2100
Morcenx **299** d.	...	1547	1549	...	|	1640	1642	1642	1725	1725	|	...	|	1847	1847	1927	1927	...	|	|	...	2047	2047	2047	|
Facture Biganos **299 306** d.	...	1619	1619	...	|	1718	1719	1719	1803	1803	|	...	|	1919	1919	1959	1959	...	|	|	...	2119	2119	2119	|
Bordeaux St Jean **299 306** a.	...	1643	1643	...	1740	1741	1741	1741	1825	1825	1840	...	1935	1941	1941	2021	2021	...	2040	2040	...	2143	2143	2143	2209
Paris Montparnasse **300** a.	...	...	...	...	1952	...	...	...	...	...	2058	...	2152	...	...	...	...	...	2259	2259	...	...	...	...	0027

A – ⑤⑦ until July 1 (also May 17, 18); daily July 7 - Sept. 3; ⑤⑦ from Sept. 8.
B – ⑥⑦ **m** until July 9; daily July 10 - Sept. 3; ⑥⑦ from Sept. 9.
C – ⑦ **n** until July 2; daily July 8 - Sept. 8; ⑦ from Sept. 10.
D – Ⓑ until July 2 (not May 18, 19); daily July 3 - Sept. 3; Ⓑ from Sept. 4.
E – By connecting trains on † (change at Dax).
F – By connecting trains on ①–④ (change at Dax).

d – Not Apr. 10, May 1, 8, 29, Aug. 15.
e – July 9 - Sept. 3 (not July 14, Aug. 14).
f – July 8 - Sept. 2 (also July 14, Aug. 14).
g – Not May 18, 19, July 14, Aug. 14.
h – Also May 17, July 13; not May 19, July 14.
j – Until Sept. 29.
k – Also Apr. 10, May 1, 8, 29, Aug. 15.
m – Also Apr. 10, May 1, 8, 18, 19, 29.
n – Not Apr. 10, May 1, 8, 29.

p – Also Apr. 10 May 1, 8, 18, 19, 29, July 14, Aug. 14, 15.
q – Not Apr. 10, May 1, 8, 18, 19, 29, July 14, Aug. 14, 15.
◨ – Other trains: Dax - Hendaye at 0631 Ⓐ, 1044 Ⓐ, 1710 Ⓐ; Dax - Bayonne at 0810 Ⓐ, 1810 Ⓐ, 1944 Ⓐ, 2038 †; Hendaye - Dax at 0638 Ⓐ, 0853 Ⓐ, 1627 Ⓐ; Bayonne - Dax at 0605 Ⓐ, 1131 †, 1631 Ⓐ, 2003 Ⓐ.

TGV – High-speed train. Ⓡ. 🍷.

COUTRAS - BORDEAUX - ARCACHON 306

TGV services are subject to alteration May 18 – 20, Sept. 23, 30, Nov. 3, 4. *TGV* timings may vary by a few minutes - please check your reservation.

km								*TGV* 8471					*TGV* 8473					*TGV* 8475					*TGV* 8477	*TGV* 8477	
		Ⓐ	Ⓐ	⚒	Ⓐ	⚒	†	⑥	Ⓐ	⑥	Ⓐ	Ⓐ		Ⓐ		Ⓒ	Ⓐ	⑦		Ⓐ	Ⓐ	Ⓒ	①–④	⑤	Ⓐ
								d					A					f					g	h	
0	**Coutras** 302 d.	...	...	0646	...	...	0911	...	...	1015	...	...	...	1311	...	1511	...	...	...	...	1911	...	...	...	...
16	Libourne 302 d.	0556	0625	0658	0723	0825	0923	...	1025	1027	1125	1225	...	1325	1425	1523	1625	...	1725	1825	1925	1925	...	...	2025
	Paris Montparnasse 300 d.	|	|	|	|	|	|	0758	|	|	|	|	1108	|	|	|	|	1508	|	|	|	|	1844	1844	|
53	**Bordeaux** St Jean 302 a.	0629	0658	0731	0758	0858	0958	1019	1058	1058	1158	1258	1314	1358	1458	1558	1658	1715	1758	1858	1958	1958	2051	2051	2058
35	**Bordeaux** St Jean 299 305 d.	0635	0704	0735	0804	0904	1004	1025	1104	1104	1204	1304	1324	1404	1504	1604	1704	1725	1804	1904	2004	2004	2057	2057	2104
93	Facture Biganos 299 305 d.	0704	0733	0804	0833	0933	1033	1047	1133	1133	1233	1333	1349	1433	1533	1633	1733	1749	1833	1933	2033	2033	2119	2119	2133
109	La Teste a.	0721	0751	0821	0851	0951	1051	1104	1151	1150	1251	1351	|	1451	1551	1651	1750	|	1851	1951	2051	2051	|	2134	2151
112	**Arcachon** a.	0725	0755	0825	0855	0955	1055	1110	1155	1155	1255	1355	1410	1455	1555	1655	1755	1810	1855	1955	2055	2055	2134	2139	2155

	TGV 8478												*TGV* 8470					*TGV* 8472				*TGV* 8476		
	①–⑥	Ⓐ	⚒	Ⓐ	⑥	Ⓐ	Ⓐ	Ⓐ	Ⓒ	Ⓐ	Ⓐ	Ⓒ	⑥	Ⓐ		Ⓐ	Ⓐ		Ⓐ	Ⓒ	Ⓐ	⑦		
	j												d					A				f		
Arcachon d.	0600	0605	0635	0705	0805	0905	1005	1105	1105	1205	1305	1305	1350	1405	1505	1605	1635	1619	1705	1705	1805	1858	1905	2105
La Teste d.	|	0609	0639	0709	0809	0909	1009	1109	1109	1209	1309	1309	1357	1409	1509	1609	1639	|	1709	1709	1809	1904	1909	2109
Facture Biganos 299 305 d.	0618	0627	0656	0727	0827	0927	1027	1127	1127	1227	1327	1327	1412	1427	1527	1627	1656	1637	1727	1727	1827	1920	1927	2127
Bordeaux St Jean 299 305 a.	0640	0656	0725	0756	0856	0956	1056	1156	1156	1256	1356	1356	1436	1456	1556	1656	1725	1702	1756	1756	1856	1944	1956	2156
Bordeaux St Jean 302 d.	0646	0702	0730	0802	0902	1002	1102	1202	1202	1302	1402	1402	1446	1502	1602	1702	1729	1708	1802	1802	1902	1950	2002	2202
Paris Montparnasse 300 a.	0854	|	|	|	|	|	|	|	|	|	|	|	1713	|	|	|	|	1926	|	|	|	2233	|	|
Libourne 302 d.	...	0735	0803	0835	0934	1035	1135	1235	1235	1336	1435	1435	...	1535	1635	1735	1802	...	1835	1835	1935	...	2035	2235
Coutras 302 a.	...	...	...	...	0945	...	...	1247	...	...	...	1447	...	...	...	...	...	...	1847	...	...	...	2047	...

Full service Bordeaux - Arcachon and v.v.: from Bordeaux at 0604 Ⓐ, 0635 Ⓐ, 0704 Ⓐ, 0735 ⚒, 0804, 0835 Ⓐ, 0904 ⚒, 1004, 1035 Ⓒ, 1104, 1204, 1304, 1404, 1504, 1535 Ⓐ, 1604, 1635 Ⓐ, 1704, 1735 Ⓐ, 1804, 1835 Ⓐ, 1904, 1935 Ⓐ, 2004, 2035 Ⓑ, 2104, 2135, 2235, 2304 ⑤; from Arcachon at 0503 Ⓐ, 0535 Ⓐ, 0605 ⚒, 0635 ⚒, 0650 Ⓐ, 0705 ⚒, 0720 Ⓐ, 0735 ⚒, 0805, 0835, 0905, 0935 Ⓐ, 1005, 1105, 1205, 1305, 1405, 1505, 1605, 1635 Ⓐ, 1705, 1735 Ⓐ, 1805, 1835 Ⓐ, 1905, 1935 Ⓐ, 2005, 2105.

A – ⑥⑦ e until July 9; daily July 10 - Sept. 3; ⑥⑦ from Sept. 9.
d – July 8 - Sept. 2 (also July 14, Aug. 14).
e – Also Apr. 10, May 1, 8, 18, 19, 29.
f – Also Apr. 10, May 1, 8, 29, Aug. 15.
g – Not Apr. 10, May 1, 8, 17, 18, 29, July 13, Aug. 14, 15, Nov. 2.
h – Also May 17, July 13; not May 19, July 14, Nov. 3.
j – Not Apr. 10, May 1, 8, 29, Aug. 15, Nov. 4, 18, 25, Dec. 2, 9.
TGV – High-speed train. 🅁. 🍸.

BORDEAUX - LE VERDON - POINTE DE GRAVE 307

SERVICE APRIL 8 - JUNE 4.

km		Ⓐ	Ⓐ	⑥	Ⓐ	†	⑥	Ⓐ		Ⓒ	Ⓐ	Ⓒ	Ⓐ	†	⑥	Ⓐ		†	Ⓐ	①–④	⑤Ⓒ	Ⓐ	†	Ⓐ
0	**Bordeaux** St Jean d.	0626	0727	0759	0858	0902	0959	1059	...	1159	1259	1359	1459	1559	1559	1658	...	1659	1759	1857	1857	1952	2025	2042
19	Blanquefort d.	0651	0755	0824	0922	0926	1024	1122	...	1225	1323	1424	1522	1624	1624	1723	...	1723	1827	1923	1927	2015	2051	2105
35	Margaux d.	0713	0814	0843	0942	0945	1043	1143	...	1244	1343	1443	1542	1643	1643	1743	...	1742	1843	1942	1943	2032	2109	2123
57	Pauillac d.	0738	0833	0905	1001	1005	1105	1205	...	1305	1404	1505	1602	1704	1705	1804	...	1802	1905	2002	2005	2052	2142	2142
76	Lesparre d.	...	0848	0920	...	1020	1120	1220	...	1320	...	1520	1617	...	1720	...	...	1817	1920	2017	2020	...	2158	...
102	Soulac sur Mer d.	...	0911	0942	...	1042	1142	1242	...	1342	...	1542	1639	...	1742	...	...	1839	1942	2040	2042	...	2220	...
109	**Le Verdon** a.	...	0918	0950	...	1050	1150	1250	...	1350	...	1550	1647	...	1750	...	...	1847	1950	2048	2049	...	2228	...
112	**Pointe de Grave** a.	...	...	...	...	...	...	...	...	...	...	...	...	...	...	...	...	...	...	...	...	...	...	...

	Ⓐ	Ⓐ	⑥		Ⓐ	⑥	Ⓐ		†	⚒	Ⓒ		Ⓐ	Ⓐ	Ⓒ		Ⓐ	Ⓒ	Ⓐ		Ⓑ	⑥	†
Pointe de Grave d.	...	...	...	...	...	...	...	...	...	...	...	...	...	...	...	...	...	...	...	...	...	...	...
Le Verdon d.	...	0553	...	...	0653	0819	...	...	0919	1018	1218	...	...	1319	1419	...	...	1619	1718	...	...	1822	1919
Soulac sur Mer d.	...	0600	...	...	0700	0826	...	...	0926	1025	1225	...	...	1326	1426	...	...	1626	1725	...	...	1829	1926
Lesparre d.	...	0623	...	...	0722	0848	...	...	0948	1048	1248	...	...	1348	1448	...	...	1648	1748	...	...	1853	1948
Pauillac d.	0610	0639	0643	...	0740	0906	0908	...	1006	1106	1306	...	1307	1406	1506	...	1643	1706	1806	...	1906	1909	2006
Margaux d.	0629	0658	0703	...	0800	0928	0928	...	1026	1128	1328	...	1328	1427	1527	...	1703	1728	1828	...	1928	1928	2029
Blanquefort d.	0652	0722	0722	...	0823	0950	0950	...	1044	1150	1348	...	1350	1447	1546	...	1722	1750	1850	...	1950	1950	2050
Bordeaux St Jean a.	0715	0749	0745	...	0846	1013	1013	...	1107	1212	1412	...	1412	1512	1612	...	1747	1813	1913	...	2012	2013	2113

⛴ **POINTE DE GRAVE - ROYAN**. Sailing time approximately 20 minutes. ✆ 0974 500 033. www.transgironde.fr
January - June and September - December: Up to 9 sailings daily. **July and August**: Every 40 – 50 minutes 0630 - 2030 (0715 - 2115 from Royan).

PÉRIGUEUX - LE BUISSON - AGEN 308

km		Ⓐ	⚒	†	Ⓐ	Ⓒ	Ⓐ	Ⓐ	Ⓒ		Ⓐ	†	⚒	⚒	Ⓑ	⑥	①–④	①–④	⑤	†	⑥	①–④	†	⑤
0	**Périgueux** d.	...	...	...	...	0825	0835	0941	1214	...	1253	1434	1518	1638	...	...	1734	...	1820	1830	1838	2000	2005	2028
40	Les Eyzies d.	...	...	...	...	0853	0909	1009	1249	...	1327	1509	1546	1715	...	...	1808	...	1857	1858	1912	2034	2040	2103
57	Le Buisson 318 d.	...	...	...	...	0911	0926	1027	1306	...	1344	1526	1604	1732	...	...	1828	...	1915	1916	1929	2051	2057	2120
90	**Sarlat** 318 a.	...	...	...	...	|	...	|	...	...	...	...	|	...	...	...	1857	...	|	|	...	...	...	...
108	Monsempron Libos d.	0634	0758	0817	0955	1005	...	1119	...	1326	...	...	1656	...	1801	1847	...	1924	2007	2008	...	...	...	...
152	**Agen** a.	0721	0845	0902	1040	1048	...	1202	...	1411	...	...	1740	...	1853	1932	...	2012	2053	2051	...	...	...	...

	①	②–⑤		Ⓐ	Ⓐ	Ⓒ	Ⓐ		Ⓒ	Ⓐ	⚒	†	†	⑥	Ⓐ		Ⓐ	⚒	⑤	Ⓑ	⑥	①–④	⑤†
Agen d.	...	...	...	0741	0900	0916	...	1232	...	...	1435	...	1556	...	1638	1706	...	1749	1749	1907	1946	2031	2106
Monsempron Libos d.	0525	...	...	0826	0944	1004	...	1316	...	...	1518	...	1640	...	1725	1751	...	1834	1834	1952	2030	2115	2151
Sarlat 318 d.	|	0548	...	...	|	|	...	...	...	...	|	...	|	...	...	...	...	...	|	...	...	...	...
Le Buisson 318 d.	0618	0618	0720	...	1037	1056	1139	...	1332	1442	1609	1627	1732	1739	...	...	1838	...	1925	...	...	...	...
Les Eyzies d.	0636	0636	0737	...	1054	1114	1156	...	1349	1459	1627	1644	1750	1756	...	...	1856	...	1943	...	...	...	...
Périgueux a.	0710	0710	0812	...	1123	1142	1231	...	1424	1534	1655	1719	1819	1831	...	...	1933	...	2017	...	...	...	...

LIMOGES - ANGOULÊME and POITIERS 309

km		Ⓐ 🚌	Ⓐ 🚌	Ⓐ		Ⓐ	⚒ 🚌	⑥		†	⑥ 🚌			† 🚌	Ⓐ 🚌	†		⚒	Ⓐ 🚌	Ⓐ			⑤Ⓒ 🚌	Ⓐ
0	**Limoges** Benedictins d.	0455	0640	0700	...	0756	0850	0911	...	1005	1140	1213	...	1240	1400	1510	...	1605	1655	1712	...	1810	1805	1920
42	St Junien d.	0535	0720	0742	...	0839	0930	0951	...	1046	1220	1253	...	1320	1440	1551	...	1646	1735	1754	...	1853	1845	2003
50	Saillat Chassenon a.	|	|	...	...	0845	|	0957	...	1052	|	1259	...	|	|	1557	...	1652	|	...	...	1858	|	2009
122	**Angoulême** a.	0720	0855	...	...	...	1115	...	...	...	1405	...	...	1505	1625	...	...	...	1910	...	...	...	2030	...

	Ⓐ	Ⓐ 🚌	Ⓐ	Ⓐ 🚌		Ⓐ	⑥	†	⑥ 🚌		Ⓐ 🚌			Ⓐ		⑥ 🚌		Ⓐ 🚌	† 🚌		Ⓐ 🚌	† 🚌	⑤⑥ 🚌
Angoulême d.	...	0545	...	0740	...	...	...	...	1205	...	1240	...	...	...	...	1655	...	1730	1900	...	2000	2120	2120
Saillat Chassenon d.	0649	|	...	|	...	0857	1007	1103	|	...	|	1404	1701	...	...	|	1908	|	|	...	|	|	|
St Junien d.	0656	0715	0752	|	...	0904	1014	1110	1345	...	1420	1412	1708	1804	...	1835	1916	1910	2040	...	2130	2300	2305
Limoges Benedictins a.	0736	0800	0833	0940	...	0944	1054	1150	1430	...	1505	1451	1749	1845	...	1920	1956	1955	2125	...	2215	2345	2355

km		Ⓐ	①		②–⑤	⑥		⑥	Ⓐ		†	Ⓒ		Ⓐ	†		Ⓐ	⑥		Ⓑ	Ⓐ		⑤	†
0	**Limoges** Benedictins d.	0503	0557	...	0602	0611	...	0748	0848	...	0958	1250	...	1252	1507	...	1543	1705	...	1738	1832	...	1936	2026
139	**Poitiers** a.	0700	0758	...	0758	0804	...	0949	1056	...	1157	1450	...	1451	1701	...	1750	1904	...	1942	2045	...	2137	2223

	Ⓐ	⑥		Ⓐ	†			†		Ⓐ	⑥		Ⓑ	Ⓐ		⑥	†		Ⓐ				
Poitiers d.	0545	0833	...	0834	0948	...	1238	1527	...	1532	1654	...	1722	1828	...	1924	2009	...	2021	...	...	...	...
Limoges Benedictins a.	0745	1036	...	1032	1146	...	1438	1720	...	1727	1851	...	1924	2030	...	2123	2205	...	2219	...	...	...	...

310 PARIS - LIMOGES - TOULOUSE

MARCH 31 - JUNE 30. **Warning!** *INTERCITÉS* (★) services are subject to a large number of complex variations. Trains may not run on all days shown and timings shown may vary by several minutes (earlier departures possible; please check your reservation for confirmed timings). See Table **320** for *TGV* services Paris - Agen - Toulouse and v.v.

km		★	★	★		★	★	★		★	★	★		★	★	★		★	★	★		■	■
		3605	**3615**	**3617**		**3619**	**3625**	**3625**		**3629**	**3635**	**3645**		**3655**	**3655**	**3655**		**3665**	**3675**	**3685**		**3751**	**3731**
		①–⑥	①–⑤	⑦						⑦				①–⑤	⑥⑦	①–⑤		⑥⑦	①–⑤			①–⑤	⑥⑦
							A	B			C			D		E						🅁	🅁
0	**Paris** Austerlitz .... **294 315** d.	0627	0740	0741	...	0826	0936	1037	...	1133	1241	1439	...	1641	1641	1741	...	1741	1841	1936	...	2142	2212
119	Les Aubrais-Orléans .... **294 315** d.	0732	|	|	...	0928	|	|	...	1230	|	1539	...	|	|	|	...	|	|	|	...	2300	2332
200	Vierzon Ville .... **315** d.	0809	0913	0912	...	1009	1113	1213	...	1307	1413	1615	...	|	1814	1912	...	1912	2012	2119	...	|	|
236	Issoudun .... d.	|	|	|	...	|	1134	1234	...	|	|	|	...	1834	1834	|	...	|	2033	|	...	|	|
263	Châteauroux .... d.	0842	0945	0945	...	1041	1149	1250	...	1339	1445	1648	...	1850	1850	1944	...	1944	2049	2151	...	|	|
294	Argenton sur Creuse .... d.	|	|	|	...	|	|	|	...	|	1501	|	...	|	|	2000	...	2000	|	2207	...	|	|
341	La Souterraine .... d.	0919	1027	1026	...	1119	1227	1327	...	1417	1526	1725	...	|	1927	2026	...	2026	2126	2232	...	|	|
400	**Limoges** Benedictins .... a.	0954	1102	1103	...	1153	1301	1401	...	1452	1602	1800	...	1957	2002	2101	...	2101	2201	2306	...	|	|
400	**Limoges** Benedictins .... d.	0957	1104	1104	...	1156	1304	1404	...	1455	1603	1803	...	2000	2005	2104	...	2104	2204	2309	...	|	|
459	Uzerche .... d.	|	1142	1142	...	|	1342	1442	...	|	|	|	...	2038	2042	|	...	|	2241	|	...	|	|
499	**Brive la Gaillarde** .... a.	1058	1209	1209	...	1257	1407	1507	...	1554	1705	1903	...	2104	2108	2203	...	2203	2306	0010	...	|	|
499	**Brive la Gaillarde** .... d.	1101	...	...	...	1300	...	...	...	...	1706	1906	...	2106	...	...	...	2206	...	...	...	|	|
536	Souillac .... d.	1127	...	...	...	1326	...	...	...	...	1732	1931	...	2132	...	...	...	2232	...	...	...	|	0401
559	Gourdon .... d.	1144	...	...	...	1342	...	...	...	...	1748	1947	...	2147	...	...	...	2248	...	...	...	|	0424
600	Cahors .... d.	1211	...	...	...	1409	...	...	...	...	1816	2014	...	2214	...	...	...	2315	...	...	...	|	0504
639	Caussade .... d.	1237	...	...	...	1435	...	...	...	...	...	2040	...	...	...	...	...	...	...	...	...	|	0548
662	Montauban .... **320** d.	1252	...	...	...	1451	...	...	...	...	...	2055	...	...	...	...	...	...	...	...	...	0625	0625
713	**Toulouse** Matabiau .... **320** a.	1324	...	...	...	1528	...	...	...	...	...	2130	...	...	...	...	...	...	...	...	...	0707	0707

	★	★	★	★	★		★	★	★	★	★		★	★	★	★		★	★	★	■	■
	3604	**3614**	**3624**	**3628**	**3634**		**3638**	**3644**	**3648**	**3650**	**3656**		**3654**	**3664**	**3654**	**3674**		**3684**	**3684**	**3694**	**3750**	**3750**
	①–⑤		①–⑥	⑦	①–⑥		⑦	①–⑥	⑦		⑥⑦			⑦				Ⓑ	⑥		①–⑤	⑥⑦
													F		A						🅁	🅁
Toulouse Matabiau .... **320** d.	...	...	...	...	...	...	...	0718	...	1022	...	...	...	...	...	...	...	...	...	1631	2200	2218
Montauban .... **320** d.	...	...	...	...	...	...	...	0753	...	1055	...	...	...	...	...	...	...	...	...	1703	2242	2247
Caussade .... d.	...	...	...	...	...	...	...	0807	...	1108	...	...	...	...	...	...	...	...	...	1717	|	2301
Cahors .... d.	...	...	...	...	0639	...	0755	0835	...	1134	1241	...	1244	...	...	...	...	...	...	1743	|	2329
Gourdon .... d.	...	...	...	...	0706	...	0822	0902	...	1201	1308	...	1311	...	...	...	...	...	...	1810	|	2356
Souillac .... d.	...	...	...	...	0723	...	0839	0920	...	1219	1325	...	1328	...	...	...	...	...	...	1827	|	0014
Brive la Gaillarde .... a.	...	...	...	...	0747	...	0903	0947	...	1245	1349	...	1353	...	...	...	...	...	...	1853	|	|
Brive la Gaillarde .... d.	0348	0451	0555	0652	0750	...	0906	0950	1105	1248	1352	...	1356	1552	1553	1654	...	1745	1750	1856	|	|
Uzerche .... d.	|	0517	0655	|	0816	...	0932	|	1130	|	1417	...	1422	|	1619	|	...	1811	1816	|	|	|
Limoges Benedictins .... a.	0448	0553	0658	0751	0852	...	1008	1051	1206	1349	1454	...	1458	1651	1655	1754	...	1848	1853	1956	|	|
Limoges Benedictins .... d.	0451	0556	0733	0754	0855	...	1011	1054	1209	1352	1457	...	1501	1654	1658	1757	...	1851	1856	1995	|	|
La Souterraine .... d.	0528	0632	0808	0829	0929	...	1045	1129	|	1426	1531	...	1535	1728	1733	1831	...	1928	1930	2304	|	|
Argenton sur Creuse .... d.	|	0656	0810	0852	0953	...	|	|	1303	|	|	...	|	1752	|	1855	...	|	|	|	|	|
Châteauroux .... d.	0605	0713	|	0910	1010	...	1123	1206	1321	1504	1609	...	1613	1809	1811	1912	...	2009	2011	2111	|	|
Issoudun .... d.	0620	|	0826	|	|	...	1138	|	1336	|	1624	...	|	|	|	|	...	2024	|	|	|	|
Vierzon Ville .... **315** d.	0643	0750	0850	|	1046	...	1201	1244	1359	1539	1647	...	1649	1844	1849	1948	...	2048	2047	2147	|	|
Les Aubrais-Orléans .... **294 315** a.	|	|	|	1017	|	...	|	1318	|	1618	|	...	|	|	|	|	...	|	|	2222	0535	0543
Paris Austerlitz .... **294 315** a.	0819	0919	1023	1117	1216	...	1331	1420	1532	1719	1821	...	1819	2032	2032	2120	...	2219	2219	2320	0650	0650

TER REGIONAL SERVICES **ORLÉANS - LIMOGES**

	⚒	⚒	Ⓐ	Ⓐ	⑥		†		⚒	Ⓒ	⚒	Ⓒ	Ⓐ	Ⓐ		⑥	Ⓑ	⑥	†	Ⓐ	Ⓐ	Ⓐ
Orléans .... **315** d.	...	...	0638	0738	0739	0908	...	...	...	1038	1311	...	...	...	...	...	1608	1634	1634	...	...	1839
Salbris .... **315** d.	...	...	0716	0818	0818	0944	...	...	...	1117	1350	...	...	...	...	...	1644	1712	1712	...	...	1917
Vierzon Ville .... **315** d.	...	0645	0733	0836	0836	0957	...	...	1044	1134	1417	...	...	1652	...	...	1658	1729	1729	1733	1834	1935
Issoudun .... d.	...	0708	0758	0858	0858	...	...	...	1105	1156	1438	...	...	1714	...	...	...	1751	1751	1755	1856	1956
Châteauroux .... d.	0627	0726	0816	0916	0916	...	1003	...	1120	1214	1455	1514	1708	1732	...	1803	...	1809	1808	1810	1911	2013
Argenton sur Creuse .... d.	0643	0743	0835	0934	0935	...	1019	...	1137	1233	...	1530	1724	1756	...	1819	...	1832	1831	1827	1928	2030
La Souterraine .... d.	0714	0811	...	...	...	...	1050	...	1206	...	...	1559	1754	...	...	1849	...	...	1900	1856	...	2059
Limoges Benedictins .... a.	0758	0853	...	...	...	...	1140	...	1255	...	...	1649	1845	...	...	1936	...	...	1943	1939	...	2144

	Ⓐ	①	⚒	†	⚒	⚒	Ⓐ	Ⓐ	⑥	Ⓐ	Ⓒ		†	Ⓐ	⑥	†	†	Ⓐ	⚒	Ⓐ	Ⓐ	Ⓑ
Limoges Benedictins .... d.	...	0531	...	0715	0722	...	0825	...	...	1319	1322	...	...	...	1601	1609	...	1617	1724	...	...	1820
La Souterraine .... d.	...	0614	...	0806	0804	...	0912	...	...	1406	1406	...	...	...	1647	1652	...	1701	1810	...	...	1908
Argenton sur Creuse .... d.	...	0643	0643	0835	0832	0920	0942	1203	...	1433	1434	...	1619	1620	1715	1720	...	1728	1837	...	1920	1937
Châteauroux .... d.	0641	0721	0721	0851	0848	0937	0958	1221	1236	1450	1450	...	136	1639	1730	1736	...	1744	1854	...	1938	1953
Issoudun .... d.	0657	0739	0739	...	0903	0954	...	1237	1253	1505	...	...	1653	1655	...	1753	...	1801	1908	...	1954	...
Vierzon Ville .... **315** d.	0721	0807	0807	...	0926	1017	...	1302	1316	1527	...	...	1717	1721	...	1823	1830	1831	1930	2004	2021	...
Salbris .... **315** d.	0739	0824	0824	...	...	1033	...	1318	1332	...	...	...	1735	1737	...	...	1847	1848	...	2018	2037	...
Orléans .... **315** a.	0818	0904	0904	...	...	1112	...	1358	1411	...	...	...	1819	1819	...	...	1930	1930	...	2055	2117	...

TER REGIONAL SERVICES **LIMOGES - BRIVE LA GAILLARDE**

	Ⓐ	Ⓐ		⑥	Ⓐ		Ⓐ	†		Ⓐ	⑥		Ⓐ	Ⓐ		Ⓒ	Ⓐ		Ⓐ			
Limoges Benedictins .... d.	0556	0614	...	0658	0708	...	0811	1010	...	1230	1236	...	1653	1728	...	1820	1845	...	2029	...	...	...
Uzerche .... d.	0635	0704	...	0748	0758	...	0901	1100	...	1320	1326	...	1743	1819	...	1910	1935	...	2118	...	...	...
Brive la Gaillarde .... a.	0702	0733	...	0817	0827	...	0930	1129	...	1349	1355	...	1812	1849	...	1940	2004	...	2148	...	...	...

	Ⓐ		⚒		Ⓐ				⑥		Ⓐ				Ⓐ		Ⓑ					
Brive la Gaillarde .... d.	0610	...	0710	...	0810	...	1225	...	1450	...	1715	...	1817	...	1915	...	2014	...	...	...	...	...
Uzerche .... d.	0640	...	0740	...	0840	...	1255	...	1520	...	1744	...	1847	...	1945	...	2041	...	...	...	...	...
Limoges Benedictins .... a.	0730	...	0830	...	0930	...	1344	...	1610	...	1834	...	1936	...	2035	...	2120	...	...	...	...	...

TER REGIONAL SERVICES **BRIVE LA GAILLARDE - TOULOUSE**

	Ⓐ	Ⓐ	†	⑥	Ⓐ	Ⓐ		Ⓒ	Ⓐ	⚒	†			⚒		†	⚒	†	Ⓐ	⚒	†	⑥
Brive la Gaillarde .... d.	...	0607	...	0620	0721	...	...	0824	0916	...	1025	...	...	1428	...	...	...	1629	1724	...	1824	2024
Souillac .... d.	...	0633	...	0645	0744	...	...	0847	0941	...	1049	...	...	1452	...	...	...	1653	1748	...	1849	2048
Gourdon .... d.	...	0648	...	0701	0759	...	...	0902	0956	...	1104	...	...	1507	...	...	...	1708	1803	...	1905	2103
Cahors .... d.	0630	0715	0732	0727	0825	0932	...	0927	1022	1128	1129	...	1332	1532	...	1532	1732	1733	1829	1930	1932	2128
Caussade .... d.	0657	0742	0801	0756	0852	0959	...	0954	...	1159	1157	...	1400	1600	...	1600	1759	1801	1857	1957	2000	2156
Montauban .... **320** d.	0715	0800	0818	0814	0910	1017	...	1011	...	1218	1215	...	1417	1617	...	1616	1817	1818	1915	2014	2018	2213
Toulouse Matabiau .... **320** a.	0747	0834	0902	0901	0943	1102	...	1058	...	1258	1300	...	1503	1703	...	1656	1858	1858	2001	2059	2106	2258

	Ⓐ	Ⓐ	Ⓒ	Ⓒ	Ⓐ	Ⓐ		Ⓐ	Ⓒ	Ⓐ	Ⓒ		Ⓐ	Ⓒ	Ⓐ	Ⓐ	Ⓒ	Ⓐ	Ⓐ	Ⓐ	Ⓐ	Ⓒ
Toulouse Matabiau .... **320** d.	0604	0701	0701	0901	0901	...	1101	1259	1301	1458	1458	...	1655	1658	1711	1814	1901	1916	1932	2007	2032	2100
Montauban .... **320** d.	0644	0738	0746	0943	0943	...	1143	1343	1343	1544	1543	...	1743	1745	1746	1847	1947	1946	2018	2046	2117	2141
Caussade .... d.	0659	0753	0802	0958	0958	...	1158	1358	1358	1559	1558	...	...	1800	1802	1902	2002	2001	...	2101	...	2157
Cahors .... d.	0727	0820	0829	1026	1031	1037	1230	1425	1426	1626	1626	...	...	1827	1833	1929	2030	2033	...	2132	...	2228
Gourdon .... d.	0753	...	...	1051	...	1103	...	1452	1453	...	1653	...	...	...	1858	1955	2055	...	...	...	...	...
Souillac .... d.	0808	...	...	1107	...	1118	...	1508	1509	...	1709	...	...	...	1913	2011	2111	...	...	...	...	...
Brive la Gaillarde .... a.	0833	...	...	1138	...	1143	...	1536	1536	...	1736	...	...	...	1943	2036	2136	...	...	...	...	...

A – ①–④ Apr. 3–27.
B – ⑤–⑦ Apr. 1–30; daily from May 1.
C – Apr. 28 - May 16 and May 31 - June 30.
D – Apr. 3–7; Apr. 24 - May 16; May 31 - June 23.
E – Apr. 3–28.
F – May 2–5, 9–12, 15–17; ①–⑤ June 1–30.

★ – *INTERCITÉS*. 🅁.

■ – *INTERCITÉS DE NUIT*. 🛏 1, 2 cl. (2). Overnight journeys only.
Timings and running days vary. For confirmed days of running and timings please consult the SNCF journey planner: www.oui.sncf/billet-train.

BRIVE - AURILLAC 311

km		Ah	Ⓐ	⑥	Ⓐ	Ⓐ 🚌 g	Ⓒ	Ⓒ	Ⓐ 🚌	
0	**Brive la Gaillarde** 316 d.	0720	1125	1131	1413	1515	1531	1715	*1935*	2216
27	St Denis-près-Martel 316 d.	0745	1147	1200	1437	|	1559	1742	2010	2240
102	**Aurillac** a.	0908	1318	1323	1557	1710	1728	1912	2201	2358

	Ⓐ	⚒ f	⚒ g	Ⓒ		Ⓐ	†	⑤	
Aurillac d.	0518	0620	0730	1036	...	1150	1434	1559	1704
St Denis-près-Martel 316 d.	0639	0744	0848	1201	...	1316	1600	1718	1828
Brive la Gaillarde 316 a.	0705	0812	0914	1229	...	1342	1626	1742	1849

A – To/from Neussargues (Table **331**). f – Until Mar. 25. g – From Mar. 27. h – Until Mar. 12.

TOULOUSE and PARIS - LATOUR DE CAROL 312

For overnight trains Paris - Latour de Carol see Table **319**. For *Le Petit Train Jaune* Latour de Carol - Villefranche see Table **354**. For services Latour de Carol - Barcelona see Table **656**.

km				Ⓐ	Ⓒ	Ⓐ	①⑤	Ⓒ	Ⓐ	Ⓐ	Ⓒ	Ⓐ	Ⓒ	Ⓑ	Ⓐ	Ⓒ	Ⓐ	Ⓒ	Ⓐ	Ⓐ	Ⓒ	Ⓒ	Ⓐ	⑤
0	**Toulouse** Matabiau ◧ d.	0647	0747	0847	0847	0947	1047	1047	1216	1247	1247	1347	1347	1447	1547	1547	1647	1747	1748	1847	1847	1947	2047	2145
65	Pamiers ◧ d.	0741	0842	0946	0944	1046	1146	1145	1315	1346	1346	1442	1442	1545	1644	1644	1746	1846	1845	1945	1945	2048	2148	2245
83	Foix ◧ d.	0757	0902	1001	1000	1100	1200	1202	1332	1400	1402	1459	1505	1601	1659	1659	1805	1902	1859	2001	2000	2107	2203	2300
123	Ax-les-Thermes d.	0840	0940	...	1039	1141	...	1243	1412	...	1442	1540	1546	...	1740	1743	1845	1942	1940	2044	...	2147	...	...
144	L'Hospitalet-près-l'Andorre d.	...	1005	...	...	1208	...	1308	...	...	...	1605	1615	...	1806	1816	...	2011	...	2110	...	...	...	...
163	**Latour de Carol** a.	...	1028	...	...	1229	...	1328	...	...	...	1626	1635	...	1827	1836	...	2032	...	2131	...	...	...	...

	⚒	⚒	Ⓐ	Ⓒ		Ⓐ	①⑤	Ⓒ		Ⓐ	Ⓒ	Ⓐ	Ⓐ	Ⓒ	Ⓐ	Ⓒ	Ⓐ	Ⓒ	Ⓐ	Ⓐ	Ⓒ	Ⓒ	Ⓐ
Latour de Carol d.	...	...	...	...	0725	...	...	...	1031	...	...	...	1331	1334	...	1524	...	...	1632	...	1725	...	1832
L'Hospitalet-près-l'Andorre d.	...	...	...	...	0750	...	...	...	1055	...	...	...	1354	1357	...	1547	...	...	1656	...	1748	...	1855
Ax-les-Thermes d.	...	0614	0718	...	0817	0919	...	1018	1121	1216	1222	...	1421	1423	1615	1615	...	1720	1722	...	1816	...	1921
Foix ◧ d.	0556	0655	0758	0800	0903	1003	1100	1104	1203	1257	1305	1401	1500	1504	1658	1658	1731	1802	1804	1900	1901	2001	2002
Pamiers ◧ d.	0613	0713	0816	0817	0919	1019	1117	1118	1220	1316	1321	1417	1518	1520	1715	1715	1745	1818	1819	1916	1917	2019	2018
Toulouse Matabiau ◧ a.	0714	0814	0914	0914	1014	1114	1214	1214	1314	1414	1414	1514	1614	1614	1814	1814	1847	1916	1915	2014	2014	2114	2114

◧ – Other trains Toulouse - Foix at 0716 Ⓐ, 1617 Ⓐ, 1647 Ⓒ, 1717 Ⓐ, 1816 Ⓐ, 1916 Ⓐ, 1947 Ⓐ; Foix - Toulouse at 0623 Ⓐ, 0724 Ⓐ, 1602 Ⓑ.

🚌 ANDORRA 🚌 313

Toulouse Matabiau d.	1100	1500	2000
Toulouse Airport ✈ d.	1130	1530	2030
Andorra bus station a.	1500	1900	2400

Andorra bus station d.	0500	1000	1500
Toulouse Airport ✈ d.	0830	1330	1830
Toulouse Matabiau a.	0845	1345	1845

Operated by ANDBUS ✆ +34 973 984 016. www.andorrabybus.com.

Andorra bus station d.	0845	and	1845
Soldeu d.	0925	hourly	1925
Pas de la Casa a.	0940	until	1940

Pas de la Casa d.	0845	and	1845
Soldeu d.	0910	hourly	1910
Andorra bus station a.	0940	until	1940

Operated by Cooperativa Interurbana (service L4). Additional services operate on ①–⑥.

TOULOUSE - CASTRES - MAZAMET 314

km		Ⓐ	Ⓐ		⚒	†					Ⓐ	† 🚌		Ⓐ	Ⓐ					⑤ 🚌				
0	**Toulouse** Matabiau d.	0541	0643	...	0750	0840	...	1143	1344	...	1543	1546	...	1643	1719	...	1740	1847	...	1940	2043	...	...	...
86	Castres a.	0654	0758	...	0903	0956	...	1251	1451	...	1656	1722	...	1749	1832	...	1854	1959	...	2103	2157	...	...	...
86	Castres d.	0704	0808	...	0913	1002	...	1301	1501	...	1702	1723	...	1759	1846	...	1908	2009	...	2104	2203	...	...	...
105	**Mazamet** a.	0722	0826	...	0930	1020	...	1320	1520	...	1720	1753	...	1817	1903	...	1926	2027	...	2134	2221	...	...	...

	Ⓐ	Ⓐ		Ⓐ			Ⓐ	Ⓑ		⚒	† 🚌					Ⓐ							
Mazamet d.	0527	0550	...	0635	0737	...	0843	1028	...	1231	1305	...	1432	1729	...	1823	1940	...	...	...	...	...	...
Castres a.	0544	0608	...	0652	0756	...	0901	1045	...	1249	1334	...	1449	1747	...	1840	1957	...	...	...	...	...	...
Castres d.	0551	0614	...	0658	0802	...	0907	1051	...	1255	1335	...	1455	1753	...	1858	2003	...	...	...	...	...	...
Toulouse Matabiau a.	0701	0730	...	0806	0910	...	1016	1201	...	1402	1505	...	1602	1906	...	2008	2114	...	...	...	...	...	...

PARIS and ORLÉANS - VIERZON - BOURGES - NEVERS and MONTLUÇON 315

km		Ⓐ	Ⓐ	⚒	⚒	⑥	Ⓐ 🚌		⚒	⚒ 🚌	③	Ⓐ	⑤			Ⓐ	† 🚌	Ⓑ	⑥ 🚌	Ⓐ	Ⓐ	Ⓐ	Ⓐ 🚌	Ⓑ	Ⓑ
0	**Paris** Austerlitz 310 d.	...	...	...	0706	...	...	...	...	...	...	...	...	1204	...	...	...	...	...	...	...	...	...	1708	...
	Orléans 310 d.	...	0607	0708	|	...	...	0908	...	...	...	...	1208	|	...	1409	...	1608	...	...	1627	1708	...	|	1809
119	Les Aubrais-Orléans 310 d.	...	|	|	0806	...	...	|	...	...	...	...	|	1305	...	|	...	|	...	...	|	|	...	1806	|
178	Salbris d.	...	0643	0745	0830	...	...	0944	...	...	...	...	1245	1329	...	1445	...	1644	...	...	1706	1744	...	1831	1846
200	Vierzon Ville 290 310 d.	...	0659	0801	0845	0856	0925	0959	1023	...	...	...	1300	1345	...	1500	...	1700	...	...	1725	1759	...	1847	1901
232	**Bourges** 290 a.	...	0726	0821	0903	|	|	1020	|	...	...	...	1321	1404	...	1528	...	1720	...	...	1753	1820	...	1906	1922
	Bourges 290 d.	...	0729	...	...	|	|	...	|	1120	...	1241	...	...	1417	...	...	1722	1735	1746	...	1822	1838	...	...
	Nevers 290 a.	...	0817	...	...	|	|	...	|	|	...	|	...	...	|	...	...	1811	|	|	...	1910	|	...	...
291*	St Amand-Montrond-Orval d.	0634	...	...	...	0949	|	...	1128	1218	1324	1329	...	...	1459	...	1720	...	1838	1836	...	...	1953	...	...
341*	**Montluçon** a.	0728	...	...	...	1036	1100	...	1215	...	1418	...	...	...	1545	...	1820	...	...	1930	...	...	...	...	...

	⑤	①–④	†	Ⓐ			⑤	†	⑤†
Paris Austerlitz 310 d.	...	...	...	...	1906	...	2054	2106	...
Orléans 310 d.	...	...	...	1912	|	...	|	|	...
Les Aubrais-Orléans 310 d.	...	...	...	|	2006	...	2159	2205	...
Salbris d.	...	...	...	1948	2031	...	2225	2231	...
Vierzon Ville 290 310 d.	...	1923	...	2003	2046	...	2241	2246	2250
Bourges 290 a.	...	|	...	2024	2105	...	2259	2304	|
Bourges 290 d.	1930	|	1945	...	...	2115	...	...	|
Nevers 290 a.	|	|	|	...	...	|	...	...	|
St Amand-Montrond-Orval d.	2025	2025	2034	...	...	2201	...	...	2344
Montluçon a.	2111	2111	2128	...	...	2248	...	...	0034

	Ⓐ	⚒	⚒	⑥	Ⓐ ⊡	⑥	Ⓐ	⚒ 🚌	Ⓐ 🚌
Montluçon d.	...	0523	...	0600	...	...	...	...	0630
St Amand-Montrond-Orval d.	...	0610	...	0646	0639	...	...	0720	0738
Nevers 290 d.	...	|	...	|	|	...	0649	|	|
Bourges 290 a.	...	|	...	|	0725	...	0734	0825	|
Bourges 290 d.	0638	|	0655	|	...	0736	0737	...	|
Vierzon Ville 290 310 d.	0700	0707	0715	0738	...	0759	0800	...	0835
Salbris d.	0712	...	0729	...	...	|	0814	...	...
Les Aubrais-Orléans 310 a.	|	...	0757	...	...	|	|	...	...
Orléans 310 a.	0748	...	|	...	...	0833	0850	...	...
Paris Austerlitz 310 a.	...	...	0854	...	...	...	...	...	...

	Ⓐ	⑥	Ⓑ		⚒	③ ⊡	⑥	Ⓐ	†	⑥ 🚌	Ⓐ	⚒	Ⓐ	Ⓐ	Ⓐ	Ⓒ			Ⓐ	Ⓐ	⑤ 🚌	†	†	Ⓐ
Montluçon d.	...	0801	0810	...	1040	1229	...	...	...	...	...	...	...	...	...	...	1712	...	1741	...	1847	1909	...	1938
St Amand-Montrond-Orval d.	...	0848	0857	...	1127	1321	...	...	...	1352	1422	...	...	...	...	...	1759	...	1837	...	2007	1956	...	2023
Nevers 290 d.	0751	|	|	...	|	▬	...	1243	...	|	|	...	...	1646	1748	...	|	...	|	1852	|	|	...	...
Bourges 290 a.	0837	0931	0940	...	|	Ⓐ	...	1329	...	1455	1512	...	...	1733	1834	...	1846	...	1926	1938	|	2042	...	...
Bourges 290 d.	0840	...	...	0950	|		...	1332	1358	...	...	1556	1637	1736	1837	1837	...	1856	...	1941	|	...	2054	...
Vierzon Ville 290 310 d.	0902	...	...	1010	1218	1302	1316	1353	1418	...	...	1615	1701	1759	1859	1902	...	1916	...	2004	2134	...	2113	...
Salbris d.	0915	...	...	1025	...	1318	1332	1409	1433	...	...	1629	1714	1812	1912	1916	...	1931	...	2018	...	...	2126	...
Les Aubrais-Orléans 310 a.	|	...	...	1054	...	|	|	|	1504	...	...	1657	|	|	|	|	...	1959	...	|	...	...	2153	...
Orléans 310 a.	0953	...	...	|	...	1357	1411	1448	|	...	...	|	1749	1851	1950	1953	...	|	...	2055	...	...	|	...
Paris Austerlitz 310 a.	...	...	...	1154	...	...	...	...	1603	...	...	1755	...	...	...	...	...	2054	...	...	...	...	2259	...

⊡ – Does not run during school holidays - please enquire locally for dates.

* – Via Bourges (Montluçon is *327 km* for trains not calling at Bourges).

316 BRIVE - RODEZ

For overnight trains Paris - Rodez - Albi see Table **319**.

km		⑥	Ⓐ	Ⓑ	Ⓐ	Ⓒ	Ⓐ	Ⓐ		Ⓑ
0	**Brive la Gaillarde** 311 d.	0541	0546	0744	1118	1329	1435	1707	1935	2225
27	St Denis-près-Martel 311 d.	0606	0610	0814	1142	1353	1501	1743	2003	2249
45	Rocamadour-Padirac d.	0622	0626	0830	1157	1408	1517	1759	2018	2304
53	Gramat d.	0629	0633	0837	1204	1415	1525	1806	2025	2311
88	Figeac 317 d.	0657	0703	0904	1233	1442	1554	1835	2053	2338
94	Capdenac 317 d.	0707	0713	0914	1243	1451	1607	1845	2103	2348
109	Viviez-Decazeville d.	0722	0728	0931	1258	1506	1622	1900	2118	0003
161	**Rodez** a.	0810	0814	1017	1343	1550	1707	1945	2203	0048

	Ⓐ	⑥	†	Ⓐ	Ⓒ	Ⓐ	Ⓐ	Ⓒ	Ⓐ	Ⓒ	
Rodez d.	0611	0720	0810	0845	1048	1052	1252	1418	1503	1614	1741
Viviez-Decazeville d.	0656	0805	0855	0930	1133	1137	1340	1507	1550	1659	1826
Capdenac 317 d.	0715	0822	0913	0947	1150	1154	1401	1524	1610	1716	1844
Figeac 317 d.	0723	0829	0920	0955	1157	1201	1408	1531	1618	1723	1852
Gramat d.	0750	0855	0947	1022	1224	1229	1437	1558	1647	1752	1918
Rocamadour-Padirac d.	0757	0902	0954	1029	1231	1236	1444	1604	1654	1759	1925
St Denis-près-Martel 311 d.	0813	0917	1009	1045	1247	1252	1500	1620	1710	1815	1941
Brive la Gaillarde 311 a.	0837	0941	1033	1109	1310	1315	1524	1643	1736	1838	2007

317 AURILLAC - TOULOUSE

km		①	Ⓐ	⚒			⚒	⚒			⚒	Ⓐ						Ⓐ				Ⓐ	①–④	
		🚌		🚌				🚌			🚌				🚌			🚌	🚌				🚌	
0	**Aurillac** d.	...	...	0629	...	...	0824	...	...	...	1025	...	...	1224	...	...	...	1325	1630	...	...	1801	1840	...
65	Figeac 316 d.	0544	...	0749	...	...	0939	0949	...	...	1145	...	...	1339	1347	...	...	1445	1750	...	...	1916	1957	...
71	Capdenac 316 d.	0559	0612	0804	...	0814	...	1004	...	1014	1200	1211	...	...	1402	1415	...	1500	1805	1815	...	...	2008	...
100	Villefranche de Rouergue d.	...	0640	...	...	0845	...	...	...	1044	...	1239	...	...	...	1445	...	...	...	1845	...	...	...	...
117	Najac d.	...	0655	...	...	0900	...	...	...	1059	...	1254	...	...	...	1500	...	...	...	1900	...	...	...	...
170	Gaillac 323 d.	...	0742	...	...	0949	...	...	...	1145	...	1341	...	...	...	1546	...	...	...	1949	...	...	...	...
224	**Toulouse** Matabiau 323 a.	...	0831	...	...	1031	...	...	...	1223	...	1423	...	...	...	1623	...	...	...	2031	...	...	...	...

	⚒	⚒	Ⓐ	Ⓐ			⚒	⚒					Ⓐ			Ⓐ	Ⓒ	Ⓐ		Ⓐ		Ⓒ	Ⓐ
		🚌					🚌	🚌			🚌		🚌			🚌	🚌			🚌		🚌	🚌
Toulouse Matabiau 323 d.	...	...	0653	...	...	0857	...	...	1303	...	...	...	...	...	1701	...	...	1811	...	...	1909	...	...
Gaillac 323 d.	...	...	0742	...	...	0937	...	...	1341	...	...	...	...	...	1742	...	...	1850	...	...	1949	...	...
Najac d.	...	...	0829	...	...	1028	...	...	1428	...	...	...	...	...	1828	...	...	1937	...	...	2035	...	...
Villefranche de Rouergue d.	...	...	0844	...	...	1043	...	...	1444	...	...	...	...	...	1844	...	...	1953	...	...	2051	...	...
Capdenac 316 d.	...	0815	0915	...	...	1109	1115	1315	1511	...	1521	...	1649	...	1911	1917	1921	2020	...	2026	2118	2123	2128
Figeac 316 d.	0604	0830	0923	1000	...	...	1130	1330	...	...	1536	1546	1704	...	...	1932	1936	...	...	2041	...	2138	2143
Aurillac a.	0719	0950	...	1116	...	...	1250	1450	...	...	...	1701	1824	...	...	2052	...	...	...	2201	...	2258	...

318 BORDEAUX - LIBOURNE - BERGERAC - SARLAT

km		⚒	⚒	Ⓐ		Ⓐ		Ⓐ	Ⓒ	Ⓐ	Ⓐ	Ⓐ	Ⓒ	Ⓒ	Ⓐ	Ⓐ	Ⓐ	Ⓒ	Ⓐ	Ⓐ	Ⓐ	⑤	Ⓒ		⑤
0	**Bordeaux** St Jean 300 302 d.	...	0551	0720	0741	0842	0941	1042	1141	1142	1242	1342	1341	1541	1601	1642	1741	1741	1819	1840	1940	1940	1941	2133	2227
37	Libourne 300 302 d.	...	0622	0745	0806	0905	1006	1105	1205	1205	1306	1405	1406	1605	1625	1706	1806	1806	1843	1903	2005	2005	2005	2157	2251
45	St Émilion d.	...	0629	0752	0813	0912	1013	1112	1212	1212	1313	1412	1414	1612	1633	1714	1813	1813	1850	1910	2013	2013	2014	2204	2258
77	Ste Foy la Grande d.	...	0702	0825	0841	0939	1039	1139	1241	1240	1339	1441	1439	1641	1701	1742	1838	1838	1923	1941	2040	2040	2042	2227	2322
99	**Bergerac** d.	0615	0721	0844	0900	0953	1059	1156	1259	1254	1359	1459	1459	1659	1720	1801	1859	1859	1940	1959	2056	2059	2057	2244	2339
135	Le Buisson 308 d.	0647	...	...	0935	...	1132	...	...	...	1434	...	1532	...	1755	...	1932	1834	...	...	...	2132	...	...	...
168	**Sarlat** 308 a.	0717	...	...	1004	...	1201	...	...	...	1503	...	1601	...	1824	...	2001	2003	...	...	...	2201	...	...	...

	Ⓐ	⚒	Ⓐ	⑥	Ⓐ	Ⓐ	Ⓐ	†	⑥	†	Ⓐ	⑥	Ⓐ	Ⓒ	Ⓐ	Ⓐ		Ⓒ	Ⓐ	Ⓑ		Ⓐ	Ⓐ	Ⓒ
Sarlat 308 d.	...	...	...	0620	0622	...	0740	0753	...	...	...	0912	...	...	1104	...	1251	...	...	...	1727	...	1904	1907
Le Buisson 308 d.	...	...	...	0651	0652	...	0810	0824	...	...	...	0943	...	...	1135	...	1322	...	...	...	1758	...	1935	1937
Bergerac d.	0533	0605	0622	0728	0728	0805	0859	0900	0901	1005	1007	1018	1105	1201	1208	1301	1359	1559	1620	1722	1835	1905	2008	2011
Ste Foy la Grande d.	0549	0621	0641	0745	0744	0824	0920	0917	0920	1022	1022	1040	1122	1220	1223	1320	1420	1618	1639	1743	1856	1922	2023	2026
St Émilion d.	0613	0645	0709	0814	0814	0848	0946	0944	0948	1046	1046	1104	1146	1250	1247	1348	1448	1650	1715	1814	1929	1946	2047	2049
Libourne 300 302 d.	0621	0653	0717	0821	0821	0856	0953	0953	0956	1054	1054	1112	1153	1258	1255	1356	1455	1658	1722	1821	1938	1953	2054	2057
Bordeaux St Jean 300 302 a.	0646	0718	0739	0844	0844	0918	1018	1016	1021	1118	1118	1137	1218	1321	1318	1418	1518	1721	1745	1844	2003	2018	2115	2120

319 OVERNIGHT TRAINS PARIS - RODEZ, LOURDES, LATOUR DE CAROL and CERBÈRE

MARCH 31 - JUNE 30. INTERCITÉS DE NUIT – 🛏 1, 2 cl. and (2). Overnight journeys only. For services to Toulouse see Table **310**.
Timings and running days may vary. For confirmed days of running and timings please consult the SNCF journey planner: www.oui.sncf/billet-train.

	3741	**3737**	**3971**	**3741**	**3737**	**3971**	**3751**	**3751**	**3751**
	①–⑤	⑤	①–⑤	⑥⑦	⑦		①–⑤	⑤	⑥⑦
		d			**e**			**f**	
Paris Austerlitz d.	2113	2113	2113	2141	2141	2141	2142	2142	2212
Les Aubrais-Orléans d.	2227	2227	2227	2249	2249	2249	2300	2300	2332
St Denis-près-Martel a.	|	|	|	|	|	|	0441	0441	0441
Rocamadour-Padirac a.	|	|	|	|	|	|	0458	0458	0458
Gramat a.	|	|	|	|	|	|	0505	0505	0505
Figeac a.	|	|	|	|	|	|	0536	0536	0536
Capdenac a.	|	|	|	|	|	|	0545	0545	0545
Viviez-Decazeville a.	|	|	|	|	|	|	0601	0601	0601
Rodez a.	|	|	|	|	|	|	0655	0655	0655
Carmaux a.	|	|	|	|	|	|	...	0840	...
Albi Ville a.	|	|	|	|	|	|	...	0902	...
Tarbes a.	0708	|	|	0709	|	|	...	...	...
Lourdes a.	0725	|	|	0726	|	|	...	...	...
Pau ⊡ a.	...	|	|	...	|	|	...	...	...
Orthez ⊡ a.	...	|	|	...	|	|	...	...	...
Dax ⊡ a.	...	|	|	...	|	|	...	...	...
Bayonne ⊡ a.	...	|	|	...	|	|	...	...	...
Biarritz ⊡ a.	...	|	|	...	|	|	...	...	...
St Jean de Luz ⊡ a.	...	|	|	...	|	|	...	...	...
Hendaye ⊡ a.	...	|	|	...	|	|	...	...	...
Pamiers a.	...	|	0638	...	|	0638	...	...	...
Foix a.	...	|	0652	...	|	0652	...	...	...
Ax-les-Thermes a.	...	|	0741	...	|	0741	...	...	...
L'Hospitalet ⊖ a.	...	|	0818	...	|	0818	...	...	...
Latour de Carol a.	...	|	0846	...	|	0846	...	...	...
Castelnaudary a.	...	0657	...	...	0657	...	...	...	...
Carcassonne a.	...	0722	...	...	0722	...	...	...	...
Lézignan a.	...	0755	...	...	0755	...	...	...	...
Narbonne a.	...	0809	...	...	0809	...	...	...	...
Perpignan a.	...	0934	...	...	0934	...	...	...	...
Argelès sur Mer a.	...	0954	...	...	0954	...	...	...	...
Collioure a.	...	1000	...	...	1000	...	...	...	...
Port Vendres a.	...	1005	...	...	1005	...	...	...	...
Banyuls sur Mer a.	...	1012	...	...	1012	...	...	...	...
Cerbère a.	...	1020	...	...	1020	...	...	...	...
Portbou a.	...	1034	...	...	1034	...	...	...	...

	3740	**3970**	**3738**	**3756**	**3758**	**3758**	**3742**	**3970**	**3738**
	①–⑤	①–⑤	⑤	①–⑤	⑥⑦	⑦	⑥⑦	⑥⑦	⑦
			d	**g**		**h**	**j**		**e**
Portbou d.	...	...	...	...	...	...	...	...	...
Cerbère d.	...	...	1832	...	...	...	...	...	1832
Banyuls sur Mer d.	...	...	1840	...	...	...	...	...	1840
Port Vendres d.	...	...	1846	...	...	...	...	...	1846
Collioure d.	...	...	1851	...	...	...	...	...	1851
Argelès sur Mer d.	...	...	1858	...	...	...	...	...	1858
Perpignan d.	...	...	1906	...	...	...	...	...	1906
Narbonne d.	...	...	2043	...	...	...	...	...	2043
Lézignan d.	...	...	2058	...	...	...	...	...	2058
Carcassonne d.	...	...	2118	...	...	...	...	...	2118
Castelnaudary d.	...	...	2137	...	...	...	...	...	2137
Latour de Carol d.	...	1842	|	...	...	...	...	1842	|
L'Hospitalet ⊖ d.	...	1909	|	...	...	...	...	1909	|
Ax-les-Thermes d.	...	1944	|	...	...	...	...	1944	|
Foix d.	...	2033	|	...	...	...	...	2033	|
Pamiers d.	...	2049	|	...	...	...	...	2049	|
Hendaye ⊡ d.	...	|	|	...	...	...	...	|	|
St Jean de Luz ⊡ d.	...	|	|	...	...	...	...	|	|
Biarritz ⊡ d.	...	|	|	...	...	...	...	|	|
Bayonne ⊡ d.	...	|	|	...	...	...	...	|	|
Dax ⊡ d.	...	|	|	...	...	...	...	|	|
Orthez ⊡ d.	...	|	|	...	...	...	...	|	|
Pau ⊡ d.	...	|	|	...	...	...	...	|	|
Lourdes d.	1948	|	|	...	...	...	2157	|	|
Tarbes d.	2003	|	|	...	...	...	2213	|	|
Albi Ville d.	|	|	|	...	...	2050	|	|	|
Carmaux d.	|	|	|	...	...	2113	|	|	|
Rodez d.	|	|	|	2238	2238	2238	|	|	|
Viviez-Decazeville d.	|	|	|	2329	2329	2329	|	|	|
Capdenac d.	|	|	|	2347	2347	2347	|	|	|
Figeac d.	|	|	|	2356	2356	2356	|	|	|
Gramat d.	|	|	|	0027	0027	0027	|	|	|
Rocamadour-Padirac d.	|	|	|	0034	0034	0034	|	|	|
St Denis-près-Martel d.	|	|	|	0051	0051	0051	|	|	|
Les Aubrais-Orléans d.	0516	0516	0516	0535	0543	0543	0608	0608	0608
Paris Austerlitz a.	0633	0633	0633	0650	0650	0650	0719	0719	0719

d – Also Apr. 10, 24–27, May 1–4, 8, 17, 29; not May 19.
e – Also Apr. 22, 29, May 6; not Apr. 9, May 28.
f – Not May 19.
g – Train **3758** on ⑤.
h – Also Apr. 10, May 1, 8, 29 (arrives Les Aubrais 0535, Paris 0650); not Apr. 9, 30, May 7, 28.
j – Departs Lourdes and Tarbes up to 75 minutes earlier Apr. 16, 30, May 7, 14, 21, June 4.
⊡ – These destinations are served in summer only.
⊖ – Full name is L'Hospitalet-près-l'Andorre.

BORDEAUX - TOULOUSE - NARBONNE 320

TGV and *INTERCITÉS* services are subject to alteration Apr. 8 – 10, 14 May 5 – 8, 18 – 21, 27 – 29, June 10, Oct. 6, 22, Nov. 11, 12, 18, 19, 25, 26, Dec. 2.
TGV and *INTERCITÉS* timings may vary by a few minutes - please check your reservation. For overnight trains Paris - Cerbère - Portbou see Table **319**.

km		★	*TGV*	★	*TGV*	★	*TGV*	★		*TGV*	★	*TGV*	*TGV*	★	*TGV*		*TGV*	★	*TGV*	★	*TGV*	*TGV*	*TGV*
		4651	**6871**	**4655**	**8501**	**4657**	**8503**	**4659**		**7671**	**4661**	**8505**	**6873**	**4663**	**6875**		**7673**	**4665**	**8509**	**4669**	**8517**	**8519**	**8523**
		①–⑤																		Ⓑ			⑤
		d			A		B	C		D ⊠							⊠	E		F	G		e
	Paris Montparnasse **300** d.	...	...	...	0606	...	0708	...	...	0907	...	1108	...	...	...	...	1231	...	1508	...	1706	1908	2002
0	**Bordeaux** St Jean d.	...	...	0627	0820	0826	0925	1027	...	1120	1228	1320	...	1426	...	...	1519	1628	1721	1828	1920	2120	2222
79	Marmande d.	...	...	|	|	0904	|	|	...	|	|	|	...	|	...	...	|	|	|	1906	|	|	|
136	Agen d.	...	...	0731	0924	|	1027	1131	...	1225	1332	1423	...	1530	...	...	1625	1732	|	|	2027	2225	2326
206	Montauban d.	...	...	0808	|	1008	|	1208	...	1304	1409	1503	...	1607	...	...	1704	1809	|	2011	2106	2305	|
257	**Toulouse** Matabiau a.	...	...	0840	1024	1040	1132	1240	...	1331	1440	1531	...	1639	...	...	1736	1840	1926	2042	2136	2336	0035
257	**Toulouse** Matabiau d.	0645	0743	0845	...	1045	...	1245	...	...	1445	...	1543	1644	1743	...	...	1845	...	2045	...	...	...
348	Carcassonne d.	0728	0827	0929	...	1129	...	1329	...	...	1530	...	1627	1729	1827	...	...	1929	...	2129	...	...	...
407	**Narbonne** a.	0758	0856	0958	...	1158	...	1358	...	...	1558	...	1656	1758	1856	...	...	1958	...	2202	...	...	...
	Montpellier Sud-de-France **355** a.	|	0955	|	...	|	...	|	...	...	|	...	|	|	2001	...	...	|	...	|	...	...	...
	Montpellier St Roch **355** a.	0853	|	1054	...	1254	...	1454	...	...	1652	...	1755	1854	|	...	...	2052	...	2255	...	...	...
	Marseille St Charles **355** a.	1033	|	1234	...	1438	...	1637	...	...	1835	...	|	2036	|	...	...	2232	...	...	...	...	...
	Lyon Part Dieu **350** a.	...	1150	...	...	...	...	...	...	...	...	...	1950	...	2150	...	...	...	...	...	...	...	...

	TGV	*TGV*	★	*TGV*	*TGV*	★	*TGV*	★	*TGV*	*TGV*	★		*TGV*	*TGV*	★	*TGV*	*TGV*	★	*TGV*	★	*TGV*	★
	8502	**8504**	**4752**	**8508**	**6821**	**4756**	**8512**	**4758**	**7672**	**6823**	**4760**		**6823**	**8514**	**4762**	**8516**	**7674**	**4764**	**8522**	**4766**	**6825**	**4770**
	①–⑥		①–⑥	Ⓑ						⑥⑦			①–⑤	⑤–⑦		Ⓑ			⑦			①–⑤
	f		F	G f	H	J			⊠	g			d	h		j	⊠		k			d
Lyon Part Dieu **350** d.	...	...	...	...	0640	...	...	...	...	1010	...	...	1210	...	...	...	...	...	...	...	1810	...
Marseille St Charles **355** d.	...	...	...	...	|	0722	...	0927	...	|	1124	...	|	...	1323	...	...	1527	...	1728	|	1923
Montpellier St Roch **355** d.	...	...	0706	...	0844	0907	...	1107	...	1206	1306	...	1409	...	1506	...	...	1707	...	1907	2007	2107
Montpellier Sud-de-France **355** d.	...	...	|	...	|	|	...	|	...	|	|	...	|	...	|	...	...	|	...	|	|	|
Narbonne d.	...	...	0802	...	0947	1004	...	1204	...	1300	1400	...	1503	...	1602	...	...	1804	...	2005	2104	2204
Carcassonne d.	...	...	0833	...	1020	1035	...	1236	...	1333	1430	...	1534	...	1633	...	...	1836	...	2036	2136	2236
Toulouse Matabiau a.	...	...	0918	...	1102	1118	...	1319	...	1417	1518	...	1619	...	1718	...	...	1918	...	2118	2219	2318
Toulouse Matabiau d.	0623	0823	0922	1035	...	1124	1227	1324	1421	...	1518	...	...	1623	1724	1719	1824	1924	1959	2124	...	...
Montauban d.	0657	0857	0951	|	...	1151	|	1352	1456	...	1550	...	...	|	1751	1753	1857	1950	|	2150	...	...
Agen d.	0735	0935	1028	|	...	1228	1335	|	1535	...	1627	...	...	1731	1828	1831	1935	|	|	2228	...	...
Marmande d.	|	|	|	|	...	|	|	1456	|	...	|	...	...	|	|	|	|	2055	|	|	...	...
Bordeaux St Jean a.	0840	1040	1132	1240	...	1337	1440	1538	1640	...	1732	...	...	1836	1942	1940	2040	2139	2213	2337	...	...
Paris Montparnasse **300** a.	1052	1252	...	1452	...	...	1713	...	1852	...	...	...	...	2058	...	2152	2315	...	0027	...	...	...

TER REGIONAL TRAINS **BORDEAUX - AGEN**

km		①	②–⑤	⚒	Ⓐ	⚒	Ⓐ	Ⓒ	Ⓐ	⑥	⚒	†	Ⓐ		⚒	†	Ⓑ	Ⓐ		Ⓐ	Ⓑ	⑥	†	⚒	Ⓑ
0	**Bordeaux** St Jean d.	0549	...	0656	0727	0833	1033	1133	1133	1233	1333	1434	1533	...	1633	1633	1733	1802	1833	1858	1927	1933	2033	2047	2135
79	Marmande d.	0636	0650	0749	0813	0919	1119	1220	1252	1351	1419	1520	1620	...	1722	1751	1819	1858	1919	1952	2022	2052	2152	2133	2221
136	**Agen** a.	0711	0724	0824	0848	0954	1154	1255	...	...	1454	1555	1655	...	1757	...	1854	...	1954	...	2058	...	...	2208	2256

	Ⓐ	Ⓐ	⚒	Ⓐ	⑥	Ⓐ	Ⓐ		Ⓒ	†	Ⓐ	Ⓐ	Ⓐ	Ⓒ	⑥	Ⓐ		Ⓑ	Ⓐ	†	⚒	Ⓑ	①–④	⑤Ⓒ
Agen d.	...	0535	0612	...	...	0712	0812	0912	1107	...	1207	...	1307	1312	...	1407	1607	1712	...	...	1807	1912	2004	2004
Marmande d.	0538	0610	0647	0700	0712	0747	0847	0947	1142	1210	1242	1319	1342	1347	1409	1442	1642	1747	1804	1809	1842	1947	2038	2039
Bordeaux St Jean a.	0645	0657	0734	0801	0825	0835	0933	1033	1228	1328	1328	1434	...	1433	1528	1528	1728	1833	1915	1927	1928	2037	...	2125

TER REGIONAL TRAINS **AGEN - TOULOUSE**

km		Ⓐ	⚒	Ⓐ	Ⓐ	⑥	Ⓐ	Ⓐ		Ⓐ	Ⓐ	Ⓐ	Ⓒ	Ⓐ						Ⓐ	Ⓐ	Ⓒ	Ⓐ	Ⓒ	Ⓐ
0	**Agen** d.	...	...	0556	...	0628	...	0651	...	...	0748	...	0828	0849	1032	1151	1427	...	1630	...	1752	1828	1856	2032	2056
70	Montauban d.	0544	0616	0644	0655	0715	0718	0739	...	0817	0836	0847	0916	0937	1121	1238	1515	...	1718	1721	1840	1921	1944	2119	2144
121	**Toulouse** Matabiau a.	0629	0702	0716	0739	0748	0803	0811	...	0902	0911	0932	0948	1009	1156	1311	1547	...	1749	1806	1912	1948	2017	2152	2216

	Ⓐ	⑥	Ⓐ	Ⓐ	Ⓐ		Ⓐ	Ⓒ					Ⓐ	Ⓐ	Ⓒ	Ⓐ	Ⓐ	Ⓐ		Ⓐ	Ⓒ	Ⓐ	Ⓐ	
Toulouse Matabiau d.	0601	0606	0628	0701	0755	...	0801	0807	1008	1207	1432	...	1557	1601	1602	1646	1732	1750	...	1757	1807	1832	1852	2007
Montauban d.	0640	0640	0713	0735	0824	...	0846	0837	1041	1240	1503	...	1626	1646	1635	1715	1817	1818	...	1842	1838	1917	1929	2037
Agen a.	0728	0728	...	0827	0915	...	...	0928	1128	1328	1553	...	1717	...	1724	1802	...	1905	...	...	1928	...	2017	2133

TER REGIONAL TRAINS **TOULOUSE - CARCASSONNE - NARBONNE**

km		Ⓐ	Ⓐ	Ⓒ	Ⓐ	Ⓐ	Ⓒ	Ⓐ	Ⓐ	Ⓐ	Ⓒ	Ⓐ	Ⓐ	Ⓒ	Ⓐ	Ⓒ	Ⓐ	Ⓐ		Ⓐ	⑤	Ⓒ	Ⓐ		Ⓐ
																			F						
0	**Toulouse** Matabiau ◧ d.	...	0605	0713	0716	0808	0917	0917	1004	1117	1117	1204	1317	1317	1414	1514	1517	1604	1650	1717	1717	1717	1751	1919	2005
55	Castelnaudary ◧ d.	0558	0653	0756	0758	0856	0956	1001	1052	1159	1200	1250	1358	1400	1502	1557	1557	1653	1736	1758	1758	1759	1844	2000	2050
91	**Carcassonne** ◧ d.	0620	0714	0818	0820	0918	1019	1023	1114	1221	1224	1312	1420	1422	1525	1619	1619	1715	1757	1820	1820	1821	1906	2021	2113
128	Lézignan d.	0639	0733	0838	0839	...	1039	1042	...	1240	1244	...	1438	1441	...	1638	1638	1734	1815	1839	1839	1839	1924	2040	...
150	**Narbonne** a.	0655	0747	0850	0852	...	1052	1055	...	1253	1257	...	1452	1453	...	1651	1651	1747	1828	1851	1851	1851	1937	2053	...
	Perpignan **355** a.	...	...	0942	0945	...	1148	1148	...	1347	1352	...	1549	1554	...	1748	1748	...	...	1948	1948	1948	...	2150	...
	Cerbère **355** a.	...	...	1026	...	...	1230	...	...	...	1435	...	...	1639	...	1830	...	...	...	...	2033	2033	...	...	...
	Portbou **355** a.	...	...	1040	...	...	1241	...	...	...	1449	...	...	1652	...	1845	...	...	...	...	...	...	...	...	...

	Ⓐ	Ⓐ	⚒	⚒	Ⓐ	Ⓐ	Ⓒ	Ⓐ	⑥	†	Ⓐ	Ⓐ	Ⓒ	Ⓐ	Ⓒ	Ⓐ	Ⓐ	Ⓐ	Ⓒ	Ⓐ	Ⓐ	Ⓒ	Ⓐ	Ⓒ
				F																F				
Portbou **355** d.	...	...	...	...	...	...	...	...	0905	...	...	...	...	...	1305	...	...	...	1505	...	...	1705	...	...
Cerbère **355** d.	...	...	...	...	...	0723	...	...	0927	0926	...	...	...	...	1329	...	...	...	1526	...	...	1727	...	...
Perpignan **355** d.	...	...	0624	...	...	0807	...	...	1010	1016	1016	1227	...	1400	1410	...	...	1609	1610	...	...	1810	1810	...
Narbonne d.	...	0623	0719	0727	0807	0906	0906	...	1113	1113	1115	1321	1321	1453	1509	...	1638	1702	1708	1727	1809	1908	1908	2009
Lézignan d.	...	0636	0733	0740	0821	0919	0919	...	1131	1131	1131	1334	1336	1507	1524	...	1651	1716	1724	1741	1822	1921	1923	2024
Carcassonne ◧ d.	0606	0656	0755	0801	0841	0939	0939	1039	1152	1152	1152	1354	1355	1526	1544	1626	1710	1736	1745	1802	1842	1941	1943	2044
Castelnaudary ◧ d.	0629	0717	0817	0822	0902	1000	1000	1101	1214	1214	1214	1416	1416	1555	1604	1655	1731	1756	1805	1824	1903	2002	2003	2104
Toulouse Matabiau ◧ a.	0721	0758	0858	0912	0948	1040	1040	1144	1256	1256	1256	1457	1457	1633	1644	1740	1815	1836	1845	1909	1950	2041	2043	2144

A – ①–⑤ until July 7 and from Sept. 4 (not Apr. 10, May 1, 8, 18, 19, 29).
B – ⑥ until July 8 (also May 18, 19); ①–⑥ July 10 - Sept. 2 (not Aug. 15); ⑥ from Sept. 9.
C – Daily until Mar. 3; ⑥⑦ Mar. 4 – 19; daily Mar. 25 - Nov. 19 and from Dec. 3.
D – Not Mar. 6 – 10, 13 – 17, 20 – 24, 27 – 31, Nov. 19 - Dec. 1.
E – Daily until Apr. 9; ⑥⑦ Apr. 15 - July 2 (also May 18, 19; not May 28) daily from July 3.
F – To / from Montpellier, Beziers or Nîmes (Table **355**).
G – Ⓑ until July 2 (not May 18, 19); daily July 3 - Sept. 3; Ⓑ from Sept. 4.
H – Not Mar. 6 – 10, 13 – 17, 20 – 24, Nov. 20 - Dec. 1.
J – Not ①–⑤ Mar. 6 – 24, ①–⑤ Nov. 20 - Dec. 1.

d – Not Apr. 10, May 1, 8, 18, 19, 29, July 14, Aug. 15.
e – Also May 17, July 13; not May 19, July 14.
f – Not Apr. 10, May 1, 8, 29, Aug. 15.
g – Also Apr. 10, May 1, 8, 18, 19, 29, July 14, Aug. 15.
h – Also Apr. 10, May 1, 8, 17, 18, 29, Aug. 14, 15.
j – Not May 18, 19, July 14, Aug. 14.
k – Also Apr. 10, May 1, 8, 29, Aug. 15.

◧ – Additional trains Toulouse - Carcassone and v.v.:
From Toulouse at 0649 Ⓐ, 0748 Ⓐ, 1807 Ⓐ, 1850 Ⓐ.
From Carcassone at 0708 Ⓐ, 1242 Ⓐ, 1445 Ⓐ.

⊠ – OUIGO low-cost TGV service. Internet booking only (www.ouigo.com).

★ – *INTERCITÉS*. Ⓡ.

TGV – High-speed train. Ⓡ. 🍸.

323 TOULOUSE - ALBI - RODEZ

km																							
		⑥ 🚌	Ⓐ			①⑤		Ⓐ					Ⓐ		Ⓐ		Ⓐ		Ⓐ	†	⚒		† 🚌
0	**Toulouse** Matabiau 317 d.	0022	0606	0715	0917	1005	1116	1231	...	1307	1411	1635	1711	1736	1752	...	1815	1837	1914	1914	1928	2123	2325
54	Gaillac 317 d.	0122	0648	0811	1004	1051	1200	1321	...	1358	1458	1726	1757	1822	1842	...	1905	1922	2005	2005	2020	2209	0025
75	**Albi** Ville d.	0152	0703	0825	1024	1104	1217	1341	...	1417	1512	1745	1819	1836	1902	...	1924	1936	2028	2029	2040	2231	0055
92	Carmaux d.	...	0721	0842	1041	1122	1234	1358	...	1433	1530	1802	...	1854	1918	...	...	1954	...	2045	2056	2247	...
158	**Rodez** a.	...	0823	0946	...	1220	1336	...	...	...	1631	...	...	1957	...	...	...	2054	...	2146	2157	...	...

	Ⓐ	⚒	Ⓐ		Ⓐ	⑥	Ⓐ		†				Ⓐ	Ⓐ					Ⓐ		†	⚒
Rodez d.	...	...	...	...	0620	0633	0739	...	...	0834	1022	...	1224	...	...	1431	...	1636	1727	1844	2102	2113
Carmaux d.	0522	0557	0617	0644	0722	0736	0843	...	0843	0934	1123	1144	1322	1454	...	1531	1650	1735	1825	1955	2210	2213
Albi Ville d.	0540	0614	0634	0704	0742	0756	0903	...	0903	0951	1141	1201	1342	1513	...	1548	1707	1754	1845	2012	2232	2232
Gaillac 317 d.	0558	0632	0657	0725	0756	0811	0918	...	0918	1004	1200	1223	1358	1533	...	1602	1726	1808	1906	2032	2245	2245
Toulouse Matabiau 317 a.	0648	0720	0744	0820	0836	0851	1000	...	1000	1044	1239	1312	1437	1619	...	1641	1820	1852	1954	2119	2324	2324

324 PAU - OLORON - CANFRANC

For connections to Zaragoza (Spain) see Table **670**.

km																							
		Ⓐ	Ⓐ 🚌	⚒	⚒ 🚌		†		© 🚌	Ⓐ		©	🚌	Ⓐ			🚌		Ⓐ	©			
0	**Pau** d.	0716	...	0916	...	...	1043	1208	...	1433	...	1433	...	1701	1740	...	...	1906	2029	2047	...	...	...
36	Oloron-Ste-Marie d.	0752	0810	0953	...	...	1119	1244	...	1508	...	1509	...	1740	1816	...	...	1942	2104	2122	...	...	...
61	Bedous (Gare) d.	...	0843	1026	1035	...	1152	1317	1343	...	...	1542	1555	...	1850	...	1856	2016	...	...	...	...	...
77	Urdos (Douane) 🏛 d.	...	0905	...	1057	...	...	...	1405	...	...	...	1617	...	...	...	1918	...	...	...	...	...	...
96	**Canfranc** (Gare) a.	...	0923	...	1115	...	...	...	1423	...	...	...	1635	...	...	...	1936	...	...	...	...	...	...

	Ⓐ	⑥	Ⓐ	†		Ⓐ	©	🚌			©	Ⓐ	🚌	Ⓐ		©	Ⓐ	🚌			🚌	
Canfranc (Gare) d.	...	...	...	...	...	...	...	1124	...	...	...	...	1436	...	...	...	...	1741	...	...	2001	...
Urdos (Douane) 🏛 d.	...	...	...	...	...	...	...	1141	...	...	...	...	1453	...	...	...	...	1758	...	...	2018	...
Bedous (Gare) d.	...	...	0718	...	...	...	0920	1204	1210	...	1435	...	1516	1536	...	1601	...	1821	1909	...	2041	...
Oloron-Ste-Marie d.	0626	0725	0756	0830	...	0957	0957	...	1248	...	1513	1525	...	1609	...	1639	1811	...	1946	...	2117	...
Pau a.	0702	0800	0832	0906	...	1033	1033	...	1324	...	1549	1601	...	1646	...	1714	1856	...	2024	...	...	...

325 TOULOUSE - TARBES - PAU - BAYONNE

SERVICE FROM APRIL 1. Please refer to earlier editions for amended service until March 31.

km																								
														14141			**14143**	**14143**					**14151**	**14151**
		①	Ⓐ	Ⓐ	⑥	©	Ⓐ	Ⓐ		Ⓐ	©			★	Ⓐ		© ★	Ⓐ ★	†	†		⑤	† ★	⚒ ★
0	**Toulouse** Matabiau d.	...	...	...	...	...	0631	0640	...	0731	0731	0831	...	0932	...	1016	1135	1135	...	...	1231	...	1330	1334
91	St Gaudens d.	...	...	...	...	...	0725	0752	...	0830	0830	0930	...	|	...	1116	1224	1224	...	...	1330	...	1419	1424
104	Montréjeau d.	...	...	...	...	...	0743	0810	...	0848	0848	0948	...	1039	...	1133	|	|	...	...	1348	...	|	|
121	Lannemezan d.	...	...	...	...	...	0756	...	...	0901	0901	1001	...	|	...	1146	|	|	...	...	1401	...	|	|
158	**Tarbes** 305 d.	0518	...	0619	0625	0748	0824	...	...	0927	0929	1027	...	1115	1200	1211	1315	1315	1338	...	1427	1432	1511	1515
179	Lourdes 305 d.	0532	...	0633	0639	0802	0839	...	...	0942	0944	...	...	1132	1214	...	1332	1332	1352	...	...	1446	1528	1532
218	**Pau** 305 d.	0601	0614	0707	0713	0832	0908	...	0919	1011	1013	...	...	1200	1244	...	1359	1359	1422	1506	...	1516	1556	1559
258	Orthez 305 d.	0625	0639	0731	0737	0856	...	...	0944	...	...	...	...	1223	1307	...	1422	1422	1446	1530	...	1540	1619	1622
272	Puyoô 305 d.	0634	0649	0741	0747	0906	...	...	0955	...	...	...	...	|	1317	...	|	|	1456	1541	...	1551	|	|
323	**Bayonne** a.	...	0730	0821	0828	...	...	...	1033	...	...	...	...	1313	...	...	1505	1519	...	1618	...	...	1702	1728

							14155						**14157**										
	Ⓐ		Ⓐ	Ⓐ		©	Ⓐ ★		Ⓐ	†	Ⓐ	⑥	© ★	Ⓐ	Ⓐ		Ⓐ	©	Ⓐ	©	Ⓐ		† 🚌
Toulouse Matabiau d.	...	1431	...	1442	1531	1631	1634	...	1642	...	...	...	1725	1735	1742	...	1831	1831	1841	1931	1931	2031	2200
St Gaudens d.	...	1526	...	1555	1625	1731	|	...	1755	...	...	...	|	1830	1854	...	1926	1930	1954	2026	2030	2130	2340
Montréjeau d.	...	1545	...	1613	1643	1749	|	...	1813	...	...	...	|	1848	1912	...	1943	1948	2012	2043	2048	2148	|
Lannemezan d.	...	1557	...	...	1656	1801	1751	...	...	...	...	...	1841	1901	...	...	1956	2001	...	2056	2101	2200	|
Tarbes 305 d.	...	1627	1639	...	1724	1826	1816	...	...	1809	...	1838	1907	1929	...	...	2024	2027	...	2124	2127	2227	0043
Lourdes 305 d.	...	...	1653	...	1739	...	1832	...	...	1824	...	1852	1923	1944	...	...	...	...	...	2139	2143	...	0118
Pau 305 d.	1710	...	1723	...	1808	...	1900	...	...	1900	1913	1923	1952	2013	...	...	...	...	...	2208	2212	...	0213
Orthez 305 d.	1735	...	1746	...	...	...	1922	...	...	1925	1937	1945	2015	...	...	...	...	...	...	...	...	...	...
Puyoô 305 d.	1746	...	1756	...	...	...	|	...	...	1936	1948	1955	|	...	...	...	...	...	...	...	...	...	...
Bayonne a.	1827	...	...	...	...	...	2005	...	...	2018	2027	...	2104	...	...	...	...	...	...	...	...	...	...

										14140	**14140**								**14142**				
	Ⓐ	Ⓐ	⚒	⑥	Ⓐ	Ⓐ	©	Ⓐ	Ⓐ	Ⓐ ★	© ★	©	©	Ⓐ	Ⓐ			†	★		Ⓐ		
Bayonne d.	...	...	...	...	...	...	...	...	0635	0700	0700	0734	...	...	0751	...	...	...	1059	...	...	...	...
Puyoô 305 d.	...	...	...	...	...	...	...	0659	0716	|	|	0815	...	...	0831	...	...	1051	|	...	1300	...	...
Orthez 305 d.	...	...	...	...	...	...	...	0710	0726	0747	0747	0826	...	...	0842	...	...	1101	1143	...	1310	...	...
Pau 305 d.	...	...	...	...	0553	...	0653	0736	0750	0811	0811	0849	...	...	0905	0954	...	1124	1207	1250	1336	...	...
Lourdes 305 d.	...	...	...	...	0622	...	0722	0807	...	0839	0839	...	...	...	...	1023	...	1155	1235	1320	1406	...	...
Tarbes 305 d.	...	0539	...	0635	0638	0734	0739	0823	...	0855	0855	...	0938	0945	...	1039	1134	1210	1251	1335	1421	1437	1536
Lannemezan d.	...	0606	...	0701	0705	0759	0806	...	...	|	|	...	1003	1010	...	1106	1200	...	|	1401	...	1505	1601
Montréjeau d.	0515	0618	0649	0713	0718	0812	0818	...	...	|	|	...	1016	1023	...	1118	1213	...	1326	1413	...	1515	1614
St Gaudens d.	0523	0626	0658	0722	0726	0821	0827	...	...	0937	0937	...	1024	1031	...	1127	1222	...	|	1422	...	1526	1623
Toulouse Matabiau a.	0644	0729	0821	0829	0829	0929	0929	...	...	1032	1033	...	1133	1140	...	1238	1329	...	1429	1529	...	1631	1731

		14148	**14148**	**14148**					**14150**	**14150**													
	Ⓐ	† ★	Ⓐ ★	⑥ ★	†	©	Ⓐ	⑥	† ★	⚒ ★	©	Ⓐ	Ⓐ	†	Ⓐ	Ⓐ	†	Ⓐ	†	⑥	†	©	⑤
Bayonne d.	1332	1441	1447	1508	...	...	...	...	1620	1624	...	...	1734	1745	...	...	...	1842	...	1924	1924	...	...
Puyoô 305 d.	1409	|	|	|	1600	...	...	1700	|	|	...	...	1812	1823	...	1910	...	1920	2003	2004	2003	2033	2110
Orthez 305 d.	1420	1554	1533	1552	1610	...	...	1710	1736	1736	...	...	1822	1833	...	1920	...	1930	2014	2015	2014	2043	2120
Pau 305 d.	1444	1618	1557	1617	1634	...	1653	1734	1805	1850	...	1852	1846	1857	...	1944	1951	1954	2038	2039	2038	2107	2144
Lourdes 305 d.	...	1647	1628	1645	1705	...	1722	1805	1833	1833	...	1921	...	...	...	2018	2021	...	2112	...	2112	2138	2215
Tarbes 305 d.	...	1708	1647	1703	1720	1735	1738	1820	1850	1850	1935	1937	...	...	...	2033	2037	...	2126	...	2126	2153	2230
Lannemezan d.	...	1735	1714	1731	...	1800	1805	...	|	|	2000	2004	...	...	...	...	2104						
Montréjeau d.	...	|	|	|	...	1813	1817	...	|	|	2013	2017	...	...	2100	...	2116						
St Gaudens d.	...	|	|	|	...	1821	1826	...	1932	1932	2021	2026	...	...	2109	...	2125						
Toulouse Matabiau a.	...	1845	1834	1844	...	1929	1929	...	2027	2027	2129	2129	...	...	2228	...	2229						

🚌 MONTRÉJEAU - LUCHON 🚌

	Ⓐ				©	⚒	Ⓐ	©		Ⓐ		
Montréjeau d.	0754	0859	...	1144	1359	1425	1600	1815	...	1858	2059	...
Luchon Gare a.	0842	0947	...	1232	1447	1514	1648	1903	...	1946	2147	...

	Ⓐ	⚒	†	⚒	†	Ⓐ	©	⚒	©	Ⓐ	©	Ⓐ
Luchon Gare d.	0617	0903	1017	1113	1248	1453	1514	1605	1708	1714	1913	1951
Montréjeau d.	0707	0953	1107	1203	1338	1543	1604	1655	1758	1807	2003	2041

★ – *INTERCITÉS*.

BRIVE LA GAILLARD and LIMOGES - USSEL - CLERMONT FERRAND 326

BRIVE and LIMOGES - USSEL ⊠

km		Ⓐ	Ⓐ	⑥ s	Ⓒ			⑤ f⊕	⑦ w	Ⓐ ⊖	⑦ w	①–④ m⊗	⑥ s	⑤ f	⑥ s		⑦ w	①–④ m	⑦ w	⑤⑥ r		①–④ m	⑤ f	⑦ w	⑤ f	Ⓑ B	Ⓑ C
	Périgueux **302** d.	...	...	...	...	...	...	...	...	...	...	...	...	...	...	...	...	...	1610	...	...	...	...	...	...	...	...
0	**Brive la Gaillarde** . **302** ◧ d.	...	0624	...	0919	...	...	1211	...	...	1314	1330	1332	1416	...	...	...	1709	1712	1750	...	1853	1914	1933	2039	...	...
26	Tulle **302** ◧ a.	...	0650	...	0945	...	...	1237	...	...	1339	1358	1357	1443	...	...	...	1735	1738	1816	...	1918	1940	2001	2104	...	...
26	Tulle d.	...	0657	...	0952	...	...	1247	...	...	1346	1404	1404	1452	...	...	...	1743	1745	1824	...	1926	1947	2008	2112	...	...
	Limoges d.	0535	|	0751	|	1005	...	|	1220	1237	|	|	|	|	1428	...	1555	|	|	|	1827	|	|	|	|	2107	2108
79	Meymac d.	0715	0756	0930	1047	1144	...	1341	1357	1416	1440	1459	1458	1548	1604	...	1732	1838	1839	1919	2005	2021	2046	2102	2205	2245	2246
92	**Ussel** a.	0727	0808	0942	1059	1156	...	1353	1409	1428	1452	1511	1510	1600	1616	...	1744	1850	1850	1931	2017	2033	2058	2114	2217	2257	2258

km		Ⓐ	Ⓐ	⑥ s	Ⓐ	⑥ s	⑦ w	Ⓒ	Ⓐ ⊙	①–⑥ d⊖	⑦ w	⑤ f	A	⑦ w	⑤ f	⑦ w	⑤ h	⑦ w	①–④ m◇	⑤ f	⑦ w	⑤⑥ r		⑦ w	①–④ m	⑤ f	⑤ f
0	**Ussel** d.	0539	0612	0646	0740	0758	0843	0954	1040	1224	1236	1251	1251	1254	1457	1507	1513	1543	1625	1629	1630	1706	1757	1901	1931	1950	2031
13	Meymac d.	0552	0625	0659	0754	0811	0856	1007	1053	1237	1249	1304	1304	1307	1510	1520	1526	1556	1637	1641	1643	1719	1810	1913	1944	2007	2049
111	**Limoges** a.	|	0804	0835	0933	|	|	1143	1233	1414	|	|	|	1443	|	|	1701	1732	|	|	|	|	1949	|	|	|	2227
	Tulle a.	0645	...	...	...	0905	0949	...	...	...	1343	1400	1402	...	1606	1613	...	...	1730	1734	1735	1812	...	2006	2040	2101	...
	Tulle **302** ◧ d.	0652	...	...	...	0912	0956	...	...	...	1350	1410	1412	...	1613	1620	...	...	1738	1740	1743	1819	...	2013	2048	2108	...
	Brive la Gaillarde . **302** ◧ a.	0718	...	...	...	0937	1021	...	...	...	1416	1435	1439	...	1641	1647	...	...	1808	1809	1810	1846	...	2039	2114	2135	...
	Périgueux **302** a.	...	...	...	...	...	...	...	...	...	...	...	...	...	...	...	...	...	...	1918	1918	...	...	...	...	...	...

🚌 USSEL - CLERMONT FERRAND 🚌

	🚌		🚌	🚌 Ⓒ		🚌 ⚒	🚌 †		🚌 ⑤	🚌	
Ussel d.	0825	...	1125	1230	...	1530	1625	...	1925	2110	...
Clermont Ferrand a.	1010	...	1310	1410	...	1715	1810	...	2110	2250	...

	🚌		🚌		🚌		🚌 Ⓐ	🚌		
Clermont Ferrand d.	0745	...	1045	...	1245	...	1645	1745	...	...
Ussel a.	0930	...	1230	...	1430	...	1830	1930	...	...

A – ①②③④⑥ (not Apr. 10, May 1, 8, 17, 29). Subject to alteration on ①–④ Mar. 20 - Apr. 20.
B – Ⓑ until Mar. 26.
C – Ⓑ from Mar. 27 (not May 18).

d – Not Apr. 10, May 1, 8, 29.
f – Also May 17.
h – Also May 17; not Apr. 28, May 5, 12.
m – Not Apr. 10, May 1, 8, 17, 18, 29.
r – Also May 17, 18.
s – Also May 18.
w – Also Apr. 10, May 1, 8, 29.

◇ – Subject to alteration Mar. 27 - Apr. 6.
⊗ – Subject to alteration Mar. 27 - Apr. 20.
⊖ – Subject to alteration Mar. 27 – 30, Apr. 3 – 6, 24 – 28, May 2 – 5, 9 – 12.
⊙ – Subject to alteration on Mar. 31, Apr. 7, 24 – 28, May 2 – 5, 9 – 12.
⊕ – Subject to alteration on Apr. 14, 21.
⊠ – Services from / to Limoges are subject to alteration on May 6, 7, 19, 20, 21, 27, 28. Timings of services from / to Limoges may vay by up to 3 minutes Jan. 9 – 29 and from May 1.
◧ – Additional local trains run Brive - Tulle and v.v.

CLERMONT FERRAND - LYON 328

For rail journeys Clermont Ferrand - St Étienne and v.v., travel via Roanne (see Table **291** for connecting services).
Timings Clermont Ferrand - Roanne - Lyon may vary by up to 3 minutes Feb. 6 - Mar. 26 (earlier departures possible); timings in the opposite direction (from Lyon) are unaffected.

km		Ⓐ	①–⑥ d		Ⓐ	①–⑥ d	①–⑥ d	⑦ w	①–⑥ d	Ⓐ	①–⑥ d		⊖				Ⓐ		Ⓑ z	①–⑥ d	Ⓑ z			Ⓑ z	⑦ w
0	**Clermont Ferrand 329 330** d.	...	...	...	...	...	0600	...	...	0704	...	...	0902	...	...	1202	...	1402	1502	...	...	1700	...	1802	1950
14	Riom-Châtel-Guyon **329 330** d.	...	...	...	...	...	0609	...	...	|	...	...	0911	...	...	1211	...	1411	1511	...	...	1711	...	1811	1959
55	Vichy **330** d.	...	...	...	...	...	0637	...	...	|	...	...	0935	...	...	1235	...	1435	1535	...	...	1733	...	1834	2022
129	Roanne **290** d.	0506	0550	0604	0635	0650	0722	0725	0735	|	0835	0935	1021	1135	1250	1321	1451	1520	1621	1650	1750	1821	1850	1921	2107
171	Tarare d.	0542	0630	0645	0711	0731	0757	0803	0811	|	0911	1011	1052	1211	1331	1352	1532	1551	1652	1731	1831	1852	1931	1952	2137
222	**Lyon** Part Dieu **290** a.	0625	|	0726	0752	|	0834	0852	0852	0918	0952	1052	1126	1252	|	1426	|	1626e	1726	|	|	1926	|	2027	2211
227	**Lyon** Perrache **290** a.	0638	0723	0738	0803	0824	0848	0903	0903	0930	1003	1103	1140	1303	1424	1440	1624	1640e	1740	1824	1924	1940	2024	2040	2222

	Ⓐ	①–⑥ d		①–⑥ d		⊙			Ⓐ		①–⑥ d			①–⑥ d					Ⓐ	Ⓐ	Ⓐ		Ⓑ z		
Lyon Perrache **290** d.	0557	0620	0657	0757	0957	1124	1157	1236	1336	1420	1457	1557	1620	1657	1720	1736	1757	1820	1836	1857	1920	1936	1957	2020	2057
Lyon Part Dieu **290** d.	0608	0634	0708	0808	1008	1136	1208	|	1348	1434	1508	1608	1634	1708	1734	|	1808	1834	|	1908	1932	|	2008	2034	2108
Tarare d.	0650	0709	0801	0850	1050	1210	1250	1329	1439	1509	1550	1650	1709	1750	1809	1829	1850	1909	1929	1950	|	2029	2050	2109	2150
Roanne **290** d.	0730	0742	0841	0925	1125	1244	1325	1409	1519	1542	1625	1725	1742	1825	1842	1909	1925	1942	2009	2025	|	2109	2125	2142	2225
Vichy **330** d.	...	0826	...	...	...	1328	...	...	...	1626	...	...	1826	...	1926	...	...	2026	...	...	|	...	...	2226	...
Riom-Châtel-Guyon **329 330** d.	...	0849	...	...	...	1351	...	...	...	1649	...	...	1849	...	1949	...	...	2049	...	...	|	...	...	2249	...
Clermont Ferrand .. **329 330** a.	...	0858	...	...	...	1400	...	...	...	1658	...	...	1859	...	1958	...	...	2058	...	...	2145	...	...	2258	...

d – Not Apr. 10, May 1, 8, 29.
e – 8 minutes later on Dec. 20, 27.
w – Also Apr. 10, May 1, 8, 29.
z – Not May 18.

⊖ – Not Jan. 30, 31, Feb. 1 – 3, 6 – 10, 13 – 17.
⊙ – Not Jan. 30, 31, Feb. 1, 2, 6 – 9, 13 – 16.

MONTLUÇON - CLERMONT FERRAND 329

Subject to alteration May 19 – 21.

km		⑥ s	Ⓐ	Ⓐ	A	②–⑤ r🚌	Ⓐ		Ⓑ z		⑦ w
0	**Montluçon 327** d.	...	0559	0702	0828	0844	1036	1220	1700	1843	1936
13	Commentry d.	...	0611	0714	0840	0909	1047	1233	1713	1856	1947
67	Gannat **327** d.	0705	0706	0807	0927	1012	1133	1326	1805	1949	2042
94	Riom-Châtel-Guyon ▷ d.	0729	0730	0826	0943	1045	1152	1345	1830	2008	2101
108	**Clermont Ferrand** ▷ a.	0741	0742	0836	0952	1110	1202	1354	1839	2018	2110

	Ⓐ	① g		①–⑥ d		Ⓑ z	①–⑥ d	Ⓑ z	⑤ f	⑦ w
Clermont Ferrand ▷ d.	0604	0635	0734	1216	1348	1647	1746	1910	2007	2012
Riom-Châtel-Guyon ▷ d.	0613	0645	0747	1228	1401	1700	1758	1922	2017	2022
Gannat **327** d.	0630	0710	0808	1247	1425	1727	1824	1950	2037	2043
Commentry d.	0721	0811	0857	1342	...	1822	1915	2040	2128	2134
Montluçon 327 a.	0734	0823	0908	1353	...	1832	1926	2053	2138	2144

A – ①⑥⑦ (also Apr. 11, May 2, 9, 18, 30).

d – Not Apr. 10, May 1, 8, 29.
f – Also May 17.
g – Also Apr. 11, May 2, 9, 30; not Apr. 10, May 1, 8, 29.
r – Not Apr. 11, May 2, 9, 18, 30.

s – Also May 18.
w – Also Apr. 10, May 1, 8, 29.
z – Not May 18.

▷ – See also Tables **328** and **330**.

330 PARIS - NEVERS - CLERMONT FERRAND

SERVICE FEBRUARY 27 - JUNE 25. On May 18 services in this table run as on ⑥. **Warning!** Subject to alteration May 18–21.

km	SEE NOTE ⊠								5951 R★	5955 R★				5959 R★	5963 R★			5967 R★		5971 R★	5973 R★		5977 R★	5979 R★	5983 R★	5983 R★
		⚒	Ⓐ B	Ⓐ	⚒	Ⓐ	⚒	Ⓑ	①–⑥ b		⚒	⚒ D	Ⓐ				Ⓐ	⑤ f	Ⓑ		Ⓐ a	†	Ⓐ r	A	H	⑤ f
0	**Paris** Bercy ▶ d.	...	...	...	...	...	...	...	0700	0900	...	...	...	1300	1400	...	...	1458	...	1600	1657	...	1757	1757	1857	1857
254	**Nevers** ‡ ▶ d.	...	...	0532	...	...	0701	...	0859	1059	...	...	...	1459	1559	...	...	1659	...	1759	1859	...	|	1959	2059	2059
314	Moulins sur Allier ‡ d.	0501g	0552	0618	0639	0714	0741	0809	0930	1130	1216	1307	1413	1530	1630	1643	1712	1730	1807	1830	1930	1934	|	2030	2130	2130
355	St Germain des Fossés ‡ d.	0534	0619	0651	0711	0746	0809	0837	|	|	1245	1338	1442	|	|	1713	1742	|	1842	|	|	2001	|	|	|	2157
365	Vichy ▷ d.	0543	0631	0700	0719	0754	0818	0846	0957	1157	1253	1347	1451	1557	1657	1722	1751	1757	1851	1857	1957	2010	|	2057z	2203	2206
406	Riom - Châtel-Guyon ▷ d.	0605	0652	0722	0741	0816	0838	0908	1019	1219	1315	1409	1513	1619	1719	1743	1813	1819	1913	1919	2019	2033	|	2119z	2225	2228
420	**Clermont Ferrand** ▷ a.	0614	0701	0732	0750	0826	0847	0917	1029	1229	1325	1421	1522	1629	1729	1752	1822	1829	1922	1929	2029	2042	2111	2129z	2234	2237

	5950 R★	5950 R★	5954 R★		5958 R★					5962 R★		5966 R★			5970 R★	5974 R★		5978 R★			5982 R★		5986 R★		5990 R★	
	① g⊖	②–⑤ p⊖	Ⓐ a⊖	Ⓐ	⑥ k⊖	Ⓐ	Ⓐ	⚒	Ⓐ	⊖	⑥	①–⑥ b⊖	⚒	⚒	⊖	⑦ d⊖	Ⓐ	⊖	Ⓐ	Ⓐ	Ⓑ h⊖	E	⑦ e⊖		⊖❋	C
Clermont Ferrand ▷ d.	0525	0528	0555	0612	0631	0643	0717	0741	0808	0831	0842	1031	1042	1241	1331	1431	1540	1631	1641	1712	1731	1738	1831	1842	1931	2024
Riom - Châtel-Guyon ▷ d.	0536	0539	|	0621	0642	0652	0726	0751	0820	0842	0850	1042	1051	1250	1342	1442	1549	1642	1649	1721	1742	1747	1842	1851	1942	2033
Vichy ▷ d.	0600	0603	|	0645	0706	0714	0747	0814	0842	0906	0912	1106	1113	1312	1406	1506	1611	1706	1711	1742	1806	1809	1906	1912	2006	2054
St Germain des Fossés ‡ d.	0609	|	|	0653	|	0723	0756	0822	0850	|	0920	|	1123	1321	|	|	1619	|	1719	1751	|	1817	|	1921	|	2103
Moulins sur Allier ‡ d.	0631	0631	|	0722	0731	0753	0826	0848	...	0931	0950	1131	1157	1352	1431	1531	1649	1731	1748	1818	1831	1848	1931	1950	2031	2130
Nevers ‡ ▶ d.	0700	0700	|	0754	0800	...	...	0918	...	1000	...	1200	...	...	1500	1600	...	1800	...	...	1900	...	2000	...	2100	...
Paris Bercy ▶ a.	0857	0857	0902	...	0957	...	...	...	...	1157	...	1357	...	...	1657	1757	...	1957	...	...	2057	...	2157	...	2257	...

ADDITIONAL TER TRAINS PARIS - NEVERS *Subject to alteration on Mar. 11, 12, 18, 19, 25, 26*

km			Ⓐ			⚒	⚒		Ⓐ	Ⓐ	Ⓒ	Ⓐ J	†
0	**Paris** Bercy d.	...	0711	0911	...	...	1411	...	1702	1802	1801	1902	2004
119	Montargis d.	...	0816	1011	...	...	1511	...	1810	1910	1910	2010	2110
155	Gien d.	...	0838	1035	...	...	1533	...	1834	1933	1934	2032	2132
196	Cosne d.	0736	0902	1059	1236	1335	1557	1747	1859	1958	1957	2056	2158
228	La Charité d.	0801	0921	1116v	1301	1401	1616	1812	1916	2015	2017	2116	2215
254	**Nevers** a.	0825	0942	1138v	1325	1424	1637	1836	1937	2036	2037	2136	2235

	Ⓐ	Ⓐ	⑥	Ⓐ	Ⓐ			Ⓐ J	†	⚒		◧
Nevers d.	0456	0556	0622	0721	0835	1023	1235	1422	1622	1635	1823	1925
La Charité d.	0518	0618	0644	0742	0859	1044	1259	1444	1645	1659	1844	1952
Cosne d.	0534	0634	0702	0801	0924	1103	1324	1501	1702	1724	1903	2017
Gien d.	0559	0659	0727	0825	...	1126	...	1525	1727	...	1926	...
Montargis d.	0623	0723	0752	0849	...	1150	...	1549	1753	...	1950	...
Paris Bercy a.	0727	0827	0850	0952	...	1251	...	1649	1851	...	2049	...

A – Ⓑ to Apr. 16; ⑦ from Apr. 23 (also May 1, 8, 29).
B – ① to Apr. 3 (also Apr. 11); ⚒ from Apr. 17.
C – Ⓒ Mar. 4 - Apr. 10; daily from Apr. 15.
D – From Dijon (Table **373**). Runs 4–7 minutes later Feb. 27 - Apr. 14.
E – To Dijon on Ⓑ (Table **373**).
H – ①②③④⑥⑦ (not May 17).
J – Ⓐ from Mar. 6.

a – Not May 19.
b – Not Apr. 10, May 1, 8, 19, 20, 29.
d – Also Apr. 10, May 1, 8, 29; not May 21.
e – Also Apr. 10, May 1, 8, 29.
f – Also May 17; not May 19.
g – ① (also Apr. 11, May 2, 9, 30; not Apr. 10, May 1, 8, 29).
h – Not May 18, 19.

k – Also May 18; not May 20.
p – Not Apr. 11, May 2, 9, 18, 19, 30.
r – Not Feb. 27 - Apr. 14, May 19.
v – 4 minutes later on Ⓒ.
z – 4–7 minutes later on Ⓐ Feb. 27 - Apr. 14.

★ – *INTERCITÉS*. 🍷.
◧ – Runs 10 minutes later on ⚒.
❋ – This service is subject to frequent alteration on ①–⑤ (departures may be up to 42 minutes **earlier** and does not call at Nevers on certain dates). Please check before travelling.
⊠ – Certain southbound departure times of TER services may be up to 3 minutes **earlier** until Apr. 16.
⊖ – Departure times may be up to 7 minutes **earlier** until May 7.
▶ – For additional trains see panel below main table.
▷ – See also Tables **328** and **329**.
‡ – See also Table **290**.

331 CLERMONT FERRAND - NEUSSARGUES - AURILLAC

On May 18 services in this table run as on ⑥.

km		Ⓐ 🚌	C	⊗	⊙	B		Ⓐ	†	⚒	†	Ⓐ	⑤† △
0	**Clermont Ferrand** ‡ d.	*0542*t	0709	1036	1303	...	1648	1748	1757	1842	1957	2012	2123
36	Issoire ‡ d.	*0610*t	0737	1104	1329	...	1716	1815	1825	1910	2025	2039	2151
61	Arvant ‡ d.	0636	0756	1123	1349	...	1736	1838	1844	1929	2045	2059	2211
85	Massiac-Blesle d.	0652	0816	1143	1409	...	1757	1902	1904	1949	2106	2118	2232
111	**Neussargues** a.	0723	0837	1204	1430	...	1817	1922	1924	2010	2126	2139	2252
111	**Neussargues** d.	0723	0840	1205	*1438*	1608	1818	1925	1925	2014	2127	2140	2253
120	Murat (Cantal) d.	0738	0849	1214	*1447*	1617	1827	1935	1934	2023	2136	2149	2301
131	Le Lioran d.	0750	0905	1226	*1459*	1630	1838	1953	1945	2035	2148	2200	2314
168	**Aurillac** a.	0837	0939	1258	*1528*	1701	1910	2025	2020	2107	2220	2233	2345

	⚒	Ⓐn 🚌	①–⑤ A	D	⊙	⊙		Ⓐ	Ⓐ	†
Aurillac d.	0551	0713	0744	0911	1026	*1330*	1633	1740	1918	1951
Le Lioran d.	0622	0800	0817	0947	1059	*1401*	1708	1814	1952	2024
Murat (Cantal) d.	0633	0812	0828	0959	1111	*1413*	1720	1829	2003	2035
Neussargues a.	0641	0827	0837	1007	1119	*1421*	1728	1837	2012	2043
Neussargues d.	0642	0827	0838	...	1120	1436	1733	1839	2013	2044
Massiac-Blesle d.	0704	0858	0900	...	1145	1458	1758	1901	2034	2107
Arvant ‡ d.	0724	0914	0919	...	1205	1517	1817	1920	2054	2128
Issoire ‡ d.	0745	*0950*r	0938	...	1223	1536	1836	1939	2112	2146
Clermont Ferrand ‡ a.	0819	*1019*r	1006	...	1251	1601	1904	2007	2140	2215

A – ①–⑤ Dec. 19–30; ①–⑤ Feb. 6 - Mar. 3.
B – Daily to Mar. 26 (not Dec. 25, Jan. 1); ⑤ from Apr. 7 (also May 17). To Brive (Table **311**).
C – Daily Dec. 17–24, 26–31; ⑥⑦ Jan. 7–29; daily Feb. 4 - Mar. 5; ⑥⑦ Mar. 11–26.

D – Dec. 17 - Mar. 26 (not Dec. 25, Jan. 1).

n – Not Dec. 19–30, Feb. 6 - Mar. 3, Apr. 11, May 2, 9, 17, 30.
r – Not Mar. 13–31. By train Arvant - Clermont.
t – By train Clermont - Arvant.

⊗ – Subject to alteration on Ⓐ Mar. 13 - Apr. 14.
⊙ – Subject to alteration on Ⓐ Mar. 27 - Apr. 14.
△ – ⑤† (also May 17; not May 18). Runs 13–15 minutes later on †.
‡ – See also Table **333**.

332 (CLERMONT FERRAND -) NEUSSARGUES - BÉZIERS

WARNING! Rail services are subject to alteration April 29 - June 24. Please check locally if travelling during this period.

km		⚒	⚒	Ⓐ	⚒	🚌 ⚒		⑤ d	🚌	🚌 ⑥	🚌 Ⓑ w
0	**Clermont Ferrand 331** d.	...	...	...	...	1050	1303	...	1650	1950	2130
111	**Neussargues** **331** d.	...	...	...	...	|	1436	...	|	|	|
130	St Flour ⊖ d.	...	...	...	...	|	1457	*1547**	|	|	|
168	St Chély d'Apcher d.	...	...	...	1130	1225	1537	1627	1830	2125	2300
201	Marvejols ♥ d.	...	...	...	1207	|	1614	1706	|	|	|
	Mende ♥ a.	...	...	...	|	1340	|	|	1945	2240	0015
243	Sévérac le Château d.	...	...	...	1257	▬	1702	1756	▬	...	...
273	Millau a.	...	...	...	1329	...	1735	1828	†	...	...
273	Millau d.	0551	...	...	1330	...	1738	1830	2105	...	...
352	Bédarieux d.	0714	0842	1243	1449	1727	1858	1954	2231	...	...
394	**Béziers** a.	0747	0915	1317	1522	1801	1932	2026	2303	...	...

	🚌 ⚒	⚒	⚒		⑤ d	Ⓐ		N	⑦ hM	⑤ d
Béziers d.	...	0639	0757	0933	...	1200	1643	1821	1901	1901
Bédarieux d.	...	0716	0830	1008	...	1233	1715	1859	1944	1947
Millau a.	...	0834	▬	1124	...	▬	▬	2016	2054	2105
Millau d.	...	0836	🚌	1126	1341	🚌	🚌	...	2059	...
Sévérac le Château d.	...	0906		1157	1411	Ⓐ	Ⓒ	...	2132	...
Mende ♥ d.	0700	|	0950	|	|	1535	1600	...	|	...
Marvejols ♥ d.	|	0954	|	1250	1458	|	|	...	2223	...
St Chély d'Apcher d.	0820	1030	1115	1328	1535	1655	1720	...	2259	...
St Flour ⊖ d.	|	...	|	1406	...	|	|	...	*2336**	...
Neussargues **331** a.	|	...	|	1427	...	|	|	...	...	...
Clermont Ferrand **331** a.	1000	...	1300	1601	...	1835	1900	...	...	...

OTHER 🚌 LINKS. See Tables **331** and **333** for connecting rail services Clermont Ferrand - Arvant / Massiac and v.v.

	🚌 Ⓐ	🚌 Ⓐ	🚌 ⑥	🚌 ⚒	🚌	🚌	🚌 Ⓑ	🚌 ⑤	🚌 Ⓐ	🚌 †
Clermont Ferrand **331 333** d.	...	...	...	1048	...	...	...	...	2130	2148
Arvant **331 333** d.	...	0741	0826	|					|	|
Massiac-Blesle **331** d.	0711	0758	0843	|	1147	1808	1910	2124	|	|
St Flour ⊖ d.	0735	0824	0909	1213	1211	1833	1935	2149	2255	2313

	🚌 ⚒	🚌 ⚒	🚌	🚌 †	🚌	🚌 ⑤	🚌 ⚒	🚌 Ⓐ	🚌 †
St Flour ⊖ d.	0628	0845	1104	1645	1718	1728	1745	1825	1930
Massiac-Blesle **331** a.	0653	|	1128	|	1742	|	|	1850	|
Arvant **331 333** a.	...	|	...	|	...	1808	|	...	|
Clermont Ferrand **331 333** a.	...	1010	...	1810	...	...	1910	...	2055

M – From Montpellier (Table **355**).
N – ①②③④⑥⑦ (also Feb. 24, Mar. 3, Apr. 28, May 5, 19; not May 17).

d – Also May 17; not Feb. 24, Mar. 3, Apr. 28, May 5, 19.
h – Also Apr. 10, May 8, 29; not Feb. 19, 26, Apr. 9, 23, 30, May 7, 28.
w – Runs 20 minutes later on †.

* – By 🚌 to / from St Chély d'Apcher.
⊖ – St Flour - Chaudes Aigues.
♥ – See Table **333** for connecting rail services Marvejols - Mende and v.v.

☛ *Bus services in this table are operated on behalf of SNCF. Rail tickets valid.*

CLERMONT FERRAND - NÎMES and LE PUY EN VELAY 333

km		Ⓐ ⊙	⑥ w	②–⑤ d	Ⓐ 🚌	Ⓐ ⊖	† ⊙	⑦ 🚌	† ⊙	⑥ ⊖	① e	🚌	⊙	🚌	🚌	⊖	⑤† h⊙	Ⓒ	Ⓐ		⑤ h⊙	🚌	⊖			⑦ b
0	**Clermont Ferrand** .. 331 ¶ d.	...	...	...	...	0645	...	...	...	0735	...	...	...	...	...	1253	...	1430	1448	...	...	...	1640	...	1937	...
36	Issoire 331 ¶ d.	...	...	...	...	0714	...	...	...	0803	...	...	...	...	...	1321	...	1509	1519	...	...	...	1708	...	2015	...
61	Arvant 331 ¶ d.	...	...	...	...	0736	...	...	...	0822	...	...	...	...	...	1341	...	1532	1540	...	...	...	1728	...	2036	...
71	Brioude ¶ d.	...	...	...	...	0745	...	...	...	0831	...	...	...	...	...	1352	...	1540	1549	...	...	...	1737	...	2045	...
95	St Georges d'Aurac ¶ d.	...	...	...	...	0803	...	...	...	0849	...	...	...	...	...	|	...	...	...	...	...	...	1806r	...	...	...
103	Langeac d.	...	...	...	...	0811	...	...	...	0857	...	...	...	...	...	1419	...	...	...	...	...	...	1814	...	...	...
170	Langogne d.	...	...	...	...	0939	...	0924	...	1026	1118	1230	...	...	...	1549r	...	...	...	...	...	...	1945r	...	...	...
	Marvejols d.	...	...	0700	*0734*	|	...	|	...	|	|	|	...	1332	...	|	...	...	...	...	1720	...	|	...	...	2233
	Mende d.	0447	...	0750	0838	|	0840	|	...	|	|	|	1150	1425	1454	|	1653	...	...	...	1832v	1834	|	...	...	2314
188	La Bastide-St Laurent d.	0600	0710	...	0948	1006r	0949	0949	1012	1048	1137	1255	1308r	...	1602	1613r	1808r	...	...	...	1940	1942	2015r	...	...	...
241	Grand Combe la Pise d.	0706	0814	...	...	1105	...	...	1116	1147	1235	...	1409	...	...	1714	1911	...	...	...	...	...	2115	...	...	...
254	Alès d.	0723	0834	...	...	1125	...	...	1134	1206	1258r	...	1430	...	...	1733	1930	...	...	...	...	...	2131	...	...	...
303	**Nîmes** Centre a.	0800	0906	...	...	1157	...	...	1207	1238	1338	...	1502	...	...	1805	2002	...	...	...	...	...	2204	...	...	...

km		Ⓐ	⑥ s			⚒ s⊗	① e	⊖	🚌		⊙	🚌	⑤ h	⚒ 🚌	Ⓐ	Ⓒ	⊖	🚌	①–④ m	⑤ h🚌	Ⓑ ⊖	①–⑥ a⊙	⑦ b⊙	🚌		⑤ h
	Nîmes Centre d.	...	...	...	...	...	0716	0815	...	...	1217	...	...	...	...	...	1421	...	...	...	1658	1815	1815	...	...	2121
	Alès d.	...	...	...	...	...	0753	0849	...	...	1253	...	...	...	...	...	1455	...	...	...	1750	1852	1852	...	...	2156
	Grand Combe la Pise d.	...	...	...	...	...	0814	0905	...	...	1310	...	...	...	...	...	1512	...	...	...	1813	1913	1912	...	...	2213
0	La Bastide-St Laurent d.	...	...	...	...	...	0917	1004	1008	...	1421r	1420	...	...	...	...	1611	1614	...	...	1917	2017r	2017r	2020	...	2316
47	Mende d.	...	...	...	...	...	|	|	1117	...	1532	|	1613	1618	...	...	|	1722	1730	1734	|	2126	2128	|	...	...
82	**Marvejols** a.	...	...	...	...	...	|	|	1202	...	...	|	1700	1655	...	...	|	...	1817	1820	|	...	2210	|	...	...
	Langogne d.	...	...	...	...	...	0936	1028	...	...	...	1444	...	...	...	...	1633	...	...	...	1939	...	...	2044	...	...
	Langeac d.	...	...	...	...	...	...	1152	...	...	...	...	...	...	...	...	1756	...	...	...	2102	...	...	...	...	...
	St Georges d'Aurac ¶ d.	...	...	...	...	...	...	1200	...	...	...	...	...	...	...	...	1805	...	...	...	2110	...	...	...	...	...
	Brioude ¶ d.	0555	0630	0707	...	1104	...	1219	...	...	...	...	...	...	1604	1604	1824	...	...	...	2129	...	...	...	...	...
	Arvant 331 ¶ d.	0603	0638	0715	...	1112	...	1228	...	...	...	...	...	...	1612	1612	1833	...	...	...	2138	...	...	...	...	...
	Issoire 331 ¶ d.	0624	0658	0735	...	1132	...	1249	...	...	...	...	...	...	1633	1633	1851	...	...	...	2156	...	...	...	...	...
	Clermont Ferrand .. 331 ¶ a.	0655	0738	0814	...	1211	...	1317	...	...	...	...	...	...	1707	1712	1916	...	...	...	2224	...	...	...	...	...

CLERMONT FERRAND - LE PUY EN VELAY

km		Ⓐ	🚌 ⚒♣ s⊡	⊗	🚌 ⊡	🚌 ⊡	⚒ s	🚌 † z	⑤ f	🚌 Ⓐ ⊡	🚌 ⑤ f	† z
0	**Clermont Ferrand** d.	0542	...	0949	...	...	1758	*1757*t	1858	...	*2012*t	2034
36	Issoire d.	0610	...	1017	...	...	1826	*1825*t	1926	...	*2039*t	2103
61	Arvant d.	0629	...	1036	...	...	1845	1900	1945	...	2103	2122
71	Brioude d.	0638	...	1045	1357	...	1854	1913	1954	2052	2118	2134
95	St Georges d'Aurac d.	0706	...	1110	|	...	1918	|	2019	|	|	2158
103	Langeac d.	|	0817	|	|	1818	|	|	|	|	2156	|
147	**Le Puy en Velay** a.	0757	0903	1201	1505	1908	2010	2021	2110	2212	2242	2250

	① g	②–⑤ k	⚒ s⊗	🚌 ⚒s ♥⊡	🚌 †z ⊡	⑥ s	🚌 Ⓐ		🚌 ⊡	🚌 Ⓐ	† z
Le Puy en Velay d.	0523	0609	0807	0945	1059	1210	1220	1601	1654	1918	1950
Langeac d.	|	|	|	|	|	|	|	|	1744	|	|
St Georges d'Aurac d.	0616	0702	0900	|	|	1303	|	1654	...	|	2043
Brioude d.	0641	0724	0921	1049	1203	1324	1326	1715	...	2026	2104
Arvant d.	0649	0733	0929	...	...	1333	1341	1724	...	2043	2112
Issoire d.	0710	0754	0950	...	...	1354	1423	1745	...	*2112*t	2133
Clermont Ferrand a.	0742	0824	1019	...	...	1422	1503	1813	...	*2140*t	2200

D – ①②③④⑥ (also Feb. 24, Mar. 3, Apr. 28, May 5, 19; not Apr. 10, May 1, 8, 17, 18, 29).

a – Also Feb. 19, 26, Apr. 9, 23, 30, May 7, 28; not Apr. 10, May 8, 29.
b – Also Apr. 10, May 8, 29; not Feb. 19, 26, Apr. 9, 23, 30, May 7, 28.
d – Not Apr. 11, May 2, 9, 18, 19, 30.
e – Also Apr. 11, May 9, 30; not Feb. 20, 27, Apr. 10, 24, May 1, 8, 29.
f – Also May 17.
g – Also Apr. 11, May 2, 9, 30; not Apr. 10, May 1, 8, 29.
h – Also May 17; not Feb. 24, Mar. 3, Apr. 28, May 5, 19.
k – Not Apr. 11, May 2, 9, 18, 30.
m – Also Feb. 24, Mar. 3, Apr. 28, May 5, 19; not Apr. 10, May 1, 8, 17, 18, 29.
r – Arrives 5–10 minutes earlier.
s – Also May 18.
t – By train Clermont Ferrand - Arvant and v.v.
v – Arrives 1808.
w – Not Feb. 25, Mar. 4, Apr. 29, May 6, 20.

z – Not May 18.

⊗ – Subject to alteration on ①–⑤ Mar. 13–31.
⊖ – Subject to alteration Feb. 18 - Mar. 5 and Mar. 13 - June 9 (rail replacement 🚌 operates for part of journey south of Langeac; extended journey time with amended timings Langeac - Nîmes and v.v.; please confirm times locally).
⊙ – Subject to alteration Feb. 18 - Mar. 5 and Apr. 22 - May 7.
♣ – On ⑥ Langeac d. 0902, Le Puy en Velay a. 0948.
♥ – On ⑥ Le Puy en Velay d. 0952, Brioude a. 1054.
⊡ – See main panel for connecting rail service from / to Clermont Ferrand.
¶ – See also panel below main table.
► – Other trains Alès - Nîmes (journey time 32–41 minutes).
From Alès at 0558 Ⓐ, 0628 Ⓐ, 0656, 0801 ⚒, 0834, 0933, 1035 Ⓐ, 1232 Ⓐ, 1258, 1534, 1637 Ⓐ, 1839 Ⓐ and 1934 **D**.
From Nîmes at 0614 Ⓐ, 0655 Ⓐ, 0716 ⚒, 0750 Ⓐ, 0921 Ⓐ, 1023, 1120 Ⓐ, 1258 Ⓐ, 1319 Ⓐ, 1521 Ⓐ, 1618, 1727 ⚒, 1936 Ⓐ and 2121.

TGV services

LYON - MASSY - LE MANS - RENNES and NANTES 335

Timings may vary by a few minutes – please check your reservation. Subject to alteration Apr. 8–10. See Table **290** for slower services via Bourges.

	TGV 5380	*TGV* 5350 A	*TGV* 5350 n		*TGV* 5376 ⊡	*TGV* 5354 ⊗	*TGV* 5382 B	*TGV* 5382 ⑥ k		*TGV* 5386		*TGV* 5358 D△	*TGV* 5358 C
Marseille St Charles **350** d.	...	...	...	...	0735	...	...	1036	...	1436	...	...	...
Avignon TGV **350** d.	...	...	...	...	0806	...	...	1115	...	1515	...	...	...
Montpellier Sud de France **355** d.	...	...	...	...	|	...	...	|	...	|	...	1641	1641
Valence TGV **355** d.	...	...	...	...	0844	...	...	|	...	|	...	1744	1744
Lyon Perrache d.	0616	0616	0616	...	|	1016	1132t	|	...	|	...	|	|
Lyon Part Dieu d.	0630	0630	0630	...	0930	1030	1146t	1230	...	1629	...	1826t	1827
Massy TGV d.	0839	0839	0843	...	1140p	1239r	1356	1440	...	1839	...	2035	2038
Versailles Chantiers a.	|	|	|	...	1155	|	|	|	...	|	...	|	|
Mantes la Jolie a.	|	|	|	...	1229	|	|	|	...	|	...	|	|
Rouen Rive Droite a.	|	|	|	...	1322	|	|	|	...	|	...	|	|
Le Havre a.	|	|	|	...	1431	|	|	|	...	|	...	|	|
St Pierre des Corps a.	|	|	0943	...	...	|	|	|	...	|	...	2128	2131
Saumur Rive Droit a.	|	|	|	...	...	|	|	|	...	|	...	2206	2205
Le Mans 280 a.	0930	0930	|	...	...	1329	1450	1531	...	1929	...	|	|
Laval 280 a.	1002	|	|	...	...	|	|	|	...	2005	...	|	|
Rennes 280 a.	1030	|	|	...	...	|	1541	1621	...	2032	...	|	|
Angers St Laud 280 a.	...	1027	1039	...	...	1409j	...	...	...	...	...	2229	2229
Nantes 280 a.	...	1108	1119	...	...	1450j	...	...	...	...	...	2309	2309

	TGV 5300 H	*TGV* 5300 C	*TGV* 5300 E	*TGV* 5332		*TGV* 5336 L	*TGV* 5336 ⑦ e	*TGV* 5306 ⑤ f	*TGV* 5306 M▽		*TGV* 5316 ⊡	*TGV* 5320	*TGV* 5338
Nantes 280 d.	0448	0451	0504	...	...	...	...	1244	1244	...	...	1705z	...
Angers St Laud 280 d.	0527	0530	0543	...	...	...	...	1327	1327	...	...	1744z	...
Rennes 280 d.	|	|	|	0731	...	1230	1230	|	|	...	...	|	1730
Laval 280 d.	|	|	|	|	...	1258	1258	|	|	...	...	|	|
Le Mans 280 d.	|	|	|	0826	...	1330	1330	|	|	...	...	|	1830
Saumur Rive Droit d.	0550	0553	|	|	...	|	|	1350	1350	...	...	|	|
St Pierre des Corps d.	0628	0628	|	|	...	|	|	1428	1428	...	...	1830	|
Le Havre d.	|	|	|	|	...	|	|	|	|	...	1541	|	|
Rouen Rive Droite d.	|	|	|	|	...	|	|	|	|	...	1639	|	|
Mantes la Jolie d.	|	|	|	|	...	|	|	|	|	...	1732	|	|
Versailles Chantiers d.	|	|	|	|	...	|	|	|	|	...	1811	|	|
Massy TGV d.	0724	0724	0726	0923	...	1424	1424	1526	1526	...	1828p	1926	1926
Lyon Part Dieu a.	0930	0930	0930	1130	...	1630	1630	1730	1730	...	2036	2130	2130
Lyon Perrache a.	|	|	|	|	...	...	|	|	1749	...	|	2147	2147
Valence TGV **355** a.	1015	1015	1015	|	...	...	1715	1815	...	...	2116	...	...
Montpellier Sud de France **355** a.	1120	1120	1120	|	...	...	1834●	|	...	...	|	...	...
Avignon TGV **350** a.	...	...	...	1245	...	...	...	1852	...	...	2152	...	...
Marseille St Charles **350** a.	...	...	...	1324	...	...	...	1927	...	...	2224	...	...

A – ①–⑤ Feb. 13 - Mar. 10 (also May 19, 20, 21, 28, 29).
B – ①④⑤⑦ to Mar. 20; Ⓑ from Mar. 23 (not May 18, 19).
C – Until Mar. 19.
D – From Mar. 20.
E – Runs on May 19, 20, 21, 28, 29 only.
H – From Mar. 20 (not May 19, 20, 21, 28, 29).
L – ①④⑤⑥⑦ to Mar. 20; daily from Mar. 23.
M – ①②③④⑥⑦ (also May 19; not May 17).

e – Also Apr. 10, May 1, 8, 29.
f – Also May 17; not May 19.
j – 10–11 minutes later Feb. 13 - Apr. 28.
k – Also May 18, 19.
n – Not Feb. 13–17, 20–24, 27, 28, Mar. 1–3, 6–10, May 19, 20, 21, 28, 29.
p – Massy **Palaiseau**.
r – 1236 Feb. 13 - Apr. 28.
t – 4 minutes later from May 15.
z – 2 minutes earlier Jan. 2 - Feb. 12.

TGV – High-speed train. Ⓡ. 🍷.

● – Montpellier Saint Roch.
⊗ – Subject to alteration Apr. 3–7, 11–14.
△ – Subject to alteration on May 18, 19, 20, 27, 28.
▽ – Subject to alteration on May 19, 20, 27, 28, 29.
⊡ – Subject to alteration on various dates (particularly on ⑥⑦ from Jan. 28). Please check before travelling.

340 PARIS - LYON and ST ÉTIENNE *TGV trains*

For Charles de Gaulle ✈ - Marne la Vallée - Lyon see Table **11**. For Paris - Lyon St Exupéry ✈ see Table **342**. For Paris - Lyon - Milano see Table **44**.
Timings may vary by up to 9 minutes from May 15 (please check your reservation for confirmed timings).

km		*TGV*	*TGV*	*TGV*	*TGV*	*TGV*	*TGV*	*TGV*	*TGV*	*TGV*	*TGV*	*TGV*	*FR*	*TGV*	*TGV*	*TGV*	*TGV*	*TGV*	*TGV*	*TGV*	*FR*	*TGV*	*TGV*	*TGV*	*TGV*
		6601	**6601**	**7801**	**6641**	**7801**	**6603**	**6643**	**6681**	**6605**	**6607**	**6607**	**6647**	**6609**	**6611**	**6613**	**7803**	**6685**	**6615**	**6617**	**6651**	**6619**	**6621**	**6687**	**6623**
			②–⑤	①	Ⓐ	⑥	①–⑥	Ⓐ	①–⑥	Ⓒ		Ⓒ													②–⑦
		H	J	⊠	s	⊠	b	s	b	w		w	♠				⊠				♠				d
0	**Paris** Gare de Lyon .. **341/2** d.	0547	0601	0606	0624	0624	0654	0719	0748	0748	0857	0857	0924	0954z	1057	1148y	1223n	1249x	1249x	1346k	1420	1459	1549	1658	1658
303	Le Creusot TGV ..... d.	0715	0729	|	|	|	|	|	0917	0917	|	|	|	|	|	1317	|	|	|	1511	|	|	1715	|	|
363	Mâcon Loché TGV .... **341/2** a.	|	|	|	|	|	|	|	|	|	|	|	|	|	|	|	|	|	|	|	|	|	1733	|	|
427	**Lyon** Part-Dieu ..... a.	0756	0808	0808	0822	0822	0856	0922	0956	0956	1056	1056	1126	1156	1256	1356	1422	1456	1456	1556	1622	1656	1803	1856	1856
	St Étienne Châteaucreux .. a.	|	|	|	|	|	|	|	1048	|	...	|	|	|	|	|	|	1548	|	|	|	|	|	1948	|
432	**Lyon** Perrache ..... a.	0810	0821	0821	0836	0836	0910	0936	...	1010	...	1110	1149	1210	1310	1410	1436	...	1510	1610	1636	1710	1817	...	1910

	TGV	*TGV*	*TGV*	*TGV*	*TGV*	*TGV*	*FR*	*TGV*	*TGV*	*TGV*	
	6663	**6627**	**7805**	**6665**	**6689**	**6669**	**6671**	**6631**	**6633**	**6633**	
	Ⓐ			Ⓑ		Ⓑ			①–④		
	v		⊠	h ◇		h	♠		D	E	
Paris Gare de Lyon ... **341/2** d.	1723	1743	1823	1828	1859	1925	1955	1959	2043	2057	...
Le Creusot TGV ..... d.	|	1915	|	|	|	|	|	|	2214	2225	...
Mâcon Loché TGV ..... **341/2** a.	|	|	|	|	|	|	|	|	2235	2244	...
Lyon Part-Dieu ..... a.	1922	1956	2022	2031	2056	2122	2152	2156	2304	2311	...
St Étienne Châteaucreux ... a.	|	|	|	|	2148	|	|	|	|	|	...
Lyon Perrache ..... a.	1936	2010	2036	2050	...	2136	2206	2210	2315f	2324	...

	TGV	*TGV*	*TGV*	*FR*	*TGV*	*TGV*	*TGV*	*TGV*	*TGV*
	6602	**6642**	**6644**	**6650**	**6690**	**6604**	**6693**	**6608**	**6610**
	Ⓐ	Ⓐ	①–④		①–⑥	⑤⑥			Ⓑ
	v	v	m	♠	b	r			h
Lyon Perrache ..... d.	0550	0624	0639	0646	...	0650	...	0750	0850
St Étienne C ⊡ ..... d.	|	|	|	|	0615	|	0643	|	|
Lyon Part-Dieu ..... d.	0604	0638	0652	0700	0704	0704	0734	0804	0904
Mâcon Loché TGV . **341/2** d.	0631	|	|	|	|	|	|	|	|
Le Creusot TGV ..... d.	0653	|	|	|	|	|	|	0846	|
Paris Gare de Lyon . **341/2** a.	0817	0836	0856	0905	0908	0908	0936	1010	1102

	TGV	*TGV*	*TGV*	*TGV*	*TGV*	*FR*	*TGV*	*TGV*	*TGV*	*TGV*	*TGV*	*TGV*	*TGV*	*TGV*	*TGV*	*FR*	*TGV*	*TGV*	*TGV*	*TGV*	*TGV*		*TGV*	*TGV*	*TGV*
	7802	**6612**	**6614**	**6616**	**6616**	**6654**	**6694**	**6618**	**6620**	**6620**	**6622**	**7804**	**6624**	**6664**	**6626**	**6656**	**6696**	**6668**	**6628**	**6630**	**6632**		**6634**	**7806**	**6676**
				Ⓐ	Ⓒ					⑥⑦				Ⓑ				⑤⑦			Ⓑ			⑤⑦	⑤⑦
	⊠			p	w	♠			A	B		⊠		h		♠		t			h			⊠	t
Lyon Perrache ..... d.	0924	0950	1050	...	1150	1242	...	1249	1350	1350	1450	1524	1550	1611	1650	1711	...	1723	1750	1850	1950	...	2049	2124	2150
St Étienne Châteaucreux ... d.	|	|	|	...	|	|	1212	|	|	|	|	|	|	|	|	|	1644	|	|	|	|	...	|	|	|
Lyon Part-Dieu ..... d.	0938	1004	1104	1134	1204	1300	1304	1304	1404	1404	1504	1538	1604	1634	1704	1734	1738	1738	1804	1904	2004	...	2103	2138	2204
Mâcon Loché TGV ..... **341/2** d.	|	|	|	|	|	|	|	|	|	|	|	|	|	|	|	|	|	|	|	|	|	...	|	|	2231
Le Creusot TGV ..... d.	|	1046	|	|	|	|	|	|	1448	1453	|	|	1648	|	|	|	|	|	1846	|	|	...	2148	|	2253
Paris Gare de Lyon ... **341/2** a.	1136	1213	1304	1334	1405	1459	1504j	1504j	1612	1619	1702	1736	1813	1838	1906	1931	1937	1937	2012	2107c	2204	...	2314	2340	0016

A – ①–⑤ until May 12; daily from May 15.
B – Until May 14.
D – ①–④ Jan. 9 - May 11 (not Apr. 10, May 1, 8). Timings may vary by up to 5 minutes.
E – Ⓑ to Jan. 8; ⑤† Jan. 13 - May 8; Ⓑ from May 12 (not May 18, 19).
Terminates at Lyon Part-Dieu on ⑤ Jan. 13 - Mar. 31. Subject to alteration on Apr. 2, 9.
H – ①–⑤ to Jan. 9; ① Jan. 16 - Apr. 24 (also Apr. 11, May 2, 9; not Apr. 10);
Ⓐ from May 15 (not May 19). Departs Paris 0544 on Apr. 11, May 9.
J – ②–⑤ Jan. 10 - May 12 (not Apr. 11, May 2, 9).

b – Not Apr. 10, May 1, 8, 29.
c – 2111 on Feb. 25, Mar. 4.
d – Also Apr. 10, May 1, 8, 29; not Apr. 11, May 2, 9, 30.
f – Apr. 4 - May 11 only.
h – Not May 18, 19.
j – 3–5 minutes later on Dec. 20, 21, Jan. 3, 4, Apr. 11, 12, 25, 26.
k – 3–5 minutes earlier on Dec. 20, 21, 27, 28, Feb. 20, 23, 24, Mar. 20, 23, 24, Apr. 11, 12, 18, 19.
m – Not Apr. 10, May 1, 8, 17, 18, 29.
n – 1219 on Dec. 27, 28, Apr. 18, 19.

p – Not Dec. 27, 28, 29, May 19.
r – Also May 17, 18.
s – Not Dec. 26 – 30, May 19.
t – Also Apr. 10, May 1, 8, 17, 29; not May 19.
v – Not May 19.
w – Also May 19.
x – 1242 on Dec. 20, 21, Apr. 11, 12; 1253 on Feb. 18.
y – 1143 on Dec. 27, 28, Apr. 18, 19; 1150 on Feb. 11, 18, 19, 26.
z – 0952 on ⑥ Feb. 4 - Mar. 4.

TGV – High-speed train. 🅁. 🍸.
FR – Italian high-speed train. 🅁. 🍸.

⊡ – St Étienne Châteaucreux.
◇ – From May 15 Paris d. 1842, Lyon Part-Dieu a. 2036, Lyon Perrache a. 2050.
♠ – *Frecciarossa* Italian high-speed train. Special fares. 🅁. 🍸.
⊠ – OUIGO low-cost TGV service. Internet bookings only at www.ouigo.com

341 PARIS - GENÈVE and ANNECY

Timings may vary by up to 8 minutes from May 15 (please check your reservation). Annecy services are subject to alteration on Mar. 25, 26. Genève services are subject to alteration May 27 – 29.
Other *TGV* services: Paris - Chambéry, see Tables **44** and **366**; Paris - Mâcon Loché, see Table **340**; Paris - Lyon St Exupéry ✈, see Table **342**.

PARIS - GENÈVE - LAUSANNE

km		*TGV*	*TGV*	*TGV*	*TGV*	*TGV*	*TGV*	*TGV*	*TGV*	*TGV*	
		9761	**9763**	**9765**	**9773**	**9775**	**9777**	**9781**	**9789**	**9789**	
		①–⑥							⑦–④		
									A	B	
0	**Paris** Gare de Lyon ... d.	0618z	0814	1015	1214	1410	1614	1814	1904	2016	...
406	Bourg-en-Bresse .. **376** d.	0812	1012	1212	1412	1612	1812	2010	2056	2212	...
439	Nurieux-Brion ..... **376** a.	|	|	|	|	|	|	2035	|	|	...
470	Bellegarde ..... **346** a.	0859	1100	1300	1500	1700	1900	2100	2151	2300	...
503	**Genève** . **346 505 570** a.	0929	1130	1330	1530	1730	1930	2130	2224	2330	...
563	**Lausanne** ..... **505 570** a.	1016r	...	...	...	1816v	2016v	...	...	...	...

	TGV		*TGV*	*TGV*	*TGV*	*TGV*	*TGV*	*TGV*	*TGV*	*TGV*
	9760		**9764**	**9768**	**9770**	**9774**	**9776**	**9780**	**9784**	**9784**
	①–⑥								①–④	
	d								L	J
Lausanne .... **505 570** d.	...	...	...	0945r	...	1345t	...	...	1845	1945
Genève 346 505 570 d.	0629	...	0824	1029	1229	1429	1624	1824	1944	2029
Bellegarde ..... **346** d.	0702	...	0900	1102	1302	1502	1702	1902	2014	2102
Nurieux-Brion ... **376** d.	|	...	0925	|	|	|	|	|	|	|
Bourg-en-Bresse . **376** d.	0752	...	0952	1152	1352	1552	1752c	1952	2103	2151
Paris Gare de Lyon .. a.	0946	...	1146	1350	1545	1750	1947	2144	2302	2346

PARIS - CHAMBÉRY - ANNECY

km		*TGV*	*TGV*		*TGV*	*TGV*		*TGV*	*TGV*	*TGV*	
		6931	**9241**		**6937**	**6941**		**6949**	**6951**	**6953**	
		①–⑥								⑤	
		b	u					s	s	f	
0	**Paris** Gare de Lyon ... d.	0639k	0639k	...	0943	1243y	...	1739	1843	2042	...
363	Mâcon Loché TGV ..... d.	0823	0823	...	1123	1423	...	1923j	2023	2219	...
441	Lyon St Exupéry ✈ .... d.	|	|	...	|	|	...	|	|	|	...
532	**Chambéry** .... **345 364** a.	0936	0936	...	1236	1536	...	2036j	2135	2334	...
546	Aix les Bains. **345 364** a.	0959	...	...	1259	1559	...	2104	2200	2357	...
585	**Annecy** ..... **345 364** a.	1028	...	...	1328	1632	...	2134	2230	0025‡	...

	TGV		*TGV*		*TGV*	*TGV*		*TGV*	*TGV*	*TGV*
	6960		**6964**		**6972**	**6972**		**6978**	**6980**	**6986**
	①–⑥					⑥			⑦	
	b		n		D	E			e	s △
Annecy ..... **345 364** d.	0529	...	0929	...	1230	1230	...	1531	1732	1832
Aix les Bains **345 364** d.	0557	...	1000	...	1259	1259	...	1559	1759	1859
Chambéry ... **345 364** d.	0622	...	1022	...	1324	1324	...	1623	1822	1922
Lyon St Exupéry ✈ ... d.	|	...	|	...	|	|	...	|	|	|
Mâcon Loché TGV .... d.	0738	...	1138	...	1438	1454	...	1738x	1938	2040
Paris Gare de Lyon .. a.	0916	...	1316	...	1617	1632	...	1916	2116	2219

A – ⑦–④ from June 4.
B – Ⓑ to June 2 (also Feb. 18, 25, Mar. 4, Apr. 22, 29, May 6); ⑤ from June 9.
D – Ⓑ to May 12; daily from May 14. On ①–⑤ Feb. 6 – 24 departs Chambéry 1322.
On ⑦ until May 14 departs Mâcon Loché TGV 1442, arrives Paris 1624.
E – ⑥ until May 13.
J – Ⓑ to Jan. 8; ⑤† Jan. 13 - May 8; Ⓑ from May 12 (not May 18, June 21). Arrives Paris 2355 on ①–④ Dec. 26 - Jan. 5. Does not run Lausanne - Genève Feb. 26 - Mar. 5.
L – ①–④ Jan. 9 - May 11 (not Apr. 10, May 1, 8). Feb. 27 - Mar. 6 does not run Lausanne - Genève and departs Genève 1942.

b – Not Apr. 10, May 1, 8, 29.
c – 1750 on ⑥ until Apr. 29.
d – Also Feb. 19, 26, Mar. 5, Apr. 23, 30, May 7.
e – Also Apr. 10, May 1, 8, 29.
f – Also May 17; not May 19.
j – Feb. 6 – 26 departs Mâcon Loché TGV 1922, arrives Chambéry 2039.
k – 0643 on ⑥ until Mar. 25 (not Feb. 11, 18, 25); 0641 on Feb. 11, 18, 25.

n – Not Dec. 25.
r – Not Feb. 27 - Mar. 7.
s – Not Dec. 24, 31.
t – Not Feb. 27 - Mar. 6.
u – Not May 6 – 11.
v – Not Feb. 26 - Mar. 6.
x – Not Feb. 11, 18, 25.
y – 1238 on Dec. 20, 21, Apr. 11, 12.
z – 0616 on Feb. 18, 25.

TGV – High-speed train. 🅁. 🍸.

△ – Timings may vary by up to 5 minutes on Feb. 25, 26, Mar. 4, 5, Apr. 2, 10, 16, 23, May 1, 8, 14.
‡ – Does not run Aix les Bains - Annecy Mar. 3 - Apr. 7 and Apr. 28 - May 12.

PARIS - GRENOBLE 342

Timings may vary by up to 5 minutes Feb. 6–26. Paris timings may vary by up to 12 minutes from May 15 (later departures / earlier arrivals). Subject to alteration on Mar. 25, 26.

km												
		TGV	*TGV*	*TGV*	*TGV*	*TGV*	*TGV*	*TGV*	*TGV*	*TGV*	*TGV*	*TGV*
		6901	**6905**	**6911**	**6917**	**6919**	**6919**	**6921**	**6923**	**6925**	**6927**	**6929**
		①							Ⓑ			⑤⑦
		g	z	H		D	E	J	h	w	L	M
0	**Paris** Gare de Lyon ..... **350/1** d.	0612	0709	1010	1208**k**	1358**n**	1414	1608	1708	1809	1911	2010
441	Lyon St Exupéry ✈ ...... **350/1** a.	0805	0905	1205	1405	1555	1605	1805	1905	2005	2105	2205
441	Lyon St Exupéry ✈ .... d.	0809	0909	1209	1409	1609	1609	1809	1909	2009**r**	2109	2209
553	**Grenoble** .... a.	0914	1013	1313	1513	1713	1713	1913	2013	2114	2213	2313

	TGV	*TGV*	*TGV*	*TGV*		*TGV*	*TGV*	*TGV*	*TGV*	*TGV*		*TGV*
	6902	**6904**	**6906**	**6908**		**6910**	**6910**	**6920**	**6922**	**6924**		**6928**
	Ⓐ	①	①–⑥				⑦					⑦
	v	C	b			G	B					e
Grenoble .... d.	0547	0647	0746	0947	...	1247	1247	1446	1647	1846	...	2047
Lyon St Exupéry ✈ .... a.	0650	0750	0849	1050	...	1350	1354	1549	1750	1949	...	2150
Lyon St Exupéry ✈ ...... **350/1** d.	0654	0758	0854	1054	...	1354	1358	1554	1754	1954	...	2154
Paris Gare de Lyon .... **350/1** a.	0851	0956	1049	1249	...	1557	1600	1758	1952	2149	...	2349**j**

B – ⑦ until May 14.
C – ① until Mar. 20.
D – Until May 14.
E – From May 15.
G – ①⑤ to May 12 (also Apr. 11, May 2, 9; not Feb. 27, Mar. 3, 10, Apr. 10); ①⑤⑦ from May 15 (also May 17, 30; not May 19, 29).
H – ①⑤⑥⑦ (also Apr. 11, May 2, 9, 17, 18, 30).
J – Ⓑ to Mar. 31; Ⓐ from Apr. 3 (not May 19).
L – Ⓑ to Mar. 30; ⑦–④ from Apr. 2 (not May 17, 18). Subject to alteration Apr. 16–27.
M – ⑤⑦ (also Apr. 10, May 1, 8, 17, 29; not Apr. 19). Subject to alteration on Mar. 5, 12, 19, 26, Apr. 16, 23.

b – Not Apr. 10, May 1, 8, 29.
e – Also Apr. 10, May 1, 8, 29.
g – Also Apr. 11, May 2, 9, 30; not Jan. 2, Apr. 10, May 1, 8, 29.
h – Not May 18, 19.
j – 2356 on May 8.
k – 1206 on Dec. 27, 28, Apr. 18, 19.
n – 1355 on Dec. 20, 21, Apr. 11, 12.
r – 2014 on ⑦ until May 14 (also Apr. 10, May 1, 8).
v – Not May 19.
w – Not Dec. 24, 31.
z – Not Dec. 25, Jan. 1.

TGV – High-speed train. 🅁. 🍷.

LYON - GRENOBLE 343

Timings may vary by 1–2 minutes Feb. 6–26. Subject to alteration on Mar. 25, 26, Apr. 8, 9. On May 18 services in this table run as on ⑥.

km																									
		⚒	Ⓐ		Ⓐ		Ⓐ		Ⓐ					Ⓐ		❖	Ⓐ					⑥		⑤†	
									z	z	z	z	z						△	n	B	🚌		f 🚌	🚌
0	**Lyon** Part-Dieu .. **344** d.	0616	0646	0716	0746	0816	0845	0916	0945	1016	1116	1216	1315	1345	1416	and at	1845	1916	2016	2116	2216	2216	...	2320	2314
41	Bourgoin-Jallieu . **344** d.	0643	0712	0743	0813	0843	0911	0943	1012	1043	1143	1243	1343	1411	1443	the same	1911	1943	2043	2143	2243	2307	...	|	0005
56	La Tour du Pin ... **344** d.	0654	0724	0754	0824	0854	0922	0954	1023	1054	1154	1254	1356	1422	1454	minutes	1922	1954	2054	2154	2253	|	...	|	0025
104	Voiron .... d.	0725	0755	0825	0855	0925	0954	1025	1054	1125	1225	1325	1425	1454	1525	past each	1954	2025	2125	2225	2325	|	...	|	0115
129	**Grenoble** .... a.	0740	0810	0840	0910	0940	1009	1040	1109	1140	1240	1340	1440	1509	1540	hour until	2010	2040	2140	2240	2340	0015	...	0050	0150

	⚒	Ⓐ				Ⓐ						Ⓐ		Ⓐ		Ⓐ		Ⓐ		Ⓐ					⑥
							z		z	z												🚌		D	🚌
Grenoble .... d.	0521	0551	0621	and at	0921	0951	1021	1121	1221	1321	1421	1451	1521	1551	1621	1651	1721	1751	1821	1851	1921	1947	2021	2121	2123
Voiron .... d.	0538	0608	0638	the same	0938	1008	1038	1138	1238	1338	1438	1508	1538	1608	1638	1708	1738	1808	1838	1908	1938	|	2038	2138	2153
La Tour du Pin ..... **344** d.	0608	0638	0708	minutes	1008	1037	1108	1208	1307	1408	1507	1537	1608	1637	1708	1737	1808	1837	1908	1937	2008	|	2108	2208	2238
Bourgoin-Jallieu ... **344** d.	0618	0648	0718	past each	1018	1048	1118	1218	1317	1418	1518	1548	1618	1648	1718	1748	1818	1848	1918	1948	2018	|	2118	2218	2300
Lyon Part-Dieu .... **344** a.	0644	0715	0744	hour until	1044	1115	1144	1244	1344	1444	1544	1615	1644	1715	1745	1815	1844	1915	1944	2015	2044	2116	2144	2246	2400

B – Ⓑ to Feb. 26; ⑤ Mar. 3–31; Ⓑ from Apr. 2 (not Apr. 16–20, 23–27).
D – Ⓑ to Apr. 2; ⑤† Apr. 7 - May 21 (also May 17; not Apr. 28, May 12, 18); Ⓑ from May 28. Runs 16–18 minutes **earlier** on ①–④ until Mar. 30.
f – Also May 17; not May 18.
n – Not Apr. 16–20, 23–27.
z – Not Feb. 27, 28, Mar. 1–3, 6–10.
❖ – Timings may vary by 1–2 minutes.
△ – Runs 8–12 minutes later Bourgoin-Jallieu - Grenoble on ①–④ Jan. 9 - May 4 (not Apr. 10, May 1).

LYON - CHAMBÉRY 344

Certain services run to / from Modane or Bourg St Maurice on ⑥⑦ until Apr. 23 (Tables **366** and **367**). Timings may vary by up to 3 minutes on certain dates. Subject to alteration on Mar. 25, 26.
Note: On May 18 services in this table run as on ⑥.

km																									
		Ⓐ	⚒	⑥		Ⓒ			Ⓐ	†	Ⓒ				Ⓒ		⑥	Ⓐ	Ⓒ						
		🚌		B	A	B	E		⊙	BV	L			D	B◇	E	B		B					M	N
0	**Lyon** Part Dieu . **343/5** d.	0620	0650	0724	0750	0849	0850	0950	1034	1043	1050	1150	1249	1350	1450	1450	1511	1550	1550	1650	1750	1850**r**	1950	2050	2150
41	Bourgoin-Jallieu ... **343** d.	|	0719	0748	0819	0913	0917	1018	|	1117	1117	1216	1314	1417	1516	1519	|	1616	1616	1719	1817	1917	2017	2117	2217
56	La Tour du Pin ..... **343** d.	|	0730	0759	0830	0924	0927	1029	|	1128	1128	1227	1325	1427	1528	1530	|	1627	1626	1730	1827	1927	2027	2128	2228
106	**Chambéry** .... **345** a.	0750	0816	0842	0916	1007	1016	1119**j**	1158	1219	1216	1316**t**	1417	1516	1617	1616	1647	1715	1726	1816**z**	1916**z**	2016	2116	2216	2312

	⚒	⚒		Ⓒ		⑥	Ⓐ	Ⓒ	Ⓒ	Ⓒ	Ⓐ	⑥		Ⓒ			Ⓒ		Ⓒ		Ⓑ		Ⓒ		
				B	E	B		B	F	B	w⊙	h		B	E		B	E	B	E		H	B	E	
Chambéry .... **345** d.	0544	0644	0744	0843	0844	0853	0944	1043	1044	1044	1137	1142**k**	1244	1340	1344	1444	1538	1544	1641	1644	1744	1844	1943	1944	2044
La Tour du Pin ...... **343** d.	0632	0732	0832	0933	0932	|	1032	1135	1135	|	|	1232	1332	1433	1432	1532	1633	1632	1733	1732	1832	1932	2034	2032	2132
Bourgoin-Jallieu .... **343** d.	0643	0743	0843	0946	0943	|	1043	1146	1147	|	|	1244	1343	1444	1443	1543	1645	1643	1743	1743	1843	1943	2045	2043	2143
Lyon Part Dieu .. **343/5** a.	0710	0811	0910	1010	1010	1020	1110	1210	1210	1210	1302	1310	1410	1510	1510	1610	1711	1710	1810	1810	1910	2010	2110	2110	2210**y**

A – Ⓐ to Apr. 21; ⚒ from Apr. 24.
B – Until Apr. 23.
D – Daily to Apr. 29; ⚒ from May 2.
E – Ⓐ to Apr. 21; daily from Apr. 24.
F – From Apr. 29.
H – Daily to Apr. 28; Ⓑ from Apr. 30.
L – ⑥ to Apr. 22; Ⓒ from Apr. 29. On ⑥ Dec. 24 - Mar. 25 Bourgoin-Jallieu d. 1127, La Tour du Pin d. 1136, Chambéry a. 1232.
M – Ⓐ to Mar. 24; ⑤ Mar. 31 - Apr. 28; Ⓐ from May 2. On ①–④ Feb. 6 - Mar. 23 Lyon Part Dieu d. 2046, Chambéry a. 2223 (not calling at not calling at Bourgoin-Jallieu or La Tour du Pin).
N – Daily to Mar. 24 (not Jan. 29); ⑤⑥ Mar. 31 - Apr. 22; daily from Apr. 28.
V – On Feb. 26 Lyon d. 1050, Chambéry a. 1243 (not calling at Bourgoin-Jallieu or La Tour du Pin).

h – Not Apr. 8.
j – 1125 on ⑥ until Apr. 22.
k – 1144 from Apr. 29.
r – 1846 on ⑥ until Apr. 22.
t – 1322 on Ⓒ until Apr. 23.
w – Not Jan. 23 - Feb. 3.
y – 2223 on Dec. 18, Jan. 15, Feb. 5, 12, Mar. 5, 12, 19, Apr. 16.
z – 5–7 minutes later on † until Apr. 23.

◇ – Timings may vary by up to 5 minutes.
⊙ – Via Aix les Bains (Table **345**).

LYON - AIX LES BAINS - ANNECY 345

Note: On May 18 services in this table run as on ⑥.

km																									
		🚌					🚌		🚌				🚌		🚌		🚌								
		Ⓐ	Ⓐ	⚒	⚒	⚒	†	Ⓐ	Ⓐ	Ⓒ	Ⓐ	Ⓐ	†	⚒	Ⓐ		Ⓐ	Ⓐ		Ⓐ		Ⓑ			
												w		w		w									
0	**Lyon** Part Dieu ..... **344 346** d.	0608	...	...	0708	0808	0808	0908	1008	1008	1034	...	1208	1208	1308	1408	1508	...	1608	...	1708	1808	...	1908	2108
46	Ambérieu .... **346** d.	|	0614	0714	0733	0833	|	0933	|	1033	|	1214	|	1233	|	1434	|	1614	1633	...	1733	1833	1914	1933	2133
96	Culoz .... **346** d.	|	0652	0752	0804	|	|	|	|	|	|	1252	|	|	|	|	|	1652	|	1752	|	|	1952	|	2204
118	Aix les Bains .... a.	|	0711	0811	0819	0918	0935	1018	|	1118	1146	1311	|	1318	|	1518	|	1711	1718	1811	1818	1918	2011	2017	2221
118	Aix les Bains .... **364** d.	|	0713	0813	*0835*	0925	0935	1025	|	1126	1148	1314	|	1325	|	1525	|	1713	*1734*	1813	*1834*	*1935*	2013	2025	2227
132	**Chambéry** .... **344 364** a.	|	0725	0825	|	|	|	|	|	|	1158	1329	|	|	|	|	|	1725	|	1825	|	|	2025	|	|
157	**Annecy** .... **364** a.	0759	...	...	*0915*	1007	1010	1107	1159	1207	...	...	1359	1407	1459	1607	1659	...	*1815*	...	*1915*	*2015*	...	2107	2307

						🚌	🚌					🚌							🚌					🚌	
	Ⓐ	Ⓐ	⚒	Ⓐ	⚒	†	Ⓐ	Ⓒ	Ⓐ	Ⓐ	⑥	Ⓑ	⚒		⚒	†	Ⓐ		⑥		Ⓑ	Ⓐ		Ⓐ	†
									w	w			w	w						●					n
Annecy .... **364** d.	...	0553	0653	...	*0743*v	0800	0900	0953	1053	...	1153	1200	...	1353	1553	1553	...	*1643*b	1700	...	*1743*	...	*1845*	2000	2053
Chambéry .... **344 364** d.	0534	|	|	0734	|	|	|	|	|	1137	|	|	1234	|	|	|	1634	|	|	1734	|	1834	|	|	|
Aix les Bains .... **364** a.	0546	0634	0734	0747	*0823*v	|	|	1033	1134	1147	1233	|	1247	1433	1633	1633	1647	*1723*b	|	1747	*1823*	1847	*1923*	|	2134
Aix les Bains .... d.	0548	0641	0741	0749	0841	|	|	1040	1141	1150	1241	|	1249	1440	1640	1640	1649	1740	|	1749	1841	1849	1941	|	2141
Culoz .... **346** d.	0608	|	|	0808	|	|	|	|	|	1206	|	|	1308	|	|	1657	1707	1756	|	1808	|	1908	|	|	|
Ambérieu .... **346** d.	0646	0728	0828	0846	0928	|	|	1128	1228	1238	1328	|	1346	1527	1727	1729	...	1828	|	1846	1928	1946	2028	|	2228
Lyon Part Dieu .... **344 346** a.	...	0752	0852	...	0952	0952	1052	1152	1252	1302	1352	1352	...	1552	1752	1752	...	1852	1852	...	1952	...	2052	2152	2252

b – Not ⑥.
n – Not Apr. 2, 9.
v – On ①–⑤ Jan. 23 - Feb. 10 connection departs Annecy *0719*, arrives Aix les Bains *0801*.
w – Not Jan. 23–27, 30, 31, Feb. 1–3.

● – Runs 2–5 minutes earlier on ⑥ until Apr. 15 (also on Feb. 26, Mar. 5).

346 LYON - BELLEGARDE - GENÈVE

km																									
		①-⑤ d	①-⑤ d	⑥	①-⑥ h		①-⑥ b	r⊗	A △	A	①-⑤ d	A △	r	A △	A	A △	r	A △	A	r	A △	A	Ⓑ v		
0	**Lyon** Part Dieu .... **345** d.	...	...	...	0638	0838	0938	1038	1038	...	...	1135f	1238	1238	...	1347	1438	1438	...	1638	1635	...	1738	1834	2038
50	Ambérieu .... **345** d.	...	...	...	0703	0903	1003	1103	1103	...	...	|	1303	1303	...	|	1503	1503	...	1703	1709t	...	|	|	2103
102	Culoz .... **345 364** d.	...	...	...	0740	0940	1041	1141	1141	...	...	|	1341	1341	...	|	1540	1540	...	1740	1745t	...	1840	1940	2140
135	Bellegarde .... **364** a.	...	...	...	0804	1004	1104	1204	1204	...	...	1252	1404	1405	...	1505	1604	1604	...	1804	1806	...	1904	2004	2204
135	Bellegarde .... **364** ◐ d.	0552	0625	0652	0807	1007	1107	1207	...	1220	1246	...	1407	...	1420	...	1607	...	1620	1807	...	1820	1907	2005	2207
168	**Genève** .... **364** ◐ a.	0629	0658	0729	0835	1035	1135	1235	...	1247	1318	...	1435	...	1447	...	1635	...	1647	1835	...	1847	1934	2034	2234

	①-⑥ b	①-⑥ d	①-⑥ b		r	A	A △	A △	A	A △	⑥⑦ c	①-⑤ a	①-⑥ b⊗	r⊗	A	A △	r	A	A △	A △	⑦ z	①-⑥ b		①-⑤ d	①-⑤ d
Genève .... **364** ◐ d.	0514	0602	0614	0714	0914	0914	...	...	1114	...	1130	1130	1225	1314j	1314	...	1514	1514	...	...	1714	1730	1914	2018	2116
Bellegarde .... **364** ◐ a.	0545	0637	0645	0742	0946	0946	...	...	1146	...	1200	1200	1254	1346j	1346	...	1546	1546	...	...	1746	1757	1946	2053	2150
Bellegarde .... **364** d.	0554	...	0650	0755	0955	...	0955	1057	...	1200	1201	1205	1256	1355	...	1401	1555	...	1556	1655	1755	1759	1955	...	...
Culoz .... **345 364** d.	0619	...	0715	0820	1020	...	1023	|	...	1222	1224	1227	1322	1420	...	1426	1620	...	1621	|	1820	1825	2020	...	...
Ambérieu .... **345** d.	0657	...	0755	0858	|	...	|	|	...	1302	1302	1302	1357	1458	...	1458	1658	...	1658	|	1858	1857	2058	...	...
Lyon Part Dieu ..... **345** a.	0722	...	0822	0922	1122	...	1122	1222	...	1326	1326	1326	1422	1522	...	1522	1722	...	1721	1815	1922	1922	2122	...	...

A – Runs on Dec. 17, 24, 31, Feb. 4, 11, 18, 25, Mar. 4 only.

a – Not Apr. 10, May 1, 8, 18, 29.
b – Not Apr. 10, May 1, 8, 29.
c – Also Apr. 10, May 1, 8, 18, 29.
d – Not Apr. 10, May 18, 29.
f – 1133 on Feb. 25.
h – Not Apr. 10, May 29.
j – 4 minutes later on Dec. 26, Jan. 2, Apr. 7.
r – Not Dec. 17, 24, 31, Feb. 4, 11, 18, 25, Mar. 4.

t – On Feb. 11, 18, 25 departs Ambérieu 1703, Culoz 1743.
v – Not May 18.
z – Also Apr. 10, May 1, 8, 29.

⊗ – Subject to alteration Jan. 23–27, 30, 31, Feb. 1–3.
△ – To/from St Gervais (Table **365**).
◐ – Additional journeys on ①-⑤ (not Apr. 10, May 18, 29):
From Bellegarde at 0725, 1725, 1825, 1925, 2025 and 2125.
From Genève at 0502, 1202, 1602, 1702, 1802 and 1902.

348 LYON - ST ÉTIENNE

TER services

For *TGV* trains Paris - St Étienne see Table **340**. On May 18 services in this table run as on ⑥.

km																								
		⚒	Ⓐ	⚒	⚒	Ⓐ	Ⓐ			Ⓐ	Ⓐ	⚒		Ⓐ			Ⓐ	⚒		Ⓐ			Ⓐ	⚒
0	**Lyon** Part-Dieu .... d.	...	0624	...	0654	...	0724	...	0754	...	0824	...	0854	0924	...	0954	1024	...	1054	1124	...	1154	1224	...
	Lyon Perrache .... d.	0531	|	0631	|	0701	|	0731	|	0801	|	0831	|	|	0931	|	|	1031	|	|	1131	|	|	1231
22	Givors Ville .... d.	0558	0641	0658	0711	0728	0741	0758	0811	0828	0841	0858	0911	0941	0958	1011	1041	1058	1111	1141	1158	1211	1241	1258
47	St Chamond .... d.	0617	0700	0717	0730	0747	0800	0817	0830	0847	0900	0917	0930	1000	1017	1030	1100	1117	1130	1200	1217	1230	1300	1317
59	**St Étienne** Châteaucreux ..... a.	0626	0710	0726	0740	0756	0810	0826	0840	0856	0910	0926	0940	1010	1026	1040	1110	1126	1140	1210	1226	1240	1310	1326

	z	Ⓐ			Ⓐ	⚒		Ⓐ			Ⓐ	Ⓐ	⚒		Ⓐ	Ⓐ			Ⓐ	Ⓐ	⚒		Ⓐ	Ⓐ
Lyon Part-Dieu .... d.	1254	1324	...	1354	1424	...	1454	1524	...	1554	...	1624	...	1654	...	1724	...	1754	...	1824	...	1854	...	1924
Lyon Perrache .... d.	|	|	1331	|	|	1431	|	|	1531	|	1601	|	1631	|	1701	|	1731	|	1801	|	1831	|	1901	|
Givors Ville .... d.	1311	1341	1358	1411	1441	1458	1511	1541	1558	1611	1628	1641	1658	1711	1728	1741	1758	1811	1828	1841	1858	1911	1928	1941
St Chamond .... d.	1330	1400	1417	1430	1500	1517	1530	1600	1617	1630	1647	1700	1717	1730	1747	1800	1817	1830	1847	1900	1917	1930	1947	2000
St Étienne Châteaucreux ...... a.	1340	1410	1426	1440	1510	1526	1540	1610	1626	1640	1656	1710	1726	1740	1756	1810	1826	1840	1856	1910	1926	1940	1956	2010

				⚒	Ⓑ	C	D	①-④ m 🚌	🚌	
Lyon Part-Dieu .... d.	...	1954	2024	...	2124	2224	2324	2324	0024	...
Lyon Perrache .... d.	1931	|	|	2031	|	|	|	|	|	...
Givors Ville .... d.	1958	2011	2041	2058	2141	2242	2342	2353	0100	...
St Chamond .... d.	2017	2030	2100	2117	2200	2301	0000	0022	0128	...
St Étienne Châteaucreux ...... a.	2026	2040	2110	2126	2210	2310	0010	0037	0142	...

	Ⓐ	Ⓐ	Ⓐ	Ⓐ	⚒	Ⓐ	Ⓐ	⚒
St Étienne Châteaucreux .... d.	0520	0534	0550	0604	0620	0634	0650	0704
St Chamond .... d.	0530	0543	0600	0613	0630	0643	0700	0713
Givors Ville .... d.	0548	0602	0618	0632	0648	0702	0718	0732
Lyon Perrache .... a.	|	0629	|	0659	|	0729	|	0759
Lyon Part-Dieu .... a.	0606	...	0636	...	0706	...	0736	...

		Ⓐ	Ⓐ			Ⓐ	Ⓐ	⚒		Ⓐ			Ⓐ	⚒		Ⓐ			Ⓐ	⚒		Ⓐ		
St Étienne Châteaucreux ...... d.	0720	0734	0750	0804	0820	0834	0850	0904	0920	0950	1004	1020	1050	1104	1120	1150	1204	1220	1250	1304	1320	1350	1404	1420
St Chamond .... d.	0730	0743	0800	0813	0830	0843	0900	0913	0930	1000	1013	1030	1100	1113	1130	1200	1213	1230	1300	1313	1330	1400	1413	1429
Givors Ville .... d.	0748	0802	0818	0832	0848	0902	0918	0932	0948	1018	1032	1048	1118	1132	1148	1218	1232	1248	1318	1332	1348	1418	1432	1448
Lyon Perrache .... a.	|	0829	|	0859	|	0929	|	0959	|	|	1059	|	|	1159	|	|	1259	|	|	1359	|	|	1459	|
Lyon Part-Dieu .... a.	0806	...	0836	...	0906	...	0936	...	1006	1036	...	1106	1136	...	1206	1236	...	1306	1336	...	1406	1436	...	1506

	Ⓐ	⚒		Ⓐ			Ⓐ	Ⓐ	⚒		Ⓐ	Ⓐ			Ⓐ	Ⓐ	⚒					Ⓑ		H
St Étienne Châteaucreux ...... d.	1450	1504	1520	1550	1604	1620	1634	1650	1704	1720	1734	1750	1804	1821	1834	1850	1904	1920	2004	2020	...	2120	...	2220
St Chamond .... d.	1500	1513	1530	1600	1613	1630	1643	1700	1713	1730	1743	1800	1813	1830	1843	1900	1913	1930	2013	2030	...	2130	...	2230
Givors Ville .... d.	1518	1532	1548	1618	1632	1648	1702	1718	1732	1748	1802	1818	1832	1849	1902	1918	1932	1949	2032	2048	...	2148	...	2249
Lyon Perrache .... a.	|	1559	|	|	1659	|	1729	|	1759	|	1829	|	1859	|	1929	|	1959	|	2059	|	...	|	...	|
Lyon Part-Dieu .... a.	1536	...	1606	1636	...	1706	...	1736	...	1806	...	1836	...	1906	...	1936	...	2006	...	2106	...	2206	...	2307

C – Daily to Apr. 2; ⑥⑦ from Apr. 8.
D – ⑤-⑦ to Apr. 2 (not Dec. 18, Jan. 15, Feb. 5, 12, Mar. 5, 12, 19); ⑥⑦ from Apr. 8 (not Apr. 16, May 14, 21, 28).
H – Daily to Feb. 11 (not Dec. 18, Jan. 1, 15, Feb. 5); ⑥⑦ from Feb. 18 (not Mar. 5, 12, 19, Apr. 16, May 14, 21, 28).

m – Not Apr. 10, May 1, 8, 17, 18, 29.
z – Not Feb 27 - Mar. 3.

349 ST ÉTIENNE - LE PUY

On May 18 train services in this table run as on ⑥.

km																
		Ⓐ	⚒	k		⚒ ◇	◇	⑥ 🚌	Ⓐ 🚌		Ⓐ	Ⓒ	Ⓐ	Ⓐ		
0	**St Étienne** Châteaucreux ..... d.	0531	0649	0855	...	1105	1252	1400	1425	1557	1717	1755	1803	1855	2014	2200
15	Firminy .... d.	0551	0711	0911	...	1121	1308	|	|	1613	1733	1811	1825	1912	2036	2222
88	**Le Puy en Velay** .... a.	0724	0824	1024	...	1227	1421	1520	1545	1720	1846	1918	1933	2019	2142	2326

	Ⓐ	Ⓐ	⚒	Ⓐ	k		◇		◇		Ⓐ	Ⓒ	Ⓐ	†	Ⓒ	Ⓑ
Le Puy en Velay .... d.	0433	0543	0642	0739	0847	...	1037	...	1234	...	1613	1639	1734	1737	1840	1938
Firminy .... d.	0538	0649	0754	0853	0953	...	1143	...	1349	...	1727	1754	1853	1853	1950	2056
St Étienne Châteaucreux ...... a.	0558	0707	0810	0909	1009	...	1205	...	1406	...	1743	1810	1910	1910	2007	2112

k – Not Mar. 26.

◇ – Subject to alteration Apr. 17–21, 24–28, May 2–5, 9–12.

PARIS / LYON - AVIGNON - MARSEILLE - TOULON - NICE 350

TGV **SERVICES FROM / TO PARIS** (see next page for services from / to / via Lyon). For other *TGV* trains Paris - Valence TGV and v.v., see Table **355**. For *TGV* trains Paris - Valence Ville - Avignon Centre, see Table **351**. For regional TER services Marseille - Nice, also overnight service Paris - Nice, see Table **361**. Paris timings may vary by up to 14 minutes from May 15 (later departures / earlier arrivals; please check your reservation).

km		*TGV* 7829	*TGV* 6101	*TGV* 6103	*TGV* 7851	*TGV* 6173	*TGV* 6155	*TGV* 6107	*TGV* 6175	*TGV* 6109	*TGV* 6165	*TGV* 6111	*TGV* 7825	*TGV* 6177
		⊠	Ⓐ v		⊠			A			C		⊠	
0	**Paris** Gare de Lyon .... 342 351 355 d.	0550y	0629	0734	0818	0907	0907	0933	0959	1034	1118	1133	1233j	1354j
441	Lyon St Exupéry ✈ .... 342 351 d.	|	|	|	|	|	|	|	|	|	|	|	|	|
527	Valence TGV .... 355 d.	|	|	|	|	|	|	|	|	|	|	|	|	|
657	**Avignon** TGV .... d.	0846	0922	1020	|	|	|	1220	|	1321	1404	1420	1520	|
731	Aix en Provence TGV .... d.	0913	0943	1044	1121	|	|	1244	|	1344	|	1444	1544	|
750	**Marseille** St Charles .... a.	0925	0956	1056	|	1215	1215	1256	1314	1356	|	1456	1556	1715
750	**Marseille** St Charles .... 360 361 d.	...	...	...	|	1228	1228	...	1328	...	|	...	...	1728
817	**Toulon** .... 360 361 a.	...	...	...	1211	1311	1311	...	1411	...	1511	...	...	1811
	Toulon .... 361 d.	...	...	...	1215	1316	1324	...	1415	...	1515	...	...	1815
	Hyères .... 360 a.	...	...	...	|	|	1340	...	|	...	|	...	...	|
885	Les Arcs-Draguignan .... 361 a.	...	...	...	|	|	...	...	1448	...	|	...	...	|
911	St Raphaël-Valescure .... 361 a.	...	...	...	1301	1401	...	...	|	...	1601	...	...	1901
943	**Cannes** .... 361 a.	...	...	...	1325	1425	...	...	1525	...	1625	...	...	1926
954	Antibes .... 361 a.	...	...	...	1339	1439	...	...	1538	...	1639	...	...	1939
974	**Nice** .... 361 a.	...	...	...	1358	1458	...	...	1557	...	1658	...	...	1958

	TGV 7827	*TGV* 7827	*TGV* 6163	*TGV* 6117	*TGV* 7853	*TGV* 6121	*TGV* 6181	*TGV* 6123	*TGV* 6153	*TGV* 6127	*TGV* 6187	*TGV* 6129	*TGV* 6131	*TGV* 6131	*TGV* 6137
	S⊠	T⊠	⑤⑥ N		⊠	Ⓑ h			Ⓑ h	B	⑤ F	n	②–④ r	D	⑤⑦ H
Paris Gare de Lyon .... 342 351 355 d.	1434	1438	1517	1538	1559	1630	1718	1728	1756	1832	1920	1937	2010	2034	2135
Lyon St Exupéry ✈ .... 342 351 d.	|	|	|	|	|	|	|	|	|	|	|	|	|	|	|
Valence TGV .... 355 d.	|	|	|	|	1829	|	|	|	|	|	|	|	|	|	|
Avignon TGV .... d.	1725	1720	1759	1820	|	1920	|	2020	|	2120	2207	2220	2254	2320	0023
Aix en Provence TGV .... d.	1750	1744	|	1844	|	1944	2020	2044	|	2144	|	2244	2318	2344	0047
Marseille St Charles .... a.	1804	1756	|	1856	|	1957	|	2056	2115	2156	|	2256	2330	2356	0059
Marseille St Charles .... 360 361 d.	...	...	|	...	|	...	|	...	2128	...	|	...	...	...	...
Toulon .... 360 361 a.	...	...	1908	...	2011	...	2111	...	2211	...	2314	...	...	...	...
Toulon .... 361 d.	...	...	1911	...	2016	...	2115	...	...	...	2318	...	...	...	...
Hyères .... 360 a.	...	...	|	...	|	...	|	...	...	...	|	...	...	...	...
Les Arcs-Draguignan .... 361 a.	...	...	|	...	2049	...	|	...	...	...	|	...	...	...	...
St Raphaël-Valescure .... 361 a.	...	...	2002	...	|	...	2202	...	...	...	0004	...	...	...	...
Cannes .... 361 a.	...	...	2027	...	2126	...	2228	...	...	...	0028	...	...	...	...
Antibes .... 361 a.	...	...	2040	...	2140	...	2241	...	...	...	0041	...	...	...	...
Nice .... 361 a.	...	...	2100	...	2159	...	2300	...	...	...	0100	...	...	...	...

	TGV 6102	*TGV* 6136	*TGV* 6150	*TGV* 6106	*TGV* 7858	*TGV* 6112	*TGV* 7822	*TGV* 6188	*TGV* 7820	*TGV* 6116	*TGV* 6116	*TGV* 6174	*TGV* 6170	*TGV* 6120
	Ⓐ v	①–④ m	Ⓐ v		⊠		⊠	P	⊠	⑥ G	E		Ⓒ Q	B
Nice .... 361 d.	...	...	...	...	0601	...	...	0757	...	...	...	0957	1054	...
Antibes .... 361 d.	...	...	...	...	0617	...	...	0814	...	...	...	1016	1116	...
Cannes .... 361 d.	...	...	...	...	0631	...	...	0828	...	...	...	1032	1133	...
St Raphaël-Valescure .... 361 d.	...	...	...	...	|	...	...	0853	...	...	...	1058	1158	...
Les Arcs-Draguignan .... 361 d.	...	...	...	...	0709	...	...	0910	...	...	...	|	|	...
Hyères .... 360 d.	...	...	...	...	|	...	...	|	...	...	...	|	|	...
Toulon .... 361 a.	...	...	...	...	0743	...	...	0944	...	...	...	1144	1243	...
Toulon .... 360 361 d.	...	...	0550	...	0747	...	...	0948	...	...	...	1148	1247	...
Marseille St Charles .... 360 361 a.	...	...	|	...	|	...	...	1033	...	...	...	1233	|	...
Marseille St Charles .... d.	0520	0604	|	0704	|	0904	0935	1047	1154	1203	1204	1247	|	1404
Aix en Provence TGV .... d.	0534	0618	0642	0718	0841	0918	|	|	1208	1217	1218	|	1356	1418
Avignon TGV .... d.	0556	0641	0705	0741	|	0941	1005	|	1231	1240	1241	|	|	1440
Valence TGV .... 355 d.	|	|	|	|	|	|	1040	|	|	|	|	|	|	|
Lyon St Exupéry ✈ .... 342 351 d.	|	|	|	|	0954	|	|	|	1325	|	|	|	|	|
Paris Gare de Lyon .... 342 351 355 a.	0841	0929	0951	1023	1151	1223	1254	1355t	1520	1525	1525	1602z	1637	1726

	TGV 6176	*TGV* 6122	*TGV* 6124	*TGV* 6128	*TGV* 7856	*TGV* 7824	*TGV* 6168	*TGV* 6132	*TGV* 6180	*TGV* 6186	*TGV* 6134	*TGV* 6144	*TGV* 6144
				B	⊠	⊠	B	n		⑦ R	⑦ e	J	⑦ L
Nice .... 361 d.	1202	...	...	...	1502	...	1601	...	1657	1739	...	...	...
Antibes .... 361 d.	1219	...	...	...	1518	...	1617	...	1718	1754	...	...	...
Cannes .... 361 d.	1233	...	...	...	1532	...	1632	...	1733	1808	...	...	...
St Raphaël-Valescure .... 361 d.	1258	...	...	...	1557	...	1658	...	|	1833	...	...	...
Les Arcs-Draguignan .... 361 d.	|	...	...	...	|	...	|	...	1810	|	...	...	...
Hyères .... 360 d.	|	...	1450	...	|	...	|	...	|	|	...	...	...
Toulon .... 361 a.	1344	...	1503	...	1643	...	1744	...	1844	1920	...	...	...
Toulon .... 360 361 d.	1348	...	1507	...	1647	...	1748	...	1848	1924	...	...	...
Marseille St Charles .... 360 361 a.	1433	...	1550	...	|	...	1833	...	|	|	...	...	...
Marseille St Charles .... d.	1447	1502	1604	1703	|	1732	1848	1904	|	|	2009	2035	2102
Aix en Provence TGV .... d.	|	1518	1619	1718	1739	1747	|	1918	|	|	2023	2049	2117
Avignon TGV .... d.	|	1541	1641	1741	|	1809	|	1941	1958	2033	2045	2111	2140
Valence TGV .... 355 d.	|	|	|	|	|	|	|	|	|	|	|	|	|
Lyon St Exupéry ✈ .... 342 351 d.	|	|	|	|	|	|	|	|	|	|	|	|	|
Paris Gare de Lyon .... 342 351 355 a.	1803	1833	1929	2032	2042	2102	2159	2229k	2246	2317	2333	2356	0026

A – ①–⑥ to Mar. 25; daily from Mar. 27.
B – Ⓑ to Mar. 24; daily from Mar. 26.
C – ⑤⑥ to Mar. 25; daily from Mar. 27.
D – ①⑤⑥⑦ (not Dec. 24, 31, Feb. 6, 13, Mar. 13, 20, 27, Apr. 3, 17).
E – Ⓑ to May 12; daily from May 14. Arrives Paris 1531 on Jan. 3, 4, Apr. 25, 26.
F – ⑤ from Mar. 31 (also May 17; not May 19).
G – Until May 13.
H – ⑤⑦ from Mar. 31 (also Apr. 10, May 1, 8, 17, 29; not May 19).
J – Runs on Apr. 10, May 1, 8, 29 only.
L – ⑦ from Apr. 2.
N – ⑤⑥ from Mar. 31 (also May 17, 18).
P – ⑥⑦ to Mar. 19; daily from Mar. 25.
Q – Ⓒ from Apr. 1 (also May 19).
R – ⑦ from Apr. 2 (also Apr. 10, May 1, 8, 29).
S – Until May 14.
T – From May 15.

e – Also Apr. 10, May 1, 8, 29.
h – Not May 18, 19.
j – 3 – 5 minutes earlier on Dec. 20, 21, 27, 28, Apr. 11, 12, 18, 19.
k – 2224 on ⑦ until Mar. 26 (not Feb. 26, Mar. 5).
m – Not Apr. 10, May 1, 8, 17, 18, 29.
n – Not Dec. 24.
r – Also Feb. 6, 13; not Mar. 14 - Apr. 20.
t – 6 – 7 minutes later on Apr. 11, 12, 25, 26.
v – Not May 19.
y – 0545 on ②–⑤ Jan. 10 - May 12 (not Apr. 11, May 2, 9); 0548 on ⑥ Jan. 14 - May 13 (not Feb. 18, 25, Apr. 1).
z – 1605 on ⑥; 1609 on ⑦.

TGV – High-speed train. 🅁. 🍷.

⊠ – OUIGO low-cost TGV service. Internet bookings only at www.ouigo.com.

350 PARIS / LYON - AVIGNON - MARSEILLE - TOULON - NICE

TGV **SERVICES FROM / TO / VIA LYON** (see previous page for services from / to Paris Gare de Lyon).
Timings may vary by up to 5 minutes from May 15 (please check your reservation).

km		TGV 6801	TGV 6805	TGV 7831	TGV 5102		TGV 9810	TGV 5332	TGV 5113	TGV 9877	TGV 6813	TGV 7841	TGV 7835	TGV 9830	TGV 5306	TGV 5537	TGV 7845	TGV 7845	TGV 9580	TGV 9835	TGV 5135	TGV 5316	TGV 5125
									⑥						⑤		A	B		⑥	⑤		Ⓑ
		d	d	⊠	D				k	L ⊡		⊠	⊠		f	◇	⊠	⊠	F ▽	k	f	❦	h ⊗
	Brussels Midi **11** d.	...	...	...	...	...	0635	...	...	...	...	...	...	1317	...	...	...	...	...	1617	...	...	...
	Lille Europe **11** d.	...	...	...	0550t	...	0724	...	0903	...	...	...	...	1402	...	...	...	...	...	1703	1703	...	1822
	Lille Flandres **11** d.	...	...	...	|	...	|	...	|	...	...	1132	1301	|	...	...	1520	1541	...	|	|	...	|
	Charles de Gaulle ✈ **11** d.	...	...	0655	0651	...	0826	...	0958	...	...	1231	1358	1457	...	...	1640	1658	...	1758	1758	...	1959
	Marne la Vallée-Chessy **11** d.	...	...	0712	0707	...	0840	...	1012	...	...	1246	1412	1512	...	...	1654	1713	...	1811	1811	...	2012
	Nantes **335** d.	...	...	|	|	...	|	...	|	...	...	|	|	|	1244	...	|	|	...	|	|	...	|
	Rennes **335** d.	...	...	|	|	...	|	0731	|	...	...	|	|	|	|	...	|	|	...	|	|	...	|
	Le Havre **335** d.	...	...	|	|	...	|	|	|	...	...	|	|	|	|	...	|	|	...	|	|	1541	|
	Massy TGV **335** d.	...	...	|	|	...	|	0923	|	...	...	|	|	|	1526	...	|	|	...	|	|	1828z	|
	Nancy **379** d.	...	...	|	|	...	|	|	|	...	...	|	|	|	|	1226	|	|	...	|	|	|	|
	Metz **379** d.	...	...	|	|	...	|	|	|	0811	...	|	|	|	|	|	|	|	...	|	|	|	|
	Strasbourg **379** d.	...	...	|	|	...	|	|	|	0904	...	|	|	|	|	1337	|	|	1615	|	|	|	|
	Dijon Ville **379** d.	...	...	|	|	...	|	|	|	1121	...	|	|	|	|	1620	|	|	|	|	|	|	|
	Genève **346** d.	...	...	|	|	...	|	|	|	|	...	|	|	|	|	|	|	|	|	|	|	|	|
0	**Lyon** Part Dieu ▶ d.	0628	0806j	|	0906	...	1036	1140	1210	1310	1406	|	1608	1706	1740	1806	|	|	2006	2010	2010	2042	2206
	Lyon St Exupéry ✈ d.	|	|	|	|	...	|	|	|	|	|	1437	|	|	|	|	1900y	1900	|	|	|	|	|
104	Valence TGV ▶ d.	0704	0848	|	|	...	1120	|	1256c	1351	|	|	|	|	1820	|	1934	1934	|	2055	2055	2121	|
	Avignon TGV d.	0739	0928	0950	1012	...	1155	1250	1331	1428	1512	1530	1715	1810	1855	1911	2009	2009	2112	2129	2129	2155	2311
	Aix en Provence TGV d.	0801	0951	1012	1034	...	|	1312	|	1452	1534	1552	|	1832	|	1933	2031	2031	2136	2151	2151	|	2335
	Marseille St Charles a.	0813	1003	1024	1046	...	1224	1324	1401	1506	1546	1608	1743	1844	1927	1944	2043	2043	2148	2203	2205	2224	2347
	Marseille St Charles **360 361** d.	0827	1020	...	...	...	...	...	...	...	1558	...	...	...	...	1957	...	...	...	...	...	...	...
	Toulon 360 361 d.	0915	1111	...	...	...	...	...	...	...	1643	...	...	...	...	2044	...	...	...	...	...	...	...
	Les Arcs-Draguignan **361** a.	0949	|	...	...	...	...	...	...	...	...	...	...	...	...	2117	...	...	...	...	...	...	...
	St Raphaël-Valescure **361** a.	1006	1202	...	...	...	...	...	...	...	...	...	...	...	...	2134	...	...	...	...	...	...	...
	Cannes 361 a.	1035	1226	...	...	...	...	...	...	...	...	...	...	...	...	2159	...	...	...	...	...	...	...
	Antibes **361** a.	1047	1239	...	...	...	...	...	...	...	...	...	...	...	...	2211	...	...	...	...	...	...	...
	Nice 361 a.	1106	1258	...	...	...	...	...	...	...	...	...	...	...	...	2230	...	...	...	...	...	...	...

	TGV 7838	TGV 9854	TGV 5376	TGV 9583		TGV 5516	TGV 7842	TGV 5382		TGV 9866		TGV 6864	TGV 5192		TGV 5386	TGV 9868	TGV 9896	TGV 7832	TGV 9882	TGV 6850	TGV 7836	TGV 6866	TGV 6852
								⑥				⑦	⑥										
	⊠		❦	F △			⊠	h				e	U				L ⊙	⊠			T ⊠	n	
Nice 361 d.	...	...	...	...	...	0700	...	...	...	...	...	...	...	...	...	...	...	...	...	1440	...	...	1727
Antibes **361** d.	...	...	...	...	...	0716	...	...	...	...	...	...	...	...	...	...	...	...	...	1456	...	...	1745
Cannes 361 d.	...	...	...	...	...	0730	...	...	...	...	...	...	...	...	...	...	...	...	...	1509	...	...	1759
St Raphaël-Valescure **361** d.	...	...	...	...	...	0755	...	...	...	...	...	...	...	...	...	...	...	...	...	1534	...	...	1823
Les Arcs-Draguignan **361** d.	...	...	...	...	...	0812	...	...	...	...	...	...	...	...	...	...	...	...	...	|	...	...	1840
Toulon 360 361 d.	...	...	...	...	...	0850	...	...	...	...	...	...	...	...	...	...	...	...	...	1623	...	1754	1918
Marseille St Charles **360 361** a.	...	...	...	...	...	0933	...	...	...	...	...	...	...	...	...	...	...	...	...	1719	...	1853	2004
Marseille St Charles d.	0613	0636	0735	0811	...	0946	1002	1036	...	1212	...	1332	1333	...	1436	1512	1556	1648	1712	1736	1825	1911	2018
Aix en Provence TGV d.	0627	0650	|	0826	...	1000	1017	1050	...	1226	...	1346	1351	...	1450	1526	1611	|	1726	1755	1840	1926	2032
Avignon TGV d.	0650	0715	0806	0848	...	1023	1040	1115	...	1249	...	1408	1413	...	1515	1549	1633	1719	1749	1817	1902	1949	2055
Valence TGV ▶ d.	|	|	0844	|	...	|	|	|	...	|	...	1443	|	...	|	|	1714	|	|	|	|	|	2129
Lyon St Exupéry ✈ a.	0741	|	|	|	...	|	1133	|	...	|	...	|	|	...	|	|	|	1811	|	|	|	|	|
Lyon Part Dieu ▶ a.	|	0820	0920	0954	...	1126	|	1220	...	1351	...	1518	1514	...	1620	1653	1750	|	1854	1920	1954	2054	2202
Genève **346** a.	|	|	|	|	...	|	|	|	...	|	...	...	|	...	|	|	|	|	|	...	|	...	...
Dijon Ville **379** a.	|	|	|	|	...	1325	|	|	...	|	...	...	|	...	|	|	1939	|	|	...	|	...	...
Strasbourg **379** a.	|	|	|	1343	...	1554	|	|	...	|	...	...	|	...	|	|	2207	|	|	...	|	...	...
Metz **379** a.	|	|	|	...	...	|	|	|	...	|	...	...	|	...	|	|	2302p	|	|	...	|	...	...
Nancy **379** a.	|	|	|	...	...	1702	|	|	...	|	...	...	|	...	|	|	...	|	|	...	|	...	...
Massy TGV **335** a.	|	|	1137z	...	...	...	|	1434	...	|	...	...	|	...	1834	|	...	|	|	...	|	...	...
Le Havre **335** a.	|	|	1431	...	...	...	|	|	...	|	...	...	|	...	|	|	...	|	|	...	|	...	...
Rennes **335** a.	|	|	...	...	...	...	|	1621	...	|	...	...	|	...	2032	|	...	|	|	...	|	...	...
Nantes **335** a.	|	|	...	...	...	...	|	...	...	|	...	...	|	...	...	|	...	|	|	...	|	...	...
Marne la Vallée-Chessy **11** a.	0935	1019	...	...	...	...	1319	...	...	1547	...	...	1709	...	...	1849	...	2010•	2049	...	2147	...	...
Charles de Gaulle ✈ **11** a.	0951	1033	...	...	...	...	1332	...	...	1601	...	...	1723	...	...	1902	...	2024•	2103	...	2202	...	...
Lille Flandres **11** a.	1048	|	...	...	...	...	1430x	...	...	|	...	...	1900	...	...	|	...	...	|	...	...	...	...
Lille Europe **11** a.	...	1127	...	...	...	...	...	...	...	1657	...	...	...	...	...	1958	...	...	2157	...	...	...	...
Brussels Midi **11** a.	...	1211	...	...	...	...	...	...	...	1743	...	...	...	...	...	2043	...	...	2243	...	...	...	...

A – Until May 14. On Apr. 9 starts from Tourcoing (d. 1530; not calling at Lille), Charles de Gaulle d. 1655, Marne la Vallée d. 1711, Lyon St Exupéry a. 1857, d. 1901, then as shown.
B – From May 15.
D – ①–⑤ to Mar. 24; ①–⑥ from Mar. 27 (not Apr. 10, May 1, 8, 29).
F – From / to Frankfurt (Table **47**).
L – From / to Luxembourg (Table **379**).
T – To Tourcoing (a. 2309).
U – From Apr. 1.

c – Arrives 1245.
d – Not Jan. 1.
e – Also Apr. 10, May 1, 8, 29.
f – Also May 17; not May 19.
h – Not May 18, 19.
j – 0804 on ⑦.
k – Also May 18, 19.
n – Not Dec. 24, 31.
p – Not ①–④ Dec. 12 - Mar. 23. 46 – 57 minutes later on Dec. 17, 24, Jan. 6, 13, 20, Apr. 3 – 7.
t – 0600 from May 15.
x – On Apr. 9 diverted to Tourcoing (a. 1438; not calling at Lille).
y – Arrives 1842.
z – Massy **Palaiseau**.

TGV – High-speed train. 🅁. 🍸.

△ – Runs 29 – 33 minutes earlier Marseille - Lyon on Jan. 29, Apr. 22, 23.
▽ – Runs 26 – 40 minutes later Lyon - Marseille on Jan. 28, Apr. 22, 23.
⊡ – On Apr. 22, 23 runs 20 – 30 minutes later Lyon - Marseille and does not call at Valence.
◇ – On Jan. 28, Apr. 22, 23 runs 26 – 65 minutes later Lyon - Nice.
⊙ – Later arrivals Dijon - Metz on Jan. 28, Apr. 22.
• – On ⑥ Dec. 31 - Apr. 15 (also Jan. 29, Mar. 26) does not call at Marne la Vallée and arrives Charles de Gaulle 2016.
⊗ – On ①–④ Mar. 13 - Apr. 20 (not Apr. 10) does not call at Avignon or Aix en Provence and arrives Marseille 0012.
❦ – Subject to alteration on various dates (particularly on ⑥⑦). Please check before travelling.
⊠ – OUIGO low-cost TGV service. Internet bookings only at www.ouigo.com.
▶ – For other trains Valence TGV - Lyon and Paris see Table **355**. For Valence Ville - Lyon see Table **351**.

LYON - VALENCE - AVIGNON - MARSEILLE via 'classic' line 351

See Table **350** for *TGV* services Paris / Lyon - Valence TGV - Avignon TGV - Marseille, Table **355** for *TGV* services Paris / Lyon - Valence TGV - Montpellier.
TGV timings may vary by up to 5 minutes (please check your reservation for confirmed timings). All TER trains are 2nd class only except through services between Lyon and Marseille.
Warning! Subject to alteration on June 10.

km		Ⓐ	Ⓐ	Ⓒ	Ⓒ	Ⓐ	Ⓐ	Ⓒ	Ⓐ	⚒	Ⓐ		Ⓐ			*TGV* **6191** ①–⑥ **b**		⚒ ⊗	⊗	⊗	⊗	Ⓐ	⊗	*TGV* **6193** **n**	⚒ ⊗
	Paris Gare de Lyon § d.	...	...	...	...	...	...	...	...	...	...	...	...	...	...	0709**z**	...	...	...	...	...	...	...	1208**k**	...
	Lyon St Exupéry TGV ✈ § d.	...	...	...	...	...	...	...	...	...	...	...	...	...	...	0914	...	...	...	...	...	...	...	1414	...
	Lyon Perrache d.	...	...	...	...	...	...	...	...	...	0639	...	0739	...	...	|	...	...	...	...	...	...	...	|	1339
0	**Lyon** Part-Dieu d.	...	...	...	...	...	...	...	...	0620	|	0720	|	...	0820	|	0920	1020	...	1120	1220	...	1320	|	|
32	Vienne d.	...	...	...	...	...	...	...	...	0639	0700	0740	0800	...	0840	|	0940	1039	...	1140	1240	...	1340	|	1400
87	Tain-l'Hermitage-Tournon d.	...	...	...	...	...	...	...	...	0718	0741	0825	0841	...	0917	|	1023	1119	...	1216	1325	...	1423	|	1441
105	**Valence** Ville a.	...	...	...	...	...	...	...	...	0728	0752	0835	0852	...	0928	0946	1034	1129	...	1227	1335	...	1432	1446	1452
105	**Valence** Ville d.	...	...	...	0606	0606	0630	0706	0706	▬	...	0837	...	0905	...	0949	1036	1130	1230	...	1337	...	1435	1449	...
150	Montélimar d.	...	...	...	0634	0634	0657	0734	0734	...	...	0900	...	0933	...	1012	1059	1158	1257	...	1400	...	1502	1512	...
202	Orange d.	...	...	...	0708	0709	0731	0808	0809	Ⓐ	...	0934	...	1008	...	1041	1132	1231	1330	...	1434	...	1535	1541	...
230	**Avignon** Centre a.	...	...	...	0730	0735	0750	0831	0834		...	0950	...	1032	...	1056	1147	1249	1352	...	1449	...	1552	1556	...
230	**Avignon** Centre d.	0552	0648	0651	0748	...	0753	0844	...	0849	...	0953	...	1040	...	...	*1155*	...	1355	...	1451	1553	...	1559	...
265	Arles 355 d.	0610	0707	0709	0807	...	0811	0904	...	0907	...	1014	...	1108	...	...	*1213*	...	1413	...	1510	1610	...	1619	...
299	Miramas 355 d.	0633	0731	0736	0834	...	0834	0929	...	0931	...	1039	...	1131	...	...	*1236*	...	1435	...	1533	1636	...	1636	...
328	Vitrolles (for ✈) ⊖ 355 d.	0650	0749	0758	0856	...	0851	0947	...	0953	...	1056	...	1149	...	...	*1258*	...	1456	...	1553	1657	...	...	...
351	**Marseille** St Charles 355 a.	0707	0805	0819	0917	...	0908	1007	...	1019	...	1115	...	1207	...	...	*1319*	...	1518	...	1612	1718	...	...	...

	⑤	Ⓒ	①–④ **m**			⑤⑥†	Ⓑ	Ⓐ	⚒		Ⓐ		⑤ **f A**		Ⓐ		Ⓐ	*TGV* **6195** Ⓐ **v**	Ⓑ	⚒	†	*TGV* **6195** ⑦ **e**			△
Paris Gare de Lyon § d.	...	...	...	...	...	...	...	...	...	...	...	...	...	...	...	...	...	1708**z**	...	...	...	1809**z**	...	...	...
Lyon St Exupéry TGV ✈ § d.	...	...	...	...	...	...	...	...	...	...	...	...	...	...	...	...	...	1918	...	...	...	2010	...	...	...
yon Perrache d.	...	...	...	...	...	...	...	1539	...	1639	...	...	...	1739	1811	...	...	|	1839	...	...	|	1939	...	...
yon Part-Dieu d.	...	...	...	1420	1520	1520	...	|	1620	|	...	1720	...	|	|	1820	...	|	|	1920	1920	|	|	2020	2120
ienne d.	...	...	...	1440	1540	1540	...	1600	1640	1700	...	1740	...	1800	1832	1840	...	|	1900	1940	1940	|	2000	2040	2140
ain-l'Hermitage-Tournon d.	...	...	...	1517	1620	1620	...	1640	1725	1741	...	1825	...	1840	1912	1921	...	|	1941	2022	2022	|	2041	2120	2221
alence Ville a.	...	...	...	1527	1631	1631	...	1651	1735	1752	...	1835	...	1851	1923	1931	...	1946	1952	2033	2032	2038	2052	2131	2232
alence Ville d.	1506	1535	...	▬	▬	1636	1705	1705	1737	...	1805	1837	1857	1905	...	1933	...	1949	...	2035	2034	2042	...	...	...
lontélimar d.	1534	1557	...	...	...	1705	1734	1734	1804	...	1834	1900	1923	1934	...	2001	...	2013	...	2058	2059	2113	...	...	...
range d.	1609	1629	...	⑤	Ⓒ	1735	1809	1809	1836	...	1909	1934	1956	2009	...	2033	...	2041	...	2132	2132	2141	...	...	...
vignon Centre a.	1634	1644	...			1758	1834	1834	1852	...	1935	1949	2013	2034	...	2048	...	2057	...	2149	2149	2157	...	...	...
vignon Centre d.	1652	1646	1704	1749	1750	...	...	*1851*	...	...	...	1951	...	...	...	...	2056	2100	...	...	*2157*	2200	...	...	...
rles 355 d.	1711	1704	1722	1807	1809	...	...	*1910*	...	...	...	2010	...	...	...	...	2114	2121	...	...	*2214*	2222	...	...	...
liramas 355 d.	1736	1727	1745	1832	1836	...	...	*1939*	...	...	...	2033	...	...	...	...	2136	2140	...	...	*2236*	2240	...	...	...
itrolles (for ✈) ⊖ 355 d.	1757	1744	1810	1849	1858	...	...	*2000*	...	...	...	2051	...	...	...	...	2158	...	...	...	*2258*	...	...	...	...
larseille St Charles 355 a.	1819	1800	1830	1906	1919	...	...	*2022*	...	...	...	2107	...	...	...	...	2219	...	...	...	*2319*	...	...	...	...

	Ⓐ	Ⓐ	⚒	⚒	Ⓐ	⑥	Ⓒ	⚒	⚒	Ⓐ	*TGV* **6194** ①–⑥ **b**	⚒	Ⓐ	⊗	Ⓐ ⊗	Ⓐ	⊗	⊗	⑥	Ⓑ ⊗	Ⓒ		⊗		Ⓑ
larseille St Charles 355 d.	...	...	...	...	...	...	...	...	...	...	...	...	...	0655	...	0741	...	0841	...	...	0939	1041	...	1141	...
itrolles (for ✈) ⊖ 355 d.	...	...	...	...	...	...	...	...	...	...	...	...	...	0710	...	0800	...	0900	...	...	0959	1100	...	1200	...
liramas 355 d.	...	...	...	...	...	...	...	...	...	...	0622	...	0645	0730	...	0826	...	0926	...	...	1024	1127	...	1229**j**	...
rles 355 d.	...	...	...	...	...	...	...	...	...	...	0643	...	0708	0751	...	0849	...	0954**j**	...	...	1048	1146	...	1248	...
vignon Centre a.	...	...	...	...	...	...	...	...	...	...	0700	...	0724	0808	...	0908	...	1013	...	...	1106	1203	...	1308	...
vignon Centre d.	...	...	...	...	0534	0534	...	0611	...	0636	0704	0708	0727	0811	...	...	...	1017	...	...	...	...	1211	1325	...
range d.	...	...	...	...	0555	0555	...	0627	...	0656	0721	0731	0751	0827	...	...	...	1041	...	...	...	...	1227	1351	...
lontélimar d.	...	0533	...	...	0630	0630	...	0701	...	0730	0748	0807	0824	0900	...	...	...	1118	...	...	...	...	1301	1426	...
alence Ville a.	...	0601	...	...	0700	0701	...	0723	...	0758	0809	0834	0851	0921	...	...	...	1149	...	...	...	...	1322	1454	...
alence Ville d.	0536	0607	0629	0637	0706	0707	0707	0725	0737	0807	0812	0836	...	0923	1032	...	1128	...	1229	1229	...	...	1324	...	1507
ain-l'Hermitage-Tournon d.	0547	0618	0640	0648	0717	0718	0718	0736	0748	0818	|	0847	...	0935	1044	...	1139	...	1240	1240	...	...	1336	...	1518
ienne d.	0627	0658	0721	0728	0758	0758	0758	0820	0828	0858	|	0927	...	1020	1120	...	1221	...	1320	1321	...	...	1421	...	1558
yon Part-Dieu a.	|	|	0740	|	|	|	|	0840	|	|	|	0948	...	1040	1140	...	1240	...	1339	1340	...	...	1440	...	|
yon Perrache a.	0649	0719	...	0749	0819	0819	0819	...	0849	0919	|	...	...	...	...	...	...	...	...	...	...	...	...	...	1619
Lyon St Exupéry TGV ✈ § a.	...	...	...	...	...	...	...	...	...	...	0841	...	...	...	...	...	...	...	...	...	...	...	...	...	...
Paris Gare de Lyon § a.	...	...	...	...	...	...	...	...	...	...	1049**y**	...	...	...	...	...	...	...	...	...	...	...	...	...	...

	TGV **6196**		⚒					Ⓐ		Ⓐ	Ⓑ	*TGV* **6198** **G**		Ⓒ	Ⓐ	⑦ **A**	Ⓐ		Ⓐ	Ⓒ	Ⓐ **w**	**B**	⑥ **d**	**C**	
larseille St Charles 355 d.	...	1255	...	1341	1441	...	...	1541	...	...	...	...	1655	...	1722	...	1755	...	1856	1840	...	...	...	...	2041
itrolles (for ✈) ⊖ 355 d.	...	1310	...	1402	1500	...	...	1600	...	...	...	...	1710	...	1735	...	1811	...	1911	1900	...	...	...	...	2100
liramas 355 d.	...	1330	...	1428	1526	...	...	1626	...	...	...	1715	1729	...	1759**j**	...	1831	...	1931	1931**j**	...	...	...	...	2126
rles 355 d.	...	1352	...	1449	1549	...	...	1649	...	...	...	1736	1751	...	1821	...	1851	...	1951	1951	...	...	...	...	2149
vignon Centre a.	...	1408	...	1508	1608	...	...	1708	...	...	...	1800	1808	...	1840	...	1912	...	2008	2008	...	...	...	...	2208
vignon Centre d.	1404	1412	...	1512	▬	1617	...	...	1707	1725	...	1804	1812	1834	1845	1904	...	1925	2011	2025	...	...	...	...	...
range d.	1421	1428	...	1541	...	1633	...	...	1727	1751	...	1821	1828	1857	1910	1919	...	1954**j**	2031	2050	...	...	...	...	...
lontélimar d.	1449	1501	...	1622	Ⓑ	1705	...	...	1801	1827	...	1849	1901	1932	1954	1953	...	2029	2107	2124	...	...	...	...	...
alence Ville a.	1510	1522	...	1654		1725	...	...	1829	1854	...	1910	1922	2000	2025	2014	...	2055	2135	2151	...	...	...	...	...
alence Ville d.	1513	1524	1607	...	1707	1727	1807	...	1832	...	1907	1913	1924	...	...	...	...	2058	...	...	2156	2156	2200	2200	...
ain-l'Hermitage-Tournon d.	|	1535	1618	...	1718	1739	1818	...	1844	...	1918	|	1936	...	...	...	...	2109	...	...	2207	2207	2211	2211	...
ienne d.	|	1621	1658	...	1758	1821	1858	...	1920	...	1958	|	2020	...	...	...	...	2142	...	...	2253**x**	|	2253	2253	...
yon Part-Dieu a.	|	1640	|	...	|	1840	|	...	1940	...	|	|	2040	...	...	...	...	2202	...	...	2315	|	2312	|	...
yon Perrache a.	|	...	1719	...	1819	...	1919	...	...	...	2019	|	...	...	...	...	...	...	...	...	...	2314	...	2311	...
Lyon St Exupéry TGV ✈ § a.	1542	...	...	...	...	...	...	...	...	...	...	1943	...	...	...	...	...	...	...	...	...	...	...	...	...
Paris Gare de Lyon § a.	1758**g**	...	...	...	...	...	...	...	...	...	...	2149**y**	...	...	...	...	...	...	...	...	...	...	...	...	...

A – To / from Annecy (Table **364**).
B – Runs Apr. 3 – 7, 11 – 13 only.
C – Runs on Feb. 25, Mar. 4 only.

b – Not Feb. 25, Mar. 4.
d – Also Apr. 10, May 1, 8, 29.
e – Also May 17.
f – 1746 from May 15.
g – Arrives 6 – 7 minutes earlier.
k – 1206 on Apr. 18, 19; 1214 from May 15.
m – Not Apr. 10, May 1, 8, 18, 29.
n – Not Apr. 24 – 28.

v – Not May 19.
w – Ⓐ until Apr. 28 (not Apr. 3 – 7, 11 – 13).
x – Not Mar. 6 – 31, Apr. 14.
y – 3 minutes earlier from May 15.
z – 5 – 6 minutes later from May 15.

TGV – High-speed train. Ⓡ. 🍸.

△ – Runs 7 – 8 minutes **earlier** on ①–⑤ from Mar. 6. Subject to alteration on Apr. 4, 5, 12.
⊗ – Subject to alteration or cancellation Apr. 24 – 28.
§ – See Table **342** for full service Paris - Lyon St Exupéry and v.v.
⊖ – Vitrolles Aéroport Marseille-Provence ✈. A shuttle bus runs to the airport terminal (journey time: 5 minutes).

351a AVIGNON TGV - AVIGNON CENTRE - CARPENTRAS

km		Ⓐ	Ⓐ		Ⓐ	Ⓐ		Ⓐ	Ⓒ							Ⓐ		Ⓐ					†		
0	**Avignon** TGV .... ◇ d.	0612	0641	0712	0741	0813	0912	1012	1112	1210	...	1321	1412	1512	...	1641	1710	1741	1812	1912	2012	...	2212	...	...
4	**Avignon** Centre .... ◇ d.	0621	0651	0721	0751	0822	0921	1021	1122	1221	...	1329	1421	1521	...	1651	1720	1751	1821	1921	2021	...	2221	...	...
31	**Carpentras** .... a.	0653	0723	0753	0823	0853	0953	1051	1153	1253	...	1400	1453	1553	...	1723	1753	1823	1853	1953	2053	...	2253	...	...

		⚒	Ⓐ	Ⓐ		Ⓐ	Ⓐ										Ⓐ								
	Carpentras .... d.	0608	0708	0738	0808	0838	0908	1008	...	1208	1308	...	1438	1508	1608	1708	1738	1808	1908	2008	2108	...	...	...	...
	Avignon Centre .... ◇ a.	0639	0739	0809	0839	0909	0939	1039	...	1239	1339	...	1509	1539	1639	1739	1809	1839	1939	2039	2139	...	...	...	...
	Avignon TGV .... ◇ a.	0650	0750	0820	0850	0920	0948	1050	...	1249	1349	...	1520	1549	1650	1750	1820	1850	1950	2050	2150	...	...	...	...

◇ – **Full service** Avignon TGV - Avignon Centre and v.v. (journey 4–6 minutes):
From Avignon TGV at 0612 Ⓐ, 0641, 0712, 0741 Ⓐ, 0813 Ⓐ, 0842, 0912, 0941, 1012 Ⓐ, 1041, 1112 Ⓒ, 1141, 1210, 1236 Ⓒ, 1238 Ⓐ, 1321, 1341, 1412, 1441 Ⓒ, 1512, 1541, 164 1710, 1741 Ⓐ, 1812, 1842, 1912, 1941, 2012, 2051 Ⓒ, 2056 Ⓐ, 2112 and 2212 **b**.
From Avignon Centre at 0544 Ⓐ, 0614 Ⓒ, 0644 †, 0713 Ⓐ, 0744 Ⓐ, 0814, 0844, 0914, 0942 Ⓐ, 1014 Ⓒ, 1044, 1114, 1142, 1212 Ⓒ, 1244, 1311, 1342, 1414 Ⓒ, 1444, 1514, 1544, 1614 Ⓒ, 1617 Ⓐ, 1644, 1714, 1744, 1816 Ⓐ, 1843 Ⓐ, 1844 Ⓒ, 1914, 1942, 2014, 2044 and 2144 **b**.

352 🚌 TOULON - ST TROPEZ - ST RAPHAËL

🚌 route **7802**: **Toulon** Gare Routière (adjacent to railway station) → **St Tropez** Gare Routière. *84 km.* Journey 1 hr 40 m - 1 hr 45 m.
From Toulon at 0620 ⚒, 0900 ⚒, 1130, 1530 ⚒ and 1815. **From St Tropez** at 0600 ⚒, 1230 ⚒, 1630, 1730 ⚒ and 1830 ⚒.

🚌 route **7601**: **St Tropez** Gare Routière → **St Raphaël** Gare Routière (adjacent to railway station). *35 km* Journey 1 hr 20 m - 1 hr 30 m.
From St Tropez at 0630, 0730, 0830, 0930, 1130, 1230 and hourly until 1930; then 2045.
From St Raphaël at 0615, 0715, 0815, 0915, 1115, 1315, 1515, 1615, 1715, 1800, 1915 and 2015.

Operator: ZOU! ✆ 0 809 400 013
https://zou.maregionsud.fr

353 LYON - BOURG EN BRESSE

Local stopping trains via Villars-les-Dombes. See Table **378** for services via Ambérieu. On May 18 services in this table run as on ⑥ (except where shown).

km		Ⓐ	Ⓐ	⚒	Ⓐ	† 🚌	Ⓐ 🚌	⚒	Ⓐ		Ⓐ	⚒	Ⓐ		Ⓐ	⚒	Ⓐ		Ⓐ	⚒	⑥	Ⓐ	E	⑤† f	Ⓐ 🚌
0	**Lyon** Perrache .... d.	0601	0631	0701	0801	...	...	1001	1101	1201	1301	1401	1501	1601	1643	1701	1731	1801	1843	1901	2001	2001	2101	2116	...
5	**Lyon** Part Dieu .... d.	0612	0642	0712	0812	0812	0912	1012	1112	1212	1312	1412	1512	1612	1656	1712	1742	1812	1856	1912	2012	2013	2112	2130	222
65	**Bourg en Bresse** .... a.	0712	0739	0812	0912	0933	1033	1112	1212	1312	1412	1512	1612	1712	1747	1812	1844	1912	1947	2012	2112	2112	2212	2230	234

		Ⓐ	⚒	† 🚌	Ⓐ	⚒	Ⓐ		Ⓐ	⚒	Ⓐ 🚌			Ⓐ	⚒	Ⓐ	Ⓐ 🚌			⚒		Ⓐ			Ⓑ
	Bourg en Bresse .... d.	0517	0548	0557	0617	0648	0714	0748	0814	0848	0927	...	1048	1148	1248	1348	1427	...	1548	1648	1748	1848	1948	...	204
	Lyon Part Dieu .... a.	0617	0648	0718	0718	0748	0804	0848	0904	0948	1048	...	1148	1248	1348	1448	1548	...	1648	1748	1848	1948	2048	...	214
	Lyon Perrache .... a.	0629	0659	...	0729	0759	0817	0859	0917	0959	...	...	1159	1259	1359	1459	...	...	1659	1759	1859	1959	2059	...	215

E – ①②③④⑥ (not Apr. 10, May 1, 8, 17, 18, 29).

f – Also May 17, 18.

353a MÂCON - BOURG EN BRESSE - AMBÉRIEU

km		🚌 Ⓒd	Ⓐn	🚌 Ⓒd	Ⓐn	z	🚌		🚌 Ⓐ	🚌 A	Ⓐn	🚌	Ⓐn	🚌 A	🚌	🚌 A	Ⓐn	Ⓐn	🚌 Ⓒd	🚌 A	Ⓐn	🚌 Ⓒd	Ⓐn	🚌 A	🚌 Ⓐ	🚌 Ⓒ
0	**Mâcon** Ville .... d.	...	0704	0727	0804	...	0904	...	1104	...	...	...	1304	1304	1504	...	...	1702	1704	...	1802	1804	1904	1904	2004	210
37	Bourg en Bresse .... a.	...	0732	0829	0833	...	1006	...	1206	...	...	...	1334	1406	1606	...	...	1730	1806	...	1830	1906	1932	2006	2106	213
37	Bourg en Bresse **378** d.	0716	0734	...	...	0843	...	1043r	...	1216	1231	1316	...	...	...	1616	1628	1732	...	1816	1832	*1916*	1934	...	...	...
68	**Ambérieu** .... **378** a.	0755	0758	...	...	0901	...	1102	...	1255	1255	1355	...	...	...	1655	1653	1755	...	1855	1855	*1955*	1958	...	...	...

	🚌 A	Ⓐn	🚌 A	🚌	Ⓐn	🚌 Ⓒd	🚌	🚌 Ⓐ	🚌 A	Ⓐn	🚌	Ⓐn	🚌 Ⓒd	🚌	🚌	Ⓐn	🚌 Ⓒd	Ⓐn	🚌 A	Ⓐn	🚌 Ⓒd	🚌 A		Ⓐn	🚌 Ⓒd	🚌
Ambérieu .... **378** d.	...	0655	0705	...	0805	0805	*0905*v	...	...	...	1205	1305	1305	...	1505	...	...	1702	1705	1805	1805	...	1858	1905	...	211
Bourg en Bresse .. **378** a.	...	0718	0745	...	0829	0845	*0945*v	...	...	...	1245	1329	1345	...	1545	...	...	1725	1745	1828	1845	...	1917	1928	...	215
Bourg en Bresse .... d.	0650	0719	...	0750	...	...	0950	1050	1215	1228	...	...	...	1350	...	1626	1650	1726	*1750*	1829	...	1850	...	1929	1950	...
Mâcon Ville .... a.	0753	0747	...	0853	...	...	1053	1153	1318	1257	...	...	...	1453	...	1654	1753	1754	*1853*	1857	...	1953	...	1957	2053	...

A – Runs Dec. 19–23, 26–30, Feb. 6–10, 13–17, Apr. 11–14, 17–21 only.
d – Ⓒ (daily Dec. 17 - Jan. 1, Feb. 4–19, Apr. 8–23).

n – Not Dec. 19–30, Feb. 6–17, Apr. 11–21.
r – 1039 Apr. 3–7, 11–14, May 2–5, 9–12.

v – ⚒ only.
z – Not Apr. 22.

353b DIJON - BOURG EN BRESSE

Subject to alteration on June 17, 18

km		Ⓐ		Ⓒ		D		Ⓐ		
0	**Dijon** Ville .... d.	0644	...	0844	...	1244	...	1744	1844	...
30	St Jean de Losne .... d.	0718	...	0918	...	1311	...	1818	1918	...
86	Louhans .... d.	0757	...	0957	...	1347	...	1857	1957	...
140	**Bourg en Bresse** .... a.	0828	...	1028	...	1418	...	1928	2028	...

	Ⓐ			E			†		
Bourg en Bresse .... d.	0532	0632	...	1132	...	1737	1832	...	...
Louhans .... d.	0605	0705	...	1205	...	1810	1905	...	...
St Jean de Losne .... d.	0644	0744	...	1244	...	1847	1944	...	...
Dijon Ville .... a.	0716	0815	...	1316	...	1916	2016	...	...

D – Daily to Apr. 2 (also Apr. 8–10); daily Apr. 15 - May 1; Ⓒ from May 6.

E – ①–⑥ to Apr. 1 (also Apr. 8); ①–⑥ Apr. 15–29; ⑥ from May 6 (not May 27).

354 PERPIGNAN - VILLEFRANCHE - LATOUR DE CAROL

km			Ⓐ	Ⓐv	Ⓐv	Ⓐv	Ⓐv	Ⓐ	Ⓐ	Ⓐ			Ⓒ	Ⓒ	Ⓒ	Ⓒ	Ⓒ	Ⓒ	†	†				
0	**Perpignan** .... d.	Ⓐ	0711	0909	1110	1311	1511	1716	1816	1916	...	Ⓒ	0811	1011	1211	1411	1611	1813	1911	2011	...	...	...	...
40	Prades-Molitg les Bains .... d.		0754	0948	1149	1350	1550	1756	1859	1955	...		0855	1050	1250	1450	1650	1852	1953	2050	...	...	...	...
46	**Villefranche-Vernet les Bains** ... a.		0801	0956	1157	1358	1558	1803	1907	2003	...		0902	1058	1258	1458	1658	1900	2001	2058	...	...	...	...

		Ⓐ	Ⓐ	Ⓐ	Ⓐv	Ⓐv	Ⓐv	Ⓐv	Ⓐ			⑥	⑥	Ⓒ	Ⓒ	Ⓒ	Ⓒ	Ⓒ	Ⓒ				
Villefranche-Vernet les Bains .... d.	Ⓐ	0611	0708	0809	1010	1210	1410	1610	1814	...	Ⓒ	0708	0809	0910	1110	1310	1510	1710	1909	...	...	...	...
Prades-Molitg les Bains .... d.		0619	0716	0817	1018	1218	1418	1618	1822	...		0716	0817	0918	1118	1318	1518	1718	1917	...	...	...	...
Perpignan .... a.		0659	0757	0859	1059	1259	1459	1659	1904	...		0757	0859	0959	1159	1359	1559	1759	1955	...	...	...	...

VILLEFRANCHE - LATOUR DE CAROL *Petit Train Jaune* Narrow gauge, 2nd class. In summer most trains include open sightseeing carriages. **No service February 27 - April 27**

km		E	H		E	J	C	D	n	
0	**Villefranche-Vernet les Bains** ..... d.	0936	0935	...	1349	1349	1547	1547	1747	...
28	Mont Louis la Cabanasse .... d.	1049	1053	...	1501	1506	1713	1713	1904	...
35	Font Romeu-Odeillo-Via .... d.	1115	1122	...	1520	1525	1732	1735	1923	...
56	Bourg Madame .... d.	1214	1220	...	...	...	...	1834	2014	...
63	**Latour de Carol** .... a.	1231	1238	...	...	...	...	1851	2031	...

	H	E	K	L	J	E	J	E	C
Latour de Carol .... d.	0804	0814	0857	0905	...	...	1521	1535	...
Bourg Madame .... d.	0822	0832	0915	0923	...	...	1539	1553	...
Font Romeu-Odeillo-Via .... d.	0929	0934	1022	1027	1549	1555	1644	1652	175
Mont Louis la Cabanasse .... d.	0958	0958	1055	1052	1618	1617	1711	1715	181
Villefranche-Vernet les Bains ... a.	1107	1109	1200	1157	1731	1731	1827	1827	192

C – ⑦ to Feb. 26; † from Apr. 30.
D – ⑤⑥ Feb. 3–25; ⑤⑥ from Apr. 28.
E – Until Feb. 26.
H – From Apr. 29.
J – From Apr. 28.

K – ⑥⑦ from Apr. 29.
L – ⑥⑦ Feb. 4–26.

n – Not Feb. 27 - Apr. 27.
v – Not Apr. 10–28.

PARIS, LYON and MARSEILLE - MONTPELLIER - PERPIGNAN - PORTBOU 355

TGV services from / to Paris. Paris timings may vary by up to 9 minutes from May 15 (later departures / earlier arrivals; please check your reservation).

km	All services 🅁	TGV 6271 Ⓐ v	TGV 6221 Ⓐ v	TGV 6221 Ⓒ w	TGV 7885 H ⊠	TGV 9713	TGV 6275	TGV 7875 ⊠	TGV 9715	TGV 6277	TGV 6223	TGV 6225	TGV 6279 A	TGV 6279 ⑤ f	TGV 6367 ①–④ B	TGV 6227 C	TGV 6227 D
0	**Paris** Gare de Lyon **342 351** d.	0649	0739	0739	0823	0938	1143y	1439	1454	1653	1653	1733	1854	1854	1906	1942	1942
441	Lyon St Exupéry ✈. **342 351** d.	|	|	|	|	|	|	1637	|	|	|	|	|	|	|	|	|
527	Valence TGV d.	0909	0958	0956	1038	1158	1400	|	1709	1911r	1916r	1958	2109	2109	2129	2158	2158
676	**Nîmes** Pont-du-Gard d.	0948	|	|	1119	|	1439	|	1749	1952	|	|	2149	2149	2209	|	2239
	Nîmes Centre d.	|	1046	1046	|	1246	|	1746	|	|	2003	2046	|	|	|	2246	|
	Montpellier Saint-Roch a.	|	1111	1111	|	1312	|	1811	|	|	2029	2111	|	|	|	2311	|
	Montpellier Saint-Roch d.	|	...	1117	|	1318	|	...	|	|	...	2117	|	|	|	...	|
730	**Montpellier** Sud-de-France a.	1008	...	|	1138	|	1459	...	1808	2011	...	|	2208	2208	2228	...	2258
	Montpellier Sud-de-France d.	1017	...	|	1143	|	1510	...	1817	2020	...	|	...	2217	...	...	...
759	Sète d.	1034	...	1134	1200	1335	1528	...	1834	2037	...	2134	...	2233	...	...	...
782	Agde d.	1051	...	1151	1217	1355	1544	...	1851	2052	...	2151	...	2249	...	...	...
803	Béziers d.	1106	...	1206	1232	1410	1559	...	1906	2106	...	2206	...	2303	...	...	...
829	**Narbonne** a.	1120	...	1220	1246	1424	1613	...	1920	2120	...	2220	...	2316	...	...	...
892	**Perpignan** a.	1156	...	1256z	1324	1458	1652	...	1956	2156	...	2256	...	2354	...	...	...
	Barcelona Sants **13 657** a.	...	...	...	...	1627	...	...	2125	...	...	...	...	...	...	...	...

All services 🅁	TGV 6200 Ⓐ v	TGV 6250 Ⓐ v	TGV 6250 ⑥ k	TGV 6202	TGV 7872 ⊠	TGV 6252 ⑦ E	TGV 6252	TGV 9708	TGV 6258 Ⓑ h	TGV 6206 ⑦ e◇	TGV 6206	TGV 7882 H ⊠	TGV 9704	TGV 6262 ⑤ F	TGV 6262 ⑦ E	TGV 6260
Barcelona Sants **13 657** d.	...	...	...	...	...	...	...	1033	...	...	...	...	1432	...	...	...
Perpignan d.	...	0604	...	0704	...	1004	...	1204	1304	1404	...	1504	1604	...	1704	1804
Narbonne d.	...	0642	...	0742	...	1042	...	1242	1342	1441	...	1542	1642	...	1742	1843
Béziers d.	...	0658	...	0758	...	1058	...	1258	1358	1457	...	1559	1658	...	1800	1900
Agde d.	...	0711	...	0811	...	1112	...	1312	1412	1511	...	1613	1711	...	1814	1914
Sète d.	...	0727	...	0827	...	1128	...	1328	1428	1527	...	1630	1727	...	1830	1930
Montpellier Sud-de-France a.	...	0743	...	|	...	1145	...	|	1443	|	...	1645	|	...	1845	1945
Montpellier Sud-de-France d.	...	0750	0752	|	...	1152	1152	|	1450	|	...	1652	|	1851	1852	1952
Montpellier Saint-Roch a.	...	|	|	0843	...	|	|	1344	|	1543	...	|	1743	|	|	|
Montpellier Saint-Roch d.	0550	|	|	0850	1024	|	|	1350	|	1550	1550	|	1751	|	|	|
Nîmes Centre d.	0619	|	|	0919	1053	|	|	1419	|	1619	1619	|	1822	|	|	|
Nîmes Pont-du-Gard d.	|	0813	0813	|	|	1214	1214	|	1516	|	|	1720	|	1913	1914	2013
Valence TGV d.	0705	0853	0853	1005	|	1253	1253	1505	1555	1704	1704	1759	1906	1952	1954	2053
Lyon St Exupéry ✈.. **342 351** d.	|	|	|	|	1202	|	|	|	|	|	|	|	|	|	|	|
Paris Gare de Lyon . **342 351** a.	0921	1107	1107	1218	1400t	1509	1509t	1721	1818	1921	1921	2022	2121	2214	2214	2308

TGV services from / to / via Lyon and Montpellier.
Timings may vary by a few minutes (please check your reservation).

km	All services 🅁	TGV 6821 ⊗	TGV 7813 ⊠	TGV 5300	TGV 6823 Ⓒ w	TGV 5521 △	TGV 7867 ⊠T	TGV 9812 Ⓒ w	TGV 9812 Ⓐ v	TGV 6823 Ⓐ v	TGV 9826	TGV 5336 ⑦ e	TGV 9879 L▽	TGV 6825	TGV 5120 G	TGV 9836 ⑤ Y	TGV 9836 ①–④ U	TGV 9836 J	TGV 9836 X
	Brussels Midi **11** d.	...	...	...	...	...	...	0817	0817	...	1017	...	...	...	...	1617	1617	1617	1617
	Lille Europe **11** d.	...	...	...	...	...	...	0903	0903	...	1103	...	...	...	1518	1703	1703	1703	1703
	Charles de Gaulle ✈ **11** d.	...	...	...	...	...	0854	0958	0958	...	1158	...	...	...	1627	1758	1758	1758	1758
	Marne la Vallée - Chessy **11** d.	...	...	...	...	...	0910	1012	1012	...	1211	...	...	...	1642	1811	1811	1811	1811
	Metz **379** d.	...	...	...	...	0546	|	|	|	...	|	...	1212	...	|	|	|	|	|
	Strasbourg **379** d.	...	...	...	...	0647	|	|	|	...	|	...	1306	...	|	|	|	|	|
	Dijon Ville **379** d.	...	...	...	...	0921	|	|	|	...	|	...	1521	...	|	|	|	|	|
	Nantes **335** d.	...	...	0448j	...	|	|	|	|	...	|	...	|	...	|	|	|	|	|
	Rennes **335** d.	...	...	|	...	|	|	|	|	...	|	1230	|	...	|	|	|	|	|
	Massy TGV d.	...	...	0724	...	|	|	|	|	...	|	1424	|	...	|	|	|	|	|
0	**Lyon** Part Dieu **350** d.	0640	0736p	0940	1010	1106	1110	1210	1210	1210	1410	1640	1710	1810	1840	2010	2010	2010	2010
	Lyon St Exupéry ✈ d.	|	|	|	|	|	|	|	|	|	|	|	|	|	|	|	|	|	|
104	Valence TGV **350** d.	0720	0818	1020	1047	|	1150	1250	1251	1251	1450	1718	1750	1850	1924	2050	2050	2050	2050
	Marseille St Charles .. **350** d.	|	|	|	|	|	|	|	|	|	|	|	|	|	|	|	|	|	|
	Aix en Provence TGV. **350** d.	|	|	|	|	|	|	|	|	|	|	|	|	|	|	|	|	|	|
	Avignon TGV **350** d.	|	|	|	|	|	|	|	|	|	|	|	|	|	|	|	|	|	|
	Nîmes Pont-du-Gard d.	|	|	1059	|	|	1232	|	|	|	1529	|	1829	|	|	2129	2130	|	|
263	**Nîmes** Centre d.	0807	0906	|	1137	1227	|	1336	1337	1337	|	1807	|	1936	2020	|	|	2136	2136
313	**Montpellier** Saint-Roch a.	0837	0931	|	1202	1254	|	1402	1402	1402	|	1834	|	2002	2054	|	|	2202	2202
	Montpellier Saint-Roch d.	0844	...	|	1206	...	|	...	...	1409	|	...	|	2007	...	|	|	2207	...
	Montpellier Sud-de-France a.	|	...	1120	|	...	1253	...	...	|	1550	...	1850	|	...	2149	2149	|	...
	Montpellier Sud-de-France d.	|	...	...	|	...	...	...	...	|	...	...	...	|	...	2154	...	|	...
340	Sète d.	0903	...	...	|	...	...	...	...	|	...	...	...	2024	...	2211	...	2224	...
363	Agde d.	|	...	...	|	...	...	...	...	|	...	...	...	|	...	2228	...	2241	...
384	Béziers d.	0930	...	...	1246	...	...	...	...	1447	...	...	...	2048	...	2241	...	2255	...
410	**Narbonne** a.	0944	...	...	1259	...	...	...	...	1500	...	...	...	2101	...	2254	...	2309	...
	Toulouse Matabiau **320** a.	1102	...	...	1415	...	...	...	...	1619	...	...	...	2219	...	|	...	|	...
473	**Perpignan** a.	...	...	...	...	...	...	...	...	...	...	...	...	...	...	2331	...	2345	...
	Barcelona Sants **13 657** a.	...	...	...	...	...	...	...	...	...	...	...	...	...	...	...	...	...	...

– ⑤⑥ Jan. 13 - Feb. 25; ①–⑥ Feb. 27 - Mar. 25; ⑤–⑦ from Mar. 31 (also Apr. 10, May 1, 8, 17, 18, 29).
– ①–④ Jan. 9 - Feb. 23; ①–④ from Mar. 27 (not Apr. 10, May 1, 8, 17, 18, 29).
– Ⓑ to Jan. 8; ⑦ Jan. 15 - Feb. 19; Ⓑ Feb. 26 - Mar. 26; ⑦ from Apr. 2 (also Apr. 10, May 1, 8).
– ⑤ Jan. 13 - Feb. 24; ①–⑤ from Mar. 27 (not Apr. 10, May 1, 8, 18, 19).
– ⑦ from Apr. 2 (also Apr. 10, May 1, 8, 29).
– ⑤ from Mar. 31 (also Apr. 17; not Apr. 19).
– ④⑤⑦ to Jan. 1; ⑤ Jan. 6 - Mar. 3; ④⑤⑦ from Mar. 9 (also Apr. 10, May 1, 8, 29; not Apr. 9, 30, May 7, 18, 19, 28).
– From Mar. 27.
– ⑤⑥ to Apr. 8; ⑥ from Apr. 15 (also May 19). Does not run Montpellier - Perpignan Feb. 17 - Mar. 4.
– From Luxembourg (Table **379**).
– From Tourcoing (d. 0744; see Table **11**).
– ①–④ from Apr. 11 (not May 1, 8, 17, 18).
– ⑦–④ to Apr. 10; ⑦ from Apr. 16 (also May 1, 8).
– ⑤ from Apr. 14 (also May 17, 18).

– Also Apr. 10, May 1, 8, 29.
– Not May 19.

h – Not May 18, 19.
j – 0451 until Mar. 19; 0504 on May 19, 20, 21, 28, 29.
k – Also May 18, 19.
p – Lyon **Perrache**.
r – Arrives 1905.
t – 6–9 minutes later on Apr. 11, 12, 25, 26.
v – Not May 19.
w – Also May 19.
y – 1136 on Apr. 18, 19.
z – 1307 on May 18, 19.

TGV – High-speed train. 🅁. 🍷.

◇ – Timings Perpiganan - Montpellier vary by up to 3 minutes on Apr. 23.
⊗ – Terminates at Montpellier Mar. 6–10, 13–17, 20–24.
△ – Runs 38–40 minutes later Lyon - Montpellier on Apr. 22, 23.
▽ – Runs 18–28 minutes later Lyon - Montpellier on Apr. 22, 23.
⊠ – OUIGO low-cost TGV service. Internet bookings only at www.ouigo.com

355 PARIS, LYON and MARSEILLE - MONTPELLIER - PERPIGNAN - PORTBOU

TGV services from / to / via Montpellier and Lyon.
Timings may vary by a few minutes (please check your reservation).

km	All services 🅁	*TGV*		*TGV*		*TGV*	*TGV*		*TGV*		*TGV*		*TGV*	*TGV*		*TGV*		*TGV*	*TGV*		*TGV*		*TGV*	*TGV*
		5156		**9898**		**9862**	**9862**		**6871**		**5158**		**5500**	**7860**		**9864**		**5358**	**5182**		**6873**		**7810**	**687**
		①⑤				①–⑤	⑥⑦				⑥													
		m		L		h	k▲				t		⊡	⊠									⊠	
	Barcelona Sants **13 657** .... d.	...	...	...	...	...	...	...	...	...	...	...	...	...	...	...	...	...	...	...	...	...	...	...
	Perpignan .... d.	...	...	...	...	...	0708	...	...	...	...	...	...	...	...	...	...	...	...	...	...	...	...	...
	Toulouse Matabiau **320** .... d.	...	...	...	...	...	|	...	0743	...	...	...	...	...	...	...	...	...	...	...	1543	...	...	174
	Narbonne .... d.	...	...	...	...	...	0749	...	0859	...	...	...	...	...	...	...	...	...	...	...	1659	...	...	185
	Béziers .... d.	...	...	...	...	...	0805	...	0915	...	...	...	...	...	...	...	...	...	...	...	1715	...	...	191
	Agde .... d.	...	...	...	...	...	0820	...	|	...	...	...	...	...	...	...	...	...	...	...	|	...	...	|
	Sète .... d.	...	...	...	...	...	0836	...	0939	...	...	...	...	...	...	...	...	...	...	...	1739	...	...	193
	Montpellier Sud-de-France .. a.	...	...	...	...	...	|	...	0955	...	...	...	...	...	...	...	...	...	...	...	|	...	...	200
	Montpellier Sud-de-France .. d.	...	...	...	...	0912	|	...	1005	...	...	...	...	1359	...	...	...	1641	1712	...	|	...	...	201
	Montpellier Saint-Roch .... a.	...	...	...	...	|	0854	...	|	...	...	...	...	|	...	...	...	|	|	...	1755	...	...	|
	Montpellier Saint-Roch .... d.	0528	...	0629	...	|	0859	...	|	...	1157	...	1358	|	...	1451	...	|	|	...	1759	...	1853	|
0	**Nîmes** Centre .... d.	0556	...	0700	...	|	0927	...	|	...	1226	...	1427	|	...	1519	...	|	|	...	1827	...	1922	|
	Nîmes Pont-du-Gard .... d.	|	...	|	...	0933	|	...	1029	...	|	...	|	1421	...	|	...	1702	1733	...	|	...	|	203
82	**Avignon** TGV .... **350** a.	|	...	|	...	|	|	...	|	...	|	...	|	|	...	|	...	|	|	...	|	...	|	|
116	Aix en Provence TGV. **350** a.	|	...	|	...	|	|	...	|	...	|	...	|	|	...	|	...	|	|	...	|	...	|	|
135	**Marseille** St Charles .. **350** a.	|	...	|	...	|	|	...	|	...	|	...	|	|	...	|	...	|	|	...	|	...	|	|
	Valence TGV .... **350** d.	0644	...	0748	...	1015	1015	...	1112	...	1313	...	1515	|	...	1615	...	1744	1815	...	1914	...	2015	211
	Lyon St Exupéry ✈ .... a.	|	...	|	...	|	|	...	|	...	|	...	|	1524	...	|	...	|	|	...	|	...	|	|
	Lyon Part Dieu .... **350** a.	0720	...	0824	...	1050	1050	...	1150	...	1347	...	1550	|	...	1649	...	1820	1850	...	1948	...	2050	215
	Massy TGV .... a.	|	...	|	...	|	|	...	...	...	|	...	|	|	...	|	...	2034	|	...	...	...	...	...
	Rennes **335** .... a.	|	...	|	...	|	|	...	...	...	|	...	|	|	...	|	...	|	|	...	...	...	...	...
	Nantes **335** .... a.	|	...	|	...	|	|	...	...	...	|	...	|	|	...	|	...	2309	|	...	...	...	...	...
	Dijon Ville **379** .... a.	|	...	0958j	...	|	|	...	...	...	|	...	1740	|	...	|	...	...	|	...	...	...	...	...
	Strasbourg **379** .... a.	|	...	1224j	...	|	|	...	...	...	|	...	2013	|	...	|	...	...	|	...	...	...	...	...
	Metz **379** .... a.	|	...	1319j	...	|	|	...	...	...	|	...	2113	|	...	|	...	...	|	...	...	...	...	...
	Marne la Vallée - Chessy **11** a.	0924	...	...	...	1251	1255	...	...	...	1547	...	...	1725	...	1849	...	...	2049	...	...	...	...	...
	Charles de Gaulle ✈ **11** .... a.	0937	...	...	...	1304	1309	...	...	...	1601	...	...	1739	...	1902	...	...	2102	...	...	...	...	...
	Lille Europe **11** .... a.	1042•	...	...	...	1424	1424	...	...	...	1657	...	...	1844•	...	1958	...	...	2157	...	...	...	...	...
	Brussels Midi **11** .... a.	...	...	...	...	1525	1525	...	...	...	...	...	...	...	...	2043	...	...	...	...	...	...	...	...

INTERCITÉS and *TER* services. See above and page 205 for *TGV* and *AVE* services. See Table **319** for overnight *Intercités de Nuit* service Paris - Portbou.
Warning! Services from Marseille are subject to alteration on June 10.

km							**4752**														**4756**				
		⑥	Ⓐ	⚒	Ⓐ	Ⓐ	①–⑥	Ⓐ	⚒	Ⓐ	⑥	Ⓐ	†	Ⓒ	Ⓐ	Ⓐ	Ⓐ	†	⚒	Ⓐ		Ⓐ	Ⓑ	Ⓒ	Ⓐ
							d													s	⊗				
							★🅁														★🅁				
0	**Marseille** St Charles .... **351** d.	...	...	...	...	...	...	...	...	...	...	...	...	...	...	0621	...	...	...	...	0722	...	...	...	...
23	Aéroport Marseille ✈ ‡ . **351** d.	...	...	...	...	...	...	...	...	...	...	...	...	...	...	0636	...	...	...	...	|	...	...	...	...
52	Miramas .... **351** d.	...	...	...	...	...	...	...	...	...	...	...	...	...	...	0656	...	...	...	...	|	...	...	...	...
86	Arles .... **351** d.	...	...	...	...	...	...	...	...	...	...	...	...	...	...	0716	...	...	...	...	0811	...	...	...	...
	Avignon Centre .... **357** d.	...	...	...	...	...	...	...	...	0615	...	0632	...	...	...	|	0717	...	0735	...	|	...	0833	...	...
100	Tarascon-sur-Rhône .... d.	...	...	...	...	...	...	...	...	0628	...	0645	...	...	...	0725	0731	...	0747	...	|	...	0845	...	...
118	**Nîmes** Pont-du-Gard .... d.	...	...	...	...	...	...	...	...	0644	...	0701	...	...	...	0739	0748	...	0803	...	|	...	0901	...	...
128	**Nîmes** Centre .... **357** d.	...	0513	0538	...	0605	0638	0651	0656	0656	...	0713	0713	...	...	0750	0759	...	0814	...	0838	0848	0913	...	...
154	Lunel .... d.	...	0530	0555	...	0631	|	0709	0716	0716	...	0731	0731	...	...	0808	0817	...	0832	...	|	0906	0931	...	...
178	**Montpellier** Saint-Roch .... a.	...	0547	0610	...	0647	0702	0725	0739	0739	...	0747	0747	...	...	0824	...	...	0847	...	0903	0922	0947	...	...
	Montpellier Saint-Roch .... d.	...	0551	0613	...	0655	0706	0729	...	0742	0751	0751	0751	...	...	0828	...	...	0853	...	0907	0926	0951	...	...
198	Frontignan .... d.	...	0603	0630	...	0706	|	0746	...	0758	0802	0802	0803	...	...	0840	...	...	0905	...	|	0940	1004	...	...
205	Sète .... d.	...	0611	0637	...	0713	|	0753	...	0804	0809	0809	0809	...	...	0847	...	...	0912	...	0923	0947	1011	...	...
228	Agde .... d.	...	0625	0653	...	0727	|	0809	...	...	0824	0824	0824	...	...	0902	...	...	0926	...	|	1001	1025	...	...
249	Béziers .... d.	...	0638	0708	...	0740	0746	0824	...	...	0837	0837	0837	...	...	0915	...	...	0939	...	|	1014	1038	...	...
	Toulouse Matabiau **320** ... d.	...	|	|	...	|	|	|	...	...	|	|	|	0713	0716	|	...	...	|	...	|	|	|	0917	091
275	**Narbonne** .... a.	...	0652	0724	...	0753	0759	0841	...	...	0850	0850	0850	0850	0852	0928	...	...	0952	...	1001	1028	1052	1052	105
	Narbonne .... d.	0703	0706	0727	0736	0807	0802	...	...	...	...	...	...	0858	0903	...	...	1006	1006	...	1004	...	...	1105	110
	Toulouse Matabiau **320** ... a.	|	|	0912	|	|	0918	...	...	...	...	...	...	|	|	...	...	|	|	...	1118	...	...	|	|
	Bordeaux St Jean **320** .❦ a.	|	|	...	|	|	1132	...	...	...	...	...	...	|	|	...	...	|	|	...	1337z	...	...	|	|
296	Port la Nouvelle .... d.	0715	0719	...	0750	0819	...	...	...	...	...	...	...	0911	0916	...	...	1019	1019	...	...	...	...	1118	111
330	Rivesaltes .... d.	0738	0742	...	0813	0842	...	...	...	...	...	...	...	0935	0939	...	...	1042	1042	...	...	...	...	1142	114
338	**Perpignan** .... a.	0744	0748	...	0820	0848	...	...	...	...	...	...	...	0942	0945	...	...	1048	1049	...	...	...	...	1148	114
	Perpignan .... d.	0751	0755	...	...	0855	...	...	...	...	...	...	...	0949	...	...	...	...	...	1055	...	...	...	1155	...
360	Argelès sur Mer .... d.	0807	0812	...	...	0910	...	...	...	...	...	...	...	1007	...	...	...	...	...	1112	...	...	...	1210	...
365	Collioure .... d.	0812	0817	...	...	0915	...	...	...	...	...	...	...	1011	...	...	...	...	...	1117	...	...	...	1215	...
368	Port Vendres .... d.	0815	0821	...	...	0919	...	...	...	...	...	...	...	1015	...	...	...	...	...	1121	...	...	...	1219	...
373	Banyuls sur Mer .... d.	0820	0827	...	...	0924	...	...	...	...	...	...	...	1020	...	...	...	...	...	1126	...	...	...	1224	...
380	Cerbère .... **657** a.	0826	0833	...	...	0929	...	...	...	...	...	...	...	1026	...	...	...	...	...	1133	...	...	...	1230	...
382	**Portbou** .... **657** a.	0840	0847	...	...	0947	...	...	...	...	...	...	...	1040	...	...	...	...	...	1147	...	...	...	1241	...

NOTES for pages 206 and 207.

B – Ⓑ Feb. 26 - May 8 (not Mar. 27–31, Apr. 3–7); ⑦ from May 14 (also May 19, 29). On ①–⑤ Feb. 27 - Mar. 24, ①–⑤ Apr. 11–28 and May 2–5 departs Avignon 2138 and does not call at Nîmes Pont-du-Gard.
H – ⑦ (also Apr. 10, May 8, 29; not Feb. 19, 26, Apr. 9, 23, 30, May 7, 28). To St Chély d'Apcher (Table **332**).
L – To Luxembourg (Table **379**).

d – Not May 29.
f – ⑤–⑦ (also Apr. 10). Departs Toulouse 1715 on Mar. 18, 19, 25, 26.
h – Not May 18, 19.
j – On Apr. 23 arrives Dijon 1027, Strasbourg 1257, Metz 1350.
k – Also May 18, 19.
m – Also Apr. 11, May 2, 9, 30; not Jan. 9 - Mar. 6, Apr. 10, May 1, 8, 19, 29.
r – Until Feb. 26 Narbonne a. 1401, d. 1404, Toulouse a. 1518.
s – Not Mar. 13–17, 20–24, 27–31, Apr. 3–7.
t – Also May 18; not May 20.
u – ①–④ (not Apr. 10). Departs Toulouse 1715 Mar. 13–23.
v – Not May 19.
y – Not Mar. 6–24.
z – 3–10 minutes earlier until Feb. 26.

TGV – High-speed train. 🅁. 🍸.

• – Lille **Flandres**.
▲ – Does not run Perpiganan - Montpellier Feb. 18 - Mar. 5.
△ – Subject to alteration on May 18, 19, 20, 27, 28.
⊡ – Subject to alteration on Apr. 22, 23.
⊗ – Does not run Narbonne - Bordeaux Mar. 6–10, 13–17, 20–24.
❦ – Journeys to / from Bordeaux are subject to alteration Apr. 8–10, May 6–8, 18–21, 27, 2
◧ – Timings may vary by up to 4 minutes on Apr. 10.
‡ – Vitrolles Aéroport Marseille-Provence ✈. A shuttle bus runs to / from the airport termina (journey time: 5 minutes).
★ – *INTERCITÉS*. 🅁. 🍸.
⊠ – OUIGO low-cost TGV service. Internet bookings only at www.ouigo.com

PORTBOU - PERPIGNAN - MONTPELLIER - MARSEILLE, LYON and PARIS 355

TER services. See pages 205 and 206 for *TGV*, *AVE* and *INTERCITÉS* services. See Table **319** for overnight *Intercités de Nuit* services Paris - Portbou and Cerbère - Paris.
Warning! Services from / to Marseille are subject to alteration on June 10.

km			Ⓐ	Ⓒ	Ⓐ	4758 ★R	Ⓐ	Ⓐ	Ⓒ		4760 ★R	Ⓐ	Ⓐ	Ⓐ	Ⓒ		Ⓑ	⑥	4762 ★R	Ⓐ	Ⓐ	Ⓐ		Ⓒ	Ⓐ
	Marseille St Charles **351** d.	0823	...	...	...	0927	...	...	...	...	1124	...	...	...	...	1222	...	...	1323	...	...	...	...	...	...
	Aéroport Marseille ✈ ‡ **351** d.	0837	...	...	...	|	...	...	...	...	|	...	...	...	...	1237	...	...	|	...	...	...	...	...	...
	Miramas **351** d.	0856	...	...	...	|	...	...	...	...	|	...	...	...	...	1256	...	...	|	...	...	...	...	...	...
	Arles **351** d.	0916	...	...	...	|	...	...	...	...	1208	...	...	...	...	1316	...	...	|	...	...	...	...	...	...
0	**Avignon** Centre **357** d.	|	...	0929	0931	|	...	...	...	1132	|	1216	...	...	...	|	1332	1332	|	...	...	...	...	...	...
21	Tarascon-sur-Rhône d.	0925	...	0944	0945	|	...	...	...	1147	|	1229	...	...	...	1325	1346	1346	|	...	...	...	...	...	...
39	**Nîmes** Pont-du-Gard d.	0939	...	1002	1002	|	...	...	...	1203	|	1244	...	...	...	1339	1402	1402	|	...	...	...	...	...	...
49	**Nîmes** Centre **357** d.	0950	...	1013	1013	1038	...	...	...	1214	1238	1257	...	...	...	1351	1414	1414	1438	...	1513	...	...	...	...
	Lunel d.	1008	1012	1031	1031	|	...	...	...	1232	|	1317	...	...	...	1409	1431	1432	|	...	1531	...	...	...	...
	Montpellier Saint-Roch a.	1025	1035	1047	1047	1103	...	...	...	1248	1302	1341	...	...	...	1425	1447	1448	1502	...	1547	...	...	...	...
	Montpellier Saint-Roch d.	...	1038	1051	1051	1107	1151	...	...	1252	1306	...	1351	...	...	1429	1451	1452	1506	...	1551	...	...	...	...
	Frontignan d.	...	1050	1103	1104	|	1203	...	...	1304	|	...	1403	...	...	1446	1504	1504	|	...	1603	...	...	...	...
	Sète d.	...	1055	1111	1111	|	1211	...	...	1311	1322	...	1411	...	...	1453	1511	1511	|	...	1611	...	...	...	...
	Agde d.	...	...	1125	1125	|	1225	...	...	1325	|	...	1425	...	...	1510	1525	1525	|	...	1625	...	...	...	...
	Béziers d.	...	...	1138	1138	1147	1238	...	...	1338	|	...	1438	...	...	1526	1538	1538	1546	...	1638	...	...	...	...
	Toulouse Matabiau **320** d.	...	...	|	|	|	|	1117	1117	|	|	...	|	1317y	1317	|	|	|	|	...	|	1518	...	1514	...
	Narbonne a.	...	...	1152	1152	1201	1255	1253	1257	1352	1357r	...	1453	1452y	1453	1542	1552	1552	1559	...	1652	1651	...	1651	...
	Narbonne d.	...	...	...	1206	1204	...	1304	1309	1406	1400r	...	...	1505	1506	...	1606	1606	1602	...	...	1704	...	1704	1737
	Toulouse Matabiau **320** a.	...	...	...	|	1319	...	|	|	|	1512r	...	...	|	|	...	|	|	1718	...	...	|	...	|	|
	Bordeaux St Jean **320** a.	...	...	...	|	1538z	...	|	|	|	1732	...	...	|	|	...	|	|	1942z	...	...	|	...	|	|
	Port la Nouvelle d.	...	...	...	1218	...	...	1317	1322	1419	...	...	...	1518	1522	...	1618	1619	...	...	...	1717	...	1719	1750
	Rivesaltes d.	...	...	...	1243	...	...	1340	1346	1442	...	...	...	1542	1546	...	1641	1642	...	...	...	1742	...	1742	1813
	Perpignan a.	...	...	...	1248	...	...	1347	1352	1448	...	...	...	1549	1554	...	1647	1648	...	...	...	1748	...	1748	1818
	Perpignan d.	...	...	...	1255	...	...	...	1400	1455	...	...	...	...	1601	...	1655	...	...	1723	...	...	1755	1755	1823
	Argelès sur Mer d.	...	...	...	1312	...	...	...	1415	1512	...	...	...	...	1618	...	1712	...	...	1739	...	...	1811	1811	1839
	Collioure d.	...	...	...	1317	...	...	...	1420	1517	...	...	...	...	1623	...	1717	...	...	1744	...	...	1816	1816	1844
	Port Vendres d.	...	...	...	1321	...	...	...	1424	1521	...	...	...	...	1627	...	1721	...	...	1748	...	...	1820	1820	1848
	Banyuls sur Mer d.	...	...	...	1326	...	...	...	1429	1526	...	...	...	...	1632	...	1726	...	...	1753	...	...	1825	1825	1853
	Cerbère **657** a.	...	...	...	1333	...	...	...	1435	1533	...	...	...	...	1639	...	1733	...	...	1800	...	...	1830	1830	1900
	Portbou **657** a.	...	...	...	1347	...	...	...	1449	1547	...	...	...	...	1652	...	1747	...	...	...	...	...	1845	1845	...

	Ⓐ	Ⓒ	4764 ★R	Ⓐ	①–④ u	⑤–⑦ f	Ⓑ	Ⓐ	⑦ H	Ⓐ	Ⓒ	Ⓐ	Ⓐ	⑥	†	Ⓐ	4766 ★R				⑥	Ⓑ	4770 Ⓐ v ★R	Ⓑ	B
Marseille St Charles **351** d.	...	...	1527	...	...	...	...	...	...	1623	1623	...	...	...	...	...	1728	...	...	1821	...	...	1923	...	...
Aéroport Marseille ✈ ‡ **351** d.	...	...	|	...	...	...	...	...	...	1637	1637	...	...	...	...	...	|	...	...	1837	...	...	|	...	...
Miramas **351** d.	...	...	|	...	...	...	...	...	...	1656	1657	...	...	...	...	...	|	...	...	1856	...	...	|	...	...
Arles **351** d.	...	...	|	...	...	...	...	...	...	1716	1717	...	...	...	...	...	|	...	...	1916	...	...	|	...	...
Avignon Centre **357** d.	1526	1531	|	...	...	...	...	1631	...	|	|	...	1719	1732	1732	1732	|	1826	...	|	1932	1932	|	...	2137
Tarascon-sur-Rhône d.	1546	1547	|	...	...	...	...	1644	...	1725	1727	...	|	1745	1745	1745	|	1845	...	1926	1947	1947	|	...	|
Nîmes Pont-du-Gard d.	1606	1603	|	...	...	...	...	1701	...	1739	1741	...	|	1801	1801	1801	|	1901	...	1940	2004	2003	|	...	2203
Nîmes Centre **357** d.	1617	1614	1638	1649	...	...	1713	1713	...	1751	1753	...	1801	1812	1814	1814	1839	1913	...	1951	2012	2014	2038	2214	2214
Lunel d.	1634	1632	|	1709	...	...	1731	1731	...	1808	1812	1812	1825	1831	1832	1835	|	1931	...	2009	...	2033	|	2232	2232
Montpellier Saint-Roch a.	1649	1648	1703	1725	...	...	1746	1746	...	1824	1829	1835	1840	1847	1849	1851	1903	1948	...	2025	...	2049	2103	2248	2248
Montpellier Saint-Roch d.	1653	1652	1707	1729	...	...	1750	1750	1755	1828	1833	1838	...	1851	1853	1855	1907	1952	...	2029	...	2053	2107	2252	2252
Frontignan d.	1704	1704	|	1740	...	...	1803	1803	1809	1840	1854	1855	...	1905	1905	1908	|	2004	...	2040	...	2105	|	2304	2304
Sète d.	1712	1712	|	1747	...	...	1811	1811	1819	1846	1901	1902	...	1911	1911	1915	|	2011	...	2047	...	2112	|	2311	2311
Agde d.	1726	1726	|	1801	...	...	1825	1825	1831	1900	1920	1919	...	1927	1927	1929	|	2025	...	2101	...	2126	|	2326	2326
Béziers d.	1739	1739	1747	1814	...	...	1838	1838	1844	1914	1935	1934	...	1942	1942	1942	1947	2038	...	2113	...	2139	2147	2340	2340
Toulouse Matabiau **320** d.	|	|	|	|	1717	1717	|	|	...	|	|	|	...	|	|	|	|	|	1919	|	...	|	|	|	|
Narbonne a.	1753	1753	1801	1828	1851	1851	1852	1852	...	1928	1951	1950	...	1956	1956	1955	2002	2052	2053	2128	...	2153	2201	2356	2356
Narbonne d.	1807	1806	1804	1835	1904	1904	...	...	...	...	...	...	...	...	2008	2006	2005	...	2108	...	...	2206	2204	...	...
Toulouse Matabiau **320** a.	|	|	1918	|	|	|	...	...	...	...	...	...	...	...	|	|	2118	...	|	...	...	|	2318	...	...
Bordeaux St Jean **320** a.	|	|	2139z	|	|	|	...	...	...	...	...	...	...	...	|	|	2337z	...	|	...	...	|	...	...	...
Port la Nouvelle d.	1820	1819	...	1847	1917	1917	...	...	...	...	...	...	...	...	2021	2019	...	...	2121	...	...	2219	...	...	...
Rivesaltes d.	1843	1844	...	1910	1941	1941	...	...	...	...	...	...	...	...	2044	2042	...	...	2144	...	...	2242	...	...	...
Perpignan a.	1848	1851	...	1916	1948	1948	...	...	...	...	...	...	...	...	2049	2048	...	...	2150	...	...	2248	...	...	...
Perpignan d.	1855	...	...	...	...	1955	...	...	...	...	...	...	...	...	...	2055	...	...	...	...	...	...	...	...	...
Argelès sur Mer d.	1912	...	...	...	...	2012	...	...	...	...	...	...	...	...	...	2111	...	...	...	...	...	...	...	...	...
Collioure d.	1917	...	...	...	...	2017	...	...	...	...	...	...	...	...	...	2116	...	...	...	...	...	...	...	...	...
Port Vendres d.	1921	...	...	...	...	2021	...	...	...	...	...	...	...	...	...	2119	...	...	...	...	...	...	...	...	...
Banyuls sur Mer d.	1926	...	...	...	...	2026	...	...	...	...	...	...	...	...	...	2124	...	...	...	...	...	...	...	...	...
Cerbère **657** a.	1933	...	...	...	...	2033	...	...	...	...	...	...	...	...	...	2130	...	...	...	...	...	...	...	...	...
Portbou **657** a.	1947	...	...	...	...	...	...	...	...	...	...	...	...	...	...	...	...	...	...	...	...	...	...	...	...

	Ⓐ	Ⓐ		Ⓐ	Ⓐ	Ⓐ	Ⓐ	Ⓐ	Ⓐ	Ⓒ	Ⓐ	Ⓐ	⚒	Ⓐ		Ⓐ	Ⓒ	4651 Ⓐ v ★R	Ⓐ	Ⓒ		Ⓐ	Ⓐ	Ⓐ	Ⓒ ◧
Portbou **657** d.	...	...	...	...	...	...	...	...	...	...	...	...	...	...	...	...	...	...	...	...	...	...	...	...	...
Cerbère **657** d.	...	...	...	...	...	...	...	...	...	...	...	0526	...	...	...	0626	...	...	...	...	...	0703	0723	...	0726
Banyuls sur Mer d.	...	...	...	...	...	...	...	...	...	...	...	0532	...	...	...	0632	...	...	...	...	...	0710	0729	...	0732
Port Vendres d.	...	...	...	...	...	...	...	...	...	...	...	0538	...	...	...	0638	...	...	...	...	...	0715	0735	...	0738
Collioure d.	...	...	...	...	...	...	...	...	...	...	...	0542	...	...	...	0642	...	...	...	...	...	0719	0739	...	0742
Argelès sur Mer d.	...	...	...	...	...	...	...	...	...	...	...	0547	...	...	...	0647	...	...	...	...	...	0724	0744	...	0747
Perpignan a.	...	...	...	...	...	...	...	...	...	...	...	0603	...	...	...	0703	...	...	...	...	...	0740	0800	...	0803
Perpignan d.	...	...	...	...	...	...	0540	...	...	...	...	...	0624	0638	...	0710	0712	...	...	...	...	0745	0807	...	0810
Rivesaltes d.	...	...	...	...	...	...	0547	...	...	...	...	...	0631	0644	...	0717	0719	...	...	...	...	0751	0814	...	0817
Port la Nouvelle d.	...	...	...	...	...	...	0611	...	...	...	...	...	0655	0709	...	0740	0743	...	...	...	...	0815	0838	...	0840
Bordeaux St Jean **320** d.	...	...	...	...	...	...	|	...	...	...	...	...	|	|	...	|	|	...	...	...	...	|	|	...	|
Toulouse Matabiau **320** d.	...	...	...	...	...	...	|	...	...	...	...	...	|	|	...	|	|	0645	...	...	...	|	|	...	|
Narbonne a.	...	...	...	...	...	...	0625	...	...	...	...	...	0710	0722	...	0754	0756	0758	←	...	...	0829	0852	...	0854
Narbonne d.	...	...	0534	...	0600	0615	...	0634	...	0646	0709	...	0719	...	...	0809	...	0801	0809	0809	...	0834	0906y	0906	0906
Toulouse Matabiau **320** a.	...	...	|	...	|	|	...	|	...	|	|	...	0858	...	...	→	...	|	|	|	...	|	1040y	|	|
Béziers d.	0443	...	0549	...	0615	0633	...	0649	...	0709	0724	...	...	...	...	...	...	0817	0824	0824	...	0849	...	0921	0921
Agde d.	0457	...	0601	...	0630	0647	...	0701	...	0729	0736	...	...	...	...	...	...	|	0836	0837	...	0901	...	0933	0933
Sète d.	0514	...	0616	...	0646	0704	...	0716	0730	0747	0751	...	...	...	...	...	...	|	0851	0851	...	0916	...	0947	0947
Frontignan d.	0520	...	0622	...	0651	0709	...	0721	0736	0753	0757	...	...	...	...	...	...	|	0857	0857	...	0922	...	0953	0953
Montpellier Saint-Roch a.	0532	...	0633	...	0709	0726	...	0734	0755	0809	0809	...	...	...	...	...	...	0853	0909	0909	...	0935	...	1004	1004
Montpellier Saint-Roch d.	0535	...	0637	0642	0713	0729	...	0738	0758	0812	0813	...	...	...	...	...	...	0857	0913	0913	...	...	...	1008	1008
Lunel d.	0552	...	0655	0659	0729	0750	...	0755	0814	0828	0830	...	...	...	...	...	...	|	0930	0930	...	...	...	1026	1026
Nîmes Centre **357** d.	0611	0642	0714	0728	0750	...	...	0814	0844	0848	0850	...	...	...	...	...	...	0924	0947	0951	...	...	...	1046	1046
Nîmes Pont-du-Gard d.	0623	0651	0724	0737	0759	...	...	0823	|	0858	0900	...	...	...	...	...	...	|	...	1004	...	...	...	1056	1056
Tarascon-sur-Rhône d.	0636	0707	0736	0752	0815	...	...	0838	|	0912	0915	...	...	...	...	...	...	|	...	1017	...	...	...	1113	1113
Avignon Centre **357** a.	|	0720	|	0804	0829	...	...	|	0922	0924	0927	...	...	...	...	...	...	|	...	|	...	...	...	1128	1128
Arles **351** d.	0645	...	0744	...	...	...	...	0846	...	...	...	...	...	...	...	...	...	|	...	1026	...	...	...	...	...
Miramas **351** d.	0706	...	0806	...	...	...	...	0908	...	...	...	...	...	...	...	...	...	|	...	1048	...	...	...	...	...
Aéroport Marseille ✈ ‡ **351** d.	0723	...	0823	...	...	...	...	0924	...	...	...	...	...	...	...	...	...	|	...	1104	...	...	...	...	...
Marseille St Charles **351** a.	0739	...	0839	...	...	...	...	0941	...	...	...	...	...	...	...	...	...	1033	...	1120	...	...	...	...	...

← FOR NOTES SEE PREVIOUS PAGE 206

355 PORTBOU - PERPIGNAN - MONTPELLIER - MARSEILLE, LYON and PARIS

TER services. See pages 205 and 206 for *TGV*, *AVE* and *INTERCITÉS* services. See Table **319** for overnight *Intercités de Nuit* service Cerbère - Paris.
Warning! Services to Marseille are subject to alteration on June 10.

		4655								4657									4659						
	Ⓐ				⑥	†	Ⓑ	Ⓐ	Ⓐ		Ⓐ	Ⓐ		Ⓐ	Ⓒ	Ⓐ	Ⓐ	⚒		Ⓐ	Ⓒ	Ⓐ	Ⓒ		Ⓐ
	⊗	⊡									s								w						
		★ [R]								★ [R]									★ [R]						
Portbou **657** d.	...	...	...	...	0905	...	...	...	...	...	1005	...	...	...	1105	...	...	1205	...	...	...	...	1305	...	...
Cerbère **657** d.	0824	...	...	...	0927	0926	...	...	...	...	1026	...	...	...	1126	...	...	1226	...	...	...	...	1329	...	...
Banyuls sur Mer d.	0830	...	...	...	0934	0934	...	...	...	...	1032	...	...	...	1132	...	...	1232	...	...	...	...	1335	...	...
Port Vendres d.	0836	...	...	...	0939	0941	...	...	...	...	1038	...	...	...	1138	...	...	1238	...	...	...	...	1340	...	...
Collioure d.	0839	...	...	...	0943	0946	...	...	...	...	1042	...	...	...	1141	...	...	1242	...	...	...	...	1344	...	...
Argelès sur Mer d.	0845	...	...	...	0948	0952	...	...	...	...	1047	...	...	...	1147	...	...	1247	...	...	...	...	1348	...	...
Perpignan a.	0903	...	...	...	1003	1009	...	...	...	...	1103	...	...	...	1203	...	...	1303	...	...	...	...	1403	...	...
Perpignan d.	0910	...	...	...	1010	1016	1016	...	...	...	...	1110	...	...	1210	...	1227	1310	...	...	...	1400	1410	...	...
Rivesaltes d.	0917	...	...	...	1017	1022	1022	...	...	...	...	1117	...	...	1216	...	1234	1317	...	...	...	1406	1417	...	...
Port la Nouvelle d.	0941	...	...	...	1040	1046	1046	...	...	...	...	1141	...	...	1240	...	1258	1340	...	...	...	1430	1441	...	...
Bordeaux St Jean **320** .. ❦ d.	|	0627	...	...	|	|	|	...	...	0826	...	|	...	...	|	...	|	|	1027	...	...	|	|	...	...
Toulouse Matabiau **320** d.	|	0845	...	...	|	|	|	...	...	1045	...	|	...	...	|	...	|	|	1245	...	...	|	|	...	...
Narbonne a.	0955	0958	...	...	1054	1102	1102	...	...	1158	...	1154	...	...	1254	...	1312	1355	1358	...	...	1444	1454	...	...
Narbonne d.	...	1001	1009	...	1113	1115	1115	...	...	1201	...	1209	...	1215	1309	1309	1321	...	1401	1434	...	1453	1509	1509	...
Toulouse Matabiau **320** a.	...	|	|	...	1256	1256	1256	...	...	|	...	|	...	|	|	|	1457	...	|	|	...	1633	1644	|	...
Béziers d.	...	1018	1024	...	...	...	...	...	...	|	...	1224	...	1233	1324	1324	...	...	1417	1448	...	...	...	1524	...
Agde d.	...	|	1036	...	...	...	...	...	...	|	...	1236	...	1248	1336	1336	...	...	|	1501	...	...	...	1536	...
Sète d.	...	|	1051	...	...	...	...	1112	...	1236	...	1251	...	1306	1351	1351	...	...	|	1515	...	...	...	1551	...
Frontignan d.	...	|	1057	...	...	...	...	1118	...	|	...	1257	...	1312	1356	1357	...	...	|	1521	...	...	...	1557	...
Montpellier Saint-Roch a.	...	1054	1109	...	...	...	...	1136	...	1254	...	1309	...	1330	1409	1409	...	...	1454	1532	...	...	...	1609	...
Montpellier Saint-Roch d.	...	1058	1113	...	...	...	...	1139	1227	1258	...	1313	1313	...	...	1413	...	...	1458	1536	1538	...	...	1613	...
Lunel d.	...	|	1130	...	...	...	...	1159	1249	|	...	1330	1330	...	...	1430	...	...	|	1553	1555	...	...	1630	1635
Nîmes Centre **357** d.	...	1125	1150	...	...	...	...	...	1313	1325	...	1350	1350	...	...	1450	...	...	1525	1613	1614	...	...	1650	1706
Nîmes Pont-du-Gard d.	...	|	1159	...	...	...	...	...	|	|	...	1359	1359	...	...	1459	...	...	|	1622	1623	...	...	1659	1714
Tarascon-sur-Rhône d.	...	|	1215	...	...	...	...	...	|	|	...	1415	1415	...	...	1515	...	...	|	1636	1636	...	...	1715	1728
Avignon Centre **357** a.	...	|	1229	...	...	...	...	...	1400	|	...	1428	1428	...	...	1530	...	...	|	|	|	...	...	1727	1742
Arles **351** d.	...	|	...	...	...	...	...	...	...	1352	...	...	...	...	...	...	...	...	|	1644	1645	...	...	...	...
Miramas **351** d.	...	|	...	...	...	...	...	...	...	|	...	...	...	...	...	...	...	...	|	1707	1708	...	...	...	...
Aéroport Marseille ✈ ‡ d.	...	|	...	...	...	...	...	...	...	|	...	...	...	...	...	...	...	...	|	1728	1727	...	...	...	...
Marseille St Charles **351** a.	...	1234	...	...	...	...	...	...	...	1438	...	...	...	...	...	...	...	...	1637	1747	1747	...	...	...	...

	4661								4663								4665							4669	
		⑥	Ⓑ		Ⓐ	Ⓒ		Ⓐ			Ⓒ	Ⓐ	Ⓒ	Ⓐ	Ⓑ	Ⓐ		Ⓐ			Ⓒ	Ⓐ		Ⓑ	Ⓐ
																r	△							▽	
	★ [R]								★ [R]								★ [R]							★ [R]	
Portbou **657** d.	...	...	1405	...	...	1505	...	...	...	1605	...	...	1705	...	...	...	...	1805	...	...	1905	...	...	...	2005
Cerbère **657** d.	...	...	1426	...	...	1526	...	...	...	1626	...	...	1727	...	...	...	...	1826	...	...	1926	...	...	...	2026
Banyuls sur Mer d.	...	...	1432	...	...	1532	...	...	...	1632	...	...	1734	...	...	...	...	1832	...	...	1932	...	...	...	2032
Port Vendres d.	...	...	1438	...	...	1538	...	...	...	1638	...	...	1739	...	...	...	...	1838	...	...	1937	...	...	...	2038
Collioure d.	...	...	1442	...	...	1542	...	...	...	1642	...	...	1743	...	...	...	...	1842	...	...	1941	...	...	...	2042
Argelès sur Mer d.	...	...	1447	...	...	1547	...	...	...	1647	...	...	1748	...	...	...	...	1847	...	...	1946	...	...	...	2047
Perpignan a.	...	...	1503	...	...	1603	...	...	...	1703	...	...	1803	...	...	...	...	1903	...	...	2002	...	...	...	2103
Perpignan d.	...	1510	1510	...	1609	1610	...	...	...	1710	...	...	1810	1810	...	...	...	1910	1910	...	2009	2010	...	...	...
Rivesaltes d.	...	1517	1517	...	1616	1617	...	...	...	1717	...	...	1817	1817	...	...	...	1917	1917	...	2016	2017	...	...	...
Port la Nouvelle d.	...	1541	1540	...	1640	1640	...	...	...	1740	...	...	1841	1841	...	...	...	1941	1941	...	2042	2041	...	...	...
Bordeaux St Jean **320** .. ❦ d.	1228	|	|	...	|	|	...	...	1426	|	...	...	|	|	...	...	1628	|	|	...	|	|	...	1828	...
Toulouse Matabiau **320** d.	1445	|	|	...	|	|	...	...	1644	|	1650	1650	|	|	...	...	1845	|	|	...	|	|	...	2045	...
Narbonne a.	1558	1554	1555	...	1653	1653	...	...	1758	1754	1828	1828	1854	1854	...	...	1958	1954	1954	...	2057	2054	...	2158	...
Narbonne d.	1601	1609	1609	1634	1702	1708	1709	1725	1801	1809	1831	1830	1908	1908	1906	1906	2001	2009	2009	...	2108	2109	...	2201	...
Toulouse Matabiau **320** a.	|	|	|	|	1836	1845	|	|	|	|	|	|	2041	2043	|	|	|	|	|	...	|	|	...	|	...
Béziers d.	1617	1624	1624	1649	...	...	1724	1743	1817	1824	1845	1845	...	...	1921	1921	2017	2024	2024	...	2124	2124	...	|	...
Agde d.	|	1636	1636	1701	...	...	1736	1758	|	1836	1857	1857	...	...	1933	1933	|	2036	2036	...	2136	2136	...	|	...
Sète d.	|	1651	1651	1716	...	...	1751	1815	|	1851	1912	1911	...	...	1948	1948	|	2051	2051	...	2151	2151	...	2236	...
Frontignan d.	|	1657	1657	1722	...	...	1757	1822	|	1857	1918	1917	...	...	1954	1954	|	2057	2057	...	2157	2157	...	|	...
Montpellier Saint-Roch a.	1652	1709	1709	1734	...	...	1809	1834	1854	1909	1929	1928	...	...	2006	2006	2052	2109	2109	...	2209	2209	...	2254	...
Montpellier Saint-Roch d.	1656	1713	1713	1738	...	...	1814	1838	1858	1913	1933	1932	...	...	2010	2010	2056	2113	2113	...	2213	2213	...	2258	...
Lunel d.	|	1730	1730	1755	...	...	1830	1855	|	1930	1951	1955	...	...	2027	2027	|	2130	2130	...	2230	2230	...	|	...
Nîmes Centre **357** d.	1723	1750	1750	1814	...	...	1850	1911	1925	1950	2009	2011	...	...	2044	2047	2123	2147	2147	...	2247	2247	...	2322	...
Nîmes Pont-du-Gard d.	|	1759	1802	1824	...	...	1859	...	|	1959	...	...	...	...	...	2056e	|	...	...	...	...	...	...	...	...
Tarascon-sur-Rhône d.	|	1815	1819	1838	...	...	1915	...	|	2015	...	...	...	...	...	2113e	|	...	...	...	...	...	...	...	...
Avignon Centre **357** a.	|	1828	1834	|	...	...	1928	...	|	2028	...	...	...	...	...	2126	|	...	...	...	...	...	...	...	...
Arles **351** d.	1750	...	...	1846	...	...	...	...	|	...	...	...	...	...	...	...	|	...	...	...	...	...	...	...	...
Miramas **351** d.	|	...	...	1907	...	...	...	...	|	...	...	...	...	...	...	...	|	...	...	...	...	...	...	...	...
Aéroport Marseille ✈ ‡ . **351** d.	|	...	...	1923	...	...	...	...	|	...	...	...	...	...	...	...	|	...	...	...	...	...	...	...	...
Marseille St Charles **351** a.	1835	...	...	1940	...	...	...	...	2036	...	...	...	...	...	...	...	2232	...	...	...	...	...	...	...	...

e – Not Apr. 11 - May 3.
r – Not May 4 - June 2.
s – Not Mar. 13 – 17, 20 – 24, 27 – 31, Apr. 3 – 7.
w – Not Mar. 6 – 10, 13 – 17, 20 – 24.

⊗ – Does not run Cerbère - Perpignan Mar. 13 – 17, 20 – 24, 27 – 31, Apr. 3 – 7.
⊡ – Does not run Bordeaux - Béziers on May 29.
△ – Does not run Béziers - Marseille Apr. 11 – 14, 17 – 21, 24 – 28, May 1 – 5, 8 – 12, 15 – 17, 22 – 26, 28 – 31, June 1, 2, 5 – 16, 19 – 23, 26 – 30.
▽ – Runs 1 – 5 minutes later Toulouse - Nîmes from Feb. 27. Subject to alteration Apr. 10 – 13. Does not run Bordeaux - Narbonne on May 28.
★ – *INTERCITÉS*. [R]. 🍸.
❦ – Journeys from Bordeaux are subject to alteration on Apr. 8, 9, 10, May 6, 7, 8, 18, 19, 20, 21, 27, 28.
‡ – Vitrolles Aéroport Marseille-Provence ✈. A shuttle bus runs to the airport terminal (journey time: 5 minutes)

356 NÎMES - LE GRAU-DU-ROI

SERVICE UNTIL APRIL 28

km		Ⓐ n		Ⓐ							
0	**Nîmes** Centre d.	1032	...	1736	...	...	...	...	...	...	...
39	Aigues-Mortes d.	1113	...	1825	...	...	...	...	...	...	...
45	**Le Grau-du-Roi** a.	1121	...	1832	...	...	...	...	...	...	...

	Ⓐ		Ⓐ d		Ⓐ					
Le Grau-du-Roi d.	0635	...	1147	...	1844	...	...	...	...	...
Aigues-Mortes d.	0643	...	1156	...	1852	...	...	...	...	...
Nîmes Centre a.	0732	...	1239	...	1937	...	...	...	...	...

APRIL 29 - JUNE 30

km				Ⓐ E	Ⓒ		Ⓒ E				
0	**Nîmes** Centre d.	1032	...	1252	1255	...	1355	...	1736	...	...
39	Aigues-Mortes d.	1113	...	1338	1336	...	1434	...	1825	...	...
45	**Le Grau-du-Roi** a.	1121	...	1345	1344	...	1441	...	1832	...	...

	Ⓐ		G	H		J		E		
Le Grau-du-Roi d.	0635	...	1140	1147	...	1610	...	1731	...	1844
Aigues-Mortes d.	0643	...	1149	1156	...	1619	...	1739	...	1852
Nîmes Centre a.	0732	...	1233	1239	...	1702	...	1832	...	1937

E – From May 27.
G – From June 3.
H – Until June 2.

J – Ⓒ to May 21; daily from May 27.

n – Not Mar. 13 – 31.

AVIGNON - PONT-SAINT-ESPRIT 357

km		⚒		†	D	E	ⒶB	†	⚒	†	
	Nîmes Centre...... **355** d.	...	...	...	...	1343	1500	...	...	...	...
	Avignon Centre .. **355** a.	...	...	...	...	1413	1540	...	...	...	...
0	**Avignon** Centre ....d.	0621	0823	1023	1223	1432	1554	1622	1822	1903	...
35	Bagnols-sur-Cèze ....d.	0644	0845	1044	1245	1454	1616	1646	1845	1925	...
47	**Pont-Saint-Esprit**.......a.	0651	0852	1051	1252	1501	1623	1653	1852	1932	...

	⚒	†	ⒶB	D	E	†	⚒			†
Pont-Saint-Esprit....d.	0706	0806	0912	1006	1203	1408	1606	1800	...	2006
Bagnols-sur-Cèze ....d.	0714	0815	0920	1014	1212	1417	1614	1809	...	2014
Avignon Centre.......a.	0740	0837	0942	1036	1233	1439	1637	1830	...	2036
Avignon Centre **355** d.	...	...	0957	...	1247	...	...	...	...	...
Nîmes Centre ... **355** a.	...	...	1029	...	1316	...	...	...	...	...

– Feb. 27 - May 12. **D** – ①–⑥ to Feb. 25; ⑥ Mar. 4 - May 13; ⚒ from May 15. **E** – Daily to Feb. 26; Ⓒ Mar. 4 - May 8; daily from May 13.

MARSEILLE, VALENCE and GRENOBLE - GAP - BRIANÇON 358

km		5789 N		Ⓐ			⚒		⑥ L	Ⓑ n	⑥ k			⑥	Ⓑ			⑤†	⑥	Ⓑ	Ⓑ	⑥	Ⓑ	Ⓑ	⑤†
0	**Marseille** St Charles..... ▷ d.	...	...	...	0741				...	...	...	1311	...	...	...	1641	...	...	1741	1741	...	...	1841	...	...
37	Aix en Provence............ ▷ d.	...	...	...	0825				...	...	...	1355	...	...	...	1724	...	...	1824	1824	...	...	1924	...	...
106	Manosque-Gréoux..............d.	...	...	...	0910				...	...	...	1437	...	...	...	1808	...	...	1907	1910	...	...	2005	...	...
139	Château Arnoux - St Auban..d.	...	...	...	0934				...	...	...	1501	...	...	...	1832	...	...	1930	1933	...	...	2031	...	...
156	Sisteron ....d.	...	...	...	0947				...	...	...	1517	...	...	...	1849	...	...	1947	1946	...	...	2045	...	...
	Paris Austerlitz ....d.	2051	...	...	|	...	...	...	...	...	...	|	...	...	...	|	...	...	|	...	...	...	|	...	...
	Valence TGV..................d.	|	...	...	|	...	0955	...	1207	...	...	|	1429	...	...	|	1751	1751	|	...	...	...	|	1958	1958
	Valence Ville **364**.........d.	|	...	...	|	...	1005	...	1220	...	...	|	1441	...	...	|	1801	1801	|	...	...	...	|	2008	2008
	Crest..............................d.	0442	...	...	|	...	1037	...	1252	...	...	|	1514	...	...	|	1835	1835	|	...	...	...	|	2039	2039
	Die..................................d.	0520	...	...	|	...	1119	...	1327	...	...	|	1553	...	...	|	1912	1912	|	...	...	...	|	2114	2114
◧	**Grenoble** ....d.	|	...	...	|	0810	|	1023	|	1254	1254	|	|	1557	1604	|	|	|	|	...	1809	1809	|	|	|
206	Veynes-Dévoluy ....a.	0627	...	...	1030	1039	1217	1234	1424	1506	1524	1559	1650	1809	1817	1931	2007	2007	2028	...	2028	2039	2127	2209	2209
206	Veynes-Dévoluy ....d.	|	...	...	1033	1047	1227	1241	1430	1507	1526	1602	1653	1810	1818	1935	2010	2010	2031	...	...	2048	2129	2212	2212
233	**Gap** ....a.	0655	...	...	1052	1107	1247	1301	1451	1528	1547j	1622	1715	1830	1838	1956	2031	2031	2051	...	...	2109	2200	2232	2232
233	**Gap** ....d.	|	...	0826	1055	...	1250	...	1507	...	...	1630	1726	...	...	2000	...	2055	2055	...	...	...	...	...	2235
270	Embrun...............................d.	0733	...	0905	1129	...	1326	...	1547	...	...	1708	1807	...	...	2051t	...	2137	2138	...	...	...	...	...	2306
287	Montdauphin-Guillestre........d.	0750	...	0919	1143	...	1341	...	1601	...	...	1724	1822	...	...	2107	...	2152	2153	...	...	...	...	...	2321
302	L'Argentière les Écrins ....d.	0804	...	0930	1155	...	1354	...	1613	...	...	1740	1833	...	...	2119	...	2203	2204	...	...	...	...	...	2333
315	**Briançon** ....a.	0822	...	0942	1208	...	1406	...	1625	...	...	1754	1845	...	...	2131	...	2216	2216	...	...	...	...	...	2345

	⚒ s	Ⓐ	⚒	Ⓐ	Ⓐ	⑥	⑥	†		Ⓑ	Ⓐ	Ⓒ			Ⓐ	⑥		🚌 ⑤†	⑥ Lc	⑤†					5790 N
riançon..............................d.	...	...	...	...	0449g	0519	...	...	...	0609	0658	0827r	0848	...	1050	...	1247	...	1338	1425	1507	...	1725	...	2003
'Argentière les Écrins ....d.	...	...	...	...	0501g	0531	...	...	...	0621	0710	0839r	0900	...	1102	...	1259	...	1356	1438	1519	...	1739	...	2019
lontdauphin-Guillestre ....d.	...	...	...	...	0511g	0541	...	...	...	0632	0721	0849r	0910	...	1112	...	1309	...	1407	1448	1530	...	1750	...	2033
mbrun...................................d.	...	...	...	...	0526g	0555	...	...	...	0647	0735	0904r	0926	...	1130	...	1325	...	1423	1502	1546	...	1805	...	2052
ap...a.	...	...	...	...	0558g	0628	...	...	...	0728	0810	0937r	0958	...	1202	...	1403	...	1457	1535	1619	...	1837	...	|
ap...d.	...	0500	...	0539	0600	0629	...	0629	0711	0731	...	0939	1001	1150	1205	1354	1406	1425	1502	1538	1625	1744	1840	1856	2134
'eynes-Dévoluy.....................a.	...	0519	...	0558	0619	0659	...	0659	0731	0751	...	0958	1021	1210	1225	1414	1428	1450	1522	1557	1646	1804	1859	1916	|
eynes-Dévoluy......................d.	...	0531	0525	0601	0622	0700	0652	0701	0735	0755	...	1001	1024	1214	1228	1415	1431	1450	1530	1600	1651	1805	1902	1917	2207
Grenoble ....a.	...	|	0743	|	|	|	|	|	0957	|	...	|	|	1432	|	1632	|	1632	|	|	|	2032	|	2149	|
Die....................................d.	...	|	...	|	0717	0754	|	|	...	0856	...	|	1121	...	1324	...	|	...	1634	|	1751	...	|	...	2312
Crest..................................d.	...	|	...	|	0752	0829	|	|	...	0937	...	|	1157	...	1401	...	|	...	1710	|	1833	...	|	...	2348
Valence Ville **364** ....a.	...	|	...	|	0822	0858	|	|	...	1008	...	|	1226	...	1431	...	|	...	1740	|	1901	...	|	...	|
Valence TGV.................a.	...	|	...	|	0832	0908	|	|	...	1017	...	|	1241	...	1443	...	|	...	1800	|	1911	...	|	...	|
Paris Austerlitz ....a.	...	|	...	|	...	...	|	|	...	...	...	|	...	...	...	...	|	...	...	|	...	...	|	...	0755
isteron..................................d.	0547	0614	...	0644	...	...	0744	0744	...	...	...	1044	...	...	...	...	1516	...	...	1642	...	...	1948	...	...
hâteau Arnoux - St Auban .. d.	0601	0628	...	0658	...	...	0758	0758	...	...	...	1058	...	...	...	...	1530	...	...	1655	...	...	2002	...	...
lanosque-Gréoux ....d.	0625	0655	...	0726	...	...	0822	0822	...	...	...	1127	...	...	...	...	1556	...	...	1718	...	...	2029	...	...
ix en Provence ....▷ d.	0710	0740	...	0810	...	...	0910	0910	...	...	...	1210	...	...	...	...	1640	...	...	1810	...	...	2111	...	...
larseille St Charles........▷ a.	0749	0819	...	0849	...	...	0949	0949	...	...	...	1249	...	...	...	...	1719	...	...	1849	...	...	2149	...	...

OTHER LOCAL TRAINS MARSEILLE - AIX EN PROVENCE (2nd class)

rom Marseille St Charles at 0623 Ⓐ, 0653, 0711 Ⓐ, 0723 Ⓐ, 0753, 0823 Ⓐ, 0853, 923 Ⓐ, 0953 Ⓒ, 1058 Ⓒ, 1124 Ⓐ, 1153, 1223 Ⓐ, 1253, 1353, 1453, 1554 Ⓐ, 623 Ⓐ, 1653, 1711 Ⓐ, 1723, 1753, 1811 Ⓐ, 1823 Ⓐ, 1853, 1953, 2053 Ⓑ, 2153.

From Aix en Provence at 0623 Ⓐ, 0640 Ⓐ, 0652 ⚒, 0653 †, 0721 Ⓐ, 0753, 0823 Ⓑ, 0853 ⚒, 0953, 1056 Ⓒ, 1123 Ⓐ, 1153, 1253, 1353, 1453, 1553, 1623 Ⓐ, 1653, 1710 Ⓐ, 1723 Ⓐ, 1740 Ⓐ, 1753, 1823, 1853 Ⓐ, 1923, 1953 ①–④ **m**, 2010 ⑤, 2023, 2123 Ⓒ, 2153 Ⓐ, 2253 †.

– Ⓐ Mar. 13 - Apr. 14.
– Ⓒ (daily Feb. 11 - Mar. 12 and from Apr. 15).
– ⑥ Dec. 17 - Mar. 25.
– Conveys 🛏 1, 2 cl. and 💺2 (reclining). Ⓡ. For overnight journeys only. **Timings may vary**. May not run on certain nights. For confirmed days of running and timings please consult the SNCF journey planner: www.sncf.com

– Not Feb. 25, Mar. 4.
– ① (also Apr. 11, May 2, 9, 30; not Apr. 10, May 1, 8, 29).
– 1557 on Feb. 26, Mar. 5.

k – Also Feb. 26, Mar. 5.
m – Not Apr. 10, May 1, 8, 18, 29.
n – Not Feb. 26, Mar. 5.
r – 28 – 33 minutes **earlier** on Mar. 11, 12, 18, 19.
s – Runs 13 – 18 minutes later on ⑥ (not Mar. 11, 18, 25). Runs 35 – 48 minutes later on Mar. 11, 18, 25.
t – Arrives 2036.

◧ – Grenoble - Veynes-Dévoluy is 109 km.
▷ – For other local trains see panel below main table.

🚌 **BRIANÇON - MODANE** *Valid until Apr. 30*

	Ⓡ	Ⓒ	C	A
Briançon rail station d.	0650	1225	1445	1645
Modane rail station . a.	0830	1405	1625	1825

	Ⓡ	Ⓒ	C	A
Modane rail station . d.	1115	1455	1715	1915
Briançon rail station a.	1240	1610	1840	2040

✆ 0809 400 013 https://zou.maregionsud.fr

NICE - ANNOT - DIGNE 359

2nd class only

km	CP ▲		⑦◇				Ⓑ
0	**Nice** (Gare CP) ....d.	0655	0837	0920	1300	1710	1809
	Plan du Var ....d.	0736	0918	1002	1342	1751	1850
41	Villars sur Var..............d.	0755	0938	1021	1401	1810	1909
58	Puget Théniers ....d.	0818	1001	1044	1424	1833	1933
64	Entrevaux ....d.	0828	1011	1054	1434	1843	1943
78	Annot...........................d.	0847	1027	1112	1452	1904	1959
96	Thorame Haute............d.	0911	...	1136	1516	1927	...
106	St André les Alpes......d.	0925	...	1151	1531	1940	...
150	**Digne** .... ★ a.	1022	...	1248	1628	2037	...

CP ▲	⚒				⑦◇	
Digne................... ★ d.	...	0710	1052	1432	...	1735
St. André les Alpes. d.	...	0809	1152	1532	...	1829
Thorame Haute ...... d.	...	0823	1206	1546	...	1841
Annot .... d.	0542	0848	1230	1610	1640	1903
Entrevaux.................. d.	0600	0906	1248	1628	1658	1921
Puget Théniers .... d.	0610	0916	1258	1638	1708	1932
Villars sur Var.......... d.	0631	0937	1319	1659	1729	1953
Plan du Var .... d.	0652	0959	1341	1720	1750	2014
Nice (Gare CP) ...... a.	0731	1038	1420	1803	1828	2053

🚂 *TRAIN DES PIGNES* steam train, **2022**
⑦ May 8 - Oct. 30 ⊠
Puget Théniers 1100 → Annot 1220
Annot 1530 → Puget Théniers 1615
Also calls at Entrevaux
www.traindespignes.fr

🚌 LER route 66, operated by Autocars Payan.

	🚌 ⚒	🚌		🚌		🚌		🚌	
)igne △ ....d.	0455	0730	...	1145	...	1330	...	1630	...
)igne (Gare).......................d.	0500	0740	...	1155	...	1340	...	1640	...
lanosque-Gréoux (Gare) ......d.	0600	0845	...	1300	...	1445	...	1750	...
ix en Provence TGV ....a.	0700	0945	...	1400	...	1545	...	1850	...
éroport Marseille ✈ ....a.	0715	1000	...	1415	...	1600	...	1905	...

	🚌 ⚒		🚌		🚌		🚌		🚌
Aéroport Marseille ✈....................d.	0955	...	1255	...	1540	...	1830	...	2105
Aix en Provence TGV ....d.	1025	...	1325	...	1610	...	1900	...	2130
Manosque-Gréoux (Gare)...............a.	1130	...	1430	...	1715	...	2005	...	2220
Digne (Gare) ....a.	1230	...	1530	...	1815	...	2100	...	2310
Digne △ ....a.	1240	...	1540	...	1825	...	2105	...	2315

△ – Gare Routière (bus station).
▲ – Narrow gauge railway, operated by Chemins de Fer de Provence. **All services are operated by 🚌 between St André les Alpes and Digne until further notice.**
★ – 🚌 Digne - Sisteron and v.v. LER route 37. Journey time: 60 minutes. From Digne (Gare CP) at 0755 ⚒, 1140, 1245 ⚒, 1610 ⑤, 1720 ⊡ and 1815. From Sisteron (Gare SNCF) at 0640 ⚒, 1105 ⚒, 1250 ⚒, 1605 and 1845.

⊠ – Also July 15, 22, 29, Aug. 4, 5, 11, 12, 18, 19, 25, 26, Nov. 5. On Sept. 18, Nov. 5 runs Puget - Annot - Le Fugeret (a. 1300) and v.v. – return train departs Le Fugeret 1525 (on Sept. 18) / 1535 (on Nov. 5), Annot 1710 (on Sept. 18) / 1640 (on Nov. 5), arrives Puget 1755 (on Sept. 18) / 1725 (on Nov. 5).
⊡ – Daily except ⑤.
◇ – ⑦ June 19 - Oct. 30, 2022. Connects with *Train des Pignes* steam train (see panel).

🚌 information: ✆ 0 809 400 013 https://zou.maregionsud.fr

360 MARSEILLE - TOULON - HYÈRES

km		Ⓐ	Ⓐ	Ⓐ		Ⓐ		Ⓐ		Ⓒ	Ⓒ	Ⓐ¶	Ⓐ	Ⓒ	Ⓐ	Ⓒ	Ⓒ	Ⓐ		Ⓐ	6155 ♥	Ⓒ	Ⓐ		Ⓐ
	Paris Gare de Lyon **350** d.	...	...	...	...	...	...	...	...	...	...	...	...	...	...	...	...	...	...	...	0907k	...	...	...	...
0	**Marseille** St Charles **361** d.	0532	...	0602	0629	0702	0732	0802	0832	0926	1002	1002	1033	1033	1046	1103	1132	1132	1202	1202	1228	1233	1233	1302	130
27	Cassis • d.	|	...	0627	0654	0727	0757	0827	0857	0952	1027	1027	1058	1058	1130	1129	1157	1157	1227	1227	|	1258	1312	1327	132
37	La Ciotat d.	0607	...	0634	0701	0735	0804	0835	0905	1000	1034	1035	1105	1106	1137	1136	1204	1205	1234	1234	|	1305	1319	1334	133
51	Bandol d.	|	...	0646	0713	0747	0816	0847	0916	1012	1046	1047	1117	1117	1148	1148	1216	1217	1246	1246	|	1317	1331	1346	134
67	**Toulon** **361** a.	0627	...	0701	0728	0801	0831	0901	0931	1027	1101	1101	1131	1132	1202	1203	1231	1231	1301	1301	1311	1331	1345	1401	140
67	**Toulon** d.	...	0634	0704	0731	...	0834	...	0934	1030	...	1104	...	1135	1205	...	1234	...	...	1304	1324	...	...	...	140
87	**Hyères** a.	...	0656	0726	0756	...	0856	...	0956	1053	...	1126	...	1157	1227	...	1256	...	...	1326	1340	...	...	...	142

	Ⓐ	Ⓒ		Ⓐ	Ⓒ	Ⓒ	Ⓐ	Ⓒ	Ⓐ	Ⓐ	Ⓒ		Ⓐ		Ⓐ		Ⓐ			Ⓐ					⑤⑥
Paris Gare de Lyon **350** d.	...	...	...	...	...	...	...	...	...	...	...	...	...	...	...	...	...	...	...	...	...	...	...	...	...
Marseille St Charles **361** d.	1331	1350	1403	1419	1433	1502	1503	1532	1532	1603	1603	1632	1703	1732	1802	1833	1902	1933	...	2012	2033	...	2132	...	223
Cassis • d.	1404	1415	1428	1458	1458	1527	1528	1557	1557	1628	1628	1657	1728	1758	1827	1858	1927	1959	...	2053	2058	...	2157	...	225
La Ciotat d.	1411	1423	1435	1505	1505	1534	1535	1604	1605	1635	1635	1704	1735	1805	1834	1905	1935	2006	...	2101	2105	...	2205	...	230
Bandol d.	1423	1434	1447	1517	1517	1546	1547	1616	1617	1647	1647	1716	1747	1817	1846	1917	1947	2018	...	2112	2117	...	2217	...	231
Toulon **361** a.	1438	1449	1501	1531	1531	1601	1602	1631	1631	1701	1702	1731	1802	1831	1900	1932	2001	2033	...	2126	2131	...	2231	...	233
Toulon d.	...	1452	...	1534	1534	...	1605	1634	...	1704	...	1734	1805	1834	1903	1935	...	2036	...	...	2134	...	...	...	...
Hyères a.	...	1516	...	1556	1556	...	1627	1656	...	1726	...	1756	1827	1856	1926	1957	...	2058	...	...	2157	...	...	...	...

		Ⓐ	Ⓐ	Ⓐ		Ⓐ	Ⓐ	Ⓐ		Ⓐ		Ⓒ			Ⓒ	Ⓒ	Ⓐ	Ⓒ	Ⓐ	Ⓒ	Ⓐ	Ⓒ	Ⓐ	Ⓒ	Ⓐ
Hyères d.	...	...	0603	...	0633	...	0703	...	0731	0803	0833	...	0933	...	1030	...	1103	1132	...	...	1203	1233	...	...	130
Toulon a.	...	...	0625	...	0655	...	0725	...	0755	0825	0855	...	0955	...	1053	...	1125	1154	...	...	1225	1255	...	...	132
Toulon **361** d.	0558	0623	0628	0652	0658	0719	0728	0751	0758	0828	0858	0928	0959	1028	1056	1128	1128	1157	1158	1228	1228	1258	1258	1328	132
Bandol d.	0613	|	0644	|	0714	|	0744	|	0814	0844	0914	0943	1016	1043	1112	1143	1144	1213	1213	1243	1243	1314	1313	1343	134
La Ciotat d.	0625	0644	0655	0713	0725	0740	0755	0812	0825	0855	0925	0955	1028	1054	1123	1155	1155	1225	1225	1254	1255	1325	1324	1355	135
Cassis • d.	0632	|	0703	|	0733	|	0803	|	0833	0903	0933	1002	1036	1101	1131	1202	1203	1232	1232	1302	1303	1333	1332	1402	140
Marseille St Charles **361** a.	0658	0714	0728	0744	0758	0811	0828	0843	0858	0928	0958	1028	1103	1128	1156	1228	1228	1258	1258	1328	1340	1358	1359	1428	145
Paris Gare de Lyon **350** a.	...	...	...	...	...	...	...	...	...	...	...	...	...	...	...	...	...	...	...	...	...	...	...	...	...

			Ⓐ	6124 ♥			Ⓐ		Ⓐ	Ⓒ	Ⓐ	Ⓐ		Ⓐ			A	B			⑤⑥†	C			
Hyères d.	...	1403	...	1450	...	1533	...	1633	1703	1730	...	1803	1833	...	1933	...	2026	2031	...	2133	2133	...	...	...	...
Toulon a.	...	1425	...	1503	...	1555	...	1655	1725	1753	...	1825	1855	...	1955	...	2048	2053	...	2155	2155	...	...	...	...
Toulon **361** d.	1358	1428	1450	1507	1528	1558	1628	1658	1728	1756	1758	1828	1858	1928	1958	...	2058	2056	...	...	2158	2228	...	...	...
Bandol d.	1413	1444	1505	|	1543	1614	1643	1714	1744	1811	1811	1846	1914	1943	2014	...	2114	2112	...	...	2214	2243	...	...	...
La Ciotat d.	1425	1455	1516	|	1555	1625	1655	1725	1755	1822	1822	1901	1925	1955	2025	...	2126	2123	...	...	2225	2254	...	...	...
Cassis • d.	1432	1503	1524	|	1602	1633	1702	1733	1803	1829	|	1908	1933	2002	2033	...	2133	2131	...	...	2233	2302	...	...	...
Marseille St Charles **361** a.	1458	1541	1555	1550	1628	1658	1728	1758	1828	1856	1858	1937	1958	2028	2058	...	2158	2158	...	...	2258	2328	...	...	...
Paris Gare de Lyon **350** a.	...	...	...	1929j	...	...	...	...	...	...	...	...	...	...	...	...	...	...	...	...	...	...	...	...	...

A – ①-⑤ from Mar. 27 (also June 10).
B – Daily to Mar. 26; ⑥⑦ from Apr. 1 (not June 10).
C – ⑥ until Apr. 15 (also Dec. 18, 25, Jan. 1); Ⓒ from Apr. 22.

j – 1922 from May 15.
k – 0910 from May 15.

¶ – Timings Marseille - Toulon are 1–2 minutes earlier Feb. 20 - Mar. 3.
• – Cassis station is located 4 km from Cassis town.
♥ – *TGV* high-speed train. Ⓡ. 🍷.

361 MARSEILLE - TOULON - CANNES - NICE - MONACO - VENTIMIGLIA

Local *TER* services. See Table **350** for long-distance *TGV* services.

km				①-⑤	①-⑤	⑥⑦	①-⑤	①-⑤	⑥⑦	①-⑤	①-⑤	⑥⑦	⑥	①-⑤	①-⑤	⑥⑦	①-⑤	Ⓐ	Ⓒ	⊖	⑥⑦		5771 ★	①-⑤	⑥⑦
0	**Marseille** St Charles **360** d.	...	...	...	...	...	...	...	...	...	...	...	...	...	...	...	...	0532	0557	...	...	...	...	...	...
	Paris Austerlitz d.	...	...	...	...	...	...	...	...	...	...	...	...	...	...	...	...	|	|	...	...	...	2051	...	...
67	**Toulon** **360** d.	...	...	...	...	...	...	...	...	...	...	...	...	...	...	...	...	0630	0642	...	...	0647	0709	...	...
100	Carnoules d.	...	...	...	...	...	...	...	...	...	...	...	...	...	...	...	...	0650	|	...	...	0719	|	...	...
135	Les Arcs-Draguignan d.	...	...	...	...	...	...	...	...	*0548*	...	...	0628	0628	...	...	...	0709	0717	...	0728	0745	0748	...	...
158	Fréjus d.	...	...	...	...	...	...	...	...	*0601*	...	...	0641	0641	...	...	...	0724	|	...	0741	...	|	...	...
161	St Raphaël-Valescure d.	...	...	...	...	...	...	...	...	*0607*	...	...	0646	0647	...	...	...	0729	0733	...	0747	...	0806	...	...
165	Boulouris sur Mer d.	...	...	...	...	...	...	...	...	*0610*	...	...	0650	0650	...	...	...	|	|	...	0750	...	|	...	...
◧	Grasse d.	...	...	...	...	...	...	...	...	|	0638	0638b	|	|	0708	...	...	|	|	0738	|	...	|	0808	...
193	**Cannes** d.	...	...	0553	0608	0616	0623	0638	0638	0653	0708	0708	0719	0723	0738	0740	0753	0801	0800	0808	0821	...	0830	0838	083
202	Juan les Pins d.	...	...	0602	0617	0625	0630	0647	0647	0700	0717	0717	...	0730	0747	0749	0800	|	|	0817	...	...	|	0846	084
204	Antibes d.	...	...	0605	0621	0628	0634	0651	0650	0704	0721	0720	...	0734	0751	0752	0804	0813	0814	0821	...	...	0843	0850	085
213	Cagnes sur Mer d.	...	...	0615	0630	0638	0642	0659	0700	0712	0730	0730	...	0742	0759	0802	0812	|	|	0830	...	...	|	0900	090
219	Nice St Augustin ✈ ⊡ d.	...	...	0625	0639	0647	0652	0707	0710	0722	0739	0740	...	0752	0808	0812	0822	0828	0829	0838	...	...	|	0909	091
224	**Nice** Ville a.	...	...	0632	0647	0655	0700	0715	0718	0730	0747	0748	...	0800	0815	0820	0830	0836	0837	0847	...	...	0908	0917	091
	Nice Ville d.	0540	0620	0635	0650	0658	0703	0718	0721	0733	0750	0751	...	0803	0818	0823	0833	...	...	0850	...	...	...	0920	092
229	Villefranche sur Mer d.	0547	0627	0643	0657	0705	0711	0726	0729	0741	0757	0758	...	0811	0826	0831	0841	...	...	0858	...	...	...	0927	092
231	Beaulieu sur Mer d.	0551	0631	0646	0701	0709	0715	0729	0732	0744	0801	0802	...	0814	0829	0834	0844	...	...	0901	...	...	...	0931	093
234	Eze d.	0554	0634	|	0704	0713	|	0733	0736	|	0804	0805	...	|	0833	0838	|	...	...	0904	...	...	...	0934	093
240	**Monaco-Monte Carlo** d.	0604	0644	0657	0714	0722	0726	0743	0746	0755	0814	0815	...	0825	0843	0848	0855	...	...	0914	...	...	...	0944	094
244	Cap Martin-Roquebrune d.	0608	0648	|	0718	0727	|	0747	0751	|	0818	0819	...	|	0848	0853	|	...	...	0918	...	...	...	0948	095
249	Menton d.	0617	0657	0709	0727	0735	0739	0757	0759	0807	0827	0827	...	0839	0857	0901	0907	...	...	0927	...	...	...	0957	095
259	**Ventimiglia** a.	0632	0712	...	0742	0753	...	...	0812	0822	0842	0842	...	...	...	0915	0922	...	...	0942	...	...	...	1012	101

	①-⑤ △		①-⑤	⑥⑦					⑥⑦													⑥⑦	①-⑤	①-⑤	
Marseille St Charles **360** d.	...	...	...	...	0757	...	...	...	...	...	0957	...	...	...	...	...	1157	...	...	...	...	...	...	...	...
Toulon **360** d.	...	...	...	...	0843	...	...	...	...	...	1043	...	...	...	...	1147	1243	...	...	1247	...	...	...	...	...
Carnoules d.	...	...	...	...	|	...	...	...	...	...	1103	...	...	...	...	1219	|	...	...	1319	...	...	...	...	...
Les Arcs-Draguignan d.	0757	...	...	...	0919	...	0928	...	...	...	1122	...	1128	...	...	1245	1319	...	1328	1345	...	...	...	...	...
Fréjus d.	0810	...	...	...	|	...	0941	...	...	...	|	...	1141	...	...	▬	|	...	1341	▬	...	...	...	...	...
St Raphaël-Valescure d.	0815	...	...	...	0935	...	0947	...	...	...	1138	...	1147	...	...	...	1335	...	1347	...	...	...	...	...	...
Boulouris sur Mer d.	0818	...	...	...	|	...	0950	...	...	...	|	...	1150	...	...	...	|	...	1350	...	...	...	...	...	...
Grasse d.	|	0838	0908	...	|	0938	|	...	1038	...	|	1138	|	...	1238	...	|	1338	|	...	1438	...	...	...	1538
Cannes d.	0849	0908	0938	0938	1001	1008	1021	1046	1108	1146	1202	1208	1221	1239	1308	1338	1401	1408	1421	1438	1508	1538	1543		1608
Juan les Pins d.	...	0917	0947	0947	|	1017	...	1055	1117	1155	|	1217	...	1248	1317	1347	|	1417	...	1446	1517	1546	1552	...	1617
Antibes d.	...	0920	0950	0951	1014	1020	...	1059	1121	1159	1214	1220	...	1251	1320	1350	1414	1420	...	1450	1520	1550	1555	...	1620
Cagnes sur Mer d.	...	0930	1000	1001	|	1030	...	1108	1131	1208	|	1230	...	1300	1330	1359	|	1430	...	1500	1530	1559	1604	...	1630
Nice St Augustin ✈ ⊡ d.	...	0939	1009	1011	1029	1039	...	1118	1141	1218	1228	1239	...	1310	1339	1409	1428	1439	...	1509	1539	1609	1614	...	1639
Nice Ville a.	...	0947	1017	1018	1037	1047	...	1125	1148	1225	1237	1247	...	1318	1347	1417	1437	1447	...	1517	1547	1617	1622	...	1647
Nice Ville d.	...	0950	1020	1021	...	1050	...	1128	1151	1228	...	1250	...	1321	1350	1420	...	1450	...	1520	1550	1620	1625	1633	1650
Villefranche sur Mer d.	...	0957	1027	1029	...	1057	...	1136	1159	1236	...	1257	...	1328	1357	1427	...	1457	...	1527	1601	1628	1633	1641	1657
Beaulieu sur Mer d.	...	1001	1031	1032	...	1101	...	1139	1202	1239	...	1301	...	1332	1401	1431	...	1501	...	1531	1604	1631	1636	1644	170
Eze d.	...	1004	1034	1036	...	1104	...	1142	1206	1242	...	1304	...	1335	1404	1434	...	1504	...	1534	1607	1634	1639	|	1704
Monaco-Monte Carlo d.	...	1014	1044	1046	...	1114	...	1152	1216	1252	...	1314	...	1345	1414	1444	...	1514	...	1544	1617	1644	1649	1656	1714
Cap Martin-Roquebrune d.	...	1018	1048	1051	...	1118	...	1157	1221	1257	...	1318	...	1350	1418	1448	...	1518	...	1548	1621	1648	1653	|	1718
Menton d.	...	1027	1057	1059	...	1127	...	1206	1229	1306	...	1327	...	1359	1427	1457	...	1527	...	1557	1627	1657	1701	1709	1727
Ventimiglia a.	...	1042	1112	1113	...	1142	...	1220	1243	1320	...	1342	...	1413	1442	1512	...	1542	...	1612	1642	1712	...	1723	1742

b – 0642 on ⑥.

△ – Runs 29–31 minutes earlier on Mar. 10.
⊖ – Certain departure times are 1–3 minutes later on ⑥⑦.

★ – Conveys 🛏 1, 2 cl. and 💺 (reclining). Also calls at Marseille-Blancarde (a. 0620). Ⓡ For overnight journeys only. **Timings may vary**. For confirmed timings and days of running, please consult the SNCF journey planner: www.sncf.com
◧ – Grasse - Cannes is *17 km*.
⊡ – Situated approximately 800 metres from Nice ✈ terminal building.

MARSEILLE - TOULON - CANNES - NICE - MONACO - VENTIMIGLIA 361

Local *TER* services. See Table **350** for long-distance *TGV* services.

		⑥⑦	①–⑤			⊖	①–⑤		①–⑤	⊖	⑥⑦	①–⑤	Ⓐ	①–⑤				①–⑤	Ⓐ				①–⑤	⑥⑦		⑥
Marseille St Charles 360 d.	...	...	...	...	1457	...	...	...	...	...	...	...	...	...	1657	...	...	1708	1757	...	...	...	...	...	...
Toulon 360 d.	...	...	...	1447	1543	...	...	...	...	...	...	...	1647	...	1743	1747	...	1818	1843	...	...	...	...	...	...
Carnoules d.	...	...	...	1519	|	...	...	...	...	...	...	...	1719	...	|	1819	...	1851	1902	...	...	...	...	...	...
Les Arcs-Draguignan d.	1528	...	...	1545	1619	...	...	...	...	...	1728	1728	1745	...	1819	1845	...	1917	1922	...	1928	...	...	...	...
Fréjus d.	1541	...	...	▬	|	...	...	...	...	...	1741	1741	▬	...	|	▬	...	▬	|	...	1941	...	...	...	...
St Raphaël-Valescure d.	1547	...	...	...	1635	...	...	...	...	...	1746	1747	...	...	1835	...	...	...	1938	...	1947	...	...	...	...
Boulouris sur Mer d.	1550	...	...	①–⑤	|	...	...	...	...	...	1749	1750	⑥⑦	...	|	...	...	⑥⑦	|	...	1950	...	...	...	...
Grasse d.	|	...	...		|	1638	...	...	...	1738	|	|		1808	|	1838	1908		|	1938	|	2008	...	2038	2038
Cannes d.	1621	1636	1640	1653	1701	1708	1725	1739	1755	1808	1819	1823	1830	1837	1901	1908	1938	1940	2001	2008	2021	2037	2039	2108	2108
Juan les Pins d.	...	1645	1648	1700	|	1717	1732	1748	1803	1817	...	1830	1840	1846	|	1917	1947	1950	|	2017	...	2046	2047	2117	2117
Antibes d.	...	1648	1651	1704	1714	1721	1735	1751	1806	1821	...	1834	1843	1850	1914	1920	1950	1953	2014	2020	...	2049	2050	2121	2121
Cagnes sur Mer d.	...	1658	1701	1712	|	1730	1743	1800	1814	1830	...	1842	1858	1900	|	1930	2000	2003	|	2030	...	2059	2059	2131	2131
Nice St Augustin ✈ ⊡ d.	...	1708	1710	1722	1728	1739	1753	1809	1824	1839	...	1852	1908	1909	1928	1939	2009	2014	2028	2039	...	2108	2108	2140	2140
Nice Ville a.	...	1715	1717	1731	1735	1747	1801	1817	1832	1847	...	1900	1915	1917	1937	1947	2017	2020	2037	2047	...	2116	2116	2148	2148
Nice Ville d.	...	1721	1720	1734	...	1750	1804	1820	1835	1850	...	...	1918	1920	...	1950	2020	2023	...	2050	...	2125	2125	...	2151
Villefranche sur Mer d.	...	1729	1727	1742	...	1757	1812	1827	1842	1857	...	...	1926	1927	...	1957	2027	2031	...	2057	...	2133	2133	...	2158
Beaulieu sur Mer d.	...	1732	1731	1745	...	1801	1815	1831	1846	1901	...	...	1929	1931	...	2001	2031	2034	...	2101	...	2136	2136	...	2202
Eze d.	...	1736	1734	|	...	1804	|	1834	|	1904	...	...	1933	1934	...	2004	2034	2037	...	2104	...	2139	2139	...	2205
Monaco-Monte Carlo d.	...	1746	1744	1756	...	1814	1826	1844	1856	1914	...	...	1943	1944	...	2014	2044	2047	...	2114	...	2149	2149	...	2214
Cap Martin-Roquebrune d.	...	1751	1748	|	...	1818	|	1848	|	1918	...	...	1948	1948	...	2018	2048	2052	...	2118	...	2154	2153	...	2219
Menton d.	...	1759	1757	1810	...	1827	1839	1857	1909	1927	...	...	1956	1957	...	2027	2057	2100	...	2127	...	2203	2202	...	2227
Ventimiglia a.	...	1813	...	1825	...	1842	...	1913	...	1942	...	...	2010	2012	...	2042	2112	2113	...	2142h	...	2217f	2216k	...	...

	⑤⑥	①–④	⑦	⑤⑥	H		G	⑦ E	⑦ E	D	C
Marseille St Charles 360 d.	...	...	...	...	...	...	...	2005	...	2057	...
Toulon 360 d.	...	...	...	...	...	1947	...	2051	...	2145	...
Carnoules d.	...	...	...	...	...	2019	...	2111	...	|	...
Les Arcs-Draguignan d.	...	...	...	...	...	2045	2127	2131	2142	2221	...
Fréjus d.	...	...	...	...	...	...	2139	|	2155	|	...
St Raphaël-Valescure d.	...	...	...	...	...	...	2144	2147	2200	2237	...
Boulouris sur Mer d.	...	...	...	...	...	...	2147	|	2204	|	...
Grasse d.	2110	2108	2110	...	...	...	|	|	|	|	2308
Cannes d.	2139	2139	2139	2208	2208	...	2217	2210	2234	2302	2340
Juan les Pins d.	2147	2148	2147	2217	2217	...	...	|	...	|	2349
Antibes d.	2150	2152	2151	2221	2220	...	...	2220	...	2312	2352
Cagnes sur Mer d.	2200	2202	2200	2230	2230	...	...	|	...	|	0002
Nice St Augustin ✈ ⊡ d.	2211	2212	2212	2240	2240	...	...	2231	...	2323	0010
Nice Ville a.	2219	2220	2220	2248	2248	...	...	2239	...	2331	0019
Nice Ville d.	2222	...	...	2251	...	...	...	...	...	...	...
Villefranche sur Mer d.	2230	...	...	2259	...	...	...	...	...	...	...
Beaulieu sur Mer d.	2233	...	...	2302	...	...	...	...	...	...	...
Eze d.	2236	...	...	2305	...	...	...	...	...	...	...
Monaco-Monte Carlo d.	2246	...	...	2315	...	...	...	...	...	...	...
Cap Martin-Roquebrune d.	2251	...	...	2319	...	...	...	...	...	...	...
Menton d.	2259	...	...	2328	...	...	...	...	...	...	...
Ventimiglia a.	2312	...	...	...	...	...	...	...	...	...	...

	Ⓐ	⚒	Ⓐ	Ⓑ	⑥	⑥⑦	①–⑤		①–⑤
Ventimiglia d.	...	...	...	...	...	0513r	...	...	...
Menton d.	...	...	...	...	...	0532	0534	...	...
Cap Martin-Roquebrune d.	...	...	...	...	...	0538	0540	...	...
Monaco-Monte Carlo d.	...	...	...	...	...	0546	0548	...	...
Eze d.	...	...	...	...	...	0553	0556	...	...
Beaulieu sur Mer d.	...	...	...	...	...	0557	0601	...	...
Villefranche sur Mer d.	...	...	...	...	...	0600	0604	...	...
Nice Ville a.	...	...	...	...	...	0607	0611	...	...
Nice Ville d.	...	...	0525e	0542	...	0610	0614	0625	...
Nice St Augustin ✈ ⊡ d.	...	...	0532e	0548	...	0618	0620	0632	...
Cagnes sur Mer d.	...	...	|	0557	...	0627	0629	|	...
Antibes d.	...	...	0545	0606	...	0637	0639	0647	...
Juan les Pins d.	...	...	|	0609	...	0640	0642	|	...
Cannes d.	...	...	0601	0622	0622	0650	0654	0701	0709
Grasse a.	...	...	|	0653	0657	...	0723	|	|
Boulouris sur Mer d.	...	...	|	▬	▬	...	▬	|	0740
St Raphaël-Valescure d.	...	...	0625	...	...	...	...	0725	0745
Fréjus d.	...	...	|	Ⓐ	...	...	Ⓐ	|	0750
Les Arcs-Draguignan d.	0540	0604	0641	0629	0658	...	0729	0741	0803
Carnoules d.	0607	0632	|	0702	0732	...	0802	|	...
Toulon 360 a.	0738	0704	0716	0734	0804	...	0834	0816	...
Marseille St Charles 360 a.	0744	...	0811	0843	...	...	...	0903	...

		①–⑤	⑥⑦	⑥⑦	①–⑤	⑥⑦	①–⑤	①–⑤	⑥⑦	①–⑤		①–⑤	①–⑤	⑥⑦	①–⑤			①–⑤	⑥⑦	①–⑤		⑥⑦	①–⑤		
Ventimiglia d.	0546	0616	0617	...	...	0638	0645	...	0713	0716	...	...	0743	0744	...	0816	...	0846	0846	0902	0916z	0943	...	1015	...
Menton d.	0604	0634	0636	...	0650	0658	0703	0721	0732	0734	...	0751	0801	0803	0819	0834	...	0904	0905	0920	0934	1002	...	1032	...
Cap Martin-Roquebrune d.	0610	0640	0642	...	|	0704	0709	|	0738	0740	...	|	0807	0809	|	0840	...	0910	0911	|	0940	1008	...	1038	...
Monaco-Monte Carlo d.	0618	0648	0650	...	0705	0712	0717	0736	0746	0748	...	0805	0815	0817	0834	0848	...	0918	0919	0935	0948	1016	...	1047	...
Eze d.	0626	0656	0657	...	|	0719	0725	|	0753	0756	...	|	0823	0824	|	0856	...	0926	0926	|	0956	1023	...	1054	...
Beaulieu sur Mer d.	0631	0701	0701	...	0715	0724	0730	0746	0757	0801	...	0816	0828	0828	0844	0901	...	0931	0930	0945	1001	1027	...	1059	...
Villefranche sur Mer d.	0634	0704	0704	...	0719	0727	0733	0750	0800	0804	...	0819	0831	0831	0848	0904	...	0934	0933	0948	1004	1030	...	1102	...
Nice Ville a.	0641	0711	0711	...	0727	0734	0740	0758	0807	0811	...	0827	0838	0838	0857	0911	...	0941	0940	0957	1011	1037	...	1109	...
Nice Ville d.	0644	0714	0714	...	0730	0737	0743	0803	0810	0814	0825	0830	0841	0841	0900	0914	...	0944	0943	...	1014	1040	1044	1112	1125
Nice St Augustin ✈ ⊡ d.	0650	0720	0722	...	0738	0744	0749	0809	0818	0821	0832	0838	0849	0849	0907	0920	...	0950	0951	...	1020	1048	1050	1118	1132
Cagnes sur Mer d.	0659	0729	0731	...	0747	0753	0757	0818	0827	0828	|	0847	0857	0858	0916	0929	...	0959	0959	...	1029	1057	1059	1127	|
Antibes d.	0709	0739	0741	...	0755	0803	0805	0826	0837	0837	0846	0855	0905	0908	0924	0939	...	1009	1009	...	1039	1107	1109	1137	1146
Juan les Pins d.	0712	0742	0744	...	0759	0806	0808	0829	0841	0840	|	0859	0908	0911	0928	0942	...	1012	1012	...	1042	1110	1112	1140	|
Cannes d.	0724	0755	0754	0809	0809	0819	0820	0837	0851	0852	0901	0907	0919	0923	0936	0955	1009	1022	1025	...	1052	1123	1124	1150	1201
Grasse a.	0753	0823	...	|	|	0853	0853	...	...	0923	|	...	...	0953	...	1023t	|	...	1053	...	...	1152	1153	...	|
Boulouris sur Mer d.	▬	...	...	0840	0840	...	...	...	...	...	|	...	...	...	...	...	1041	...	...	...	...	...	...	...	|
St Raphaël-Valescure d.	...	...	...	0845	0845	...	...	...	...	...	0925	...	...	...	...	...	1046	...	...	...	...	...	...	...	1225
Fréjus d.	...	...	...	0849	0850	...	...	...	...	...	|	...	...	...	...	...	1050	...	...	...	...	...	...	...	|
Les Arcs-Draguignan d.	0858	...	...	0903	0903	...	...	...	...	...	0941	...	...	...	...	...	1103	...	...	...	...	...	...	...	1241
Carnoules d.	0932	...	...	...	...	...	...	...	...	...	|	...	...	...	...	...	...	...	...	...	...	...	...	...	|
Toulon 360 a.	1004	...	...	...	...	...	...	...	...	...	1015	...	...	...	...	...	...	...	...	...	...	...	...	...	1316
Marseille St Charles 360 a.	...	...	...	...	...	...	...	...	...	...	1107	...	...	...	...	...	...	...	...	...	...	...	...	...	1403

					⑥⑦	◧											⑥⑦	①–⑤					①–⑤	⑥⑦	①–⑤
Ventimiglia d.	...	...	1046	1116	1146	1214	...	...	...	1245	1316	...	1344	1417	...	1445	1516	1516	...	...	...	1546	...	1608	1616
Menton d.	...	...	1105	1135	1205	1231	...	...	...	1303	1334	...	1404	1435	...	1504	1534	1534	...	...	...	1604	1620	1627	1634
Cap Martin-Roquebrune d.	...	...	1111	1141	1211	1237	...	...	...	1309	1340	...	1410	1441	...	1510	1540	1540	...	...	...	1610	|	1633	1640
Monaco-Monte Carlo d.	...	...	1120	1149	1219	1246	...	...	...	1317	1349	...	1419	1449	...	1519	1548	1548	...	...	...	1618	1635	1641	1648
Eze d.	...	...	1127	1156	1226	1253	...	...	...	1325	1356	...	1425	1456	...	1526	1555	1556	...	...	...	1626	|	1648	1655
Beaulieu sur Mer d.	...	...	1131	1201	1231	1258	...	...	...	1330	1401	...	1430	1501	...	1530	1600	1601	...	...	...	1631	1646	1652	1700
Villefranche sur Mer d.	...	...	1134	1204	1234	1301	...	...	...	1333	1404	...	1433	1504	...	1533	1603	1604	...	...	...	1634	1650	1655	1703
Nice Ville a.	...	...	1141	1211	1240	1308	...	...	...	1340	1411	...	1440	1511	...	1540	1610	1611	...	...	...	1641	1659	1702	1710
Nice Ville d.	...	...	1144	1214	1243	1311	1325	...	...	1343	1414	1425	1443	1514	...	1543	1613	1614	1625	...	...	1644	1702	1705	1713
Nice St Augustin ✈ ⊡ d.	...	...	1151	1220	1250	1318	1332	...	...	1350	1421	1432	1450	1520	...	1550	1620	1620	1633	...	...	1651	1709	1713	1720
Cagnes sur Mer d.	...	...	1200	1229	1259	1327	|	...	...	1355	1429	|	1459	1529	...	1559	1629	1629	|	...	...	1659	1717	1722	1727
Antibes d.	...	...	1209	1239	1308	1337	1346	...	...	1408	1439	1446	1508	1539	...	1609	1638	1639	1647	...	...	1709	1725	1732	1736
Juan les Pins d.	...	...	1213	1242	1312	1340	|	...	...	1411	1442	|	1512	1542	...	1612	1642	1642	|	...	...	1712	1729	1736	1739
Cannes d.	...	1209	1224	1253	1323	1350	1401	...	1409	1423	1451	1501	1523	1552	1609	1623	1651	1655	1701	...	1709	1724	1739	1745	1751
Grasse a.	...	|	1253	1321t	1353	...	|	...	|	1453	...	|	1553	▬	|	1653	...	1723	|	...	|	1753	|	...	1823
Boulouris sur Mer d.	...	1240	...	...	...	...	|	...	1440	...	...	|	...	...	1640	...	...	...	|	...	1740	...	1811	...	...
St Raphaël-Valescure d.	...	1245	...	...	...	...	1426	...	1445	...	...	1525	...	...	1645	...	...	...	1725	...	1745	...	1816	...	...
Fréjus d.	...	1249	...	...	...	...	|	...	1450	...	...	|	...	...	1650	...	...	...	|	...	1750	...	1820	...	...
Les Arcs-Draguignan d.	1258	1303	...	...	...	...	1442	1446	1503	...	...	1541	...	1658	1703	...	...	...	1741	1758	1803	...	1833	...	...
Carnoules d.	1332	...	...	...	...	...	|	1513	...	...	...	|	...	1732	...	...	...	...	|	1832	...	...	...	...	...
Toulon 360 a.	1404	...	...	...	...	...	1516	1544	...	...	...	1616	...	1804	...	...	...	...	1816	1904	...	...	...	...	...
Marseille St Charles 360 a.	...	...	...	...	...	...	1603	...	...	...	...	1706	...	...	...	...	...	...	1922	...	...	...	...	...	...

C – ⑥⑦ to Mar. 5; ⑥ Mar. 11 - May 20; ⑥⑦ from May 27.
D – ⑤–⑦ to Mar. 5; ⑤⑥ Mar. 10 - May 20 (also Apr. 10, May 1, 8, 18); ⑤⑥† from May 26.
E – ⑦ Mar. 12 - May 21.
G – Daily to Mar. 11; ①–⑥ Mar. 13 - May 20; daily from May 22.
H – ⑦–④ to Mar. 12; ④ Mar. 16 - May 18 (also Apr. 10, May 1, 8); ⑦–④ from May 25.

e – ①–⑤ to Mar. 10 (also Apr. 11, May 2, 9, 19); ①–⑤ from May 30.

f – ⑤ only.
h – ⑤⑥ only.
k – ⑥ only.
r – ⑦ only.
t – ①–⑤ only.
z – ⑥⑦ only.

⊖ – Certain departure times are 1 – 3 minutes later on ⑥⑦.
◧ – Runs 2 – 3 minutes later on ⑥⑦.
⊡ – Situated approximately 800 metres from Nice ✈ terminal building.

361 VENTIMIGLIA - MONACO - NICE - CANNES - TOULON - MARSEILLE

Local *TER* services. See Table **350** for long-distance *TGV* services.

	Ⓐ	①–⑤	⑥⑦	Ⓒ	①–⑤	①–⑤	⑥⑦	⑥⑦	①–⑤			**5772** ★		①–⑤		①–⑤					⑥	⑦ M	⑤	⑥	⑤⑥
Ventimiglia d.	...	1646	1646	...	...	1716	1717	...	...	1746	1816	...	...	...	1846	...	1916	...	1946	2016	2131	...	2246	2247	2317
Menton d.	1650	1705	1705	...	1720	1735	1736	...	1750	1805	1834	...	...	1851	1904	1920	1934	...	2004	2035	2153	...	2304	2306	2338
Cap Martin-Roquebrune d.	|	1711	1711	...	|	1741	1742	...	|	1811	1840	...	...	|	1910	|	1940	...	2010	2041	2159	...	2310	2312	2344
Monaco-Monte Carlo d.	1705	1719	1719	...	1735	1749	1750	...	1805	1819	1848	...	...	1905	1918	1935	1948	...	2018	2049	2208	...	2318	2320	2353
Eze d.	|	1726	1726	...	|	1756	1757	...	|	1826	1855	...	...	|	1926	|	1956	...	2026	2056	2215	...	2326	2327	0000
Beaulieu sur Mer d.	1715	1731	1730	...	1745	1801	1801	...	1815	1830	1900	...	...	1916	1930	1945	2001	...	2031	2100	2220	...	2331	2331	0005
Villefranche sur Mer d.	1719	1734	1733	...	1749	1804	1804	...	1819	1833	1903	...	...	1919	1933	1949	2004	...	2034	2103	2223	...	2334	2334	0008
Nice Ville a.	1727	1741	1740	...	1757	1811	1811	...	1827	1841	1911	...	...	1927	1941	1957	2011	...	2041	2110	2230	...	2343	2341	0015
Nice Ville d.	1733	1744	1743	1755	1800	1814	1814	...	1830	1843	1914	1911	1925	1930	1943	2000	2014	...	2044	2113	2233	2244	...	2344	...
Nice St Augustin ✈ ⊡ d.	1740	1751	1751	1802	1808	1821	1822	...	1838	1851	1921	|	1932	1938	1950	2008	2020	...	2050	2120	2240	2252	...	2352	...
Cagnes sur Mer d.	1748	1759	1800	|	1817	1829	1831	...	1847	1859	1929	|	|	1947	1959	2017	2029	...	2059	2129	2249	2301	...	0001	...
Antibes d.	1756	1808	1810	1817	1825	1838	1841	...	1855	1908	1939	1934	1946	1955	2008	2025	2039	...	2109	2139	2257	2311	...	0011	...
Juan les Pins d.	1759	1811	1813	|	1829	1841	1845	...	1859	1911	1943	|	|	1959	2011	2029	2042	...	2112	2142	2300	2314	...	0014	...
Cannes d.	1809	1824	1826	1831	1837	1855	1854	1910	1909	1924	1953	1946	2002	2009	2025	2037	2052	2117	2125	2152	2327v	2327	...	0024	...
Grasse a.	|	1853	1853	|	...	1923	...	|	|	1953	...	|	|	|	2055	...	...	|	2153	...	2352	2353	...	...	...
Boulouris sur Mer d.	|	...	...	|	...	...	...	1940	1940	...	...	|	|	2040	...	...	...	2150	...	...	...	...	...	...	...
St Raphaël-Valescure d.	1836	...	...	1855	...	...	...	1945	1945	...	...	2013	2027	2045	...	...	...	2155	...	...	...	...	...	...	...
Fréjus d.	1841	...	...	|	...	...	...	1949	1950	...	...	|	|	2050	...	...	...	2159	...	...	...	...	...	...	...
Les Arcs-Draguignan d.	1856	...	...	1911	...	...	...	2002	2003	...	...	2030	2043	2103	...	...	...	2212	...	...	...	...	...	...	...
Carnoules d.	1921	...	...	|	...	...	...	...	...	...	...	|	2102	...	...	...	...	...	...	...	...	...	...	...	...
Toulon 360 a.	1939	...	...	1946	...	...	...	...	...	...	...	2112d	2120	...	...	...	...	...	...	...	...	...	...	...	...
Paris Austerlitz a.	|	...	...	|	...	...	...	...	...	...	...	0755	|	...	...	...	...	...	...	...	...	...	...	...	...
Marseille St Charles 360 a.	2033	...	...	2033	...	...	...	...	...	...	...	...	2213	...	...	...	...	...	...	...	...	...	...	...	...

M – ⑦ to Mar. 5 and from May 28.

d – Departure time.
v – Arrives 2310.

★ – Conveys 🛏 1, 2 cl. and 2 (reclining). Also calls at Marseille-Blancarde (d. 2200). Ⓡ. For overnight journeys only. **Timings may vary** (earlier departures possible). For confirmed timings and days of running, please consult the SNCF journey planner: www.sncf.com
⊡ – Situated approximately 800 metres from Nice ✈ terminal building.

363 BELLEGARDE and GENÈVE - ANNEMASSE - ÉVIAN LES BAINS

See Table **346** for connecting trains Lyon Part Dieu - Bellegarde and v.v. French holiday dates apply. Subject to alteration on Mar. 25, 26.

km				①–⑤ a	Ⓐ			①–⑤ a			Ⓑ ⊙	⑥⑦ z	①–⑤ a	🚌 ①–⑤ a	TGV 6501 ⑥ M		Ⓒ	🚌 Ⓐ	Ⓑ ⊖	◇		△⊗	☆	TGV 6503 C
	Paris Gare de Lyon 341 d.	...	...	...	...	...	...	...	...	...	...	...	...	...	0649	...	...	...	...	...	...	...	...	1027
	Bellegarde 365 d.	...	...	...	0715	...	...	...	...	0815	0915	...	...	...	0950	...	1015	1015	1115	...	...	1215	...	1339
0	**Genève** 365 ‡ d.	0632	...	0702	|	0732	0802	...	0832	|	|	0932	0932	...	|	1032	|	|	|	1132	1232	|	1332	|
9	Genève Eaux Vives 365 ‡ d.	0647	...	0717	|	0747	0817	...	0847	|	|	0947	0947	...	|	1047	|	|	|	1147	1247	|	1347	|
17	Annemasse 365 ‡ a.	0655	...	0725	0755	0755	0825	...	0855	0855	0955	0955	0955	...	1034	1055	1055	1105	1155	1155	1255	1255	1355	1418
17	Annemasse d.	...	0701	0731	...	0801	...	0830	...	0901	...	1001	1001	...	|	...	1101	1105	...	1201	...	1301	1401	|
47	Thonon les Bains d.	...	0731	0801	...	0831	...	0902	...	0931	...	1031	1030	1039	1104	...	1131	1150	...	1231	...	1331	1431	1506
56	**Évian les Bains** a.	...	0739	0809	...	0839	...	0909	...	0939	...	1039	...	1059	1115	...	1139	1210	...	1239	...	1339	1439	1517

		△♡			△	①–⑤ a			①–⑤ a		△	①–⑤ a			TGV 6511 ⑤ M				⊕		⊕		J	🚌 ⑤
Paris Gare de Lyon 341 d.	...	...	...	...	...	...	...	...	...	...	...	...	...	...	1703	...	...	...	...	...	...	...	...	...
Bellegarde 365 ‡ d.	...	1415	...	...	1615	...	1715	...	...	...	1815	...	1915	...	1950	...	2015	2115	...	...	2215	...	...	2315
Genève 365 ‡ d.	1432	|	1532	1632	|	1702	|	1732	1802	1832	|	1902	|	1932	|	2032	|	|	2132	2232	|	...	2332	|
Genève Eaux Vives 365 ‡ d.	1447	|	1547	1647	|	1717	|	1747	1817	1847	|	1917	|	1947	|	2047	|	|	2147	2247	|	...	2347	|
Annemasse 365 a.	1455	1455	1555	1655	1655	1725	1755	1755	1825	1855	1855	1925	1955	1955	2034	2055	2055	2155	2155	2255	2255	...	2355	0003
Annemasse d.	...	1501	1601	...	1701	1731	...	1801	1831	...	1901	1931	...	2001	|	...	2101	...	2201	...	2301	...	...	0003
Thonon les Bains d.	...	1531	1631	...	1731	1801	...	1831	1901	...	1931	2001	...	2031	2110	...	2131	...	2231	...	2331	...	...	0048
Évian les Bains a.	...	1539	1639	...	1739	1809	...	1839	1909	...	1939	2009	...	2039	2121	...	2139	...	2239	...	2339	...	...	0108

	①–⑥ a	L	①–⑤ a			①–⑤ a			①–⑤ a	△			Ⓒ △	Ⓐ ♧		🚌 Ⓐ	⑥⑦ z		①–⑤ a◇		△♤		⑥⑦ z	①–⑤ a☆
Évian-les-Bains d.	0521	...	0551	0621	...	0648	0721	...	0751	0821	...	0921	1021	1021	...	1045	1121	...	...	...	1221	...	1251	1321
Thonon-les-Bains d.	0530	...	0600	0630	...	0700	0730	...	0800	0830	...	0930	1030	1030	...	1105	1130	...	1141	...	1230	...	1300	1330
Annemasse a.	0559	...	0629	0659	...	0729	0759	...	0829	0859	...	0959	1100	1100	...	1150	1159	...	1214	...	1259	...	1329	1359
Annemasse 365 ‡ d.	0605	0605	0635	0705	0705	0735	0805	0805	0835	0905	0905	1005	1105	1112	1105	1150	1205	1205	...	1220	1305	1305	1335	1405
Genève Eaux Vives 365 ‡ d.	0613	|	0643	|	0713	0743	0813	|	0843	|	0913	1013	|	|	1113	|	1213	1213	...	1228	|	1313	1343	1413
Genève 365 ‡ a.	0627	|	0657	|	0727	0757	0827	|	0857	|	0927	1027	|	|	1127	|	1227	1227	...	1242	|	1327	1357	1427
Bellegarde 365 a.	...	0642	...	0742	...	...	...	0842	...	0942	...	...	1142	1157	...	1240	...	...	...	...	1342	...	...	...
Paris Gare de Lyon 341 a.	...	...	...	...	...	...	...	...	...	...	...	...	...	...	...	...	...	...	...	...	...	...	...	...

	Ⓑ ⊡	TGV 6504 ⑥ G	TGV 6504 ⑦ H	Ⓐ ☆	Ⓒ △		☆	Ⓑ ⊙			TGV 6506 ⑦ D	①–⑤ a	TGV 6506 F	①–⑤ a	Ⓐ	TGV 6506 ⑥⑦ E	①–⑥ a							Ⓑ ⊕
Évian-les-Bains d.	...	1314	1340	1421	1421	...	1521	...	1621	...	1645	1651	1700	1721	...	1720	1751	1821	...	1921	...	2021	...	2151
Thonon-les-Bains d.	...	1331	1353	1430	1430	...	1530	...	1630	...	1658	1700	1711	1730	...	1733	1800	1830	...	1930	...	2030	...	2200
Annemasse a.	...	|	|	1459	1459	...	1559	...	1659	...	|	1729	|	1759	...	|	1829	1859	...	1959	...	2059	...	2230
Annemasse 365 ‡ d.	1405	1428	1434	...	1505	1505	1605	1605	1705	1705	1734	1735	1756	1805	1805	1822	1835	1905	1905	2005	2005	2105	2105	2235
Genève Eaux Vives 365 ‡ d.	|	|	|	...	|	1512	1613	|	|	1713	|	1743	|	1813	|	|	1843	|	1913	2013	|	|	2113	2243
Genève 365 ‡ a.	|	|	|	...	|	1527	1627	|	|	1727	|	1757	|	1827	|	|	1857	|	1927	2027	|	|	2127	2257
Bellegarde 365 a.	1442	1505	1518	...	1542	...	...	1642	1742	...	1818	...	1845	...	1842	1923	...	1942	...	...	2042	2142	...	...
Paris Gare de Lyon 341 a.	...	1818	1823	...	...	...	...	...	...	...	2126	...	2134	...	...	2234	...	...	...	...	...	...	...	...

C – ⑥⑦ to Mar. 26; ⑥ from Apr. 1 (also May 18, 19).
D – ⑦ from Apr. 2 (not May 28).
E – ⑥⑦ until Mar. 26 (not Dec. 24, 31, Feb. 18, 25, 26, Mar. 4, 5). Arrives Paris 2225 on ⑥.
F – Runs on Feb. 18, 25, 26, Mar. 4, 5, Apr. 10, May 1, 8, 28, 29 only. Arrives Paris 2159 on Feb. 25, Mar. 4.
G – ⑥ until Mar. 25 (also May 28).
H – ⑦ from Apr. 2 (also Apr. 10, May 1, 8, 29; not May 28). Arrives Paris 1843 on Apr. 10, May 1, 8. Arrives Paris 1834 on May 29.
J – Daily to Apr. 1; ⑤⑥ from Apr. 7.
L – Daily to Apr. 2; Ⓒ Apr. 8–23 (also Apr. 11); daily from Apr. 29.
M – Until Mar. 25.

a – Not Apr. 10, May 18, 29.
z – Also Apr. 10, May 18, 29.

TGV – High-speed train. Ⓡ. 🍷. Only for journeys from/to Paris. Timings may vary by a few minutes – please check your reservation.

△ – Change trains at Annemasse on Dec. 17, 24, 31, Feb. 4, 11, 18, 25, Mar. 4.
♧ – Subject to alteration Feb. 27, 28, Mar. 1–3, 6–10, 27–31, Apr. 17–21, 24–28.
⊡ – Subject to alteration Feb. 20–24, Mar. 20–24, 27–31, Apr. 3–7, 17–21.
⊗ – Subject to alteration Feb. 27, 28, Mar. 1–3, 6–10, Apr. 17–21, 24–28.
⊖ – Subject to alteration Mar. 6–10, 20–24, 27–31, Apr. 3–7, 17–21.
♤ – Subject to alteration Feb. 27, 28, Mar. 1–3, Apr. 17–21, 24–28.
⊙ – Subject to alteration Mar. 20–24, 27–31, Apr. 3–7.
♡ – Subject to alteration Apr. 17–21, 24–28.
⊕ – Subject to alteration on ①–⑤ Mar. 20 - Apr. 14.
◇ – Subject to alteration Feb. 27 - Mar. 3, Apr. 24–28.
☆ – Subject to alteration Apr. 24–28.
‡ – Frequent additional services (every 15 minutes during the day) operate Genève - Annemasse and v.v.

GENÈVE and ANNECY - CHAMBÉRY - GRENOBLE - VALENCE 364

On May 18 services run as on ⑥ (except where shown).

km		Ⓐ	⚒	Ⓐ	⚒		⚒	Ⓐ	⚒	⊙		Ⓒ	Ⓒ	◇	☆	Ⓒ	⊙					Ⓐ	A	Ⓑ	Ⓐ
0	**Genève** 341 346 d.	...	...	...	...	...	...	...	0659	...	...	...	...	1000	...	...	...	1159	...	...	...	1459	...	...	...
33	Bellegarde 341 346 d.	...	...	...	...	...	...	...	0729	...	...	...	...	1029	...	...	...	1229	...	...	...	1529	...	...	...
66	Culoz 346 d.	...	...	...	...	...	...	...	|	...	...	...	...	|	...	...	...	|	...	...	...	|	...	...	...
	Annecy 341 345 d.	...	...	...	0543	...	0643	0719	|	0743	0843	0843	0953	|	1043	1143	...	|	1243	1343	1443	|	1543	1643	1718
88	Aix les Bains 341 345 d.	...	...	...	0626	...	0726	0803	0806	0826	0926	0926	1033	1107	1126	1226	...	1307	1327	1426	1526	1607	1626	1726	1800
102	**Chambéry** 341 345 a.	...	...	...	0637	...	0737	0814	0818	0837	0937	0937	...	1117	1136	1237	...	1318	1337	1437	1537	1618	1637	1737	1810
102	**Chambéry** d.	...	0540	*0557*	0640	...	0740	...	0821c	0840	...	0940	...	1120	1140	1240	1240	1321	1340	1440	1540	1621	1640	1740	...
116	Montmélian d.	...	0551	*0606*	0651	...	0751	...	|	0851	...	0951	...	|	1151	1251	1251	|	1351	1451	1551	|	1651	1751	...
165	**Grenoble** a.	...	0627	*0651*	0727	...	0827	...	0902c	0927	...	1027	...	1201	1227	1327	1327	1402	1427	1527	1627	1702	1727	1827	...
165	**Grenoble** d.	0601	0630	0704	0730	0730	0830	...	...	0930	...	1030	...	1204	1230	1330	1330	...	1430	1530	1630	1705	1730	1830	...
242	Romans-Bourg de Péage d.	0658	0727	0758	0827	0827	0927	...	...	1027	...	1128	...	1259	1327	1427	1427	...	1527	1627	1727	1758	1827	1927	...
249	Valence TGV a.	0704	0733	0804	0833	0833	0933	...	...	1033	...	1134	...	1306	1333	1433	1433	...	1533	1633	1733	1805	1833	1933	...
259	**Valence** Ville a.	0715	0743	0814	0843	0843	0943	...	...	1043	...	1144	...	1316	1342	1442	1442	...	1543	1643	1743	1814	1843	1943	...

		⑤⑥† d		⚒			Ⓐ		🚌
Genève 341 346 d.	1642	1642	...	...	...	1842	...	...	...
Bellegarde 341 346 d.	1711	1711	...	...	...	1911	...	...	...
Culoz 346 d.	1746	1746	...	...	...	1943	...	...	...
Annecy 341 345 d.	|	|	1743	...	1845	|	1918	1943	2038
Aix les Bains 341 345 d.	1806	1806	1826	...	1926	2003	2007	2026	2136
Chambéry 341 345 a.	1816	1816	1837	...	1937	2013	2019	2037	2208
Chambéry d.	1821	1821	1840	...	1940	2021	...	2040	...
Montmélian d.	|	|	1850	...	1951	|	...	2051	...
Grenoble a.	1902	1902	1926	...	2027	2102	...	2127	...
Grenoble d.	...	1905	1930	1941	2030	...	...	...	...
Romans-Bourg de Péage d.	...	1957	2027	2059	2127	...	...	...	...
Valence TGV a.	...	2004	2033	2105	2133	...	...	...	...
Valence Ville a.	...	2013	2043	2114	2143	...	...	...	...

	①–⑤ b	⚒	⚒	Ⓐ	Ⓐ	⚒	①–⑥ b	Ⓐ		Ⓐ	
Valence Ville d.	...	...	...	...	...	0524	...	...	...	0617	0645
Valence TGV d.	...	...	...	...	...	0532	...	...	...	0627	0655
Romans-Bourg de Péage d.	...	...	...	...	...	0540	...	...	...	0635	0703
Grenoble a.	...	...	...	...	...	0647	...	...	...	0730	0755
Grenoble d.	0507	...	0539	...	0633	...	0658	...	0733	0733	0758
Montmélian d.	0544	...	0626	...	0710	...	|	...	0810	0810	|
Chambéry a.	0554	...	0635	...	0719	...	0739	...	0819	0819	0839
Chambéry 341 345 d.	0557	0622	...	0645	0722	...	0742	0800	0822	0822	0842
Aix les Bains 341 345 d.	0609	0635	...	0658	0735	...	0754	0813	0835	0835	0855
Annecy 341 345 a.	|	0715	...	0733	0815	...	|	0856	0915	0915	|
Culoz 346 d.	0632	...	...	...	...	...	|	...	...	...	|
Bellegarde 341 346 d.	0702	...	...	...	...	...	0833	...	...	...	0933
Genève 341 346 a.	0731	...	...	...	...	...	0900	...	...	...	1001

	Ⓐ	⊗	Ⓐ	⊖			⊙	⊙	⊙	⊙	Ⓐ				Ⓐ					⑦ A	Ⓐ ⊡		Ⓒ	🚌	Ⓑ t
Valence Ville d.	0717	0817	0917	1017	...	...	1217	1317	1346	1417	...	1517	1617	1645	...	1710	1745	1816	1916	2017	2017	2117	2117	...	2217
Valence TGV d.	0727	0827	0927	1027	...	...	1227	1327	1356	1427	...	1527	1627	1655	...	1725	1755	1827	1926	2027	2027	2127	2127	...	2227
Romans-Bourg de Péage d.	0735	0835	0935	1035	...	...	1235	1335	1404	1435	...	1535	1635	1703	...	1733	1803	1835	1934	2035	2035	2135	2135	...	2235
Grenoble a.	0830	0930	1030	1130	...	...	1330	1430	1455	1530	...	1630	1730	1755	...	1830	1855	1930	2030	2130	2130	2230	2230	...	2330
Grenoble d.	▬	0933	...	1133	1158	1233	1333	1433	1458	1533	...	1633	1733	1758	...	1833	*1909*	1933	2033	2133	2133	...	2233	...	...
Montmélian d.	...	1010	...	1210	|	1310	1410	1510	|	1610	...	1710	1810	|	...	1910	*1954*	2010	2110	2210	2210	...	2310	...	...
Chambéry a.	...	1020	...	1219	1239	1320	1419	1519	1539	1619	...	1719	1819	1839	...	1919	*2003*	2019	2119	2219	2219	...	2319	...	...
Chambéry 341 345 d.	⚒	1023	...	1222	1242	1323	1422	1522	1542	1622	1700	1722	1822	1842	1901	1923	...	2022	2122	2222	2224	...	...	2330	...
Aix les Bains 341 345 d.	0925	1036	...	1234	1255	1335	1435	1534	1555	1635	1712	1734	1834	1855	1913	1935	...	2035	2135	2235	2235	...	...	2350	...
Annecy 341 345 a.	1007	1115	...	1315	|	1415	1515	1615	|	1715	1755	1815	1915	|	1956	2015	...	2115	2215	2315	2315	...	...	0022	...
Culoz 346 d.	...	...	...	...	|	...	...	...	|	...	...	...	...	|	...	...	...	...	...	...	...	...	...	...	...
Bellegarde 341 346 d.	...	...	...	...	1333	...	...	...	1633	...	...	...	...	1933	...	...	...	...	...	...	...	...	...	...	...
Genève 341 346 a.	...	...	...	...	1400	...	...	...	1701	...	...	...	...	2001	...	...	...	...	...	...	...	...	...	...	...

A – To / from Avignon (Table **351**).

b – Not Apr. 10, May 18, 29.

c – 2 – 3 minutes later on ⑥ until Apr. 22.

d – Also May 17.

t – Not Mar. 12 – 16, 19 – 23, 26 – 30, Apr. 16 – 20, 23 – 27, May 18, 28 – 31, June 1, 4 – 8.

⊡ – Subject to alteration on ①–④ Mar. 13 – 30 and ①–④ May 2 – 17.

◇ – Subject to alteration Apr. 24 – 28, May 27, 28.

☆ – Subject to alteration Apr. 24 – 28, May 2 – 4.

⊗ – Subject to alteration Apr. 24 – 27, May 2 – 4.

⊖ – Subject to alteration on ①–⑤ Jan. 23 - Mar. 10, Apr. 24 – 28, May 26 – 29.

⊙ – Subject to alteration Apr. 24 – 28.

365 BELLEGARDE / GENÈVE / ANNECY - LA ROCHE SUR FORON - ST GERVAIS

See panel below main table for *TGV* services from / to Paris. French holiday dates apply. Subject to alteration on Mar. 25, 26.

km		Ⓐ			Ⓑ		◇ ⊙		Ⓑ ⊙	Ⓒ	⊙	Ⓐ 🚌		Ⓑ ⊖	⑥ 🚌	n ⊕	n ¶⊙	Ⓐ 🚌	D		D	Ⓐ 🚌	n ♡	n △¶	D
	Lyon Part-Dieu **346** d.	...	...	...	...	...	...	...	...	...	...	...	...	...	...	...	...	...	1038	...	1135j	...	...	...	1238
0	**Bellegarde** 363 d.	...	...	...	0715t	0815	...	...	0915	1015	...	1015	...	1115	1115	1215	...	1215	1215	...	1312	...	1415	...	1415
	Genève 363 ▷ d.	...	0632	0732	|	|	0832	0932	|	|	1032	|	1132	|	|	|	1232	|	|	1332	|	...	|	1432	|
	Genève Eaux Vives 363 ▷ d.	...	0647	0747	|	|	0847	0947	|	|	1047	|	1147	|	|	|	1247	|	|	1347	|	...	|	1447	|
38	Annemasse 363 ▷ a.	...	0655	0755	0755t	0855	0855	0955	0955	1055	1055	|	1155	1155	|	1255	1255	|	1255	1355	1355	...	1455	1455	1455
38	Annemasse ▷ d.	...	0702	...	0802	...	0902	...	1002	...	1102	|	...	1202	|	...	1302	|	1302	▬	1402	1405	...	1502	1502
•	**Annecy** ▷ d.	...	|	...	|	...	|	...	|	...	|	|	...	|	|	...	|	|	|	...	|	|	...	|	|
55	La Roche sur Foron ▷ a.	...	0719	...	0819	...	0919	...	1019	...	1119	1106	...	1219	1206	...	1319	1306	1319	Ⓐ	1419	1432	...	1519	1519
55	La Roche sur Foron d.	0624	0724	...	0824	...	0924	...	1024	...	1124	1106	...	1224	1206	...	1324	1306	1324	🚌	1424	1432	...	1524	1524
77	Cluses (Haute-Savoie) d.	0653	0753	...	0854	...	0953	...	1053	...	1153	1150	...	1253	1250	...	1353	1350	1354	1400	1454	1516	...	1553	1554
96	Sallanches Megève d.	0710	0810	...	0909	...	1010	...	1110	...	1210	1214	...	1310	1314	...	1410c	1414	1412	1424	1512	1540	...	1610	1612
102	**St Gervais-les-Bains** a.	0714	0815	...	0915	...	1016	...	1116	...	1216	1230	...	1316	1330	...	1416c	1430	1418	1440	1517	1556	...	1616	1618

		n	D		Ⓐ ⊡	n	n	D	Ⓐ	Ⓐ				Ⓐ	n	n	D				⑥	Ⓑ 🚌		⑤	⑦–④ 🚌
Lyon Part-Dieu **346** d.	...	...	1347	...	...	...	...	1438	...	...	...	...	...	...	...	...	1635	...	...	...	...	...	...	...	...
Bellegarde 363 d.	...	...	1515	...	...	1615	...	1615	...	...	...	1715	...	...	1815	...	1815	...	1915	2015	...	2015	...	2115	2115
Genève 363 ▷ d.	1532	...	|	1547	...	|	1632	|	1647	...	1732	|	1747	...	|	1832	|	1932	|	|	2032	|	2132	|	|
Genève Eaux Vives 363 ▷ d.	1547	...	|	1602	...	|	1647	|	1702	...	1747	|	1802	...	|	1847	|	1947	|	|	2047	|	2147	|	|
Annemasse 363 ▷ a.	1555	...	1555	1610	...	1655	1655	1655	1710	...	1755	1755	1810	...	1855	1855	1855	1955	1955	2055	2055	2105	2155	2155	|
Annemasse ▷ d.	...	1602	1602	1619	...	...	1702	1702	1719	...	...	1802	1819	...	...	1902	1902	...	2002	...	2102	2105	...	2202	|
Annecy ▷ d.	...	|	|	|	1552	...	|	|	|	1652	...	|	|	1752	...	|	|	...	|	...	|	|	...	|	|
La Roche sur Foron ▷ a.	...	1619	1619	1638	1633	...	1719	1719	1738	1733	...	1819	1838	1833	...	1919	1919	...	2019	...	2119	2132	...	2219	2206
La Roche sur Foron d.	...	1624	1624	...	1645	...	1724	1724	...	1745	...	1824	...	1845	...	1924	1924	...	2024	...	2124	2132	...	2224	2206
Cluses (Haute-Savoie) d.	...	1653	1655	...	1712	...	1753	1754	...	1812	...	1853	...	1912	...	1953	1955	...	2053	...	2153	2216	...	2253	2250
Sallanches Megève d.	...	1710	1713	...	1725	...	1810	1812	...	1825	...	1910	...	1925	...	2010	2013	...	2108	...	2210	2240	...	2310	2314
St Gervais-les-Bains a.	...	1716	1718	...	1731	...	1816	1818	...	1830	...	1916	...	1930	...	2016	2018	...	2114	...	2216	2256	...	2316	2330

	L		Ⓐ				Ⓐ				Ⓐ		D	n	n	D	Ⓒ n		⑥ n 🚌	Ⓑ ⊙	D	Ⓒ n	Ⓐ ♧	⚒ 🚌	d ⊙
St Gervais-les-Bains d.	0450	...	0520	...	0549	...	0633	...	0649	...	0733	...	0747	0749	...	0847	0849	...	0930	0949	0947	...	...	1030	1049
Sallanches Megève d.	0455	...	0525	...	0555	...	0638	...	0654	...	0739	...	0754	0755	...	0854	0854	...	0946	0955	0954	...	...	1046	1054
Cluses (Haute-Savoie) d.	0511	...	0541	...	0611	...	0654	...	0710	...	0754	...	0811	0811	...	0911	0911	...	1010	1011	1011	...	...	1110	1111
La Roche sur Foron a.	0537	...	0604	...	0637	...	0716	...	0737	...	0816	...	0837	0837	...	0937	0937	...	1054	1037	1037	...	...	1154	1137
La Roche sur Foron ▷ d.	0541	...	...	0623	0641	...	0727	0723	0741	...	0827	0823	0841	0841	...	0941	0941	...	1054	1041	1041	...	...	1154	1141
Annecy ▷ a.	|	...	...	|	|	...	0806	|	|	...	0906	|	|	|	...	|	|	...	|	|	|	...	...	|	|
Annemasse ▷ a.	0558	...	...	0640	0658	...	...	0740	0758	...	...	0840	0858	0858	...	0958	0958	...	|	1058	1055	...	...	|	1158
Annemasse 363 ▷ d.	0605	0605	...	0650	0705	0705	...	0750	0805	0805	...	0850	0905	0905	0905	1005	...	1005	|	1105	1105	1105	1112	|	*1205*
Genève Eaux Vives 363 ▷ d.	|	0613	...	0658	0713	|	...	0758	|	0813	...	0858	|	0913	|	|	...	1013	|	1113	|	|	|	|	*1213*
Genève 363 ▷ a.	|	0627	...	0712	0727	|	...	0812	|	0827	...	0912	|	0927	|	|	...	1027	|	1127	|	|	|	|	*1227*
Bellegarde 363 a.	0642	...	...	...	...	0742	...	...	0842	...	...	...	0942	...	0942	1042	...	...	1145	...	1141	1142	1157	1245	...
Lyon Part-Dieu **346** a.	...	...	...	...	...	...	...	...	...	...	...	...	1122	...	...	1222	...	...	...	...	1326	...	...	...	...

	⑥ n 🚌	D	Ⓑ ¶⊙	n ♤	Ⓑ ⊗		Ⓐ 🚌	D	Ⓒ n	Ⓒ n	D	Ⓑ ⊙				Ⓐ							Ⓑ		
St Gervais-les-Bains d.	1125	1145	1149	...	1249	...	1259	1346	1349	...	1446	1449	...	1549	...	1649	...	1749	...	1849	...	...	1949	...	...
Sallanches Megève d.	1141	1153	1155	...	1254	...	1315	1354	1355	...	1454	1454	...	1555	...	1655	...	1755	...	1854	...	...	1954	...	...
Cluses (Haute-Savoie) d.	1205	1212	1211	...	1311	...	1339	1411	1411	...	1512	1511	...	1611	...	1711	...	1811	...	1911	...	...	2011	...	...
La Roche sur Foron a.	1249	1237	1237	...	1337	...	1423	1437	1437	...	1537	1537	...	1637	...	1737	...	1837	...	1937	...	...	2037	...	...
La Roche sur Foron ▷ d.	1249	1241	1241	...	1341	...	1423	1441	1441	...	1541	1541	...	1641	...	1741	...	1841	...	1941	...	...	2041	...	...
Annecy ▷ a.	|	|	|	...	|	...	|	|	|	...	|	|	...	|	...	|	...	|	...	|	...	...	|	...	...
Annemasse ▷ a.	|	1258	1258	...	1358	...	1450	1459	1458	...	1558	1558	...	1658	...	1758	...	1858	...	1958	...	...	2058	...	...
Annemasse 363 ▷ d.	|	1305	1305	1305	1405	1405	1450	1506	1505	1505	1605	1605	1605	1705	1705	1805	1805	1905	1905	2005	2005	...	...	2105	2105
Genève Eaux Vives 363 ▷ d.	|	|	1313	|	|	1413	|	|	1513	|	|	|	1613	1713	|	|	1813	1913	|	|	2013	...	...	|	2113
Genève 363 ▷ a.	|	|	1327	|	|	1427	|	|	1527	|	|	|	1627	1727	|	|	1827	1927	|	|	2027	...	...	|	2127
Bellegarde 363 a.	1340	1342	...	1342	1442	...	1540	1543	...	1542	1642	1642	...	...	1742	1842	...	...	1942	2042	...	...	...	2142	...
Lyon Part-Dieu **346** a.	...	1522	...	...	...	...	...	1721	...	...	1815	...	...	...	...	...	...	...	...	...	...	...	...	...	...

ANNECY - ANNEMASSE - GENÈVE

	Ⓐ		Ⓐ		Ⓐ			Ⓑ ⊡	⊡	Ⓑ ⊡	¶⊡	Ⓐ	†	Ⓐ	Ⓒ	Ⓑ ⊡	Ⓐ ⊡			Ⓑ	Ⓐ			Ⓑ	
Annecy d.	*0510**	0544	*0610**	0644	*0710**	0744	0844	0944	1044	1144	1244	*1340**	1344	*1440**	1444	1544	1552	...	1644	1744	1752	...	1844	1944	2044
La Roche sur Foron a.	|	0619	|	0719	|	0819	0919	1019	1119	1219	1319	|	1419	|	1519	1619	1633	...	1719	1819	1833	...	1919	2019	2119
La Roche sur Foron d.	|	0623	|	0723	|	0823	0923	1023	1123	1223	1323	|	1423	|	1523	1623	...	1641	1723	1823	...	1841	1923	2023	2123
Annemasse a.	*0610**	0640	*0710**	0740	*0810**	0840	0942	1040	1140	1240	1340	*1440**	1440	*1540**	1540	1640	...	1658	1740	1840	...	1858	1940	2040	2140
Annemasse ◧ d.	0620	0650	0720	0750	0820	0850	0950	1050	1150	1250	1350	1450	1450	1550	1550	1650	...	1705	1750	1850	...	1905	1950	2050	2150
Genève Eaux Vives ◧ d.	0628	0658	0728	0758	0828	0858	0958	1058	1158	1258	1358	1458	1458	1558	1558	1658	...	1713	1758	1858	...	1913	1958	2058	2158
Genève ◧ a.	0642	0712	0742	0812	0842	0912	1012	1112	1212	1312	1412	1512	1512	1612	1612	1712	...	1727	1812	1912	...	1927	2012	2112	2212

	Ⓑ		Ⓐ		Ⓑ	⊡	Ⓑ ⊡	⊡	†	Ⓐ	¶⊡	†	Ⓐ	⊡		Ⓐ	Ⓐ		Ⓐ			Ⓑ	⑥		⚒
Genève ◧ d.	0547	0632	...	0647	0747	0847	0947	1047	1147	1147	1247	1347	1347	1447	1547	1647	1717	1747	1817	1847	1947	2047	2047	...	2148
Genève Eaux Vives ◧ d.	0602	0647	...	0702	0802	0902	1002	1102	1202	1202	1302	1402	1402	1502	1602	1702	1732	1802	1832	1902	2002	2102	2102	...	2203
Annemasse ◧ a.	0610	0655	...	0710	0810	0910	1010	1110	1210	1210	1310	1410	1410	1510	1610	1710	1740	1810	1840	1910	2010	2110	2110	...	2211
Annemasse d.	0619	0702	...	0719	0819	0919	1019	1119	1219	*1220**	1319	1419	*1420**	1519	1619	1719	*1750**	1819	*1850**	1919	2019	2119	*2120**	...	*2220**
La Roche sur Foron a.	0638	0719	...	0738	0838	0938	1038	1138	1238	|	1338	1438	|	1538	1638	1738	|	1838	|	1938	2038	2138	|	...	|
La Roche sur Foron d.	0642	...	0727	0742	0842	0942	1042	1142	1242	|	1342	1442	|	1542	1642	1742	|	1842	|	1942	2042	2142	|	...	|
Annecy a.	0716	...	0806	0816	0916	1016	1116	1216	1316	*1320**	1416	1516	*1520**	1616	1716	1816	*1850**	1916	*1950**	2016	2116	2216	*2220**	...	*2320**

TGV services from / to Paris. Timings may vary by a few minutes (please check your reservation for confirmed timings). For other services Paris - Bellegarde, see Table **341**.

Services run until Mar. 26	*TGV* **6467** ⑦ v	*TGV* **6467** ⑥		*TGV* **6473** ⑥	*TGV* **6473** ⑦		*TGV* **6477** ⑤		
Paris Gare de Lyon d.	0634	0649	...	1027	1029	...	1703	...	...
Bellegarde a.	0927	0950	...	1340	1339	...	1950	...	...
Annemasse a.	1027	1034	...	1423	1418	...	2034	...	...
Cluses (Haute-Savoie) a.	1110	1136	...	1509	1509	...	2128	...	...
Sallanches Megève a.	1124	1151	...	1528	1528	...	2143	...	...
St Gervais-les-Bains a.	1133	1201	...	1536	1536	...	2151	...	...

Services run until Mar. 26	*TGV* **6480** ⑥		*TGV* **6482** ⑥	*TGV* **6482** ⑦		*TGV* **6484** H	*TGV* **6484** G	*TGV* **6484** J	*TGV* **6484** ⑦ e	*TGV* **6484** ⑥ w	
St Gervais-les-Bains d.	0928	...	1301	1300	...	1631	1633	1633	1633	1633	...
Sallanches Megève d.	0936	...	1311	1311	...	1639	1641	1641	1641	1641	...
Cluses (Haute-Savoie) d.	0954	...	1325	1326	...	1704	1701	1701	1701	1701	...
Annemasse d.	1038	...	1428	1425	...	1756	1801	1801	1822	1822	...
Bellegarde d.	1119	...	1505	1508	...	1845	1846	1845	1919	1923	...
Paris Gare de Lyon a.	1431	...	1818	1823	...	2159	2134	2159	2234	2225	...

D – Runs on Dec. 17, 24, 31, Feb. 4, 11, 18, 25, Mar. 4 only.
G – Runs on Feb. 26, Mar. 5 only.
H – Runs on Feb. 18, 25 only.
J – Runs on Mar. 4 only.
L – Daily to Apr. 2; Ⓒ Apr. 8–23 (also Apr. 11); daily from Apr. 29.

c – Cluses - St Gervais on Ⓒ only.
d – Not Feb. 18, 19, 25, 26.
e – Not Feb. 26, Mar. 5.
j – 1133 on Feb. 25.
n – Not Dec. 17, 24, 31, Feb. 4, 11, 18, 25, Mar. 4.

t – Ⓐ only.
v – Not Dec. 25, Jan. 1.
w – Not Dec. 24, 31, Feb. 18, 25, Mar. 4.

TGV – High-speed train. 🅁. 🍸. Only for journeys from / to Paris.

* – By 🚌.
◇ – Change trains at Annemasse on ⑥.
△ – Change trains at Annemasse on Ⓐ.
¶ – Subject to alteration Feb. 20–24.
♡ – Subject to alteration Apr. 17–21, 24–28.
⊡ – Subject to alteration Mar. 6–10, 13–17, 20–24.

⊙ – Subject to alteration Mar. 20–24, 27–31, Apr. 3–7.
♤ – Subject to alteration Feb. 27, 28, Mar. 1–3, Apr. 17–21, 24–28.
⊖ – Subject to alteration Mar. 6–10, 20–24, 27–31, Apr. 3–7, 17–21.
⊕ – Subject to alteration Feb. 27, 28, Mar. 1–3, 6–10, Apr. 17–21, 24–28.
♧ – Subject to alteration Feb. 27, 28, Mar. 1–3, 6–10, 27–31, Apr. 17–21, 24–28.
⊗ – Subject to alteration Feb. 20–24, Mar. 20–24, 27–31, Apr. 3–7, 17–21.
• – Annecy to La Roche sur Foron is 39 km.
▷ – For other trains Genève - Annemasse - La Roche sur Foron - Annecy see panel below the main table (see also note ◧).
◧ – Frequent services (every 15 minutes during the day) operate Genève - Annemasse and v.v.

ST GERVAIS - CHAMONIX - VALLORCINE (- MARTIGNY) 365a

Mont-Blanc Express. For full details of journeys Vallorcine - Martigny and v.v., see Table **572**. **SERVICE UNTIL APRIL 16.**

km																									
												A					Ⓐe								
0	**St Gervais** d.	0628	0705	0808	...	0928	1028	1128	1228	1328	1428	1528	...	...	1628	1728	1805	1828	1928	2028	...	...	...	...	...
9	Les Houches d.	0654	0733	0836	...	0954	1054	1154	1254	1354	1454	1554	...	...	1654	1754	1833	1854	1954	2054	...	...	...	...	...
20	**Chamonix** Mont-Blanc a.	0713	0750	0852	...	1013	1113	1213	1313	1413	1513	1613	...	...	1713	1813	1851	1913	2013	2113	...	...	...	...	...
20	**Chamonix** Mont-Blanc d.	0728	0828	0928	...	1028	1128	1228	1328	1428	1528	1628	...	1658	1728	1828	1857	1928	2028	...	...	...	...	...	...
24	Les Tines d.	0737	0837	0937	...	1037	1137	1237	1337	1437	1537	1637	...	1707	1737	1837	1906	1937	2037	...	...	...	...	...	...
28	Argentière Haute Savoie d.	0746	0846	0946	...	1046	1146	1246	1346	1446	1546	1646	...	1716	1746	1846	1916	1946	2046	...	...	...	...	...	...
35	**Vallorcine** a.	0801	0901	1001	...	1101	1201	1301	1401	1501	1601	1701	...	1731	1801	1901	1931	2001	2101	...	...	...	...	...	...
	Change trains																								
35	**Vallorcine** ★ **572** d.	0810	0910	1010	...	1110	1210	1310	1410	1510	1610	...	1710	...	1810	1910	...	2010	2110	...	...	...	...	...	...
56	**Martigny** **572** a.	0859	0959	1059	...	1159	1259	1359	1459	1559	1659	...	1759	...	1859	1959	...	2059	2159	...	...	...	...	...	...
											A														
	Martigny **572** d.	...	...	0718	0818	0918	1018	1118	1218	1318	...	1518	1618	1718	1818	1918	...	...	...	...	...	...	...	...	...
	Vallorcine ★ **572** a.	...	...	0805	0905	1005	1105	1205	1305	1405	...	1605	1705	1805	1905	2005	...	...	...	...	...	...	...	...	...
	Change trains																								
	Vallorcine d.	0640	0710	0810	0910	1010	1110	1210	1310	1410	1510	1610	1710	1810	1910	2010	...	...	...	...	...	...	...	...	...
	Argentière Haute Savoie d.	0654	0727	0827	0927	1027	1127	1227	1327	1427	1527	1627	1727	1827	1927	2027	...	...	...	...	...	...	...	...	...
	Les Tines d.	0703	0737	0837	0937	1037	1137	1237	1337	1437	1537	1637	1737	1837	1937	2037	...	...	...	...	...	...	...	...	...
	Chamonix Mont-Blanc a.	0710	0745	0845	0945	1045	1145	1245	1345	1445	1545	1645	1745	1845	1945	2045	...	...	...	...	...	...	...	...	...
	Chamonix Mont-Blanc d.	0715	0755	0855	0955	1055	1155	1255	1355	1455	1615	1715	1815	1915	1955	...	...	...	...	...	...	...	...	...	...
	Les Houches d.	0732	0814	0914	1014	1114	1214	1314	1414	1514	1632	1732	1832	1932	2014	...	...	...	...	...	...	...	...	...	...
	St Gervais a.	0757	0840	0940	1040	1140	1240	1340	1440	1540	1657	1757	1857	1957	2040	...	...	...	...	...	...	...	...	...	...

A – Until Apr. 2. e – Not Dec. 19 – 30, Feb. 6 – 17, Apr. 10 – 14. ★ – 🏛 is at Le Châtelard Frontière (see Table **572**).

(PARIS -) CHAMBÉRY - ALBERTVILLE - BOURG ST MAURICE 366

Timings may vary by up to 4 minutes on certain dates. See panel below main table for *TGV* services from / to Paris. On May 18 services in this table run as on ⑥.

km																									
		🚌 Ⓐ	Ⓐ	🚌 Ⓐ	⑥ E	🚌 Ⓐ	† E	G	⑥ E	H	🚌 Ⓐ	Ⓒ E	G	Ⓒ E	Ⓐ	⑥ E	H	Ⓒ E	G	Ⓒ E	⑥ E	H	⑥ E	A	🚌 ⚒
	Lyon Part Dieu **344** d.	...	...	...	0650	...	...	...	0950	...	...	1150	...	1350	...	1511	...	1550	...	...	1750	...	1846	...	...
	Aix les Bains **345 364** d.	...	...	...	|	...	0917	0939	|	...	...	|	1339	|	1539	1637	1640	|	1739	1818	|	1939	|	2039	...
0	**Chambéry** **345 364 367** d.	0551	0653	...	0819	0808	0931	0952	1131	1153	1251	1331	1353	1531	1553	1650	1653	1731	1753	1832	1920	1953	2053	2053	2200
13	Montmélian **367** d.	0621	0703	...	0829	0838	0941	1003	1141	1203	|	1342	1403	1542	1603	1701	1703	1741	1803	1841	1932	2003	2103	2103	2230
25	St Pierre d'Albigny **367** d.	0639	0714	...	0839	0853	0950	1014	1150	1214	|	1350	1414	1551	1614	1715	1713	1750	1814	1850	1943	2014	2112	2114	2245
48	Albertville a.	0717	0737	...	0857	0918	1015	1037	1211	1237	1351	1415	1437	1615	1637	1737	1737	1812	1837	1915	2014	2037	2137	2137	2310
48	Albertville d.	0717	0744	...	0904	0918	1022	1044	1222	1244	1351	1422	1444	1622	1644	1748	1744	1822	1844	1922	2022	2044	2144	2144	2310
76	**Moûtiers-Salins** d.	0747	0810	0845	0930	0948	1050	1113	1248	1313	1421	1449	1513	1648	1713	1815	1813	1850	1913	1954	2050	2113	2212	2213	2345
91	Aime la Plagne d.	0802	...	0900	0950	1003	1106	1129	1304	1329	|	1505	1529	1707	1729	1831	1829	1909	1929	2012	2106	2129	2228	2229	0000
98	Landry d.	0812	...	0910	1000	1013	1116	1138	1315	1338	|	1515	1538	1717	1738	1841	1838	1919	1938	2022	2116	2138	2238	2238	0011
105	**Bourg St Maurice** a.	0824	...	0922	1007	1025	1123	1145	1322	1345	1451	1522	1545	1723	1745	1849	1845	1926	1945	2029	2123	2145	2245	2245	0025

	🚌 Ⓐ	D	⑥ E	B	⑥ E	🚌 †	🚌 Ⓐ	Ⓐ n	Ⓒ E	🚌 Ⓐ	G	⑥ E	† E		H	Ⓒ E		G	Ⓒ E		A	Ⓒ E△	🚌 Ⓐ	A	Ⓒ E
Bourg St Maurice d.	0419	0513	0538	0613	0638	0717	0759	...	0838	0841	1013	1038	1045	...	1213	1238e	...	1413	1442	...	1613	1640	1641	1813	1832f
Landry d.	|	0521	0546	0621	0648	0728	0810	...	0848	0852	1021	1048	1054	...	1221	1248	...	1421	1452	...	1621	1650	1653	1821	1842f
Aime la Plagne d.	|	0532	0557	0632	0659	0740	0822	...	0859	0904	1032	1059	1104	...	1232	1301	...	1432	1503	...	1632	1701	1705	1832	1853
Moûtiers-Salins d.	0449	0549	0614	0649	0717	0802	0839	0849	0917	0921	1049	1117	1121	...	1249	1317	...	1449	1520	...	1649	1717	1722	1849	1915
Albertville a.	0524	0615	0640	0715	0740	0847	...	0915	0940	0956	1115	1140	1140	...	1315	1340	...	1515	1543	...	1715	1740	1757	1915	1940
Albertville d.	0524	0622	0647	0722	0748	0847	...	0922	0947	0956	1122	1150	1147	...	1322	1347	...	1522	1550	...	1722	1747	1757	1922	1947
St Pierre d'Albigny **367** d.	0544	0648	0712	0748	0815	0915	...	0948	1013	1026	1148	1211	1211	...	1348	1413	...	1548	1612	...	1748	1810	1822	1948	2013
Montmélian **367** d.	0559	0658	0721	0758	0826	0930	...	0958	1023	1041	1158	1221	1221	...	1358	1423	...	1558	1622	...	1758	1819j	1837	1958	2023
Chambéry **345 364 367** a.	0629	0707	0732	0807	0837	1000	...	1007	1032g	1111	1207	1232	1232	...	1407	1432	...	1607	1629	...	1807	1827j	1907	2007	2032
Aix les Bains **345 364** a.	...	...	|	0821	0903	...	...	...	1054	...	...	|	|	...	1421	|	...	1621	|	...	1821	|	...	2019	|
Lyon Part Dieu **344** a.	...	...	0910	...	1020	...	...	...	1210	...	...	1410	1410	...	...	1610	...	...	1810	...	...	2010	...	...	2210v

TGV services from / to Paris. Timings may vary by a few minutes (please check your reservation for confirmed timings). For ski trains from / to Lille, Brussels, Amsterdam and London, see Table **9**.

	TGV **6417**	*TGV* **6419**	*TGV* **6429**	*TGV* **6435**	*TGV* **6437**	*TGV* **6439**	*TGV* **6443**	*TGV* **6455**	*TGV* **6447**	*TGV* **6453**
	⑥	Ⓒ	⑤–①	⑥⑦	⑥		⑥	⑤	⑤	④⑤
	L	Ps	Ls	L	L	N	L	L	P	L
Paris Gare de Lyon **341** d.	0638	0743k	0838r	0949	1052	1138	1322	1544	1555	1751
Chambéry **341** a.	0952	1054	1154	1301	1355	1441	1626	1854	1917	2120
Albertville a.	1026	1138	1244	1342	1439	1518	1707	1950	2001	2202
Moûtiers-Salins a.	1110	1209	1324	1419	1515	1550	1740	2024	2034	2235
Aime la Plagne a.	1127	1231	1341	1437	1537	1607	1801	2041	2050	2252
Landry a.	1138	1243	1352	1449	1549	1618	1812	2052	2102	2302
Bourg St Maurice a.	1148	1253	1402	1500	1600	1627	1822	2102	2112	2312

	TGV **6420**	*TGV* **6422**	*TGV* **6426**	*TGV* **6434**	*TGV* **6434**	*TGV* **6436**	*TGV* **6436**	*TGV* **6438**	*TGV* **6446**	*TGV* **6442**
		⑥⑦	⑥	⑥		①⑤	⑥	⑥⑦	⑦	Ⓒ
	N	L	L	L	M	L	L¶	Lz	L	P‡
Bourg St Maurice d.	0912	0947	1324	1403	1507	1600	1612	1648	1813	1908
Landry d.	0921	0957	1334	1413	1517	1610	1622	1658	1824	1918
Aime la Plagne d.	0932	1007	1345	1425	1527	1621	1633	1708	1835	1929
Moûtiers-Salins d.	0950	1031	1408	1448	1542	1639	1651	1726	1851	1947
Albertville d.	1028t	1110	1453	1523	1616	1712	1725	1758	1932	2020
Chambéry **341** d.	1112t	1155	1538	1605	1655	1801	1804	1839	2010	2055
Paris Gare de Lyon ... **341** a.	1416t	1454	1845	1911	2006	2126	2126	2214c	2317	0001

A – Ⓐ to Apr. 21; daily from Apr. 24.
B – Ⓑ to Apr. 21; daily from Apr. 23.
D – Ⓐ to Apr. 21; ⚒ from Apr. 24.
E – Until Apr. 23.
G – Ⓐ to Apr. 7; daily from Apr. 29.
H – Ⓐ to Apr. 7; ⚒ from Apr. 29.
L – Until Mar. 26.
M – ⑦ to Mar. 26; ⑥ Apr. 1 – 29.
N – ⑥⑦ to Mar. 26; ⑥ Apr. 1 – 29.
P – Until May 1.

c – 2203 on ⑥.
e – 1235 on Feb. 18, 25.
f – 4 – 6 minutes earlier on Feb. 19, 26.
g – 1037 on Dec. 17, 24, 31, Feb. 11.
j – 4 – 5 minutes later on Apr. 1, 8, 10, 15, 22.

k – 0719 on Apr. 22.
n – Not Apr. 11 – 14, 17 – 21, 24 – 28.
r – 0843 on ⑥ (not Feb. 11, 18, 25).
s – Not Jan. 1.
t – On Apr. 29 Albertville d. 1023, Chambéry d. 1101, Paris a. 1410.
v – 2223 on Dec. 18, Jan. 15, Feb. 5, 12, Mar. 5, 12, 19, Apr. 16.
z – Not Dec. 24.

TGV – High-speed train. Ⓡ. 🍸. Only for journeys from / to Paris.

△ – Departure times Bourg St Maurice - Moûtiers-Salins may be up to 12 minutes earlier on Feb. 11, 18, 25, Mar. 4.
¶ – Not Dec. 24. Departure times Bourg St Maurice - Albertville are up to 8 minutes earlier on Feb. 11, 28, 25, Mar. 4.
‡ – Not Dec. 24, 31. Departs Bourg st Maurice 1903 on Feb. 25. Departure times are up to 15 minutes earlier on Apr. 29.

FRANCE

367 CHAMBÉRY - MODANE

See Table **44** for *TGV* services Paris - Modane - Milano and v.v. Timings may vary by 1–2 minutes on certain dates. On May 18 services in this table run as on ⑥.

km					🚌																				
								TGV 6401									*TGV* 6407							
		M	⑥ T	Ⓐ		⑥ T	Ⓐ	Ⓒ T	⑥ Y	L	G	† Bm	⑥ B	D	Ⓒ R		Ⓒ T	⑥⑦ U	Ⓒ T¶	Ⓐ	⑥ T	M	⑥ Tn	† T	J
	Paris Gare de Lyon **341** ... d.	...	...	...	...	...	...	...	0743	...	...	...	...	...	...	...	...	1138	...	...	...	...	...	...	...
	Lyon Part Dieu **344** ... d.	...	...	...	...	0724	...	0849	|	...	1043	1043	1050	1050	...	...	1249	|	1450	...	...	...	1650	1650	1650
0	**Chambéry** ... **364 366** d.	0629	0629	0729	...	0846	0833	1011	1054	1130	1223	1229	1236j	1248	1248	...	1429	1441	1620	1648	1748	1748	1816	1825	1836
14	Montmélian ... **364 366** d.	0640	0640	0739	...	0858	|	1022	|	1140	1233	1239	1247	1259	1259	...	1440	|	1632	1658	1758	1758	1832	1835	1847
26	St Pierre d'Albigny ... **366** d.	0649	0652	0749	...	0914	|	1031	|	1150	1242	1249	1303	1308	1308	...	1452	|	1641	1706	1807	1808	1844	1845	1856
61	St Avre la Chambre ... d.	0720	0721	0819	...	0941	0956	1056	1142	1220	1306	1321	1327	1331	1339	...	1516	1526	1705	1737	1831	1839	1914	1914	1918
71	St Jean de Maurienne ... d.	0729	0731	0828	...	0952	1011	1106	1153	1235	1317	1332	1338	1342	1348	...	1527	1536	1715	1746	1841	1848	1925	1925	1928
83	St Michel-Valloire ... d.	0742	0746	0841	...	1008	1027	1121	1209	1248	1332	1347	1353	1357	1404	...	1542	1553	1730	1759	1856	1901	1940	1940	1941
99	**Modane** ... a.	0756	0800	0856	...	1026	1047	1136	1226	1302	1345	1400	1407	1411	1418	...	1556	1611	1746	1813	1911	1915	1954	1954	1955

						🚌				🚌	🚌	
	N	† T	P §	†	⑤ f	①–④ t	† T	⑤ T	Q	⑥	⑤	
Paris Gare de Lyon **341** ... d.	...	...	...	...	...	...	...	...	...	...	...	...
Lyon Part Dieu **344** ... d.	...	1750	...	...	...	...	1950	...	...	...	...	...
Chambéry ... **364 366** d.	1829	1928	1929	2046	2046	2051	2121	2150	2150	2154	2231	
Montmélian ... **364 366** d.	1839	1939	1940	2056	2056	|	2137	2201	2201	2224	2301	
St Pierre d'Albigny ... **366** d.	1847	1951	1949	2106	2106	|	2207z	2210	2212	2240	2317	...
St Avre la Chambre ... d.	1917	2016	2020	2136	2136	2214	2236	2240	2241	2315	2352	...
St Jean de Maurienne ... d.	1926	2027	2029	2145	2145	2229	2246	2249	2250	2330	0011	...
St Michel-Valloire ... d.	1939	2042	2042	2158	2158	2245	2301	2302	2303	2346	0023	...
Modane ... a.	1952	2056	2056	2211	2213	2305	2315	2317	2317	0006	0043	...

	🚌			🚌				🚌
	Ⓐ		⚒	†	Ⓒ T	M		Ⓐ
Modane ... d.	0436	...	0550	0601	0700	0701	...	0753
St Michel-Valloire ... d.	0456	...	0606	0621	0718	0718	...	0813
St Jean de Maurienne ... d.	0512	...	0619	0637	0730	0730	...	0829
St Avre la Chambre ... d.	0527	...	0628	0652	0742	0739	...	0844
St Pierre d'Albigny ... **366** d.	|	...	0657	0743	0809	0809	...	|
Montmélian ... **364 366** d.	|	...	0706	0759	0819	0819	...	|
Chambéry ... **364 366** a.	0629	...	0715	0829	0828	0828	...	1007
Lyon Part Dieu **344** ... a.	...	...	...	...	1010	...	...	...
Paris Gare de Lyon **341** a.	...	...	...	...	...	...	...	...

								🚌																	
											TGV 6406	*TGV* 6406					*TGV* 6414								
	Ⓒ T	N	† T	⑥ Th		K	Ⓒ T	Ⓐ		Ⓒ T	⑥ U	⑥ W	⑥ T	† T	N		⑥⑦ U	Ⓐ	Ⓒ Tk	A	B	N		† T	S
Modane ... d.	0854	0939	0959	1001	...	1128	1159	1205	...	1359	1435	1534	1559	1559	1601	...	1716	1716	1809	1809	1811	1822	...	2003	2009
St Michel-Valloire ... d.	0911	0954	1017	1020	...	1147	1217	1225	...	1416	1452	1550	1617	1617	1618	...	1732	1732	1826	1825	1829	1837	...	2022	2025
St Jean de Maurienne ... d.	0926	1006	1033	1035	...	1218	1231	1241	...	1431	1508	1607	1629	1629	1630	...	1746	1745	1841	1839	1843	1850	...	2037	2038
St Avre la Chambre ... d.	0936	1024	1044	1046	...	1228	1241	1256	...	1441	1519	1617	1642	1641	1639	...	1756	1753	1851	1848	1853	1858	...	2047	2046
St Pierre d'Albigny ... **366** d.	1003	1104v	1109	1110	...	1258	1309	1347	...	1510	|	|	1710	1710	1709	...	|	1823	1915	1918	1918	1929	...	2107	2117
Montmélian ... **364 366** d.	1016	1113v	1119	1120	...	1307	1319	1403	...	1519	|	|	1719	1719	1719	...	|	1836	1925	1928	1928	1938	...	2116	2125
Chambéry ... **364 366** a.	1028	1121v	1128	1136	...	1316	1328	1423	...	1528	1605	1655	1727	1728	1730	...	1839	1846	1935	1937	1938	1947	...	2128	2134
Lyon Part Dieu **344** ... a.	1210	...	...	1310	...	...	1510	...	...	1711	|	|	...	1910	...	...	|	...	2110	2110	2110	...	...	...	...
Paris Gare de Lyon **341** ... a.	...	...	...	...	...	...	...	...	...	...	1911	2006	...	...	...	...	2214e	...	...	...	...	...	...	...	...

A – Feb. 5, 11, 12, 18, 19 only.
B – Feb. 25 only.
D – Feb. 26 only.
G – Mar. 5 only.
J – Apr. 8, 15 only.
K – ①–⑤ until Jan. 13; ①–⑤ Feb. 13 - Mar. 10 (also Apr. 17–21, 24–28); Ⓒ from Apr. 29.
L – ①–⑤ until Jan. 13; ①–⑤ Feb. 13 - Mar. 10 (also Apr. 21, 28); Ⓒ from Apr. 29.
M – Ⓐ to Apr. 21; ⚒ from Apr. 24.
N – Ⓐ to Apr. 21; daily from Apr. 24.
P – ⚒ to Apr. 22; daily from Apr. 24.
Q – ①–④ to Apr. 20 (not Apr. 10); Ⓑ from Apr. 24.
R – Ⓒ from Apr. 30.

S – Ⓐ to Apr. 21; Ⓑ from Apr. 24.
T – Until Apr. 23.
U – Until Mar. 26.
W – ⑥ Apr. 1–29.
Y – Until Apr. 29.

e – 2203 on ⑥ (not Feb. 25); 2140 on Feb. 25.
f – Also May 17.
h – Not Apr. 8.
j – 1232 on Apr. 1, 8, 15, 22.
k – Not Feb. 5, 11, 12, 18, 19, 25.
m – Not Feb. 26, Mar. 5.
n – Not Apr. 8, 15.
r – 0719 on Apr. 22.

t – Not Apr. 10, May 1, 8, 17, 18, 29.
v – 4–5 minutes later Jan. 16 - Feb. 10, Mar. 13 - Apr. 14 and on ①–⑤ from May 1.
z – Arrives 2147.

TGV – High-speed train. Ⓡ. 🍸. Only for journeys from / to Paris.

¶ – On Dec. 17, 24, 31, Mar. 11 runs 5–12 minutes later Chambéry - Modane. On Apr. 10 Chambéry d. 1621, Montmélian d. 1636, St Pierre d'Albigny d. 1656, St Avre la Chambre d. 1720, St Jean de Maurienne d. 1730, St Michel-Valloire d. 1745, Modane a. 1759.
§ – Runs 2 minutes later on ⑤.

*See Table **44** for TGV services Paris - Modane - Milano and v.v.*

368 🚌 CHAMONIX - MONT BLANC TUNNEL - COURMAYEUR

SAT / Arriva Italia

By 🚌. Journey 45 minutes. Service confirmed until April 10, 2023.

Dec. 17 - Apr. 10: From Chamonix (Avenue de Courmayeur) at 0830, 0930, 1100, 1500, 1615, 1730. From Courmayeur (Piazzale Monte Bianco) at 0815, 0945, 1200, 1400, 1615, 1730.
Apr. 11 - June 23: From Chamonix (Avenue de Courmayeur) at 0830, 1815. From Courmayeur (Piazzale Monte Bianco) at 0945, 1700.
June 24 - Sept. 10: From Chamonix (Avenue de Courmayeur) at 0830, 1245, 1530, 1800. From Courmayeur (Piazzale Monte Bianco) at 0945, 1145, 1545, 1800.
Sept. 11 - Oct. 15: From Chamonix (Avenue de Courmayeur) at 0830, 1815. From Courmayeur (Piazzale Monte Bianco) at 0945, 1700.

Arriva Italia

🚌 COURMAYEUR - PRÉ ST DIDER - AOSTA

Courmayeur △ ... d.	0645	0745	0835	0935	and	1935	2035	2135	...	...
Pré St Didier ... d.	0653	0753	0843	0943	hourly	1943	2043	2143	...	...
Aosta ⊡ ... a.	0745	0845	0935	1035	until	2035	2135	2235	...	...

Aosta ⊡ ... d.	0645	0745	0845	0945	1045	1145	1245	1335	1445	and	2145
Pré St Didier ... d.	0737	0837	0937	1037	1137	1237	1337	1427	1537	hourly	2237
Courmayeur △ ... a.	0745	0845	0945	1045	1145	1245	1345	1435	1545	until	2245

△ – P. le Monte Bianco.
⊡ – Autostazione (bus station).

Operators: SAT Mont-Blanc ✆ +33 (0)450 780 533 sat-montblanc.com
Arriva Italia Aosta ✆ +39 02 841 21000 aosta.arriva.it

369 CORSICAN RAILWAYS

Narrow gauge. 2nd class.

SERVICE FEBRUARY 27 - JUNE 25

km		Ⓐ	⚒	Ⓐ	Ⓐ	⚒	Ⓐ			⚒	⚒		⚒		⚒		⚒		Ⓐ			Ⓐ			⚒	Ⓑ h	⚒
0	**Bastia** ... d.	...	...	0550	0600	0612	0629	0712	0756	0825	...	0916	0957	1025	1130	1213	1318	1430	1514	1541	1615	1707	1721	...	1805	1839	1933
10	Biguglia ... d.	...	...	0605	0613	0627	0645	0729	0811	0841	...	0931	1013	1040	1144	1228	1334	1446	1530	1555	1633	1725	1735	...	1823	1857	1948
22	Casamozza ... d.	...	...	0619	0628	0642	0659	0743	0827	0855	...	0947	1027	1055	1159	1242	1348	1500	1544	1611	1648	1740	1750	...	1838	1913	2002
47	Ponte Leccia ... d.	...	...	▬	0711	...	...	...	0906	...	...	1025	...	...	1234	...	▬	▬	▬	1646	...	▬	1831f	1830	...	1950	...
98	Ile Rousse ▽ d.	...	...	...	|	...	...	...	|	...	...	1140	...	...	|	...	...	...	...	|	...	...	|	1945	...	|	...
120	**Calvi** ... ▽ a.	...	...	...	|	...	...	...	|	...	...	1215	...	...	|	...	...	...	...	|	...	...	|	2030	...	|	...
74	Corté ... d.	...	...	...	0800e	...	...	...	0947	...	...	...	...	...	1312	...	...	...	...	1726	...	...	1909	...	...	2024	...
90	Vivario ... d.	...	...	...	0831	...	...	...	1018	...	...	...	...	...	1343	...	...	...	...	1757	...	...	1940	...	...	...	...
107	Vizzavona ... d.	...	...	⚒	0853	...	...	...	1037	...	...	...	...	...	1402	...	⚒	⚒	⚒	1818	...	⚒	1959	...	...	...	...
145	Mezzana ... d.	0715	0825	0915	0941	...	...	...	1127	...	1320	...	...	...	1450	...	1640	1755	1844	1906	...	2000	2047	...	...	...	...
158	**Ajaccio** ... a.	0735	0845	0935	1001	...	...	...	1147	...	1340	...	...	...	1510	...	1700	1815	1904	1926	...	2020	2104	...	...	...	...

	Ⓐ	⚒	⚒		⚒	Ⓐ	Ⓐ	Ⓒ		Ⓐ		⚒	⚒	⚒	⚒		⚒		Ⓐ			⚒	⚒		⚒	⚒	⚒
Ajaccio ... d.	...	...	...	...	...	...	0600	...	...	0645	0741	0800	0850	...	1105	...	1215	...	...	...	1521	...	1615	1706	1730	1820	1935
Mezzana ... d.	...	...	...	...	...	...	0618	...	...	0705	0801	0820	0910	...	1128	...	1235	...	...	...	1542	...	1635	1727	1750	1840	1955
Vizzavona ... d.	...	...	...	...	...	...	0706	...	...	▬	0852	▬	▬	...	1216	...	▬	...	...	...	1630	...	▬	1817	...	...	...
Vivario ... d.	...	...	...	...	...	...	0725	...	...	...	0911	...	...	...	1235	...	...	...	...	...	1649	...	...	1836	...	...	...
Corté ... d.	...	...	0632	...	...	...	0803	...	...	...	0946	...	...	...	1313	...	...	...	...	...	1725	...	...	1910	...	...	...
Calvi ... ▽ d.	...	...	|	...	...	0635	|	0700	...	...	|	...	...	...	|	...	...	...	...	1605	|	...	...	|	...	...	...
Ile Rousse ▽ d.	...	...	|	...	...	0721	|	0746	...	...	|	...	...	...	|	...	...	...	...	1641	|	...	...	|	...	...	...
Ponte Leccia ... d.	...	...	0710	...	...	0835	0839	0900	0910	⚒	1023	...	...	...	1347	...	Ⓐ	...	...	1755	1801	...	⚒	1949	...	...	...
Casamozza ... d.	0629	0701	0745	0813	0906	...	0916	...	0948	1042	1058	1120	1309	1353	1422	1505	1618	1710	1757	...	1840	1859	2006	2024	...	...	...
Biguglia ... d.	0645	0716	0800	0829	0920	...	0931	...	1002	1057	1113	1134	1323	1407	1436	1519	1633	1725	1811	...	1857	1914	2020	2038	...	...	...
Bastia ... a.	0701	0734	0818	0847	0936	...	0945	...	1018	1112	1127	1150	1339	1422	1450	1535	1648	1741	1827	...	1914	1929	2035	2051	...	...	...

A – ①–⑤ to Mar. 31; daily from Apr. 3.

e – Arrives 0745.

f – Arrives 1827.
h – Ⓑ (not Apr. 9, 30, May 7, 28). On May 17 does not run Casamozza - Corté.

▽ – **Additional journeys** Ile Rousse - Calvi and v.v.:
From Ile Rousse at 0850 **A**, 1050 **A**, 1350, 1650 **A** and 1850 **A**.
From Calvi at 0750 **A**, 0950 **A**, 1250, 1450 **A** and 1750 **A**.

PARIS - DIJON - BESANÇON - MULHOUSE - BASEL — 370

TGV Rhin-Rhône

Regional TER services: Table **371** Paris - Dijon; Table **374** Dijon - Besançon; Table **378** Besançon - Belfort; Table **378a** Belfort - Mulhouse; Table **385** Mulhouse - Basel.
Paris timings may vary by up to 9 minutes from May 15 (please check your reservation). **Warning!** Subject to alteration on Mar. 11, 12, 18, 19.

km		*TGV* 6701	*TGV* 9203	*TGV* 9261	*TGV* 6703	*TGV* 6703	*TGV* 6703	*TGV* 9211	*TGV* 6705	*TGV* 9269	*TGV* 9213		*TGV* 9215	*TGV* 6743	*TGV* 9219	*TGV* 6745	*TGV* 6709	*TGV* 9277	*TGV* 9223	*TGV* 6711		*TGV* 6715	*TGV* 6753
		Ⓐ				Ⓒ								Ⓑ		Ⓑ						Ⓑ	⑤⑦
		v		L	A	w	B	⊗⊕	⊕	⊕L	⊕			h◇		h◇		L				h	f◧
0	**Paris** Gare de Lyon ... **375** d.	0645	0715	0753	0853	0917**g**	0918	1020	1113	1154**y**	1219**y**	...	1415	1449	1619	1643	1713	1747	1819	1849	...	2021	2116
212	Montbard ... d.	0757	|	|	|	1024**g**	|	|	|	|	|	...	|	1557	|	1757	|	|	|	1956	...	|	2223
287	**Dijon** Ville ... **375** a.	0831	|	0931	1037	1058	1057	1157	1252	1331	1357	...	|	1631	|	1835	1852	1930	1957	2031	...	2158	2257
287	**Dijon** Ville ... **375 377 379** d.	0835	|	0935	1044	1102	1104	1201	1256	1335	1401	...	|	1635	|	1839	1856	1933	2001	2035	...	2202	2301
333	Dole ... **375** a.	|	|	0958	|	|	|	|	|	1358	|	...	|	1658	|	1901	|	1955	|	|	...	|	2325
364	**Besançon** Franche-Comté TGV. **379** d.	0905**a**	|	...	1138**r**	1132	1138	|	1325	...	|	...	|	|	|	|	1925	...	|	2108	...	2231	|
377	Besançon Viotte ... a.	0919	|	...	|	|	|	|	|	...	|	...	|	1727	|	1927	|	...	|	|	...	|	2351
446	Belfort Montbéliard TGV ... **379** d.	...	0941	...	1210	1156	1210	|	1349	...	|	...	1640	...	1841	...	1949	...	|	2132	...	2255	...
491	**Mulhouse** ... **379** a.	...	1003	...	1239	1218	1239	1303	1412	...	1503	...	1703	...	1903	...	2012	...	2103	2155	...	2320	...
525	**Basel** SBB ... a.	...	1026	...	...	...	...	1326	...	...	1526	...	1726	...	1926	...	...	...	2126	...	...	...	...
	Zürich HB **510** ... ▷ a.	...	1126	...	...	...	...	1426	...	...	1626	...	1826**c**	...	2026	...	...	...	2226	...	...	...	...

	TGV 6760	*TGV* 6700	*TGV* 6700	*TGV* 6762		*TGV* 6702	*TGV* 9264	*TGV* 9206		*TGV* 9210		*TGV* 6704	*TGV* 9218	*TGV* 9268		*TGV* 9222	*TGV* 6706	*TGV* 9226	*TGV* 9270	*TGV* 6708	*TGV* 6766	*TGV* 6766	*TGV* 9234
	Ⓐ	①–⑥	⑦	①–⑥													Ⓑ				Ⓐ	⑦	
	v	b	e¶	b‡			L	⊗		⊕		⊕		L			h		L⊡		v	e◇	
Zürich HB **510** ... ▷ d.	...	...	...	...	...	...	...	0734	...	0934	...	...	1134	...	...	1334	...	1534	...	...	...	...	1834
Basel SBB ... d.	...	...	...	...	...	...	...	0834	...	1034	...	...	1234	...	...	1434	...	1634	...	...	...	...	1934
Mulhouse ... **379** d.	...	0547	0605	...	...	0746	...	0856	...	1056	...	1205	1256	...	...	1456	1540	1656	...	1746	...	...	1956
Belfort Montbéliard TGV ... **379** d.	...	0611	0630	...	...	0811	...	0920	...	|	...	1231	1320	...	...	|	1605	|	...	1811	...	...	2021
Besançon Viotte ... d.	0532	|	|	0636	...	|	...	|	...	|	...	|	|	...	...	|	|	|	...	|	1932	1937	|
Besançon Franche-Comté TGV .. **379** d.	|	0635	0656	0653	...	0834	...	|	...	|	...	1254	|	...	...	|	1628	|	...	1834	|	1953	|
Dole ... **375** d.	0558	|	|	|	...	|	0902	|	...	|	...	|	|	1400	...	|	|	|	1800	|	1959	|	|
Dijon Ville ... **375 377 379** a.	0622	0702	0725	0722	...	0902	0926	|	...	1158	...	1323	|	1424	...	1558	1656	1758	1824	1902	2023	2022	|
Dijon Ville ... **375** d.	0626	0706	0729	0726	...	0906	0930	|	...	1202	...	1327	|	1428	...	1602	1700	1802	1828	1906	2027	2026*	|
Montbard ... d.	0704	|	0805	0805	...	|	|	|	...	|	...	1405	|	|	...	|	1738	|	|	|	|	2103*	|
Paris Gare de Lyon ... **375** a.	0813	0846	0911	0912	...	1044	1112	1141	...	1340**j**	...	1514**k**	1540	1607**z**	...	1741**t**	1849	1942	2009	2047	2209	2209*	2251

LOCAL CONNECTING TRAINS BESANÇON FRANCHE-COMTÉ TGV - BESANÇON VIOTTE (see note ⊠)

km		⚒													Ⓑ					⚒	Ⓑ	⑥		D
0	Besançon Viotte ... d.	0604	...	0807	...	1011	...	1140	1229	...	1338	1414	1516	1603	...	1735	1807	1905	1937	2025	2046	...	2209
13	Besançon Franche-Comté TGV ... a.	0619	...	0820	...	1026	...	1153	1243	...	1355	1427	1528	1616	...	1748	1822	1917	1950	2042	2058	...	2221

	⚒												Ⓑ					⚒			D		
Besançon Franche-Comté TGV ... d.	0651	...	0843	...	1054	...	1210	...	1339	1430	1451	1539	1637	...	1807	1841	1931	2026	2114	...	2241	...	...
Besançon Viotte ... a.	0705	...	0858	...	1108	...	1224	...	1354	1445	1504	1552	1652	...	1822	1854	1948	2039	2127	...	2256	...	...

A – ②⑤ (also Mar. 6, May 15, 17; not Mar. 7, 14, 21, 28, 31, Apr. 18, May 16, 19). On Apr. 4, 7, 11, 14, 21, 28 Dijon a. 1049, d. 1056. On Mar. 6 departs Paris 0842. On Apr. 25 Paris d. 0841, Dijon a. 1020, d. 1029 and then as shown.
B – ①–⑤ to Dec. 30; ①③④ Jan. 2 - Mar. 2 (also Mar. 31, Apr. 3, 5, 6, 12, 13, 24); ③④ Apr. 26 - May 11 (also May 16); ①③④ from May 22 (not May 29).
D – Ⓑ to Apr. 23; ⑦ from Apr. 30 (also May 19).
L – *TGV Lyria*. To/from Lausanne (Table **375**).

b – Not Apr. 10, May 1, 8, 29.
c – ⑥⑦ (also Apr. 7, 10, May 18, 19, 29).
e – Also Apr. 10, May 1, 8, 29.
f – Also Apr. 10, May 1, 8, 17, 29; not Apr. 9, 30, May 7, 28.
g – 2–6 minutes earlier on ⑥ Jan. 24 - Apr. 15 (also May 19).
h – Not May 18, 19.
j – 1346 on Apr. 25, 26.
k – 1521 on Apr. 11, 12.
r – 1131 from June 6.
t – 1746 on Feb. 25, Mar. 4.

v – Not May 19.
w – Also May 19.
y – 3–6 minutes earlier on Dec. 27, 28, Apr. 18, 19.
z – 1612 on ⑥ until May 13; 1614 on ⑦ until May 14.

TGV – High-speed train. Ⓡ. ♀.

* – On May 21, 29, June 11, 18, 25 Dijon d. 2025, Montbard d. 2101, Paris a. 2204.
◧ – Runs 23–24 minutes earlier on Apr. 16, May 14. Timings may vary by a few minutes on certain other dates.
¶ – Runs 1–3 minutes earlier Belfort - Paris from May 21.
▷ – Zürich timings vary on Dec. 11.
⊗ – Subject to alteration Mar. 6–9, 13–16, 20–23, 27–30, Apr. 17–20.
⊕ – Subject to alteration May 22–25, June 5–8, 12–15.
⊡ – Subject to alteration Mar. 6–9, 11, 13–16, 18, 20–23.
◇ – Subject to alteration on May 7, 28, June 4.
‡ – Subject to alteration on Apr. 22, May 27.
⊠ – Subject to alteration on Apr. 22, May 6, 7, 27, 28, June 4.

MULHOUSE - FREIBURG — 370a

km		①–⑤ a							🚌	
0	**Mulhouse** ... d.	0633	0831	1031	1231	1431	1631	1831	2015	...
19	Neuenburg 🏛 ... d.	0653	0851	1051	1251	1451	1651	1851	2047	...
22	Müllheim (Baden) ... a.	0657	0856	1055	1255	1455	1655	1855	2053	...
51	Müllheim (Baden) ... **912** d.	*0705*	*0904*	*1104***n**	*1306*	*1501*	*1707*	*1907*	...	2104
51	**Freiburg** (Brsg) Hbf ... **912** a.	*0724*	*0924*	*1124***n**	*1325*	*1523*	*1726*	*1926*	...	2124

	①–⑤ a	①–⑥	⑦							🚌
Freiburg (Brsg) Hbf ... **912** d.	*0627*	*0918*	0936	*1034*	*1238*	*1432*	*1632*	*1832*	2033	...
Müllheim (Baden) ... **912** a.	*0648*	*0936*	0955	*1052*	*1257*	*1451*	*1651*	*1851*	2052	...
Müllheim (Baden) ... d.	0703	0945	0956	1103	1308	1503	1703	1903	...	2103
Neuenburg 🏛 ... d.	0708	0950	1000	1108	1313	1508	1708	1908	...	2109
Mulhouse ... a.	0727	1012	1019	1127	1332	1527	1727	1927	...	2135

a – Not Apr. 7, 10, May 1, 18, 29.

n – On ⑦ (also Apr. 7, 10, May 1, 18, 29, June 8) Müllheim d. *1102*, Freiburg a. *1121*.

BELFORT - MEROUX - DELLE — 370b

See Table **515** for full service Meroux - Delle - Biel/Bienne and v.v. French holiday dates apply.

km		Ⓐ	⚒	⚒	Ⓐ	Ⓐ	⑥		Ⓐ	Ⓐ			⚒		Ⓐ		Ⓐ	†	⑥	Ⓐ	Ⓑ		Ⓑ	Ⓐ		D
0	**Belfort** Ville ... d.	0442	0548	...	0704	0748	*0748*	*0848*	1002	...	1142	...	1248	...	1348	...	1543	1548	1602	1644	1719	*1848*	*1948*	2027	2114	...
7	Meroux TGV ⊡ ... a.	0451	0556	...	0712	0756	*0757*	*0856*	1010	...	1151	...	1256	...	1356	...	1551	1556	1611	1652	1726	*1856*	*1956*	2034	2122	...
7	Meroux TGV ⊡ .. **515** d.	0452	...	0603	0714	0801	0803	0903	...	1103	...	1203	...	1303	...	1403	1552	...	1612	1659	1727	1903	2003	...	...	2203
21	**Delle** 🏛 ... **515** a.	0509	...	0619	0730	0817	0819	0919	...	1119	...	1219	...	1319	...	1419	1610	...	1630	1715	1745	1919	2019	...	...	2219
	Biel/Bienne **515** ... a.	...	...	0741	...	...	0941	1041	...	1241	...	1341	...	1441	...	1541	...	...	...	...	...	2041	2141	...	...	...

	⚒ D	Ⓐ	⚒	Ⓐ	⑥			Ⓐ		⚒		Ⓐ		Ⓐ	†	⚒	Ⓑ		Ⓑ	Ⓐ			†	†	†	Ⓐ
Biel/Bienne **515** ... d.	...	...	...	...	0619	0719	...	0919	1019	...	1119	...	1219	...	1519	...	...	1719	1819	...	...	...	...	2119	...	...
Delle 🏛 ... **515** d.	0541	...	0655	0743	0741	0841	...	1041	1141	...	1241	...	1341	1441	1641	1643	1746	1841	1941	...	...	...	2226	2241	...	2248
Meroux TGV ⊡ ... **515** a.	0556	...	0711	0759	0756	0856	...	1056	1156	...	1256	...	1356	1457	1656	1659	1802	1856	1956	...	...	...	2242	2256	...	2304
Meroux TGV ⊡ ... d.	...	0603	0713	0804	*0806*	...	0943	*1107*	...	1232	...	1327	*1403*	1503	*1701*	1701	1803	*1903*	*2006*	2050	2140	...	...	...	2300	2307
Belfort Ville ... a.	...	0612	0723	0813	*0815*	...	0952	*1116*	...	1241	...	1337	*1412*	1512	*1711*	1710	1812	*1914*	*2015*	2059	2149	...	...	...	2310	2316

D – To/from Delémont (Table **515**).

⊡ – Meroux station platforms are located directly above Belfort-Montbéliard TGV station.

371 PARIS - SENS - AUXERRE and DIJON *TER services*

For *TGV* services Paris - Dijon see Table **370**. **WARNING!** Timings may vary by up to 4 minutes (particularly during the period Mar. 6–26); earlier departures possible. Subject to alteration on Mar. 11, 12, 18, 19. Journeys to/from Lyon are subject to alteration on Apr. 22, 23.

km		Ⓐ	⚒	⑥	Ⓐ	⚒	Ⓐ	Ⓐ	Ⓑ	⑥		r	⑥	Ⓐ ⊗	⑥	Ⓑ r	Ⓒ	Ⓐ	Ⓐ 🚌	r	Ⓐ	†	⑥	Ⓒ		
0	**Paris** Bercy d.	...	...	...	...	...	0611	...	...	...	0735	...	0833	0836	...	...	0920	0920	...	...	1033	1033	1033	...	...	1233
113	Sens d.	...	...	0621	0624	...	0721	...	...	...	0833	...	0931	0933	...	...	1027	1027	...	...	1131	1131	1131	...	...	1331
147	Joigny d.	...	...	0648	0651	...	0747	...	...	...	0851	...	0948	0950	...	...	1047	1047	...	...	1147	1149	1147	...	...	1348
	Auxerre d.	0534	0635	|	|	...	|	*0739*	0835	0837	|	...	|	|	1037	1039	|	|	...	...	|	|	|	*1139*	...	|
156	Laroche Migennes a.	0553	0653	0654	0658	...	0755	*0752*	0853	0853	0858	...	0955	0957	1054	1053	1055	1055	...	...	1155	1155	1155	*1152*	...	1355
156	Laroche Migennes d.	0558	...	0658	0702	0707	0757	0801	...	...	0902	0907	0957	0959r	...	...	1059	...	1110	1107	1158r	1157	1205	1202	...	1405r
175	**Auxerre** a.	|	...	|	|	0725	0810	|	...	...	|	0920	1010	1014r	...	...	|	...	|	1125	1211r	1210	1218	|	...	1418r
197	Tonnerre d.	0625	...	0722	0723	...	...	0824	...	...	0924	...	...	...	...	...	1123	...	1219	...	...	...	...	1225	...	...
243	Montbard d.	0650	...	0748	0750	...	...	0850	...	...	0950	...	...	...	...	...	1150	...	1317	...	...	...	...	1251	...	...
315	**Dijon** Ville a.	0727	...	0827	0827	...	...	0927	...	...	1027	...	...	...	...	...	1227	...	1446	...	...	...	...	1328	...	...
	Lyon Part Dieu **377** a.	...	...	1043	1042	...	...	...	...	...	1243	...	...	...	...	...	1443	...	...	...	...	...	...	...	...	...

	†	Ⓐ x	Ⓑ v¶	x	⚒	x	Ⓐ ⊗	Ⓐ	†				⑥	†	Ⓐ	Ⓑ		†	⚒		Ⓑ	⚒	†	⑥	†	Ⓐ
Paris Bercy d.	...	...	...	...	1335	...	1433	...	...	...	1534	...	1627	1627	1627f	...	...	...	...	1727	1727	...	...	1827	1827	1827
Sens d.	...	...	...	...	1434	...	1531	...	...	...	1634	...	1731	1731	1732	...	...	...	...	1834	1834	...	...	1932	1932	1932
Joigny d.	...	...	...	...	1452	...	1549	...	...	...	1652	...	1749	1749	1748	...	...	...	...	1851	1851	...	...	1948	1948	1948
Auxerre d.	1335	1337	...	1435	|	...	|	1535	*1540*	1635	|	...	|	|	|	1735	...	1832	1839	|	|	...	...	|	|	|
Laroche Migennes a.	1353	1351	...	1453	1458	...	1555	1551	*1555*	1653	1658	...	1755	1755	1755	1753	...	1846	1853	1858	1858	...	...	1955	1955	1955
Laroche Migennes d.	...	...	1402	...	1502	1507	1607	1600	1558	...	1702	1707	1757	1805	1805	1758	...	...	...	1902	1902	1907	1916	1957	2005	*2007*
Auxerre a.	...	...	|	...	|	1525	1620	|	|	...	|	1725	1810	1819	1818	|	...	...	...	|	|	1921	1934	2010	2018	*2022*
Tonnerre d.	...	...	1427	...	1524	...	...	1626	1625	...	1724	...	...	...	...	1825	...	...	...	1924	1924	...	...	...	...	...
Montbard d.	...	...	1452	...	1550	...	...	1650	1650	...	1750	...	...	...	...	1849	...	...	...	1950	1950	...	...	...	...	...
Dijon Ville a.	...	...	1529	...	1627	...	...	1727	1727	...	1827	...	...	...	...	1926	...	...	...	2027	2027	...	...	...	...	...
Lyon Part Dieu **377** a.	...	...	...	...	1843	...	...	...	...	...	2042	...	...	...	...	...	...	...	...	...	2244p	...	...	...	...	...

	†	Ⓐ	Ⓑ			⑤–⑦	①–④				
Paris Bercy d.	...	...	...	...	1927	...	...	2033	...	2240	...
Sens d.	...	...	...	...	2034	...	...	2131	...	2355	...
Joigny d.	...	...	...	...	2051	...	...	2149	...	0023	...
Auxerre d.	1943	1946	...	2035	|	...	...	|	...	|	...
Laroche Migennes a.	1956	2002	...	2053	2058	...	...	2155	...	0031	...
Laroche Migennes d.	...	...	2011	...	2102	2107	2107	2157	...	...	...
Auxerre a.	...	...	|	...	|	2120	2125	2210	...	...	...
Tonnerre d.	...	...	2035	...	2124	...	...	...	...	...	...
Montbard d.	...	...	2101	...	2150	...	...	...	...	...	...
Dijon Ville a.	...	...	2138	...	2227	...	...	...	...	...	...
Lyon Part Dieu **377** a.	...	...	...	...	...	...	...	...	...	...	...

	Ⓐ		Ⓐ	⑥	Ⓐ		⚒	⑥	Ⓐ	⚒
Lyon Part Dieu **377** d.	...	...	...	...	...	...	...	...	...	...
Dijon Ville d.	...	...	...	...	...	...	...	0533	0533	...
Montbard d.	...	...	...	...	...	...	...	0609	0611	...
Tonnerre d.	...	...	...	...	...	...	...	0635	0636	...
Auxerre d.	0450	...	0534	0550	...	...	0635	|	|	...
Laroche Migennes a.	0503	...	0553	0603	...	...	0653	0657	0658	...
Laroche Migennes d.	0505	...	...	0605	0607	...	...	0701	0702	0707
Auxerre a.	|	...	...	|	|	...	...	|	|	0725
Joigny d.	0513	...	...	0613	0615	...	...	0708	0710	...
Sens d.	0530	...	...	0630	0632	...	...	0729	0728	...
Paris Bercy a.	0633	...	...	0727	0732	...	...	0827	0833	...

	Ⓑ	⚒	†	Ⓑ	⑥	⚒	r	Ⓐ	⑥	⚒	⑥	Ⓑ r	Ⓐ ⊙	Ⓒ	r			Ⓐ A	Ⓒ	Ⓐ	†	⑥		x		x
Lyon Part Dieu **377** d.	...	...	...	...	...	0518g	...	...	...	...	...	...	...	0717	...	...	...	...	...	...	...	...	...	...	1118	...
Dijon Ville d.	0631	...	...	...	...	0733	...	0833	0833	...	...	...	...	0933	...	...	...	1207	1233	...	...	...	...	...	1331	...
Montbard d.	0708	...	...	...	...	0811	...	0910	0910	...	...	...	...	1011	...	...	...	1306	1310	...	...	...	...	...	1411	...
Tonnerre d.	0733	...	...	...	...	0836	...	0936	0936	...	...	...	...	1036	...	...	...	1334	1336	...	...	...	...	...	1436	...
Auxerre d.	|	0739	0748	0835	0837	|	...	|	|	0950x	1037	1039	...	|	...	1139r	...	|	|	1337x	1335	1340	...	1435	|	...
Laroche Migennes a.	0800	0752	0801	0853	0853	0858	...	1000	1003	1003x	1054	1053	...	1058	...	1152r	...	1359	1400	1351x	1353	1355	...	1453	1501	...
Laroche Migennes d.	0807	0805	0804	...	...	0902	0907	...	1010	1005	...	...	1102	1102	1107	1204	...	*1405*	*1405*	1402	1405	1404	...	...	1502	1507
Auxerre a.	0825	|	|	...	...	|	0920	...	1026	|	...	...	|	|	1125	|	...	*1418*	*1418*	|	|	|	...	...	|	1525
Joigny d.	...	0813	0812	...	...	0909	...	...	...	1013	...	...	1109	1109	...	1213	...	...	...	1411	1413	1413	...	...	1510	...
Sens d.	...	0830	0830	...	...	0927	...	...	...	1030	...	...	1127	1127	...	1230	...	...	...	1429	1430	1430	...	...	1528	...
Paris Bercy a.	...	0934	0934	...	...	1025	...	...	...	1133	...	...	1225	1225	...	1327	...	...	...	1527c	1527	1527	...	...	1637	...

	Ⓐ	Ⓒ				Ⓑ	Ⓒ	Ⓐ	†	⚒		⚒	†		⑥	Ⓑ	†	Ⓐ	†	Ⓐ			⑤–⑦	①–④		Ⓑ
Lyon Part Dieu **377** d.	...	...	...	1318	...	...	...	...	...	...	1516z	...	...	...	...	...	...	...	...	...	...	1718	...	...	...	...
Dijon Ville d.	...	...	...	1533	...	1633	...	...	...	...	1733	...	...	...	1833	1833	...	...	...	...	...	1933	...	...	...	2037y
Montbard d.	...	...	...	1611	...	1710	...	...	...	...	1811	...	...	...	1910	1910	...	...	...	...	...	2011	...	...	...	2129
Tonnerre d.	...	...	...	1636	...	1736	...	...	...	...	1836	...	...	...	1936	1939t	...	...	...	...	...	2036	...	...	...	2154
Auxerre d.	*1535*	1540	1635	|	...	|	1749	1750	1832	1839	|	...	...	...	|	|	...	...	1943	1946	2035	|	...	...	...	|
Laroche Migennes a.	*1551*	1555	1653	1658	...	1759	1802	1803	1846	1853	1858	...	...	...	2002	2000	...	...	1956	2002	2053	2058	...	...	...	2221
Laroche Migennes d.	1605	1605	...	1702	1707	*1805*	1805	1820	...	...	1902	1907	1916	...	2007	...	2005	2007	2005	2005	...	2102	2107	2107	...	2228
Auxerre a.	|	|	...	|	1725	*1819*	|	|	...	...	|	1921	1934	...	2025	...	2018	2022	|	|	...	|	2120	2125	...	2244
Joigny d.	1613	1613	...	1709	...	...	1813	1828	...	...	1909	...	...	...	...	...	...	...	2014	2013	...	2109	...	...	...	...
Sens d.	1630	1630	...	1727	...	...	1830	1854	...	...	1927	...	...	...	...	...	...	...	2040	2040	...	2127	...	...	...	...
Paris Bercy a.	1727	1727	...	1824	...	...	1927	2013	...	...	2025	...	...	...	...	...	...	...	2147	2150	...	2225	...	...	...	...

LOCAL TRAINS PARIS - LAROCHE MIGENNES. For faster trains see the main part of Table **371** above.

km							†	⑥	Ⓐ				Ⓐ	Ⓒ	Ⓐ	Ⓐ	Ⓒ	Ⓐ	Ⓐ	Ⓒ	Ⓐ		Ⓐ	Ⓒ		
0	**Paris** Gare de Lyon d.	0646	0746	0846	1046	1146	1246	1246	1246	1346	1446	1546	1621	1646	1712	1721	1746	1812	1821	1846	1912	1946	2046	2046	2146	2246
45	Melun d.	0713	0810	0913	1113	1213	1313	1313	1313	1413	1513	1613	1647	1713	|	1748	1813	|	1849	1913	|	2013	2113	2113	2213	2313
60	Fontainebleau-Avon d.	0726	0823	0926	1126	1226	1326	1326	1326	1426	1526	1626	1700	1725	|	1801	1826	|	1901	1926	|	2027	2126	2126	2226	2326
79	Montereau d.	0746	0844	0945	1145	1244	1345	1345	1345	1444	1546	1644	1722	1746	1806	1823	1846	1906	1923	1946	2006	2046	2144	2146	2244	2344
113	Sens a.	0816	...	1014	1213	...	1413	1413	1416	...	1614	...	1749	1813	1833	1850	1914	1933	1950	2013	2033	2114	...	2213	...	...
113	Sens d.	0835	...	1035	1215	...	1415	1434	1437	...	1634	...	1751	1834	1835	1852	1935	1935	1952	2034	2035	2135	...	2215	...	...
147	Joigny d.	0902	...	1102	1243	...	1443	1502	1504	...	1702	...	1818	1902	1902	1918	2002	2002	2018	2102	2102	2202	...	2243	...	...
156	**Laroche Migennes** a.	0909	...	1109	1250	...	1450	1509	1511	...	1709	...	1825	1909	1909	1925	2009	2009	2025	2109	2109	2209	...	2250	...	...

		Ⓐ	⑥	Ⓐ	Ⓐ	Ⓒ	Ⓐ	Ⓐ	†	⑥							⚒	†		⚒	†	Ⓒ	Ⓐ			
Laroche Migennes d.	0410	0451	0510	0539	0551	0610	0639	0651	...	0651	0750	1012	...	1210	...	1410	...	1449	1551k	...	1651	1810	1820	...	...	...
Joigny d.	0419	0500	0519	0547	0600	0619	0647	0700	...	0700	0759	1021	...	1219	...	1419	...	1457	1600k	...	1700	1819	1828	...	...	...
Sens a.	0444	0525	0544	0611	0625	0643	0711	0725	...	0724	0824	1044	...	1244	...	1441	...	1524	1625k	...	1725	1844	1852	...	...	...
Sens d.	0446	0527	0546	0614	0627	0645	07114	0727	...	0745	0844	1045	...	1246	...	1443	...	1544	1645	...	1746	1846	1854	...	...	...
Montereau d.	0515	0557	0614	0643	0655	0715	0745	0756	0814	0815	0914	1116	1214	1314	1414	1513	1613	1613	1714	1814	1815	1915	1921	2014	2114	2214
Fontainebleau-Avon d.	0533	|	0632	0702	|	0733	0802	|	0832	0832	0931	1134	1232	1332	1432	1531	1630	1632	1732	1832	1833	1932	|	2032	2132	2232
Melun d.	0546	|	0645	0714	|	0745	0814	|	0845	0845	0944	1147	1247	1345	1447	1545	1645	1645	1745	1847	1845	1945	|	2045	2145	2245
Paris Gare de Lyon a.	0613	0648	0713	0743	0748	0813	0843	0848	0913	0913	1013	1215	1313	1413	1513	1613	1713	1713	1813	1913	1913	2013	2013b	2113	2213	2313

A – Ⓐ to Mar. 3 (also Mar. 13–17, Apr. 3–7).
b – Paris **Bercy**.
c – On Feb. 28, Mar. 21, 22 arrives Paris **Gare de Lyon** (a. 1530; not Bercy).
f – On Mar. 21, 22 departs Paris **Gare de Lyon** (d. 1625; not Bercy).
g – ① (also Apr. 11, May 2, 9, 30; not Apr. 10, May 1, 8, 29). On Feb. 27, Mar. 6 starts from Lyon Perrache (d. 0500), not calling at Lyon Part Dieu.
k – 16–18 minutes later on ①–⑤ Mar. 2–31.
p – 2242 on †. On ①–⑤ Mar. 6–24 diverted to Lyon Perrache (a. 2245).
r – Not Apr. 17–21, 24–28.

t – 1936 on ④.
v – Not Mar. 13–17.
x – Not Apr. 24–28
y – 2031 Mar. 6–26.
z – 1518 on Ⓐ.

⊗ – Subject to alteration Mar. 2–31.
⊙ – Subject to alteration Apr. 6, 24–28. Departure times are 4 minutes earlier on Apr. 3–5, 7, May 30, 31, June 2.
¶ – Runs 11–22 minutes later on certain dates from Apr. 3.

DIJON and CHALON SUR SAÔNE - MONTCHANIN - NEVERS 373

Westbound timings Chalon sur Saône - Montchanin may vary by up to 3 minutes Jan. 9 - Mar. 26 (earlier departures possible). Subject to alteration on Mar. 18, 19, Apr. 15, 16, 22, 23.

km		Ⓐ	Ⓐ	Ⓐ	⚒	⚒	Ⓐ	Ⓑ		⚒ ⊖	Ⓐ		⊗	⚒ ⊗	⚒		Ⓑ	Ⓑ	⚒	⚒	Ⓑ	Ⓑ	†		
0	**Dijon** Ville 377 d.	...	...	0612	...	0711c	...	0812	...	0954	...	...	1212	...	1412	...	1546	...	...	1712	...	1812	1812	...	1912
37	Beaune 377 d.	...	...	0632	...	0731	...	0832	...	1016	...	...	1231	...	1432	...	1608z	...	...	1732	...	1832	1832	...	1931
	Chalon sur Saône 377 d.	...	*0556*	|	0710	|	0810	|	...	|	1017	...	|	1410	|	...	|	1610	1710	|	1810	|	|	1910	|
	Chagny 377 d.	...	0622	|	0722	|	0822	|	...	|	1028	...	|	1422	|	...	|	1622	1722	|	1822	|	|	1922	|
81	**Montchanin** d.	...	0648	0658	0748	0758	0848	0858	...	1046	1054	...	1258	1448	1459	...	1635	1648	1748	1758	1848	1858	1858	1948	1958
89	Le Creusot Ville d.	...	...	0706	...	0805	...	0906	...	1054	...	...	1305	...	1505	...	1642	...	...	1805	...	1905	1905	...	2005
111	Étang ★ d.	0605	...	0721	...	0821	...	0921	...	1110	...	...	1321	...	1521	...	1658	...	...	1821	...	1920	1921	...	2021
	Autun ★ a.	|	...	|	...	|	...	|	...	|	...	...	|	...	|	...	|	...	...	|	...	...	|	...	|
179	Decize d.	0647	...	0804	...	0903	...	1004	...	1152	...	...	1403	...	1603	...	1740	...	...	1903	...	...	2004	...	2103
216	**Nevers** a.	0719	...	0829	...	0929	...	1029	...	1217	...	...	1429	...	1629	...	1806	...	...	1929	...	...	2029	...	2129

km		Ⓐ	① g	⚒	⚒	⚒	Ⓑ	Ⓐ	● ⊗	⊗	⊗		Ⓐ	Ⓐ			Ⓑ	⚒		Ⓑ	Ⓑ	⑥	⑥	Ⓐ	Ⓑ ⊖
	Nevers d.	...	0531	...	0631	...	0731	...	0931	...	1057	...	1331	...	...	1541	...	...	...	1731	...	1844	...	1848	1931
	Decize d.	...	0556	...	0657	...	0757	...	0957	...	1122	...	1357	...	...	1604	...	...	...	1757	...	1911	...	1920	1958
0	Autun ★ d.	...	|	...	|	...	|	...	|	...	|	...	|	...	...	|	...	...	...	|	...	|	...	...	|
15	Étang ★ d.	0640	0640	...	0740	...	0840	...	1040	...	1205	...	1440	...	...	|	...	...	...	1840	...	1954	...	2003	2041
	Le Creusot Ville d.	0655	0655	...	0755	...	0855	...	1055	...	1221	...	1456	...	...	1657	...	...	...	1855	...	2010	...	...	2057
0	**Montchanin** d.	0703	0703	0712	0803	0812	0903	0912	1103	1112	1227	...	1503	1512	...	1704	1712	1812	...	1903	1912	2017	2024	...	2118k
29	Chagny 377 d.	|	|	0738	|	0838	|	0938	|	1138	|	...	|	1540	...	|	1739	1839	...	|	1938	|	2050	...	|
44	**Chalon sur Saône** 377 a.	|	|	0750	|	0850	|	0950	|	1150	|	...	|	1551	...	|	1750	1850	...	|	1950	|	2100	...	|
	Beaune 377 d.	0729	0729	...	0829	...	0929	...	1129	...	1253	...	1529	...	...	1729	...	...	...	1929	...	2043	...	...	2144
	Dijon Ville 377 a.	0748	0748	...	0848	...	0948	...	1148	...	1315	...	1548	...	...	1748	...	...	...	1948	...	2102	...	...	2204

MONTCHANIN - PARAY LE MONIAL - MOULINS SUR ALLIER ⊡

km		Ⓐ	⚒	†	⚒		⚒	Ⓑ		Ⓑ	
	Dijon Ville (see above) d.	...	...	...	0954	...	...	...	...	...	...
0	**Montchanin** ▷ d.	0708	0808	0908	1107	1308	1508	1708	1808	1908	2005
15	Montceau les Mines ▷ d.	0722	0822	0922	1120	1322	1522	1722	1822	1922	2019
50	Paray le Monial 290 ▷ d.	0752	0852	0952	1156j	1352	1552	1752	1852	1952	2050
61	Digoin 290 d.	...	...	...	1210	...	...	...	...	...	...
117	**Moulins sur Allier** 290 a.	...	...	...	1300	...	...	...	...	...	...
	Clermont Ferrand 330 a.	...	...	...	1421h	...	...	...	...	...	...

	Ⓐ	⚒			⚒		Ⓑ		Ⓑ
Clermont Ferrand 330 d.	...	...	...	...	...	...	...	...	1738
Moulins sur Allier 290 d.	...	...	...	...	...	...	...	...	1905
Digoin 290 d.	...	...	...	...	...	...	...	...	1948
Paray le Monial 290 ▷ d.	0608	0708	1009	1211	1408	1608	1808	1908	2008j
Montceau les Mines ▷ d.	0638	0738	1039	1239	1438	1638	1838	1938	2039
Montchanin ▷ a.	0652	0752	1052	1253	1452	1652	1852	1952	2052
Dijon Ville (see above) a.	...	...	...	...	...	...	...	...	2204

c – 0704 on ⑤ (also on ④ Mar. 30 - Apr. 20 and on ④ May 4 – 25).
g – Also Apr. 11, May 2, 9, 30; not Apr. 10, May 1, 8, 29.
h – 1427 Feb. 27 - Apr. 14.
j – Arrives 7 – 10 minutes earlier.
k – Arrives 2103.
w – ①②④⑤⑥ (not Apr. 10, May 1, 8, 18, 29).
z – ⑦–④ (not May 17).

⊡ – Subject to alteration from Apr. 22.
⊗ – Subject to alteration Apr. 11 – 14, 17 – 21, 24 – 28.
● – Runs 5 – 9 minutes **earlier** Feb. 6 - Mar. 22 (also on Mar. 25).
⊖ – Conveys (12) Dijon - Montchanin - Clermont Ferrand and v.v. (see panel below main table).
▷ – Additional journeys Montchanin - Paray and v.v. on Ⓐ: **From Montchanin** at 1608. **From Paray le Monial** at 1708.
★ – 🚌 **ÉTANG - AUTUN** and v.v. Journey time 21 minutes: **From Étang** at 0645 ① **g**, 0725 Ⓐ, 0825 ⑥, 0925 Ⓑ, 1045 Ⓐ, 1210 Ⓒ, 1325, 1525 Ⓐ, 1701 Ⓑ, 1801 ⚒, 1825 ⚒, 1845 Ⓐ, 1925 Ⓑ, 2045 Ⓑ. **From Autun** at 0534 Ⓐ, 0609 Ⓐ, 0650 Ⓐ, 0712 ① **g**, 0809 Ⓐ, 0850 †, 1009, 1134 **w**, 1216 ③, 1449 Ⓐ, 1626, 1749 ⚒, 1809 Ⓑ, 1849 †, 1923 ⑥, 1950 †.

DIJON - DOLE - BESANÇON 374

For *TGV* services see Table **370** (Paris - Dijon - Besançon - Basel) and Table **379** (Strasbourg - Besançon - Dijon). Subject to alteration on Apr. 22.

km		Ⓐ		Ⓐ		Ⓐ	¶					Ⓐ		Ⓐ	Ⓐ		Ⓐ		Ⓐ		Ⓐ			Ⓑ			
0	**Dijon** Ville 375 d.	0509	0614	0642	0709	0742	0807	0909	1012	1109	1209	1309	1346	1409	1509	1542	1609	1642	1711	1741	1809	1842	1909	1942	2009	2109	2209
32	Auxonne d.	0529	0635	0701	0730	0801	0827	0929	1032	1129	1230	1329	1408	1429	1529	1604	1629	1704	1730	1804	1829	1904	1929	2004	2029	2129	2230
46	Dole Ville 375 d.	0539	0646	0711	0742	0811	0838	0939	1042	1139	1242	1339	1418	1439	1539	1614	1639	1714	1740	1814	1839	1914	1939	2014	2039	2139	2241
91	**Besançon** Viotte a.	0604	0722	0736	0814	0836	0905	1004	1107	1204	1314	1404	1450	1504	1604	1647	1704	1746	1804	1846	1904	1946	2004	2046	2104	2204	2315

	Ⓐ		Ⓐ	Ⓐ				Ⓐ				Ⓐ		Ⓐ					Ⓑ		Ⓐ		Ⓐ		Ⓐ		⊙
Besançon Viotte d.	0456	0556	0625	0656	0714	0756	0856	0914	0956	1056	...	1206	1225	1256	1356	1456	1556	1611	1655	1714	1756	1814	1856	1914	1956	2056	2156
Dole Ville 375 d.	0530	0622	0659	0722	0747	0823	0921	0947	1021	1121	...	1233	1259	1322	1422	1522	1622	1647	1721	1747	1822	1847	1921	1947	2022	2121	2221
Auxonne d.	0540	0631	0708	0731	0756	0832	0930	0956	1030	1130	...	1242	1308	1331	1431	1531	1631	1656	1730	1756	1831	1856	1930	1956	2031	2130	2231
Dijon Ville 375 a.	0602	0651	0730	0751	0819	0853	0951	1018	1051	1151	...	1301	1330	1351	1451	1551	1651	1721	1750	1818	1851	1918	1951	2018	2051	2151	2251

¶ – On ① (also Apr. 11, May 2, 9, 30; not Apr. 10, May 1, 8, 29) Dijon d. 0809, Auxonne d. 0829, Dole d. 0839, Besançon a. 0914.
⊙ – Daily to Apr. 23; † from Apr. 30 (not May 18).

PARIS - DIJON - LAUSANNE and NEUCHÂTEL 375

TGV timings may vary by up to 9 minutes from May 15 (please check your reservation for confirmed timings). **Warning!** *TGV* services via Dijon are subject to alteration on Mar. 11, 12, 18, 19.

km										*TGV* 9761	*TGV* 9261				*TGV* 9269				*TGV* 9775				*TGV* 9777	*TGV* 9277	
		①–⑤ a¶		①–⑤ a		Ⓐ	Ⓐ	⑥	Ⓐ	①–⑥ z					⊙	s	①–⑤ c¶		w	①–⑤ b¶	Ⓐ		w		
0	**Paris** Gare de Lyon 370 d.	...	...	...	...	...	...	...	...	0618v	0753	...	...	...	1154f	...	...	...	1410	...	...	...	1614	1747	...
287	**Dijon** Ville 370 374 d.	...	...	...	...	...	*0509*	...	*0640*	|	0935	...	...	*1012*	1335	...	...	...	|	...	...	1734	|	1933	...
333	Dole Ville 374 376 d.	...	...	...	...	...	0616	0616	0715	|	1000	...	1014	1114	1400	...	...	...	|	...	...	1816k	|	1957	...
359	Arc-et-Senans d.	...	...	...	...	...	0638	0640	|	|	|	...	1034	1133	|	...	...	...	|	...	...	1834	|	|	...
365	Mouchard 376 d.	...	...	...	...	...	0647	0647	0740	|	|	...	1040	1142	|	...	...	...	|	...	...	1844	|	2015	...
389	Andelot 376 d.	...	...	...	...	...	0705	0706	...	◐	|	...	1058	1205	|	...	...	...	◐	...	...	1903	◐	|	...
410	Frasne d.	0517	...	0620	...	0717	...	0722	...	|	1044	1053	...	1220	1444	1453	1620	...	|	1718	1806	1918	|	2044	2053
426	Pontarlier 🛃 a.	|	...	|	...	0732	...	0737	...	|	|	1104	...	1235	|	1504	|	...	|	1729	1822	1933	|	|	2104
490	**Neuchâtel** a.	|	...	|	...	...	...	...	...	|	|	1153	...	...	|	1553	|	...	|	...	...	...	|	|	2153
434	Vallorbe 🛃 ▷ a.	0536	0540	0637	0640	...	...	...	...	|	1057	...	...	...	1457	...	1636	1640	|	...	...	...	|	2057	...
480	**Lausanne** ▷ a.	...	0625	...	0725	...	...	...	...	1016	1152	...	...	...	1537	...	...	1725	1816	...	...	...	2016	2137	...

								TGV 9264	*TGV* 9768				*TGV* 9268	*TGV* 9774					*TGV* 9270					*TGV* 9782	*TGV* 9784
	①–⑤ a¶	Ⓐ		①–⑤ a	①–⑤ a	①–⑤ a		z			⚒	s		y	①–⑤ c¶	①–⑤ a	①–⑤ b¶	s	⊗		①–⑤ b	Ⓐ		①–④ L	J
Lausanne ▷ d.	...	...	0502	...	0602	...	...	0723	0945	...	...	...	1223	1345	...	1602	...	...	1623	1633	...	...	...	1845	1945
Vallorbe 🛃 ▷ d.	...	...	0549	0558	0649	0655	...	0800	|	...	...	...	1300	|	...	1649	1652	...	1700	1718	1723	...	...	|	|
Neuchâtel d.	...	...	▬	|	...	|	0706	|	|	...	...	1206	|	|	...	...	|	1606	|	...	|	...	...	|	|
Pontarlier 🛃 d.	0503	0555	⚒	|	...	|	0755	|	|	...	1128	1255	|	|	...	...	|	1655	|	...	|	1736	1829	|	|
Frasne d.	0513	0611	d	0615	...	0711	0806	0815	|	...	1145	1306	1315	|	1606	...	1710	1706	1715	...	1742	1752	1845	|	|
Andelot 376 d.	...	0624	0759	...	...	...	...	|	◐	1202	1202	...	|	◐	1616	...	...	...	|	...	...	...	1901	◐	◐
Mouchard 376 d.	...	0650r	0817	...	...	...	...	0845	|	1220	1220	...	|	|	...	...	...	...	|	...	...	...	1918	|	|
Arc-et-Senans d.	...	0655	0823	...	...	...	...	|	|	1226	1226	...	|	|	...	...	...	...	|	...	...	...	1924	|	|
Dole Ville 374 376 d.	...	0729k	0841	...	...	...	...	0902	|	1245	1245	...	1400	|	...	...	...	...	1800	...	...	...	1941	|	|
Dijon Ville 370 374 d.	...	0755	...	...	...	...	...	0930	|	*1330*	*1330*	...	1428	|	...	...	...	...	1828	...	...	...	*2018*	|	|
Paris Gare de Lyon 370 a.	...	...	...	...	...	...	...	1112	1342	...	...	...	1607t	1750	...	...	...	...	2009	...	...	...	...	2302	2346

J – Ⓑ to Jan. 8; ⑤† Jan. 13 - May 8 (not Feb. 26 - Mar. 5); Ⓑ from May 12 (not May 18, June 21). Arrives Paris 2355 on ①–④ Dec. 26 - Jan. 5.
L – ①–④ Jan. 9 - May 11 (not Feb. 27 - Mar. 6, Apr. 10, May 1, 8).

a – Not Apr. 7, 10, May 18, 29.
b – Not Mar. 6 – 9, 13 – 16, 20 – 23, Apr. 7, 10, May 18, 29.
c – Not Mar. 6 – 9, 13 – 16, 20 – 23, 27 – 31, Apr. 7, 10, May 18, 29.
d – Not Apr. 11 – 14, 17 – 21.
f – 1151 on Apr. 18, 19.

k – Arrives 16 – 17 minutes earlier.
r – Arrives 0643.
s – Not Mar. 27 – 31.
t – 1612 on ⑥ until May 13; 1614 on ⑦ until May 14.
v – 0616 on Feb. 18, 25.
w – Not Feb. 26 - Mar. 6.
y – Not Feb. 27 - Mar. 6.
z – Not Feb. 27 - Mar. 7.

TGV – *TGV Lyria*. High-speed train. Ⓡ. 🍸.
¶ – (12) Pontarlier - Frasne - Vallorbe and v.v.
⊗ – Subject to alteration Mar. 6 – 9, 11, 13 – 16, 18, 20 – 23.
⊙ – Subject to alteration May 22 – 25, June 5 – 8, 12 – 15.
◐ – Via Genève (Table **341**).
▷ – Additional local services Vallorbe - Lausanne and v.v. (journey time ±45 minutes):
From Vallorbe at 0740 and hoourly until 2340.
From Lausanne at 0533 and hourly until 2333.

376 DOLE / BESANÇON - MOREZ - ST CLAUDE - BOURG EN BRESSE

km												
		⑥	Ⓐ				🚌 ⑤ f	⑤ f	D	⑤† f	🚌 ⊖	🚌 ⑤† f
0	**Dole** Ville .... 375 d.	0616	0616	...	1014	*1114*	1612	...	1816	...	...	...
	Besançon ◇ . 378 d.	|	|	...	|	|	|	1639	|	...	...	...
26	Arc-et-Senans 375/8 d.	0640	0638	...	1034	*1133*	|	1702	1834	...	...	...
32	Mouchard .... 375/8 d.	0647	0647	...	1040	*1142*	1659	1709	1844	...	...	2045
56	Andelot .... 375 d.	0705	0710	0710	1103	1209	...	1734	1902	1910	1910	|
70	Champagnole .... d.	...	0740j	0740j	1120	1221	...	1746	...	1923	1930	2127
105	Morez ....d.	...	0832	0832	1213	1312	...	1844	...	2015	2017	2209
128	**St Claude** ....a.	...	0859	0859	1240	1340	...	1912	...	2042	2057	2249

	① g	⚒ s		⑤ f	🚌 ⑤ f	①–④ p	🚌 Ⓐ		Ⓑ	
St Claude .... d.	0443	0617	0954	1510	...	1551	...	1725	1725	...
Morez .... d.	0515	0649	1029	1545	...	1626	...	1758	1758	...
Champagnole .... d.	0602	0736	1146t	1632	...	1712	1735	1845	1845	...
Andelot .... 375 a.	0613	0753	1157	1642	...	...	1755	1856	1856k	1901
Mouchard .... 375/8 a.	0636	0816	*1219*	1705	1715	...	1825	...	1925	1917
Arc-et-Senans .... 375/8 a.	*0654*	0822	*1225*	1713	|	...	|	...	1930	1923
Besançon-Viotte . 378 a.	|	|	|	1738	|	...	|	...	1957	|
Dole Ville .... 375 a.	*0712*	0841	*1245*	...	1802	...	1912	...	...	1941

ST CLAUDE - OYONNAX - BOURG EN BRESSE ✣

km												
		⚒	⚒	🚌	🚌 ⚒	Ⓐ	🚌	🚌 ⚒	🚌 Ⓐ	🚌	🚌	†
0	**St Claude** ..... 🚌 ⊠ d.	*0550*a	*0645*	*0840*	*0940*	*1140*	*1235*c	*1440*a	...	*1630*a	*1725*	...
32	Oyonnax .... 🚌 ⊠ d.	*0626*a	*0721*	*0916*	*1016*	*1216*	*1311*c	*1516*a	...	*1706*a	*1801*	...
32	Oyonnax .... d.	0638	0733	0925	1025	1238	1320	1525	1610	1725	1810	1838
45	Brion Montréal ⊡ ..... d.	0654	0749	0942	1042	1254	1343	1542	1634	1742	1827	1854
48	Nurieux Brion .... d.	0658	0753	|	|	1258	|	|	|	|	|	1858
81	**Bourg en Bresse** ▷ a.	0733	0833	1022	1122	1332	1423	1622	1714	1822	1907	1932
	Lyon Part Dieu .... ▷ a.	0830	...	...	...	...	...	...	...	...	...	...

	🚌 Ⓐ	Ⓐ	🚌 ⑥	🚌	🚌 ⚒	🚌 ⚒	Ⓑ		🚌	🚌 Ⓑ
Lyon Part Dieu .... ▷ d.	...	...	...	...	...	...	...	...	...	...
Bourg en Bresse ...... ▷ d.	0645	0844	0850	1030	1235	1430	1730	1837r	1930	2025
Nurieux Brion .... d.	|	0925	|	|	|	|	1808	1916	|	|
Brion Montréal ⊡ .... d.	0725	0929	0930	1110	1315	1510	1812	1919	2010	2105
Oyonnax .... a.	0742	0944	0947	1134	1332	1527	1827	1935	2027	2129
Oyonnax .... 🚌 ⊠ d.	*0750*	*0955*	*0955*	*1143*	*1340*	*1535*	*1838*a	*1948*a	*2038*	...
St Claude .... 🚌 ⊠ a.	*0826*	*1031*	*1031*	*1219*	*1416*	*1611*	*1914*a	*2024*a	*2114*	...

D – From Dijon (d. 1734).

a – Ⓐ only.

c – ⑥⑦ only.

f – Also May 17.

g – Also Apr. 11, May 2, 9, 30; not Apr. 10, May 1, 8, 29.

j – Arrives 0721.

k – Departs 1908.

p – Not Apr. 10 – 20, May 1, 8, 17, 18, 29.

r – 1841 on Feb. 25, Mar. 4.

s – By 🚌 in amended timings Apr. 11 – 14, 17 – 21 (St Claude d. 0517, Morez d. 0552, Champagnole d. 0642, Andelot a. 0702, Mouchard a. 0732, Arc-et-Senans a. 0745, Dole a. 0841).

t – Arrives 1115.

⊖ – ①②③④⑥ (not Apr. 10, May 1, 8, 17, 18, 29).

✣ – On May 18 services run as on ⑥.

⊠ – All services St Claude - Oyonnax and v.v. are by 🚌.

⊡ – Brion Montréal la Cluse.

◇ – Besançon-Viotte.

▷ – See Tables **353** and **378** for full service Bourg en Bresse - Lyon and v.v.

376a BESANÇON - LE LOCLE - LA CHAUX DE FONDS

km											
		①–⑤ a	①–⑤ a						Ⓐ		
0	**Besançon** Viotte .... d.	...	...	...	0931	...	1409	...	1737	1934	...
32	La Valdahon .... d.	0449	0538	...	1015	...	1450	1543	1830	2019	...
66	Morteau .... d.	0528	0627	0728	1055	...	1528	1628	1907	2058	...
79	Le Locle .... 512 d.	0544	0644	0744	1113	...	1544	1644	...	2114	...
87	**La Chaux de Fonds** 512 a.	0553	0653	0753	1122	...	1553	1653	...	2123	...

	①–⑤ a	①–⑤ a						Ⓐ		⑦–④
La Chaux de Fonds .. 512 d.	0600	0700	0800	1200	...	1600	1700	...	2131	2131
Le Locle .... 512 d.	0607	0709	0809	1209	...	1609	1709	...	2140	2140
Morteau .... d.	0622	0724	0826	1226	...	1626	1726	1914	2155	2157
La Valdahon .... d.	0700	...	0903	1303	...	1704	1803	1952	...	2233
Besançon Viotte .... a.	0737	...	0943	1343	...	1750	1853	2037	...	...

a – Not Apr. 7, 10, May 18, 29.

377 DIJON - CHALON SUR SAÔNE - MÂCON - LYON

TER Services

For *TGV* services Dijon - Lyon, see Table **379**. **WARNING! Timings may vary by up to 4 minutes until Mar. 25** (earlier departures possible). Subject to alteration on Apr. 22, 23. Journeys from / to Paris are subject to alteration on Mar. 11, 12, 18, 19

km																									
		Ⓐ	⚒	Ⓐ	Ⓐ		⚒	Ⓐ	S		Ⓐ			Ⓐ	⚒		Ⓐ			†	Ⓐ	Ⓐ	Ⓒ		
	Paris Bercy **371** .... d.	...	...	...	...	...	...	...	...	...	...	0735	...	...	...	0920c	...	...	...	...	...	...	...	1335r	...
0	**Dijon** Ville .... 373 d.	...	...	0541	...	0641	0725	0741	0841	0850	0941	1041	...	1141	1146	1241	1341	1350	1441	...	1541	...	1550	1641	...
37	Beaune .... 373 d.	...	...	0602	...	0702	0750	0802	0902	0920	1002	1102	...	1202	1215	1302	1402	1420	1502	...	1602	...	1620	1702	...
52	Chagny .... d.	...	...	0612	...	0712	0759	0812	0912	0931	1012	1112	...	1212	1224	1312	1412	1431	1512	...	1612	...	1631	1712	...
67	**Chalon sur Saône** .... d.	...	...	0623	...	0723	0813	0823	0923	0946	1023	1123	...	1223	1235	1323	1423	1446	1523	...	1623	...	1708b	1723	...
125	Mâcon Ville .... d.	0600	0636	0655	0728	0755	...	0855	0955	...	1055	1155	1236	1255	1314	1355	1455	...	1555	1655	1655	1736	1751	1755	1836
163	Villefranche sur Saône .... d.	0632	0707	0720	0752	0820	...	0920	1019	...	1120	1220	1307	1320	...	1419	1520	...	1620	1720	1720	1807	...	1819	1907
197	**Lyon** Part Dieu .... a.	0656	|	0743	0814	0844	...	0942	1043	...	1142	1243	|	1342	...	1443	1542	...	1644	1742	1743	|	...	1843	|
	Lyon Perrache .... a.	...	0734	...	0825	...	...	...	...	...	...	...	1334	...	...	...	...	...	...	...	...	1834	...	...	1934

	Ⓐ			Ⓐ	⑥	⑦	†	Ⓐ	⚒	
Paris Bercy **371** .... d.	...	...	1534	...	...	...	1727	1727	...	...
Dijon Ville .... 373 d.	1741	1752	1841	1941	1950	2013	2041	2041	2050	2212
Beaune .... 373 d.	1801	1821	1902	2002	2018	2042	2102	2102	2120	2241
Chagny .... d.	1812	1833	1911	2012	2030	2054	2111	2112	2131	2254
Chalon sur Saône .... d.	1823	1847	1922	2023	2043	2109	2122	2123	2140	2307
Mâcon Ville .... d.	1855	...	1955	2055	...	...	2155	2155	...	...
Villefranche sur Saône ..... d.	1920	...	2018	2120	...	...	2219	2218	...	...
Lyon Part Dieu .... a.	1942	...	2042	2142	...	...	2242	2244n	...	...
Lyon Perrache .... a.	...	...	...	...	...	...	2258	2245p	...	...

	⚒	Ⓑ	⚒	① g	⚒	Ⓐ		Ⓐ		Ⓐ
Lyon Perrache .... d.	...	...	...	0500	...	0605	...	...	...	0726
Lyon Part Dieu .... d.	...	...	...	0518e	...	0618	0717	...	...	|
Villefranche sur Saône ...... d.	...	...	...	0543	...	0643	0743	...	...	0754
Mâcon Ville .... d.	...	...	0607	0607	...	0707	0807	0818	...	0824
Chalon sur Saône .... d.	0556	0614	0639	0639	0714	0739	0839	0856	0913	...
Chagny .... d.	0606	0624	0649	0649	0724	0749	0849	0906	0923	...
Beaune .... 373 d.	0615	0635	0659	0659	0737	0759	0859	0915	0941	...
Dijon Ville .... 373 a.	0639	0707	0719	0719	0807	0819	0919	0942	1010	...
Paris Bercy **371** .... a.	...	...	1025	1025	...	...	1225c	...	...	...

	Ⓐ				Ⓐ			Ⓐ		Ⓐ	Ⓐ			Ⓐ			⚒	Ⓐ	Ⓐ	†	Ⓐ		Ⓐ		Ⓑ k
Lyon Perrache .... d.	...	0826	...	...	...	...	...	...	...	1326	...	...	...	...	...	...	1726	1736	...	...	1836	...	...	2106	2206
Lyon Part Dieu .... d.	0818	|	0918	...	1018	1118	...	1218	1318	|	1418	1516j	...	1618	1718	...	|	1746	1818	...	1846	1918	2018	2116	2216
Villefranche sur Saône ..... d.	0843	0854	0943	...	1043	1143	...	1243	1343	1354	1443	1543	...	1643	1743	...	1757	1809	1843	...	1909	1943	2043	2139	2239
Mâcon Ville .... d.	0907	0924	1007	...	1107	1207	...	1307	1407	1424	1507	1607	...	1707	1807	1823c	1825	1832	1907	1920	1932	2007	2107	2202	2302
Chalon sur Saône .... d.	0939	...	1039	1114	1139	1239	1248	1339	1439	...	1539	1639	1714	1739	1839	1914	...	...	1939	2002	...	2039	2139	...	...
Chagny .... d.	0949	...	1049	1124	1149	1249	1303	1349	1449	...	1549	1649	1724	1749	1849	1929	...	...	1949	2013	...	2049	2149	...	...
Beaune .... 373 d.	0959	...	1059	1137	1159	1259	1315	1359	1459	...	1559	1659	1736	1759	1859	1941	...	...	1959	2022	...	2059	2159	...	...
Dijon Ville .... 373 a.	1019	...	1119	1207	1219	1319	1344	1419	1519	...	1619	1719	1807	1819	1919	2010	...	...	2019	2049	...	2119	2219	...	...
Paris Bercy **371** .... a.	...	...	...	...	...	1637	...	...	1824	...	...	2025	...	...	2225	...	...	...	...	...	...	...	...	...	...

PARIS - DIJON - LYON

Ouigo Classique. Low-cost traditional loco-hauled train. Internet bookings only: www.ouigo.com. All services are subject to frequent variations – SEE NOTE ▲.

	5763	5765	5765
		Ⓒ	Ⓐ
Paris Bercy .... d.	1152	1811	1817
Melun .... d.	1233	1841	1846
Dijon Ville .... a.	1458	2104	2104
Dijon Ville .... d.	1501	2107	2107
Chalon sur Saône .... d.	1540	2146	2146
Mâcon Ville .... d.	1613	2217	2217
Lyon Part Dieu .... a.	1652	2257	2252
Lyon Perrache .... a.	1704	...	...

	5756		5774
Lyon Perrache .... d.	0608	...	1806
Lyon Part Dieu .... d.	|	...	|
Mâcon Ville .... d.	0651	...	1848
Chalon sur Saône ...... d.	0723	...	1930
Dijon Ville .... a.	0814	...	2014
Dijon Ville .... d.	0817	...	2017
Melun .... a.	1029	...	2229
Paris Bercy .... a.	1108	...	2308

S – From Sens on ⚒ (Table **371**).

b – Arrives 1646.

c – Ⓒ only.

e – Not Feb. 27, Mar. 6.

g – Also Apr. 11, May 2, 9, 30; not Apr. 10, May 1, 8, 29.

j – 1518 on Ⓐ.

k – Not May 18.

n – Not Mar. 6 – 24.

p – Mar. 6 – 24 only.

r – ⚒ only.

▲ – Sample timings are shown in this table. All services are subject to frequent variations and may not run on certain dates. Departure / arrival stations at Paris and Lyon may also vary. Please check carefully when booking.

LYON - LONS-LE-SAUNIER - BESANÇON - BELFORT 378

See Table **379** for *TGV* services Lyon - Besançon Franche-Comté TGV - Belfort Montbéliard TGV. **Warning!** Subject to alteration on Apr. 22, May 6.

km																										
		⚒	⚒	Ⓐ	Ⓐ	Ⓐ		Ⓐ	Ⓒ			Ⓐ	⚒	⚒ m			Ⓐ			Ⓐ	Ⓑ	Ⓐ	Ⓒ	⚒ m	Ⓐ	⑤† f
0	**Lyon** Perrache... **353** d.	...	...	...	0601	...	0716	...	...	...	...	1301	...	1401	...	...	...	...	1616	1616	1716	1816	1816	1901	...	2116
5	**Lyon** Part-Dieu .. **353** d.	...	...	...	0612	...	0730	0942**k**	0942	...	...	1312	...	1412	...	...	...	...	1630	1630	1733	1830	1830	1912	...	2130
	Ambérieu ‡ d.	...	...	...	|	...	|	|	|	...	...	|	...	|	...	...	...	...	|	|	1759	1858	1859	|	...	|
65	Bourg-en-Bresse **353** ‡ d.	...	...	...	0712	0719	0819	1021**k**	1023	...	...	1412	1418**n**	1512	1523	...	...	...	1719	1719	1819	1918	1919	2012	2038	2232
129	**Lons-le-Saunier** d.	0544	0616	0645	▬	0800	0901	1101	1100	...	1215	▬	1501	▬	1602	...	1701	1715	1801	1801	1859	2001	2001	...	2122	2312
178	Mouchard d.	0627	0702	0722	...	0839	0938	1137	1137	...	1302	...	1538	...	1639	...	1738	1802	1838	1838	...	2038	2038	...	...	...
184	Arc-et-Senans d.	0634	0707	0729	Ⓐ	0845	0943	1145	1145	...	1307	⚒	1543	...	1644	...	1743	1807	1843	1843	...	2043	2043	...	...	...
218	**Besançon** Viotte a.	0710	0742	0755		0909	1009	1209	1209	...	1342		1609	...	1710	...	1809	1842	1909	1909	...	2109	2109	...	...	...
218	**Besançon** Viotte ▷ d.	0714	...	...	0814	...	1014	1214	...	1232	...	1514	...	1614	...	1732	1814	...	...	1914	...	...	2114	...	...	...
297	Montbéliard ▷ d.	0810	...	...	0910	...	1110	1310	...	1341	...	1610	...	1710	...	1841	1910	...	...	2010	...	...	2210	...	...	...
315	**Belfort** Ville ▷ a.	0824	...	...	0924	...	1124	1324	...	1356	...	1624	...	1724	...	1856	1924	...	...	2024	...	...	2224	...	...	...

	⚒	Ⓐ	Ⓐ		Ⓐ		†	⚒		⚒	⚒ n	Ⓐ	⚒ n	† w			Ⓐ	⑥	Ⓐ	†	Ⓐ	Ⓐ		Ⓐ		
Belfort Ville ▷ d.	...	...	0535	...	0604	0604	...	0736	0936	...	...	...	...	...	1204	1336	...	1536	1536	1536	1636	...	...	*1736*	1836	2036
Montbéliard ▷ d.	...	...	0549	...	0620	0620	...	0751	0951	...	...	...	...	...	1220	1351	...	1551	1551	1551	1651	...	...	*1750*	1851	2051
Besançon Viotte ... ▷ a.	...	...	0646	...	0728	0728	...	0846	1046	...	...	...	...	...	1328	1446	...	1646	1646	1646	1746	...	...	*1849*	1946	2146
Besançon Viotte d.	...	0601	...	0651	0731	...	0846	0851	...	1051	...	...	1251	1318	▬	1451	1518	1651	1651	1651	▬	1751	1818	1900	1951	...
Arc-et-Senans d.	...	0633	...	0713	0755	...	0913	0913	...	1113	...	...	1323	1350	...	1513	1552	1713	1713	1713	...	1813	1852	1932	2014	...
Mouchard d.	...	0640	...	0721	0801	...	0920	0920**j**	...	1120	...	...	1328	1357	...	1520	1600	1720	1720	1720	Ⓐ	1820	1900	1938	2022	...
Lons-le-Saunier d.	0601	0730	...	0801	0844	...	1001	1001**j**	...	1159	1301	...	1406	1437	...	1601	1645	1759	1801	1801		1859	1945	2022	2101	...
Bourg-en-Bresse **353** ‡ d.	0643	...	...	0843	...	...	1043	1043**j**	...	...	1341	1348	1442	1514	1548	1643	...	...	1841	1843	1848	...	...	...	2143	...
Ambérieu ‡ d.	|	...	...	0902	...	...	1103	1103	...	...	...	|	...	...	|	|	...	...	...	|	|	...	...	...	|	...
Lyon Part-Dieu .... **353** a.	0730	...	...	0930	...	...	1130	1130	...	...	...	1448	...	...	1648	1731	...	...	...	1930	1948	...	...	...	2230	...
Lyon Perrache .. **353** a.	0744	...	...	...	...	...	1145	1144	...	...	...	1459	...	...	1659	1745	...	...	...	...	1959	...	...	...	2244	...

OTHER SERVICES **BESANÇON - BELFORT**

	Ⓐ	Ⓐ	Ⓑ	†		Ⓐ	Ⓐ	Ⓒ		Ⓐ		Ⓐ
Besançon Viotte d.	0532	0614	0632	0714	0732	1114	1314	1332	1632	1714	1832	2012
Montbéliard d.	0641	0715	0741	0810	0841	1210	1410	1441	1742	1810	1941	2110
Belfort Ville a.	0656	0728	0756	0824	0856	1224	1424	1456	1757	1824	1956	2125

	Ⓐ	Ⓐ	Ⓐ	Ⓐ	Ⓐ				
Belfort Ville d.	0636	0704	0836	1136	1236	1304	1704	1819	1936
Montbéliard d.	0651	0720	0851	1151	1250	1320	1720	1833	1951
Besançon Viotte a.	0746	0828	0946	1246	1348	1428	1828	1943	2046

f – Also May 17.
j – Apr. 3–7, 11–14, May 2–5, 9–12, 15–17, 19, 22–26 departs Mouchard 0919, Lons-le-Saunier 0958, Bourg-en-Bresse 1039.
k – Apr. 11–14 departs Lyon Part Dieu 0933, Bourg-en-Bresse 1019.
m – Also May 18.
n – Not Apr. 3–7, 11–14, May 2–5, 9–12, 15–17, 19, 22–26.
w – Also Apr. 11–14, May 2–5, 9–12, 15–17, 19, 22–26.
‡ – See also Table **353a**.
▷ – See also panel below main table.

Local trains BELFORT - MULHOUSE 378a

See also Table 380

	Ⓐ	⚒	Ⓐ	⚒	Ⓐ	Ⓒ	Ⓐ	Ⓐ	Ⓒ	Ⓐ	Ⓐ	Ⓒ	Ⓐ	Ⓒ	Ⓐ	Ⓐ		Ⓐ	†	Ⓐ	⚒	†	Ⓐ	Ⓐ	⑥	†	Ⓐ¶ 🚌
Belfort Ville d.	0531	0555	0631	0701	0734	0736	0806	0906	1004	1006	1202	1210	1304	1404	1506	1606	1706	1736	1800	1806	1848	1900	1907	2006	2016	2055	2055
Altkirch d.	0551	0619	0653	0723	0755	0758	0826	0927	1024	1026	1222	1232	1326	1426	1526	1626	1726	1758	1822	1828	1910	1922	1929	2026	2036	2117	2146
Mulhouse a.	0609	0637	0710	0740	0811	0815	0839	0939	1039	1039	1234	1247	1339	1439	1539	1639	1740	1810	1839	1840	1922	1939	1940	2040	2050	2133	2209

	Ⓐ	⚒	Ⓐ	Ⓐ			Ⓐ	Ⓐ	Ⓒ	Ⓐ	Ⓐ	Ⓒ		Ⓐ		†	⚒	Ⓐ	Ⓐ		Ⓐ	Ⓐ		Ⓐ			Ⓐ 🚌
Mulhouse d.	0620	0650	0723	0802	0823	...	0923	1023	1122	1220	1310	1315	...	1423	...	1559	1619	1650	1719	1751	1823	1901	1929	2020	2056	...	2225
Altkirch d.	0632	0704	0735	0816	0835	...	0935	1035	1136	1235	1322	1332	...	1435	...	1616	1636	1707	1736	1808	1838	1915	1946	2037	2110	...	2249
Belfort Ville a.	0654	0727	0758	0840	0857	...	0956	1056	1159	1256	1343	1355	...	1456	...	1640	1659	1730	1800	1831	1901	1939	2010	2100	2132	...	2340

¶ – Runs 13 minutes later on ⑤.

LUXEMBOURG - METZ - STRASBOURG - DIJON - LYON 379

Timings may vary by up to 7 minutes – please check your reservation for confirmed timings. **Warning!** Subject to alteration on Apr. 22, 23.

km		*TGV* **5521**	*TGV* **9877**	*TGV* **9879**	*TGV* **5537**		*TGV* **9580**	*TGV* **5535**	
							♣	⑤⑦ d	
0	**Luxembourg** **384** d.	...	0724**k**	1124	...	...	...	...	...
34	Thionville **384** d.	...	0750**k**	1149	...	...	...	...	...
64	**Metz** **383 384** d.	0546	0811	1212	...	...	...	...	...
	Nancy ▷ d.	|	|	|	1226	...	...	...	...
209	**Strasbourg** **383** a.	0640	0858	1300	1329	...	...	...	...
209	**Strasbourg** **385** d.	0647	0904	1306	1337	...	1615	1903	...
274	Colmar **385** d.	|	|	|	1405	...	|	1933	...
315	**Mulhouse** **370 385** d.	0752	0957	1357	1440	...	1709	2004	...
360	Belfort Montbéliard TGV **370** d.	0817	1021	1421	1506	...	1734	2029	...
442	**Besançon** Franche-Comté TGV **370** d.	0841	1044	1444	1536	...	1758	2052	...
519	**Dijon** Ville **370** ▷ a.	0911	1111	1511	1604	...	|	2119	...
519	**Dijon** Ville **377** d.	0921	1121	1521	1620	1752	|	2129	...
556	Beaune **377** d.	|	|	|	1642	1821	|	|	...
586	**Chalon sur Saône** **377** d.	0956	|	|	|	1848	1856	|	...
644	Mâcon Ville **377** d.	|	1222	1621	|	...	|	2229**r**	...
716	**Lyon** Part Dieu **11 377** a.	1056	1300	1656	1756	...	1956	2304**r**	...
	Lyon Perrache a.	|	|	|	|	...	|	2318**r**	...
	Valence TGV **350** a.	|	1346	1745	|	...	|	...	...
	Avignon TGV **350** a.	|	1425	|	1908	...	2109	...	...
	Aix en Provence TGV **350** a.	|	1449	|	1930	...	2133	...	...
	Marseille St Charles **350** a.	|	1506	|	1944	...	2148	...	...
	Nice Ville **360** a.	|	...	|	2230	...	...	...	...
	Nîmes Centre **355** a.	1224	...	1826•	...	...	...	...	...
	Montpellier Saint-Roch **355** a.	1254	...	1850•	...	...	...	...	...

	TGV **5514**	*TGV* **9898**	*TGV* **9583**	*TGV* **5512**		*TGV* **5516**	*TGV* **5500**	*TGV* **9896**
	① g		♣	⑥ s				⊙
Montpellier Saint-Roch **355** d.	...	0629	...	...	...	...	1358	...
Nîmes Centre **355** d.	...	0700	...	...	...	...	1427	...
Nice Ville **360** d.	...	|	...	...	...	0700	|	...
Marseille St Charles **350** d.	...	|	0811	...	...	0946	|	1556
Aix en Provence TGV **350** d.	...	|	0826	...	...	1000	|	1611
Avignon TGV **350** d.	...	|	0848	...	...	1023	|	1633
Valence TGV **350** d.	...	0748	|	...	...	|	1515	1714
Lyon Perrache d.	...	|	|	0942	...	|	|	|
Lyon Part Dieu **11 377** d.	0546	0834	1004	1004	...	1132	1604	1800
Mâcon Ville **377** d.	0604	|	|	|	...	1212	1641	|
Chalon sur Saône **377** d.	0641	|	1106	1106	1114	1244	|	|
Beaune **377** d.	|	|	|	|	1137	1306	|	|
Dijon Ville **377** a.	0740	0958	|	|	1207	1325	1740	1939
Dijon Ville **370** ▷ d.	0800	1008	|	|	...	1337	1750	1949
Besançon Franche-Comté TGV ... **370** d.	0838	1036	1204	1204	...	1409	1822	2019
Belfort Montbéliard TGV **370** d.	0905	1059	1227	1227	...	1433	1847	2045
Mulhouse **370 385** d.	0935	1124	1254	1254	...	1459	1912	2112
Colmar **385** d.	|	1152	|	|	...	1527	1944	|
Strasbourg **385** a.	1027	1224	1343	1343	...	1554	2013	2207
Strasbourg **383** d.	...	1231	...	...	...	1600	2024	2214**z**
Nancy ▷ a.	...	|	...	...	...	1702	|	|
Metz **383 384** a.	...	1319	...	...	...	...	2113	2302**z**
Thionville **384** a.	...	1347	...	...	...	...	...	2323**c**
Luxembourg **384** a.	...	1415**p**	...	...	...	...	...	2349**c**

A – Daily to Mar. 26; Ⓒ from Apr. 1.

c – ⑥⑦ to Apr. 2; daily from Apr. 8. Terminates at Thionville on May 28.
d – Also Apr. 10, May 1, 8, 17, 29; not Apr. 9, 30, May 7, 19, 28.
g – Also Apr. 11, May 2, 9, 30; not Apr. 10, May 1, 8, 29.
k – ①⑥⑦ to Mar. 20; daily from Mar. 25 (not May 27–29).
p – Not May 27, 28, 29.
r – Timings Mâcon - Lyon may vary (please check your reservation). Terminates at Lyon Part Dieu on ⑤ Jan. 13 - Mar. 31. Does not call at Mâcon on Apr. 21.
s – Also May 18; not May 20.
v – Not Mar. 10, 13–17.
z – Not ①–④ Dec. 12 - Mar. 23.

TGV – High-speed train. 🅁. 🍷.

♣ – From / to Frankfurt (Tables **48** and **912**).
◐ – Runs 8–9 minutes **earlier** on ⑥.
◧ – Runs 3–5 minutes **earlier** on ⑥.
⊙ – Later arrivals at Metz, Thionville and Luxembourg Apr. 3–7.
▷ – See panel below main table for other TER services Nancy - Dijon and v.v.
• – Arrives Nîmes **Pont-du-Gard** (not Centre) and Montpellier **Sud-de-France** (not Saint-Roch).

TER services **NANCY - NEUFCHÂTEAU - DIJON**

	A	⚒◐	
Nancy **382** d.	0754	1307	1654
Toul **382** d.	0816	1329	1714
Neufchâteau d.	0842	1353	1738
Culmont Chalindrey a.	0934	...	1826
Culmont Chalindrey **380 381a** d.	0944**v**	...	1833
Dijon Ville **380 381a** a.	1031**v**	...	1927

	⚒◧	A	
Dijon Ville **380 381a** d.	...	1100**v**	2005
Culmont Chalindrey **380 381a** a.	...	1145**v**	2053
Culmont Chalindrey d.	...	1155	2058
Neufchâteau d.	0655	1245	2151
Toul **382** a.	0720	1311	2219
Nancy **382** a.	0745	1336	2239

380 PARIS - TROYES - MULHOUSE

SERVICE UNTIL JUNE 4. Timings may vary by up to 5 minutes (earlier departures possible). Readers are advised to check timings locally before travelling.
Warning! A revised timetable from / to Paris operates on Mar. 18, 19, May 6 – 8 with a much reduced service; trains that do run are retimed and diverted between Paris and Chaumont, not calling at Nogent, Romilly, Troyes or Bar sur Aube – please check locally for journeys on these dates.

km		Ⓐ	⚒	Ⓐ	Ⓐ	⑥	Ⓐ	⑥	Ⓐ		Ⓐ △	†	⑥	⚒	⑥	Ⓐ	⑥	†	⚒	Ⓐ	⑦	⑥		Ⓐ	①–④ m
0	**Paris** Est d.	...	...	...	...	...	0542	0642	0642	0742	0842	0842	0842	0942	1042	1142	1142	1142	1242r	1342	1342	1342	...	...	1508
110	Nogent sur Seine d.	...	...	...	...	...	0644	0739	0740	0840	0940	0939	0940	1040	1140	1240	1240	1240	1340	1440	1439	1440	...	...	1610
129	Romilly sur Seine d.	...	...	...	...	...	0656	0750	0751	0851	0951	0950	0951	1051	1151	1251	1251	1251	1351	1451	1450	1451	...	...	1621
166	**Troyes** d.	...	...	...	0507	0639	0716	0810	0811	0912	1011	1010	1017	1111	1211	1311	1315	1316	1411	1511	1516	1515	...	...	1649
221	Bar sur Aube d.	...	...	...	0538	0709	0746	0840	0841	0943c	1041	1040	1048	▬	▬	1341	1345	1347	▬	1541	1547	1547	...	...	1719
262	Chaumont 381a d.	...	...	...	0600	0730	0808	0901	0902	1004c	1102	1101	1109	...	...	1402	1407	1408	...	1604	1608	1609	...	...	1740
296	Langres 381a d.	...	...	...	0623	0753	0832	0924	0924	1027c	1124	1122	1130	...	...	1426	1430	1432	...	1625	1630	1633	...	...	1805
307	Culmont Chalindrey 381a ‡ d.	...	...	...	0632	0800	0840	0932	0933	1034c	1133	1131	1140	Ⓐ	...	1435	1440	1441	Ⓐ	1635	1639	1642	...	...	1815
	Dijon Ville 381a ‡ a.	...	...	...	0726	...	...	...	|	...	|	|	|	w	w	1521	1525	...		|	|	|	...	...	...
380	Vesoul d.	0639	0739	0839	...	...	...	...	1010	...	1211	1208	1217	1239	1339	...	...	...	1639	1713	1716	1719	1739	1839	...
410	Lure 382 d.	0656	0756	0856	...	...	...	...	1027	...	1228	1226	1234	1256	1356	...	...	...	1656	1730	1733	1736	1756	1856	...
442	**Belfort** Ville 378a 382 d.	0725	0825	0925	...	...	...	...	1048	...	1246	1249	1255	1325	1425	...	...	...	1725	1748	1751	1754	1825	1925	...
490	**Mulhouse** 378a a.	...	...	...	...	...	...	...	1115	...	...	1316	1323	...	...	...	...	...	...	...	...	...	...	...	...

	Ⓒ	⑤	†	A	⑤	Ⓐ	⚒	Ⓑ		Ⓑ		
Paris Est d.	1512	1512	1642	1642	1642	1712	1742	1812	1842	1942	2042	2212j
Nogent sur Seine d.	1610	1610	1738	1738	1740	1814	1840	1914t	1939	2040	2138	2310
Romilly sur Seine d.	1621	1621	1749	1749	1751	1825	1851	1925t	1950	2051	2149	2321
Troyes d.	1651	1651	1809	1812	1817	1844	1911	1944t	2011	2111	2209	2341
Bar sur Aube d.	1721	1722	1839	1844	1851	...	...	...	2041	...	2240	...
Chaumont 381a d.	1742	1743	1900	1906	1913	...	...	...	2102	...	2302	...
Langres 381a d.	1807	1806	1921	1927	1936	...	...	...	2123	...	2324	...
Culmont Chalindrey 381a ‡ d.	1815	1822	1936	1936	1946	...	...	...	2132	...	2334	...
Dijon Ville 381a ‡ a.	...	...	|	|	|	...	...	...	|	...	...	...
Vesoul d.	...	...	2013	2013	2024	...	...	...	2210	...	...	...
Lure 382 d.	...	...	2031	2031	2042	...	...	...	2227	...	...	...
Belfort Ville 378a 382 d.	...	...	2051	2051	2102	...	...	...	2249	...	...	...
Mulhouse 378a a.	...	...	2117	2117	2130	...	...	...	2315	...	...	...

	Ⓐ	⚒	Ⓐ	⚒	Ⓐ	Ⓐ	⑥	Ⓐ
Mulhouse 378a d.	...	...	...	...	...	...	...	0518
Belfort Ville 378a 382 d.	...	...	...	...	...	...	...	0546
Lure 382 d.	...	...	...	...	...	...	...	0604
Vesoul d.	...	...	...	...	...	...	...	0623
Dijon Ville 381a ‡ d.	...	...	...	...	...	...	...	|
Culmont Chalindrey 381a ‡ d.	...	...	...	...	0545	...	0610	0701
Langres 381a d.	...	...	...	...	0555	...	0619	0709
Chaumont 381a d.	...	...	...	...	0617	...	0640	0731
Bar sur Aube d.	...	...	...	...	0637	...	0701	0751
Troyes d.	0517	0547	0613	0647	0712	0747	0747	0820
Romilly sur Seine d.	0537	0607	0634	0707	0733	0807	0808	0839
Nogent sur Seine d.	0549	0619	0646	0719	0745	0819	0820	0851
Paris Est a.	0646	0716	0746	0816	0846	0916	0916	0947

	†	⑥	Ⓐ	⚒	Ⓐ		Ⓐ	Ⓒ	Ⓐ	Ⓐ	Ⓒ	†	Ⓐ	⑥	⚒ w	Ⓐ	⑥	⑤	z	Ⓐ	Ⓐ			†	Ⓑ
Mulhouse 378a d.	0518	...	...	...	...	0742	...	...	...	...	...	1235	...	...	...	...	...	1535	1535	...	...	...	...	...	...
Belfort Ville 378a 382 d.	0547	...	0635	0735	...	0811	0935	...	...	...	...	1303	1311	...	1335	...	...	1604	1604	...	1635	1735	1809	...	1839
Lure 382 d.	0605	...	0704	0804	...	0829	1004	...	...	...	...	1322	1329	...	1404	...	...	1622	1622	...	1704	1805	1827	...	1908
Vesoul d.	0623	...	0721	0821	...	0846	1021	...	...	...	...	1340	1346	...	1421	...	...	1639	1639	...	1721	1822	1845	...	1925
Dijon Ville 381a ‡ d.	|	...	▬	...	0813	|	▬	...	...	...	...	|	|	...	▬	...	1617	|	|	1706	▬	...	|	...	...
Culmont Chalindrey 381a ‡ d.	0702	0723	...	...	0918	0925	...	1125	1225	...	1326	1427	1425	1426	...	1551	1719	1724	1730	1820	...	...	1924	2108	...
Langres 381a d.	0709	0732	...	...	...	0934	...	1134	1234	...	1335	1435	1434	1434	...	1600	▬	1732	1738	1830	...	...	1934	2117	...
Chaumont 381a d.	0730	0754	⚒	...	...	0955	⚒	1156	1255	...	1356	1457	1455	1455	⑥	1621	...	1753	1759	1851	Ⓑ	...	1955	2138	...
Bar sur Aube d.	0751	0816		...	...	1016		1216	1316	...	1416	1518	1516	1516		1641	...	1813	1820	1912		...	2015	2158	...
Troyes d.	0821	0847	0947	...	...	1047	1147	1247	1347	1447	1447	1549	1547	1546	1636	1717	1747	1848	1849	1941	1947	...	2049	2228	...
Romilly sur Seine d.	0840	0907	1007	...	...	1108	1207	1306	1407	1507	1507	1609	1608	1605	1656	1737	1807	1908	1908	...	2007	...	2108	...	...
Nogent sur Seine d.	0853	0920	1019	...	...	1120	1219	1318	1419	1519	1519	1620	1620	1617	1708	1749	1819	1920	1920	...	2019	...	2120	...	...
Paris Est a.	0947	1016	1117	...	...	1216	1316	1416	1516	1616	1616	1716	1716	1716	1816	1846	1917	2016	2016	...	2116	...	2216	...	...

A – ①②③④⑥ (not Apr. 10, May 1, 8, 18, 29).

c – Troyes - Culmont Chalindrey on Ⓒ only.
j – 2210 on †.
m – Not Apr. 10, May 1, 8, 18, 29.
r – 1234 on ⑤.

t – 4 minutes earlier on †.
w – Not Mar. 13 – 17, 20 – 24, 27 – 31, Apr. 3 – 7, 11 – 14.
z – Not ⑤.

△ – Terminates at Vesoul May 22 – 26.
‡ – See also panel below Table **379**.

381 PARIS - CHÂLONS EN CHAMPAGNE - BAR LE DUC - NANCY and ST DIZIER

TER services

Warning! Subject to alteration on Mar. 11, 12, Apr. 15, 16, May 19.

km		Ⓐ	Ⓐ	⑥	Ⓐ	⑥	†	Ⓐ v	Ⓐ T⊖	⑥	†	⑥	Ⓐ A	⑥	Ⓐ D	Ⓒ	⑥	Ⓐ E	Ⓐ M	Ⓐ	F	⑦	⑥	⑥ w
0	**Paris** Est 390 d.	...	0636	...	0736	0836	0836	0836	0836	0936	1036	1036	1036	1136	1236	1236	1436	1436	...	1636	1636	1636	1636	...
95	Château Thierry d.	...	0731	...	0826	0929	0931	0931	0931	1031	1131	1131	1131	1231	1331	1324	1531	1531	...	1723	1724	1728	1731	...
	Reims ♠ d.	...	|	...	|	|	|	|	|	|	|	|	|	|	|	|	|	|	...	|	|	|	|	1749
142	Épernay ♠ d.	0644	0759	0816	0854	0957	0959	0956	0958	1059	1159	1159	1159	1259	1358	1352	1559	1559	1614	1750	1752	1759	1759	1817
172*	**Châlons en Champagne** 381a d.	0704	0823	0832	0912	1015	1017	...	1023	1115	1215	1217	1217	1316	1413	1409	1614	1616	1632	1807	1809	1817	1816	1835
205	Vitry le François 381a d.	0723	0842	0848	0931	1033	1035	...	1042	...	...	1235	1235	1334	...	1427	...	1634	1649	1824	1827	1835	1833	1853
234	**St Dizier** 381a a.	|	0900	|	|	|	|	...	1059	...	...	1255	|	|	...	1446	...	1653	|	|	|	|	|	|
255	**Bar le Duc** ♣ d.	0754	...	0914	0957	1058	1059	...	...	...	...	...	1300	1359	...	...	...	...	1714	1848	1852	1905	1859	1920
295	Commercy ♣ d.	0815	...	0939	1020	1119	...	...	...	...	...	...	...	...	...	...	...	...	...	1910	1920	1929	...	1944
321	Toul ♣ d.	0830	...	0957	1036	1134	...	...	...	...	...	...	...	...	...	...	...	...	...	1925	1941	1945	...	2001
354	**Nancy** ♣ a.	0854	...	1025	1056	1153	...	...	...	...	...	...	...	...	...	...	...	...	...	1944	2004	2004	...	2029
	Strasbourg 383 a.	...	...	...	1237	1318	...	...	...	...	...	...	...	...	...	...	...	...	...	2121	2138	2141	...	...

	Ⓐ	† ⊡		2785 Ⓑ h♥	Ⓐ	⑤	Ⓒ	①–④ m	⑤ △	† ▽	
Paris Est 390 d.	1736	...	1835	1928	1936	1936	2036	2136	2136	2236	...
Château Thierry d.	1831	...	1931	|	2031	2031	2131	2231	2231	2331	...
Reims ♠ d.	|	1831	|	◐	|	|	|	|	|	|	...
Épernay ♠ d.	1859	1912	1959	|	2058	2058	2159	2259	2259	2359	...
Châlons en Champagne 381a d.	1916	1930	2016	2035	2114	2115	2215	2315	2316	0015	...
Vitry le François 381a d.	1934	1946	2034	2055	...	2133	...	...	2334	...	...
St Dizier 381a a.	1953	|	2052	|	...	2152	...	...	|	...	...
Bar le Duc ♣ d.	...	2014	...	2119	...	...	...	...	2359	...	...
Commercy ♣ d.	...	2040	...	...	...	...	...	...	...	...	...
Toul ♣ d.	...	2059	...	...	...	...	...	...	...	...	...
Nancy ♣ a.	...	2126	...	...	...	...	...	...	...	...	...
Strasbourg 383 a.	...	...	...	...	...	...	...	...	...	...	...

	Ⓐ		⚒	2778 ①–⑥ b♥	Ⓐ	Ⓒ	Ⓐ d
Strasbourg 383 d.	...	...	...	...	...	...	0444
Nancy ♣ d.	...	...	...	...	...	...	0616
Toul ♣ d.	...	...	...	...	...	...	0640
Commercy ♣ d.	...	...	...	...	...	...	0659
Bar le Duc ♣ d.	...	...	...	0610	...	...	0722
St Dizier 381a d.	...	...	0533	|	0633	0709‡	|
Vitry le François 381a d.	...	...	0553	0636	0653	0730‡	0752
Châlons en Champagne 381a d.	0512	...	0611	0655	0711	0748	0812
Épernay ♠ d.	0529	...	0629	|	0729	0805	0830
Reims ♠ a.	|	...	|	◧	|	|	|
Château Thierry d.	0559	...	0659	|	0759	0834	0859
Paris Est 390 a.	0653	...	0753	0801	0853	0923	0953

	†	⑥	①–⑤ T	⑥	†	Ⓐ r	①–⑤ G	⑥	Ⓐ B	⑥	Ⓒ	Ⓐ	Ⓒ	†	Ⓐ	⑥	Ⓐ	†	⑦	①–⑤	⑦	⑥		⑤ p
Strasbourg 383 d.	...	...	...	0818	...	...	...	...	...	...	...	...	...	...	...	...	...	...	...	1619	1619	...	...	...
Nancy ♣ d.	...	...	...	1002	...	...	...	...	...	...	...	...	1436	...	...	...	...	1620	...	1746	1755	...	...	2035
Toul ♣ d.	...	...	...	1024	...	...	...	...	...	...	...	...	1459	...	...	...	...	1652	...	1808	1816	...	...	2058
Commercy ♣ d.	...	...	...	1039	...	...	...	...	...	...	...	...	1514	...	...	...	...	1710	...	1825	1832	...	...	2112
Bar le Duc ♣ d.	...	0905	...	1102	1105	...	...	...	1329	1406	...	...	1534	...	...	...	...	1735	...	1847	1855	1906	...	2133
St Dizier 381a d.	...	|	0933	|	|	...	1133	...	|	|	1508	...	|	...	1633	...	1733	|	1809	|	|	|	...	|
Vitry le François 381a d.	...	0930	0954	1127	1130	...	1154	...	1354	1430	1530	...	1600	...	1654	...	1754	1806k	1830	1911	1925	1930	...	2201
Châlons en Champagne 381a d.	0941	0948	1012	1149	1148	...	1212	1248	1412	1449	1548	1612	1616	1650	1712	1750	1812	1829k	1848	1932	1943	1948	...	2218
Épernay ♠ d.	1006	1005	1029	1207	1205	1229	1229	1307	1429	1506	1606	1629	1641z	1707	1730	1807	1830	1849k	1906	1949	2000	2005	...	2235
Reims ♠ a.	|	|	|	|	|	|	|	|	|	|	|	|	1702	|	|	|	|	...	|	|	|	|	...	...
Château Thierry d.	1035	1034	1059	1236	1234	1244	1244	1335	1459	1534	1635	1659	...	1736	1759	1835	1859	...	1935	2020	2029	2034	...	...
Paris Est 390 a.	1123	1123	1153	1323	1323	1353	1353	1423	1553	1623	1723	1753	...	1823	1853	1923	1953	...	2023	2123	2124	2123	...	...

FOR NOTES AND OTHER TER SERVICES BETWEEN BAR LE DUC AND NANCY, SEE NEXT PAGE →

PARIS - CHÂLONS EN CHAMPAGNE - BAR LE DUC - NANCY and ST DIZIER 381

OTHER TER SERVICES **BAR LE DUC - NANCY**

	Ⓐ	Ⓐ	⚒		†	Ⓐ		Ⓐ	ⒶN	Ⓐ	ⒶR	†	Ⓐ	ⒶQ		ⒶS	⑥	Ⓐ	ⒶQ	†	Ⓐ	ⒶR	Ⓐ	⑥	†		Ⓐ
Bar le Duc ....d.	0554	0613	0725	...	0926	1005c	...	...	1125	...	1213	1225	...	1306	...	1425	1427	...	1525	1525	...	1625	1725	1721	1826	...	2125
Commercy ....d.	0615	0639	0746	...	0947	1026	...	1146	1146	1239	1239	1246	1326	1326	...	1446	1447	1546	1546	1546	1646	1646	1746	1746	1847	...	2146
Toul ....d.	0630	0658	0801	...	1001	1041	...	1201	1201	1258	1258	1300	1341	1341	...	1501	1502	1601	1601	1601	1701	1701	1801	1804	1901	...	2201
Nancy ....a.	0654	0725	0825	...	1025	1105	...	1225	1225	1325	1325	1324	1405	1405	...	1525	1525	1625	1625	1625	1725	1725	1825	1829	1925	...	2225

	⑥	Ⓐ	⑥	Ⓐ	Ⓐ	ⒶN	†	Ⓐ	ⒶR	Ⓐ	ⒶQ	Ⓒ	Ⓐ	ⒶR	Ⓐ	ⒶH	Ⓐ	⑥	Ⓐ	Ⓐ	⑥	†	Ⓐ	⑥	Ⓐ	†	Ⓐ
Nancy ....d.	0646	0735	0801	0835	0935	0935	1000	1035	1035	1135	1135	1234	1334	1334	1435	1435	1535	1607	1634	1706	1801	1834	1835	1934	1935	2034	2034
Toul ....d.	0710	0758	0825	0858	0958	0958	1024	1058	1058	1158	1158	1300	1400	1400	1458	1458	1558	1631	1658	1733	1824	1858	1858	2000	2000	2058	2058
Commercy ....d.	0724	0812	0840	0913	1012	1013	1039	1111	1112	1211	1212	1319	1418	1419	1511	1512	1613	1646	1713	1752	1839	1912	1913	2019	2019	2112	2112
Bar le Duc ....a.	0747	0833	0859	0934x	...	1034	1059	...	1133	...	1233	1344	...	1445	...	1533	1633	1708	1735	1818	1859	1934	1934	2045	2045	2134	2133

A – Dec. 26 - Jan. 6, May 15–19 and from May 25. Also runs Paris - Épernay until Dec. 23, Jan. 9 - Mar. 3 and Mar. 20–24.
B – Bar le Duc - Épernay on ①–⑤ Dec. 26 - Jan. 6; Épernay - Paris on Ⓐ until Mar. 3 (also Mar. 20–24).
D – Paris - Épernay on Ⓐ (not Mar. 27 - Apr. 17); Épernay - Châlons Dec. 12–16, 26–30, Jan. 2–6, Apr. 18–21 and from May 9.
E – Paris - Épernay on Ⓐ (not Apr. 11–17); Épernay - St Dizier on Ⓐ to Jan. 6 / from Apr. 3 (not Apr. 11–17).
F – Apr. 10, May 1, 8, 18, 29 only.
G – Dec. 12–16, 26–30, Jan. 2–6, Apr. 18–21 and from May 9 (does not run St Dizier - Châlons Apr. 18–21).
H – Dec. 12–23, Jan. 2–6, Jan. 23 - Feb. 24 and from May 12.
M – Ⓐ Dec. 26 - Jan. 6; Ⓐ from Apr. 3. To Metz (a. 1816).
N – Dec. 12–23, Jan. 2–6 and from May 2.
Q – Dec. 12–23, Jan. 2–6 and from May 15.
R – Until Jan. 6 and from May 15.
S – Dec. 26 - Jan. 6 and from May 15.
T – Dec. 12–16, 26–30, Jan. 2–6, Apr. 18–21 and from May 4.

b – ①–⑥ (not Apr. 10, May 1, 8, 29). On Apr. 15 does not run Bar le Duc - Châlons.
c – Not Jan. 9 - Mar. 10, Apr. 24–28.
d – Not Dec. 12–15, Feb. 14–16, 21–23.
h – Ⓑ (not Apr. 9, 30, May 7, 28). On Apr. 14 does not run Châlons - Bar le Duc.
k – 8–10 minutes later on Apr. 10, May 1, 8, 18, 29.
m – Not Apr. 10, May 1, 8, 17, 18, 29.
p – Not Mar. 17, 24, Apr. 7, 14.

r – Not Mar. 27 - Apr. 17.
v – Not Apr. 11–17.
w – Not Feb. 18, Mar. 11, Apr. 15.
x – Not Mar. 13 - Apr. 21.
z – Arrives 1632.

⊡ – Runs 33–40 minutes later on Apr. 10, May 1, 8, 18, 29.
△ – Runs one hour **earlier** on Mar. 24, 31, Apr. 7, 14.
▽ – Runs one hour **earlier** on Apr. 10.
⊖ – Terminates at Châlons Apr. 18–21.
‡ – 7–10 minutes earlier on Apr. 10, May 8.
◐ – Via Champagne-Ardenne TGV (d. 2011).
◧ – Via Champagne-Ardenne TGV (a. 0715).
* – *188 km* via high-speed line.
♣ – See panel above for other TER services Bar le Duc - Nancy and v.v.
♥ – *TGV* train. 🅁. 🍷.
♠ – **ÉPERNAY - REIMS**. *31 km*. Journey: 33–40 minutes.
From Épernay: On Ⓐ at 0632, 0649, 0732, 0802, 0832, 0902, 1002, 1101, 1159, 1300, 1402, 1432, 1602, 1632, 1702, 1731, 1802, 1832, 1902, 2002 and 2102⑤. On Ⓒ at 0642⑥, 0802⑥, 1002, 1159, 1402, 1602, 1802 and 2002.
From Reims: On Ⓐ at 0548, 0649, 0720, 0749, 0820, 0849, 0948, 1048, 1148, 1248, 1348, 1420, 1548, 1620, 1648, 1720, 1748, 1820, 1849, 1949 and 2048⑤. On Ⓒ at 0718⑥, 0918, 1118, 1248⑥, 1318†, 1518, 1719 and 1922.

REIMS - CHÂLONS EN CHAMPAGNE - DIJON 381a

Subject to alteration on ⑥⑦ Apr. 15–30.

km		Ⓐ	Ⓐ	Ⓐ	Ⓒ	Ⓐ	Ⓐ⊗		Ⓐ	Ⓒ	Ⓐ◇	⚒	Ⓐ⊙	Ⓒ	Ⓐ	Ⓒ	Ⓐ	Ⓐ	Ⓐ	⑥	†	Ⓐ	Ⓒ	Ⓐ	Ⓐ
0	**Reims** ....d.	...	0620	0705	0738	0740	0835	0935	1035	1135	1135	1235	1335	1335	1435	1502	1535	1635	1735	1735	1738	1835	1935	1935	2035
58	**Châlons en Champagne** ....a.	...	0655	0748	0812	0815	0909	1018	1109	1209	1209	1318	1409	1410	1518	1536	1609	1709	1818	1817	1820	1918	2010	2018	2109
58	**Châlons en Champagne**. **381** d.	...	0657	...	0825	...	0923	...	...	1223	1223	...	1423	...	...	1550	1623	1723	1823	1823	1826	1923	...	2023	...
91	Vitry le François .... **381** d.	...	0718	...	0843	...	0941	...	...	1241	1241	...	1441	...	...	1608	1641	1741	1841	1842	1845	1941	...	2041	...
120	St Dizier .... **381** d.	0622	0737	...	0902	...	1001	...	...	1301	1301	...	1501	...	...	1627	1701	1801	1900	1901	1904	2001	...	2100	...
193	Chaumont .... **380** d.	0719	0824	...	0957	...	1055	...	...	1347	1355	...	1549	...	...	1714	1747	1855	...	1958	2001	2048	...	...	...
227	Langres .... **380** d.	0743	...	...	...	...	...	...	...	...	...	...	1612	...	...	...	...	...	...	2020	2023	2111	...	...	...
238	Culmont Chalindrey ... **379 380** d.	0752	...	...	...	...	...	...	...	...	...	...	1624	...	...	...	...	...	...	2028	2036	2120	...	...	...
315	**Dijon** Ville .... **379 380** a.	...	...	...	...	...	...	...	...	...	...	...	1710	...	...	...	...	...	...	...	2123	...	...	...	...

	Ⓐ	Ⓐ	⑥	Ⓐ	Ⓒ	Ⓐ	Ⓐ	Ⓒ	Ⓐ	Ⓐ⊖	Ⓒ	Ⓐ	Ⓐ◇	Ⓒ	Ⓐ	⑥	⊡	Ⓐ	Ⓐ	Ⓐ	Ⓒ	Ⓐ	Ⓐ		Ⓐ
Dijon Ville .... **379 380** d.	...	...	...	...	...	...	...	...	...	...	...	...	...	...	...	...	...	...	...	...	...	...	...	...	1805
Culmont Chalindrey .... **379 380** d.	...	...	...	0539	...	0629	...	0733	...	...	...	...	...	...	...	...	...	1458	...	...	...	...	1639r	...	1904
Langres .... **380** d.	...	...	...	0548	...	0638	...	0742	...	...	...	...	...	...	...	...	...	1507	...	...	...	...	1648r	...	1913
Chaumont .... **380** d.	...	...	...	0612	...	0701	...	0805	...	1013	...	...	1204	1214	...	...	1411	1529	...	...	...	...	1711	1802	1935
St Dizier .... **381** d.	...	0557	...	0700	...	0757	...	0901	...	1100	...	...	1300	1300	...	...	1458	1616	...	...	...	...	1800	1859	2024
Vitry le François .... **381** d.	...	0617	...	0720	...	0817	...	0920	...	1120	...	...	1320	1320	...	...	1518	...	...	...	...	...	1820	1919	2044
Châlons en Champagne. **381** a.	...	0637	...	0737	...	0837	...	0937	...	1137	...	...	1337	1337	...	...	1535	...	...	...	...	...	1837	1937	2104
Châlons en Champagne .... d.	0612	0643	0646	0742	0800	0850	0942	0950	1050	1150	1200	1242	1350	1350	1442	1450	1550	...	1612	1712	1742	1812	1850	1950	2106
Reims .... a.	0655	0730	0730	0825	0835	0925	1025	1025	1125	1225	1235	1325	1425	1425	1525	1525	1625	...	1655	1755	1825	1855	1925	2025	2141

r – Not Apr. 11–21.
⊗ – Subject to alteration Mar. 13–17, 27–31, Apr. 13, 14 and from May 4.
◇ – Subject to alteration from Mar. 6.
⊙ – Subject to alteration Apr. 3–28 and from May 4.
⊖ – Subject to alteration Mar. 13 - Apr. 28.
⊡ – Subject to alteration Mar. 6–10, 13–17 and on ①–⑤ Mar. 27 - May 5.

☛ Other services Reims - Châlons en Champagne and v.v.:
From Reims at 0809Ⓐ, 1605Ⓐ, 1705Ⓐ, 1803Ⓐ and 2226†.
From Châlons en Champagne at 0720Ⓐ, 0820Ⓐ, 1650Ⓐ and 1750Ⓐ.

STRASBOURG - ST DIÉ - ÉPINAL - BELFORT 382

STRASBOURG - ST DIÉ - ÉPINAL ⊠

km		(Ⓐ)	Ⓐ	Ⓐ	Ⓐn	Ⓐn	Ⓐn	Ⓐn	Ⓐ	Ⓐ	Ⓐ	Ⓐ	Ⓐ	Ⓐ		(⑥)	⑥	⑥	⑥	⑥	⑥	⑥	⑥	⑥
0	**Strasbourg** .... ▷ d.		...	0540	0706	0906	1140	1306	...	1544t	1614	1706	1806	1944	...		...	0706	0906	1206	...	1506	1714	1806
9	Entzheim Aéroport ✈ .... ▷ d.		...	0548	0715	0915	1148	1316	...	|	1622	1715	|	1952	...		...	0715	0915	1215	...	1515	1722	1815
19	Molsheim .... ▷ d.		...	0556	0725	0924	1155	1323	...	1558t	1629	1723	1824	1959	...		...	0724	0824	1224	...	1524	1731	1824
87	**St Dié** .... a.		...	0727	0832	1029	1300	1429	...	1658t	1747	1846	1923	2112	...		...	0829	1029	1329	...	1629	1856	1929
	St Dié .... d.		0633	0736	0839	1036	1307	1435	1603	1704	1757	...	1929	...	...		0605	0836	1036	1336	1502	1636	...	1936
147	**Épinal** .... a.		0726	0830	0932	1130	1403	1526	1656	1758	1849	...	2020	...	...		0656	0930	1129	1431	1556	1731	...	2031

	⑥		(†)	†	†	†	†	†	†	†
Strasbourg .... ▷ d.	2014	...		...	0806	1130	1336	1414	1606	1814
Entzheim Aéroport ✈ .... ▷ d.	2022	...		...	0814	1138	1344	1422	1615	1822
Molsheim .... ▷ d.	2029	...		...	0821	1145	1351	1430	1624	1829
St Dié .... a.	2136	...		...	0929	1300	1457	1550	1730	1938
St Dié .... d.	2144	...		0732	0937	1307	1504	...	1737	1946
Épinal .... a.	2237	...		0825	1030	1359	1557	...	1829	2038

	(Ⓐ)	Ⓐ	Ⓐ	Ⓐr	Ⓐn	Ⓐn	Ⓐn	Ⓐn	Ⓐ
Épinal .... d.		...	0630	0732	1035	1204	1304	1508	1559
St Dié .... a.		...	0723	0825	1126	1257	1358	1600	1653
St Dié .... d.		0540	0730t	0836t	1133	1304	...	1612	1701
Molsheim .... ▷ d.		0708	0838t	0938t	1239	1408	...	1731	1810
Entzheim Aéroport ✈ ..... ▷ d.		0715	0846t	0946t	1246	1416	...	1738	1817
Strasbourg .... ▷ a.		0724	0854t	0954t	1254	1424	...	1746	1824

	Ⓐ	Ⓐ	Ⓐz		(⑥)	⑥	⑥	⑥	⑥	⑥	⑥	⑥	⑥	⑥		(†)	†	†	†	†	†	†	†	†
Épinal .... d.	1701	1834	2051	...		...	0640	0734	1035	1234	1502	1633	1834	2050	...		...	0834	1037	1409	1633	...	1843	2052
St Dié .... a.	1754	1926	2142	...		...	0730	0825	1126	1325	1553	1726	1925	2141	...		...	0925	1127	1500	1724	...	1934	2145
St Dié .... d.	1800	1935	...	...		0611	...	0833	1133	1333	...	1733	1933	2149	...		0757	0933	1134	1507	1733	1816	1941	...
Molsheim .... ▷ d.	1909	2039	...	...		0730	...	0939	1239	1439	...	1839	2039	2257	...		0909	1039	1239	1614	1839	1931	2046	...
Entzheim Aéroport ✈ .... ▷ d.	1916	2047	...	...		0738	...	0946	1246	1446	...	1846	2046	2305	...		0916	1046	1246	1622	1846	1938	2053	...
Strasbourg .... ▷ a.	1924	2054	...	...		0746	...	0954	1254	1454	...	1854	2054	2313	...		0924	1054	1254	1630	1854	1946	2101	...

ÉPINAL - BELFORT

km	See note ❖	Ⓐ		ⒶX							
0	**Épinal** .... d.	0626	...	0958	...	1455	...	1858	...	...	...
58	Luxeuil les Bains .... d.	0715	...	1043	...	1540	...	1943	...	...	...
76	Lure .... **380** d.	0728	...	1056	...	1553	...	1956	...	...	...
108	**Belfort** Ville .... **380** a.	0757	...	1125	...	1622	...	2025	...	...	...

	Ⓐ		X		Ⓑ					
Belfort Ville ...... **380** d.	0558	...	1105	...	1705	...	2005	...	...	...
Lure .... **380** d.	0627	...	1134	...	1734	...	2034	...	...	...
Luxeuil les Bains ...... d.	0640	...	1147	...	1747	...	2047	...	...	...
Épinal .... a.	0730	...	1234	...	1834	...	2134	...	...	...

X – Not Feb. 13–17, 20–24, Mar. 13–17, 20–24, 27–31, Apr. 3–7, 11–14, 17–21, 24–28.
n – Not Feb. 13–17, 20–24, Apr. 17–21, 24–28.
r – Not Feb. 13–17, 20–24.
t – Not Apr. 17–21, 24–28.
z – From Apr. 11 Épinal d. 2054, St Dié a. 2145.
⊠ – On Apr. 7 services Strasbourg - St Dié and v.v. run as on ⑦.
❖ – Timings Épinal - Belfort may vary by up to 4 minutes on certain dates.
▷ – Additional trains run Strasbourg - Entzheim Aéroport (300 metres from terminal) - Molsheim and v.v.: 3–4 per hour on Ⓐ, 1–2 per hour on ⑥, hourly on †.

FRANCE

383 METZ and NANCY - STRASBOURG

On Apr. 7 *TER* services run as on ⑦ (unless indicated otherwise). Timings may vary by 1 – 2 minutes on certain dates. For faster *TGV* services Paris - Strasbourg, see Table **390**.

km		Ⓐ c	*TGV* **5521** Ⓐ 🅁	⑥	Ⓐ	Ⓐ	⚒	⚒	*TGV* **9877** 🅁	⚒		Ⓐ	Ⓐ	Ⓒ	⑥	Ⓐ	*TGV* **2587** ⑦ e 🅁	Ⓐ w	†	*TGV* **9879** 🅁	⑥	Ⓐ	*TGV* **5537** 🅁	Ⓒ	Ⓐ	⑥
0	**Metz** ▷ d.	...	0546	...	...	...	0642	...	0811	0747	...	0842	...	0943	...	1034	...	...	...	1212	...	...	...	1221	...	...
	Paris Est **381** d.	...	|	...	...	...	|	...	|	|	...	|	...	|	...	|	0913	0736	...	|	0836t	...	...	|	...	...
Δ	**Nancy** **387** d.	...	|	...	...	0612	|	0713	|	|	0813	|	0914	|	1010	|	1100	1100	1115	|	1157	1213	1226	|	1313	1316
	Lunéville **387** d.	...	|	...	...	0630	|	0731	|	|	0831	|	0932	|	1028	|	|	1122	1133	|	1215	1231	|	|	1331	1335
88	Sarrebourg ▷ d.	0531	|	0603	0617	0653	|	0755	|	0848	0854	|	0955	|	1051	|	1141	1147	1156	|	1239	1255	|	|	1356	1358
91	Réding d.	0536	|	0607	0622	0657	0730	|	|	...	|	0930	|	1032	|	1125	|	|	|	|	|	|	|	1310	|	|
114	Saverne d.	0552	|	0623	0639	0715	0745	0815	|	...	0914	0945	1015	1047	1110	1144	1159	1205	1215	|	1255	1315	|	1328	1412	1417
159	**Strasbourg** a.	0631	0640	0703	0708	0740	0810	0840	0858	...	0940	1010	1041	1113	1138	1210	1222	1237	1240	1300	1318	1340	1329	1405	1441	1443

	Ⓐ	⑥		Ⓐ	⚒	Ⓐ	†	Ⓑ	Ⓑ	Ⓐ	⑥	⑥	⚒	†	Ⓑ	Ⓑ	Ⓐ	Ⓒ	⚒	Ⓐ w	†	† z¶	⑥	Ⓑ	*TGV* **2583** ①–⑤ v 🅁	*TGV* **2583** ⑦ A 🅁
Metz ▷ d.	1310	1344	...	1442	...	1517	1547	...	1642	...	1647	...	1742	1746	...	1842	...	...	1944	...	1948	...	...	2042	...	...
Paris Est **381** d.	|	|	...	|	...	|	|	...	|	...	|	...	|	|	...	|	...	...	|	1636	|	1636	...	|	1943	2007
Nancy **387** d.	|	|	1414	|	1516	|	|	1613	|	1714	|	1715	|	|	1813	|	1916	1916	|	1948	|	2015	2016	|	2124	2150
Lunéville **387** d.	|	|	1432	|	1536	|	|	1631	|	1731	|	1733	|	|	1831	|	1934	1934	|	2007	|	2035	2034	|	2146	2211
Sarrebourg ▷ d.	|	1445	1455	|	1559	1618	1648	1655	|	1757	1747	1759	|	1848	1855	|	1957	1957	|	2034	2048	2059	2056	|	2211	2236
Réding d.	1423	...	|	1530	|	...	...	|	1730	|	...	|	1829	...	|	1930	|	|	2032	|	...	|	|	2130	|	|
Saverne d.	1442	...	1514	1545	1618	...	...	1714	1745	1814	...	1816	1845	...	1915	1945	2015	2017	2046	2055	...	2116	2113	2145	2229	2254
Strasbourg a.	1510	...	1540	1610	1646	...	...	1740	1810	1840	...	1842	1910	...	1941	2010	2040	2042	2111	2121	...	2141	2139	2210	2254	2317

	Ⓐ w	*TGV* **2584** ①–⑥ b 🅁	⚒	Ⓐ	Ⓐ	⚒	E	⚒	Ⓑ	⑥ t		Ⓐ	⑥	Ⓒ		Ⓐ	Ⓐ	⑥		*TGV* **9898** 🅁	†	Ⓐ	Ⓐ	†	⑥	Ⓐ
Strasbourg d.	0444	0541	...	0615	0647	0717	0727	0748	0818	0818	...	0849	0919	0949	1019	1049	1119	1149	1219	1231	...	1249	1315	1349	1419	1426
Saverne d.	0507	0606	...	0643	0713	0746	0754	0815	0846	0846	...	0915	0945	1014	1046	1115	1146	1215	1246	|	...	1315	1341	1414	1447	1454
Réding d.	|	|	...	|	0729	|	|	0829	|	|	...	0929	|	1029	|	1129	|	1229	|	|	...	1329	|	1429	|	|
Sarrebourg ▷ d.	0524	0624	0636	0700	|	0802	0810	|	0905	0903	0910	|	1003	|	1104	|	1204	|	1305	|	1310	|	1358	|	1505	1513
Lunéville **387** d.	0550	0649	|	0725	|	0829	0834	|	0928	0928	|	|	1026	|	1128	|	1229	|	1328	|	|	|	1420	|	1532	1536
Nancy **387** a.	0612	0709	|	0744	|	0847	0853	|	0947	0952	|	|	1044	|	1147	|	1247	|	1347	|	|	|	1440	|	1551	1554
Paris Est **381** a.	0953	0846	|	...	|	...	...	|	...	1323	|	|	...	|	...	|	...	|	...	|	|	|	...	|	...	...
Metz ▷ a.	...	...	0736	...	0816	...	...	0916	...	...	1011	1016	...	1116	...	1216	...	1316	...	1319	1410	1416	...	1516	...	...

	Ⓐ	⑥	Ⓐ	Ⓐ	*TGV* **2588** ⑦ e ⊡ 🅁	†	*TGV* **5516** 🅁	Ⓑ	†	⑥	Ⓐ		⑥	Ⓑ		† z		Ⓐ	Ⓐ	⑥	†	Ⓐ	*TGV* **5500** 🅁	Ⓐ	†	*TGV* **9896** x 🅁
Strasbourg d.	1449	1518	1519	...	1547	1551	1600	1619	...	1647	1648	1719	...	1749	1819	...	1849	1919	...	1946	1948j	1949	2024	2049	2054	2214
Saverne d.	1515	1546	1546	...	1613	1622	|	1643	...	1713	1714	1745	...	1815	1846	...	1914	1946	...	2012	2014	2015	|	2115	2138	|
Réding d.	1529	|	|	...	|	1642	|	|	...	1727	1732	|	...	1830	|	...	1929	|	...	|	|	2034	|	2129	2153	|
Sarrebourg ▷ d.	|	1605	1605	1606	1631	|	|	1700	1711	|	1744	1804	1808	|	1905	1911	|	2005	2009	2030	2030	2038	|	|	2157	|
Lunéville **387** d.	|	1629	1629	|	|	|	|	1724	|	|	|	1829	|	|	1929	|	|	2029	|	2053	2055	...	|	|	...	|
Nancy **387** a.	|	1647	1647	|	1710	|	1702	1745	|	|	|	1847	|	|	1947	|	|	2047	|	2111	2113	...	|	|	...	|
Paris Est **381** a.	|	...	...	|	1846	|	...	2124	|	|	|	...	|	|	...	|	|	...	|	...	...	...	|	|	...	|
Metz ▷ a.	1616	...	...	1710	...	1735	...	...	1812	1815	1835	...	1907	1917	...	2011	2016	...	2059	...	...	...	2113	2216	...	2302

A – ⑦ (also Apr. 10, May 1, 8, 29; not Feb. 5 - Mar. 12, Apr. 9, 30, May 7, 28).
E – Runs on Mar. 11 and Apr. 15 only.

b – Not Apr. 10, May 1, 8, 19, 20, 29.
c – Not ②-④ Feb. 28 - Mar. 16.
e – Also Apr. 10, May 1, 8, 29.
j – 1944 on Apr. 7, 10, May 1, 8, 18, 29.

t – Not Mar. 11, Apr. 15.
v – Not Apr. 10, May 1, 8, 18, 19, 29.
w – Also Apr. 7.
x – Not ①-④ Dec. 12 - Mar. 23. Later Metz arrival Apr. 3 – 7.
z – Not Apr. 7.

TGV – High-speed train. 🅁. 🍸.

⊡ – Runs 21 – 27 minutes earlier Strasbourg - Nancy on Apr. 10, May 1, 8, 29.
¶ – Runs up to 9 minutes earlier Nancy - Strasbourg on Apr. 10, May 1, 8, 18, 29.
▷ – Other trains Metz - Sarrebourg (journey ± 60 minutes): **From Metz** at 0617 Ⓐ, 0917 Ⓐ, 1017 Ⓐ, 1026 Ⓒ, 1403 Ⓐ, 1717 Ⓐ, 1817 Ⓐ, 1917 ⑥ and 2017 Ⓐ. **From Sarrebourg** at 0736 Ⓐ, 1036 Ⓐ, 1136 Ⓐ, 1211 ⑥, 1456 ⑥, 1636 Ⓐ and 1836 Ⓐ.
Δ – Nancy - Sarrebourg: *80 km*.

384 Regional trains NANCY - METZ - LUXEMBOURG

French holiday dates apply, but with variations on May 9, June 23 (see shaded box below). See Table **390** for *TGV* trains Paris - Metz - Luxembourg.
Services in this table are subject to considerable alteration with numerous timing variations; readers planning journeys are strongly advised to confirm timings before travelling.

km		Ⓐ	Ⓐ	⚒	Ⓐ		Ⓐ	Ⓐ		⚒	Ⓐ		Ⓐ	†	⑥	Ⓐ		❖	Ⓐ		⑥⑦		Ⓐ🚌	⑥
0	**Nancy** d.	0528	0620	0650	0720	0748	0806	0820	0828	0850	0920	0949	1020	1028	1050	1120	1150	and in the	2020	2050	2150	...	2237	2250
28	Pont-à-Mousson d.	0553	0637	0706	0737	0805	0823	0837	0853	0907	0937	1006	1036	1052	1107	1137	1206	same hourly	2037	2107	2207	...	2331	2306
37	Pagny sur Moselle d.	0602	0644	0713	0744	0812	0830	0844	0902	0913	0945	1013	1043	1101	1114	1145	1213	pattern until	2044	2113	2213	...	2350	2313
57	**Metz** a.	0625	0702	0730	0802	0833	0846	0901	0925	0932	1002	1031	1100	1122	1130	1201	1230		2101	2131	2230	...	0024	2330

	Ⓐ	⚒	Ⓐ	Ⓑ	⑥	Ⓐ		Ⓐ	⚒	Ⓐ		Ⓐ	⚒	Ⓐ		⊠	Ⓐ			Ⓑ		Ⓐ🚌	Ⓒ	Ⓒ🚌
Metz d.	0559	0629	0658	0729	0736	0758	0830	0859	0929	0959	1033	1100	1128	1159	1228	and in the	2000	2029	2035	2128	...	2225	2232	2339
Pagny sur Moselle d.	0615	0645	0715	0745	0758	0814	0846	0915	0945	1016	1048	1117	1144	1215	1244	same hourly	2016	2045	2058	2144	...	2259	2245	0009
Pont-à-Mousson d.	0622	0652	0722	0752	0807	0822	0853	0923	0953	1023	1055	1124	1152	1223	1252	pattern until	2023	2052	2107	2152	...	2318	2252	0024
Nancy a.	0640	0711	0740	0810	0832	0840	0910	0940	1011	1041	1115	1141	1210	1240	1312		2040	2112	2132	2210	...	0012	2312	0116

(NANCY -) METZ - LUXEMBOURG

km		Ⓐ	Ⓐ	⚒	Ⓐ	⚒	Ⓐ		Ⓐ	⚒	Ⓐ	†	⑥	⚒	Ⓑ				Ⓐ	Ⓐ	Ⓒ	Ⓐ		Ⓐ		Ⓐ
	Nancy ★ d.	...	...	...	0558	0650k	...	0748c	...	0850k	...	0949	...	1050k	...	1150c	1249c	1348c	...	...	...	...	1549c	...	1626	...
0	**Metz** d.	0531	0604	0629	0700	0730	0800	0830	0903	0931	1029	1031	1042	1131	1144	1230	1330	1430	1443	1528	1545	1603	1629	1700	1729	1801
18	Hagondange d.	0542	0620	0641	0711	0741	0812	0842	0915	0942	1042	1043	1101	1142	1200	1241	1342	1442	1501	1540	1602	1616	1640	1712	1744	1812
30	Thionville d.	0554	0632	0653	0727	0757	0824	0857	0932	0954	1054	1057	1115	1154	1215	1257	1357	1457	1514	1552	1615	1632	1652	1725	1757	1825
64	**Luxembourg** a.	0622	0703	0722	0752	0822	0915	0922	1003	1022	1122	1122	1145	1222	1245	1322	1422	1522	1545	1645	1645	1703	1745	1752	1822	1915

		Ⓐ			⚒	⑦	Ⓒ	Ⓐ	⑥	⑤†
Nancy ★ d.	1750c	1758	1850c	1950c	2050k	...	2150	...	...	...
Metz d.	1831	1900	1932	2032	2133	2146	2232	2246	2314	2316
Hagondange d.	1842	1914	1943	2043	2144	2202	2243	2303	2330	2332
Thionville d.	1854	1930	1954	2055	2157	2216	2257	2314	2340	2343
Luxembourg a.	1922	2003	2022	2122	2222	2245	2322	...	...	...

	Ⓐ	⚒	Ⓐ	Ⓐ	Ⓐ	⑥	Ⓐ	Ⓐ		Ⓐ		⚒	Ⓐ
Luxembourg d.	0516	0539k	0546	...	0616	0628	...	0709	0739	0809	0816	0839	...
Thionville d.	0547	0604	0616	0634	0648	0700	0658	0737	0807	0837	0847	0907	0924
Hagondange d.	0557	0616	0626	0644	0658	0712	0710	0748	0818	0848	0859	0918	0934
Metz a.	0614	0627	0642	0656	0715	0729	0725	0800	0830	0859	0917	0930	0954
Nancy ★ a.	...	0711	...	0740	...	0811	0810	0902	0912c	...	...	1011k	1041

		Ⓒ	Ⓐ		Ⓐ		Ⓐ		Ⓑ	⑥	Ⓐ		Ⓐ			Ⓐ	⑥	Ⓐ	Ⓒ	Ⓐ	⑦		Ⓐ	Ⓒ	Ⓐ	⑥⑦
Luxembourg d.	0939	1016	1039	1139	1216	1239	1258	1339	1416	1439	1439	1539	1558	1616	1739	1816	1839	1858	1939	2009	2016	...	2139	2139	2239	2256
Thionville d.	1007	1046	1109	1207	1247	1308	1335	1407	1447	1507	1507	1608	1629	1707	1807	1908	1910	1931	2007	2034	2048	...	2204	2207	2304	2328
Hagondange d.	1018	1057	1120	1218	1257	1318	1347	1418	1459	1518	1518	1618	1640	1718	1818	1918	1921	1942	2018	2046	2059	...	2216	2218	2316	2338
Metz a.	1031	1116	1133	1230	1319	1330	1400	1432	1517	1530	1531	1633	1651	1730	1830	1931	1933	2000	2030	2100	2117	...	2230	2230	2327	2355
Nancy ★ a.	1115	...	1232	1312c	1410	...	...	1511c	...	1611	...	1715c	...	1812c	1912c	...	2016	...	2112	...	...	...	...	2312	...	...

c – Ⓒ only.
k – ⑥ only.

❖ – Timings vary (please check).
⊠ – Timings vary (please check). The 1428 from Metz runs on Ⓒ only.
★ – See upper panel for full service Nancy - Metz and v.v.

PUBLIC HOLIDAY ALTERATIONS

*On May 9, June 23 (public holidays in Luxembourg) many services to / from Luxembourg operate as on Ⓒ / †. On May 8 (public holiday in France) many services to / from Luxembourg operate as on Ⓐ / ⚒. **Please check locally if travelling on these dates.***

STRASBOURG - MULHOUSE - BASEL 385

French holiday dates apply

For *TGV* trains Paris - Strasbourg - Colmar see Table **390**. For *TGV* trains Luxembourg - Metz - Strasbourg - Mulhouse - Lyon - Marseille / Montpellier see Table **379**.
On Apr. 7 services in this table run as on ⑦.

km		Ⓐ	Ⓐ	⚒	Ⓐ	⑥ 2	Ⓐ	Ⓒ	Ⓐ	Ⓒ 2		Ⓐ	⑥ 2		Ⓐ	⑥ 2	⚒	† 2	Ⓐ		Ⓐ	Ⓒ 2		Ⓐ	⑥ 2		Ⓐ
0	**Strasbourg** d.	...	0519	0551	0621	0621	0651	0651	0721	0721	0751	0821	0821	0851	0921	0921	0951	0951	1021	1051	1121	1121	1151	1221	1221	1251	1321
43	Sélestat d.	...	0539	0611	0641	0645	0711	0713	0741	0743	0811	0841	0843	0911	0941	0943	1011	1016	1041	1111	1141	1143	1211	1241	1243	1311	1341
65	Colmar d.	...	0550	0623	0653	0659	0723	0723	0753	0758	0823	0853	0858	0923	0953	0958	1023	1028	1053	1123	1153	1158	1223	1253	1258	1323	1353
106	**Mulhouse** ‡ d.	0546	0616	0646	0716	0728	0746	0749	0816	0825	0846	0916	0925	0946	1016	1025	1046	1055	1116	1146	1216	1225	1246	1314	1325	1346	1416
133	St Louis (Haut Rhin) ‡ d.	0559	0629	0659	0729	...	0759	0812	0829	...	0859	0929	...	0959	1029	...	1059	...	1129	1159	1229	...	1259	...	...	1359	1429
140	**Basel** SBB ‡ a.	0608	0638	0708	0738	...	0808	0820	0840	...	0908	0938	...	1008	1040	...	1108	...	1138	1208	1240	...	1308	...	...	1408	1440

	⚒	† 2	⑥ 2		Ⓐ	⑥ 2		Ⓑ	⑥ 2		Ⓐ	⑥ 2		Ⓑ	⑥ 2		Ⓑ	⑥ 2		Ⓑ	⑥ 2	Ⓐ 2	⚒	† 2	¶2	† 2	⚒⊖ 2
Strasbourg d.	1351	1351	1421	1451	1521	1521	1551	1621	1621	1651	1721	1721	1751	1821	1821	1851	1921	1921	1951	2021	2021	2051	2121	2121	2221	2251	2320
Sélestat d.	1411	1416	1443	1511	1541	1543	1610	1641	1643	1711	1741	1743	1811	1841	1843	1911	1941	1942	2011	2041	2043	2114	2141	2143	2242	2311	2346
Colmar d.	1423	1428	1456	1523	1553	1558	1622	1653	1658	1723	1753	1758	1823	1853	1858	1923	1953	1954	2023	2053	2058	2128	2153	2158	2255	2323	0000
Mulhouse ‡ d.	1446	1455	1525	1546	1616	1625	1646	1716	1725	1746	1816	1825	1846	1916	1925	1946	2016	2021	2046	2116	2125	2155	2216	2225**z**	2320**r**	2344**z**	0022
St Louis (Haut Rhin) ‡ d.	1459	...	...	1559	1629	...	1659	1729	...	1759	1829	...	1859	1929	...	1959	2029	...	2058	2129	...	...	2229	...	...	...	...
Basel SBB ‡ a.	1508	...	...	1608	1640	...	1709	1738	...	1808	1838	...	1908	1940	...	2008	2038	...	2108	2138	...	...	2238	...	...	...	...

	Ⓐ 2	⑥ 2	Ⓐ	Ⓐ		† 2	⑥ 2	Ⓐ		⑥ 2	Ⓐ		Ⓐ		⑥ 2		⑥ 2	Ⓐ	† 2	⚒	Ⓐ		Ⓐ		Ⓐ	† 2	⚒
Basel SBB ‡ d.	...	...	0521	0537	0621	...	...	0651	0721	...	0751	0821	0851	0921	...	1021	...	1051	...	1121	1151	1221	1251	1321	...	...	1421
St Louis (Haut Rhin) ‡ d.	...	...	0530	0546	0630	...	...	0700	0730	...	0800	0830	0900	0930	...	1030	...	1100	...	1130	1200	1230	1300	1330	...	...	1430
Mulhouse ‡ d.	0457	0535	0546	0601	0646	0700	0704	0716	0746	0803	0816	0846	0916	0946	1005	1046	1104	1116	1135	1146	1216	1246	1316	1346	1416	1435	1446
Colmar d.	0518	0604	0606	0629	0706	0727	0732	0736	0806	0832	0836	0906	0936	1006	1033	1106	1131	1136	1203	1206	1236	1306	1336	1406	1436	1503	1506
Sélestat d.	0530	0616	0619	0642	0719	0739	0743	0749	0819	0844	0849	0919	0949	1019	1046	1119	1144	1149	1216	1219	1249	1319	1349	1419	1449	1516	1519
Strasbourg a.	0556	0639	0639	0709	0739	0804	0809	0809	0839	0909	0909	0939	1009	1039	1109	1139	1209	1209	1239	1239	1309	1339	1409	1439	1509	1539	1539

	⑥ 2	Ⓐ	† 2	⚒	⑥ 2	Ⓐ		†	⑥ 2	Ⓐ		⑥	Ⓑ		⑥ 2	Ⓐ		⑥ 2	Ⓑ	† △2	⚒ d	⑥ ▽2	Ⓐ d	†	Ⓐ	⑥ 2	Ⓑ 2◇
Basel SBB ‡ d.	...	1451	...	1521	...	1551	1621	1639	...	1651	1721	...	1751	1821	...	1851	1921	...	1951	...	2021	...	2038	2121	2151	...	...
St Louis (Haut Rhin) ‡ d.	...	1500	...	1530	...	1600	1630	1647	...	1700	1730	...	1800	1830	...	1900	1930	...	2000	...	2030	...	2046	2130	2200	...	...
Mulhouse ‡ d.	1514	1516	1535	1546	1603	1616	1646	1702	1705	1716	1746	1805	1816	1846	1904	1916	1946	2004	2016	2035	2046	2103	2113	2145	2216	2234**z**	2330**v**
Colmar d.	1535	1536	1603	1606	1633	1636	1706	1730	1733	1736	1806	1833	1836	1906	1932	1936	2006	2032	2036	2103	2106	2130	2139	2207	2236	2302	2359
Sélestat d.	1547	1549	1616	1619	1646	1649	1719	1742	1746	1749	1819	1846	1849	1919	1943	1949	2019	2043	2049	2116	2119	2142	2152	2219	2249	2313	0012
Strasbourg a.	1609	1609	1639	1639	1709	1709	1739	1809	1809	1809	1839	1909	1909	1939	2009	2009	2039	2109	2109	2139	2139	2211	2214	2239	2309	2339	0040

d – Runs daily Basel - Mulhouse.
r – ①–⑤ until Mar. 3; daily from Mar. 6. Arrives 2325 on ⑥ (also Feb. 27, Mar. 1).
v – Not ⑦ Jan. 22 - Mar. 5.
z – Not Jan. 21 - Mar. 5.

⊖ – Terminates at Colmar on Jan. 21, 25, 28, Feb. 4, 11, 18, 25, Mar. 4.
¶ – Runs 10 – 13 minutes later on Feb. 28.
△ – Runs 12 – 16 minutes later Jan. 22 - Mar. 5.
▽ – Departure times may be up to 8 minutes **earlier** on Jan. 21, 28, Feb. 11, 18, 25, Mar. 4.

◇ – On † from Mar. 12 Mulhouse d. 2338, Colmar d. 0002, Sélestat d. 0014, Strasbourg a. 0040. Runs 2 – 3 minutes earlier Colmar - Strasbourg Feb. 20 – 22, Mar. 6, 7.
‡ – **Other local trains Mulhouse - Basel** (journey 30 – 32 minutes). On Apr. 7, 10, May 18, 29 services run as on ⑦. Subject to alteration on Mar. 11, 12.
From Mulhouse at 0449 ①–⑤, 0549 ①–⑤, 0619 ①–⑥, 0649 ①–⑤, 0719 ①–⑥, 0749, 0819 ①–⑤, 0919, 1119, 1219 ①–⑤, 1319, 1419 ①–⑥, 1519 ⑥⑦, 1549 ①–⑤, 1619 ①–⑥, 1649 ①–⑤, 1719 ①–⑥, 1749 ①–⑤, 1819, 1849 ①–⑤, 1919 ①–⑥, 1949 Ⓑ and 2019 ①–⑤.
From Basel SBB at 0608 ①–⑤, 0638 ①–⑤, 0708 ①–⑥, 0738 ①–⑤, 0808 ①–⑥, 0839, 1039, 1138 ①–⑤, 1239, 1338 ①–⑤, 1439 ⑥⑦, 1538 ①–⑥, 1608 ①–⑤, 1639 ①–⑥, 1708 ①–⑤, 1738, 1808 ①–⑤, 1838 ①–⑥, 1908 Ⓑ, 1939 ①–⑤, 2138 ①–⑤ and 2238 ①–⑤.

NANCY - ÉPINAL - REMIREMONT 386

Warning! Timings may vary by up to 5 minutes from Apr. 11 (earlier departures possible). Subject to alteration on May 27, 28, June 3, 4.

km		Ⓐ	Ⓐ	⚒	⚒	Ⓐ	Ⓒ	Ⓐ ⊗	Ⓑ ⊗	⑥	Ⓐ ⊗	⑥	†	Ⓐ ⊗	†	⚒ ⊗	⊡ ⊗	⚒ ⊗	⊗	2571 ♥	Ⓒ	Ⓐ		Ⓐ	Ⓐ	Ⓒ	Ⓐ
	Paris Est **390** d.	...	...	...	...	...	...	...	...	...	...	...	...	...	...	...	...	...	...	1223	...	...	...	...	...	...	...
0	**Nancy** d.	0555	0620	0655	0720	0755	0820	0820	0855	0926	0931	1020	1020	1055	1120	1120	1220	1255	1320	1406	1420	1420	1520	1555	1620	1622	1655
74	Épinal a.	0651	0720	0752	0818	0853	0909	0918	0951	1018	1022	1104	1113	1152	1204	1218	1318	1353	1418	1448	1512**f**	1518	1618	1652	1718	1713	1751
74	Épinal d.	...	0722	...	0820	...	0911	0920	...	...	1024	...	1115	...	...	1220	1320	...	1420**r**	1451	...	1520	1620	...	1720	...	...
100	**Remiremont** a.	...	0754	...	0850	...	0934	0951	...	...	1054	...	1143	...	...	1251	1351	...	1451**r**	1512	...	1551	1651	...	1751	...	...

			⚒	Ⓐ		2573 ♥	◧	△	⑥	Ⓐ ▽	†
Paris Est **390** d.	...	...	...	...	...	1810	...	...	...	...	...
Nancy d.	1720	1755	1820	1857	1920	1958	2020	2120	2205	2220	2255
Épinal a.	1818	1851	1918	1953	2018	2039	2118	2218	2301	2318	2358
Épinal d.	1820	...	1920	...	2020**v**	2042	...	2220	...	...	...
Remiremont a.	1851	...	1951	...	2051**v**	2105	...	2251	...	...	...

	Ⓐ	⚒	2574 ⚒ ♥	†	⚒	⚒	Ⓐ	⑥	Ⓐ		Ⓐ ⊗	2578 † ♥
Remiremont d.	...	0512**t**	0600	...	0615	...	0711	...	...	0812	...	0859
Épinal a.	...	0541**t**	0621	...	0643	...	0741	...	...	0841	...	0920
Épinal d.	0500	0543**j**	0624	0648	0645	0706	0743	0746	0806	0843	0906	0923
Nancy a.	0559	0640	0705	0740	0740	0803	0840**k**	0841	0902	0940	1002	1005
Paris Est **390** a.	...	...	0846	...	...	...	...	...	...	...	...	1150

	Ⓐ ⊗	Ⓒ	Ⓐ ⊗	Ⓐ ⊗	Ⓒ	⚒ ⊗	⊗	Ⓐ ⊗	Ⓐ ⊗	⑥	⊗	Ⓒ ⊖	Ⓐ	2580 ♥		Ⓐ	⚒	†	Ⓑ		⑥	Ⓐ	†	Ⓐ	⑥	Ⓐ	†
Remiremont d.	0912	...	1012	...	1033	...	1212	...	1312	...	1412	...	1514	1556	1612	...	1712	...	1812	...	1903	1912	1930	...	2012	2012	...
Épinal a.	0941	...	1041	...	1102	...	1241	...	1340	...	1441	...	1542	1620	1641	...	1741	...	1841	...	1924	1941	1951	...	2043	2041	...
Épinal d.	0943	0946**h**	1043	1106	1104	1142	1242	1321	1342	1356	1446	1543	1544	1623	1643	1706	1743	1756	1843	1905	1926	1943	1953	2006	2045	2043	2148
Nancy a.	1040	1040	1140	1202	1202	1240	1341	1408	1436	1440	1542	1640	1640	1706	1739	1802	1840	1840	1940	2002	2016	2040	2040	2102	2140	2150	2240
Paris Est **390** a.	...	...	...	...	...	...	...	...	...	...	...	...	...	1846	...	...	...	...	...	...	...	...	...	...	...	...	...

f – 1504 on † until Apr. 10.
h – 0955 on †.
j – 0547 on ⑥.
k – 0844 on ④ (not Mar. 2, 9).
r – ⚒ only.

t – Ⓐ only.

◧ – On ⑥ Nancy d. 2025, Épinal a. 2109.
⊖ – On ⑥ Épinal d. 1553, Nancy a. 1637.
⊡ – On ⑥ Épinal a. 1324, d. 1326, Remiremont a. 1356.

⊗ – Subject to alteration Feb. 13 – 17, 20 – 24, Apr. 17 – 21, 24 – 28.
△ – By 🚌 on Ⓐ from Mar. 20 (Nancy d. 2101, Épinal d. 2225, Remiremont a. 2308).
▽ – By 🚌 on Ⓐ from Mar. 20 (Nancy d. 2220, Épinal a. 2339).
♥ – *TGV* train. Ⓡ. 🍸.

NANCY - LUNÉVILLE - ST DIÉ 387

km		Ⓐ	Ⓐ		⑥	Ⓐ	Ⓐ ⊗	⑥	†	Ⓐ ⊗	⑥	⑥	⑥	†	Ⓐ ⊗		Ⓐ	⑥	2591 ⑦ e♥	Ⓐ	⑥	Ⓐ	⑥	†	Ⓐ	⚒	†
	Paris Est **390** d.	...	...	...	...	...	...	...	...	...	...	...	...	...	...	...	...	...	1358	...	...	...	...	...	...	...	...
0	**Nancy** 383 d.	0542	0650	0750	0855	0859	0926	0950	0955	1027	1054	1136	1250	1250	1308	1410	1450	1453	1554	1550	1553	1649	1653	1652	1711	1750	1759
33	Lunéville 383 d.	0604	0711	0811	0914	0921	0951	1009	1013	1100	1112	1155	1312	1315	1330	1429	1511	1512	1615	1611	1614	1710	1711	1710	1730	1811	1820
84	**St Dié** a.	0703	0755	0854	0953	1002	1031	1055	1055	1143	1152	1237	1355	1355	1415	1512	1553	1551	1647	1653	1654	1753	1751	1759	1831	1853	1900

	⑥	Ⓐ	Ⓐ	2593 ①–⑤ t♥	⑥	†	Ⓐ		2595 ⑦ z♥	Ⓐ	
Paris Est **390** d.	...	...	...	1810	...	...	...	...	2007	...	...
Nancy 383 d.	1850	1850	1909	1954	2002	2002	2002	...	2154	2158	...
Lunéville 383 d.	1910	1912	1931	|	2021	2021	2031	...	|	2217	...
St Dié a.	1952	1952	2028	2047	2059	2102	2117	...	2245	2258	...

	Ⓐ		⑥	Ⓐ	Ⓐ	†	2596 ①–⑥ b♥	Ⓐ	Ⓐ	⑥	Ⓐ	Ⓒ
St Dié d.	0505	...	0557	0606	0631	0701	0715	0732	0807	0808	0905	0908
Lunéville 383 d.	0546	...	0640	0652	0729	0742	|	0832	0850	0854	0951	0951
Nancy 383 a.	0605	...	0658	0713	0749	0803	0809	0851	0911	0912	1012	1010
Paris Est **390** a.	...	...	...	...	...	...	0946	...	...	...	...	...

b – Not Apr. 10, May 1, 8, 19, 20, 29.
e – Also Apr. 10, May 1, 8, 29.
t – Not Apr. 10, May 1, 8, 18, 19, 29.
z – ⑦ (also Apr. 10, May 1, 8, 29; not Apr. 9, 30, May 7, 28).
⊗ – Subject to alteration Feb. 13 – 17, 20 – 24, Apr. 17 – 21, 24 – 28.
♥ – *TGV* train. Ⓡ. 🍸.

387 NANCY - LUNÉVILLE - ST DIÉ

																	2598									
	⑥	Ⓐ	Ⓒ	⑥	Ⓐ	Ⓒ		⑥	Ⓐ	⑥	Ⓐ	†	⑥	Ⓐ	Ⓐ	⑥	⑦	†	Ⓐ	⑥	⑥	†	Ⓐ	Ⓐ	†	⑥
		⊗			⊗												e♥									
St Dié d.	1000	1046	1108	1208	1226	1252	...	1403	1442	1520	1557	1557	1610	1632	1708	1708	1711	1730	1807	1808	1908	1922	1930	2005	2005	2015
Lunéville **383** d.	1037	1131	1149	1249	1310	1349	...	1446	1530	1601	1639	1642	1651	1729	1749	1750	1746	1815	1850	1851	1949	2008	2032	2052	2104	2100
Nancy **383** a.	1055	1151	1210	1310	1333	1410	...	1504	1550	1619	1657	1659	1710	1748	1807	1810	1804	1833	1910	1910	2007	2032	2051	2110	2124	2120
Paris Est **390** a.	...	...	...	...	...	...	...	...	...	...	...	...	...	...	...	...	1950	...	...	...	...	...	...	...	...	...

e – Also Apr. 10, May 1, 8, 29.

⊗ – Subject to alteration Feb. 13 – 17, 20 – 24, Apr. 17 – 21, 24 – 28.

♥ – *TGV* train. 🅁. 🍷.

389 PARIS - REIMS - CHARLEVILLE MÉZIÈRES - SEDAN

km																									
						TGV 2707		*TGV* 2709	*TGV* 2715					*TGV* 2719				*TGV* 2721							*TGV* 2733
		⚒	Ⓐ	⚒	Ⓐ	Ⓐ		①–⑥	⑦	Ⓐ	⑥	†	⚒	①–⑥	⑥	Ⓐ	Ⓐ	⑦	†	Ⓐ	⑥	Ⓐ	Ⓐ	⑥	⑤
						r		b	e					b				e							f
0	**Paris Est** **390** d.	...	...	...	...	0739	...	0828	0828	...	...	...	...	1028	...	...	...	1058	...	...	...	...	...	...	1258
136	Champagne Ard □ **390 391a** d.	...	...	...	0740	|	0810j	|	|	...	0910	1010	1010	|	1110	1110	1140	|	1210	1210	1210	1240	1309	1310	|
147	**Reims** **391a** a.	...	...	...	0752	0825	0822j	0914	0914	...	0924	1022	1022	1114	1122	1122	1152	1144	1221	1222	1222	1252	1321	1322	1344
147	**Reims** d.	0630	0700	0735	0800	...	0830	0919	0919	0930	0932	1030	1030	...	1130	1130	1200	...	1229	1230	1230	1300	1329	1330	...
186	Rethel d.	0653	0723	0758	0824	...	0853	0942	0942	0953	0956	1053	1054	...	1153	1154	1224	...	1253	1254	1253	1323	1353	1353	...
235	**Charleville-Mézières** a.	0725	0751	0830	0852	...	0925	1010	1010	1025	1027	1125	1126	...	1225	1226	1252	...	1325	1326	1325	1351	1425	1425	...
235	**Charleville-Mézières** **389a** d.	0730	...	0835	...	...	0930	1019x	...	1030x	1032	...	1131x	...	1230	1231x	...	...	...	1331x	1330	...	1430	1430	...
255	**Sedan** **389a** a.	0751y	...	0855	...	...	0950q	1035x	...	1051x	1052	...	1152x	...	1250	1257x	...	...	...	1351x	1356	...	1458	1450	...

	TGV 2735					*TGV* 2743		*TGV* 2743				*TGV* 2747				*TGV* 2751	*TGV* 2753				*TGV* 2757	*TGV* 2759		🚌	*TGV* 2765
	⑥		⑥	†	Ⓐ				Ⓐ		Ⓐ		⑥	Ⓑ	Ⓐ		⑤	⚒	†	⚒	⑤⑦		Ⓐ	⑥	⑤⑦
	s					A		B								D	E				t	C			t
Paris Est **390** d.	1325	...	...	...	...	1528	...	1558	...	...	...	1728	...	...	...	1828	1828	...	...	...	2028	2058	...	...	2128
Champagne Ard □ **390 391a** d.	|	1410	1510	1510	1519	|	1610	|	1640	1710	1740	|	1810	1810	1840	|	|	1910	2010	2016	|	|	...	...	|
Reims **391a** a.	1411	1422	1521	1522	1527	1614	1622	1645	1652	1723	1752	1814	1821	1822	1852	1914	1914	1922	2021	2028	2114	2144	...	...	2214
Reims d.	...	1430	1529	1530	1530	...	1630	...	1700	1724	1800	...	1829	1830	1900	1920	1920	1930	2029	2030	...	...	2200	2200	2219
Rethel d.	...	1453	1552	1553	1553	...	1653	...	1724	1749	1823	...	1853	1854	1924	1943	1943	1954	2053	2053	...	...	2223	|	2242
Charleville-Mézières a.	...	1525	1624	1625	1625	...	1726	...	1751	1823	1856	...	1925	1926	1952	2011	2011	2026	2125	2125	...	...	2255	2320	2311
Charleville-Mézières **389a** d.	...	1530	1629	...	1630	...	1731	...	1800	1828	...	...	...	1931	...	2020	...	2031	2130	...	...	...	...	...	2320
Sedan **389a** a.	...	1550	1651	...	1649	...	1758	...	1826	1853	...	...	...	1957	...	2035	...	2052	2155	...	...	...	...	...	2335

		TGV 2706				*TGV* 2712		*TGV* 2714			*TGV* 2716	*TGV* 2720						*TGV* 2722	*TGV* 2726					*TGV* 2730	*TGV* 2738
	Ⓐ	Ⓐ	Ⓐ	Ⓐ	⑥	Ⓐ	Ⓐ	①–⑥	⑥	Ⓐ	Ⓐ	⑦	Ⓐ	⑥	Ⓐ		⚒	Ⓑ	⑥		Ⓐ	⚒	Ⓐ	Ⓐ	⑦
		r				r		b			r	e						h	s¶					r	e
Sedan **389a** d.	...	...	0535	0605	0604	...	0638	0649	0710	0705	...	0723	0735	...	0800	0911z	1011	...	1053	1111x	...	1205x	...	1253x	...
Charleville-Mézières **389a** a.	...	...	0600	0624	0630	...	0657	0703	0730	0730	...	0737	0800	...	0827	0930	1030	...	1107	1130x	...	1230x	...	1307x	...
Charleville-Mézières d.	0535	...	0608	0629	0635	...	0704	0715	0735	0735	...	0747	0808	0830	0832	0935	1035	...	1116	1135	1208	1235	1305	1317	...
Rethel d.	0606	...	0636	0702	0709	...	0736	0747	0807	0808	...	0818	0836	0905	0905	1007	1109	...	1148	1207	1236	1307	1337	1348	...
Reims a.	0630	...	0701	0725	0733	...	0800	0809	0830	0833	...	0839	0900	0930	0929	1031	1132	...	1209	1230	1300	1330	1401	1409	...
Reims **391a** d.	0635	0645	0706	0735	0738	0745	0805	0815	0835	0838	0845	0845	0905	0935	0934	1035	1137	1201	1215	1235	1305	1335	1406	1415	1415
Champagne Ard □ **390 391a** d.	0648	|	0719	0748	0750	|	0818	|	0848	0851	|	|	0918	0948	0948	1049	1150	|	|	1248	1318	1348	1418	|	|
Paris Est **390** a.	...	0731	...	...	...	0831	...	0901	...	...	0931	0931	...	...	...	...	...	1247	1301	...	...	...	...	1501	1501

					TGV 2750		*TGV* 2752	*TGV* 2754						*TGV* 2756		*TGV* 2760			*TGV* 2762						*TGV* 2766
	†	⚒	⑥	Ⓐ	⑥		Ⓐ	⑦	Ⓒ	Ⓐ	Ⓐ	†	⚒	⑤⑦	Ⓐ		⑥	Ⓑ	⑤⑦	Ⓐ	⑥	Ⓐ	Ⓒ	Ⓐ	⑦
					s		r	e						t		C			t				g		e
Sedan **389a** d.	1305	1311x	1404	1411x	...	1511	...	...	1604k	1611	1635	1705	1711	...	1735	...	1805	1811	...	*1834*	...	*1905*	2010	*2019*	2053
Charleville-Mézières **389a** a.	1329	1330x	1430	1430x	...	1530	...	...	1629k	1630	1700	1730	1730	...	1800	...	1829	1830	...	*1902*	...	*1930*	2034	*2034*	2107
Charleville-Mézières d.	1334	1335	1435	1435	...	1535	...	1617	1634	1635	1708	1735	1735	...	1808	...	1834	1835	...	1908	1934	2005	2039	2105	2117
Rethel d.	1407	1409	1508	1507	...	1609	...	1648	1706	1707	1736	1808	1807	...	1836	...	1908	1908	...	1936	2006	2037	2112	2138	2148
Reims a.	1431	1432	1531	1530	...	1632	...	1709	1730	1730	1800	1831	1830	...	1900	...	1931	1932	...	2000	2030	2101	2136	2202	2209
Reims **391a** d.	1436	1437	1536	1535	1615	1637	1715	1715	1735	1735	1805	1836	1835	1845	1905	1915	1936	1937	1945	...	...	...	...	...	2215
Champagne Ard □ **390 391a** d.	1448	1450	1548	1548	|	1650	|	|	1748	1748	1818	1849	1848	|	1918	|	1948	1950	|	...	...	...	...	...	|
Paris Est **390** a.	...	...	...	...	1701	...	1801	1801	...	...	...	...	...	1931	...	2001	...	...	2031	...	...	...	...	...	2301

A – ①②④⑦ to Jan. 26; ①②④⑤⑦ Jan. 29 - Mar. 16; ①②④⑦ Mar. 19 - May 16; ①②④⑤⑦ from May 21 (also June 28).
B – ③⑤ to Jan. 27; ③ Feb. 1 - Mar. 8; ③⑤ Mar. 15 - May 12; ③ May 17 - June 21.
C – ①②③④⑥ (also May 19; not Apr. 10, May 1, 8, 17, 29).
D – ①②③④⑥⑦ to Mar. 23; daily from Mar. 25.
E – ⑤ to Mar. 24.

b – Not Apr. 10, May 1, 8, 29.
e – Also Apr. 10, May 1, 8, 29.
f – Also May 17; not May 19.
g – Not Apr. 23.
h – Not May 18, 19.
j – ⚒ only.
k – ⑥ only.

q – 0955 on Ⓒ.
r – Not May 19.
s – Also May 18, 19.
t – Also Apr. 10, May 1, 8, 17, 29; not May 19.
u – Also May 17, 18.
x – Not ①–⑤ Feb. 20 - Mar. 31.
y – 0755 on ⑥.
z – 0905 on †.

TGV – High-speed train. 🅁. 🍷.

¶ – Runs 13 – 15 minutes **earlier** on May 19.
□ – Champagne Ardenne TGV.

389a CHARLEVILLE MÉZIÈRES - LONGUYON - LONGWY and THIONVILLE

km													
		Ⓐ	Ⓐ	Ⓐ	Ⓐ	Ⓐ	⑥	Ⓐ	†		Ⓐ	†	
			v		v			d					◧
0	**Charleville-Mézières** **389** d.	0520	...	0620	...	...	0920	1120	1330	...	1720	1818	...
20	**Sedan** **389** d.	0536	...	0636	...	...	0935	1136	1345	...	1736	1835	...
69	Montmédy ▷ d.	0607	...	0707	...	...	1006	1207	1416	...	1807	1909	...
	Longwy **392** d.	|	0614	|	...	0815	|	|	|	...	|	|	...
91	Longuyon **392** ▷ a.	0621	0626	0721	...	0827	1020	1221	1430	...	1821	1922	...
91	Longuyon **392** ▷ d.	0630	0629	0730	0729	0828	1025	1230z	1435	...	1830	1923	2002
	Longwy **392** ▷ a.	0643	|	0742	|	|	1038	1243z	1447	...	1843	|	2014
132	Hayange d.	...	0701	...	0801	0901	...	...	...	...	...	1954	...
140	**Thionville** a.	...	0709	...	0809	0910	...	...	...	...	...	2002	...

	Ⓐ	Ⓐ		Ⓐ	⑥		†	Ⓐ	Ⓐ	Ⓐ	Ⓐ	†
		v		B						v		
Thionville d.	...	0635	...	...	...	...	1619	1710	...	1841	...	...
Hayange d.	...	0643	...	...	...	...	1628	1718	...	1849	...	...
Longwy **392** d.	0654	|	...	1316	1426	...	|	|	1816	|	1916	2022
Longuyon **392** a.	0706	0716	...	1328	1439	...	1658	1750	1828	1921	1928	2034
Longuyon **392** d.	0711	...	...	1333	1444	...	1659	1751	1833	1922	1933	2039
Longwy **392** a.	|	...	...	|	|	...	|	1805	|	1936	|	|
Montmédy d.	0725	...	...	1349	1459	...	1712	...	1847	...	1947	2053
Sedan **389** d.	0757k	...	...	1419	1532	...	1743k	...	1919k	...	2019k	2126
Charleville-Mézières **389** a.	0812h	...	...	1434	1547	...	1758k	...	1934k	...	2034k	2143

B – Ⓐ until Jan. 13 (also Apr. 11); Ⓐ May 2 – 26; ①–⑤ June 5 – 23.

d – Not Jan. 16 - Apr. 7.
h – Arrives 0818 Jan. 23 - Feb. 24.
k – 2 – 3 minutes later Jan. 23 - Feb. 26.
v – Not Dec. 26 – 30.
z – Not Apr. 12 – 14, 17 – 21, 24 – 28.

◧ – Runs 2 minutes later Mar. 6 - Apr. 23.
▷ – Timings Montmédy - Longwy may be up to 3 minutes later Jan. 23 - Feb. 26.

PARIS - STRASBOURG, NANCY, METZ and LUXEMBOURG 390

Warning! Timings may vary by up to 6 minutes (please check your reservation for confirmed timings). Subject to alteration Feb. 25, 26, May 12 – 15.
Journeys to / from Luxembourg are subject to alteration May 27 – 29. See Tables **30** and **32** for full details of international *TGV / ICE* services between Paris and Germany (including services via Forbach and Saarbrücken). See Table **391** for other *TGV* services Marne la Vallée - Paris Charles de Gaulle ✈ - Champagne-Ardenne - Meuse - Lorraine - Strasbourg and v.v.

km			*ICE*	*TGV*	*TGV*	*TGV*	*TGV*	*TGV*	*TGV*	*TGV*	*TGV*	*TGV*	*TGV*	*TGV*	*TGV*	*TGV*	*TGV*	*TGV*	*ICE*		*TGV*	*TGV*	*TGV*	*TGV*	*TGV*	*TGV*
			9571	**2601**	**2501**	**9561**	**2363**	**2801**	**2503**	**2407**	**9403**	**2807**	**2503**	**2587**	**2365**	**7691**	**2505**	**2815**	**9573**		**2571**	**9401**	**2421**	**2817**	**9575**	**2369**
				①	①–⑤	①–⑥	①–⑥	①–⑤	⑥	Ⓑ	⑥	①–⑥	①–⑤	⑦	①–⑤		①–⑥		◐			⑤				Ⓑ
			♧	g	v	u⊡	b	v	k	h	p⊖	b	z	e	v	☒	b	▲	♧		♤	a⊖	E	▲	♧	h
0	**Paris** Est	d.	0655	0658	0707	0720	0720	0725	0728	0758	0758	0812	0838	0913	0925	1008	1013	1025	1055	...	1223	1246j	1252	1327	1355	1355
136	Champagne-Ardenne TGV	d.	|	|	0749	|	|	|	0812	0841	0841	0854	0921	|	|	|	|	|	|	...	1306	|	|	|	|	|
236	Meuse TGV	d.	|	|	|	|	|	|	0840	0908	|	|	|	1016	|	|	|	|	|	...	|	|	|	|	|	|
330	**Nancy**	a.	|	|	0844	|	|	|	0916	|	|	|	1016	1051	|	|	1144	|	|	...	1400	|	|	|	|	|
315	**Metz** 384	a.	|	0824	...	|	|	0852	...	|	|	0946	...	|	|	|	...	1204	|	...	...	|	|	1454	|	|
345	Thionville 384	a.	|	...	...	|	|	0914	...	|	|	1010	...	|	|	|	...	1227	|	...	...	|	|	1519	|	|
379	**Luxembourg** 384	a.	|	...	...	|	|	0944	...	|	|	1038	...	▽	|	|	...	1252	|	...	...	|	|	1552	|	|
304	Lorraine TGV	d.	|	...	...	|	|	...	...	|	0922	...	...	|	|	|	...	...	|	...	...	1402	|	...	|	|
439	**Strasbourg** 385	a.	0841	...	...	0906	0906	...	...	0959	0959	...	...	1222	1111	1154	...	...	1241	...	...	1438	1438	...	1541	1541
482	Sélestat 385	a.	...	...	...	...	|	...	...	...	...	...	...	...	|	...	...	...	...	...	...	...	...	...	...	|
504	**Colmar** 385	a.	...	...	...	...	0942	...	...	...	...	...	...	...	1144	...	...	...	...	...	...	...	...	...	...	1626

		TGV	*TGV*	*TGV*	*TGV*	*ICE*	*TGV*	*TGV*	*TGV*	*TGV*	*TGV*	*TGV*	*TGV*	*TGV*	*TGV*	*TGV*	*TGV*	*TGV*	*TGV*	*TGV*	*TGV*	*TGV*	*TGV*	*TGV*	*TGV*	*TGV*
		2509	**2591**	**2431**	**2509**	**9563**	**2613**	**9577**	**2513**	**7693**	**2443**	**2443**	**2515**	**9591**	**2833**	**9579**	**2573**	**2593**	**2625**	**2625**	**2377**	**2785**	**2839**	**2583**	**2583**	**2595**
		①–⑤	⑦	⑤	⑥			Ⓑq			⑤⑦	①–④	①–⑤					①–⑤	⑤	①–④		Ⓑ		①–⑤	⑦	⑦y
		v	e♡	f	k	⊡	D	⊙	R	☒	d	n	v	⊖	▲	⊕	♤	v♡	t	x		o B	▲	v	e	♡
Paris Est	d.	1358	1358	1455	1458	1521	1524	1555	1607	1616	1643	1655	1713	1725	1740	1755	1810	1810	1840	1840	1855	1928	1940	1943	2007	2007
Champagne-Ardenne TGV	d.	1441	1441	|	1541	|	|	|	1649	|	|	|	|	|	|	|	|	|	|	1922	|	2008	|	|	|	|
Meuse TGV	d.	1508	1509	|	1609	|	|	|	|	|	|	|	|	|	|	|	1913	1913	|	|	|	...	|	|	2109	2109
Nancy	a.	1544	1544	|	1644	|	|	|	1744	|	|	|	1844	|	|	|	1948	1948	|	|	|	...	|	2119	2144	2144
Metz 384	a.	...	...	|	...	|	1654	|	...	1744*	|	|	...	|	1907	|	...	...	2012	2014	|	...	2107	|	|	...
Thionville 384	a.	...	...	|	...	|	...	|	...	|	|	|	...	|	1934	|	...	...	...	...	|	...	2130	|	|	...
Luxembourg 384	a.	...	...	|	...	|	...	|	...	|	|	|	...	|	2005	|	...	...	...	...	|	...	2158	▽	▽	...
Lorraine TGV	d.	...	...	|	...	|	...	|	...	|	|	|	...	|	...	|	...	...	...	...	|	...	...	|	|	...
Strasbourg 385	a.	...	...	1641	...	1707	...	1741	...	1900	1829	1841	...	1911	...	1941	...	...	...	...	2041	...	...	2254	2317¦	...
Sélestat 385	a.	...	...	...	...	...	...	...	...	...	...	...	...	...	...	...	...	...	...	...	2106	...	...	...	...	...
Colmar 385	a.	...	...	...	...	...	...	...	...	...	...	...	...	...	...	...	...	...	...	...	2119	...	...	...	...	...

		TGV	*TGV*	*TGV*	*TGV*	*TGV*	*TGV*	*TGV*	*TGV*	*TGV*	*TGV*
		2519	**2643**	**2465**	**2465**	**2843**	**2519**	**2527**	**2647**	**2471**	**2471**
		⑥	①–⑤	⑤–⑦	①–④	⑥⑦	Ⓑ	⑤⑦	⑦	⑤⑦	⑤⑦
		k	N☆	c	m	e	T	d	Q	L	H
Paris Est	d.	2007	2008	2025	2025	2040	2044	2112	2140	2155	2206
Champagne-Ardenne TGV	d.	|	|	|	|	|	|	|	|	|	|
Meuse TGV	d.	2109	|	|	2128	|	2146	|	|	|	|
Nancy	a.	2144	|	|	|	|	2229	2244	|	|	|
Metz 384	a.	...	2136	|	|	2207	...	...	2307	|	|
Thionville 384	a.	...	...	|	|	2229	...	...	...	|	|
Luxembourg 384	a.	...	...	|	|	2257	...	...	...	|	|
Lorraine TGV	d.	...	...	2141	2149	...	...	...	...	|	|
Strasbourg 385	a.	...	...	2224	2225	...	...	...	...	2341	2357
Sélestat 385	a.	...	...	...	...	...	...	...	...	...	...
Colmar 385	a.	...	...	...	...	...	...	...	...	...	...

		TGV	*TGV*	*TGV*	*TGV*	*TGV*	*TGV*	*TGV*	*TGV*	*TGV*	*TGV*
		2530	**2650**	**2778**	**2400**	**2852**	**2404**	**2574**	**2584**	**2854**	**2654**
		①–⑤	①–⑤	①–⑥	①	①–⑤	①–⑤	⚒	①–⑥	Ⓐ	⑥
		v	v	b B	g	N	v	♤	Y		p
Colmar 385	d.	...	...	...	...	...	...	...	...	...	...
Sélestat 385	d.	...	...	...	...	...	...	...	...	...	...
Strasbourg 385	d.	...	...	...	0623	...	0640	...	0541	...	...
Lorraine TGV	d.	...	...	...	|	...	|	...	|	...	...
Luxembourg 384	d.	...	...	...	|	0559	|	...	▽	0634	...
Thionville 384	d.	...	...	...	|	0627	|	...	|	0701	...
Metz 384	d.	...	0620	...	|	0650	|	...	|	0724	0726
Nancy	d.	0612	|	...	|	|	|	0716	0716	|	|
Meuse TGV	d.	|	|	...	|	0723	0733	|	|	|	|
Champagne-Ardenne TGV	d.	|	|	0718	|	|	|	|	|	|	|
Paris Est	a.	0746	0750	0801	0816	0821	0835	0846	0846	0850	0852

		TGV	*TGV*	*TGV*	*TGV*	*TGV*	*TGV*	*TGV*	*TGV*	*TGV*	*ICE*		*TGV*	*TGV*	*TGV*	*TGV*	*TGV*	*ICE*		*ICE*	*TGV*	*TGV*	*TGV*	*TGV*	*TGV*	*TGV*
		2350	**9590**	**2596**	**2534**	**9578**	**9588**	**2352**	**2656**	**2860**	**9568**		**2536**	**2578**	**2356**	**9576**	**2864**	**9566**		**9574**	**2540**	**7692**	**2542**	**2870**	**2430**	**2358**
		①–⑥	①–⑤	①–⑥	⑦	①–⑥	⑥⑦	⑦	Ⓐ	Ⓒ	Ⓑq		⚒	†	①–⑥			⑥r					⑤⑦		⑥	①–⑤
		b	v⊖	b♡	e	u♧	w■	s		▲	⊡			♤	b	⊙		⊡		♧		☒	d	▲	k	v
Colmar 385	d.	0638	...	...	...	...	⊖	0737	...	...	...	...	...	...	1001	...	...	...	...	...	...	...	...	...	...	1416
Sélestat 385	d.	0652	...	...	...	...	...	0750	...	...	...	...	...	...	|	...	...	...	...	...	...	...	...	...	...	|
Strasbourg 385	d.	0719	0749	...	...	0820	0820	0820	...	...	0852	...	...	...	1044	1044	...	1052	...	1219	...	1250	...	...	1449	1449
Lorraine TGV	d.	0759	|	...	...	|	|	|	...	...	|	...	...	...	|	|	...	|	...	|	...	|	...	...	|	|
Luxembourg 384	d.	|	|	...	...	|	|	|	...	0759	|	...	...	...	|	|	1010	|	...	|	...	|	...	1410	|	|
Thionville 384	d.	|	|	...	...	|	|	|	...	0826	|	...	...	...	|	|	1039	|	...	|	...	|	...	1434	|	|
Metz 384	d.	|	|	...	...	|	|	|	0847	0850	|	...	...	...	|	|	1108•	|	...	|	...	1352	...	1503	|	|
Nancy	d.	|	|	0816	0816	|	|	|	|	|	|	...	1011	1011	|	|	|	|	...	|	1255	|	1430	|	|	|
Meuse TGV	d.	|	|	|	|	|	|	|	0920	0923	|	...	|	|	|	|	|	|	...	|	1332	|	|	|	|	|
Champagne-Ardenne TGV	d.	|	|	|	|	|	|	|	|	|	|	...	1108	1108	|	|	|	|	...	|	1401	|	|	|	|	|
Paris Est	a.	0916	0935	0946	0946	1005	1005	1005	1020	1023	1038	...	1150	1150	1231	1231	1237•	1238	...	1405	1442	1528*	1601	1631	1635	1638

		TGV	*TGV*	*ICE*	*TGV*	*TGV*	*TGV*	*TGV*	*TGV*	*TGV*	*TGV*	*TGV*	*TGV*	*TGV*	*TGV*	*TGV*	*TGV*	*TGV*	*TGV*	*TGV*	*TGV*	*TGV*	*TGV*	*TGV*	*TGV*	*TGV*
		2440	**2544**	**9572**	**2872**	**2580**	**2588**	**2680**	**2450**	**2362**	**2548**	**2598**	**2454**	**9402**	**9402**	**9560**	**2550**	**2886**	**2552**	**9570**	**2552**	**2892**	**7694**	**2552**	**2470**	**2474**
			①–⑤	◧			⑦	Ⓑ	⑥	Ⓑ	①–⑤	⑦	①–④	⑤	⑦		⑥		⑦		①–⑤	⑦		⑦	⑤	⑦
		G	v	♧	▲	♤	e	h	p	h	v	e♡	m	a⊖	e⊖	⊡	p	▲		♧	h	y	☒⊗	e	f	e
Colmar 385	d.	...	...	...	...	...	...	...	...	1645	...	...	...	...	...	...	...	...	...	...	...	...	...	...	...	...
Sélestat 385	d.	...	...	...	...	...	...	...	...	|	...	...	...	...	...	...	...	...	...	...	...	...	...	...	...	...
Strasbourg 385	d.	1544	...	1619	...	...	1547◊	...	1718	1719	...	...	1819	1819	1819	1857	...	...	...	2020	...	...	2001	...	2119	2149
Lorraine TGV	d.	|	...	|	...	...	|	...	|	|	...	...	|	|	1857	|	...	...	...	|	...	...	|	...	|	|
Luxembourg 384	d.	|	...	|	1610	...	▽	...	|	|	...	...	|	|	|	|	...	1847	...	|	...	2010	|	...	|	|
Thionville 384	d.	|	...	|	1632	...	|	...	|	|	...	...	|	|	|	|	...	1917	...	|	...	2034	|	...	|	|
Metz 384	d.	|	...	|	1654	...	|	1725	|	|	...	...	|	|	|	|	...	1944	...	|	...	2057	2106	...	|	|
Nancy	d.	|	1611	|	|	1716	1716	|	|	|	1811	1811	|	|	|	|	1920	|	2014	|	2024	|	|	2116	|	|
Meuse TGV	d.	|	|	|	|	|	|	|	|	|	1848	1848	|	|	|	|	1956	|	|	|	|	|	|	|	|	|
Champagne-Ardenne TGV	d.	|	1708	|	|	|	|	1820	|	|	|	|	1930	1930	1938	|	2023	2038	2110	|	2130	|	|	|	|	|
Paris Est	a.	1735	1750	1805	1831	1846	1846	1901	1903	1905	1950	1950	2012	2012	2020	2041	2105	2119	2151	2205	2212	2220	2232	2246	2305	2335

B – To / from Bar le Duc (Table **381**).
D – Ⓑ to Jan. 8; ②③④⑤⑦ Jan. 10 - Mar. 12; Ⓑ from Mar. 14 (not May 18, 19). From May 14 Paris d. 1540, Metz a. 1704.
E – ⑥⑦ to Mar. 12 (also Dec. 12 – 15, 22, Jan. 2); ①②③④⑥⑦ from Mar. 14 (not May 17).
G – ⑤⑦ to Mar. 12 (also Dec. 12 – 15, 22, Jan. 2); Ⓑ from Mar. 14 (not May 18, 19).
H – ⑤⑦ Jan. 20 - May 12 (also Apr. 10, May 1, 8).
L – ⑤⑦ to Jan. 15; ⑤⑦ from May 14 (also May 17, 29; not May 19).
N – ①–⑤ from Mar. 27 (not Apr. 10, May 1, 8, 18, 19, 29).
Q – ⑦ (not Apr. 23). Departs Paris 2124 on May 29.
R – ⑦–④ to Mar. 9 (also Dec. 16, 23); Ⓑ from Mar. 12 (not May 18, 19).
T – Ⓑ from Mar. 27 (not May 18, 19).
Y – Not Dec. 23, 24, 30, 31, Apr. 10, May 1, 8, 19, 20, 29.

a – Also May 17.
b – Not Apr. 10, May 1, 8, 29.
c – Also Apr. 10, May 1, 8, 17, 18, 29.
d – Also Apr. 10, May 1, 8, 17, 29; not May 19.
e – Also Apr. 10, May 1, 8, 29.
f – Also May 17; not May 19.
g – Also Apr. 11, May 2, 9, 30; not Dec. 19, 26, Apr. 10, May 1, 8, 29.
h – Not May 18, 19.
j – 1228 on Apr. 28.
k – Also May 18, 19.
m – Not Apr. 10, May 1, 8, 17, 18, 29.
n – Not Dec. 19 – 21, 26 – 29, Apr. 10, May 1, 8, 17, 18, 29.
o – Not Apr. 9, 30, May 7, 8.
p – Also May 18.
q – Not Apr. 9, 30, May 28.
r – Also Apr. 9, 30, May 28.
s – Also Apr. 10, May 1, 29.
t – Also May 17; not Dec. 30, May 19.
u – Not Apr. 10, May 1, 29.
v – Not Apr. 10, May 1, 8, 18, 19, 29.
w – Also Apr. 10, May 1, 8, 18, 19, 29.
x – Not Dec. 26 – 29, Apr. 10, May 1, 8, 17, 18, 29.
y – Also Apr. 10, May 1, 8, 29; not Apr. 9, 30, May 7, 28.
z – Not Dec. 26 – 30, Apr. 10, May 1, 8, 18, 19, 29.

TGV – High-speed train. Ⓡ. 🍷.
ICE – German high-speed train. Ⓡ. ✕.

¦ – Not Feb. 5 - Mar. 12, Apr. 9, 30, May 7, 28.
■ – Train number **9408** on ⑦ (also Apr. 10, May 1, 29).
◧ – Runs as *TGV* **9592** on ⑥ (also Apr. 9, 30, May 28).
◐ – Runs as *TGV* **9593** on ⑥ (also Apr. 9, 30, May 28).
⊕ – 🚌 Paris - Stuttgart (- München ⑥r). See Table **32**.
☆ – From May 15 Paris d. 2040, Metz a. 2204.

• – 10 – 17 minutes earlier May 2 – 5, 27 – 29 and from June 1.
⊗ – On ①–⑤ Feb. 20 - Mar. 24 does not call at Metz and arrives Paris 2152.
◊ – 1521 on Apr. 10, May 1, 8, 29.
▽ – Via Saverne (Table **383**).
⊙ – To / from München (Table **32**).
⊡ – To / from Frankfurt (Table **30**).
♧ – To / from Stuttgart (Table **32**).
⊖ – From / to Freiburg (Brsg) Hbf (Table **32**).
♤ – To / from Remiremont (Table **386**).
♡ – To / from St Dié (Table **387**).
▲ – **WARNING!** Service subject to frequent timing variations and may not run Metz - Luxembourg and v.v. on certain dates. Please check before travelling and refer to your reservation for confirmed timings.
* – Arrival time may vary.
☒ – OUIGO low-cost TGV. Internet bookings only: www.ouigo.com

391 STRASBOURG - BRUSSELS, NANTES, RENNES and BORDEAUX

Timings may vary by a few minutes on certain dates – please check your reservation.

	TGV	*TGV*	*TGV*		*TGV*		*TGV*	*TGV*		*TGV*	*TGV*	*TGV*	
	9890	**5487**	**5487**		**5470**		**9404**	**5454**		**9894**	**9894**	**5488**	
							⑥	Ⓑ		①–⑥	⑦	Ⓑ	
		r	**H**				**k**	**h**		**b** ◇	**e** ⊙	**m**	
Freiburg (Brsg) Hbf d.	...	...	...	...	...	...	1222p	...	...	...	...	...	...
Offenburg d.	...	...	...	...	...	...	1311p	...	...	...	...	...	...
Strasbourg d.	0601	0731	0731	...	1001	...	1356	1401	...	1701	1701	1701	...
Lorraine TGV ★ d.	0638	0809	0809	...	1040	...	1438	1439	...	1742	1742	1742	...
Meuse TGV ★ d.	0659	|	|	...	1101	...	1505	1505	...	1809	1809	1809	...
Champagne-Ardenne TGV a.	0723	0847	0847	...	1125	...	1529	1531	...	1832	1832	1832	...
Champagne-Ardenne TGV d.	0726	0858	0858	...	1128	...	1534	1534	...	1835	1835	1835	...
Paris Charles de Gaulle ✈ a.	0756	0928	0928	...	1201	...	1605	1605	...	1906	1906	1906	...
Paris Charles de Gaulle ✈ d.	0807	0945	0945	...	1216	...	1619	1619	...	1912	1912	1921	...
Lille Europe a.	0856	|	|	...	|	...	|	|	...	2008	2019v	|	...
Brussels Midi/Zuid a.	0943	|	|	...	|	...	|	|	...	2101	2109	|	...
Marne la Vallée - Chessy § a.	...	0955	0955	...	1226	...	1628	1628	...	...	...	1931	...
Marne la Vallée - Chessy § d.	...	1002	1002	...	1235	...	1633	1633	...	...	...	1935	...
Massy TGV a.	...	1035	1034	...	1304	...	1704	1704	...	...	...	2004	...
St Pierre des Corps a.	...	1132	|	...	|	...	1806	1806	...	...	...	|	...
Le Mans a.	...	|	1128	...	1359	...	|	|	...	...	...	2100	...
Angers a.	...	1236	1237	...	|	...	|	|	...	...	...	2140	...
Nantes a.	...	1319	1319	...	|	...	|	|	...	...	...	2219	...
Rennes a.	...	...	...	...	1448t	...	|	|	...	...	...	...	...
Poitiers a.	...	...	...	...	...	...	1840	1840	...	...	...	...	...
Angoulême a.	...	...	...	...	...	...	1922	1922	...	...	...	...	...
Bordeaux St Jean a.	...	...	...	...	...	...	2002	2002	...	...	...	...	...

	TGV		*TGV*		*TGV*	*TGV*		*TGV*		*TGV*		*TGV*	
	9870		**5482**		**5440**	**9406**		**9874**		**5480**		**5460**	
			①–⑥		①–⑥	⑦							
			n		**b** ⊗	**e**		⊖					
Bordeaux St Jean d.	...	...	...	...	0854	0854	...	...	...	...	...	...	...
Angoulême d.	...	...	...	...	0935	0936	...	...	...	...	...	...	...
Poitiers d.	...	...	...	...	1019	1019	...	...	...	...	...	...	...
Rennes d.	...	...	...	...	|	|	...	...	...	...	...	1603c	...
Nantes d.	...	...	0809f	...	|	|	...	...	...	1409f	...	|	...
Angers d.	...	...	0848f	...	|	|	...	...	...	1449f	...	|	...
Le Mans d.	...	...	0930	...	|	|	...	...	...	1530	...	1657	...
St Pierre des Corps d.	...	...	|	...	1054	1054	...	...	...	|	...	|	...
Massy TGV d.	...	...	1025f	...	1155	1155	...	...	...	1626	...	1754	...
Marne la Vallée - Chessy § a.	...	...	1055	...	1224	1224	...	...	...	1657	...	1823	...
Marne la Vallée - Chessy § d.	...	...	1100	...	1228	1228	...	...	...	1703	...	1828	...
Brussels Midi/Zuid d.	0717	...	|	...	|	|	...	1317	...	|	...	|	...
Lille Europe d.	0802	...	|	...	|	|	...	1402	...	|	...	|	...
Paris Charles de Gaulle ✈ a.	0853	...	1109	...	|	|	...	1452	...	1713	...	1837	...
Paris Charles de Gaulle ✈ d.	0859	...	1122	...	|	|	...	1457	...	1729	...	1853	...
Champagne-Ardenne TGV a.	0928	...	1152	...	1255	1255	...	1555	...	1800	...	1929	...
Champagne-Ardenne TGV d.	0934	...	1155	...	1258	1258	...	1604	...	1810	...	1935	...
Meuse TGV ★ a.	1000	...	|	...	1323	1323	...	|	...	|	...	2000	...
Lorraine TGV ★ a.	1025	...	1232	...	1349	1349	...	1648	...	1848	...	2025	...
Strasbourg a.	1105	...	1312	...	1429	1429	...	1737	...	1929	...	2104	...
Offenburg a.	...	...	...	...	...	1455q	...	...	...	...	...	...	...
Freiburg (Brsg) Hbf a.	...	...	...	...	...	1543q	...	...	...	...	...	...	...

H – Runs Feb. 13 – 17, 20 – 24, 27, 28, Mar. 1 – 3, 6 – 10, May 19 – 21, 27 – 29 only.

b – Not Apr. 10, May 1, 8, 29.
c – Not Apr. 8, 9.
e – Also Apr. 10, May 1, 8, 29.
f – 3 – 5 minutes **earlier** Jan. 2 - Feb. 12.
h – Not May 18.
k – Also May 18.
m – Not May 19.
n – Not May 20.
p – Not Mar. 4, 11.
q – Not Mar. 5, 12.
r – Not Feb. 13 – 17, 20 – 24, 27, 28, Mar. 1 – 3, 6 – 10, May 19 – 21, 27 – 29.
t – Not Apr. 8, 9.
v – 2027 on Apr. 30, May 7.

TGV – High-speed train. Ⓡ. 🍷.

◇ – Also calls at Haute Picardie (a. 1938).
⊙ – Also calls at Haute Picardie (a. 1944).
⊖ – Also calls at Marne la Vallée - Chessy (a. 1507, d. 1523).
⊗ – Subject to alteration on Apr. 11, May 2, 9, 20, 30.
§ – Station for Disneyland Paris.
★ – Connecting 🚌 services operate on the following routes:
Nancy - Lorraine TGV (journey 35 minutes);
Metz - Lorraine TGV (journey 25 minutes);
Verdun - Meuse TGV (journey 25 minutes).

391a REIMS - CHAMPAGNE ARDENNE TGV

	⚒	Ⓐ	Ⓐ	⑥	Ⓑ	⑥	Ⓐ	Ⓐ	Ⓐ	⑥	Ⓐ	⚒	†	Ⓐ	⚒	Ⓐ	m	Ⓐ	k	Ⓐ	†	⚒	Ⓐ	⑥	Ⓐ
Reims d.	0635	0706	0735	0738	0805	0835	0838	0905	0934	0935	1005	1035	1036	1105	1137	1205	1235	1305	1335	1406	1436	1437	1535	1536	1605
Champagne-Ardenne TGV a.	0648	0719	0748	0750	0818	0848	0851	0918	0948	0948	1018	1048	1049	1118	1150	1218	1248	1318	1348	1418	1448	1450	1548	1548	1618

		Ⓐ		Ⓐ	⚒	†	Ⓐ	⑥	Ⓑ	Ⓐ	†	
Reims d.	1637	1705	1735	1805	1835	1836	1905	1936	1937	2035	2105	...
Champagne-Ardenne TGV a.	1650	1718	1748	1818	1848	1849	1918	1948	1950	2048	2117	...

	⚒	Ⓐ	⚒	Ⓑ	Ⓐ	⑥	Ⓐ
Champagne-Ardenne TGV d.	0710	0740	0810	0840	0910	0910	0940
Reims a.	0722	0752	0822	0852	0923	0924	0952

		Ⓐ	⚒m	Ⓐ	m	Ⓐ	Ⓐ	Ⓒ	Ⓐ		Ⓐ	Ⓒ	Ⓐ		Ⓐ		Ⓐ		Ⓐ		Ⓐ	†	⚒	Ⓐ	†
Champagne-Ardenne TGV d.	1010	1040	1110	1140	1210	1240	1309	1310	1340	1410	1440	1510	1519	1610	1640	1710	1740	1810	1840	1910	1940	2010	2016	2110	2147
Reims a.	1022	1052	1122	1152	1222	1252	1321	1322	1352	1422	1452	1522	1527	1622	1652	1723	1752	1822	1852	1922	1952	2021	2028	2122	2159

k – Not ①–⑤ Feb. 13 - Mar. 31.
m – Not ①–⑤ Feb. 20 - Mar. 31.

392 LONGWY - NANCY / LUXEMBOURG

LONGWY - NANCY (see note ⊖)

km		Ⓐ	⚒		Ⓒ	①–⑤ E	①–⑤ E	Ⓒ		†w V	†	
0	**Longwy** 389a d.	0541	0640	...	1047	1247	1447	1641	...	...	1917	...
16	Longuyon 389a d.	0554	0654	...	1100	1300	1500	1654	...	...	1931	...
57	Conflans-Jarny d.	0627	0729	...	1133	1330	1530	1728	...	1924	2003	...
100	Pont-à-Mousson 384 d.	0701	0800	...	1206	1400	1601	1801	...	1959	2037	...
128	**Nancy** 384 a.	0720	0820	...	1223	1420	1620	1818	...	2016	2054	...

	⚒ s		H		†	Ⓐ			⑤f V
Nancy 384 d.	0839	...	1239	...	1639	1739	1839	...	1944
Pont-à-Mousson 384 d.	0859	...	1259	...	1659	1759	1859	...	2001
Conflans-Jarny d.	0934	...	1334z	...	1733	1833z	1933z	...	2029
Longuyon 389a d.	1003	...	1403z	...	1803	1902z	2002z	...	...
Longwy 389a a.	1016	...	1415z	...	1816	1914z	2014z	...	...

LONGWY - LUXEMBOURG (see note ◇)

km		①–⑤ b	①–⑥ b	①–⑤ b	①–⑥ b	①–⑤ b	①–⑤ b	①–⑤ b	①–⑤ b	①–⑤ b	①–⑤ b	①–⑤ b	①–⑤ b	⑥	①–⑤ b	①–⑤ b	①–⑥ b
0	**Longwy** d.	0620	0650	0720	0748c	0820	0850	1320	1350	1650	1720	1750	1820	1850	*1850*	*1920*	1950
8	Rodange 🛃 ⊡ d.	0629	0659	0729	0759	0829	0859	1329	1359	1659	1729	1759	1829	1859	1911	1941	1959
10	Pétange ⊡ d.	0634	0704	0734	0804	0834	0904	1334	1404	1704	1734	1804	1834	1904	1916	1946	2004
27	**Luxembourg** ⊡ a.	0657	0727	0757	0827	0857	0927	1357	1427	1727	1757	1827	1857	1927	1940	2010	2027

	①–⑤ b	①–⑥ b	①–⑤ b	①–⑥ b	①–⑤ b	①–⑤ b		①–⑤ b	①–⑤ b	①–⑤ b	①–⑤ b	①–⑤ b	①–⑤ b	①–⑥ b	①–⑤ b	①–⑥ b
Luxembourg ⊡ d.	*0520*	0604	*0620*	0704	0734	0804	...	1204	1234	1604	1634	1704	1734	1804	1834	1904
Pétange ⊡ d.	*0544*	0627	*0644*	0727	0757	0827	...	1227	1257	1627	1657	1727	1757	1827	1857	1927
Rodange 🛃 ⊡ d.	0602	0632	0702	0732	0802	0832	...	1232	1302	1632	1702	1732	1802	1832	1902	1932
Longwy a.	0609	0639	0709	0739	0809	0839	...	1239	1309	1639	1709	1739	1809	1839	1909	1939

LONGWY - METZ 🚌 service (journey 55 minutes):
From Longwy at 0505 Ⓐ, 0630 Ⓐ, 0740, 0945 ⚒, 1235 ⑥, 1242 Ⓐ, 1335 †, 1445 ⚒, 1545 Ⓐ, 1615 ⑥, 1620 Ⓑ, 1745 ⑥, 1823 Ⓐ, 1925 Ⓐ and 1930 Ⓒ.
From Metz at 0635 Ⓐ, 0838 Ⓐ, 0920 ⚒, 1020 †, 1220 ⚒, 1430 ⑥, 1520 Ⓑ, 1620 ⚒, 1720 Ⓐ, 1820 Ⓐ, 1830 Ⓒ, 2026 Ⓐ, 2030 ⑥, 2120 †, 2218 ⑥ and 2237 Ⓐ.

E – ①–⑤ until Jan. 6.
H – Daily until Jan. 8; Ⓒ from Jan. 14.
V – From / to Verdun (Table **393a**).

b – Not Apr. 10, May 1, 9, 18, 29.

c – 0750 from May 8.
f – Not Feb. 17, 24, Apr. 21, 28.
s – Not ①–⑤ Mar. 6 - Apr. 14.
w – Not Apr. 9 – 30, May 7, 28. Conflans d. 1928 from May 14.
z – 2 – 3 minutes later Mar. 6 - Apr. 23.

⊖ – Journeys between Longwy and Nancy are also possible via Metz (see Longwy - Metz 🚌 panel together with Table **384**).
◇ – Service until June 10.
⊡ – Additional trains run Rodange - Luxembourg and v.v. (see Table **449**).

393 🚌 CHÂLONS EN CHAMPAGNE - VERDUN 🚌

Journey time: 1 hour 48 minutes

From Châlons en Champagne at 0820 Ⓐ, 1025 Ⓒ, 1230 Ⓐ, 1425 Ⓒ, 1430 Ⓐ, 1830 Ⓐ, 1840 †, 2025 Ⓒ and 2030 Ⓐ.
From Verdun at 0512 Ⓐ, 0742 Ⓒ, 1014 Ⓐ, 1209 Ⓐ, 1222 Ⓒ, 1509 Ⓐ, 1622 †, 1732 †, 1734 Ⓐ and 1742 ⑥.

VERDUN - METZ 393a

Warning! Timings may vary by up to 4 minutes.

km		⑥	Ⓐ	Ⓐ m	Ⓐ 🚌	⑥⑦ w	Ⓐ 🚌	Ⓐ n	⑥	Ⓐ	†k N	†
0	**Verdun** d.	...	0636	0738	0905	1038	1205	1638	1640	1813	1847	1934
40	Conflans-Jarny d.	0631	0716	0815	0955	1115	1255	1715	1717	1850	1922	2010
66	Hagondange . **384** d.	0709	|	0847	|	1147	|	1742	1747	|	...	|
84	**Metz** **384** a.	0722	0758	0903	1035	1202	1355	*1800*r	1801	1937	...	2051

	Ⓐ	Ⓐ 🚌	Ⓐ p	⑥ s	⑥⑦ w	Ⓐ 🚌	Ⓐ m	⑦	Ⓐ	⑥	⑤f N
Metz **384** d.	0555	0708	*0830*	0852	1255	1345	1637	1636	1821	1855	...
Hagondange **384** d.	|	|	0911	0907	1310	|	1651	1650	|	1908	...
Conflans-Jarny d.	0634	0753	0943	0939	1343	1430	1723	1727	1859	1940	2034
Verdun a.	0716	0840	1019	1014	1417	1517	1759	*1818*	1933	2015	2110

N – To/from Nancy (Table **392**).

f – Not Feb. 17, 24, Apr. 21, 28.
k – Not Apr. 9–30, May 7, 28. From May 14 Verdun d. 1851, Conflans a. 1926.
m – Not Mar. 6 - Apr. 14.
n – Not Mar. 6 - Apr. 14.
p – Not Feb. 13–24, Mar. 6 - Apr. 28.
r – *1816* on May 9.
s – Not Mar. 25.
w – Also May 1, 8; not Mar. 25, 26.

METZ - FORBACH - SAARBRÜCKEN 394

French holiday dates apply

On Apr. 7 services in this table run as on ⑦.

km		Ⓐ	Ⓐ	⑥	Ⓐ	Ⓐ	⑥	Ⓐ	⚒	†	Ⓐ	⑥	Ⓐ n	Ⓒ	Ⓐ n	Ⓐ n	Ⓒ e	Ⓐ n	⑥	Ⓐ	Ⓐ	†	⑥	⚒		Ⓐ	Ⓐ
0	**Metz** d.	...	0538	0608	0638	0704	0738	0738	0838	0838	0938	0938	1038	1038	1138	1238	1238	1338	1338	1438	1538	1538	1538	1638	...	1713	1733
50	St Avold d.	...	0609	0640	0709	0739	0812	0809	0911	0911	1010	1012	1111	1111	1215	1311	1314	1409	1410	1510	1609	1612	1613	1709	...	1746	1809
70	Forbach a.	...	0625	0656	0725	0753	0825	0825	0927	0926	1024	1025	1128	1125	1226	1325	1325	1425	1425	1524	1625	1625	1626	1725	...	1800	1825
70	Forbach d.	0531	*0631*	0700	*0731*	...	...	*0831*	0932	*0931*	*1031*	...	1130	*1131*e	*1231*	*1331*	1330	*1431*	*1431*	*1531*	*1631*	*1631*	1631	...	1731	...	*1831*
81	**Saarbrücken** a.	0542	*0642*	0709	*0742*	...	...	*0842*	0940	*0942*	*1042*	...	1140	*1142*e	*1242*	*1342*	1340	*1442*	*1442*	*1542*	*1642*	*1642*	1642	...	1742	...	*1842*

	Ⓒ	Ⓐ		Ⓑ	Ⓐ	Ⓐ	Ⓒ	Ⓐ	Ⓐ	Ⓒ	Ⓐ	† e
Metz d.	1733	1813	1838	...	1910	1938	1938	2038	...	2138	2238	2238
St Avold d.	1811	1850	1909	...	1946	2009	2011	2109	...	2209	2309	2311
Forbach a.	1825	1904	1925	...	2000	2025	2025	2125	...	2225	2325	2327
Forbach d.	*1831*	...	...	1931	...	*2031*	*2031*	*2131*	2244	...	*2344*	2330
Saarbrücken a.	*1842*	...	...	1942	...	*2042*	*2042*	*2142*	2255	...	*2355*	2340

	Ⓐ	D	⑥ B	⑥ A	Ⓐ	Ⓐ	⚒	Ⓐ	Ⓑ	⑥	Ⓐ	Ⓐ
Saarbrücken d.	0446	...	0450	0450	...	0616	...	...	*0716*	0721	...	0816
Forbach a.	0456	...	0500	0500	...	0626	...	...	*0726*	0731	...	0826
Forbach d.	...	0503	0503	0521	0607	...	0633	0707	0733	0733	0801	...
St Avold d.	...	0519	0520	0538	0621	...	0647	0723	0749	0750	0815	...
Metz a.	...	0550	0555	0614	0656	...	0720	0756	0820	0822	0847	...

	⚒	Ⓐ	Ⓑ	⑥	Ⓐ n	Ⓐ n	Ⓒ	Ⓐ n	⑥	C	⑦ e	⑥	Ⓐ n	Ⓐ	⑥	Ⓑ		Ⓐ	Ⓒ	Ⓐ		⑥	Ⓑ	Ⓑ	Ⓐ	Ⓐ	Ⓐ
Saarbrücken d.	...	0921	*1016*	*1016*	*1116*	1221	...	*1316*	1321	1421	1421	*1416*	*1416*	*1516*	1521	*1616*	*1716*	...	*1816*	*1816*	*1916*	*2016*	*2016*	2116	...	2225	2325
Forbach a.	...	0931	*1026*	*1026*	*1126*	1231	...	*1326*	1331	1431	1429	*1426*	*1426*	*1526*	1531	*1626*	*1726*	...	*1826*	*1826*	*1926*	*2026*	*2026*	2126	...	2235	2335
Forbach d.	0834	0933	1033	1033	1133	1233	1233	1333	1333	1433	1431	1433	1433	1534	1533	1633	1733	1808	1833	1836	1933	2033	2033	...	2134	...	...
St Avold d.	0850	0949	1049r	1047	1149	1247	1247	1348	1350	1447	1447	1447	1449	1549	1547	1649r	1749	1823	1847	1852	1948	2047	2049	...	2149	...	...
Metz a.	0920	1021	1120	1120	1220	1323f	1320	1420	1422	1522	1525	1520	1520	1620	1621	1720	1820	1857	1921	1925	2020	2120	2120	...	2220	...	...

A – Mar. 18 - May 13 (also on Feb. 4).
B – Feb. 11 - Mar. 11 and from May 20.
C – Runs on Apr. 10, May 1, 8, 18, 29 only.
D – ①–⑤ Feb. 6 - Mar. 10; ① Mar. 13 - Apr. 24 (also Apr. 11, May 2, 9; not Apr. 10); Ⓐ May 15 - June 16; ① from June 19.
e – Not Apr. 7.
f – 1320 from June 1.
n – Not Feb. 13 - Mar. 3, Apr. 3–21, June 12–16.
r – 2 minutes earlier on †.

STRASBOURG - SAARBRÜCKEN 395

French holiday dates apply

On Apr. 7 services in this table run as on ⑦.

km		Ⓐ	Ⓐ ⊙		⚒ ⊙		†	⚒ ⊗		Ⓐ ⊗		⊗		Ⓐ ⊗	†		⑥	Ⓐ	Ⓑ	Ⓐ	⚒		Ⓑ	⑥	Ⓑ
0	**Strasbourg** d.	0534	0634	...	0734	...	0849	0934	...	1134	...	1234	...	1430	1434	...	1534	1534	1634	1704	1734	...	1834	1934	2004
71	Diemeringen a.	0626	0726	...	0826	...	0941	1026	...	1226	...	1326	...	1524	1525	...	1626	1626	1726	1756	1826	...	1926	2026	2056
97	Sarreguemines a.	0653	0753	...	0853	...	1008	1053	...	1253	...	1353	...	1551	1553	...	1653	1653	1753	1823	1853	...	1953	2053	2123
	Sarreguemines 🚉 ▲ d.	...	...	...	0911v	...	1011	...	...	1311	...	...	...	...	...	...	1711	...	...	...	...	...	...	2111	...
115	**Saarbrücken** Hbf ▲ a.	...	...	...	0927v	...	1027	...	...	1327	...	...	...	...	...	...	1727	...	...	...	...	...	...	2127	...

	Ⓐ	Ⓐ	⚒	Ⓐ	⚒	†	⚒ ⊗		†	⚒ ⊗		⚒ ⊗	†		⑥	Ⓐ ⊗	Ⓐ ⊙	Ⓑ ⊙	Ⓑ		⑥	Ⓑ		Ⓒ 🚌
Saarbrücken Hbf ▲ d.	...	...	...	...	...	0654t	...	...	...	0939	...	...	1139	...	...	1339	...	...	...	...	1739	...	...	...
Sarreguemines 🚉 ▲ a.	...	...	...	...	...	0713t	...	...	...	1000	...	...	1200	...	...	1401	...	...	...	...	1800	...	...	...
Sarreguemines d.	0502	0532	0602	0632	0702	0714	0802	...	1002	1002	...	1202	1202	...	1402	1402	1502	1602	1702	...	1802	1832	...	1910
Diemeringen d.	0531	0601	0631	0701	0730	0743	0831	...	1030	1030	...	1230	1230	...	1430	1430	1530	1630	1730	...	1830	1900	...	1940
Strasbourg a.	0625	0655	0725	0755	0825	0837	0925	...	1125	1125	...	1325	1325	...	1525	1525	1625	1725	1825	...	1925	1955	...	2115

SAARBAHN LIGHT RAIL SERVICE **S1 SARREGUEMINES - SAARBRÜCKEN** ⊡

	⚒	Ⓐ	⚒	Ⓐ				
Sarreguimes (Bahnhof) d.	0516	0546	0616	0646	0716	hourly ◐	2316	0016
Saarbrücken Hbf a.	0545	0615	0645	0715	0745	until	2345	0045

	⚒	Ⓐ	⚒	Ⓐ	⚒	Ⓐ			
Saarbrücken Hbf d.	0440	0510	0540	0610	0640	0710	0740	hourly ◧	2340
Sarreguimes (Bahnhof) a.	0510	0540	0610	0640	0710	0740	0810	until	0010

t – Not Apr. 7, 10, May 1, 8, 18, 29.
v – Not Apr. 17–21, 24–28.

⊗ – Subject to alteration Feb. 13–17, 20–24, Apr. 17–21, 24–28.
⊙ – Subject to alteration Feb. 13–17, 20–24.

▲ – For additional light rail service Sarreguemines - Saarbrücken see below main table.
⊡ – Operated by Saarbahn (www.saarbahn.de). In Saarbrücken also serves city centre.
◐ – Every 30 minutes 0716 - 0916 and 1216 - 2116 on Ⓐ, 0816 - 1816 on ⑥, 1216 - 1816 on †.
◧ – Every 30 minutes 0740 - 0840 and 1140 - 2040 on Ⓐ, 0740 - 1740 on ⑥, 1140 - 1740 on †.

STRASBOURG - WISSEMBOURG 396

Additional trains run Strasbourg - Haguenau and v.v.

On Apr. 7 services in this table run as on ⑦. See Table **918** for connecting trains Wissembourg - Neustadt (Weinstr) and v.v.

km			Ⓐ	Ⓐ	Ⓐ ¶	Ⓐ ‡	Ⓐ ¶	Ⓐ ¶	Ⓐ	Ⓐ	Ⓐ	Ⓐ	Ⓐ	Ⓐ	Ⓐ	Ⓐ 🚌	
0	**Strasbourg** d.	Ⓐ	0635	0740	0927	1127	1235	1327	1605	1705	1727	1805	1835	1905	2110	...	...
34	Haguenau a.		0657	0813	0952	1152	1257	1353	1626	1726	1749	1827	1856	1927	2147	2157	...
66	**Wissembourg** a.		0729	0841	1019	1220	1340	1420	1656	1754	1830	1906	1930	2006	...	2234	...

		⑥	⑥	⑥	⑥	⑥	⑥	⑥	⑥
Strasbourg d.	⑥	0705	0757	0927	1128	1235	1327	1605	1727
Haguenau a.		0727	0819	0949	1150	1256	1348	1626	1749
Wissembourg a.		0757	0849	1019	1220	1331	1419	1702	1830

	⑥	⑥			†	†	†	†	†	†	†	
Strasbourg d.	1827	2005	...	†	0827	1127	1327	1627	1727	1814	2012	...
Haguenau a.	1850	2027	...		0848	1148	1348	1648	1748	1835	2033	...
Wissembourg a.	1919	2101	...		0916	1216	1416	1717	1816	1912	2110	...

		Ⓐ	Ⓐ	Ⓐ	Ⓐ	Ⓐ ¶	Ⓐ ‡	Ⓐ ¶	Ⓐ ¶	Ⓐ
Wissembourg d.	Ⓐ	0600	0629	0737	0848	1041	1230	1430	1600	1701
Haguenau d.		0633	0702	0809	0913	1109	1301	1500	1631	1729
Strasbourg a.		0655	0725	0833	0935	1133	1325	1525	1655	1755

	Ⓐ	Ⓐ	Ⓐ			⑥	⑥	⑥	⑥		⑥	⑥	⑥	⑥	⑥	
Wissembourg d.	1800	1836	1936	...	⑥	0601	0725	0906	1043	...	1258	1443	1557	1800	1942	...
Haguenau d.	1830	1903	2003	...		0633	0803	0932	1110	...	1341	1509	1631	1830	2010	...
Strasbourg a.	1855	1925	2025	...		0655	0825	0955	1133	...	1420	1533	1655	1855	2033	...

		†	†	†		†	†	†	†	†
Wissembourg d.	†	0739	0945	1044	...	1301	1444	1647	1839	2037
Haguenau d.		0811	1011	1110	...	1333	1510	1723	1912	2110
Strasbourg a.		0833	1033	1133	...	1355	1533	1745	1933	2133

¶ – Subject to alteration May 2–12.
‡ – Subject to alteration on ②④⑤ May 2–12.

397 PRIVATE TOURIST RAILWAYS

MER DE GLACE - TRAIN DE MONTENVERS

✆ 04.50.53.22.75. www.compagniedumontblanc.fr

From Chamonix (200 metres from SNCF station) to Montenvers 'Mer de Glace' (altitude 1913 metres). Journey time: 20 minutes. Services generally run every 30 minutes (except where shown). A more frequent service (every 20 minutes) is provided during periods of high demand. **2023 service confirmed until April 30.**

A cable car takes visitors to the ice grotto inside the glacier (please check for opening dates).

Dec. 17 - Mar. 17: from Chamonix 1000 - 1600; returning until 1630. See note ⊡.
Mar. 18 - Apr. 30: from Chamonix 1000 - 1630; returning until 1700. See note ⊡.
May 1 - July 8: from Chamonix 0830 - 1630 ‡; returning until 1700.
July 9 - Aug. 28: from Chamonix 0830 - 1700; returning until 1730.
Aug. 29 - Sept. 18: from Chamonix 0830 - 1630 ‡; returning until 1700.
Sept. 19 - Oct. 2: from Chamonix 0930 - 1600; returning until 1630.
Oct. 22 - Nov. 6: from Chamonix 0930 - 1600; returning until 1630.

⊡ – Hourly until 1300; every 30 minutes from 1300.
‡ – Departure from Chamonix at 0900 (also 0930 return service) runs if sufficient demand.

PANORAMIQUE DES DÔMES

Electric rack railway from the foot to the summit of Le puy de Dôme. Journey: 15 minutes. **2023 service**. No service Mar. 20 – 24, Nov. 13 – 17. www.panoramiquedesdomes.fr

Until Mar. 19 (does **not** run on ①②): Hourly departures 1000 - 1700, returning 1030 - 1730.
Mar. 25 - June 30: Departures every 40 minutes 0900 - 1900, returning 0920 - 1920.
July 1 - Aug. 31: Departures every 20 minutes 0900 - 2000, returning 0920 - 2020.
Sept. 1 - Nov. 5: Departures every 40 minutes 0900 - 1900, returning 0920 - 1920.
From Nov. 8 (does **not** run on ①②): Hourly departures 1000 - 1700, returning 1030 - 1730.

TRAMWAY DU MONT BLANC

The highest rack railway in France. www.compagniedumontblanc.fr
✆ 04.50.53.22.75.

Winter: December 17, 2022 - March 26, 2023 (not Mar. 6 – 10, 13 – 17, 20 – 24).
Running dates are subject to confirmation; please confirm locally.
Runs from St Gervais Le Fayet (opposite SNCF station) to Bellevue (altitude 1794 metres). Journey 60 minutes.

Mondays to Fridays until March 3 (not school holidays):
Depart St Gervais: 0830, 1045, 1245 and 1415.
Depart Bellevue: 0935, 1200, 1420 and 1630.

Saturdays and Sundays (also during school holidays):
Depart St Gervais: 0830, 0930, 1045, 1245, 1415 and 1515.
Depart Bellevue: 0935, 1035, 1200, 1345, 1520 and 1630.

Summer: June 11 - September 18, 2022
From St Gervais Le Fayet (opposite SNCF station) to Nid d'Aigle (altitude 2372 metres). Journey 70 – 80 minutes.

June 11 - July 8 and August 29 - September 18
Depart St Gervais: 0820, 0930, 1030¶, 1110, 1230, 1340¶, 1445, 1525.
Depart Nid d'Aigle: 0940, 1050, 1205¶, 1240, 1355, 1505¶, 1615, 1640.

July 9 - August 28:
Depart St Gervais: 0700, 0800, 0910¶, 0945, 1100, 1210¶, 1315, 1355, 1515¶, 1620, 1700.
Depart Nid d'Aigle: 0815, 0920, 1040¶, 1110, 1225, 1330¶, 1450, 1525, 1635¶, 1755, 1815.

¶ – Subject to cancellation (please check locally).

398 PARIS - PARIS AÉROPORTS

See page 31 for plan of central Paris

CHARLES DE GAULLE - PARIS

VAL shuttle train: air terminals - RER / TGV station.

Roissyrail (RER line B): Aéroport Charles de Gaulle 2 TGV - Paris Châtelet les Halles. Frequent service 0450 - 2400.

Journey time from Charles de Gaulle :

Gare du Nord	35 minutes
Châtelet les Halles ★	38 minutes
St Michel Notre Dame	40 minutes
Antony (for Orly , see middle panel)	58 minutes

★ Cross - platform interchange with *RER* for Gare de Lyon.

ORLY - PARIS (*VAL + RER B*)

VAL light rail : Orly Sud - Orly Ouest - Antony (7 minutes). Frequent service ① - ⑤: 0600 - 2230; ⑦: 0700 - 2300. Cross platform interchange with RER line B (below).

RER line B : Antony - Paris. Frequent service 0510 - 0010.

Journey time from Antony :

St Michel Notre Dame	20 minutes
Châtelet les Halles ☆	25 minutes
Gare du Nord	29 minutes

☆ Interchange with *RER* for Gare de Lyon.

ORLY - PARIS (*Orlyrail*)

🚌 : Orly (Ouest and Sud) - Pont de Rungis Aéroport d'Orly station. Frequent shuttle service.

RER line C : Pont de Rungis Aéroport d'Orly - Paris. Every 15 minutes approx. 0500 - 2330 (0530 - 2400 from Paris).

Journey time from Pont de Rungis Aéroport d'Orly :

Paris Austerlitz	24 minutes
St Michel Notre Dame	27 minutes
Musée d'Orsay	31 minutes
Champ de Mars Tour Eiffel	39 minutes

399 🚌 SAVOIE SKI BUSES

Winter 2022 / 2023

A network of bus services links the airports at Genève and Lyon with most ski resorts in the Savoie area during the ski season. A selection of services is shown below but details should be confirmed before booking. Further details of services from Genève can be found on the Genève bus station website www.gare-routiere.com where online bookings can be made; for telephone bookings ✆ +41 22 732 02 30. Bookings can also be made through the websites and offices of the operators and at tourist offices in the ski resorts.

A minimum of one hour should be allowed between aircraft and bus and vice versa. Reservation is recommended or compulsory, and in most cases journeys from the resort to the airport should be confirmed at the local tourist office or bus station (generally 24 or 48 hours in advance) when timings will be given. Most services do not operate on December 25.

🚌 GENÈVE AÉROPORT - ST GERVAIS - CHAMONIX

Departures from Genève Gare Routière and Genève ✈ (Arrivals terminal) to St Gervais (Gare SNCF) and Chamonix Sud (Ave Courmayeur) at least six times daily. Journey 2 hours 10 minutes. Operator: www.ouibus.com. Connections at St Gervais Gare SNCF are available to / from St Gervais (Le Pont), Combloux, Megève, Praz sur Arly and Les Contamines.

🚌 GENÈVE AÉROPORT - TARENTAISE SKI RESORTS

🚌 Genève ✈ (Secteur International) - Moûtiers - Aime - Bourg St Maurice - Tignes - Val d'Isère. Journey approximately 4 hours. Reservations : www.altibus.com

Connections (with through fares) are available to most ski resorts in the area, including Pralognan, Brides les Bains, St Martin de Belleville, Les Ménuires, Val Thorens, Méribel, La Tania, Le Praz, Courchevel, Plagne and Les Arcs. Additional direct services are operated by Voyages Loyet to St Martin de Belleville, Les Ménuires and Val Thorens.

🚌 OTHER SERVICES FROM GENÈVE AÉROPORT ✈

GRENOBLE Daily services to Grenoble. Connections available to l'Alpe d'Huez, Stations de l'Isère, Briancon and Serre Chevalier. Reservations: www.ouibus.com

AVORIAZ via Thonon (connections for Abondance and Châtel), Saint Jean d'Aulps, Morzine. Runs on ⑥ during ski season. Reservations www.sat-autocars.com

LA CLUSAZ via Le Grand Bornand, St Jean de Sixt. Runs on ⑤⑥⑦ during ski season. Reservations www.ballanfat-autocars.fr

For further ski resorts see www.altibus.com

🚌 LYON ✈ / CHAMBÉRY ✈ - SAVOIE SKI RESORTS

Bus services operate from Lyon St Exupéry airport and Chambéry airport to most Savoie ski resorts from late December to mid April. Book on-line at www.altibus.com or ✆ +33 479 68 32 96. Reservations are compulsory, at least 48 hours in advance.

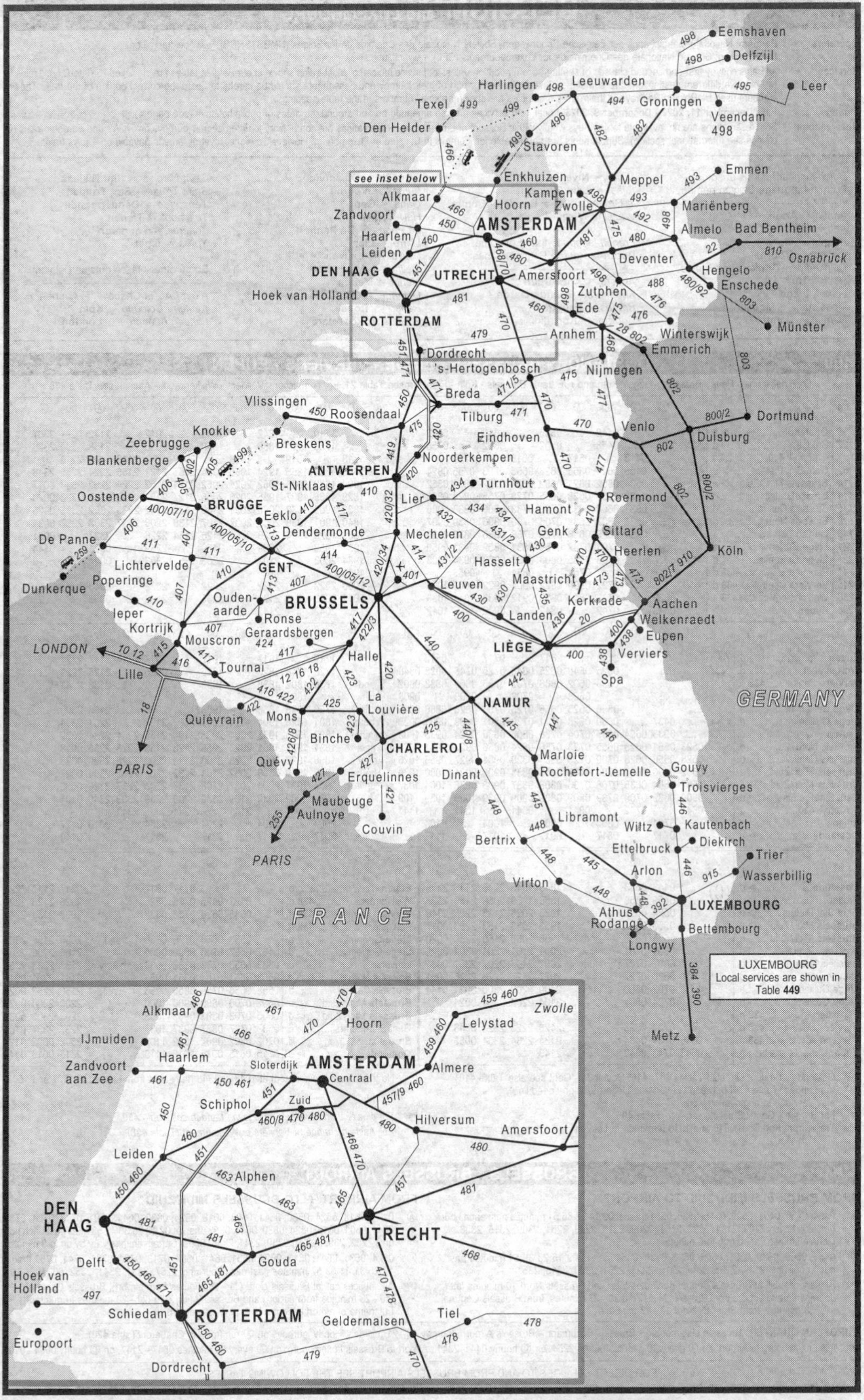
Eemshaven
Delfzijl
Harlingen
Leeuwarden
Groningen
Leer
Texel
Den Helder
Stavoren
Veendam
Enkhuizen
Emmen
Meppel
Mariënberg
Kampen
Zwolle
Alkmaar
Hoorn
Zandvoort
AMSTERDAM
Almelo
Bad Bentheim
Haarlem
Leiden
Osnabrück
DEN HAAG
UTRECHT
Amersfoort
Deventer
Hengelo
Enschede
Hoek van Holland
Zutphen
Ede
Münster
ROTTERDAM
Arnhem
Winterswijk
Emmerich
Dordrecht
's-Hertogenbosch
Nijmegen
Vlissingen
Breda
Roosendaal
Tilburg
Dortmund
Knokke
Breskens
Eindhoven
Venlo
Duisburg
Zeebrugge
Blankenberge
Noorderkempen
ANTWERPEN
Oostende
St-Niklaas
Turnhout
BRUGGE
Lier
Roermond
Eeklo
Hamont
De Panne
Dendermonde
Mechelen
Genk
Sittard
Heerlen
Köln
Lichtervelde
GENT
Hasselt
Dunkerque
Poperinge
Leuven
Maastricht
Oudenaarde
BRUSSELS
Kerkrade
Ieper
Aachen
Kortrijk
Ronse
Landen
Welkenraedt
Geraardsbergen
Eupen
Mouscron
LONDON
LIÈGE
Verviers
Halle
Lille
Tournai
Spa
GERMANY
La Louvière
NAMUR
Quiévrain
Mons
Binche
CHARLEROI
Marloie
Gouvy
Rochefort-Jemelle
PARIS
Quévy
Troisvierges
Erquelinnes
Dinant
Maubeuge
Aulnoye
Libramont
Wiltz
Kautenbach
Couvin
Bertrix
Diekirch
Ettelbruck
PARIS
Trier
Arlon
Wasserbillig
Virton
FRANCE
Athus
Rodange
LUXEMBOURG
Bettembourg
Longwy
LUXEMBOURG
Local services are shown in Table 449
Metz
see inset below
Alkmaar
Hoorn
Lelystad
Zwolle
IJmuiden
Haarlem
Zandvoort aan Zee
Sloterdijk
AMSTERDAM
Centraal
Almere
Schiphol
Zuid
Hilversum
Amersfoort
Leiden
Alphen
DEN HAAG
UTRECHT
Delft
Gouda
Hoek van Holland
Schiedam
ROTTERDAM
Geldermalsen
Tiel
Europoort
Dordrecht

BELGIUM and LUXEMBOURG

Operators: **Belgium**: Nationale Maatschappij der Belgische Spoorwegen / Société Nationale des Chemins de fer Belges (NMBS / SNCB). www.belgianrail.be
Luxembourg: Société Nationale des Chemins de fer Luxembourgeois (CFL). www.cfl.lu

Services: All trains convey first and second classes of seating accommodation unless otherwise indicated. Most trains shown in our Belgian tables are classified *IC* (InterCity). Trains for two or more different destinations are sometimes linked together for part of their journey and passengers should be careful to board the correct portion of the train. The line numbers used by Belgian Railways in their public timetables are shown as small numbers in the table headings.

Timings: Valid **December 11, 2022 - December 9, 2023**. Local train services may be amended on and around the dates of public holidays (see page 4).

Reservations: Seat reservations are not available for journeys wholly within Belgium or Luxembourg. Reservations are compulsory for international journeys on *Thalys* and *Eurostar* trains (for timings see International section). Supplements are not payable for journeys in Belgium or Luxembourg. However, a higher level of fares is payable on *Thalys* trains.

Dutch-language forms of some **French-language** Belgian names

Aarlen = **Arlon**
Aat = **Ath**
Bergen = **Mons**
Doornik = **Tournai**
Duinkerke = **Dunkerque** (France)
Hoei = **Huy**
Luik = **Liège**
Moeskroen = **Mouscron**
Namen = **Namur**
Nijvel = **Nivelles**
Rijsel = **Lille** (France)
's Gravenbrakel = **Braine le Comte**
Wezet = **Visé**

French-language forms of some **Dutch-language** Belgian names

Anvers = **Antwerpen**
Audenarde = **Oudenaarde**
Bruges = **Brugge**
Courtrai = **Kortrijk**
Dixmude = **Diksmuide**
Furnes = **Veurne**
Gand = **Gent**
Hal = **Halle**
La Panne = **De Panne**
Lierre = **Lier**
Louvain = **Leuven**
Malines = **Mechelen**
Menin = **Menen**
Ostende = **Oostende**
Renaix = **Ronse**
Roulers = **Roeselare**
Saint Nicolas = **Sint Niklaas**
Saint Trond = **Sint Truiden**
Termonde = **Dendermonde**
Tirlemont = **Tienen**
Tongres = **Tongeren**
Ypres = **Ieper**

Some other places outside Belgium

Aken / Aix la Chapelle = **Aachen**
Keulen / Cologne = **Köln**
Londen / Londres = **London**

400 OOSTENDE - BRUSSELS - LIÈGE - VERVIERS - EUPEN

Lines 50a, 36, 37

For *Thalys* trains Paris - Brussels - Liège - Köln and *ICE* trains Brussels - Köln - Frankfurt see Table **21**. For connections Verviers - Welkenraedt - Aachen see Table **438**

km																									
			Ⓐ	Ⓐ	Ⓐ	Ⓐ	Ⓐ	Ⓐ	Ⓐ	Ⓐ	Ⓐ		Ⓐ	Ⓐ	Ⓐ	Ⓐ	Ⓐ	Ⓐ	Ⓐ	Ⓐ	Ⓐ	Ⓐ	Ⓐ	Ⓐ	
										⊡												△		△	
0	**Oostende** ▶ d.	Ⓐ	...	...	0442	...	0536	...	0636	...	0742		...	1740	...	1842	...	1942	...	2042	...	2142	...	2307	...
22	Brugge ▷ d.		...	...	0458	...	0552	...	0652	...	0758		...	1756	...	1858	...	1958	...	2058	...	2158	...	2323	...
	Kortrijk **410** d.		...	0418	|	0517	|	0618	|	0717	|	and	1718	|	1819	|	1918	|	2018	|	2118	|	2218	|	...
62	Gent Sint-Pieters ▷ d.		...	0455	0524	0555	0623	0655	0723	0755	0824	at	1755	1824	1855	1924	1955	2024	2055	2124	2155	2224	2255	2348	...
114	**Brussels** Midi / Zuid ▷ a.		...	0524	0552	0624	0652	0724	0752	0824	0852	the	1824	1852	1924	1952	2024	2052	2124	2152	2224	2252	2324	0017	...
114	**Brussels** Midi / Zuid d.		...	0526	0555	0628	0655	0728	0755	0828	0855	same	1828	1855	1927	1955	2026	2055	2127	2157	2228	2257	2328	0020	...
116	Brussels Central d.		...	0531	0600	0633	0700	0733	0800	0833	0900	minutes	1833	1900	1932	2000	2031	2100	2132	2202	2233	2302	2333	0025	...
118	Brussels Nord d.		...	0537	0607	0639	0706	0739	0806	0839	0907	past	1840	1907	1938	2007	2037	2107	2138	2208	2237	2308	2337	0031	...
148	Leuven d.		...	0554	0625	0658	0726	0758	0826	0858	0926	each	1859	1926	1954	2026	2054	2126	2154	2226	...	2327	...	0051	...
221	**Liège** Guillemins a.		...	...	0701	0732	0759	0831	0859	0931	0959	hour	1931	1959	...	2059	...	2159	...	2259	...	0021	...	0144	...
221	**Liège** Guillemins d.		...	...	0703	0735	0803	0836	0903	0934	1003	until	1934	2003	...	2103	...	2203	...	2303	...	0024	...	...	...
241	Pepinster **438** d.		...	...	|	0752	|	0854	|	0953	|		1953	|	...	|	...	|	...	|	...	|	...	...	...
245	**Verviers** Central **438** d.		...	...	0722	0800	0822	0901	0922	1000	1022		2000	2022	...	2122	...	2222	...	2322	...	0043	...	...	...
258	Welkenraedt **438** a.		0636	...	0733	0812	0833	0912	0933	1011	1033		2011	2033	...	2133	...	2233	...	2333	...	0053	...	...	...
264	**Eupen** a.		0643	...	0742	...	0842	...	0942	...	1042		...	2042	...	2142	...	...	...	...	...	...	...	...	...

		Ⓐ	Ⓐ	Ⓐ	Ⓐ	Ⓐ	Ⓐ	Ⓐ	Ⓐ	Ⓐ	Ⓐ	Ⓐ		Ⓐ	Ⓐ	Ⓐ	Ⓐ	Ⓐ	Ⓐ	Ⓐ	Ⓐ	Ⓐ	Ⓐ		
			△									⊙											△		
Eupen d.	Ⓐ	...	...	...	...	...	0617	...	0717	...	0812	...		1717	...	1817	...	1917	...	2017	...	2117	2221	...	...
Welkenraedt **438** d.		...	...	...	0525	0548	0625	0648	0725	0746	0825	0848		1725	1748	1825	...	1925	...	2025	...	2125	2229	...	...
Verviers Central **438** d.		...	...	...	0538	0602	0638	0702	0738	0803	0838	0902	and	1738	1802	1838	...	1938	...	2038	...	2138	2241	...	...
Pepinster **438** d.		...	...	...	|	0608	|	0708	|	0809	|	0908	at	|	1808	|	...	|	...	|	...	|	|	...	...
Liège Guillemins a.		...	...	...	0556	0625	0656	0725	0756	0826	0856	0925	the	1756	1825	1856	...	1956	...	2056	...	2156	2300	...	...
Liège Guillemins d.		...	0437	...	0600	0628	0701	0730	0801	0829	0901	0928	same	1801	1828	1901	...	2001	...	2101	...	2201	2304	...	...
Leuven d.		...	0533	0604	0635	0704	0736	0806	0836	0904	0933	1003	minutes	1833	1903	1933	2004	2035	2104	2135	2204	2234	2359	...	...
Brussels Nord d.		0523	0551	0623	0655	0723	0756	0824	0856	0922	0951	1021	past	1851	1921	1951	2023	2055	2123	2155	2223	2255	0018	...	...
Brussels Central d.		0528	0556	0628	0700	0728	0801	0829	0901	0927	0956	1026	each	1856	1926	1956	2028	2100	2128	2200	2228	2300	0023	...	...
Brussels Midi / Zuid a.		0532	0600	0632	0704	0732	0805	0833	0905	0931	1000	1030	hour	1900	1930	2000	2032	2104	2132	2204	2232	2304	0027	...	...
Brussels Midi / Zuid ▷ d.		0537	0604	0635	0708	0736	0808	0837	0908	0936	1004	1037	until	1904	1937	2004	2037	2108	2137	2208	2237	2308	0030	...	...
Gent Sint-Pieters ▷ d.		0609	0639	0709	0739	0809	0839	0909	0939	1009	1039	1109		1939	2009	2039	2109	2139	2209	2239	2309	2340	0101	...	...
Kortrijk **410** a.		0641	|	0742	|	0841	|	0941	|	1041	|	1141		|	2041	|	2141	|	2241	|	2341	|	|	...	...
Brugge ▷ d.		...	0704	...	0804	...	0904	...	1004	...	1104	...		2004	...	2104	...	2204	...	2304	...	0010	0127	...	...
Oostende ▶ a.		...	0717	...	0817	...	0917	...	1017	...	1117	...		2017	...	2117	...	2217	...	2317	...	0023	0140	...	...

		Ⓒ	Ⓒ	Ⓒ		Ⓒ	Ⓒ	Ⓒ	Ⓒ	Ⓒ	
									△	△
Oostende ▶ d.	Ⓒ	...	0443	0543		1843	1943	2043	2143	2308
Brugge ▷ d.		...	0459	0559		1859	1959	2059	2159	2323
Gent Sint-Pieters ▷ d.		...	0524	0625		1925	2025	2125	2225	2348
Brussels Midi / Zuid ▷ a.		...	0553	0653		1953	2053	2153	2253	0017
Brussels Midi / Zuid d.		...	0556	0656	and	1956	2056	2156	2256	0020
Brussels Central d.		...	0601	0701		2001	2101	2201	2301	0025
Brussels Nord d.		...	0607	0707	hourly	2007	2107	2207	2307	0031
Leuven d.		...	0626	0727		2027	2127	2226	2326	0051
Liège Guillemins a.		...	0702	0800	until	2100	2200	2300	0021	0144
Liège Guillemins d.		...	0704	0804		2104	2204	2304	0024	...
Pepinster **438** d.		...	|	|		|	|	|	|	...
Verviers Central **438** d.		...	0723	0823		2123	2223	2323	0043	...
Welkenraedt **438** a.		0636	0734	0834		2134	2234	2334	0053	...
Eupen a.		0643	0743	0843		2143	...	...	...	...

	Ⓒ	Ⓒ	Ⓒ	Ⓒ	Ⓒ		Ⓒ	Ⓒ	Ⓒ
	△								△
Eupen d.	...	...	...	0717	0817		2017	2117	2221
Welkenraedt **438** d.	...	0522	0625	0725	0825		2025	2125	2229
Verviers Central **438** d.	...	0535	0638	0738	0838		2038	2138	2241
Pepinster **438** d.	...	|	|	|	|		|	|	|
Liège Guillemins a.	...	0553	0656	0756	0856	and	2056	2156	2300
Liège Guillemins d.	0437	0557	0700	0800	0900		2100	2200	2304
Leuven d.	0533	0633	0733	0833	0933	hourly	2133	2233	2359
Brussels Nord d.	0553	0651	0751	0851	0951		2151	2251	0018
Brussels Central d.	0558	0656	0756	0856	0956	until	2156	2256	0023
Brussels Midi / Zuid a.	0602	0700	0800	0900	1000		2200	2300	0027
Brussels Midi / Zuid ▷ d.	0605	0703	0803	0903	1003		2203	2303	0030
Gent Sint-Pieters ▷ d.	0637	0737	0837	0937	1037		2237	2337	0101
Brugge ▷ d.	0702	0802	0902	1002	1102		2302	0002	0127
Oostende ▶ a.	0715	0815	0915	1015	1115		2315	0015	0140

▶ – Oostende - Brugge: see also Tables **407**, **410**; Oostende - Gent see also Table **410**.
△ – Via Landen (Table **430**) between Leuven and Liège (not high-speed line). May vary due to engineering work.
▷ – For Brugge - Gent - Brussels see also Table **405**.
⊡ – Trains from Kortrijk at 0816 and 1018 terminate at Leuven.
⊙ – No trains from Welkenraedt at 1048 or 1348 (they start from Leuven at 1207 and 1503).

☛ *For slower trains Brussels - Liège via Landen see Table **430**.*
*For Aachen change at Verviers or Welkenraedt (Table **438**).*

401 BRUSSELS - BRUSSELS AIRPORT ✈

Line 36c

FROM BRUSSELS MIDI / ZUID TO AIRPORT ✈

Ⓐ: 0404, 0436, 0451, 0509, 0515, 0536, 0551 then at 09 14 23 36 51 minutes past each hour until 2051 then 2109, 2114, 2123, 2151, 2209, 2215, 2223, 2251, 2309, 2315, 2323. Certain timings vary by up to 3 minutes.

Ⓒ: 0451, 0509, 0539, 0551, 0609, 0623, 0639, 0651 then at 09 15 23 39 51 minutes past each hour until 2139, 2151, 2209, 2215, 2223, 2251, 2309, 2315, 2351.

☛ All services call at Brussels Central 4 minutes later and Brussels Nord 10 minutes later. Journey time to airport: from Brussels Midi / Zuid 20 – 27 minutes, from Brussels Centraal 16 – 23 minutes, from Brussels Nord 10 – 17 minutes.

FROM AIRPORT ✈ TO BRUSSELS MIDI / ZUID

Ⓐ: 0431, 0513, 0524, 0530, 0541, 0603, 0613, 0624, 0630, 0641, 0701, 0713, 0724, 0730, 0741, 0801, 0813, 0824, 0830, 0841, 0853 then at 02 13 25 30 41 53 mins past each hour until 2253, 2302, 2324, 2330, 2341, 2348, 0002. Certain timings vary by up to 3 minutes.

Ⓒ: 0524, 0531, 0541, 0613, 0624, 0631, 0641, 0657, 0713, 0724, 0731, 0741, 0757 then at 13 25 31 41 53 57 minutes past each hour until 2257, 2331, 2341, 2352, 0031.

☛ All services call at Brussels Nord (11 – 18 minutes from airport), Brussels Centraal (16 – 23 minutes from airport) and Brussels Midi / Zuid (21 – 28 minutes from airport). Full name of airport is Brussels Airport - Zaventem.

EUROPEAN QUARTER: Brussels Luxembourg - Brussels Schumann - Brussels Airport. Journey 18 – 21 minutes. Hourly journeys on Ⓐ run from / to Charleroi (Table **420**).
Brussels Luxembourg to Airport: on Ⓐ every 30 minutes 0654 – 2254, on Ⓒ hourly 0441 – 2341. Airport to Brussels Luxembourg: on Ⓐ every 30 minutes 0547 – 2147, on Ⓒ hourly 0604 – 0104.

FOR DIRECT SERVICES TO AND FROM BRUSSELS AIRPORT SEE THE FOLLOWING TABLES:
Aalst **412**, Antwerpen **420** / **432**, Brugge **405**, Charleroi **420**, Denderleeuw **412**, Gent **405**, Hasselt **432**, Kortrijk **407**, Leuven **430** / **432**, Mechelen **432**, Mons **422**, Namur **440**, Tournai **417**.

ZEEBRUGGE - BRUGGE 402

Line 50a

km			Ⓐ	Ⓐ	Ⓐ	Ⓐ		Ⓐ	Ⓐ	Ⓐ	Ⓐ	Ⓐ				Ⓒ	Ⓒ	Ⓒ		Ⓒ	Ⓒ	Ⓒ	
0	Zeebrugge Strand ❦ d.	Ⓐ	...	...	...	...	and	...	...	...	...	...	...	...	Ⓒ	0807	0907	1007	and	1807	1907	2007	...
0	Zeebrugge Dorp ❦ d.		0708	0808	0908	1008	hourly	1608	1708	1808	1908	2008	...	...		|	|	|	hourly	|	|	|	...
15	Brugge a.		0724	0824	0924	1024	until	1624	1724	1824	1924	2024	...	...		0824	0924	1024	until	1824	1924	2024	...

		Ⓐ	Ⓐ	Ⓐ	Ⓐ		Ⓐ	Ⓐ	Ⓐ	Ⓐ	Ⓐ	Ⓐ				Ⓒ	Ⓒ	Ⓒ		Ⓒ	Ⓒ	Ⓒ	
Brugge d.	Ⓐ	0636	0736	0836	0936	and	1436	1536	1636	1736	1836	1936	...	...	Ⓒ	0736	0836	0936	and	1736	1836	1936	...
Zeebrugge Dorp ❦ a.		0652	0752	0852	0952	hourly	1452	1552	1652	1752	1852	1952	...	...		|	|	|	hourly	|	|	|	...
Zeebrugge Strand ❦ a.		...	...	...	...	until	...	...	...	...	...	...	...	...		0753	0853	0953	until	1753	1853	1953	...

❦ – On certain high summer dates during July and August trains on Ⓐ serve Zeebrugge Strand (not Zeebrugge Dorp). Please enquire locally.

☛ Most trains continue beyond Brugge as stopping services to Gent (not shown). Change at Brugge for Brussels and faster service to Gent (Tables **400**/**405**).

KNOKKE and BLANKENBERGE - BRUGGE - GENT - BRUSSELS 405

Line 50a

For additional trains Brugge - Gent - Brussels see Table **400**. For Brugge - Gent (- Antwerpen) see Table **410**.

km			Ⓐ	Ⓐ	Ⓐ	Ⓐ ◧	Ⓐ		Ⓐ	Ⓐ	Ⓐ	Ⓐ		Ⓒ	Ⓒ	Ⓒ	Ⓒ	Ⓒ	Ⓒ		Ⓒ	Ⓒ	Ⓒ n
0	**Knokke** d.	Ⓐ	...	...	...	0506	...	and	2006	...	2121	2221	Ⓒ	...	...	...	...	0707	...	and	2007	...	2221
•	Blankenberge d.		...	...	...	|	0551	at	|	2051	|	|		...	...	...	...	|	0754	at	|	2054	|
22	Brugge a.		...	...	...	0527	0602	the	2028	2102	2143	2243		...	...	...	...	0728	0805	the	2028	2105	2242
22	Brugge d.		0406	0431	0508	0531	0606	same	2031	2108	...	...		0509	0609	...	0709	0731	0809	same	2031	2109	...
62	**Gent** Sint-Pieters d.		0439	0500	0539	0600	0636	minutes	2100	2139	...	...		0540	0640	0703	0740	0803	0840	minutes	2103	2140	...
119	**Brussels** Midi / Zuid a.		0508	0529	0607	0629	0705	past	2129	2207	...	...		0608	0708	0731	0808	0831	0908	past	2131	2208	...
121	Brussels Central a.		0515	0540	0615	0640	0714	each	2140	2215	...	...		0616	0716	0743	0816	0843	0916	each	2143	2216	...
123	Brussels Nord a.		0520	0545	0620	0645	0719	hour	2145	2220	...	...		0621	0721	0748	0821	0848	0921	hour	2148	2221	...
135	**Brussels Airport** ✈ a.		▽	0559	▽	0657	▽	until	2157	▽	...	...		▽	▽	0802	▽	0902	▽	until	2202	▽	...

		Ⓐ n	Ⓐ	Ⓐ ❦	Ⓐ		Ⓐ	Ⓐ	Ⓐ	Ⓐ	Ⓐ	Ⓐ	Ⓐ		Ⓒ n	Ⓒ n	Ⓒ	Ⓒ		Ⓒ	Ⓒ	Ⓒ	Ⓒ
Brussels Airport ✈ d.	Ⓐ	...	▽	0603	▽	and	2003	▽	2103	▽	2203	▽	2302	Ⓒ	...	...	0657	▽	and	2057	▽	▽	▽
Brussels Nord d.		...	0540	0615	0640	at	2015	2040	2115	2140	2215	2240	2315		...	...	0712	0740	at	2112	2140	2240	2340
Brussels Central d.		...	0545	0620	0645	the	2020	2045	2120	2145	2220	2245	2320		...	...	0717	0745	the	2117	2145	2245	2345
Brussels Midi / Zuid d.		...	0553	0629	0653	same	2029	2053	2129	2153	2229	2253	2327		...	...	0727	0752	same	2127	2152	2252	2352
Gent Sint-Pieters d.		...	0625	0702	0727	minutes	2102	2125	2202	2225	2302	2325	0003		...	...	0803	0823	minutes	2203	2223	2324	0030
Brugge a.		...	0651	0730	0753	past	2130	2151	2230	2251	2330	2351	0030		...	...	0830	0848	past	2230	2249	2350	0056
Brugge d.		0633	0655	0733	0757	each	2133	2155	2233	...	...	...	...		0733	0753	0833	0853	each	2233	2253	...	...
Blankenberge a.		|	0706	|	0808	hour	|	2206	|	...	...	...	...		|	0804	|	0905	hour	|	2304	...	...
Knokke a.		0653	...	0753	...	until	2153	...	2253	...	...	...	...		0753	...	0853	...	until	2253	...	...	...

n – An additional journey runs one hour earlier.

▽ – To / from Leuven, Hasselt / Genk (Table **430**).

• – Blankenburg - Brugge: *15 km*.

◧ – No journeys on Ⓐ at 1006, 1106 (local trains run Knokke to Brugge at 1006, 1105).

❦ – 0701Ⓐ, 1203Ⓐ and 1303Ⓐ from Brussels Airport require a change at Brugge for Knokke.

KNOKKE - OOSTENDE - DE PANNE (Coastal Tramway) 406

De Lijn 'Kusttram'

KNOKKE railway station - **OOSTENDE** railway station *Journey 65 minutes*

Ⓐ: 0445, 0545, 0645, 0715, 0735, 0755, 0825, 0840, 0855, 0910, 0925, and every 15 minutes until 1800, 1815, 1830, 1845, 1900, 1920, 1945, 2002, 2024, 2124, 2224, 2324.

Ⓒ: 0445⑥, 0545, 0645, 0715, 0755⑥, 0825, 0840⑥, 0855, 0910, 0925, 0940, 0955, 1010 and every 15 minutes until 1845, 1900, 1920, 1940, 2002, 2024, 2124, 2224, 2324.

Calls at Heist (+6 minutes), Zeebrugge (+13 minutes), Blankenberge (+25 minutes).

OOSTENDE railway station - **DE PANNE** railway station *Journey 79 minutes*

Ⓐ: 0452, 0552, 0652, 0707, 0727, 0740, 0752, 0822, 0842, 0902, 0917, 0932, 0947, 1002, 1017 and every 15 minutes until 1832, 1902, 1932, 2027, 2127, 2227, 2327.

Ⓒ: 0452⑥, 0552⑥, 0652, 0707⑥, 0727, 0740⑥, 0752, 0822, 0842, 0902, 0917, 0932, 0947, 1002 and every 15 minutes until 1837, 1907, 1937, 2007, 2027, 2127, 2227, 2327.

Calls at Middelkerke (+23 minutes), Nieuwpoort (+41 minutes), Koksijde (+60 minutes).

DE PANNE railway station - **OOSTENDE** railway station *Journey 79 minutes*

Ⓐ: 0419, 0519, 0619, 0716, 0734, 0816, 0831, 0846, 0901 and every 15 minutes until 1701, 1716, 1731, 1746, 1819, 1836, 1854, 1909, 1924, 1949, 2014, 2114, 2214, 2314.

Ⓒ: 0419⑥, 0519⑥, 0619, 0716, 0734⑥, 0816, 0831, 0846⑥, 0901 and every 15 minutes until 1701, 1716, 1731, 1746, 1803, 1819, 1836, 1854, 1909, 1924, 1944, 2014, 2114, 2214, 2314.

Calls at Koksijde (+19 minutes), Nieuwpoort (+38 minutes), Middelkerke (+56 minutes).

OOSTENDE railway station - **KNOKKE** railway station *Journey 65 minutes*

Ⓐ: 0452, 0532, 0552, 0632, 0652, 0712, 0732, 0752, 0812, 0832, 0852, 0915, 0937, 0952, 1007, 1022 and every 15 minutes until 1907, 1937, 2007, 2037, 2127, 2227, 2327.

Ⓒ: 0452⑥, 0532⑥, 0632⑥, 0652, 0732, 0752, 0812, 0832, 0852, 0915, 0937, 0952, 1007, 1022 and every 15 minutes until 1852, 1907, 1937, 2007, 2037, 2127, 2227, 2327.

A change of tram may be necessary at Oostende. In July and August trams run every 10 minutes during the day.

Connections with rail services are available at Knokke (Table **405**), Zeebrugge (Table **402**), Blankenberge (Table **405**), Oostende (Tables **400/07/10**) and De Panne (Table **411**).

OOSTENDE - BRUGGE - KORTRIJK - BRUSSELS 407

Lines 66, 89

For direct trains Oostende - Brugge - Brussels via Gent (also Kortrijk - Gent - Brussels) see Table **400**. For direct trains Brugge - Brussels - Brussels Nationaal ✈ see Table **405**.

km			Ⓐ	Ⓐ	Ⓐ	Ⓐ	Ⓐ	Ⓐ	Ⓐ	Ⓐ	Ⓐ	Ⓐ		Ⓐ	Ⓐ	Ⓐ		Ⓒ	Ⓒ	Ⓒ	Ⓒ		Ⓒ	Ⓒ
0	**Oostende** ▷ d.	Ⓐ	...	...	...	...	0558	...	...	0657	0758	0858		1958	2058	2158	Ⓒ	...	...	...	0648		1948	2148
22	Brugge ▷ d.		...	...	...	...	0616	...	...	0716	0816	0916		2016	2116	2216		...	...	...	0705		2005	2205
39	Torhout d.		...	...	...	...	0632	...	...	0732	0832	0932		2032	2132	2232		...	...	...	0721		2021	2221
44	Lichtervelde § d.		...	...	...	...	0637	...	...	0737	0837	0937		2037	2137	2237		...	...	...	0735		2035	2235
52	Roeselare d.		...	...	...	...	0644	...	...	0745	0844	0944	and	2044	2144	2244		...	...	...	0743	and	2043	2243
73	**Kortrijk** a.		...	...	...	...	0705	...	...	0805	0905	1005		2105	2205	2305		...	...	...	0803		2103	2303
73	**Kortrijk** d.		0512	0543	0611	0643	0711	0744	0812	0816	0911	1011	hourly	2111	2211	...		0511	0611	0711	0811	hourly	2111	...
98	Oudenaarde d.		0533	0603	0632	0703	0732	0803	0833	|	0933	1033		2133	2233	...		0531	0631	0731	0831		2131	...
115	Zottegem d.		0547	0617	0645	0717	0745	0818	0847	◇	0947	1047	until	2147	2247	...		0547	0647	0747	0847	until	2147	...
136	Denderleeuw d.		0605	0639	0705	0739	0804	0837	0905	|	1005	1105		2205	2305	...		0605	0705	0805	0905		2205	...
158	**Brussels** Midi / Zuid a.		0620	0656	0720	0756	0819	0853	0920	0924	1020	1120		2220	2320	...		0620	0720	0820	0920		2220	...
160	Brussels Central a.		0627	0705	0727	0805	0826	0900	0927	0932	1027	1127		2227	2327	...		0627	0727	0827	0927		2227	...
162	Brussels Nord a.		0632	0710	0732	0810	0831	0905	0932	0937	1032	1132		2232	2332	...		0632	0732	0832	0932		2232	...
174	**Brussels Airport** ✈ a.		0647	...	0747	...	0847	...	0947	...	1047	1147		2247	2347	...		0646	0746	0846	0946		2246	...

		Ⓐ	Ⓐ	Ⓐ	Ⓐ		Ⓐ	Ⓐ	Ⓐ	Ⓐ	Ⓐ	Ⓐ	Ⓐ	Ⓐ		Ⓐ		Ⓒ	Ⓒ		Ⓒ	Ⓒ	Ⓒ	Ⓒ
Brussels Airport ✈ d.	Ⓐ	...	...	0513	0613		1613	1713	1813	...	1913	2013	2113	2213	...	...	Ⓒ	...	0613		1913	2013	2113	2213
Brussels Nord d.		...	...	0527	0627		1627	1727	1827	1921	1927	2027	2127	2227	...	2319		...	0627		1927	2027	2127	2227
Brussels Central d.		...	...	0532	0632		1632	1732	1832	1926	1932	2032	2132	2232	...	2323		...	0632		1932	2032	2132	2232
Brussels Midi / Zuid d.		...	...	0539	0639		1639	1739	1839	1937	1939	2039	2139	2242	...	2329		...	0639		1939	2039	2139	2239
Denderleeuw d.		...	...	0558	0658		1658	1758	1858	|	1958	2058	2158	2303	...	2348		...	0659		1959	2059	2159	2259
Zottegem d.		...	...	0615	0715	and	1715	1815	1915	◇	2015	2115	2215	2319	...	0015		...	0715	and	2015	2115	2215	2315
Oudenaarde d.		...	...	0630	0731		1732	1832	1932	|	2032	2132	2232	2333	...	0030		...	0731		2031	2131	2231	2331
Kortrijk a.		...	...	0647	0749	hourly	1749	1849	1949	2041	2049	2151	2249	2351	...	...		...	0749	hourly	2049	2149	2249	2349
Kortrijk d.		0455	0555	0655	0755		1755	1855	1955	2055	...	2155	...	...	...	...		0657	0757		2057	2157	...	...
Roeselare d.		0517	0617	0717	0817	until	1817	1917	2017	2117	...	2217	...	...	...	...		0718	0818	until	2118	2218	...	...
Lichtervelde § d.		0524	0624	0724	0824		1824	1924	2024	2125	...	2224	...	...	...	...		0735	0835		2135	2235	...	...
Torhout d.		0529	0629	0729	0829		1829	1929	2029	2130	...	2229	...	...	...	...		0740	0840		2140	2240	...	...
Brugge ▷ a.		0544	0644	0744	0844		1844	1944	2044	2146	...	2245	...	...	...	...		0755	0855		2156	2255	...	...
Oostende ▷ a.		0602	0702	0802	0902		1904	2002	2102	2202	...	2302	...	...	...	...		0811	0911		2211	2311	...	...

◇ – Via Gent (Table **400**). To Leuven / from Welkenraedt.

▷ – See also Tables **400** and **410**.

§ – On Ⓒ trains arrive 10 minutes earlier.

ADDITIONAL TRAINS *Journey 47 minutes*

Brugge - Kortrijk: Ⓐ hourly 0557 - 2257; Ⓒ every 2 hours 0737 - 1937.

Kortrijk - Brugge: Ⓐ hourly 0516 - 2116; Ⓒ every 2 hours 0635 - 2035.

410 POPERINGE - KORTRIJK - GENT - ANTWERPEN

Lines 69, 75, 59

km		Ⓐ	Ⓐ	Ⓐ	Ⓐ				Ⓐ										Ⓐ	Ⓐ	Ⓐ			
0	**Poperinge** d.	...	0407	...	...	0507	...		...	1909	...	2007	...	2107	...	2207	...		0549	0649	0735	...	...	...
10	Ieper d.	...	0415	...	...	0515	...		...	1917	...	2015	...	2115	...	2215	...		0558	0658	0743	...	...	...
23	Comines / Komen d.	...	0425	...	...	0525	...	and	...	1927	...	2025	...	2125	...	2225	...		0608	0708	0753	...	...	...
32	Menen d.	...	0435	...	...	0535	...	at	...	1937	...	2035	...	2135	...	2235	...		0619	0719	0802	...	...	...
43	**Kortrijk** a.	...	0450	...	...	0550	...	the	...	1952	...	2050	...	2150	...	2250	...	A	0633	0736	0817	...	...	...
43	**Kortrijk** d.	...	0458	...	...	0558	...	same	...	1959	...	2058	...	2158	...	2258	...	L	0640	0740	...	...	...	...
	Oostende ▷ d.	...	|	...	...	|	0610	minutes	...	|	2010	|	2110	|	2210	|	...	S	|	|	...	...	...	...
	Brugge ▷ d.	...	|	...	△	|	0625	past	△	|	2025	|	2125	|	2225	|	...	O	|	|	...	...	...	...
85	**Gent** Sint-Pieters ▷ a.	...	0524	...	0607	0624	0649	each	2007	2024	2049	2124	2149	2224	2249	2324	...		0711	0811	...	...	...	...
85	**Gent** Sint-Pieters d.	0427	0527	0553	0611	0627	0653	hour	2011	2027	2053	2127	2153	2227	2253	2327	...		0716	0815	...	...	...	...
112	Lokeren d.	0449	0549	0615	0633	0649	0715	until	2033	2049	2115	2149	2215	2249	2315	2349	...		▽	▽	...	...	...	...
125	Sint-Niklaas d.	0500	0600	0626	0644	0700	0726		2044	2100	2126	2200	2226	2300	2326	2400	...		...	...	...	...	...	...
148	Antwerpen Berchem a.	0517	0617	0648	0703	0717	0748		2103	2117	2148	2217	2248	2317	2348	0017	...		...	...	...	...	...	...
151	**Antwerpen** Centraal a.	0523	0623	0654	0709	0723	0754		2109	2123	2154	2223	2254	2323	2354	0023	...		...	...	...	...	...	...

	Ⓐ					Ⓐ			Ⓐ				Ⓐ				Ⓐ	Ⓒ			Ⓐ	Ⓐ	Ⓐ	
Antwerpen Centraal d.	0437	0506	0537	0606	0637	0649	0706	0737	0751		2006	2037	2051	2106	2137	2237	2337	2337	...		...	...	...	...
Antwerpen Berchem d.	0442	0512	0543	0612	0643	0654	0712	0743	0756		2012	2043	2056	2112	2143	2243	2343	2343	...		...	...	...	...
Sint-Niklaas d.	0502	0536	0602	0636	0702	0715	0736	0802	0817	and	2036	2102	2117	2136	2202	2302	0002	0002	...		...	...	...	...
Lokeren d.	0512	0546	0612	0646	0712	0725	0746	0812	0828	at	2046	2112	2128	2146	2212	2312	0012	0012	...		...	▽	▽	...
Gent Sint-Pieters a.	0533	0606	0633	0706	0733	0749	0807	0833	0850	the	2107	2133	2149	2207	2233	2333	0033	0033	...	A	...	1638	1744	...
Gent Sint-Pieters ▷ d.	0536	0609	0636	0710	0736	0753	0810	0836	0853	same	2110	2136	2152	2210	2236	2336	...	0039	...	L	...	1641	1748	...
Brugge ▷ a.	|	0635	|	0735	|	△	0835	|	△	minutes	2135	|	△	2235	|	|	...	|	...	S	...	|	|	...
Oostende ▷ a.	|	0650	|	0750	|	...	0850	|	...	past	2150	|	...	2250	|	|	...	|	...	O	...	|	|	...
Kortrijk a.	0601	...	0701	...	0801	...	...	0901	...	each	...	2201	...	...	2301	0011	...	0113	...		...	1711	1819	...
Kortrijk d.	0604	...	0708	...	0810	...	...	0910	...	hour	...	2210	...	...	2310	...	...	...	...		1641	1719	1822	...
Menen d.	0619	...	0723	...	0825	...	...	0925	...	until	...	2225	...	...	2327	...	...	...	...		1656	1736	1838	...
Comines / Komen d.	0629	...	0733	...	0835	...	...	0935	...		...	2235	...	...	2337	...	...	...	...		1705	1747	1849	...
Ieper d.	0639	...	0743	...	0845	...	...	0945	...		...	2245	...	...	2347	...	...	...	...		1715	1757	1859	...
Poperinge a.	0647	...	0751	...	0853	...	...	0953	...		...	2253	...	...	2354	...	...	...	...		1722	1805	1907	...

ADDITIONAL TRAINS KORTRIJK - GENT

		Ⓐ§		Ⓐ§		Ⓒ		Ⓒ
Kortrijk d.	Ⓐ	0418	hourly	2218	Ⓒ	0523	hourly	2223
Gent Sint-Pieters a.		0451	until	2251		0554	until	2254

		Ⓐ§		Ⓐ§		Ⓒ		Ⓒ
Gent Sint-Pieters d.	Ⓐ	0609	hourly	2309	Ⓒ	0606	hourly	2306
Kortrijk a.		0641	until	2341		0637	until	2337

△ – From / to De Panne (Table **411**).
▽ – To / from Brussels (Table **400**).
▷ – See also Table **400** (also **407** Oostende - Brugge).
§ – Most journeys continue to / from Brussels (Table **400**).
☛ *Between Kortrijk and Antwerpen most trains are attached to Lille - Kortrijk - Antwerpen trains (Table **415**).*

411 DE PANNE - LICHTERVELDE - GENT

Line 73

km			Ⓐ		Ⓐ ◧		Ⓒ △		Ⓒ △
0	**De Panne** § d.	Ⓐ	0452		1852	Ⓒ	0552		2052
5	Veurne d.		0501	and	1901		0601	and	2101
20	Diksmuide d.		0513		1913		0613		2113
39	Lichtervelde d.		0530	hourly	1930		0630	hourly	2130
56	Tielt d.		0542		1943		0642		2142
86	**Gent** Sint-Pieters a.		0607	until	2007		0707	until	2207
	Antwerpen **410** a.		0709		2109		|		|
	Brussels Midi / Zuid a.		...		...		0812		2312
	Brussels Airport ✈ a.		...		...		0835		2335

		Ⓐ ◐		Ⓐ		Ⓒ △		Ⓒ △
Brussels Airport ✈ d.	Ⓐ	...		...	Ⓒ	0524		2025
Brussels Midi / Zuid d.		...		...		0548		2048
Antwerpen **410** d.		0649	and	2051		|	and	|
Gent Sint-Pieters d.		0753		2152		0653		2153
Tielt d.		0819	hourly	2219		0719	hourly	2219
Lichtervelde d.		0832		2232		0732		2232
Diksmuide d.		0849	until	2249		0749	until	2249
Veurne d.		0901		2301		0801		2301
De Panne § a.		0908		2308		0808		2308

△ – To / from Leuven or Landen (Table **430**). Runs Gent - Brussels and v.v. via Aalst (Table **412**).
◧ – Also De Panne - Gent at 1952Ⓐ, 2052Ⓐ.
◐ – Also Gent - De Panne at 0553Ⓐ, 0653Ⓐ.
§ – De Panne railway station is situated in Adinkerke. Connection available with the coastal tramway (Table **406**).

412 GENT - AALST - DENDERLEEUW - BRUSSELS

Line 50

For direct trains Gent - Brussels see Tables **400** and **405**

km		Ⓐ	Ⓐ △	Ⓐ		△		Ⓐ	Ⓒ	△
0	**Gent** Sint-Pieters d.	0441	0512	0540	0541	0612	and at	2141	2141	2226
28	Aalst d.	0513	0543	0613	0612	0643	the same	2213	2212	|
35	Denderleeuw d.	0523	0553	0623	0625	0653	minutes	2223	2223	2254
58	**Brussels** Midi / Zuid a.	0541	0611	0641	0642	0711	past	2241	2242	2312
60	Brussels Central a.	0548	0617	0648	0649	0718	each	2248	2249	2318
62	Brussels Nord a.	0553	0622	0653	0654	0723	hour	2253	2254	2323
74	**Brussels Airport** ✈ a.	⊡	0635	⊡	...	0736	until	⊡	...	2335

	Ⓐ △	Ⓐ	Ⓒ	△	Ⓐ		Ⓒ	△	Ⓐ
Brussels Airport ✈ d.	0524	⊡	...	0624	⊡	and at	...	2224	⊡
Brussels Nord d.	0537	0607	0606	0637	0707	the same	2206	2237	2307
Brussels Central d.	0541	0612	0610	0641	0712	minutes	2210	2241	2312
Brussels Midi / Zuid d.	0549	0619	0618	0649	0719	past	2218	2249	2319
Denderleeuw d.	0609	0639	0642	0709	0739	each	2242	2309	2339
Aalst d.	0619	0648	0651	0719	0748	hour	2251	2319	2349
Gent Sint-Pieters a.	0648	0719	0719	0747	0818	until	2319	2347	0020

△ – To / from Leuven or Landen (Table **430**). On Ⓒ most journeys run from / to De Panne (Table **411**).
⊡ – To / from Hasselt or Tongeren (Table **431**).

413 EEKLO - GENT - OUDENAARDE - RONSE

Line 86

km			Ⓐ		Ⓐ‡		Ⓒ		Ⓒ	⑥‡
0	**Eeklo** d.	Ⓐ	0510		2011	Ⓒ	0711	and hourly	1911	2011
27	**Gent** St-Pieters a.		0545	and	2045		0745	on ⑥,	1945	2045
27	**Gent** St-Pieters d.		0557	hourly	2057		0757	every two	1957	2057
52	Oudenaarde a.		0627	until	2127		0827	hours on †	2027	2127
52	Oudenaarde d.		0633	△	2135		0835	until	2035	2135
66	**Ronse** a.		0644		2146		0846		2046	2146

		Ⓐ		Ⓐ		Ⓒ		Ⓒ	⑥§
Ronse d.	Ⓐ	0514		2014	Ⓒ	0714	and hourly	1914	2014
Oudenaarde a.		0525	and	2025		0725	on ⑥,	1925	2025
Oudenaarde d.		0533	hourly	2033		0733	every two	1933	2033
Gent St-Pieters a.		0603	until	2103		0803	hours on †	2003	2103
Gent St-Pieters d.		0615	▽	2115		0815	until	2015	2115
Eeklo a.		0649		2149		0849		2049	2149

△ – Also Gent - Ronse at 1728Ⓐ, 1828Ⓐ.
▽ – Also Ronse - Gent at 0547Ⓐ, 0645Ⓐ, 2114Ⓐ, 2214Ⓐ.
‡ – Also Eeklo - Gent - Oudenaarde at 2111, 2211Ⓐ.
§ – Also Ronse - Gent at 2114Ⓒ.

414 GENT - MECHELEN - LEUVEN

Line 53

For Mechelen - Leuven via Brussels Nationaal ✈ see Table **432**

km			Ⓐ	Ⓐ	Ⓐ	Ⓐ	Ⓐ	Ⓐ	Ⓐ		Ⓐ	Ⓐ	Ⓐ	Ⓐ	Ⓐ
0	**Gent** St-Pieters d.	Ⓐ	0421	...	...	0521	0557	...	0619	and at the same	2057	...	2121	2157	2257
30	Dendermonde d.		0500	0524	...	0600	0624	...	0700	minutes	2124	...	2200	2224	2320
57	Mechelen d.		0528	0548	0622	0628	0648	0722	0728	past each	2148	2222	2228	2253	...
82	**Leuven** a.		...	0613	0653	...	0713	0753	...	hour until	2213	2253	...	2317	...

		Ⓒ	Ⓒ	Ⓒ	Ⓒ		Ⓒ	Ⓒ	Ⓒ
Gent St-Pieters d.	Ⓒ	...	0657	...	0757	and at the same	...	2157	...
Dendermonde d.		...	0728	...	0828	minutes	...	2228	...
Mechelen d.		0735	0754	0835	0854	past each	2235	2254	2335
Leuven a.		0804	...	0904	...	hour until	2304	...	0004

		Ⓐ	Ⓐ	Ⓐ	Ⓐ	Ⓐ	Ⓐ	Ⓐ		Ⓐ	Ⓐ	Ⓐ	Ⓐ
Leuven d.	Ⓐ	0506	0547	...	0606	0647	...	0706	and at the same	2147	...	2206	2247
Mechelen d.		0538	0615	0631	0638	0715	0731	0738	minutes	2215	2231	2238	2315
Dendermonde d.		...	0639	0702	...	0740	0802	...	past each	2239	2302	...	2336
Gent St-Pieters a.		...	0703	0740	...	0804	0840	...	hour until	2303	2340	...	...

		Ⓒ	Ⓒ	Ⓒ	Ⓒ	Ⓒ		Ⓒ	Ⓒ	Ⓒ	Ⓒ
Leuven d.	Ⓒ	...	...	0654	...	0754	and at the same	...	2054	2154	2254
Mechelen d.		0606	0706	0723	0806	0823	minutes	2106	2123	2223	2323
Dendermonde d.		0634	0734	...	0834	...	past each	2134	...	...	...
Gent St-Pieters a.		0701	0802	...	0902	...	hour until	2202	...	...	...

LILLE - MOUSCRON - KORTRIJK 415

Line 75

See Table **410** for connecting trains Kortrijk - Gent - Antwerpen and v.v. **Warning!** Lille - Mouscron is subject to alteration on French and Belgian public holidays

km		Ⓐ	⚒	⚒	Ⓐ					Ⓐ		Ⓒ	Ⓐ	Ⓒ	⑥	Ⓑ		Ⓐ	†	⚒					
0	**Lille** Flandres ▷ d.	0627	0709	0809	0830	0909	1009	1109	1209	1227	1309	1403	1409	1509	1603	1609	1709	1727	1803	1809	1909	2009	2109	2209	...
10	Roubaix ▷ d.	0637	0723	0823	0840	0919	1019	1119	1219	1240	1319	1417	1419	1519	1617	1619	1723	1737	1817	1822	1919	2019	2119	2219	...
12	Tourcoing 🏨 ▷ d.	0641	0727	0827	0844	0924	1024	1124	1224	1244	1324	1422	1424	1524	1622	1624	1727	1741	1822	1827	1924	2024	2124	2224	...
18	Mouscron a.	...	0733	0833	...	0929	1029	1129	1229	...	1329	1427	1430	1530	1627	1630	1733	...	1827	1832	1930	2029	2129	2229	...
18	Mouscron **417** d.	...	0736	0836	...	0936	1036	1136	1236	...	1336	1436	1436	1536	1636	1636	1736	...	1833	1836	1936	2036	2136	2236	...
30	**Kortrijk** **417** a.	...	0745	0845	...	0945	1045	1145	1245	...	1345	1445	1445	1545	1645	1646	1745	...	1845	1845	1945	2045	2145	2245	...
	Gent Sint-P. **410** a.	...	...	...	...	...	...	...	...	...	...	...	...	...	...	...	...	...	...	...	...	...	...	...	...
	Antwerpen **410** a.	...	...	...	...	...	...	...	...	...	...	...	...	...	...	...	...	...	...	...	...	...	...	...	...

	⚒	Ⓐ	⚒		Ⓐ					Ⓐ						Ⓐ									
Antwerpen **410** d.	...	...	...	...	...	...	...	...	...	...	...	...	...	...	...	...	...	...	...	...	...	...	...	...	...
Gent Sint-P. **410** d.	...	...	...	...	...	...	...	...	...	...	...	...	...	...	...	...	...	...	...	...	...	...	...	...	...
Kortrijk **417** d.	0613	...	0713	0813	...	0913	1002	1113	1213	...	1313	1401	1513	1613	1713	...	1813	1913	2013	2113	...	...	...	...	...
Mouscron **417** a.	0623	...	0723	0824	...	0923	1023	1123	1223	...	1323	1423	1523	1623	1723	...	1823	1923	2023	2123	...	...	...	...	...
Mouscron d.	0630	...	0727	0827	...	0930	1030	1130	1230	...	1327	1430	1530	1630	1727	...	1827	1930	2030	2130	...	...	...	...	...
Tourcoing 🏨 ▷ d.	0637	0720	0733	0833	0916	0937	1037	1137	1237	1320	1333	1437	1537	1637	1733	1816	1833	1937	2037	2137	...	...	...	...	...
Roubaix ▷ d.	0641	0724	0737	0837	0920	0941	1041	1141	1241	1324	1337	1441	1541	1641	1737	1821	1837	1941	2041	2141	...	...	...	...	...
Lille Flandres ▷ a.	0651	0733	0751	0851	0929	0951	1051	1151	1251	1333	1351	1451	1551	1651	1751	1830	1851	1951	2051	2151	...	...	...	...	...

▷ – Frequent services Lille Flandres - Lille Europe - Roubaix/Tourcoing are operated by the Lille *VAL* métro (Line 2) or by tram.

LILLE - TOURNAI - MONS 416

Lines 78, 118

km			Ⓐ	Ⓐ	Ⓐ d	Ⓐ	Ⓐ d	Ⓐ	Ⓐ	Ⓐ	Ⓐ	Ⓐ	Ⓐ	Ⓐ	Ⓐ	Ⓐ	Ⓐ	Ⓐ	Ⓐ	Ⓐ	Ⓐ	Ⓐ	Ⓐ	Ⓐ	Ⓐ
0	**Lille** Flandres § d.	Ⓐ	...	0601	...	0708	...	0729	*0808*	*0908*	*1008*	...	*1208*	*1308*	...	*1508*	*1608*	*1708*	1732	*1808*	*1908*	*2008*	...	...	2208
	Mouscron **417** d.		0522	|	0622	|	0717	|	|	|	|	...	|	|	...	|	|	|	|	|	|	|	...	...	|
25	**Tournai** **417** a.		0539	0630	0639	0739	0733	0755	*0837*	*0936*	*1036*	...	*1237*	*1336*	...	*1536*	*1636*	*1736*	1805	*1836*	*1937*	*2036*	...	...	2236
25	**Tournai** d.		0543	...	0643	...	0743	...	0843	0943	1043	1143	1243	1343	1443	1543	1643	1743	...	1843	1943	2043	2143	2223	...
64	Saint-Ghislain d.		0603	...	0703	...	0802	...	0903	1003	1103	1203	1303	1403	1503	1603	1703	1803	...	1903	2003	2104	2203	2253	...
73	**Mons** a.		0613	...	0713	...	0813	...	0913	1013	1113	1213	1313	1413	1513	1613	1713	1813	...	1913	2013	2113	2214	2308	...
	Charleroi Sud **425** a.		0647	...	0747	...	0847	...	0947	1047	1147	1247	1347	1447	1547	1647	1747	1847	...	1947	2047	2147	2247	...	...
	Namur **425** a.		0722	...	0822	...	0922	...	1022	1122	1222	1322	1422	1522	1622	1722	1822	1922	...	2022	2122	2222	2322	...	...

		Ⓐ	Ⓐ	Ⓐ	Ⓐ	Ⓐ	Ⓐ	Ⓐ	Ⓐ	Ⓐ	Ⓐ	Ⓐ	Ⓐ	Ⓐ	Ⓐ	Ⓐ	Ⓐ k	Ⓐ	Ⓐ k	Ⓐ	Ⓐ	Ⓐ	Ⓐ	Ⓐ	Ⓐ
Namur **425** d.	Ⓐ	...	...	...	0538	...	0638	0738	0838	0938	1038	1138	1238	1338	1438	...	1538	...	1638	...	1738	1838	1938	2038	2138
Charleroi Sud **425** d.		...	...	...	0614	...	0714	0814	0914	1014	1114	1214	1314	1414	1514	...	1614	...	1714	...	1814	1914	2014	2114	2214
Mons d.		0450	...	0550	0646	...	0746	0846	0946	1046	1146	1246	1346	1446	1546	...	1646	...	1746	...	1846	1946	2046	2146	2246
Saint-Ghislain d.		0504	...	0604	0656	...	0756	0856	0956	1056	1156	1256	1356	1456	1556	...	1656	...	1757	...	1857	1956	2056	2156	2256
Tournai a.		0533	...	0633	0715	...	0815	0915	1015	1115	1215	1315	1415	1515	1615	...	1715	...	1818	...	1918	2015	2115	2215	2321
Tournai **417** d.		...	0622	*0644*	0722	0805	*0822*	*0922*	*1022*	*1122*	*1222*	*1322*	...	*1522*	*1622*	1649	1719	1723	1826	1822	*1923*	*2021*	*2121*	...	...
Mouscron **417** a.		...	|	|	|	|	|	|	|	|	|	|	...	|	|	|	1736	|	1843	|	|	|	|	...	...
Lille Flandres § a.		...	0652	*0719*	0752	0832	*0852*	*0952*	*1052*	*1152*	*1252*	*1352*	...	*1552*	*1652*	1722	...	1752	...	1852	*1952*	*2052*	*2152*	...	...

		Ⓒ	Ⓒ	Ⓒ		Ⓒ	Ⓒ	Ⓒ	
Mouscron **417** d.	Ⓒ	0613	0713	0813		2013	2113	2213	...
Tournai **417** d.		0629	0729	0829	and	2029	2129	2229	...
Saint-Ghislain d.		0658	0758	0858	hourly	2058	2158	2258	...
Mons a.		0712	0812	0912	until	2112	2212	2312	...
Charleroi Sud **425** a.		0751	0851	0951		2151	2251	...	...
Namur **425** a.		0830	0930	1030		2230	2330	...	...
Liège Guillemins **442** a.		0917	1017	1117		2317	...	...	...

		Ⓒ	Ⓒ	Ⓒ	Ⓒ		Ⓒ	Ⓒ	
Liège Guillemins **442** d.	Ⓒ	...	...	0640	0740		1940	2040	...
Namur **425** d.		...	0629	0729	0829	and	2029	2129	...
Charleroi Sud **425** d.		0609	0709	0808	0908	hourly	2108	2208	...
Mons d.		0648	0748	0848	0948	until	2148	2248	...
Saint-Ghislain d.		0702	0802	0902	1002		2202	2301	...
Tournai **417** a.		0730	0830	0930	1030		2230	2330	...
Mouscron **417** a.		0746	0846	0946	1046		2246	2346	...

		⑥	⑥	Ⓒ		Ⓒ	Ⓒ	Ⓒ	
Lille Flandres § d.	Ⓒ	0653	0749	0849	hourly	1953	2053	2153	...
Tournai a.		0721	0821	0921	until	2021	2121	2221	...

		⑥	⑥	Ⓒ		Ⓒ	Ⓒ	Ⓒ	
Tournai d.	Ⓒ	0636	0736	0836	hourly	1936	2036	2144	...
Lille Flandres § a.		0704	0809	0904	until	2004	2104	2213	...

d – From Kortrijk (depart 0608 and 0705).
k – To Kortrijk (arrive 1749 and 1854).

§ – 🏨 between Lille and Tournai = Blandain.

KORTRIJK - MOUSCRON - TOURNAI - BRUSSELS - SINT NIKLAAS 417

Lines 94, 60

For direct trains Kortrijk - Brussels see Table **400** (via Gent) and Table **407** (via Oudenaarde)

km			Ⓐ	Ⓐ	Ⓐ	Ⓐ	Ⓐ	Ⓐ	Ⓐ	Ⓐ	Ⓐ	Ⓐ	Ⓐ	Ⓐ	Ⓐ		Ⓐ	Ⓐ	Ⓐ		Ⓒ		Ⓒ
0	**Kortrijk** **415** d.	Ⓐ	...	...	...	...	...	...	...	...	0638	...	...	0739	...		2038	...	2138	Ⓒ	...		...
13	Mouscron **415/6** d.		...	...	...	...	0549	0607	...	...	0649	0706	...	0751	...		2049	...	2149		...		...
32	**Tournai** **416** d.		0444	0509	0544	0557	0609	0627	0644	0657	0709	0727	0744	0810	0844	and	2109	2144	2209		0544		2244
50	Leuze d.		0456	0522	0556	0610	0622	0639	0656	0710	0722	0739	0756	0822	0856	at	2122	2156	2222		0557		2257
62	Ath d.		0507	0533	0607	0621	0633	0650	0707	0721	0733	0750	0807	0833	0907	the	2133	2207	2233		0609	and	2308
100	Halle d.		0537	0603	0637	|	0703	|	0737	|	0803	|	0837	0902	0937	same	2203	2237	2303		0637		2337
116	**Brussels** Midi/Zuid a.		0548	0613	0648	0700	0715	0728	0748	0800	0815	0828	0848	0914	0948	minutes	2215	2248	2315		0648	hourly	2348
116	**Brussels** Midi/Zuid d.		0551	0617	0651	0702	0718	0730	0751	0802	0818	0830	0853	0917	0951	past	2218	2251	2318		0651		2351
118	Brussels Central d.		0556	0622	0656	0707	0723	0735	0756	0807	0823	0835	0858	0922	0956	each	2223	2256	2323		0656	until	2356
120	Brussels Nord d.		0604	0629	0704	0713	0729	0739	0802	0813	0829	0839	0905	0929	1004	hour	2229	2304	2329		0704		0004
132	**Brussels Airport** ✈ a.		0624	|	0724	n	|	...	0824	n	|	...	0924	|	1024	until	|	2324	|		0724		0024
154	Dendermonde a.		...	0656	...	...	0756	...	...	...	0856	...	...	0956	...		2256	...	0012		...		...
168	Lokeren **410** a.		...	0721	...	...	0821	...	...	...	0921	...	...	1021	...		2321	...	...		...		...
181	**Sint-Niklaas** **410** a.		...	0736	...	...	0836	...	...	...	0936	...	...	1036	...		2336	...	...		...		...

		Ⓐ	Ⓐ	Ⓐ	Ⓐ	Ⓐ		Ⓐ	Ⓐ	Ⓐ	Ⓐ	Ⓐ	Ⓐ	Ⓐ		Ⓐ	Ⓐ	Ⓐ	Ⓐ		Ⓒ		Ⓒ
Sint-Niklaas **410** d.	Ⓐ	...	...	0524	...	0624		...	1924	...	2024	...	2124	2224		...	...	...	...	Ⓒ	...		...
Lokeren **410** d.		...	...	0539	...	0639		...	1939	...	2039	...	2139	2239		...	...	...	...		...		...
Dendermonde d.		...	...	0603	...	0703	and	...	2003	...	2103	...	2203	2303		...	...	...	...		...		...
Brussels Airport ✈ d.		...	0541	|	0641	|	at	1941	|	2041	|	2141	|	|		n	...	n	...		0541		2241
Brussels Nord d.		...	0601	0633	0701	0732	the	2001	2034	2101	2133	2201	2233	2333	A	1549	1616	1649	1717		0600	and	2300
Brussels Central d.		...	0606	0638	0706	0737	same	2006	2039	2106	2138	2206	2238	2338	L	1554	1621	1654	1722		0605		2305
Brussels Midi/Zuid a.		...	0610	0642	0710	0741	minutes	2010	2043	2110	2142	2210	2242	2342	S	1558	1625	1658	1726		0609	hourly	2309
Brussels Midi/Zuid d.		0513	0613	0647	0713	0747	past	2013	2047	2113	2147	2213	2247	2347	O	1600	1627	1700	1728		0613		2313
Halle d.		0524	0624	0658	0724	0758	each	2024	2058	2124	2158	2224	2258	2358		|	|	|	|		0624	until	2324
Ath d.		0553	0653	0729	0753	0829	hour	2053	2129	2153	2226	2253	2329	0026		1640	1706	1740	1806		0654		2354
Leuze d.		0602	0702	0738	0802	0838	until	2102	2138	2202	...	2302	2338	...		1649	1716	1749	1815		0703		0003
Tournai **416** d.		0615	0715	0753	0815	0853		2115	2152	2215	...	2315	2350	...		1702	1730	1802	1830		0715		0016
Mouscron **415/6** d.		...	...	0812	...	0912		...	2211	...	...	...	...	...		...	1750	...	1850		...		...
Kortrijk **415** a.		...	...	0822	...	0922		...	2220	...	...	...	...	...		...	...	...	...		...		...

n – To/from Namur and Liège via Brussels Luxembourg (Table **440**).

419 ROOSENDAAL - ESSEN - ANTWERPEN
Line 12

km			Ⓐ	Ⓐ ♡	Ⓐ	Ⓐ ♡	Ⓐ	Ⓐ ♡	Ⓐ		Ⓐ ♡	Ⓐ	Ⓐ	Ⓐ		Ⓒ b	Ⓒ b	Ⓒ b		Ⓒ b	Ⓒ
0	**Roosendaal** d.	Ⓐ	...	...	0620	...	0720	...	...	and at the		...	2220	2320	Ⓒ	...	0720	0820	and	2120	2220
8	Essen 🏛 d.		0505	0546	0631	0646	0731	0746	0805	same minutes	2046	2146	2231	2331		0631	0731	0831	hourly	2131	2231
26	Kapellen d.		0522	0606	0651	0706	0751	0806	0823	past each	2106	2206	2251	2351		0651	0751	0851	until	2151	2251
41	**Antwerpen** Centraal a.		0537	0622	0710	0722	0810	0822	0841	hour until	2122	2222	2310	0010		0720	0818	0918		2218	2314

		Ⓐ ♡	Ⓐ	Ⓐ	Ⓐ ♡	Ⓐ	Ⓐ		Ⓐ ♡	Ⓐ	Ⓐ ♡	Ⓐ	Ⓐ ♡		Ⓒ	Ⓒ	Ⓒ b		Ⓒ b	Ⓒ b	Ⓒ b
Antwerpen Centraal d.	Ⓐ	0537	0550	0619	0638	0650	0719	and at the	2038	2050	2138	2150	2238	Ⓒ	0546	0646	0742	and	2142	2242	2342
Kapellen d.		0555	0609	0637	0656	0709	0737	same minutes	2056	2109	2156	2209	2256		0609	0709	0809	hourly	2209	2309	0009
Essen 🏛 d.		0613	0631	0655	0713	0731	0755	past each	2113	2131	2213	2231	2313		0631	0731	0831	until	2231	2329	0029
Roosendaal a.		...	0639	...	...	0739	...	hour until	...	2139	...	2233	...		0638	0739	0839		2239	...	...

b – To / from Antwerpen Berchem.
♡ – To / from Brussels (Table **420**); most continue to / from Charleroi.

420 BREDA - ANTWERPEN - BRUSSELS - CHARLEROI
Lines 25, 124

For *Thalys* services Paris - Brussels - Antwerpen - Amsterdam see Table **18**. For additional trains Antwerpen - Brussels Nationaal ✈ see Table **432**.

km			Ⓐ	Ⓐ	Ⓐ	Ⓐ	Ⓐ ♡	Ⓐ	Ⓐ	Ⓐ ♡	Ⓐ ♡	Ⓐ	Ⓐ ♥	Ⓐ ♡	Ⓐ ♡	△	Ⓐ	Ⓐ ♥	Ⓐ ♡	Ⓐ	Ⓐ	Ⓐ ♥	Ⓐ	Ⓐ
0	**Breda** 🏛 d.	Ⓐ	...	...	...	...	...	...	...	...	...	...	0742	...	...		...	2042	...	...	...	2142	...	...
33	Noorderkempen (Brecht) d.		...	...	...	...	...	...	0700	...	...	...	0801	...	...		...	2101	...	...	...	2201	...	...
57	**Antwerpen** Centraal a.		...	...	...	...	...	...	0717	...	...	...	0816	...	...	and	...	2116	...	...	...	2216	...	...
57	**Antwerpen** Centraal 432 d.		0454	...	0554	0625	0654	0708	0719	0725	0754	0808	0819	0825	0854	at	2106	2119	2125	2154	2205	2219	2225	2254
59	Antwerpen Berchem d.		0459	...	0559	0630	0659	0713	0724	0730	0759	0813	0825	0830	0859	the	2111	2125	2130	2159	2210	2225	2230	2259
81	Mechelen 432 d.		0514	...	0614	0644	0714	0735	0739	0744	0814	0835	0839	0844	0914	same	2133	2139	2144	2214	2247	2239	2244	2314
	Brussels Airport ✈ 432 a.		|	...	|	|	|	|	0751	|	|	|	0850	|	|	minutes	|	2150	|	|	|	2250	|	|
101	Brussels Nord d.		0532	0602	0632	0702	0732	0756	...	0802	0832	0856	0908	0902	0932	past	2154	2208	2202	2232	2317	2308	2302	2332
103	Brussels Central d.		0537	0607	0637	0707	0737	0801	...	0807	0837	0901	0913	0907	0937	each	2159	2213	2207	2237	2321	2313	2307	2337
105	**Brussels** Midi / Zuid a.		0541	0611	0641	0711	0741	0805	...	0811	0841	0905	0917	0911	0941	hour	2203	2217	2211	2241	2325	2317	2311c	2341
105	**Brussels** Midi / Zuid d.		0545	0615	0645	0715	0745	...	...	0815	0845	...	...	0915	0945	until	...	...	2215	2245	2332	...	...	...
134	Nivelles d.		0610	0641	0710	0741	0810	...	...	0841	0910	...	...	0941	1010		...	...	2241	2310	|	...	...	...
160	**Charleroi** Sud a.		0636	0707	0736	0807	0836	...	...	0907	0936	...	...	1007	1036		...	...	2307	2336	0027	...	...	...

	Ⓐ	Ⓐ ♡	Ⓐ ♥	Ⓐ					Ⓒ	Ⓒ	Ⓒ	Ⓒ	Ⓒ	Ⓒ	Ⓒ	Ⓒ ♥	Ⓒ		Ⓒ	Ⓒ ♥	Ⓒ	Ⓒ	Ⓒ ♥	
Breda 🏛 d.	...	...	2242	...	...	...	...	Ⓒ	...	...	...	...	...	...	...	0742	...		...	2142	...	...	2242	...
Noorderkempen (Brecht) d.	...	...	2300	...	...	...	...		...	...	...	...	...	...	...	0801	...		...	2201	...	...	2301	...
Antwerpen Centraal a.	...	...	2316	...	...	...	...		...	...	...	...	...	...	...	0816	...	and	...	2216	...	...	2316	...
Antwerpen Centraal 432 d.	2305	2325	2319	0005	...	...	...		...	0540	0609	0640	0709	0740	0809	0819	0840	at	2209	2219	2240	2309	2319	...
Antwerpen Berchem d.	2310	2330	2325	0010	...	...	...		...	0545	0614	0645	0714	0745	0814	0825	0845	the	2214	2225	2245	2314	2325	...
Mechelen 432 d.	2347	2344	2338	0047	...	...	...		...	0603	0632	0703	0732	0803	0832	0839	0903	same	2232	2239	2303	2332	2339	...
Brussels Airport ✈ 432 a.	|	|	2352	|	...	...	...		...	|	|	|	|	|	|	0850	|	minutes	|	2250	|	|	2350	...
Brussels Nord d.	0013	0002	|	|	...	...	...		0555	0624	0655	0724	0755	0824	0855	0907	0924	past	2255	2307	2324	2355	0006	...
Brussels Central d.	0017	0007	|	|	...	...	...		0600	0627	0700	0727	0800	0828	0900	0912	0928	each	2300	2312	2328	2400	0011	...
Brussels Midi / Zuid a.	0021	0011c	0017	0120	...	...	...		0604	0632	0704	0732	0803	0832	0904	0916	0932	hour	2304	2316	2332	0004	0015	...
Brussels Midi / Zuid d.	0024	...	...	...	...	...	...		0607	...	0707	...	0806	...	0907	...	...	until	2307	...	...	...	...	...
Nivelles d.	|	...	...	...	...	...	...		0631	...	0731	...	0831	...	0931	...	...		2331	...	...	...	...	...
Charleroi Sud a.	0122	...	...	...	...	...	...		0658	...	0758	...	0858	...	0958	...	...		2358	...	...	...	...	...

		Ⓐ ♡	Ⓐ	Ⓐ ⊡	Ⓐ ♥	Ⓐ ♡	Ⓐ	Ⓐ	Ⓐ ♥	Ⓐ ♡	Ⓐ	Ⓐ	Ⓐ ♥	Ⓐ ♡		Ⓐ ♥	Ⓐ ♡	Ⓐ	Ⓐ	Ⓐ ♥	Ⓐ ♡	Ⓐ	Ⓐ ♡	Ⓐ
Charleroi Sud d.	Ⓐ	...	...	0425	...	...	...	0524	...	0553	...	0624	...	0653		...	1853	...	1924	...	1953	2024	2053	2124
Nivelles d.		...	...	0456	...	...	...	0551	...	0620	...	0651	...	0720		...	1920	...	1951	...	2020	2051	2120	2151
Brussels Midi / Zuid a.		...	...	0535	...	...	...	0616	...	0645	...	0716	...	0745	and	...	1945	...	2016	...	2045	2116	2145	2216
Brussels Midi / Zuid d.		0449	0519	0538	0545	0549	0556	0619	0645	0649	0659	0718	0744	0747	at	1945	1949	1956	2019	2045	2049	2119	2149	2219
Brussels Central d.		0454	0524	0542	0550	0554	0601	0624	0650	0654	0704	0723	0749	0752	the	1950	1954	2001	2024	2050	2054	2124	2154	2224
Brussels Nord d.		0502	0530	0549	0556	0602	0608	0630	0656	0702	0710	0730	0756	0802	same	1956	2002	2008	2030	2056	2102	2132	2202	2230
Brussels Airport ✈ 432 d.		|	|	|	0611	|	|	|	0711	|	|	|	0811	|	minutes	2011	|	|	|	2111	|	|	|	|
Mechelen 432 d.		0518	0546	0616	0624	0618	0629	0646	0724	0718	0731	0746	0824	0818	past	2024	2018	2029	2046	2124	2118	2148	2218	2246
Antwerpen Berchem d.		0531	0559	0651	0638	0631	0649	0659	0738	0731	0752	0759	0838	0831	each	2038	2031	2049	2059	2138	2131	2201	2231	2300
Antwerpen Centraal 432 a.		0535	0603	0655	0642	0635	0653	0703	0742	0735	0756	0803	0842	0835	hour	2042	2035	2053	2103	2142	2135	2205	2235	2304
Antwerpen Centraal d.		...	...	...	0644	...	...	...	0744	...	...	...	0844	...	until	2044	...	...	...	2144	...	...	...	...
Noorderkempen (Brecht) d.		...	...	...	0701	...	...	...	0801	...	...	...	0901	...		2101	...	...	...	2201	...	...	...	...
Breda 🏛 a.		...	...	...	0718	...	...	...	0818	...	...	...	0918	...		2118	...	...	...	2218	...	...	...	...

	Ⓐ	Ⓐ	Ⓐ	Ⓐ					Ⓒ ♥	Ⓒ	Ⓒ	Ⓒ ♥	Ⓒ	Ⓒ		Ⓒ ♥	Ⓒ	Ⓒ	Ⓒ	Ⓒ	Ⓒ	Ⓒ	⑥ ⊡	
Charleroi Sud d.	2153	...	2224	...	...	...	...	Ⓒ	...	0505	...	...	0605	...		...	2005	...	2105	...	2205	...	...	...
Nivelles d.	2220	...	2251	...	...	...	...		...	0532	...	...	0632	...		...	2032	...	2132	...	2232	...	2304	...
Brussels Midi / Zuid a.	2245	...	2317	...	...	...	...		...	0556	...	...	0656	...	and	...	2056	...	2156	...	2257	...	2341	...
Brussels Midi / Zuid d.	2249	2256	2319	2356	...	...	...		0544	0559	0627	0644	0659	0727	at	2044	2059	2127	2159	2227	2259	2327	2343	...
Brussels Central d.	2254	2301	2324	0001	...	...	...		0549	0604	0631	0649	0704	0731	the	2049	2104	2131	2204	2231	2304	2331	2347	...
Brussels Nord d.	2302	2308	2328	0008	...	...	...		0556	0610	0638	0656	0710	0738	same	2056	2110	2138	2210	2238	2310	2338	2353	...
Brussels Airport ✈ 432 d.	|	|	...	|	...	...	...		0611	|	|	0711	|	|	minutes	2111	|	|	|	|	|	|	|	...
Mechelen 432 d.	2318	2329	...	0029	...	...	...		0624	0630	0659	0724	0730	0759	past	2124	2130	2159	2230	2259	2330	2359	0020	...
Antwerpen Berchem d.	2331	2349	...	0049	...	...	...		0638	0647	0716	0738	0747	0816	each	2138	2147	2216	2247	2316	2347	0016	0051	...
Antwerpen Centraal 432 a.	2335	2353	...	0053	...	...	...		0642	0651	0720	0742	0751	0820	hour	2142	2151	2220	2251	2320	2351	0020	0055	...
Antwerpen Centraal d.	...	...	...	...	...	...	...		0644	...	...	0744	...	...	until	2144	...	...	...	...	...	...	...	...
Noorderkempen (Brecht) d.	...	...	...	...	...	...	...		0701	...	...	0801	...	...		2201	...	...	...	...	...	...	...	...
Breda 🏛 a.	...	...	...	...	...	...	...		0718	...	...	0818	...	...		2218	...	...	...	...	...	...	...	...

c – Connects with train to Charleroi in preceding column.

△ – No service from Antwerpen at 2036.
♥ – From / to Amsterdam or Den Haag via Rotterdam (Table **18**).
♡ – From / to Essen (Belgium), Table **419**.
⊡ – Local train.

BRUSSELS AIRPORT ✈ - CHARLEROI
Runs Ⓐ only

	Ⓐ		Ⓐ	
Brussels Airport ✈ d.	0547		2147	...
Brussels Schuman d.	0603	and	2203	...
Brussels Luxembourg d.	0610	hourly	2210	...
Nivelles d.	0652	until	2252	...
Charleroi Sud a.	0722		2322	...

	Ⓐ		Ⓐ	
Charleroi Sud d.	0538		2138	...
Nivelles d.	0608	and	2208	...
Brussels Luxembourg d.	0654	hourly	2254	...
Brussels Schuman d.	0657	until	2257	...
Brussels Airport ✈ a.	0712		2312	...

421 CHARLEROI - MARIEMBOURG - COUVIN
Line 132

km			Ⓐ	Ⓐ	Ⓐ		Ⓐ	Ⓐ		Ⓒ		Ⓒ
0	**Charleroi** Sud d.	Ⓐ	0542	0656	0821		2121	2221	Ⓒ	0815		2215
18	Berzée d.		0606	0720	0841	every	2141	2241		0837	every	2237
22	Walcourt d.		0615	0730	0848	hour	2148	2248		0846	**two**	2246
35	Philippeville d.		0629	0744	0903	until	2203	2303		0900	hours	2300
48	Mariembourg ▲ d.		0641	0754	0915	△	2215	2315		0912	until	2312
53	**Couvin** a.		0647	0800	0921		2221	2321		0918		2318

		Ⓐ	Ⓐ		Ⓐ	Ⓐ		Ⓒ		Ⓒ
Couvin d.	Ⓐ	0724	0907		1607	2107	Ⓒ	0640		2040
Mariembourg ▲ d.		0733	0916	every	1616	2116		0649	every	2049
Philippeville d.		0746	0927	hour	1627	2127		0702	**two**	2102
Walcourt d.		0800	0942	until	1641	2141		0716	hours	2116
Berzée d.		0807	0947	▽	1647	2146		0723	until	2123
Charleroi Sud a.		0829	1008		1713	2207		0746		2143

△ – Also from Charleroi Sud at 1653, 1744, 1839.
▽ – Also from Couvin at 0429, 0449, 0524, 0609, 0633, 1643, 1804, 1907, 2007.

▲ – For MARIEMBOURG - TREIGNES heritage railway operated by *Chemin de Fer à Vapeur des 3 Vallées* (CFV3V). For days of running and timings see www.cfv3v.eu

BRUSSELS - MONS - QUIÉVRAIN 422

Lines 96, 97

Warning! Engineering work may affect services in this table on Ⓒ.

km			Ⓐ	Ⓐ ◇	Ⓐ	Ⓐ ◇	Ⓐ		Ⓐ ◇	Ⓐ	Ⓐ ◇	Ⓐ	Ⓐ ◇	Ⓐ	Ⓐ ◇	Ⓐ	Ⓐ ◇	Ⓐ			Ⓒ		Ⓒ
0	**Brussels Airport** ✈ d.	Ⓐ	0530	...	0630	...	0729		...	1930	...	2030	...	2130	...	2230	...	2330	...	Ⓒ	0531		2231
12	Brussels Nord 423 d.		0543	0613	0643	0712	0743	and	1913	1943	2013	2043	2113	2143	2213	2243	2313	2343	...		0543		2243
14	Brussels Central 423 d.		0548	0618	0648	0717	0748	at	1918	1948	2018	2048	2118	2148	2218	2248	2318	2348	...		0548		2248
16	**Brussels** Midi / Zuid 423 d.		0556	0625	0655	0725	0756	the	1925	1956	2025	2055	2125	2156	2225	2256	2325	2356	...		0556	and	2256
32	Halle 423 d.		|	0635	|	0735	|	same	1935	|	2035	|	2135	|	2235	|	2335	|	...		|	hourly	|
45	Braine-le-Comte 423 d.		0617	0647	0717	0747	0819	minutes	1947	2017	2047	2118	2147	2217	2247	2317	2347	0018	...		0617	until	2317
51	Soignies d.		0624	0654	0724	0754	0825	past	1954	2024	2054	2125	2154	2224	2254	2324	2354	0025	...		0624		2324
76	**Mons** a.		0643	0712	0743	0812	0844	each	2012	2043	2112	2143	2212	2243	2312	2343	0012	0043	...		0643		2343
76	**Mons** d.		...	0715	...	0814	...	hour	2015	...	2115	...	2215	...	2315	...	...	...	...		⊡		⊡
86	Saint-Ghislain a.		...	0729	...	0829	...	until	2029	...	2129	...	2229	...	2329	...	...	...	...		⊡		⊡
96	**Quiévrain** a.		...	0750	...	0851	...		2047	...	...	...	...	...	...	...	...	...	...		⊡		⊡

		Ⓐ	Ⓐ ◇	Ⓐ	Ⓐ ◇	Ⓐ	Ⓐ ◇	Ⓐ	Ⓐ ◇	Ⓐ		Ⓐ ◇	Ⓐ	Ⓐ ◇	Ⓐ	Ⓐ				Ⓒ		Ⓒ	
Quiévrain d.	Ⓐ	...	...	...	0513	...	0613	...	0713	...		1913	...	2013	...	...	...	...	Ⓒ	⊡		⊡	...
Saint-Ghislain d.		...	...	...	0530	...	0630	...	0730	...	and	1930	...	2030	...	...	...	...		⊡		⊡	...
Mons a.		...	...	...	0545	...	0645	...	0745	...	at	1945	...	2045	...	...	...	...		⊡		⊡	...
Mons d.		0419	0450	0519	0550	0618	0650	0718	0750	0819	the	1950	2019	2050	2119	2219	...	...		0518	and	2218	...
Soignies d.		0440	0509	0540	0609	0638	0709	0738	0809	0840	same	2009	2040	2109	2140	2240	...	...		0540	hourly	2240	...
Braine-le-Comte 423 d.		0447	0516	0547	0616	0645	0716	0745	0816	0847	minutes	2016	2047	2116	2147	2247	...	...		0547	until	2247	...
Halle 423 d.		|	0526	|	0626	|	0727	|	0827	|	past	2026	|	2126	|	|	...	...		0553		|	...
Brussels Midi / Zuid 423 a.		0506	0535	0605	0635	0703	0736	0804	0836	0905	each	2035	2105	2135	2205	2305	...	...		0605		2305	...
Brussels Central 423 a.		0513	0542	0613	0642	0710	0742	0810	0842	0913	hour	2042	2113	2142	2213	2313	...	...		0613		2313	...
Brussels Nord 423 a.		0518	0547	0618	0647	0715	0747	0815	0847	0918	until	2047	2118	2147	2218	2318	...	...		0618		2318	...
Brussels Airport ✈ a.		0531	...	0631	...	0728	...	0828	...	0931		...	2131	...	2231	2331	...	...		0631		2331	...

◇ – From / to Liège via Landen (Table **430**).

⊡ – MONS - QUIÉVRAIN LOCAL TRAINS ON Ⓒ: from Mons hourly 0654Ⓒ - 2054Ⓒ, from Quiévrain hourly 0737Ⓒ - 2137Ⓒ.

BRUSSELS - LA LOUVIÈRE - BINCHE 423

Lines 96, 108

Warning! Engineering work may affect services in this table on Ⓒ. For additional trains Brussels - Halle - Braine-le-Comte see Table **422**

km			Ⓐ		Ⓐ	Ⓐ	Ⓐ		Ⓒ		Ⓒ
0	**Brussels** Nord d.	Ⓐ	0618		2018	2118	2218	Ⓒ	0618		2218
2	Brussels Central d.		0623		2023	2123	2223		0622		2222
4	**Brussels** Midi / Zuid d.		0630	and	2030	2130	2230		0630	and	2230
20	Halle d.		0641	hourly	2041	2141	2241		0643	hourly	2243
33	Braine-le-Comte d.		0658	until	2058	2158	2258		0700	until	2300
52	**La Louvière** Centre d.		0718		2118	2218	2318		0721		2321
55	La Louvière Sud a.		0722		2122	2222	2322		0725		2325
64	**Binche** a.		0740		2140	...	...		0748		2348

		Ⓐ		Ⓐ		Ⓒ	Ⓒ		Ⓒ
Binche d.	Ⓐ	0520		2120	Ⓒ	0512	0612		2212
La Louvière Sud d.		0538		2138		0535	0635		2235
La Louvière Centre d.		0544	and	2144		0541	0641	and	2241
Braine-le-Comte d.		0606	hourly	2206		0604	0704	hourly	2304
Halle d.		0620	until	2220		0620	0720	until	2320
Brussels Midi / Zuid a.		0630		2230		0630	0730		2330
Brussels Central a.		0637		2237		0636	0736		2336
Brussels Nord a.		0642		2242		0641	0741		2341

☛ On Ⓐ trains run beyond Brussels to / from Turnhout (Table **434**).

BRUSSELS - GERAARDSBERGEN 424

Lines 94, 123 (S6)

km			Ⓐ		Ⓐ		Ⓒ		Ⓒ
0	**Brussels** Nord d.	Ⓐ	0442		2042	Ⓒ	0742		2042
2	Brussels Centraal d.		0446	and	2046		0746	and	2046
4	**Brussels** Midi / Zuid d.		0453	hourly	2053		0753	hourly	2053
18	Halle d.		0504	until	2104		0804	until	2104
33	Edingen d.		0515		2115		0815		2115
49	**Geraardsbergen** a.		0534		2134		0834		2134

		Ⓐ		Ⓐ		Ⓒ		Ⓒ
Geraardsbergen d.	Ⓐ	0425		2025	Ⓒ	0725		2025
Edingen d.		0446	and	2046		0746	and	2046
Halle d.		0458	hourly	2057		0758	hourly	2058
Brussels Midi / Zuid a.		0507	until	2107		0807	until	2107
Brussels Centraal a.		0513		2113		0813		2113
Brussels Nord a.		0518		2118		0818		2118

MONS - CHARLEROI - NAMUR 425

Lines 118, 130

km			Ⓐ	Ⓐ	Ⓐ	Ⓐ ♡	Ⓐ	Ⓐ	Ⓐ		Ⓐ	Ⓐ	Ⓐ	Ⓐ	Ⓐ	Ⓐ		Ⓒ	Ⓒ ♡	Ⓒ ♡		Ⓒ ♡	Ⓒ ♡
	Tournai 416 d.	Ⓐ	...	...	...	0543	...	0643	...	and at	1943	...	2043	...	2143	...	Ⓒ	...	0629	0729		2029	2129
0	**Mons** d.		0437	...	0539	0615	0639	0715	0739	the same	2015	2039	2116	2139	2216	2239		0614	0714	0814		2114	2214
20	La Louvière Sud d.		0452	...	0557	0630	0657	0730	0757	minutes	2030	2057	2130	2157	2230	2257		0632	0732	0832	and	2132	2232
41	**Charleroi** Sud d.		0513	0550	0619	0650	0719	0750	0819	past	2050	2119	2150	2219	2250	2316		0654	0754	0854	hourly	2154	2254
56	Tamines d.		0526	0602	0630	0702	0730	0802	0830	each	2102	2130	2202	2232	2302	...		0707	0807	0907	until	2207	2307
78	**Namur** a.		0550	0622	0650	0722	0750	0822	0850	hour	2122	2150	2222	2256	2322	...		0730	0830	0930		2230	2330
	Liège Guillemins 442 a.		0635	...	0735	...	0835	...	0935	until	...	2235	...	...	...	...		0817	0917	1017		2317	...

		Ⓐ	Ⓐ	Ⓐ	Ⓐ	Ⓐ	Ⓐ	Ⓐ		Ⓐ	Ⓐ	Ⓐ	Ⓐ	Ⓐ	Ⓐ	Ⓐ		Ⓒ ♡	Ⓒ ♡	Ⓒ ♡		Ⓒ ♡	Ⓒ
Liège Guillemins 442 d.	Ⓐ	...	...	...	0524	...	0624	...	and at	1924	...	2024	...	2124	...	2224	Ⓒ	...	...	0640		2040	2140
Namur d.		...	0505	0538	0611	0638	0711	0738	the same	2011	2038	2111	2138	2210	2238	2310		...	0629	0729		2129	2229
Tamines d.		...	0530	0559	0632	0659	0732	0759	minutes	2033	2059	2132	2159	2234	2259	2334		...	0653	0753	and	2153	2253
Charleroi Sud d.		0443	0545	0614	0645	0714	0745	0814	past	2045	2114	2145	2214	2249	2310	2346		0609	0709	0808	hourly	2209	2306
La Louvière Sud d.		0505	0606	0630	0706	0730	0806	0830	each	2106	2130	2206	2230	2309	...	...		0630	0730	0830	until	2230	...
Mons a.		0521	0621	0644	0721	0744	0821	0844	hour	2121	2144	2221	2244	2327	...	...		0646	0746	0846		2246	...
Tournai 416 a.		...	...	0715	...	0815	...	0915	until	...	2215	...	2321	...	...	...		0730	0830	0930		2330	...

♡ – From / to Mouscron (Table **416**).

MONS - QUÉVY 426

Line 96

km		Ⓐ	Ⓐ	Ⓐ		Ⓐ	Ⓐ§	Ⓐ§	Ⓐ	Ⓐ	Ⓐ
0	Mons d.	0723	0822	0922	hourly	1622	1729	1810	1922	2022	2122
18	Quévy a.	0738	0838	0938	until	1638	1748	1830	1938	2038	2138

	Ⓐ	Ⓐ‡	Ⓐ	Ⓐ	Ⓐ‡	Ⓐ	Ⓐ		Ⓐ	Ⓐ
Quévy d.	0520	0557	0620	0651	0712	0820	0920	hourly	1920	2020
Mons a.	0538	0615	0638	0709	0731	0838	0938	until	1938	2038

§ – From Brussels (depart Brussels Midi 1640 and 1717).

‡ – To Brussels (arrive Brussels Midi 0703 and 0819).

No service on Ⓒ.

CHARLEROI - MAUBEUGE 427

	Ⓐ								Ⓐ	Ⓒ
Charleroi Sud d.	0524	0618**d**	0824	1024	1224	1424	1624	1824	1924	2024
Erquelinnes d.	0607	0707	0907	1107	1307	1507	1707	1909	2007	2107
Maubeuge 🚌 a.	0620	0720	0920	1120	1320	1520	1720	1921	2020	2120

	Ⓐ							e	Ⓐ	Ⓒ
Maubeuge 🚌 d.	0643	0743	0943	1143	1343	1543	1743	1953	2053	2143
Erquelinnes d.	0659	0759	0956	1156	1356	1556	1806	2006	2106	2156
Charleroi Sud a.	0741	0838	1038	1238	1438	1638	1848	2048	2148	2238

d – 0624 on Ⓒ.

e – 10 minutes earlier on Ⓒ.

☛ For connections Maubeuge - Paris see Table **255**.

430 BRUSSELS - LANDEN - HASSELT, GENK and LIÈGE

Lines 36, 21

For direct services Brussels - Liège via high-speed line see Table **400**. For other services Brussels - Hasselt on Ⓐ (via Aarshot) see Table **431**.

km			Ⓐ	Ⓐ	Ⓐ	Ⓐ	Ⓐ	Ⓐ		Ⓐ	Ⓐ	Ⓐ	Ⓐ	Ⓐ	Ⓐ				Ⓐ	Ⓐ	Ⓐ	Ⓐ		
			♡		•	♡	△	•		♡	△	•	♡	△	△									
0	**Brussels** Midi / Zuid d.	Ⓐ	0511	0515	0538	0611	0614	0638		2111	2114	2138	2211	2215	2315	...	...		1603	1631	1707	1801	...	...
2	Brussels Central d.		0516	0519	0543	0616	0618	0643	and	2116	2118	2143	2216	2219	2319	...	...		1608	1636	1712	1806	...	...
4	Brussels Nord d.		0522	0525	0549	0622	0625	0649	at	2122	2125	2149	2222	2225	2325	...	...		1614	1642	1718	1812	...	...
16	**Brussels Airport** ✈ d.		|	0537	|	|	0637	|	the	|	2137	|	|	2237	2337	...	...	A	|	|	|	|	...	...
33	Leuven d.		0542	0553	0610	0642	0653	0710	same	2142	2153	2210	2242	2253	2353	...	...	L	1636	1703	1738	1834	...	...
64	Tienen d.		0556	0609	0625	0656	0709	0725	minutes	2155	2209	2225	2256	2309	0009	...	...	S	1651	1718	1753	1850	...	...
64	Landen d.		0606	0622	0634	0706	0722	0734	past	2206	2222	2234	2306	2322	0022	...	...	O	1700	1729	1803	1859	...	...
75	Sint-Truiden d.		0615	...	|	0715	...	|	each	2215	...	|	2315	...	...	...	...		|	1744	|	...	...	...
92	**Hasselt** a.		0630	...	|	0731	...	|	hour	2230	...	|	2330	...	...	...	...		|	1800	|	...	...	...
108	Genk a.		0651	...	|	0751	...	|	until	2251	...	|	...	...	...	...	...		|	...	|	...	...	...
103	**Liège** Guillemins a.		...	...	0706	...	...	0809		...	...	2306	...	...	...	...	...		1737	...	1837	...	...	...

		Ⓒ	Ⓒ	Ⓒ	Ⓒ	Ⓒ	Ⓒ	Ⓒ	Ⓒ		Ⓒ	Ⓒ	Ⓒ	Ⓒ	Ⓒ	Ⓒ	Ⓒ	Ⓒ					
		♡		♡		△	♡		△		♡		△	♡	△	b	△	b					
Brussels Midi / Zuid d.	Ⓒ	0612	...	0712	...	0715	0812	...	0815		2111	...	2115	2212	2215	2256	2315	0020	...	...	...	...	...
Brussels Central d.		0617	...	0717	...	0719	0817	...	0819	and	2116	...	2119	2217	2219	2301	2319	0025	...	...	...	...	...
Brussels Nord d.		0623	...	0723	...	0725	0823	...	0825	at	2122	...	2125	2223	2225	2307	2325	0031	...	...	...	...	...
Brussels Airport ✈ d.		|	...	|	...	0738	|	...	0838	the	|	...	2138	|	2238	|	2338	|	...	...	...	...	...
Leuven d.		0642	...	0742	...	0754	0842	...	0854	same	2142	...	2154	2242	2254	2327	2352	0051	...	...	...	...	...
Tienen d.		0656	...	0756	...	0810	0856	...	0910	minutes	2156	...	2210	2256	2310	2342	...	0106	...	...	...	...	...
Landen d.		0706	0710	0806	0810	0823	0906	0910	0923	past	2206	2210	2223	2306	2323	2351	...	0115	...	...	...	...	...
Sint-Truiden d.		0715	|	0815	|	...	0915	|	...	each	2215	|	...	2315	...	|	...	|	...	...	...	...	...
Hasselt a.		0730	|	0830	|	...	0930	|	...	hour	2230	|	...	2330	...	|	...	|	...	...	...	...	...
Genk a.		0751	|	0851	|	...	0951	|	...	until	2251	|	...	2351	...	|	...	|	...	...	...	...	...
Liège Guillemins a.		...	0754	...	0854	...	...	0954	...		...	2255	...	...	...	0021	...	0144	...	...	...	...	...

		Ⓐ	Ⓐ	Ⓐ	Ⓐ	Ⓐ	Ⓐ	Ⓐ	Ⓐ	Ⓐ	Ⓐ	Ⓐ	Ⓐ		Ⓐ	Ⓐ	Ⓐ			Ⓐ	Ⓐ	Ⓐ		
		△	♡	b	•	△	♡	•		△	♡	•	△		♡	•								
Liège Guillemins d.	Ⓐ	...	...	0437	0454	...	...	0553	...	...	...	0655	...		...	2156	...	...		0623	...	0722	...	...
Genk d.		...	...	|	|	...	0507	|	0534	...	0607r	|	...	and	2107	|	...	...		|	0638	|	...	...
Hasselt d.		...	0428	|	|	...	0528	|	0555	...	0628	|	...	at	2128	|	...	...		|	0659	|	...	...
Sint-Truiden d.		...	0444	|	|	...	0544	|	0616	...	0644	|	...	the	2144	|	...	...	A	|	0718	|	...	...
Landen d.		0435	0454	0507	0527	0535	0554	0624	0629	0633	0654	0726	0735	same	2154	2227	2235	...	L	0701	0730	0801	...	...
Tienen d.		0452	0506	0518	0539	0552	0606	0636	0644	0650	0706	0738	0752	minutes	2206	2239	2252	...	S	0713	0744	0813	...	...
Leuven d.		0508	0521	0533	0553	0608	0621	0653	0659	0707	0722	0754	0808	past	2221	2253	2308	...	O	0727	0759	0827	...	...
Brussels Airport ✈ a.		0521	|	|	|	0621	|	|	|	0721	|	|	0821	each	|	|	2321	...		|	|	|	...	...
Brussels Nord a.		0534	0538	0549	0611	0634	0638	0710	0717	0734	0740	0813	0834	hour	2238	2311	2334	...		0744	0817	0844	...	...
Brussels Central a.		0540	0544	0555	0617	0640	0644	0716	0723	0739	0748	0819	0839	until	2244	2317	2340	...		0751	0823	0851	...	...
Brussels Midi / Zuid a.		0545	0549	0600	0622	0645	0649	0721	0728	0744	0753	0824	0844		2249	2322	2345	...		0756	0828	0856	...	...

		Ⓒ	Ⓒ	Ⓒ	Ⓒ	Ⓒ	Ⓒ	Ⓒ	Ⓒ	Ⓒ	Ⓒ	Ⓒ	Ⓒ		Ⓒ	Ⓒ	Ⓒ	Ⓒ	Ⓒ	Ⓒ	Ⓒ	Ⓒ	
		△	b	△	△	♡	△		♡	△		♡	△			♡	△		♡		♡	b	
Liège Guillemins d.	Ⓒ	...	0437	...	...	...	...	0705	...	...	0805	...	...		2005	...	...	2105	...	2205	...	2304	...
Genk d.		...	|	...	...	...	...	|	0707	...	|	0807	...	and	|	2007	...	|	2107	|	2204	|	...
Hasselt d.		...	|	...	...	0628	...	|	0728	...	|	0828	...	at	|	2028	...	|	2128	|	2228	|	...
Sint-Truiden d.		...	|	...	...	0644	...	|	0744	...	|	0844	...	the	|	2044	...	|	2144	|	2244	|	...
Landen d.		...	0506	0535	0635	0654	0735	0748	0754	0835	0848	0854	0936	same	2048	2054	2135	2148	2154	2248	2254	2333	...
Tienen d.		...	0517	0552	0652	0706	0752	...	0806	0852	...	0906	0952	minutes	...	2106	2152	...	2206	...	2306	2345	...
Leuven d.		0507	0533	0608	0708	0721	0808	...	0821	0908	...	0921	1008	past	...	2121	2208	...	2221	...	2321	2359	...
Brussels Airport ✈ a.		0521	|	0621	0721	|	0821	...	|	0921	...	|	1021	each	...	|	2221	...	|	...	|	|	...
Brussels Nord a.		0534	0550	0634	0735	0738	0835	...	0838	0935	...	0938	1034	hour	...	2138	2234	...	2238	...	2338	0016	...
Brussels Central a.		0540	0557	0640	0740	0744	0840	...	0844	0940	...	0944	1040	until	...	2144	2240	...	2244	...	2344	0022	...
Brussels Midi / Zuid a.		0545	0602	0645	0745	0749	0845	...	0849	0945	...	0949	1045		...	2149	2245	...	2249	...	2349	0027	...

b – From / to Brugge and Oostende (Table **400**).
r – Journey at 0907 departs Genk at 0856 (arrives Hasselt 0915).

♡ – From / to Brugge and Gent, Table **405** (most trains also from / to Blankenberge).
△ – From / to Gent via Aalst, Table **412** (on Ⓒ most trains also from / to De Panne, Table **411**).
• – From / to Mons and Quiévrain (Table **422**).

431 BRUSSELS - AARSCHOT - HASSELT - TONGEREN

Line 35

No service on Ⓒ via this route. For other trains Brussels - Hasselt (via Landen) see Table **430**.

km			Ⓐ	Ⓐ	Ⓐ		Ⓐ	Ⓐ	Ⓐ
	Gent **412** ▷ d.	Ⓐ	0441	0540	0639		1941	2041	2141
0	**Brussels** Midi / Zuid d.		0544	0644	0743		2044	2144	2244
2	Brussels Central d.		0549	0649	0748	and	2049	2149	2249
4	Brussels Nord d.		0555	0655	0755	hourly	2055	2155	2255
46	Aarschot **432** d.		0621	0721	0821	until	2121	2221	2321
63	Diest **432** d.		0634	0734	0834		2134	2234	2334
84	**Hasselt** **432** a.		0648	0748	0848		2148	2248	2348
110	Tongeren **435** a.		0721	0821	0921		2221	...	...

		Ⓐ	Ⓐ	Ⓐ	Ⓐ		Ⓐ	Ⓐ
Tongeren **435** d.	Ⓐ	...	0538	0638	0738		2038	2138
Hasselt **432** d.		0511	0611	0711	0811		2111	2211
Diest **432** d.		0527	0627	0727	0827	and	2127	2227
Aarschot **432** d.		0541	0641	0741	0841	hourly	2141	2241
Brussels Nord a.		0605	0705	0805	0905	until	2205	2305
Brussels Central a.		0611	0711	0812	0911		2211	2311
Brussels Midi / Zuid a.		0616	0716	0817	0916		2216	2316
Gent **412** ▷ a.		0719	0818	0920	1020		2320	0020

▷ – Gent to Brussels is via Aalst and Denderleeuw (Table **412**).

432 ANTWERPEN - BRUSSELS NATIONAAL ✈ - AARSCHOT - HASSELT

Lines 35, 36c, 16

For Antwerpen - Hasselt via Mol see Table **434**. For additional trains Brussels Nationaal ✈ - Leuven see Table **430**.

km	*Via Airport*		Ⓐ		Ⓐ		Ⓒ		Ⓒ	Ⓒ
0	**Antwerpen** Centraal **420** d.	Ⓐ	0449		2249	Ⓒ	0536		2136	2236
24	Mechelen **420** d.		0508		2308		0556		2156	2256
40	**Brussels Airport** ✈ **420** d.		0521	and	2321		0610	and	2210	2310
59	Leuven d.		0542	hourly	2342		0633	hourly	2233	2333
75	Aarschot d.		0556	until	2356		0647	until	2247	2347
92	Diest d.		0609		0009		0706		2306	0006
113	**Hasselt** a.		0622		0022		0723		2323	0023

		Ⓐ		Ⓐ		Ⓒ	Ⓒ		Ⓒ
						‡			
Hasselt d.	Ⓐ	0436		2236	Ⓒ	...	0637		2237
Diest d.		0450		2250		...	0655		2255
Aarschot d.		0502	and	2302		...	0714	and	2314
Leuven d.		0524	hourly	2324		0536	0736	hourly	2336
Brussels Airport ✈ **420** a.		0539	until	2339		0550	0750	until	2350
Mechelen **420** a.		0552		2352		0604	0804		0004
Antwerpen Centraal **420** a.		0611		0011		0624	0824		0024

km	*Via Lier*		Ⓐ		Ⓐ		Ⓒ		Ⓒ	Ⓒ
0	**Antwerpen** Centraal d.	Ⓐ	0617		2017	Ⓒ	0628		2128	2228
14	Lier d.		0635	and	2035		0643	and	2143	2243
41	Aarschot d.		|	hourly	|		0717	hourly	2217	2317
59	Diest d.		0704	until	2104		0730	until	2230	2330
80	**Hasselt** a.		0717		2117		0743		2243	2343

		Ⓐ		Ⓐ		Ⓒ	Ⓒ		Ⓒ
Hasselt d.	Ⓐ	0541		1941	Ⓒ	0618	0718		2218
Diest d.		0555	and	1955		0633	0733	and	2233
Aarschot d.		|	hourly	|		0655	0755	hourly	2255
Lier d.		0625	until	2025		0717	0817	until	2317
Antwerpen Centraal a.		0640		2040		0731	0831		2331

km	*Via Lier*		Ⓐ		Ⓐ		Ⓒ		Ⓒ	
0	**Antwerpen** Centraal d.	Ⓐ	0632	and	2232	Ⓒ	0646	and	2246	...
14	Lier d.		0649	hourly	2249		0706	hourly	2306	...
41	Aarschot d.		0712	until	2312		0735	until	2335	...
57	**Leuven** a.		0724		2324		0748		2348	...

		Ⓐ		Ⓐ		Ⓒ		Ⓒ	
Leuven d.	Ⓐ	0636	and	2036	Ⓒ	0611	and	2211	...
Aarschot d.		0650	hourly	2050		0625	hourly	2225	...
Lier d.		0713	until	2113		0656	until	2256	...
Antwerpen Centraal a.		0728		2128		0714		2314	...

‡ – Also at 0636.

Line 15 — BRUSSELS and ANTWERPEN - LIER - TURNHOUT / HASSELT / HAMONT — 434

km			Ⓐ	Ⓐ	Ⓐ	Ⓐ	Ⓐ	Ⓐ		Ⓐ	Ⓐ	Ⓐ	Ⓐ	Ⓐ	Ⓐ	Ⓐ	Ⓐ	Ⓐ	Ⓐ	Ⓐ	Ⓐ	Ⓐ	
	Brussels Midi / Zuid ▷ d.	Ⓐ	...	...	...	0633	...	...		1833	...	...	1933	...	...	2033	...	...	2133	...	2233	...	...
	Brussels Central ▷ d.		...	...	...	0638	...	...		1838	...	...	1938	...	...	2038	...	...	2138	...	2238	...	...
	Brussels Nord ▷ d.		...	...	...	0644	...	...	and	1844	...	...	1944	...	...	2044	...	...	2144	...	2244	...	...
	Mechelen ▷ d.		...	...	...	0705	...	...	at	1904	...	...	2004	...	...	2104	...	...	2204	...	2304	...	...
0	**Antwerpen** Centraal d.		0547	0609	0646	|	0709	0747	the	|	1909	1947	|	2009	2047	|	2109	2147	|	2225	|	2325	...
2	Antwerpen Berchem d.		0552	0615	0652	|	0715	0752	same	|	1915	1952	|	2015	2052	|	2115	2152	|	2230	|	2330	...
15	Lier d.		0603	0627	0703	0723	0727	0803	minutes	1922	1927	2003	2022	2027	2103	2122	2127	2203	2222	2244	2322	2345	...
34	Herentals d.		0622	0643	0722	0739	0743	0822	past	1938	1943	2022	2038	2043	2122	2138	2143	2222	2238	2307	2338	0008	...
	Turnhout a.		0638	|	0738	0754	|	0838	each	1953	|	2038	2053	|	2138	2153	|	2238	2253	|	2353	|	...
46	Geel d.		...	0655	...	...	0755	...	hour	...	1955	...	...	2055	...	...	2155	...	...	2319	...	0020	...
56	Mol a.		...	0702	...	...	0802	...	until	...	2002	...	...	2102	...	...	2202	...	...	2326	...	0028	...
99	**Hasselt** a.		...	0752**r**	...	...	0852**r**	...		...	2052**r**	...	...	2153**r**	...	...	2253**r**	...	...	|	...	...	...
77	Overpelt a.		...	0722	...	...	0826	...		...	2026	...	...	2122	...	...	2222	...	...	2343	...	...	...
79	Neerpelt a.		...	0726	...	...	0828	...		...	2028	...	...	2126	...	...	2226	...	...	2346	...	...	...
87	**Hamont** a.		...	0738	...	...	0838	...		...	2038	...	...	2138	...	...	2238	...	...	...	...	...	...

km			Ⓐ	Ⓐ	Ⓐ	Ⓐ	Ⓐ	Ⓐ	Ⓐ	Ⓐ	Ⓐ	Ⓐ	Ⓐ		Ⓐ	Ⓐ	Ⓐ	Ⓐ	Ⓐ	Ⓐ	Ⓐ	Ⓐ
	Hamont d.	Ⓐ	...	...	...	0528	...	...	0619	...	...	0715	...		...	1919	...	...	2019	...	2119	...
	Neerpelt d.		...	...	...	0538	...	...	0634	...	...	0727	...		...	1934	...	...	2030	...	2130	...
	Overpelt d.		...	...	...	0541	...	...	0638	...	...	0731	...	and	...	1938	...	...	2033	...	2133	...
	Hasselt d.		...	...	...	|	...	...	0607**s**	...	...	0707**s**	...	at	...	1907**s**	...	...	2008**s**	...	2108**s**	2208
	Mol d.		0458	...	...	0558	...	...	0658	...	...	0758	...	the	...	1958	...	...	2058	...	2158	2252
	Geel d.		0506	...	...	0606	...	...	0706	...	...	0806	...	same	...	2006	...	...	2106	...	2206	...
0	**Turnhout** d.		|	0458	0521	|	0604	0621	|	0704	0721	|	0804	minutes	1921	|	2004	2021	|	2104	|	...
18	Herentals d.		0519	0523	0543	0619	0623	0642	0719	0723	0742	0819	0823	past	1943	2019	2023	2043	2119	2123	2219	...
38	Lier d.		0535	0539	0558	0635	0639	0658	0735	0739	0758	0835	0839	each	1958	2035	2039	2058	2135	2139	2235	...
	Antwerpen Berchem a.		0545	|	0608	0645	|	0708	0745	|	0808	0845	|	hour	2008	2045	|	2108	2145	|	2245	...
	Antwerpen Centraal a.		0551	|	0613	0651	|	0713	0751	|	0813	0851	|	until	2013	2051	|	2113	2151	|	2251	...
55	Mechelen ▷ d.		...	0558	...	...	0658	...	...	0758	...	...	0858		...	...	2058	...	...	2158	...	...
75	Brussels Nord ▷ a.		...	0616	...	...	0716	...	...	0816	...	...	0916		...	...	2116	...	...	2216	...	...
77	Brussels Central ▷ a.		...	0622	...	...	0722	...	...	0822	...	...	0922		...	...	2122	...	...	2222	...	...
79	**Brussels** Midi / Zuid ▷ a.		...	0627	...	...	0727	...	...	0827	...	...	0927		...	...	2127	...	...	2227	...	...

		Ⓒ	Ⓒ	Ⓒ	Ⓒ		Ⓒ	Ⓒ △	Ⓒ ▽	Ⓒ
Antwerpen C. d.	Ⓒ	0609	0709	0751	0809		2009	2051	2109	2309
Ant. Berchem d.		0615	0715	0800	0815	and	2015	2100	2115	2315
Lier d.		0627	0727	0810	0827	at	2027	2110	2127	2327
Herentals d.		0643	0743	0833	0843	the	2043	2133	2143	2343
Turnhout a.		|	|	0848	|	same	|	2148	|	|
Geel d.		0655	0755	...	0855	minutes	2055	...	2155	2355
Mol a.		0702	0802	...	0902	past	2102	...	2202	0002
Hasselt a.		0752**x**	0852**x**	...	0952**x**	each	2152**x**	...	|	|
Overpelt a.		0726	0826	...	0926	hour	2126	...	2226	0026
Neerpelt a.		0728	0828	...	0928	until	2128	...	2228	0028
Hamont a.		0738	0838	...	0938		2138	...	2238	0038

		Ⓒ ⊙	Ⓒ ⊡	Ⓒ	Ⓒ	Ⓒ		Ⓒ	Ⓒ	Ⓒ	Ⓒ	Ⓒ
Hamont d.	Ⓒ	0628	...	0719	...	0819		...	2019	...	2119	...
Neerpelt d.		0637	...	0730	...	0830	and	...	2030	...	2130	...
Overpelt d.		0640	...	0733	...	0833	at	...	2033	...	2133	...
Hasselt d.		|	...	|	...	0808**z**	the	...	2008**z**	...	2108**z**	...
Mol d.		0658	...	0758	...	0858	same	...	2058	...	2158	...
Geel d.		0706	...	0806	...	0906	minutes	...	2106	...	2206	...
Turnhout d.		|	0717	|	0817	|	past	2017	|	2117	|	2217
Herentals d.		0719	0733	0819	0833	0919	each	2033	2119	2133	2219	2233
Lier d.		0735	0752	0835	0852	0935	hour	2052	2135	2152	2235	2252
Ant. Berchem a.		0745	0801	0845	0901	0945	until	2101	2145	2201	2245	2301
Antwerpen C. a.		0751	0810	0851	0910	0951		2110	2151	2210	2251	2310

r – Portion for Hasselt is detached from the main train at Mol (departs Mol xx07 or xx08).
s – Portion from Hasselt attaches to the main train at Mol (arrives Mol xx53; Hamont portion arrives xx49).
x – Hourly on ⑥. On ⑦ Hasselt is served every **two** hours (from Antwerpen even hours 0609 - 2009). Note **r** applies.
z – Hourly on ⑥. On ⑦ Hasselt is served every **two** hours (departing on even hours 0808 - 2008). Note **s** applies.

▷ – See also Table **420**.
△ – Also at 2151, 2251, 2351.
▽ – Also at 2209.
⊡ – Also at 0617.
⊙ – Also runs Mol - Antwerpen at 0449 and Neerpelt - Antwerpen at 0537.

☛ *On Ⓐ Turnhout trains run beyond Brussels to / from Binche (Table **423**).*

Line 34 — LIÈGE - HASSELT — 435

km			Ⓐ ◇		Ⓐ ◇		Ⓒ ♡		Ⓒ ♡
0	**Liège** Guillemins d.	Ⓐ	0723	and	2123	Ⓒ	0613	and	2113
27	Tongeren 431 d.		0759	hourly	2159		0652	hourly	2152
53	**Hasselt** 431 a.		0823	until	2223		0715	until	2215

		Ⓐ ◇		Ⓐ ◇		Ⓒ ♡		Ⓒ ♡		
Hasselt 431 d.	Ⓐ	0637	and	2037	Ⓒ	0546	and	2046	...	...
Tongeren 431 d.		0701	hourly	2101		0610	hourly	2110	...	...
Liège Guillemins a.		0737	until	2137		0647	until	2147	...	...

◇ – From / to Maastricht (Table **436**).

♡ – Most journeys on Ⓒ run beyond Hasselt to / from Antwerpen (Table **432**).

Line 40 — LIÈGE - MAASTRICHT — 436

km			Ⓐ	Ⓐ	Ⓐ ◇	Ⓐ ◇		Ⓐ ◇	Ⓐ ◇	Ⓐ					⑥	Ⓒ	Ⓒ	Ⓒ		Ⓒ	Ⓒ		
0	**Liège** Guillemins d.	Ⓐ	0609	0639	0739	0839	and	2039	2139	2239	...	...	...	Ⓒ	0608	0708	0808	0908	and	2108	2208	...	...
19	Visé 🏛 d.		0627	0658	0758	0858	hourly	2058	2158	2258	...	...	...		0627	0727	0827	0927	hourly	2127	2227	...	...
32	**Maastricht** a.		0642	0713	0813	0913	until	2113	2213	2313	...	...	...		0642	0742	0842	0942	until	2142	2242	...	...

		Ⓐ	Ⓐ	Ⓐ ◇	Ⓐ	Ⓐ ◇	Ⓐ ◇		Ⓐ ◇	Ⓐ	Ⓐ	Ⓐ		⑥	Ⓒ	Ⓒ	Ⓒ		Ⓒ	Ⓒ		
Maastricht d.	Ⓐ	...	...	0648	...	0748	0848	and	2048	2148	2248	2348	Ⓒ	0718	0818	0918	1018	and	2218	2318	...	...
Visé 🏛 d.		0615	0646	0704	0727	0804	0904	hourly	2104	2204	2304	0004		0733	0833	0933	1033	hourly	2233	2333	...	...
Liège Guillemins a.		0633	0703	0721	0746	0821	0921	until	2121	2221	2321	0021		0752	0852	0952	1052	until	2252	2352	...	...

◇ – To / from Hasselt (Table **435**).

Lines 37, 44 — SPA - VERVIERS - AACHEN — 438

For international trains Brussels - Aachen and beyond see Tables **20** / **21**.

km		Ⓐ	Ⓐ ⊡				Ⓐ	Ⓒ	Ⓒ	
0	Spa Géronstère d.	0538	0638	0738		1938	2038	2038	2138	...
1	**Spa** d.	0541	0641	0741	and	1941	2041	2041	2141	...
13	Pepinster d.	0600	0700	0800	hourly	2000	2100	2100	2200	...
17	**Verviers** Central a.	0605	0705	0805	until	2005	2105	2106	2205	...
17	**Verviers** Central 400 d.	0627	0727	0827		2027	2127	2127	2227	...
31	Welkenraedt 🏛 400 d.	0641	0741	0841		2041	2140	2141	2240	...
50	**Aachen** Hbf a.	0656	0756	0856		2056	...	2156	...	...

		Ⓐ	Ⓒ				Ⓐ
Aachen Hbf d.	...	0704	...	0804		2004	2104
Welkenraedt 🏛 400 d.	0620	0720	0720	0820	and	2020	2119
Verviers Central 400 a.	0633	0733	0733	0833	hourly	2033	...
Verviers Central d.	0654	0754	0754	0854	until	2054	...
Pepinster d.	0701	0801	0801	0901		2101	...
Spa d.	0720	0820	0820	0920		2120	...
Spa Géronstère a.	0722	0822	0822	0922		2122	...

△ – Also 2204Ⓒ to Welkenraedt.

⊡ – Runs daily Welkenraedt - Aachen.

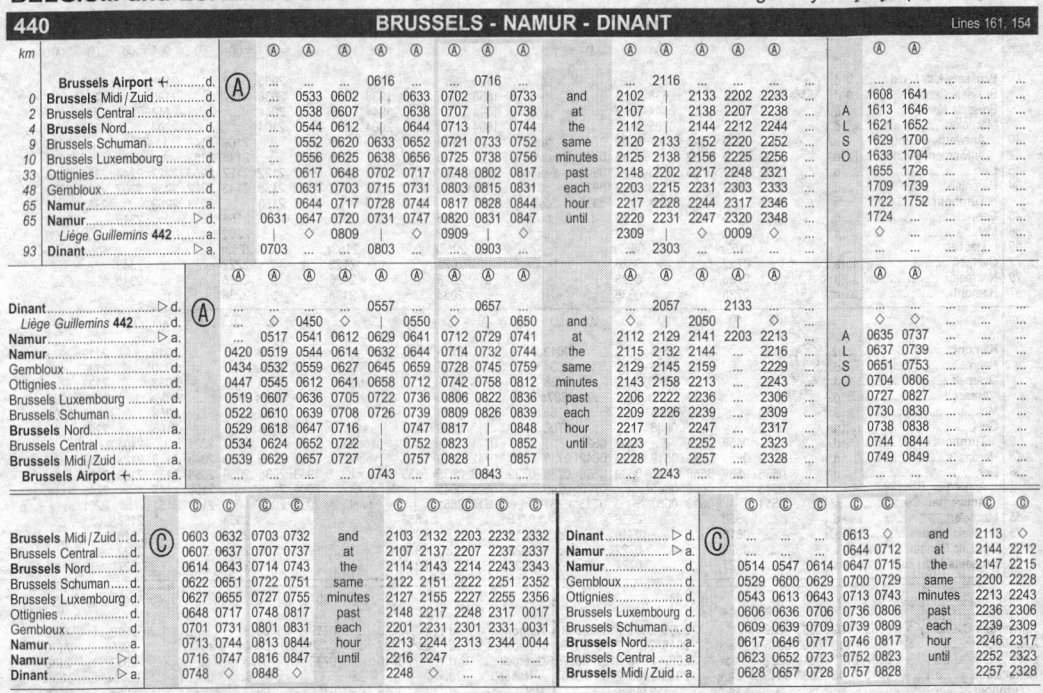

440 BRUSSELS - NAMUR - DINANT

Lines 161, 154

km			Ⓐ	Ⓐ	Ⓐ	Ⓐ	Ⓐ	Ⓐ	Ⓐ	Ⓐ		Ⓐ	Ⓐ	Ⓐ	Ⓐ	Ⓐ			Ⓐ	Ⓐ		
	Brussels Airport ✈ d.	Ⓐ	...	...	...	0616	...	...	0716	...		...	2116	...	...	...	...		...	...	...	...
0	**Brussels** Midi / Zuid d.		...	0533	0602	|	0633	0702	|	0733	and	2102	|	2133	2202	2233	...		1608	1641	...	...
2	Brussels Central d.		...	0538	0607	|	0638	0707	|	0738	at	2107	|	2138	2207	2238	...	A	1613	1646	...	...
4	**Brussels** Nord d.		...	0544	0612	|	0644	0713	|	0744	the	2112	|	2144	2212	2244	...	L	1621	1652	...	...
9	Brussels Schuman d.		...	0552	0620	0633	0652	0721	0733	0752	same	2120	2133	2152	2220	2252	...	S	1629	1700	...	...
10	Brussels Luxembourg d.		...	0556	0625	0638	0656	0725	0738	0756	minutes	2125	2138	2156	2225	2256	...	O	1633	1704	...	...
33	Ottignies d.		...	0617	0648	0702	0717	0748	0802	0817	past	2148	2202	2217	2248	2321	...		1655	1726	...	...
48	Gembloux d.		...	0631	0703	0715	0731	0803	0815	0831	each	2203	2215	2231	2303	2333	...		1709	1739	...	...
65	**Namur** a.		...	0644	0717	0728	0744	0817	0828	0844	hour	2217	2228	2244	2317	2346	...		1722	1752	...	...
65	**Namur** ▷ d.		0631	0647	0720	0731	0747	0820	0831	0847	until	2220	2231	2247	2320	2348	...		1724	...	...	...
	Liège Guillemins **442** a.		|	◇	0809	|	◇	0909	|	◇		2309	|	◇	0009	◇	...		◇	...	...	...
93	**Dinant** ▷ a.		0703	...	...	0803	...	...	0903	...		...	2303	...	...	...	...		...	...	...	...

		Ⓐ	Ⓐ	Ⓐ	Ⓐ	Ⓐ	Ⓐ	Ⓐ	Ⓐ	Ⓐ		Ⓐ	Ⓐ	Ⓐ	Ⓐ	Ⓐ			Ⓐ	Ⓐ		
Dinant ▷ d.	Ⓐ	...	...	...	...	0557	...	...	0657	...		...	2057	...	2133	...	...		...	...	...	...
Liège Guillemins **442** d.		...	◇	0450	◇	|	0550	◇	|	0650	and	◇	|	2050	|	◇	...		◇	◇	...	...
Namur ▷ a.		...	0517	0541	0612	0629	0641	0712	0729	0741	at	2112	2129	2141	2203	2213	...	A	0635	0737	...	...
Namur d.		0420	0519	0544	0614	0632	0644	0714	0732	0744	the	2115	2132	2144	...	2216	...	L	0637	0739	...	...
Gembloux d.		0434	0532	0559	0627	0645	0659	0728	0745	0759	same	2129	2145	2159	...	2229	...	S	0651	0753	...	...
Ottignies d.		0447	0545	0612	0641	0658	0712	0742	0758	0812	minutes	2143	2158	2213	...	2243	...	O	0704	0806	...	...
Brussels Luxembourg d.		0519	0607	0636	0705	0722	0736	0806	0822	0836	past	2206	2222	2236	...	2306	...		0727	0827	...	...
Brussels Schuman d.		0522	0610	0639	0708	0726	0739	0809	0826	0839	each	2209	2226	2239	...	2309	...		0730	0830	...	...
Brussels Nord a.		0529	0618	0647	0716	|	0747	0817	|	0848	hour	2217	|	2247	...	2317	...		0738	0838	...	...
Brussels Central a.		0534	0624	0652	0722	|	0752	0823	|	0852	until	2223	|	2252	...	2323	...		0744	0844	...	...
Brussels Midi / Zuid a.		0539	0629	0657	0727	|	0757	0828	|	0857		2228	|	2257	...	2328	...		0749	0849	...	...
Brussels Airport ✈ a.		...	...	...	...	0743	...	...	0843	...		...	2243	...	...	...	...		...	...	...	...

		Ⓒ	Ⓒ	Ⓒ	Ⓒ		Ⓒ	Ⓒ	Ⓒ	Ⓒ	Ⓒ
Brussels Midi / Zuid d.	Ⓒ	0603	0632	0703	0732	and	2103	2132	2203	2232	2332
Brussels Central d.		0607	0637	0707	0737	at	2107	2137	2207	2237	2337
Brussels Nord d.		0614	0643	0714	0743	the	2114	2143	2214	2243	2343
Brussels Schuman d.		0622	0651	0722	0751	same	2122	2151	2222	2251	2352
Brussels Luxembourg d.		0627	0655	0727	0755	minutes	2127	2155	2227	2255	2356
Ottignies d.		0648	0717	0748	0817	past	2148	2217	2248	2317	0017
Gembloux d.		0701	0731	0801	0831	each	2201	2231	2301	2331	0031
Namur a.		0713	0744	0813	0844	hour	2213	2244	2313	2344	0044
Namur ▷ d.		0716	0747	0816	0847	until	2216	2247	...	...	...
Dinant ▷ a.		0748	◇	0848	◇		2248	◇	...	...	...

		Ⓒ	Ⓒ	Ⓒ	Ⓒ	Ⓒ		Ⓒ	Ⓒ
Dinant ▷ d.	Ⓒ	...	...	...	0613	◇	and	2113	◇
Namur ▷ a.		...	...	...	0644	0712	at	2144	2212
Namur d.		0514	0547	0614	0647	0715	the	2147	2215
Gembloux d.		0529	0600	0629	0700	0729	same	2200	2228
Ottignies d.		0543	0613	0643	0713	0743	minutes	2213	2243
Brussels Luxembourg d.		0606	0636	0706	0736	0806	past	2236	2306
Brussels Schuman d.		0609	0639	0709	0739	0809	each	2239	2309
Brussels Nord a.		0617	0646	0717	0746	0817	hour	2246	2317
Brussels Central a.		0623	0652	0723	0752	0823	until	2252	2323
Brussels Midi / Zuid a.		0628	0657	0728	0757	0828		2257	2328

◇ – To / from Arlon, Luxembourg or other destinations in Table **445**.

▷ – See also Table **448**.

442 NAMUR - LIÈGE

Line 125

km			Ⓐ	Ⓐ	Ⓐ	Ⓐ	Ⓐ	Ⓐ		Ⓐ	Ⓐ	Ⓐ	Ⓐ	Ⓐ		Ⓒ	Ⓒ	Ⓒ ▽	Ⓒ ▽		Ⓒ ▽	Ⓒ ▽	Ⓒ ▽
	Mons **425** d.	Ⓐ	0437	...	0539	...	0639	...	and at	1939	...	2039	...	...	Ⓒ	...	0614	0714	0814		1914	2014	2114
	Charleroi Sud **425** d.		0513	...	0619	...	0719	...	the	2019	...	2119	...	...		...	0654	0754	0854		1954	2054	2154
	Brussels Midi / Zuid **440** § d.		|	...	|	0602	|	0702	same	|	2002	|	2102	2202		...	|	|	|	and	|	|	|
0	**Namur** d.		0553	0620	0653	0720	0753	0820	minutes	2053	2120	2153	2220	2320		0629	0732	0832	0932	hourly	2032	2132	2232
20	Andenne d.		0606	0635	0706	0735	0806	0835	past	2106	2135	2206	2235	2335		0643	0746	0846	0946	until	2046	2146	2246
31	Huy d.		0615	0646	0715	0746	0815	0846	each	2115	2146	2215	2246	2346		0654	0757	0857	0957		2057	2157	2257
60	**Liège** Guillemins a.		0635	0709	0735	0809	0835	0909	hour	2135	2209	2235	2309	0009		0716	0817	0917	1017		2117	2217	2317
63	Liège St Lambertus a.		0646	0720	0746	0820	0846	0920	until	2146	2220	2246	2320	0020		0727	0828	0928	1028		2128	2228	2328

		Ⓐ	Ⓐ	Ⓐ	Ⓐ	Ⓐ	Ⓐ	Ⓐ		Ⓐ	Ⓐ	Ⓐ	Ⓐ	Ⓐ		Ⓒ ▽	Ⓒ ▽	Ⓒ ▽	Ⓒ ▽		Ⓒ ▽	Ⓒ	Ⓒ
Liège St Lambertus d.	Ⓐ	0439	0513	0540	0613	0640	0713	0740	and at	2013	2040	2113	2140	2213	Ⓒ	0630	0730	0830	0930		2030	2130	2235
Liège Guillemins d.		0453	0524	0550	0624	0650	0724	0750	the	2024	2050	2124	2150	2224		0640	0740	0840	0940		2040	2140	2245
Huy d.		0514	0545	0613	0645	0713	0746	0813	same	2045	2113	2145	2213	2245		0701	0801	0901	1001	and	2101	2201	2307
Andenne d.		0525	0554	0625	0654	0725	0754	0825	minutes	2054	2125	2154	2225	2254		0712	0812	0912	1012	hourly	2112	2212	2318
Namur a.		0541	0608	0641	0708	0741	0808	0841	past	2108	2141	2208	2241	2308		0726	0826	0926	1026	until	2126	2226	2331
Brussels Midi / Zuid **440** § a.		0657	|	0757	|	0857	|	0957	each	|	2257	|	...	|		|	|	|	|		|	|	...
Charleroi Sud **425** a.		...	0642	...	0742	...	0842	...	hour	2142	...	2246	...	2346		0806	0906	1007	1107		2206	2306	...
Mons **425** a.		...	0721	...	0821	...	0921	...	until	2221	...	2327	...	...		0846	0946	1046	1146		2246	...	...

§ – For direct trains Brussels - Liège see Table **400**.

▽ – From / to Mouscron via Tournai (Table **416**).

☛ On Ⓒ trains continue beyond Liège to / from Liers.

445 (BRUSSELS -) NAMUR - LUXEMBOURG

Line 162

km			Ⓐ	Ⓐ	Ⓐ	Ⓐ		Ⓐ	Ⓐ	Ⓐ	Ⓐ		Ⓐ	Ⓐ			Ⓒ	Ⓒ		Ⓒ	Ⓒ	Ⓒ	Ⓒ
	Brussels Midi / Zuid **440** d.	Ⓐ	...	...	0533	0633		1933	2033	2133	2233		1609	1807	...	Ⓒ	0632	0732		1832	1932	2032	2132
	Brussels Nord **440** d.		...	...	0544	0644		1944	2044	2144	2244		1621	1821	...		0643	0743		1843	1943	2043	2143
	Brussels Luxembourg **440** d.		...	...	0556	0656		1956	2056	2156	2256		1633	1833	...		0655	0755		1855	1955	2055	2155
0	**Namur** d.		0536	0603	0647	0747	and	2047	2147	2247	2348	A	1724	1922	...		0747	0847	and	1947	2047	2147	2247
29	Ciney d.		0556	0621	0704	0804	hourly	2104	2204	2304	0003	L	1759	1938	...		0803	0903	hourly	2003	2104	2203	2303
52	Marloie d.		0616	0644	0722	0822	until	2122	2222	2322	...	S	1817	1959	...		0821	0921	until	2021	2122	2221	2321
58	Rochefort-Jemelle d.		0622	0649	0729	0829	⊡	2129	2228	2327	...	O	1822	2005	...		0828	0928	⊡	2028	2128	2229	2326
90	Libramont d.		0656	0718	0756	0856		2156	2255	...	...		...	...	...		0856	0956		2056	2156	2256	...
137	Arlon a.		0722	0751	0822	0922		2222	2322	...	...		...	...	...		0922	1022		2122	2222	2322	...
137	Arlon ▷ d.		0729	0801	0829	0929		2229	2329	...	...		...	...	...		0929	1029		2129	2229	*2329*	...
165	**Luxembourg** ▷ a.		0749	0825	0849	0949		2249	2349	...	...		...	...	...		0949	1049		2149	2249	*2349*	...

		Ⓐ	Ⓐ	Ⓐ	Ⓐ	Ⓐ	Ⓐ	Ⓐ	Ⓐ		Ⓐ	Ⓐ	Ⓐ	Ⓐ	Ⓐ	Ⓐ		Ⓒ	Ⓒ	Ⓒ		Ⓒ	Ⓒ
Luxembourg ▷ d.	Ⓐ	...	...	...	*0511*	...	*0611*	0711	0811		1911	2011	2111	2211	2311	2400	Ⓒ	...	0611	0711		2011	*2111*
Arlon ▷ a.		...	...	...	*0531*	...	*0631*	0731	0831		1931	2031	2131	2231	2331	0030		...	0631	0731		2031	*2131*
Arlon d.		...	0436	...	0536	...	0636	0736	0836		1936	2036	2136	...	...	...		...	0636	0736		2036	2136
Libramont d.		...	0509	...	0608	...	0709	0808	0908	and	2008	2108	2209	...	...	...		...	0708	0808	and	2108	2208
Rochefort-Jemelle d.		0437	0533	0554	0632	0640	0733	0832	0932	hourly	2032	2132	2233	...	...	...		0632	0732	0832	hourly	2132	2231
Marloie d.		0444	0540	0602	0639	0649	0740	0839	0939	until	2039	2139	2240	...	...	...		0639	0739	0839	until	2139	...
Ciney d.		0502	0557	0619	0656	0718	0757	0856	0957	♡	2056	2157	2257	...	...	...		0656	0756	0856	♡	2156	...
Namur a.		0517	0612	0637	0712	0734	0813	0912	1013		2112	2213	2312	...	...	...		0712	0812	0912		2212	...
Brussels Luxembourg **440** a.		0606	0703	0726	0804	0826	0905	1004	1104		2204	2304	...	...	...	...		0805	0905	1005		2305	...
Brussels Nord **440** a.		0618	0716	0738	0817	0838	0917	1017	1117		2217	2317	...	...	...	...		0817	0917	1017		2317	...
Brussels Midi / Zuid **440** a.		0629	0727	0749	0828	0849	0928	1028	1128		2228	2328	...	...	...	...		0828	0928	1028		2328	...

⊡ – A change of train at Arlon is also required for the following departures from Brussels: Ⓐ – 0833, 1532, 1632, 1733; Ⓒ – 2032; ⑦ – 1032, 1332, 1432, 1832.

♡ – A change of train at Arlon is also required for the departures from Luxembourg: Ⓐ – 1211; ⑦ – 0611, 1411, 1511, 1611, 1711, 1811.

▷ – Additional local trains run Arlon - Kleinbettingen 🚌 - Luxembourg (journey time: 20–30 minutes).

LIÈGE - GOUVY - CLERVAUX - LUXEMBOURG 446

Line 43 / L10

km		Ⓐ	Ⓒ				A		A		A		A		A		A		A		A				
0	**Liège** Guillemins .. **447** d.	...	...	...	...	0607	0707	0807	0907	1007	1107	1207	1307	1407	1507	1607	1707	1807	1907	2007	2107	2207	...	...	...
23	Rivage .... **447** d.	...	...	...	...	0631	0731	0831	0931	1031	1131	1231	1331	1431	1531	1631	1731	1831	1931	2031	2131	2231	...	...	...
31	Aywaille .... d.	...	...	...	...	0639	0739	0839	0939	1039	1139	1239	1339	1439	1539	1639	1739	1839	1939	2039	2139	2239	...	...	...
58	Trois-Ponts .... d.	...	...	...	...	0702	0802	0902	1002	1102	1202	1302	1402	1502	1602	1702	1802	1902	2002	2102	2202	2302	...	...	...
70	Vielsalm .... d.	...	...	...	...	0712	0812	0912	1012	1112	1212	1312	1412	1512	1612	1712	1812	1912	2014	2114	2214	2312	...	...	...
81	Gouvy 🏛 .... d.	...	...	0524**a**	0624**a**	0724	0824	0924	1024	1124	1224	1324	1424	1524	1624	1724	1824	1924	2024	2124	2224	2321	...	...	...
91	Troisvierges .... d.	0435	0505	0535	0635	0735	0835	0935	1035	1135	1235	1335	1435	1535	1635	1735	1835	1935	2035	2135	2235	...	...	...	...
99	**Clervaux** .... d.	0444	0514	0545	0644	0744	0844	0944	1044	1144	1244	1344	1444	1544	1644	1744	1844	1944	2044	2144	2244	...	...	...	...
114	Kautenbach .... d.	0501	0531	0601	0701	0801	0901	1001	1101	1201	1301	1401	1501	1601	1701	1801	1901	2001	2101	2201	2301	...	...	...	...
129	Ettelbruck .... d.	0516	0546	0616	0716	0816	0916	1016	1116	1216	1316	1416	1516	1616	1716	1816	1916	2016	2116	2216	2316	...	...	...	...
141	Mersch .... d.	0528	0556	0626	0726	0828	0928	1028	1128	1228	1328	1428	1528	1628	1728	1828	1928	2028	2128	2228	2328	...	...	...	...
160	**Luxembourg** .... a.	0546	0615	0646	0743	0846	0946	1046	1146	1246	1346	1446	1546	1646	1746	1846	1946	2046	2146	2246	2346	...	...	...	...

	Ⓐ	Ⓐ	B	Ⓐ	B		B		B		B		B		B		B		B						
Luxembourg .... d.	...	...	0516	...	0616	0716	0816	0916	1016	1116	1216	1316	1416	1516	1616	1716	1816	1916	2016	2116	2216	2316	...	...	...
Mersch .... d.	...	...	0533	...	0633	0733	0833	0933	1033	1133	1233	1333	1433	1533	1633	1733	1833	1933	2033	2133	2233	2333	...	...	...
Ettelbruck .... d.	...	...	0545	...	0645	0745	0845	0945	1045	1145	1245	1345	1445	1545	1645	1745	1845	1945	2045	2145	2245	2345	...	...	...
Kautenbach .... d.	...	...	0559	...	0659	0759	0859	0959	1059	1159	1259	1359	1459	1559	1659	1759	1859	1959	2059	2159	2300	2400	...	...	...
Clervaux .... d.	...	...	0616	...	0716	0816	0916	1016	1116	1216	1316	1416	1516	1616	1716	1816	1916	2016	2116	2216	2315	0015	...	...	...
Troisvierges .... d.	...	...	0633	...	0733	0833	0933	1033	1133	1233	1333	1433	1533	1633	1733	1833	1933	2033	2133	2233	2324	0024	...	...	...
Gouvy 🏛 .... d.	0505	0543	0643	0712	0743	0843	0943	1043	1143	1243	1343	1443	1543	1643	1743	1843	1943	2043	2143	2243	...	...	...	...	...
Vielsalm .... d.	0515	0552	0652	0722	0752	0852	0952	1052	1152	1252	1352	1452	1552	1652	1752	1852	1952	2052	2152	2252	...	...	...	...	...
Trois-Ponts .... d.	0526	0602	0702	0733	0802	0902	1002	1102	1202	1302	1402	1502	1602	1702	1802	1902	2002	2102	2202	2302	...	...	...	...	...
Aywaille .... d.	0550	0625	0725	0803	0825	0925	1025	1125	1225	1325	1425	1525	1625	1725	1825	1925	2025	2125	2225	2325	...	...	...	...	...
Rivage .... **447** d.	0558	0633	0733	0811	0833	0933	1033	1133	1233	1333	1433	1533	1633	1733	1833	1933	2033	2133	2233	2333	...	...	...	...	...
Liège Guillemins ... **447** a.	0621	0655	0755	0834	0855	0955	1055	1155	1255	1355	1455	1555	1655	1755	1855	1955	2055	2155	2255	2355	...	...	...	...	...

A – Runs ①–⑤ (not Belgian holidays) Liège - Troisvierges; daily Troisvierges - Luxembourg.
B – Runs daily Luxemourg - Troisvierges; ①–⑤ (not Belgian holidays) Troisvierges - Liège.

a – ①–⑤ (not Belgian holidays).

ADDITIONAL TRAINS TROISVIERGES - CLERVAUX - LUXEMBOURG:
From Troisvierges hourly 0405Ⓐ - 2205Ⓐ. From Luxembourg hourly 0544Ⓐ - 2344Ⓐ.

CONNECTING TRAINS KAUTENBACH - WILTZ (journey 12 – 14 minutes):
From Kautenbach: On Ⓐ every 30 minutes 0533 - 2303; on Ⓒ hourly 0603, 0703, 0804 - 2304.
From Wiltz: On Ⓐ every 30 minutes 0416 - 2246; on Ⓒ hourly 0546 - 0746 and 0842 - 2342.

LIÈGE - MARLOIE - ROCHEFORT JEMELLE 447

Line 43

km			Ⓐ	Ⓐ		Ⓐ	Ⓐ	Ⓐ	Ⓐ	Ⓐ	Ⓐ	Ⓐ	Ⓐ		Ⓒ	Ⓒ	Ⓒ	Ⓒ	Ⓒ	Ⓒ	Ⓒ	Ⓒ	
	Liège St Lambertus ◇ .... d.	Ⓐ	0606	0703		1603	1624	1703	1803	1903	2003	2103	2203	Ⓒ	0805	1005	1205	1405	1605	1805	2005	2205	...
0	**Liège** Guillemins .... **446** d.		0616	0716	and	1616	1647	1716	1816	1916	2016	2116	2216		0816	1016	1216	1416	1616	1816	2016	2216	...
23	Rivage .... **446** d.		0643	0743	hourly	1643	1716	1743	1843	1943	2043	2143	2243		0843	1043	1243	1443	1643	1843	2043	2243	...
43	Barvaux .... d.		0705	0805	until	1705	1738	1805	1905	2005	2105	2205	2305		0905	1105	1305	1505	1705	1905	2105	2305	...
65	Marloie .... **445** a.		0723	0823		1723	1758	1823	1923	2023	2123	2223	2323		0923	1123	1323	1523	1723	1923	2123	2323	...
71	**Rochefort-Jemelle** .... **445** a.		...	...		...	1807	...	...	...	2130	2231	2331		...	...	...	...	...	...	...	2331	...

		Ⓐ	Ⓐ	Ⓐ	Ⓐ	Ⓐ	Ⓐ	Ⓐ		Ⓐ	Ⓐ			Ⓒ	Ⓒ	Ⓒ	Ⓒ	Ⓒ	Ⓒ	Ⓒ	Ⓒ		
Rochefort-Jemelle .... **445** d.	Ⓐ	0426	0526	0603	0625	...	...	...		...	...	...	Ⓒ	0728	...	...	...	...	...	...	...	...	...
Marloie .... **445** d.		0435	0535	0613	0635	0735	0835	0935	and	1935	2035	...		0735	0935	1135	1335	1535	1735	1935	2135	...	...
Barvaux .... d.		0452	0552	0631	0652	0752	0852	0952	hourly	1952	2052	...		0752	0952	1152	1352	1552	1752	1952	2152	...	...
Rivage .... **446** d.		0515	0615	0654	0715	0815	0915	1015	until	2015	2115	...		0815	1015	1215	1415	1615	1815	2015	2215	...	...
Liège Guillemins .... **446** a.		0543	0643	0722	0743	0843	0943	1043		2043	2143	...		0843	1043	1243	1443	1643	1843	2043	2243	...	...
Liège St Lambertus ◇ .... a.		0555	0655	0736	0755	0855	0955	1055		2055	2155	...		0854	1054	1254	1454	1654	1854	2054	2254	...	...

◇ – Most trains continue beyond Liège St Lambertus to / from Liers.

ARDENNES LOCAL SERVICES 448

Lines 154, 166, 165

km			Ⓐ	Ⓐ		Ⓐ		Ⓒ		Ⓒ
0	**Namur** .... **440** d.	Ⓐ	0552	0650		1952	Ⓒ	0552		1952
28	Dinant .... **440** d.		0623	0723		2023		0623	and	2023
43	Houyet .... d.		0639	0739	and	2039		0639	every	2039
52	Beauraing .... d.		0647	0747	hourly	2047		0647	**two**	2047
100	Bertrix .... a.		0727	0827	until	2127		0727	hours	2127
100	Bertrix .... d.		0735	0835		2135		0735	until	2135
108	**Libramont** .... a.		0745	0845		2145		0745		2145

		Ⓐ	Ⓐ		Ⓐ		Ⓒ		Ⓒ
Libramont .... d.	Ⓐ	0614	0714		1914	Ⓒ	0714		1914
Bertrix .... a.		0623	0723		1923		0723	and	1923
Bertrix .... d.		0631	0731	and	1931		0731	every	1931
Beauraing .... d.		0711	0811	hourly	2011		0811	**two**	2011
Houyet .... d.		0720	0820	until	2020		0820	hours	2020
Dinant .... **440** d.		0737	0837		2037		0837	until	2037
Namur ...... **440** a.		0808	0908		2108		0908		2108

km			Ⓐ		Ⓐ	Ⓐ‡		Ⓒ		Ⓒ
0	**Libramont** .... d.	Ⓐ	0657		2057	2157	Ⓒ	0757	and	2157
8	Bertrix .... d.		0707	and	2107	2206		0807	every	2207
33	Florenville .... d.		0721	hourly	2121	...		0821	**two**	2221
57	Virton .... d.		0740	until	2140	...		0840	hours	2240
85	Athus .... ▷ d.		0801		2201	...		0901	until	2301
98	**Arlon** .... a.		0818		2218	...		0918		2318

		Ⓐ		Ⓐ			Ⓒ		Ⓒ
Arlon .... d.	Ⓐ	0641		2132	...	Ⓒ	0541		1941
Athus .... ▷ d.		0700	and	2151	...		0601	and	2001
Virton .... d.		0721	hourly	2221	...		0622	every	2022
Florenville .... d.		0738	until	2238	...		0639	**two**	2039
Bertrix .... d.		0753		2253	...		0654	hours	2054
Libramont .... a.		0803		2303	...		0704	until	2104

▷ – Athus - Luxembourg: see Table **449**. ‡ – Also 2257Ⓐ to Bertrix.

LUXEMBOURG – local services 449

Operator: CFL

		⚒	every	⚒		†		†	every	†
Luxembourg ..... **446** d.	⚒	0455	30	2355	†	0455	and	1155	30	2355
Ettelbruck .... **446** d.		0536	minutes	0037		0536	hourly	1236	mins	0037
Diekirch .... a.		0542	until	0042		0542	until	1242	until	0042

		⚒		⚒		†		†		†
Diekirch .... d.	⚒	0420	every	2320	†	0450	and	1050	every	2320
Ettelbruck .... **446** d.		0426	30	2326		0456	hourly	1056	30	2326
Luxembourg ... **446** a.		0508	minutes	0008		0538	until	1138	minutes	0008

		⚒		⚒		†		†		†
Luxembourg .... d.	⚒	0520	every	2350	†	0550	and	1150	every	2350
Pétange .... d.		0544	30	0014		0614	hourly	1214	30	0014
Rodange .... d.		0550	minutes	0020		0620	until	1220	minutes	0020
Athus (Belgium) .. ▷ a.		0555		0025		0625		1225		0025

		⚒		⚒		†		†		†
Athus (Belgium) . ▷ d.	⚒	0435	every	2335	†	0635	and	1135	every	2335
Rodange .... d.		0440	30	2340		0640	hourly	1140	30	2340
Pétange .... d.		0445	mins	2345		0645	until	1145	minutes	2345
Luxembourg .... a.		0510		0010		0710		1210		0010

Luxembourg → Bettembourg → Esch-sur-Alzette → Pétange → **Rodange** (journey 12 mins to Bettembourg, 25 mins to Esch, 45 – 50 mins to Pétange, 50 – 55 mins to Rodange):
⚒: 0521 and approx every 30 minutes to 1921, 1932 and every 30 minutes until 2332, 0002.
†: 0502, and hourly to 2302, 0002.

Rodange → Pétange → Esch-sur-Alzette → Bettembourg → **Luxembourg** (5 – 7 mins to Pétange, 26 – 32 mins to Esch, 39 – 45 mins to Bettembourg, 50 – 55 mins to Luxembourg):
⚒: 0451, 0551, 0651, 0721, and every 30 minutes to 1921, 2033 and every 30 minutes 0003.
†: 0432, 0532 and hourly to 2303, 0003.

Luxembourg → **Wasserbillig** (journey 35 – 42 minutes):
Trains run approx. every 30 minutes (some continue to Trier, Table **915**).

Wasserbillig → **Luxembourg** (journey 35 – 42 minutes):
Trains run approx. every 30 minutes (some from Trier, Table **915**).

Luxembourg → **Kleinbettingen** (journey 18 – 19 minutes) ⊠:
Ⓐ: 0525 and approx. every 30 minutes to 2055, 2120, 2220, 2320, 2400.
Ⓒ: 0545 and hourly to 2245.

Kleinbettingen → **Luxembourg** (journey 18 – 19 minutes) ⊠:
Ⓐ: 0445 and approx. every 30 mins to 2115, 2150, 2250, 2350.
Ⓒ: 0615 and hourly to 2315.

Bettembourg → Dudelange → **Volmerange-les-Mines** (journey 17 minutes):
Approx. every 30 mins. On † runs only to Dudelange Usines, hourly (afternoon every 30 mins).

Volmerange-les-Mines → Dudelange → **Bettembourg** (journey 14 minutes):
Approx. every 30 mins. On † runs from Dudelange Usines, hourly (afternoon every 30 mins).

▷ – For connections to / from Arlon see Table **448**.

⊠ – Certain trains continue to / from Arlon.

NETHERLANDS

SEE MAP PAGE 231

Operator: NS – Nederlandse Spoorwegen (unless otherwise indicated) www.ns.nl

Services: Trains convey first- and second-class seated accommodation, unless otherwise indicated in the tables. Some trains consist of portions for two or more destinations, and passengers should be careful to join the correct part of the train. The destination of each train portion is normally indicated beside the entrance doors.

Timings: Valid **until December 9**, 2023.

Holidays: Unless otherwise indicated, services marked ⚒ do not run on ⑦ or on Dec. 26, Apr. 10, May 29.
those marked Ⓐ do not run on ⑥⑦ or on Dec. 26, Apr. 10, 27, May 18, 29.
those marked Ⓑ do not run on ⑥ or on Apr. 27, May 18.
those marked † run on ⑦ and on Dec. 26, Apr. 10, May 29.
those marked Ⓒ run on ⑥⑦ and on Apr. 10, 27, May 18, 29.
those marked ⑥ also run Apr. 27, May 18.

No trains, other than international services, will run between ± 2000 hours on Dec. 31 and ± 0200 on Jan. 1.

Tickets: A nationwide smartcard system called *OV-chipkaart* is used for all public transport in the Netherlands. Personalised and anonymous cards are available (€7.50 on-line, €10.50 paper application) which can be loaded and topped up with travel credit. Disposable single use cards can also be purchased from ticket machines and ticket offices for full fare single / return journeys and day tickets (a €1 supplement is payable for single use cards). You must always check-in and check-out your OV-chipkaart for each journey. Alternatively, e-tickets for full fare single and return journeys may be purchased on-line and printed yourself.

Supplements: A supplement is payable for journeys on *Intercity direct* services (except for local journeys Amsterdam - Schiphol and Rotterdam - Breda), also for internal journeys on *ICE* trains between Amsterdam and Arnhem. In both cases the single journey supplement is €2.60 (off-peak discounts are available). Supplements may be purchased from special Supplement Pillars (using your OV-chipkaart) or from ticket machines.

450 AMSTERDAM - DEN HAAG - ROTTERDAM - ROOSENDAAL - VLISSINGEN

See Table **451** for faster *Intercity direct* services Amsterdam - Schiphol ✈ - Rotterdam via the high-speed line.
See Tables **452** and **460** for services from / to Amsterdam Zuid. See Table **18** for International services to / from Brussels.

km		④⑤z	⊖	⊖			Ⓐ	Ⓐ	Ⓐ	⑥	⚒	Ⓐ	Ⓒ		Ⓐ	Ⓒ			Ⓐ	Ⓒ			
0	**Amsterdam** Centraal ...... **461** d.	0005	0005	0035	...	...	...	...	...	...	0535	0605	...	0635	0705	0705	0735	and at the same minutes past each hour until	1905	1905	1935	2005	2035
5	Amsterdam Sloterdijk .... d.	0010	0010	0040	...	...	...	...	...	...	0540	0610	...	0640	0710	0710	0740		1910	1910	1940	2010	2040
19	**Haarlem** .... **461** d.	0021	0021	0051	...	...	...	...	...	...	0551	0621	...	0651	0721	0721	0751		1921	1921	1951	2021	2051
47	Leiden Centraal .... a.	0040	0040	0110	...	...	...	...	...	...	0610	0640	...	0710	0740	0740	0810		1940	1940	2010	2040	2110
47	Leiden Centraal ...... **460** d.	0043	0045	0115	...	...	...	...	...	...	0615	0645	...	0715	0745	0745	0815		1945	1945	2015	2045	2115
63	**Den Haag** HS ...... **460 471** d.	0057	0059	0129	...	...	...	...	...	...	0629	0659	...	0729	0759	0759	0829		1959	1959	2029	2059	2129
71	Delft .... **460 471** d.	0103	0105	0135	...	...	...	...	...	...	0635	0705	...	0735	0805	0805	0835		2005	2005	2035	2105	2135
81	Schiedam Centrum ...... **460** d.	0111	0114	0144	...	...	...	...	...	...	0643	0713	...	0743	0813	0813	0843		2013	2013	2043	2113	2143
85	**Rotterdam** Centraal **460 471** a.	0116	0120	0150	...	...	...	...	...	...	0648	0718	...	0748	0818	0818	0848		2018	2018	2048	2118	2148
85	**Rotterdam** Centraal **460 471** d.	...	...	...	...	...	...	...	0621	...	0651	0721	...	0751	0821	0821	0851		2021	2021	2051	2121	2151
105	Dordrecht .... **460 471** d.	...	...	...	...	...	...	...	0637	...	0707	0737	...	0807	0837	0837	0907		2037	2037	2107	2137	2207
143	**Roosendaal** .... a.	...	...	...	...	...	...	...	0700	...	0730	0800	...	0830	0900	0900	0930		2100	2100	2130	2200	2230
143	**Roosendaal** .... d.	...	...	...	...	...	0606	0636	0703	0706	0736	0803	0806	0836	0903	0906	0936		2103	2106	2136	2206	2236
156	Bergen op Zoom .... d.	...	...	...	...	...	0615	0645	0712	0715	0745	0812	0815	0845	0912	0915	0945		2112	2115	2145	2215	2245
193	Goes .... d.	...	...	...	...	...	0646	0716	0732	0746	0816	0832	0846	0916	0932	0946	1016		2132	2146	2216	2246	2316
212	Middelburg .... d.	...	...	...	...	...	0701	0731	0744	0801	0831	0844	0901	0931	0944	1001	1031		2144	2201	2231	2301	2331
218	**Vlissingen** .... a.	...	...	...	...	...	0709	0739	0751	0809	0839	0851	0909	0939	0951	1009	1039		2151	2209	2239	2309	2339

						⑦–②		③–⑥	
Amsterdam Centraal ...... **461** d.	2105	2135	2205	2235	2305	2305	2335	2335	...
Amsterdam Sloterdijk .... d.	2110	2140	2210	2240	2310	2310	2340	2340	...
Haarlem .... **461** d.	2120	2151	2221	2251	2321	2321	2351	2351	...
Leiden Centraal .... a.	2140	2210	2240	2310	2340	2340	0010	0010	...
Leiden Centraal ...... **460** d.	2145	2215	2245	2315	2345	2345	0015	0015	...
Den Haag HS ...... **460 471** d.	2159	2229	2259	2329	2359	2359	0029	0029	...
Delft .... **460 471** d.	2205	2235	2305	2335	0005	0005	0035	0035	...
Schiedam Centrum ...... **460** d.	2213	2243	2313	2343	0013	0013	0043	0043	...
Rotterdam Centraal **460 471** a.	2218	2248	2318	2348	0018	0018	0048	0048	...
Rotterdam Centraal **460 471** d.	2221	2251	2321	2351	0021	0021	0051	0051	...
Dordrecht .... **460 471** d.	2237	2307	2337	0007	0036	0037	0106	0107	...
Roosendaal .... a.	2300	2330	2400	0030	...	0109	...	0139	...
Roosendaal .... d.	2306	2336	0006	...	...	...	...	...	...
Bergen op Zoom .... d.	2315	2345	0015	...	...	...	...	...	...
Goes .... d.	2346	0016	0046	...	...	...	...	...	...
Middelburg .... d.	0001	0031	0101	...	...	...	...	...	...
Vlissingen .... a.	0009	0039	0109	...	...	...	...	...	...

	A	④v	⚒	Ⓐ	⚒	Ⓐ		Ⓐ	†
Vlissingen .... d.	...	...	...	...	...	...	...	0540	...
Middelburg .... d.	...	...	...	...	...	...	...	0546	...
Goes .... d.	...	...	...	...	...	...	...	0558	...
Bergen op Zoom .... d.	...	...	...	...	...	0547	...	0617	...
Roosendaal .... a.	...	...	...	...	...	0557	...	0627	...
Roosendaal .... d.	...	...	...	0531	...	0601	...	0631	...
Dordrecht .... **460 471** d.	...	...	...	0554	0554	0624	0624	0654	0654
Rotterdam Centraal ...... **460 471** a.	...	...	...	0608	0608	0638	0638	0708	0708
Rotterdam Centraal ...... **460 471** d.	0512	0515	0542	0612	0612	0642	0642	0712	0712
Schiedam Centrum .... **460** d.	0516	0521	0546	0616	0616	0646	0646	0716	0716
Delft .... **460 471** d.	0525	0528	0554	0624	0624	0654	0654	0724	0724
Den Haag HS .... **460 471** d.	0533	0536	0603	0633	0633	0703	0703	0733	0733
Leiden Centraal .... **460** a.	0545	0548	0615	0645	0645	0715	0715	0745	0745
Leiden Centraal .... d.	0550	0550	0620	0650	0650	0720	0720	0750	0750
Haarlem .... **461** d.	0610	0610	0640	0710	0710	0740	0740	0810	0810
Amsterdam Sloterdijk .... d.	0619	0619	0649	0719	0719	0749	0749	0819	0819
Amsterdam Centraal .... **461** a.	0625	0625	0655	0725	0725	0755	0755	0825	0825

	⑥	Ⓐ	†	⚒		Ⓒ	Ⓐ			Ⓒ	Ⓐ												
Vlissingen .... d.	0551	0610	...	0621	...	0651	0710	0721	and at the same minutes past each hour until	1851	1910	1921	1951	2021	2051	2121	2151	2221	2251	2321	...	...	...
Middelburg .... d.	0559	0616	...	0629	...	0659	0716	0729		1859	1916	1929	1959	2029	2059	2129	2159	2229	2259	2329	...	...	...
Goes .... d.	0614	0628	...	0644	...	0714	0728	0744		1914	1928	1944	2014	2044	2114	2144	2214	2244	2314	2344	...	...	...
Bergen op Zoom .... d.	0644	0647	...	0714	...	0744	0747	0814		1944	1947	2014	2044	2114	2144	2214	2244	2314	2344	0014	...	...	...
Roosendaal .... a.	0654	0657	...	0724	...	0754	0757	0824		1954	1957	2024	2054	2124	2154	2224	2254	2324	2354	0024	...	...	...
Roosendaal .... d.	0701	0701	...	0731	...	0801	0801	0831		2001	2001	2031	2101	2131	2201	2231	2301	2331	0001	...	...	...	...
Dordrecht .... **460 471** d.	0724	0724	0724	0754	0754	0824	0824	0854		2024	2024	2054	2124	2154	2224	2254	2324	2354	0024	...	...	...	...
Rotterdam Centraal **460 471** a.	0738	0738	0738	0808	0808	0838	0838	0908		2038	2038	2108	2138	2208	2238	2308	2338	0008	0038	...	...	...	...
Rotterdam Centraal **460 471** d.	0742	0742	0742	0812	0812	0842	0842	0912		2042	2042	2112	2142	2212	2242	2312	2342	0012	...	...	...	...	...
Schiedam Centrum ...... **460** d.	0746	0746	0746	0816	0816	0846	0846	0916		2046	2046	2116	2146	2216	2246	2316	2346	0016	...	...	...	...	...
Delft .... **460 471** d.	0754	0754	0754	0824	0824	0854	0854	0924		2054	2054	2124	2154	2224	2254	2324	2354	0024	...	...	...	...	...
Den Haag HS ...... **460 471** d.	0803	0803	0803	0833	0833	0903	0903	0933		2103	2103	2133	2203	2233	2303	2333	0003	0033	...	...	...	...	...
Leiden Centraal ...... **460** a.	0815	0815	0815	0845	0845	0915	0915	0945		2115	2115	2145	2215	2245	2315	2345	0015	0045	...	...	...	...	...
Leiden Centraal .... d.	0820	0820	0820	0850	0850	0920	0920	0950		2120	2120	2150	2220	2250	2320	2350	0020	0050	...	...	...	...	...
Haarlem .... **461** d.	0840	0840	0840	0910	0910	0940	0940	1010		2140	2140	2210	2240	2310	2340	0010	0040	0110	...	...	...	...	...
Amsterdam Sloterdijk .... d.	0849	0849	0849	0919	0919	0949	0949	1019		2149	2149	2219	2249	2319	2349	0019	0049	0119	...	...	...	...	...
Amsterdam Centraal ...... **461** a.	0855	0855	0855	0925	0925	0955	0955	1025		2155	2155	2225	2255	2325	2355	0025	0055	0125	...	...	...	...	...

AMSTERDAM - DEN HAAG CENTRAAL *See note* ❖

km		①–④ b	①–④ b	①–④ b	①–④ b	①–④ b	①–④ b	①–④ b		①–④ b	①–④ b	①–④ b	①–④ b	①–④ b	①–④ b	①–④ b	①–④ b	①–④ b						
0	**Amsterdam** Centraal ...... **461** d.	0620	0650	0720	0750	0820	0850	0920	...	1520	1550	1620	1650	1720	1750	1820	1850	1920	...	...	...	...	...	...
5	Amsterdam Sloterdijk .... d.	0625	0655	0725	0755	0825	0855	0925	...	1525	1555	1625	1655	1725	1755	1825	1855	1925	...	...	...	...	...	...
19	**Haarlem** .... **461** d.	0637	0707	0737	0807	0837	0907	0937	...	1537	1607	1637	1707	1737	1807	1837	1907	1937	...	...	...	...	...	...
47	Leiden Centraal .... a.	0657	0727	0757	0827	0857	0927	0957	...	1557	1627	1657	1727	1757	1827	1857	1927	1957	...	...	...	...	...	...
47	Leiden Centraal ...... **460** d.	0700	0730	0800	0830	0900	0930	1000	...	1600	1630	1700	1730	1800	1830	1900	1930	2000	...	...	...	...	...	...
62	**Den Haag** Centraal ...... **460** a.	0711	0741	0811	0841	0911	0941	1011	...	1611	1641	1711	1741	1811	1841	1911	1941	2011	...	...	...	...	...	...

	①–④ b	①–④ b	①–④ b	①–④ b	①–④ b	①–④ b	①–④ b	①–④ b		①–④ b	①–④ b	①–④ b	①–④ b	①–④ b	①–④ b	①–④ b	①–④ b	①–④ b						
Den Haag Centraal ...... **460** d.	0617	0649	0719	0749	0819	0849	0919	0949	...	1549	1619	1649	1719	1749	1819	1849	1917	1947	...	...	...	...	...	...
Leiden Centraal ...... **460** a.	0631	0701	0731	0801	0831	0901	0931	1001	...	1601	1631	1701	1731	1801	1831	1901	1929	1959	...	...	...	...	...	...
Leiden Centraal .... d.	0633	0703	0733	0803	0833	0903	0933	1003	...	1603	1633	1703	1733	1803	1833	1903	1933	2003	...	...	...	...	...	...
Haarlem .... **461** d.	0655	0725	0755	0825	0855	0925	0955	1025	...	1625	1655	1725	1755	1825	1855	1925	1955	2025	...	...	...	...	...	...
Amsterdam Sloterdijk .... d.	0704	0734	0804	0834	0904	0934	1004	1034	...	1634	1704	1734	1804	1834	1904	1934	2004	2034	...	...	...	...	...	...
Amsterdam Centraal ...... **461** a.	0710	0740	0810	0840	0910	0940	1010	1040	...	1640	1710	1740	1810	1840	1910	1940	2010	2040	...	...	...	...	...	...

A – ①②③⑤ (not Apr. 10, May 29).

b – Not Apr. 10, 27, May 18, 29.
v – Not Apr. 27, May 18.
z – Not Apr. 28, May 19.

⊖ – ①②③⑥⑦ (also Apr. 28, May 19).
❖ – Direct *Intercity* services Amsterdam Centraal - Den Haag Centraal only run on ①–④ as shown. At other times use Vlissingen services in the main table and change trains at Leiden (see Table **460** for connecting trains between Leiden and Den Haag Centraal).

AMSTERDAM - ROTTERDAM - BREDA 451

Intercity direct services via the high-speed line. Supplement payable (except for local journeys Amsterdam - Schiphol and Rotterdam - Breda).
See Table **471** for other connecting services Rotterdam - Breda and v.v.

km		1010	910	9212	912	1014	914	1016	9216	916	1018		958	1060	9260	960	1062		1064	9264	1066	1068	9268
		⚒	Ⓐ	B	Ⓐ		Ⓐ		B	Ⓐ			Ⓐ		B	Ⓐ				B			B
0	**Amsterdam** Centraal .... ★ d.	0553	0608	0628	0638	0655	0708	0725	0728	0738	0755	and at the same minutes past each hour until	1808	1825	1828	1838	1855	...	1925	1928	1953	2025	2028
17	**Schiphol** ✈ .... ★ d.	0610	0623	0643	0653	0710	0723	0740	0743	0753	0810		1823	1840	1843	1853	1910	...	1940	1943	2010	2040	2043
70	**Rotterdam** Centraal .... a.	0636	0649	0709	0719	0736	0749	0806	0809	0819	0836		1849	1906	1909	1919	1936	...	2006	2009	2036	2106	2109
70	**Rotterdam** Centraal .... **471** d.	...	...	0711	...	...	...	...	0811	...	...		...	...	1911	...	...	...	...	2011	...	...	2111
117	**Breda** .... **471** a.	...	...	0734	...	...	...	...	0834	...	...		...	...	1934	...	...	...	...	2034	...	...	2134

	1070		1072	9272	1074		1076	1076	1078	
				B			Ⓐ	Ⓒ		
Amsterdam Centraal .... ★ d.	2055	...	2125	2128	2153	...	2223	2225	2253	...
Schiphol ✈ .... ★ d.	2110	...	2140	2143	2210	...	2240	2240	2310	...
Rotterdam Centraal .... a.	2136	...	2206	2209	2236	...	2306	2306	2336	...
Rotterdam Centraal .... **471** d.	...	...	...	2211	...	...	...	...	2341	...
Breda .... **471** a.	...	...	...	2234	...	...	...	...	0005	...

	1003		1005		905	1007	907	1009	9211
	⚒		⚒		Ⓐ		Ⓐ	Ⓐ	B
Breda .... **471** d.	...	...	...	...	...	...	...	...	0726
Rotterdam Centraal .... **471** a.	...	...	...	...	...	...	...	...	0750
Rotterdam Centraal .... d.	0624	...	0651	...	0711	0724	0741	0751	0754
Schiphol ✈ .... ★ d.	0651	...	0718	...	0738	0751	0808	0818	0821
Amsterdam Centraal ..... ★ a.	0705	...	0732	...	0752	0805	0822	0832	0835

	909	1011	911	1013	9215		953	1055	955	1057	9259		1059	1061	9263	1063	1065	9267	1067	1069	9271		1073
	Ⓐ		Ⓐ		B		Ⓐ		Ⓐ		B				B			B			B		
Breda .... **471** d.	...	...	...	...	0826	and at the same minutes past each hour until	...	...	...	...	1926	...	...	...	2026	...	...	2126	...	...	2226	...	...
Rotterdam Centraal .... **471** a.	...	...	...	...	0850		...	...	...	...	1950	...	...	...	2050	...	...	2150	...	...	2250	...	...
Rotterdam Centraal .... d.	0811	0824	0841	0851	0854		1911	1924	1941	1951	1954	...	2024	2051	2054	2124	2151	2154	2224	2251	2254	...	2341
Schiphol ✈ .... ★ d.	0838	0851	0908	0918	0921		1938	1951	2008	2018	2021	...	2051	2118	2121	2151	2218	2221	2251	2318	2321	...	0008
Amsterdam Centraal .... ★ a.	0852	0905	0922	0932	0935		1952	2007	2022	2032	2035	...	2105	2132	2135	2205	2232	2235	2305	2332	2335	...	0022

B – To / from Brussels (Table **18**).

★ – Additional local trains run up to 4 times per hour Amsterdam Centraal - Schiphol and v.v.

DORDRECHT - ROTTERDAM - SCHIPHOL ✈ - AMSTERDAM ZUID - LELYSTAD 452

For services Amsterdam Centraal - Almere - Zwolle and v.v., see Table **459**. For services via Amersfoort and Utrecht, see Table **481**.
No service on Ⓒ.

	①-④ b	⑤	①-④ b	⑤	①-④ b	⑤		①-④ b	⑤	①-④ b	⑤	Ⓐ	Ⓐ		Ⓐ	Ⓐ	①-④ b	⑤	①-④ b	⑤	
Dordrecht .... **450** d.	...	...	0604	0604	0634	0634	and at the same minutes past each hour until	0834	0834	0904	0904	0934	1004	and at the same minutes past each hour until	1304	1334	1404	1404	1434	1434	and at the same minutes past each hour until
Rotterdam Centraal .... **450** d.	0551	0551	0621	0621	0651	0651		0851	0851	0921	0921	0951	1021		1321	1351	1421	1421	1451	1451	
Schiedam Centrum .... **450** d.	0556	0556	0626	0626	0656	0656		0856	0856	0926	0926	0956	1026		1326	1356	1426	1426	1456	1456	
Delft .... **450** d.	0604	0604	0634	0634	0704	0704		0904	0904	0934	0934	1004	1034		1334	1404	1434	1434	1504	1504	
Den Haag HS .... **450** d.	0613	0613	0643	0643	0713	0713		0913	0913	0943	0943	1013	1043		1343	1413	1443	1443	1513	1513	
Leiden Centraal .... **450 460** d.	0627	0627	0657	0657	0727	0727		0927	0927	0957	0957	1027	1057		1357	1427	1457	1457	1527	1527	
Schiphol ✈ .... **460** d.	0644	0645	0714	0715	0744	0745		0944	0945	1014	1015	1045	1115		1415	1445	1514	1515	1544	1545	
Amsterdam Zuid .... **460** a.	0650	0651	0720	0721	0750	0751		0950	0951	1020	1021	1051	1121		1421	1451	1520	1521	1550	1551	
Amsterdam Zuid .... **460** d.	0656	...	0726	...	0756	...		0956	...	1026	...	...	...		...	...	1526	...	1556	...	
Duivendrecht .... d.	0701	...	0731	...	0801	...		1001	...	1031	...	...	...		...	...	1531	...	1601	...	
Almere Centrum ..... **459 460** d.	0719	...	0749	...	0819	...		1019	...	1049	...	...	...		...	...	1549	...	1619	...	
Almere Buiten .... **459** d.	0724	...	0754	...	0824	...		1024	...	1054	...	...	...		...	...	1554	...	1624	...	
Lelystad Centrum ... **459 460** a.	0736	...	0806	...	0836	...		1036	...	1106	...	...	...		...	...	1606	...	1636	...	

	①-④ b	⑤	①-④ b	⑤		Ⓐ	Ⓐ		
Dordrecht .... **450** d.	1734	1734	1804	1804	...	1839	1909	...	...
Rotterdam Centraal .... **450** d.	1751	1751	1821	1821	...	1857	1927	...	...
Schiedam Centrum .... **450** d.	1756	1756	1826	1826	...	1901	1931	...	...
Delft .... **450** d.	1804	1804	1834	1834	...	1909	1939	...	...
Den Haag HS .... **450** d.	1813	1813	1843	1843	...	1918	1948	...	...
Leiden Centraal .... **450 460** d.	1827	1827	1857	1857	...	1931	2001	...	...
Schiphol ✈ .... **460** d.	1844	1845	1914	1915	...	1949	2019	...	...
Amsterdam Zuid .... **460** a.	1850	1851	1920	1921	...	1955	2025	...	...
Amsterdam Zuid .... **460** d.	1856	...	1926	...	...	...	...	...	...
Duivendrecht .... d.	1901	...	1931	...	...	...	...	...	...
Almere Centrum ..... **459 460** d.	1919	...	1949	...	...	...	...	...	...
Almere Buiten .... **459** d.	1924	...	1954	...	...	...	...	...	...
Lelystad Centrum ... **459 460** a.	1936	...	2006	...	...	...	...	...	...

	Ⓐ		⑤	①-④ b	⑤	①-④ b		⑤	①-④ b
Lelystad Centrum **459 460** d.	...	...	...	0624	...	0654	and at the same minutes past each hour until	...	0854
Almere Buiten .... **459** d.	...	...	...	0636	...	0706		...	0906
Almere Centrum .. **459 460** d.	...	...	...	0642	...	0712		...	0912
Duivendrecht .... d.	...	...	...	0659	...	0729		...	0929
Amsterdam Zuid .... a.	...	...	...	0704	...	0734		...	0934
Amsterdam Zuid .... **460** d.	0639	...	0708	0709	0738	0739		0938	0938
Schiphol ✈ .... **460** d.	0647	...	0717	0717	0747	0747		0947	0946
Leiden Centraal .... **450 460** d.	0705	...	0735	0735	0805	0805		1005	1005
Den Haag HS .... **450** d.	0719	...	0749	0749	0819	0819		1019	1019
Delft .... **450** d.	0725	...	0755	0755	0825	0825		1025	1025
Schiedam Centrum ...... **450** d.	0733	...	0803	0803	0833	0833		1033	1033
Rotterdam Centraal .... **450** a.	0738	...	0808	0808	0838	0838		1038	1038
Dordrecht .... **450** a.	0756	...	0826	0826	0856	0856		1056	1056

	⑤	①-④ b	Ⓐ	Ⓐ		Ⓐ	Ⓐ	⑤	①-④ b	⑤	①-④ b		⑤ v	①-④ b	⑤ v	①-④ b	⑤ v	①-④ b	⑤ v	①-④ b		Ⓐ
Lelystad Centrum ... **459 460** d.	...	0924	...	...	and at the same minutes past each hour until	...	...	...	1424	...	1454	and at the same minutes past each hour until	...	1654	...	1724	...	1754	...	1824	...	...
Almere Buiten .... **459** d.	...	0936	...	...		...	...	...	1436	...	1506		...	1706	...	1736	...	1806	...	1836	...	...
Almere Centrum ..... **459 460** d.	...	0942	...	...		...	...	...	1442	...	1512		...	1712	...	1742	...	1812	...	1842	...	...
Duivendrecht .... d.	...	0959	...	...		...	...	...	1459	...	1529		...	1729	...	1759	...	1829	...	1859	...	...
Amsterdam Zuid .... a.	...	1004	...	...		...	...	...	1504	...	1534		...	1734	...	1804	...	1834	...	1904	...	...
Amsterdam Zuid .... **460** d.	1008	1009	1038	1108		1408	1438	1508	1509	1538	1539		1738	1739	1808	1809	1838	1838	1908	1909	...	1935
Schiphol ✈ .... **460** d.	1017	1017	1047	1117		1417	1447	1517	1517	1547	1547		1747	1747	1817	1817	1846	1846	1917	1917	...	1942
Leiden Centraal .... **450 460** d.	1035	1035	1105	1135		1435	1505	1535	1535	1605	1605		1805	1805	1835	1835	1905	1905	1935	1935	...	2000
Den Haag HS .... **450** d.	1049	1049	1119	1149		1449	1519	1549	1549	1619	1619		1819	1819	1849	1849	1919	1919	1949	1949	...	2014
Delft .... **450** d.	1055	1055	1125	1155		1455	1525	1555	1555	1625	1625		1825	1825	1855	1855	1925	1925	1955	1955	...	2020
Schiedam Centrum .... **450** d.	1103	1103	1133	1203		1503	1533	1603	1603	1633	1633		1833	1833	1903	1903	1933	1933	2003	2003	...	2028
Rotterdam Centraal .... **450** a.	1108	1108	1138	1208		1508	1538	1608	1608	1638	1638		1838	1838	1908	1908	1938	1938	2008	2008	...	2033
Dordrecht .... **450** a.	1126	1126	1156	1226		1526	1556	1626	1626	1656	1656		1857	1857	1926	1926	1957	1957	...	...	...	...

b – Not Apr. 10, 27, May 18, 29.

ALMERE - UTRECHT 457

km		Ⓐ	Ⓐ	Ⓐ	⚒	†	Ⓐ		⚒			⚒					A	④d				
0	**Almere** Centrum .... d.	0551	0621	0651	0721	0721	0751	0821	0851	and at the same minutes past each hour until	1921	1951	2021	...	2121	...	2221	2221	...	2321	...	...
20	Naarden-Bussum .... **480** d.	0611	0642	0712	0742	0741	0812	0842	0912		1942	2012	2041	...	2141	...	2241	2241	...	2341	...	...
26	Hilversum .... **480** d.	0617	0648	0718	0748	0747	0818	0848	0918		1948	2018	2047	2117	2147	2217	2247	2253	2317	2347	...	...
43	**Utrecht** Centraal .... a.	0636	0705	0735	0805	0806	0835	0905	0935		2005	2035	2106	2136	2206	2236	2306	2312	2336	0006	...	...

		⑥⑦c		Ⓐ	⚒	Ⓐ	⚒		⚒			⚒							④d	A		
Utrecht Centraal .... d.	0024	0054	...	0626	0656	0726	0756	0826	0856	and at the same minutes past each hour until	1926	1956	2024	2054	2124	2154	2224	...	2247	2254	2324	2354
Hilversum .... **480** d.	0042	0113	...	0643	0713	0743	0813	0843	0913		1943	2013	2043	2112	2143	2212	2243	...	2305	2312	2343	0013
Naarden-Bussum .... **480** d.	...	0121	...	0651	0721	0751	0821	0851	0921		1951	2021	2051	...	2151	...	2251	...	...	...	2351	0021
Almere Centrum .... a.	...	0138	...	0708	0738	0808	0838	0908	0938		2008	2038	2108	...	2208	...	2308	...	...	...	0008	0038

A – ①②③⑤⑥⑦ (also Apr. 27, May 18). **c** – Also Apr. 28, May 19. **d** – Not Apr. 27, May 18.

459 AMSTERDAM - ALMERE - ZWOLLE

See Table 460 for fast services via Amsterdam Zuid

km		Ⓐ	Ⓐ	⑥	Ⓐ	Ⓐ	⚒	Ⓐ	⚒	†	⚒	⚒													
0	**Amsterdam** Centraal .... d.	...	...	...	0553	0608	...	0623	0638	...	0653	0708	0723	0738	0753	0808	and at the same minutes past each hour until	2223	2238	2253	2308	2323	2338	2353	0008
14	Weesp .... d.	...	...	...	0610	|	...	0640	|	...	0710	|	0740	|	0810	|		2240	|	2310	|	2340	|	0010	|
30	**Almere** Centrum .... 460 d.	...	...	...	0625	0628	...	0655	0658	...	0725	0728	0755	0758	0825	0828		2255	2258	2325	2328	2355	2358	0024	0028
36	Almere Buiten .... 460 d.	...	...	...	0631	...	...	0701	...	...	0731	...	0801	...	0831	...		2301	...	2331	...	0001	...	0030	...
54	**Lelystad** Centrum .. 460 d.	0541	0611	0641	0654	...	0724	0724	...	0741	0754	...	0824	...	0854	...		2324	...	2354	...	0020	...	0044	...
75	Dronten .... d.	0553	0623	0653	0706	...	0736	0736	...	0753	0806	...	0836	...	0906	...		2336	...	0006	...	...	...	...	...
88	Kampen Zuid .... d.	0602	0632	0702	0714	...	0744	0744	...	0802	0814	...	0844	...	0914	...		2344	...	0014	...	...	...	...	...
104	**Zwolle** .... 460 a.	0613	0643	0713	0724	...	0754	0754	...	0813	0824	...	0854	...	0924	...		2354	...	0024	...	...	...	...	...

	Ⓐ	Ⓐ		Ⓐ		Ⓐ		⚒		⚒													⑥⑦c		
Zwolle .... 460 d.	...	...	...	...	0537a	...	0607a	...	0637a	...	0707r	...	0737r	...	0807	...	0837	and at the same minutes past each hour until	...	2237	...	2307	...	2337	0007
Kampen Zuid .... d.	...	...	...	...	0546a	...	0617a	...	0646a	...	0717r	...	0746r	...	0817	...	0846		...	2246	...	2317	...	2346	0017
Dronten .... d.	...	...	...	...	0555a	...	0625a	...	0655a	...	0725r	...	0755r	...	0825	...	0855		...	2255	...	2325	...	2355	0025
Lelystad Centrum .... 460 d.	0514	...	0540	...	0610	...	0640	...	0710	...	0740	...	0810	...	0840	...	0910		...	2310	...	2340	...	0010	0037
Almere Buiten .... 460 d.	0528	...	0558	...	0628	...	0658	...	0728	...	0758	...	0828	...	0858	...	0928		...	2328	...	2358	...	0028	...
Almere Centrum .... 460 d.	0536	0602	0606	0632	0636	0702	0706	0732	0736	0802	0806	0832	0836	0902	0906	0932	0936		2332	2336	0002	0006	0032	0036	...
Weesp .... d.	0551	|	0621	|	0651	|	0721	|	0751	|	0821	|	0851	|	0921	|	0951		|	2351	|	0021	|	0051	...
Amsterdam Centraal .... a.	0607	0622	0637	0652	0707	0722	0737	0753	0807	0822	0837	0852	0908	0922	0937	0952	1007		2352	0007	0022	0037	0052	0107	...

a – Ⓐ only. c – Also Apr. 28, May 19. r – ⚒ only.

460 DEN HAAG - SCHIPHOL ✈ - AMSTERDAM ZUID - ALMERE - ZWOLLE

For services Amsterdam Centraal - Almere - Zwolle and v.v., see Table **459**. For services via Amersfoort and Utrecht, see Table **481**.

km		⑥	Ⓐ	⚒	⚒													⑤⑥c						
0	**Den Haag** Centraal .... 450 d.	...	0533	0603	0633	0703	0733	0803	0833	and at the same minutes past each hour until	2003	2033	2103	2133	2203	2233	2303	2303	2333	...	...	...	...	...
15	Leiden Centraal .... 450 452 d.	...	0547	0617	0647	0717	0747	0817	0847		2017	2047	2117	2147	2217	2247	2317	2317	2347	...	...	...	...	...
42	**Schiphol** ✈ .... 452 d.	...	0605	0635	0705	0735	0805	0835	0904		2035	2105	2135	2205	2235	2305	2335	2335	0003	...	...	...	...	...
51	**Amsterdam** Zuid .... 452 d.	...	0612	0642	0712	0742	0812	0842	0912		2042	2112	2142	2212	2242	2312	2342	2342	...	...	...	...	...	...
80	**Almere** Centrum .... 452 459 d.	...	0632	0702	0732	0802	0832	0902	0932		2102	2132	2202	2232	2302	2332	0002	0002	...	...	...	...	...	...
104	**Lelystad** Centrum. 452 459 d.	0641	0647	0717	0747	0817	0847	0917	0947		2117	2147	2217	2247	2317	2347	0017	0017	...	...	...	...	...	...
154	**Zwolle** .... 459 a.	0713	0713	0743	0813	0843	0913	0943	1013		2143	2213	2243	2313	2343	0015	0043	0043	...	...	...	...	...	...
	Leeuwarden 482 .... a.	...	|	0843	|	0943	|	1043	|		2243	|	2351	|	0051	|	...	0151	...	...	...	...	...	...
	Groningen 482 .... a.	...	0811	...	0911	...	1011	...	1111		...	2311	...	0023	...	0123	...	...	...	...	...	...	...	...

	⚒	Ⓐ		Ⓐ		Ⓐ		⚒		⚒	Ⓐ											⑤⑥		
Groningen 482 .... d.	...	...	...	...	...	...	...	0536b	...	...	...	0649h	...	0749t	...	0849	...	and at the same minutes past each hour until	2149	...	2249	2326	...	...
Leeuwarden 482 .... d.	...	...	...	...	...	0507	...	|	...	...	0617	|	0717v	|	0817	|	0917		|	2217	|	|	...	...
Zwolle .... 459 d.	...	...	...	0547	...	0617	...	0647	...	0717	0717	0747	0817	0847	0917	0947	1017		2247	2317	2347	0037	...	...
Lelystad Centrum .. 452 459 d.	...	0543	...	0613	...	0643	...	0713	...	0743	0743	0813	0843	0913	0943	1013	1043		2313	2343	0013	0108	...	...
Almere Centrum .... 452 459 d.	...	0558	...	0628	0658	0658	...	0728	0758	0758	0758	0828	0858	0928	0958	1028	1058		2328	2358	0028	0122	...	...
Amsterdam Zuid .... 452 d.	...	0618	...	0648	0718	0718	...	0748	0818	0818	0818	0848	0918	0948	1018	1048	1118		2348	0018	0048	0142z	...	...
Schiphol ✈ .... 452 d.	0556	0626	0656	0656	0726	0726	0756	0756	0826	0826	0826	0856	0926	0956	1026	1057	1126		2356	0026	0056	...	...	...
Leiden Centraal .... 450 452 d.	0615	0645	0715	0715	0745	0745	0815	0815	0845	0845	0845	0915	0945	1015	1045	1115	1145		0015	0045	0115	...	...	...
Den Haag Centraal .... 450 a.	0626	0656	0726	0726	0756	0756	0826	0826	0856	0856	0856	0926	0956	1026	1056	1126	1156		0026	0056	0126c	...	...	...

b – 0549 on ⑥ (also Apr. 27, May 18).
c – Mornings of ⑥⑦ (also Apr. 28, May 19).
h – 0636 on ⑥ (also Apr. 27, May 18).
t – 0736 on †.
v – 0706 on †.
z – Amsterdam **Centraal**.

461 AMSTERDAM - HAARLEM - HOORN and ZANDVOORT AAN ZEE

km		Ⓐ¶	Ⓐ	⑥	Ⓐ	Ⓒ	⑥	Ⓐ	⑥	⚒	†	⚒	†	⚒	†	⚒	†						†	⚒
	Amsterdam Centraal ... 450 d.	0526	0556	...	0626	...	0626	0656	0656	0726	0726	0756	0756	0826	0826	0856	0856	0926	0956	and every 30 minutes until	1726	1756	1826	1826
	Amsterdam Sloterdijk ... 450 d.	0531	0601	...	0631	...	0631	0701	0701	0731	0731	0801	0801	0831	0831	0901	0901	0931	1001		1731	1801	1831	1831
0	**Haarlem** .... 450 d.	0545	0615	...	0645	0645	0645	0715	0715	0745	0745	0815	0815	0845	0845	0915	0915	0945	1015		1745	1815	1845	1845
11	Beverwijk .... d.	0602	0632	...	0702	0702	0702	0732	0732	0802	0802	0832	0832	0902	0902	0932	0932	1002	1032		1802	1832	1902	1902
22	Castricum .... 466 d.	0615	0645	0649	0715	0719	0719	0745	0749	0815	0819	0845	0849	0915	0919	0945	0949	1015	1045		1815	1845	1915	1919
34	**Alkmaar** .... 466 a.	0626	0656	0700	0726	0730	0730	0756	0800	0826	0830	0856	0900	0926	0930	0956	1000	1026	1056		1826	1856	1926	1930
34	**Alkmaar** .... 466 d.	0631	0701	0701	0731	0731	0731	0801	0801	0831	0831	0901	0901	0931	0931	1001	1001	1031	1101		1831	1901	1931	1931
40	Heerhugowaard .... 466 d.	0639	0709	0709	0739	0739	0739	0809	0809	0839	0839	0909	0909	0939	0939	1009	1009	1039	1109		1839	1909	1939	1939
57	**Hoorn** .... a.	0654	0724	0724	0754	0754	0754	0824	0824	0854	0854	0924	0924	0954	0954	1024	1024	1054	1124		1854	1924	1954	1954

	†	⚒										
Amsterdam Centraal .... 450 d.	1856	1856	1926	1956	2026	2056	2126	2156	2226	2256	2326	2356
Amsterdam Sloterdijk .... 450 d.	1901	1901	1931	2001	2031	2101	2131	2201	2231	2301	2331	0001
Haarlem .... 450 d.	1915	1915	1945	2015	2045	2115	2145	2215	2245	2315	2345	0015
Beverwijk .... d.	1932	1932	2002	2032	2102	2132	2202	2232	2302	2332	0002	0032
Castricum .... 466 d.	1945	1949	2019	2049	2119	2149	2219	2249	2319	2349	0019	0049
Alkmaar .... 466 a.	1956	2000	2030	2100	2130	2200	2230	2300	2330	2400	0030	0100
Alkmaar .... 466 d.	2001	2001	2031	...	2131	...	2231	...	2331	...	0031t	...
Heerhugowaard .... 466 d.	2009	2009	2039	...	2139	...	2239	...	2339	...	0039t	...
Hoorn .... a.	2024	2024	2054	...	2154	...	2254	...	2354	...	0054t	...

	Ⓐ	⚒	⑥	Ⓐ	Ⓒ	Ⓐ	⑥	Ⓑ
Hoorn .... d.	...	...	...	0606	...	0636	0706	0706
Heerhugowaard .... 466 d.	...	...	...	0621	...	0651	0721	0721
Alkmaar .... 466 a.	...	...	...	0629	...	0659	0729	0729
Alkmaar .... 466 d.	0530	0600	0630	0634	0700	0704	0730	0734
Castricum .... 466 d.	0540	0610	0640	0644	0710	0714	0740	0744
Beverwijk .... d.	0558	0629	0658	0658	0728	0728	0758	0758
Haarlem .... 450 d.	0617	0648	0717	0717	0747	0747	0817	0817
Amsterdam Sloterdijk. 450 a.	0630	0700	0730	0730	0800	0800	0830	0830
Amsterdam Centraal .. 450 a.	0635	0706	0735	0735	0805	0805	0835	0835

	†	⚒	†	⚒	†	⚒	†	⚒																
Hoorn .... d.	...	0736	0806	0806	...	0836	0906	0906	0936	1006	and every 30 minutes until	1736	1806	1836	1906	1936	2006	...	2106	...	2206	...	2306	...
Heerhugowaard .... 466 d.	...	0751	0821	0821	...	0851	0921	0921	0951	1021		1751	1821	1851	1921	1951	2021	...	2121	...	2221	...	2321	...
Alkmaar .... 466 a.	...	0759	0829	0829	...	0859	0929	0929	0959	1029		1759	1829	1859	1929	1959	2029	...	2129	...	2229	...	2329	...
Alkmaar .... 466 d.	0800	0804	0830	0834	0900	0904	0930	0934	1004	1034		1804	1834	1900	1930	2000	2030	2100	2130	2200	2230	2300	2330	2400
Castricum .... 466 d.	0810	0814	0840	0844	0910	0914	0940	0944	1014	1044		1814	1844	1910	1940	2010	2040	2110	2140	2210	2240	2310	2340	0010
Beverwijk .... d.	0828	0828	0858	0858	0929	0929	0958	0958	1028	1058		1828	1858	1928	1958	2028	2058	2129	2158	2228	2258	2328	2358	0028
Haarlem .... 450 d.	0847	0847	0917	0917	0948	0948	1017	1017	1047	1117		1847	1917	1947	2017	2047	2117	2148	2217	2247	2317	2347	0017	0047
Amsterdam Sloterdijk .... 450 a.	0900	0900	0930	0930	1000	1000	1030	1030	1100	1130		1900	1930	2000	2030	2100	2130	2200	2230	2300	2330	2400	0030	0059
Amsterdam Centraal .... 450 a.	0905	0905	0935	0935	1006	1006	1035	1035	1105	1135		1905	1935	2006	2035	2105	2135	2206	2235	2305	2335	0006	0035	0105

AMSTERDAM - ZANDVOORT AAN ZEE

km		Ⓐ	Ⓐ	⑥	Ⓐ	Ⓒ	Ⓐ	Ⓒ	Ⓐ	Ⓒ		Ⓐ	Ⓒ	Ⓐ	Ⓒ									
0	**Amsterdam** Centraal ... 450 d.	...	...	...	0641	...	0711	...	0741	...	and every 30 minutes until	1911	...	1941	...	...	...	...	...	...	...	...	...	...
5	Amsterdam Sloterdijk ... 450 d.	...	...	...	0646	...	0716	...	0746	...		1916	...	1946	...	...	...	...	...	...	...	...	...	...
19	**Haarlem** .... 450 d.	0600	0630	0635	0700	0705	0730	0735	0800	0805		1930	1935	2000	2005	2035	2105	2135	2205	2235	2305	2335	0005	0035
27	**Zandvoort** aan Zee .... a.	0610	0640	0645	0710	0715	0740	0745	0810	0815		1940	1945	2010	2015	2045	2115	2145	2215	2245	2315	2345	0015	0045

	Ⓐ	Ⓐ	⑥	Ⓐ	⑥	Ⓐ	Ⓒ	Ⓐ	Ⓒ	Ⓐ		Ⓒ	Ⓐ	Ⓒ	Ⓐ									
Zandvoort aan Zee .... d.	0550	0620	0650	0650	0720	0720	0750	0750	0820	0820	and every 30 minutes until	1850	1850	1920	1920	1950	2020	2050	2120	2150	2220	2250	2320	2350
Haarlem .... 450 d.	0602	0632	0701	0702	0731	0732	0801	0802	0831	0832		1901	1902	1931	1932	2001	2031	2101	2131	2201	2231	2301	2331	0001
Amsterdam Sloterdijk .... 450 d.	0615	0645	...	0715	...	0745	...	0815	...	0845		...	1915	...	1945	...	...	...	...	...	...	...	...	...
Amsterdam Centraal .... 450 a.	0620	0650	...	0720	...	0750	...	0820	...	0850		...	1920	...	1950	...	...	...	...	...	...	...	...	...

t – Mornings of ⑥⑦ (also Apr. 27, May 18). ¶ – 3 minutes later Amsterdam - Alkmaar on ④⑤.

LEIDEN - ALPHEN - UTRECHT and GOUDA 463

Additional services run on Ⓐ

km		Ⓐ	⚒	⚒								
0	**Leiden** Centraal .... d.	0553	0623	0653	0723	0753	and every	2323	2353	0023	...	...
15	Alphen a/d Rijn .... d.	0609	0639	0709	0739	0809	30 minutes	2339	0009	0039	...	...
34	Woerden .... d.	0625	0655	0725	0755	0825	until	2355	0025	0055	...	...
50	**Utrecht** Centraal .... a.	0635	0705	0735	0805	0835		0005	0035	0105	...	...

	Ⓐ	⚒	⚒								
Utrecht Centraal .... d.	0555	0625	0655	0725	0755	and every	2325	2355	0025	...	...
Woerden .... d.	0606	0636	0706	0736	0806	30 minutes	2336	0006	0036	...	...
Alphen a/d Rijn .... d.	0624	0654	0724	0754	0824	until	2354	0024	0054	...	...
Leiden Centraal .... a.	0637	0707	0737	0807	0837		0007	0037	0107	...	...

ALPHEN A/D RIJN - GOUDA and v.v. *17 km*. Journey: 22 – 29 minutes.

From Alphen a/d Rijn at 0610 Ⓐ, 0640 Ⓐ, 0710 ⚒, 0740 ⚒, 0810, 0840 and every 30 minutes until 0010, 0040; then 0108.

From Gouda at 0551 Ⓐ, 0628 ⚒, 0658 ⚒, 0728, 0758, 0821, 0858, 0928, 0958, 1021, 1058, 1128, 1158, 1221, 1258, 1328, 1358, 1421, 1458, 1528, 1558, 1621 ©, 1627 Ⓐ, 1658, 1728, 1758, 1821 ©, 1827 Ⓐ, 1858, 1928, 1958, 2021, 2058, 2128, 2158, 2221 Ⓐ, 2228 ©, 2258, 2328, 2358 and 0028.

AMSTERDAM - GOUDA - ROTTERDAM 465

For fast trains **Amsterdam** - **Rotterdam**, see Tables **450** and **451**. For other trains **Gouda** - **Rotterdam**, see Table **481**.

km		Ⓐ	⚒	⚒	⚒					
0	**Amsterdam** Centraal ..... d.	0549	0619	0649	0719	0749	0819		2319	2349
6	Amsterdam Amstel .... d.	0558	0627	0658	0728	0758	0828	and every	2328	2358
9	Duivendrecht .... d.	0601	0631	0701	0731	0801	0831	30 minutes	2331	0001
27	Breukelen .... d.	0618	0648	0718	0748	0818	0848		2348	0018
40	Woerden .... d.	0628	0658	0728	0758	0828	0858	until	2358	0028
56	**Gouda** .... d.	0641	0711	0741	0811	0841	0911		0011	0041
70	Rotterdam Alexander ..... d.	0654	0724	0754	0824	0854	0924		0024	0054
80	**Rotterdam** Centraal .... a.	0704	0734	0804	0834	0904	0934		0034	0104

	Ⓐ	Ⓐ	⚒	⚒					
Rotterdam Centraal .... d.	0524	0554	0624	0654	0724	0754		2254	2324
Rotterdam Alexander .... d.	0534	0604	0634	0704	0734	0804	and every	2304	2334
Gouda .... d.	0549	0619	0649	0719	0749	0819	30 minutes	2319	2349
Woerden .... d.	0601	0632	0702	0732	0802	0832		2331	0001
Breukelen .... d.	0611	0641	0711	0741	0811	0841	until	2341	0011
Duivendrecht .... d.	0628	0658	0728	0758	0828	0858		2358	0028
Amsterdam Amstel ...... d.	0632	0702	0732	0802	0832	0902		0002	0032
Amsterdam Centraal .. a.	0641	0711	0741	0811	0841	0911		0011	0041

AMSTERDAM - ALKMAAR - DEN HELDER 466

km		⑥⑦c		Ⓐ	⚒	Ⓐ	Ⓐ					†	⚒									
	Nijmegen 468 .... d.	...	...	...	...	...	...	0536a	0613r	0643r	0713	0736	0743	0813	0843		2013	2043	2113	2143	2213	2243
	Arnhem Centraal 468 .... d.	...	...	...	...	...	...	0602a	0632r	0702r	0732	0801	0802	0832	0902		2032	2101	2131	2201	2231	2301
0	**Amsterdam** Centraal **461 470** d.	0114	...	0529	...	0609	0639	0709	0739	0809	0839	0909	0909	0939	1009	and every	2139	2209	2239	2309	2339	0009
5	Amsterdam Sloterdijk **461 470** d.	0119	...	0535	...	0615	0645	0715	0745	0815	0845	0915	0915	0945	1015		2145	2215	2245	2315	2345	0015
12	Zaandam .... **470** d.	0125	...	0542	...	0622	0652	0722	0752	0822	0852	0922	0922	0952	1022	30 minutes	2152	2222	2252	2322	2352	0022
29	Castricum .... **461 470** d.	0148	...	0606	...	0634	0704	0734	0804	0834	0904	0934	0934	1004	1034		2204	2234	2304	2334	0004	0034
41	**Alkmaar** .... **461 470** a.	0159	...	0618	...	0646	0716	0746	0816	0846	0916	0946	0946	1016	1046	until	2216	2246	2316	2346	0016	0046
41	**Alkmaar** .... **461** d.	0201	...	0619	0649	0649	0719	0749	0819	0849	0919	0949	0949	1019	1049		2219	2249	2319	2349	0019	0049**b**
48	Heerhugowaard .... **461** d.	0209	...	0628	0658	0658	0728	0757	0828	0858	0928	0958	0958	1028	1058		2228	2258	2328	2358	0028	0058**b**
83	**Den Helder** .... a.	0235	...	0656	0726	0726	0756	0826	0856	0926	0956	1026	1026	1056	1126		2256	2326	2356	0033	0056	0126**b**

	Ⓐ	Ⓐ	†	⑥	Ⓐ	Ⓐ	⚒	Ⓐm														
Den Helder .... d.	...	0504	...	...	0534	0604	0634	0646	0704	0734	0804	0834	0904	0934		2004	2034	2104	2134	2204	2304	2357
Heerhugowaard .... **461** d.	...	0531	...	...	0601	0631	0701	0715	0731	0801	0831	0901	0931	1001		2031	2101	2131	2201	2231	2331	0024
Alkmaar .... **461** a.	...	0541	...	...	0611	0641	0711	0724	0741	0811	0841	0911	0941	1011	and every	2041	2111	2141	2211	2241	2341	0031
Alkmaar .... **461 470** d.	0502	0544	0603	0600	0614	0644	0714	0727	0744	0814	0844	0914	0944	1014		2044	2114	2144	2214	2244	2344	0032
Castricum .... **461 470** d.	0512	0555	0613	0610	0625	0655	0725	0735	0755	0825	0855	0925	0955	1025	30 minutes	2055	2125	2155	2225	2255	2355	0043
Zaandam .... **470** d.	0536	0608	0635	|	0638	0708	0738	0749	0808	0838	0908	0938	1008	1038		2108	2138	2208	2238	2308	0008	0103
Amsterdam Sloterdijk . **461 470** d.	0542	0615	0641	0700	0645	0715	0745	0755	0815	0845	0915	0945	1015	1045	until	2115	2145	2215	2245	2315	0015	0109
Amsterdam Centraal. **461 470** a.	0547	0621	0647	0705	0651	0721	0751	0801	0821	0851	0921	0951	1021	1051		2121	2151	2221	2251	2321	0021	0115
Arnhem Centraal 468 .... a.	...	0728	...	...	0758	0828	0858	...	0930	1000	1030	1100	1128	1158		2228	2258	2330	2400	0030	0132	...
Nijmegen 468 .... a.	...	0747	...	...	0817	0847	0917	...	0947	1017	1047	1117	1147	1217		2247	2317	2347	0024	0049	...	...

a – Ⓐ only.
b – Mornings of ①④⑤⑥⑦ (also Apr. 11, May 30).
c – Also Apr. 27, May 18.
m – To Maastricht (Table **470**).
r – ⚒ only.

AMSTERDAM and SCHIPHOL ✈ - ARNHEM - NIJMEGEN 468

Many trains from / to Amsterdam Centraal start from / continue to Den Helder (see Table **466**). For international trains **Amsterdam** – **Arnhem** – **Köln**, see Table **28**.

km		Ⓐ	Ⓐ	Ⓐ		Ⓐ	Ⓐ	Ⓐ	⚒	Ⓐ		Ⓐ		Ⓐ		Ⓐ		Ⓐ		Ⓐ			Ⓐ
0	**Amsterdam** Centraal...... **470** d.	...	...	...	...	...	0624	...	0654	...	0724	...	0754	...	0824	...	0854	...	0924	...	and at	1254	...
6	Amsterdam Amstel .... **470** d.	...	...	...	...	...	0632	...	0702	...	0732	...	0802	...	0832	...	0902	...	0932	...	the same	1302	...
	Schiphol ✈ .... **470** d.	...	...	...	...	0618	|	...	|	0703	|	0733	|	0803	|	0833	|	0903	|	0933		|	1303
	Amsterdam Zuid......... **470** d.	...	...	...	...	0626	|	...	|	0710	|	0740	|	0810	|	0840	|	0910	|	0940		|	1310
39	**Utrecht** Centraal............ **470** a.	...	...	...	...	0648	0651	...	0721	0738	0751	0808	0821	0839	0851	0908	0921	0938	0951	1008	minutes	1321	1338
39	**Utrecht** Centraal.................. d.	0553	0623	0639	...	...	0653	0709	0723	0742	0753	0812	0823	0842	0853	0913	0923	0942	0953	1012	past each	1323	1342
79	Ede-Wageningen .... d.	0620	0650	0703	...	...	0718	0733	0748	0805	0818	0835	0848	0905	0918	0934	0948	1005	1018	1035	hour until	1348	1405
96	**Arnhem** Centraal................. a.	0630	0700	0714	...	...	0729	0744	0758	0815	0829	0845	0858	0915	0928	0945	0958	1015	1028	1045		1358	1415
96	**Arnhem** Centraal........... **475** d.	0635	0705	0720	...	...	0735	0750	0805	0820	0835	0850	0905	0920	0935	...	1005	...	1035	...		1405	...
114	**Nijmegen** .... **475** a.	0647	0717	0732	...	...	0747	0802	0817	0832	0847	0902	0917	0932	0947	...	1017	...	1047	...		1417	...

		Ⓐ		Ⓐ		Ⓐ			Ⓐ		Ⓐ		Ⓐ										
Amsterdam Centraal...... **470** d.	1324	...	1354	...	1424	...		1824	...	1854	...	1924	...	1954	2024	2054	2124	2154	2224	2254	2324	...	0024
Amsterdam Amstel.......... **470** d.	1332	...	1402	...	1432	...	and at	1832	...	1902	...	1932	...	2002	2032	2102	2132	2202	2232	2302	2332	...	0032
Schiphol ✈ .... **470** d.	|	1333	|	1403	|	1433	the same	|	1833	|	1903	|	1933	|	|	|	|	|	|	|	|	...	|
Amsterdam Zuid........ **470** d.	|	1340	|	1410	|	1440		|	1841	|	1910	|	1940	|	|	|	|	|	|	|	|	...	|
Utrecht Centraal............ **470** a.	1351	1408	1421	1438	1451	1508	minutes	1851	1908	1921	1938	1951	2004	2021	2051	2121	2151	2221	2251	2321	2351	...	0051
Utrecht Centraal.................. d.	1353	1412	1423	1442	1453	1512	past each	1853	1914	1923	1942	1953	2009	2023	2053	2123	2153	2223	2253	2323	2353	...	0053
Ede-Wageningen .... d.	1418	1435	1448	1505	1518	1535	hour until	1918	1935	1948	2005	2020	2033	2050	2120	2150	2220	2250	2320	2350	0020	...	0119
Arnhem Centraal.................. a.	1428	1445	1458	1515	1528	1545		1928	1945	1958	2015	2030	2044	2100	2130	2200	2230	2300	2330	2400	0030	...	0132
Arnhem Centraal........... **475** d.	1435	...	1505	1520	1535	1550		1935	1950	2005	2020	2035	...	2105	2135	2205	2235	2305	2335	0005	0035	...	...
Nijmegen .... **475** a.	1447	...	1517	1532	1547	1602		1947	2002	2017	2032	2047	...	2117	2147	2217	2247	2317	2347	0024	0049	...	...

km		Ⓐ	Ⓐ	Ⓐ	⚒	Ⓐ	⚒	†	Ⓐ		Ⓐ	†	⚒			Ⓐ		Ⓐ		Ⓐ		Ⓐ		Ⓐ	
	Nijmegen .... **475** d.	...	0536	...	0613	0628	0643	...	0658	0713	0728	0736	0743	0758	0813	0828	0843	0858	0913	0928	0943	...	1013	...	1043
	Arnhem Centraal......... **475** a.	...	0556	...	0626	0640	0656	...	0710	0726	0740	0756	0756	0810	0826	0840	0856	0910	0926	0940	0956	...	1026	...	1056
	Arnhem Centraal.................. d.	0546	0602	0616	0632	0645	0701	...	0715	0732	0745	0801	0802	0815	0832	0845	0902	0915	0932	0945	1002	1015	1032	1045	1102
	Ede-Wageningen................... d.	0556	0612	0626	0642	0655	0711	...	0725	0742	0755	0811	0812	0825	0842	0855	0912	0925	0942	0955	1012	1025	1042	1055	1112
	Utrecht Centraal.................. a.	0621	0637	0651	0707	0718	0738	...	0748	0807	0817	0838	0837	0847	0907	0918	0937	0948	1008	1018	1037	1048	1107	1118	1137
0	**Utrecht** Centraal.......... **470** d.	0626	0639	0656	0709	0722	0739	0738	0752	0809	0822	0839	0839	0852	0909	0922	0939	0952	1009	1022	1039	1052	1109	1122	1139
36	**Amsterdam** Zuid...... **470** d.	0651	|	0721	|	0751	|	|	0821	|	0851	|	|	0921	|	0951	|	1021	|	1051	|	1121	|	1151	|
45	**Schiphol** ✈ .... **470** a.	0657	|	0727	|	0757	|	|	0827	|	0857	|	|	0927	|	0957	|	1027	|	1057	|	1127	|	1157	|
	Amsterdam Amstel....... **470** d.	...	0657	...	0727	...	0757	0759	...	0827	...	0858	0858	...	0927	...	0957	...	1027	...	1057	...	1127	...	1157
	Amsterdam Centraal ... **470** a.	...	0705	...	0735	...	0805	0807	...	0835	...	0905	0905	...	0935	...	1005	...	1035	...	1105	...	1135	...	1205

		Ⓐ		Ⓐ		Ⓐ		Ⓐ			Ⓐ		Ⓐ										
Nijmegen .... **475** d.		...	1443	...	1513	1528	1543	1558	1613		1758	1813	1828	1843	1913	1943	2013	2043	2113	2143	2213	2243	2313
Arnhem Centraal.......... **475** a.	and at	...	1456	...	1526	1540	1556	1610	1626	and at	1810	1826	1840	1856	1926	1956	2026	2056	2126	2156	2226	2256	2326
Arnhem Centraal.................. d.	the same	1445	1502	1515	1532	1545	1602	1615	1632	the same	1815	1832	1846	1901	1931	2001	2031	2101	2131	2201	2231	2301	2331
Ede-Wageningen .... d.		1455	1512	1525	1542	1555	1612	1625	1642		1825	1842	1856	1911	1941	2011	2041	2111	2141	2211	2241	2311	2341
Utrecht Centraal.................. a.	minutes	1518	1537	1548	1607	1618	1637	1648	1707	minutes	1848	1907	1921	1938	2008	2038	2108	2138	2208	2238	2308	2338	0008
Utrecht Centraal........... **470** d.	past each	1522	1539	1552	1609	1622	1639	1652	1709	past each	1852	1909	1926	1939	2009	2039	2109	2139	2209	2239	2309	2339	...
Amsterdam Zuid....... **470** d.		1551	|	1621	|	1651	|	1721	|		1921	|	1951	|	|	|	|	|	|	|	|	|	...
Schiphol ✈ .... **470** a.	hour until	1557	|	1627	|	1657	|	1727	|	hour until	1927	|	1957	|	|	|	|	|	|	|	|	|	...
Amsterdam Amstel......... **470** d.		...	1557	...	1627	...	1657	...	1727		...	1927	...	1957	2027	2057	2127	2157	2227	2257	2327	2357	...
Amsterdam Centraal.... **470** a.		...	1605	...	1635	...	1705	...	1735		...	1935	...	2005	2035	2105	2135	2205	2235	2305	2335	0005	...

470 ENKHUIZEN - AMSTERDAM - EINDHOVEN - MAASTRICHT, VENLO and HEERLEN

km		Ⓐ	Ⓐ	Ⓐ	⚒	⚒	Ⓐ	Ⓐ	Ⓒ	⑥		Ⓐ	Ⓐ	Ⓒ		Ⓐ	Ⓐh	⑥		Ⓐ	⚒	†		⚒	⚒
0	**Enkhuizen** d.	...	...	0509	...	0539	0539	...	...	0609	...	0609	...	0639	...	0639	...	0709	...	0709	...	0739	...	0739	...
18	Hoorn d.	...	...	0535	...	0605	0605	...	...	0635	...	0640	...	0705	...	0710	...	0735	...	0740	...	0805	...	0810	...
	Alkmaar 466 d.	...	...	|	...	|	|	0627	...	|	...	|	0657	|	...	|	0727	|	...	|	0757t	|	...	|	0827t
	Castricum 466 d.	...	...	|	...	|	|	0635	...	|	...	|	0705	|	...	|	0735	|	...	|	0805t	|	...	|	0835t
	Zaandam 466 d.	...	...	|	...	|	|	0649	...	|	...	|	0719	|	...	|	0749	|	...	|	0819t	|	...	|	0849t
57	Amsterdam Sloterdijk 466 d.	...	...	0600	...	0630	0630	0655	...	0700	...	0705	0725	0730	...	0735	0755	0800	...	0805	0825t	0830	...	0835	0855t
62	**Amsterdam** Centraal 466 a.	...	...	0606	...	0636	0636	0701	...	0706	...	0711	0731	0736	...	0741	0801	0806	...	0811	0831t	0836	...	0841	0901t
62	**Amsterdam** Centraal 468 d.	...	...	0610	...	▬	0641	0705	...	0710	...	0715	0735	0740	...	0745	0804	0811	...	0816	0835	0840	...	0845	0905
68	Amsterdam Amstel 468 d.	...	...	0618	...	...	0649	0713	...	0718	...	0723	0743	0748	...	0753	0812	0819	...	0824	0843	0848	...	0853	0913
101	**Utrecht** Centraal 468 d.	...	0609	0639	...	...	0709	0733	...	0739	...	0744	0803	0809	...	0814	0833	0839	...	0844	0903	0909	...	0914	0933
149	's-Hertogenbosch d.	...	0639	0709	...	...	0739	0806	...	0809	...	0815	0836	0839	...	0845	0906	0909	...	0915	0936	0939	...	0945	1006
181	**Eindhoven** Centraal a.	...	0658	0728	...	Ⓒ	0758	0824	...	0828	...	0834	0854	0858	...	0904	0924	0928	...	0934	0954	0958	...	1004	1024
181	**Eindhoven** Centraal d.	0629	0659	0729	0729	0757	0759	0827	0829	0829	0838	0838	0857	0859	0908	0908	0927	0929	0938	0938	0957	0959	1008	1008	1027
210	Weert d.	0646	0716	0746	0746	0815	0816	0845	0846	0846	0856	0856	0915	0916	0926	0926	0945	0946	0956	0956	1015	1016	1026	1026	1045
234	Roermond d.	0700	0730	0800	0800	0830	0830	0900	0900	0900	0910	0910	0930	0930	0940	0940	1000	1000	1010	1010	1030	1030	1040	1040	1100
258	Sittard ★ d.	0716	0746	0816	0816	0846	0846	0916	0916	0916	0926	0926	0946	0946	0956	0956	1016	1016	1026	1026	1046	1046	1056	1056	1116
277	**Heerlen** ★ a.	|	|	|	|	|	|	|	|	|	0941	0941	|	|	1011	1011	|	|	1041	1041	|	|	1111	1111	|
280	**Maastricht** a.	0730	0800	0830	0830	0900	0900	0930	0930	0930	...	...	1000	1000	...	...	1030	1030	...	...	1100	1100	...	...	1130

	†		⚒	⚒	†		⚒	⚒	†		⚒										†	⚒	†	†
Enkhuizen d.	0809	...	0809	...	0839	...	0839	...	0909	...	0909	...	0939	...	1009	and at the same minutes past each hour until	...	1739	...	1809	...	1839	1839	...
Hoorn d.	0835	...	0840	...	0905	...	0910	...	0935	...	0940	...	1010	...	1040		...	1810	...	1840	...	1905	1909	...
Alkmaar 466 d.	|	...	|	0857t	|	...	|	0927t	|	...	|	0957t	|	1027t	|		1757t	|	1827t	|	...	|	|	...
Castricum 466 d.	|	...	|	0905t	|	...	|	0935t	|	...	|	1005t	|	1035t	|		1805t	|	1835t	|	...	|	|	...
Zaandam 466 d.	|	...	|	0919t	|	...	|	0849t	|	...	|	1019t	|	1049t	|		1819t	|	1849t	|	...	|	|	...
Amsterdam Sloterdijk 466 d.	0900	...	0905	0925t	0930	...	0935	0955t	1000	...	1005	1025t	1035	1055t	1105		1825t	1835	1855t	1905	...	1930	1935	...
Amsterdam Centraal 466 a.	0906	...	0911	0931t	0936	...	0941	1001t	1006	...	1011	1031t	1041	1101t	1111		1831t	1841	1901t	1911	...	1936	1941	...
Amsterdam Centraal 468 d.	0910	...	0914	0935	0940	...	0945	1005	1010	...	1014	1034	1046	1105	1115		1834	1846	1905	1915	1935	1940	1945	2005
Amsterdam Amstel 468 d.	0918	...	0922	0943	0948	...	0953	1013	1018	...	1022	1042	1054	1113	1123		1842	1854	1913	1922	1943	1948	1953	2013
Utrecht Centraal 468 d.	0939	...	0944	1003	1009	...	1014	1033	1039	...	1044	1103	1114	1133	1144		1903	1914	1933	1944	2003	2009	2014	2033
's-Hertogenbosch d.	1009	...	1015	1036	1039	...	1045	1106	1109	...	1115	1136	1145	1206	1215		1935	1945	2005	2015	2036	2039	2045	2106
Eindhoven Centraal a.	1028	...	1034	1054	1058	...	1104	1124	1128	...	1134	1154	1204	1224	1234		1954	2004	2024	2034	2054	2058	2104	2124
Eindhoven Centraal d.	1029	1038	1038	1057	1059	1108	1108	1127	1129	1138	1138	1157	1208	1227	1238		1957	2008	2027	2038	2057	2059	2108	2127
Weert d.	1046	1056	1056	1115	1116	1126	1126	1145	1146	1156	1156	1215	1226	1245	1256		2015	2026	2045	2056	2115	2116	2126	2145
Roermond d.	1100	1110	1110	1130	1130	1140	1140	1200	1200	1210	1210	1230	1240	1300	1310		2030	2040	2100	2110	2130	2130	2140	2200
Sittard ★ d.	1116	1126	1126	1146	1146	1156	1156	1216	1216	1226	1226	1246	1256	1316	1326		2046	2056	2116	2126	2146	2146	2156	2216
Heerlen ★ a.	|	1141	1141	|	|	1211	1211	|	|	1241	1241	|	1311	|	1341		|	2111	|	2141	|	|	2211	|
Maastricht a.	1130	...	...	1200	1200	...	...	1230	1230	...	...	1300	...	1330	...		2100	...	2130	...	2200	2200	...	2230

	⚒	†								
Enkhuizen d.	1909	1909	1939	2009	2039	2109	2139	2209	2239	2309
Hoorn d.	1935	1940	2005	2035	2105	2135	2205	2235	2305	2335
Alkmaar 466 d.	|	|	|	|	|	|	|	|	|	|
Castricum 466 d.	|	|	|	|	|	|	|	|	|	|
Zaandam 466 d.	|	|	|	|	|	|	|	|	|	|
Amsterdam Sloterdijk 466 d.	2000	2005	2030	2100	2130	2200	2230	2300	2330	0000
Amsterdam Centraal 466 a.	2006	2011	2036	2106	2136	2206	2236	2306	2336	0006
Amsterdam Centraal 468 d.	2010	2014	2040	2110	2140	2210	2240	2310	2340	...
Amsterdam Amstel 468 d.	2018	2022	2048	2118	2148	2218	2248	2318	2348	...
Utrecht Centraal 468 d.	2039	2044	2109	2139	2209	2239	2309	2341	0011	...
's-Hertogenbosch d.	2109	2115	2139	2209	2239	2309	2339	0009	0039	...
Eindhoven Centraal a.	2128	2134	2158	2228	2258	2328	2358	0028	0058	...
Eindhoven Centraal d.	2129	2138	2159	2229	2259	2329	2359	...	...	...
Weert d.	2146	2156	2216	2246	2316	2346	0016	...	...	...
Roermond d.	2200	2210	2230	2300	2330	2400	0030	...	...	...
Sittard ★ d.	2216	2226	2246	2316	2346	0016	0046	...	...	...
Heerlen ★ a.	|	2241	|	|	|	|	|	...	...	...
Maastricht a.	2230	...	2300	2330	2400	0030	0100	...	...	...

	Ⓐ	Ⓐ	Ⓐ	⚒		Ⓐ	Ⓐ	Ⓐ	⑥	Ⓒ
Maastricht d.	...	...	...	...	...	...	0531	...	...	...
Heerlen ★ d.	...	...	...	...	...	...	|	0549	...	...
Sittard ★ d.	...	...	...	...	...	...	0547	0605	...	...
Roermond d.	...	...	...	...	...	...	0602	0620	...	...
Weert d.	...	...	...	...	...	...	0616	0634	...	...
Eindhoven Centraal a.	...	...	...	...	...	...	0632	0651	...	...
Eindhoven Centraal d.	...	0534	0604	...	...	0627	0636	0657	0704	...
's-Hertogenbosch d.	...	0553	0623	...	...	0648	0658	0718	0723	...
Utrecht Centraal 468 d.	...	0623	0653	0653	...	0719	0729	0749	0753	...
Amsterdam Amstel 468 d.	...	0641	0711	0711	...	0737	0747	0807	0811	...
Amsterdam Centraal 468 a.	...	0649	0719	0719	...	0745	0755	0815	0819	...
Amsterdam Centraal 466 d.	0623	0652	0722	0722	0722	0749	0759	0819	0823	0823
Amsterdam Sloterdijk 466 d.	0629	0658	0728	0728	0728	0755	0805	0825	0829	0829
Castricum 466 d.	|	|	|	|	|	|	0812	|	|	|
Zaandam 466 d.	|	|	|	|	|	|	0824	|	|	|
Alkmaar 466 a.	|	|	|	|	|	|	0833	|	|	|
Hoorn d.	0659	0729	0759	0759	0759	0829	...	0859	0859	0859
Enkhuizen a.	0723	0753	0823	0823	0823	0853	...	0923	0923	0923

	Ⓐ	Ⓐ	⑥	Ⓐ	Ⓐ	Ⓒ	Ⓐ	⚒	†	⚒	⚒	†	⚒	⚒	†	⚒								
Maastricht d.	0601	...	0631	0631	...	0701	0701	...	0731	0731	...	0801	0801	...	0831	0831	...	0901	...	0931	and at the same minutes past each hour until	...	1631	...
Heerlen ★ d.	|	0619	|	|	0649	|	|	0719	|	|	0749	|	|	0819	|	|	0849	|	0919	|		1619	|	1649
Sittard ★ d.	0617	0635	0647	0647	0705	0717	0717	0735	0747	0747	0805	0817	0817	0835	0847	0847	0905	0917	0935	0947		1635	1647	1705
Roermond d.	0632	0650	0702	0702	0720	0732	0732	0750	0802	0802	0820	0832	0832	0850	0902	0902	0920	0932	0950	1002		1650	1702	1720
Weert d.	0646	0704	0716	0716	0734	0746	0746	0804	0816	0816	0834	0846	0846	0904	0916	0916	0934	0946	1004	1016		1704	1716	1734
Eindhoven Centraal a.	0702	0721	0732	0732	0751	0802	0802	0821	0832	0832	0851	0902	0902	0921	0932	0932	0951	1002	1021	1032		1721	1732	1751
Eindhoven Centraal d.	0706	0727	0734	0736	0757	0804	0806	0827	0834	0836	0857	0904	0906	0927	0934	0936	0957	1006	1027	1036		1727	1736	1757
's-Hertogenbosch d.	0728	0748	0753	0758	0818	0823	0828	0848	0853	0858	0918	0923	0928	0948	0953	0958	1018	1028	1048	1058		1748	1758	1818
Utrecht Centraal 468 d.	0759	0819	0823	0829	0849	0853	0859	0919	0923	0929	0949	0953	0959	1019	1023	1029	1049	1059	1119	1129		1819	1829	1849
Amsterdam Amstel 468 d.	0817	0837	0841	0847	0908	0911	0917	0937	0941	0947	1007	1011	1017	1037	1041	1047	1107	1117	1137	1147		1837	1847	1907
Amsterdam Centraal 468 a.	0825	0845	0849	0855	0917	0919	0925	0945	0949	0955	1015	1019	1025	1045	1049	1055	1115	1125	1145	1155		1845	1855	1915
Amsterdam Centraal 466 d.	0828	0849	0853	0858	0919	0923	0929	0949	0953	0959t	1019	1023	1029t	1049	1053	1059t	1119	1129t	1149	1159t		1849	1859t	1919
Amsterdam Sloterdijk 466 d.	0835	0855	0859	0905	0925	0929	0935	0955	0959	1005t	1025	1029	1035t	1055	1059	1105t	1125	1135t	1155	1205t		1855	1905t	1925
Castricum 466 d.	0842	|	|	0912	|	|	0942	|	|	1012t	|	|	1042t	|	|	1112t	|	1142t	|	1212t		|	1912t	|
Zaandam 466 d.	0854	|	|	0924	|	|	0954	|	|	1024t	|	|	1054t	|	|	1124t	|	1154t	|	1224t		|	1924t	|
Alkmaar 466 a.	0903	|	|	0933	|	|	1003	|	|	1033t	|	|	1103t	|	|	1133t	|	1203t	|	1233t		|	1933t	|
Hoorn d.	...	0929	0929	...	0959	0959	...	1029	1029	...	1059	1059	...	1129	1129	...	1159	...	1229	...		1929	...	1959
Enkhuizen a.	...	0953	0953	...	1023	1023	...	1053	1053	...	1123	1123	...	1153	1153	...	1223	...	1253	...		1953	...	2023

			⚒	†		⚒	†		⚒	†		⚒	†	†	⚒	†						⑤⑥f			
Maastricht ◐ d.	1701	...	1731	1731	...	1801	1801	...	1831	1831	...	1901	1901	...	1931	1931	2001	2031	2101	2131	2201	2231	2231	2301	0001
Heerlen ★ d.	|	1719	|	|	1749	|	|	1819	|	|	1849	|	|	1919	|	|	|	|	|	|	|	|	|	|	|
Sittard ◐ ★ d.	1717	1735	1747	1747	1805	1817	1817	1835	1847	1847	1905	1917	1917	1935	1947	1947	2017	2047	2117	2147	2217	2247	2247	2317	0017
Roermond ◐ d.	1732	1750	1802	1802	1820	1832	1832	1850	1902	1902	1920	1932	1932	1950	2002	2002	2032	2102	2132	2202	2232	2302	2302	2332	0032
Weert ◐ d.	1746	1804	1816	1816	1834	1846	1846	1904	1916	1916	1934	1946	1946	2004	2016	2016	2046	2116	2146	2216	2246	2316	2316	2346	0046
Eindhoven Centraal ◐ a.	1802	1821	1832	1832	1851	1902	1902	1921	1932	1932	1951	2002	2002	2021	2032	2032	2102	2132	2202	2232	2302	2332	2332	0002	0105
Eindhoven Centraal d.	1806	...	1834	1836	...	1904	1906	...	1934	1936	...	2004	2006	...	2034	2036	2104	2134	2204	2234	2304	2334	2334	...	...
's-Hertogenbosch d.	1828	...	1853	1858	...	1923	1928	...	1953	1958	...	2023	2028	...	2053	2058	2123	2153	2223	2253	2323	2353	2353	...	...
Utrecht Centraal 468 d.	1859	...	1923	1929	...	1953	1959	...	2023	2029	...	2053	2059	...	2123	2129	2153	2223	2253	2323	2353	0023	0023	...	...
Amsterdam Amstel 468 d.	1917	...	1941	1947	...	2011	2017	...	2041	2047	...	2111	2117	...	2141	2147	2211	2241	2313	2343	0013	0043	0043	...	...
Amsterdam Centraal 468 a.	1925	...	1949	1955	...	2019	2025	...	2049	2055	...	2119	2125	...	2149	2155	2219	2249	2321	2351	0021	0051	0051	...	...
Amsterdam Centraal 466 d.	1929t	...	1953	...	...	2023	...	...	2053	...	...	2123	...	...	2153	...	2223	2253	2323	2353	0023	0053	...	...	...
Amsterdam Sloterdijk 466 d.	1935t	...	1959	...	...	2029	...	...	2059	...	...	2129	...	...	2159	...	2229	2259	2329	2359	0029	0059	...	...	...
Castricum 466 d.	1942t	...	|	...	...	|	...	...	|	...	...	|	...	...	|	...	|	|	|	|	|	|	...	...	...
Zaandam 466 d.	1954t	...	|	...	...	|	...	...	|	...	...	|	...	...	|	...	|	|	|	|	|	|	...	...	...
Alkmaar 466 a.	2003t	...	|	...	...	|	...	...	|	...	...	|	...	...	|	...	|	|	|	|	|	|	...	...	...
Hoorn d.	...	...	2029	...	...	2059	...	...	2129	...	...	2159	...	...	2229	...	2259	2329	2359	0025	0105	0135	...	...	...
Enkhuizen a.	...	...	2053	...	...	2123	...	...	2153	...	...	2223	...	...	2253	...	2323	2353	0023	...	0127c	0157	...	...	...

c – Mornings of ⑥⑦ (also Apr. 28, May 19).
f – Also Apr. 27, May 18.
h – From Den Helder (Table **466**).
t – Ⓐ only.

★ – Additional local trains Sittard - Heerlen and v.v. (operated by Arriva; journey 20 minutes):
From Sittard at 0618 Ⓐ, 0648 ⚒, 0718 ⚒, 0748, 0818 and every 30 minutes until 0048.
From Heerlen at 0552 Ⓐ, 0622 ⚒, 0652 ⚒, 0722, 0752 and every 30 minutes until 0022.

ENKHUIZEN - AMSTERDAM - EINDHOVEN - MAASTRICHT, VENLO and HEERLEN 470

SCHIPHOL - AMSTERDAM ZUID - EINDHOVEN - VENLO

km		Ⓐ	Ⓐ	⚒	⚒	Ⓐ	⚒	Ⓐ														⑥	Ⓑ
0	**Schiphol** ✈ ... **468** ▷ d.	...	...	...	...	0618	...	0645	0715	0745		1815	1845	1915	1949	2019	2049	2119	2149	2219	...	2249	2315	2318
9	**Amsterdam** Zuid . **468** d.	...	...	...	...	0626	...	0655	0725	0755	and every	1825	1855	1925	1956	2026	2056	2126	2156	2226	...	2256	2325	2326
45	**Utrecht** Centraal.. **468** a.	...	...	...	...	0648	...	0718	0748	0818		1848	1918	1948	2018	2048	2118	2148	2218	2248	...	2318	2348	2348
45	**Utrecht** Centraal.........d.	...	...	*0609*a	...	0654	...	0724	0754	0824	30 minutes	1854	1924	1954	2024	2054	2125	2154	2224	2254	*2309*	*2341*	*0009*	*0011*
93	's-Hertogenbosch.........d.	...	...	*0639*a	...	0725	...	0755	0825	0854		1925	1955	2025	2054	2124	2154	2224	2254	2324	*2339*	*0009*	*0039*	*0039*
125	**Eindhoven** Centraal ... a.	...	...	*0658*a	...	0743	...	0813	0843	0913	until	1943	2013	2043	2113	2143	2213	2243	2313	2343	*2358*	*0028*	*0058*	*0058*
125	**Eindhoven** Centraal ... d.	0619	0649	0719	0749	0749	0819	0819	0849	0919		1949	2019	2049	2119	2149	2219	2249	2319	...	0019	...	...	...
138	Helmond.....................d.	0628	0658	0728	0758	0758	0828	0828	0858	0928		1958	2028	2058	2128	2158	2228	2258	2328	...	0028	...	...	...
176	**Venlo**.........................a.	0658	0728	0758	0828	0828	0858	0858	0928	0958		2028	2058	2128	2158	2228	2258	2328	2358	...	0058	...	...	...

	Ⓐ	Ⓐ	Ⓐ	⚒														†			†		Ⓑ	⑥	
Venlo..........................d.	...	0533	0603	0633	0703	0733		1633	1703	1733	1803	1833	1903	1933	2003	...	2033	2033	...	2103	2103	...	...	...
Helmond.........................d.	...	0602	0632	0702	0732	0802	and every	1702	1732	1802	1832	1902	1932	2002	2032	...	2102	2102	...	2132	2132	...	...	...
Eindhoven Centraal ....a.	...	0611	0641	0711	0741	0811		1711	1741	1811	1841	1911	1941	2011	2041	...	2111	2111	...	2141	2141	...	...	...
Eindhoven Centraal ....d.	0547	0617	0647	0717	0747	0817	30 minutes	1717	1747	1817	1847	1917	1947	2017	2047	...	2117	...	...	2147	...	*2204*	*2204*	*2234*
's-Hertogenbosch..........d.	0608	0638	0708	0738	0808	0838		1738	1808	1838	1908	1938	2008	2038	2108	...	2138	...	...	2208	...	*2223*	*2223*	*2253*
Utrecht Centraal..........a.	0635	0705	0735	0805	0839	0905	until	1805	1835	1904	1934	2004	2034	2104	2134	...	2205	...	...	2235	...	*2249*	*2251*	*2321*
Utrecht Centraal... **468** d.	0642	0712	0742	0812	0842	0912		1812	1842	1912	1942	2012	2042	2112	2142	...	2212	...	...	2242	...	2312	2312	2342
Amsterdam Zuid .. **468** a.	0705	0735	0805	0835	0904	0934		1838	1908	1935	2005	2035	2105	2135	2205	...	2235	...	...	2305	...	2334	2334	0004
Schiphol ✈..... **468** ▽ a.	0711	0741	0811	0841	0914	0944		1844	1914	1941	2011	2041	2111	2141	2211	...	2241	...	...	2311	...	2341	2344	0011

a – Ⓐ only.

▷ – Departure times at Schiphol may be up to 4 minutes later.

▽ – Arrival times at Schiphol may be up to 3 minutes earlier.

DEN HAAG - EINDHOVEN 471

km		Ⓐ	Ⓐ	⚒	Ⓐ	Ⓐ	⚒		⚒		Ⓐ◇				◇							
0	**Den Haag** Centraal......................... d.	...	...	...	0546	...	0616	...	0646	...	...	0716	...	0746		2216	...	2246	...	...	...	...
2	**Den Haag** HS.................. **450 460** d.	0523	...	...	0553	...	0623	...	0653	...	...	0723	...	0753	and at	2223	...	2253	...	...	...	...
10	Delft .... **450 460** d.	0530	...	...	0600	...	0630	...	0700	...	...	0730	...	0800		2230	...	2300	...	...	...	...
24	**Rotterdam** Centraal ...**450 451 460** d.	0544	...	...	0614	...	0644	...	0714	0714	...	0744	...	0814	the same	2244	...	2314	...	...	...	...
◐	Dordrecht......................... **450 460** d.	|	0558	0558	|	0628	|	0658	|	|	0728	|	0758	|	minutes	|	2258	|	2358	...	...	...
71	Breda .... **451** a.	0607	0621	0621	0637	0651	0707	0721	0737	0737	0751	0807	0821	0837		2307	2321	2337	0021	...	...	...
71	Breda .... **475** d.	0608	0623	...	0638	0653	0708	0723**r**	0738	0738	0753	0808	0823	0838	past each	2308	2323	2340	0023	...	...	...
92	Tilburg.. **475** d.	0624	0642	...	0654	0712	0724	0742**r**	0754	0754	0812	0824	0842	0854	hour until	2324	2342	2355	0042	...	...	...
	's-Hertogenbosch............... **475** a.	|	0658	...	|	0728	|	0758**r**	|	|	0828	|	0858	|		|	2358	|	0058	...	...	...
129	**Eindhoven** Centraal........................a.	0646	...	...	0716	...	0746	...	0816	0816	...	0846	...	0916		2346	...	0016	...	...	...	...

	Ⓐ	⚒	Ⓐ	Ⓐ	⚒	Ⓐ	⚒			Ⓐ				Ⓐ⊡	⊡							
Eindhoven Centraal.........................d.	0544	...	0614	...	0644	...	0714	...	0744	...	0814	...	0844	...		2214	...	2244	2314	...	2344	...
's-Hertogenbosch................ **475** d.	|	0603**a**	|	0633	|	0703	|	0733	|	0803	|	0833	|	0903	and at	|	2233	|	|	2333	|	...
Tilburg... **475** d.	0609	0619**a**	0639	0649	0709	0719	0739	0749	0809	0819	0839	0849	0909	0919		2239	2249	2309	2339	2349	0009	...
Breda .... **475** a.	0621	0637**a**	0651	0707	0721	0737	0751	0807	0821	0837	0851	0907	0921	0937	the same	2251	2307	2321	2351	0007	0021	...
Breda ....**451** ★ d.	0623	0639	0653	0709	0723	0739	0753	0809	0823	0839	0853	0909	0923	0939		2253	2309	2323	2353	0009	0023	0039
Dordrecht...................**450 460** ★ a.	|	0702	|	0732	|	0802	|	0832	|	0902	|	0932	|	1002	minutes	|	2332	|	|	0032	|	0102
Rotterdam Centraal ... **450 451 460** d.	0648	...	0718	...	0748	...	0818	...	0848	...	0918	...	0948	...	past each	2318	...	2348	0018	...	0050	...
Delft .... **450 460** d.	0659	...	0729	...	0759	...	0829	...	0859	...	0929	...	0959	...		2329	...	2359	0029	...	...	...
Den Haag HS.................. **450 460** a.	0706	...	0736	...	0806	...	0836	...	0906	...	0936	...	1006	...	hour until	2336	...	0006	0036	...	...	...
Den Haag Centraal..........................a.	0714	...	0742	...	0812	...	0842	...	0912	...	0942	...	1012	...		2342	...	0011	0041	...	...	...

a – Ⓐ only.
r – ⚒ only.

◐ – Dordrecht - Breda is 30 km.
◇ – The xx28 Ⓐ from Dordrecht to 's-Hertogenbosch runs hourly until 1928.
⊡ – The xx03 Ⓐ from 's-Hertogenbosch to Dordrecht runs hourly until 1903.

Operated by Arriva (NS tickets valid) MAASTRICHT - HEERLEN - AACHEN 473

km		①–⑤ d	⑥ e	①–⑤ d		①–⑥ e				
0	**Maastricht** .... **472** d.	...	...	0624	...	0724	0824	and	2324	...
11	Valkenburg .... **472** d.	...	...	0636	...	0736	0836	hourly	2336	...
24	**Heerlen**.......................... **472** d.	0548	0648	0648	0748	0748	0848	until	2348	...
34	Herzogenrath 🏛 .... **802** d.	0600	0700	0700	0800	0800	0900		2400	...
48	**Aachen** Hbf..................... **802** a.	0612	0712	0712	0812	0812	0912		0012	...

	①–⑤ d	①–⑥ e					
Aachen Hbf.............. **802** d.	0547	0646	0746	0847	and	2247	2347
Herzogenrath 🏛 .... **802** d.	0600	0700	0800	0900	hourly	2300	2400
Heerlen....................... **472** d.	0614	0714	0814	0914	until	2314	0012
Valkenburg .... **472** d.	0624	0724	0824	0924		2324	...
Maastricht................... **472** a.	0635	0735	0835	0935		2335	...

Other trains MAASTRICHT - HEERLEN - KERKRADE

km		Ⓐ	⚒	⚒						
0	**Maastricht** ....d.	0542	0612	0642	0712	0742	and every	2242	2312	2342
11	Valkenburg ....d.	0555	0625	0655	0725	0755	30 minutes	2255	2325	2355
24	**Heerlen**...d.	0615	0645	0715	0745	0815	until	2315	2345	0015
33	**Kerkrade Centrum**..............d.	0627	0657	0727	0757	0827		2327	2357	0027

	Ⓐ	⚒	⚒					
Kerkrade Centrum...d.	0605	0635	0705	0735	0805	and every	2335	0005
Heerlen ....d.	0619	0649	0719	0749	0819	30 minutes	2349	0019
Valkenburg ....d.	0636	0706	0736	0806	0836	until	0006	0036
Maastricht.................a.	0649	0719	0749	0819	0849		0019	0049

d – Not Apr. 10, 27, May 18, 29.

e – Not Apr. 10, May 29.

ROOSENDAAL - 's-HERTOGENBOSCH - NIJMEGEN - ARNHEM - ZWOLLE 475

km		Ⓐ	Ⓐ	Ⓐ	⚒	⚒	Ⓐ	⑥	†	Ⓐ	†	⚒	†	⚒										
0	**Roosendaal** ....d.	...	...	...	...	...	0527	...	...	0557	...	0627	0654	0657	0727	0757		2127	2157	2227	2257	2327	...	...
23	Breda.......................... **471** d.	...	...	...	...	...	0550	...	...	0620	...	0650	0713	0720	0750	0820		2150	2220	2250	2320	2350	...	...
44	Tilburg .... **471** d.	...	...	...	...	...	0603	...	...	0633	...	0703	0733	0733	0803	0833		2203	2233	2303	2333	0004	...	...
67	**'s-Hertogenbosch**....... **471** a.	...	...	...	...	...	0619	...	...	0649	...	0719	0749	0749	0819	0849	and every	2219	2249	2319	2349	0019	...	...
67	**'s-Hertogenbosch**.................d.	...	...	...	...	...	0624	...	...	0654	...	0724	0754	0754	0824	0854		2224	2254	2324	2354	...	...	...
86	Oss..d.	...	...	...	...	...	0635	...	...	0705	...	0735	0805	0805	0835	0905	30 minutes	2235	2305	2335	0005	...	...	...
110	**Nijmegen** ....a.	...	...	...	...	...	0652	...	...	0722	...	0752	0822	0822	0852	0922		2252	2322	2352	0022	...	...	...
110	**Nijmegen** .... **468** d.	...	...	0624	...	0654	0654	*0713*	*0713*	0724	*0736*	0754	0824	0824	0854	0924	until	2254	2324	2354	0024	...	...	...
129	**Arnhem** Centraal......... **468** a.	...	...	0637	...	0707	0707	*0726*	*0726*	0737	*0756*	0807	0837	0837	0907	0937		2307	2337	0007	0037	...	...	...
129	**Arnhem** Centraal.................d.	...	0559	0641	...	0711	0711	0741	0730	0741	0811	0811	0841	0841	0911	0941		2311	2341	...	...	...	...	...
145	Dieren.......................................d.	...	0620	0653	...	0723	0723	0753	0751	0753	0823	0823	0853	0853	0923	0953		2323	2353	...	...	...	...	...
159	Zutphen ....d.	0603	0633	0703	0703	0733	0733	0803	0803	0803	0833	0833	0903	0903	0933	1003		2333	0003	...	...	...	...	...
174	Deventer...................................d.	0616	0646	0716	0716	0746	0746	0816	0816	0816	0846	0846	0916	0916	0946	1016		2346	0016	...	...	...	...	...
204	**Zwolle** ....a.	0640	0710	0740	0740	0810	0810	0840	0840	0840	0910	0910	0940	0940	1010	1040		0010	0040	...	...	...	...	...

	Ⓐ	Ⓐ	Ⓐ		⚒	Ⓐ	⚒	Ⓐ	†	⚒	⚒											
Zwolle................................d.	...	...	...	...	...	...	...	0620	...	0650	0720	0750	0820	0850		2120	2150	2220	2250	2320	2350	...
Deventer.................................d.	...	...	...	...	...	...	...	0645	...	0715	0745	0815	0845	0915		2145	2215	2245	2315	2345	0015	...
Zutphen ....d.	...	...	...	...	...	0547	...	0658	...	0728	0758	0828	0858	0928		2158	2228	2258	2328	2358	0028	...
Dieren.....................................d.	...	...	...	...	...	0559	...	0707	...	0737	0807	0837	0907	0937		2207	2237	2307	2337	0007	0037	...
Arnhem Centraal...................a.	...	...	...	...	...	0619	...	0719	...	0749	0819	0849	0919	0949		2219	2249	2319	2349	0019	0049	...
Arnhem Centraal.......... **468** d.	...	...	0553	...	...	0623	0653	0723	0753	0753	0823	0853	0923	0953	and every	2223	2253	2323	2353	*0035*	...	...
Nijmegen .... **468** a.	...	...	0606	...	...	0636	0706	0736	0806	0806	0836	0906	0936	1006	30 minutes	2236	2306	2336	0006	*0049*	...	...
Nijmegen ....d.	...	...	0609	...	...	0639	0709	0739	0809	0809	0839	0909	0939	1009	until	2239	2309	2339	...	...	...	...
Oss ....d.	...	...	0625	...	...	0655	0725	0755	0825	0825	0855	0925	0955	1025		2255	2325	2355	...	...	...	...
's-Hertogenbosch ....a.	...	...	0637	...	...	0707	0737	0807	0837	0837	0907	0937	1007	1037		2307	2337	0007	...	...	...	...
's-Hertogenbosch .... **471** d.	...	0612	0642	...	0712	0712	0742	0812	0842	0842	0912	0942	1012	1042		2312	2342	0012	...	...	...	...
Tilburg .... **471** d.	...	0628	0658	...	0728	0728	0758	0828	0858	0858	0928	0958	1028	1058		2328	2358	0028	...	...	...	...
Breda .... **471** d.	0615	0645	0715	0745	0745	0745	0815	0845	0915	0915	0945	1015	1045	1115		2345	0015	0049	...	...	...	...
Roosendaal..............................a.	0633	0703	0733	0803	0803	0803	0833	0903	0933	0933	1003	1033	1103	1133		0003	0033	0107	...	...	...	...

476 ARNHEM and ZUTPHEN - WINTERSWIJK

Operated by **Arriva** (NS tickets valid) 2nd class only

ARNHEM - WINTERSWIJK

km		Ⓐ	⚒	⚒		⚒		⚒		⚒		⚒					⊡				Ⓐ				
0	**Arnhem** Cen... d.	0605	0705	0731	0805	0835	0901	0935	1005	1035	1105	1131	1205	1235	1305	1331	and at the same	1905	1931	2005	2031	2105	2205	2305	0005
14	Zevenaar .... d.	0620	0720	0741	0820	0850	0920	0950	1020	1050	1120	1150	1220	1250	1320	1350	minutes past	1920	1950	2020	2050	2120	2220	2320	0020
30	Doetinchem..... d.	0637	0737	0807	0837	0907	0937	1007	1037	1107	1137	1207	1237	1307	1337	1407	each hour until	1937	2007	2037	2107	2137	2237	2337	0037
64	**Winterswijk**.... a.	0710	0810	0840	0910	0940	1013	1040	1110	1140	1210	1240	1310	1340	1410	1440		2010	2042	2110	2140	2210	2310	0010	0110

	Ⓐ	Ⓐ	⚒	Ⓐ		⚒		⚒		⚒		⚒		⚒							Ⓐ		Ⓐ		
Winterswijk......d.	0520	0550	0620	0650	0720	0750	0820	0850	0920	0950	1020	1050	1120	1150	1220	1250	and at the same	1920	1950	2020	2050	2120	2150	2220	2320
Doetinchem ......d.	0553	0623	0653	0723	0753	0823	0853	0923	0953	1023	1053	1123	1153	1223	1253	1323	minutes past	1953	2023	2053	2123	2153	2223	2253	2353
Zevenaar ....d.	0610	0640	0710	0740	0810	0840	0910	0940	1010	1040	1110	1140	1210	1240	1310	1340	each hour until	2010	2040	2110	2140	2210	2240	2310	0010
Arnhem Cen ....a.	0625	0655	0725	0756	0825	0856	0925	0955	1025	1055	1125	1155	1225	1255	1325	1355		2025	2055	2125	2155	2225	2255	2325	0025

ZUTPHEN - WINTERSWIJK

km		Ⓐ	Ⓐ	Ⓐ	⑥	Ⓐ		Ⓐ		Ⓐ		Ⓐ		Ⓐ							Ⓐ				
0	**Zutphen** .... d.	0632	0702	0732	0737	0802	0837	0907	0937	1007	1037	1107	1137	1207	1237	1307	and at the same	1937	2007	2038	2107	2137	2237	2337	0019
22	Ruurlo............. d.	0648	0718	0748	0751	0818	0851	0921	0951	1021	1051	1121	1151	1221	1251	1321	minutes past	1951	2021	2052	2121	2152	2251	2351	0033
43	**Winterswijk**.... a.	0707	0737	0807	0810	0840	0910	0940	1010	1040	1110	1140	1210	1240	1311	1340	each hour until	2010	2040	2111	2140	2211	2311	0011	0052

	Ⓐ	Ⓐ	⑥	Ⓐ	Ⓐ	Ⓒ	Ⓐ		Ⓐ		Ⓐ		Ⓐ		Ⓐ							Ⓐ		
Winterswijk......d.	0555	0617	0620	0647	0717	0720	0747	0820	0850	0920	0950	1020	1050	1120	1150	1220	1250	and at the same	1920	1950	2020	2050	2120	2220	2320
Ruurlo................d.	0612	0635	0638	0705	0735	0738	0805	0838	0908	0938	1008	1038	1108	1138	1208	1238	1308	minutes past	1938	2008	2038	2108	2138	2238	2338
Zutphen...........a.	0628	0651	0653	0721	0751	0753	0821	0853	0923	0953	1023	1053	1123	1153	1223	1253	1323	each hour until	1953	2023	2053	2124	2154	2254	2353

⊡ – Arnhem d. 1435 / 1635 / 1835 (not 1431 / 1631 / 1831).

477 NIJMEGEN - VENLO - ROERMOND

Operated by **Arriva** (NS tickets valid)

km		⚒	⚒								
0	**Nijmegen** ....d.	0538a	0608a	0638r	0708r	0738	0808	and every	2238	2308	2338
24	Boxmeer...........d.	0601a	0631a	0701r	0731r	0801	0831	30 minutes	2301	2331	0001
39	Venray..............d.	0615a	0645a	0715r	0745r	0815	0845	until	2315	2345	0015
61	**Venlo** ....d.	0633	0703	0733	0803	0833	0903		2333	0003	0031
84	**Roermond** ....a.	0655	0725	0755	0825	0855	0925		2355	0025	...

	⚒	⚒								
Roermond.....d.	...	0603a	0633a	0703r	0733r	0803	0833	and every	2233	2303
Venlo ....d.	0559	0629	0659	0729	0759	0829	0859	30 minutes	2259	2329
Venray............d.	0615	0645	0715	0745	0815	0845	0915	until	2315	2345
Boxmeer.........d.	0630	0700	0730	0800	0830	0900	0930		2330	0000
Nijmegen ......a.	0652	0722	0752	0822	0852	0922	0952		2352	0022

a – Ⓐ only. r – ⚒ only.

478 ARNHEM - TIEL - GELDERMALSEN - UTRECHT and 's-HERTOGENBOSCH

km		Ⓐ	Ⓐ	⚒	⚒					
0	**Tiel**..........................d.	0553	0623	0653	0723	0753	0823	and every	2323	2353
12	Geldermalsen ....d.	0612	0642	0712	0742	0812	0842	30 minutes	2342	0012
38	**Utrecht** Centraal.........a.	0638	0708	0738	0808	0838	0908	until	0007	0038

	Ⓐ	Ⓐ	⚒						
Utrecht Centraal......d.	0552	0622	0652	0722	0752	and every	2322	2352	...
Geldermalsen............d.	0624	0654	0724	0754	0824	30 minutes	2354	0024	...
Tiel.........................a.	0635	0705	0735	0805	0835	until	0005	0035	...

km		Ⓐ	Ⓐ	⚒						
0	Geldermalsen ....d.	0612	0641	0711	...	0741	0811	and every 30 minutes	2342	0011
22	**'s-Hertogenbosch** .....a.	0628	0657	0727	...	0757	0827	until	2358	0027

	Ⓐ	⚒	⚒						
's-Hertogenbosch...d.	0603	0633	0703	0733	0803	and every 30 minutes	2333	0003	...
Geldermalsen...........a.	0618	0648	0718	0748	0818	until	2348	0018	...

ARNHEM - TIEL and v.v. Operated by **Arriva** (NS tickets valid). 2nd class only. *44 km.* Journey time: 35 – 36 minutes.

From Arnhem at 0608 Ⓐ 0638 Ⓐ, 0708 Ⓐ, 0738 Ⓐ, 0808 Ⓐ, 0838 ⚒, 0908 Ⓐ, 0938, 1008 Ⓐ, 1038, 1138, 1238, 1338, 1408 Ⓐ, 1438, 1508 Ⓐ, 1538, 1608 Ⓐ, 1638, 1708 Ⓐ, 1738, 1808 Ⓐ, 1838, 1938, 2038, 2138, 2238 and 2338. **From Tiel** at 0617 Ⓐ, 0647 Ⓐ, 0717 Ⓐ, 0747 ⚒, 0817 Ⓐ, 0847, 0917 Ⓐ, 0947, 1047, 1147, 1247, 1317 Ⓐ, 1347, 1417 Ⓐ, 1447, 1517 Ⓐ, 1547, 1617 Ⓐ, 1647, 1717 Ⓐ, 1747, 1847, 1947, 2017 Ⓐ, 2047, 2147, 2247 and 2347 ⑥.

479 DORDRECHT - GELDERMALSEN

Operated by **R-net** (NS tickets valid); 2nd class only

km		Ⓐ	⑥	Ⓐ	⑥	Ⓐ	⑥	Ⓐ	Ⓒ	Ⓐ	⑥	Ⓐ		Ⓒ	Ⓐ	⑥	Ⓐ	Ⓐ						
0	**Dordrecht**........d.	0508	0541	0548	0611	0616	0641	0648	0711	0718	0741	0748	and at same	1911	1918	1941	1948	2007	2011	2111	2211	2311	...	0011
10	Sliedrecht ....d.	0520	0553	0600	0623	0628	0653	0700	0723	0730	0753	0800	minutes past	1923	1930	1953	2000	2021	2023	2123	2223	2323	...	0023
24	Gorinchem........d.	0544	0610	0614	0640	0645	0710	0714	0740	0744	0810	0814	each hour	1940	1944	2010	2014	2040	2040	2140	2240	2340	...	0040
49	**Geldermalsen**..a.	0607	0634	0637	0704	0707	0734	0737	0804	0807	0834	0837	until	2004	2008	2034	2037	2105	2104	2204	2304	0004	...	0103

	Ⓐ	⑥	Ⓐ	⑥	Ⓐ	⑥	Ⓐ	Ⓒ	Ⓐ		⑥	Ⓐ	Ⓒ	Ⓐ	⑥	Ⓐ	Ⓒ	Ⓐ	⑥	Ⓐ				
Geldermalsen...d.	0614	0641	0644	0711	0714	0741	0744	0811	0814	and at same	1841	1844	1911	1914	1941	1944	2011	2013	2041	2042	2111	2211	2311	0011
Gorinchem.........d.	0646	0709	0716	0739	0746	0809	0816	0839	0846	minutes past	1909	1916	1939	1946	2009	2016	2039	2039	2109	2109	2139	2239	2339	0039
Sliedrecht ....d.	0700	0723	0730	0753	0800	0823	0830	0853	0900	each hour	1923	1930	1953	2000	2023	2031	2053	2053	2123	2123	2153	2253	2353	0053
Dordrecht.........a.	0712	0735	0742	0805	0812	0835	0842	0905	0912	until	1935	1942	2005	2012	2035	2042	2105	2105	2135	2135	2205	2305	0005	0105

480 AMSTERDAM and SCHIPHOL ✈ - AMERSFOORT - DEVENTER - ENSCHEDE

AMSTERDAM CENTRAAL - AMERSFOORT

km		Ⓐ	Ⓐ	Ⓐ	⚒			Ⓐ		⚒					✣									
0	**Amsterdam** Centraal......d.	0600	0611	0630	0641	0700	0711	0730	0741	0800	0811	0830	0841	0900	and at	2241	2300	2311	2330	2341	...	...	...	...
14	Weesp.............................d.	|	0629	|	0659	|	0729	|	0759	|	0829	|	0859	|	the same	2259	|	2329	|	2359	...	...	...	...
23	Naarden-Bussum ..... **457** d.	|	0635	|	0705	|	0735	|	0805	|	0835	|	0905	|	minutes	2305	|	2335	|	0005	...	...	...	...
29	Hilversum .... **457** d.	0622	0645	0652	0715	0722	0745	0752	0815	0822	0845	0852	0915	0922	past each	2315	2322	2345	2352	0015	...	...	...	...
36	Baarn...............................d.	|	0650	|	0720	|	0750	|	0820	|	0850	|	0920	|	hour until	2320	|	2350	|	0020	...	...	...	...
45	**Amersfoort** Centraal ......a.	0634	0658	0704	0728	0734	0758	0804	0828	0834	0858	0904	0928	0934		2328	2334	2358	0004	0028	...	...	...	...

		Ⓐ	Ⓐ	Ⓐ	Ⓐ		Ⓐ		⚒		⚒		⚒				◇	◇						
Amersfoort Centraal.......d.	0448	0501	0531	0601	0626	0631	0656	0701	0726	0731	0756	0801	0826	0831	0856	0901	0926	and at	2231	2256	2301	2326	2356	0001
Baarn ....d.	0455	0508	0538	0608	|	0638	|	0708	|	0738	|	0808	|	0838	|	0908	|	the same	2238	|	2308	|	|	0008
Hilversum .... **457** d.	0502	0516	0546	0616	0640	0646	0710	0716	0740	0746	0810	0816	0840	0846	0910	0916	0940	minutes	2246	2310	2316	2340	0010	0016
Naarden-Bussum...... **457** d.	0511	0525	0555	0625	|	0655	|	0725	|	0755	|	0825	|	0855	|	0925	|	past each	2255	|	2325	|	|	0025
Weesp...............................d.	0521	0533	0603	0633	|	0703	|	0733	|	0803	|	0833	|	0903	|	0933	|	hour until	2303	|	2333	|	|	0033
Amsterdam Centraal ......a.	0537	0549	0619	0649	0700	0719	0730	0750	0800	0819	0830	0849	0900	0919	0930	0949	1000		2319	2330	2349	2400	0030	0049

SCHIPHOL ✈ - AMSTERDAM ZUID - AMERSFOORT - ENSCHEDE

km		Ⓐ	Ⓐ	⚒H	⚒	⚒	H				H				H			H			H			
0	**Schiphol** ✈...................d.	0538	0608	...	0638	0708	...	0738	...	0808	...	0838		2108	...	2138	2208	...	2238	2308	...	2338	...	...
9	Amsterdam Zuid ....d.	0545	0615	...	0645	0715	...	0745	...	0815	...	0845	and at	2115	...	2145	2215	...	2245	2315	...	2345	...	...
14	Duivendrecht....................d.	0550	0620	...	0650	0720	...	0750	...	0820	...	0850	the same	2120	...	2150	2220	...	2250	2320	...	2350	...	...
37	Hilversum ....d.	0607	0637	...	0707	0737	...	0807	...	0837	...	0907		2137	...	2207	2237	...	2307	2337	...	0007	...	...
53	**Amersfoort** Centraal ......a.	0618	0649	...	0718	0748	...	0819	...	0848	...	0918	minutes	2148	...	2218	2248	...	2318	2348	...	0018	...	...
53	**Amersfoort** Centraal ......d.	0622	...	0652	0722	...	0752	0822	...	...	0852	0922		...	2152	2222	...	2252	2322	...	2352	...	...	...
96	Apeldoorn ....d.	0647	...	0717	0747	...	0817	0847	...	...	0917	0947	past each	...	2217	2247	...	2317	2347	...	0017	...	...	...
111	**Deventer** ....d.	0700	...	0730	0800	...	0830	0900	...	...	0930	1000		...	2230	2300	...	2330	2400	...	0030	...	...	...
149	Almelo .... **492** d.	0725	...	0755	0825	...	0855	0925	...	...	0955	1025	hour until	...	2255	2325	...	2355	0025	...	0055	...	...	...
164	**Hengelo** .... **492** a.	0737	...	0806	0836	...	0906	0936	...	...	1006	1036		...	2306	2336	...	0006	0036	...	0106	...	...	...
172	**Enschede** .... **492** a.	0744	...	0814	0844	...	0914	0944	...	...	1014	1044		...	2314	2344	...	0014	0044	...	0114	...	...	...

H – From Den Haag (Table **481**).

CONTINUES ON NEXT PAGE →

✣ – The 1900 from Amsterdam runs on dates as shown in the Amsterdam Centraal - Hengelo panel.
◇ – The 0926 from Amersfoort runs on ⚒ only (subsequent services from Amersfoort at xx26 run daily).

AMSTERDAM and SCHIPHOL ✈ - AMERSFOORT - DEVENTER - ENSCHEDE 480

ENSCHEDE - AMERSFOORT - AMSTERDAM ZUID - SCHIPHOL ✈

	ⒶH	Ⓐ	Ⓐ	⚒	ⒶH	⚒H		⚒		⚒H	H		⚒		H				H			J		
Enschede 492 d.	0446	...	0516	...	0546	...	...	0616	...	0646	...	...	0716	...	0746	...	0816	and at the same minutes past each hour until	2146	...	2216	2246	...	...
Hengelo 492 d.	0454	...	0524	...	0554	...	...	0624	...	0654	...	...	0724	...	0754	...	0824		2154	...	2224	2254	...	...
Almelo 492 d.	0506	...	0536	...	0606	...	...	0636	...	0706	...	...	0736	...	0806	...	0836		2206	...	2236	2306	...	...
Deventer d.	0532	...	0602	...	0632	0632	...	0702	...	0732	0732	...	0802	0802	0832	...	0902		2232	...	2302	2332	...	...
Apeldoorn d.	0544	...	0614	...	0644	0644	...	0714	...	0744	0744	...	0814	0814	0844	...	0914		2244	...	2314	2344	...	...
Amersfoort Centraal a.	0608	...	0638	...	0708	0708	...	0738	...	0808	0808	...	0838	0838	0908	...	0938		2308	...	2338	0008	...	...
Amersfoort Centraal d.	...	0611	0641	0641	...	...	0711	0741	0741	...	...	0811	0841	0841	...	0911	0941		...	2311	2341	...	0011	...
Hilversum d.	...	0624	0654	0654	...	...	0724	0754	0754	...	...	0824	0854	0854	...	0924	0954		...	2324	2354	...	0024	...
Duivendrecht d.	...	0640	0710	0710	...	...	0740	0810	0810	...	...	0840	0910	0910	...	0940	1010		...	2340	0010	...	0040	...
Amsterdam Zuid a.	...	0645	0715	0715	...	...	0745	0815	0815	...	...	0845	0915	0915	...	0945	1015		...	2345	0015	...	0045	...
Schiphol ✈ a.	...	0652	0722	0722	...	...	0752	0822	0822	...	...	0852	0922	0922	...	0952	1022		...	2352	0022	...	0052	...

Through trains **AMSTERDAM CENTRAAL - DEVENTER - HENGELO**

	F♥		♥			♥	Ⓐ	♥⊡	Ⓐ	♥	Ⓐ	♥		Ⓒ	♥		E♥	⑥							
Amsterdam Centraal d.	0502	...	0700	...	0900	0910	1000	1100	1200	1300	1400	1500	...	1700	1710	...	1900	1900	...	...	...	...	...	...	...
Hilversum d.	0525	...	0722	...	0922	0932	1022	1122	1222	1322	1422	1522	...	1722	1732	...	1922	1922	...	...	...	...	...	...	...
Amersfoort Centraal d.	0540	...	0736	...	0936	0945	1036	1136	1236	1336	1436	1536	...	1736	1745	...	1936	1936	...	...	...	...	...	...	...
Apeldoorn d.	0605	...	0809	...	1002	1010	1102	1201	1302	1401	1502	1601	...	1802	1810	...	2001	2002	...	...	...	...	...	...	...
Deventer d.	0617	...	0821	...	1012	1022	1112	1218	1312	1418	1512	1618	...	1812	1821	...	2018	2019	...	...	...	...	...	...	...
Almelo d.	0642	...	0846	...	...	1047	...	1246	...	1446	...	1646	...	...	1847	...	2046	2046	...	...	...	...	...	...	...
Hengelo a.	0653	...	0857	...	...	1057	...	1257	...	1457	...	1657	...	...	1857	...	2057	2056	...	...	...	...	...	...	...

	⑥	G♥	Ⓐ	L♥	†	Ⓐ	♥	Ⓐ	♥⊖	Ⓐ	♥			♥		♥		♥							
Hengelo d.	...	0802	...	0902	0904	...	1102	...	1302	...	1502	...	...	1702	...	1902	...	2102	...	...	...	...	...	...	...
Almelo d.	...	0815	...	0915	0916	...	1115	...	1315	...	1514	...	...	1715	...	1915	...	2115	...	...	...	...	...	...	...
Deventer d.	0848	0848	0918	0948	0948	1048	1148	1248	1348	1448	1538	1548	...	1748	...	1948	...	2148	...	...	...	...	...	...	...
Apeldoorn d.	0900	0900	0930	1000	1000	1100	1200	1300	1400	1500	|	1600	...	1800	...	2000	...	2200	...	...	...	...	...	...	...
Amersfoort Centraal d.	0926	0926	0656	1026	1026	1126	1226	1326	1426	1526	1616	1626	...	1826	...	2026	...	2226	...	...	...	...	...	...	...
Hilversum d.	0940	0940	1010	1040	1040	1140	1240	1340	1440	1540	1629	1640	...	1840	...	2040	...	2240	...	...	...	...	...	...	...
Amsterdam Centraal a.	1000	1000	1029	1100	1100	1200	1300	1400	1500	1600	1649	1700	...	1900	...	2100	...	2300	...	...	...	...	...	...	...

E – ⑧ to Apr. 2; ⑦ Apr. 10 - Aug. 27 (also Apr. 10, May 1, 29; not Apr. 30, May 28); ⑧ from Sept. 4.
F – ①–⑥ Apr. 3 - Sept. 2 (not Apr. 10, May 1, 29).
G – ① Apr. 3 - Aug. 28 (also Apr. 11, May 2, 30; not Apr. 10, May 1, 29).
H – To Den Haag (Table **481**).
J – Continues to Den Haag on dates in Table **481**.
L – ①–⑥ (not Apr. 10, May 1, 29).
⊖ – June 11 - Sept. 3 runs up to 12 minutes **earlier** and does not call at Apeldoorn.
⊡ – June 11 - Sept. 3 runs up to 10 minutes later.
♥ – *IC* service to / from Germany via Bad Bentheim. Conveys 🍸. See Table **22** for further details.

ROTTERDAM and DEN HAAG - UTRECHT - ZWOLLE 481

Additional fast trains run Rotterdam / Den Haag - Utrecht and v.v. at peak times.

km		⑥	†				Ⓐ	⚒	Ⓐ	⚒	Ⓐ	Ⓐ	⚒	①–④ b	⚒	⚒		⚒		①–④ b				
0	**Rotterdam** Centraal d.	0005	0005	0005	...	...	...	...	...	...	0605	...	0635	0650	...	0705	...	...	0735	0750	...	0805	...	0835
10	Rotterdam Alexander d.	0013	0013	0013	...	...	...	...	...	...	0613	...	0643	0658	...	0713	...	...	0743	0758	...	0813	...	0843
	Den Haag Centraal d.	|	|	|	...	...	...	...	0555	...	|	0625	|	|	0655	|	...	0725	|	|	0755	|	0825	|
24	Gouda d.	0024	0024	0024	...	...	...	...	0614	...	0624	0644	0654	0709	0714	0724	...	0744	0754	0809	0814	0824	0844	0854
56	**Utrecht** Centraal a.	0042	0042	0042	...	...	...	...	0632	...	0642	0702	0712	0727	0732	0742	...	0802	0812	0827	0832	0842	0902	0912
56	**Utrecht** Centraal d.	0049	0049	0049	...	...	0619	0637	0637	0649	0649	0707	0719	...	0737	0749	...	0807	0819	...	0837	0849	0907	0919
77	**Amersfoort** Centraal a.	0102	0102	0102	...	...	0632	0650	0650	0702	0702	0720	0732	...	0750	0802	...	0820	0832	...	0850	0902	0920	0932
77	**Amersfoort** Centraal d.	0106	0106	...	...	...	0634	0652	0652	0704	0704	...	0734	...	0752	0804	0804	...	0834	...	0852	0904	...	0934
	Deventer **480** a.	|	|	...	...	...	|	0728	0728	|	|	...	|	...	0828	|	|	...	|	...	0928	|	...	|
	Enschede **480** a.	|	|	...	...	...	|	0814	0814	|	|	...	|	...	0914	|	|	...	|	...	1014	|	...	|
144	**Zwolle** a.	0141	0141	...	...	...	0709	...	...	0739	0739	...	0809	...	...	0839	0839	...	0909	...	...	0939	...	1009
	Leeuwarden **482** a.	|	...	...	...	...	0813	...	...	|	|	...	0913	...	...	|	|	...	1013	...	...	|	...	1113
	Groningen **482** a.	0251	...	...	...	...	...	...	...	0842	0842	...	...	...	...	0942	0942	...	...	...	...	1042	...	...

	①–④ b																	⚒					
Rotterdam Centraal d.	0850	...	0905	...	0935	...	and at the same minutes past each hour until	2105	...	2135	...	...	2205	...	2235	...	...	2305	2305	...	2335	...	...
Rotterdam Alexander d.	0858	...	0913	...	0943	...		2113	...	2143	...	...	2213	...	2243	...	...	2313	2313	...	2343	...	...
Den Haag Centraal d.	|	0855	|	0925	|	0955		|	2125	|	2155	...	|	2225	|	2255	...	|	|	2325	|	...	2355
Gouda d.	0909	0914	0924	0944	0954	1014		2124	2144	2154	2214	...	2224	2244	2254	2314	...	2324	2324	2344	2354	...	0014
Utrecht Centraal a.	0927	0932	0942	1002	1012	1032		2142	2202	2212	2232	...	2242	2302	2312	2332	...	2342	2342	0002	0012	...	0032
Utrecht Centraal d.	...	0937	0949	1007	1019	1037		2149	2207	2219	2237	...	2249	2307	2319	2337	...	2349	2349	0007	0019	...	0037
Amersfoort Centraal a.	...	0950	1002	1020	1032	1050		2202	2220	2232	2250	...	2302	2320	2332	2350	...	0002	0002	0020	0032	...	0050
Amersfoort Centraal d.	...	0952	1004	...	1034	1052		2204	...	2234	2252	...	2304	...	2334	2352	...	0004	0004	...	...	...	...
Deventer **480** a.	...	1028	|	...	|	1128		|	...	|	2328	...	|	...	|	0028	...	|	|	...	...	...	...
Enschede **480** a.	...	1114	|	...	|	1214		|	...	|	0014	...	|	...	|	0114	...	|	|	...	...	...	...
Zwolle a.	...	...	1039	...	1109	...		2239	...	2309	...	...	2339	...	0009	...	...	0046	0046	...	...	...	...
Leeuwarden **482** a.	...	...	|	...	1213	...		|	...	0013	...	...	|	...	...	...	...	|	...	...	...	...	...
Groningen **482** a.	...	...	1142	...	...	...		2342	...	...	...	...	0042	...	...	...	...	0158	...	...	...	...	...

km		Ⓐ	①–④ b	Ⓐ	Ⓐ		Ⓐ	①–④ b	Ⓐ	⚒	Ⓐ	⚒	Ⓐ	⚒	Ⓐ	①–④ b	⚒	Ⓐ	⚒		⚒		⚒	①–④ b
	Groningen **482** d.	...	...	...	...	...	...	...	...	...	...	...	0506	...	...	...	...	...	...	...	0606	...	...	...
	Leeuwarden **482** d.	...	...	...	...	...	...	...	...	...	...	...	|	...	...	...	...	0547	...	...	|	...	...	...
	Zwolle d.	...	...	...	...	...	...	...	0550	...	...	...	0620	...	...	...	0650	0650	...	...	0720	...	...	...
	Enschede **480** d.	...	...	...	...	...	0446	...	|	...	...	...	|	...	0546	...	|	|	...	...	|	...	0646	...
	Deventer **480** d.	...	...	...	...	...	0532	...	|	...	...	...	|	0632	0632	...	|	|	...	...	|	0732	0732	...
	Amersfoort Centraal a.	...	...	...	...	...	0608	...	0625	...	...	...	0655	0708	0708	...	0725	0725	...	...	0755	0808	0808	...
	Amersfoort Centraal d.	...	...	...	...	...	0610	...	0628	...	0640	...	0658	0710	0710	...	0728	0728	0740	...	0758	0810	0810	...
	Utrecht Centraal a.	...	...	...	...	...	0623	...	0641	...	0653	...	0711	0723	0723	...	0741	0741	0753	...	0811	0823	0823	...
	Utrecht Centraal d.	0558	0603	0613	0618	...	0628	0633	0648	0658	0658	0718	0718	0728	0728	0733	0748	0748	0758	0818	0818	0828	0828	0833
0	Gouda d.	0617	0622	0632	0636	...	0647	0652	0706	0717	0717	0736	0736	0747	0747	0752	0806	0806	0817	0836	0836	0847	0847	0852
28	**Den Haag** Centraal a.	0636	|	0651	|	...	0706	|	|	0736	0736	|	|	0806	0806	|	|	|	0836	|	|	0908	0908	|
	Rotterdam Alexander d.	...	0631	...	0646	...	...	0701	0716	...	...	0746	0746	...	...	0801	0816	0816	...	0846	0846	...	...	0901
	Rotterdam Centraal a.	...	0640	...	0655	...	...	0710	0725	...	...	0755	0755	...	...	0810	0825	0825	...	0855	0855	...	...	0910

		⚒		Ⓒ	Ⓐ		†	⚒														⑤⑥ f	
Groningen **482** d.	...	...	...	0706	0718	...	...	...	...	0818	...	...	...	and at the same minutes past each hour until	2118	...	...	...	2218	...	...	...	...
Leeuwarden **482** d.	...	0647	...	|	|	...	0736	0747	...	|	...	0847	...		|	...	2147	...	|	...	...	...	2236
Zwolle d.	0750	0750	...	0820	0820	...	0850	0850	...	0920	...	0950	...		2220	...	2250	...	2320	...	...	...	2350
Enschede **480** d.	|	|	...	|	|	0746	|	|	...	|	0846	|	...		|	2146	|	...	|	...	2246	2246	|
Deventer **480** d.	|	|	...	|	|	0832	|	|	...	|	0932	|	...		|	2232	|	...	|	...	2332	2332	|
Amersfoort Centraal a.	0825	0825	...	0855	0855	0908	0925	0925	...	0955	1008	1025	...		2255	2308	2325	...	2355	...	0008	0008	0025
Amersfoort Centraal d.	0828	0828	0840	0858	0858	0910	0928	0929	0940	0958	1010	1028	1040		2258	2310	2328	2340	2358	...	0010	0010	0028
Utrecht Centraal a.	0841	0841	0853	0911	0912	0923	0941	0942	0953	1011	1023	1041	1053		2311	2323	2341	2353	0011	...	0023	0023	0041
Utrecht Centraal d.	0848	0848	0858	0918	0918	0928	0948	0948	0958	1018	1028	1048	1058		2318	2328	2348	2358	0018	...	...	0028	...
Gouda d.	0906	0906	0917	0936	0936	0947	1006	1006	1017	1036	1047	1106	1117		2336	2347	0006	0017	0036	...	...	0047	...
Den Haag Centraal a.	|	|	0936	|	|	1006	|	|	1036	|	1106	|	1136		|	0006	|	0036	|	...	...	0106	...
Rotterdam Alexander d.	0916	0916	...	0946	0946	...	1016	1016	...	1046	...	1116	...		2346	...	0016	...	0046	...	...	...	...
Rotterdam Centraal a.	0925	0925	...	0955	0955	...	1025	1025	...	1055	...	1125	...		2355	...	0025	...	0055	...	...	...	...

b – Not Apr. 10, 27, May 18, 29.
f – Also Apr. 27, May 18.

482 ZWOLLE - GRONINGEN and LEEUWARDEN

km		⑥		Ⓐ	Ⓐ	ⒶL	Ⓐ	Ⓐ	Ⓐ	⚒M	⚒		Ⓐ	⚒	Ⓐ	⚒	⚒			⚒			⚒	†N
	Rotterdam Centraal **481** d.	0005	...	...	...	...	...	...	...	...	...	...	...	...	...	...	0605a	...	...	...	...	...	...	...
	Utrecht Centraal **481** d.	0049	...	...	...	...	...	...	...	...	...	...	...	...	0619	...	0649	...	...	...	...	...	...	...
	Amersfoort Centraal **481** d.	0106	...	...	...	...	...	...	...	...	...	...	...	...	0634	...	0704	...	...	...	...	...	...	...
	Den Haag Centraal **460** d.	|	...	...	...	...	...	...	...	...	...	...	0533	...	|	...	|	...	...	0603	...	...	0633	...
	Schiphol + **460** d.	|	...	...	...	...	...	...	...	...	...	...	0605	...	|	...	|	...	...	0635	...	...	0705	...
	Amsterdam Zuid **460** d.	|	...	...	...	...	...	...	...	...	...	...	0612	...	|	...	|	...	...	0642	...	...	0712	...
	Zwolle **460 481** a.	0141	...	...	...	...	...	...	...	...	...	...	0713	...	0709	...	0739	...	...	0743	...	...	0813	...
0	**Zwolle** d.	0145	...	0548	0552	0615	0618	0622	0645	0648	0652	...	0715	0718	0718	0722	0745	0745	0748	0748	0752	...	0815	0815
27	Meppel d.	0200	...	0604	0607	|	0634	0637	|	0704	0707	...	|	0734	0734	0737	|	|	0804	0804	0807	...	|	|
41	Steenwijk d.	|	...	0613	|	|	0643	|	|	0713	|	...	|	0743	0743	|	|	|	0813	0813	|	...	|	|
65	Heerenveen d.	|	...	0629	|	|	0656	|	|	0726	|	...	|	0756	0756	|	|	|	0826	0826	|	...	|	|
94	**Leeuwarden** a.	|	...	0651	|	|	0713	|	|	0743	|	...	|	0813	0813	|	|	|	0843	0843	|	...	|	|
47	Hoogeveen d.	0212	...	...	0619	|	...	0649	|	...	0719	...	|	...	...	0749	|	|	...	...	0819	...	|	|
77	Assen d.	0231	...	...	0637	0655	...	0707	0725	...	0737	...	0755	...	...	0807	0825	0825	...	...	0837	...	0855	0855
104	**Groningen** a.	0251	...	...	0657	0712	...	0727	0742	...	0757	...	0812	...	...	0827	0842	0842	...	...	0857	...	0912	0912

		⚒	⚒	⚒					⚒						⚒◐							
Rotterdam Centraal **481** d.	...	0635	...	0705	...	...	...	...	0735	...	0805	...	...	...	0835	...		1805	...	...	...	1835	...
Utrecht Centraal **481** d.	...	0719	...	0749	...	...	...	...	0819	...	0849	...	...	...	0919	...	and at	1849	...	...	...	1919	...
Amersfoort Centraal **481** d.	...	0734	...	0804	0804	...	...	...	0834	...	0904	...	...	...	0934	...		1904	...	...	...	1934	...
Den Haag Centraal **460** d.	...	|	...	|	|	0703	...	0733	|	...	|	0803	...	0833	|	...	the	|	1803	...	1833	|	...
Schiphol + **460** d.	...	|	...	|	|	0735	...	0805	|	...	|	0835	...	0905	|	...	same	|	1835	...	1905	|	...
Amsterdam Zuid **460** d.	...	|	...	|	|	0742	...	0812	|	...	|	0842	...	0912	|	...		|	1842	...	1912	|	...
Zwolle **460 481** a.	...	0809	...	0839	0839	0843	...	0913	0909	...	0939	0943	...	1013	1009	...	minutes	1939	1943	...	2013	2009	...
Zwolle d.	0818	0818	0822	0845	0845	0848	0852	0915	0918	0922	0945	0948	0952	1015	1018	1022	past	1945	1948	1952	2015	2018	2022
Meppel d.	0833	0834	0837	|	|	0904	0907	|	0934	0937	|	1004	1007	|	1034	1037		|	2004	2007	|	2034	2037
Steenwijk d.	0843	0843	|	|	|	0913	|	|	0943	|	|	1013	|	|	1043	|	each	|	2013	|	|	2043	|
Heerenveen d.	0856	0856	|	|	|	0926	|	|	0956	|	|	1026	|	|	1056	|	hour	|	2026	|	|	2056	|
Leeuwarden a.	0913	0913	|	|	|	0943	|	|	1013	|	|	1043	|	|	1113	|		|	2043	|	|	2113	|
Hoogeveen d.	...	...	0849	|	|	...	0919	|	...	0949	|	...	1019	|	...	1049	until	|	...	2019	|	...	2049
Assen d.	...	...	0907	0925	0925	...	0937	0955	...	1011	1025	...	1037	1055	...	1107		2025	...	2037	2055	...	2107
Groningen a.	...	...	0927	0942	0942	...	0957	1012	...	1031	1042	...	1057	1112	...	1127		2042	...	2057	2112	...	2127

																						⑤⑥	
Rotterdam Centraal **481** d.	1905	...	...	...	1935	...	2005	...	...	...	2035	...	2105	...	...	2135	...	2205	...	...	...	...	2305	...
Utrecht Centraal **481** d.	1949	...	...	...	2019	...	2049	...	...	...	2119	...	2149	...	...	2219	...	2249	...	...	...	...	2349	...
Amersfoort Centraal **481** d.	2004	...	...	...	2034	...	2104	...	...	...	2134	...	2204	...	...	2234	...	2304	...	...	...	...	0004	...
Den Haag Centraal **460** d.	|	1903	...	1933	|	...	|	2003	...	2033	|	...	|	2103	2133	|	...	|	2203	...	2233	...	|	2303
Schiphol + **460** d.	|	1935	...	2005	|	...	|	2035	...	2105	|	...	|	2135	2205	|	...	|	2235	...	2305	...	|	2335
Amsterdam Zuid **460** d.	|	1942	...	2012	|	...	|	2042	...	2112	|	...	|	2142	2212	|	...	|	2242	...	2312	...	|	2342
Zwolle **460 481** a.	2039	2043	...	2113	2109	...	2139	2143	...	2213	2209	...	2239	2243	2313	2309	...	2339	2343	...	0013	...	0046	0043
Zwolle d.	2045	2048	2052	2115	2118	2122	2145	2148	2152	2215	2218	2222	2245	2248	2315	2318	...	2345	2348	...	0015	...	0049	0048
Meppel d.	|	2104	2107	|	2134	2137	|	2204	2207	|	2234	2237	|	2304	2330	2334	...	|	0004	...	0031	...	0107	0104
Steenwijk d.	|	2113	|	|	2143	|	|	2213	|	|	2243	|	|	2313	|	2343	...	|	0013	...	|	...	|	0113
Heerenveen d.	|	2126	|	|	2156	|	|	2226	|	|	2256	|	|	2329	|	2356	...	|	0029	...	|	...	|	0129
Leeuwarden a.	|	2143	|	|	2213	|	|	2243	|	|	2313	|	|	2351	|	0013	...	|	0051	...	|	...	|	0151
Hoogeveen d.	|	...	2119	|	...	2149	|	...	2219	|	...	2249	|	...	2342	...	...	|	...	...	0043	...	0118	...
Assen d.	2125	...	2137	2155	...	2207	2225	...	2237	2255	...	2307	2325	...	0001	...	...	0025	...	...	0102	...	0137	...
Groningen a.	2142	...	2157	2212	...	2227	2242	...	2257	2312	...	2327	2342	...	0023	...	...	0042	...	...	0123	...	0158	...

	Ⓐ	Ⓐ		Ⓐ	Ⓐ	⑥	Ⓐ	⚒	Ⓐ	⚒	⑥	Ⓑ	Ⓐ	†	⚒	Ⓒ	Ⓐ	⚒	†	⚒	†	⚒	⚒	
Groningen d.	...	0506	...	...	0536	0548	...	0606	0633	...	0636	0648	0703	...	...	0706	0718	0733	...	...	0736	0748	0803	...
Assen d.	...	0528	...	...	0558	0604	...	0628	0653	...	0658	0704	0723	...	...	0728	0734	0753	...	...	0758	0804	0823	...
Hoogeveen d.	...	0548	...	...	0618	|	...	0648	0711	...	0718	|	0741	...	...	0747	|	0811	...	...	0818	|	0841	...
Leeuwarden d.	0507	|	...	0547	|	|	0617	|	|	0647	|	|	|	0706	0717	|	|	|	0736	0747	|	|	|	0817
Heerenveen d.	0529	|	...	0604	|	|	0634	|	|	0704	|	|	|	0728	0734	|	|	|	0759	0804	|	|	|	0834
Steenwijk d.	0546	|	...	0617	|	|	0647	|	|	0717	|	|	|	0746	0747	|	|	|	0816	0817	|	|	|	0847
Meppel d.	0556	0600	...	0626	0630	|	0656	0700	0722	0726	0730	|	0752	0755	0756	0800	|	0822	0825	0826	0830	|	0852	0856
Zwolle a.	0612	0615	...	0642	0645	0645	0712	0715	0738	0742	0745	0745	0808	0812	0812	0815	0815	0838	0841	0842	0845	0845	0908	0912
Zwolle **460 481** d.	0617	0620	...	0650	0647	0647	0717	0720	...	0750	0747	0747	...	0817	0817	0820	0820	...	0850	0850	0847	0847	...	0917
Amsterdam Zuid **460** a.	0717	|	...	|	0747	0747	0817	|	...	|	0847	0847	...	0917	0917	|	|	...	|	|	0947	0947	...	1017
Schiphol + **460** a.	0724	|	...	|	0754	0754	0824	|	...	|	0854	0854	...	0924	0924	|	|	...	|	|	0954	0954	...	1024
Den Haag Centraal **460** a.	0756	|	...	|	0826	0826	0856	|	...	|	0926	0926	...	0956	0956	|	|	...	|	|	1026	1026	...	1056
Amersfoort Centraal **481** a.	...	0655	...	0725	...	...	...	0755	...	0825	...	...	...	...	...	0855	0855	...	0925	0925	...	...	...	...
Utrecht Centraal **481** a.	...	0711	...	0741	...	...	...	0811	...	0841	...	...	...	...	...	0911	0911	...	0941	0942	...	...	...	...
Rotterdam Centraal **481** a.	...	0755	...	0825	...	...	...	0855	...	0925	...	...	...	...	...	0955	0955	...	1025	1025	...	...	...	...

					⚒◧		⊠																
Groningen d.	0818	0833	...	0848	0903	...		1718	1733	...	1748	1803	...	1818	1833	...	1848	1903	...	1918	1933	...	1948
Assen d.	0834	0853	...	0904	0923	...	and at	1734	1753	...	1804	1823	...	1834	1853	...	1904	1923	...	1934	1953	...	2004
Hoogeveen d.	|	0911	...	|	0941	...		|	1811	...	|	1841	...	|	1910	...	|	1941	...	|	2011	...	|
Leeuwarden d.	|	|	0847	|	|	0917	the	|	|	1747	|	|	1817	|	|	1847	|	|	1917	|	|	1947	|
Heerenveen d.	|	|	0904	|	|	0934		|	|	1804	|	|	1834	|	|	1904	|	|	1934	|	|	2004	|
Steenwijk d.	|	|	0917	|	|	0947	same	|	|	1817	|	|	1847	|	|	1917	|	|	1947	|	|	2017	|
Meppel d.	|	0922	0926	|	0952	0956	minutes	|	1822	1826	|	1852	1856	|	1922	1926	|	1952	1956	|	2022	2026	|
Zwolle a.	0915	0938	0942	0945	1008	1012	past	1815	1838	1842	1845	1908	1912	1915	1938	1942	1945	2008	2012	2015	2038	2042	2045
Zwolle **460 481** d.	0920	...	0950	0947	...	1017		1820	...	1850	1847	...	1917	1920	...	1950	1947	...	2017	2020	...	2050	2047
Amsterdam Zuid **460** a.	|	...	|	1047	...	1117	each	|	...	|	1947	...	2017	|	...	|	2047	...	2117	|	...	|	2147
Schiphol + **460** a.	|	...	|	1054	...	1124		|	...	|	1954	...	2024	|	...	|	2054	...	2124	|	...	|	2154
Den Haag Centraal **460** a.	|	...	|	1126	...	1156	hour	|	...	|	2026	...	2056	|	...	|	2126	...	2156	|	...	|	2226
Amersfoort Centraal **481** a.	0955	...	1025	...	...	...	until	1855	...	1925	...	...	...	1955	...	2025	...	...	...	2055	...	2125	...
Utrecht Centraal **481** a.	1011	...	1041	...	...	...		1911	...	1941	...	...	...	2011	...	2041	...	...	...	2111	...	2141	...
Rotterdam Centraal **481** a.	1055	...	1125	...	...	...		1955	...	2025	...	...	...	2055	...	2125	...	...	...	2155	...	2225	...

																					⑤	⑥	
Groningen d.	2003	...	2018	2033	...	2048	2103	...	2118	2133	...	2148	...	2203	...	2218	2233	...	...	2248	...	2326	2326	2330
Assen d.	2023	...	2034	2053	...	2104	2123	...	2134	2153	...	2204	...	2223	...	2234	2253	...	...	2304	...	2348	2348	2353
Hoogeveen d.	2041	...	|	2111	...	|	2141	...	|	2211	...	|	...	2241	...	|	2311	...	...	|	...	0007	0007	0011
Leeuwarden d.	|	2017	|	|	2047	|	|	2117	|	|	2147	|	...	|	2217	|	|	...	2236	|	2324	|	|	|
Heerenveen d.	|	2034	|	|	2104	|	|	2134	|	|	2204	|	...	|	2234	|	|	...	2259	|	2346	|	|	|
Steenwijk d.	|	2047	|	|	2117	|	|	2147	|	|	2217	|	...	|	2247	|	|	...	2316	|	0003	|	|	|
Meppel d.	2052	2056	|	2122	2126	|	2152	2156	|	2222	2226	|	...	2252	2256	|	2322	...	2326	|	0012	0019	0019	0022
Zwolle a.	2108	2112	2115	2138	2142	2145	2208	2212	2215	2238	2242	2245	...	2308	2312	2315	2338	...	2342	2345	0028	0035	0035	0038
Zwolle **460 481** d.	...	2117	2120	...	2150	2147	...	2217	2220	...	2250	2247	...	...	2317	2320	...	...	2350	2347	...	0037	0037	...
Amsterdam Zuid **460** a.	...	2217	|	...	|	2247	...	2317	|	...	|	2347	...	...	0017	|	...	...	|	0047	...	0142‡	0155‡	...
Schiphol + **460** a.	...	2224	|	...	|	2254	...	2324	|	...	|	2354	...	...	0024	|	...	...	|	0054	...	...	...	...
Den Haag Centraal **460** a.	...	2256	|	...	|	2326	...	2356	|	...	|	0026	...	...	0056	|	...	...	|	...	...	...	...	...
Amersfoort Centraal **481** a.	...	...	2155	...	2225	...	...	...	2255	...	2325	...	...	...	...	2355	...	...	0025	...	...	...	...	...
Utrecht Centraal **481** a.	...	...	2211	...	2241	...	...	...	2311	...	2341	...	...	...	...	0011	...	...	0041	...	...	...	...	...
Rotterdam Centraal **481** a.	...	...	2255	...	2325	...	...	...	2355	...	0025	...	...	...	...	0055	...	...	...	...	...	...	...	...

J – ①②③④⑦.
L – From Lelystadt Centrum (d. 0541).
M – From Lelystadt Centrum on Ⓐ (d. 0611).
N – From Lelystadt Centrum (d. 0741).

a – Ⓐ only.
c – Mornings of ⑥⑦ (also Apr. 28, May 27, June 7; not Dec. 26, Jan. 1).

⊠ – Groningen d. 0930 (not 0933). On ⚒ Groningen d. 1330 (not 1333). On ②⑤ Groningen d. 1631 (not 1633).
◐ – The 1522, 1622, 1722, 1822 and 1922 from Zwolle run daily. The 1822 from Zwolle arrives Groningen 1931.
◧ – The 1603 and 1703 from Groningen run daily.
‡ – Amsterdam **Centraal**.

OLDENZAAL - HENGELO - ZUTPHEN — 488

Operated by **Blauwnet** (NS tickets valid) 2nd class only

km		Ⓐ	†	Ⓐ	⚒												Ⓑ		⚒		†	⚒	†		D	
0	**Oldenzaal**...★ d.	0602	...	0632	0702	0732	and at	1402	1432	1502	1532	and at	2002	2032	2102	2132	2132	2202	2232	2232	2302	2332	2332	0002	0032
11	**Hengelo** .....★ a.	0612	...	0642	0712	0742	the same	1412	1442	1512	1542	the same	2012	2042	2112	2142	2142	2212	2242	2242	2312	2342	2342	0012	0042
11	**Hengelo** .... d.	0616	...	0646	0716	0746	minutes	1416	1446	1516	1546	minutes	2016	2046	2116	2146	...	2216	...	2246	2316	2346	...	0016	0046
26	Goor .... d.	0630	0700	0700	0730	0800	past each	1430	1500	1530	1600	past each	2030	2100	2130	2200	...	2230	...	2300	2330	2400	...	0030	0100
39	Lochem............ d.	0639	0709	0709	0739	0809	hour until	1439	1509	1539	1609	hour until	2039	2109	2139	2209	...	2239	...	2309	2339	...	...	0039	...
56	**Zutphen** .... a.	0653	0721	0723	0753	0823		1453	1523	1553	1623		2053	2122	2153	2221	...	2253	...	2321	2353	...	...	0050	...

	Ⓐ	Ⓐ	Ⓐ	⚒	Ⓐ		⚒		⚒			⚒									Ⓐ				D
Zutphen ....d.	...	...	0609	...	0636	...	0706j	0736t	0806	0836t	and at	1306	1336t	1406	1436t	1506	1536	and at	2006	2036	2106	2136	2236t	2336t	0009
Lochem ....d.	...	...	0621	...	0651	...	0721	0751	0821	0851	the same	1321	1351	1421	1451	1521	1551	the same	2021	2051	2121	2151	2251	2350	0021
Goor...................d.	0530	0600	0630	0630	0700	0700	0730	0800	0830	0900	minutes	1330	1400	1430	1500	1530	1600	minutes	2030	2100	2130	2200	2300	0000	0029
Hengelo ....a.	0544	0614	0644	0644	0714	0714	0744	0814	0844	0914	past each	1344	1414	1444	1514	1544	1614	past each	2044	2114	2144	2214	2314	0014	...
Hengelo ...... ★ d.	0548	0618	0648	0648	0718	0718	0748	0818	0848	0918	hour until	1348	1418	1448	1518	1548	1618	hour until	2048	2118	2148	2218	2318	0018	...
Oldenzaal ... ★ a.	0558	0628	0658	0658	0728	0728	0758	0828	0858	0928		1358	1428	1458	1528	1558	1628		2058	2128	2158	2228	2328	0028	...

D – Mornings of ②–⑦.

j – 0709 on ⑥.
t – 3 minutes later on †.

★ – See Table **811** for other journeys Bad Bentheim - Oldenzaal - Hengelo and v.v.

ZWOLLE - ENSCHEDE — 492

Operated by **Blauwnet** (NS tickets valid)

km		Ⓐ	Ⓐ	⚒	⚒						
0	**Zwolle**.............d.	0551	0621	0651	0721	0751	0822	and at	2251	2321	2351
18	Raalte................d.	0608	0636	0708	0736	0808	0836	the same	2308	2336	0008
32	Nijverdal ....d.	0618	0647	0718	0747	0818	0847	minutes	2318	2347	0018
44	Almelo .... 480 d.	0630	0700	0730	0800	0830	0900	past each	2330	0000	0030
59	Hengelo...... **480** d.	0647	0717	0747	0817	0847	0917	hour until	2348	0018	0044z
67	**Enschede** . **480** a.	0656	0726	0756	0826	0856	0926		2357	0027	0053z

	Ⓐ	Ⓐ	Ⓐ	⚒	⚒					
Enschede 480 d.	0506	0534	0604	0634	0704	0734	0804	and at	2304	2334
Hengelo ... **480** d.	0517	0547	0617	0647	0717	0747	0817	the same	2317	2346
Almelo ...... **480** d.	0530	0600	0630	0700	0730	0800	0830	minutes	2330	0000
Nijverdal ....d.	0543	0616	0643	0716	0743	0816	0843	past each	2343	0016
Raalte...............d.	0554	0624	0654	0724	0754	0824	0854	hour until	2354	0024
Zwolle...............a.	0609	0638	0709	0739	0809	0838	0909		0009	0039

z – 4 minutes later on the mornings of ③⑤⑥⑦ (also Apr. 28, June 7; not Dec. 26, Jan. 2).

☛ Additional trains run on Ⓐ.

ZWOLLE - EMMEN — 493

Operated by **Blauwnet** (NS tickets valid)

km		Ⓐ	Ⓐ	Ⓐ	⑥	Ⓐ																	⚒	⚒	D
0	**Zwolle**............ d.	0553	0623	0653	0653	0723	0753	0823	0853	0923	and at	1523	1553	1623	1653	1723	1753	1823	1853	and at	2223	2253	2323	2355	0023
23	Ommen............ d.	0607	0637	0707	0707	0737	0807	0837	0907	0937	the same	1537	1607	1637	1707	1737	1807	1837	1908	the same	2237	2308	2337	0009	0037
34	Mariënberg........ d.	0614	0644	0714	0714	0744	0814	0844	0914	0944	minutes	1544	1614	1644	1714	1743	1814	1844	1915	minutes	2244	2315	2344	0016	0044
55	Coevorden .... d.	0630	0700	0730	0735	0800	0835	0900	0935	1000	past each	1600	1635	1700j	1735	1800j	1835	1900	1935	past each	2300	2336	2400	0036	0100
75	**Emmen** .... a.	0650	0720	0750	0750	0815	0850	0915	0953	1015	hour until	1615	1650	1715j	1750	1815j	1850	1915	1950	hour until	2315	2351	0015	0054	0119

	Ⓐ	Ⓐ	Ⓐ		Ⓐ	⑥																	⚒		⚒	D
Emmen ....d.	0512	0542	0610	0641	0711	0715	0741	0815	0841	and at	1615	1641	1711f	1741	1811f	1841	1915	1941	2015	2041	2115	2141	2215	2241	2315	0019
Coevorden........ d.	0530	0600	0630	0700	0730	0731	0800	0832	0900	the same	1632	1700	1730	1800	1830	1900	1931	2000	2031	2100	2131	2200	2231	2300	2333	0036
Mariënberg .... d.	0546	0616	0646	0716	0746	0746	0816	0846	0916	minutes	1646	1716	1746	1816	1846	1916	1946	2016	2046	2116	2146	2216	2246	2316	2348	0052
Ommen ....d.	0553	0623	0653	0723	0753	0753	0823	0853	0923	past each	1653	1723	1753	1823	1853	1923	1953	2023	2053	2123	2153	2223	2253	2323	2355	0059
Zwolle...............a.	0608	0638	0708	0738	0808	0808	0838	0908	0938	hour until	1708	1738	1808	1838	1908	1938	2008	2038	2108	2138	2208	2238	2308	2338	0011	0114

D – Mornings of ②–⑦ (not Apr. 11, May 30).

f – 4 minutes later on †.

j – On Ⓐ departs Coevorden 5 minutes later, arrives Emmen 8 minutes later.

LEEUWARDEN - GRONINGEN — 494

Operated by **Arriva** (NS tickets valid)

km		Ⓐ	⚒	Ⓐ		⚒	Ⓐ			⚒	⚒				⚒	⚒										
0	**Leeuwarden** d.	0550	0620	0647	0650	0720	0747	0750	0817	0820	0847	0850	and at the same	1917	1920	1947	1950	2017	2050	2117	2150	2217	2250	2317	2356	0055
25	Buitenpost.... d.	0614	0644	|	0714	0744	|	0814	0833	0844	|	0914	minutes past	1933	1944	|	2014	2033	2114	2133	2214	2233	2314	2333	0018	0117
54	**Groningen**... a.	0636	0706	0721	0736	0806	0821	0836	0851	0906	0921	0936	each hour until	1951	2006	2021	2036	2051	2136	2151	2236	2251	2336	2351	0040	0139

	Ⓐ	⚒	Ⓐ		Ⓐ	⚒	Ⓐ		⚒	⚒				⚒	⚒											
Groningen ....d.	0554	0624	0639	0654	0709	0724	0739	0754	0809	0824	0839	0854	and at the same	1909	1924	1939	1954	2039	2054	2139	2154	2239	2254	2339	2354	0054
Buitenpost .....d.	0616	0646	0656	0716	|	0746	0756	0816	|	0846	0856	0916	minutes past	|	1946	1956	2016	2056	2116	2156	2216	2256	2316	2356	0016	0115
Leeuwarden..a.	0640	0710	0714	0740	0744	0810	0814	0840	0844	0910	0914	0940	each hour until	1944	2010	2014	2040	2113	2140	2214	2240	2314	2340	0019	0040	0139

GRONINGEN - BAD NIEUWESCHANS - LEER — 495

Operated by **Arriva** (NS tickets valid); 2nd class only

km		Ⓐ	⚒	†		⚒	†	⚒	†	⚒	†	⚒											
0	**Groningen** .... **498** d.	0514	0617	0653	and at	1717	1753	1817	1853	1917	1953	1953	2053	2153	2253	2353	0023	...	...	...	...	...	...
15	Hoogezand-Sappemeer .. **498** d.	0530	0633	0709	the same	1733	1809	1833	1909	1933	2009	2010	2109	2209	2309	0009	0039	...	...	...	...	...	...
34	Winschoten..........................d.	0547	0650	0731	minutes	1750	1831	1850	1931	1950	2031	2037	2131	2231	2331	0027	0056	...	...	...	...	...	...
46	**Bad Nieuweschans** 🏛..........d.	0559	0701	0741	past each	1801	1841	1901	1941	2001	2041	2047	2141	2241	2341	...	0106	...	...	...	...	...	...
56	Weener 🏛..........................a.	0607	0710	0750	hour until	1810	1850	1910	1950	2010	2050	2056	2150	2250	...	...	...	...	...	...	...	...	...

	Ⓐ	Ⓐ	Ⓐ	⚒	†	⚒	†	⚒		†	⚒	†	⚒	†	⚒								
Weener 🏛...............................d.	...	...	0618	...	...	0718	0810	0818	and at	1810	1818	1910	1918	2010	2017	2110	2310	...	...	...	...	...	...
Bad Nieuweschans 🏛..........d.	...	...	0628	...	...	0728	0820	0828	the same	1820	1828	1920	1928	2020	2027	2120	2320	0005	0111	...	...	...	...
Winschoten..............................d.	0537	0608	0640	0710	0740	0740	0834	0840	minutes	1834	1840	1934	1940	2034	2040	2134	2334	0016	0120	...	...	...	...
Hoogezand-Sappemeer .. **498** d.	0554	0624	0656	0726	0756	0756	0850	0856	past each	1850	1856	1950	1956	2050	2056	2150	2351	0033	0137	...	...	...	...
Groningen........................ **498** a.	0611	0641	0713	0743	0813	0813	0908	0913	hour until	1908	1913	2008	2013	2108	2113	2208	0008	0050	0154	...	...	...	...

	①–⑥ b 🚌	⑦ b 🚌	①–⑥ b 🚌		⑦ b 🚌	①–⑥ b 🚌	🚌	🚌	🚌				①–⑥ d 🚌	🚌		🚌
Groningen.....d.	...	...	...	and at the same	...	...	...	...	...	...	...	A	0630	0830	and every	2030
Weener 🏛.........d.	0612	0800	0812	minutes past	2000	2012	2100	2200	2300	...	...	L S	|	|	**two** hours	|
Leer ....a.	0630	0820	0830	each hour until	2020	2030	2120	2220	2320	...	...	O	0725	0925	until	2125

	①–⑤ b 🚌	①–⑥ b 🚌	⑦ b 🚌	①–⑥ b 🚌		⑦ b 🚌	①–⑥ b 🚌	🚌	🚌	🚌			①–⑥ d 🚌	🚌		🚌
Leer ....d.	0542	0642	0730	0742	and at the same	1930	1942	2030	2130	2230	...	A L	0730	0930	and every	2130
Weener 🏛.........a.	0602	0702	0750	0802	minutes past	1942	2002	2050	2154	2250	...	S	|	|	**two** hours	|
Groningen.....a.	...	...	...	...	each hour until	...	...	...	...	...	...	O	0825	1025	until	2225

b – Please check timings on and around Dutch and German holidays.
d – Not Apr. 10, May 29.

☛ Dutch public holiday dates apply for rail services (see page 242). Additional trains run Groningen - Winschoten and v.v. on ⚒.

LEEUWARDEN - STAVOREN — 496

Operated by **Arriva** (NS tickets valid); 2nd class only

km		Ⓐ	Ⓐ	⚒	Ⓐ	⚒					Ⓐ		Ⓐ		Ⓐ							⑤⑥			
0	**Leeuwarden**.....d.	0522	0552	0622	0652	0722	0822	and	1422	1522	1552	1622	1652	1722	1752	1822	1922	2022	2122	2222	2322	2323	...	...	...
22	Sneek...............a.	0542	0612	0642	0712	0742	0842	hourly	1442	1542	1612	1642	1712	1742	1812	1842	1942	2042	2142	2242	2342	2342	...	...	...
22	Sneek...............d.	0546	0616	0646	0716	0746	0846	until	1446	1546	1616	1646	1716	1746	1816	1846	1946	2046	2146	2246	...	2346	...	...	...
51	**Stavoren**..........a.	0613	0643	0713	0743	0813	0913		1513	1613	1643	1713	1743	1813	1843	1913	2013	2113	2213	2313	...	0013	...	...	...

	⑥⑦		Ⓐ	⚒	⚒	Ⓐ	⚒				Ⓐ		Ⓐ		Ⓐ										
Stavoren...........d.	0018	...	0618	0648	0718	0748	0818	0918	and	1618	1648	1718	1748	1818	1848	1918	2018	2118	2218	2318	...	...	...	...	...
Sneek.................a.	0044	...	0644	0714	0744	0814	0844	0944	hourly	1644	1714	1744	1814	1844	1914	1944	2044	2144	2244	2345	...	...	...	...	...
Sneek.................d.	0046	...	0648	0718	0748	0818	0848	0948	until	1648	1718	1748	1818	1848	1918	1948	2048	2148	2248	2348	...	...	...	...	...
Leeuwarden......a.	0108	...	0708	0738	0808	0838	0908	1008		1708	1738	1808	1838	1908	1938	2008	2108	2208	2308	0008	...	...	...	...	...

☛ Additional trains run Leeuwarden - Sneek and v.v. on ⚒.

497 SCHIEDAM - HOEK VAN HOLLAND

Services are operated by *Rotterdamse Elektrische Tram N.V.* (RET). Local RET fares apply.

Metro line **B**: (Nesselande -) Schiedam Centrum - Hoek van Holland. Journey time: 24 minutes. All services call at Vlaardingen Centrum and Maassluis Centrum.

Departures from Schiedam Centrum:

On Ⓐ at 0018, 0518, 0548, 0603, 0619, 0641, 0648, 0718, 0736, 0756, 0816 and every 20 minutes until 1856; 1917, 1948, 2018 and every 30 minutes until 2348.

On ⑥ at 0018, 0619, 0648, 0718 and every 30 minutes until 1118; 1133, 1156, 1216, 1236 and every 20 minutes until 1816; 1847, 1918, 1948 and every 30 minutes until 2348.

On ⑦ at 0018, 0748, 0818 and every 30 minutes until 2348.

Departures from Hoek van Holland Haven:

On Ⓐ at 0018, 0048, 0547, 0617, 0631, 0651, 0711 and every 20 minutes until 1851; 1918, 1929, 1948, 2018 and every 30 minutes until 2348.

On ⑥ at 0018, 0048, 0648, 0718 and every 30 minutes until 1048; 1111, 1131, 1151 and every 20 minutes until 1851; 1918, 1948 and every 30 minutes until 2348.

On ⑦ at 0018, 0048, 0747, 0817 and every 30 minutes until 1847; 1918, 1948 and every 30 minutes until 2348.

498 OTHER BRANCH LINES

ALMELO – MARIËNBERG Operated by **Blauwnet** (NS tickets valid)

19 km. Journey time: 17 – 19 minutes.

From Almelo:

0618 Ⓐ, 0648 Ⓐ, 0718 Ⓐ, 0748 ⚒, 0818 Ⓐ, 0848, 0948, 1048, 1148, 1248, 1318 ⚒, 1348, 1418 ⚒, 1448, 1518 ⚒, 1548, 1618 ⚒, 1648, 1718 ⚒, 1748, 1818 ⚒, 1848, 1918, 1949, 2048, 2148, 2248 and 2351.

From Mariënberg:

0555 Ⓐ, 0625 Ⓐ, 0655 Ⓐ, 0725 ⚒, 0755 Ⓐ, 0825, 0855 Ⓐ, 0925, 1025, 1125, 1225, 1325, 1355 ⚒, 1425, 1455 ⚒, 1525, 1555 ⚒, 1625, 1655 ⚒, 1725, 1755 ⚒, 1825, 1855, 1925, 2025, 2125, 2225 and 2325.

AMERSFOORT – EDE-WAGENINGEN Operated by **Connexxion** (NS tickets valid)

34 km. Journey time: 35 – 38 minutes.

From Amersfoort Centraal:

0509 Ⓐ, 0535 ⚒, 0609 ⚒, 0639 ⚒, 0709, 0739, 0809, 0839 and every 30 minutes until 2339.

All trains call at Barneveld Centrum (17 minutes from Amersfoort)

From Ede-Wageningen:

0553 Ⓐ, 0623 ⚒, 0653 ⚒, 0723 ⚒, 0753, 0823, 0853 and every 30 minutes until 0023.

All trains call at Barneveld Centrum (20 minutes from Ede-Wageningen)

APELDOORN – ZUTPHEN Operated by **Arriva** (NS tickets valid)

18 km. Journey time: 13 – 20 minutes.

From Apeldoorn:

0636 Ⓐ, 0705 Ⓐ, 0735 Ⓐ, 0805 ⚒, 0806 †, 0823 Ⓒ, 0835 Ⓐ, 0905 Ⓐ, 0906 Ⓒ, 0923 Ⓒ, 0935 Ⓐ and at 05 Ⓐ, 06 Ⓒ, 23 Ⓒ and 35 Ⓐ minutes past each hour until 1905 Ⓐ, 1906 Ⓒ, 1923 Ⓒ, 1935 Ⓐ; then 2004, 2024, 2101, 2123, 2201, 2223, 2301, 2323, 2400.

From Zutphen:

0612 Ⓐ, 0636 Ⓐ, 0706 Ⓐ, 0736 Ⓐ, 0737 Ⓒ, 0754 Ⓒ, 0806 Ⓐ, 0836 Ⓐ, 0837 Ⓒ, 0854 Ⓒ and at 06 Ⓐ, 36 Ⓐ, 37 Ⓒ and 54 Ⓒ minutes past each hour until 1806 Ⓐ, 1836 Ⓐ, 1837 Ⓒ, 1854 Ⓒ; then 1906 Ⓐ, 1936 Ⓐ, 1937 Ⓒ, 2007, 2037, 2104, 2137, 2205, 2237, 2304 and 2337.

GRONINGEN – DELFZIJL Operated by **Arriva** (NS tickets valid)

38 km. Journey time: 37 – 38 minutes. 2nd class only.

From Groningen:

0518 Ⓐ, 0548 ⚒, 0618, 0648 ⚒, 0718, 0748 ⚒ and at 18 and 48 ⚒ minutes past each hour until 2018, 2048 ⚒; then 2118, 2218, 2318 and 0031.

From Delfzijl:

0600 Ⓐ, 0630 ⚒, 0700, 0730 ⚒, 0800, 0830 ⚒ and at 00 and 30 ⚒ minutes past each hour until 2100, 2130 ⚒; then 2200, 2300, 0001 and 0114.

GRONINGEN – EEMSHAVEN ⊡ Operated by **Arriva** (NS tickets valid)

36 km. Journey time: 51 – 53 minutes. 2nd class only.

From Groningen:

0752 ⑥, 0922 ⚒, 0952 ⚒, 1052 ⚒, 1122 ⚒, 1252 ⚒, 1322 ⚒ 1422 †, 1652 ⑥.

From Eemshaven:

0848 ⑥, 1018 ⚒, 1048 ⚒, 1148 ⚒, 1218 ⚒, 1348 ⚒, 1418 ⚒, 1518 †, 1748 ⑥.

GRONINGEN – VEENDAM 🚂 Operated by **Arriva** (NS tickets valid)

29 km. Journey time: 28 minutes. 2nd class only.

From Groningen:

0459 Ⓐ, 0529 Ⓐ, 0559 ⚒, 0629 ⚒, 0659 ⚒, 0723 †, 0729 ⚒, 0759 ⚒, 0823 †, 0829 ⚒ and at 59 ⚒, 23 † and 29 ⚒ minutes past each hour until 1859 ⚒, 1923 †, 1929 ⚒; then 2023, 2123, 2223, 2323 and 0046.

All trains call at Hoogezand-Sappemeer (16 minutes from Groningen)

From Veendam:

0532 Ⓐ, 0602 Ⓐ, 0632 ⚒, 0702 ⚒, 0732 ⚒, 0802 ⚒, 0807 †, 0832 ⚒, 0902 ⚒, 0907 †, 0932 ⚒ and at 02 ⚒, 07 † and 32 ⚒ minutes past each hour until 1902 ⚒, 1907 †, 1932 ⚒; then 2002 ⚒, 2007 †, 2107, 2207, 2307, 2400 and 0119.

All trains call at Hoogezand-Sappemeer (12 minutes from Veendam)

LEEUWARDEN – HARLINGEN Haven ★ Operated by **Arriva** (NS tickets valid)

26 km. Journey time: 25 – 30 minutes. 2nd class only.

From Leeuwarden:

0540 Ⓐ, 0549 Ⓐ, 0619 Ⓐ, 0640 ⑥, 0649 ⚒, 0719, 0749, 0819, 0849, 0919, 0949 and every 30 minutes until 2019; then 2119, 2219 and 2319.

From Harlingen Haven:

0616 Ⓐ, 0646 Ⓐ, 0716 ⚒, 0746 ⚒, 0816, 0846 and every 30 minutes until 2116; then 2152, 2252 and 2352.

ZWOLLE – KAMPEN Operated by **Blauwnet** (NS tickets valid)

13 km. Journey time: 11 minutes.

From Zwolle:

0547 Ⓐ, 0617 Ⓐ, 0647 ⚒, 0717, 0747 and every 30 minutes until 0017.

From Kampen:

0602 Ⓐ, 0632 Ⓐ, 0702 ⚒, 0732, 0802, 0832 and every 30 minutes until 0032.

⊡ – **Timings valid until March 18**. Additional trains run Groningen - Roodeschool and v.v. Eemshaven is the station for ⛴ to / from Borkum. See www.ag-ems.de for latest sailing times.

★ – For ⛴ to / from Terschelling and Vlieland. All trains also call at Harlingen (station for the town centre), 3 minutes from Harlingen Haven.

🚂 – Station for *Museumspoorlijn S.T.A.R.* Steam trains operate to / from Stadskanaal on ⑦ May - September. www.stadskanaalrail.nl

499 OTHER 🚌 and ⛴ LINES

Subject to confirmation

ALKMAAR – LEEUWARDEN 🚌 *Arriva Qliner* route **350**

Journey time: 1 hr 41 m – 2 hrs 28 m

From Alkmaar rail station:

On Ⓐ at 0528, 0623, 0723, 0826, 0928, 1028, 1128, 1228, 1328, 1426, 1524, 1619, 1719, 1827, 1930, 2030 and 2130.

On ⑥ at 0631, 0731, 0830, 0930, 1030, 1128, and hourly until 1728; then 1829, 1929, 2029 and 2129.

On † at 0831, 0931, 1031, 1131, 1229, 1329, 1429 and hourly until 2229.

From Leeuwarden bus station:

On Ⓐ at 0611, 0711, 0813, 0915 and hourly until 1515; then 1614, 1714, 1818, 1919, 2019, 2119, and 2219.

On ⑥ at 0717, 0817, 0915, 1015 and hourly until 1715; then 1818, 1919, 2019, 2119 and 2219.

On † at 0818, 0918, 1018, 1118, 1215, 1315, 1415, 1515, 1615, 1715, 1818, 1919, 2019, 2119, and 2219.

DEN HELDER – TEXEL ⛴ *TESO*: ✆ +31 (0) 222 36 96 00

🚌 route **33**: Den Helder rail station (departs 18 minutes before ships sail) to Havenhoofd.

From Den Helder Havenhoofd: 0630 ⚒, 0730 ⚒, 0830 and hourly until 2130.

Journey time: 20 minutes

From Texel ('t Horntje ferryport): 0600 ⚒, 0700 ⚒, 0800 and hourly until 2100.

🚌 route **33**: Den Helder Havenhoofd to rail station (journey: 7 minutes).

ENKHUIZEN – STAVOREN ⛴ *Rederij V & O* ▲: ✆ +31 (0) 228 32 66 67

From Enkuizen Spoorhaven: 0845 **A**, 1245 **A**, 1645**A**.

Journey time: ± 90 minutes

From Stavoren: 1025 **A**, 1425 **A**, 1825 **A**.

VLISSINGEN – BRESKENS ⛴ *Westerschelde Ferry* ▲ Journey time: 23 minutes

0548 Ⓐ, 0648 Ⓐ, 0748, 0848 and hourly until 2048, 2148 Ⓐ.

Additional sailings operate June - August.

BRESKENS ferryport **– BRUGGE** rail station 🚌 *Connexxion* **42** Journey time: 84 minutes

0614 Ⓐ, 0714 Ⓐ, 0715 ⑥, 0815, 0915, 1015 and hourly until 2215.

BRUGGE rail station **– BRESKENS** ferryport 🚌 *Connexxion* **42** Journey time: 82 minutes

0648 ⚒, 0748 ⚒, 0848, 0948 and hourly until 1948; then 2048 ⚒.

BRESKENS – VLISSINGEN ⛴ *Westerschelde Ferry* ▲ Journey time: 23 minutes

0618 Ⓐ, 0718 Ⓐ, 0818, 0918 and hourly until 2118, 2218 Ⓐ.

Additional sailings operate June - August.

A – ②–⑦ Apr. 29 - June 25 (also Apr. 22, 23); daily June 27 - Sept. 3; ②–⑦ Sept. 5 – 30.

▲ – Conveys foot passengers, cycles and mopeds only.

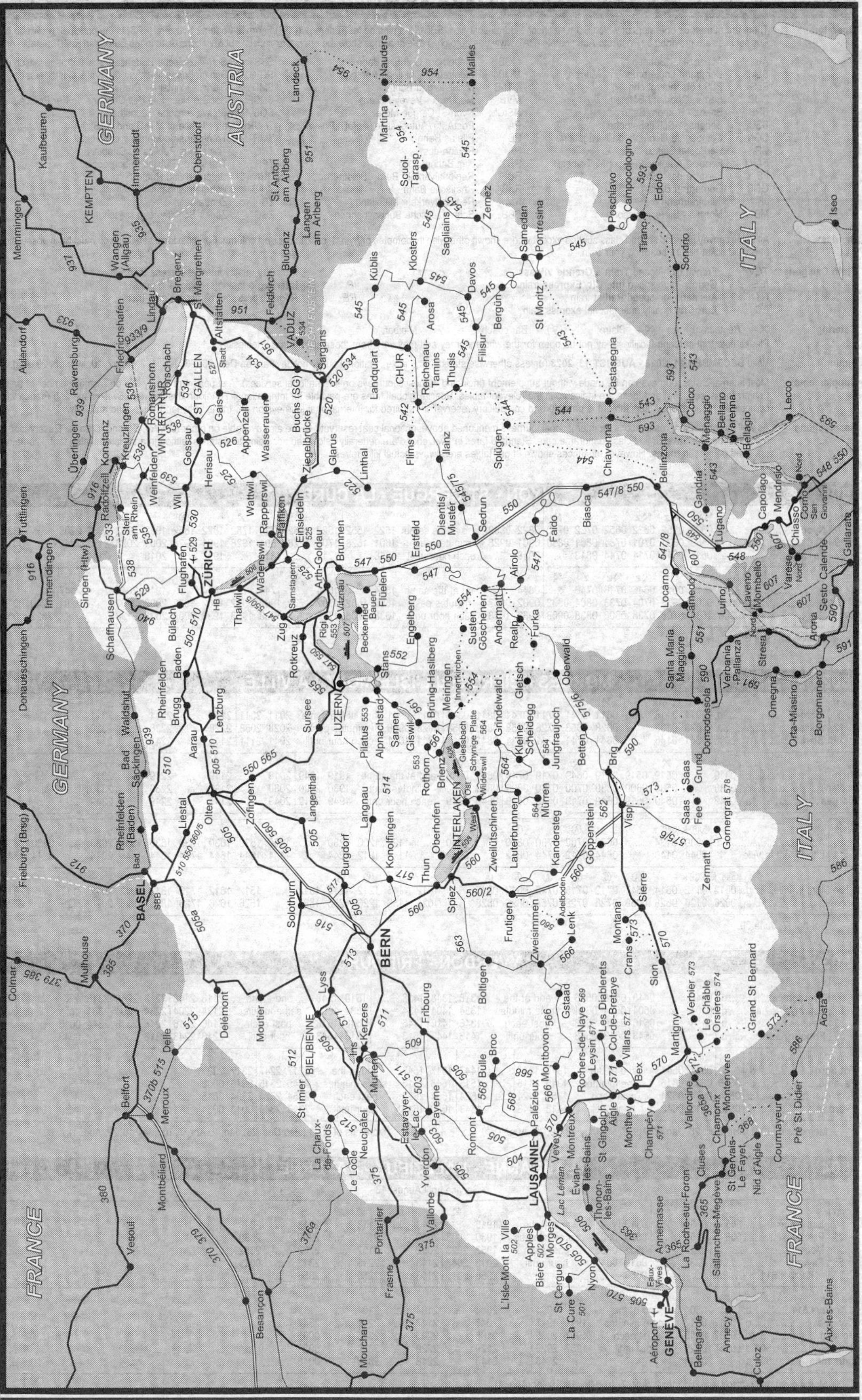
FRANCE
GERMANY
AUSTRIA
ITALY
LIECHTENSTEIN
BASEL
ZÜRICH
BERN
LUZERN
LAUSANNE
GENÈVE
ST GALLEN
CHUR
INTERLAKEN
BIEL/BIENNE
WINTERTHUR
Schaffhausen
Singen (Htw)
Konstanz
Kreuzlingen
Romanshorn
Rorschach
St Margrethen
Bregenz
Lindau
Friedrichshafen
Ravensburg
Kempten
Memmingen
Kaufbeuren
Immenstadt
Oberstdorf
Wangen (Allgäu)
Landeck
St Anton am Arlberg
Langen am Arlberg
Bludenz
Feldkirch
Buchs (SG)
Sargans
VADUZ
Landquart
Klosters
Davos
Filisur
Bergün
Samedan
Pontresina
St Moritz
Scuol-Tarasp
Zernez
Sagliains
Martina
Nauders
Malles
Poschiavo
Campocologno
Tirano
Edolo
Sondrio
Iseo
Lecco
Colico
Chiavenna
Castasegna
Splügen
Thusis
Reichenau-Tamins
Ilanz
Flims
Arosa
Disentis/Mustér
Sedrun
Andermatt
Göschenen
Airolo
Faido
Biasca
Bellinzona
Locarno
Lugano
Chiasso
Como
Mendrisio
Capolago
Varese
Gallarate
Sesto Calende
Arona
Stresa
Verbania-Pallanza
Domodossola
Omegna
Borgomanero
Luino
Brig
Visp
Zermatt
Gornergrat
Saas Fee
Sierre
Sion
Martigny
Montana
Crans
Verbier
Le Châble
Orsières
Grand St Bernard
Aosta
Pré St Didier
Courmayeur
Chamonix
St Gervais-Le Fayet
Sallanches-Megève
Cluses
La Roche-sur-Foron
Annemasse
Annecy
Aix-les-Bains
Culoz
Bellegarde
Aéroport
Nyon
St Cergue
La Cure
Morges
Bière
Apples
L'Isle-Mont la Ville
Vallorbe
Frasne
Pontarlier
Mouchard
Besançon
Vesoul
Belfort
Montbéliard
Meroux
Delle
Delémont
Moutier
Mulhouse
Colmar
Freiburg (Brsg)
Rheinfelden (Baden)
Bad Säckingen
Waldshut
Donaueschingen
Tuttlingen
Immendingen
Radolfzell
Überlingen
Aulendorf
Liestal
Olten
Aarau
Brugg
Baden
Lenzburg
Zofingen
Langenthal
Burgdorf
Solothurn
Lyss
Kerzers
Murten
Ins
Neuchâtel
La Chaux-de-Fonds
Le Locle
St Imier
Yverdon
Estavayer-le-Lac
Payerne
Fribourg
Romont
Palézieux
Vevey
Montreux
Bulle
Broc
Montbovon
Gstaad
Zweisimmen
Lenk
Boltigen
Spiez
Thun
Frutigen
Kandersteg
Goppenstein
Lauterbrunnen
Mürren
Grindelwald
Kleine Scheidegg
Jungfraujoch
Wengen
Meiringen
Brienz
Brünig-Hasliberg
Sarnen
Alpnachstad
Pilatus
Engelberg
Stans
Arth-Goldau
Zug
Rigi
Vitznau
Flüelen
Erstfeld
Brunnen
Einsiedeln
Rapperswil
Pfäffikon
Wädenswil
Thalwil
Ziegelbrücke
Glarus
Linthal
Gossau
Wil
Herisau
Appenzell
Wasserauen
Gais
Altstätten
Weinfelden
Bülach
Flughafen
Oberwald
Realp
Furka
Gletsch
Aigle
Bex
Monthey
Champéry
Leysin
Les Diablerets
Villars
St Gingolph
Évian-les-Bains
Thonon-les-Bains
Lac Léman
Vallorcine
Montenvers
Nid d'Aigle
Langnau
Konolfingen
Sursee
Rotkreuz
Oberhofen
Zweilütschinen
Wilderswil
Schynige Platte
Giessbach
Rothorn

SWITZERLAND

Operators: There are numerous operators of which Schweizerische Bundesbahnen (SBB)/Chemins de fer Féderaux (CFF)/Ferrovie Federali Svizzere (FFS) is the principal: www.sbb.ch. Bus services are provided by PostAuto/Autopostale (PA): www.postauto.ch. Table headings show the operators' initials; abbreviations used in the European Rail Timetable are.

AB	Appenzeller Bahnen	MGB	Matterhorn Gotthard Bahn	SBS	Schweizerische Bodensee-Schifffahrtsgesellschaft
BLM	Bergbahn Lauterbrunnen - Mürren	MOB	Montreux - Oberland Bernois	SGV	Schifffahrtsgesellschaft des Vierwaldstättersees
BLS	BLS Lötschbergbahn	MThB	Mittelthurgau Bahn	SMC	Sierre - Montana - Crans
BOB	Berner Oberland Bahnen	MVR	Montreux - Vevey Riviera	SNCF	Société Nationale des Chemins de Fer Francais
BRB	Brienz - Rothorn Bahn	NStCM	Nyon-St Cergue-Morez	SOB	Schweizerische Südostbahn
BSB	Bodensee-Schiffsbetriebe	PA	PostAuto / Autopostale / AutoDaPosta	THURBO	an alliance of MThB and SBB
CGN	Compagnie Générale de Navigation	PB	Pilatus Bahn	TMR	Transports de Martigny et Régions
CP	CarPostal Suisse	RA	RegionAlps	TPC	Transports Publics du Chablais
FART	Ferrovie Autolinee Regionali Ticinesi	RB	Rigi Bahnen	TPF	Transports Publics Fribourgeois
FS	Ferrovie dello Stato	RBS	Regionalverkehr Bern - Solothurn	URh	Untersee und Rhein
GGB	Gornergrat Bahn	RhB	Rhätische Bahn	WAB	Wengernalpbahn
JB	Jungfraubahn	RM	Regionalverkehr Mittelland	ZB	Zentralbahn
MBC	Morges - Bière - Cossonay	SBB	Schweizerische Bundesbahnen	ZSG	Zürich Schifffahrtsgesellschaft

Services: All trains convey first and second class seating except where shown otherwise in footnotes or by a '1' or '2' in the train column. For most local services you must be in possession of a valid ticket before boarding your train.

Train Categories:

TGV	French high-speed **Train à Grande Vitesse**.	*IC*	**InterCity** quality internal express train.
ICE	German high-speed **InterCity Express** train.	*IR*	**InterRegio** fast inter-regional train.
RJ	Austrian high-speed **Railjet** train.	*RE*	**RegioExpress** semi-fast regional train.
EC	**EuroCity** quality international express train.		

Catering: ✕ – Restaurant; ⊗ – Bistro; (🍸) – Bar coach; 🍸 – Minibar.
Please note that catering facilities may not be open for the whole journey and may vary from those shown in our tables.

Timings: Valid **DECEMBER 11, 2022 - AUGUST 13, 2023** (unless otherwise stated in the table). National public holidays are on Dec. 25, 26, Jan. 1, 2, Apr. 7, 10, May 18, 29, Aug. 1

Supplements: Most internal Swiss journeys can be made without supplement (including domestic journeys on international services). A supplement is payable on a small number of trains (mainly tourist services) and these are indicated in the relevant tables. Special 'global' fares are payable for international *TGV* journeys between Switzerland and France with compulsory reservation. A supplement is payable and compulsory reservation required for international journeys on *EC* trains between Switzerland and Italy.

Reservations: As well as compulsory reservations for international journeys mentioned above, optional seat reservations are also available on other *ICE*, *RJ*, *EC* and *IC* trains. Reservation is recommended for travel in first class panorama cars. Standard fares in Switzerland are generally calculated according to distance, although artificially inflated tariff-kilometres are used on certain routes. However, distances shown in our tables are always actual kilometres.

501 NYON - ST CERGUE - LA CURE

Narrow gauge 2nd class only NStCM

km																								
		Ⓐ	⚒z	⚒z	z		⚒							⚒		⚒		Ⓐ		Ⓐ				
0	**Nyon** d.	0522	0552	0622	0652	0722	0752	0822	0852	and at the same	1522	1552	1622	1652	1722	1752	1822	1852	1922	1952	2052	2209	...	2339
19	St Cergue d.	0559	0631	0701	0731	0801	0830	0901	0928	minutes past	1601	1628	1701	1728	1801	1828	1901	1928	2001	2028	2131	2240	...	0010
27	**La Cure** a.	*0614*	0644	0714	0744	0818	...	0918	...	each hour until	1618	...	1718	...	1818	...	1918	...	2018	...	2144	...	...	...

	Ⓐ		Ⓐ	⚒z	⚒z	z	⚒							⚒		⚒		Ⓐ					
La Cure d.	...	...	*0616*	0646	0716	0746	...	0844	...	and at the same	1544	...	1644	...	1744	...	1844	...	1944	2044	...	2147	...	...
St Cergue d.	0533	0604	0633	0704	0733	0804	0832	0902	0932	minutes past	1602	1632	1702	1732	1802	1832	1902	1932	2002	2102	...	2201	2249	0019
Nyon a.	0608	0638	0708	0738	0808	0838	0908	0938	1008	each hour until	1638	1708	1738	1808	1838	1908	1938	2008	2038	2138	...	...	2323	0053

z – Change trains at St Cergue on Ⓐ.

502 MORGES - BIÈRE and L'ISLE MONT LA VILLE

Narrow gauge 2nd class only MBC

km																							
			⑤⑥k		⚒	⚒		⚒		⚒		Ⓐ			Ⓐ								
0	**Morges** d.	0011	0116	...	0611	0641	0711	0741	0811	0841	0911	0941	and at the same	2011	2041	2111	...	2211	...	2311	...	...	...
12	Apples a.	0028	0133	...	0628	0658	0728	0758	0828	0858	0928	0958	minutes past	2028	2058	2128	...	2228	...	2328	...	...	...
19	**Bière** a.	0041	0146	...	0641	0711	0741	0811	0841	0911	0941	1011	each hour until	2041	2111	2141	...	2241	...	2341	...	...	...

	⑤⑥k		⚒	⚒		⚒		⚒		Ⓐ			Ⓐ										
Bière d.	0019	...	0519	0549	0619	0649	0719	0749	0819	0849	and at the same	1919	1949	2019	...	2119	...	2219	...	2319	...	...	...
Apples d.	0030	...	0530	0600	0630	0700	0730	0800	0830	0900	minutes past	1930	2000	2030	...	2130	...	2230	...	2330	...	...	...
Morges a.	0049	...	0549	0619	0649	0719	0749	0819	0849	0919	each hour until	1949	2019	2049	...	2149	...	2249	...	2349	...	...	...

km																										
		⑤⑥k	⑤⑥k			Ⓐ		Ⓐ					Ⓐ													
0	Apples d.	0030	0134	...	0630	0700	0730	0800	...	0930	...	1130	1200	1230	...	1430	1530	1630	1730	1830	1930	2030	...	2230	2330
11	L'Isle Mont la Ville a.	0044	0148	...	0644	0712	0744	0812	...	0944	...	1144	1212	1244	...	1444	1544	1644	1744	1844	1944	2044	...	2244	2344

	⑤⑥k	⑤⑥k		Ⓐ	Ⓒ	Ⓐ	Ⓐ	Ⓒ	Ⓐ			Ⓐ	Ⓒ	Ⓐ										
L'Isle Mont la Ville d.	0012	0112	0614	0645	0712	0715	0745	0812	0815	...	1012	1145	1212	1215	1312	...	1512	1612	1712	1812	1912	2012	2112	...	2312
Apples a.	0026	0126	0628	0658	0726	0728	0758	0826	0828	...	1026	1158	1226	1228	1326	...	1526	1626	1726	1826	1926	2026	2126	...	2326

k – Not Apr. 7, June 30.

503 YVERDON - FRIBOURG

SBB

km																						
		⑥⑦c																		⑥⑦e		
0	**Yverdon** d.	0048	...	0448	0518	0548	and at the	1318	1348	1418	...	1518	1548	and at the	2118	2148	2218	2248	2318	...	...	...
18	Estavayer-le-Lac d.	0104	...	0504	0534	0604	same minutes	1334	1404	1434	...	1534	1604	same minutes	2134	2204	2234	2304	2334	...	...	...
28	Payerne d.	0114	...	0516	0546	0616	past each	1346	1416	1446	...	1546	1616	past each	2146	2216	2246	2316	2344	0016	...	...
50	**Fribourg** a.	...	...	0543	0613	0643	hour until	1413	1443	1513	...	1613	1643	hour until	2213	2243	2313	2348	...	0043	...	...

Fribourg d.	...	0517	0547	and at the	1317	1347	...	1447	1517	1547	and at the	2217	2247	2317	2338	...	...	...	...	...	...	...
Payerne d.	0515	0545	0615	same minutes	1345	1415	...	1515	1545	1615	same minutes	2245	2315	2345	0006	...	...	...	...	...	...	...
Estavayer-le-Lac d.	0524	0554	0624	past each	1354	1424	...	1524	1554	1624	past each	2254	2324	2354	0015	...	...	...	...	...	...	...
Yverdon a.	0543	0613	0643	hour until	1413	1443	...	1543	1613	1643	hour until	2313	2343	0013	0034	...	...	...	...	...	...	...

c – Mornings of ⑥⑦ (also Dec. 26, Jan. 2, Apr. 7, 10, May 18, 19, 29, Aug. 1). **e** – Mornings of ⑥⑦ (also Dec. 26, Jan. 2, Apr. 7, 10, May 18, 29, Aug. 1).

504 LAUSANNE - PALÉZIEUX - PAYERNE

SBB

Service until August 13

km																							
		⑥⑦c			⚒			⚒															
0	**Lausanne** 505 d.	0133	...	0513	...	and at the	1913	...	2013	...	2113	...	2213	...	2313	...	...	...	...	...	...	...	...
21	Palézieux 505 d.	0155	...	0530	0603	same minutes	1930	2003	2030	...	2130	...	2230	...	2330	...	...	...	...	...	...	...	...
38	Moudon d.	0213	...	0552	0623	past each	1952	2023	2052	...	2152	...	2252	...	2352	...	...	...	...	...	...	...	...
58	**Payerne** a.	0232	...	0613	0643	hour until	2013	2043	2113	...	2213	...	2313	...	0013	...	...	...	...	...	...	...	...
	Kerzers **511** a.	...	...	0656	...		2056	...	2156	...	2256	...	2356	...	...	...	...	...	...	...	...	...	...

	⚒			⚒																			
Kerzers **511** d.	...	0504	and at the	...	1904	...	2004	...	2104	...	2204	...	...	...	...	...	...	...	...	...	...	...	...
Payerne d.	0517	0547	same minutes	1917	1947	...	2047	...	2147	...	2247	...	2347	...	...	...	...	...	...	...	...	...	...
Moudon d.	0537	0605	past each	1937	2005	...	2105	...	2205	...	2305	...	0005	...	...	...	...	...	...	...	...	...	...
Palézieux 505 d.	0557	0629	hour until	1957	2029	...	2129	...	2229	...	2329	...	0029	...	...	...	...	...	...	...	...	...	...
Lausanne 505 a.	...	0648		...	2048	...	2148	...	2248	...	2348	...	0048	...	...	...	...	...	...	...	...	...	...

c – Mornings of ⑥⑦ (also Dec. 26, Jan. 2, Apr. 7, 10, May 18, 19, 29, Aug. 1).

SBB GENÈVE - LAUSANNE - BERN / BIEL - ZÜRICH 505

km		RE 18493	IR 2503	IR 2155	IR 2155	IR 2353	IR 2353	IC 703	IC 1507	IR 2159	IC 507	IR 2357	IR 2505	IR 2505	IC 805	IR 2809	IC 705	IC 1509	IR 1805	IC 509	IR 2359	IR 2507	IC 807	RE 18455
		⑥⑦	⑥⑦	②–⑦	①	①	②–⑦					Ⓐ	②–⑦	①										
				e	d	dH	eH	✕	✕		R✕	§			✕	⊙	✕	✕		R✕	H◇	🍸	B✕	
0	Genève Aéroport ✈ 570 d.	0011	...	...	...	◇	◇	...	...	...	...	...	...	...	...	...	...	...	...	...	...	...	...	0511
6	**Genève** 570 d.	0020	...	...	...	...	...	...	...	...	...	...	...	...	...	...	...	...	0447	...	...	...	...	0520
27	Nyon 570 d.	0036	...	...	...	...	...	...	...	...	...	...	...	...	...	...	...	...	0502	...	...	...	...	0536
53	Morges 570 d.	0055	...	...	...	...	...	...	...	...	...	...	...	...	...	...	...	...	0521	...	...	...	...	0555
66	**Lausanne** 570 a.	0108	...	...	...	...	...	...	...	...	...	...	...	...	...	...	...	...	0537	...	...	...	...	0608
66	**Lausanne** d.	...	0130	...	...	...	...	...	...	...	...	...	...	0444	...	...	...	...	▬	0542	...	0544	...	▬
	Yverdon d.	...	|	...	...	...	...	...	...	...	...	...	...	|	...	...	...	...	...	0606	...	|	...	...
	Neuchâtel d.	...	|	...	...	...	...	...	...	...	...	...	...	|	...	...	...	...	...	0626	...	|	...	...
	Biel / Bienne a.	...	|	...	...	...	...	...	...	...	...	...	...	|	...	...	...	...	...	0642	...	|	...	...
	Biel / Bienne d.	...	|	...	...	...	...	...	0516	...	0543	...	...	|	...	...	...	0616	...	0644	...	|	...	...
	Solothurn d.	...	|	...	...	...	...	...	0534	...	0601	...	...	|	...	...	...	0634	...	0701	...	|	...	...
87	Palézieux d.	...	0146	...	...	...	...	...	|	...	|	...	...	0500	...	...	...	|	*IR*	|	...	0600	...	*IR*
106	Romont 568 d.	...	0202	...	...	...	...	...	|	...	|	...	...	0516	...	...	...	|	**2161**	|	...	0616	...	**2811**
132	Fribourg 568 d.	...	0219	...	...	...	...	...	|	...	|	...	0534	0534	...	...	0604	|	|	|	...	0634	...	
163	**Bern** 568 a.	...	...	...	...	...	...	...	|	...	|	...	0556	0556	...	...	0626	|	|	|	...	0656	...	⊙
163	**Bern** d.	...	...	0418h	*0359z*	*0431z*	0438b	0529j	|	...	|	0538	0600	0600	0602	0607	0631	|	0633	|	0638	0700	0702	0707
	Luzern 565 a.	...	...	|	|	|	|	|	|	...	|	|	0701	0701	|	|	|	|	|	|	|	0801	|	|
186	Burgdorf d.	...	...	|	|	0454	0454b	|	|	...	|	0553	...	...	|	0621	|	|	|	|	0653	...	|	0721
210	Langenthal d.	...	...	|	|	0512	0512	|	|	...	|	0612	...	...	|	0641	|	|	|	|	0712	...	|	0741
230	**Olten** a.	...	...	0444	0444	0524	0524	0555	0557	...	0618	0624	...	...	0628	0654	|	0657	0700	0718	0724	...	|	0754
230	**Olten** d.	...	...	0446	0446	0526	0526	0557	0559	0602	0620	0626	...	...	0631	...	|	0659	0702	0720	0730	...	|	...
243	Aarau 510 d.	...	...	0456	0456	0536	0536	|	|	0614	0631	0640	...	...	|	...	|	|	0714	0731	|	...	|	...
253	Lenzburg 510 d.	...	...	0503	0503	0542	0542	|	|	|	|	0647	...	...	|	...	|	|	|	|	|	...	|	...
	Brugg 510 d.	...	...	|	|	|	|	|	|	0630	|	|	...	...	|	...	|	|	0730	|	|	...	|	...
	Baden 510 a.	...	...	|	|	|	|	|	|	0638	|	|	...	...	|	...	|	|	0738	|	|	...	|	...
285	**Zürich** HB 510 a.	...	...	0528	0528	0606	0606	0628	0630	0654	0656	0713	...	...	0702	...	0728	0730	0754	0756	0806	...	0758	...
	Zürich Flughafen ✈ 530/5 a.	...	...	0541	0541	...	...	0651	0642a	...	0712	...	...	...	0714	...	0751	...	...	0812	...	...	0814	...
	St Gallen 530 a.	...	...	...	...	...	...	0752	0732a	...	0802	...	...	...	|	...	0852	...	...	0902	...	...	...	...
	Romanshorn 535 a.	...	...	...	...	...	...	...	...	...	...	...	...	...	0812	...	...	...	...	...	...	...	0912	...

km		IC 1511	IC 707	IR 2163		IR 2509	IC 511	IC 809	RE 18457	IC 1513	IC 709	IR 2165		IR 2511	IC 513	IC 811	RE 18459	IC 1515	IC 711	IR 2167		IR 2513	IC 515	IC 813
		✕	✕			🍸	R✕	A✕		✕	✕			🍸	R✕	B✕		✕	✕			🍸	R✕	A✕
	Genève Aéroport ✈ 570 d.	...	0531	...		0549	0602	...	0611	...	0632	...		0649	0705	...	0711c	...	0732	...		0749	0805	...
	Genève 570 d.	...	0542	...		0559	0612	...	0620	...	0642	...		0659	0715	...	0720	...	0742	...		0759	0815	...
	Nyon 570 d.	...	|	...		0613	0626	...	0636	...	|	...		0713	|	...	0736	...	|	...		0813	|	...
0	Morges 570 d.	...	|	...		0630	0642	...	0655	...	|	...		0730	0742	...	0755	...	|	...		0830	0842	...
	Lausanne 570 a.	...	0617	...		0641	|	...	0708	...	0717	...		0741	|	...	0808	...	0817	...		0841	|	...
0	**Lausanne** d.	0615	0620	...	0625	0644	|	...	▬	0715	0720	...	0725	0744	|	...	▬	0815	0820	...	0825	0844	|	...
39	Yverdon d.	0637	|	...	0658	|	0706	...	...	0737	|	...	0758	|	0806	...	...	0837	|	...	0858	|	0906	...
75	Neuchâtel d.	0658	|	...	▬	|	0726	...	...	0758	|	...	▬	|	0826	...	...	0858	|	...	▬	|	0926	...
105	**Biel / Bienne** a.	0715	|	...	...	|	0743	...	...	0815	|	...	...	|	0843	...	...	0915	|	...	...	|	0943	...
105	**Biel / Bienne** d.	0717	|	...	...	|	0746	...	...	0817	|	...	...	|	0846	...	...	0917	|	...	...	|	0946	...
130	Solothurn d.	0734	|	...	...	|	0801	...	...	0834	|	...	...	|	0901	...	...	0934	|	...	...	|	1001	...
	Palézieux d.	|	|	...	*IR*	0700	|	...	*IR*	|	|	...	*IR*	0800	|	...	*IR*	|	|	...	*IR*	0900	|	...
	Romont 568 d.	|	|	...	**2361**	0716	|	...	**2813**	|	|	...	**2363**	0816	|	...	**2815**	|	|	...	**2365**	0916	|	...
	Fribourg 568 d.	|	0704	...		0734	|	...		|	0804	...		0834	|	...		|	0904	...		0934	|	...
	Bern 568 a.	|	0726	...	H⊡	0756	|	...	⊙	|	0826	...	H◇	0856	|	...	⊙	|	0926	...	H⊡	0956	|	...
	Bern d.	|	0731	0733	0738	0800	|	0802	0807	|	0831	0833	0838	0900	|	0902	0907	|	0931	0933	0938	1000	|	1002
	Luzern 565 a.	|	|	|	|	0901	|	|	|	|	|	|	|	1001	|	|	|	|	|	|	|	1101	|	|
	Burgdorf d.	|	|	|	0753	...	|	|	0821	|	|	|	0853	...	|	|	0921	|	|	|	0953	...	|	|
	Langenthal d.	|	|	|	0812	...	|	|	0841	|	|	|	0912	...	|	|	0941	|	|	|	1012	...	|	|
165	**Olten** a.	0757	|	0800	0824	...	0818	|	0854	0857	|	0900	0924	...	0918	|	0954	0957	|	1000	1024	...	1018	|
165	**Olten** d.	0759	|	0802	0830	...	0820	|	...	0859	|	0902	0930	...	0920	|	...	0959	|	1002	1030	...	1020	|
178	Aarau 510 d.	|	|	0814	|	...	0831	|	...	|	|	0914	|	...	0931	|	...	|	|	1014	|	...	1031	|
	Lenzburg 510 d.	|	|	|	|	...	|	|	...	|	|	|	|	...	|	|	...	|	|	|	|	...	|	|
196	Brugg 510 d.	|	|	0830	|	...	|	|	...	|	|	0930	|	...	|	|	...	|	|	1030	|	...	|	|
205	Baden 510 a.	|	|	0838	|	...	|	|	...	|	|	0938	|	...	|	|	...	|	|	1038	|	...	|	|
227	**Zürich** HB 510 a.	0830	0828	0854	0906	...	0856	0858	...	0930	0928	0954	1006	...	0956	0958	...	1030	1028	1054	1106	...	1056	1058
	Zürich Flughafen ✈ 530/5 a.	0842a	0851	...	...	...	0912	0914	...	...	0951	...	...	...	1012	1014	...	...	1051	...	...	...	1112	1114
	St Gallen 530 a.	0932a	0952	...	...	...	1002	|	...	...	1052	...	...	...	1102	|	...	...	1152	...	...	...	1202	|
	Romanshorn 535 a.	...	...	...	...	...	...	1012	...	...	...	...	...	...	...	1112	...	...	...	...	...	...	...	1212

	RE 18461	IC 1517	IC 713	IR 2169		IR 2515	IC 517	IC 815	RE 18463	IC 1519	IC 715	IR 2171		IR 2517	IC 519	IC 817	RE 18465	IC 1521	IC 717	IR 2173		IR 2519	IC 521	IC 819
		✕	♣✕			🍸	R✕	B✕		✕	✕			🍸	R✕	A✕		✕	✕			🍸	R✕	B✕
Genève Aéroport ✈ 570 d.	0811c	...	0832	...		0849	0905	...	0911c	...	0932	...		0949	1005	...	1011c	...	1032	...		1049	1105	...
Genève 570 d.	0820	...	0842	...		0859	0915	...	0920	...	0942	...		0959	1015	...	1020	...	1042	...		1059	1115	...
Nyon 570 d.	0836	...	|	...		0913	|	...	0936	...	|	...		1013	|	...	1036	...	|	...		1113	|	...
Morges 570 d.	0855	...	|	...		0930	0942	...	0955	...	|	...		1030	1042	...	1056	...	|	...		1130	1142	...
Lausanne 570 a.	0908	...	0917	...		0941	|	...	1008	...	1017	...		1041	|	...	1108	...	1117	...		1141	|	...
Lausanne d.	▬	0915	0920	...	0925	0944	|	...	▬	1015	1020	...	1025	1044	|	...	▬	1115	1120	...	1125	1144	|	...
Yverdon d.	...	0937	|	...	0958	|	1006	...	...	1037	|	...	1058	|	1106	...	...	1137	|	...	1158	|	1206	...
Neuchâtel d.	...	0958	|	...	▬	|	1026	...	...	1058	|	...	▬	|	1126	...	...	1158	|	...	▬	|	1226	...
Biel / Bienne a.	...	1015	|	...	...	|	1043	...	...	1115	|	...	...	|	1143	...	...	1215	|	...	...	|	1243	...
Biel / Bienne d.	...	1017	|	...	...	|	1046	...	...	1117	|	...	...	|	1146	...	...	1217	|	...	...	|	1246	...
Solothurn d.	...	1034	|	...	...	|	1101	...	...	1134	|	...	...	|	1201	...	...	1234	|	...	...	|	1301	...
Palézieux d.	*IR*	|	|	...	*IR*	1000	|	...	*IR*	|	|	...	*IR*	1100	|	...	*IR*	|	|	...	*IR*	1200	|	...
Romont 568 d.	**2817**	|	|	...	**2367**	1016	|	...	**2819**	|	|	...	**2369**	1116	|	...	**2821**	|	|	...	**2371**	1216	|	...
Fribourg 568 d.		|	1004	...		1034	|	...		|	1104	...		1134	|	...		|	1204	...		1234	|	...
Bern 568 a.	⊙	|	1026	...	H◇	1056	|	...	⊙	|	1126	...	H◇	1156	|	...	⊙	|	1226	...	H◇	1256	|	...
Bern d.	1007	|	1031	1033	1038	1100	|	1102	1107	|	1131	1133	1138	1200	|	1202	1207	|	1231	1233	1238	1300	|	1302
Luzern 565 a.	|	|	|	|	|	1201	|	|	|	|	|	|	|	1301	|	|	|	|	|	|	|	1401	|	|
Burgdorf d.	1021	|	|	|	1053	...	|	|	1121	|	|	|	1153	...	|	|	1221	|	|	|	1253	...	|	|
Langenthal d.	1041	|	|	|	1112	...	|	|	1141	|	|	|	1212	...	|	|	1241	|	|	|	1312	...	|	|
Olten a.	1054	1057	|	1100	1124	...	1118	|	1154	1157	|	1200	1224	...	1218	|	1254	1257	|	1300	1324	...	1318	|
Olten d.	...	1059	|	1102	1130	...	1120	|	...	1159	|	1202	1230	...	1220	|	...	1259	|	1302	1330	...	1320	|
Aarau 510 d.	...	|	|	1114	|	...	1131	|	...	|	|	1214	|	...	1231	|	...	|	|	1314	|	...	1331	|
Lenzburg 510 d.	...	|	|	|	|	...	|	|	...	|	|	|	|	...	|	|	...	|	|	|	|	...	|	|
Brugg 510 d.	...	|	|	1130	|	...	|	|	...	|	|	1230	|	...	|	|	...	|	|	1330	|	...	|	|
Baden 510 a.	...	|	|	1138	|	...	|	|	...	|	|	1238	|	...	|	|	...	|	|	1338	|	...	|	|
Zürich HB 510 a.	...	1130	1128	1154	1206	...	1156	1158	...	1230	1228	1254	1306	...	1256	1258	...	1330	1328	1354	1406	...	1356	1358
Zürich Flughafen ✈ 530/5 a.	...	...	1151a	...	...	...	1212	1214	...	...	1251	...	...	...	1312	1314	...	...	1351	...	...	...	1412	1414
St Gallen 530 a.	...	...	1252a	...	...	...	1302	|	...	...	1352	...	...	...	1402	|	...	...	1452	...	...	...	1502	|
Romanshorn 535 a.	...	...	...	...	...	...	...	1312	...	...	...	...	...	...	...	1412	...	...	...	...	...	...	...	1512

A – From Interlaken (Table **560**).
B – From Brig (Table **560**).
H – To Chur (Table **520**).
R – To Rorschach (Table **530**).

a – Ⓐ only.
b – 2 minutes earlier on Ⓒ.

c – Ⓒ only.
d – Not Dec. 26, Jan. 2, Apr. 10, May 8, 29, June 12, 26, Aug. 21, 28, Oct. 2, 9.
e – Also Dec. 26, Jan. 2, Apr. 10, May 8, 29, June 12, 26, Aug. 21, 28, Oct. 2, 9.
h – 0404 on Mar. 25, 26, June 3, 4, June 20 – 23, 26 – 30, Sept. 9, 10, 26 – 29, Oct. 2 – 6, 28, 29.
j – 0513 on Feb. 6, 27, Mar. 27, May 8, June 5, 19 – 23, 26 – 30, July 24, Sept. 4, 11, 25 – 29, Oct. 2 – 6, 30, Dec. 4.
z – Change trains at Zollikofen (departs Zollikofen 11 minutes later).

§ – Runs as *RE* **4509** Olten - Zürich.
♣ – On Ⓒ runs as *IC* **903** and continues to Chur (Table **520**).
⊙ – Operated by BLS.
◇ – Operated by SOB.
⊡ – Operated by SBB on Ⓐ, by SOB on Ⓒ.

505 GENÈVE - LAUSANNE - BERN / BIEL - ZÜRICH

SBB

	RE 18467	IC 1523	IC 719	IR 2175		IR 2521	IC 523	IC 821	RE 18469	IC 1525	IC 721	IR 2177		IR 2523	IC 525	IC 823	RE 18471	IC 1527	IC 723	IR 2179		IR 2525	IC 527	IC 825
		✕	♠✕			🍷	R✕	B✕		✕	✕			🍷	R✕	A✕		✕	✕			🍷	R✕	B✕
Genève Aéroport ✈ 570 d.	1111c	...	1132	...	...	1149	1205	...	1211c	...	1232	...	...	1249	1305	...	1311c	...	1332	...	...	1349	1405	...
Genève 570 d.	1120	...	1142	...	...	1159	1215	...	1220	...	1242	...	...	1259	1315	...	1320	...	1342	...	...	1359	1415	...
Nyon 570 d.	1136	...	|	...	...	1213	|	...	1236	...	|	...	...	1313	|	...	1336	...	|	...	...	1413	|	...
Morges 570 d.	1155	...	|	...	...	1230	1242	...	1256	...	|	...	...	1330	1342	...	1355	...	|	...	...	1430	1442	...
Lausanne 570 a.	1208	...	1217	...	...	1241	|	...	1308	...	1317	...	...	1341	|	...	1408	...	1417	...	...	1441	|	...
Lausanne d.	▬	1215	1220	...	1225	1244	|	...	▬	1315	1320	...	1325	1344	|	...	▬	1415	1420	...	1425	1444	|	...
Yverdon d.	...	1237	|	...	1258	|	1306	...	...	1337	|	...	1358	|	1406	...	...	1437	|	...	1458	|	1506	...
Neuchâtel d.	...	1258	|	...	▬	|	1326	...	...	1358	|	...	▬	|	1426	...	...	1458	|	...	▬	|	1526	...
Biel / Bienne a.	...	1315	|	...	...	|	1343	...	...	1415	|	...	...	|	1443	...	...	1515	|	...	...	|	1543	...
Biel / Bienne d.	...	1317	|	...	...	|	1346	...	...	1417	|	...	...	|	1446	...	...	1517	|	...	...	|	1546	...
Solothurn d.	...	1334	|	...	...	|	1401	...	...	1434	|	...	...	|	1501	...	...	1534	|	...	...	|	1601	...
Palézieux d.	*IR*	|	|	...	*IR*	1300	|	...	*IR*	|	|	...	*IR*	1400	|	...	*IR*	|	|	...	*IR*	1500	|	...
Romont 568 d.	**2823**	|	|	...	**2373**	1316	|	...	**2825**	|	|	...	**2375**	1416	|	...	**2827**	|	|	...	**2377**	1516	|	...
Fribourg 568 d.		|	1304	...		1334	|	...		|	1404	...		1434	|	...		|	1504	...		1534	|	...
Bern 568 a.	⊙	|	1326	...	H◇	1356	|	...	⊙	|	1426	...	H◇	1456	|	...	⊙	|	1526	...	H⊡	1556	|	...
Bern d.	1307	|	1331	1333	1338	1400	|	1402	1407	|	1431	1433	1438	1500	|	1502	1507	|	1531	1533	1538	1600	|	1602
Luzern 565 a.	|	|	|	|	|	1501	|	|	|	|	|	|	|	1601	|	|	|	|	|	|	|	1701	|	|
Burgdorf d.	1321	|	|	|	1353	...	|	|	1421	|	|	|	1453	...	|	|	1521	|	|	|	1553	...	|	|
Langenthal d.	1341	|	|	|	1412	...	|	|	1441	|	|	|	1512	...	|	|	1541	|	|	|	1612	...	|	|
Olten a.	1354	1357	|	1400	1424	...	1418	|	1454	1457	|	1500	1524	...	1518	|	1554	1557	|	1600	1624	...	1618	|
Olten d.	...	1359	|	1402	1430	...	1420	|	...	1459	|	1502	1530	...	1520	|	...	1559	|	1602	1630	...	1620	|
Aarau 510 d.	...	|	|	1414	|	...	1431	|	...	|	|	1514	|	...	1531	|	...	|	|	1614	|	...	1631	|
Lenzburg 510 d.	...	|	|	|	|	...	|	|	...	|	|	|	|	...	|	|	...	|	|	|	|	...	|	|
Brugg 510 d.	...	|	|	1430	|	...	|	|	...	|	|	1530	|	...	|	|	...	|	|	1630	|	...	|	|
Baden 510 a.	...	|	|	1438	|	...	|	|	...	|	|	1538	|	...	|	|	...	|	|	1638	|	...	|	|
Zürich HB 510 a.	...	1430	1428	1454	1506	...	1456	1458	...	1530	1528	1554	1606	...	1556	1558	...	1630	1628	1654	1706	...	1656	1658
Zürich Flughafen ✈ 530/5 a.	...	...	1451a	...	...	...	1512	1514	...	...	1551	...	...	...	1612	1614	...	1642a	1651	...	...	...	1712	1714
St Gallen 530 a.	...	...	1552a	...	...	...	1602	|	...	...	1652	...	...	...	1702	|	...	1732a	1752	...	...	...	1802	|
Romanshorn 535 a.	...	...	...	...	...	...	...	1612	...	...	...	...	...	...	...	1712	...	...	...	...	...	...	...	1812

	RE 18473	IC 1529	IC 725	IR 2181		IR 2527	IC 529	IC 827	RE 18475	IC 1531	IC 727	IR 2183		IR 2529	IC 531	IC 829	RE 18477	IC 1533	IC 729	IR 2185		IR 2531	IC 533	IC 831
		✕	✕			🍷	R✕	A✕		✕	✕			🍷	R✕	B✕		✕	✕			🍷	✕	A✕
Genève Aéroport ✈ 570 d.	1411c	...	1432	...	...	1449	1505	...	1511c	...	1532	...	...	1549	1605	...	1611c	...	1632	...	...	1649	1705	...
Genève 570 d.	1420	...	1442	...	...	1459	1515	...	1520	...	1542	...	...	1559	1615	...	1620	...	1642	...	...	1659	1715	...
Nyon 570 d.	1436	...	|	...	...	1513	|	...	1536	...	|	...	...	1613	|	...	1636	...	|	...	...	1713	|	...
Morges 570 d.	1456	...	|	...	...	1530	1542	...	1555	...	|	...	...	1630	1642	...	1655	...	|	...	...	1730	1742	...
Lausanne 570 a.	1508	...	1517	...	...	1541	|	...	1608	...	1617	...	...	1641	|	...	1708	...	1717	...	...	1741	|	...
Lausanne d.	▬	1515	1520	...	1525	1544	|	...	▬	1615	1620	...	1625	1644	|	...	▬	1715	1720	...	1725	1744	|	...
Yverdon d.	...	1537	|	...	1558	|	1606	...	...	1637	|	...	1658	|	1706	...	...	1737	|	...	1758	|	1806	...
Neuchâtel d.	...	1558	|	...	▬	|	1626	...	...	1658	|	...	▬	|	1726	...	...	1758	|	...	▬	|	1826	...
Biel / Bienne a.	...	1615	|	...	...	|	1643	...	...	1715	|	...	...	|	1743	...	...	1815	|	...	...	|	1843	...
Biel / Bienne d.	...	1617	|	...	...	|	1646	...	...	1717	|	...	...	|	1746	...	...	1817	|	...	...	|	1846	...
Solothurn d.	...	1634	|	...	...	|	1701	...	...	1734	|	...	...	|	1801	...	...	1834	|	...	...	|	1901	...
Palézieux d.	*IR*	|	|	...	*IR*	1600	|	...	*IR*	|	|	...	*IR*	1700	|	...	*IR*	|	|	...	*IR*	1800	|	...
Romont 568 d.	**2829**	|	|	...	**2379**	1616	|	...	**2831**	|	|	...	**2381**	1716	|	...	**2833**	|	|	...	**2383**	1816	|	...
Fribourg 568 d.		|	1604	...		1634	|	...		|	1704	...		1734	|	...		|	1804	...		1834	|	...
Bern 568 a.	⊙	|	1626	...	H◇	1656	|	...	⊙	|	1726	...	H⊡	1756	|	...	⊙	|	1826	...	H◇	1856	|	...
Bern d.	1607	|	1631	1633	1638	1700	|	1702	1707	|	1731	1733	1738	1800	|	1802	1807	|	1831	1833	1838	1900	|	1902
Luzern 565 a.	|	|	|	|	|	1801	|	|	|	|	|	|	|	1901	|	|	|	|	|	|	|	2001	|	|
Burgdorf d.	1621	|	|	|	1653	...	|	|	1721	|	|	|	1753	...	|	|	1821	|	|	|	1853	...	|	|
Langenthal d.	1641	|	|	|	1712	...	|	|	1741	|	|	|	1812	...	|	|	1841	|	|	|	1912	...	|	|
Olten a.	1654	1657	|	1700	1724	...	1718	|	1754	1757	|	1800	1824	...	1818	|	1854	1857	|	1900	1924	...	1918	|
Olten d.	...	1659	|	1702	1730	...	1720	|	...	1759	|	1802	1830	...	1820	|	...	1859	|	1902	1930	...	1920	|
Aarau 510 d.	...	|	|	1714	|	...	1731	|	...	|	|	1814	|	...	1831	|	...	|	|	1914	|	...	1931	|
Lenzburg 510 d.	...	|	|	|	|	...	|	|	...	|	|	|	|	...	|	|	...	|	|	|	|	...	|	|
Brugg 510 d.	...	|	|	1730	|	...	|	|	...	|	|	1830	|	...	|	|	...	|	|	1930	|	...	|	|
Baden 510 a.	...	|	|	1738	|	...	|	|	...	|	|	1838	|	...	|	|	...	|	|	1938	|	...	|	|
Zürich HB 510 a.	...	1730	1728	1754	1806	...	1756	1758	...	1830	1828	1854	1906	...	1856	1858	...	1930	1928	1954	2006	...	1956	1958
Zürich Flughafen ✈ 530/5 a.	...	...	1751	...	...	...	1812	1814	...	1842a	1851	...	...	...	1912	1914	...	...	1951	...	...	...	2012	2014
St Gallen 530 a.	...	...	1852	...	...	...	1902	|	...	1932a	1952	...	...	...	2002	|	...	...	2052	...	...	...	2102	|
Romanshorn 535 a.	...	...	...	...	...	...	...	1912	...	...	...	...	...	...	...	2012	...	...	...	...	...	...	...	2112

	RE 18479	IC 1535	IC 731	IR 2187		IR 2533	IC 535	IC 833	RE 18481	IC 1537	IC 733	IR 2189		IR 2535	IC 537	IC 835	RE 18483	IC 1539	IC 735 ⑤⑥	IC 735 ⑦–④	IR 2191		IR 2537	IC 539
		✕	✕			🍷	✕	B✕		✕	✕				✕	A✕		◐	n✕	r✕	✕			◐
Genève Aéroport ✈ 570 d.	1711c	...	1732	...	...	1749	1805	...	1811c	...	1832	...	...	1849	1905	...	1911c	...	1932	1932	...	...	1949	2005
Genève 570 d.	1720	...	1742	...	...	1759	1815	...	1820	...	1842	...	...	1859	1915	...	1920	...	1942	1942	...	...	1959	2015
Nyon 570 d.	1736	...	|	...	...	1813	|	...	1836	...	|	...	...	1913	|	...	1936	...	|	|	...	...	2013	|
Morges 570 d.	1755	...	|	...	...	1830	1842	...	1855	...	|	...	...	1930	1942	...	1955	...	|	|	...	...	2030	2042
Lausanne 570 a.	1808	...	1817	...	...	1841	|	...	1908	...	1917	...	...	1941	|	...	2008	...	2017	2017	...	...	2041	|
Lausanne d.	▬	1815	1820	...	1825	1844	|	...	▬	1915	1920	...	1925	1944	|	...	▬	2015	2020	2020	...	2025	2044	|
Yverdon d.	...	1837	|	...	1858	|	1906	...	...	1937	|	...	1958	|	2006	...	...	2037	|	|	...	2058	|	2106
Neuchâtel d.	...	1858	|	...	▬	|	1926	...	...	1958	|	...	▬	|	2026	...	...	2058	|	|	...	▬	|	2126
Biel / Bienne a.	...	1915	|	...	...	|	1943	...	...	2015	|	...	...	|	2043	...	...	2115	|	|	...	...	|	2143
Biel / Bienne d.	...	1917	|	...	...	|	1946	...	...	2017	|	...	...	|	2046	...	...	2117	|	|	...	...	|	2146
Solothurn d.	...	1934	|	...	...	|	2001	...	...	2034	|	...	...	|	2101	...	...	2134	|	|	...	...	|	2201
Palézieux d.	*IR*	|	|	...	*IR*	1900	|	...	*IR*	|	|	...	*IR*	2000	|	...	*IR*	|	|	|	...	*IR*	2100	|
Romont 568 d.	**2835**	|	|	...	**2385**	1916	|	...	**2837**	|	|	...	**2387**	2016	|	...	**2839**	|	|	|	...	**2389**	2116	|
Fribourg 568 d.		|	1904	...		1934	|	...		|	2004	...		2034	|	...		|	2104	2104	...		2134	|
Bern 568 a.	⊙	|	1926	...	H◇	1956	|	...	⊙	|	2026	...	◇	2056	|	...	⊙	|	2126	2126	...	◇	2156	|
Bern d.	1907	|	1931	1933	1938	2000	|	2002	2007	|	2031	2033	2038	2100	|	2102	2107	|	2131	2131	2133n	2138	2200	|
Luzern 565 a.	|	|	|	|	|	2101	|	|	|	|	|	|	|	2201	|	|	|	|	|	|	|	|	2301	|
Burgdorf d.	1921	|	|	|	1953	...	|	|	2021	|	|	|	2053	...	|	|	2121	|	|	|	|	2154	...	|
Langenthal d.	1941	|	|	|	2012	...	|	|	2041	|	|	|	2112	...	|	|	2141	|	|	|	|	2212	...	|
Olten a.	1954	1957	|	2000	2024	...	2018	|	2054	2057	|	2100	2124	...	2118	|	2154	2157	|	2157	2200n	2225	...	2218
Olten d.	...	1959	|	2002	2030	...	2020	|	...	2059	|	2102	...	...	2120	|	...	2159n	|	2200	2202	...	...	2220
Aarau 510 d.	...	|	|	2014	|	...	2031	|	...	|	|	2114	...	...	2131	|	...	|	|	|	2214	...	...	2231
Lenzburg 510 d.	...	|	|	|	|	...	|	|	...	|	|	|	...	...	|	|	...	|	|	|	|	...	...	|
Brugg 510 d.	...	|	|	2030	|	...	|	|	...	|	|	2130	...	...	|	|	...	|	|	|	2230	...	...	|
Baden 510 a.	...	|	|	2038	|	...	|	|	...	|	|	2138	...	...	|	|	...	|	|	|	2238	...	...	|
Zürich HB 510 a.	...	2030	2028	2054	2106	...	2056	2058	...	2130	2128	2154	...	...	2156	2158	...	2230n	2228	2231	2254	...	...	2256
Zürich Flughafen ✈ 530/5 a.	...	...	2051	...	...	...	...	2114	...	...	2151	...	...	...	...	2214	...	...	2251	2251	...	...	...	...
St Gallen 530 a.	...	...	2152	...	...	...	...	|	...	...	2252	...	...	...	...	|	...	...	2352	2352	...	...	...	...
Romanshorn 535 a.	...	...	...	...	...	...	...	2212	...	...	...	...	...	...	...	2312	...	...	...	...	...	...	...	...

A – From Interlaken (Table **560**).
B – From Brig (Table **560**).
H – To Chur (Table **520**).
R – To Rorschach (Table **534**).

a – Ⓐ only.
c – Ⓒ only.
n – ⑤⑥ (not Dec. 24, Apr. 7).
r – Also Dec. 24, Apr. 7.

♠ – On Ⓒ runs as *IC* **909** and continues to Chur (Table **520**).
◐ – Conveys ✕ until Biel/Bienne.
⊙ – Operated by BLS.
◇ – Operated by SOB.
⊡ – Operated by SBB on Ⓐ, by SOB on Ⓒ.

SBB GENÈVE - LAUSANNE - BERN / BIEL - ZÜRICH 505

	IC 837	RE 18485	IC 1541 ▽	IC 737		RE 18439	IR 2539 ⑦–④	IR 2539 ⑤⑥	IC 839	IC 541	RE 4793	RE 18487	IC 1543	IC 739	RE 18441	IR 2541	IC 841	IC 543	RE 18489	IC 1545	RE 18443	IR 2543	RE 18491	IC 1547
			◐	✕						◐			◐	◧						D				
Genève Aéroport ✈ 570 d.	...	2011c	...	2032	...	...	...	2049	...	2102k	...	2111c	...	...	...	...	...	...	2210	...	...	...	2310	...
Genève 570 d.	...	2020	...	2042	...	2050	...	2059	...	2112k	...	2120	...	...	2150	...	...	...	2220	...	2250	...	2320	...
Nyon 570 d.	...	2036	...	|	...	2106	...	2113	...	2126k	...	2136	...	...	2206	...	...	...	2236	...	2306	...	2336	...
Morges 570 d.	...	2056	...	|	...	2125	...	2130	...	2142	...	2156	...	...	2225	...	...	...	2256	...	2325	...	2356	...
Lausanne 570 a.	...	2108	...	2117	...	2138	...	2141	...	|	...	2208	...	...	2238	...	...	...	2310	...	2338	...	0010	...
Lausanne d.	...	▬	2115	2120	2125	...	2144	2144	...	|	...	▬	2215	2220	...	2244	...	...	▬	2315	...	2344	▬	0015
Yverdon d.	...	...	2137	|	2158	...	|	|	...	2204	...	...	2237	|	...	|	...	...	...	2337	...	|	...	0037
Neuchâtel d.	...	...	2158	|	▬	...	|	|	...	2226	...	...	2258	|	...	|	...	...	...	2358	...	|	...	0058
Biel / Bienne a.	...	...	2215	|	...	...	|	|	...	2243	...	...	2315	|	...	|	...	...	...	0015	...	|	...	0115
Biel / Bienne d.	...	...	2217	|	...	...	|	|	...	2246	...	...	2317	|	...	|	...	2346	...	...	...	|	...	▬
Solothurn d.	...	...	2234	|	...	...	|	|	...	2305	...	...	2334	|	...	|	...	0005	...	...	...	|	...	...
Palézieux d.	...	*IR*	|	|	*IR*	...	2200	2200	...	|	...	*IR*	|	|	...	2300	...	|	*IR*	...	...	0000	*IC*	*IR*
Romont 568 d.	...	**2841**	|	|	**2351**	...	2216	2216	...	|	...	**2845**	|	|	...	2316	...	|	**2399**	...	...	0016	**843**	**2847**
Fribourg 568 d.	...		|	2204		...	2234	2234	...	|	...		|	2304	...	2334	...	|		...	...	0034	⑥⑦	⑥⑦
Bern 568 a.	...	⊙	|	2226		...	2256	2256	...	|	...	⊙	|	2326	...	2356	...	|	◇	...	...	0100	**h**	**h**⊙
Bern d.	2202	2206	|	2231	2233	...	2300	2300	2302	|	...	2306	|	2331	...	...	0002	|	0006	...	...	...	0106	0109
Luzern **565** a.	|	|	|	|	|	...	0001	0001	|	|	...	|	|	|	...	...	|	|	|	...	...	...	|	|
Burgdorf d.	|	2222	|	|	2251	...	...	...	|	|	...	2322	|	|	...	...	|	|	0022	...	...	...	|	0125
Langenthal d.	|	2241	|	|	2312	...	...	...	|	|	...	2341	|	|	...	...	|	|	0041	...	...	...	|	0144
Olten a.	2228	2254	2257	2257	2325	...	...	...	2328	2330	...	2355	2357	2357	...	...	0028	0030	0054	...	...	...	0132	0157
Olten d.	2230	...	2302	2300	...	...	...	...	2330	2333	2335	...	...	0002	...	...	0035	0037	...	...	...	...	0134	...
Aarau 510 d.	|	...	2314	|	...	...	...	...	|	2344	2345	...	...	0012	...	...	|	0047	...	...	...	...	0145	...
Lenzburg 510 d.	|	...	|	|	...	...	...	...	|	|	|	...	...	0019	...	...	|	0054	...	...	...	...	|	...
Brugg 510 d.	|	...	2330	|	...	...	...	...	|	|	0003	...	...	|	...	...	|	|	...	...	...	...	|	...
Baden 510 a.	|	...	2338	|	...	...	...	...	|	|	0013	...	...	|	...	...	|	|	...	...	...	...	|	...
Zürich HB 510 a.	2302	...	2354	2331	...	...	...	...	0001	0010	0042	...	...	0040	...	...	0106	0114	...	...	...	...	0210	...
Zürich Flughafen ✈ **530/5** a.	2314	...	...	...	...	...	...	...	...	...	...	...	...	...	...	...	...	...	...	...	...	...	...	...
St Gallen **530** a.	|	...	...	...	...	...	...	...	...	...	...	...	...	...	...	...	...	...	...	...	...	...	...	...
Romanshorn **535** a.	0012	...	...	...	...	...	...	...	...	...	...	...	...	...	...	...	...	...	...	...	...	...	...	...

km ♥		RE 18400 ⑥⑦	RE 18402	RE 18450	RE 18404	RE 18452	IC 504	IR 2504		IC 702	IC 1504	RE 18454	IR 2806 Ⓐ	IR 2506	IR 2352	IC 704	IC 1506	IR 2808	IC 804	IR 2508	IR 2354	IC 508	IR 2158	IC 706
										✕	✕		⊙		◇	✕	⊖	⊙	A✕	🍷	⊡	✕		✕
	Romanshorn d.	...	...	...	...	...	...	...	...	...	...	...	...	...	...	...	...	...	...	...	...	...	...	...
	St Gallen **530** d.	...	...	...	...	...	...	...	...	...	...	...	...	...	...	...	...	...	...	...	...	...	...	0507
	Zürich Flughafen ✈ **530/5** d.	...	...	...	...	...	...	...	...	...	...	...	...	...	...	...	...	...	...	...	...	...	...	0608
0	**Zürich** HB 510 d.	...	...	...	...	...	...	...	...	...	...	...	...	...	...	0519	...	...	0602	...	0553	0604	0606	0632
	Baden 510 d.	...	...	...	...	...	...	...	...	...	...	...	...	...	...	|	...	...	|	...	|	|	0621	|
	Brugg 510 d.	...	...	...	...	...	...	...	...	...	...	...	...	...	...	|	...	...	|	...	|	|	0632	|
32	Lenzburg 510 d.	...	...	...	...	...	...	...	...	...	...	...	...	...	...	0540	...	...	|	...	|	|	|	|
42	Aarau 510 d.	...	...	...	...	...	...	...	...	...	...	...	...	...	...	0548	...	...	|	...	|	0630	0646	|
55	**Olten** a.	...	...	...	...	...	...	...	...	...	...	...	...	...	...	0557	...	...	|	...	0628	0638	0655	|
55	**Olten** d.	...	...	...	...	...	...	...	...	...	...	...	0506	...	0536	0602	0602	0606	|	...	0636	0640	0656	|
	Langenthal d.	...	...	...	...	...	...	...	...	...	...	...	0518	...	0548	|	|	0618	|	...	0648	|	|	|
	Burgdorf d.	...	...	...	...	...	...	...	...	...	...	...	0538	...	0606	|	|	0638	|	...	0706	|	|	|
	Luzern **565** d.	...	...	...	...	...	...	...	...	...	...	...	|	...	|	|	|	|	|	0600	|	|	|	|
117	**Bern** a.	...	...	...	...	...	...	...	...	...	...	...	0553	...	0621	0628	|	0653	0658	0700	0721	|	0724	0728
	Bern 568 d.	...	...	...	...	...	...	0504	...	0534	...	...	▬	0604	▬	0634	|	▬	...	0704	...	|	▬	0734
	Fribourg 568 d.	...	...	...	...	...	...	0526	...	0556	...	...	...	0626	...	0656	|	...	...	0726	...	|	...	0756
	Romont 568 d.	...	...	...	...	...	...	0544	...	|	...	...	*IC*	0644	...	|	|	...	...	0744	...	|	...	|
	Palézieux d.	...	...	...	...	...	...	0600	...	|	...	...	**1606**	0700	...	|	|	...	...	0800	...	|	...	|
	Solothurn d.	...	...	...	...	...	...	|	...	|	...	...		|	...	|	0626	...	...	|	...	0658	...	|
	Biel / Bienne a.	...	...	...	...	...	...	|	...	|	...	...	**D**✕	|	...	|	0643	...	...	|	...	0713	...	|
	Biel / Bienne d.	...	...	...	...	...	0514	|	...	|	0545	...	0616	|	...	|	0645	*RE*	...	|	...	0716	...	|
	Neuchâtel d.	...	...	...	...	...	0533	|	...	|	0603	...	0634	|	...	|	0703	**18456**	...	|	...	0734	...	|
	Yverdon d.	...	...	...	...	...	0554	|	0600	|	0623	...	0654	|	0700	|	0723		...	|	...	0754	0800	|
	Lausanne a.	...	...	...	...	...	|	0616	0634	0640	0645	...	|	0716	0734	0740	0745		...	0816	...	|	0834	0840
	Lausanne 570 d.	0251	0351	0451	0521	0551	|	0619	...	0643	...	0651	|	0719	...	0743	...	0751	...	0819	...	|	...	0843
	Morges 570 d.	0303	0404	0505	0535	0605	0618	0629	...	|	...	0705	0718	0729	...	|	...	0805	...	0829	...	0818	...	|
	Nyon 570 d.	0324	0425	0525e	0555	0625	|	0646	...	|	...	0725	|	0746	...	|	...	0825	...	0846	...	|	...	|
	Genève 570 a.	0339	0450	0542e	0610	0640	0647	0704	...	0720	...	0740	0747	0804	...	0820	...	0840	...	0904	...	0847	...	0918
	Genève Aéroport ✈ 570 a.	...	0456	0549e	...	...	0656	0711	...	0727	...	0749c	0756	0811	...	0827	...	0849c	...	0911	...	0856	...	0927

km ♥		IC 1508	IR 2810	IC 806	IR 2510	IR 2356	IC 510	IR 2160	IC 708	IC 1510	IR 2812	IC 808	IR 2512	IR 2358	IC 512	IR 2162	IC 710	IC 1512	IR 2814	IC 810	IR 2514	IR 2360	IC 514	IR 2164
		✕	⊙	B✕	🍷	H◇	R✕		✕	✕	⊙	A✕	🍷	H⊡	R✕		✕	✕	⊙	B✕	🍷	H◇	R✕	
	Romanshorn **535** d.	...	...	0548	...	...	...	...	...	...	...	0648	...	...	...	...	...	...	...	0748	...	...	...	...
	St Gallen **530** d.	...	...	|	...	...	0558	...	0607	0628a	...	|	...	...	0658	...	0707	...	...	|	...	...	0758	...
	Zürich Flughafen ✈ **530/5** d.	...	...	0645	...	...	0648	...	0708	0718a	...	0745	...	...	0748	...	0808	...	...	0845	...	...	0848	...
	Zürich HB 510 d.	0630	...	0702	...	0653	0704	0706	0732	0730	...	0802	...	0753	0804	0806	0832	0830	...	0902	...	0853	0904	0906
	Baden 510 d.	|	...	|	...	|	|	0722	|	|	...	|	...	|	|	0822	|	|	...	|	...	|	|	0922
	Brugg 510 d.	|	...	|	...	|	|	0732	|	|	...	|	...	|	|	0832	|	|	...	|	...	|	|	0932
	Lenzburg 510 d.	|	...	|	...	|	|	|	|	|	...	|	...	|	|	|	|	|	...	|	...	|	|	|
	Aarau 510 d.	|	...	|	...	|	0730	0746	|	|	...	|	...	|	0830	0846	|	|	...	|	...	|	0930	0946
	Olten a.	0700	...	|	...	0728	0738	0755	|	0800	...	|	...	0828	0838	0855	|	0900	...	|	...	0928	0938	0955
0	**Olten** d.	0702	0706	|	...	0736	0740	0756	|	0802	0806	|	...	0836	0840	0856	|	0902	0906	|	...	0936	0940	0956
	Langenthal d.	|	0718	|	...	0748	|	|	|	|	0818	|	...	0848	|	|	|	|	0918	|	...	0948	|	|
	Burgdorf d.	|	0738	|	...	0806	|	|	|	|	0838	|	...	0906	|	|	|	|	0938	|	...	1006	|	|
	Luzern **565** d.	|	|	|	0700	|	|	|	|	|	|	|	0800	|	|	|	|	|	|	|	0900	|	|	|
	Bern a.	|	0753	0758	0800	0821	|	0824	0828	|	0853	0858	0900	0921	|	0924	0928	|	0953	0958	1000	1021	|	1024
	Bern 568 d.	|	▬	...	0804	...	|	▬	0834	|	▬	...	0904	...	|	▬	0934	|	▬	...	1004	...	|	▬
	Fribourg 568 d.	|	...	...	0826	...	|	...	0856	|	...	...	0926	...	|	...	0956	|	...	...	1026	...	|	...
	Romont 568 d.	|	...	...	0844	...	|	...	|	|	...	...	0944	...	|	...	|	|	...	...	1044	...	|	...
	Palézieux d.	|	...	...	0900	...	|	...	|	|	...	...	1000	...	|	...	|	|	...	...	1100	...	|	...
36	Solothurn d.	0726	...	...	|	...	0758	...	|	0826	...	...	|	...	0858	...	|	0926	...	...	|	...	0958	...
61	**Biel / Bienne** a.	0743	...	...	|	...	0813	...	|	0843	...	...	|	...	0913	...	|	0943	...	...	|	...	1013	...
	Biel / Bienne d.	0745	*RE*	...	|	...	0816	...	|	0845	*RE*	...	|	...	0916	...	|	0945	*RE*	...	|	...	1016	...
	Neuchâtel d.	0803	**18458**	...	|	...	0834	...	|	0903	**18460**	...	|	...	0934	...	|	1003	**18462**	...	|	...	1034	...
	Yverdon d.	0823		...	|	...	0854	0900	|	0923		...	|	...	0954	1000	|	1023		...	|	...	1054	1100
	Lausanne a.	0845		...	0916	...	|	0934	0940	0945		...	1016	...	|	1034	1040	1045		...	1116	...	|	1134
	Lausanne 570 d.	...	0851	...	0919	...	|	...	0943	...	0951	...	1019	...	|	...	1043	...	1051	...	1119	...	|	...
	Morges 570 d.	...	0905	...	0929	...	0918	...	|	...	1005	...	1029	...	1018	...	|	...	1105	...	1129	...	1118	...
	Nyon 570 d.	...	0925	...	0946	...	|	...	|	...	1025	...	1046	...	|	...	|	...	1125	...	1146	...	|	...
	Genève 570 a.	...	0940	...	1001	...	0947	...	1018	...	1040	...	1101	...	1047	...	1118	...	1140	...	1201	...	1147	...
	Genève Aéroport ✈ 570 a.	...	0949c	...	1011	...	0956	...	1027	...	1049c	...	1111	...	1056	...	1127	...	1149c	...	1211	...	1156	...

A – To Interlaken (Table **560**).
B – To Brig (Table **560**).
D – From / to Delémont (Table **505a**).
H – From Chur (Table **520**).
R – From Rorschach (Table **530**).

a – Ⓐ only.

c – © only.
e – 1–3 minutes later on Ⓐ.
h – Mornings of ⑥⑦ (not Dec. 25, Apr. 8).
k – ⑤⑥ only.
▽ – Runs as *IR* **2193** Olten - Zürich.
◐ – Conveys ✕ until Biel/Bienne.

⊖ – Conveys ✕ from Biel/Bienne.
◧ – Conveys ✕ Lausanne - Bern.
⊙ – Operated by BLS.
◇ – Operated by SOB.
⊡ – Operated by SBB on Ⓐ, by SOB on ©.
♥ – Kilometres via the high-speed line.

505 ZÜRICH - BIEL / BERN - LAUSANNE - GENÈVE SBB

	IC 712	IC 1514	IR 2816	IC 812	IR 2516	IR 2362	IC 516	IR 2166	IC 714	IC 1516	IR 2818	IC 814	IR 2518	IR 2364	IC 518	IR 2168	IC 716	IC 1518	IR 2820	IC 816	IR 2520	IR 2366	IC 520	IR 2170
	✕	✕	⊙	B✕	🍸	H◇	R✕		✕	✕	⊙	A✕	🍸	H◇	R✕		✕	✕	⊙	B✕	🍸	H◇	R✕	
Romanshorn **535** d.	...	...	...	0848	...	...	...	...	...	...	...	0948	...	...	...	...	...	...	...	1048	...	...	...	...
St Gallen **530** d.	0807	...	...	|	...	...	0858	...	0907	...	...	|	...	...	0958	...	1007	...	...	|	...	...	1058	...
Zürich Flughafen + **530/5** d.	0908	...	...	0945	...	...	0948	...	1008	...	...	1045	...	...	1048	...	1108	...	...	1145	...	...	1148	...
Zürich HB **510** d.	0932	0930	...	1002	...	0953	1004	1006	1032	1030	...	1102	...	1053	1104	1106	1132	1130	...	1202	...	1153	1204	1206
Baden **510** d.	|	|	...	|	...	|	|	1022	|	|	...	|	...	|	|	1122	|	|	...	|	...	|	|	1222
Brugg **510** d.	|	|	...	|	...	|	|	1032	|	|	...	|	...	|	|	1132	|	|	...	|	...	|	|	1232
Lenzburg **510** d.	|	|	...	|	...	|	|	|	|	|	...	|	...	|	|	|	|	|	...	|	...	|	|	|
Aarau **510** d.	|	|	...	|	...	|	1030	1046	|	|	...	|	...	|	1130	1146	|	|	...	|	...	|	1230	1246
Olten a.	|	1000	...	|	...	1028	1038	1055	|	1100	...	|	...	1128	1138	1155	|	1200	...	|	...	1228	1238	1255
Olten d.	|	1002	1006	|	...	1036	1040	1056	|	1102	1106	|	...	1136	1140	1156	|	1202	1206	|	...	1236	1240	1256
Langenthal d.	|	|	1018	|	...	1048	|	|	|	|	1118	|	...	1148	|	|	|	|	1218	|	...	1248	|	|
Burgdorf d.	|	|	1038	|	...	1106	|	|	|	|	1138	|	...	1206	|	|	|	|	1238	|	...	1306	|	|
Luzern **565** d.	|	|	|	|	1000	|	|	|	|	|	|	|	1100	|	|	|	|	|	|	|	1200	|	|	|
Bern a.	1028	|	1053	1058	1100	1121	|	1124	1128	|	1153	1158	1200	1221	|	1224	1228	|	1253	1258	1300	1321	|	1324
Bern **568** d.	1034	|	▬	...	1104	...	|	▬	1134	|	▬	...	1204	...	|	▬	1234	|	▬	...	1304	...	|	▬
Fribourg **568** d.	1056	|	...	...	1126	...	|	...	1156	|	...	...	1226	...	|	...	1256	|	...	...	1326	...	|	...
Romont **568** d.	|	|	...	...	1144	...	|	...	|	|	...	...	1244	...	|	...	|	|	...	...	1344	...	|	...
Palézieux d.	|	|	...	...	1200	...	|	...	|	|	...	...	1300	...	|	...	|	|	...	...	1400	...	|	...
Solothurn d.	|	1026	...	...	|	...	1058	...	|	1126	...	...	|	...	1158	...	|	1226	...	...	|	...	1258	...
Biel / Bienne a.	|	1043	...	...	|	...	1113	...	|	1143	...	...	|	...	1213	...	|	1243	...	...	|	...	1313	...
Biel / Bienne d.	|	1045	RE	...	|	...	1116	...	|	1145	RE	...	|	...	1216	...	|	1245	RE	...	|	...	1316	...
Neuchâtel d.	|	1103	18464	...	|	...	1134	...	|	1203	18466	...	|	...	1234	...	|	1303	18468	...	|	...	1334	...
Yverdon d.	|	1123	...	...	|	...	1154	1200	|	1223	...	...	|	...	1254	1300	|	1323	...	...	|	...	1354	1400
Lausanne a.	1140	1145	...	...	1216	...	|	1234	1240	1245	...	...	1316	...	|	1334	1340	1345	...	...	1416	...	|	1434
Lausanne **570** d.	1143	...	1151	...	1219	...	|	...	1243	...	1251	...	1319	...	|	...	1343	...	1351	...	1419	...	|	...
Morges **570** d.	|	...	1205	...	1229	...	1218	...	|	...	1305	...	1329	...	1318	...	|	...	1405	...	1429	...	1418	...
Nyon **570** d.	|	...	1225	...	1246	...	|	...	|	...	1325	...	1346	...	|	...	|	...	1425	...	1446	...	|	...
Genève **570** a.	1218	...	1240	...	1301	...	1247	...	1318	...	1340	...	1401	...	1347	...	1418	...	1440	...	1501	...	1447	...
Genève Aéroport + **570** a.	1227	...	1249c	...	1311	...	1256	...	1327	...	1349c	...	1411	...	1356	...	1427	...	1449c	...	1511	...	1456	...

	IC 718	IC 1520	IR 2822	IC 818	IR 2522	IR 2368	IC 522	IR 2172	IC 720	IC 1522	IR 2824	IC 820	IR 2524	IR 2370	IC 524	IR 2174	IC 722	IC 1524	IR 2826	IC 822	IR 2526	IR 2372	IC 526	IR 2176
	✕	✕	⊙	A✕	🍸	H◇	R✕		✕	✕	⊙	B✕	🍸	H⊡	R✕		♣✕	✕	⊙	A✕	🍸	H◇	R✕	
Romanshorn **535** d.	...	...	...	1148	...	...	...	...	...	...	...	1248	...	...	...	...	...	...	...	1348	...	...	...	...
St Gallen **530** d.	1107	...	...	|	...	...	1158	...	1207	...	...	|	...	...	1258	...	1307a	...	...	|	...	...	1358	...
Zürich Flughafen + **530/5** d.	1208	...	...	1245	...	...	1248	...	1308	...	...	1345	...	...	1348	...	1408a	...	...	1445	...	...	1448	...
Zürich HB **510** d.	1232	1230	...	1302	...	1253	1304	1306	1332	1330	...	1402	...	1353	1404	1406	1432	1430	...	1502	...	1453	1504	1506
Baden **510** d.	|	|	...	|	...	|	|	1322	|	|	...	|	...	|	|	1422	|	|	...	|	...	|	|	1522
Brugg **510** d.	|	|	...	|	...	|	|	1332	|	|	...	|	...	|	|	1432	|	|	...	|	...	|	|	1532
Lenzburg **510** d.	|	|	...	|	...	|	|	|	|	|	...	|	...	|	|	|	|	|	...	|	...	|	|	|
Aarau **510** d.	|	|	...	|	...	|	1330	1346	|	|	...	|	...	|	1430	1446	|	|	...	|	...	|	1530	1546
Olten a.	|	1300	...	|	...	1328	1338	1355	|	1400	...	|	...	1428	1438	1455	|	1500	...	|	...	1528	1538	1555
Olten d.	|	1302	1306	|	...	1336	1340	1356	|	1402	1406	|	...	1436	1440	1456	|	1502	1506	|	...	1536	1540	1556
Langenthal d.	|	|	1318	|	...	1348	|	|	|	|	1418	|	...	1448	|	|	|	|	1518	|	...	1548	|	|
Burgdorf d.	|	|	1338	|	...	1406	|	|	|	|	1438	|	...	1506	|	|	|	|	1538	|	...	1606	|	|
Luzern **565** d.	|	|	|	|	1300	|	|	|	|	|	|	|	1400	|	|	|	|	|	|	|	1500	|	|	|
Bern a.	1328	|	1353	1358	1400	1421	|	1424	1428	|	1453	1458	1500	1521	|	1524	1528	|	1553	1558	1600	1621	|	1624
Bern **568** d.	1334	|	▬	...	1404	...	|	▬	1434	|	▬	...	1504	...	|	▬	1534	|	▬	...	1604	...	|	▬
Fribourg **568** d.	1356	|	...	...	1426	...	|	...	1456	|	...	...	1526	...	|	...	1556	|	...	...	1626	...	|	...
Romont **568** d.	|	|	...	...	1444	...	|	...	|	|	...	...	1544	...	|	...	|	|	...	...	1644	...	|	...
Palézieux d.	|	|	...	...	1500	...	|	...	|	|	...	...	1600	...	|	...	|	|	...	...	1700	...	|	...
Solothurn d.	|	1326	...	...	|	...	1358	...	|	1426	...	...	|	...	1458	...	|	1526	...	...	|	...	1558	...
Biel / Bienne a.	|	1343	...	...	|	...	1413	...	|	1443	...	...	|	...	1513	...	|	1543	...	...	|	...	1613	...
Biel / Bienne d.	|	1345	RE	...	|	...	1416	...	|	1445	RE	...	|	...	1516	...	|	1545	RE	...	|	...	1616	...
Neuchâtel d.	|	1403	18470	...	|	...	1434	...	|	1503	18472	...	|	...	1534	...	|	1603	18474	...	|	...	1634	...
Yverdon d.	|	1423	...	...	|	...	1454	1500	|	1523	...	...	|	...	1554	1600	|	1623	...	...	|	...	1654	1700
Lausanne a.	1440	1445	...	...	1516	...	|	1534	1540	1545	...	...	1616	...	|	1634	1640	1645	...	...	1716	...	|	1734
Lausanne **570** d.	1443	...	1451	...	1519	...	|	...	1543	...	1551	...	1619	...	|	...	1643	...	1651	...	1719	...	|	...
Morges **570** d.	|	...	1505	...	1529	...	1518	...	|	...	1605	...	1629	...	1618	...	|	...	1705	...	1729	...	1718	...
Nyon **570** d.	|	...	1525	...	1546	...	|	...	|	...	1625	...	1646	...	|	...	|	...	1725	...	1746	...	|	...
Genève **570** a.	1518	...	1540	...	1601	...	1547	...	1618	...	1640	...	1701	...	1647	...	1718	...	1740	...	1801	...	1747	...
Genève Aéroport + **570** a.	1527	...	1549c	...	1611	...	1556	...	1627	...	1649c	...	1711	...	1656	...	1727	...	1749c	...	1811	...	1756	...

	IC 724	IC 1526	IR 2828	IC 824	IR 2528	IR 2374	IC 528	IR 2178	IC 726	IC 1528	IR 2830	IC 826	IR 2530	IR 2376	IC 530	IR 2180	IC 728	IC 1530	IR 2832	IC 828	IR 2532	IR 2378	IC 532	IR 2182
	✕	✕	⊙	B✕	🍸	H⊡	R✕		✕	✕	⊙	A✕	🍸	H◇	R✕		♠✕	✕	⊙	B✕		H◇	R✕	
Romanshorn **535** d.	...	...	...	1448	...	...	...	...	...	...	...	1548	...	...	...	...	...	...	...	1648	...	...	...	...
St Gallen **530** d.	1407	...	...	|	...	...	1458	...	1507	...	...	|	...	...	1558	...	1607a	1628a	...	|	...	...	1658	...
Zürich Flughafen + **530/5** d.	1508	...	...	1545	...	...	1548	...	1608	...	...	1645	...	...	1648	...	1708a	1718a	...	1745	...	...	1748	...
Zürich HB **510** d.	1532	1530	...	1602	...	1553	1604	1606	1632	1630	...	1702	...	1653	1704	1706	1732	1730	...	1802	...	1753	1804	1806
Baden **510** d.	|	|	...	|	...	|	|	1622	|	|	...	|	...	|	|	1722	|	|	...	|	...	|	|	1822
Brugg **510** d.	|	|	...	|	...	|	|	1632	|	|	...	|	...	|	|	1732	|	|	...	|	...	|	|	1832
Lenzburg **510** d.	|	|	...	|	...	|	|	|	|	|	...	|	...	|	|	|	|	|	...	|	...	|	|	|
Aarau **510** d.	|	|	...	|	...	|	1630	1646	|	|	...	|	...	|	1730	1746	|	|	...	|	...	|	1830	1846
Olten a.	|	1600	...	|	...	1628	1638	1655	|	1700	...	|	...	1728	1738	1755	|	1800	...	|	...	1828	1838	1855
Olten d.	|	1602	1606	|	...	1636	1640	1656	|	1702	1706	|	...	1736	1740	1756	|	1802	1806	|	...	1836	1840	1856
Langenthal d.	|	|	1618	|	...	1648	|	|	|	|	1718	|	...	1748	|	|	|	|	1818	|	...	1848	|	|
Burgdorf d.	|	|	1638	|	...	1706	|	|	|	|	1738	|	...	1806	|	|	|	|	1838	|	...	1906	|	|
Luzern **565** d.	|	|	|	|	1600	|	|	|	|	|	|	|	1700	|	|	|	|	|	|	|	1800	|	|	|
Bern a.	1628	|	1653	1658	1700	1721	|	1724	1728	|	1753	1758	1800	1821	|	1824	1828	|	1853	1858	1900	1921	|	1924
Bern **568** d.	1634	|	▬	...	1704	...	|	▬	1734	|	▬	...	1804	...	|	▬	1834	|	▬	...	1904	...	|	▬
Fribourg **568** d.	1656	|	...	...	1726	...	|	...	1756	|	...	...	1826	...	|	...	1856	|	...	...	1926	...	|	...
Romont **568** d.	|	|	...	...	1744	...	|	...	|	|	...	...	1844	...	|	...	|	|	...	...	1944	...	|	...
Palézieux d.	|	|	...	...	1800	...	|	...	|	|	...	...	1900	...	|	...	|	|	...	...	2000	...	|	...
Solothurn d.	|	1626	...	...	|	...	1658	...	|	1726	...	...	|	...	1758	...	|	1826	...	...	|	...	1858	...
Biel / Bienne a.	|	1643	...	...	|	...	1713	...	|	1743	...	...	|	...	1813	...	|	1843	...	...	|	...	1913	...
Biel / Bienne d.	|	1645	RE	...	|	...	1716	...	|	1745	RE	...	|	...	1816	...	|	1845	RE	...	|	...	1916	...
Neuchâtel d.	|	1703	18476	...	|	...	1734	...	|	1803	18478	...	|	...	1834	...	|	1903	18480	...	|	...	1934	...
Yverdon d.	|	1723	...	...	|	...	1754	1800	|	1823	...	...	|	...	1854	1900	|	1923	...	...	|	...	1954	2000
Lausanne a.	1740	1745	...	...	1816	...	|	1834	1840	1845	...	...	1916	...	|	1934	1940	1945	...	...	2016	...	|	2034
Lausanne **570** d.	1743	...	1751	...	1819	...	|	...	1843	...	1851	...	1919	...	|	...	1943	...	1951	...	2019	...	|	...
Morges **570** d.	|	...	1805	...	1829	...	1818	...	|	...	1905	...	1929	...	1918	...	|	...	2005	...	2029	...	2018	...
Nyon **570** d.	|	...	1825	...	1846	...	|	...	|	...	1925	...	1946	...	|	...	|	...	2025	...	2046	...	|	...
Genève **570** a.	1818	...	1840	...	1901	...	1847	...	1918	...	1940	...	2001	...	1947	...	2018	...	2040	...	2101	...	2047	...
Genève Aéroport + **570** a.	1827	...	1849c	...	1911	...	1856	...	1927	...	1949c	...	2011	...	1956	...	2027	...	2049c	...	2111	...	2056	...

A – To Interlaken (Table **560**).
B – To Brig (Table **560**).
H – From Chur (Table **520**).
R – From Rorschach (Table **530**).

a – Ⓐ only.
c – Ⓒ only.

⊙ – Operated by BLS.
◇ – Operated by SOB.
⊡ – Operated by SBB on Ⓐ, by SOB on Ⓒ.
♣ – On Ⓒ run as *IC* **902** and starts from Chur (Table **520**).
♠ – On Ⓒ run as *IC* **908** and starts from Chur (Table **520**).

SBB ZÜRICH - BIEL / BERN - LAUSANNE - GENÈVE 505

	IC 730	IC 1532	IR 2834	IC 830	IR 2534	IR 2380	IC 534	IR 2184	RE 18436 ⑦–④		IC 732	IR 1734 ⑤⑥	IC 1534	IR 2836	IC 832	IR 2536	IR 2382	IC 536	RE 18438	IR 2186	IC 734	IC 1536	IR 2838	IC 834
	✗	✗	⊙	A ✗		H ◇	R ✗				✗		✗	⊙	✗		H ◇	R ◐			✗	◐	⊙	✗
Romanshorn **535** d.	...	...	...	1748	...	...	...	...	...	...	...	...	...	...	1848	...	...	...	...	...	...	...	...	1948
St Gallen **530** d.	1707	...	...	|	...	...	1758	...	...	...	1807	...	1828a	...	|	...	...	1858	...	...	1907	...	...	|
Zürich Flughafen ✈ **530/5** d.	1808	...	...	1845	...	...	1848	...	...	...	1908	...	1918a	...	1945	...	...	1948	...	...	2008	...	...	2045
Zürich HB **510** d.	1832	1830	...	1902	...	1853	1904	1906	...	...	1932	...	1930	...	2002	...	1953	2004	...	2006	2032	2030	...	2102
Baden **510** d.	|	|	...	|	...	|	|	1922	...	...	|	...	|	...	|	...	|	|	...	2022	|	|	...	|
Brugg **510** d.	|	|	...	|	...	|	|	1932	...	...	|	...	|	...	|	...	|	|	...	2032	|	|	...	|
Lenzburg **510** d.	|	|	...	|	...	|	|	|	...	...	|	...	|	...	|	...	|	|	...	|	|	|	...	|
Aarau **510** d.	|	|	...	|	...	|	1930	1946	...	...	|	...	|	...	|	...	|	2030	...	2046	|	|	...	|
Olten a.	|	1900	...	|	...	1928	1938	1955	...	...	|	...	2000	...	|	...	2028	2038	...	2055	|	2100	...	|
Olten d.	|	1902	1906	|	...	1936	1940	1956	...	...	|	...	2002	2006	|	...	2036	2040	...	2056	|	2102	2106	|
Langenthal d.	|	|	1918	|	...	1948	|	|	...	...	|	...	|	2018	|	...	2048	|	...	|	|	|	2118	|
Burgdorf d.	|	|	1938	|	...	2006	|	|	...	...	|	...	|	2038	|	...	2106	|	...	|	|	|	2138	|
Luzern **565** d.	|	|	|	|	1900	|	|	|	...	...	|	...	|	|	|	2000	|	|	...	|	|	|	|	|
Bern a.	1928	|	1953	1958	2000	2021	|	2024	...	...	2028	...	|	2053	2058	2100	2121	|	...	2124	2128	|	2153	2158
Bern **568** d.	1934	|	▬	...	2004	...	|	▬	...	...	2034	...	|	▬	▬	2104	...	|	...	▬	2134	|	▬	▬
Fribourg **568** d.	1956	|	...	...	2026	...	|	...	...	...	2056	...	|	...	...	2126	...	|	...	...	2156	|	...	...
Romont **568** d.	|	|	...	...	2044	...	|	...	...	...	|	...	|	...	...	2144	...	|	...	...	|	|	...	...
Palézieux d.	|	|	...	...	2100	...	|	...	...	...	|	...	|	...	...	2200	...	|	...	...	|	|	...	...
Solothurn d.	|	1926	...	...	|	...	1958	...	...	...	|	...	2026	...	...	|	...	2058	...	...	|	2126	...	...
Biel / Bienne a.	|	1943	...	...	|	...	2013	...	...	...	|	...	2043	...	...	|	...	2113	...	...	|	2143	...	...
Biel / Bienne d.	|	1945	*RE*	...	|	...	2016	*RE*	...	...	|	...	2045	*RE*	*RE*	|	...	2116	...	...	|	2145	*RE*	*RE*
Neuchâtel d.	|	2003	**18482**	...	|	...	2034	**18436**	...	...	|	...	2103	**18484**	**18484**	|	...	2134	...	...	|	2203	**18486**	**18486**
Yverdon d.	|	2023		...	|	...	2054	⑤⑥	...	2100	|	...	2123	⑤⑥	⑦–④	|	...	2154	...	2200	|	2223	⑤⑥	⑦–④
Lausanne a.	2040	2045		...	2116	...	|		...	2134	2140	...	2145			2216	...	|	...	2234	2240	2245		
Lausanne **570** d.	2043	...	2051	...	2119k	...	|	2121	2121	...	...	2148	...	2151	2151	...	...	|	2221	...	2243k	...	2251	2251
Morges **570** d.	|	...	2105	...	2129k	...	2118	2135	2135	...	...	2159	...	2205	2205	...	...	2218	2235	...	|	...	2305	2305
Nyon **570** d.	|	...	2125	...	2146k	...	|	2155	2200	...	...	2216	...	2225	2229	...	...	2233k	2255t	...	|	...	2325	2329
Genève **570** a.	2118	...	2144	...	2201k	...	2147k	2210	2223	...	...	2231	...	2240	2254	...	...	2247k	2310t	...	2318k	...	2340	2349
Genève Aéroport ✈ **570** a.	2127	...	2149c	...	2211k	...	...	...	...	...	...	2241	...	2249	2300	...	...	...	2318t	...	2327k	...	2349	2357

	IR 2538	IR 2386	RE 18440 ⑦–④	IC 538	IR 2188	IC 736	IC 1538	IR 2840	IC 836	IR 2540	IR 2394	IC 540	IR 2190	IC 738	IC 838	IR 2502	IR 2502	IR 2396	IC 542	IR 2192	IC 740	IC 842	IR 2846 ⑥⑦	IC 844 ⑥⑦
	¶			R		✗		⊙			◇			✗			★	◇					h ⊙	h
Romanshorn **535** d.	...	...	...	...	...	...	...	...	2048	...	...	...	...	...	2148	...	...	...	...	...	...	...	...	...
St Gallen **530** d.	...	...	...	1958	...	2007	...	...	|	...	...	...	...	2107	|	...	...	...	...	...	...	...	...	...
Zürich Flughafen ✈ **530/5** d.	...	...	...	2048	...	2108	...	...	2145	...	...	...	...	2208	2245	...	...	...	...	...	...	...	...	...
Zürich HB **510** d.	...	2055	...	2104	2106	2132	2130	...	2202	...	...	2204	2206	2232	2302	...	...	...	2304	2306	2332	0002	...	0102
Baden **510** d.	...	|	...	|	2122	|	|	...	|	...	...	|	2222	|	|	...	...	...	|	2322	|	|	...	|
Brugg **510** d.	...	|	...	|	2132	|	|	...	|	...	...	|	2232	|	|	...	...	...	|	2332	|	|	...	|
Lenzburg **510** d.	...	|	...	|	|	|	|	...	|	...	...	|	|	|	|	...	...	...	|	|	|	|	...	|
Aarau **510** d.	...	|	...	2130	2146	|	|	...	|	...	...	2230	2246	|	|	...	...	...	2330	2346	|	|	...	|
Olten a.	...	2128	...	2138	2155	|	2200	...	2232	...	...	2238	2256	2302	2332	...	...	...	2338	2356	0002	0032	...	0132
Olten d.	...	2136	...	2140	2156	|	2202	2206	2235	...	2237	2240	▬	2304	2335	...	...	2337	2340	▬	0004	0035	0037	0135
Langenthal d.	...	2148	...	|	|	|	|	2218	|	...	2249	|	...	|	|	...	...	2349	|	...	|	|	0049	|
Burgdorf d.	...	2209	...	|	|	|	|	2236	|	...	2309	|	...	|	|	...	...	0009	|	...	|	|	0110	|
Luzern **565** d.	2100	|	...	|	|	|	|	|	|	2200	|	|	...	|	|	...	...	|	|	...	|	|	|	|
Bern a.	2200	2226	...	|	2224	2228	|	2253	2302	2300	2326	|	...	2331	0002	...	...	0026	|	...	0031	0104g	0126	0204
Bern **568** d.	2204	▬	...	|	...	2234	|	▬	▬	2308	...	|	...	▬	...	0008	0008	...	|	...	...	...	...	...
Fribourg **568** d.	2226	...	...	|	...	2256	|	...	...	2330	...	|	...	...	...	0032	0033	...	|	...	...	...	...	...
Romont **568** d.	2244	...	...	|	...	...	|	...	...	2348	...	|	...	...	...	...	0050	...	|	...	...	...	...	...
Palézieux d.	2300	...	...	|	...	...	|	...	...	0004	...	|	...	...	...	...	0106	...	|	...	...	...	...	...
Solothurn d.	|	...	...	2158	...	...	2226	...	...	|	...	2257	...	...	...	...	|	...	0005	...	...	...	...	...
Biel / Bienne a.	|	...	...	2213	...	...	2243	...	...	|	...	2314	...	...	...	...	|	...	0022	...	...	...	...	...
Biel / Bienne d.	|	*RE*	...	...	...	...	2245	*RE*	*RE*	|	...	2316	*RE*	*RE*	...	...	|	...	0024h	*RE*	...	...	...	...
Neuchâtel d.	|	**18440**	...	...	...	...	2303	**18488**	**18488**	|	...	2334	**18442**	**18444**	...	...	|	...	0042h	**18446**	...	...	...	...
Yverdon d.	|	⑤⑥	...	...	...	...	2323	⑤⑥	⑦–④	|	...	2354	①–⑤	⑥⑦	...	...	|	...	0102h	⑥⑦	...	...	...	...
Lausanne a.	2316		...	...	...	...	2345			0020	...	0016			...	...	0122	...	0125h		...	...	...	...
Lausanne **570** d.	...	2321	2321	...	...	...	...	2351	2351	...	...	...	0025	0051	...	...	...	...	...	0135	...	...	...	...
Morges **570** d.	...	2335	2335	...	...	...	...	0005	0005	...	...	...	0039	0105	...	...	...	...	...	0148	...	...	...	...
Nyon **570** d.	...	2355	0000	...	...	...	...	0025	0029	...	...	...	0101	0125	...	...	...	...	...	0208	...	...	...	...
Genève **570** a.	...	0010	0017	...	...	...	...	0042	0045	...	...	...	0117	0140	...	...	...	...	...	0224	...	...	...	...
Genève Aéroport ✈ **570** a.	...	...	...	...	...	...	...	0049	...	...	...	...	...	...	...	...	...	...	...	...	...	...	...	...

A – To Interlaken (Table **560**).
H – From Chur (Table **520**).
R – From Rorschach (Table **530**).

a – Ⓐ only.
c – Ⓒ only.
g – On the mornings of ① (not Dec. 26, Jan. 2, Apr. 10, May 8, 29, June 12, 26, Aug. 14, 21, Oct. 2, 9) change trains at Zollikofen (a. 0109, d. *0114*), Bern a. *0122*.
h – Mornings of ⑥⑦ (not Dec. 25, Apr. 8).

k – ⑤⑥ only.
t – 4 – 13 minutes later on ⑦–④.

★ – Mornings of ①⑥⑦.
◐ – Conveys ✗ until Biel/Bienne.
¶ – Runs as *IC* **1490** on † Feb 12 - June 4.
⊙ – Operated by BLS.
◇ – Operated by SOB.

SBB BIEL/BIENNE and PORRENTRUY - BASEL 505a

km		IC 1545	⑥⑦			IC 1607			IC 1609			IC 1611				IC 1637			IC 1639			IC 1641		
		L	c					D			D				D			D			D			
0	**Biel / Bienne** **515** d.	0019	0121	...	...	0549	...	0619	0649	...	0719	0749	and at	...	2019	2049	...	2119	2149	...	2219	2249	...	2319
24	Moutier **515** d.	0039	0138	...	...	0608	...	0638	0708	...	0738	0808	the same	...	2038	2108	...	2138	2208	...	2238	2308	...	2338
	Porrentruy **515** d.	|	|	...	0508	|	0610	|	|	0710	|	|	minutes	2010	|	|	2110	|	|	2210	|	|	2310	|
35	Delémont **515** a.	0048	0148	...	0539	0618	0639	0648	0718	0739	0748	0818	past each	2039	2048	2118	2139	2148	2218	2239	2248	2318	2339	2348
	Delémont d.	...	...	...	0543	0623	0643	...	0723	0743	...	0823	hour until	2043	...	2123	2143	...	2223	2243	...	2323	2343	...
74	**Basel** SBB a.	...	...	...	0623	0655	0723	...	0755	0823	...	0855		2123	...	2155	2223	...	2255	2323	...	2355	0028	...

			IC 1606			IC 1608			IC 1610				IC 1636			IC 1638			IC 1640		IC 1642	⑤⑥		
			G	D			D			D				D			D					k		
Basel SBB d.	...	0457	...	...	0537	0603	...	0637	0703	...	0737	and at	2003	...	2037	2103	...	2137	2203	2237	2303	...	2342	0042
Delémont a.	...	0537	...	...	0617	0637	...	0717	0737	...	0817	the same	2037	...	2117	2137	...	2217	2237	2317	2337	...	0022	0122
Delémont **515** d.	0512	*0551*	0542	0612	0621	0642	0712	0721	0742	0812	0821	minutes	2042	2111	2121	2142	2212	2221	2242	2321	*2351*	2342	0023	...
Porrentruy **515** a.	|	*0620*	|	|	0650	|	|	0750	|	|	0850	past each	|	|	2150	|	|	2250	|	2350	*0020*	|	0052	...
Moutier **515** d.	0522	...	0552	0622	...	0652	0722	...	0752	0822	...	hour until	2052	2122	...	2152	2222	...	2252	...	...	2354	...	...
Biel / Bienne **515** d.	0541	...	0610	0641	...	0710	0741	...	0810	0841	...		2110	2141	...	2210	2241	...	2310	...	...	0013	...	...

D – To / from Delle (Table **515**).
G – To Genève Aéroport (Table **505**).
L – From Lausanne (Table **505**).

c – Not Dec. 25, Apr. 8.
k – Not Dec. 24, Apr. 7.

506 LAC LÉMAN CGN

GENÈVE - YVOIRE - LAUSANNE ⊡

	⛴ D	⛴ G	A	C	⛴ E	ⒸE	⛴ D	⛴ G	J	⛴ E	⛴ E
Genève Mont-Blanc d.	1045	1045	1235	...	...	...	1445	1445	...	...	...
Genève Jardin-Anglais d.	|	|	|	1235	1235	...	|	|	1900	1900	...
Nyon d.	1205	1205	1345	|	|	...	|	|	|	|	...
Yvoire (France) d.	1225	1245	...	1400	1400	1445	1610	1615	2032	2032	2037
Morges d.	...	1356	...	...	...	1556	...	1731	...	...	2152
Lausanne-Ouchy a.	...	1433	...	...	...	1633	...	1808	...	...	2230

	⛴ G	⛴ D	A	C	⛴ E	ⒸE	⛴ G	⛴ D	⛴ E	⛴ E	J
Lausanne-Ouchy d.	1055	...	...	...	...	1255	1455	...	1855	...	...
Morges d.	1131	...	...	...	...	1331	1531	...	1931	...	...
Yvoire (France) d.	1250	1250	...	1405	1405	1441	1645	1645	2030	2035	2035
Nyon d.	1315	1315	1350	|	|	...	1712	1712	...	2055	2055
Genève Jardin-Ang. a.	|	|	|	1520	1520	...	|	|	...	2220	2220
Genève Mont-Blanc a.	1430	1413	1505	...	...	...	1835	1835	...	...	...

LAUSANNE - ST GUINGOLPH

	D	⛴ E	D	A		⛴ C	E	AD		E	⛴ H	A	⛴ E	AD		⛴ D	E	⛴ E	A	D		E		⛴ D		
Lausanne-Ouchy d.	0910	0940	←	...	...	1040	1040	...	...	1240	1240	1240	1245	...	...	1445	1450	1545	...	...	...	1650	...	1815	...	...
Vevey-Marché d.	1000	|	1002	...	...	1131	1131	1145	...	|	|	1338	|	1345	...	|	|	|	1545	1545	...	1745	...	1905	...	...
Vevey-La Tour d.	→	|	|	...	...	...	...	1150	...	1333	1343	|	|	1350	...	|	1543	|	1550	1550	...	|	...	|	...	...
Montreux d.	...	|	1025	...	...	...	...	1220	...	...	...	|	|	1420	...	|	...	|	1620	1620	...	1808	...	1925	...	...
Territet d.	...	|	|	...	...	...	...	1227	...	...	...	|	|	1427	...	|	...	|	1627	1627	...	|	...	...	...	...
Château-de-Chillon d.	...	|	1035	...	...	...	...	1235	...	...	...	|	|	1435	...	|	...	|	1635	1635	...	|	...	...	...	...
Villeneuve d.	...	|	1043	...	...	...	...	1243	...	...	...	1404	|	1443	...	|	...	|	1643	1643	...	1822	...	...	...	...
Bouveret d.	...	|	1105	1105	...	...	...	1305	...	...	...	...	|	1505	...	|	...	|	1705	1705	...	1844	...	...	...	...
St Gingolph a.	...	1030	1118	1118	...	...	...	1318	...	...	...	...	1335	1518	...	1535	...	1635	...	1718	...	...	...	...	...	...

	E		⛴ C	E	⛴ E	AD		AD	⛴ H	E		⛴ E	A		AD	E		⛴ D		⛴ E	D		⛴ D			
St Gingolph d.	...	...	...	...	1030	1118	...	1318	...	...	...	1335	...	...	1518	...	...	1535	...	1635	1718	...	...	...	...	...
Bouveret d.	0905	...	...	...	1043	|	...	|	...	...	...	1348	...	...	|	...	...	1548	...	1648	|	...	...	...	...	...
Villeneuve d.	|	...	...	...	1104	|	...	|	...	...	...	1409	1409	...	|	...	...	|	...	1709	|	...	...	...	...	...
Château-de-Chillon d.	|	...	...	...	1112	|	...	|	...	...	...	1417	1417	...	|	...	...	1617	...	1717	1744	...	...	...	...	...
Territet d.	|	...	...	...	|	|	...	|	...	...	...	|	|	...	|	...	...	|	...	|	|	...	...	...	...	...
Montreux d.	0930	...	...	...	1130	|	...	|	...	...	...	1430	1430	...	|	...	...	1630	...	1730	1755	...	1927	...	...	...
Vevey-La Tour d.	|	...	...	...	|	|	...	|	1345	1345	...	|	|	...	|	1545	...	|	...	|	|	...	|	...	...	...
Vevey-Marché d.	0952	...	1135	1135	1152	1140	...	1340	1352	1352	...	1452	1452	...	1540	1552	...	1652	...	1752	1815	...	|	...	...	...
Lausanne-Ouchy a.	1037	...	1227	1227	1237	...	...	...	1442	1442	...	1537	1555	...	...	1644	...	1755	...	1842	1905	...	2030	...	...	...

LAUSANNE - ÉVIAN-LES-BAINS (France) *See notes ⊡ and ⊠*

	L									M	N
Lausanne-Ouchy d.	0740	0925	1100	1230	1400	1530	1715	1840	2000	2130	2235
Évian les Bains a.	0815	1000	1135	1305	1435	1605	1750	1915	2035	2150	2255

	L									M	N
Évian les Bains d.	0820	1005	1145	1315	1445	1615	1800	1920	2045	2200	2256
Lausanne-Ouchy a.	0855	1040	1220	1350	1520	1650	1835	1955	2120	2220	2345

A – ⑦ to Apr. 16 (also Jan. 2, Apr. 7, 10); ⑦ from Oct. 29.
C – Ⓒ Apr. 22 - June 17; ⑥⑦ Sept. 9 - Oct. 22 (also Sept. 18).
D – Apr. 22 - Oct. 22.
E – June 18 - Sept. 3.
G – Ⓒ Apr. 22 - June 11; daily June 17 - Sept. 3; ⑥⑦ Sept. 9 - Oct. 22 (also Sept. 18).
H – Apr. 22 - June 17 and Sept. 4 - Oct. 22.
J – May 25 - June 17 and Sept. 4 – 23.
L – ⚒ to June 10 (also Dec. 26); daily June 12 - Sept. 3.
M – Ⓐ to Apr. 14 (also Dec. 26); ⚒ Apr. 17 - June 10; daily June 12 - Sept. 3.
N – Ⓐ to June 16 (also Dec. 26); daily June 18 - Sept. 3.
P – ①–⑥ June 19 - Sept. 3 (not Aug. 1).
Q – Mornings of Ⓑ June 20 - Sept. 4 (not Aug. 2).

r – Also Dec. 26. t – Not Sept. 18.

⊡ – **Service shown in the table is valid until September 3** (Swiss holiday dates apply). A more frequent service is planned **from Sept. 4** as follows: **From Lausanne** at 0445 ⚒ t, 0530 Ⓐ t, 0615 ⚒ t, 0700 Ⓐ t, 0805, 0905 Ⓐ t, 1005, 1105 Ⓐ t, 1205, 1305 Ⓐ t, 1405, 1505 Ⓐ t, 1605, 1650 Ⓐ t, 1735, 1820 Ⓐ t, 1905, 1950 Ⓐ t, 2035, 2135 and 2235 Ⓐ t. **From Évian les Bains** at 0530 ⚒ t, 0615 Ⓐ t, 0700 ⚒ t, 0745 Ⓐ t, 0845, 0945 Ⓐ t, 1045, 1145 Ⓐ t, 1245, 1345 Ⓐ t, 1445, 1545 Ⓐ t, 1645, 1730 Ⓐ t, 1815, 1900 Ⓐ t, 1945, 2030 Ⓐ t, 2105, 2205 and 2305 Ⓐ t.
⊠ – Additional sailings: **From Lausanne** at 0455 ⚒ r, 0620 ⚒ r and 2350 **P**. **From Évian-les-Bains** at 0010 **Q**, 0540 ⚒ r and 0700 ⚒ r.
⛴ – Normally operated by historic steamship.

Operator: CGN – Compagnie Générale de Navigation ✆ +41 (0) 848 811 848 (www.cgn.ch).

507 VIERWALDSTÄTTERSEE SGV

SERVICE UNTIL APRIL 14

	Ⓐ						c				Ⓐ
Luzern (Bahnhofquai) d.	0620	0912	1012	1112	1200	...	1300	1412	1512	1612	1712
Verkehrshaus Lido d.	|	0922	1022	1122	1210	...	|	1422	1522	1622	|
Weggis d.	0659	0953	1053	1153	1240	...	|	1453	1553	1653	1747
Vitznau d.	▬	1010	1110	1209	1254	1309	1348	1510	1610	1710	...
Beckenried a.	...	1026	1126	...	...	1325	...	1526	1626	1726	...
Beckenried d.	...	*1027*	1127	...	...	1326	...	...	*1627*	*1727*	...
Gersau d.	...	*1045*	1145	...	...	1344	...	...	*1645*	*1745*	...
Treib d.	0902	*1102*	1202	...	...	1401	...	...	*1702*	*1802*	...
Brunnen d.	0911	*1111*	1211	...	...	1410	...	...	*1709*	*1809*	...
Rütli d.	0921	*1121*	1221	...	...	1420**c**	...	...	...	...	...
Sisikon d.	...	...	|	...	...	|	...	...	...	...	...
Tellsplatte d.	...	...	|	...	...	|	...	...	...	...	...
Bauen d.	...	...	1235	...	...	1434**c**	...	...	...	...	...
Flüelen a.	...	...	1255	...	...	1456**c**	...	...	...	...	...

	Ⓐ						c			Ⓐ	
Flüelen d.	...	...	...	...	...	...	1300	...	1500**c**	...	...
Bauen d.	...	...	...	...	...	...	|	...	1521**c**	...	...
Tellsplatte d.	...	...	...	...	...	...	1316	...	|	...	...
Sisikon d.	...	...	...	...	...	...	1324	...	|	...	...
Rütli d.	...	...	...	...	...	...	1336	...	1536	...	...
Brunnen d.	...	*0949*	...	1149	...	...	1349	...	1549	...	...
Treib d.	...	*0957*	...	1157	...	...	1357	...	1557	...	...
Gersau d.	...	*1014*	...	1214	...	...	1414	...	1614	...	...
Beckenried a.	...	*1026*	...	1226	...	...	1426	...	1626	...	...
Beckenried d.	...	1032	...	1232	...	...	1432	1532	*1632*	...	1732
Vitznau d.	...	1049	1210	1248	1256	1349	1449	1549	*1649*	...	1749
Weggis d.	0707	1105	|	...	1312	1405	1505	1605	*1705*	1749	1805
Verkehrshaus Lido d.	|	|	|	...	1335	1435	1535	1635	*1735*	|	|
Luzern (Bahnhofquai) a.	0742	1141	1255	...	1347	1447	1547	1647	*1747*	1825	1841

SERVICE APRIL 15 - MAY 26

	Ⓐ			⊙		⛴									
Luzern (Bahnhofquai) d.	0620	...	...	0912	1012	1112	1200	...	1312	1412	1512	...	1612	1712	...
Verkehrshaus Lido d.	|	...	...	0922	1022	1122	1210	...	1322	1422	1522	...	1622	|	...
Weggis d.	0659	...	...	0953	1053	1153	1240	...	1353	1453	1553	...	1653	1747	...
Vitznau d.	...	...	...	1010	1110	1210	1254	1310	1410	1510	1610	...	1710	...	...
Beckenried d.	...	...	...	1027	1127	1227	...	1327	1427	1527	1626	1627	1800	...	...
Gersau d.	...	...	...	1045	1145	1245	...	1345	1445	1545	...	1645	1817	...	...
Treib d.	...	0828	...	1102	1202	1302	...	1402	1502	1602	...	1702	1834	...	...
Brunnen d.	...	0836	...	1111	1211	1311	...	1411	1511	1611	...	1709	1841	...	...
Rütli d.	...	0846	...	1121	1221	1321	...	1421	1521	1621	...	...	...	...	...
Sisikon d.	...	...	...	|	|	1332	...	|	|	1632	...	...	...	...	...
Tellsplatte d.	...	...	...	|	|	1339	...	|	|	1639	...	...	...	...	...
Bauen d.	...	...	...	1135	1235	|	...	1435	1535	1649	...	...	...	...	...
Flüelen a.	...	...	...	1155	1255	1355t	...	1455	1555	1708	...	...	...	...	...

	Ⓐ							⊙		⛴					
Flüelen d.	...	...	...	...	0948	...	...	1200t	1300	1400	1500	...	...	1600	...
Bauen d.	...	...	...	...	1008	...	...	|	1321	1421	1521	...	...	1621	...
Tellsplatte d.	...	...	...	...	1018	...	...	1216	|	|	|	...	...	|	...
Sisikon d.	...	...	...	...	1025	...	...	1224	|	|	|	...	...	|	...
Rütli d.	...	...	...	...	1036	...	...	1236	1336	1436	1536	...	...	1636	...
Brunnen d.	...	...	0919	...	1049	1149	...	1249	1349	1449	1549	...	...	1649	...
Treib d.	...	...	0927	...	1057	1157	...	1257	1357	1457	1557	...	...	1657	...
Gersau d.	...	...	0942	...	1114	1214	...	1314	1414	1514	1614	...	...	1714	...
Beckenried d.	...	...	1000	...	1132	1232	...	1332	1432	1532	1626	1632	...	1732	...
Vitznau d.	...	...	1049	...	1149	1248	1256	1349	1449	1549	...	1649	...	1749	...
Weggis d.	0707	...	1105	...	1205	...	1312	1405	1505	1605	...	1705	1749	1805	...
Verkehrshaus Lido d.	|	...	|	...	1235	...	1335	1435	1535	1635	...	1735	|	1835	...
Luzern (Bahnhofquai) a.	0742	...	1147	...	1247	...	1347	1447	1547	1647	...	1747	1825	1847	...

c – ⑥⑦ to Mar. 5 (daily Dec. 24 - Jan. 2); daily from Mar. 11.
t – Connects with Gotthard Panorama Express train service to/from Lugano on ②–⑦ Apr. 15 - Oct. 22 (see panel in Table **547**). All-inclusive tour packages available.

¶ – Sails daily Vitznau - Brunnen.
⊙ – Operated by ⛴ on ✝.
⛴ – Normally operated by historic steamship.

Operator: SGV – Schifffahrtsgesellschaft Vierwaldstättersee ✆ +41 (0) 41 367 67 67 (www.lakelucerne.ch).

OTHER SWISS LAKES 508

ZÜRICHSEE (operator: ZSG)

	B	†w	C	A	D	L		D	R	R
Zürich (Bürkliplatz) d.	0920	1010	1020	1120	1120	1220	1320	1420	1520	1730
Erlenbach d.	0956	|	|	|	1156	|	1356	|	1556	|
Thalwil d.	|	|	1054	1154	|	1254	|	1454	|	1805
Wädenswil d.	1038	1118	|	|	1238	|	1438	|	1638	1900
Rapperswil a.	1125	...	1220	1320	1325	1420	1525	1620	1725	1950

	†w	U	C	A	D	L		D	C	R
Rapperswil d.	...	1135	1230	1330	1335	1430	1535	1630	1735	1955
Wädenswil d.	1119	1220	|	|	1420	|	1620	|	1820	2046
Thalwil d.	|	|	1357	1457	|	1557	|	1757	|	2133
Erlenbach d.	|	1302	|	|	1502	|	1702	|	1902	|
Zürich (Bürkliplatz) a.	1230	1335	1430	1530	1535	1630	1735	1830	1935	2210

BRIENZERSEE (operator: BLS)

	S	K	S ⛴	S	K	K	S ⛴	K	S	T ⛴
Interlaken Ost d.	0907	1007	1107	1207	1207	1307	1407	1507	1607	1907
Iseltwald d.	0952	1046	1152	1246	1252	1352	1452	1552	1652	1952
Brienz a.	1020	1120	1220	1320	1320	1420	1520	1620	1720	2020

	S	K	S ⛴	K	P	S ⛴	K	S		T ⛴
Brienz d.	1040	1140	1240	1340	1440	1540	1640	1740	...	2040
Iseltwald d.	1117	1208	1308	1408	1517	1608	1708	1817	...	2108
Interlaken Ost a.	1153	1253	1353	1453	1553	1653	1753	1853	...	2153

THUNERSEE (operator: BLS)

	F	⑦H	Q	M		N ⛴	M	J	F	F	E ⛴
Thun d.	0840	0940	0940	1040	1140	1240	1340	1440	1440	1540	1840
Oberhofen d.	|	1003	1003	1106	1203	1303	1406	|	1503	1603	1903
Spiez d.	0928	1024	1028	1150	1228	1328	1450	1528	1528	1628	1928
Beatenbucht d.	0954	...	1102	...	1302	1402	...	1552	1602	1702	2002
Interlaken West a.	1049	...	1149	...	1349	1449	...	...	1649	1749	...

	⑦H	M	F	Q	M		J	N ⛴	F	F	E ⛴
Interlaken West d.	...	...	1110	1210	...	1410	...	1510	1710	1810	...
Beatenbucht d.	...	...	1158	1258	...	1458	1553	1558	1758	1910	2004
Spiez d.	1026	1200	1234	1334	1500	1534	1614	1634	1834	1934	2034
Oberhofen d.	1047	1241	1257	1357	1541	1557	1649	1657	|	1957	2057
Thun a.	1110	1310	1320	1420	1610	1620	1712	1720	1920	2015	2120

A – Until Apr. 1 and from Oct. 23.
B – © Apr. 2 - June 25 (also May 1); daily July 1 - Aug. 31; ⑥⑦ Sept. 2 - Oct. 22.
C – © Apr. 2–23; daily Apr. 29 - Oct. 1; ⑥⑦ Oct. 7–22.
D – Apr. 2 - Oct. 22.
E – ②–⑥ May 18 - Sept. 16 (also May 6, 13; not Aug. 1).
F – May 18 - Oct. 22.
H – ⑦ Dec. 11 - Apr. 2 (not Jan. 1); ⑦ Nov. 19 - Dec. 3.
J – Apr. 7 - May 17 and Oct. 23 - Nov. 12.
K – Apr. 7 - May 17 and Sept. 18 - Oct. 22.
L – July 1 - Aug. 31.
M – ⑤–⑦ Feb. 17 - Apr. 2.
N – Daily Dec. 25 - Jan. 2; ⑥⑦ May 6–14; daily May 18 - Oct. 22.
P – Apr. 7 - Oct. 22.
Q – Apr. 7 - Nov. 12.
R – May 1 - Sept. 30.
S – May 18 - Sept. 17.
T – ⑥ June 17 - Aug. 26.
U – © May 6 - June 25 (also May 1); daily July 1 - Aug. 31; ⑥⑦ Sept. 2–30.
w – Also May 1; not Dec. 25, Jan. 1.
⛴ – Operated by historic steamship.

Operators:
BLS – Schifffahrt Berner Oberland ✆ +41 (0) 58 327 48 11 (www.bls.ch).
ZSG – Zürichsee Schifffahrtsgesellschaft ✆ +41 (0) 44 487 13 33 (www.zsg.ch).

TPF FRIBOURG - MURTEN - INS - NEUCHÂTEL 509

Warning! Services are subject to alteration March 20 - August 23.

km		⚒	⚒								
0	**Fribourg** d.	0454	0531	0601	0631	and at the	2101	2131	2201	2231	2334
22	Murten d.	0525	0602	0632	0702	same minutes	2132	2202	2232	2302	0005
32	Ins 511 d.	0539	0612	0644	0712	past each	2144	2212	2244	2314	0017z
45	**Neuchâtel** 511 a.	...	0625	...	0725	hour until	...	2225	...	...	...

	⚒		⚒						
Neuchâtel 511 d.	*0532*	...	0634	...	0734	and at the	...	2234	...
Ins 511 d.	0546	0612	0646	0712	0746	same minutes	2212	2246	2319
Murten d.	0556	0626	0656	0726	0756	past each	2226	2256	2330
Fribourg a.	0630	0700	0730	0800	0830	hour until	2300	2330	0001

z – Murten - Ins on the mornings of ⑥⑦ only.

SBB BASEL - ZÜRICH 510

Non-stop *IC*, *ICE* and *TGV* services.

km		*IC* 551	*IC* 1251	*IC* 559	*IC* 1253	*IC* 561	*ICE* 3	*IC* 1255	*IC* 563	*ICE* 271 1271	*IC* 565	*IC* 767	*TGV* 9203	*IC* 769	*IC* 569	*IC* 771	*IC* 591	*IC* 571	*ICE* 71	*TGV* 9211	*IC* 775	*IC* 575	*ICE* 73	*ICE* 73	*TGV* 9213	*EC* 9	*IC* 579
			✕	✕	✕	✕	①–⑤ L✕	⑥⑦ c✕	✕	G✕	✕	✕	P⊗	✕	✕		Ⓐ ✕	© ✕	G✕	P⊗	✕	✕	© G✕	Ⓐ G✕	P⊗	G✕	✕
0	**Basel** SBB d.	0533	0606	0633	0706	0733	0806	0806	0833	0906	0933	1006	1033	1106	1133	1206	1233	1233	1306	1333	1406	1433	1506	1506	1533	1606	1633
91	**Zürich** HB a.	0626	0700	0726	0800	0826	0900	0900	0926	1000	1026	1100	1126	1200	1226	1300	1326	1326	1400	1426	1500	1526	1600	1600	1626	1700	1726
	Chur 520 a.	...	...	0852	0922	0952	1022z	1022v	1052	1122	1152	...	...	...	1352	...	...	1452	1522	...	...	1652	1722	...	...	...	1852

	ICE 75	*IC* 581	*IC* 595	*TGV* 9215	*IC* 783	*IC* 583	*ICE* 77	*TGV* 9219	*IC* 787	*IC* 587	*ICE* 79	*TGV* 9223	*IC* 791	*IC* 793
	G✕	Ⓐd ✕	T	©s P⊗		✕	G✕	P⊗	✕	✕	G	P⊗	⑤⑥ k	⑤⑥ k
Basel SBB d.	1706	1733	1733	1733	1806	1833	1906	1933	2006	2033	2106	2133	2206	2306
Zürich HB a.	1800	1826	1826	1826	1900	1926	2000	2026	2100	2126	2200	2226	2300	2400
Chur 520 a.	1922	1952	...	...	...	2052	...	...	...	2252r	...	...	...	...

	ICE 78		*IC* 556	*IC* 556	*IC* 760	*TGV* 9206	*ICE* 76	*IC* 560	*IC* 764
	G		✕	⚒ ✕	✕	P	G	✕	✕
Chur 520 d.	...	...	...	0508	...	...	...	0708	...
Zürich HB d.	0559	...	0634	0634	0659	0734	0759	0834	0859
Basel SBB a.	0653	...	0728	0728	0753	0828	0853	0928	0953

	IC 552	*TGV* 9210	*ICE* 74	*IC* 564	*EC* 8	*TGV* 9218	*ICE* 72	*IC* 568	*IC* 772	*TGV* 9222	*ICE* 70	*IC* 572	*IC* 776	*TGV* 9226	*IC* 576	*ICE* 272 292	*IC* 578	*IC* 578	*IC* 782	*TGV* 9234	*ICE* 4	*ICE* 4	*IC* 582	*IC* 584	*IC* 60470	*IC* 1258	*IC* 792
	Q	w P	G	✕	G✕	P	G	✕	✕	P	G	✕		P	✕	G	✕	Ⓐ ✕	✕	P	G✕	© G✕	✕	✕	G		⑤⑥ k
Chur 520 d.	...	...	...	0908	...	...	1037	1108	...	...	1237	1308	...	...	1508	...	...	1608	...	...	...	1737	1808	1908	...	2008	...
Zürich HB d.	0934	0934	0959	1034	1059	1134	1159	1234	1259	1334	1359	1434	1459	1534	1634	1659	1734	1734	1759	1834	1859	1859	1934	2034	2059	2134	2259
Basel SBB a.	1028	1028	1053	1128	1153	1228	1253	1328	1353	1428	1453	1528	1553	1628	1728	1753	1828	1828	1853	1928	1953	1953	2028	2128	2153	2228	2353

IR and *RE* services

km																							
0	**Basel** SBB d.	0437	...	0511	0537	0543	...	and at	1911	1937	1943	...	2011	2043	...	2111	2143	...	2211	2243	...	2311	...	0011
17	Rheinfelden d.	0450	...	0525	0550	|	...	the same	1925	1950	|	...	2025	|	...	2125	|	...	2225	|	...	2325	...	0025
57	Brugg 505 d.	0520	...	0600	0620	|	...		2000	2020	|	...	2100	|	...	2200	|	...	2300	|	...	0000	...	0100
66	Baden 505 d.	0529	...	0608	0629	|	...	minutes	2008	2029	|	...	2108	|	...	2208	|	...	2308	|	...	0008	...	0108
	Liestal d.	|	...	|	|	0554	...		|	|	1954	...	|	2054	...	|	2154	...	|	2254	...	|	...	|
	Aarau 505 d.	|	...	|	|	0623	0654	past each	|	|	2023	2054	|	2123	2154	|	2223	2254	|	2323	...	|	...	|
	Lenzburg 505 d.	|	...	|	|	0630	0701	hour until	|	|	2030	2101	|	2130	2201	|	2230	2301	|	2330	...	|	...	|
88	**Zürich** HB 505 530 535 a.	0549	...	0624	0649	0652	0722		2024	2049	2052	2122	2124	2152	2222	2224	2252	2322	2324	2352	...	0024	...	0124
	Zürich Flughafen ✈ 530 535 a.	0604	...	...	0704	...	...		...	2104	...	...	...	...	...	...	...	...	...	...	...	...	...	...

km		⑥⑦ j																						
	Zürich Flughafen ✈ 530 535 d.	...	...	...	...	0556	...	...	...	0656	...	...		...	2056	...	...	...	...	...	...	...	...	...
0	**Zürich** HB 505 530 535 d.	0108	0508	0535	0608	0610	0636	0638	0708	0710	0736	0738	and at	2108	2110	2136	2138	2208	2236	2238	2308	2336	2338	0008
32	Lenzburg 505 d.	0129	0529	|	0629	|	|	0659	0729	|	|	0759	the same	2129	|	|	2159	2229	|	2259	2329	|	2359	0029
41	**Aarau** 505 d.	0136	0536	|	0636	|	|	0705	0736	|	|	0805		2136	|	|	2205	2236	|	2305	2336	|	0005	0036
77	Liestal d.	0202	0602	|	0702	|	|	...	0802	|	|	...	minutes	2202	|	|	...	2302	|	...	0002	|	...	0102
	Baden 505 d.	|	|	0551	|	0632	0652	...	|	0732	0752	...	past each	|	2132	2152	...	|	2252	...	|	2352	...	|
	Brugg 505 d.	|	|	0600	|	0641	0702	...	|	0741	0802	...		|	2141	2202	...	|	2302	...	|	0002	...	|
	Rheinfelden d.	|	|	0634	|	0713	0734	...	|	0810	0834	...	hour until	|	2210	2234	...	|	2334	...	|	0034	...	|
91	**Basel** SBB a.	0213	0613	0650	0713	0732	0748	...	0813	0824	0848	...		2213	2224	2248	...	2313	2348	...	0013	0048	...	0113

G – International service from / to stations in Germany (see Table **912**).
L – ①–⑤ (not Dec. 26, Apr. 7, 10, May 1, 29). From Karlsruhe (Table **912**).
P – From / to Paris (Table **370**). 🅁 for international journeys.
Q – Aug. 1–27 only.
T – © Aug. 1–26.
c – ⑥⑦ (also Dec. 26, Apr. 7, 10, May 1, 29).
d – Not Dec. 27–30, May 19.
j – Not Dec. 25, Apr. 8.
k – Not Dec. 24, Apr. 7.
r – ⑦–④ (also Apr. 7).
s – Also Dec. 27–30, May 19; not Aug. 1–26.
v – Not May 1.
w – Not Aug. 1–27.
z – Jan. 2, May 18, Aug. 1 only.

511 BERN - PAYERNE and NEUCHÂTEL

SBB, BLS

km			⚒	Ⓐ		C				C			D		C				C						
0	**Bern** d.	...	...	...	*0534*	0553	0608	0608	*0634*	0653	0708	0708		*2134*	2153	2208	2208	*2234*	2253	2308	2308	2337	...	0008	0008
22	Kerzers ▲ d.	0504	...	0532	0604	0611	0631	0634	0704	0711	0731	0734	and at	2204	2211	2231	2234	2304	2311	2331	2334	0003	...	0034	0036
	Murten d.	0521f	0542	0542	0621f	│	│	0643	0721f	│	│	0743	the same	2221f	│	│	2243	2321f	│	│	2342	│	...	│	0045
	Avenches d.	0529	0549	0549	0629	│	│	0649	0729	│	│	...	minutes	2229	│	│	...	2329	│	│	2350	│	...	│	...
	Payerne a.	0541	0557	0557	0641	│	│	0657	0741	│	│	...	past each	2241	│	│	...	2341	│	│	0001	│	...	│	...
	Lausanne **504** ● a.	0648	...	...	0748	│	│	...	0848	│	│	...	hour until	2348	│	│	...	...	│	│	...	│	...	│	...
30	Ins **508** d.	...	...	...	...	0617	0640	...	...	0717	0740	...		...	2217	2240	...	...	2317	2340	...	0013	...	0041	...
43	**Neuchâtel 508** a.	...	...	...	...	0627	0656	...	...	0727	0756	...		...	2227	2256	...	...	2327	2356	...	0026	...	0056	...

km		C		⚒		C		Ⓐ			C				E	C				C					
	Neuchâtel 508 d.	0532	...	...	0601	0632	...	0656	...	0701	0732	...	...	0801		2232	...	...	2301	2332	...	...	...	...	0009
	Ins **508** d.	0543	...	...	0617	0642	...	0708	...	0717	0742	...	...	0817	and at	2242	...	...	2317	2342	...	...	...	...	0025
	Lausanne **504** ● d.	│	...	...	│	│	0513	│	...	│	│	0613	...	│	the same	│	2113	...	│	│	2213	...	...	...	│
0	**Payerne** d.	│	...	0600	│	│	0618	│	0700	│	│	0718	...	│	minutes	│	2218	...	│	│	2318	...	...	0006	│
11	Avenches d.	│	...	0608	│	│	0630	│	0708	│	│	0730	...	│	past each	│	2230	...	│	│	2330	...	...	0017	│
18	Murten d.	│	0617	0617	│	│	0647f	│	0717	│	│	0747f	0817	│	hour until	│	2247f	2317	│	│	2347f	...	...	0025	│
26	Kerzers ▲ d.	0548	0630	0630	0630	0648	0656	0719	0730	0730	0748	0756	0830	0830		2248	2256	2330	2330	2348	2356	0004	...	0038	0038
	Bern a.	0606	0652	0652	0652	0706	*0726*	0738	0752	0752	0806	*0826*	0852	0852		2306	*2326*	2352	2352	0006	...	0030	...	0103	0103

C – To / from La Chaux de Fonds (Table **512**).
D – On Ⓐ the 0804 from Kerzers departs Murten 0815.
E – On Ⓐ the 1413 from Lausanne departs Avenches 1537.
f – Arrives 8–9 minutes earlier.
● – Services to / from Lausanne are subject to alteration from Aug. 14.
▲ – Connecting services **KERZERS** - **LYSS**. *17 km*. Journey: 19–20 minutes. From **Kerzers**: 0606 and hourly until 2306. From **Lyss**: 0535 and hourly until 2235; then 2336 and 0009.

512 NEUCHÂTEL and BIEL / BIENNE - LA CHAUX DE FONDS - LE LOCLE

SBB, BLS

NEUCHÂTEL - LA CHAUX DE FONDS - LE LOCLE

km					⊠											
	Bern **511** d.	...	...	0553	and at	...	1853	...	1953	...	2053	...	2153	...	2253	...
0	**Neuchâtel** d.	0529	0600	0629	the same	1900	1929	2000	2029	2100	2129	2200	2229	2300	2329	0000
29	**La Chaux de Fonds** a.	0557	0627	0657	minutes	1927	1957	2027	2057	2127	2157	2227	2257	2327	2357	0027
	La Chaux de Fonds d.	*0607*	0631	*0707*	past each	1931	*2003*	2037	*2103*	2137	*2203*	2237	*2303*	2337	...	0037
37	**Le Locle** a.	*0615*	0640	*0715*	hour until	1940	*2011*	2046	*2111*	2146	*2211*	2246	*2311*	2346	...	0046

Le Locle d.	*0450*	0520	and at	*2251*	2320
La Chaux de Fonds a.	*0459*	0529	the same	*2259*	2329
La Chaux de Fonds d.	0502	0532	minutes	2302	2332
Neuchâtel a.	0530	0600	past each	2330	2400
Bern **511** a.	0606	...	hour until	0006	...

BIEL / BIENNE - LA CHAUX DE FONDS

km		Ⓐ												
0	**Biel / Bienne** d.	0518	0547	0620f	0647	0720	and at the same	1847	1920	1947	2047	2147	2247	2347
28	St Imier d.	0600	0613	0700	0713	0800	minutes past	1913	2000	2017	2117	2217	2317	0017
44	**La Chaux de Fonds** a.	0617	0628	0717	0728	0817	each hour until	1928	2017	2034	2134	2234	2334	0034

	Ⓐ												A	B
La Chaux de Fonds d.	0441	0532	0542	0632	0642	and at the same	1932	1942	2042	2142	2242	...	2342	2342
St Imier d.	0457	0545	0559	0645	0659	minutes past	1945	1959	2059	2159	2259	...	2359	2359
Biel / Bienne a.	0539	0612	0640	0712	0741	each hour until	2012	2041	2141	2241	2341	...	0041	0047

A – ⑦–④ (also Apr. 7).
B – ⑤⑥ (not Apr. 7).
f – 0616 from June 26.
⊠ – Certain connecting trains La Chaux de Fonds (d. *xx07*) - Le Locle (a. *xx15*) run 4 minutes earlier (subsequent departures from La Chaux de Fonds are at *0807*, *0903*, *1003*, *1103*, *1207*, *1303*, *1403*, *1503*, *1607*, *1707*, *1803* and *1903*).

513 BERN - BIEL

SBB

km			⑥⑦n		Ⓐ																		
0	**Bern** d.	0012	0112	...	0500	0530	...	0612	0642	and at the same	2012	2042	...	2112	2132	...	2212	2232	...	2312	2332	...	...
23	Lyss d.	0030	0135	...	0522	0552	...	0630	0700	minutes past	2030	2100	...	2130	2154	...	2230	2254	...	2330	2354	...	...
34	**Biel / Bienne** a.	0038	0143	...	0535	0605	...	0638	0708	each hour until	2038	2108	...	2138	2207	...	2238	2307	...	2338	0007	...	...

	⑥⑦n																					
Biel / Bienne d.	0026	...	0518	0552	...	0622	0652	and at the same	2022	2052	...	2122	2154	...	2222	2254	...	2322	2354	...	...	...	...
Lyss d.	0035	...	0531	0601	...	0631	0701	minutes past	2031	2101	...	2131	2207	...	2231	2307	...	2331	0007	...	...	...	...
Bern a.	0052	...	0554	0618	...	0648	0718	each hour until	2048	2118	...	2148	2230	...	2248	2330	...	2348	0030	...	...	...	...

n – Not Dec. 25, Apr. 8.

☛ Additional stopping services operate.

514 BERN - LUZERN via Langnau

BLS

For fast services via Zofingen see Table **565**.

km											
0	**Bern** d.	0536a	...	0612	0636	and at	2136	...	2212	2236	2342
21	Konolfingen d.	0552a	...	0634	0652	the same	2152	...	2234	2252	0005
38	Langnau d.	0606	0636	0652	0706	minutes	2206	2236	2252	2306	0023
75	Wolhusen d.	0645	0720	...	0745	past each	2245	2320	...	2346	...
96	**Luzern** a.	0703	0743	...	0803	hour until	2303	2343	...	0010	...

	Ⓐ										
Luzern d.	0450	...	0557	...	0616	and at	2157	...	2216	2257	...
Wolhusen d.	0514	...	0615	...	0644	the same	2215	...	2244	2315	...
Langnau d.	0554	0607	0654	0707	0722	minutes	2254	2307	2322	2351	0007
Konolfingen d.	0607	0626	0707	0726	...	past each	2307	2326	...	...	0026
Bern a.	0626	0648	0726	0748	...	hour until	2326	2348	...	...	0049

a – Ⓐ only.

☛ Additional stopping services operate.

515 BIEL/BIENNE - DELÉMONT - DELLE - MEROUX

SBB

km																								
0	**Biel / Bienne** 505a d.	...	...	...	...	0619	0719	0819	0919	1019	1119	1219	1319	1419	1519	1619	1719	1819	1919	2019	2119	2219	...	2319
24	Moutier 505a d.	...	...	...	...	0638	0738	0838	0938	1038	1138	1238	1338	1438	1538	1638	1738	1838	1938	2038	2138	2238	...	2338
35	Delémont 505a d.	0417	0449	...	0551	0651	0751	0851	0951	1051	1151	1251	1351	1451	1551	1651	1751	1851	1951	2051	2151	2251	...	2351
63	Porrentruy 505a d.	0448	0520	...	0622	0722	0822	0922	1022	1122	1222	1322	1422	1522	1622	1722	1822	1922	2022	2122	2222	2322	...	0020
75	**Delle** 🏛 a.	0504	0536	...	0638	0738	0838	0938	1038	1138	1238	1338	1438	1538	1638	1738	1838	1938	2038	2138	2238	2338	...	...
75	**Delle** 🏛 370b d.	...	0541r	...	...	0741k	0841	0941	1041e	1141	1241	1341	...	...	1641v	1741t	1841	1941b	...	2141	2241v	...	...	...
89	Meroux TGV ⊡ 370b d.	...	0556r	...	...	0756k	0856	0956	1056e	1156	1256	1356	...	...	1656v	1756t	1856	1956b	...	2156	2256v	...	...	...

Meroux TGV ⊡ 370b d.	...	...	0603r	...	0803k	0903	1003	1103e	1203	1303	1403	...	...	1703v	1803t	1903	2003b	...	2203	2303v	...	...	...
Delle 🏛 370b a.	...	...	0619r	...	0819k	0919	1019	1119e	1219	1319	1419	...	...	1719v	1819t	1919	2019b	...	2219	2319v	...	...	...
Delle 🏛 d.	...	0518	0621	0721	0821	0921	1021	1121	1221	1321	1421	1521	1621	1721	1821	1921	2021	2121	2221	2321	0022	...	...
Porrentruy 505a d.	0436	0540	0640	0740	0840	0940	1040	1140	1240	1340	1440	1540	1640	1740	1840	1940	2040	2140	2240	2340	0042	...	...
Delémont 505a d.	0512	0612	0712	0812	0912	1012	1112	1212	1312	1412	1512	1612	1712	1812	1912	2012	2112	2212	2309	0009	0110	...	...
Moutier 505a a.	0521	0621	0721	0821	0921	1021	1121	1221	1321	1421	1521	1621	1721	1821	1921	2021	2121	2221	...	...	...	...	...
Biel / Bienne 505a a.	0541	0641	0741	0841	0941	1041	1141	1241	1341	1441	1541	1641	1741	1841	1941	2041	2141	2241	...	...	...	...	...

b – Ⓑ.
e – ①–⑤ (not Apr. 10, May 1, 8, 18, 29, July 3 - Aug. 25, Nov. 1).
k – ⑥ to July 1; ①–⑥ July 3 - Aug. 26 (not July 14, Aug. 15); ⑥ from Sept. 2.
r – ①–⑥ (not Apr. 10, May 1, 8, 18, 29, July 14, Aug. 15, Nov. 1).
t – ⑥ only.
v – ⑦ (also Apr. 10, May 1, 8, 18, 29, July 14, Aug. 15, Nov. 1).
⊡ – Meroux station platforms are located directly above the Belfort-Montbéliard TGV platforms.

516 BERN - SOLOTHURN

Narrow gauge. RBS

km		⚒	⚒											Ⓐ	Ⓐ	Ⓐ	Ⓐ	Ⓐ	Ⓐ	Ⓐ	Ⓐ	Ⓐ
0	**Bern** RBS d.	0511	0550	0605	0635	and at the same	2205	2235	2305	2335	0011	...	Additional	0620	0650	0720	0750	0820	1650	1720	1750	1820
14	Jegenstorf d.	0530	0604	0619	0649	minutes past	2219	2249	2319	2349	0030	...	services	0634	0704	0734	0804	0834	1704	1734	1804	1834
34	**Solothurn** a.	0555	0625	0640	0710	each hour until	2240	2310	2340	0013	0054	...	on Ⓐ	0655	0725	0755	0825	0855	1725	1755	1825	1855

												Ⓐ	Ⓐ	Ⓐ	Ⓐ	Ⓐ		Ⓐ	Ⓐ	Ⓐ	Ⓐ	Ⓐ
Solothurn d.	0516	0548	0618	0648	and at the same	2218	2248	2318	2350	...	Additional	0603	0633	0703	0733	0803	...	1633	1703	1733	1803	1833
Jegenstorf d.	0538	0608	0638	0708	minutes past	2238	2308	2338	0012	...	services	0623	0653	0723	0753	0823	...	1653	1723	1753	1823	1853
Bern RBS a.	0552	0622	0652	0722	each hour until	2252	2322	2352	0030	...	on Ⓐ	0637	0707	0737	0807	0837	...	1707	1737	1807	1837	1907

BLS SOLOTHURN - BURGDORF - THUN 517

km		⚒	Ⓐ	⚒		Ⓐ																	
0	**Solothurn** d.	...	...	0514	0542	0611	0646	0717	and at the same minutes past each hour until	1846	1917	1946	2017	...	...	2117	...	...	2217	...	...	2317	...	0017
5	Biberist Ost d.	...	...	0520	0547	0616	0650	0722		1850	1922	1950	2022	...	...	2122	...	...	2222	...	...	2322	...	0022
21	**Burgdorf** a.	...	...	0545	0612	0645	0712	0745		1912	1945	2012	2045	...	...	2145	...	...	2245	...	...	2345	...	0045
21	**Burgdorf** 505 d.	0448	0515	0551	0625	0651	0725	0751		1925	1951	2025	2051	*2049*	2125	2151	*2149*	2225	2251	*2249*	2325	2351	*2349*	▬
28	Hasle-Rüegsau d.	0501	0525	|	0638	|	0738	|		1938	|	2038	|	2102	2138	|	2202	2238	|	2302	2338	|	0001	...
46	Konolfingen a.	0522	0549	|	0700	|	0800	|		2000	|	2100	|	2123	2200	|	2223	2300	|	2323	2400	|	0023	...
46	Konolfingen d.	*0535*	0558	|	0701	|	0801	|		2001	|	2101	|	...	2201	|	...	2301	|	...	0001	|	...	0036
	Bern 505 560 a.	|	|	0611	|	0711	|	0811		|	2011	|	2111	...	|	2211	...	|	2311	...	|	0011	...	|
61	**Thun** 560 a.	*0556*	0619	0651	0719	0751	0819	0851		2019	2051	2119	2151	...	2219	2251	...	2319	2351	...	0019	0059	...	0057

				Ⓐ																					
Thun 560 d.	...	0502	...	0539	0608	0639	and at the same minutes past each hour until	1808	1839	...	1939	...	2008	2039	...	2108	2139	...	2208	2239	...	2308	2339	...	*0003*
Bern 505 560 d.	...	0550	...	|	0650	|		1850	|	...	|	...	2050	|	...	2150	|	...	2250	|	...	2350	|	...	|
Konolfingen a.	...	|	...	0558	|	0658		|	1858	...	1958	...	|	2058	...	|	2158	...	|	2258	...	|	2358	...	*0024*
Konolfingen d.	...	|	...	0600	|	0700		|	1900	*1936*	2000	*2036*	|	2100	*2136*	|	2200	*2236*	|	2300	*2336*	|	0000	...	0037
Hasle-Rüegsau d.	...	|	...	0622	|	0722		|	1922	1957	2022	2057	|	2122	2157	|	2222	2257	|	2322	0001	|	0022	...	0058
Burgdorf 505 a.	...	0608	...	0632	0708	0732		1908	1932	2011	2032	2111	2108	2132	2211	2208	2232	2311	2308	2332	0011	0008	0032	...	0107
Burgdorf d.	0528	0615	0647	0647	0715	0747		1915	1947	...	2047	...	2115	...	...	2215	...	...	2315	...	...	0015	...	...	...
Biberist Ost d.	0550	0635	0706	0706	0735	0806		1935	2006	...	2105	...	2135	...	...	2235	...	...	2335	...	...	0035	...	...	...
Solothurn a.	0557	0642	0713	0713	0742	0812		1942	2012	...	2112	...	2142	...	...	2242	...	...	2342	...	...	0042	...	...	...

SBB ZÜRICH - SARGANS - CHUR 520

km		IR 2395		IR 2353	IC 557	RJX 161	IC 911	IR 2355	IC 559	IC 1253	IC 913	IR 2359	IC 561	EC 163	IC 1255	IR 2361	IC 563	ICE 271 1271	IR 2363	IC 565	RJX 165	IR 2365	IC 567	IC 903	IC 921
		⑥⑦ z◇		B◇	✕	E✕	✕	◇	✕	Ⓐ ✕	Ⓒ ✕	B◇	✕	E✕	Ⓒ ‡✕	B⊡	✕	G✕	B◇	✕	H✕	B⊡	Ⓐ ✕	Ⓒ Y✕	✕
	Basel SBB 510 d.	...	...	...	...	...	...	...	0633	0706	...	...	0733	...	0806	...	0833	0906	...	0933	...	...	...	...	...
0	**Zürich HB** 522 555 d.	0020	...	0612	0638	0640	0707	0712	0738	0807	0807	0812	0838	0840	0907	0912	0938	1007	1012	1038	1040	1112	1138	1138	1207
12	Thalwil 555 d.	0028	...	0621	|	|	|	0721	|	|	|	0821	|	|	|	0921	|	|	1021	|	|	1121	|	|	|
24	Wädenswil 522 d.	0037	...	0631	|	|	|	0731	|	|	|	0831	|	|	|	0931	|	|	1031	|	|	1131	|	|	|
33	Pfäffikon 522 d.	0045	...	0641	|	|	|	0741	|	|	|	0841	|	|	|	0941	|	|	1041	|	|	1141	|	|	|
57	Ziegelbrücke 522 d.	0100	...	0700	|	|	|	0800	|	|	|	0900	|	|	|	1000	|	|	1100	|	|	1200	|	|	|
90	**Sargans** 534 d.	0120	...	0723	0734	0736	0803	0823	0834	0903	0903	0923	0934	0936	1003	1023	1034	1103	1123	1133	1136	1223	1234	1234	1303
106	Buchs 534 a.	|	...	|	|	0748	|	|	|	|	|	|	|	0948	|	|	|	|	|	|	1148	|	|	|	|
103	Landquart 534 545 d.	0131	...	0734	0743	...	0813	0834	0843	0913	0913	0934	0942	...	1013	1034	1043	1113	1134	1143	...	1234	1243	1243	1313
116	**Chur** 534 545 a.	0138	...	0743	0752	...	0822	0843	0852	0922	0922	0943	0952	...	1022	1043	1052	1122	1143	1152	...	1243	1252	1252	1322

	IR 2367	IC 569	RJX 167	IR 2369	IC 571	ICE 71	IR 2371	IC 573	IC 909	RJX 169	IR 2373	IC 575	IC 929	ICE 73	IR 2375	IC 577	RJX 367	IC 931	IR 2377	IC 579	ICE 75	IR 2379	IC 581	RJX 369	IR 2381
	B◇	✕	J✕	B◇	✕	G✕	B◇	Ⓐ ✕	Ⓒ Y✕	E✕	B◇	✕	Ⓐ ✕	Ⓒ ✕	B◇	✕	E✕	✕	B⊡	✕	G✕	B◇	✕	E✕	B⊡
Basel SBB 510 d.	...	1133	...	...	1233	1306	...	...	...	...	...	1433	...	1506	...	...	...	...	...	1633	1706	...	1733	...	...
Zürich HB 522 555 d.	1212	1238	1240	1312	1338	1407	1412	1438	1438	1440	1512	1538	1607	1607	1612	1638	1640	1707	1712	1738	1807	1812	1838	1840	1912
Thalwil 555 d.	1221	|	|	1321	|	|	1421	|	|	|	1521	|	|	|	1621	|	|	|	1721	|	|	1821	|	|	1921
Wädenswil 522 d.	1231	|	|	1331	|	|	1431	|	|	|	1531	|	|	|	1631	|	|	|	1731	|	|	1831	|	|	1931
Pfäffikon 522 d.	1241	|	|	1341	|	|	1441	|	|	|	1541	|	|	|	1641	|	|	|	1741	|	|	1841	|	|	1941
Ziegelbrücke 522 d.	1300	|	|	1400	|	|	1500	|	|	|	1600	|	|	|	1700	|	|	|	1800	|	|	1900	|	|	2000
Sargans 534 d.	1323	1334	1336	1423	1434	1503	1523	1533	1533	1536	1623	1634	1703	1703	1723	1734	1736	1803	1823	1834	1903	1923	1934	1936	2023
Buchs 534 a.	|	|	1348	|	|	|	|	|	|	1548	|	|	|	|	|	|	1748	|	|	|	|	|	|	1948	|
Landquart 534 545 d.	1334	1343	...	1434	1443	1513	1534	1543	1543	...	1634	1643	1713	1713	1734	1743	...	1813	1834	1843	1913	1934	1943	...	2034
Chur 534 545 a.	1343	1352	...	1443	1452	1522	1543	1552	1552	...	1643	1652	1722	1722	1743	1752	...	1822	1843	1852	1922	1943	1952	...	2043

	IC 583	IR 2383	IC 585	NJ 465	IR 2385	IC 597	IC 587	NJ 467	IR 2391	IC 589	IR 2393
	✕	B◇	✕	Ⓡ N	B◇	⑤⑥ e	⑦–④ d	Ⓡ W	◇		⊙
Basel SBB 510 d.	1833	...	...	...	...	...	2033	...	...	...	...
Zürich HB 522 555 d.	1938	2012	2038	2040	2112	2138	2138	2140	2212	2238	2312
Thalwil 555 d.	|	2021	|	|	2121	|	|	|	2221	|	2321
Wädenswil 522 d.	|	2031	|	|	2131	|	|	|	2231	|	2331
Pfäffikon 522 d.	|	2041	|	|	2141	|	|	|	2241	|	2341
Ziegelbrücke 522 d.	|	2100	|	|	2200	|	|	|	2300	|	0000
Sargans 534 d.	2034	2128	2134	2136	2228	2234	2234	2236	2328	2336	0031
Buchs 534 a.	|	|	|	2148	|	|	|	2248	|	|	|
Landquart 534 545 d.	2043	2138	2143	...	2238	2243	2243	...	2339	2349	0042
Chur 534 545 a.	2052	2147	2152	...	2247	2252	2252	...	2348	2357	0051

	IC 556	IR 2356	IC 558	IR 2358	IC 912	NJ 466	IC 560	IR 2360	NJ 464
	⚒ ✕	B◇		B⊡	Ⓐ ✕	Ⓡ W	✕	B◇	Ⓡ N
Chur 534 545 d.	0508	0516	0608	0616	0637	...	0708	0716	...
Landquart 534 545 d.	0518	0525	0618	0625	0647	...	0718	0725	...
Buchs 534 d.	|	|	|	|	|	0712	|	|	0812
Sargans 534 d.	0526	0535	0626	0635	0656	0724	0726	0735	0824
Ziegelbrücke 522 d.	|	0600	|	0700	|	|	|	0800	|
Pfäffikon 522 d.	|	0619	|	0719	|	|	|	0819	|
Wädenswil 522 d.	|	0629	|	0729	|	|	|	0829	|
Thalwil 555 d.	|	0639	|	0739	|	|	|	0839	|
Zürich HB 522 555 a.	0622	0648	0722	0748	0753	0820	0822	0848	0920
Basel SBB 510 a.	0728	...	...	...	...	...	0928	...	...

	IC 562	IR 2362	IC 916	IC 564	IR 2364	IC 918	RJX 366	IC 566	IC 596	IR 2366	ICE 72	IC 568	IR 2368	RJX 368	IC 570	IR 2370	ICE 70	IC 572	IC 902	IR 2372	RJX 160	IC 574	IR 2374	IC 928	IC 576
	✕	B◇	✕	✕	B◇	Ⓒ	E✕	Ⓐ ✕	Ⓒ ✕	B◇	G	✕	B◇	E✕	✕	B⊡	G	Ⓐ ✕	Ⓒ Y✕	B◇	J✕	✕	B⊡	✕	✕
Chur 534 545 d.	0808	0816	0837	0908	0916	0937	...	1008	1008	1016	1037	1108	1116	...	1208	1216	1237	1308	1308	1316	...	1408	1416	1437	1508
Landquart 534 545 d.	0818	0825	0847	0918	0925	0947	...	1018	1018	1025	1047	1118	1125	...	1218	1225	1247	1318	1318	1325	...	1418	1425	1447	1518
Buchs 534 d.	|	|	|	|	|	|	1011	|	|	|	|	|	|	1211	|	|	|	|	|	|	1411	|	|	|	|
Sargans 534 d.	0826	0835	0856	0926	0935	0956	1023	1026	1026	1035	1056	1126	1135	1223	1226	1235	1256	1326	1326	1335	1423	1426	1435	1456	1526
Ziegelbrücke 522 d.	|	0900	|	|	1000	|	|	|	|	1100	|	|	1200	|	|	1300	|	|	|	1400	|	|	1500	|	|
Pfäffikon 522 d.	|	0919	|	|	1019	|	|	|	|	1119	|	|	1219	|	|	1319	|	|	|	1419	|	|	1519	|	|
Wädenswil 522 d.	|	0929	|	|	1029	|	|	|	|	1129	|	|	1229	|	|	1329	|	|	|	1429	|	|	1529	|	|
Thalwil 555 d.	|	0939	|	|	1039	|	|	|	|	1139	|	|	1239	|	|	1339	|	|	|	1439	|	|	1539	|	|
Zürich HB 522 555 a.	0922	0948	0953	1022	1048	1053	1120	1122	1122	1148	1153	1222	1248	1320	1322	1348	1353	1422	1422	1448	1520	1522	1548	1553	1622
Basel SBB 510 a.	...	...	...	1128	...	...	...	...	...	...	1253	1328	...	...	...	...	1453	1528	...	...	...	...	...	...	1728

	IR 2376	RJX 162	IC 578	IC 908	IR 2378	IC 1256	IC 932	IC 580	IR 2380	IC 934	ICE 4	EC 164	IC 582	IR 2382	IC 936	IC 584	IR 2384	RJX 166	IC 1258	IR 2388	IC 588	IR 2390	RJX 168	IR 2392	IR 2398
	B◇	H✕	Ⓐ ✕	Ⓒ Y✕	B◇	Ⓐ ✕	Ⓒ ✕	✕	B◇	Ⓐ ✕	Ⓒ G✕	E✕	✕	B◇	✕	✕	⊡	E✕		◇	✕	⊡	E✕	◇	⑤⑥ v◇
Chur 534 545 d.	1516	...	1608	1608	1616	1637	1637	1708	1716	1737	1737	...	1808	1816	1837	1908	1916	...	2008	2016	2108	2114	...	2214	2314
Landquart 534 545 d.	1525	...	1618	1618	1625	1647	1647	1718	1725	1747	1747	...	1818	1825	1847	1918	1925	...	2018	2025	2118	2122	...	2222	2322
Buchs 534 d.	|	1611	|	|	|	|	|	|	|	|	|	1811	|	|	|	|	|	2011	|	|	|	|	2211	|	|
Sargans 534 d.	1535	1623	1626	1626	1635	1656	1656	1726	1735	1756	1756	1823	1826	1835	1856	1926	1935	2023	2026	2035	2126	2135	2223	2235	2337
Ziegelbrücke 522 d.	1600	|	|	|	1700	|	|	|	1800	|	|	|	|	1900	|	|	2000	|	|	2100	|	2200	|	2300	0000
Pfäffikon 522 d.	1619	|	|	|	1719	|	|	|	1819	|	|	|	|	1919	|	|	2019	|	|	2119	|	2219	|	2319	0019
Wädenswil 522 d.	1629	|	|	|	1729	|	|	|	1829	|	|	|	|	1929	|	|	2029	|	|	2129	|	2229	|	2329	0029
Thalwil 555 d.	1639	|	|	|	1739	|	|	|	1839	|	|	|	|	1939	|	|	2039	|	|	2139	|	2239	|	2339	0039
Zürich HB 522 555 a.	1648	1720	1722	1722	1748	1753	1753	1822	1848	1853	1853	1920	1922	1948	1953	2022	2048	2120	2122	2148	2222	2248	2320	2348	0048
Basel SBB 510 a.	...	...	1828	...	...	...	...	...	...	...	1953	...	2028	...	...	2128	...	...	2228	...	...	...	...	...	...

Other connecting services **SARGANS - BUCHS**

Sargans d.	0500	0536	and at the same minutes past each hour until	2200	2236	2300	2339	0000
Buchs a.	0512	0545		2212	2245	2312	2347	0012

	⚒							
Buchs d.	0512	0615	0647	and at the same minutes past each hour until	2315	2347	0018	0047
Sargans a.	0524	0624	0701		2325	0001	0028	0101

B – From/to Bern (Table **505**). Most convey (🍸).
E – International service to/from stations in Austria (Tables **86** and **951**).
G – International service from/to stations in Germany (Tables **73** and **912**).
H – (12) ✕ Budapest - Wien - Zürich and v.v. (Table **86**).
J – (12) ✕ Bratislava - Wien - Zürich and v.v. (Table **86**).
N – 🛏 1, 2 cl. ▬ 2 cl. and (2) Zürich - Graz and v.v. Also conveys through cars to/from Zagreb (Table **86**).

W – 🛏 1, 2 cl. ▬ 2 cl. and (2) Zürich - Wien - Budapest and v.v. (Table **86**).
Y – From/to Genève (Table **505**).

d – Also Apr. 7.
e – Not Apr. 7.
v – Not Dec. 24, Apr. 7.

z – Not Dec. 25, Apr. 8.
‡ – Runs as *ICE* 3 on Jan. 2, May 18, Aug. 1.
◇ – Operated by SOB.
⊡ – Operated by SBB on Ⓐ, by SOB on Ⓒ.
⊙ – Operated by SBB on ⑦–④ (also Dec. 24, Apr. 7), by SOB on ⑤⑥ (not Dec. 24, Apr. 7).

522 (ZÜRICH -) ZIEGELBRÜCKE - LINTHAL — SBB, SOB

km												
	Zürich HB ... **520** d.	...	...	...	0643		1743	...	1843	...		...
	Wädenswil ... **520** d.	...	...	...	0700	and	1800	...	1900	...	and	...
	Pfäffikon ... **520** d.	...	...	...	0707		1807	...	1907	...		...
0	**Ziegelbrücke** ... **520** d.	0434	0534	0634	0734	hourly	1834	1901	1934	2001	hourly	2301
11	Glarus ... d.	0446	0546	0646	0746		1846	1916	1946	2016		2316
16	Schwanden ... d.	0459	0559	0659	0759	until	1859	1929	1954	2029	until	2329
27	**Linthal** ... a.	0516	0616	0716	0816		1916	1946	...	2046		2346

	Ⓐ								
Linthal ... d.	0442	0542		1842	...	1946	2012		0012
Schwanden ... d.	0504	0604	and	1904	1934	2004	2034	and	0034
Glarus ... d.	0514	0614		1914	1944	2014	2044		0044
Ziegelbrücke ... **520** a.	0525	0625	hourly	1925	1957	2025	2057	hourly	0057
Pfäffikon ... **520** a.	0552	0652		1952	...	...	...		...
Wädenswil ... **520** a.	0600	0700	until	2000	...	...	...	until	...
Zürich HB ... **520** a.	0617	0717		2017	...	...	...		...

525 LUZERN - ARTH GOLDAU - ST GALLEN — SOB

km			IR 2009 V			IR 2011 V					IR 2013 V			IR 2015 V	⊠			IR 2039 V		IR 2041		IR 2043	⑤⑥ k	
0	**Luzern** ... **547 550** d.	...	...	...	...	...	0539	...	...	0639	...	...	...	0739	and at	...	...	1939	...	*2039*	...	*2139*	*2218*	*2218*
16	Küssnacht am Rigi ... d.	...	...	...	...	...	0558	...	...	0658	...	...	...	0800		...	...	2000	...	*2059*	...	*2159*	|	|
28	**Arth Goldau 547 550** a.	...	...	...	...	...	0610	...	...	0710	...	...	...	0811		...	...	2011	...	*2111*	...	*2211*	*2245*	*2245*
28	**Arth Goldau** ... d.	...	...	...	...	...	*0615*	...	...	*0715*	...	...	...	0816	the same	...	...	2016	...	2116	...	2216	2315	2315
	Einsiedeln ... ● d.	0516	...	0541r	0616	...	|	0645	0711	|	...	0746	0811	|		1946	2011	|	2111	|	2211	|	|	|
48	Biberbrugg ... ● d.	0523	0538a	0550r	0625	0638	*0643*	0652	0725f	*0737*	0738	0752	0825f	0837	minutes	1952	2025f	2037	2125f	2137	2225f	2237	2339	2339
54	Samstagern ... ● d.	0533	|	0601	0633	|	...	0701	0733	...	|	0801	0833	|		2001	2033	|	2133	2144	2233	2244	2348	2348
62	Pfäffikon ... d.	0546	0554a	0616	0646	0654	...	0716	0746	...	0754	0816	0846	0854	past each	2016	2046	2054	2146	2154	2246	2254	0001	0001
66	**Rapperswil** ... a.	0553	0600a	0623	0653	0700	...	0723	0753	...	0800	0823	0853	0900		2023	2053	2100	2153	2200	2253	2303	0006	0006
66	**Rapperswil** ... d.	...	0603	...	...	0703	...	...	...	...	0803	...	...	0903	hour until	...	...	2103	...	2203	...	2303	0006	...
94	Wattwil ... d.	...	0627	...	...	0727	...	...	...	...	0827	...	...	0927		...	...	2127	...	2227	...	2327	0029	...
117	Herisau ... d.	...	0647	...	...	0747	...	...	...	...	0847	...	...	0947		...	...	2147	...	2247	...	2347	0048	...
125	**St Gallen** ... a.	...	0655	...	...	0755	...	...	...	...	0855	...	...	0955		...	...	2155	...	2255	...	2355	0056	...

	Ⓐ			IR 2006 V			IR 2008 V				IR 2010 V		⊠		IR 2034 V			IR 2036		IR 2038		IR 2040	IR 2042	IR 2044
St Gallen ... d.	...	...	...	0505	...	...	0605	...	...	...	0705	...		...	1905	...	...	2005	...	2105	...	2205	2305	0005
Herisau ... d.	...	...	...	0513	...	...	0613	...	...	...	0713	...	and at	...	1913	...	...	2013	...	2113	...	2213	2313	0013
Wattwil ... d.	...	...	...	0532	...	...	0632	...	...	...	0732	...		...	1932	...	...	2032	...	2132	...	2232	2332	0032
Rapperswil ... a.	...	...	...	0557	...	...	0657	...	...	...	0757	...	the same	...	1957	...	...	2057	...	2157	...	2257	2357	0057
Rapperswil ... d.	0506	...	0536	0559	0606	...	0659	...	0706	0736	0759	0806		1936	1959	2006	2036	2059	2106	2159	2206	2257	0006	...
Pfäffikon ... d.	0511	...	0541	0603	0611	...	0703	...	0711	0741	0803	0811	minutes	1941	2003	2011	2041	2103	2111	2203	2211	2301	0011	...
Samstagern ... ● d.	0523	...	0555	|	0625	...	|	...	0725	0755	|	0825		1955	|	2025	2055	2112	2125	2212	2225	2313	0023	...
Biberbrugg ... ● d.	0531	...	0603	0619	0638j	0643	0719	0738	0739j	0805	0820	0839j	past each	2005	2020	2039j	2105	2120	2139j	2222	2239j	2322	...	...
Einsiedeln ... ● a.	|	...	|	▬	0645	|	▬	|	0746	0812	|	0846		2012	|	2046	2112	|	2146	|	2246	|	...	...
Arth Goldau ... a.	*0607*	...	*0635*	...		0711	...	0811	...	...	0845	...	hour until	...	2045	...	...	2145	...	2248	...	2349	...	...
Arth Goldau . **547 550** d.	...	0620	...	0646	...	*0715*	0747	*0815*	...	...	0849	...		...	2049	...	...	*2149*	...	*2315*	...	...	...	...
Küssnacht am Rigi ... d.	...	0632	...	0700	...	|	0800	|	...	...	0901	...		...	2101	...	...	*2201*	...	|	...	...	...	...
Luzern ... **547 550** a.	...	0653	...	0721	...	*0741*	0821	*0841*	...	...	0921	...		...	2121	...	...	*2221*	...	*2341*	...	...	...	...

EINSIEDELN - BIBERBRUGG - WÄDENSWIL

km		Ⓐ										
0	**Einsiedeln** ... d.	0454	0524	0557	0624	0657	0724	0759	and at the same	2224	2259	2324
6	Biberbrugg ... d.	0501	0532	0607	0632	0707	0732	0807	minutes	2232	2307	2332
11	Samstagern ... d.	0509	0541	0617	0641	0717	0741	0817	past each	2241	2317	2341
17	**Wädenswil** ... a.	0518	0550	0626	0650	0726	0750	0826	hour until	2250	2326	2350

	Ⓐ								
Wädenswil ... d.	0541	0610	0634	0710	0734	and at the same	2310	2334	0015
Samstagern ... d.	0550	0617	0641	0717	0741	minutes	2317	2341	0025
Biberbrugg ... d.	0558	0626	0651	0726	0752	past each	2326	2352	0033
Einsiedeln ... a.	0606	0633	0657	0733	0759	hour until	2333	2359	0040

V – VORALPEN EXPRESS – Most convey (🍸).
a – Ⓐ only.
f – Arrives 7 minutes earlier.
j – Arrives 4–5 minutes earlier.
k – Also Apr. 6, 9, 30, May 17, 18, 28, July 31; not Dec. 24, 31.
r – On Ⓒ departs Einsiedeln 0546, Biberbrugg 0552.
⊠ – Train numbers increase by 2 each hour.
● – See panel below main table for services Einsiedeln - Samstagern - Wädenswil and v.v.

526 GOSSAU - APPENZELL - WASSERAUEN — Narrow gauge. AB

km		Ⓐ	e																								
0	**Gossau** ... ▷ d.	0551	0621	0651	0721	0751	and at	1021	1051	1121	1151	1221	1321	1351	1421	1451	1521	1551	1621	1651	1721	1751	1851	1951	2051	2151
5	Herisau ... ▷ d.	0558	0628	0658	0728	0758	the same	1028	1058	1128	1158	1228	1328	1358	1428	1458	1528	1558	1628	1658	1728	1758	1858	1958	2058	2158
15	Urnäsch ... ▷ d.	0613	0643	0713	0743	0813	minutes	1043	1113	1143	1213	1243	1343	1413	1443	1513	1543	1613	1643	1713	1743	1813	1913	2013	2113	2213
26	**Appenzell** ... ▷ a.	0630	0700	0730	0800	0830	past each	1100	1130	1200	1230	1300	1400	1430	1500	1530	1600	1630	1700	1730	1800	1830	1930	2030	2130	2230
32	**Wasserauen** ... a.	0643	0712	0743	0812t	0842	hour until	1112t	1142	1212	1242	1312	1412	1442t	1512	1542t	1612	1642	1712	1742	1812	1842	*1947**	*2047**	*2147*‡	...

Wasserauen ... d.	...	0648a	0718e	0748	0818t	and at	1118t	1148	1218	1248	1318	1418	1448t	1518	1548t	1618	1648	1718	1748	1818	1848	...	*1947**	*2047**	*2147*‡	...
Appenzell ... ▷ d.	0630	0700	0730	0800	0830	the same	1130	1200	1230	1300	1330	1430	1500	1530	1600	1630	1700	1730	1800	1830	1900	1930	2000	2100	2200	2300
Urnäsch ... ▷ d.	0645	0715	0745	0815	0845	minutes	1145	1215	1245	1315	1345	1445	1515	1545	1615	1645	1715	1745	1815	1845	1915	1945	2015	2115	2215	2315
Herisau ... ▷ d.	0702	0732	0802	0832	0902	past each	1202	1232	1302	1332	1402	1502	1532	1602	1632	1702	1732	1802	1832	1902	1932	2002	2032	2132	2232	2332
Gossau ... ▷ a.	0708	0738	0808	0838	0908	hour until	1208	1238	1308	1338	1408	1508	1538	1608	1638	1708	1738	1808	1838	1908	1938	2008	2038	2138	2238	2338

a – Ⓐ only.
e – Ⓐ to Apr. 28; ⚒ Apr. 29 - Dec. 8; not Nov. 4, 11, 18, 25, Dec. 2.
t – Apr. 29 - Oct. 29.
* – By 🚌 from/to Appenzell.
‡ – Apr. 29 - Oct. 29. By 🚌 from/to Appenzell.
▷ – **Additional journeys** Gossau - Appenzell:
From Gossau at 1251, 1821, 1921, 2021, 2251 and 2351.
From Appenzell at 0500 ⚒, 0530 Ⓑ, 0600 **e** and 1400.

527 ST GALLEN - APPENZELL — Narrow gauge rack railway. AB

km		⑥⑦ z 🚌	⑥⑦ z 🚌	⑥⑦ z 🚌		⚒	Ⓒ	Ⓐ		⑥	Ⓐ						♣							
0	**St Gallen** ... d.	0026	0137	0243	...	0520	0550	0550	0620	0650	0650	0720	0750	...	0826	0856	and every	2226	2256	...	2326	...	...	...
7	Teufen ... d.	0038	0149	0255	...	0534	0604	0604	0634	0704	0704	0734	0804	...	0841	0911	30 minutes	2241	2311	...	2341	...	...	...
14	Gais ▲ ... d.	0048	0159	0305	...	0547	0617	0619	0647	0717	0719	0747	0817	...	0854	0924	until	2254	2324	...	2354	...	...	...
20	**Appenzell** ... a.	0059	0210	0316	...	0558	0628	0630	0658	0728	0730	0758	0828	...	0905	0935		2305	2335	...	0005	...	...	...

	⑥⑦ z 🚌	⑥⑦ z 🚌		⚒		Ⓐ	⚒		Ⓐ						♠						⑤⑥ k 🚌		
Appenzell ... d.	0104	0210	...	0508	0538	0558	0608	0638	0658	0708	0738	...	0814	0844	and every	2214	2244	...	2314	...	2353	...	...
Gais ▲ ... d.	0113	0219	...	0521	0551	0607	0621	0651	0707	0721	0751	...	0827	0857	30 minutes	2227	2257	...	2327	...	0002	...	...
Teufen ... d.	0123	0229	...	0534	0604	0618	0634	0704	0718	0734	0804	...	0840	0910	until	2240	2310	...	2340	...	0012	...	...
St Gallen ... a.	0137	0243	...	0550	0620	0633	0650	0720	0733	0750	0820	...	0856	0926		2256	2326	...	2356	...	0026	...	...

k – Also Apr. 6, 9, 30, May 17, 18, 28, July 31, Oct. 31; not Dec. 24.
z – Also Apr. 7, 10, May 1, 18, 19, 29, Aug. 1, Nov. 1; not Dec. 25.
♣ – On Ⓐ the 1726 and 1826 from St Gallen run 2 minutes later Gais - Appenzell.
♠ – On Ⓐ the 1714 and 1814 from Appenzell depart Gais 3 minutes **earlier**. On Ⓐ Appenzell d. 1747/1847 (not 1744/1844).
▲ – Rail service **Gais - Altstätten Stadt** and v.v. *8 km*. Journey time: 20–23 minutes. **Operator**: AB.
From **Gais** at 0620 Ⓐ, 0720, 0824 and hourly until 1824; then 1924 🚌 and 2024 🚌.
From **Altstätten Stadt** at 0654 Ⓐ, 0754, 0900 and hourly until 1900; then 2000 🚌 and 2100 🚌.
A connecting 🚌 service operates Altstätten Stadt - Altstätten SBB station (in Table **534**). Journey time: 6 minutes.

529 WINTERTHUR - SCHAFFHAUSEN — SBB

km																								
0	**Winterthur** ... d.	0542	0606	0619	0642	and at the same	2106	2119	2142	2206	2242	2306	2342	0012	...	...	...	...	...	...	...	...
26	Schloss Laufen am Rheinfall . d.	0606	0630	|	0706	minutes past	2130	|	2206	2230	2306	2330	0006	0036	...	...	...	...	...	...	...	...
30	**Schaffhausen** ... a.	0613	0638	0646	0713	each hour until	2138	2146	2213	2238	2313	2338	0013	0043	...	...	...	...	...	...	...	...

Schaffhausen ... d.	0515	0521	0546	and at the same	2015	2021	2046	2121	2146	2221	2246	2321	2347	...	...	...	...	...	...	...	...
Schloss Laufen am Rheinfall ... d.	|	0526	0550	minutes past	|	2026	2050	2126	2150	2226	2250	2326	2351	...	...	...	...	...	...	...	...
Winterthur ... a.	0542	0554	0619	each hour until	2042	2054	2119	2154	2219	2254	2319	2354	0023	...	...	...	...	...	...	...	...

SBB ZÜRICH - ST GALLEN 530

km		IR 3251			IR 3253	IC 701 ✕	IC 505 ✕	IR 3255	IC 1507 Ⓐ ✕	IC 703 ✕	IC 507 ✕	IR 3257	EC 97 v M✕	IC 705 F✕	IC 509 ✕	IR 3259	IC 1511 Ⓐ ✕	IC 707 ✕	IC 511 ✕	IR 3261	EC 99 M✕	IC 709 ✕	IC 513 ✕	IR 3263
	Genève **505** ▷ d.	...	...	...	...	...	...	...	...	...	...	...	...	...	...	...	...	0542	0612	...	...	0642	0715	...
	Lausanne **505** d.	...	...	...	...	...	...	...	...	...	...	...	...	...	0542	...	0615	0620	|	...	...	0720	|	...
	Biel/Bienne **505** d.	...	...	...	...	...	...	...	0516	...	0543	...	...	...	0644	...	0717	|	0746	...	...	|	0846	...
	Bern **505** d.	...	...	...	...	...	...	...	|	0529j	|	...	...	0631	|	...	|	0731	|	...	...	0831	|	...
0	**Zürich** HB ● **535** d.	...	...	...	...	0539	0603	0609	0633	0639	0703	0709	0733	0739	0803	0809	0833	0839	0903	0909	0933	0939	1003	1009
10	**Zürich** Flughafen ✈ ● **535** d.	...	...	...	...	0553	0613	0623	0643	0653	0713	0723	0743	0753	0813	0823	0843	0853	0913	0923	0943	0953	1013	1023
30	Winterthur **535** d.	...	...	0511	...	0608	0629	0638	0659	0708	0729	0738	0758	0808	0829	0838	0859	0908	0929	0938	0958	1008	1029	1038
57	Wil d.	0456	...	0542	0556	0626	|	0656	|	0726	|	0756	|	0826	|	0856	|	0926	|	0956	|	1026	|	1056
78	Gossau d.	0515	...	...	0615	0645	|	0715	|	0745	|	0815	|	0845	|	0915	|	0945	|	1015	|	1045	|	1115
87	**St Gallen** **534** a.	0522	...	...	0622	0652	0702	0722	0732	0752	0802	0822	0830	0852	0902	0922	0932	0952	1002	1022	1030	1052	1102	1122
103	Rorschach **534** a.	0539	...	...	0639	...	0721	0739	...	...	0821	0839	...	...	0921	0939	...	...	1021	1039	...	...	1121	1139
	Chur **534** a.	0648	...	...	0748	...	...	0848	...	...	...	0948	...	...	...	1048	...	...	...	1148	...	...	...	1248

	IC 711 ✕	IC 515 ✕	IR 3265	EC 191 M✕	IC 713 ✕	IC 713 Ⓐ ✕	IC 517 ✕	IR 3267	IC 715 ✕	IC 519 ✕	IR 3269	EC 193 M✕	IC 717 ✕	IC 521 ✕	IR 3271	IC 719 ✕	IC 719 Ⓐ ✕	IC 523 ✕	IR 3273	IC 721 ✕	IC 525 ✕	IR 3275	IC 1527 Ⓐ ✕	IC 723 ✕
Genève **505** ▷ d.	0742	0815	...	...	...	0842	0915	...	0942	1015	...	...	1042	1115	...	...	1142	1215	...	1242	1315	...	...	1342
Lausanne **505** d.	0820	|	...	...	...	0920	|	...	1020	|	...	...	1120	|	...	...	1220	|	...	1320	|	...	1415	1420
Biel/Bienne **505** d.	|	0946	...	...	...	|	1046	...	|	1146	...	...	|	1246	...	...	|	1346	...	|	1446	...	1517	|
Bern **505** d.	0931	|	...	...	...	1031	|	...	1131	|	...	...	1231	|	...	...	1331	|	...	1431	|	...	|	1531
Zürich HB ● **535** d.	1039	1103	1109	1133	1139	1139	1203	1209	1239	1303	1309	1333	1339	1403	1409	1439	1439	1503	1509	1539	1603	1609	1633	1639
Zürich Flughafen ✈ ● **535** d.	1053	1113	1123	1143	1153	1153	1213	1223	1253	1313	1323	1343	1353	1413	1423	1453	1453	1513	1523	1553	1613	1623	1643	1653
Winterthur **535** d.	1108	1129	1138	1158	1208	1208	1229	1238	1308	1329	1338	1358	1408	1429	1438	1508	1508	1529	1538	1608	1629	1638	1659	1708
Wil d.	1126	|	1156	|	1226	1226	|	1256	1326	|	1356	|	1426	|	1456	1526	1526	|	1556	1626	|	1656	|	1726
Gossau d.	1145	|	1215	|	1245	1245	|	1315	1345	|	1415	|	1445	|	1515	1545	1545	|	1615	1645	|	1715	|	1745
St Gallen **534** a.	1152	1202	1222	1230	1252	1252	1302	1322	1352	1402	1422	1430	1452	1502	1522	1552	1552	1602	1622	1652	1702	1722	1732	1752
Rorschach **534** a.	...	1221	1239	...	...	...	1321	1339	...	1421	1439	...	...	1521	1539	...	...	1621	1639	...	1721	1739	...	...
Chur **534** a.	...	...	1348	...	...	...	...	1448	...	...	1548	...	...	...	1648	...	...	...	1748	...	...	1848	...	...

	IC 527 ✕	IR 3277	EC 197 M✕	IC 725 ✕	IC 529 ✕	IR 3279	IC 1531 Ⓐ ✕	IC 727 ✕	IC 531 ✕	IR 3281 S	EC 199 n M✕	IC 729 ✕	IC 533 ✕	IR 3283	IC 731 ✕	IR 3285	IC 733 ✕	IR 3287	IC 735	IR 3289		◇		IR 3293
Genève **505** ▷ d.	1415	...	...	1442	1515	...	...	1542	1615	...	...	1642	1715	...	1742	...	1842	...	1942	...	...	...	...	...
Lausanne **505** d.	|	...	...	1520	|	...	1615	1620	|	...	...	1720	|	...	1820	...	1920	...	2020	...	...	...	...	...
Biel/Bienne **505** d.	1546	...	...	|	1646	...	1717	|	1746	...	...	|	1846	...	|	...	|	...	|	...	...	...	...	...
Bern **505** d.	|	...	...	1631	|	...	|	1731	|	...	...	1831	|	...	1931	...	2031	...	2131	...	...	...	...	...
Zürich HB ● **535** d.	1703	1709	1733	1739	1803	1809	1833	1839	1903	1909	1933	1939	2003	2009	2039	2109	2139	2209	2239	2309	...	2339	...	0017
Zürich Flughafen ✈ ● **535** d.	1713	1723	1743	1753	1813	1823	1843	1853	1913	1923	1943	1953	2013	2023	2053	2123	2153	2223	2253	2323	...	2353	...	0030
Winterthur **535** d.	1729	1738	1758	1808	1829	1838	1859	1908	1929	1938	1958	2008	2029	2038	2108	2138	2208	2238	2308	2338	...	0009	...	0045
Wil d.	|	1756	|	1826	|	1856	|	1926	|	1956	|	2026	|	2056	2126	2156	2226	2256	2326	2356	...	0031	...	0103
Gossau d.	|	1815	|	1845	|	1915	|	1945	|	2015	|	2045	|	2115	2145	2215	2245	2315	2345	0015	...	0048	...	0120
St Gallen **534** a.	1802	1822	1830	1852	1902	1922	1932	1952	2002	2022	2030	2052	2102	2122	2152	2222	2252	2322	2352	0022	...	0055	...	0128
Rorschach **534** a.	1821	1839	...	...	1921	1939	...	...	2021	2039	...	...	...	...	...	...	...	...	...	...	...	...	...	...
Chur **534** a.	...	1948	...	...	...	2048	...	...	...	...	...	...	...	...	...	...	...	...	...	...	...	...	...	...

	IR 3292	⑥⑦ c ◇	⑥⑦ c		IR 3252	IC 706 ✕	IR 3254	IC 510 ✕	IC 708 ✕	IC 1510 Ⓐ ✕	IR 3256 S	IC 512 ✕	IC 710 ✕	EC 290 ①–⑤ L✕	IR 3258	IC 514 ✕	IC 712 ✕	IR 3260	IC 516 ✕	IC 714 ✕	EC 198 v M✕	IR 3262	IC 518 ✕	IC 716 ✕
Chur **534** d.	...	...	...	...	...	...	...	...	...	...	...	...	...	...	0611	...	...	0711	...	...	...	0811	...	...
Rorschach **534** d.	...	...	...	...	...	...	...	0539	...	...	0621	0639	...	...	0721	0739	...	0821	0839	...	...	0921	0939	...
St Gallen **534** d.	0037	...	...	...	0437	0507	0537	0558	0607	0628	0637	0658	0707	0729	0737	0758	0807	0837	0858	0907	0929	0937	0958	1007
Gossau d.	0044	...	...	...	0444	0514	0544	|	0614	|	0644	|	0714	|	0744	|	0814	0844	|	0914	|	0944	|	1014
Wil d.	0102	0105	...	...	0504	0534	0604	|	0634	|	0704	|	0734	|	0804	|	0834	0904	|	0934	|	1004	|	1034
Winterthur **535** d.	...	0127	0135	...	0524	0554	0624	0633	0654	0703	0724	0733	0754	0803	0824	0833	0854	0924	0933	0954	1003	1024	1033	1054
Zürich Flughafen ✈ ● **535** a.	...	...	|	...	0536	0606	0636	0646	0706	0716	0736	0746	0806	0816	0836	0846	0906	0936	0946	1006	1016	1036	1046	1106
Zürich HB ● **535** a.	...	...	0158	...	0551	0621	0651	0657	0721	0727	0751	0757	0821	0827	0851	0857	0921	0951	0957	1021	1027	1051	1057	1121
Bern **505** a.	...	...	...	...	...	0728	...	|	0828	|	...	|	0928	...	...	|	1028	...	|	1128	...	...	|	1228
Biel/Bienne **505** a.	...	...	...	...	...	|	...	0813	|	0843	...	0913	|	...	...	1013	|	...	1113	|	...	...	1213	|
Lausanne **505** a.	...	...	...	...	...	0840	...	|	0940	0945	...	|	1040	...	...	|	1140	...	|	1240	...	...	|	1340
Genève **505** ▷ a.	...	...	...	...	...	0918	...	0947	1018	...	...	1047	1118	...	...	1147	1218	...	1247	1318	...	...	1347	1418

	IR 3264	IC 520 ✕	IC 718 ✕	EC 196 M✕	IR 3266	IC 522 ✕	IC 720 ✕	IR 3268	IC 524 ✕	IC 722 Ⓐ ✕	IC 742 Ⓒ ✕	IR 3270	IC 526 ✕	IC 724 ✕	IR 3272	IC 528 ✕	IC 726 ✕	EC 192 M✕	IR 3274	IC 530 ✕	IC 728 Ⓐ ✕	IC 748 Ⓒ ✕	IC 1530 Ⓐ ✕	IR 3276
Chur **534** d.	0911	...	...	...	1011	...	...	1111	...	...	...	1211	...	...	1311	...	...	...	1411	...	...	...	...	1511
Rorschach **534** d.	1021	1039	...	...	1121	1139	...	1221	1239	...	...	1321	1339	...	1421	1439	...	...	1521	1539	...	...	...	1621
St Gallen **534** d.	1037	1058	1107	1129	1137	1158	1207	1237	1258	1307	1307	1337	1358	1407	1437	1458	1507	1529	1537	1558	1607	1607	1628	1637
Gossau d.	1044	|	1114	|	1144	|	1214	1244	|	1314	1314	1344	|	1414	1444	|	1514	|	1544	|	1614	1614	|	1644
Wil d.	1104	|	1134	|	1204	|	1234	1304	|	1334	1334	1404	|	1434	1504	|	1534	|	1604	|	1634	1634	|	1704
Winterthur **535** d.	1124	1133	1154	1203	1224	1233	1254	1324	1333	1354	1354	1424	1433	1454	1524	1533	1554	1603	1624	1633	1654	1654	1703	1724
Zürich Flughafen ✈ ● **535** a.	1136	1146	1206	1216	1236	1246	1306	1336	1346	1406	1406	1436	1446	1506	1536	1546	1606	1616	1636	1646	1706	1706	1716	1736
Zürich HB ● **535** a.	1151	1157	1221	1227	1251	1257	1321	1351	1357	1421	1421	1451	1457	1521	1551	1557	1621	1627	1651	1657	1721	1721	1727	1751
Bern **505** a.	...	|	1328	...	...	|	1428	...	|	1528	...	...	|	1628	...	|	1728	...	...	|	1828	...	|	...
Biel/Bienne **505** a.	...	1313	|	...	...	1413	|	...	1513	|	...	...	1613	|	...	1713	|	...	...	1813	|	...	1843	...
Lausanne **505** a.	...	|	1440	...	...	|	1540	...	|	1640	...	...	|	1740	...	|	1840	...	...	|	1940	...	1945	...
Genève **505** ▷ a.	...	1447	1518	...	...	1547	1618	...	1647	1718	...	...	1747	1818	...	1847	1918	...	...	1947	2018	...	...	...

	IC 532 ✕	IC 730 ✕	EC 190 M✕	IR 3278	IC 534 ✕	IC 732 ✕	IC 1534 Ⓐ ✕	IR 3280	IC 536 ✕	IC 734 ✕	EC 98 M✕	IR 3282	IC 538 ✕	IC 736 F✕	IR 3284		IC 738 ✕	EC 96 n M✕	IR 3286	◇	IR 3288		IR 3290
Chur **534** d.	...	...	...	1611	...	...	...	1711	...	...	...	1811	...	...	1911	...	...	...	2011	...	...	...	...
Rorschach **534** d.	1639	...	...	1721	1739	...	...	1821	1839	...	...	1921	1939	...	2021	...	...	...	2121	...	...	...	...
St Gallen **534** d.	1658	1707	1729	1737	1758	1807	1828	1837	1858	1907	1929	1937	1958	2007	2037	...	2107	2129	2137	2213	2237	...	2337
Gossau d.	|	1714	|	1744	|	1814	|	1844	|	1914	|	1944	|	2014	2044	...	2114	|	2144	2222	2244	...	2344
Wil d.	|	1734	|	1804	|	1834	|	1904	|	1934	|	2004	|	2034	2104	...	2134	|	2204	2239	2304	...	0004
Winterthur **535** d.	1733	1754	1803	1824	1833	1854	1903	1924	1933	1954	2003	2024	2033	2054	2124	...	2154	2203	2224	2301	2324	...	0028
Zürich Flughafen ✈ ● **535** a.	1746	1806	1816	1836	1846	1906	1916	1936	1946	2006	2016	2036	2046	2106	2136	...	2206	2216	2236	2314	2336	...	0040
Zürich HB ● **535** a.	1757	1821	1827	1851	1857	1921	1927	1951	1957	2021	2027	2051	2057	2121	2151	...	2221	2227	2251	2325	2351	...	0053
Bern **505** a.	|	1928	...	...	|	2028	|	...	|	2128	...	...	|	2228	...	...	2331	...	...	...	...	...	...
Biel/Bienne **505** a.	1913	|	...	...	2013	|	2043	...	2113	|	...	...	2213	...	...	...	...	...	...	...	...	...	...
Lausanne **505** a.	|	2040	...	...	|	2140	2145	...	|	2240	...	...	...	...	...	...	...	...	...	...	...	...	...
Genève **505** ▷ a.	2047	2118	...	...	2147k	...	...	...	2247k	2318k	...	...	...	...	...	...	...	...	...	...	...	...	...

F – From/to Fribourg (Table **505**).
L – ①–⑤ (not Dec. 26, Apr. 7, 10, May 1, 18, 19, 29, Sept. 18, 25, Oct. 2). From Lindau (Table **75**).
M – From/to München (Table **75**).
S – From/to Sargans (Table **534**).

c – Also Apr. 7, 10, May 1, 18, 19, 29, Aug. 1, Nov. 1; not Dec. 25.
j – 0513 on Feb. 6, 27, Mar. 27, May 8, June 5, 19–23, 26–30, July 24, Sept. 4, 11, 25–29, Oct. 2–6, 30, Dec. 4.
k – ⑤⑥ only.
n – Not Dec. 24, 31.
v – Not Dec. 25, Jan. 1.

◇ – Operated by THURBO.
▷ – Most Genève services start from/continue to Genève Aéroport (see Table **505**).
● – Frequent services operate **Zürich - Zürich Flughafen** and v.v. (up to 13 trains per hour 0600 - 2400).

533 SCHAFFHAUSEN - KREUZLINGEN *URh*

	✕A		✕B		✕A		✕A		
Schaffhausen d.	0910	...	1110	...	1318	...	1518	...	...
Stein am Rhein d.	1115	...	1315	...	1523	...	1723	...	...
Kreuzlingen Hafen a.	1355	...	1555	...	1805	...	2005j	...	...

	✕A		✕D	✕F		✕A		✕E	
Kreuzlingen Hafen d.	0900	...	1100	1200	...	1427	...	1627	...
Stein am Rhein d.	1130	...	1330	1530h	...	1657	...	1857	...
Schaffhausen a.	1245	...	1445	1645	...	1815	...	2015j	...

A – ④–⑦ Apr. 7 – 23 (also Apr. 10); daily Apr. 27 - Oct. 1.
B – ⑦ Apr. 9 - June 11 (also Apr. 7, 10, May 18, 29, June 8); daily June 24 - Sept. 10 (also Sept. 17, 24); daily Oct. 1 – 15.
D – ④–⑦ Apr. 17 – 23 (also Apr. 10); daily Apr. 27 - Oct. 15.
E – ⑦ Apr. 9 - June 11 (also Apr. 7, 10, May 18, 29, June 8); daily June 24 - Sept. 10 (also Sept. 17, 24, Oct. 1).
F – ④ June 29 - Sept. 7.
h – Arrives 1425.
j – Not Aug. 12.

534 WIL - ST GALLEN - BUCHS - CHUR *SBB*

Warning! Subject to alteration February 27 - October 29 (trains replaced by 🚌 Altstätten - Buchs). See page 561 for amended service during this period.

km		*IR* 3251 W	*IR* 3253 W	*IR* 3255	*IR* 3257	*EC* 97 pM	*IR* 3259	*IR* 3261	*EC* 99 M	*IR* 3263	*IR* 3265	*EC* 191 M	*IR* 3267	*IR* 3269	*EC* 193 M	*IR* 3271	*IR* 3273	*IR* 3275	*IR* 3277	*EC* 197 M	*IR* 3279	*IR* 3281	*EC* 199 nM	◇	◇	◇	◇
	Zürich HB **530** d.	...	...	0609	0709	0733	0809	0909	0933	1009	1109	1133	1209	1309	1333	1409	1509	1609	1709	1733	1809	1909	1933	...	...	...	...
0	**St Gallen** **530** d.	0525	0625	0725	0825	0832	0925	1025	1032	1125	1225	1232	1325	1425	1432	1525	1625	1725	1825	1832	1925	2025	2032	2125	2225	2325	0026
16	Rorschach **530** d.	0539	0639	0739	0839	|	0939	1039	|	1139	1239	|	1339	1439	|	1539	1639	1739	1839	|	1939	2039	|	2139	2239	2339	0043
27	**St Margrethen** d.	0547	0647	0747	0847	0849	0947	1047	1049	1147	1247	1249	1347	1447	1449	1547	1647	1747	1847	1849	1947	2047	2049	2147	2247	2347	0053
39	Altstätten d.	0559	0659	0759	0859	...	0959	1059	...	1159	1259	...	1359	1459	...	1559	1659	1759	1859	...	1959	2059	...	2159	2259	0002	0107
65	**Buchs** **520** d.	0615	0715	0815	0915	...	1015	1115	...	1215	1315	...	1415	1515	...	1615	1715	1815	1915	...	2015	2115	...	2215	2315	0018	...
81	Sargans ⊖ **520** a.	0624	0724	0824	0924	...	1024	1124	...	1224	1324	...	1424	1524	...	1624	1724	1824	1924	...	2024	2124	...	2225	2325	0028	...
93	Landquart **520** a.	0638	0737	0837	0937	...	1037	1137	...	1237	1337	...	1437	1537	...	1637	1737	1837	1937	...	2037	*2148*	...	*2248*	*2339*	*0042*	...
107	**Chur** **520** a.	0648	0748	0848	0948	...	1048	1148	...	1248	1348	...	1448	1548	...	1648	1748	1848	1948	...	2048	*2156*	...	*2256*	*2348*	*0051*	...

	IC 556 ⚒	*IR* 3256	*EC* 290 L	*IR* 3258	*IR* 3260	*EC* 198 pM	*IR* 3262	*IR* 3264	*EC* 196 M	*IR* 3266	*IR* 3268	*IR* 3270	*IR* 3272	*EC* 192 M	*IR* 3274	*IR* 3276	*EC* 190 M	*IR* 3278	*IR* 3280	*EC* 98 M	*IR* 3282	*IR* 3284	*EC* 96 nM	*IR* 3286	◇	◇	◇
Chur **520** d.	0508	...	...	0611	0711	...	0811	0911	...	1011	1111	1211	1311	...	1411	1511	...	1611	1711	...	1811	1911	...	2011	*2114*	*2214*	*2301*
Landquart **520** d.	0518	...	...	0621	0721	...	0821	0921	...	1021	1121	1221	1321	...	1421	1521	...	1621	1721	...	1821	1921	...	2021	*2122*	*2222*	*2309*
Sargans ⊖ **520** d.	0526	0536	...	0636	0736	...	0836	0936	...	1036	1136	1236	1336	...	1436	1536	...	1636	1736	...	1836	1936	...	2036	2136	2236	2339
Buchs **520** d.	...	0545	...	0645	0745	...	0845	0945	...	1045	1145	1245	1345	...	1445	1545	...	1645	1745	...	1845	1945	...	2045	2145	2245	2348
Altstätten d.	...	0601	...	0701	0801	...	0901	1001	...	1101	1201	1301	1401	...	1501	1601	...	1701	1801	...	1901	2001	...	2101	2201	2301	0003
St Margrethen d.	...	0613	0710	0713	0813	0910	0913	1013	1110	1113	1213	1313	1413	1510	1513	1613	1710	1713	1813	1910	1913	2013	2110	2113	2213	2313	0013
Rorschach **530** d.	...	0621	|	0721	0821	|	0921	1021	|	1121	1221	1321	1421	|	1521	1621	|	1721	1821	|	1921	2021	|	2121	2221	2321	0021
St Gallen **530** a.	...	0635	0728	0735	0835	0928	0935	1035	1128	1135	1235	1335	1435	1528	1535	1635	1728	1735	1835	1928	1935	2035	2128	2135	2234	2334	0034
Zürich HB **530** a.	...	0751	0827	0851	0951	1027	1051	1151	1227	1251	1351	1451	1551	1627	1651	1751	1827	1851	1951	2027	2051	2151	2227	2251	...	...	...

🚌 FELDKIRCH (AUSTRIA) - VADUZ (LIECHTENSTEIN) - SARGANS 🚌. Line number **11**.

	①–⑤ z	①–⑥ v	①–⑥ v																				
Feldkirch (Bahnhof) d.	...	...	...	...	0624	0654	and at the	1724	1754	1824	1854	1924	1954	2024	2054	2124	2154	2224	2254	...	...	...	...	...
Schaan (Bahnhof) d.	0515	0530	0600	0630	0700	0730	same minutes	1800	1830	1900	1930	2000	2030	2100	2130	2200	2230	2300	2330	...	...	...	...	...
Vaduz Post d.	0526	0541	0611	0641	0711	0741	past each	1811	1841	1909	1941	2009	2041	2109	2141	2209	2239	2309	2339	...	...	...	...	...
Sargans (Bahnhof) a.	0557	0612	0642	0712	0742	0812	hour until	1842	1912	...	2012	...	2112	...	2212	...	...	...	...	...	...	...	...	...

	①–⑤ z	①–⑥ v		①–⑤ z		①–⑤ z			①–⑤ z															
Sargans (Bahnhof) d.	...	...	...	0544	...	0614	0644	...	0714	0744	0814	and at the	1844	1914	1944	...	2044	...	2144	...	2244	...	...	...
Vaduz Post d.	0518	0548	0618	0618	0648	0648	0718	0748	0748	0818	0848	same minutes	1918	1948	2018	2048	2118	2148	2218	2248	2318	...	...	...
Schaan (Bahnhof) d.	0530	0600	0630	0630	0700	0700	0730	0800	0800	0830	0900	past each	1930	2000	2030	2100	2130	2200	2230	2300	2326	...	...	...
Feldkirch (Bahnhof) a.	0606	0636	0706	0706	0736	0736	0806	0836	0836	0906	0936	hour until	2006	2036	2106	2136	2206	2236	2306	2336	...	...	...	...

L – ①–⑤ (not Dec. 26, Apr. 7, 10, May 1, 18, 19, 29, Sept. 18, 25, Oct. 2). From Lindau (Table **75**).
M – 12 ✕ Zürich - Bregenz - München and v.v.
W – From Wil (Table **530**).
n – Not Dec. 24, 31.
p – Not Dec. 25, Jan. 1.
v – Also Feb. 19; not Dec. 24, 26, Feb. 2, Apr. 10, May 1, 18, 29, June 8, Aug. 15, Nov. 1.
z – Not Dec. 26, Jan. 6, Feb. 2, Apr. 7, 10, May 1, 18, 29, June 8, Aug. 15, Sept. 8, Nov. 1.
◇ – Operated by THURBO.
⊖ – See panel below main table for 🚌 links to / from Vaduz.

535 ZÜRICH - KONSTANZ and ROMANSHORN *SBB, THURBO*

km		◇	*RE* 2103 Ⓐ	R	*IC* 803 ✕	◇	*IR* 2107	R	*IC* 805 ✕	◇	*IR* 2109	R	*IC* 807 A✕	◇	*IR* 2111	R	*IC* 809 A✕	◇	*IR* 2113	R	⊡ ⊠	*IC* 831 A✕	◇	*IR* 2135	R	*IC* 833 A✕
	Bern **505 560** d.	...	...	...	...	...	...	...	0602	...	...	...	0702	...	...	...	0802	...	...	...		1902	...	...	...	2002
	Luzern **555** d.	...	...	...	...	...	0535	...	|	...	0635	...	|	...	0735	...	|	...	0835	...	and at	|	...	1935	...	|
0	**Zürich** HB ‡ **530** d.	...	*0525*	...	0605	...	0635	...	0705	...	0735	...	0805	...	0835	...	0905	...	0935	...	the same	2005	...	2035	...	2105
10	**Zürich** Flug ✈ ‡ **530** d.	...	|	...	0616	...	0646	...	0716	...	0746	...	0816	...	0846	...	0916	...	0946	...	minutes	2016	...	2046	...	2116
30	Winterthur **530** d.	...	0601	...	0631	...	0701	...	0731	...	0801	...	0831	...	0901	...	0931	...	1001	...	past each	2031	...	2101	...	2131
46	Frauenfeld d.	...	0612	...	0642	...	0712	...	0742	...	0812	...	0842	...	0912	...	0942	...	1012	...	hour until	2042	...	2112	...	2142
64	Weinfelden **538/9** d.	0606	0625	0627	0655	0706	0725	0727	0755	0806	0825	0827	0855	0906	0925	0927	0955	1006	1025	1027		2055	2106	2125	2127	2155
87	Kreuzlingen a.	0631	0643	|	|	0731	0743	|	|	0831	0843	|	|	0931	0943	|	|	1031	1043	|		|	2131	2143	|	|
88	**Konstanz** a.	0634	0650	|	|	0742	0750	|	|	0834	0850	|	|	0934	0950	|	|	1034	1050	|		|	2134	2150	|	|
86	**Romanshorn** **538/9** a.	...	...	0642	0712	...	...	0742	0812	...	...	0842	0912	...	...	0942	1012	...	...	1042		2112	...	...	2142	2212

	◇	*IR* 2137	R	*IC* 835 A	◇	*IR* 2139 ¶	R	*IC* 837	◇	*RE* 2145 ◇	*RE* 3547 ◇	◇
Bern **505 560** d.	...	...	...	2102	...	...	...	2202	...	...	...	...
Luzern **555** d.	...	...	...	|	...	...	...	|	...	...	...	...
Zürich HB ‡ **530** d.	...	2135	...	2205	...	2235	...	2305	...	2339	0008	...
Zürich Flug ✈ ‡ **530** d.	...	2146	...	2216	...	2246	...	2316	...	2353	0019	...
Winterthur **530** d.	...	2201	...	2231	...	2301	...	2331	...	0008	0034	...
Frauenfeld d.	...	2212	...	2242	...	2312	...	2342	...	0018	0045	...
Weinfelden **538/9** d.	2206	2225	2227	2255	2306	2325	2327	2355	0006	0030	0100	0106
Kreuzlingen a.	2231	2243	|	|	2331	2343	|	|	0030	0048	|	0130
Konstanz a.	2234	2250	|	|	2334	2350	|	|	0034	0051	|	0135
Romanshorn **538/9** a.	...	...	2242	2312	...	...	2342	0012	...	...	0117	...

	R	*IR* 2106	◇	*IC* 806 A✕	R	*IR* 2108	◇	*IC* 808 A✕	⊡ ❖
Romanshorn **538/9** d.	0517	...	...	0548	0617	...	...	0648	
Konstanz d.	|	0509	0524	|	|	0609	0624	|	and at
Kreuzlingen d.	|	0516	0527	|	|	0616	0627	|	
Weinfelden **538/9** d.	0533	0536	0554	0606	0633	0636	0654	0706	the same
Frauenfeld d.	...	0548	...	0618	...	0648	...	0718	minutes
Winterthur **530** d.	...	0601	...	0631	...	0701	...	0731	
Zürich Flughafen ✈ ‡ **530** a.	...	0614	...	0644	...	0714	...	0744	past each
Zürich HB ‡ **530** a.	...	0625	...	0655	...	0725	...	0755	hour until
Luzern **555** d.	...	0725	...	|	...	0825	...	|	
Bern **505 560** a.	...	...	...	0758	...	...	...	0858	

	R	*IR* 2130	◇	*IC* 830 A✕	R	*IR* 2132	◇	*IC* 832 ✕	R	*IR* 2134	◇	*IC* 834 ✕	R	*IR* 2136	◇	*IC* 836 ✕	R	*IR* 2138 §	◇	*IC* 838	R	*RE* 2142 ◇	◇	*IC* 840	R	*RE* 2146 ◇	◇
Romanshorn **538/9** d.	1717	...	...	1748	1817	...	...	1848	1917	...	...	1948	2017	...	...	2048	2117	...	...	2148	2217	...	...	2248	2317	...	...
Konstanz d.	|	1709	1724	|	|	1809	1824	|	|	1909	1924	|	|	2009	2024	|	|	2109	2124	|	|	2209	2224	|	|	2309	0009
Kreuzlingen d.	|	1716	1727	|	|	1816	1827	|	|	1916	1927	|	|	2016	2027	|	|	2116	2127	|	|	2216	2227	|	|	2316	0020
Weinfelden **538/9** d.	1733	1736	1754	1806	1833	1836	1854	1906	1933	1936	1954	2006	2033	2036	2054	2106	2133	2136	2154	2206	2233	2236	2254	2306	2333	2336	0047
Frauenfeld d.	...	1748	...	1818	...	1848	...	1918	...	1948	...	2018	...	2048	...	2118	...	2148	...	2218	...	2248	...	2318	...	2348	...
Winterthur **530** d.	...	1801	...	1831	...	1901	...	1931	...	2001	...	2031	...	2101	...	2131	...	2201	...	2231	...	2301	...	2331	...	2359	...
Zürich Flug ✈ ‡ **530** a.	...	1814	...	1844	...	1914	...	1944	...	2014	...	2044	...	2114	...	2144	...	2214	...	2244	...	2314	...	2344	...	|	...
Zürich HB ‡ **530** a.	...	1825	...	1855	...	1925	...	1955	...	2025	...	2055	...	2125	...	2155	...	2225	...	2255	...	2325	...	2355	...	*0035*	...
Luzern **555** d.	...	1925	...	|	...	2025	...	|	...	2125	...	|	...	...	...	|	...	...	...	|	...	...	...	...	...	...	...
Bern **505 560** a.	...	...	...	1958	...	...	...	2058	...	...	...	2158	...	...	...	2302	...	...	...	0002	...	...	...	...	...	...	...

A – From / to stations in Table **560**.
R – To / from Rorschach (Table **538**). Operated by THURBO.
§ – On ①②③④⑦ (also Dec. 24, Apr. 7) runs as *RE* **2140** ◇.
¶ – On ①②③④⑦ (also Dec. 24, Apr. 7) runs as *RE* **2141** ◇.
❖ – The 1609 from Konstanz terminates at Zürich HB.
⊠ – Passengers travelling on the 1635 from Luzern must change trains at Zürich HB.
⊡ – Train numbers increase by 2 each hour.
‡ – Frequent services operate **Zürich - Zürich Flughafen** and v.v. (up to 13 trains per hour 0600 - 2400).
◇ – Operated by THURBO.

BSB / SBS — ROMANSHORN - FRIEDRICHSHAFEN ferry service — 536

	h	h	e	e				f	f
Romanshorn Autoquai ..... d.	0524	0624	0724	0824	0924	and hourly until	1824	1924	2024
Friedrichshafen Fähre ..... a.	0608	0708	0808	0908	1008		1908	2008	2108

	h	h	e	e				f	f
Friedrichshafen Fähre .... d.	0520	0620	0720	0820	0920	and hourly until	1820	1920	2020
Romanshorn Autoquai ...... a.	0604	0704	0804	0904	1004		1904	2004	2104

e – ①–⑥ to Mar. 25 (not Dec. 24, 26, 31, Jan. 2, 6); daily Mar. 27 - Nov. 11; ①–⑥ from Nov. 13.
f – ①–⑤ to Mar. 24 (not Dec. 26 - Jan. 6); daily Mar. 27 - Nov. 10; ①–⑤ from Nov. 13.
h – ①–⑤ (not Dec. 26 - Jan. 6, Apr. 7, 10, May 18, 29, Aug. 1).

Operator: BSB / SBS ✆ 071 466 78 88.

THURBO — SCHAFFHAUSEN - ROMANSHORN - RORSCHACH and ST GALLEN — 538

km								⚒																
0	**Schaffhausen** .... d.	...	...	...	...	...	...	...	...	0519	...	0549	...	...	0619	...	and at the same minutes past each hour until	1949	...	...	2019	...	2049	...
20	Stein am Rhein .... d.	...	...	...	...	0513	...	...	...	0543	...	0613	...	...	0643	...		2013	...	...	2043	...	2113	...
46	**Kreuzlingen** .... d.	0445	...	0515	...	0545	...	...	...	0615	...	0645	...	...	0715	...		2045	...	...	2115	...	2145	...
	Konstanz .... d.	|	...	|	...	|	...	...	0609	|	...	|	...	0709	|	...		|	...	2109	|	...	|	...
47	Kreuzlingen Hafen .... d.	0447	...	0517	...	0547	...	...	0612	0617	...	0647	...	0712	0717	...		2047	...	2112	2117	...	2147	...
	Weinfelden .... **535 539** d.	|	...	|	...	|	...	0557	|	|	0627	|	*0655*	|	|	0727		|	*2055*	|	|	2127	|	*2155*
65	**Romanshorn** .... **535 539** a.	0512	...	0542	...	0612	...	0612	0625	0642	0642	0712	*0712*	0725	0742	0742		2112	*2112*	2125	2142	2142	2212	*2212*
65	**Romanshorn** .... d.	0514	0516	0544	0546	0614	0616	0616	0626	0644	0646	0714	0716	0726	0744	0746		2114	2116	2126	2144	2146	2214	2216
	St Gallen .... a.	0541	|	0611	|	0641	|	|	0644	0711	|	0741	|	0744	0811	|		2141	|	2144	2211	|	2241	|
73	Arbon .... a.	...	0525	...	0555	...	0625	0625	...	...	0655	...	0725	...	...	0755		...	2125	...	...	2155	...	2225
80	**Rorschach** .... a.	...	0536	...	0606	...	0636	0636	...	...	0706	...	0736	...	...	0806		...	2136	...	...	2206	...	2236

											⑥⑦j
Schaffhausen .... d.	2119	...	2149	...	2219	...	2249	...	2319	2349	...
Stein am Rhein .... d.	2143	...	2213	...	2243	...	2313	...	2343	0013	...
Kreuzlingen .... d.	2215	...	2245	...	2315	...	2345	...	0015	0044	0105
Konstanz .... d.	|	...	|	...	|	...	|	...	|	...	|
Kreuzlingen Hafen .... d.	2217	...	2247	...	2317	...	2347	...	0017	...	0107
Weinfelden .... **535 539** d.	|	2227	|	*2255*	|	2327	|	*2355*	|	...	|
Romanshorn .... **535 539** a.	2242	2242	2312	*2312*	2342	2342	0012	*0012*	0042	...	0128
Romanshorn .... d.	2244	2246	2314	2316	2344	2346	0014	0017	...	...	*0134*
St Gallen .... a.	2311	|	2341	|	0011	|	0041	|	...	...	*0158*
Arbon .... a.	...	2255	...	2325	...	2355	...	0025	...	...	...
Rorschach .... a.	...	2306	...	2336	...	0006	...	0036	...	...	...

				Ⓐ					
Rorschach .... d.	...	...	...	...	...	0454	...	0524	...
Arbon .... d.	...	...	...	...	...	0504	...	0534	...
St Gallen .... d.	...	...	...	...	...	|	...	|	0519
Romanshorn .... a.	...	...	...	...	...	0513	...	0542	0546
Romanshorn ...... **535 539** d.	...	...	...	0448	...	0517	0518	*0548*	0548
Weinfelden .... **535 539** a.	...	...	...	|	...	0533	|	*0605*	|
Kreuzlingen Hafen .... d.	...	...	...	0511	...	...	0541	...	0611
Konstanz .... a.	...	...	...	|	...	...	|	...	|
Kreuzlingen .... d.	0446	...	0515	0515	...	...	0546	...	0615
Stein am Rhein .... d.	0516	...	0546	0546	...	...	0616	...	0646
Schaffhausen .... a.	0541	...	0613	0613	...	...	0643	...	0713

																					⑤⑥k			
Rorschach .... d.	0554	...	...	0624	...	0654	...	and at the same minutes past each hour until	...	2124	...	2154	...	2224	...	2254	...	...	2324	...	...	...	2354	...
Arbon .... d.	0604	...	...	0634	...	0704	...		...	2134	...	2204	...	2234	...	2304	...	...	2334	...	...	...	0004	...
St Gallen .... d.	|	0549	0615	|	0619	|	0649		2115	|	2119	|	2149	|	2219	|	2249	...	|	2319	2319	...	|	2349
Romanshorn .... a.	0613	0616	0633	0643	0646	0713	0716		2133	2143	2146	2213	2216	2243	2246	2313	2316	...	2343	2346	2346	...	0013	0016
Romanshorn .... **535 539** d.	0617	0618	0633	*0648*	0648	0717	0718		2133	*2148*	2148	2217	2218	*2248*	2248	2317	2318	...	...	2348	2348	...	...	0018
Weinfelden ..... **535 539** a.	0633	|	|	*0705*	|	0733	|		|	*2205*	|	2233	|	*2305*	|	2333	|	...	...	|	|	...	...	|
Kreuzlingen Hafen .... d.	...	0641	0647	...	0711	...	0741		2147	...	2211	...	2241	...	2311	...	2341	...	...	0011	0011	...	...	0041
Konstanz .... a.	...	|	0649	...	|	...	|		2149	...	|	...	|	...	|	...	|	...	...	|	|	...	...	|
Kreuzlingen .... d.	...	0646	...	...	0715	...	0746		...	...	2215	...	2246	...	2315	...	2346	...	...	0013	0015	...	...	0044
Stein am Rhein .... d.	...	0716	...	...	0746	...	0816		...	...	2246	...	2316	...	2346	...	0016	...	...	...	0046	...	...	...
Schaffhausen .... a.	...	0743	...	...	0813	...	0843		...	...	2313	...	2343	...	0013	...	0043	...	...	...	0111	...	...	...

j – Mornings of ⑥⑦ (also Apr. 7, 10, May 1, 18, 19, 29, Aug. 1; not Dec. 25).
k – Also Apr. 6, 9, 30, May 17, 18, 28, July 31; not Dec. 23.

THURBO — ROMANSHORN - WEINFELDEN - WIL — 539

km			Ⓐ			Ⓐ					
0	**Romanshorn** ‡ d.	...	0507	0537	and at the same minutes past each hour until	1907	1937	2037	2137	2237	2337
22	Weinfelden ... ‡ d.	0502	0532	0602		1932	2002	2102	2202	2302	0002
41	**Wil** .... a.	0527	0557	0627		1957	2027	2127	2227	2327	0027

	Ⓐ			Ⓐ					
Wil .... d.	0502	0532	and at the same minutes past each hour until	1902	1932	2032	2132	2232	2332
Weinfelden ..... ‡ a.	0530	0559		1930	1959	2059	2159	2259	2359
Romanshorn ‡ a.	0553	0623		1953	2023	2123	2223	2323	0023

‡ – See also Tables **535** and **538**.

PA — CHUR - FLIMS — 542

Chur (Postautostation) - **Flims** Dorf (Post). Journey time: 26–41 minutes. Additional journeys operate until Apr. 18 and June 11 - Oct. 23.

From **Chur** at 0600, 0630, 0658, 0728, 0758, 0828, 0858 and at 28 and 58 minutes past each hour until 1828, 1858; then 1928, 1958, 2058, 2158 and 2258.

From **Flims** Dorf at 0527, 0557 ⚒, 0629, 0659, 0713 Ⓐ, 0729, 0759, 0829, 0859, 0929, 0959, 1029, 1059, 1129, 1159, 1229, 1259, 1329, 1359 and at 29 and 59 minutes past each hour until 1929, 1959; then 2029, 2127, 2227 and 2327.

PA, RhB* — ST MORITZ and TIRANO - CHIAVENNA - LUGANO — 543

				PⓇ	BⓇ					
St Moritz, Bahnhof .... d.	0815	0915	1020	1025	...	1115	✣	1815	1915	2015
Silvaplana .... d.	0827	0927	1032	1034**u**	...	1127		1827	1926	2026
Sils / Segl Maria, Posta .... d.	0836	0936	1041	1041**u**	...	1136	and	1836	1934	2034
Maloja, Posta .... d.	0848	0948	1053	1053**u**	...	1148		1848	1945	2045
Castasegna 🏛 .... d.	0929	1029	1134	1126**u**	...	1229	hourly	1929	2024	2124
Chiavenna, Stazione ...... d.	0953	1053	1158	1206**u**	...	1253		1953	2048	2139
Tirano, Stazione .... d.	...	...	...	|	1420	...	until	...	...	...
Menaggio .... d.	...	...	...	1311	|	...		...	...	...
Lugano, Stazione ◐ .... a.	...	...	...	1416	1730	...		...	...	...

							BⓇ	PⓇ		
Lugano, Stazione ◐ .... d.	...	...	...		...	...	1000	1531	...	...
Menaggio .... d.	...	...	...		...	...	|	1618	...	...
Tirano, Stazione .... a.	...	...	...	and	...	...	1300	|	...	...
Chiavenna, Stazione .... d.	0709	...	0907		1607	1707	...	1725**s**	1807	1914
Castasegna 🏛 .... d.	0725	0823	0923	hourly	1623	1723	...	|	1823	1930
Maloja, Posta .... d.	0811	0911	1011		1711	1811	...	1823**s**	1911	2011
Sils / Segl Maria, Posta ..... d.	0824	0924	1024	until	1724	1824	...	1834**s**	1924	2024
Silvaplana .... d.	0832	0932	1032		1732	1832	...	1840**s**	1932	2032
St Moritz, Bahnhof .... a.	0841	0941	1041		1741	1845	...	1856	1945	2045

A – June 18 - Oct. 23.
B – *Bernina Express*: ④–⑦ Feb. 16 - Apr. 2; daily Apr. 3 - Oct. 22; ④–⑦ Oct. 26 - Nov. 26.
P – *Palm Express*: ⑤⑥† to June 4 (daily Dec. 16 - Jan. 2); daily June 9 - Oct. 22; ⑤–⑦ from Oct. 27.

s – Stops to set down only.
u – Stops to pick up only.

✣ – The 1515 from St Moritz runs 6 minutes later Maloja - Chiavenna.
◐ – 🏛 is at Gandria.

* – **Operators**: Tirano - Lugano RhB. ✆ (081) 288 65 65; St Moritz - Chiavenna - Lugano PA. ✆ (058) 341 34 92.

☛ **Additional journeys** St Moritz - Chiavenna and v.v.
From St Moritz at 0720 and 1815 **A**.
From Chiavenna at 0615 and 2014 **A**.

PA — CHUR - BELLINZONA and CHIAVENNA — 544

km				S A	BⓇ A	BⓇ	BⓇ		S A	BⓇ ⑥A	BⓇ										S A			BⓇ		
0	**Chur** Postautostation .... d.	0658	...	...	0758	0808	0858	...	...	0958	1008	1058	...	1208	1258	...	1408	1458	...	1608	...	1658	...	1808	...	2008
40	Thusis Bahnhof .... ⊡ d.	0725	0735	...	0825	0835	0925	0935	...	1025	1035	1125	1135	1235	1325	1335	1435	1525	1535	1635	...	1725	1735	1835	1935	2035
64	Splügen Dorf .... d.	0754	0816	0820	|	0906	0954	1016	1020	|	1106	1154	1216	1306	1354	1416	1506	1554	1616	1706	1715	1754	1816	1906	2016	2106
	San Bernardino Villaggio ..... a.	0810	0836	|	0910	0924	1010	1036	|	1110	1124	1210	1236	1324	1410	1436	1524	1610	1636	1724	|	1810	1836	1924	2036	2124
	Chiavenna Stazione ◐ .... a.	|	...	1020	|	|	|	...	1220	|	|	|	...	|	|	...	|	|	...	|	1915	|	...	|	...	|
179	**Bellinzona** Stazione .... a.	0904	...	...	1004	1020	1104	...	...	1204	1220	1304	...	1420	1504	...	1620	1704	...	1820	...	1904	...	2020	...	2220

				S A												S A	BⓇ		BⓇ	S A	BⓇ	BⓇ A		BⓇ	⑥A	
Bellinzona Stazione .... d.	...	...	0742	...	...	0856	0942	...	1056	1142	...	1256	1342	...	1456	...	1542	...	1656	...	1742	1756	...	1856	1956	2056
Chiavenna Stazione ◐ .. d.	...	...	|	0745	...	|	|	...	|	|	...	|	|	...	|	1445	|	...	|	1645	|	|	...	|	|	|
San Bernardino Villaggio ... d.	0633	0722	0833	|	0922	0952	1033	1122	1152	1233	1322	1352	1433	1522	1552	|	1633	1722	1752	|	1833	1852	1922	1952	2052	2144
Splügen Dorf .... d.	0653	0743	0853	0940	0943	1010	1053	1143	1210	1253	1343	1410	1453	1543	1610	1640	1653	1743	1810	1840	1853	1910	1943	2010	2110	2201
Thusis Bahnhof .... ⊙ a.	0724	0823	0928	...	1023	1039	1128	1223	1239	1328	1423	1439	1528	1623	1639	...	1728	1823	1839	...	1928	1939	2023	2039	2143	2228
Chur Postautostation .... a.	0753	...	0953	...	...	1104	1153	...	1304	1353	...	1504	1553	...	1704	...	1753	...	1904	...	1953	2004	...	2104	2208	...

A – June 10 - Oct. 22.
B – San Bernardino Route Express.
S – Splügen Pass service.

⊡ – Stops to pick up only.
⊙ – Stops to set down only.
◐ – 🏛 is at Splügen Pass.

Reservations: ✆ +41 58 341 34 87 up to one hour before departure from origin.

545 RHÄTISCHE BAHN (RhB) services — Narrow gauge

DISENTIS / MUSTÉR - CHUR

km		Ⓐ		⚒						
0	**Disentis / Mustér** d.	*0439**	0544	0615	0644	0744	and	1944	2044	2224	...
12	Trun d.	*0453**	0602	0631	0702	0802	hourly	2002	2102	2239	...
30	Ilanz d.	0524	0624	0653	0724	0824	until	2024	2124	2259	2340
49	Reichenau-Tamins d.	0549	0649	0718	0749	0849		2049	2149	2323	0001x
59	**Chur** a.	0603	0703	0732	0803	0902		2102	2203	2333	0011

		⚒									
Chur d.	0610	0652	0755	and	1955	2059	2159	2259	A	1725	1825
Reichenau-Tamins d.	0622	0703	0805	hourly	2005	2112	2211	2311	L	|	|
Ilanz d.	0653	0733	0833	until	2033	2141	2235	2335	S	1802	1902
Trun d.	0715	0754	0854		2054	2200	*2259**	*2359**	O	1825	1925
Disentis / Mustér a.	0731	0811	0911		2111	2215	*2318**	*0018**		1841	1941

CHUR - LANDQUART - KLOSTERS - SCUOL TARASP / DAVOS

km		Ⓐ M	⚒	⚒	⚒	Ⓐ						M✤			✤	M						M			M
0	**Chur** 520 534 d.	...	*0452*	*0519*	...	*0550*	0621a	...	*0650*	*0721*	...	*0753*	*0821*	...		*1453*	*1521*	...	*1553*	*1621*	...	*1653*	*1721*	...	*1753*
14	**Landquart** 520 534 a.	...	*0509*	*0541*	...	*0610*	0641a	...	*0710*	*0741*	...	*0810*	*0841*	...	and at	*1510*	*1541*	...	*1610*	*1641*	...	*1710*	*1741*	...	*1810*
14	**Landquart** d.	0454	0513	0550	...	0620	0647	...	0720	0747	0750	0820	0847	0850		1520	1547	1550	1620	1647	1650	1720	1747	1750	1820
35	Küblis d.	0514	0539	0614	...	0646	0714	...	0743	0810	0814	0843	0910	0914	the same	1543	1610	1614	1643	1710	1714	1743	1810	1814	1843
44	Klosters Dorf d.	|	0553	0627	...	0659	0727	...	|	0823	|	|	0923	|		|	1623	|	|	1723	|	|	1823	|	
46	**Klosters** Platz a.	0528	0556	0630	...	0702	0729	...	0758	0825	0829	0858	0925	0929	minutes	1558	1625	1629	1658	1725	1729	1758	1825	1829	1858
46	**Klosters** Platz 🚗 d.	...	0558	0630	0632	0703	0732	0731	0802	0829	0832	0902	0929	0932		1602	1629	1632	1702	1729	1732	1802	1829	1832	1902
61	**Davos** Dorf d.	...	0630	0654	|	0726	|	0754	0829	0853	|	0929	0953	|	past each	1629	1653	|	1729	1753	|	1826	1853	|	1926
64	**Davos** Platz a.	...	0633	0657	|	0729	|	0757	0833	0857	|	0933	0957	|		1633	1657	|	1733	1757	|	1829	1857	|	1929
68	Sagliains ¶ 🚗 a.	...	...	...	0658	...	0758	...	...	...	0855	...	...	0955	hour until	...	...	1655	...	...	1755	...	...	1855	...
77	Ardez ⊗ a.	...	...	...	0708	...	0808	...	...	...	0906	...	...	1006		...	...	1706	...	...	1806	...	...	1906	...
85	**Scuol-Tarasp** a.	...	...	...	0718	...	0818	...	...	...	0915	...	...	1015		...	...	1715	...	...	1815	...	...	1915	...

			R										
Chur 520 534 d.	*1821*	...	*1853*	*1921*	...	...	*2015**	...	*2115**	...	*2215**	...	*2315**
Landquart 520 534 a.	*1841*	...	*1910*	*1941*	...	...	*2043**	...	*2143**	...	*2243**	...	*2343**
Landquart d.	1847	1850	1920	1947	1950	...	2047	...	2147	...	2247	...	2355
Küblis d.	1910	1914	1943	2013	2017	...	2113	...	2215	...	2313	...	0021
Klosters Dorf d.	1923	|	|	2026	|	...	2126	...	2233	...	2326	⑤⑥	0033
Klosters Platz a.	1925	1929	1958	2029	2031	...	2129	...	2236	...	2329	e	0036
Klosters Platz 🚗 d.	1929	1932	2002	2030	2035	2035	2130	2135	2238	2238	2330	2335	0037
Davos Dorf d.	1953	|	2026	2054	|	|	2154	|	2301	|	2354	|	0059
Davos Platz a.	1957	|	2030	2058	|	|	2158	|	2305	|	2358	|	0105
Sagliains ¶ 🚗 a.	...	1955	...	...	2058	2058	...	2158	...	2258	...	2358	...
Ardez ⊗ a.	...	2006	...	...	2109	2109	...	2209	...	2309	...	0009	...
Scuol-Tarasp a.	...	2015	...	...	2118	2118	...	2218	...	2318	...	0018	...

	⚒		Ⓐ E		⚒		Ⓐ G	Ⓐ H	
Scuol-Tarasp d.	...	...	...	...	0541	...	...	...	...
Ardez ⊗ d.	...	...	...	...	0549	...	...	...	...
Sagliains ¶ 🚗 d.	...	...	...	...	0603	...	...	...	...
Davos Platz d.	0500	...	...	...	|	0600	0610	0626	...
Davos Dorf d.	0504	...	...	...	|	0604	0614	0631	...
Klosters Platz 🚗 a.	0526	...	...	...	0623	0626	0643	0655	...
Klosters Platz d.	0528	...	0556	...	...	0629	0647	0656	...
Klosters Dorf d.	0531	...	|	...	...	0632	0650	0659	...
Küblis d.	0545	...	0614	...	...	0646	0714	0714	...
Landquart a.	0613	...	0643	...	...	0713	0738	0738	...
Landquart 520 534 d.	...	0619	...	0648	...	*0717*	...	...	0748
Chur 520 534 a.	...	0636	...	0706	...	*0736*	...	...	0806

	⚒		M						M⊗	⊗			M			Ⓒ M									
Scuol-Tarasp d.	0641	...	...	0741	...	...	0841	...	...		1641	...	...	1741	...	...	1841	...	...	1941	2041	...	...	2141	...
Ardez ⊗ d.	0649	...	...	0749	...	...	0849	...	...	and at	1649	...	...	1749	...	...	1849	...	...	1949	2049	...	...	2149	...
Sagliains ¶ 🚗 d.	0703	...	...	0803	...	...	0903	...	...		1703	...	...	1803	...	...	1903	...	...	2003	2103	...	...	2203	...
Davos Platz d.	|	0700	0729	|	0802	0826	|	0902	0926	the same	|	1702	1726	|	1802	1830	|	1902	2000	|	|	2100	2150	|	2222
Davos Dorf d.	|	0704	0733	|	0806	0830	|	0906	0930		|	1706	1730	|	1806	1834	|	1906	2004	|	|	2103	2154	|	2226
Klosters Platz 🚗 a.	0723	0727	0755	0823	0828	0855	0923	0929	0954	minutes	1723	1729	1754	1823	1828	1854	1923	1929	2027	2026	2123	2127	2218	2220	2250
Klosters Platz d.	...	0728	0759	0825	0831	0859	0925	0931	0959		1725	1731	1759	1825	1831	1859	1925	1931	...	2029	...	2128	...	2222	2253
Klosters Dorf d.	...	0731	|	...	0834	|	...	0934	|	past each	...	1734	|	...	1834	|	...	1934	...	2032	...	2132	...	2225	2257
Küblis d.	...	0745	0816	0844	0850	0616	0944	0950	1016		1744	1750	1816	1844	1850	1916	1944	1950	...	2046	...	2145	...	2239	2312
Landquart a.	...	0813	0837	0910	0913	0937	1010	1013	1037	hour until	1810	1813	1837	1910	1913	1937	2010	2013	...	2113	...	2213	...	2305	2335
Landquart 520 534 d.	...	*0817*	*0848*	...	*0917*	*0948*	...	*1017*	*1048*		...	*1817*	*1848*	...	*1917*	*1948*	...	*2017*	...	*2117**	...	*2217**	...	*2317**	*2352*
Chur 520 534 a.	...	*0836*	*0906*	...	*0936*	*1006*	...	*1036*	*1106*		...	*1836*	*1906*	...	*1936*	*2006*	...	*2036*	...	*2143**	...	*2243**	...	*2343**	*0022*

SCUOL TARASP and KLOSTERS - ST MORITZ and PONTRESINA

km		Ⓐ		⚒	†	⚒	⚒											Ⓒ				Ⓒ				
0	**Scuol-Tarasp** d.	...	...	0601	0641	*0641*	...	*0741*	0834	...	0934	...	1034	...	1134	...	1234	...	1334	...	1434	...	1534	...	1634	1734
8	Ardez ⊗ d.	...	...	0611	0649	*0649*	...	*0749*	0843	...	0943	...	1043	...	1143	...	1243	...	1343	...	1443	...	1543	...	1643	1743
	Landquart ◐ d.	0454	...	|	|	|	...	|	|	0820	|	0920	|	1020	|	1120	|	1220	|	1320	|	1420	|	1520	|	|
	Klosters Platz d.	0530	...	|	|	|	...	|	|	0900	|	1000	|	1100	|	1200	|	1300	|	1400	|	1500	|	1600	|	|
17	Sagliains ¶ a.	|	...	|	0701	*0701*	...	*0800*	0854	|	0954	|	1054	|	1154	|	1254	|	1354	|	1454	|	1554	|	1654	1754
	Sagliains ¶ d.	|	...	|	0703	0703	...	0803	0855	|	0955	|	1055	|	1155	|	1255	|	1355	|	1455	|	1555	|	1655	1755
19	Susch ⊗ d.	0553	...	0623	0705	0705	...	0805	0858	0919	0958	1019	1058	1119	1158	1219	1258	1319	1358	1419	1458	1519	1558	1619	1658	1758
25	Zernez ⊖ d.	0602	...	0633	0713	0713	...	0813	0907	0929	1007	1026	1107	1129	1207	1226	1307	1329	1407	1426	1507	1529	1607	1626	1707	1807
42	Zuoz d.	0622	0633r	0653	0733	0733	0755	0834	0927	0955	1027	1046	1127	1156	1227	1246	1327	1356	1427	1446	1527	1558	1627	1646	1727	1827
52	Samedan a.	0633	0646r	0706	0746	0746	0811	0847	0942	1008	1042	1057	1142	1207	1242	1257	1342	1407	1442	1457	1542	1608	1642	1657	1742	1842
52	Samedan ▲ d.	0636	0648	0709	0748	0748	0812	0850	0948	1010	1048	1059	1148	1209	1248	1259	1348	1409	1448	1459	1548	1609	1648	1659	1748	1848
	St Moritz ▲ a.	0643	|	0716	|	|	0819	|	|	1018	|	1109	|	1217	|	1309	|	1417	|	1509	|	1617	|	1709	|	|
57	**Pontresina** a.	...	0657	...	0757	0757	...	0857	0957	...	1057	...	1157	...	1257	...	1357	...	1457	...	1557	...	1657	...	1757	1857

						Ⓒ			⑤⑥ e	
Scuol-Tarasp d.	...	1834	...	1934	...	...	*2041*	*2141*	2241	...
Ardez ⊗ d.	...	1843	...	1943	...	...	*2049*	*2149*	2249	...
Landquart ◐ d.	1720	|	1820	|	...	1920	|	|	...	...
Klosters Platz d.	1800	|	1900	|	2000	2000	|	|	...	...
Sagliains ¶ a.	|	1854	|	1954	|	|	*2101*	*2201*	2301	...
Sagliains ¶ d.	|	1855	|	1955	|	|	2103	2203	...	2303
Susch ⊗ d.	1819	1858	1919	1958	2021	2021	2105	2206	...	2306
Zernez ⊖ d.	1826	1907	1926	2007	2032	2032	2113	2213	...	2313
Zuoz d.	1846	1927	1946	2027	2054	2054	2133	2233	...	2333
Samedan a.	1857	1942	1959	2042	2107	2107	2146	2246	...	2345
Samedan ▲ d.	1859	1948	2001	2048	...	2110	2150	2250	...	2346
St Moritz ▲ a.	1909	|	2009	|	...	2118	|	|	...	2354
Pontresina a.	...	1957	...	2057	...	...	2157	2257	...	...

	Ⓐ	⚒	⚒	†	†T 🚌	⚒			⚒		
Pontresina d.	...	...	0542	0558	...	...	...	0702	...	0802	...
St Moritz ▲ d.	...	0445	|	|	...	...	0645	|	0723	|	0845
Samedan ▲ a.	...	0452	0548	0604	...	...	0651	0708	0729	0808	0853
Samedan d.	0454	0513	0553	0608	...	0608	0652	0713	0730	0813	0858
Zuoz d.	0507	0526	0607	0622	...	0622	0703	0726	0744	0827	0910
Zernez ⊖ d.	0526	0546	...	0646	...	0646	0729	0746	...	0849	0929
Susch ⊗ d.	0533	0553	...	0653	0655	0653	0737	0753	...	0858	0937
Sagliains ¶ a.	|	0556	...	0656	|	0656	|	0756	...	0901	|
Sagliains ¶ d.	|	0601	...	0703	|	*0658*	|	*0758*	...	0902	|
Klosters Platz a.	0550	|	...	0723	|	|	0757	|	...	|	0957
Landquart ◐ a.	0643	|	...	...	|	|	0837	|	...	|	1037
Ardez ⊗ d.	...	0611	...	...	0709	*0708*	...	*0808*	...	0914	...
Scuol-Tarasp a.	...	0623	...	...	0717	*0718*	...	*0818*	...	0923	...

		Ⓒ				Ⓒ				Ⓒ								Ⓒ							⑤⑥ e	
Pontresina d.	0902	...	1002	...	1102	...	1202	...	1302	...	1402	...	1502	...	1602	...	1702	...	1802	1902	2002	2102	2202	...	2302	2302
St Moritz ▲ d.	|	0937	|	1047	|	1137	|	1247	|	1337	|	1447	|	1537	|	1647	|	1737	|	|	|	|	|	...	|	|
Samedan ▲ a.	0908	0944	1008	1056	1108	1144	1208	1256	1308	1344	1408	1456	1508	1544	1608	1656	1708	1744	1808	1908	2007	2107	2208	...	2308	2308
Samedan d.	0913	0945	1013	1058	1113	1145	1213	1258	1313	1345	1413	1458	1513	1545	1613	1658	1713	1745	1813	1913	2013	2113	2213	...	2313	...
Zuoz d.	0927	0956	1027	1110	1127	1156	1227	1310	1327	1356	1427	1510	1527	1559	1627	1710	1727	1756	1827	1927	2027	2127	2227	...	2327	...
Zernez ⊖ d.	0949	1029	1049	1129	1149	1229	1249	1329	1349	1429	1449	1529	1549	1629	1649	1729	1749	1829	1849	1949	2046	2146	2246	...	2346	...
Susch ⊗ d.	0958	1037	1058	1137	1158	1237	1258	1337	1358	1437	1458	1537	1558	1637	1658	1737	1758	1837	1858	1958	2053	2153	2253	...	2353	...
Sagliains ¶ a.	1001	|	1101	|	1201	|	1301	|	1401	|	1501	|	1601	|	1701	|	1801	|	1901	2001	2056	2156	2256	...	2356	...
Sagliains ¶ d.	1002	|	1102	|	1202	|	1302	|	1402	|	1502	|	1602	|	1702	|	1802	|	1902	2002	*2058*	*2158*	*2258*	...	*2358*	...
Klosters Platz a.	|	1057	|	1157	|	1257	|	1357	|	1457	|	1557	|	1657	|	1757	|	1857	|	|	|	|	|	...	|	...
Landquart ◐ a.	|	1137	|	1237	|	1337	|	1437	|	1537	|	1637	|	1737	|	1837	|	1937	|	|	|	|	|	...	|	...
Ardez ⊗ d.	1014	...	1114	...	1214	...	1314	...	1414	...	1514	...	1614	...	1714	...	1814	...	1914	2014	*2109*	*2209*	*2309*	...	*0009*	...
Scuol-Tarasp a.	1023	...	1123	...	1223	...	1323	...	1423	...	1523	...	1623	...	1723	...	1823	...	1923	2023	*2118*	*2218*	*2318*	...	*0018*	...

FOR NOTES SEE NEXT PAGE →

Narrow gauge

RHÄTISCHE BAHN (RhB) services 545

CHUR - ST MORITZ

km																										
							951						955													
													Z									D		⑤⑥		
		⚒	⚒	⚒		🍷	B🍷	🍷					B🍷	🍷	🍷									d		
0	**Chur** d.	0428	0509	0604	0658	0758	0828	0858	0958	1058	1158	1258	1334	1358	1458	1558	1658	1758	1858	1958	2056	2056	2156	2156	2256	0001
10	Reichenau-Tamins d.	0440	0518	0617	0708	0808	|	0908	1008	1108	1208	1308	|	1408	1508	1608	1708	1808	1908	2008	2108	2108	2209	2209	2306	0011
27	Thusis d.	0503	0541	0640	0729	0829	0859	0929	1029	1129	1229	1329	1411	1429	1529	1629	1729	1829	1929	2029	2133	2133	2231	2233	2329	0034
41	Tiefencastel d.	▬	0557	▬	0746	0846	0918	0946	1046	1146	1246	1346	1428	1446	1546	1646	1746	1846	1946	2046	2149	2149	...	2249	▬	...
51	**Filisur** d.	...	0613	...	0801	0901	0933	1001	1101	1201	1301	1401	|	1501	1601	1701	1801	1901	2001	2101	2204	2204	...	2304	...	...
59	Bergün / Bravuogn d.	...	0630	...	0814	0914	0947	1014	1114	1214	1314	1414	1457	1514	1614	1714	1814	1914	2014	2114	2217	2217	...	2315	...	...
72	Preda d.	...	0647	...	0832	0932	|	1032	1132	1232	1332	1432	|	1532	1632	1732	1832	1932	2032	2132	2234	2234	...	2331	...	...
84	**Samedan** a.	...	0700	...	0846	0945	|	1045	1145	1245	1345	1445	|	1545	1645	1745	1845	1945	2045	2145	2248	2248	...	2344	...	...
84	**Samedan** d.	0556	*0709*	0749	0853	0949	|	1049	1149	1249	1349	1449	|	1549	1649	1749	1849	1949	2049	2149	...	2250	...	...	2346	...
	Pontresina a.	|	|	|	|	|	1020	|	|	|	|	|	1533	|	|	|	|	|	|	|	...	|	...	...	|	...
87	Celerina d.	0601	*0713*	0753	0856	0953	...	1053	1153	1253	1353	1453	...	1553	1653	1753	1853	1953	2053	2153	...	2253	...	...	2350	...
89	**St Moritz** a.	0606	*0716*	0800	0901	1000	...	1100	1200	1300	1400	1500	...	1600	1700	1800	1900	2000	2100	2200	...	2300	...	...	2354	...

											950							952							
											Z												⑤⑥		
	⚒	⚒	Ⓐ	⚒	⚒	†					B🍷	🍷	🍷					B🍷	🍷	🍷			d		
St Moritz d.	...	...	*0445*	0541	...	0558	0702	0802	0902	1002	...	1102	1202	1302	1402	1502	1602	...	1702	1802	1902	2002	2102	2102	2202	2359
Celerina d.	...	...	*0448*	0545	...	0601	0706	0805	0905	1005	...	1105	1205	1305	1405	1505	1605	...	1705	1805	1905	2005	2105	2105	2205	0003
Pontresina d.	...	...	|	|	...	|	|	|	|	|	1027	|	|	|	|	|	|	1624	|	|	|	|	|	|	|	|
Samedan a.	...	...	*0452*	0548	...	0605	0709	0809	0909	1009	|	1109	1209	1309	1409	1509	1609	|	1709	1809	1909	2009	2109	2109	2209	0007
Samedan d.	...	...	0511	0550	...	0607	0715	0815	0915	1015	|	1115	1215	1315	1415	1515	1615	|	1715	1815	1915	2015	2115	▬	▬	▬
Preda d.	...	...	|	0603	...	0620	0729	0829	0929	1029	|	1129	1229	1329	1429	1529	1629	|	1729	1829	1929	2029	2129	...	...	...
Bergün / Bravuogn d.	...	...	0541	0620	...	0637	0747	0847	0947	1047	1102	1147	1247	1347	1447	1547	1647	1704	1747	1847	1947	2047	2147	...	...	...
Filisur d.	...	...	0554	0634	...	0651	0801	0901	1001	1101	1117	1201	1301	1401	1501	1601	1701	1718	1801	1901	2001	2101	2202	...	...	...
Tiefencastel d.	...	...	0611	0651	...	0707	0815	0915	1015	1115	1132	1215	1315	1415	1515	1615	1715	1732	1815	1915	2015	2116	2217	...	...	...
Thusis d.	0509	0608	0627	0709	0728	0728	0833	0933	1033	1133	|	1233	1333	1433	1533	1633	1733	|	1833	1933	2033	2133	2233	2233	2333	0040
Reichenau-Tamins d.	0534	0632	0653	|	0753	0753	0852**s**	0952**s**	1052**s**	1152**s**	|	1252**s**	1352**s**	1452**s**	1552**s**	1652**s**	1752**s**	|	1852**s**	1952**s**	2052**s**	2156	2256	2256	2356	0102
Chur a.	0548	0646	0705	0742	0805	0805	0904	1004	1104	1204	1222	1304	1404	1504	1604	1704	1804	1822	1904	2004	2104	2209	2310	2310	0010	0112

ST MORITZ - TIRANO

km																										
								971		951				973			955		975					🚌		🚌
					⚒			Z						Z			Z		L				Ⓐ			
							△	A🍷	▷	B🍷	△			A🍷	◇	▽▷	B🍷	△	A🍷	▷						W
0	**St Moritz** d.	...	...	...	0643	0748	0848	0917	0948	...	1048	1148	1248	1317	1348	1448	...	1548	1614	1648	1748	1848	1948	...	2020	...
6	**Pontresina** a.	...	...	...	0652	0757	0857	0925	0957	...	1057	1157	1257	1325	1357	1457	...	1557	1622	1657	1757	1857	1957	...	2029	...
6	**Pontresina** d.	...	...	...	0702	0808	0904	0928	1008	1025	1104	1208	1304	1328	1408	1504	1541	1605	1623	1704	1808	1904	2004	...	...	2122
12	Morteratsch ⊗ d.	...	...	...	0711	0818	0913	|	1018	|	1113	1218	1313	|	1418	1513	|	1618	|	1713	1818	1913	2013	...	...	2128
17	Bernina Diavolezza ⊗ d.	...	...	...	0720	0828	0923	|	1028	1042	1123	1228	1323	|	1428	1523	1606	1628	1639	1723	1828	1922	2022	...	...	|
22	Ospizio Bernina d.	...	...	...	0731	0838	0933	|	1038	|	1133	1238	1333	|	1438	1533	1619	1638	1652	1733	1838	1932	2032	...	...	2144
27	Alp Grüm a.	...	...	...	0740	0849	0942	1006	1049	1101	1142	1249	1342	1407	1449	1542	1628	1649	1700	1742	1849	1942	2042	...	...	|
27	Alp Grüm d.	...	...	...	0744	0853	0944	1018	1053	1115	1144	1253	1344	1418	1453	1544	1640	1653	1716	1744	1853	1946	2046	...	...	|
44	**Poschiavo** a.	...	...	...	0830	0941	1022	1054	1141	1201	1222	1341	1422	1453	1541	1622	1715	1741	1800	1822	1932	2023	2123	...	...	2210s
44	**Poschiavo** d.	0620	0742	0834	0834	0942	1023	1056	1142	1210	1223	1342	1423	1455	1542	1623	1724	1742	1801	1823	*1934**	*2034**	...	2134	...	|
48	Le Prese d.	0627	0749	0841	0841	0949	1030	1103	1149	1221	1230	1349	1430	1502	1549	1630	1732	1749	|	1830	*1940**	*2040**	...	2140	...	2217s
51	Miralago ⊗ d.	0633	0754	0847	0847	0954	1035	|	1154	|	1235	1354	1435	|	1554	1635	|	1754	|	1835	*1944**	*2044**	...	2144	...	2221s
54	Brusio ⊗ d.	0642	0803	0857	0857	1002	1043	|	1202	|	1243	1402	1443	|	1602	1643	|	1802	|	1843	*1948**	*2048**	...	2148	...	2225s
58	Campocologno 🏛 d.	0654	0814	0908	0908	1014	1052	|	1214	|	1252	1414	1452	|	1614	1652	|	1814	|	1852	*1952**	*2052**	...	2152	...	2229s
61	**Tirano** a.	0703	0823	0917	0917	1023	1100	1132	1223	1249	1300	1423	1500	1531	1623	1700	1759	1823	1839	1900	*2000**	*2100**	...	2200	...	2236

	🚌		🚌			950			972				974		952			976				🚌		🚌	🚌	🚌
	J	⚒				Z			L				Z					Z								
						B🍷	◇	▽▷	A🍷	△	▷	▷	A🍷		B🍷	△	△	A🍷				S				
Tirano d.	0540	...	0653	...	0741	0806	0900	0941	1006	1100	1141	1300	1317	1341	1424	1500	1541	1606	1700	1741	1900	...	1939	2002	2102	2202
Campocologno 🏛 d.	0546	...	0659	...	0752	|	0908	0952	|	1108	1152	1308	|	1352	|	1508	1552	|	1708	1752	1910	...	1947	2008	2108	2208
Brusio ⊗ d.	0550	...	0706	...	0802	|	0916	1002	|	1116	1202	1316	|	1402	|	1516	1602	|	1716	1802	1920	...	1956	2012	2112	2212
Miralago ⊗ d.	0555	...	0710	...	0810	|	0923	1010	|	1123	1210	1323	|	1410	|	1523	1610	|	1723	1810	1927	...	2003	2015	2115	2215
Le Prese d.	0559	...	0712	...	0815	0835	0928	1015	1041	1128	1215	1328	1344	1415	1455	1528	1615	1640	1728	1815	1932	...	2007	2018	2218**y**	2218**y**
Poschiavo a.	0605	...	0728	...	0825	0845	0936	1025	1048	1136	1225	1336	1353	1425	1506	1536	1625	1647	1736	1825	1940	...	2016	2028	2128**y**	2228**y**
Poschiavo d.	0607	0628	...	0732	0828	0847	0937	1028	1050	1137	1228	1337	1357	1428	1510	1537	1628	1648	1737	1828	...	2005	...	...	...	...
Alp Grüm a.	|	0706	...	0811	0906	0923	1010	1106	1126	1210	1306	1410	1442	1506	1544	1610	1706	1727	1810	1906	...	|	...	...	...	...
Alp Grüm d.	|	0708	...	0813	0908	0948	1013	1108	1142	1213	1308	1413	1459	1508	1545	1613	1708	1742	1813	1908	...	|	...	...	...	...
Ospizio Bernina d.	0638	0715	...	0820	0915	0958	1020	1115	|	1220	1315	1420	|	1515	|	1620	1715	|	1820	1915	...	2036	...	...	...	...
Bernina Diavolezza ⊗ d.	0643	0726	...	0833	0927	|	1034	1127	1200	1233	1327	1434	|	1527	|	1634	1727	|	1834	1927	...	2041	...	...	...	...
Morteratsch ⊗ d.	0649	0738	...	0844	0940	|	1047	1140	|	1244	1340	1444	|	1540	|	1644	1740	|	1844	1940	...	2047	...	...	...	...
Pontresina a.	0703	0748	...	0856	0951	1025	1056	1151	1225	1253	1351	1453	1534	1551	1622	1653	1751	1815	1853	1951	...	2101	...	...	...	...
Pontresina d.	...	0801	...	0901	1001	...	1101	1201	1227	1301	1401	1501	1536	1601	...	1701	1801	1817	1901	2001	...	...	...	...	...	...
St Moritz a.	...	0811	...	0911	1011	...	1111	1211	1235	1311	1411	1511	1545	1611	...	1711	1811	1825	1911	2011	...	...	...	...	...	...

DAVOS - FILISUR

km		⚒			♣					
0	Davos Platz d.	0605	...	0731	and hourly	2031	...	...	...	...
16	**Filisur** a.	0630	...	0756	until	2056	...	...	...	...

	⚒			♣						
Filisur d.	0634	...	0804	and hourly	2104	...	...	...	...	...
Davos Platz a.	0658	...	0829	until	2129	...	...	...	...	...

CHUR - AROSA

km		⚒								●
0	**Chur** d.	0508	0620	0708	and	1908	2006	2100	...	2300
18	Langwies d.	0550	0705	0750	hourly	1950	2044	2140	...	2341
26	**Arosa** a.	0609	0722	0809	until	2009	2102	2157	...	2358

	⚒	Ⓐ	Ⓒ							
Arosa d.	0549	0623	0649	0749	and	1749	1849	1949	2107	2203
Langwies d.	0605	0638	0705	0805	hourly	1805	1905	2004	2123	2219
Chur a.	0651	0720	0751	0851	until	1851	1948	2045	2205	2300

A – BERNINA EXPRESS – (12) [panorama car]. Ⓡ for travel in panorama car.
B – BERNINA EXPRESS – (12) [panorama car] Chur - Pontresina - Tirano and v.v. Ⓡ for travel in panorama car.
D – Daily to Mar. 12; ⑤⑥ from Mar. 17 (also Apr. 6, 9, May 17, 28, July 31).
E – From Samedan (see lower panel on page 268).
G – Until Nov. 3.
H – From Nov. 6.
J – Ⓐ (daily May 22 - Nov. 3). To Samedan (a. 0706).
L – Dec. 26 - Jan. 8, Apr. 7 - Oct. 22 (also Dec. 7 – 9, 2023).
M – Conveys (12) Landquart - Klosters - St Moritz and v.v. (see lower panel on page 268).
R – On Ⓒ conveys (12) Landquart - Klosters - St Moritz (see lower panel on page 268).

S – To Samedan (a. 2104).
T – May 14 - Oct. 22.
U – May 6 - Oct. 29.
W – From Samedan (d. 2115).
Z – May 13 - Oct. 22.

a – Ⓐ only.
d – Also Apr. 6, May 17; not Dec. 24, Apr. 7.
e – ⑤⑥ (also Dec. 26 – 29, Jan. 1, Apr. 6, May 17; not Dec. 24, Apr. 7).

f – ⑤ (not Apr. 7).
r – ⚒ only.
s – Calls to set down only.
x – Calls on request.
y – 3 – 7 minutes later on ⑥ (also Apr. 6, May 17, July 31).

* – By 🚌.
⊗ – Request stop.
◐ – See upper panel on page 268.

▷ – Conveys open car June 26 - Sept. 3 (subject to fine weather).
△ – Conveys panorama car (Ⓡ) until Mar. 26.
◇ – Conveys panorama car (Ⓡ) Jan. 9 - Mar. 26.
▽ – Conveys panorama car (Ⓡ) until Mar. 26 and from Oct. 23.
❖ – The 1020 from Landquart requires a change of trains at Klosters Platz. The 1220 and 1420 from Landquart run on Ⓒ only and require a change of trains at Klosters Platz.
⊠ – The 1026, 1226 and 1426 from Davos Platz run on Ⓒ only and require a change of trains at Klosters Platz.
▲ – See Chur - St Moritz panel on page 269 for connecting trains Samedan - St Moritz and v.v.
♣ – Variations May 13 - Oct. 29: The 1031 and 1531 from Davos are retimed to depart at 1018 and 1518 (Filisur a. 1053, 1553); the 1104 and 1604 from Filisur are retimed to depart at 1106, 1606 (Davos a. 1150, 1650). These retimed services are operated with historic rolling stock (including open cars).
● – Operated by 🚌 in similar timings on ①–④ Apr. 11 - Nov. 23 (not May 18, 29, July 31, Aug. 1).
¶ – Sagliains station can only be used for changing trains.
⊖ – 🚌 **ZERNEZ - MALLES**. Operator: AutoDaPosta ✆ +41 (0) 81 856 10 90. Journey ± 1 h 30 m. **From Zernez** at 0715, 0815, 0915, 1015 **U**, 1032, 1115, 1215 **U**, 1315, 1415 **U**, 1515, 1615, 1715, 1815 **U** and 1915. **From Malles / Mals** at 0610, 0803, 0903, 1003 **U**, 1103, 1203 **U**, 1303, 1403 **U**, 1503, 1545 **U**, 1603, 1703, 1803 and 1903.
🚗 – Car-carrying operates operates Klosters Selfranga - Sagliains and v.v. ✆ +41 (0) 81 288 37 37 (www.rhb.ch/en/car-transporter).

547 LUZERN and ZÜRICH - BELLINZONA - LOCARNO (via Gotthard pass)

SBB, SO[cut]

See Table **550** for faster services via the Gotthard and Ceneri Base tunnels. **Warning!** Journeys to / from Locarno are subject to alteration Jan. 7 - Feb. 12 (see note ▲).

km		C	⊙	*IC* ◇¶	⊙	*IC* ◇	⊙		*EC* ◇	⊙	*IC* ◇	⊙	*IC* ◇	⊙	*IC* ◇	⊙	*IC* ◇	⊙	*IC/IR* ◇	⊙	*IC* ◇	⊙	*IC/IR* ◇	*IR* ◇	
	Basel SBB **565** d.	...	...	0503	...	...	0603		1503	...	...	1603	1703	...	...	1803	1903	...	...	2003	2103	...	...	2203f	...
	Luzern **525 550** d.	...	...	0618	...	...	0718		1618	...	...	1718	1818	...	...	1918	2018	...	...	2118	2218	...	...	2318	...
0	**Zürich** HB **550** d.	...	...	│	0605	0705	│		│	1605	1705	│	│	1805	1905	│	│	2005	2105	│	│	2205	2305	│	...
29	Zug **550** d.	...	...	│	0630	0730	│		│	1630	1730	│	│	1830	1930	│	│	2030	2130	│	│	2230	2330	│	...
45	**Arth-Goldau 525 550** a.	...	...	0645	0645	0745	0745	and in	1645	1645	1745	1745	1845	1845	1945	1945	2145	2045	2145	2145	2245	2245	2345	2345	...
45	**Arth-Goldau** **550** d.	...	...	▬	0654	▬	0754	the same	▬	1654	▬	1754	▬	1854	▬	1954	▬	2054	▬	2154	...	2254	...	...	235
53	Schwyz d.	...	...	...	0702	...	0802		...	1702	...	1802	...	1902	...	2002	...	2102	...	2202	...	2302	...	...	000
56	Brunnen d.	...	...	...	0706	...	0806	pattern	...	1706	...	1806	...	1906	...	2006	...	2106	...	2206	...	2306	...	...	000
68	Flüelen d.	...	...	...	0715	...	0815		...	1715	...	1815	...	1915	...	2015	...	2115	...	2215	...	2315	...	...	001
71	Altdorf **550** d.	...	...	...	0718	...	0818	every **two**	...	1718	...	1818	...	1918	...	2018	...	2118	...	2218	...	2318	...	...	001
77	**Erstfeld** d.	...	0625	...	0725	...	0825	hours until	...	1725	...	1825	...	1925	...	2025	...	2125	...	2224	...	2324	...	...	002
106	Göschenen d.	...	0651	...	0751	...	0851		...	1751	...	1851	...	1951	...	2051	...	2151	...	▬	...	...	...	...	...
122	Airolo d.	0612	0702	...	0802	...	0902		...	1802	...	1902	...	2002	...	2102	...	2202	...	...	...	...	...	...	...
142	Faido d.	0630	0721	...	0821	...	0921		...	1821	...	1921	...	2021	...	2121	...	2221	...	...	...	...	...	...	...
168	Biasca **548** d.	0655	0745	...	0845	...	0945		...	1845	...	1945	...	2045	...	2145	...	2245	...	...	...	...	...	...	...
187	**Bellinzona** ... **548 550** a.	0709	0800	...	0900	...	1000		...	1900	...	2000	...	2100	...	2200	...	2300	**E**	**E**	...	...	...	...	...
187	**Bellinzona** ▷ d.	*0719*	0804	0819	0904	0919	1004		1819	1904	1919	2004	2019	...	2119	...	2219	...	2319	2349	...	...	...	...	...
208	**Locarno** ▷ a.	*0744*	0825	0844	0925	0944	1025		1844	1925	1944	2025	2044	...	2144	...	2244	...	2344	0014	...	...	...	...	...

km		⊙	*IC* ◇ ①–⑥	⊙	*IC* ◇			⊙		⊙		⊙		⊙		★	⊙		⊙					**E**	**E**
	Locarno ▷ d.	...	...	...	...	0435	0515	...	0615	...	0715	0735	0815	0835	0915		1935	2015	2035	2115	2145	2215	2245	2315	234
	Bellinzona ▷ a.	...	...	...	...	0501	0541	...	0641	...	0741	0755	0841	0855	0941		1955	2041	2055	2141	2211	2241	2311	2341	001
	Bellinzona ... **548 550** d.	...	0507	...	...	...	...	0559	▬	0659	▬	0759	▬	0859	▬		1959	▬	2059	▬	▬	▬	▬	...	...
	Biasca **548** d.	...	0521	...	...	...	...	0614	...	0714	...	0814	...	0914	...		2014	...	2114	...	...	...	...	...	...
	Faido d.	...	│	...	...	...	...	0639	...	0739	...	0839	...	0939	...	and in	2039	...	2139	...	...	...	...	...	...
	Airolo d.	...	│	...	...	...	...	0658	...	0758	...	0858	...	0958	...		2058	...	2158	...	...	...	...	...	...
	Göschenen d.	...	│	...	...	...	...	0709	...	0809	...	0909	...	1009	...	the same	2109	...	2209	...	...	...	...	...	...
	Erstfeld d.	0531	│	0631	...	...	...	0734	...	0834	...	0934	...	1034	...	pattern	2134	...	2234	...	...	...	...	...	...
	Altdorf **550** d.	0537	0550	0637	...	...	...	0739	...	0839	...	0939	...	1039	...		2139	...	2239	...	...	...	...	...	...
	Flüelen d.	0541	│	0641	...	...	...	0744	...	0844	...	0944	...	1044	...	every **two**	2144	...	2244	...	...	2309	...	...	...
	Brunnen d.	0554	│	0654	...	...	...	0755	...	0855	...	0955	...	1055	...	hours until	2155	...	2255	...	2307	2320	...	...	...
	Schwyz d.	0558	│	0658	...	...	...	0759	*IC*	0859	*IC*	0959	*IC*	1059	*EC*		2159	*IC*	2259	*IC*	2310	2323	...	...	...
	Arth-Goldau **550** a.	0607	0611	0707	...	...	...	0807	◇	0907	◇	1007	◇	1107	◇		2207	◇	2307	◇	2319	2331	...	...	...
0	**Arth-Goldau 525 550** d.	0615	0615	0715	0715	...	...	0815	0815	0915	0915	1015	1015	1115	1115		2215	2215	2315	2315	2320	2332	...	...	...
	Zug **550** a.	│	0630	0730	│	...	...	│	0830	0930	│	│	1030	1130	│		│	2230	2330	│	│	2353	2358	...	...
	Zürich HB **550** a.	│	0655	0755	│	...	...	│	0855	0955	│	│	1055	1155	│		│	2255	2355	│	│	...	0025	...	...
28	**Luzern** **525 550** a.	0641	...	...	0741	...	...	0841	...	...	0941	1041	...	...	1141		2241	...	...	2341	2353	...	...	...	...
	Basel SBB **565** a.	0756	...	...	0856	...	...	0956	...	...	1056	1156	...	...	1256		0001	...	...	0102	...	...	...	...	...

C – To Chiasso (Table **548**).

E – Daily to Jan. 7; ⑤⑥ Jan. 13 - June 10 (also Feb. 16, 19–21, Apr. 6, 9, 10, May 18, 28, June 8); daily June 16 - Sept. 9; ⑤⑥ from Sept. 15 (also Oct. 31).

f – On ⑦–④ from Jan. 30 departs *2156* (change trains at Olten).

⊙ – *TRENO GOTTARDO*. Operated by SOB. Conveys (🍷).

◇ – Service shown here for connecting purposes only. Most run to / from Bellinzona via the Gotthard Base Tunnel (see Table **550** for full details).

★ – Late evening Basel arrivals (from 2156) may be up 5 minutes later on ⑦–④ from Jan. 30.

¶ – The 0503 from Basel departs 2 minutes earlier on ①–⑤ from Jan. 31 (other services in the regular pattern depart Basel at xx03 on a daily basis).

▲ – Journeys to / from Locarno are subject to alteration Jan. 7 - Feb. 12. During this period trains are replaced by 🚌 Tenero (*km 204*) - Locarno and v.v. with journey times extended by up to 18 minutes (earlier Locarno departures).

▷ – Other services Bellinzona - Locarno and v.v. (see also note ▲): **From Bellinzona** at 0449, 0519, 0549, 0619, 0649, 0704, 0749, 0849 and hourly until 2149; then 2249 **E**. **From Locarno** at 0545, 0645 and hourly until 2045.

GOTTHARD PANORAMA EXPRESS

	3093 ♣🍷		**309**[cut] ♣
Arth-Goldau d.	1315	**Lugano** d.	091
Flüelen d.	1409	**Bellinzona** d.	094
Göschenen d.	1453	Airolo d.	104
Airolo d.	1510	Göschenen d.	110
Bellinzona a.	1607	Flüelen d.	114
Lugano a.	1641	**Arth-Goldau** a.	120

♣ – ②–⑦ Apr. 15 - Oct. 22 (also May 29). Conveys panorama car. Supplement payable. All-inclusive train/ferry tour packages available (see Table **507** for connecting ferry services Flüelen - Luzern).

548 Local services BIASCA and LOCARNO - LUGANO - MILANO

SBB

km										A														
0	Biasca **547** d.	...	...	0515	...	0555	...	0625	...	0655	...	0721d	...	0755	...	0825		...	1925	...	1955	...	2025	...
19	**Bellinzona** **547** a.	...	...	0529	...	0609	...	0639	...	0709	...	0735d	...	0809	...	0839		...	1939	...	2009	...	2039	...
19	**Bellinzona** **607** d.	0433	0517	0532	...	0616	...	0641	...	0716	...	0746	...	0816	...	0846	and at	...	1946	...	2016	...	2046	...
	Locarno ▲ d.	│	│	│	0555	│	0625	│	0655	│	0725	│	0755	│	0825	│	the same	1925	│	1955	│	2025	│	205
	Cadenazzo **607** d.	│	│	│	0609	│	0639	│	0709	│	0739	│	0809	│	0839	│		1939	│	2009	│	2039	│	210
48	**Lugano** **607** a.	0505	0551	0604	0624	0635	0654	0658	0724	0735	0754	0805	0824	0835	0854	0905	minutes	1954	2005	2024	2035	2054	2105	212
48	**Lugano** **607** d.	0506	0602	0606	...	0636	0702	0706	0725	0736	0802	0806	0825	0836	0902	0906		2002	2006	2025	2036	2102	2106	...
67	Mendrisio **607** d.	0532	0619	0632	...	0658	0719	0732	0742	0758	0819	0832	0841	0858	0919	0932	past each	2019	2032	2041	2058	2119	2132	...
74	**Chiasso** **607** a.	0540	0626	0640	...	0706	0726	0740	0750	0806	0826	0840	0949	0906	0926	0940	hour until	2026	2040	2049	2106	2126	2140	...
74	**Chiasso** 🛃 **607** d.	0543	0631	0647	...	...	0731	0743	...	...	0831	0843	...	...	0931	0943		2031	2043	...	...	...	...	...
78	Como S. Glovanni **607** d.	0554	0636	0654	...	...	0736	0750	...	...	0836	0850	...	...	0936	0950		2036	2050	...	...	...	...	...
125	**Milano** Centrale a.	...	0717	...	...	...	0817	...	...	...	0917	...	...	...	1017	...		2117	...	...	...	...	...	...

Biasca **547** d.	2055	...	2125	...	2155	...	2225	...	2255	...	2325	...
Bellinzona **547** a.	2109	...	2139	...	2209	...	2239	...	2309	...	2339	...
Bellinzona **607** d.	2116	...	2146	...	2216	...	2246	...	2316	...	2346	...
Locarno ▲ d.	│	2125	│	2155	│	2225	│	2255	│	2325e	│	...
Cadenazzo **607** d.	│	2139	│	2209	│	2239	│	2309	│	2339	│	...
Lugano **607** a.	2135	2154	2205	2224	2235	2254	2305	2324	2335	2354	0005	...
Lugano **607** d.	2136	2155	2206	...	2236	2255	2306	...	2336	2355	0006	...
Mendrisio **607** d.	2158	2216	2232	...	2258	2316	2332	...	2358	0016	0032	...
Chiasso **607** a.	2206	2224	2240	...	2306	2329	2344	...	0006	0029	0040	...
Chiasso 🛃 **607** d.	...	...	...	...	...	...	...	...	...	...	...	...
Como S. Glovanni **607** d.	...	...	...	...	...	...	...	...	...	...	...	...
Milano Centrale a.	...	...	...	...	...	...	...	...	...	...	...	...

Milano Centrale d.	...	...	...	...	...	...	...	...
Como S. Glovanni **607** d.	...	...	...	0511	...	...	...	061
Chiasso 🛃 **607** a.	...	...	...	0517	...	...	...	061
Chiasso **607** d.	0402b	...	0452	0520	0534	0554	...	062
Mendrisio **607** d.	0411	...	0500	0534	0543	0604	...	063
Lugano **607** a.	0431	...	0520	0554	0604	0624	...	065
Lugano **607** d.	0432	...	0521	0603	0605	0625	0635	065
Cadenazzo **607** d.	│	...	│	│	0620	│	0650	│
Locarno ▲ a.	│	...	│	│	0635	│	0705	│
Bellinzona **607** a.	0503	...	0554	0619	...	0643	...	071
Bellinzona **547** d.	0509	...	0556	0620	...	0650	...	072
Biasca **547** a.	0524	...	0610	0627	...	0707	...	073

km																										
	Milano Centrale d.	...	...	...	...	0643	...		...	...	1943	...	...	...	2043	...	...	...	2143	...	...	...	2243c	...
	Como S. Glovanni **607** d.	...	...	...	0710	0723	...		...	2010	2023	...	...	2110	2123	...	...	...	2223	...	...	...	2323c	...
	Chiasso 🛃 **607** a.	...	...	...	0717	0729	...	and at	...	2017	2029	...	...	2117	2129	...	...	...	2229	...	...	...	2329c	...
	Chiasso **607** d.	0634	0654	0711	0720	0734	0754	the same	2011	2020	2034	2054	...	2120	2134	2154	...	2220	2234	2254	...	2320	2334	2354
	Mendrisio **607** d.	0642	0704	0718	0734	0742	0804		2018	2034	2042	2104	...	2134	2142	2204	...	2234	2243	2304	...	2334	2243	0004
	Lugano **607** a.	0658	0724	0734	0754	0758	0824	minutes	2034	2054	2058	2124	...	2154	2158	2224	...	2254	2304	2324	...	2354	0004	0024
0	**Lugano** **607** d.	0705	0725	0735	0755	0805	0825		2035	2055	2105	2125	2135	2155	2205	2225	2235	2255	2305	2325	2335	2355	0005	0025
30	Cadenazzo **607** d.	0720	│	0750	│	0820	│	past each	2050	│	2120	│	2150	│	2220	│	2250	│	2320	│	2350	│	0020	│
42	**Locarno** ▲ a.	0735	│	0805	│	0835	│	hour until	2105	│	2135	│	2205	│	2235	│	2305e	│	2335e	│	0005h	│	0035h	│
	Bellinzona **607** a.	...	0743	...	0813	...	0843		...	2113	...	2143	...	2213	...	2243	...	2313	...	2343	...	0030	...	0056
	Bellinzona **547** d.	...	0750	...	0820	...	0850		...	2120	...	2150	...	2220	...	2250	...	2320	...	2350	...	...	...	...
	Biasca **547** a.	...	0807	...	0837	...	0907		...	2137	...	2207	...	2237	...	2307	...	2337	...	0007	...	...	...	...

A – From Airolo (Table **547**).

b – ②–⑦ (also Dec. 26, Apr. 10, May 1, 29).

c – ⑥⑦ only.

d – 4 minutes later on ⑥⑦ (also Dec. 26, Jan. 6, Apr. 10, May 1, 18, 29, June 8, 29, Aug. 1, 15, Nov. 1, Dec. 8, 9).

e – Daily to Jan. 7; ⑤⑥ Jan. 13 - June 10 (also Feb. 16, 19–21, Apr. 6, 9, 10, May 18, 28, June 8); daily June 16 - Sept. 9; ⑤⑥ from Sept. 15 (also Oct. 31).

h – To Locarno on mornings daily to Jan. 8, ⑥⑦ Jan. 14 - June 11 (also Feb. 17, 20–22, Apr. 7, 10, 11, May 19, 29, June 9), daily June 17 - Sept. 10, ⑥⑦ from Sept. 16 (also Nov. 1).

▲ – Journeys to / from Locarno are subject to alteration Jan. 7 - Feb. 12. During this period trains are replace[d] by 🚌 Tenero (*km 204*) - Locarno and v.v. with journe[y] times extended by up to 23 minutes (earlier Locarno departures).

SBB, FS — ZÜRICH and LUZERN - LUGANO - MILANO (via Gotthard and Ceneri Base Tunnels) — 550

See Table 547 for slower services via the classic Gotthard route.

km		IR 2409	IC 659	EC 307	IR 2311	IC 861	EC 313	IR 2413	IC 663	EC 311	IR 2315	IC 865	EC 315	IR 2417	IC 667	EC 327	IR 2319	IC 869	EC 317	IR 2421	EC 151	IR 2323	IC 873	EC 319
				◧			◧			◧			◧			◧			◧					◧
		★	✕	B✕	★	✕	✕	★	✕	V✕	★	✕	✕	★	✕	G✕	★	✕	✕	★	F✕	★	✕	¶✕
0	**Zürich** HB 547 555 d.	0605	...	0633	...	0705	0733	0805	...	0833	...	0905	0933	1005	...	1033	...	1105	1133	1205	...	...	1305	1333
29	Zug 547 555 d.	0630	...	0700	...	0730	0800	0830	...	0900	...	0930	1000	1030	...	1100	...	1130	1200	1230	...	...	1330	1400
	Basel SBB **565** d.	|	0501	|	0603	|	|	|	0703	|	0803	|	|	|	0903	|	1003	|	|	|	1103	1203	|	|
	Luzern 525 547 d.	|	0618	|	0718	|	⊙	|	0818	⊙	0918	|	⊙	|	1018	⊙	1118	|	⊙	|	1218	1318	|	⊙
45	**Arth-Goldau** 525 547 a.	0645	0645	0716	0745	0745	0816	0845	0845	0916	0945	0945	1016	1045	1045	1116	1145	1145	1216	1245	1245	1345	1345	1416
45	**Arth-Goldau** 547 d.	...	0649	0718	...	0749	0818	...	0849	0918	...	0949	1018	...	1049	1118	...	1149	1218	...	1249	...	1349	1418
51	Altdorf 547 d.	...	0708	|	...	|	|	...	0908	|	...	|	|	...	1108	|	...	|	|	...	1308	...	|	|
165	Bellinzona ▲ 547 a.	...	0742	0812	...	0842	0912	...	0942	1012	...	1042	1112	...	1142	1212	...	1242	1312	...	1342	...	1442	1512
165	Bellinzona 548 607 d.	...	0744	0814	...	0844	0914	...	0944	1014	...	1044	1114	...	1144	1214	...	1244	1314	...	1344	...	1444	1514
186	**Lugano** 548 607 a.	...	0758	0830	...	0858	0930	...	0958	1030	...	1058	1130	...	1158	1230	...	1258	1330	...	1358	...	1458	1530
186	**Lugano** 548 607 d.	...	...	0832	...	...	0932	...	...	1032	...	...	1132	...	...	1232	...	...	1332	...	1410	...	...	1532
212	**Chiasso** 🏛 548 607 d.	...	...	0902	...	...	1002	...	...	1102	...	...	1202	...	...	1302	...	...	1402	...	1455	...	...	1602
216	Como S. Giovanni 548 607 d.	...	...	0910	...	...	1010	...	...	1110	...	...	1210	...	...	1310	...	...	1410	...	1503	...	...	1610
263	**Milano** Centrale 548 a.	...	...	|	...	...	1050	...	...	1150	...	...	1250	...	...	|	...	...	1450	...	1550	...	...	1650
	Milano Rogoredo a.	...	...	1020	...	...	...	...	...	...	...	...	...	...	...	1418	...	...	...	...	...	...	...	...

	IR 2425	IC 675	IR 2327	IC 877	EC 321	IR 2429	EC 153	IR 2331	IC 881	EC 323	IR 2433	IC 683	IR 2335	IC 885	EC 325	IR 2437	IC 687	IC 1487	IR 2339	IC 889	IR 2441	IC 691	IC 893	IC 895
					◧					◧					◧			⑥⑦		①–⑤			①–⑤	⑥
	★	✕	★	✕	✕	★	✕	★	✕	✕	★	✕	★	✕	✕	★	✕	✕	★	✕	★	✕		
ürich HB 547 555 d.	1405	...	...	1505	1533	1605	...	...	1705	1733	1805	...	...	1905	1933	2005	...	2033	...	2105	2205	...	2305	2305
ug 547 555 d.	1430	...	...	1530	1600	1630	...	...	1730	1800	1830	...	...	1930	2000	2030	...	2100	...	2130	2230	...	2330	2330
Basel SBB **565** d.	|	1303	1403	|	|	|	1503	1603	|	|	|	1703	1803	|	|	|	1903	|	2003	|	|	2103	|	|
Luzern 525 547 d.	|	1418	1518	|	⊙	|	1618	1718	|	⊙	|	1818	1918	|	⊙	|	2018	|	2118	|	|	2218	|	|
rth-Goldau 525 547 a.	1445	1445	1545	1545	1616	1645	1645	1745	1745	1816	1845	1845	1945	1945	2016	2045	2045	2116	2145	2145	2245	2245	2345	2345
rth-Goldau 547 d.	...	1449	...	1549	1618	...	1649	...	1749	1818	...	1849	...	1949	2018	...	2049	2118	...	2149	...	2249	2349	2349
ltdorf 547 d.	...	1508	...	|	|	...	1708	...	|	|	...	1908	...	|	|	...	2108	|	...	|	...	2308	|	0008
ellinzona ▲ 547 a.	...	1542	...	1642	1712	...	1742	...	1842	1912	...	1942	...	2042	2112	...	2142	2212	...	2242	...	2342	0047	0055
ellinzona 548 607 d.	...	1544	...	1644	1714	...	1744	...	1844	1914	...	1944	...	2044	2114	...	2144	2214	...	2244	...	2344	...	0057
ugano 548 607 a.	...	1558	...	1658	1730	...	1758	...	1858	1930	...	1958	...	2058	2130	...	2158	2228	...	2258	...	2358	...	0111
ugano 548 607 d.	...	...	...	...	1732	...	1800	...	...	1932	...	...	...	...	2132	...	2202	...	...	2302	...	0002	...	...
hiasso 🏛 548 607 d.	...	...	...	...	1802	...	1855	...	...	2002	...	...	...	...	2202	...	2230	...	...	2333	...	0033	...	...
omo S. Giovanni 548 607 d.	...	...	...	...	1810	...	1903	...	...	2010	...	...	...	...	2210	...	...	...	...	...	...	...	...	...
ilano Centrale 548 a.	...	...	...	...	1850	...	1950	...	...	2050	...	...	...	...	2250	...	...	...	...	...	...	...	...	...
Milano Rogoredo a.	...	...	...	...	...	...	...	...	...	...	...	...	...	...	...	...	...	...	...	...	...	...	...	...

	IC 862	IR 2308	IC 664	IR 2410	IC 866	IR 2312	IC 668	IR 2414	EC 312	IC 870	IR 2316	EC 156	IR 2418	EC 314	IC 874	IR 2320	EC 158	IR 2422	EC 316	IC 878	IR 2324	IC 680	IR 2426	EC 318
	①–⑥								◧					◧			◧		◧					◧
		★		★	✕	★	✕	★	✕	✕	★	✕	★	✕	✕	★	✕	★	✕	✕	★	✕	★	✕
Milano Rogoredo d.	...	...	...	...	...	...	...	...	...	...	...	...	...	...	...	...	...	...	...	...	...	...	...	...
ilano Centrale 548 d.	...	...	...	...	...	...	...	...	0710	...	...	0810	...	0910	...	...	1010	...	1110	...	...	...	...	1310
omo S. Giovanni 548 607 d.	...	...	...	...	...	...	...	...	0754	...	...	0904	...	0950	...	...	1059	...	1150	...	...	...	...	1350
hiasso 🏛 548 607 d.	...	...	0530	...	...	...	...	...	0805	...	...	0924	...	1005	...	...	1124	...	1205	...	...	...	...	1405
ugano 548 607 a.	...	...	0558	...	...	...	...	...	0828	...	...	0950	...	1028	...	...	1150	...	1228	...	...	...	...	1428
ugano 548 607 d.	...	...	0600	...	0702	...	0802	...	0830	0902	...	1002	...	1030	1102	...	1202	...	1230	1302	...	1402	...	1430
ellinzona 548 607 a.	...	...	0615	...	0716	...	0816	...	0846	0916	...	1016	...	1046	1116	...	1216	...	1246	1316	...	1416	...	1446
ellinzona ▲ 547 d.	0507	...	0617	...	0717	...	0817	...	0847	0917	...	1017	...	1047	1117	...	1217	...	1247	1317	...	1417	...	1447
ltdorf 547 d.	0550	...	0650	...	|	...	0850	...	|	|	...	1050	...	|	|	...	1250	...	|	|	...	1450	...	|
rth-Goldau 547 a.	0611	...	0715	...	0811	...	0915	...	0942	1011	...	1115	...	1142	1211	...	1315	...	1342	1411	...	1515	...	1542
rth-Goldau 525 547 d.	0615	0615	0715	0715	0815	0815	0915	0915	0945	1015	1015	1115	1115	1145	1215	1215	1315	1315	1345	1415	1415	1515	1515	1545
Luzern 525 547 a.	|	0641	0741	|	|	0841	0941	|	⊙	|	1041	1141	|	⊙	|	1241	1341	|	⊙	|	1441	1541	|	⊙
Basel SBB **565** a.	|	0756	0856	|	|	0956	1056	|	|	|	1156	1256	|	|	|	1356	1456	|	|	|	1556	1656	|	|
ug 547 555 a.	0630	...	...	0730	0830	...	...	0930	1000	1030	...	...	1130	1200	1230	...	...	1330	1400	1430	...	...	1530	1600
ürich HB 547 555 a.	0655	...	...	0755	0855	...	...	0955	1027	1055	...	...	1155	1227	1255	...	...	1355	1427	1455	...	...	1555	1627

	IC 882	IR 2328	IR 2682	IC 1482	IC 684	IR 2430	EC 320	IC 886	IR 2332	EC 308	IC 688	IR 2434	EC 322	IC 890	IR 2336	EC 310	IC 692	IR 2438	EC 324	IC 894	IR 2340	EC 326	IC 696	IR 2442
			Ⓐ	A			◧			◧			‡◧			◧			◧			◧		
	✕	★		✕	✕	★	✕	✕	★	B✕	✕	★	✕	✕	★	V✕	✕	★	✕	✕	★	G✕		★
Milano Rogoredo d.	...	...	...	...	...	...	...	...	...	1540	...	...	...	...	...	...	...	...	...	...	...	1942	...	...
ilano Centrale 548 d.	...	...	...	...	...	...	1510	...	...	|	...	...	1710	...	...	1810	...	...	1910	...	...	|	...	...
omo S. Giovanni 548 607 d.	...	...	...	...	...	...	1550	...	...	1650	...	...	1750	...	...	1850	...	...	1950	...	...	2050	...	...
hiasso 🏛 548 607 d.	...	...	...	...	...	...	1605	...	...	1705	...	...	1805	...	...	1905	...	...	2005	...	...	2105	...	...
ugano 548 607 a.	...	...	...	...	...	...	1628	...	...	1728	...	...	1828	...	...	1928	...	...	2028	...	...	2128	...	...
ugano 548 607 d.	1502	...	...	1530	1602	...	1630	1702	...	1730	1802	...	1830	1902	...	1930	2002	...	2030	2102	...	2130	2202	...
ellinzona 548 607 a.	1516	...	...	1546	1616	...	1646	1716	...	1746	1816	...	1846	1916	...	1946	2016	...	2046	2116	...	2146	2216	...
ellinzona ▲ 547 d.	1517	...	...	1547	1617	...	1647	1717	...	1747	1817	...	1847	1917	...	1947	2017	...	2047	2117	...	2147	2217	...
ltdorf 547 d.	|	...	...	|	1650	...	|	|	...	|	1850	...	|	|	...	|	2050	...	|	|	...	|	2250	...
rth-Goldau 547 a.	1611	...	...	1642	1715	...	1742	1811	...	1842	1915	...	1942	2011	...	2042	2115	...	2142	2211	...	2242	2315	...
rth-Goldau 525 547 d.	1615	1615	1645	1645	1715	1715	1745	1815	1815	1845	1915	1915	1945	2015	2015	2045	2115	2115	2145	2215	2215	2245	2315	2315
Luzern 525 547 a.	|	1641	|	⊙	1741	|	⊙	|	1841	⊙	1941	|	⊙	|	2041	⊙	2141	|	|	|	2241	|	2341	|
Basel SBB **565** a.	|	1756	|	|	1856	|	|	|	1956	|	2056	|	|	|	2156**x**	|	2300**z**	|	|	|	0001	|	0102**y**	|
ug 547 555 a.	1630	...	1700	1700	...	1730	1800	1830	...	1900	...	1930	2000	2030	...	2100	...	2130	2200	2230	...	2300	...	2330
ürich HB 547 555 a.	1655	...	1727	1727	...	1755	1827	1855	...	1927	...	1955	2027	2055	...	2127	...	2155	2227	2255	...	2327	...	2355

– ✝ to Apr. 2; ⑥⑦ Apr. 8 - Oct. 29 (also Apr. 10, May 29, Aug. 1); ⑦ from Nov. 5.
– To / from Bologna (Table **600**).
– From Frankfurt (Table **912**).
– To / from Genova (Table **610**).
– To / from Venezia (Table **605**).
– On ⑦–④ from Jan. 30 change trains at Olten (arrives Basel *2201*).
– 0105 on the mornings of ①–⑤ from Jan. 31.

z – 2305 on ⑦–④ from Jan. 30.
¶ – Train number **329** on ⑤–⑦ (also Dec. 26, Jan 2, Apr. 10, May 18, 29, Aug. 1).
‡ – Train number **332** on ⑤–⑦ (also Dec. 26, Jan 2, Apr. 10, May 18, 29, Aug. 1).
◧ – Supplement payable in Italy and for international journeys.
★ – Operated by SOB. See Table **547** for full details.
⊙ – See Table **525** for connecting service from / to Luzern.
▲ – For connecting services Bellinzona - Locarno and v.v. see Table **547**.

FART — LOCARNO - DOMODOSSOLA — 551

km				C		C		C 🍷			V 🍷		C 🍷	V 🍷		V 🍷		V 🍷		C 🍷				⑤⑦	
0	**Locarno** d.	0538	...	0648	0709	0748	0809	0848	...	0953	1048	1118	1148	1248	1348	1448	1513	1548	1619	1648	...	1748	1819	1848	1920
20	Camedo 🏛 d.	0619	...	0724	0750	0824	0850	0924	...	1038	1124**u**	1204	1224	1324**u**	1432	1524**u**	1554	1624	1704	1724	...	1824	1905	1925	2000
26	Re d.	...	...	0740	...	0840**x**	...	0940**x**	...	1056	1140**x**	...	1240**x**	1340**x**	...	1540**x**	...	1640**x**	...	1740**x**	...	1840**x**	...	1941**x**	...
34	S. Maria Maggiore d.	...	...	0753	...	0853**x**	...	0953**x**	...	1110	1153**x**	...	1253**x**	1353**x**	...	1553**x**	...	1653**x**	...	1753**x**	...	1853**x**	...	1955**x**	...
53	**Domodossola** a.	...	...	0836	...	0936	...	1036	...	1149	1236	...	1336	1436	...	1636	...	1736	...	1836	...	1936	...	2036	...

						C 🍷	C	V 🍷	V 🍷			V 🍷				V 🍷		C 🍷		C		C			C ⑤⑦
omodossola d.	...	...	...	...	0825	0925	1003	1025	1125	...	1225	1325	...	...	...	1525	...	1625	...	1725	...	1900	...	...	2025
. Maria Maggiore d.	...	...	...	...	0910**x**	1010**x**	1045	1110**x**	1210**x**	...	1310	1410**x**	...	...	...	1610**x**	...	1710**x**	...	1810	...	1943	...	...	2109**x**
e d.	...	...	...	...	0922**x**	1022**x**	1057	1122**x**	1222**x**	...	1322	1422**x**	...	...	...	1622**x**	...	1722**x**	...	1822	...	1955	...	...	2122**x**
amedo 🏛 d.	0625	0656	0756	0856	0939	1038	1109	1139	1239	1255	1339	1438**s**	1447	...	1607	1638**s**	1723	1739	...	1839	1924	2008**s**	2019	...	2137**s**
ocarno a.	0708	0741	0841	0941	1019	1117	1155	1216	1317	1341	1421	1519	1535	...	1655	1717	1808	1819	...	1919	2009	2046	2106	...	2217

– CENTOVALLI EXPRESS.
– TRENO PANORAMICO VIGEZZO VISION – Conveys panorama car. Supplement payable.

s – Stops to set down only.
u – Stops to pick up only.
x – Stops only on request.

552 LUZERN - STANS - ENGELBERG

Narrow gauge rack railway. ZE

km																							
		E			E				E			E		🚌				🚌					©T	©
0	**Luzern** 561 d.	0504	0527	0557	0610	0627		2057	2110	2127	2157	2210	2227	...	2257	2310	2327	...	2357	0032	0102		0836	093
9	Hergiswil 561 d.	0514	0540	0610	|	0640	and at	2110	|	2140	2210	|	2240	...	2310	2318	2340	...	0010	0045	0114	EXTRA	0847	094
11	Stansstad d.	0518	0544	0614	|	0644	the same	2114	|	2144	2214	|	2244	...	2314	2322	2344	...	0014	0050	0118	SERVICES	0851	095
14	Stans d.	0522	0548	0618	0624	0648	minutes	2118	2124	2148	2218	2224	2248	...	2318	2326	2348	...	0018	0054	0122	▶▶▶	0854	095
18	Dallenwil d.	0529	0552	...	0629	0652	past each	...	2129	2152	...	2229	2252	2255	2322	...	2352	2355	0022	0059	...		|	|
21	Wolfenschiessen d.	0533	0557	...	0633	0657	hour until	...	2133	2157	...	2233	2257	|	...	...	2357	|	0027	0103	...		|	|
33	**Engelberg** ⊡ a.	0553	...	...	0653	...		...	2153	...	...	2253	...	2316	...	...	...	0016	...	...	...		0921	102

		🚌			E				E			E			E		🚌		🚌			©T	©
Engelberg ⊡ d.	...	0500	...	...	0602	...		...	2102	...	...	2202	...	...	2302	...	2330	...	0018	...		1624	172
Wolfenschiessen d.	0453	|	0522	0601	0622	...	and at	2101	2122	...	2201	2222	...	2301	2322	...	|	0001	|	0038	EXTRA	|	|
Dallenwil d.	0456	0523	0527	0604	0629	...	the same	2104	2129	...	2204	2229	...	2304	2329	2334	2353	0004	0038	0041	SERVICES	|	|
Stans d.	0501	...	0532	0610	0634	0640	minutes	2110	2134	2140	2210	2234	2240	2310	2334	2340	...	0010	...	0047	▶▶▶	1701	180
Stansstad d.	0505	...	0535	0614	|	0644	past each	2114	|	2144	2214	|	2244	2314	|	2344	...	0014	...	0051		1705	180
Hergiswil 561 d.	0509	...	0540	0618	|	0648	hour until	2118	|	2148	2218	|	2248	2318	|	2348	...	0018	...	0055		1709	180
Luzern 561 a.	0522	...	0549	0631	0649	0701		2131	2149	2201	2231	2249	2301	2331	2349	0001	...	0031	...	0109		1719	181

E – LUZERN - ENGELBERG EXPRESS. Conveys panorama cars. T – © Dec. 11 - Mar. 26 (also Dec. 27–30); © May 13 - Oct. 29. ⊡ – Station for Titlis, accessible by cable-ca

553 MOUNTAIN RAILWAYS IN CENTRAL SWITZERLAND

RB (2nd class only

ARTH-GOLDAU - RIGI KULM

km						C					C	F
0	Arth-Goldau d.	0755	0908	1008	1108	1208	1308	1423	1523	1623	1723	1823
9	Rigi Kulm a.	0840	0947	1047	1147	1247	1347	1502	1602	1702	1802	1902

				C						C	F
Rigi Kulm d.	0858	1001	1101	1201	1301	1416	1516	1616	1716	1816	191
Arth-Goldau a.	0948	1048	1148	1248	1348	1503	1603	1703	1803	1903	200

RIGI KULM - VITZNAU

km										S 🚂	A	W 🚂														
0	Rigi Kulm d.	...	...	0900	1000	1100	1200	1300	1400	1415	1430	1430	1500	1600	1700	...	1820t	...	2000t	...	2240h	...	...	...	...	...
2	Rigi Staffelhöhe d.	0715	...	0910	1010	1110	1210	1310	1410	1428	1446	1447	1510	1610	1710	...	1830	...	2010	...	2250	...	...	...	...	...
7	Vitznau a.	0749	...	0940	1040	1140	1240	1340	1440	1506	1513	1539	1540	1640	1740	...	1900	...	2040	...	2320	...	...	...	...	...

						⑦D	S 🚂		W 🚂	A															
Vitznau d.	0635	...	0815	0915	1015	1050	1051	1115	1116	1150	1215	1315	1415	1515	1615	...	1740	...	1915	...	2205	...	...	...	...
Rigi Staffelhöhe d.	0659	...	0837	0937	1037	1115	1158	1137	1217	1215	1237	1337	1437	1537	1637	...	1801	...	1937	...	2227	...	...	...	...
Rigi Kulm a.	...	...	0847	0947	1047	1125	1221	1147	1234	1225	1247	1347	1447	1547	1647	...	1811g	...	1947g	...	2237h	...	...	...	...

ALPNACHSTAD - PILATUS KULM. Narrow gauge rack railway. *5 km*. Journey time: 30 minutes uphill, 40 minutes downhill. **Operator**: PB ✆ 041 329 11 11.
Services run daily May 18 - November 11 (weather permitting). **No winter service**.

From **Alpnachstad** at 0810 **r**, 0845, 0920, 0955, 1030, 1105, 1140, 1215, 1250, 1325, 1400, 1435, 1510, 1545, 1620, 1655 **r** and 1730 **r**.

From **Pilatus Kulm** at 0844 **r**, 0919, 0954, 1029, 1104, 1139, 1214, 1249, 1324, 1359, 143 1509, 1544, 1619, 1654, 1729 **r** and 1804 **r**.

BRIENZ - BRIENZER ROTHORN. Narrow gauge rack railway. *8 km*. Most services operated by 🚂. Journey time: 55–60 minutes uphill, 60–70 minutes downhill.
Operator: BRB, ✆ 033 952 22 22. Services run **June 5 - October 24** (subject to demand and weather conditions on the mountain). Extra trains may run at busy times. **No winter service**

From **Brienz**: 0736 **B**, 0836, 0940, 1045, 1145, 1258, 1358, 1458 and 1636.

From **Brienzer Rothorn**: 0906 **B**, 0938, 1115, 1220, 1328, 1428, 1528, 1628 and 1740.

A – ⑦ May 21 - Sept. 10 (daily July 8 - Aug. 20).
B – ⑥⑦ July 1 - Sept. 30.
C – © (daily Dec. 24 - Mar. 5, May 1 - Oct. 22).
D – ⑦ May 21 - Sept. 10.
F – ⑤ to Apr. 21 (also Apr. 6; not Apr. 7); ⑤–⑦ Apr. 28 - Oct. 22 (also May 17, 18, 29, June 7, 8, Aug. 1, 15); ⑤ from Oct. 27.
S – Summer service. Running dates to be confirmed.
W – Winter service. Running dates to be confirmed.
g – ⑤⑥ Dec. 30 - Mar. 4; daily Apr. 29 - Oct. 22; ⑤⑥ Oct. 27 - Dec. 2.
h – ⑤⑥ Apr. 29 - May 20; daily May 21 - Sept. 10; ⑤⑥ Sept. 15 - Oct. 21.
r – May 18 - Oct. 29.
t – Apr. 29 - Oct. 22.
🚂 – Steam train. Supplement payable for uphill journe to Rigi Kulm (no supplement for downhill journeys Reservations: www.rigi.ch ✆ 041 399 87 87

554 🚌 MEIRINGEN - ANDERMATT

PA

Service operates **June 10 - October 15** (no winter service). Reservations: ✆ +41 (0) 848 100 222.

	A					A	©			A	
Meiringen Bahnhof d.	...	0850	...	0925	...	1050	1055	1325	1322	1520	...
Steingletscher, Susten d.	...	0941	1000	|	...	|	1146	|	1419	|	...
Susten Passhöhe d.	...	▬	1010	|	...	|	...	|	1429	|	...
Göschenen Bahnhof d.	...	...	1049	|	...	|	...	|	1508	|	...
Grimsel Passhöhe d.	0912	...	|	1055	...	1205	...	1440	|	1635	...
Gletsch Post d.	0922	...	|	1105	...	1215	...	1450	|	1645	...
Oberwald Bahnhof a.	0937	...	|	1120	...	1230	...	1505	|	1700	...
Oberwald Bahnhof d.	...	0942	|	...	1220	...	...	...	|	...	*1704*
Gletsch Post a.	...	0954	|	...	1232	...	...	...	|	...	*1716*
Gletsch Post d.	...	0954	|	...	1318	...	...	...	|	...	1720
Furka Passhöhe d.	...	1010	|	...	1340	...	...	...	|	...	1740
Realp Post d.	...	...	|	...	1404	...	...	...	|	...	1804
Andermatt Bahnhof a.	...	...	1104	...	1423	...	...	...	1523	...	1823

		A		A	B	©	A				A
Andermatt Bahnhof d.	...	...	0830	...	...	...	...	...	1534	1551	...
Realp Post d.	...	...	0842	...	...	...	...	...	1546	|	...
Furka Passhöhe d.	...	...	0906	...	...	...	...	...	1610	|	...
Gletsch Post a.	...	...	0935	...	...	...	...	...	1639	|	...
Gletsch Post d.	...	...	1005	...	...	...	...	...	*1645*	|	...
Oberwald Bahnhof a.	...	...	1020	...	...	...	...	...	*1700*	|	...
Oberwald Bahnhof d.	...	0845	...	1030	1104	...	1250	1530	...	|	170
Gletsch Post d.	...	0857	...	1042	1116	...	1302	1542	...	|	17
Grimsel Passhöhe d.	...	0911	...	1113	1133	...	1333	1613	...	|	173
Göschenen Bahnhof d.	0911	▬	...	|	|	...	|	|	...	1611	|
Susten Passhöhe d.	0946	...	...	|	|	...	|	|	...	1646	|
Steingletscher, Susten d.	0956	1000	...	|	|	1150	|	|	...	1720	|
Meiringen Bahnhof a.	...	1051	...	1214	1234	1241	1434	1714	...	1811	183

A – June 24 - Oct. 8.

B – June 10–23 and Oct. 9–15 only.

555 ZÜRICH FLUGHAFEN ✈ - ZÜRICH - LUZERN

SBB (train category *IR*

km		B	⑥⑦b	⑥⑦d	⑥⑦d	⑥⑦d	⑥⑦d												A			Ⓐe		
	Konstanz 535 d.	...	...	...	...	...	...	...	...	...	0509	...	0609	...	0709		...	1509	...	...	...	...	...	170
0	**Zürich** Flughafen ✈ ‡ d.	...	...	...	...	...	...	...	...	...	0615	...	0715	...	0815	and at	...	1615	...	...	...	...	...	181
10	**Zürich** HB 520 ‡ d.	0008	0010	0035	0135	0235	0335	...	0535	0610	0635	0710	0735	0810	0835	the same	1610	1635	1639	1710	1735	1739	1810	183
22	Thalwil 520 d.	0017	|	0045	|	|	|	...	0545	|	0645	|	0745	|	0845	minutes	|	1645	|	|	1745	|	|	184
39	Zug d.	0035	0032	0102	0157	0257	0357	...	0603	0632	0703	0732	0803	0832	0903	past each	1632	1703	1712	1732	1803	1812	1832	190
49	Rotkreuz d.	0046	|	0109	0206	0306	0406	...	0611	|	0711	|	0811	|	0911	hour until	|	1711	1722	|	1811	1822	|	191
67	**Luzern** a.	0107	0051	0123	0223	0323	0423	...	0625	0651	0725	0751	0825	0851	0925		1651	1725	1739	1751	1825	1839	1851	192

Konstanz 535 d.	...	1809	...	1909	...	...	...	...	...	...
Zürich Flughafen ✈ ‡ d.	...	1915	...	2015	...	...	...	...	...	...
Zürich HB 520 ‡ d.	1910	1935	2010	2035	2110	2135	2210	2235	2310	2335
Thalwil 520 d.	|	1945	|	2045	|	2145	|	2245	|	2345
Zug d.	1932	2003	2032	2103	2132	2203	2232	2303	2332	0003
Rotkreuz d.	|	2011	|	2111	|	2211	|	2311	|	0011
Luzern a.	1951	2025	2051	2125	2151	2225	2251	2325	2351	0025

	⑥⑦d	⑥⑦d	⑥⑦d	⑥⑦d					Ⓐe	
Luzern d.	0035	0135	0235	0335	...	0452	0535	0609	0620	063
Rotkreuz d.	0048	0151	0251	0351	...	0513	0548	|	0635	064
Zug d.	0057	0200	0300	0400	...	0526	0558	0629	0647	065
Thalwil 520 d.	0114	0216	0316	0416	...	0543	0614	|	|	071
Zürich HB 520 ‡ a.	0123	0225	0325	0425	...	0555	0625	0650	0720	072
Zürich Flughafen ✈ ‡ a.	...	...	...	...	...	...	0644	...	...	074
Konstanz 535 d.	...	...	...	...	...	...	0750	...	...	085

		Ⓐe																						
Luzern d.	0709	0720	0735	0809	0835		1509	1535	1609	1635	1709	1735	1809	1835	1909	1935	2009	2035	2109	2135	2209	2235	2309	233
Rotkreuz d.	|	0735	0748	|	0848	and at	|	1548	|	1648	|	1748	|	1848	|	1948	|	2048	|	2148	|	2248	|	234
Zug d.	0729	0747	0758	0829	0858	the same	1529	1558	1629	1658	1729	1758	1829	1858	1929	1958	2029	2058	2129	2158	2229	2258	2329	235
Thalwil 520 d.	|	|	0814	|	0914	minutes	|	1614	|	1714	|	1814	|	1914	|	2014	|	2114	|	2214	|	2314	|	001
Zürich HB 520 ‡ a.	0750	0820	0825	0850	0925	past each	1550	1625	1650	1725	1750	1825	1850	1925	1950	2025	2050	2125	2150	2225	2250	2325	2350	002
Zürich Flughafen ✈ ‡ a.	...	...	0844	...	0944	hour until	...	1644	...	...	...	1844	...	1944	...	2044	...	...	...	...	...	...	...	...
Konstanz 535 d.	...	...	0950	...	1050		...	1750	...	...	...	1950	...	2050	...	2150	...	...	...	...	...	...	...	...

A – Ⓐ to Apr. 5 (not Dec. 27 - Jan. 6); ①–④ Apr. 11 - Oct. 26 (not May 17, 18, 29, July 24 - Aug. 3); ①–⑤ from Oct. 30.
B – ①–⑤ (also Apr. 8).
b – Not Apr. 8.
d – Also Apr. 7, 10, May 18, 19, 29, Aug. 1; not Dec. 25.
e – Not Dec. 27 - Jan. 6, May 19, July 24 - Aug. 4.
‡ – See also Tables **530** and **535**. Frequent services operate **Zürich - Zürich Flughafen** and v.v. (up to 13 trains per hour 0600 - 2400).

SBB

BASEL - BERN - INTERLAKEN and BRIG 560

See Table 562 for services via Kandersteg.

km		IC 993 ⑥⑦ z		IC 955	IC 802 ✕	IC 1057 ✕	IC 957 ⊗	IC 804 ✕	EC 51 ◧ ✕		IC 959 ⊗	IC 806 ✕	IC 333 ✕		IC 961 ✕	IC 808 ✕	IC 1063 ✕	IC 963 ✕	IC 810 ✕	IC 1065 ⊗	IC 965 ✕	IC 812 ✕	EC 53 ◧ ✕	IC 967 ⊗	IC 814 ✕	IC 1069 ✕
	Romanshorn **535** d.	...	...	...	...	...	...	...	...	...	...	0548	...	...	...	0648	...	...	0748	...	...	0848	...	...	0948	...
	Zürich Flughafen ✈ **535** d.	...	...	...	...	...	...	...	...	...	...	0645	...	...	...	0745	...	...	0845	...	...	0945	...	...	1045	...
	Zürich HB **505** d.	...	...	...	...	...	...	0602	...	...	...	0702	...	...	...	0802	...	...	0902	...	...	1002	...	...	1102	...
0	**Basel** SBB **565** d.	...	...	...	...	0522	0556	|	0628	...	0656	|	0728	...	0756	|	0828	0856	|	0928	0956	|	1028	1056	|	1128
39	Olten **505 565** d.	...	...	...	...	0558	0629	|	0658	...	0729	|	0758	...	0829	|	0858	0929	|	0958	1029	|	1058	1129	|	1158
101	**Bern** **505** a.	...	...	...	...	0626	0656	0658c	0726	...	0756	0758c	0826	...	0856	0858c	0926	0956	0958c	1026	1056	1058c	1126	1156	1158c	1226
101	**Bern** d.	0109	...	0604	0607	0634	0707	0704	0734	...	0804	0807	0834	...	0907	0904	0934	1004	1007	1034	1104	1107	1134	1207	1204	1234
132	Thun d.	0136	...	0624	0626	0654	0726	0724	0754	...	0824	0826	0854	...	0926	0924	0954	1024	1026	1054	1124	1126	1154	1226	1224	1254
142	**Spiez** ▷ d.	0147	...	0634	0636	0704	0736	0734	0805	...	0834	0836	0904	...	0936	0934	1005	1034	1036	1104	1134	1136	1205	1236	1234	1304
158	Interlaken West ▷ a.	0202	...	0651	|	0722	|	0751	|	...	0851	|	0922	...	|	0951	|	1051	|	1122	1151	|	|	|	1251	1322
160	**Interlaken** Ost ▷ a.	0208	...	0658	|	0728	|	0758	|	...	0858	|	0928	...	|	0958	|	1058	|	1128	1158	|	|	|	1258	1328
197	Visp **570** d.	...	...	...	0703	...	0803	...	0833	...	...	0903	...	...	1003	...	1033	...	1103	...	...	1203	1233	1303	...	...
206	**Brig** **570 590** a.	...	...	...	0711	...	0811	...	0841	...	...	0911	...	...	1011	...	1040	...	1111	...	...	1211	1241	1311	...	...
	Domodossola 🏛 **590** a.	...	...	...	...	...	...	...	0912	...	...	...	...	...	...	...	...	...	...	...	...	...	1312	...	...	...
	Milano Centrale **590** a.	...	...	...	...	...	...	...	1040	...	...	...	...	...	...	...	...	...	...	...	...	...	1440	...	...	...

	ICE 275 G✕	IC 816 ✕	EC 57 ◧ ✕	IC 971 ⊗	IC 818 ✕	IC 1073 ✕	EC 7 G✕	IC 820 ✕	IC 1075 ✕	IC 975 ✕	IC 822 ✕	IC 1077 ⊗	IC 977 ⊗	IC 824 ✕	IC 1079 ⊗	IC 979 ✕	IC 826 ✕	EC 59 ◧ ✕	ICE 371 G✕	IC 828 ✕	IC 1083 ⊗	IC 983 ✕	IC 830 ✕	IC 1085 ✕	ICE 373 G✕	IC 1087 ①–⑥ ✕
Romanshorn **535** d.	...	1048	...	...	1148	...	...	1248	...	...	1348	...	...	1448	...	...	1548	...	...	1648	...	...	1748	...	...	...
Zürich Flughafen ✈ **535** d.	...	1145	...	...	1245	...	...	1345	...	...	1445	...	...	1545	...	...	1645	...	...	1745	...	...	1845	...	...	...
Zürich HB **505** d.	...	1202	...	...	1302	...	...	1402	...	...	1502	...	...	1602	...	...	1702	...	...	1802	...	...	1902	...	...	...
Basel SBB **565** d.	1156	|	1228	1256	|	1328	1356	|	1428	1456	|	1528	1556	|	1628	1656	|	1728	1756	|	1828	1856	|	1928	1956	2028
Olten **505 565** d.	1229	|	1258	1329	|	1358	1429	|	1458	1529	|	1558	1629	|	1658	1729	|	1758	1829	|	1858	1929	|	1958	2029	2058
Bern **505** a.	1256	1258c	1326	1356	1358c	1426	1456	1458c	1526	1556	1558c	1626	1656	1658c	1726	1756	1758c	1826	1856	1858c	1926	1956	1958c	2026	2056	2126
Bern d.	1304	1307	1334	1407	1404	1434	1504	1507	1534	1607	1604	1634	1704	1707	1734	1807	1804	1834	1904	1907	1934	2007	2004	2034	2107	2134
Thun d.	1324	1326	1354	1426	1424	1454	1524	1526	1554	1626	1624	1654	1724	1726	1754	1826	1824	1854	1924	1926	1954	2026	2024	2054	2126	2154
Spiez ▷ d.	1334	1336	1405	1436	1434	1504	1534	1536	1605	1636	1634	1704	1734	1736	1805	1836	1834	1905	1934	1936	2004	2036	2034	2105	2137	2205
Interlaken West ▷ a.	1352	|	|	|	1451	1522	1551	|	|	|	1651	1722	1751	|	|	|	1851	|	1952	|	2022	|	2050	|	2154	|
Interlaken Ost ▷ a.	1358	|	|	|	1458	1528	1558	|	|	|	1658	1728	1758	|	|	|	1858	|	1958	|	2028	|	2056	|	2159	|
Visp **570** d.	...	1403	1433	1503	...	...	...	1603	1633	1703	...	...	...	1803	1833	1903	...	1933	...	2003	...	2103	...	2133	...	2233
Brig **570 590** a.	...	1411	1441	1511	...	...	...	1611	1640	1711	...	...	...	1811	1841	1911	...	1941	...	2011	...	2111	...	2141	...	2241
Domodossola 🏛 **590** a.	...	...	1512	...	...	...	...	...	...	...	...	...	...	...	...	...	...	2012	...	...	...	...	...	...	...	...
Milano Centrale **590** a.	...	...	1640	...	...	...	...	...	...	...	...	...	...	...	...	...	...	2140	...	...	...	...	...	...	...	...

	IC 1089 ⑦ ✕	IC 987	IC 1091	IC 1093 ①–⑥ ⊖	IC 1095 ⑦	IC 989	IC 1097	RE 4293	IC 838	IC 991
Romanshorn **535** d.	...	...	...	...	...	...	...	...	...	...
Zürich Flughafen ✈ **535** d.	...	...	...	...	...	...	...	...	...	...
Zürich HB **505** d.	...	...	...	...	...	...	...	...	...	...
Basel SBB **565** d.	2028	2056	2128	...	...	2156	2228e	...	*2256*	...
Olten **505 565** d.	2058	2129	2158	...	...	2229	2258	...	2335	...
Bern **505** a.	2126	2156	2226	...	...	2256	2326	...	0002	...
Bern d.	2134	2207	...	2234	2234	2308	2339	...	...	0008
Thun d.	2154	2226	...	2254	2254	2327	2359	...	...	0030
Spiez ▷ d.	2205	2237	...	2305	2305	2338	0009	0015	...	0040
Interlaken West ▷ a.	|	2252	...	|	|	2355	0024	|	...	0056
Interlaken Ost ▷ a.	|	2258	...	|	⊙	2400	0030	⊙	...	0101
Visp **570** d.	|	...	...	2336	|	...	...	|	...	...
Brig **570 590** a.	2303h	...	...	2344	0013	...	...	0123	...	...
Domodossola 🏛 **590** a.	...	...	...	...	...	...	...	...	...	...
Milano Centrale **590** a.	...	...	...	...	...	...	...	...	...	...

	IC 956	IC 1056 ✕	ICE 372 G✕	IC 807 ⊖✕	IC 1058 ⊗	IC 960 ⊗	IC 809 ✕	IC 1060 ✕	IC 962 ✕	IC 811 ✕	IC 1062 ⊗
Milano Centrale **590** d.	...	...	...	...	...	...	...	...	...	...	...
Domodossola 🏛 **590** d.	...	...	...	...	...	...	...	...	...	...	...
Brig **570 590** d.	...	...	...	0546	...	0648	...	0718	...	0748	...
Visp **570** d.	...	...	...	0554	...	0657	...	0727	...	0757	...
Interlaken Ost ▷ d.	0458	0531	0558	|	0630	|	0700	|	0800	|	0830
Interlaken West ▷ d.	0503	0536	0603	|	0635	|	0705	|	0805	|	0835
Spiez ▷ d.	0520	0554	0622	0625	0654	0725	0722	0754	0822	0823	0854
Thun d.	0530	0604	0633	0636	0704	0736	0733	0804	0833	0834	0904
Bern a.	0552	0624	0652	0654c	0724	0754	0752c	0824	0852	0854c	0924
Bern **505** d.	0604	0636	0704	0702	0736	0804	0802	0836	0904	0902	0936
Olten **505 565** a.	0630	0703	0730	|	0803	0830	|	0903	0930	|	1003
Basel SBB **565** a.	0701	0732	0801	|	0832	0901	|	0932	1001	|	1032
Zürich HB **505** a.	...	...	...	0758	...	...	0858	...	...	0958	...
Zürich Flug ✈ **535** a.	...	...	...	0814	...	...	0914	...	...	1014	...
Romanshorn **535** a.	...	...	...	0912	...	...	1012	...	...	1112	...

	IC 964 ✕	IC 813 ✕	EC 50 ◧ ✕	ICE 278 G✕	IC 815 ✕	IC 1066 ⊗	IC 968 ✕	IC 817 ✕	IC 1068 ✕	EC 6 G✕	IC 819 ✕	IC 1070 ✕	IC 972 ⊗	IC 821 ✕	EC 52 ◧ G✕	IC 974 ⊗	IC 823 ✕	IC 1074 ✕	ICE 376 G✕	IC 825 ✕	IC 1076 ✕	IC 978 ¶ ⊗	IC 827 ✕	IC 1078 ✕	IC 980 ✕	IC 829 ‡ ✕
Milano Centrale **590** d.	...	...	0720	...	...	...	...	...	...	...	...	...	...	...	1120	...	...	...	...	...	...	...	...	...	...	...
Domodossola 🏛 **590** d.	...	...	0848	...	...	...	...	...	...	...	...	...	...	...	1248	...	...	...	...	...	...	...	...	...	...	...
Brig **570 590** d.	0848	...	0918	...	0948	...	1048	...	1118	...	1148	...	...	1248	1318	1348	...	...	...	1448	1518	1548	...	...	...	1648
Visp **570** d.	0857	...	0927	...	0957	...	1057	...	1127	...	1157	...	...	1257	1327	1357	...	...	...	1457	1527	1557	...	...	...	1657
Interlaken Ost ▷ d.	|	0900	|	1000	|	1030	|	1100	|	1200	|	1230	1300	|	|	|	1400	1430	1500	|	|	|	1600	1630	1700	|
Interlaken West ▷ d.	|	0905	|	1005	|	1035	|	1105	|	1205	|	1235	1305	|	|	|	1405	1435	1505	|	|	|	1605	1635	1705	|
Spiez ▷ d.	0923	0922	0954	1022	1023	1054	1123	1122	1154	1222	1223	1254	1322	1323	1354	1423	1422	1454	1522	1523	1554	1623	1622	1654	1722	1723
Thun d.	0934	0933	1004	1033	1034	1104	1134	1133	1204	1233	1234	1304	1333	1334	1404	1434	1433	1504	1533	1534	1604	1634	1633	1704	1733	1734
Bern a.	0954	0952c	1024	1052	1054c	1124	1154	1152c	1224	1252	1254c	1324	1352	1354c	1424	1454	1452c	1524	1552	1554c	1624	1654	1652c	1724	1752	1754c
Bern **505** d.	1004	1002	1036	1104	1102	1136	1204	1202	1236	1304	1302	1336	1404	1402	1436	1504	1502	1536	1604	1602	1636	1704	1702	1736	1804	1802
Olten **505 565** a.	1030	|	1103	1130	|	1203	1230	|	1303	1330	|	1403	1430	|	1503	1530	|	1603	1630	|	1703	1730	|	1803	1830	|
Basel SBB **565** a.	1101	|	1132	1201	|	1232	1301	|	1332	1401	|	1432	1501	|	1532	1601	|	1632	1701	|	1732	1801	|	1832	1901	|
Zürich HB **505** a.	...	1058	...	...	1158	...	...	1258	...	...	1358	...	...	1458	...	...	1558	...	...	1658	...	...	1758	...	...	1858
Zürich Flughafen ✈ **535** a.	...	1114	...	...	1214	...	...	1314	...	...	1414	...	...	1514	...	...	1614	...	...	1714	...	...	1814	...	...	1914
Romanshorn **535** a.	...	1212	...	...	1312	...	...	1412	...	...	1512	...	...	1612	...	...	1712	...	...	1812	...	...	1912	...	...	2012

	EC 54 Ⓐ◧ ✕	EC 54 Ⓒ◧ ✕		IC 982 § ✕	IC 831 ✕	IC 1082 ⊗	IC 984 ⊗	IC 833 ✕	IC 1084 ⊗	IC 986 ✕	IC 835 ✕		EC 56 ◧ ✕	IC 336	IC 837	IC 1088	IC 338	IC 990	IC 839	IC 1090 ①–⑥	IC 1096	IC 992	IC 1092 ⑦	IC 841		IC 1094 ⑤⑥ k
Milano C **590** d.	1520	1520	...	...	...	...	...	...	...	...	...	...	1820	...	...	...	...	...	...	...	...	...	...	...	...	...
Domodossola 🏛 **590** d.	1648	1648	...	...	...	...	...	...	...	...	...	...	1948	...	...	...	...	...	...	...	...	...	...	...	...	...
Brig **570 590** d.	1718	1720	...	1748	...	...	...	1848	1918	1948	...	...	2019	...	...	2118	...	...	...	2218	...	...	2226	...	...	...
Visp **570** d.	1727	1729	...	1757	...	...	...	1857	1927	1957	...	...	2028	...	...	2127	...	...	...	2227	...	...	|	...	...	...
Interlaken Ost ▷ d.	|	|	...	|	1800	1830	1900	|	|	|	2000	...	|	2100	...	|	...	2200	...	|	...	2300	|	...	...	2333
Interlaken West ▷ d.	|	|	...	|	1805	1835	1905	|	|	|	2005	...	|	2105	...	|	...	2205	...	|	...	2305	|	...	...	2338
Spiez ▷ d.	1754	1756	...	1823	1822	1854	1922	1923	1954	2023	2022	...	2054	2122	...	2154	...	2222	...	2254	...	2322	2325	...	...	2357
Thun d.	1804	1807	...	1834	1833	1904	1933	1934	2004	2034	2033	...	2104	2133	...	2204	...	2233	...	2304	...	2333	2336	...	...	0007
Bern a.	1824	1828	...	1854	1852c	1924	1952	1954c	2024	2054	2052c	...	2124	2152	...	2224	...	2252	...	2324	...	2352	2354	...	...	0027
Bern **505** d.	1836	1836	...	1904	1902	1936	2004	2002	2036	2104	2102	...	2136	...	2202	...	2236	...	2302	...	2336	...	...	0002	...	...
Olten **505 565** a.	1903	1903	...	1930	|	2003	2030	|	2103	2130	|	...	2203	...	2228	...	2303	...	2328	...	0003	...	...	0028	...	...
Basel SBB **565** a.	1932	1932	...	2001	|	2032	2101	|	2132	2201	|	...	2232f	...	*2300*f	...	2337f	...	*0001*	...	0037r	...	...	*0102*r	...	...
Zürich HB **505** a.	...	...	...	...	1958	...	...	2058	...	...	2158	...	...	...	...	...	...	...	...	...	...	...	...	...	...	...
Zürich Flughafen ✈ **535** a.	...	...	...	...	2014	...	...	2114	...	...	2214	...	...	...	...	...	...	...	...	...	...	...	...	...	...	...
Romanshorn **535** a.	...	...	...	...	2112	...	...	2212	...	...	2312	...	...	...	...	...	...	...	...	...	...	...	...	...	...	...

– From/to stations in Germany (Table **912**).
– From June 11.
– Connects with train in previous column.
– 2223 on ⑦–④ Jan. 30 - June 29; 2217 on ⑦–④ July 2 - Dec. 7.
– 4–5 minutes later on ⑦–④ from Jan. 30.
– 2309 Jan. 8 - July 16.
– ⑤⑥ (not Dec. 24, Apr. 7).

r – 3–4 minutes later on the mornings of ①–⑤ from Jan. 31.
z – ⑥⑦ (not Dec. 25, Apr. 8).
¶ – Runs 1–2 minutes later Spiez - Bern on ⑦ Jan. 8 - Mar. 19.
§ – Runs 1–2 minutes later Spiez - Bern on ⑦ Jan. 8 - Mar. 12.
‡ – Runs 1–2 minutes later Spiez - Bern on † Jan. 2 - Apr. 2 (also Apr. 10, May 21, 29) and ⑦ June 18 - Oct. 22.
⊙ – Via Kandersteg (Table **562**).
⊖ – Also calls at Frutigen (Table **562**).

◧ – Supplement payable for journeys to/from Milano.
▷ – Other trains Spiez - Interlaken West - Interlaken Ost and v.v. (operated by BLS):
From Spiez at 0555, 0805, 1005, 1023 **J**, 1205, 1223, 1405, 1523 **J**, 1605, 1723 **J**, 1805 and 1905.
From Interlaken Ost at 0730, 0908, 0930, 1108 **J**, 1130, 1330, 1408 **J**, 1530, 1608 **J**, 1730 and 1930.

561 LUZERN - INTERLAKEN

Narrow gauge rack railway. Z.

km		Ⓐ	Ⓐ			L			L				L			L			L			L		
0	**Luzern** 552 d.	...	...	...	0542	0606	0612	0642	0706	0712	0742		1706	1712	1742	1806	1812	1842	1906	1912	1942	2006	2012	204
9	Hergiswil 552 d.	...	...	...	0554	|	0624	0654	|	0724	0754		|	1724	1754	|	1824	1854	|	1924	1954	|	2024	205
13	Alpnachstad ⊙ d.	...	...	...	0559	|	0629	0659	|	0729	0759	and at	|	1729	1759	|	1829	1859	|	1929	1959	|	2029	205
15	Alpnach Dorf d.	...	...	...	0601	|	0631	0701	|	0731	0801		|	1731	1801	|	1831	1901	|	1931	2001	|	2031	210
21	Sarnen d.	...	...	...	0609	0624	0639	0709	0724	0739	0809	the same	1724	1739	1809	1824	1839	1909	1924	1939	2009	2024	2039	210
23	Sachseln d.	...	...	...	0613	0628	0643	0713	0728	0743	0813		1728	1743	1813	1828	1843	1913	1928	1943	2013	2028	2043	211
29	Giswil d.	...	...	...	0621	0637	0651	0721	0737	0751	0821	minutes	1737	1751	1821	1837	1851	1921	1937	1951	2021	2037	2051	212
36	Lungern d.	...	...	...	▬	0651	...	▬	0751	...	▬		1751	...	▬	1851	...	...	1951	▬	...	2051	▬	...
40	Brünig Hasliberg d.	...	...	...	...	0703	...	...	0803	...	...	past each	1803	...	...	1903	...	...	2003	...	...	2103	...	...
45	**Meiringen** ● a.	...	...	...	...	0716	...	...	0816	...	...		1816	...	...	1916	...	...	2016	...	...	2116	...	...
45	**Meiringen** ● d.	0515	0545	0614	0651	0722	...	0751	0822	...	0851	hour until	1822	...	1851	1922	...	...	...	2020	...	...	2120	...
58	**Brienz** ⊡ d.	0527	0556	0628	0702	0733	...	0802	0837	...	0902		1837	...	1902	1935	...	...	...	2032	...	...	2132	...
65	Oberried d.	0537	0608	0639	0712	0744	...	0812	|	...	0912		|	...	1912	1944	...	...	...	2042	...	...	2142	...
74	**Interlaken** Ost a.	0550	0620	0651	0724	0754	...	0824	0855	...	0924		1855	...	1924	1955	...	...	...	2055	...	...	2155	...

	L		⑤⑥ k								
Luzern 552 d.	2106	2112	...	2142	2212	2242	2312	2342	0012	0042	...
Hergiswil 552 d.	|	2124	...	2154	2224	2254	2324	2354	0024	0056	...
Alpnachstad ⊙ d.	|	2129	...	2159	2229	2259	2329	2359	0029	0100	...
Alpnach Dorf d.	|	2131	...	2201	2231	2301	2331	0001	0031	0102	...
Sarnen d.	2124	2139	...	2209	2239	2309	2339	0009	0039	0110	...
Sachseln d.	2128	2143	...	2213	2243	2313	2343	0013	0043	0113	...
Giswil d.	2137	2151	...	2221	2251	2321	2351	0021	0051	0121	...
Lungern d.	2151	▬	...	...	...	...	...	...	...	...	...
Brünig Hasliberg d.	2203	...	...	...	...	...	...	...	...	...	...
Meiringen ● a.	2216	...	...	...	...	...	...	...	...	...	...
Meiringen ● d.	...	2220	2320	...	...	...	...	...	...	...	...
Brienz ⊡ d.	...	2232	2332	...	...	...	...	...	...	...	...
Oberried d.	...	2242	2342	...	...	...	...	...	...	...	...
Interlaken Ost a.	...	2255	2355	...	...	...	...	...	...	...	...

	⑥⑦ z				L		Ⓐ	L	
Interlaken Ost d.	0006	...	...	...	...	...	0557	...	...
Oberried d.	0017	...	...	...	...	...	0609	...	...
Brienz ⊡ d.	0026	...	...	...	...	...	0618	...	...
Meiringen ● a.	0039	...	...	...	...	...	0631	...	...
Meiringen ● d.	...	...	...	...	0541	...	▬	0641	...
Brünig Hasliberg d.	...	...	...	...	0551	...	...	0651	...
Lungern d.	...	...	...	...	0604	...	...	0704	...
Giswil d.	...	0505	0535	0605	0621	0635	0705	0721	073
Sachseln d.	...	0513	0543	0613	0629	0643	0713	0729	074
Sarnen d.	...	0519	0549	0619	0635	0649	0719	0735	074
Alpnach Dorf d.	...	0524	0554	0624	|	0654	0724	|	075
Alpnachstad ⊙ d.	...	0529	0559	0629	|	0659	0729	|	075
Hergiswil 552 d.	...	0533	0603	0633	|	0703	0733	|	080
Luzern 552 a.	...	0546	0616	0646	0655	0716	0746	0755	081

	Ⓐ	L			L				L			L			L △								
Interlaken Ost d.	0627	0704	...	0733	0804	...	0833		1804	...	1833	1904	...	1933	2004	...	2104	...	...	2204	...	...	2304	...
Oberried d.	0640	0714	...	0745	|	...	0844		|	...	1844	|	...	1946	2015	...	2115	...	...	2215	...	...	2315	...
Brienz ⊡ d.	0650	0725	...	0754	0825	...	0854	and at	1825	...	1854	1925	...	1956	2025	...	2124	...	...	2224	...	...	2324	...
Meiringen ● a.	0703	0735	...	0807	0835	...	0907		1835	...	1907	1935	...	2009	2036	...	2137	...	...	2237	...	...	2337	...
Meiringen ● d.	▬	0741	...	▬	0841	...	▬	the same	1841	...	▬	1941	...	▬	2041	...	...	...	...	...	...	...	...	...
Brünig Hasliberg d.	...	0751	...	...	0851	...	...		1851	...	...	1951	...	...	2051	...	...	...	...	...	...	...	...	...
Lungern d.	...	0804	...	...	0904	...	...	minutes	1904	...	...	2004	...	...	2104	...	...	...	...	...	...	...	...	...
Giswil d.	0805	0821	0835	0905	0921	0935	1005		1921	1935	2005	2021	2035	2105	2121	2135	...	2205	2235	...	2305	2335	...	000
Sachseln d.	0813	0829	0843	0913	0929	0943	1013	past each	1929	1943	2013	2029	2043	2113	2129	2143	...	2213	2243	...	2313	2343	...	001
Sarnen d.	0819	0835	0849	0919	0935	0949	1019		1935	1949	2019	2035	2049	2119	2135	2149	...	2219	2249	...	2319	2349	...	001
Alpnach Dorf d.	0824	|	0854	0924	|	0954	1024	hour until	|	1954	2024	|	2054	2124	|	2154	...	2224	2254	...	2324	2354	...	002
Alpnachstad ⊙ d.	0829	|	0859	0929	|	0959	1029		|	1959	2029	|	2059	2129	|	2159	...	2229	2259	...	2329	2359	...	002
Hergiswil 552 d.	0833	|	0903	0933	|	1003	1033		|	2003	2033	|	2103	2133	|	2203	...	2233	2303	...	2333	0003	...	003
Luzern 552 a.	0846	0855	0916	0946	0955	1016	1046		1955	2016	2046	2055	2116	2146	2155	2216	...	2246	2316	...	2346	0016	...	004

L – LUZERN - INTERLAKEN EXPRESS. (12) [panorama cars]. The following services convey ✕: From Luzern 0806 - 1506 (0706 - 1706 May 14 - Oct. 30). From Interlaken 1004 - 1704 (0904 - 1904 May 14 - Oct. 30).

k – ⑤⑥ (not Dec. 24, Apr. 7).
z – ⑥⑦ (not Dec. 25, Apr. 8).

△ – Change trains at Meiringen on ④ (except on May 18).
⊙ – Station for Pilatusbahn (Table **553**).
⊡ – Station for Brienz Rothorn Bahn (Table **553**).

● – Rail service **Meiringen** - **Innertkirchen** and v.v. Narrow gauge. 2nd class only. *5 km.* Journey time: 11 minutes. **Operator**: ZB.
From Meiringen at 0612 Ⓐ, 0634 Ⓐ, 0656 Ⓐ, 0718 Ⓐ, 0745, 0818 Ⓐ, 0845, 0945, 1045, 1118 Ⓐ, 1145, 1218 Ⓐ, 1245, 1318 Ⓐ, 1345, 1445, 1545, 1618 Ⓐ, 1645, 1718 Ⓐ, 174 1818 Ⓐ, 1845, 1918 Ⓐ, 1945, 2045, 2145 and 2245 ⑤⑥ **k**.
From Innertkirchen Kraftwerk at 0558 Ⓐ, 0623 Ⓐ, 0629 Ⓒ, 0645 Ⓐ, 0707, 0729 Ⓐ, 0802, 0829 Ⓐ, 0902, 1002, 1102, 1129 Ⓐ, 1202, 1229 Ⓐ, 1302, 1329 Ⓐ, 1402, 1502, 1602, 1629 Ⓐ, 1702, 1729 Ⓐ, 1802, 1829 Ⓐ, 1902, 1929 Ⓐ, 2002, 2102 and 2202 ⑤⑥

562 BERN - SPIEZ - BRIG (via Lötschberg pass)

BLS

Services from / to Bern (except *IC* / *EC* trains) also convey (12) Bern - Spiez - Zweisimmen (Table **563**).
Passengers from Bern and Thun should ensure they join the correct portion for their destination. See Table **560** for faster services via the Lötschberg Base Tunnel.

km																		*IC*		*IC*		*IC*	*IC*	*IC*	
																		1085		**1087/9**		**1093**	**1095**	**1097**	
													Ⓐ	Ⓒ								①-⑥	⑦		
0	**Bern** 560 d.	...	0639	0739	0839	0939	1039	1139	1239	1339	1439	1539	1639	1639	1739	1839	1939	2034	...	2134	...	2234	2234	2339	...
31	Thun 560 d.	...	0701	0801	0901	1001	1101	1201	1301	1401	1501	1601	1701	1701	1801	1901	2001	2054	...	2154	...	2254	2254	2359	...
41	**Spiez** 560 a.	...	0710	0810	0910	1010	1110	1210	1310	1410	1510	1610	1710	1710	1810	1910	2010	2105	...	2202	...	2302	2302	0008	...
41	**Spiez** d.	0612	0712	0812	0912	1012	1112	1212	1312	1412	1512	1612	1712	1712	1812	1912	2012	2105	2112	2205	2212	2305	2305	...	001
55	Frutigen ● d.	0624	0724	0824	0924	1024	1124	1224	1324	1424	1524	1624	1724	1724	1824	1924	2024	|	2124	|	2224	2317	2317	...	002
72	Kandersteg 🚗 d.	0640	0740	0840	0940	1040	1140	1240	1340	1440	1540	1640	1740	1740	1840	1940	2040	|	2140	|	2240v	|	2335	...	004
89	Goppenstein 🚗 d.	0654	0754	0854	0954	1054	1154	1254	1354	1454	1554	1654	1754	1754	1854	1954	2054	|	2154	|	2254v	|	2348	...	005
115	**Brig** 560 a.	0718	0820	0918	1020	1118	1220	1318	1420	1518	1620	1718	1818	1820	1918	2020	2120	2141	2218	2241z	2320v	2344	0013	...	012
	Domodossola 590 a.	...	...	...	...	...	...	...	...	...	...	...	...	...	...	...	...	...	...	...	...	...	...	...	...

		IC																*IC*			*EC*		*IC*		*IC*
		807																**1084**			**56**		**1088**		**992**
		R✕			Ⓒ	Ⓐ													Ⓒ	Ⓐ					
Domodossola 590 d.	...	...	...	...	...	...	...	...	...	...	...	...	...	...	...	...	...	...	...	...	1948	...	...	...	...
Brig 560 d.	0514	0546	...	0636	0734	0736	0836	0934	1036	1134	1236	1334	1436	1534	1636	1734	1836	1918	1934	1936	2019	2036	2118	2205	...
Goppenstein 🚗 d.	0538	|	...	0700	0800	0800	0900	1000	1100	1200	1300	1400	1500	1600	1700	1800	1900	|	2000	2000	|	2100	|	2231	...
Kandersteg 🚗 d.	0553	|	←	0715	0815	0815	0915	1015	1115	1215	1315	1415	1515	1615	1715	1815	1915	|	2015	2015	|	2115	|	2247	...
Frutigen ● d.	0609	0612	0631	0731	0831	0831	0931	1031	1131	1231	1331	1431	1531	1631	1731	1831	1931	|	2031	2031	|	2131	|	2303	...
Spiez a.	→	0624	0644	0744	0844	0844	0944	1044	1144	1244	1344	1444	1544	1644	1744	1844	1944	1953	2044	2044	2053	2144	2153	2316	...
Spiez 560 d.	...	0625	0650	0750	0850	0850	0950	1050	1150	1250	1350	1450	1550	1650	1750	1850	...	1954	...	...	2054	...	2154	...	232
Thun 560 a.	...	0634	0658	0758	0858	0858	0958	1058	1158	1258	1358	1458	1558	1658	1758	1858	...	2003	...	...	2103	...	2203	...	233
Bern 560 a.	...	0654	0721	0821	0921	0921	1021	1121	1221	1321	1421	1521	1621	1721	1821	1921	...	2024	...	...	2124	...	2224	...	235

R – (12) Brig - Zürich - Romanshorn.

v – 6–8 minutes later on ⑦ Jan. 8 - July 16.
z – 2303 on ⑦ to Jan. 7 / from July 23; 2309 on ⑦ Jan. 8 - July 16.

🚗 – Car-carrying shuttle available. ✆ +41 (0) 58 327 41 14.
www.bls.ch/en/fahren/unterwegs-mit/autoverlad/kandersteg-goppenstein

● – 🚌 **SERVICE FRUTIGEN - ADELBODEN**. 20 km. Journey ±30 minutes.
Operator: Autoverkehr Frutigen-Adelboden (AFA). ✆ +41 (0) 33 673 74 74.
From Frutigen at 0615 Ⓐ, 0632, 0700 Ⓐ, 0732, 0800, 0832, 0900 Ⓒ, 0932, 1000 Ⓒ, 1032, 1132 and hourly until 1532; then 1603 Ⓒ, 1632, 1700, 1732, 1800, 1832, 1900 Ⓐ, 1932, 2032, 2132, 2232 and 2325.
From Adelboden (Post) at 0537 Ⓐ, 0551, 0622 Ⓐ, 0651, 0725, 0751, 0825 Ⓒ, 0851, 0925 Ⓒ, 0951, 1051 and hourly until 1451; then 1525 Ⓒ, 1551, 1625, 1651, 1725, 1751 1825 Ⓐ, 1851, 1951, 2051, 2151 and 2225.

BLS — INTERLAKEN - SPIEZ - ZWEISIMMEN — 563

km				Ⓐ		Ⓒ		★			B	A★					B	A★		B		B	A★	
	Interlaken Ost ◇	**560** d.	...	...	...	...	...	0908	...	...	...	1108	...	...	...	...	...	1408	...	...	...	...	1608	...
	Bern **560 562** △	d.	...	0639	...	0739	...	0839	|	0939	1039	...	|	1139	1239	...	1339	...	|	1439	...	1539	...	|	1639
0	**Spiez**	**560** d.	0612	0712	0738	0812	0838	0912	0938	1012	1112	1138	1138	1212	1312	1338	1412	1438	1438	1512	1538	1612	1638	1638	1712
11	Erlenbach im Simmental	d.	0629	0729	0753	0829	0853	0929	0953	1029	1129	1153	1153	1229	1329	1353	1429	1453	1453	1529	1553	1629	1653	1653	1729
26	Boltigen	d.	0649	0749	0811	0849	0911	0949	1011	1049	1149	1211	1211	1249	1349	1411	1449	1511	1511	1549	1611	1649	1711	1711	1749
35	**Zweisimmen**	a.	0659	0759	0820	0859	0920	0959	1020	1059	1159	1220	1220	1259	1359	1420	1459	1520	1520	1559	1620	1659	1720	1720	1759
	Montreux **566**	a.	...	...	...	...	...	...	1220	...	...	...	1420	...	...	...	...	...	1720	...	...	...	...	1720	...

		Ⓐ								
Interlaken Ost ◇	**560** d.	...	...	...	...	...	...	...	...	...
Bern **560 562** △	d.	...	1739	...	1839	1939	...	...	...	...
Spiez	**560** d.	1738	1812	1838	1912	2012	2106	2206	2306	0016
Erlenbach im Simmental	d.	1753	1829	1853	1929	2029	2121	2221	2321	0032
Boltigen	d.	1811	1849	1911	1949	2049	2141	2241	2341	0051
Zweisimmen	a.	1820	1859	1920	1959	2059	2152	2252	2352	0102
Montreux **566**	a.	...	...	...	...	...	...	...	...	...

		Ⓐ	Ⓐ	Ⓒ	Ⓐ				Ⓐ		B
Montreux **566**	d.	...	...	...	...	...	...	...	...	...	...
Zweisimmen	d.	0539	0554	0602	0639	0702	0739	0802	0839	0902	0939
Boltigen	d.	0548	0602	0610	0648	0710	0748	0810	0848	0910	0948
Erlenbach im Simmental	d.	0605	0622	0630	0705	0730	0805	0830	0905	0930	1005
Spiez	**560** a.	0621	0639	0647	0721	0747	0821	0847	0921	0947	1021
Bern **560 562**	a.	...	0721	0721	...	0821	...	0921	...	1021	...
Interlaken Ost ◇	**560** a.	...	...	...	...	...	...	...	...	...	...

		A★			★		Ⓒ			B	A★				B	A★		B							
Montreux **566**	d.	0735	...	...	0935	...	...	...	...	...	1235	...	...	...	...	1435	...	...	...	...	...	...	...	...	...
Zweisimmen	d.	0939	1002	1102	1139	1202	1239	1302	1402	1439	1439	1502	1539	1602	1639	1639	1702	1739	1802	1902	2002	2104	2204	2304	0013
Boltigen	d.	0948	1010	1110	1148	1210	1248	1310	1410	1448	1448	1510	1548	1610	1648	1648	1710	1748	1810	1910	2012	2114	2214	2314	0023
Erlenbach im Simmental	d.	1005	1030	1130	1205	1230	1305	1330	1430	1505	1505	1530	1605	1630	1705	1705	1730	1805	1830	1930	2031	2134	2234	2334	0045
Spiez	**560** a.	1021	1047	1147	1221	1247	1321	1347	1447	1521	1521	1547	1621	1647	1721	1721	1747	1821	1847	1947	2047	2150	2250	2350	0101
Bern **560 562**	a.	|	1121	1221	|	1321	...	1421	1521	...	|	1621	...	1721	...	|	1821	...	1921	...	...	...	...	...	...
Interlaken Ost ◇	**560** a.	1050	...	...	1250	...	...	...	...	...	1550	...	...	...	...	1750	...	...	...	...	...	...	...	...	...

A – From June 11.
B – Until June 10.
★ – GOLDEN PASS EXPRESS – Conveys panorama cars. Reservation recommended. Also conveys Prestige class (🅁 and supplement payable).
◇ – Trains also call at Interlaken West.
△ – Trains from Bern convey portions for Zweisimmen and Brig; please ensure you join the correct portion.

Narrow gauge rack railway. BOB, WAB, JB — INTERLAKEN - KLEINE SCHEIDEGG - JUNGFRAUJOCH — 564

INTERLAKEN - LAUTERBRUNNEN / GRINDELWALD

km																			🚌	🚌					
0	**Interlaken** Ost	d.	0605	0605	0635	0635		2005	2005	2035	2035	2105	2105	...	2205	2205	...	2304	2305	...	...	...	...	...
3	Wilderswil ⊡	d.	0610	0610	0640	0640	and every	2010	2010	2040	2040	2110	2110	...	2210	2210	...	2311	2312	...	...	...	...	...
8	Zweilütschinen	d.	0616	0617	0646	0647	30 minutes	2016	2017	2046	2047	2116	2117	...	2216	2217	...	2318	2319	...	...	...	...	...
	Grindelwald Terminal 🚡	a.	|	0635	|	0705		|	2035	|	2105	|	2135	...	|	2235	...	|	|	...	...	...	...	...
19	**Grindelwald**	a.	|	0639	|	0709	until	|	2039	|	2109	|	2139	...	|	2239	...	|	2337	...	...	...	...	...
	Lauterbrunnen ⊙	a.	0625	...	0655	...		2025	...	2055	...	2125	...	...	2225	...	...	2325	...	...	...	...	...	...

km																			🚌	🚌		🚌			
0	**Lauterbrunnen** ⊙	d.	...	0532	...	0602	...	0632		...	2002	...	2032	...		2132	...	...	2230	...	2330	...	...	...
	Grindelwald	d.	0518	|	0548	|	0618	|	and every	1948	|	2018	|	...	2118	|	...	2218	|	...	|	...	...	...
	Grindelwald Terminal 🚡	d.	0522	|	0552	|	0622	|	30 minutes	1952	|	2022	|	...	2122	|	...	|	|	...	|	...	...	...
4	Zweilütschinen	d.	0542	0542	0612	0612	0642	0642		2012	2012	2042	2042	...	2142	2142	...	2236	2236	...	2336	...	...	...
9	Wilderswil ⊡	d.	0548	0548	0618	0618	0648	0648	until	2018	2018	2048	2048	...	2148	2148	...	2243	2245	...	2345	...	...	...
12	**Interlaken** Ost	a.	0552	0552	0623	0623	0653	0653		2023	2023	2053	2053	...	2153	2153	...	2252	2254	...	2354	...	...	...

GRINDELWALD - KLEINE SCHEIDEGG *No service May 8 – 17 and Oct. 23 - Nov. 5*

km				b			b		b	u		r		r										
0	**Grindelwald**	d.	0745	0815	0845	and at the same	1615	1645	1715	1715	1745	1745	1815	1915	...	...	...	...	...	...	...	...	...	...
1	Grindelwald Grund	d.	0753	0823	0853	minutes past	1623	1653	1720	1723	1750	1753	1820	1920	...	...	...	...	...	...	...	...	...	...
9	**Kleine Scheidegg**	a.	0817	0847	0917	each hour until	1647	1717	...	1747	...	1817	...	...	...	...	...	...	...	...	...	...	...	...

			b		b		b			b			u	r									
Kleine Scheidegg	d.	...	...	...	0831	0901	0931	and at the same	1601	1631	1701	1731	1801	1831	...	...	...	...	...	...	...	...	...
Grindelwald Grund	d.	0736	0806	0836	0906	0936	1006	minutes past	1636	1706	1736	1806	1836	1906	...	...	...	...	...	...	...	...	...
Grindelwald	a.	0740	0810	0840	0910	0940	1010	each hour until	1640	1710	1740	1810	1840	1910	...	...	...	...	...	...	...	...	...

LAUTERBRUNNEN - WENGEN - KLEINE SCHEIDEGG (SEE NOTE ▲)

km																										
0	**Lauterbrunnen** ⊙	d.	0600	0630	0700	0730	0800	0830	0900	0930	1000	1030	1100	1130	1200	1230	1300	1330	1400	1430	1500	1530	1600	1630	1700	1730
4	Wengen	a.	0611	0641	0711	0742	0812	0842	0912	0942	1012	1042	1112	1142	1212	1242	1312	1342	1412	1442	1512	1542	1612	1642	1712	1742
4	Wengen ▲	d.	...	...	...	0746	0816v	0846	0916v	0946	1016v	1046	1116v	1146	1216v	1246	1316v	1346	1416	1446v	1516	1546v	1616	1646v	1716r	1746r
11	**Kleine Scheidegg** ▲	a.	...	...	...	0808	0838v	0908	0938v	1008	1038v	1108	1138v	1208	1238v	1308	1338v	1408	1438	1508v	1538	1608v	1638	1708v	1738r	1808r

Lauterbrunnen ⊙	d.	1800	1830	1900	1930	2000	2030	2100	2130	2230	2330
Wengen	a.	1812	1842	1912	1941	2011	2041	2111	2141	2241	2341
Wengen ▲	d.	1816t	...	...	...	...	...	...	...	...	...
Kleine Scheidegg ▲	a.	1838t	...	...	...	...	...	...	...	...	...

Kleine Scheidegg ▲	d.	...	...	...	...	...	...	...	0814v	0844	0914v
Wengen ▲	a.	...	...	...	...	...	...	...	0839v	0909	0939v
Wengen	d.	0504	0540	0613	0643	0713	0742	0812	0842	0912	0942
Lauterbrunnen ⊙	a.	0517	0553	0626	0656	0726	0755	0825	0855	0925	0955

Kleine Scheidegg ▲	d.	0944	1014v	1044	1114v	1144	1214v	1244	1314	1344v	1414	1444v	1514	1544v	1614	1644v	1714	1744r	1814r	1844t	...	...	...	...	...	...
Wengen ▲	a.	1009	1039v	1109	1139v	1209	1239v	1309	1339	1409v	1439	1509v	1539	1609v	1639	1709v	1739	1809r	1839r	1909t	...	...	...	...	...	...
Wengen	d.	1012	1042	1112	1142	1212	1242	1312	1342	1412	1442	1512	1542	1612	1642	1712	1742	1812	1842	1912	1943	2013	2043	2113	2213	2313
Lauterbrunnen ⊙	a.	1025	1055	1125	1155	1225	1255	1325	1355	1425	1455	1525	1555	1625	1655	1725	1755	1825	1855	1925	1956	2026	2056	2126	2226	2326

KLEINE SCHEIDEGG - JUNGFRAUJOCH. SEE NOTE ▲. See note 🚡 for *Eiger Express* gondola service Grindelwald Terminal - Eigergletscher.

km			a	a		‡	¶	‡	¶	‡	¶	‡	¶	‡	¶	‡	¶	‡	¶	n	m	m		t	t
0	**Kleine Scheidegg** ▲	d.	...	...	*0827*	0900c	0930e	1000c	1030e	1100c	1130e	1200c	1230e	1300c	1330e	1400c	1430e	1500c	1530e	1600r	1630r	1700r	...	...	...
2	Eigergletscher 🚡 ▲	a.	...	...	*0832*	0905c	0935e	1005c	1035e	1105c	1135e	1205c	1235e	1305c	1335e	1405c	1435e	1505c	1535e	1605r	1635r	1705r	...	...	...
	Eigergletscher	d.	0745	0815	0845	0915	0945	1015	1045	1115	1145	1215	1245	1315	1345	1415	1445	1515	1545	1615	1645	1715	...	1745	1815
9	**Jungfraujoch**	a.	0811	0841	0911	0941	1011	1041	1111	1141	1211	1241	1311	1341	1411	1441	1511	1541	1611	1641	1711	1741	...	1811	1841

		a	a			‡	¶	‡	¶	‡	¶	‡	¶	‡	¶	‡	¶	‡	¶	n	m	m		t	t
Jungfraujoch	d.	0817	0847	...	0917	0947	1017	1047	1117	1147	1217	1247	1317	1347	1417	1447	1517	1547	1617	1647	1717	1747	...	1817	1847
Eigergletscher	a.	0841	0911	...	0941	1011	1041	1111	1141	1211	1241	1311	1341	1411	1441	1511	1541	1611	1641	1711	1741	1811	...	1841	1911
Eigergletscher 🚡 ▲	d.	*0846*	...	...	*0946*	1016k	1046	1116k	1146	1216k	1246	1316k	1346	1416k	1446	1516k	1546	1616k	1646	1716r	1746r	1816r	...	...	...
Kleine Scheidegg ▲	a.	*0854*	...	...	*0954*	1024k	1054	1124k	1154	1224k	1254	1324k	1354	1424k	1454	1524k	1554	1624k	1654	1724r	1754r	1824r	...	...	...

a – May 6 - Oct. 22.
b – Dec. 17 - Apr. 23, July 1 - Oct. 22 and Nov. 6 – 10.
c – Dec. 17 - Apr. 23 and June 17 - Oct. 22. 3 minutes earlier Dec. 17 - Apr. 23.
e – 3 minutes earlier until Apr. 23 and from Dec. 2.
k – Dec. 17 - Apr. 23 and June 17 - Oct. 22.
m – May 18 - Oct. 22.
n – May 6 - Nov. 5.
r – June 17 - Oct. 22.
t – July 1 - Aug. 20.
u – July 1 - Oct. 22.
v – Dec. 17 - Apr. 23 and May 18 - Oct. 22.
* – Via Wengen (*28 km* via Grindelwald).
¶ – Change trains at Eigergletscher until Apr. 23 and from Dec. 2.
‡ – Change trains at Eigergletscher Dec. 17 - Apr. 23.
◇ – Additional journeys operate until Apr. 10 and from June 3.

▲ – No service Wengen - Kleine Scheidegg - Eigergletscher and v.v. Apr. 24 - May 5 and Nov. 6 - Dec. 1.
🚡 – *Eiger Express* gondola service Grindelwald Terminal - Eigergletscher and v.v. Journey time 20 minutes. Regular departures as follows: Until Apr. 23 0800 - 1650; Apr. 24 - May 17 0715 - 1720; May 18 - June 30 0715 - 1820; July 1 - Aug. 20 0715 - 1920; Aug. 21 - Oct. 22 0715 - 1820; Oct. 23 - Nov. 5 0800 - 1720. **Closed Nov. 6 – 10.**
⊙ – Cableway **Lauterbrunnen - Grütschalp**, and narrow gauge railway **Grütschalp - Mürren**. Total distance: *5 km*. Operator: BLM. Journey time: 20 minutes including connection. **Operates Dec. 11 - May 7 and June 3 - Oct. 1.**
From Lauterbrunnen at 0631, 0701, 0731, 0801, 0838, 0908, 0938 and every 30 minutes ◇ until 1938.
From Mürren at 0606, 0636, 0706, 0736, 0806, 0828, 0858, 0928, 0958 and every 30 minutes ◇ until 1858.
Cableway **Mürren - Schilthorn**. **Operates Dec. 11 - Apr. 23 and Apr. 29 - Nov. 12**. Operator: Schilthornbahn.
From Mürren at 0810, 0840 and every 30 minutes until 1610.
From Schilthorn at 0903, 0933 and every 30 minutes until 1633.
⊡ – Narrow gauge rack railway **Wilderswil - Schynige Platte**. **Operates July 1 - Oct. 22.** *7 km*. Journey time: 52 minutes. Operator: BOB. **Service may be suspended in bad weather.**
From Wilderswil at 0725, 0845, 0925, 1005, 1045, 1125, 1205, 1245, 1325, 1405, 1445, 1525, 1605 and 1645.
From Schynige Platte at 0821, 0941, 1021, 1101, 1141, 1221, 1301, 1341, 1421, 1501, 1541, 1621, 1701 and 1753.

565 BASEL and BERN - LUZERN

SBB, SOB

km		IR 2349	IC 659	IR 2457	RE 4709	IR 2505	IR 2311	IR 2459	RE 4711	IR 2507	IC 663	IR 2461	RE 4713	IR 2509	IR 2315	IR 2463	RE 4715	IR 2511	IC 667	IR 2465	RE 4717	IR 2513	IR 2319	IR 2467	RE 4719	IR 2515
		⑥⑦ t	✕	Ⓐ			★ L			🍷	✕			🍷	★ L			🍷	✕			🍷	★ L			🍷
0	**Basel** SBB 560 d.	0100	0503r	...	...	...	0603	0616	...	...	0703	0716	...	...	0803	0816	...	...	0903	0916	...	...	1003	1016	...	...
14	Liestal d.	0110	|	...	...	...	|	0627	...	...	|	0727	...	...	|	0827	...	...	|	0927	...	...	|	1027	...	...
21	Sissach d.	0116	|	...	...	...	|	0633	...	...	|	0733	...	...	|	0833	...	...	|	0933	...	...	|	1033	...	...
39	**Olten** 560 d.	0137h	0530	0549	0606	...	0630	0649	0706	...	0730	0749	0806	...	0830	0849	0906	...	0930	0949	1006	...	1030	1049	1106	...
	Genève Aéroport ✈ **505** d.	|	|	|	|	...	|	|	|	...	|	|	|	0549	|	|	|	0649	|	|	|	0749	|	|	|	0849
	Genève **505** d.	|	|	|	|	...	|	|	|	...	|	|	|	0559	|	|	|	0659	|	|	|	0759	|	|	|	0859
	Lausanne **505** d.	|	|	|	|	0444g	|	|	|	0544	|	|	|	0644	|	|	|	0744	|	|	|	0844	|	|	|	0944
	Bern d.	|	|	|	|	0600	|	|	|	0700	|	|	|	0800	|	|	|	0900	|	|	|	1000	|	|	|	1100
47	Zofingen d.	0144	|	0558	0613	0629	|	0658	0713	0729	|	0758	0813	0829	|	0858	0913	0929	|	0958	1013	1029	|	1058	1113	1129
69	Sursee d.	0158	|	0612	0631	0642	|	0712	0731	0742	|	0812	0831	0842	|	0912	0931	0942	|	1012	1031	1042	|	1112	1131	1142
95	**Luzern** a.	0216	0605	0630	0655	0701	0705	0730	0755	0801	0805	0830	0855	0901	0905	0930	0955	1001	1005	1030	1055	1101	1105	1130	1155	1201
	Lugano **550** a.	...	0758	...	...	...	...	...	...	...	0958	...	...	...	...	...	...	...	1158	...	...	...	...	...	...	...

	EC 151	IR 2469	RE 4721	IR 2517	IR 2323	IR 2471	RE 4723	IR 2519	IC 675	IR 2473	RE 4725	IR 2521	IR 2327	IR 2475	RE 4727	IR 2523	EC 153	IR 2477	RE 4729	IR 2525	IR 2331	IR 2479	RE 4731	IR 2527	IC 683	IR 2481
	F✕			🍷	★ L			🍷	✕			🍷	★ L			🍷	M✕			🍷	★ L			🍷	✕	
Basel SBB 560 d.	1103	1116	...	...	1203	1216	...	...	1303	1316	...	...	1403	1416	...	...	1503	1516	...	...	1603	1616	...	...	1703	1716
Liestal d.	|	1127	...	...	|	1227	...	...	|	1327	...	...	|	1427	...	...	|	1527	...	...	|	1627	...	...	|	1727
Sissach d.	|	1133	...	...	|	1233	...	...	|	1333	...	...	|	1433	...	...	|	1533	...	...	|	1633	...	...	|	1733
Olten 560 d.	1130	1149	1206	...	1230	1249	1306	...	1330	1349	1406	...	1430	1449	1506	...	1530	1549	1606	...	1630	1649	1706	...	1730	1749
Genève Aéroport ✈ **505** d.	|	|	|	0949	|	|	|	1049	|	|	|	1149	|	|	|	1249	|	|	|	1349	|	|	|	1449	|	|
Genève **505** d.	|	|	|	0959	|	|	|	1059	|	|	|	1159	|	|	|	1259	|	|	|	1359	|	|	|	1459	|	|
Lausanne **505** d.	|	|	|	1044	|	|	|	1144	|	|	|	1244	|	|	|	1344	|	|	|	1444	|	|	|	1544	|	|
Bern d.	|	|	|	1200	|	|	|	1300	|	|	|	1400	|	|	|	1500	|	|	|	1600	|	|	|	1700	|	|
Zofingen d.	|	1158	1213	1229	|	1258	1313	1329	|	1358	1413	1429	|	1458	1513	1529	|	1558	1613	1629	|	1658	1713	1729	|	1758
Sursee d.	|	1212	1231	1242	|	1312	1331	1342	|	1412	1431	1442	|	1512	1531	1542	|	1612	1631	1642	|	1712	1731	1742	|	1812
Luzern a.	1205	1230	1255	1301	1305	1330	1355	1401	1405	1430	1455	1501	1505	1530	1555	1601	1605	1630	1655	1701	1705	1730	1755	1801	1805	1830
Lugano **550** a.	1358	...	...	...	...	...	...	...	1558	...	...	...	...	...	...	...	1758	...	...	...	...	...	...	...	1958	...

	RE 4733	IR 2529	IR 2335	IR 2483	RE 4735	IR 2531	IC 687	IR 2485	RE 4737	IR 2533	IR 2339	IR 2487	RE 4739	IR 2535	IC 691	IR 2489	RE 4741	IR 2537	IR 2343	IR 2491	RE 4743	IR 2539	IR 2345	IR 2493	RE 4745	IR 2347
		🍷	★ B			🍷	C✕			🍷	★ E			🍷	C✕				★ A	⑤⑥ s				⑤⑥ s		★
Basel SBB 560 d.	...	...	1803	1816	...	...	1903	1916	...	...	2003	2016	...	...	2103	2116	...	...	2203z	2216	...	...	2258v	2316	...	0004
Liestal d.	...	...	|	1827	...	...	|	1927	...	...	|	2027	...	...	|	2127	...	...	|	2227	...	...	2308v	2327	...	0014
Sissach d.	...	...	|	1833	...	...	|	1933	...	...	|	2033	...	...	|	2133	...	...	|	2233	...	...	|	2333	...	|
Olten 560 d.	1806	...	1830	1849	1906	...	1930	1949	2006	...	2030	2049	2106	...	2130	2149	2206	...	2230	2249	2307	...	2330j	2348	0007	0035j
Genève Aéroport ✈ **505** d.	|	1549	|	|	|	1649	|	|	|	1749	|	|	|	1849	|	|	|	1949	|	|	|	2049k	|	...	|	|
Genève **505** d.	|	1559	|	|	|	1659	|	|	|	1759	|	|	|	1859	|	|	|	1959	|	|	|	2059k	|	...	|	|
Lausanne **505** d.	|	1644	|	|	|	1744	|	|	|	1844	|	|	|	1944	|	|	|	2044	|	|	|	2144	|	...	|	|
Bern d.	|	1800	|	|	|	1900	|	|	|	2000	|	|	|	2100	|	|	|	2200	|	|	|	2300	|	...	|	|
Zofingen d.	1813	1829	|	1858	1913	1929	|	1958	2013	2029	|	2058	2113	2129	|	2158	2213	2229	|	2256	2314	2329	|	...	0014	0042
Sursee d.	1831	1842	|	1912	1931	1942	|	2012	2031	2042	|	2112	2131	2142	|	2212	2231	2242	|	...	2332	2342	|	...	0033	0056
Luzern a.	1855	1901	1905	1930	1955	2001	2005	2030	2055	2101	2105	2130	2155	2201	2205	2230	2255	2301	2305	...	2355	0001	0005	...	0055	0116
Lugano **550** a.	...	...	...	...	...	...	2158	...	...	...	...	...	...	...	2358	...	...	...	...	...	...	...	...	...	...	...

km		IR 2344	IR 2304	RE 4706	IR 2456	IR 2306	IR 2508	RE 4708	IR 2458	IR 2308	IR 2510	RE 4710	IR 2460	IC 664	IR 2512	RE 4712	IR 2462	IR 2312	IR 2514	RE 4714	IR 2464	IC 668	IR 2516	RE 4716	IR 2466	IR 2316
		⑥⑦ t	★				🍷			★ E	🍷			C	🍷			★ B	🍷			✕	🍷			★ L
	Lugano **550** d.	...	...	...	...	...	...	...	...	...	...	...	...	0600	...	...	...	...	...	...	...	0802	...	...	...	...
0	**Luzern** d.	0047	0454	0458	0530a	0554	0600	0605	0630	0654	0700	0705	0730	0754	0800	0805	0830	0854	0900	0905	0930	0954	1000	1005	1030	1054
26	Sursee d.	0107	|	0524	0548a	|	0618	0627	0648	|	0718	0727	0748	|	0818	0827	0848	|	0918	0927	0948	|	1018	1027	1048	|
48	Zofingen d.	0120	|	0545	0603a	|	0632	0645	0703	|	0732	0745	0803	|	0832	0845	0903	|	0932	0945	1003	|	1032	1045	1103	|
111	**Bern** a.	|	|	|	|	|	0700	|	|	|	0800	|	|	|	0900	|	|	|	1000	|	|	|	1100	|	|	|
	Lausanne **505** a.	|	|	|	|	|	0816	|	|	|	0916	|	|	|	1016	|	|	|	1116	|	|	|	1216	|	|	|
	Genève **505** a.	|	|	|	|	|	0901	|	|	|	1001	|	|	|	1101	|	|	|	1201	|	|	|	1301	|	|	|
	Genève Aéroport ✈ **505** a.	|	|	|	|	|	0911	|	|	|	1011	|	|	|	1111	|	|	|	1211	|	|	|	1311	|	|	|
	Olten 560 d.	0137h	0530	0552	0612	0630	...	0652	0712	0730	...	0752	0812	0830	...	0852	0912	0930	...	0952	1012	1030	...	1052	1112	1130
	Sissach d.	|	|	...	0627	|	...	...	0727	|	...	...	0827	|	...	...	0927	|	...	...	1027	|	...	...	1127	|
	Liestal d.	0153	|	...	0634	|	...	...	0734	|	...	...	0834	|	...	...	0934	|	...	...	1034	|	...	...	1134	|
	Basel SBB 560 a.	0204	0556	...	0645	0656	...	...	0745	0756	...	...	0847	0856	...	...	0947	0956	...	...	1045	1056	...	...	1145	1156

	IR 2518	RE 4718	IR 2468	EC 156	IR 2520	RE 4720	IR 2470	IR 2320	IR 2522	RE 4722	IR 2472	EC 158	IR 2524	RE 4724	IR 2474	IR 2324	IR 2526	RE 4726	IR 2476	IC 680	IR 2528	RE 4728	IR 2478	IR 2328	IR 2530	RE 4730
	🍷			M✕	🍷			★ L	🍷			M✕	🍷			★ L	🍷			✕	🍷			★ L	🍷	
Lugano **550** d.	...	...	...	1002	...	...	...	...	...	...	...	1202	...	...	...	...	...	...	...	1402	...	...	...	...	...	...
Luzern d.	1100	1105	1130	1154	1200	1205	1230	1254	1300	1305	1330	1354	1400	1405	1430	1454	1500	1505	1530	1554	1600	1605	1630	1654	1700	1705
Sursee d.	1118	1127	1148	|	1218	1227	1248	|	1318	1327	1348	|	1418	1427	1448	|	1518	1527	1548	|	1618	1627	1648	|	1718	1727
Zofingen d.	1132	1145	1203	|	1232	1245	1303	|	1332	1345	1403	|	1432	1445	1503	|	1532	1545	1603	|	1632	1645	1703	|	1732	1745
Bern a.	1200	|	|	|	1300	|	|	|	1400	|	|	|	1500	|	|	|	1600	|	|	|	1700	|	|	|	1800	|
Lausanne **505** a.	1316	|	|	|	1416	|	|	|	1516	|	|	|	1616	|	|	|	1716	|	|	|	1816	|	|	|	1916	|
Genève **505** a.	1401	|	|	|	1501	|	|	|	1601	|	|	|	1701	|	|	|	1801	|	|	|	1901	|	|	|	2001	|
Genève Aéroport ✈ **505** a.	1411	|	|	|	1511	|	|	|	1611	|	|	|	1711	|	|	|	1811	|	|	|	1911	|	|	|	2011	|
Olten 560 d.	...	1152	1212	1230	...	1252	1312	1330	...	1352	1412	1430	...	1452	1512	1530	...	1552	1612	1630	...	1652	1712	1730	...	1752
Sissach d.	...	...	1227	|	...	...	1327	|	...	...	1427	|	...	...	1527	|	...	...	1627	|	...	...	1727	|	...	...
Liestal d.	...	...	1234	|	...	...	1334	|	...	...	1434	|	...	...	1534	|	...	...	1634	|	...	...	1734	|	...	...
Basel SBB 560 a.	...	...	1245	1256	...	...	1345	1356	...	...	1445	1456	...	...	1545	1556	...	...	1645	1656	...	...	1745	1756	...	...

	IR 2480	IC 684	IR 2532	RE 4732	IR 2482	IR 2332	IR 2534	RE 4734	IR 2484	IC 688	IR 2536	RE 4736	IR 2486	IR 2336	IR 2538	RE 4738	IR 2488	IC 692	IR 2540	RE 4740	IR 2490	IR 2340	IR 2542	RE 4742	IC 696	RE 4744
		✕	🍷			★ L				✕				★ L	¶		⑤⑥ s	✕			⑤⑥ s	★ L				
Lugano **550** d.	...	1602	...	...	...	...	...	...	...	1802	...	...	...	...	...	...	...	2002	...	...	...	...	...	...	2202	...
Luzern d.	1730	1754	1800	1805	1830	1854	1900	1905	1930	1954	2000	2005	2030	2054	2100	2105	2130	2154	2200	2205	...	2254	2300	2305	2354	0005
Sursee d.	1748	|	1818	1827	1848	|	1918	1927	1948	|	2018	2027	2048	|	2118	2127	2148	|	2218	2227	...	|	2318	2327	|	0028
Zofingen d.	1803	|	1832	1845	1903	|	1932	1945	2003	|	2032	2045	2103	|	2132	2145	2203	|	2232	2245	2303	|	2332	2345	|	0046
Bern a.	|	|	1900	|	|	|	2000	|	|	|	2100	|	|	|	2200	|	|	|	2300	|	|	|	2400	|	|	|
Lausanne **505** a.	|	|	2016	|	|	|	2116	|	|	|	2216	|	|	|	2316	|	|	|	0020	|	|	|	...	|	|	|
Genève **505** a.	|	|	2101	|	|	|	2201k	|	|	|	...	|	|	|	...	|	|	|	...	|	|	|	...	|	|	|
Genève Aéroport ✈ **505** a.	|	|	2111	|	|	|	2211k	|	|	|	...	|	|	|	...	|	|	|	...	|	|	|	...	|	|	|
Olten 560 d.	1812	1830	...	1852	1912	1930	...	1952	2012	2030	...	2052	2112	2130	...	2152	2212	2233j	...	2253	2312	2333j	...	2353	0035h	0055
Sissach d.	1827	|	...	...	1927	|	...	...	2027	|	...	...	2127	|	...	...	2227	|	...	...	2327	|	...	...	|	...
Liestal d.	1834	|	...	...	1934	|	...	...	2034	|	...	...	2134	|	...	...	2234	2249x	...	...	2334	2349	...	...	0051q	...
Basel SBB 560 a.	1845	1856	...	...	1945	1956	...	...	2045	2056	...	...	2145	2156y	...	...	2245	2300x	...	...	2345	0001	...	...	0102q	...

A – To Arth-Goldau (Table **547**).
B – To / from Bellinzona via Göschenen (Table **547**).
C – To / from Chiasso (Table **550**).
E – To / from Erstfeld (Table **547**).
F – [12] ✕ Frankfurt - Basel - Luzern - Milano ◧.
L – To / from Locarno via Göschenen (Table **547**).
M – To / from Milano ◧ (Table **550**).

a – Ⓐ only.
g – ① only.
h – Arrives 7 – 9 minutes earlier.
j – Arrives 5 – 6 minutes earlier.
k – ⑤⑥ only.
q – 2 – 3 minutes later on ①–⑤ from Jan. 31.

r – 0501 on ①–⑤ from Jan. 31.
s – Not Apr. 7.
t – Not Dec. 25, Apr. 8.
v – 2 minutes earlier on ⑦–④ from Jan. 30.
x – 4 – 5 minutes later on ⑦–④ from Jan. 30.
y – On ⑦–④ from Jan. 30 change trains at Olten and arrive *2201*.

z – On ⑦–④ from Jan. 30 depart *2156* and change trains at Olten.
¶ – Runs as *IC* **1490** on † Feb. 12 - June 4.
★ – Operated by SOB. Conveys (🍷).
◧ – Supplement payable for journeys to / from Italy.

Narrow gauge. MOB — LENK - ZWEISIMMEN - MONTREUX — 566

km		2201	2203	2205	2207	2209	2211	2213	2215	4065	2217	2219	4069	2221	2223	2225	4075	2227	2229	4079	2231	2233	2235	2237	2239	2241
													S				S			S						
							P	P	P	E🍸	P	B	E🍸	P	P	P	E🍸	P	B	E🍸						
	Interlaken Ost 563 . d.	...	...	...	...	...	...	...	...	0908	...	...	1108	...	...	...	1408	...	...	1608	...	...	...	...	...	...
	Spiez 563 d.	...	...	...	...	...	...	...	...	0938	...	...	1138	...	...	...	1438	...	...	1638	...	...	...	...	...	...
0	**Zweisimmen** ★ ‡ d.	...	...	0502a	0602	0702	0802	0902	1002	1030	1102	1202	1230	1302	1402	1502	1530	1602	1702	1730	1802	1902	2002	2102	2202	2302
9	Saanenmöser ‡ d.	...	...	0517a	0617	0717	0817	0917	1017	1044	1117	1217	1244	1317	1417	1517	1544	1617	1717	1744	1817	1917	2017	2117	2217	2317
11	Schönried ‡ d.	...	...	0522a	0622	0722	0822	0922	1022	1047	1122	1222	1247	1322	1422	1522	1547	1622	1722	1747	1822	1922	2022	2122	2222	2322
16	**Gstaad** ‡ d.	...	0436	0536	0636	0736	0836	0936	1036	1100	1136	1236	1300	1336	1436	1536	1600	1636	1736	1800	1836	1936	2036	2136	2236	2336
19	Saanen d.	...	0440	0540	0640	0740	0840	0940	1040	|	1140	1240	|	1340	1440	1540	|	1640	1740	|	1840	1940	2040	2140	2240	2340
23	Rougemont d.	...	0445	0545	0645	0745	0845	0945	1045	|	1145	1245	|	1345	1445	1545	|	1645	1745	|	1845	1945	2045	2145	2245	2345
29	Château d'Oex d.	0432	0503	0603	0659	0803	0903	1003	1103	1118	1203	1303	1318	1403	1503	1603	1618	1703	1803	1818	1903	2003	2103	2203	2303	2359
40	**Montbovon** d.	0449	0523	0623	0723	0823	0923	1023	1123	1136	1223	1323	1336	1423	1523	1623	1636	1723	1823	1836	1923	2023	2123	2223	2323	...
51	Les Avants § d.	0513	0545	0645	0745	0845	0945	1045	1145	|	1245	1345	|	1445	1545	1645	|	1745	1845	|	1945	2045	2145	2245	2345	...
55	Chamby ⊗ § d.	0519	0552	0652	0752	0852	0952	1052	1152	|	1252	1352	|	1452	1552	1652	|	1752	1852	|	1952	2052	2152	2252	2352	...
58	Chernex § d.	0528	0601	0701	0801	0901	1001	1101	1201	|	1301	1401	|	1501	1601	1701	|	1801	1901	|	2001	2100	2200	2300	0000	...
62	**Montreux** § a.	0540	0611	0711	0811	0911	1011	1111	1211	1220	1311	1411	1420	1511	1611	1711	1720	1811	1911	1920	2011	2113	2213	2313	0013	...

	2202	2204	2206	2208	4064	2210	2212	4068	2214	2216	2218	4074	2220	2222	4078	2224	2226	2326	2228	2230	2232	2234	2236	2238	2240	2242
	Ⓐ				S							S			S			Ⓐd								
					E🍸	P	P	E🍸	B	P	P	E🍸	P	P	E🍸	B	P		P	P						
Montreux § d.	...	0450	0550	0650	0735	0750	0850	0935	0950	1050	1150	1235	1250	1350	1435	1450	1550	1621	1650	1750	1850	1950	2049	2149	2249	2349
Chernex § d.	...	0500	0600	0700	|	0800	0900	|	1000	1100	1200	|	1300	1400	|	1500	1600	1632	1700	1800	1900	2000	2100	2200	2300	0000
Chamby ⊗ § d.	...	0505	0605	0705	|	0805	0905	|	1005	1105	1205	|	1305	1405	|	1505	1605	1637	1705	1805	1905	2005	2105	2205	2305	0005
Les Avants § d.	...	0511	0611	0711	|	0811	0911	|	1011	1111	1211	|	1311	1411	|	1511	1611	1656v	1711	1811	1911	2011	2111	2211	2311	0011
Montbovon d.	...	0538	0638	0738	0823	0838	0938	1023	1038	1138	1238	1323	1338	1438	1523	1538	1638	1722	1738	1838	1938	2038	2138	2238	2338	0038
Château d'Oex d.	0500	0600	0700	0800	0841	0900	1000	1041	1100	1200	1300	1341	1400	1500	1541	1600	1700	1738	1800	1900	2000	2100	2200	2300	0000	0055
Rougemont d.	0513	0614	0714	0814	|	0914	1014	|	1114	1214	1314	|	1414	1514	|	1614	1714	...	1814	1914	2014	2114	2214	2314	0014	...
Saanen d.	0519	0619	0719	0819	|	0919	1019	|	1119	1219	1319	|	1419	1519	|	1619	1719	...	1819	1919	2019	2119	2219	2319	0019	...
Gstaad ‡ d.	0523	0625	0725	0825	0902	0925	1025	1102	1125	1225	1325	1402	1425	1525	1602	1625	1725	...	1825	1925	2025	2125	2225	2325	0023	...
Schönried ‡ d.	0530	0632	0732	0832	0909	0932	1032	1109	1132	1232	1332	1409	1432	1532	1609	1632	1732	...	1832	1932	2032	2132	2232	2332	...	...
Saanenmöser ‡ d.	0536	0641	0741	0841	0916	0941	1041	1116	1141	1241	1341	1416	1441	1541	1616	1641	1741	...	1841	1941	2041	2141	2241	2341	...	...
Zweisimmen ★ ‡ a.	0550	0657	0757	0857	0929	0957	1057	1129	1157	1257	1357	1429	1457	1557	1629	1657	1757	...	1857	1957	2057	2157	2257	2357	...	...
Spiez 563 a.	...	...	...	...	1021	...	...	1221	...	...	...	1521	...	...	1721	...	...	...	...	...	...	...	...	...	...	...
Interlarken Ost 563 a.	...	...	...	...	1050	...	...	1250	...	...	...	1550	...	...	1750	...	...	...	...	...	...	...	...	...	...	...

B – GOLDEN PASS BELLE ÉPOQUE – Conveys Belle Époque carriages.
E – GOLDEN PASS EXPRESS – Conveys panorama cars. Reservation recommended. Also conveys Prestige class (🄿 and supplement payable).
P – GOLDEN PASS PANORAMIC – Conveys panorama cars.
Q – Daily to June 11; Ⓒ from June 17.
R – Daily to June 10; Ⓐ from June 12.
S – From June 11.
U – Until June 10.

a – Ⓐ only.
d – Runs daily Montreux - Les Avants.
h – Also Apr. 7, May 18, 29, Aug. 1, Sept. 18.
t – ⑤⑥ until June 10 (not Apr. 7).
v – Arrives 1645.

⊗ – Chamby is a request stop.
‡ – Additional local trains Zweisimmen - Gstaad and v.v.:
From Zweisimmen at 0630 Ⓐ, 0730 Ⓐ, 0830 **R**, 1130 Ⓒ **S**, 1230 **U**, 1430 **Q**, 1530 Ⓒ **U**, 1630, 1730 **U** and 1830 **R**.
From Gstaad at 0503 Ⓐ, 0603 Ⓐ **S**, 0703 Ⓐ, 0803 Ⓐ, 0903 **U**, 1203 Ⓒ **S**, 1303 **U**, 1503, 1603 Ⓒ **U**, 1703 and 1903 ⑤⑥ **t**.
§ – Additional local trains Les Avants - Montreux and v.v.:
From Les Avants at 0617, 0717 and hourly until 2017.
From Montreux at 0049 ⑥⑦ **h**, 0621, 0721 and hourly until 2021.
★ – Local trains Lenk - Zweisimmen and v.v. (*13 km*, journey time 18 minutes):
From Lenk at 0533 Ⓐ, 0637, 0737, 0837, 0937, 1005 Ⓒ, 1037, 1137, 1237, 1337, 1437, 1537, 1637, 1737, 1837, 1905 Ⓐ, 1937, 2037, 2137, 2237 and 2337 ⑤⑥.
From Zweisimmen at 0505 Ⓐ, 0605. 0705, 0805, 0905, 1005, 1037 Ⓒ, 1105, 1205, 1305, 1405, 1505, 1605, 1705, 1805, 1837 Ⓐ, 1905, 2005, 2105, 2205, 2305 ⑤⑥.

TPF — MONTBOVON - BULLE - PALÉZIEUX and ROMONT — 568

MONTBOVON - BULLE - PALÉZIEUX *Narrow gauge*

km																							
		⚒	Ⓐ		Ⓐ	Ⓐ	⚒	Ⓐ		Ⓐ			Ⓐ		Ⓐ	⑤⑥		Ⓐ					
0	**Montbovon** d.	...	...	...	0537	...	0645	...	0717	...	0837		...	2137	...	2237	2237	...	2337	...	...	...	...
13	Gruyères d.	...	...	...	0558	0632	0706	0732	0737	0832	0858	and at the	2132	2158	2232	2258	2258	2332	2358	...	...	...	...
17	**Bulle** a.	...	...	...	0607	0638	0715	0738	0747	0838	0907	same minutes	2138	2207	2238	2307	2307	2338	0007	...	...	...	...
17	**Bulle** d.	0519	0546	0616	0616	0646	0716	0746	0816	0846	0916	past each	2146	2216	2246	2316	...	...	...	...	...	...	...
37	Châtel-St Denis a.	0542	0611	0641	0641	0711	0741	0811	0841	0911	0941	hour until	2211	2241	2311	2341	...	...	...	...	...	...	...
37	Châtel-St Denis d.	0543	0615	0645	0645	0715	0745	0815	0845	0915	0945		2215	2245	2315	2345	...	...	...	...	...	...	...
41	**Palézieux** a.	0556	0625	0655	0655	0725	0755	0825	0855	0925	0955		2225	2255	2325	2355	...	...	...	...	...	...	...

	⑥⑦		Ⓐ	⚒	Ⓐ		⚒	Ⓐ		Ⓐ			Ⓐ		Ⓐ							
Palézieux d.	0010	...	...	...	...	...	0604	0634	0704	0734		2204	2234	2304	2334	...	...	...	...	...	...	...
Châtel-St Denis a.	0020	...	...	...	...	...	0614	0644	0714	0744	and at the	2214	2244	2314	2344	...	...	...	...	...	...	...
Châtel-St Denis d.	0020	...	...	...	...	...	0618	0648	0718	0748	same minutes	2218	2248	2318	2348	...	...	...	...	...	...	...
Bulle a.	0046	...	...	...	...	...	0644	0714	0744	0814	past each	2244	2314	2344	0014	...	...	...	...	...	...	...
Bulle d.	...	...	0450	0550	0620	0645	0645	0720	0750	0820	hour until	2250	2320	...	...	...	...	...	...	...	...	...
Gruyères d.	...	...	0458	0558	0627	0652	0652	0727	0758	0827		2258	2327	...	...	...	...	...	...	...	...	...
Montbovon a.	...	...	0519	0619	...	0713	0713	...	0819	...		2319	...	...	...	...	...	...	...	...	...	...

BROC - BULLE - ROMONT - FRIBOURG - BERN

km																							
0	**Broc** Fabrique d.	...	...	0603	0633		1803	1833	1903	1933	2003	2033	2103	2133	2203	2233	2303	2333	...	...	...	...	...
1	Broc Village d.	...	...	0605	0635	and at the	1805	1835	1905	1935	2005	2035	2105	2135	2205	2235	2305	2335	...	...	...	...	...
5	**Bulle** a.	...	...	0613	0643	same minutes	1813	1843	1913	1943	2013	2043	2113	2143	2213	2243	2313	2343	...	...	...	...	...
5	**Bulle** d.	0520	0550	0620	0650	past each	1820	1850	1920	1950	2020	2050	2120	2150	2220	2250	2320	2350	...	...	...	...	...
23	Romont 505 a.	0537	0607	0637	0707	hour until	1837	1907	1937	2007	2037	2107	2137	2207	2237	2307	2337	0007	...	...	...	...	...
49	Fribourg 505 a.	0555	0625	0655	0725		1855	1925	1955	2025	2055	2125	2155	2225	2255	2325	2355	0025	...	...	...	...	...
80	**Bern** 505 a.	...	0651	...	0751		...	1951	...	...	...	...	...	...	...	...	...	...	...	...	...	...	...

			Ⓐ																		
Bern 505 d.	...	...	...	...	...	...	0709		...	2009	...	...	...	...	...	...	...	...	...	...	...
Fribourg 505 d.	...	...	0534	0604	0634	0704	0734	and at the	2004	2034	2104	2134	2204	2234	2304	2334	...	...	...	...	...
Romont 505 d.	...	...	0553	0623	0653	0723	0753	same minutes	2023	2053	2123	2153	2223	2253	2323	2353	0036	...	...	...	...
Bulle a.	...	...	0611	0641	0711	0741	0811	past each	2041	2111	2141	2211	2241	2311	2341	0011	0053	...	...	...	...
Bulle d.	0547	0617	0617	0647	0717	0747	0817	hour until	2047	2117	2147	2217	2247	2317	...	...	...	...	...	...	...
Broc Village d.	0555	0625	0625	0655	0725	0755	0825		2055	2125	2155	2225	2255	2325	...	...	...	...	...	...	...
Broc Fabrique a.	0557	0627	0627	0657	0727	0757	0827		2057	2127	2157	2227	2257	2327	...	...	...	...	...	...	...

Narrow gauge rack railway. 2nd class only. MVR — MONTREUX - CAUX - ROCHERS DE NAYE — 569

Services do not run Haut-de-Caux - Rochers de Naye and v.v. on ①② Jan. 9 - Feb. 7 and ①② Feb. 20 - Mar. 28.

km													
0	**Montreux** d.	0544	0644	0744	0819		1519	1619	1719	1819	1919		2319
3	Glion ▲ d.	0554	0654	0754	0829	and	1529	1629	1729	1829	1929	and	2329
5	Caux a.	0604	0704	0804	0841	hourly	1541	1641	1741	1841	1939	hourly	2339
6	Haut-de-Caux a.	0608	0808	0808	0846	until	1546	1646	1746	1846	1944	until	2344
10	**Rochers de Naye** a.	...	...	...	0907		1607	1707b	1807b	...	...		...

Rochers de Naye d.	...	...	...	0912		1612	1712b	1812b	...	...		...
Haut-de-Caux d.	0609	0709	0809	0934	and	1634	1734	1834	...	1945	and	2345
Caux d.	0613	0713	0813	0942	hourly	1642	1742	1842	...	1949	hourly	2349
Glion ▲ d.	0625	0725	0831	0953	until	1653	1753	1853	...	2001	until	0001
Montreux a.	0638	0738	0843	1008		1708	1808	1908	...	2013		0013

b – May 18 - Oct. 29.

▲ – Funicular railway operates **Glion** - **Territet** and v.v. Journey: 6 minutes. **Operator**: MVR ✆ 021 989 81 90. No service Apr. 18 – 20, Oct. 16 – 21. Simultaneous departures from both **Glion** and **Territet** at 0516, 0531, 0546, 0601 and every 15 minutes until 2116; then 2146 and every 30 minutes until 0046.
Note: Local stopping trains run hourly from Territet to Montreux, Vevey, Lausanne and Aigle.

570 GENÈVE - LAUSANNE - SION - BRIG SBB

km		IR 1705	IR 1805		RE 18455	EC 35	IR 1707	IR 1807	RE 18457	IR 1709	IR 1809	RE 18459	EC 37	IR 1711	IR 1811	RE 18461	IR 1713		IR 1829	RE 18479	IR 1731	IR 1831	RE 18481	EC 41
		①–⑤				◧ V ✕							◧ ¶ ✕					❖						◧ ✕
0	**Genève** Aéroport ✈ 505 d.	...	...	...	0511	...	0519	...	0611	0619	0701	0711c	...	0719	0801	0811c	0819		1701	1711c	1719	1801	1811c	...
6	**Genève** 505 d.	...	0447	...	0520	0539	0529	0609	0620	0629	0710	0720	0739	0729	0810	0820	0829		1710	1720	1729	1810	1820	1839
27	Nyon 505 d.	...	0502	...	0536	|	0544	|	0636	0644	|	0736	|	0744	|	0836	0844		|	1736	1744	|	1836	|
53	Morges 505 d.	...	0521	...	0555	|	0600	|	0655	0700	|	0755	|	0800	|	0855	0900		|	1756	1800	|	1855	|
66	**Lausanne** 505 a.	...	0535	...	0608	0615	0611	0647	0708	0711	0747	0808	0815	0811	0847	0908	0911	and at	1747	1808	1811	1847	1908	1915
66	**Lausanne** ▷ d.	0452	0547	0600	0611	0618	0621	0650	0711	0721	0750	0811	0818	0821	0850	0911	0921		1750	1811	1821	1850	1911	1918
84	Vevey ▷ d.	0510	0602	0617	0626	|	0636	0705	0726	0736	0805	0826	|	0836	0905	0926	0936	the same	1805	1826	1836	1905	1926	|
91	**Montreux** ▷ d.	0518	0609	0625	0632	0637	0643	0711	0732	0743	0811	0832	0837	0843	0911	0932	0943		1811	1832	1843	1911	1932	1937
95	Villeneuve ▷ d.	0524	|	0630	|	|	|	|	0736	|	|	|	|	|	|	0936	|	minutes	|	1836	|	|	|	|
105	Aigle ▷ d.	0533	0620	0637	0642	|	0653	0722	0743	0753	0822	0842	|	0853	0922	0943	0953		1822	1843	1853	1922	1942	|
114	Bex d.	0540	|	...	0648	|	|	|	0749	|	|	0848	|	|	|	0949	|	past each	|	1849	|	|	1948	|
118	St Maurice d.	0558	0629	...	0653	|	|	0732	0753	|	0832	0853	|	|	0932	0953	|		1832	1853	|	1932	1953	|
133	Martigny d.	0609	0640	...	...	|	0711	0743	...	0811	0843	...	|	0911	0943	...	1011	hour until	1843	...	1911	1943	...	|
158	**Sion** d.	0623	0655	...	...	0713	0725	0757	...	0825	0857	...	0913	0925	0957	...	1025		1857	...	1925	1957	...	2013
174	Sierre / Siders d.	0634	0705	...	...	|	0735	0807	...	0835	0908	...	|	0935	1008	...	1035		1908	...	1935	2008	...	|
184	Leuk d.	0641	0713	...	...	|	0742	|	...	0842	|	...	|	0942	|	...	1042		|	...	1942	|	...	|
203	Visp 560 d.	0655	0725	...	...	|	0755	0825	...	0855	0925	...	|	0955	1025	...	1055		1925	...	1955	2025	...	|
212	**Brig** 560 a.	0702	0732	...	...	0740	0802	0832	...	0902	0932	...	0940	1002	1032	...	1102		1932	...	2002	2032	...	2040
	Milano Centrale 590 a.	...	...	...	...	0940	...	...	...	...	...	...	1140	...	...	...	...		...	...	...	...	...	2240

	IR 1733	IR 1833	RE 18483	IR 1735	IR 1835	RE 18485	IR 1737	IR 1737	IR 1837	IR 1837	RE 18487	RE 18487	IR 1739	RE 3579	IR 1739	RE 3579	IR 1839	IR 1839	IR 1741	RE 3591	IR 1841	IR 1743		EC 39	IR 1929
			A		⊙	⑤⑥ m	⑤⑥	⑦–④	⑦–④ ⊙	⑤⑥	⑤⑥		⑤⑥	⑤⑥	⑦–④	⑦	⑤⑥	⑦–④	⑤⑥	⑤⑥	⑦–④			◧ ✕	Ⓐ n
Genève Aéroport ✈ 505 d.	1816t	1901	1911c	1919	2001	2011e	2019	2019	...	2058	2111e	2111c	2119	...	...	...	2201	2149	2219	...	2249	*2310*		...	...
Genève 505 d.	1826t	1910	1920	1929	2010	2020	2029	2029	2104	2108	2120	2120	2129	...	...	...	2210	2159	2229	*2250*	2259	*2320*		1339	1704
Nyon 505 d.	1841t	|	1936	1944	|	2036	2044	2044	2119	|	2136	2136	2144	...	...	...	|	2213	2243	*2306*	2313	*2336*		|	|
Morges 505 d.	1900	|	1955	2000	|	2056	2100	2100	2135	|	2156	2156	2200	...	...	...	|	2230	2300	*2325*	2330	*2356*		|	1738
Lausanne 505 a.	1911	1947	2008	2011	2047	2108	2111	2111	2147	2147	2208	2208	2211	...	...	...	2247	2241	2312	*2338*	2341	*0010*	A	1415	1751
Lausanne ▷ d.	1921	1950	2011	2021	2050	2111	2121	2121	2150	2150	2211	...	2221	...	2221	...	2250	2256	2321	2350	2356	0025		1418	1756
Vevey ▷ d.	1936	2005	2026	2036	2105	2126	2136	2140	2204	2205	2226	...	2236	...	2241	...	2305	2312	2336	0005	0011	0040	L	|	1811
Montreux ▷ d.	1943	2011	2032	2043	2111	2132	2143	2147	2211	2211	2232	...	2243	...	2247	...	2311	2318	2343	0011	0017	0046		1437	1818
Villeneuve ▷ d.	|	|	2036	|	|	2136	|	|	|	|	2236	...	|	...	|	...	|	|	|	|	|	|	S	|	1823
Aigle ▷ d.	1953	2022	2043	2053	2122	2143	2153	2157	2222	2222	2243	...	2253	...	2257	...	2322	2329	2353	0021	0028	0056		|	1832
Bex d.	|	|	2049	|	|	2149	|	|	|	|	2249	...	|	...	|	...	|	|	0000	0027	0034	0103	O	|	1839
St Maurice d.	|	2032	2053	|	2132	2153	|	|	2232	2232	2253	...	|	...	|	...	2332	2338	0006	0031	0039	0107		|	1844
Martigny d.	2011	2043	2104y	2111	2143	...	2211	2214	2243	2243	...	...	2311	...	2314	...	2343	2348	0016	...	0050	0118		|	1858
Sion d.	2025	2057	2116y	2125	2157	...	2225	2228	2259	2257	...	...	2324	2329	2328	2332	2357	0002	0031	...	0103	0132		1513	1916
Sierre / Siders d.	2035	2108	...	2135	2208	...	2235	2238	2310	2308	...	...	...	2339	2338z	2342	0008	0013	0041	...	0114	...		|	...
Leuk d.	2042	|	...	2142	|	...	2242	2245	|	|	...	...	...	2346	2345z	2349	|	0020	0048	...	0121	...		|	...
Visp 560 d.	2055	2125	...	2155	2225	...	2255	2257	2327	2325	...	...	...	2357	2357z	2400	0025	0031	0100	...	0133	...		|	...
Brig 560 a.	2102	2132	...	2202	2232	...	2302	2304	2338	2332	...	...	...	0004	0004z	0007	0032	0040	0108	...	0141	...		1540	...
Milano Centrale 590 a.	...	...	...	...	...	...	...	...	...	...	...	...	...	...	...	...	...	...	...	...	...	...		1740	...

	RE 3590		IR 1702	IR 1804	IR 1704	RE 18454	IR 1904	IR 1806	IR 1706	RE 18456	RE 18456	IR 1808	IR 1708	RE 18458	IR 1810	IR 1710	RE 18460		IR 1830	IR 1730	RE 18480	IR 1832	IR 1732	EC 36
	⑥⑦						Ⓐ n			Ⓒ	Ⓐ						△	⊠						◧ ‡ ✕
Milano Centrale 590 d.	...	...	...	...	...	...	...	...	...	...	...	...	...	...	...	...	...		...	...	...	...	...	1720
Brig 560 d.	...	...	...	0420	*0438*	...	...	0524	0557	...	...	0624	0657	...	0726	0757	...		1726	1757	...	1826	1857	1916
Visp 560 d.	...	...	...	0429	*0444*	...	...	0532	0606	...	...	0632	0706	...	0735	0806	...		1735	1806	...	1835	1906	|
Leuk d.	...	...	...	0439	*0500*	...	...	0542	0616	...	...	0642	0716	...	|	0816	...		|	1816	...	|	1916	|
Sierre / Siders d.	...	...	...	0447	*0507*	...	...	0550	0624	...	...	0650	0724	...	0750	0824	...	and at	1750	1824	...	1850	1924	|
Sion d.	...	...	0424	0458	0529	...	0550	0601	0634	...	0637	0701	0734	...	0801	0834	...		1801	1834	...	1901	1934	1947
Martigny d.	...	...	0438	0513	0543	...	0605	0616	0648	...	0652	0716	0748	...	0816	0848	...	the same	1816	1848	...	1916	1948	|
St Maurice d.	0039	...	0449	0524	0554	0604	0616	0627	|	0704	0704	0727	|	0804	0827	|	0904		1827	|	1904	1927	|	|
Bex d.	0043	...	0454	0529	0559	0608	0621	|	|	0708	0708	|	|	0808	|	|	0908	minutes	|	|	1908	|	|	|
Aigle ▷ d.	0049	...	0502	0538	0606	0615	0629	0638	0706	0715	0715	0738	0806	0815	0837	0906	0915		1837	1906	1915	1937	2006	|
Villeneuve ▷ d.	0056	...	|	|	|	0622	|	|	|	0722	0722	|	|	0822	|	|	0922	past each	|	|	1922	|	|	|
Montreux ▷ d.	0101	...	0513	0548	0617	0627	0641	0648	0717	0727	0727	0748	0817	0827	0848	0917	0927		1848	1917	1927	1948	2017	2022
Vevey ▷ d.	0108	...	0521	0555	0624	0632	0649	0655	0724	0732	0732	0755	0824	0832	0855	0924	0932	hour until	1855	1924	1932	1955	2024	|
Lausanne ▷ a.	0123	...	0537	0610	0639	0648	0704	0710	0739	0748	0748	0810	0839	0848	0910	0939	0948		1910	1939	1948	2010	2039	2042
Lausanne 505 d.	*0135*	...	0548	0613	0648	0651	0708	0713	0748	0751	0751	0813	0848	0851	0913	0948	0951		1913	1948	1951	2013	2048	2045
Morges 505 d.	*0148*	...	0559	|	0659	0705	0724	|	0759	0805	0805	|	0859	0905	|	0959	1005		|	1959	2005	|	2059	|
Nyon 505 d.	*0208*	...	0616	|	0716	0725	|	|	0816	0825	0825	|	0916	0925	|	1016	1025		|	2016	2025	|	2116	|
Genève 505 a.	*0224*	...	0634	0652	0734	0740	0756	0752	0834	0840	0840	0852	0934	0940	0952	1034	1040		1952	2034	2040	2052	2131	2121
Genève Aéroport ✈ 505 a.	...	...	0641	0659	0741	0749c	...	0759	0841	0849	...	0859	0941	0949c	0959	1041	1049c		1959	2041	2049c	2059	2141k	...

	RE 18482	IR 1834	IR 1834	IR 1734	IR 1734	RE 18484	RE 18484	IR 1836	IR 1836	IR 1736	IR 1736	EC 42	RE 18486	RE 18486	RE 3592	IR 1838	EC 44	RE 18488	RE 18488	IR 1840	IR 1840	RE 18442		EC 32	EC 34
		⑤⑥	⑦–④	⑤⑥		⑤⑥	⑦–④	⑤⑥	⑦–④	⑤⑥		⑤⑥ ◧ V	⑤⑥	⑦–④	⑦–④	⑤⑥	⑦–④ ◧ V	⑤⑥	⑦–④	⑤⑥	⑦–④	①–⑤		◧ ✕	◧ ✕
Milano Centrale 590 d.	...	...	...	...	...	...	...	...	...	...	...	1920	...	...	...	...	1920	...	...	...	...	...		0820	1320
Brig 560 d.	...	1926	1926	1957	1957	...	...	2026	2026	2057	2057	2116	...	...	...	2126	2126	...	...	2226	2226	...		1016	1516
Visp 560 d.	...	1935	1935	2006	2006	...	...	2035	2035	2106	2106	|	...	...	...	2135	2134	...	...	2235	2235	...		|	|
Leuk d.	...	|	|	2016	2016	...	...	|	|	2116	2116	|	...	...	...	|	|	...	...	|	|	...		|	|
Sierre / Siders d.	...	1950	1950	2024	2024	...	...	2050	2050	2124	2124	|	...	...	...	2150	2149	...	...	2250	2250	...	A	|	|
Sion d.	...	2001	2001	2034	2034	...	...	2101	2101	2134	2134	2147	...	...	...	2201	2201	...	...	2301	2301	...		1047	1547
Martigny d.	...	2016	2016	2048	2048	...	...	2116	2116	2148	2148	|	...	...	...	2216	2215	...	...	2316	2316	...	L	|	|
St Maurice d.	2001	2027	2027	|	|	2104	...	2127	2127	|	|	|	2201	...	2211	2227	2226	2304	...	2327	2327	...		|	|
Bex d.	2011	|	|	|	|	2108	...	|	|	|	|	|	2211	...	2215	|	|	2308	...	|	|	...	S	|	|
Aigle ▷ d.	2018	2037	2036	2106	2106	2115	...	2137	2136	2206	2206	|	2218	...	2223	2237	2236	2315	...	2336	2336	...		|	|
Villeneuve ▷ d.	|	|	|	|	|	2122	...	|	|	|	|	|	|	...	2229	|	|	2322	...	|	|	...	O	|	|
Montreux ▷ d.	2028	2048	2047	2116	2116	2127	...	2148	2147	2216	2216	2222	2228	...	2233	2248	2247	2327	...	2347	2347	...		1122	1622
Vevey ▷ d.	2033	2055	2053	2123	2123	2133	...	2155	2153	2223	2223	|	2233	...	2242	2255	2253	2332	...	2353	2353	...		|	|
Lausanne ▷ a.	2048	2110	2110	2139	2139	2149	...	2210	2210	2239	2239	2242	2248	...	2300	2310	2310	2348	...	0010	0010	...		1142	1642
Lausanne 505 d.	2051	2113	2113	2148	...	2151	2151	2213	2213	2248	...	2245	2251	2251	...	2313	2313	2351	2351	0013	...	0025		1145	1645
Morges 505 d.	2105	|	2125	2159	...	2205	2205	|	2224r	2259	...	|	2305	2305	...	|	2324r	0005	0005	0025	...	0039		|	|
Nyon 505 d.	2125	|	2141	2216	...	2225	2229	|	2240r	2316	...	|	2325	2329	...	|	2339r	0025	0029	0041	...	0101		|	|
Genève 505 a.	2142	2154	2157	2234	...	2242	2251	2253	2257r	2334	...	2321	2342	2351	...	2352	2358r	0042	0045	0059	...	0117		1221	1721
Genève Aéroport ✈ 505 a.	2149h	2200	2204	2241	...	2249	2257	2259	2304r	2341	...	...	2349	2357	...	2359	0003r	0049	...	0105	...	...		...	...

A – ⑤⑥† (daily Jan. 6 - Apr. 30, May 2–7, 9–29).
V – [12] and ✕ Genève - Milano - Venezia and v.v.

c – Ⓒ only.
e – ⑥ only.
h – ⑥⑦ only.
k – ⑤⑥ only.
m – Not Apr. 7.
n – Not Dec. 27 - Jan. 16, May 19.
r – 5–12 minutes later from July 9.
t – 2–3 minutes later on Ⓒ.
y – St Maurice - Sion on ①–④ Jan. 9 - May 25 (not Apr. 10, May 1, 8, 18).
z – Not ⑦.

⊙ – Runs up to 6 minutes later Vevey - Brig on ⑦–④ Mar. 12 - Sept. 7.
❖ – Train numbers increase by 2 each hour. See later columns for additional trains within the hourly pattern. The 1320 from Genève (1311 Ⓒ from Genève Aéroport) does not call at Villeneuve.
⊠ – Train numbers increase by 2 each hour. See later columns for additional trains within the hourly pattern. Timing variations for St Maurice to Genève services: St Maurice d. 1101 / 1601 (not 1104 / 1604) then retimed at Bex (d. 1111 / 1611), Aigle (d. 1118 / 1618), not calling at Villeneuve.
△ – Timings may vary by 1–2 minutes on certain dates.
▷ – Hourly stopping trains also run Lausanne - Aigle and v.v.
◧ – Supplement payable for journeys from / to Italy.
‡ – Train number **46** on Ⓒ.
¶ – Train number **47** on Ⓒ.

Local services from VEVEY, AIGLE and BEX — 571

2nd class only

VEVEY - BLONAY - LES PLÉIADES: Narrow gauge (rack Blonay - Les Pléiades). **Operator**: MVR. Additional services run Vevey - Blonay and v.v. on Ⓐ. On Sept. 18 services run as on Ⓒ.

km																							
					Ⓐ		Ⓒ			✥												⑤⑥	⑦–④
0	Vevey d.	0556	0641	0711	0726	0741	0741	0811	0841	and at the same	1811	1841	1911	1941	2011	2041	2111	2141	2211	2245	...	2341	2355
6	Blonay a.	0612	0657	0727	0742	0757	0757	0827	0857	minutes past	1827	1857	1927	1957	2027	2057	2127	2157	2227	2301	...	2357	0011
10	Les Pléiades a.	...	...	...	0759	...	0819	...	0919	each hour until	...	1919	...	...	...	...	...	...	...	...	...	...	...

					Ⓐ		Ⓐ		Ⓐ			Ⓒ									
Les Pléiades d.	...	...	...	...	0637	...	0719	...	0802	...	...	0835	...	0935	and at the same	...	1935	...	...	...	...	...
Blonay d.	0531	0601	0631	0701	0701	0731	0746	0801	0826	0831	0901	0901	0931	1001	minutes past	1931	2001	2031	2116	2131	2216	2320
Vevey a.	0546	0616	0646	0716	0716	0746	0801	0816	...	0846	0916	0915	0946	1016	each hour until	1946	2016	2046	2131	2146	2231	2335

AIGLE - LEYSIN: Narrow gauge rack railway. *6 km*. Journey time: 29–39 minutes. The Leysin terminus station is Grand Hotel, but all trains also call at Feydey station. **Operator**: TPC.

From Aigle at 0545, 0656 Ⓒ, 0756 Ⓒ, 0805 Ⓐ, 0856, 0956 and hourly until 2156. Also **Aigle - Leysin Feydey** at 0622 Ⓐ, 0713 Ⓐ, 0832 Ⓒ, 1532 Ⓒ, 1732 Ⓐ, 1832 Ⓐ and 2303.

From Leysin Grand Hotel at 0521, 0619 Ⓐ, 0653 Ⓒ, 0753 Ⓒ, 0853, 0953 and hourly until 1653; then 1727 Ⓐ, 1753 Ⓒ, 1853, 1953, 2053, 2153 and 2238. Also **Leysin Feydey - Aigle** at 0654 Ⓐ, 0746 Ⓐ, 0932 Ⓒ, 1632 Ⓒ, 1759 Ⓐ, 1916 Ⓐ and 2334.

AIGLE - LES DIABLERETS: Narrow gauge. *23 km*. Journey time: 50–54 minutes. **Operator**: TPC.

From Aigle at 0525, 0625, 0725, 0829, 0929 and hourly until 2229.

From Les Diablerets at 0607, 0707, 0734, 0834 and hourly until 2234.

AIGLE - CHAMPÉRY: Narrow gauge rack railway. 2nd class only. **Operator**: TPC. Additional trains operate Aigle - Monthey and v.v. on ⚒.

km																										
		A			⚒																	⑤⑥t		⑤⑥t		⑤⑥t
0	**Aigle** d.	0022	...	...	0507	0619	0732	0829	0932	1028	1132	1228	1332	1428	1532	1628	1728	1828	1928	2033	2130	2233	2233	2303	2303	2358
11	Monthey Ville a.	0041	...	...	0526	0639	0752	0849	0952	1049	1152	1249	1352	1449	1552	1649	1749	1849	1949	2052	2149	2252	2252	2322	2322	0017
11	Monthey Ville d.	...	...	0512	0528	0641	0800	0851	1000	1100	1200	1251	1400	1451	1600	1700	1800	1900	1951	2100	2151	2259	...	2324	...	...
23	**Champéry** a.	...	...	0545	0601	0717	0834	0924	1034	1134	1234	1324	1434	1524	1634	1734	1834	1934	2024	2134	2224	2332	...	2357	...	...

	⚒		Ⓐ		⚒	Ⓐ		⚒																⑤⑥t
Champéry d.	...	...	0524	0602	...	0627	...	0656	0756	0903	0956	1056	1156	1303	1356	1503	1556	1656	1756	1856	2003	2056	2203	2226	2337
Monthey Ville a.	...	...	0558	0635	...	0701	...	0730	0830	0937	1030	1130	1230	1337	1430	1537	1630	1730	1830	1930	2037	2130	2237	2259	0010
Monthey Ville d.	0435	0540	0603	0640	0705	0705	0739	0739	0837	0940	1037	1140	1237	1340	1437	1540	1637	1737	1837	1937	2040	2137	2240	2302	...
Aigle a.	0455	0600	0624	0701	0729	0729	0800	0800	0857	1000	1057	1200	1257	1400	1457	1600	1657	1757	1857	1957	2100	2157	2300	2322	...

BEX - VILLARS-SUR-OLLON - COL-DE-BRETAYE: Narrow gauge rack railway. 2nd class only. **Operator**: TPC. Additional trains operate Villars - Col-de-Bretaye and v.v. (see note ⊡).

km																										
			C													C		D				D				
0	**Bex** d.	0623	0715	0715	0802	0902	1002	1102	1202	1311	...	1402	1502	1602	1702	...	1802	...	1902	2002	2102	...	...	...	...	...
3	Bévieux ⊗ d.	0633	0725	0725	0812	0912	1012	1112	1212	1321	...	1412	1512	1612	1712	...	1812	...	1912	2012	2112	...	...	...	...	...
12	Villars-sur-Ollon a.	0701	0753	0753	0840	0940	1040	1140	1240	1349	...	1440	1540	1640	1740	...	1840	...	1940	2040	2140	...	...	...	...	...
12	Villars-sur-Ollon d.	...	0805	...	0850	0950	*1050*	*1150*	*1250*	...	1420	*1450*	*1550*	*1650*	...	1750	...	1914	...	...	...	2204	...	...	...	...
17	**Col-de-Bretaye** a.	...	0823	...	0908	1008	*1108*	*1208*	*1308*	...	1438	*1508*	*1608*	*1708*	...	1808	...	1932	...	...	...	2222	...	...	...	...

					C												C		D			D		
Col-de-Bretaye d.	...	...	...	...	0830	...	*0945*	*1045*	*1145*	1215	...	*1345*	*1445*	1545	1645	1745	1815	...	1935	...	...	2225	...	...	...
Villars-sur-Ollon a.	...	...	...	...	0850	...	*1005*	*1105*	*1205*	1235	...	*1405*	*1505*	1605	1705	1805	1835	...	1955	...	...	2245	...	...	...
Villars-sur-Ollon d.	0510	0616	0708	0813	...	0913	1013	1113	1213	...	1304	1413	1513	1613	1713	1813	...	1913	...	2013	2113	...	...	...	...
Bévieux ⊗ d.	0543	0649	0741	0846	...	0946	1046	1146	1246	...	1337	1446	1546	1646	1746	1846	...	1946	...	2046	2146	...	...	...	...
Bex a.	0554	0700	0752	0857	...	0957	1057	1157	1257	...	1348	1457	1557	1657	1757	1857	...	1957	...	2057	2157	...	...	...	...

A – ①–⑤ (also Apr. 8).
C – Daily Dec. 18 - Apr. 10 and July 1 - Sept. 3; ⑥⑦ Sept. 9–24.
D – ⑤⑥ Dec. 23 - Apr. 8; ⑤⑥ July - Sept. 2; ⑥ Sept. 9–23.

t – Not Apr. 7.

⊗ – Trains call at Bévieux on request.

✥ – Certain Les Pléiades arrivals are up to 7 minutes later on Ⓐ.
⊡ – Additional trains operate Villars - Col-de-Bretaye and v.v. Dec. 17 - Apr. 10 and July 1 - Sept. 3.

MARTIGNY - VALLORCINE — 572

TMR (2nd class only). Narrow gauge rack railway

For services Vallorcine - Chamonix - St Gervais and v.v. see Table **365a**.

km					❦					
0	**Martigny** d.	0518	0618	0718		1918	2018	2118	2218	...
7	Salvan d.	0533	0633	0733	and	1935	2035	2133	2233	...
9	Les Marécottes d.	0538	0638	0738	hourly	1938	2038	2138	2238	...
14	Finhaut d.	0550	0650	0750	until	1950	2050	2150	2250	...
18	Le Châtelard Frontière 🏛 d.	0600	0700	0800		2000	2100	2200	2300	...
21	**Vallorcine** a.	...	...	0805		2005	...	...	...	...

	Ⓐ		Ⓐ						
Vallorcine d.	...	...	...	...	0810		2110	...	...
Le Châtelard Frontière 🏛 d.	0516	0616	0640	0716	0816	and	2116	2216	2316
Finhaut d.	0526	0626	0650	0726	0826	hourly	2126	2226	2326
Les Marécottes d.	0539	0639	0702	0739	0839	until	2139	2239	2339
Salvan d.	0543	0643	0706	0743	0843		2143	2243	2343
Martigny a.	0559	0659	0729	0759	0859		2159	2259	2359

❦ – The 1418 from Martigny terminates at Le Châtelard Frontière.

SION VALLEY RESORTS — 573

🚌 **LE CHÂBLE - VERBIER**. Journey time: ± 25 minutes. **Operator**: PA.

From Le Châble Gare at 0648 Ⓐ **h**, 0748, 0948, 1045 Ⓒ, 1145 Ⓐ **h**, 1321 Ⓒ, 1448, 1721 Ⓐ **h**, 1821 Ⓒ, 1848 Ⓐ **h** and 1948.

From Verbier Post at 0607 Ⓐ **h**, 0717 Ⓐ **h**, 0817, 1017, 1117 Ⓒ, 1217 Ⓐ **h**, 1417 Ⓒ, 1517, 1650, 1750 Ⓐ **h**, 1850 Ⓒ, 1917 Ⓐ **h** and 2017.

🚌 **MARTIGNY - AOSTA** via Grand St Bernard tunnel. Journey time: ± 1 hour 50 minutes. **Operator**: TMR / SAVDA.

From Martigny Gare at 0830 ②⑤ (not Apr. 7, Aug. 1) and 1830 ②⑤⑦ (not Apr. 7)..

From Aosta Autostazione at 1100 ②⑤ (not Apr. 7, Aug. 1) and 1600 ②⑤⑦ (not Apr. 7).

🚌 **SION - CRANS-SUR-SIERRE**. Journey time: ± 45 minutes. On June 6, Aug. 15, Nov. 1, Dec. 8 services run as on ⑦. On Apr. 7 services run as on Ⓐ. **Operator**: PA.

From Sion Gare at 0610 Ⓐ, 0645 ⚒, 0745, 0840 ⚒, 0905 Ⓐ, 1000, 1045 ⚒, 1145 Ⓒ, 1150 Ⓐ, 1230 ⚒, 1345, 1510, 1540 Ⓐ, 1648 ⚒, 1710 †, 1810, 1910 and 2105 ⚒.

From Crans-sur-Sierre Post at 0643, 0700 Ⓐ, 0740 ⚒, 0835, 0930 ⚒, 1005 Ⓐ, 1050, 1135 ⚒, 1235 Ⓒ, 1245 Ⓐ, 1335 ⚒, 1545, 1605 Ⓐ, 1635, 1805, 1905 and 2005 ⚒.

SIERRE - MONTANA. Funicular railway. *4 km*. Journey time: 13–14 minutes. **Closed for maintenance Apr. 24–29, Oct. 30, 31.** 🚌 services also available. **Operator**: SMC.

From **Sierre** (SMC) at 0622, 0642 and at 22 and 42 minutes past each hour until 2122, 2142 (also at 0702, 0902, 1002, 1202, 1302, 1402, 1502, 1702, 1802, 1902, 2102, 2202 and 2222).

From **Montana** Gare at 0622, 0642 and at 22 and 42 minutes past each hour until 2122, 2142 (also at 0702, 0902, 1002, 1202, 1302, 1402, 1502, 1702, 1802, 1902, 2102, 2202 and 2222).

🚌 **BRIG - SAAS-FEE**. Journey time: 68–89 minutes. Services call at **Visp** (Bahnhof Süd) ± 20 minutes from Brig, and **Saas Grund** (Post) ± 10 minutes from Saas Fee. **Operator**: PA.

From Brig Bahnhof at 0420, 0515, 0545 and every 30 minutes until 1115; then 1140, 1215, 1247, 1315, 1345 and every 30 minutes until 1845; then 1945, 2045 and 2215.

From Saas-Fee Busterminal at 0530, 0600, 0630, 0700, 0730, 0752, 0822, 0852 and every 30 minutes until 1852; then 1930, 1957, 2130 and 2330.

h – Not June 8, Aug. 15, Nov. 1, Dec. 8.

MARTIGNY - LE CHÂBLE and ORSIÈRES — 574

RA

km																										
												✥										b	b		b	b
0	**Martigny** d.	0605	...	0715	...	0749	...	0815	...	0849	...	and	2049	...	2152	...	2319	...		A	1615	...	and	2015	...
13	Sembrancher a.	0622	0623	0731	0732	0805	0807	0830	0832	0905	0907	hourly	2105	2107	2208	2210	2335	2337	...	L	1630	1632	hourly	2030	2032
19	**Orsières** a.	|	0632	|	0740	|	0816	|	0840	|	0916	until	|	2116	|	2219	|	2346		S	|	1640	until	|	2040
19	**Le Châble** a.	0632	...	0741	...	0815	...	0839	...	0915	...		2115	...	2218	...	2345	...		O	1639	...		2039	...

													⊠								b	b		b	b
Le Châble d.	...	0533	...	0637	...	0709	...	0746	...	0821	...	0846	and	...	2046	...	...	2242	...	A	...	1621	and	...	2021
Orsières d.	0532	|	0636	|	0708	|	0744	|	0820	|	0844	|	hourly	2044	|	...	2240	|	...	L	1620	|	hourly	2020	|
Sembrancher d.	0541	0542	0645	0646	0717	0720	0753	0755	0828	0830	0853	0855	until	2053	2055	...	2249	2251	...	S	1628	1630	until	2028	2030
Martigny a.	...	0558	...	0704	...	0736	...	0811	...	0845	...	0911		...	2111	...	...	2307	...	O	...	1645		...	2045

b – Not Sept. 29 - Oct. 8.

✥ – The 1149 from Martigny to Le Châble (and connecting train 1207 from Sembrancher to Orsières) run 11 minutes later on ③ (except on Dec. 28, Jan. 4, Feb. 22, Apr. 12, June 28, July 5, 12, 19, 26, Aug. 2, 9, 16, Oct. 25, Nov. 1 when normal timings apply).

⊠ – The 1146 from Le Châble to Martigny (and connecting train 1144 from Orsières to Sembrancher) run 4–5 minutes **earlier** on ③ (except on Dec. 28, Jan. 4, Feb. 22, Apr. 12, June 28, July 5, 12, 19, 26, Aug. 2, 9, 16, Oct. 25, Nov. 1 when normal timings apply). No service from Le Châble to Martigny at 1246 (this service is retimed to run 12 minutes later with the connecting train from Orsières running 10 minutes later).

575 GLACIER EXPRESS

MGB, RhB*

Glacier Express through services. [R]. Supplement payable. For local services see Tables **545** and **576**. Narrow gauge railway (part rack).

km		WINTER SERVICE ▶▶▶	902 [R] ✕	904 [R] A ✕	SUMMER SERVICE ▶▶▶	900 [R] ✕	902 [R] ✕	904 [R] ✕	906 [R] ✕
0	**Zermatt** d.		0852	0952		0752	0852	0952	...
45	**Brig** Bahnhofplatz a.		1010	1110		0910	1010	1110	...
45	**Brig** Bahnhofplatz d.		1018	1118		0918	1018	1118	1418
113	**Andermatt** a.	Dec. 11	1146	1246	May 13	1046	1146	1246	1546
113	**Andermatt** d.	to	1154	1254	to	1054	1154	1254	1554
142	**Disentis / Mustér** a.	May 12	1256	1356	Oct. 15	1154	1256	1356	1654
142	**Disentis / Mustér** d.		1311	1411		1219	1311	1411	1711
201	**Chur** ▽ a.		1425	1525		1325	1425	1525	1825
242	Tiefencastel ▽ a.		1528	1628		...	1528	1628	1946
252	**Filisur** ▽ a.		1543	1643		...	1543	1643	2001
285	**Samedan** ▽ a.		1631	1731		...	1631	1731	2049
290	**St Moritz** a.		1637	1737		...	1637	1737	2100

	WINTER SERVICE ▶▶▶	923 [R] ✕	925 [R] A ✕	SUMMER SERVICE ▶▶▶	901 [R] ✕	903 [R] ✕	905 [R] ✕	907 [R] ✕
St Moritz d.		0851	0948		0702	0851	0948	...
Samedan △ d.		0901	0958		0715	0901	0958	...
Filisur △ d.		0949	1043		0801	0949	1043	...
Tiefencastel △ d.	Dec. 11	1007	1100	May 13	0815	1007	1100	...
Chur △ d.	to	1105	1214	to	0926	1105	1214	1426
Disentis / Mustér a.	May 12	1218	1328	Oct. 15	1028	1218	1328	1528
Disentis / Mustér d.		1237	1337		1037	1237	1337	1537
Andermatt a.		1352	1452		1152	1352	1452	1652
Andermatt d.		1354	1454		1208	1408	1508	1708
Brig Bahnhofplatz a.		1540	1640		1340	1540	1640	1840
Brig Bahnhofplatz d.		1550	1650		...	1550	1650	1850
Zermatt a.		1710	1810		...	1710	1810	2010

All Glacier Express trains convey (12) [panorama cars]. Reservations can be made at any Swiss station. Reservations for ✕ are obligatory and must be made in advance of travel: RhB, ✆ 081 288 65 65. Meals are served between 1100 and 1330 at your seat. Further information: www.glacierexpress.ch

A – Apr. 6 - May 12.
△ – Calls to pick up only.
▽ – Calls to set down only.

* – Operators: MGB: Zermatt - Brig - Andermatt - Disentis; RhB: Disentis - Chur - St Moritz.

576 Local services ZERMATT - BRIG - ANDERMATT - DISENTIS (also ANDERMATT - GÖSCHENEN)

MGB

Narrow gauge railway (part rack). For *Glacier Express* through services see Table **575**

ZERMATT - VISP - BRIG

km							J 🚌				J 🚌												
0	**Zermatt** d.	0537	0613	0637	0737	0813	...	0837	and at	1713	...	1737	1813	1837	1913	1937	2013	...	2113	...	2213	...	...
8	Täsch d.	0548	0625	0648	0748	0825	...	0848	the same	1725	...	1748	1825	1848	1925	1948	2025	...	2125	...	2223	...	...
21	St Niklaus d.	0613	0650	0713	0813	0850	...	0913	minutes	1750	...	1813	1850	1913	1950	2013	2050	...	2150	...	2244	...	...
29	Stalden-Saas d.	0635	0710	0735	0835	0910	...	0935	past each	1810	...	1835	1910	1935	2010	2035	2110	...	2210	...	2305	...	...
36	Visp a.	0646	0722	0746	0846	0922	...	0946	hour until	1822	...	1846	1922	1946	2022	2046	2122	...	2222	...	2316	...	...
36	Visp 560 570 d.	0650	0725	0750	*0908*	0925t	0926	*1008*		1825t	1826	*1908*	1925	1950	2025	2050	2125	...	2225	...	2318	...	...
45	**Brig** Bahnhofplatz 560 570 a.	0702	0737	0802	*0920*	0937t	0937	*1020*		1837t	1837	*1920*	1937	2002	2037	2102	2137	...	2237	...	2328	...	...

									J 🚌				J 🚌							①–⑥	⑦	
Brig Bahnhofplatz 560 570 d.	0517	0552	0627	0652	0727	0752	0827	*0838*	0927	0927t	and at	*1738*	1827	1827t	*1838*	...	1952	...	2052	...	2227	2317	...
Visp 560 570 a.	0528	0603	0638	0703	0738	0803	0838	*0850*	0937	0938t	the same	*1750*	1837	1838t	*1850*	...	2003	...	2103	...	2238	2328	...
Visp d.	0530	0608	0641	0708	0741	0808	0841	0908	...	0941	minutes	1808	...	1841	1908	...	2008	...	2108	...	2241	2329	...
Stalden-Saas d.	0539	0618	0651	0718	0751	0818	0851	0918	...	0951	past each	1818	...	1851	1918	...	2018	...	2118	...	2249	2338	...
St Niklaus d.	0555	0636	0711	0736	0811	0836	0911	0936	...	1011	hour until	1836	...	1911	1936	...	2036	...	2136	...	2308	2355	...
Täsch d.	0620	0700	0736	0800	0836	0900	0936	1000	...	1036		1900	...	1936	2000	...	2100	...	2200	...	2336	0017	...
Zermatt a.	0635	0714	0751	0814	0851	0914	0951	1014	...	1051		1914	...	1951	2014	...	2114	...	2214	...	2348	0028	...

VISP - BRIG - ANDERMATT

km				△				①–⑥	⑦	
	Visp d.	...	0708		1908	2008	2108	2238	2255	...
0	**Brig** Bahnhofplatz d.	0623	0723	and	1923	2023	2123	2250	2316	...
7	Mörel d.	0633	0733		1933	2033	2133	2300	2325	...
10	Betten d.	0639	0739	hourly	1939	2039	2139	2306	2332	...
17	Fiesch d.	0656	0756		1956	2056	2155	2322	2349	...
41	Oberwald 🚗 d.	0742	0842	until	2042	2139	*2235**	...	...	...
59	Realp 🚗 ⊗ d.	0805	0905		2105	...	...	...	...	...
68	**Andermatt** a.	0820	0920		2120	...	...	...	...	...

										①–⑥	⑦
Andermatt d.	...	...	0737		1637	1737	1837	1925	2025	...	...
Realp 🚗 ⊗ d.	...	...	0750	and	1650	1750	1850	1936	2036	...	...
Oberwald 🚗 d.	*0612**	0712	0812		1712	1812	1912	1956	2056	*2250**	*2250**
Fiesch d.	0655	0755	0855	hourly	1755	1855	1955	2031	2131	2325	2353
Betten d.	0715	0815	0915		1815	1915	2015	2048	2148	2344	0010
Mörel d.	0722	0822	0922	until	1822	1922	2022	2057	2157	2351	0017
Brig Bahnhofplatz a.	0733	0833	0933		1833	1933	2033	2106	2206	0001	0026
Visp a.	0750	0850	0950		1850	*1950*	*2050*	2138	2222	...	...

ANDERMATT - GÖSCHENEN

km																							
	Realp d.	...	0616	...	...	0731	...	0831	...	0931	...	...	and at the same	...	...	...	1831	...	...	...	...	...	2131	2231
0	**Andermatt** d.	0550	0629	0650	0729	0750	0829	0850	0929	0950	1029	1050	minutes past	1729	1750	1829	1850	1929	1950	2029	2050	2129	2150	2250
4	**Göschenen** a.	0605	0644	0705	0744	0806	0844	0906	0944	1006	1044	1106	each hour until	1744	1806	1844	1906	1944	2006	2044	2106	2144	2206	2306

Göschenen d.	0608	0654	0714	0754	0814	0854	0914	0954	and at the same	1614	1654	1714	1754	1812	1854	1914	1954	2014	2054	2114	2154	2214	2314
Andermatt a.	0618	0706	0724	0806	0824	0906	0924	1006	minutes past	1624	1706	1724	1806	1822	1906	1922	2006	2022	2106	2124	2206	2224	2324
Realp a.	...	0721	...	0821	...	0921	...	...	each hour until	...	...	...	1821	...	...	...	...	...	2121	...	2221	...	...

ANDERMATT - DISENTIS

km		B				🚌 C	🚌 A	🚌	
0	**Andermatt** 🚗 d.	0621	0728	and	1928	...	2124	...	...
10	Oberalppass d.	0639	0750	hourly	1950	...	2139	...	...
19	Sedrun 🚗 d.	0707	0816	until	2016	2101	2201	2201	...
29	**Disentis / Mustér** a.	0727	0839		2039	2118	2218	2218	...

	B					🚌	🚌 A	🚌 C		🚌
Disentis / Mustér d.	0620	0708r	0814	and	1914	2022	2022	2122	...	2222
Sedrun 🚗 d.	0637	0731	0831	hourly	1931	2040	2040	2140	...	2239
Oberalppass d.	0656	0753	0853	until	1953	...	2102	...	...	...
Andermatt 🚗 a.	0722	0822	0922		2022	...	2117	...	...	...

REALP - FURKA - OBERWALD ⊡

km		H		H 🚂		H		D 🚂		
0	**Realp** DFB d.	0915	...	1020	...	...	...	1420	...	...
7	Furka DFB a.	0940	...	1105	...	...	...	1505	...	...
7	Furka DFB d.	0950	...	1130	...	...	...	1530	...	...
13	Gletsch d.	1020	...	1210	...	1320	...	1610	...	...
18	**Oberwald** a.	1045	...	1235	...	1345	...	1635	...	...

	E 🚂		H		H 🚂		H	H			
Oberwald d.	1050	...	1145	...	1350	...	1445	...	...	...	...
Gletsch d.	1120	...	1205	...	1420	...	1505	1615	...	...	...
Furka DFB a.	1155	...	...	...	1455	...	...	1640	...	...	...
Furka DFB d.	1220	...	...	...	1520	...	...	1650	...	...	...
Realp DFB a.	1305	...	...	...	1605	...	...	1720	...	...	...

A – May 1 - Oct. 31.
B – May 13 - Oct. 15.
C – Until Apr. 30 and from Nov. 1.
D – ④–⑥ June 29 - Sept. 23 (also Aug. 13–16).
E – ⑤–⑦ June 30 - Sept. 24 (also Aug. 14–17).
H – ④–⑦ June 29 - Sept. 24 (also Aug. 14–16).

J – Until May 12.
r – 0714 May 13 - Oct. 15.
t – From May 13.
* – By 🚌 from / to Fiesch.
⊗ – Realp is a request stop.

🚂 – Steam train. [R]. Special fares.
⊡ – Summer only tourist service. Special fares. Operator: Dampfbahn Furka-Bergstrecke ✆ 0848 000 144. www.dfb.ch
△ – The 0908 and 1808 departures from Visp require a change of trains at Brig.
🚗 – Car-carrying shuttle available. ✆ +41 (0) 848 642 442. www.matterhorngotthardbahn.ch

578 ZERMATT - GORNERGRAT

Narrow gauge rack railway. GGB

Journey ±33 minutes uphill, ±44 minutes downhill, *9 km*. *Services may be suspended in bad weather.*

UNTIL APR. 23. From Zermatt at 0824, 0848, 0912, 0936, 1000, 1024, 1048, 1112, 1136, 1200, 1224, 1248, 1312, 1336, 1400, 1424, 1448, 1512, 1536, 1600, 1624, 1724 and 1824. **From Gornergrat** at 0735, 0907, 0931, 0955, 1019, 1043, 1107, 1131, 1155, 1219, 1243, 1307, 1331, 1355, 1419, 1443, 1507, 1531, 1555, 1619, 1638, 1718, 1818, 1918 and 2007 **b**.

APR. 24 - JUNE 9 and OCT. 16 - NOV. 1. From Zermatt at 0700, 0805, 0835, 0910, 0945, 1020, 1055, 1130, 1205, 1240, 1315, 1350, 1425, 1500, 1535, 1610, 1645 and 1740. **From Gornergrat** at 0742, 0847, 0922, 0957, 1032, 1107, 1142, 1217, 1252, 1327, 1402, 1437, 1512, 1547, 1622, 1657, 1732 and 1837.

JUNE 10 - OCT. 15. From Zermatt at 0700, 0800, 0824, 0848, 0912, 0936, 1000, 1024, 1048, 1112, 1136, 1200, 1224, 1248, 1312, 1336, 1400, 1424, 1448, 1512, 1536, 1600, 1624, 1724 and 1824. **From Gornergrat** at 0735, 0843, 0907, 0931, 0955, 1019, 1043, 1107, 1131, 1155, 1219, 1243, 1307, 1331, 1355, 1419, 1443, 1507, 1531, 1555, 1619, 1638, 1718, 1818, 1918 and 2007 **c**.

NOV. 2 - DEC. 1: From Zermatt at 0700 Ⓐ, 0824, 1024, 1136, 1224, 1336, 1424 and 1624. **From Gornergrat** at 0735 Ⓐ, 0931, 1131, 1219, 1331, 1419, 1531 and 1718.

b – Until Apr. 16.
c – June 23 - Sept. 25.

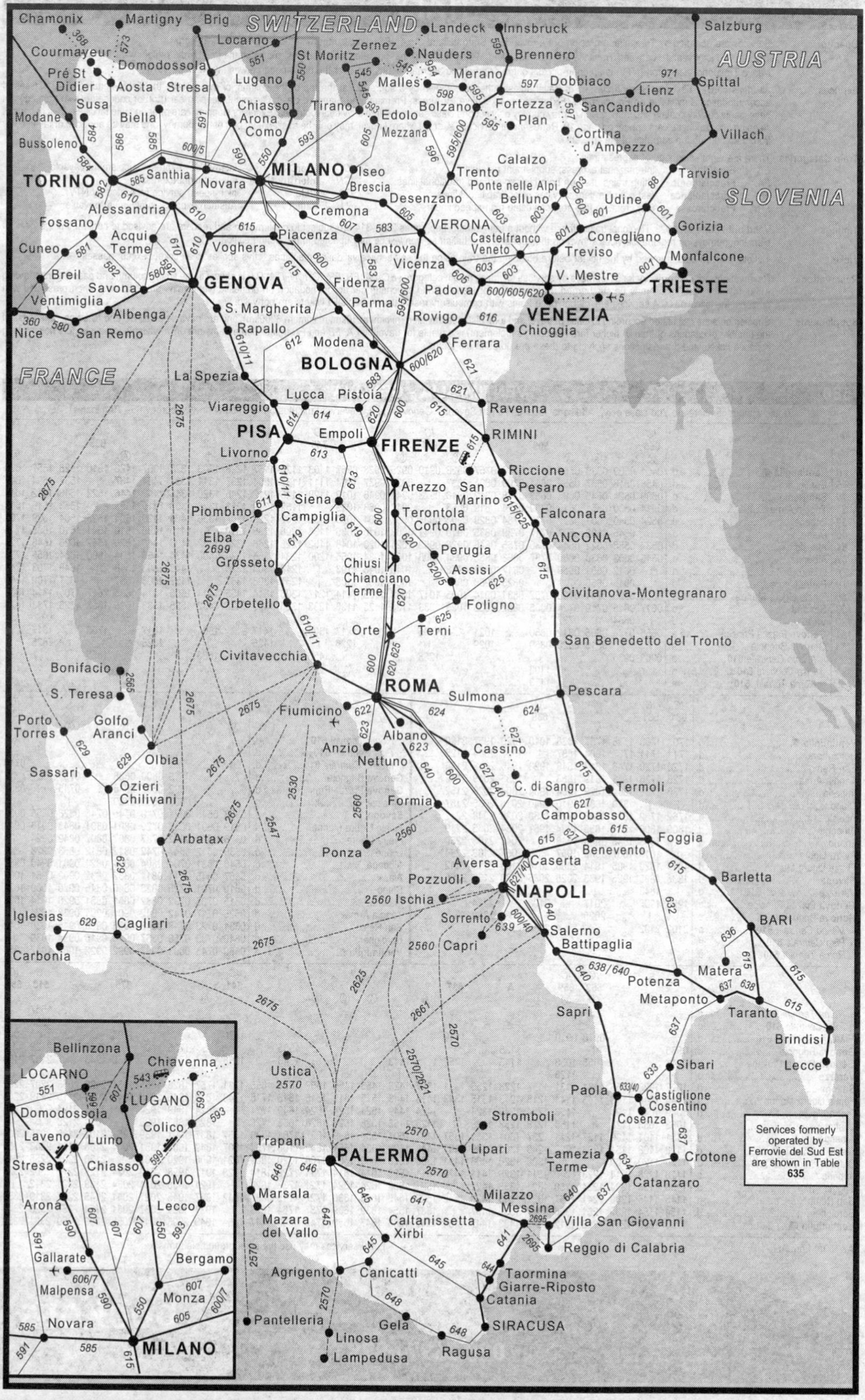
SWITZERLAND
AUSTRIA
SLOVENIA
FRANCE
Chamonix
Martigny
Brig
Locarno
Landeck
Innsbruck
Salzburg
Zernez
St Moritz
Nauders
Brennero
Courmayeur
Domodossola
Pré St Didier
Aosta
Stresa
Lugano
Malles
Merano
Dobbiaco
Lienz
Spittal
Susa
Biella
Chiasso
Arona
Como
Tirano
Edolo
Mezzana
Bolzano
Fortezza
SanCandido
Plan
Modane
Bussoleno
Cortina d'Ampezzo
Villach
MILANO
Iseo
Brescia
Calalzo
Tarvisio
TORINO
Santhia
Novara
Trento
Ponte nelle Alpi
Belluno
Udine
Alessandria
Cremona
Desenzano
Fossano
Acqui Terme
Voghera
Piacenza
Mantova
VERONA
Castelfranco Veneto
Treviso
Conegliano
Gorizia
Cuneo
Breil
Savona
GENOVA
Fidenza
Parma
Vicenza
Padova
V. Mestre
Monfalcone
TRIESTE
Ventimiglia
Albenga
S. Margherita
Rapallo
Rovigo
VENEZIA
Chioggia
Nice
San Remo
Modena
Ferrara
BOLOGNA
La Spezia
Lucca
Pistoia
Ravenna
Viareggio
PISA
Empoli
FIRENZE
RIMINI
Livorno
Arezzo
San Marino
Riccione
Pesaro
Siena
Piombino
Campiglia
Terontola Cortona
Falconara
ANCONA
Elba
Perugia
Grosseto
Chiusi Chianciano Terme
Assisi
Orbetello
Foligno
Civitanova-Montegranaro
Orte
Terni
San Benedetto del Tronto
Civitavecchia
Bonifacio
S. Teresa
ROMA
Sulmona
Pescara
Fiumicino
Porto Torres
Golfo Aranci
Albano
Anzio
Nettuno
Cassino
Olbia
Sassari
Ozieri Chilivani
C. di Sangro
Termoli
Formia
Campobasso
Arbatax
Ponza
Benevento
Foggia
Aversa
Caserta
Pozzuoli
NAPOLI
Barletta
Ischia
Iglesias
Sorrento
Cagliari
Salerno
Battipaglia
BARI
Carbonia
Capri
Matera
Potenza
Metaponto
Taranto
Sapri
Brindisi
Lecce
Ustica
Sibari
Paola
Castiglione Cosentino
Cosenza
Stromboli
Trapani
Lipari
PALERMO
Lamezia Terme
Crotone
Catanzaro
Marsala
Milazzo
Messina
Mazara del Vallo
Caltanissetta Xirbi
Villa San Giovanni
Reggio di Calabria
Agrigento
Canicattì
Taormina Giarre-Riposto
Catania
Pantelleria
Gela
SIRACUSA
Linosa
Ragusa
Lampedusa
Bellinzona
Chiavenna
LOCARNO
LUGANO
Domodossola
Colico
Laveno
Luino
Stresa
Chiasso
COMO
Arona
Lecco
Gallarate
Bergamo
Malpensa
Monza
Novara
MILANO
Services formerly operated by Ferrovie del Sud Est are shown in Table 635

ITALY

Operator: Services are operated by Trenitalia, a division of Ferrovie dello Stato Italiane S.p.a. (FS), unless otherwise noted: www.trenitalia.com.
Trenord is a joint venture between Trenitalia and Ferrovie Nord Milano (LeNord) that operates local services, mainly in the Lombardia region: www.trenord.it.
Nuovo Trasporto Viaggiatori (NTV) is an open-access operator providing alternative services over the high-speed network: www.italotreno.it.

Services: All trains convey First and Second classes of travel unless otherwise shown by a figure "2" at the top of the column, or in a note in the Table heading. Four classes of accommodation is available on Frecciarossa (*FR*) services: Executive, Business, Premium and Standard class. Overnight sleeping car (🛏) or couchette (🛏) trains do not necessarily convey seating accommodation or may convey only second class seats - refer to individual footnotes. Excelsior sleeping cars offer en-suite facilities. Descriptions of sleeping and couchette cars appear on page 10. Refreshment services (✕ or 🍸) where known, may only be available for part of the journey, and may be added to or taken away from trains during the currency of the timetable.

Train Categories: There are eight categories of express train:

EC	**EuroCity**	international express; supplement payable.	*IC*	**InterCity**	internal day express; supplement payable.
FA	**Frecciargento**	tilting trains used on both high-speed and traditional lines.	*ICN*	**InterCity Notte**	internal night express.
FB	**Frecciabianca**	fast premium fare services using traditional lines.	*ITA*	**.italo**	high-speed service (operated by NTV).
FR	**Frecciarossa**	fast premium fare services using high-speed lines.	*RJ*	**Railjet**	Austrian express; supplement payable.

Timings: **Valid until June 10**, 2023. Regional trains (those without a train number) on pages 294–314 are subject to confirmation and readers are advised to confirm timings locally if planning journeys on regional services shown on these pages. The Italian section will be fully updated in the Spring edition.

Tickets: Tickets must be date-stamped by the holder before boarding the train using the self-service validating machines – this applies to all tickets except passes.

Reservations: Reservations are **compulsory** for all journeys by services for which a train category (*EC, FA, FB, FR, IC, ICN, ITA, RJ*) is shown in the timing column and passengers boarding without a prior reservation may be surcharged. Reservations for sleeping and couchette car accommodation on domestic night trains are valid only when presented with personal identification. *ITA* services are 'global' price trains with compulsory reservation - Trenitalia tickets are not valid.

Supplements: Supplements are calculated according to class of travel and total distance travelled (minimum 10km, maximum 3000km), and are payable on all *EC* and *IC* trains, regardless of the number of changes of train. A higher fare (including supplement) is payable for travel by *FA, FB* and *FR* trains. Some trains are only available to passengers holding long distance tickets and the restrictions applying to these are noted in the tables.

580 VENTIMIGLIA - GENOVA

Trains without numbers are 2nd class only. Additional local trains run Savona - Genova and v.v. every 30 minutes on Ⓐ / hourly on Ⓒ (journey 65–70 minutes).

km			IC 655				IC 505				IC 631				IC 745				IC 655				IC 635			
			⚒		Ⓐ	Ⓐ				Ⓐ		Ⓒ	Ⓐ					Ⓐ	†			Ⓐ				Ⓐ
0	**Ventimiglia** 🏛	d.	0451	0509	0530	0550	0637	0700	0757	0828	0910	0925	0928	0957	1103	1128	1157	1228	1303	1328	1357	1428	1510	1528	1557	1628
5	Bordighera	d.	0458	0516	0537	0558	0644	0709	0804	0837	|	0933	0937	1004	1111	1137	1204	1237	1311	1337	1404	1437	|	1537	1604	1637
16	San Remo	d.	0508	0524	0545	0606	0653	0718	0812	0846	0923	0941	0946	1012	1120	1146	1212	1246	1320	1346	1412	1446	1523	1546	1612	1646
24	Taggia Arma	d.	0514	0530	0551	0612	0700	0724	0819	0853	|	0947	0953	1019	|	1152	1219	1253	1326	1353	1419	1453	|	1553	1619	1653
39	Imperia	d.	0524	0540	0601	0622	0710	0734	0829	0904	0935	0957	1004	1029	1132	1202	1229	1304	1336	1404	1429	1504	1535	1604	1629	1704
46	Diano	d.	|	0545	0606	0627	0717	0739	0835	0910	0941	1003	1010	1035	1138	1208	1235	1310	|	1410	1435	1510	1541	1610	1635	1710
61	Alassio	d.	0537	0556	0622	0644	0730	0755	0848	0926	0952	1021	1026	1048	1152	1225	1248	1326	1352	1426	1448	1526	1552	1626	1648	1726
67	Albenga	d.	0545	0603	0630	0650	0737	0803	0855	0934	1000	1027	1034	1055	1200	1234	1255	1334	1400	1434	1455	1534	1600	1634	1655	1734
76	Loano	d.	|	0612	0651	0659	|	0817	0903	0948	|	1040	1048	1103	|	1248	1303	1348	|	1448	1503	1548	|	1648	1703	1748
79	Pietra Ligure	d.	|	0616	0655	|	|	0823	0908	0957	|	1050	1057	1108	|	1257	1308	1357	|	1457	1508	1557	|	1657	1708	1800
85	Finale Ligure Marina	d.	0600	0623	0701	0708	0752	0831	0914	1005	1017	1059	1105	1114	1217	1305	1314	1405	1414	1505	1514	1605	1617	1705	1714	1805
108	**Savona**	d.	0617	0645	0719	0724	0805	0852	0933	1025	1033	1125	1125	1133	1233	1325	1333	1425	1432	1525	1533	1625	1633	1725	1733	1825
120	Varazze	d.	|	0654	|	0732	|	...	|	...	|	...	...	|	|	...	|	...	|	...	|	...	|	...	|	...
151	**Genova** Piazza Principe	§ a.	0655	0738	0805	0812	0850	...	1021	...	1105	...	...	1217	1305	...	1417	...	1504	...	1617	...	1705	...	1817	...
154	**Genova** Brignole	a.	|	|	0813	0820	0859	...	1029	...	|	...	...	1225	|	...	1425	...	|	...	1625	...	|	...	1825	...
	Milano Centrale **610**	a.	0903	0935	...	...	|	...	...	...	1255	...	...	...	1455	...	...	...	1653	...	...	...	1855	...	...	...
	Pisa Centrale **610**	a.	...	...	...	...	1103	...	...	...	...	...	...	...	...	...	...	...	...	...	...	...	...	...	...	...
	Roma Termini **610**	a.	...	...	...	...	1433	...	...	...	...	...	...	...	...	...	...	...	...	...	...	...	...	...	...	...

		IC 681	IC 681				IC 639				
		Ⓐ	Ⓒ			Ⓐ					
Ventimiglia 🏛	d.	1703	1703	1728	1757	1828	1910	1928	1957	2120	...
Bordighera	d.	1711	1711	1737	1804	1837	|	1937	2004	2128	...
San Remo	d.	1720	1720	1746	1812	1846	1923	1946	2012	2136	...
Taggia Arma	d.	1726	1726	1753	1819	1853	|	1953	2019	2142	...
Imperia	d.	1736	1736	1804	1829	1904	1934	2004	2029	2152	...
Diano	d.	|	|	1810	1835	1910	1940	2010	2035	2157	...
Alassio	d.	1752	1752	1826	1848	1926	1950	2026	2048	2212	...
Albenga	d.	1800	1800	1834	1855	1934	1957	2034	2055	2219	...
Loano	d.	|	1808	1848	1903	1948	|	2048	2103	2230	...
Pietra Ligure	d.	|	1813	1857	1908	1957	|	2057	2108	2234	...
Finale Ligure Marina	d.	1814	1820	1905	1914	2005	2018	2105	2114	2242	...
Savona	d.	1833	1835	1925	1933	2025	2035	2125	2133	2305	...
Varazze	d.	|	1843	...	|	...	|	...	2146	...	...
Genova Piazza Principe	§ a.	1908	1908	...	2017	...	2108	...	2224	...	...
Genova Brignole	a.	|	|	...	2025	...	|	...	2232	...	...
Milano Centrale **610**	a.	2102	2102	...	...	...	2253	...	...	...	...
Pisa Centrale **610**	a.	...	...	...	...	...	...	...	...	...	...
Roma Termini **610**	a.	...	...	...	...	...	...	...	...	...	...

										IC 633
		Ⓐ	Ⓐ			⚒	†	Ⓐ		
Roma Termini **610**	d.	...	...	...	...	...	...	...	...	...
Pisa Centrale **610**	d.	...	...	...	...	...	...	...	...	...
Milano Centrale **610**	d.	...	...	...	...	...	...	...	...	0710
Genova Brignole	d.	...	...	0515	0600	0638	...	0737	...	|
Genova Piazza Principe	§ d.	...	...	0522	0607	0646	...	0745	...	0858
Varazze	d.	...	...	0605	0653	0729	...	|	...	|
Savona	d.	0503	0545	0621	0710	0745	0745	0828	0855	0931
Finale Ligure Marina	d.	0519	0601	0636	0729	0801	0801	0843	0915	0943
Pietra Ligure	d.	0526	0607	0642	0737	0807	0807	0849	0924	|
Loano	d.	0530	0612	0647	0742	0812	0812	0853	0928	|
Albenga	d.	0546	0631	0704	0804	0824	0824	0901	0940	0957
Alassio	d.	0557	0645	0711	0811	0832	0832	0908	0951	1007
Diano	d.	0610	0701	0725	0825	0846	0846	0920	1009	1021
Imperia	d.	0615	0705	0732	0832	0851	0851	0928	1014	1028
Taggia Arma	d.	0625	0717	0742	0842	0901	0901	0938	1024	|
San Remo	d.	0631	0723	0748	0848	0906	0906	0945	1030	1042
Bordighera	d.	0640	0733	0756	0857	0915	0915	0954	1039	|
Ventimiglia 🏛	a.	0650	0745	0803	0903	0922	0922	1003	1047	1054

					IC 659	IC 659		A		IC 637								IC 641				IC 675			IC 518	IC 689
		Ⓐ	Ⓒ		Ⓐ	Ⓒ	Ⓐ				Ⓐ		Ⓐ	Ⓒ	Ⓐ				Ⓐ							
Roma Termini **610**	d.	...	...	...	...	...	...	...	...	...	...	...	...	...	...	...	...	...	...	...	...	...	...	...	1557	...
Pisa Centrale **610**	d.	...	...	...	...	...	...	...	...	...	...	...	...	...	...	...	...	...	...	...	...	...	...	...	1903	...
Milano Centrale **610**	d.	...	...	...	0910	0910	...	...	...	1110	...	...	...	...	...	...	...	1510	...	...	...	1705	...	...	|	2005
Genova Brignole	d.	0935	...	...	|	|	...	1135	...	|	...	1335	...	...	...	1535	...	|	...	1735	...	|	1935	...	2129	|
Genova Piazza Principe	§ d.	0943	...	...	1058	1058	...	1143	...	1258	...	1343	...	...	...	1543	...	1658	...	1743	...	1858	1943	...	2137	2158
Varazze	d.	|	...	...	|	1123	...	|	...	|	...	|	...	...	...	|	...	|	...	|	...	|	|	...	|	|
Savona	d.	1028	1028	1055	1131	1131	1157	1228	1255	1331	1357	1428	1455	1455	1557	1628	1655	1731	1757	1828	1855	1931	2028	2055	2207	2232
Finale Ligure Marina	d.	1043	1043	1115	1143	1144	1218	1243	1315	1343	1418	1443	1515	1515	1618	1643	1715	1743	1818	1843	1915	1943	2046	2115	2219	2245
Pietra Ligure	d.	1049	1049	1124	|	1153	1224	1249	1324	|	1424	1449	1524	1524	1624	1649	1724	|	1824	1849	1924	|	2051	2124	|	|
Loano	d.	1053	1053	1128	|	1159	1228	1253	1328	|	1428	1453	1528	1528	1628	1653	1728	|	1828	1853	1928	|	2054	2128	|	|
Albenga	d.	1101	1101	1139	1157	1211	1237	1301	1339	1357	1437	1501	1539	1539	1637	1701	1739	1757	1837	1901	1939	1957	2102	2139	2235	2301
Alassio	d.	1108	1108	1151	1208	1226	1249	1308	1349	1407	1449	1508	1551	1551	1649	1708	1751	1807	1849	1908	1951	2004	2108	2151	2243	2308
Diano	d.	1120	1120	1209	|	|	1306	1320	1406	1421	1506	1520	1609	1609	1706	1720	1809	1821	1906	1920	2007	|	2120	2207	2255	2319
Imperia	d.	1128	1128	1214	1223	1240	1311	1328	1411	1428	1511	1528	1614	1614	1711	1728	1814	1828	1911	1928	2012	2024	2128	2212	2302	2326
Taggia Arma	d.	1138	1138	1224	1234	1250	1321	1338	1421	|	1521	1538	1624	1624	1721	1738	1824	|	1921	1938	2021	2034	2138	2221	2312	|
San Remo	d.	1145	1145	1230	1241	1257	1327	1345	1428	1442	1527	1545	1630	1630	1727	1745	1830	1842	1927	1945	2027	2041	2145	2227	2319	2339
Bordighera	d.	1154	1154	1239	1251	1306	1337	1354	1437	|	1537	1554	1639	1639	1737	1754	1839	|	1937	1954	2037	2051	2154	2237	2328	2349
Ventimiglia 🏛	a.	1203	1203	1247	1258	1312	1349	1403	1447	1454	1549	1603	1647	1650	1749	1803	1847	1854	1949	2003	2047	2058	2203	2250	2334	2358

A – Ⓑ from Apr. 1.

§ – Local services may use the underground platforms.

VENTIMIGLIA and NICE - CUNEO — 581

2nd class

km																										
			Ⓐ				🚌										Ⓐ	Ⓐ 🚌			Ⓒ 🚌		Ⓐ	Ⓐ 🚌			
	Ventimiglia ......d.	0618	...	...	...	...	...	...	...	1039	...	...	...	...	...	...	...	...	...	...	1849	...	...	...	...	...
0	**Nice** Ville ......d.	|	0545	...	0723	0813	...	...	0908	|	...	1208	...	1458	...	1541	...	...	1720	...	|	1810	...	1909	1943	...
34	Sospel..........d.	|	0649	...	0820	0906	...	...	1012	|	...	1304	...	1552	...	1643	...	...	1818	...	|	1919	...	2023	2041	...
43	Breil sur Roya...a.	0655	0702	...	0832	0918	...	...	1027	1117	...	1316	...	1604	...	1655	...	...	1830	...	1925	1928	...	2035	2053	...
43	Breil sur Roya...d.	0656	0726	...	...	...	0935	...	1039	1119	...	1327	...	1610	...	...	1725	...	...	1914	1926	...	1935	...	...	...
71	Tende..............d.	0751	0826	0840	...	...	1034	1155	1133	1220	...	1429	1442	1710	1754	...	1824	...	...	2013	2017	...	2034	...	...	...
89	Limone ▦.. **582** d.	0840	...	0910	...	...	...	1225	...	1247	...	...	1512	...	1828	...	...	...	...	...	2046	...	...	...	...	...
118	**Cuneo**....... **582** a.	0919	...	...	...	...	...	...	...	1319	...	...	...	...	...	...	...	...	...	...	2119	...	...	...	...	...

km																										
		Ⓐ	Ⓐ 🚌	Ⓐ	Ⓐ 🚌			Ⓐ	Ⓒ 🚌	Ⓒ									Ⓐ 🚌							
0	**Cuneo**....... **582** d.	...	...	...	...	...	0641	...	...	...	...	...	...	...	...	...	1441	...	...	...	...	...	1715	...	...	...
29	Limone ▦.. **582** d.	...	...	...	...	...	0720	...	...	...	...	...	1107	...	1400	...	1520	...	...	...	1700	...	1756	...	...	...
47	Tende..............d.	...	0530	...	0620	...	0750	0900	0800	...	...	...	1137	1145	1430	1444	1550	...	1630	...	1730	1734	1828	...	...	...
76	Breil sur Roya...a.	...	0630	...	0711	...	0841	0954	0907	...	...	...	...	1239	...	1536	1641	...	1721	...	...	1831	1922	...	...	...
76	Breil sur Roya...d.	0600	...	0636	...	0734	0842	0958	...	0958	...	1101	...	1242	...	1539	1643	...	...	1732	...	1832	1927	1940	...	...
	Sospel..........d.	0612	...	0649	...	0747	|	1011	...	1011	...	1113	...	1304	...	1552	|	...	...	1745	...	1846	|	1952	...	...
	Nice Ville ......a.	0706	...	0756	...	0847	|	1103	...	1103	...	1209	...	1356	...	1650	|	...	...	1844	...	1944	|	2048	...	...
96	**Ventimiglia** ......a.	...	...	...	...	...	0921	...	...	...	...	...	...	...	...	...	1721	...	...	...	...	...	2005	...	...	...

☛ French holiday dates apply.

TORINO - CUNEO, LIMONE and SAVONA — 582

2nd class

km																								
				⚒			⚒			⚒	⚒		Ⓑ		⚒			Ⓑ	†					
0	**Torino** Porta Nuova............d.	...	0525	...	0625	...	0641	0722	...	...	...	0825	...	0925	...	1025	...	...	...	1125	...	1225	...	1325
52	Savigliano...........................d.	...	0603	...	0703	...	0734	0803	...	...	...	0903	...	1003	...	1103	...	...	...	1203	...	1303	...	1403
64	Fossano ....d.	...	0612	0622	0713	0725	0745	0812	...	...	0822	0913	0925	1012	1022	1113	...	...	1125	1212	...	1313	1325	1412
90	Cuneo .... **581** d.	0550	0636	|	|	0750	...	0836	...	0841	|	|	0950	1036	|	|	...	1150	1150	1236	...	|	1350	1436
119	**Limone** .... **581** a.	0628	...	|	|	0828	...	...	...	0919	|	|	1028	...	|	|	...	1228	1228	...	...	|	1428	...
83	Mondovi..............................d.	...	...	0640	0728	...	...	...	...	...	0840	0928	...	...	1040	1128	...	...	...	...	...	1328	...	...
103	Ceva ....d.	...	...	0700	0742	...	...	...	...	...	0900	0942	...	...	1100	1142	...	...	...	...	...	1342	...	...
132	S.Giuseppe di Cairo.............d.	...	...	0730	0813	...	...	...	...	...	0929	1013	...	...	1129	1213	...	...	...	...	...	1413	...	...
153	**Savona** ....a.	...	...	0752	0836	...	...	...	...	...	...	1036	...	...	...	1236	...	...	...	...	...	1436	...	...

	⚒							Ⓐ		Ⓐ			Ⓐ	Ⓐ		⚒				⚒			
Torino Porta Nuova.......................d.	...	1425	...	1525	...	...	1625	...	1725	...	...	...	1750	...	1825	...	1855	...	1925	1955	2025	...	2125
Savigliano.......................................d.	...	1503	...	1603	...	...	1703	...	1803	...	...	...	1829	...	1903	...	1931	...	2003	2032	2103	...	2203
Fossano ....d.	1422	1513	1525	1612	1622	...	1713	1725	1812	...	1822	...	1837	1845	1913	1925	1941	...	2012	2041	2113	...	2212
Cuneo .... **581** d.	|	|	1550	1636	|	...	|	1750	1836	1841	|	...	1901	|	|	1950	|	...	2036	|	|	...	2236
Limone .... **581** a.	|	|	1628	...	|	...	|	1828	...	1919	|	...	...	|	|	2028	|	...	...	|	|	...	...
Mondovi..d.	1440	1528	...	...	1640	...	1728	...	...	...	1840	...	...	1858	1928	...	1956	...	...	2100	2128	...	...
Ceva..d.	1500	1542	...	...	1700	...	1742	...	...	...	1900	...	...	1912	1942	...	2018	...	...	2120	2142	...	...
S.Giuseppe di Cairo..........................d.	1529	1613	...	...	1729	...	1813	...	...	...	1929	...	...	...	2013	...	2049	...	...	...	2213	...	...
Savona ....a.	...	1636	...	...	...	...	1836	...	...	...	...	...	...	...	2036	...	2112	...	...	...	2236	...	...

				⚒	⚒	⚒	⚒		⚒	Ⓐ	†			⚒	†	⚒				Ⓐ		Ⓑ	
Savona ....d.	...	...	0531	...	...	...	...	...	...	...	...	...	0731	0808	...	...	...	...	0931	...	...	...	1131
S.Giuseppe di Cairo..........................d.	...	...	0553	...	...	0631	...	...	...	...	...	...	0753	0831	0831	...	...	...	0953	1031	...	...	1153
Ceva..d.	...	...	0617	...	0650	0700	...	...	...	0738	...	...	0817	0900	0900	...	...	...	1017	1100	...	...	1217
Mondovi..d.	...	...	0632	...	0706	0720	...	...	...	0752	...	...	0832	0920	0920	...	...	...	1032	1120	...	...	1232
Limone .... **581** d.	...	...	|	...	|	|	0640	...	...	|	0732	...	|	|	|	0855	...	0932	|	|	...	1132	|
Cuneo .... **581** d.	0524	0612	|	0654	|	|	0719	0724	0751	|	0812	...	|	|	|	0934	0924	1012	|	|	1124	1212	|
Fossano ....d.	0544	0635	0644	0714	0722	0738	...	0744	0814	0805	0835	...	0844	0938	0938	...	0944	1035	1044	1138	1144	1235	1244
Savigliano.......................................d.	0552	...	0652	0722	0731	...	...	0752	0822	...	...	...	0852	...	...	...	0952	...	1052	...	1152	...	1252
Torino Porta Nuova.......................a.	0635	...	0735	0805	0815	...	...	0835	0905	...	...	...	0935	...	...	...	1035	...	1135	...	1235	...	1335

	⚒		Ⓑ						⚒					⚒	†	Ⓐ		Ⓐ				⚒	
Savona ....d.	...	...	...	1330	...	...	...	1531	...	...	...	...	1731	1800	...	...	...	...	1931	...	...	...	2131
S.Giuseppe di Cairo..........................d.	1231	...	...	1353	1431	...	...	1553	1631	...	...	...	1753	1831	1831	...	...	...	1953	2031	...	...	2153
Ceva..d.	1300	...	...	1417	1500	...	...	1617	1700	...	...	...	1817	1900	1900	...	...	...	2017	2100	...	...	2217
Mondovi..d.	1320	...	...	1432	1520	...	...	1632	1720	...	...	...	1832	1920	1920	...	...	...	2032	2120	...	...	2232
Limone .... **581** d.	|	...	1332	|	|	...	1532	|	|	...	1732	...	|	|	|	1840	...	1932	|	|	...	2132	|
Cuneo .... **581** d.	|	1324	1412	|	|	1524	1612	|	|	1724	1812	...	|	|	|	1919	1924	2012	|	|	2124	2212	|
Fossano ....d.	1338	1344	1435	1444	1538	1544	1635	1644	1738	1744	1835	...	1844	1938	1938	...	1944	2035	2044	2138	2144	2235	2244
Savigliano.......................................d.	...	1352	...	1452	...	1552	...	1652	...	1752	...	...	1852	...	...	...	1952	...	2052	...	2152	...	2252
Torino Porta Nuova.......................a.	...	1435	...	1535	...	1635	...	1735	...	1835	...	...	1935	...	...	...	2035	...	2135	...	2235	...	2340

MANTOVA and PORRETTA TERME — 583

2nd class

BOLOGNA - PORRETTA TERME
59 km Journey 60 – 72 minutes

From **Bologna** Centrale: 0552 ⚒, 0630 ⚒, 0704, 0804 ⚒, 0904, 1004 ⚒, 1104, 1204, 1304, 1404, 1504, 1604, 1704, 1737, 1804, 1837 Ⓐ, 1904, 1937 Ⓐ, 2004, 2104, 2204.

From **Porretta Terme**: 0500 ⚒, 0550, 0608, 0640, 0718, 0750 ⚒, 0822, 0922 ⚒, 1022, 1122 ⚒, 1222, 1322, 1422, 1522, 1622, 1720, 1821, 1921, 2021, 2050 Ⓐ, 2122 Ⓐ.

MANTOVA - MODENA
61 km Journey 60 – 90 minutes

From **Mantova**: 0535 ⚒, 0629, 0732 ⚒, 0829, 0929, 1129, 1229 ⚒, 1329, 1429 ⚒, 1529, 1629 ⚒, 1729, 1829 ⚒, 1929, 2029 ⚒, 2129.

From **Modena**: 0547 ⚒, 0630 ⚒, 0707, 0807 ⚒, 0907, 1107 †, 1207 ⚒, 1307, 1407 ⚒, 1507, 1607 ⚒, 1707, 1807 ⚒, 1907, 2007, 2107 ⚒, 2207.

PORRETTA TERME - PISTOIA
40 km Journey 60 – 75 minutes

From **Porretta Terme**: 0655 ⚒, 0715⚒, 0926 ⚒, 1322, 1524, 1824.

From **Pistoia**: 0600, 0823 ⚒, 1220, 1420, 1721, 1926.

VERONA - MANTOVA
37 km Journey 45 – 50 minutes

From **Verona** Porta Nuova: 0631 ⚒, 0731 ⚒, 0831 ⚒, 0931, 1231 ⚒, 1331, 1431 ⚒, 1531, 1631 ⚒, 1731, 1831 ⚒, 1931, 2031 ⚒, 2131 †.

From **Mantova**: 0629 ⚒, 0729 ⚒, 0829, 0929 ⚒, 1229, 1329 ⚒, 1429, 1529 ⚒, 1629, 1729 ⚒, 1829, 1929 ⚒, 2029.

584 TORINO - SUSA and BARDONECCHIA — 2nd class

For Italy - France *Frecciarossa* and *TGV* services via Oulx and Modane see Table **44**. For domestic high-speed trains see Table **600**.

km																								
		⚒	⚒	†	⚒	⚒		⚒	†	⚒	⚒		⚒	†	⚒	⚒		⚒	†	⚒	⚒		⚒	†
0	**Torino** Porta Nuova d.	0445	0515	0545	0545	0615	0645	0715	0745	0745	0815	0845	0915	0945	0945	1015	1045	1115	1145	1145	1215	1245	1315	1345
46	Bussoleno d.	0543	0559	0632	0643	0712	0743	0759	0832	0843	0859	0943	0959	1032	1043	1059	1143	1159	1232	1243	1259	1343	1359	1432
54	**Susa** a.	0553	|	|	0653	|	0753	|	|	0853	|	0953	|	|	1053	|	1153	|	|	1253	|	1353	|	|
76	Oulx-Claviere ▲ d.	...	0628	0701	...	0742	...	0828	0901	...	0928	...	1028	1101	...	1128	...	1228	1301	...	1328	...	1428	1501
87	**Bardonecchia** ♣ a.	...	0641	0714	...	0755	...	0841	0914	...	0941	...	1041	1114	...	1146	...	1246	1314	...	1341	...	1441	1514
107	**Modane** 🚌 ♣ a.	...	...	...	...	...	...	...	...	...	...	...	...	...	...	...	...	...	...	...	...	...	...	...

	⚒	⚒		⚒	†	⚒	⚒		⚒	†	⚒	⚒		⚒	†	⚒	⚒		⚒	†	⚒	⚒	
Torino Porta Nuova d.	1345	1415	1445	1515	1545	1545	1615	1645	1715	1745	1745	1815	1845	1915	1945	1945	2015	2045	2115	2145	2145	2215	2245
Bussoleno d.	1443	1459	1543	1559	1632	1643	1704	1743	1759	1832	1843	1859	1943	1959	2032	2043	2059	2143	2159	2232	2243	2259	2342
Susa a.	1453	|	1553	|	|	1653	|	1753	|	|	1853	|	1953	|	|	2053	|	2153	|	|	2253	|	...
Oulx-Claviere-Sestriere ▲ d.	...	1528	...	1628	1701	...	1733	...	1828	1901	...	1928	...	2028	2101	...	2128	...	2228	2301	...	2328	...
Bardonecchia ♣ a.	...	1541	...	1641	1714	...	1745	...	1841	1914	...	1941	...	2041	2114	...	2141	...	2241	2314	...	2341	...
Modane 🚌 ♣ a.	...	...	...	...	...	...	...	...	...	...	...	...	...	...	...	...	...	...	...	...	...	...	...

	†	⚒	†	⚒	⚒	⚒	⚒	†	⚒		⚒	⚒	†	⚒		⚒	⚒	†	⚒		⚒	⚒	†
Modane 🚌 ♣ d.	...	...	...	...	...	...	...	...	...	...	...	...	...	...	...	...	...	...	...	...	...	...	...
Bardonecchia ♣ d.	...	...	0509	0521	...	0621	...	0648	0721	...	0821	...	0848	0921	...	1021	...	1048	1121	...	1215	...	1248
Oulx-Claviere-Sestriere ▲ d.	...	...	0522	0534	...	0634	...	0701	0734	...	0834	...	0901	0934	...	1034	...	1101	1134	...	1227	...	1301
Susa d.	0439	0509	|	|	0609	|	0709	|	|	0809	|	0909	|	|	1009	|	1109	|	|	1209	|	1309	|
Bussoleno d.	0449	0519	0549	0601	0619	0701	0719	0728	0801	0819	0901	0919	0928	1001	1019	1101	1119	1128	1201	1219	1301	1319	1328
Torino Porta Nuova a.	0545	0615	0645	0645	0715	0745	0815	0815	0845	0915	0945	1015	1015	1045	1115	1145	1215	1215	1245	1315	1345	1415	1415

	⚒		⚒	⚒	†	⚒		⚒	⚒	†	⚒		⚒	⚒	†	⚒		⚒	⚒	†	⚒		⚒
Modane 🚌 ♣ d.	...	...	...	...	...	...	...	...	...	...	...	...	...	...	...	...	...	...	...	...	...	...	...
Bardonecchia ♣ d.	1307	...	1421	...	1448	1521	...	1621	...	1648	1721	...	1821	...	1848	1921	...	2015	...	2048	2121	...	2221
Oulx-Claviere-Sestriere ▲ d.	1320	...	1434	...	1501	1534	...	1634	...	1701	1734	...	1834	...	1901	1934	...	2027	...	2101	2134	...	2234
Susa d.	|	1409	|	1509	|	|	1609	|	1709	|	|	1809	|	1909	|	|	2009	|	2109	|	|	2209	|
Bussoleno d.	1349	1419	1501	1519	1528	1601	1619	1701	1719	1728	1801	1819	1901	1919	1928	2001	2019	2101	2119	2128	2201	2219	2301
Torino Porta Nuova a.	1445	1515	1545	1615	1615	1645	1715	1745	1815	1815	1845	1915	1945	2015	2015	2045	2115	2145	2215	2215	2245	2315	2345

▲ – Station for Cesana, Claviere and Sestriere.

♣ – A cross-border 🚌 service is available Bardonecchia - Modane and v.v. Journey time 30 minutes. www.gherra.it
From **Bardonecchia** at 0800 Ⓐ, 1200 Ⓐ, 1500 Ⓐ, 1900 Ⓐ. From **Modane** at 0730 Ⓐ, 0930 Ⓐ, 1330 Ⓐ, 1630 Ⓐ.

585 TORINO - MILANO

For Italy - France *Frecciarossa* and *TGV* services via Oulx and Modane see Table **44**. For domestic high-speed trains see Table **600**.

km																								
																					IC **509**		*ICN* **797** ✣B		
0	**Torino** Porta Nuova 586 d.	0454	0554	0654	0754	0854	...	1054	1154	1254	1354	1454	...	...	1554	1654	1754	1854	...	1905	1954	2030	2054	...
6	**Torino** Porta Susa 586 d.	0505	0605	0705	0805	0905	...	1105	1205	1305	1405	1505	...	...	1605	1705	1805	1905	...	1916u	2005	2040u	2105	...
29	Chivasso 586 d.	0520	0620	0720	0820	0920	...	1120	1220	1320	1420	1520	...	...	1620	1720	1820	1920	...	|	2020	|	2120	...
60	Santhià d.	0538	0638	0738	0838	0938	...	1138	1238	1338	1438	1538	...	...	1638	1738	1838	1938	...	|	2038	|	2138	...
79	Vercelli d.	0549	0649	0749	0849	0949	...	1149	1249	1349	1449	1549	...	...	1649	1749	1849	1949	...	2001	2049	2120	2149	...
101	Novara d.	0605	0705	0805	0905	1005	...	1205	1305	1405	1505	1605	...	...	1705	1805	1905	2005	...	2015	2105	2137	2205	...
140	Rho Fiera Milano d.	0633	0733	0833	0933	1033	...	1233	1333	1433	1533	1633	...	...	1733	1833	1933	2033	...	|	2133	|	2233	...
153	**Milano** Centrale a.	0645	0745	0845	0945	1045	...	1245	1345	1445	1545	1645	...	...	1745	1845	1945	2045	...	2055	2145	2210g	2245	...

		IC **508**		*ICN* **798** ✣B																			
Milano Centrale d.	0615	0620	0715	0658g	0815	...	0915	1115	1215	1315	1415	...	...	1515	1615	1715	1815	...	1915	2015	2115	2215	...
Rho Fiera Milano d.	0625	|	0725	|	0825	...	0925	1125	1225	1325	1425	...	...	1525	1625	1725	1825	...	1925	2025	2125	2225	...
Novara d.	0656	0702	0756	0802	0856	...	0956	1156	1256	1356	1456	...	...	1556	1656	1756	1856	...	1956	2056	2156	2256	...
Vercelli d.	0709	0716	0809	0816	0909	...	1009	1209	1309	1409	1509	...	...	1609	1709	1809	1909	...	2009	2109	2209	2309	...
Santhià d.	0721	|	0821	|	0921	...	1021	1221	1321	1421	1521	...	...	1621	1721	1821	1921	...	2021	2121	2221	2321	...
Chivasso 586 d.	0742	|	0842	|	0942	...	1042	1242	1342	1442	1542	...	...	1642	1742	1842	1942	...	2042	2142	2242	2342	...
Torino Porta Susa 586 a.	0754	0805s	0854	0905s	0954	...	1058	1254	1354	1454	1554	...	...	1654	1754	1854	1954	...	2054	2154	2254	2354	...
Torino Porta Nuova 586 a.	0806	0820	0906	0920	1006	...	1110	1306	1406	1506	1606	...	...	1706	1806	1906	2006	...	2106	2206	2306	0006	...

km	2nd class	Ⓐ	Ⓐ	Ⓒ	Ⓐ	Ⓐ	Ⓒ	Ⓐ	Ⓐ	Ⓒ	Ⓐ	Ⓐ	Ⓒ	Ⓐ	Ⓐ	Ⓒ	Ⓐ	Ⓐ	Ⓒ	Ⓐ	Ⓐ	Ⓐ	Ⓐ	Ⓒ	Ⓐ
0	**Santhià** d.	0648	0750	0750	0850	0931	0950	0950	1150	1250	1250	1350	1450	1450	1550	1650	1650	1750	1850	1850	1932	1950	2050	2050	2150
27	**Biella S. Paola** a.	0710	0818	0815	0918	0949	1015	1018	1218	1315	1318	1418	1515	1518	1618	1715	1718	1818	1915	1918	1949	2018	2118	2115	2218

2nd class	Ⓐ	Ⓒ	Ⓐ	Ⓐ	Ⓒ	Ⓐ	Ⓐ	Ⓒ	Ⓐ	Ⓐ	Ⓐ	Ⓒ	Ⓐ	Ⓐ	Ⓒ	Ⓐ	Ⓐ	Ⓒ	Ⓐ	Ⓐ	Ⓒ	Ⓐ	Ⓐ	Ⓐ
Biella S. Paola d.	0641	0648	0713	0751	0848	0851	0951	1148	1151	1227	1251	1348	1351	1451	1548	1551	1651	1748	1751	1851	1948	1951	2051	2151
Santhià a.	0707	0712	0730	0813	0912	0913	1013	1212	1213	1244	1313	1412	1413	1513	1612	1613	1713	1812	1813	1913	2012	2013	2113	2213

B – 🛏 1, 2 cl., 🛏 2 cl. (4 berth) Torino - Salerno and v.v.

g – Milano **Porta Garibaldi**.

s – Stops to set down only.

u – Stops to pick up only.

✣ – Running days, timings and numbers of *ICN* trains may vary - please check your reservation. For confirmed timings please consult the *Trenitalia* journey planner at www.trenitalia.com

586 TORINO - AOSTA — 2nd class

km																									
		⚒	†	⚒	†	⚒	†	⚒	†	⚒	†	⚒	†	†	⚒	⚒	†	⚒	†	⚒	†	⚒	†	⚒	†
0	**Torino** Porta Nuova 585 d.	0525	0525	0725	0725	0825	0825	0925	0925	1125	1125	1325	1325	1425	1425	1625	1625	1725	1725	1825	1825	2025	2025	2225	2225
6	**Torino** Porta Susa 585 d.	0534	0534	0734	0734	0834	0834	0934	0934	1134	1134	1334	1334	1434	1434	1634	1634	1734	1734	1834	1834	2034	2034	2234	2234
29	Chivasso 585 d.	0552	0552	0752	0752	0852	0852	0952	0952	1152	1152	1352	1352	1452	1452	1652	1652	1752	1752	1852	1852	2052	2052	2252	2352
62	Ivrea a.	0613	0613	0822	0822	0922	0922	1022	1022	1222	1222	1422	1422	1517	1522	1722	1722	1822	1817	1922	1922	2122	2122	2322	2322
62	Ivrea d.	0614	0614	0823	0823	0923	0923	1023	1023	1223	1223	1423	1423	1518	1523	1723	1723	1823	1818	1923	1923	2123	2123	2323	2323
79	Pont Saint Martin d.	0634	0637	0837	0842	0937	0937	1037	1037	1237	1237	1437	1437	1537	1537	1737	1737	1837	1837	1937	1942	2137	2142	2337	2337
91	Verrès d.	0646	0650	0848	0855	0948	0950	1048	1050	1248	1250	1448	1450	1550	1548	1748	1750	1848	1850	1948	1955	2148	2155	2348	2350
104	Chatillon-Saint Vincent d.	0700	0702	0900	0913	1000	1002	1100	1102	1300	1302	1500	1502	1602	1600	1800	1802	1900	1902	2000	2013	2200	2207	0000	0002
129	**Aosta** a.	0720	0722	0920	0934	1020	1022	1120	1122	1320	1322	1520	1522	1622	1620	1820	1822	1920	1922	2020	2034	2220	2227	0020	0022

	†	⚒	⚒	†	†	⚒	†	⚒	⚒	†	⚒	†	⚒	†	⚒	†	⚒	†	⚒	†	†	⚒	⚒	†
Aosta d.	0537	0540	0640	0641	0737	0740	0837	0840	1040	1041	1240	1241	1440	1441	1540	1541	1740	1741	1840	1841	1937	1940	2040	2044
Chatillon-Saint Vincent d.	0558	0600	0700	0702	0758	0800	0858	0900	1100	1102	1300	1302	1500	1502	1600	1602	1800	1802	1900	1902	1958	2000	2100	2106
Verrès d.	0611	0612	0718	0714	0811	0812	0911	0912	1112	1114	1312	1314	1512	1514	1612	1614	1812	1814	1912	1914	2011	2012	2112	2118
Pont Saint Martin d.	0623	0622	0728	0726	0823	0822	0923	0922	1122	1126	1322	1326	1522	1526	1622	1626	1822	1826	1922	1926	2023	2026	2122	2130
Ivrea a.	0640	0640	0740	0740	0840	0840	0940	0940	1140	1140	1340	1340	1540	1540	1640	1640	1840	1840	1940	1940	2040	2040	2140	2140
Ivrea d.	0641	0641	0741	0741	0841	0841	0941	0941	1141	1141	1341	1341	1541	1541	1641	1641	1841	1841	1941	1941	2041	2041	2141	2141
Chivasso 585 a.	0706	0706	0806	0806	0906	0906	1006	1006	1206	1206	1406	1406	1606	1606	1706	1706	1906	1906	2006	2006	2106	2106	2206	2206
Torino Porta Susa 585 a.	0725	0725	0830	0825	0925	0925	1025	1025	1225	1225	1425	1425	1625	1625	1725	1725	1925	1925	2025	2025	2125	2125	2225	2225
Torino Porta Nuova 585 a.	0735	0735	0840	0835	0935	0935	1035	1035	1235	1235	1435	1435	1635	1635	1735	1735	1935	1935	2035	2035	2135	2135	2235	2235

BRIG - STRESA - MILANO 590

EC services convey ✕ and are Ⓡ (inclusive of supplement).

km		EC 35	EC 51	EC 37	EC 47	EC 53	EC 57	EC 39	EC 59	EC 41	
				①–⑤	⑥⑦						
				V c	V e						
	Genève 570 d.	0539	...	0739	0739	...	...	1339	...	1839	...
	Lausanne **570** d.	0618	...	0818	0818	...	...	1418	...	1918	...
	Basel **560** d.	|	0628	|	|	1028	1228	|	1728	|	...
	Bern **560** d.	|	0734	|	|	1134	1334	|	1834	|	...
0	**Brig** 🏛 d.	0744	0844	0944	0944	1244	1444	1544	1944	2044	...
42	**Domodossola** 🏛 § a.	0812	0912	1012	1011u	1312	1512	1612	2012	2112	...
42	**Domodossola** d.	0817	0917	1017	1017u	1317	1517	1617	2017	2117	...
81	Stresa d.	|	0941	1041	1041	|	1541	1641	|	2141	...
124	Gallarate d.	0907	|	|	|	1407	|	|	2107	|	...
167	**Milano** Centrale a.	0940	1040	1140	1140	1440	1640	1740	2140	2240	...

	EC 50	EC 32	EC 52	EC 34	EC 54	EC 36	EC 46	EC 56	EC 42	EC 44
						①–⑤	⑥⑦		⑤⑥	⑦–④
			F			c	e		V	V
Milano Centrale d.	0720	0820	1120	1305	1520	1720	1720	1820	1920	1920
Gallarate d.	0754	|	|	|	1554	|	|	|	1954	1954
Stresa d.	|	0920	1220	1416	|	1820	1820	1920	|	|
Domodossola a.	0843	0943	1243	1443	1643	1843	1843s	1943	2043	2043
Domodossola 🏛 § d.	0848	0948	1248	1448	1648	1848	1847s	1948	2048	2048
Brig 🏛 a.	0916	1014	1316	1514	1716	1914	1914	2016	2114	2114
Bern **560** a.	1024	|	1424	|	1824h	|	|	2124	|	|
Basel **560** a.	1132	|	1532	|	1932	|	|	2232f	|	|
Lausanne **570** a.	...	1142	...	1642	...	2042	2042	...	2242	2310
Genève **570** a.	...	1221	...	1721	...	2121	2121	...	2321	2356

LOCAL TRAINS **DOMODOSSOLA - MILANO** (SEE NOTE ♠)

km						⚒	†	⚒		⚒				⚒			⚒					⚒			⚒
0	**Domodossola** d.	0456	0556	0601	0654	0720	0801	...	0856	...	1001	1201	1256	...	1401	1456	...	1601	1656	1801	1856	...	2001	2056	...
30	Verbània-Pallanza d.	0516	0616	0627	0716	0743	0827	...	0916	...	1027	1227	1316	...	1427	1516	...	1627	1716	1827	1916	...	2027	2116	...
35	Baveno d.	|	|	0632	|	|	0832	...	|	...	1032	1232	|	...	1432	|	...	1632	|	1832	|	...	2032	|	...
39	Stresa d.	0523	0623	0636	0723	0751	0836	...	0923	...	1036	1236	1323	...	1436	1523	...	1636	1723	1836	1923	...	2036	2123	...
56	Arona d.	0537	0637	0704	0737	0806	0906	0906	0937	1006	1106	1306	1337	1406	1506	1537	1606	1706	1737	1906	1937	2006	2106	2137	2206
82	Gallarate d.	0559	0659	0733	0759	0835	0935	0935	0959	1035	1135	1335	1359	1435	1535	1559	1635	1735	1759	1935	1959	2035	2135	2159	2235
89	Busto Arsizio FS d.	0605	0705	0739	0805	0841	0941	0941	1005	1041	1141	1341	1405	1441	1541	1605	1641	1741	1805	1941	2005	2041	2141	2205	2241
112	Rho-Fiera Milano d.	0621	0721	0801	0821	0901	1001	1001	1021	1101	1200	1401	1421	1501	1601	1621	1701	1801	1821	2001	2020	2101	2201	2221	2301
123	**Milano** P Garibaldi a.	|	|	0814	|	0914	1014	1014	|	1114	1214	1414	|	1514	1614	|	1714	1814	|	2014	|	2114	2214	|	2314
125	**Milano** Centrale a.	0637	0737	...	0835	...	...	...	1035	...	...	...	1435	...	...	1635	...	...	1837	...	2037	...	...	2235	...

					⚒			⚒			⚒			⚒				⚒			⚒		⚒	
Milano Centrale d.	...	0725	...	0825	...	0925	...	...	1325	...	...	1525	...	...	1725	...	1825	...	1925	...	...	2125	...	...
Milano Porta Garibaldi d.	0612	|	0746	|	0846	|	1146	1246	|	1346	1446	|	1546	1646	|	1746	|	1846	|	1946	2046	|	2146	2246
Rho-Fiera Milano d.	0623	0736	0757	0836	0857	0936	1157	1257	1336	1357	1457	1536	1557	1657	1736	1757	1836	1857	1936	1957	2057	2136	2157	2257
Busto Arsizio FS d.	0644	0754	0818	0854	0918	0954	1218	1318	1354	1418	1518	1554	1618	1718	1754	1818	1854	1918	1954	2018	2118	2154	2218	2318
Gallarate d.	0650	0800	0824	0900	0924	1000	1224	1324	1400	1424	1524	1600	1624	1724	1800	1824	1900	1924	2000	2024	2124	2200	2224	2324
Arona d.	0721	0820	0854	0920	0954	1020	1254	1354	1420	1454	1554	1620	1654	1754	1820	1854	1920	1954	2020	2054	2154	2220	2254	2354
Stresa d.	0741	0833	0915	0933	...	1033	1315	...	1433	1515	...	1633	1715	...	1833	1915	1933	...	2033	2115	...	2233	...	...
Baveno d.	0745	|	0919	|	...	|	1319	...	|	1519	...	|	1719	...	|	1919	|	...	|	2119	...	|	...	...
Verbània-Pallanza d.	0750	0842	0924	0942	...	1042	1324	...	1442	1524	...	1642	1724	...	1842	1924	1942	...	2042	2124	...	2242	...	...
Domodossola a.	0823	0904	0959	1004	...	1104	1359	...	1504	1551	...	1704	1759	...	1904	1959	2004	...	2104	2159	...	2304	...	...

OTHER TRAINS **BRIG - DOMODOSSOLA**

km						Ⓐ						③–⑦								Ⓐ				
0	**Brig** 🚗 d.	0022	...	0522	...	0622	...	0722	...	0922	...	1122	...	1322	...	1522	...	1722	...	1822	...	1922	...	2222
23	Iselle di Trasquera § 🚗 d.	0036	...	0536	...	0636	...	0736	...	0936	...	1136	...	1336	...	1536	...	1736	...	1836	...	1936	...	2236
42	**Domodossola** a.	0054	...	0554	...	0654	...	0754	...	0954	...	1154	...	1354	...	1554	...	1754	...	1854	...	1954	...	2254

					Ⓐ						③–⑦								Ⓐ				
Domodossola d.	0434	...	0558	...	0658	...	0758	...	0958	...	1158	...	1358	...	1558	...	1758	...	1858	...	1958	...	2258
Iselle di Trasquera § 🚗 d.	0452	...	0615	...	0715	...	0815	...	1015	...	1215	...	1415	...	1615	...	1815	...	1915	...	2015	...	2316
Brig 🚗 a.	0510	...	0632	...	0732	...	0832	...	1032	...	1232	...	1432	...	1632	...	1832	...	1932	...	2032	...	2333

F – To Frankfurt (Tables **560** and **912**).
V – To / from Venezia (Table **605**).
c – Not Jan. 2, Apr. 7, 10, May 18, 29.
e – Also Jan. 2, Apr. 7, 10, May 18, 29.
f – 2237 on ⑦–④ from Jan. 30.
h – 1828 on ⑥⑦ (also Swiss public holidays).

s – Calls to set down only.
u – Calls to pick up only.
♠ – Most services (2) only. Certain trains are operated by Trenord.
§ – Ticket point is **Iselle**.
🚗 – Car-carrying shuttle available. www.bls.ch.

2nd class — DOMODOSSOLA and ARONA - NOVARA - ALESSANDRIA 591

km		Ⓐ	⚒			⚒	⚒				
0	**Domodossola** d.	0520	0617	0648	1245	1343	1545	1747	1848	...	...
38	Omegna d.	0614	0657	0752	1337	1444	1641	1842	1940	...	...
44	Pettenasco d.	0621	0704	0759	1343	1451	1648	1849	1947	...	...
47	Orta-Miasino d.	0626	0712	0804	1351	1456	1653	1854	1952	...	...
60	Borgomanero d.	0641	0724	0815	1406	1507	1704	1905	2004	...	...
90	**Novara** a.	0716	0754	0843	1437	1541	1740	1943	2039	...	...

	⚒		†	⚒			⚒		
Novara d.	0546	0645	1223	1345	1515	1734	1915	...	...
Borgomanero d.	0621	0725	1249	1420	1550	1811	1950	...	...
Orta-Miasino d.	0645	0740	1306	1432	1608	1826	2006	...	...
Pettenasco d.	0649	0744	1311	1437	1613	1831	2011	...	...
Omegna d.	0656	0751	1318	1443	1619	1843	2018	...	...
Domodossola a.	0748	0849	1417	1542	1714	1938	2114	...	...

ARONA - NOVARA

km		⚒	⚒	†A	Ⓐ	⚒	⚒	⚒	†A	⚒	†
0	**Arona** d.	0648	0748	0915	1348	1548	1748	1848	1915	1948	2115
20	Oleggio d.	0712	0812	0932	1412	1612	1812	1912	1932	2012	2132
37	**Novara** a.	0732	0832	0948	1432	1632	1832	1932	1948	2032	2148

	⚒	Ⓐ	†B	⚒	⚒	⚒	†B	⚒	⚒	†
Novara d.	0650	0750	0812	1423	1523	1723	1812	1823	1923	2012
Oleggio d.	0713	0813	0826	1441	1541	1741	1826	1841	1941	2026
Arona a.	0739	0839	0845	1512	1612	1812	1845	1912	2012	2045

NOVARA - ALESSANDRIA

km		⚒	⚒	†	⚒	†	⑥	Ⓐ🚌	Ⓐ	⑥	Ⓐ🚌	⚒	⚒	†	⚒	⚒	⚒	†	⚒	⚒	Ⓐ	†	⚒	⚒	Ⓐ
0	**Novara** d.	0608	0708	...	0808	0808	0908	0908	...	1208	1208	...	1344	1408	1423	1608	1708	...	1727	1827	...	1908	...	2027	...
25	Mortara a.	0632	0732	...	0832	0832	0932	0950	...	1235	1249	...	1411	1432	1452	1632	1732	...	1754	1854	...	1932	...	2054	...
25	Mortara d.	...	0732	0732	0832	0832	0932	...	1000	...	...	1328	...	1432	1452	...	1732	1732	...	...	1900	1932	2000	...	2100
67	**Alessandria** a.	...	0814	0814	0914	0914	1014	...	1042	...	...	1414	...	1514	1532	...	1814	1814	...	...	1943	2020	2043	...	2143

	⚒	⚒	Ⓐ	⚒	†	⚒	⚒	Ⓐ	⚒		⚒	⚒	⚒	†		⚒	Ⓐ	Ⓐ						
Alessandria d.	0511	...	0608	...	0645	...	0650	0723	...	1245	...	1545	...	1645	...	1845	1945	2045	...	...	...	...	...	...
Mortara a.	0555	...	0651	...	0728	...	0736	0753	...	1328	...	1633	...	1728	...	1928	2028	2128	...	...	...	...	...	...
Mortara d.	...	0612	...	0705	0728	0728	...	...	0828	1328	1428	...	1728	1728	1828	1928	2028	2128	...	...	...	...	...	...
Novara a.	...	0640	...	0733	0752	0752	...	...	0852	1352	1452	...	1752	1752	1852	1952	2052	2152	...	...	...	...	...	...

A – Additional services Arona - Novara at 1115†, 1315†, 1515†, 1715†.

B – Additional services Novara - Arona at 1012†, 1212†, 1412†, 1612†.

2nd class — ACQUI TERME 592

km					⚒	⚒			⚒	⚒	
0	**Alessandria** d.	...	0740	0935	1140	...	1340	1540	1740	1940	...
34	**Acqui Terme** d.	0545	0817	1017	1217	1324	1417	1617	1817	2017	...
84	S. Giuseppe di Cairo d.	0652	0922	1122	1322	1437	1522	1722	1922	2122	...
105	**Savona** a.	0717	0947	1150	1347	1500	1547	1748	1947	2147	...

	⚒	⚒	⚒	†			⚒			
Savona d.	0611	0800	0959	1010	...	1207	1407	1611	1811	2000
S. Giuseppe di Cairo d.	0639	0839	1039	1039	...	1239	1439	1639	1839	2039
Acqui Terme a.	0736	0937	1136	1136	...	1336	1536	1736	1936	2137
Alessandria a.	0820	...	1220	1220	...	1420	1620	1820	2020	...

km			⚒						ⒶC		
0	**Acqui Terme** d.	0607	0703	0917	...	1217	1317	1617	1717	1817	2040
59	**Genova** P Principe a.	0727	0825	1043	...	1343	1443	1743	1843	1942	2157
61	**Genova** Brignole a.	0735	0833	1051	...	1351	1451	1751	1851	1950	2206

			⚒			ⒶD				
Genova Brignole d.	0706	0913	1013	...	1313	1413	1613	1813	1913	2035
Genova P Principe d.	0714	0921	1021	...	1321	1421	1621	1821	1921	2043
Acqui Terme a.	0835	1039	1139	...	1439	1539	1739	1939	2039	2202

C – Additional services Acqui Terme - Genova Brignole at 0515Ⓐ, 0740Ⓐ, 1417Ⓐ.

D – Additional services Genova Brignole - Acqui Terme at 0600Ⓐ, 1213Ⓐ, 1713Ⓐ.

593 MILANO - COLICO - TIRANO and COLICO - CHIAVENNA

Trenord

Additional local trains are available Milano Porta Garibaldi - Lecco and v.v. (line S8), and Lecco - Sondrio and v.v.

km																							
		2	⚒ 🚌											🚌		c	c	🚌	c	🚌	2 e	2 e	
0	**Milano** Centrale d.	...	...	0620	0720	0820	0920	1020	1220	1320	1420	1620	1720	...	1820	1920	2020	...	2120	...	2252	2322	...
12	Monza d.	...	...	0632	0732	0832	0932	1032	1232	1332	1432	1632	1732	...	1832	1932	2032	...	2132	...	2309	2339	...
50	Lecco d.	...	...	0702	0802	0902	1002	1102	1302	1402	1502	1702	1802	...	1902	2002	2102	...	2201	2206	2354	0024	...
72	Varenna-Esino d.	...	...	0725	0825	0925	1025	1125	1325	1425	1525	1725	1825	...	1925	2025	2125	...	...	2247	...	...	...
75	Bellano-Tartavalle Terme d.	...	...	0730	0830	0930	1030	1130	1330	1430	1530	1730	1830	...	1930	2030	2130	...	...	2254	...	...	...
89	**Colico** a.	...	...	0746	0846	0946	1046	1146	1346	1446	1546	1746	1846	...	1946	2046	2146	...	...	2317	...	...	...
130	Sondrio a.	0520	0641	0820	0920	1020	1120	1220	1420	1520	1620	1820	1921	1930	2020	2119	2221	2225	...	0013	...	...	...
156	**Tirano** a.	0555	0722	0852	0952	1052	1205	1252	1452	1605	1652	1852	...	2012	2052	2152	...	2307	...	...	...	...	...
		† 🚌	† c	⚒ 🚌	⚒																2	2	
	Tirano d.	...	...	...	...	...	0612	0700	...	0908	1108	1208	1308	1508	1608	...	1708	1808	1908	2008	...	...	...
	Sondrio d.	0334	...	0356	...	0530	0641	0741	...	0941	1141	1241	1341	1541	1641	...	1741	1841	1941	2041	...	...	...
	Colico d.	0440	...	0452	...	0601	0715	0815	...	1015	1215	1315	1415	1615	1715	...	1815	1915	2015	2115	...	...	...
	Bellano-Tartavalle Terme d.	0503	...	0515	...	0615	0730	0830	...	1030	1230	1330	1430	1630	1730	...	1830	1930	2030	2130	...	...	...
	Varenna-Esino d.	0510	...	0522	...	0620	0735	0835	...	1035	1235	1335	1435	1635	1735	...	1835	1935	2035	2135	...	...	...
	Lecco d.	0544	0549	0556	0601	0654	0801	0901	...	1101	1301	1401	1501	1701	1801	...	1901	2001	2101	2201	2206	2306	...
	Monza d.	...	0623	...	0626	0727	0827	0927	...	1127	1327	1427	1527	1727	1827	...	1927	2027	2127	2227	2251	2351	...
	Milano Centrale a.	...	0640	...	0640	0740	0840	0940	...	1140	1340	1440	1540	1740	1840	...	1940	2040	2140	2240	2308**p**	0008**p**	...

COLICO - CHIAVENNA

2nd class

km																								
		🚌	⚒	†	⚒				† c															🚌
0	**Colico** d.	0553	0618	0653	0701	...	0753	0853	0930	0953	...	1053	1153	1253	1353	...	1453	1553	1653	1753	...	1853	1953	2053
27	**Chiavenna** a.	0629	0649	0725	0732	...	0825	0925	1006	1025	...	1125	1225	1325	1425	...	1525	1625	1725	1825	...	1925	2025	2129

	Ⓐ 🚌	⚒ 🚌	⚒	†	⚒	†	⚒													† c			
Chiavenna d.	0519	0544	0614	0635	0657	0735	0740	0835	...	0935	1035	1135	1235	...	1335	1435	1535	1635	1735	1745	1835	1935	2031
Colico a.	0555	0620	0646	0707	0729	0807	0807	0907	...	1007	1107	1207	1307	...	1407	1507	1607	1707	1807	1830	1907	2007	2107

b – Runs 25 minutes later on school days.
c – Not Feb. 5, 19, Mar. 19, Apr. 2.
e – Not Feb. 4, 5, 18, 19, Mar. 18, 19, Apr. 1, 2.
p – Milano **Porta Garibaldi**.

🚌 TIRANO - EDOLO

	⚒	⚒	⚒	⚒	⚒ b		⚒	⚒	⚒	⚒	⚒
Tirano Stazione d.	0840	1040	1245	1435	1635	**Edolo** d.	0615	0915	1115	1515	1715
Aprica S Pietro d.	0920	1120	1320	1510	1715	Aprica S Pietro d.	0650	0940	1140	1540	1740
Edolo a.	0945	1145	...	1540	1745	**Tirano** Stazione a.	0730	1020	1220	1620	1820

595 INNSBRUCK - BOLZANO / BOZEN - VERONA - BOLOGNA

For high-speed trains Bolzano - Verona - Milano / Bologna / Roma and v.v. see Table **600**. For other local trains see next page.

km																							
		2	2 ⚒	2	2	2 ⚒	*EC* **81** ①–⑤ ✕ ♠	*EC* **1281** ⑥⑦ ✕ ♠	2	2	*EC* **83** ✕ ♠♦	2		*EC* **85** ✕ ♠	2	*EC* **87** ✕ ♠	2	*EC* **89** ✕ ♠	2	2	*ICN* **763** ⑥⑦ ❖♦	*EC* **185** ✕ ♦	2
	München Hbf **951** d.	...	...	...	...	...	0734	0734	...	...	0934	...	...	1132	...	1334	...	1534	...	...	...	...	...
0	**Innsbruck** Hbf d.	...	...	...	0549	...	0924	0924	...	...	1124	...	...	1324	...	1524	...	1724	...	...	...	2004	2105
37	**Brennero / Brenner** 🏨 a.	...	...	...	0629	...	1000	1000	...	...	1200	...	...	1400	...	1600	...	1800	...	...	...	2040	2145
37	**Brennero / Brenner** 🏨 d.	...	...	0608	0632	0708	1014	1010	1038	...	1214	1300	...	1414	1508	1614	1708	1814	...	1908	...	2050	2151
60	Vipiteno / Sterzing d.	...	...	0627	0652	0727	|	|	1057	...	|	1320	...	|	1527	|	1727	|	...	1927	...	2116	2210
78	Fortezza / Franzensfeste d.	...	0536	0645	0709	0745	1046	1046	1115	...	1246	1338	...	1446	1545	1646	1745	1846	...	1945	...	2134	2228
89	Bressanone / Brixen d.	...	0545	0655	0719	0755	1056	1056	1125	...	1256	1348	...	1456	1555	1656	1755	1856	...	1955	...	2144	2238
99	Chiusa / Klausen d.	...	0553	0703	0728	0803	|	|	1133	...	|	1356	...	|	1603	|	1803	|	...	2003	...	|	2246
127	**Bolzano / Bozen** a.	...	0617	0729	0753	0829	1127	1127	1159	...	1327	1423	...	1527	1629	1727	1829	1927	...	2029	...	2215	2310
127	**Bolzano / Bozen** 600 d.	0500	0620	0731	...	0831	1131	1131	...	1231	1331	1425	...	1531	1631	1731	1831	1931	...	2031	2130	...	2315
143	Ora / Auer d.	0512	0633	0743	...	0843	|	|	...	1243	|	1437	...	|	1643	|	1843	|	...	2043	2144	...	2331
165	Mezzocorona d.	0525	0650	0756	...	0856	|	|	...	1256	|	1450	...	|	1656	|	1856	|	...	2056	2200	...	2351
182	Trento 600 d.	0537	0705	0810	...	0910	1204	1204	...	1310	1404	1504	...	1604	1710	1804	1910	2004	...	2110	2216	...	0009
206	Rovereto 600 d.	0551	0720	0825	...	0925	1219	1219	...	1325	1419	1519	...	1619	1725	1819	1925	2019	...	2125	2232	...	...
274	**Verona** Porta Nuova 600 a.	0646	0814	0914	...	1014	1256	1256	...	1414	1458	1614	...	1658	1814	1858	2014	2056	←	2214	2316	...	...
274	**Verona** Porta Nuova 600 d.	0703	...	...	...	...	1313	1313	...	1426	1522	1626	...	1710	1826	1915	→	...	2104	...	2336	...	...
388	**Bologna** Centrale 600 a.	0837	...	...	...	...	1410	|	...	1558	1619	1758	...	|	1958	2016	...	...	2230	...	⊖	...	...
	Venezia Santa Lucia **605** a.	...	...	...	...	...	...	1428	...	...	...	...	...	1825	...	...	...	...	...	...	|	...	...
	Roma Termini **620** a.	...	...	...	...	...	...	...	...	...	...	...	...	...	...	...	...	...	...	...	0606	...	...

	2 Ⓐ		2	*EC* **184** ✕ ♦	*ICN* **764** ⑤⑥ ❖♦	2	2	*EC* **88** ✕ ♠	*EC* **86** ✕ ♠	2 Ⓐ	2 Ⓒ		*EC* **84** ✕ ♠♦	2 Ⓐ	*EC* **82** ✕ ♠	2	*EC* **80** ①–⑤ ✕ ♠	*EC* **1280** ⑥⑦ ✕ ♠	2	2 Ⓐ	2	2
Roma Termini **620** d.	...	...	...	...	2300	...	...	...	...	...	...	...	...	...	...	...	...	...	...	...	...	...
Venezia S Lucia **605** d.	...	...	...	...	|	...	...	...	...	...	...	...	...	...	1335	...	...	1535	...	...	...	...
Bologna Centrale 600 d.	...	...	...	...	●	0605	...	0745	...	...	1010	...	1152	1205	|	1410	1550	|	1610	...	1810	2005
Verona Porta Nuova 600 a.	...	...	...	...	0530	0743	...	0847	...	...	1135	...	1247	1335	1450	1535	1645	1650	1735	...	1935	2135
Verona Porta Nuova 600 d.	...	...	...	...	0600	...	0750	0901	1101	1150	1150	...	1301	1350	1501	1550	1701	1701	1750	...	1950	2155
Rovereto 600 d.	...	...	...	...	0701	...	0839	0943	1143	1239	1239	...	1343	1439	1543	1639	1743	1743	1839	...	2039	2246
Trento 600 d.	0528	...	0640	...	0717	...	0854	0959	1159	1254	1254	...	1359	1454	1559	1654	1759	1759	1854	...	2054	2301
Mezzocorona d.	0544	...	0653	...	0730	...	0905	|	|	1305	1305	...	|	1505	|	1705	|	|	1905	...	2105	2312
Ora / Auer d.	0603	...	0711	...	0747	...	0919	|	|	1319	1319	...	|	1519	|	1719	|	|	1919	...	2119	2326
Bolzano / Bozen 600 a.	0618	...	0728	...	0805	...	0930	1031	1231	1330	1330	...	1431	1530	1631	1730	1831	1831	1930	...	2130	2339
Bolzano / Bozen d.	0632	...	0732	0750	...	...	0932	1034	1234	1332	1332	...	1434	1532	1634	1732	1834	1834	1932	2032	2132	...
Chiusa / Klausen d.	0655	...	0755	|	...	...	0955	|	|	1355	1355	...	|	1555	|	1755	|	|	1955	2055	2155	...
Bressanone / Brixen d.	0703	...	0803	0818	...	...	1003	1104	1304	1403	1403	...	1504	1603	1704	1803	1904	1904	2003	2103	2203	...
Fortezza / Franzensfeste d.	0715	...	0815	0829	...	...	1015	1115	1315	1415	1415	...	1515	1615	1715	1815	1915	1915	2015	2115	2215	...
Vipiteno / Sterzing d.	0733	...	0833	0847	...	...	1033	|	|	1433	1433	...	|	1633	|	1833	|	|	2033	2133	2233	...
Brennero / Brenner 🏨 a.	0752	...	0852	0910	...	...	1056	1148	1348	1456	1456	...	1548	1656	1748	1856	1948	1948	2056	2151	2256	...
Brennero / Brenner 🏨 d.	...	...	0902	0920	...	...	...	1200	1400	...	...	...	1600	...	1800	...	2000	2000	...	2154	...	...
Innsbruck Hbf a.	...	...	0938	0956	...	...	...	1236	1436	...	...	...	1636	...	1836	...	2036	2036	...	2230	...	...
München Hbf **951** a.	...	...	...	...	...	...	...	1427	1627	...	...	...	1827	...	2026	...	2227	2227	...	...	...	...

♦ – NOTES (LISTED BY TRAIN NUMBER)

83 – (12) ✕ München - Bolgona (- Rimini a. 1733 May 25 - June 10).
84 – (12) ✕ (May 26 - Sept. 10: Rimini d. 1034 -) Bolgona - München.
184 – (12) ✕ Bolzano - Innsbruck - Wien. Train classification *RJX* in Austria (Tables **950** / **951**).
185 – (12) ✕ Wien - Innsbruck - Bolzano. Train classification *RJX* in Austria (Tables **950** / **951**).
763 – From Bolzano on ⑥⑦: 🛏 1, 2 cl., ▬ 2 cl. (4 berth) (2) Bolzano - Roma.
764 – From Roma on ⑤⑥: 🛏 1, 2 cl., ▬ 2 cl. (4 berth) (2) Roma - Bolzano.

⊖ – Via Orvieto (d. 0510).
● – Via Orte (d. 2341) and Orvieto (d. 0013).
♠ – Also available to passengers without reservation.
❖ – Running days, timings and numbers of *ICN* trains may vary - please check your reservation. For confirmed timings please consult the *Trenitalia* journey planner at www.trenitalia.com.

2nd class INNSBRUCK - BRENNERO - BOLZANO - MERANO, VERONA and BOLOGNA 595

Local trains - for long distance trains and through trains Brennero - Bolzano - Verona - Bologna see previous page.
Innsbruck - Brennero trains are subject to alteration on and around Austrian holiday dates.

INNSBRUCK - BRENNERO

km																								
			①–⑥	A				①–⑥													B	①–⑥		
0	**Innsbruck** Hbf d.	0005	0519	0549	0619	0649	0749	0819	0849	0949	1049	1149	1249	1349	1449	1549	1649	1749	1849	1949	2105	2205	2305	...
18	Matrei d.	0022	0537	0607	0636	0706	0806	0836	0906	1006	1106	1206	1306	1406	1506	1606	1706	1806	1906	2006	2123	2222	2322	...
23	Steinach in Tirol d.	0027	0542	0612	0641	0711	0811	0841	0911	1011	1111	1211	1311	1411	1511	1611	1711	1811	1911	2011	2128	2227	2327	...
37	**Brennero / Brenner** a.	0044	0559	0629	0658	0728	0828	0858	0928	1028	1128	1228	1328	1428	1528	1628	1728	1828	1928	2028	2145	2244	2344	...

		①–⑥		①–⑥			B														C		
Brennero / Brenner d.	0527	0558	0628	0703	0733	0833	0902	0933	1033	1133	...	1233	1333	1433	1533	1633	1733	1833	1933	2033	2154	2303	...
Steinach in Tirol d.	0546	0617	0647	0720	0750	0850	0917	0950	1050	1150	...	1250	1350	1450	1550	1650	1750	1850	1950	2050	2209	2320	...
Matrei d.	0550	0621	0651	0724	0754	0854	0921	0954	1054	1154	...	1254	1354	1454	1554	1654	1754	1854	1954	2054	2213	2324	...
Innsbruck Hbf a.	0607	0638	0708	0742	0811	0911	0938	1013	1111	1213	...	1311	1413	1511	1613	1711	1813	1911	2011	2111	2230	2341	...

BRENNERO - BOLZANO - MERANO

km																								
		⚒	Ⓐ		⚒			Ⓐ	⚒	Ⓒ									⚒				D	
0	**Brennero / Brenner** d.	0534	...	0608	...	0708	0738	0808	...	0838	0938	1038	1138	1238	1338	1438	1538	1638	...	1738	1838	1938	...	2108
23	Vipiteno / Sterzing d.	0553	...	0627	...	0727	0757	0827	...	0857	0957	1057	1157	1257	1357	1457	1557	1657	...	1757	1857	1957	...	2127
41	Fortezza / Franzensfeste d.	0611	0640	0645	0715	0745	0815	0845	...	0915	1015	1115	1215	1315	1415	1515	1615	1715	...	1815	1915	2015	2122	2145
52	Bressanone / Brixen d.	0621	0649	0655	0725	0755	0825	0855	...	0925	1025	1125	1225	1325	1425	1525	1625	1725	...	1825	1925	2025	2130	2155
62	Chiusa / Klausen d.	0629	0657	0703	0733	0803	0833	0903	...	0933	1033	1133	1233	1333	1433	1533	1633	1733	...	1833	1933	2033	2138	2203
90	**Bolzano / Bozen** a.	0653	0723	0729	0759	0829	0859	0929	...	0959	1059	1159	1259	1359	1459	1559	1659	1759	...	1859	1959	2059	2159	2229
90	**Bolzano / Bozen** ◧ d.	0655	0735	...	0801	...	0901	...	0935	1001	1101	1201	1301	1401	1501	1601	1701	1801	1835	1901	2001	2101	2203	...
122	**Merano / Meran** ◧ a.	0743	0815	...	0845	...	0945	...	1015	1045	1145	1245	1345	1445	1545	1645	1745	1845	1915	1944	2044	2144	2244	...

	⚒	⚒	†	⚒		⚒			Ⓒ								Ⓐ				C		
Merano / Meran ◧ d.	...	0600	...	0633	0713	0746	0816	0916	1016	1116	1216	1316	1416	1516	1616	1716	1746	1816	1916	...	1946	2046	2146
Bolzano / Bozen ◧ a.	...	0650	...	0718	0800	0826	0900	1000	1100	1200	1300	1400	1500	1600	1700	1800	1825	1900	2000	...	2027	2126	2226
Bolzano / Bozen d.	0602	0702	0702	...	0802	...	0902	1002	1102	1202	1302	1402	1502	1602	1701	1802	1827	1902	...	2002	2032	...	...
Chiusa / Klausen d.	0625	0725	0725	...	0825	...	0925	1025	1125	1225	1325	1425	1525	1625	1722	1825	1849	1925	...	2025	2055	...	...
Bressanone / Brixen d.	0633	0733	0733	...	0833	...	0933	1033	1133	1233	1333	1433	1533	1633	1730	1833	1857	1933	...	2033	2103	...	...
Fortezza / Franzensfeste d.	0645	0745	0745	...	0845	...	0945	1045	1145	1245	1345	1445	1545	1645	1745	1845	1907	1945	...	2045	2115	...	...
Vipiteno / Sterzing d.	0703	0803	0803	...	0903	...	1003	1103	1203	1303	1403	1503	1603	1703	1803	1903	1932	2003	...	2103	2133	...	...
Brennero / Brenner a.	0722	0822	0822	...	0922	...	1022	1122	1222	1322	1422	1522	1622	1722	1822	1922	1958	2022	...	2122	2151	...	...

BOLZANO - PLAN 🚌

Service 350 (♥)																							
	⚒																						
Bolzano / Bozen bus station d.	0628	0728	...	0828	0928	...	1028	1128	...	1228	1328	...	1428	1528	...	1628	1728	...	1828	1928	...	...	...
Ponte Gardena / Waidbruck d.	0657	0757	...	0857	0957	...	1057	1157	...	1257	1357	...	1457	1557	...	1657	1757	...	1857	1957	...	...	...
Ortisei / St Ulrich d.	0727	0827	...	0927	1027	...	1127	1227	...	1327	1427	...	1527	1627	...	1727	1827	...	1927	2027	...	...	...
Santa / St Cristina d.	0736	0836	...	0936	1036	...	1136	1236	...	1336	1436	...	1536	1636	...	1736	1836	...	1936	2036	...	...	...
Selva / Wolkenstein d.	0748	0848	...	0948	1048	...	1148	1248	...	1348	1448	...	1548	1648	...	1748	1848	...	1948	2048	...	...	...
Plan a.	0752	0852	...	0952	1052	...	1152	1252	...	1352	1452	...	1552	1652	...	1752	1852	...	1952	2052	...	...	...

Service 350 (♥)																							
Plan d.	0634	0732	...	0834	0934	...	1034	1134	...	1234	1334	...	1434	1534	...	1634	1734	...	1834	...	...	...	...
Selva / Wolkenstein d.	0637	0735	...	0837	0937	...	1037	1137	...	1237	1337	...	1437	1537	...	1637	1737	...	1837	...	...	...	...
Santa / St Cristina d.	0649	0749	...	0849	0949	...	1049	1149	...	1249	1349	...	1449	1549	...	1649	1749	...	1849	...	...	...	...
Ortisei / St Ulrich d.	0701	0801	...	0901	1001	...	1101	1201	...	1301	1401	...	1501	1601	...	1701	1801	...	1901	...	...	...	...
Ponte Gardena / Waidbruck a.	0729	0829	...	0929	1029	...	1129	1229	...	1329	1429	...	1529	1629	...	1729	1829	...	1929	...	...	...	...
Bolzano / Bozen bus station a.	0757	0857	...	0957	1057	...	1157	1257	...	1357	1457	...	1557	1657	...	1757	1857	...	1957	...	...	...	...

BOLZANO - VERONA

km																								
		Ⓐ	⚒		Ⓐ	Ⓒ		Ⓒ		⚒		Ⓐ			Ⓐ		Ⓐ	Ⓐ			Ⓐ		†	
0	**Bolzano / Bozen** d.	0536	0634	0736	0836	0936	...	1031	1136	1236	1336	1434	...	1536	1636	1736	1836	1906	...	1936	2036	...	2136	...
16	Ora / Auer d.	0555	0651	0755	0855	0955	...	1043	1155	1255	1355	1452	...	1555	1655	1755	1855	1922	...	1955	2055	...	2155	...
38	Mezzocorona d.	0616	0712	0816	0916	1016	...	1056	1216	1316	1416	1513	...	1616	1716	1816	1916	1942	...	2016	2116	...	2216	...
55	Trento d.	0633	0733	0833	0937	1033	...	1110	1233	1333	1433	1535	...	1633	1733	1833	1933	1955	...	2033	2133	...	2233	...
79	Rovereto d.	0647	0747	0847	0951	1047	...	1125	1247	1347	1447	1549	...	1647	1747	1847	1947	2010	...	2047	2147	...	2247	...
147	**Verona** Porta Nuova a.	0751	0854	0954	1058	1151	...	1214	1351	1454	1551	1655	...	1751	1854	1951	2051	2108	...	2151	2251	...	2348	...

	⚒	⚒	Ⓐ	⚒			Ⓐ	⑥	†	⚒			⚒		Ⓐ			Ⓐ		Ⓐ		Ⓐ	
Verona Porta Nuova d.	0520	0606	0627	0706	...	0806	0850	0906	0953	1106	...	1206	1306	1406	1506	1606	...	1706	1806	1906	2006	2106	...
Rovereto d.	0607	0707	0732	0807	...	0907	0937	1007	1042	1207	...	1307	1407	1507	1607	1707	...	1807	1907	2007	2107	2207	...
Trento d.	0632	0732	0749	0832	...	0932	0952	1032	1057	1232	...	1332	1432	1532	1632	1732	...	1832	1932	2032	2132	2232	...
Mezzocorona d.	0646	0746	0802	0846	...	0946	1005	1046	1108	1246	...	1346	1446	1546	1646	1746	...	1846	1946	2046	2146	2246	...
Ora / Auer d.	0706	0806	0817	0906	...	1006	1020	1106	1122	1306	...	1406	1506	1606	1706	1806	...	1906	2006	2106	2206	2306	...
Bolzano / Bozen a.	0724	0823	0830	0923	...	1023	1039	1123	1133	1323	...	1423	1523	1623	1723	1823	...	1923	2023	2123	2223	2327	...

VERONA - BOLOGNA

km																								
			⚒			Ⓒ					†			⚒			⚒							
0	**Verona** Porta Nuova d.	0518	0605	...	0703	1026	...	1226	1326	...	1345	1426	...	1514	1626	...	1717	1826	...	2104	...	...	...	...
114	**Bologna** Centrale a.	0653	0739	...	0837	1151	...	1358	1458	...	1524	1558	...	1655	1758	...	1857	1958	...	2230	...	...	...	...

					Ⓒ		⚒	Ⓐ		Ⓒ						Ⓑ							
Bologna Centrale d.	0605	0710	...	0810	1010	...	1110	1205	...	1210	1410	...	1610	1810	...	1910	2005	...	2105	...	...	...	...
Verona Porta Nuova a.	0743	0835	...	0935	1135	...	1240	1335	...	1338	1535	...	1735	1935	...	2048	2135	...	2235	...	...	...	...

A – (2) Innsbruck - Bolzano.
B – (2) Innsbruck - Trento and v.v.
C – (2) Merano - Innsbruck.
D – (2) Lienz - Merano (Table **597**).

◧ – Additional trains: Bolzano - Merano at 0545 ⚒, 0624 ⚒, 0655 †, 0735 ⑥, 0801 †, 0835 ⚒, 1135 ⚒, 1335 ⚒, 1635 Ⓐ; Merano - Bolzano at 0846 ⚒, 1046 ⚒, 1246 ⚒, 1446 ⚒, 1946 Ⓐ.

♥ – For more information www.suedtirolmobil.info.

596 TRENTO - MALÉ - MEZZANA

Trentino Trasporti

Service until June 23. Mezzocorona Ferrovia is adjacent to Mezzocorona FS station. Operator: Trentino Trasporti www.trentinotrasporti.it.

km		⚒	⚒	⚒	⚒	⚒	⚒	⚒	⚒	⚒	⚒	⚒	⚒	⚒	⚒	⚒	†	†	†	†	†	†	†	†
0	**Trento** d.	0612	0710	0810	0932	1021	1104	1206	1244	1345	1555	1633	1718	1727	1842	1935	0610	0810	1010	1210	1410	1610	1810	2010
17	Mezzocorona Ferrovia d.	0639	0738	0839	0958	1047	1130	1232	1311	1414	1622	1700	1739	1754	1908	2001	0637	0837	1037	1237	1437	1637	1837	2037
22	Mezzolombardo d.	0647	0753	0847	1006	1055	1138	1240	1319	1422	1631	1708	1746	1802	1916	2008	0644	0844	1044	1244	1444	1644	1844	2044
45	Cles d.	0729	0831	0925	1043	1132	1222	1320	1357	1459	1709	1746	1819	1840	1953	2044	0722	0922	1122	1322	1522	1722	1922	2122
56	Malé d.	0755	0857	0951	1109	1157	1250	1347	1421	1527	1736	1810	1840	1904	2016	2104	0746	0946	1146	1346	1546	1746	1944	2144
66	**Mezzana** a.	...	0913	1007	1125	1213	1309	1408	...	1544	1753	...	1857	...	...	...	0803	1003	1203	1403	1603	1803	...	...

	⚒	⚒	⚒	⚒	⚒	⚒	⚒	⚒	⚒	⚒	⚒	⚒	⚒	⚒	⚒	⚒	†	†	†	†	†	†	†	†
Mezzana d.	...	0600	...	0657	...	0933	1036	1137	1230	1346	1425	...	1619	1715	1806	1921	...	0842	1042	1242	1442	1642	1842	...
Malé d.	0530	0618	0644	0717	0820	0953	1055	1156	1251	1407	1444	1530	1639	1735	1825	1943	0600	0900	1100	1300	1500	1700	1900	2000
Cles d.	0550	0637	0709	0755	0847	1019	1121	1223	1319	1433	1512	1554	1707	1801	1853	2008	0624	0924	1124	1324	1524	1724	1924	2024
Mezzolombardo d.	0626	0711	0749	0832	0926	1056	1159	1302	1359	1512	1550	1632	1747	1842	1931	2044	0701	1001	1201	1401	1601	1801	2001	2101
Mezzocorona Ferrovia d.	0633	0717	0756	0840	0933	1103	1207	1310	1406	1520	1557	1639	1755	1849	1938	2052	0708	1008	1208	1408	1608	1808	2008	2108
Trento a.	0700	0737	0825	0906	0959	1129	1233	1339	1434	1544	1623	1705	1824	1915	2004	2117	0734	1034	1234	1434	1634	1834	2034	2134

597 FORTEZZA / FRANZENSFESTE - S. CANDIDO / INNICHEN - LIENZ

2nd class ÖBB, SAD

Trains to Lienz are subject to alteration on and around Italian and Austrian holiday dates. Additional trains run Fortezza - S. Candido and v.v. on Ⓐ.

km		Ⓐ		△	△	△	△	△	△	△					Ⓐ B	Ⓒ										
0	**Fortezza / Franzensfeste** d.	0547	...	0650	0750	0850	0950	1050	1150	1250	1350	1450	1550	1650	1750	1850	1950	2050	...	...	...	...	...	...	...	...
33	Brunico / Bruneck d.	0630	...	0730	0830	0930	1030	1130	1230	1330	1430	1530	1630	1730	1830	1930	2030	2130	...	...	...	...	...	...	...	...
61	Dobbiaco / Toblach d.	0706	...	0806	0906	1006	1106	1206	1306	1406	1506	1606	1706	1806	1906	2006	2106	2206	...	...	...	...	...	...	...	...
65	**S. Candido / Innichen** a.	0710	...	0810	0910	1010	1110	1210	1310	1410	1510	1610	1710	1810	1910	2010	2110	2210	...	...	...	...	...	...	...	...
65	**S. Candido / Innichen** 🏛 d.	...	0716	0816	0916	1016	1116	1216	1316	1416	1516	1616	1716	1816	1916	2016	...	...	...	...	...	...	...	...	...	...
78	Sillian 🏛 d.	...	0730	0830	0930	1030	1130	1230	1330	1430	1530	1630	1730	1830	1930	2030	...	...	...	...	...	...	...	...	...	...
108	**Lienz** a.	...	0809	0909	1009	1109	1209	1309	1409	1509	1609	1709	1809	1909	2009	2109	...	...	...	...	...	...	...	...	...	...

	Ⓐ	⚒	△	△	△	△	△	△	△							D									
Lienz d.	...	...	0550	0645	0750	0850	0950	1050	1150	1250	1350	1450	1550	1650	1750	1850	1950	...	...	...	...	...	...	...	...
Sillian d.	...	...	0630	0730	0830	0930	1030	1130	1230	1330	1430	1530	1630	1730	1830	1930	2030	...	...	...	...	...	...	...	...
S. Candido / Innichen 🏛 a.	...	...	0643	0743	0843	0943	1043	1143	1243	1343	1443	1543	1643	1743	1843	1943	2043	...	...	...	...	...	...	...	...
S. Candido / Innichen 🏛 d.	0521	0550	0650	0750	0850	0950	1050	1150	1250	1350	1450	1550	1650	1750	1850	1950	2050	...	...	...	...	...	...	...	...
Dobbiaco / Toblach d.	0526	0555	0655	0755	0855	0955	1055	1155	1255	1355	1455	1555	1655	1755	1855	1955	2055	...	...	...	...	...	...	...	...
Brunico / Bruneck d.	0600	0631	0731	0831	0931	1031	1131	1231	1331	1431	1531	1631	1731	1831	1931	2031	2131	...	...	...	...	...	...	...	...
Fortezza / Franzensfeste a.	0634	0710	0810	0910	1010	1110	1210	1310	1410	1510	1610	1710	1810	1910	2010	2110	2210	...	...	...	...	...	...	...	...

🚌 DOBBIACO / TOBLACH - CORTINA 🚌

Service 445 (♠)									
Dobbiaco / Toblach bus station d.	0705	0905	1105	1405	1605	1805	...	...	...
Dobbiaco / Toblach Bahnhof d.	0710	0910	1110	1410	1610	1810	...	...	...
Cortina a.	0755	0955	1155	1455	1655	1855	...	...	...

Service 445 (♠)									
Cortina d.	0805	1005	1305	1505	1705	1905	...	...	...
Dobbiaco / Toblach Bahnhof a.	0845	1045	1345	1545	1745	1945	...	...	...
Dobbiaco / Toblach bus station a.	0850	1050	1350	1550	1750	1950	...	...	...

B – From Bolzano.
D – 🚃 Lienz - Merano (Table 595).

△ – Subject to alteration Fortezza - S. Candido and v.v. Mar. 26 - May 14.
♠ – For more information www.suedtirolmobil.info.

598 MERANO / MERAN - MALLES / MALS

2nd class SAD

'Ferrovia della Val Venosta'. Operator: SAD www.sad.it.

km		⚒																								
0	**Merano / Meran** d.	0532*	0636*	0709*	0739*	0809*	0909*	0939*	1009*	1109*	1139*	1209*	1309*	1339*	1409*	1509*	1539*	1609*	1709*	1739*	1809*	1909*	1949*	2049*	2149*	2249*
	Töll d.	0548	0652	0731	0802	0835	0931	1002	1035	1131	1202	1235	1331	1402	1435	1531	1602	1635	1731	1802	1835	1931	2000	2100	2200	2300
37	Silandro / Schlanders d.	0623	0729	0810	0832	0910	1010	1032	1110	1210	1232	1310	1410	1432	1510	1610	1632	1710	1810	1832	1910	2010	2032	2132	2232	2332
60	**Malles / Mals** a.	0653	0754	0838	0855	0938	1038	1055	1138	1238	1255	1338	1438	1455	1538	1638	1655	1738	1838	1855	1938	2038	2055	2155	2255	2355

	⚒																								
Malles / Mals d.	0518	0540	0616	0701	0720	0820	0903	0920	1020	1103	1120	1220	1303	1320	1420	1503	1520	1620	1703	1720	1820	1903	1920	2020	2120
Silandro / Schlanders d.	0540	0603	0641	0727	0748	0848	0927	0948	1048	1127	1148	1248	1327	1348	1448	1527	1548	1648	1727	1748	1848	1927	1948	2048	2148
Töll a.	0612	0637	0716	0757	0825	0925	0957	1025	1125	1157	1225	1325	1357	1425	1525	1557	1625	1725	1757	1825	1925	1957	2025	2125	2225
Merano / Meran a.	0626*	0651*	0734*	0811*	0839*	0939*	1011*	1039*	1139*	1211*	1239*	1339*	1411*	1439*	1539*	1611*	1639*	1739*	1811*	1839*	1939*	2011*	2039*	2139*	2239*

* – Connection by 🚌.

599 ITALIAN LAKES (LAGO MAGGIORE, GARDA, COMO)

Lago Maggiore: ⛴ services link Arona, Stresa, Baveno, Laveno, Luino and Locarno throughout the year on an irregular schedule.
Operator: Navigazione sul Lago Maggiore, P. le Baracca 1, 28041 Arona, Italy. ✆ +39 (0)322 233 200. www.navigazionelaghi.it

---

Lago di Garda: ⛴ services link Desenzano, Peschiera, Garda, Salo, Gardone and Riva, (April to October only), on an irregular schedule with a very limited service at other times.
Operator: Navigazione sul Lago di Garda, Piazza Matteotti 1, 25015 Desenzano del Garda, Italy. ✆ +39 (0)30 914 9511. www.navigazionelaghi.it

---

Lago di Como: ⛴ services link Como, Bellagio, Menaggio, Varenna, Bellano and Colico (April to September only) on an irregular schedule.
Operator: Navigazione Lago di Como, Via Per Cernobbio 18, 22100 Como, Italy. ✆ +39 (0)31 579 211. www.navigazionelaghi.it

Hydrofoil service (valid until March 25, 2023):

	⚒	†	⚒	⚒	⚒	†	⚒	⚒	†	⚒	⚒
Como d.	0733	1110	1225	1330	1420	1540	1710	1810	1850	1910	1920
Tremezzo d.	0819	1146	1302	1419	1457	1617	1746	1857	1927	1957	1956
Bellagio d.	|	1155	1309	1429	1504	1624	1752	1904	1933	2004	2002
Menaggio d.	0808	1202	1316	1437	1511	1631	1758	1912	1939	2012	2008
Bellagio a.	0813	|	...	|	...	...	|	...	|	|	|
Bellano d.	...	1211	...	1453	...	...	1808	...	1951	2028	2018
Colico a.	...	1238	...	1525	...	...	...	...	2014	2058	2043

	⚒	⚒	†	⚒	⚒	†	⚒	⚒	†	⚒	⚒
Colico d.	0606	...	0722	...	...	1355	...	1605	...	...	...
Bellano d.	0628	...	0753	...	...	1422	...	1638	...	...	1808
Bellagio d.	|	0700	|	...	...	|	...	|	...	...	|
Menaggio d.	0641	0709	0803	0808	1316	1434	1511	1655	1709	1758	1835
Bellagio d.	0647	|	0812	0814	1330	1442	1525	1704	1716	1810	1841
Tremezzo d.	0653	0718	0818	0820	1336	1448	1531	1710	1723	1816	1846
Como a.	0730	0805	0905	0857	1412	1525	1607	1754	1800	1851	1916

Italo, Trenitalia — HIGH-SPEED SERVICES — 600

All trains 🅁 and 🍸. *FA*, *FB* and *FR* trains are operated by Trenitalia (www.trenitalia.com). *ITA* trains are operated by Italo (www.italotreno.it).
Trenitalia tickets and passes are not valid on Italo trains. Trains may use different numbers for part of their journey.

km		*FR* 9503 ①–⑥	*ITA* 9907	*FR* 9401	*FR* 9303	*FR* 9603 Ⓐ	*FR* 9511 L	*ITA* 9967 ①–⑥	*FR* 9605 ⚒	*FR* 8505	*ITA* 8111 R	*ITA* 9969	*FR* 9403	*FR* 9607	*ITA* 8951	*FR* 9515	*ITA* 9971	*FR* 9604	*FA* 8801 L	*ITA* 8903	*ITA* 9915 A	*FR* 9405	*FR* 9611	*ITA* 8953
0	**Torino** Porta Nuova 605 d.	...	...	...	...	...	...	...	...	...	...	...	...	0550	...	...	0600	...	...	...	0625	...	0650	...
6	**Torino** Porta Susa △ 605 d.	...	...	...	...	...	...	...	...	...	...	...	...	0600	...	...	0610	...	...	...	0635	...	0700	...
	Bergamo d.	...	...	...	...	...	...	...	0545	...	...	...	...	|	0543	...	|	...	...	...	|	...	|	...
	Brescia 605 d.	...	...	...	...	...	...	...	|	...	...	...	...	|	0627	...	|	0642	...	...	|	...	|	...
	Desenzano-Sirmione 605 d.	...	...	...	...	...	...	...	|	...	...	...	...	|	0643	...	|	|	...	...	|	...	|	...
	Peschiera del Garda 605 d.	...	...	...	...	...	...	...	|	...	...	...	...	|	0652	...	|	|	...	...	|	...	|	...
	Bolzano / Bozen 595 d.	...	...	...	...	...	...	...	|	0512	...	...	...	|	|	...	|	|	...	...	|	...	|	0642
	Trento 595 d.	...	...	...	...	...	...	...	|	0543	...	...	...	|	|	...	|	|	...	...	|	...	|	0714
	Rovereto 595 d.	...	...	...	...	...	...	...	|	0557	...	...	...	|	|	...	|	|	...	...	|	...	|	0728
	Verona Porta Nuova 595 a.	...	...	...	...	...	...	...	|	0640	...	...	...	|	0711	...	|	|	...	...	|	...	|	0810
	Verona Porta Nuova 605 d.	...	...	...	...	...	...	...	|	0652	...	...	...	|	0722	...	|	|	...	...	|	...	|	0822
148	**Milano** Centrale 605 a.	...	...	...	...	...	...	...	0625	|	...	...	...	0650	|	...	0657	0720	...	...	0730	...	0750	|
148	**Milano** Centrale d.	...	0540	...	0545	0600	0610	0615	0635	|	0640	0645	...	0700	|	0710	0715	0730	...	...	0740	...	0800	|
158	Milano Rogoredo d.	...	0550	...	0557u	|	0620u	0626	|	|	|	|	...	|	|	0720u	0726	0740	...	...	|	...	|	|
299	Reggio Emilia AV d.	...	0628	...	|	|	0656	|	|	|	0728	|	...	|	|	0756	|	|	...	...	0828	...	|	|
	Venezia Santa Lucia d.	...	|	0526	|	|	|	|	|	|	|	|	0626	|	|	|	|	|	0653	0705	|	0726	|	|
	Venezia Mestre △ 620 d.	...	|	0538	|	|	|	|	|	|	|	|	0638	|	|	|	|	|	0705	0717	|	0738	|	|
	Padova 620 d.	...	|	0556	|	|	|	|	|	|	|	|	0656	|	|	|	|	|	0723	0735	|	0756	|	|
	Rovigo 620 d.	...	|	0617	|	|	|	|	|	|	|	|	|	|	|	|	|	|	0747	|	|	0816	|	|
	Ferrara 620 d.	...	|	|	|	|	|	|	|	|	|	|	0729	|	|	|	|	|	0805	0811	|	|	|	|
363	**Bologna** Centrale ● 620 a.	...	0654	0659	0809	0704	0724	|	|	0744	0754	0749	0759	0804	0814	0824	|	|	0842	0839	0854	0859	0904	0914
363	**Bologna** Centrale ● 620 d.	...	0657	0702	0812	0707	0727	|	|	0747	0757	0752	0802	0807	0817	0827	|	|	...	0842	0857	0902	0907	0917
455	**Firenze** SMN 620 a.	...	0735	0739	0850	|	0804	|	|	0824	0835	|	0839	|	0854	0904	|	|	...	0920	0935	0939	|	0954
455	**Firenze** SMN 620 d.	0600	0743	0748	0859	|	0814	|	|	0833	0843	|	0848	|	0903	0914	|	|	...	0928	0943	0948	|	1003
	Roma Tiburtina 620 a.	0739	0910	0914s	1023s	|	0941	|	|	1001s	1009	0950	1014	|	|	1039	|	|	...	1054	1109	1114	|	|
716	**Roma** Termini 620 a.	0749	0919	0928	1035	0910	0949	0924	0934	1010	1019	1000	1025	1011	1035	1049	1025	1040	...	1105	1119	1122	1110	1135
716	**Roma** Termini 640 d.	0800	0930h	...	...	0925	...	0941	0953	...	1030	...	1035	1025	...	1100	1040	1053	...	1115	...	1135	1125	...
926	**Napoli** Afragola a.	0856s	1027h	...	...	|	...	|	1051s	...	|	...	|	|	...	1156	1139	1148s	...	|	...	|	|	...
938	**Napoli** Centrale 640 a.	0913	1043h	...	...	1033	...	1053	1103	...	1143	...	1148	1138	...	1213	1153	1203	...	1228	...	1248	1233	...
938	**Napoli** Centrale 640 d.	...	...	...	...	...	...	...	...	...	1200	...	...	...	...	1225	1205	...	...	...	...	...	...	...
988	**Salerno** 640 a.	...	...	...	...	...	...	...	...	...	1242	...	...	...	...	1302	1250	...	...	...	...	...	...	...

	FR 9519	*ITA* 9973 G	*FR* 9613 Ⓑ	*ITA* 8905	*FA* 8507	*FA* 9466 T	*ITA* 9919	*FR* 9583 R	*ITA* 9975	*FR* 9409 U	*FR* 9617	*ITA* 8907 U	*FR* 8503	*ITA* 9923	*ITA* 9923	*FR* 9411	*FR* 9311	*FR* 9527	*ITA* 9977	*ITA* 8902 T	*ITA* 9927	*FR* 9413	*FR* 9623 Ⓐ
Torino Porta Nuova 605 d.	0700	...	...	...	...	...	0730	0800	...	...	...	...	...	0830	...	...	0840	...	...	...	0930	...	...
Torino Porta Susa △ 605 d.	0710	...	...	...	...	...	0740	0810	...	...	...	...	...	0840	...	...	0850	...	...	...	0940	...	...
Bergamo d.	|	...	...	...	...	...	|	|	...	...	...	...	0800	|	...	...	|	...	...	...	|	...	...
Brescia 605 d.	|	...	...	...	...	...	|	|	...	...	...	...	0847	|	...	...	|	...	...	...	|	...	...
Desenzano-Sirmione 605 d.	|	...	...	...	...	...	|	|	...	...	...	...	|	|	...	...	|	...	...	...	|	...	...
Peschiera del Garda 605 d.	|	...	...	...	...	...	|	|	...	...	...	...	0909	|	...	...	|	...	...	...	|	...	...
Bolzano / Bozen 595 d.	|	...	...	...	0712	...	|	|	...	...	...	...	|	|	...	...	|	...	...	...	|	...	...
Trento 595 d.	|	...	...	...	0743	...	|	|	...	...	...	...	|	|	...	...	|	...	...	...	|	...	...
Rovereto 595 d.	|	...	...	...	0757	...	|	|	...	...	...	...	|	|	...	...	|	...	...	...	|	...	...
Verona Porta Nuova 595 a.	|	...	...	...	0840	...	|	|	...	...	...	...	0924	|	...	...	|	...	...	...	|	...	...
Verona Porta Nuova 605 d.	|	...	...	...	0852	...	|	|	...	...	...	...	0937	|	...	...	|	...	...	...	|	...	...
Milano Centrale 605 a.	0800	...	...	...	|	...	0830	0902	...	...	...	...	|	0930	...	...	|	...	...	...	1030	...	...
Milano Centrale d.	0810	0815	0830	...	|	...	0840	0910	0915	...	0935	...	|	0940	0940	...	|	1010	1015	...	1040	...	1058
Milano Rogoredo d.	0820	0826	|	...	|	...	0850	0920	0926	...	|	...	|	0950	0950	...	1004	1020u	1026	...	1050	...	|
Reggio Emilia AV d.	0856	|	|	...	|	...	0928	0956	|	...	|	...	|	1028	1028	...	1042	1056	|	...	1128	...	|
Venezia Santa Lucia d.	|	|	|	0805	|	...	|	|	|	...	|	...	|	|	|	0926	|	|	|	...	|	1026	|
Venezia Mestre △ 620 d.	|	|	|	0817	|	0834	|	|	|	0840	|	0920	|	|	|	0938	|	|	|	1017	|	1038	|
Padova 620 d.	|	|	|	0835	|	0850	|	|	|	0856	|	0935	|	|	|	0956	|	|	|	1035	|	1056	|
Rovigo 620 d.	|	|	|	0857	|	|	|	|	|	|	|	|	|	|	|	|	|	|	|	|	|	|	|
Ferrara 620 d.	|	|	|	|	|	|	|	|	|	0929	|	1011	|	|	|	1029	|	|	|	1110	|	1129	|
Bologna Centrale ● 620 a.	0924	|	0934	0939	0944	0949	0954	1024	|	0959	|	1039	1044	1054	1054	1059	1109	1124	|	1139	1154	1159	1204
Bologna Centrale ● 620 d.	0927	|	0937	0942	0947	0952	0957	1027	|	1002	|	1042	1047	1057	1057	1102	1112	1127	|	1142	1157	1202	1207
Firenze SMN 620 a.	1004	|	|	1020	1024	|	1035	1104	|	1039	|	1120	1124	1135	1135	1139	1150	1204	|	1220	1235	1239	|
Firenze SMN 620 d.	1014	|	|	1028	1033	|	1043	1114	|	1048	|	1128	1133	1143	1143	1148	1159	1214	|	1228	1243	1248	|
Roma Tiburtina 620 a.	1139	|	|	1154	1159s	1149s	1209	1240	|	1214	|	1254	|	1309	1309	1314	1322	1340	|	1354	1409	1414	|
Roma Termini 620 a.	1149	1125	1140	1205	1210	1200	1219	1249	1225	1225	1234	1305	1305	1319	1319	1325	1335	1349	1325	1405	1419	1425	1410
Roma Termini 640 d.	1200	1140	1155	...	...	...	1230	1300	1240	1250	...	1330	...	...	...	1335	1353	1400	1340	1415	1430	1438	1425
Napoli Afragola a.	1257	1237	|	...	...	...	1327	1356	|	|	...	|	...	...	...	|	1448s	1456	1437	|	1527	|	|
Napoli Centrale 640 a.	1315	1253	1300	...	...	...	1343	1413	1353	1403	...	1443	...	...	...	◧	1503	1512	1453	1528	1543	1548	1533
Napoli Centrale 640 d.	1325	...	...	...	...	...	...	1425	...	...	...	...	...	...	...	...	...	1525	1505	...	...	...	...
Salerno 640 a.	1406	...	...	...	...	...	...	1504	...	...	...	...	...	...	...	...	...	1606	1552	...	...	...	...

	FR 9587 R	*ITA* 9979	*ITA* 8911 g	*ITA* 9931	*FR* 9627 Ⓐ	*FR* 9415	*FR* 9721	*FR* 9535 d	*FR* 9535 e	*ITA* 9981	*ITA* 9935	*FR* 8419 R	*FR* 9631 Ⓑ	*ITA* 9983	*ITA* 8913	*ITA* 9939 A	*FR* 9421	*ITA* 8959	*FR* 9543	*ITA* 9985	*FR* 9639 R	*ITA* 8915	*FA* 8519 S	*ITA* 8153 R
Torino Porta Nuova 605 d.	1000	...	...	...	...	...	...	1100	1100	...	1130	...	...	...	...	1220	...	...	1300	...	...	...	...	1320
Torino Porta Susa △ 605 d.	1010	...	...	...	...	...	...	1110	1110	...	1141	...	...	...	...	1230	...	...	1310	...	...	...	...	1330
Bergamo d.	|	...	...	...	...	...	...	|	|	...	|	...	...	...	...	|	...	...	|	...	...	...	...	|
Brescia 605 d.	|	...	...	...	...	...	...	|	|	...	|	...	...	...	...	|	...	1329	|	...	...	...	...	|
Desenzano-Sirmione 605 d.	|	...	...	...	...	...	...	|	|	...	|	...	...	...	...	|	...	1344	|	...	...	...	...	|
Peschiera del Garda 605 d.	|	...	...	...	...	...	...	|	|	...	|	...	...	...	...	|	...	1353	|	...	...	...	...	|
Bolzano / Bozen 595 d.	|	...	...	...	...	...	0845	|	|	...	|	...	...	...	...	|	...	|	|	...	...	...	1312	|
Trento 595 d.	|	...	...	...	...	...	0919	|	|	...	|	...	...	...	...	|	...	|	|	...	...	...	1343	|
Rovereto 595 d.	|	...	...	...	...	...	0934	|	|	...	|	...	...	...	...	|	...	|	|	...	...	...	1357	|
Verona Porta Nuova 595 a.	|	...	...	...	...	...	1020	|	|	...	|	...	...	...	...	|	...	1411	|	...	...	...	1440	|
Verona Porta Nuova 605 d.	|	...	...	...	...	...	1032	|	|	...	|	...	...	...	...	|	...	1422	|	...	...	...	1452	|
Milano Centrale 605 a.	1102	...	...	...	...	...	1145	1202	1202	...	1230	...	...	...	...	1330	...	|	1402	...	...	...	|	1430
Milano Centrale d.	1110	1115	...	1140	1158	...	...	1210	1210	1215	1240	...	1300	1320	...	1340	...	|	1410	1420	1430	...	|	1440
Milano Rogoredo d.	1120	1126	...	1150	|	...	...	1220	1220	1226	1250	...	|	1329	...	|	...	|	1420	1429	|	...	|	|
Reggio Emilia AV d.	1156	|	...	1228	|	...	...	1256	1256	|	1328	...	|	|	...	1428	...	|	1456	|	|	...	|	1528
Venezia Santa Lucia d.	|	|	1105	|	|	1126	...	|	|	|	|	1226	|	|	1305	|	1326	|	|	|	|	1405	|	|
Venezia Mestre △ 620 d.	|	|	1117	|	|	1138	...	|	|	|	|	1238	|	|	1317	|	1338	|	|	|	|	1417	|	|
Padova 620 d.	|	|	1135	|	|	1156	...	|	|	|	|	1256	|	|	1335	|	1356	|	|	|	|	1435	|	|
Rovigo 620 d.	|	|	1157	|	|	|	...	|	|	|	|	|	|	|	|	|	1417	|	|	|	|	|	|	|
Ferrara 620 d.	|	|	|	|	|	1229	...	|	|	|	|	1329	|	|	1411	|	|	|	|	|	|	1511	|	|
Bologna Centrale ● 620 a.	1224	|	1239	1254	1304	1259	...	1324	1324	|	1354	1359	1404	|	1439	1454	1459	1514	1524	|	1534	1539	1544	1554
Bologna Centrale ● 620 d.	1227	|	1242	1257	1307	1302	...	1327	1327	|	1357	1402	1407	|	1442	1457	1502	1517	1527	|	1537	1542	1547	1557
Firenze SMN 620 a.	1304	|	1320	1335	|	1339	...	1404	1404	|	1435	1439	|	|	1520	1535	1539	1554	1604	|	|	1620	1624	1635
Firenze SMN 620 d.	1314	|	1328	1343	|	1348	...	1414	1414	|	1443	1448	|	|	1528	1543	1548	1603	1614	|	|	1628	1633	1643
Roma Tiburtina 620 a.	1440	|	1454	1509	|	1514s	...	1540	|	|	1609	1614	1604	|	1653	1709	1714	|	1740	|	|	1754	1759	1809
Roma Termini 620 a.	1449	1425	1505	1519	1510	1525	...	1549	1549	1525	1619	1624	1615	1625	1705	1719	1724	1735	1749	1725	1740	1805	1810	1819
Roma Termini 640 d.	1500	...	...	1530	1525	...	...	1600	1600	1540	1630	1635	1625	...	1715	...	1735	...	1800	...	1753	1815	1820	1830
Napoli Afragola a.	1556	...	...	1625	|	...	...	1656s	1656s	|	1727	1736	|	...	1816	...	|	...	1856	...	1848	|	1921	1928
Napoli Centrale 640 a.	1612	...	...	1643	1633	...	...	1712	1712	1653	1743	|	1733	...	|	...	1848	...	1913	...	|	1928	|	|
Napoli Centrale 640 d.	1625	...	...	1700	...	...	...	...	...	...	...	|	...	...	|	...	...	...	1925	...	|	...	|	|
Salerno 640 a.	1706	...	...	1739	...	...	...	...	...	...	...	1809	...	...	1854	...	...	...	2005	...	1919	...	1948	2016

FOR FOOTNOTES SEE NEXT PAGE →

600 HIGH-SPEED SERVICES

Italo, Trenitalia

All trains ® and 🍸. *FA*, *FB* and *FR* trains are operated by Trenitalia (www.trenitalia.com). *ITA* trains are operated by Italo (www.italotreno.it).
Trenitalia tickets and passes are not valid on Italo trains. Trains may use different numbers for part of their journey.

	FR 9425	*FR* 9641	*FR* 9547 N	*ITA* 9987	*FR* 9643 Ⓑ	*FR* 8815 L	*ITA* 8919	*ITA* 9947	*FR* 9427	*FR* 9645	*ITA* 8963	*FR* 9551	*ITA* 9989	*FR* 9647	*ITA* 8923	*FR* 8525	*ITA* 9951	*FR* 9431	*FR* 9325 ①–④	*FR* 9325 ⑤–⑦	*FR* 9555 B	*ITA* 9991 C	*FR* 9651
Torino Porta Nuova .... 605 d.	...	1350	...	...	...	...	...	1430	...	1450	...	...	...	...	...	...	1530	...	1540	⊕	...	...	...
Torino Porta Susa △ .... 605 d.	...	1400	...	...	...	...	...	1440	...	1500	...	...	...	...	...	...	1540	...	1550	1550	...	...	...
Bergamo .... d.	...	|	...	...	...	...	...	|	...	|	...	...	...	...	...	...	|	...	|	|	...	...	...
Brescia .... 605 d.	...	|	...	...	...	...	...	|	...	|	...	...	...	...	...	...	|	...	|	|	...	...	...
Desenzano-Sirmione .... 605 d.	...	|	...	...	...	...	...	|	...	|	...	...	...	...	...	...	|	...	|	|	...	...	...
Peschiera del Garda .... 605 d.	...	|	...	...	...	...	...	|	...	|	...	...	...	...	...	...	|	...	|	|	...	...	...
Bolzano / Bozen .... 595 d.	...	|	...	...	...	...	...	|	...	|	1442	...	...	...	...	1512	|	...	|	|	...	...	...
Trento .... 595 d.	...	|	...	...	...	...	...	|	...	|	1514	...	...	...	...	1543	|	...	|	|	...	...	...
Rovereto .... 595 d.	...	|	...	...	...	...	...	|	...	|	1528	...	...	...	...	1557	|	...	|	|	...	...	...
Verona Porta Nuova .... 595 a.	...	|	...	...	...	...	...	|	...	|	1610	...	...	...	...	1640	|	...	|	|	...	...	...
Verona Porta Nuova .... 605 d.	...	|	...	...	...	...	...	|	...	|	1620	...	...	...	...	1652	|	...	|	|	...	...	...
Milano Centrale .... 605 a.	...	1450	...	...	...	...	...	1530	...	1550	|	...	...	...	...	|	1630	...	|	|	...	...	...
Milano Centrale .... d.	...	1500	1510	1515	1525	...	...	1540	...	1600	|	1610	1615	1630	...	|	1640	...	|	|	1710	1715	1735
Milano Rogoredo .... d.	...	|	1520u	1526	1538u	...	...	1550	...	|	|	1620u	1626	1640u	...	|	1650	...	1704	1704	1720u	1726	|
Reggio Emilia AV .... d.	...	|	1556	|	|	...	...	1628	...	|	|	1656	|	|	...	|	1728	...	1742	1742	1756	|	|
Venezia Santa Lucia .... d.	1426	|	|	|	|	1452	1505	|	1526	|	|	|	|	|	1605	|	|	1626	|	|	|	|	|
Venezia Mestre △ .... 620 d.	1438	|	|	|	|	1504	1517	|	1538	|	|	|	|	|	1617	|	|	1638	|	|	|	|	|
Padova .... 620 d.	1456	|	|	|	|	1521	1535	|	1556	|	|	|	|	|	1635	|	|	1656	|	|	|	|	|
Rovigo .... 620 d.	|	|	|	|	|	1546	|	|	|	|	|	|	|	|	1656	|	|	1717	|	|	|	|	|
Ferrara .... 620 d.	1529	|	|	|	|	1602	1611	|	1629	|	|	|	|	|	|	|	|	|	|	|	|	|	|
Bologna Centrale ● .... 620 a.	1559	1604	1624	|	1634	1637	1639	1654	1659	1704	1714	1724	|	|	1739	1744	1754	1759	1809	1809	1824	|	|
Bologna Centrale ● .... 620 d.	1602	1607	1627	|	1637	...	1642	1657	1702	1707	1717	1727	|	|	1742	1747	1757	1802	1812	1812	1827	|	|
Firenze SMN .... 620 a.	1639	|	1704	|	|	...	1720	1735	1739	|	1754	1804	|	|	1820	1824	1835	1839	1850	1850	1904	|	|
Firenze SMN .... 620 d.	1648	|	1714	|	|	...	1728	1743	1748	|	1803	1814	|	|	1828	1833	1843	1848	1859	1859	1914	|	|
Roma Tiburtina .... 620 a.	1814	|	1840	|	|	...	1854	1909	1914	|	|	1940	|	|	1954	1959	2009	2014	2024	2024	2043	|	|
Roma Termini .... 620 a.	1825	1810	1849	1825	1840	...	1905	1919	1925	1910	1935	1949	1925	1940	2005	2010	2019	2025	2035	2035	2050	2025	2034
Roma Termini .... 640 d.	1835	...	1900	1840	1853	...	1915	1930	1935	...	...	2000	1940	...	2015	2025	2030	2035	2053	2053	2100	...	...
Napoli Afragola .... a.	|	...	1956	|	1948s	...	|	2025	|	...	...	2056	2038	...	|	|	2125	|	2148s	2148s	2156	...	...
Napoli Centrale .... 640 a.	1948	...	2010	1953	2003	...	2028	2043	2048	...	...	2113	2053	...	2147	2133	2143	2148	2203	2203	2213	...	...
Napoli Centrale .... 640 d.	...	...	2020	...	...	...	2040	2055	2101	...	...	2125	...	...	...	...	2155	...	...	...	2223	...	...
Salerno .... 640 a.	...	...	2057	...	...	...	2117	2132	2138	...	...	2205	...	...	...	...	2232	...	...	...	2300	...	...

	ITA 8925	*FA* 8527	*ITA* 9955	*ITA* 9993	*FR* 9433	*FR* 9653	*ITA* 8967	*FR* 9559	*ITA* 9995	*FR* 9657	*FA* 8529	*ITA* 9959	*ITA* 9997 Ⓑ	*FR* 9435	*FR* 9329 Ⓑ P	*FR* 9663	*ITA* 9961 Ⓑ	*FR* 9437		*FR* 9567 Ⓑ	*FR* 9681 ①–⑤ j	*ITA* 9963	
Torino Porta Nuova .... 605 d.	...	...	1630	...	...	...	...	1700	...	...	...	1720	...	...	1740	...	...	...	...	1900	...	1925	...
Torino Porta Susa △ .... 605 d.	...	...	1640	...	...	...	...	1710	...	...	...	1730	...	...	1750	...	...	...	...	1910	...	1935	...
Bergamo .... d.	...	1600	|	...	...	...	...	|	...	...	...	|	...	...	|	...	...	...	...	|	...	|	...
Brescia .... 605 d.	...	1700	|	...	...	...	1729	|	...	...	...	|	...	...	|	...	...	...	...	|	...	|	...
Desenzano-Sirmione .... 605 d.	...	|	|	...	...	...	1743	|	...	...	...	|	...	...	|	...	...	...	...	|	...	|	...
Peschiera del Garda .... 605 d.	...	1725	|	...	...	...	1752	|	...	...	...	|	...	...	|	...	...	...	...	|	...	|	...
Bolzano / Bozen .... 595 d.	...	|	|	...	...	...	|	|	...	...	1710	|	...	...	|	...	...	...	...	|	...	|	...
Trento .... 595 d.	...	|	|	...	...	...	|	|	...	...	1743	|	...	...	|	...	...	...	...	|	...	|	...
Rovereto .... 595 d.	...	|	|	...	...	...	|	|	...	...	1757	|	...	...	|	...	...	...	...	|	...	|	...
Verona Porta Nuova .... 595 a.	...	1741	|	...	...	...	1811	|	...	...	1840	|	...	...	|	...	...	...	...	|	...	|	...
Verona Porta Nuova .... 605 d.	...	1752	|	...	...	...	1822	|	...	...	1852	|	...	...	|	...	...	...	...	|	...	|	...
Milano Centrale .... 605 a.	...	|	1730	...	...	...	|	1802	...	...	|	1830	...	...	|	...	...	...	...	2002	...	2030	...
Milano Centrale .... d.	...	|	1740	1745	...	1800	|	1810	1820	1830	|	1840	1845	...	|	1935	1940	...	...	2010	...	2040	...
Milano Rogoredo .... d.	...	|	1750	|	...	|	|	1820	1829	|	|	|	|	...	1904	|	1950	...	...	2020	2044	|	...
Reggio Emilia AV .... d.	...	|	1828	|	...	|	|	1856	|	|	|	1928	|	...	1942	|	2028	...	...	2056	|	2128	...
Venezia Santa Lucia .... d.	1705	|	|	|	1726	|	|	|	|	|	|	|	|	1826	|	|	|	1926	...	|	|	|	...
Venezia Mestre △ .... 620 d.	1717	|	|	|	1738	|	|	|	|	|	|	|	|	1838	|	|	|	1938	...	|	|	|	...
Padova .... 620 d.	1735	|	|	|	1756	|	|	|	|	|	|	|	|	1856	|	|	|	1956	...	|	|	|	...
Rovigo .... 620 d.	|	|	|	|	|	|	|	|	|	|	|	|	|	|	|	|	|	|	...	|	|	|	...
Ferrara .... 620 d.	1811	|	|	|	1829	|	|	|	|	|	|	|	|	1929	|	|	|	2029	...	|	|	|	...
Bologna Centrale ● .... 620 a.	1839	1844	1854	1849	1859	1904	1914	1924	|	1934	1944	1954	1949	1959	2009	|	2054	2059	...	2124	|	2154	...
Bologna Centrale ● .... 620 d.	1842	1847	1857	1852	1902	1907	1917	1927	|	1937	1947	1957	1952	2002	2012	|	2057	2102	...	2127	|	2157	...
Firenze SMN .... 620 a.	1920	1924	1935	|	1939	|	1954	2004	|	|	2024	2035	|	2039	2050	|	2135	2139	...	2204	|	2235	...
Firenze SMN .... 620 d.	1928	1933	1943	|	1948	|	2003	2014	|	|	2033	2043	|	2048	...	|	2143	2148	...	2214	|	2243	...
Roma Tiburtina .... 620 a.	2054	2059s	2109	2049	2114s	|	2132	2140	|	|	2159s	2209	2149	2214	...	|	2309	2314s	...	2340s	2329	0009	...
Roma Termini .... 620 a.	2105	2110	2119	2100	2125	2110	2143	2149	2125	2140	2210	2219	2200	2225	...	2234	2319	2325	...	2349	...	0019	...
Roma Termini .... 640 d.	2115	...	2130	...	...	2125	2205	2200	2140	2153	...	2230	...	2235	...	2245	...	...	...	...	...	...	...
Napoli Afragola .... a.	|	...	2225	...	...	|	|	2256s	2237	2248s	...	|	...	2334s	...	|	...	...	...	...	...	...	...
Napoli Centrale .... 640 a.	2228	...	2243	...	...	2233	2318	2313	2253	2303	...	2343	...	2348	...	2353	...	...	...	...	...	...	...
Napoli Centrale .... 640 d.	...	...	...	...	...	2245	...	...	...	...	...	...	...	...	...	...	...	...	...	...	...	...	...
Salerno .... 640 a.	...	...	...	...	...	2322	...	...	...	...	...	...	...	...	...	...	...	...	...	...	...	...	...

NOTES for pages 289 and 290.

A – To Bari (Tables **615**).
B – To Battipaglia (Table **640**).
C – To Caserta (Table **615**).
G – From Genova (Table **610**).
L – To Lecce (Tables **615**).
N – To Taranto (Tables **615**).
P – To Perugia (Table **620**).
R – To Reggio di Calabria (Table **640**).
S – To Sibari (Tables **640**).
T – From Trieste (Table **601**).
U – From Udine (Table **601**).

d – Not Dec. 12, 22, 23, Jan. 8, 9.
e – Runs Dec. 12, 22, 23, Jan. 8, 9 only.
f – Train **8139** on Ⓒ.
g – ①④⑤⑥⑦ only.
h – ⑦ only.
j – Not Apr. 6, 10, 11, 12, 25, 26, May 1, 2, June 2, 5.
s – Calls to set down only.
u – Calls to pick up only.

◧ – To Fiumicino Aeroporto ✈ (a. 1407).
⊕ – From Bardonecchia (d. 1440) and Oulx (d. 1451).
△ – Most trains call to pick up only.
● – Most services use underground platforms 16 – 19; allow a minimum of 10 minutes when connecting with services from / to the main station.

All trains 🅁 and 🍸. *FA*, *FB* and *FR* trains are operated by Trenitalia (www.trenitalia.com). *ITA* trains are operated by Italo (www.italotreno.it).
Trenitalia tickets and passes are not valid on Italo trains. Trains may use different numbers for part of their journey.

km		FR	ITA	FR	FR	FR	FR	ITA	FR	FR	ITA	FR	ITA	FR	FA	ITA	FR	FR	ITA	FR	FR	ITA	FR	ITA
		9782	9900	9600	9300	9682	9400	9904	9508	9606	9966	9404	9908	9608	8502	9968	9512	9610	8954	9304	9304	9970	9406	9912
		①–⑤	①–⑥		①–⑥	①–⑤		①–⑥		①–⑤	①–⑥			①–⑥				①–⑥	①–⑤	①–④	⑤–⑦			
					P	j													b					
	Salerno 640 d.	...	...	...	...	...	...	...	...	...	...	...	...	0515	...	...	...	...	...	...	...	...	...	...
	Napoli Centrale 640 a.	...	...	...	...	...	...	...	...	...	...	...	...	|	...	...	...	...	...	...	...	...	...	...
	Napoli Centrale 640 d.	...	...	...	...	...	...	...	...	0509	...	...	0514	|	...	0535	...	...	0550	0523	0523	0602	0609	0620
	Napoli Afragola d.	...	...	...	...	...	...	...	...	0521u	...	...	0529	0542	...	0550	...	...	|	⊖	⊖	0616	|	|
0	**Roma** Termini 640 a.	...	...	...	...	...	...	...	...	0615	...	...	0630	0640	...	0646	...	...	0705	0715	0715	0720	0725	0730
4	**Roma** Termini 620 d.	...	...	...	...	...	0535	0540	0600	0625	0630	0635	0640	0650	0645	0705	0710	0720	0725	0725	0725	0730	0735	0740
261	**Roma** Tiburtina 620 d.	...	...	...	...	0530	0545u	0550	0610u	|	0638	0643u	0648	|	0655u	|	0720u	|	|	0735	0735	0740	0745	0750
—	**Firenze** SMN 620 a.	...	...	...	...	|	0711	0717	0746	|	|	0811	0817	|	0827	|	0846	|	0857	0901	0901	|	0911	0917
	Firenze SMN 620 d.	...	...	...	0710	|	0720	0725	0755	|	|	0820	0825	|	0836	|	0855	|	0905	0910	0910	|	0920	0925
	Bologna Centrale ● 620 a.	...	...	...	0748	|	0758	0803	0833	|	0838	0858	0903	0853	0913	0908	0933	0923	0943	0948	0948	|	0958	1003
0	**Bologna** Centrale ● 620 d.	...	...	...	0751	|	0801	0806	0836	|	0841	0901	0906	0856	0916	0911	0936	0926	0946	0951	0951	|	1001	1006
47	Ferrara 620 d.	...	...	...	|	|	0829	|	|	|	|	0929	|	|	|	|	|	|	|	|	|	|	1029	|
79	Rovigo 620 d.	...	...	...	|	|	|	|	|	|	|	|	|	|	|	|	|	|	|	|	|	|	|	|
123	Padova 620 d.	...	...	...	|	|	0906	|	|	|	|	1006	|	|	|	|	|	|	|	|	|	|	1106	|
151	**Venezia** Mestre ▽ 620 a.	...	...	...	|	|	0923	|	|	|	|	1023	|	|	|	|	|	|	|	|	|	|	1123	|
160	**Venezia** Santa Lucia a.	...	...	...	|	|	0934	|	|	|	|	1034	|	|	|	|	|	|	|	|	|	|	1134	|
	Reggio Emilia AV d.	...	...	...	0815	|	...	0830	0900	|	|	...	0930	|	|	|	1000	|	|	1015	1015	|	...	1030
	Milano Rogoredo a.	...	...	...	0854	0815	...	0908	0938	|	|	...	|	|	|	|	1038s	1020s	|	1055	1055	1032	...	|
	Milano Centrale a.	...	...	...	|	...	...	0920	0950	0924	0945	...	1020	1000	|	1015	1050	1035	|	|	|	1045	...	1120
	Milano Centrale 605 d.	0653	0730	0753	|	...	...	0930	1002	...	...	...	1030	...	|	...	...	...	|	|	|	...	...	1130
114	**Verona** Porta Nuova 605 a.	|	|	|	|	...	...	|	|	...	...	...	|	...	1008	...	...	...	1038	|	|	...	...	|
114	**Verona** Porta Nuova 595 d.	|	|	|	|	...	...	|	|	...	...	...	|	...	1020	...	...	...	1050	|	|	...	...	|
182	Rovereto 595 d.	|	|	|	|	...	...	|	|	...	...	...	|	...	1103	...	...	...	1132	|	|	...	...	|
206	Trento 595 d.	|	|	|	|	...	...	|	|	...	...	...	|	...	1117	...	...	...	1146	|	|	...	...	|
261	**Bolzano / Bozen** 595 a.	|	|	|	|	...	...	|	|	...	...	...	|	...	1151	...	...	...	1218	|	|	...	...	|
137	Peschiera del Garda 605 d.	|	|	|	|	...	...	|	|	...	...	...	|	...	...	...	...	...	...	|	|	...	...	|
151	Desenzano-Sirmione 605 d.	|	|	|	|	...	...	|	|	...	...	...	|	...	...	...	...	...	...	|	|	...	...	|
179	**Brescia** 605 a.	|	|	|	|	...	...	|	|	...	...	...	|	...	...	...	...	...	...	|	|	...	...	|
229	**Bergamo** a.	|	|	|	|	...	...	|	|	...	...	...	|	...	...	...	...	...	...	|	|	...	...	|
	Torino Porta Susa ▽ 605 a.	0743	0818	0843	1008	...	...	1018	1053	...	...	...	1124	...	...	...	...	...	...	1208	1208	...	...	1229
	Torino Porta Nuova 605 a.	0755	0830	0855	1020	...	...	1030	1105	...	...	...	1135	...	...	...	...	...	...	1220	⊙	...	...	1240

	ITA	ITA	FR	FR	ITA	FR	ITA	FR	FR	ITA	ITA	FR	FR	FR	ITA	FA	ITA	ITA	FR	FR	FR	FR	ITA	FA
	8904	9972	9516	9616	8956	9490	9916	9618	8506	8906	9974	9520	9620	9414	9920	8508	8908	9976	9524	9624	9310	9416	9924	8509
				①–⑥	①–⑤																			
		C	B		b																			S
Salerno 640 d.	...	...	0550	...	...	0610	0620	...	...	...	...	...	...	0713	0720	...	...	...	0744	...	...	...	...	0913
Napoli Centrale 640 a.	...	...	0628	...	...	0647	0658	...	...	...	...	...	...	0753	0758	...	...	...	0822	...	...	...	...	|
Napoli Centrale 640 d.	0607	...	0640	0655	0702	0709	0720	...	0730	...	0740	0745	...	0809	0820	...	0830	...	0840	...	0855	...	0920	|
Napoli Afragola d.	|	...	0658	0710u	|	|	0735	...	|	...	|	0801	...	|	0835	...	|	...	0855	...	0910u	...	0934	0941
Roma Termini 640 a.	0735	...	0755	0804	0815	0820	0830	...	0840	...	0851	0900	...	0925	0930	...	0945	...	0950	...	1008	...	1030	1040
Roma Termini 620 d.	0755	0805	0810	0820	0825	0835	0840	0850	0850	0855	0905	0910	0925	0935	0943	0950	0955	1005	1010	1020	1025	1035	1040	1050
Roma Tiburtina 620 d.	0805	|	0820	|	|	0845	0850	|	0900u	0905	|	0920	|	0945	0951	1000u	1005	|	1020	|	1035	1045u	1050	1100
Firenze SMN 620 a.	0931	|	0946	|	0957	1011	1017	|	1027	1031	|	1046	|	1111	1117	1127	1131	|	1146	|	1201	1211	1217	1227
Firenze SMN 620 d.	0939	|	0955	|	1005	1020	1025	|	1036	1039	|	1055	|	1120	1125	1136	1139	|	1155	|	1210	1220	1225	1236
Bologna Centrale ● 620 a.	1018	1008	1033	1023	1043	1058	1103	1053	1113	1118	1108	1133	|	1158	1203	1213	1218	1208	1233	1223	1248	1258	1303	1313
Bologna Centrale ● 620 d.	1021	1011	1036	1026	1046	1101	1106	1056	1116	1121	1111	1136	|	1201	1206	1216	1221	1211	1236	1226	1251	1301	1306	1316
Ferrara 620 d.	|	|	|	|	|	|	|	|	|	1149	|	|	|	1229	|	|	1249	|	|	|	|	1329	|	|
Rovigo 620 d.	1106	|	|	|	|	1145	|	|	|	|	|	|	|	|	|	|	|	|	|	|	|	|	|	|
Padova 620 d.	1127	|	|	|	|	1206	|	|	|	1227	|	|	|	1306	|	|	1327	|	|	|	|	1406	|	|
Venezia Mestre ▽ 620 a.	1142	|	|	|	|	1223	|	|	|	1242	|	|	|	1323	|	|	1342	|	|	|	|	1423	|	|
Venezia Santa Lucia a.	1155	|	|	|	|	1234	|	|	|	1255	|	|	|	1334	|	|	1355	|	|	|	|	1434	|	|
Reggio Emilia AV d.	...	|	1100	|	|	...	1130	|	|	...	|	1200	|	...	1230	|	...	|	1300	|	1315	...	1330	|
Milano Rogoredo a.	...	|	1138	1120s	|	...	1208	|	|	...	|	1238s	|	...	1308	|	...	|	1338s	1320s	1355	...	|	|
Milano Centrale a.	...	1115	1150	1135	|	...	1220	1200	|	...	1215	1250	1224	...	1320	|	...	1315	1350	1335	|	...	1420	|
Milano Centrale 605 d.	...	...	1202	...	|	...	1230	...	|	...	...	...	...	...	1330	|	...	...	...	...	|	...	1430	|
Verona Porta Nuova 605 a.	...	...	|	...	1138	...	|	...	1208	...	...	...	...	...	|	1308	...	...	...	...	|	...	|	1408
Verona Porta Nuova 595 d.	...	...	|	...	1149	...	|	...	1220	...	...	...	...	...	|	1320	...	...	...	...	|	...	|	1420
Rovereto 595 d.	...	...	|	...	|	...	|	...	1303	...	...	...	...	...	|	|	...	...	...	...	|	...	|	1503
Trento 595 d.	...	...	|	...	|	...	|	...	1317	...	...	...	...	...	|	|	...	...	...	...	|	...	|	1517
Bolzano / Bozen 595 a.	...	...	|	...	|	...	|	...	1348	...	...	...	...	...	|	|	...	...	...	...	|	...	|	1548
Peschiera del Garda 605 d.	...	...	|	...	1207	...	|	...	...	...	...	...	...	...	|	1336	...	...	...	...	|	...	|	...
Desenzano-Sirmione 605 d.	...	...	|	...	1216	...	|	...	...	...	...	...	...	...	|	|	...	...	...	...	|	...	|	...
Brescia 605 a.	...	...	|	...	1231	...	|	...	...	...	...	...	...	...	|	1400	...	...	...	...	|	...	|	...
Bergamo a.	...	...	|	...	...	...	|	...	...	...	...	...	...	...	|	1500	...	...	...	...	|	...	|	...
Torino Porta Susa ▽ 605 a.	...	...	1249	...	...	...	1318	...	...	...	...	...	...	...	1418	...	...	...	...	...	1508	...	1520	...
Torino Porta Nuova 605 a.	...	...	1300	...	...	...	1330	...	...	...	...	...	...	...	1430	...	...	...	...	...	1520	...	1530	...

	ITA	ITA	FR	FR	FR	ITA	FA	ITA	ITA	FR	ITA	FR	ITA	FR	ITA	ITA	FR	FR	ITA	ITA	FR	FA	FR	FR
	8910	9978	9514	9628	8418	9928	8816	8914	9980	9532	8960	9420	9932	9634	8916	9982	9584	9422	8134	9984	9638	9751	9540	9640
				①–⑤																	①–⑤			⑥
			N		R	A	L								g		R		R					
Salerno 640 d.	0838	...	0846	...	0959	...	...	...	...	...	...	...	...	...	...	...	1051	...	1122	...	...	...	...	...
Napoli Centrale 640 a.	0923	...	0928	...	|	...	...	...	...	...	...	...	...	...	...	...	1127	...	1158	...	...	...	...	...
Napoli Centrale 640 d.	0935	...	0940	1030	|	...	...	...	1035	1040	...	1109	1120	1130	...	1135	1140	1209	1215	...	1230	...	1240	1255
Napoli Afragola d.	|	...	0958	|	1025	...	...	...	|	1057u	...	|	1135	|	...	|	1158	|	1230	...	|	...	1258u	|
Roma Termini 640 a.	1045	...	1055	1140	1125	...	...	...	1145	1200	...	1219	1230	1239	...	1245	1300	1320	1330	...	1340	...	1355	1405
Roma Termini 620 d.	1055	1105	1110	1150	1135	1140	...	1155	1210	1210	1225	1236	1240	1250	1255	1305	1310	1335	1340	1410	1350	...	1410	1420
Roma Tiburtina 620 d.	1105	|	1120	|	1145	1150	...	1203	|	1220	|	1245	1250	|	1305	|	1320	1345	1350	|	|	...	1420	|
Firenze SMN 620 a.	1231	|	1246	|	1311	1317	...	1331	|	1346	1357	1411	1417	|	1431	|	1446	1511	1517	|	|	...	1546	|
Firenze SMN 620 d.	1239	|	1255	|	1320	1325	...	1339	|	1355	1405	1420	1425	|	1439	|	1455	1520	1525	|	|	...	1555	|
Bologna Centrale ● 620 a.	1318	1308	1333	1353	1358	1403	...	1418	|	1433	1443	1458	1503	1453	1518	1508	1533	1558	1603	|	1553	...	1633	|
Bologna Centrale ● 620 d.	1321	1311	1336	1356	1401	1406	1418	1421	|	1436	1446	1501	1506	1456	1521	1511	1536	1601	1606	|	1556	...	1636	|
Ferrara 620 d.	1349	|	|	|	1429	|	1440	|	|	|	|	|	|	|	1552	|	|	1629	|	|	|	...	|	|
Rovigo 620 d.	|	|	|	|	|	|	1457	1506	|	|	|	1545	|	|	|	|	|	|	|	|	|	...	|	|
Padova 620 d.	1427	|	|	|	1506	|	1533	1527	|	|	|	1606	|	|	1627	|	|	1706	|	|	|	...	|	|
Venezia Mestre ▽ 620 a.	1442	|	|	|	1523	|	1556	1542	|	|	|	1623	|	|	1642	|	|	1723	|	|	|	...	|	|
Venezia Santa Lucia a.	1455	|	|	|	1534	|	1608	1555	|	|	|	1634	|	|	1655	|	|	1734	|	|	|	...	|	|
Reggio Emilia AV d.	...	|	1400	|	...	1435	...	...	|	1500	|	...	1530	|	...	|	1600	...	1635	|	|	...	1700	|
Milano Rogoredo a.	...	|	1438	|	...	|	...	...	1502	1538	|	...	1608	|	...	|	1638	...	|	1702	|	...	1738s	1718s
Milano Centrale a.	...	1415	1450	1458	...	1520	...	...	1515	1550	|	...	1620	1600	...	1615	1650	...	1720	1715	1658	...	1750	1730
Milano Centrale 605 d.	...	...	1502	...	...	1530	...	...	...	1602	|	...	...	...	...	...	1702	...	1730	...	...	1745	...	...
Verona Porta Nuova 605 a.	...	...	|	...	...	|	...	...	...	|	1538	...	...	...	...	...	|	...	|	...	...	1858	...	...
Verona Porta Nuova 595 d.	...	...	|	...	...	|	...	...	...	|	1549	...	...	...	...	...	|	...	|	...	...	1920	...	...
Rovereto 595 d.	...	...	|	...	...	|	...	...	...	|	|	...	...	...	...	...	|	...	|	...	...	2003	...	...
Trento 595 d.	...	...	|	...	...	|	...	...	...	|	|	...	...	...	...	...	|	...	|	...	...	2017	...	...
Bolzano / Bozen 595 a.	...	...	|	...	...	|	...	...	...	|	|	...	...	...	...	...	|	...	|	...	...	2048	...	...
Peschiera del Garda 605 d.	...	...	|	...	...	|	...	...	...	|	1607	...	...	...	...	...	|	...	|	...	...	...	...	...
Desenzano-Sirmione 605 d.	...	...	|	...	...	|	...	...	...	|	1616	...	...	...	...	...	|	...	|	...	...	...	...	...
Brescia 605 a.	...	...	|	...	...	|	...	...	...	|	1631	...	...	...	...	...	|	...	|	...	...	...	...	...
Bergamo a.	...	...	|	...	...	|	...	...	...	|	...	...	...	...	...	...	|	...	|	...	...	...	...	...
Torino Porta Susa ▽ 605 a.	...	...	1549	...	...	1629	...	...	...	1649	...	...	...	...	...	...	1749	...	1824	...	...	...	...	...
Torino Porta Nuova 605 a.	...	...	1600	...	...	1640	...	...	...	1700	...	...	...	...	...	...	1800	...	1835	...	...	...	...	...

FOR FOOTNOTES SEE NEXT PAGE →

600 HIGH-SPEED SERVICES

Italo, Trenitalia

All trains 🅁 and 🍸. *FA*, *FB* and *FR* trains are operated by Trenitalia (www.trenitalia.com). *ITA* trains are operated by Italo (www.italotreno.it).
Trenitalia tickets and passes are not valid on Italo trains. Trains may use different numbers for part of their journey.

	FR 9423	*ITA* 9940	*FR* 9642	*ITA* 8918	*ITA* 9986	*FR* 9544	*FR* 9644	*FR* 9320		*FR* 9426	*ITA* 9946		*ITA* 9950	*FR* 9588	*FR* 9648	*FA* 9480	*FR* 9428	*ITA* 9948	*FR* 8524	*ITA* 8920	*ITA* 9990	*FR* 9552	*FR* 9652 Ⓑ	*FR* 9430
				T							**R**			**R**		**T**				**U**				**U**
Salerno 640 d.	...	...	...	...	...	1250	...	...	...	...	1324	...	1343	1354	...	...	...	...	...	...	...	1445	...	...
Napoli Centrale 640 a.	...	...	...	...	...	1328	...	...	...	...	1358	...	1423	1428	...	...	...	...	...	...	...	1523	...	...
Napoli Centrale 640 d.	⊡	1320	1330	1335	...	1340	...	1355	...	1410	1420	...	1435	1440	1500	...	1509	1520	...	1535	...	1540	1555	1609
Napoli Afragola d.	|	1335	|	|	...	1358	...	1410u	...	|	|	...	|	1458	1515u	...	|	1535	...	|	...	1558	1610u	|
Roma Termini 640 a.	1425	1430	1435	1446	...	1455	...	1505	...	1520	1530	...	1545	1555	1610	...	1620	1630	...	1645	...	1700	1705	1719
Roma Termini 620 d.	1435	1440	1450	1455	1505	1510	1520	1525	...	1535	1540	...	1610	1610	1625	1630	1635	1640	1650	1655	1705	1710	1720	1735
Roma Tiburtina 620 d.	1445	1450	|	1505	|	1520	|	1535	...	1545	1550	...	|	1620	|	1640u	1645	1650	1700u	1705	|	1720	|	1745
Firenze SMN 620 a.	1611	1617	|	1631	|	1646	|	1701	...	1711	1717	...	|	1746	|	|	1811	1817	1827	1831	|	1846	|	1911
Firenze SMN 620 d.	1620	1625	|	1639	|	1655	|	1710	...	1720	1725	...	|	1755	|	|	1820	1825	1836	1839	|	1855	|	1920
Bologna Centrale ● 620 a.	1658	1703	1653	1718	1708	1733	|	1748		1758	1803		|	1833	|	1838	1858	1903	1913	1918	1908	1933	1923	1958
Bologna Centrale ● 620 d.	1701	1706	1656	1721	1711	1736	|	1751	...	1801	1806	...	|	1836	|	1841	1901	1906	1916	1921	1911	1936	1926	2001
Ferrara 620 d.	|	|	|	1752	|	|	|	|	...	1829	|	...	|	|	|	|	1929	|	|	1949	|	|	|	|
Rovigo 620 d.	1745	|	|	|	|	|	|	|	...	|	|	...	|	|	|	|	|	|	|	|	|	|	|	2045
Padova 620 d.	1806	|	|	1827	|	|	|	|	...	1906	|	...	|	|	|	1942	2006	|	|	2027	|	|	|	2106
Venezia Mestre ▽ 620 a.	1823	|	|	1842	|	|	|	|	...	1923	|	...	|	|	|	1956	2023	|	|	2040	|	|	|	2123
Venezia Santa Lucia a.	1834	|	|	...	|	|	|	|	...	1934	|	...	|	|	|	...	2034	|	|	...	|	|	|	...
Reggio Emilia AV d.	...	1730	|	...	|	1800	|	1815	...	...	1835	...	|	1900	|	...	...	1930	|	...	|	2000	|	...
Milano Rogoredo a.	...	1808	|	...	|	1838s	1818s	1855	...	...	|	...	1902	1938	|	...	...	2008	|	...	|	2038	|	...
Milano Centrale a.	...	1820	1800	...	1815	1850	1830	|	...	...	1920	...	1915	1950	1924	...	...	2020	|	...	2015	2050	2030	...
Milano Centrale 605 d.	...	1830	1810	...	...	...	...	|	...	...	1930	...	...	2002	...	...	...	...	|	...	...	2102	2053	...
Verona Porta Nuova 605 a.	...	|	|	...	...	...	...	|	...	...	|	...	...	|	...	...	...	...	2008	...	...	|	|	...
Verona Porta Nuova 595 d.	...	|	|	...	...	...	...	|	...	...	|	...	...	|	...	...	...	...	2020	...	...	|	|	...
Rovereto 595 d.	...	|	|	...	...	...	...	|	...	...	|	...	...	|	...	...	...	...	2103	...	...	|	|	...
Trento 595 d.	...	|	|	...	...	...	...	|	...	...	|	...	...	|	...	...	...	...	2117	...	...	|	|	...
Bolzano / Bozen 595 a.	...	|	|	...	...	...	...	|	...	...	|	...	...	|	...	...	...	...	2148	...	...	|	|	...
Peschiera del Garda 605 d.	...	|	|	...	...	...	...	|	...	...	|	...	...	|	...	...	...	...	...	...	...	|	|	...
Desenzano-Sirmione 605 d.	...	|	|	...	...	...	...	|	...	...	|	...	...	|	...	...	...	...	...	...	...	|	|	...
Brescia 605 a.	...	|	|	...	...	...	...	|	...	...	|	...	...	|	...	...	...	...	...	...	...	|	|	...
Bergamo a.	...	|	|	...	...	...	...	|	...	...	|	...	...	|	...	...	...	...	...	...	...	|	2143	...
Torino Porta Susa ▽ 605 a.	...	1918	1859	...	...	...	...	2008	...	...	2029	...	...	2049	...	...	...	...	...	...	...	2149	...	...
Torino Porta Nuova 605 a.	...	1930	1910	...	...	...	...	2020	...	...	2040	...	...	2100	...	...	...	...	...	...	...	2200	...	...

	ITA 9952	*FR* 9658	*FR* 8828	*ITA* 8922	*ITA* 9992	*FR* 9556	*FR* 9660	*ITA* 8966	*FR* 9432	*ITA* 9954	*FR* 9662	*ITA* 9994	*FR* 8528	*FR* 9560	*ITA* 8968	*FR* 9434	*ITA* 8158	*FR* 9668 Ⓑ	*FR* 9330		*ITA* 9996 Ⓑ	*ITA* 9962		*FR* 9568 Ⓑ
	A	**R**	**L**		**G**									**L**			**R**							
Salerno 640 d.	...	1617	...	...	...	...	...	...	...	1625	...	...	...	...	...	...	1722	...	...	...	...	1814	...	...
Napoli Centrale 640 a.	...	|	...	...	...	...	...	...	...	1705	...	...	...	...	...	...	1758	...	...	...	...	1858	...	...
Napoli Centrale 640 d.	...	|	...	1635	1620	1640	1655	...	1705	1720	1725	1730	...	...	1755	1809	1820	1830	...	...	1835	1920	...	1940
Napoli Afragola d.	...	1641	...	|	|	1658u	1709u	...	|	1734	|	1748	...	...	|	|	|	|	...	...	|	1935	...	1958u
Roma Termini 640 a.	...	1740	...	1745	1730	1755	1805	...	1815	1830	1835	1846	...	...	1910	1920	1930	1940	...	...	1946	2030	...	2055
Roma Termini 620 d.	1740	1750	...	1755	1805	1810	1820	1825	1835	1840	1850	1905	1850	1911	1925	1935	1940	1950	1950	...	2005	2040	...	2110
Roma Tiburtina 620 d.	1750	|	...	1805	|	1819	|	|	1847	1851	|	|	1901u	1920	|	1945	1950	|	2000u	...	|	2050	...	2120
Firenze SMN 620 a.	1917	|	...	1931	|	1946	|	1957	2032	2017	|	|	2027	2046	2057	2111	2117	|	2127	...	|	2217	...	2258
Firenze SMN 620 d.	1925	|	...	1939	|	1955	|	2005	2041	2025	|	|	2036	2055	2105	2120	2125	|	2136	...	|	2225	...	...
Bologna Centrale ● 620 a.	2003	1953	...	2018	|	2033	2023	2043	2118	2103	2053	2108	2113	2133	2143	2158	2203	2153	2213	...	|	2303	...	...
Bologna Centrale ● 620 d.	2006	1956	2018	2021	|	2036	2026	2046	2121	2106	2056	2111	2116	2136	2146	2201	2206	2156	2216	...	|	2306	...	...
Ferrara 620 d.	|	|	2042	|	|	|	|	|	2152	|	|	|	|	|	|	2229	|	|	|	...	|	|	...	...
Rovigo 620 d.	|	|	2108	2101	|	|	|	|	|	|	|	|	|	|	|	|	|	|	|	...	|	|	...	...
Padova 620 d.	|	|	2140	2127	|	|	|	|	2229	|	|	|	|	|	|	2306	|	|	|	...	|	|	...	...
Venezia Mestre ▽ 620 a.	|	|	2156	2142	|	|	|	|	2242	|	|	|	|	|	|	2323	|	|	|	...	|	|	...	...
Venezia Santa Lucia a.	|	|	2209	2155	|	|	|	|	2255	|	|	|	|	|	|	2334	|	|	|	...	|	|	...	...
Reggio Emilia AV d.	2030	|	...	...	|	2100	|	|	...	2130	|	|	|	2200	|	...	2235	|	|	...	|	2330	...	...
Milano Rogoredo a.	|	|	...	...	2103	2138s	|	|	...	2208	|	|	|	2238s	|	...	|	|	|	...	2302	0008	...	...
Milano Centrale a.	2120	2100	...	...	2115	2150	2130	|	...	2220	2200	2215	|	2250	|	...	2320	2300	0015	...	2315	0020	...	...
Milano Centrale 605 d.	2130	...	...	...	...	...	2145	|	...	...	2210	2230	|	...	|	...	...	...	...	...	...	...	...	...
Verona Porta Nuova 605 a.	|	...	...	...	...	...	|	2138	...	...	|	|	2208	...	2238	...	...	...	...	...	...	...	...	...
Verona Porta Nuova 595 d.	|	...	...	...	...	...	|	2150	...	...	|	|	2220	...	2249	...	...	...	...	...	...	...	...	...
Rovereto 595 d.	|	...	...	...	...	...	|	2232	...	...	|	|	|	...	|	...	...	...	...	...	...	...	...	...
Trento 595 d.	|	...	...	...	...	...	|	2246	...	...	|	|	|	...	|	...	...	...	...	...	...	...	...	...
Bolzano / Bozen 595 a.	|	...	...	...	...	...	|	2318	...	...	|	|	|	...	|	...	...	...	...	...	...	...	...	...
Peschiera del Garda 605 d.	|	...	...	...	...	...	|	...	...	...	|	|	|	...	2307	...	...	...	...	...	...	...	...	...
Desenzano-Sirmione 605 d.	|	...	...	...	...	...	|	...	...	...	|	|	|	...	2316	...	...	...	...	...	...	...	...	...
Brescia 605 a.	|	...	...	...	...	...	2223	...	...	...	|	|	2300	...	2331	...	...	...	...	...	...	...	...	...
Bergamo a.	|	...	...	...	...	...	...	...	...	...	|	|	2340	...	0010	...	...	...	...	...	...	...	...	...
Torino Porta Susa ▽ 605 a.	2229	...	...	...	...	...	...	...	...	...	2259	2319	...	...	...	...	...	...	...	...	...	...	...	...
Torino Porta Nuova 605 a.	2240	...	...	...	...	...	...	...	...	...	2310	2330	...	...	...	...	...	...	...	...	...	...	...	...

NOTES for pages 291 and 292.

- **A** – From Bari (Tables **615**).
- **B** – From Battipaglia (Table **640**).
- **C** – From Caserta (Table **615**).
- **G** – To Genova (Table **610**).
- **L** – From Lecce (Tables **615**).
- **N** – From Taranto (Tables **615**).
- **P** – From Perugia (Table **620**).
- **R** – From Reggio di Calabria (Table **640**).
- **S** – From Sibari (Tables **640**).
- **T** – To Trieste (Table **601**).
- **U** – To Udine (Table **601**).

- **b** – Timings may vary by up to 10 minutes due to engineering work.
- **g** – ①④⑤⑥⑦ only.
- **j** – Not Apr. 6, 10, 11, 12, 25, 26, May 1, 2, June 2, 5.
- **s** – Calls to set down only.
- **u** – Calls to pick up only.

- ⊡ – From Fiumicino Aeroporto ✈ (a. 1353).
- ⊖ – Via Cassino (d. 0605).
- ⊙ – To Oulx (a. 1312) and Bardonecchia (a. 1325).
- ▽ – Most trains call to set down only.
- ● – Most services use underground platforms 16 – 19; allow a minimum of 10 minutes when connecting with services from / to the main station.

VENEZIA - UDINE and TRIESTE — 601

For Venezia / Udine / Trieste - Ljubljana trains see Table **87**. For Udine - Villach trains see Table **88**.

km		ICN 774	FR 9707	IC 588	ITA 8918	FA 9480	IC 592	FR 9759		
		A ❖			B					
	Roma Termini **600 620** d.	2235	...	1022	1455	1630	1530	...	...	...
	Bologna C **600 620** d.	0333	...	1446	1721	1841	2000	...	...	...
	Torino P Nuova **605** d.	|	...	|	|	|	|	1840	...	...
	Milano Centrale **605** d.	|	0745	|	|	|	|	|	...	...
	Milano P Garibaldi **605** d.	|	|	|	|	|	|	1943	...	...
0	**Venezia** Mestre d.	0525	1011	1640	1855	2010	2151	2205	...	...
33	S. Dona di Piave-Jesolo ◧ d.	|	1039	1705	1926	|	2212	|	...	...
60	Portogruaro-Caorle d.	|	1057	1728	1949	|	2237	|	...	...
74	Latisana-Lignano-Bibione d.	●	1108	1739	1958	|	2249	2242	...	...
103	Cervignano-Aquileia-Grado d.	|	1126	1757	|	|	2307	2301	...	...
115	Trieste Airport ✈ d.	|	1135	1807	2024	2125	2317	2310	...	...
	Gorizia Centrale ⊡ d.	0816	|	|	|	|	|	|	...	...
120	Monfalcone d.	0834	1142	1814	2032	|	2324	2317	...	...
148	**Trieste** Centrale a.	0901	1205	1837	2056	2155	2347	2340	...	...

	FR 9712	FA 9466	IC 584	ITA 8902	IC 594	FA 9758	ICN 770		
				B			A ❖		
Trieste Centrale d.	0600	0642	0721	0802	1327	1705	1950	...	...
Monfalcone d.	0625	|	0747	0827	1352	1730	2014	...	...
Gorizia Centrale ⊡ d.	|	|	|	|	|	|	2038	...	...
Trieste Airport ✈ d.	0631	0707	0753	0834	1358	1736	|	...	...
Cervignano-Aquileia-Grado d.	0639	|	0802	|	1407	1743	|	...	...
Latisana-Lignano-Bibione d.	0655	|	0822	0900	1424	1759	●	...	...
Portogruaro-Caorle d.	|	|	0834	0910	1434	1809	|	...	...
S. Dona di Piave-Jesolo ◧ d.	|	|	0852	0929	1452	1825	|	...	...
Venezia Mestre a.	0741	0819	0919	0955	1514	1850	2315	...	...
Milano P Garibaldi **605** a.	0955	|	|	|	|	|	|	...	...
Milano Centrale **605** a.	|	|	|	|	|	2115	|	...	...
Torino P Nuova **605** a.	1100	|	|	|	|	...	|	...	...
Bologna C **600 620** a.	...	0949	1112	1139	1721	...	0109	...	...
Roma Termini **600 620** a.	...	1200	1535	1405	2135	...	0635	...	...

km		ICN 774	RJ 132	RJ 130	ITA 8993	ITA 8920	FA 9755	FR 9430		
		A ❖				C		C		
	Roma Termini **600 620** d.	2235	...	...	...	1655	...	1735	...	...
	Bologna C **600 620** d.	0333	...	...	...	1921	...	2001	...	...
	Milano Centrale **605** d.	|	...	...	1735	|	1845	|	...	...
0	**Venezia** Santa Lucia d.	0548	0955	1555	|	|	|	|	...	...
9	**Venezia** Mestre d.	|	1007	1607	2000	2051	2110	2137	...	...
30	Treviso Centrale d.	0614	1030	1630	2028	2109	2130	2156	...	...
57	Conegliano d.	0634	|	|	2046	2127	2148	2215	...	...
74	Sacile d.	0654	|	|	|	|	|	|	...	...
87	Pordenone d.	0705	1107	1707	2106	2147	2208	2236	...	...
136	**Udine** a.	0743	1144	1744	2140	2217	2237	2305	...	...
	Wien Hbf **88** a.	...	1742	2342	...	...	...	...	...	...

	FA 9713	FR 9409	ITA 8971	ITA 8907	RJ 131	RJ 133	ICN 770		
		C		D			A ❖		
Wien Hbf **88** d.	...	...	...	...	0618	1218	...	...	...
Udine d.	0615	0647	0716	0727	1218	1818	2059	...	...
Pordenone d.	0646	0721	0749	0800	1251	1851	2133	...	...
Sacile d.	|	|	|	|	|	|	2143	...	...
Conegliano d.	0706	0750	0812	0823	|	|	2156	...	...
Treviso Centrale d.	0731	0813	0831	0845	1332	1932	2215	...	...
Venezia Mestre a.	0749	0825	0855	0908	1353	1953	|	...	...
Venezia Santa Lucia a.	|	|	|	|	1405	2005	2238	...	...
Milano Centrale **605** a.	1015	|	1125	|	...	...	|	...	...
Bologna C **600 620** a.	...	0959	...	1039	...	...	0109	...	...
Roma Termini **600 620** a.	...	1225	...	1305	...	...	0635	...	...

km																								
		⚒																					Ⓑ	
0	**Venezia** Santa Lucia d.	...	...	...	0639	0739	...	0939	1039	...	1239	1339	...	1439	1539	...	1639	1739	...	1839	1939	...	2101	2239
9	**Venezia** Mestre d.	...	0551	...	0651	0751	...	0951	1051	...	1251	1351	...	1451	1551	...	1651	1751	...	1851	1951	...	2114	2251
42	S. Dona di Piave-Jesolo ◧ d.	...	0615	...	0715	0815	...	1015	1115	...	1315	1415	...	1515	1615	...	1715	1815	...	1915	2015	...	|	2315
69	Portogruaro-Caorle d.	0529	0635	...	0735	0835	...	1035	1135	...	1335	1435	...	1535	1635	...	1735	1835	...	1935	2035	...	|	2335
83	Latisana-Lignano-Bibione d.	0540	0646	...	0746	0846	...	1046	1146	...	1346	1446	...	1546	1646	...	1746	1846	...	1946	2046	...	2154	2346
101	S. Giorgio di Nogaro d.	0552	0658	...	0758	0858	...	1058	1158	...	1358	1458	...	1558	1658	...	1758	1858	...	1958	2058	...	2204	2358
112	Cervignano-Aquileia-Grado d.	0601	0707	...	0807	0907	...	1107	1207	...	1407	1507	...	1607	1707	...	1807	1907	...	2007	2107	...	2212	0007
124	Trieste Airport ✈ d.	0609	0715	...	0815	0915	...	1115	1215	...	1415	1515	...	1615	1715	...	1815	1915	...	2015	2115	...	2220	0015
129	Monfalcone d.	0615	0721	...	0821	0921	...	1121	1221	...	1421	1521	...	1621	1721	...	1821	1921	...	2021	2121	...	2226	0021
157	**Trieste** Centrale a.	0642	0744	...	0844	0944	...	1144	1244	...	1444	1544	...	1644	1744	...	1844	1944	...	2044	2144	...	2255	0044

																				Ⓐ			
Trieste Centrale d.	0516	0616	...	0716	0816	...	0916	1216	...	1316	1416	...	1516	1616	...	1716	1816	...	1916	2016	...	2116	2206
Monfalcone d.	0540	0640	...	0740	0840	...	0940	1240	...	1340	1440	...	1540	1640	...	1740	1840	...	1940	2040	...	2140	2229
Trieste Airport ✈ d.	0545	0645	...	0745	0845	...	0945	1245	...	1345	1445	...	1545	1645	...	1745	1845	...	1945	2045	...	2145	2234
Cervignano-Aquileia-Grado d.	0553	0653	...	0753	0853	...	0953	1253	...	1353	1453	...	1553	1653	...	1753	1853	...	1953	2053	...	2153	2242
S. Giorgio di Nogaro d.	0601	0701	...	0801	0901	...	1001	1301	...	1401	1501	...	1601	1701	...	1801	1901	...	2001	2101	...	2201	2249
Latisana-Lignano-Bibione d.	0614	0714	...	0814	0914	...	1014	1314	...	1414	1514	...	1614	1714	...	1814	1914	...	2014	2114	...	2214	2300
Portogruaro-Caorle d.	0625	0725	...	0825	0925	...	1025	1325	...	1425	1525	...	1625	1725	...	1825	1925	...	2025	*2139*	...	*2239*	2310
S. Dona di Piave-Jesolo ◧ d.	0643	0743	...	0843	0943	...	1043	1343	...	1443	1543	...	1643	1743	...	1843	1943	...	2043	*2203*	...	*2302*	2327
Venezia Mestre a.	0709	0809	...	0909	1009	...	1109	1409	...	1509	1609	...	1709	1809	...	1909	2009	...	2109	*2238*	...	*2338*	2350
Venezia Santa Lucia a.	0721	0821	...	0921	1021	...	1121	1421	...	1521	1621	...	1721	1821	...	1921	2021	...	2121	*2251*	...	*2351*	...

km																								
		Ⓐ	Ⓐ	Ⓐ	⚒		⚒	†					Ⓐ			Ⓐ	†		Ⓐ		†			
0	**Venezia** Santa Lucia d.	0501	0513	0601	0701	...	0713	0801	1001	1201	...	1401	1501	1601	...	1701	1701	1801	1901	...	1901	2001	2201	2301
9	**Venezia** Mestre d.	0514	0526	0614	0714	...	0726	0814	1014	1214	...	1414	1514	1614	...	1714	1714	1814	1914	...	1914	2014	2214	2314
30	Treviso Centrale d.	0534	0552	0634	0734	...	0752	0834	1034	1234	...	1434	1534	1634	...	1734	1734	1834	1934	...	1934	2034	2235	2335
57	Conegliano d.	0552	0619	0652	0752	...	0819	0852	1052	1252	...	1452	1552	1652	...	1752	1752	1852	1952	...	1952	2052	2253	2353
74	Sacile d.	0603	0634	0703	0803	...	0834	0903	1103	1303	...	1503	1603	1703	...	1803	1803	1903	2003	...	2003	2103	2304	0004
87	Pordenone d.	0615	0648	0715	0815	...	0848	0915	1115	1315	...	1515	1615	1715	...	1815	1815	1915	2015	...	2015	2115	2316	0016
136	**Udine** a.	0651	0728	0751	0851	...	0928	0951	1151	1351	...	1551	1651	1751	...	1851	1851	1951	2051	...	2051	2151	2353	0053
136	**Udine** d.	0654	0732	*0808*	0854	...	0938	0954	1154	1354	...	1554	1654	1754	...	1854	*1908*	1954	*2120*	...	2120	2154	2355	...
169	Gorizia Centrale ⊡ d.	0718	0803	*0839*	0918	...	1009	1018	1218	1418	...	1618	1718	1818	...	1918	*1939*	2018	*2151*	...	2151	2218	0026	...
192	Monfalcone d.	0739	0827	*0903*	0939	...	1033	1039	1239	1439	...	1639	1739	1839	...	1939	*2003*	2041	*2215*	...	2215	2239	0049	...
219	**Trieste** Centrale a.	0802	0856	*0932*	1002	...	1102	1102	1302	1502	...	1702	1802	1902	...	2002	*2032*	2104	*2244*	...	2244	2302	0118	...

		⚒	⚒			†			Ⓐ		⚒		Ⓐ			Ⓐ	Ⓐ			Ⓐ		Ⓐ	
Trieste Centrale d.	...	0528	0548	0658	...	*0728*	0858	1058	1128	...	*1222*	1258	1332	...	1458	*1552*	*1558*	1658	...	1758	1858	*1928*	2032
Monfalcone d.	...	0558	0618	0722	...	*0758*	0922	1122	1158	...	*1246*	1322	1402	...	1522	*1616*	*1628*	1722	...	1822	1922	*1958*	2058
Gorizia Centrale ⊡ d.	...	0620	0645	0743	...	*0820*	0943	1143	1220	...	|	1343	1424	...	1543	|	*1650*	1743	...	1843	1943	*2020*	2120
Udine a.	...	0652	0719	0806	...	*0852*	1006	1206	1252	...	*1324*	1406	1456	...	1606	*1654*	*1722*	1806	...	1906	2006	*2052*	2152
Udine d.	0601	0658	0732	0809	...	0909	1009	1209	1305	...	1332	1409	1509	...	1609	1709	1732	1809	...	1909	2009	2109	2209
Pordenone d.	0636	0737	0811	0844	...	0944	1044	1244	1340	...	1411	1444	1544	...	1644	1744	1811	1844	...	1944	2044	2144	2244
Sacile d.	0647	0752	0825	0855	...	0955	1055	1255	1351	...	1425	1455	1555	...	1655	1755	1825	1855	...	1955	2055	2155	2254
Conegliano d.	0659	0803	0841	0907	...	1007	1107	1307	1403	...	1441	1507	1607	...	1707	1807	1841	1907	...	2007	2107	2207	2307
Treviso Centrale d.	0723	0823	0907	0927	...	1027	1127	1327	1423	...	1507	1527	1627	...	1727	1827	1907	1927	...	2027	2127	2227	2327
Venezia Mestre a.	0746	0846	0934	0946	...	1046	1146	1346	1444	...	1534	1546	1646	...	1746	1846	1934	1946	...	2046	2146	2246	2346
Venezia Santa Lucia a.	0759	0859	0947	0959	...	1059	1159	1359	1459	...	1547	1559	1659	...	1759	1859	1947	1959	...	2059	2159	2259	2359

🚋 service **Trieste** (Piazza Oberdan) - **Villa Opicina** (Stazione Trenovia) and v.v. *Linea Tranviaria.* Operator: Trieste Trasporti S.p.A. Service currently suspended, replacement 🚌 (Line **2**).
From **Trieste**: 0711, 0731, 0751 and every 20 minutes until 2011. From **Villa Opicina**: 0700, 0720, 0740 and every 20 minutes until 2000. Journey 15 minutes.
Walking times: Trieste Centrale railway station - Piazza Oberdan ± 10 minutes; Villa Opicina Stazione Trenovia - Villa Opicina railway station ± 20 minutes.

A – 🛏 1, 2 cl., 🛏 2 cl. (4 berth) (2.) Trieste - Udine - Venezia - Roma and v.v.
B – (12.) 🍷 Napoli - Milano - Venezia - Trieste and v.v. (Table **600**).
C – (12.) 🍷 Napoli - Roma - Bologna - Venezia - Udine and v.v. (Table **600**).
D – (12.) 🍷 Udine - Venezia - Bologna - Roma - Napoli - Salerno (Table **600**).

◧ – A 🚌 service operates 0600 - 1930 to Lido di Jesolo; 1 – 2 per hour. Journey 35 minutes.
● – Via Udine and Venezia (see Udine - Venezia sub-table).

⊡ – An international 🚌 service operates between Gorizia Centrale and Nova Gorica (Slovenia; bus stop 100 metres from station on Italian side) stations. Total journey time ± 20 minutes.
❖ – Running days, timings and numbers of *ICN* trains may vary - please check your reservation. For confirmed timings please consult the *Trenitalia* journey planner at www.trenitalia.com.

603 NORTH EAST ITALY LOCAL SERVICES

2nd class

BELLUNO - CALALZO (see note △)

km																								
		⚒s	🚌⚒	s	🚌	Ⓐv	🚌Ⓑ	Ⓒs	🚌Ⓒ	🚌Ⓐ	s	🚌	⚒s	🚌⚒	s	🚌	s	🚌	🚌Ⓐ	🚌Ⓐ	s	🚌	Ⓑv	🚌Ⓑ
0	**Belluno** d.	0730	0753	0830	0853	0930	0953	1030	1030	1230	1330	1353	1430	1453	1530	1553	1730	1753	1830	1853	1930	1953	2030	2053
7	Ponte nelle Alpi-Polpet a.	0738	0806	0838	0906	0938	1006	1038	1043	1241	1338	1406	1438	1506	1538	1606	1738	1806	1841	1906	1938	2006	2038	2106
7	Ponte nelle Alpi-Polpet d.	0739	0806	0839	0906	0939	1006	1039	1043	1241	1339	1406	1439	1506	1539	1606	1739	1806	1841	1906	1939	2006	2039	2106
44	**Calalzo** ● a.	0827	0857	0927	0957	1027	1057	1127	1134	1326	1427	1457	1527	1557	1627	1657	1827	1857	1926	1957	2027	2057	2127	2157

	⚒s	🚌⚒	s	🚌	s	🚌Ⓐ	🚌⚒	⚒s	🚌	s	🚌Ⓐ	🚌Ⓑ	Ⓑv	🚌⚒	⑥s	🚌Ⓑ	Ⓑv	🚌	s	s	🚌		
Calalzo ● d.	0628	0648	0728	0858	0928	1058	1158	1228	1258	1328	1358	1458	1528	1558	1628	1658	1728	1758	1828	1928	1928	...	...
Ponte nelle Alpi-Polpet a.	0708	0734	0808	0944	1008	1144	1244	1308	1344	1408	1444	1544	1608	1644	1708	1744	1808	1844	1908	2008	2014	...	...
Ponte nelle Alpi-Polpet d.	0710	0734	0810	0944	1010	1144	1244	1310	1344	1410	1444	1544	1610	1644	1710	1744	1810	1844	1910	2010	2014	...	...
Belluno a.	0718	0752	0818	1002	1018	1202	1302	1318	1402	1418	1502	1602	1618	1702	1718	1802	1818	1902	1918	2018	2032	...	...

CALALZO - CORTINA

km	🚌 service 30 (♠)																							
		⚒		⚒		⚒	⚒	⑥		Ⓐ	⚒	⚒				⚒		⚒	⚒	†		⚒	⚒	
0	**Calalzo** Stazione FS d.	0622	0658	0740	...	0820	0935	1100	...	1110	1215	1310	...	1400	...	1450	...	1635	1740	1835	...	1900	2035	...
35	**Cortina** Autostazione a.	0718	0756	0838	...	0918	1033	1158	...	1208	1313	1408	...	1458	...	1548	...	1733	1838	1933	...	1958	2128	...

🚌 service 30 (♠)																						
	⚒	⚒	⚒		⚒	⚒	⚒		⚒		⚒		⚒		⚒		⚒	⚒	⚒				
Cortina Autostazione d.	0545	0623	0650	...	0820	0930	1115	...	1220	1240	1315	...	1402	1505	1620	...	1705	1755	1920	...	1940	2010	...
Calalzo Stazione FS a.	0643	0721	0748	...	0918	1028	1213	...	1318	1338	1413	...	1500	1603	1718	...	1803	1853	2018	...	2035	2103	...

VENZIA - CONEGLIANO - BELLUNO

km																								
		⚒		Ⓐ	Ⓒ			Ⓐ🚌	Ⓐ🚌			⚒				Ⓐ		⚒			Ⓑ			🚌
0	**Venezia** Santa Lucia d.	...	...	0743	0748	...	0843	...	...	...	...	...	...	...	...	1443	...	1643	1743	...	1843	...	1931	...
9	**Venezia** Mestre d.	...	...	0756	0800	...	0856	...	...	...	...	...	...	...	...	1456	...	1656	1756	...	1856	...	1944	...
30	Treviso Centrale d.	...	...	0822	0821	...	0922	...	...	...	...	...	...	...	...	1522	...	1722	1822	...	1922	...	2007	...
57	**Conegliano** d.	0639	0741	0840	0841	...	0940	1040	1140	1241	...	1341	...	1441	...	1540	1641	1740	1846	...	1940	...	2031	2201
71	Vittorio Veneto d.	0657	0802	0902	0902	...	1002	1103	1203	1302	...	1402	...	1502	...	1602	1702	1802	1903	...	2002	...	2047	2224
98	Ponte nelle Alpi-Polpet a.	0731	0831	0931	0931	...	1031	1148	1248	1331	...	1431	...	1531	...	1631	1731	1831	1931	...	2031	...	2115	2309
98	Ponte nelle Alpi-Polpet d.	0739	0839	0939	0939	...	1039	1148	1248	1339	...	1439	...	1539	...	1639	1739	1839	1939	...	2039	...	2116	2310
105	**Belluno** a.	0747	0847	0947	0947	...	1047	1201	1301	1347	...	1447	...	1547	...	1647	1747	1847	1947	...	2047	...	2124	2322

	⚒	⚒	†	⚒			Ⓐ🚌		Ⓐ🚌		Ⓐ				⚒	Ⓐ					Ⓒ		🚌
Belluno d.	0536	0615	0620	0720	...	0820	0920	1020	1120	...	1220	1320	1420	...	1520	1620	1720	...	...	...	1820	1920	2020
Ponte nelle Alpi-Polpet a.	0544	0623	0628	0728	...	0828	0933	1028	1133	...	1228	1328	1428	...	1528	1628	1728	...	...	...	1828	1928	2033
Ponte nelle Alpi-Polpet d.	0545	0624	0633	0733	...	0833	0933	1033	1133	...	1233	1333	1433	...	1533	1633	1733	...	...	...	1833	1933	2033
Vittorio Veneto d.	0613	0656	0701	0759	...	0901	1011	1101	1211	...	1301	1401	1501	...	1601	1701	1801	...	...	...	1904	2001	2111
Conegliano d.	0631	0712	0719	0817	...	0921	1041	1119	1241	...	1318	1418	1521	...	1618	1721	1819	...	...	...	1919	2018	2141
Treviso Centrale d.	0653	0737	0737	0837	...	0940	...	1137	...	...	...	...	1540	...	...	1740	1837	...	...	...	1940	...	...
Venezia Mestre a.	0716	0804	0804	0904	...	1004	...	1204	...	...	...	...	1604	...	...	1804	1904	...	...	...	2004	...	...
Venezia Santa Lucia a.	0729	0817	0817	0917	...	1017	...	1217	...	...	...	...	1617	...	...	1817	1917	...	...	...	2017	...	...

PADOVA - CASTELFRANCO VENETO - MONTEBELLUNA

km																								
		Ⓐ	⚒		†			⚒C	⚒			⚒		⚒	ⒶC			Ⓑ				C	🚌	
0	**Padova** d.	0607	0704	0804	0904	...	1104	1125	1204	1304	...	1404	1504	1604	1625	...	1704	1804	1904	2004	...	2125	2246	...
31	Castelfranco Veneto d.	0636	0736	0836	0936	...	1136	1152	1236	1336	...	1436	1536	1636	1652	...	1736	1836	1936	2036	...	2156	2347	...
48	**Montebelluna** a.	0652	0752	0852	0952	...	1153	1205	1252	1352	...	1452	1552	1652	1705	...	1752	1852	1952	2052	...	2209	0017	...

	⚒C		⚒	†C			⚒C	†			⚒		⚒C	⚒			⚒	Ⓑ					
Montebelluna d.	0541	0708	0808	0808	...	0908	0946	1008	1208	...	1308	1408	1457	1508	...	1608	1708	1808	1908	...	2008	2108	...
Castelfranco Veneto d.	0554	0725	0825	0825	...	0925	0959	1025	1225	...	1325	1425	1510	1525	...	1625	1725	1825	1925	...	2025	2125	...
Padova a.	0628	0756	0856	0853	...	0956	1033	1056	1256	...	1356	1456	1534	1556	...	1656	1756	1856	1956	...	2056	2156	...

TRENTO - BASSANO DEL GRAPPA

km																								
		⚒		⚒						⚒		⚒				⚒		⚒		⚒		⚒		
0	**Trento** d.	0505	...	0535	...	0605	...	0905	...	1105	...	1205	...	1305	...	1605	...	1635	...	1705	...	1805	...	1905
31	Levico Terme d.	0552	...	0622	...	0652	...	0952	...	1152	...	1252	...	1352	...	1652	...	1722	...	1752	...	1852	...	1952
44	Borgo Valsugana Centro d.	0608	...	0638	...	0710	...	1008	...	1208	...	1308	...	1408	...	1708	...	1738	...	1808	...	1908	...	2008
97	**Bassano del Grappa** a.	0712	...	...	...	0816	...	1116	...	1316	...	1416	...	1516	...	1816	...	...	...	1916	...	2016	...	2116

	⚒		⚒		⚒		†		⚒		⚒		⚒				⚒				⚒		
Bassano del Grappa d.	0500	...	0725	...	0825	...	0925	...	1125	...	1325	...	1425	...	1525	...	...	...	1925	...	2025	...	2125
Borgo Valsugana Centro d.	0558	...	0828	...	0928	...	1028	...	1228	...	1428	...	1528	...	1628	...	1821	...	2028	...	2128	...	2228
Levico Terme d.	0612	...	0842	...	0942	...	1042	...	1242	...	1442	...	1542	...	1642	...	1842	...	2042	...	2142	...	2242
Trento a.	0659	...	0929	...	1029	...	1129	...	1329	...	1529	...	1629	...	1729	...	1929	...	2129	...	2229	...	2329

TREVISO - MONTEBELLUNA - BELLUNO *SEE NOTE* ⊡

km																								
		⚒	⚒		⚒	⚒		†	⚒		⚒				Ⓐ									
0	**Treviso** Centrale d.	*0535*	*0635*	...	*0735*	*0935*	...	*1135*	*1235*	...	*1335*	*1435*	...	*1535*	*1658*	...	*1735*	*1835*	*1935*	...	...	...		...
21	Montebelluna d.	0609	0709	...	0809	1009	...	1209	1309	...	1409	1509	...	1609	1809	...	1809	1909	2009	...	...	...		...
56	Feltre d.	0639	0806	...	0906	1106	...	1306	1406	...	1506	1606	...	1706	1906	...	1906	2006	2106	...	...	...		...
87	**Belluno** a.	0751	0851	...	0951	1151	...	1351	1451	...	1551	1651	...	1751	1951	...	1951	2051	2151	...	...	...		...

	⚒	⚒		⚒			†						⚒	Ⓑ									
Belluno d.	0352	0507	...	0607	0707	...	0807	1007	...	1207	1407	...	1507	1607	...	1707	1807	1907	...	...	...		...
Feltre d.	0439	0554	...	0654	0754	...	0854	1054	...	1254	1454	...	1554	1654	...	1754	1854	1954	...	...	...		...
Montebelluna a.	0531	0651	...	0751	0851	...	0951	1151	...	1351	1551	...	1651	1751	...	1851	1951	2051	...	...	...		...
Treviso Centrale a.	*0625*	*0725*	...	*0825*	*0925*	...	*1025*	*1225*	...	*1425*	*1625*	...	*1725*	*1825*	...	*1925*	*2025*	*2125*	...	...	...		...

VENEZIA - CASTELFRANCO VENETO - BASSANO DEL GRAPPA

km									
		⚒	⚒	⚒					
0	**Venezia** Santa Lucia d.	0527	0557	0627	0657	0757	and	2057	2157
9	**Venezia** Mestre d.	0540	0609	0640	0709	0809	hourly	2109	2210
45	Castelfranco Veneto d.	0628	0646	0728	0746	0846	until	2146	2252
64	**Bassano del Grappa** a.	0644	0711	0744	0811	0911		2211	2314

	⚒	⚒		⚒				
Bassano del Grappa d.	0521	0546	0621	0646	0721	and	2021	2121
Castelfranco Veneto d.	0545	0604	0646	0704	0746	hourly	2046	2146
Venezia Mestre a.	0621	0650	0721	0750	0821	until	2121	2226
Venezia Santa Lucia a.	0633	0703	0733	0803	0833		2133	2239

VICENZA - CASTELFRANCO VENETO - TREVISO

km																								
		⚒			⚒	†		Ⓐ			⚒			⚒			⚒	⚒						
0	**Vicenza** d.	0614	0714	...	0814	0914	...	1114	1214	...	1314	1414	...	1514	1614	...	1714	1814	...	1914	2014	...	...	...
24	Cittadella d.	0639	0739	...	0839	0939	...	1139	1239	...	1339	1439	...	1539	1639	...	1739	1839	...	1939	2039	...	...	...
36	Castelfranco Veneto d.	0655	0755	...	0855	0955	...	1155	1255	...	1355	1455	...	1555	1655	...	1755	1855	...	1955	2055	...	...	...
60	**Treviso** Centrale a.	0722	0822	...	0922	1022	...	1222	1322	...	1422	1522	...	1622	1722	...	1822	1922	...	2022	2122	...	...	...

	⚒	⚒			⚒		†	Ⓑ		⚒			⚒			⚒			⚒				
Treviso Centrale d.	0538	0638	...	0738	0838	...	0938	1138	...	1238	1338	...	1438	1538	...	1638	1738	...	1838	2038	...	...	...
Castelfranco Veneto d.	0607	0707	...	0807	0907	...	1007	1207	...	1307	1407	...	1507	1607	...	1707	1807	...	1907	2107	...	...	...
Cittadella d.	0621	0721	...	0821	0921	...	1021	1221	...	1321	1421	...	1521	1621	...	1721	1821	...	1921	2121	...	...	...
Vicenza a.	0646	0746	...	0846	0946	...	1046	1246	...	1346	1446	...	1546	1646	...	1746	1846	...	1946	2146	...	...	...

C – Padova - Montebelluna - Belluno and v.v.

s – Runs until Apr. 1.

v – Runs until Mar. 31.

△ – Additional 🚌 services available.

♠ – Operator: Dolomitibus. www.dolomitibus.it. Subject to confirmation.

● – Full name of station is Calalzo-Pieve di Cadore-Cortina.

⊡ – All services Montebelluna - Belluno and v.v. are currently operated by 🚌 (connecting services Treviso - Montebelluna and v.v. are by train). 🚌 timings at Feltre are at the bus station.

🍷 on all *FA*, *FR* and *ITA* trains

TORINO - MILANO - VERONA - VENEZIA

605

km		*ITA*	*FR*	*FR*	*FR*	*ITA*	*EC*	*ITA*	*FR*	*EC*	*EC*	*ITA*	*FR*		*FR*	*FR*	*EC*	*FR*	*ITA*	*FR*	*ITA*	*FR*	*ITA*
		8973	**9707**	**9709**	**9710**	**8977**	**35**	**8981**	**9723**	**1281**	**311**	**8983**	**9731**		**9735**	**9741**	**85**	**9747**	**8993**	**9751**	**8995**	**9755**	**8997**
		④–①								⑥⑦						Ⓑ		Ⓑ					
					A		**D**			**C**♠	**B**						**C**♠			**E**			
0	**Milano** Centrale .... **600** d.	0735	0745	0815	0845	0935	1005	1135	1145	...	1205	1235	1345	...	1445	1545	...	1645	1735	1745	1835	1845	1935
83	Brescia .... **600** d.	0813	0823	0853	0923	1013	1053	1213	1223	...	1253	1313	1423	...	1523	1623	...	1723	1813	1823	1913	1923	2013
111	Desenzano-Sirmione .... **600** d.	|	|	0908	|	1027	|	|	1238	...	|	1327	|	...	1538	|	...	|	1827	|	|	|	2027
125	Peschiera del Garda ‡ .... **600** d.	0833	0844	|	0944	|	1114	1234	|	...	1314	|	1444	...	|	1644	...	1744	|	1844	1934	1944	|
148	**Verona** Porta Nuova .... **600** a.	0847	0858	0928	0958	1047	1128	1247	1258	...	1328	1347	1458	...	1558	1658	...	1758	1847	1858	1947	1958	2047
148	**Verona** Porta Nuova .... d.	0849	0900	0930	1000	1049	1130	1249	1300	1313	1330	1349	1500	...	1600	1700	1710	1800	1849	...	1949	2000	2049
200	Vicenza .... d.	0917	0927	0957	1027	1117	1157	1317	1327	1338**s**	1357	1417	1527	...	1627	1727	1735**s**	1827	1917	...	2017	2027	2117
230	Padova .... **600** d.	0934	0946	1016	1046	1134	1216	1334	1346	1358**s**	1416	1434	1546	...	1646	1746	1756**s**	1846	1934	...	2034	2046	2134
258	**Venezia** Mestre .... **600** a.	0952**s**	1000	1030**s**	1100**s**	1152**s**	1230**s**	1352**s**	1400**s**	1414**s**	1430**s**	1452**s**	1600**s**	...	1700**s**	1800**s**	1812**s**	1900**s**	1950	...	2052**s**	2100	2152**s**
267	**Venezia** Santa Lucia .... **600** a.	1003	|	1042	1112	1203	1242	1403	1412	1428	1442	1503	1612	...	1712	1812	1825	1912	|	...	2103	|	2203
	Udine **601** .... a.	...	|	...	...	...	...	...	...	...	...	...	...	...	...	...	...	...	2140	...	...	2237	...
	Trieste Centrale **601** .... a.	...	1205	...	...	...	...	...	...	...	...	...	...	...	...	...	...	...	...	...	...	...	...

	ITA	*FR*	*FR*	*FR*	*ITA*	*ITA*	*FR*	*FR*		*FR*	*EC*	*FR*	*ITA*	*ITA*	*EC*	*EC*	*FR*	*ITA*	*EC*	*FR*	*ITA*	*FR*
	8970	**9706**	**9708**	**9713**	**8974**	**8971**	**9721**	**9724**		**9728**	**82**	**9736**	**8984**	**8986**	**310**	**1280**	**9744**	**8988**	**42/44**	**9748**	**8992**	**9758**
		①–⑥														⑥⑦					④–①	
							E				**C**♠				**B**	**C**♠	**A**		**D**			
Trieste Centrale **601** .... d.	...	...	...	...	...	...	...	...	...	...	...	...	...	...	...	...	...	...	...	...	...	1705
Udine **601** .... d.	...	...	...	0615	...	0716	...	...	...	...	...	...	...	...	...	...	...	...	...	...	...	|
Venezia Santa Lucia .... **600** d.	0557	0648	0718	|	0757	|	...	1048	...	1148	1335	1348	1357	1457	1518	1535	1548	1557	1618	1648	1757	|
Venezia Mestre .... **600** d.	0609**u**	0700**u**	0730**u**	0800	0809**u**	0909	...	1100**u**	...	1200**u**	1347**u**	1400**u**	1409**u**	1509**u**	1530**u**	1547**u**	1600**u**	1609**u**	1630**u**	1700**u**	1809**u**	1900
Padova .... **600** d.	0626	0716	0746	0816	0826	0926	...	1116	...	1216	1403**u**	1416	1426	1526	1546	1603**u**	1616	1626	1646	1716	1826	1916
Vicenza .... d.	0644	0734	0804	0834	0844	0944	...	1134	...	1234	1424**u**	1434	1444	1544	1604	1624**u**	1634	1644	1704	1734	1844	1934
Verona Porta Nuova .... a.	0710	0800	0830	0900	0910	1010	...	1200	...	1300	1453	1500	1510	1610	1630	1654	1700	1710	1730	1800	1910	2000
Verona Porta Nuova .... **600** d.	0712	0802	0832	0902	0912	1012	1032	1202	...	1302	...	1502	1512	1612	1632	...	1702	1712	1732	1802	1912	2002
Peschiera del Garda ‡ .... **600** d.	|	|	0848	|	0926	|	1048	|	...	1318	...	|	|	1626	1648	...	|	|	1748	|	1926	2018
Desenzano-Sirmione .... **600** d.	0733	0823	|	0923	|	1033	|	1223	...	|	...	1523	1533	|	|	...	1723	1733	|	1823	|	|
Brescia .... **600** d.	0749	0839	0909	0939	0949	1049	1109	1239	...	1339	...	1539	1549	1649	1709	...	1739	1749	1809	1839	1949	2039
Milano Centrale .... **600** a.	0825	0915	0945	1015	1025	1125	1145	1315	...	1415	...	1615	1625	1725	1755	...	1815	1825	1855	1915	2025	2115

	FR	*FR*	*FR*					
	9743	**9753**	**9759**					
Torino Porta Nuova .... **600** d.	1510	1710	1840	...	...	...	...	...
Torino Porta Susa .... **600** d.	1520**u**	1720**u**	1850**u**	...	...	...	...	...
Rho-Fiera Milano .... d.	1558	1756	1926	...	...	...	...	...
Milano Porta Garibaldi .... a.	1610	1810	1940	...	...	...	...	...
Milano Porta Garibaldi .... d.	1613	1813	1943	...	...	...	...	...
Brescia .... **600** d.	1653	1853	2023	...	...	...	...	...
Desenzano-Sirmione .... **600** d.	1708	1908	|	...	...	...	...	...
Peschiera del Garda ‡ .... **600** d.	|	|	|	...	...	...	...	...
Verona Porta Nuova .... **600** a.	1728	1928	2053	...	...	...	...	...
Verona Porta Nuova .... d.	1730	1930	2055	...	...	...	...	...
Vicenza .... d.	1757	1957	|	...	...	...	...	...
Padova .... **600** d.	1816	2016	|	...	...	...	...	...
Venezia Mestre .... **600** a.	1830**s**	2030**s**	2155	...	...	...	...	...
Venezia Santa Lucia .... **600** a.	1842	2042	|	...	...	...	...	...
Trieste Centrale **601** .... a.	...	...	2340	...	...	...	...	...

	FR	*FR*	*FR*				
	9702	**9712**	**9716**				
Trieste Centrale **601** .... d.	...	0600	...	...	...	...	...
Venezia Santa Lucia .... **600** d.	0618	|	0818	...	...	...	...
Venezia Mestre .... **600** d.	0630**u**	0749	0830**u**	...	...	...	...
Padova .... **600** d.	0646	|	0846	...	...	...	...
Vicenza .... d.	0704	|	0904	...	...	...	...
Verona Porta Nuova .... a.	0730	0844	0930	...	...	...	...
Verona Porta Nuova .... **600** d.	0732	0846	0932	...	...	...	...
Peschiera del Garda ‡ .... **600** d.	0748	|	0948	...	...	...	...
Desenzano-Sirmione .... **600** d.	|	|	|	...	...	...	...
Brescia .... **600** d.	0809	|	1009	...	...	...	...
Milano Porta Garibaldi .... a.	0847	0955	1047	...	...	...	...
Milano Porta Garibaldi .... d.	0850	0958	1050	...	...	...	...
Rho-Fiera Milano .... d.	0903	|	1103	...	...	...	...
Torino Porta Susa .... **600** a.	0938**s**	1048**s**	1138**s**	...	...	...	...
Torino Porta Nuova .... **600** a.	0950	1100	1150	...	...	...	...

MILANO - VERONA - VENEZIA LOCAL TRAINS

2nd class Trenord

	Ⓐ	⚒	⚒	†					Ⓒ														Ⓒ
Milano Centrale .... d.	...	...	...	...	0625	0725	0825	...	0925	...	1125	1225	1325	1425	1525	1625	1725	1825	1925	2025	2125	2225	2325
Milano Lambrate .... d.	...	...	...	...	0633	0733	0833	...	0933	...	1133	1233	1333	1433	1533	1633	1733	1833	1933	2033	2133	2233	2333
Treviglio .... d.	...	...	...	...	0656	0756	0856	...	0956	...	1156	1256	1356	1456	1556	1656	1756	1856	1956	2056	2156	2256	2356
Brescia .... d.	...	...	0631	...	0733	0833	0933	...	1033	...	1233	1333	1433	1533	1633	1733	1833	1933	2033	2133	2233	2333	0033
Desenzano-Sirmione .... d.	...	...	0654	...	0749	0849	0949	...	1049	...	1249	1349	1449	1549	1649	1749	1849	1949	2049	2149	2249	2349	0049
Peschiera del Garda ‡ .... d.	...	...	0703	...	0758	0858	0958	...	1058	...	1258	1359	1458	1558	1658	1758	1858	1958	2058	2158	2258	2358	0058
Verona Porta Nuova .... a.	...	...	0720	...	0817	0917	1017	...	1117	...	1317	1417	1517	1617	1717	1817	1917	2017	2117	2217	2317	0017	0117
			|																				
Verona Porta Nuova .... d.	0522	0622	0722	0722	0822	0922	1022	1122	...	1222	1322	1422	1522	1622	1722	1822	1922	2041	...	2222	...	...	...
Vicenza .... d.	0603	0703	0803	0803	0903	1003	1103	1203	...	1303	1403	1503	1603	1703	1803	1903	2003	2141	...	2303	...	...	...
Padova .... **600** d.	0622	0722	0822	0822	0922	1022	1122	1222	...	1322	1422	1522	1622	1722	1822	1922	2022	2210	...	2322	...	...	...
Venezia Mestre .... **600** a.	0637	0737	0837	0837	0937	1037	1137	1237	...	1337	1437	1537	1637	1737	1837	1937	2037	2243	...	2337	...	...	...
Venezia Santa Lucia .... **600** a.	0650	0750	0850	0850	0950	1050	1150	1250	...	1350	1450	1550	1650	1750	1850	1950	2050	2256	...	2350	...	...	...

			⚒		⚒							Ⓐ											Ⓒ
Venezia Santa Lucia .... **600** d.	...	...	0504	...	0610	...	0710	0810	0910	1010	1110	1210	...	1310	1410	1510	1610	1710	1810	1910	2010	2110	2134
Venezia Mestre .... **600** d.	...	...	0517	...	0623	...	0723	0823	0923	1023	1123	1223	...	1323	1423	1523	1623	1723	1823	1923	2023	2123	2147
Padova .... **600** d.	...	...	0546	...	0640	...	0740	0840	0940	1040	1140	1240	...	1340	1440	1540	1640	1740	1840	1940	2040	2140	2220
Vicenza .... d.	...	...	0612	...	0658	...	0758	0858	0958	1058	1158	1258	...	1358	1458	1558	1658	1758	1858	1958	2058	2158	2252
Verona Porta Nuova .... a.	...	...	0720	...	0738	...	0838	0938	1038	1138	1238	1338	...	1438	1538	1638	1738	1838	1938	2038	2138	2238	2334
										Ⓒ													
Verona Porta Nuova .... d.	0543	0643	...	0743	...	0839	...	0943	...	1143	1243	...	1343	1443	1543	1643	1743	1843	1943	2043	2143	...	...
Peschiera del Garda ‡ .... d.	0557	0657	...	0757	...	0853	...	0957	...	1157	1257	...	1357	1457	1557	1657	1757	1857	1957	2057	2157	...	...
Desenzano-Sirmione .... d.	0607	0707	...	0807	...	0901	...	1007	...	1207	1307	...	1407	1507	1607	1707	1807	1907	2007	2107	2207	...	...
Brescia .... d.	0628	0728	...	0828	...	0928	...	1028	...	1228	1328	...	1428	1528	1628	1728	1828	1928	2028	2128	2228	...	...
Treviglio .... d.	0705	0801	...	0905	...	1005	...	1105	...	1305	1405	...	1505	1605	1705	1805	1905	2005	2105	2205	2305	...	...
Milano Lambrate .... d.	0728	0828	...	0928	...	1028	...	1128	...	1328	1428	...	1528	1628	1728	1828	1928	2028	2128	2228	2328	...	...
Milano Centrale .... a.	0735	0835	...	0935	...	1035	...	1135	...	1335	1435	...	1535	1635	1735	1835	1935	2035	2135	2235	2335	...	...

BRESCIA - EDOLO

2nd class Trenord

km		⚒	†						Ⓐ	
0	**Brescia** .... d.	0555	0707	0907	1107	1307	1507	1707	1758	1907
	Iseo .... d.	0633	0733	0933	1133	1333	1533	1733	1831	1933
103	**Edolo** ⊖ .... a.	0834	0907	1107	1307	1507	1707	1907	2018	2107

	⚒	⚒							†
Edolo ⊖ .... d.	0554	0647	0754	0954	1154	1354	1554	1754	1954
Iseo .... d.	0731	0833	0931	1131	1331	1531	1731	1931	2136
Brescia .... a.	0754	0903	0954	1154	1354	1554	1754	1954	2200

A – (12) 🍷 Genova - Venezia and v.v.
B – (12) ✕ Zürich - Milano - Venezia and v.v. Ⓡ inclusive of supplement.
C – (12) ✕ München - Verona - Venezia and v.v.
D – (12) 🍷 Genève - Milano - Venezia and v.v. Ⓡ inclusive of supplement.
E – (12) 🍷 Milano - Bolzano and v.v.

s – Stops to set down only.
u – Stops to pick up only.
♠ – Also available to passengers without reservation.
‡ – Station for Gardaland Park. Free shuttle bus available.
⊖ – For 🚌 Edolo - Tirano see Table **593**.

606 MILANO MALPENSA AEROPORTO ✈ — Trenord

Milano Centrale .... d.	0525	0555	0625	and at	1955	2025	2125	2225	2325
Milano Porta Garibaldi .... d.	0535	0605	0635	the same	2005	2035	2135	2235	2335
Milano Bovisa .... d.	0542	0612	0642	minutes	2012	2042	2142	2242	2342
Busto Arsizio FN .... d.	0607	0637	0707	past each	2037	2107	2207	2307	0007
Malpensa Aeroporto T1 ✈ ..... a.	0616	0646	0716	hour until	2046	2116	2216	2316	0016

Malpensa Aeroporto T1 ✈ . d.	0543	0613	0643	and at	2043	2113	2143	2243
Busto Arsizio FN .... d.	0552	0622	0652	the same	2052	2122	2152	2252
Milano Bovisa .... a.	0618	0648	0718	minutes	2118	2148	2218	2318
Milano Porta Garibaldi .... a.	0625	0655	0725	past each	2125	2155	2225	2325
Milano Centrale .... a.	0637	0707	0737	hour until	2137	2207	2237	2335

All services below operate as *Malpensa Express*. Special fare payable.

Milano Cadorna .... d.	0457	0527	0557	0627	and at the same	2157	2227	2257	2327
Milano Bovisa .... d.	0503	0533	0603	0633	minutes	2203	2233	2303	2333
Busto Arsizio FN .... d.	0525	0555	0625	0655	past each	2225	2255	2325	2355
Malpensa Aeroporto T1 ✈ ..... a.	0534	0604	0634	0704	hour until	2234	2304	2334	0004

Malpensa Aeroporto T1 ✈ . d.	0556	0626	0656	0726	and at the same	2256	2326	2356
Busto Arsizio FN .... d.	0603	0633	0703	0733	minutes	2303	2333	0003
Milano Bovisa .... a.	0626	0656	0726	0756	past each	2326	2356	0026
Milano Cadorna .... a.	0634	0704	0734	0804	hour until	2334	0004	0034

607 MILANO LOCAL SERVICES — Trenord

Subject to alteration on and around Italian and Swiss public holidays. See Table **548** for services Locarno - Cadenazzo - Lugano and v.v.

MILANO and MALPENSA AEROPORTO - PORTO CERESIO, COMO and BELLINZONA

km				①–⑥			①–⑥			①–⑥				①–⑥						①–⑥			①–⑥
0	**Milano** Porta Garibaldi .... d.	...	...	...	...	0532	...	...	0632	...	...	0732		...	...	1932	...	2032	...	2104	...	2234	...
13	Rho-Fiera Milano .... d.	...	...	...	...	0543	...	...	0643	...	...	0743	and	...	...	1943	...	2043	...	2117	...	2247	...
	Malpensa Aeroporto T1 ✈ d.	...	...	...	...	|	...	0619	|	...	0719	|	at	...	1919	|	2019	|	2119	|	2219	|	2319
	Busto Arsizio FN .... d.	...	...	...	...	|	...	0630	|	...	0730	|	the	...	1930	|	2030	|	2130	|	2230	|	2330
36	Busto Arsizio FS .... d.	...	...	...	...	0559	...	0638	0701	...	0738	0801	same	...	1938	2001	2038	2101	2138	2143	2238	2313	2338
44	Gallarate .... d.	...	...	...	...	0605	...	0644	0707	...	0744	0807	minutes	...	1944	2007	2044	2107	2144	2150	2244	2320	2344
63	Varese .... d.	0500	0525	0536	0606	0625	0636	0706	0725	0736	0806	0825	past	1936	2006	2025	2106	2125	2206	2217	2306	2347	0006
77	**Porto Ceresio** .... a.	|	0545	|	|	0645	|	|	0745	|	|	0845	each	|	|	2045	|	2145	|	...	|	...	|
75	Stabio .... d.	0516	...	0553	0623	...	0653	0723	...	0753	0823	...	hour	1953	2023	...	2123	...	2223	...	2323	...	0023
79	Mendrisio .... **550** a.	0520	...	0557	0627	...	0657	0727	...	0757	0827	...	until	1957	2027	...	2127	...	2227	...	2327	...	0027
86	Chiasso .... **550** a.	|	...	0610	|	...	0710	|	...	0810	|	...		2010	|	...	|	...	|	...	|	...	|
90	**Como** San Giovanni .... a.	|	...	0624	|	...	0724	|	...	0824	|	...		2024	|	...	|	...	|	...	|	...	|
98	Lugano .... **550** a.	0554	...	...	0654	...	...	0747e	...	...	0854	...		...	2054	...	2154	...	2254	...	2354	...	0054
127	**Bellinzona** .... **550** a.	0619	...	...	0713	...	...	0807e	...	...	0913	...		...	2113	...	2213	...	2313	...	0030	...	0126

km				①–⑥			①–⑥			①–⑥			①–⑥				①–⑥					①–⑥	
108	**Bellinzona** .... **550** d.	...	0433	...	...	0532	...	...	0641	...	...	0746	...		...	1846	...	...	1946	...	...	...	2046
79	Lugano .... **550** d.	...	0506	...	...	0606	...	...	0706	...	...	0806	...	and	...	1906	...	...	2006	...	...	...	2106
71	**Como** San Giovanni .... d.	...	|	0541	...	|	0636	...	|	0736	...	|	0836	at	...	|	1936	...	|	...	...	...	|
67	Chiasso .... **550** d.	...	|	0550	...	|	0650	...	|	0750	...	|	0850	the	...	|	1950	...	|	...	...	...	|
60	Mendrisio .... **550** d.	...	0533	0603	...	0633	0703	...	0733	0803	...	0833	0903	same	...	1933	2003	...	2033	...	...	...	2133
56	Stabio .... d.	...	0537	0607	...	0637	0707	...	0737	0807	...	0837	0907	minutes	...	1937	2007	...	2037	...	...	...	2137
	Porto Ceresio .... d.	0516	|	|	0616	|	|	0716	|	|	0816	|	|	past	1916	|	|	2016	|	...	2116	...	|
44	Varese .... d.	0536	0600	0624	0636	0700	0724	0736	0800	0824	0836	0900	0924	each	1936	2000	2024	2036	2100	...	2136	2143	2200
25	Gallarate .... d.	0552	0616	...	0704	0716	...	0752	0816	...	0852	0916	...	hour	1952	2016	...	2052	2116	...	...	2210	2216
17	Busto Arsizio FS .... d.	0558	0625	...	|	0725	...	0758	0825	...	0858	0925	...	until	1958	2025	...	2058	2125	...	...	2216	2225
	Busto Arsizio FN .... d.	|	0631	...	|	0731	...	|	0831	...	|	0931	...		|	2031	...	|	2131	...	...	|	2231
0	**Malpensa** Aeroporto T1 ✈ a.	|	0641	...	|	0741	...	|	0841	...	|	0941	...		|	2041	...	|	2141	...	...	|	2241
	Rho-Fiera Milano .... d.	0616	...	...	0731	...	...	0816	...	...	0916	...	...		2016	...	...	2116	...	...	...	2241	...
	Milano Porta Garibaldi .... a.	0628	...	...	0741	...	...	0828	...	...	0928	...	...		2028	...	...	2128	...	...	...	2255	...

GALLARATE - LUINO - CADENAZZO - BELLINZONA

km		①–⑥		①–⑤														①–⑤		①–⑥				
0	**Gallarate** .... d.	0608	...	0719	0819	...	0842	...	...	1419	...	1519	1619	...	1719	1819	...	1842	1919	1942	2019	...	2219	...
31	Laveno Mombello .... d.	0644	...	0800	0901	...	0927	...	...	1501	...	1601	1701	...	1801	1901	...	1927	2001	2027	2101	...	2301	...
46	**Luino** .... d.	0703	0718	0815	0918	...	0943	1118	1318	1518	...	1615	1718	...	1815	1918	...	1943	2015	2043	2118	...	2315	...
59	Pino-Tronzano 🏨 .... d.	...	0730	...	0930	...	...	1130	1330	1530	...	...	1730	...	...	1930	...	...	...	...	2130	...	...	...
77	**Cadenazzo** .... a.	...	0756	...	0956	1001	...	1156	1356	1556	1601	...	1756	1801	...	1956	2001	...	...	...	2156	2201	...	...
86	**Bellinzona** .... a.	...	*0811*	...	...	1011	...	*1211*	*1411*	...	1611	...	...	1811	...	...	2011	...	...	...	...	2211	...	...

	①–⑥	①–⑤		⑥⑦	①–⑤		①–⑥																
Bellinzona .... d.	...	...	0553	...	...	...	...	*0749*	0949	...	1149	...	...	*1349*	...	*1549*	...	*1749*	...	1949	...	...	...
Cadenazzo .... d.	...	...	0604	...	...	...	...	0804	0959	...	1159	1204	...	1404	...	1604	...	1804	...	1959	2004	...	...
Pino-Tronzano 🏨 .... d.	...	...	0628	...	...	...	...	0828	...	...	...	1228	...	1428	...	1628	...	1828	...	...	2028	...	...
Luino .... d.	0500	0534	0645	0604	0619	...	0718	0845	...	...	...	1242	1345	1445	1545	1645	1745	1845	1945	...	2042	2045	...
Laveno Mombello .... d.	0516	0550	0705	0617	0640	...	0733	0900	...	...	...	...	1400	1500	1600	1700	1800	1900	2000	...	...	2100	...
Gallarate .... a.	0552	0629	0741	0651	0718	...	0806	0935	...	...	...	...	1441	1541	1641	1741	1841	1941	2041	...	...	2141	...

MILANO - CREMONA - MANTOVA

km											
0	**Milano** Centrale .... d.	0620	0820	1020	1220	1420	1620	1715	1820	1915	2020
60	Codogno .... d.	0702	0902	1102	1302	1502	1702	1758	1902	1958	2102
88	Cremona .... d.	0730	0930	1130	1330	1530	1730	1823	1930	2023	2130
151	**Mantova** .... a.	0818	1018	1218	1418	1618	1818	1918	2018	2118	2218

Mantova .... d.	0518	0607	0642	0842	1042	1242	1442	1642	1842	2042
Cremona .... d.	0613	0653	0730	0930	1130	1330	1530	1730	1930	2130
Codogno .... d.	0639	0718	0753	0953	1153	1353	1553	1753	1953	2153
Milano Centrale .... a.	0730	0810	0842	1040	1240	1440	1640	1840	2040	2240

MILANO - BERGAMO — *56 km* Journey 55–60 minutes 2nd class

From **Milano** Centrale at 0535, 0605, 0705, 0805, 0905, 1005, 1105, 1205, 1305, 1405, 1505, 1605, 1705, 1805, 1905, 2005, 2105, 2205, 2340.

From **Bergamo** at 0500, 0602, 0702, 0735 Ⓐ, 0802, 0902, 0957 Ⓒ, 1002 Ⓐ, 1057 Ⓒ, 1102 Ⓐ, 1202, 1302, 1402, 1502, 1602, 1702, 1802, 1902, 2002, 2102, 2202, 2300 Ⓒ.

MILANO - COMO LAGO — *46 km* Journey: 1 hour. 2nd class

From **Milano** Cadorna: 0613 ⚒, 0643, 0716, 0743 and hourly until 2043, 2143, 2243.

From **Como** Lago: 0516, 0616, 0716 and hourly until 2016, 2116, 2216.

Additional services operate on ⚒. A reduced service may operate in peak summer.

MILANO - VARESE - LAVENO — *72 km* Journey: 87–107 mins 2nd class

From **Milano** Cadorna: 0609 ⚒, 0639, 0752, 0852, 0939, 1039, 1139, 1239, 1352, 1439, 1539, 1652, 1722 Ⓐ, 1752, 1822 Ⓐ, 1852, 1909 Ⓐ, 1939 Ⓒ, 1952 Ⓐ, 2039.

From **Laveno-Mombello** FN: 0538 Ⓐ, 0608 ⚒, 0638, 0708 ⚒, 0738, 0808 ⚒, 0838, 0938, 1038, 1138, 1238, 1338, 1438, 1538, 1638, 1738, 1838, 1938, 2038.

A reduced service may operate in peak summer.

e – On ⑥⑦ arrives Lugano 0754, Bellinzona 0813.

🍷 on all *EC*, *FA*, *FB*, *FR* and *ITA* trains

TORINO and MILANO - GENOVA - PISA - ROMA 610

km		IC 501	FB 8601	FA 8583 ①–⑥ ♦		FB 8605	FA 8551 ①–⑥	IC 651		IC 503	IC 505 A	IC 633 A	NJ 40295 233 D	IC 657 Ⓐ	IC 657 Ⓒ	IC 659 Ⓐ A		IC 659 Ⓒ A	FB 8613	IC 511	IC 637 A	IC 665	FB 8619
0	**Torino** Porta Nuova d.	...	...	...	...	...	...	...	...	0605	...	...	...	...	...	...	...	...	...	1040	...	...	...
56	Asti d.	...	...	...	...	...	...	...	...	0641	...	...	...	...	...	...	...	...	...	1113	...	...	...
91	Alessandria d.	...	...	...	...	...	...	...	...	0702	...	...	...	...	...	...	...	...	...	1136	...	...	...
112	Novi Ligure d.	...	...	...	...	...	...	...	...	0718	...	...	...	...	...	...	...	...	...	|	...	...	...
	Milano Centrale d.	...	...	...	...	...	...	0610	...	|	...	0710	0744r	0805	0805	0910	...	0910	...	|	1110	1210	1310
	Pavia d.	...	...	...	...	...	...	0635	...	|	...	0735	0804	0835	0835	0935	...	0935	...	|	1135	1235	1335
	Voghera d.	...	...	...	...	...	...	|	...	|	...	0751	|	0851	0851	|	...	|	...	|	1151	|	|
	Tortona d.	...	...	...	...	...	...	0659	...	|	...	|	|	|	|	0959	...	0959	...	|	|	1259	|
166	**Genova** Piazza Principe a.	...	...	...	...	...	...	0744	...	0803	...	0844	0938	0944	0944	1044	...	1044	...	1221	1244	1344	1437
166	**Genova** Piazza Principe d.	...	0515	0553	...	0705	0720	0747	...	...	0853	...	0941	0947	0947	...	...	...	1210	1224	...	1347	1502
169	**Genova** Brignole d.	...	0522u	0600u	...	0712u	0728u	0756	...	...	0901	...	|	0956	0956	...	...	...	1217u	1233	...	1356	1512
194	S. Margherita-Portofino d.	...	|	|	...	|	|	0824	...	...	|	...	|	1016	1016	...	...	...	|	|	...	1416	|
196	Rapallo d.	...	|	|	...	0737	0757	0829	...	...	0922	...	1014	1021	1021	...	...	...	|	1304	...	1421	1537
205	Chiavari d.	...	0547	|	...	0746	|	0838	...	...	0931	...	|	1030	1030	...	...	...	1246	1313	...	1430	1546
212	Sestri Levante d.	0505	|	|	...	|	|	0845	...	...	0938	...	|	1039	1039	...	...	...	|	1321	...	1438	|
235	Levanto d.	0522	|	|	...	|	|	0901	...	...	|	...	1046	1100	1100	...	...	...	|	|	...	1501	|
240	Monterosso d.	0528	|	|	...	|	|	0907	...	...	|	...	|	1107	1107	...	...	...	|	|	...	1507	|
256	La Spezia Centrale d.	0544	0618	0651	...	0816	0832	0923	...	...	1013	...	1110	1123	1123	...	...	...	1316	1352	...	1521	1616
272	Sarzana d.	0557	|	|	...	|	|	|	...	...	|	...	...	|	|	...	...	...	|	|	...	...	|
282	Carrara-Avenza d.	0606	|	|	...	|	|	|	...	...	|	...	...	|	1141	...	...	...	|	1411	...	...	|
289	Massa Centro d.	0614	0638	|	...	0836	|	0945	...	...	1035	...	...	1145	1148	...	...	...	1336	1419	...	...	1636
310	Viareggio d.	0628	0650	|	...	0848	|	1000	...	...	1048	...	...	1200	1209	...	...	...	1348	1434	...	...	1648
331	**Pisa** Centrale a.	0644	0704	0730	...	0904	0912	1017	...	...	1103	...	...	1217	1223	...	...	...	1404	1447	...	...	1704
331	**Pisa** Centrale d.	0647	0707	0733	...	0907	0915	1020	...	...	1111	...	...	1220	1226	...	...	...	1407	1450	...	...	1707
	Firenze Campo di Marte d.	|	|	0826	...	|	1006	|	...	...	|	...	...	|	|	...	...	...	|	|	...	...	|
351	**Livorno** Centrale a.	0701	0720	|	...	0920	|	1035	...	...	1124	...	...	1235	1240	...	...	...	1420	1502	...	...	1720
351	**Livorno** Centrale d.	0703	0722	|	...	0922	|	...	...	...	1126	...	...	1255	1255	...	...	...	1422	1504	...	...	1722
385	Cecina d.	0728	|	|	...	|	|	...	...	...	1150	...	...	1326	1323	...	...	...	|	|	...	...	|
420	Campiglia Marittima d.	0747	0757	|	...	0957	|	...	...	...	|	...	...	1350	1341	...	...	...	1457	1540	...	...	1757
437	Follonica d.	0758	|	|	...	|	|	...	...	...	1215	...	...	1401	1352	...	...	...	|	1552	...	...	|
479	Grosseto d.	0819	0824	|	...	1024	|	...	...	...	1235	...	...	1433	1425	...	...	...	1524	1614	...	...	1824
589	Civitavecchia d.	0924	0916	|	...	1116	|	...	...	...	1326	...	...	...	...	...	...	...	1616	1708	...	...	1916
660	**Roma** Ostiense a.	1015	|	|	...	|	|	...	...	...	1420s	...	...	...	...	...	...	...	|	1752	...	...	|
667	**Roma** Termini a.	|	1003	1000	...	1203	1132	...	...	...	1433	...	...	...	...	...	...	...	1703	1803	...	...	2003
	Napoli Centrale **640** a.	1229	...	...	...	...	...	...	...	...	...	...	...	...	...	...	...	...	...	2029	...	...	...
	Salerno **640** a.	...	...	...	...	...	...	...	...	...	...	...	...	...	...	...	...	...	...	2124	...	...	...

	IC 669	EC 327 ⊖ ♦	IC 641 A		FB 8623	IC 673	FA 8591		IC 675 A	IC 679	FA 9745 ♦		IC 519	IC 685	IC 689 A		ICN 1963 ❖♦	IC 687	ITA 9992 ♦		ICN 899 B ❖♦	ICN 799 C ❖♦
Torino Porta Nuova d.	...	...	...	...	1520	...	...	...	...	...	...	...	1805	...	...	...	...	...	...	...	2015	2155
Asti d.	...	...	...	...	1555	...	...	...	...	...	...	...	1841	...	...	...	...	...	...	...	2056	2236
Alessandria d.	...	...	...	...	1616	...	...	...	...	...	...	...	1902	...	...	...	...	...	...	...	2116	2259
Novi Ligure d.	...	...	...	...	|	...	...	...	...	...	...	...	1916	...	...	...	...	...	...	...	|	|
Milano Centrale d.	1405	1420r	1510	...	|	1605	...	...	1705	1805	1825	...	|	1905	2005	...	2010	2110	2130	...	|	|
Pavia d.	1435	1441	1535	...	|	1635	...	...	1735	1835	1857	...	|	1935	2035	...	2041	2135	|	...	|	|
Voghera d.	1451	|	1551	...	|	1651	...	...	1751	1851	|	...	|	1951	2051	...	2057	2151	|	...	|	|
Tortona d.	|	1513	|	...	|	|	...	...	|	1902	|	...	|	|	|	...	2108	|	|	...	|	|
Genova Piazza Principe a.	1544	1552	1644	...	1700	1744	...	...	1844	1944	1955s	...	2002s	2044	2144	...	2153	2244	2309s	...	2205	2350
Genova Piazza Principe d.	1547	...	...	...	1705	1747	1835	...	...	1947	1955s	...	2002s	2047	...	...	2156	2247	2311s	...	2208	2353
Genova Brignole d.	1556	...	...	...	1712	1756	1842u	...	...	1956	2006	...	2012	2056	...	...	2205	2256	2318	...	2217	0002
S. Margherita-Portofino d.	|	...	...	...	|	1816	|	...	...	2016	...	...	...	|	...	...	|	2319	...	...	|	|
Rapallo d.	1621	...	...	...	1737	1821	|	...	...	2021	...	...	...	2126	...	...	|	2324	...	...	2242	0028
Chiavari d.	1630	...	...	...	1746	1830	|	...	...	2030	...	...	...	2135	...	...	|	2333	...	...	2251	0038
Sestri Levante d.	1638	...	...	...	|	1838	|	...	...	2038	...	...	...	2142	...	...	|	2345	...	...	|	|
Levanto d.	1701	...	...	...	|	1901	|	...	...	2100	...	...	...	|	...	...	|	0001	...	...	|	|
Monterosso d.	1707	...	...	...	|	1907	|	...	...	2107	...	...	...	|	...	...	|	0007	...	...	|	|
La Spezia Centrale d.	1724	...	...	...	1816	1923	1948	...	...	2123	...	...	...	2223	...	...	2309	0025	...	...	2353	0127
Sarzana d.	|	...	...	...	1828	|	2000	...	...	|	...	...	...	2235	...	...	|	...	...	...	|	|
Carrara-Avenza d.	1746	...	...	...	|	1942	|	...	...	|	...	...	...	2243	...	...	|	...	...	...	|	|
Massa Centro d.	1754	...	...	...	1840	1949	2012	...	...	2145	...	...	...	2250	...	...	|	...	...	...	|	|
Viareggio d.	1809	...	...	...	1852	2002	|	...	...	2200	...	...	...	2303	...	...	2341	...	...	...	|	|
Pisa Centrale a.	1824	...	...	...	1908	2017	2036	...	...	2217	...	...	...	2317	...	...	2356	...	...	...	0051	0216
Pisa Centrale d.	1826	...	...	...	1911	2020	2038	...	...	2220	...	...	...	2320	...	...	2359	...	...	...	0154	0221
Firenze Campo di Marte d.	|	...	...	...	|	|	2131	...	...	|	...	...	...	|	...	...	|	...	...	...	|	|
Livorno Centrale a.	1842	...	...	...	1924	2035	|	...	...	2235	...	...	...	2335	...	...	0014	...	...	...	0210	0237
Livorno Centrale d.	...	...	...	...	1926	...	|	...	...	...	...	...	...	...	...	...	0017	...	...	...	0240	0240
Cecina d.	...	...	...	...	1948	...	|	...	...	...	...	...	...	...	...	...	|	...	...	...	|	|
Campiglia Marittima d.	...	...	...	...	2006	...	|	...	...	...	...	...	...	...	...	...	|	...	...	...	|	|
Follonica d.	...	...	...	...	|	...	|	...	...	...	...	...	...	...	...	...	|	...	...	...	|	|
Grosseto d.	...	...	...	...	2033	...	|	...	...	...	...	...	...	...	...	...	|	...	...	...	0407	0407
Civitavecchia d.	...	...	...	...	2121	...	|	...	...	...	...	...	...	...	...	...	|	...	...	...	0500	0500
Roma Ostiense a.	...	...	...	...	|	...	|	...	...	...	...	...	...	...	...	...	|	...	...	...	0543	0543
Roma Termini a.	...	...	...	...	2203	...	2256	...	...	...	...	...	...	...	...	...	|	...	...	...	|	|
Napoli Centrale **640** a.	...	...	...	...	...	...	...	...	...	...	...	...	...	...	...	...	|	...	...	...	0817	0817
Salerno **640** a.	...	...	...	...	...	...	...	...	...	...	...	...	...	...	...	...	0613	...	...	...	0911	0911

km		2	2	ICN 757 ❖♦					
0	**Torino** Porta Nuova d.	...	...	2050	...	...	...	...	...
56	Asti d.	...	...	2129	...	...	...	...	...
91	Alessandria d.	...	...	2152	...	...	...	...	...
	Genova Brignole d.	1117	1706	|	...	...	...	...	...
	Genova Piazza Principe d.	1125	1714	|	...	...	...	...	...
113	Tortona d.	1241	1848	2207	...	...	...	...	...
130	Voghera d.	1253	1902	2218	...	...	...	...	...
188	Piacenza a.	1340	1947	2255	...	...	...	...	...
335	**Bologna** Centrale a.	*1525*	2125	0022	...	...	...	...	...

	ICN 754 ❖♦	2	2					
Bologna Centrale d.	0535	0633	*1150*	...	...	...	...	...
Piacenza d.	0710	0809	1409	...	...	...	...	...
Voghera d.	0757	0856	1456	...	...	...	...	...
Tortona d.	0808	0907	1507	...	...	...	...	...
Genova Piazza Principe a.	|	1014	1612	...	...	...	...	...
Genova Brignole a.	|	1024	1620	...	...	...	...	...
Alessandria d.	0825	...	...	...	...	...	...	...
Asti d.	0847	...	...	...	...	...	...	...
Torino Porta Nuova a.	0925	...	...	...	...	...	...	...

♦ – **NOTES** (LISTED BY TRAIN NUMBER)

326 – [12] ✕ Genova - Milano - Zürich (Table **550**).
327 – [12] ✕ Zürich - Milano - Genova (Table **550**).
754 – 🛏 1, 2 cl., 🛏 2 cl. (4 berth) Lecce - Torino.
757 – 🛏 1, 2 cl., 🛏 2 cl. (4 berth) Torino - Lecce.
796 – 🛏 1, 2 cl., 🛏 2 cl. (4 berth) and [2] Salerno - Torino.
799 – 🛏 1, 2 cl., 🛏 2 cl. (4 berth) and [2] Torino - Salerno.
1962 – 🛏 1, 2 cl., 🛏 2 cl. (4 berth) Siracusa - Milano; 🛏 1, 2 cl., 🛏 2 cl. (4 berth) Palermo (**1964**) - Messina - Milano.
1963 – 🛏 1, 2 cl., 🛏 2 cl. (4 berth) Milano - Siracusa; 🛏 1, 2 cl., 🛏 2 cl. (4 berth) Milano - Messina (**1965**) - Palermo.
8583 – [12] 🍷 Genova - Roma (**8586**) - Fiumicino Airport ✈ (a. 1022).
8596 – [12] 🍷 Fiumicino Airport ✈ (**8595**, d. 1953) - Roma - Genova.
9710 – [12] 🍷 Genova - Milano (**9711**) - Venezia.
9745 – [12] 🍷 Venezia (**9744**) - Milano - Genova.
9992 – [12] 🍷 Napoli - Milano - Genova.
9998 – [12] 🍷 Genova - Milano - Napoli.

A – To / from Ventimiglia (Table **580**).
B – ①–⑤ until May. 5.
C – ⑥⑦ until Mar. 26.
D – *ÖBB nightjet* – 🛏 1, 2 cl., 🛏 2 cl. (4, 6 berth), [2] München - Villach - Tarvisio 🏛 - Milano - Genova - La Spezia and v.v. Conveys 🛏 1, 2 cl., 🛏 2 cl. (4, 6 berth), [2] 🍷 Wien - Milano - Genova - La Spezia and v.v. Special fares apply.

r – Milano **Rogoredo**.
s – Calls to set down only.
t – Roma **Tiburtina**.
u – Calls to pick up only.

⊖ – Ⓡ for international journeys.
❖ – Running days, timings and numbers of *ICN* trains vary - please check your reservation. For confirmed timings please consult the *Trenitalia* journey planner at www.trenitalia.com.

610 ROMA - PISA - GENOVA - MILANO and TORINO

🍷 on all *EC*, *FA*, *FB*, *FR* and *ITA* trains

km			*ICN* 796 ⑥⑦ ✣♦	*ITA* 9998 ♦	*IC* 652	*IC* 500	*FR* 9710 ♦		*ICN* 796 ③–⑤ ✣♦	*ICN* 796 ①② ✣♦	*IC* 655 ①–⑥ A	*IC* 658	*ICN* 1962 ⑥⑦ ✣♦		*IC* 662	*IC* 504	*ICN* 1962 ①–⑤ ✣♦	*FA* 8588	*IC* 631 A	*IC* 666	*FB* 8606	*IC* 745 A	*IC* 670	*IC* 655 † A
	Salerno **640**	d.	2052	...	...	...	...	...	2052	2052	...	...	2333	...	...	...	2333	...	...	...	...	...	...	...
	Napoli Centrale **640**	d.	2146	...	...	...	...	...	2146	2146	...	...	|	...	...	...	|	...	...	...	...	...	...	...
0	**Roma** Termini	d.	|	...	...	...	...	...	|	|	...	...	|	...	...	...	|	0623	...	...	0657	...	...	...
7	**Roma** Ostiense	d.	0011	...	...	...	...	...	0011	0014	...	...	|	...	...	...	|	|	...	...	|	...	...	...
81	Civitavecchia	d.	0053	...	...	...	...	...	0335	0335	...	...	|	...	...	...	|	|	...	...	0746	...	...	...
188	Grosseto	d.	0153	...	...	...	...	...	0431	0431	...	...	|	...	...	...	|	|	...	...	0839	...	...	...
230	Follonica	d.	|	...	...	...	...	...	|	|	...	...	|	...	...	...	|	|	...	...	|	...	...	...
247	Campiglia Marittima	d.	|	...	...	...	...	...	|	|	...	...	|	...	...	...	|	|	...	...	0905	...	...	...
282	Cecina	d.	|	...	...	...	...	...	|	|	...	...	|	...	...	...	|	|	...	...	0920	...	...	...
316	**Livorno** Centrale	a.	0306	...	...	...	...	...	0540	0540	...	...	|	...	...	...	|	|	...	...	0939	...	...	...
316	**Livorno** Centrale	d.	0309	...	...	...	...	...	0543	0543	...	0525	|	...	0625	...	|	|	...	0835	0941	...	1124	...
	Firenze Campo di Marte	d.	|	...	...	...	...	...	|	|	...	|	0536	...	|	...	0536	0754	...	|	|	...	|	...
336	**Pisa** Centrale	a.	0323	...	...	...	...	...	0557	0557	...	0539	0647	...	0639	...	|	0848	...	0855	0953	...	1139	...
336	**Pisa** Centrale	d.	0326	...	...	...	...	...	0600	0600	...	0542	0647	...	0642	...	|	0850	...	0857	0956	...	1142	...
357	Viareggio	d.	|	...	...	...	...	...	|	|	...	0557	0711	...	0657	...	|	|	...	0923	1012	...	1200	...
378	Massa Centro	d.	|	...	...	...	...	...	|	|	...	0613	|	...	0709	...	|	0916	...	0937	1025	...	1212	...
385	Carrara-Avenza	d.	|	...	...	...	...	...	|	|	...	|	|	...	0716	...	|	|	...	0952	|	...	1219	...
395	Sarzana	d.	|	...	...	...	...	...	|	|	...	|	|	...	0724	...	|	|	...	|	|	...	|	...
411	La Spezia Centrale	d.	0425	...	0456	...	...	...	0656	0656	...	0638	0807	...	0738	...	|	0939	...	1010	1046	...	1238	...
418	Monterosso	d.	|	...	0514	...	...	...	|	|	...	0654	|	...	|	...	|	|	...	1033	|	...	1255	...
423	Levanto	d.	|	...	0521	...	...	...	|	|	...	0700	|	...	0757	...	|	|	...	1040	|	...	1302	...
446	Sestri Levante	d.	|	...	0540	...	...	...	|	|	...	0716	|	...	0814	...	|	|	...	1122	|	...	1324	...
453	Chiavari	d.	0512	...	0552	...	...	...	0743	0743	...	0724	|	...	0824	...	|	|	...	1132	1117	...	1332	...
462	Rapallo	d.	0521	...	0601	...	...	...	0752	0752	...	0733	|	...	0833	...	|	|	...	1141	|	...	1341	...
464	S. Margherita-Portofino	d.	|	...	0607	...	...	...	|	|	...	0739	|	...	...	...	|	|	...	...	|	...	1346	...
498	**Genova** Brignole	d.	0555	0608	0635	0648	0658	...	0833	0833	...	0810	0936	...	0909	...	|	1038s	...	1210	1145	...	1410	...
501	**Genova** Piazza Principe	a.	0601	0612u	0641	0656u	0705u	...	0839	0839	...	0816	0950	...	0915	...	|	1045	...	1216	1150	...	1416	...
501	**Genova** Piazza Principe	d.	0606	0614u	0644	0656u	0705u	...	0842	0842	0719	0819	0950	...	0918	0923	|	...	1119	1219	1159	1319	1419	1520
573	Tortona	d.	|	|	|	|	|	...	|	|	|	0900	1028	...	|	|	|	...	|	|	|	|	|	|
590	Voghera	d.	|	|	0734	|	|	...	|	|	0808	0910	1039	...	1008	|	|	...	1208	1308	|	1408	1508	1608
616	Pavia	d.	|	|	0751	|	0806	...	|	|	0826	0926	1055	...	1026	|	|	...	1226	1325	|	1426	1526	1626
655	**Milano** Centrale	a.	|	0805	0825	|	0835	...	|	|	0903	1003	1122	...	1058	|	1010	...	1258	1356	|	1458	1556	1656
	Novi Ligure	d.	|	...	...	0734	...	...	|	|	...	...	...	...	...	|	...	...	...	...	|	...	...	...
	Alessandria	d.	0657	...	...	0748	...	...	0937	0937	...	...	...	...	...	1010	...	...	...	...	1244	...	...	...
	Asti	d.	0723	...	...	0807	...	...	1001	1001	...	...	...	...	...	1029	...	...	...	...	1302	...	...	...
	Torino Porta Nuova	a.	0810	...	...	0845	...	...	1040	1040	...	...	...	...	...	1110	...	...	...	...	1340	...	...	...

		IC 510	*EC* 326 ⊖♦	*IC* 674	*FB* 8616		*IC* 635 A	*IC* 680	*NJ* 40235 235 D	*FB* 8620	*IC* 681 Ⓐ A	*IC* 681 Ⓒ A	*IC* 684 Ⓒ	*IC* 684 Ⓐ	*IC* 639 A		*IC* 518 A	*FA* 8556 Ⓑ	*FB* 8626	*FB* 8630		*FA* 8596 Ⓑ ♦	*IC* 522
Salerno **640**	d.	0626	...	...	...	...	...	...	...	...	...	...	...	...	...	...	...	...	...	...	...	...	...
Napoli Centrale **640**	d.	0731	...	...	...	...	...	...	...	...	...	...	...	...	...	...	...	...	...	...	...	...	1731
Roma Termini	d.	0957	...	...	1157	...	...	...	...	1357	...	...	...	...	...	...	1557	1620	1657	1827	...	2032	|
Roma Ostiense	d.	1007	...	...	|	...	...	...	...	|	...	...	...	...	...	...	1607	|	|	|	...	|	1943
Civitavecchia	d.	1047	...	...	1246	...	...	...	...	1446	...	...	...	...	...	...	1647	|	1746	1916	...	|	2023
Grosseto	d.	1139	...	...	1339	...	...	...	...	1539	...	...	1604	1610	...	...	1739	|	1838	2007	...	|	2121
Follonica	d.	1158	...	...	|	...	...	...	...	|	...	...	1624	1631	...	...	1759	|	|	|	...	|	2141
Campiglia Marittima	d.	1209	...	...	1405	...	...	...	...	1605	...	...	1636	1642	...	...	|	|	1907	2032	...	|	2151
Cecina	d.	|	...	...	|	...	...	...	...	|	...	...	1655	1700	...	...	1823	|	|	|	...	|	2210
Livorno Centrale	a.	1243	...	...	1438	...	...	...	...	1638	...	...	1716	1722	...	...	1844	|	1938	2105	...	|	2234
Livorno Centrale	d.	1245	...	1324	1440	...	...	...	...	1640	...	...	1718	1724	...	...	1846	|	1940	2107	...	|	2236
Firenze Campo di Marte	d.	|	...	|	|	...	...	...	...	|	...	...	|	|	...	...	|	1744	|	|	...	2150	|
Pisa Centrale	a.	1259	...	1339	1453	...	...	...	...	1653	...	...	1733	1739	...	...	1900	1837	1953	2120	...	2240	2250
Pisa Centrale	d.	1302	...	1342	1456	...	...	...	...	1656	...	...	1736	1742	...	...	1903	1840	1956	2123	...	2243	2253
Viareggio	d.	1317	...	1402	1512	...	...	...	...	1712	...	...	1753	1802	...	...	1919	|	2012	2140	...	|	2310
Massa Centro	d.	1330	...	1414	1525	...	...	...	...	1725	...	...	1814	1814	...	...	1935	|	2025	2154	...	|	2323
Carrara-Avenza	d.	1339	...	|	|	...	...	...	...	|	...	...	1821	|	...	...	|	|	|	|	...	|	2331
Sarzana	d.	|	...	|	|	...	...	...	...	|	...	...	|	|	...	...	|	|	|	|	...	|	2340
La Spezia Centrale	d.	1405	...	1438	1546	...	...	1638	1710	1746	...	...	1838	1838	...	...	2003	1927	2046	2216	...	2327	0008
Monterosso	d.	|	...	1455	|	...	...	1655	|	|	...	...	1855	1855	...	...	|	|	|	|	...	|	0024
Levanto	d.	|	...	1502	|	...	...	1702	1737	|	...	...	1902	1902	...	...	|	|	|	|	...	|	0031
Sestri Levante	d.	1444	...	1524	|	...	...	1725	|	|	...	...	1925	1925	...	...	2030	|	|	|	...	|	0049
Chiavari	d.	1451	...	1532	1616	...	...	1732	|	1817	...	...	1932	1932	...	...	2038	|	|	2246	...	|	...
Rapallo	d.	1500	...	1541	1625	...	...	1741	1834	|	...	...	1941	1941	...	...	2046	2002	2123	|	...	|	...
S. Margherita-Portofino	d.	|	...	1546	|	...	...	1746	|	|	...	...	1946	1946	...	...	|	|	|	|	...	|	...
Genova Brignole	d.	1529	...	1608	1651s	...	...	1809	|	1847	...	...	2010	2010	...	...	2129	2023s	2143s	2313s	...	0022s	...
Genova Piazza Principe	a.	1535	...	1614	1658	...	...	1815	1934	1852	...	...	2016	2016	...	...	2134	2032	2150	2320	...	0030	...
Genova Piazza Principe	d.	1538	1809	1619	...	...	1719	1818	1950	1854	1922	1922	2019	2019	2122	...	...	...	...	...	...	...	...
Tortona	d.	|	1854	1700	...	...	|	1900	|	|	2000	2000	|	|	|	...	...	...	...	...	...	...	...
Voghera	d.	|	|	|	...	...	1808	|	|	|	|	|	2108	2108	2208	...	...	...	...	...	...	...	...
Pavia	d.	|	1920	1726	...	...	1826	1926	2106	2006	2026	2026	2126	2126	2226	...	...	...	...	...	...	...	...
Milano Centrale	a.	|	1940r	1756	...	...	1858	2000	2124r	2043	2105	2100	2156	2156	2256	...	...	...	...	...	...	...	...
Novi Ligure	d.	|	...	...	...	...	...	...	...	...	...	...	...	...	...	...	...	...	...	...	...	...	...
Alessandria	d.	1636	...	...	...	...	...	...	...	...	...	...	...	...	...	...	...	...	...	...	...	...	...
Asti	d.	1700	...	...	...	...	...	...	...	...	...	...	...	...	...	...	...	...	...	...	...	...	...
Torino Porta Nuova	a.	1740	...	...	...	...	...	...	...	...	...	...	...	...	...	...	...	...	...	...	...	...	...

FOR FOOTNOTES SEE PREVIOUS PAGE.

611 TORINO and MILANO - GENOVA - PISA - ROMA

2nd class

Regional trains. For long distance trains see Table **610**.

TORINO - GENOVA

km												
0	**Torino** Porta Nuova	d.	0530	0630	0730	0830	and	1730	1830	1930	2130
56	Asti	d.	0607	0707	0807	0907	hourly	1807	1907	2007	2207
91	Alessandria	d.	0631	0731	0831	0931	hour	1831	1931	2031	2231
112	Novi Ligure	d.	0644	0744	0844	0944	until	1844	1944	2044	2244
166	**Genova** Piazza Principe	a.	0733	0830	0933	1030	◧	1933	2030	2130	2330

Genova Piazza Principe	d.	0527	0627	0727	0827	and	1727	1827	2027	2127
Novi Ligure	d.	0614	0714	0814	0914	hourly	1814	1914	2114	2214
Alessandria	d.	0631	0731	0831	0931	hour	1831	1931	2131	2231
Asti	d.	0654	0754	0854	0954	until	1854	1954	2154	2254
Torino Porta Nuova	a.	0730	0830	0930	1030	◧	1930	2030	2230	2335

MILANO - GENOVA

km			⚒		⚒			Ⓐ	Ⓒ			
0	**Milano** Centrale	d.	0625	0725	0830	1225	1425	1625	1625	1825	2025	...
10	**Milano** Rogoredo	d.	0638	0738	0844	1238	1438	1638	1638	1840	2038	...
39	Pavia	d.	0659	0759	0905	1259	1459	1659	1659	1903	2059	...
65	Voghera	d.	0716	0816	0923	1316	1516	1716	1716	1918	2116	...
82	Tortona	d.	0726	0826	0935	1326	1526	1726	1726	1929	2126	...
154	**Genova** Piazza Principe	a.	0818	0908	1025	1418	1618	1818	1814	2021	2218	...
157	**Genova** Brignole	a.	0826	0920	...	1427	...	1827	...	2030	...	...

		②–⑥		Ⓐ	Ⓒ	Ⓐ	Ⓒ			⚒	Ⓑ
Genova Brignole	d.	0536	...	1336	...	...	...	...	1936	...	...
Genova Piazza Principe	d.	0544	0750	1344	1344	1544	1546	1744	1944	2035	2144
Tortona	d.	0632	0832	1432	1432	1632	1632	1832	2032	2123	2232
Voghera	d.	0643	0843	1443	1443	1643	1643	1843	2043	2134	2243
Pavia	d.	0701	0901	1501	1501	1701	1701	1901	2101	2151	2301
Milano Rogoredo	a.	0720	0918	1520	1520	1720	1720	1920	2120	2210	2320
Milano Centrale	a.	0735	0935	1535	1535	1735	1735	1935	2135	2225	2335

◧ – No train from Torino at 0930, 1630; no train from Genova at 1127, 1527. Some trains continue to / from Genova Brignole. Timings may vary by 2–3 minutes.

2nd class

TORINO and MILANO - GENOVA - PISA - ROMA

611

Regional trains. For long distance trains see Table **610**.

GENOVA - SESTRI LEVANTE - LA SPEZIA

km																								
				⚒		†				Ⓐ		Ⓐ			Ⓐ	Ⓐ						Ⓒ	Ⓒ	
0	**Genova** Brignole d.	0500	0606	0720	...	0720	1045	1245	...	1322	1445	1620	...	1645	1738	1819	...	1845	1930	2045	...	2045	2300	...
25	S. Margherita-Portofino d.	0528	0637	0757	...	0759	1115	1315	...	1403	1515	1702	...	1715	1809	1903	...	1915	2009	2112	...	2112	2336	...
27	Rapallo d.	0532	0641	0801	...	0803	1119	1319	...	1408	1519	1708	...	1719	1814	1908	...	1919	2014	2116	...	2116	2340	...
36	Chiavari d.	0540	0650	0811	...	0811	1127	1327	...	1418	1527	1716	...	1727	1823	1918	...	1927	2023	2125	...	2125	2348	...
43	**Sestri Levante** a.	0548	0659	0825	...	0819	1134	1334	...	1428	1534	1728	...	1734	1832	1932	...	1936	2031	2132	...	2134	2358	...
43	**Sestri Levante** d.	0549	0700	0826	...	0820	1135	1335	...	1429	1535	1740	...	1735	1840	1941	...	1937	2032	2133	...	2135	2359	...
66	Levanto d.	0615	0725	0853	...	0847	1150	1350	...	1511	1550	1814	...	1750	1914	2015	...	1952	2052	2148	...	2150	0021	...
71	Monterosso d.	0620	0730	0858	...	0853	|	1355	...	1517	1555	1819	...	1755	1919	2020	...	1957	2057	2153	...	2155	0026	...
80	Riomaggiore d.	0635	|	0908	...	0909	1203	|	...	1533	1604	1834	...	|	1935	2035	...	2004	2106	2202	...	2203	0041	...
87	**La Spezia** Centrale a.	0645	0745	0914	...	0917	1210	1410	...	1540	1610	1845	...	1810	1942	2045	...	2010	2112	2210	...	2210	0052	...
					Ⓐ	†		Ⓐ														Ⓒ	Ⓒ	
	La Spezia Centrale d.	0508	...	...	0540	0600	...	0625	0706	...	0750	...	0950	1150	...	1350	1550	...	1750	1945	...	2145	2310	...
	Riomaggiore d.	0517	...	...	0549	0608	...	|	0714	...	|	...	|	|	...	1358	1558	...	1758	1953	...	2153	2319	...
	Monterosso d.	0533	...	...	0604	0623	...	|	0729	...	|	...	|	|	...	1406	1606	...	|	2005	...	2201	2335	...
	Levanto d.	0538	...	...	0609	0628	...	0641	0734	...	0811	...	1011	1211	...	1411	1611	...	1811	2011	...	2206	2340	...
	Sestri Levante a.	0604	...	...	0635	0655	...	0655	0759	...	0825	...	1025	1225	...	1425	1625	...	1825	2035	...	2223	0004	...
	Sestri Levante d.	0605	...	...	0636	0657	...	0657	0800	...	0826	...	1026	1226	...	1426	1626	...	1826	2036	...	2224	0005	...
	Chiavari d.	0617	...	...	0645	0707	...	0706	0808	...	0833	...	1033	1234	...	1434	1634	...	1834	2044	...	2231	0014	...
	Rapallo d.	0628	...	...	0656	0716	...	|	0816	...	0841	...	1041	1242	...	1442	1642	...	1842	2055	...	2239	0025	...
	S. Margherita-Portofino d.	0632	...	...	0700	0720	...	|	0820	...	0845	...	1045	1246	...	1446	1646	...	1846	2059	...	2243	0029	...
	Genova Brignole a.	0709	...	...	0753	0753	...	0740	0856	...	0915	...	1115	1315	...	1515	1715	...	1915	2139	...	2309	0123	...

LA SPEZIA - PISA

km																								
			⚒	⚒	†	⚒	⚒		†	⚒		⚒			†	Ⓐ			Ⓐ			⚒		
0	**La Spezia** Centrale d.	0512	0600	0656	0712	0715	0740	0821	0915	0915	1021	1215	1319	1415	1440	1515	1540	1621	1705	1740	1821	1916	2015	2226
16	Sarzana d.	0530	0615	0717	0733	0736	0800	0838	0932	0931	1036	1228	1335	1430	1500	1531	1600	1637	1720	1800	1837	1933	2031	2241
26	Carrara-Avenza d.	0538	0623	0725	0743	0746	0807	0847	0940	0939	1044	1236	1343	1440	1508	1538	1608	1645	1728	1808	1845	1948	2039	2249
33	Massa Centro d.	0544	0630	0732	0749	0753	0814	0853	0946	0946	1050	1242	1349	1446	1514	1544	1614	1651	1734	1814	1850	1954	2045	2256
54	Viareggio d.	0604	0653	0755	0810	0814	0825	0913	1007	1010	1110	1259	1406	1503	1533	1603	1633	1708	1753	1833	1907	2013	2105	2316
75	**Pisa** Centrale a.	0624	0721	0818	0827	0832	0849	0940	1038	1043	1140	1322	1427	1527	1552	1625	1652	1727	1816	1852	1927	2032	2127	2339
		⚒	⚒			⚒			⚒		⚒				Ⓑ			Ⓐ	Ⓒ	†	Ⓑ	⚒		⚒
	Pisa Centrale d.	0526	0622	0702	0736	0819	...	1106	1134	1234	1306	1334	1433	1506	1538	1634	1706	1736	1743	1806	1834	1934	2034	2140
	Viareggio d.	0546	0641	0724	0758	0837	...	1123	1155	1254	1323	1357	1452	1523	1558	1655	1723	1757	1804	1823	1859	1954	2055	2201
	Massa Centro d.	0608	0701	0745	0821	0858	...	1144	1215	1312	1344	1415	1510	1544	1615	1712	1744	1817	1822	1844	1917	2012	2113	2221
	Carrara-Avenza d.	0616	0707	0751	0828	0905	...	1150	1221	1318	1350	1421	1516	1550	1621	1718	1750	1823	1828	1850	1923	2018	2119	2231
	Sarzana d.	0623	0715	0802	0837	0913	...	1158	1229	1326	1358	1430	1525	1558	1628	1726	1758	1830	1836	1858	1932	2031	2128	2239
	La Spezia Centrale a.	0650	0731	0826	0858	0933	...	1220	1258	1341	1420	1458	1539	1620	1645	1739	1820	1858	1858	1920	1958	2058	2143	2258

PISA - ROMA

km										
		Ⓒd	Ⓐ							
0	**Pisa** Centrale d.	...	...	0545	0745	1145	1343	1545	1745	1945
20	**Livorno** Centrale d.	...	...	0603	0803	1203	1400	1603	1803	2003
43	Rosignano d.	...	...	0620	0820	1220	1416	1620	1820	2020
54	Cecina d.	...	...	0629	0829	1229	1424	1629	1829	2029
89	Campiglia Marittima d.	...	...	0650	0851	1251	1445	1651	1851	2051
106	Follonica d.	...	...	0700	0902	1302	1455	1702	1902	2102
148	Grosseto d.	0615	0629	0728	0930	1330	1530	1730	1930	2130
186	Orbetello-Monte Argentario d.	0643	0657	0751	0953	1353	1553	1753	1953	2153
225	Tarquinia d.	0716	0730	0827	1029	1429	1629	1829	2029	2229
255	Civitavecchia d.	0730	0744	0842	1044	1444	1644	1844	2044	2244
264	S. Marinella d.	0737	0751	0849	1051	1451	1651	1851	2051	2251
286	Ladispoli-Cerveteri d.	0754	0807	0904	1105	1505	1705	1905	2105	2305
329	**Roma** Ostiense a.	0838	0837	0936	1136	1536	1736	1936	2136	2336
336	**Roma** Termini a.	0850	0850	0948	1148	1548	1747	1948	2148	2348

	⚒								
Roma Termini d.	...	0612	1012	1212	1412	1612	1812	2012	2112
Roma Ostiense d.	...	0623	1023	1223	1423	1623	1823	2023	2121
Ladispoli-Cerveteri d.	...	0651	1051	1251	1451	1651	1855	2052	2155
S. Marinella d.	...	0707	1107	1307	1507	1707	1911	2107	2211
Civitavecchia d.	...	0715	1115	1315	1515	1715	1924	2115	2220
Tarquinia d.	...	0728	1128	1328	1528	1728	1936	2128	2233
Orbetello-Monte Argentario d.	0602	0800	1201	1401	1601	1801	2009	2201	2306
Grosseto d.	0628	0823	1226	1426	1626	1826	2033	2226	2330
Follonica d.	0652	0845	1250	1450	1650	1850	2057	2250	...
Campiglia Marittima d.	0704	0855	1301	1501	1701	1901	2108	2301	...
Cecina d.	0729	0916	1324	1524	1724	1924	2128	2324	...
Rosignano d.	0737	0927	1332	1532	1732	1932	2136	2333	...
Livorno Centrale a.	0753	0952	1355	1555	1755	1955	2155	2355	...
Pisa Centrale a.	0811	1018	1415	1615	1815	2015	2215	0015	...

d – Runs 4–5 minutes later on ⑦.

CAMPIGLIA - PIOMBINO

km										
		⚒	⑥	⚒			Ⓐ			
0	**Campiglia** Marittima d.	0556	1003	1336	1533	1645	1736	1804	...	...
14	**Piombino** a.	0608	1019	1352	1547	1700	1752	1816	...	...
16	**Piombino** Marittima a.	0624	1032	1405	1600	1713	1802	1831	...	...

	⚒		Ⓒ		⚒			Ⓐ	
Piombino Marittima d.	0632	0920	1053	...	1519	1608	1724	1812	1845
Piombino d.	0643	0931	1104	...	1531	1619	1736	1820	1856
Campiglia Marittima a.	0659	0947	1120	...	1552	1635	1753	1838	1909

2nd class

PARMA - LA SPEZIA

612

For other trains Pontremoli - S. Stefano di Magra and v.v. see next page.

km																							
		⚒						⚒			⚒			⚒			⚒			⚒			†
0	**Parma** d.	...	0514	...	0627	0745	...	...	...	...	1226	1344	...	...	1553	...	...	1747	...	1946	2057	...	2244
23	Fornovo d.	...	0532	...	0650	0812	...	...	...	...	1247	1407	...	...	1620	...	...	1813	...	2014	2124	...	2307
61	Borgo Val di Taro d.	...	0609	...	0731	0846	...	...	...	...	1323	1445	...	...	1653	...	...	1850	...	2045	2202	...	2340
79	Pontremoli d.	0535	0627	...	0749	0904	...	0942	1315	...	1342	1503	...	1543	1711	...	1807	1908	...	2103	2220	...	2359
100	Aulla Lunigiana d.	0556	0652	...	0819	0922	...	1010	1336	...	1410	1524	...	1610	1730	...	1829	1927	...	2124	2238	...	0021
108	S. Stefano di Magra d.	0603	0659	...	0825	0930	...	1016	1342	...	1416	1534	...	1616	1738	...	1836	1934	...	2131	2246	...	0028
120	**La Spezia** Centrale a.	0621	0722	...	0851	0944	...	1033	1400	...	1433	1556	...	1633	1758	...	1852	1952	...	2154	2306	...	0045
					⚒	⚒								⚒			⚒			⚒			
	La Spezia Centrale d.	0540	0612	...	0810	0927	...	1015	1226	...	1325	1408	...	1527	1604	...	1657	1808	...	1927	2009	...	2114
	S. Stefano di Magra d.	0551	0629	...	0827	0945	...	1032	1243	...	1343	1423	...	1545	1623	...	1716	1826	...	1945	2028	...	2125
	Aulla Lunigiana d.	0558	0637	...	0834	0952	...	1038	1249	...	1351	1430	...	1551	1632	...	1723	1834	...	1952	2037	...	2132
	Pontremoli d.	0625	0657	...	0856	1015	...	1058	1308	...	1413	1457	...	1613	1654	...	1746	1855	...	2015	2057	...	2152
	Borgo Val di Taro d.	0644	0717	...	0915	...	...	1116	1325	...	...	1514	...	...	1712	...	1804	1912	...	...	2116	...	2209
	Fornovo d.	0720	0750	...	0952	...	...	1150	1404	...	...	1552	...	...	1747	...	1845	1946	...	...	2148	...	2244
	Parma a.	0744	0813	...	1016	...	...	1209	1431	...	...	1614	...	...	1814	...	1910	2011	...	...	2214	...	2314

612 MILANO - PISA - FIRENZE — 2nd class

For other trains Pontremoli - S. Stefano di Magra and v.v. see previous page.

km			A		⚒		Ⓐ	⑥		
0	**Milano** Centrale d.	...	0650	...	...	...	...	...	1705r	...
10	**Milano** Rogoredo d.	...	0701	...	...	...	...	...	1741	...
72	Piacenza d.	...	0759	...	...	...	...	...	1842	...
107	Fidenza d.	...	0821	...	...	...	...	...	1906	...
132	Fornovo d.	...	0842	...	...	...	...	...	1926	...
170	Borgo Val di Taro d.	0541	0933	...	...	...	...	...	2007	...
188	Pontremoli d.	0601	0953	1221	1421	...	1621	1621	2026	...
209	Aulla Lunigiana d.	0623	1021	1243	1447	...	1643	1643	2059	...
217	S. Stefano di Magra d.	0631	1028	1251	1453	...	1651	1651	2106	...
225	Sarzana a.	0639	1043	1300	1500	...	1659	1659	2115	...
235	Carrara-Avenza d.	0647	1052	1308	1509	...	1708	1708	2124	...
242	Massa Centro d.	0653	1100	1314	1515	...	1714	1714	2130	...
263	Viareggio d.	0714	1124	1333	1534	...	1733	1733	2150	...
284	**Pisa** Centrale 613 d.	0744	1145	1354	1554	...	1754	1754	2212	...
304	**Livorno** Centrale a.	│	...	│	│	...	│	│	2230c	...
331	Empoli 613 d.	0815	...	1432	1632	...	1832	1836	...	...
	Firenze Rifredi 613 a.	0839	...	1459	1659	...	1859	1912	...	...
365	**Firenze** SMN 613 a.	0848	...	1508	1708	...	1908	1919	...	...

		†	⚒	⚒		⚒			
Firenze SMN 613 d.	...	0850	1053	1253	...	1653	...	1853	...
Firenze Rifredi 613 d.	...	0856	1059	1259	...	1659	...	1859	...
Empoli 613 d.	...	0925	1127	1327	...	1728	...	1927	...
Livorno Centrale d.	0548e	│	│	│	...	│	...	│	...
Pisa Centrale 613 d.	0606	1006	1206	1406	...	1806	1907	2006	...
Viareggio d.	0624	1023	1223	1423	...	1823	1926	2023	...
Massa Centro d.	0641	1044	1244	1444	...	1844	1943	2044	...
Carrara-Avenza d.	0647	1050	1250	1450	...	1850	1948	2050	...
Sarzana d.	0656	1058	1258	1458	...	1858	1956	2058	...
S. Stefano di Magra d.	0711	1109	1309	1507	...	1911	2015	2109	...
Aulla Lunigiana d.	0718	1116	1316	1514	...	1918	2023	2116	...
Pontremoli d.	0739	1140	1341	1540	...	1942	2043	2142	...
Borgo Val di Taro d.	0802	...	...	...	...	...	2104	...	...
Fornovo d.	0845	...	...	...	...	...	2136	...	...
Fidenza d.	0905	...	...	...	...	...	2158	...	...
Piacenza d.	0930	...	...	...	...	...	2225	...	...
Milano Rogoredo a.	1015	...	...	...	...	...	2310	...	...
Milano Centrale a.	1041r	...	...	...	...	...	2322	...	...

A – Not Mar. 4–6, Apr. 22–24, 29, 30, May 1.

c – Not Mar. 11. Arrives 2235 on ⑤⑦ Mar. 5 - Apr. 2 (also Mar. 18, Apr. 25).

e – Departs 0538 on ⑥⑦ Mar. 18 - Apr. 2.

r – Milano **Porta Garibaldi**.

613 FIRENZE - SIENA, PISA and LIVORNO — 2nd class

km			⚒	†					⚒		⚒									⚒	⚒	⚒	†	
0	**Firenze** SMN 614 d.	0535	0620	0620	0653	0728	0810	0828	0910	0928	1010	1028	1100	...	1110	1128	1138	1210	1228	1300	1310	1328	1338	1410
	Firenze Rifredi 614 d.	0540	0626	0626	0659	0734	0816	0834	0916	0934	1016	1034	│	...	1116	1134	1144	1216	1234	│	1316	1334	1344	1416
34	Empoli d.	0601	0650	0650	0730	0758	0840	0858	0940	0958	1040	1058	1123	...	1140	1157	1213	1240	1258	1323	1340	1358	1413	1440
72	Poggibonsi-S. Gimignano d.	│	0729	0724	│	│	0915	│	1015	│	1115	│	│	...	1215	│	│	1315	│	│	1415	│	│	1514
97	**Siena** a.	│	0755	0747	│	│	0938	│	1040	│	1140	│	│	...	1238	│	│	1340	│	│	1440	│	│	1537
81	**Pisa** Centrale 614 d.	0637	...	...	0809	0837	...	0932	...	1032	...	1132	1154	...	...	1227	1302	...	1332	1354	...	1432	1509	...
101	**Livorno** Centrale a.	0651	...	...	0826	0851	...	0948	...	1048	...	1148	1211	...	...	1242	1320	...	1348	1411	...	1448	1526	...

			⚒		⚒	⚒	⚒									⑥			†	⚒	⚒		
Firenze SMN 614 d.	1428	1500	1510	1528	1610	1628	1700	1710	1728	1738	1810	1828	...	1910	1928	1953	2010	2053	2128	2128	2138	2200	2307
Firenze Rifredi 614 d.	1434	│	1516	1534	1616	1634	│	1716	1734	1744	1816	1834	...	1916	1934	1959	2016	2059	2134	2134	2144	2206	2313
Empoli d.	1458	1523	1540	1558	1640	1658	1723	1740	1758	1813	1840	1858	...	1940	1958	2027	2040	2127	2200	2200	2208	2236	2343
Poggibonsi-S. Gimignano d.	│	│	1615	│	1715	│	│	1815	│	│	1915	│	...	2015	│	│	2115	│	│	│	2246	│	│
Siena a.	│	│	1640	│	1738	│	│	1840	│	│	1938	│	...	2040	│	│	2137	│	│	│	2316	│	│
Pisa Centrale 614 d.	1532	1554	...	1632	...	1732	1754	...	1832	1858	...	1932	...	...	2032	2106	...	2206	2232	2239	...	2327	0032
Livorno Centrale a.	1548	1611	...	1648	...	1748	1811	...	1846	1912	...	1948	...	...	2048	2124	...	2224	2248	2257	...	2344	0050

	⚒		⚒		⚒	†	⚒	⚒	⚒	†						⚒	†	⚒	⚒		⚒		
Livorno Centrale d.	0500	0519	...	0612	...	...	...	0716	...	...	0730	0742	0812	...	0849	0912	0912	...	1012	1110	...	1212	...
Pisa Centrale 614 d.	0519	0539	...	0629	...	...	...	0738	...	...	0754	0803	0832	...	0909	0932	0932	...	1032	1130	...	1232	...
Siena d.	│	│	0543	│	0613	0636	0636	│	0702	0715	│	│	│	0818	│	│	│	0918	│	│	1118	│	1218
Poggibonsi-S. Gimignano d.	│	│	0606	│	0648	0658	0659	│	0728	0742	│	│	│	0842	│	│	│	0942	│	│	1142	│	1242
Empoli d.	0602	0618	0645	0659	0723	0735	0750	0808	0820	0820	0832	0847	0904	0921	0937	1004	1017	1021	1104	1202	1221	1304	1321
Firenze Rifredi 614 a.	0631	0645	0713	0720	0744	0753	0822	0829	0850	0850	0859	0915	0925	0943	│	1025	1038	1043	1125	1226	1243	1325	1343
Firenze SMN 614 a.	0639	0653	0723	0728	0754	0804	0832	0838	0859	0859	0908	0923	0933	0952	1001	1033	1047	1052	1133	1233	1252	1333	1352

						⚒	⚒	⚒				⚒							⚒				
Livorno Centrale d.	1249	1312	...	1343	1412	...	1449	1512	...	...	1540	1612	...	1649	1712	...	1812	...	1849	...	2012	...	2112	...
Pisa Centrale 614 d.	1309	1332	...	1401	1432	...	1509	1532	...	...	1601	1632	...	1709	1732	...	1832	...	1909	...	2032	...	2132	...
Siena d.	│	│	1318	│	│	1418	│	│	1518	│	│	1618	│	│	1718	│	1818	│	1918	│	2018	│	2140
Poggibonsi-S. Gimignano d.	│	│	1342	│	│	1442	│	│	1542	│	│	1642	│	│	1742	│	1842	│	1942	│	2042	│	2207
Empoli d.	1337	1404	1421	1447	1504	1521	1537	1604	1621	1647	1704	1721	1737	1804	1821	1904	1921	1937	2021	2107	2121	2204	2241
Firenze Rifredi 614 a.	│	1425	1443	1516	1525	1543	│	1625	1643	1716	1725	1743	│	1825	1843	1925	1943	│	2043	2129	2143	2225	2310
Firenze SMN 614 a.	1401	1433	1452	1525	1533	1552	1601	1633	1652	1725	1733	1752	1801	1833	1852	1933	1952	2001	2052	2139	2152	2233	2319

614 FIRENZE - PRATO - BOLOGNA, VIAREGGIO and PISA — 2nd class

km		⚒	⚒				†	⚒	⚒			†			Ⓐ🚌	†	Ⓐ🚌	Ⓐ			†			⚒
0	**Firenze** SMN 613 d.	0510	...	...	...	0709	...	...	...	0809	...	...	0909	...	...	1009	...	...	1209	...	...	1309	...	...
	Firenze Rifredi 613 d.	0516	...	...	...	0715	...	...	...	0815	...	...	0915	...	...	1015	...	...	1215	...	...	1315	...	...
17	Prato Centrale d.	0533	...	...	0615	0728	...	...	0738	0830	...	0908	0930	...	1005	1030	1105	...	1230	...	1240	1330	...	1340
	Bologna Centrale a.	│	...	...	0727	│	...	...	0850	│	...	1020	│	...	1150	│	1250	...	│	...	1352	│	...	1456
34	Pistoia d.	0551	...	...	...	0745	...	...	...	0844	...	...	0944	...	...	1044	...	...	1244	...	...	1344	...	...
47	Montecatini Centro d.	0604	...	...	...	0801	...	...	...	0901	...	...	1001	...	...	1101	...	...	1301	...	...	1401	...	...
78	Lucca d.	0646	0652	0755	...	0830	0842	0849	...	0930	0942	...	1033	1042	...	1130	...	1242	1330	1340	...	1430	1442	...
101	**Viareggio** a.	0707	│	│	...	0850	│	│	...	0950	│	...	1056	│	...	1150	...	│	1350	│	...	1450	│	...
102	**Pisa** Centrale 613 a.	...	0717	0825	...	...	0913	0916	...	...	1013	...	...	1111	...	...	...	1313	...	1413	...	...	1513	...

					⚒					⚒			†	⚒	⚒			⚒		Ⓐ	⚒		
Firenze SMN 613 d.	1409	...	1509	...	...	1609	...	...	1709	...	...	1809	...	...	...	1909	...	...	2009	...	2109	2209	...
Firenze Rifredi 613 d.	1415	...	1515	...	...	1615	...	...	1715	...	...	1815	...	...	...	1915	...	...	2015	...	2115	2215	...
Prato Centrale d.	1430	...	1530	...	1540	1630	...	1640	1730	...	1740	1830	...	...	1910	1930	...	2008	2030	...	2130	2230	2249
Bologna Centrale a.	│	...	│	...	1656	│	...	1752	│	...	1852	│	...	...	2022	│	...	2120	│	...	│	│	2350
Pistoia d.	1444	...	1544	...	...	1644	...	...	1744	...	...	1844	...	...	...	1944	...	...	2044	...	2144	2246	...
Montecatini Centro d.	1501	...	1601	...	...	1701	...	...	1801	...	...	1901	...	...	...	2001	...	...	2101	...	2200	2301	...
Lucca d.	1530	1542	1630	1642	...	1730	1742	...	1830	1842	...	1930	1941	1945	...	2030	2042	...	2130	2142	2249	2330	...
Viareggio a.	1550	│	1650	│	...	1750	│	...	1850	│	...	1950	│	│	...	2050	│	...	2150	│	2309	2350	...
Pisa Centrale 613 a.	...	1613	...	1713	...	...	1813	...	...	1917	...	...	2013	2015	...	...	2113	...	...	2213	...	...	...

	⑥		⚒	⚒		⚒		⚒					⚒			Ⓐ🚌	⚒				⚒		
Pisa Centrale 613 d.	...	0525	...	0613	...	...	...	...	0750	...	0850	...	...	0950	...	...	1020	...	1250	...	...	1343	...
Viareggio d.	...	│	0545	│	0628	...	0710	...	│	0810	│	0910	...	│	1010	...	│	1207	│	1310	...	│	1410
Lucca d.	...	0559	0609	0640	0648	...	0727	...	0823	0831	0920	0931	...	1018	1032	...	1048	1231	1317	1331	...	1409	1431
Montecatini Centro d.	...	...	0641	...	0715	...	0753	...	...	0857	━	0957	...	...	1057	...	...	1257	━	1357	...	...	1457
Pistoia d.	...	...	0709	...	0732	...	0813	...	...	0913	...	1013	...	...	1113	...	...	1313	...	1413	...	...	1513
Bologna Centrale d.	0608	...	│	...	│	0708	│	0808	...	│	0908	│	1008	...	│	1210	...	│	...	│	1408	...	│
Prato Centrale d.	0720	...	0728	...	0747	0820	0830	0920	...	0930	1024	1030	1120	...	1130	1355	...	1330	...	1430	1520	...	1530
Firenze Rifredi 613 a.	...	...	0746	...	0801	...	0846	...	...	0946	...	1046	...	...	1146	...	...	1346	...	1446	...	...	1546
Firenze SMN 613 a.	...	...	0752	...	0807	...	0852	...	...	0952	...	1052	...	...	1152	...	...	1352	...	1452	...	...	1552

							⚒						⚒					⚒		⚒	⚒		
Pisa Centrale 613 d.	...	1450	...	...	1550	...	...	1650	...	...	1750	...	...	1850	...	1950	...	...	2050	...	...	2150	...
Viareggio d.	...	│	1510	...	│	1610	...	│	1710	...	│	1810	...	│	1910	│	2010	...	│	2110	...	│	2210
Lucca d.	...	1517	1531	...	1617	1631	...	1717	1731	...	1817	1831	...	1917	1931	2017	2031	...	2118	2131	...	2217	2231
Montecatini Centro d.	...	...	1557	...	...	1657	...	...	1757	...	...	1857	...	...	1957	...	2057	...	...	2157	...	...	2257
Pistoia d.	...	...	1613	...	...	1713	...	...	1813	...	...	1913	...	...	2013	...	2113	...	...	2213	...	...	2313
Bologna Centrale d.	1508	...	│	1608	...	│	1708	...	│	1808	...	│	1838	...	│	...	│	2038	...	│	2208	...	│
Prato Centrale d.	1620	...	1630	1724	...	1730	1824	...	1830	1924	...	1930	1950	...	2030	...	2130	2151	...	2230	2320	...	2330
Firenze Rifredi 613 a.	...	...	1646	...	...	1746	...	...	1846	...	...	1946	...	...	2046	...	2146	2202	...	2246	...	...	2344
Firenze SMN 613 a.	...	...	1652	...	...	1752	...	...	1852	...	...	1952	...	...	2052	...	2152	2210	...	2252	...	...	2350

🍸 on *FA*, *FB*, *FR* and *ITA* trains — MILANO, BOLOGNA, RIMINI, ANCONA and ROMA - BARI - LECCE — 615

High-speed and long-distance trains. For local trains Milano - Bologna see Table **620**. For other local trains see page 303.

km		*ITA* 8141	*FA* 8303	*IC* 703	*FR* 9511	*FR* 9803	*FR* 8801	*IC* 603	*FR* 8803	*ITA* 9915	*IC* 605	*FA* 8311	*IC* 607	*FR* 8807		*FA* 8315	*FR* 8809	*IC* 1545	*EC* 307		*FR* 8811	*IC* 609	
				B			V			T		Ⓑ						⑥	A				
0	**Milano** Centrale .... **600 620** d.	...	...	...	0610	0705	...	...	0805	0740	0705	...	0910**g**	1105	...	...	1205	1000	...	...	1305	...	...
10	**Milano** Rogoredo △ .... **600 620** d.	...	...	...	0620	|	...	...	|	|	0716	...	0933	|	...	...	|	1013	1022	...	|	...	...
72	Piacenza .... **620** d.	...	...	...	|	|	...	...	|	|	0808	...	1020	|	...	...	|	1048	1101	...	|	...	...
107	Fidenza .... **620** d.	...	...	...	|	|	...	...	|	|	0827	...	1042	|	...	...	|	1105	|	...	|	...	...
129	Parma .... **620** d.	...	...	...	◧	◧	...	...	0854	◧	0840	...	1054	1154	...	...	1254	1118	1133	...	1354	...	...
157	Reggio Emilia .... **620** d.	...	...	...	|	|	...	...	0908	|	0855	...	1109	1208	...	...	1308	1133	1151	...	1408	...	...
	Reggio Emilia AV .... **600** d.	...	...	...	0656	|	...	...	|	0828	|	...	|	|	...	...	|	|	|	...	|	...	...
182	Modena .... **620** d.	...	...	...	|	|	...	...	0921	|	0926	...	1126	1221	...	...	1321	1149	1209	...	1421	...	...
219	**Bologna** Centrale .... **600 620** a.	...	...	...	0724	0812	...	...	0942	0854	0954	...	1156	1242	...	...	1342	1219	1230	...	1442	...	...
219	**Bologna** Centrale .... d.	...	...	...	0727	0815	0845	0800	0945	0857	0958	...	1200	1245	...	...	1345	1225	...	...	1445	1400	...
269	Faenza .... d.	...	...	...	|	|	|	0828	|	|	1028	...	1228	|	...	...	|	1256	...	...	|	1428	...
284	Forlì .... d.	...	...	...	|	|	|	0838	|	|	1038	...	1238	|	...	...	1416	1306	...	...	|	1438	...
302	Cesena .... d.	...	...	...	|	|	|	0851	|	|	1052	...	1251	1324	...	...	|	1319	...	...	|	1451	...
331	**Rimini** ● .... a.	...	...	...	|	0915	0938	0911	1038	|	1113	...	1313	1341	...	...	1441	1348	...	...	1541	1513	...
331	**Rimini** ● .... d.	...	...	...	|	0917	0940	0919	1040	|	1115	...	1315	1343	...	...	1443	1351	...	...	1543	1515	...
340	Riccione .... d.	...	...	...	|	0925	|	0930	1045	|	1124	...	1324	|	...	...	|	1400	...	...	|	1524	...
364	Pesaro .... d.	...	...	...	◧	0942	1002	0947	1102	◧	1142	...	1342	1402	...	...	1502	1418	...	...	1602	1542	...
376	Fano .... d.	...	...	...	|	|	|	0956	|	|	1151	...	1351	|	...	...	|	1427	...	...	|	1551	...
398	Senigallia .... d.	...	...	...	|	|	|	1010	|	|	1203	...	1403	|	...	...	|	1439	...	...	|	1603	...
423	**Ancona** .... a.	...	...	...	|	1013	1031	1036	1131	|	1223	...	1423	1431	...	...	1531	1456	...	...	1631	1623	...
423	**Ancona** .... d.	...	...	...	|	...	1034	1039	1134	|	1226	...	1426	1434	...	...	1534	1458	...	...	1634	1626	...
466	Civitanova Marche-Montegranaro .... d.	...	...	...	|	...	|	1101	1157	|	1255	...	1452	|	...	...	|	1523	...	...	|	1652	...
508	S. Benedetto del Tronto .... d.	...	...	...	|	...	|	1126	|	|	1323	...	1523	1513	...	...	1613	1548	...	...	|	1723	...
569	**Pescara** Centrale .... a.	...	...	...	|	...	1144	1201	1244	|	1359	...	1559	1544	...	...	1644	1631	...	...	1744	1759	...
569	**Pescara** Centrale .... d.	...	...	...	|	...	1147	1203	1247	|	1401	...	1601	1547	...	...	1647	1635	...	...	1747	1801	...
659	Termoli .... d.	...	...	...	|	...	1236	1254	1336	|	1452	...	1652	1636	...	...	1736	1750	...	...	1836	1852	...
	Roma Termini .... d.	0745	0805	0728	1000	...	|	|	|	1145	|	1305	|	|	...	1505	|	|	...	...	|	|	...
	Caserta .... d.	0855	0914	1008	1108	...	|	|	|	1253	|	1414	|	|	...	1614	|	|	...	...	|	|	...
	Benevento .... d.	0946	1002	1104	1152	...	|	|	|	1337	|	1503	|	|	...	1702	|	|	...	...	|	|	...
746	**Foggia** .... a.	1045	1105	1225	1254	...	1319	1349	1419	1445	1549	1606	1741	1719	...	1755	1819	1848	...	...	1919	1949	...
746	**Foggia** .... d.	1054	1114	1236	1303	...	1322	1352	1422	1454	1552	1615	1744	1722	...	1804	1822	1851	...	...	1922	1952	...
814	Barletta .... d.	1123	1143	1306	1333	...	1354	1421	1451	1522	1621	1644	1819	1751	...	1834	1851	1927	...	...	1951	2021	...
869	**Bari** Centrale .... a.	1205	1211	1354	1410	...	1431	1505	1527	1610	1705	1714	1858	1827	...	1905	1927	2016	...	...	2027	2105	...
869	**Bari** Centrale .... d.	...	1215	...	1418	...	1435	1509	...	...	1717	...	1902	1840	...	1909	1931	2020	...	...	2031	2109	...
923	Gioia del Colle .... d.	...	|	...	|	...	|	|	...	...	1751	...	|	1912	...	|	|	|	...	...	|	|	...
984	**Taranto** .... a.	...	|	...	|	...	|	|	...	...	1826	...	|	1946	...	|	|	|	...	...	|	|	...
910	Monopoli .... d.	...	|	...	|	...	|	1537	...	...	...	...	1927	...	...	|	|	2042	...	...	|	2137	...
924	Fasano .... d.	...	|	...	|	...	|	1549	...	...	...	...	1937	...	...	|	|	2054	...	...	|	2148	...
944	Ostuni .... d.	...	|	...	|	...	|	1604	...	...	...	...	1954	...	...	|	|	2113	...	...	|	2201	...
980	**Brindisi** .... d.	...	1312	...	1527	...	1538	1627	...	...	1936	...	2018	...	...	2007	2026	2139	...	...	2126	2225	...
1019	**Lecce** .... a.	...	1335	...	1550	...	1558	1651	...	...	1955	...	2040	...	...	2029	2050	2201	...	...	2150	2249	...

	FA 8319	*FR* 8813	*ITA* 9939		*IC* 705	*FA* 8323	*FR* 9547		*FR* 8815	*FR* 9809	*IC* 611	*IC* 613		*FR* 8819	*FR* 9811	*FA* 8823	*FR* 8825	*FR* 8829	*ICN* 789	*ICN* 765	*ICN* 755	*ICN* 757
			T		⑤				V										⑤ ❖	❖	❖	T ❖
Milano Centrale .... **600 620** d.	...	1405	1340	...	...	...	1510	...	...	1535	...	1505	...	1605	1730	1750	1850	2005	...	2115	2150	...
Milano Rogoredo △ .... **600 620** d.	...	|	|	...	...	...	1520	...	...	|	...	1516	...	|	|	|	|	|	...	|	|	...
Piacenza .... **620** d.	...	|	|	...	...	...	|	...	...	|	...	1608	...	|	|	1820	1920	|	...	2201	2235	...
Fidenza .... **620** d.	...	|	|	...	...	...	|	...	...	|	...	1627	...	|	|	|	|	|	...	|	|	...
Parma .... **620** d.	...	1454	◧	...	...	...	◧	...	...	◧	...	1642	...	1654	◧	1846	1954	2054	...	2233	2307	...
Reggio Emilia .... **620** d.	...	1508	|	...	...	...	|	...	...	|	...	1659	...	1708	|	1903	2008	2108	...	2251	2325	...
Reggio Emilia AV .... **600** d.	...	|	1428	...	...	...	1556	...	...	1621	...	|	...	|	1814	|	|	|	...	|	|	...
Modena .... **620** d.	...	1521	|	...	...	...	|	...	...	|	...	1716	...	1721	|	1919	2021	2121	...	2308	2341	...
Bologna Centrale .... **600 620** a.	...	1542	1454	...	...	...	1624	...	...	1650	...	1750	...	1742	1842	1942	2042	2142	...	2335	0006	...
Bologna Centrale .... d.	...	1545	1457	...	...	...	1627	...	1645	1655	1600	1758	...	1745	1845	1945	2045	2145	...	2339	0010	0027
Faenza .... d.	...	|	|	...	...	...	|	...	|	|	1628	1828	...	1808	|	2008	2108	|	...	0010	0040	|
Forlì .... d.	...	|	|	...	...	...	|	...	|	|	1638	1838	...	1817	1916	2017	2117	2216	...	0024	0058	|
Cesena .... d.	...	1624	|	...	...	...	|	...	|	|	1651	1851	...	1829	|	2029	2129	|	...	0038	0112	|
Rimini ● .... a.	...	1641	|	...	...	...	|	...	1741	1754	1713	1913	...	1849	1941	2049	2149	2241	...	0109	0140	0148
Rimini ● .... d.	...	1643	|	...	...	...	|	...	1743	1756	1715	1915	...	1851	1943	2051	2151	2243	...	0119	0155	0201
Riccione .... d.	...	1650	|	...	...	...	|	...	|	|	1724	1924	...	|	|	2059	|	|	...	|	|	|
Pesaro .... d.	...	1706	◧	...	...	...	◧	...	1802	|	1742	1942	...	1910	2002	2114	2210	2302	...	0158	|	|
Fano .... d.	...	|	|	...	...	...	|	...	|	|	1751	1951	...	|	|	|	|	|	...	|	|	|
Senigallia .... d.	...	|	|	...	...	...	|	...	|	|	1803	2003	...	|	|	|	|	|	...	|	|	|
Ancona .... a.	...	1734	|	...	...	...	|	...	1833	1847	1823	2023	...	1939	2031	2142	2242	2338	...	0242	0247	0252
Ancona .... d.	...	1737	|	...	...	...	|	...	1836	1850	1826	2026	...	1942	2034	2145	...	...	...	0246	0250	0256
Civitanova Marche-Montegranaro .... d.	...	|	|	...	...	...	|	...	|	|	1852	2052	...	|	|	|	...	...	...	|	|	|
S. Benedetto del Tronto .... d.	...	1816	|	...	...	...	|	...	|	|	1928	2129	...	2022	2115	2225	...	...	...	|	|	|
Pescara Centrale .... a.	...	1847	|	...	...	...	|	...	1944	1957	2008	2205	...	2054	2148	2305	...	...	...	0404	0411	0426
Pescara Centrale .... d.	...	1850	|	...	...	...	|	...	1947	2000	2010	...	...	2057	...	...	...	...	...	0406	0413	0428
Termoli .... d.	...	1939	|	...	...	...	|	...	2036	2048	2102	...	...	2145	...	...	...	...	...	|	0513	|
Roma Termini .... d.	1705	|	1743	...	1601	1805	1900	...	|	|	|	...	...	|	...	...	...	...	2358	|	|	
Caserta .... d.	1819	|	1857	...	1755	1917	|	...	|	|	|	...	...	|	...	...	...	...	0236	|	|	
Benevento .... d.	1900	|	1942	...	1905	2002	|	...	|	|	|	...	...	|	...	...	...	...	0324	|	|	
Foggia .... a.	2005	2021	2045	...	2037	2102	|	...	2119	2129	2151	...	...	2228	...	...	...	...	0449	0544	0606	0617
Foggia .... d.	2014	2024	2054	...	2049	2111	|	...	2122	2132	2156	...	...	2231	...	...	...	...	0504	0547	0609	0638
Barletta .... d.	2044	2053	2128	...	2120	2142	|	...	2151	|	2227	...	...	2300	...	...	...	...	0537	0618	0652	0721
Bari Centrale .... a.	2114	2130	2207	...	2202	2212	|	...	2222	2232	2308	...	...	2336	...	...	...	...	0627	0654	0740	0810
Bari Centrale .... d.	2118	2134	...	...	2224	2215	|	...	2226	...	...	...	...	...	...	...	...	...	0631	0705	0744	0814
Gioia del Colle .... d.	|	|	...	...	2301	|	|	...	|	...	...	...	...	...	...	...	...	...	|	0740	|	|
Taranto .... a.	|	|	...	...	2335	|	0007	...	|	...	...	...	...	...	...	...	...	...	|	0815	|	|
Monopoli .... d.	|	|	...	...	...	|	...	...	|	...	...	...	...	...	...	...	...	...	0656	|	0819	0852
Fasano .... d.	|	|	...	...	...	|	...	...	|	...	...	...	...	...	...	...	...	...	0707	|	0828	0904
Ostuni .... d.	|	|	...	...	...	|	...	...	|	...	...	...	...	...	...	...	...	...	0720	|	0841	0919
Brindisi .... d.	2243	2234	...	...	...	2315	...	...	2321	...	...	...	...	...	...	...	...	...	0742	0932	0907	0945
Lecce .... a.	2306	2256	...	...	...	2338	...	...	2345	...	...	...	...	...	...	...	...	...	0810	1002	0930	1010

A – (12) ✕ Zürich - Milano - Bologna and v.v. Ⓡ inclusive of supplement. Also available to passengers without reservation.
B – Also calls at Cassino (d. 0912) and Vairano-Caianello (d. 0935).
C – Also calls at Vairano-Caianello (d. 2029) and Cassino (d. 2049).
T – To / from Torino (*ITA* trains Table **600**; *ICN* trains Table **610**).
V – To / from Venezia (Table **600**).

g – Milano **Porta Garibaldi**.

◧ – Via Table **600**.
△ – Most trains call here to pick up only.
▽ – Most trains call here to set down only.
● – For 🚌 service to **San Marino** see next page.
❖ – 🛏 1, 2 cl., 🛏 2 cl. (4 berth). Running days, timings and numbers of *ICN* trains may vary - please check your reservation.
For confirmed timings please consult the *Trenitalia* journey planner at www.trenitalia.com.

615 LECCE - BARI - ROMA, ANCONA, RIMINI, BOLOGNA and MILANO

🍸 on *FA*, *FB*, *FR* and *ITA* trains

High-speed and long-distance trains. For local trains Bologna - Milano see Table **620**. For other local trains see page 303.

km		*FA* 8802	*FR* 9802	*FA* 8804	*FA* 8806	*FR* 8300	*ITA* 9972	*IC* 604	*FR* 8810	*FA* 8348	*FR* 9806	*IC* 606	*FR* 8814	*FR* 9514	*ITA* 9928	*FA* 8302	*FR* 8816	*IC* 608	*FA* 8306	*FR* 8818	*FR* 8820	*IC* 610	
						①–⑥				①–⑥													
														T	T		V						
0	**Lecce** d.	...	...	...	...	...	...	...	...	...	...	...	0555	...	...	0605	0700	0623	0710	0806	...	0820	...
39	**Brindisi** d.	...	...	...	...	...	...	...	...	...	...	...	0617	...	...	0628	0723	0647	0734	0829	...	0842	...
75	Ostuni d.	...	...	...	...	...	...	...	...	...	...	...	|	...	...	|	|	0710	|	|	...	0904	...
95	Fasano d.	...	...	...	...	...	...	...	...	...	...	...	|	...	...	|	|	0723	|	|	...	0917	...
109	Monopoli d.	...	...	...	...	...	...	...	...	...	...	...	|	...	...	|	|	0733	|	|	...	0928	...
	Taranto d.	...	...	...	...	...	...	...	...	...	...	...	|	0527	...	|	|	|	|	|	0916	...	...
	Gioia del Colle d.	...	...	...	...	...	...	...	...	...	...	...	|	|	...	|	|	|	|	|	0948	...	...
150	**Bari** Centrale a.	...	...	...	...	...	...	...	...	...	...	...	0726	|	...	0732	0826	0802	0834	0926	1020	0951	...
150	**Bari** Centrale d.	...	...	...	...	...	...	...	0530	0610	0635	0555	0730	|	0650	0746	0830	0806	0846	0930	1030	0955	...
205	Barletta d.	...	...	...	...	...	...	...	0606	0644	|	0634	0806	|	0737	0815	0906	0851	0915	1006	1106	1038	...
273	**Foggia** a.	...	...	...	...	...	...	...	0633	0711	0736	0707	0833	|	0806	0844	0933	0918	0944	1033	1133	1107	...
273	**Foggia** d.	...	...	...	...	0455	...	...	0636	0720	0739	0710	0836	|	0815	0853	0936	0921	0953	1036	1136	1110	...
374	Benevento d.	...	...	...	...	0554	...	...	|	0818	|	|	|	|	0922	1000	|	|	1107	|	|	|	...
437	Caserta d.	...	...	...	...	0632	0645	...	|	0856	|	|	|	|	1006	1048	|	|	1147	|	|	|	...
653	**Roma** Termini a.	...	...	...	...	0745	0750	...	|	1003	|	|	|	1055	1115	1155	|	|	1255	|	|	|	...
	Termoli d.	...	...	...	...	...	|	...	0720	...	0824	0805	0920	|	|	...	1020	1009	...	1120	1220	1205	...
	Pescara Centrale a.	...	...	...	...	...	|	...	0807	...	0909	0900	1007	|	|	...	1107	1100	...	1207	1307	1300	...
	Pescara Centrale d.	...	0500	...	0600	...	|	0702	0810	...	0912	0902	1010	|	|	...	1110	1102	...	1210	1310	1302	...
	S. Benedetto del Tronto d.	...	0532	...	0636	...	|	0736	0841	...	|	0936	|	|	|	...	|	1148	...	1241	1341	1348	...
	Civitanova d.	...	|	...	|	...	|	0809	|	...	|	1009	1057	|	|	...	|	1213	...	|	|	1413	...
	Ancona a.	...	0612	...	0717	...	|	0835	0922	...	1025	1035	1122	|	|	...	1222	1235	...	1322	1422	1435	...
	Ancona d.	0520	0615	0620	0720	...	◧	0838	0925	...	1028	1038	1125	◧	◧	...	1225	1238	...	1325	1425	1438	...
	Senigallia d.	|	|	|	|	...	|	0856	|	...	|	1056	|	|	|	...	|	1256	...	|	|	1456	...
	Fano d.	|	|	|	|	...	|	0909	|	...	|	1109	|	|	|	...	|	1309	...	|	|	1509	...
	Pesaro d.	0547	0641	0647	0749	...	|	0919	0952	...	|	1119	1152	|	|	...	1252	1317	...	1352	1452	1517	...
	Riccione d.	|	|	|	0804	...	|	0938	1006	...	|	1138	|	|	|	...	|	1338	...	|	|	1538	...
	Rimini ● a.	0608	0701	0708	0810	...	|	0945	1015	...	1118	1145	1213	|	|	...	1313	1345	...	1413	1513	1545	...
	Rimini ● d.	0610	0703	0710	0812	...	|	0947	1017	...	1120	1147	1215	|	|	...	1315	1347	...	1415	1515	1547	...
	Cesena d.	0627	|	0727	0828	...	|	1009	|	...	|	1207	|	|	|	...	|	1407	...	|	1532	1607	...
	Forlì d.	0640	0733	0739	0840	...	|	1021	1042	...	|	1219	|	|	|	...	|	1419	...	1442	|	1619	...
	Faenza d.	0649	|	0749	0849	...	|	1031	|	...	|	1229	|	|	|	...	|	1429	...	|	|	1629	...
	Bologna Centrale a.	0715	0810	0815	0915	...	1008	1101	1115	...	1215	1300	1315	1333	1403	...	1415	1500	...	1515	1615	1700	...
	Bologna Centrale 600 620 d.	0718	0813	0818	0918	...	1011	1105	1118	...	1218	...	1318	1336	1406	...	...	...	...	1518	1618	...	...
	Modena 620 d.	0737	|	0837	0937	...	|	1133	1137	...	|	...	1337	|	|	...	...	...	...	1537	1637	...	...
	Reggio Emilia AV 600 d.	|	0844	|	|	...	|	|	|	...	1242	...	|	1400	1435	...	...	...	...	|	|	...	...
	Reggio Emilia 620 d.	0752	|	0853	0953	...	|	1204	1153	...	|	...	1353	|	|	...	...	...	...	1553	1653	...	...
	Parma 620 d.	0807	|	0909	1009	...	◧	1220	1209	...	◧	...	1409	◧	◧	...	...	...	...	1609	1709	...	...
	Fidenza 620 d.	|	|	|	|	...	|	1232	|	...	|	...	|	|	|	...	...	...	...	|	|	...	...
	Piacenza 620 d.	0833	|	|	|	...	|	1252	|	...	|	...	|	|	|	...	...	...	...	|	|	...	...
	Milano Rogoredo ▽ 600 620 a.	0904	|	|	|	...	|	|	|	...	|	...	|	1438	|	...	...	...	...	|	|	...	...
	Milano Centrale 600 620 a.	0915	0935	0954	1054	...	1115	1340	1254	...	1325	...	1505	1450	1520	...	...	...	...	1654	1754	...	...

	FA 8312	*FA* 8312	*FR* 8824	*EC* 326	*IC* 1546	*IC* 612	*FA* 8314	*ITA* 9952	*FR* 8828	*IC* 614	*FR* 9810	*FR* 9560	*IC* 704	*FR* 8830	*IC* 710	*ITA* 8140	*FA* 8326	*ICN* 752	*ICN* 758	*ICN* 754	*ICN* 754	*ICN* 788
	①	⑥			⑦										⑦					①–⑥	⑦	⑦
				A				T	V				C					❖	❖	T ❖	T ❖	❖
Lecce d.	...	0941	1006	...	0935	0835	1115	...	1257	1154	...	1310	...	...	...	...	1715	1950	1831	2025	2025	2215
Brindisi d.	...	1004	1029	...	0956	0900	1138	...	1320	1214	...	1331	...	...	...	...	1738	2019	1901	2053	2053	2240
Ostuni d.	...	|	|	...	1018	|	|	...	|	1235	...	|	...	...	...	...	|	2044	|	2116	2116	2302
Fasano d.	...	|	|	...	1030	|	|	...	|	1247	...	|	...	...	...	...	|	2059	|	2131	2131	2315
Monopoli d.	...	|	|	...	1040	|	|	...	|	1257	...	|	...	...	...	...	|	2109	|	2140	2140	2326
Taranto d.	...	|	|	...	|	1032	|	...	|	|	...	|	...	...	1540	...	|	|	2001	|	|	|
Gioia del Colle d.	...	|	|	...	|	1109	|	...	|	|	...	|	...	...	1612	...	|	|	2034	|	|	|
Bari Centrale a.	1101	1101	1126	...	1105	1143	1242	...	1426	1344	...	1444	...	...	1649	...	1842	2137	2115	2206	2206	2355
Bari Centrale d.	1105	1105	1130	...	1108	1155	1246	1300	1430	1355	...	1455	1605	1630	1700	1750	1846	2145	2125	2210	2210	0000
Barletta d.	1134	1134	1206	...	1151	1238	1315	1337	1506	1438	...	1527	1648	1706	1734	1837	1915	2238	2213	2246	2256	0048
Foggia a.	1206	1206	1233	...	1221	1307	1344	1406	1533	1507	...	1554	1728	1733	1809	1906	1944	2315	2249	2321	2328	0140
Foggia d.	1215	1215	1236	...	1223	1310	1353	1415	1536	1510	...	1603	1741	1736	1820	1915	1953	2318	2303	2325	2331	0200
Benevento d.	1316	1316	|	...	|	|	1500	1522	|	|	...	1702	1855	|	1953	2028	2100	|	|	|	|	0321
Caserta d.	1404	1404	|	...	|	|	1545	1609	|	|	...	1746	1958	|	2049	2109	2145	|	|	|	|	0407
Roma Termini a.	1515	1515	|	...	|	|	1655	1715	|	|	...	1855	2220	|	2300	2215	2255	|	|	|	|	0610
Termoli d.	...	...	1320	...	1332	1405	...	|	1620	1605	...	|	...	1820	...	...	...	0015	|	|	0021	...
Pescara Centrale a.	...	...	1407	...	1430	1500	...	|	1707	1700	...	|	...	1907	...	...	...	0114	0105	0122	0122	...
Pescara Centrale d.	...	...	1410	...	1432	1502	...	|	1710	1702	...	|	...	1910	...	...	...	0117	0108	0126	0126	...
S. Benedetto del Tronto d.	...	...	1441	...	1512	1536	...	|	|	1748	...	|	...	|	...	...	...	0200	|	|	|	...
Civitanova d.	...	...	|	...	1539	1606	...	|	|	1813	...	|	...	|	...	...	...	|	|	|	|	...
Ancona a.	...	...	1522	...	1610	1635	...	|	1822	1835	...	|	...	2022	...	...	...	0303	0256	0309	0309	...
Ancona d.	...	...	1525	...	1614	1638	...	◧	1825	1838	1910	◧	...	2025	...	...	...	0312	0306	0317	0317	...
Senigallia d.	...	...	|	...	1630	1656	...	|	|	1856	|	|	...	|	...	...	...	|	|	|	|	...
Fano d.	...	...	|	...	1643	1709	...	|	|	1909	|	|	...	|	...	...	...	|	|	|	|	...
Pesaro d.	...	...	1552	...	1655	1717	...	|	1852	1917	1946	|	...	2052	...	...	...	|	|	0351	|	...
Riccione d.	...	...	|	...	1718	1738	...	|	|	1938	2004	|	...	2104	...	...	...	|	|	|	|	...
Rimini ● a.	...	...	1613	...	1727	1745	...	|	1913	1945	2012	|	...	2113	...	...	...	0407	0357	0417	0417	...
Rimini ● d.	...	...	1615	...	1729	1747	...	|	1915	1947	2014	|	...	2115	...	...	...	0409	0359	0419	0419	...
Cesena d.	...	...	|	...	1747	1807	...	|	|	2007	|	|	...	|	...	...	...	|	|	0440	|	...
Forlì d.	...	...	1642	...	1759	1819	...	|	|	2019	|	|	...	|	...	...	...	|	|	0453	|	...
Faenza d.	...	...	|	...	1810	1829	...	|	|	2029	|	|	...	|	...	...	...	|	|	0503	|	...
Bologna Centrale a.	...	...	1715	...	1840	1901	...	2003	2015	2100	2115	2133	...	2215	...	...	...	0502	0452	0530	0530	...
Bologna Centrale 600 620 d.	...	...	1718	1726	1845	1905	...	2006	...	2104	2118	2136	...	2218	...	...	...	0506	0456	...	...	...
Modena 620 d.	...	...	1737	1749	1913	1936	...	|	...	2135	|	|	...	2237	...	...	...	0526	|	...	...	...
Reggio Emilia AV 600 d.	...	...	|	|	|	|	...	2030	...	|	2142	2200	...	|	...	...	...	|	|	...	...	...
Reggio Emilia 620 d.	...	...	1753	1805	1926	1956	...	|	...	2151	|	|	...	2253	...	...	...	0539	|	...	...	...
Parma 620 d.	...	...	1809	1825	1941	2013	...	◧	...	2210	◧	◧	...	2309	...	...	...	0554	|	...	...	...
Fidenza 620 d.	...	...	|	|	1954	2025	...	|	...	2224	|	|	...	|	...	...	...	|	|	...	...	...
Piacenza 620 d.	...	...	|	1859	2019	2046	...	|	...	2243	|	|	...	|	...	...	...	0628	|	...	...	...
Milano Rogoredo ▽ 600 620 a.	...	...	|	1935	2104	2126	...	|	...	2328	|	2238	...	|	...	...	...	|	|	...	...	...
Milano Centrale 600 620 a.	...	...	1855	...	2115	2140	...	2120	...	2340	2225	2250	...	2355	...	...	...	0712	0705	...	...	...

🚌 service **RIMINI - SAN MARINO**. *27 km*, journey 50 – 55 minutes. Operator: BonelliBus s.a.s. ✆ +39 0541 662 069. www.bonellibus.it
From Rimini (FS railway station) at 0810 ⚒, 1015 ⚒, 1700 ⚒, 1915 ⚒. **From San Marino** (Piazzale Calcigni) at 0810 ⚒, 1015 ⚒, 1700 ⚒, 1915 ⚒.

FOR FOOTNOTES SEE PREVIOUS PAGE.

PIACENZA - BOLOGNA - ANCONA - PESCARA and BARI - TARANTO - LECCE 615

Local trains. For high-speed and long-distance trains see previous two pages.

km			⚒				Ⓒ	Ⓐ			A											⚒
0	**Piacenza** d.	...	...	...	0530	0649	0749	0849	0849	0949	1049	1149	...	1249	1345	1449	1549	1649	1749	1849	1909	1949	2055	2148
35	Fidenza d.	...	...	...	0558	0714	0814	0914	0914	1014	1114	1214	...	1314	1412	1514	1614	1714	1814	1914	1937	2014	2118	2213
57	Parma d.	...	...	...	0615	0727	0827	0927	0927	1027	1127	1227	...	1327	1427	1527	1627	1727	1827	1927	2000	2027	2133	2226
85	Reggio Emilia d.	...	...	...	0642	0744	0844	0944	0944	1044	1144	1244	...	1344	1444	1544	1644	1744	1844	1944	2018	2044	2149	2243
110	Modena d.	...	...	...	0700	0758	0858	0958	0958	1058	1158	1258	...	1358	1458	1558	1658	1801	1858	1958	2035	2058	2204	2258
147	**Bologna** Centrale a.	...	...	...	0729	0825	0925	1025	1025	1125	1225	1325	...	1425	1525	1625	1725	1825	1925	2025	2108	2125	2233	2328
147	**Bologna** Centrale d.	0500	0555	0634	0734	0834	0934	1034	1034	1134	1234	1334	...	1434	1534	1634	1734	1834	1934	2034	2112	2134	...	...
182	Imola d.	0527	0622	0655	0802	0855	0955	1058	1058	1155	1255	1355	...	1455	1555	1655	1756	1855	1955	2055	2131	2155	...	...
189	Castelbolognese-Riolo Terme d.	0533	0628	0702	0808	0902	1002	1104	1104	1202	1302	1402	...	1502	1602	1702	1802	1902	2002	2102	2138	2202	...	...
195	Faenza d.	0539	0635	0717	0817	0917	1017	1117	1115	1217	1317	1417	...	1517	1617	1717	1817	1917	2017	2117	|	2217	...	...
210	Forlì d.	0548	0644	0728	0828	0928	1033	1128	1129	1228	1328	1428	...	1528	1628	1734	1828	1928	2029	2128	|	2228	...	...
228	Cesena d.	0603	0659	0742	0842	0942	1059	1142	1156	1244	1342	1442	...	1542	1642	1748	1844	1942	2046	2142	|	2245	...	...
257	**Rimini** a.	0630	0725	0801	0901	1001	1120	1201	1219	1309	1403	1501	...	1601	1701	1805	1901	2001	2112	2201	2318	2322	...	...
257	**Rimini** d.	...	...	0803	0903	1003	...	1203	1221	1319	1405	1503	...	1603	1703	1807	1903	2003	...	2203	...	...	...	...
266	Riccione d.	...	...	0812	0912	1012	...	1212	1230	1331	1414	1511	...	1612	1713	1815	1910	2012	...	2212	...	...	...	...
275	Cattolica-Gabicce d.	...	...	0820	0920	1020	...	1220	1238	1341	1422	1519	...	1620	1722	1823	1919	2020	...	2220	...	...	...	...
290	Pesaro d.	...	...	0830	0930	1030	...	1230	1248	1352	1432	1530	...	1630	1735	1834	1931	2030	...	2230	...	...	...	...
302	Fano d.	...	...	0838	0938	1038	...	1238	1258	1402	1439	1539	...	1638	...	1842	1939	2038	...	2238	...	...	...	...
324	Senigallia d.	...	...	0853	0954	1053	...	1253	1319	1425	1454	1554	...	1653	...	1857	1952	2053	...	2252	...	...	...	...
341	Falconara Marittima d.	...	...	0906	1011	1104	...	1304	1342	1439	1504	1607	...	1704	...	1911	2006	2104	...	2306	...	...	...	...
349	**Ancona** a.	...	...	0920	1022	1116	...	1316	1355	1450	1516	1620	...	1716	...	1922	2020	2116	...	2318	...	...	...	...

																B	C			B	C		
Ancona d.	...	...	0445	...	0545	0645	0745	0845	...	1045	1145	...	1245	...	1445	...	...	...	1645	...	...	...	1845
Falconara Marittima d.	...	...	0454	...	0555	0655	0756	0854	...	1054	1154	...	1256	...	1455	...	...	...	1654	...	...	...	1855
Senigallia d.	...	...	0505	...	0605	0707	0808	0904	...	1104	1204	...	1305	...	1505	...	...	...	1704	...	...	...	1905
Fano d.	...	...	0519	...	0620	0720	0822	0919	...	1119	1219	...	1319	...	1518	...	...	...	1719	...	...	...	1918
Pesaro d.	...	...	0527	...	0628	0728	0830	0927	...	1127	1227	...	1327	...	1526	...	1613	...	1727	...	1737	1823	1926
Cattolica-Gabicce d.	...	...	0538	...	0639	0739	0841	0938	...	1138	1238	...	1338	...	1536	...	1624	...	1738	...	1748	1834	1936
Riccione d.	...	...	0546	...	0645	0748	0847	0946	...	1146	1246	...	1347	...	1544	...	1633	...	1746	...	1756	1842	1944
Rimini a.	...	...	0556	...	0652	0759	0856	0956	...	1156	1256	...	1356	...	1556	...	1644	...	1756	...	1805	1853	1956
Rimini d.	...	...	0558	...	0654	0801	0858	0958	1041	1158	1258	...	1358	1441	1558	1640	1646	...	1758	...	1807	1854	1958
Cesena d.	...	...	0618	...	0709	0819	0919	1019	1110	1219	1319	...	1419	1510	1619	1708	1711	...	1819	...	1830	1919	2019
Forlì d.	...	...	0631	...	0720	0831	0931	1033	1127	1231	1331	...	1431	1528	1631	1726	1726	...	1831	...	1853	1933	2031
Faenza d.	...	...	0641	...	0730	0841	0941	1043	1140	1241	1341	...	1441	1540	1641	1735	1735	...	1841	...	1903	1943	2041
Castelbolognese-Riolo Terme d.	...	...	0647	...	0743	0847	0947	1049	1147	1247	1347	...	1447	1548	1647	1748	1748	...	1847	...	1909	1949	2047
Imola d.	...	...	0700	...	0800	0900	1000	1100	1200	1300	1400	...	1500	1600	1700	1756	1756	...	1900	...	1916	2000	2100
Bologna Centrale a.	...	...	0726	...	0826	0926	1026	1126	1226	1326	1426	...	1526	1626	1726	1826	1826	...	1926	...	1948	2026	2126
Bologna Centrale d.	0500	0633	0733	0750	0833	0933	1033	1133	1233	1333	1433	...	1533	1633	1733	1833	1833	1850	1933	1950	1954	2033	2133
Modena d.	0530	0702	0802	0824	0902	1002	1102	1202	1302	1402	1502	...	1602	1702	1802	1902	1902	1924	2002	2024	2024	2102	2202
Reggio Emilia d.	0545	0719	0817	0842	0917	1017	1117	1217	1317	1417	1517	...	1617	1717	1817	1917	1917	1942	2017	2042	2042	2117	2217
Parma d.	0600	0734	0833	0903	0933	1033	1133	1233	1333	1433	1533	...	1633	1733	1833	1933	1933	2003	2033	2103	2103	2133	2233
Fidenza d.	0612	0746	0845	0926	0947	1045	1145	1245	1345	1445	1545	...	1645	1745	1845	1945	1945	2017	2045	2126	2126	2145	2245
Piacenza a.	0635	0807	0910	0948	1013	1113	1210	1310	1410	1510	1610	...	1710	1810	1912	2010	2010	2051	2110	2148	2148	2210	2310

km		⚒	⚒		⚒	†							⑥		Ⓑ			Ⓐ		⚒				
0	**Ancona** d.	0515	0625	...	0733	0810	...	1145	...	1345	...	...	1440	...	1445	...	1645	1745	...	1841	1945	...		...
43	Civitanova ◧ d.	0549	0700	...	0808	0845	...	1221	...	1421	...	...	1516	...	1521	...	1722	1821	...	1922	2020	...		...
85	S. Benedetto del Tronto d.	0621	0732	...	0840	0919	...	1253	...	1454	...	...	1554	...	1554	...	1756	1854	...	1954	2053	...		...
146	**Pescara** Centrale a.	0720	0824	...	0917	1010	...	1350	...	1540	...	...	1656	...	1656	...	1856	1941	...	2050	2145	...		...

	⚒			⚒	†		⚒				⚒		†	⚒			Ⓐ		†	⚒			
Pescara Centrale d.	0505	0550	...	0653	0915	...	1015	...	1158	...	1415	...	1520	1602	...	1720	1817	...	1913	1915	...		...
S. Benedetto del Tronto d.	0556	0649	...	0752	1007	...	1102	...	1256	...	1506	...	1612	1700	...	1813	1908	...	2007	2007	...		...
Civitanova ◧ d.	0626	0723	...	0825	1039	...	1135	...	1330	...	1539	...	1644	1732	...	1848	1938	...	2039	2039	...		...
Ancona a.	0705	0802	...	0907	1115	...	1217	...	1410	...	1615	...	1730	1809	...	1930	2010	...	2120	2120	...		...

km		⚒	⚒	⚒		†	⚒	⚒		⚒	⚒			⚒	†	⚒		⚒		⚒			Ⓐ	⑥
0	**Bari** d.	0530	0623	0720	...	0815	0950	1050	...	1305	1335	1437	...	1524	1600	1625	...	1740	1820	1945	...	2050	2239	2350
54	Gioia del Colle d.	0612	0706	0802	...	0858	1033	1132	...	1349	1418	1520	...	1606	1641	1707	...	1822	1900	2027	...	2133	2321	0033
115	**Taranto** a.	0652	0745	0842	...	0937	1112	1212	...	1422	1457	1559	...	1646	1722	1747	...	1902	1940	2107	...	2212	2359	0112

	⚒	⚒			⚒	⚒	⚒		†	⚒	⚒		⚒	⚒	⚒			⚒	†		⚒	⚒	⚒
Taranto d.	0440	0540	0620	...	0705	0756	0955	...	1040	1135	1300	...	1345	1432	1535	...	1650	1805	1910	...	1930	2015	2100
Gioia del Colle d.	0514	0619	0659	...	0744	0836	1027	...	1119	1213	1340	...	1425	1512	1615	...	1730	1838	1950	...	2005	2055	2140
Bari a.	0554	0702	0742	...	0827	0918	1103	...	1202	1254	1420	...	1507	1554	1657	...	1810	1922	2032	...	2047	2137	2222

km		⚒	⚒	⚒	⚒	⚒	⚒	⚒	⚒	
0	**Taranto** d.	0535	0608	0845	1244	1402	1523	1652	1849	...
34	Francavilla Fontana d.	0602	0637	0913	1312	1429	1551	1722	1915	...
70	**Brindisi** a.	0635	0719	0954	1350	1506	1634	1759	2001	...

	⚒	⚒	⚒	⚒	⚒	⚒	⚒	⚒	
Brindisi d.	0645	0754	1100	1401	1519	1644	1809	2018	...
Francavilla Fontana d.	0722	0833	1138	1440	1554	1719	1846	2051	...
Taranto a.	0750	0907	1206	1513	1625	1755	1922	2123	...

km		Ⓐ	Ⓒ	Ⓐ		Ⓐ	⑥	Ⓐ		⑥	Ⓐ	†		Ⓐ	Ⓒ	Ⓐ		Ⓒ	Ⓒ	Ⓐ		Ⓐ	Ⓐ	⑥
0	**Bari** Centrale d.	0502	0520	0602	...	0632	0708	0732	...	0801	0802	0802	...	0902	0902	1002	...	1035	1220	1232	...	1302	1332	1335
41	Monopoli d.	0537	0555	0629	...	0659	0745	0802	...	0838	0830	0838	...	0930	0939	1029	...	1112	1257	1259	...	1329	1359	1412
55	Fasano d.	0546	0604	0637	...	0707	0754	0811	...	0848	0838	0847	...	0938	0948	1037	...	1121	1306	1307	...	1337	1407	1421
75	Ostuni d.	0559	0618	0651	...	0718	0808	0825	...	0903	0852	0901	...	0952	1001	1048	...	1136	1321	1318	...	1351	1418	1436
111	**Brindisi** d.	0622	0642	0714	...	0744	0831	0845	...	0927	0916	0924	...	1016	1026	1113	...	1158	1343	1344	...	1413	1444	1458
150	**Lecce** a.	0655	0712	0743	...	0813	0901	0915	...	0955	0945	0956	...	1045	1058	1143	...	1228	1413	1413	...	1443	1513	1528

	Ⓐ	Ⓒ	Ⓐ		⑥	Ⓐ	Ⓐ		Ⓒ	Ⓐ	⑥		Ⓐ	Ⓒ	Ⓐ		Ⓒ	Ⓐ	Ⓒ		Ⓐ		
Bari Centrale d.	1402	1440	1502	...	1535	1602	1632	...	1635	1702	1735	...	1802	1818	1832	...	1950	2040	2040	...	2102	...	2302
Monopoli d.	1429	1517	1529	...	1612	1629	1659	...	1712	1729	1820	...	1829	1854	1859	...	2026	2111	2117	...	2129	...	2339
Fasano d.	1437	1526	1537	...	1621	1637	1707	...	1721	1737	1829	...	1837	1902	1907	...	2034	2120	2125	...	2137	...	2347
Ostuni d.	1451	1541	1551	...	1636	1651	1720	...	1736	1748	1843	...	1851	1917	1918	...	2049	2133	2139	...	2151	...	0001
Brindisi d.	1515	1603	1615	...	1658	1715	1744	...	1758	1812	1905	...	1915	1942	1944	...	2113	2157	2203	...	2215	...	0025
Lecce a.	1543	1633	1645	...	1728	1743	1813	...	1828	1845	1938	...	1943	2013	2013	...	2144	2225	2234	...	2243	...	0055

		Ⓐ	Ⓒ		Ⓐ	Ⓐ	Ⓒ		Ⓐ		⑥		Ⓐ	Ⓒ	Ⓐ		Ⓐ	Ⓒ	Ⓐ		⑥		Ⓐ
Lecce d.	0447	0611	0628	...	0640	0725	0725	...	0753	...	0847	...	1017	1017	1120	...	1217	1217	1317	...	1317	...	1347
Brindisi d.	0515	0639	0658	...	0706	0754	0756	...	0820	...	0918	...	1045	1048	1147	...	1246	1248	1345	...	1348	...	1416
Ostuni d.	0539	0659	0720	...	0728	0816	0818	...	0840	...	0941	...	1107	1111	1209	...	1307	1311	1407	...	1411	...	1439
Fasano d.	0554	0713	0734	...	0740	0828	0832	...	0900	...	0955	...	1121	1125	1223	...	1321	1325	1421	...	1425	...	1451
Monopoli d.	0602	0722	0743	...	0749	0838	0840	...	0910	...	1003	...	1130	1133	1231	...	1330	1333	1430	...	1433	...	1500
Bari Centrale a.	0638	0759	0821	...	0822	0908	0919	...	0944	...	1041	...	1158	1211	1300	...	1358	1411	1458	...	1511	...	1528

	Ⓐ	Ⓒ	Ⓐ		Ⓒ				Ⓒ	Ⓐ	Ⓐ		Ⓒ		Ⓒ		Ⓐ	⚒	Ⓒ		Ⓐ		⚒
Lecce d.	1417	1417	1517	...	1517	...	1547	...	1605	1617	1720	...	1725	...	1800	...	1817	1905	2000	...	2017	...	2117
Brindisi d.	1445	1448	1545	...	1548	...	1615	...	1635	1645	1747	...	1752	...	1832	...	1845	1933	2032	...	2045	...	2146
Ostuni d.	1507	1511	1607	...	1611	...	1637	...	1658	1707	1809	...	1815	...	1855	...	1907	1956	2055	...	2107	...	2207
Fasano d.	1521	1525	1621	...	1625	...	1651	...	1712	1721	1823	...	1831	...	1909	...	1921	2010	2109	...	2121	...	2218
Monopoli d.	1530	1533	1630	...	1633	...	1700	...	1720	1730	1831	...	1839	...	1917	...	1930	2019	2117	...	2130	...	2227
Bari Centrale a.	1558	1611	1658	...	1711	...	1728	...	1758	1758	1900	...	1918	...	1954	...	1958	2058	2154	...	2158	...	2311

A – By connecting trains on † (change at Bologna).
B – Not May 27, 28, June 2–4, 10.
C – Runs May 27, 28, June 2–4, 10.

◧ – Full name is Civitanova Marche-Montegranaro.

616 ROVIGO - CHIOGGIA

Sistemi Territoriali

km																							
		⚒	†		†	⚒🚌	⚒		Ⓑ	⑥	†		⚒	⚒	†		⚒	Ⓑ	Ⓐ🚌			Ⓐ🚌	†
0	**Rovigo** d.	0609	...	...	0709	0709	0809	...	0909	...	1109	...	1309	1409	1509	...	1609	1715	1809	...	1915	2009	2055
25	Adria d.	0636	0636	...	0736	0757	0836	...	0936	1136	1136	...	1336	1436	1536	...	1636	1742	1857	...	1942	2057	2121
57	**Chioggia** a.	0719	0719	...	0819	0850	0919	...	1019	1219	1219	...	1419	1519	1619	...	1719	1825	1950	...	2025	2150	...

	⚒🚌	⚒🚌	†	⚒		⚒🚌	⑥	Ⓑ	†	⚒	†	⚒	⑥	Ⓐ	†	Ⓐ🚌		Ⓐ	Ⓐ🚌	†	Ⓑ	⑥
Chioggia d.	...	0510	...	0629	0729	0829	0929	0929	1029	1229	1329	1429	1529	1529	...	...	1735	1835	1929	1935	2035	2035
Adria d.	0551	0604	0608	0708	0808	0921	1007	1008	1107	1308	1408	1508	1607	1608	1608	1722	1814	1914	2022	2014	2113	2114
Rovigo a.	0639	0639	0639	0739	0839	...	...	1039	...	1339	1439	1539	...	1639	1639	1810	1845	1945	2110	2045	...	2145

619 SIENA - GROSSETO and CHIUSI

2nd class

km																							
		⚒	⚒	†	⚒	†🚌	⚒	†	⚒	⚒	†	⚒		⚒	†	⚒	†	⚒	†🚌	⚒	†	⚒	
0	**Siena** d.	0545	0627	0725	0735	0755	0810	0943	1010	1209	1243	1355	...	1542	1544	1705	1738	1745	1846	1850	1943	1943	...
29	Buonconvento a.	0622	0655	0800	0805	0835	0844	1011	1041	1237	1311	1430	...	1609	1612	1740	1814	1826	1919	1933	2012	2023	...
102	**Grosseto** a.	*0757**	...	...	...	0945	*1008**	*1131**	...	*1357**	*1431**	...	...	*1730**	*1732**	...	*1934**	*1946**	2024	...	*2134**	*2143**	...

	†	⚒	⚒🚌	⚒	⚒		🚌	⚒	⚒	†	⚒	†	⚒	⚒	†	†🚌	⚒		⚒	🚌	🚌	
Grosseto d.	*0439**	...	0601	...	...	*0700**	0746	...	...	...	...	*1315**	*1321**	...	...	1640	...	*1746**	...	1949	1954	...
Buonconvento d.	0559	0554	|	0703	0718	0818	|	0900	1102	1107	1250	1435	1441	1625	1650	|	1755	1906	1953	|	|	2100
Siena a.	0629	0623	0735	0732	0757	0846	0856	0935	1140	1137	1325	1508	1513	1700	1725	1815	1832	1940	2030	2100	2104	2120

km																							
		⚒	†	†	⚒		†	⚒	⚒	⚒		†	⚒		⚒		⚒	†	⚒	⚒		†	⚒
0	**Siena** d.	0554	0600	0802	0813	...	1002	1215	1325	1352	...	1402	1443	1602	1648	...	1743	1802	1816	1926	...	2002	2023
89	**Chiusi-Chianciano Terme** a.	0717	0724	0927	0936	...	1127	1336	1448	1525	...	1523	1612	1727	1813	...	1904	1927	1944	2055	...	2127	2147

	⚒	†	⚒	⚒		†	⚒	†	⚒		†	⚒	⚒	†		⚒	†	⚒	⚒		†	⚒
Chiusi-Chianciano Terme d.	0556	0629	0645	0710	...	0830	0900	1030	1046	...	1230	1348	1511	1632	...	1713	1830	1835	1955	...	2030	2153
Siena a.	0728	0748	0756	0835	...	0950	1027	1150	1201	...	1352	1522	1636	1752	...	1841	1950	2006	2125	...	2150	2310

* – By 🚌.

620 VENEZIA and MILANO - BOLOGNA - FIRENZE - ROMA

Long-distance trains. For high-speed trains see Table **600**. For other long-distance trains Milano - Bologna see Table **615**. For other local trains see next page.

km		*IC*	*FR*			*IC*		*IC*		*IC*			*IC*		*IC*			*ICN*	*FR*		*IC*	*ICN*	*ICN*
		581	**9503**	2	2	**583**	2	**1589**		**584**	2	2	**594**	2	**597**		2	**795**	**9329**	2	**599**	**770**	**797**
		①–⑥	①–⑥					⑥											Ⓑ				
								A										**B** ❖	**C**		**D**	**E** ❖	**F** ❖
	Trieste Centrale **601** d.	...	...	...	...	...	...	...	...	0721	...	...	1327	...	...	...	...	...	...	...	...	1950	...
0	**Venezia** Santa Lucia d.	...	...	...	...	...	...	...	...	|	...	...	|	...	...	...	...	...	...	...	...	2305	...
9	**Venezia** Mestre d.	...	...	...	...	...	...	...	...	0934	...	...	1534	...	...	...	...	...	...	...	...	2317	...
37	Padova d.	...	...	...	...	...	...	...	...	0950	...	...	1550	...	...	...	...	...	...	...	...	2338	...
81	Rovigo d.	...	...	...	...	...	...	...	...	1023	...	...	1630	...	...	...	...	...	...	...	...	0013	...
113	Ferrara d.	...	...	...	...	...	...	...	...	1042	...	...	1650	...	...	...	...	...	...	...	...	0032	...
	Milano Centrale d.	...	...	...	...	0650	...	0655	...	|	...	...	|	...	1348	...	...	1535g	1848g	...	1740	|	2213g
	Milano Rogoredo △ d.	...	...	...	...	0700	...	0705	...	|	...	...	|	...	1357	...	...	|	1904	...	1756	|	|
	Piacenza d.	...	...	...	...	0738	...	0744	...	|	...	...	|	...	1437	...	...	1630	|	...	1836	|	2319
	Fidenza d.	...	...	...	...	0758	...	0805	...	|	...	...	|	...	1455	...	...	|	|	...	1852	|	|
	Parma d.	...	...	...	...	0811	...	0819	...	|	...	...	|	...	1508	...	...	1707	|	...	1904	|	2352
	Reggio Emilia d.	...	...	...	...	0830	...	0835	...	|	...	...	|	...	1525	...	...	1726	1942v	...	1920	|	|
	Modena d.	...	...	...	...	0848	...	0853	...	|	...	...	|	...	1547	...	...	1744	|	...	1936	|	|
160	**Bologna** Centrale a.	...	...	...	...	0914	...	0933	...	1112	...	...	1721	...	1614	...	...	1814	2009	...	2000	0109	|
160	**Bologna** Centrale d.	...	...	...	...	0918	...	0937	...	1118	...	...	1725	...	1618	...	...	1818	2012	...	2004	0151	|
241	Prato Centrale d.	...	...	...	...	1005	...	1057	...	1210	...	...	1814	...	1710	...	...	1910	|	...	2105	|	|
	Firenze Rifredi d.	...	...	...	...	1017	...	1116	...	1230	...	...	1828	...	1730	...	...	1934f	|	...	|	|	|
257	**Firenze** SMN d.	0545	0600	0640	0904	|	1114	|	...	|	1314	1514	|	1714	|	...	1914	|	2059	2114	2152	|	|
345	Arezzo d.	0625	0633	0743	1007	1113	1217	|	...	1312	1417	1617	1907	1817	1811	...	2017	|	2133	2217	2230	0425	|
363	Castiglion Fiorentino d.	|	|	0755	1020	|	1228	|	...	|	1428	1628	|	1828	|	...	2028	|	|	2228	|	|	|
379	Terontola-Cortona d.	0645	|	0808	1035	1134	1241	|	...	1330	1441	1641	1929	1842	1835	...	2042	|	2154	2241	2251	0445	|
422	**Perugia** d.	|	|	|	|	|	|	|	...	|	|	|	|	|	|	...	|	|	2230	|	2317	|	|
390	Castiglione del Lago d.	|	◧	0810	1042	|	1248	|	...	|	1448	1648	|	1849	|	...	2049	|	...	2248	...	|	|
408	Chiusi-Chianciano Terme d.	0704	|	0831	1054	1152	1301	1230	...	1349	1500	1700	1950	1900	1856	...	2102	|	...	2259	...	0507	|
458	Orvieto d.	0725	|	0857	1120	1217	1327	|	...	1413	1527	1727	2015	*1943*	1921	...	2129	|	...	2325	...	|	0448
490	Orte d.	|	|	0938	1155	1249	1401	|	...	1450	1611	1811	2051	*2021*	1952	...	2211	|	...	2358	...	|	|
568	**Roma** Tiburtina a.	|	0739	1049	1236	1327	1430	1336	...	|	1648	1848	|	*2118*	2035	...	2243	2321	...	0034	...	|	0553
573	**Roma** Termini a.	0820	0749	...	1248	|	1448	|	...	1535	1705	1900	2135	*2130*	2100	...	2300	...	...	0055	...	0635	|
	Napoli Centrale **640** a.	...	0913	...	...	1529	...	1609	...	...	...	...	...	...	2330	...	...	...	...	...	...	...	0846

km		*FR*	*IC*	*ICN*				*IC*		*IC*				*IC*	*IC*	*IC*		*IC*	*FR*		*FR*	*ICN*	*ICN*
		9300	**580**	**794**	2	2	2	**588**	2	**590**	2	2	2	**592**	**596**	**1588**	2	**598**	**9432**	2	**9568**	**774**	**798**
		①–⑥									⚒	†				⑦		Ⓑ			Ⓑ		
		C	**D**	**B** ❖												**A**						**E** ❖	**F** ❖
	Napoli Centrale **640** d.	...	...	...	...	...	...	...	...	1031	...	...	...	...	1420	1446	...	...	1705	...	1940	...	2135
0	**Roma** Termini d.	...	...	...	0606	0702	0902	1022	...	|	1302	1302	1502	1530	|	|	1720	1815	1835	2002	2110	2235	|
5	**Roma** Tiburtina d.	...	...	0609	0615	0713	0912	|	1111	1240	1313	1313	1513	|	1635	1712	1730	|	1847	2012	2120	|	2355
83	Orte d.	...	...	|	0650	0747	0952	1102	1149	1314	1346	1346	1552	1613	1705	|	1804	1854	|	2047	|	|	0027
115	Orvieto d.	...	...	|	0724	0820	1029	1139	1229	1345	1419	1421	1626	1648	1743	1814	1837	1923	|	2121	|	|	0103
165	Chiusi-Chianciano Terme d.	...	...	|	0758	0848	1058	1210	1258	1410	1514	1511	1658	1717	1814	1842	1906	1946	|	2149	|	0007	|
183	Castiglione del Lago d.	...	...	|	0809	0900	1109	|	1310	|	1531	1529	1709	|	|	|	1918	|	◧	2200	◧	|	|
	Perugia d.	0524	0638	|	|	|	|	|	|	|	|	|	|	|	|	|	|	|	|	|	|	|	|
194	Terontola-Cortona d.	0556	0710	|	0819	0908	1119	1230	1319	1427	1540	1536	1719	1737	1836	1901	1927	2004	|	2207	|	0025	|
210	Castiglion Fiorentino d.	|	|	|	0831	0923	1131	|	1332	|	...	1549	1731	|	|	|	1939	|	|	2220	|	|	|
228	Arezzo d.	0625	0732	|	0844	0943	1145	1252	1345	1452	...	1603	1744	1802	1901	1927	1952	2026	1959	2233	2225	0047	|
316	**Firenze** SMN d.	0710	0821	|	0952	1048	1250	|	1448	|	...	...	1848	|	|	|	2055	2125	2041	2342	2258	|	|
	Firenze Rifredi d.	|	|	1007f	...	...	...	1333	...	1533	...	...	...	1845	1941	2017	...	...	|	...	...	0203f	|
332	Prato Centrale d.	|	0833	1030	...	...	...	1352	...	1552	...	...	...	1901	1952	2038	...	...	|	...	...	|	|
413	**Bologna** Centrale a.	0748	0942	1138	...	...	...	1442	...	1642	...	...	...	1956	2042	2130	...	...	2118	...	...	0328	|
413	**Bologna** Centrale d.	0751	0946	1145	...	...	...	1446	...	1646	...	...	...	2000	2046	2139	...	...	2121	...	...	0443	|
450	Modena d.	|	1010	1213	...	...	...	|	...	1708	...	...	...	|	2110	2209	...	...	|	...	...	|	|
475	Reggio Emilia d.	0815v	1024	1231	...	...	...	|	...	1724	...	...	...	|	2124	2225	...	...	|	...	...	|	|
503	Parma d.	|	1039	1250	...	...	...	|	...	1741	...	...	...	|	2140	2243	...	...	|	...	...	|	0524
525	Fidenza d.	|	1054	|	...	...	...	|	...	1755	...	...	...	|	2154	2304	...	...	|	...	...	|	|
560	Piacenza d.	|	1119	1328	...	...	...	|	...	1819	...	...	...	|	2219	2322	...	...	|	...	...	|	0556
622	**Milano** Rogoredo ▽ a.	0854	1204	|	...	...	...	|	...	1904	...	...	...	|	2304	0001	...	...	|	...	...	|	|
632	**Milano** Centrale a.	0912g	1215	1425g	...	...	...	|	...	1917	...	...	...	|	2317	0015	...	...	|	...	...	|	0655g
	Ferrara d.	...	...	...	...	...	...	1513	...	...	...	...	...	2034	...	...	...	...	2152	...	...	0512	...
	Rovigo d.	...	...	...	...	...	...	1530	...	...	...	...	...	2053	...	...	...	...	|	...	...	0531	...
	Padova d.	...	...	...	...	...	...	1600	...	...	...	...	...	2122	...	...	...	...	2229	...	...	0609	...
	Venezia Mestre a.	...	...	...	...	...	...	1616	...	...	...	...	...	2136	...	...	...	...	2242s	...	...	0626	...
	Venezia Santa Lucia a.	...	...	...	...	...	...	|	...	...	...	...	...	|	...	...	...	...	2255	...	...	0638	...
	Trieste Centrale **601** a.	...	...	...	...	...	...	1837	...	...	...	...	...	2347	...	...	...	...	...	...	...	0956	...

A – [12] Milano - Reggio di Calabria and v.v.
B – 🛏 1, 2 cl., ▬ 2 cl. (4 berth) Torino - Reggio di Calabria and v.v.
C – [12] 🍸 Torino - Perugia and v.v.
D – [12] Milano - Terni and v.v.
E – 🛏 1, 2 cl., ▬ 2 cl. (4 berth) [2] Trieste - Udine - Venezia - Roma and v.v.
F – 🛏 1, 2 cl., ▬ 2 cl. (4 berth) Torino - Salerno and v.v.

f – Firenze **Campo di Marte**.
g – Milano **Porta Garibaldi**.
s – Calls to set down only.
v – Reggio Emilia **AV**.

◧ – Via Table **600**.
△ – Trains call here to pick up only.
▽ – Trains call here to set down only.
❖ – Running days, timings and numbers of *ICN* trains may vary - please check your reservation. For confirmed timings please consult the *Trenitalia* journey planner at www.trenitalia.com.

2nd class VENEZIA / MILANO - BOLOGNA and FIRENZE - PERUGIA - FOLIGNO 620

Local trains. For long-distance trains see previous page.

VENEZIA - BOLOGNA

km			⚒																				
0	**Venezia** Santa Lucia d.	...	0534	0640	0740	0840	0940	1040	1140	1240	1340	1440	1540	1640	1740	1840	1940	...	2140	...	...	...	...
9	**Venezia** Mestre d.	...	0553	0653	0753	0853	0953	1053	1153	1253	1353	1453	1553	1653	1753	1853	1953	...	2153	...	...	...	...
37	Padova d.	...	0612	0709	0809	0909	1009	1109	1209	1309	1409	1509	1609	1709	1809	1909	2009	...	2210	...	...	...	...
81	Rovigo d.	0550	0647	0758	0844	0958j	1044	1144	1244	1344	1444	1558k	1644	1744	1858	1946	2046	...	2248	...	...	...	...
113	Ferrara d.	0609	0705	0818	0905	1018	1105	1205	1305	1405	1505	1618	1705	1805	1918	2014	2111	...	...	...	...	...	...
160	**Bologna** Centrale a.	0647	0746	0855	0946	1048	1146	1246	1346	1446	1546	1650	1746	1846	1948	2046	2146	...	...	...	...	...	...

			Ⓐ	⚒																		
Bologna Centrale d.	...	...	...	0612	0712	0812	0912	1012	1112	1212	1312	1425	1512	1612	1712	1812	1912	...	2112	...	...	...	...
Ferrara d.	...	...	0615	0648	0748	0844	0954	1044	1144	1244	1344	1500	1544	1644	1744	1844	1944	...	2144	...	...	...	...
Rovigo d.	0611	0634	0634	0708	0808	0903	1014	1103	1203	1303	1403	1518	1603	1703	1803	1903	2003	...	2203	...	...	...	...
Padova d.	0651	0721	0721	0753	0853	0953	1053	1153	1253	1353	1453	1553	1653	1753	1853	1953	2053	...	2253	...	...	...	...
Venezia Mestre a.	0707	0756	0756	0807	0907	1007	1107	1207	1307	1407	1507	1607	1707	1807	1907	2007	2107	...	2307	...	...	...	...
Venezia Santa Lucia a.	0720	0809	0809	0820	0920	1020	1120	1220	1320	1420	1520	1620	1720	1820	1920	2020	2120	...	2320	...	...	...	...

MILANO - BOLOGNA

km				①	⑥⑦																			❖
0	**Milano** Centrale d.	0515	...	0615	0630	0720	0920	1120	1320	1520	1615	...	1720	1815	1920	...	...	2120	2205g	...		...		...
10	**Milano** Rogoredo d.	0527	...	0627	|	0732	0932	1132	1332	1532	1627	...	1732	1827	1932	...	...	2133	2227	...		...		...
72	Piacenza d.	0609	0715	0715	0727	0814	1014	1214	1414	1614	1707	...	1814	1909	2014	2055	2148	2214	2305	...	A	0649	and	1949
107	Fidenza d.	0632	0742	0742	0751	0845	1037	1245	1437	1637	1727	...	1843	1937	2037	2118	2213	2240	|	...	L	0714		2014
129	Parma d.	0647	0755	0755	0806	0900	1100	1300	1500	1700	1743	1758	1906n	2000	2100	2133	2226	2257	2334	...	S	0727	hourly	2027
157	Reggio Emilia d.	0706	0814	0814	0821	0920	1120	1320	1520	1719	...	1819	1927	2018	2118	2149	2243	...	2349	...	O	0744	until	2044
182	Modena d.	0724	0834	0834	0840	0938	1138	1338	1538	1738	...	1838	1946	2035	2138	2204	2258t	...	0005	...		0758		2058
219	**Bologna** Centrale a.	0805	0910	0910	0904	1010	1210	1410	1610	1810	...	1910	2016	2108	2210	2233	2328t	...	0033	...		0825		2125

		⚒												⑤		w	⑥⑦						△
Bologna Centrale d.	0528	0540	0550	0658	0750	0950	1150	...	1350	1550	...	1750	1833	1850	1950	...	2050	2229	...		0733		2133
Modena d.	0555	0607	0624	0731	0824	1024	1224	...	1424	1624	...	1824	1902	1924	2024	...	2118	2256	...	A	0802	and	2202
Reggio Emilia d.	0610	0622	0642	0800	0842	1042	1242	...	1442	1642	...	1842	1917	1942	2042	...	2136	2310	...	L	0817		2217
Parma d.	0627	0640	0703	0818	0903	1103	1305	1415	1503	1703	1815	1903	1933	2003	2103	...	2152	2325	...	S	0833	hourly	2233
Fidenza d.	0639	0656	0726	0830	0926	1126	1326	1429	1524	1726	1829	1926	1945	2017	2126	2158	2206	...	...	O	0845	until	2245
Piacenza d.	0706	0725	0753	0853	0950	1150	1350	1453	1550	1750	1853	1950	2012	2053	2150	2225	2231	...	...		0910		2310
Milano Rogoredo a.	0747	0803	0836	0936	1033	1233	1433	1533	1633	1833	1933	2033	2046	2133	2233	2312	2319	...	...		...		...
Milano Centrale a.	0800	0834g	0850	0950	1045	1245	1445	1545	1645	1845	1945	2045	2110g	2145	2245	2322	2330	...	...		...		...

FIRENZE - PERUGIA - FOLIGNO

km		⚒	⚒		⚒		⚒	⚒	⚒		Ⓐ🚌	⚒R		Ⓐ			Ⓐ		†	⚒		⑥	Ⓑ
0	**Firenze** SMN d.	...	...	0640	...	0802	0948	...	...	1214	...	...	1414	...	1614	1714	...	...	1814	1814	...	2014	2014
88	Arezzo d.	...	...	0743	...	0913	1049	...	...	1317	...	...	1517	...	1717	1817	...	...	1917	1917	...	2117	2117
106	Castiglion Fiorentino d.	...	...	0755	...	0924	1102	...	...	1328	...	...	1528	...	1728	1828	...	...	1928	1928	...	2128	2128
122	Terontola-Cortona d.	0625	0710	0809	0830	0941	1121	1139	1226	1341	1450	...	1541	1620	1741	1841	1850	...	1941	1941	...	2141	2141
134	Passignano sul Trasimeno d.	0639	0721	...	0841	0950	...	1149	1235	1350	1507	...	1550	1629	1750	...	1900	...	1950	1950	...	2151	2150
165	**Perugia** 625 d.	0718	0805	...	0914	1019	...	1227	1316	1427	1540	1555	1623	1703	1828	...	1941	...	2024	2024	...	2221	2239r
176	**Perugia** Ponte San Giovanni 625 d.	0727	0814	...	0924	1030	...	1236	1327	1436	...	1606	1632	1714	1839	...	1950	...	2035	2036	...	2230	2248
189	Assisi 625 d.	0739	0828	...	0938	1043	...	1247	1343	1448	...	1627	1645	1728	1852	...	2001	...	2047	2048	...	2242	2259
200	Spello 625 d.	0749	0840	...	0946	1052	...	1255	1354	1459	...	1637	1654	1737	1906	...	2010	...	2056	2057	...	2251	2307
205	**Foligno** 625 a.	0758	0850	...	0952	1057	...	1301	1402	1508	...	1643	1703	1744	1915	...	2016	...	2107	2112	...	2257	2315

	⚒	†	⚒		⚒T				⚒			⚒		⚒		Ⓐ			Ⓐ		⚒R	⑥R
Foligno 625 d.	0530	0617	0636	...	0722	...	0910	1108	1150	...	1303	1345	...	1417	1456	1533	...	1706	1810	1903	2053	2053
Spello 625 d.	0536	0622	0641	...	0728	...	0915	1114	1156	...	1309	1351	...	1424	1502	1538	...	1711	1816	1909	2100	2100
Assisi 625 d.	0545	0632	0649	...	0742	...	0924	1122	1205	...	1317	1404	...	1436	1511	1549	...	1721	1824	1917	2110	2110
Perugia Ponte San Giovanni 625 d.	0600	0647	0708	...	0753	...	0936	1134	1216	...	1330	1417	...	1451	1526	1603	...	1733	1842	1929	2124	2124
Perugia 625 d.	0615	0702	0718	...	0804	...	0950	1144	1227	...	1341	1427	...	1505	1540	1627n	...	1744	1853	1941	2135	2137
Passignano sul Trasimeno d.	0642	...	0753	...	0838	...	1019	1212	1256	...	1409	1459	...	...	1609	1658	...	1812	1922	2009	...	2207
Terontola-Cortona d.	0656	...	0805	0819	0855	0908	1036k	1221	1309	1319	1419	1511	1517	...	1619	1714	1719	1825	1933	2019	...	2220
Castiglion Fiorentino d.	0710	...	...	0831	...	0923	|	1234	...	1332	1431	...	1531	...	1631	...	1731	1837	...	2031	...	...
Arezzo d.	0725	...	...	0844	...	0943	1100	1245	...	1345	1444	...	1543	...	1644	...	1744	1849	...	2044	...	...
Firenze SMN a.	0838	...	...	0952	...	1048	1155	1351	...	1448	1548	...	1648	...	1757	...	1848	1952	...	2150	...	...

R – To / from Roma (Table **625**).
T – From Terni (Table **625**).

g – Milano **Porta Garibaldi**.
j – Arrives 0947.

k – Arrives 6 minutes earlier.
n – Arrives 8–9 minutes earlier.
r – Arrives 2218.
t – On † Modena d. 2257, Bologna a. 2324.
w – Until May 9 (not Mar. 3–5, Apr. 21–23, 28–30).

❖ – Piacenza d. 1345 (not 1349), Fidenza d. 1412 (not 1414), then follows the regular pattern.
△ – Timings at Fidenza and Piacenza may vary by up to 3 minutes.

2nd class FERRARA and BOLOGNA - RAVENNA - RIMINI 621

km							⚒		⚒		†	⚒	⚒		⚒	⚒		†	⚒	†A		ⒸA	†B
0	**Ferrara** d.	...	...	0520	...	0546	...	...	0610	...	...	...	0709	...	...	...	...	0827	0827	...	...	...	...
	Bologna Centrale d.	...	...	|	...	|	0555	...	|	...	...	0650	|	0702	...	...	0806	|	|	...	0906	0906	...
	Imola d.	...	...	|	...	|	0622	...	|	...	...	0712	|	0729	...	...	0827	|	|	...	0927	0927	...
	Castelbolognese-Riolo Terme d.	...	...	|	...	|	0627	0640	|	...	...	0719	|	0734	0750	...	0834	|	|	...	0934	0934	...
	Lugo d.	...	...	|	...	|	...	0657	|	...	...	0734	|	...	0802	...	0848	|	|	...	0948	0948	...
74	**Ravenna** a.	...	...	0622	...	0702	...	0730	0733	...	...	0805	0833	...	0834	...	0915	0942	0943	...	1016	1016	...
74	**Ravenna** d.	0533	...	...	0628	...	...	...	...	0747	0819	...	...	...	...	0847	0919	...	0947	0947	...	1019	1020
95	Cervia-Milano Marittima d.	0551	...	...	0646	...	...	...	...	0808	0838	...	...	...	...	0908	0938	...	1008	1008	...	1038	1038
103	Cesenatico d.	0559	...	...	0652	...	...	...	...	0816	0846	...	...	...	...	0916	0946	...	1016	1016	...	1046	1046
124	**Rimini** a.	0630	...	...	0723	...	...	...	...	0842	0912	...	...	...	...	0942	1017	...	1042	1042	...	1117	1117

	⚒		†		⚒				⚒							⚒							
Ferrara d.	0917	...	1005	...	1137	...	1235	...	1335	...	1435	...	...	1637	...	1737	...	1835	...	...	2037	...	...
Bologna Centrale d.	|	1006	|	1106	|	1206	|	1306	|	1406	|	1506	1606	|	1706	|	1806	|	1906	2006	|	2112	2206
Imola d.	|	1027	|	1127	|	1227	|	1327	|	1427	|	1527	1627	|	1727	|	1827	|	1927	2027	|	2131	2239
Castelbolognese-Riolo Terme d.	|	1034	|	1134	|	1234	|	1334	|	1434	|	1534	1634	|	1734	|	1834	|	1934	2034	|	2138	2245
Lugo d.	|	1048	|	1148	|	1248	|	1348	|	1448	|	1548	1648	|	1748	|	1848	|	1948	2048	|	2152	2301
Ravenna a.	1027	1115	1113	1216	1248	1316	1348	1416	1448	1516	1548	1616	1716	1748	1816	1848	1916	1950	2016	2116	2150	2216	2330
Ravenna d.	...	...	1119	1219	...	1319	...	1419	...	1519	...	1619	1719	...	1819	...	1919	...	2019	2119	...	2219	...
Cervia-Milano Marittima d.	...	...	1138	1238	...	1338	...	1438	...	1538	...	1638	1738	...	1838	...	1938	...	2038	2137	...	2237	...
Cesenatico d.	...	...	1146	1246	...	1346	...	1446	...	1546	...	1646	1746	...	1846	...	1946	...	2046	2143	...	2244	...
Rimini a.	...	...	1217	1317	...	1417	...	1517	...	1617	...	1717	1817	...	1917	...	2017	...	2117	2217	...	2318	...

A – From May 27.
B – Until May 21.

FOR RETURN SERVICE, SEE NEXT PAGE. →

621 RIMINI - RAVENNA - BOLOGNA and FERRARA

2nd class

km																						
			⚒	⚒		⚒				⚒	⚒	⚒			†		⚒			†		†	⚒
	Rimini d.	...	...	...	0520	...	0606	...	0654	...	0735	...	...	0843	...	0918	...	...	...	1043	...	...	...
	Cesenatico d.	...	...	...	0544	...	0636	...	0721	...	0800	...	...	0916	...	0946	...	...	...	1116	...	...	...
	Cervia-Milano Marittima d.	...	...	...	0551	...	0647	...	0727	...	0809	...	...	0922	...	0952	...	...	...	1122	...	...	...
	Ravenna a.	...	...	...	0612	...	0707	...	0746	...	0831	...	...	0941	...	1014	...	...	...	1140	...	...	...
0	**Ravenna** d.	0503	0545	...	0627	0626	...	0712	0755	0757	...	0843	0844	0944	0955	...	1040	1045	...	...	1144	1147	1210
28	Lugo d.	0528	0612	...	0657	|	...	|	0815	|	...	|	0912	1012	|	...	|	1112	...	...	1212	|	|
42	Castelbolognese-Riolo Terme d.	0546	0627	0631	0714	|	...	|	|	|	...	|	0928	1028	|	...	|	1128	...	...	1228	|	|
50	Imola d.	0555	...	0637	0721	|	...	|	|	|	...	|	0934	1034	|	...	|	1134	...	...	1234	|	|
84	**Bologna** Centrale a.	0626	...	0710	0743	|	...	|	0854	|	...	|	0954	1054	|	...	|	1154	...	...	1254	|	|
	Ferrara a.	...	...	...	...	0740	...	0824	...	0904	...	0955	...	...	1107	...	1200	...	...	...	...	1259	1324

		©A					⚒						⚒										
Rimini d.	...	1143	...	1243	...	1343	...	1443	1520	1543	...	1643	...	1743	...	1843	...	1943	...	2043	...	2143	2243
Cesenatico d.	...	1216	...	1316	...	1416	...	1516	1546	1616	...	1716	...	1816	...	1916	...	2016	...	2116	...	2216	2315
Cervia-Milano Marittima d.	...	1222	...	1322	...	1422	...	1522	1552	1622	...	1722	...	1822	...	1922	...	2022	...	2122	...	2222	2321
Ravenna a.	...	1241	...	1341	...	1441	...	1541	1612	1641	...	1741	...	1841	...	1941	...	2041	...	2141	...	2241	2340
Ravenna d.	1244	1244	1310	1344	1425	1444	1512	1544	1616	1645	1712	1744	1812	1844	...	1944	2012	2044	...	2145	2212	...	...
Lugo d.	1312	1312	|	1412	|	1512	|	1612	|	1712	|	1812	|	1912	...	2012	|	2112	...	2220	|	...	...
Castelbolognese-Riolo Terme d.	1328	1328	|	1428	|	1528	|	1628	|	1728	|	1828	|	1928	...	2028	|	2128	...	2234	|	...	...
Imola d.	1334	1334	|	1434	|	1534	|	1634	|	1734	|	1834	|	1934	...	2034	|	2134	...	2240	|	...	...
Bologna Centrale a.	1354	1354	|	1454	|	1554	|	1654	|	1754	|	1854	|	1954	...	2054	|	2154	...	2300	|	...	...
Ferrara a.	...	...	1424	...	1546	...	1624	...	1724	...	1824	...	1924	...	...	...	2124	...	...	...	2322	...	...

← FOR RETURN SERVICE AND FOOTNOTES, SEE PREVIOUS PAGE.

622 ROMA AIRPORTS ✈

ROMA FIUMICINO AIRPORT ✈. *Leonardo Express* rail service Roma Termini - Roma Fiumicino ✈ and v.v. *31 km.* Journey time: 32 minutes. Special fare payable.

From **Roma** Termini: 0450, 0520, 0550, 0605, 0620, 0635, 0650, 0705, 0735, 0750, 0805, 0820, 0835, 0905, 0920, 0935, 0950, 1020, 1035, 1050, 1105, 1120, 1135, 1205, 1220, 1235, 1250, 1320, 1350, 1405, 1420, 1435, 1450, 1505, 1520, 1535, 1550, 1605, 1620, 1635, 1650, 1705, 1720, 1735, 1750, 1805, 1820, 1835, 1850, 1920, 1935, 1950, 2005, 2020, 2035, 2050, 2105, 2120, 2135, 2150, 2205, 2235 and 2305.

From **Roma Fiumicino**: 0538, 0608, 0638, 0653, 0708, 0723, 0738, 0753, 0823, 0838, 0853, 0908, 0923, 0953, 1008, 1023, 1038, 1108, 1123, 1138, 1153, 1208, 1223, 1253, 1308, 1323, 1338, 1408, 1438, 1453, 1508, 1523, 1538, 1553, 1608, 1623, 1638, 1653, 1708, 1723, 1738, 1753, 1808, 1823, 1838, 1853, 1908, 1923, 1938, 2008, 2023, 2038, 2053, 2108, 2123, 2138, 2153, 2208, 2223, 2238, 2253 and 2353.

Additional suburban rail services operate Roma Tiburtina - Roma Ostiense - Fiumicino ✈. *39 km.* Journey time: Tiburtina - Fiumicino ✈ ± 45 minutes; Ostiense - Fiumicino ✈ ± 30 minutes. From Roma Tiburtina 0545 - 2200 (approx. every 15 minutes on Ⓐ / every 30 minutes on ©); from Roma Fiumicino ✈ 0557 - 2242 (approx. every 15 minutes on Ⓐ / every 30 minutes on ©).

ROMA CIAMPINO AIRPORT ✈. Rail service Roma Termini - Ciampino and v.v. (Table **623**). A 🚌 connects Ciampino station and the airport. Overall journey time approximately 60 minutes.

623 ROMA - ALBANO LAZIALE and ANZIO

2nd class

km																								
		⚒				⚒			⚒	†	⚒	⚒	†	⚒	Ⓐ	⑥	†	⚒	⚒		†	⚒		⚒
0	**Roma** Termini d.	0542	...	0721	0821	0900	...	1221	1321	1421	1421	1521	1621	1621	1721	1721	1821	1821	1921	...	2021	2021	...	2121
14	Ciampino d.	0558	...	0740	0837	0918	...	1237	1337	1437	1437	1537	1637	1637	1737	1742	1837	1837	1937	...	2037	2037	...	2137
23	Marino Laziale d.	0614	...	0801	0857	0936	...	1257	1400	1456	1500	1600	1656	1700	1800	1802	1856	1900	2000	...	2056	2100	...	2157
26	Castel Gandolfo d.	0621	...	0807	0904	0942	...	1303	1406	1503	1507	1606	1703	1706	1806	1809	1903	1906	2007	...	2102	2106	...	2204
29	**Albano Laziale** a.	0627	...	0815	0912	0951	...	1312	1415	1511	1515	1615	1711	1715	1815	1817	1911	1915	2015	...	2111	2115	...	2213

	⚒	⚒	⚒					⚒			⚒		⚒		Ⓑ	⑥		⚒		⚒		⚒	†
Albano Laziale d.	0629	0700	0743	0838	...	1023	...	1144	...	1343	1443	1543	1643	...	1743	1743	...	1843	1943	2043	...	2140	2145
Castel Gandolfo d.	0636	0707	0750	0845	...	1030	...	1151	...	1351	1451	1551	1651	...	1751	1751	...	1851	1951	2051	...	2148	2152
Marino Laziale d.	0643	0720	0802	0858	...	1036	...	1157	...	1359	1459	1559	1659	...	1759	1803	...	1859	1959	2059	...	2158	2158
Ciampino d.	0703	0739	0823	0917	...	1057	...	1218	...	1419	1519	1619	1719	...	1819	1823	...	1919	2019	2119	...	2219	2219
Roma Termini a.	0720	0754	0841	0934	...	1113	...	1234	...	1434	1534	1634	1734	...	1834	1838	...	1934	2034	2134	...	2234	2234

ROMA - ANZIO *57 km* Journey 59 – 77 minutes. All services continue to Nettuno (*3 km* and 4 – 7 minutes from Anzio).

From **Roma** Termini: 0506 ⚒, 0640, 0742 ⚒, 0812, 0942, 1042 ⚒, 1142, 1242 ⚒, 1342, 1412 Ⓐ, 1442, 1542 ⚒, 1642, 1742 ⚒, 1812 Ⓐ, 1842, 1912 Ⓐ, 1942, 2042 ⚒ and 2142.

From **Anzio**: 0455 ⚒, 0559 ⚒, 0635, 0703 Ⓐ, 0731 †, 0733 ⚒, 0816 ⚒, 0912, 1012, 1112 ⚒, 1212 ⚒, 1310 †, 1312 ⚒, 1412 ⚒, 1510 †, 1512 ⚒, 1612 ⚒, 1630 Ⓐ, 1705 †, 1712 ⚒, 1810 †, 1812 ⚒, 1912 ⚒, 2010 †, 2012 ⚒, 2112 Ⓐ and 2201.

624 ROMA - PESCARA

2nd class

km																									
			†	⚒	⚒		⚒	†		⚒			⚒	†	†	⑥	Ⓑ		⚒		⚒		⚒		⚒
0	**Roma** Termini d.	...	...	0715	...	0903	...	...	...	...	...	1310	1420	1420	...	...	...	1640	...	...	...	1847	...	...	...
	Roma Tiburtina ◧ d.	...	0710	|	0810	|	...	...	1110	...	...	|	|	|	...	1510	1515	|	...	...	1715	|	1915	2010	2050
40	Tivoli d.	...	0811	0828	0901	0951	...	...	1211	...	...	1405b	1457	1458	...	1604	1604	1720	...	...	1759	1922	2000	2101	2136
108	Avezzano d.	0630	0920	0947	1023	1106	*1247*	...	1319	1349	...	1517	1601	1602	*1615*	1740	1740	1819	1845	...	1914	2020	2110	2215	2246
172	Sulmona ⊖ d.	0740	1020	...	...	...	1402	1405	...	1512	1557	...	1652	...	1750	...	...	1908	1956	2001	...	2111	...	...	...
226	Chieti d.	0849	1059	...	...	...	1505	1457	...	...	1647	...	1737	...	1843	...	...	1951	...	2054	...	2156	...	...	...
240	**Pescara** Centrale a.	0905	1117	...	...	...	1521	1515	...	...	1712	...	1750	...	1900	...	...	2006	...	2112	...	2209	...	...	...

	⚒		⚒	†	⚒		†	⚒		⚒	⚒		†	⚒	⚒	⚒	†	⚒	⚒	†	⚒	⚒			
Pescara Centrale d.	...	...	...	...	0523	0730	...	0925	...	...	1119	...	1215	1215	...	...	1438	1510	...	1627	1715	1821	...	1916	2020
Chieti d.	...	...	...	...	0536	0744	...	0937	...	...	1138	...	1232	1241	...	...	1458	1532	...	1648	1738	1842	...	1937	2040
Sulmona ⊖ d.	...	...	...	0619	0619	0826	...	1019	...	...	1232	...	1325	1340	1410	...	1542	1627	*1700*	1736	1845	1943	...	2040	2147
Avezzano d.	0508	0545	0624	0711	0712	0919	1112	1112	1145	1320	1339	1345	...	...	1530	1604	1637	...	1835	1837	2010	*2050**	2112	...	...
Tivoli d.	0610	0700	0736	0810	0812	1023	1210	1211	1300	1438	...	1532	...	...	1642	1721	1750	...	2001	1951	...	...	2232	...	...
Roma Tiburtina ◧ a.	0700	0806	0833	|	|	1055	|	|	|	1536	...	|	...	...	1736	|	|	...	2053	2035	...	...	|	...	...
Roma Termini a.	...	...	...	0845	0845	...	1250	1250	1350	...	...	1624	...	...	...	1826	1825	...	...	...	...	...	2315	...	...

b – 1359 on †. * – By 🚌 Sulmona - Avezzano. ◧ – Roma **Tiburtina Piazzale Est**. ⊖ – For 🚌 service Sulmona - Castel di Sangro see Table **627**.

625 ROMA - PERUGIA, RAVENNA and ANCONA

km																									
			IC						*IC*								*IC*		*FB*					*IC*	
		2	**580**	2	2	2		2	**534**					2			**540**		**8852**					**546**	
		⚒	A	†	⚒	⚒T		Ⓐ		⚒	†	⚒	†	⚒						Ⓑ	⚒	†	⚒C	Ⓑ	
0	**Roma** Termini 620 d.	...	...	...	...	...	0547	...	0750	0802	0815	0930	1005	*1158*	1322	1428	1522	1558	1725	1800	1832	1855	1902	1955	*2102*
5	**Roma** Tiburtina 620 d.	...	...	...	...	...	0557	...	0758u	0813	0824	0938	1013	*1207*	1331	1436	1529u	1609	|	1812	1842	1906	1912	2006u	*2112*
83	Orte 620 d.	...	...	...	...	...	0634	...	0830	0847	0858	1013	1047	*1243*	1405	1509	1601	1644	|	1846	1917	1940	1946	2037	*2148*
112	Terni d.	...	0505	...	...	0620	0653	0735	0852	0908	0919	1036	1107	*1308*	1428	1529	1622	1706	1830	1910	1938	2001	2008	2056	*2212*
141	Spoleto d.	...	0537	...	...	0656	0717	0814	0917	0934	0952	1103	1139	*1333*	1457	1556	1648	1739	1853	1942	2005	2028	2033	2130	*2238*
167	**Foligno** a.	...	0557	...	...	0720	0740	0835	0933	0953	1011	1126	1154	*1352*	1518	1612	1704	1757	1907	1959	2023	2046	2051	2145	*2256*
167	**Foligno** 620 d.	0545	0559	0615	0640	0722	0742	0837	0935	0955	1013	1128	1156	1417	1520	1614	1706	1759	1909	2001	2025	2048	2053	2147	2303
172	Spello 620 d.	|	|	|	|	0728	|	0843	|	|	|	|	|	|	|	1620	|	|	|	2007	|	|	2100	|	|
183	Assisi 620 d.	|	0615	|	|	0742	|	0853	|	1011	1028	|	1210	|	|	1630	|	|	|	2017	|	|	2110	2200	|
196	**Perugia** Ponte SG ⊡ 620 d.	|	0626	|	|	0753	|	0906	|	1029	1049	|	1220	|	|	1644	|	|	|	2033	|	|	2124	2209s	|
207	**Perugia** 620 a.	|	0636	|	|	0802	|	0915	|	1044	1059	|	1230	|	|	1658	|	|	|	2046	|	|	2135	2222	|
224	Fabriano d.	0647	...	0714	0736	...	0837	...	1031	...	...	1226	...	1523	1614	...	1755	1848	1950	...	2123	2139	...	...	2357
268	Jesi d.	0733	...	0756	0821	...	0914	...	1101	...	...	1310	...	1606	1706	...	1828	1923	2020	...	2200	2213	...	...	0033
286	Falconara Marittima d.	0751	...	0813	0839	...	0927	...	1115	...	...	1328	...	1626	1727	...	1852	1940	2042	...	2213	2232	...	...	0048
	Pesaro d.	|	...	|	|	...	|	...	|	...	...	|	...	|	|	...	|	|	2105	...	|	|	...	...	|
	Rimini d.	|	...	|	|	...	|	...	|	...	...	|	...	|	|	...	|	|	2129	...	|	|	...	...	|
	Ravenna a.	|	...	|	|	...	|	...	|	...	...	|	...	|	|	...	|	|	2205	...	|	|	...	...	|
295	**Ancona** a.	0805	...	0828	0855	...	0940	...	1125	...	...	1340	...	1637	1740	...	1905	1956	...	...	2225	2245	...	...	0100

A – To Milano (Table **620**).
C – To Terontola-Cortona on ⑥ (Table **620**).
T – To Terontola-Cortona (Table **620**).
s – Calls to set down only.
u – Calls to pick up only.
⊡ – Full name is Perugia Ponte San Giovanni.

ANCONA, RAVENNA and PERUGIA - ROMA — 625

					IC		*IC*	*IC*		*FB*										*IC*					*IC*
				2	**531**	2	**533**	**533**		**8851**										**541**				2	**599**
		⚒	①–⑥	⚒	①–⑥	⚒	†	⚒	†		Ⓐ		⚒	†	⚒	†	⚒		⚒						**A**
Ancona d.	0333	...	...	0505	...	...	0550	0550	...	...	...	0905	...	...	...	...	1250	1350	...	1555	...	1850	1950	2130	...
Ravenna d.	|	...	...	|	...	...	|	|	...	0615	...	|	...	...	...	...	|	|	...	|	...	|	|	|	...
Rimini d.	|	...	...	|	...	...	|	|	...	0652	...	|	...	...	...	...	|	|	...	|	...	|	|	|	...
Pesaro d.	|	...	...	|	...	...	|	|	...	0716	...	|	...	...	...	...	|	|	...	|	...	|	|	|	...
Falconara Marittima d.	0346	...	...	0513	...	...	0600	0600	...	0750	...	0914	...	...	...	...	1305	1403	...	1604	...	1900	2001	2139	...
Jesi d.	0400	...	...	0526	...	...	0614	0614	...	0807	...	0928	...	...	...	...	1323	1417	...	1616	...	1914	2016	2153	...
Fabriano d.	0434	...	...	0605	...	...	0651	0651	...	0838	...	1007	...	...	...	...	1412	1457	...	1652	...	1952	2052	2235	...
Perugia 620 d.	|	...	0552	|	0640	0652	|	|	0723	|	0953	|	1105	1120	1347	1402	|	|	1555	|	1815	|	|	|	2319
Perugia Ponte SG ⊡ 620 d.	|	...	0603	|	0651**u**	0705	|	|	0732	|	1002	|	1115	1131	1357	1412	|	|	1606	|	1825	|	|	|	2329
Assisi 620 d.	|	...	0615	|	0703	0720	|	|	0745	|	1014	|	1130	1146	1413	1423	|	|	1627	|	1838	|	|	|	2339
Spello 620 d.	|	...	0626	|	|	0731	|	|	0754	|	1025	|	1138	1158	1427	|	|	|	1637	|	1848	|	|	|	|
Foligno 620 a.	0520	...	0633	0705	0715	0735	0740	0740	0800	0918	1033	1102	1148	1207	1436	1436	1509	1552	1643	1756	1854	2044	2145	2327	2350
Foligno d.	0522	0555	0636	...	0717	0737	0750	0750	0802	0920	...	1105	1150	1209	1438	1438	*1515*	1554	1645	1758	1856	2046	2147	...	2354
Spoleto d.	0540	0616	0659	...	0736	0759	0810	0814	0822	0938	...	1124	1214	1233	1500	1500	*1537*	1614	1705	1815	1912	2059	2205	...	|
Terni d.	0610	0648	0740	...	0801	0828	0835	0843	0846	1002	...	1152	1247	1302	1527	1527	*1610*	1647	1734	1853	1938	2126	2238	...	0040
Orte 620 d.	0633	|	0805	...	0818	...	0858	0900	0905	|	...	1216	1313	1327	1555	1555	*1632*	1710	1756	1914	2001	2147	2259	...	...
Roma Tiburtina 620 a.	0708	0743	0839	...	0845**s**	...	|	|	0936	1045**s**	...	1248	1345	1400	1629	1629	...	1748	1830	|	2039	2221	2329	...	...
Roma Termini 620 a.	0718	0800	0852	...	0855	...	0938	0942	0955	1100	...	1300	1355	1415	1643	1643	...	1758	1845	1950	2050	2232	2342	...	...

A – From Milano (Table **620**). **s** – Calls to set down only. **u** – Calls to pick up only. ⊡ – Full name is Perugia Ponte San Giovanni.

ROMA and NAPOLI - CAMPOBASSO - TERMOLI — 627

2nd class

km				⚒	⑤†	⚒	†	⚒	†	Ⓐ	⑥
0	**Roma** Termini ∇ d.	0615	0907	1307	1435	1732**t**	1740	1935	2014	2035	2042
138	Cassino ∇ d.	0742	1033	1445	1603	|	|	|	|	|	|
162	Venafro d.	0808	1056	1502	1624	1933	1931	2128	2205	2219	2226
169	Rocca Ravindola d.	|	1105	|	|	1941	|	|	|	|	|
187	Isernia d.	0829	*1130**	1524	*1700**	*2005**	*2005**	*2200**	*2235**	*2250**	*2257**
246	**Campobasso** a.	*0935**	*1235**	*1635**	*1800**	*2110**	*2110**	*2300**	*2335**	*2350**	*2350**

			⚒	⚒	†	Ⓐ	⑥			⚒🚌
Campobasso d.	*0535**	...	*1215**	*1400**	...	*1640**	...	...	*1920**	2010
Isernia d.	*0620**	...	*1315**	1503	...	1800	...	...	2032	2125
Rocca Ravindola d.	0655	...	|	|	...	|	...	...	|	...
Venafro d.	0704	...	1358	1531	1744	1822	1822	...	2055	...
Cassino ∇ a.	0723	...	1416	1549	1804	1840	1842	...	2116	...
Roma Termini ∇ a.	0853	...	1553**t**	1727	1934	2025	2026	...	2254	...

km		⚒	†	⑥	Ⓐ	†	⚒	Ⓒ	Ⓐ	†	⚒
0	**Napoli** Centrale ∇ d.	...	...	1206	1206	1400	1400	1706	1706	1930	1930
34	Caserta ∇ d.	0805	0845	1241	1241	1440	1440	1739	1739	2003	2003
80	Vairano-Caianello ∇ d.	0850	0929	1322	1322	1516	1516	1824	1824	2044	2044
101	Venafro d.	0910	0948	1342	1342	1538	1538	1843	1843	2104	2104
108	Rocca Ravindola d.	|	0956	1348	1349	1545	|	1850	1850	2112	|
126	Isernia d.	*0950**	1015	*1420**	1407	*1610**	1601	*1915**	1906	*2135**	2127
185	**Campobasso** a.	*1050**	*1125**	*1530**	*1530**	*1715**	*1715**	*2020**	*2020**	*2235**	*2235**

	⚒	⚒	†	†	†	⑥	Ⓐ	⚒	†	⚒
Campobasso d.	*0450**	*0605**	*0705**	*1205**	*1230**	*1235**	*1245**	...	*1720**	*1745**
Isernia d.	*0550**	*0705**	*0805**	1328	*1345**	*1350**	1411	...	*1835**	1909
Rocca Ravindola d.	|	|	0846	|	*1405**	1427	1427	...	*1900**	1925
Venafro d.	0628	0750	0854	1352	1434	1435	1434	1713	1930	1932
Vairano-Caianello ∇ d.	0646	0809	0913	1411	1455	1455	1455	1731	1954	1954
Caserta ∇ a.	0716	0847	0944	1449	1529	1529	1529	1811	2030	2030
Napoli Centrale ∇ a.	0754	0929	1020	...	1609	1609	1609	...	2106	2106

km				🚌		⚒🚌				🚌	
0	**Campobasso** d.	0600	...	1000	...	1414	...	1825	...	2100	...
87	**Termoli** a.	0750	...	1145	...	1600	...	2018	...	2245	...

					⚒🚌		🚌		🚌	
Termoli d.	0605	...	1200	...	1410	...	1750	...	2100	...
Campobasso a.	0750	...	1355	...	1555	...	1935	...	2245	...

ROMA - CASSINO (- CASERTA) ⊡

	⚒		†	⚒	⚒	†		†	⚒	⚒		⚒				⚒	†	Ⓐ				⚒		Ⓐ	⑥	
Roma Termini d.	0535	0615	0707	0742	0800	0800	0907	1014	1014	1235	1242	1307	1342	1435	1542	1642	1655	1707	1742**v**	1807	1842	1907	1942	2042	2049	2128
Cassino d.	0736	0741	0857	0942	0947	1014	1032	1227	1245	1406	1440	1444	1540**v**	1602	1740**v**	1858	1857	1844	1940	1946	2040	2045	2142	2248	2305	2340
Vairano-C ⊖ a.	...	...	...	...	...	...	...	...	...	1429	...	...	...	...	...	1927	1927	...	...	2008	...	...	...	...	...	...
Caserta a.	...	...	...	...	...	...	...	...	...	1505	...	...	...	...	...	2020	2018	...	...	2045	...	...	...	...	...	...

		⚒	†			⚒	†	⚒		⚒	†		⚒	†	⚒				⑥	†	Ⓐ	†	⚒	Ⓑ		Ⓐ
Caserta d.	...	0500	0512	0610	...	0730	...	...	...	...	...	...	...	...	...	...	...	...	...	...	...	...	...	...	...	...
Vairano-C ⊖ d.	...	0547	0557	0646	...	0808	...	...	...	...	...	...	...	...	...	...	...	...	...	...	...	...	...	...	...	...
Cassino d.	0608	0618	0627	0711	0724	0837	0850	0913	1018	1218	1231	1320**r**	1422	1458	1518	1550	1620	1720**k**	1758	1805	1808	1822	1841	1932**v**	2018	2120
Roma Termini a.	0748	0820	0834	0848	0853	1013	1107	1107	1147	1448	1448	1520	1620	1720	1720	1727	1820	1920	2020	1934	2020	2020	2026	2148	2241	2334

CASSINO - NAPOLI

km		⚒	⚒	⚒	⚒	†	⚒	⚒	⚒	Ⓐ		Ⓐ
0	**Cassino** d.	0550	0703	0838	1005	1305	1435	1514	...	1710	...	*2100*
32	Vairano-C ⊖ d.	0621	0736	0911	1033	1338	1506	1547	1605	1742	1954	*2126*
78	Caserta d.	0705	0820	0955	1117	1422	1550	1635	1650	1826	2031	2209
112	**Napoli** Centrale a.	0746	0905	1040	...	1505	1635	...	1735	1910	2106	2252

	⚒	⚒		⚒	⚒	⚒	†	Ⓐ	⚒	Ⓐ
Napoli Centrale d.	0510	*0642*	0755	1154	*1242*	*1442*	1550	1712	1755	1955
Caserta d.	0551	0730	0836	1235	1336	1536	1631	1754	1838	2038
Vairano-C ⊖ d.	0638	0808	0920	1317	1419	1619	1713	1836	1920	2120
Cassino a.	*0710*	0835	0957	1355	1453	1656	1750	1913	1957	2157

OTHER 🚌 SERVICES

CAMPOBASSO - BENEVENTO and v.v. : **From Campobasso** at 0620 ⚒, 1305 ⚒, 1416 ⚒ and 1750 ⚒. **From Benevento** at 0640 ⚒, 0740 ⚒, 1420 ⚒ and 1740 ⚒. Journey time: ±70 minutes.
SULMONA - CASTEL DI SANGRO and v.v. : **From Sulmona** at 1030 and 1950 ⚒. **From Castel di Sangro** at 0555 ⚒, 1615 † and 1640 ⚒. Journey time: 60–70 minutes.

k – 1715 on †. **t** – Roma **Tiburtina**. ***** – Connection is by 🚌. ∇ – See also panels below main table.
r – 1318 on ⑥. **v** – 2–4 minutes later on †. ⊖ – Vairano-Caianello. ⊡ – See Table **615** for other fast services Roma - Caserta.

SARDINIA — 629

2nd class

CAGLIARI - CARBONIA and IGLESIAS

km		⚒	⚒	Ⓐ					⚒	⚒	Ⓑ	Ⓑ	⚒	⚒	Ⓑ	Ⓑ	⚒	⚒			⚒	⚒🚌	⚒	⚒			Ⓑ
0	**Cagliari** d.	0526	0545	0614	0644	...	0744	...	0844	...	0944	...	1044	...	1145	...	1244	...	1344	...	1418	...	1444	...	1544	...	1644
7	Elmas Aeroporto ✈ d.	0532	0551	0620	0650	...	0750	...	0850	...	0950	...	1050	...	1150	...	1250	...	1350	...	1424	...	1450	...	1550	...	1650
17	Decimomannu d.	0541	0604	0635	0704	...	0804	...	0903	...	1003	...	1103	...	1203	...	1304	...	1403	...	1432	...	1503	...	1603	...	1703
46	Villamassargia a.	0603	0635	0703	0731	0734	0831	0834	0931	0934	1031	1034	1131	1134	1231	1234	1331	1334	1431	1434	1500	1504	1531	1534	1631	1634	1731
69	**Carbonia** Serbariu a.	|	0651	|	|	0751	0847	|	|	0951	1047	|	|	1150	1247	|	|	1350	1447	|	|	1527	|	1550	1647	|	|
55	**Iglesias** a.	0611	...	0712	0741	...	...	0843	0940	...	...	1043	1140	...	...	1243	1340	...	...	1443	1509	...	1540	...	...	1643	1740

	Ⓑ			Ⓐ	Ⓐ🚌	Ⓐ	Ⓐ				🚌
Cagliari d.	...	1744	...	1810	...	1844	...	1944	...	2044	...
Elmas Aeroporto ✈ d.	...	1750	...	1816	...	1850	...	1950	...	2050	...
Decimomannu d.	...	1803	...	1830	...	1903	...	2004	...	2103	...
Villamassargia a.	1734	1831	1834	1858	1901	1931	1934	2031	2034	2130	2135
Carbonia Serbariu a.	1750	1847	|	|	1924	|	1950	2047	|	|	2158
Iglesias a.	...	...	1843	1906	...	1940	...	...	2043	2140	...

	Ⓐ🚌	⚒	⚒	⚒	†	⚒🚌	⚒	⚒		Ⓐ	
Iglesias d.	...	0553	0623	...	0627	...	0653	...	0721	0754	0818
Carbonia Serbariu d.	0532	|	|	0613	|	0632	|	0710	|	|	|
Villamassargia d.	0558	0603	0630	0635	0636	0658	0703	0726	0731	0803	0826
Decimomannu d.	...	0633	...	0702	0703	...	0732	...	0756	0831	...
Elmas Aeroporto ✈ d.	...	0645	...	0717	0716	...	0744	...	0807	0844	...
Cagliari a.	...	0652	...	0724	0723	...	0750	...	0815	0850	...

		⚒	⚒	Ⓑ	Ⓑ	⚒	⚒	Ⓑ	Ⓑ	⚒	⚒		†	⚒	⚒	⚒	⚒			Ⓑ	Ⓑ			Ⓐ	Ⓐ		
Iglesias d.	...	...	0921	1018	...	...	1121	1218	...	...	1321	1418	...	...	...	1521	1552	1618	...	...	1721	1818	...	...	1921	2018	...
Carbonia Serbariu d.	0810	0910	|	|	1010	1110	|	|	1210	1310	|	|	1410	1410	1510	|	|	|	1610	1710	|	|	1810	1910	|	|	2010
Villamassargia d.	0831	0926	0931	1026	1031	1126	1131	1226	1231	1326	1331	1426	1431	1431	1526	1531	1601	1626	1631	1726	1731	1826	1831	1926	1931	2026	2031
Decimomannu d.	0856	...	0956	...	1057	...	1156	...	1257	...	1356	...	1456	1500	...	1556	1631	...	1656	...	1756	...	1857	...	1956	...	2059
Elmas Aeroporto ✈ d.	0909	...	1009	...	1009	...	1208	...	1310	...	1409	...	1509	1515	...	1607	1639	...	1711	...	1807	...	1911	...	2009	...	2113
Cagliari a.	0915	...	1015	...	1117	...	1215	...	1317	...	1415	...	1516	1522	...	1614	1645	...	1717	...	1814	...	1917	...	2015	...	2120

Narrow gauge services on Sardinia are operated by ARST (www.arst.sardegna.it). Regular services operate on the following routes: Alghero - Sassari, Sassari - Sorso, Macomer - Nuoro and Monserrato Gottardo - Isili. Tram connections are available Monserrato Gottardo - Cagliari Repubblica and v.v. *Trenino Verde della Sardegna* operates tourist trains (www.treninoverde.com).

629 SARDINIA 2nd class

FOR CAGLIARI - CARBONIA / IGLESIAS, SEE PREVIOUS PAGE.

CAGLIARI - SASSARI - GOLFO ARANCI

km		⚒		⚒	⚒	†	†	†	⚒	⚒	⚒🚌	†	†	†	⚒	⚒	⚒	†	†	⚒	⚒	⚒	⚒	†	⚒	⚒	⚒
0	**Cagliari** d.	...	...	...	...	...	...	...	0630	...	...	0624	...	...	0722	0835	0925	0933	1014	...	...	...	1040	1110	1112	...	...
7	Elmas Aeroporto ✈ d.	...	...	...	...	...	...	...	│	...	...	0630	...	...	0729	0842	0931	0939	1020	...	...	...	1046	1116	1117	...	...
17	Decimomannu d.	...	...	...	...	...	...	...	0641	...	...	0638	...	...	0737	│	0939	0947	1032	...	...	...	│	1129	1131	...	...
95	**Oristano** d.	...	...	...	...	...	...	...	0730	...	...	0730	...	...	0830	0931	1048	1046	1136	...	...	...	1134	1225	1232	...	...
154	Macomer d.	...	...	...	...	...	...	...	0824	...	...	0821	...	...	▬	1024	1144	1142	...	...	...	...	1227	▬	...	...	...
	Sassari d.	...	...	0600	...	...	...	...	│	...	...	...	...	...	...	│	▬	...	...	1120	...	...	│	...	...	...	...
214	Ozieri-Chilivani a.	...	...	0639	...	...	...	...	0903	...	...	0904	...	...	...	1104	⚒	...	...	1210	...	...	│	...	...	...	...
214	Ozieri-Chilivani d.	...	...	0644	0645	0745	...	0748	0906	0910	...	0914	0912	1105	...	1109	1109	...	...	1212	...	...	│	⚒	...	1441	...
261	**Sassari** d.	...	0650	│	0742	0824	0835	│	│	0950	...	0952	│	│	...	│	1149	...	...	│	...	...	1339	1345	...	1525	1530
280	Porto Torres a.	...	0704	│	0801	...	0848	│	│	...	...	...	│	│	...	│	...	...	...	│	...	...	...	1400	...	...	1545
281	Porto Torres Marittima a.	...	0707	│	0804	...	0852	│	│	...	...	...	│	│	†	│	...	...	...	│	...	...	...	1404	...	...	1549
285	Olbia a.	0640	...	0747	...	...	...	0852	1002	...	1010	...	1015	1211	1227	1206	...	...	...	1316	1337	1450	...	...	...	...	...
306	**Golfo Aranci** a.	0704	...	...	...	...	...	...	...	...	1042	...	...	...	1252	...	...	...	...	...	1402	1514	...	...	...	...	...

	†	†	⚒	⚒	⚒	†	†	⚒	⚒	Ⓐ	⚒	⚒	⚒	†	†	†	⚒	†	⚒	⚒	†	⚒	⚒🚌	⚒	†		🚌
Cagliari d.	1222	...	1222	...	1325	1413	...	1430	...	...	1522	1630	...	1640	...	1713	1720	1820	1830	...	1915	1920	...	2035	2040	2200	...
Elmas Aeroporto ✈ d.	1229	...	1229	...	1332	1419	...	1437	...	...	1529	1636	...	1647	...	1719	1726	1826	1836	...	1921	1926	...	2041	2046	2208	...
Decimomannu d.	1238	...	1237	...	1341	1428	...	│	...	...	1537	│	...	│	...	1732	1739	1834	│	...	1934	1940	...	2050	2055	2226	2231
Oristano d.	1331	...	1330	...	1438	1531	...	1534	...	...	1632	1731	...	1742	...	1829	1841	1928	1936	...	2034	2050	2056	2154	2201	...	0021
Macomer d.	1431	...	1431	...	1535	1629	...	1631	...	...	▬	1819	...	1830	...	▬	...	2028	2024	2036	▬	▬	2216	...	...	...	...
Sassari d.	│	...	│	...	▬	│	1630	│	1628	...	...	│	...	│	...	...	...	│	│	│	...	...	...	...	...	...	...
Ozieri-Chilivani a.	1516	...	1516	...	...	1712	1712	1709	1708	...	...	1858	...	1908	...	†	...	2117	│	2123	⚒	†	...	...	...	...	...
Ozieri-Chilivani d.	1521	1521	1524	1522	...	1719	1718	1717	1714	...	...	1901	1903	1915	1913	1954	...	2125	│	2125	2128	2130	...	...	...	...	...
Sassari d.	│	1600	│	1601	...	1800	│	1759	│	...	...	│	1947	1954	│	2030	...	...	2134	│	2208	2210	...	...	...	...	...
Porto Torres a.	│	...	│	...	...	1812	│	1811	│	...	Ⓒ	│	...	...	│	...	...	...	...	│	...	...	...	...	...	...	...
Porto Torres Marittima a.	│	...	│	...	...	1816	│	1816	│	...	🚌	│	...	...	│	...	...	...	...	│	...	...	...	...	...	...	...
Olbia a.	1623	...	1634	...	1650	...	1823	...	1825	1830	1830	1959	...	...	2016	...	...	2224	...	2228	...	...	...	...	...	...	...
Golfo Aranci a.	...	...	...	...	1714	...	...	...	...	1854	1902	...	...	...	...	...	...	...	...	...	...	...	...	...	...	...	...

		⚒🚌	⚒	⚒🚌	⚒	†	⚒	⚒	⚒	†	†		⚒	†	†	⚒	⚒	†	†	⚒	⚒	⚒	†	⚒🚌	†	⚒	†
Golfo Aranci d.	...	...	...	...	...	...	...	...	...	...	...	...	...	...	...	0715	...	...	...	...	...	...	...	1050	...	...	...
Olbia d.	...	...	...	...	...	...	...	0537	...	0632	...	...	...	...	0757	0738	0803	...	0946	1004	...	...	...	1122	...	...	...
Porto Torres Marittima d.	...	...	...	...	...	...	...	│	...	│	...	0718	...	...	│	...	...	...	│	│	0952	...	1005	▬	...	...	...
Porto Torres d.	...	...	...	...	...	...	...	│	...	│	...	0721	...	...	│	...	...	...	│	│	0955	...	1008	...	...	...	...
Sassari d.	...	...	...	...	...	...	0600	│	0630	│	0704	0736	0820	0826	│	...	0924	...	│	│	1010	1023	1022	...	...	...	...
Ozieri-Chilivani a.	...	...	...	...	...	...	0639	0640	│	0740	0742	▬	0859	0905	0909	...	0902	1013	1101	1103	...	1100	1100	...	...	...	...
Ozieri-Chilivani d.	...	...	...	...	...	...	...	0644	│	...	0750	...	...	...	0911	...	0905	...	1105	1109	...	1108	1108	...	...	...	...
Sassari a.	...	...	...	...	...	...	...	│	│	...	│	...	...	...	│	...	│	...	1146	1149	...	│	│	...	...	...	...
Macomer d.	...	0510	...	0605	...	...	...	0731	0743	...	0839	⚒	...	...	0956	...	0945	...	...	...	...	1146	1151	⚒	...	1341	...
Oristano d.	0530	0620	0630	0725	0730	0730	...	...	0831	...	0925	0930	...	...	1046	...	1031	...	...	...	...	1233	1237	1330	1430	1437	1530
Decimomannu d.	0629	...	0721	...	0821	0829	...	...	│	...	1015	1027	...	...	1144	...	│	...	...	...	...	│	1343	1422	1530	1538	1624
Elmas Aeroporto ✈ d.	0637	...	0729	...	0830	0837	...	...	0921	...	1022	1041	...	...	1152	...	1118	...	...	...	...	1320	1351	1430	1545	1546	1639
Cagliari a.	0643	...	0737	...	0837	0843	...	...	0928	...	1029	1048	...	...	1159	...	1125	...	...	...	...	1327	1358	1438	1552	1554	1646

	⚒	†	†	†	⚒	⚒	⚒	⚒	†	⚒	⚒	⚒	†	⚒		⚒	⚒	†	⚒	†	†	Ⓐ	Ⓒ🚌	⚒	⚒	†	†
Golfo Aranci d.	...	1301	...	...	...	...	...	1415	...	...	1525	...	...	...	1725	...	...	...	...	...	...	1905	1905	...	...	...	...
Olbia d.	1330	1325	1410	...	1415	...	...	1439	...	...	1549	1608	1554	...	1749	1757	...	...	...	1838	...	1929	1937	...	2015	...	2018
Porto Torres Marittima d.	│	...	│	...	│	1415	...	▬	...	1605	▬	│	│	...	▬	│	1830	1840	...	│	...	...	...	...	│	...	│
Porto Torres d.	│	...	│	...	│	1418	...	...	...	1608	⚒	│	│	...	⚒	│	1833	1843	...	│	...	...	...	...	│	...	│
Sassari d.	│	...	│	1433	│	1433	1439	...	...	1623	1628	│	│	...	1815	│	1848	1858	1900	│	1904	...	...	2031	│	2032	│
Ozieri-Chilivani a.	1439	...	1514	1511	1520	...	1518	...	...	...	1708	1707	1712	...	1855	1856	...	...	│	1949	1949	...	...	2120	2123	2113	2124
Ozieri-Chilivani d.	1441	...	1521	1519	1522	...	1525	...	...	...	...	1713	▬	...	...	1900	...	...	│	...	1956	...	...	...	2128	...	2130
Sassari a.	1525	...	1600	│	1601	...	│	⚒	...	...	...	│	...	...	...	│	...	...	│	...	│	...	...	...	2208	...	2210
Macomer d.	...	...	...	1558	...	...	1605	1632	1729	...	...	1752	†	...	...	1940	...	...	2024	...	2048	...	...	...	...	...	...
Oristano d.	...	...	...	1654	...	...	1649	1732	1830	...	...	1848	1930	1936	...	2032	...	...	2116	...	2137	...	...	...	...	...	...
Decimomannu d.	...	...	...	1745	...	...	│	1833	1936	...	...	│	2029	2036	...	│	...	...	2216	...	2235	...	...	...	...	...	...
Elmas Aeroporto ✈ d.	...	...	...	1752	...	...	1737	1847	1944	...	...	1936	2043	2043	...	2121	...	...	2225	...	2242	...	...	...	...	...	...
Cagliari a.	...	...	...	1800	...	...	1744	1853	1951	...	...	1943	2050	2049	...	2128	...	...	2232	...	2249	...	...	...	...	...	...

632 FOGGIA - POTENZA 2nd class

km				⚒	⚒	†			†	⚒🚌	⚒	†	⚒🚌	⚒			⚒🚌	⚒	⚒	†	⚒				🚌
0	**Foggia** d.	0506	0534	0620	0645	0645	...	0842	1029	1120	...	1137	1300	...	1424	...	1630	...	1752	1752	1830	...	2057	...	2250
67	Melfi d.	0555	0633	0723	0757	0748	...	0942	1124	1210	1238	1232	1410	1420	1534	...	1720	1729	1849	1850	1930	...	2156	...	2340
119	**Potenza** Centrale a.	0705	0758	0837	0917	0919	...	1101	1237	...	1347	1347	...	1530	1644	...	...	1850	2000	2000	2051	...	2256	...	0053

		⚒	†	⚒	⚒🚌		⚒	†		⚒	⚒🚌			⚒	⚒🚌	⚒	†						
Potenza Centrale d.	0528	0618	0715	0715	...	...	0840	0842	...	0936	...	...	1128	1234	...	1330	1330	...	1704	1816	...	2010	...	2111
Melfi d.	0636	0726	0826	0847	0856	...	0945	0945	...	1055	1110	...	1229	1350	1410	1448	1452	...	1815	1933	...	2119	...	2224
Foggia a.	0746	0823	0935	...	0946	...	1040	1040	...	...	1200	...	1329	...	1500	1558	1558	...	1931	2032	...	2222	...	2321

633 PAOLA - COSENZA - SIBARI 2nd class

km		⚒	⚒	⚒◇	⚒			Ⓒ			⑥	Ⓐ		⚒	◇	⚒		Ⓑ	⚒	⚒◇	Ⓐ	Ⓐ	Ⓑ	Ⓑ	
	Napoli Centrale **640** d.	...	...	...	...	...	...	0650	...	0850	...	...	...	...	...	...	1250	...	...	...	...	...	...	...	1914
0	**Paola** d.	0651	0718	0748	0816	0916	1016	1026	...	1216	1306	1345	1416	1519	1546	1616	1646	1716	1819	1846	1916	1948	2015	2129	2258
21	Castiglione Cosentino d.	0705	0734	0803	0831	0931	1031	1040	...	1231	1321	1400	1431	1534	1601	1631	1701	1731	1834	1901	1931	2001	2031	2144	2313
26	**Cosenza** a.	0712	0739	0809	0837	0937	1037	1047	...	1236	1327	1406	1437	1540	1607	1637	1707	1737	1840	1907	1937	2007	2037	2150	2320

	⚒		⚒△		Ⓐ	Ⓑ		⚒	⚒	Ⓐ	Ⓒ	Ⓐ	Ⓒ	⚒	Ⓐ		⚒	Ⓐ	⚒	⚒	†			Ⓐ
Cosenza d.	0523	0558	0615	0623	0723	0823	0923	1050	1123	1223	1314	1320	1323	1353	1423	1453	1523	1623	1653	1723	1753	1823	1853	2023
Castiglione Cosentino d.	0530	0604	0621	0630	0732	0830	0930	1057	1130	1230	1321	1327	1330	1400	1430	1459	1533	1630	1700	1730	1800	1833	1900	2030
Paola a.	0545	0620	0637	0645	0747	0845	0945	1112	1145	1245	1337	1342	1345	1414	1445	1514	1548	1645	1715	1745	1815	1847	1915	2045
Napoli Centrale **640** a.	...	1010	...	...	...	...	...	...	...	...	1738	...	...	...	...	1908	...	...	...	...	...	...	2258b	...

km			⚒		Ⓑ		⚒	Ⓐ		Ⓑ	
0	**Cosenza** d.	0516	0716	...	1142	...	1415	1542	1742	1942	...
5	Castiglione Cosentino d.	0522	0726	...	1148	...	1421	1548	1748	1948	...
70	**Sibari** a.	0614	0813	...	1235	...	1510	1635	1835	2035	...

	Ⓐ				⚒	Ⓑ		⚒	Ⓑ
Sibari d.	0525	0640	0825	...	1325	1525	...	1725	1925
Castiglione Cosentino d.	0618	0725	0910	...	1411	1618	...	1818	2018
Cosenza a.	0625	0732	0917	...	1418	1625	...	1825	2025

b – 2308 until Mar. 26.

◇ – 2–4 minutes later on ⚒ until Mar. 25.

△ – 5–7 minutes **earlier** on ⚒ until Mar. 25.

☛ Certain services Cosenza - Paola and v.v. run to / from Reggio di Calabria (see Table **640**).

☛ For *FA* train Bolzano - Roma - Paola - Sibari, see Tables **600** and **640**.

634 CATANZARO - LAMEZIA TERME 2nd class

km		⚒		⚒			Ⓐ	†		⚒	†	⚒	Ⓐ			Ⓐ			Ⓐ					
0	**Catanzaro** Lido d.	0528	0628	0735	0829	0935	1028	1035	...	1335	1428	1431	1528	1628	1735	1828	1935	...	2128	...	...	...	...	...
9	Catanzaro d.	0536	0636	0743	0837	0943	1036	1043	...	1343	1436	1439	1536	1636	1743	1836	1943	...	2136	...	...	...	...	...
47	**Lamezia Terme** Centrale a.	0620	0720	0820	0920	1020	1122	1120	...	1420	1520	1520	1620	1720	1820	1920	2020	...	2213	...	...	...	...	...

	⚒	⚒			†	Ⓐ			⚒	Ⓑ	Ⓑ	⚒		⚒	Ⓐ								
Lamezia Terme Centrale d.	0540	0640	0740	0840	0940	1040	...	1240	1340	1435	1540	1640	1740	1840	1940	2040	...	...	...	...	...	...	...
Catanzaro d.	0616	0716	0820	0916	1021	1116	...	1316	1421	1516	1616	1716	1819	1916	2021	2116	...	...	...	...	...	...	...
Catanzaro Lido a.	0625	0725	0828	0925	1030	1125	...	1325	1430	1525	1625	1725	1827	1925	2030	2125	...	...	...	...	...	...	...

NO SERVICE ON SUNDAYS OR PUBLIC HOLIDAYS

SUD EST SERVICES

Line 1 : BARI - TARANTO

km			⚒	⚒	⚒	⚒	⚒	⚒	⚒	⚒	⚒	⚒		⚒	⚒	⚒🚌	⚒	⚒	⚒	⚒🚌	⚒		⚒	⚒	⚒
0	**Bari** Centrale	d.	...	...	...	...	...	0521	...	0621	...	0721	...	0821	...	0835	...	0921	...	...	1021	...	1121	...	...
1	Bari Sud Est	d.	...	...	...	...	...	0525	...	0625	...	0725	...	0825	...	0839	...	0925	...	...	1025	...	1125	...	...
4	Mungivacca	d.	...	...	...	...	...	0535	...	0635	...	0735	...	0835	...	|	...	0935	...	...	1035	...	1135	...	...
	Casamassima	d.	...	...	...	...	...	0608	...	0708	...	0808	...	0908	...	|	...	1008	...	...	1108	...	1208	...	...
43	Putignano	a.	...	0501	...	0630	...	0639	0709	0739	0744	0839	...	0939	0944	1000	1013	1039	1047	...	1139	...	1239	1248	...
78	Martina Franca **2**	d.	0530	0556	0637	0730	0741	...	0801	...	0841	...	...	...	1035	...	1108	...	1139	1210	...	...	...	1345	1353
113	**Taranto**	a.	0625	...	0733	...	0839	...	...	...	...	...	...	...	...	...	...	...	...	1302	...	...	...	...	1449

km			⚒	⚒	⚒	⚒	⚒	⚒	⚒	⚒	⚒🚌	⚒	⚒	⚒	⚒🚌	⚒	⚒	⚒	⚒	⚒	⚒	⚒	⚒	⚒	⚒
	Bari Centrale	d.	1221	...	...	1321	...	1421	...	...	1455	...	...	1521	1550	...	1621	1721	...	1821	...	1921	...	2021	2051
	Bari Sud Est	d.	1225	...	...	1325	...	1425	...	...	1459	...	...	1525	1554	...	1625	1725	...	1825	...	1925	...	2025	2055
0	Mungivacca	d.	1235	...	...	1335	...	1435	...	...	|	...	...	1535	|	...	1635	1735	...	1835	...	1935	...	2035	2105
20	Casamassima	d.	1308	...	...	1408	...	1508	...	...	|	...	...	1608	|	...	1708	1808	...	1908	...	2008	...	2108	2138
44	Putignano	a.	1339	1349	...	1439	1515	1539	1555	...	1620	1625	...	1639	1715	1730	1739	1839	1855	1939	1955	2039	2101	2139	2209
	Martina Franca **2**	d.	...	1446	1500	...	1612	...	1648	1705	...	1716	1755	...	...	1822	...	...	1951	...	2051	...	2153	...	...
	Taranto	a.	...	...	1556	...	...	...	...	1801	...	...	1851	...	...	...	...	...	...	...	...	...	...	...	...

		⚒	⚒	⚒	⚒	⚒	⚒	⚒	⚒🚌	⚒	⚒	⚒	⚒	⚒	⚒🚌	⚒	⚒	⚒	⚒	⚒		⚒	⚒	⚒
Taranto	d.	...	...	...	...	...	...	...	...	...	...	...	0635	...	...	...	0740	0846	...	...	...	...	...	...
Martina Franca **2**	d.	...	0442	...	0511	...	...	0611	...	...	0708	...	0735	0820	...	...	0836	0938	0950	...	...	...	1147	...
Putignano	d.	0518	0533	0554	0605	0613	0654	0704	0715	0754	0816	0854	...	0910	0925	0954	...	...	1043	1054	...	1154	1239	1254
Casamassima	d.	0547	...	0628	...	0646	0728	...	|	0828	...	0928	...	...	|	1028	...	...	...	1128	...	1228	...	1328
Mungivacca	d.	0634	...	0704	...	0734	0804	...	|	0904	...	1004	...	...	|	1104	...	...	...	1204	...	1304	...	1404
Bari Sud Est	a.	0640	...	0710	...	0740	0810	...	0836	0910	...	1010	...	...	1046	1110	...	...	...	1210	...	1310	...	1410
Bari Centrale	a.	0644	...	0714	...	0744	0814	...	0840	0914	...	1014	...	...	1050	1114	...	...	...	1214	...	1314	...	1414

		⚒	⚒	⚒	⚒	⚒	⚒	⚒	⚒	⚒	⚒	⚒🚌	⚒	⚒	⚒	⚒	⚒	⚒🚌	⚒	⚒	⚒	⚒	⚒🚌	⚒
Taranto	d.	...	...	...	...	...	...	...	...	1515	...	...	...	1602	...	...	...	...	...	1812	1900	...	...	...
Martina Franca **2**	d.	1223	...	1325	1400	...	1456	...	...	1617	1625	...	...	1658	1735	...	1835	...	...	1912	1956	2005	...	2131
Putignano	d.	1320	1354	1421	1451	1454	1549	1554	1654	...	1726	1735	1754	...	1830	1854	1927	1935	1954	...	...	2055	2100	2228
Casamassima	d.	...	1428	...	...	1528	...	1628	1728	...	...	|	1828	...	...	1928	...	|	2028	...	...	...	|	...
Mungivacca	d.	...	1504	...	...	1604	...	1704	1804	...	...	|	1904	...	...	2004	...	|	2104	...	...	...	|	...
Bari Sud Est	a.	...	1510	...	...	1610	...	1710	1810	...	...	1856	1910	...	...	2010	...	2056	2110	...	...	...	2221	...
Bari Centrale	a.	...	1514	...	...	1614	...	1714	1814	...	...	1900	1914	...	...	2014	...	2100	2114	...	...	...	2225	...

Line 2 : MARTINA FRANCA - LECCE

km			⚒		⚒		⚒		⚒		⚒		⚒	⚒		⚒		⚒		⚒						
0	**Martina Franca 1**	d.	0457	...	0540	...	0713	...	0854	...	1155	...	1308	...	...	1519	...	1740	...	1833	...	...	...	...	...	...
41	Francavilla Fontana	d.	0556	...	0646	...	0819	...	0954	...	1254	...	1408	1414	...	1621	...	1838	...	1934	...	...	...	...	...	...
92	Novoli **3**	d.	0720	...	0809	...	0937	...	1133	...	1418	...	...	1537	...	1750	...	1957	...	2054	...	...	...	...	...	...
103	**Lecce 5**	a.	0737	...	0825	...	0952	...	1149	...	1434	...	...	1552	...	1805	...	2012	...	2110	...	...	...	...	...	...

		⚒		⚒		⚒		⚒		⚒	⚒		⚒		⚒		⚒		⚒						
Lecce 5	d.	0417	...	0551	...	0704	...	0905	...	1230	...	...	1347	...	1440	...	1655	...	1832	...	...	...	...	...	...
Novoli **3**	d.	0433	...	0606	...	0719	...	0921	...	1246	...	...	1402	...	1455	...	1710	...	1848	...	...	...	...	...	...
Francavilla Fontana	d.	0557	...	0730	...	0903	...	1047	...	1405	1411	...	1527	...	1620	...	1839	...	2017	...	...	...	...	...	...
Martina Franca 1	a.	0655	...	0828	...	1005	...	1148	...	...	1511	...	1630	...	1721	...	1947	...	2114	...	...	...	...	...	...

Line 3 : LECCE - NOVOLI - NARDÒ - GAGLIANO

km			⚒	⚒	⚒	⚒	⚒	⚒	⚒	⚒		⚒	⚒G
0	**Lecce 5**	d.	0516	...	0833	1007	1118	1305	1500	1611	...	1925	2035
11	Novoli **2**	d.	0536	0726	0853	1027	1138	1325	1529	1631	...	1945	2101
36	Nardò Centrale **5**	d.	0619	0813	0941	1110	1224	1409	1616	1716	...	2033	2149
60	Casarano **4**	d.	0717	0856	1026	1157	1311	1451	1703	1804	...	2116	...
85	**Gagliano Leuca 6**	a.	0759	0937	1108	1239	1353	1532	1746	1855	...	2157	...

		⚒	⚒	⚒	⚒	⚒	⚒	⚒	⚒		⚒	⚒
Gagliano Leuca 6	d.	...	0634	0811	0943	1114	1248	1406	1543	...	1752	1906
Casarano **4**	d.	0550	0716	0857	1025	1156	1335	1452	1625	...	1834	1948
Nardò Centrale **5**	d.	0632	0800	0940	1111	1238	1421	1535	1717	...	1917	2034
Novoli **2**	d.	0714	0848	1028	1200	1327	1515	1627	1808	...	2013	2123
Lecce 5		...	0903	1044	1216	1342	1532	1643	1824	...	2028	2139

Line 4 : CASARANO - GALLIPOLI

km			⚒		⚒		⚒	⚒		⚒	⚒		⚒
0	Casarano **3**	d.	0719	...	0919	...	1325	1459	...	1639	1819	...	1959
22	Gallipoli **5**	a.	0755	...	0955	...	1401	1535	...	1715	1855	...	2035

		⚒	⚒	⚒		⚒		⚒	⚒		⚒	⚒
Gallipoli **5**	d.	0503	0633	0813	...	1233	...	1413	1553	...	1733	1913
Casarano **3**	a.	0539	0710	0850	...	1310	...	1450	1630	...	1810	1950

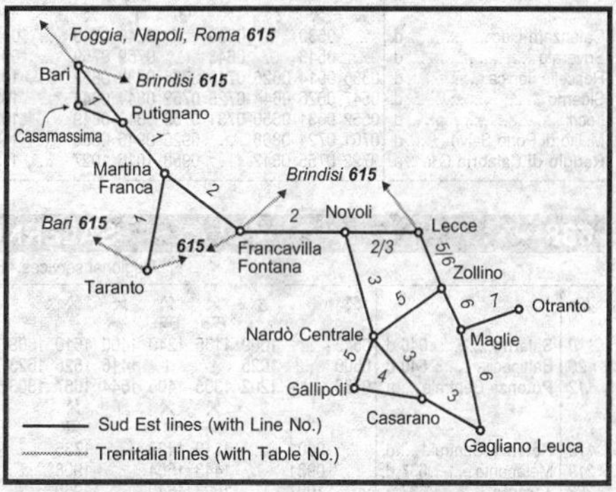

Line 5 : LECCE - GALLIPOLI

km			⚒	⚒		⚒	⚒	⚒		⚒	⚒	⚒		⚒	⚒	⚒		⚒	⚒							
0	**Lecce 2**	d.	0600	0700	...	0900	1000	1103	...	1303	1400	1500	...	1703	1800	1900	...	2035	2100	...	...	...	...	...	...	...
19	Zollino **6**	d.	0635	0737	...	0939	1039	1139	...	1339	1443	1539	...	1739	1839	1939	...	|	2139	...	...	...	...	...	...	...
36	Nardò Centrale **3**	d.	0709	0809	...	1009	1109	1209	...	1409	1511	1609	...	1809	1909	2009	...	2149	2209	...	...	...	...	...	...	...
53	**Gallipoli 4**	a.	0743	0843	...	1040	1143	1240	...	1443	1543	1640	...	1843	1943	2043	...	2217	2240	...	...	...	...	...	...	...

		⚒	⚒	⚒	⚒		⚒		⚒	⚒	⚒		⚒	⚒	⚒	⚒									
Gallipoli 4	d.	0607	0707	0807	0907	...	1107	...	1307	1407	1505	...	1707	1807	1907	2007	...	...	...	...	...	...	...	...	...
Nardò Centrale **3**	d.	0637	0737	0837	0937	...	1137	...	1337	1437	1538	...	1737	1837	1937	2037	...	...	...	...	...	...	...	...	...
Zollino **6**	d.	0706	0812	0912	1012	...	1212	...	1412	1512	1612	...	1812	1912	2012	2112	...	...	...	...	...	...	...	...	...
Lecce 2	a.	0750	0850	0947	1050	...	1250	...	1447	1550	1650	...	1847	1950	2047	2147	...	...	...	...	...	...	...	...	...

Line 6 : LECCE - ZOLLINO - GAGLIANO

km			⚒		⚒	⚒		⚒	⚒		⚒	⚒	⚒	⚒		⚒	⚒		⚒	⚒		⚒				
0	**Lecce 2**	d.	0530	...	0700	...	...	0900	...	...	1030	1130	1230	1330	...	1530	1630	...	1800	...	...	1930	...	...	...	...
19	Zollino **5**	d.	0604	...	0735	0738	...	0938	0948	...	1105	1215	1305	1409	...	1613	1707	...	1838	1842	...	2015	...	...	...	...
29	Maglie **7**	d.	0624	...	...	0758	...	...	1007	...	1127	1235	1325	1428	...	1632	1725	...	...	1901	...	2035	...	...	...	...
66	**Gagliano Leuca 3**	a.	0729	...	...	0911	...	...	1119	...	1244	1344	1443	1548	...	1738	...	...	...	2009	...	2140	...	...	...	...

		⚒	⚒	⚒	⚒	⚒		⚒		⚒		⚒	⚒	⚒		⚒	⚒	⚒		⚒	⚒H				
Gagliano Leuca 3	d.	0515	0533	...	0626	...	...	0809	...	1014	...	1207	1305	1405	...	1634	...	...	...	1809					
Maglie **7**	d.	0625	0642	...	0733	...	...	0916	...	1121	...	1322	1425	1516	...	1744	...	1823	...	1919	2018	...	...	...	...
Zollino **5**	d.	0642	0701	0706	0755	0812	...	0941	...	1142	...	1342	1442	1541	...	1803	1812	1842	...	1941	2042	...	...	...	...
Lecce 2	a.	0720	...	0750	...	0850	...	1020	...	1218	...	1420	1520	1617	...	...	1847	1920	...	2017	2120	...	...	...	...

Line 7 : MAGLIE - OTRANTO.

km			⚒	⚒	⚒	⚒	⚒	⚒	⚒	⚒	⚒	
0	Maglie **6**	d.	0630	0805	1010	1130	1331	1520	1635	1748	1905	...
18	Otranto	a.	0659	0834	1039	1159	1400	1549	1704	1817	1934	...

		⚒	⚒		⚒	⚒	⚒	⚒	⚒	⚒	⚒H
Otranto	d.	0707	0842	...	1047	1244	1442	1558	1711	1827	1948
Maglie **6**	a.	0736	0911	...	1116	1313	1511	1627	1740	1856	2017

G – To Gallipoli (Line 5).

H – 🚌 Otranto - Maglie - Lecce.

636 BARI - MATERA
2nd class FAL

km																										
		⚒		⚒		⚒			⚒	⚒	⚒		⚒	⚒	⚒	⚒	⚒	⚒	⚒	⚒		⚒	⚒	⚒	⚒	⚒
0	**Bari** Centrale d.	0506	...	0617	...	0751	...	...	0959	1048	1139	...	1248	1339	1410	1513	1558	1653	1742	1808	...	1917	2003	2059	2122	2210
48	Altamura a.	0619	...	0731	...	0902	...	...	1110	1204	1256	...	1403	1450	1520	1630	1710	1806	1852	1920	...	2030	2112	2215	2234	2320
		⚒	⚒	⚒		⚒		⚒	⚒	⚒	⚒		⚒		⚒	⚒	⚒	⚒		⚒		⚒	⚒	⚒		⚒🚌
48	Altamura d.	0623	0701	0737	...	0909	...	1031	1117	1212	1258	...	1412	...	1522	1633	1714	1808	...	1924	...	2035	2119	2218	...	2323
76	**Matera** Centrale a.	0652	0732	0805	...	0937	...	1059	1148	1242	1326	...	1441	...	1551	1701	1746	1836	...	1954	...	2106	2150	2246	...	2351

			⚒	⚒	⚒	⚒	⚒		⚒		⚒	⚒		⚒	⚒	⚒	⚒		⚒		⚒	⚒		⚒	⚒
Matera Centrale d.	...	...	0549	0622	0704	0753	0837	...	1002	...	1114	1205	...	1341	1428	1521	1605	...	1717	...	1824	1923	...	2038	2122
Altamura a.	...	...	0616	0653	0733	0823	0904	...	1029	...	1143	1235	...	1408	1457	1552	1632	...	1745	...	1854	1953	...	2107	2151
	⚒	⚒	⚒	⚒	⚒	⚒	⚒	⚒	⚒		⚒	⚒		⚒	⚒	⚒	⚒		⚒		⚒	⚒		⚒	⚒
Altamura d.	0452	0602	0624	0657	0739	0827	0906	0948	1035	...	1147	1239	...	1413	1500	1556	1635	...	1749	...	1900	1957	...	2113	2155
Bari Centrale a.	0603	0714	0735	0807	0851	0939	1015	1101	1152	...	1301	1352	...	1528	1614	1709	1755	...	1905	...	2017	2112	...	2224	2310

Operator: Ferrovie Appulo Lucane. ✆ (+39) 800 050 500. www.ferrovieappulolucane.it

637 REGGIO DI CALABRIA - SIBARI - TARANTO
2nd class

km											*IC* **564**				*IC* **562**												
						⚒		⚒	Ⓐ			Ⓐ				⚒	†	⚒	Ⓐ	⚒	Ⓐ		⚒	⚒	Ⓐ	⚒	Ⓑ
0	**Reggio di Calabria** C.le d.	...	...	...	0500	...	...	0547	0547	0708	0800	0808	...	1108	1210	1308	1308	1408	1508	...	1608	1708	...	1808	1925	...	2008
30	Melito di Porto Salvo d.	...	...	...	0523	...	...	0619	0619	0731	0828	0839	...	1131	1235	1331	1331	1439	1531	...	1639	1731	...	1839	1950	...	2039
96	Locri d.	...	...	...	0616	0652	...	0735	0735	0824	0923	0953	...	1218	1328	1424	1424	1553	1624	1650	1755	1824	1852	1954	2050	2117	2154
101	Siderno d.	...	...	...	0627	0659	...	0740	0740	0830	0929	0959	...	1223	1336	1430	1430	1559	1630	1657	1800	1830	1859	2000	2058	2127	2200
112	Roccella Jonica d.	...	...	...	0642	0714	...	0755	0756	0847	0944	1015	...	1235	1354	1444	1442	1615	1642	1710	1818	1842	1914	2015	2114	2142	2215
160	Soverato d.	...	...	...	0717	0759	...	...	0835	0918	1028	...	...	1313	1426	1518	1519	▬	1713	1803	▬	1917	1959	▬	2146	...	...
178	Catanzaro Lido a.	...	...	...	0730	0818	...	...	0850	0930	1042	...	...	1330	1439	1530	1533	...	1730	1818	...	1930	2018	...	2200	...	...
			⚒		⚒		Ⓑ				|			⚒	|	⚒	†	Ⓐ	Ⓐ			Ⓐ	⚒	Ⓐ			
178	Catanzaro Lido d.	...	0540	0635	0740	...	0840	...	...	...	1044	...	1240	1340	1441	1540	1540	1630	1740	...	1835	1940	2040	2127	...	...	...
238	**Crotone** d.	0500	0624	0734	0830	...	0930	...	...	...	1139	...	1324	1430	1530	1632	1632	1730	1831	...	1926	2030	2125	2212	...	...	...
325	Rossano d.	0557	0753	0858	...	...	...	...	...	...	1241	...	1439	1554	1643	1745	1747	1851	1950	...	2053	2142	...	...	...	...	...
336	Corigliano Calabro d.	0605	0802	0907	...	...	...	...	...	...	1256	...	1453	1603	1658	1758	1756	1900	2001	...	2102	2151	...	...	...	...	...
351	**Sibari** a.	0617	0815	0920	...	...	...	...	...	...	1307	...	1505	1615	1712	1815	1810	1915	2015	...	2115	2204	...	...	...	...	...
351	**Sibari** d.	...	...	...	...	...	...	...	...	...	1309	...	...	...	1714	...	...	...	...	...	...	...	...	...	...	...	...
366	Trebisacce d.	...	...	...	...	...	...	...	...	...	1321	...	...	...	1726	...	...	...	...	...	...	...	...	...	...	...	...
430	Metaponto 638 d.	...	...	...	...	...	...	...	...	...	1404	...	...	...	1812	...	...	...	...	...	...	...	...	...	...	...	...
473	**Taranto** 638 a.	...	...	...	...	...	...	...	...	...	1437	...	...	...	1850	...	...	...	...	...	...	...	...	...	...	...	...

												IC **558**							*IC* **566**								
				⚒			⚒	⚒			Ⓑ			Ⓐ		⚒		Ⓐ			⚒	Ⓑ	Ⓐ	Ⓐ	Ⓒ	Ⓐ	
Taranto 638 d.	...	...	...	...	...	...	...	...	...	...	...	0830	...	...	...	...	...	...	1306	...	...	...	...	...	...	...	...
Metaponto 638 d.	...	...	...	...	...	...	...	...	...	...	...	0859	...	...	...	...	...	...	1335	...	...	...	...	...	...	...	...
Trebisacce d.	...	...	...	...	...	...	...	...	...	...	...	0941	...	...	...	...	...	...	1429	...	...	...	...	...	...	...	...
Sibari a.	...	...	...	...	...	...	...	...	...	...	...	0953	...	...	...	...	...	...	1440	...	...	...	...	...	...	...	...
Sibari d.	...	...	...	...	...	...	0505	0550	0700	...	...	0955	...	...	...	...	1245	1345	1442	...	1545	1645	...	1745	1845	1845	2241
Corigliano Calabro d.	...	...	...	...	...	...	0517	0606	0712	...	...	1008	...	...	...	...	1256	1357	1453	...	1603	1657	...	1757	1857	1900	2254
Rossano d.	...	...	...	...	...	...	0526	0617	0720	...	...	1017	...	...	...	...	1304	1405	1502	...	1612	1705	...	1805	1908	1911	2302
Crotone d.	...	...	...	0535	...	...	0639	0733	0835	...	0935	1120	...	1235	...	1335	1430	1530	1611	...	1730	1831	...	1943	2030	2030	2359
Catanzaro Lido a.	...	...	...	0625	...	...	0725	0820	0925	...	1025	1208	...	1325	...	1425	1520	1620	1709	...	1820	1920	...	2039	2120	2120	...
												|				▬			|							
	⚒	⚒	⚒	⚒	Ⓑ	†	⚒		⚒	†		|	⚒	⚒		Ⓐ		Ⓐ	|		Ⓑ	⚒				
Catanzaro Lido d.	...	0530	...	0630	...	0740	0740	...	0935	0935	...	1212	...	1335	1425	...	...	1635	1711	1735	1830	1935	2030	...	...	...	...
Soverato d.	...	0543	...	0643	...	0759	0759	...	0948	0948	...	1228	...	1355	1444	...	...	1649	1731	1749	1843	1959	2043	...	...	...	...
Roccella Jonica d.	0535	0614	0625	0713	0735	0832	0832	...	1019	1019	...	1306	1333	1444	1514	1625	...	1736	1803	1822	1914	2042	2114	...	...	...	...
Siderno d.	0547	0626	0644	0725	0752	0844	0844	...	1033	1033	...	1319	1353	1456	1526	1642	...	1749	1816	1840	1926	2059	2126	...	...	...	...
Locri d.	0552	0631	0650	0731	0759	0849	0849	...	1038	1038	...	1327	1358	1505	1531	1648	...	1755	1825	1845	1931	2107	2131	...	...	...	...
Melito di Porto Salvo d.	0701	0724	0808	...	0926	0946	0950	...	1127	1131	...	1417	1523	...	1622	1807	...	1904	1924	1937	2025	...	2225	...	...	...	...
Reggio di Calabria C.le a.	0722	0755	0842	...	0958	1016	1027	...	1150	1156	...	1440	1553	...	1647	1840	...	1937	1950	2000	2050	...	2255	...	...	...	...

638 SALERNO - POTENZA - TARANTO

Regional services. For long-distance *FR* and *IC* trains, see Table **640**.

km												
		⚒		†	⚒🚌	⚒🚌	⚒	⚒		A	⚒	†
0	**Salerno** 640 d.	0545	...	1009	1135	1240	1400	1510	1608	1703	1954	2023
20	Battipaglia 640 d.	0600	...	1025	|	|	1415	1525	1623	1717	2010	2038
112	**Potenza** Centrale a.	0753	...	1202	1305	1405	1544	1657	1806	1846	2139	2210
					⚒🚌	⚒		⚒🚌		|		
112	**Potenza** Centrale d.	...	0801	...	1310	1428	...	1735	...	1848	...	...
219	Metaponto 637 d.	...	0931	...	1443	1604	...	1908	...	2007	...	...
263	**Taranto** 637 a.	...	1007	...	1523	1640	...	1950	...	2045	...	...

	⚒	†	⚒🚌	A	⚒		⚒🚌				
Taranto 637 d.	...	...	0535	1010	1101	...	1230	...	...	...	1830
Metaponto 637 d.	...	...	0615	1047	1136	...	1310	...	...	...	1904
Potenza Centrale a.	...	...	0748	1215	1315	...	1445	...	...	...	2048
			⚒🚌	|	◧	⚒🚌		⚒	⚒	†	⚒
Potenza Centrale d.	0625	0658	0800	1217	1325	1420	...	1729	1858	1928	2113
Battipaglia 640 d.	0804	0845	|	1345	1501	1541	...	1913	2028	2108	2250
Salerno 640 a.	0821	0903	0930	1358	1520	1620	...	1930	2045	2134	2306

A – To/from Napoli Centrale (Table **640**).

◧ – Runs daily Potenza - Salerno.

639 NAPOLI - SORRENTO, BAIANO and SARNO
2nd class Circumvesuviana Ferrovia

km	*See note* ⊡																											
	Napoli Porta Nolana d.	0554	0648	0800	0818	0906	0930	1018	1106	1154	1218	1242	1306	1336	1418	1442	1512	1618	1706	1736	1818	1906	1930	1954	2018	2042	2130
0	**Napoli** P. Garibaldi d.	0557	0650	0802	0821	0909	0933	1021	1109	1157	1221	1245	1309	1338	1421	1445	1514	1621	1709	1738	1821	1909	1933	1957	2021	2045	2133
10	Ercolano Scavi d.	0613	0704	0816	0837	0925	0949	1037	1125	1213	1237	1301	1325	1352	1437	1501	1528	1637	1725	1752	1837	1925	1949	2013	2037	2101	2149
23	Pompei S. Villa Misteri d.	0635	0723	0835	0859	0947	1011	1059	1147	1235	1259	1323	1347	1411	1459	1523	1547	1659	1747	1811	1859	1947	2011	2035	2059	2123	2211
29	Castellammare d.	0648	0736	0848	0912	1000	1024	1112	1200	1248	1312	1336	1400	1424	1512	1536	1600	1712	1800	1824	1912	2000	2024	2048	2112	2136	2224
42	**Sorrento** a.	0710	0758	0910	0934	1022	1046	1134	1222	1310	1334	1358	1422	1446	1534	1558	1622	1734	1822	1846	1934	2022	2046	2110	2134	2158	2246

See note ⊙																										
Sorrento d.	0600	0712	0800	0848	0936	1000	1048	1112	1200	1248	1336	1400	1448	1512	1536	1600	1624	1648	1736	1800	1824	1912	2000	2024	2048	2112	2136
Castellammare d.	0623	0735	0823	0911	0959	1023	1111	1135	1223	1311	1359	1423	1511	1535	1559	1623	1647	1711	1759	1823	1847	1935	2023	2047	2111	2135	2159
Pompei S. Villa Misteri d.	0636	0748	0836	0924	1012	1036	1124	1148	1236	1324	1412	1436	1524	1548	1612	1636	1700	1724	1812	1836	1900	1948	2036	2100	2124	2148	2212
Ercolano Scavi d.	0657	0809	0855	0943	1031	1057	1145	1207	1255	1343	1433	1455	1545	1609	1631	1657	1721	1745	1833	1855	1921	2007	2057	2121	2145	2209	2233
Napoli P. Garibaldi a.	0714	0826	0908	0956	1044	1114	1202	1220	1308	1356	1450	1508	1602	1626	1644	1714	1738	1802	1850	1908	1938	2020	2114	2138	2202	2226	2250
Napoli Porta Nolana a.	0715	0827	0910	0958	1046	1115	1203	1222	1310	1358	1451	1510	1603	1627	1646	1715	1739	1803	1851	1910	1939	2022	2115	2139	2203	2227	2251

NAPOLI - BAIANO Journey 71 minutes.

From Napoli Porta Nolana* at 0626, 0650⚒, 0714, 0802, 0850, 0938, 1002⚒, 1026, 1114, 1202, 1226, 1250, 1338, 1402, 1426, 1514, 1602, 1714⚒, 1738, 1826, 1850, 1914⚒, 1938.

From Baiano at 0608, 0632⚒, 0656, 0720⚒, 0744, 0808, 0832⚒, 0856, 0944, 1032, 1120, 1144⚒, 1208, 1256, 1344, 1408, 1432, 1520, 1544, 1608, 1656, 1744, 1920, 2008.

NAPOLI - SARNO Journey 74 minutes. All services call at Poggiomarino (58 minutes from Napoli, 16 minutes from Sarno).

From Napoli Porta Nolana* at 0628, 0652⚒, 0716, 0740, 0828, 0916, 0940⚒, 1004, 1028⚒, 1052, 1140, 1204⚒, 1228, 1316⚒, 1404, 1452, 1540, 1628, 1716, 1740⚒, 1804, 1828, 1852, 1940, 2004 **p**.

From Sarno at 0608, 0632⚒, 0656, 0720, 0808, 0832⚒, 0858, 0920, 1008, 1056, 1120⚒, 1144, 1208⚒, 1232, 1320, 1344⚒, 1408, 1456⚒, 1544, 1632, 1720, 1808, 1856, 1944, 2010.

p – To Poggiomarino only.

⊡ – Additional trains (journey 76 minutes): From Napoli Porta Nolana at 0618, 0706, 0730, 0954, 1042, 1354 and 1554.
⊙ – Additional trains (journey 75 minutes): From Sorrento at 0624, 0824, 0912, 1136, 1224 and 1424.
* – Trains call at Napoli Porta Garibaldi 2–3 minutes later.

Operator: Circumvesuviana Ferrovia. www.eavsrl.it.

☛ SITA operates 🚌 services along the Amalfi Coast between Sorrento and Salerno. A change of buses at Amalfi is necessary. (www.sitasudtrasporti.it).

🍷 on all *FA*, *FR* and *ITA* services.

ROMA - NAPOLI - TARANTO and REGGIO DI CALABRIA 640

km		*ICN* 1963	*ICN* 1965		*ICN* 799	*ICN* 797	*ITA* 8191	*IC* 701	*FR* 9501	*IC* 721	*IC* 723	*FA* 8333	*ITA* 9903		*IC* 551	*IC* 501	*ITA* 8111	*IC* 727	*IC* 729	*IC* 553	*FR* 9583	*IC* 583	2	*IC* 1589
					①⑦				①–⑥															⑥
		❖	❖		❖	❖										A								
	Torino Porta Nuova **600 610** d.	...	...	...	2155	2030	...	...	...	...	...	...	...	...	...	...	...	...	...	...	0800	...	...	...
	Milano Centrale **600 620** d.	2010	2010	...	|	2213g	...	...	...	...	...	...	...	...	...	...	0640	...	...	...	0910	0650	...	0655
	Bologna Centrale **600 620** d.	|	|	...	|	|	...	...	...	...	...	...	...	...	...	...	0757	...	...	...	1027	0918	...	0937
0	**Roma** Termini **600** d.	|	|	...	0546o	0558t	0600	0626	0700	0726	0726	0730	0740	...	0926	1018o	1030	1126	1126	1226	1300	1329t	...	1346t
62	Latina d.	|	|	...	0637	|	|	0700	|	0800	0800	|	|	...	1000	1057	|	1200	1200	1300	|	1400	...	1428
129	Formia-Gaeta d.	|	|	...	0717	|	|	0735	|	0835	0835	|	|	...	1035	1134	|	1235	1235	1335	|	1435	...	1507
195	Aversa d.	|	|	...	0758	|	|	0811	|	0911	0911	|	|	...	1111	1209	|	1311	1311	1411	|	1511	...	1545
	Napoli Afragola **600** a.	|	|	...	|	|	|	|	0756s	|	|	0832	|	...	|	|	|	|	|	|	1356	|	...	|
	Napoli Afragola **600** d.	|	|	...	|	|	|	|	0756s	|	|	0834	|	...	|	|	|	|	|	|	1358	|	...	|
214	**Napoli** Centrale **600** a.	|	|	...	0817	0846	0712	0829	0812	0929	0929	|	0854	...	1129	1229	1143	1329	1329	1429	1413	1529	...	1609
214	**Napoli** Centrale **600** d.	|	|	...	0835	0905	0725	0845	...	0950	0950	|	...	...	1145	...	1200	1345	1345	1445	1425	...	1614	1630
268	**Salerno** **600** a.	0613	0613	...	0911	0945	0802	0923	...	1037	1037	0905	...	...	1219	...	1242	1421	1421	1524	1504	...	1658	1715
268	**Salerno** **638** d.	0616	0616	...	...	...	0805	0925	...	1039	1039	0908	...	...	1222	...	1245	1424	1424	1526	1507	...	1703	1718
288	Battipaglia **638** d.	0630	0630	...	...	...	|	0939	...	|	|	|	...	...	1235	...	|	|	|	1538	|	...	1717	|
380	Potenza Centrale **638** d.	|	|	...	...	...	|	1102	...	|	|	|	...	...	|	...	|	|	|	|	|	...	1848	|
487	Metaponto **638** d.	|	|	...	...	...	|	1223	...	|	|	|	...	...	|	...	|	|	|	|	|	...	2007	|
531	**Taranto** **638** a.	|	|	...	...	...	|	1255	...	|	|	|	...	...	|	...	|	|	|	|	|	...	2045	|
318	Agropoli-Castellabate d.	0650	0650	...	...	...	0830	...	...	|	|	|	...	...	1255	...	1310	|	|	1606	|	...	...	|
395	Sapri d.	0745	0745	...	...	...	0916	...	...	1147	1147	|	...	...	1347	...	1355	1533	1533	1709	|	...	...	1836
489	Paola d.	0846	0846	...	...	...	1003	...	...	1240	1240	1100	...	...	1453	...	1445	1632	1632	1808	1702	...	...	1927
546	**Lamezia Terme** Centrale a.	0929	0929	...	...	...	1030	...	...	1306	1306	1126	...	...	1523	...	1512	1658	1658	1839	1728	...	...	1956
546	**Lamezia Terme** Centrale d.	0932	0932	...	...	...	1033	...	...	1308	1308	1129	...	...	1526	...	1515	1701	1701	1842	1730	...	...	1959
606	Rosarno d.	1006	1000	...	...	...	1105	...	...	|	|	1157	...	...	1559	...	1551	|	|	1915	1758	...	...	2035
616	Gioia Tauro d.	1014	1014	...	...	...	|	...	...	1344	1344	|	...	...	1608	...	|	1735	1735	1923	|	...	...	2044
652	Villa S. Giovanni a.	1040	1040	...	...	...	1135	...	...	1410	1410	1227	...	...	1632	...	1619	1805	1805	1947	1828	...	...	2107
652	Villa S. Giovanni d.	1105	1105	...	...	...	1138	...	...	1430	1430	1230	...	...	1635	...	1622	1825	1825	1950	1830	...	...	2210
667	**Reggio di Calabria** Centrale a.	|	|	...	...	...	1200	...	...	|	|	1250	...	...	1650	...	1642	|	|	2007	1848	...	...	2125
	Siracusa **641** a.	1548	|	...	...	...	...	...	...	1833	|	...	...	...	...	...	...	2253	|	...	...	...	...	...
	Palermo Centrale **641** a.	...	1655	...	...	...	...	...	...	...	1925	...	...	...	...	...	...	...	2305	...	...	...	...	...

	FA 8867	*IC* 555	*FR* 9587	*IC* 707	*IC* 561	*FR* 8419	*IC* 591	*FR* 9639	*FA* 8519	*IC* 511	*ITA* 8143	*FR* 9547	*IC* 511	*FR* 9551	*ICN* 1975	*ICN* 1957	*IC* 597	*ICN* 1955	*ICN* 1957	*ICN* 1955	*ICN* 1957	*ICN* 1959	*ICN* 1961	*ICN* 795
															①–④	①–④		⑤	⑤	⑥⑦	⑥⑦			
						B			C						❖	❖		❖	❖	❖	❖	❖	❖	❖
Torino Porta Nuova **600 610** d.	...	...	1000	...	...	...	...	...	...	1040	1320	...	...	...	...	...	...	...	...	...	...	...	...	1335
Milano Centrale **600 620** d.	...	...	1110	...	...	...	...	1430	...	|	1440	1510	...	1610	...	...	1348	...	...	...	...	...	...	1535g
Bologna Centrale **600 620** d.	...	...	1227	...	...	1402	...	1537	1547	|	1557	1627	...	1727	...	...	1618	...	...	...	...	...	...	1818
Roma Termini **600** d.	1405	1426	1500	1526	1626	1635	1726	1753	1820	1826	1830	1900	...	2000	2031	2031	2115	2106	2106	2131	2131	2300	2300	2324t
Latina d.	|	1500	|	1557	1700	|	1800	|	|	1900	|	|		|	2107	2107	2156	2140	2140	2207	2207	|	|	|
Formia-Gaeta d.	|	1535	|	1635	1735	|	1835	|	|	1935	|	|		|	2144	2144	2235	2220	2220	2244	2244	|	|	|
Aversa d.	|	1611	|	1711	1811	|	1911	|	|	2011	|	|	...	|	|	|	2311	|	|	|	|	|	|	|
Napoli Afragola **600** a.	1507	|	1556	|	|	1736	|	1848	1921	|	1928	1956	...	2056	|	|	|	|	|	|	|	|	|	|
Napoli Afragola **600** d.	1509	|	1558	|	|	1738	|	1850	1923	|	1930	1958	←	2058	|	|	|	|	|	|	|	|	|	|
Napoli Centrale **600** a.	|	1629	1612	1729	1829	|	1929	|	|	2029	|	2010	2029	2113	2308	2308	2330	2350	0006	0006	0006	|	|	|
Napoli Centrale **600** d.	|	1645	1625	1745	1855	|	1945	|	|	→	|	2020	2045	2125	2324	2324	2346	0006	0022	0022	0022	|	|	|
Salerno **600** a.	1539	1726	1706	1823	1932	1809	2030	1919	1948	...	2016	2057	2124	2205	0001	0001	0022	0053	0053	0053	0053	|	|	0227
Salerno **638** d.	1541	1729	1709	1826	1934	1811	...	1921	1950	...	2019	2059	...	...	0004	0004	...	0055	0055	0055	0055	|	|	0231
Battipaglia **638** d.	1553	1743	|	1840	1948	|	...	|	|	...	|	|	...	...	|	|	...	|	|	|	|	|	|	|
Potenza Centrale **638** d.	|	|	|	2008	|	|	...	|	|	...	|	2224	...	...	|	|	...	|	|	|	|	|	|	|
Metaponto **638** d.	|	|	|	2128	|	|	...	|	|	...	|	2338	...	...	|	|	...	|	|	|	|	|	|	|
Taranto **638** a.	|	|	|	2200	|	|	...	|	|	...	|	0007	...	...	|	|	...	|	|	|	|	|	|	|
Agropoli-Castellabate d.		1806	1736	...	|	|	...	|	|	...	2045	...	...	...	|	|	...	|	|	|	|	|	|	|
Sapri d.	1649	1906	1823	...	2102	|	...	|	|	...	2130	...	...	...	|	|	...	|	|	|	|	|	|	0353
Paola d.	1745	2014	1917	...	2205	2000	...	2115	2138	...	2223	...	...	...	|	|	...	|	|	|	|	|	|	0451
Lamezia Terme Centrale a.	1813	2044	1945	...	2236	2026	...	2142	...	...	2249	...	...	...	|	|	...	|	|	|	|	0459	0459	0530
Lamezia Terme Centrale d.	1816	2047	1948	...	2239	2029	...	2145	...	...	2252	...	...	...	|	|	...	|	|	|	|	0502	0502	0533
Rosarno d.	1847	2122	2020	...	2311	2059	...	2215	...	...	2322	...	...	...	|	|	...	|	|	|	|	|	|	0652
Gioia Tauro d.	1855	2130	|	...	2319	|	...	|	...	...	|	...	...	...	|	|	...	|	|	|	|	|	|	0701
Villa S. Giovanni a.	1919	2156	2051	...	2341	2127	...	2244	...	...	2351	...	...	...	0330	0330	...	0425	0425	0425	0425	0610	0610	0731
Villa S. Giovanni d.	1922	2159	2054	...	2344	2130	...	2247	...	...	2354	...	...	...	0350	0350	...	0445	0445	0445	0445	0635	0635	0734
Reggio di Calabria Centrale a.	1937	2214	2110	...	2359	2145	...	2305	...	...	0008	...	...	...	|	|	...	|	|	|	|	|	|	0757
Siracusa **641** a.	...	...	...	...	...	...	...	...	...	...	...	...	...	...	0901	|	...	0936	|	0936	|	1129	|	...
Palermo Centrale **641** a.	...	...	...	...	...	...	...	...	...	...	...	...	...	...	...	0924	...	...	1007	...	1007	...	1157	...

REGIONAL TRAINS

2nd class

km			⚒	†	⚒	Ⓐ	†	⚒	†	⚒	†	Ⓐ	⑥	⚒	Ⓐ	†	⚒	†	⚒	†	⚒	† w	⚒		⚒
0	**Roma** Termini d.	0531	0656	0736	0736	0750t	1036	1036	1136	1156	1238	1256	1256	1453	1441t	1536	1556	1636	1656	1736	1756	1836	1856	1956	2056h
62	Latina d.	0608	0731	0818	0818	0839	1118	1118	1218	1233	1323	1331	1331	1530	1537	1618	1631	1718	1731	1818	1832	1918	1931	2032	2131k
129	Formia-Gaeta d.	0657	0821	0906	0912	0925	1207	1212	1311	1321	1413	1421	1421	1610	1623	1707	1721	1807	1821	1907	1921	2007	2021	2110	2221k
195	Aversa d.	0750	0914	1006	1013	|	1302	1314	1402	1414	1507	1514	|	|	1715	1806	1814	1902	1914	2006	2014	2102	2114	|	|
216	**Caserta** **626** a.	|	|	|	|	1025	|	|	|	|	|	|	1515	1708j	|	|	|	|	|	|	|	|	|	2208	2322
214	**Napoli** Centrale **626** a.	0812	0950	1038	1036	1116	1323	1340	1423	1440	1535	1548	1551	...	1743	1843	1840	1923	1940	2043	2040	2123	2140	2252	2355

km				Ⓐ	Ⓒ				Ⓐ △	⊡		⚒ D	⚒ E		⚒ E	⚒ D	⚒	Ⓐ	Ⓐ		Ⓑ				Ⓑ
0	**Napoli** Centrale **638** d.	...	0540	0650	0650	0735	0750	0850	...	...	1250	...	...	1350	...	...	1514	...	...	1714	...	1814	1914	2025	2116
54	Salerno **638** d.	0551	0637	0733	0733	0818	0833	0935	...	...	1333	...	...	1433	...	...	1601	...	1712	1803	...	1903	2001	2108	2203
74	Battipaglia **638** d.	0610	0652	0749	0749	0835	0849	0949	...	...	1348	...	...	1448	...	...	1616	...	1731	1827	...	1918	2016	2126	2221
104	Agropoli-Castellabate d.	0632	0715	0810	0810	0857	0911	1011	...	...	1411	...	...	1510	...	...	1639	...	1754	1850	...	1946	2048	2150	2241
135	Ascea d.	0656	0741	0834	0834	0922	0936	1036	...	...	1435	...	...	1535	...	...	1704	...	1819	1914	...	2011	2112	2216	2304
181	Sapri d.	0737r	0825	0906	0906	1006	1027	1110	1315	1410	1514	1544	1622	1628	1722	1722	1745	1826	1900	1954	2002	2049	2147	2250	2340
193	Maratea d.	0748r	...	0917	0918	...	...	1122	1328	1423	1526	1558	1634	...	1735	1735	...	1838	...	...	2014	...	2159	...	...
241	Belvedere Marittimo d.	0831	...	0957	0956	...	...	1153	1404	1502	|	1637	1721	...	1811	1815	...	1914	...	...	2049	...	2230	...	...
275	Paola **633** d.	0905	...	1024	1026	...	...	1216	1437	1532	1646	1720	1753	...	1846	1848	...	1948	...	...	2129	...	2258	...	...
301	**Cosenza** **633** a.	...	...	...	1047	...	...	1236	...	...	1707	...	...	...	1907	1910	...	2007	...	...	2150	...	2320	...	...

km		⚒	⚒	Ⓐ	⚒		⚒	Ⓐ	†			⚒		Ⓐ		⚒	Ⓐ	⚒	Ⓑ	Ⓐ	⚒				Ⓐ
0	**Cosenza** **633** d.	...	...	...	0523	0623	...	0723	...	...	0923	...	...	1223	1320	...	1423	1523	...	1623	1723	...	1823	...	...
26	Paola **633** d.	...	0515	...	0555	0655	...	0757	...	...	0955	...	...	1255	1355	...	1455	1558	...	1655	1755	...	1857	...	...
83	**Lamezia Terme** Centrale d.	0525	0552	0510z	0632	0732	0637z	0832	0757z	...	1026	1037z	...	1332	1437	1337z	1532	1633	1537z	1736	1832	1741z	1932	...	1937z
143	Rosarno d.	0558	0625	0636	0705	0805	0815	0905	0935	...	1114	1215	...	1405	1507	1514	1605	1706	1715	1810	1905	1919	2005	...	2108
153	Gioia Tauro d.	0605	0632	0644	0712	0812	0823	0912	0944	...	1121	1223	...	1412	1514	1523	1612	1713	1723	1817	1912	1928	2012	...	2116
189	Villa S. Giovanni d.	0637	0704	0719	0744	0844	0858	0944	1019	...	1154	1258	...	1444	1546	1558	1644	1745	1758	1852	1944	2003	2044	...	2152
204	**Reggio di Calabria** Centrale a.	0653	0720	0745	0802	0902	0925	1002	1046	...	1210	1325	...	1502	1603	1625	1702	1802	1825	1910	2002	2030	2102	...	2228

A – (12) Sestri Levante - Napoli.
B – (12) 🍷 Venezia - Reggio di Calabria.
C – (12) 🍷 Bolzano - Sibari (a. 2231).
D – Until Mar. 25.
E – From Mar. 27.
g – Milano Porta Garibaldi.
h – 2054 on ⑥.

j – 1719 on ⑤.
k – On ⑤ Latina d. 2128, Formia-Gaeta d. 2215.
o – Roma Ostiense.
r – 1–2 minutes earlier on †.
s – Calls to set down only.
t – Roma Tiburtina.
w – Not May 1.
z – Via Tropea (coastal route; 22 km longer).

△ – Runs 3–5 minutes earlier until Mar. 24.
⊡ – Runs 5–9 minutes later on ⚒ until Mar. 25.
❖ – 🛏 1, 2 cl., 🛏 2 cl. (4 berth). Running days, timings and numbers of *ICN* trains may vary (please check your reservation). For confirmed timings please consult the *Trenitalia* journey planner at www.trenitalia.com.

640 REGGIO DI CALABRIA and TARANTO - NAPOLI - ROMA

🍷 on all *FA*, *FR* and *ITA* services

	IC	*FR*	*IC*		*FR*	*IC*	*FA*	*FR*	*IC*	*IC*	*FR*	*ITA*	*IC*	*IC*	*FA*		*IC*	*IC*	*FR*		*IC*	*IC*	*IC*	*FR*
	582	**9516**	**510**		**9514**	**590**	**8509**	**8418**	**590**	**550**	**9584**	**8134**	**700**	**552**	**8862**		**596**	**1588**	**9588**	2	**556**	**728**	**722**	**9658**
																		⑦						
							C	**B**																
Palermo Centrale **641** d.	...	...	...	...	...	...	...	...	...	...	...	...	...	...	...	...	...	...	...	...	...	0650	...	...
Siracusa **641** d.	...	...	...	...	...	...	...	...	...	...	...	...	...	...	...	...	...	...	...	...	...	|	0732	...
Reggio di Calabria Centrale d.	...	...	...	...	...	...	...	0607	...	0617	0644	0724	...	0756	0858	...	...	0925	1008	...	1000	|	|	1230
Villa S. Giovanni a.	...	...	...	...	...	...	...	0622	...	0635	0658	0739	...	0811	0912	...	...	0938	1023	...	1016	1120	1120	1244
Villa S. Giovanni d.	...	...	...	...	...	...	...	0625	...	0637	0701	0742	...	0813	0915	...	...	0941	1026	...	1018	1150	1150	1247
Gioia Tauro d.	...	...	...	...	...	...	...	|	...	0701	|	|	...	0840	0941	...	...	1007	|	...	1052	1217	1217	|
Rosarno d.	...	...	...	...	...	...	...	0652	...	0709	0730	0814	...	0848	0950	...	...	1015	1055	...	1105	|	|	1317
Lamezia Terme Centrale a.	...	...	...	...	...	...	...	0725	...	0741	0802	0845	...	0919	1019	...	...	1046	1122	...	1138	1253	1253	1349
Lamezia Terme Centrale d.	...	...	...	...	...	...	...	0728	...	0744	0805	0847	...	0922	1022	...	...	1049	1125	...	1141	1256	1256	1352
Paola d.	...	...	...	...	...	...	0718	0759	...	0817	0835	0917	...	0958	1054	...	...	1122	1154	...	1214	1329	1329	1423
Sapri d.	...	...	...	...	...	...	|	|	...	0922	0934	1010	...	1058	1143	...	...	1222	|	...	1312	1420	1420	|
Agropoli-Castellabate d.	...	...	...	...	...	...	|	|	...	|	1023	1055	...	1144	|	...	...	|	|	...	1404	|	|	|
Taranto **638** d.	...	...	...	...	0527	...	|	|	...	|	|	|	0801	|	|	...	...	|	|	1010	|	|	|	|
Metaponto **638** d.	...	...	...	...	0600	...	|	|	...	|	|	|	0835	|	|	...	...	|	|	1047	|	|	|	|
Potenza Centrale **638** d.	...	...	...	...	0717	...	|	|	...	|	|	|	0956	|	|	...	...	|	|	1217	|	|	|	|
Battipaglia **638** d.	...	0530	...	...	|	...	|	|	...	1025	|	|	1127	1208	1244	...	...	|	|	1345	1424	|	|	|
Salerno **638** a.	...	0545	...	...	0844	...	0910	0956	...	1038	1048	1119	1138	1220	1256	...	...	1334	1351	1358	1434	1534	1534	1614
Salerno **600** d.	0528	0550	0626	...	0846	0858	0913	0959	...	1041	1051	1122	1140	1223	1258	...	...	1337	1354	1401	1437	1537	1537	1617
Napoli Centrale **600** a.	0606	0628	0705	...	0928	0948	|	|	←	1117	1127	1158	1218	1305	|		...	1418	1428	1438	1517	1617	1617	|
Napoli Centrale **600** d.	0631	0640	0731	...	0940	1031	|	|	1031	1131	1140	1215	1231	1331	|	...	1420	1446	1440	...	1531	1631	1631	|
Napoli Afragola **600** a.	|	0656	|	...	0956	→	0939	1023	|	|	1156	1228	|	|	1322		|	|	1456	...	|	|	|	1639
Napoli Afragola **600** d.	|	0658	|	...	0958	...	0941	1025	|	|	1158	1230	|	|	1324		|	|	1458	...	|	|	|	1641
Aversa d.	0648	|	0749	...	|	...	|	|	1049	1149	|	|	1249	1349	|	...	1438	1506	|	...	1549	1649	1649	|
Formia-Gaeta d.	0722	|	0822	...	|	...	|	|	1122	1222	|	|	1322	1422	|	...	1513	1545	|	...	1622	1722	1722	|
Latina d.	0800	|	0900	...	|	...	|	|	1200	1300	|	|	1400	1500	|	...	1551	1625	|	...	1700	1800	1800	|
Roma Termini **600** a.	0834	0755	0934	...	1055	...	1040	1125	1237t	1332	1300	1330	1434	1534	1425	...	1633t	1705t	1555	...	1734	1834	1834	1740
Bologna Centrale **600 620** a.	...	1033	|	...	1333	...	1313	1358	1642	...	1533	1603	...	...	...	...	2042	2130	1833	...	...	...	...	1953
Milano Centrale **600 620** a.	...	1150	|	...	1450	...	...	...	1917	...	1650	1720	...	...	...	...	2317	0015	1950	...	...	...	...	2100
Torino Porta Nuova **600 610** a.	...	1300	1740	...	1600	...	...	...	...	...	1800	1835	...	...	...	...	...	...	2100	...	...	...	...	...

	IC	*ITA*	*IC*	*FA*	*IC*	*IC*	*FA*	*IC*		*ICN*	*ICN*		*ITA*		*ICN*	*ICN*		*ICN*		*ICN*	*ICN*		*ICN*	*ICN*
	522	**8158**	**702**	**8868**	**730**	**724**	**8332**	**560**		**798**	**796**		**8192**		**1964**	**1962**		**794**		**1954**	**1956**		**1958**	**1960**
											⑥⑦													
	A									❖	❖				❖	❖		❖		❖	❖		❖	❖
Palermo Centrale **641** d.	...	...	...	...	1000	...	...	...	...	...	...	...	...	...	1235	...	...	...	...	1848	...	...	2055	...
Siracusa **641** d.	...	...	...	...	|	1010	...	...	...	...	...	...	...	...	|	1335	...	...	...	|	1910	...	|	2145
Reggio di Calabria Centrale d.	...	1328	...	1347	|	|	1515	1508	...	...	...	...	1734	...	|	|	...	2143	...	|	|	...	|	|
Villa S. Giovanni a.	...	1344	...	1402	1420	1420	1530	1523	...	...	...	...	1750	...	1815	1815	...	2200	...	2335	2335	...	|	|
Villa S. Giovanni d.	...	1347	...	1405	1450	1450	1533	1526	...	...	...	...	1753	...	1845	1845	...	2203	...	0005	0005	...	|	|
Gioia Tauro d.	...	|	...	1430	1515	1515	|	1557	...	...	...	...	|	...	1914	1914	...	2237	...	|	|	...	|	|
Rosarno d.	...	1416	...	1438	|	|	1601	1607	...	...	...	...	1821	...	1922	1922	...	2247	...	|	|	...	|	|
Lamezia Terme Centrale a.	...	1450	...	1510	1559	1559	1626	1638	...	...	...	...	1854	...	1957	1957	...	0007	...	0105	0105	...	|	|
Lamezia Terme Centrale d.	...	1452	...	1513	1601	1601	1629	1640	...	...	...	...	1856	...	2000	2000	...	0010	...	0108	0108	...	|	|
Paola d.	...	1521	...	1544	1639	1639	1700	1713	...	...	...	...	1927	...	2052	2052	...	0054	...	|	|	...	|	|
Sapri d.	...	1610	...	1635	1729	1729	|	1813	...	...	...	...	2013	...	2156	2156	...	0153	...	|	|	...	|	|
Agropoli-Castellabate d.	...	1655	...	|	|	|	|	1901	...	...	...	...	2058	...	2254	2254	...	|	...	|	|	...	|	|
Taranto **638** d.	...	|	1350	|	|	|	|	|	...	...	...	...	|	...	|	|	...	|	...	|	|	...	|	|
Metaponto **638** d.	...	|	1430	|	|	|	|	|	...	...	...	...	|	...	|	|	...	|	...	|	|	...	|	|
Potenza Centrale **638** d.	...	|	1548	|	|	|	|	|	...	...	...	...	|	...	|	|	...	|	...	|	|	...	|	|
Battipaglia **638** d.	...	|	1717	1731	|	|	|	1922	...	...	...	...	|	...	2315	2315	...	|	...	|	|	...	|	|
Salerno **638** a.	...	1719	1730	1743	1837	1837	1852	1934	...	...	...	...	2125	...	2330	2330	...	0307	...	|	|	...	0642s	0642s
Salerno **600** d.	...	1722	1733	1745	1839	1839	1854	1937	...	2038	2052	...	2128	...	2333	2333	...	0310	...	|	|	...	0642s	0642s
Napoli Centrale **600** a.	...	1758	1817	|	1918	1918	|	2017	...	2120	2128	...	2208	...	|	|	...	|	...	|	|	...	0722s	0722s
Napoli Centrale **600** d.	1731	1820	1831	|	1931	1931	|	2031	...	2135	2146	...	2218	...	|	|	...	|	...	|	|	...	0722s	0722s
Napoli Afragola **600** a.	|	|	|	1810	|	|	1920	|	...	|	|	...	|	...	|	|	...	|	...	|	|	...	|	|
Napoli Afragola **600** d.	|	|	|	1812	|	|	1922	|	...	|	|	...	|	...	|	|	...	|	...	|	|	...	|	|
Aversa d.	1749	|	1849	|	1949	1949	|	2049	...	|	2205	...	|	...	|	|	...	|	...	|	|	...	|	|
Formia-Gaeta d.	1822	|	1922	|	2028	2028	|	2122	...	|	2243	...	|	...	|	|	...	0454	...	0549s	0549s	...	0831s	0831s
Latina d.	1900	|	2000	|	2105	2105	|	2200	...	|	2321	...	|	...	|	|	...	0530	...	0629s	0629s	...	0910s	0910s
Roma Termini **600** a.	1941o	1930	2034	1915	2138	2138	2025	2234	...	2349t	0008o	...	2330	...	|	|	...	0606o	...	0718	0718	...	0951	0951
Bologna Centrale **600 620** a.	...	2203	...	...	...	...	...	...	...	|	|	...	...	...	0707s	0707s	...	|	...	...	...	...	...	...
Milano Centrale **600 620** a.	...	2320	...	...	...	...	...	...	...	0655g	|	...	...	...	1010	1010	...	|	...	...	...	...	...	...
Torino Porta Nuova **600 610** a.	...	...	...	...	...	...	...	...	...	0920	0810	...	...	...	...	...	...	1440	...	...	...	...	...	...

REGIONAL TRAINS

2nd class

	⚒	⚒	⚒	⚒		Ⓑ	Ⓐ		⚒			⚒	⚒	⚒	Ⓐ	Ⓑ	Ⓑ	Ⓒ	⚒	Ⓑ	Ⓐ	Ⓑ	⚒	⚒	Ⓐ
			E	**D**												**E**	**D**								
Reggio di Calabria Centrale d.	0500	0535	0555	0555	0658	0735	0800	...	1035	...	1158	1235	1258	1358	1435	1453	1453	1535	1558	1635	1658	1758	1835	1858	1958
Villa S. Giovanni d.	0518	0605	0613	0613	0716	0805	0819	...	1105	...	1216	1305	1316	1416	1505	1511	1511	1605	1616	1705	1716	1816	1905	1916	2016
Gioia Tauro d.	0549	0638	0644	0652	0747	0835	0850	...	1139	...	1247	1339	1347	1447	1536	1542	1544	1639	1647	1739	1747	1847	1939	1947	2047
Rosarno d.	0555	0648	0650	0659	0755	0843	0856	...	1148	...	1255	1348	1355	1455	1548	1548	1550	1648	1655	1748	1755	1855	1948	1955	2055
Lamezia Terme Centrale d.	0632	0823z	0725	0734	0832	1008z	0932	...	1323z	...	1332	1523z	1440v	1532	1723z	1625	1621	1823z	1740v	1923z	1832	1932	2123z	2032	2130
Paola **633** a.	0705	...	0806	0806	0905	...	1005	...	...	...	1405	...	1509	1606	...	1658	1653	...	1809	...	1905	2005	...	2105	...
Cosenza **633** a.	0739	...	0837	0837	0937	...	1037	...	...	...	1437	...	1540	1637	...	1737	1737	...	1840	...	1937	2037	...	...	...

	①–⑥						Ⓑ		⚒	⚒		⚒	Ⓒ	Ⓐ	⚒			⚒	†	⚒	⚒	†			Ⓐ
									E	**D**														△	
Cosenza **633** d.	...	...	...	...	0558	...	0823	...	...	...	...	...	1314	...	1353	1453	...	1653	...	...	...	1753	...	1853	2023
Paola **633** d.	...	...	...	...	0622	...	0847	...	1146	1224	1245h	...	1339	1347	1425	1525	...	1725	1725	...	1815	1816	...	1930	2055
Belvedere Marittimo d.	...	...	...	...	0648	...	0917	...	1210	1249	1311h	...	1408	1419k	1456	1554h	...	1755r	1753f	...	1845	1846	...	1956	2123p
Maratea d.	...	...	...	...	0721	...	1005	...	1247	1320	1349h	...	1443	1454	1533	1637	...	1832r	1836	...	1924	1923	...	2028	2155p
Sapri d.	0420	0540	0600	0642	0734	1016	1019	1255	1257	1330	1400j	1428	1455	1512k	1547	1650	1714	1845r	1850	1850	1936	1936	2016	2040	2205p
Ascea d.	0457	0618	0638	0718	0808	1056	...	1347	...	...	1450	1511	1539	1550	...	1722	1803	...	1923	1924	...	...	2055	2112	...
Agropoli-Castellabate d.	0523	0644	0705	0744	0833	1119	...	1414	...	...	1517	1539	1612	1616	...	1747	1836	...	1947	1948	...	...	2120	2136	...
Battipaglia **638** d.	0545	0706	0729	0810	0910	1144	...	1440	...	...	1540	1610	1641	1641	...	1809	1901	...	2011	2011	...	...	2144	2159	...
Salerno **638** d.	0604	0728	0750	0831	0931	1203	...	1501	...	...	1601	1626	1701	1701	...	1831	1920	...	2031	2031	...	...	2201	2217	...
Napoli Centrale **638** a.	0642	0807	0827	0908	1010	1243	...	1538	...	...	1638	...	1738	1738	...	1908	1958	...	2108	2108	...	...	2238	2258	...

	⚒	⚒	†	⚒	⚒	†	⚒	†	Ⓐ	†	⚒	⚒	⚒	†	⚒	†	⚒	†	†	⚒	⚒	⚒	†	Ⓑ	
																w									
Napoli Centrale **626** d.	0405	0500	0500	...	0620	0637	0820	0830	0935	1117	1120	1220	1325	1345	1425	1430	1520	1540	1617	1620	1720	1820	1817	1952	2045
Caserta **626** d.	|	|	|	0609	|	|	|	|	|	|	|	|	|	|	|	|	|	|	|	|	|	|	|	|	|
Aversa d.	0428	0525	0528	|	0638	0659	0838	0856	0952	1145	1138	1238	1345	1403	1445	1456	1538	1559	1645	1638	1738	1838	1845	2017	2109
Formia-Gaeta d.	0514	0611	0614	0705	0738	0752	0938	0949	1041	1249	1238	1340	1443	1454	1540	1553	1638	1652	1752	1738	1838	1938	1952	2113	2209
Latina d.	0551	0655	0710	0743	0828	0842	1028	1041	1115	1338	1337	1438	1528	1542	1628	1640	1728	1742	1842	1828	1937	2028	2042	...	2257
Roma Termini a.	0630	0734	0754	0827	0904	0924	1104	1124	1153t	1422	1422	1524	1604	1624	1712	1724	1804	1824	1924	1904	2024	2112	2131	...	2340

A – (12) Napoli - Sestri Levante.
B – (12) 🍷 Reggio di Calabria - Venezia.
C – (12) 🍷 Sibari (d. 0627) - Bolzano.
D – Until Mar. 26.
E – From Mar. 27.
f – 1759 until Mar. 26.
g – Milano Porta Garibaldi.
h – 2 minutes earlier until Mar. 26.

j – 2–3 minutes later on †.
k – Until Mar. 24 Belvedere Marittimo d. 1414, Sapri d. 1515.
o – Roma Ostiense.
p – 11 minutes later until Mar. 24.
r – 3–4 minutes later until Mar. 25.
s – Calls to set down only.
t – Roma Tiburtina.

v – Arrives 10 minutes earlier.
w – Not May 1.
z – Via Tropea (coastal route; 22 km longer).
△ – Until Mar. 26 runs 6 minutes later Belvedere Marittimo - Salerno and arrives Napoli 2308.
❖ – 🛏 1, 2 cl., 🛌 2 cl. (4 berth). Running days, timings and numbers of *ICN* trains may vary (please check your reservation). For confirmed timings please consult the *Trenitalia* journey planner at www.trenitalia.com.

VILLA SAN GIOVANNI - MESSINA - SIRACUSA and PALERMO — 641

2nd class (unless otherwise noted)

km																									
			ICN 1955				*ICN* 1959						*ICN* 1963			*IC* 721							*IC* 727		
		⚒		†	⚒					⚒	⚒	⚒		⚒					⚒			⚒			
			❖				❖		P				❖			R					P		R		
0	**Villa S. Giovanni** ▲ d.	...	0350	...	...	...	0635	...	...	...	...	...	1105	...	...	1430	...	...	...	...	...	...	1825	...	...
9	**Messina** Centrale ▲ a.	...	0515	...	...	...	0805	...	...	...	...	...	1245	...	...	1535	...	...	...	...	...	...	1935	...	...
9	**Messina** Centrale ⊡ d.	0513	0550	0652	0726	0755	0845	0915	...	1025	1115	1200	1315	1320	*1435*	1605	1618	1715	1745	1825	...	1927	2015	2018	2134
56	Taormina-Giardini ⊡ d.	0552	0649	0756	0806	0902	0932	1001	...	1121	1156	1310	1356	1405	*1539*	1642	1723	1758	1850	1932	...	2028	2058	2127	2238
74	Giarre-Riposto ⊡ d.	0610	0714	0814	0820	0929	0948	1016	...	1140	1216	1331	1410	1422	*1601*	1658	1741	1813	1909	1950	...	2052	2115	2144	2256
104	**Catania** Centrale ⊡ a.	0630	0740	0852	0840	1000	1010	1035	...	1213	1236	1403	1432	1443	*1632*	1725	1820	1832	1934	2022	...	2117	2137	2218	2329
104	**Catania** Centrale **645** d.	0635	0750	...	0845	...	1016	...	1050	...	1240	...	1435	1503	1650	1728	...	1837	...	...	2059	...	2140	...	...
110	Catania Fontanarossa ✈ **645** d.	0646	|	...	0854	...	|	...	1058	...	1249	...	|	1513	1658	|	...	1845	...	...	2108	...	|	...	...
160	Augusta d.	0730	0838	...	0933	...	1109	...	1145	...	1333	...	1526	1551	1748**r**	1814	...	1931	...	...	2143	...	2226	...	...
191	**Siracusa** a.	0755	0901	...	0955	...	1129	...	1210	...	1400	...	1548	1610	1808**r**	1833	...	2000	...	...	2210	...	2253	...	...

						IC 722		*IC* 724						*ICN* 1962									*ICN* 1956		*ICN* 1960
	⚒	⚒			⚒				⚒	†	⚒	⚒			⚒		⚒			⚒	⚒			⚒	
				P		R		R						❖				P					❖		❖
Siracusa d.	...	0506	...	0552	0640	0732	0844	1010	...	...	...	1253	...	1335	1415	...	...	1601	...	...	1712	1820	1910	1925	2145
Augusta d.	...	0525	...	0613	0706	0753	0914	1031	...	...	...	1316	...	1400	1434	...	...	1622	...	...	1733	1841	1932	1957	2206
Catania Fontanarossa ✈ **645** d.	...	0604	...	0651	0758	|	1004	|	...	...	...	1356	...	|	1522	...	...	1701	...	1735	1820	1919	|	2035	|
Catania Centrale **645** a.	...	0612	...	0705	0806	0838	1010	1115	...	...	...	1406	...	1451	1528	...	...	1708	...	1745	1829	1928	2019	2044	2255
Catania Centrale ⊡ d.	0501	0617	0626	...	0808	0841	1015	1118	1104	1123	1254	1410	1424	1454	1531	1540	1624	...	1719	1747	1836	1933	2026	*2109*	2258
Giarre-Riposto ⊡ d.	0530	0640	0653	...	0831	0904	1037	1142	1131	1150	1327	1432	1457	1522	1552	1613	1656	...	1741	1824	1900	1955	2051	*2134*	2320
Taormina-Giardini ⊡ d.	0552	0701	0715	...	0848	0918	1103	1156	1207	1211	1352	1448	1522	1539	1610	1643	1723	...	1758	1850	1919	2011	2112	*2153*	2335
Messina Centrale ⊡ a.	0703	0751	0833	...	0942	0953	1159	1245	1303	1307	1506	1546	1617	1625	1655	1759	1807	...	1840	1953	2000	2108	2150	*2240*	0015
Messina Centrale ▲ d.	...	...	...	...	...	1010	...	1310	...	...	...	...	...	1645	...	...	...	...	...	...	...	...	2210	...	0035
Villa S. Giovanni ▲ a.	...	...	...	...	...	1120	...	1420	...	...	...	...	...	1815	...	...	...	...	...	...	...	...	2335	...	◧

km																									
				ICN 1957				*ICN* 1961							*ICN* 1965			*IC* 723						*IC* 729	
		⚒	⚒		⚒	†	⚒			⚒	†	⚒	⚒	⚒			⚒		†	⚒		⚒	†		⚒
				❖				❖							❖			R						R	
0	**Villa S. Giovanni** ▲ d.	...	...	0350	...	...	...	0635	...	...	...	...	...	...	1105	...	...	1430	...	...	...	...	...	1825	...
9	**Messina** Centrale ▲ a.	...	...	0515	...	...	...	0805	...	...	...	...	...	...	1245	...	...	1535	...	...	...	...	...	1935	...
9	**Messina** Centrale d.	0453	...	0555	0636	0745	0756	0837	1005	1043	...	...	1227	...	1320	1437	...	1615	1708	1714	...	*1805*	1857	2005	2152
45	Milazzo d.	0511	...	0617	0659	0804	0817	0859	1036	1101	...	...	1246	...	1343	1453	...	1637	1725	1731	...	*1835*	1915	2026	2223
115	S. Agata di Militello d.	0604	0651	0722	0755	0909	0916	1002	1138	1159	1207	1217	1352	1415	1444	1545	1600	1728	1818	1832	1850	1950	2021	2119	2319
173	Cefalù d.	0657	0804	0827	0843	1009	1004	1100	...	1242	1307	1318	1437	1525	1557	1638	1715	1835	1905	1920	2004	2058	2118	2214	...
204	Termini Imerese **645** d.	0720	0827	0854	0902	1026	1022	1120	...	1303	1330	1342	1455	1555	1618	1700	1737	1856	1925	1936	2034	2123	2136	2238	...
241	**Palermo** Centrale **645** a.	0747	0907	0924	0929	1055	1052	1157	...	1332	1400	1412	1523	1622	1655	1729	1805	1925	1955	2005	2106	2154	2205	2305	...

				IC 728					*IC* 730				*ICN* 1964							*ICN* 1954				*ICN* 1958	
	⚒		⚒		⚒	⚒				⚒	⚒	⚒		⚒		⚒	⚒				⚒	⚒	†		⚒
				R					R				❖							❖				❖	
Palermo Centrale **645** d.	0507	...	0622	0650	...	0700	0827	0938	1000	...	1138	...	1235	1338	1430	1628	...	1738	1833	1848	1938	2033	2033	2055	2135
Termini Imerese **645** d.	0532	...	0649	0715	...	0737	0851	1006	1035	...	1206	...	1305	1406	1458**t**	1653	...	1806	1858	1917	2006	2058	2058	2122	2203
Cefalù d.	0548	...	0707	0735	...	0800	0913	1027	1059	...	1242	...	1335	1438	1526	1714	...	1834**v**	1919	1936	2029	2116	2119	2143	2227
S. Agata di Militello d.	0641	0654	0758	0824	0840	...	1004	1130	1142	1206	1344	1413	1443	1539	1623	1812	1913	1944	2007	2021	2133	2210	2211	2250	2325
Milazzo d.	0735	0758	0856	0917	0944	...	1051	...	1234	1308	...	1521	1558	...	1712	1900	2020	...	2054	2125	...	2256	2300	2350	...
Messina Centrale a.	0754	0831	0920	0940	1017	...	1111	...	1255	1342	...	1553	1620	...	1732	1920	2051	...	2116	2155	...	2320	2322	0020	...
Messina Centrale ▲ d.	...	...	...	1010	...	...	...	...	1310	...	...	...	1645	...	...	...	...	...	...	2210	...	...	...	0035	...
Villa S. Giovanni ▲ a.	...	...	...	1120	...	...	...	...	1420	...	...	...	1815	...	...	...	...	...	...	2335	...	...	...	◧	...

P – Until Mar. 12 runs to / from Palermo (Table **645**).
R – To / from Roma (Table **640**).

r – On † Augusta d. 1743, Siracusa a. 1805.
t – 1501 on †.
v – 1832 on †.

◧ – To Roma (Table **640**), not calling at Villa S. Giovanni.
▲ – Through trains are conveyed by ⛴ Villa S. Giovanni - Messina and v.v. See Table **2695** for other sailings.
⊡ – Other trains Messina - Catania and v.v.: **From Messina Centrale** at 0539 ⚒, 1335 ⚒ and 1415 ⚒. **From Catania Centrale** at 0529 ⚒, 1327 ⚒, 1745 † and 1939.
❖ – 🛏 1, 2 cl., 🛏 2 cl. (4 berth). For origin see Table **640**. Running days, timings and numbers of *ICN* trains may vary (please check your reservation). For confirmed timings please consult the *Trenitalia* journey planner at www.trenitalia.com.

CATANIA - RANDAZZO - RIPOSTO — 644

Ferrovia Circumetnea

km		⚒	⚒	⚒	⚒	⚒	⚒	⚒	⚒	⚒	⚒
0	**Catania** Borgo ⊙ d.	...	0646	0805	...	0920	1220	...	1350	1530	1623
20	Paternò ⊙ d.	...	0722	0841	...	0956	1256	...	1426	1608	1658
36	Adrano Nord d.	...	0752	0909	...	1024	1325	...	1453	1636	...
52	Bronte d.	...	0816	0936	...	...	1352	...	...	1703	...
71	**Randazzo** a.	...	0843	1003	...	...	1419	...	...	1730	...
71	**Randazzo** d.	0632	...	...	1215	...	...	1506	...	...	...
109	Giarre a.	0739	...	...	1323	...	...	1614	...	...	...
111	**Riposto** a.	0744	...	...	1327	...	...	1618	...	...	...

	⚒	⚒	⚒	⚒	⚒	⚒	⚒	⚒	⚒	⚒
Riposto d.	...	...	...	0855	...	...	...	1350	...	1626
Giarre d.	...	...	...	0859	...	...	...	1354	...	1630
Randazzo a.	...	...	...	1004	...	...	...	1459	...	1735
Randazzo d.	0557	0715	...	...	1058	1230	...	...	1501	▬
Bronte d.	0626	0744	...	...	1127	1259	...	...	1530	...
Adrano Nord d.	0651	0809	1100	...	1152	1324	1508	...	1555	⚒
Paternò ⊙ d.	0723	0840	1131	...	1223	1353	1536	...	1626	1713
Catania Borgo ⊙ a.	0759	0915	1206	...	1300	1430	1611	...	1703	1750

Metropolitana di Catania operates a metro service Nesima - San Nullo - Milo - Catania Borgo - Giuffrida - Galatea - Giovanni XXIII (for Catania Centrale) - Stesicoro and v.v. (*8.8 km*).
From Nesima every 10 – 15 minutes 0640 ⚒/0830 † - 2200; **from Stesicoro** every 10 – 15 minutes 0700 ⚒/0855 † - 2230.

⊙ – Other trains: Catania Borgo - Paternò at 0558 ⚒, 1136 ⚒ and 1305 ⚒; Paternò - Catania Borgo at 0640 ⚒, 1308 ⚒ and 1438 ⚒.

645 Service from March 13 — PALERMO and AGRIGENTO - CATANIA — 2nd class

km		⚒	⚒	†	⚒	⚒	⚒		⚒	⚒	⚒	⚒	†	⚒	⚒n	⚒	⚒	†	⚒	⚒	†	†	⚒	⚒	⚒	⚒
0	**Palermo** Centrale ▽ 641 d.	...	...	...	...	...	...	0731	0931	...	...	...	...	1327	...	...	...	1531	1531	...	...	1731	1731	...	...	1945
37	Termini Imerese ▽ 641 d.	...	...	...	...	...	...	0756	0956	...	...	...	...	1353	...	...	...	1555	1555	...	...	1755	1755	...	...	2012
70	Roccapalumba-Alia ▽ d.	...	...	...	0620	...	0730	|	|	...	...	...	...	1416	...	1519	1553	|	1617	...	...	|	1817	...	1954	2036
	Agrigento Centrale d.	...	...	...	|	...	|	|	|	...	1250	...	...	|	1350	|	|	|	|	...	1700	|	|	1912	|	|
	Aragona-Caldare d.	...	...	...	|	...	|	|	|	...	1306	...	...	|	1406	|	|	|	|	...	1716	|	|	1928	|	|
	Canicattì d.	...	...	...	|	...	|	|	|	...	1347	...	...	|	1443	|	|	|	|	...	1758	|	|	2007	|	|
	Caltanissetta Xirbi a.	...	...	...	0718	...	0821	0900	1100	...	|	...	...	1500	|	1616	1643	1700	1700	...	|	1900	1900	|	2044	2119
	Caltanissetta Centrale d.	0430	0515	0705	0737	0800	0838	|	|	1306	1415	1420	1512	|	1512	1634	...	|	|	1721	1828	|	|	2037	2100	|
127	Caltanissetta Xirbi d.	0439	0525	0713	...	0808	...	0901	1101	1314	...	1428	1521	1501	...	...	...	1701	1701	1729	...	1905	1905	...	...	2120
154	Enna d.	0505	0556	0739	...	0834	...	0926	1124	1342	...	1501	1546	1524	...	...	...	1723	1723	1752	...	1927	1927	...	...	2144
175	Dittaino a.	0525	0618	0759	...	0855	...	0947	1145	1403	...	1522	1606	1545	...	...	...	1745	1745	1812	...	1947	1947	...	...	2205
237	Catania Fontanarossa ✈ 641 a.	0642*	0726*	0916*	...	1012*	...	1044*	1242*	1511*	...	1630*	1723*	1642*	...	...	...	1842*	1842*	1929*	...	2044*	2044*	...	...	2302*
243	**Catania** Centrale 641 a.	0707*	0751*	0941*	...	1037*	...	1109*	1307*	1536*	...	1655*	1748*	1707*	...	...	...	1907*	1907*	1954*	...	2109*	2109*	...	...	2327*

km		⚒	⚒	⚒	⚒n		†	⚒	⚒	⚒	⚒	⚒	⚒	⚒		⚒	†	⚒	⚒	⚒	⚒	†	†	⚒		⚒
	Catania Centrale 641 d.	...	...	0409*	...	0643*	0823*	0851*	0913*	...	...	...	...	1251*	...	1510*	1449*	1449*	...	1715*	1651*	1651*	...	...	1933*	2042*
	Catania Fontanarossa ✈ 641 d.	...	...	0434*	...	0708*	0848*	0916*	0938*	...	...	...	...	1316*	...	1535*	1514*	1514*	...	1740*	1716*	1716*	...	...	1958*	2107*
	Dittaino d.	...	...	0536	...	0810	1010	1018	1100	1155	...	...	...	1418	...	1657	1616	1616	...	1902	1818	1818	...	...	2120	2220
	Enna d.	...	...	0555	...	0835	1030	1037	1125	1215	...	...	...	1437	...	1724	1635	1635	...	1928	1837	1837	...	...	2145	2241
0	Caltanissetta Xirbi a.	...	...	0617	...	0900	1056	1100	1149	1240	...	...	...	1500	...	1757	1700	1700	...	1953	1900	1900	...	...	2209	2306
6	**Caltanissetta** Centrale d.	0502	0558	|	0646	|	1104	|	1158	1248	1256	1405	1523	|	...	1805	|	|	1806	2000	|	|	1923	1935	2220	2314
	Caltanissetta Xirbi d.	0517	|	0618	|	0901	...	1101	...	...	1311	1423	|	1501	...	...	1701	1701	1822	...	1901	1901	|	|	...	...
35	Canicattì d.	|	0635	|	0725	|	...	|	...	...	|	|	1605	|	...	...	|	|	|	...	|	|	2005	2015	...	...
65	Aragona-Caldare d.	|	0705	|	0754	|	...	|	...	...	|	|	1643	|	...	...	|	|	|	...	|	|	2043	2052	...	...
78	**Agrigento** Centrale a.	|	0730	|	0810	|	...	|	...	...	|	|	1659	|	...	...	|	|	|	...	|	|	2059	2109	...	...
	Roccapalumba-Alia ▽ d.	0609	...	0709	...	|	...	|	...	...	1405	1533	...	|	...	...	1743	|	1928	...	|	1943	...	...	...	...
	Termini Imerese ▽ 641 d.	...	...	0732	...	1005	...	1205	...	...	...	...	...	1605	...	...	1807	1805	...	...	2012	2012	...	...	...	...
	Palermo Centrale ▽ 641 a.	...	...	0759	...	1029	...	1229	...	...	...	...	...	1629	...	...	1831	1829	...	...	2037	2037	...	...	...	...

DIRECT TRAINS PALERMO - AGRIGENTO

km		⚒	⚒		Ⓐ	⚒	Ⓐ			Ⓐ	⚒				
0	**Palermo** Centrale 641 d.	0543	0743	0843	1043	1143	1243	1343	1443	1543	1643	1743	1843	...	2043
37	Termini Imerese 641 d.	0612	0812	0912	1112	1212	1312	1418	1512	1612	1712	1812	1912	...	2112
70	Roccapalumba-Alia d.	0643	0843	0943	1143	1243	1343	1443	1543	1643	1743	1843	1943	...	2143
125	Aragona-Caldare ⊠ d.	0732	0932	1032	1232	1332	1432	1532t	1632	1732	1832	1932	2032	...	2232
139	**Agrigento** Centrale ⊠ a.	0747	0947	1047	1247	1347	1447	1547t	1647	1747	1847	1947	2047	...	2247

	⚒	⚒	⚒	Ⓐ			Ⓐ	⚒	⚒	Ⓑ	†			⚒
Agrigento Centrale ⊠ d.	0454	0522	0615	0715	0815	1015	1215	1315	1415	1515	1615	1715	1815	2015
Aragona-Caldare ⊠ d.	0508	0536	0632	0732	0832	1032	1232	1332	1432	1532	1632	1732	1832	2032
Roccapalumba-Alia d.	0552	0617	0717	0817	0917	1117	1317	1417	1517	1617	1717	1817	1917	2117
Termini Imerese 641 d.	0623	0651	0749	0849	0949	1149	1349	1449	1549	1649	1749	1849	1949	2149
Palermo Centrale 641 a.	0655	0717	0822	0917	1017	1217	1417	1517	1617	1717	1817	1917	2017	2217

n – Not Apr. 6 – 11.
t – On ①–⑥ Feb. 27 - Apr. 8 Aragona-Caldare d. 1545, Agrigento Centrale a. 1600.
* – Connection is by 🚌.
⊠ – Timings at Aragona-Caldare and Agrigento Centrale may vary by up to 5 minutes Feb. 27 - Apr. 9 (earlier departures possible).
▽ – See also panel below main table.

646 PALERMO - TRAPANI — 2nd class

km		⚒	⚒	⚒	⚒	†	⚒	†	†	⚒	⚒	⚒	†	†	⚒	⚒	⚒	⚒	†	⚒		†	⚒	†	⚒
0	**Palermo** Centrale d.	...	...	...	...	...	...	0808	...	1012	...	...	1108	...	...	1412	...	...	1708	1712	...	2008	2012	...	...
32	Piraineto d.	...	...	...	...	...	...	0859	0930	1108	1121	...	1159	1231	...	1508	1525	...	1759	1808	1835	2059	2108	2122	2135
73	Castellammare del Golfo d.	...	...	...	0730	...	...	...	1013	...	1201	...	...	1311	...	...	1605	...	▬	▬	1917	...	...	2201	2214
79	Alcamo Diramazione d.	...	...	...	0738	...	...	...	1021	...	1209	...	...	1318	1503	...	1616	...	†	⚒	1925	...	...	2208	2221
121	Castelvetrano d.	0520	0620	0728	0824	0830	0949	...	1104	...	1247	1414	...	1359	1540	...	1702	1735	1755	1910	2010	...	...	2250	2303
144	Mazara del Vallo d.	0542	0652	0755	0846	0852	1010	...	1126	...	1318	1445	...	...	1609	...	...	1801	1820	1940	2033	...	...	...	...
165	Marsala d.	0605	0725	0821	0913	0913	1031	...	1155	...	1349	1514	...	...	1635	...	...	1824	1848	2002	2057	...	...	...	...
196	**Trapani** a.	0638	0758	0855	0941	0955	1107	...	1230	...	1422	1545	...	...	1705	...	...	1900	1920	2035	2134	...	...	...	...

	⚒C	⚒	†	†	⚒	⚒	⚒	†	†	⚒	⚒	⚒	⚒	⚒	⚒	⚒	†	†	⚒			†	⚒	⚒	
Trapani d.	...	0549	0555	...	0650	...	0809	0910	...	1022	1153	...	1241	1338	1438	...	1520	...	1604	...	1815	...	...	1952	2046
Marsala d.	...	0627	0629	...	0724	...	0846	0945	...	1058	1225	...	1314	1416	1515	...	1553	...	1636	...	1847	...	...	2029	2124
Mazara del Vallo d.	...	0651	0652	...	0756	...	0913	1007	...	1123	1246	...	1346	1444	1537	...	1615	...	1657	...	1908	...	...	2058	2148
Castelvetrano d.	0500	0718	0718	...	0823	...	0939	1029	...	1152	1314	...	1412	1510	1606	...	1645	...	1724	...	1937	...	...	2128	2216
Alcamo Diramazione d.	0542	...	0756	...	0901	...	...	1111	...	...	1353	...	1452	...	1647	...	1724	...	...	...	2015	...	...	...	...
Castellammare del Golfo d.	0550	...	0803	...	0908	...	...	1119	...	...	1401	...	...	...	1654	...	1731	...	...	...	2022	...	...	...	...
Piraineto d.	0649	...	0848	0925	0953	1051	...	1205	1225	...	1444	1451	...	...	1735	1751	1815	1825	...	...	2109	2125	2151	...	...
Palermo Centrale a.	0747	...	...	1017	...	1147	...	...	1317	...	...	1547	...	...	...	1847	...	1917	...	...	...	2217	2247	...	...

C – Change trains at Cinisi-Terrasini (a. 0627, d. 0640).

648 Service from March 13 — SIRACUSA - GELA - CALTANISSETTA — 2nd class

km		⚒		⚒ 🚌	Ⓐ d		⚒ 🚌		⚒ 🚌	⚒		⚒ 🚌		⚒ 🚌		⚒ 🚌		⚒ 🚌						
0	**Siracusa** d.	...	...	0505	...	...	...	...	1019	...	...	1410	...	1535	...	1741	...	2019	...	...	...	...	...	...
62	Pozzallo d.	...	...	0611	...	...	...	...	1125	...	...	1516	...	1641	...	1847	...	2125	...	...	...	...	...	...
92	Modica d.	0531	...	0715	0738	...	0844	...	1229	1342	...	1620	...	1745	...	1951	...	2226	...	...	...	...	...	...
112	Ragusa d.	0553	...	0747	0800	...	0916	...	1311	1406	...	1702	...	1827	...	2023	...	...	...	...	...	...	...	...
153	Vittoria d.	0633	...	...	0842	...	1010	...	1405	1445	...	1756	...	1921	...	...	...	...	...	...	...	...	...	...
183	**Gela** d.	0657	...	...	0907	...	1053	...	1448	1508	...	1839	...	...	...	...	...	...	...	...	...	...	...	...
218	Licata d.	0725	...	...	0934	...	...	...	...	1534	...	...	...	...	...	...	...	...	...	...	...	...	...	...
264	Canicattì 645 d.	0806	...	...	1013	...	...	...	...	1615	...	...	...	...	...	...	...	...	...	...	...	...	...	...
293	**Caltanissetta** Centrale 645 a.	0836	...	...	1040	...	...	...	...	1642	...	...	...	...	...	...	...	...	...	...	...	...	...	...
299	**Caltanissetta** Xirbi 645 a.	0850	...	...	1053	...	...	...	...	1655	...	...	...	...	...	...	...	...	...	...	...	...	...	...

	⚒ 🚌		⚒ 🚌		⚒	⚒		⚒ 🚌		⚒ 🚌		⚒ 🚌		Ⓐ d	⚒ 🚌		⚒						
Caltanissetta Xirbi 645 d.	...	...	...	...	...	...	...	...	...	...	...	...	...	1710	...	...	1910	...	...	...	...	...	...
Caltanissetta Centrale 645 d.	...	...	...	...	0510	...	...	...	...	...	...	...	...	1721	...	...	1921	...	...	...	...	...	...
Canicattì 645 d.	...	...	...	...	0537	...	...	...	...	...	...	...	...	1746	...	...	1947	...	...	...	...	...	...
Licata d.	...	...	...	...	0615	...	...	...	...	...	...	...	...	1822	...	...	2025	...	...	...	...	...	...
Gela d.	...	...	...	...	0645	0727	...	1230	...	1420	...	1704	...	1849	...	...	2052	...	...	...	...	...	...
Vittoria d.	...	...	...	...	...	0751	...	1313	...	1503	...	1747	...	1912	1934	...	2116	...	...	...	...	...	...
Ragusa d.	...	...	0711	...	...	0844	...	1417	...	1607	...	1851	...	1959	2028	...	2158	...	...	...	...	...	...
Modica d.	0530	...	0743	...	...	0907	...	1449	...	1639	...	1923	...	2020	2100	...	2220	...					
Pozzallo d.	0631	...	0844	...	...	...	...	1550	...	1740	...	2024	...	...	...	...	...	...					
Siracusa a.	0737	...	0950	...	...	...	...	1656	...	1846	...	2130	...	...	...	...	...	...					

d – Not Apr. 24, June 1.

MALTA

Bus services on Malta and Gozo are operated by Malta Public Transport www.publictransport.com.mt. Travellers will also find useful information on the unofficial website www.maltabybus.com.

649 PRINCIPAL BUS SERVICES

Routes from Valletta: **X4** Airport - Hal Far, **1** L'Isla (Senglea), **2/4** Birgu (Vittoriosa), **3** Birgu - Smart City - Rinella - Kalkara, **13-15** Sliema - San Giljan (St Julian's), **13** Bahar ic-Caghaq, **31/45/48** Mosta - Bugibba (**45** via Qawra seafront), **31/43/45** Naxxar, **41/42** Mosta - St Paul's Bay - Mellieha - Ghadira - Cirkewwa (for Gozo ferry), **44** Ghajn Tuffieha (Golden Bay), **49** Armier Bay (summer), **51-53** Rabat / Mdina, **52/56** Dingli, **61** Zebbug, **62** Siggiewi, **71/73** Zurrieq, **72** Qrendi, **74** Hagar Qim - Blue Grotto, **80/82/X4** Birzebbuga, **81/85** Marsaxlokk, **91-93** Marsaskala, **94** Xghajra.

Other routes: **X1** Airport - Cirkewwa, **X2** Airport - Sliema, **X3** Airport - Rabat - Bugibba, **186** Bugibba - Ta' Qali - Rabat, **202** Sliema - Naxxar - Mosta - Rabat, **203** Sliema - Naxxar - Mosta - Bugibba, **212** Sliema - San Giljan - Bugibba, **221** Bugibba - Mellieha - Cirkewwa, **222** Sliema - St Paul's Bay - Mellieha - Cirkewwa, **223** Bugibba - Ghajn Tuffieha, **225** Sliema - St Paul's Bay - Ghajn Tuffieha.

Gozo: routes from Rabat (Victoria): **301/303** Mgarr (for Cirkewwa ferry), **302** Ramla, **305** Sannat, **306/330** Xlendi, **307** Xaghra, **308** Ta' Pinu - Ghasri, **309** Zebbug, **310** Marsalforn, **311** Dwejra.

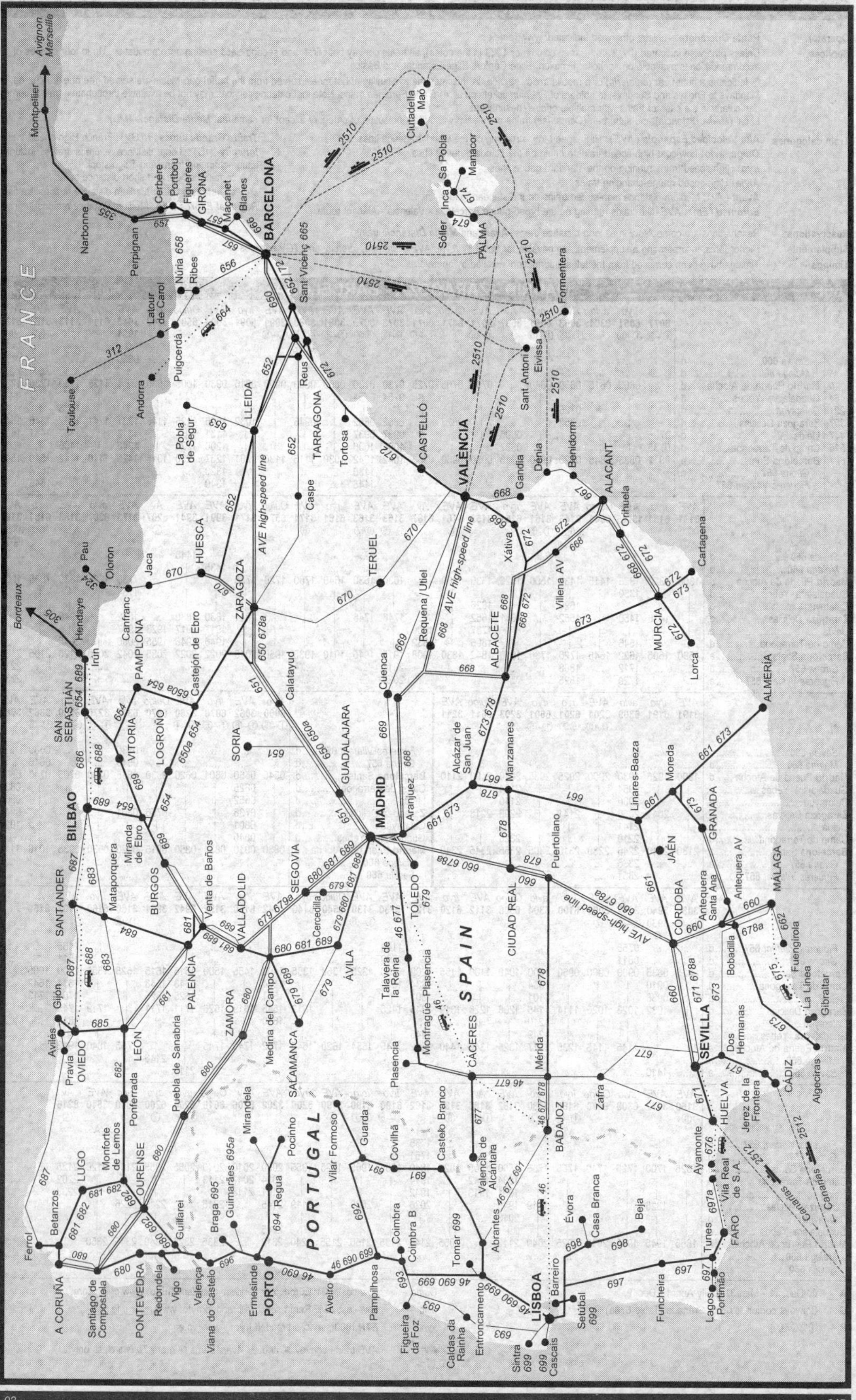
FRANCE
SPAIN
PORTUGAL
Montpellier
Avignon Marseille
Narbonne
Toulouse
Perpignan
Cerbère
Portbou
Figueres
GIRONA
Maçanet
Blanes
BARCELONA
Latour de Carol
Núria 658
Ribes
Puigcerdà
Andorra
La Pobla de Segur
LLEIDA
Reus
Sant Vicenç 665
TARRAGONA
Tortosa
Caspe
CASTELLÓ
VALÈNCIA
Ciutadella
Maó
Sa Pobla
Manacor
Inca
Sóller
PALMA
Formentera
Eivissa
Sant Antoni
Gandia
Dénia
Benidorm
ALACANT
Orihuela
Xàtiva
Cartagena
MURCIA
Lorca
Villena AV
ALBACETE
Requena / Utiel
TERUEL
Cuenca
Pau
Oloron
Jaca
Canfranc
HUESCA
ZARAGOZA
Bordeaux
Hendaye
Irún
SAN SEBASTIÁN
PAMPLONA
Castejón de Ebro
VITORIA
LOGROÑO
SORIA
Calatayud
GUADALAJARA
MADRID
Aranjuez
TOLEDO
BILBAO
Miranda de Ebro
SANTANDER
Mataporquera
BURGOS
Venta de Baños
VALLADOLID
PALENCIA
SEGOVIA
Cercedilla
ÁVILA
Medina del Campo
SALAMANCA
ZAMORA
Puebla de Sanabria
LEÓN
Ponferrada
Gijón
Avilés
OVIEDO
Pravia
Ferrol
A CORUÑA
Betanzos
LUGO
Monforte de Lemos
OURENSE
Santiago de Compostela
PONTEVEDRA
Redondela
Vigo
Valença
Viana do Castelo
Guillarei
Braga 695
Guimarães 695a
Mirandela
Ermesinde
PORTO
Regua
Pocinho
Aveiro
Vilar Formoso
Guarda
Covilhã
Castelo Branco
Coimbra B
Coimbra
Pampilhosa
Figueira da Foz
Caldas da Rainha
Entroncamento
Tomar 699
Abrantes
Valencia de Alcántara
LISBOA
Sintra 699
Cascais 699
Barreiro
Setúbal 699
Évora
Casa Branca
Beja
Funcheira
Tunes
Lagos
Portimão
FARO
Vila Real de S.A.
Ayamonte
HUELVA
Plasencia
Monfragüe - Plasencia
CÁCERES
Talavera de la Reina
Mérida
BADAJOZ
Zafra
CIUDAD REAL
Puertollano
Alcázar de San Juan
Manzanares
Linares-Baeza
JAÉN
CÓRDOBA
SEVILLA
Dos Hermanas
Jerez de la Frontera
CÁDIZ
Algeciras
Gibraltar
La Línea
Fuengirola
MÁLAGA
Bobadilla
Antequera Santa Ana
Antequera AV
GRANADA
Moreda
ALMERÍA
AVE high-speed line
Canarias

SPAIN

Operator: **Renfe Operadora** – unless otherwise indicated. www.renfe.es

Services: Unless otherwise indicated (by '2' in the train column or (2) in the notes), all trains convey both first- and second-class seating accommodation. Up to four classes of accommodation is available on services: Prémium, Elige Confort, Elige Estándar and Básico.

🍸 indicates a buffet car (*cafetería*) or a mobile trolley service. ✕ indicates the availability of hot meals served from the buffet car. Meals are served free of extra charge, on Mondays to Fridays and Sundays, to holders of *Prémium* tickets on all *AVE* and *Euromed* trains. Note that catering services may not be available throughout a train's journey, particularly in the case of trains with multiple origins / destinations.

Local (*Media Distancia*) and suburban (*Cercanías*) trains are shown without an indication of category except for some fast ***Media Distancia*** (*MD*).

Train categories:

Alta Velocidad Española (*AVE*): High-speed trains running on the standard-gauge lines.
Ouigo, avlo: Low-cost high-speed trains running on the standard-gauge lines.
iryo: High-speed trains running on the standard-gauge lines.
Alvia: High-speed gauge-changing trains.
Avant (*Av*): Medium-distance high-speed trains on the standard-gauge lines.
Euromed (*Em*): *AVE*-like trains running on the broad-gauge Barcelona - València - Alacant route.
Train à Grande Vitesse (*TGV*): French High-speed trains.
Intercity (*IC*): Long distance express trains, including gauge-changing trains and Talgo stock. Also certain medium and short distance trains.
Media Distancia (*MD*): Medium distance regional trains.
Regional Exprés (*RE*): Medium distance regional trains.

Reservations: Reservations are compulsory in all long distance trains, ***Avant*** and ***Media Distancia*** trains.

Supplements: Higher fares, incorporating a supplement, are payable for travel by *Alvia*, *AVE*, *Euromed*, *Intercity* and *TGV* services.

Timings: Timings have been compiled from the latest information supplied by operators.

650 MADRID - ZARAGOZA - BARCELONA — High-speed services

km		*Av* 8077 ①–⑤	*iryo* 6051 ①–⑤	*avlo* 6301	*AVE* 3063 ①–⑤	*iryo* 6061 ①–⑤	*Av* 8087	*AVE* 3071 ①–⑤	*Ouigo* 6471	*iryo* 6071 ①–⑤	*AVE* 3073 ①–⑤	*AVE* 3073 ⑥⑦	*AVE* 3081 ①–⑤	*AVE* 3083 ①②③④⑥⑦	*AVE* 3091 ①–⑤	*iryo* 6091	*AVE* 3093	*Ouigo* 6501	*avlo* 6303	*AVE* 3943 3991 G	*iryo* 6111	*AVE* 3113	*AVE* 3123 Ⓑ	*AVE* 3123 ⑥
	Sevilla **660** d.	...	...	...	...	...	...	...	...	...	...	...	...	...	...	...	...	...	...	0850	...	...	...	...
	Málaga **660** d.	...	...	...	...	...	...	...	...	...	...	...	...	...	...	...	...	...	...	|	...	...	...	...
0	**Madrid** Puerta de Atocha d.	...	0605	0615	0630	0640	...	0700	0705	0725	0730	0730	0800	0830	0900	0916	0930	1005	1030	|	1125	1130	1230	1230
64	Guadalajara - Yebes d.	...	|	|	|	|	...	|	|	|	0754	0754	|	|	|	|	|	|	|	|	|	|	|	|
221	Calatayud d.	...	|	|	0726	|	...	|	|	|	|	|	|	|	|	|	|	|	|	|	|	1226	|	|
307	**Zaragoza** Delicias d.	...	|	|	0752	|	...	|	0823	|	0852	0852	|	0946	|	1032	1046	1125	1146	1237	1241	1252	1346	1346
447	Lleida d.	0705	|	|	|	|	0805	|	|	|	0937	0937	|	|	|	|	1131	|	|	1319	|	1337	1431	1431
526	Camp de Tarragona d.	0735	|	|	|	|	0837	|	|	|	1006	1006	|	|	|	|	1200	1224	|	1346	|	1406	|	|
621	**Barcelona** Sants a.	0811	0835	0845	0920	0910	0913	0930	0950	0955	1042	1042	1030	1115	1130	1201	1237	1250	1315	1420	1410	1442	1540	1540
	Girona **657** a.	...	...	...	...	...	...	...	...	...	...	1130	...	...	...	...	1323	...	...	...	...	...	1628	...
	Figueres Vilafant **657** a.	...	...	...	...	...	...	...	...	...	...	1145	...	...	...	...	1340	...	...	...	...	...	1645	...

	AVE 3131 ①②③④⑦	*iryo* 6131	*AVE* 19725	*Ouigo* 6541	*AVE* 3143 Ⓑ	*AVE* 3151 ①–⑤	*iryo* 6151	*AVE* 3153	*AVE* 3161 Ⓑ	*Av* 8187	*AVE* 3163 ①–⑤	*AVE* 3163 ⑥⑦	*iryo* 6161	*AVE* 3171 Ⓑ	*Ouigo* 6571	*iryo* 6171	*AVE* 3991	*AVE* 3941	*Av* 8207 Ⓐ	*AVE* 3173	*avlo* 6307	*AVE* 3183	*iryo* 6181	*AVE* 3191 ①②③④⑦
Sevilla **660** d.	...	...	...	...	...	...	...	...	...	...	...	...	...	...	...	...	...	1448	...	...	...	...	...	...
Málaga **660** d.	...	...	...	...	...	...	...	...	...	...	...	...	...	...	...	...	1435	|	...	...	...	...	...	...
Madrid Puerta de Atocha d.	1300	1320	1325	1415	1430	1500	1525	1530	1600	...	1630	1630	1640	1700	1720	1725	|	|	...	1730	1800	1830	1835	1900
Guadalajara - Yebes d.	|	|	1350	|	|	|	|	|	|	...	|	|	|	|	|	|	|	|	...	1754	|	|	|	|
Calatayud d.	|	|	|	|	1526	|	|	1626	|	...	|	|	|	|	|	|	|	|	...	|	|	|	|	|
Zaragoza Delicias d.	|	1436	1450	|	1552	|	1641	1652	|	...	1746	1746	|	|	|	1841	1830	1830	...	1852	|	1946	|	|
Lleida d.	|	|	|	|	|	|	|	1737	|	1800	|	|	|	|	|	|	1917	1917	1923	1937	|	|	|	|
Camp de Tarragona d.	|	|	1546	|	|	|	|	1806	|	1832	|	|	|	|	|	|	1946	1946	1955	2006	|	2045	|	|
Barcelona Sants a.	1530	1605	1622	1645	1720	1730	1810	1842	1830	1908	1915	1915	1910	1930	1950	2010	2022	2022	2035	2042	2030	2120	2105	2130
Girona **657** a.	...	...	1712	...	1808	...	...	...	...	...	2011	...	...	...	...	...	...	...	...	...	...	...	...	2218
Figueres Vilafant **657** a.	...	...	1729	...	1825	...	...	...	...	...	2028	...	...	...	...	...	...	...	...	...	...	...	...	2235

	AVE 3191 ⑤	*iryo* 6191	*avlo* 6309	*AVE* 3201 ①–⑤	*iryo* 6201 ⑥⑦	*iryo* 6601 ①–⑤	*AVE* 3203	*Ouigo* 6611	*AVE* 3211 A
Sevilla **660** d.	...	...	...	...	...	...	...	...	...
Málaga **660** d.	...	...	...	...	...	...	...	...	...
Madrid Puerta de Atocha d.	1900	1925	1930	2000	2025	2035	2040	2100	2110
Guadalajara - Yebes d.	|	|	1954	|	|	|	2104	|	|
Calatayud d.	|	|	2030	|	|	|	2140	|	|
Zaragoza Delicias d.	|	2041	2056	|	2141	|	2206	2218	|
Lleida d.	|	|	2141	|	|	|	2251	|	|
Camp de Tarragona d.	|	|	2210	|	|	|	2320	|	|
Barcelona Sants a.	2130	2210	2246	2230	2310	2305	2355	2345	2340
Girona **657** a.	...	...	2336	...	...	...	...	...	...
Figueres Vilafant **657** a.	...	...	2351	...	...	...	...	...	...

	iryo 6060 ①–⑤	*AVE* 3062 ①–⑥	*iryo* 6070 ①–⑤	*AVE* 3260 ①–④	*Ouigo* 6470	*avlo* 6302	*AVE* 3270 ①–④	*iryo* 6080 ①–⑤	*AVE* 3662 ①–⑤	*AVE* 3082
Figueres Vilafant **657** d.	...	...	...	...	...	0530	...	...	0630	...
Girona **657** d.	...	...	...	...	...	0546	...	...	0646	...
Barcelona Sants d.	0545	0550	0604	0620	0630	0635	0700	0705	0740	0800
Camp de Tarragona d.	|	0625	|	|	|	|	|	|	|	0834
Lleida d.	|	0652	|	|	|	|	|	|	|	0901
Zaragoza Delicias d.	|	0736	|	|	0756	0801	|	|	|	0945
Calatayud d.	|	0801	|	|	|	|	|	|	|	1010
Guadalajara - Yebes d.	|	0840	|	|	|	|	|	|	|	|
Madrid Puerta de Atocha a.	0830	0910	0834	0850	0915	0920	0930	0935	1010	1112
Málaga **660** a.	...	...	...	...	...	...	...	...	...	...
Sevilla **660** a.	...	...	...	...	...	...	...	...	...	...

	AVE 3080 ①–⑤	*AVE* 3940 3930 G	*AVE* 3092 ①–⑥	*AVE* 3092 ⑦	*iryo* 6100	*avlo* 6304	*Ouigo* 6500	*AVE* 3112	*iryo* 6120	*AVE* 3122	*AVE* 19730	*AVE* 3130 ①–⑤	*Ouigo* 6540	*iryo* 6140	*AVE* 3142	*iryo* 6150	*AVE* 3152	*AVE* 3942	*AVE* 3991	*AVE* 3150 ①–⑤	*iryo* 6160	*AVE* 3162	*Av* 8166	
Figueres Vilafant **657** d.	...	...	0755	...	...	...	...	...	...	...	1143	...	...	...	...	...	...	...	...	...	...	1455	...	...
Girona **657** d.	...	...	0811	...	...	...	...	...	...	...	1200	...	...	...	...	...	...	...	...	...	...	1511	...	...
Barcelona Sants d.	0825	0835	0900	0900	0950	1000	1040	1100	1155	1200	1250	1325	1350	1355	1400	1455	1500	1515	1515	1525	1555	1600	1605	...
Camp de Tarragona d.	|	0910	|	|	|	1034	|	|	|	1234	1322	|	|	|	1434	|	|	1548	1548	|	|	1634	1642	...
Lleida d.	|	0938	|	|	|	1101	|	|	|	1301	|	|	|	|	1501	|	|	1625	1625	|	|	1701	1713	...
Zaragoza Delicias d.	|	1032	1026	1026	1114	1145	1206	1226	1319	1345	1425	|	|	1519	1545	1619	1626	1711	1711	|	1719	1745	...	...
Calatayud d.	|	|	|	|	|	1210	|	|	|	|	|	|	|	|	1610	|	|	|	|	|	|	1810	...	...
Guadalajara - Yebes d.	|	|	|	|	|	1249	|	|	|	1445	|	|	|	|	|	|	|	|	|	|	|	|	...	...
Madrid Puerta de Atocha a.	1055	|	1145	1145	1235	1317	1325	1345	1440	1512	1545	1554	1620	1640	1712	1740	1745	|	|	1755	1840	1912	...	...
Málaga **660** a.	...	|	...	...	...	...	...	...	...	...	...	...	...	...	...	...	...	|	2146	...	...	...	...	...
Sevilla **660** a.	...	1410	...	...	...	...	...	...	...	...	...	...	...	...	...	...	...	2115	...	...	...	...	...	...

	AVE 3160 Ⓑ	*AVE* 3172	*avlo* 6308	*Ouigo* 6570	*iryo* 6180 ①–⑤	*iryo* 6180 ⑥⑦	*AVE* 3182	*Av* 8186 ①–⑤	*AVE* 3180 Ⓑ	*AVE* 3192	*iryo* 6190 ①–⑤	*iryo* 6190 ⑥⑦	*AVE* 3190 Ⓑ	*iryo* 6200	*AVE* 3202	*Av* 8206	*Ouigo* 6610	*iryo* 6200 ①–⑥	*iryo* 6200 ⑦	*avlo* 6310	*AVE* 3610 A	*Av* 8216 Ⓐ		
Figueres Vilafant **657** d.	...	...	...	...	...	...	...	...	...	1735	...	...	...	...	...	...	...	...	...	...	...	...	...	...
Girona **657** d.	...	...	...	...	...	...	...	...	...	1751	...	...	...	...	...	...	...	...	...	...	...	...	...	...
Barcelona Sants d.	1625	1700	1725	1740	1755	1755	1800	1805	1825	1840	1905	1905	1925	1955	2000	2010	2040	2055	2055	2100	2120	2125	...	...
Camp de Tarragona d.	|	|	|	|	|	|	1834	1842	|	1914	|	|	|	|	2034	2047	2113	|	|	|	|	2202	...	...
Lleida d.	|	|	|	|	|	|	1901	1913	|	1942	|	|	|	|	2101	2118	|	|	|	|	|	2233	...	...
Zaragoza Delicias d.	|	1826	|	|	|	1919	1945	...	|	2026	|	2029	|	2119	2145	...	2215	|	2219	2226	|	...	...	...
Calatayud d.	|	|	|	|	|	|	2010	...	|	|	|	|	|	|	|	...	|	|	|	|	|	...	...	...
Guadalajara - Yebes d.	|	|	|	|	|	|	|	...	|	|	|	|	|	|	2245	...	|	|	|	|	|	...	...	...
Madrid Puerta de Atocha a.	1855	1945	1955	2010	2025	2040	2112	...	2055	2145	2135	2150	2155	2240	2312	...	2335	2325	2340	2345	2350	...	...	...
Málaga **660** a.	...	...	...	...	...	...	...	...	...	...	...	...	...	...	...	...	...	...	...	...	...	...	...	...
Sevilla **660** a.	...	...	...	...	...	...	...	...	...	...	...	...	...	...	...	...	...	...	...	...	...	...	...	...

A – Ⓑ Dec. 11 - Mar. 31. Daily Apr. 1 - Dec. 9.
G – Conveys portion to / from Granada (Table **678a**).
P – ①②③④⑥.

Ouigo – Low-cost ***TGV*** Euroduplex services branded **Ouigo**: www.ouigo.com
avlo – Low-cost ***AVE*** Renfe services branded **avlo**: www.avlorenfe.com
iryo – ***ETR*** 1000 services branded **iryo**: www.iryo.eu
☛ *AVE* trains convey ✕ and 🍸. *Avant* trains (*Av*) are *Turista* class only.

MADRID – LOGROÑO, PAMPLONA / IRUÑA, HUESCA – BARCELONA 650a

	IC	IC	Alvia	Alvia	Alvia	Alvia	Alvia	Alvia	Alvia	AVE	IC	Alvia	Alvia	Alvia	Alvia	Alvia	Alvia	Alvia	AVE	Alvia			
	635	10655	533	433	601	705	603	605	661	3363	563	631	621 625	537	437	609	613	701	3393	801			
	①–⑤	⑥		②④⑥	①–⑤	⑥⑦	⑥	Ⓑ	①–⑥	⑤⑦	⑦						⑤⑦			Ⓑ			
		y	K	F					G			B	J	K	F								
Madrid Puerta de Atocha d.	...	...	...	...	0735	0805	0935	1135	...	1605	...	...	...	...	...	1505	1735	1815	1905	1935	...	...	...
Guadalajara - Yebes d.	...	...	...	...	|	0831	1002	1201	...	|	...	...	...	...	...	1531	|	1840	1928	|	...	...	...
Calatayud d.	...	...	...	...	|	0917	1106	1248	...	|	...	...	...	...	...	1619	|	1934	2006	|	...	...	...
Logroño **654** a.	...	...	...	0904	|	1132	|	|	...	|	...	...	...	...	1753	|	|	2142	|	|	...	...	...
Pamplona / Iruña **654** a.	0625	0812	0905	|	1042	...	1303	1452	1508	|	1610	1729	1729	1754	|	1828	2043	...	|	2240	...	...	...
Zaragoza Delicias d.	0810	1003	1109	1109	...	...	...	...	1701	1727	1747	1924	1924	1952	1952	...	...	...	2033	...	...	...	...
Huesca **670** a.	|	|	|	|	...	...	...	...	|	1810	|	|	|	|	|	...	...	...	2118	...	...	...	...
Lleida d.	0900	1056	1200	1200	...	...	...	...	1754	...	1839	2014	2014	2051	2057	...	...	...	...	...	...	...	...
Camp de Tarragona d.	0930	1127	1233	1233	...	...	...	...	1827	...	1910	2053	2053	2128	2133	...	...	...	...	...	...	...	...
Barcelona Sants a.	1010	1205	1309	1309	...	...	...	...	1903	...	1955	2135	2135	2209	2214	...	...	...	...	...	...	...	...

	Alvia	AVE	Alvia	Alvia	Alvia	Alvia	Alvia	Alvia	Alvia	Alvia	IC	Alvia	Alvia	Alvia	Alvia	AVE	Alvia	Alvia	Alvia	Alvia	IC	IC	IC
	802	3272	702	800	600	534	602	438	632	622 626	10560	606	664	530	430	3592	608	612	706	610	562	562	562
	①–⑤			①	⑥		Ⓑ				⑥				①③⑤	⑤⑦	⑤	⑦	⑥⑦	Ⓑ	⑤	①–④	⑦
						K		F	B	J	b		G	K	F								
Barcelona Sants d.	...	...	...	...	...	0730	...	0850	0930	0930	1005	...	1210	1530	1530	...	...	...	...	...	1845	1840	1930
Camp de Tarragona d.	...	...	...	...	...	0808	...	0927	1006	1006	1043	...	1248	1608	1608	...	...	...	...	...	1922	1918	2008
Lleida d.	...	...	...	...	...	0844	...	0959	1038	1038	1115	...	1322	1639	1639	...	...	...	...	...	1954	1950	2041
Huesca **670** d.	...	0815	...	...	...	|	...	|	|	|	|	...	|	|	|	1935	...	...	...	...	|	|	|
Zaragoza Delicias d.	...	0900	...	...	...	0934	...	1048	1131	1131	1204	...	1414	1729	1729	2020	...	...	...	...	2048	2102	2134
Pamplona / Iruña **654** d.	0640	|	...	0810	0900	1117	1130	|	1324	1324	1354	1537	1606	1925	|	|	1828	1828	...	1935	2232	2244	2328
Logroño **654** d.	|	|	0730	|	|	...	|	1242	...	...	...	|	...	...	1936	|	|	|	1845	|	...	...	...
Calatayud d.	|	0925	0936	|	1113	...	1323	...	...	...	...	|	...	...	...	|	|	|	2055	2131	...	...	...
Guadalajara - Yebes d.	|	1005	1022	|	1202	...	1411	...	...	...	...	|	...	...	...	|	|	|	2157	2221	...	...	...
Madrid Puerta de Atocha a.	0950	1035	1050	1124	1230	...	1448	...	...	...	...	1845	...	...	...	2140	2135	2135	2225	2250	...	...	...

B – [12] Salamanca - Valladolid - Barcelona and v.v. (Tables **654, 689**).
F – [12] Bilbao - Barcelona and v.v. (Table **654**).
G – [12] Gijón - Barcelona and v.v. (Table **685**).
J – [12] Vigo / A Coruña - Barcelona and v.v. (Table **680**).
K – [12] San Sebastián / Donostia - Barcelona and v.v. (Table **654**).

b – To Irún (Table **654**).
y – From Vitoria / Gasteiz (Table **654**).

☛ **Shaded services are suspended until further notice.**

MADRID - SORIA and ZARAGOZA 651

km	*For high-speed trains see Tables **650** and **650a***		2 Ⓐ		2 Ⓒ	2 Ⓐ H	2 Ⓐ	2 Ⓒ	2 Ⓒ	2 Ⓐ		2 ⑤	2 w		2 ⑦		2	2 ⑦	2 Ⓐ	
0	**Madrid**-Chamartín-Clara Campoamor d.	...	...	...	...	0715	0747	0814	0915	...	...	1543	1547	...	...	...	1900	1907	1952	...
55	Guadalajara d.	...	...	...	...	0757	0826	0854	0959	...	...	1629	1642	...	...	...	1939	2038	2050	...
138	Sigüenza d.	...	...	...	...	0859	0920	0944	1102	...	...	1717	1743	...	...	...	2030	2142	2153	...
248	**Soria** a.	...	...	...	...	|	1030	1054	|	...	...	1823	|	...	...	...	2136	...	...	...
178	Arcos de Jalón d.	...	0650	...	0850	0936	...	...	1140	...	...	...	1815	...	...	...	...	...	...	...
241	Calatayud d.	...	0736	...	0936	1016	...	...	1221	1321	...	...	1859	...	2023	...	...	...	...	...
339	**Zaragoza** Delicias ♣ a.	...	0855	...	1101	1118	...	...	1325	1438	...	...	2011	...	2149	...	...	...	...	...

*For high-speed trains see Tables **650** and **650a***		2 Ⓐ		2 Ⓐ		2 Ⓒ		2		2 H		2 Ⓑ	2 ⑦		2		2			
Zaragoza Delicias ♥ d.	...	...	...	...	...	...	...	0857	...	1409	...	1620	...	...	...	...	2036	...	...	...
Calatayud d.	...	...	...	...	...	...	...	1022	...	1508	...	1742	...	...	...	...	2157	...	...	...
Arcos de Jalón d.	...	...	...	...	...	...	...	1108	...	1545	...	...	...	...	...	...	2244	...	...	...
Soria d.	...	...	...	0653	...	0830	...	|	...	|	...	...	1644	...	1900	...	...	...	...	...
Sigüenza d.	...	0648	...	0826	...	1008	...	1144	...	1620	...	...	1817	...	2033	...	...	...	...	...
Guadalajara d.	...	0754	...	0923	...	1056	...	1248	...	1723	...	...	1908	...	2126	...	...	...	...	...
Madrid-Chamartín-Clara Campoamor a.	...	0913	...	1006	...	1137	...	1336	...	1809	...	...	1950	...	2206	...	...	...	...	...

H – To / from Barcelona (Table **652**).
w – To Lleida on Ⓑ (Table **652**).
♥ – All services call 7 – 8 minutes earlier at Zaragoza **Goya** and 5 minutes earlier at Zaragoza **Portillo**.
♣ – All services call 4 – 5 minutes later at Zaragoza **Portillo** and 6 – 8 minutes later at Zaragoza **Goya**.

ZARAGOZA - BARCELONA 652

km	*For high-speed trains see Tables **650** and **650a***	2 ⚒	2	2	2 ⚒	2	2	2	2	2	2	2 ⑥	2 ⑦	2	2 Ⓐ	2 Ⓒ	2	2	2 Ⓐ	2 ⚒	2 †	2	2	2 Ⓑ	2
	Madrid Chamartín ‡ **651** d.	...	...	...	...	...	...	...	...	...	...	...	...	...	0715	...	...	...	...	...	...	...	...	1547	...
0	**Zaragoza** Delicias ♣ d.	...	...	...	...	...	...	...	...	...	...	0857	1027	...	1116	1116	...	...	1515	...	...	1630	...	2012	2015
114	Caspe d.	...	...	...	...	...	0705	...	...	...	...	|	|	...	1252	1252	...	...	|	...	...	1800	...	|	2152
★	Lleida d.	...	...	...	0623	0715	|	...	...	...	...	1121	1237	1310	|	|	1545	...	1727	1748	1748	|	...	2240	...
239	Reus d.	0537	0641	0733	0743	|	0906	...	1107	1139	1308	...	...	1437	1454	1454	1714	1836	...	|	|	2005	2122	...	...
257	Tarragona **672** d.	0555	0659	0749	0800	|	0926	1021	1125	1158	1326	...	...	1455	1512	1512	1730	1858	...	|	|	2027	2140	...	...
282	Sant Vicenç de Calders **672** d.	0616	0719	0810	0831	0847	0948	1043	1145	1218	1347	...	...	1517	1536	1536	1750	1919	...	1913	1923	2046	2200	...	...
342	**Barcelona** Sants **672** a.	0720	0809	0909	0934	0939	1040	1138	1240	1309	1440	...	...	1610	1637	1640	1840	2013	...	2010	2019	2139	2304	...	...
345	Barcelona Pass. de Gràcia a.	0725	0814	0914	0939	0944	1045	1143	1245	1314	1445	...	...	1615	1644	1645	1845	2018	...	2015	2024	2144	2309	...	...
350	**Barcelona** França a.	0735	0824	0925	0949	0954	1055	1155	1255	1325	1455	...	...	1625	1655	1655	1855	2028	...	2025	2034	2154	2319	...	...

*For high-speed trains see Tables **650** and **650a***	2 Ⓐ	2 Ⓐ	2	2 Ⓒ	2	2	2	2		2	2	2	2 ⑦	2 Ⓐ	2	2	2	2	2	2	2 Ⓑ	2			
Barcelona França d.	...	...	0613	...	0647	0713	0843	0913	...	1143	1313	1343	...	1513	1543	1643	1713	1843	1847	1940	2010	2113	...	...	...
Barcelona Pass. de Gràcia d.	...	...	0624	...	0659	0724	0854	0924	...	1154	1324	1354	...	1524	1554	1654	1724	1854	1858	1952	2021	2124	...	...	...
Barcelona Sants **672** d.	...	...	0630	...	0706	0730	0903	0930	...	1203	1330	1403	...	1533	1603	1703	1730	1903	1904	1957	2027	2130	...	...	...
Sant Vicenç de Calders **672** d.	...	...	0724	...	0807	0822	0950	1017	...	1248	1420	1449	...	1619	1649	1747	1820	1948	2005	2046	2115	2222	...	...	...
Tarragona **672** d.	...	...	0746	...	|	0844	1011	1042	...	1308	1441	1511	...	1640	1710	1809	1841	|	2037	2107	2136	2243	...	...	...
Reus d.	...	...	0803	...	|	0900	1028	1048	...	1326	1458	1531	...	1656	1727	1827	1855	|	2052	2124	2152	2259	...	...	...
Lleida d.	...	0625	...	...	0956	...	|	...	...	1455	...	1650	1515	...	|	1955	|	2112	...	...	...	...	...	...	...
Caspe d.	0653	|	...	1039	...	...	1229	...	...	...	...	...	|	...	1944	...	2108	...	...	...	...	...	...	...	...
Zaragoza Delicias ♥ a.	0825	0856	...	1212	...	...	1405	...	...	...	...	...	1731	...	2114	...	...	...	...	...	...	...	...	...	...
Madrid Chamartín ‡ **651** a.	...	1329	...	...	...	...	1807	...	...	...	...	...	...	...	...	...	...	...	...	...	...	...	...	...	...

★ – Leida - Reus: *90 km.*
Zaragoza - Lleida: *189 km.*
Lleida - Sant Vicenç: *106 km.*

♥ – All trains call 5 – 8 minutes earlier at Zaragoza **Goya** and 3 – 5 minutes earlier at Zaragoza **Portillo**.
♣ – All trains call 4 – 5 minutes later at Zaragoza **Portillo** and 6 – 8 minutes later at Zaragoza **Goya**.
‡ – Full name is Madrid-Chamartín-Clara Campoamor.

LLEIDA - LA POBLA DE SEGUR 653

FGC 2nd class

km						A	Ⓑ			†	①–④	
0	**Lleida** d.	...	0620	0747	0905	1040	1047	...	1330	1705	1730	...
27	Balaguer d.	...	0646	0815	0931	1110	1115	...	1356	1731	1756	...
77	Tremp d.	...	...	0909	...	|	1209	...	...	1825	1850	...
90	**La Pobla de Segur** a.	...	...	0922	...	1235	1222	...	...	1838	1903	...

	Ⓐ	Ⓑ	Ⓑ	⑦	⑥	Ⓐ	A	Ⓒ	①–④	B	
La Pobla de Segur d.	0708	1008	...	1515	...	1530	1700	1900	1930	...	...
Tremp d.	0719	1019	...	1526	...	1541	|	1911	1941	...	...
Balaguer d.	0815	1115	1408	1622	1623	1637	1830f	2007	2037	2202	...
Lleida a.	0841	1141	1434	1648	1649	1703	1900	2033	2103	2228	...

A – Tren dels Llacs: Dates of running in 2023 have not yet been published.
B – Runs 19 minutes earlier on ⑥.
f – Arrive 1815.

654 ZARAGOZA - IRÚN and BILBAO

km		18071	16071	Alvia 601	Alvia 534	Alvia 438	Alvia 603	Alvia 622	Alvia 632	Alvia 605	IC 10560	18021	IC 282	Alvia 664	18073	16015	Alvia 609	18023	Alvia 530	16017	Alvia 430	Alvia 613	18075	
		2	2					626				2			2	2		2		2	①③		2	
		①–⑥	①–⑤	①–⑤			⑥	J	S	Ⓑ	⑥			A				⑤		①–⑥	⑤	⑤⑦		
	Barcelona Sants **652** d.	...	...	...	0730	0850	...	0930	0930	...	1005	...	...	1210	...	...	...	...	1530	...	1530	...	...	...
	Madrid PA ‡ **650a** d.	...	...	0735	|	|	0935	|	|	1135	|	...	...	|	...	...	1505	...	|	...	|	1735	...	...
0	**Zaragoza** Delicias d.	0625	...	|	0934	1048	|	1131	1131	|	1204	1309	...	1414	1435	...	|	1652	1729	...	1729	|	1742	...
94	Castejón de Ebro ★ d.	0729	0730	0944	1028	1148	1210	1233	1233	|	1259	1417	...	|	1540	...	|	1748	1828	...	1845	|	1849	...
182	**Pamplona / Iruña** d.	0837	|	1042	1119	|	1303	1326	1326	1452	1356	1526	...	1608	|	1642	1828	1859	1930	1958	|	2043	|	...
234	Altsasu **689** d.	0918t	|	...	1150	|	...	|	|	...	|	...	...	|	|	1718t	...	...	1959	2034t	|	...	|	...
275	Vitoria / Gasteiz **689** d.	0950	|	...	|	|	...	1419	1419	...	|	...	1645	1702	|	1753	...	...	|	2107	|	...	|	...
321	San Seb / Don ❖ d.	|	|	...	1303	|	...	|	|	...	1550	...	1821	|	|	|	...	...	2116	...	|	...	|	...
337	**Irún** **689** a.	|	|	...	...	|	...	|	|	...	...	...	1844	|	|	|	...	...	...	...	|	...	|	...
171	**Logroño 650a** d.	|	0829	...	...	1242	...	|	|	...	...	...	...	|	1635	|	...	...	...	...	1938	...	1945	...
242	Miranda de Ebro **689** d.	1016	...	...	...	1341	...	1439	1439	...	...	...	...	1722	...	1820	...	...	...	...	2032	...	...	...
347	**Bilbao** Abando **689** a.	...	...	...	...	1522	...	...	...	...	...	...	...	...	...	...	...	...	...	...	2209	...	...	...

	16027	18077	IC 562	IC 562	Alvia 701	Alvia 801	18079	IC 562	
	2	2					2		
	⑦		①–④	⑤	Ⓑ	Ⓑ	⑤⑥⑦	⑦	
Barcelona Sants **652** d.	...	...	1840	1845	...	...	...	1930	...
Madrid PA ‡ **650a** d.	...	...	|	|	1815	1935	...	|	...
Zaragoza Delicias d.	...	1921	2102	2048	|	|	2109	2134	...
Castejón de Ebro ★ d.	1852	2031	|	2141	|	|	2215	|	...
Pamplona / Iruña d.	2005	2138	2244	2232	|	2240	|	2328	...
Altsasu **689** d.	2046t	...	...	...	|	...	|	...	...
Vitoria / Gasteiz **689** d.	2118	...	...	...	|	...	|	...	...
San Seb / Don ❖ d.	|	...	...	...	|	...	|	...	...
Irún **689** a.	|	...	...	...	|	...	|	...	...
Logroño 650a d.	|	...	...	...	2136	...	2312	...	...
Miranda de Ebro **689** d.	2143	...	...	...	...	...	...	...	...
Bilbao Abando **689** a.	...	...	...	...	...	...	...	...	...

	18068	IC 635	18072	Alvia 802	Alvia 702	18074	Alvia 800	IC 10655	Alvia 600	
	2		2			2				
	①–⑤	①–⑤	①–⑤	①–⑤	①–⑥		①	⑥	⑥	
Bilbao Abando **689** d.	...	...	...	...	...	...	...	...	...	...
Miranda de Ebro **689** d.	...	...	...	...	...	...	...	...	...	...
Logroño 650a d.	...	...	0615	...	0735	...	...	...	...	...
Irún **689** d.	...	...	|	...	|	...	...	...	...	...
San Seb / Don ❖ d.	...	...	|	...	|	...	...	...	...	...
Vitoria / Gasteiz **689** d.	...	...	|	...	|	...	...	0718	...	...
Altsasu **689** d.	...	...	|	...	|	...	...	|	...	...
Pamplona / Iruña d.	...	0625	|	0640	|	0743z	0810	0812	0900	...
Castejón de Ebro d.	0605	0717	0720e	0730	|	0850	|	|	0952	...
Zaragoza Delicias a.	0715	0807	0836	|	|	0956	|	1000	|	...
Madrid PA ‡ **650a** a.	...	|	...	0950	1050	...	1124	|	1230	...
Barcelona Sants **652** a.	...	1010	...	...	...	...	...	1205	...	...

	Alvia 533	Alvia 433	16019	Alvia 602		18076	IC 281	Alvia 661	Alvia 606	IC 563	18070	18029	Alvia 621	Alvia 631	Alvia 537	Alvia 437	Alvia 608	Alvia 612	Alvia 610	16111	16011	18078		
		②④	2 b			2		A			2	2	625							2	2	2		
		⑥	①–⑥	Ⓑ				①–⑥		⑦	⑤⑥⑦	b	J	S			⑤	⑦	Ⓑ	①–⑥	⑦			
Bilbao Abando **689** d.	...	0630	...	...	...	...	...	...	...	...	...	...	...	...	...	1520	...	...	...	...	...	...	...	...
Miranda de Ebro **689** d.	...	0805	0925	...	...	...	...	1347	...	...	...	1501	1602	1602	...	1652	...	...	...	...	...	...	...	...
Logroño 650a d.	...	0904	|	...	...	1415	...	|	...	...	1642	|	|	|	...	1753	...	...	...	...	...	2023	...	...
Irún **689** d.	...	|	|	...	...	|	1154	|	...	...	|	|	|	|	...	|	...	...	...	...	...	|	...	...
San Seb / Don ❖ d.	0710	|	|	...	...	|	1221	|	...	...	|	|	|	|	1610	|	...	...	...	...	...	|	...	...
Vitoria / Gasteiz **689** d.	|	|	0952	...	...	|	1358	1411	...	...	|	1530	1632	1632	|	|	...	...	...	1900	1921	|	...	...
Altsasu **689** d.	0830	|	1025t	...	...	|	...	|	...	...	|	1601t	|	|	1722	|	...	...	...	1931t	1952t	|	...	...
Pamplona / Iruña d.	0905	|	1057	1130	...	|	...	1508	1537	1610	|	1638	1729	1729	1754	|	1828	1828	1935	2015	2026	|	...	...
Castejón de Ebro d.	1002	1002	...	|	...	1510	...	1602	|	1659	1741	1744	1826	1826	1854	1854	|	|	|	2111	2123	2127	...	...
Zaragoza Delicias a.	1106	1106	...	|	...	1611	...	1659	|	1744	...	1851	1921	1921	1950	1950	|	|	|	...	2217	2235	...	...
Madrid PA ‡ **650a** a.	|	|	...	1448	...	...	...	|	1845	|	...	...	|	|	|	|	2135	2135	2250	...	...	...	...	...
Barcelona Sants **652** a.	1309	1309	...	...	...	...	...	1903	...	1955	...	...	2135	2135	2214	2214	...	...	...	...	...	...	...	...

A – 🚃12 Barcelona - Gijón and v.v. (Table **685**).
C – 🚃12 Barcelona - Valladolid - Salamanca and v.v. (Tables **650a, 689**).
J – 🚃12 🍷 Barcelona - Vigo / A Coruña and v.v. (Table **680**).
S – 🚃12 Salamanca - Valladolid - Barcelona and v.v. (Tables **680, 689**).

b – From Burgos Rosa Manzano on ①–⑥ (Table **689**).
e – Arrive 0709.
t – Altsasu Pueblo (*230 km*).
z – ①–⑤.

★ – Calatayud - Castejón: *140 km.*
‡ – Full name is Madrid Puerta de Atocha.
❖ – Full name is San Sebastián / Donostia.
☛ **Shaded services are suspended until further notice.**

656 BARCELONA - PUIGCERDÀ - LATOUR DE CAROL

2nd class

km		Ⓐ													Ⓐ	Ⓒ								
0	**Barcelona** Sants d.	0501	0531	0601	0701	0731	0801	0831	0931	1031	1131	1201	1231	1301	1331	1331	1431	1501	1531	1631	1701	1731	1801	1831
	La Sagrera-Meridiana d.	0515	0545	0615	0715	0745	0815	0845	0945	1045	1145	1215	1245	1315	1345	1345	1445	1515	1545	1645	1715	1745	1815	1845
	Sant Andreu Arenal d.	0518	0548	0618	0718	0748	0818	0848	0948	1048	1148	1218	1248	1318	1348	1348	1448	1518	1548	1648	1718	1748	1848	1848
33	Granollers - Canovelles d.	0545	0615	0645	0745	0815	0845	0915	1015	1115	1215	1245	1315	1345	1415	1415	1515	1545	1615	1715	1745	1815	1845	1915
74	Vic d.	0622	0652	0723	0823	0852	0922	0953	1053	1153	1253	1322	1353	1422	1453	1453	1553	1622	1653	1753	1822	1853	1923	1952
90	Torelló d.	...	...	0738	0838	...	...	1008	1108	1208	1308	...	1408	...	1508	1508	1608	...	1708	1808	...	1908	1938	...
110	Ripoll d.	...	...	0805	0906	...	...	1035	1137	1237	1335	...	1437	...	1536	1536	1635	...	1737	1835	...	1942	2005	...
124	Ribes de Freser **658** a.	...	...	0826	0921	...	...	1056	...	...	1356	...	...	...	...	1551	1656	...	...	1856	...	...	2026	...
145	La Molina a.	...	...	0853	...	...	...	1126	...	...	1426	...	...	...	...	...	1726	...	...	1923	...	...	2053	...
159	Puigcerdà a.	...	...	0912	...	...	...	1145	...	...	1445	...	...	...	...	...	1745	...	...	1941	...	...	2111	...
163	**Latour de Carol** 🏛 **312** a.	...	...	0918	...	...	...	1151	...	...	1451	...	...	...	...	...	1751	...	...	...	...	...	...	...

	Ⓐ								
Barcelona Sants d.	1852	1901	1931	2001	2031	2101	2131	2231	...
La Sagrera-Meridiana d.	1906	1915	1945	2015	2045	2115	2145	2245	...
Sant Andreu Arenal d.	1908	1918	1948	2018	2048	2118	2148	2248	...
Granollers - Canovelles d.	1930	1946	2015	2045	2115	2145	2215	2315	...
Vic d.	2009	2022	2052	2123	2152	2223	2252	2352	...
Torelló d.	2021	...	...	2138	...	2238	...	...	...
Ripoll d.	2047	...	...	2207	...	2307	...	...	...
Ribes de Freser **658** a.	2104	...	...	...	...	...	...	...	...
La Molina a.	2131	...	...	...	...	...	...	...	...
Puigcerdà a.	2150	...	...	...	...	...	...	...	...
Latour de Carol 🏛 **312** a.	...	...	...	...	...	...	...	...	...

	Ⓐ				Ⓐ				
Latour de Carol 🏛 **312** d.	...	...	...	...	...	...	...	...	...
Puigcerdà d.	...	...	...	...	0524	...	...	...	0703
La Molina d.	...	...	...	...	0544	...	...	...	0723
Ribes de Freser **658** d.	...	...	...	...	0611	...	...	...	0750
Ripoll d.	...	...	0539	...	0629	...	0710	...	0809
Torelló d.	...	...	0606	...	0650	...	0737	...	0837
Vic d.	0524	0554	0623	0654	0705	0724	0754	0824	0854
Granollers - Canovelles d.	0601	0631	0701	0731	0745	0801	0831	0901	0931
Sant Andreu Arenal a.	0629	0659	0729	0759	0808	0829	0859	0929	0959
La Sagrera-Meridiana a.	0632	0702	0732	0802	0811	0832	0902	0932	1002
Barcelona Sants a.	0646	0716	0746	0816	0825	0846	0916	0946	1016

												Ⓒ	Ⓐ											
Latour de Carol 🏛 **312** d.	...	0825	...	1025	...	...	...	...	1325	...	...	...	...	...	1625	...	...	...	1855	...	...	...	...	...
Puigcerdà d.	...	0832	...	1032	...	...	...	...	1332	...	...	...	...	...	1632	...	...	...	1902	...	...	...	...	...
La Molina d.	...	0852	...	1052	...	...	...	...	1352	...	...	...	...	...	1652	...	...	...	1922	...	...	...	...	...
Ribes de Freser **658** d.	...	0919	1021	1121	...	...	...	...	1421	...	...	1621	...	...	1721	...	...	...	1949	...	...	...	...	...
Ripoll d.	...	0941	1039	1140	...	1239	...	1339	1440	...	1539	1639	1639	...	1740	...	1907	...	2008	...	2109	...	...	...
Torelló d.	...	1007	1107	1207	...	1307	...	1407	1507	...	1607	1707	1707	...	1807	...	1937	...	2038	...	2137	...	...	...
Vic d.	0954	1024	1124	1224	1254	1324	1354	1424	1524	1554	1624	1724	1724	1754	1824	1854	1954	2024	2054	2124	2154	2224	...	...
Granollers - Canovelles d.	1031	1101	1201	1301	1331	1401	1431	1501	1601	1631	1701	1801	1801	1831	1901	1931	2031	2101	2131	2201	2231	2301	...	...
Sant Andreu Arenal a.	1059	1129	1229	1329	1359	1429	1459	1529	1629	1659	1729	1829	1829	1859	1929	1959	2059	2129	2159	2229	2259	2329	...	...
La Sagrera-Meridiana a.	1102	1132	1232	1332	1402	1432	1502	1532	1632	1702	1732	1832	1832	1902	1932	2002	2102	2132	2202	2232	2302	2332	...	...
Barcelona Sants a.	1116	1146	1246	1346	1416	1446	1516	1546	1646	1716	1746	846	1846	1916	1946	2016	2116	2146	2216	2246	2316	2346	...	...

BARCELONA - GIRONA - FIGUERES - PORTBOU / PERPIGNAN 657

Reservations are not compulsory on *Media Distancia* (*MD*) services on the Barcelona - Girona - Portbou - Cebère route. All stopping services convey 2nd class only.

km	km		*MD* Ⓐ	Ⓐ	*MD* Ⓐ	*Av* **34609***		*AVE* **10737** D	*MD*	Ⓐ	Ⓒ	*Av* **34063***	*MD* Ⓐ	*TGV* **9708** P	*MD* Ⓒ	*AVE* **3073** **34073*** ⑥⑦	Ⓐ	Ⓒ	*MD* Ⓐ	*MD* Ⓒ	*AVE* **3093** **34093***	*MD* Ⓐ	Ⓐ	Ⓒ	*TGV* **9704** P	*MD* Ⓐ	*Av* **34023***
		Madrid ⊠ **660** ..... d.	...	...	...	...	...	...	...	...	...	...	...	...	...	0730	...	...	...	...	0930	...	...	...	...	...	...
0	0	**Barcelona** Sants ... **666** d.	...	...	...	0705	...	0822	...	...	...	0930	...	1033	...	1050	...	...	...	...	1245	...	...	...	1432	...	1450
		Barcelona Sant AC ¶ .... d.	0602	0617	0647	|	0747	|	0832	0917	0932	|	1017	|	1032	|	1102	1132	1147	1232	|	1247	1317	1332	|	1417	|
31		Granollers Centre .... d.	0625	0640	0710	|	0809	|	0855	0940	0955	|	1040	|	1055	|	1125	1155	1210	1255	|	1310	1340	1355	|	1440	|
72		Maçanet - Massanes **666** d.	0700	0714	0743	|	0842	|	0921	1013	1028	|	1106	|	1122	|	1158	1228	1235	1322	|	1335	1413	1428	|	1505	|
86		Caldes de Malavella ..... d.	0717	0731	0757	|	0855	|	0934	1026	1041	|	1119	|	1135	|	1211	1241	1248	1335	|	1348	1426	1441	|	1518	|
102	95	**Girona** .... d.	0730	0748	0810	0746	0911	0903	0947	1042	1058	1011	1132	1114	1148	1130	1227	1258	1301	1347	1325	1401	1442	1458	1513	1531	1531
118		Flaçà .... d.	0743	0804	0823	|	0926	|	1000	1057	1113	|	1145	|	1201	|	1242	1313	1314	1400	|	1414	1457	1513	|	1544	|
143		Figueres .... § d.	0800	0827	0841	|	0949	|	1017	1120	1136	|	1202	|	1218	|	1305	1336	1331	1417	|	1431	1520	1536	|	1601	|
	129	Figueres Vilafant .... § d.	...	|	...	0800	|	0919	|	|	|	1025	|	1131	|	1145	|	|	...	...	1340	...	|	|	1530	...	1545
162		Llançà .... d.	...	0841	...	...	1003	...	1029	1134	1150	...	1214	|	1230	...	1319	1350	...	...	...	...	1534	1550	|	...	...
169		**Portbou** 🏛 .... **355** a.	...	0850	...	...	1012	...	1036	1143	1159	...	1221	|	1237	...	1328	1359	...	...	...	...	1543	1559	|	...	...
171		**Cerbère** 🏛 .... **355** a.	...	0854	...	...	1016	...	...	1147	1203	...	...	|	...	...	1332	1403	...	...	...	...	1547	1603	|	...	...
	177	**Perpignan** .... **355** a.	...	...	...	...	...	...	...	...	...	...	...	1155	...	...	...	...	...	...	...	...	...	...	1554	...	...

	MD Ⓒ	Ⓐ	Ⓒ	*AVE* **3123** **34123*** Ⓑ	*TGV* **9706** Q P	*MD* Ⓐ	*MD* Ⓒ		*AVE* **19725** **34725*** C	*AVE* **3143** **34143*** Ⓑ	*MD* Ⓐ	*MD* Ⓒ	*MD* Ⓐ	Ⓒ	*AVE* **34153*** ①–④ ⑦	*MD* Ⓐ	Ⓒ	Ⓐ	*AVE* **3163** **34163*** ①–⑤	*MD*	*MD*	*AVE* **3191** **34191*** S	*MD* Ⓐ	*MD* Ⓒ	*avlo* **6309**
Madrid ⊠ **660** .... d.	...	...	...	1230	...	...	...	...	1325	1430	...	...	...	...	...	...	...	...	1630	...	...	1900	...	...	1930
Barcelona Sants ... **666** d.	...	...	...	1550	1610	...	...	...	1634	1730	...	...	...	...	1830	...	...	...	1925	...	...	2140	...	...	2256
Barcelona Sant AC ¶ .... d.	1432	1517	1532	|	|	1617	1632	1717	|	|	1747	1747	1817	1832	|	1847	1932	1947	|	2017	2117	|	2217	2224	|
Granollers Centre .... d.	1455	1540	1555	|	|	1640	1655	1740	|	|	1810	1810	1840	1855	|	1910	1955	2010	|	2040	2140	|	2240	2246	|
Maçanet - Massanes . **666** d.	1522	1613	1628	|	|	1705	1722	1813	|	|	1836	1837	1905	1928	|	1936	2036	2043	|	2107	2206	|	2305	2312	|
Caldes de Malavella...... d.	1535	1626	1641	|	|	1718	1735	1826	|	|	1849	1850	1918	1941	|	1949	2049	2056	|	2120	2221	|	2318	2327	|
Girona .... d.	1547	1642	1658	1630	1651	1731	1747	1842	1715	1810	1902	1902	1931	1958	1911	2002	2106	2112	2013	2132	2234	2220	2329	2338	2336
Flaçà .... d.	1600	1657	1713	|	|	1744	1800	1857	|	|	1915	1915	1944	2013	|	2015	2121	2127	|	2145	2247	|	...	...	|
Figueres .... § d.	1617	1720	1736	|	|	1801	1817	1920	|	|	1932	1932	2001	2036	|	2033	2144	2150	|	2202	2305	|	...	...	|
Figueres Vilafant......... § d.	...	|	|	1645	1708	...	...	|	1729	1825	|	...	...	...	1925	...	|	|	2028	...	...	2235	...	...	2351
Llançà .... d.	...	1734	1750	...	|	...	...	1934	...	...	1944	...	...	...	...	...	2206	2204	...	...	...	...	...	...	...
Portbou 🏛 .... **355** a.	...	1743	1759	...	|	...	...	1942	...	...	1951	...	...	...	...	...	...	2212	...	...	...	...	...	...	...
Cerbère 🏛 .... **355** a.	...	1747	1803	...	|	...	...	...	...	...	...	...	...	...	...	...	...	...	...	...	...	...	...	...	...
Perpignan .... **355** a.	...	...	...	...	1732	...	...	...	...	...	...	...	...	...	...	...	...	...	...	...	...	...	...	...	...

	avlo **6302**	*MD* Ⓐ	*MD* Ⓐ	*MD* Ⓒ	*AVE* **3662** **34662*** ①–⑤	*Em/Av* **1081** **34082*** ①–⑤	*MD* Ⓒ	*MD* Ⓐ	*MD* Ⓐ	Ⓐ	Ⓒ	*AVE* **3092** **34092*** ①–⑥	*MD* ⚒	*Em/Av* **1101** **34102***		*MD* Ⓐ	*MD* Ⓒ		*AVE* **19730** **34730*** B	*TGV* **9711** Q P	*MD* Ⓒ	*MD* Ⓐ	*Av* **34394***	Ⓒ	Ⓐ	*MD* Ⓐ	*MD* Ⓒ
Perpignan .... **355** d.	...	...	...	...	...	...	...	...	...	...	...	...	...	...	...	...	...	...	...	1203	...	...	...	...	...	...	...
Cerbère 🏛 .... **355** d.	...	...	...	...	...	...	...	...	...	...	...	...	...	...	...	...	...	...	...	|	...	...	...	...	...	...	...
Portbou 🏛 .... **355** d.	...	...	...	...	...	...	...	...	...	0705	0720	...	...	...	0820	...	...	1020	...	|	1138	1154	...	1220	1235	1324	1337
Llançà .... d.	...	...	...	...	...	...	...	...	...	0713	0728	...	...	...	0828	...	...	1028	...	|	1145	1201	...	1228	1243	1331	1344
Figueres Vilafant......... § d.	0530	...	...	...	0630	0710	...	...	...	|	|	0755	...	0910	|	...	...	|	1143	1228	|	|	1310	|	|	|	|
Figueres .... § d.	|	...	0542	0603	|	|	0624	0644	0713	0729	0744	|	0813	|	0844	0943	0959	1044	|	|	1200	1215	|	1244	1259	1345	1359
Flaçà .... d.	|	...	0603	0623	|	|	0644	0704	0733	0754	0809	|	0833	|	0909	1003	1019	1109	|	|	1219	1233	|	1309	1324	1403	1418
Girona .... d.	0546	0604	0618	0637	0646	0726	0658	0718	0747	0811	0826	0811	0847	0926	0926	1017	1033	1126	1200	1245	1233	1248	1326	1326	1341	1418	1432
Caldes de Malavella...... d.	|	0616	0631	0650	|	|	0711	0730	0759	0825	0840	|	0900	|	0940	1029	1046	1140	|	|	1246	1301	|	1340	1355	1431	1445
Maçanet - Massanes **666** d.	|	0630	0645	0701	|	|	0724	0743	0811	0837	0852	|	0911	|	0952	1041	1057	1152	|	|	1257	1312	|	1352	1407	1442	1456
Granollers Centre .... d.	|	0705	0715	0730	|	|	0758	0813	0841	0911	0926	|	0941	|	1026	1111	1126	1226	|	|	1326	1341	|	1426	1441	1511	1526
Barcelona Sant AC ¶ .... a.	|	0730	0740	0754	|	|	0820	0837	0905	0935	0950	|	1005	|	1050	1135	1150	1250	|	|	1350	1405	|	1450	1505	1535	1550
Barcelona Sants ... **666** a.	0625	...	...	...	0725	0805	...	...	...	...	...	0850	...	1005	...	...	...	...	1238	1325	...	...	1405	...	...	...	...
Madrid ⊠ **660** .... a.	0920	...	...	...	1010	...	...	...	...	...	...	1145	...	...	...	...	...	...	1545	...	...	...	...	...	...	...	...

	MD Ⓐ	*AVE* **3162** **34262***	Ⓒ	Ⓐ	*TGV* **9713** P	*MD* Ⓐ	*MD* Ⓒ		*Av* **34182***	*MD*	*AVE* **3192** **34192***	*MD* Ⓐ	*MD* Ⓒ	Ⓐ	*AVE* **10742** **34742*** D	*MD*	*AVE* **34292*** Ⓑ	*TGV* **9715** P	Ⓐ	Ⓒ	*MD* Ⓐ	Ⓐ	Ⓒ				
Perpignan .... **355** d.	...	...	...	...	1505	...	...	...	...	...	...	...	...	...	...	...	...	2003	...	...	...	...	...	...	...	...	...
Cerbère 🏛 .... **355** d.	...	...	...	...	|	...	...	...	...	...	...	...	...	...	...	...	...	|	...	...	...	...	...	...	...	...	...
Portbou 🏛 .... **355** d.	...	...	1420	1435	|	...	...	1605	...	...	...	...	1720	1735	...	...	...	|	1850	...	...	2027	2103	...	...	...	...
Llançà .... d.	...	...	1428	1443	|	...	...	1613	...	...	...	...	1728	1743	...	...	...	|	1858	...	...	2034	2111	...	...	...	...
Figueres Vilafant......... § d.	...	1455	|	|	1530	...	...	|	1710	...	1735	...	|	|	1837	...	1935	2028	|	...	...	|	|	...	...	...	...
Figueres .... § d.	1413	|	1444	1459	|	1543	1559	1629	|	1713	|	...	1744	1759	|	1843	|	|	1914	1958	2019	2048	2127	...	...	...	...
Flaçà .... d.	1433	|	1509	1524	|	1603	1619	1654	|	1733	|	...	1809	1824	|	1903	|	|	1939	2018	2039	2106	2152	...	...	...	...
Girona .... d.	1447	1511	1526	1541	1546	1617	1633	1711	1726	1747	1751	1817	1826	1841	1851	1917	1952	2045	1956	2032	2053	2120	2209	...	...	...	...
Caldes de Malavella...... d.	1500	|	1540	1555	|	1630	1646	1725	|	1800	|	1830	1840	1855	|	1930	|	|	2010	2045	2106	2133	2223	...	...	...	...
Maçanet - Massanes **666** d.	1511	|	1552	1607	|	1641	1657	1737	|	1811	|	1841	1852	1907	|	1941	|	|	2022	2056	2117	2145	2237	...	...	...	...
Granollers Centre .... d.	1541	|	1626	1641	|	1711	1726	1811	|	1841	|	1911	1926	1941	|	2011	|	|	2056	2126	2147	2217	2311	...	...	...	...
Barcelona Sant AC ¶ .... a.	1605	|	1650	1705	|	1735	1750	1835	|	1905	|	1935	1950	2005	|	2035	|	|	2120	2150	2211	2241	2335	...	...	...	...
Barcelona Sants ... **666** a.	...	1550	...	...	1627	...	...	...	1805	...	1830	...	...	...	1932	...	2030	2125	...	...	...	...	...	...	...	...	...
Madrid ⊠ **660** .... a.	...	1912	...	...	...	...	...	...	...	...	2145	...	...	...	...	...	...	...	...	...	...	...	...	...	...	...	...

	Ⓐ		Ⓐ	Ⓒ	Ⓐ	Ⓒ	Ⓐ	Ⓒ	Ⓐ	Ⓒ	
Portbou 🏛 ..... d.	0850	1012	1143	1159	1328	1359	1543	1559	1743	1759	...
Cerbère 🏛 ..... a.	0854	1016	1147	1203	1332	1403	1547	1603	1747	1803	...

	Ⓐ		Ⓐ	Ⓒ	Ⓐ	Ⓒ		Ⓐ	Ⓒ		Ⓐ	Ⓒ		
Cerbère 🏛 .. d.	0902	1024	1155	1211	1340	1411	...	1555	1611	...	1755	1811	...	...
Portbou 🏛 a.	0906	1028	1159	1215	1344	1415	...	1559	1615	...	1759	1815	...	...

B – Daily. From Marseille ②③④⑤ until Apr. 23, daily Apr. 24 - Dec. 9 (Table **13**). Start date from Marseille is subject to confirmation.
C – Daily. To Marseille ①②③④ until Apr. 23, daily Apr. 24 - Dec. 9 (Table **13**). Start date to Marseille is subject to confirmation.
D – Daily. To / from Lyon ①–⑤ until Apr. 23, daily Apr. 24 - Dec. 9 (Table **13**). Start date to / from Lyon is subject to confirmation.

P – To / from Paris (Table **13**).
Q – July 8 - Sept. 3.
S – ①②③④⑦.

⊠ – Madrid Puerta de Atocha.
¶ – Barcelona Sant Andreu Comtal.
* – Train number for *Turista class (classified Av)*.

§ – **FIGUERES VILAFANT - FIGUERES BUS STATION (150m from Figueres)**. *5 km.* By 🚌. Journey time: 15 – 20 minutes.

From **Figueres Vilafant**: 0810, 0915, 1010, 1030 Ⓐ, 1150, 1345, 1600, 1655 Ⓑ, 1745, 1840, 1935 ①②③④⑦, 2035 Ⓐ, 2105, 2245 ①②③④⑦, 0000.

From **Figueres Bus Station**: 0505, 0605 Ⓐ, 0645 Ⓐ, 0725 ⚒, 0840, 0940, 1110, 1240, 1425 ⚒, 1515, 1635 Ⓐ, 1725, 1810, 1910 Ⓑ.

2nd class VALL DE NÚRIA 658

Ribes Enllaç - **Ribes** Vila - **Queralbs** - **Núria** rack railway

HIGH SEASON:

⑥⑦ from June 4 (also June 24, July 30 - Sept. 4, also Oct. 31, Nov. 1):

From **Ribes** Enllaç: 0730 **v**, 0930, 1020, 1110, 1205, 1250, 1340, 1435, 1540, 1625, 1720, 1930 ⑤.
From **Núria**: 0820, 1020, 1110, 1205, 1250, 1340, 1435, 1540, 1625, 1710, 1830, 2015 ⑤.

LOW SEASON:

①–⑤ from June 1 (not June 24, July 30 - Sept. 4, Oct. 31, Nov. 1):

From **Ribes** Enllaç: 0730 **v**, 0930, 1110, 1250, 1435, 1625.
From **Núria**: 0820, 1020, 1205, 1340, 1540, 1710.

Journey times **Ribes** – **Queralbs** (*6 km*) 24 minutes, **Ribes** – **Núria** (*12 km*) 44 minutes.

Ferrocarrils de la Generalitat de Catalunya (FGC) ✆ +34 972 732 020. www.valldenuria.cat

v – From Ribes Vila.

2nd class AEROPORT BARCELONA 659

Local rail service *Cercanías* (suburban) line **R2 Nord**. *14km*

Aeroport - Barcelona Sants – Barcelona Passeig de Gràcia

Journey time: 19 minutes Sants, 26 minutes Passeig de Gràcia

From Aeroport del Prat:

0542, 0608, 0638, 0708, 0738 and every 30 minutes until 2208, 2238, 2308, 2338.

From Barcelona Sants:

0513, 0535, 0609, 0639, 0709 and every 30 minutes until 2139, 2209, 2239, 2314.

660 MADRID - CÓRDOBA - SEVILLA and MÁLAGA — High-speed services

km		Av	iryo	AVE	Alvia	AVE	AVE	AVE	iryo	AVE	AVE	iryo	AVE	AVE	Alvia	IC	AVE	AVE	iryo	AVE	AVE	AVE	AVE	AVE	AVE	Alvia	iryo	AVE	
		2260	**6066**	**2070**	**2074**	**2072**	**2076**	**2072**	**6078**	**2080**	**2082**	**6086**	**2090**	**2092**	**2394**	**2494**	**2100**	**3982**	**6106**	**2110**	**2112**	**3940**	**3930**	**2310**	**2122**	**2134**	**6136**	**2140**	
		①–⑤				①–⑤		⑥⑦		①–⑤	①–④		①–④		⑥														
		⇊	A		✣				A			G				B		V	D							✣	C		
	Barcelona Sants **650** . d.	...	...	...	...	...	...	...	...	...	...	...	...	...	...	...	...	...	...	...	...	0835	0835	...	...	...	...	...	...
0	**Madrid** Puerta de Atocha d.	0620	0655	0700	0705	0735	0735	0735	0755	0800	0825	0855	0905	0935	0945	0945	1000	...	1050	1100	1135	|	|	1150	1235	1305	1353	1400	...
171	Ciudad Real d.	0720	|	0751	0759	|	|	|	|	|	|	|	|	1026	|	|	|	1127t	|	|	|	1225	1225	1241	|	1356	|	|	...
210	Puertollano d.	0738	|	0807	0816	|	|	|	|	|	|	|	|	1044	|	|	|	1145	|	|	|	1241	1241	1257	|	1410	|	|	...
345	**Córdoba** d.	0830	0845	0856	0906	0919	0919	0917	0941	0947	|	1045	|	1129	1134	1136	1147	1233	1240	1245	1321	1327	1336	1346	1419	1454	1545	1547	...
470	**Sevilla** a.	0916	0929	0940	0955	|	|	|	|	1034	|	1129	1128	|	|	1220	1234	1330	1324	1332	|	1410	|	1430	|	1542	1627	1634	...
	Cádiz **671** a.	...	...	...	1129	|	|	|	|	...	|	...	...	|	|	|	...	...	...	...	|	...	|	...	|	1717	...	...	...
	Huelva **671** a.	...	...	...	...	|	|	|	|	...	|	...	...	|	1331	1402	...	...	...	...	|	...	|	...	|	...	...	...	...
419	Puente Genil - Herrera ¶ a.	...	...	...	...	0940	0940	0940	|	...	|	...	...	|	...	...	...	...	...	...	|	...	|	...	1440	...	...	...	...
455	Antequera - Santa Ana § a.	...	...	...	...	0956	0956	0956	1001	...	|	...	...	1200	...	...	...	...	...	...	|	...	1408	...	1456	...	...	...	...
	Algeciras **673** a.	...	...	...	...	|	|	|	|	...	|	...	...	|	...	...	...	...	...	...	|	...	|	...	|	...	...	...	...
	Granada **678a** a.	...	...	...	...	|	1100	|	|	...	|	...	...	|	...	...	...	...	...	...	|	...	1503	...	|	...	...	...	...
513	**Málaga** María Zambrano a.	...	...	...	...	1025	...	1025	1030	...	1051	...	...	1226	...	...	...	...	...	...	1410	...	...	...	1525	...	...	...	...

	AVE	AVE	iryo	AVE	IC	AVE	AVE	Alvia	AVE	AVE	AVE	AVE	iryo	AVE	Alvia	AVE	AVE	AVE	AVE	AVE	AVE	AVE	AVE	AVE	AVE	Av	AVE		
	2142	**2146**	**xxxx**	**2150**	**9330**	**2152**	**2160**	**2164**	**2360**	**2162**	**2170**	**2172**	**6176**	**2180**	**2384**	**2182**	**3942**	**3992**	**3974**	**2380**	**2190**	**2192**	**2196**	**2202**	**2210**	**2410**	**2212**		
				Ⓑ					Ⓑ		Ⓑ			Ⓑ	Ⓑ	Ⓑ			①⑤⑦	④⑤⑦							⑤		
			A		◐			✣					A		J				E							⇊			
Barcelona Sants **650** .. d.	...	...	...	...	...	...	...	...	...	...	...	...	...	...	...	...	1515	1515	...	...	...	...	...	...	...	...	...	...	...
Madrid Puerta de Atocha d.	1435	1435	1455	1500	1505	1535	1600	1610	1630	1635	1700	1735	1755	1800	1805	1830	|	|	...	1835	1900	1935	1935	2030	2100	2125	2130	...	...
Ciudad Real d.	|	|	|	|	|	|	|	|	|	1726	|	|	|	|	|	|	1916	1916	1942	|	1951	2026	2026	|	2150	2219	|	...	...
Puertollano d.	|	|	|	|	|	|	|	|	|	1742	|	|	|	|	|	|	|	|	1957	|	2007	2042	2042	|	2207	2234	|	...	...
Córdoba d.	1621	1621	1641	1647	1710	|	1747	|	|	1827	1847	1921	1945	1947	2000	|	2027	2043	2045	|	2056	2131	2131	2214	2256	2324	|	...	...
Sevilla a.	|	|	|	1734	|	|	1834	|	1853	|	1934	|	2029	2034	|	|	2115	|	|	2109	2140	|	|	|	2340	0010	|	...	...
Cádiz **671** a.	|	|	|	...	|	|	...	2019	...	|	...	|	...	...	|	|	...	|	|	...	...	|	|	|	...	...	|	...	...
Huelva **671** a.	|	|	|	...	|	|	...	...	...	|	...	|	...	...	2154	|	...	|	|	...	...	|	|	|	...	...	|	...	...
Puente Genil - Herrera ¶. a.	|	|	|	...	|	|	...	...	...	1848	...	|	...	...	...	|	...	2106	2110	...	...	|	|	2235	...	...	|	...	...
Antequera - Santa Ana §. a.	1654	1654	1701	...	1755	|	...	...	...	1901	...	|	...	...	...	|	...	2121	2125	...	...	2201	2201	2248	...	...	|	...	...
Algeciras **673** a.	|	|	|	...	2032	|	...	...	...	|	...	|	...	...	...	|	...	|	|	...	...	|	|	|	...	...	|	...	...
Granada **678a** a.	|	1757	|	...	...	|	...	...	...	|	...	|	...	...	...	|	...	|	|	...	...	|	2306	|	...	...	|	...	...
Málaga María Zambrano . a.	1723	...	1730	...	...	1808	...	...	...	1927	...	2010	...	...	...	2058	...	2146	2151	...	...	2230	...	2314	...	...	2359	...	...

	Av	AVE	AVE	AVE	AVE	AVE	AVE	AVE	iryo	AVE	AVE	AVE	AVE	Alvia	AVE	AVE	iryo	AVE	AVE	AVE	iryo	Alvia	AVE	AVE	iryo	AVE	Alvia	AVE	AVE
	2261	**2063**	**2061**	**2073**	**2071**	**2273**	**2077**	**2083**	**xxxx**	**2075**	**2081**	**3931**	**3943**	**2285**	**2093**	**2091**	**6107**	**3971**	**2103**	**2101**	**xxxx**	**2205**	**2111**	**2123**	**6127**	**2131**	**2135**	**2143**	**2141**
	①–⑤	①–⑤	①–④	①–④				①–④			①–⑤			①–⑤		①–⑥		⑤⑥				⑥							
	★								A	✣							A	U			A				C		✣		
Málaga María Zambrano . d.	...	0628	...	0710	...	0705	...	0808	0810	...	...	...	...	...	0858	...	...	0945	1028	...	1130	...	...	1158	...	...	...	1358	...
Granada **678a** d.	...	|	...	|	...	|	0700	|	|	...	...	0810	...	...	|	...	...	|	|	...	|	...	...	|	...	...	...	|	...
Algeciras **673** d.	...	|	...	|	...	|	|	|	|	...	...	|	...	...	|	...	...	|	|	...	|	...	...	|	...	...	...	|	...
Antequera - Santa Ana §. d.	...	|	...	|	...	0729	0804	|	1155	...	...	0906	...	...	0924	...	...	1008	|	...	1155	...	...	|	...	...	...	1423	...
Puente Genil - Herrera ¶. d.	...	|	...	|	...	0742	|	|	|	...	...	|	...	...	0938	...	...	1021	|	...	|	...	...	|	...	...	...	1437	...
Huelva **671** d.	...	|	...	|	...	|	|	|	|	...	...	|	...	0800	|	...	...	|	|	...	|	1025	...	|	...	...	...	|	...
Cádiz **671** d.	...	|	...	|	...	|	|	|	|	0640	...	|	...	|	|	...	...	|	|	...	|	|	...	|	...	...	1220	|	...
Sevilla d.	0610	|	0643	|	0708	|	|	|	|	0815	0843	|	0850	|	|	0945	1015	|	|	1043	|	|	1143	|	1215	1340	1345	|	1443
Córdoba d.	0653	0722	0727	|	0754	0807	0835	|	1224	0906	0927	0942	0942	0950	1003	1028	1029	1051	1122	1127	1224	1218	1227	1249	1259	|	1441	1502	1527
Puertollano d.	0744	|	|	|	0841	|	0919	|	|	0957	|	|	|	|	1047	1111	|	1135	|	|	|	|	|	|	|	|	1526	1546	|
Ciudad Real d.	0759	|	|	|	0857	|	0938	|	|	1015	|	1040	1040	|	1103	1126	|	1148	|	|	|	|	|	|	|	|	1541	1602	|
Madrid Puerta de Atocha a.	0858	0910	0915	0938	0952	0952	1030	1038	1049	1109	1115	|	|	1143	1156	1223	1247	...	1309	1316	1409	1410	1417	1435	1447	1610	1636	1655	1715
Barcelona Sants **650** .. a.	...	...	...	...	...	...	...	...	...	...	...	1420	1420	...	...	...	...	...	...	...	...	...	...	...	...	...	...	...	...

	AVE	AVE	AVE	AVE	AVE	AVE	AVE	AVE	AVE	iryo	AVE	Alvia	AVE	IC	AVE	AVE	AVE	AVE	AVE	IC	AVE	Alvia	AVE	AVE	AVE	iryo	AVE	iryo	AVE
	3991	**3941**	**2153**	**2151**	**2161**	**2167**	**2163**	**2361**	**3973**	**6177**	**2173**	**2365**	**2171**	**9331**	**2371**	**3981**	**2183**	**2181**	**2193**	**2375**	**2191**	**2175**	**2391**	**2197**	**2203**	**xxxx**	**2211**	**6217**	**2213**
				Ⓑ	Ⓑ			Ⓑ	⑦			⑦			④⑤⑦		Ⓑ	Ⓑ		★			④⑤⑦						⑦
									F	C				★		V				B		✣				A		A	
Málaga María Zambrano . d.	1435	...	1458	...	...	...	1613	...	1638	...	1658	...	...	...	...	...	1800	...	1858	...	...	...	...	...	2000	2045	...	...	2118
Granada **678a** d.	|	...	|	...	...	1533	|	...	|	...	|	...	...	...	...	...	|	...	|	...	...	...	...	1918	|	|	...	...	|
Algeciras **673** d.	|	...	|	...	...	|	|	...	|	...	|	...	...	1503	...	...	|	...	|	...	...	...	...	|	|	|	...	...	|
Antequera - Santa Ana §. d.	1459	...	|	...	...	1643	1643	...	1701	...	1722	...	...	1738	...	...	|	...	|	...	...	...	...	2025	2025	2110	...	...	|
Puente Genil - Herrera ¶. d.	1512	...	|	...	...	|	|	...	1714	...	1735	...	...	|	...	...	|	...	|	...	...	...	...	2046	2046	|	...	...	|
Huelva **671** d.	|	...	|	...	...	|	|	...	|	...	|	1615	...	|	...	...	|	...	|	1750	...	...	...	|	|	|	...	...	|
Cádiz **671** d.	|	...	|	...	...	|	|	...	|	...	|	|	...	|	...	...	|	...	|	|	...	1810	...	|	|	|	...	...	|
Sevilla d.	|	1448	|	1543	1613	|	|	1643	|	1710	|	|	1728	|	1743	1801	|	1843	|	1924	1943	|	2015	|	|	|	2058	2115	|
Córdoba d.	1540	1540	|	1627	|	1719	1719	1727	1743	1753	1800	1808	1813	1820	1827	1849	1854	1927	1952	2014	2027	|	|	2111	2111	2139	2143	2159	|
Puertollano d.	1624	1624	|	|	|	|	|	|	1827	|	|	|	1900	1920	|	1948	|	|	2036	|	|	|	|	|	|	|	2230	|	|
Ciudad Real d.	1640	1640	|	|	|	|	|	|	1843	|	|	|	1915	1937	|	2005t	|	|	2052	|	|	|	|	|	|	|	2247	|	|
Madrid Puerta de Atocha a.	|	|	1742	1815	1840	1911	1911	1917	...	1942	1945	2003	2010	2040	2017	...	2045	2117	2144	2212	2217	2222	2236	2300	2300	2324	2342	2347	235[illegible]
Barcelona Sants **650** .. a.	2022	2022	...	...	...	...	...	...	...	...	...	...	...	...	...	...	...	...	...	...	...	...	...	...	...	...	...	...	...

A – From Mar. 31.
B – June 13 - Sept. 11.
C – From May 5.
D – From May 19.
E – ①⑤⑦ (Ⓑ July 14 - Sept. 10). From València (Table **668**).
F – ⑦. To València (Table **668**).
G – May 8 – 18.
J – Ⓑ (daily June 13 - Sept. 11).

U – ⑤⑥ (②③④⑤⑥ July 14 - Sept. 15). To València (Table **668**).
V – From / to València (Table **668**). Timings differ before Mar. 5.

f – Arrive 23 minutes earlier.
j – 15 minutes earlier on ⑥.
t – From Mar. 5.

§ – ± *17 km* from Antequera.
¶ – ± *8 km* from Puente Genil.

★ – Also calls at Villanueva de CLP (⊠), 23 – 25 mins. after departing Córdoba.
◐ – Also calls at Villanueva de CLP (⊠), 100 mins. after departing Madrid.
⇊ – Also calls at Villanueva de CLP (⊠), 25 – 28 mins. after departing Puertollano.
⊠ – Full name: Villanueva de Córdoba-Los Pedroches.
iryo – ***ETR*** 1000 services branded **iryo**: www.iryo.eu
✣ – Subject to alteration from Mar. 5. See Table **671** for timings.
☛ All trains convey 🍸. *AVE* trains also convey ✕.
☛ **Shaded services are suspended until further notice.**

Avant high-speed shuttle services — Málaga – Córdoba – Sevilla — *Turista* class; 🍸

	8654	**8664**	**8694**		**8744**	**8764**	**8784**	**8704**	
	Ⓐ	Ⓐ				Ⓐ			
Málaga María Zambrano d.	...	0643	0910	...	1415	1628	1818	2013	...
Antequera - Santa Ana § d.	...	0709	0936	...	1441	1654	1842	2039	...
Puente Genil - Herrera ¶ d.	...	0723	0950	...	1455	1708	1856	2053	...
Córdoba a.	...	0748	1015	...	1520	1732	1920	2118	...
Córdoba d.	0650	0753	1020	...	1525	1737	1928	2123	...
Sevilla a.	0738	0838	1105	...	1610	1823	2013	2208	...

	8075	**8085**		**8125**	**8155**	**8175**	**8195**	**8215**		
	Ⓐ					Ⓐ		Ⓐ		
Sevilla d.	0650	0800	...	1252	1530	1755	1935	2135	...	...
Córdoba a.	0735	0845	...	1336	1612	1840	2020	2220	...	...
Córdoba d.	0740	0850	...	1341	1617	1845	2025	...	...	...
Puente Genil - Herrera ¶ d.	0803	0913	...	1407	1650	1915	2050	...	...	...
Antequera - Santa Ana § d.	0817	0927	...	1428	1704	1929	2104	...	...	...
Málaga María Zambrano a.	0845	0955	...	1456	1730	1955	2132	...	...	...

§ – ± *17 km* from Antequera. ¶ – ± *8 km* from Puente Genil.

Avant high-speed shuttle services — Madrid – Puertollano — *Turista* class; 🍸

		8260		**8080**		**8100**		**8130**	**8140**		**8150**		**8170**	**8180**	**8190**	**8200**	**8220**							
		Ⓐ		Ⓐ					Ⓐ					Ⓐ		Ⓑ								
Madrid Puerta de Atocha d.	...	0640	...	0805	...	1035	...	1315	1415	...	1545	...	1720	1815	1915	2015	2215	...	...	...	...	...	...	...
Ciudad Real d.	...	0736	...	0901	...	1131	...	1411	1511	...	1641	...	1817	1911	2011	2110	2311	...	...	...	...	...	...	...
Puertollano a.	...	0758	...	0918	...	1148	...	1428	1528	...	1658	...	1833	1928	2028	2128	2328	...	...	...	...	...	...	...

		8261		**8271**	**8471**	**8081**	**8081**		**8101**		**8111**			**8151**	**8161**	**8171**	**8181**	**8191**		**8211**			
		Ⓐ		Ⓐ	Ⓐ	Ⓐ	Ⓒ							⚒	Ⓐ		⑦			Ⓑ			
Puertollano d.	...	0625	...	0700	0725	0815	0820	...	1015	...	1120	...	...	1515	1615	1715	1828	1915	...	2120	...	...	...
Ciudad Real d.	...	0642	...	0717	0742	0832	0840	...	1032	...	1137	...	...	1532	1632	1732	1845	1932	...	2137	...	...	...
Madrid Puerta de Atocha a.	...	0742	...	0813	0838	0928	0944	...	1131	...	1236	...	...	1628	1728	1828	1940	2028	...	2233	...	...	...

MADRID - ALMERÍA and JAÉN 661

For other trains Madrid – Córdoba – Granada / Málaga and v.v. via the AVE high-speed line, see Table **660**

km		MD	MD	MD	IC	MD	MD		MD	MD		MD	IC	MD	IC	MD		MD		MD		MD	
		17008	**13331**	**13079**	**276**	**18030**	**18030**		**18170**	**13083**		**13035**	**697**	**13073**	**278**	**18032**		**18034**		**18036**		**17000**	
		2	2	2		2	2		2	2		2	🍸	2	🍸	2		2		2		2	
		①–⑤	①–⑤			Ⓐ	Ⓒ									Ⓐ		Ⓑ					
				E					C	E		E	T	E				A					
0	**Madrid** Chamartín ‡ .... **669 672b** d.	...	...	...	0758	0823	0916	...	...	...	...	...	...	...	1456	1545	...	1720	...	1918	...	2114	...
8	**Madrid** Atocha Cercanías **669 672b** d.	0713	...	...	0817	0836	0929	...	1310	...	...	...	...	...	1513	1559	...	1734	...	1932	...	2128	...
57	Aranjuez .... **669 672b** d.	0751	...	...	|	0916	1004	...	1343	...	...	...	...	...	|	1634	...	|	...	2010	...	2207	...
	Barcelona Sants **672** .... d.	|	...	...	|	|	|	...	|	...	...	...	0830	...	|	|	...	|	...	|	...	|	...
	València Nord **668** .... d.	|	...	...	|	|	|	...	|	...	...	...	1200	...	|	|	...	|	...	|	...	|	...
157	Alcázar de San Juan .... **678** d.	0840	...	...	0937	1010	1058	...	1440	...	...	...	1510	...	1634	1723	...	1856	...	2101	...	2301	...
206	Manzanares .... **678** d.	...	...	...	|	1034	1122	...	1505	...	...	...	1540	...	1657	1747	...	1921	...	2124	...	...	...
323	Linares - Baeza .... a.	...	...	...	1119	1212	1246	...	...	...	...	...	1701	...	1811	1912	...	2044	...	2241	...	...	...
323	Linares - Baeza .... d.	...	...	...	1121	1213	1247	...	...	...	...	...	1703	...	1813	1913	...	2045	...	2242	...	...	...
441	Moreda .... d.	...	...	...	|	|	|	...	...	...	...	...	|	...	1951	|	...	|	...	|	...	...	...
466	Guadix .... **673** d.	...	...	...	1314	|	|	...	...	...	...	...	|	...	2013	|	...	|	...	|	...	...	...
565	**Almería** .... **673** a.	...	...	...	1427	|	|	...	...	...	...	...	|	...	2129	|	...	|	...	|	...	...	...
¶	**Jaén** .... d.	...	0540	0635	...	1254	1328	...	...	1432	...	1652	|	1832	...	1954	...	2126	...	2323	...	...	...
371	Andújar .... d.	...	0621	0716	...	...	...	...	...	1514	...	1737	1741	1913	...	...	...	...	...	...	...	...	...
450	**Córdoba** .... a.	...	0712	0810	...	...	...	...	...	1610	...	1828	1831	2007	...	...	...	...	...	...	...	...	...

	MD		MD		MD	IC	MD		MD	IC	MD	MD	MD		MD	MD	MD	MD	MD	IC		MD	
	18047		**18031**		**18033**	**277**	**13337**		**13001**	**694**	**18171**	**13003**	**17041**		**18035**	**18035**	**13009**	**18037**	**13011**	**279**		**13017**	
	2		2		2		2		2	🍸	2	2	2		2	2	2	2	2	🍸			
	①–⑤		Ⓐ				①–⑤		①–⑤			⑥⑦			Ⓒ	Ⓐ							
									E	T		E	C				E		N			E	
Córdoba .... d.	...	...	...	...	...	...	0732	...	0906	1011	...	1002	...	...	...	...	1451	...	1626	...	...	2105	...
Andújar .... d.	...	...	...	...	...	...	0836	...	0959	1105	...	1056	...	...	...	...	1544	...	1720	...	...	2157	...
Jaén .... d.	...	...	0612	...	0832	...	0928	...	1047	|	...	1141	...	...	1522	1628	1627	1720	1810	...	...	2243	...
Almería .... **673** d.	...	...	|	...	|	0732	...	...	...	|	...	...	...	...	|	|	...	|	...	1605	...	...	...
Guadix .... **673** d.	...	...	|	...	|	0849	...	...	...	|	...	...	...	...	|	|	...	|	...	1719	...	...	...
Moreda .... d.	...	...	|	...	|	0910	...	...	...	|	...	...	...	...	|	|	...	|	...	|	...	...	...
Linares - Baeza .... a.	...	...	0650	...	0912	1041	...	...	...	1139	...	...	...	...	1602	1705	...	1800	...	1914	...	...	...
Linares - Baeza .... d.	...	...	0651	...	0913	1043	...	...	...	1142	...	...	...	...	1603	1706	...	1801	...	1916	...	...	...
Manzanares .... **678** d.	...	...	0807	...	1032	|	...	...	...	1302	...	...	1501	...	1723	1827	...	1921	...	2035	...	...	...
Alcázar de San Juan .... **678** d.	0527	...	0832	...	1055	1223	...	...	...	1329	1355	...	1527	...	1745	1848	...	1946	...	2059	...	...	...
València Nord **668** .... a.	|	...	|	...	|	|	...	...	...	1630	|	...	|	...	|	|	...	|	...	|	...	...	...
Barcelona Sants **672** .... a.	|	...	|	...	|	|	...	...	...	2005	|	...	|	...	|	|	...	|	...	|	...	...	...
Aranjuez .... **669 672b** d.	0621	...	0918	...	1143	...	...	...	...	...	1447	...	1624	...	1830	1934	...	2032	...	|	...	...	...
Madrid Atocha Cercanías **669 672b** a.	0656	...	0959	...	1213	1343	...	...	...	...	1526	...	1704	...	1905	2008	...	2109	...	2219	...	...	...
Madrid Chamartín ‡ .... **669 672b** a.	...	...	1013	...	1227	1359	...	...	...	...	1541	...	1718	...	1919	2022	...	2122	...	2233	...	...	...

C – To / from Ciudad Real (Table **678**).
E – To / from Cádiz (Table **671**).
N – Daily from Sevilla. From Cádiz on ①–⑤. Table **671**.
T – TORRE DEL ORO – (12) 🍸 Barcelona - València - Córdoba - Sevilla - Cádiz and v.v. (Table **672a**).
¶ – Linares - Jaen: *59 km.* Jaen - Andújar: *54 km.*
‡ – Full name is Madrid-Chamartín-Clara Campoamor.
☛ **Shaded services are suspended until further notice.**

2nd class MÁLAGA - TORREMOLINOS - FUENGIROLA 662

km												
						❦						
0	**Málaga** María Zambrano .d.	0523	0558	0633	0653	and	2133	2203	2233	2303	2333	...
8	Málaga Aeropuerto ✈ .....d.	0532	0607	0642	0702	every	2142	2212	2242	2312	2342	...
16	**Torremolinos** ....d.	0543	0618	0653	0713	20	2153	2223	2253	2323	2353	...
20	Benalmádena ....d.	0554	0629	0704	0724	mins.	2204	2234	2304	2334	0004	...
31	**Fuengirola** ....a.	0606	0641	0716	0736	until	2216	2246	2316	2346	0016	...

					❦						
Fuengirola .... d.	0610	0645	0720	0740	and	2220	2250	2320	2350	0020	...
Benalmádena .... d.	0624	0659	0734	0754	every	2234	2304	2334	0004	0034	...
Torremolinos .... d.	0633	0708	0743	0803	20	2243	2313	2343	0013	0043	...
Málaga Aeropuerto ✈ .. d.	0644	0719	0754	0814	mins.	2254	2324	2354	0024	0054	...
Málaga María Zambrano a.	0652	0727	0802	0822	until	2302	2332	0002	0032	0102	...

❦ – 0653, 0733, 0813 from Málaga and 0740, 0820, 0900 from Fuengirola do not run on ⑥⑦.

🚌 BARCELONA - ANDORRA 664

From **Barcelona** Nord bus station: 0630 *, 0700, 0730 *, 1030, 1500, 1700 *, 1900.
From **Andorra la Vella** bus station: 0600, 0815 *, 1100, 1500, 1700 *, 1915.
Journey 3 hr 15 min (* 4 hours). Operator: Alsina Graells, Barcelona (ALSA) ✆ (+34) 91 327 05 40.

From **Barcelona Airport** ✈ (T1 and T2): 0730, 0930, 1100, 1300, 1500, 1730, 2000, 2130, 2300.
From **Barcelona** Sants railway station: 0615, 0815, 1015, 1145, 1345, 1545, 1815, 2045, 2215, 2345.
From **Andorra la Vella** bus station: 0330, 0615, 0815, 1115, 1315, 1515, 1630, 1815, 2015, 2215.
Journey 3 hours (3 hrs 30 mins to / from Barcelona ✈). Operator: Autocars Nadal ✆ +376 805 151.

2nd class BARCELONA - SITGES - SANT V de CALDERS 665

Local rail service **Barcelona - Sitges - Sant Vicenç de Calders**.
From Barcelona Sants: 0606, 0636 and every 30 minutes until 2206; then 2306.
From Sant Vicenç: 0601, 0616 ⚒, 0631 Ⓐ, 0659, 0729, 0751, 0831, 0902, 0932 and every 30 minutes until 2102, 2132 Ⓐ, then 2200.

Additional trains operate **Barcelona - Sitges** and v.v.

Journey times: **Barcelona** – **Sitges** (*34 km*) 30 minutes,
Barcelona – **Sant Vicenç** (*60 km*) 57 minutes.

2nd class BARCELONA - MATARÓ, BLANES and MAÇANET 666

Cercanías (suburban) line **R1**. For faster services Barcelona - Maçanet via Granollers, see Table **657**.

Approximate journey times (in mins) to / from **Barcelona** Sants: Mataró (46), Arenys de Mar (57), Calella (69), Pineda de Mar (73), Malgrat de Mar (79), Blanes (84), Maçanet - Massanes (97).

Barcelona Sants – **Mataró** and v.v. *35 km*
Ⓐ: 4 – 6 trains per hour.
From Barcelona 0555 – 2318; from Mataró 0501 – 2301.
Ⓒ: 2 – 4 trains per hour.
From Barcelona 0555 – 2318; from Mataró 0501 – 2231.

Barcelona Sants – **Blanes** *67 km*
0555, 0625 and every 30 mins. until 2155 Ⓒ, 2255 Ⓐ.

Blanes - Barcelona Sants
Daily: 0603, 0623 and every 30 mins. until 2153.

Barcelona Sants – Blanes – **Maçanet - Massanes** *82 km*
Daily: 0555, 0655 and every 30 mins. until 2155.

Maçanet - Massanes – Blanes – **Barcelona** Sants
Ⓐ: 0609, 0639 and every 30 mins until 1109 then hourly until 1909, 1939, 2009, 2039, 2109, 2139.
Ⓒ: 0609, 0639, 0709 and hourly until 1909, 2009, 2139.

2nd class ALACANT - BENIDORM - DÉNIA 667

◐ *By tram (route L1)*	①–⑤								
Alacant Luceros ⊙ .....d.	...	0541	0611	0711	every	1911	2011	2111	2211
El Campello ....d.	...	0609	0639	0739	30 mins.	1939	2039	2139	2239
La Vila Joiosa ....d.	0612	0635	0705	0805	◐	2005	2105	2205	2305
Benidorm ....a.	0630	0653	0723	0823	until	2023	2123	2223	2323

✣ *By tram (route L1)*	①–⑤								
Benidorm ....d.	0635	0705	0805	every	1905	2005	2105	2205	2235
La Vila Joiosa ....d.	0653	0723	0823	30 mins.	1923	2023	2123	2223	2253
El Campello ....d.	0723	0753	0853	✣	1953	2053	2153	2253	...
Alacant Luceros ⊙ ....a.	0751	0821	0921	until	2021	2121	2221	2321	...

By train (route L9)									
Benidorm ....d.	0507	0607	0707		1907	2007	2107	2207	...
Altea ....d.	0522	0622	0722	every	1922	2022	2122	2222	...
Calpe ....d.	0544	0644	0744	hour	1944	2044	2144	...	...
Teulada ....d.	0603	0703	0803	◐	2003	2103	2203	...	...
Gata .... 🚌 d.	*0620*	*0720*	*0820*	until	*2020*	*2120*	*2220*	...	...
Dénia .... 🚌 a.	*0646*	*0746*	*0846*		*2046*	*2146*	*2246*	...	...

By train (route L9)									
Dénia .... 🚌 d.	*0540*	*0640*	*0740*		*1940*	*2040*	...	*2140*	...
Gata ....d.	0617	0717	0817	every	2017	2117	...	2217	...
Teulada ....a.	0625	0725	0825	hour	2025	2125	...	2225	...
Calpe ....d.	0645	0745	0845	◐	2045	2145	...	2245	...
Altea ....d.	0706	0806	0906	until	2106	2206	2230	2306	...
Benidorm ....a.	0721	0821	0921		2121	2221	2245	2321	...

◐ – Alacant - Benidorm runs every 30 minutes 0641 - 2141 (also 0025, 0155 night of ⑤⑥ June 30 - Aug. 26).
✣ – Benidorm - Alacant runs every 30 minutes 0635 - 2205 (also 0211, 0441 night of ⑤⑥ June 30 - Aug. 26).
⊙ – ± 400 m from Alacant Renfe station.
Operator: Tram Metropolitano / FGV ✆ 900 72 04 72 www.fgvalicante.com

668 MADRID - ALBACETE, ALACANT and VALÈNCIA

km		AVE		avlo	iryo		AVE	Ouigo	AVE	AVE	AVE	AVE	AVE	AVE	Ouigo	AVE	iryo	MD	MD	AVE	Alvia	AVE	IC	avlo	IC	Ouigo
		5662	18024	5064	6061	18018	5072	xxxx	5070	5080	5092	5962	5890	5102	xxxx	5100	6102	14404	18081	5110	4072	5312	5710	5124	694	xxxx
		①–⑥	①–⑤		①–⑤	⑥⑦	①–⑥		①–⑤							①–⑤		①–⑥	2	①–⑤		⑥⑦			🍷	
			B			J				C	V								h		S	N	Z		T	
	Madrid Chamartín ¶ d.	...	...	0630	0645	...	0700	0720	0730	0830	0900	0915	...	1000	1015	1030	1045	...	...	1130	1145	1200	1210	1228	...	1345
0	**Madrid** Puerta de Atocha d.	0630	...	|	|	...	|	|	|	|	|	|	0940	|	|	|	|	...	...	|	|	|	|	|	...	|
189	Cuenca Fernando Zóbel d.	0726	...	0735	|	...	0804	|	0835	|	1005	|	1037	|	|	1134	1150	...	...	|	1257	1301	1320	1333	...	|
321	Requena / Utiel d.	|	...	|	|	...	|	|	0911	|	|	|	1114	|	|	1209	|	...	...	|	|	|	1359	1408	...	|
322*	**Albacete** d.	0800	0806	|	|	0918	0839	|	|	|	1039	|	|	|	|	|	|	1100	1229	|	1342	1335	|	|	1441	|
436	Villena AV d.	0834	|	|	|	|	0913	|	|	|	|	|	|	|	|	|	|	|	|	|	1420	|	|	|	|	|
486	**Alacant** Terminal d.	0901	|	|	|	|	0932	|	|	|	1124	|	|	1217	|	|	|	|	1400	|	1440	1420	|	|	|	|
	Elche AV / Elx AV d.	0923	|	|	|	|	...	|	|	|	...	1132	|	...	|	|	|	|	...	|	...	...	|	|	|	|
	Orihuela d.	0938	|	|	|	|	...	|	|	|	...	1147	|	...	|	|	|	|	...	|	...	...	|	|	|	|
477	**Murcia** a.	0955	|	|	|	|	...	|	|	|	...	1212	|	...	|	|	|	|	...	|	...	...	|	|	|	|
391	Xátiva d.	...	0931	|	|	1042	...	|	|	|	...	...	|	...	|	|	|	1206	...	|	...	...	|	|	1545	|
	València Joaquín Sorolla a.	...	|	0826	0834	|	...	0910	0933	1019	...	...	1135	...	1205	1230	1240	|	...	1319	...	...	1422	1429	|	1535
	València Nord △ a.	...	1014	...	...	1118	...	...	...	...	...	...	|	...	...	...	...	1245	...	...	...	...	|	...	1630	...
	Castelló de la Plana **672** a.	...	...	...	...	...	...	...	...	...	...	...	1235	...	...	...	...	...	...	...	...	...	1521	...	1727	...

	AVE	AVE	AVE	AVE	MD	AVE	Alvia	AVE	iryo	AVE	MD	Ouigo	AVE	AVE	Av	avlo	iryo	AVE	Ouigo	AVE	AVE	AVE	Alvia	AVE	AVE	AVE
	5142	5140	5742	5150	14406	5162	4110	5160	6162	5172	18181	xxxx	5170	5182	8173	5184	6182	5382	xxxx	5990	5792	5212	4140	5200	3981	5210
	①–⑤					Ⓑ		Ⓑ			2				Ⓐ						Ⓑ	Ⓑ		Ⓑ		
							G				h				H			Y					G		P	
Madrid Chamartín ¶ d.	1400	1424	...	1530	...	1600	1615	1630	1645	1700	...	1720	1730	1800	...	1830	1845	1900	1925	...	1930	1955	2005	2030	...	2100
Madrid Puerta de Atocha d.	|	|	1425	|	...	|	|	|	|	|	...	|	|	|	1810	|	|	|	|	1925	|	|	|	|	...	|
Cuenca Fernando Zóbel d.	|	1529	1521	|	...	1705	1726	|	1750	|	...	|	|	|	1921	|	|	2005	|	2022	|	2100	2116	|	2139	2205
Requena / Utiel d.	|	1604	|	|	...	|	|	|	|	|	...	|	|	|	|	|	|	|	|	2059	|	|	|	|	|	2241
Albacete d.	1537	|	1555	|	1650	1739	|	|	|	1833	1849	|	|	1933	2000	|	|	2039	|	|	|	2134	2156	|	|	|
Villena AV d.	1611	|	1629	|	|	1813	|	|	|	|	|	|	|	|	...	|	|	|	|	|	|	2207	2234	|	|	|
Alacant Terminal d.	1630	|	1656	|	|	1833	|	|	|	1920	2031	|	|	2020	...	|	|	2126	|	|	|	2226	2254	|	|	|
Elche AV / Elx AV d.	...	|	1718	|	|	...	|	|	|	...	...	|	|	...	...	|	|	...	|	|	2146	...	...	|	|	|
Orihuela d.	...	|	1733	|	|	...	|	|	|	...	...	|	|	...	...	|	|	...	|	|	2202	...	...	|	|	|
Murcia a.	...	|	1750	|	|	...	|	|	|	...	...	|	|	...	...	|	|	...	|	|	2219	...	...	|	|	|
Xátiva d.	...	|	...	|	1800	...	|	|	|	...	...	|	|	...	...	|	|	...	|	|	...	...	...	|	|	|
València Joaquín Sorolla a.	...	1625	...	1719	|	...	1832	1819	1840	...	...	1910	1919	...	...	2019	2034	...	2115	2120	...	...	...	2219	2230	2303
València Nord △ a.	...	...	...	...	1840	...	|	...	...	...	...	...	...	...	...	...	...	...	...	|	...	...	...	...	...	...
Castelló de la Plana **672** a.	...	...	...	...	...	...	1931	...	...	...	...	...	...	...	...	...	...	...	...	2220	...	...	...	...	...	...

	Av	AVE	AVE	iryo	AVE	AVE	Av	AVE	Ouigo	AVE	AVE	AVE	AVE	AVE	AVE	avlo	iryo	Ouigo	AVE	AVE	MD	Alvia	Alvia	AVE	AVE	IC
	8072	5063	5061	6063	5773	5763	8082	5871	xxxx	5273	5071	5073	5081	3982	5083	5095	6103	xxxx	5093	5101	18183	4143	4111	5121	5803	697
	①–⑤	①–⑤	①–④	①–⑤	⑥	Ⓐ	⑥⑦					①–④	①–⑥							①–⑥	2			①–⑤		🍷
	H						H			Y				P							h	S	G			T
Castelló de la Plana **672** d.	...	...	...	...	...	...	...	0605	...	...	...	...	...	...	...	...	...	...	...	...	...	...	1107	...	...	1056
València Nord △ d.	...	...	...	...	...	...	...	|	...	...	...	...	...	...	...	...	...	...	...	...	...	...	|	...	...	1200
València Joaquín Sorolla d.	...	...	0635	0655	...	...	...	0700	0735	...	0750	...	0845	0900	...	0935	1000	1010	...	1035	...	...	1209	1245	...	|
Xátiva d.	...	...	|	|	...	...	...	|	|	...	|	...	|	|	...	|	|	|	...	|	...	...	|	|	...	1248
Murcia d.	...	...	|	|	0615	0625	...	|	|	...	|	...	|	|	...	|	|	|	...	|	...	...	|	|	1150	|
Orihuela d.	...	...	|	|	0631	0641	...	|	|	...	|	...	|	|	...	|	|	|	...	|	...	...	|	|	1206	|
Elche AV / Elx AV d.	...	...	|	|	0646	0655	...	|	|	...	|	...	|	|	...	|	|	|	...	|	...	...	|	|	1220	|
Alacant Terminal d.	...	0555	|	|	|	|	...	|	|	0720	|	0740	|	|	0835	|	|	|	0940	|	1012	1035	|	|	1255	|
Villena AV d.	...	0615	|	|	|	|	...	|	|	|	|	|	|	|	0855	|	|	|	1000	|	|	1057	|	|	1315	|
Albacete d.	0545	0648	|	|	0734	|	0650	|	|	0808	|	|	|	|	0929	|	|	|	1034	|	1150	1133	|	|	1349	1356
Requena / Utiel d.	|	|	0659	|	|	|	|	0726	|	|	0814	|	|	|	|	0959	|	|	|	1059	...	|	1239	|	|	...
Cuenca Fernando Zóbel d.	0628	0722	0735	|	0808	|	0732	0803	|	0842	0850	|	|	0952	1003	1035	|	|	|	1135	...	1212	1320	|	1423	...
Madrid Puerta de Atocha a.	0738	|	|	|	|	|	0840	0858	|	|	|	|	|	...	|	|	|	|	|	|	...	|	|	|	1548	...
Madrid Chamartín ¶ a.	...	0825	0838	0851	0912	0910	...	...	0925	0945	0954	1000	1038	...	1108	1138	1153	1200	1208	1238	...	1322	1430	1435	...	...

	Ouigo	AVE	MD	iryo	AVE	AVE	AVE	avlo	Alvia	AVE	AVE	Ouigo	MD		AVE	AVE	AVE	AVE	AVE	Ouigo	iryo	AVE	IC	AVE	avlo	MD
	xxxx	5131	14405	6143	5843	5951	5143	5155	4181	5153	5161	xxxx	18083	18027	5171	5183	5181	5193	5191	xxxx	6203	5203	5201	5903	5215	1440
										Ⓑ			2		Ⓑ			⑤⑦	Ⓑ					Ⓑ		Ⓑ
									G				h	A	D	N							Q			
Castelló de la Plana **672** d.	...	...	...	...	...	1414	...	...	...	...	...	...	...	...	...	...	...	...	...	...	...	...	1908	...	...	...
València Nord △ d.	...	...	1345	...	...	|	...	...	...	...	...	...	...	1725	...	...	...	...	...	...	...	...	|	...	...	205
València Joaquín Sorolla d.	1330	1345	|	1400	...	1510	...	1545	...	...	1645	1650	...	|	1740	...	1845	...	1945	2000	2000	...	2012	...	2110	|
Xátiva d.	|	|	1426	|	...	|	...	|	...	...	|	|	...	1807	|	...	|	...	|	|	|	...	|	...	|	212
Murcia d.	|	|	|	|	1355	|	...	|	...	...	|	|	...	|	|	...	|	...	|	|	|	...	|	1925	|	|
Orihuela d.	|	|	|	|	1411	|	...	|	...	...	|	|	...	|	|	...	|	...	|	|	|	...	|	1940	|	|
Elche AV / Elx AV d.	|	|	|	|	1425	|	...	|	...	...	|	|	...	|	|	...	|	...	|	|	|	...	|	1954	|	|
Alacant Terminal d.	|	|	|	|	|	|	1435	|	1520	1530	|	|	1700	|	|	1740	|	1845	|	|	|	1945	|	2024	|	223
Villena AV d.	|	|	|	|	|	|	1455	|	1542	1550	|	|	|	|	|	|	|	|	|	|	|	|	|	2044	|	...
Albacete d.	|	|	1537	|	|	|	1529	|	1621	1625	|	|	1838	1928	|	1828	|	1933	|	|	|	2036	|	2118	|	...
Requena / Utiel d.	|	|	...	|	|	1534	|	|	|	|	|	|	...	...	1804	|	|	|	|	|	|	|	2038	|	2134	...
Cuenca Fernando Zóbel d.	|	|	...	|	|	1611	|	|	1705	1700	|	|	...	...	1840	1902	|	|	|	|	|	|	2116	2152	2210	...
Madrid Puerta de Atocha a.	|	|	...	|	|	1706	|	|	|	|	|	|	...	...	|	|	|	|	|	|	|	|	|	2247	|	...
Madrid Chamartín ¶ a.	1520	1535	...	1553	1640	...	1708	1738	1815	1803	1835	1840	...	...	1944	2008	2035	2108	2135	2150	2155	2208	2227	...	2312	...

A – To Alcázar de San Juan on Ⓑ. To Ciudad Real on ⑥ (Table **678**).
B – From Alcázar de San Juan on ①–⑤. From Ciudad Real on ① (Table **678**).
C – On ①–⑥ from Burgos (Table **689**).
D – On Ⓑ to Burgos (Table **689**).
G – From / to Gijón (Table **685**).
H – From / to Toledo (Table **679**).
J – From Alcázar de San Juan.
N – From / to Leon (Table **682**).
P – From / to Sevilla (Table **660**).
Q – On ⑤⑦ from Vinaròs (Table **672**).
S – From / to Santander (Table **684**).
T – TORRE DEL ORO – 12 🍷 Barcelona - Cádiz and v.v. (Table **672a**).
V – On ①–⑤ from / to Leon (Table **682**).
Y – From / to Ourense (Table **680**).
Z – On ⑤⑦ to Vinaròs (Table **672**).
h – From/to Ciudad Real (Table **678**).
* – Albacete - Xátiva - València: *203 km*.
¶ – Full name is Madrid-Chamartín-Clara Campoamor.

Av – ***Avant*** high-speed services. Single clas
avlo – Low-cost ***AVE*** Renfe services branded **avlo**: www.avlorenfe.com
Ouigo – Low-cost ***TGV*** services branded **Ouigo** www.ouigo.com
iryo – ***ETR*** 1000 services branded **iryo**: www.iryo.eu
☛ **Shaded services are suspended unti further notice.**

△ – *Cercanías* (suburban) line **C1**: **València** - **Gandia** and v.v. *62 km* 2nd class. Journey time: 54 - 60 minutes.

From **València** Nord

Ⓐ: 0611, 0641 and every 30 minutes until 1941; then 1956, 2033, 2041, 2111, 2141, 2211, 2241.
Ⓒ: 0641, 0741 and hourly until 2241.

From **Gandia**

Ⓐ: 0605, 0640, 0655, 0710, 0725, 0740, 0755, 0825, 0840, 0855, 0915, 092 0955 and every 30 minutes until 2225.
Ⓒ: 0655, 0755 and hourly until 2055; then 2225.

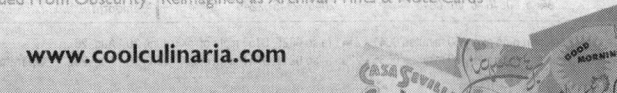

MADRID - CUENCA - VALÈNCIA — 669

2nd class

🚌 subject to confirmation from March 4. 🚌 Cuenca - Utiel withdrawn from March 4.

km			🚌			🚌 Ⓑ			🚌	
0	**Madrid** Atocha Cercanías . d.	0655	...	...	1048	...	...	1441	...	...
8	Villaverde Bajo .... d.	0703	...	...	1056	...	...	1449	...	...
49	Aranjuez **661 672b** .... a.	0740	...	...	1133	...	...	1526	...	...
	Aranjuez **661 672b** ... 🚌 d.	...	0806	...	...	1154	...	...	1548	...
	Cuenca .... 🚌 d.	...	1122	...	...	1510	...	...	1902	...
	Cuenca Fernando Zóbel 🚌 d.	...	1136	...	...	1524	...	...	1916	...
	Utiel .... a.	...	...	...	...	...	...	...	...	...
	Utiel .... d.	...	...	1410	...	...	1745	...	...	2135
	València Nord .... a.	...	...	1613	...	...	1925	...	...	2307

	Ⓐ	🚌 Ⓐ	Ⓐ	Ⓒ	🚌 Ⓒ	Ⓒ		🚌 Ⓑ			🚌	
València Nord .... d.	0638	...	...	0714	...	...	1107	...	...	1258	...	...
Utiel .... a.	0830	...	...	0910	...	...	1315	...	...	1458	...	...
Utiel .... d.	...	...	...	...	...	...	...	...	...	...	...	...
Cuenca Fernando Zóbel 🚌 d.	...	1045	...	...	1125	...	...	1536	...	...	1733	...
Cuenca .... 🚌 d.	...	1059	...	...	1139	...	...	1550	...	...	1747	...
Aranjuez **661 672b**. 🚌 a.	...	1415	...	...	1455	...	...	1906	...	...	2103	...
Aranjuez **661 672b** .... d.	...	...	1420	...	...	1510	...	...	1920	...	...	2131
Villaverde Bajo .... a.	...	...	1457	...	...	1547	...	...	1957	...	...	2208
Madrid Atocha Cercanías. a.	...	...	1505	...	...	1555	...	...	2005	...	...	2216

VALÈNCIA - TERUEL - ZARAGOZA - HUESCA - CANFRANC — 670

2nd class (except *AVE* trains)

km		Ⓐ	Ⓒ	Ⓐ		*MD* 18502		*MD* 18504 A		*AVE* 3393	*MD* 18506		
0	**València** Nord .... d.	...	...	...	...	0935	...	1213	...	...	1622	...	...
34	Sagunt .... d.	...	...	...	...	1005	...	1248	...	...	1654	...	...
65	Segorbe .... d.	...	...	...	...	1033	...	1317	...	...	1721	...	...
171	**Teruel** .... d.	...	...	...	0640	1215	...	1451	...	...	1850	...	...
242	Calamocha .... d.	...	...	...	0727	1304	...	1535	...	...	1939	...	...
305	Cariñena .... d.	...	...	...	0817	1355	...	1625	...	...	2041	...	...
	Madrid ◇ **650** ...... d.	...	...	...	|	|	...	|	...	1905	|	...	...
359	**Zaragoza** Delicias .... d.	0624	0648	0843	0901	1432	1542	1702	1902	2033	2119	2139	...
361	**Zaragoza** Portillo ..... d.	0627	0651	0848	0911	1436	1546	1705	1905	|	2123	2142	...
363	**Zaragoza** Goya .... d.	0629	0653	0851	0913	1439	1549	1707	1907	|	2125	2144	...
417	Tardienta .... d.	0709	0734	0931	...	1512	1629	...	1948	2103	...	2223	...
439	**Huesca** .... a.	0724	0750	0946	...	1528	1644	...	2003	2118	...	2238	...
439	**Huesca** .... d.	...	...	0951	...	...	1650	...	...	...	...	...	...
474	Ayerbe .... d.	...	...	1030	...	...	1730	...	...	...	...	...	...
533	Sabiñánigo .... d.	...	...	1137	...	...	1837	...	...	...	...	...	...
549	Jaca .... d.	...	...	1154	...	...	1858	...	...	...	...	...	...
574	**Canfranc 324** .... a.	...	...	1229	...	...	1937	...	...	...	...	...	...

	Ⓐ	*MD* 18511	Ⓐ	*AVE* 3272	Ⓒ	Ⓐ		Ⓒ	*MD* 18515			
Canfranc 324 .... d.	...	...	...	...	...	0605	...	0850	...	...	1750	...
Jaca .... d.	...	...	...	...	...	0640	...	0925	...	...	1825	...
Sabiñánigo .... d.	...	...	...	...	...	0655	...	0940	...	...	1840	...
Ayerbe .... d.	...	...	...	...	...	0802	...	1052	...	...	1951	...
Huesca .... a.	...	...	...	...	...	0845	...	1133	...	...	2032	...
Huesca .... d.	0623	...	0738	0815	0833	0850	...	1138	1602	1838	2037	...
Tardienta .... d.	0638	...	0753	0827	0850	0905	...	1154	1618	1856	2053	...
Zaragoza Goya .... d.	0716	0808	0831	|	0932	0949	1109	1236	1702	1941	2138	...
Zaragoza Portillo .. d.	0719	0811	0833	|	0935	0952	1112	1239	1705	1943	2142	...
Zaragoza Delicias d.	0723	0815	0836	0900	0938	0955	1120	1243	1725	1948	2147	...
Madrid ◇ **650** ... a.	...	|	...	1035	...	...	|	...	|	|	...	...
Cariñena .... d.	...	0859	...	...	...	...	1201	...	1813	2036	...	...
Calamocha .... d.	...	0959	...	...	...	...	1250	...	1910	2132	...	...
Teruel .... d.	...	1049	...	...	...	...	1337	...	2000	2221	...	...
Segorbe .... d.	...	1220	...	...	...	...	1511	...	2132	...	...	...
Sagunt .... d.	...	1250	...	...	...	...	1543	...	2203	...	...	...
València Nord ...... a.	...	1323	...	...	...	...	1614	...	2232	...	...	...

A – From Cartagena on ①–⑤. From Murcia on ⑥ (Table **672**).   ◇ – Madrid Puerta de Atocha.   ☛ See Table **324** for 🚌 Canfranc - Bedous for connections to / from Pau.

CÓRDOBA - SEVILLA - HUELVA and CÁDIZ — 671

km		*MD* 13000 2 Ⓐ	*MD* 13002 2 ⚒	*MD* 13030 2 Ⓐ	*MD* 13030 2 Ⓒ	*MD* 13099 2 Ⓒ	*MD* 13079 2 J	*Alvia* 2074 P	*Alvia* 2074 Q	*MD* 13037 2 Ⓐ	*MD* 13020 2
	Madrid PA ❖ **660** .... d.	...	...	...	...	...	...	0705	0730	...	...
0	**Córdoba** .... **660** d.	...	...	0700	...	...	0812	0906	0930	...	0908
51	Palma del Río .... d.	...	...	0729	...	...	0845	|	|	...	0943
129	**Sevilla** .... **660** a.	...	...	0821	...	...	0937	0955	1036	...	1032
129	**Sevilla** .... **673** § d.	0640	0745	0832	0832	0845	0945	0957	1038	1000	1045
204	La Palma del Condado .... d.	|	|	|	|	0949	|	|	|	1108	|
244	**Huelva** .... a.	|	|	|	|	1020	|	|	|	1138	|
145	Dos Hermanas .... **673** § d.	0654	0758	0846	0846	...	0958	|	|	...	1058
162	Utrera .... § d.	0705	|	0858	0858	...	1008	|	|	...	1108
224	Aeropuerto de Jerez....... ▲ d.	0739	|	0933	0933	...	|	|	|	...	1143
236	Jerez de la Frontera....... ▲ d.	0746	0846	0940	0940	...	1045	1053	1128	...	1151
251	Puerto de Santa María .... d.	0756	0855	0950	0950	...	1056	1103	1139	...	1200
270	San Fernando - Bahía Sur ... d.	0809	0911	1006	1006	...	1112	1118	1153	...	1214
285	**Cádiz** .... a.	0826	0923	1017	1017	...	1126	1129	1207	...	1226

km			*IC* 2494	*MD* 13008 2 Ⓐ		*MD* 13010 2	*Alvia* 2134 Q	*MD* 13032 2 Ⓒ	*MD* 13032 2 Ⓐ	*Alvia* 2134 P	*MD* 13032 2 Ⓐ	*MD* 13014 2	*MD* 13039 2	*MD* 13083 2 J	
	Madrid PA ❖ **660** .... d.	...	0945	...	...	...	1205	...	...	1305	...	...	...	...	...
0	**Córdoba** .... **660** d.	...	1136	...	...	...	1355	1400	1400	1454	...	...	...	1612	...
51	Palma del Río .... d.	...	|	...	...	...	|	1431	1431	|	←	...	...	1643	...
129	**Sevilla** .... **660** a.	...	1220	...	...	...	1453	1520	1520	1542	1520	...	...	1730	...
129	**Sevilla** .... **673** § d.	...	1240	1245	...	1445	1455	...	1549	1545	1549	1645	1700	1745	...
204	La Palma del Condado .... d.	...	1335	|	...	|	|	...	→	|	|	|	1758	|	...
244	**Huelva** .... a.	...	1402	|	...	|	|	...	...	|	|	|	1834	|	...
145	Dos Hermanas .... **673** § d.	...	...	1258	...	1500	|	...	...	|	1603	1658	...	1758	...
162	Utrera .... § d.	...	...	1308	...	|	|	...	...	|	1613	|	...	1808	...
224	Aeropuerto de Jerez....... ▲ d.	...	...	1345	...	1540	|	...	...	|	|	1741	...	1844	...
236	Jerez de la Frontera....... ▲ d.	...	...	1353	...	1548	1555	...	...	1642	1655	1749	...	1852	...
251	Puerto de Santa María .... d.	...	...	1402	...	1558	1605	...	...	1651	1704	1758	...	1901	...
270	San Fernando - Bahía Sur ... d.	...	...	1418	...	1615	1620	...	...	1706	1718	1813	...	1917	...
285	**Cádiz** .... a.	...	...	1430	...	1627	1631	...	...	1717	1730	1825	...	1930	...

	Alvia 2164 Q	*Alvia* 2164 P	*MD* 13035 2 J	*IC* 697 A	*MD* 13394 2	*Alvia* 2384	*MD* 13095 2	*MD* 13073 2 J			
Madrid PA ❖ **660** .... d.	1605	1610	...	...	...	1805	...	...	...	...	...
Córdoba .... **660** d.	|	|	1830	1836	...	2000	...	2010	...	...	...
Palma del Río .... d.	|	|	1905	|	...	|	...	2042	...	...	...
Sevilla .... **660** a.	|	|	1956	1925	...	|	...	2128	...	...	...
Sevilla .... **673** § d.	|	|	2010	1930	2045	|	2050	2150	...	...	...
La Palma del Condado ..... d.	|	|	|	|	|	2128	2149	|	...	...	...
Huelva .... a.	|	|	|	|	|	2154	2218	|	...	...	...
Dos Hermanas .... **673** § d.	|	|	2023	|	2058	...	...	2203	...	...	...
Utrera .... § d.	|	|	|	|	2109	...	...	2213	...	...	...
Aeropuerto de Jerez .... ▲ d.	|	|	|	|	|	...	...	2248	...	...	...
Jerez de la Frontera .... ▲ d.	1944	1942	2113	2032	2148	...	...	2256	...	...	...
Puerto de Santa María .... d.	1955	1952	2122	2043	2157	...	...	2305	...	...	...
San Fernando - Bahía Sur .... d.	2011	2007	2137	2059	2212	...	...	2321	...	...	...
Cádiz .... a.	2024	2019	2150	2110	2223	...	...	2335	...	...	...

	MD 13001 2 J Ⓐ	*Alvia* 2075 Q	*Alvia* 2075 P	*MD* 13041 2	*Alvia* 2285 Ⓐ	*MD* 13003 2 M	*IC* 694 A	*MD* 13005 2	*MD* 13007 2 Ⓐ
Cádiz .... d.	0540	0635	0640	...	...	0645	0735	0840	0940
San Fernando - Bahía Sur. d.	0553	0647	0652	...	...	0656	0748	0851	0951
Puerto de Santa María ..... d.	0608	0702	0705	...	...	0711	0804	0905	1006
Jerez de la Frontera .... ▲ d.	0617	0712	0715	...	...	0720	0814	0914	1015
Aeropuerto de Jerez .... ▲ d.	0624	|	|	...	...	0728	|	|	1023
Utrera .... § d.	0702	|	|	...	...	0806	|	|	|
Dos Hermanas .... **673** § d.	0712	|	|	...	...	0816	|	1005	1107
Huelva .... d.	|	|	|	0655	0800	|	|	|	|
La Palma del Condado . d.	|	|	|	0725	0824	|	|	|	|
Sevilla .... **673** § a.	0728	0805	0812	0825	|	0832	0908	1020	1120
Sevilla .... **660** d.	0740	0808	0815	...	|	0841	0912	...	...
Palma del Río .... d.	0828	|	|	...	|	0929	|	...	...
Córdoba .... **660** a.	0904	0903	0904	...	0948	1000	1006	...	...
Madrid PA ❖ **660** .... a.	...	1110	1109	...	1143	...	...	...	...

	Alvia 2205 ⑥	*MD* 13009 2 J	*Alvia* 2135 P	*MD* 13011 2J Ⓐ	*MD* 13011 2J Ⓒ	*Alvia* 2135 Q	*MD* 13393 2	*MD* 13013 2 Ⓐ	*MD* 13043 2	*Alvia* 2365 ⑦	*MD* 13015 2
Cádiz .... d.	...	1140	1220	1240	...	1330	1412	1440	...	...	1540
San Fernando - Bahía Sur ... d.	...	1151	1231	1251	...	1341	1423	1451	...	...	1551
Puerto de Santa María .... d.	...	1206	1244	1306	...	1355	1436	1506	...	...	1606
Jerez de la Frontera .... ▲ d.	...	1215	1253	1315	...	1406	1445	1515	...	...	1615
Aeropuerto de Jerez .... ▲ d.	...	1223	|	|	...	|	|	1523	...	...	1623
Utrera .... § d.	...	|	|	1356	...	|	1525	|	...	...	1700
Dos Hermanas .... **673** § d.	...	1306	|	1406	...	|	1535	1606	...	...	1710
Huelva .... d.	1025	|	|	|	...	|	|	|	1500	1615	|
La Palma del Condado .... d.	1047	|	|	|	...	|	|	|	1530	1642	|
Sevilla .... **673** § a.	|	1320	1343	1420	...	1455	1549	1620	1627	|	1725
Sevilla .... **660** d.	|	1330	1345	1503	1503	1457	...	...	...	|	1735
Palma del Río .... d.	|	1415	|	1551	1551	|	...	...	...	|	1824
Córdoba .... **660** a.	1216	1449	1439	1624	1624	1552	...	...	...	1806	1903
Madrid PA ❖ **660** .... a.	1410	...	1636	...	...	1755	...	...	...	2003	...

		IC 2375	*MD* 13017 2 J	*Alvia* 2175 P	*Alvia* 2175 QR	*Alvia* 2175 ⑤⑦ Q	*MD* 13031 2	*MD* 13049 2	*MD* 13019 2	*MD* 13021 2				
Cádiz .... d.	...	...	1740	1810	1810	1810	1840	...	1940	2040	...	...	...	...
San Fernando - Bahía Sur ... d.	...	...	1751	1822	1822	1822	1851	...	1951	2052	...	...	...	...
Puerto de Santa María .... d.	...	...	1805	1836	1837	1837	1905	...	2006	2106	...	...	...	...
Jerez de la Frontera .... ▲ d.	...	...	1814	1847	1848	1848	1914	...	2015	2115	...	...	...	...
Aeropuerto de Jerez .... ▲ d.	...	...	1822	|	|	|	1921	...	|	|	...	...	...	...
Utrera .... § d.	...	...	|	|	|	|	|	...	2102	2156	...	...	...	...
Dos Hermanas .... **673** § d.	...	...	1906	|	|	|	2005	...	2112	2206	...	...	...	...
Huelva .... d.	...	1750	|	|	|	|	|	1900	|	|	...	...	...	...
La Palma del Condado .... d.	...	1817	|	|	|	|	|	1930	|	|	...	...	...	...
Sevilla .... **673** § a.	...	1914	1920	|	|	|	2017	2030	2128	2220	...	...	...	...
Sevilla .... **660** d.	...	1924	1940	|	|	|	2030	...	...	...	...	...	...	...
Palma del Río .... d.	...	|	2027	|	|	|	2117	...	...	...	...	...	...	...
Córdoba .... **660** a.	...	2012	2102	|	2034	|	2148	...	...	...	...	...	...	...
Madrid PA ❖ **660** .... a.	...	2212	...	2222	2235	2235	...	...	...	...	...	...	...	...

A – TORRE DEL ORO – 🚃12 🍸 Barcelona - València - Córdoba - Sevilla - Cádiz and v.v. (Table **672a**).
J – From / to Jaén (Table **661**).
M – To Jaén on Ⓒ (Table **661**).
P – Until Mar. 4.
Q – From Mar. 5.
R – ①②③④⑥.
t – ①–⑤.
❖ – Madrid Puerta de Atocha.
§ – Frequent suburban services operate Sevilla - Utrera and v.v.
▲ – Additional suburban services operate Jerez de la Frontera - Aeropuerto de Jerez and v.v.: depart Aeropuerto 0720 Ⓐ, 0820 Ⓒ, 1325, 1920; depart Jerez 0657 Ⓐ, 0757 Ⓒ, 1257, 1857.

672 BARCELONA - VALÈNCIA - ALACANT - CARTAGENA

km		MD 14123 2	AVE 5871	Ⓐ 2	⑥ 2	⚒ 2	Em 1071 ①–⑤	IC 1307 ⑥	Em 1081 ①–⑤	Em 1081 ⑥	Alvia 4111 ①–⑥ G	2	IC 697 A	Em 1101	2	Ⓑ 2	AVE 5149	Ⓐ 2	Ⓒ 2	IC 463 🍷	IC 11463	2
	Figueres Vilafant d.	...	...	...	...	...	...	...	0710	...	...	...	...	0910	...	...	...	...	...	...	...	...
	Girona d.	...	...	...	...	...	...	...	0726	...	...	...	...	0926	...	...	...	...	...	...	...	...
0	**Barcelona** França d.	...	...	...	...	0543	...	...	|	...	...	0743	...	|	0943	...	...	1043	1043	...	...	...
5	Barcelona Passeig de Gràcia d.	...	...	...	...	0554	...	...	|	...	...	0754	...	|	0956	...	...	1054	1054	...	...	...
8	**Barcelona** Sants **652** d.	...	...	...	...	0600	0715	0725	0815	0815	...	0803	0830	1015	1000	...	...	1103	1103	1200	...	...
68	Sant Vicenç de Calders **652** d.	...	...	...	...	0650	|	|	|	|	...	0848	|	|	1049	...	...	|	1148	|	...	...
82	Altafulla - Tamarit d.	...	...	...	...	0702	|	|	|	|	...	0901	|	|	1102	...	...	|	1200	|	...	...
	Camp de Tarragona d.	...	...	...	...	|	0751	|	0851	0851	...	|	0907	1051	|	...	...	|	|	|	...	...
93	Tarragona **652** d.	...	...	...	...	0712	|	0834	|	|	...	0912	|	|	1112	...	...	1202	1210	1259	...	...
103	Vila–Seca ¶ d.	...	...	...	...	0722	|	|	|	|	...	0922	|	|	1122	...	...	1212	1220	|	...	...
105	Cambrils-AV d.	...	...	...	...	0733	|	|	|	|	...	0934	0929	|	1134	...	...	1224	1231	1318	...	...
	Tortosa d.	...	...	0635	0758	|	|	|	|	|	...	|	|	|	|	...	...	|	|	|	...	1335
163	L'Aldea - Amposta d.	...	...	0648	0811	0815	|	|	|	|	...	1014	0954	|	1212	...	...	1301	1311	1340	...	1350
176	Tortosa a.	...	...	|	|	0826	|	|	|	|	...	1025	|	|	1223	...	...	1312	1322	|	...	|
202	Vinaròs d.	...	...	0710	0833	...	|	|	|	|	...	...	1011	|	1308	...	...	...	...	1356	...	1412
208	Benicarló - Peñíscola d.	...	...	0716	0839	...	|	|	|	|	...	...	1019	|	1314	...	...	...	...	1402	...	1418
268	Benicàssim d.	...	...	0754	0924	...	|	|	|	|	...	...	|	|	1351	...	...	...	...	1430	...	1455
280	Castelló de la Plana d.	...	0605	0805	0935	...	0915	1008	1015	1015	1107	...	1056	1215	1400	...	1414	...	...	1439	...	1504
353	**València** Nord a.	...	|	0905	1038	...	|	1054	|	|	|	...	1155	|	1508	...	|	...	...	1530	...	1608
353	**València** Nord **668** d.	0701	|	...	...	...	|	1104	|	|	|	...	1200	|	...	1445	|	...	...	1542	...	...
	València Joaquín Sorolla a.	|	0652	...	...	...	1002	|	1104	1104	1159	...	|	1307	...	|	1500	...	...	|	...	...
	València Joaquín Sorolla **668** d.	|	0700	...	...	...	1012	|	...	...	1209	...	|	1317	...	|	1510	...	...	|	...	...
409	Xátiva **668** d.	0740	|	...	...	...	|	|	...	...	|	...	1248	|	...	1522	|	...	...	1624	...	...
	Madrid P de Atocha **668** a.	|	0858**t**	...	...	...	|	|	...	...	1430**t**	...	|	|	...	|	1706	...	...	|	...	...
	Cádiz **671** a.	|	...	...	...	...	|	|	...	...	...	...	2110	|	...	|	...	...	...	|	...	...
495	Elda - Petrer d.	0842	...	...	...	...	|	|	...	...	...	...	...	|	...	1620	...	...	...	1704	...	...
536	**Alacant** a.	0917	...	...	...	...	1210	1258	...	...	...	...	...	1512	...	1653	...	...	...	1734	...	...
536	**Alacant** d.	0924	...	...	...	...	...	...	...	...	...	...	...	...	...	...	...	...	...	1750	...	...
614	Murcia **673** a.	1101	...	...	...	...	...	...	...	...	...	...	...	...	...	...	...	...	...	1920	1940	...
677	**Lorca** Sutullena a.	...	...	...	...	...	...	...	...	...	...	...	...	...	...	...	...	...	...	...	2104	...
679	**Cartagena** **673** a.	...	...	...	...	...	...	...	...	...	...	...	...	...	...	...	...	...	...	...	...	...

	IC 1131 ⑤⑦	2	MD 18523 2 f	⑤ 2	Em 1141 Ⓑ	IC 165	2	IC 1351 ⑤	Em 1161	Ⓐ 2	Ⓒ 2	⑤ 2	IC 5201	IC 1371 ⑤	IC 5811	2	Em 1171 Ⓑ	Em 1181	2	IC 1201 Ⓑ	2	2
Figueres Vilafant d.	...	...	...	...	1310	...	...	...	...	...	...	...	...	...	...	...	...	...	...	...	...	...
Girona d.	...	...	...	...	1326	...	...	...	...	...	...	...	...	...	...	...	...	...	...	...	...	...
Barcelona França d.	...	1243	...	...	|	...	1443	...	...	1540	1540	...	...	...	...	...	...	...	1743	...	1943	2043
Barcelona Passeig de Gràcia d.	...	1256	...	...	|	...	1454	...	...	1551	1551	...	...	...	...	...	...	...	1755	...	1955	2054
Barcelona Sants **652** d.	1300	1303	...	...	1415	1500	1503	1530	1610	1557	1557	...	...	1700	...	...	1715	1815	1800	1930	2000	2103
Sant Vicenç de Calders **652** d.	|	1349	...	...	|	|	1547	|	|	|	1643	...	...	|	...	...	|	|	1847	|	2049	2148
Altafulla - Tamarit d.	|	1401	...	...	|	|	1559	|	|	|	1656	...	...	|	...	...	|	|	1859	|	2102	2201
Camp de Tarragona d.	|	|	...	...	1451	|	|	|	1648	|	|	...	...	|	...	...	1751	1851	|	|	|	|
Tarragona **652** d.	1359	1411	...	...	|	1558	1609	1630	|	1657	1706	...	...	1800	...	...	|	|	1910	2032	2111	2212
Vila–Seca ¶ d.	|	1421	...	...	|	|	1618	|	|	1706	1716	...	...	|	...	...	|	|	1920	|	2119	2222
Cambrils-AV d.	1418	1433	...	...	|	1615	1629	|	|	1716	1728	...	...	1818	...	...	|	|	1932	|	2130	2234
Tortosa d.	|	|	...	...	|	|	|	|	|	|	|	...	...	|	...	1902	|	|	|	|	|	|
L'Aldea - Amposta d.	1439	1513	...	...	|	1637	1720	|	|	1751	1806	...	...	1839	...	1919	|	|	2015	|	2210	2315
Tortosa a.	|	1524	...	...	|	|	1733	|	|	1802	1821	...	...	|	...	|	|	|	2026	|	2225	2326
Vinaròs d.	1454	...	...	...	|	1654	...	|	|	...	...	...	1814**j**	1854	...	1942	|	|	...	|	2305	...
Benicarló - Peñíscola d.	1500	...	...	...	|	1700	...	|	|	...	...	...	1821**j**	1900	...	1947	|	|	...	|	...	...
Benicàssim d.	1531	...	...	...	|	1729	...	|	|	...	...	...	1856**j**	1930	...	2026	|	|	...	|	...	...
Castelló de la Plana d.	1540	...	...	...	1612	1739	...	|	1810	...	...	...	1908	1940	2007	2036	1912	2015	...	2200	...	...
València Nord a.	1648	...	...	...	|	1837	...	1848	|	...	...	...	|	2033	|	2155	|	|	...	|	...	...
València Nord **668** d.	...	...	1628	1705	|	1847	...	1858	|	...	...	1944	|	2045	|	...	|	|	...	|	...	...
València Joaquín Sorolla a.	...	...	|	|	1655	|	...	|	1857	...	...	|	1959	|	2055	...	1955	2102	...	2252	...	...
València Joaquín Sorolla **668** d.	...	...	|	|	...	|	...	|	1907	...	...	|	2012	|	2105	...	...	2112	...	...	...	...
Xátiva **668** d.	...	...	1711	1741	...	1929	...	1948	|	...	...	2028	|	2128	|	...	...	|	...	...	...	...
Madrid P de Atocha **668** a.	...	...	|	|	...	|	...	|	|	...	...	|	2227**t**	|	2332	...	...	|	...	...	...	...
Cádiz **671** a.	...	...	|	|	...	|	...	|	|	...	...	|	...	|	...	...	...	|	...	...	...	...
Elda - Petrer d.	...	...	1753	1831	...	2016	...	|	|	...	...	2119	...	2212	...	...	...	|	...	...	...	...
Alacant a.	...	...	1825	1911	...	2042	...	2055	2105	...	...	2150	...	2245	...	...	...	2314	...	...	...	...
Alacant d.	...	...	1831	...	...	2054	...	...	...	...	...	...	...	...	...	...	...	...	...	...	...	...
Murcia **673** a.	...	...	1945	...	...	2221	...	...	...	...	...	...	...	...	...	...	...	...	...	...	...	...
Lorca Sutullena a.	...	...	|	...	...	|	...	...	...	...	...	...	...	...	...	...	...	...	...	...	...	...
Cartagena **673** a.	...	...	2047	...	...	2330	...	...	...	...	...	...	...	...	...	...	...	...	...	...	...	...

	Ⓐ 2	⑥ 2	IC 1262 ①–⑥	IC 1072 ①–⑥	2	Em 1082 ①–⑥	2	Em 1092	2	2	IC 1102	Em 1112	AVE 5890	Ⓒ 2	Ⓐ 2	MD 18504 ①–⑥ 2f	IC 11460	IC 460	2	IC 5710	IC 1342 ⑦	2
Cartagena **673** d.	...	...	...	...	...	...	...	...	...	...	...	...	...	...	...	0650**z**	...	...	...	...	...	...
Lorca Sutullena d.	...	...	...	...	...	...	...	...	...	...	...	...	...	...	...	|	0711	...	...	...	...	...
Murcia **673** d.	...	...	...	...	...	...	...	...	...	...	0630	...	...	...	...	0752	0835	0855	...	...	...	...
Alacant a.	...	...	...	...	...	...	...	...	...	...	0744	...	...	...	...	0909	...	1013	...	...	...	...
Alacant d.	...	...	...	...	...	...	...	0720	...	...	0800	0920	...	...	...	0917	...	1029	...	...	...	...
Elda - Petrer d.	...	...	...	...	...	...	...	|	...	...	0828	|	...	...	...	0956	...	1057	...	...	...	...
Cádiz **671** d.	...	...	...	...	...	...	...	|	...	...	|	|	...	...	...	|	...	|	...	...	...	...
Madrid P de Atocha **668** d.	...	...	...	...	...	...	...	|	...	...	|	|	0940	...	...	|	...	|	...	1210**t**	...	...
Xátiva **668** d.	...	...	...	...	...	...	...	|	...	...	0917	|	|	...	...	1046	...	1152	...	|	...	...
València Joaquín Sorolla **668** a.	...	...	...	...	...	...	...	0905	...	...	|	1110	1135	...	...	|	...	|	...	1422	...	...
València Joaquín Sorolla d.	...	...	...	...	...	0815	...	0915	...	...	|	1120	1145	...	...	|	...	|	...	1428	...	...
València Nord **668** a.	...	...	...	...	...	|	...	|	...	...	0954	|	|	...	...	1132	...	1236	...	|	...	...
València Nord d.	...	...	0620	0705	...	|	...	|	0755	...	1005	|	|	...	...	...	...	1251	...	|	1400	1417
Castelló de la Plana d.	...	...	0711	0750	...	0855	...	0959	0907	...	1052	1203	1235	...	...	...	...	1348	...	1523	1452	1526
Benicàssim d.	...	...	0719	|	...	|	...	|	0920	...	1100	|	...	...	...	...	...	1403	...	1536**j**	1500	1535
Benicarló - Peñíscola d.	...	...	0747	|	...	|	...	|	0957	...	1129	|	...	...	...	...	...	1429	...	1617**j**	1528	1617
Vinaròs d.	...	...	0752	|	0653	|	...	|	1003	...	1135	|	...	...	...	...	...	1434	...	1624**j**	1533	1622
Tortosa d.	0600	0605	|	|	0740	|	0936	|	|	1145	|	|	...	1346	1403	...	...	|	1545	...	|	|
L'Aldea - Amposta d.	0612	0619	0810	|	0751	|	0950	|	1029	1156	1151	|	...	1357	1413	...	...	1450	1556	...	1551	1641
Tortosa a.	|	|	|	|	|	|	|	|	1040	|	|	|	...	|	|	...	...	|	|	...	|	1707
Cambrils-AV d.	0648	0707	0838	|	0832	|	1033	|	...	1236	1220	|	...	1439	1448	...	...	1520	1639	...	1619	...
Vila–Seca ¶ d.	0659	0717	|	|	0843	|	1044	|	...	1247	|	|	...	1449	1457	...	...	|	1649	...	|	...
Tarragona **652** d.	0710	0726	0900	0913	0854	|	1056	|	...	1258	1238	|	...	1500	1508	...	...	1541	1659	...	1638	...
Camp de Tarragona d.	|	|	|	|	|	1018	|	1127	...	|	|	1332	...	|	|	...	...	|	|	...	|	...
Altafulla - Tamarit d.	|	0734	|	|	0902	|	1105	|	...	1306	|	|	...	1507	|	...	...	|	1707	...	|	...
Sant Vicenç de Calders **652** d.	|	0747	|	|	0915	|	1119	|	...	1319	|	|	...	1520	|	...	...	|	1720	...	|	...
Barcelona Sants **652** a.	0812	0837	1010	1010	1009	1055	1211	1216	...	1412	1340	1415	...	1612	1612	...	...	1640	1810	...	1740	...
Barcelona Passeig de Gràcia a.	0817	0842	...	...	1014	...	1216	...	...	1417	...	...	...	1617	1617	...	...	...	1815	...	...	...
Barcelona França a.	0827	0852	...	...	1025	...	1227	...	...	1428	...	...	...	1627	1627	...	...	...	1825	...	...	...
Girona a.	...	...	...	...	...	...	...	...	...	...	...	...	...	...	...	...	...	...	...	...	...	...
Figueres Vilafant a.	...	...	...	...	...	...	...	...	...	...	...	...	...	...	...	...	...	...	...	...	...	...

FOR NOTES SEE NEXT PAGE →

CARTAGENA - ALACANT - VALÈNCIA - BARCELONA 672

	Em 1152 Ⓑ	Alvia 1162 ①–⑤	2	IC 694 A	IC 264	2	2	Em 1182 ⑦	Alvia 4110 G	IC 1382 ⑦	Em 1192	2	IC 1402 ⑦	IC 1402 ⑤	2	Ⓑ 2	IC 1402 ⑤	MD 14202 2	①–⑤ 2	⑥ 2	AVE 5198	
Cartagena 673 ¦ d.	...	...	...	...	1200	...	...	...	...	...	...	...	...	...	...	...	...	1613	...	...	...	...
Lorca Sutullena ¦ d.	...	...	...	...	|	...	...	...	...	...	...	...	...	...	...	...	...	|	...	...	...	...
Murcia 673 ¦ d.	...	...	...	...	1307	...	...	...	...	...	...	...	...	...	...	...	...	1710	...	...	...	...
Alacant ¦ a.	...	...	...	...	1429	...	...	...	...	...	...	...	...	...	...	...	...	1830	...	...	...	...
Alacant d.	...	1410	...	...	1444	...	...	...	...	...	1718	...	1811	...	1755	...	...	1837	1928	1926	...	...
Elda - Petrer d.	...	|	...	...	1527	...	...	...	...	...	|	...	1838	...	1829	...	...	1909	2004	2003	...	...
Cádiz **671** d.	...	|	...	0735	|	...	...	...	...	...	|	...	|	...	|	...	...	|	|	|	...	...
Madrid P de Atocha **668** d.	...	|	...	|	|	...	...	...	1615‡	...	|	...	|	...	|	...	...	|	|	|	1925	...
Xátiva 668 d.	...	|	...	1545	1613	...	...	...	|	...	|	...	1922	...	1922	...	...	2013	2103	2101	|	...
València Joaquín Sorolla 668 a.	...	1553	...	|	|	...	...	...	1832	...	1905	...	|	...	|	...	...	|	|	|	2120	...
València Joaquín Sorolla d.	1518	1603	...	|	|	...	...	1803	1842	...	1915	...	|	...	|	...	...	|	|	|	2130	...
València Nord 668 a.	|	|	...	1630	1658	...	...	|	|	...	|	...	2005	...	2002	...	...	2054	2143	2141	|	...
València Nord ¦ d.	|	|	...	1635	1703	...	1638	|	|	1850	|	...	2015	2022	...	2007	2022	...	...	...	|	...
Castelló de la Plana ¦ d.	1602	1645	...	1729	1748	...	1750	1844	1931	1940	1955	...	2104	2111	...	2109	2111	...	...	...	2220	...
Benicàssim ¦ d.	|	|	...	|	1756	...	1758	|	...	|	|	...	2116	2123	...	2122	2123	...	...	...	...	...
Benicarló - Peñíscola ¦ d.	|	|	...	1807	1823	...	1837	|	...	|	|	...	2146	2153	...	2158	2153	...	...	...	...	...
Vinaròs ¦ d.	|	|	...	1814	1829	...	1843	|	...	|	|	...	2152	2159	...	2204	2159	...	...	...	...	...
Tortosa d.	|	|	1644	|	|	1842	1938	|	...	|	|	2052	|	|	...	|	|	...	...	...	...	...
L'Aldea - Amposta d.	|	|	1655	1831	1845	1855	1950	|	...	|	|	2106	2208	2215	...	2225	2215	...	...	...	...	...
Tortosa a.	|	|	|	|	|	|	|	|	...	|	|	|	|	|	...	2246	|	...	...	...	...	...
Cambrils-AV d.	|	|	1736	1905	1914	1937	2030	|	...	|	|	2147	2241	2247	...	...	2247	...	...	...	...	...
Vila–Seca ¶ d.	|	|	1747	|	|	1947	2042	|	...	|	|	2159	|	|	...	...	|	...	...	...	...	...
Tarragona 652 d.	|	|	1758	|	1937	1958	2053	|	...	2104	|	2210	2302	2307	...	...	2307	...	...	...	...	...
Camp de Tarragona d.	1732	1818	|	1928	|	|	|	2018	...	|	2125	|	|	|	...	...	|	...	...	...	...	...
Altafulla - Tamarit d.	|	|	1807	|	|	2006	2102	|	...	|	|	|	|	|	...	...	|	...	...	...	...	...
Sant Vicenç de Calders 652 d.	|	|	1820	|	|	2019	2116	|	...	|	|	2230	|	|	...	...	|	...	...	...	...	...
Barcelona Sants 652 a.	1819	1858	1912	2005	2040	2110	2210	2057	...	2213	2204	2323	2359	2359	...	...	2359	...	...	...	...	...
Barcelona Passeig de Gràcia a.	...	...	1917	...	...	2115	2215	...	...	...	...	2330	...	...	...	...	...	...	...	...	...	...
Barcelona França a.	...	...	1927	...	...	2125	2225	...	...	...	...	2340	...	...	...	...	...	...	...	...	...	...
Girona a.	...	...	...	...	...	...	...	...	...	...	...	...	...	...	...	...	...	...	...	...	...	...
Figueres Vilafant a.	...	...	...	...	...	...	...	...	...	...	...	...	...	...	...	...	...	...	...	...	...	...

Alacant - Orihuela – Murcia – Cartagena

	Ⓐ 2	Av 33075 Ⓐ	Av 33085	Av 33662 ⚒	⚒ 2	MD 14123	Av 33105	2	2	IC 11092 q 🚌	Av 33125	Ⓐ 2	Av 33155 Ⓐ	Av 33742	Ⓐ 2	Av 33175	2	IC 463 B	MD 18523 f	Av 33195	IC 11182 q 🚌	IC 165 B	Ⓑ 2	Av 33215
Alacant Terminal d.	...	0700	0840	0901	...	0924	1010	...	...	...	1250	...	1515	1656	...	1715	...	1750	1836	1955	...	2054	...	2155
Elche AV / Elx AV d.	...	0720	0900	0923	...	1005p	1030	...	...	...	1310	...	1535	1718	...	1735	...	1824p	1908p	2015	...	2131p	...	2215
Orihuela d.	...	0734	0914	0938	...	1040	1044	...	...	...	1324	...	1549	1733	...	1749	...	1854	1949	2029	...	2204	...	2229
Murcia d.	0720	0753	0933	0955	1015	1101	1105	1158	1235	1307	1343	1430	1608	1750	1755	1808	1810	1920	2011	2048	2155	2230	2239	2248
Cartagena a.	0825	...	...	...	1116	...	...	1304	1338	1435	...	1529	...	...	1856	...	1913	...	2105	...	2315	2330	2341	...

	⑥ 2	Ⓐ 2	Av 33067	IC 11093 q 🚌	MD 18504 Ⓐ f	Av 33087	IC 460 B	Av 33107	2	Av 33803	Av 33127	IC 264 B	2	Av 33157 Ⓐ	IC 11183 q 🚌	Av 33167	MD 14202		Ⓑ 2	Av 33903 Ⓑ	Av 33197	Av 33217		2
Cartagena d.	0500	0509	...	0625	0650	...	...	...	1030	...	...	1200	1235	...	1420	...	1613	...	1810	...	...	...	...	2115
Murcia d.	0556	0605	0640	0754	0752	0815	0855	1010	1128	1150	1245	1307	1333	1500	1545	1650	1710	...	1906	1925	1950	2120	...	2214
Orihuela d.	...	...	0657	...	0811	0832	0912	1027	...	1206	1302	1328	...	1517	...	1707	1728	...	...	1940	2006	2137	...	...
Elche AV / Elx AV d.	...	...	0711	...	0843p	0846	0940p	1041	...	1220	1316	1352p	...	1531	...	1721	1758p	...	...	1954	2020	2151	...	...
Alacant Terminal a.	...	...	0732	...	0909	0907	1013	1102	...	1241	1337	1429	...	1552	...	1742	1830	...	...	2014	2042	2212	...	...

A – TORRE DEL ORO – 🛏12 🍷 Barcelona - València - Córdoba - Sevilla - Cádiz and v.v. (Table **672a**).
B – From / to Barcelona.
G – To / from Gijón (Tables **681**, **685**).

f – From / to Zaragoza (Table **670**).
j – ⑤⑦.
p – Elche Parque / Elx Parc.
q – From / to Albacete (Table **673**).
t – Depart / arrive Madrid ‡.

x – 🚌.
y – ⑦.
z – Ⓐ.

¦ – Additional local trains operate between these stations.
¶ – Station for Port Aventura.
‡ – Madrid-Chamartín-Clara Campoamor.
☛ – **Shaded services are suspended until further notice.**

BARCELONA - SEVILLA - CADIZ 672a

	IC 697 A
Barcelona Sants d.	0830
Camp de Tarragona d.	0907
Cambrils-AV d.	1012
L'Aldea - Amposta d.	0929
Vinaròs d.	1011
Benicarló - Peñíscola d.	1019
Castelló de la Plana d.	1056
València Nord a.	1155
València Nord d.	1200
Xátiva d.	1248
Albacete d.	1401
Alcázar de San Juan d.	1510
Manzanares d.	1540
Linares - Baeza a.	1701
Linares - Baeza d.	1703
Andújar d.	1741
Córdoba a.	1831
Córdoba d.	1836
Sevilla a.	1925
Sevilla d.	1930
Jerez de la Frontera d.	2032
Puerto de Santa María d.	2043
San Fernando - Bahía Sur d.	2059
Cádiz a.	2110

	IC 694 A
Cádiz d.	0735
San Fernando - Bahía Sur d.	0748
Puerto de Santa María d.	0804
Jerez de la Frontera d.	0814
Sevilla a.	0908
Sevilla d.	0912
Córdoba a.	1006
Córdoba d.	1011
Andújar d.	1105
Linares - Baeza a.	1139
Linares - Baeza d.	1142
Manzanares d.	1302
Alcázar de San Juan d.	1329
Albacete d.	1441
Xátiva d.	1545
València Nord a.	1630
València Nord d.	1635
Castelló de la Plana d.	1729
Benicarló - Peñíscola d.	1807
Vinaròs d.	1814
L'Aldea - Amposta d.	1831
Cambrils-AV d.	1905
Camp de Tarragona d.	1928
Barcelona Sants a.	2005

A – TORRE DEL ORO – 🛏12 🍷 Barcelona - Cádiz and v.v. (Tables **661**, **668**, **671**, **672**, **678**).

MADRID - CARTAGENA 672b

km		AVE 5092	IC 11092 🚌		MD 18040	IC 10146 ⑤	88146 🚌 ⑤	AVE 5182	IC 11182 🚌	MD 18044 ⑤	MD 18042 Ⓑ
0	**Madrid** Chamartín ¶ ‡ d.	0900	...	...	1419	1540	...	1800	...	1643	1818
8	**Madrid** Atocha C ◧ ‡ d.	|	...	...	1432	1602	...	|	...	1657	1832
57	Aranjuez ‡ d.	|	...	...	1509	1639	...	|	...	1731	1908
157	Alcázar de San Juan ‡ d.	|	...	...	1604	|	...	|	...	1828	2000
288	**Albacete** d.	1037	1055	...	1715	1821	...	1931	1945	1941	2106
354	Hellín d.	...	1140	...	...	|	...	...	2030	...	...
	Archena-Fortuna d.	...	1240	...	...	1940	1953	...	2130	...	...
450	Murcia 672 ¦ d.	...	1307	...	...	...	2025	...	2155	...	...
	Lorca Sutullena ¦ a.	...	|	...	...	...	2146	...	|	...	...
562	Aguilas ¦ a.	...	|	...	...	...	2220	...	|	...	...
515	**Cartagena** 672 ¦ a.	...	1435	...	...	...	...	...	2315	...	...

	MD 18041 Ⓐ	MD 18049 ⑥	MD 18049 ⑦	IC 11093 🚌	AVE 5093		MD 18043	IC 11183 🚌	AVE 5183	88418 🚌 ⑦	IC 10418 ⑦	
Cartagena 672 ¦ d.	...	...	...	0625	...	...	...	1420	...	...	...	...
Aguilas ¦ d.	...	...	...	|	...	...	...	|	...	1510	...	...
Lorca Sutullena ¦ d.	...	...	...	|	...	...	...	|	...	1545	...	...
Murcia 672 ¦ d.	...	...	...	0755	...	...	...	1550	...	1710	...	...
Archena-Fortuna d.	...	...	...	0825	...	...	...	1620	...	1740	1753	...
Hellín d.	...	...	...	0925	...	...	...	1720	...	...	|	...
Albacete d.	0605	0730	...	1015	1034	...	1740	1813	1828	...	1915	...
Alcázar de San Juan ‡ d.	0711	0837	0837	...	|	...	1851	...	|	...	|	...
Aranjuez ‡ d.	0807	0933	0933	...	|	...	1948	...	|	...	2100	...
Madrid Atocha C ◧ ‡ a.	0844	1008	1008	...	|	...	2022	...	|	...	2144	...
Madrid Chamartín ¶ ‡ a.	0858	1022	1022	...	1208	...	2036	...	2008	...	2159	...

‡ – See also Table **661**. ◧ – Madrid **Atocha Cercanías**. ¶ – Full name is Madrid-Chamartín-Clara Campoamor. ¦ – Additional local trains operate between these stations.

673 SEVILLA and ALGECIRAS - MÁLAGA, GRANADA and ALMERÍA

2nd class

For trains **Sevilla** – **Málaga** and v.v. via **Córdoba**, see Table **660**. For trains **Sevilla** – **Granada** and v.v. via **Córdoba**, see Table **678a**.

km		*MD* 13063	*MD* 13900	*MD* 13940	*MD* 13902		*MD* 13065	*MD* 13942	*MD* 13904	*IC* 9331		*MD* 13906 ⑤⑦	*MD* 13944	*MD* 13077	*MD* 13908	*MD* 13946	*MD* 13910				
0	**Sevilla** d.	...	0714	...	0825	...	...	...	1140	...	...	1630	...	...	1848	...	1958	...	...	...	...
15	Dos Hermanas d.	...	0729	...	0842	...	...	...	1155	...	...	1645	...	...	1906	...	2013	...	...	...	...
	Algeciras d.	0620	|	...	|	...	1030	...	|	1503	...	|	...	1704	|	...	|	...	...	...	...
	San Roque - La Línea d.	0635	|	...	|	...	1046	...	|	1518	...	|	...	1725	|	...	|	...	...	...	...
	Ronda d.	0758	|	...	|	...	1224	...	|	1631	...	|	...	1855	|	...	|	...	...	...	...
	Antequera - Santa Ana § d.	|	0901	...	1019	...	|	...	1329	|	...	1816	...	|	2044	...	2143	...	...	...	...
167	Bobadilla d.	0851	0907	...	1025	...	1319	...	1335	|	...	1822	...	1949	2050	...	2153	...	...	...	...
236	**Málaga** M. Zambrano a.	|	1006	...	1117	...	|	...	1434	|	...	1918	...	|	2146	...	2247	...	...	...	...
	Antequera - Santa Ana § a.	0856	...	...	...	...	1325	...	...	1737	...	...	...	1954	...	...	...	...	...	...	...
	Madrid Pta de Atocha **660** a.	...	...	...	...	...	...	...	...	2040	...	...	...	...	...	...	...	...	...	...	...
183	Antequera AV d.	...	...	...	...	...	...	...	...	...	...	...	...	...	...	...	...	...	...	...	...
290	**Granada** a.	...	...	1110	...	...	...	1512	...	...	...	...	1812	...	...	2205	...	...	...	...	...
372	Guadix **661** d.	...	...	1220	...	...	...	1621	...	...	...	...	1928	...	...	2313	...	...	...	...	...
471	**Almería** **661** a.	...	...	1332	...	...	...	1752	...	...	...	...	2044	...	...	0032	...	...	...	...	...

km		*MD* 13901		*MD* 13951	*MD* 13903	*MD* 13062	*MD* 13953		*MD* 13905	*MD* 13064		*MD* 13907 ⑥⑦	*IC* 9330	*MD* 13955	*MD* 13909		*MD* 13957	*MD* 13076	*MD* 13911		
0	**Almería** **661** d.	...	...	0620	...	...	1035	...	...	...	...	...	...	1428	...	...	1804	...	...	...	...
99	Guadix **661** d.	...	...	0740	...	...	1149	...	...	...	...	...	...	1544	...	...	1927	...	...	...	...
181	**Granada** d.	...	...	0846	...	...	1255	...	...	...	...	...	...	1651	...	...	2036	...	...	...	...
288	Antequera AV d.	...	...	...	...	...	...	...	...	...	...	...	...	...	...	...	...	...	...	...	...
	Madrid Pta de Atocha **660** d.	...	...	...	...	...	...	...	...	...	...	...	1505	...	...	...	...	...	...	...	...
	Antequera - Santa Ana § d.	...	...	...	...	1009	...	...	...	1433	...	...	1756	...	...	...	...	2055	...	...	...
	Málaga M. Zambrano d.	0637	...	...	0858	|	...	...	1321	|	...	1558	|	...	1719	...	...	|	2037	...	...
304	Bobadilla d.	0734	...	...	0954	1014	...	...	1419	1440	...	1657	|	...	1816	...	...	2101	2135	...	...
	Antequera - Santa Ana § d.	0740	...	...	1000	|	...	...	1425	|	...	1703	|	...	1828	...	...	|	2141	...	...
376	Ronda d.	|	...	...	|	1108	...	...	|	1534	...	|	1900	...	|	...	...	2204	|	...	...
468	San Roque - La Línea d.	|	...	...	|	1233	...	...	|	1707	...	|	2018	...	|	...	...	2328	|	...	...
480	**Algeciras** a.	|	...	...	|	1248	...	...	|	1721	...	|	2032	...	|	...	...	2343	|	...	...
456	Dos Hermanas a.	0920	...	...	1136	...	...	...	1556	...	...	1832	...	...	1957	...	...	...	2311	...	...
471	**Sevilla** a.	0938	...	...	1156	...	...	...	1617	...	...	1850	...	...	2014	...	...	...	2327	...	...

§ – ± *17 km* from Antequera.

For Granada - Córdoba - Sevilla *Avant* **services, see Table 678a.**

674 PALMA DE MALLORCA - INCA - SA POBLA and MANACOR

SFM 2nd class

km			Ⓐ	Ⓐ	Ⓐ	Ⓐ	Ⓐ	Ⓐ	Ⓐ	Ⓐ	Ⓐ	and at	Ⓐ	Ⓐ	Ⓐ	Ⓐ	Ⓐ			©	©	and at	©	©	
0	**Palma** d.	Ⓐ	0546	0617	0632	0717	0732	0750	0817	0832	0850	the same minutes	2032	2050	2117	2132	2220	...	©	0610	0640	minutes	2140	2210	...
7	Marratxi d.		0600	0625	0646	0725	0746	0804	0825	0846	0904	past	2046	2104	2125	2146	2235	...		0624	0654	past	2154	2224	...
29	**Inca** d.		0620	0645	0707	0745	0807	0824	0845	0907	0924	each	2107	2124	2145	2207	2255	...		0645	0715	each	2215	2245	...
*****	sa Pobla a.		0637	|	0724	|	0824	...	|	0924	...	hour	2124	...	|	2224	|	...		|	0732	hour	2232	|	...
64	**Manacor** a.		...	0718	...	0816	...	...	0916	...	...	until	...	...	2216	...	2326	...		0715	...	until	...	2315	...

		Ⓐ	Ⓐ	Ⓐ	Ⓐ	Ⓐ	Ⓐ	Ⓐ	Ⓐ	Ⓐ	Ⓐ	and at	Ⓐ	Ⓐ	Ⓐ	Ⓐ			©	©	©	and at	©	©	
Manacor d.	Ⓐ	...	0625	...	...	0725	...	...	0825	...	...	the same minutes	...	2125	...	2228	...	©	0624	0724	...	minutes	...	2224	...
sa Pobla d.		0605	|	0700	...	|	0800	...	|	0900	...	past	...	|	2200	|	...		|	|	0807	past	2207	|	...
Inca d.		0621	0656	0716	0739	0756	0816	0839	0856	0916	0936	each	2136	2156	2216	2258	...		0655	0755	0823	each	2224	2255	...
Marratxi d.		0641	0716	0736	0759	0816	0836	0859	0916	0936	0956	hour	2156	2216	2236	2318	...		0715	0815	0844	hour	2244	2315	...
Palma a.		0655	0724	0750	0813	0824	0850	0913	0924	0950	1010	until	2210	2230	2250	2333	...		0729	0829	0858	until	2258	2329	...

*** – *19 km* Inca - sa Pobla.

Operator: Serveis Ferroviaris de Mallorca (SFM) ✆ +34 971 752 245.

PALMA DE MALLORCA - SÓLLER *28 km* Journey time: 55 minutes. **Operator**: Ferrocarril de Sóller (FS) ✆ +34 971 752 051. **SÓLLER - PALMA DE MALLORCA**

Nov. - Mar.: 1000, 1250, 1510, 1800. Apr. - Oct.: 1000, 1040, 1730, 1830.

Nov. - Mar.: 0900, 1140, 1400, 1700. Apr. - Oct.: 0830, 0900, 1630, 1730.

A connecting tram service operates **Sóller** - **Port de Sóller**. *5 km*. Journey time: 15–20 minutes. Not all services shown.

From Sóller: 0800, 0900, 1000, 1100, 1200, 1300, 1330, 1400, 1430, 1500, 1530, 1600, 1700, 1800, 1900.
From Port de Sóller: 0830, 0930, 1030, 1130, 1230, 1300, 1430, 1500, 1530, 1630, 1700, 1730, 1830, 1930, 2000.

675 🚌 MÁLAGA and ALGECIRAS - LA LÍNEA (for Gibraltar)

There are no cross-border 🚌 services: passengers to / from Gibraltar must cross the frontier on foot (walking-time about 5 minutes) and transfer to / from Gibraltar local 🚌 services

🚌 **MÁLAGA** bus stn – **LA LÍNEA** bus station (for **Gibraltar**)

From Málaga: 0830, 1130 ▽, 1315, 1430, 1545, 1730, 2025.
From La Línea: 0745, 1105, 1235, 1530, 1630 ▽, 1925, 2015.

Journey time: 3 hours. Operator: Avanza, Málaga ✆ (+34) 91 272 28 32.

▽ – Journey operated by ALSA (see Table **664** for contact details).

🚌 **ALGECIRAS** bus station - **LA LÍNEA** bus station (for **Gibraltar**) Route M-120

From Algeciras: Ⓐ: 0700 and every 30 minutes until 2130, also 2230.
⑥: every 45 mins 0700 – 2115, also 2230. †: every 45 mins 0800 – 2130, also 2230.

From La Línea: Ⓐ: 0645, 0745 and every 30 minutes until 2215, also 2315.
⑥: every 45 mins 0700 – 2200, also 2315. †: 0700, 0845 then every 45 mins until 2215, also 2315.

Journey time: 45 mins. Operator: Transportes Generales Comes SA, Algeciras ✆ (+34) 902 450 550.

676 🚌 SEVILLA - AYAMONTE - FARO - LAGOS

DAMAS ☆

	Summer	⚒	†	⚒		Ⓐ	©		⚒			Winter		⚒		Ⓐ	⑥	⑦	Ⓐ		Ⓑ	⑥	†	⚒
Sevilla ⊖ d.	July 1 -	0730	...	0930	1130	...		1530	1730	1930	...	Sept. 6 -	0730	0930	1130	...	1300	...	...	1530	...	1730	1900	1930
Huelva d.	Sept. 4	0900	0900	1100	1300	1400	1500	1700	1900	2100	...	June 30,	0900	1100	1300	1400	1430	1430	1530	1700	1900	1900	2030	2100
Ayamonte a.	2022	1000	1000	1200	1400t	1505	1600t	1800	2000	2240	...	2022	1015j	1215	1415f	1500	1545	1555	1630	1815z	2000x	2015	2145	2215

	Summer	⚒	⚒	⚒			⚒			Ⓐ	©	Winter	⚒	Ⓐ			Ⓐ	⑥	†	Ⓐ	⑥	⑥	Ⓑ	
Ayamonte d.	July 1 -	0640	0700	0800	0930h	1100	1230	1500	1730	2000	2000	Sept. 6 -	0640	0830	0930	1145	1400	1500	1515	1545	1615	1715	1730	1930
Huelva d.	Sept. 4	0800	0900	1000	1100	1300	1400	1700	1900	2100	2130	June 30,	0740x	0930	1030j	1245j	1500	1600	1615	1645	1715	1830	1845	2045j
Sevilla ⊖ a.	2022	0915	1015	1115	1215	1415	1515	1815	2015	...	2245	2022	0910	...	1215	...	...	1715	1745	1815	1845	1945	...	2230

f – 15 mins. later on †. **h** – 30 mins. earlier on ⑦. **j** – 15 mins. later on ©. **t** – 30 mins. later on ⑦. **x** – 20–25 mins. later on ⑥. **z** – 15 mins. later on ⑥.

⛴ **Ayamonte - Vila Real de Santo António Guadiana** Journey time: 10 minutes. ✆ (+34) 959 470 617.
Sept. 16 - Apr. 30: hourly from Ayamonte 1000 - 1900 ⚒, 1100 - 1800 †. From Vila Real de Santo António Guadiana 0945 then hourly 1030 - 1730, 1900 ⚒, 1100 - 1800 †.

INTERNATIONAL 🚌 SERVICE Joint ALSA △ / REDE EXPRESSOS ☆ service *for international journeys only* No service Dec. 25, Jan. 1

	→ Summer July 1 - Sept. 4, 2022					→ Winter 2022-2023		
Sevilla Santa Justa d.		0930	1130	1530	1800		0930	1530
Huelva, Estación de Autobuses d.		|	1315	|	|		|	|
Ayamonte 🏛 ES d.		|	|	|	|		|	|
Vila Real de Santo António 🏛 PT a.		|	|	|	|		|	|
Faro, Aeroporto a.		1115	1400	1745	2015		1145	1745
Albufeira, Terminal Rodoviário a.		1215	1500	1845	2115		1245	1845
Portimão, Av. Guanaré a.		1315	1530	1915	2145		1315	1915
Lagos, Terminal Rodoviário a.		1345	1600	1945	2215		1345	1945

	→ Summer July 1 - Sept. 4, 2022					→ Winter 2022-2023		
Lagos, Terminal Rodoviário d.		0800	1030	1530	1700		0800	1530
Portimão, Av. Guanaré d.		0830	1100	1600	1730		0830	1600
Albufeira, Terminal Rodoviário d.		0900	1130	1630	1800		0900	1630
Faro, Aeroporto d.		0945	1215	1715	1845		0945	1715
Vila Real de Santo António 🏛 PT d.		|	|	|	|		|	|
Ayamonte 🏛 ES a.		|	|	|	|		|	|
Huelva, Estación de Autobuses a.		|	|	|	2145		|	|
Sevilla Santa Justa a.		1415	1645	2145	2330		1415	2145

☆ – REDE EXPRESSOS ✆ +707 22 33 44. www.rede-expressos.pt
△ – ALSA, ✆ +34 919 914 030. www.alsa.com

ES – Spain (Central European Time).
PT – Portugal (West European Time).

Huelva bus station is ± 1.7 km from the rail station.
Ayamonte bus station is ± 1.5 km from the ferry terminal.

MADRID - CÁCERES - BADAJOZ - LISBOA 677

km						IC 190	5500	IC 512		MD 17902	17028		4432
		2	2	2	🚌	2	2	🅁	🚌	2	2	2	2
		Ⓐ	Ⓐ	Ⓒ	⚒	⚒			⚒		③⑤⑦		
0	**Madrid** Chamartín ‡ d.	...	...	...	...	0828	...	...	...	...	...	...	...
8	**Madrid** Atocha Cercanías d.	...	...	...	...	0850	...	...	...	1055	...	...	...
146	Talavera de la Reina d.	...	...	...	...	1015	...	...	...	1222	...	...	...
	Navalmoral de La Mata d.	...	...	...	...	1053	...	...	...	1257	...	...	...
	Plasencia d.	...	...	...	1045	|	...	...	...	|	...	...	...
	Monfragüe–Plasencia d.	...	...	...	1109	1123	...	...	1135	1325	...	...	...
278	Plasencia a.	...	...	...	▬	|	...	...	1159	1339	...	...	...
278	Plasencia d.	0630	...	0735	...	|	...	...	▬	1343	...	...	...
343*	**Cáceres** d.	0709	...	0815	...	1201	...	...	...	1425	1436	...	...
	San Vicente de Alcántara d.	|	...	|	...	|	...	...	...	|	1550	...	...
430	Valencia de Alcántara d.	|	...	|	Ⓒ	|	...	...	...	|	1605	...	...
409	Mérida a.	0748	...	0854	2	1237	...	...	...	1505	▬	...	...
409	Mérida 678 d.	0754	0755	0900	0907	1247	...	...	...	1522	...	1531	...
469	**Badajoz** 🏛 678 ES a.	|	0841	|	0952	1324	1409	...	IC	|	...	1611	...
	Elvas 🏛 PT a.	|	...	|	▬	...	1325	...	523	|	...	...	...
	Abrantes 691 a.	|	...	|	...	...	1520	...	🅁	|	...	...	...
	Entroncamento 691 a.	|	...	|	...	...	1552	1600	1630	|	...	...	1844
	Coimbra B 690 a.	|	...	|	...	...	...	|	1730	|	...	...	|
	Aveiro 690 a.	|	...	|	...	...	...	|	1802	|	MD	...	|
	Porto Campanhã 690 a.	|	...	|	...	...	...	|	1852	|	13086	...	|
	Lisboa Oriente 691 a.	|	...	|	...	...	...	1652	...	|	2	...	2013
742	**Lisboa** S Apolónia 691 a.	|	...	|	...	...	...	1700	...	|	⑤⑥⑦	...	2020
475	Zafra d.	0846	...	0955	13084	...	...	...	...	1616	1625	...	...
649	Sevilla a.	1117	...	1231	2	...	...	...	...	1858	|	...	...
521	Fregenal de la Sierra d.	...	...	...	⚒	...	...	...	...	...	1704	...	...
	Jabugo-Galaroza d.	...	...	...	0735	...	...	...	...	...	1745	...	...
660	Huelva a.	...	...	...	0932	...	...	...	...	...	1938	...	...

km		AP 126		5502	IC 528	MD 17012		Alvia 194		17823	17018	17702	17706
			2	2	🅁	2	🚌			2	2	2	2
		Ⓑ	Ⓑ			Ⓑ			🚌	Ⓑ	Ⓑ	①–④	
0	**Madrid** Chamartín ‡ d.	...	...	...	...	...	...	1617	...	...	...	...	...
8	**Madrid** Atocha Cercanías d.	...	...	...	...	1450	...	1638	...	...	1815	1908	2109
146	Talavera de la Reina d.	...	...	...	...	1615	...	1800	...	...	1948	2037	2237
	Navalmoral de La Mata d.	...	...	...	...	1652	...	1835	...	...	2039	...	...
	Plasencia d.	...	...	...	...	|	1825	|	...	...	|	...	...
	Monfragüe–Plasencia d.	...	...	...	...	1734	1849	1902	1915	...	2110	...	...
278	Plasencia a.	...	...	...	...	1748	▬	|	1939	...	2125	...	...
278	Plasencia d.	...	...	...	...	1751	...	|	...	...	2128	...	...
343*	**Cáceres** d.	...	...	...	...	1831	...	1943	...	...	2236	...	...
	San Vicente de Alcántara d.	...	...	...	...	|	...	|	...	...	...	...	...
430	Valencia de Alcántara d.	...	...	...	...	|	...	|	...	...	...	...	...
409	Mérida a.	...	...	...	...	1911	...	2020	...	...	...	...	...
409	Mérida 678 d.	...	1814	...	...	▬	...	2025	...	2034	...	...	...
469	**Badajoz** 🏛 678 ES a.	...	1900	1941	...	IC	...	2055	...	|	...	...	...
	Elvas 🏛 PT a.	...	...	1857	...	529	...	...	...	|	...	...	...
	Abrantes 691 a.	...	...	2053	...	🅁	...	...	...	|	...	...	...
	Entroncamento 691 a.	1942	...	2137	2201	2300	...	...	...	|	...	...	...
	Coimbra B 690 a.	|	...	...	|	2359	...	...	...	|	...	...	...
	Aveiro 690 a.	|	...	...	|	0030	...	...	...	|	...	...	...
	Porto Campanhã 690 a.	|	...	...	|	0123	...	...	...	|	...	...	...
	Lisboa Oriente 691 a.	2032	...	...	2252	...	...	...	...	|	...	...	...
742	**Lisboa** S Apolónia 691 a.	2040	...	...	2300	...	...	...	...	|	...	...	...
475	Zafra d.	...	...	...	...	...	...	...	...	2124	...	...	...
649	Sevilla a.	...	...	...	...	...	...	...	...	...	...	...	...
521	Fregenal de la Sierra d.	...	...	...	...	...	...	...	...	...	...	...	...
	Jabugo-Galaroza d.	...	...	...	...	...	...	...	...	...	...	...	...
660	Huelva a.	...	...	...	...	...	...	...	...	...	...	...	...

	17703	17021	17705			Alvia 197		Alvia 199		17026	IC 520	4407
	2	2	2	2					2	2	🅁	2
	Ⓐ	⚒	⑦	⚒	🚌	Ⓐ	🚌	Ⓒ	⚒	Ⓑ	①–⑥	
Huelva d.	...	...	...	...	...	...	...	...	...	...	...	...
Jabugo-Galaroza d.	...	...	...	...	...	...	...	...	...	...	...	...
Fregenal de la Sierra d.	...	...	...	...	...	...	...	...	...	...	...	...
Sevilla d.	...	...	...	...	...	...	...	...	...	...	...	...
Zafra d.	...	...	...	0655	...	...	...	...	...	...	...	...
Lisboa S Apolónia 691 d.	...	...	...	|	...	...	...	...	...	...	...	0745
Lisboa Oriente 691 d.	...	...	...	|	...	...	...	...	...	...	...	0753
Porto Campanhã 690 d.	...	...	...	|	...	...	...	...	...	...	0637	|
Aveiro 690 d.	...	...	...	|	...	...	...	...	...	...	0732	|
Coimbra B 690 d.	...	...	...	|	...	...	...	...	...	...	0804	|
Entroncamento 691 d.	...	...	...	|	...	...	...	...	...	...	0900	0919
Abrantes 691 d.	...	...	...	|	...	...	...	...	...	...	...	...
Elvas 🏛 PT d.	...	...	...	|	...	...	...	...	...	...	...	...
Badajoz 🏛 678 ES d.	...	...	...	|	...	0725	...	0830	1200	...	...	...
Mérida 678 a.	...	...	...	0743	...	0754	...	0859	1243	...	...	...
Mérida d.	...	...	...	...	...	0759	...	0904	...	1255	...	...
Valencia de Alcántara d.	...	...	...	...	...	|	...	|	...	|	...	...
San Vicente de Alcántara d.	...	...	...	...	...	|	...	|	...	|	...	...
Cáceres d.	...	0615	...	...	...	0839	...	0944	...	1334	...	...
Plasencia a.	...	0721	...	...	...	|	...	|	...	1412	...	...
Plasencia d.	...	0725	...	...	0840	|	...	|	...	1416	...	...
Monfragüe–Plasencia d.	...	0741	...	...	0904	0916	0925	1021	...	1432	...	...
Plasencia a.	...	|	...	...	...	|	0949	|	...	|	...	...
Navalmoral de La Mata d.	...	0809	...	...	...	0944	...	1048	...	1459	...	...
Talavera de la Reina d.	0623	0844	0844	...	...	1020	...	1129	...	1534	...	...
Madrid Atocha Cercanías a.	0751	1016	1016	...	...	1143	...	1253	...	1711	...	...
Madrid Chamartín ‡ a.	...	...	...	...	...	1205	...	1311	...	...	...	...

	IC 541	5501	MD 13087	MD 17907	17029	IC 720	IC 513	5503	IC 193				13089
	🅁	2	2	2	2	🅁	🅁	2	2	🚌	2	2	2
			⑤⑥⑦		③⑤⑦				Ⓑ	Ⓑ			Ⓑ
Huelva d.	...	...	1058	...	...	...	...	...	...	...	...	...	1940
Jabugo-Galaroza d.	...	...	1254	...	...	...	...	...	...	...	...	...	2133
Fregenal de la Sierra d.	...	...	1337	...	...	...	...	...	...	...	...	...	...
Sevilla d.	...	...	|	1200	...	...	...	...	...	...	...	1654	...
Zafra d.	...	...	1418	1425	...	...	...	...	...	...	...	1925	...
Lisboa S Apolónia 691 d.	0815	...	▬	|	...	...	1230	...	...	...	...	|	...
Lisboa Oriente 691 d.	0823	...	...	|	...	...	1239	...	...	...	...	|	...
Porto Campanhã 690 d.	|	...	...	|	...	1038	|	...	...	...	...	|	...
Aveiro 690 d.	|	...	...	|	...	1131	|	...	...	...	...	|	...
Coimbra B 690 d.	|	...	...	|	...	1202	|	...	...	...	...	|	...
Entroncamento 691 d.	0923	0928	...	|	...	1300	1329	1336	...	...	...	|	...
Abrantes 691 d.	...	0959	...	|	...	▬	...	1407	...	...	...	|	...
Elvas 🏛 PT d.	...	1159	...	|	...	...	...	1612	...	...	...	|	...
Badajoz 🏛 678 ES d.	...	1313	1430	|	...	...	...	1726	1736	...	1945	|	...
Mérida 678 a.	...	...	1516	1513	...	...	...	...	1810	...	2036	2015	...
Mérida d.	...	...	...	1521	...	...	...	...	1820	...	...	2039	...
Valencia de Alcántara d.	...	...	...	|	1720	...	...	...	|	...	...	|	...
San Vicente de Alcántara d.	...	...	...	|	1735	...	...	...	|	...	...	|	...
Cáceres d.	...	...	...	1603	1849	🚌	...	...	1901	...	...	2119	...
Plasencia a.	...	...	...	1644	...	Ⓑ	...	...	|	...	...	2158z	...
Plasencia d.	...	...	...	1647	...	1900	...	...	|	...	...	...	...
Monfragüe–Plasencia d.	...	...	...	1704	...	1924	...	...	1938	1950	...	...	...
Plasencia a.	...	...	...	|	...	...	...	...	|	2014	...	...	...
Navalmoral de La Mata d.	...	...	...	1731	...	...	...	...	2005	...	...	...	...
Talavera de la Reina d.	...	...	...	1818	...	...	...	...	2041	...	...	...	...
Madrid Atocha Cercanías a.	...	...	...	1938	...	...	...	...	2204	...	...	...	...
Madrid Chamartín ‡ a.	...	...	...	...	...	...	...	...	2221	...	...	...	...

x – ⚒. ⁂ – Connection not guaranteed. ‡ – Full name is Madrid-Chamartín-Clara Campoamor. ES – Spain (Central European Time).
z – Ⓑ. * – Madrid - Cáceres via Plasencia *363 km*. PT – Portugal (West European Time).

ALCÁZAR DE SAN JUAN - BADAJOZ 678

km		MD 17042	MD 17044				MD 18183	IC 697	MD 18330	MD 18083	18027	
		2	2	2	2	2	2		2	2	2	
		Ⓐ	Ⓒ	Ⓐ	Ⓒ		w	T		w	A	
	Madrid AC § **661 668** d.	...	...	...	...	...	...	...	...	...	...	...
	Albacete **672b** d.	...	...	...	...	...	1150	1401	...	1838	1929	...
0	**Alcázar de San Juan** 661 d.	0715	0845	...	...	...	1302	1510	1535	1950	2053	...
50	Manzanares 661 d.	0740	0910	...	...	...	1327	1538	1559	2017	2120	...
114	Ciudad Real 660 d.	0820	0950	...	...	...	1408	...	1647	2058	2200	...
153	Puertollano 660 d.	...	...	...	...	1200	...	...	1712	...	...	...
265	Cabeza del Buey d.	...	...	0617	0725	1346	...	...	1859	...	...	...
392	Mérida 677 d.	...	...	0755	0907	1531	...	...	2038	...	...	...
451	**Badajoz** 677 a.	...	...	0841	0952	1611	...	...	2130	...	...	...

	18024	MD 18081	IC 694	MD 18331	MD 18181				
	2B	2		2	2	2		2	
	Ⓐ	w	T		w				
Badajoz 677 d.	...	...	...	0658	...	1430	...	1945	...
Mérida 677 d.	...	...	...	0750	...	1525	...	2053	...
Cabeza del Buey d.	...	...	...	0921	...	1708	...	2227	...
Puertollano 660 d.	...	...	...	1106	...	1906	...	...	...
Ciudad Real 660 d.	0536	1012	...	1135	1624	...	...	...	...
Manzanares 661 d.	0614	1052	1302	1224	1710	...	...	...	...
Alcázar de San Juan 661 a.	0642	1117	1324	1250	1733	...	...	...	...
Albacete **672b** a.	0806	1227	1436	...	1847	...	...	...	...
Madrid AC § **661 668** a.	...	...	...	...	...	...	...	...	...

A – 2 València - Albacete - Ciudad Real (Table **668**).
B – 2 Ciudad Real - Albacete - València (Table **668**).
T – TORRE DEL ORO – 12 🍸 Barcelona - València - Córdoba - Sevilla - Cádiz and v.v. (Table **672a**).
w – From/to Alacant (Table **668**).
§ – Madrid Atocha Cercanías.
☛ **Shaded services are suspended until further notice.**

GRANADA - MÁLAGA / CÓRDOBA - SEVILLA 678a

Avant high-speed shuttle services, *Turista* class

For trains **Sevilla** – **Málaga** and v.v. via **Córdoba**, see Table **660**. For trains **Sevilla** – **Málaga** and v.v. via **Dos Hermanas**, see Table **673**.

	8475	8915		8935	8525		8575	8955		8505	
Granada d.	0635	0736	...	1306	1315	...	1726	1846	...	2002	...
Loja d.	0657	0758	...	1328	1337	...	1753	1908	...	2025	...
Antequera AV d.	0724	0827	...	1356	1404	...	1820	1936	...	2054	...
Málaga M. Zambrano a.	|	0854	...	1422	|	...	|	2003	...	|	...
Antequera - Santa Ana § d.	0734	...	...	...	1414	...	1829	...	...	2105	...
Puente Genil - Herrera ¶ d.	0749	...	...	...	1430	...	1844	...	...	2122	...
Córdoba a.	0813	...	...	...	1455	...	1907	...	...	2149	...
Córdoba d.	0818	...	...	...	1500	...	1912	...	...	2154	...
Sevilla a.	0907	...	...	...	1546	...	1956	...	...	2241	...

	8275	8815		8295		8335	8835		8855	8395	
Sevilla d.	0739	...	...	0913	...	1208	...	...	...	1920	...
Córdoba a.	0820	...	...	0956	...	1252	...	...	...	2005	...
Córdoba d.	0825	...	...	1001	...	1257	...	...	...	2010	...
Puente Genil - Herrera ¶ d.	0903	...	...	1032	...	1325	...	...	...	2039	...
Antequera - Santa Ana § d.	0920	...	...	1049	...	1341	...	...	...	2055	...
Málaga M. Zambrano d.	|	0925	...	|	...	|	1550	...	2025	|	...
Antequera AV d.	0935	0953	...	1059	...	1355	1619	...	2053	2107	...
Loja d.	1004	1021	...	1126	...	1425	1646	...	2120	2136	...
Granada a.	1026	1043	...	1148	...	1446	1708	...	2142	2157	...

§ – ± *17 km* from Antequera. ¶ – ± *8 km* from Puente Genil.

679 MADRID - TOLEDO, SEGOVIA, VALLADOLID, SALAMANCA and EL ESCORIAL

2nd class

km		*Av*	*Av*	*Av*	*Av*	*Av*	*Av*	*Av*	*Av*		*Av*	*Av*	*Av*	*Av*	*Av*	*Av*	*Av*	*Av*				
		8062	**8072**	**8082**	**8082**	**8292**	**8102**	**8312**	**8322**		**8132**	**8142**	**8152**	**8162**	**8172**	**8182**	**8192**	**8212**				
		Ⓐ	B Ⓐ	Ⓐ	B Ⓒ							Ⓐ		Ⓐ		Ⓐ						
0	**Madrid** Puerta de Atocha d.	0655	0750	0850	0850	0920	1020	1120	1220	...	1350	1450	1550	1650	1750	1850	1945	2050	...	...	...	...
75	**Toledo** a.	0728	0823	0923	0923	0953	1052	1153	1253	...	1423	1523	1623	1723	1823	1923	2018	2123	...	...	...	...

	Av	*Av*	*Av*	*Av*		*Av*	*Av*		*Av*	*Av*		*Av*	*Av*	*Av*	*Av*	*Av*	*Av*	*Av*				
	8063	**8273**	**8073**	**8283**		**8093**	**8103**		**8123**	**8133**		**8153**	**8163**	**8173**	**8183**	**8193**	**8203**	**8213**				
	Ⓐ	Ⓐ	Ⓐ	Ⓐ									Ⓐ	B								
Toledo d.	0625	0650	0725	0755	...	0925	1025	...	1225	1325	...	1525	1613	1725	1825	1920	2025	2130	...	...	...	...
Madrid Puerta de Atocha a.	0658	0723	0758	0828	...	0959	1059	...	1258	1358	...	1558	1646	1759	1858	1954	2058	2203	...	...	...	...

km	km		*Av*	*Av*	*Av*	*Alvia*	*Av*	*Alvia*	*Av*	*Alvia*	*Av*	*Av*	*Av*	*Av*	*Alvia*	*Av*	*Av*	*Av*	*Av*	*Av*	*Av*	*Av*	*Av*	*Alvia*	*Av*
			8069	**31071**	**8079**	**4899**	**8109**	**4809**	**8129**	**4929**	**8139**	**34149**	**8159**	**8359**	**4969**	**31267**	**8169**	**8179**	**8389**	**8189**	**8199**	**8209**	**34209**	**4909**	**8219**
			Ⓐ	Ⓐ	Ⓐ	Ⓐ		Ⓒ		①–⑤	⑤	Ⓑ	⑤				Ⓐ		Ⓑ	A	Ⓐ		Ⓑ		
0	0	**Madrid** Chamartín ‡ d.	0640	0708	0752	0850	1015	1035	1205	1240	1340	1440	1510	1540	1550	1610	1626	1700	1810	1845	1925	2000	2025	2040	2130
68	68	**Segovia** Guiomar d.	0708	|	0820	0918	1043	1103	1233	1308	1408	1508	1548	1608	1618	1640	1654	1728	1838	1913	1954	2028	|	2108	2158
		Medina del Campo AV d.	|	|	|	0947	|	1131	|	1336	|	|	|	|	1647	|	|	|	|	|	|	|	|	2137	|
180		**Valladolid** ⊠ a.	0748	0807	0857	|	1120	|	1310	|	1445	1539	1615	1645	|	1726	1731	1805	1915	1950	2031	2105	2118	|	2235
	230	**Salamanca** a.	...	...	...	1031	...	1216	...	1421	...	...	...	...	1731	...	...	...	...	...	...	...	...	2221	...

	Av	*Av*	*Alvia*	*Av*	*Av*	*Av*	*Av*	*Alvia*	*Av*	*Alvia*	*Av*	*Av*	*Av*	*Alvia*	*Av*	*Av*	*Av*	*Alvia*	*Av*	*Av*			
	8058	**8068**	**4868**	**8078**	**8278**	**34078**	**8088**	**4898**	**8098**	**4918**	**8118**	**8148**	**8158**	**4958**	**8168**	**8178**	**34178**	**4988**	**8198**	**8208**			
	Ⓐ	Ⓐ	Ⓐ	Ⓐ		Ⓐ	Ⓐ	Ⓒ	Ⓒ	①–⑤	Ⓐ	Ⓐ			⑤⑦		Ⓑ						
Salamanca d.	...	...	0625	...	...	...	...	0820	...	1050	...	...	...	1530	...	...	...	1820	...	...	...	...	...
Valladolid ⊠ d.	0623	0645	|	0715	0755	0816	0845	|	0950	|	1130	1405	1520	|	1622	1750	1836	|	1946	2035	...	...	...
Medina del Campo AV d.	|	|	0708	|	|	|	|	0904	|	|	|	|	|	1614	|	|	|	1903	|	|	...	...	...
Segovia Guiomar d.	0700	0722	0738	0752	0832	|	0922	0934	1027	1159	1207	1442	1557	1644	1659	1827	1911	1933	2023	2112	...	...	...
Madrid Chamartín ‡ a.	0728	0750	0805	0820	0900	0908	0950	1000	1055	1226	1235	1510	1625	1711	1727	1855	1937	2000	2051	2140	...	...	...

km		Ⓐ	Ⓒ	Ⓒ	Ⓐ	Ⓒ		⑤	Ⓒ	Ⓐ	Ⓒ
0	**Madrid** Chamartín ‡ d.	...	0845	1015	1116	1215	...	1531	1615	1815	1915
58	Cercedilla d.	0648	0950	1134	1230	1332	...	1659	1732	1930	2031
100	**Segovia** a.	0730	1032	1215	1312	1414	...	1740	1813	2014	2115

	Ⓐ	Ⓒ	Ⓒ			⑤	Ⓒ	Ⓐ	Ⓒ	
Segovia d.	0743	1042	1243	1442	...	1746	1843	2046	2125	...
Cercedilla a.	0827	1126	1324	1524	...	1833	1924	2128	2207	...
Madrid Chamartín ‡ a.	0935	1234	1436	1635	...	1936	2034	2235	2309	...

km		*MD*	*MD*	*MD*	*MD*	*MD*	*MD*	*MD*	*MD*		
		18001	**18901**	**18921**	**18903**	**18905**	**18907**	**18913**	**18909**		
		Ⓐ	Ⓐ	Ⓒ		Ⓐ					
0	**Madrid** Principe Pio ◧ d.	0643	0740	0828	1110	1340	1525	1754	1937	2153**q**	...
122	Ávila ◧ d.	0822	0908	0955	1239	1510	1711	1936	2112	2341	...
233	**Salamanca** a.	...	1040	1123	1353	1619	1828	2046	2221	...	...

			MD	*MD*	*MD*	*MD*	*MD*	*MD*	*MD*	*MD*
			18900	**18912**	**18902**	**18004**	**18904**	**18006**	**18906**	**18908**
	Ⓐ	Ⓐ				Ⓐ			Ⓐ	
Salamanca d.	...	...	0732	0941	1228	...	1644	...	1802	1958
Ávila ◧ d.	0555	0630	0840	1058	1339	1547	1812	1900	1912	2106
Madrid Principe Pio ◧ a.	0742	0813	1011	1233	1512	1731	1948	2048	2056	2244

MADRID ATOCHA CERCANÍAS - VILLALBA - EL ESCORIAL. *45 km.* Line C8. Journey time: Villalba, 53 minutes; El Escorial, 66-67 minutes. Depart 14 minutes later from Madrid Chamartín; arrive 15 minutes earlier at Madrid Charmartín. Additional services operate.

From **Madrid Atocha Cercanías**: 0621 Ⓐ, 0635 Ⓒ, 0651 Ⓐ, 0709 Ⓐ, 0723 Ⓐ, 0737 Ⓒ, 0750 Ⓐ, 0835 Ⓒ, 0839 Ⓐ, 0935 Ⓒ, 0941 Ⓐ, 1036, 1135, 1235, 1335, 1407 Ⓐ, 1436 Ⓒ, 1450 Ⓐ, 1521 Ⓐ, 1536 Ⓒ, 1547 Ⓐ, 1635, 1715 Ⓐ, 1736 Ⓒ, 1745 Ⓐ, 1827 Ⓐ, 1836 Ⓒ, 1847 Ⓐ, 1920, 1936, Ⓒ, 1944 Ⓐ, 2036 Ⓐ, 2042 Ⓒ, 2139, 2236, 2334.

From **El Escorial**: 0548, 0616 Ⓒ, 0631 Ⓐ, 0658 Ⓐ, 0706 Ⓐ, 0716 Ⓒ, 0736 Ⓐ, 0802 Ⓐ, 0817 Ⓒ, 0831 Ⓐ, 0915, 1015, 1115, 1215, 1315, 1414, 1515, 1601 Ⓐ, 1615 Ⓒ, 1624 Ⓐ, 1713, 1815, 1858 Ⓐ, 1912 Ⓐ, 1915 Ⓒ, 1930 Ⓐ, 1959 Ⓐ, 2013 Ⓒ, 2029 Ⓐ, 2115, 2215.

A – ①②③④⑥.
B – From / to Albacete (Table **668**).
q – Madrid-Chamartín-Clara Campoamor.
MD – Medium Distance Plus.
Av – ***Avant*** high-speed services. Single class.
◧ – See also Tables **680**, **681**, **689**.
⊠ – Full name is Valladolid Campo Grande.
‡ – Full name is Madrid-Chamartín-Clara Campoamor.
☛ **Shaded services are suspended until further notice.**

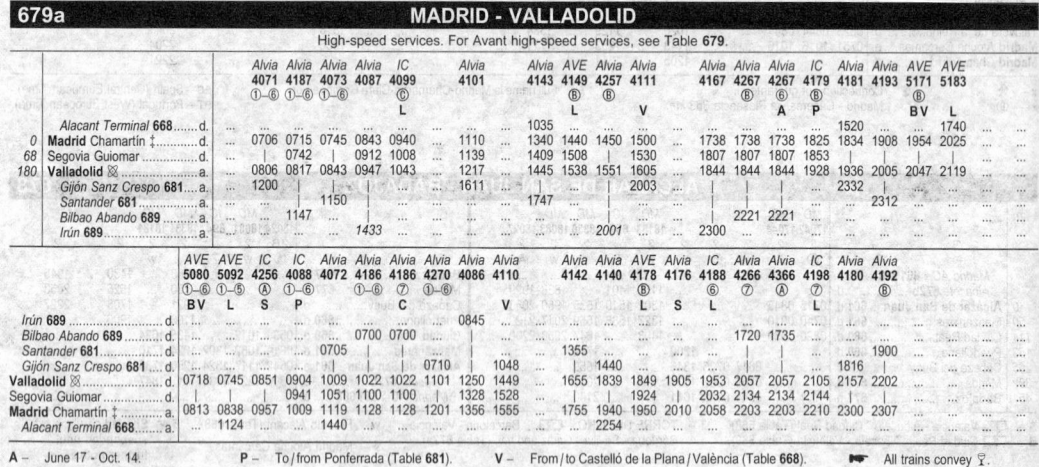

679a MADRID - VALLADOLID

High-speed services. For Avant high-speed services, see Table **679**.

km			*Alvia*	*Alvia*	*Alvia*	*Alvia*	*IC*		*Alvia*		*Alvia*	*AVE*	*Alvia*	*Alvia*		*Alvia*	*Alvia*	*Alvia*	*IC*	*Alvia*	*Alvia*	*AVE*	*AVE*		
			4071	**4187**	**4073**	**4087**	**4099**		**4101**		**4143**	**4149**	**4257**	**4111**		**4167**	**4267**	**4267**	**4179**	**4181**	**4193**	**5171**	**5183**		
			①–⑥	①–⑥	①–⑥		Ⓒ					Ⓑ	Ⓑ				Ⓑ	⑥	Ⓑ			Ⓑ			
							L					**L**		**V**				**A**	**P**			**B V**	**L**		
	Alacant Terminal **668** d.	...	...	...	...	...	...	...	...	...	1035	...	...	...	...	...	...	...	...	1520	...	...	1740	...	...
0	**Madrid** Chamartín ‡ d.	...	0706	0715	0745	0843	0940	...	1110	...	1340	1440	1450	1500	...	1738	1738	1738	1825	1834	1908	1954	2025	...	...
68	Segovia Guiomar d.	...	|	0742	|	0912	1008	...	1139	...	1409	1508	|	1530	...	1807	1807	1807	1853	|	|	|	|	...	...
180	**Valladolid** ⊠ a.	...	0806	0817	0843	0947	1043	...	1217	...	1445	1538	1551	1605	...	1844	1844	1844	1928	1936	2005	2047	2119	...	...
	Gijón Sanz Crespo **681** a.	...	1200	|	|	|	...	...	1611	...	|	...	|	2003	...	|	|	|	...	2332	|	...	...	...	...
	Santander **681** a.	...	...	|	1150	|	...	...	...	...	1747	...	|	...	...	|	|	|	...	...	2312	...	...	...	...
	Bilbao Abando **689** a.	...	...	1147	...	|	...	...	...	...	...	...	|	...	...	|	2221	2221	...	...	...	...	...	...	...
	Irún **689** a.	...	...	...	...	*1433*	...	...	...	...	...	...	*2001*	...	...	2300	...	...	...	...	...	...	...	...	...

	AVE	*AVE*	*IC*	*IC*	*Alvia*	*Alvia*	*Alvia*	*Alvia*	*Alvia*	*Alvia*		*Alvia*	*Alvia*	*AVE*	*Alvia*	*IC*	*Alvia*	*Alvia*	*IC*	*Alvia*	*Alvia*			
	5080	**5092**	**4256**	**4088**	**4072**	**4186**	**4186**	**4270**	**4086**	**4110**		**4142**	**4140**	**4178**	**4176**	**4188**	**4266**	**4366**	**4198**	**4180**	**4192**			
	①–⑥	①–⑤	Ⓐ	①–⑥		①–⑥	⑦	①–⑥						Ⓑ		⑥	⑦	Ⓐ	⑦		Ⓑ			
	B V	**L**	**S**	**P**			**C**			**V**				**L**	**S**	**L**			**L**					
Irún **689** d.	...	...	...	...	...	...	...	...	0845	...	...	...	...	...	...	...	...	...	...	...	...	...	...	...
Bilbao Abando **689** d.	...	...	...	...	...	0700	0700	...	|	...	...	...	...	...	...	...	1720	1735	...	...	...	...	...	...
Santander **681** d.	...	...	...	...	0705	|	|	...	|	...	...	1355	...	...	...	...	|	|	...	...	1900	...	...	...
Gijón Sanz Crespo **681** d.	...	...	...	...	|	|	|	0710	|	1048	...	|	1440	...	...	...	|	|	...	1816	|	...	...	...
Valladolid ⊠ d.	0718	0745	0851	0904	1009	1022	1022	1101	1250	1449	...	1655	1839	1849	1905	1953	2057	2057	2105	2157	2202	...	...	...
Segovia Guiomar d.	|	|	|	0941	1051	1100	1100	|	1328	1528	...	|	|	1924	|	2032	2134	2134	2144	|	|	...	...	...
Madrid Chamartín ‡ a.	0813	0838	0957	1009	1119	1128	1128	1201	1356	1555	...	1755	1940	1950	2010	2058	2203	2203	2210	2300	2307	...	...	...
Alacant Terminal **668** a.	...	1124	...	1440	...	...	...	...	...	...	...	...	2254	...	...	...	...	...	...	...	...	...	...	...

A – June 17 - Oct. 14.
B – To / from Burgos (Table **689**).
C – June 18 - Oct. 15.
L – To / from León (Table **681**).
P – To / from Ponferrada (Table **681**).
S – From San Sebastián / Donostia (Table **689**).
V – From / to Castelló de la Plana / València (Table **668**).
⊠ – Full name is Valladolid Campo Grande.
‡ – Full name is Madrid-Chamartín-Clara Campoamor.
☛ All trains convey 🍷. *AVE* trains also convey ✕.

MADRID - ZAMORA - VIGO, PONTEVEDRA and A CORUÑA — 680

For services to / from A Coruña via León, see Table **682**

Additional connections between Vigo and Ourense can be made by changing trains at Santiago de Compostela

km		12512	9480	9072	9480	9082	4254	12526	9112	12623	12528	4275	9090	9132	4095	5273	9120	4115	9140	9550	12538	4325	9160	9162	4145
			Av	*MD*	*Av*	*MD*	*Alvia*		*MD*			*Alvia*	*Av*	*MD*	*Alvia*	*AVE*	*Av*	*Alvia*	*Av*	*Av*		*Alvia*	*Av*	*MD*	*Alvia*
		R		R		R		R	R	R	R			R			2				R		R	R	
		2	2	2	2	2	Z	2	2	2	2	X	2	2	b	B		X	2	2	2	q	2	2	
		①–⑤										①–⑤	①–⑤		①–⑥			①–⑥		①–⑤					Ⓑ
0	**Madrid** Chamartín ‡ **681 689** d.	...	...	...	...	...	...	...	...	...	...	0620	...	...	0800	1000	...	1120	...	...	...	1315	...	...	1430
68	Segovia Guiomar **679 679a** d.	...	...	...	...	...	...	...	...	...	...	0650	...	...	|	|	...	|	...	...	...	1346	...	...	|
	Irún **689** d.	...	...	...	...	...	...	...	...	...	...	|	...	...	|	|	...	|	...	...	...	|	...	...	|
	Barcelona Sants **650a** d.	...	...	...	...	...	...	...	...	...	...	|	...	...	|	|	...	|	...	...	...	|	...	...	|
	Miranda de Ebro **681 689** d.	...	...	...	...	...	...	...	...	...	...	|	...	...	|	|	...	|	...	...	...	|	...	...	|
207*	Medina AV **681 689** d.	...	...	...	...	...	...	...	...	...	...	0719	...	...	|	|	...	|	...	...	...	1415	...	...	|
297	**Zamora** d.	...	...	...	...	...	...	...	...	...	...	0747	...	...	0914	1102	...	1234	...	...	...	1442	...	...	1544
404	Sanabria AV a.	...	...	...	...	...	...	...	...	...	...	0825	...	...	|	|	...	|	...	...	...	1514	...	...	|
547	**Ourense** d.	...	0645	...	0755	...	...	...	...	1005	...	0930	0940	...	1038	1211	1225	1401	1415	1535	...	1617	1635	...	1708
641	Guillarei d.	...	|	...	|	...	...	...	...	1127	...	|	|	...	|	...	|	|	|	|	...	...	|	...	|
	Vigo Urzáiz d.	0505**c**	|	0640	|	0800	0920	0913**c**	1100	|	1230**c**	1100	|	1340	|	...	|	1538	|	|	1502**c**	...	|	1635	|
666	Redondela AV d.	0518**r**	|	0648	|	|	|	0926**r**	|	1150**r**	1243**r**	|	|	1348	|	...	|	|	|	|	1513**r**	...	|	|	|
678	**Vigo** Guixar a.	|	|	|	|	|	|	|	|	1205	|	|	|	|	|	...	|	|	|	|	|	...	|	|	|
684	**Pontevedra** d.	0536	|	0659	|	0815	0936	0945	1115	...	1302	1044	|	1401	|	...	|	1522	|	|	1534	...	|	1650	|
717	Vilagarcía de Arousa d.	0553	|	0716	|	0830	0953	1003	1130	...	1320	...	|	1418	|	...	|	...	|	|	1552	...	|	1705	|
677§	Santiago de Compostela d.	0637	0725	0742	0835	0852	1020	1050	1152	...	1405	...	1020	1444	1122	...	1305	...	1455	1615	1636	...	1715	1727	1749
751§	**A Coruña** a.	0716	0753	0813	0903	0920	...	1126	1220	...	1442	...	1048	1512	1202	...	1333	...	1523	1643	1713	...	1743	1755	1818

	4184	9172	9182	12488	4165	9590	283	9192	4175	12554	622	626	18322	9212	4185	12560	4205	31456
	Alvia	*MD*	*MD*		*Alvia*	*Av*	*IC*	*MD*	*Alvia*		*Alvia*	*Alvia*	*RE*	*MD*	*Alvia*		*AVE*	*Av*
		R	R	R			🍷	R		R	🍷	🍷		R				
	Z	2	2	2	X	2	2	2	b	2	P	Q	2	2	Z	2		2
	Ⓑ		Ⓑ				A				✣	✣	J				Ⓑ	Ⓑ
Madrid Chamartín ‡ **681 689** d.	...	...	...	...	1600	...	...	...	1745	...	...	...	...	...	1915	...	2035	...
Segovia Guiomar **679 679a** d.	...	...	...	...	|	...	...	...	1815	...	...	...	...	...	|	...	|	...
Irún **689** d.	...	...	...	...	|	...	0910	...	|	...	...	...	...	...	|	...	|	...
Barcelona Sants **650a** d.	...	...	...	...	|	...	|	...	|	...	0930	0930	...	...	|	...	|	...
Miranda de Ebro **681 689** d.	...	...	...	...	|	...	1140	...	|	...	1441	1441	...	...	|	...	|	...
Medina AV **681 689** d.	...	...	...	...	|	...	|	...	1844	...	|	|	1759**x**	...	|	...	|	...
Zamora d.	...	...	...	...	1714	...	|	...	1910	...	|	|	1852	...	2029	...	2141	...
Sanabria AV a.	...	...	...	...	|	...	|	...	1944	...	|	|	2014**p**	...	2103	...	|	...
Ourense d.	...	...	...	...	1839	1900	1908	...	2048	...	2149	2149	...	...	2208	...	2250	2258
Guillarei d.	...	...	...	...	|	|	|	...	|	...	2259	|	...	...	|	...	...	|
Vigo Urzáiz d.	1708	1730	1815	1820**c**	2012	|	|	1925	|	2025**c**	|	|	...	2135	|	...	...	|
Redondela AV d.	|	|	|	1833**r**	|	|	|	|	|	2038**r**	2324**r**	|	...	2143	|	...	...	|
Vigo Guixar a.	|	|	|	|	|	|	|	|	|	|	2335	|	...	|	|	...	...	|
Pontevedra d.	1724	1745	1830	1852	1956	|	|	1940	|	2057	...	|	...	2156	2331	...	...	|
Vilagarcía de Arousa d.	1742	1800	1845	1914	...	|	|	1955	|	2116	...	|	...	2213	|	...	...	|
Santiago de Compostela d.	...	1822	1907	1956	...	1940	2001	2017	2131	2200	...	2229	...	2239	2251	2305	...	2337
A Coruña a.	...	1850	1935	...	...	2008	2033	2045	2209	2236	...	2259	...	2307	...	2338	...	0005

km		31455	4054	18321	18321	9061	4484	12411	9073	4064	9083	621	625	9093	9581	4254	280	12421	9113	9111	4114	9123	12453	9131	4354
		Av	*AVE*	*RE*	*RE*	*Av*	*Alvia*		*MD*	*Alvia*	*MD*	*Alvia*	*Alvia*	*MD*	*Av*	*Alvia*	*IC*		*MD*	*Av*	*Alvia*	*MD*		*Av*	*Alvia*
				2	2			R	R		R	🍷	🍷	R			🍷	R	R			R			
		2		J	J	2	X	2	2	b	2	R	S	2	2	Z	2	2	2	2	q	2	2	2	X
		①–⑥	①–⑥	Ⓐ	Ⓒ	①–⑤	①–⑤	①–⑤		①–⑥		✣	✣		⑥⑦		A		①–⑤					①–⑤	
0	**A Coruña** d.	0508	...	...	...	0555	...	0535	0700	0716	0800	...	0805	0900	0920	...	0930	0930	1100	1130	...	1200	1240	1330	...
74	Santiago de Compostela d.	0538	...	...	...	0625	...	0614	0730	0747	0830	...	0834	0930	0949	1020	1006	1012	1130	1200	...	1230	1322	1400	...
116	Vilagarcía de Arousa d.	|	...	...	...	|	...	0651	0756	|	0850	...	|	0950	|	|	|	1050	1150	|	...	1250	1405	|	...
149	**Pontevedra** d.	|	...	...	...	|	0606	0711	0813	|	0906	...	|	1006	|	0936	|	1108	1206	|	...	1306	1423	|	1336
	Vigo Guixar d.	|	...	...	...	|	|	|	|	|	|	0742	|	|	|	|	|	|	|	|	...	|	|	|	|
167	Redondela AV d.	|	...	...	...	|	|	0730**r**	0825	|	|	0753**r**	|	|	|	|	|	1127**r**	|	|	...	|	1441**r**	|	|
179	**Vigo** Urzáiz d.	|	...	...	...	|	0550	0741**c**	0833	|	0920	|	|	1020	|	|	|	1140**c**	1220	|	...	1320	1454**c**	|	1320
192	Guillarei d.	|	...	...	...	|	|	...	...	|	...	0810	|	...	|	|	|	...	...	|	...	...	...	|	|
	Ourense d.	0616	0630	...	...	0703	0718	...	...	0827	...	0920	0920	...	1026	1102	1110	...	...	1238	1258	...	...	1438	1450
	Sanabria AV d.	...	|	0702**p**	0730**p**	...	0821	...	...	0934	...	|	|	...	...	|	|	...	...	...	1403	...	...	...	|
	Zamora d.	...	0741	0826	0854	...	0902	...	...	1008	...	|	|	...	...	1230	|	...	...	...	1439	...	...	...	1620
	Medina AV **681 689** d.	...	|	0919**x**	0947**x**	...	|	...	...	1036	...	|	|	...	...	|	|	...	...	...	1507	...	...	...	|
	Miranda de Ebro **681 689** a.	...	|	...	...	...	|	...	...	|	...	1600	1600	...	...	|	1842	...	...	...	|	...	...	...	|
	Barcelona Sants **650a** a.	...	|	...	...	...	|	...	...	|	...	2135	2135	...	...	|	|	...	...	...	|	...	...	...	|
	Hendaye **689** a.	...	|	...	...	...	|	...	...	|	...	...	...	...	...	|	2122	...	...	...	|	...	...	...	|
	Segovia Guiomar **679 679a** d.	...	|	...	...	...	|	...	...	1106	...	...	...	...	...	|	...	...	...	...	1537	...	...	...	|
	Madrid Chamartín ‡ **681 689** a.	...	0845	...	...	...	1020	...	...	1106	...	...	...	...	...	1342	...	...	...	...	1606	...	...	...	1736

		9133	4115	9153	9351	5182	12431	4134	12967	9173	9171	4184	9183	12441	4204	9201	12459	9213	12461	12561	4185
		MD	*Alvia*	*MD*	*Av*	*AVE*	*MD*	*Alvia*		*MD*	*Av*	*Alvia*	*MD*		*Alvia*	*Av*		*MD*			*Alvia*
		R		R			R		R	R	2		R	R		2	R	R	R		
	2	2	X	2	2	B	2	b	2	2		X	2	2			2	2	2	2	Z
	h		①–⑥									Ⓑ	Ⓑ		Ⓑ						
A Coruña d.	...	1400	...	1500	1510	...	1550	1626	...	1700	1720	...	1800	1908	1935	1950	...	2115	...	2210	...
Santiago de Compostela d.	...	1430	...	1530	1540	...	1632	1656	1725	1730	1750	...	1830	1950	2006	2020	2025	2147	2200	2243	2251
Vilagarcía de Arousa d.	...	1455	1504	1550	|	...	1709	|	|	1750	|	...	1850	2033	|	|	2105	2213	2241	...	2314
Pontevedra d.	...	1512	1522	1606	|	...	1727	|	|	1806	|	1724	1906	2054	|	|	2123	2231	2259	...	2331
Vigo Guixar d.	1410	|	|	|	|	...	|	|	|	|	|	|	|	|	|	|	|	|	|	...	|
Redondela AV d.	1423**r**	1522	|	|	|	...	1745**r**	|	|	|	|	|	|	2115**r**	|	|	2143**r**	2243	2319**r**	...	|
Vigo Urzáiz d.	|	1529	1538	1620	|	...	1759**c**	|	|	1820	|	1708	1920	2126**c**	|	|	2156**c**	2251	2332**c**	...	2346
Guillarei d.	1444	...	...	...	|	...	...	|	|	...	|	|	...	...	|	|	...	...	...	...	...
Ourense d.	1610	...	...	...	1618	1625	...	1733	1906	...	1828	1844	...	...	2047	2058	...	...	...	...	...
Sanabria AV d.	...	...	...	...	...	|	...	|	...	...	...	1947	...	...	|	...	...	...	...	...	...
Zamora d.	...	...	...	...	...	1736	...	1903	...	...	...	2024	...	...	2213	...	...	...	...	...	...
Medina AV **681 689** d.	...	...	...	...	...	|	...	|	...	...	...	2052	...	...	|	...	...	...	...	...	...
Miranda de Ebro **681 689** a.	...	...	...	...	...	|	...	|	...	...	...	|	...	...	|	...	...	...	...	...	...
Barcelona Sants **650a** a.	...	...	...	...	...	|	...	|	...	...	...	|	...	...	|	...	...	...	...	...	...
Hendaye **689** a.	...	...	...	...	...	|	...	|	...	...	...	|	...	...	|	...	...	...	...	...	...
Segovia Guiomar **679 679a** d.	...	...	...	...	...	|	...	|	...	...	...	2123	...	...	|	...	...	...	...	...	...
Madrid Chamartín ‡ **681 689** a.	...	...	...	...	...	1840	...	2018	...	...	...	2152	...	...	2329	...	...	...	...	...	...

A – CAMINO DE SANTIAGO – ⊏2⊐ 🍷 Irún / Hendaye - Miranda de Ebro - A Coruña and v.v.
B – From / to Alacant (Table **668**).
J – ⊏2⊐ Valladolid - Medina del Campo - Puebla de Sanabria and v.v. (Table **689**).
P – ③⑤⑦ ⊏12⊐ 🍷 Barcelona - Ourense - Vigo ✣.
Q – ①②④⑥ ⊏12⊐ 🍷 Barcelona - Ourense - A Coruña ✣.
R – ①④⑥ ⊏12⊐ 🍷 Vigo - Ourense - Barcelona ✣.
S – ②③⑤⑦ ⊏12⊐ 🍷 A Coruña - Ourense - Barcelona ✣.
X – Routeing is Madrid - Ourense - Pontevedra - Vigo and v.v.
Z – Routeing is Madrid - Ourense - Santiago de Compostela - Pontevedra - Vigo and v.v. See opposite direction for further stops.

b – To / from Ferrol (Table **682**).
c – Vigo **Guixar**.
h – To Ponferrada (Table **682**).
p – Puebla de Sanabria
q – To / from Lugo (Table **682**).
r – Redondela **de Galica**.
x – Medina del Campo.
◐ – Via Lugo (Table **682**).
‡ – Full name is Madrid-Chamartín-Clara Campoamor.

* – *153 km* Madrid - Medina del Campo via high-speed line.
§ – *636 km* Madrid - Santiago de Compostela via high-speed line. *697 km* Madrid - A Coruña via high-speed line.
✣ – On days of indirect service, connections are available between Ourense and Vigo / A Coruña and v.v. in similar timings.

☛ **Shaded services are suspended until further notice.**

681 MADRID - LEÓN

km	km via HSL				Alvia	Alvia		IC		Alvia	IC	Alvia	Alvia	AVE	Alvia	Alvia	MD	IC	IC	Alvia	MD	Alvia	AVE			
					4071	4073	18101	4099		4101	283	4143	622	4149	4111	664	18003	4171	4179	4181	18005	4193	5183			
			Ⓐ	Ⓒ	①–⑥	①–⑥	2	Ⓒ			2🍷		626	Ⓑ			2	⑤	Ⓑ		2					
			2	2							B	E	L		P			2		Q			Q			
0	0	**Madrid** Chamartín ¶ ... 680 689 d.	...	...	0706	0745	...	0940	...	1110	...	1340	...	1440	1500	...	1628p	1715	1825	1834	1827p	1908	2025	...	...	...
121		Ávila ... 680 689 d.	...	...	│	│	...	│	...	│	...	│	...	│	│	...	1759	│	│	│	2009	│	│	...	...	...
207		Medina del Campo .. 680 689 d.	...	...	│	│	...	│	...	│	...	│	...	│	│	...	1845	│	│	│	2054	│	│	...	...	...
249	180	**Valladolid** C. Grande ... 689 d.	0700	0718	0808	0845	0955	1045	...	1217	...	1448	...	1540	1607	...	1913	│	1930	1938	2120	2007	2121	...	...	...
286		Venta de Baños ... 689 d.	0733	0751	│	│	1027	│	...	│	...	│	...	│	│	...	1938	│	│	│	2147	│	│	...	...	...
		Barcelona Sants **652** ... d.	│	│	│	│	│	│	...	│	...	│	0930	│	│	1210	│	│	│	│	│	│	│	...	...	...
		Irún **689** ... d.	│	│	│	│	│	│	...	│	0910	│	│	│	│	│	│	│	│	│	│	│	│	...	...	...
		Miranda de Ebro ... 689 d.	│	│	│	│	│	│	...	│	1140	│	1441	│	│	1723	│	│	│	│	│	│	│	...	...	...
		Burgos Rosa Manzano 689 d.	│	│	│	│	│	│	...	│	1234	│	1546	│	│	1816	│	│	│	│	│	│	│	...	...	...
		Palencia ... 689 d.	0747	0805	0834	0917	1038	1110	...	1243	1323	1519	1622	1606	1633	1906	1949	│	1957	2005	2158	2039	2145	...	...	...
297	233	*Santander* **684** ... a.	│	│	│	1150	1344	│	...	│	│	1747	│	│	│	│	│	│	│	│	│	2312	│	...	...	...
		León ... a.	0923	0927	0918	...	...	1148	...	1328	1428	...	1707	1641	1716	2014	2102	1927	2044	2048	2307	...	2221	...	...	...
420	345	*Gijón Sanz Crespo* **685** ... a.	1246	1246	1200	...	...	...	...	1611	│	...	│	...	2003	2312x	...	2213	│	2332	...	...	...	...	...	...
		Ponferrada **682** ... a.	...	...	...	...	...	...	...	...	1614	...	1841	...	...	...	...	...	2232	...	...	...	...	...	...	...
		Vigo Guixar **682** ... a.	...	...	...	...	...	...	...	...	│	...	2335	...	...	...	...	...	...	...	...	...	...	...	...	...
		A Coruña **682** ... a.	...	...	...	...	...	...	...	...	2033	...	2259	...	...	...	...	...	...	...	...	...	...	...	...	...
		Ferrol **682** ... a.	...	...	...	...	...	...	...	...	...	...	...	...	...	...	...	...	...	...	...	...	...	...	...	...

	MD	AVE	IC	Alvia	AVE	Alvia	Alvia		Alvia	Alvia	IC	Alvia	MD	IC	Alvia	AVE			IC	IC	IC	Alvia	Alvia			
	18002	5092	4088	4072	5122	4270	661		4110	625	280	4142	18006	4540	4140	4178			4188	4160	4198	4180	4192			
	2	①–⑤	①–⑥		⑥⑦	①–⑤				621	2🍷		2	⑦		Ⓑ	†	⚒	⑥	⑦	⑦		Ⓑ			
	w	Q		E	Q				P	L	B			2	Q		2	2		2						
Ferrol **682** ... d.	...	...	...	...	...	...	...	...	...	...	...	...	...	...	...	...	...	...	...	...	...	...	...	...	...	...
A Coruña **682** ... d.	...	...	...	...	...	...	...	...	...	0805	0930	...	...	...	...	...	...	...	...	...	...	...	...	...	...	...
Vigo Guixar **682** ... d.	...	...	...	...	...	...	...	...	...	0742	│	...	...	...	...	...	...	...	...	...	...	...	...	...	...	...
Ponferrada **682** ... d.	...	...	0605	...	...	...	...	...	...	1211	1344	...	...	...	...	...	1620	...	...	...	...	...	...	...	...	...
Gijón Sanz Crespo **685** ... d.	...	...	│	...	...	0710	0757	...	1048	│	│	...	...	1403	1440	...	│	1515	...	1605	...	1816	...	...	...	...
León ... d.	0640	0645	0741	...	0950	0951	1044	...	1339	1345	1544	...	1542	1656	1728	1748	1841	1843	1845	1857	1958	2049	...	...	...	...
Santander **684** ... d.	│	│	│	0705	│	│	│	...	│	│	│	1355	│	│	│	│	│	│	│	│	│	│	1900	...	...	...
Palencia ... 689 d.	0750	0721	0831	0935	1025	1036	1157	...	1424	1430	1655	1623	1654	1746	1813	1824	2007	2005	1927	│	2038	2131	2131	...	...	...
Burgos Rosa Manzano . 689 d.	│	│	│	│	│	│	1252	...	│	1505	1746	│	│	│	│	│	│	│	│	│	│	│	│	...	...	...
Miranda de Ebro ... 689 a.	│	│	│	│	│	│	1345	...	│	1600	1842	│	│	│	│	│	│	│	│	│	│	│	│	...	...	...
Hendaye **689** ... a.	│	│	│	│	│	│	│	...	│	│	2122	│	│	│	│	│	│	│	│	│	│	│	│	...	...	...
Barcelona Sants **652** ... a.	│	│	│	│	│	│	1903	...	│	2135	...	│	│	│	│	│	│	│	│	│	│	│	│	...	...	...
Venta de Baños ... 689 d.	0803	│	│	│	│	│	...	...	│	...	...	│	1706	│	│	│	2023	2018	│	│	│	│	│	...	...	...
Valladolid C. Grande ... 689 d.	0833	0745	0904	1009	1048	1101	...	...	1449	...	...	1655	1742	1813	1839	1849	2057	2054	1953	│	2105	2157	2202	...	...	...
Medina del Campo ... 680 689 a.	0859	│	│	│	│	│	...	...	│	...	...	│	1807	│	│	│	...	...	│	│	│	│	│	...	...	...
Ávila ... 680 689 a.	0943	│	│	│	│	│	...	...	│	...	...	│	1852	│	│	│	...	...	│	│	│	│	│	...	...	...
Madrid Chamartín ¶ ... 680 689 a.	1126p	0838	1009	1119	1140	1201	...	...	1555	...	...	1755	2041p	1917	1940	1950	...	...	2058	2107	2210	2300	2307	...	...	...

☛ **FOR NOTES**, SEE TABLE **682** BELOW.

682 LEÓN - VIGO, FERROL and A CORUÑA

km		MD	MD	MD				Alvia	MD	IC	MD	Alvia		Alvia		Alvia	Alvia		MD	IC		IC			
		37064	12681	12641				4095	12694	283	12687	4325		4175		626	622		12646	4179		560			
		2	2	2	2	2	2	①–⑥	2	2	2			Ⓑ	2			2	2	Ⓑ	2	Ⓑ			
		①–⑥			X			A	JZ	B		MZ		A		LX	LX	⑤	HX			2JZ			
	Madrid Chamartín ¶ ‡ d.	...	...	...	...	...	...	0800	...	...	...	1315	...	1745	...	...	...	...	...	1825	...	...	...	...	...
	Barcelona Sants ... ‡ d.	...	...	...	...	...	...	│	...	...	...	│	...	│	...	0930	0930	...	...	│	...	...	...	...	...
	Irún ... ‡ d.	...	...	...	...	...	...	│	...	0910	...	│	...	│	...	│	│	...	...	│	...	...	...	...	...
	Bilbao Abando ... ‡ d.	...	...	...	...	...	...	│	...	│	...	│	...	│	...	│	│	...	...	│	...	...	...	...	...
0	**León** ... d.	...	...	...	...	...	0705	│	...	1443	...	│	...	│	1700	1709	1709	1805	...	2046	2235	...	...	...	...
52	Astorga ... d.	...	...	...	...	...	0752	│	...	1515	...	│	...	│	1733	1741	1741	1851	...	2120	2322	...	...	...	...
128	**Ponferrada** ... d.	...	...	...	0615	...	0901	│	...	1616	...	│	...	│	1834	1842	1842	2008	...	2232	0031	...	...	...	...
238	Monforte de Lemos ... a.	...	...	...	0801	...	...	│	...	1753	...	1720	...	│	2016	2019	2019	...	...	...	...	...	...	...	...
238	Monforte de Lemos ... d.	...	...	0711	0810	...	...	│	1316	1809	...	1722	...	│	2021	2034	2034	...	2042	...	...	2342	...	...	...
285	Ourense ... **680** d.	...	...	│	0900	1005	...	1038	1230	1908	...	1632	...	2048	2100	2149	2149	...	1940	...	...	2300	...	...	...
416	**Vigo** Guixar ... **680** a.	...	...	│	...	1205	...	│	│	│	...	│	...	│	2249	│	2335	...	│	...	...	│	...	...	...
309	Lugo ... d.	...	...	0815	...	...	...	│	1416	│	...	1825	...	│	...	│	...	...	2148	...	...	0035	...	...	...
445	**Ferrol** ... d.	0720	0840	│	...	...	...	│	...	▲	1915	...	...	│	...	▲	...	...	│	...	...	...	...	...	...
402	Betanzos - Infesta ... d.	0806	0929	0946	...	...	...	1232	...	│	2006	...	...	2238	...	│	...	...	2303	...	...	...	...	...	...
428	**A Coruña** ... **680** a.	0828	0954	1012	...	...	...	1202	...	2033	2037	...	...	2209	...	2259	...	...	2331	...	...	...	...	...	...
445	**Ferrol** ... a.	...	...	...	...	...	...	1312	...	...	...	...	...	2323	...	...	...	...	...	...	...	...	...	...	...

		IC		Alvia		MD	MD	Alvia	Alvia		Alvia	IC	MD				Alvia	MD		IC	MD	MD			
		4088		4064		12644	12680	621	625		4114	280	12696				4134	12696		558	12642	37145			
	2	①–⑥	2	①–⑥	2	2	2					2	2	2	2	2		2		Ⓑ	2	2			
	Ⓐ		Ⓒ	A		HX		LX	LX		MZ	B	JZ		†y	X	A			2JZ					
Ferrol ... d.	...	...	...	0555	...	...	...	...	...	...	...	...	...	...	...	...	1510	...	...	...	...	...	...	...	...
A Coruña ... **680** d.	...	...	...	0716	...	0706	0645	...	0805	...	...	0930	...	...	...	...	1626	1720	...	...	1935	2209	...	...	...
Betanzos - Infesta ... d.	...	...	...	0641	...	0735	0716	...	│	...	...	│	...	...	...	...	1553	1751	...	...	2004	2238	...	...	...
Ferrol ... a.	...	...	...	│	...	│	0803	...	▲	...	...	▲	...	...	...	...	│	1838	...	...	│	2323	...	...	...
Lugo ... d.	...	...	...	│	...	0854	...	...	│	...	1050	│	1425	...	...	...	│	...	...	1845	2127	...	...	...	...
Vigo Guixar ... **680** d.	...	...	...	│	0705	│	...	0742	│	...	│	│	│	...	...	1410	│	...	...	│	│	...	...	...	...
Ourense ... **680** d.	...	...	...	0827	0858	1046	...	0920	0920	...	1258	1110	1615	...	...	1630	1733	...	...	2030	│	...	...	...	...
Monforte de Lemos ... a.	...	...	...	│	0946	0954	...	1010	1010	...	1151	1148	1526	...	...	1722	│	...	...	1946	2220	...	...	...	...
Monforte de Lemos ... d.	...	...	...	│	0951	...	...	1035	1035	...	1153	1208	...	...	...	1722	│	...	...	...	...	...	...	...	...
Ponferrada ... d.	0515	0605	0645	│	1144	...	...	1211	1211	...	│	1344	...	1515	1620	1907	│	...	...	...	...	...	...	...	...
Astorga ... d.	0619	0707	0749	│	...	...	...	1311	1311	...	│	1453	...	1630	1740	...	│	...	...	...	...	...	...	...	...
León ... a.	0656	0741	0828	│	...	...	...	1342	1342	...	│	1528	...	1710	1836	...	│	...	...	...	...	...	...	...	...
Bilbao Abando ... ‡ a.	...	│	...	│	...	...	...	│	│	...	│	│	...	...	...	...	│	...	...	...	...	...	...	...	...
Hendaye ... ‡ a.	...	│	...	│	...	...	...	│	│	...	│	2122	...	...	...	...	│	...	...	...	...	...	...	...	...
Barcelona Sants ... ‡ a.	...	│	...	│	...	...	...	2135	2135	...	│	...	...	...	...	...	│	...	...	...	...	...	...	...	...
Madrid Chamartín ¶ ‡ a.	...	1009	...	1134	...	...	...	...	...	...	1606	...	...	...	...	...	2018	...	...	...	...	...	...	...	...

A – [12] Madrid - Zamora - Ourense - A Coruña - Betanzos - Ferrol and v.v. (Table **680**).
B – CAMINO DE SANTIAGO – [2] 🍷 Irún / Hendaye - Monforte de Lemos - Santiago - A Coruña and v.v.
E – [12] Alacant - Madrid - Santander and v.v.
H – Routeing is A Coruña - Lugo - Monforte de Lemos - Ourense and v.v., with connections at Ourense to and from Madrid (Table **680**).
J – Routeing is Ourense - Monforte de Lemos - Lugo and v.v.
L – [12] 🍷 Barcelona - A Coruña and Vigo and v.v. 🚌 until July 2023: Monforte de Lemos - Ourense. For days of running see Table **680**.
M – [12] Madrid - Zamora - Ourense - Monforte de Lemos - Lugo and v.v. (Table **680**).
P – From / to Castelló de la Plana and València (Table **668**).

Q – From / to Alacant (Table **668**).
X – Until July 2023: 🚌 Ourense - Monforte de Lemos and v.v.
Z – Until July 2023: 🚌 Ourense - Lugo and v.v.

p – Madrid **Principe Pio**.
w – Runs 10 minutes later on Ⓒ.
x – Not ⑥.
y – To Valladolid (Table **681**).

▲ – Via Santiago (Table **680**).
‡ – See Table **681**.
¶ – Full name is Madrid-Chamartín-Clara Campoamor.

☛ **Shaded services are suspended until further notice.**

683 LEÓN - BILBAO

FEVE narrow-gauge

1350 ✣ →	1410 →	1445 →	1535 →	1636 →	1715 →	1801 →	1935 →	2044 →	2134
León	San Feliz	La Vecilla	Cistierna	Guardo	Vado Cervera	Mataporquera	Espinosa	Balmaseda	**Bilbao** Concordia
2203 ✣	← 2138	← 2059	← 2018	← 1921	← 1841	← 1800	← 1623	← 1520	← 1430

✣ – Journey may be by 🚌 between León and Asunción-Universidad y León, due to construction of a new tunnel.

PALENCIA - SANTANDER 684

km		Alvia 4073 ①–⑥	2		Alvia 4143 A		①–⑥ 2	⑦ 2	Alvia 4193	
	Madrid CCC ¶ **681 689** ..... d.	0745	...	...	1340	...	...	...	1908	...
	Valladolid C G **681 689** ..... d.	0845	0955	...	1448	...	1829	1829	2007	...
0	**Palencia** ..... d.	0917	1038	...	1519	...	1915	1915	2039	...
98	Aguilar de Campoo ..... d.	1012	1152	...	|	...	2028	2028	2132	...
'10	Mataporquera **683** ‡ ..... d.	|	1201	...	|	...	2042	2042	|	...
'29	Reinosa ..... § d.	1035	1216	...	|	...	2058	2058	2157	...
'88	Torrelavega ..... § d.	1124	1315	...	1721	...	2153	2157	2246	...
?18	**Santander** ..... § a.	1150	1344	...	1747	...	2222	2226	2312	...

	🚌 ⑥⑦ 2	⑥⑦ 2	Alvia 4072 A	①–⑤ 2		Alvia 4142	2	Alvia 4192 Ⓑ	
Santander ..... § d.	0700	...	0705	0919	...	1355	1538	1900	...
Torrelavega ..... § d.	0728	0745	0729	0953	...	1419	1609	1923	...
Reinosa ..... § d.	...	0839	0815	1056	...	|	1702	2010	...
Mataporquera **683** ‡ ..... d.	...	0855	|	1112	...	|	1723	|	...
Aguilar de Campoo ..... d.	...	0905	0838	1122	...	|	1733	2032	...
Palencia ..... a.	...	1022	0933	1234	...	1621	1844	2129	...
Valladolid C G **681 689** ..... a.	...	1108	1005	1320	...	1653	1930	2200	...
Madrid CCC ¶ **681 689** ..... a.	...	...	1119	...	...	1755	...	2307	...

– From / to Alacant (Table **668**).
‡ – Narrow gauge station is 600 metres.
§ – Additional local services operate between these stations.
¶ – Full name is Madrid-Chamartín-Clara Campoamor.

LEÓN - OVIEDO - GIJÓN 685

km		Alvia 4071 ①–⑥	Ⓐ 2 A	Ⓒ 2 A		Alvia 4101		Alvia 4111 V	IC 4171 ⑤ 2	Alvia 4181 C	
	Barcelona Sants **681** d.	...	...	...	...	...	...	...	...	...	...
	Madrid CCC ¶ **681** .. d.	0706	...	...	...	1110	...	1500	1715	1834	...
0	**León** ..... d.	0920	0925	0929	...	1330	...	1720	1929	2050	...
109	Pola de Lena ..... § a.	|	1138	1138	...	1508	...	1903	|	|	...
140	**Oviedo** ▽ ..... § a.	1130	1217	1217	...	1541	...	1936	2143	2305	...
172	**Gijón** Sanz Crespo.. § a.	1200	1246	1246	...	1611	...	2003	2213	2332	...

	Alvia 4270 ①–⑥		Alvia 4110 V		Alvia 4140 C	2 ⚒ A	IC 4160 ⑦ 2	Alvia 4180	⑦ 2	
Gijón Sanz Crespo § d.	0710	...	1048	...	1440	1515	1605	1816	2025	...
Oviedo ▽ ..... § d.	0737	...	1116	...	1509	1544	1632	1845	2055	...
Pola de Lena ..... § d.	|	...	1156	...	1548	1622	|	|	2130	...
León ..... a.	0949	...	1337	...	1726	1841	1855	2047	2352	...
Madrid CCC ¶ **681** . a.	1201	...	1555	...	1940	...	2107	2300	...	...
Barcelona Sants **681** a.	...	...	...	...	...	...	...	...	...	...

– From / to Valladolid (Table **681**).
– From / to Alacant (Table **668**).
V – To / from València and Castelló de la Plana (Table **668**).
¶ – Full name is Madrid-Chamartín-Clara Campoamor.

▽ – **OVIEDO – AVILÉS** and v.v. ***Renfe Cercanías*** (suburban) service. *31 km.* Journey time: ± 38 minutes. **Additional services on** Ⓐ.
From Oviedo: Approximately 1 train each hour 0550 Ⓐ, 0616 Ⓐ, then 0716 until 2216. **From Avilés**: Approximately 1 train each hour 0641 Ⓐ, 0741 Ⓐ, then 0841 until 2311.

– **GIJÓN – OVIEDO – POLA de LENA** and v.v. ***Renfe Cercanías*** (suburban) service. *63 km.* Journey time: ± 78 minutes.
From Pola de Lena: Approximately 1–2 trains each hour from 0630 until 2200. **From Gijón**: Approximately 1–2 trains each hour from 0600 until 2230.

SAN SEBASTIÁN - BILBAO 686

Euskotren (narrow gauge)

	Ⓐ	Ⓐ	Ⓒ					
an Sebastián ⊡ Amara ..... d.	0550	0650	0650	0750	0850		1950	2050
arautz ..... d.	0620	0720	0720	0820	0920		2020	2120
umaia ..... d.	0629	0729	0729	0829	0929	and	2029	2129
bar ..... d.	0711	0811	...	0911	1011	hourly	2111	2211
urango ..... d.	0741	0841	...	0941	1041	until	2141	2241
lbao Casco Viejo § ⊖ ..... a.	0821	0921	...	1021	1121		2221	2321**z**
lbao Matiko ..... a.	0825	0925	...	1024	1124		2225	2325**z**

	Ⓐ	Ⓐ	Ⓒ					
Bilbao Matiko ..... d.	...	0555	...	0655**x**	0755**x**		1855**x**	1955**x**
Bilbao Casco Viejo § ⊖ ..... d.	...	0558	...	0658**x**	0758**x**		1858**x**	1958**x**
Durango ..... d.	0539	0639	...	0739	0839	and	1939	2039
Eibar ..... d.	0614	0714	...	0814	0914	hourly	2014	2114
Zumaia ..... d.	0700	0800	0800	0900	1000	until	2100	2200
Zarautz ..... d.	0708	0808	0808	0908	1008		2108	2208
San Sebastián ⊡ Amara ..... a.	0738	0838	0838	0938	1038		2138	2238

– 3 mins. earlier on Ⓒ.
– Ⓒ.
⊡ – San Sebastián / Donostia.
⊖ – Metro interchange.
§ – Bilbao Casco Viejo ⇆ Bilbao Abando (*Renfe*): ± *400 m.* Linked by tram approx every 3 - 5 minutes, journey 2 minutes.
Operator: Euskotren. 2nd class, narrow gauge. Distance: San Sebastian - Bilbao *108* km.

BILBAO - SANTANDER - OVIEDO - FERROL 687

FEVE (narrow gauge)

			Ⓐ		Ⓐ					
ilbao Concordia § ..... d.	...	...	...	0800	...	...	1300	...	1934	...
arrón ..... d.	...	...	0710	0942	...	...	1439	...	2115	...
reto ..... d.	...	...	0721	0953	...	...	1450	...	2126	...
antander ..... a.	...	...	0830	1056	...	...	1556	...	2230	...
antander ..... ▽ d.	...	0829	...	...	...	1528	...	...	...	...
orrelavega ..... ▽ d.	...	0900	...	...	...	1559	...	...	...	...
abezón de la Sal ..... ▽ d.	...	0941	...	...	...	1634	...	...	...	...
nquera ..... d.	...	1023	...	...	...	1718	...	...	...	...
anes ..... d.	0710	1101	...	...	1427	1758	...	...	...	...
ibadesella ..... d.	0749	1138	...	...	1506	1837	...	...	...	...
viedo ..... a.	1022	1356	...	...	1731	2101	...	...	...	...

					Ⓐ			Ⓐ		
Oviedo ..... d.	...	...	0757	...	1110	...	1444	...	1839	...
Ribadesella ..... d.	...	...	1021	...	1337	...	1712	...	2105	...
Llanes ..... d.	...	...	1104	...	1416	...	1754	...	2144	...
Unquera ..... d.	...	...	1134	...	...	...	1824	...	...	...
Cabezón de la Sal ..... ▽ d.	...	...	1221	...	...	...	1909	...	...	...
Torrelavega ..... ▽ d.	...	...	1302	...	...	...	1947	...	...	...
Santander ..... ▽ a.	...	...	1334	...	...	...	2019	...	...	...
Santander ..... d.	0754	...	...	1400	...	1900	...	2037	...	...
Treto ..... d.	0858	...	...	1507	...	2003	...	2144	...	...
Marrón ..... d.	0910	...	...	1519	...	2014	...	2155	...	...
Bilbao Concordia § ..... a.	1108	...	...	1659	...	2205	...	...	...	...

viedo ..... △ d.	...	...	0719	...	...	...	...	...	1418	...
Gijón Sanz Crespo . △ d.	...	0701	|	0931	...	1131	...	1421	|	1831
Avilés ..... △ d.	...	0740	|	1018	...	1218	...	1500	|	1918
ravia ..... △ d.	...	0812	0839	1048	...	1248	...	1529	1540	1948
uarca ..... d.	...	...	1003	...	...	...	...	...	1708	...
avia ..... d.	...	...	1033	...	...	...	...	...	1739	...
ibadeo ..... d.	0655	...	1134	...	1500	...	...	...	1840	...
veiro ..... d.	0803	...	1244	...	1609	...	...	...	1949	...
rtigueira ..... d.	0843	...	1324	...	1650	...	1840	...	2028	...
errol ..... a.	1000	...	1444	...	1810	...	1957	...	2144	...

Ferrol ..... d.	...	...	0820	...	1045	...	1445	1530	...	1905
Ortigueira ..... d.	...	...	0938	...	1204	...	1601	1649	...	2027
Viveiro ..... d.	...	...	1018	...	1245	...	...	1729	...	2106
Ribadeo ..... d.	...	...	1130	...	1353	...	...	1842	...	2218
Navia ..... d.	...	...	1225	...	...	...	...	1940	...	...
Luarca ..... d.	...	...	1256	...	...	...	...	2012	...	...
Pravia ..... △ d.	0848	1148	1428	1448	...	1648	...	2152	2155	...
Avilés ..... △ d.	0926	1226	|	1526	...	1726	...	|	2229	...
Gijón Sanz Crespo ... △ a.	1008	1308	|	1608	...	1808	...	|	2309	...
Oviedo ..... △ a.	...	...	1542	...	...	...	...	2305	...	...

▽ – Additional trains run Santander - Cabezón de al Sal and v.v.
△ – Additional trains run Oviedo / Gijón - Pravia and v.v.
§ – Bilbao Concordia is adjacent to Bilbao Abando (*Renfe*).
Operator: FEVE. 2nd class, narrow gauge.

🚌 IRÚN - BILBAO - SANTANDER - GIJÓN 688

ALSA ★

🚌	▽ ①–⑥			♡ Ⓑ	♡ ⑥	①–⑥	⑦				♡ Ⓑ	⑥		♡ Ⓑ		♡	⑤⑦					⊖ ⑤⑦		⑦	
ún RENFE rail station ..... d.	...	...	...	0645	...	0745	...	...	0845	...	...	...	1100	...	1345	1445	...	...	1615	...	1830	...	2045	2115	2355
an Sebastián / Donostia ..... d.	...	...	...	0710	...	0810	...	...	0910	...	...	...	1125	...	1410	1510	...	...	1640	...	1855	...	2110	2140	0020
ilbao TermiBus ..... d.	0600	...	0700	0830	0830	0930	0930	1000	1030	1130	1230	1230	1330	1430	1530	1630	1730	1730	1800	1845	2030	2115	2230	2300	0145
antander ..... d.	0715	0830	0830	0950	0950	1100	1115	1130	1215	1300	1350	1400	1530	1550	1700	1750	1900	1900	1930	2015	2200	2235	2350	0020	0330
viedo ..... a.	1000*	1145	...	1205	1205	...	...	...	1530	...	1605	...	1845	1805	...	2005	2145	...	2230	2230	...	0050	...	...	0600
ijón ..... a.	0930	1215	...	1230	1230	...	...	...	1600	...	1635	...	1915	1835	...	2030	2215	...	2300	2300	...	0120	...	...	0700

🚌		①–⑥			①–⑥	♡	♡ ①–⑥	⑤	⑦	①–⑥	♡ ①–⑥		⑤⑦	♡			⑥	♡ Ⓑ				▽ Ⓑ	⑤⑦	▽ ⑤	▽ ⑦
ijón ..... d.	0014	...	...	...	...	0715	...	...	0815	0815	0915	1130	...	1315	...	1515	1545	1630	...	1715	...	1915	2015	2115	2115
viedo ..... d.	0100	...	...	...	...	0745	...	...	0845	0845	0945	|	...	1345	...	|	1615	1700	...	1745	...	1945	2045	2145	2145
antander ..... d.	0345	0600	0700	0800	0930	1005	1200	...	1200	1230	1200	1400	1545	1605	1700	1900	1900	1920	...	2030	2100	2205	2340	0005	2359
ilbao TermiBus ..... d.	0515	0730	0840	0930	1100	1120	1315	1400	1400	1415	1315	1530	1745	1720	1830	2045	2030	2035	2045	2200	2230	2320	...	0120	0115
an Sebastián / Donostia ..... a.	0640	0845	1000	...	1210	1230	...	1510	1600	1615	...	...	1855	1830**z**	1940	2155	...	2145**r**	2155	2310	...	...	...	...	0225
ún RENFE rail station ..... a.	0700	0915	1030	...	1240	1305	...	1545	1630	1645	...	...	1925	1905**z**	2010	2225	...	2220**r**	2225	2340	...	...	...	...	0300

♡ – *Clase Supra+* luxury coach.
▽ – *Clase Supra Economy* luxury coach.
⊖ – *Supra+ on ⑤, Supra Economy on ⑦.*
r – ①–④ only.
z – ⑥ only.
* – Calls after Gijon.
★ – ALSA: ✆ +34 913 270 540 www.alsa.es
Frequent services operate Bilbao - Santander and Oviedo - Gijon.

689 MADRID and SALAMANCA - BILBAO and IRÚN

km		RE	RE	RE			RE	Alvia	MD	Alvia		RE	RE	RE	Alvia	Alvia	MD			MD			
△		16207	16001	16019	17227	17201	18302	4187	18001	4087		18321	17203	18321	438	661	18061	18029		18011			
		2	2	2	2	2	2		2			Y 2	2	Y 2		A	2	2	2	2			
		Ⓐ		N		Ⓐ		⚒	Ⓐ			Ⓐ	Ⓒ	Ⓒ		⚒		Z		Ⓒ			
0	**Madrid** Chamartín ‡ .... **680 681** d.	...	...	...	...	...	...	0715	0643**p**	0843	...	...	...	...	...	...	0907**p**	...	...	0940**p**	...	...	...
121	Ávila .... **680 681** d.	...	...	...	...	0645	...	|	0823	|	...	...	0833	...	...	...	1038	...	...	1118	...	...	...
	Salamanca .... d.	...	...	...	...	|	0715	|	|	|	...	...	|	...	...	...	|	...	...	|	...	...	...
207	Medina del Campo .... **680 681** d.	...	...	...	0655	0733	0802	|	0911	|	...	0920	0923	0948	...	...	1125	...	...	1206	...	...	...
250	**Valladolid** Campo Grande .... **681** d.	...	...	...	0730	0807	0828	0819	0939	0949	...	0955	0959	1025	...	...	1150	...	1225	1235	...	...	...
286	Venta de Baños .... **681** d.	...	...	...	...	...	...	|	...	|	...	...	...	...	...	...	1215	...	1300	...	...	...	...
298	Palencia .... **681** d.	...	...	...	...	...	...	|	...	|	...	...	...	...	...	1157	1229	...	1313	...	...	...	...
371	**Burgos** Rosa Manzano .... **681** d.	...	...	0823	...	...	...	0910	...	1037	...	...	...	...	...	1252	1320	...	...	...	...	...	...
460	Miranda de Ebro .... **654** d.	0720	0825	0925	...	...	...	1010	...	1137	...	...	...	...	1341	1347	1419	1501	...	...	...	...	...
565	**Bilbao** Abando .... **654** a.	|	|	|	...	...	...	1147	...	|	...	...	...	...	1522	|	|	|	...	...	...	...	...
494	Vitoria / Gasteiz .... **654** d.	0747	0857	0952	...	...	...	...	...	1158	...	...	...	...	...	1411	1442	1530	...	...	...	...	...
	Barcelona Sants **653** .... a.	...	|	|	...	...	...	...	...	|	...	...	...	...	...	1903	|	|	...	...	...	...	...
537	Altsasu .... **654** d.	...	0926	1025**n**	...	...	...	...	...	|	...	...	...	...	...	...	1511	1601**n**	...	...	...	...	...
624	**San Sebastián / Donostia** .... ▲ **654** a.	...	1048	...	...	...	...	...	...	1337	1406	...	...	...	...	...	1708	...	...	...	...	...	...
641	**Irún** .... ▲ **654** a.	...	1137	...	...	...	...	...	...	...	1433	...	...	...	...	...	1735	...	...	...	...	...	...
643	Hendaye .... ▲ **654** a.	...	...	...	...	...	...	...	...	...	...	...	...	...	...	...	...	...	...	...	...	...	...

	Alvia	Alvia	IC	IC	MD	MD	MD	IC		IC	MD	RE	MD		RE	Alvia	Alvia	MD	AVE	MD	RE	MD	
	631	621 625	280	282	18063	18063	18306	4257		280	18905	17221	18314	16111	18009	4167	4267	18065	5171	18065	18312	18007	
					2	2	2	2		2	2	2	2	2	2			2	V	2	2	2	
		Q			Ⓑ	⑥		Ⓑ		D	Ⓐ			Z	⑤		H	Ⓑ	Ⓑ	Ⓑ		Ⓑ	
Madrid Chamartín ‡ .... **680 681** d.	...	...	...	...	1226**p**	1226**p**	...	1450	...	...	1340**p**	...	...	...	1455**p**	1738	1738	1712**p**	1954	...	...	2028**p**	...
Ávila .... **680 681** d.	...	...	...	...	1405	1405	...	|	...	...	1510	1535	...	...	1641	|	|	1850	|	...	...	2209	...
Salamanca .... d.	1248	...	...	...	|	|	1400	|	...	...	1619	|	1604	...	|	|	|	|	|	...	2053	|	...
Medina del Campo .... **680 681** d.	1327	...	...	...	1452	1452	1504	|	...	...	...	1624	1644	...	1734	|	|	1938	|	...	2148	2256	...
Valladolid Campo Grande .... **681** d.	1353	...	...	...	1517	1517	1528	1551	...	...	...	1657	1712	...	1806	1844	1844	2006	2049	...	2223	2321	...
Venta de Baños .... **681** d.	|	...	...	...	1542	1542	1605	|	...	...	...	...	...	...	1834	|	|	2031	|	...	...	2347	...
Palencia .... **681** d.	|	1430	...	...	1557	1557	1617	|	...	1655	...	...	...	...	|	|	|	2050	|	←	...	2358	...
Burgos Rosa Manzano .... **681** d.	1502	1505	...	...	1645	1652	...	1639	...	1746	...	...	...	...	1927	1934	1934	2142	2127	2143	...	...	...
Miranda de Ebro .... **654** d.	1602	1602	1625	...	1750	1759	...	1739	...	1850	...	...	...	...	2027	2038	2043	→	...	2239	...	...	...
Bilbao Abando .... **654** a.	|	|	1815	...	|	|	...	|	...	|	...	...	...	...	|	|	2221	...	...	|	...	...	...
Vitoria / Gasteiz .... **654** d.	1632	1632	...	1645	1811	1819	...	1801	...	1911	...	...	...	1900	2050	2100	...	...	...	2300	...	...	...
Barcelona Sants **653** .... a.	2135	2135	...	|	|	|	...	|	...	|	...	...	...	|	...	|	...	...	...	...	...	...	...
Altsasu .... **654** d.	...	...	...	1711	1838	1848	...	|	...	1934	...	...	...	1931**n**	...	|	...	...	...	...	...	...	...
San Sebastián / Donostia .... ▲ **654** a.	...	...	...	1835	1959	2011	...	1942	2010	2051	...	...	...	...	...	2240	...	...	...	...	...	...	...
Irún .... ▲ **654** a.	...	...	...	...	2037	2116	...	...	2037	2116	...	...	...	...	...	2300	...	...	...	...	...	...	...
Hendaye .... ▲ **654** a.	...	...	...	...	...	...	...	...	...	2122	...	...	...	...	...	...	...	...	...	...	...	...	...

km		MD	AVE	MD	IC	MD		MD	Alvia	RE	RE	RE	Alvia	IC	MD	MD	MD	MD	IC	IC	Alvia	Alvia	
		18066	5080	18300	4256	18304		18010	4186	17218	16000	18071	4086	283	18308	18004	18012	18012	281	283	622 626	632	
		2	V	2	2	2	2	2		2	2	Z 2		2	2	2	2	2		2			
		⚒	⚒	Ⓐ	Ⓐ			⚒	J		⚒	⚒		D			⚒	†			Q		
0	**Irún** .... ▲ **654** d.	...	...	...	...	...	...	...	...	...	0551	...	0845	0910	...	...	1023	1023	...	...	...	...	...
17	**San Sebastián / Donostia** .... ▲ **654** d.	...	...	...	0502	...	...	...	...	...	0618	...	0902	0933	...	...	1122	1114	1213	...	...	...	...
104	Altsasu .... **654** d.	...	...	...	|	...	...	...	...	...	0736	0918**n**	|	1046	...	...	1245	1237	1334	...	...	...	...
	Barcelona Sants **653** .... d.	...	...	...	|	...	...	...	...	...	|	|	|	|	...	...	|	|	|	...	0930	0930	...
147	Vitoria / Gasteiz .... **654** d.	...	...	...	0645	...	...	0740	...	...	0808	0950	1043	1108	...	...	1315	1307	1358	...	1419	1419	...
	Bilbao Abando .... **654** d.	...	...	...	|	...	...	|	0700	...	...	|	|	|	...	...	|	|	...	1215	|	|	...
180	Miranda de Ebro .... **654** d.	...	...	...	0706	...	0716	0801	0837	...	...	1016	1105	1140	...	...	1335	1327	...	1404	1441	1500	...
270	**Burgos** Rosa Manzano .... **681** d.	...	0640	...	0803	...	0816	0900	0934	...	...	...	1202	1233	...	...	1432	1435	...	...	1546	1555	...
353	Palencia .... **681** d.	0545	|	...	|	...	...	0959	|	...	...	...	|	1321	1335	...	1524	1533	...	...	1620	|	...
355	Venta de Baños .... **681** d.	0558	|	...	|	...	...	1011	|	...	...	...	|	...	1348	...	1535	1544	...	...	...	|	...
391	**Valladolid** Campo Grande .... **681** d.	0626	0718	0735	0851	0940	...	1038	1022	1300	...	...	1250	...	1419	1424	1602	1610	...	...	...	1701	...
434	Medina del Campo .... **680 681** d.	0652	|	0814	|	1007	...	1105	|	1338	...	...	|	...	1448	1500	1628	1635	...	...	...	1730	...
511	**Salamanca** .... a.	|	|	0911	|	1046	...	|	|	|	...	...	|	...	1548	|	|	|	...	...	...	1810	...
	Ávila .... **680 681** d.	0740	|	...	|	...	...	1155	|	1429	...	...	|	...	...	1547	1718	1721	...	...	...	...	...
	Madrid Chamartín ‡ .... **680 681** a.	0928**p**	0813	...	0957	...	...	1325**p**	1128	...	...	...	1356	...	...	1731**p**	1855**p**	1909**p**	...	...	...	...	...

		RE	MD	RE	Alvia		IC	Alvia	Alvia	RE	RE			Alvia	Alvia	Alvia				RE	RE		
		18322	18014	18318	437		4276	4176	664	17200	18008	16015		4166	4266	4366	17226	16017	16027	16004	16004		
	2	2	2	2			2			2	2	2					2	2 N	2 b	2	2		
		Y					⑦	①–⑥	A		†	N	⑦	⑦	⑦	Ⓐ		⚒	†	Ⓑ	⑥		
Irún .... ▲ **654** d.	...	...	1317	...	...	1437	...	...	...	...	...	...	1617	...	...	...	...	...	...	1916	1954	...	...
San Sebastián / Donostia .... ▲ **654** d.	...	...	1404	...	...	1502	1517	1517	...	...	...	...	1643	1703	...	...	...	...	...	2012	2040	...	...
Altsasu .... **654** d.	...	...	1527	...	...	...	|	|	...	...	...	1715**n**	...	|	...	...	...	2034**n**	2047**n**	2131	2200	...	...
Barcelona Sants **653** .... d.	...	...	|	...	...	...	|	|	1210	...	...	|	...	|	...	...	...	|	|	|	|	...	...
Vitoria / Gasteiz .... **654** d.	...	...	1557	...	...	...	1659	1659	1702	...	1720	1750	...	1845	...	...	...	2107	2119	2205	2234	...	...
Bilbao Abando .... **654** d.	...	...	|	...	1520	...	|	|	|	...	|	|	...	|	1720	1735	...	...	|	|	|	...	...
Miranda de Ebro .... **654** d.	...	...	1617	...	1650	...	1719	1719	1723	...	1744	1817	...	1910	1910	1910	...	...	2144	2230	2259	...	...
Burgos Rosa Manzano .... **681** d.	...	...	1716	...	...	...	1817	1817	1816	...	1843	...	...	2008	2008	2008	...	...	...	...	...	...	...
Palencia .... **681** d.	1633	...	1805	...	...	...	|	|	1904	...	|	...	...	|	|	|	...	...	...	...	...	...	...
Venta de Baños .... **681** d.	1646	...	1817	...	...	...	|	|	...	...	1933	...	...	|	|	|	...	...	...	...	...	...	...
Valladolid Campo Grande .... **681** d.	1720	1734	1845	1856	...	...	1905	1905	...	1948	2005	...	...	2057	2057	2057	2240	...	...	...	...	...	...
Medina del Campo .... **680 681** d.	...	1758	1916	1934	...	...	|	|	...	2025	2040	...	...	|	|	|	2314	...	...	...	...	...	...
Salamanca .... a.	...	...	|	2027	...	...	|	|	...	|	|	...	...	|	|	|	...	...	...	...	...	...	...
Ávila .... **680 681** d.	...	...	2003	...	...	...	|	|	...	2115	2137	...	...	|	|	|	...	...	...	...	...	...	...
Madrid Chamartín ‡ .... **680 681** a.	...	...	2142**p**	...	...	...	2010	2010	...	...	2340**p**	...	...	2203	2203	2203	...	...	...	...	...	...	...

A – 🚃12 Gijón - Barcelona and v.v. (Table **685**).
D – CAMINO DE SANTIAGO – 🚃2 A Coruña - Palencia - Irún / Hendaye and v.v.
H – Ⓑ (daily July 22 - Oct. 12).
J – ⚒ (daily June 18 - Oct. 15).
N – To / from Pamplona (Table **654**).
Q – 🚃12 Vigo / A Coruña - Palencia - Barcelona and v.v. (Table **680**).
V – From / to València (Table **668**).
Y – 🚃2 Puebla de Sanabria - Medina del Campo - Valladolid and v.v. (Table **680**).
Z – To / from Pamplona and Zaragoza (Table **654**).

b – From / to Castejón de Ebro and Pamplona / Iruña (Table **654**
n – Altsasu Pueblo.
p – Madrid **Principe Pio**.

△ – Km's via Ávila.
‡ – Full name is Madrid-Chamartín-Clara Campoamor.

☛ **Shaded services are suspended until further notice.**

▲ – **SAN SEBASTIÁN - IRÚN** and v.v. ***Renfe Cercanías*** (suburban) service. Additional journeys can be made by changing trains at Pasaia. *17 km.* Journey time: ± 27 minutes
From San Sebastián: 0626 ⑦, 0701 ⚒, 0726 Ⓒ, 0751 Ⓐ, 0816 ⑥, 0838 Ⓐ, 0946 ⑦, 0951 ⚒, 1036 ⚒, 1100 ⑦, 1116 ⑥, 1126 ⑦, 1146 Ⓐ, 1218 ⑦, 1226 ⚒, 1346, 1421 ⚒, 1516 ⚒, 1546 1639 Ⓑ, 1648 ⑥, 1743, 1816 ⑦, 1931 ⚒, 1954 ⑦, 2001 ⚒, 2046 ⚒, 2144.
From Irún: 0648 ⚒, 0738 Ⓐ, 0810 ⑥, 0828 Ⓑ, 0928 Ⓑ, 1028 ⚒, 1042 ⑦, 1128 Ⓐ, 1158 Ⓒ, 1218 Ⓐ, 1258 Ⓒ, 1333, 1453, 1535 ⑦, 1618, 1713 ⑦, 1723 ⑥, 1727 Ⓐ, 1733 ⑦, 1813 ⑥ 1858 Ⓑ, 1918, 2033, 2128, 2215.

▲ – **SAN SEBASTIÁN / DONOSTIA** (Amara) - **IRÚN** (Colón, near Renfe station) - **HENDAYE** (SNCF station) and v.v. ***EuskoTren*** (narrow-gauge) service. *22 km.* Journey time: ± 37 mins
From San Sebastián: 0615 Ⓐ, 0645 Ⓐ, 0715, 0745 and every 30 mins until 2215, 2245. **From Hendaye** (⊙): 0533 Ⓐ, 0603 Ⓐ, 0633 Ⓐ, 0703, 0733 and every 30 mins until 2233.
⊙ – 4 minutes later from Irún.

PORTUGAL

SEE MAP PAGE 315

perator: CP – Comboios de Portugal (www.cp.pt).

ain categories: ***Alfa Pendular*** – *AP* – high-quality tilting express trains. ***Intercidades*** – *IC* – high-quality express trains linking the main cities. ***Interregional*** – *IR* – 'semi-fast' links usually calling at principal stations only. ***Celta*** – International services between Porto and Vigo. ***Regional*** and ***Suburbano*** – local stopping trains (shown without train numbers). Higher fares are payable for travel by *AP* and *IC* trains, and there is an additional supplement for travel by *AP* trains.

rvices: All services shown with a train number convey first and second class accommodation (on *Alfa Pendular* trains termed, respectively, *Conforto* and *Turística*) unless otherwise indicated. *Regional* and *Suburbano* trains convey second-class seating only. *AP*, *IC*, *IR* and international trains convey a buffet car (*carruagem-bar*) and there is an at-seat service of meals to passengers in 1st class on *AP* and certain *IC* trains.

servations: Reservations are **compulsory** for travel by *AP*, *IC* and international trains. Seat reservation is not normally available on other services.

mings: Timings are the latest received. Amendments to timetables may come into effect at short notice, especially during the Christmas and New Year period.

LISBOA - COIMBRA - PORTO 690

Subject to alteration on and around public holidays (see page 4). Reservations are compulsory on *AP* and *IC* trains. Local trains Aveiro - Porto run approx hourly.

km		*IR*	*IC*	*AP*	*AP*	*AP*	*IC*	*AP*	*IC*	*AP*	*AP*	*IR*	*IC*		*AP*	*IC*	*AP*	*IC*	*IC*	*AP*	*AP*	*IC*		*IC*
		831	**521**	**131**	**121**	**123**	**721**	**182**	**621**	**125**	**133**	**821**	**523**		**135**	**525**	**127**	**527**	**731**	**137**	**186**	**723**		**529**
			①–⑥			Ⓐ				⚒		⑤			Ⓑ	⑤		⑥	Ⓑ				Ⓑ	
		⊡		△			△	♧	☆		△				△				⊡	△	♧	△		
0	**Lisboa** S Apolónia ▷ d.	...	0630	0700	0800	0900	0930	...	1130	1200	1400	...	1530	...	1600	1630	1700	1730	1730	1800	...	1930	...	2200
7	**Lisboa** Oriente ▷ d.	...	0639	0709	0809	0909	0939	1009	1139	1209	1409	...	1539	...	1609	1639	1709	1739	1739	1809	1909	1939	...	2209
31	Vila Franca de Xira ▷ d.	...	0652	|	|	|	0952	|	1152	|	|	...	1552	...	|	1652	|	1752	1752	|	|	1952	...	2222
75	Santarém ▷ d.	...	0713	|	0839	|	1013	|	1213	|	|	...	1613	...	|	1713	|	1813	1813	|	|	2013	...	2243
07	**Entroncamento** ▷ d.	...	0733	|	0858	|	1033	|	1233	|	|	1405	1630	...	|	1733	|	1833	1833	|	|	2033	2127	2303
40	Caxarias ▷ d.	...	|	|	|	|	1051	|	|	|	|	1428	|	...	|	1751	|	1851	1851	|	|	|	2157	2321
71	Pombal ▷ d.	...	0805	|	0927	|	1108	|	1306	|	|	1448	1706	...	|	1808	|	1908	1908	|	|	2105	2220	2338
99	Alfarelos ▷ d.	...	|	|	|	|	|	|	1320	|	|	1505	1720	...	|	|	|	|	|	|	|	|	2243	|
218	**Coimbra** B ▷ d.	0725	0830	0844	0950	1044	1132	1144	1333	1344	1544	1519	1733	...	1744	1832	1844	1932	1932	1944	2044	2130	2307	0002
232	Pampilhosa ▷ d.	0736	|	|	|	|	|	|	1343	|	|	1530	1743	...	|	|	|	|	|	|	|	|	2319	|
273	Aveiro ▷ d.	0803	0900	0911	1016	1111	1200	1211	1402	1411	1611	1603	1802	...	1811	1900	1911	2000	2000	2011	2111	2200	2352	0030
318	Espinho d.	0831	0924	|	1037	|	1224	|	1424	|	|	1640	1824	...	|	1924	|	2024	2024	|	|	2224	0021	0054
334	Vila Nova de Gaia d.	0849	0940	0947	1052	1146	1241	1246	1441	1446	1647	1659	1840	...	1847	1940	1946	2040	2040	2047	2146	2241	0040	0110
337	**Porto** Campanhã a.	0900	0953	1000	1105	1158	1255	1258	1455	1458	1700	1711	1852	...	1900	1953	1958	2053	2053	2100	2158	2255	0052	0123

			AP	*AP*	*IC*	*IC*	*IC*	*AP*	*IC*	*AP*	*IC*	*AP*	*AP*		*IC*	*AP*	*IC*	*AP*	*IC*	*AP*	*IC*	*IR*	*IR*	*AP*
			180	**130**	**520**	**522**	**730**	**120**	**720**	**122**	**524**	**132**	**184**		**722**	**124**	**526**	**126**	**620**	**134**	**528**	**820**	**830**	**136**
		①–⑥			①–⑥	⑦	①–⑥	⚒		Ⓑ							⑦	Ⓑ				⑦		Ⓑ
			♧	△			⊡		△			△	♧		△				☆	△			⊡	△
	orto Campanhã d.	0100	0532	0632	0637	0837	0837	0932	1038	1132	1237	1332	1432	...	1438	1632	1637	1732	1737	1832	1937	1944	2015	2032
	a Nova de Gaia d.	0106	0537	0637	0642	0842	0842	0937	1043	1137	1242	1337	1437	...	1443	1637	1642	1737	1742	1837	1942	1949	2021	2037
	spinho d.	0135	|	|	0702	0902	0902	|	1103	|	1302	|	|	...	1503	|	1702	1756	1802	|	2002	2010	2041	|
	eiro ▷ d.	0217	0620	0720	0731	0931	0931	1020	1130	1220	1331	1420	1520	...	1530	1720	1731	1821	1831	1920	2031	2044	2126	2120
	ampilhosa ▷ d.	0247	|	|	|	|	|	|	1148	|	|	|	|	...	1548	|	|	|	|	|	|	2109	2154	|
	oimbra B ▷ d.	0257	0646	0746	0800	0959	0959	1046	1200	1246	1359	1446	1546	...	1600	1746	1759	1845	1859	1946	2059	2120	2205	2146
	farelos ▷ d.	0311	|	|	|	|	|	|	1212	|	|	|	|	...	1612	|	|	|	|	|	|	2133	...	|
	ombal ▷ d.	0330	|	|	0826	1024	1024	|	1226	|	1424	|	|	...	1626	|	1824	1909	1924	|	2124	2150	...	|
	axarias ▷ d.	0350	|	|	|	1040	1040	|	|	|	1440	|	|	...	|	|	1840	|	1940	|	2140	|	...	|
	ntroncamento ▷ d.	0415	|	|	0859	1059	1059	|	1259	|	1459	|	|	...	1659	|	1859	1940	1959	|	2159	2236	...	|
	antarém ▷ d.	0442	|	|	0919	1119	1119	|	1319	|	1519	|	|	...	1719	|	1919	1959	2019	|	2219	2258	...	|
	a Franca de Xira ▷ d.	0525	|	|	0939	1139	1139	|	1339	|	1539	|	|	...	1739	|	1939	|	2039	|	2239	2326	...	|
	sboa Oriente ▷ a.	0552	0823	0922	0952	1152	1152	1222	1352	1422	1552	1622	1723	...	1752	1922	1952	2032	2052	2122	2252	2343	...	2322
	sboa S Apolónia ▷ a.	0600	...	0930	1000	1200	1200	1230	1400	1430	1600	1630	...	...	1800	1930	2000	2040	2100	2130	2300	2350	...	2330

– Lisboa - Porto - Braga and v.v. (Table **695**).
– Lisboa - Porto - Guimarães and v.v. (Table **695a**).
⊡ – To / from Valença (Table **696**).
♧ – Faro - Lisboa - Porto and v.v. (Table **697**).
▷ – See also Tables **691**, **692**, **699**.

inha da Beira Baixa

LISBOA - ENTRONCAMENTO - COVILHÃ - GUARDA 691

Subject to alteration on and around public holidays (see page 4). Reservations are compulsory on *IC* trains.

km					*IC* **541**		*IC* **543**			*IC* **545**	
		Ⓐ									
0	**Lisboa** Sta Apolónia ▷ d.	0550	...	...	0815	_0945_	1315	1615	_1745_	1915	_1945_
7	**Lisboa** Oriente ▷ d.	0558	...	...	0823	_0953_	1323	1623	_1753_	1923	_1953_
31	Vila Franca de Xira ▷ d.	0616	...	...	0838	_1011_	1338	1639	_1811_	1938	_2011_
75	Santarém ▷ d.	0653	...	...	0904	_1054_	1404	1706	_1854_	2004	_2054_
07	**Entroncamento** ▷ a.	0719	...	...	0923	_1120_	1425	1728	_1920_	2025	_2120_
07	**Entroncamento** d.	...	...	0746	0924	1128	1426	1729	1936	2026	2154
35	Abrantes d.	...	...	0817	0945	1204	1446	1804	2009	2046	2230
99	Ródão d.	...	...	0921	1043	1304	1536	1904	2113	2143	...
29	Castelo Branco a.	...	...	0949	1106	1332	1605	1938	2141	2206	...
29	Castelo Branco d.	...	0644	0954	1107	1439	1606	1945	...	2207	...
83	Fundaõ d.	...	0732	1042	1142	1533	1641	2033	...	2242	...
01	**Covilhã** a.	...	0748	1058	1156	1549	1655	2049	...	2256	...
01	**Covilhã** d.	...	0800	...	1204	1550	1656	...	...	2257	...
47	**Guarda** a.	...	0844	...	1257	1634	1742	...	...	2343	...

				IC **540**			*IC* **542**			*IC* **544**
	①	Ⓐ	①–⑥							
Guarda d.	...	...	...	0707	...	1159	1407	...	1743	1807
Covilhã a.	...	...	...	0752	...	1242	1452	...	1826	1852
Covilhã d.	0450	...	...	0753	0850	1256	1453	...	1827	1853
Fundaõ d.	0506	...	...	0807	0906	1312	1507	...	1843	1907
Castelo Branco a.	0553	...	...	0842	0953	1401	1542	...	1931	1942
Castelo Branco d.	...	...	0556	0843	1010	1403	1543	1817	...	1943
Ródão d.	...	...	0624	0907	1043	1431	1607	1846	...	2007
Abrantes d.	...	0540	0721	1002	1141	1535	1701	1949	...	2101
Entroncamento a.	...	0613	0758	1020	1217	1606	1720	2021	...	2120
Entroncamento ▷ d.	...	_0625_	0807	1021	_1236_	_1636_	1721	_2041_	...	2121
Santarém ▷ d.	...	_0647_	0829	1041	_1303_	_1703_	1741	_2108_	...	2141
Vila Franca de Xira ▷ d.	...	_0717_	0856	1101	_1347_	_1747_	1801	_2147_	...	2201
Lisboa Oriente ▷ a.	...	_0734_	0912	1113	_1406_	_1806_	1813	_2206_	...	2213
Lisboa Sta Apolónia ▷ a.	...	_0741_	0920	1120	_1413_	_1813_	1820	_2213_	...	2220

km			
0	**Entroncamento** d.	0928	1336
28	Abrantes d.	0959	1407
110	Portalegre d.	1115	1528
159	Elvas 🏛 d.	1159	1612
169	**Badajoz** 🏛 ⊙ a.	1313	1726

Badajoz 🏛 ⊙ d.	1409	1941
Elvas 🏛 d.	1325	1857
Portalegre d.	1410	1942
Abrantes d.	1521	2052
Entroncamento a.	1552	2137

⊙ – Spanish time (one hour ahead of Portugal).
▷ – See also Tables **690**, **692**, **699**.

inha da Beira Alta

LISBOA - COIMBRA - GUARDA - VILAR FORMOSO 692

Subject to alteration on and around public holidays (see page 4). Reservations are compulsory on *IC* trains. Local trains run Coimbra B - Coimbra and v.v.

km		*IC* **511**	🚌	🚌	🚌	*IC* **513**	🚌	🚌	🚌	🚌	*IC* **515**
				⚒			Ⓐ	Ⓑ			
	Lisboa S Apolónia ▷ d.	0730	...	...	...	1230	...	...	...	...	1830
	Lisboa Oriente ▷ d.	0739	...	...	...	1239	...	...	...	...	1839
	Vila Franca de Xira ▷ d.	0752	...	...	...	1252	...	...	...	...	1852
	Santarém ▷ d.	0813	...	...	...	1313	...	...	...	...	1913
	Entroncamento ▷ d.	0833	...	...	...	1333	...	...	...	...	1933
	Fátima ✣ d.	0846	...	...	...	1346	...	...	...	...	1946
	Caxarias d.	0853	...	...	...	1353	...	...	...	...	1953
	Pombal d.	0910	...	...	...	1410	...	...	...	...	2010
	Alfarelos d.	0924	...	...	...	1424	...	...	...	...	2024
0	**Coimbra** d.	|	...	1216	1216	|	1615	1615	1826	1826	|
2	**Coimbra** B d.	0935	...	1225	1225	1435	1625	1625	1835	1835	2035
16	Pampilhosa d.	|	...	|	1245	|	|	1645	|	1855	|
51	Santa Comba Dão d.	_1030_*	...	1325	1340	_1530_*	1725	1740	1935	1950	_2130_*
83	Nelas d.	_1055_*	...	1400	1425	_1555_*	1800	1830	2010	2040	_2155_*
95	Mangualde d.	_1115_*	...	1420	1445	_1615_*	1820	1850	2030	2100	_2215_*
71	**Guarda** ● a.	_1215_*	1300	1520	1600	_1715_*	1920	2005	2130	2230	_2315_*
218	Vilar Formoso 🏛 ● a.	...	1420	...	...	...	...	...	...	...	...

	🚌	🚌	🚌	*IC* **510**	🚌	*IC* **512**	🚌	🚌		*IC* **514**
	⚒		⚒				⑦	①–⑥	⑦	
Vilar Formoso 🏛 ● d.	...	...	0515	...	...	...	...	...	...	...
Guarda ● d.	0415	0600	0635	_0640_*	0900	_1210_*	1515	1530	_1545_*	_1740_*
Mangualde d.	0530	0715	...	_0740_*	1030	_1310_*	1645	1645	_1655_*	_1840_*
Nelas d.	0550	0735	...	_0800_*	1050	_1330_*	1705	1705	_1715_*	_1900_*
Santa Comba Dão d.	0640	0810	...	_0825_*	1140	_1355_*	1750	1750	_1750_*	_1925_*
Pampilhosa d.	0735	|	...	|	1235	|	1845	1845	|	|
Coimbra B d.	0750	0910	...	0921	1250	1454	1900	1900	1914	2020
Coimbra a.	0800	...	...	|	1300	|	...	1910	|	|
Alfarelos d.	...	...	...	0937	...	1506	...	...	1928	2035
Pombal d.	...	...	...	0951	...	1521	...	...	1945	2049
Caxarias d.	...	...	...	1007	...	1538	...	...	2005	2106
Fátima ✣ d.	...	...	...	1014	...	1545	...	...	2012	2114
Entroncamento ▷ d.	...	...	...	1028	...	1559	...	...	2036	2128
Santarém ▷ d.	...	...	...	1048	...	1619	...	...	2059	2148
Vila Franca de Xira ▷ d.	...	...	...	1109	...	1639	...	...	2126	2209
Lisboa Oriente ▷ a.	...	...	...	1122	...	1652	...	...	2143	2222
Lisboa S Apolónia ▷ a.	...	...	...	1130	...	1700	...	...	2150	2230

– Also from Guarda at 1805 🚌; also from Vilar Formoso at 0735 † 🚌, 1615 🚌.
– See also Tables **690**, **691**, **699**.
✣ – Chão de Maçãs - Fátima (*20 km* from Fátima).
* – By 🚌.

693 LISBOA - CALDAS DA RAINHA - FIGUEIRA DA FOZ and COIMBRA *Linha do Oeste*

For connecting suburban services Lisboa - Mira Sintra - Meleças see Table **699**.

km								*IR* **811**	*IR* **813**		
								Ⓐ	Ⓒ		
	Lisboa Santa Apolónia d.	0535	...	...	1150	...	...	1653	1653	...	...
0	Entrecampos d.	0545	...	...	1201	...	...	1703	1703	...	...
2	Sete Rios d.	0549	...	...	1204	...	...	1707	1707	...	...
15	Agualva - Cacém d.	0604	...	...	1221	...	...	1725	1725	...	...
19	Mira Sintra - Meleças d.	0609	0735	0927	1227	...	1408	1730	1730	1833	1930
65	Torres Vedras d.	0720	0836	1027	1327	1415	1511	1821	1821	1935	2031
88	Bombarral d.	0746	0859	1049	1354	1438	1533	1843	1843	2002	2053
107	**Caldas da Rainha** a.	0808	0921	1111	1416	1459	1555	1859	1859	2023	2115

		IR **810**								
Caldas da Rainha d.	0520	0621	0725	1116	1230	...	1316	1616	1735	192
Bombarral d.	0541	0638	0747	1138	1252	...	1337	1638	1756	194
Torres Vedras d.	0603	0700	0809	1200	1313	...	1400	1700	1820	200
Mira Sintra - Meleças d.	0703	0754	0916	1302	...	...	1502	1803	1923	211
Agualva - Cacém d.	...	0758	...	...	...	...	1507	...	...	211
Sete Rios a.	...	0813	...	...	...	...	1523	...	...	213
Entrecampos a.	...	0816	...	...	...	...	1527	...	...	213
Lisboa S Apolónia a.	...	0830	...	...	...	...	1541	...	...	214

km		*IR* **801**			*IR* **803**				*IR* **805**		
		①–⑥						⊡			
0	**Caldas da Rainha** d.	0613	...	0830	1115	...	1420	...	1612	...	1906
12	São Martinho do Porto d.	0621	...	0841	1123	...	1430	...	1620	...	1916
46	Marinha Grande d.	0650	...	0920	1152	...	1503	...	1649	...	1949
56	Leiria d.	0658	...	0928	1200	...	1511	...	1657	...	1957
109	Verride a.	0743	...	...	1245	...	|	...	1743	...	2042
109	Verride d.	0744	0752	...	1248	1348	|	1624	1748	1748	2047
123	Bifurcação de Lares a.	|	0759	...	|	1355	1553	1615	|	1755	|
129	**Figueira da Foz** a.	|	0811	...	|	1409	1601	|	|	1809	|
117	Alfarelos d.	0752	...	...	1257	...	...	1634	1756	...	2056
136	**Coimbra** B a.	0805	...	...	1310	...	...	1701	1812	...	2113

			IR **800**			*IR* **802**				*IC* **804**
	●						Ⓐ⊡			Ⓑ
Coimbra B d.	0515	...	0852	...	...	1350	1608	...	...	193
Alfarelos d.	0530	...	0907	...	...	1405	1636	...	...	195
Figueira da Foz d.	|	0858	|	...	1358	|	|	1717	1858	|
Bifurcação de Lares d.	|	0911	|	...	1411	|	1655	1726	1911	|
Verride a.	0537	0918	0915	...	1418	1413	1646	|	1918	195
Verride d.	0537	...	0921	...	...	1419	...	|	...	195
Leiria d.	0623	...	1009	1213	...	1510	...	1813	...	210
Marinha Grande d.	0634	...	1019	1224	...	1519	...	1823	...	210
São Martinho do Porto d.	0711	...	1046	1256	...	1547	...	1854	...	212
Caldas da Rainha a.	0723	...	1055	1308	...	1557	...	1905	...	213

LOCAL TRAINS **FIGUEIRA DA FOZ - COIMBRA**

km		⚒	Ⓐ	A		⚒	Ⓐ																	
0	**Figueira da Foz** d.	0558	0630	0647	...	0656	0736	0858	...	0958	1058	1158	...	1258	1358	1458	...	1602	1658	1758	...	1858	1958	215
8	Bifurcação de Lares d.	0610	0640	|	...	0709	0746	0911	...	1014	1111	1211	...	1311	1411	1511	...	1615	1714	1811	...	1911	2011	220
20	Verride d.	0619	0648	|	...	0718	0753	0920	...	1022	1120	1220	...	1320	1420	1520	...	1624	1722	1820	...	1920	2020	221
28	Alfarelos **699** d.	0630	0658	0707	...	0731	0803	0939	...	1034	1134	1233	...	1334	1433	1535	...	1634	1734	1834	...	1933	2034	222
47	**Coimbra** B **699** a.	0657	0716	0720	...	0758	0820	1006	...	1101	1200	1300	...	1400	1500	1601	...	1701	1800	1900	...	2000	2101	225
49	**Coimbra** **699** a.	0706	0725	...	...	0810	0834	1015	...	1110	1210	1309	...	1410	1509	1612	...	1710	1810	1913	...	2009	2110	230

		⚒			Ⓐ								Ⓐ			Ⓑ	Ⓐ			A		
Coimbra **699** d.	0016	0525	0655	...	0755	0855	0952	...	1158	1300	1358	...	1455	1600	1658	...	1758	1904	1954	...	...	...	223
Coimbra B **699** d.	0025	0533	0703	...	0803	0903	1001	...	1206	1308	1406	...	1503	1608	1706	...	1806	1914	2002	...	2206	...	224
Alfarelos **699** d.	0055	0602	0731	...	0834	0939	1034	...	1235	1336	1435	...	1535	1636	1735	...	1835	1934	2036	...	2225	...	231
Verride d.	0106	0617	0752	...	0849	0952	1047	...	1248	1348	1448	...	1551	1648	1748	...	1848	1942	2047	...	|	...	232
Bifurcação de Lares d.	0114	0625	0759	...	0856	0959	1054	...	1255	1355	1455	...	1559	1655	1755	...	1855	|	2055	...	|	...	233
Figueira da Foz a.	0126	0640	0811	...	0909	1013	1109	...	1309	1409	1509	...	1613	1709	1809	...	1909	1956	2107	...	2244	...	234

A – (2) Valença - Porto - Figueira da Foz and v.v. (trains *IR* **830** / **831**).

⊡ – Calling order is Bifurcação de Lares - Verride - Alfarelos - Coimbra B and v.v.

● – Runs up to 9 minutes later Alfarelos - São Martinho do Porto on ②–⑥.

694 PORTO - RÉGUA - TUA - POCINHO *Linha do Douro*

km				*IR* **861**	*IR* **21861**		*IR* **865**			*IR* **867**		*IR* **869**					*IR* **871**	*IR* **873**	*IR* **875**				*IR* **877**	
		⚒	⚒		⑥⑦								H											
0	**Porto** São Bento ◧ d.	0630	...		0820	...	0920	0930	...		...	1320	...	1330	...	...	1520	...		...	1830	...	1920	222
3	**Porto** Campanhã ◧ d.	0635	...	0725	0825	...	0925	0935	...	1125	...	1325	...	1335	...	...	1525	...	1725	...	1835	...	1925	222
12	Ermesinde ◧ d.	0647	...	0736	0836	...	0936	0947	...	1136	...	1336	...	1347	...	...	1536	...	1736	...	1847	...	1936	223
50	Caíde ◧ d.	0722	...	0812	0911	...	1009	1023	...	1212	...	1409	...	1422	...	...	1609	...	1816	...	1922	...	2008	231
59	Livração ◧ d.	0734	...	0822	0920	...	1019	1034	...	1221	...	1419	...	1437	...	...	1619	...	1826	...	1936	...	2017	232
64	Marco de Canaveses ◧ d.	0739	0743	0828	0926	...	1025	1042	1050	1228	...	1426	...	1442	...	1450	1625	...	1832	...	1942	1950	2023	233
107	**Régua** a.	...	0836	0916	1019	...	1111	...	1150	1316	...	1514	...	...	...	1548	1711	...	1923	...	...	2045	2108	002
107	**Régua** d.	...	...	0918	1020	...	1112	...	...	...	...	1516	1528	...	...	...	...	1717	1927	...	...	...	...	...
130	Pinhão d.	...	...	0946	1047	...	1138	...	...	...	...	1543	1615	...	...	...	...	1743	1954	...	...	...	...	...
143	Tua d.	...	...	1001	1103	...	1155	...	...	...	...	1559	1635	...	...	...	...	1759	2010	...	...	...	...	...
175	**Pocinho** a.	...	...	1045	1150	...	1238	...	...	...	...	1641	...	...	...	...	...	1841	2053	...	...	...	...	...

		IR **860**	*IR* **862**				*IR* **864**	*IR* **866**				*IR* **868**	*IR* **21860**		*IR* **874**					*IR* **876**			
				⚒									⑥⑦					H					
Pocinho d.	...	...	0708	...	...	...	...	1108	...	...	...	1308	1512	...	...	...	...	...	...	1714	1926	...	...
Tua d.	...	...	0750	...	...	...	...	1153	...	...	...	1350	1604	...	...	...	...	1706	...	1758	2009	...	...
Pinhão d.	...	...	0806	...	...	...	...	1209	...	...	...	1406	1621	...	...	...	...	1750	...	1814	2024	...	...
Régua a.	...	...	0832	...	...	...	...	1235	...	...	...	1433	1648	...	...	...	...	1826	...	1839	2050	...	...
Régua d.	0530	0648	0837	0917	...		1049	1236	1317	...	...	1434	1649	...	1712	1808	...	...	...	1840	...	2109	...
Marco de Canaveses ◧ d.	0625	0739	0925	1013	...	1014	1139	1325	1412	...	1414	1524	1740	...	1759	1906	1913	...	...	1928	...	2205	220
Livração ◧ d.	0634	0745	0936	...	...	1020	1145	1335	...	...	1420	1535	1746	...	1805	...	1919	...	...	1935	...	...	221
Caíde ◧ d.	0647	0755	0947	...	...	1037	1155	1347	...	...	1437	1547	1758	...	1816	...	1934	...	...	1945	...	...	222
Ermesinde ◧ d.	0725	0829	1021	...	...	1114	1227	1421	...	...	1514	1626	1836	...	1849	...	2010	...	...	2017	...	...	231
Porto Campanhã ◧ a.	0735	0839	1030	...	...	1125	1235	1430	...	...	1525	1635	1845	...	1900	...	2020	...	...	2025	...	...	232
Porto São Bento ◧ a.	...	0845	...	...	...	1130	1240	...	...	...	1530	...	1850	...	1905	...	2025	...	...	2030	...	...	233

H – COMBOIO HISTORICO – 2022 dates: ⑥ June 4 - Oct. 29 (also ⑦ July 3 - Oct. 9). Steam-hauled tourist train. Ⓡ. Special fare payable.

◧ – Local trains run hourly Porto São Bento - Marco de Canaveses and v.v.

695 PORTO - BRAGA

Subject to alteration on and around public holidays (see page 4). Reservations are compulsory on *AP* and *IC* trains. Additional local trains run on Ⓐ.

km						*AP* **131**				*IC* **721**					*AP* **133**				*AP* **135**				*AP* **137**		*IC* **723**	
																		Ⓐ	Ⓑ							
	Lisboa Sta Ap. **690**. d.	...	...	...	...	0700	...	...	...	0930	...	...	...	...	1400	...	...	...	1600	...	...	...	1800	...	1930	...
0	**Porto** São Bento **696** d.	0050	0645	0745	0845	|	1000	1045	1145	|	1240	1345	1455	1545	|	1645	1740	1815	|	1840	1915	1945	|	2105	|	230
3	**Porto** Campanhã **696** d.	0055	0650	0750	0850	1000	1005	1050	1150	1255	1245	1350	1500	1550	1700	1650	1745	1820	1900	1845	1920	1950	2100	2110	2255	231
12	Ermesinde **696** d.	0107	0702	0802	0902	|	1018	1102	1202	|	1304	1402	1512	1602	|	1709	1757	1832	|	1857	1932	2002	|	2122	|	232
26	Trofa **696** d.	0120	0716	0816	0916	|	1032	1116	1216	|	1320	1416	1526	1616	|	1725	1811	1844	|	1908	1946	2016	|	2136	|	233
35	Famalicão **696** d.	0128	0727	0827	0927	1021	1043	1127	1227	1317	1331	1427	1537	1627	1721	1736	1822	1852	1921	1923	1957	2027	2121	2147	2317	234
42	Nine **696** d.	0133	0735	0835	0935	1026	1051	1135	1235	1323	1339	1435	1545	1635	1726	1744	1830	1857	1926	1932	2002	2035	2126	2155	2323	235
57	**Braga** a.	0153	0756	0856	0956	1037	1112	1156	1257	1333	1359	1456	1606	1656	1737	1804	1851	1909	1937	1953	2014	2056	2137	2216	2333	001

		AP **130**							*IC* **720**				*AP* **132**		*IC* **722**					*AP* **134**			*AP* **136**		
				Ⓐ	Ⓒ																		Ⓑ		
Braga d.	0434	0554	0629	0721	0734	0804	0834	0937	0959	1039	1134	1229	1254	1337	1359	1439	1534	1644	1735	1754	1834	1935	1954	2039	233
Nine **696** d.	0454	0604	0649	0733	0754	0824	0854	0957	1010	1059	1154	1249	1304	1357	1410	1459	1554	1704	1755	1804	1854	1955	2004	2059	235
Famalicão **696** d.	0502	0609	0657	0738	0802	0832	0902	1005	1015	1107	1202	1257	1309	1405	1415	1507	1602	1712	1811	1809	1902	2011	2009	2107	235
Trofa **696** d.	0513	|	0708	0746	0813	0844	0913	1016	|	1118	1213	1308	|	1416	|	1518	1613	1723	1823	|	1913	2023	|	2118	000
Ermesinde **696** d.	0529	|	0729	0759	0834	0859	0929	1039	|	1134	1229	1329	|	1439	|	1533	1629	1739	1839	|	1929	2039	|	2133	001
Porto Campanhã **696** a.	0541	0632	0741	0811	0846	0911	0941	1051	1038	1146	1241	1341	1332	1451	1438	1545	1641	1751	1851	1832	1941	2051	2032	2145	003
Porto São Bento **696** a.	0545	|	0745	0815	0850	0915	0945	1055	|	1150	1245	1345	|	1455	|	1550	1645	1755	1855	|	1945	2055	|	2150	003
Lisboa Sta Ap. **690** a.	...	0930	...	...	...	...	...	...	1400	...	...	...	1630	...	1800	...	...	...	...	2130	...	...	2330	...	...

PORTO - GUIMARÃES 695a

0 km

							IC 621				
			Ⓐ							Ⓐ	
Lisboa Sta Ap. **690** . d.	...	...	...	...	...	...	1130	...	...	...	...
rto São Bento ... ▷ d.	0725	0825	0925	1025	1225	1420	|	1620	1825	1910	2020
rto Campanhã ... ▷ d.	0730	0830	0930	1030	1230	1425	1455	1625	1830	1915	2025
mesinde .... ▷ d.	0742	0842	0940	1042	1242	1437	|	1637	1842	1925	2037
ofa .... ▷ d.	0757	0857	0951	1057	1257	1452	1514	1652	1857	1936	2052
uimarães .... a.	0837	0941	1027	1138	1341	1532	1549	1744	1943	2009	2138

								IC 620			
	Ⓐ	Ⓐ							Ⓐ	Ⓐ	
Guimarães .... d.	0553	0702	0853	0953	1153	1353	1553	1641	1813	2020	2148
Trofa .... ▷ d.	0633	0739	0933	1036	1233	1433	1633	1716	1900	2105	2229
Ermesinde .... ▷ d.	0649	0751	0949	1053	1249	1449	1649	|	1918	2122	2247
Porto Campanhã ... ▷ a.	0701	0801	1001	1106	1301	1501	1701	1737	1931	2136	2301
Porto São Bento ... ▷ a.	0705	0805	1005	1110	1305	1505	1705	|	1935	2140	2305
Lisboa Sta Ap. **690** . a.	...	...	...	...	...	...	...	2100	...	...	...

her trains: **Porto - Guimarães** at 0620 Ⓐ, 1125 Ⓐ, 1725 Ⓐ, 1925 Ⓐ, 2120 Ⓒ, 2225 Ⓐ, 2320; **Guimarães - Porto** at 0653 Ⓒ, 0802 Ⓐ, 1253 Ⓐ, 1707 Ⓐ, 1758 Ⓒ, 1921 Ⓐ, 1953 Ⓒ, 2247.

– See also Tables **695** and **696**.

PORTO - VIANA DO CASTELO - VALENÇA - VIGO 696

inha do Minho

km																									
		IR 851					421	*IR* 831			*IR* 853					*IR* 855			*IR* 857	423				*IC* 731	
			Ⓐ			①–⑥	C	D					Ⓐ							C				Ⓑ	
	Lisboa Sta Apolónia **690** .. d.	...	...	...	...	...	...	...	...	...	...	...	...	...	...	...	...	...	...	...	...	...	...	1730	...
	Coimbra B **690** .... d.	...	...	...	...	...	...	0725	...	...	...	...	...	...	...	...	...	...	...	...	...	...	...	1932	...
0	**Porto** São Bento .... **695** d.	...	0615	...	0645	...	...	|	1000	...	1305	1345	...	1455	...	...	1645	...	...	...	1915	...	...	|	...
3	**Porto** Campanhã .... **695** d.	0605	0620	...	0650	...	0813	0901	1005	...	1310	1350	...	1500	...	1610	1650	...	1815	1910	1920	...	...	2103	2210
15	Ermesinde .... **695** d.	0615	0632	...	0702	...	|	0910	1018	...	1321	1402	...	1512	...	1621	1709	...	1825	|	1932	...	...	|	2220
26	Trofa .... **695** d.	0625	0644	...	0716	...	|	0924	1032	...	1332	1416	...	1526	...	1631	1725	...	1835	|	1946	...	...	2122	2231
35	Famalicão .... **695** d.	0632	0652	...	0727	...	|	0935	1043	...	1340	1427	...	1537	...	1638	1736	...	1842	|	1957	...	...	2129	2238
42	**Nine** .... **695** a.	0637	0656	...	0735	...	0842	0944	1051	...	1345	1435	...	1545	...	1643	1743	...	1848	1939	2002	...	...	2134	2243
42	**Nine** .... d.	0638	...	0659	...	0746	0842	0952	...	1054	1346	...	1503	...	1558	1644	...	1746	1849	1940	...	2006	...	2135	2244
54	Barcelos .... d.	0647	...	0711	...	0804	|	1002	...	1106	1355	...	1515	...	1610	1653	...	1758	1858	|	...	2017	...	2145	2300
85	**Viana do Castelo** .... d.	0725	...	0804	...	0850	0916	1038	...	1145	1427	...	1556	...	1650	1723	...	1840	1932	2014	...	2058	2131	2216	2336
19	Vila Nova de Cerveira .... d.	0752	...	0847	...	...	|	1107	...	1223	1500	...	...	...	1727	1751	...	1917	2004	|	...	...	2208	2241	...
33	**Valença** .... 🏛 PT d.	0802	...	0900	...	...	0957	1116	...	1236	1510	...	...	...	1740	1800	...	1930	2014	2050	...	...	2221	2250	...
37	Tui .... 🏛 ES d.	...	...	...	...	...	|	...	...	...	...	...	...	...	...	...	...	...	...	|	...	...	...	...	...
65	Redondela **680** .... d.	...	...	...	...	...	|	...	...	...	...	...	...	...	...	...	...	...	...	|	...	...	...	...	...
77	**Vigo** Guixar **680** .... a.	...	...	...	...	...	1135	...	...	...	...	...	...	...	...	...	...	...	...	2234	...	...	...	...	...

					IC 730	*IR* 850	420			*IR* 852						*IR* 854					*IR* 830		422	*IR* 856
			①–⑥		①–⑥		C							Ⓐ							D		C	
go Guixar **680** .... d.	...	...	...	...	...	...	0858	...	...	...	...	...	...	...	...	...	...	...	...	...	...	...	1956	...
edondela **680** .... d.	...	...	...	...	...	...	|	...	...	...	...	...	...	...	...	...	...	...	...	...	...	...	|	...
i .... 🏛 ES d.	...	...	...	...	...	...	|	...	...	...	...	...	...	...	...	...	...	...	...	...	...	...	|	...
lença .... 🏛 PT d.	...	...	...	0549	0650	0721	0836	...	...	0926	1140	...	1245	...	...	1425	1448	...	...	...	1802	1834	1933	2023
a Nova de Cerveira .... d.	...	...	...	0602	0700	0731	|	...	...	0939	1153	...	1258	...	...	1435	1502	...	...	...	1812	1847	|	2038
ana do Castelo .... d.	0511	...	0559	0642	0726	0803	0917	0941	...	1009	1236	...	1337	1348	...	1508	1608	...	1755	...	1848	1931	2014	2109
rcelos .... d.	0548	...	0634	0733	0754	0832	|	1021	...	1038	1314	...	...	1429	...	1538	1654	...	1834	...	1929	...	|	2145
ne .... a.	0600	...	0652	0744	0802	0840	0950	1033	...	1046	1326	...	...	1441	...	1547	1707	...	1846	...	1937	...	2048	2155
ne .... **695** d.	...	0649	...	0745	0803	0841	0951	...	1059	1047	...	1357	...	...	1459	1548	...	1755	...	1854	1938	...	2048	2156
malicão .... **695** d.	...	0657	...	0751	0810	0847	|	...	1107	1053	...	1405	...	...	1507	1554	...	1811	...	1902	1944	...	|	2203
ofa .... **695** d.	...	0708	...	0758	0817	0854	|	...	1118	1100	...	1416	...	...	1518	1601	...	1823	...	1913	1951	...	|	2210
mesinde .... **695** d.	...	0729	...	0810	|	0906	|	...	1134	1112	...	1439	...	...	1533	1612	...	1839	...	1929	2002	...	|	2220
rto Campanhã .... **695** a.	...	0740	...	0820	0834	0915	1020	...	1145	1120	...	1450	...	...	1544	1620	...	1850	...	1940	2010	...	2118	2230
rto São Bento .... **695** a.	...	0745	...	0825	|	...	...	...	1150	1125	...	1455	...	...	1550	...	...	1855	...	1945	|	...	...	...
Coimbra B **690** .... a.	...	...	...	...	0957	...	...	...	...	...	...	...	...	...	...	...	...	...	...	...	2205	...	...	...
Lisboa Sta Apolónia **690** .... a.	...	...	...	...	1200	...	...	...	...	...	...	...	...	...	...	...	...	...	...	...	...	...	...	...

– *Celta.* 2 Ⓡ.
– 2 Valença - Porto - Figueira da Foz and v.v.

ES – Spain (Central European Time).
PT – Portugal (West European Time).

LISBOA - PINHAL NOVO - TUNES - FARO 697

km										
			AP 180		*IC* 570	*IC* 572		*AP* 184	*IC* 574	
	Porto Campanhã **690** .... d.	...	0532	...	...	...	...	1432	...	...
	Coimbra B **690** .... d.	...	0646	...	...	...	...	1546	...	...
0	**Lisboa** Oriente .... ⊙ d.	...	0823	...	1002	1402	...	1723	1832	...
7	Entrecampos .... ⊙ d.	...	0831	...	1010	1410	...	1731	1840	...
9	Sete Rios .... ⊙ d.	...	|	...	1014	1414	...	|	1844	...
18	Pragal .... ⊙ d.	...	|	...	1026	1426	...	|	1855	...
47	Pinhal Novo .... ⊙ d.	...	0906	...	1048	1448	...	1806	1918	...
118	Grândola .... d.	...	|	...	1119	1516	...	|	1945	...
180	Funcheira .... d.	...	|	...	1157	1554	...	|	2024	...
264	**Tunes** .... ▷ d.	...	1054	...	1302	1707	...	1955	2134	...
269	Albufeira .... ▷ d.	...	1101	...	1307	1712	...	2002	2139	...
286	Loulé .... ▷ d.	...	1113	...	1319	1724	...	2014	2151	...
302	**Faro** .... ▷ a.	...	1123	...	1330	1735	...	2023	2202	...

		AP 182		*IC* 670	*IC* 672		*AP* 186		*IC* 674
Faro .... ▷ d.	...	0700	...	0822	1415	...	1600	...	1815
Loulé .... ▷ d.	...	0710	...	0833	1426	...	1611	...	1825
Albufeira .... ▷ d.	...	0723	...	0845	1438	...	1624	...	1837
Tunes .... ▷ d.	...	0729	...	0851	1444	...	1630	...	1844
Funcheira .... d.	...	0821	...	1001	1554	...	|	...	1954
Grândola .... d.	...	0855	...	1039	1638	...	|	...	2033
Pinhal Novo .... ⊙ d.	...	0923	...	1108	1707	...	1823	...	2105
Pragal .... ⊙ a.	...	|	...	1130	1734	...	|	...	2134
Sete Rios .... ⊙ a.	...	|	...	1143	1744	...	|	...	2144
Entrecampos .... ⊙ a.	...	0957	...	1146	1747	...	1857	...	2147
Lisboa Oriente .... ⊙ a.	...	1005	...	1156	1756	...	1905	...	2156
Coimbra B **690** .... a.	...	1144	...	...	...	...	2044	...	...
Porto Campanhã **690** ...... a.	...	1258	...	...	...	...	2158	...	...

LOCAL TRAINS **LAGOS - TUNES - FARO**

			⚒		Ⓐ					Ⓐ	
0	**Lagos** .... d.	0610	0654	0747	0903	1110	1323	1509	1720	1827	2011
18	Portimão .... d.	0631	0714	0806	0923	1130	1349	1529	1744	1847	2031
29	Silves .... d.	0648	0731	0823	...	1148	1405	1547	1801	1905	2049
42	Algoz .... d.	0704	0747	0840	...	1205	1422	1604	1818	1926	2105
46	**Tunes** .... ▷ d.	0711	0754	0851	...	1212	1428	1611	1824	1933	2112
52	Albufeira .... ▷ d.	0722	0800	0858	...	1219	1438	1623	1837	1939	2123
69	Loulé .... ▷ d.	0743	0815	0919	...	1242	1453	1638	1859	1955	2138
85	**Faro** .... ▷ a.	0759	0835	0934	...	1257	1508	1654	1916	2010	2154

	⚒	Ⓐ						Ⓐ		
Faro .... ▷ d.	0711	...	0902	1023	1225	1617	1741	1825	1918	2050
Loulé .... ▷ d.	0728	...	0919	1039	1242	1638	1758	1842	1935	2107
Albufeira .... ▷ d.	0743	...	0935	1100	1307	1655	1814	1900	2001	2123
Tunes .... ▷ d.	0754	...	0942	1106	1313	1707	1824	1908	2007	2133
Algoz .... d.	0800	...	0947	1112	1318	1713	1830	1914	2013	2138
Silves .... d.	0823	...	1004	1129	1334	1729	1846	1933	2029	2152
Portimão .... d.	0838	0931	1020	1148	1349	1744	1906	1948	2049	2207
Lagos .... a.	0858	0951	1040	1209	1410	1805	1926	2008	2109	2226

– Also see other section of table above or below.

⊙ – See Table **698** for other fast trains, Table **699** for local services, including connections Barreiro - Pinhal Novo.

FARO - VILA REAL DE SANTO ANTÓNIO 697a

			Ⓐ			Ⓐ						
0	**Faro** .... d.	0720	0857	0955	1130	1300	1515	1713	1753	1927	2030	2216
10	Olhão .... d.	0735	0908	1006	1141	1311	1531	1729	1804	1939	2040	2227
32	Tavira .... d.	0806	0939	1033	1208	1342	1558	1756	1831	2010	2106	2254
56	**Vila Real** §......... a.	0834	1008	1102	1237	1412	1627	1825	1900	2039	2135	2319

										Ⓐ	
Vila Real § ..... d.	0548	0639	0706	0840	1108	1243	1430	1633	1753	1910	2107
Tavira .... d.	0617	0708	0735	0909	1135	1312	1504	1702	1831	1940	2138
Olhão .... d.	0644	0735	0802	0936	1204	1339	1531	1729	1901	2006	2201
Faro .... a.	0654	0746	0813	0946	1214	1349	1542	1739	1912	2017	2211

– ± 1500 metres from bus station / ferry terminal.

ADDITIONAL JOURNEYS: Faro - Villa Real at 1355, 1826 Ⓐ; Villa Real - Faro at 1524 Ⓐ.

LISBOA - PINHAL NOVO - ÉVORA and BEJA 698

inha do Alentejo

km										
		IC 590	*IC* 592	*IC* 594	*IC* 790	*IC* 596	*IC* 598			
		Ⓐ	Ⓐ	Ⓒ	Ⓐ					
0	**Lisboa** Oriente .... ▷ d.	0702	0902	0952	1332	1702	1902	...	...	...
7	Entrecampos .... ▷ d.	0710	0910	1000	1340	1710	1910	...	...	...
9	Sete Rios .... ▷ d.	0714	0914	1004	1344	1714	1914	...	...	...
18	Pragal .... ▷ d.	0726	0926	1015	1356	1726	1926	...	...	...
47	**Pinhal Novo** .... ▷ d.	0748	0948	1032	1418	1748	1948	...	...	...
88	Vendas Novas .... d.	0818	1010	1102	1440	1810	2010	...	...	...
122	Casa Branca .... d.	0832	1024	1116	1454	1824	2024	...	...	...
148	Évora .... a.	0842	1035	1126	1505	1835	2035	...	...	...
185	**Beja** .... a.	*0926**	*1118**	*1210**	*1551**	*1920**	*2116**	...	...	...

	IC 690	*IC* 692	*IC* 698	*IC* 694	*IC* 696				
	Ⓐ		Ⓐ						
Beja .... d.	*0623**	*0822**	*1045**	*1611**	*1815**	...	...	...	...
Évora .... d.	0706	0906	1135	1657	1906	...	...	...	...
Casa Branca .... d.	0717	0917	1146	1708	1917	...	...	...	...
Vendas Novas .... d.	0731	0931	1200	1722	1931	...	...	...	...
Pinhal Novo .... ▷ d.	0753	0953	1223	1751	1953	...	...	...	...
Pragal .... ▷ a.	0814	1014	1244	1814	2014	...	...	...	...
Sete Rios .... ▷ a.	0824	1024	1254	1824	2024	...	...	...	...
Entrecampos .... ▷ a.	0828	1028	1258	1828	2028	...	...	...	...
Lisboa Oriente .... ▷ a.	0836	1036	1306	1836	2036	...	...	...	...

– See Table **697** for other fast trains and Table **699** for local services, including connections Barreiro - Pinhal Novo.

* – Change at Casa Branca. *IC* train. Ⓡ.

699 OTHER LOCAL SERVICES

LISBOA - ESTORIL - CASCAIS

km									
0	**Lisboa** Cais do Sodre ◧ d.	0530	0600	0630	and at least	2200	2230	2300	2330
24	Estoril ◧ d.	0606	0636	0706	every 30	2236	2306	2336	0006
26	**Cascais** ◧ a.	0610	0640	0710	minutes until	2240	2310	2340	0010

Cascais ◧ d.	0530	0600	0630	and at least	2200	2230	2300	233
Estoril ◧ d.	0534	0604	0634	every 30	2204	2234	2304	233
Lisboa Cais do Sodre ◧ a.	0610	0640	0710	minutes until	2240	2310	2340	001

◧ – Also from Lisboa and Cascais at 0000, 0030, 0100, 0130.

LISBOA ORIENTE - SINTRA

km		Ⓐ	Ⓒ	Ⓐ	Ⓒ				
0	**Lisboa Oriente** ⊡ d.	0558	0608	0618	0638	and	2308	2338	...
	Roma Areeiro ⊡ d.	0605	0615	0625	0645	at	2315	2345	...
	Entrecampos ⊡ d.	0607	0617	0627	0647	least	2317	2347	...
	Sete Rios ⊡ d.	0610	0620	0630	0650	every	2320	2350	...
	Monte Abraão ⊡ d.	0625	0635	0645	0705	30	2335	0005	...
	Agualva - Cacém ⊡ d.	0631	0641	0651	0711	minutes	2341	0011	...
	Sintra ⊡ a.	0645	0655	0705	0725	until	2355	0025	...

Sintra ⊡ d.	0506	0536	and	2306	2336	...	...	...
Agualva - Cacém ⊡ d.	0519	0549	at	2319	2349	...	...	...
Monte Abraão ⊡ d.	0524	0554	least	2324	2354	...	...	...
Sete Rios ⊡ d.	0539	0609	every	2339	0009	...	...	...
Entrecampos ⊡ d.	0542	0612	30	2342	0012	...	...	...
Roma Areeiro ⊡ d.	0544	0614	minutes	2344	0014	...	...	...
Lisboa Oriente ⊡ a.	0552	0622	until	2352	0022	...	...	...

⊡ – Also from Lisboa at 0008, 0038, 0108; also from Sintra at 0006.

LISBOA ROSSIO - SINTRA and MIRA SINTRA-MELEÇAS

km		Ⓐ	Ⓒ	Ⓐ	Ⓒ		Ⓐ	Ⓒ	Ⓐ	Ⓒ
0	**Lisboa Rossio** d.	0541	0601	0626	0631	and	1941	2001	2026	2031
	Monte Abraão d.	0601	0621	0646	0651	hourly	2001	2021	2046	2051
	Agualva - Cacém d.	0607	0627	0652	0657	until	2007	2027	2052	2057
	Mira Sintra - M'ças a.	|	|	0655	0700	⊖	|	|	2055	2100
	Sintra a.	0621	0641	...	...		2021	2041	...	...

	Ⓐ	Ⓒ	Ⓒ	Ⓐ		Ⓐ	Ⓒ	Ⓒ	Ⓐ
Sintra d.	0640	0650	...	...	and	1940	1950	...	...
Mira Sintra - M'ças d.	|	|	0730	0735	hourly	|	|	2030	203
Agualva - Cacém d.	0653	0703	0733	0738	until	1953	2003	2033	204
Monte Abraão d.	0659	0709	0739	0744	●	1959	2009	2039	204
Lisboa Rossio a.	0719	0729	0759	0804		2019	2029	2059	210

⊖ – Lisboa Rossio - Mira Sintra - Meleças trains run 5 minutes earlier 1021 Ⓐ - 1621 Ⓐ. Other trains: **Lisboa Rossio - Sintra** at 0001, 0031, 0101, 0611 Ⓐ, 0711 Ⓐ, 0811 Ⓐ, 0911 Ⓐ, 1001 Ⓐ, 1101 Ⓐ, 1201 Ⓐ, 1301 Ⓐ, 1401 Ⓐ, 1501 Ⓐ, 1601 Ⓐ, 1711 Ⓐ, 1811 Ⓐ, 1911 Ⓐ, 2011 Ⓐ, 2041 Ⓐ, 2101, 2131, 2201, 2231, 2301, 2331; **Lisboa Rossio - Mira Sintra - Meleças** at 0656 Ⓐ, 0756 Ⓐ, 0856 Ⓐ, 1656 Ⓐ, 1756 Ⓐ, 1856 Ⓐ, 1956 Ⓐ.

● – Mira Sintra - Meleças - Lisboa Rossio trains run 5 minutes earlier 1030 Ⓐ - 1630 Ⓐ. Other trains: **Sintra - Lisboa Rossio** at 0020, 0520, 0550, 0620, 0710 Ⓐ, 0810 Ⓐ, 0910 Ⓐ, 1000 Ⓐ, 1100 Ⓐ, 1200 Ⓐ, 1300 Ⓐ, 1400 Ⓐ, 1500 Ⓐ, 1600 Ⓐ, 1710 Ⓐ, 1810 Ⓐ, 1910 Ⓐ, 2010 Ⓐ, 2050, 2120, 2150, 2220, 2250, 2320, 2350; **Mira Sintra - Meleças - Lisboa Rossio** at 0705 Ⓐ, 0805 Ⓐ, 0905 Ⓐ, 1705 Ⓐ, 1805 Ⓐ, 1905 Ⓐ, 2005 Ⓐ.

LISBOA - PINHAL NOVO - SETÚBAL

Fertagus (CP tickets not valid)

km										
0	**Roma-Areeiro** d.	0643	0743	0843	0943		1943	2043	2143	2243
	Entrecampos d.	0645	0745	0845	0945	and	1945	2045	2145	2245
	Sete Rios d.	0649	0749	0849	0949	hourly	1949	2049	2149	2249
	Pragal d.	0700	0800	0900	1000	until	2000	2100	2200	2300
	Pinhal Novo d.	0728	0828	0928	1028	⊙	2028	2128	2228	2328
	Setúbal a.	0741	0841	0941	1041		2041	2141	2241	2341

				Ⓒ	Ⓐ		Ⓒ	Ⓐ
Setúbal d.	0658		1858	1958	2018		2258	231
Pinhal Novo d.	0712	and	1912	2012	2032	and	2312	233
Pragal d.	0739	hourly	1939	2039	2059	hourly	2339	235
Sete Rios d.	0750	until	1950	2050	2110	until	2350	001
Entrecampos d.	0754	⊙	1954	2054	2114	⊙	2354	001
Roma-Areeiro a.	0756		1956	2056	2116		2356	001

⊙ – Also from Roma-Areeiro at 0043 Ⓐ, 0543 Ⓐ, 2343 Ⓒ, 2358 Ⓐ; from Setúbal at 0018 Ⓐ, 0548 Ⓐ, 0558 Ⓒ, 1928 Ⓐ.
Additional trains run every 10 – 20 minutes (every 30 mins evenings and Ⓒ) Roma-Areeiro - Pragal - Coina and v.v.

Catamaran LISBOA - BARREIRO

Transtejo Soflusa — Certain Ⓐ peak journeys do not run in July and Augus

From Lisboa Terreiro do Paço: By ⛴ journey time 20 - 25 minutes. *10* km

Ⓐ: 0000, 0030, 0100, 0200, 0530, 0550, 0620, 0640, 0700 and every 5 – 15 minutes until 0920, 0940, 0955 and every 30 minutes until 1455, 1520, 1535, 1600, 1625, 1640 and every 5 – 15 minutes until 2035, 2100, 2125, 2155, 2230, 2255, 2330.

Ⓒ: 0000, 0030, 0100, 0200, 0545, 0615, 0647, 0715, 0755, 0825 ⑥, 0855, 0925 ⑥, 0955, 1025 ⑥, 1055, 1155, 1255, 1355, 1455, 1525, 1555, 1625, 1655, 1725, 1755, 1825, 1855, 1925, 1955, 2055, 2125, 2155, 2255.

From Barreiro Barcos: By ⛴ journey time 20 - 25 minutes. *10* km

Ⓐ: 0005, 0030, 0130, 0505, 0520, 0555, 0615, 0635 and every 5 – 15 minutes until 0910, 0925, 0940, 0955, 1025 and every 30 minutes until 1455, 1510, 1535, 1600 and ever 5 – 15 minutes until 1950, 2010, 2035, 2100, 2125, 2200, 2225, 2300, 2330.

Ⓒ: 0005, 0030, 0130, 0515, 0545, 0622, 0650, 0725, 0755 ⑥, 0825, 0855⑥, 0925, 0955 (1025, 1125, 1225, 1325, 1425, 1455, 1525, 1555, 1625, 1655, 1725, 1755, 1825, 185 1925, 2025, 2055, 2125, 2225, 2330.

BARREIRO - SETÚBAL

km		Ⓐ				Ⓐ	Ⓒ	
0	**Barreiro** d.	0555	0625	and every	2125	2232	2232	2325
15	Pinhal Novo d.	0614	0644	30 mins	2144	2251	2251	2344
28	**Setúbal** d.	0626	0656	(hourly on Ⓒ)	2156	2303	2303	2356
	Praias do Sado A. a.	0633	0703	until	2203	2310	...	...

	Ⓒ	Ⓐ				Ⓐ			Ⓐ	Ⓒ
P. do Sado A. d.	0540	0610	0640	and every	2040	2114	2144	2240	2340	...
Setúbal d.	0548	0618	0648	30 mins	2048	2122	2151	2248	2348	234
Pinhal Novo d.	0600	0630	0700	(hourly on Ⓒ)	2100	2136	2202	2300	0000	000
Barreiro a.	0618	0648	0718	until	2118	2154	2220	2318	0018	001

LISBOA - ENTRONCAMENTO - TOMAR

Local trains — For fast trains see Table 69

km		Ⓐ	⚒			Ⓐ		Ⓐ	Ⓐ			Ⓐ		Ⓐ				Ⓐ§			Ⓐ§					Ⓐ	
0	**Lisboa** S. Apolónia d.	0550	0645	0745	...	0845	0945	1045	1145	...	1245	1345	1445	1545	...	1615	1645	1715	...	1745	1815	1845	1945	...	2045	2145	224
7	**Lisboa** Oriente d.	0558	0653	0753	...	0853	0953	1053	1153	...	1253	1353	1453	1553	...	1623	1653	1723	...	1753	1823	1853	1953	...	2053	2153	225
31	Vila Franca de Xira d.	0616	0711	0811	...	0911	1011	1111	1211	...	1311	1411	1511	1611	...	1639	1711	1739	...	1811	1838	1911	2011	...	2111	2211	231
75	Santarém d.	0653	0754	0854	...	0957	1054	1148	1254	...	1348	1454	1549	1654	...	1706	1754	1806	...	1854	1907	1954	2054	...	2149	2259	234
107	Entroncamento a.	0719	0820	0919	...	1023	1120	1214	1321	...	1414	1520	1615	1720	...	1728	1820	1828	...	1920	1929	2020	2120	...	2215	2325	001
130	**Tomar** a.	0751	0847	0946	...	...	1151	1242	...	...	1442	1551	1643	1751	...	...	1851	1859	...	1947	1958	2051	2148	...	2246	2352	004

	Ⓐ	Ⓐ§	⚒	†	Ⓐ§	⚒	†	①–⑥		Ⓐ		⚒	†			Ⓐ					Ⓐ	⑦		Ⓐ	⑦§	
Tomar d.	0510	0604	0614	...	0650	0711	...	...	0801	...	1009	1111	...	...	1313	...	1511	1600	1711	1811	1903	...	2011	...	...	220
Entroncamento d.	0541	0625	0641	0641	0710	0741	0741	0807	0836	0941	1036	1141	1141	1236	1341	1436	1541	1636	1741	1841	1942	2036	2041	2141	2236	224
Santarém d.	0608	0647	0708	0708	0733	0808	0808	0829	0903	1008	1103	1208	1208	1303	1408	1503	1607	1703	1808	1908	2009	2059	2108	2205	2258	230
Vila Franca de Xira d.	0647	0717	0747	0747	0802	0847	0847	0856	0947	1047	1147	1247	1247	1347	1447	1547	1654	1747	1847	1956	2055	2126	2147	2247	2326	234
Lisboa Oriente d.	0706	0734	0806	0806	0819	0906	0906	0912	1006	1106	1206	1306	1306	1406	1506	1606	1713	1806	1906	2013	2113	2143	2206	2306	2343	000
Lisboa S. Apolónia a.	0713	0741	0813	0813	0828	0913	0913	0920	1013	1113	1213	1313	1313	1413	1513	1613	1720	1813	1913	2020	2120	2150	2213	2313	2350	001

§ – *IR* train.

ENTRONCAMENTO - COIMBRA

Local trains — For fast trains see Table 69

km		†	Ⓐ		Ⓐ						Ⓐ		Ⓑ
0	**Entroncamento** d.	...	0555	0640	0740	0843	1037	1237	1537	1737	1840	1940	2127
24	Fátima ⊙ d.	...	0616	0700	0807	0910	1057	1257	1557	1757	1907	2007	2148
64	Pombal d.	...	0649	0733	0840	0943	1135	1336	1630	1836	1940	2039	2220
91	Alfarelos d.	0712	0713	0756	0903	1007	1158	1359	1654	1859	2003	2103	2243
111	**Coimbra B** a.	0733	0733	0816	0924	1027	1218	1420	1714	1920	2024	2123	2305
111	**Coimbra B** d.	0739	0739	0821	0929	1032	1223	1425	1719	1926	2030	2131	...
113	**Coimbra** a.	0743	0743	0825	0933	1037	1228	1429	1724	1930	2034	2135	...

	①–⑥	Ⓐ					Ⓐ			Ⓑ
Coimbra d.	0606	0707	0810	1016	1322	1620	1715	1815	1915	201
Coimbra B a.	0609	0710	0813	1019	1325	1624	1718	1818	1918	201
Coimbra B d.	0614	0715	0818	1024	1330	1631	1724	1824	1924	202
Alfarelos d.	0637	0738	0840	1047	1353	1653	1746	1846	1946	204
Pombal d.	0701	0801	0904	1118	1417	1717	1818	1917	2019	210
Fátima ⊙ d.	0742	0852	0945	1150	1459	1750	1850	1958	2051	213
Entroncamento a.	0803	0912	1006	1211	1519	1810	1911	2018	2111	220

⊙ – Station is *20 km* from Fátima (full name of station is Chão de Maças - Fátima).

AVEIRO - COIMBRA

Local trains — For fast trains see Table 69

km					Ⓐ		Ⓐ		Ⓐ				
0	**Aveiro** d.	0645	0748	0948	1048	1135	1224	1348	1448	1535	1748	1948	2152
41	Pampilhosa d.	0723	0824	1024	1124	1213	1300	1424	1524	1613	1824	2026	2231
55	**Coimbra B** a.	0737	0839	1039	1139	1229	1315	1439	1539	1628	1839	2040	2245
57	**Coimbra** a.	0752	0853	1044	1148	1234	1320	1444	1554	1634	1852	2050	2254

		⚒								
Coimbra d.	0635	0734	0845	1053	1343	1449	1642	1834	1949	220
Coimbra B d.	0639	0738	0851	1057	1348	1454	1647	1846	1954	221
Pampilhosa d.	0655	0755	0907	1114	1404	1512	1703	1903	2015	223
Aveiro a.	0734	0834	0945	1153	1444	1551	1740	1940	2054	230

Additional trains: **Aveiro - Coimbra** at 0545 ⚒, 0735 Ⓐ, 0848 Ⓐ, 1648 Ⓐ, 1849 Ⓐ, 2048 Ⓐ; **Coimbra - Aveiro** at 0536 Ⓐ, 1006 Ⓐ, 1135 Ⓐ, 1238 Ⓐ, 1532 Ⓐ, 1732 Ⓐ, 2042 Ⓐ.

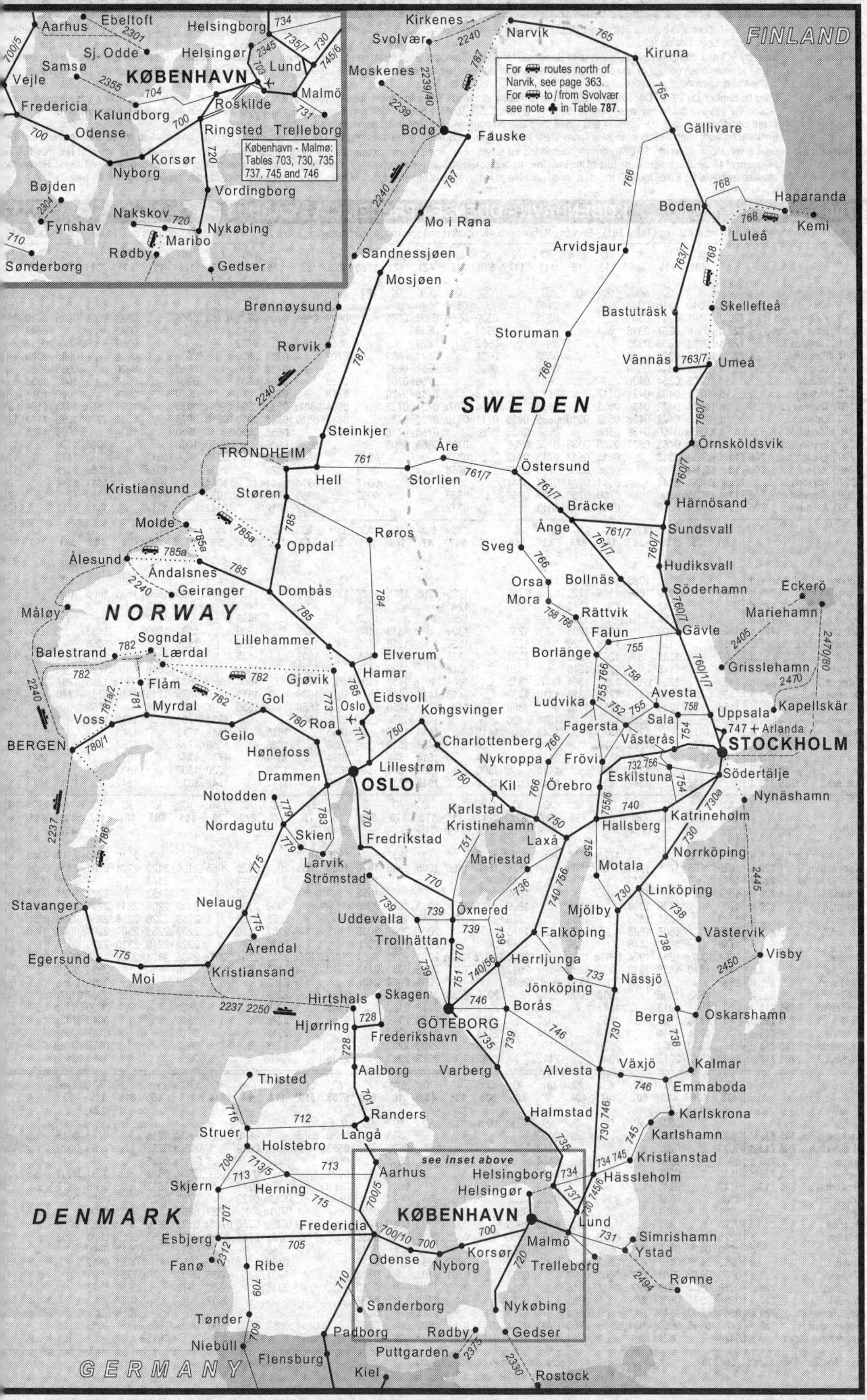
FINLAND
SWEDEN
NORWAY
DENMARK
GERMANY
For routes north of Narvik, see page 363. For to/from Svolvær see note ♣ in Table 787.
København - Malmö: Tables 703, 730, 735 737, 745 and 746
see inset above
KØBENHAVN
STOCKHOLM
OSLO
GÖTEBORG
BERGEN
TRONDHEIM
Kirkenes
Svolvær
Narvik
Kiruna
Moskenes
Bodø
Fauske
Gällivare
Boden
Haparanda
Kemi
Luleå
Mo i Rana
Sandnessjøen
Mosjøen
Arvidsjaur
Brønnøysund
Bastuträsk
Skellefteå
Storuman
Rørvik
Vännäs
Umeå
Steinkjer
Örnsköldsvik
Åre
Östersund
Hell
Storlien
Kristiansund
Støren
Bräcke
Härnösand
Ånge
Sundsvall
Molde
Røros
Oppdal
Sveg
Ålesund
Åndalsnes
Hudiksvall
Orsa
Bollnäs
Mora
Söderhamn
Geiranger
Dombås
Eckerö
Måløy
Rättvik
Mariehamn
Falun
Gävle
Sogndal
Lillehammer
Balestrand
Lærdal
Borlänge
Elverum
Grisslehamn
Hamar
Flåm
Gjøvik
Avesta
Eidsvoll
Ludvika
Myrdal
Gol
Kapellskär
Kongsvinger
Sala
Uppsala
Voss
Roa
Fagersta
Arlanda
Geilo
Charlottenberg
Västerås
Hønefoss
Nykroppa
Frövi
Lillestrøm
Eskilstuna
Södertälje
Drammen
Kil
Örebro
Notodden
Nynäshamn
Karlstad
Katrineholm
Kristinehamn
Hallsberg
Nordagutu
Skien
Laxå
Fredrikstad
Norrköping
Larvik
Mariestad
Strömstad
Motala
Linköping
Stavanger
Nelaug
Öxnered
Mjölby
Uddevalla
Västervik
Trollhättan
Falköping
Arendal
Visby
Egersund
Herrljunga
Moi
Kristiansand
Jönköping
Nässjö
Hirtshals
Skagen
Borås
Berga
Oskarshamn
Hjørring
Frederikshavn
Varberg
Alvesta
Växjö
Kalmar
Thisted
Aalborg
Emmaboda
Randers
Halmstad
Karlskrona
Struer
Langå
Karlshamn
Holstebro
Kristianstad
Aarhus
Helsingborg
Hässleholm
Skjern
Herning
Helsingør
Fredericia
Lund
Esbjerg
Malmö
Simrishamn
Odense
Korsør
Ystad
Fanø
Ribe
Nyborg
Trelleborg
Rønne
Sønderborg
Nykøbing
Tønder
Niebüll
Padborg
Rødby
Gedser
Flensburg
Puttgarden
Kiel
Rostock
Ebeltoft
Sj. Odde
Samsø
Vejle
Kalundborg
Roskilde
Ringsted
Bøjden
Fynshav
Nakskov
Maribo
Vordingborg
Nykøbing

DENMARK

Operators: The principal operator is Danske Statsbaner (*DSB*): www.dsb.dk. Arriva Tog (*AT*) operate many local services in Jutland: www.arriva.dk. Local trains over the Øresund bridge a marketed as Øresundståg (*Øtåg*).

Services: InterCity (*IC*) and InterCityLyn (*Lyn*) trains offer *Business* (1st class), *Standard* (2nd class), and on some services *Hvilepladser* ('quiet' seats) and *Familiepladser* ('family' sea These services often consist of two or more portions for different destinations and care should be taken to join the correct portion. Other trains convey 1st and 2nd (standa classes of accommodation unless otherwise shown.

Timings: Valid **December 11**, 2022 - **December 9**, 2023 (unless otherwise stated). Readers should note, however, that minor amendments may be made at any time, especially on a around the dates of public holidays (Dec. 25, 26, Jan. 1, Apr. 6, 7, 9, 10, May 5, 18, 28, 29) and during the Summer mid June - mid August when fewer trains run. In our Danish tables Ⓐ = ①–⑤, Ⓒ = ⑥⑦. See the panel on page 343 for service provision on holiday dates. Engineering work often affects schedules (particularly late evening / early morning services and also during the summer months) and readers are advised to check locally.

Reservations: Seat reservations (currently 30 DKK) are recommended for travel on *IC* and *Lyn* trains (especially at peak times) and may be purchased a maximum of two months anc minimum of 15 minutes before departure of the train from its *originating* station. Passengers may board the train without a reservation but are not guaranteed a seat. Reservatio are also available on EuroCity (*EC*) trains. It is not possible to reserve seats on other types of train. Special reservation rules may apply during holiday periods.

700 KØBENHAVN - ODENSE - FREDERICIA - AARHUS

Most Aarhus services run to / from Aalborg (Table **701**). Services København - Middelfart and v.v. run to / from Esbjerg (Table **705**). For other through cars see Tables **710**, **712** and **715**

km		*IC* 401	*IC* 409	*IC* 409	*IC* 113	*Lyn* 15	*IC* 117	*IC* 117	*IC* 819	*Lyn* 19	*IC* 421	*IC* 121	*IC* 5750	*IC* 823	*Lyn* 23	*IC* 125	*IC* 827	*Lyn* 27	*IC* 129	*IC* 131	*IC* 831	*Lyn* 31	*IC* 133	*IC* 835	*Ly* 35
			Ⓐ	⑥⑦	Ⓐ	Ⓐ	Ⓐ		Ⓐ	Ⓐ	Ⓒ	Ⓐ	Fj	Ⓐ											
	København Lufthavn ✈ d.	0040	0216	0236	...	...	0440	...	...	0528	0540	...	...	...	0628	...	...	0728	...	...	...	0832	...	...	092
0	**København** H ... § **720** d.	0101	0241	0301	...	...	0505	...	0529	0556	0601	0605	...	0629	0656	0705	0729	0756	0805	...	0829	0856	0905	0929	095
20	Høje Taastrup .... § **720** d.	0116	0257	0316	...	...	|	...	0543	|	0616	|	...	0643	|	|	0743	|	|	...	0843	|	|	0943	|
31	Roskilde .... § **720** d.	0123	0306	0323	...	...	|	...	0552	|	0624	|	...	0652	|	|	0752	|	|	...	0852	|	|	0952	|
64	Ringsted .... **720** d.	0140	0324	0340	...	...	0539	...	0608	|	0641	0639	...	0709	|	0739	0809	|	0839	...	0909	|	0939	1009	|
93	Slagelse .... d.	0159	0344	0359	...	...	0558	...	0626	|	0657	0658	...	0726	|	0758	0826	|	0858	...	0926	|	0958	1026	|
108	Korsør .... d.	0208	0354	0408	...	...	0607	...	0635	|	0706	0707	...	0735	|	0807	0835	|	0907	...	0935	|	1007	1035	|
132	Nyborg .... d.	0221	0408	0421	0517	...	0620	...	0648	|	0718	0720	...	0748	|	0820	0848	|	0920	...	0948	|	1020	1048	|
160	**Odense** .... a.	0234	0422	0434	0533	...	0633	...	0704	0707**c**	0734	0733	...	0804	0807**c**	0833	0904	0907**c**	0933	...	1004	1007**c**	1033	1104	110
160	**Odense** .... d.	0236	0424	0436	0535	0610	0635	0635	0711	0710	0735	0735	...	0813	0810	0835	0913	0910	0935	...	1013	1010	1035	1113	111
210	Middelfart .... d.	0259**k**	0450	0459	0558	|	0658	0658	0736	|	0758	0758	...	0836	|	0858	0936	|	0958	...	1036	|	1058	1136	|
220	**Fredericia** .... a.	0307**k**	0458	0507	0606	0638	0706	0706	...	0738	0806	0806	...	...	0838	0906	...	0938	1006	...	...	1038	1106	...	113
220	**Fredericia** .... **705 715** d.	0320**k**	0513	...	0613	0643	0713	0713	...	0743	...	...	0816	...	0843	0913	...	0943	...	1013	...	1043	1113	...	114
246	Vejle .... **705 715** d.	0344**k**	0528	...	0628	0658	0728	0728	...	0758	...	...	0831	...	0858	0928	...	0958	...	1028	...	1058	1128	...	115
277	Horsens .... **705** d.	0406**k**	0544	...	0644	0714	0744	0744	...	0814	...	...	0847	...	0914	0944	...	1014	...	1044	...	1114	1144	...	121
306	Skanderborg . **705 713** d.	0420**k**	0600	...	0700	0730	0800	0800	...	0830	...	...	0902	...	0930	1000	...	1030	...	1100	...	1130	1200	...	123
329	**Aarhus** .... **705 713** a.	0445**k**	0612	...	0712	0742	0812	0812	...	0842	...	...	0914	...	0942	1012	...	1042	...	1112	...	1142	1212	...	124

	IC 137	*IC* 139	*IC* 839	*Lyn* 39	*IC* 141	*IC* 843	*Lyn* 43	*IC* 145	*IC* 147	*IC* 847	*Lyn* 47	*IC* 149	*IC* 851	*Lyn* 51	*IC* 153	*IC* 155	*IC* 855	*Lyn* 55	*IC* 157	*IC* 859	*Lyn* 59	*IC* 161	*Lyn* 361	*IC* 163	
																							Ⓑn		
København Lufthavn ✈ d.	...	...	...	1028	...	...	1128	...	...	...	1228	...	...	1328	...	...	...	1428	...	...	1528	...	1604	...	
København H ... § **720** d.	1005	...	1029	1056	1105	1129	1156	1205	...	1229	1256	1305	1329	1356	1405	...	1429	1456	1505	1529	1556	1605	1626	...	
Høje Taastrup .... § **720** d.	|	...	1043	|	|	1143	|	|	...	1243	|	|	1343	|	|	...	1443	|	|	1543	|	|	|	...	
Roskilde .... § **720** d.	|	...	1052	|	|	1152	|	|	...	1252	|	|	1352	|	|	...	1452	|	|	1552	|	|	|	...	
Ringsted .... **720** d.	1039	...	1109	|	1139	1208	|	1239	...	1309	|	1339	1409	|	1439	...	1509	|	1539	1609	|	1639	|	...	...
Slagelse .... d.	1058	...	1126	|	1158	1226	|	1258	...	1326	|	1358	1426	|	1458	...	1526	|	1558	1626	|	1658	|	...	...
Korsør .... d.	1107	...	1135	|	1207	1235	|	1307	...	1335	|	1407	1435	|	1507	...	1535	|	1607	1635	|	1707	|	...	...
Nyborg .... d.	1120	...	1148	|	1220	1248	|	1320	...	1348	|	1420	1448	|	1520	...	1548	|	1620	1648	|	1720	|	...	...
Odense .... a.	1133	...	1204	1207**c**	1233	1304	1307**c**	1333	...	1404	1407**c**	1433	1504	1507**c**	1533	...	1604	1607**c**	1633	1704	1707**c**	1733	1737	...	...
Odense .... d.	1135	...	1213	1210	1235	1313	1310	1335	...	1413	1410	1435	1513	1510	1535	...	1613	1610	1635	1713	1710	1735	1740	...	...
Middelfart .... d.	1158	...	1236	|	1258	1336	|	1358	...	1436	|	1458	1536	|	1558	...	1636	|	1658	1736	|	1758	|	...	...
Fredericia .... a.	1206	...	...	1238	1306	...	1338	1406	...	...	1438	1506	...	1538	1606	...	...	1638	1706	...	1738	1806	|	...	...
Fredericia ..... **705 715** d.	...	1213	...	1243	1313	...	1343	...	1413	...	1443	1513	...	1543	...	1613	...	1643	1713	...	1743	...	|	1813	...
Vejle .... **705 715** d.	...	1228	...	1258	1328	...	1358	...	1428	...	1458	1528	...	1558	...	1628	...	1658	1728	...	1758	...	|	1828	...
Horsens .... **705** d.	...	1244	...	1314	1344	...	1414	...	1444	...	1514	1544	...	1614	...	1644	...	1714	1744	...	1814	...	|	1844	...
Skanderborg .. **705 713** d.	...	1300	...	1330	1400	...	1430	...	1500	...	1530	1600	...	1630	...	1700	...	1730	1800	...	1830	...	|	1900	...
Aarhus .... **705 713** a.	...	1312	...	1342	1412	...	1442	...	1512	...	1542	1612	...	1642	...	1712	...	1742	1812	...	1842	...	1905	1912	...

	IC 863	*Lyn* 63	*IC* 165	*IC* 867	*Lyn* 67	*IC* 169	*IC* 167	*IC* 871	*Lyn* 71	*Lyn* 71	*IC* 173	*IC* 175	*IC* 875	*Lyn* 75	*Lyn* 75	*IC* 177	*IC* 879	*Lyn* 79	*IC* 181	*IC* 883	*IC* 187	*IC* 187	*IC* 489 437	*IC* 431	
							⑤⑥		⑤⑥	⑦–④	⑤⑥	⑦–④		⑤⑥	⑦–④							⑤⑥			
København Lufthavn ✈ d.	...	1628	...	...	1728	...	...	...	1828	...	...	1832	...	1928	1928	...	...	2028	...	...	2140	2140	2240	2340	...
København H ... § **720** d.	1629	1656	1705	1729	1756	1805	...	1829	1856	1856	1905	1905	1929	1956	1956	2005	2029	2056	2105	2129	2201	2201	2301	0001	...
Høje Taastrup .... § **720** d.	1643	|	|	1743	|	|	...	1843	|	|	|	|	1943	|	|	|	2043	|	|	2143	|	|	2316	0016	...
Roskilde .... § **720** d.	1652	|	|	1752	|	|	...	1852	|	|	|	|	1952	|	|	|	2052	|	|	2152	|	2224	2324	0024	...
Ringsted .... **720** d.	1709	|	1739	1809	|	1839	...	1909	|	|	1939	1939	2009	|	|	2039	2109	|	2139	2209	2241	2241	2341	0041	...
Slagelse .... d.	1726	|	1758	1826	|	1858	...	1926	|	|	1958	1958	2026	|	|	2058	2126	|	2158	2226	2258	2258	2358	0058	...
Korsør .... d.	1735	|	1807	1835	|	1907	...	1935	|	|	2007	2007	2035	|	|	2107	2135	|	2207	2235	2307	2307	0006	0106	...
Nyborg .... d.	1748	|	1820	1848	|	1920	...	1948	|	|	2020	2020	2048	|	|	2120	2148	|	2220	2248	2320	2320	0019	0119	...
Odense .... a.	1804	1807**c**	1833	1904	1907**c**	1933	...	2004	2007**c**	2007**c**	2033	2033	2104	2107**c**	2107**c**	2133	2204	2207**c**	2235	2304	2333	2333	0035	0135	...
Odense .... d.	1813	1810	1835	1913	1910	1935	...	2013	2010	2010	2035	2035	2113	2110	2110	2136	...	2210	2236	...	...	2336	0036	...	...
Middelfart .... d.	1836	|	1858	1936	|	1959	...	2036	|	|	2058	2058	2136	|	|	2158	...	|	2258	...	...	2359	0059	...	...
Fredericia .... a.	...	1838	1906	...	1938	2006	...	...	2038	2038	2106	2106	...	2138	2138	2206	...	2238	2306	...	...	0007	0107**p**	...	...
Fredericia ..... **705 715** d.	...	1843	1913	...	1943	...	2013	...	2043	...	2113	2120	...	2143	...	2220	...	...	2320	...	...	0020	0119**p**	...	...
Vejle .... **705 715** d.	...	1858	1928	...	1958	...	2028	...	2058	...	2128	2146	...	2158	...	2246	...	...	2346	...	...	0046	0143**p**	...	...
Horsens .... **705** d.	...	1914	1944	...	2014	...	2044	...	2114	...	2144	2212	...	2214	...	2312	...	...	0012	...	...	0112	0206**p**	...	...
Skanderborg .. **705 713** d.	...	1930	2000	...	2030	...	2100	...	2130	...	2200	2232	...	2230	...	2332	...	...	0032	...	...	0132	0228**p**	...	...
Aarhus .... **705 713** a.	...	1942	2012	...	2042	...	2112	...	2142	...	2212	2247	...	2243	...	2347**b**	...	...	0053	...	...	0153	0249**p**	...	...

	IC 438	*IC* 400	*IC* 402	*IC* 802	*IC* 104	*IC* 404	*Lyn* 6	*IC* 806	*Lyn* 308	*IC* 108	*IC* 408	*Lyn* 10	*IC* 810	*IC* 5753	*Lyn* 310	*IC* 112	*Lyn* 14	*IC* 814	*IC* 116	*Lyn* 18	*IC* 818	*IC* 118 120	*Lyn* 22		
		Ⓐ	Ⓒ	Ⓐ	Ⓐ	Ⓒ	Ⓐ	Ⓐ	Ⓐn	Ⓐ	Ⓒ	Ⓐ	Ⓐ	ⒶF	Ⓐ										
Aarhus .... **705 713** d.	0007	...	0209	...	...	...	0400	...	...	...	...	0515	...	0539	0555	...	0615	...	0645**a**	0715	...	0745	0815	...	...
Skanderborg .. **705 713** d.	0030	...	0232	...	...	...	0416	...	...	...	...	0529	...	0553	|	...	0629	...	0659**a**	0729	...	0759	0829	...	...
Horsens .... **705** d.	0049	...	0254	...	...	...	0434	...	...	...	...	0545	...	0608	|	...	0645	...	0714**a**	0745	...	0814	0845	...	...
Vejle .... **705 715** d.	0115	...	0317	...	...	...	0454	...	...	...	...	0602	...	0624	|	...	0702	...	0731**a**	0802	...	0831	0902	...	...
Fredericia ..... **705 715** a.	0142	...	0343	...	...	...	0512	...	...	...	...	0617	...	0640	|	...	0717	...	0745**a**	0817	...	0845	0917	...	...
Fredericia .... d.	0153	...	0353	...	...	...	0523	...	...	0553	0553	0623	...	...	|	0653**a**	0723	...	0753	0823	...	0853	0923	...	...
Middelfart .... d.	0201	...	0401	...	...	...	|	0523	...	0601	0601	|	0624	...	|	0701**a**	|	0723	0801	|	0823	0901	|	...	...
Odense .... a.	0223	...	0423	...	...	...	0550	0548**c**	...	0623	0623	0650	0648**c**	...	0719	0723**a**	0750	0748**c**	0823	0850	0848**c**	0923	0950	...	...
Odense .... d.	0225	0412	0425	0456	0525	0525	0553	0556	0622	0625	0625	0653	0656	...	0722	0725	0753	0756	0825	0853	0856	0925	0953	...	...
Nyborg .... d.	0239	0426	0439	0513	0540	0541	|	0613	|	0640	0642	|	0713	...	|	0740	|	0813	0840	|	0913	0940	|	...	...
Korsør .... d.	0252	0439	0452	0525	0552	0554	|	0625	|	0652	0654	|	0725	...	|	0752	|	0825	0852	|	0925	0952	|	...	...
Slagelse .... d.	0302	0448	0501	0535	0601	0602	|	0635	|	0701	0703	|	0735	...	|	0801	|	0835	0901	|	0935	1001	|	...	...
Ringsted .... **720** a.	0318	0504	0518	0550	0618	0618	|	0650	|	0718	0719	|	0750	...	|	0818	|	0850	0918	|	0950	1018	|	...	...
Roskilde .... § **720** a.	0335	0521	0535	0607	|	0635	|	0707	|	|	0735	|	0807	...	|	|	|	0907	|	|	1007	|	|	...	...
Høje Taastrup .... § **720** a.	0344	0530	0544	0615	|	0644	|	0715	|	|	0744	|	0815	...	|	|	|	0915	...	|	1015	|	|	...	...
København H ... § **720** a.	0400	0548	0600	0631	0655	0700	0703	0731	0734	0755	0800	0803	0831	...	0834	0855	0903	0931	0955	1003	1031	1055	1103	...	...
København Lufthavn ✈ a.	0424	...	0624	...	...	0724	0725	...	0756	...	0824	0825	...	...	0856	...	0925	...	...	1025	...	...	1125	...	...

F – To / from Flensburg (Table **710**).

a – Ⓐ only.

b – 2355 ⑦–④.

c – Connects with train in previous column.

j – 2–4 minutes earlier June 17 - Aug. 19.

k – 3–10 minutes earlier ①–⑤.

p – 1–4 minutes later ⑤⑥.

n – Not July 1 - Aug. 6.

§ – *IC* and *Lyn* trains are not available for local journeys. Frequent local trains run between Roskilde and København.

AARHUS - FREDERICIA - ODENSE - KØBENHAVN 700

Most services from Aarhus start from Aalborg (Table **701**). Services Middelfart - København start from Esbjerg (Table **705**). For other through cars see Tables **710**, **712** and **715**.

	IC 822	*IC* 124	*Lyn* 26	*IC* 826	*IC* 383	*IC* 126	*IC* 128	*Lyn* 30	*IC* 830	*IC* 132	*Lyn* 34	*IC* 834	*IC* 134	*IC* 136	*Lyn* 38	*IC* 838	*IC* 140	*Lyn* 42	*IC* 842	*IC* 385	*IC* 142	*IC* 144	*Lyn* 344	*Lyn* 46	*IC* 846
					H d															H d			Ⓑ n		
Aarhus 705 713 d.	...	0845	0915	...	0939	0945	...	1015	...	1045	1115	...	1145	...	1215	...	1245	1315	...	1339	1345	...	1355	1415	...
Skanderborg 705 713 d.	...	0859	0929	...	0953	0959	...	1029	...	1059	1129	...	1159	...	1229	...	1259	1329	...	1353	1359	...	|	1429	...
Horsens 705 d.	...	0914	0945	...	1008	1014	...	1045	...	1114	1145	...	1214	...	1245	...	1314	1345	...	1408	1414	...	|	1445	...
Vejle 705 715 d.	...	0931	1002	...	1024	1031	...	1102	...	1131	1202	...	1231	...	1302	...	1331	1402	...	1424	1431	...	|	1502	...
Fredericia 705 715 a.	...	0945	1017	...	1040	1045	...	1117	...	1145	1217	...	1245	...	1317	...	1345	1417	...	1440	1445	...	|	1517	...
Fredericia d.	...	0953	1023	...	...	...	1053	1123	...	1153	1223	...	...	1253	1323	...	1353	1423	...	...	...	1453	|	1523	...
Middelfart d.	0923	1001	|	1023	...	...	1101	|	1123	1201	|	1223	...	1301	|	1323	1401	|	1423	...	...	1501	|	|	1523
Odense a.	0948c	1023	1050	1048c	...	...	1123	1150	1148c	1223	1250	1248c	...	1323	1350	1348c	1423	1450	1448c	...	...	1523	1519	1550	1548c
Odense d.	0956	1025	1053	1056	...	...	1125	1153	1156	1225	1253	1256	...	1325	1353	1356	1425	1453	1456	...	...	1525	1522	1553	1556
Nyborg d.	1013	1040	|	1113	...	...	1140	|	1213	1240	|	1313	...	1340	|	1413	1440	|	1513	...	...	1540	|	|	1613
Korsør d.	1025	1052	|	1125	...	...	1152	|	1225	1252	|	1325	...	1352	|	1425	1452	|	1525	...	...	1552	|	|	1625
Slagelse d.	1035	1101	|	1135	...	...	1202	|	1235	1301	|	1335	...	1401	|	1435	1501	|	1535	...	...	1601	|	|	1635
Ringsted 720 a.	1050	1118	|	1150	...	...	1218	|	1250	1318	|	1350	...	1418	|	1450	1518	|	1550	...	...	1618	|	|	1650
Roskilde § 720 a.	1107	|	|	1207	...	...	|	|	1307	|	|	1407	...	|	|	1507	|	|	1607	...	...	|	|	|	1707
Høje Taastrup § 720 a.	1115	|	|	1215	...	...	|	|	1315	|	|	1415	...	|	|	1515	|	|	1615	...	...	|	|	|	1715
København H § 720 a.	1131	1155	1203	1231	...	...	1255	1303	1331	1355	1403	1431	...	1455	1503	1531	1555	1603	1631	...	...	1655	1634	1703	1731
København Lufthavn ✈ a.	...	...	1225	...	...	...	...	1325	...	...	1425	...	...	...	1525	...	...	1625	...	...	...	...	1656	1725	...

	IC 148	*Lyn* 50	*IC* 850	*IC* 150	*IC* 152	*Lyn* 54	*IC* 854	*IC* 156	*Lyn* 58	*IC* 858	*IC* 160	*Lyn* 62	*IC* 862	*IC* 164	*Lyn* 66	*IC* 866	*IC* 168	*Lyn* 70	*Lyn* 70	*IC* 470	*IC* 472	*IC* 476	*IC* 478	*IC* 480	*IC* 180
																		⑦–④	⑤⑥	⑦–④	⑤⑥	⑦–④	⑤⑥	⑤⑥	⑦–④
Aarhus 705 713 d.	1445	1515	...	1545	...	1615	...	1645	1715	...	1745	1815	...	1845	1915	...	1945f	...	2015	2013	2045	2113	2138	2213	2205
Skanderborg 705 713 d.	1459	1529	...	1559	...	1629	...	1659	1729	...	1759	1829	...	1859	1929	...	1959f	...	2029	2030	2059	2130	2151	2230	2230
Horsens 705 d.	1514	1545	...	1614	...	1645	...	1714	1745	...	1814	1845	...	1914	1945	...	2014f	...	2045	2049	2014	2149	2206	2249	2249
Vejle 705 715 d.	1531	1602	...	1631	...	1702	...	1731	1802	...	1831	1902	...	1931	2002	...	2031f	...	2102	2115	2131	2215	2223	2315	2315
Fredericia 705 715 a.	1545	1617	...	1645	...	1717	...	1745	1817	...	1845	1917	...	1945	2017	...	2045f	...	2117	2143	2145	2243	2238	2343	2345
Fredericia d.	1553	1623	...	...	1653	1723	...	1753	1823	...	1853	1923	...	1953	2023	...	2053	2123	2123	2153	2153	2253	2253	2353	2353
Middelfart d.	1601	|	1623	...	1701	|	1723	1801	|	1823	1901	|	1923	2001	|	2023	2101	|	|	2201	2201	2301	2301	0001	0001
Odense a.	1623	1650	1648c	...	1723	1750	1748c	1823	1850	1848c	1923	1950	1948c	2023	2050	2048c	2123	2150	2150	2223	2223	2323	2323	0023	0023
Odense d.	1625	1653	1656	...	1725	1753	1756	1825	1853	1856	1925	1953	1956	2025	2053	2056	2125	2153	2153	2225	2225	2325	2325	0025	...
Nyborg d.	1640	|	1713	...	1740	|	1813	1840	|	1913	1940	|	2013	2040	|	2113	2141	|	|	2242	2242	2342	2342	0042	...
Korsør d.	1652	|	1725	...	1752	|	1825	1852	|	1925	1952	|	2025	2052	|	2125	2154	|	|	2254	2254	2354	2354	0054	...
Slagelse d.	1701	|	1735	...	1801	|	1835	1901	|	1935	2001	|	2035	2101	|	2135	2202	|	|	2303	2303	0003	0003	0103	...
Ringsted 720 a.	1718	|	1750	...	1818	|	1850	1918	|	1950	2018	|	2050	2118	|	2150	2218	|	|	2319	2319	0019	0019	0119	...
Roskilde § 720 a.	|	|	1806	...	|	|	1907	|	|	2007	|	|	2107	|	|	2207	|	|	|	2335	2335	0035	0035	0135	...
Høje Taastrup § 720 a.	|	|	1814	...	|	|	1915	|	|	2015	|	|	2115	|	|	2215	|	|	|	2344	2344	0044	0044	0144	...
København H § 720 a.	1755	1803	1831	...	1855	1903	1931	1955	2003	2031	2055	2103	2131	2155	2203	2231	2255	2303	2303	2400	2400	0100	0100	0200	...
København Lufthavn ✈ a.	...	1825	...	...	...	1925	...	...	2025	...	...	2125	...	...	2225	...	...	2325	2325	0024	0024	0124	0124	0224	...

H – (12) Ÿ Aarhus - Hamburg (Table **710**).
c – Connects with train in previous column.
d – Dec. 11 - June 16, Aug. 21 - Dec. 9.
f – 6–8 minutes earlier ⑦–④.
n – Not July 3 - Aug. 6.
§ – *IC* and *Lyn* trains are not available for local journeys. Frequent local trains run between Roskilde and København.

AARHUS - AALBORG 701

km		*IC* 101		*IC* 105 Ⓐ	*Lyn* 7 Ⓐ	*IC* 109	*Lyn* 11 Ⓐ	*IC* 113 Ⓐ	*IC* 115 ⑥⑦	*Lyn* 15 Ⓐ	*IC* 117 Ⓐ	*IC* 117	*Lyn* 19 Ⓐ	*Lyn* 19	*IC* 123	*Lyn* 23	*IC* 125	*Lyn* 27	*IC* 131	*Lyn* 31	*IC* 133	*Lyn* 35	*IC* 139
	København H **700** d.	...	...	...	...	...	...	...	...	...	0505	...	0556	...	...	0656	0705	0756	...	0856	0905	0956	...
	Odense **700** d.	...	...	...	...	...	...	0535	...	0610	0635	0635	0710	...	...	0810	0835	0910	...	1010	1035	1110	...
	Fredericia **700** d.	...	...	...	...	...	...	0613	...	0643	0713	0713	0743	...	...	0843	0913	0943	1013	1043	1113	1143	1213
0	**Aarhus** 712 d.	0420	...	0520	0549	0620	0649	0720	0722	0750	0820	0820	0850	0850	0920	0950	1020	1050	1120	1150	1220	1250	1320
46	Langå 712 d.	0446	...	0546	|	0646	|	0746	0748	|	0846	0846	|	|	0946	|	1046	|	1146	|	1246	|	1346
59	Randers d.	0456	...	0556	0620	0656	0720	0756	0758	0821	0856	0856	0921	0921	0956	1021	1056	1121	1156	1221	1256	1321	1356
91	Hobro d.	0512	...	0612	0636	0712	0736	0812	0814	0837	0912	0912	0937	0937	1012	1037	1112	1137	1212	1237	1312	1337	1412
140	**Aalborg** a.	0551	...	0651	0706	0751	0806	0851	0853	0906	0951	0951	1006	1006	1051	1106	1151	1206	1251	1306	1351	1406	1451

	Lyn 39	*IC* 141	*Lyn* 43	*IC* 147	*Lyn* 47	*IC* 149	*Lyn* 51	*IC* 155	*Lyn* 55	*IC* 157	*Lyn* 59	*IC* 163	*Lyn* 63	*IC* 165	*Lyn* 67	*IC* 167 ⑤⑥	*IC* 167 Ⓐ	*IC* 171 n	*IC* 173 ⑤⑥	*IC* 175 p	*IC* 181 ⑤⑥	*IC* 187 ⑤⑥	
København H **700** d.	1056	1105	1156	...	1256	1305	1356	...	1456	1505	1556	...	1656	1705	1756	...	...	1805	1905	1905	2005	2201	...
Odense **700** d.	1210	1235	1310	...	1410	1436	1510	...	1610	1636	1710	...	1810	1836	1910	...	...	1935	2035	2035	2136	2336	...
Fredericia **700** d.	1243	1313	1343	1413	1443	1513	1543	1613	1643	1713	1743	1813	1843	1913	1943	2013	...	2020	2113	2120	2220	0020	...
Aarhus 712 d.	1350	1420	1450	1520	1550	1620	1650	1720	1750	1820	1850	1920	1950	2020	2050	2120	2120	2210	2220	2310	0010	0210	...
Langå 712 d.	|	1446	|	1546	|	1646	|	1746	|	1846	|	1946	|	2046	|	2146	2146	2236	2246	2336	0036	0236	...
Randers d.	1421	1456	1521	1556	1621	1656	1721	1756	1821	1856	1921	1956	2021	2056	2121	2156	2156	2246	2256	2346	0046	0246	...
Hobro d.	1437	1512	1537	1612	1637	1712	1737	1812	1837	1912	1937	2012	2037	2112	2137	2212	2212	2302	2312	0002	0102	0302	...
Aalborg a.	1506	1551	1606	1651	1706	1751	1806	1851	1906	1951	2006	2051	2106	2151	2206	2251	2251	2341	2351	0041	0141	0341	...

	IC 192 402	*IC* 194		*Lyn* 14 Ⓐ	*IC* 116 Ⓐ	*Lyn* 18 Ⓐ	*IC* 118	*IC* 120	*Lyn* 22	*IC* 124	*Lyn* 26	*IC* 126	*IC* 128	*Lyn* 30	*IC* 132	*Lyn* 34	*IC* 134	*IC* 136	*Lyn* 38	*IC* 140	*Lyn* 42	*IC* 142	*Lyn* 46
Aalborg d.	0005	0105	...	0450	0505	0550	0605	...	0650	0705	0750	0805	...	0850	0905	0950	1005	...	1050	1105	1150	1205	1250
Hobro d.	0044	0144	...	0519	0544	0619	0644	...	0719	0744	0819	0841	...	0919	0944	1019	1044	...	1119	1141	1219	1244	1319
Randers d.	0101	0201	...	0535	0601	0635	0701	...	0735	0801	0835	0901	...	0935	1001	1035	1101	...	1135	1201	1235	1301	1335
Langå 712 d.	0109	0209	...	|	0609	|	0709	...	|	0809	|	0909	...	|	1009	|	1109	...	|	1209	|	1309	|
Aarhus 712 a.	0138	0236	...	0608	0638	0708	0738	...	0808	0838	0908	0938	...	1008	1038	1108	1138	...	1208	1238	1308	1338	1408
Fredericia **700** a.	0343j	...	...	0717	0745	0817	0845	0853	0917	0945	1017	1045	1053	1117	1145	1217	1245	1253	1317	1345	1417	1445	1517
Odense **700** a.	0423j	...	...	0750	0823	0850	...	0923	0950	1023	1050	...	1123	1150	1223	1250	...	1323	1350	1423	1450	...	1550
København H **700** a.	0600j	...	...	0903	0955	1003	...	1055	1103	1155	1203	...	1255	1303	1355	1403	...	1455	1503	1555	1603	...	1703

	IC 148	*Lyn* 50	*IC* 150	*Lyn* 54	*IC* 156	*Lyn* 58	*IC* 160	*Lyn* 62	*IC* 164	*Lyn* 66	*IC* 166 Ⓐ	*IC* 168 ⑤⑥	*Lyn* 70	*IC* 474 ⑦–④	*IC* 472 ⑤⑥	*IC* 172 ⑦–④	*IC* 476 ⑦–④	*IC* 478 ⑤⑥	*IC* 180 ⑦–④	*IC* 480 ⑤⑥	*IC* 182 184	*IC* 438	*IC* 190
Aalborg d.	1305	1350	1405	1450	1505	1550	1605	1650	1705	1750	1759	1805	1850j	1848	1905	1905	1948	2005	2022	2022	2122	2222	2305
Hobro d.	1344	1419	1444	1519	1544	1619	1644	1719	1744	1819	1838	1844	1919j	1917	1944	1945	2017	2035	2102	2101	2202	2302	2344
Randers d.	1401	1435	1501	1535	1601	1635	1701	1735	1801	1835	1854	1901	1935j	1933	2001	2001	2033	2051	2118	2118	2228	2318	0001
Langå 712 d.	1409	|	1509	|	1609	|	1709	|	1809	|	1903	1909	|	|	2009	2010	|	|	2127	2126	2227	2327	0009
Aarhus 712 a.	1438	1508	1538	1608	1638	1708	1738	1808	1838	1908	1931	1938	2008j	2006	2038	2038	2106	2124	2155	2155	2255	2355	0036
Fredericia **700** a.	1545	1617	1645	1717	1745	1817	1845	1917	1945	2017	2038	2045	2117j	2143	2145	...	2243	2238	2345	2343	0043	0142	...
Odense **700** a.	1623	1650	...	1750	1823	1850	1923	1950	2023	2050	2123	2123	2150	2223	2223	...	2323	2323	0023	0023	...	0223	...
København H **700** a.	1755	1803	...	1903	1955	2003	2055	2103	2155	2203	2255	2255	2303	2400	2400	...	0100	0100	0200	0200	...	0400	...

j – ⑥⑦ only.
n – Not June 15 - Aug. 20.
p – On ⑤⑥ departs København H at 1956 and runs 20–35 minutes later to Aarhus.

703 HELSINGØR - KØBENHAVN - KØBENHAVN LUFTHAVN ✈ - MALMÖ

EASTBOUND

Services operate every 20 minutes (less frequent 0000 - 0400 hours) **Helsingør** - Østerport - København H - København Lufthavn ✈ - **Malmö C**.

Journey times:

Helsingør - København H: 47 minutes;
København H - København Lufthavn ✈: 13 minutes;
København Lufthavn ✈ - Malmö C: 26 minutes.

København H - København Lufthavn ✈ services operate every 10 minutes.

WESTBOUND

Services operate every 20 minutes (less frequent 0000 - 0400 hours) **Malmö C** - København Lufthavn ✈ - København H - Østerport - **Helsingør**.

Journey times:

Malmö C - København Lufthavn ✈: 21 minutes;
København Lufthavn ✈ - København H: 13 minutes;
København H - Helsingør: 46 minutes.

København Lufthavn ✈ - København H services operate every 10 minutes.

704 KØBENHAVN - KALUNDBORG

km		Ⓐ	Ⓐ	Ⓐ	Ⓐ	Ⓐ	Ⓒ	Ⓐ	Ⓐ	Ⓐ	Ⓒ	Ⓐ	Ⓐ	Ⓐ	Ⓒ		Ⓐ	Ⓒ		Ⓒ				
0	**København H** ▷ d.	0514	0534	0544	0614	0634	0634	0644	0714	0734	0734	0744	0814	0834	0848	and at	2034	2048	2134	2148	2234	2334	0034	...
20	Høje Taastrup ▷ d.	0529	0546	0559	0629	0646	0649	0659	0729	0746	0749	0759	0829	0846	0900	the same	2046	2100	2149	2200	2249	2349	0049	...
31	**Roskilde** ▷ d.	0538	0555	0608	0638	0655	0656	0708	0738	0755	0757	0808	0838	0855	0908	minutes	2055	2108	2156	2208	2256	2356	0056	...
67	Holbæk ▷ a.	0608	0613	0638	0708	0713	0725	0738	0808	0813	0825	0838	0908	0913	0929	past each	2113	2129	2225	2229	2325	0025	0125	...
67	Holbæk d.	...	0615	...	...	0715	0731	...	...	0815	...	...	...	0915	0931	hour until	2115	2131	2231**a**	2231	2328	0028	0128**c**	...
111	**Kalundborg** a.	...	0655	...	...	0754	0813	...	...	0855	...	...	...	0955	1013		2154	2213	2313**a**	2313	0008	0106	0208**c**	...

	Ⓐ	Ⓒn	Ⓐ	Ⓐp	Ⓐ	Ⓒ	Ⓐ	Ⓐp	Ⓐ	Ⓒ	Ⓐ	Ⓐp	Ⓒ	Ⓐ	Ⓒ	Ⓐ		Ⓒ	Ⓐ	Ⓐ	Ⓒ		
Kalundborg d.	...	...	0508	0536	...	0554	0603	0629	...	0654	0703	0729	0749	0803	0849	0903	and at	2049	2103	...	2149	2156**a**	2249	...
Holbæk a.	...	...	0548	0610	...	0631	0644	0706	...	0731	0744	0806	0828	0844	0928	0944	the same	2128	2144	...	2228	2231**a**	2328	...
Holbæk ▷ d.	0521	0534	0551	0612	0621	0634	0646	0712	0721	0734	0746	0812	0830	0846	0930	0946	minutes	2130	2146	2151	2230	2234	2334	...
Roskilde ▷ d.	0552	0603	0622	0635	0652	0703	0705	0735	0752	0803	0805	0835	0852	0905	0952	1005	past each	2152	2205	2222	2252	2303	0004	...
Høje Taastrup ▷ a.	0559	0610	0629	0642	0659	0710	0712	0742	0759	0810	0812	0842	0859	0912	0959	1012	hour until	2159	2212	2229	2259	2310	0009	...
København H ▷ a.	0616	0626	0646	0656	0716	0726	0726	0756	0816	0826	0826	0856	0913	0926	1013	1026		2213	2226	2246	2313	2326	0026	...

a – ①–⑤ only. **c** – ⑥⑦ only. **n** – Not Apr. 10, May 29. **p** – Not Apr. 3–5, May. 19. ▷ – Additional trains run København - Holbæk and v.v.

705 AARHUS - FREDERICIA - ESBJERG

km		2 Ⓐ	2	*IC* 815 Ⓐ	2	*IC* 819 Ⓐ	2	*IC* 823 Ⓐ	2	*IC* 827	2	*IC* 831	2	*IC* 835	2	*IC* 839	2	*IC* 843	2	*IC* 847	2	*IC* 851	2	*IC* 855	2	*IC* 859
	Aarhus 700 713 d.	...	...	...	0558**a**	...	0658**f**	...	0758	...	0858	...	0958	...	1058	...	1158	...	1258	...	1358	...	1458	...	1558	...
	Skanderborg 700 713 d.	...	...	...	0614**a**	...	0714**f**	...	0814	...	0914	...	1014	...	1114	...	1214	...	1314	...	1414	...	1514	...	1614	...
	Horsens 700 d.	...	...	...	0629**a**	...	0729**f**	...	0829	...	0929	...	1029	...	1129	...	1229	...	1329	...	1429	...	1529	...	1629	...
	Vejle 700 715 d.	...	...	...	0649**a**	...	0749	...	0849	...	0949	...	1049	...	1149	...	1249	...	1349	...	1449	...	1549	...	1649	...
	København H 700 d.	...	...	...	|	0529	|	0629	|	0729	|	0829	|	0929	|	1029	|	1129	|	1229	|	1329	|	1429	|	1529
	Odense 700 d.	...	...	0613	|	0713	|	0813	|	0913	|	1013	|	1113	|	1213	|	1313	|	1413	|	1513	|	1613	|	1713
0	Middelfart 700 d.	...	...	0636	|	0736	|	0836	|	0936	|	1036	|	1136	|	1236	|	1336	|	1436	|	1536	|	1636	|	1736
	Fredericia 700 710/5 d.	0513	0613	|	0713	|	0813	|	0913	|	1013	|	1113	|	1213	|	1313	|	1413	|	1513	|	1613	|	1713	|
23	Kolding 710 d.	0528	0628	0652	0728	0752	0828	0852	0928	0952	1028	1052	1128	1152	1228	1252	1328	1352	1428	1452	1528	1552	1628	1652	1728	1752
36	Lunderskov 710 d.	0536	0636	0700	0736	0800	0836	0900	0936	1000	1036	1100	1136	1200	1236	1300	1336	1400	1436	1500	1536	1600	1636	1700	1736	1800
47	Vejen d.	0544	0644	0707	0744	0808	0844	0908	0944	1008	1044	1108	1144	1208	1244	1308	1344	1408	1444	1508	1544	1608	1644	1708	1744	1808
75	Bramming 709 d.	0607	0707	0729	0807	0822	0907	0922	1007	1022	1107	1122	1207	1222	1307	1322	1407	1422	1507	1522	1607	1622	1707	1722	1807	1822
91	**Esbjerg** 709 a.	0618	0718	0739	0818	0832	0918	0932	1018	1032	1118	1132	1218	1232	1318	1332	1418	1432	1518	1532	1618	1632	1718	1732	1818	1832

	2	*IC* 863	2	*IC* 867	2	*IC* 871	⑤⑥ 2	*IC* 875	⑤⑥ 2	⑤⑥ 2
Aarhus 700 713 d.	1658	...	1758	...	1858	...	1958	...	2058	2138
Skanderborg 700 713 d.	1714	...	1814	...	1914	...	2014	...	2114	2151
Horsens 700 d.	1729	...	1829	...	1929	...	2029	...	2129	2206
Vejle 700 715 d.	1749	...	1849	...	1949	...	2049	...	2149	2223
København H 700 d.	|	1629	|	1729	|	1829	|	1929	|	**b**
Odense 700 d.	|	1813	|	1913	|	2013	|	2113	|	|
Middelfart 700 d.	|	1836	|	1936	|	2036	|	2136	|	|
Fredericia 700 710/5 d.	1813	|	1913	|	2013	|	2113	|	2213	2323
Kolding 710 d.	1828	1852	1928	1952	2028	2052	2128	2152	2228	2338
Lunderskov 710 d.	1836	1900	1936	2000	2036	2100	2136	2200	2236	2346
Vejen d.	1844	1908	1944	2008	2044	2108	2144	2208	2244	2354
Bramming 709 d.	1907	1922	2007	2022	2107	2122	2207	2222	2307	0017
Esbjerg 709 a.	1918	1932	2018	2032	2118	2132	2218	2232	2318	0028

	IC 806 Ⓐ	Ⓐ	*IC* 810 Ⓐ	2 Ⓐ	*IC* 814	d 2	*IC* 818	2	*IC* 822	2	*IC* 826
Esbjerg 709 d.	...	...	0526	0543	0627**a**	0641	0727	0741	0827	0841	0927
Bramming 709 d.	...	...	0538	0554	0638**a**	0652	0738	0752	0838	0852	0938
Vejen d.	...	...	0552	0616	0652**a**	0714	0752	0814	0852	0914	0952
Lunderskov 710 d.	...	...	0559	0624	0659**a**	0722	0759	0822	0859	0922	0959
Kolding 710 d.	0509	...	0609	0633	0709	0731	0809	0831	0909	0931	1009
Fredericia 700 710 715 d.	|	0620	|	0650	|	0750	|	0850	|	0950	|
Middelfart 700 d.	0523	|	0623	|	0723	|	0823	|	0923	|	1023
Odense 700 a.	0548	|	0648	|	0748	|	0848	|	0948	|	1048
København H 700 a.	0731	|	0831	|	0931	|	1031	|	1131	|	1231
Vejle 700 715 d.	...	0640	...	0710	...	0810	...	0910	...	1010	...
Horsens 700 d.	...	0700	...	0730	...	0830	...	0930	...	1030	...
Skanderborg 700 713 d.	...	0715	...	0745	...	0845	...	0945	...	1045	...
Aarhus 700 713 a.	...	0732	...	0802	...	0902	...	1002	...	1102	...

	2	*IC* 830	2	*IC* 834	2	*IC* 838	2	*IC* 842	2	*IC* 846	2	*IC* 850	2	*IC* 854	2	*IC* 858	2	*IC* 862	2	*IC* 866	2	*IC* 870	2	2	2	2
Esbjerg 709 d.	0941	1027	1041	1127	1141	1227	1241	1327	1341	1427	1441	1527	1541	1627	1641	1727	1741	1827	1841	1927	1941	2027	2041	2141	2241	2341
Bramming 709 d.	0952	1038	1052	1138	1152	1238	1252	1338	1352	1438	1452	1538	1552	1638	1652	1738	1752	1838	1852	1938	1952	2038	2052	2152	2252	2352
Vejen d.	1014	1052	1114	1152	1214	1252	1314	1352	1414	1451	1514	1551	1614	1651	1714	1751	1814	1851	1914	1951	2014	2051	2114	2214	2314	0014
Lunderskov 710 d.	1022	1059	1122	1159	1222	1259	1322	1359	1422	1459	1522	1559	1622	1659	1722	1759	1822	1859	1922	1959	2022	2059	2122	2222	2322	0022
Kolding 710 d.	1031	1109	1131	1209	1231	1309	1331	1409	1431	1509	1531	1609	1631	1709	1731	1809	1831	1909	1931	2009	2031	2109	2131	2231	2331	0031
Fredericia 700 710/5 d.	1050	|	1150	|	1250	|	1350	|	1450	|	1550	|	1650	|	1750	|	1850	|	1950	|	2050	|	2148	2248	2348	0048
Middelfart 700 d.	|	1123	|	1223	|	1323	|	1423	|	1523	|	1623	|	1723	|	1823	|	1923	|	2023	|	2123	...	...	...	...
Odense 700 d.	|	1148	|	1248	|	1348	|	1448	|	1548	|	1648	|	1748	|	1848	|	1948	|	2048	|	2148	...	...	...	...
København H 700 a.	|	1331	|	1431	|	1531	|	1631	|	1731	|	1831**c**	|	1931	|	2031	|	2131	|	2231	|	*2400***e**	...	...	...	...
Vejle 700 715 d.	1110	...	1210	...	1310	...	1410	...	1510	...	1610	...	1710	...	1810	...	1910	...	2010	...	2110	...	...	...	...	...
Horsens 700 d.	1130	...	1230	...	1330	...	1430	...	1530	...	1630	...	1730	...	1830	...	1930	...	2030	...	2130	...	...	...	...	...
Skanderborg 700 713 d.	1145	...	1245	...	1345	...	1445	...	1545	...	1645	...	1745	...	1845	...	1945	...	2045	...	2145	...	...	...	...	...
Aarhus 700 713 a.	1202	...	1302	...	1402	...	1502	...	1602	...	1702	...	1802	...	1902	...	2002	...	2102	...	2202	...	...	...	...	...

a – ①–⑤ only.
b – Connecting train from København (to Fredericia) departs at 2105 (Table **700**).
d – Change trains at Fredericia on ⑥⑦.
e – Connecting train departs Odense at 2225.
f – 0648 on ⑥⑦.

707 ESBJERG - SKJERN

Operator: *AT*; 2nd class only

km			Ⓐ	Ⓐ	Ⓐ	Ⓐ	Ⓐ		Ⓐ	Ⓐ	Ⓐ	Ⓐ	Ⓐ	Ⓐ	Ⓐ			⑥	Ⓒ	⑥	Ⓒ		Ⓒ	Ⓒ	Ⓒ
0	**Esbjerg** ▷ d.	Ⓐ	0442	0537	0641	0802	0903		1603	1641	...	1839	2039	2239	2330	...	Ⓒ	...	...	0617	0817		2017	2217	2317
17	Varde ▷ d.		0501	0555	0702	0829	0929	and	1629	1700	1729	1857	2057	2257	2349	...		0437	0637	0637	0837	and every	2037	2237	2336
60	**Skjern** a.		0538	0633	0739	0910	1010	hourly	1710	...	1810	1934	2134	2334	...	...		0513	0713	0713	0913	**two** hours	2113	2313	...
	Herning 713 a.		0621	0723	0823	0954	1056	until	1756	...	...	2014	2214	0023	...	...		0555	0755	0755	0955	until	2155	2355	...
	Aarhus 713 a.		...	...	...	1136	1236		1936	...	...	2139	2239	...	...	...		...	...	0930	1130		2330	...	...

		Ⓐ	Ⓐ	Ⓐ	Ⓐ	Ⓐ		Ⓐ	Ⓐ	Ⓐ	Ⓐ	Ⓐ	Ⓐ				⑥	⑥	⑦	Ⓒ		Ⓒ	Ⓒ		
Aarhus 713 d.	Ⓐ	...	...	...	0623	0726		1326	1426	1526	1726	1918	...	...	...	Ⓒ	...	0530	0730	0930		1930	...	...	...
Herning 713 d.		...	0554	0655	0755	0902	and	1502	1602	1702	1902	2102	...	...	...		0502	0702	0902	1102	and every	2102	2302	...	...
Skjern d.		0602	0650	0742	0842	0942	hourly	1542	1642	1742	1942	2142	2342	...	...		0543	0743	0943	1143	**two** hours	2143	2343	...	...
Varde ▷ d.		0645	0740	0822	0922	1022	until	1622	1720	1820	2019	2219	0018	...	...		0620	0820	1020	1220	until	2220	0019	...	...
Esbjerg ▷ a.		0703	0801	0839	0940	1040		1640	1738	1838	2037	2237	...	...	...		0638	0838	1038	1238		2238	...	...	...

▷ – Additional services operate Esbjerg - Varde and v.v.

SKJERN - HOLSTEBRO 708

Operator: *MIDTTRAFIK* 2nd class only

km			Ⓐ	Ⓐ	Ⓐ	Ⓐ	Ⓐ	Ⓐ	Ⓐ		Ⓐ	Ⓐ	Ⓐ	Ⓐ	Ⓐ	Ⓐ				Ⓒ		Ⓒ	Ⓒ
0	**Skjern** d.	Ⓐ	0504	0619	0715	0801	0906	1044	1138	and	1638	1740	1911	2011	2139	2345	...	...	Ⓒ	0715	and every	2215	2315
23	Ringkøbing d.		0523	0639	0736	0819	0924	1102	1156	hourly	1656	1758	1930	2030	2156	0002	...	...		0735	**two** hours	2235	2333
71	**Holstebro** a.		0605	0720	0818	0857	1007	1140	1240	until	1735	1838	2008	2109	2234	...	...	...		0814	until	2314	...

		Ⓐ	Ⓐ	Ⓐ	Ⓐ	Ⓐ	Ⓐ	Ⓐ	Ⓐ		Ⓐ	Ⓐ	Ⓐ	Ⓐ	Ⓐ				Ⓒ	Ⓒ		Ⓒ
Holstebro d.	Ⓐ	0445	0534	0638	0737	0936	1021	1108	1208	and	1608	1808	1852	2025	2244	...	...	Ⓒ	0737	0837	and every	2137
Ringkøbing d.		0524	0620	0716	0819	1015	1102	1157	1257	hourly	1657	1848	1931	2107	2323	...	...		0824	0916	**two** hours	2216
Skjern a.		0542	0637	0734	0837	1032	1120	1214	1314	until	1714	1906	1948	2125	2340	...	...		0841	0933	until	2233

ESBJERG - TØNDER - NIEBÜLL 709

Operator: *AT* 2nd class only

ESBJERG - TØNDER

km			Ⓐ	Ⓐ	Ⓐ	Ⓐ		Ⓐ	Ⓐ	Ⓐ	Ⓐ	Ⓐ				⑦	⑥	Ⓒ		Ⓒ	Ⓒ	Ⓒ	Ⓒ
0	**Esbjerg** ▷ d.	Ⓐ	0425	0531	0631	0756	and	1756	1956	2046	2156	2256	...	...	Ⓒ	...	0557	0757	and every	1957	2055	2157	2255
16	Bramming ▷ d.		0440	0546	0646	0812	hourly	1812	2012	2101	2212	2312	...	...		...	0612	0812	**two** hours	2012	2110	2212	2310
33	Ribe ▷ d.		0458	0603	0705	0831	until	1831	2031	2118	2231	2328	...	...		0635	0635	0835	until	2035	2127	2235	2327
80	**Tønder** a.		0546	0651	0754	0922		1922	2122	...	2319	...	...	...		0722	0722	0922		2122	...	2322	...

		Ⓐ	Ⓐ	Ⓐ		Ⓐ		Ⓐ	Ⓐ	Ⓐ				⑥	Ⓒ		Ⓒ	Ⓒ	Ⓒ		
Tønder d.	Ⓐ	0554	0657	0827	and	1927	...	2127	...	2327	...	...	Ⓒ	0527	0727	and every	2127	...	2327	...	...
Ribe ▷ d.		0645	0750	0914	hourly	2014	2124	2214	2333	0013	...	...		0614	0814	**two** hours	2214	2332	0013	...	...
Bramming ▷ d.		0712	0812	0932	until	2032	2142	2232	2351	...	...	...		0632	0832	until	2231	2351	...	...	...
Esbjerg ▷ a.		0726	0826	0947		2047	2157	2247	0006	...	...	...		0647	0847		2247	0006	...	...	...

TØNDER - NIEBÜLL ★

17 km. Journey time: 17 – 19 minutes. Operated by Norddeutsche Eisenbahn.

From Tønder: On ①–⑤ at 0706, 0832, 1032, 1232, 1432, 1532, 1632, 1832, 1932 and 2132; on ⑥ at 0732 and every **two** hours until 2132; on ⑦ at 0932 and every **two** hours until 2132.

From Niebüll: On ①–⑤ at 0636, 0733, 1007, 1207, 1407, 1507, 1607, 1807, 1907 and 2107; on ⑥ at 0707 and every **two** hours until 2107; on ⑦ at 0907 and every **two** hours until 2107.

▷ – Additional services operate Esbjerg - Ribe and v.v. See Table **705** for other services Esbjerg - Bramming and v.v.

★ – Danish public holiday dates apply.

FREDERICIA - SØNDERBORG and FLENSBURG 710

See Table **705** for other *IC* services København - Odense - Kolding - Lunderskov and v.v.

km		*IC*		*Lyn*	*Lyn*	*IC*	*IC*	*IC*	*Lyn*	*Lyn*	*Lyn*		*IC*	*IC*	*IC*	*Lyn*	*Lyn*	*IC*	*IC*	*Lyn*	*Lyn*		*IC*	*IC*
		5751		**911**	**6**	**5753**	**5753**	**1191**	**919**	**19**	**116**		**5755**	**1183**	**393**	**27**	**124**	**383**	**1193**	**35**	**132**		**79**	**395**
								j		**919**	**919**		**d**	**5755**	**p**	**927**	**927**	**5757**	**j**	**935**	**935**		**5759**	
		Ⓐ		Ⓐ	Ⓐ		Ⓐ	**R**	Ⓒ	Ⓐ			Ⓐ	Ⓒ**d**	**R**			**R**	**R**					**R**
	København H **700** d.	...	...	...	...	...	...	0526		0556	...	...	...	...	0726	0756	...	...	0926	0956	...	...	...	1126
	Odense **700** d.	...	...	0513	...	...	...	|	0700	0710	...	...	...	...	|	0910	...	...	|	1110	...	...	...	|
	Aarhus **700** d.	...	...	|	0400	...	0539	|	|	|	0645	...	0732	0739	|	|	0845	0939	|	|	1045	...	1115	|
0	**Fredericia** **705** d.	0445	...	0550	0550	0645	0645	|	0750	0750	0750	...	0845	0845	|	0950	0950	1045	|	1150	1150	...	1245	|
20	Kolding **705** d.	0458	...	0603	0603	0658	0658	0718	0803	0803	0803	...	0858	0858	0918	1003	1003	1058	1118	1203	1203	...	1258	1318
33	Lunderskov **705** d.	0506	...	0611	0611	0706	0706	|	0811	0811	0811	...	0906	0906	|	1011	1011	1106	|	1211	1211	...	1306	|
60	Vojens d.	0523	...	0628	0628	0723	0723	|	0828	0828	0828	...	0923	0923	|	1028	1028	1123	|	1228	1228	...	1323	|
95	Tinglev d.	0544	...	0649	0649	0744	0744	|	0849	0849	0849	...	0944	0944	|	1049	1049	1144	|	1249	1249	...	1344	|
136	**Sønderborg** a.	|	...	0722	0722	|	|	|	0922	0922	0922	...	|	|	|	1122	1122	|	|	1322	1322	...	|	|
110	Padborg 🏛 a.	0553	...	...	...	0753	0753	0759	...	...	...	...	0953	0953	0959	...	...	1153	1159	...	...	...	1353	1359
122	**Flensburg** 🏛 a.	0607	...	...	...	0807	0807	|	...	...	...	...	1007	1007	|	...	...	1207	|	...	...	...	1407	|
302	*Hamburg Hbf* **823** a.	...	...	...	...	...	...	1005	...	...	...	...	...	1202j	1205	...	...	1402p	1406	...	...	...	...	1602

	Lyn	*Lyn*	*IC*	*IC*	*Lyn*	*Lyn*	*IC*	*IC*	*IC*	*Lyn*	*Lyn*	*IC*	*IC*	*Lyn*	*Lyn*	*IC*	*Lyn*	*Lyn*	*IC*	*IC*	*Lyn*	*IC*	*IC*
	43	**140**	**385**	**1197**	**51**	**148**	**1187**	**1187**	**397**	**59**	**156**	**5765**	**1199**	**67**	**164**	**5767**	**75**	**472**	**177/9**	**181**	**983**	**399**	**399**
	943	**943**	**5761**	**j**	**951**	**951**	**5763**	**j**	**p**	**959**	**959**		**j**	**967**	**967**		**975**	**975**	**3374**	**3390**		**m**	**j**
			R	**R**				**R**	**R**				**R**					⑤⑥				**R**	**R**
København H **700** d.	1156	...	...	1326	1356	...	...	...	1526	1556	...	...	1726	1756	...	...	1956	...	2005	2105	...	0001	0001
Odense **700** d.	1310	...	...	|	1510	...	...	...	|	1710	...	...	|	1910	...	...	2110	...	2135	2235	...	0137	0137
Aarhus **700** d.	|	1245	1339	|	|	1445	1515	1539	|	|	1645	1739	|	|	1845	1915n	|	2045	|	|	...	|	|
Fredericia **705** d.	1350	1350	1445	|	1550	1550	1645	1645	|	1750	1750	1845	|	1950	1950	2045	2150	2150	2213	2323	2358	0221	0221
Kolding **705** d.	1403	1403	1458	1518	1603	1603	1658	1658	1718	1803	1803	1858	1918	2003	2003	2058	2203	2203	2228	2338	0011	|	|
Lunderskov **705** d.	1411	1411	1506	|	1611	1611	1706	1706	|	1811	1811	1906	|	2011	2011	2106	2211	2211	2236	2346	0019	|	|
Vojens d.	1428	1428	1523	|	1628	1628	1723	1723	|	1828	1828	1923	|	2028	2028	2123	2228	2228	...	...	0036	|	|
Tinglev d.	1449	1449	1544	|	1649	1649	1744	1744	|	1849	1849	1944	|	2049	2049	2144	2249	2249	...	...	0057	|	|
Sønderborg a.	1522	1522	|	|	1722	1722	|	|	|	1922	1922	|	|	2122	2122	|	2322	2322	...	...	0130	|	|
Padborg 🏛 a.	...	...	1553	1559	...	...	1753	1753	1759	...	...	1953	1959	...	...	2153	...	...	...	...	...	0325	0325
Flensburg 🏛 a.	...	...	1607	|	...	...	1807	1807	|	...	...	2007	|	...	...	2207	...	...	...	...	...	0340	0340
Hamburg Hbf **823** a.	...	...	1802p	1804	...	...	...	2002	2002	...	...	...	2158	...	...	...	...	...	...	...	...	0624	0618b

	Lyn	*Lyn*	*Lyn*	*Lyn*	*IC*	*IC*	*IC*	*Lyn*	*Lyn*	*IC*	*IC*	*Lyn*	*Lyn*	*IC*	*IC*	*IC*	*Lyn*	*Lyn*	*IC*	*IC*	*Lyn*	*Lyn*	*IC*
	910	**910**	**914**	**914**	**3321**	**5750**	**5750**	**922**	**922**	**1198**	**5752**	**930**	**930**	**396**	**1186**	**5754**	**938**	**938**	**1196**	**386**	**946**	**946**	**394**
	10	**113**	**14**	**117**	**116**			**22**	**125**	**j**	**31**	**30**	**133**	**p**	**j**	**39**	**38**	**141**	**j**	**5756**	**46**	**149**	
	Ⓐ	Ⓐ	Ⓐ	Ⓐ	Ⓒ	⚒	⑦			**R**				**R**	**R**				**R**	**R**			**R**
Hamburg Hbf **823** d.	...	...	...	...	...	...	...	...	...	0652b	...	...	...	0856	0853	...	...	...	1053	1053p	...	...	1253
Flensburg 🏛 ★ d.	...	...	...	...	...	0650	...	...	...	|	0850	...	...	|	1050	1050	...	...	|	1250	...	...	|
Padborg 🏛 d.	...	...	...	...	...	0706	...	...	...	0859	0906	...	...	1059	1106	1106	...	...	1259	1306	...	...	1459
Sønderborg d.	0435	0435	0535	0535	...	|	...	0735	0735	|	|	0935	0935	|	|	|	1135	1135	|	|	1335	1335	|
Tinglev d.	0510	0510	0610	0610	...	0716	0716	0810	0810	|	0916	1010	1010	|	1116	1116	1210	1210	|	1316	1410	1410	|
Vojens d.	0529	0529	0629	0629	...	0736	0736	0829	0829	|	0936	1029	1029	|	1136	1136	1229	1229	|	1336	1429	1429	|
Lunderskov **705** d.	0545	0545	0645	0645	0722	0753	0753	0845	0845	|	0953	1045	1045	|	1153	1153	1245	1245	|	1353	1445	1445	|
Kolding **705** d.	0555	0555	0655	0655	0731	0802	0802	0855	0855	0943	1002	1055	1055	1143	1202	1202	1255	1255	1343	1402	1455	1455	1543
Fredericia **705** a.	0607	0607	0723	0723	0748	0814	0814	0907	0907	|	1014	1107	1107	|	1214	1214	1307	1307	|	1414	1507	1507	|
Aarhus **700** a.	|	0712	|	0812	|	0914	0914	|	1012	|	1142	|	1212	|	1318	1342	|	1412	|	1520	|	1612	|
Odense **700** a.	0650	...	0750	...	0823	...	...	0950	...	|	...	1150	...	|	...	...	1350	...	|	...	1550	...	|
København H **700** a.	0803	...	0903	...	0955	...	...	1103	...	1133	...	1303	...	1334	...	...	1503	...	1534	...	1703	...	1734

	IC	*Lyn*	*Lyn*	*IC*	*IC*	*Lyn*	*Lyn*	*IC*	*IC*	*IC*	*IC*	*IC*	*Lyn*	*Lyn*	*IC*	*IC*	*IC*	*IC*	*Lyn*	*Lyn*	*IC*	*IC*	*IC*
	5758	**954**	**954**	**1192**	**384**	**962**	**962**	**392**	**1182**	**5762**	**5762**	**5762**	**970**	**970**	**3375**	**1190**	**5764**	**3379**	**978**	**978**	**5766**	**398**	**390**
	55	**54**	**157**	**j**	**5760**	**62**	**165**	**p**	**j**		**71**	**171**	**70**	**173**	**472**	**j**	**177/9**	**476**	**78**	**181**		**e**	**f**
				R	**R**			**R**	**R**	⑥	⑤	⑦–④		⑦–④		**R**						**R**	**R**
Hamburg Hbf **823** d.	...	...	...	1453	1450p	...	...	1654	1652	...	...	...	...	...	...	1853	...	...	...	...	...	2356	2356
Flensburg 🏛 ★ d.	1450	...	...	|	1650	...	...	|	1850	1850	1850	1850	...	...	...	|	2050	...	...	...	2250	0250	0250
Padborg 🏛 d.	1506	...	...	1659	1706	...	...	1859	1906	1906	1906	1906	...	...	...	2059	2106	...	...	...	2306	0340	0340
Sønderborg d.	|	1535	1535	|	|	1735	1735	|	|	|	|	|	1935	1935	...	|	|	...	2135	2135	|	|	|
Tinglev d.	1516	1610	1610	|	1716	1810	1810	|	1916	1916	1916	1916	2010	2010	...	|	2116	...	2210	2210	2316	|	|
Vojens d.	1536	1629	1629	|	1736	1829	1829	|	1936	1936	1936	1936	2029	2029	...	|	2136	...	2229	2229	2336	|	|
Lunderskov **705** d.	1553	1645	1645	|	1753	1845	1845	|	1953	1953	1953	1953	2045	2045	2122	|	2153	2222	2245	2245	2353	|	|
Kolding **705** d.	1602	1655	1655	1743	1802	1855	1855	1943	2002	2002	2002	2002	2055	2055	2131	2143	2202	2231	2255	2255	0002	|	|
Fredericia **705** a.	1614	1707	1707	|	1814	1907	1907	|	2014	2014	2014	2014	2107	2107	2148	|	2214	2248	2307	2307	0014	0439	0439
Aarhus **700** a.	1742	|	1812	|	1920	|	2012	|	2119	2119	2142	2147	|	2247	|	|	2355	|	|	0053	0153	|	|
Odense **700** a.	...	1750	...	|	...	1950n	...	...	...	...	...	...	2150n	...	2223	|	...	2323	2348	...	...	0516	0516
København H **700** a.	...	1903n	...	1934	...	2103n	...	2134	...	...	...	...	2303n	...	2400	2334	...	0100	...	...	...	0655	0700

R – 🅁 for international journeys.

b – Hamburg **Altona**.

d – Not Apr. 3 – 5.

e – ①–④⑦ June 18 - Sept. 10.

f – ⑤⑥ June 16 - Sept. 9.

j – June 17 - Aug. 20.

m – Aug. 20 - Sept. 10.

p – Dec. 11 - June 16, Aug. 21 - Dec. 9.

★ – Danish public holiday dates apply.

712 AARHUS - VIBORG - STRUER

Operator: *AT* 2nd class only

km	Ⓐ	Ⓐ	Ⓐ	Ⓐ	Ⓐ	Ⓐ	Ⓐ	Ⓐ	Ⓐ	Ⓐ	Ⓐ	Ⓐ	Ⓐ	Ⓐ	Ⓐ	Ⓐ	Ⓐ	Ⓐ	Ⓐ	Ⓐ	Ⓐ		
0	**Aarhus** 701 ▷ d.	0432	0523	0623	0654	0755	0854	0954	1054	1154	1254	1354	1454	1554	1654	1754	1854	1954	2054	2154	2329	...	...
46	Langå 701 ▷ a.	0502	0553	0653	0724	0825	0924	1024	1124	1224	1324	1424	1524	1624	1724	1824	1924	2024	2124	2224	2359	...	...
46	Langå ▷ d.	0507	0558	0658	0730	0830	0930	1030	1130	1230	1330	1430	1530	1630	1730	1830	1930	2030	2130	2230	0004	...	...
86	Viborg ▷ d.	0539	0645j	0730	0802	0905	1005	1105	1205	1305	1405	1505	1605	1705	1805	1905	2005	2105	2205	2305	0034	...	...
116	Skive d.	0608	0716	0754	0826	0929	1029	1129	1226	1329	1429	1529	1629	1729	1829	1929	2029	2128	2229	2329	...	...	...
148	**Struer** a.	0630	0741	0815	0852	0952	1052	1152	1252	1352	1452	1552	1652	1752	1852	1952	2052	...	2252	2352	...	...	...

Ⓒ	⑥	⑥	⑥	Ⓒ	Ⓒ	Ⓒ	Ⓒ	⑦	⑥	Ⓒ	Ⓒ	Ⓒ	Ⓒ	Ⓒ	Ⓒ	Ⓒ	⑥	⑦	Ⓒ	⑥	⑦	Ⓒ	Ⓒ	
Aarhus 701 ▷ d.	...	0455	0555	0655	0755	0855	0955	1055	1055	1155	1255	1355	1455	1555	1655	1755	1855	1855	1955	2055	2055	2155	2301	...
Langå 701 ▷ a.	...	0525	0625	0725	0825	0925	1025	1125	1125	1225	1325	1425	1525	1625	1725	1825	1925	1925	2025	2125	2125	2225	2331	...
Langå ▷ d.	...	0530	0630	0730	0830	0930	1030	1130	1130	1230	1330	1430	1530	1630	1730	1830	1930	1930	2030	2130	2130	2230	2336	...
Viborg ▷ d.	0505	0605	0705	0805	0905	1005	1105	1205	1205	1305	1405	1505	1605	1705	1805	1905	2005	2005	2105	2205	2205	2305	0006	...
Skive d.	0529	0628	0729	0829	0929	1029	1129	1228	1229	1329	1429	1529	1629	1729	1829	1929	2028	2029	2129	2228	2229	2329	...	...
Struer a.	0552	...	0752	0852	0952	1052	1152	...	1252	1352	1452	1552	1652	1752	1852	1952	...	2052	2152	...	2252	2352	...	...

Ⓐ	Ⓐ	Ⓐ	Ⓐ	Ⓐ	Ⓐ	Ⓐ	Ⓐ	Ⓐ	Ⓐ	Ⓐ	Ⓐ	Ⓐ	Ⓐ	Ⓐ	Ⓐ	Ⓐ	Ⓐ	Ⓐ	Ⓐ	Ⓐ	Ⓐ			
Struer d.	...	0450	0515	0546	0639	0707	0816	0915	1015	1115	1215	1315	1415	1515	1615	1715	1815	1915	2015	...	2215	...	...	...
Skive d.	...	0512	0537	0608	0701	0729	0839	0941	1041	1141	1241	1341	1441	1541	1641	1741	1841	1941	2041	2141	2241	...	...	...
Viborg ▷ d.	0437	0538	0607	0637	0739k	0808	0909	1009	1109	1209	1309	1409	1509	1609	1709	1809	1909	2009	2109	2209	2309	...	...	...
Langå ▷ a.	0506	0610	0640	0710	0813	0842	0943	1043	1143	1243	1343	1443	1543	1643	1743	1843	1943	2043	2143	2243	2338	...	...	...
Langå 701 ▷ d.	0511	0615	0647	0715	0818	0847	0948	1048	1148	1248	1348	1448	1548	1648	1748	1848	1948	2048	2148	2248	2343	...	...	...
Aarhus 701 ▷ a.	0542	0647	0720	0746	0849	0918	1019	1119	1219	1319	1419	1519	1619	1719	1819	1919	2019	2119	2219	2319	0014	...	...	...

Ⓒ	⑥	⑥	⑥	Ⓒ	Ⓒ	Ⓒ	Ⓒ	Ⓒ	⑥	⑦	Ⓒ	Ⓒ	Ⓒ	Ⓒ	Ⓒ	Ⓒ	Ⓒ	⑥	⑦	Ⓒ	⑥	⑦	Ⓒ	
Struer d.	...	0515	...	0715	0815	0915	1015	1115	1215	...	1315	1415	1515	1615	1715	1815	1915	...	2015	2115	...	2215	2315	...
Skive d.	...	0541	0641	0741	0841	0941	1041	1141	1241	1241	1341	1441	1541	1641	1741	1841	1941	2041	2041	2141	2241	2241	2341	...
Viborg ▷ d.	0511	0611	0711	0811	0911	1011	1111	1211	1311	1311	1411	1511	1611	1711	1811	1911	2011	2111	2111	2211	2311	2311	0005	...
Langå ▷ a.	0543	0643	0743	0843	0943	1043	1143	1243	1343	1343	1443	1543	1643	1743	1843	1943	2043	2143	2143	2243	2348	2348	...	...
Langå 701 ▷ d.	0548	0648	0748	0848	0948	1048	1148	1248	1348	1348	1448	1548	1648	1748	1848	1948	2048	2148	2148	2248	2353	2353	...	...
Aarhus 701 ▷ a.	0619	0719	0819	0919	1019	1119	1219	1319	1419	1419	1519	1619	1719	1819	1919	2019	2119	2219	2219	2319	0024	0024	...	...

j – Arrives 0628. k – Arrives 0725. ▷ – Additional services operate Aarhus - Viborg and v.v.

713 AARHUS - HERNING - SKJERN and STRUER

Operator: *AT*; 2nd class only

km	Ⓐ	Ⓐ	Ⓐ	Ⓐ	Ⓐ	Ⓐ	Ⓐ	Ⓐ	Ⓐ	Ⓐ		Ⓐ	Ⓐ	Ⓐ	Ⓐ	Ⓐ	Ⓐ	Ⓐ	Ⓐ	Ⓐ	Ⓐ	Ⓐ	Ⓐ
0	**Aarhus** 700 705 d.	...	...	0457	...	0601	0623	0706	0726	0802	and at	1502	1526	1602	1702	1726	1802	1826	1918	2018	2118	2218	2337
23	Skanderborg 700 705 d.	...	...	0516	...	0620	0642	0725	0745	0821	the same	1521	1545	1621	1721	1745	1821	1845	1937	2037	2137	2237	2356
53	Silkeborg d.	...	...	0542	...	0644	0711	0753	0814	0849	minutes	1549	1614	1649	1749	1814	1853	1914	2011	2111	2211	2307	0022
94	**Herning** a.	...	...	0619	...	0725	0752	0825	0853	0924	past each	1624	1653	1724	1824	1853	1925	1953	2052	2152	2252	2343	0058
94	**Herning** 715 d.	0458	0554	0627	0655	0727	0755	0827	0902	0927	hour until	1627	1702	1727	1827	1902	...	...	2102	2159	2302	...	...
	Holstebro 715 d.	|	|	0705	|	0818	|	0905	|	1005		1705	|	1805	1905	|	...	...	|	2234	|	...	...
	Struer 715 a.	|	|	0718	|	0831	|	0918	|	1018		1718	|	1818	1918	|	...	...	|	2247	|	...	...
136	**Skjern** a.	0535	0628	...	0729	...	0829	...	0936	...		...	1736	...	...	1936	...	...	2136	...	2336	...	...
	Esbjerg 707 a.	...	0801	...	0839	...	0940	...	1040	...		...	1838	...	...	2037	...	...	2237	...	...	...	...

Ⓒ	⑥	⑥	⑦	⑥	Ⓒ	Ⓒ	Ⓒ	Ⓒ	Ⓒ	Ⓒ	Ⓒ	Ⓒ	Ⓒ	Ⓒ	Ⓒ	Ⓒ	Ⓒ	Ⓒ	Ⓒ	Ⓒ	Ⓒ			
Aarhus 700 705 d.	...	0530	...	0630	0730	0830	0930	1030	1130	1230	1330	1430	1530	1630	1730	1830	1930	2030	2130	2230	2336	...	...	...
Skanderborg 700 705 d.	...	0550	...	0650	0750	0850	0950	1050	1150	1250	1350	1450	1550	1650	1750	1850	1950	2050	2150	2250	2355	...	...	...
Silkeborg d.	...	0617	...	0717	0817	0917	1017	1117	1217	1317	1417	1517	1617	1717	1817	1917	2017	2117	2217	2318	0022	...	...	...
Herning a.	...	0653	...	0753	0853	0953	1053	1153	1253	1353	1453	1553	1653	1753	1853	1953	2053	2153	2253	2354	0058	...	...	...
Herning 715 d.	0502	0702	0702	...	0902	...	1102	...	1302	...	1502	...	1702	...	1902	...	2102	...	2302	...	...	...	...	...
Holstebro 715 d.	|	|	|	...	|	...	|	...	|	...	|	...	|	...	|	...	|	...	|	...	...	...	...	...
Struer 715 a.	|	|	|	...	|	...	|	...	|	...	|	...	|	...	|	...	|	...	|	...	...	...	...	...
Skjern a.	0537	0737	0737	...	0937	...	1137	...	1337	...	1537	...	1737	...	1937	...	2137	...	2337	...	...	...	...	...
Esbjerg 707 a.	0638	0838	0838	...	1038	...	1238	...	1438	...	1638	...	1838	...	2038	...	2238	...	...	...	...	...	...	...

Ⓐ	Ⓐ	Ⓐ	Ⓐ	Ⓐ	Ⓐ	Ⓐ	Ⓐ	Ⓐ	Ⓐ	Ⓐ	Ⓐ	Ⓐ	Ⓐ	Ⓐ	Ⓐ		Ⓐ	Ⓐ	Ⓐ	Ⓐ	Ⓐ	Ⓐ	Ⓐ
Esbjerg 707 d.	...	...	0442	...	...	0537	...	...	0641	...	...	...	0802	...	0903		...	1503	...	1603	...	1839	...
Skjern d.	...	0517	0543	...	...	0645	...	...	0745	...	...	...	0918	...	1018	and at	...	1618	...	1718	...	1939	...
Struer 715 d.	...	|	|	0532	...	|	0632	...	|	0723	...	0832	|	0932	|	the same	1532	|	1632	|	...	|	...
Holstebro 715 d.	...	|	|	0548	...	|	0648	...	|	0748	...	0848	|	0948	|		1548	|	1648	|	...	|	...
Herning 715 a.	...	0552	0621	0623	...	0723	0725	...	0823	0825	...	0925	0954	1025	1054	minutes	1625	1654	1725	1754	...	2014	...
Herning d.	0519	0555	...	0624	0702	...	0731	0802	...	0831	0902	0931	1002	1031	1102	past each	1631	1702	1731	1802	1902	2015	2115
Silkeborg d.	0555	0632	...	0657	0739	...	0812	0847	...	0912	0947	1012	1047	1112	1147	hour until	1712	1747	1812	1847	1944	2053	2153
Skanderborg 700 705 d.	0619	0703	...	0720	0806	...	0838	0916	...	0938	1016	1038	1116	1138	1216		1738	1816	1838	1816	2011	2120	2220
Aarhus 700 705 a.	0639	0723	...	0739	0825	...	0857	0936	...	0957	1036	1057	1136	1157	1236		1757	1836	1857	1936	2031	2139	2239

	Ⓐ	Ⓐ	Ⓐ	Ⓒ	⑥	⑥	Ⓒ	⑥	⑦	Ⓒ	Ⓒ	Ⓒ	Ⓒ	Ⓒ	Ⓒ	Ⓒ	Ⓒ	Ⓒ	Ⓒ	Ⓒ	Ⓒ	Ⓒ	Ⓒ	Ⓒ	Ⓒ
Esbjerg 707 d.	2039	...	2239		...	...	...	0617	...	...	0817	...	1017	...	1217	...	1417	...	1617	...	1817	...	2017	...	2217
Skjern d.	2139	...	2345		...	0518	...	0718	0718	...	0918	...	1118	...	1318	...	1518	...	1718	...	1918	...	2118	...	2318
Struer 715 d.	|	...	|		...	|	...	|	|	...	|	...	|	...	|	...	|	...	|	...	|	...	|	...	|
Holstebro 715 d.	|	...	|		...	|	...	|	|	...	|	...	|	...	|	...	|	...	|	...	|	...	|	...	|
Herning 715 a.	2214	...	0023		...	0555	...	0755	0755	...	0955	...	1155	...	1355	...	1555	...	1755	...	1955	...	2155	...	2355
Herning d.	2215	2329	...		0502	0602	0702	0802	0802	0902	1002	1102	1202	1302	1402	1502	1602	1702	1802	1902	2002	2102	2202	2329	...
Silkeborg d.	2253	0007	...		0542	0642	0742	0842	0842	0942	1042	1142	1242	1342	1442	1542	1642	1742	1842	1942	2042	2142	2242	0007	...
Skanderborg 700 705 d.	2320	0036	...		0611	0711	0811	0911	0911	1011	1111	1211	1311	1411	1511	1611	1711	1811	1911	2011	2111	2211	2311	0036	...
Aarhus 700 705 a.	2339	0055	...		0630	0730	0830	0930	0930	1030	1130	1230	1330	1430	1530	1630	1730	1830	1930	2030	2139	2230	2330	0055	...

715 VEJLE - HERNING - STRUER

Operators: *AT (2nd class only)*, DSB

km		2	2	2	2	2		*Lyn* 23 **723**	2	*Lyn* 31 **731**	2	2	2		*Lyn* 47 **747**	2	2	2		*Lyn* 63 **763**	2	2	2	2
	København H 700 d.	...	...	...	...	...	...	0656	...	0856	...	...	...	...	1256	...	...	...	...	1656	...	...	...	...
	Odense 700 d.	...	...	...	...	...	...	0810	...	1010	...	...	...	...	1410	...	...	...	...	1810	...	...	...	...
	Fredericia 700 d.	...	...	...	...	...	...	0846	...	1046	...	...	...	...	1446	...	...	...	...	1846	...	...	...	...
0	**Velje** d.	...	0503	0603	0703	0803	...	0903	1003	1103	1203	1303	1403	...	1503	1603	1703	1803	...	1903	2003	2103	2203	2303
73	Herning a.	...	0557	0657	0757	0857	...	0957	1057	1157	1257	1357	1457	...	1557	1657	1757	1857	...	1957	2057	2157	2257	2357
73	Herning 713 d.	0459	0559	0659	0759	0859	...	0959	1059	1159	1259	1359	1459	...	1559	1659	1759	1859	...	1959	2059	2159	2309	...
114	Holstebro 708 713 d.	0534	0534	0738	0834	0934	...	1034	1134	1234	1334	1434	1534	...	1634	1734	1834	1934	...	2034	2134	2234	2346	...
129	**Struer** 708 713 a.	0547	0647	0750	0847	0947	...	1047	1147	1247	1347	1447	1547	...	1647	1747	1847	1947	...	2047	2147	2247	2359	...

	2	2	2	2		*Lyn* 726 **26**	2	2	2		*Lyn* 742 **42**	2		*Lyn* 750 **50**	2	2	2		*Lyn* 766 **66**	2	2	2	2	2
Struer 708 713 d.	...	0504	0604	0704	...	0804	0904	1004	1104	...	1204	1304	...	1404	1504	1604	1704	...	1804	1904	2004	2104	2204	2304
Holstebro 708 713 d.	...	0518	0618	0718	...	0818	0918	1018	1118	...	1218	1318	...	1418	1518	1618	1718	...	1818	1918	2018	2118	2218	2318
Herning 713 a.	...	0552	0652	0752	...	0852	0952	1052	1152	...	1252	1352	...	1452	1552	1652	1752	...	1852	1952	2052	2152	2252	2350
Herning d.	0456	0558	0658	0758	...	0858	0958	1058	1158	...	1258	1358	...	1458	1558	1658	1758	...	1858	1958	2058	2158	2258	...
Vejle a.	0555	0655	0755	0855	...	0956	1055	1155	1255	...	1356	1455	...	1556	1655	1755	1855	...	1956	2055	2155	2255	2356	...
Fredericia 700 a.	...	...	...	...	...	1017	...	...	...	...	1417	...	...	1617	...	...	...	...	2017	...	...	...	...	...
Odense 700 a.	...	...	...	...	...	1050	...	...	...	...	1450	...	...	1650	...	...	...	...	2050	...	...	...	...	...
København H 700 a.	...	...	...	...	...	1203	...	...	...	...	1603	...	...	1803	...	...	...	...	2203	...	...	...	...	...

STRUER - THISTED 716

Operator: *AT* 2nd class only

km				Ⓐ	Ⓐ	Ⓐ	Ⓐ		Ⓐ	Ⓐ	Ⓐ	Ⓐ	Ⓐ	Ⓐ	Ⓐ	Ⓐ	Ⓐ			⑥	©		©	⑦	⑥
0	**Struer**	d.	Ⓐ	0415	0514	0606	0708	...	1007	1207	1307	1407	1507	1607	1807	2007	2207	...	©	0511	0706	and every	2104	2220	2304
74	**Thisted**	a.		0532	0634	0737	0839	...	1124	1324	1424	1524	1624	1724	1924	2124	2324	...		0627	0823	**two** hours until	2221	2340	0021

			Ⓐ	Ⓐ	Ⓐ	Ⓐ	Ⓐ	Ⓐ	Ⓐ	Ⓐ	Ⓐ	Ⓐ	Ⓐ	Ⓐ	Ⓐ			⑥	©		©	©	⑦	⑥
Thisted	d.	Ⓐ	0537	0639	0742	0844	1134	1329	1429	1529	1629	1735	1935	2135	2329	...	©	0633	0830	and every	2030	2229	2346	0029
Struer	a.		0653	0755	0858	1000	1254	1454	1554	1654	1745	1854	2054	2254	0045	...		0753	0951	**two** hours until	2151	2351	0102	0145

KØBENHAVN - NYKØBING 720

km			⑦–①	©p	Ⓐ	Ⓐ	©	Ⓐ	Ⓐ	Ⓐ	Ⓐ			Ⓐ		Ⓐ		m		m		m		m
0	**København** H	700 704 ▷ d.	0026	0426	0507	...	0606	0607	...	0637	0640	0707	...	0740	0807	0840	0907	0940	1007	1040	1107	1140	1207	1240
20	Høje Taastrup	700 704 ▷ d.	0040	0440	0521	...	0621	0621	...	0651	|	0721	...	|	0821	|	0921	|	1021	|	1121	|	1221	|
31	Roskilde	700 704 ▷ d.	0054	0454	0531	...	0634	0631	...	0701	|	0731	...	|	0831	|	0931	|	1031	|	1131	|	1231	|
64	Ringsted	700 ▷ d.	0117	0516	0554	...	0657	0654	...	0724	0714	0754	...	0814	0854	0914	0954	1014	1054	1114	1154	1214	1254	1314
91	Næstved	▷ d.	0132	0532	0609	0614	0714	0709	0714	0739	0728	0809	0814	0828	0909	0928	1009	1028	1109	1128	1209	1228	1309	1328
118	Vordingborg	d.	...	...	...	0631	0731	...	0730	...	0742	...	0831	0842	...	0942	...	1042	...	1142	...	1242	...	1342
147	**Nykøbing** (Falster)	⊙ a.	...	...	...	0652	0752	...	0752	...	0757	...	0852	0857	...	0957	...	1057	...	1157	...	1257	...	1357

			m		m		Ⓐ	m		Ⓐ	m		Ⓐ	m		Ⓐ	m		m		m			
København H	700 704 ▷ d.	1307	1340	1407	1440	1507	1537	1540	1607	1637	1640	1707	1737	1740	1807	1837	1840	1907	1940	2007	2040	2144	2253	2353
Høje Taastrup	700 704 ▷ d.	1321	|	1421	|	1521	1551	|	1621	1751	|	1721	1751	|	1821	1851	|	1921	|	2021	|	|	|	|
Roskilde	700 704 ▷ d.	1331	|	1431	|	1531	1601	|	1631	1701	|	1731	1801	|	1831	1901	|	1931	|	2031	|	|	|	|
Ringsted	700 ▷ d.	1354	1414	1454	1514	1554	1624	1614	1654	1724	1714	1754	1824	1814	1854	1924	1914	1954	2014	2054	2114	2218	2327	0027
Næstved	▷ d.	1409	1428	1509	1528	1609	1639	1628	1709	1839	1728	1809	1839	1828	1909	1939	1928	2009	2028	2109	2128	2235	2344	0044
Vordingborg	d.	...	1442	...	1542	...	...	1642	...	...	1742	...	...	1842	...	...	1942	...	2042	...	2142	2252	0001	0101
Nykøbing (Falster)	⊙ a.	...	1457	...	1557	...	...	1657	...	...	1757	...	...	1857	...	...	1957	...	2057	...	2157	2313	0022	0122

		Ⓐ	Ⓐ	©	Ⓐ	Ⓐ	Ⓐq	Ⓐ	©	Ⓐr	Ⓐ	Ⓐ	©	©	Ⓐr	Ⓐr		s		s		s		s
Nykøbing (Falster)	⊙ d.	0438	...	0448	0508	...	0538	...	0548	0603	0608	...	0648	...	0703	0803	...	0903	...	1003	...	1103	...	1203
Vordingborg	d.	0459	...	0509	0529	...	0559	...	0609	0618	0629	...	0709	...	0718	0818	...	0918	...	1018	...	1118	...	1218
Næstved	▷ d.	0515	0520	0528	0545	0550	0615	0620	0628	0633	0645	0650	0725	0733	0733	0833	0850	0933	0950	1033	1050	1133	1150	1233
Ringsted	700 ▷ d.	...	0537	0544	...	0607	...	0637	0644	0647	...	0707	...	0749	0747	0847	0907	0947	1007	1047	1107	1147	1207	1247
Roskilde	700 704 ▷ d.	...	0558	0608	...	0628	...	0658	0708	|	...	0728	...	0811	|	|	0928	|	1028	|	1128	|	1228	|
Høje Taastrup	700 704 ▷ a.	...	0607	0607	...	0637	...	0707	0719	|	...	0737	...	0823	|	|	0937	|	1037	|	1137	|	1237	|
København H	700 704 ▷ a.	...	0623	0635	...	0653	...	0723	0735	0720	...	0753	...	0838	0820	0920	0953	1020	1053	1120	1153	1220	1253	1320

			s		s		Ⓐ	s		Ⓐ	s		Ⓐ	s		s		s		s		s	s	
Nykøbing (Falster)	⊙ d.	...	1303	...	1403	...	...	1503	...	...	1603	...	...	1703	...	1803	...	1903	...	2003	...	2051	2151	2321
Vordingborg	d.	...	1318	...	1418	...	...	1518	...	...	1618	...	...	1718	...	1818	...	1918	...	2018	...	2112	2212	2342
Næstved	▷ d.	1250	1333	1350	1433	1450	1520	1533	1550	1620	1633	1650	1720	1733	1750	1833	1850	1933	1950	2033	2050	2130	2230	2400
Ringsted	700 ▷ d.	1307	1347	1407	1447	1507	1537	1547	1607	1637	1647	1707	1737	1747	1807	1847	1907	1947	2007	2047	2107	2148	2248	0016
Roskilde	700 704 ▷ d.	1328	|	1428	|	1528	1558	|	1628	1658	|	1728	1758	|	1828	|	1928	|	2028	|	2128	|	|	|
Høje Taastrup	700 704 ▷ a.	1337	|	1437	|	1537	1607	|	1637	1707	|	1737	1807	|	1837	|	1937	|	2037	|	2137	|	|	|
København H	700 704 ▷ a.	1353	1420	1453	1520	1553	1623	1620	1653	1723	1720	1753	1823	1820	1853	1920	1953	2020	2053	2120	2153	2221	2321	0050

m – Dec. 12 - Apr. 10.
p – Also May 19, (Not Apr. 10, May 29).
q – Dec. 12 - June 30, (Not Apr. 3 – 5, May 19).
r – Dec. 12 - Apr. 5.
s – Dec. 11 - Apr. 10.

▷ – Additional trains run København - Næstved and v.v.
⊙ – **NYKØBING - NAKSKOV** and v.v. Journey time: 46 – 47 minutes. Operator: Lokaltog A/S.
All trains call at Maribo (25 minutes from Nykøbing / 22 minutes from Nakskov); operates every 30 minutes on Ⓐ, hourly on ©, connecting with most rail services listed below (journey time: 40 minutes).
From Nykøbing on Ⓐ at 0507, 0533 and every 30 minutes until 1903, 1933; then 2007, 2107, 2207, 2321 and 0026.
From Nykøbing on © at 0707, 0807 and hourly until 2207; then 2321 and 0026.
From Nakskov on Ⓐ at 0415, 0438, 0508 and every 30 minutes until 1908; then 1955, 2055, 2224 and 2324.
From Nakskov on © at 0557, 0708 and hourly until 1908; then 1955, 2055, 2224 and 2324.

AALBORG - SKAGEN and HIRTSHALS 728

Nordjyske Jernbaner (2nd class only)

km				Ⓐ	Ⓐ	Ⓐ	Ⓐ	Ⓐ	Ⓐ	Ⓐ		Ⓐ	Ⓐ	Ⓐ	Ⓐ	Ⓐ	Ⓐ	Ⓐ	Ⓐ	Ⓐ	Ⓐ	Ⓐ	Ⓐ	Ⓐ	Ⓐ
0	**Aalborg**	d.	Ⓐ	...	...	0404	...	...	0514	0544	★ ♥	1614	1644	1714	...	1814	...	1914	...	2014	...	2114	...	2214	...
48	Hjørring	a.		...	...	0439	...	...	0549	0619	and at	1649	1719	1749	...	1849	...	1949	...	2049	...	2149	...	2249	...
48	Hjørring	d.		...	...	0454	0455	0524	0554	0627	the same	1654	1727	1754	1755	1854	1902	1957	2002	2057	2102	2157	2202	2257	2302
66	**Hirtshals**	a.		...	...	|	0517	|	|	0649	minutes	|	1750	|	1819	|	1924	|	2024	|	2124	|	2224	|	2324
85	**Frederikshavn**	a.		...	...	0526	...	0556	0626	...	past each	1726	...	1826	...	1925	...	2025	...	2125	...	2225	...	2325	...
85	**Frederikshavn**	d.		0435	0505	0535	...	0605	0635	...	hour until	1735	...	1838	...	1938	...	2038	...	2138	...	2238	...	2338	...
125	**Skagen**	a.		0512	0542	0612	...	0642	0712	...		1812	...	1915	...	2015	...	2115	...	2215	...	2315	...	0015	...

			©	©	⑥	©	©		©	©
Aalborg	d.	©	0414	...	...	0614	...		2214	...
Hjørring	a.		0449	...	...	0649	...	and at	2249	...
Hjørring	d.		0457	0557	0602	0657	0702	the same	2257	2302
Hirtshals	a.		|	|	0624	|	0724	minutes	|	2324
Frederikshavn	a.		0525	0625	...	0725	...	past each	2325	...
Frederikshavn	d.		0538	0638	...	0738	...	hour until	2338	...
Skagen	a.		0615	0715	...	0815	...		0015	...

			Ⓐ	Ⓐ	Ⓐ	Ⓐ		Ⓐ	Ⓐ	Ⓐ	Ⓐ
Skagen	d.	Ⓐ	...	...	...	0520	♣	...	1720	...	1750
Frederikshavn	a.		...	...	...	0600	and at	...	1800	...	1830
Frederikshavn	d.		...	0512	...	0612	the same	...	1812	...	1842
Hirtshals	d.		0518	|	0549	|	minutes	1750	|	1829	|
Hjørring	a.		0543	0545	0613	0645	past each	1813	1845	1851	1915
Hjørring	d.		...	0549	0619	0649	hour until	1819	1849	...	1919
Aalborg	a.		...	0627	0657	0727		1857	1927	...	1957

		Ⓐ	Ⓐ	Ⓐ	Ⓐ	Ⓐ	Ⓐ	Ⓐ	Ⓐ	Ⓐ	Ⓐ	Ⓐ	Ⓐ	
Skagen	d.	...	1842	...	1942	...	2042	...	2142	...	2242	...	2342	...
Frederikshavn	a.	...	1919	...	2019	...	2119	...	2219	...	2319	...	0019	...
Frederikshavn	d.	...	1927	...	2027	...	2127	...	2227	...	2327	...	0027	...
Hirtshals	d.	1929	|	2029	|	2129	|	2229	|	2329	|	0029	|	...
Hjørring	a.	1951	1955	2051	2055	2151	2155	2251	2255	2351	2355	0051	0055	...
Hjørring	d.	...	2002	...	2102	...	2202	...	2302	...	0002	...	...	...
Aalborg	a.	...	2043	...	2143	...	2243	...	2343	...	0043	...	...	...

			©	⑥	©	©	©		©	©	©	©
Skagen	d.	©	...	...	...	...	0642		...	2242	...	2342
Frederikshavn	a.		...	...	...	...	0719	and at	...	2319	...	0019
Frederikshavn	d.		0527	...	0627	...	0727	the same	...	2327	...	0027
Hirtshals	d.		|	0629	|	0729	|	minutes	2329	|	0029	|
Hjørring	a.		0555	0651	0655	0851	0755	past each	2351	2355	0051	0055
Hjørring	d.		0602	...	0702	...	0802	hour until	...	0002	...	...
Aalborg	a.		0643	...	0743	...	0843		...	0043	...	...

★ – Hjørring d. 0957 / 1057 / 1157 / 1257 (not 0954 / 1054 / 1154 / 1254).
♥ – Additional trains on Ⓐ: Hjørring - Frederikshavn - Skagen at 0624, 0724, 1324, 1424, 1524 and 1624 (departing Frederikshaven at 0705, 0805, 1405, 1505, 1605 and 1705); Frederikshavn - Skagen at 1305; Hjørring - Hirtshals at 0002, 0427, 0527, 0555, 0655, 0755, 1355, 1455, 1555 and 1655.
♣ – Additional trains on Ⓐ: Skagen - Frederikshavn - Hjørring at 0550, 0650, 0750, 1350, 1450, 1550 and 1650 (departing Frederikshavn at 0642, 0742, 1442, 1542, 1642 and 1742); Skagen - Frederikshavn at 0042, 0750 and 0850; Hirtshals - Hjørring at 0618, 0718, 0818, 1419, 1519, 1619, 1719 and 1819.

TRAIN SERVICES IN DENMARK ON AND AROUND PUBLIC HOLIDAYS

On the following dates the service provided is as per the day of the week indicated

Date	DSB	Arriva	Date	DSB	Arriva	Date	DSB	Arriva
Dec. 23	⑤	⑤	Apr. 5	⑤	⑦	May 4	⑤	⑤
Dec. 24	⑥	⑦	Apr. 6	⑥	⑦	May 5	⑥	⑦
Dec. 25	⑦	⑦	Apr. 7	⑥	⑥	May 17	⑤	⑦
Dec. 26	⑦	⑦	Apr. 8	⑥	⑦	May 18	⑥	⑦
Dec. 31	⑥	⑦	Apr. 9	⑦	⑦	May 28	⑦	⑥
Jan. 1	⑦	⑦	Apr. 10	⑦	⑦	May 29	⑦	⑦

ICELAND

There are no railways in Iceland but bus services serve most major settlements. Principal services along road number 1 around the country and some other important routes are shown below. Buses have scheduled stops in all settlements (often at N1 filling stations) but stops at other points along the route are possible with prior agreement with the operator. For comprehensive information on all bus routes, including local services and ferries, see www.publictransport.is and the websites of operators (see bottom of page). Confirm all timings with operators as schedules may change at short notice. Buses may be cancelled, delayed or run to amended schedules during adverse weather conditions, particularly in winter.

Scheduled public bus services (*STR*, *FAS*) and buses to Keflavík airport run all year, though there are no long-distance *STR* services on Dec. 24, 25, 31, Jan. 1. Tickets can be purchased from the driver or obtained beforehand. Travelling a full circle around the country by bus is only possible in summer and involves use of local buses in the east. Summer 2023 schedules are not yet available, but are expected to be similar to those that operated in 2022.

Scheduled touristic buses operated by private companies (*RE*, *TRX* and *SCA*) run only in summer, serving a few popular tourist destinations in the highlands. These have to be pre-booked, although tickets can also be obtained from the driver if there is space available. Tourist excursions and day tours to other destinations are available all year.

Public holidays in 2023: Jan. 1, Apr. 6, 7, 9, 10, 20, May 1, 18, 28, 29, June 17, Aug. 7, Dec. 25, 26.
No services run on Dec. 25, Jan. 1. Only a limited service runs on Dec. 24, 31.

729 PRINCIPAL BUS SERVICES

REYKJAVÍK - AKUREYRI - EGILSSTADIR

km	*STR Route 57*		④‡	x	⑥‡	⑥‡	†		Ⓑ
0	Reykjavík (BSÍ terminal) ■ ▷ d.	...	*0832*c	*0832*c	*0832*c	...	0840	...	*1658*c
7	Reykjavík (Mjódd) ■ ▷ d.	...	0900	0900	0900	...	0900	...	1730
89	Borgarnes (N1) ▷ d.	...	1021	1028	1021b	1028	1028	...	1858
426	Akureyri (Hof) a.	...	...	1529	...	1529	1529	...	2359
	STR Route 56 ⊙	v							
426	Akureyri (Hof) d.	0800	...	...	...	...	...	...	...
513	Reykjahlíd (Mývatn) N1 d.	0915	...	...	...	...	...	...	...
676	Egilsstadir (Campsite) d.	1122	...	...	...	...	...	...	...

STR Route 56 ⊙			v					
Egilsstadir (Campsite) d.	...	...	1230	...	...	...	...	...
Reykjahlíd (Mývatn) N1 d.	...	...	1436	...	...	...	...	...
Akureyri (Hof) a.	...	...	1551b	...	...	...	...	...
STR Route 57	Ⓑ			y	④‡			
Akureyri (Hof) d.	1015	...	...	1620	...	...	...	...
Borgarnes (N1) ▷ d.	1523	...	...	2128	2128	...	...	...
Reykjavík (Mjódd) ■ ▷ a.	1643	...	...	2248	2248	...	...	...
Reykjavík (BSÍ terminal) ■ ▷ a.	*1702*c	...	...	*2301*c	*2301*c	...	...	...

EGILSSTADIR - HÖFN

No winter service Breiddalsvík - Djúpivogur and v.v.

km	*STR/FAS Route 91*			Ⓐ	⑥			Ⓐ	
0	Egilsstadir (Campsite) d.	...	...	0902	1002	...	...	1602	...
36	Reydarfjördur (Molinn) a.	...	...	0935	1035	...	...	1635	...
	STR Route 96		Ⓐ	▬	▬	Ⓐ	Ⓐ	Ⓐ	Ⓐ
36	Reydarfjördur (Molinn) d.	...	0757	...	...	1506	1624	1744	1917
56	Fáskrúdsfjördur (Kirkjugardur) a.	...	0817	...	...	1526	1644b	1804b	1937
	STR Route 92	Ⓐ	▬			▬	Ⓐ	Ⓐg	
56	Fáskrúdsfjördur (Kirkjugardur) d.	0715	...	...	...	...	1648	1815	...
105	Breiddalsvík (Kaupfjelagid) a.	0755	...	...	...	...	1728	1855	...
	STR Route 94	▬	④R	†R	zA	†A			
105	Breiddalsvík (Kaupfjelagid) d.	wR	...	...	1325	1800	...	...	...
166	Djúpivogur (Hótel Framtíd) d.	0810	1245	1315	1430	1900	...	...	...
269	Höfn í Hornafirdi ★ a.	1010	1440	1515	1545	2020	...	...	...

STR Route 94			wR	zA	④R	†R		†A
Höfn í Hornafirdi ★ d.	...	...	1010	1012	1440	1515	...	1520
Djúpivogur (Hótel Framtíd) d.	...	...	1130	1230	1610	1645	...	1700
Breiddalsvík (Kaupfjelagid) a.	...	...	▬	1325	▬	▬	...	1800
STR Route 92	Ⓐ			▬		Ⓐg	Ⓐg	
Breiddalsvík (Kaupfjelagid) d.	0625	...	...	...	...	1600	1730	...
Fáskrúdsfjördur (Kirkjugardur) a.	0705b	...	...	...	...	1640	1810b	...
STR Route 96	Ⓐ		Ⓐ	Ⓐ	Ⓐ	Ⓐ	Ⓐ	
Fáskrúdsfjördur (Kirkjugardur) d.	0712	...	0822	1432	1552	1722	1812	...
Reydarfjördur (Molinn) a.	0722b	...	0842	1452	1612	1742	1822	...
STR/FAS Route 91	Ⓐ	⑥	Ⓐ					
Reydarfjördur (Molinn) d.	0735	0853	1433	...	...	...	...	...
Egilsstadir (Campsite) a.	0805	0926	1506	...	...	...	...	...

HÖFN - REYKJAVÍK

km	*operator*	*RE*	*STR*	*STR*	*STR*	*STR*	*STR*	*STR*	*RE*
	route number	HB03	51	51	51	51	51	51	HB03
		B [R]	†	Ⓒ	Ⓒ	u	Ⓐ	Ⓐ	B [R]
0	Höfn í Hornafirdi ★ d.	...	1025	...	...	1155	...	...	...
79	Jökulsárlón glacier lagoon d.	...	1125	...	...	1255	...	...	...
135	Skaftafell (Service centre) d.	...	1220	...	...	1350	...	...	...
274	Vík í Mýrdal (N1) d.	...	1415b	1442	...	1545b	1600	...	...
308	Skógar (Waterfall) ● d.	1015	...	1507	...	...	1625	...	...
357	Hvolsvöllur (N1) ● ▷ d.	1115r	...	1547	...	...	1705	...	1750
405	Selfoss (N1) ▷ d.	...	...	1627b	1629	...	1745b	1750	1830
458	Reykjavík (Mjódd) ■ ▷ a.	...	...	...	1724	...	...	1845	|
465	Reykjavík (BSÍ) ■ ▷ a.	...	...	...	*1802*c	...	...	*1902*c	1930

operator	*RE*	*STR*	*STR*	*STR*	*STR*	*STR*	*STR*	
route number	HB03	51	51	51	51	51	51	
	B [R]	Ⓒ	Ⓒ	†	Ⓐ	Ⓐ	u	
Reykjavík (BSÍ) ■ ▷ d.	0700	*1102*c	...	...	*1232*c	...	...	...
Reykjavík (Mjódd) ■ ▷ d.	|	1130	...	...	1300	...	...	...
Selfoss (N1) ▷ d.	0740	1224b	1227	...	1354b	1357	...	...
Hvolsvöllur (N1) ● ▷ d.	0900	...	1307	...	...	1437	...	...
Skógar (Waterfall) ● d.	0945	...	1342	...	...	1512	...	...
Vík í Mýrdal (N1) d.	...	...	1412b	1445	...	1542b	1615	...
Skaftafell (Service centre) d.	...	...	...	1650	...	...	1820	...
Jökulsárlón glacier lagoon d.	...	...	...	1735	...	...	1905	...
Höfn í Hornafirdi ★ a.	...	...	...	1835	...	...	2005	...

OTHER SERVICES

Reykjavík - Keflavík Airport: *50 km*, journey ±50 minutes. From BSÍ terminal ■: *flybus*, operator *RE*, connecting with all flights. From Klettagardar 4: *Grayline*, operator *GL*. From Reykjavík Terminal, Skógarhlíd 10: *Airport Direct Economy*, operator *AD*. All operators offer connecting shuttle services to/from hotels and other places in the Reykjavík area. Additional stopping services: *STR* route 55, BSÍ (Vatnsmýrarvegur ■) - KEF Airport and v.v. on Ⓐ peak hours only. During off-peak hours and on Ⓒ route 55 only operates Hafnarfjördur (Fjördur) – KEF Airport and v.v. From Reykjavík, use *STR* city route 1 from Hlemmur via Gamla Hringbraut ■ direction Hfj. Skardshlíd and change to route 55 at Hafnarfjördur (Fjördur). 7 – 13 services per day with a total journey time of 75 – 90 minutes.

Reykjavík - Blue Lagoon: 48 *km*, journey ±45 minutes. From BSÍ terminal ■: operator *RE*, daily, [R]. From Reykjavík Terminal (Skógarhlíd 10) ■: 'Destination Blue Lagoon', operator *BL*, daily, [R]. Both operators also provide infrequent services KEF Airport - Blue Laggon and v.v.

Egilsstadir - Seydisfjördur: *27 km*, journey ±40 minutes, *STR* route 93, operated by *FAS*. Services connect with Smyril Line ferry (Table **2285**). Confirm departure point with operator. Summer (June 9 - Aug. 18, 2022): From **Egilsstadir** (Campsite) at 0900 Ⓐ, 1005 ⑥, 1050 ④, 1605 Ⓐ. From **Seydisfjördur** (Herdubreid, Austurvegur 4) at 0745 Ⓐ, 0845 ⑥, 1000 ④ **s**, 1430 Ⓐ. Winter (Aug. 19, 2022 - ca. May 31, 2023): From **Egilsstadir** (Campsite) at 0900 Ⓐ, 1005 ⑥, 1105 ② **D**, 1605 Ⓐ. From **Seydisfjördur** (Herdubreid, Austurvegur 4) at 0745 Ⓐ, 0845 ⑥, 1010 ② **Ds**, 1430 Ⓐ.

LAUGAVEGUR HIKING TRAIL. Reykjavík - Landmannalaugar (*215 km*, journey ± 4 h 15 m): *RE Highland Bus* daily June 15 - Sept. 11, 2023; *TRX Highland Bus* daily June 16 - Sept. 8, 2023. **Reykjavík - Thórsmörk** (*158 km*, journey ± 4 h 30 m): *RE Highland Bus* daily May 26 - Sept. 15, 2023; *TRX Highland Bus* daily June 19 - Sept. 11, 2023. **Hvolsvöllur - Thórsmörk - Skógar**: *SCA* daily May 1 - Nov. 1, 2023. [R] on all routes with operation dependent on weather and highland road conditions (*RE* services are cancelled if no bookings received 24 hours before departure).

A – May 15 - Aug. 15, 2022 (please confirm with operator).
B – June 15 - Sept. 11, 2023 (service cancelled if no bookings received 24 hours before departure).
D – ② Aug. 23 - Dec. 20, 2022; ② Mar. 21 - May 30, 2023. Connects with Smyril Line ferry; confirm with operator.
R – Sept. 29, 2022 - ca. May 14, 2023.

b – Passengers connecting with onward services should inform operator/bus driver.
c – Connection with *STR* city route 3 from/to Gamla Hringbraut (next to BSÍ), change at Mjódd (see ■).
g – Runs on demand only. ✆ +354 892 0955 at least six hours before departure.
r – Continues to Reykjavík at 1750 (see later column).
s – Seydisfjördur Smyril Line terminal.

u – ①②④⑤ (not holidays)
v – ①②⑤†.
w – ①③⑤.
x – ①②③⑤ (not holidays).
y – ①②③⑤⑥⑦ (also holidays).
z – ①③④⑤.

‡ – Not holidays.
★ – Höfn swimming pool.
● – Additional *SCA* services operate.
▷ – Additional *STR* services operate.
⊙ – Operated by *SBA*.

N1 – Bus stop is at N1 filling station.

■ – Reykjavík 🚌 terminals

BSÍ/Umferdarmidstödin (city centre, south side)
○ BSÍ terminal (*RE*, also certain *STR* services on route 57)
○ bus stop "BSÍ" 50 m north of BSÍ at Vatnsmýrarvegur (STR route 55)
○ bus stop "Gamla Hringbraut" 100 m north of BSÍ (STR city buses)

Hlemmur (*STR* city services; city centre, east side)

Mjódd bus terminal (7 km southeast of city centre)
○ *STR* long-distance routes 51, 52, 27 and *STR* city services 3, 11, 12, 17.

Connections city centre - BSÍ - Mjódd: City service 3 runs every 30 minutes from Hlemmur to Sel/Fell via Gamla Hringbraut (at BSÍ) and Mjódd. Journey to Mjódd 25 – 32 minutes from Hlemmur, 14 – 21 minutes from Gamla Hringbraut. Connections Mjódd - city centre: *STR* city service 3 (direction Hlemmur), departs at xx21 and xx51 past each hour. Note: no city services on ⑦ and public holiday mornings before 0950.

Operators:

AD	Airport Direct ✆ +354 497 8000 www.airportdirect.is	*SBA*	SBA Nordurleid ✆ +354 550 0700 www.sba.is
BL	Destination Blue Lagoon ✆ +354 420 8800 www.destinationbluelagoon.is	*SCA*	Southcoast Adventure ✆ +354 867 3535 www.southadventure.is
FAS	Ferdathjónusta Austurlands ✆ +354 472 1515 www.straeto.is	*STR*	Straetó ✆ +354 540 2700 www.straeto.is
GL	Gray Line Iceland ✆ +354 540 1313 www.grayline.is	*TRX*	TREX ✆ +354 587 6000 www.trex.is
RE	Reykjavik Excursions ✆ +354 580 5400 www.re.is or www.ioyo.is		

SWEDEN

SEE MAP PAGE 337

Operators: Most services are operated by Swedish State Railways (SJ): www.sj.se. There are, however, a number of other operators that run services and these are indicated by their initials in the relevant table heading, or at the top of each train column where more than one operator runs services on the same route.

AEX – Arlanda Express; *FLX* – FlixTrain; *IB* – Inlandsbanan AB; *MTR* – MTRX; *NT* – Norrtåg; *Øtåg* – Øresundståg; *ST* – Snälltåget; *Tågab* – Tågåkeriet i Bergslagen AB; Vy – Vy Tåg AB

The Regional Public Transport Authority is responsible for many local services, known collectively as Länstrafik (*LT*). Those shown within these pages are abbreviated as follows: *Krösa* – Krösatågen; *M* – Mälartåg; Skåne – Skånetrafiken; *V* – Västtågen; *VTAB* – Värmlandstrafik; *XT* – X-Trafik

Services: Trains convey first and second classes of accommodation, unless otherwise shown. The fastest SJ trains are classified *Snabbtåg (Sn)* and *InterCity (IC)*. On overnight trains, sleeping cars (🛏) offer the following accommodation: First-class compartments (one or two berths) with shower and WC. These can only be booked as a private compartment and include breakfast in either the bistro car or at a nearby hotel at your destination. Second-class compartments (three berths) have shared shower and WC facilities in each coach. These can be booked as a private compartment for one, two or three persons, or as a single berth in a shared compartment (male or female). Couchette cars (▬) have six berths which can be booked as a single berth in a shared compartment or as a private compartment when four or more passengers are travelling together.

Timings: **Valid until June 22, 2023** (unless otherwise stated). Services may be amended on and around the dates of public holidays.

Catering: Most long-distance services convey a bistro-car (🍷) serving drinks, snacks and light meals. First-class tickets on *Sn* services includes access to complimentary tea, coffee and snacks with breakfast also served on departures before 0900. First-class tickets on *MTR* services include a complimentary meal and drinks.

Tickets: Travellers should ensure they are in possession of a valid ticket before joining a train as penalties can be severe. Local operators issue tickets on board the train where stations have no ticket machines.

Reservations: Seat reservation is compulsory on all *Snabbtåg*, *InterCity*, *MTRX*, *Snälltåget* and overnight trains. Reserved seats are not labelled and, if occupied, should be claimed by presenting the seat ticket on the train.

STOCKHOLM - MALMÖ - KØBENHAVN 730

On Apr. 7 services in this table run as on ⑥. See Table **730a** for other regional and *IC* services Stockholm - Norrköping - Linköping.
Trains in this table are not available for local journeys Stockholm - Södertälje Syd and v.v. or København Lufthavn ✈ - København H and v.v.

km	All trains 🅁		*Sn* 519	*Sn* 521	*Sn* 523	*Sn* 525	*Sn* 527	*ST* 3941	*Sn* 529	*Sn* 531	*Sn* 533	*Sn* 535	*Sn* 537	*Sn* 539	*Sn* 541	*ST* 3943	*Sn* 543
			🍷 Ⓐ	🍷 ⚒	🍷 Ⓑ	🍷	🍷	🍴	🍷	🍷 Ⓐ	🍷	🍷 Ⓐ	🍷	🍷 Ⓑ	🍷	🍴★	🍷 Ⓑ
0	**Stockholm** Central	d.	0521	0615	0720	0821	0922	0928	1021	1121	1220	1321	1422	1522	1611	1623	1722
36	Södertälje Syd	d.	|	0636	|	|	0941	0945	|	1141	|	1340	|	|	1631	1640	|
162	**Norrköping** 754	d.	0633	0733	0833	0933	1039	1055	1133	1238	1333	1438	1534	1635	1731	1742	1838
209	Linköping 754	d.	0659	0759	0859	0959	1103	1122	1159	1303	1359	1503	1559	1659	1759	1807	1903
241	**Mjölby**	d.	|	0814	|	1015	|	|	1214	|	1414	|	1614	|	1814	|	|
277	Tranås	d.	|	|	0928	|	|	|	|	|	|	|	|	|	|	|	|
329	**Nässjö** 733	d.	0749	0853	0953	1053	1152	1216	1253	1353	1453	1553	1653	1751	1853	1906	1953
	Jönköping 733	a.	|	|	|	|	|	|	|	|	|	|	|	|	|	|	|
416	Alvesta 746	d.	0823	0927	1027	1127	1227	1251	1327	1427	1527	1627	1727	1825	1927	1945	2027
463	Älmhult 746	d.	0842	|	|	|	|	|	|	|	|	|	|	1844	|	|	|
514	Hässleholm 745 746	a.	0905	1005	1105	1205	1305	1330s	1405	1505	1605	1705	1805	1905	2005	2025s	2105
581	Lund 745 746 ●	a.	0934	1034	1134	1234	1334s	1410s	1434	1534s	1634	1734s	1834	1934s	2034	2105s	2134s
597	**Malmö** C ●	a.	0948	1048	1148	1248	1348	1425	1448	1548	1648	1748	1848	1948	2048	2120	2148
626	København Lufthavn ✈ ●	a.	1010	1110	1210	1310	1410	...	1510	...	1710	...	1910	...	2110	...	...
638	**København** H ●	a.	1025	1125	1225	1325	1425	...	1525	...	1725	...	1925	...	2125	...	...

All trains 🅁		*Sn* 545	*Sn* 547	*Sn* 549	*ST* 3939	1	*ST* 3901
		🍷	🍷 Ⓑ	🍷 B	④† E	¶ Ⓑ vA	④⑦ G
Stockholm Central	d.	1822	1921	2028	2310	2317	2355
Södertälje Syd	d.	|	1941	|	2334	|	|
Norrköping 754	d.	1936	2038	2141	0100	0106	0200
Linköping 754	d.	2000	2103	2207	0136	0208	0235
Mjölby	d.	2015	|	2222	|	|	|
Tranås	d.	|	|	|	|	|	|
Nässjö 733	d.	2053	2153	2259	|	0311	0350
Jönköping 733	a.	|	|	|	|	|	|
Alvesta 746	d.	2127	2227	2332	|	0357	0435
Älmhult 746	d.	|	|	|	|	|	|
Hässleholm 745 746	a.	2205	2305	0010	0553s	0449s	0600s
Lund 745 746 ●	a.	2234s	2334s	0038s	0646s	0632s	0650s
Malmö C ●	a.	2248	2348	0052	0708	0648	0710
København Lufthavn ✈ ●	a.	...	...	...	...	...	...
København H ●	a.	...	...	...	...	...	...

All trains 🅁		*Sn* 520	*Sn* 522	*Sn* 524	*Sn* 526	*Sn* 528
		🍷 Ⓐ	🍷 Ⓐ	🍷 Ⓐ	🍷	🍷 ⚒
København H ●	d.	...	...	...	...	0721
København Lufthavn ✈ ●	d.	...	...	...	...	0735
Malmö C ●	d.	0404	0504	0604	0704	0804
Lund 745 746 ●	d.	0418u	0518u	0618u	0718u	0818
Hässleholm 745 746	d.	0450	0548	0648	0748	0848
Älmhult 746	d.	0512	|	0709	|	|
Alvesta 746	d.	0533	0628	0730	0828	0928
Jönköping 733	d.	|	|	|	|	|
Nässjö 733	d.	0606	0701	0804	0901	1001
Tranås	d.	0630	|	|	|	|
Mjölby	a.	|	0738	|	0939	|
Linköping 754	a.	0702	0757	0856	0956	1052
Norrköping 754	a.	0730	0822	0921	1021	1117
Södertälje Syd	a.	|	0921	|	|	1217
Stockholm Central	a.	0843	0941	1034	1136	1236

All trains 🅁		*Sn* 530	*ST* 3940	*Sn* 532	*Sn* 534	*Sn* 536	*Sn* 538	*Sn* 540	*Sn* 542	*Sn* 544	*ST* 3942	*Sn* 546	*Sn* 548	*Sn* 550	2	*ST* 3938
		🍷	🍴★ H	🍷	🍷	🍷 Ⓑ	🍷	🍷 Ⓑ	🍷	🍷 Ⓑ	🍴	🍷	🍷 B	🍷 Ⓑ	Ⓑ wA	J
København H ●	d.	...	...	0921	...	1121	1221	1321	1421	1521	...	1621	...	1821	...	...
København Lufthavn ✈ ●	d.	...	...	0935	...	1135	1235	1335	1435	1535	...	1635	...	1835	...	...
Malmö C ●	d.	0904	0918	1004	1104	1204	1304	1404	1504	1604	1610	1704	1804	1904	2232	2255
Lund 745 746 ●	d.	0918u	0930u	1018	1118u	1218	1318	1418	1518	1618	1625u	1718	1817u	1918	2246u	2310
Hässleholm 745 746	d.	0948	1005u	1048	1148	1248	1348	1448	1548	1648	1656u	1748	1848	1948	0026u	2359
Älmhult 746	d.	|	|	|	|	|	|	|	|	1710	|	|	|	|	|	|
Alvesta 746	d.	1028	1045	1128	1228	1328	1428	1528	1628	1730	1735	1828	1928	2028	0117	|
Jönköping 733	d.	|	|	|	|	|	|	|	|	|	|	|	|	|	|	|
Nässjö 733	d.	1101	1120	1201	1301	1401	1501	1601	1701	1804	1810	1901	2001	2102	0205	|
Tranås	d.	|	|	|	|	|	|	1626	|	|	|	|	|	2126	|	|
Mjölby	d.	1139	|	|	1340	|	1540	|	1739	|	|	1939	|	|	|	|
Linköping 754	a.	1156	1222	1251	1357	1452	1557	1657	1756	1854	1905	1956	2053	2158	0310	0400
Norrköping 754	a.	1222	1247	1316	1422	1517	1622	1721	1821	1919	1930	2022	2118	2223	0340	0435
Södertälje Syd	a.	|	1350	1415	|	1620	|	1818	|	|	2035	2119	2217	2320	|	0620
Stockholm Central	a.	1334	1410	1434	1534	1638	1737	1838	1936	2034	2055	2138	2237	2339	0537	0645

A – Conveys 🛏, ▬ and (2).
B – ④⑤⑦ (also Apr. 10, May 1, 17, June 6; not Apr. 7).
E – From May 1.
G – ④⑦ until Apr. 30 (also Feb. 27, Apr. 10).
H – Daily until Mar. 31; ⑦ Apr. 2 - May 21.
J – ①⑦ Jan. 29 - Feb. 27; ①⑦ Mar. 26 - Apr. 24 (also Apr. 11; not Apr. 9); ①④⑤⑦ from Apr. 30 (also May 2, 13, 17). Subject to alteration.

s – Calls to set down only.
u – Calls to pick up only.
v – Also Feb. 25, Mar. 4, 11, 18; not Apr. 7.
w – Not Apr. 5 - 9.

¶ – Train number **67** on ⑦ Feb. 12 - Apr. 16 (also Apr. 6, 10).
★ – Conveys ▬ (**300/1**) from / to Berlin and Hamburg (Table **50**).
● – See also Tables **735, 737, 745** and **746** for other trains Lund - Malmö - København and v.v.

☛ **First-class tickets**: On *Sn* services includes complimentary tea, coffee and snacks with breakfast served on departures before 0900

730a (GÄVLE -) STOCKHOLM - LINKÖPING

See Table **730** for other fast services Stockholm - Linköping and v.v. *IC* train numbers may vary on certain dates. **Note**: On Apr. 7 services run as on ⑥.

	◇ Ⓐ 2	*IC* **257** ⚒ 🅁	◇ Ⓐ 2	*IC* **259** Ⓐ 🅁	◇ 2	*IC* **261** ⚒ 🅁	◇ Ⓐ 2	◇ 2	*IC* **265** Ⓒ 🅁	◇ Ⓐ 2	◇ 2	*IC* **269** 🅁	◇ Ⓐ 2	◇ 2	*IC* **273** Ⓑ 🅁	◇ Ⓐ 2	◇ 2	*IC* **277** 🅁	◇ Ⓐ 2	*IC* **279** Ⓐ 🅁	◇ 2	*IC* **281** † 🅁	◇ Ⓐ 2	◇ Ⓑ 2	◇ A 2	*IC* **287** Ⓐ 🅁
Gävle C **761** d.	...	...	...	0603	...	0704	...	...	0904	...	...	1104	...	...	1304	...	...	1504	...	1602	...	1704	...	...	...	2004
Stockholm Central d.	0543	0638	0643	0740	0743	0837	0843	0943	1037	1043	1143	1237	1243	1343	1437	1443	1541	1639	1643	1737	1744f	1838	1843	1943	2043	2137
Flemingsberg d.	0554	0650	0654	0752	0755	0849	0854	0955	1049	1054	1154	1249	1254	1354	1448	1454	1552	1651	1654	1749	1755f	1849	1854	1954	2054	2149
Södertälje Syd d.	0604	0700	0704	0802	0805	0859	0904	1005	1059	1104	1204	1259	1304	1405	1459	1504	1604	1701	1703	1759	1805f	1859	1904	2004	2104	2159
Nyköping d.	0646	|	0745	|	0845	|	0945	1045	|	1145	1245	|	1345	1445	|	1545	1644	|	1745	|	1845	|	1945	2046	2145	|
Norrköping 754 a.	0727	0807	0826	0906	0926	1003	1029	1126	1203	1226	1327	1403	1426	1526	1603	1626	1726	1804	1827	1903	1926	2005	2026	2126	2226	2303
Linköping 754 a.	...	0835	...	0938	...	1031	...	...	1230	...	...	1429	...	...	1634	...	...	1837	...	1931	...	2031	...	...	...	2329

	IC **262** Ⓐ 🅁	◇ Ⓐ 2	*IC* **264** Ⓐ 🅁	◇ 2	*IC* **266** ⑥ 🅁	*IC* **266** † 🅁	◇ 2	◇ Ⓐ 2	*IC* **270** ⚒ 🅁	◇ 2	◇ Ⓐ 2	*IC* **274** 🅁	◇ 2	◇ Ⓐ 2	*IC* **278** 🅁	◇ 2	◇ Ⓐ 2	*IC* **282** Ⓐ 🅁	◇ 2	◇ Ⓐ 2	*IC* **286** 🅁	◇ 2	◇ Ⓐ 2	*IC* **290** ⑦e 🅁	◇ 2	◇ Ⓐ 2
Linköping 754 d.	0528	...	0624	...	0721	0728	...	...	0929	...	...	1131	...	...	1329	...	...	1526	...	...	1726	...	...	1928	...	...
Norrköping 754 d.	0555	0634	0653	0734	0748	0755	0834	0934	0956	1034	1134	1157	1234	1333	1356	1434	1534	1556	1634	1734	1754	1834	1934	1954	2034	2134
Nyköping d.	|	0714	|	0814	|	|	0914	1014	|	1114	1214	|	1314	1414	|	1514	1614	|	1714	1814	|	1914	2016	|	2114	2214
Södertälje Syd d.	0701	0751	0758	0853	0856	0900	0952	1051	1101	1152	1251	1302	1355	1451	1502	1552	1654	1701	1751k	1852	1903	1951	2051	2102	2151	2252
Flemingsberg d.	0711	0801	0808	0902	0906	0910	1002	1100	1111	1201	1301	1312	1405	1501	1512	1602	1704	1711	1801k	1902	1913	2001	2101	2114	2201	2301
Stockholm Central a.	0722	0812	0819	0913	0917	0921	1013	1111	1122	1212	1311	1323	1415	1512	1523	1612	1714	1722	1812k	1912	1924	2011	2112	2125	2212	2312
Gävle C **761** a.	0856	...	0956	...	1056	1056	...	...	1256	...	...	1456	...	...	1656	...	...	1856	...	...	2056	...	...	...	...	...

A – ①②③④⑥ (also Apr. 7; Apr. 6, 10, May 1, 17, 18, June 6).

e – Also Apr. 10, May 1; not Apr. 9, 30.
f – 3–5 minutes earlier on ⑦ (also Apr. 10, May 1, 18, June 6; not Apr. 9, 30).
k – 4–5 minutes later on Ⓒ to Mar. 12 and on ⑥ from Mar. 18 (also Apr. 7).

◇ – Operated by Mälartåg.

731 MALMÖ - YSTAD - SIMRISHAMN and TRELLEBORG

Operator: *Skåne*

km		Ⓐ	Ⓐ	⚒	Ⓐ		Ⓐ		⚒							⚒		⚒		⚒	⚒		⚒		
0	**Malmö C** d.	...	0507	...	0537	0607	0637	0707	0737	0807	0837	and at the same	1907	1937	2007	2037	2107	2137	2207	2207	2237	2307	2307	...	2337f
70	Ystad d.	0458	0558	0558	0626	0658	0726	0758	0826	0858	0926	minutes past	1958	2026	2058	2126	2158	2226	2256	2258	2326	2356	2358	...	0026
116	**Simrishamn** a.	0538	0638	0638	...	0738	...	0838	...	0938	...	each hour until	2038	...	2138	...	2238	...	...	2338	...	...	0038	...	...

	Ⓐ	Ⓐ		Ⓐ	Ⓐ		Ⓐ	⚒		Ⓐ							⚒		⚒		⚒		⚒	⚒	⑤⑥t
Simrishamn d.	...	...	...	...	0547	...	...	0647	...	...	0747	...	and at the same	1847	...	1947	...	2047	...	2147	...	2247	2247	2347	2347
Ystad d.	0430	0500	0530	0600	0630	0630	0700	0730	0730	0800	0830	0900	minutes past	1930	2000	2030	2100	2130	2200	2230	2300	2326	2330	0026	0030
Malmö C a.	0520	0550	0620	0650	0720	0720	0750	0820	0820	0850	0920	0950	each hour until	2020	2050	2120	2150	2220	2250	2320j	2350	...	0020	...	0120

km									
0	**Malmö C** d.	0547	0620	0647	and at the same minutes past	2220	2247	2320f	2347f
44	**Trelleborg C** a.	0619	0652	0719	each hour until	2252	2319	2352	0019

										D	⑤⑥t
Trelleborg C d.	0507	0540	and at the same minutes past	2107	2140	2207	2240	2307	2340	2340
Malmö C a.	0539	0612	each hour until	2139	2212	2239	2312j	2339r	0005	0012

D – ⑦–④ also Apr. 7.
f – 3 minutes later on ⑦–④ also Apr. 7.
j – 5–7 minutes earlier on ⑦–④ also Apr. 7.
r – 2332 on †.
t – Not Apr. 7.

732 STOCKHOLM - ESKILSTUNA - ARBOGA - ÖREBRO

Operator: *Mälartåg* (2nd class only)

Timings may vary by 1–2 minutes. See Table **756** for other connecting services Arboga - Örebro and v.v. **Note**: On Apr. 7 services run as ⑥.

km		Ⓐ	Ⓐ	Ⓒ	Ⓐ	Ⓐ		⑥	Ⓐ		Ⓐ		Ⓐd		Ⓐ		Ⓐ	Ⓐ	Ⓒ	Ⓐ	Ⓐ		Ⓐ		Ⓐ	Ⓐw
0	**Stockholm** Central d.	...	0555	0642	0655	0755	0855	0953	0955	1055	1155	1255	1355	1455	1511	1554	1610	1655	1658	1713	1755	1855	1955	2055	2155	2255
36	Södertälje Syd d.	...	0616	0703	0716	0816	0916	1017	1016	1116	1216	1317	1416	1518	|	1616	|	1718	1718	|	1816	1916	2016	2116	2216	2316
67	Läggesta ● d.	...	0633	0720	0733	0833	0933	1033	1033	1133	1233	1333	1433	1533	|	1633	|	1733	1733	|	1833	1933	2033	2133	2233	2333
83	Strängnäs d.	...	0641	0730	0741	0841	0941	1041	1041	1141	1241	1341	1441	1541	|	1641	|	1741	1741	|	1841	1941	2041	2141	2241	2341
115	Eskilstuna a.	...	0657	0745	0757	0857	0958	1056	1056	1156	1256	1356	1456	1556	1602	1657	1701	1757	1756	1802	1856	1956	2056	2156	2256	2356
115	Eskilstuna d.	0602	0702j	0759	0759	0859	0959	...	1059	1159	1259	1359	1459	1559c	1603	...	1703	...	1759	1803	1859	1959	2059	2159	2259	2359
141	Kungsör d.	0618	0718	0815	0815	0916	1015	...	1115	1215	1316	1415	1515	1615c	1619	...	1719	...	1815	1819	1915	2015	2115	2215	2315	0015
159	Arboga 756 a.	0628	0728	0825	0825	0926	1025	...	1125	1225	1326	1425	1525	1625c	1629	...	1729	...	1825	1829	1925	2025	2125	2225	2325	0025
205	**Örebro C** 756 a.	0649r	0750r	...	0845r	...	...	...	...	...	...	...	1545r	...	1650r	...	1750r	...	...	1850r	1945r	2045e	2145r	2246e	2345r	0045z

	Ⓐv	Ⓐh	Ⓐ	Ⓐ		Ⓐ		⑥	Ⓐ		⚒				†	Ⓐ	Ⓐ	Ⓒ	Ⓐ	†	Ⓐ	Ⓒt	Ⓐ		Ⓐ	x
Örebro C 756 d.	0413	0510r	...	0608r	...	0704r	...	...	0813r	...	...	...	...	...	...	...	1513r	...	1608r	...	1708r	...	1808r	1913e	2014r	2113a
Arboga 756 d.	0434	0531	...	0629	...	0729	0734c	...	0834	0934	1034a	1134	1234a	1334	...	1434	1534	1534	1629	...	1729	1734	1829	1932	2034	2134
Kungsör d.	0445	0542	...	0640	...	0740	0745c	...	0845	0945	1045a	1145	1245a	1345	...	1445	1545	1545	1640	...	1740	1745	1840	1943	2045	2146
Eskilstuna a.	0500	0557	...	0655	...	0755	0800c	...	0900	1000	1100a	1200	1300a	1400	...	1500	1600	1600	1655	...	1755	1800	1855	2000	2100	2200
Eskilstuna d.	0504	0559	0604	0700	0704	0800	0804	0904	0904	1004	1104	1204	1304	1404	1504	1504	1601	1604	1702	1704	1804	1804	1904	2004	2104	2204
Strängnäs d.	0518	|	0618	|	0718	|	0818	0918	0918	1018	1118	1218	1318	1418	1518	1518	1617	1618	1716	1718	1818	1818	1918	2018	2118	2218
Läggesta ● d.	0527	|	0627	|	0727	|	0827	0927	0927	1027	1127	1227	1327	1427	1527	1527	1625	1627	1725	1727	1827	1827	1927	2027	2127	2227
Södertälje Syd d.	0544	|	0644	|	0744	|	0843	0946	0947	1044	1144	1244	1344	1444	1545	1546	1644	1644	1744	1744	1845	1845	1944	2044	2144	2243
Stockholm Central a.	0605	0648	0705	0748	0805	0850	0903	1005	1006	1105	1205	1305	1405	1505	1605	1605	1705	1705	1805	1805	1905	1905	2005	2105	2205	2303

a – Ⓐ only.
c – Ⓒ only.
d – Runs daily Stockholm - Eskilstuna.
e – Ⓐ (not Mar. 13 - May 15).
h – Not Feb. 13–24.
j – 0659 from May 24.

r – Not Mar. 13 - May 15.
t – Not Mar. 4.
v – Not Mar. 27 - May 15. Starts from Arboga Mar. 13–24. Runs up to 5 minutes later Eskilstuna - Stockholm Jan. 2 - Feb. 24.
w – Not ①–④ Jan. 23 - Mar. 16; not Feb. 17, 24. Also runs Stockholm - Eskilstuna on † to Feb. 19 / from Apr. 2.

x – Does not run on Ⓐ Mar. 13 - May 15.
z – Not mornings Mar. 18 - May 16.

● – Narrow gauge service operates Mariefred - Läggesta (nedre) - Taxinge-Näsby. Summer only. Operator: Östra Södermanlands Järnväg, Box 53, SE-647 22 Mariefred. ✆ +46 (0) 159 210 00.

733 SKÖVDE - JÖNKÖPING - NÄSSJÖ

Operator: Västtågen; 2nd class only

km		Ⓐ	Ⓐ	Ⓐ	⚒	Ⓐ		⚒	Ⓐ	Ⓒ	Ⓐ		⑥	Ⓐ		Ⓐ		n	Ⓒ	Ⓐ	Ⓑ	n	Ⓐ	Ⓑ	Ⓐd	⑥c
0	**Skövde** 740 d.	0443	0551	0624	0656	0800	0857	*0951*	1056	1059	1155	1249	1348	1350	...	1424	1456	1551	1648	1653	1753	1858	1952	*2050*	...	2159
30	Falköping 740 a.	0500	0608	0641	0713	0818	0914	*1008*	1113	1116	1212	1306	1405	1408	...	1441	1513	1610	1711	1710	1810	1915	2014	*2107*	...	2216
30	Falköping d.	0502	0612	0642	0717	0820	0916	1016	1116	1118	1215	1315	...	...	1414	1444	1515	1615	1717	1714	1816	1918	2016	2116	...	2219
100	Jönköping a.	0544	0656	0728	0800	0902	1001	1100	1201	1201	1300	1401	...	...	1459	1526	1559	1703	1804	1804	1904	2002	2101	2200	...	2303
100	Jönköping d.	0546	0704	*0738*	0807	0909	1004	1104	1207	1207	1307	1407	...	...	1506	*1535*n	1607	1707	1806	1806	1906	2004	2106	2209	2300	2310
143	**Nässjö** a.	0617	0738	*0814*	0839	0941	1038	1137	1240	1240	1339	1438	...	...	1541	*1608*n	1639	1740	1840	1841	1940	2035	2140	2240	2331	2341

	Ⓐe	Ⓐ	⑥c	Ⓐ	Ⓐ	⑥	⚒	†	Ⓐ		Ⓐ	⑥	Ⓐ	Ⓒ	Ⓑ	⑥v	†w	Ⓐ	n		†	Ⓐ	Ⓑ	⑥n	Ⓐ	n
Nässjö d.	0422	0555	0714	0715	0820	0820	0915	0920	1018	1118	1219	1219	1316	1317	1416	1514	1514	1528	1619	1720	1820	1820	1919	1919	2021	2120
Jönköping a.	0459	0626	0750	0749	0852	0852	0954	0952	1049	1153	1250	1250	1349	1349	1447	1547	1547	1601	1652	1753	1851	1851	1958	1955	2058	2151
Jönköping d.	0501	0628	0800	0800	0902	0931	1001	1001	1100	1201	1300	1301	1401	1401	1459	1603	1603	1603	1703	1804	1904	1904	2002	2002	2101	2201r
Falköping a.	0544	0716	0845	0846	0944	1012	1046	1046	1144	1245	1344	1344	1444	1444	1543	1646	1647	1646	1746	1846	1945	1947	2046	2046	2145	2247
Falköping 740 d.	0549	0721	0856	0852	0946	*1020*	1052	1054	...	1248j	1346	1352	1450	1446	*1553*	1649	1653	1654	1758	1848	*1954*	...	2050	*2107*	*2205*t	2249
Skövde 740 a.	0605	0737	0912	0908	1002	*1036*	1108	1110	...	1305j	1402	1408	1506	1502	*1609*	1705	1709	1710	1814	1904	*2010*	...	2106	*2123*	*2222*t	2305

c – Not Mar. 11, 25.
d – Not Mar. 20–23.
e – Not Mar. 6 - May 12.
j – 3 minutes later on Ⓒ.
r – 2204 on ⑤⑥ (also Apr. 6, May 17; not Apr. 7).

t – Not Feb. 24.
v – Also Apr. 7.
w – Not Apr. 7.

KRISTIANSTAD - HÄSSLEHOLM - HELSINGBORG 734

Operator: *Skåne*

km		Ⓐ	Ⓐ	Ⓐ	Ⓐ	Ⓐ	⚒	Ⓐ		Ⓐ		Ⓐ				Ⓐ			Ⓐ						
0	**Kristianstad** ..... 745 d.	...	0401	...	*0501*	0540	*0601*	0639	*0701*	0739	*0801*	0839	*0901*	and at	*1401*	1439	*1501*	and at	1739	*1801*	*1901*	*2001*	*2101*	*2201*	*2301*
30	Hässleholm .... 745 a.	...	0423	...	*0523*	0600	*0623*	0700	*0723*	0800	*0823*	0900	*0923*	the same	*1423*	1500	*1523*	the same	1800	*1823*	*1923*	*2023*	*2123*	*2223*	*2323*
30	Hässleholm ....d.	...	...	0500	0530	0600	0630	0700	0730	0800	0830	0900	0930	minutes	1430	1500	1530	minutes	1800	1830	1930	2030	2130	2230	2330
83	Åstorp ....d.	0510	...	0540	0610	0640	0710	0740	0810	0840	0910	0940	1010	past each	1510	1540	1610	past each	1840	1910	2010	2110	2210	2310	0010
107	**Helsingborg** ....a.	0535	...	0605	0635	0705	0735	0805	0835	0905	0935	1005	1035	hour until	1535	1605	1635	hour until	1905	1935	2035	2135	2235	2335	0035

	Ⓐ	Ⓐ	Ⓐ	⚒	Ⓐ	Ⓐ		Ⓐ		Ⓐ				Ⓐ			Ⓐ							⚒
Helsingborg ....d.	...	0416	0447	0516	...	0547	0616	0647	0716	0747	0816	and at	1316	1347	1416	and at	1647	1716	1816	1916	2016	2116	2216	2316
Åstorp ....d.	...	0439	0510	0539	...	0610	0639	0710	0739	0810	0839	the same	1339	1410	1439	the same	1710	1739	1839	1939	2039	2139	2239	2339
Hässleholm ....a.	...	0518	0548	0618	...	0648	0718	0748	0818	0848	0918	minutes	1418	1448	1518	minutes	1748	1818	1918	2018	2118	2218	2318	0018
Hässleholm .... 745 d.	0450	*0532*	0550	...	0632	0650	*0732*	0750	*0832*	0850	*0932*	past each	*1432*	1450	*1532*	past each	1750	*1832*	*1932*	*2032*	*2132*	*2232*	*2332*	...
Kristianstad .... 745 a.	0514	*0554*	0614	...	0654	0714	*0754*	0814	*0854*	0914	*0954*	hour until	*1454*	1514	*1554*	hour until	1814	*1854*	*1954*	*2054*	*2154*	*2254*	*2354*	...

GÖTEBORG - MALMÖ - KØBENHAVN 735

Operator: *Øtåg* (except *Sn* trains)

WARNING! From March 13 to April 6 all southbound services are diverted Ängelholm - Lund (not calling at Helsingborg or Landskrona).
Sn services in both directions are diverted March 13 - Apr. 6 and do not call at Helsingborg (certain services also diverted Apr. 7 – 10).

km		Ⓐ	Ⓐ	Ⓐ	⑥	*Sn* 481 Ⓐ R 🍷		*Sn* 483 ⑥v R 🍷		*Sn* 485 Ⓐ R 🍷				*Sn* 487 R 🍷						*Sn* 491 R 🍷				*Sn* 493 Ⓐ R 🍷	
0	**Göteborg** C ....d.	...	...	0540	...	0624	0640	0724	0740	0824	0840	...	0940	1024	1040	...	1140	...	1240	1324	1340	...	1440	1524	1540
28	Kungsbacka ....d.	...	...	0559	...	|	0659	|	0759	|	0859	...	0959	|	1059	...	1159	...	1259	|	1359	...	1459	|	1559
76	Varberg ....d.	...	...	0629	...	|	0729	|	0829	|	0929	...	1029	|	1129	...	1229	...	1329	|	1429	...	1529	|	1629
106	Falkenberg ....d.	...	...	0645	...	|	0745	|	0845	|	0945	...	1045	|	1145	...	1245	...	1345	|	1445	...	1545	|	1645
150	**Halmstad** ....d.	0504	0604	0704	0705	0737	0804	0837	0904	0937	1004	...	1104	1137	1204	...	1304	...	1404	1437	1504	...	1604	1637	1704
173	Laholm ....d.	0515	0615	0715	0715	|	0815	|	0915	|	1015	...	1115	|	1215	...	1315	...	1415	|	1515	...	1615	|	1715
185	Båstad ....d.	0522	0622	0722	0722	|	0822	|	0922	|	1022	...	1122	|	1222	...	1322	...	1422	|	1522	...	1622	|	1722
210	Ängelholm ....d.	0534	0634	0734	0734	|	0834	|	0934	|	1034	...	1134	|	1234	...	1334	...	1434	|	1534	...	1634	|	1734
237	**Helsingborg** ....a.	0608	0708	0808	0808	0818	0908	0918	1008	1018	1108	...	1208	1218	1308	...	1408	...	1508	1518	1608	...	1708	1718	1808
237	**Helsingborg** .... 737 d.	0610	0710	0810	0810	0819	0910	0919	1010	1019	1110	...	1210	1219	1310	...	1410	...	1510	1519	1610	...	1710	1719	1810
259	Landskrona .... 737 d.	0621	0721	0821	0821	|	0921	|	1021	|	1121	...	1221	|	1321	...	1421	...	1521	|	1621	...	1721	|	1821
290	Lund .... ● d.	0639	0739	0839	0839	0846**s**	0939	0946**s**	1039	1046**s**	1139	...	1239	1246**s**	1339	...	1439	...	1539	1546**s**	1639	...	1739	1746**s**	1839
306	**Malmö** C .... ● a.	0651	0751	0851	0851	0900	0951	1000	1051	1100	1151	...	1251	1300	1351	...	1451	...	1551	1600	1651	...	1751	1800	1851
306	**Malmö** C .... ● d.	0653	0753	0853	0853	...	0953	...	1053	...	1153	...	1253	...	1353	...	1453	...	1553	...	1653	...	1753	...	1853
335	København Lufthavn ✈ .. ● a.	0714	0814	0914	0914	...	1014	...	1114	...	1214	...	1314	...	1414	...	1514	...	1614	...	1714	...	1814	...	1914
347	**København** H .... ● a.	0729	0829	0929	0929	...	1029	...	1129	...	1229	...	1329	...	1429	...	1529	...	1629	...	1729	...	1829	...	1929

		Sn 495 R 🍷			*Sn* 405 Ⓑz R 🍷					
Göteborg C ....d.	1640	1724	1740	1840	1923	1940	2040	2140	2240	2340
Kungsbacka ....d.	1659	|	1759	1859	|	1959	2059	2159	2259	2359
Varberg ....d.	1729	|	1829	1929	|	2029	2129	2229	2329	0029
Falkenberg ....d.	1745	|	1845	1945	|	2045	2145	2245	2345	0045
Halmstad ....d.	1804	1837	1904	2004	2037	2104	2204	2304	0003	0103
Laholm ....d.	1815	|	1915	2015	|	2115	2215	2315	...	...
Båstad ....d.	1822	|	1922	2022	|	2122	2222	2322	...	...
Ängelholm ....d.	1834	|	1934	2034	|	2134	2234	2334	...	...
Helsingborg ....a.	1908	1918	2008	2108	2118	2208	2308	0008	...	...
Helsingborg .... 737 d.	1910	1919	2010	2110	2119	2210	2310	...	...	...
Landskrona .... 737 d.	1921	|	2021	2121	|	2221	2321	...	...	...
Lund .... ● d.	1939	1946**s**	2039	2139	2146**s**	2239	2339	...	...	...
Malmö C .... ● a.	1951	2000	2051	2151	2200	2251	2351	...	...	...
Malmö C .... ● d.	1953	...	2053	2153	...	2253	...	...	...	...
København Lufthavn ✈ ... ● a.	2014	...	2114	2214	...	2314	...	...	...	...
København H .... ● a.	2029	...	2129	2229	...	2329	...	...	...	...

	Ⓐ	Ⓐ	Ⓒ	Ⓐ	*Sn* 426 Ⓐ R 🍷		⚒	*Sn* 418 ⑥k R 🍷	*Sn* 482 Ⓐ R 🍷	
København H .... ● d.	...	...	...	...	...	...	0527	...	...	0627
København Lufthavn ✈ .. ● d.	...	...	...	...	...	...	0542	...	...	0642
Malmö C .... ● a.	...	...	...	...	...	...	0606	...	...	0706
Malmö C .... ● d.	...	...	...	0508	0517	...	0608	0624	0701	0708
Lund .... ● d.	...	...	...	0522	0531**u**	...	0622	0638**u**	0715**u**	0722
Landskrona .... 737 d.	...	...	...	0536	|	...	0636	|	|	0736
Helsingborg .... 737 a.	...	...	...	0549	0602	...	0649	0701	0740	0749
Helsingborg .... d.	...	0454	...	0554	0603	...	0654	0702	0740	0754
Ängelholm ....d.	...	0524	...	0618	|	...	0724	|	|	0824
Båstad ....d.	...	0536	...	0630	|	...	0736	|	|	0836
Laholm ....d.	...	0543	...	0637	|	...	0743	|	|	0843
Halmstad ....d.	0445	0556	0656	0656	0651	0756	0756	0749	0821	0856
Falkenberg ....d.	0502	0613	0713	0713	|	0813	0813	|	|	0913
Varberg ....d.	0519	0633	0733	0735	|	0833	0833	|	|	0933
Kungsbacka ....d.	0544	0659	0759	0759	|	0859	0859	|	|	0959
Göteborg C ....a.	0605	0720	0820	0820	0805	0920	0920	0905	0935	1020

			Sn 486 R 🍷				*Sn* 488 Ⓐ R 🍷				*Sn* 490 R 🍷						*Sn* 492 R 🍷				*Sn* 494 Ⓑb R 🍷				
København H .... ● d.	0727	0827	...	0927	...	1027	...	1127	...	1227	...	1327	...	1427	...	1527	...	1627	...	1727	...	1827	1927	2027	2227
København Lufthavn ✈ ... ● d.	0742	0842	...	0942	...	1042	...	1142	...	1242	...	1342	...	1442	...	1542	...	1642	...	1742	...	1842	1942	2042	2242
Malmö C .... ● a.	0806	0906	...	1006	...	1106	...	1206	...	1306	...	1406	...	1506	...	1606	...	1706	...	1806	...	1906	2006	2106	2306
Malmö C .... ● d.	0808	0908	1001	1008	...	1108	1201	1208	...	1308	1401	1408	...	1508	...	1608	1701	1708	...	1808	1901	1908	2008	2108	2308
Lund .... ● d.	0822	0922	1015**u**	1022	...	1122	1215**u**	1222	...	1322	1415**u**	1422	...	1522	...	1622	1715**u**	1722	...	1822	1915**u**	1922	2022	2122	2322
Landskrona .... 737 d.	0836	0936	|	1036	...	1136	|	1236	...	1336	|	1436	...	1536	...	1636	|	1736	...	1836	|	1936	2036	2136	2336
Helsingborg .... 737 a.	0849	0949	1040	1049	...	1149	1240	1249	...	1349	1440	1449	...	1549	...	1649	1740	1749	...	1849	1940	1949	2049	2149	2349
Helsingborg ....d.	0854	0954	1041	1054	...	1154	1241	1254	...	1354	1441	1454	...	1554	...	1654	1741	1754	...	1854	1941	1954	2054	2154	2354
Ängelholm ....d.	0924	1024	|	1124	...	1224	|	1324	...	1424	|	1524	...	1624	...	1724	|	1824	...	1924	|	2024	2124	2224	0014
Båstad ....d.	0936	1036	|	1136	...	1236	|	1336	...	1436	|	1536	...	1636	...	1736	|	1836	...	1936	|	2036	2136	2236	0026
Laholm ....d.	0943	1043	|	1143	...	1243	|	1343	...	1443	|	1543	...	1643	...	1743	|	1843	...	1943	|	2043	2143	2243	0033
Halmstad ....d.	0956	1056	1121	1156	...	1256	1322	1356	...	1456	1521	1556	...	1656	...	1756	1821	1856	...	1956	2021	2056	2156	2256	0044
Falkenberg ....d.	1013	1113	|	1213	...	1313	|	1413	...	1513	|	1613	...	1713	...	1813	|	1913	...	2013	|	2113	2213	2313	...
Varberg ....d.	1033	1133	|	1233	...	1333	|	1433	...	1533	|	1633	...	1733	...	1833	|	1933	...	2033	|	2133	2233	2333	...
Kungsbacka ....d.	1059	1159	|	1259	...	1359	|	1459	...	1559	|	1659	...	1759	...	1859	|	1959	...	2059	|	2159	2259	2359	...
Göteborg C ....a.	1120	1220	1235	1320	...	1420	1435	1520	...	1620	1635	1720	...	1820	...	1920	1935	2020	...	2120	2135	2220	2320	0020	...

b – Not Apr. 7, June 5.
k – Also Apr. 7, May 18, June 6.
s – Calls to set down only.
u – Calls to pick up only.
v – Also Apr. 7.
z – Not Apr. 7, 9, 30.
● – See also Tables **737**, **745** and **746**.

ÖREBRO - HALLSBERG - HERRLJUNGA - GÖTEBORG 736

Operator: *Västtågen* (2nd class only)

km		Ⓐ		Ⓐ	⑥	Ⓐ	Ⓐ	⑥	†	Ⓐ	⑥	†	Ⓐ	⑥	Ⓐ	†	⑥	†	Ⓐ	⑥	Ⓐ	†	Ⓐ	⑥	†	⑥	Ⓐp
	Örebro C .... 755 756 d.	...	...	...	...	...	...	...	...	0746	...	...	...	...	...	...	...	...	...	...	...	...	1637	...	...	...	...
0	**Hallsberg** 740 755 756 d.	...	...	...	...	...	...	...	...	0814	...	...	...	1123	...	1253	...	...	...	...	...	...	1657	1710	1838	...	1955
30	Laxå ....756 d.	...	...	...	...	...	...	...	...	0830	...	...	...	1138	1200	1309	...	...	...	...	...	...	1717	1728	1853	...	2013
92	Mariestad ....d.	...	...	0524	...	0656	0756	0817	0819	0923**j**	...	...	1119	1225	1256**j**	1354	1406	1407	1445	1608	1625	1703	1810**j**	1816	1952**h**	...	2107**j**
146	Lidköping ....a.	...	...	0606	...	0746	0851	0902	0901	1013	...	...	1205	1312	1343	...	1450	1449	1531	1657	1713	1750	1856	1902	2039	...	2153
146	Lidköping ....d.	0520	...	0618	0713	0750	0904	0904	0904	1023	1116	1149	1211	1327	1353	...	1453	1452	1536	...	1718	1752	1911	1918	...	2209	2209
201	**Herrljunga** ..... 740 756 a.	0606	...	0701	0759	0837	0953	0948	0948	1110	1203	1236	1258	1416	1441	...	1538	1536	1624	...	1804	1837	1957	2005	...	2255	2256
	Göteborg C ... 740 756 a.	...	...	0755	...	0931	...	1040	1040	1205	...	1340	...	1510	1540	...	1635	1640	...	...	...	1931	...	...	...	...	...

	Ⓐ	Ⓐ	Ⓐ	⑥	†	Ⓐ	⑥	Ⓐ	Ⓐ	†	⑥	⑥	Ⓐ	⑥	Ⓐ	†	†	⑥	Ⓐ	⑥	Ⓐ	†	Ⓐ	†	⑥	Ⓐp	⚒
Göteborg C..... 740 756 d.	...	...	...	...	...	0835	...	...	1030	1130	1130	...	...		1350	1420	...	1530	...	1725	1730	1730	...	1950			
Herrljunga ...... 740 756 d.	...	...	0701	...	...	0921	0956	1036	1117	1215	1218	...	1304	1400	1442	1516	...	1617	1631	1814	1817	1816	1925	2051	2058	2103	2301
Lidköping ....a.	...	...	0749	...	...	1008	1044	1124	1159	1304	1302	...	1350	1446	1528	1604	...	1704	1716	1859	1858	1905	2012	2135	2144	2149	2346
Lidköping ....d.	0440	0607	0753	0807	0936	1014	1046	...	1206	1307	1312	...	1356	1451	1532	1607	...	1708	1719	1904	1901**r**	1908	2014	...	...	...	...
Mariestad ....d.	0547**f**	0651	0844	0906	1025	1105	1132	...	1248	1349	1354	1405	1457**h**	1538	1620	1655	1706	1753	1808	1947	1944**r**	1950	2100	...	...	...	...
Laxå .... 756 d.	0633	...	...	0950	1110	1150	...	...	...	...	...	1500**j**	1542	...	...	...	1750	...	1857	...	...	...	...	...	...	...	...
Hallsberg . 740 755 756 a.	0650	...	...	1007	1126	...	...	...	...	...	...	1516	1559	...	...	...	1806	...	1915	...	...	...	...	...	...	...	...
Örebro C......... 755 756 a.	0715	...	...	...	...	...	...	...	...	...	...	...	1621	...	...	...	...	...	...	...	...	...	...	...	...	...	...

f – Arrives 0523.
h – Arrives 16 minutes earlier.
j – Arrives 8 – 10 minutes earlier.
p – Not Mar. 20 – 23.
r – 3 minutes later on ⑤ (also Apr. 6, May 17).

737 KØBENHAVN - MALMÖ - HELSINGBORG

Operators: *Skåne; Øtåg*

Local trains between Malmö and Helsingborg are 2nd class only. For other trains see Tables **735**, **745** and **746**.

	⑥⑦		ⒶeØ	Ⓐ		dØ	Ⓐ	ØⒶ		bØ	Ⓐ	AØ		AØ	bØ	Ⓐ	AØ		AØ	bØ	Ⓐ	ⒶØ		bØ	Ⓐ	AØ
København H d.	...	...	...	...	...	0527	...	...	...	0627	...	0656	...	0716f	0727	...	0756	...	0816f	0827	...	0856	...	0927	...	0956
København Lufthavn ✈ d.	...	...	...	...	...	0542	...	...	...	0642	...	0711	...	0731f	0742	...	0811	...	0831f	0842	...	0911	...	0942	...	1011
Malmö C d.	0014	...	0508	0514	0541	0608	0614	0638	0641	0708	0714	0738	0741	0758	0808	0814	0838	0841	0858	0908	0914	0938	0941	1008	1014	1038
Lund d.	0030	...	0522	0530	0557	0622	0630	0653	0657	0722	0730	0753	0757	0812	0822	0830	0853	0857	0912	0922	0930	0953	0957	1022	1030	1053
Landskrona d.	0052	...	0536	0556	0620	0636	0652	0707	0720	0736	0752	0807	0820	0833	0836	0852	0907	0920	0933	0936	0952	1007	1020	1036	1052	1107
Helsingborg a.	0110	...	0549	0613	0638	0649	0710	0722	0738	0749	0810	0822	0838	0846	0849	0910	0922	0938	0946	0949	1010	1022	1038	1049	1110	1122

		bØ	Ø			bØ	Ø		bØ	Ⓐ	Ø		AØ	bØ	Ⓐ	Ø		AØ	bØ	Ⓐ	Ø		bØ	Ⓐ	AØ
København H d.	...	1027	1056	...	and at	1427	1456	...	1527	...	1556	...	1616f	1627	...	1656	...	1716f	1727	...	1756	...	1827	...	1856
København Lufthavn ✈ d.	...	1042	1111	...	the same	1442	1511	...	1542	...	1611	...	1631f	1642	...	1711	...	1731f	1742	...	1811	...	1842	...	1911
Malmö C d.	1041	1108	1138	1141	minutes	1508	1538	1541	1608	1614	1638	1641	1658	1708	1714	1738	1741	1758	1808	1814	1838	1841	1908	1914	1938
Lund d.	1057	1122	1153	1157	past each	1522	1553	1557	1622	1630	1653	1657	1712	1722	1730	1753	1757	1812	1822	1830	1853	1857	1922	1930	1953
Landskrona d.	1120	1136	1207	1220	hour until	1536	1607	1620	1636	1652	1707	1720	1733	1736	1752	1807	1820	1833	1836	1852	1907	1920	1936	1952	2007
Helsingborg a.	1138	1149	1222	1238		1549	1622	1638	1649	1710	1722	1738	1746	1749	1810	1822	1838	1846	1849	1910	1922	1938	1949	2010	2022

		bØ		bØ		Ø		bØ	⚒	Ø
København H d.	...	1927	...	2027	...	2127	...	2227	...	2329
København Lufthavn ✈ d.	...	1942	...	2042	...	2142	...	2242	...	2344
Malmö C d.	1941	2008	2041	2108	2141	2208	2241	2308	2341	0008
Lund d.	1957	2022	2057	2122	2157	2222	2257	2322	2357	0022
Landskrona d.	2020	2036	2120	2136	2220	2236	2320	2336	0020	0036
Helsingborg a.	2038	2049	2138	2149	2238	2249	2338	2349	0038	0049

	Ⓐ	ⒶØ	Ⓐ	AØ		eØ	AØ	Ⓐ	AØ		eØ
Helsingborg d.	0450	0510	0523	0535	0550	0610	0613	0623	0635	0650	0710
Landskrona d.	0506	0521	0539	0547	0606	0621	0625	0639	0647	0706	0721
Lund d.	0531	0539	0604	0609	0631	0639	0645	0704	0709	0731	0739
Malmö C d.	0545	0553	0618	0630	0645	0653	0659	0718	0723	0745	0753
København Lufthavn ✈ a.	...	0614	...	0644	...	0714	0721f	...	0744	...	0814
København H a.	...	0629	...	0659	...	0729	0736f	...	0759	...	0829

	AØ	Ⓐ	AØ		dØ	Ⓐ	AØ		bØ	Ⓐ	Ø		bØ	Ø			bØ	Ø		bØ	Ⓐ	Ø		bØ	AØ
Helsingborg d.	0713	0723	0735	0750	0810	0823	0835	0850	0910	0923	0935	0950	1010	1035	1050	and at	1310	1335	1350	1410	1423	1435	1450	1510	1513
Landskrona d.	0725	0739	0747	0806	0821	0839	0847	0906	0921	0939	0947	1006	1021	1047	1106	the same	1321	1347	1406	1421	1439	1447	1506	1521	1525
Lund d.	0745	0804	0809	0831	0839	0904	0909	0931	0939	1004	1009	1031	1039	1109	1131	minutes	1339	1409	1431	1439	1504	1509	1531	1539	1545
Malmö C d.	0759	0818	0823	0845	0853	0918	0923	0945	0953	1018	1023	1045	1053	1123	1145	past each	1353	1423	1445	1453	1518	1523	1545	1553	1559
København Lufthavn ✈ a.	0821f	...	0844	...	0914	...	0944	...	1014	...	1044	...	1114	1144	...	hour until	1414	1444	...	1514	...	1544	...	1614	1621f
København H a.	0836f	...	0859	...	0929	...	0959	...	1029	...	1059	...	1129	1159	...		1429	1459	...	1529	...	1559	...	1629	1636f

	Ⓐ	Ø		bØ	AØ	Ⓐ	Ø		bØ	Ⓐ	Ø		bØ	Ⓐ		bØ	Ⓐ		bØ		bØ		bØ		bØ	⚒
Helsingborg d.	1523	1535	1550	1610	1613	1623	1635	1650	1710	1723	1735	1750	1810	1823	1850	1910	1923	1950	2010	2050	2110	2150	2210	2250	2310	2350
Landskrona d.	1539	1547	1606	1621	1625	1639	1647	1706	1721	1739	1747	1806	1821	1839	1906	1921	1939	2006	2021	2106	2121	2206	2221	2306	2321	0006
Lund d.	1604	1609	1631	1639	1645	1704	1709	1731	1739	1804	1809	1831	1839	1904	1931	1939	2004	2031	2039	2131	2139	2231	2239	2331	2338	0031
Malmö C d.	1618	1623	1645	1653	1659	1718	1723	1745	1753	1818	1823	1845	1853	1918	1945	1953	2018	2045	2053	2145	2153	2245	2253	2345	2351	0045
København Lufthavn ✈ a.	...	1644	...	1714	1721f	...	1744	...	1814	...	1844	...	1914	...	...	2014	...	...	2114	...	2214	...	2314	...	...	...
København H a.	...	1659	...	1729	1736f	...	1759	...	1829	...	1859	...	1929	...	...	2029	...	...	2129	...	2229	...	2329	...	...	...

A – ①–⑤ (not Apr. 7, 10, May 18).
b – Not Mar. 13 - Apr. 6.
d – Not Mar. 13–18, 20–25, 27–31, Apr. 1, 3–6.
e – Not Mar. 13–17, 20–24, 27–31, Apr. 3–6.
f – Not Apr. 6, May 5.

738 South-eastern SECONDARY LINES

Operator: *Krösatågen*

km		Ⓐ								Ⓑc	
0	**Västervik** d.	0541	0735	...	1007	1207	1407	1605	1807	2007	...
77	Åtvidaberg d.	0646	0840	...	1113	1313	1513	1713	1913	2113	...
116	**Linköping** a.	0721	0921	...	1151	1351	1551	1749	1951	2151	...

	Ⓐ										Ⓑc
Linköping d.	0544	...	0757	...	1008	1208	1409	1608	1809	...	2008
Åtvidaberg d.	0616	...	0841	...	1042	1243	1444	1643	1844	...	2044
Västervik a.	0725	...	0946	...	1150	1350	1550	1750	1950	...	2150

km		Ⓐ	Ⓐ	⑥z						Ⓑc	Ⓑb
0	**Linköping** d.	...	0523	...	0819	1020	1220	1420	1621	1821	2022
41	Rimforsa d.	...	0602	...	0901	1101	1301	1501	1701	1901	2101
123	Hultsfred d.	0609	0705	0705	1005	1205	1405	1605	1805	2005	2204
159	Berga ▷ a.	0634	0733	0733	1030	1230	1430	1630	1830	2030	...
159	Berga ▷ d.	0639	0738	0738	1035	1235	1435	1635	1835	2035	...
235	**Kalmar** a.	0738	0838	0838	1138	1338	1538	1738	1938	2138	...

	Ⓐx	Ⓐ	⑥z							Ⓑc	Ⓑb
Kalmar d.	...	0539	...	...	0830	1036	1236	1436	1636	1836	2035
Berga ▷ a.	...	0637	...	...	0933	1133	1333	1533	1733	1933	2134
Berga ▷ d.	...	0642	...	...	0938	1138	1338	1538	1738	1938	2139
Hultsfred d.	0531	0706	0706	...	1004	1204	1404	1604	1804	2004	2202
Rimforsa d.	0632	0805	0806	...	1102	1302	1502	1702	1902	2102	...
Linköping a.	0710	0842	0842	...	1140	1339	1539	1740	1941	2139	...

b – Not Apr. 7, 9, 30.
c – Not Apr. 7.
x – Not ②⑤ Feb. 28 - Mar. 24.
z – Also Apr. 7, May 18; not Apr. 8.

▷ – Connecting 🚌 services **Berga - Oskarshamn** and v.v. (operated by Länsbuss).
29 km. Journey 31–40 minutes. **Subject to confirmation.**
From Berga at 0640 Ⓐ, 0739 Ⓐ, 0740 ⑥, 1035 Ⓒ, 1235 Ⓒ, 1435, 1635, 1835 and 2035 Ⓑ.
From Oskarshamn at 0555 Ⓐ, 0855 Ⓒ, 1055, 1255, 1430 Ⓐ, 1455 Ⓒ, 1655, 1855 Ⓑ and 2055 Ⓑ.

739 VARBERG - UDDEVALLA

Operator: *Västtågen* (2nd class only).

km		*Sn* **462** Ⓐ¶	Ⓐ	Ⓐ	*Sn* **460** ⑥q¶	Ⓐ	Ⓒ	Ⓐ	Ⓐs	†	Ⓒ	Ⓐ	†	Ⓐ	⑥	Ⓐ	⚒	Ⓐ	Ⓐ	†A	Ⓐ	Ⓐ	⑥	†	Ⓐp	Ⓑ△
0	**Varberg** d.	...	...	...	...	*0606*	...	0703	0809	...	1039	1041	...	...	1239	1341	1441	...	1538	1639	1640	1740	1839	1839	1841	2040
84	Borås a.	...	...	...	...	*0724*	...	0828	0934	...	1200	1158	...	...	1400	1458	1559	...	1702	1800	1802	1909	2000	2000	2002	2205
84	Borås d.	0548	0558	0657	0728	0755	0805	0918	...	1002	1203	1205	1401	1402	1403	1502	1603	1645	...	1802	1804	...	...	2002	2004	...
127	**Herrljunga** a.	0625	0633	0735	0759	0834	0840	0953	...	1040	1238	1240	1439	1440	1441	1540	1640	1723	...	1842	1842	...	...	2037	2041	...
127	**Herrljunga** d.	0637	0641	0756	0807	0839	0928	...	...	1121	1333	1333	1543	1532	1539	*1624*	...	1732	...	1857	1857	...	...	2120	2120	...
	Stockholm C **740** a.	0917	|	|	1051	|	|	...	...	|	|	|	|	|	|	|	...	|	...	|	|	...	...	|	|	...
191	Vänersborg d.	...	0731	0852	...	0925	1019	...	...	1213	1419	1420	1630	1620	1625	*1711*	...	1825	...	1943	1943	...	...	2208	2210	...
195	Öxnered d.	...	0738	0858	...	0931	1025	...	...	1221	1425	1425	1636	1630	1632	*1717*	...	1832	...	1950	1949	...	...	2218	2218	...
217	**Uddevalla C** a.	...	0753	0914	...	0947	1040	...	...	1237	1440	1441	1652	1649	1648	*1732*	...	1849	...	2005	2003	...	...	2232	2232	...

	Ⓐ	Ⓐ	Ⓐ	⑥	Ⓐs	Ⓐs	Ⓒ	Ⓐ	Ⓐv	Ⓒ	⑥	Ⓐ	Ⓒ	Ⓐ	Ⓒ	Ⓐ	Ⓐ	Ⓒ	Ⓐ	†	*Sn* **467** Ⓑe¶	Ⓐ	Ⓒ	†	Ⓐ	†
Uddevalla C d.	...	...	0517	...	0628	0659	0729	0817	...	0920	0920	1119	1136	1317	1317	...	1458	1527	1611	1619	...	...	...	...	...	1933
Öxnered d.	...	...	0532	...	0643	0715	0744	0833	...	0936	0936	1135	1153	1336	1336	...	1513	1543	1628	1635	...	...	...	...	...	1949
Vänersborg d.	...	...	0538	...	0652	0721	0751	0840	...	0942	0942	1142	1159	1341	1342	...	1522	1549	1633	1641	...	...	...	...	...	1955
Stockholm C **740** d.	...	...	|	...	|	|	|	|	...	|	|	|	|	|	|	...	|	|	|	|	1604	...	...	...	...	|
Herrljunga a.	...	...	0624	...	0740	0811	0838	0937	...	1029	1029	1231	1249	1429	1429	...	1612	1638	1719	1727	1847	...	...	...	...	2041
Herrljunga d.	...	0548	0644	...	0752	0835	0922	1026	1124	1122	1122	1321	1320	1524	1523	1605	...	1726	1724	...	1854	1920	1922	1922	2105	2121
Borås a.	...	0624	0722	...	0830	0911	1000	1104	1159	1200	1200	1356	1355	1602	1601	1641	...	1801	1802	...	1925	1958	1957	1957	2140	2156
Borås d.	0525	0625	0727	0759	0836	0959	1003	...	1201	...	1203	1458	1402	...	1603j	1703	...	1803	1805	...	...	2003	...	2002	...	...
Varberg a.	0646	0746	0849	0920	0953	1120	1120	...	1318	...	1320	1619	1525	...	1720j	1821	...	1920	1922	...	...	2120	...	2119	...	...

GÖTEBORG - UDDEVALLA - STRÖMSTAD *Subject to alteration from April 14*

km		⑥	Ⓐ		†◧	Ⓐ		†c	Ⓐ	⑥	Ⓑ	
0	**Göteborg C** ▲ d.	0710	0840	1040	1240	1240	1440	1640	1645	1840	1840	...
89	Uddevalla C ▲ a.	0826	0953	1153	1353	1353	1553	1753	1743	1953	1953	...
89	Uddevalla C d.	0828	1005	1210	1405	1410	1602	1808	1750	2001	2015	...
173	Skee d.	0939	1121	1323	1520	1525	1717	1923	1906	2112	2126	...
180	**Strömstad** a.	0945	1127	1329	1527	1531	1723	1930	1912	2118	2132	...

	Ⓐ	Ⓐ	⑥		Ⓒ	Ⓐ	b		Ⓐd	Ⓒh
Strömstad d.	0527	0642	0647	...	1031	1229	1430	1627	1818	1834
Skee d.	0533	0648	0653	...	1037	1235	1436	1633	1823	1840
Uddevalla C a.	0645	0800	0805	...	1149	1351	1552	1747	1939	1954
Uddevalla C ▲ d.	0648	0807	0807	...	1207	1407	1607	1807	1954	2007
Göteborg C ▲ a.	0745	0920	0920	...	1320	1520	1720	1920	2110	2120

A – Until Feb. 12.
b – Not Mar. 26.
c – Not Apr. 7.
d – Not Feb. 24.
e – Not Apr. 7, 9, 30, May 17, June 5.
f – Also Apr. 6; not Feb. 24, 25.
h – Not Feb. 25, Mar. 26.
p – Not Feb. 27, 28, Mar. 1, 2, 6–9, 13–16, 20–23.
q – Also Apr. 7, May 18, June 6; not Apr. 8.

s – Not Feb. 23.
u – Not Feb. 26.
v – Not Feb. 28, Mar. 1, 2.
x – Not Feb. 24, 25.
y – Not Feb. 25.
z – Not Apr. 6.
¶ – Conveys (12) and 🍸. Ⓡ.
△ – On † Varberg d. 2042, Borås a. 2159.

◧ – On Apr. 10 Göteborg d. 1310, Uddevalla a. 1401, d. 1404, Skee d. 1521, Strömstad a. 1527.
▲ – Other services Göteborg - Uddevalla and v.v.: *Subject to alteration from April 14.*
From Göteborg C at 0525 Ⓐ, 0640 Ⓐ, 0740 Ⓐ, 0840 Ⓒ **u**, 0940 ⚒, 1140, 1240 ⑥, 1340, 1540, 1640 ⚒, 1710 Ⓐ, 1740 **j**, 1940 **j**, 2040 **j**, 2140 ⑥ **y**, 2240 ⑤⑥ **f** and 2340 ⑦–④ **z**.
From Uddevalla C at 0507 Ⓐ, 0534 Ⓐ, 0607 Ⓐ, 0637 Ⓐ, 0707 ⚒, 0807 † **u**, 0907 ⚒, 1007, 1107, 1207 Ⓐ, 1307, 1407 Ⓒ, 1507, 1707 **j**, 1907 **j**, 2107 **x** and 2207 **x**.

STOCKHOLM - GÖTEBORG 740

See Table **756** for slower regional services via Västerås and Örebro. FlixTrain also run a number of services on this route (internet bookings only: www.flixtrain.com).
Warning! Timings may vary by up to 5 minutes until Feb. 26. *MTR* train numbers may also vary until Feb. 26 (an extra digit '1' is usually added to the front of the number).

km	All trains [R]	*Sn*	*MTR*	*Sn*	*MTR*	*Sn*		*MTR*	*Sn*		*Sn*	*MTR*	*MTR*		*Sn*	*MTR*	*Sn*	*Sn*	*MTR*	*Sn*		*Sn*	*Sn*	*IC*
		401	**2021**	**421**	**2023**	**423**		**2025**	**425**		**427**	**2017**	**2027**		**429**	**2029**	**431**	**403**	**2033**	**433**		**435**	**435**	**105**
		🍷	🍷	🍷	🍷	🍷		🍷	🍷		🍷	🍷	🍷		🍷	🍷	🍷	🍷	🍷	🍷		🍷	🍷	🍷
		Ⓐ	Ⓐ	⚒	①–③	Ⓐ					Ⓑ	Ⓒ	⑥				Ⓑ	⑤				Ⓐ	†	⑤
			a	k	r			A			b	B	C			D	b	f	x				b	f
0	**Stockholm** C .... 750/6 d.	0600	0607	0627	0708	0734	...	0812	0834	...	0930	0953	0953	...	1030	1058	1134	1208	1211	1230	...	1329	1333	1340
36	Södertälje Syd △ .... 750 d.	|	|	|	|	|	...	|	|	...	0949	1014	|	...	|	|	|	|	|	1249	...	|	|	1400
131	Katrineholm .... 750 d.	|	0704	0722	0806	0825	...	0909	0926	...	1026	|	|	...	1121	|	1226	|	1309	1326	...	1421	1425	|
197	**Hallsberg** .... 750 756 d.	|	|	0748	|	|	...	|	|	...	|	|	|	...	|	|	|	|	|	|	...	|	|	1511
272	Töreboda .... 756 d.	|	|	|	|	|	...	|	|	...	|	|	|	...	|	|	|	|	|	|	...	|	|	|
311	**Skövde** .... 756 d.	|	0809	0829	0911	0928	...	1016	1030	...	1129	1156	1154	...	1225	1258	1328	|	1412	1430	...	1525	1528	1607
341	Falköping .... 756 d.	|	0824	|	|	|	...	|	|	...	|	|	1209	...	|	|	|	|	1427	|	...	|	|	|
375	Herrljunga .... 756 d.	0815	|	|	|	|	...	|	|	...	|	1227	|	...	1252	1323	|	|	|	|	...	1553	|	1640
410	Alingsås ▽ .... 756 a.	0835	|	|	|	|	...	1106	|	...	|	1243	|	...	|	|	|	|	1500	|	...	|	|	|
455	**Göteborg** C .... 756 a.	0905	0925	0935	1030	1040	...	1135	1135	...	1240	1310	1310	...	1335	1410	1440	1510	1530	1540	...	1640	1635	1745

All trains [R]	*MTR*	*Sn*		*Sn*	*MTR*	*Sn*	*Sn*	*Sn*	*Sn*	*MTR*	*Sn*	*Sn*	*MTR*		*Sn*	*Sn*	*MTR*	*Sn*		*MTR*	*MTR*	*Sn*		*MTR*
	2037	**437**		**439**	**2009**	**405**	**467**	**411**	**441**	**2041**	**407**	**443**	**2043**		**445**	**445**	**2045**	**447**		**2047**	**2057**	**449**		**2051**
	🍷	🍷		🍷	🍷	🍷	🍷	🍷	🍷	🍷	🍷	🍷	🍷		🍷	🍷	🍷	🍷		🍷	🍷	🍷		🍷
				Ⓑ	Ⓑ	Ⓑ	Ⓑ	⑥	Ⓑ		Ⓐ		†		⑥	Ⓑ	⑥	Ⓑ		Ⓑ	Ⓑ	Ⓑ		
	E			b	b‡	d	e	k	b	F			b◧		k	b	k	b		H	G	b		J
Stockholm C .... 750/6 d.	1425	1434	...	1527	1545	1551	1604	1629	1632	1649	1716	1728	1742	...	1814	1829	1853	1929	...	1952	1952	2034	...	2123
Södertälje Syd △ .... 750 d.	1443	|	...	|	|	1611	|	|	|	1708	|	1747	|	...	|	|	|	1948	...	|	|	|	...	|
Katrineholm .... 750 d.	1523	1527	...	1619	|	|	|	1727	1727	1747	|	1824	1838	...	1913	1921	|	2026	...	|	|	2126	...	2219
Hallsberg .... 750 756 d.	|	|	...	|	|	1715	|	|	|	|	|	|	|	...	|	|	|	|	...	|	|	|	...	|
Töreboda .... 756 d.	|	|	...	|	|	|	1801	|	|	|	|	|	|	...	|	|	|	|	...	|	|	|	...	|
Skövde .... 756 d.	1626	1630	...	1725	1745	1756	1816	1828	1829	1851	|	1929	1945	...	2022	2025	2048	2130	...	2155	2155	2230	...	2325
Falköping .... 756 d.	|	|	...	|	1800	|	1832	|	|	|	|	|	2000	...	|	|	2103	|	...	2209	2209	|	...	|
Herrljunga .... 739 756 d.	|	|	...	|	1818	|	1854j	1853	|	|	|	|	|	...	|	2053	|	|	...	|	2229	|	...	|
Borås .... 739 a.	|	|	...	|	|	|	1925	|	|	|	|	|	|	...	|	|	|	|	...	|	|	|	...	|
Alingsås ▽ .... 756 a.	1707	|	...	|	1838	1843	...	|	|	1938	|	|	2039	...	2108	|	2136	|	...	2240	|	|	...	0006
Göteborg C .... 756 a.	1733	1740	...	1835	1905	1915	...	1936	1935	2005	2010	2040	2105	...	2140	2140	2205	2240	...	2308	2350	2340	...	0033
Trollhättan .... a.	...	...	...	...	...	...	...	...	...	...	2048	...	...	...	...	...	...	...	...	...	...	...	...	...
Uddevalla .... a.	...	...	...	...	...	...	...	...	...	...	2108	...	...	...	...	...	...	...	...	...	...	...	...	...

All trains [R]	*Sn*	*Sn*	*MTR*	*MTR*	*Sn*	*MTR*	*Sn*	*Sn*	*MTR*	*Sn*	*Sn*	*MTR*	*Sn*	*Sn*	*Sn*		*Sn*	*SN*	*Sn*		*Sn*	*MTR*	*Sn*	*MTR*
	420	**400**	**2000**	**2012**	**462**	**2022**	**422**	**404**	**2024**	**424**	**460**	**2026**	**426**	**416**	**426**		**428**	**428**	**428**		**430**	**2032**	**432**	**2034**
	🍷	🍷	🍷	🍷	🍷	🍷	🍷	🍷	🍷	🍷	🍷	🍷	🍷	🍷	🍷		🍷	🍷	🍷		🍷	🍷	🍷	🍷
	Ⓐ	Ⓐ		②③	Ⓐ		⚒	Ⓐ	①–④	Ⓐ	⑥	②–⑥	Ⓐ	⑥	⑦		⑥	⑦	Ⓐ				Ⓑ	⑦
			L	B		M	k		m		q	p		q	s		t	u					b	N
Uddevalla .... d.	...	...	...	...	...	...	...	0546	...	...	...	...	...	0718	...	...	...	...	...	...	...	...	...	...
Trollhättan .... d.	...	...	...	...	...	...	...	0606	...	...	...	...	...	0738	...	...	...	...	...	...	...	...	...	...
Göteborg C .... 756 d.	0459	0539	0550	0550	...	0554	0624	0644	0654	0724	...	0754	0819	0819	0824	...	0919	0924	0924	...	1024	1054	1124	1154
Alingsås △ .... 756 d.	0525	|	0615	0615	...	|	|	0714	0720	|	...	0820	|	0849	|	...	|	0949	|	...	|	|	|	1220
Borås .... 739 d.	|	|	|	|	0548	|	|	|	|	|	0728	|	|	|	|	...	|	|	|	...	|	|	|	|
Herrljunga .... 739 756 d.	0543	|	|	0632	0637	0634	|	|	|	|	0807	|	|	|	0904	...	|	|	1004	...	|	1134	|	|
Falköping .... 756 d.	0558	|	|	0648	0653	0649	|	|	|	|	0823	|	|	|	|	...	|	|	|	...	|	1149	|	|
Skövde .... 756 d.	0613	|	0656	0703	0708	0703	0725	|	0801	0825	0838	0901	0926	0930	0930	...	1026	1029	1030	...	1125	1203	1225	1301
Töreboda .... 756 d.	0629	|	|	|	|	|	|	|	|	|	|	|	|	|	|	...	|	|	|	...	|	|	|	|
Hallsberg .... 750 756 d.	0700	|	|	|	0754	|	|	|	|	|	0924	|	1010	|	|	...	1110	|	|	...	|	|	|	|
Katrineholm .... 750 d.	0726	|	|	0811	|	0811	0831	|	|	0933	|	1009	1037	1037	1037	...	1137	1137	1137	...	1231	1312	1333	|
Södertälje Syd ▽ .... 750 a.	0804	|	|	|	|	|	0910	|	0950	|	1032	1049	|	|	|	...	|	|	|	...	|	|	1409	|
Stockholm C .... 750/6 a.	0823	0832	0854	0909	0917	0909	0930	0947	1009	1026	1051	1108	1130	1130	1130	...	1230	1230	1230	...	1325	1411	1429	1508

All trains [R]	*Sn*	*Sn*	*MTR*	*Sn*		*Sn*		*Sn*	*Sn*	*MTR*		*IC*	*Sn*	*Sn*	*Sn*	*MTR*	*Sn*		*Sn*	*MTR*		*MTR*	*Sn*	*MTR*
	434	**412**	**2036**	**436**		**438**		**440**	**440**	**2040**		**104**	**442**	**442**	**408**	**2044**	**444**		**446**	**2046**		**2050**	**450**	**2052**
	🍷	🍷	🍷	🍷		🍷		🍷	🍷	🍷		🍷	🍷	🍷	🍷	🍷	🍷		🍷	🍷		🍷	🍷	🍷
		⑤		Ⓑ				Ⓑ	⑥			†	Ⓑ	⑥	Ⓑ		Ⓑ						Ⓑ	
		f		b				b	k	Q		b	b	k	b	R	b			T		W	b	Y
Göteborg C .... 756 d.	1224	1249	1254	1324	...	1424	...	1524	1524	1529	...	1554	1624	1624	1649	1654	1724	...	1824	1829	...	1954	2024	2054
Alingsås △ .... 756 d.	|	|	1319	|	...	|	...	|	|	1555	...	|	|	1649	1717	|	|	...	|	1855	...	|	|	2120
Herrljunga .... 756 d.	1303	|	|	|	...	|	...	|	|	|	...	|	|	1708	1737	1739	|	...	|	|	...	|	|	|
Falköping .... 756 d.	|	|	1350	|	...	|	...	|	|	|	...	|	|	|	|	1754	|	...	|	|	...	2046	|	|
Skövde .... 756 d.	1329	1355	1403	1428	...	1525	...	1625	1631	1636	...	1707	1725	1734	|	1808	1825	...	1925	1936	...	2101	2125	2201
Töreboda .... 756 d.	|	|	|	|	...	|	...	|	|	|	...	|	|	|	|	|	|	...	|	|	...	|	|	|
Hallsberg .... 750 756 d.	|	1439	|	|	...	|	...	|	|	|	...	1757	|	|	|	|	1909	...	|	|	...	|	2210	|
Katrineholm .... 750 d.	1438	|	|	1533	...	1632	...	1733	1744	1745	...	|	1833	1845	|	|	1936	...	2033	2045	...	|	2237	|
Södertälje Syd ▽ .... 750 a.	|	|	1549	1609	...	|	...	1809	1825	|	...	1908	|	|	|	|	|	...	2111	|	...	|	|	|
Stockholm C .... 750/6 a.	1531	1601	1607	1628	...	1726	...	1829	1845	1846	...	1931	1927	1939	1953	2020	2029	...	2131	2143	...	2306	2330	0003

A – ④–⑥ to Mar. 11; ④–⑦ from Mar. 16 (also May 1, 17, June 6).
B – Until Mar. 12.
C – ⑥ from Mar. 18 (also Apr. 7).
D – Ⓐ (daily from Mar. 13).
E – ①④⑤⑥⑦ to Feb. 26 (also Mar. 5, 6); daily from Mar. 9.
F – ②③⑥⑦ to Mar. 8 (not Feb. 22, 28, Mar. 1, 4); daily from Mar. 11.
G – Ⓑ from Mar. 24 (also Mar. 19).
H – Ⓑ until Mar. 12 (also Mar. 17).
J – ④⑤† (also May 17; not Feb. 26, Mar. 10, 23, 24, Apr. 7, 9, 30, May 18, 19, June 4).
L – ① to Mar. 6; ①–③ from Mar. 13 (not Apr. 10, May 1, 17, June 5, 6).
M – ①④⑤ to Mar. 10; Ⓐ from Mar. 14 (not May 19, June 5).
N – ⑦ from Mar. 19 (also Apr. 10, May 1, 18, June 6).
Q – Ⓐ to Mar. 10; Ⓑ from Mar. 13 (not Apr. 7).
R – Ⓑ (daily from Mar. 12).
T – ①④⑤⑥⑦ (daily from Mar. 9).
W – ②③④⑤⑦ to Mar. 5; Ⓑ from Mar. 7 (not Apr. 7).
Y – ⑦ to Feb. 26; ④⑤⑦ from Mar. 2 (also Apr. 10, May 1, 17, June 6; not Apr. 7, 9, 30, May 18, 19, June 4).

a – Not May 19, June 5.
b – Not Apr. 7.
d – Not Apr. 7, 9, 30.
e – Not Apr. 7, 9, 30, May 17, June 5.
f – Also Apr. 6, May 17; not Apr. 7.
j – Arrives 1847.
k – Also Apr. 7.
m – Also May 19; not Apr. 6, 10, May 1, 17, June 6.
p – Not May 2, 18, 19, June 6.
q – Also Apr. 7, May 18, June 6; not Apr. 8.
r – Not Apr. 10, May 1, 17, June 6.
s – Also Apr. 8, 10, May 1.
t – Also Apr. 7, May 18, June 6.
u – Also Apr. 10, May 1.
x – Not Feb. 27 - Mar. 4.

‡ – Train number **2039** on †.
◧ – Train number **2053** Mar. 19 - May 21.
△ – Trains call to pick up only.
▽ – Trains call to set down only.

☛ **First-class tickets**: On *Sn* services includes complimentary tea, coffee and snacks with breakfast served on departures before 0900. On *MTR* services a complimentary meal and drink is included.

745 KØBENHAVN - MALMÖ - KRISTIANSTAD - KARLSKRONA

Operators: Øtåg; Skåne

For other trains København - Lund, see Tables **735** and **737**. For other trains København - Hässleholm, see Tables **730** and **746**.

km		②–⑦		Ⓐ	Ⓐ	Ⓐ	Ⓐ	⚒																		
0	**København** H ... d.	z	...	...	...	...	0447	0547	0547	0647	0747	0847	0947	1047	1147	1247	1347	1447	1547	1647	1747	1847	1947	2047	2147	2249
12	København Lufthavn ✈ ... d.	...	...	...	...	...	0502	0602	0602	0702	0802	0902	1002	1102	1202	1302	1402	1502	1602	1702	1802	1902	2002	2102	2202	2304
47	**Malmö** C ... a.	...	...	...	...	...	0526	0626	0626	0726	0826	0926	1026	1126	1226	1326	1426	1526	1626	1726	1826	1926	2026	2126	2226	2326
47	**Malmö** C ... d.	0052	...	...	...	0425	0528	0628	0628	0728	0828	0928	1028	1128	1228	1328	1428	1528	1628	1728	1828	1928	2028	2128	2228	2328
63	Lund ... d.	0107	...	...	...	0445	0542	0642	0642	0742	0842	0942	1042	1142	1242	1342	1442	1542	1642	1742	1842	1942	2042	2142	2242	2342
130	Hässleholm ... **734** d.	0152	...	...	0511	0532	0611	0711	0711	0811	0911	1011	1111	1211	1311	1411	1511	1611	1711	1811	1911	2011	2111	2211	2312	0011
160	**Kristianstad** ... **734** a.	...	...	...	0531	0554	0631	0731	0731	0831	0931	1031	1131	1231	1331	1431	1531	1631	1731	1831	1931	2031	2131	2231	2331	0031
160	**Kristianstad** ... d.	...	...	0502	0537	*0602*	0637	0737	...	0837	0937	1037	1137	1237	1337	1437	1537	1637	1737	1837	1937	2037	2137	2237	...	...
191	Sölvesborg ... d.	...	...	0525	0558	*0625*	0658	0758	...	0858	0958	1058	1158	1258	1358	1458	1558	1658	1758	1858	1958	2058	2158	2258	...	...
222	**Karlshamn** ... d.	...	...	0550	0620	*0650*	0720	0820	...	0920	1020	1120	1220	1320	1420	1520	1620	1720	1820	1920	2020	2120	2220	2320	...	...
260	Ronneby ... d.	...	...	...	0646	...	0746	0846	...	0946	1046	1146	1246	1346	1446	1546	1646	1746	1846	1946	2046	2146	2246	2346	...	...
290	**Karlskrona** ... a.	...	...	...	0712	...	0812	0912	...	1012	1112	1212	1312	1412	1512	1612	1712	1812	1912	2012	2112	2212	2312	0012	...	...

	②–⑦		Ⓐ				Ⓐ		⚒		⚒															
Karlskrona ... d.	z	...	...	...	...	...	0447	...	0547	...	0647	0747	0847	0947	1047	1147	1247	1347	1447	1547	1647	1747	1847	1947	2047	2147
Ronneby ... d.	...	...	...	...	...	...	0507	...	0607	...	0707	0807	0907	1007	1107	1207	1307	1407	1507	1607	1707	1807	1907	2007	2107	2207
Karlshamn ... d.	...	...	...	...	...	...	0535	...	0635	...	0735	0835	0935	1035	1135	1235	1335	1435	1535	1635	1735	1835	1935	2035	2135	2235
Sölvesborg ... d.	...	...	...	...	...	...	0557	...	0657	...	0757	0857	0957	1057	1157	1257	1357	1457	1557	1657	1757	1857	1957	2057	2157	2257
Kristianstad ... a.	...	...	...	...	...	...	0619	...	0719	...	0819	0919	1019	1119	1219	1319	1419	1519	1619	1719	1819	1919	2019	2119	2219	2319
Kristianstad ... **734** d.	0001	...	0401	...	0524	0624	0624	0724	0724	0824	0824	0924	1024	1124	1224	1324	1424	1524	1624	1724	1824	1924	2024	2124	2224	2324
Hässleholm ... **734** d.	0028	...	0428	0506	0545	0645	0645	0745	0745	0845	0845	0945	1045	1145	1245	1345	1445	1545	1645	1745	1845	1945	2045	2145	2245	2345
Lund ... d.	0115	...	0515	0552	0619	0719	0719	0819	0819	0919	0919	1019	1119	1219	1319	1419	1519	1619	1719	1819	1919	2019	2119	2219	2319	0019
Malmö C ... a.	0127	...	0527	0605	0631	0731	0731	0831	0831	0931	0931	1031	1131	1231	1331	1431	1531	1631	1731	1831	1931	2031	2131	2231	2331	0031
Malmö C ... d.	...	...	...	...	0633	0733	0733	0833	0833	0933	0933	1033	1133	1233	1333	1433	1533	1633	1733	1833	1933	2033	2133	2233	2333	0033
København Lufthavn ✈ ... a.	...	...	...	...	0654	0754	0754	0854	0854	0954	0954	1054	1154	1254	1354	1454	1554	1654	1754	1854	1954	2054	2154	2254	2354	0055
København H ... a.	...	...	...	...	0709	0809	0809	0909	0909	1009	1009	1109	1209	1309	1409	1509	1609	1709	1809	1909	2009	2109	2209	2309	0009	0110

z – Not Apr. 8, 11, May 2, 19, June 7.

746 KØBENHAVN, MALMÖ and GÖTEBORG - KALMAR

Other trains: København - Lund see Tables **735** and **737**; København - Lund - Hässleholm see Table **745**; København - Lund - Hässleholm - Alvesta see Table **730**.

km		*Øtåg* Ⓐ	*Øtåg* Ⓐ	*Øtåg* Ⓐ	Ⓐ	*Øtåg*	*Øtåg* Ⓐ	*Øtåg*	⑥k	*Øtåg*	*Øtåg* Ⓐ	*Øtåg*	⚒k	*Øtåg*	*Øtåg* Ⓐ	*Øtåg*	*Øtåg*	*Øtåg* Ⓑ	*Øtåg* Ⓐ	†n	*Øtåg*	*Øtåg*	*Øtåg* Ⓐ	*Øtåg*	*Øtåg*	*Øtåg* Ⓑ
0	**København** H ... d.	...	...	0507	...	0607	0607	0707	...	0807	0807	0907	...	1007	1007	1107	1207	1207	1207	...	1307	1407	1407	1507	1607	1607
12	København Lufthavn ✈ ... d.	...	...	0522	...	0622	0622	0722	...	0822	0822	0922	...	1022	1022	1122	1222	1222	1222	...	1322	1422	1422	1522	1622	1622
47	**Malmö** C ... a.	...	...	0546	...	0646	0646	0746	...	0846	0846	0946	...	1046	1046	1146	1246	1246	1246	...	1346	1446	1446	1546	1646	1646
47	**Malmö** C ... d.	...	...	0548	...	0648	0648	0748	...	0848	0848	0948	...	1048	1048	1148	1248	1248	1248	...	1348	1449	1448	1548	1648	1648
63	Lund ... d.	...	...	0602	...	0702	0702	0802	...	0902	0902	1002	...	1102	1102	1202	1302	1302	1302	...	1402	1502	1502	1602	1702	1702
80	Eslöv ... d.	...	...	0610	...	0710	0710	0810	...	0910	0910	1010	...	1110	1110	1210	1310	1310	1310	...	1410	1510	1510	1610	1710	1710
130	Hässleholm ... d.	...	...	0639	...	0735	0739	0839	...	0935	0939	1039	...	1135	1139	1239	1335	1339	1339	...	1439	1539	1539	1639	1735	1739
181	Älmhult ... d.	...	...	0702	...	...	0802	0902	...	...	1002	1102	...	...	1202	1302	...	1402	1402	...	1502	1602	1602	1702	...	1802
	Göteborg C ... d.	...	...	│	0604	...	│	│	0804	...	│	│	1004	...	│	│	...	│	│	1159	│	│	│	│	...	│
	Borås ... d.	...	...	│	0659	...	│	│	0859	...	│	│	1059	...	│	│	...	│	│	1259	│	│	│	│	...	│
	Limmared ... d.	...	...	│	0729	...	│	│	0929	...	│	│	1129	...	│	│	...	│	│	1329	│	│	│	│	...	│
	Värnamo ... d.	...	...	│	0811	...	│	│	1011	...	│	│	1211	...	│	│	...	│	│	1411	│	│	│	│	...	│
228	Alvesta ... a.	...	...	0723	0836	...	0823	0923	1036	...	1023	1123	1236	...	1223	1323	...	1423	1423	1438	1523	1623	1623	1723	...	1823
228	Alvesta ... d.	...	0631	0736	0837	...	0843	0936	1037	...	1036	1136	1237	...	1237	1336	...	1436	1436	1442	1536	1636	1636	1736	...	1836
245	**Växjö** ... d.	0549	0648	0749	0850	...	0855	0949	1050	...	1049	1149	1250	...	1252	1349	...	1448	1449	1453	1549	1649	1649	1749	...	1848
302	Emmaboda ... ▽ a.	0625	0724	0825	0928	...	...	1025	1128	...	1125	1225	1329	...	...	1425	...	...	1525	1528	1625	...	1725	1825	...	...
302	Emmaboda ... ▽ d.	0630	0730	0830	0930	...	...	1030	1129	...	1130	1230	1330	...	...	1430	...	...	1530	1530	1630	...	1730	1830	...	...
330	Nybro ... d.	0643	0743	0843	0944	...	...	1043	1144	...	1143	1243	1344	...	...	1443	...	...	1543	1544	1643	...	1743	1843	...	...
359	**Kalmar** ... a.	0659	0759	0859	1005	...	...	1059	1205	...	1159	1259	1405	...	...	1459	...	...	1559	1605	1659	...	1759	1859	...	...

		Øtåg	*Øtåg*	*Øtåg* Ⓑ	Ⓑn	*Øtåg*	*Øtåg*	*Øtåg* Ⓑ	*Øtåg*
København H ... d.	...	1707	1807	1807	...	1907	2007	2007	2107
København Lufthavn ✈ ... d.	...	1722	1822	1822	...	1922	2022	2022	2122
Malmö C ... a.	...	1746	1846	1846	...	1946	2046	2046	2146
Malmö C ... d.	...	1748	1848	1848	...	1948	2048	2048	2148
Lund ... d.	...	1802	1902	1902	...	2002	2102	2102	2202
Eslöv ... d.	...	1810	1910	1910	...	2010	2110	2110	2210
Hässleholm ... d.	...	1839	1935	1939	...	2039	2135	2139	2246j
Älmhult ... d.	...	1902	...	2002	...	2102	...	2202	2309
Göteborg C ... d.	1604	│	...	│	1804	│	...	│	│
Borås ... d.	1702	│	...	│	1859	│	...	│	│
Limmared ... d.	1733	│	...	│	1929	│	...	│	│
Värnamo ... d.	1817	│	...	│	2011	│	...	│	│
Alvesta ... a.	1843	1923	...	2023	2038	2123	...	2223	2328
Alvesta ... d.	1851	1936	...	2037	2042	2136	...	2238	2341
Växjö ... d.	1907	1949	...	2048	2053	2149	...	2248	2352
Emmaboda ... ▽ a.	1945	2025	...	...	2128	2224	...	...	...
Emmaboda ... ▽ d.	1947	2030	...	...	2130	2226	...	...	...
Nybro ... d.	2001	2043	...	...	2144	2240	...	...	...
Kalmar ... a.	2020	2059	...	...	2205	2256	...	...	...

km		*Øtåg* Ⓐ	Ⓐ	*Øtåg* Ⓐ	*Øtåg* Ⓐ	*Øtåg* ⑥	*Øtåg*	*Øtåg*	⑥k	*Øtåg* Ⓐ	*Øtåg* ⑥	*Øtåg*
	Kalmar ... d.	...	0456	...	0600	...	...	0700	0756	0800	...	...
	Nybro ... d.	...	0514	...	0615	...	...	0715	0813	0815	...	...
	Emmaboda ... ▽ a.	...	0528	...	0629	...	...	0729	0828	0829	...	...
	Emmaboda ... ▽ d.	...	0530	...	0631	...	...	0731	0830	0831	...	...
	Växjö ... d.	0511	0606	0613	0711	0711	...	0807	0906	0907	0911	...
	Alvesta ... a.	0521	0618	0624	0722	0721	...	0818	0918	0918	0921	...
0	Alvesta ... d.	0532	0619	0632	0732	0732	...	0832	0919	0932	0932	...
49	Värnamo ... d.	│	0647	│	│	│	...	│	0948	│	│	...
110	Limmared ... d.	│	0728	│	│	│	...	│	1029	│	│	...
149	Borås ... d.	│	0800	│	│	│	...	│	1100	│	│	...
222	**Göteborg** C ... a.	│	0855	│	│	│	...	│	1155	│	│	...
	Älmhult ... d.	0552	...	0652	0752	0752	...	0852	...	0952	0952	...
	Hässleholm ... d.	0623	...	0723	0823	0823	0823	0923	...	1023	1023	1023
	Eslöv ... d.	0646	...	0746	0846	0846	0846	0946	...	1046	1046	1046
	Lund ... d.	0659	...	0759	0859	0859	0859	0959	...	1059	1059	1059
	Malmö C ... a.	0711	...	0811	0911	0911	0911	1011	...	1111	1111	1111
	Malmö C ... d.	0713	...	0813	0913	0913	0913	1013	...	1113	1113	1113
	København Lufthavn ✈ ... a.	0734	...	0834	0934	0934	0934	1034	...	1134	1134	1134
	København H ... a.	0749	...	0849	0949	0949	0949	1049	...	1149	1149	1149

	Øtåg		*Øtåg* ⚒	*Øtåg*	*Øtåg*	Ⓑn	*Øtåg* Ⓐ	*Øtåg*	*Øtåg*	*Øtåg* Ⓐ	*Øtåg* †	*Øtåg*	*Øtåg*	⚒k	*Øtåg* Ⓐ	*Øtåg*	*Øtåg*	†n	*Øtåg* Ⓐ	*Øtåg* †	*Øtåg*	*Øtåg*	*Øtåg* Ⓐ	*Øtåg* †	*Øtåg*	*Øtåg* Ⓐ
Kalmar ... d.	0900	0956	...	...	1100	1156	...	...	1300	1400	...	...	1500	1554	...	...	1700	1756	1800	...	...	1900	2000	...	...	2100
Nybro ... d.	0915	1013	...	...	1115	1213	...	...	1315	1415	...	...	1515	1613	...	...	1715	1813	1815	...	...	1915	2015	...	...	2115
Emmaboda ... ▽ a.	0929	1028	...	...	1129	1228	...	...	1329	1429	...	...	1529	1628	...	...	1729	1828	1829	...	...	1929	2029	...	...	2129
Emmaboda ... ▽ d.	0931	1030	...	...	1131	1230	...	...	1331	1431	...	...	1531	1630	...	...	1731	1830	1831	...	...	1931	2033	...	...	2131
Växjö ... d.	1007	1106	1111	...	1207	1305	1313	...	1410	1510	1511	...	1610	1706	1713	...	1807	1906	1907	1911	...	2007	2109	2111	...	2206
Alvesta ... a.	1018	1118	1121	...	1218	1318	1324	...	1421	1521	1521	...	1621	1718	1724	...	1818	1918	1918	1921	...	2018	2121	2121	...	...
Alvesta ... d.	1032	1119	1132	...	1232	1319	1332	...	1432	1532	1532	...	1632	1719	1732	...	1832	1919	1932	1932	...	2032	2132	2132	...	...
Värnamo ... d.	│	1147	│	...	│	1347	│	...	│	│	│	...	│	1747	│	...	│	1947	│	│	...	│	│	│	...	...
Limmared ... d.	│	1229	│	...	│	1429	│	...	│	│	│	...	│	1829	│	...	│	2027	│	│	...	│	│	│	...	...
Borås ... d.	│	1300	│	...	│	1500	│	...	│	│	│	...	│	1900	│	...	│	2103	│	│	...	│	│	│	...	...
Göteborg C ... a.	│	1355	│	...	│	1555	│	...	│	│	│	...	│	1955	│	...	│	2200	│	│	...	│	│	│	...	...
Älmhult ... d.	1052	...	1152	...	1252	...	1352	...	1452	1552	1552	...	1652	...	1752	...	1852	...	1952	1952	...	2052	2152	2152	...	...
Hässleholm ... d.	1123	...	1223	1223	1323	...	1423	1423	1523	1623	1623	1623	1723	...	1823	1823	1923	...	2023	2023	2023	2123	2223	2223	2223	...
Eslöv ... d.	1146	...	1246	1246	1346	...	1446	1446	1546	1646	1646	1646	1746	...	1846	1846	1946	...	2046	2046	2046	2146	2246	2246	2246	...
Lund ... d.	1159	...	1259	1259	1359	...	1459	1459	1559	1659	1659	1659	1759	...	1859	1859	1959	...	2059	2059	2059	2159	2259	2259	2259	...
Malmö C ... a.	1211	...	1311	1311	1411	...	1511	1511	1611	1711	1711	1711	1811	...	1911	1911	2011	...	2111	2111	2111	2211	2311	2311	2311	...
Malmö C ... d.	1213	...	1313	1313	1413	...	1513	1513	1613	1713	1713	1713	1813	...	1913	1913	2013	...	2113	2113	2113	2213	2313	2313	2313	...
København Lufthavn ✈ ... a.	1234	...	1334	1334	1434	...	1534	1534	1634	1734	1734	1734	1834	...	1934	1934	2034	...	2134	2134	2134	2234	2334	2334	2334	...
København H ... a.	1249	...	1349	1349	1449	...	1549	1549	1649	1749	1749	1749	1849	...	1949	1949	2049	...	2149	2149	2149	2249	2349	2349	2349	...

EMMABODA - KARLSKRONA (2nd class only) — Operator: *Krösatågen*

km		Ⓐ	⚒k	⚒k	⚒k		⚒k				Ⓑn		Ⓑn		Ⓑn		Ⓑn
0	Emmaboda ... d.	0634	0734	0834	0934	1034	1134	1234	1334	1434	1534	1634	1734	1834	1952	2034	2134
57	Karlskrona ... a.	0716	0816	0916	1016	1116	1216	1316	1416	1516	1616	1716	1816	1916	2034	2116	2216

	Ⓐ	⚒k	⚒k	⚒k		⚒k				Ⓑn		Ⓑn		Ⓑn		Ⓑn
Karlskrona ... a.	0542	0642	0742	0842	0942	1042	1142	1242	1342	1442	1542	1642	1742	1842	1942	2042
Emmaboda ... d.	0625	0725	0825	0925	1025	1125	1225	1325	1425	1525	1625	1725	1825	1925	2025	2125

j – Arrives 2238.
k – Also Apr. 7.
n – Not Apr. 7.
▽ – See panel below main table for connecting trains Emmaboda - Karlskrona and v.v.

STOCKHOLM - STOCKHOLM ARLANDA ✈ 747

Operator: A-Train AB (*AEX*) Arlanda Express

Journey time: 18 minutes. All services stop at Arlanda Södra (17 minutes from Stockholm, 2 minutes from Arlanda Norra). Södra serves terminals 2, 3 and 4; Norra serves terminal 5.
Note: Certain services do not run on Dec. 24, 25, 31, Jan. 1, Apr. 7, 8.

From **Stockholm** Central: 0420, 0435, 0450, 0505, 0520, 0535, 0550 and every 15 minutes until 2335; then 0005 and 0035.

From **Arlanda** Norra: 0450, 0505, 0520, 0535, 0550 and every 15 minutes until 2350; then 0005, 0035 and 0105.

STOCKHOLM - HALLSBERG - KARLSTAD - OSLO 750

SERVICE UNTIL MAY 22. Swedish holiday dates apply. **Note**: On Apr. 7 services run as on ⑥. Subject to alteration on Feb. 25, 26.

km		*VTAB*	*VTAB*	*VTAB*	*VTAB*	*VTAB*	*Sn*	*VTAB*	*VTAB*	*VTAB*	*IC*	*VTAB*	*VTAB*	*VTAB*	*Sn*	*VTAB*	*Sn*	*VTAB*	*VTAB*	*VTAB*	*VTAB*	*IC*	*VTAB*	*VTAB*	*VTAB*	*VTAB*	*Sn*
							621				**623**				**627**		**629**					**635**					**639**
		Ⓐ	Ⓐ	⑥	Ⓐ	†a	Ⓐ	⑥d	†a	Ⓐd		Ⓐd	⑥d	†	Ⓐ	Ⓐb		⑥w	Ⓐd	†a	Ⓐd		⑥h	Ⓐd	Ⓐd	†	⑥
		2	2	2	2	2	🅁🍷	2	2	2	🅁🍷	2	2	2	🅁🍷	2	🅁🍷	2	2	2	2	🅁🍷	2	2	2	2	🅁🍷
0	**Stockholm** C △ d.	...	...	...	...	...	0602	...	...	...	0737	...	...	...	0950	...	1051	...	...	...	...	1257	...	...	...	...	1529
36	Södertälje Syd △ d.	...	...	...	...	...	|	...	...	...	0758u	...	...	...	1009u	...	1109u	...	...	...	...	1320u	...	...	...	...	1548u
131	Katrineholm △ d.	...	...	...	...	...	|	...	...	...	0840	...	...	...	1047	...	1151	...	...	...	...	1401	...	...	...	...	1626
197	**Hallsberg** △ d.	...	...	...	...	...	0725	...	...	...	0911	...	...	...	1113	...	1220	...	...	...	...	1431	...	...	...	...	1652
261	Degerfors d.	...	...	...	0704	...	0754	...	...	...	0946	...	...	...	1140	1208	1250	...	...	...	...	1501	...	...	...	...	1720
287	Kristinehamn d.	...	0607	0644	0721	...	0809	0817	0826	0904	1001	1005	1056	1139	1154	1222	1305	1312	1402	1442	1458	1522	1542	1602	1637	1704	1734
327	**Karlstad** a.	...	0644	0708	0750	...	0832	0843	0855	0929	1029	1105	1121	1203	1214	1247	1327	1336	1434	1509	1523	1544	1607	1628	1701	1734	1759
327	**Karlstad** **751** d.	0532	0644	0709	0751	0759	0834	0850	0856	0929	1032	1106	1122	1205	...	1249	1329	1338	1436	1517	1523	...	1608	1630	1702	1744	...
347	Kil **751** d.	0545	0703	0723	0817t	0814	|	0904	0909	0949	|	1119	1135	1218	...	1301	|	1353	1448	1530	1538	...	1622	1642	1716	1759	...
395	Arvika d.	0621	0742	0800	0850	0850	0913	0946	0947	1037t	1111	1154	1212	1253	...	1339	1408	1445t	1524	1606	1614	...	1708	1723	1753	1843	...
430	Charlottenberg 🏛 a.	0648	0815	0824	0914	0914	|	1012	1013	1103	|	1218	1236	1320	...	1404	|	1510	1549	1634	1638	...	1733	1747	1816	1906	...
472	Kongsvinger a.	0723	...	0850	...	...	|	...	1051	...	|	...	...	...	...	...	|	1554	...	1702	...	...	...	1819	...	...	...
572	**Oslo** Sentral a.	...	...	1008	...	...	1110	...	1200	...	1310	...	...	...	...	...	1614	1710	...	1829	...	...	...	...	...	...	...

	IC	*VTAB*	*VTAB*	*Sn*	*VTAB*	*VTAB*	*Sn*	*VTAB*	*VTAB*	*VTAB*	*IC*	*VTAB*
	639			**643**			**645**				**647**	
	Ⓑ	†p	Ⓐ	Ⓑ	Ⓐ	†p		⑥g	†	Ⓐ	Ⓑ	Ⓐ
	🅁🍷	2	2	🅁🍷	2	2	🅁🍷	2	2	2	🅁🍷	2
Stockholm C △ d.	1530	...	...	1655	...	...	1809	...	...	...	1939	...
Södertälje Syd △ d.	1550u	...	...	1715u	...	...	1827u	...	...	...	1958u	...
Katrineholm △ d.	1633	...	...	1757u	...	...	1909	...	...	...	2041	...
Hallsberg △ d.	1705	...	...	1824	...	...	1936	...	...	...	2113	...
Degerfors d.	1736	...	1832	1853	...	...	2007	...	...	...	2144	...
Kristinehamn d.	1751	...	1847	1908	1918	...	2022	2056	2118	2128	2200	2220
Karlstad a.	1816	...	1912	1930	1947	...	2045	2122	2146	2153	2223	2244
Karlstad **751** d.	1817	1907	1912	...	1948	2003	2047	2125	2147	2156	...	2248
Kil **751** d.	|	1921	1929	...	2007	2016	|	2146	2200	2209	...	2301
Arvika d.	1904	1959	2003	...	2051	2051	2126	2222	2240	2305t	...	2336
Charlottenberg 🏛 a.	|	2024	...	...	2116	...	|	2246	2310	2337	...	0001
Kongsvinger a.	1957	...	...	...	...	...	|	...	...	...	...	...
Oslo Sentral a.	2124	...	...	...	...	...	2324	...	...	...	...	...

	VTAB	*Sn*	*VTAB*	*IC*	*Sn*	*VTAB*	*VTAB*	*VTAB*	*VTAB*	*Sn*	*VTAB*
		620		**624**	**622**					**626**	
	Ⓐ	Ⓐ	Ⓐ	Ⓐ	⑥	Ⓐ	†a	Ⓐ	⑥d	Ⓐ	Ⓐb
	2	🅁🍷	2	🅁🍷	🅁🍷	2	2	2	2	🅁🍷	2
Oslo Sentral d.	...	...	...	...	...	...	...	...	...	0556	...
Kongsvinger d.	...	...	...	...	...	...	...	...	...	|	0828
Charlottenberg 🏛 d.	...	...	0535	...	...	0628	0636	0655	0710	|	0852
Arvika d.	0508	...	0559	...	...	0652	0700	0720	0734	0750	0916
Kil **751** d.	0545	...	0636	...	...	0735	0737	0757	0818	|	0953
Karlstad **751** a.	0558	...	0648	...	...	0748	0749	0813	0832	0831	1006
Karlstad d.	0558	0611	0649	0656	0718	0749	0750	0815	0833	0833	1009
Kristinehamn d.	0628	0632	0714	0719	0739	0820	0816	0843	0859	0855	1038
Degerfors d.	0643	0648	...	0737	0755	...	...	...	...	0911	1053
Hallsberg △ d.	...	|	...	0815	0824	...	...	...	...	0945	...
Katrineholm △ a.	...	|	...	0846	0850	...	...	...	...	1014	...
Södertälje Syd △ a.	...	|	...	0929s	0928s	...	...	...	...	1055s	...
Stockholm C △ a.	...	0827	...	0952	0948	...	...	...	...	1114	...

	IC	*VTAB*	*VTAB*	*VTAB*	*Sn*	*VTAB*	*VTAB*	*Sn*	*VTAB*	*VTAB*	*VTAB*	*VTAB*	*IC*	*IC*	*VTAB*	*VTAB*	*IC*	*VTAB*	*VTAB*	*VTAB*	*Sn*	*VTAB*	*VTAB*	*VTAB*		*VTAB*	*VTAB*
	630				**634**			**638**					**642**	**642**			**644**				**648**						
		Ⓐd	⑥d	†	Ⓑ	Ⓐd	⑥		Ⓐd	†	⑥h	Ⓐd	⑥	Ⓑ	†a	Ⓐ	Ⓑ	Ⓐ	Ⓐ	⑥		†	⑥g	Ⓐ		Ⓐ	†a
	🅁🍷	2	2	2	🅁🍷	2	2	🅁🍷	2	2	2	2	🅁🍷	🅁🍷	2	2	🅁🍷	2	2	2	🅁🍷	2	2	2		2	2
Oslo Sentral d.	0652j	...	...	...	...	...	1052	1146	...	...	...	...	...	...	1332	...	1436	...	...	...	1636	...	1756	...	...	...	1936
Kongsvinger d.	0858	...	...	...	...	...	1211	|	...	...	...	...	...	...	1454	...	1555	...	...	...	|	...	1906	...	...	...	2058
Charlottenberg 🏛 d.	|	1005	1026	1110	...	1134	1235	|	1340	1344	1345	1438	...	...	1518	1529	|	1640	1727	1802	|	1915	1931	1938	...	2058	2122
Arvika d.	0944	1029	1049	1139	...	1155	1300	1343	1408	1410	1409	1503	...	...	1546	1554	1640	1703	1753	1826	1844	1938	1956	2003	...	2123	2154
Kil **751** d.	|	1113	1129	1219	...	1234	1346	|	1449	1444	1445	1539	...	...	1624	1642t	|	1745	1828	1902	|	2015	2033	2042	...	2208	2229
Karlstad **751** a.	1023	1126	1142	1232	...	1247	1359	1430	1502	1457	1457	1555	...	...	1636	1656	1720	1758	1841	1915	1924	2028	2046	2058	...	2221	2243
Karlstad d.	1024	1127	1144	1233	1244	1248	1400	1432	1503	1458	1458	1556	1614	1616	1638	1657	1722	1759	1842	1916	1929	2028	2048	2058	...	...	2250
Kristinehamn d.	1048	1152	1218	1258	1305	1316	1425	1453	1534	1523	1523	1623	1638	1640	1707	1723	1749	1824	1908	1942	1951	2055	2114	2127	...	...	2320
Degerfors d.	1105	...	...	...	1321	...	...	1509	...	...	...	...	1654	1656	...	1738	1806	...	...	...	2007	...	...	...	...	...	...
Hallsberg △ d.	1137	...	...	...	1350	...	...	1541	...	...	...	...	1732	1728	...	...	1840	...	...	...	2039	...	...	...	...	...	...
Katrineholm △ a.	1207	...	...	...	1416	...	...	1609	...	...	...	...	1802	1758	...	...	1911	...	...	...	2107	...	...	...	...	...	...
Södertälje Syd △ a.	1254s	...	...	...	1456s	...	...	1650s	...	...	...	...	1848s	1841s	...	...	1954s	...	...	...	2148s	...	...	...	...	...	...
Stockholm C △ a.	1314	...	...	...	1514	...	...	1709	...	...	...	...	1908	1901	...	...	2013	...	...	...	2208	...	...	...	...	...	...

Mälartåg; 2nd class	Ⓐ	⚒	†	Ⓐ	Ⓒ	Ⓐ	Ⓐ	Ⓐ		Ⓐ	Ⓐ	Ⓐ		⑤	⑦–④
													A	f	q
Stockholm C d.	0633	0751	0903	1101	1140	1249	1459	1537	1557	1700	1750	1858	1958	2058	2158
Flemingsberg d.	0644	0802	0915	1112	1150	1300	1510	1548	1609	1712	1803	1909	2009	2110	2209
Södertälje Syd d.	0654	0811	0925	1122	1200	1309	1521	1558	1618	1721	1813	1919	2019	2120	2219
Flen **754** d.	0729	0845	0959	1156	1233	1342	1554	1636	1652	1755	1847	1954	2054	2155	2254
Katrineholm **754** d.	0741	0857	1011	1208	1246	1354	1606	1650	1708	1809	1859	2006	2106	2206	2306
Hallsberg a.	0811	0926	1041	1239	1315	1426	1635	1720	1740	1839	1929	2036	2136	2237	2336

Mälartåg; 2nd class	Ⓐ	Ⓐ	⑥	Ⓐ	Ⓒ	⑥	Ⓐ	⑥	†	Ⓐ	Ⓐ		Ⓐ	Ⓑ	Ⓑ
Hallsberg d.	0507*	0622	0749	0821	0913	1020	1222	1310	1322	1422	1522	1622	1722	1819	2022
Katrineholm d.	0554	0654	0820	0858	0944	1054	1255	1342	1354	1453	1554	1654	1753	1850	2054
Flen **754** d.	0605	0705	0832	0911	0955	1105	1306	1353	1405	1505	1605	1705	1804	1902	2105
Södertälje Syd **754** d.	0641	0741	0906	0943	1029	1141	1341	1427	1441	1538	1641	1740	1838	1938	2141
Flemingsberg a.	0651	0751	0915	0953	1038	1151	1351	1436	1451	1548	1651	1751	1847	1948	2151
Stockholm C a.	0702	0802	0925	1003	1049	1202	1402	1446	1502	1602	1702	1802	1857	1958	2202

A – ①②③④⑥† (not Apr. 6, May 17).
a – Not Apr. 9.
b – Not Mar. 8, 15, 20–24.
d – Not Mar. 20–25.
f – Also Apr. 6, May 17; not Jan. 6, Apr. 7.
g – Not Apr. 8.
h – Not Mar. 25.
j – 0732 on ⑥⑦ (also Apr. 3–7, 10, May 1, 17–19, June 6).
p – Not Apr. 9, 30.
q – Not Apr. 6, 9, 30, May 17.
s – Calls to set down only.
t – Arrives 9–15 minutes earlier.
u – Calls to pick up only.
w – Not Mar. 25, Apr. 8.
***** – 0522 on ③–⑤.
△ – See also Table **740** and panel below main table.

KARLSTAD - GÖTEBORG 751

Note: On Apr. 7 services run as on ⑥

km		Ⓐ		⑥	Ⓐ			Ⓑ	*Tågab* ⑥H	*Tågab* ⑦k		*Tågab* ⑦G	J
0	**Karlstad** **750** d.	0613	0812	1006	1010	1212	1411	1611	1648	1727	1813	2017	2232
19	Kil **750** d.	0626	0827	1025	1027	1226	1426	1625	1701	1741	1830	2035	2245
70	Säffle d.	0659	0900	1101	1100	1258	1459	1700	1734	|	1901	2110	2317
87	Åmål d.	0710	0910	1111	1110	1310	1511	1710	1746	1817	1912	2120	2327
128	Mellerud d.	0736	0936	1135	1135	1336	1536	1737	1811	|	1938	2143	2352
169	Öxnered d.	0759	0959	1159	1159	1359	1559	1759	|	|	2000	2207	0014
179	Trollhättan a.	0805	1005	1205	1205	1405	1605	1805	1835	1925	2006	2212	0020
251	**Göteborg** C a.	0845	1040	1240	1240	1440	1645	1845	1915	2010	2040	2245	0050

	Ⓐ	Ⓐ		⚒	*Tågab* ⑦G	*Tågab* ①L	*Tågab* ⑤z			Ⓑ		*Tågab* ⑦k
Göteborg C d.	0514	0714	0914	1114	1140	1145	1235	1314	1514	1714	1914	2040
Trollhättan d.	0548	0753	0953	1151	1213	1218	1308	1346	1553	1752	1945	2113
Öxnered d.	0555	0759	1000	1158	1220	1225	|	1359	1559	1758	1957	|
Mellerud d.	0617	0821	1022	1221	1240	1245	1332	1420	1622	1823	2020	2139
Åmål d.	0641	0845	1046	1245	1305	1313	1359	1444	1646	1847	2044	2206
Säffle d.	0659	0859	1059	1258	1318	1323	|	1459	1659	1859	2056	2216
Kil **750** a.	0730	0931	1133	1330	1346	1351	1441	1531	1731	1932	2128	2246
Karlstad **750** a.	0744	0945	1147	1350	1359	1405	1454	1543r	1746	1947	2143	2304

G – ⑦ to May 21 (also Apr. 10, May 1; not Feb. 26, Apr. 9, 30).
H – ⑥ to May 20 (not Apr. 7, 8).
J – ⑦–④ from Apr. 2 (not Apr. 6, 9, 30, May 17, June 5).
L – ① to May 22 (not Mar. 20, Apr. 10, May 1).
k – Also Apr. 10, May 1; not Feb. 26, Apr. 9, 30.
r – 1546 on ⑥.
z – Not Apr. 7, May 19.

VÄSTERÅS - LUDVIKA 752

2nd class only **Note**: On Apr. 7 services run as on ⑥

km		Ⓐ	Ⓐ	⑥c	Ⓐ	Ⓐ	Ⓒj	Ⓐ	Ⓐ	Ⓒ	Ⓐ	Ⓐ	Ⓒ	Ⓐ	Ⓐ	†	Ⓐ	Ⓐ	⑥	Ⓐ	†	Ⓐ	Ⓐ	Ⓒt	Ⓐ	Ⓐ	Ⓐ
0	**Västerås** d.	0533	0651	0723	0741	0842	0927	0944	1044	1127	1144	1244	1327	1344	1443	1527	1547	1617	1627	1648	1726	1750	1849	1927	1949	2047	2221
80	Fagersta C d.	0634	0751	0824	0839	0939	1026	1042	1141	1226	1241	1341	1426	1441	1540	1626	1645	1716	1729	1745	1826	1847	1947	2027	2046	2144	2318
129	**Ludvika** a.	0717	...	0914	0923	...	1114	1126	...	1314	...	1423	1514	...	1624	1714	...	...	1813t	1827	1910	...	2031	2111	...	2228	...

	Ⓐ	Ⓐ		Ⓐ	Ⓐ	⑥c	Ⓐ	Ⓐ	Ⓒ	Ⓐ	Ⓐ	Ⓒ	Ⓐ	Ⓐ	Ⓒ	Ⓐ	Ⓐ	Ⓒ	Ⓐ	Ⓐ	Ⓒt	Ⓐ	Ⓐ	†	Ⓐ	Ⓐ	Ⓐ
Ludvika d.	...	0524	...	...	...	0653	0728	...	0845c	0932	...	1045j	...	1232	1245	...	1432	1445	...	1636	1645	...	1837	1837	...	*2052*	2055
Fagersta C d.	0539	0610	...	0641	0712	0739	0814	0916	0931	1018	1117	1131	1217	1318	1331	1417	1518	1531	1622	1722	1731	1822	1923	1931	2021	2143	2143
Västerås a.	0636	0707	...	0736	0810	0839	0911	1013	1031	1115	1214	1231	1314	1415	1431	1514	1616	1631	1719	1819	1830	1919	2020	2031	2118	2240	2240

c – Not Apr. 8.
j – Not Apr. 9.
t – Not Apr. 7, 8.

754 LINKÖPING - NORRKÖPING - VÄSTERÅS - SALA

Operator: *Mälartåg* (2nd class only)

km		Ⓐ	Ⓐ	Ⓐd	Ⓐdn	n	Ⓐdn	n	Ⓐdn	n	Ⓐd		Ⓐd	Ⓐ		Ⓐd		Ⓐ		Ⓐ
	Linköping 730 d.	...	...	0610	0710	0810	0910	1010	...	1210	1310	1410	1510	...	1610	1710	1810	1910	2010	...
0	**Norrköping** 730 d.	...	0538	0638	0738	0838	0938	1038	1138	1238	1338	1437	1538	1608	1638	1738	1838	1938	2038	2138
48	Katrineholm 750 d.	...	0604	0704	0804	0904	1004	1104	1204	1304	1404	1503	1604	1634	1704	1803	1904	2004	2104	2204
71	Flen 750 d.	...	0615	0715	0815	0915	1015	1115	1215	1315	1415	1515	1615	1647	1715	1815	1915	2015	2115	2215
112	Eskilstuna d.	0552	0652	0752	0852	0952	1052	1152	1252	1352	1452	1552	1652	1722	1752	1852	1952	2052	2152	2252
160	**Västerås** d.	0626	0726	0826	0926	1026	1126	1226	1326	1426	1526	1626	1726	1756	1826	1926	2026	2126	2226	2326
199	Sala a.	0654	0754	0854	0954	1054	1154	1254	1354	1454	1554	1654	1754	1824	1854	1954	2053	*2158*	...	...

	Ⓐ		Ⓐ		Ⓐd	n	Ⓐdn	n	Ⓐdn	n	Ⓐdn		Ⓐ	Ⓐd		Ⓐd		Ⓐd		Ⓐ
Sala d.	...	...	0603	0703	0803	0903	1003	1103	1203	1303	1403	1503	1532	1603	1703	1803	1903	2005	2105	2205
Västerås d.	0528	...	0634	0734	0834	0934	1034	1134	1234	1334	1434	1534	1604	1634	1734	1834	1934	2034	2134	2234
Eskilstuna d.	0608j	...	0708	0808	0908	1008	1108	1208	1308	1408	1508	1608	1638	1708	1808	1908	2008	2108	2207	2307
Flen 750 d.	0642	...	0742	0842	0944	1042	1142	1242	1342	1442	1542	1642	1712	1742	1842	1942	2042	2142	...	...
Katrineholm 750 d.	0658	...	0758	0858	0955	1058	1158	1258	1358	1458	1558	1658	1724	1758	1858	1958	2058	2158	...	...
Norrköping 730 a.	0723	...	0823	0923	1022	1123	1222	1323	1423	1523	1623	1723	1752	1823	1923	2023	2123	2223	...	...
Linköping 730 a.	0750	...	0850	0950	...	1150	1250	1349	1450	1549	1650	1754	...	1850	1950	2050	2150	...	...	...

d – Runs daily Eskilstuna - Sala and v.v.
j – Arrives 0601.
n – Not Feb. 27 - Mar. 3.

755 MJÖLBY - HALLSBERG - ÖREBRO - GÄVLE

2nd class only

WARNING! From March 11 to May 16 service is subject to major alteration in the Frövi and Örebro area. **Please check timings locally if travelling during this period.**

km		Ⓐ	Ⓐ	Ⓐ	Ⓐ	⑥	Ⓐ	Ⓐ	⑥	⚒	Ⓐ	⚒	†	Ⓐ		⑥	Ⓐ	Ⓐ	⊖	Ⓐ		Ⓐ	†	Ⓑ		Ⓑ	Ⓑc	Ⓑ
0	**Mjölby** d.	...	...	...	...	...	...	...	...	...	...	0801	...	...	1001	...	...	...	1201	...	1401	...	...	...	1601	1801	...	2001
27	Motala d.	...	...	...	...	...	...	...	...	...	...	0818	...	...	1018	...	...	...	1218	...	1418	...	...	...	1618	1818	...	2018
96	**Hallsberg** a.	...	...	...	...	...	...	...	...	...	...	0907	...	...	1107	...	...	...	1307	...	1507	...	...	...	1701	1910	...	2107
	Hallsberg 756 d.	...	...	...	0515	0525	0618	0730	0739	0827t	0831	0916	0935	*1020*	1116	*1220*	*1220*	1242	1316	1431	1516	*1620*	*1620*	1643t	1711	1927	1949	2116
121	**Örebro** C 756 a.	...	...	...	0535	0545	0638	0750	0759	0847t	0853	0936	0955	*1041*	1136	*1241*	*1241*	1302	1336	1451	1536	*1641*	*1641*	1703t	1731	1946	2009	2136
	Örebro C d.	...	...	...	0549	0546	0650	0751	0800	0848	0853	0952	0957	1053	1152	1249	1253	1304	1350	1453	1551	1649	1651	1705	1740	1951	2011	2153
146	Frövi d.	...	...	...	0604	0601	0705	0807	0815	0903	0909	1007	1012	1108	1207	1312	1308	1319	1406	1508	1608	1708	1707	1724	1755	2006	2026	2208
204	Kopparberg d.	...	...	...	0647	0644	0751	0854	0858	|	0954	1054	1056	1157	1257	|	1356	|	1451	1552	1659	1801	|	|	1838	2049	|	2251
232	Grängesberg d.	...	...	...	0710	0705	0812	0919	0919	|	1015	1123	1123	1219	1323	|	1417	|	1512	1614	1721	1824	|	|	1859	2110	|	2312
247	Ludvika d.	...	...	0631	0724	0717	0825	0937	0931	|	1027	1136	1137	1231	1335	|	1436	|	1524	1632	1733	1835	|	|	1911z	2127	|	2323
295	**Borlänge** a.	...	...	0659	0752	0745	0902	1007	0959	|	1103	1204	1204	1302	1404	|	1505	|	1552	1700	1804	1904	|	|	1939z	2154	|	0002
	Borlänge 758 d.	0524	...	0700	0759	0804	0907	1008	1008	|	1104	1205	1205	1304	1406	|	1509	|	1605	1701	1806	1913	|	|	2010	...	|	...
317	Falun 758 d.	0548	...	0719	0822	0822	0925	1028	1028	|	1122	1225	1225	1328	1427	|	1528	|	1627	1719	1826	1931	|	|	2028	...	|	...
	Fagersta d.	|	0600	|	|	|	|	|	|	0949	|	|	|	|	|	1358	|	1408	|	|	|	|	1753	1807	|	...	2112	...
	Avesta Krylbo d.	|	0627	|	|	|	|	|	|	1016	|	|	|	|	|	1424	|	1434	|	|	|	|	1820	1833	|	...	2137	...
371	Storvik d.	0628	0706	0800	0903	0903	1005	1105	1105	1056	1203	1306	1306	1405	1505	1503	1605	1513	1705	1803	1905	2007	1859	1924	2104q	...	2217	...
385	Sandviken d.	0639	0717	0811	0914	0914	1016	1116	1116	1107	1213	1316	1316	1416	1516	1513	1616	1524	1716	1815	1916	2018	1910	1936	2115q	...	2228	...
408	**Gävle** a.	0655	0736	0826	0930	0930	1036	1136	1132	1121	1229	1336r	1332	1436	1535	1527	1636	1543	1736e	1829	1931	2034	1924	1955	2131q	...	2243	...

km		Ⓐ	Ⓐ	Ⓐ	⑥	Ⓐ		⚒	Ⓐ	Ⓑ	⑥	Ⓐ	†	⚒	†	Ⓐ	Ⓐ		Ⓐ		Ⓐ		Ⓐ	†		†	Ⓐ	Ⓑ
0	**Gävle** d.	...	0422	0409	...	0511	0607t	0817	0714	*0822*t	0822	0924	1025	1021	1035	1211	1121	1224	1321	1421	1521	1621	1628	1631	1821	1827	1921	2017
23	Sandviken d.	...	0438	0424	...	0527	0623t	0833	0731	*0838*t	0838	0940	1041	1037	1051	1232	1137	1240	1337	1437	1537	1637	1644	1647	1837	1843	1937	2037
37	Storvik d.	...	0448	0434	...	0537	0638t	0843	0742	*0848*t	0848	0950	1051	1047	1101	1242	1147	1250	1347	1447	1547	1647	1654	1657	1847	1858	1947	2047
95	Avesta Krylbo d.	...	0527	|	...	|	|	0924	|	|	|	|	1132	|	|	1323	|	|	|	|	|	|	1734	1737	|	1945	2027	|
130	Fagersta d.	...	0553	|	...	|	|	0951	|	|	|	|	1156	|	|	1348	|	|	|	|	|	|	1805	1805	|	2010	2052	|
	Falun 758 d.	...	|	0515	...	0619	0721t	|	0824	*0926*t	0926	1030	|	1139f	1139	|	1229	1331	1428	1529	1636f	1729	|	|	1930	...	...	2132
	Borlänge 758 a.	...	|	0540	...	0642	0739t	|	0840	*0943*t	0943	1047	|	1156	1156	|	1248	1348	1445	1546	1653	1746	|	|	1950	...	...	2149
	Borlänge d.	...	|	0548	0602	0643	0758	|	0849	0954	0959	1050	|	1159	1159	|	1249	1349	1446	1559	1700	1751	|	|	2010b	...	...	...
	Ludvika d.	...	|	0617	0631	0719	0827	|	0922	1024	1028	1120	|	1231	1231	|	1318	1421	1521	1629	1730	1820	|	|	2042b	...	...	...
	Grängesberg d.	...	|	0629	0644	0731	0839	|	0934	1037	1040	1135	|	1243	1243	|	1334	1433	1534	1640	1743	1834	|	|	2054b	...	...	...
	Kopparberg d.	...	|	0649	0708	0752	0859	|	0954	1057	1100	1159	|	1303	1303	|	1355	1453	1554	1701	1803	1859	|	|	2118b	...	...	...
202	Frövi d.	...	0639	0740	0752	0839	0943	1035	1041	1142	1144	1243	1241	1347	1347	1433	1440	1538	1640	1749	1851	1946	1855	1856	2210b	...	...	...
228	**Örebro** C a.	...	0659	0758	0808	0855	1002	1050	1057	1201	1200	1302	1258	1405	1405	1450	1500	1554	1656	1806	1912	2006	1916	1916	2225b	...	...	...
	Örebro C 756 d.	0617	0659	0817	0817	0857	1017	1051t	*1110*	1219	1217	*1316*	*1316*	1417	1417	1450	...	1622	*1704*	1817	*1917*	2017	1921	1921	2226b	...	...	...
252	**Hallsberg** 756 a.	0637	0717	0837	0837	0916	1037	1111t	*1131*	1237	1237	*1337*	*1337*	1437	1437	1510	...	1642	*1745*	1837	*1938*	2037	1941	1941	2246b	...	...	...
	Hallsberg d.	0646	...	0846	0846	...	1046	...	...	1246	1246	...	...	1446	1446	...	...	1644	...	1846b	...	2046b	...	...	...	...	...	...
	Motala d.	0728	...	0928	0928	...	1128	...	...	1328	1328	...	...	1528	1528	...	...	1728	...	1928b	...	2128b	...	...	...	...	...	...
	Mjölby a.	0744	...	0944	0944	...	1144	...	...	1344	1344	...	...	1544	1544	...	...	1744	...	1944b	...	2144b	...	...	...	...	...	...

b – Ⓑ only.
c – Not Mar. 6 – 10.
e – 1731 on ©.
f – Arrives 7 – 8 minutes earlier.
q – Not ⑥.
r – 1332 on ⑥.
t – Ⓐ only.
z – 7 minutes later on †.
⊖ – Change trains at Borlänge on ⚒.

756 STOCKHOLM - VÄSTERÅS - ÖREBRO - HALLSBERG - GÖTEBORG

See Table **740** for fast services Stockholm - Skövde - Göteborg and v.v. See Table **732** for Stockholm - Örebro via Eskilstuna. **Note**: On Apr. 7 services run as ⑥.
Warning! Subject to alteration Mar. 13 – 20, Apr. 11 – 20 (also late evening on Mar. 12, Apr. 10 / early morning on Mar. 21, Apr. 21). Timings may vary by up to 5 minutes on certain other dates.

km		Ⓐ	Ⓐ	⑥	⚒	†	⑥	Ⓐ	⚒							Ⓑ	⑥		Ⓐ		Ⓑ	v	⑦ e	⚒	Ⓑ d
0	**Stockholm** C ‡ d.	...	...	...	0614	...	0714	0714	0814	0914	1014	1114	1214	1314	1414	1514	1514	1614	1636	1714	1814	1914	1958	2014	2214
72	Enköping ‡ d.	...	...	...	0655	...	0755	0755	0855	0955	1055	1155	1255	1355	1455	1555	1555	1655	1725	1755	1855	1955	2042	2055	2255
107	**Västerås** ‡ d.	0512	0612	0636	0712	0812	0812	0812	0912	1012	1112	1212	1312	1412	1512	1612	1612	1712	1744	1812	1912	2012	2109	2112	2312
141	Köping d.	0529	0629	0653	0729	0829	0829	0829	0929	1029	1129	1229	1329	1429	1529	1629	1629	1729	1804	1829	1929	2029	2128	2129	2329
159	Arboga d.	0542	0641	0705	0741	0841	0841	0841	0941	1041	1141	1241	1341	1441	1541	1641	1641	1741	1817	1841	1941	2041	2139	2140	2340
205	**Örebro** C a.	0602	0704	0726	0804	0904	0904	0910	1002	1105	1204	1302	1402	1502	1602	1702	1702	1803	1842	1903	2002	2102	2203	2203	0002
205	**Örebro** C 755 d.	0609	0728	0728	0812	0915	0915	0916	1003	1110	1213	1316	1403	1512	1604	1704	1714t	1803	1843	1917	2003	2103	2204	2203	0003
230	**Hallsberg** 736 755 d.	0632	0751	0751	0835	0939	0939	0939	1025	1133	1235	1339	1424	1535	1634k	1737k	1737t	1824	1904	1950k	2024	2124	2225	2224	0025
260	Laxå 736 d.	0647	0806	0806	0850	0954	0954	0954	...	1148	1250	1353	...	1549	1648	1752	1752t	...	...	2004	...	...	...	...	...
305	Töreboda d.	0706	0825	0825	0909	1023	1023	1023	...	1219	1309	1421	...	1608	1716	1823	1823	...	...	2023	...	...	...	...	...
344	**Skövde** d.	0723	0841	0841	0936	1039	1039	1039	...	1239	1337	1439	...	1639	1736	1840	1840	...	...	2039	...	...	...	...	...
374	Falköping a.	0739	0856	0856	0951	1054	1054	1054	...	1254	1352	1454	...	1654	1751	1855	1855	...	...	2054	...	...	...	...	...
408	Herrljunga 736 a.	0803	0912	0912	1010	1110	1110	1110	...	1310	1411	1510	...	1710	1810	1911	1911	...	...	2110	...	...	...	...	...
443	Alingsås a.	0825	0933	0933	1032	1132	1132	1132	...	1332	1432	1532	...	1732	1832	1932	1932	...	...	2131	...	...	...	...	...
488	**Göteborg** C a.	0905	1000	1000	1100	1200	1200	1200	...	1400	1500	1600	...	1800	1900	2000	2000	...	...	2200	...	...	...	...	...

	Ⓐ	Ⓐ	⚒	⑥	Ⓑ	⚒	†	⚒								Ⓐ	⑥	†	⑥	Ⓑ	Ⓑ	⑥	Ⓑ	⑦–④ ¶	Ⓑ
Göteborg C d.	...	...	...	...	...	0559	...	0659	0759	...	0959	1059	1159	...	1359	1459	1459	1459	1559	1559	1659	1759	...	1855	...
Alingsås d.	...	...	...	...	...	0627	...	0726	0826	...	1026	1125	1226	...	1426	1526	1525	1525	1626	1626	1726	1826	...	1921	...
Herrljunga 736 d.	...	...	...	...	...	0649	...	0748	0849	...	1049	1146	1249	...	1449	1549	1547	1547	1649	1649	1748	1849	...	1942	...
Falköping d.	...	...	...	...	...	0705	...	0805	0905	...	1105	1205	1305	...	1505	1605	1605	1605	1706	1706	1805	1905	...	2002	...
Skövde d.	...	...	...	...	...	0720	...	0820	0920	...	1120	1220	1320	...	1520	1620	1620	1620	1721	1721	1820	1920	...	2020	...
Töreboda d.	...	...	...	...	...	0742	...	0843	0936j	...	1142	1242	1336	...	1543	1642	1636	1642	1736	1743	1843	1943	...	2043	...
Laxå 736 d.	...	...	...	...	...	0802	...	0903	1003	...	1202	1302	1402	...	1602	1702	1656	1702	1755	1802	1902	2002	...	2102	...
Hallsberg 736 755 d.	0534	0554	0634	0731	0734	0820	0834	0920	1020	1134	1220	1320	1420	1534	1620	1720	1720k	1734z	1813	1820	1920	2020	2034	2120	2220
Örebro C 755 a.	0555	0615	0655	0752	0755	0841	0855	0941	1041	1155	1241	1341	1441	1555	1641	1741	1741	1755	1834	1841	1941	2041	2055	2141	2242
Örebro C d.	0557	0617	0657	0754	0757	0856	0857	0957	1057	1157	1257	1357	1457	1557	1657	1757	1757	1757	1857	1857	1957	2057	2055	2157	2243
Arboga d.	0620	0642	0718	0817	0820	0920	0918	1018	1118	1220	1318	1418	1518	1620	1719	1818	1818	1818	1918	1918	2018	2118	2118	2218	2307
Köping d.	0630	0657	0729	0828	0830	0930	0929	1029	1129	1230	1329	1429	1529	1630	1729	1829	1829	1829	1929	1929	2029	2129	2129	2229	2317
Västerås ‡ d.	0648	0717	0748	0847	0848	0948	0948	1048	1148	1248	1348	1448	1548	1648	1747	1848	1848	1848	1948	1948	2048	2148	2148	2248	2337
Enköping ‡ d.	0703	0735	0803	0905	0903	1003	1003	1103	1203	1303	1403	1503	1603	1703	1803	1903	1903	1903	2003	2003	2103	2203	2203	2303p	...
Stockholm C ‡ a.	0744	0821	0844	0951	0944	1044	1044	1144	1244	1344	1444	1544	1644	1744	1844	1944	1944	1944	2044	2044	2144	2244	2244	2344p	...

d – Not Apr. 9.
e – Also Apr. 10, May 1; not Apr. 9, 30.
j – 0943 on Ⓐ.
k – Arrives 8 – 12 minutes earlier.
p – † (not Apr. 9, 30).
t – 12 minutes later Mar. 25 - May 13.
v – Not Apr. 7.
z – Arrives 1718.
¶ – Not Apr. 6, 9, 30, May 17.
‡ – Additional trains operate Stockholm - Västerås and v.v.

Note: On Apr. 7 services run as ⑥

STOCKHOLM - BORLÄNGE - FALUN and MORA 758

km				*Sn* 52		*IC* 14		*IC* 42	*Tågab*		*IC* 18		*IC* 20	*IC* 46	*Tågab*		*IC* 22	*Sn* 54	*IC* 48			*IC* 26		8202
		Ⓐ	Ⓐ	Ⓐ		⚒			⑦ d	Ⓐ			⚒	†	⑦ d			Ⓑ				Ⓑ		Ⓐ
		2	2	🅁🍷		🅁🍷		🅁🍷		2	🅁🍷		🅁🍷	🅁🍷			🅁🍷	🅁🍷	🅁🍷	2		🅁🍷		2
0	**Stockholm** C ♠ d.	...	...	0613	...	0740	...	0944	...	...	1144	...	1342	1344	...	...	1546	1646	1744	...	...	1944	...	2221
39	Arlanda C ✈ ♠ d.	...	...	0633u	...	0800	...	1006	...	...	1206	...	1404	1406	...	...	1605	1707u	1806	...	...	2006	...	2242
69	Uppsala ♠ d.	...	...	0651u	...	0825	...	1025	...	...	1225	...	1423	1425	...	...	1625	1725u	1825	...	...	2025	...	2301
131	Sala d.	0604	...	0739	...	0901	...	1100	...	...	1300	...	1458	1500	...	...	1700	1803	1900	...	...	2101	...	2338
164	Avesta Krylbo d.	0634	...	0759	...	0920	...	1120	...	...	1320	...	1518	1520	...	...	1719	1822	1920	...	...	2121	...	2358
229	**Borlänge** 755 ▽ d.	0719	0759	0837	...	1010	...	1212	1241	1304	1409	...	1608	1612	1624	...	1810	1857	2004	2010	...	2203	...	0044
253	**Falun** 755 a.	...	0821	0857	...	1030	...	|	1258	1326	1428	...	1626	|	1640	...	1828	1922	|	2027	...	2221	...	0103
	Leksand ▽ d.	...	...	...	...	...	...	1249	...	...	...	...	...	1649	...	...	...	...	2041	...	...	...	...	...
	Rättvik ▽ d.	...	...	...	...	...	...	1307	...	...	...	...	...	1707	...	...	...	...	2059	...	...	...	...	...
	Mora ▽ a.	...	...	...	...	...	...	1340f	...	...	...	...	...	1732	...	...	...	...	2124	...	...	...	...	...

	IC 13	*Sn* 51	*Sn* 51		*IC* 41	*IC* 15			*IC* 43	*IC* 17		*IC* 45	*IC* 19		*Sn* 53	*IC* 21			*IC* 47	8201	*IC* 25		*IC* 49	*IC* 27
	Ⓐ	Ⓐ	⑥	Ⓐ	Ⓐ	⑥		⚒	⑥	Ⓑ		†	⚒		Ⓐ	Ⓒ				Ⓐ			†	①–④ e
	🅁🍷	🅁🍷	🅁🍷	2	🅁🍷	🅁🍷		2	🅁🍷	🅁🍷		🅁🍷	🅁🍷		🅁🍷	🅁🍷		2	🅁🍷	2	🅁🍷		🅁🍷	🅁🍷
Mora ▽ d.	...	...	...	...	0628	...	...	...	0828	...	...	1030	...	...	...	...	...	...	1431	...	...	...	1822	...
Rättvik ▽ d.	...	...	...	...	0652	...	...	...	0852	...	...	1054	...	...	...	...	...	...	1455	...	...	...	1846	...
Leksand ▽ d.	...	...	...	...	0710	...	...	...	0910	...	...	1112	...	...	...	...	...	...	1513	...	...	...	1906	...
Falun 755 d.	0532	0612	0612	0721	|	0736	...	0926	|	0934	...	|	1135	...	1335	1335	...	1529	|	1629	1733	...	|	1929
Borlänge 755 ▽ d.	0552	0631	0630	0739	0750	0756	...	0943	0954	0954	...	1154	1154	...	1354	1354	...	1546	1553	1648	1753	...	1948	1948
Avesta Krylbo d.	0635	0707	0711	...	0838	0838	...	...	1036	1036	...	1236	1236	...	1434	1436	...	...	1637	1741	1839	...	2035	2034
Sala d.	0654	|	0730	...	0900	0900	...	...	1100	1100	...	1300	1300	...	1457	1459	...	...	1700	1807	1900	...	2100	2100
Uppsala ♠ d.	0734	0804s	0804s	...	0935	0935	...	...	1135	1135	...	1335	1335	...	1533s	1535	...	...	1735	1902	1934	...	2135	2138
Arlanda C ✈ ♠ a.	0756	0822s	0822s	...	0952	0952	...	...	1152	1152	...	1353	1353	...	1553s	1553	...	...	1753	1923	1951	...	2153	2154
Stockholm C ♠ a.	0820	0843	0843	...	1015	1015	...	...	1215	1215	...	1415	1415	...	1615	1615	...	...	1815	1945	2015	...	2215	2216

Other local services **BORLÄNGE - MORA** (2nd class only) ❖

km		Ⓐ	Ⓐ	⚒	⊖	Ⓐ		⚒ g	Ⓒ	Ⓐ	Ⓐ	Ⓑ v
0	**Borlänge** d.	0557	0752	0853	1018	1129	1421	1620	1818	1820	1917	2220
43	Leksand d.	0634	0825	0926	1051	1202	1454	1653	1851	1855	1950	2253
63	Rättvik d.	0649	0842	0941	1106	1217	1501	1709	1906	1912	2005	2311
103	**Mora** a.	0715	0907	1004	1129	1245	1543	1737	1929	1935	2037	2334
104	Morastrand a.	0719	0913	1010	1133	1249	1547	1740	1933	1939	2041	2338

	Ⓐ	⑥	Ⓑ	Ⓐ	⑥		⊙	Ⓐ	⑥	Ⓑ v	Ⓐ
Morastrand d.	0459	0626	0812	1003	1018	1217	1606	1807	1818	2009	2212
Mora d.	0504	0631	0820	1008	1023	1222	1611	1812	1823	2014	2217
Rättvik d.	0528	0655	0844	1033	1047	1246	1635	1842	1847	2038	2241
Leksand d.	0543	0710	0859	1048	1107	1305	1651	1857	1905	2057	2256
Borlänge a.	0614	0741	0933	1122	1141	1336	1724	1933	1936	2128	2327

d – Also Apr. 10, May 1; not Apr. 9, 30.
e – Not Apr. 6, May 17, June 22.
f – 1332 on Ⓒ.
g – Not May 15, June 17.
s – Calls to set down only.
u – Calls to pick up only.
v – Not Apr. 7, 9, June 24.

⊖ – Runs 2–5 minutes later on †.
⊙ – Runs 12–14 minutes later on †.
▽ – See also panel below main table.
♠ – Frequent local services operate Stockholm - Uppsala and v.v.
❖ – Additional trains Borlänge - Morastrand on Ⓐ:
From Borlänge at 0507, 0701, 1318, 1504 and 1727.
From Morastrand at 0534, 0708, 0906, 1058, 1300, 1514 and 1707.

STOCKHOLM - SUNDSVALL - UMEÅ 760

For additional services Stockholm - Gävle and v.v. see Table **761**. For sleeper services see Table **767**.

km		*NT*	*NT*	*Sn* 590	*NT*	*Sn* 560	*NT*	*NT*	*Sn* 562	*Sn* 564	*NT*	*Sn* 568	*NT*	*Sn* 570	*NT*	*Sn* 572	*IC* 10	*NT*	*Sn* 576	*NT*	*Sn* 578	*Sn* 580	*Sn* 580	*NT*	*Sn* 582	*Sn* 584	*Sn* 588
		2	2	🅁🍷	2	🅁🍷	2	2	🅁🍷	🅁🍷	2	🅁🍷	2	🅁🍷	2	🅁🍷	🅁🍷	2	🅁🍷	2	🅁🍷	🅁🍷	🅁🍷	2	🅁🍷	🅁🍷	🅁🍷
		Ⓐ	Ⓐ	Ⓐ		⚒ v	Ⓐ	⑥ v	Ⓐ	A		⑥ v		Ⓑ w	Ⓑ w		⊙	Ⓐ		Ⓒ	Ⓑ w	⑥ p	Ⓑ w	⑤ f	Ⓑ w		⑦ c
0	**Stockholm** C d.	...	...	0350	...	0621	...	...	0722	0821	...	1021	...	1121	...	1221	1311	...	1421	...	1521	1621	1621	...	1721	1821	2021
39	Arlanda C ✈ ◧ d.	...	...	|	...	0641	...	...	0741	0842	...	1042	...	1142	...	1242	1334	...	1442	...	1542	1641	1641	...	1742	1842	2042
69	Uppsala ◧ d.	...	...	0428	...	0700	...	...	0801	0900	...	1100	...	1200	...	1300	1355	...	1500	...	1600	1700	1700	...	1800	1900	2100
182	**Gävle** C d.	...	...	0512	...	0745	...	...	0845	0945	...	1145	...	1245	...	1345	1447	...	1545	...	1645	1745	1745	...	1845	1945	2145
260	Söderhamn d.	...	...	0556	...	0830	...	...	0930	1030	...	1230	...	1330	...	1430	1528	...	1630	...	1727	1830	1830	...	1930	2028	2227
314	Hudiksvall d.	...	...	0631	...	0858	...	...	0958	1058	...	1258	...	1358	...	1458	1600	...	1658	...	1758	1858	1858	...	1958	2056	2255
402	**Sundsvall** C a.	...	...	0740	...	0953	...	...	1053	1156	...	1353	...	1456	...	1553	1706	...	1756	...	1853	1953	1953	...	2053	2151	2350
402	**Sundsvall** C d.	0513	0713	...	0913	0957	1013	1112	...	...	1213	...	1413	...	1513	1557	...	1712	...	1813	1858	1957	...	2013	2058	...	...
470	Härnösand d.	0605	0805	...	1002	1044	1107	1203	...	...	1307	...	1505	...	1605	1645	...	1811	...	1907	1950	2044	...	2102	2148	...	...
516	Kramfors d.	0633	0832	...	1028	1108	1130	1233	...	...	1332	...	1531	...	1631	1708	...	1836	...	1934	2013	2108	...	2125	2214	...	...
603	Örnsköldsvik C d.	0718	0918	...	1112	1144	1216	1313	...	...	1413	...	1615	...	1720	1744	...	1916	...	2015	2049	2146	...	2210	2248	...	...
713	**Umeå** Östra ◐ a.	0816	1019	...	1210	1229	1319	1419	...	...	1519	...	1719	...	1818	1829	...	2019	...	2113	2134	2231	...	2325	2333	...	...
715	**Umeå** C a.	0820	1023	...	1214	1236	1323	1424	...	...	1524	...	1723	...	1822	1833	...	2023	...	2118	2140	2235	...	2329	2337	...	...

	Sn 561	*Sn* 563	*Sn* 565	*NT*	*Sn* 567	*Sn* 569	*NT*	*Sn* 571	*Sn* 573	*Sn* 573	*NT*	*Sn* 575	*Sn* 575	*Sn* 577	*NT*	*Sn* 579	*IC* 11	*NT*	*Sn* 583	*NT*	*Sn* 585	*Sn* 587	*NT*	*Sn* 589	*NT*	*NT*	*NT*
	🅁🍷	🅁🍷	🅁🍷	2	🅁🍷	🅁🍷	2	🅁🍷	🅁🍷	🅁🍷	2	🅁🍷	🅁🍷	🅁🍷	2	🅁🍷	🅁🍷	2	🅁🍷	2	🅁🍷	🅁🍷	2	🅁🍷	2	2	2
	Ⓐ	⚒ v	Ⓐ	Ⓐ		Ⓐ	Ⓐ	Ⓒ	† w	Ⓐ	⚒ v	Ⓐ	Ⓒ	† w			⊙		B	⑥ v	Ⓑ w	⑥ p	Ⓑ w	Ⓑ w	⚒ v	Ⓑ w	† w
Umeå C d.	...	...	0421	0436	...	0617	0635	0720	...	0821	0836	...	0913	*0936*	1036	...	...	1236	...	1336	1421	1513	1536	...	1636	1734	1836
Umeå Östra ◧ d.	...	...	0425	0439	...	0621	0638	0724	...	0825	0839	...	0917	*0939*	1039	...	...	1241	...	1339	1425	1517	1539	...	1639	1739	1839
Örnsköldsvik C d.	...	...	0508	0538	...	0709	0736	0807	...	0908	0937	...	1000	*1036*	1142	...	...	1338	...	1439	1508	1601	1635	...	1734	1836	1935
Kramfors d.	...	...	0544	0623	...	0744	0814	0843	...	0944	1019	...	1038	*1124*	1224	...	...	1419	...	1518	1544	1645	1730	...	1817	1925	2023
Härnösand d.	...	...	0607	0649	...	0807	0839	0906	...	1005	1043	...	1104	*1149*	1248	...	...	1443	...	1547	1607	1714	1754	...	1844	1949	2047
Sundsvall C a.	...	...	0658	0748	...	0858	0934	0957	...	1100	1144	...	1200	*1246*	1344	...	...	1548	...	1645	1659	1800	1848	...	1953	2048	2147
Sundsvall C d.	0509	0606	0702	...	0806	0902	...	1006	1106	1106	...	1206	1206	1303	...	1406	1455	...	1606	...	1706	1804	...	1903	...	...	...
Hudiksvall d.	0603	0700	0800	...	0900	1000	...	1100	1200	1200	...	1300	1300	1400	...	1500	1557	...	1700	...	1800	1858	...	2000	...	...	...
Söderhamn d.	0631	0728	0828	...	0928	1028	...	1128	1228	1228	...	1328	1328	1428	...	1528	1629	...	1728	...	1831	1926	...	2028	...	...	...
Gävle C d.	0716	0816	0915	...	1016	1116	...	1216	1316	1316	...	1416	1416	1516	...	1616	1727	...	1816	...	1916	2016	...	2116	...	...	...
Uppsala ◐ a.	0759	0859	0959	...	1059	1159	...	1259	1359	1359	...	1459	1459	1559	...	1659	1820	...	1859	...	1959	2059	...	2201	...	...	...
Arlanda C ✈ ◐ a.	0819	0917	1017	...	1117	1217	...	1317	1417	1417	...	1517	1517	1617	...	1717	1838	...	1917	...	2017	2117	...	2217	...	...	...
Stockholm C a.	0838	0938	1038	...	1138	1238	...	1338	1438	1438	...	1538	1538	1638	...	1738	1902	...	1938	...	2038	2138	...	2238	...	...	...

Other local services **GÄVLE - SUNDSVALL** (operated by *XT*, 2nd class only)

	Ⓐ	† w	⑥ v	Ⓐ	Ⓐ	⑥ v	Ⓐ	† w	Ⓐ	⊖	† w	⚒ v
Gävle C d.	0613	0745	0851	0920	1142	1300	1311	1507	1612	1708	2112	2116
Söderhamn d.	0704	0828	0941	1006	1227	1346	1401	1557	1700	1756	2159	2158
Hudiksvall d.	0736	0859	1012	1039	1259	1415	1431	1637	1742	1828	2234	2226
Sundsvall C a.	0842	0957	1118	1143	1358	1519	1545	1743	1842	1936	2332	2324

	Ⓐ	Ⓒ ◇	Ⓐ	† w	Ⓐ	⑥ v	Ⓑ w §	⑥ v	Ⓐ	† w	⊡	Ⓐ
Sundsvall C d.	0533	0841	0931	1028	1232	1305	1424	1531	1615	1756	1954	2134
Hudiksvall d.	0634	0944	1036	1130	1331	1411	1530	1634	1716	1856	2054	2244
Söderhamn d.	0704	1012	1104	1202	1403	1446	1602	1704	1744	1928	2126	2312
Gävle C a.	0746	1109	1149	1248	1449	1535	1652	1746	1837	2028	2214	2359

A – ⑥ to May 20 (also Apr. 7); Ⓒ from May 27.
B – Ⓑ to May 19 (not Apr. 7); daily from May 21.

c – Also Apr. 10, May 1; not Apr. 9, 30.
f – Also Apr. 6, May 17; not Apr. 7.
p – Also Apr. 7.
v – Also Apr. 7.
w – Not Apr. 7.

◧ – Trains call to pick up only.
◐ – Trains call to set down only.
⊙ – To / from Duved (Table **761**).
§ – Runs 12–16 minutes later on †.
⊡ – On ⑥ (also Apr. 7) departs Sundsvall 1959, Hudiksvall 2057, then as shown.
On † (not Apr. 7) Sundsvall d. 2008, Hudiksvall d. 2115, Söderhamn d. 2148, Gävle a. 2235.
⊖ – On ⑥ (also Apr. 7) Gävle d. 1658, Söderhamn d. 1757, Hudiksvall d. 1826, Sundsvall a. 1936.
◇ – On ⑥ (also Apr. 7) Sundsvall d. 0841, Hudiksvall d. 0941, Söderhamn d. 1013, Gävle a. 1105.

761 STOCKHOLM and SUNDSVALL - ÖSTERSUND - TRONDHEIM

See Table **760** for other fast services Stockholm - Gävle - Sundsvall and v.v. For sleeper services see Table **767**. **Note:** On Apr. 7 services run as on ⑥.

km		*NT*	*NT*		*NT*	*NT*		*NT*		*NT*	*NT*	*IC* **80**	*NT*	*NT*		*NT*		*NT*	*NT*	*NT*	*IC* **10**		*NT*		*NT*	*Sn* **598**	*NT*
		Ⓒ	Ⓐ		⑥	Ⓐ		Ⓐ		Ⓐ	Ⓒ		†	⑥				†	⑥	Ⓐ			Ⓐ		†		Ⓐ
		2	2	2	2	2		2		2	2	🅁🍷	2	2		2	2	2	2	2	🅁🍷		2		2	🅁🍷	2
0	**Stockholm** C ◇ d.	...	...	...	...	...	...	...	...	...	...	0748	...	...	...	...	...	...	...	...	1311	...	...	...	...	1659	...
39	Arlanda C ✈ ◇ d.	...	...	...	...	...	...	...	...	...	...	0820	...	...	...	...	...	...	...	...	1334	...	...	...	...	1720**u**	...
69	Uppsala ◇ d.	...	...	...	...	...	...	...	...	...	...	0837	...	...	...	...	...	...	...	...	1355	...	...	...	...	1738**u**	...
182	**Gävle** C ◇ d.	...	...	...	...	...	...	...	...	...	...	0928	...	...	...	...	...	...	...	...	1447	...	...	...	...	1827	...
281	Bollnäs d.	...	...	...	...	...	...	...	...	...	...	1033	...	...	...	...	...	...	...	...	|	...	...	...	...	1917	...
344	Ljusdal d.	...	...	...	...	...	...	...	...	...	...	1113	...	...	...	...	...	...	...	...	|	...	...	...	...	1952	...
	Sundsvall d.	...	0456	...	0609	0609	...	0810	...	1008	1009	|	1210	1210	...	1410	...	1603	1609	1639	1710	...	1809	...	1909	|	2009
450	Ånge d.	...	0607	...	0723	0723	...	0924	...	1124	1124	1213	1323	1323	...	1524	...	1714	1722	1756	1820	...	1927	...	2022	2051	2121
480	Bräcke d.	...	0626	...	0741	0741	...	0942	...	1142	1142	1233	1341	1341	...	1542	...	1731	1739	1814	1842	...	1944	...	2040	2109	2139
551	**Östersund** C a.	...	0722	...	0833	0837	...	1034	...	1237	1237	1317	1432	1433	...	1631	...	1822	1843	1905	1927	...	2035	...	2143	2202	2232
551	**Östersund** C d.	0720	0722	...	0842	...	...	1038	...	1238	...	1323	...	1433	...	1631	...	1822	...	...	1929	...	2035	...	...	...	...
656	Åre d.	0833	0836	...	1010	...	...	1159	...	1359	...	1441	...	1546	...	1744	...	1938	...	...	2047	...	2150	...	...	...	...
665	Duved d.	0841	0844	...	1018	...	...	...	...	1407	...	1454	...	1554	...	1752	...	1946	...	...	2100	...	2158	...	...	...	...
713	Storlien 🏛 a.	0914	0916	0929	...	...	...	...	...	...	...	...	...	...	...	1825	1849	...	...	...	...	...	...	...	...	...	...
819	**Trondheim** a.	...	...	1104	...	...	...	...	...	...	...	...	...	...	...	...	2028	...	...	...	...	...	...	...	...	...	...

km		*NT*	*Sn* **591**	*NT*	*Sn* **597**	*Sn* **595**	*NT*	*NT*	*NT*		*NT*	*IC* **11**		*NT*	*NT*	*NT*		*NT*	*NT*	*NT*	*IC* **85**	*NT*		*NT*		*NT*	*NT*
		Ⓐ	Ⓐ	Ⓐ	⑥	†	⑥	†	Ⓐ	2				⑥	Ⓐ	†		⑥	Ⓐ	†		⑥		Ⓐ	2	Ⓑ	
		2	🅁🍷	2	🅁✕	🅁✕	2	2	2		2	🅁🍷		2	2	2		2	2	2	🅁🍷	2		2		2	2
	Trondheim d.	...	...	...	...	...	...	...	...	0731	...	...	...	...	...	...	...	...	...	...	...	...	...	...	1648	...	...
	Storlien 🏛 d.	...	...	...	...	...	...	...	...	0909	0931	...	...	...	...	...	...	...	...	...	...	...	...	...	1827	1839	1839
	Duved d.	...	...	0600	...	0800**r**	0802	...	...	...	1004	1030	...	1204	...	...	...	...	1506	...	1532	1613	...	...	...	1912	1912
	Åre d.	...	...	0607	...	0812**r**	0809	...	...	...	1011	1048	...	1210	1212	...	...	...	1512	...	1550	1619	...	...	...	1919	1919
	Östersund C a.	...	...	0721	...	0919**r**	0928	...	...	...	1125	1213	...	1324	1324	...	...	...	1628	...	1715	1738	...	...	...	2035	2035
	Östersund C d.	0513	0604	0727	0733	0922	0928	0929	0930	...	1127	1217	...	1327	1325	1327	...	1527	1630	1632	1720	1738	...	1927	...	2035	...
	Bräcke d.	0602	0645	0818	0814	1003	1018	1018	1018	...	1217	1306	...	1417	1417	1417	...	1616	1719	1719	1804	1828	...	2018	...	2127	...
0	Ånge d.	0623	0703	0837	0832	1020	1037	1037	1037	...	1233	1325	...	1435	1435	1435	...	1632	1735	1735	1824	1844	...	2035	...	2143	...
94	**Sundsvall** a.	0738	|	0954	|	|	1153	1153	1153	...	1353	1450	...	1553	1553	1553	...	1752	1851	1851	|	2001	...	2152	...	2257	...
	Ljusdal a.	...	0802	...	0932	1126	...	...	...	...	...	|	...	...	...	...	...	...	...	...	1925	...	...	...	...	...	...
	Bollnäs a.	...	0836	...	1007	1201	...	...	...	...	...	|	...	...	...	...	...	...	...	...	2010	...	...	...	...	...	...
	Gävle C ◇ a.	...	0929	...	1109	1258	...	...	...	...	...	1722	...	...	...	...	...	...	...	...	2106	...	...	...	...	...	...
	Uppsala ◇ a.	...	1016**s**	...	1159**s**	1347**s**	...	...	...	...	...	1820	...	...	...	...	...	...	...	...	2158	...	...	...	...	...	...
	Arlanda C ✈ ◇ a.	...	1033**s**	...	1217**s**	|	...	...	...	...	...	1838	...	...	...	...	...	...	...	...	2223	...	...	...	...	...	...
	Stockholm C ◇ a.	...	1058	...	1238	1422	...	...	...	...	...	1902	...	...	...	...	...	...	...	...	2246	...	...	...	...	...	...

Other *IC* services **STOCKHOLM - GÄVLE** ⊠

km	All 🅁	*IC* **262**	*IC* **264**	*IC* **266**	*IC* **268**	*IC* **270**		*IC* **274**	*IC* **278**	*IC* **280**	*IC* **282**	*IC* **286**	
			Ⓐ	Ⓒ	Ⓐ	⚒				Ⓐ	Ⓑ		
0	**Stockholm** C d.	0730	0830	0931	1030	1131	...	1331	1531	1631	1730	1931	...
39	Arlanda C ✈ d.	0752	0852	0952	1051	1151	...	1352	1552	1651	1751	1951	...
69	Uppsala d.	0810	0910	1010	1109	1210	...	1410	1610	1710	1809	2010	...
182	**Gävle** C a.	0856	0956	1056	1156	1256	...	1456	1656	1756	1856	2056	...

All 🅁	*IC* **259**	*IC* **261**	*IC* **265**	*IC* **269**	*IC* **273**	*IC* **277**	*IC* **279**	*IC* **281**	*IC* **283**	*IC* **285**	*IC* **287**
	Ⓐ	⚒	Ⓒ		Ⓑ		Ⓐ	†	⚒		Ⓐ
Gävle C d.	0603	0704	0904	1104	1304	1504	1602	1704	1803	1903	2004
Uppsala d.	0651	0751	0951	1151	1351	1551	1651	1751	1851	1951	2051
Arlanda C ✈ a.	0708	0808	1008	1208	1408	1608	1708	1808	1908	2008	2108
Stockholm C a.	0728	0828	1028	1228	1428	1628	1728	1828	1928	2028	2128

r – Until May 1.
s – Calls to set down only.
u – Calls to pick up only.

◇ – For other *IC* trains Stockholm - Gävle and v.v. see panel below main table.
⊠ – Most services run from / to Linköping (see Table **730a**). On Apr. 7 services run as on ⑥.

763 UMEÅ - LULEÅ

Operator: *NT (2nd class only)*

km		⚒v		Ⓑw		
0	**Umeå** Östra ♣ d.	0808	...	1324	1839	...
2	**Umeå** C ♣ d.	0811	...	1329	1843	...
33	Vännäs ♣ d.	0841	...	1358	1911	...
142	Bastuträsk d.	0951	...	1509	2023	...
269	Älvsbyn d.	1108	...	1630	2141	...
315	Boden 765 a.	1136	...	1656	2209	...
351	**Luleå** 765 a.	1222	...	1731	2245	...

	⚒v	z	Ⓑw	
Luleå 765 d.	0830	1333	1856	...
Boden 765 d.	0912	1405	1937	...
Älvsbyn d.	0937	1429	2005	...
Bastuträsk d.	1049	1542	2119	...
Vännäs ♣ d.	1205	1703	2241	...
Umeå C ♣ a.	1228	1728	2305	...
Umeå Östra ♣ a.	1233	1733	2309	...

♣ – Other local journeys Umeå Östra - Umeå C - Vännäs and v.v.:
From Umeå Östra at 0521 Ⓐ, 0632 Ⓐ, 0704 ⑥ **v**, 0751 Ⓐ, 1006 † **w**, 1040 Ⓐ, 1136 ⑥ **v**, 1220 Ⓑ **w**, 1432 Ⓐ, 1613 Ⓐ, 1629 ⑥ **v**, 1633 Ⓑ **w**, 1725 Ⓐ, 1918 Ⓐ and 2146 Ⓐ.
From Vännäs at 0558 Ⓐ, 0710 Ⓐ, 0837 Ⓐ, 0842 ⑥ **v**, 1133 Ⓐ, 1204 † **w**, 1331 ⑥ **v**, 1350 Ⓐ, 1531 Ⓐ, 1555 Ⓑ **w**, 1647 Ⓐ, 1810 Ⓐ, 1822 ⑥ **v z**, 1954 Ⓐ, 2034 Ⓑ **w** and 2325.

v – Also Apr. 7. **w** – Not Apr. 7. **z** – Not Mar. 18.

765 LULEÅ - NARVIK

km		*Vy* **94**	*Vy* **94**	*NT*		*Vy* **96**	*NT*		*NT*	
		🅁✕	🅁✕	⚒		🅁🍷	Ⓑ			
		☉	◐	v2			w2		2	
0	**Luleå** 763 d.	...	0513	0609	...	0959	1116	...	1628	...
36	Boden 763 a.	...	0537	0635	...	1023	1143	...	1658	...
36	Boden d.	0611	0611	0635	...	1031	1143	...	1701	...
204	Gällivare d.	0807	0807	0847	...	1301**r**	1354	...	1901	...
304	**Kiruna** a.	0914	0914	0951	...	1427	1514	...	2022	...
304	**Kiruna** d.	0929	0929	...	...	1452	...	...	...	...
397	Abisko Östra d.	1059	1059	...	...	1556	...	...	...	...
406	Björkliden d.	1117	1117	...	...	1610	...	...	...	...
426	Vassijaure d.	|	|	...	...	1638	...	...	...	...
433	Riksgränsen 🏛 a.	1147	1147	...	...	1650	...	...	...	...
473	**Narvik** a.	1235	1235	...	...	1743	...	...	...	...

	NT		*NT*	*NT*		*Vy* **95**	*NT*	*Vy* **93**	*Vy* **93**
						🅁🍷		🅁✕	🅁✕
	⚒		†	⚒			Ⓑ		
	v2		w2	v2			w2	☉	◧
Narvik d.	...	...	...	...	...	1039	...	1511	1511
Riksgränsen 🏛 d.	...	...	...	...	...	1125	...	1558	1558
Vassijaure d.	...	...	...	...	...	1139	...	|	|
Björkliden d.	...	...	...	...	...	1214	...	1630	1630
Abisko Östra d.	...	...	...	...	...	1233	...	1646	1646
Kiruna a.	...	...	...	...	...	1349	...	1754	1754
Kiruna d.	0554	...	1041	1045	...	1406	1609	1829	1829
Gällivare d.	0711	...	1159	1200	...	1528**t**	1719	1957	1957
Boden a.	0908	...	1358	1355	...	1740	1923	2149	2149
Boden 763 d.	0908	...	1358	1358		1752	1928	...	2157
Luleå 763 a.	0937	...	1425	1427	...	1825	2005	...	2223

r – Arrives 1244.
t – Arrives 1513.
v – Also Apr. 7.
w – Not Apr. 7.
◐ – Train number **3964** Luleå - Boden.
◧ – Train number **3963** Boden - Luleå.
☉ – Overnight service from / to Stockholm (see Table **767**).

766 *2022 service* KRISTINEHAMN - MORA - ÖSTERSUND - GÄLLIVARE

INLANDSBANAN

km		⊡ H	⊡ L	⊡ M	C
	Göteborg d.	0710	0715	...	...
0	**Kristinehamn 750** d.	|	|	0920	...
131	Grängesberg d.	|	|	1104	...
146	Ludvika d.	1130	1126	1118	...
192	Borlänge d.	1207	1212	1210**j**	...
296	**Mora 758** d.	1320	1320	1320**j**	1340
310	Orsa d.	...	...	...	1354
433	Sveg d.	...	...	...	1621
617	**Östersund** C **761** a.	...	...	...	2030

	C	⊡ K	⊡ J	⊡ M◇
Östersund C **761** d.	0723	...	...	...
Sveg d.	1013	...	...	...
Orsa d.	1212	...	...	...
Mora 758 d.	1229	1402	1402	1405**f**
Borlänge d.	...	1518	1518	1517
Ludvika d.	...	1556	1556	1551
Grängesberg d.	...	1606	1606	|
Kristinehamn 750 a.	...	1844	|	|
Göteborg a.	...	...	2010	2005**f**

km		D	
0	**Östersund** C **761** d.	0756	...
115	Ulriksfors d.	0940	...
244	Vilhelmina d.	1217**v**	...
312	Storuman d.	1319	...
384	Sorsele d.	1441	...
420	Slagnäs d.	1515	...
473	Arvidsjaur d.	1703**t**	...
646	Jokkmokk d.	1957	...
746	**Gällivare 765** a.	2147	...

	E	
Gällivare 765 d.	0730	...
Jokkmokk d.	0921	...
Arvidsjaur d.	1244**z**	...
Slagnäs d.	1337	...
Sorsele d.	1426	...
Storuman d.	1537	...
Vilhelmina d.	1713**r**	...
Ulriksfors d.	1907	...
Östersund C **761** a.	2052	...

C – June 20 - Aug. 28.
D – June 20 - Aug. 27.
E – June 21 - Aug. 28.
H – ①④⑤ July 4 - Aug. 8.
J – ④⑤ July 7 - Aug. 5.
K – ①⑥ July 4 - Aug. 8.
L – ⑥ July 9 - Aug. 6.
M – ⑦ June 26 - Aug. 7.
f – On June 26 Mora d. 1400, Göteborg a. 2040.
j – 10 minutes earlier on June 26.
r – Arrives 1643.
t – Arrives 1608.
v – Also calls at Vilhelmina norra (a. 1138, d. 1217).
z – Arrives 1159.

⊡ – Operated by *Tågab*.

Operator: Inlandsbanan AB, Box 561, 831 27 Östersund
✆ +46 (0) 771 53 53 53.

LONG DISTANCE SLEEPER TRAINS 767

All services 🅁	*Vy* 94	*Vy* 94 3965	*Vy* 92		*SJ* 70/74	*SJ* 74	*SJ* 70	*SJ* 74/70	*SJ* 70	*SJ* 74/70	
							M	M	⑤f	⑤f	
	A	B	D		G	F	E	H	E	H	
Göteborg d.	...	...	...	...	...	1929	...	1929	...	1929	...
Herrljunga △ d.	...	...	...	...	...	2015	...	2015	...	2015	...
Skövde △ d.	...	...	...	...	...	2047	...	2047	...	2047	...
Hallsberg △ d.	...	...	...	...	...	2139	...	2139	...	2139	...
Örebro C △ d.	...	...	...	...	...	2200	...	2200	...	2200	...
Stockholm C d.	1810	1810	2156	...	2239	|	2239	|	2239	|	...
Arlanda C ✈ △ d.	1835	1835	2222	...	2303	|	2303	|	2303	|	...
Uppsala △ d.	1902	1902	2242	...	2325	|	2325	|	2325	|	...
Gävle △ d.	2001	2001	2352	...	0029	|	0029	|	0029	|	...
Söderhamn d.	2056	2056	0042	...	0120	|	0120	|	0120	|	...
Hudiksvall d.	2136	2136	0123	...	0212	|	0212	|	0212	|	...
Sundsvall a.	2232	2232	0224	...	0314	0330	0314	0330	0314	0330	...
Sundsvall d.	2244	2244	0236	...	0415	0415	0356	0356	0356	0356	...
Härnösand d.	2340	2340	0332	...	0514	0514	|	|	|	|	...
Kramfors d.	0010	0010	0408	...	0554	0554	|	|	|	|	...
Ånge a.	|	|	|	...	|	|	0514	0514	0514	0514	...
Bräcke a.	|	|	|	...	|	|	0539	0539	0539	0539	...
Östersund C a.	|	|	|	...	|	|	0645	0645	0645	0645	...
Åre a.	|	|	|	...	|	|	0859	0859	0916	0916	...
Duved a.	|	|	|	...	|	|	0917	0917	0934	0934	...
Örnsköldsvik d.	0056	0056	0454	...	0644	0644	...	...	...	...	...
Umeå C a.	0207	0207	0614	...	0758	0758	...	...	...	...	...
Umeå C d.	0212	0212	0622	...	...	...	...	...	...	...	...
Bastuträsk d.	0351	0351	0813	...	...	...	...	...	...	...	...
Älvsbyn d.	0516	0516	0934	...	...	...	...	...	...	...	...
Boden a.	0547	0547	1003	...	...	...	...	...	...	...	...
Luleå a.	|	0642	1100	...	...	...	...	...	...	...	...
Narvik **765** a.	1235	...	...	...	...	...	...	...	...	...	...

All services 🅁	*SJ* 77/71	*SJ* 77	*SJ* 71	*SJ* 71/77		*Vy* 91		*Vy* 3962 93	*Vy* 93
		❖		❖					
	G	F	E	H		D		C	A
Narvik **765** d.	...	...	...	...	...	...	...	...	1511
Luleå d.	...	...	...	...	...	1657	...	2110	|
Boden d.	...	...	...	...	...	1754	...	2213	2213
Älvsbyn d.	...	...	...	...	...	1822	...	2243	2244
Bastuträsk d.	...	...	...	...	...	1939	...	0007	0007
Umeå C a.	...	...	...	...	...	2109	...	0135	0135
Umeå C d.	1941	1941	...	...	...	2117	...	0144	0144
Örnsköldsvik d.	2051	2051	...	...	...	2234	...	0242	0242
Duved d.	|	|	1901	1901	...	|	...	|	|
Åre d.	|	|	1936	1936	...	|	...	|	|
Östersund C d.	|	|	2122	2122	...	|	...	|	|
Bräcke d.	|	|	2214	2214	...	|	...	|	|
Ånge d.	|	|	2236	2236	...	|	...	|	|
Kramfors d.	2140	2140	|	|	...	2327	...	0330	0330
Härnösand d.	2210	2210	|	|	...	0007	...	0401	0401
Sundsvall a.	2320	2320	2343	2343	...	0102	...	0500	0500
Sundsvall d.	0023	0014	0023	0014	...	0117	...	0512	0512
Hudiksvall d.	0126	|	0126	|	...	0248	...	0610	0610
Söderhamn d.	0201	|	0201	|	...	0322	...	0644	0644
Gävle ▽ a.	0250	|	0250	|	...	0410	...	0729	0729
Uppsala ▽ a.	0412	|	0412	|	...	0532	...	0836	0836
Arlanda C ✈ ▽ a.	0447r	|	0447r	|	...	0558	...	0900	0900
Stockholm C a.	0516	|	0516	|	...	0630	...	0926	0926
Örebro C ▽ a.	...	0516	...	0516	...	...	...	...	...
Hallsberg ▽ a.	...	0534	...	0534	...	...	...	...	...
Skövde ▽ a.	...	0642	...	0642	...	...	...	...	...
Herrljunga ▽ a.	...	0715	...	0715	...	...	...	...	...
Göteborg a.	...	0815	...	0815	...	...	...	...	...

A – 🛏, 🛏, [2] and ✕ Stockholm - Boden - Narvik and v.v.
B – 🛏, 🛏, [2] and ✕ Stockholm (**94**) - Boden (**3965**) - Luleå.
C – 🛏, 🛏, [2] and ✕ Luleå (**3962**) - Boden (**93**) - Stockholm.
D – 🛏, 🛏, [2] and ✕ Stockholm - Boden - Luleå and v.v.
E – 🛏, 🛏, [2] and ✕ Stockholm - Sundsvall - Duved and v.v.
F – 🛏, 🛏, [2] and ✕ Göteborg - Sundsvall - Umeå and v.v.
G – 🛏, 🛏, [2] and ✕ Stockholm - Sundsvall - Umeå and v.v.
H – 🛏, 🛏, [2] and ✕ Göteborg - Sundsvall - Duved and v.v.
M – ①②③④⑥⑦ (not Apr. 6).

f – Also Apr. 6.
r – 0436 from Mar. 27.

△ – Trains call to pick up only.
▽ – Trains call to set down only.
❖ – Arrival times Örebro - Göteborg may vary by up to 27 minutes (please check your reservation for confirmed timings).

UMEÅ - LULEÅ - HAPARANDA-TORNIO - KEMI 768

Rail service **LULEÅ - BODEN - HAPARANDA** (operated by Norrtåg). **Note**: On Apr. 7 train services run as on ⑥.

km		Ⓐ	⑥	†	Ⓐ	⑥	⑥	Ⓑ		†	
0	**Luleå** 763 765 d.	0528	*0830*	1007	1123	1315	*1628*	1634	...	2200	...
36	**Boden** 763 765 a.	0555	*0901*	1044	1150	1343	*1658*	1713	...	2231	...
	Boden d.	0555	0915	1044	1151	1343	1707	1713	...	2231	...
195	**Haparanda** a.	0726	1039	1210	1319	1515	1831	1840	...	2357	...

	Ⓐ	⑥	Ⓐ	†	⑥	†	Ⓐ	⑥		†
Haparanda d.	0554	0729	0734	0757	1049	1230	1428	1524	...	1854
Boden a.	0720	0854	0900	0923	1214	1355	1553	1649	...	2020
Boden 763 765 d.	0720	*0908*	0900	0925	1214	1400	1553	*1658*	...	2020
Luleå 763 765 a.	0756	*0937*	0929	0953	1243	1430	1625	*1731*	...	2047

🚌 **UMEÅ - LULEÅ - HAPARANDA-TORNIO** ⊠ — Länstrafiken Norrbotten, routes 20 / Express 100

	20 Ⓐ		100	20 Ⓐ	20 Ⓐ	20 Ⓒ		20 Ⓐ	20 Ⓒ	20 Ⓐ	20 †	20 ⚒	20 Ⓐ	100 Ⓐ	100 Ⓒ	100 Ⓒ	20 †	20 Ⓐ	100 Ⓒ	100 Ⓐ	20 Ⓐ		100 Ⓒ	100 Ⓐ	100
Umeå d.	...	...	...	...	0505	0545	...	0720	0730	0850	0900	...	...	1315	1315	1430	...	1525	1630	1630	1725	...	1930	2000	2100
Skellefteå d.	...	...	0535	0635	0740	0800	...	0955	0950	1125	1115	...	...	1530	1520	1635	...	1805	1835	1845	1955	...	2135	2215	2300
Piteå d.	...	...	0700	0805	0910	0925	...	1125	1115	1250	1240	...	...	1645	1635	1750	...	1935	1950	2000	2120	...	2250	2330	...
Luleå a.	...	...	0800	0905	1010	1025	...	1220	1210	1345	1335	...	...	1735	1725	1840	...	2025	2040	2050	2225	...	2340	0020	...
Luleå d.	0515	...	0820	0950	1050	1050	...	1245	1230	1400	1350	1510	1635	1745	1735	...	1855	...	2050	2100	...	...	...	...	...
Haparanda-Tornio 🏢 § d.	0800	...	1040	1220	1325	1315	...	1525	1500	1650	1635	1750v	1850	2005	1950	...	2110	...	2305	2320	...	...	...	...	...

	100		100 Ⓐ	100		20 Ⓐ	20 ⑥	100 Ⓐ	100 Ⓒ	20 Ⓐ	100 Ⓒ		100 Ⓐ	100 Ⓒ	20 †	20 Ⓐ	20 Ⓒ		20 Ⓐ	20 Ⓐ	20 Ⓐ	20 Ⓒ	20 Ⓐ	20 †	20 Ⓐ
Haparanda-Tornio 🏢 § d.	...	...	0525	...	...	0640	0725	0805	0810	0950	1050	...	1225	1230	...	1335	1345	...	1510	...	1605	1710	1715	1810	2015
Luleå a.	...	...	0750	...	...	0940	0950	1030	1030	1235	1310	...	1450	1450	...	1605	1610	...	1755	...	1845	1945	1955	2045	2235
Luleå d.	0540	...	0800	0800	...	0955	...	1040	1040	1300	1320	...	1500	1500	...	1635	1635	...	1810	...	1910	2005	2010	2055	...
Piteå d.	0635	...	0855	0855	...	1100	...	1135	1135	1405	1415	...	1555	1555	...	1750	1750	...	1915	...	2010	2105	2110	2150	...
Skellefteå d.	0750	...	1015	1015	...	1225	...	1250	1250	1535	1530	...	1715	1715	1830	1925	1925	...	2025	2030	2130	2225	2230	2300	...
Umeå a.	0955t	...	1220	1210	...	1445	...	1455	1445	1750	1725	...	1920	1910	2035	2140	2130	...	...	2245	2350	0030	...	...	...

🚌 **HAPARANDA-TORNIO - KEMI** ⊠

	ESK Ⓐ		*RO* Ⓐ		*RO* Ⓐ		*EJK* Ⓐ		*ORA* ⑦		*NET* ⑦		*ORA* ①–⑤		*EJK* Ⓐ		*NET* ⑦		*ESK* Ⓐ		*ESK* ⑦		*NET* ⑦		*EJK* ①–⑤
			s		bs		s				b		s		s		b						a		s
Haparanda-Tornio 🏢 § ⊡ d.	0645	...	0752	...	0945	...	1200	...	1200	...	1210	...	1250	...	1400	...	1410	...	1500	...	1540	...	1550	...	1623
Kemi ⊡ a.	0715	...	0830	...	1015	...	1240	...	1230	...	1245	...	1325	...	1435	...	1445	...	1530	...	1605	...	1625	...	1650

	ORA Ⓐ		*EJK* Ⓐ		*RO* Ⓐ		*ORA* ⑥		*ORA* ①		*ORA* ②–⑤		*NET* ⑦		*ORA* ⑥		*ESK* Ⓐ		*NET* ⑦		*NET* ⑦		*ORA* ⑦		*ESK* ⑦
	s		s		s								a		c		a				a				
Kemi ⊡ d.	0720	...	0810	...	0900	...	1105	...	1105	...	1145	...	1300	...	1325	...	1410	...	1500	...	1630	...	1755	...	2015
Haparanda-Tornio 🏢 § ⊡ a.	0755	...	0845	...	0940	...	1135	...	1135	...	1215	...	1335	...	1405	...	1445	...	1535	...	1705	...	1825	...	2045

a – Calls at Kemi railway station 1 minute later.
b – Calls at Kemi railway station upon request.
c – Calls at Kemi railway station at 1330.
s – On school days.
t – 0945 on ⑥⑦.
v – 1745 on ⑥.

⊠ – All stops refer to bus stations except where shown otherwise.
⊡ – Finnish time, one hour later than Swedish time.

§ – Swedish name: Haparanda-Tornio. Finnish name: Tornio-Haaparanta.

☛ Haparanda-Tornio bus station is located on the Swedish side of the border (distance to border approximately 200 metres). Note that most services run from Tornio Centre Puutarhakatu street. Walking distance between Haparanda-Tornio bus station and the Tornio Centre Puutarhakatu stop is 600 metres. Walking distance between Kemi bus and rail stations is 200 metres. See www.matkahuolto.fi for all Finnish long-distance bus services, including extra services on the Haparanda-Tornio - Kemi route.

Operators:
EJK – E. Jusila Ky: www.jussilanbussilla.fi
ESK – J. M. Eskelisen Lapin Linjat: www.eskelisen.fi
NET – NET-Matkat: www.netmatkat.com
ORA – Orajärven Bussit: www.orajarvenbussit.fi
RO – Rajalinjat Oy: ✆ 040 565 5711

NORWAY

SEE MAP PAGE 337

Operator: The principal and national operator is Vy (www.vy.no). Long distance services (and connecting local trains) between Oslo and Stavanger are operated by GoAhead Nordic (www.go-aheadnordic.no). Services Oslo - Åndalsnes / Trondheim, Hamar - Røros - Trondheim and Trondheim - Bodø are operated by SJ NORD (www.sj.no).

Services: All trains convey second class seating accommodation. Many services, as identified in the notes, also convey *Komfort* accommodation (see below). Sleeping-cars (🛏) have one and two-berth compartments; the sleeper supplement is 950 NOK per compartment (for two people travelling together, or sole use for single travellers). Most long distance express trains convey a bistro car (✕) serving hot and cold meals, drinks and snacks. 🍷 indicates that drinks and light refreshments are available from automatic vending machines.

Timings: **Valid until June 23, 2023** (unless otherwise shown). Dec. 25, 26, Jan. 1, Apr. 6, 7, 9, 10, May 1, 17, 18, 28, 29 are Norwegian public holidays and services are subject to alteration on and around these dates. Alterations to internal Norwegian services during holiday periods are not usually shown in the tables and readers are advised to confirm timings before travelling (✆ +47 61 05 19 10).

Reservations: Seat reservation is highly recommended on long-distance routes Oslo - Kristiansand - Stavanger (Table **775**), Oslo - Bergen (Table **780**), Oslo - Trondheim / Åndalsnes (Table **785**) and Trondheim - Bodø (Table **787**).

Komfort class: *Vy Komfort / Go Ahead Komfort / SJ NORD Premium* is a dedicated area provided on many trains with complimentary tea / coffee and newspapers; a supplement of 100 NOK is payable per single journey.

770 OSLO - HALDEN - GÖTEBORG

All trains convey Vy Komfort and 🍷

Warning! Until further notice, trains depart Oslo up to 12 minutes earlier and arrive Oslo up to 11 minutes later.

km	Norwegian train number	103	105	107	107	109	111	111	113	115	117	119	121	141	123	143	125	145	127	129	131	133	135	137	139
	Swedish train number	391			393		395					397							399						
		Ⓐ	⚒	Ⓑ	⑥		Ⓑ	⑥						Ⓐ		Ⓐ		Ⓐ							
0	**Oslo** Sentral d.	0608	0708	0808	0801	0908	1010	1010	1110	1210	1310	1410	1510	1538	1610	1638	1710	1738	1810	1910	2010	2110	2210	2310	0020
60	Moss d.	0642	0742	0844	0844	0946	1044	1044	1146	1244	1346	1444	1546	1613	1646	1714	1746	1814	1844	1946	2044	2146	2244	2346	0100
69	Rygge ✈ d.	0649	0749	0851	0851	0953	1051	1051	1153	1251	1353	1451	1553	1620	1653	1721	1753	1821	1851	1953	2051	2153	2251	2353	0107
94	Fredrikstad d.	0710	0814	0911	0911	1014	1111	1111	1214	1311	1414	1511	1614	1642	1715	1742	1814	1842	1911	2014	2111	2214	2311	0014	0127
109	Sarpsborg d.	0726	0829	0925	0925	1029	1125	1125	1229	1325	1432	1526	1632	1657	1734	1756	1829	1855	1926	2029	2125	2229	2324	0027	0140
137	**Halden** ★ d.	0747	0848	0944	0947	1048	1147	1144	1248	1344	1451	1547	1651	1721	1753	1821	1848	1919	1947	2048	2144	2248	2342	0046	0158
268	Öxnered **751** d.	0904	...	...	1103	...	1303	...	...	...	...	1702	...	...	...	...	...	...	2103	...	...	...	...	...	...
278	Trollhättan **751** d.	0910	...	...	1109	...	1309	...	...	...	...	1708	...	...	...	...	...	...	2109	...	...	...	...	...	...
350	**Göteborg 751** a.	0945	...	...	1145	...	1345	...	...	...	...	1740	...	...	...	...	...	...	2145	...	...	...	...	...	...

Swedish train number								390				392			394				396				398		
Norwegian train number	102	104	142	106	144	108	146	110	110	112	114	114	116	118	118	120	122	124	126	128	130	132	134	136	138
	Ⓐ	⚒	Ⓐ		Ⓐ		Ⓐ	Ⓐ	Ⓒ		Ⓑ	⑥		⑥	Ⓑ										
Göteborg 751 d.	...	...	...	...	...	...	...	0610	...	...	...	0755	...	...	1015	...	...	...	1415	...	...	...	1810	...	...
Trollhättan **751** d.	...	...	...	...	...	...	...	0645	...	...	...	0823	...	...	1044	...	...	...	1444	...	...	...	1843	...	...
Öxnered **751** d.	...	...	...	...	...	...	...	0651	...	...	...	0831	...	...	1050	...	...	...	1450	...	...	...	1850	...	...
Halden ★ d.	0406	0506	0537	0605	0637	0707	0731	0811	0811	0902	1010	1010e	1102	1211	1211	1302	1410	1502	1611	1704	1810	1902	2011	2102	2210
Sarpsborg d.	0427	0527	0558	0626	0658	0728	0757	0831	0831	0924	1031	1031	1124	1231	1231	1324	1431	1524	1631	1725	1831	1924	2031	2124	2231
Fredrikstad d.	0441	0541	0612	0640	0712	0742	0812	0844	0844	0939	1044	1044	1139	1244	1244	1339	1444	1539	1643	1740	1844	1939	2044	2139	2244
Rygge ✈ d.	0459	0559	0630	0701	0730	0759	0830	0903	0903	0958	1103	1103	1158	1303	1303	1358	1503	1558	1701	1758	1857	1958	2103	2158	2303
Moss d.	0508	0608	0640	0710	0740	0808	0840	0912	0912	1008	1112	1112	1208	1312	1312	1408	1512	1611	1712	1812	1912	2008	2112	2208	2312
Oslo Sentral a.	0541	0641	0713	0742	0813	0841	0913	0941	0942	1041	1142	1142	1241	1342	1342	1441	1543	1643	1743	1842	1942	2041	2142	2241	2342

e – Arrives 0947.

★ – 🏛 at Kornsjø (*km169*).

771 OSLO - OSLO LUFTHAVN GARDERMOEN ✈

See also Tables 783 and 785

Operated by Flytoget AS.
Special fares apply.
✆ +47 23 15 90 00
www.flytoget.no

Daily services (journey time: 19 – 22 minutes)
Trains call at Lillestrøm 10 minutes from Oslo.
From Oslo Sentral Services every 20 minutes 0440 - 2400.
From Gardermoen Services every 20 minutes 0530 - 2350 (also at 0010, 0030, 0050).

773 OSLO - GJØVIK

All trains convey 🍷

km		Ⓐ									⚒	
0	**Oslo** Sentral d.	0604	0704	0904	1104	1304	1504	1704	1904	2104	2304	0004
56	Roa d.	0703	0803	1003	1203	1403	1603	1800	2003	2201	0005	0105
70	Jaren d.	0719	0819	1019	1219	1419	1619	1819	2019	2219	0021	0121
99	Eina d.	0746	0846	1046	1246	1446	1646	1843	2043	2243	0044	0144
110	Raufoss d.	0756	0856	1056	1256	1456	1656	1853	2053	2253	0054	0154
122	**Gjøvik** a.	0806	0906	1106	1306	1506	1706	1903	2103	2303	0104	0204

	Ⓐ		Ⓐ		Ⓐ							
Gjøvik d.	0427	0532	0632	0724	0824	0932	1132	1332	1524	1724	1932	2132
Raufoss d.	0438	0543	0642	0735	0835	0943	1143	1343	1535	1735	1943	2143
Eina d.	0448	0553	0653	0746	0846	0953	1153	1353	1546	1746	1953	2153
Jaren d.	0511	0617	0718	0818	0918	1018	1218	1418	1618	1818	2019	2219
Roa d.	0530	0634	0735	0836	0936	1036	1236	1436	1634	1835	2035	2235
Oslo Sentral a.	0632	0732	0832	0932	1032	1132	1332	1532	1732	1932	2132	2332

☛ Additional trains on Ⓐ: **From Oslo S** at 1404 and 1604. **From Gjøvik** at 0331.

775 OSLO - KRISTIANSAND - STAVANGER

Long distance services are not available for local journeys Oslo - Drammen and v.v. or Sandnes - Stavanger and v.v.
Operated by GoAhead Nordic (except for local trains Oslo - Kongsberg shown in notes § and ‡).

km		701	705	705	707	709	711	713	715	719	721	725
		Ⓐ	Ⓒ	Ⓐ			Ⓑ	⚒			⑦	Ⓑ
		⊡	✕⊡	✕⊡	✕⊡	✕⊡	✕⊡	✕⊡	✕⊡	✕⊡	✕⊡	♣✕
0	**Oslo** Sentral § d.	...	...	0419	0725	0925	1125	1325	1525	1825	2125	2225
41	Drammen § d.	...	...	0454	0800	1000	1200	1400	1600	1900	2200	2300
87	Kongsberg § d.	...	...	0530	0836	1036	1236	1436	1648	1947	2247	2343
134	Nordagutu d.	...	...	0604	0909	|	1312	1513	1730	2020	2326	0020x
151	Bø d.	...	...	0619	0923	1124	1326	1527	1744	2035	2341	0036
209	Neslandsvatn ⊗ d.	...	...	0711	1006	1208	1409	1609	1827	2118	0023	0124x
270	Nelaug d.	...	...	0756	1052	1255	1455	1656	1911	2215	0111	0216x
353	**Kristiansand** a.	...	...	0853	1151	1358	1553	1753	2009	2312	0207	0329
353	**Kristiansand** d.	0502	0905	0905	1200	1414	1608	1801	2016	...	...	0346
457	Sira d.	0622	1025	1025	1325	1543	1728	1921	2136	...	...	0512x
465	Moi ⊗ d.	0629	1032	1032	1332	1551	1735	1928	2143	...	...	0520x
514	Egersund ◇ d.	0705	1107	1107	1406	1635	1814	2007	2217	...	...	0607
573	Sandnes S ◇ a.	0752	1152	1152	1452	1734	1904	2102	2300	...	...	0704
587	**Stavanger** ◇ a.	0805	1205	1205	1505	1749	1919	2115	2313	...	...	0720

	702	704	706	708	710	712	714	716	716	720	726
	Ⓐ	A	B				⑦	Ⓑ	⑥	Ⓐ	Ⓑ
	⊡	✕⊡	✕⊡	✕⊡	✕⊡	✕⊡	✕⊡	✕⊡	✕⊡	✕⊡	♣✕
Stavanger ◐ d.	...	0431	0647	0847	1016	1247	1447	1647	1647	1936	2232
Sandnes S ◐ d.	...	0445	0701	0901	1031	1301	1500	1700	1700	1950	2248
Egersund ◐ d.	...	0535	0744	0943	1118	1342	1547	1754	1754	2032	2335
Moi ⊗ d.	...	0616	0819	1019	1158	1423	1630	1830	1830	2110	0015x
Sira d.	...	0623	0826	1026	1206	1430	1637	1837	1837	2117	0025x
Kristiansand a.	...	0742	0942	1143	1331	1545	1802	1952	1952	2239	0152
Kristiansand d.	0448	0751	0954	1155	1347	1556	1812	1959	...	...	0217
Nelaug d.	0546	0854	1054	1254	1456	1655	1910	2058	...	...	0329x
Neslandsvatn. ⊗ d.	0630	0938	1140	1341	|	1740	|	2141	...	...	0419x
Bø d.	0713	1022	1226	1427	1628	1828	2034	2223	...	...	0507
Nordagutu d.	0727	1036	1240	1441	1642	1842	2049	2239	...	...	0522x
Kongsberg ‡ d.	0802	1117	1317	1517	1718	1917	2126	2317	...	...	0610
Drammen ‡ a.	0851	1151	1351	1551	1751	1951	2207	2352	...	...	0650
Oslo S ‡ a.	0925	1225	1425	1625	1825	2025	2245	0026	...	...	0726

Nelaug - Arendal

km		Ⓐ	⚒									
0	Nelaug d.	0700	0900	1100	...	1300	1500	1700	...	1915	2220	...
36	Arendal a.	0737	0937	1137	...	1337	1537	1737	...	1952	2257	...

	Ⓐ	⚒							Ⓑ	⑥	
Arendal d.	0503	0810	1010	...	1210	1410	1610	1825	2010	2120	...
Nelaug a.	0540	0847	1047	...	1247	1447	1647	1902	2047	2157	...

A – Stavanger - Kristiansand on Ⓐ; Kristiansand - Oslo on ⚒.
B – Stavanger - Kristiansand on ⚒; Kristiansand - Oslo daily.

x – Calls on request.

⊗ – Trains call on request.
♣ – Conveys 🛏 and [2] Reservation recommended.
⊡ – Reservation recommended. Conveys *Go Ahead Komfort.*

§ – Other local trains (operated by Vy) **Oslo** S - **Drammen** (35 minutes) - **Kongsberg** (75 – 81 minutes): 0009, 0609 Ⓐ, 0709, 0809 and hourly until 2309.

‡ – Other local trains (operated by Vy) **Kongsberg** - **Drammen** (43 – 44 minutes) - **Oslo** S (77 – 78 minutes): 0334 Ⓐ, 0434 Ⓐ, 0534, 0634, 0734, 0835, 0934, 1035, 1134, 1235, 1334, 1435, 1534, 1633, 1734, 1834, 1934 2034, 2134 and 2234.

◇ – Other local trains **Egersund** - **Sandnes** S (51 – 58 minutes) - **Stavanger** (67 – 71 minutes): 0453 Ⓐ, 0522 Ⓐ, 0550 Ⓐ, 0620 ⚒, 0650 Ⓐ, 0717 ⚒, 0817 ⚒, 0916, 1019, 1118, 1220, 1316, 1418, 1449 Ⓐ, 1519, 1549 Ⓐ, 1619, 1649 Ⓐ, 1720, 1818, 1920, 2018, 2122, 2221 and 2320.

◐ – Other local trains **Stavanger** - **Sandnes** S (16 minutes) - **Egersund** (67 – 71 minutes): 0449 Ⓐ, 0524 Ⓐ, 0554 ⚒, 0654 ⚒, 0754 ⚒, 0854, 0954, 1054, 1154, 1254, 1324 Ⓐ, 1354, 1424 Ⓐ, 1454, 1524 Ⓐ, 1554, 1624 Ⓐ, 1654, 1754, 1854, 1954, 2054, 2154, 2254 and 2354.

PORSGRUNN - NOTODDEN 779

km		Ⓐ	Ⓐ	Ⓐ	Ⓐ	Ⓐ	Ⓐ	Ⓐ	Ⓐ
0	**Porsgrunn** ..... 783 d.	...	0639	0749	1151	1307	1441	1605	1751
9	Skien .... 783 d.	0527	0649	0759	1201	1321	1455	1618	1801
43	Nordagutu ....a.	0557	0719	0829	1231	1351	1528	1649	1831
43	Nordagutu ....d.	0606	0720	0830	1232	1352	1529	1650	1832
62	**Notodden** ....a.	0626	0740	0850	1252	1412	1549	1710	1852

	Ⓐ	Ⓐ	Ⓐ	Ⓐ	Ⓐ	Ⓐ	Ⓐ	Ⓐ
Notodden ....d.	0636	0807	0907	1309	1448	1606	1809	2009
Nordagutu ....a.	0655	0826	0926	1328	1507	1625	1828	2028
Nordagutu ....d.	0656	0829	0927	1329	1508	1626	1831	2029
Skien .... 783 a.	0730	0859	0957	1403	1539	1700	1901	2059
Porsgrunn ... 783 a.	0739	0908	1006	1412	1552	1709	1910	...

☛ No service on Ⓒ.

OSLO - BERGEN 780

km		61	1821	63	1825	603	601	65	67	605	
		A				⑦		E		Ⓑ	
		✕⊡	A	✕⊡	A	B	✕⊡	✕⊡	✕⊡	♥✕	
0	**Oslo** Sentral .... 783 d.	0625	...	0825	...	...	1203	1425	1625	2303	...
41	Drammen .... 783 d.	0700u	...	0900u	...	...	1238u	1500u	1700u	2338u	...
112	Hønefoss ....d.	0759	...	0955	...	...	1339	1600	1801	0041	...
208	Nesbyen ....d.	0907	...	1103	...	...	1451	1708	1912	0155	...
225	Gol ....d.	0920	...	1116	...	1310	1504	1721	1928	0207	...
250	Ål ....d.	0939	...	1135	...	1329	1526	1740	1949	0229	...
275	Geilo ....d.	0959	...	1156	1314	1351	1549	1801	2012	0307	...
286	Ustaoset ....d.	|	...	1208	1324	1402	1602	1812	2023	0319	...
324	Finse ....d.	1052	1120	1237	1352	1435	1635	1856	2050	0349	...
354	**Myrdal** .... 781 d.	1121	1152	1306	1422	1502	1704	1925	2119	0421	...
403	**Voss** .... 781 d.	1205	1256	1351	1509	1609r	1754	2011	2205	0523k	...
443	Dale .... 781 a.	|	1329	|	1541	1644	1825	2049	2233	0551s	...
480	Arna .... 781 a.	1259s	1406	1449s	1620	1716s	1855s	2123s	2307s	0633s	...
489	**Bergen** .... 781 a.	1310	1414	1500	1628	1727	1902	2133	2318	0644	...

	62	1840	1810	602	604	64	66	66		606
					⑤		E	A		Ⓑ
	✕⊡	A	A	✕⊡	F	✕⊡	✕⊡	✕⊡		♥✕
Bergen .... 781 d.	0814	0829	0928	1143	1335	1541	1645	1645	...	2300
Arna .... 781 d.	0823u	0837	0936	1152u	1343u	1550u	1654u	1654u	...	2310u
Dale .... 781 d.	|	0912	1009	1230	1420	|	|	|	...	2344
Voss .... 781 d.	0922	0951	1103	1301	1504	1657	1807	1807	...	0028
Myrdal .... 781 d.	1004	1045	1205	1352	1548	1740	1852	1856	...	0120
Finse ....d.	1033	1114	|	1420	1616	1806	1927	1927	...	0200
Ustaoset ....d.	1059	...	1300	1450	1655	1835	1959	|	...	0230
Geilo ....d.	1112	...	1309	1504	1710	1849	2013	2013	...	0242
Ål ....d.	1135	...	...	1525	1738	1909	2033	2033	...	0306
Gol ....d.	1154	...	...	1545	1756	1928	2055	2055	...	0325
Nesbyen ....d.	1206	...	...	1558	...	1941	2109	2109	...	0337
Hønefoss ....d.	1317	...	...	1718	...	2057	2226	2226	...	0454
Drammen .... 783 a.	1427s	...	...	1828s	...	2151s	2327s	2327s	...	0551s
Oslo Sentral ..... 783 a.	1505	...	...	1905	...	2227	0005	0005	...	0627

A – From May 1.
B – ⑦ Jan. 15 - Apr. 2 (also Apr. 10, 16).
E – ⑤⑦ until Apr. 30 (also Feb.27, 28, Mar. 1, 2, Apr. 3–6).
F – ⑤ Jan. 13 - Mar. 31 (also Apr. 1, 5, 14).

k – Arrives 0505.
r – Arrives 1546.
s – Calls to set down only.
u – Calls to pick up only.

♥ – Conveys 🛏 and 2nd class couchette. Reservation recommended.
⊡ – Reservation recommended. Conveys *Vy Komfort*.

Local services MYRDAL - VOSS - BERGEN and FLÅM 781

See Table **780** for long-distance services

km		⚒		Ⓐ		Ⓐ				C						A	Ⓐ	Ⓐ	Ⓒ		Ⓐ					
0	**Myrdal** ....d.	...	...	...	...	...	...	...	...	0930	...	1152	...	1313	...	1422	...	1600	1600	...	...	...	...	1848	...	...
18	Mjølfjell ....d.	...	...	...	...	0746	...	...	...	|	...	1214	...	1335	...	|	...	1618x	1618x	...	...	...	...	1907	...	...
49	**Voss** ....a.	...	...	...	...	0821	...	...	...	1022	...	1254	...	1403	...	1507	...	1653	1653	...	...	...	...	1942	...	...
49	**Voss** ....d.	0508	0605	0647	0747	0832	...	1005	1054	1054	...	1256	...	1406	1509	1509	1607	1657	1701	...	1812	...	1913	1951	...	2301
89	Dale ....d.	0540	0636	0721	0823	0913	...	1040	1133	1133	...	1329	...	1438	1541	1541	1643	1733	1733	...	1843	...	1950	2030	...	2342
104	Vaksdal ....d.	0555	0654	0737	0841	0935	...	1101	1149	1149	...	1347	...	1454	1557	1557	1658	1752	1752	...	1858	...	2013	2047	...	2358
126	Arna ....‡ d.	0614	0714	0756	0901	0956	...	1120	1212	1212	...	1406	...	1518	1620	1620	1717	1811	1811	...	1917	...	2032	2109	...	0017
135	**Bergen** ....‡ a.	0622	0722	0804	0909	1004	...	1128	1220	1220	...	1414	...	1526	1628	1628	1725	1819	1819	...	1925	...	2040	2117	...	0025

	Ⓐ	Ⓐ		C		B	C		A				A	A	D	Ⓐ			Ⓐ		Ⓐ		Ⓑ	⑥		
Bergen ....‡ d.	...	0605	0707	0707	...	0829	0829	0928	0928	1035	...	1229	1229	1320	1320	1423	1528	1629	1726	1826	1925	2040	2134	2234	...	0038
Arna ....‡ d.	...	0614	0715	0715	...	0837	0837	0936	0936	1043	...	1237	1237	1328	1328	1431	1536	1637	1734	1834	1933	2048	2143	2244	...	0047
Vaksdal ....d.	...	0633	0736	0736	...	0857	0857	0954	0954	1102	...	1259	1259	1347	1347	1453	1557	1658	1753	1858	1955	2106	2201	2307	...	0109
Dale ....d.	...	0650	0751	0751	...	0912	0912	1009	1009	1117	...	1314	1314	1402	1402	1508	1612	1715	1808	1913	2010	2124	2216	2324	...	0124
Voss ....a.	...	0721	0823	0823	...	0943	0943	1040	1040	1148	...	1346	1346	1439	1439	1542	1644	1749	1844	1948	2046	2155	2251	2356	...	0155
Voss ....d.	0705	...	...	0825	...	0951	0951	...	1103	1203	...	...	1414	1441	1441	...	...	1751	...	...	...	...	...	...	...	...
Mjølfjell ....d.	0739	...	...	0859x	...	1025x	|	...	1136	1236x	...	...	1452x	1513x	1517	...	...	1822x	...	...	...	...	...	...	...	...
Myrdal ....a.	...	...	...	0917	...	1043	1036	...	1152	1255	...	...	1511	1533	1535	...	...	1840	...	...	...	...	...	...	...	...

MYRDAL - FLÅM *Service until March 31*

km								H	F			
0	Myrdal ....d.	1015	...	1315	...	1540	...	1805	1933	...	...	...
20	Flåm ....a.	1105	...	1405	...	1630	...	1855	2023	...	...	...

Flåm ....d.	0900	...	1145	...	1430	...	1655	...	...	...	...
Myrdal ....a.	0944	...	1228	...	1514	...	1736	...	...	...	...

MYRDAL - FLÅM *Service from April 1*

km						A			A	G	E	
0	Myrdal ....d.	0925	1041	1156	1313	1428	1552	1712	1827	1933	1942	...
20	Flåm ....a.	1023	1139	1254	1411	1526	1650	1810	1925	2023	2038	...

					A				G	A	E
Flåm ....d.	0825	0930	1045	1200	1320	1435	...	1600	1720	1720	1835
Myrdal ....a.	0913	1028	1143	1301	1416	1531	...	1655	1815	1815	1930

A – From May 1.
B – Until Mar. 31.
C – From Apr. 1.
D – Until Apr. 30.
E – From June 1.

F – ⑤⑦ until Mar. 31 (also Feb. 27, 28, Mar. 1, 2).
H – ①②③④⑥ until Mar. 30 (not Feb. 20–23, 27, 28, Mar. 1, 2).
G – Runs Apr. 2–7, 9, 10, 14, 16, 21, 23, 28, 30 only.

x – Request stop.

◇ – Reservation recommended.
‡ – Additional local services operate.
⊠ – **Operator**: Flåm Utvikling AS. www.norwaysbest.com
✆ + 47 57 63 14 00. 30% discount for rail pass holders.

Service until April 30 🚢 FLÅM - GUDVANGEN and 🚌 GUDVANGEN - VOSS 781a

	🚢	🚌	🚢	🚌
Flåm .... d.	0930	...	1500	...
Gudvangen ferjekai .... a.	1130	...	1700	...
Gudvangen ferjekai .... d.	...	1140	...	1725
Voss .... a.	...	1255	...	1900

	🚌	🚢	🚌 Ⓐ	🚢
Voss .... d.	1010	...	1610	...
Gudvangen ferjekai a.	1135	...	1710	...
Gudvangen ferjekai d.	...	1200	...	1730
Flåm .... a.	...	1400	...	1930

🚌 operator Skyss ✆ +47 55 55 90 70.
🚢 operator Fjord1 ✆ +47 57 75 70 00.

Service until March 31 🚢 / 🚌 LILLEHAMMER and GOL - FLÅM - BALESTRAND - BERGEN 782

	🚢 ⚒	🚌 ⑦	🚌 Ⓐ	🚌 Ⓐ	🚌 ⚒	🚌 Ⓑ	🚢 ⑦		🚌	🚌 ⑥	🚌 ⑦	🚌
Lillehammer skysst. d.	...	...	...	...	0915	...	...	...	...	...	1305	...
Gjøvik skysstasjon .. d.	...	...	...	...	1000	...	...	...	...	...	1350	...
Sogndal ⊕ ....d.	...	...	...	0630	|	...	...	...	...	...	|	...
Kaupangsenteret.... d.	...	...	...	0645	|	...	...	...	...	...	|	...
Gol Skysstasjon ...... d.	...	...	...	|	|	...	...	...	1320	...	|	1845
Lærdal Rådhus .... d.	...	...	...	0725	|	...	...	...	1525	...	|	2045
Kaupangsenteret...... d.	...	...	...	|	|	...	...	...	1600	...	|	2125
Sogndal ⊕ .... a.	...	...	...	|	|	...	...	...	1615	...	|	2140
Sogndal ⊕ .... d.	0705	0820	0855	|	|	1450	1540	...	...	1620	|	...
Flåm .... d.	|	|	|	0810	1455	|	|	...	...	|	1845	...
Leikanger Kai........... d.	0730	0845	0920	|	|	1515	1605	...	...	1645	|	...
Balestrand Kai .... d.	0750	0925	1010	|	|	1605	1625	...	...	1735	|	...
Voss .... 781 d.	|	...	...	0920	1605	...	|	...	...	...	1955	...
Bergen ⊡ .... 781 a.	1150	...	...	1100	1744	...	2015	...	...	...	2135	...

	🚌	🚌		🚌	🚌	🚌	🚌 Ⓑ	🚢 ⑥	🚢 Ⓑ	🚌 Ⓐ	🚌
Bergen ⊡.........781 d.	...	...	...	0915	...	...	...	1415	1630	...	...
Voss ....781 d.	...	...	...	1052	...	...	...	|	|	1715	...
Balestrand Kai..........d.	1005	...	...	|	1310	...	1815	1820	2030	|	...
Leikanger Kai ....d.	1055	...	...	|	1355	...	1900	1835	2050	|	...
Flåm ....a.	|	...	...	1200	|	...	|	|	|	1830	...
Sogndal ⊕ ....a.	1125	...	...	|	1425	...	1930	1900	2120	|	...
Sogndal ⊕ ....d.	...	1130	...	|	...	1430	...	...	...	|	2230
Kaupangsenteret.......d.	...	1145	...	|	...	1445	...	...	...	|	2245
Lærdal Rådhus ....d.	...	1225	...	|	...	1525	...	...	...	1920	2325
Gol skysstasjon ....a.	...	1415	...	|	...	1715	...	...	...	|	0120
Kaupangsenteret....a.	...	...	...	|	...	...	...	...	...	2000	...
Sogndal ⊕ ....a.	...	...	...	|	...	...	...	...	...	2017	...
Gjøvik skysstasjon...a.	...	...	...	1705	...	...	...	...	...	...	...
Lillehammer skysst .a.	...	...	...	1750	...	...	...	...	...	...	...

⊕ – 🚌: Sogndal skysstasjon. 🚢: Sogndal kai.
⊡ – 🚌: Bus station. 🚢: Strandkaiterminal.

🚌 operators: Vy Buss AS ✆ +47 4070 5070.
Nor-way Bussekspress ✆ +47 815 44 444.
🚢 operator: Norled AS ✆ +47 5186 8700.

783 EIDSVOLL - OSLO - SKIEN

All trains convey *Vy Komfort* and 🍷

SERVICE UNTIL APRIL 9

km		Ⓐ	⚒		⚒		⚒				Ⓐ		Ⓐ	Ⓐ		Ⓐ	Ⓐ			Ⓑ		Ⓑ		Ⓑ	
0	**Eidsvoll** 785 d.	0501	0601	0701	0801	0901	1001	1101	1201	1301	...	1401	...	...	1501	...	...	1601	1701	1801	1901	2001	2101	2201	2301
16	Oslo Lufthavn ✈ ¶ 785 d.	0513	0613	0713	0813	0913	1013	1113	1213	1313	...	1413	...	...	1513	...	...	1613	1713	1813	1913	2013	2113	2213	2313
47	Lillestrøm 785 d.	0526	0626	0726	0826	0926	1026	1126	1226	1326	...	1426	...	...	1526	...	...	1626	1726	1826	1926	2026	2126	2226	2326
68	**Oslo** S 785 a.	0536	0636	0736	0836	0936	1036	1136	1236	1336	...	1436	...	...	1536	...	...	1636	1736	1836	1936	2036	2136	2236	2336
68	**Oslo** S 785 d.	0539	0639	0739	0839	0939	1039	1139	1239	1339	1405	1439	1505	1533	1539	1605	1633	1639	1739	1839	1939	2039	2139	2239	2339
108	Drammen 785 d.	0614	0714	0814	0914	1014	1114	1214	1314	1414	1445	1514	1545	|	1614	1645	|	1714	1814	1914	2014	2114	2214	2314	0014
142	Holmestrand d.	0638	0733	0833	0933	1033	1133	1233	1333	1433	1506	1533	1606	|	1633	1706	|	1733	1833	1933	2033	2133	2233	2333	0033
156	Skoppum d.	0650	0741	0841	0941	1041	1141	1241	1341	1441	1518	1541	1618	|	1641	1718	|	1741	1841	1941	2041	2141	2241	2341	0041
172	Tønsberg d.	0706	0752	0852	0952	1052	1152	1252	1352	1452	1529	1552	1629	1643**z**	1652	1729	1743**z**	1752	1852	1952	2052	2152	2252	2352	0052
191	Torp ✈ d.	0721	0812	0912	1012	1112	1212	1312	1412	1512	|	1612	|	|	1712	|	|	1812	1912	2012	2112	2212	2312	0011	|
196	**Sandefjord** d.	0727	0818	0918	1018	1118	1218	1318	1418	1518	1548	1618	1648	1705	1718	1748	1805	1818	1918	2018	2118	2218	2318	0016	0111
215	Larvik d.	0746	0833	0933	1033	1133	1233	1333	1433	1533	1602	1633	1702	1719	1733	1802	1819	1833	1933	2033	2133	2233	2333	0030	0125
240	Porsgrunn 779 d.	0758	0845	0945	1045	1145	1245	1345	1445	1545	1618	1645	1718	1731	1745	1818	1831	1845	1945	2045	2145	2245	2345	0042	0137
249	**Skien** 779 a.	0807	0853	0953	1053	1153	1253	1353	1453	1553	1626	1653	1726	1739	1753	1826	1839	1853	1953	2053	2153	2253	2353	0050	0145

	Ⓐ	Ⓐ	⚒	Ⓐ	Ⓐ		Ⓐ	Ⓐ	⚒		⚒										Ⓑ		Ⓑ	
Skien 779 d.	0410	0427	0511	0525	0544	0610	0620	0628	0709	0809	0909	1009	1109	1209	1309	1409	1509	1607	1707	1807	1909	2009	2109	2209
Porsgrunn 779 d.	0418	0435	0519	0533	0552	0618	0628	0636	0717	0817	0917	1017	1117	1217	1317	1417	1517	1617	1717	1817	1917	2017	2117	2217
Larvik d.	0431	0449	0532	0547	0605	0631	0642	0650	0732	0832	0932	1032	1132	1232	1332	1432	1532	1632	1732	1832	1932	2032	2132	2232
Sandefjord d.	0446	0504	0547	0602	0620	0647	0656	0704	0747	0847	0947	1047	1147	1247	1347	1447	1547	1647	1747	1847	1947	2047	2147	2247
Torp ✈ d.	0450	0508	0551	0606	|	0651	|	0708	0751	0851	0951	1051	1151	1251	1351	1451	1551	1651	1751	1851	1951	2051	2151	2251
Tønsberg d.	0508	0528	0608	0626	0640	0708	0719	0728	0808	0908	1008	1108	1208	1308	1408	1508	1608	1708	1808	1908	2008	2108	2208	2308
Skoppum d.	0518	0538	0618	0636	|	0718	|	0740	0818	0918	1018	1118	1218	1318	1418	1518	1618	1718	1818	1918	2018	2118	2218	2318
Holmestrand d.	0526	0547	0626	0645	|	0726	|	0749	0826	0926	1026	1126	1226	1326	1426	1526	1626	1726	1826	1926	2026	2126	2226	2326
Drammen 785 d.	0547	0609	0647	0710	|	0747	|	0812	0847	0947	1047	1147	1247	1347	1447	1547	1647	1747	1847	1947	2047	2147	2247	2347
Oslo S 785 a.	0621	0645	0721	0745	0747	0821	0825	0845	0921	1021	1121	1221	1321	1421	1521	1621	1721	1821	1921	2021	2121	2221	2321	0021
Oslo S 785 d.	0624	...	0724	...	0752	0824	...	...	0924	1024	1124	1224	1324	1424	1524	1624	1724	1824	1924	2024	2124	2224	2324	0024
Lillestrøm 785 d.	0635	...	0735	...	0801	0835	...	...	0935	1035	1135	1235	1335	1435	1535	1635	1735	1835	1935	2035	2135	2235	2335	0035
Oslo Lufthavn ✈ ¶ 785 d.	0649	...	0749	...	...	0849	...	...	0949	1049	1149	1249	1349	1449	1549	1649	1749	1849	1949	2049	2149	2249	2349	0049
Eidsvoll 785 a.	0700	...	0759	...	...	0859	...	...	0959	1059	1159	1259	1359	1459	1559	1659	1759	1859	1959	2059	2159	2259	2359	0059

z – Arrives 6 minutes earlier.

¶ – Oslo Lufthavn Gardermoen ✈.

784 HAMAR - RØROS - TRONDHEIM

Operated by SJ NORD

km		Ⓐ	Ⓐ	⚒	Ⓐ	⑦	⑥			Ⓑ		Ⓑ
0	**Hamar** d.	...	0809	1009	1209	1209	...	...	1611	1809	...	2009
32	Elverum d.	...	0834	1034	1234	1234	...	...	1636	1834	...	2034
64	Rena d.	...	0859	1059	1257	1257	...	...	1658	1901	...	2057
120	Koppang d.	...	0940	1140	1338	1338	...	...	1741	1944	...	2139
273	**Røros** a.	...	1133	1335	1535	1535	...	...	1934	2137	...	2332
273	**Røros** d.	0506	...	...	1550	1605	1630	...	1953	...	...	...
384	Støren 785 d.	0647	...	...	1727	1740	1803	...	2128	...	...	...
435	**Trondheim** S 785 a.	0739	...	...	1823	1839	1856	...	2227	...	...	...

	Ⓐ	⚒	Ⓐ	Ⓐ	Ⓒ	Ⓑ		⑦	Ⓐ	⑦	
Trondheim S 785 d.	...	...	0537	0922	0933	...	...	1330	1621	2019	...
Støren 785 d.	...	...	0640	1019	1030	...	...	1428	1724	2127	...
Røros a.	...	...	0814	1153	1206	...	...	1603	1857	2300	...
Røros d.	0418	0623	0821	1218	1218	1418	...	1619	...	...	...
Koppang d.	0612	0817	1018	1416	1416	1613	...	1820	...	...	...
Rena d.	0654	0900	1100	1458	1458	1658	...	1902	...	...	...
Elverum d.	0716	0922	1122	1520	1520	1720	...	1924	...	...	...
Hamar a.	0740	0946	1146	1544	1544	1745	...	1947	...	...	...

785 OSLO - LILLEHAMMER - ÅNDALSNES and TRONDHEIM

Services to / from Trondheim and Åndalsnes are operated by SJ NORD. Local services Drammen - Oslo - Lillehammer are operated by Vy.

km		407		43	2343	311	2345	47	2347	49	2349	51	331	405	
		Ⓐ					Ⓐ			Ⓑ	Ⓑ	Ⓑ	Ⓑ	Ⓑ	
				R	R	◇	R	R	R	R	R	R	◇	RN	
				✕⊙	🍷	🍷⊡	🍷	✕⊙	🍷	✕⊙	🍷	✕⊙	🍷⊡	✕	
0	**Oslo** Sentral ★ d.	...	...	0802	...	0934	...	1402	...	1602	...	1802	1934	2250	...
21	Lillestrøm ★ d.	...	...	0813u	...	0945	...	1413u	...	1613u	...	1812u	1945	2320u	...
52	Oslo ✈ ⊖ ★ d.	...	...	0828u	...	0959	...	1429u	...	1629u	...	1828u	1959	2338u	...
127	**Hamar** ★ d.	...	...	0921	...	1052	...	1522	...	1722	...	1923	2052	0033	...
185	**Lillehammer** ★ d.	...	...	1009	...	1140	...	1613	...	1810	...	2020	2149	0124	...
243	Ringebu d.	...	...	1052	...	...	...	1656	...	1851	...	2102	2231	0210	...
267	Vinstra d.	...	...	1109	...	...	...	1718	...	1914	...	2119	2246	0229	...
298	Otta d.	...	...	1132	...	...	...	1741	...	1938	...	2143	2309	0258	...
344	Dombås d.	...	...	1204	1208	...	1435	1813	1817	2011	2015	2220	2341	0336	...
458	**Åndalsnes** ♥ a.	...	...	|	1328	...	1603	|	1937	|	2135	|	...	|	...
430	Oppdal ♥ d.	0634	...	1301	...	...	...	1910	...	2114	...	2317	...	0438	...
502	Støren 784 d.	0723	...	1351	...	...	...	2007	...	2209	...	0009	...	0533	...
553	**Trondheim** S 784 a.	0828	...	1439	...	...	...	2053	...	2254	...	0053	...	0624	...

	308		2340	316	2342	42	44		2346	46	2348	48		406	
	⚒		Ⓐ				Ⓑ		Ⓑ	Ⓑ				Ⓑ	
	◇		R	◇	R	R	R		R	R	R	R		RN	
	🍷⊡		🍷	🍷⊡	🍷	✕⊙	✕⊙		🍷	✕⊙	🍷	✕⊙		✕	
Trondheim S 784 d.	...	...	...	...	...	0817	1018	...	...	1318	...	1523	...	2317	...
Støren 784 d.	...	...	...	...	...	0903	1108	...	...	1413	...	1615	...	0009	...
Oppdal ♥ d.	...	...	...	...	...	0957	1205	...	...	1506	...	1710	...	0110	...
Åndalsnes ♥ d.	...	...	0710	...	0925	|	|	...	1431	|	1630	|	...	|	...
Dombås d.	0517	...	0832	...	1049	1057	1308	...	1555	1603	1752	1810	...	0226	...
Otta d.	0549	...	...	...	...	1130	1339	...	...	1634	...	1840	...	0306	...
Vinstra d.	0613	...	...	...	...	1153	1403	...	...	1657	...	1902	...	0330	...
Ringebu d.	0629	...	...	...	...	1210	1420	...	...	1714	...	1918	...	0348	...
Lillehammer ★ d.	0714	...	...	1114	...	1254	1503	...	...	1807	...	2001	...	0437	...
Hamar ★ d.	0807	...	...	1207	...	1347	1551	...	...	1852	...	2051	...	0531	...
Oslo ✈ ⊖ ★ a.	0903	...	...	1303	...	1432s	1632s	...	...	1945s	...	2132s	...	0617s	...
Lillestrøm ★ a.	0916	...	...	1316	...	1449s	1648s	...	...	1959s	...	2148s	...	0635s	...
Oslo Sentral ★ a.	0926	...	...	1326	...	1502	1702	...	...	2014	...	2202	...	0650	...

N – Conveys 🛏 and [2].
R – Reservation recommended.

s – Stops to set down only.
u – Stops to pick up only.

◇ – Operated by Vy.
⊡ – Conveys *Vy Komfort*.
⊙ – Conveys *SJ NORD Premium*.
⊖ – Oslo Lufthavn Gardermoen.
★ – See also panel below main table.
♥ – See Table **785a** for connecting 🚌 services to / from Molde, Ålesund and Kristiansund.

Local services Drammen - Oslo - Lillehammer (operated by Vy). **SERVICE UNTIL MARCH 31**.

	Ⓐ	Ⓐ		⚒		⚒		⚒			Ⓐ			Ⓐ		Ⓑ		Ⓑ		Ⓑ			①–④	⑦	
Drammen 783 d.	...	0557	0657	0757	0857	0957	1057	1157	1257	1357	...	1457	1557	...	1657	1757	1857	1957	2057	2157	2257	...	2347	2347	...
Oslo Sentral 771 783 d.	...	0634	0734	0834	0934	1034	1134	1234	1334	1434	1502	1534	1634	1702	1734	1834	1934	2034	2134	2234	2334	...	0024	0024	...
Lillestrøm 783 d.	...	0645	0745	0845	0945	1045	1145	1245	1345	1445	1513	1545	1645	1713	1745	1845	1945	2045	2145	2245	2345	...	0035	0035	...
Oslo ✈ ⊖ 771 783 d.	...	0659	0759	0859	0959	1059	1159	1259	1359	1459	1529	1559	1659	1729	1759	1859	1959	2059	2159	2259	2359	...	0049	0049	...
Eidsvoll 783 d.	...	0709	0809	0909	1009	1109	1209	1309	1409	1509	1538	1609	1709	1739	1809	1909	2009	2109	2209	2309	0009	...	0102	0102	...
Hamar a.	...	0750	0850	0948	1048	1148	1247	1346	1450	1550	1620	1650	1750	1821	1847	1947	2046	2146	2247	2347	0046	...	0141	0141	...
Hamar d.	0652	0752	0852	0952	1052	1152	1252	1348	1452	1552	...	1652	1752	...	1853	1952	2052	2152	2252	2352	0051	...	0145	...	...
Lillehammer a.	0740	0840	0937	1041	1140	1241	1340	1442	1540	1640	...	1737	1841	...	1940	2043	2141	2237	2337	0040	0137	...	0230	...	...

	Ⓐ	Ⓐ		Ⓐ	⚒	Ⓐ		⚒		⚒								Ⓑ		Ⓑ					
Lillehammer d.	0333	0414	0521	...	0614	...	0714	0814	0907	1014	1114	1215	1309	1411	1509	1614	1707	1812	1908	2017	2110	...	...	...	...
Hamar a.	0419	0500	0607	...	0706	...	0805	0905	1005	1105	1205	1305	1405	1505	1605	1705	1805	1905	2005	2106	2205	...	...	...	...
Hamar d.	0421	0502	0609	0631	0708	0728	0807	0907	1007	1107	1207	1307	1407	1507	1607	1707	1809	1908	2007	2108	2208	...	...	...	...
Eidsvoll 783 d.	0501	0542	0652	0712	0752	0811	0852	0952	1052	1152	1252	1352	1452	1552	1652	1752	1852	1952	2052	2152	2252	...	...	...	...
Oslo ✈ ⊖ 771 783 d.	0513	0603	0703	0723	0803	0823	0903	1003	1103	1203	1303	1403	1503	1603	1703	1803	1903	2003	2103	2203	2303	...	...	...	...
Lillestrøm 783 d.	0526	0616	0716	0738	0816	0838	0916	1016	1116	1216	1316	1416	1516	1616	1716	1816	1916	2016	2116	2216	2316	...	...	...	...
Oslo Sentral 771 783 a.	0536	0626	0726	0748	0826	0848	0926	1026	1126	1226	1326	1426	1526	1626	1726	1826	1926	2026	2126	2226	2326	...	...	...	...
Drammen 783 a.	0612	0702	0802	...	0902	...	1002	1102	1202	1302	1402	1502	1602	1702	1802	1902	2002	2102	2202	2302	0002	...	...	...	...

🚌 ÅNDALSNES - MOLDE and ÅLESUND; 🚌 OPPDAL - KRISTIANSUND 785a

ÅNDALSNES - MOLDE and ÅLESUND

🚌	⑦	Ⓐ	Ⓐ				Ⓐ		Ⓐ		⑥⑦		⑥	Ⓐ		Ⓐ	⑦					Ⓑ		
Åndalsnes Stasjon d.	0605	0610	0725	...	1000	...	1140	...	1330	1340	1400	...	1600	1620	...	1820	1820	...	1950	1955	...	2155	...	...
Molde Trafikkterminal a.	0732	0742	0854	...	1127	...	1307	...	1512	|	1518	...	1727	1747	...	1942	1947	...	|	2117	...	2317	...	...
Ålesund Rutebilstasjon a.	...	...	...	...	...	...	...	...	...	1545	...	...	...	...	...	...	...	...	2155	...	...	...	...	...

🚌		Ⓐ	⑥⑦	⚒		⑦	Ⓐ	⑦		Ⓐ	⑥⑦	Ⓐ	⑥		Ⓐ	Ⓐ		⑥⑦		Ⓐ	Ⓑ			
Ålesund Rutebilstasjon d.	...	0705	0710	...	...	...	...	1155	...	...	...	1400	1410	...	...	...	...	...	...	...	...	...	...	...
Molde Trafikkterminal d.	0750	|	|	0955	...	1235	1255	|	...	1430	1435	|	|	...	1545	1630	...	1755	...	1935	2030	...	2150	...
Åndalsnes Stasjon a.	0915	0910	0915	1115	...	1355	1415	1414	...	1555	1555	1605	1615	...	1715	1755	...	1912	...	2055	2150	...	2307	...

OPPDAL - KRISTIANSUND

🚌	Ⓐ	⑥		Ⓐ		⑦	Ⓐ		⑤⑦		Ⓑ	
Oppdal skysstasjon d.	0515	0530	...	1050	...	1315	1315	...	1810	...	2120	...
Kristiansund a.	0855	0845	...	1425	...	1625	1631	...	2125	...	0025	...

🚌	Ⓐ		Ⓐ	⑥		Ⓑ		⑤⑦		Ⓑ
Kristiansund d.	0630	...	1045	1125	...	1330	...	1640	...	2125
Oppdal skysstasjon a.	0940	...	1445	1445	...	1645	...	2005	...	0035

SOUTHWEST NORWAY 🚌 LINKS 786

BERGEN - TRONDHEIM ❦ Operator: NOR-WAY Bussekspress ✆ +47 2231 3150.
Ⓑ Bergen ⊡ d. 1630 → Otta ⊕ a. 0159 → Oppdal ⊕ a. 0440 → Trondheim a. 0642.
①②③④⑦: Trondheim d. 2000 → Oppdal ⊕ d. 2205 → Otta ⊕ d. 0045 → Bergen ⊡ a. 0940. ⑤⑥: Trondheim d. 2230 → Oppdal ⊕ d. 0032 → Otta ⊕ d. 0305 → Bergen ⊡ a. 1210.

BERGEN - ÅLESUND Operator: Vy Buss express ✆ +47 4070 5070. Bergen ⊡ d. 0800 → Ålesund a. 1730. Ålesund d. 1055 ⑥⑦ / 1105Ⓐ → Bergen ⊡ a. 2045.

BERGEN - STAVANGER Operator: NOR-WAY Bussekspress ✆ +47 2231 3150. *Journey time: 4½ – 5½ hours.*
From Bergen ⊡ at 0715 Ⓐ, 0840 Ⓐ, 0920 Ⓐ 0935 ⑥, 0940 ⑦, 1050 ⑥, 1040 ⑦, 1120 Ⓐ, 1230 ⑥, 1240, 1320 ⑥⑦, 1400 Ⓐ, 1435 ⚒, 1440 ⑦, 1520 ⑦, 1550 ⑥ 1635 Ⓐ, 1655 Ⓐ, 1740 ⑥⑦.
From Stavanger ⊙ at 0545 Ⓐ, 0830 Ⓐ, 0915 ⑦, 0935 ⑥, 0945 Ⓐ, 1015 ⑥, 1045 ⑦, 1130 Ⓐ, 1145 ⑦, 1215 ⑥, 1230 ⑦, 1345 Ⓐ, 1400 ⑦, 1530 Ⓑ, 1555 ⑥, 1615 ⑥, 1630 ⑦, 1700 ⑦, 1800 Ⓐ.

⊡ – Bus station. ⊙ – Stavanger Byterminalen. ⊕ – Skysstasjon. ❦ – Currently suspended.

TRONDHEIM - BODØ and NARVIK 787

Operated by SJ NORD

km		1795		1781	1783	475	🚌		1785	483	473		1787	1789	1791	471	481	🚌	1793		479	477			
		⑥⑦		Ⓐ	Ⓐ	N R ✕	◇		Ⓐ	⑥R	ⒶR		Ⓐ	Ⓐ	Ⓐ	ⒶR ✕⊙	ⒸR ✕⊙	◇	Ⓐ		ⒷR	ⒷR			
0	**Trondheim** S d.	...	...	...	...	2305	...	...	...	...	...	...	...	...	...	0749	0758	...	...	...	...	1603	...	...	...
33	Trondheim ✈ ‡ d.	...	...	...	...	2337	...	...	...	...	...	...	...	...	...	0824	0824	...	...	...	...	1636u	...	...	...
34	Stjørdal d.	...	...	...	...	2341	...	...	...	...	...	...	...	...	...	0828	0828	...	...	...	...	1641u	...	...	...
126	Steinkjer d.	...	...	...	...	0057	...	...	...	...	...	...	...	...	...	0951	0951	...	...	...	...	1807u	...	...	...
220	Grong d.	...	...	...	...	0207	...	...	...	...	...	...	...	...	...	1100	1100	...	...	...	...	1916	...	...	...
406	Mosjøen d.	...	...	...	...	0444	...	...	...	0640	0652	...	...	...	...	1320	1320	...	...	...	1657	2143z	...	...	...
498	Mo i Rana d.	...	...	...	...	0555	...	...	...	0747	0759	...	...	...	...	1431	1431	...	...	...	1801	2248	...	...	...
648	Rognan d.	0205	...	0535	0631	0750	...	...	...	0933	0944	...	1124	...	...	1631	1624	...	1801	...	2001	...	...	...	...
	Bodø ⊖ d.	|	...	|	|	|	0722	...	...	|	|	...	|	...	...	|	|	1642	|	...	|	...	...	...	...
674	Fauske d.	0225	...	0555	0651	0819	0850	...	0913	0954	1006	...	1144	1424	1612	1659	1649	1809	1830	...	2020	...	...	...	...
	Narvik ⊡ ♣ a.	|	...	|	|	|	1335	...	|	|	|	...	|	|	|	|	|	2315	|	...	|	...	...	...	...
729	**Bodø** a.	0306	...	0636	0732	0905	...	...	0956	1035	1054	...	1225	1505	1659	1744	1734	...	1910	...	2101	...	...	...	...

	1794		478		470	1782		1784		🚌	472	1786		1788	1790		474		🚌	476	1792			
	⑥⑦		⚒R		ⒶR	Ⓐ		Ⓐ		◇	R ✕⊙	Ⓐ		Ⓐ	Ⓐ		R		◇	N R ✕	M			
Bodø d.	0055	...	...	...	0734	0818	...	1012	...	...	1227	1335	...	1513	1616	...	1746	...	...	2110	2355	...	...	...
Narvik ⊡ ♣ d.	|	...	...	...	|	|	...	|	...	0705	|	|	...	|	|	...	|	...	1625	|	|	...	...	...
Fauske d.	0137	...	...	...	0817	0905	...	1056	...	1210	1316	1416	...	1555	1700	...	1828	...	2125	2202	0037	...	...	...
Bodø ⊖ a.	|	...	...	...	|	...	...	|	...	1310	|	...	...	...	|	...	|	...	2225	|	|	...	...	...
Rognan d.	0156	...	...	...	0835	...	...	1115	...	...	1336	...	...	...	1719	...	1852	...	...	2222	0056	...	...	...
Mo i Rana d.	...	...	0811	...	1023	...	...	...	...	...	1543	...	...	...	...	...	2035	...	...	0024	...	...	...	...
Mosjøen d.	...	...	0916	...	1126	...	...	...	...	...	1653	...	...	...	...	...	2138	...	...	0140	...	...	...	...
Grong d.	...	...	1129	...	...	...	...	...	...	...	1914	...	...	...	...	...	...	...	...	0405	...	...	...	...
Steinkjer a.	...	...	1231x	...	...	...	...	...	...	...	2024	...	...	...	...	...	...	...	...	0517	...	...	...	...
Stjørdal a.	...	...	1342x	...	...	...	...	...	...	...	2145	...	...	...	...	...	...	...	...	0640	...	...	...	...
Trondheim ✈ ‡ a.	...	...	1344x	...	...	...	...	...	...	...	2148	...	...	...	...	...	...	...	...	0643	...	...	...	...
Trondheim a.	...	...	1413	...	...	...	...	...	...	...	2213	...	...	...	...	...	...	...	...	0715	...	...	...	...

Local services Trondheim - Steinkjer and v.v.

km		Ⓐ	Ⓐ	⚒	Ⓐ	⚒	Ⓐ	⚒	Ⓐ	⚒	Ⓐ	Ⓐ		Ⓐ	Ⓐ		Ⓐ		Ⓐ		Ⓐ	Ⓑ			
0	**Trondheim** S d.	0509	0616	0715	0817	0917	1017	1117	1217	1317	1417	1442	1517	1542	1617	1717	1817	1917	2017	2117	2217	2317	...	...	...
31	Hell ● d.	0543	0650	0750	0850	0950	1050	1150	1250	1350	1450	1520	1550	1620	1650	1750	1850	1950	2051	2150	2250	2350	...	...	...
33	Trondheim ✈ ‡ d.	0546	0653	0753	0853	0953	1053	1153	1253	1353	1453	1523	1553	1623	1653	1753	1853	1953	2054	2153	2253	2353	...	...	...
34	Stjørdal d.	0552	0657	0759	0900	1000	1100	1200	1300	1400	1500	1528	1600	1628	1700	1800	1900	2000	2101	2200	2300	2356	...	...	...
126	**Steinkjer** a.	0722	0821	0922	1024	1124	1225	1324	1424	1524	1624	1651	1724	1751	1824	1924	2024	2124	2226	2320	0020	0115	...	...	...

	Ⓐ	Ⓐ	⚒	Ⓐ	Ⓐ		Ⓐ		Ⓐ	⚒	Ⓐ	Ⓑ	Ⓐ		Ⓐ		Ⓐ		Ⓐ					
Steinkjer d.	0431	0506	0534	0602	0632	0734	0833	0930	1037	1137	1238	1337	1437	1537	1632	1732	1837	1932	2037	2134	...	...	...	...
Stjørdal d.	0552	0623	0657	0724	0759	0900	1000	1100	1200	1300	1400	1500	1600	1700	1800	1900	2000	2101	2200	2300	...	...	...	...
Trondheim ✈ ‡ d.	0554	0626	0700	0727	0802	0903	1003	1103	1203	1303	1403	1503	1603	1703	1803	1903	2003	2104	2203	2303	...	...	...	...
Hell ● d.	0557	0629	0703	0730	0805	0906	1006	1106	1206	1306	1406	1506	1606	1706	1806	1906	2009	2107	2206	2306	...	...	...	...
Trondheim S a.	0629	0703	0741	0803	0841	0941	1041	1141	1241	1341	1441	1541	1641	1741	1841	1941	2043	2141	2241	2341	...	...	...	...

M – ②③④⑦ only.
N – Conveys 🛏, (2) and ✕.
R – Reservation recommended.

u – Calls to pick up only.
x – Calls on request.
z – Arrives 2127.

⊙ – Conveys *SJ NORD Premium*.
● – Trains call at Hell on request.
‡ – Trondheim Lufthavn (station for Trondheim Værnes Airport).
☛ – Most trains have automatic vending machines on board.
⊡ – Bus station.
⊖ – Bodø Sentrumsterminalen buss.
◇ – Operator: Nordlandsbuss.
♣ – 🚌 **Narvik - Svolvær** (Lofoten) *253 km*.
From Narvik bussterminal at 0955 and 1550.
From Svolvær sentrum at 0940 and 1515.

FINLAND

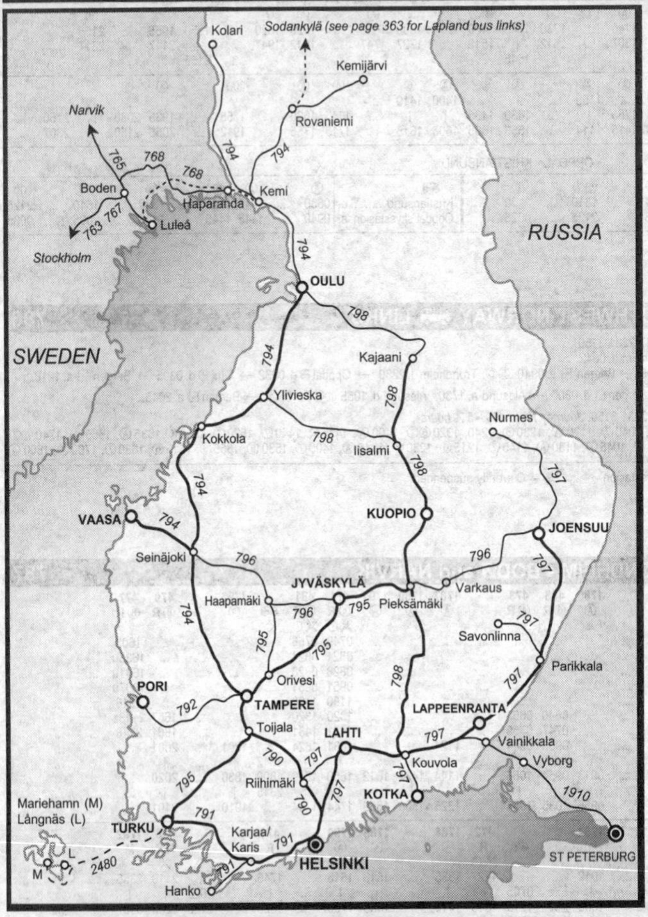

Operator: VR – VR-Yhtymä Oy www.vr.fi

Tickets and train types: Travel classes in Finland are referred to as *Extra* (1st) and *Eco* (2nd). For all except purely local journeys, tickets are always sold for travel by a specific train or combination of trains with seat reservations included. Standard *Eco* fares are referred to as 'Basic', whilst cheaper advance puchase 'Saver' fares are also available in limited numbers. In both cases tickets can be changed to a different date / departure time for a €5 fee (plus any price difference). Both ticket types can be upgraded to a seat in *Extra* class for a variable fee (€4 – 17, dependent on the length of journey). Tickets may be purchased on board long-distance trains (also regional trains outside of the Helsinki area), although an additional charge of €3 (for short journeys up to 76km) or €6 (for journeys over 76km) will be added to the 'Basic' fare. Please note that cash is no longer accepted for on board ticket purchase (only debit / credit cards are accepted). On board ticket purchase is **not** permitted on local trains (shown as 2nd class only in tables) Helsinki - Riihimäki - Tampere (Table **790**), Helsinki - Lahti - Kouvola - Kotka (Table **797**) and Riihimäki - Lahti (Table **797**).

▶ **S Pendolino** (e.g. *S* **123**) – high-speed tilting trains, with *Extra* and *Eco* class seats, all reservable.

▶ **InterCity** (e.g. *IC* **124**) – quality fast trains between major centres, with *Eco* class seats (most also convey *Extra* class seats), all reservable.

▶ **Express**, *pikajunat* (train number only shown, e.g. **128**) – other fast trains, with *Eco* class seats, all reservable. Night expresses convey sleeping-cars and *Eco* class seats only (marked ★ in the tables).

▶ **Regional**, *taajamajunat* (no train number shown) – stopping-trains, normally with *Eco* class seats only. Regional fares apply.

Rail tickets are **not** valid on 🚌 services (except Seinäjoki - Vaasa).

Services: ✕ indicates a train with a restaurant car. Trains marked 🍸 convey a *MiniBistro* trolley. A variable supplement is payable for travel in sleeping-cars (🛏) in addition to the relevant *Eco* class fare – the price to be paid depends on the date of travel and the type of accommodation required. A higher supplement is charged for occupancy of a single-berth cabin.

Timings: **Valid until March 25**, 2023.
In these tables Ⓐ = ①–⑤, ⚒ = ①–⑥, Ⓑ = ①–⑤ and ⑦.
Changes to the normal service pattern are likely to occur on and around the dates of public holidays (see page 4).

790 HELSINKI - TAMPERE

See next page for other regional services Helsinki - Riihimäki

For through journeys to / from **Oulu** and **Rovaniemi**, see Table **794**. For through journeys to / from **Jyväskylä** and **Pieksämäki**, see Table **795**.

km		*S* 35	*S*	*IC* 21	*IC* 155	*S* 155	*IC* 41		*S* 165	*IC* 23	*IC* 93	*IC* 43		*S* 33	*S* 143	*IC* 143	*IC* 45		*IC* 171	*IC* 25	*IC* 145	*IC* 37		*S* 87	*IC* 175	*IC* 87	*IC* 27
		⚒	⚒	⚒	Ⓑ	⑥	⚒	⚒	Ⓐ					m	①–④	⑤–⑦			⑤⑦					⑤	⑥	⑦–④	
		✕	2	✕	✕	✕	✕◐	2	✕	✕	✕◐	✕	2	✕	✕	✕	✕	2	✕	✕	✕	✕	2	✕	✕P	✕	✕
0	**Helsinki** d.	0503	0510	0623	0703	0703	0723	0710	0803	0824	0903	0924	0910	1003	1024	1024	1103	1110	1203	1224	1303	1324	1310	1403	1403	1403	1424
3	Pasila d.	0509	0515	0629	0709	0709	0729	0715	0809	0830	0909	0930	0915	1009	1030	1030	1109	1115	1209	1230	1309	1330	1315	1409	1409	1409	1430
16	Tikkurila d.	0519	0524	0639	0719	0719	0739	0724	0819	0841	0919	0941	0924	1019	1041	1041	1119	1124	1219	1241	1319	1341	1324	1419	1419	1419	1441
71	Riihimäki d.	0552	0625j	|	0752	0752	|	0815j	0852	|	0952	|	1012j	1052	|	|	1152	1215j	1252	|	1352	|	1415j	1452	1452	1452	|
108	Hämeenlinna d.	0611	0648	|	0811	0811	|	0838	0911	|	1011	|	1035	1111	|	|	1211	1238	1311	|	1411	|	1438	1511	1511	1511	|
147	Toijala d.	0631	0711	|	0831	0831	|	0901	0931	|	1031	|	1101	1131	|	|	1231	1301	1331	|	1431	|	1501	1531	1531	1531	|
187	**Tampere** a.	0653	0735	0758	0853	0853	0858	0925	0953	0958	1053	1058	1125	1153	1158	1158	1253	1325	1353	1358	1453	1458	1525	1553	1553	1553	1558

	IC 151	*IC* 47		*IC* 147	*IC* 51	*S* 59	*S* 59	*IC* 177	*S* 177	*IC* 49		*S* 89	*IC* 89	*IC* 29	*IC* 149	*S* 149		*IC* 265	*IC* 183	*S* 53	269		*IC* 187		*IC* 273		
	Ⓑ	Ⓑ				⑦	Ⓐ	Ⓑ	⑥			Ⓑ	⑥		Ⓑ	⑥				Ⓑ							
	✕	✕	2	✕	✕	✕	✕	✕	✕	✕	2	✕	✕	✕◐	✕	✕	2	★	✕	✕	★	2	✕	2	★		
Helsinki d.	1503	1524	1510	1603	1624	1630	1640	1703	1703	1724	1710	1803	1803	1824	1903	1903	1910	1929	2003	2024	2029	2110	2203	2240	2313	...	...
Pasila d.	1509	1530	1515	1609	1630	1636	1646	1709	1709	1730	1715	1809	1809	1830	1909	1909	1915	1937	2009	2030	2036	2115	2209	2245	2320	...	...
Tikkurila d.	1519	1541	1524	1619	1641	|	|	1719	1719	1741	1724	1819	1819	1841	1919	1919	1924	2030	2019	2041	2114	2124	2219	2254	0001	...	...
Riihimäki d.	1552	|	1615j	1652	|	1725j	1725	1752	1752	|	1815j	1852	1852	|	1952	1952	2015j	2116	2052	|	2158	2215j	2251	2345j	0044	...	...
Hämeenlinna d.	1611	|	1638	1711	|	1745	1745	1811	1811	|	1838	1911	1911	|	2011	2011	2038	2140	2111	|	2224	2238	2311	0008	0106	...	...
Toijala d.	1631	|	1701	1731	|	|	|	1831	1831	|	1901	1931	1931	|	2031	2031	2101	|	2131	|	|	2301	2331	0031	0130	...	...
Tampere a.	1653	1658	1725	1753	1758	1821	1821	1853	1853	1858	1925	1953	1953	1958	2053	2053	2125	2231	2153	2158	2313	2325	2353	0055	0155	...	...

	IC 266	*IC* 160	*IC* 162	*IC* 166	*IC* 274		*IC* 40	*IC* 80	276	*IC* 42	*S* 140	*IC* 140		*IC* 150	*S* 44	*IC* 44	*IC* 20		*IC* 36	*IC* 142	*IC* 22	*IC* 94	*S* 94		*S* 46	*IC* 46	*IC* 38
		Ⓐ	⚒	Ⓐ			Ⓐ			⚒	Ⓐ	⑥		⚒	⚒	⑦	⚒		Ⓐ			Ⓐ	⑥⑦		Ⓐ	⑥⑦	
	★	✕	✕	✕	★	2	✕	✕	★	✕	✕	✕	2	✕	✕		✕	2	✕◐	✕	✕	✕	✕	2	✕	✕	✕
Tampere d.	0345	0504	0545	0622	0608	0635	0700	0704	0734	0800	0804	0804	0835	0900	0904	0904	1000	1035	1100	1104	1200	1204	1204	1235	1300	1300	1400
Toijala d.	0412	0526	0607	|	0642j	0700	|	0726	0802	|	0826	0826	0900	|	0926	0926	|	1100	|	1126	|	1226	1226	1300	|	|	|
Hämeenlinna d.	0438	0547	0629	0700	0708	0722	|	0747	0850k	|	0847	0847	0922	|	0947	0947	|	1122	|	1147	|	1247	1247	1322	|	|	|
Riihimäki d.	0503	0608	0649	0720	0739	0755j	|	0808	0917	|	0908	0908	0955j	|	1008	1008	|	1155j	|	1208	|	1308	1308	1355j	|	|	|
Tikkurila d.	0547	0640	0721	0755	0831	0835	0821	0840	1001	0921	0940	0940	1035	1021	1040	1040	1121	1235	1221	1240	1321	1340	1340	1435	1421	1421	1521
Pasila d.	0621	0649	0730	0804	0909	0844	0830	0849	1040	0930	0949	0949	1044	1030	1049	1049	1130	1244	1230	1249	1330	1349	1349	1444	1430	1430	1530
Helsinki a.	0627	0654	0735	0810	0915	0849	0835	0854	1045	0935	0954	0954	1049	1035	1054	1054	1135	1249	1235	1254	1335	1354	1354	1449	1435	1435	1535

	IC 178	*S* 178		*IC* 48	*IC* 144	*S* 144	*IC* 24	*IC* 86	*S* 86		*IC* 50	*IC* 180		*IC* 26	*S* 146	*IC* 146		*IC* 54	*S* 34	*S* 88	*IC* 186	*IC* 88		*S* 56	*IC* 56	*IC* 28	*S* 58
	①–④	⑤⑦			Ⓑ	⑥		Ⓑ	⑥			⑤–⑦	Ⓐ		①–④	⑤–⑦	⑥⑦		m	⑤	P⑥	⑦–④		Ⓑ	⑥		⑤⑦
	✕P	✕P	2	✕	✕	✕	✕	✕	✕	2	✕	✕	2	✕	✕	✕	2	✕	✕	✕	✕	✕	2	✕	✕	✕	✕
Tampere d.	1404	1404	1435	1500	1504	1504	1600	1604	1604	1635	1700	1704	1735	1800	1804	1804	1835	1900	2000	2004	2004	2004	2035	2100	2100	2200	2300
Toijala d.	1426	1426	1500	|	1526	1526	|	1628	1628	1700	|	1728	1800	|	1826	1826	1848	|	|	2026	2026	2026	2100	|	|	|	|
Hämeenlinna d.	1447	1447	1522	|	1547	1547	|	1649	1649	1722	|	1749	1822	|	1847	1847	1922	|	|	2047	2047	2047	2122	|	|	|	|
Riihimäki d.	1508	1508	1555j	|	1608	1608	|	1708	1708	1755j	|	1808	1855j	|	1908	1908	1955j	|	|	2108	2108	2108	2155j	|	|	|	|
Tikkurila d.	1540	1540	1635	1621	1640	1640	1721	1740	1740	1835	1821	1840	1935	1921	1940	1940	1935	2021	2121	2140	2140	2140	2235	2221	2221	2321	0021
Pasila d.	1549	1549	1644	1630	1649	1649	1730	1749	1749	1844	1830	1849	1944	1930	1949	1949	1944	2030	2130	2149	2149	2149	2244	2230	2230	2330	0030
Helsinki a.	1554	1554	1649	1635	1654	1654	1735	1754	1754	1849	1835	1854	1949	1935	1954	1954	2049	2035	2135	2154	2154	2154	2249	2235	2235	2335	0035

FOR NOTES AND OTHER REGIONAL SERVICES, SEE TOP OF NEXT PAGE →

HELSINKI - TAMPERE 790

Other selected regional trains HELSINKI - RIIHIMÄKI (2nd class only)

km													
		Ⓐ	⚒										
0	**Helsinki** d.	0610	0640	0740	1040		1940	2010	2140	2340	...	...	...
3	Pasila d.	0615	0645	0745	1045	and	1945	2015	2145	2345	...	...	...
16	Tikkurila d.	0624	0654	0754	1054	hourly	1954	2024	2154	2354	...	...	...
37	Järvenpää d.	0640	0710	0810	1110	until	2010	2040	2210	0010	...	...	...
59	Hyvinkää d.	0656	0726	0826	1126		2026	2056	2226	0026	...	...	...
71	**Riihimäki** a.	0705	0735	0835	1135		2035	2105	2235	0035	...	...	...

	Ⓐ	Ⓐ		⑦							
Riihimäki d.	0525	0620	0655	0755	0925		1725	1925	2125	...	...
Hyvinkää d.	0533	0630	0703	0803	0933	and	1733	1933	2133	...	...
Järvenpää d.	0548	0648	0718	0818	0948	hourly	1748	1948	2148	...	...
Tikkurila d.	0605	0705	0735	0835	1015	until	1805	2005	2215	...	...
Pasila d.	0614	0715	0744	0844	1014		1814	2014	2214	...	...
Helsinki a.	0619	0720	0749	0849	1019		1819	2019	2219	...	...

P – To/from Pori (Table **792**).

j – Arrives 7 – 20 minutes earlier.
k – Arrives 0827.
m – ③④⑤⑦.

◐ – Train classification *S* on ⑥.
★ – Overnight train to/from northern Finland. For through cars and days of running see Table **794**.

HELSINKI - KARJAA - TURKU and KARJAA - HANKO 791

km		*IC* 941	*IC* 943	*S* 945	*IC* 945	*IC* 947	*IC* 949	*S* 949	*IC* 951	*IC* 953	*IC* 955	*IC* 957	*IC* 959	*IC* 961	*IC* 963	*IC* 965	*IC* 971	*S* 971	*S* 967	*IC* 967						
			Ⓐ	⑦	⚒	Ⓐ	①–⑤	⑥		⑤		Ⓑ	⚒	Ⓑ		Ⓑ	⑤	⑥	①–④	⑤–⑦						
		✕	🍸	🍸	🍸	🍸	🍸	✕	✕	✕	✕	🍸	🍸	🍸	🍸	🍸	🍸	🍸	🍸	✕						
0	**Helsinki** d.	0528	0628	0833	0836	0936	1036	1036	1136	1236	1336	1436	1536	1636	1736	1836	1936	1936	2106	2106	...	...	...	...	...	...
3	Pasila d.	0534	0634	0839	0842	0942	1042	1042	1142	1242	1342	1442	1542	1642	1742	1842	1942	1942	2112	2112	...	...	...	...	...	...
87	Karjaa/Karis d.	0626	0726	0932	0932	1032	1132	1132	1232	1332	1432	1532	1632	1732	1832	1932	2032	2032	2202	2202	...	...	...	...	...	...
138	Salo d.	0655	0755	1001	1001	1101	1201	1201	1301	1401	1501	1601	1701	1801	1901	2001	2101	2101	2231	2231	...	...	...	...	...	...
191	Kupittaa ▶ a.	0719	0819	1025	1025	1125	1225	1225	1325	1425	1525	1625	1725	1825	1925	2025	2125	2125	2255	2255	...	...	...	...	...	...
194	**Turku** ▶ a.	...	...	...	...	...	...	...	...	...	...	...	...	...	...	...	...	...	...	...	...	...	...	...	...	...
197	Turku satama ▶ a.	...	...	...	...	...	...	...	...	...	...	...	...	...	...	...	...	...	...	...	...	...	...	...	...	...

	IC 942	*S* 942	*IC* 944	*IC* 946	*IC* 948	*IC* 950	*IC* 954	*IC* 956	*S* 956	*IC* 958	*S* 958	*IC* 960	*IC* 962	*IC* 964	*IC* 966	*IC* 968	*IC* 972								
	①	②–⑤	Ⓐ	⚒		⚒		⚒	⑦	⑤⑦	⑥	Ⓑ				Ⓐ									
	✕	✕	🍸	🍸	✕	🍸	🍸	🍸	✕	🍸	🍸	🍸	✕	🍸	🍸	🍸	🍸								
Turku satama ▶ d.	...	...	...	...	...	...	...	...	...	...	...	...	...	...	...	...	...	...	...	...	...	...	...	...	...
Turku ▶ d.	...	...	...	...	...	...	...	...	...	...	...	...	...	...	...	...	...	...	...	...	...	...	...	...	...
Kupittaa ▶ d.	0531	0531	0631	0731	0831	0931	1131	1231	1231	1331	1331	1431	1531	1631	1731	1831	2056	...	...	...	...	...	...	...	...
Salo d.	0556	0556	0656	0756	0859	0959	1159	1259	1259	1359	1459	1459	1559	1659	1759	1859	2129	...	...	...	...	...	...	...	...
Karjaa/Karis d.	0628	0628	0728	0828	0928	1028	1228	1328	1328	1428	1528	1528	1628	1728	1828	1928	2158	...	...	...	...	...	...	...	...
Pasila d.	0718	0718	0818	0918	1018	1118	1318	1418	1418	1518	1618	1618	1718	1818	1921	2018	2251	...	...	...	...	...	...	...	...
Helsinki a.	0723	0723	0823	0923	1023	1123	1323	1423	1423	1523	1623	1623	1723	1823	1926	2023	2256	...	...	...	...	...	...	...	...

KARJAA/KARIS - HANKO *All services are currently operated by* 🚌.

km												
		Ⓐ										
0	**Karjaa/Karis** d.	0731	0936	...	1236	1436	1636	...	1836	...	2206	...
16	Tammisaari d.	0750	0955	...	1255	1455	1655	...	1855	...	2225	...
49	**Hanko** a.	0825	1030	...	1330	1530	1730	...	1930	...	2300	...

	Ⓐ										
Hanko d.	0625	0825	...	1120	1320	1520	...	1720	...	2050	...
Tammisaari d.	0655	0855	...	1155	1355	1555	...	1755	...	2125	...
Karjaa/Karis a.	0720	0920	...	1220	1420	1620	...	1820	...	2150	...

▶ – Kupittaa - Turku is currently closed to rail traffic. Please use frequent local 🚌 services (www.foli.fi).

TAMPERE - PORI 792

Most trains convey ✕

km		*IC* 477	*IC* 461	*IC* 165	*S* 165	*IC* 465	*IC* 467	*IC* 469	*IC* 175	*IC* 471	*IC* 473	*IC* 475
		Ⓐ	⚒	①–④	⑤			Ⓑ	⑥		Ⓑ	
	Helsinki **790** d.	...	...	0803	0803	...	...	...	1403	...	...	...
0	**Tampere** d.	0557	0806	1009	1009	1209	1409	1609	1609	1809	2009	2209
17	Nokia d.	0615	0824	1027	1027	1227	1427	1627	1627	1827	2027	2228
59	Vammala d.	0658	0854	1102	1102	1258	1458	1658	1658	1858	2059	2257
135	**Pori** a.	0747	0940	1148	1148	1344	1544	1744	1744	1944	2145	2343

	IC 460	*IC* 462	*IC* 466	*IC* 476	*IC* 464	*IC* 474	*IC* 178	*IC* 468	*IC* 470	*IC* 472	*IC* 186
	⚒	⚒		Ⓐ		①–④	⑤			Ⓑ	⑥
Pori d.	0517	0612	0717	0804	1003	1212	1212	1412	1612	1812	1812
Vammala d.	0604	0659	0804	0853	1050	1259	1259	1459	1659	1859	1859
Nokia d.	0633	0728	0838	0922	1119	1328	1328	1528	1728	1928	1928
Tampere a.	0650	0745	0855	0939	1136	1345	1345	1545	1745	1945	1945
Helsinki **790** a.	...	...	...	...	...	...	1554	...	...	...	2154

☛ Frequent 🚌 services operate Turku - Rauma - Pori and v.v. See www.matkahuolto.fi.

TAMPERE - VAASA, OULU, KOLARI and ROVANIEMI 794

km		*S* 35	*S* 55	*IC* 21	*IC* 711	*IC* 41	*IC* 23	*IC* 43	*IC* 45	*IC* 25	*IC* 413	*IC* 37	*IC* 37	*S* 445	*IC* 27	*IC* 37	*IC* 415	*IC* 47	*IC* 51	*S* 447	*S* 59	*S* 59	*IC* 49	*IC* 29	*S* 53	*IC* 265	269	*IC* 273
		⚒	Ⓐ	⚒		⚒					Ⓑ		Ⓑ			Ⓑ	⑥	Ⓑ			Ⓐ	⑦			Ⓑ			
		✕	✕	✕	K✕	✕◐	✕	✕	✕	✕	🍸	✕	✕	✕◧	✕	✕	🍸	✕	✕	✕◧	✕	✕	✕	✕◐	✕	★	★	★
	Helsinki **790** d.	0503	...	0623	...	0723	0824	0924	1103	1224	...	1324	1324	...	1424	...	...	1524	1624	...	1640h	1630	1724	1824	2024	1929	2029	2313
0	**Tampere** d.	0702	...	0802	...	0902	1002	1102	1302	1402	...	1502	1502	...	1602	...	...	1702	1802	...	1825	1825	1902	2002	2202	2305	2359	0230
75	Parkano d.	0744	...	|	...	|	|	1144	|	|	...	1545	1545	...	|	...	...	1735	|	...	1858	1858	|	2035	2235	0001	|	0323
159	Seinäjoki a.	0827	...	0918	...	1007	1105	1229	1416	1509	...	1625	1625	...	1713	...	...	1810	1905	...	1933	1933	2013	2117	2307	0056	0138	0411
159	Seinäjoki d.	0834	0837	0922	...	1011	1109	1234	1420	1513	...	1635	1635	1632	1725	...	...	1814	1909	1927	1937	1937	2016	2129	2310	0107	0155	0415
233	**Vaasa** a.	|	0927	|	...	1107	|	1324	1517	|	...	|	|	1728	|	...	...	1910	|	2017	|	|	2106	|	2359	|	|	|
292	Kokkola d.	0949	...	1040	...	...	1229	...	...	1616	...	1750	1750	...	1828	...	...	...	2014	...	2057	2057	...	2233	...	0238	0334	0551
371	Ylivieska d.	1030	...	1120	...	...	1309	...	...	1653	...	1830	1830	...	1905	...	...	...	2055	...	...	...	...	2310	...	0326	0424	0642
493	**Oulu** a.	1142	...	1216	...	...	1422	...	...	1748	...	1951	1951	...	2012	←	...	...	2215	...	...	...	...	0016	...	0444	0542	0806
493	**Oulu** d.	...	...	...	1223	...	1427	...	...	...	1800	...	→	...	...	2020	2020	...	...	...	...	...	...	...	...	0456	0630	0826
599	Kemi d.	...	...	...	1326	...	1531	...	...	...	1909	...	...	...	...	2126	2126	...	...	...	...	...	...	...	...	0602	0756	0936
808	**Kolari** a.	...	...	...	|	...	|	...	...	...	|	...	...	...	...	|	|	...	...	...	...	...	...	...	...	|	1055	|
713	**Rovaniemi** a.	...	...	...	1445	...	1646	...	...	...	2023	...	...	...	...	2245	2245	...	...	...	...	...	...	...	...	0720	...	1103
796	Kemijärvi a.	...	...	...	...	...	...	...	...	...	...	...	...	...	...	...	...	...	...	...	...	...	...	...	...	0850	...	...

	IC 40	*S* 52	*IC* 42	*S* 44	*IC* 20	*IC* 36	*S* 36	*IC* 22	*IC* 22	*S* 46	*IC* 46	*S* 444	*IC* 38	*IC* 48	*IC* 24		*IC* 50	*IC* 26	*IC* 54	*IC* 416	*S* 442	*S* 56	*IC* 710	*IC* 28	*S* 58	*IC* 266	*IC* 274	276
	Ⓐ	Ⓐ	⚒		⚒	Ⓐ	⑥		⚒	Ⓐ	⑥⑦	②–⑦		Ⓐ											⑤⑦			
	✕	✕	✕	✕●	✕	✕	✕	✕	✕	✕	✕	✕◧	✕	✕	✕		✕	✕	✕	🍸	✕◧	✕◧	K✕	✕	✕	★	★	★
Kemijärvi d.	...	...	...	...	...	...	...	...	...	...	...	...	...	...	...	...	...	...	...	...	...	...	...	...	...	...	1915	...
Rovaniemi d.	...	...	...	...	...	...	...	...	0515	...	...	...	...	...	0922	...	...	...	...	1310	...	...	1535	...	...	1745	2057	...
Kolari d.	...	...	...	...	...	...	...	...	|	...	...	...	...	...	|	...	...	...	...	|	...	...	|	...	...	|	|	1942
Kemi d.	...	...	...	...	...	...	...	...	0639	...	...	...	...	...	1040	...	...	...	...	1432	...	...	1659	...	...	1917	2228	2250
Oulu a.	...	...	...	...	...	...	...	...	0737	...	...	...	...	...	1140	...	...	...	...	1543	...	...	1800	...	...	2020	2349	0010
Oulu d.	...	...	...	...	0521	0620	...	0749	0749	...	...	...	0916	...	1155	...	...	1333	...	...	...	1611	...	1808	...	2055	2353	0057
Ylivieska d.	...	...	...	...	0643	0735	...	0848	0848	...	...	...	1030	...	1259	...	...	1441	...	...	...	1725	...	1904	...	2231	0109	0244
Kokkola d.	...	0517	...	...	0727	0815	0815	0927	0927	...	...	...	1117	...	1338	...	...	1521	...	...	...	1806	...	1941	...	2331	0157	0335
Vaasa d.	0444	|	0544	0644	|	|	|	|	|	1035	1035	1135	|	1247	|	...	1445	|	1625	...	1807	|	...	|	2031	|	|	|
Seinäjoki a.	0533	0626	0633	0733	0831	0922	0922	1031	1031	1124	1124	1223	1227	1343	1434	...	1534	1623	1714	...	1857	1921	...	2041	2124	0058	0345	0509
Seinäjoki d.	0537	...	0637	0737	0838	0926	0926	1035	1035	1128	1128	...	1235	1347	1438	...	1538	1628	1724	...	...	1928	...	2044	2130	0115	0356	0519
Parkano d.	0612	...	0712	0812	|	|	|	|	|	1204	1204	...	1314	|	|	...	1612	1709	|	...	...	2008	...	|	|	0209	|	|
Tampere a.	0656	...	0751	0850	0951	1051	1051	1151	1151	1251	1251	...	1355	1454	1551	...	1651	1751	1856	...	...	2051	...	2151	2249	0259	0535	0713
Helsinki **790** a.	0835	...	0935	1054	1135	1235	1235	1335	1335	1435	1435	...	1535	1635	1735	...	1835	1935	2035	...	...	2235	...	2335	0035	0627	0915	1045

K – From/to Kuopio (Table **798**).

h – 1630 on ⑦.

◐ – Train classification *S* on ⑥.
◧ – Train classification *IC* on ⑥.
● – Train classification *IC* on ⑦.

★ – Conveys 🛏, 🛋2 and ✕.

FINLAND

795 TURKU - TAMPERE - PIEKSÄMÄKI

km		IC 81		IC 905	IC 155		IC 909	IC 93		S 143	IC 143	IC 917	IC 145	IC 87		IC 921	IC 151	IC 923	IC 147	IC 927	S 89	IC 149	IC 931		IC 933
		Ⓐ	⚒	⚒						①–④	⑤–⑦			Ⓑ		⑤⑦	Ⓑ				Ⓑ				
		✕	2	🍷	✕◐	2	🍷	✕◐	2	✕	✕	🍷	✕	✕◧	2	🍷	✕	🍷	K🍷	🍷	✕	✕◐	🍷	2	🍷
	Turku satama .... d.	...	...	...	...	...	0810	...	...	...	...	...	...	...	...	...	...	...	...	1730	...	...	...	...	2020
0	**Turku** .... d.	...	...	0654	...	...	0905	...	...	...	...	1305	...	...	...	1456	...	1605	...	1805	...	...	2005	...	2100
66	Loimaa .... d.	...	...	0740	...	...	0944	...	...	...	...	1344	...	...	...	1542	...	1644	...	1844	...	...	2044	...	2142
86	Humppila .... d.	...	...	0753	...	...	0959	...	...	...	...	1357	...	...	...	1559	...	1659	...	1859	...	...	2057	...	2159
	Helsinki **790** .... d.	...	...	|	0703	...	|	0903	...	1024	1024	|	1303	1403	...	|	1503	|	1603	|	1803	1903	|	...	|
128	Toijala .... **790** d.	...	...	0819	0831	...	1025	1031	...	|	|	1425	1431	1531	...	1625	1631	1725	1731	1925	1931	2031	2123	...	2225
168	**Tampere** .... **790** a.	...	...	0842	0853	...	1047	1053	...	1158	1158	1447	1453	1553	...	1647	1653	1747	1753	1947	1953	2053	2145	...	2247
168	**Tampere** .... d.	0707	0806	...	0907	...	...	1107	1206	1212	1212	...	1507	1607	1616	...	1706	...	1807	...	2007	2107	...	2207	...
210	Orivesi .... d.	0731	0832	...	0932	...	...	1132	1232	1237	1237	...	1532	1632	1642	...	1730	...	1832	...	2032	2132	...	2233	...
	Vilppula .... d.	|	0907	...	|	...	...	|	1307	|	|	...	|	|	1717	...	|	...	|	...	|	|	...	2308	...
	Haapamäki .... a.	|	0925	...	|	1103	...	|	1325	|	|	...	|	|	1735	...	|	...	|	...	|	|	...	2326	...
266	Jämsä .... d.	0813	...	...	1012	|	...	1207	...	1312	1312	...	1607	1714	...	...	1805	...	1912	...	2108	2213	...	|	...
323	Jyväskylä .... **796** d.	0843	...	...	1041	1208	...	1240	...	1343	1343	...	1640	1744	...	...	1833	...	1941	...	2135	2243	...	0039	...
403	**Pieksämäki** .... **796** a.	...	...	...	1128	...	...	...	...	1430	1430	...	1729	...	...	...	...	...	2034	...	...	...	...	...	...

km		IC 904	IC 80		S 140	IC 140	IC 150	IC 910	IC 142		IC 94	IC 916	IC 920	IC 144	IC 922		IC 86	IC 924	S 146	IC 146	IC 928	IC 88		IC 148	IC 934
			Ⓐ	⚒	Ⓐ	⑥	⚒			⚒			⑤⑦						①–④	⑤–⑦		Ⓑ			Ⓑ
		🍷	✕	2	✕	✕	✕	🍷	K✕	2	✕●	🍷	🍷	✕◐	🍷	2	🍷◐	🍷	✕	✕	🍷	✕◧	2	✕	🍷
	Pieksämäki .... **796** d.	...	...	...	...	...	...	...	0830	...	...	...	...	1220	...	...	...	...	1523	1523	...	...	...	1811	...
	Jyväskylä .... **796** d.	...	0524	0505	0617	0617	0719	...	0919	...	1015	...	...	1315	...	...	1420	...	1612	1612	...	1810	...	1915	...
	Jämsä .... d.	...	0555	|	0648	0648	0748	...	0948	...	1051	...	...	1352	...	...	1451	...	1650	1650	...	1848	...	1951	...
0	**Haapamäki** .... d.	...	|	0619	|	|	|	...	|	1019	|	...	...	|	...	1419	|	...	|	|	...	|	1831	|	...
25	Vilppula .... d.	...	|	0640	|	|	|	...	|	1040	|	...	...	|	...	1440	|	...	|	|	...	|	1852	|	...
72	Orivesi .... d.	...	0630	0715	0725	0725	0825	...	1023	1115	1126	...	...	1427	...	1515	1526	...	1725	1725	...	1923	1927	2026	...
114	**Tampere** .... a.	...	0654	0740	0749	0749	0849	...	1049	1140	1150	...	...	1451	...	1540	1550	...	1749	1749	...	1949	1955	2050	...
	Tampere .... **790** d.	0550	0704	...	0804	0804	0900	0910	1104	...	1204	1210	1410	1504	1510	...	1604	1610	1804	1804	1810	2004	...	...	2112
	Toijala .... **790** d.	0614	0726	...	0826	0826	|	0935	1126	...	1226	1235	1435	1526	1535	...	1628	1635	1826	1826	1835	2026	...	...	2135
	Helsinki **790** .... a.	|	0854	...	0954	0954	1035	|	1254	...	1354	|	|	1654	|	...	1754	|	1954	1954	|	2154	...	...	|
	Humppila .... d.	0641	...	...	...	...	...	1000	...	...	...	1300	1500	...	1600	...	...	1700	...	...	1900	...	...	...	2200
	Loimaa .... d.	0655	...	...	...	...	...	1013	...	...	...	1313	1513	...	1613	...	...	1713	...	...	1915	...	...	...	2213
	Turku .... a.	0733	...	...	...	...	...	1050	...	...	...	1355	1550	...	1655	...	...	1750	...	...	1955	...	...	...	2250
	Turku satama .... a.	0752	...	...	...	...	...	...	...	...	...	...	...	...	1707	...	...	...	...	...	2005	...	...	...	...

K – To / from Kuopio (Table **798**). ◐ – Train classification *S* on ⑥. ● – Train classification *S* on ⑥⑦. ◧ – Train classification *S* on ⑤.

796 JOENSUU - PIEKSÄMÄKI - JYVÄSKYLÄ - SEINÄJOKI

km						IC 142			IC 148		
		2Ⓐ	2⚒	2⑦	2	✕	2	2	✕	2	
0	**Joensuu** .... d.	...	...	...	0608	...	...	1540	...	...	...
134	Varkaus .... d.	...	...	...	0745	...	...	1717	...	...	...
183	**Pieksämäki** .... **795** d.	...	...	...	0820	0830	...	1752	1811	...	...
263	**Jyväskylä** .... **795** d.	...	0505	0805	...	0919	1223	...	1915	1947	...
	Tampere **795** .... a.	...	|	|	...	1049	|	...	2050	|	...
341	Haapamäki .... d.	...	0611	0911	...	...	1330	...	...	2054	...
414	Alavus .... d.	0657	...	...	...	...	1430	...	...	2155	...
459	**Seinäjoki** .... d.	0729	...	...	...	...	1502	...	...	2227	...

		IC 155			S 143	IC 145			IC 147			
	2Ⓐ	✕◐	2	2	✕♤	✕	2⑥	2	✕	2Ⓑ		
Seinäjoki .... d.	0525	...	...	0930	...	...	...	1652	...	...	...	...
Alavus .... d.	0557	...	...	1001	...	...	...	1724	...	...	...	...
Haapamäki .... d.	...	...	...	1103	...	...	...	1827	...	...	...	...
Tampere **795** ..... d.	...	0907	...	|	1212	1507	...	|	1807	...	...	...
Jyväskylä ...... **795** d.	...	1041	...	1208	1343	1640	...	1932	1941	...	...	...
Pieksämäki .... **795** d.	...	1128	1142	...	1430	1729	1807	...	2034	2039	...	...
Varkaus .... d.	...	...	1219	...	...	...	1844	...	...	2114	...	...
Joensuu .... a.	...	...	1353	...	...	...	2018	...	...	2249	...	...

◐ – Train classification *S* on ⑥. ♤ – Train classification *IC* on ⑥⑦.

797 HELSINKI - KOUVOLA - JOENSUU - NURMES

km			S 61	IC 1			IC 63	IC 3		IC 65	IC 5			S 109	S 67	S 7	IC 9	S 9		IC 111	IC 11		IC 73	IC 115		
		⚒	⚒											⑤⑦		Ⓑ	Ⓑ	⑥	Ⓑ	Ⓑ						
		2	✕	✕	2	2	K✕	✕	2	K✕	✕	2	2	✕	K✕	✕	✕	✕	2	✕	✕	2	K✕	🍷◐	2	
0	**Helsinki** .... ▷ d.	...	0557	0657	...	...	0819	1019	...	1119	1319	...	...	1356	1419	1519	1619	1619	...	1719	1829	...	1919	2019	0010	...
3	Pasila .... ▷ d.	...	0603	0703	...	...	0825	1025	...	1125	1325	...	...	1402	1425	1525	1625	1625	...	1725	1835	...	1925	2025	0015	...
16	Tikkurila .... ▷ d.	...	0613	0714	...	...	0836	1036	...	1136	1336	...	...	1413	1436	1536	1636	1636	...	1736	1845	...	1936	2036	0024	...
104	**Lahti** .... ▷ d.	...	0651	0751	...	...	0913	1113	...	1216	1413	...	...	1451	1513	1613	1713	1713	...	1813	1923	...	2013	2113	0117	...
166	**Kouvola** .... a.	...	0719	0819	...	...	0941	1141	...	1245	1441	...	...	1519	1541	1641	1741	1741	...	1841	1951	...	2041	2141	0158	...
166	**Kouvola** .... d.	...	...	0823	...	...	...	1143	...	...	1443	...	...	...	...	1645	1744	1744	...	1844	2000	...	...	...	...	...
252	Lappeenranta ..... d.	...	...	0909	...	...	...	1223	...	...	1523	...	...	...	...	1723	1827	1827	...	1927	2046	...	...	...	...	...
288	Imatra .... d.	...	...	0940	...	...	...	1254	...	...	1554	...	...	...	...	1750	1858	1855	...	1955	2116	...	...	...	...	...
352	Parikkala .... d.	0730	...	1022	1026	...	...	1333	1337	...	1633	1637	...	...	...	|	1940	...	1944	...	2157	2202	...	...	...	...
411	Savonlinna ..... a.	0823	...	|	1119	...	...	|	1430	...	|	1730	...	...	...	|	|	...	2037	...	|	2255	...	...	...	...
482	**Joensuu** .... d.	...	...	1141	...	1154	...	1451	...	...	1751	...	1800	...	...	1938	2058	...	...	...	2315	...	...	...	...	...
586	Lieksa .... d.	...	...	...	...	1315	...	...	...	...	...	...	1921	...	...	...	...	...	...	...	...	...	...	...	...	...
642	**Nurmes** .... a.	...	...	...	...	1400	...	...	...	...	...	...	2006	...	...	...	...	...	...	...	...	...	...	...	...	...

			IC 102	IC 104		S 2	IC 62		IC 4	S 100	S 64	IC 64			IC 6		IC 8	S 114	IC 68	IC 10	S 72		IC 70		IC 12	
	Ⓐ	Ⓐ	⚒	⚒	①⑥	⚒	⚒	②–⑤	⚒	⑦	⚒	⑦						⑤⑦			Ⓑ					Ⓑ
	2	2	✕	✕	2	✕	K✕	2	✕	✕	K✕	K✕	2	2	✕	K✕	✕	✕	K✕	✕	✕	2	K✕	2	✕	2
Nurmes .... d.	...	...	...	...	...	...	...	...	...	...	...	...	0635	...	...	...	...	...	...	...	...	1540	...	...	...	...
Lieksa .... d.	...	...	...	...	...	...	...	...	...	...	...	...	0722	...	...	...	...	...	...	...	...	1626	...	...	...	...
Joensuu .... d.	...	...	...	...	...	0458	...	...	0558	...	...	...	0850	...	0900	...	1211	...	...	1511	...	1745	...	...	1813	...
Savonlinna ..... d.	...	...	...	...	0513	|	...	0622	|	...	...	...	...	0919	|	...	|	...	...	|	...	...	...	1837	|	2058
Parikkala .... d.	...	...	...	...	0606	0612	...	0715	0721	...	...	...	...	1012	1020	...	1331	...	...	1631	...	...	...	1930	1938	2151
Imatra .... d.	...	...	0502	0602	...	0656	...	...	0802	0802	...	...	...	...	1102	...	1409	...	...	1709	...	...	...	...	2020	...
Lappeenranta ..... d.	...	...	0531	0631	...	0721	...	...	0831	0831	...	...	...	...	1131	...	1436	...	...	1744	...	...	...	...	2049	...
Kouvola .... a.	...	...	0615	0715	...	0805	...	...	0915	0915	...	...	...	...	1215	...	1515	...	...	1858	...	...	...	...	2133	...
Kouvola .... d.	0450	0527	0619	0719	...	0809	0819	...	0919	0919	1119	1119	...	...	1219	1419	1519	1708	1719	1824	1915	...	2015	...	2136	...
Lahti .... ▷ d.	0529	0613	0649	0749	...	0840	0849	...	0949	0949	1149	1149	...	...	1249	1449	1549	1738	1749	1854	1947	...	2047	...	2210	...
Tikkurila .... ▷ a.	0619	0709	0725	0825	...	0915	0925	...	1025	1025	1225	1225	...	...	1325	1525	1625	1815	1825	1930	2026	...	2130	...	2247	...
Pasila .... ▷ a.	0628	0719	0734	0834	...	0924	0934	...	1034	1034	1234	1234	...	...	1334	1534	1634	1824	1834	1939	2035	...	2139	...	2257	...
Helsinki .... ▷ a.	0634	0725	0740	0840	...	0930	0940	...	1040	1040	1240	1240	...	...	1340	1540	1640	1829	1840	1945	2040	...	2145	...	2303	...

Local trains **LAHTI - KOUVOLA - KOTKA** and v.v. 2nd class only.

km		⚒			Ⓐ	⑥⑦						Ⓐ	⑥⑦			
	Lahti .... d.	...	...	...	0711	...	...	...	...	...	...	1500	...	...	...	1930
0	**Kouvola** .... d.	0600	0653	...	0800	0800	0900	...	1200	...	1527	1618	1618	1718	...	2037
51	**Kotka** .... a.	0644	0737	...	0844	0844	0944	...	1244	...	1611	1702	1702	1802	...	2121
52	**Kotka** satama.... a.	0647	0740	...	0847	0847	0947	...	1247	...	1614	1705	1705	1805	...	2124

	⚒						Ⓐ	⑥⑦				Ⓐ	⑥⑦			
Kotka satama.... d.	0654	0752	0855	...	...	1200	...	...	...	1513	1621	1712	1712	...	2033	2215
Kotka .... d.	0657	0755	0858	...	...	1203	...	...	...	1516	1624	1715	1715	...	2036	2218
Kouvola .... a.	0742	0840	0943	1030	...	1248	1317	1333	...	1601	1709	1800	1800	...	2121	2303
Lahti .... a.	0834	...	...	1113	...	...	1400	1417	...	1652	...	1845	...	...	...	...

Local trains **RIIHIMÄKI - LAHTI** and v.v. 2nd class only.
59 km. Journey time: 42 – 43 minutes.
From Riihimäki at 0435 Ⓐ, 0513 ⑥, 0613 ⚒, 0613 ⑦, 0701 Ⓐ, 0713 ⑥, 0813 and hourly until 2213.
From Lahti at 0535 ⚒, 0704 ⚒, 0804 and hourly until 2004; then 2204.

K – To / from stations in Table **798**.

◐ – Train classification *S* on ⑥.

▷ – Other local journeys Helsinki - Lahti and v.v. (2nd class only, journey 63 – 72 minutes):
From Helsinki at 0110 ⑥⑦, 0510 ⚒, 0635 Ⓐ, 0640 ⑥⑦, 0735 ⚒, 0835 ⚒, 0935 and hourly until 2135; then 2310.
From Lahti at 0024, 0614 ⑥⑦, 0713 Ⓐ, 0714 ⑥⑦, 0757 Ⓐ, 0814 ⑦, 0819 ⑥, 0919 and hourly until 2219; then 2314.

KOUVOLA - KUOPIO - OULU 798

km		IC711		S61 ⚒ ✕	IC63 ✕	IC713 🍷◐		IC65 ✕		S67 ✕	S67 Ⓑ ✕		S69 Ⓑ ✕	IC147 ✕		IC73 ✕	IC73 Ⓑ ✕
	Helsinki **797** d.	...	...	0557	0819	...	...	1119	...	1419	1419	...	1619	1603	...	1919	1919
0	**Kouvola** d.	...	...	0731	0950	...	...	1303	...	1550	1550	...	1748	|	...	2051	2051
113	Mikkeli d.	...	...	0843	1057	...	...	1406	...	1654	1654	...	1853	|	...	2154	2154
	Tampere **795** d.	...	...	|	|	...	...	|	...	|	|	...	|	1807	...	|	|
184	Pieksämäki d.	...	...	0923	1137	...	...	1445	...	1737	1737	...	1932	2036	...	2233	2233
273	**Kuopio** a.	...	...	1012	1229	...	...	1535	...	1830	1830	...	2024	2128	...	2325	2325
273	**Kuopio** d.	0719	...	...	...	1239	...	1539	...	1838	1838	...	2029	...	...	...	2329
358	Iisalmi d.	0823	...	...	...	1340	...	1642	...	1937	1937	...	2128	...	...	...	0033
441	**Kajaani** a.	0911	...	...	...	1428	...	1732	...	2032	2032	...	2219	...	...	...	0122
441	**Kajaani** d.	0917	...	...	...	1432	...	1736	...	...	2108	...	...	...	...	...	...
484	Paltamo d.	0952	...	...	...	1501	...	1807	...	...	2144	...	...	...	...	...	...
633	**Oulu** a.	1136	...	...	...	1639	...	1945	...	...	2321	...	...	...	...	...	...
	Rovaniemi **794** a.	1445	...	...	...	...	...	...	...	...	...	...	...	...	...	...	...

	IC62 ⚒ ✕		IC142 ✕	S64 ⚒ ✕	IC64 ⑦ ✕		S66 ⚒ ✕	S66 ✕		IC716 ⚒ 🍷	S716 ⑦ 🍷	IC68 ✕		S72 Ⓑ ✕	IC70 ✕		IC710 ✕
Rovaniemi **794** d.	...	...	...	...	...	...	...	...	...	...	...	...	...	...	...	...	1535
Oulu d.	...	...	...	...	...	...	0710	...	...	1003	1003	...	...	...	1224	...	1812
Paltamo d.	...	...	...	...	...	...	0847	...	...	1140	1140	...	...	...	1357	...	1959
Kajaani a.	...	...	...	...	...	...	0917	...	...	1210	1210	...	...	...	1430	...	2031
Kajaani d.	0340	...	...	0633	...	...	0923	0923	...	1217	1217	...	...	...	1433	...	2037
Iisalmi d.	0432	...	...	0725	...	...	1014	1014	...	1308	1308	...	...	...	1535	...	2128
Kuopio a.	0528	...	...	0821	...	...	1111	1111	...	1407	1407	...	...	...	1642	...	2224
Kuopio d.	0532	...	0738	0826	0826	...	1115	1115	...	...	...	1420	...	1614	1700	...	...
Pieksämäki d.	0628	...	0830	0920	0920	...	1213	1213	...	...	...	1520	...	1709	1804	...	...
Tampere **795** a.	|	...	1049	|	|	...	|	|	...	...	...	|	...	|	|	...	...
Mikkeli d.	0709	...	|	1000	1000	...	1253	1253	...	...	...	1600	...	1755	1851	...	...
Kouvola a.	0811	...	|	1109	1109	...	1403	1403	...	...	...	1711	...	1903	1952	...	...
Helsinki **797** a.	0940	...	1254	1240	1240	...	1540	1540	...	...	...	1840	...	2040	2145	...	...

IISALMI - YLIVIESKA

km		①–④ n 🚌	m 2	p 2	①–④ n 🚌
0	**Iisalmi** d.	0740	0830	1645	1645
99	Haapajärvi d.	0925	0937	1748	1830
154	**Ylivieska** a.	1015	1013	1824	1920

	①–④ n 🚌	p 2	q 2	①–④ n 🚌
Ylivieska d.	1240	1337	1912	2000
Haapajärvi d.	1330	1413	1948	2050
Iisalmi a.	1515	1518	2055	2235

m – ⚒ Dec. 16 - Jan. 7; ⑤⑥ from Jan. 13.
n – Not Dec. 19 - Jan. 5.
p – ⑤–⑦ (daily Dec. 16 - Jan. 8).
q – ⑤⑦ (Ⓑ Dec. 16 - Jan. 8).

◐ – Train classification *S* on ⑥.

LAPLAND 🚌 LINKS 799

Subject to alteration on and around public holiday dates

Narvik – Tromsø – Alta

Operator: Torghatten www.tromskortet.no

km		①–⑤	⑥	①–⑤	Ⓑ		Ⓑ			⑦	⑦
0	**Narvik** bus station d.	0535	...	...	...	1310	...	...	1545	...	1900
181	Nordkjosbotn balsfjord d.	0825	0825	1030	1320	1620	1620	...	1845	2035	2200
252	**Tromsø** Prostneset d.	0930	0930	1130	1425	1725	|	1600	1950	|	2306
241	Lyngseidet ferjekai d.	...	...	...	...	...	1730	1740	...	2145	...
465	**Alta** sentrum a.	...	...	...	...	...	...	2220	...	...	...

km		①–⑤		⑤	①–⑥	Ⓑ□		⑦	⑦	⑦
0	**Alta** sentrum d.	...	...	...	1055	...	...	1415	...	...
224	Lyngseidet ferjekai d.	...	...	...	1555	1550	...	1925	1925	...
293	**Tromsø** Prostneset d.	0620	1030	1240	1730	|	1600	2100	|	1930
	Nordkjosbotn balsfjord d.	0725	1135	1342	...	1657	1705	...	2032	2035
	Narvik bus station a.	1010	1420	...	...	...	1950	...	...	2320

Alta – Hammerfest – Karasjok – Kirkenes

Operator: Snelandia www.snelandia.no

km		①–⑤	①–⑤	⑦	⑦	①–⑤	①–⑤	Ⓑ		⑤⑦	①–⑤ ◧	⑦
0	**Alta** sentrum d.	0640	...	0900	...	...	1145	...	1430	1550	1700	1745
	Hammerfest d.	|	0700	|	1140	1225	|	1515	|	|	|	|
87	Skaidi d.	0819	0820	1045	1300	1325	1330	1615	1615	|	1830	1915
144	Hammerfest a.	|	|	|	|	|	|	|	|	|	1930	2015
112	Olderfjord d.	0845	0845	1115	1325	1400	1400	1655	1655	|	...	...
212	Honningsvåg ★ a.	1045	|	1315	|	|	1545	|	1835	|	...	...
	Nordkapp a.	1120**d**	|	1350**d**	|	|	...	|	...	|	...	...
174	Lakselv d.	...	0945	...	1440	1515	...	1755	...	|	...	...
248	Karasjok d.	...	|	...	|	1620	...	1900	...	1915	...	...
429	Tana bru d.	...	1400	...	1845	...	...	...	...	...	...	...
571	**Kirkenes** AMFI ♠ a.	...	1646	...	2103	...	...	...	...	...	...	...

	①–⑤	①–⑤		⑦	①–⑤	①–⑤	①–⑤	⑦	Ⓑ	Ⓑ	⑦	⑤⑦
Kirkenes AMFI ♠ d.	...	...	...	...	...	0605	...	...	...	...	1120	...
Tana bru d.	...	...	...	...	...	0920	...	...	...	...	1415	...
Karasjok d.	...	0615	...	...	...	|	...	...	...	1430	|	1930
Lakselv d.	...	0730	...	...	...	1305	...	...	...	1545	1755	|
Nordkapp d.	...	|	...	...	...	|	...	...	1420**d**	|	|	|
Honningsvåg ★ d.	0655	|	...	0920	...	|	1220	..	1510	|	|	|
Olderfjord d.	0845	0845	...	1115	...	1400	1400	...	1655	1655	1855	|
Hammerfest d.	|	|	...	|	1100	|	|	1340	|	|	|	|
Skaidi d.	0910	0915	...	1145	1220	1425	1430	1500	1725	1725	1915	|
Hammerfest a.	|	1015	...	|	|	1525	|	|	|	1825	2015	|
Alta sentrum a.	1037	...	...	1312	1340	...	1557	1620	1852	...	...	2245

Rovaniemi – Muonio – Tromsø

www.matkahuolto.fi

km	Operator:	*G* g	*E* k	*G* b
0	**Rovaniemi** bus station d.	0900	1140	1710
	Rovaniemi rail station d.	0840*	1125*	1720
153	Kittilä d.	1055	1335	1925
232	Muonio d.	1230	1505	2030
319	Karesuvanto d.	...	1630	...
428	Kilpisjärvi ⊡ FI d.	...	1805	...
535	Nordkjosbotn ⊕ NO d.	...	1825**n**	...
608	**Tromsø** Prostneset a.	...	1930**n**	...

	G c	*E* p	*G* g
Tromsø Prostneset d.	...	0725**n**	...
Nordkjosbotn ⊕ NO d.	...	0820**n**	...
Kilpisjärvi ⊡ FI d.	...	1050	...
Karesuvanto d.	...	1230	...
Muonio d.	0855	1400	1615
Kittilä d.	1010	1525	1740
Rovaniemi rail station a.	1210**x**	1720	1940**x**
Rovaniemi bus station a.	1215	1725	1945

Rovaniemi – Karasjok and Nordkapp

www.matkahuolto.fi

km	Operator:	*G* g		*E* k		*J* ①–⑤		*E*		*L* ⑦–④	
0	**Rovaniemi** bus station d.	0900	...	1145	...	1315	...	1720	...	2035	...
	Rovaniemi rail station d.	0840*	...	1125*	...	|	...	1705*	...	2045	...
130	Sodankylä d.	1100	...	1345	...	1505	...	1905	...	2230	...
305	Ivalo, MH FI d.	1325	...	1630**j**	...	...	...	2115	...	0030	...
346	Inari, K-market FI d.	...	...	1710	...	...	...	2150	...	...	...
461	Karasjok ⊖ NO a.	...	...	1745	...	...	...	...	...	...	...
536	Lakselv, Circle K a.	...	...	1855**r**	...	...	...	...	...	...	...
	Honningsvåg ◇ a.	...	...	2135**r**	...	...	...	...	...	...	...
735	**Nordkapp** a.	...	...	2215**r**	...	...	...	...	...	...	...

Operator:	*J* ①–⑤		*E* p		*L* ①–⑤		*E*		*G* g	
Nordkapp d.	...	...	...	...	...	...	0100**s**	...	...	...
Honningsvåg ◇ d.	...	...	...	...	...	...	0135**s**	...	...	...
Lakselv, Circle K d.	...	...	...	...	...	...	0510**s**	...	...	...
Karasjok ⊖ NO d.	...	...	...	...	...	...	0915	...	...	...
Inari, K-market FI d.	...	...	0720	...	...	...	1210	...	...	...
Ivalo, MH FI d.	...	...	0810	...	1210	...	1315**e**	...	1600	...
Sodankylä d.	0910	...	1030	...	1445**h**	...	1540	...	1830	...
Rovaniemi rail station a.	1105**x**	...	1210	...	1640•	...	1715	...	2015	...
Rovaniemi bus station a.	1110	...	1215	...	1635	...	1725	...	2020	...

Operator codes:

E – J M Eskelisen Lapin Linjat Oy.
G – OnniBus FLEX / Gold Line.
L – Liikenne O. Niemelä Oy.
J – Jbus Oy.

Time Zones:

FI – Finland (East European Time).
NO – Norway (Central European Time).

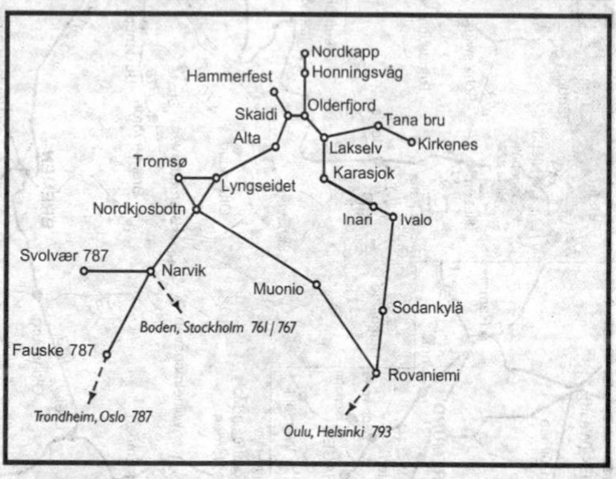

b – Until June 4.
c – Until June 5.
d – May 1 - Sept. 30.
e – Arrives at 1245.
g – Until May 1.
h – Arrives at 1425.
j – Arrives at 1600.
k – Until Mar. 9.
n – June 1 - Sept. 15.
p – Until Mar. 31.
r – June 27 - Aug. 12.
s – June 28 - Aug. 13.
x – Stops on request.

* – Serves Rovaniemi rail station before bus station.
• – Serves Rovaniemi rail station after bus station.
◧ – Runs 45 minutes later on ⑦.
□ – Runs 50 minutes earlier on ⑦.
◇ – Scandic Hotel, stops by request.
⊕ – Nordkjosbotn Gjestgiveri.
⊡ – Trekking centre (Retkeilykeskus).
⊖ – Karasjok, Scandic Hotel.
★ – Honningsvåg Nordkapphuset.
Honningsvåg - Nordkapp and v.v. *34 km*.
Journey: 35 minutes. Operates May 1 - Sept. 30.
From Honningsvåg at 1145¶.
From Nordkapp at 1430¶.

¶ – Service operated by North Cape Tours (from Honningsvåg tourist information office). Timings may vary. Special fares apply. www.northcapetours.com

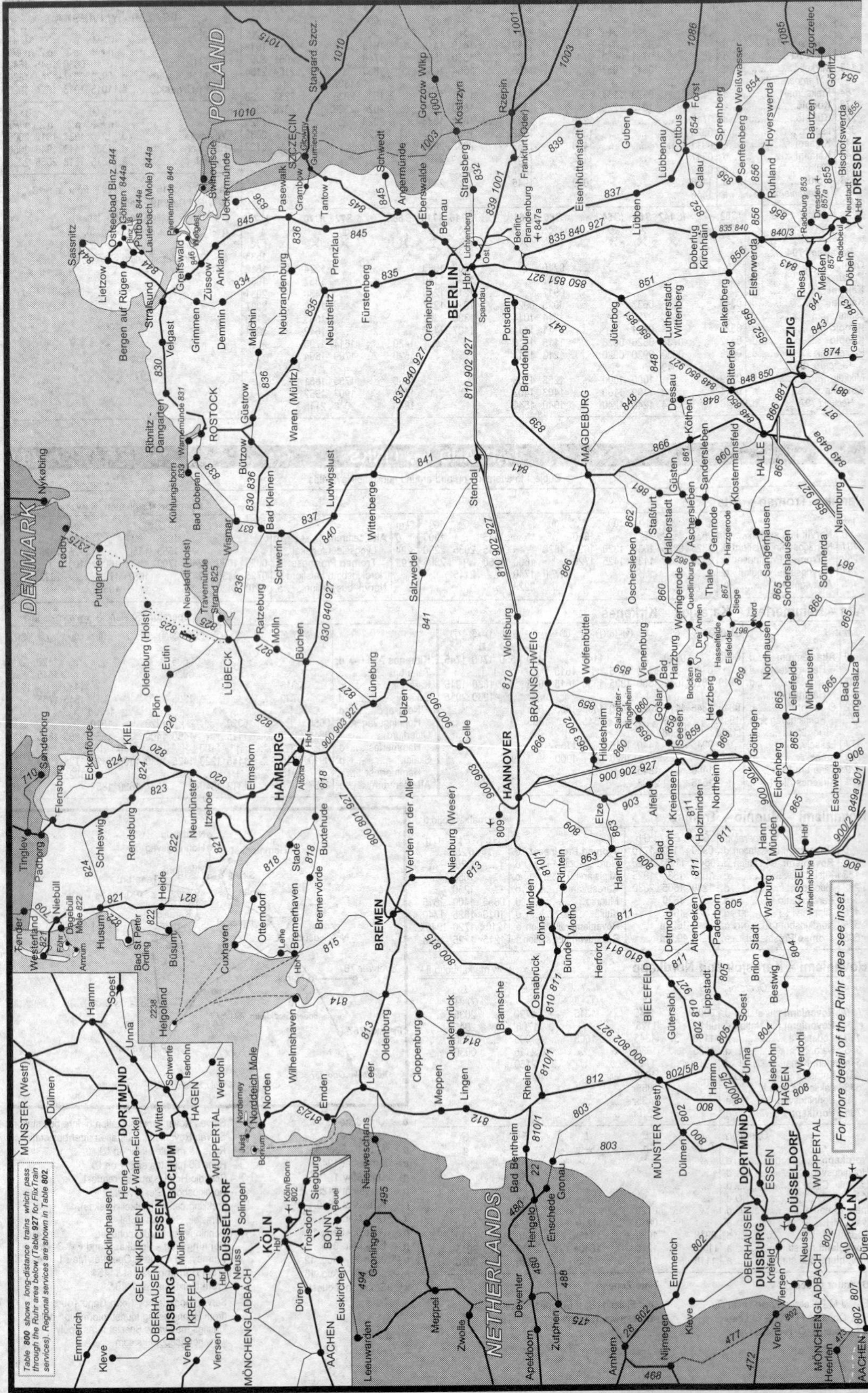
DENMARK
POLAND
NETHERLANDS
Table 800 shows long-distance trains which pass through the Ruhr area below (Table 927 for FlixTrain services). Regional services are shown in Table 802.
For more detail of the Ruhr area see inset
BERLIN
HAMBURG
HANNOVER
BREMEN
LEIPZIG
DRESDEN
MAGDEBURG
HALLE
KÖLN
DÜSSELDORF
DORTMUND
ESSEN
DUISBURG
BOCHUM
KIEL
LÜBECK
ROSTOCK
BRAUNSCHWEIG
KASSEL
BIELEFELD
MÜNSTER (Westf)
SZCZECIN
Frankfurt (Oder)
Göttingen
Osnabrück
Oldenburg
Cottbus
Potsdam
Wolfsburg
Stralsund
Schwerin
Wismar
Flensburg
Cuxhaven
Bremerhaven
Emden
Norden
Rheine
Paderborn
Hamm
AACHEN
MÖNCHENGLADBACH
WUPPERTAL
HAGEN
BONN

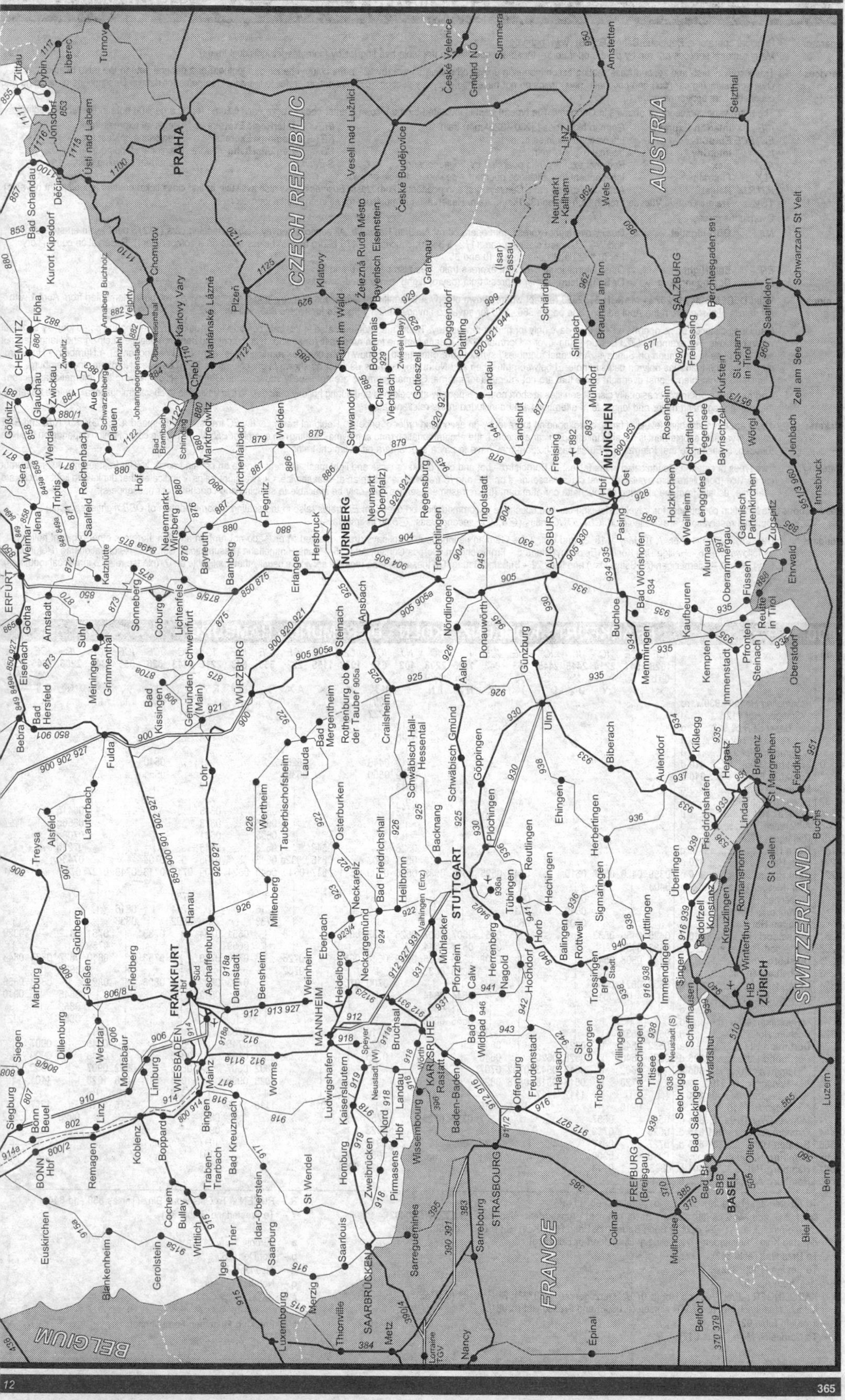
CZECH REPUBLIC
AUSTRIA
SWITZERLAND
FRANCE
BELGIUM
PRAHA
MÜNCHEN
NÜRNBERG
FRANKFURT
STUTTGART
MANNHEIM
KARLSRUHE
AUGSBURG
WÜRZBURG
SALZBURG
LINZ
STRASBOURG
SAARBRÜCKEN
BASEL
ZÜRICH
WIESBADEN
CHEMNITZ
ERFURT
BONN Hbf
Koblenz
Trier
Luxembourg
Metz
Nancy
Freiburg (Breisgau)
Ulm
Regensburg
Passau
Innsbruck
Bregenz
Lindau
Konstanz
Fulda
Kassel
Gießen
Marburg
Mainz
Heidelberg
Ingolstadt
Bamberg
Hof
Plzeň
Cheb
Karlovy Vary
Děčín
Liberec
Zittau
Mulhouse
Colmar
Belfort
Bern
Luzern
Olten

GERMANY

SEE MAP ON PAGES 364/5

Operator: Principal operator is Deutsche Bahn AG (DB) www.bahn.de
Many regional services are run by private operators – these are specified in the table heading (or by footnotes for individual trains).

Services: Trains convey first- and second-class seating accommodation unless otherwise shown (by '2' in the column heading, a footnote or a general note in the table heading). Overnight sleeping car (🛏) and couchette (▬) trains do not necessarily convey seating accommodation - refer to individual footnotes for details. Descriptions of sleeping and couchette cars appear on page 10.

There are various categories of trains in Germany. The type of train is indicated by the following letter codes above each column (or by a general note in the table heading):

ICE	**InterCity Express**	German high-speed (230–320 km/h) train.
EC / ECE	**EuroCity**	International express train.
IC	**InterCity**	Internal express train.
ALX	**alex**	Regional express train operated by *Vogtlandbahn*.
FLX	**Flixtrain**	Independent long-distance operator – see special table below.
RJ / RJX	**Railjet**	Austrian express train. Conveys first and economy (2nd) class. *Business class* also available to first class ticket holders (supplement payable).
TGV	**Train à Grande Vitesse**	French high-speed (320 km/h) train. Reservation compulsory for all international journeys.
IRE	**InterRegio Express**	Regional express train.
RE	**Regional Express**	Regional semi-fast train.
RB	**Regional Bahn**	Regional stopping train.
S-Bahn		Suburban stopping train.

Overnight services:

NJ	**ÖBB nightjet**	Quality overnight express train operated by Austrian Railways. All services convey *Deluxe* sleeping cars (1/2/3 berth) with en-suite shower and WC, standard sleeping cars (1/2/3 berth), couchettes (4/6 berth) and 2nd class seats (in a compartment). Reservation compulsory. For further details see pages 10 and 35.
EN	**EuroNight**	Other international overnight express train. See also pages 10 and 35.
D	**Durchgangszug**	Or **Schnellzug** – other express train (day or night); rarely used nowadays.

Timings: **Valid DECEMBER 11, 2022 - MARCH 31, 2023** (except where shown otherwise). Significant alterations to many long-distance services will be implemented from April 1 with full details published from the April edition. See pages 566–570 for advance timings April 1 - May 26 for Tables **850**, **900** and **902**.

Many long distance trains operate on selected days only for part of the journey. These are often indicated in the train composition footnote by showing the dated journey segment within brackets. For example '(12) Leipzig - Hannover (- Dortmund ⑦)' means that the train runs daily (or as shown in the column heading) between Leipzig and Hannover, but only continues to Dortmund on Sundays. Additional footnotes / symbols are often used to show more complex running dates, e.g. '(12) (München ⊡ -) Nürnberg - Hamburg' means that the train runs only on dates in note ⊡ between München and Nürnberg, but runs daily (or as shown in the column heading) between Nürnberg and Hamburg.
Please note that international overnight trains that are not intended for internal German journeys are not usually shown in the German section (refer to the International section).

Engineering work may occasionally disrupt services at short notice (especially at weekends and during holiday periods), so it is advisable to check timings locally before travelling. Information regarding major and longer-term alterations will be included in the relevant tables.

Tickets: There are three standard levels of fares, corresponding to travel by (in ascending order of price): ○ Regional trains. ○ *IC / EC* trains. ○ High-speed *ICE*, *TGV*, *RJ / RJX* and *ECE* trains. A variable supplement is payable for sleeping car and couchette accommodation (and sometimes seating) on overnight *EN / NJ* trains, the cost of which depends on the type required. Please note that Interrail and Eurail pass holders may have to pay a special fare on overnight trains.

Catering: Two types of catering are indicated in the tables: 🍷 Bordbistro – hot and cold drinks, snacks and light meals (at-seat service on certain trains); ✕ Bordrestaurant – full restaurant car service (bordbistro also available). First class passengers on *ICE* and *IC* trains benefit from an at-seat service. On overnight trains 🍷 indicates that drinks and light snacks are available, usually from the sleeping or couchette car attendant (the refreshment service may only be available to sleeping and couchette car passengers).

Reservations: Reservation compulsory for travel in sleeping car and couchette accommodation on overnight *EN* trains (also in the seating accommodation of *ÖBB nightjet* services). Optional reservations are available on *ICE / EC / IC* trains (€ 4,50 in second class, € 5,90 in first class).

Holidays: Dec. 25, 26, Jan. 1, Apr. 7, 10, May 1, 18, 29 and Oct. 3 are German national public holidays (trains marked ⚒ or Ⓐ do not run). In addition there are other regional holidays as follows: Jan. 6 – Heilige Drei Könige (Epiphany), June 8 – Fronleichnam (Corpus Christi), Aug. 15 – Mariä Himmelfahrt (Assumption), Oct. 31 – Reformationstag (Reformation Day), Nov. 1 – Allerheiligen (All Saints Day) and Nov. 22 – Buß und Bettag. On these days the regional service is usually that applicable on ⑦ (please refer to individual footnotes).

800 FRANKFURT - KOBLENZ - KÖLN - DORTMUND - HAMBURG

km		*ICE*	*ICE*	*IC*	*IC*	*IC*	*ICE*	*ICE*	*ICE*	*IC*	*NJ*	*ICE*	*ICE*	*ICE*	*ICE*	*ICE*	*ICE*	*IC*	*IC*	*ICE*	*ICE*	*ICE*	*IC*	*ICE*	*IC*
		1028	**541**	**2214**	**2445**	**2445**	**853**	**843**	**1108**	**2208**	**402**	**618**	**1038**	**1155**	**222**	**553**	**543**	**2212**	**2443**	**826**	**855**	**845**	**2206**	**1545**	**2306**
		Ⓑb	⚒		⚒		⚒		⑥h	④⑤														⚒	⑥h
		✕	✕	Y	D🍷	D🍷	✕	✕	N✕	FN	B	K✕	✕	✕	A✕	✕	✕	R🍷	D🍷	✕	✕	✕	N	G🍷	E
	München Hbf **904 930** d.	...	...	...	...	...	...	...	...	...	...	0001	...	...	...	...	...	...	...	...	...	...	...	...	...
	Stuttgart Hbf **912** d.	...	...	...	...	...	...	...	...	...	...	0222	...	...	...	...	...	...	...	...	...	...	...	...	...
	Basel SBB 🏛 **912** d.	...	...	...	...	...	...	...	...	...	2313	|	...	...	...	...	...	...	...	...	...	...	...	...	...
	Karlsruhe Hbf **912** d.	...	...	...	...	...	...	...	...	...	0120	|	...	...	...	...	...	...	...	...	...	...	...	...	...
	Nürnberg Hbf **920** d.	...	...	...	...	...	...	...	...	...	|	|	...	...	...	...	...	...	...	...	...	...	...	...	...
0	**Frankfurt** (Main) Hbf **910** d.	...	...	...	...	...	...	...	...	...	0313	0446	...	...	0526a	...	...	...	...	0540	...	...	...	...	...
11	**Frankfurt** Flugh. ✈ § **910** d.	...	...	...	...	...	...	...	...	...	0329	0500	...	...	0539a	...	...	...	...	0551	...	...	...	...	...
37	**Mainz** Hbf d.	...	...	...	...	...	...	...	...	...	0348	|	...	...	|	...	...	...	...	|	...	...	...	...	...
67	Bingen (Rhein) Hbf d.	...	...	...	...	...	...	...	...	...	|	|	...	...	|	...	...	...	...	|	...	...	...	...	...
128	**Koblenz** Hbf d.	...	...	...	...	...	...	...	...	...	0443	|	...	...	|	0543	...	0605	...	|	...	...	0641q	...	...
146	Andernach d.	...	...	...	...	...	...	...	...	...	|	|	...	...	|	0555	...	0618	...	|	...	...	0656q	...	...
167	Remagen d.	...	...	...	...	...	...	...	...	...	|	|	...	...	|	0608	...	0631	...	|	...	...	0708q	...	...
187	**Bonn** Hbf d.	...	...	...	...	...	...	...	...	...	0526	|	...	0548	|	0623	...	0645	...	|	...	...	0723q	...	...
221	**Köln** Hbf **910** a.	...	...	...	...	...	...	...	...	...	0553	0603	...	0615	0632a	0643	...	0705	...	0704	...	...	0743q	...	...
221	**Köln** Hbf **910** d.	0358	0426	0507	0510	...	0542	0525	0539	0539	0556	0609	0611	0617	0640	0648	0624	0709	0713	0713	0748	0727	0746	...	0801
222	**Köln** Messe/Deutz d.	0403	|	|	|	...	|	|	|	|	|	|	|	|	|	|	|	|	|	|	|	|	|	...	|
	Solingen Hbf d.	|	|	|	0529	...	0603	|	|	|	|	|	|	|	|	|	|	|	0730	|	|	|	|	...	|
	Wuppertal Hbf d.	|	|	|	0543	...	0616	|	|	|	|	|	|	|	|	0716	|	|	0744	|	0816	|	|	...	|
	Hagen Hbf d.	|	|	|	0601	...	0633	|	|	|	|	|	|	|	|	0733	|	|	0802	|	0833	|	|	...	|
261	**Düsseldorf** Hbf **910** d.	0425	0450	0533	|	...	|	0551	0607	0607	0625	0633	0638	|	0708	|	0651	0734	|	0738	|	0751	0812	...	0829
268	Düsseldorf Flughafen ✈ d.	0433	0458	|	|	...	|	0558	0614	0614	|	|	|	|	|	|	0659	|	|	|	|	0759	|	...	|
285	**Duisburg** Hbf d.	0443	0508	0547	|	...	|	0608	0625	0625	0639	0648	0651	|	0726	|	0710	0749	|	0753	|	0810	0827	0835	0843
293	Oberhausen Hbf d.	|	|	|	|	...	|	|	0633	0633	...	|	|	|	0732	|	|	|	|	|	|	|	0834	|	|
304	**Essen** Hbf d.	0500	0521	0600	|	...	|	0621	|	|	...	0700	0704	|	...	|	0723	0802	|	0805	|	0823	|	0848	0856
	Gelsenkirchen Hbf d.	|	|	0610	|	...	|	|	0644	0644	...	|	|	|	...	|	|	0812	|	...	|	|	0845	|	0910
	Wanne-Eickel Hbf d.	|	|	|	|	...	|	|	0651	0651	...	|	|	|	...	|	|	|	|	...	|	|	0852	|	|
	Recklinghausen Hbf d.	|	|	|	|	...	|	|	0658	0658	...	|	|	|	...	|	|	|	|	...	|	|	0859	|	0921
320	Bochum Hbf d.	0510	0531	|	|	...	|	0631	|	|	...	0710	|	|	...	|	0733	|	|	...	|	0833	|	|	|
338	**Dortmund** Hbf a.	0522	0543	|	0621	...	|	0643	|	|	...	0722	|	|	...	|	0745	|	0821	...	|	0845	|	0907	|
338	**Dortmund** Hbf **805** d.	0525	0546	|	0628	0628	|	0646	|	|	...	0725	|	|	...	|	0748	|	0828	...	|	0848	|	0909	|
	Hamm (Westf) **805** a.	|	0602	|	0643	0643	0702	0707	|	|	...	|	|	|	...	0802	0807	|	0843	...	0902	0907	|	0932	|
	Hannover Hbf **810** a.	|	0728	|	0818	0818	0828	0828	|	|	...	|	|	|	...	0928	0928	|	1018	...	1028	1028	|	1101	|
	Leipzig Hbf **849a 866** a.	|	|	|	1117	1117	|	|	|	|	...	|	|	|	...	|	|	|	1319	...	|	|	|	|	|
	Berlin Hbf **810** a.	|	0915	|	...	...	1015	1015	|	|	...	|	|	1015	...	1115	1115	|	...	...	1215	1215	|	1257	|
394	Münster (Westf) Hbf **801** d.	0556	...	0657	...	...	...	...	0727	0728	...	0757	|	...	...	...	...	0857	...	...	...	...	0928	...	0952
444	Osnabrück Hbf **801 815** d.	0623	...	0723	...	...	...	...	...	...	...	0823	|	...	...	...	...	0923	...	...	...	...	...	...	...
566	**Bremen** Hbf **801 815** d.	0727	...	0817	...	...	...	...	...	...	...	0917	|	...	...	...	...	1017	...	...	...	...	...	...	...
669	**Hamburg** Harburg a.	0818	...	0900	...	...	...	...	...	...	...	1000	|	...	...	...	...	1101	...	...	...	...	...	...	...
681	**Hamburg** Hbf **801** a.	0833r	...	0914	...	...	...	...	...	...	...	1014	0951	...	...	...	...	1116	...	...	...	...	...	...	...
688	**Hamburg** Altona a.	0849r	...	...	...	...	...	...	...	...	...	...	1005	...	...	...	...	...	...	...	...	...	...	...	...

A – To Amsterdam (Table **28**). Subject to alteration Feb. 11–24.
B – 🛏 1, 2 cl. and ▬ 2 cl. (Ⓡ) Zürich - Basel - Utrecht - Amsterdam. Also conveys (2) (*IC* **60402**). On mornings Feb. 11–24 calls at Bonn-**Beuel** (not Bonn Hbf), Köln Hbf a. 0557, d. 0602, then is diverted Köln - Amsterdam (not calling at Düsseldorf or Duisburg).
D – To Dresden (Table **842**).
E – To Emden (Table **812**).
F – ④⑤ from Apr. 6.
G – KAROLINGER – From Aachen Hbf (d. 0707), Herzogenrath (d. 0723), Rheydt Hbf (d. 0752), Mönchengladbach Hbf (d. 0758), Viersen (d. 0806) and Krefeld Hbf (d. 0818).
K – To Kiel (Table **820**).
N – To Norddeich Mole (Table **812**).
R – RÜGEN – To Ostseebad Binz (Tables **830** and **844**).
Y – To Westerland (Table **821**).

a – Ⓐ only.
b – Not Dec. 25.
h – Also Dec. 25.
q – Not Jan. 6 - Apr. 1.
r – ①④⑦ only.

§ – Frankfurt Flughafen Fernbahnhof.

FRANKFURT - KOBLENZ - KÖLN - DORTMUND - HAMBURG 800

	IC 2026	ICE 616	ICE 824 ⚒	ICE 1223 Ⓐ	ICE 1223 Ⓒ	ICE 555	ICE 545	ICE 220	ICE 757	IC 2310	IC 2441 ⊙	ICE 206	ICE 822	IC 2155	ICE 857	ICE 847	IC 2204	IC 5107	ICE 759	IC 2408	ICE 614	ICE 1022	ICE 820 ⚒	ICE 557	ICE 547
	U	✕	R✕	M✕	M✕	✕	✕	A✕	B✕	Y	D🍷	✕	✕	G	✕	✕	E	X	O✕	L	✕	✕	✕	✕	✕
*München Hbf **904 930*** d.	...	0332	...	...	...	...	...	...	...	...	...	...	0449e	...	...	...	...	...	...	...	0533	...	0553r	...	...
*Stuttgart Hbf **912*** d.	...	0551	...	...	...	...	...	...	...	...	...	...	│	...	...	...	...	...	...	...	0751	...	│	...	...
*Basel SBB 🚌 **912*** d.	...	│	...	...	...	...	...	...	...	...	...	0513	│	...	...	...	...	...	...	...	│	...	│	...	...
*Karlsruhe Hbf **912*** d.	...	│	...	...	...	...	...	...	...	...	...	0700	│	...	...	...	...	...	...	...	│	...	│	...	...
*Nürnberg Hbf **920*** d.	...	│	...	...	...	...	...	...	...	...	...	│	0600e	...	...	...	...	...	...	...	│	0528	0702	...	...
Frankfurt (Main) Hbf **910** d.	0542	│	0709	...	...	...	...	0728	...	...	0644	│	0809	...	...	...	...	...	...	...	│	0742	0909	...	...
Frankfurt Flughafen ✈ § **910** d.	0557	0706	0721	0710	...	...	...	0742	...	...	0657	0807	0821	...	...	...	...	...	...	...	0907	0758	0922	...	...
Mainz Hbf d.	0617	│	│	│	...	...	...	│	...	...	0717	│	│	...	...	...	...	...	...	...	│	0820	│	...	...
Bingen (Rhein) Hbf d.	0634	│	│	│	...	...	...	│	...	...	│	│	│	...	...	...	...	...	...	...	│	│	│	...	...
Koblenz Hbf d.	0713	│	│	│	...	...	...	│	...	...	0813	│	│	...	...	...	...	0841	...	...	│	0913	│	...	...
Andernach d.	│	│	│	│	...	...	...	│	...	...	│	│	│	...	...	...	...	0856	...	...	│	│	│	...	...
Remagen d.	│	│	│	│	...	...	...	│	...	...	│	│	│	...	...	...	...	0908	...	...	│	│	│	...	...
Bonn Hbf d.	0745	│	│	│	...	0822	...	│	...	...	0846	│	│	...	...	...	...	0923	...	...	│	0945	│	...	...
Köln Hbf **910** a.	0805	0804	│	│	...	0844	...	0833	...	...	0905	0904	│	...	...	...	...	0943	...	...	1004	1005	│	...	...
Köln Hbf **910** d.	0809	0811	│	│	...	0848	0828	0841	0844	0906	0909	0910	│	0917	0948	0925	0938	0946	0930	1004	1011	1009	│	1048g	1028z
Köln Messe/Deutz d.	│	│	0817	0824	...	│	│	│	│	│	│	│	0917	│	│	│	│	│	│	│	│	│	1018	│	│
Solingen Hbf d.	0829	│	│	│	...	│	│	│	│	│	│	0929	│	│	│	│	│	│	│	│	1029	│	│	│	│
Wuppertal Hbf d.	0843	│	│	│	...	0916	│	│	│	│	│	0943	│	│	1016	│	│	│	│	│	1043	│	│	1116	│
Hagen Hbf d.	0901	│	│	│	...	0933	│	│	│	│	│	1001	│	│	1033	│	│	│	│	│	1101	│	│	1133	│
Düsseldorf Hbf **910** d.	│	0834	0842	0848	...	│	0852	0908	0915	0929	0934	│	0938	0943	│	0951	1011	1012	1016v	1029	│	1033	1039	│	1052
Düsseldorf Flughafen ✈ d.	│	│	│	│	...	│	0900	│	│	│	│	│	│	0950	│	0959	│	...	│	│	│	│	│	│	1059
Duisburg Hbf d.	│	0848	│	0902	...	│	0910	0926	0930	0943	0948	│	0954	1003	│	1010	1026	...	1030	1043	│	1047	1053	│	1110
Oberhausen Hbf d.	│	│	│	│	0900	│	│	0932	│	│	│	│	│	│	│	│	1034	...	│	│	│	│	│	│	│
Essen Hbf d.	│	0900	0905	0917	0917	│	0923	...	│	0957	1000	│	1005	1017	│	1023	│	...	1047	1058	│	1100	1104	│	1123
Gelsenkirchen Hbf d.	│	│	...	│	│	│	│	...	0946	│	│	│	...	│	│	│	1045	...	│	│	│	│	...	│	│
Wanne-Eickel Hbf d.	│	│	...	│	│	│	│	...	│	│	│	│	...	│	│	│	1052	...	│	│	│	│	...	│	│
Recklinghausen Hbf d.	│	│	...	│	│	│	│	...	0957	│	│	│	...	│	│	│	1059	...	│	│	│	│	...	│	│
Bochum Hbf d.	│	0909	...	0928	0928	│	0934	...	│	│	1009	│	...	1030	│	1033	│	...	1058	│	│	1109	...	│	1133
Dortmund Hbf a.	0921	0922	...	0940	0940	│	0946	...	│	│	1021	1021	...	1042	│	1045	│	...	1109	│	1121	1121	...	│	1145
Dortmund Hbf **805** d.	...	0925	...	0942	0942	│	0948	...	│	│	1028	1025	...	1044	│	1048	│	...	1112	│	1125	...	...	│	1148
Hamm (Westf) **805** a.	...	│	...	1002	1002	1002	1007	...	│	│	1043	│	...	1101	1102	1107	│	...	1132	│	│	...	...	1202	1207
*Hannover Hbf **810*** a.	...	│	...	...	...	1128	1128	...	│	│	1218	│	...	...	1228	1228	│	...	1301	│	│	...	...	1328	1328
*Leipzig Hbf **849a 866*** a.	...	│	...	...	...	│	│	...	│	│	1517	│	...	...	│	│	│	...	│	│	│	...	...	...	│
*Berlin Hbf **810*** a.	...	│	...	...	...	1315	1315	...	│	│	...	│	...	...	1415	1415	│	...	1448	│	│	...	...	1515	1515
Münster (Westf) Hbf **801** d.	...	0957	...	...	...	...	...	...	1028	1047	...	1057	...	...	...	...	1128	...	...	1147	1157	...	...	...	...
Osnabrück Hbf **801 815** d.	...	1023	...	...	...	...	...	...	1051	│	...	1123	...	...	...	...	...	...	...	│	1223	...	...	...	...
Bremen Hbf **801 815** d.	...	1117	...	...	...	...	...	...	...	│	...	1217	...	...	...	...	...	...	...	│	1317	...	...	...	...
Hamburg Harburg a.	...	1200	...	...	...	...	...	...	...	1244	...	1300	...	...	...	...	...	...	...	│	1400	...	...	...	...
Hamburg Hbf **801** a.	...	1214	...	...	...	...	...	...	...	1258	...	1314	...	...	...	...	...	...	...	1350	1414	...	...	...	...
Hamburg Altona a.	...	1230	...	...	...	...	...	...	...	...	...	1330	...	...	...	...	...	...	...	...	1430	...	...	...	...

	ICE 128	ICE 1012 J	ICE 1110 ⑥h	IC 2010 ⑤	IC 2010 Ⓐ	ICE 202	IC 2049	ICE 728	ICE 859	ICE 849		IC 2202 Ⓐd	IC 2202	ICE 1020	ICE 612	ICE 1157	ICE 726	ICE 559	ICE 549	ICE 126	ICE 1010 ①–⑥	ICE 1055 ⑤⑦	ICE 200	IC 2047	ICE 724
	A✕	✕	N△ ✕	△	♠	✕	D🍷	✕	✕	✕		H	H	P✕	K✕	✕	✕	✕	✕	A✕	s✕	wT ✕	✕	D🍷	✕
*München Hbf **904 930*** d.	...	0626		...	...	...	...	0648	...	...	...	...	...	...	0728	...	0747	...	...	...	0828		...	...	0848
*Stuttgart Hbf **912*** d.	...	0839	0713	0714	0714	...	0736	│	...	...	...	...	...	...	0951	...	│	...	...	...	1037	...	...	0937	│
*Basel SBB 🚌 **912*** d.	...	│	│	│	│	0713	│	│	...	...	...	...	...	...	│	...	│	...	...	...	│	...	0913	│	│
*Karlsruhe Hbf **912*** d.	...	│	│	│	│	0900	│	│	...	...	...	...	...	...	│	...	│	...	...	...	│	...	1100	│	│
*Nürnberg Hbf **920*** d.	...	│	│	│	│	│	│	0800	...	...	...	...	...	0730	│	...	0859	...	...	...	│	...	│	│	1000
Frankfurt (Main) Hbf **910** d.	0926	│	│	│	│	│	*0842**	1009	...	...	...	...	...	0942	│	...	1109	...	...	1126	│	...	│	*1042**	1209
Frankfurt Flugh. ✈ § **910** d.	0942	0953	│	│	│	1007	*0856**	1021	...	...	...	...	...	0957	1107	...	1121	...	...	1142	1153	...	1207	*1056**	1223
Mainz Hbf d.	│	│	0849	0849	0849	│	0920	│	...	...	...	...	...	1020	│	...	│	...	...	│	│	...	│	1120	│
Bingen (Rhein) Hbf d.	│	│	0907	0907	0907	│	│	│	...	...	...	...	...	│	│	...	│	...	...	│	│	...	│	│	│
Koblenz Hbf d.	│	│	0944	0944	0944	│	1013	│	...	...	...	1044	...	1113	│	...	│	...	...	│	│	...	│	1213	│
Andernach d.	│	│	0956	0956	0956	│	│	│	...	...	...	1056	...	│	│	...	│	...	...	│	│	...	│	│	│
Remagen d.	│	│	1008	1008	1008	│	│	│	...	...	...	1108	...	│	│	...	│	...	...	│	│	...	│	│	│
Bonn Hbf d.	│	│	1022	1023	1023	│	1046	│	...	...	...	1123	...	1145	│	1149	│	1222	...	│	│	...	│	1246	│
Köln Hbf **910** a.	1033	│	1043	1043	1043	1104	1106	│	...	...	...	1143	...	1205	1205	1215	│	1243	...	1233	│	...	1304	1305	│
Köln Hbf **910** d.	1041	│	1046	1048	...	1111	1109	│	1148	1127z	...	1146	1146	1209	1211	1217	│	1248	1224z	1241	│	1236	1311	1309	│
Köln Messe/Deutz d.	│	1050j	│	│	...	│	│	1117	│	│	...	│	│	│	│	│	1217	│	│	│	1250	│	│	│	1317
Solingen Hbf d.	│	│	│	1109	...	│	1130	│	│	│	...	│	│	│	1229	│	│	│	│	│	│	│	│	1328	│
Wuppertal Hbf d.	│	│	│	1123	...	│	1143	│	1216	│	...	│	│	│	1243	│	│	1316	│	│	│	│	│	1343	│
Hagen Hbf d.	│	│	│	1142	...	│	1201	│	1233	│	...	│	│	│	1301	│	│	1333	│	│	│	│	│	1401	│
Düsseldorf Hbf **910** d.	1107	1112	1117	│	...	1134	│	1138	│	1153	...	1212	1212	1233	│	│	1241	│	1252	1308	1314	1318	1334	│	1338
Düsseldorf Flughafen ✈ d.	│	│	│	│	...	│	│	│	│	│	...	│	│	│	│	│	│	│	│	│	│	│	│	│	│
Duisburg Hbf d.	1126	1128	│	│	...	1147	│	1152	│	1208	...	1227	1227	1247	│	│	1255	│	1310	1326	1328	1334	1347	│	1352
Oberhausen Hbf d.	1132	│	│	│	...	│	│	│	│	│	...	1234	1234	│	│	│	│	│	│	1332	│	│	│	│	│
Essen Hbf d.	...	1141	│	│	...	1200	│	1203	│	1223	...	│	│	1300	│	│	1306	│	1323	...	1341	1347	1400	│	1403
Gelsenkirchen Hbf d.	...	│	1147	│	...	│	│	...	│	│	...	1244	1244	│	│	│	...	│	│	...	│	│	│	│	│
Wanne-Eickel Hbf d.	...	│	│	│	...	│	│	...	│	│	...	1251	1251	│	│	│	...	│	│	...	│	│	│	│	│
Recklinghausen Hbf d.	...	│	1158	│	...	│	│	...	│	│	...	1258	1258	│	│	│	...	│	│	...	│	│	│	│	│
Bochum Hbf d.	...	1153	│	│	...	1210	│	...	│	1233	...	│	│	│	│	│	...	│	1333	...	1353	│	1410	│	...
Dortmund Hbf a.	...	1205	│	1203	...	1222	1221	...	│	1245	...	│	│	│	1321	│	...	│	1345	...	1404	1408	1422	1421	...
Dortmund Hbf **805** d.	...	...	│	1210	...	1225	1228	...	│	1248	...	│	│	│	1325	│	...	│	1348	...	...	1410	1425	1428	...
Hamm (Westf) **805** a.	...	...	│	1231	...	│	1243	...	1302	1307	...	│	│	│	│	│	...	1402	1407	...	...	1432	│	1443	...
*Hannover Hbf **810*** a.	...	...	│	1401	...	│	1418	...	1428	1428	...	│	│	│	│	│	...	1528	1528	...	...	1601	│	1618	...
*Leipzig Hbf **849a 866*** a.	...	...	│	│	...	│	1717	...	│	│	...	│	│	│	│	│	...	│	│	...	...	│	│	1917	...
*Berlin Hbf **810*** a.	...	...	│	1557	...	│	...	...	1615	1615	...	│	│	│	│	1613	...	1715	1715	...	...	1747	│	...	...
Münster (Westf) Hbf **801** d.	...	...	1227	...	...	1257	...	...	...	...	...	1330	1330	1347	1357	...	...	...	...	...	...	...	1457	...	...
Osnabrück Hbf **801 815** d.	...	...	...	...	...	1323	...	...	...	...	...	1356	1356	│	1423	...	...	...	...	...	...	...	1523	...	...
Bremen Hbf **801 815** d.	...	...	...	...	...	1417	...	...	...	...	...	1457	1457	│	1517	...	...	...	...	...	...	...	1617	...	...
Hamburg Harburg a.	...	...	...	...	...	1500	...	...	...	...	...	...	...	1539	1600	...	...	...	...	...	...	...	1700	...	...
Hamburg Hbf **801** a.	...	...	...	...	...	1514	...	...	...	...	...	...	...	1550	1614	...	...	...	...	...	...	...	1714	...	...
Hamburg Altona a.	...	...	...	...	...	1530	...	...	...	...	...	...	...	1606	...	...	...	...	...	...	...	...	1730	...	...

A – To Amsterdam (Table **28**). Subject to alteration Feb. 11 – 24.
B – To Berlin (Table **810**).
D – To Dresden (Table **842**).
E – To Emden (Table **812**).
G – To Gera via Paderborn and Kassel (Tables **805** and **849a**).
H – OSTFRIESLAND – To Bremerhaven on dates in Table **815**.
J – ①②③④⑥ (not Dec. 26).
K – To Kiel (Table **820**).
L – To Lübeck Hbf (a. 1442).
M – To München via Paderborn and Kassel (Tables **805** and **900**).
N – To Norddeich Mole (Table **812**).
O – To Ostseebad Binz (Tables **844** and **845**).
P – From Passau via Regensburg (Table **920**).
R – From Würzburg on Ⓐ (Table **920**).
T – To Stralsund (Table **845**).
U – Daily to Jan. 6; Ⓑ from Jan. 8.
X – From Luxembourg (Table **915**).
Y – To Westerland (Table **821**).

d – Not Jan. 6 - Mar. 31.
e – ⚒ only.
g – 1045 on ⑤.
h – Also Dec. 25.
j – 1045 on ⑥.
r – From Feb. 11.
s – Also Dec. 25; not Dec. 26.
t – Ⓐ only.
v – Arrives 0957.
w – Also Dec. 26; not Dec. 25.
z – † only.

***** – Connecting *ICE* train (change trains at Mainz).
♠ – Ⓐ to Jan. 5. LORELEY. From Tübingen (Table **936**).
△ – Does not run Stuttgart - Köln Jan. 6 - Mar. 25.
⊙ – Also calls at Boppard Hbf (d. 0758).
§ – Frankfurt Flughafen Fernbahnhof.

800 FRANKFURT - KOBLENZ - KÖLN - DORTMUND - HAMBURG

	ICE 951	ICE 941	IC 2200	IC 1916	ICE 928	ICE 610	ICE 722	ICE 651	ICE 641	ICE 1059	ICE 124	ICE 918	ICE 108	IC 2045	ICE 720	IC 2157	ICE 953	ICE 943	IC 2006	IC 2004	IC 2014	ICE 1151	ICE 1030	ICE 228	ICE 518
				⑤⑦ r															⑥	⑦–④	⑤				
	✕	✕	N	■	P✕	✕	✕	✕	✕	B✕	A✕	✕	✕	D🍷	✕	♦	✕	✕	🍷♦	🍷♦	🍷♦	✕		E✕	✕
München Hbf **904 930** d.	...	...	...	...	...	0928	0951	...	...	...	...	1028y	...	...	1051	...	...	...	...	...	...	...	...	...	1128
Stuttgart Hbf **912** d.	...	...	...	1008	...	1151	|	...	...	...	...	1238	...	1137	|	...	...	...	...	...	1208	...	...	...	1351
Basel SBB 🚉 **912** d.	...	...	...	|	...	|	|	...	...	...	...	|	1113	|	|	...	...	...	...	...	|	...	...	...	|
Karlsruhe Hbf **912** d.	...	...	...	|	...	|	|	...	...	...	...	|	1300	|	|	...	...	...	1223	1223w	|	...	...	...	|
Nürnberg Hbf **920** d.	...	...	...	|	0930	|	1100	...	...	...	...	|	|	|	1159	...	...	...	|	|	|	...	...	1130	|
Frankfurt (Main) Hbf **910** d.	...	...	...	|	1142	|	1309	...	...	...	1326	|	|	*1242**	1409	...	...	...	|	|	|	...	...	1342	|
Frankfurt Flugh. ✈ § **910** d.	...	...	...	|	1157	1307	1321	...	...	...	1342	1353	1407	*1256**	1421	...	...	...	|	|	|	...	...	1358	1507
Mainz Hbf d.	...	...	...	1144	1220	|	|	...	...	...	|	|	|	1320	|	...	...	...	1344	1344w	1344	...	...	1420	|
Bingen (Rhein) Hbf d.	...	...	...	1207	|	|	|	...	...	...	|	|	|	|	|	...	...	...	1407	1407w	1407	...	...	|	|
Koblenz Hbf d.	...	...	...	1244	1313	|	|	...	...	...	|	|	|	1413	|	...	...	...	1444	1444	1444	...	...	1513	|
Andernach d.	...	...	...	1256	|	|	|	...	...	...	|	|	|	|	|	...	...	...	1456	1456	1456	...	...	|	|
Remagen d.	...	...	...	1308	|	|	|	...	...	...	|	|	|	|	|	...	...	...	1508	1508	1508	...	...	|	|
Bonn Hbf d.	...	...	...	1323	1345	|	|	1422	...	...	|	|	|	1446	|	...	...	...	1523	1523	1523	...	...	1545	|
Köln Hbf **910** a.	...	...	...	1343	1405	1404	|	1443	...	...	1432	|	1504	1505	|	...	...	...	1543	1543	1543	...	...	1605	1605
Köln Hbf **910** d.	1348	...	1343‡	1346	1409	1411	|	1448	...	1436	1441	|	1510	1509	|	1518	1548	...	1546	1546	1546	1537	1604	1609	1611
Köln Messe/Deutz d.	|	...	|	|	|	|	1417	|	...	|	|	1450	|	|	1517	|	|	...	|	|	|	|	|	|	|
Solingen Hbf d.	|	...	|	|	|	1429	|	|	...	|	|	|	|	1528	|	|	|	...	|	|	|	|	|	1628	|
Wuppertal Hbf d.	1416	...	|	|	|	1443	|	1515	...	|	|	|	|	1543	|	|	1615	...	|	|	|	|	|	1643	|
Hagen Hbf d.	1433	...	|	|	|	1501	|	1533	...	|	|	|	|	1602	|	|	1633	...	|	|	|	|	|	1701	|
Düsseldorf Hbf **910** d.	|	1352	1412‡	1414	1433	|	1438	|	1449	1509	1512	1517	1534	|	1538	1543	|	1549	1612	1612	1612	1616	1629	|	1634
Düsseldorf Flughafen ✈ d.	|	1400u	|	|	|	|	|	|	1458u	|	|	|	|	|	|	1550	|	1558u	|	|	|	|	|	|	|
Duisburg Hbf d.	|	1410	1427	1429	1447	|	1452	|	1509	1523	1527	1531	1547	|	1552	1602	|	1609	1626	1626	1626	1631	1643	|	1647
Oberhausen Hbf d.	|	|	1434	|	|	|	|	|	|	|	1533	|	|	|	|	|	|	|	1634	1634	1634	|	|	|	|
Essen Hbf d.	|	1423	|	1445	1500	|	1503	|	1522	1535	...	1543	1600	|	1603	1616	|	1622	|	|	|	1644	1656	|	1700
Gelsenkirchen Hbf d.	|	|	1445	|	|	|	...	|	|	1546	...	|	|	|	...	|	|	|	1645	1645	1645	|	|	|	|
Wanne-Eickel Hbf d.	|	|	1452	|	|	|	...	|	|	|	...	|	|	|	...	|	|	|	1652	1652	1652	|	|	|	|
Recklinghausen Hbf d.	|	|	1459	|	|	|	...	|	|	1558	...	|	|	|	...	|	|	|	|	1659	1659	|	|	|	|
Bochum Hbf d.	|	1433	|	1456	|	|	...	|	1533	|	...	1555	1610	|	...	1628	|	1633	|	|	|	1655	|	|	1709
Dortmund Hbf a.	|	1445	|	1508	|	1521	...	|	1545	|	...	1606	1622	1621	...	1639	|	1645	1708	|	|	1708	|	1721	1722
Dortmund Hbf **805** d.	|	1448	|	1510	|	1524	...	|	1547	|	...	...	1625	1628	...	1641	|	1647	...	|	|	1710	|	...	1725
Hamm (Westf) **805** a.	1502	1507	|	1531	|	|	...	1602	1607	|	...	...	|	1643	...	1701	1702	1707	...	|	|	1732	|	...	|
Hannover Hbf **810** a.	1628	1628	|	1701	|	|	...	1728	1728	|	...	...	|	1818	...	...	1828	1828	...	|	|	1901	|	...	|
Leipzig Hbf **849a 866** a.	|	|	|	|	|	|	...	|	|	|	...	...	|	2117	...	...	|	|	...	|	|	|	|	...	|
Berlin Hbf **810** a.	1815	1815	|	1857	|	|	...	1915	1915	|	...	...	|	...	...	...	2015	2015	...	|	|	2057	|	...	|
Münster (Westf) Hbf **801** d.	...	...	1528	...	1548	1557	...	...	...	1630	...	...	1657	...	...	...	...	...	...	1728	1728	...	|	...	1757
Osnabrück Hbf **801 815** d.	...	...	...	...	|	1623	...	...	...	1654	...	...	1723	...	...	...	...	...	...	...	...	...	|	...	1823
Bremen Hbf **801 815** d.	...	...	...	...	|	1717	...	...	...	...	...	...	1817	...	...	...	...	...	...	...	...	...	|	...	1917
Hamburg Harburg a.	...	...	...	...	1738	1800	...	...	...	...	...	...	1900	...	...	...	...	...	...	...	...	...	|	...	2001
Hamburg Hbf **801** a.	...	...	...	...	1753	1814	...	...	...	...	...	...	1914	...	...	...	...	...	...	...	...	...	1949	...	2014
Hamburg Altona a.	...	...	...	...	1805	1830	...	...	...	...	...	...	1930	...	...	...	...	...	...	...	...	...	2005	...	2030

	ICE 628	ICE 653	ICE 643	ICE 1153	IC 2012	EC 8	IC 2043	ICE 626	ICE 122	ICE 955	ICE 945	IC 2002	IC 2400	ICE 28	ICE 516	ICE 1159	ICE 624	ICE 655	ICE 645	ICE 914	IC 118	EC 6	ICE 204	ICE 104	IC 2041
											Ⓑ b												Ⓐ		†
	✕	✕	✕	✕	🍷♦	✕♦	🍷♦	✕	A✕	✕	✕	M	✕	E✕	✕	✕	✕	✕	✕	✕	♦	✕♦	✕	A✕	🍷
München Hbf **904 930** d.	1151	...	...	...	...	...	...	1250	...	...	...	...	...	...	1328	...	1351	...	...	1428	...	...	...	...	...
Stuttgart Hbf **912** d.	|	...	...	...	1312	...	...	|	...	...	...	...	...	...	1551	...	|	...	...	1637	1512	...	...	...	...
Basel SBB 🚉 **912** d.	|	...	...	...	|	1220	...	|	...	...	...	...	...	...	|	...	|	...	...	|	|	1427	1513	1513	...
Karlsruhe Hbf **912** d.	|	...	...	...	|	1412	...	|	...	...	...	...	...	...	|	...	|	...	...	|	|	1613	1700	1700	...
Nürnberg Hbf **920** d.	1257	...	...	...	|	|	...	1400	...	...	...	...	...	1330	|	...	1500	...	...	|	|	|	|	|	...
Frankfurt (Main) Hbf **910** d.	1509	...	...	...	|	*1442**	...	1609	1628	...	...	...	...	1542	|	...	1709	...	...	|	|	*1642**	|	|	...
Frankfurt Flugh. ✈ § **910** d.	1521	...	...	...	|	*1456**	...	1621	1642	...	...	...	...	1557	1707	...	1721	...	...	1753	|	*1656**	1807	1807	...
Mainz Hbf d.	|	...	...	...	1449	1520	...	|	|	...	...	...	...	1620	|	...	|	...	...	|	1649	1720	|	|	...
Bingen (Rhein) Hbf d.	|	...	...	...	1507	|	...	|	|	...	...	...	...	|	|	...	|	...	...	|	1707	|	|	|	...
Koblenz Hbf d.	|	...	...	...	1544	1613	...	|	|	...	...	...	...	1713	|	...	|	...	...	|	1744	1813	|	|	...
Andernach d.	|	...	...	...	1556	|	...	|	|	...	...	...	...	|	|	...	|	...	...	|	1756	|	|	|	...
Remagen d.	|	...	...	...	1608	|	...	|	|	...	...	...	...	|	|	...	|	...	...	|	1808	|	|	|	...
Bonn Hbf d.	|	...	...	...	1623	1645	...	|	|	...	...	...	...	1745	|	1748	|	1825j	...	|	1823	1845	|	|	...
Köln Hbf **910** a.	|	...	...	...	1643	1705	...	|	1733	...	...	...	...	1805	1804	1814	|	1845j	...	|	1842	1905	1904	1904	...
Köln Hbf **910** d.	|	1648	...	1638c	1646	1709	1713	|	1746	1748	...	1741	1804	1811	1811	1817	|	1848	...	|	1845	1909	1911	1914	1913
Köln Messe/Deutz d.	1617	|	...	|	|	|	|	1717	|	|	...	|	|	|	|	|	1819	|	...	1850	|	|	|	|	|
Solingen Hbf d.	|	|	...	|	|	|	1730	|	|	|	...	|	|	|	1829	|	|	|	...	|	|	|	1928	|	1930
Wuppertal Hbf d.	|	1715	...	|	|	|	1744	|	|	1816	...	|	|	|	1843	|	|	1916	...	|	|	|	1942	|	1944
Hagen Hbf d.	|	1733	...	|	|	|	1802	|	|	1833	...	|	|	|	1901	|	|	1933	...	|	|	|	2001	|	2002
Düsseldorf Hbf **910** d.	1641	|	1649	1709	1714	1733	|	1738	1811	|	1751	1813g	1829	1834	|	|	1842	|	1851	1914	1910	1933	|	1938	|
Düsseldorf Flughafen ✈ d.	|	|	1658u	|	|	|	|	|	|	|	1759u	|	|	|	|	|	|	|	1859u	|	1921	|	|	|	|
Duisburg Hbf d.	1655	|	1709	1723	1732	1747	|	1752	1826	|	1810	1829	1844	1848	|	|	1900	|	1910	1929	1933	1947	|	1951	|
Oberhausen Hbf d.	|	|	|	|	|	|	|	|	1832	|	|	1836	|	|	|	|	|	|	|	|	|	|	|	1957	|
Essen Hbf d.	1706	|	1722	1737	1745	1802	|	1816f	...	|	1823	|	1857	1900	|	|	1917	|	1923	1941	1947	2000	|	...	|
Gelsenkirchen Hbf d.	...	|	|	|	|	1811	|	|	...	|	|	1846	|	|	|	|	|	|	|	|	|	|	|	...	|
Wanne-Eickel Hbf d.	...	|	|	|	|	|	|	|	...	|	|	|	|	|	|	|	|	|	|	|	|	|	|	...	|
Recklinghausen Hbf d.	...	|	|	|	|	|	|	|	...	|	|	1858	|	|	|	|	|	|	|	|	|	|	|	...	|
Bochum Hbf d.	...	|	1733	1751	1756	|	|	1828	...	|	1833	|	|	1910	|	|	1928	|	1933	1952	1956	2009	|	...	|
Dortmund Hbf a.	...	|	1745	1803	...	|	1821	1841	...	|	1845	|	|	1922	1921	|	1939	|	1945	2005	...	2022	2021	...	2021
Dortmund Hbf **805** d.	...	|	1747	1806	...	|	1828	...	...	|	1848	|	|	...	1925	|	...	|	1948	...	...	2025	...	...	2028
Hamm (Westf) **805** a.	...	1802	1807	1831	...	|	1843	...	...	1902	1907	|	|	...	|	|	...	2002	2007	...	...	|	...	...	2043
Hannover Hbf **810** a.	...	1928	1928	2001	...	|	2018	...	...	2028	2028	|	|	...	|	|	...	2128	2128	...	...	|	...	...	2218
Leipzig Hbf **849a 866** a.	...	|	|	|	...	|	2317r	...	...	|	|	|	|	...	|	|	...	|	|	...	...	|	...	...	...
Berlin Hbf **810** a.	...	2115	2115	2157	...	|	...	...	...	2227	2227	|	|	...	|	2221	...	2311	2311	...	...	|	...	...	...
Münster (Westf) Hbf **801** d.	...	...	...	...	...	1857	...	...	...	...	...	1928	1947	...	1957	...	...	...	...	...	...	2057	...	...	...
Osnabrück Hbf **801 815** d.	...	...	...	...	...	1923	...	...	...	...	...	...	|	...	2023	...	...	...	...	...	...	2123	...	...	...
Bremen Hbf **801 815** d.	...	...	...	...	...	2017	...	...	...	...	...	...	|	...	2117	...	...	...	...	...	...	2219	...	...	...
Hamburg Harburg a.	...	...	...	...	...	2100	...	...	...	...	...	...	|	...	2200	...	...	...	...	...	...	2302	...	...	...
Hamburg Hbf **801** a.	...	...	...	...	...	2114	...	...	...	...	...	...	2150	...	2214	...	...	...	...	...	...	2316	...	...	...
Hamburg Altona a.	...	...	...	...	...	2132	...	...	...	...	...	...	2205	...	2230	...	...	...	...	...	...	2332	...	...	...

♦ – **NOTES** (LISTED BY TRAIN NUMBER)

6 – [12] ✕ Interlaken - Bern - Basel - Hamburg.

8 – [12] ✕ Zürich - Basel - Hamburg.

118 – BODENSEE – [12] Innsbruck - Lindau - Ulm - Stuttgart - Bochum.

2004 – ⑦–④ (not Dec. 25). SCHWARZWALD – [12] 🍷 (Konstanz - Karlsruhe ⑦ **w** -) Koblenz - Emden. Does not run Konstanz - Koblenz - Köln Jan. 8 - Mar. 30.

2006 – ⑥ (also Dec. 25; not Jan. 7 - Apr. 1). SCHWARZWALD – [12] 🍷 Konstanz - Karlsruhe - Dortmund.

2012 – Not Jan. 6 - Apr. 1. ALLGÄU – [12] 🍷 Oberstdorf - Ulm - Stuttgart - Bochum.

2014 – [12] 🍷 Stuttgart - Mannheim - Münster - Emden.

2043 – [12] Köln - Hannover (- Magdeburg Ⓑ **b**) (- Leipzig ⑤⑦ **r**).

2157 – [12] Köln - Paderborn - Kassel - Erfurt (- Gera Ⓑ **b**).

A – To Amsterdam (Table **28**). Subject to alteration Feb. 11–24.
B – To Berlin (Table **810**).
D – To Dresden (Table **842**).
E – From Wien (Tables **920/950**).
M – To Emden (Table **812**).
N – To Norddeich Mole (Table **812**).

P – From Passau via Regensburg (Table **920**).

b – Not Dec. 25.
c – Not Mar. 31.
f – Arrives 1803.
g – Arrives 1805.
j – ①②③④⑥ (also Dec. 25; not Dec. 26).
r – ⑤⑦ (also Dec. 26; not Dec. 25).
u – Calls to pick up only.
w – ⑦ (also Dec. 26; not Dec. 25).
y – 1030 on ⑥⑦.

* – Connecting *ICE* train (change trains at Mainz).
‡ – On ⑤⑦ (also Dec. 26; not Dec. 25) Köln d. 1337, Düsseldorf d. 1409.
■ – Runs as *ICE* **1116** (✕) on ⑦ (also Dec. 26). Does not run Stuttgart - Köln on ⑦ Jan. 8 - Mar. 26.
§ – Frankfurt Flughafen Fernbahnhof.

FRANKFURT - KOBLENZ - KÖLN - DORTMUND - HAMBURG 800

	ICE 622	ICE 957	ICE 947	EC 114	ICE 812	ICE 26	ICE 514	ICE 620	ICE 120	ICE 912	ICE 657	ICE 1549	IC 1941	ICE 528	ICE 1222	ICE 512	ICE 526	IC 1910	IC 2343	ICE 100	ICE 949	ICE 524	ICE 22	ICE 522	ICE 920
	✕	⑤⑦ y✕	✕	🍷♦	①–④ m✕	E✕	✕	✕	✕♦	✕	⑤⑦ L✕	✕	d	G✕	✕	✕	✕	⑦w 🍷	🍷	Ⓑb ✕			s E✕	⑦–④ T	
München Hbf **904 930** d.	1451	...	...	1347	...	...	1528	1551	...	1627	...	...	...	1649	1618	1728	1752r	1614	...	...	...	1851	...	1948	...
Stuttgart Hbf **912** d.		...	...	1607	...	...	1751		...	1838	...	1737	...			1951		1905	1915j	...	...		...		...
Basel SBB 🚉 **912** d.		...	...		...	...			...		...		...							1913	...		...		...
Karlsruhe Hbf **912** d.		...	...		...	...			...		...		...							2100	...		...		...
Nürnberg Hbf **920** d.	1600	...	...		...	1531		1657	...		...		...	1800	1736		1903				...	2000	1931	2057	...
Frankfurt (Main) Hbf **910** d.	1809	...	...		1816	1742		1909	1928		...	*1842**	...	2009	1942		2109		*2042**		...	2209	2145	2309	2324
Frankfurt Flugh. ✈ § **910** d.	1821	...	...		1831	1758	1907	1921	1942	1953	...	*1856**	...	2023	1957	2106	2121		*2058**	2207	...	2221	2158	2322	2339
Mainz Hbf d.		...	...	1744		1820					...	1920	...		2020			2049	2120		...		2220	2350	0001
Bingen (Rhein) Hbf d.		...	...	1807							...		...					2107			...				0018
Koblenz Hbf d.		...	...	1844		1913					...	2013	...		2113			2144	2213		...		2313	0043	0058
Andernach d.		...	...	1856							...		...					2156			...				
Remagen d.		...	...	1908							...		...					2208			...				0122
Bonn Hbf d.		...	...	1923		1945					...	2045	...		2145			2223	2245		2248		2345	0122	0138
Köln Hbf **910** a.		...	...	1943		2005	2004		2033		...	2105	...		2205	2206		2243	2305	2307	2309		0005	0150	0205
Köln Hbf **910** d.		1948	1928**q**	1946		2009	2011		2041		2048	2109	2113		2210	2212		2246	...	2313	2315		0013	...	0209
Köln Messe/Deutz d.	1923				1951			2027		2050				2116			2217		...			2338		...	
Solingen Hbf d.							2029						2130		2229				...	2332				...	
Wuppertal Hbf d.		2016			2017		2043				2116		2144		2244				...	2346				...	
Hagen Hbf d.		2033			2036		2101				2133		2202		2301				...	0003				...	
Düsseldorf Hbf **910** d.	1946		1952	2010		2033		2049	2108	2113		2133		2137		2235	2239	2309	...		2338	2359	0036	...	0233
Düsseldorf Flughafen ✈ d.			2000																...		2346			...	0240
Duisburg Hbf d.	2003		2010	2027		2046		2104	2126	2128		2147		2151		2249	2252	2323	...		2357	0013	0049	...	0251
Oberhausen Hbf d.									2132										...					...	
Essen Hbf d.	2017		2023	2043		2059		2117	...	2142		2159		2204		2308**h**	2304**p**	2340	...		0009	0026	0102	...	0306
Gelsenkirchen Hbf d.									...							2320			...					...	
Wanne-Eickel Hbf d.									...										...					...	
Recklinghausen Hbf d.									...							2335			...					...	
Bochum Hbf d.	2029		2033	2053		2109		2128	...	2153		2209		2214			2314	2350	...		0019	0035	0112	...	0316
Dortmund Hbf a.	2042		2045	2104	2107	2121	2121	2140	...	2205		2222	2221	2227	2321		2326	0002	...	0024	0032	0048	0125	...	0328
Dortmund Hbf **805** d.	...		2048	...	...	...	2125	2144**k**	...	...		...	2226	...	...		...	...	...	...	0034	...	...	...	0332
Hamm (Westf) **805** a.	...	2102	2107	...	...	...		2206**k**	...	...	2202	...	2243	...	...		...	...	...	...	0049	...	...	...	0350
Hannover Hbf **810** a.	...	2228	2228	...	...	...		...	...	...	2328	...	0018	...	...		...	...	...	...	0223	...	...	...	
Leipzig Hbf **849a 866** a.	...			...	...	...		...	...	...		...	...	...	...		...	...	...	...		...	...	...	
Berlin Hbf **810** a.	...	0014	0014	...	...	...		...	...	...	0114	...	...	...	...		...	...	...	...	0535	...	...	...	
Münster (Westf) Hbf **801** d.	...	...	...	...	...	...	2157	...	...	...	...	...	...	...	...	0002	...	...	...	...	...	...	...	...	0415
Osnabrück Hbf **801 815** d.	...	...	...	...	...	...	2223	...	...	...	...	...	...	...	...	...	...	...	...	...	...	...	...	...	0450
Bremen Hbf **801 815** d.	...	...	...	...	...	...	2317	...	...	...	...	...	...	...	...	...	...	...	...	...	...	...	...	...	0553
Hamburg Harburg a.	...	...	...	...	...	...	0001	...	...	...	...	...	...	...	...	...	...	...	...	...	...	...	...	...	0637
Hamburg Hbf **801** a.	...	...	...	...	...	...	0015	...	...	...	...	...	...	...	...	...	...	...	...	...	...	...	...	...	0650
Hamburg Altona a.	...	...	...	...	...	...	0031	...	...	...	...	...	...	...	...	...	...	...	...	...	...	...	...	...	0706

	ICE 523	ICE 23	ICE 525	ICE 101	ICE 1548	ICE 948	ICE 913	IC 2003	ICE 813	ICE 527	ICE 1621	ICE 513	ICE 815	EC 115	ICE 529	IC 2040	EC 7	ICE 915	IC 119	ICE 121	ICE 646	ICE 656	ICE 621	ICE 1158	ICE 1031
	⚒ ✕	t E✕	✕	⚒ ✕	✕		⚒ ✕	Ⓐ	Ⓐ ✕	✕	✕	✕	Ⓐ ✕	🍷♦	b G✕	🍷	✕♦	✕	♦	A✕	⚒ ✕	⚒ ✕	✕	✕	①–④ m
Hamburg Altona d.	...	...	...	...	...	...	...	...	...	...	...	...	...	...	...	...	0421	...	...	...	...	...	...	...	0555
Hamburg Hbf **801** d.	...	...	...	...	...	...	...	...	...	...	...	...	...	...	...	...	0437	...	...	...	...	...	...	...	0611
Hamburg Harburg d.	...	...	...	...	...	...	...	...	...	...	...	...	...	...	...	...	0449	...	...	...	...	...	...	...	
Bremen Hbf **801 815** d.	...	...	...	...	...	...	...	...	...	...	...	...	...	...	...	...	0540	...	...	...	...	...	...	...	
Osnabrück Hbf **801 815** d.	...	...	...	...	...	...	...	...	...	...	...	...	...	...	...	...	0636	...	...	...	...	...	...	...	
Münster (Westf) Hbf **801** d.	...	...	...	...	0502	...	...	...	...	...	...	0602	...	0629	...	...	0702	...	...	...	...	...	...	...	
Berlin Hbf **810** d.	...	...	...	...		0022	...	...	...	...	...		...		...	...		...	...	...	0425	0425	...	0533	
Leipzig Hbf **849a 866** d.	...	...	...	...			...	...	...	...	...		...		...	...		...	...	...			...		
Hannover Hbf **810** d.	...	...	...	...		0340	...	...	...	...	...		...		...	0540		...	...	...	0621	0621	...		
Hamm (Westf) **805** d.	...	...	...	...		0512	...	...	...	...	...		...		...	0716		...	...	...	0751	0754	...		
Dortmund Hbf **805** a.	...	...	...	...	0533		...	...	...	...	...	0633	...		...	0734		...	...	...	0810		...		
Dortmund Hbf d.	0401	0431	0522	0528	0536		0547	0549	0558	0622	0629	0636	0649		0722	0736		0756	0751	...	0813		...		
Bochum Hbf d.	0415	0444	0535		0547		0603			0636		0648	0704		0736					...	0825		...		
Recklinghausen Hbf d.														0701						...			...		
Wanne-Eickel Hbf d.								0609						0709						...			...		
Gelsenkirchen Hbf d.								0614						0715			0743			...			...		
Essen Hbf d.	0427	0457	0549		0600		0615			0651		0700	0715		0750		0757	0815		...	0837		0839		0856
Oberhausen Hbf d.								0626						0726						0826					
Duisburg Hbf d.	0440	0510	0603				0628	0633		0704			0728	0734	0803		0810	0827		0834	0851		0855		
Düsseldorf Flughafen ✈ d.																									
Düsseldorf Hbf **910** d.	0454	0524	0617		0624		0645	0648		0718		0724	0745	0749	0818		0824	0843		0851	0904		0910		0920
Hagen Hbf d.				0557		0550			0619		0657					0758			0815		...	0823			
Wuppertal Hbf d.				0615		0609			0636		0714					0814			0834		...	0840			
Solingen Hbf d.				0627					0648		0727					0826					...				
Köln Messe/Deutz a.	0518		0642				0709			0742			0809		0842			0909			...		0933		
Köln Hbf **910** a.		0550		0646	0650	0657		0715	0708		0747	0749		0815		0846	0850		0912	0919	...	0909		0941	0946
Köln Hbf **910** d.		0553		0655	0653	...		0717**e**	0719		0753	0755		0817		...	0853		0917	0928	...	...		0945	...
Bonn Hbf d.		0614			0714	...		0737**e**			0814			0837		...	0914		0938		...	...		1016	...
Remagen d.						...		0751**e**						0852		...			0952		...	...		...	...
Andernach d.						...		0804**e**						0904		...			1004		...	...		...	...
Koblenz Hbf d.		0648			0748	...		0816**e**			0848			0918		...	0948		1018		...	...		...	...
Bingen (Rhein) Hbf d.						...		...						0952		...			1052		...	...		...	...
Mainz Hbf a.		0738			0839	...		...			0939			1015		...	1039		1111		...	...		...	...
Frankfurt Flugh. ✈ § **910** a.	0634	0759	0733	0750	*0859**	...	0807	...	0826	0833	0959	0850	0926		0933	...	*1059**	1007		1017	...	...	1033	...	...
Frankfurt (Main) Hbf **910** a.	0648	0813	0748		*0913**	...		...	0841	0848	1013		0941		0948	...	*1113**			1031	...	...	1048	...	...
Nürnberg Hbf **920** a.	0900	1028	0958			...		...	...	1100	1224		...		1158	...				...	...	...	1259	...	...
Karlsruhe Hbf **912** a.		...		0858		...		...	...				...			...	1147			...	...	...		...	...
Basel SBB 🚉 **912** a.		...		1047		...		...	...				...			...	1333			...	...	...		...	...
Stuttgart Hbf **912** a.		...		...	1024	...	0922	...	...			1008	...	1153		...	...	1122	1248	...	...	...		...	...
München Hbf **904 930** a.	1006	...	1110	...	...	...	1126	...	...	1206	1338	1226	...	1410	1306	...	...	1326	...	...	...	...	1406	...	...

♦ – **NOTES** (LISTED BY TRAIN NUMBER)

7 – [12] ✕ Hamburg - Basel - Bern - Interlaken.
114 – WÖRTHERSEE – [12] 🍷 Klagenfurt - Salzburg - München - Dortmund.
115 – WÖRTHERSEE – [12] 🍷 Münster - München - Salzburg - Klagenfurt.
119 – BODENSEE – [12] Dortmund - Stuttgart - Ulm - Lindau - Innsbruck.
120 – [12] ✕ Frankfurt - Amsterdam (Table **28**). Does not run Köln - Amsterdam Feb. 10 – 23.

A – From Amsterdam (Table **28**). Subject to alteration Feb. 11 – 24.
E – From / to Wien (Tables **920**/**950**).
G – From / to Garmisch on ⑥ (Table **895**).
L – ⑤⑦ (also Dec. 26; not Dec. 25). From Aachen Hbf (d. 1959) and Düren (d. 2027).
T – ⑦–④ Jan. 9 - Mar. 30.

b – Not Dec. 25.
d – Not Dec. 26. Train number **2341** on ⑦ (not Dec. 25).
e – Not Jan. 6 - Mar. 31.
h – Arrives 2300.

j – 1937 on ⑤–⑦ (also Dec. 26).
k – ⑤⑦ only.
m – Not Dec. 26.
p – Connects at Essen with train **512** in preceding column.
q – ①②③④⑥ (also Dec. 25; not Dec. 24, 26).
r – From Feb. 11.
s – Not Dec. 24, 25, 31.
t – Not Dec. 25, 26, Jan. 1.
w – Also Dec. 26; not Dec. 25, Jan. 8 - Apr. 2.
y – Also Dec. 24, 26; not Dec. 25.
z – Not Dec. 25.

* – Connecting *ICE* train (change trains at Mainz).
§ – Frankfurt Flughafen Fernbahnhof.

800 HAMBURG - DORTMUND - KÖLN - KOBLENZ - FRANKFURT

	ICE	ICE	IC	ICE	ICE	ICE	ICE	IC	EC	IC	ICE	ICE	ICE	ICE	ICE	ICE	ICE	IC	ICE	ICE	IC	ICE		IC	ICE
	27	515	2005	946	956	623	105	2042	9	2013	644	654	625	29	517	731	1152	2009	944	954	2156	627		2044	107
			①–⑥	⚒							⚒														
	E ✕	✕	🍷 ♦	✕	✕	✕	A ✕	🍷 ♦	✕ ♦	🍷 ♦	✕	✕	✕	E ✕	✕	✕	✕	M	✕	✕	♦	✕		D 🍷	✕
Hamburg Altona d.	...	0529	...	...	...	...	...	...	0629	...	...	...	...	...	0728	0738	...	...	...	...	...	...	...	...	0829
Hamburg Hbf **801** d.	...	0545	...	...	...	...	...	...	0645	...	...	...	...	...	0745	0754	...	...	...	...	...	...	...	...	0845
Hamburg Harburg d.	...	0558	...	...	...	...	...	...	0657	...	...	...	...	...	0757	|	...	...	...	...	...	...	...	...	0857
Bremen Hbf **801 815** d.	...	0644	...	...	...	...	...	...	0744	...	...	...	...	...	0844	0852	...	...	...	...	...	...	...	...	0944
Osnabrück Hbf **801 815** d.	...	0737	...	...	...	...	...	...	0836	...	...	...	...	...	0937	|	...	...	...	...	...	...	...	...	1037
Münster (Westf) Hbf **801** d.	...	0802	0832	...	...	...	...	...	0903	...	...	...	...	...	1002	1009	...	1032	...	...	...	...	...	...	1102
Berlin Hbf **810** d.	...	|	|	0529	0529	...	...	...	|	...	0646	0646	...	...	|	|	0659	|	0746	0746	...	...	...	...	|
Leipzig Hbf **849a 866** d.	...	|	|	|	|	...	...	0441g	|	...	|	|	...	...	|	|	|	|	|	|	...	...	...	0638	|
Hannover Hbf **810** d.	...	|	|	0731	0731	...	...	0740	|	...	0831	0831	...	...	|	|	0856	|	0931	0931	...	...	...	0940	|
Hamm (Westf) **805** d.	...	|	|	0851	0854	...	...	0916	|	...	0951	0954	...	...	|	|	1026	|	1051	1054	1056	...	...	1116	|
Dortmund Hbf **805** a.	...	0832	|	0910	|	...	...	0933	|	...	1010	|	...	...	1032	|	1048	|	1110	|	1114	...	...	1133	|
Dortmund Hbf d.	0829	0835	|	0912	|	0912v	...	0936	|	0949	1013	|	...	1029	1035	|	1051	|	1112	|	1116	1122v	...	1135	|
Bochum Hbf d.	0847	|	|	0924	|	0926v	...	|	|	1004	1025	|	...	1047	|	|	1103	|	1124	|	1130	1137v	...	|	|
Recklinghausen Hbf d.	|	|	0900	|	|	|	...	|	|	|	|	|	...	|	|	1038	|	1100	|	|	|	|	...	|	|
Wanne-Eickel Hbf d.	|	|	0909	|	|	|	...	|	|	|	|	|	...	|	|	|	|	1109	|	|	|	|	...	|	|
Gelsenkirchen Hbf d.	|	|	0914	|	|	|	...	|	0942	|	|	|	...	|	|	1049	|	1114	|	|	|	|	...	|	1140
Essen Hbf d.	0900	|	|	0937	|	0941	...	|	0957	1016	1038	|	1051	1100	|	1104	1114	|	1137	|	1142	1150	...	|	1157
Oberhausen Hbf d.	|	|	0926	|	|	|	0958	|	|	|	|	|	|	|	|	|	|	1126	|	|	|	|	...	|	|
Duisburg Hbf d.	|	|	0933	0950	|	0955	|	|	1010	1030	1051	|	1104	|	|	1118	1130	1134	1150	|	1155	1203	...	|	1209
Düsseldorf Flughafen ✈ d.	|	|	|	|	|	|	|	|	|	|	1100s	|	|	|	|	|	|	|	|	|	|	|	...	|	|
Düsseldorf Hbf **910** d.	0924	|	0947	1002	|	1010	1019	|	1024	1044	1108	|	1118	1124	|	1132	1144	1149	1203	|	1211	1217	...	|	1223
Hagen Hbf d.	|	0857	|	...	0923	|	|	0958	|	|	...	1023	|	|	1057	|	|	|	...	1123	|	|	...	1157	|
Wuppertal Hbf d.	|	0914	|	...	0940	|	|	1014	|	|	...	1040	|	|	1114	|	|	|	...	1140	|	|	...	1214	|
Solingen Hbf d.	|	0927	|	...	|	|	|	1026	|	|	...	|	|	|	1127	|	|	|	...	|	|	|	...	1226	|
Köln Messe/Deutz a.	|	|	|	...	|	1032	|	|	|	|	...	|	1142	|	|	|	|	|	...	|	|	1242	...	|	|
Köln Hbf **910** a.	0950	0949	1014	...	1009	|	1045	1046	1050	1113	...	1109	|	1150	1146	1158	1212	1216	...	1209	1240	|	...	1246	1249
Köln Hbf **910** d.	0953	0955	1017	...	...	|	1055	...	1053	1117	...	...	|	1153	1155	...	...	...	...	...	...	|	...	1253	1255
Bonn Hbf d.	1014	|	1037	...	...	|	|	...	1114	1138	...	...	|	1214	|	...	...	...	...	...	...	|	...	1314	|
Remagen d.	|	|	1051	...	...	|	|	...	|	1152	...	...	|	|	|	...	...	...	...	...	...	|	...	|	|
Andernach d.	|	|	1104	...	...	|	|	...	|	1204	...	...	|	|	|	...	...	...	...	...	...	|	...	|	|
Koblenz Hbf d.	1048	|	1118	...	...	|	|	...	1148	1218	...	...	|	1248	|	...	...	...	...	...	...	|	...	1348	|
Bingen (Rhein) Hbf d.	|	|	1153h	...	...	|	|	...	|	1252	...	...	|	|	|	...	...	...	...	...	...	|	...	|	|
Mainz Hbf a.	1139	|	1215h	...	...	|	|	...	1239	1311	...	...	|	1339	|	...	...	...	...	...	...	|	...	1439	|
Frankfurt Flugh. ✈ § **910** a.	1159	1050	|	...	...	1133	1150	...	*1259**	|	...	...	1233	1359	1250	...	...	...	...	...	...	1333	...	*1459**	1350
Frankfurt (Main) Hbf **910** a.	1212	|	|	...	...	1148	|	...	*1313**	|	...	...	1248	1413	|	...	...	...	...	...	...	1348	...	*1513**	|
Nürnberg Hbf **920** a.	1427	|	|	...	...	1404	|	...	|	|	...	...	1500	1627	|	...	...	...	...	...	...	1559	...	|	|
Karlsruhe Hbf **912** a.	...	|	1334h	...	...	|	1258	...	1347	|	...	...	|	...	|	...	...	...	...	...	...	|	...	|	1458
Basel SBB 🏛 **912** a.	...	|	...	...	...	|	1447	...	1536	|	...	...	|	...	|	...	...	...	...	...	...	|	...	|	1647
Stuttgart Hbf **912** a.	...	1208	...	...	...	|	...	...	...	1450	...	...	|	...	1408	...	...	...	...	...	...	|	...	1622	...
München Hbf **904 930** a.	...	1426	...	...	...	1509	...	...	...	...	...	...	1606	...	1626	...	...	...	...	...	...	1706	...	...	...

	IC	IC	ICE	ICE	ICE	ICE	ICE	ICE	ICE	IC	ICE	IC	ICE	ICE	ICE	IC	ICE	IC	IC	ICE	ICE	ICE	ICE	ICE	ICE
	1915	2015	123	1150	642	652	629	229	519	5106	1058	2201	942	952	721	2046	109	2011	2011	1011	640	650	125	723	1156
	⑦w	⑤d																Ⓐ	⑦w	Y					
	🍷	🍷	A ✕	B ✕	✕	✕	✕	E ✕	✕	L	✕	H	✕	✕	✕	D 🍷	✕	♠	♥	✕	✕	✕	A ✕	✕	✕
Hamburg Altona d.	...	...	...	...	...	...	...	...	0929	...	...	...	...	...	...	...	1029	...	...	...	...	...	...	...	...
Hamburg Hbf **801** d.	...	...	...	...	...	...	...	...	0945	...	...	...	...	...	...	...	1045	...	...	...	...	...	...	...	...
Hamburg Harburg d.	...	...	...	...	...	...	...	...	0957	...	...	...	...	...	...	...	1057	...	...	...	...	...	...	...	...
Bremen Hbf **801 815** d.	...	...	...	...	...	...	...	...	1044	...	...	1054	...	...	...	...	1144	...	...	...	...	...	...	...	...
Osnabrück Hbf **801 815** d.	...	...	...	1106	...	...	...	...	1137	...	...	1157	...	...	...	...	1236	...	...	...	...	...	...	...	...
Münster (Westf) Hbf **801** d.	...	...	...	1132	...	...	...	...	1202	...	...	1232	...	...	...	...	1302	...	...	...	...	...	...	...	...
Berlin Hbf **810** d.	...	...	...	|	0846	0846	...	...	|	...	0900	|	0946	0946	...	...	|	...	0955	...	1046	1046	...	...	1142
Leipzig Hbf **849a 866** d.	...	...	...	|	|	|	...	...	|	...	|	|	|	|	...	0838	|	...	|	...	|	|	...	...	|
Hannover Hbf **810** d.	...	...	...	|	1031	1031	...	...	|	...	1056	|	1131	1131	...	1140	|	...	1156	...	1231	1231	...	...	|
Hamm (Westf) **805** d.	...	...	...	|	1151	1154	...	...	|	...	1226	|	1251	1254	...	1316	|	...	1326	...	1351	1354	...	...	|
Dortmund Hbf **805** a.	...	...	...	|	1210	|	...	...	1233	...	1249	|	1310	|	...	1333	|	...	1349	...	1410	|	...	...	|
Dortmund Hbf d.	1149	1151	...	|	1213	|	...	1229	1236	...	1251	|	1313	|	...	1336	|	...	1351	1349	1413	|	...	...	|
Bochum Hbf d.	1203	1204	...	|	1225	|	...	|	1247	...	1303	|	1325	|	...	|	|	...	|	1404	1425	|	...	...	|
Recklinghausen Hbf d.	|	|	...	1203	|	|	...	|	|	...	|	1300	|	|	...	|	|	...	|	|	|	|	...	...	|
Wanne-Eickel Hbf d.	|	|	...	|	|	|	...	|	|	...	|	1309	|	|	...	|	|	...	|	|	|	|	...	...	|
Gelsenkirchen Hbf d.	|	|	...	|	|	|	...	|	|	...	|	1314	|	|	...	|	1340	...	|	|	|	|	...	...	|
Essen Hbf d.	1214	1215	...	1225	1237	|	1251	|	1300	...	1315	|	1338	|	1351	|	1357	...	|	1415	1437	|	...	1451	|
Oberhausen Hbf d.	|	|	1226	|	|	|	|	|	|	...	|	1326	|	|	|	|	|	...	|	|	|	|	1426	|	|
Duisburg Hbf d.	1229	1231	1234	1238	1250	|	1304	|	|	...	1331	1334	1351	|	1404	|	1410	...	|	1428	1450	|	1434	1504	|
Düsseldorf Flughafen ✈ d.	|	|	|	|	1258s	|	|	|	|	...	|	|	1359s	|	|	|	|	...	|	|	1459s	|	|	|	|
Düsseldorf Hbf **910** d.	1244	1244	1248	1252	1307	|	1318	|	1324	1345	1348	1351	1408	|	1418	|	1423	...	|	1445	1508	|	1450	1518	|
Hagen Hbf d.	|	|	|	|	...	1223	|	1257	|	|	|	|	...	1323	|	1358	|	...	1416	|	...	1423	|	|	|
Wuppertal Hbf d.	|	|	|	|	...	1240	|	1315	|	|	|	|	...	1340	|	1414	|	...	1434	|	...	1440	|	|	|
Solingen Hbf d.	|	|	|	|	...	|	|	1326	|	|	|	|	...	|	|	1426	|	...	|	|	...	|	|	|	|
Köln Messe/Deutz a.	|	|	|	|	...	|	1342	|	|	|	|	|	...	|	1442	|	|	...	|	1509	...	|	|	1542	|
Köln Hbf **910** a.	1312	1312	1315	1319	...	1309	|	1346	1349	1414	1426c	1418	...	1409	|	1446	1449	...	1512	|	...	1509	1519	|	1541
Köln Hbf **910** d.	1317	1317	1321	...	...	1312	|	1353	1355	1417	...	...	...	...	|	1453	1455	1517	1517	|	...	...	1528	|	1543
Bonn Hbf d.	1338	1338	|	...	...	1333	|	1414	|	1438	...	...	...	...	|	1514	|	1538	1538	|	...	...	|	|	1615
Remagen d.	1352	1352	|	...	...	...	|	|	|	1451	...	...	...	...	|	|	|	1552	1552	|	...	...	|	|	...
Andernach d.	1404	1404	|	...	...	...	|	|	|	1503	...	...	...	...	|	|	|	1604	1604	|	...	...	|	|	...
Koblenz Hbf d.	1418	1418	|	...	...	...	|	1448	|	1516	...	...	...	...	|	1548	|	1618	1618	|	...	...	|	|	...
Bingen (Rhein) Hbf d.	1452	1452	|	...	...	...	|	|	|	...	...	...	...	...	|	|	|	1652	1652	|	...	...	|	|	...
Mainz Hbf a.	1511	1511	|	...	...	...	|	1539	|	...	...	...	...	...	|	1639	|	1711	1711	|	...	...	|	|	...
Frankfurt Flugh. ✈ § **910** a.	|	|	1417	...	...	...	1433	1559	1450	...	...	...	...	...	1533	*1659**	1550	|	|	1607	...	...	1617	1633	...
Frankfurt (Main) Hbf **910** a.	|	|	1431	...	...	...	1448	1613	|	...	...	...	...	...	1548	*1713**	|	|	|	|	...	...	1631	1648	...
Nürnberg Hbf **920** a.	|	|	...	...	...	...	1658	1827	|	...	...	...	...	...	1759	|	|	|	|	|	...	...	...	1859	...
Karlsruhe Hbf **912** a.	|	|	...	...	...	...	|	...	|	...	...	...	...	...	|	|	1658	|	|	|	...	...	...	|	...
Basel SBB 🏛 **912** a.	|	|	...	...	...	...	|	...	|	...	...	...	...	...	|	|	1847	|	|	|	...	...	...	|	...
Stuttgart Hbf **912** a.	1656	1649	...	...	...	...	|	...	1608	...	...	...	...	...	|	1827	...	1846	1846	1721	...	...	...	|	...
München Hbf **904 930** a.	...	...	...	...	...	...	1807	...	1826	...	...	...	...	...	1911	...	...	...	...	1927	...	...	...	2007	...

♦ – **NOTES** (LISTED BY TRAIN NUMBER)

9 – [12] ✕ Hamburg - Basel - Zürich.
2005 – ①–⑥ (also Dec. 25; not Dec. 26). SCHWARZWALD – [12] 🍷 Emden - Münster - Köln - Koblenz (- Karlsruhe - Konstanz ⑤⑥ **h**). Does not run Köln - Koblenz - Karlsruhe Jan. 6 - Mar. 31.
2013 – Not Jan. 5 - Mar. 31. ALLGÄU – [12] 🍷 Dortmund - Mainz - Mannheim - Stuttgart - Oberstdorf.
2042 – [12] 🍷 (Leipzig ① **g** -) (Magdeburg ⚒ -) Hannover - Köln.
2156 – [12] (Gera ⚒ -) Erfurt - Kassel - Paderborn - Köln.

A – From Amsterdam (Table **28**). Subject to alteration Feb. 11 – 24.
B – From Berlin (Table **810**).
D – From Dresden (Table **842**).
E – To Wien (Tables **920**/**950**).
H – OSTFRIESLAND – From Bremerhaven on dates in Table **815**.
L – To Luxembourg (Table **915**).
M – From Emden (Table **812**).
Y – ①②③④⑥ (also Dec. 25; not Dec. 26).

c – Not Mar. 31.
d – Not Jan. 6 - Mar. 31.
g – ① (also Dec. 27; not Dec. 26).
h – ⑤⑥ (also Dec. 25).
s – Calls to set down only.
v – ✝ only.
w – Also Dec. 26; not Dec. 25.

* – Connecting *ICE* train (change trains at Mainz Hbf).
♠ – Ⓐ until Jan. 4. LORELEY. To Tübingen (Table **936**) on ①–④.
♥ – To Tübingen (Table **936**) until Jan. 1. Does not run Köln - Stuttgart - Tübingen Jan. 8 - Mar. 26.
§ – Frankfurt Flughafen Fernbahnhof.

HAMBURG - DORTMUND - KÖLN - KOBLENZ - FRANKFURT 800

	ICE 611	ICE 927	ICE 1103	IC 2203	ICE 940	ICE 950	ICE 725	IC 2048	ICE 201	IC 2311	ICE 1013	IC 1917	ICE 717	ICE 127	IC 2305	ICE 548	ICE 558	ICE 1224	ICE 727	ICE 929	ICE 613	ICE 1050	IC 2205	ICE 848	ICE 858
			⑥h	Ⓑb								⑦w	⑤		⑥h										
	✕	P✕	✕N	N	✕	✕	✕	D🍷	✕	Y	✕	🍷	✕	A✕	E	✕	✕	M✕	✕	P✕	K✕	✕	N	✕	✕
Hamburg Altona ... d.	1129	1137	△	...	...	...	...	...	1229	...	...	...	...	...	...	...	...	...	...	...	...	...	...	...	...
Hamburg Hbf ... **801** d.	1145	1153	...	...	...	...	...	...	1245	1250	...	...	...	...	...	...	...	...	...	...	1345	...	...	...	...
Hamburg Harburg ... d.	1157	│	...	...	...	...	...	...	1257	│	...	...	...	...	...	...	...	...	...	...	1357	...	...	...	...
Bremen Hbf ... **801 815** d.	1244	1252	...	...	...	...	...	...	1344	1349	...	...	...	...	...	...	...	...	...	...	1444	...	...	...	...
Osnabrück Hbf ... **801 815** d.	1337	│	...	...	...	...	...	...	1437	│	...	...	...	...	...	...	...	...	...	...	1537	...	...	...	...
Münster (Westf) Hbf ... **801** d.	1402	1409	1431	1432	...	...	...	...	1502	1509	...	...	...	...	1530	...	...	...	...	...	1602	...	1632	...	...
Berlin Hbf **810** ... d.	│	│	│	│	1146	1146	...	...	│	│	...	1159	1159	...	│	1246	1246	...	...	...	│	1306	│	1346	1346
Leipzig Hbf **849a 866** d.	│	│	│	│	│	│	...	1038	│	│	...	│	│	...	│	│	│	...	...	...	│	│	│	│	│
Hannover Hbf **810** ... d.	│	│	│	│	1331	1331	...	1340	│	│	...	1356	1356	...	│	1431	1431	...	...	...	│	1456	│	1531	1531
Hamm (Westf) ... **805** d.	│	│	│	│	1451	1454	...	1516	│	│	...	1533	1533	...	│	1551	1554	1558	...	...	│	1626	│	1651	1654
Dortmund Hbf ... **805** a.	1432	│	│	│	1510	│	...	1533	│	│	...	│	│	...	│	1610	│	│	...	...	1632	1649	│	1710	│
Dortmund Hbf ... d.	1435	│	│	│	1512	│	...	1536	│	│	1549	│	│	...	│	1613	│	│	...	1629	1635	1651	│	1712	│
Bochum Hbf ... d.	│	│	│	│	1524	│	...	│	│	│	1604	│	│	...	│	1625	│	│	...	1647	│	1704	│	1724	│
Recklinghausen Hbf ... d.	│	1437	1500	1500	│	│	...	│	│	1539	│	│	│	...	1559	│	│	│	...	│	│	│	1700	│	│
Wanne-Eickel Hbf ... d.	│	│	1509	1509	│	│	...	│	│	│	│	│	│	...	1609	│	│	│	...	│	│	│	1709	│	│
Gelsenkirchen Hbf ... d.	│	│	1514	1514	│	│	...	│	1540	│	│	│	│	...	1614	│	│	1645j	...	│	│	│	1714	│	│
Essen Hbf ... d.	│	│	│	│	1536	│	1549	│	1556	1603	1615	│	│	...	1626	1637	│	│	1649	1700	│	1715	│	1737	│
Oberhausen Hbf ... d.	│	1503	1527	1526	│	│	│	│	│	│	│	│	│	1626	│	│	│	1703	│	│	│	│	1726	│	│
Duisburg Hbf ... d.	│	1510	│	│	1550	│	1604	│	1609	1616	1628	│	│	1634	1638	1650	│	...	1704	│	│	1734	│	1750	│
Düsseldorf Flughafen ✈ ... d.	│	│	│	│	│	│	│	│	│	│	│	│	│	│	│	1658s	│	...	│	│	│	│	│	│	│
Düsseldorf Hbf ... **910** d.	│	1524	1545	1545	1604	│	1618	│	1623	1630	1644	│	│	1650	1654	1707	│	...	1718	1724	│	1749	1745	1806	│
Hagen Hbf ... d.	1457	│	│	│	...	1523	│	1558	│	│	│	1609	1609	│	│	...	1623	...	│	│	1657	│	│	│	1723
Wuppertal Hbf ... d.	1514	│	│	│	...	1540	│	1614	│	│	│	1630	1630	│	│	...	1640	...	│	│	1714	│	│	│	1740
Solingen Hbf ... d.	1527	│	│	│	...	│	│	1626	│	│	│	│	│	│	│	...	│	...	│	│	1727	│	│	│	│
Köln Messe/Deutz ... a.	│	│	│	│	...	│	1642	│	│	│	1708	│	│	│	│	...	│	...	1742	│	│	│	│	│	│
Köln Hbf ... **910** a.	1546	1550	1614	1614	...	1609	│	1646	1649	1657	│	1712	1712	1716	1719	...	1709	...	│	1750	1746	1819c	1814	1832r	1809
Köln Hbf ... **910** d.	1555	1553	1617	...	...	...	│	1653	1655	...	│	1717	1717	1728	...	...	1716y	...	│	1753	1755	...	1817e	...	...
Bonn Hbf ... d.	│	1614	1637	...	...	...	│	1714	│	...	│	1738	1738	│	...	...	1736y	...	│	1814	│	...	1837e	...	...
Remagen ... d.	│	│	1651	...	...	...	│	│	│	...	│	1752	1752	│	...	...	...	...	│	│	│	...	1851e	...	...
Andernach ... d.	│	│	1704	...	...	...	│	│	│	...	│	1804	1804	│	...	...	...	...	│	│	│	...	1904e	...	...
Koblenz Hbf ... d.	│	1648	1718	...	...	...	│	1748	│	...	│	1818	1818	│	...	...	...	...	│	1848	│	...	1916e	...	...
Bingen (Rhein) Hbf ... d.	│	│	1753	...	...	...	│	│	│	...	│	1852	1852	│	...	...	...	...	│	│	│	...	...	...	...
Mainz Hbf ... a.	│	1739	1815	...	...	...	│	1839	│	...	│	1911	1911	│	...	...	...	...	│	1939	│	...	...	...	...
Frankfurt Flugh. ✈ § ... **910** a.	1650	1759	│	...	...	...	1733	*1859**	1750	...	1807	│	│	1817	...	...	...	...	1833	1959	1850	...	...	...	...
Frankfurt (Main) Hbf ... **910** a.	│	1813	│	...	...	...	1748	*1913**	│	...	│	│	│	1832	...	...	...	...	1848	2013	│	...	...	...	...
Nürnberg Hbf **920** ... a.	│	2028	│	...	...	...	1959	│	│	...	│	│	│	...	...	...	...	...	2100	2228	│	...	...	...	...
Karlsruhe Hbf **912** ... a.	│	...	│	...	...	...	│	│	1858	...	│	│	│	...	...	...	...	...	│	...	│	...	...	...	...
Basel SBB 🏛 **912** ... a.	│	...	│	...	...	...	│	│	2047	...	│	│	│	...	...	...	...	...	│	...	│	...	...	...	...
Stuttgart Hbf **912** ... a.	1808	...	1946	...	...	...	│	2023	...	...	1922	2047	2048	...	...	...	...	...	│	...	2008	...	...	...	...
München Hbf **904 930** ... a.	2026	...	...	...	...	...	2111	...	...	...	2126	...	...	...	...	...	...	...	2206	...	2226	...	...	...	...

	IC 2152	ICE 729	IC 2213	IC 2440	ICE 1659	ICE 1015	ICE 758	ICE 129	ICE 821	ICE 546	ICE 556	ICE 615	ICE 1021	ICE 1021	ICE 1546	IC 2207	ICE 846	ICE 856	ICE 823	ICE 205	IC 2442	IC 2215	ICE 221	ICE 544	ICE 554
					Ⓑb	Ⓑ	⑥						T	U	Ⓑb	E									
	G	✕	O🍷	D🍷		✕	O✕	A✕	✕	✕	✕	✕	✕	✕	F🍷		H✕	✕	✕	✕	D🍷	Y	A✕	✕	✕
Hamburg Altona ... d.	...	...	...	...	...	...	...	...	...	...	...	1529	1555	...	...	...	...	...	...	1629	...	...	...	...	...
Hamburg Hbf ... **801** d.	...	...	1444	...	...	...	...	...	...	...	...	1545	1610	1610	...	...	...	...	...	1645	...	1650	...	...	...
Hamburg Harburg ... d.	...	...	1458	...	...	...	...	...	...	...	...	1558	│	│	...	...	...	...	...	1658	...	│	...	...	...
Bremen Hbf ... **801 815** d.	...	...	1544	...	...	...	...	...	...	...	...	1644	│	│	...	...	...	...	...	1744	...	1749	...	...	...
Osnabrück Hbf ... **801 815** d.	...	...	1636	...	...	...	...	...	...	...	...	1737	│	│	...	...	...	...	...	1837	...	1842	...	...	...
Münster (Westf) Hbf ... **801** d.	...	...	1703	...	...	...	...	...	...	...	...	1802	│	│	...	1832	...	...	...	1902	...	1909	...	...	...
Berlin Hbf **810** ... d.	...	...	│	...	...	...	1353	...	...	1446	1446	│	│	│	1500	│	1546	1546	...	│	...	│	...	1646	1646
Leipzig Hbf **849a 866** d.	...	...	│	1238	...	...	│	...	...	│	│	│	│	│	│	│	│	│	...	│	1438	│	...	│	│
Hannover Hbf **810** ... d.	...	...	│	1540	...	...	1556	...	...	1631	1631	│	│	│	1656	│	1731	1731	...	│	1740	│	...	1831	1831
Hamm (Westf) ... **805** d.	1656	...	│	1716	...	...	1726	...	...	1751	1754	│	│	│	1826	│	1851	1854	...	│	1916	│	...	1951	1954
Dortmund Hbf ... **805** a.	1714	...	│	1733	...	...	1748	...	...	1810	│	1832	│	│	1848	│	1910	│	...	│	1933	│	...	2010	│
Dortmund Hbf ... d.	1716	...	│	1736	...	1750	1751	...	...	1813	│	1835	│	│	1851	│	1913	│	...	│	1936	│	...	2012	│
Bochum Hbf ... d.	1730	...	│	│	...	1804	1803	...	...	1825	│	│	│	│	1904	│	1925	│	...	│	│	│	...	2024	│
Recklinghausen Hbf ... d.	│	...	│	│	...	│	│	...	...	│	│	│	│	│	│	1900	│	│	...	│	│	1938	...	│	│
Wanne-Eickel Hbf ... d.	│	...	│	│	...	│	│	...	...	│	│	│	│	│	│	1909	│	│	...	│	│	│	...	│	│
Gelsenkirchen Hbf ... d.	│	...	1742	│	...	│	│	...	...	│	│	│	│	│	│	1914	│	│	...	1941	│	1949	...	│	│
Essen Hbf ... d.	1740	1749	1757	│	...	1815	1814	...	1837	1842j	│	│	1854	1854	1915	│	1938	│	1941	1955	│	2003	...	2037	│
Oberhausen Hbf ... d.	│	│	│	│	...	│	│	1826	│	│	│	│	│	│	│	1926	│	│	│	│	│	│	2026	│	│
Duisburg Hbf ... d.	1755	1804	1810	│	...	1828	1830	1834	1851	1855	│	│	1909	1909	1926	1933	1951	│	1954	2008	│	2016	2034	2050	│
Düsseldorf Flughafen ✈ ... d.	1806	│	│	│	...	│	│	│	│	│	│	│	│	│	...	│	│	│	│	│	│	│	│	│	│
Düsseldorf Hbf ... **910** d.	1811	1818	1824	│	...	1844	1844	1849	1905	1907	│	│	1923	1923	...	1948	2015	│	2008	2022	│	2030	2048	2104	│
Hagen Hbf ... d.	...	│	│	1758	...	│	│	│	│	...	1823	1857	│	│	...	│	...	1923	│	│	1958	│	│	│	2023
Wuppertal Hbf ... d.	...	│	│	1814	...	│	│	│	│	...	1840	1914	│	│	...	│	...	1940	│	│	2014	│	│	│	2040
Solingen Hbf ... d.	...	│	│	1826	...	│	│	│	│	...	│	1927	│	│	...	│	...	│	│	│	2026	│	│	│	│
Köln Messe/Deutz ... a.	...	1842	│	│	...	1909	│	│	1928	...	│	│	│	│	...	│	...	│	2031	│	│	│	│	│	│
Köln Hbf ... **910** a.	...	│	1850	1846	...	│	1913	1915	│	...	1909	1947	1949	1949	...	2015	...	2009	│	2049	2046	2057	2115	2132	2111
Köln Hbf ... **910** d.	...	│	...	1853	...	│	...	1921	│	...	1912	1955	1953	1953	...	...	...	...	│	2055	2053	...	2128	...	2117
Bonn Hbf ... d.	...	│	...	1914	...	│	...	│	│	...	1937	│	2014	2014	...	...	...	...	│	│	2114	...	│	...	2142
Remagen ... d.	...	│	...	│	...	│	...	│	│	...	1951	│	│	│	...	...	...	...	│	│	│	...	│	...	...
Andernach ... d.	...	│	...	│	...	│	...	│	│	...	2004	│	│	│	...	...	...	...	│	│	│	...	│	...	...
Koblenz Hbf ... d.	...	│	...	1948	...	│	...	│	│	...	2016	│	2048	2048	...	...	...	...	│	│	2148	...	│	...	...
Bingen (Rhein) Hbf ... d.	...	│	...	│	...	│	...	│	│	...	...	│	2123	2123	...	...	...	...	│	│	│	...	│	...	...
Mainz Hbf ... a.	...	│	...	2039	2043	│	...	│	│	...	...	│	2142	2142	...	...	...	...	│	│	2239	...	│	...	...
Frankfurt Flugh. ✈ § ... **910** a.	...	1933	...	│	2059	2007	...	2017	2034	...	...	2050	2159	2159	...	...	...	...	2134	2150	2259	...	2217	...	...
Frankfurt (Main) Hbf ... **910** a.	...	1948	...	│	2113	│	...	2031	2048	...	...	│	2213	2213	...	...	...	...	2148	│	2312	...	2231	...	...
Nürnberg Hbf **920** ... a.	...	2159	...	│	...	│	...	...	2259	...	...	│	0042	0042	...	...	...	...	...	│	...	...	...	...	...
Karlsruhe Hbf **912** ... a.	...	│	...	│	...	│	...	...	│	...	...	│	...	...	...	...	...	...	...	2259	...	...	...	...	...
Basel SBB 🏛 **912** ... a.	...	│	...	│	...	│	...	...	│	...	...	│	...	...	...	...	...	...	...	0059	...	...	...	...	...
Stuttgart Hbf **912** ... a.	...	│	...	2223	...	2122	...	...	│	...	...	2208	...	...	...	...	...	...	...	...	...	...	...	...	...
München Hbf **904 930** ... a.	...	2311	...	...	...	2326	...	...	0019	...	...	0028	...	...	...	...	...	...	...	...	...	...	...	...	...

A – From Amsterdam (Table **28**). Subject to alteration Feb. 11 – 24.
D – From Dresden (Table **842**).
E – From Emden (Table **812**).
F – KAROLINGER – To Krefeld Hbf (a. 1941), Viersen (a. 1953), Mönchengladbach Hbf (a. 2001), Rheydt Hbf (a. 2007), Herzogenrath (a. 2037) and Aachen Hbf (a. 2052).
G – From Gera via Kassel and Paderborn (Tables **849a** and **805**).
H – Continues to Neuss Hbf (a. 2028) and Mönchengladbach Hbf (a. 2042). On ⑦ (also Dec. 26; not Dec. 25) continues further to Aachen Hbf (a. 2133).
K – From Kiel (Table **820**).
M – From München via Kassel and Paderborn (Tables **900** and **805**).
N – From Norddeich Mole (Table **812**).
O – From Ostseebad Binz (Tables **844** and **845**).
P – To Passau via Regensburg (Table **920**).
T – ✕ to Feb. 25; ①–⑤ from Feb. 27.
U – ⑦ to Feb. 26; ⑥⑦ from Mar. 4. From Stralsund / Rostock (Table **830**).
Y – From Westerland (Table **821**).

b – Not Dec. 25.
c – Not Mar. 31.
e – Not Jan. 5 - Mar. 31.
h – Also Dec. 25.
j – Arrives 5 – 7 minutes earlier.
r – ①②③④⑥ (also Dec. 25; not Dec. 24, 26).
s – Calls to set down only.
w – Also Dec. 26; not Dec. 25.
y – ①②③④⑥ (also Dec. 25; not Dec. 26).

△ – Does not run Köln - Stuttgart Jan. 7 - Mar. 25.
* – Not Dec. 24, 31. Connecting *ICE* train (change trains at Mainz).
§ – Frankfurt Flughafen ✈ Fernbahnhof.

800 HAMBURG - DORTMUND - KÖLN - KOBLENZ - FRANKFURT

	ICE 1154	IC 2027	ICE 754	ICE 617	IC 2409	ICE 1107	IC 2209	ICE 844	ICE 854	IC 2444	IC 2307		ICE 750	ICE 542	ICE 552	ICE 552	NJ 403	ICE 619		ICE 1019	ICE 872	ICE 842		ICE 840	ICE 921
		R				⑥h	⑤⑦						⑤⑦			⑦w		A			⑦w	¶		⑤⑥†	
	✕		B✕	✕	L	N✕	wN	✕	✕	D🍷			S✕	✕	✕	✕△	C	K✕		✕	✕	✕			
Hamburg Altona ... d.	...	...	...	1729	...	...	...	...	...	...	1829v	...	...	...	...	...	...	...	...	2029	...	...	...	...	2229
Hamburg Hbf ... 801 d.	...	...	...	1745	1808	...	...	...	...	...	1845v	...	...	...	...	...	...	1945	...	2045	...	...	...	...	2246
Hamburg Harburg ... d.	...	...	...	1757	|	...	...	...	...	...	1857	...	...	...	...	...	...	1957	...	2057	...	...	...	...	2258
Bremen Hbf ... 801 815 d.	...	...	...	1844	|	...	...	...	...	...	1944	...	...	...	...	...	...	2044	...	2144	...	...	...	...	2344
Osnabrück Hbf ... 801 815 d.	...	...	1905	1937	|	...	...	...	...	...	2036	...	...	...	...	...	...	2137	...	2237	...	...	...	...	0037
Münster (Westf) Hbf ... 801 d.	...	...	1932	2002	|	2031	2032	...	...	...	2103	...	...	...	...	...	...	2203	...	2303	...	...	...	...	0104
Berlin Hbf 810 ... d.	1741	...	|	|	|	|	|	1746	1746	...	|	...	1812•	1846	1846	1846	...	|	...	|	1946	1946	...	2127	|
Leipzig Hbf 849a 866 d.	|	...	|	|	|	|	|	|	|	1638	|	...	|	|	|	|	...	|	...	|	|	|	...	|	|
Hannover Hbf 810 ... d.	|	...	|	|	|	|	|	1931	1931	1940	|	...	1956	2031	2031	2031	...	|	...	|	2131	2136	...	2331	|
Hamm (Westf) ... 805 d.	|	...	|	|	|	|	|	2051	2054	2116	|	...	2126	2151	2154	2154	...	|	...	|	2252	2315	...	0101	0124
Dortmund Hbf ... 805 a.	|	...	|	2032	|	|	|	2110	|	2133	|	...	2149	2210	|	|	...	2233	...	2333	|	2332	...	0119	0143
Dortmund Hbf ... d.	|	2029	|	2036	|	|	|	2113	|	2136	|	...	2151	2212	|	|	...	2236	...	2336	|	2338	...	0122	0145
Bochum Hbf ... d.	|	|	|	2047	|	|	|	2125	|	|	|	...	2203	2224	|	|	...	2248	...	|	|	2350	...	0134	0157
Recklinghausen Hbf ... d.	|	|	2001	|	|	2100	2100	|	|	|	|	...	|	|	|	|	...	|	...	|	|	|	...	|	|
Wanne-Eickel Hbf ... d.	|	|	|	|	|	2109	2109	|	|	|	|	...	|	|	|	|	...	|	...	|	|	|	...	|	|
Gelsenkirchen Hbf ... d.	|	|	2014	|	|	2114	2114	|	|	|	2143	...	|	|	|	|	...	|	...	|	|	|	...	|	|
Essen Hbf ... d.	|	|	2025	2100	2054	|	|	2138	|	|	2156	...	2215	2237	|	|	...	2300	...	|	|	0002	...	0146	0209
Oberhausen Hbf ... d.	|	|	|	|	|	2127	2127	|	|	|	|	...	|	|	|	|	...	|	...	|	|	|	...	|	|
Duisburg Hbf ... d.	|	|	2051	|	2114t	2134	2134	2151	|	|	2209	...	2231	2250	|	|	2301	|	...	|	|	0016	...	0159	0222
Düsseldorf Flughafen ✈ ... d.	|	|	|	|	|	|	|	|	|	|	|	...	|	|	|	|	|	|	...	|	|	|	...	0209	0231
Düsseldorf Hbf ... 910 d.	|	|	2115	2123	2128	2149	2149	2205	|	|	2223	...	2245	2305	|	|	2316	2324	...	|	|	0030	...	0218	0239
Hagen Hbf ... d.	|	2057	...	|	|	|	|	|	2123	2158	|	...	|	|	2223	2223	|	|	...	2357	2322	|	...		|
Wuppertal Hbf ... d.	|	2114	...	|	|	|	|	|	2140	2214	|	...	|	|	2240	2240	|	|	...	0014	2339	|	...		|
Solingen Hbf ... d.	|	2126	...	|	|	|	|	|	|	2226	|	...	|	|	2253	2253	|	|	...	0026	|	|	...		|
Köln Messe/Deutz ... a.	|	|	...	|	|	|	|	|	|	|	|	...	|	|	|	|	|	|	...	|	|	|	...		|
Köln Hbf ... 910 a.	2141	2146	...	2149	2157	2215	2215	2232	2209	2246	2250	...	2316	2331	2313	2313	2345	2349	...	0047	0010	0056	...	0244	0304
Köln Hbf ... 910 d.	2143	2153	...	2155	...	...	...	...	...	...	2253	...	...	...	2320b	2320	2353	2355	...	...	...	...	...	...	0349
Bonn Hbf ... d.	2209	2214	...	|	...	...	...	...	...	...	2315	...	...	...	2343b	2345	0014	|	...	...	...	...	...	...	0414
Remagen ... d.	...	|	...	|	...	...	...	...	...	...	2329	...	...	...	...	0004	|	|	...	...	...	...	...	...	0430
Andernach ... d.	...	|	...	|	...	...	...	...	...	...	2342	...	...	...	...	0018	|	|	...	...	...	...	...	...	|
Koblenz Hbf ... d.	...	2248	...	|	...	...	...	...	...	...	2355	...	...	...	...	0031	0049	|	...	...	...	...	...	...	0530r
Bingen (Rhein) Hbf ... d.	...	|	...	|	...	...	...	...	...	...	...	...	...	...	...	...	|	|	...	...	...	...	...	...	0609
Mainz Hbf ... a.	...	2339z	...	|	...	...	...	...	...	...	...	...	...	...	...	...	0140	|	...	...	...	...	...	...	0627
Frankfurt Flugh. ✈ § ... 910 a.	...	2359z	...	2254	...	...	...	...	...	...	...	...	...	...	...	...	0204	0054	...	...	...	...	...	...	0646
Frankfurt (Main) Hbf ... 910 a.	...	0013z	...	|	...	...	...	...	...	...	...	...	...	...	...	...	0220	0110	...	...	...	...	...	...	0702
Nürnberg Hbf 920 ... a.	...	...	...	|	...	...	...	...	...	...	...	...	...	...	...	...	|	|	...	...	...	...	...	...	...
Karlsruhe Hbf 912 ... a.	...	...	...	|	...	...	...	...	...	...	...	...	...	...	...	...	0401	|	...	...	...	...	...	...	...
Basel SBB 🏛 912 ... a.	...	...	...	|	...	...	...	...	...	...	...	...	...	...	...	...	0620	|	...	...	...	...	...	...	...
Stuttgart Hbf 912 ... a.	...	...	...	0008	...	...	...	...	...	...	...	...	...	...	...	...	...	0333	...	...	...	...	...	...	...
München Hbf 904 930 ... a.	...	...	...	...	...	...	...	...	...	...	...	...	...	...	...	...	...	0603	...	...	...	...	...	...	...

A – Runs Kiel - Hamburg - Köln daily; runs Köln - München daily to Jan. 8, ⑤⑥ from Jan. 13.
B – From Berlin (Table **810**).
C – 🛏 1, 2 cl. and 🛌 2 cl. (Ⓡ) Amsterdam - Utrecht - Basel - Zürich. Also conveys 💺2 (*IC* **60403**). Feb. 10 – 23 does not call at Duisburg or Düsseldorf, then Köln Hbf a. 2338, d. 2342, Bonn-**Beuel** d. 0003 (not Bonn Hbf), then as shown.
D – From Dresden (Table **842**).
K – From Kiel (Table **820**). ✕ Kiel - Köln.
L – From Lübeck Hbf (d. 1718).
N – From Norddeich Mole (Table **912**).

R – Daily to Jan. 6; Ⓑ from Jan. 8.
S – ⑤⑦ (also Dec. 26; not Dec. 25). From Stralsund (Table **845**).

b – Ⓑ (not Dec. 25).
h – Also Dec. 25.
r – Arrives 0458.
t – Arrives 2107.
v – ①⑥⑦ only.

w – Also Dec. 26; not Dec. 25.
z – On Mar. 31 Mainz a. 2343, Frankfurt Hbf a. 0029 (not calling at Frankfurt Flughafen).

△ – Does not run Bonn - Koblenz Jan. 8 - Mar. 26.
• – Berlin **Spandau** (not Hbf).
¶ – Train number **892** on ⑦ **w**.
§ – Frankfurt Flughafen Fernbahnhof.

801 Local services BREMEN - HAMBURG

See Table **800** for fast trains

BREMEN - **HAMBURG** and v.v. Operated by *metronom*. Journey time: 70 – 90 minutes. Trains call at **Rotenburg** (Wümme), 21 – 30 minutes from Bremen, 47 – 56 minutes from Hamburg.

From Bremen Hbf at 0015 Ⓒ, 0114 Ⓒ, 0314 Ⓒ, 0432 Ⓐ, 0458, 0528 Ⓐ, 0558, 0626 Ⓐ, 0633 Ⓒ, 0658, 0733, 0758, 0833, 0858 and at 33 and 58 minutes past each hour until 2033, 2058; then 2133 ⑤⑥ (also Apr. 6, 9, 30, May 17, 28), 2158 and 2312.

From Hamburg Hbf at 0057 Ⓒ, 0256 Ⓒ, 0457, 0537, 0558 Ⓐ, 0615 Ⓒ, 0637, 0715, 0737, 0815, 0837 and at 15 and 37 minutes past each hour until 2115, 2137; then 2237 and 2337.

802 RHEIN – RUHR LOCAL SERVICES

RE | *RB* services

Services in this table (pages 372 – 375) are shown route by route. Sub-headings indicate the route number and principal stations served.

RE1 Aachen - Köln - Düsseldorf - Dortmund - Hamm ♣ ⊡ *RE6* Köln - Düsseldorf - Bielefeld (- Minden) ♣ ⊡

km		⚒m		m			Ⓐm		m		m				m		m									
0	**Aachen** Hbf ... 807 d.	...	...	...	...	...	...	0451t	...	0551	...	0651	▲	...	1851	...	1951	...	2051	...	2151	...	2251	...	2351
31	Düren ... 807 d.	...	...	...	...	...	...	0517t	...	0617	...	0717		...	1917	...	2017	...	2117	...	2217	...	2317	...	0017
	Köln/Bonn Flug ✈ . d.	...	0320	...	...	0448	0448	|	0548	|	0648	|		1848	|	1947	|	2048	|	2148	|	2248	|	2348	|
70	**Köln** Hbf ... 807 a.	...	0335	...	...	0500	0500	0544t	0602	0644	0701	0744		1901	1944	2001	2043	2101	2143	2201	2244	2301	2344	0001	0044
70	**Köln** Hbf ... d.	...	0349	...	0449	0507	0507	0549	0607	0649	0707	0749	and at	1907	1949	2007	2049	2107	2149	2207	2249	2307	2349	0007	0049
71	**Köln** Messe/Deutz ... d.	...	0353	...	0453	|	|	0552	|	0653	|	0752		|	1953	|	2052	|	2152	|	2252	|	2353	|	0053
83	Leverkusen Mitte ... d.	...	0404	...	0504	|	|	0604	|	0704	|	0804	the same	|	2004	|	2104	|	2204	|	2304	|	0004	|	0104
	Neuss Hbf ... d.	...	|	...	|	0536	0536	|	0636	|	0736	|		1936	|	2036	|	2136	|	2236	|	2336	|	0036	|
110	**Düsseldorf** Hbf ... a.	...	0419	...	0519	0548	0548	0619	0647	0719	0747	0819	minutes	1947	2019	2047	2119	2147	2219	2247	2319	2347	0019	0047	0119
110	**Düsseldorf** Hbf ... ▷ d.	...	0422	...	0522	▬	0554	0622	0653	0722	0754	0822		1954	2022	2054	2122	2154	2222	2254	2322	2354	0022	0054	0122
117	Düsseldorf Flug ✈ . ▷ d.	...	0428	...	0528	...	0602	0628	0701	0728	0802	0828	past each	2002	2028	2102	2128	2202	2228	2302	2328	0002	0028	0102	0128
134	**Duisburg** Hbf ... ▷ d.	...	0438	...	0538	...	0615	0638	0716	0738	0815	0838		2014	2038	2115	2138	2215	2238	2315	2338	0017	0038	0115	0138
144	Mülheim (Ruhr) Hbf ▷ d.	...	0444	...	0544	...	0621	0644	0723	0744	0821	0844	hour until	2021	2044	2121	2144	2221	2244	2321	2344	0023	0044	0121	0144
153	**Essen** Hbf ... ▷ d.	...	0452	...	0552	Ⓒ	0629	0652	0731	0752	0829	0852		2029	2052	2129	2152	2229	2252	2329	2352	0031	0052	0129	0152
169	Bochum Hbf ... ▷ d.	...	0503	...	0603	m	0642	0703	0742	0803	0842	0903		2042	2103	2142	2203	2242	2303	2342	0003	0043	0103	0142	0203
187	**Dortmund** Hbf ... ▷ d.	0455t	0516	0555	0616	0655	0656	0716	0755	0816	0855	0916		2055	2117	2155	2216	2255	2316	2354	0016	0055	0116	0152	0216
218	**Hamm** (Westf) 810 ▷ d.	0515	0541	0615	0641	0715	0715	0741	0814	0840	0915	0940		2115	2140	2215	2241	2315	2341	...	0041	...	0141z	...	0241
268	Gütersloh Hbf ... 810 d.	0549	...	0649	...	0749	0749	...	0849	...	0949	...		2149	...	2249	...	2349	...	...	...	...	...	...	...
285	**Bielefeld** Hbf ... 810 a.	0558	...	0658	...	0758	0758	...	0858	...	0958	...		2158	...	2258	...	0001	...	...	...	...	...	...	...

	Ⓒ	Ⓐ					Ⓐ			⚒		Ⓒ	Ⓐ	m		m			m		m		m		m
Bielefeld Hbf ... 810 d.	...	...	...	...	...	...	...	...	...	0459	...	...	...	0559	...	0659	▲ ⊠	...	1959	...	2059	...	2159	...	2259
Gütersloh Hbf ... 810 d.	...	...	...	...	...	...	...	...	...	0508	...	...	...	0608	...	0708		...	2011	...	2108	...	2208	...	2308
Hamm (Westf) .. 810 ▷ d.	0018	...	...	0318	...	0418	...	...	0518	0544	...	0618	0620	0644	0720	0744		2020	2047	2120	2144	2218	2244	2319	2344
Dortmund Hbf ... ▷ d.	0046	0046	...	0346	...	0446	0507	...	0546	0607	...	0646	0646	0707	0746	0807		2046	2107	2146	2207	2246	2307	2346	0007
Bochum Hbf ... ▷ d.	0057	0057	...	0357	...	0457	0519	...	0557	0619	...	0656	0657	0719	0757	0819	and at	2057	2119	2157	2219	2257	2319	2357	0019
Essen Hbf ... ▷ d.	0110	0110	...	0410	...	0510	0532	...	0610	0632	...	0708	0710	0732	0810	0832		2110	2132	2210	2232	2310	2332	0010	0032
Mülheim (Ruhr) Hbf. ▷ d.	0116	0116	...	0416	...	0516	0538	...	0616	0638	...	0714	0716	0738	0816	0838	the same	2116	2138	2216	2238	2316	2338	0016	0038
Duisburg Hbf ... ▷ d.	0123	0123	...	0423	...	0523	0548	...	0623	0648	...	0722	0723	0748	0823	0848		2123	2148	2223	2248	2323	2348	0023	0048
Düsseldorf Flug ✈ .. ▷ d.	0132	0132	...	0432	...	0532	0557	...	0632	0657	...	0731	0732	0757	0832	0857	minutes	2132	2157	2233	2257	2332	2357	0032	0057
Düsseldorf Hbf ... ▷ a.	0137	0137	...	0437	...	0537	0605	...	0636	0705	...	0736	0737	0805	0837	0905		2137	2205	2237	2305	2337	0005	0037	0105
Düsseldorf Hbf ... d.	0139	0139	0413	0440	0513	0540	0613	0613	0640	0713	0713	0739	0740	0813	0840	0913	past each	2140	2213	2239	2313	2339	...	...	...
Neuss Hbf ... d.	|	|	0424	|	0524	|	0624	0624	|	0724	0724	|	|	0824	|	0924		|	2224	|	2324	|	...	...	...
Leverkusen Mitte ... d.	0155	0155	|	0455	|	0555	|	|	0654	|	|	0755	0755	|	0855	|	hour until	2155	|	2255	|	2355	...	...	...
Köln Messe/Deutz ... d.	0209	0209	|	0509	|	0609	|	|	0708	|	|	0808	0809	|	0908	|		2208	|	2308	|	0009	...	...	...
Köln Hbf ... a.	0212	0212	0450	0512	0552	0612	0650	0650	0712	0752	0752	0812	0812	0852	0912	0950		2212	2252	2312	2352	0012	...	...	...
Köln Hbf ... 807 d.	0215	0222	0457	0515t	0556	0615	0652	0652	0715	0758	0758	0815	0815	0858	0915	0952		2215	2258	2315	2358	0015	...	...	...
Köln/Bonn Flug ✈ .. a.	|	0234	0509	|	0609	|	0705	0705	|	0811	0811	|	|	0911	|	1005		|	2311	|	0011	|	...	...	...
Düren ... 807 d.	0239	...	...	0539t	...	0639	...	...	0739	...	...	0839	0839	...	0939	...		2239	...	2341	...	0039	...	...	...
Aachen Hbf ... 807 a.	0307	...	...	0607t	...	0707	...	...	0807	...	...	0907	0907	...	1007	...		2307	...	0009	...	0109	...	...	...

FOR NOTES SEE NEXT PAGE →

RE / RB services **RHEIN – RUHR LOCAL SERVICES** **802**

Services in this table (pages 372–375) are shown route by route. Sub-headings indicate the route number and principal stations served.

RE2 Düsseldorf - Essen - Gelsenkirchen - Münster ⊡ *RE42* Mönchengladbach - Essen - Münster

km		⚒	⚒	⚒																	◇			
0	**Düsseldorf** Hbf d.	...	0506	...	0606r	...	0706	...	0806	...	0906	●	...	1906	...	2006	...	2106	...	2206	...	...	2306	0006
7	Düsseldorf Flughafen ✈ d.	...	0513	...	0613r	...	0713	...	0813	...	0913		...	1913	...	2013	...	2113	...	2213	...	...	2313	0013
	Mönchengladbach d.	...	│	0522	│	0622	│	0722	│	0822	│		1822	│	1922	│	2022	│	2122	│	...	2222	│	│
	Viersen d.	...	│	0531	│	0631	│	0731	│	0831	│		1831	│	1931	│	2031	│	2131	│	...	2231	│	│
	Krefeld Hbf d.	...	│	0541	│	0641	│	0741	│	0841	│	and at	1841	│	1941	│	2041	│	2141	│	...	2241	│	│
24	**Duisburg** Hbf d.	...	0524	0602	0624r	0702	0724	0802	0824	0902	0924	the same	1902	1924	2002	2024	2102	2124	2202	2224	...	2302	2324j	0024
34	Mülheim (Ruhr) Hbf d.	...	0530	0609	0630r	0709	0730	0809	0830	0909	0930	minutes	1909	1930	2009	2030	2109	2130	2209	2230	...	2309	2330j	0030
43	**Essen** Hbf d.	0446	0541	0617	0641	0717	0741	0817	0841	0917	0941		1917	1941	2017	2041	2117	2141	2217	2241	...	2317	2346	0046
53	Gelsenkirchen Hbf d.	0455	0550	0626	0650	0726	0750	0826	0850	0926	0950	past each	1926	1950	2026	2050	2126	2150	2226	2250	...	2326	2354	0054
58	Wanne-Eickel Hbf d.	0500	0556	0631	0656	0731	0756	0831	0856	0931	0956	hour until	1931	1956	2031	2056	2131	2156	2231	2256	...	2331	0000	0100
68	Recklinghausen Hbf d.	0509	0604	0639	0704	0739	0804	0839	0904	0939	1004		1939	2004	2039	2104	2139	2204	2239	2304	...	2339	0009	0109
84	Haltern am See d.	0519	0613	0650	0713	0750	0813	0850	0913	0950	1013		1950	2013	2050	2113	2151	2213	2251	2313	...	2351	0020	0120
97	Dülmen d.	0528	0620	0659	0720	0759	0820	0859	0920	0959	1020		1959	2020	2059	2120	...	2220	...	2320	...	...	0029	0129
126	**Münster** (Westf) Hbf ★ d.	0550	0637	0722	0737	0822	0837	0922	0937	1022	1037		2022	2037	2122	2137	...	2237	...	2335	0003	...	0053	0153
176	**Osnabrück** Hbf ★ a.	...	0712	...	0819	...	0910	...	1015	...	1110		...	2110	...	2215	...	2310f	...	...	0039	...	...	...

		Ⓐ	⚒	⚒	⚒																		⑤⑥f	
Osnabrück Hbf ★ d.	...	...	...	...	...	...	0545r	...	0648	...	0748	...	0849	♥	...	1948	...	2049	...	...	2145	...	...	...
Münster (Westf) Hbf ★ d.	0209	...	0425	...	0525	0536t	0625	0636r	0725	0736r	0825	0836	0925		1936	2025	2036	2125	...	2209	2222	2309	2309	0007
Dülmen d.	0232	...	0439	...	0539	0558t	0639	0658r	0739	0758r	0839	0858	0939		1958	2039	2058	2139	...	2232	...	2332	2332	0029
Haltern am See d.	0244	...	0446	0507	0546	0607	0646	0707	0746	0807	0846	0907	0946	and at	2007	2046	2107	2146	2207	2244	...	2344	2344	0039
Recklinghausen Hbf d.	0255	...	0455	0519	0555	0619	0655	0719	0755	0819	0855	0919	0955		2019	2055	2119	2155	2219	2255	...	2355	2355	0050
Wanne-Eickel Hbf d.	0304	...	0503	0528	0603	0628	0703	0728	0803	0828	0903	0928	1003	the same	2028	2103	2128	2203	2228	2304	...	0004	0004	0059
Gelsenkirchen Hbf d.	0309	...	0509	0533	0609	0633	0709	0733	0809	0833	0909	0933	1009	minutes	2033	2109	2133	2209	2233	2309	...	0009	0009	0104
Essen Hbf d.	0321	...	0521	0545	0621	0645	0721	0745	0821	0845	0921	0945	1021		2045	2121	2145	2221	2245	2321	...	0019	0021	0114
Mülheim (Ruhr) Hbf d.	0327	...	0527	0552	0627	0652	0727	0752	0827	0852	0927	0952	1027	past each	2052	2127	2152	2227	2252	2327	...	...	0027	...
Duisburg Hbf d.	0336	0505	0536	0601	0636	0701	0736	0801	0836	0901	0936	1001	1036	hour until	2101	2136	2201	2236	2301	2336	...	...	0036	...
Krefeld Hbf d.	│	0530	│	0618	│	0718	│	0818	│	0918	│	1018	│		2118	│	2218	│	2318	│	...	...	│	...
Viersen d.	│	0543	│	0633	│	0733	│	0833	│	0933	│	1033	│		2133	│	2233	│	2333	│	...	...	│	...
Mönchengladbach a.	│	0551	│	0642	│	0742	│	0842	│	0942	│	1042	│		2142	│	2242	│	2342	│	...	...	│	...
Düsseldorf Flughafen ✈ d.	0346	...	0546	...	0646	...	0746	...	0846	...	0946	...	1046		...	2146	...	2246	...	2346	...	...	0046	...
Düsseldorf Hbf a.	0353	...	0553	...	0653	...	0753	...	0853	...	0953	...	1053		...	2153	...	2253	...	2353	...	...	0053	...

RE3 Düsseldorf - Duisburg - Gelsenkirchen - Dortmund - Hamm ⊡ ◇

km											
0	**Düsseldorf** Hbf d.	0445	0545	0645	✤	1845	1945	2045	2145	2245	2345
7	Düsseldorf Flughafen ✈ d.	0453	0553	0653		1853	1953	2053	2153	2253	2353
24	**Duisburg** Hbf d.	0510	0610	0710	and	1910	2010	2110	2210	2310	0010
32	Oberhausen Hbf d.	0516	0616	0716	hourly	1916	2016	2116	2216	2316	0016
48	Gelsenkirchen Hbf d.	0529	0629	0729		1929	2029	2129	2229	2329	0029
53	Wanne-Eickel Hbf d.	0534	0634	0734	until	1934	2034	2134	2234	2334	0034
57	Herne d.	0538	0638	0738		1938	2038	2138	2238	2338	0038
78	**Dortmund** Hbf d.	0557	0702	0757		1957	2057	2157	2257	2357	0057
109	**Hamm** (Westf) a.	0629t	0729r	0829		2029	...	...	...	...	...

Hamm (Westf) d.	...	0530t	0630t	0730r	0830		2030	...	...
Dortmund Hbf d.	0503	0603	0703	0803	0903		2103	2203	2303
Herne d.	0519	0619	0719	0819	0919	and	2119	2219	2319
Wanne-Eickel Hbf d.	0524	0624	0724	0824	0924		2124	2224	2324
Gelsenkirchen Hbf d.	0529	0629	0729	0829	0929	hourly	2129	2229	2329
Oberhausen Hbf d.	0543	0643	0743	0843	0943	until	2143	2243	2343
Duisburg Hbf d.	0553	0653	0753	0853	0953		2153	2253	2353
Düsseldorf Flughafen d.	0604	0704	0804	0904	1004		2204	2304	0004
Düsseldorf Hbf a.	0612	0712	0812	0912	1012		2212	2312	0012

RE4 Aachen - Mönchengladbach - Düsseldorf - Wuppertal - Dortmund ♣ ⊡ *RE13* Venlo - Mönchengladbach - Düsseldorf - Wuppertal - Hamm ◇ ⊡

km			Ⓐ	⚒	Ⓐ	⚒	⚒		⚒															
0	**Aachen** Hbf 473 d.	0253	0422	0422	...	...	0522	0522	...	0622	...		1722	...	1822	...	1922	...	2022	...	2122	...	2236	2337
14	Herzogenrath 473 d.	0307	0437	0437	...	...	0537	0537	...	0637	...	⊖	1737	...	1837	...	1937	...	2036	...	2137	...	2252	2352
58	Rheydt Hbf d.	0343	0506	0506	...	...	0606	0606	...	0706	...		1806	...	1906	...	2006	...	2106	...	2206	...	2332	0032
	Venlo ▦ d.	...	│	│	0505	0505	│	│	0605	│	0705	and at	│	1805	│	1905	│	2005	│	2105	│	2205	│	│
	Kaldenkirchen d.	...	│	│	0510	0510	│	│	0610	│	0710		│	1810	│	1910	│	2010	│	2110	│	2210	│	│
	Viersen d.	...	│	│	0527	0527	│	│	0627	│	0727	the same	│	1827	│	1927	│	2027	│	2127	│	2227	│	│
62	**Mönchengladbach** Hbf a.	0348	0511	0511	0536	0536	0611	0611	0636	0711	0736		1811	1836	1911	1936	2011	2036	2111	2136	2211	2236	2337	0037
62	**Mönchengladbach** Hbf d.	0350	0512	0512	0545	0545	0612	0612	0645	0712	0745	minutes	1812	1845	1912	1945	2012	2045	2112	2145	2212	...	...	...
79	Neuss Hbf d.	0403	0527	0527	0557	0557	0627	0627	0657	0727	0757		1827	1857	1927	1957	2027	2057	2128	2157	2227	...	...	...
90	**Düsseldorf** Hbf a.	0413	0539	0539	0609	0609	0639	0639	0709	0739	0809	past each	1839	1909	1939	2009	2039	2109	2139	2209	2239	...	...	...
90	**Düsseldorf** Hbf d.	d	0542	...	0612	...	0642	—	0712	0742	0812		1842	1912	1942	2012	2042	...	2142	...	2242	...	...	...
117	**Wuppertal** Hbf d.	...	0602	...	0632	...	0702	...	0732	0802	0832	hour until	1902	1932	2002	2032	2102	...	2202	...	2302	...	...	...
144	**Hagen** Hbf 804 d.	...	0627	...	0657	...	0727	0758	0758	0827	0858		1927	1958	2027	2055	2127	...	2227	...	2327	...	...	...
159	Witten Hbf d.	...	0641	...	│	...	0741	│	│	0841	│		1941	│	2041	...	2141	...	2241	...	2341	...	...	...
175	**Dortmund** Hbf d.	...	0650	...	│	...	0750	│	│	0850	│		1950	│	2050	...	2150	...	2250	...	2350	...	...	...
	Schwerte 804 d.	...	...	...	0706	...	...	0808	0808	...	0908		...	2008	...	...	...	...	...	...	...	...	...	...
	Unna d.	...	...	...	0720	...	...	0820	0820	...	0920		...	2020	...	...	...	...	...	...	...	...	...	...
	Hamm (Westf) a.	...	...	...	0734	...	...	0834	0834	...	0934		...	2034	...	...	...	...	...	...	...	...	...	...

km		⚒	Ⓐ	⚒	⚒			⚒																
0	**Hamm** (Westf) d.	...	...	...	...	...	...	0625	...	...	0725r	...	0822	...	0925		...	1825	...	1925	...	...	...	...
19	Unna d.	...	...	...	...	...	...	0637	...	...	0737r	...	0834	...	0937	⊗	...	1837	...	1937	...	...	...	...
35	Schwerte 804 d.	...	...	...	...	...	...	0649	...	...	0749r	...	0850	...	0949		...	1849	...	1949	...	...	...	...
	Dortmund Hbf d.	...	...	...	...	...	0610t	│	...	0710r	│	0810	│	0910	│	and at	1810	│	1910	│	2010	...	2110	2210
	Witten Hbf d.	...	...	...	...	...	0620t	│	...	0720r	│	0820	│	0920	│		1820	│	1920	│	2020	...	2120	2220
48	**Hagen** Hbf 804 d.	...	...	...	...	0602t	0634t	0702	...	0734r	0802	0834	0902	0934	1002	the same	1833	1902	1933	2002	2033	...	2133	2233
75	**Wuppertal** Hbf d.	...	...	...	...	0625t	0658t	0725	...	0758r	0825	0858	0925	0958	1025		1858	1925	1958	2025	2058	...	2158	2258
102	**Düsseldorf** Hbf a.	...	...	...	...	0646t	0718t	0746	...	0818r	0846	0918	0946	1018	1046	minutes	1918	1946	2018	2046	2118	...	2218	2318
102	**Düsseldorf** Hbf d.	...	0521	0548	0621	0648r	0721	0748	0748	0821	0848	0921	0948	1021	1048		1921	1948	2022	2048	2122	2148	2221	2321
113	Neuss Hbf d.	...	0536	0601	0636	0701r	0736	0801	0801	0836	0901	0936	1001	1036	1101	past each	1936	2001	2036	2101	2136	2201	2236	2336
130	**Mönchengladbach** Hbf a.	...	0548	0611	0648	0711r	0748	0811	0811	0848	0911	0948	1011	1048	1111		1948	2011	2048	2111	2148	2211	2248	2348
130	**Mönchengladbach** Hbf d.	0525	0550	0625	0650	0725	0750	0825	0825	0850	0925	0950	1025	1050	1125	hour until	1950	2025	2050	2125	2150	2225	2250	2350
139	Viersen d.	0533	│	0633	│	0733	│	0833	0833	│	0933	│	1033	│	1133		│	2033	│	2133	│	2233	│	│
157	Kaldenkirchen d.	0550	│	0650	│	0750	│	0850	0850	│	0950	│	1050	│	1150		│	2050	│	2150	│	2251	│	│
167	**Venlo** ▦ a.	0556	│	0656	│	0756	│	0856	0856	│	0956	│	1056	│	1156		│	2056	│	2156	│	2256	│	│
	Rheydt Hbf d.	...	0554	...	0654	...	0754	...	...	0854	...	0954	...	1054	...		1954	...	2054	...	2154	...	2254	2354
	Herzogenrath 473 d.	...	0623	...	0723	...	0823	...	...	0923	...	1023	...	1123	...		2023	...	2123k	...	2223	...	2323	0023
	Aachen Hbf 473 a.	...	0643	...	0743p	...	0843h	...	...	0943h	...	1043h	...	1143	...		2043	...	2137k	...	2243n	...	2337	0037

d – To Düsseldorf Flughafen Terminal (a. 0425).
f – ⑤⑥ (also Apr. 6, 9, 30, May 17, 28).
h – 6 minutes earlier on ©.
j – On ⑦ (also Apr. 10, May 1, 29; not Apr. 9, 30, May 28) Duisburg d. 2329, Mülheim d. 2336.
k – On © Herzogenrath d. 2126, Aachen Hbf a. 2143.
m – To / from Minden (Table 811).
n – 2236 on Ⓐ.
p – 0737 on ⑥.
r – ⚒ only.
t – Ⓐ only.
z – © only.

▲ – Timings may vary by up to 3 minutes (earlier departures possible).
⊠ – The 0759, 0959, 1159, 1459, 1559, 1659 and 1759 from Bielefeld run up to 6 minutes later Köln Hbf - Köln/Bonn Flughafen.
● – Certain Duisburg and Mülheim timings vary by up to 3 minutes. Osnabrück arrivals vary – subsequent arrivals are at 1219, 1310, 1419, 1510, 1619, 1711, 1819, 1910 and 2019.
♥ – Osnabrück departures vary – subsequent departures are at 0947, 1047, 1145, 1249, 1347, 1449, 1547, 1649, 1747 and 1849.
✤ – The 0945, 1345 and 1745 from Düsseldorf arrive Dortmund Hbf 5 minutes later.
⊖ – The 1105 and 1705 from Venlo depart Hagen and Schwerte 1–2 minutes earlier.
⊗ – Hamm d. 1422 (not 1425) / Unna d. 1434 (not 1437).
◇ – Operated by *eurobahn*.
♣ – Operated by National Express.
▷ – See Table **805** for *RE11* services Düsseldorf - Hamm - Paderborn - Kassel and v.v.
⊡ – See shaded panel on page 375 for a summary of the principal Rhein-Ruhr *RE* routes.
★ – Additional trains (◇) Münster - Osnabrück and v.v. (journey time 36 minutes):
From Münster at 0503 Ⓐ, 0603 ⚒, 0704, 0803 and hourly until 2303.
From Osnabrück at 0519 Ⓐ, 0619 ⚒, 0719 and hourly until 2119; then 2217 and 2319.

802 RHEIN – RUHR LOCAL SERVICES *RE / RB services*

Services in this table (pages 372–375) are shown route by route. Sub-headings indicate the route number and principal stations served.

RE5 Koblenz - Bonn - Köln - Düsseldorf - Duisburg - Wesel ♣ ⊡ *RE19* Düsseldorf - Emmerich - Arnhem ⊙

km				⚒◐	⚒	Ⓐ		◐		⚒									h	⑤⑥f				◐
0	**Koblenz** Hbf d.	...	...	0426	...	0516	...	0526	...	0616	...	0716	...	◇	1916	...	2016	...	2116	2116	...	2216	...	2326
18	Andernach d.	...	...	0444	...	0528	...	0544	...	0628	...	0728	...		1928	...	2028	...	2128	2128	...	2228	...	2344
29	Bad Breisig d.	...	...	0454	...	0534	...	0554	...	0634	...	0734	...	and at	1934	...	2034	...	2134	2134	...	2234	...	2354
39	Remagen d.	...	...	0511j	...	0544	...	0611j	...	0644	...	0744	...		1944	...	2044	...	2144	2144	...	2244	...	0011j
59	**Bonn** Hbf d.	...	...	0533	...	0604	...	0633	...	0704	...	0804	...	the same	2004	...	2104	...	2204	2204	...	2304	...	0033
93	**Köln** Hbf d.	...	...	0602a	0631	0631	...	0702a	0731	0731	...	0831	...		2031	...	2131	...	2228a	2231	*2249*	2328a	2349	0102a
94	**Köln** Messe/Deutz d.	...	...	0608	0634	0634	...	0708	0734	0734	...	0834	...	minutes	2034	...	2134	...	2233	2234	*2252*	2333	2353	0108
106	Leverkusen Mitte d.	...	...	...	0645	0645	...	...	0745	0745	...	0845	...		2045	...	2145	...	...	2245	*2304*	...	0004	━━
133	**Düsseldorf** Hbf d.	...	0626	...	0703	0703	0726	...	0803	0803	0826	0903	0926	past each	2103	2126	2203	2226	...	2303	2326	...	0022	...
140	Düsseldorf Flughafen ✈ d.	...	0633	...	0709	0709	0733	...	0809	0809	0833	0909	0933		2109	2133	2209	2233	...	2309	2333	...	0028	...
157	**Duisburg** Hbf d.	0544	0646	...	0719	0719	0744	...	0819	0819	0844	0919	0944	hour until	2119	2144	2219	2244	...	2317	2344	...	0036	0044
165	Oberhausen Hbf d.	0550	0652	...	0727	0727	0752	...	0827	0827	0850	0927	0950		2127	2150	2227	2250	...	...	2350	...	...	0050
192	Wesel d.	0616	0716	...	0748	0748	0816	...	0853	0853	0916	0948	1016		2148	2216	2254	2316	...	...	0016	...	...	0116
226	**Emmerich** 🏛 d.	0646b	0746	...	...	...	0846	...	...	...	0946	...	1046		...	2246	2316h	2346	...	...	0045	...	...	0145
256	**Arnhem** Centraal a.	0713b	0813	...	...	...	0913	...	...	...	1013	...	1113		...	2313	...	0013	...	...	...	...	...	...

	Ⓐ	◐		⚒	◐			⚒												◐				
Arnhem Centraal d.	...	...	...	...	...	...	...	...	0545r	...	0645	...	0745	...	▽	1845	...	1945	...	...	2045	2145	...	2245
Emmerich 🏛 d.	...	...	0409	...	...	0509	...	0539t	0609	...	0709	...	0809	...		1909	...	2009	...	...	2109	2209	...	2309
Wesel d.	...	...	0443	0507t	...	0543	...	0607	0643	0707	0743	0811	0843	0907	and at	1943	2011	2043	2111	...	2143	2243	...	2343
Oberhausen Hbf d.	...	...	0508	0533t	...	0608	...	0633	0708	0733	0808	0833	0908	0933		2008	2033	2108	2133	...	2208	2308	...	0008
Duisburg Hbf d.	...	...	0516	0542	...	0616	...	0642	0716	0742	0816	0842	0916	0942	the same	2016	2042	2116	2142	...	2216	2315	2323	0015
Düsseldorf Flughafen ✈ d.	...	...	0525	0550	...	0625	...	0650	0725	0750	0825	0850	0925	0950		2025	2050	2125	2150	...	2225	━━	2332	...
Düsseldorf Hbf d.	...	...	0533	0558	...	0633	...	0658	0733	0758	0833	0858	0933	0958	minutes	2033	2058	2133	2158	...	2233	...	2339	...
Leverkusen Mitte d.	...	...	...	0613	...	...	...	0713	...	0813	...	0913	...	1013		...	2113	...	2213	...	...	◐	2355	...
Köln Messe/Deutz d.	0526	0550	...	0626	0650	...	0726	0726	...	0826	...	0926	...	1026	past each	...	2126	...	2226	2250	...	2350	0009	...
Köln Hbf d.	0532	0556	...	0632	0656	...	0732	0732	...	0832	...	0932	...	1032		...	2132	...	2232	2256	...	2356	0012	...
Bonn Hbf d.	0557	0627	...	0657	0727	...	0757	0757	...	0857	...	0957	...	1057	hour until	...	2157	...	2257	2327	...	0027	...	...
Remagen d.	0615	0654j	...	0716	0754j	...	0816	0816	...	0916	...	1016	...	1116		...	2216	...	2316	2354j	...	0054j	...	...
Bad Breisig d.	0622	0702	...	0723	0802	...	0823	0823	...	0923	...	1023	...	1123		...	2223	...	2323	0002	...	0102	...	...
Andernach d.	0629	0712	...	0730	0813	...	0830	0830	...	0930	...	1030	...	1130		...	2230	...	2330	0012	...	0112	...	...
Koblenz Hbf a.	0642	0727	...	0742	0828	...	0842	0842	...	0942	...	1042	...	1142		...	2242	...	2342	0031	...	0132	...	...

RE7 Krefeld - Köln - Wuppertal - Hagen - Hamm - Münster (- Rheine: Table 812) ♣ ⊡

km		Ⓐ								⑤⑥f	
0	**Krefeld** Hbf d.	...	...	0535r	0635		2035	2135	2235	2235	...
18	Neuss Hbf d.	...	...	0553r	0653		2053	2153	2253	2253	...
54	**Köln** Hbf d.	...	0521t	0621r	0721	and	2121	2221	2318	2321	2352
55	**Köln** Messe/Deutz d.	...	0524t	0625r	0724		2124	2224	...	2324	2355
82	Solingen Hbf d.	...	0543t	0643r	0743	hourly	2143	2243	...	2343	0020
100	**Wuppertal** Hbf d.	...	0556t	0656r	0756		2156	2256	...	2356	0036
127	**Hagen** Hbf d.	0522	0622	0722	0822	until	2222	2322	...	0022	...
140	Schwerte (Ruhr) 808 d.	0533	0633	0733	0833		2233	2333	...	0033	...
156	Unna 808 d.	0544	0644	0744	0844		2244	2344	...	0044	...
175	**Hamm** (Westf) 805/8 d.	0559	0659	0759	0859		2259	2357	...	0057	...
211	**Münster** Hbf 805/8 a.	0622	0722	0822	0922		2322	...	...	...	...

	Ⓐ	⚒d							⑤⑥f	
Münster Hbf 805/8 d.	...	...	0529t	0634	0734		2034	2134	2134	2234
Hamm (Westf) 805/8 d.	...	0500	0600	0700	0800		2100	2200	2200	2300
Unna 808 d.	...	0513	0613	0713	0813	and	2113	2213	2213	2313
Schwerte (Ruhr) 808 d.	...	0525	0625	0725	0825		2125	2225	2225	2325
Hagen Hbf d.	0439	0539	0639	0739	0839	hourly	2139	2237	2239	2337
Wuppertal Hbf d.	0504	0604	0704	0804	0904		2204	━━	2304	...
Solingen Hbf d.	0515	0615	0715	0815	0915	until	2215	...	2315	...
Köln Messe/Deutz d.	0535	0635	0735	0835	0935		2235	...	2335	...
Köln Hbf d.	0542	0642	0742	0842	0942		2242	2342	2342	...
Neuss Hbf d.	0607	0707	0807	0907	1007		2307	0007	0007	...
Krefeld Hbf a.	0624	0724	0824	0923	1024		2324	0024	0024	...

Düsseldorf - Krefeld - Kleve ⊖

km		Ⓐ	⚒	Ⓐ		Ⓐ		♥		
0	**Düsseldorf** Hbf d.	0538	0608	0638	0708	0738	0808		2308	...
27	**Krefeld** Hbf d.	0606	0636	0706	0736	0806	0836	and	2336	...
57	Geldern d.	0631	0701	0731	0801	0831	0901		0001	...
66	Kevelaer d.	0638	0708	0738	0808	0838	0908	hourly	0008	...
72	Weeze d.	0645	0715	0745	0815	0845	0915		0015	...
79	Goch d.	0651	0721	0751	0821	0851	0921	until	0021	...
92	**Kleve** a.	0705	0735	0805	0835	0905	0935		0035	...

	Ⓐ	⚒	Ⓐ		Ⓐ		●		⑤⑥f
Kleve d.	0424	0524	0554	0624	0654	0724		2224	2354
Goch d.	0438	0538	0608	0638	0708	0738	and	2238	0008
Weeze d.	0445	0545	0615	0645	0715	0745		2245	0015
Kevelaer d.	0451	0551	0621	0651	0721	0751	hourly	2251	0021
Geldern d.	0458	0558	0628	0658	0728	0758		2258	0028
Krefeld Hbf d.	0526	0626	0656	0726	0756	0826	until	2326	0056
Düsseldorf Hbf a.	0553	0653	0723	0753	0823	0853		2353	0123

RE8 / RB27 Mönchengladbach - Köln - Königswinter - Koblenz

km		Ⓒ	Ⓐ	⚒		⚒	⚒	Ⓐ			⚒				⚒						⑤⑥f			⑤⑥f
0	**Mönchengladbach** Hbf d.	0041	...	...	...	0441	...	0507	0541	...	0607	0641	⊠	...	2007	2041	...	2141	...	2241	2241	...	2341	2341
3	Rheydt Hbf d.	0046	...	...	...	0446	...	0512	0546	...	0612	0646		...	2012	2046	...	2146	...	2246	2246	...	2346	2346
22	Grevenbroich d.	0103	...	...	...	0503	...	0529	0603	...	0629	0703	and at	...	2029	2103	...	2203	...	2303	2303	...	0003	0003
56	**Köln** Hbf a.	0135	...	...	...	0535	...	0600	0635	...	0700	0735		...	2100	2135	...	2235	...	2335	2335	...	0035	0035
56	**Köln** Hbf 807 d.	0138	...	...	...	0538	0603	0603	0638	0703	0703	0738	the same	2103	2103	2138	2203	2238	2303	2338	2338	0002	0038	0038
57	**Köln** Messe/Deutz d.	0141	...	...	...	0541	0607	0607	0641	0707	0707	0741		2107	2107	2141	2207	2241	2307	2341	2341	0006	0041	0041
71	Köln/Bonn Flughafen ✈ d.	0151	...	...	...	0551	|	|	0651	|	|	0751	minutes	|	|	2151	|	2251	|	2351	2351	|	0051	0051
83	Troisdorf 807 d.	0200	...	...	...	0600	0623	0623	0700	0723	0723	0800		2123	2123	2200	2223	2300	2323	0000	0000	0023	0100	0100
92	**Bonn** Beuel d.	0211	...	...	...	0612	0635	0635	0712	0735	0735	0812	past each	2135	2135	2212	2235	2312	2335	0012	0012	0035	0111	0111
100	Königswinter d.	0221	...	...	...	0621	0644	0644	0721	0744	0744	0821		2144	2144	2221	2244	2321	2344	0021	0021	0047	0121	0121
105	Bad Honnef d.	0226	...	...	...	0626	0651	0651	0726	0751	0751	0826	hour until	2151	2151	2226	2251	2326	2351	0026	0026	0051	0126	0126
115	Linz (Rhein) d.	0236	0437	0537	0637	0637	0701	0701	0737	0801	0801	0837		2201	2201	2237	2301	2337	2400	0036	0037	0100	0136	0137
122	Bad Hönningen d.	...	0444	0544	0644	0644	0706	0706	0744	0806	0806	0844		2206	2206	2244	2306	2344	...	...	0044	...	...	0144
138	Neuwied 914 d.	...	0458	0558	0658	0658	0719	0719	0758	0819	0819	0858		2219	2219	2258	2319	2358	...	...	0058	...	...	0158
153*	**Koblenz** Hbf 914 a.	...	0512	0612	0712	0712	0737	0737	0812	0837	0837	0912		2237	2237	2312	2337	0012	...	...	0112	...	...	0212

	Ⓒ	⚒		⚒	⚒		Ⓐ	⑥	Ⓒ		⚒				⚒								
Koblenz Hbf 914 d.	0047	...	...	0447t	0518t	0547r	0618	0619	...	0647	0719	0719	⇊	1747	1819	1819	1847	1919	1947		2219	2247	2347
Neuwied 914 d.	0101	...	...	0501t	0535t	0601r	0633	0635	...	0701	0735	0735		1801	1835	1835	1901	1935	2001		2235	2301	0001
Bad Hönningen d.	0114	...	...	0514t	0547t	0614r	0645	0647	...	0714	0747	0747	and at	1814	1847	1847	1914	1947	2014	and at	2247	2314	0014
Linz (Rhein) d.	0122	...	...	0522	0553	0622	0652	0653	0653	0722	0753	0753		1822	1853	1853	1922	1953	2022		2253	2322	0022
Bad Honnef d.	0132	...	...	0532	0602	0632	0702	0702	0702	0732	0802	0802	the same	1832	1902	1902	1932	2002	2032	the same	2302	2332	0032
Königswinter d.	0138	...	...	0538	0608	0638	0708	0708	0708	0738	0808	0808		1838	1908	1908	1938	2008	2038		2308	2338	0038
Bonn Beuel d.	0147	...	...	0547	0617	0647	0717	0717	0717	0747	0817	0817	minutes	1847	1917	1917	1947	2017	2047	minutes	2317	2347	0047
Troisdorf 807 d.	0159	...	...	0559	0628	0659	0728	0728	0728	0759	0828	0828		1859	1928	1928	1959	2028	2059		2328	2359	0059
Köln/Bonn Flughafen ✈ d.	0209	...	...	0609	|	0709	|	|	|	0809	|	|	past each	1909	|	|	2009	|	2109	past each	|	0009	0109
Köln Messe/Deutz d.	0219	0519	0619	0619	0650	0719	0750	0750	0750	0819	0850	0850		1919	1950	1950	2019	2050	2119		2350	0019	0119
Köln Hbf 807 a.	0222	0522	0622	0622	0653	0722	0753	0753	0753	0822	0853	0853	hour until	1922	1953	1953	2022	2053	2122	hour until	2353	0022	0122
Köln Hbf d.	...	0525	0625	0625	0659	0725	0759	0759	...	0825	0859	...		1925	1959	...	2025	...	2125		...	0025	0125c
Grevenbroich d.	...	0555	0655	0655	0729	0755	0829	0829	...	0855	0929	...		1955	2029	...	2055	...	2155		...	0055	0155c
Rheydt Hbf d.	...	0612	0712	0712	0746	0812	0846	0846	...	0912	0946	...		2012	2046	...	2115	...	2212		...	0112	0212c
Mönchengladbach Hbf a.	...	0619	0719	0719	0751	0819	0851	0851	...	0919	0951	...		2019	2052	...	2121	...	2219		...	0119	0219c

a – Arrival time.
b – On ⑦ Emmerich a. 0644, d. 0707, Arnhem a. 0729.
c – Mornings of Ⓒ only.
d – Runs daily Köln Messe/Deutz - Krefeld.
f – Also Dec. 25, Apr. 6, 9, 30, May 17, 28.
h – ⑦–④ (not Dec. 25, Apr. 6, 9, 30, May 17, 28).
j – Arrives 8 minutes earlier.
r – ⚒ only.
t – Ⓐ only.
▽ – Wesel d. 1211 / 1411 / 1611 / 1811 (not xx07).
◇ – Wesel a. 1053 / 1253 / 1453 / 1653 / 1753 / 1953 / 2053 (not xx48).

♥ – On Ⓐ trains run every 30 minutes until 2008.
● – On Ⓐ trains run every 30 minutes until 1824.
⇊ – Koblenz Hbf d. 0940 (not 0947), Neuwied d. 1000 (not 1001) then follows regular pattern.
⊠ – On Feb. 11, 18, Apr. 1, 3–6, 8, 11–15, 22, 29, May 6, 13, 22–26 the 1007 from Mönchengladbach is retimed to depart Mönchengladbach 0956, Rheydt 1000 (other timings follow the regular pattern).
⊙ – *RE19* operated by VIAS Rail.
◐ – Operated by Mittelrheinbahn.
♣ – Operated by National Express.
⊖ – Operated by Rhein Ruhr Bahn (additional services run on Ⓐ).
⊡ – See shaded panel on page 375 for a summary of the principal Rhein-Ruhr *RE* routes.
* – Via Koblenz-Lützel (*159 km* via Ehrenbreitstein).

RE / RB services — RHEIN – RUHR LOCAL SERVICES — 802

S-Bahn 19 Köln - Köln/Bonn Flughafen ✈ - Troisdorf

		Ⓐ	Ⓐ		Ⓐ		⑥		⑥	⑥		⑥		†		†	D			
Köln Hbf ... d.	Ⓐ	0401	0421	and every	2041	⑥	0411	and every	0811	0821	and every	2041	†	0411	and every	2041	A	2111	and every	0341
Köln Messe/Deutz ... d.		0403	0423	20 minutes	2043		0413	30 minutes	0813	0823	20 minutes	2043		0413	30 minutes	2043	I	2113	30 minutes	0343
Köln/Bonn Flughafen ✈ d.		0416	0436	until	2056		0426	until	0826	0836	until	2056		0426	until	2056	L	2126	until	0356
Troisdorf ... a.		0427	0447		2107		0437		0837	0847		2107		0437		2107	Y	2137		0407

		Ⓐ	Ⓐ		Ⓐ		⑥		⑥	⑥		⑥		†		†	D			
Troisdorf ... d.	Ⓐ	0432	0452	and every	2112	⑥	0442	and every	0712	0752	and every	2112	†	0442	and every	2112	A	2142	and every	0412
Köln/Bonn Flughafen ✈ d.		0443	0503	20 minutes	2123		0453	30 minutes	0723	0803	20 minutes	2123		0453	30 minutes	2123	I	2153	30 minutes	0423
Köln Messe/Deutz ... a.		0456	0516	until	2136		0506	until	0736	0816	until	2136		0506	until	2136	L	2206	until	0436
Köln Hbf ... a.		0459	0519		2139		0509		0739	0819		2139		0509		2139	Y	2209		0439

Dortmund - Unna - Soest ◇

km		⚒		⚒	Ⓐ		Ⓐ		Ⓐ		Ⓐ		⚒			⚒							
0	**Dortmund** Hbf ... 805 d.	0504	...	0604	0645	0704	0745	0804	0845	0904	0945	1004	1045	and at the same	1904	1945	2004	...	2104	2204	2304	...	0004
8	**Dortmund** Hörde ... d.	0513	...	0613	0653	0713	0753	0813	0853	0913	0953	1013	1053	minutes past	1913	1953	2013	...	2113	2213	2313	...	0013
23	Unna ... d.	0530	...	0630	0707	0730	0807	0830	0907	0930	1007	1030	1107	each hour until	1930	2007	2030	...	2130	2230	2330	...	0030
53	**Soest** ... 805 a.	0552	...	0652	0729	0752	0829	0852	0929	0952	1029	1052	1129		1952	2029	2052	...	2152	2252	2352	...	0052

	⚒	Ⓐ	⚒	Ⓐ		Ⓐ		Ⓐ		⚒			⚒										
Soest ... 805 d.	0504	0544	0604	0644	0704	0744	0804	0844	0904	0944	and at the same	1804	1844	1904	...	2004	...	2104	2204	2304	...	0004
Unna ... d.	0528	0608	0628	0708	0728	0808	0828	0908	0928	1008	minutes past	1828	1908	1928	...	2028	...	2128	2228	2328	...	0028
Dortmund Hörde ... d.	0544	0624	0644	0724	0744	0824	0844	0924	0944	1024	each hour until	1844	1924	1944	...	2044	...	2144	2244	2344	...	0044
Dortmund Hbf ... 805 a.	0551	0631	0651	0731	0751	0831	0851	0931	0951	1031		1851	1931	1951	...	2051	...	2151	2251	2351	...	0051

RB 53 Dortmund - Schwerte - Iserlohn

km		Ⓒ	Ⓒ	Ⓐ	Ⓐ		⚒		⊡	
0	**Dortmund** Hbf ... d.	0023	0123	0523	0553	0623	0623	0723	and	2323
8	**Dortmund** Hörde ... d.	0032	0132	0532	0602	0632	0632	0732	hourly	2332
18	Schwerte (Ruhr) ... d.	0045	0145	0545	0615	0642	0645	0745	until	2345
38	**Iserlohn** ... a.	0109	0209	0609	0639	...	0709	0809		0009

	Ⓒ	Ⓐ	Ⓐ		⚒		⊙		⑤⑥f
Iserlohn ... d.	0051	0521	0621	...	0651	0751	and	2251	2351
Schwerte (Ruhr) ... d.	0120	0550	0650	0720	0720	0820	hourly	2320	0020
Dortmund Hörde ... d.	0130	0600	0700	0730	0730	0830	until	2330	0030
Dortmund Hbf ... a.	0138	0608	0708	0738	0738	0838		2338	0038

Summary of principal Rhein - Ruhr *RE* routes

	RE1	*RE2*	*RE3*	*RE4*	*RE5*	*RE6*	*RE7*	*RE11*	*RE13*	*RE42*
Aachen Hbf	●	...	...	●	...	...	...	...	...	...
Köln Hbf	●	...	...	|	●	●	●	...	...	...
Mönchengladbach Hbf	|	...	...	●	|	|	|	...	●	●
Düsseldorf Hbf	●	●	●	●	●	●	|	●	●	|
Duisburg Hbf	●	●	●	|	●	●	|	●	|	●
Essen Hbf	●	●	|	|	...	●	|	●	|	●
via Gelsenkirchen	|	●	●	|	...	|	|	|	|	●
via Wuppertal and Hagen	|	|	|	●	...	|	●	|	●	|
Dortmund Hbf	●	|	●	●	...	●	|	●	|	|
Hamm (Westf)	●	|	●	...	...	●	●	●	●	|
Münster (Westf) Hbf	...	●	...	...	...	...	●	...	...	●

OTHER S-BAHN LINKS

Services operate every 20 – 30 minutes

Service	*Route (journey time in minutes)*
S 1	Solingen Hbf - Düsseldorf Hbf (22) - Düsseldorf Flughafen ✈ (35) - Duisburg Hbf (53) - Essen Hbf (72) - Bochum Hbf (90) - Dortmund Hbf (113).
S 3	Oberhausen Hbf - Mülheim Hbf (8) - Essen Hbf (17).
S 9	Essen Hbf - Wuppertal Hbf (46).
S11	Düsseldorf Flughafen Terminal ✈ - Düsseldorf Hbf (12) - Neuss Hbf (31) - Köln Hbf (82).

f – Also Dec. 25, Apr. 6, 9, 30, May 17, 28.

◇ – Operated by *eurobahn* (2nd class only).
⊡ – On Ⓐ trains run every 30 minutes 0653 - 1723.
⊙ – On Ⓐ trains run every 30 minutes 0721 - 1751.

2nd class only; German holiday dates apply — DORTMUND and MÜNSTER - ENSCHEDE — 803

km		⑥	Ⓐ	⚒						
0	**Dortmund** Hbf ... d.	...	0552	0652	0752r	0852		2052	2152	2252
44	Dülmen ... d.	...	0640	0740	0840r	0940	and	2140	2240	2340
61	Coesfeld (Westf) ... a.	...	0653	0753	0853r	0953		2153	2253	2353
61	Coesfeld (Westf) ... d.	0700	0705	0800	0900	1000	hourly	2200	...	...
96	Gronau (Westf) ... a.	0733	0738	0833	0933	1033		2233	...	...
96	Gronau (Westf) ... 🚌 d.	0745	0745	0845	0945	1045	until	2245	...	...
103	**Enschede** ... a.	0756	0756	0856	0956	1056		2256	...	...

	Ⓐ	⚒	⚒		Ⓐ	⑥			
Enschede ... d.	...	...	0556t	...	0656	0702	0802		2102
Gronau (Westf) ... 🚌 a.	...	...	0607t	...	0707	0713	0813	and	2113
Gronau (Westf) ... d.	...	0524t	0620	...	0708	0720	0820		2120
Coesfeld (Westf) ... a.	...	0557t	0657	...	0757	0757	0857	hourly	2157
Coesfeld (Westf) ... d.	0506	0603	0703	0803	0803	0803	0903		2203
Dülmen ... d.	0520	0617	0717	0817	0817	0817	0917	until	2217
Dortmund Hbf ... a.	0607	0707	0807	0907	0907	0907	1007		2307

km			Ⓒ		Ⓐ	Ⓐ	⚒			
0	**Münster** (Westf) Hbf ... d.	0008	0008	...	0508	0608	0708	0808	and	2308
56	Gronau (Westf) ... a.	0105	0105	...	0605	0705	0805	0905	hourly	0005
56	Gronau (Westf) ... 🚌 d.	...	0115	...	0609	0715	0815	0915	until	0015
63	**Enschede** ... a.	...	0126	...	0620	0726	0826	0926		0026

	Ⓐ	⚒	⚒						⑤⑥f
Enschede ... d.	...	...	0626	0732r	0832	and	2232	2332	2332
Gronau (Westf) ... 🚌 a.	...	...	0637	0743r	0843	hourly	2243	2343	2343
Gronau (Westf) ... d.	0445	0545	0645	0745	0845	until	2245	...	2345
Münster (Westf) Hbf . a.	0544	0644	0744	0844	0944		2344	...	0044

f – Also Dec. 25, Apr. 6, 9, 30, May 17, 28. r – ⚒ only. t – Ⓐ only.

RE services — HAGEN - KASSEL and DORTMUND - BRILON — 804

km		Ⓐ	⑥		⚒																			
0	**Hagen** Hbf ... 802 d.	0503	...	...	0603	...	0717	0817	0917	1017	1117	1215	1317	1417	1517	1615	1717	1817	1917	2017	...	*2122*	*2222*	*2322*
14	Schwerte (Ruhr) ... 802 d.	0513	...	...	0613	...	0728	0828	0928	1028	1128	1228	1328	1428	1528	1628	1728	1828	1928	2028	...	2149	2249	2349
57	Arnsberg (Westf) ... d.	0542	...	...	0642	...	0758	0858	0958	1058	1158	1258	1358	1458	1558	1658	1758	1858	1958	2058	...	2221	2321	0021
77	Meschede ... d.	0600	0609	...	0700	...	0816	0916	1016	1116	1216	1316	1416	1516	1616	1716	1816	1916	2016	2116	...	2239	2339	0039
85	Bestwig ... d.	0608	0616	...	0708	...	0823	0923	1023	1123	1223	1323	1423	1523	1623	1723	1823	1923	2022	2123	...	2246	2345	0045
100	Brilon Wald ... d.	0622	0629	...	0732h	...	0837	0937	1037	1137	1237	1337	1437	1537	1637	1737	1837	1937	...	2137	...	2259	...	...
126	Marsberg ... d.	0650	0700	...	0800	...	0900	1000	1100	1200	1300	1400	1500	1600	1700	1800	1900	2000	...	2200	...	...	...	...
151	Warburg (Westf) ... 805 d.	0721h	0721	...	0819	...	0921	1019	1119	1219	1321	1419	1521	1619	1721	1819	1921	2019	...	2219	...	...	...	...
177	Hofgeismar ... 805 d.	0737	0737	...	...	...	0937	...	...	...	1337	...	1537	...	1737	...	1937	...	...	...	...	...	...	...
202	**Kassel** Wilhelmshöhe ... 805 a.	0756	0755	...	...	...	0956	...	...	...	1356	...	1556	...	1755	...	1955	...	...	...	...	...	...	...

	⚒	⚒	⚒		Ⓐ	⑥																	
Kassel Wilhelmshöhe ... 805 d.	...	...	...	...	...	...	...	...	0803	...	1003	...	1203	...	...	...	1603	...	1803	...	...	2003	...	...
Hofgeismar ... 805 d.	...	...	...	...	...	...	...	...	0820	...	1020	...	1220	...	...	...	1620	...	1820	...	...	2020	...	...
Warburg (Westf) ... 805 d.	...	...	0535	...	0630	0635	...	0738	0838	0938	1038	1138	1238	1338	1438	1538	1638	1738	1838	1938	...	2038	...	2138
Marsberg ... d.	...	...	0555	...	0651	0655	...	0758	0859	0958	1059	1158	1259	1358	1459	1558	1659	1758	1859	1958	...	2059	...	2159
Brilon Wald ... d.	...	...	0621	...	0719	0721	...	0821	0921	1021	1121	1221	1321	1421	1521	1621	1721	1821	1921	2021	...	2125	2149	2225
Bestwig ... d.	0434	0534	0634	0634	0734	0734	0734	0834	0934	1034	1134	1234	1334	1434	1534	1634	1734	1834	1934	2034	...	2138	2210k	2238
Meschede ... d.	0441	0541	0641	0641	0741	0741	0741	0841	0941	1041	1141	1241	1341	1441	1541	1641	1741	1841	1941	2041	...	2145	2217	2245
Arnsberg (Westf) ... d.	0459	0559	0659	0659	0759	0759	0759	0859	0959	1059	1159	1259	1359	1459	1559	1659	1759	1859	1959	2059	...	...	2234	...
Schwerte (Ruhr) ... 802 a.	0528	0628	0728	0728	0828	0828	0828	0928	1028	1128	1228	1328	1428	1528	1628	1728	1828	1928	2028	2128	...	...	2303	...
Hagen Hbf ... 802 a.	0542	0642	0742	0742	0842	0842	0842	0942	1042	1142	1242	1342	1442	1542	1642	1742	1842	1942	2042	2142	...	...	2313	...

DORTMUND - BRILON WALD - BRILON STADT

km						Ⓐd		Ⓐd			
0	**Dortmund** Hbf ... d.	0741	0941	1141	1341	1441	1541	1641	1741	1941	2123
59	Arnsberg (Westf) ... d.	0825	1025	1225	1425	1525	1625	1725	1825	2025	2221
79	Meschede ... d.	0842	1042	1242	1442	1542	1642	1742	1842	2042	2239
87	Bestwig ... d.	0854	1054	1254	1454	1554	1654	1754	1854	2054	2246
102	Brilon Wald ... d.	0908	1108	1308	1508	1614k	1708	1814k	1908	2108	2301
106	**Brilon Stadt** ... a.	0916	1116	1316	1516	1622	1716	1822	1916	2116	2309

	Ⓐ¶						Ⓐd		Ⓐd	
Brilon Stadt ... d.	0543	0739	0939	1139	1339	1539	1629	1739	1829	1939
Brilon Wald ... d.	0552	0749	0949	1149	1349	1549	1649h	1749	1849h	1949
Bestwig ... d.	0610	0810k	1010k	1210k	1410k	1610k	1710k	1810k	1910k	2010k
Meschede ... d.	0617	0817	1017	1217	1417	1617	1717	1817	1917	2017
Arnsberg (Westf) ... d.	0634	0834	1034	1234	1434	1634	1734	1834	1934	2034
Dortmund Hbf ... a.	0720	0920	1120	1320	1520	1720	1820	1920	2020	2120

d – Runs daily Dortmund - Brilon Wald and v.v. h – Arrives 10 – 12 minutes earlier. k – Arrives 8 – 9 minutes earlier. ¶ – Additional train runs one hour later.

805 DÜSSELDORF and MÜNSTER - PADERBORN - KASSEL

SERVICE UNTIL APRIL 14

km								ICE	ICE		IC						IC								
		⊙		⊙	⊙	⊙	⊙	1223	1223	⊙	2155	⊙	⊙	⊙	⊙	⊙	2157	⊙	⊙	⊙	⊙				
		Ⓐ		Ⓒ	Ⓐ			Ⓐ	Ⓒ																
								M✕	M✕		G						G								
	Köln Hbf ... **800 802** d.	...	...	...	...	...	...	0824•	...	...	0918	...	...	...	...	...	1518	...	...	...	...	...	...	...	...
	Düsseldorf Hbf ... **800 802** d.	...	...	...	0536	0636	0736	0848	...	0836	0943	1036	1136	1236	1336	1436	1543	1636	1736	1836	1936	...	...	...	...
	Düsseldorf Flug ✈ **800 802** d.	...	...	...	0542	0642	0742	|	...	0842	0950	1042	1142	1242	1342	1442	1550	1642	1742	1842	1942	...	...	...	...
	Duisburg Hbf ... **800 802** d.	...	...	...	0557	0700	0758	0902	...	0858	1003	1058	1157	1259	1357	1457	1602	1659	1757	1857	1959	...	...	...	...
	Mülheim (Ruhr) Hbf ... **802** d.	...	...	...	0604	0706	0805	|	...	0904	|	1104	1204	1305	1404	1504	|	1706	1804	1904	2005	...	...	...	...
	Essen Hbf ... **800 802** d.	...	...	...	0613	0713	0813	0917	0917	0913	1017	1113	1213	1313	1413	1513	1616	1714	1813	1913	2013	...	...	...	...
	Bochum Hbf ... **800 802** d.	...	...	...	0624	0724	0824	0928	0928	0924	1030	1124	1224	1323	1424	1524	1628	1724	1824	1924	2024	...	...	...	...
0	**Dortmund** Hbf ... **800 802** d.	0433	...	0637	|	|	|	0942	0942	|	1044	|	|	|	|	|	1641	|	|	|	|	...	...	...	...
	Dortmund Hörde ★ ... d.	|	...	|	0645	0745	0845	|	|	0945	|	1145	1245	1345	1445	1545	|	1745	1845	1945	2045	...	...	...	...
31	Hamm (Westf) ... **800 802** a.	0453	...	0657	|	|	|	1002	1002	|	1101	|	|	|	|	|	1701	|	|	|	|	...	...	...	...
31	Hamm (Westf) ... d.	0501	...	0707	|	|	|	1007	1007	|	1107	|	|	|	|	|	1707	|	|	|	|	...	...	...	...
57	Soest ... **802** d.	0516	...	0722	0722	0822	0921	1022	1022	1026	1122	1221	1322	1421	1522	1621	1722	1819	1922	2021	2122	...	...	...	...
77	Lippstadt ... d.	0526	...	0732	0732	0832	0932	1032	1032	1037	1132	1232	1332	1432	1532	1632	1732	1830	1932	2032	2132	...	...	...	...
109	**Paderborn** Hbf ... **809 811** d.	0543	...	0748	0748	0848	0948	1049	1049	1054	1148	1247	1348	1447	1548	1647	1748	1845	1948	2047	2148	...	...	...	...
126	Altenbeken ... **809 811** d.	0556	...	0802	0802	...	1002	1103	1103	...	1202	...	1402	...	1602	...	1802	...	2002	...	2202	...	...	...	...
163	Warburg (Westf) ... **804** d.	0618	...	0824	0824	...	1024	1126	1126	...	1224	...	1424	...	1624	...	1824	...	2024	...	2224	...	...	...	...
189	Hofgeismar ... **804** d.	0634	...	0839	0839	...	1039	|	|	...	|	...	1439	...	1639	...	|	...	2038	...	2239	...	...	...	...
214	**Kassel** Wilhelmshöhe .. **804** a.	0652	...	0856	0856	...	1056	1156	1156	...	1255	...	1456	...	1656	...	1857	...	2054	...	2256	...	...	...	...

							IC							ICE	IC									
	⊙	⊙	⊙		⊙	⊙	2156		⊙	⊙	⊙	⊙	⊙	1224	2152		⊙	⊙	⊙	⊙	⊙				
	Ⓐ	Ⓐ																							
							G							M✕	G										
Kassel Wilhelmshöhe ... **804** d.	...	0555	...	...	0703	...	0902	...	...	1103	...	1303	...	1403	1502	...	...	1703	...	1903	2103	...	...	...	...
Hofgeismar ... **804** d.	...	0611	...	...	0720	...	|	...	...	1120	...	1320	...	|	|	...	...	1720	...	1920	2120	...	...	...	...
Warburg (Westf) ... **804** d.	0535	0635	...	...	0735	...	0934	...	...	1135	...	1335	...	1434	1534	...	...	1735	...	1935	2135	...	...	...	...
Altenbeken ... **809 811** d.	0558	0658	...	...	0758	...	0956	...	...	1158	...	1358	...	1456	1556	...	...	1758	...	1958	2159	...	...	...	...
Paderborn Hbf ... **809 811** d.	0609	0709	0709	...	0809	0909	1010	...	1109	1209	1309	1409	1504	1510	1610	...	1709	1809	1909	2009	2210	...	...	...	...
Lippstadt ... d.	0625	0725	0725	...	0825	0925	1026	...	1125	1225	1325	1425	1520	1525	1626	...	1725	1825	1925	2025	2226	...	...	...	...
Soest ... **802** d.	0635	0735	0735	...	0835	0935	1037	...	1135	1235	1335	1435	1530	1537	1637	...	1735	1835	1935	2036	2236	...	...	...	...
Hamm (Westf) ... a.	|	|	|	...	|	|	1050	...	|	|	|	|	|	1551	1650	...	|	|	|	|	|	...	...	...	...
Hamm (Westf) ... **800 802** d.	|	|	|	...	|	|	1056	...	|	|	|	|	|	▽	1656	...	|	|	|	|	|	...	...	...	...
Dortmund Hörde ★ ... d.	0711	0811	0811	...	0911	1011	|	...	1211	1311	1411	1511	1611	...	|	...	1811	1911	2011	2111	2311	...	...	...	...
Dortmund Hbf ... **800 802** d.	|	|	|	...	|	|	1116	...	|	|	|	|	|	...	1716	...	|	|	|	|	2317	...	...	...	...
Bochum Hbf ... **800 802** d.	0733	0833	0833	...	0933	1033	1130	...	1234	1333	1434	1533	1634	...	1730	...	1833	1933	2033	2133	...	...	...	...	...
Essen Hbf ... **800 802** d.	0747	0847	0847	...	0947	1047	1142	...	1247	1347	1447	1547	1647	...	1740	...	1846	1947	2047	2147	...	...	...	...	...
Mülheim (Ruhr) Hbf ... **802** d.	0753	0853	0853	...	0953	1053	|	...	1253	1353	1453	1553	1653	...	|	...	1852	1953	2053	2153	...	...	...	...	...
Duisburg Hbf ... **800 802** d.	0807	0907	0907	...	1007	1107	1155	...	1307	1407	1507	1607	1707	...	1755	...	1906	2007	2107	2207	...	...	...	...	...
Düsseldorf Flug ✈ .. **800 802** d.	0816	0916	0916	...	1016	1116	|	...	1316	1416	1516	1616	1716	...	1806	...	1915	2016	2116	2216	...	...	...	...	...
Düsseldorf Hbf ... **800 802** a.	0824	0924	0924	...	1024	1124	1208	...	1324	1424	1524	1624	1724	...	1811	...	1923	2023	2124	2224	...	...	...	...	...
Köln Hbf ... **800 802** a.	...	...	...	...	...	...	1240	...	...	...	...	...	...	...	...	...	...	...	...	...	...	...	...	...	...

MÜNSTER - HAMM - PADERBORN - WARBURG *Operated by eurobahn (2nd class only)*

	⚒		Ⓐ	⊗		⊖							⊖											⑤⑥ f	
Münster (Westf) Hbf ... **802** d.	0510	0609	0640	0710	0740t	0810	0840t	0908	1010	1110	1210	1310	1410	1510	1610	1710	1740t	1810	1840t	1910	2010	*2134*	*2234*	*2234*	2310
Hamm (Westf) ... **802** a.	0537	0636	0707	0737	0807t	0837	0907t	0937	1037	1137	1237	1337	1436	1537	1637	1737	1807t	1835	1907t	1937	2037	*2157*	*2257*	*2257*	2337
Hamm (Westf) ... d.	0546	0646	0717	0747	0817	0847	0917	0947	1046	1146	1247	1346	1446	1547	1646	1747	1817	1846	1917	1947	2047	2209	2309	2309	0009
Soest ... **802** d.	0603	0702	0734	0803	0834	0903	0934	1003	1103	1203	1303	1403	1503	1603	1703	1803	1834	1903	1934	2003	2103	2226	2326	2326	0026
Lippstadt ... d.	0615	0714	0745	0815	0846	0915	0946	1015	1115	1215	1315	1415	1515	1615	1715	1815	1846	1915	1946	2015	2115	2238	2338	2338	0038
Paderborn Hbf ... **809 811** d.	0642	0739	0810	0842	0910	0940	1010	1042	1140	1242	1340	1442	1540	1642	1740	1842	1910	1940	2010	2040	2140	2303	0001	0002	0103
Altenbeken ... **809 811** d.	0654	...	...	0854	...	...	...	1054	...	1254	...	1454	...	1654	...	1854	...	...	...	...	...	...	...	0014	...
Warburg (Westf) ... a.	0716	...	...	0916	...	...	...	1116	...	1316	...	1516	...	1716	...	1916	...	...	...	...	...	...	...	0036	...

	⚒					⊖		⊗							⊖										
Warburg (Westf) ... d.	...	...	...	...	...	0839	...	...	1039	...	1239	...	1439	...	...	...	1639	...	...	...	1839	...	2039	...	...
Altenbeken ... **809 811** d.	...	...	...	...	...	0902	...	...	1102	...	1302	...	1502	...	...	...	1702	...	...	...	1902	...	2102	...	...
Paderborn Hbf ... **809 811** d.	0521	0621	0721	0821	0851	0921j	0951	1021	1121j	1221	1321j	1421	1521j	1551	1621	1651	1721j	1751	1821	1851	1921j	2015	2115	2215	2315
Lippstadt ... d.	0544	0644	0744	0844	0914	0944	1014	1044	1144	1244	1344	1444	1544	1614	1644	1714	1744	1814	1844	1914	1944	2038	2138	2238	2338
Soest ... **802** d.	0556	0656	0756	0856	0926	0956	1026	1056	1156	1256	1356	1456	1556	1626	1656	1726	1756	1826	1856	1926	1956	2050	2150	2250	2350
Hamm (Westf) ... a.	0614	0714	0814	0914	0944	1014	1044	1114	1214	1314	1414	1514	1614	1644	1714	1744	1814	1844	1914	1944	2014	2108	2208	2308	0008
Hamm (Westf) ... **802** d.	0620	0720	0820	*0920*	0950t	1020	1050t	1122	1220	1320	1420	1520	1620	1650t	1720	1750t	1820	1850t	1922	*1959*	2020	2120	2220	2320	0010
Münster (Westf) Hbf ... **802** a.	0647	0747	0847	*0947*	1017t	1047	1117t	1147	1247	1347	1447	1547	1647	1717t	1747	1817t	1847	1917t	1947	*2022*	2047	2147	2247	2347	0040

G – To/from Gera via Weimar (Table **849a**).
M – To/from München (Table **900**).

f – Also Apr. 6, 9, 30, May 17, 28.
j – Arrives 5–6 minutes earlier.
t – Ⓐ only.

• – Köln **Messe/Deutz**.
⊗ – Change trains at Hamm on Ⓑ.
⊖ – Change trains at Hamm on Ⓐ.
⊙ – Operated by National Express.

▽ – Continues to Oberhausen (Table **800**).
★ – Most regional services are temporarily diverted via Dortmund Hörde. See Table **802** (Dortmund - Soest/Iserlohn panels) on page 375 for connections from/to Dortmund Hbf.

806 FRANKFURT - GIESSEN - KASSEL and SIEGEN

ICE/IC trains **KARLSRUHE - FRANKFURT - GIESSEN - KASSEL - HAMBURG - STRALSUND** (see next page for regional services).

ICE/IC trains	*ICE*	*ICE*	*ICE*	*IC*	*IC*	*ICE*	*ICE*	*ICE*	*ICE*	*ICE*
	1676	**1674**	**1672**	**2374**	**2374**	**1578**	**1576**	**1574**	**1572**	**1570**
	①g	⚒		Ⓐ	Ⓒ				n	Ⓑb
		✕	O✕	A🍷	A🍷	✕	✕	✕	✕	✕
Stuttgart Hbf **912** ... d.	...	...	...	0855	...	...	...	...	...	...
Karlsruhe Hbf **912** ... d.	...	...	0702**e**	|	0910	1110	1310	1510	1710	1910
Heidelberg Hbf **912** .. d.	...	...	0746**e**	0946	0946	1146	1346	1546	1746	1946
Frankfurt (Main) Hbf ... d.	0344	0649	0851	1051	1051	1251	1448	1648	1848	2051
Friedberg (Hess) ... d.	0423	0716	0916	1116	1116	1316	1516	1716	1916	2116
Gießen ... d.	0442	0734	0934	1134	1134	1334	1534	1734	1934	2134
Marburg (Lahn) ... d.	0459	0750	0950	1151	1151	1350	1550	1750	1950	2150
Treysa ... d.	0526	0815	1016	1216	1216	1416	1616	1816	2017	2216
Wabern ... d.	0543	0833	1034	1234	1234	|	1634	1834	2034	|
Kassel Wilhelmshöhe .. a.	0611	0854	1054	1254	1254	1454	1654	1854	2054	2255
Hannover Hbf **900** ... a.	0756	0957	1156	1356	1356	1556	1756	1956	2156	0010j
Hamburg Hbf **900** ... a.	0932	1130	1330	1530	1530	1732	1929	2129	2329**r**	...
Rostock Hbf **830** ... a.	1132	...	1532	...	...	1933	2133**b**	2333**z**	...	...
Stralsund Hbf **830** ... a.	1229**v**	...	1630**v**	...	...	2029**v**	2229**z**	...	...	...

ICE/IC trains	*ICE*	*ICE*	*ICE*	*ICE*	*ICE*	*ICE*	*IC*	*ICE*	*ICE*	*ICE*
	1571	**1573**	**1575**	**1577**	**1579**	**1671**	**2375**	**1595**	**1675**	**1677**
	Ⓐ	⚒	⚒					⑦w		⑤⑦
	✕	✕	✕	✕	✕	O✕	A🍷	B🍷	✕	w✕
Stralsund Hbf **830** ... d.	...	...	...	0521**k**	0727**p**	0926**v**	...	...	1326**v**	1526**v**
Rostock Hbf **830** ... d.	...	...	...	0625**a**	0825**h**	1025	...	...	1425	1625
Hamburg Hbf **900** ... d.	...	...	0624	0828	1028	1228	1427	...	1628	1828
Hannover Hbf **900** ... d.	...	0557**a**	0801	1001	1201	1401	1601	1702	1801	2001
Kassel Wilhelmshöhe ... d.	0459	0701	0903	1104	1303	1503	1703	1811	1903	2103
Wabern ... d.	0519	0720	|	1123	|	1523	1722	|	1923	2122
Treysa ... d.	0536	0737	0937	1140	1337	1540	1739	|	1940	2139
Marburg (Lahn) ... d.	0604	0804	1004	1205	1404	1604	1805	1906	2004	2204
Gießen ... d.	0622	0823	1023	1223	1423	1623	1823	1925	2023	2223
Friedberg (Hess) ... d.	0642	0842	1042	1242	1442	1642	1842	|	2042	2242
Frankfurt (Main) Hbf ... a.	0709	0910	1110	1309	1509	1709	1909	2014	2109	2309
Heidelberg Hbf **912** ... a.	0812	1013	1213	1413	1613	1813	2013	2112	...	...
Karlsruhe Hbf **912** ... a.	0850	1050	1250	1450	1650	1852	2053	|	...	...
Stuttgart Hbf **912** ... a.	...	...	...	...	...	...	...	2155	...	...

A – WATTENMEER – To/from Westerland on dates in Table **821**.
B – From Berlin (Table **810**).
O – To/from Ostseebad Binz on dates in Table **844**.

a – Ⓐ only.
b – Ⓑ (not Dec. 25).
c – Ⓒ only.
e – ⚒ only.
g – Also Dec. 27; not Dec. 26.

h – ⑥ (also Dec. 25).
j – Kassel - Hannover on ⑦ (also Dec. 26; not Dec. 25).
k – Ⓐ until Mar. 3.
n – Not Dec. 24.
p – ⑥ until Feb. 25 (also Dec. 25).
r – ⑤–⑦ (also Dec. 26; not Dec. 24).
v – Until Mar. 3.
w – Also Dec. 26; not Dec. 25.
z – ⑦ until Feb. 26 (also Dec. 26; not Dec. 25).

FRANKFURT - GIESSEN - KASSEL and SIEGEN 806

Regional trains **FRANKFURT - GIESSEN - KASSEL / SIEGEN** (see previous page for *ICE / IC* services to / from Kassel). See Table **808** for other *IC* services Frankfurt - Wetzlar - Siegen and v.v.

km		†	⚒	◇ ⚒	Ⓐ	◇ Ⓐ	◇ Ⓐ	◇ Ⓒ	◇ Ⓒ		◇ ⚒	⚒	◇	◇		◇	⚒	◇	◇		◇		◇	◇		◇
0	**Frankfurt (Main)** Hbf d.	0508	0521	...	0551	...	0616	0621	...	0717	...	0745	0815n	0815k	0919	...	0951	1021	1021	1119	...	1151	1221	1221	1319	...
34	Friedberg (Hess) d.	0533	0545	...	0615	...	0645	0645	...	0745	...	0815	0845	0845r	0945	...	1015	1045	1045	1145	...	1215	1245	1245	1345	...
39	Bad Nauheim d.	0537	│	...	0619	...	│	│	...	│	...	0819	│	│	│	...	1020	│	│	│	...	1220	│	│	│	...
66	**Gießen** a.	0603	0603	...	0635	...	0702	0702	...	0803	...	0835	0902	0902r	1003	...	1035	1102	1102	1203	...	1235	1302	1302	1403	...
66	**Gießen** 906 d.	0604	0604	0609	0640	0652	0703	0705	0709	0804	0815	0840	0905	0909	1004	1015	1040	1105	1109	1204	1215	1240	1305	1309	1404	1415
79	Wetzlar 906 d.	│	│	0624	0650	0703	│	│	0718	│	0824	0850	│	0918	│	1024	1050	│	1118	│	1224	1250	│	1318	│	1424
101	Herborn d.	│	│	0637	0712	0730	│	│	0733	│	0837	0912	│	0933	│	1037	1112	│	1133	│	1237	1312	│	1333	│	1437
107	Dillenburg d.	│	│	0642	0722	0738	│	│	0738	│	0843	0922	│	0938	│	1043	1122	│	1138	│	1243	1322	│	1338	│	1443
139	**Siegen** Hbf a.	│	│	0711	...	0805	│	│	0805	│	0912	...	│	1005	│	1112	...	│	1205	│	1312	...	│	1405	│	1512
96	Marburg (Lahn) d.	0620	0620	...	...	...	0720	0720	...	0820	...	...	0920	...	1020	...	...	1120	...	1220	...	...	1320	...	1420	...
118	Stadtallendorf d.	0636	0636	...	...	...	0737	0737	...	0836	...	...	0937	...	1036	...	...	1137	...	1236	...	...	1337	...	1436	...
138	Treysa d.	0649	0649	...	...	...	0755	0755	...	0849	...	...	0955	...	1049	...	...	1155	...	1249	...	...	1355	...	1449	...
166	Wabern d.	0707	0707	...	...	...	0818	0818	...	0907	...	...	1018	...	1107	...	...	1218	...	1307	...	...	1418	...	1507	...
196	**Kassel** Wilhelmshöhe a.	0726	0726	...	...	...	0846	0846	...	0926	...	...	1046	...	1126	...	...	1246	...	1326	...	...	1446	...	1526	...
200	**Kassel** Hbf a.	0734	0734	...	...	...	0854	0854	...	0934	...	...	1055	...	1134	...	...	1254	...	1334	...	...	1454	...	1534	...

		◇	◇		◇		◇	◇		◇ Ⓒ	◇ Ⓐ		◇	◇		◇		◇	◇		◇		◇	◇	D	◇
Frankfurt (Main) Hbf d.	1351	1421	1421	1519	...	1551	1620	1620	1719	...	1731	1751	1820	1820	1919	...	1951	2021	2021	2121	...	2151	2221	2221	2321	...
Friedberg (Hess) d.	1415	1445	1445	1545	...	1615	1645	1645	1745	...	│	1815	1845	1845	1945	...	2015	2045	2045	2145	...	2215	2245	2245	2345	...
Bad Nauheim d.	1420	│	│	│	...	1620	│	│	│	...	1800	1820	│	│	│	...	2020	│	│	│	...	2219	│	│	│	...
Gießen a.	1435	1502	1502	1603	...	1635	1702	1702	1803	...	│	1835	1902	1902	2003	...	2035	2102	2102	2203	...	2235	2302	2302	0005	...
Gießen 906 d.	1440	1505	1509	1604	1615	1640	1705	1709	1804	1815	⊙	1840	1905	1909	2004	2015	2040	2105	2109	2204	2209	2240	2305	2309	0007	0011
Wetzlar 906 d.	1450	│	1518	│	1624	1650	│	1718	│	1824	1824	1850	│	1918	│	2024	2050	│	2118	│	2218	2250	│	2318	│	0021
Herborn d.	1512	│	1533	│	1637	1712	│	1733	│	1838	1838	1912	│	1933	│	2037	2112	│	2133	│	2233	2312	│	2333	│	0043
Dillenburg d.	1522	│	1538	│	1643	1722	│	1738	│	1843	1843	1922	│	1938	│	2043	2122	│	2138	│	2238	2322	│	2338	│	0050
Siegen Hbf a.	...	│	1605	│	1712	...	│	1805	│	1912	1912	...	│	2005	│	2111	...	│	2205	│	2302	...	│	0005	│	0120
Marburg (Lahn) d.	...	1520	...	1620	...	...	1720	...	1820	...	...	...	1920	...	2020	...	...	2120	...	2220	...	...	2320	...	0031	...
Stadtallendorf d.	...	1537	...	1636	...	...	1737	...	1836	...	...	...	1937	...	2036	...	...	2140	...	2236	...	...	2340	...	0050	...
Treysa d.	...	1555	...	1649	...	...	1758	...	1849	...	...	...	1955	...	2049	...	...	2155	...	2249	...	...	2355	...	0105	...
Wabern d.	...	1618	...	1707	...	...	1819	...	1907	...	...	...	2018	...	2107	...	...	2218	...	2307	...	...	0018	...	0123	...
Kassel Wilhelmshöhe a.	...	1646	...	1726	...	...	1846	...	1927	...	...	...	2047	...	2126	...	...	2245	...	2326	...	...	0048	...	0144	...
Kassel Hbf a.	...	1655	...	1734	...	...	1854	...	1934	...	...	...	2054	...	2134	...	...	2251	...	2334	...	...	0054	...	0151	...

	Ⓐ	Ⓒ	◇ Ⓐ	◇ ⑥	◇ Ⓒ	Ⓐ	◇ Ⓐ	⚒	◇ ⑥	Ⓐ	Ⓒ	◇ Ⓐ A	◇	◇ †	◇ ⚒		◇		◇	◇		◇		◇	◇	
Kassel Hbf d.	0400	0423	...	...	...	...	...	...	...	0608	0615	...	...	...	0705	...	...	0823	...	0905	...	...	1023	...	1105	...
Kassel Wilhelmshöhe d.	0405	0429	...	...	...	...	...	...	...	0613	0620	...	...	...	0710	...	...	0829	...	0910	...	...	1029	...	1110	...
Wabern d.	0423	0448	...	...	...	...	...	...	...	0637	0645	...	...	...	0738	...	...	0848	...	0938	...	...	1048	...	1138	...
Treysa d.	0441	0505	...	...	0559	0557	...	...	...	0657	0702	...	...	0753	0805j	...	...	0905	...	1005	...	...	1105	...	1205	...
Stadtallendorf d.	0454	0519	...	...	0614	0611	...	...	...	0713	0717	...	...	0808	0819j	...	...	0919	...	1019	...	...	1119	...	1219	...
Marburg (Lahn) d.	0512	0535	...	...	0635	0634	...	...	...	0733	0735	...	...	0835	0835	...	...	0935	...	1035	...	...	1135	...	1235	...
Siegen Hbf d.	│	│	0458	0554	│	│	0600	...	0645	│	│	0645	0754	│	│	...	0845	│	0954	│	...	1045	│	1154	│	
Dillenburg d.	│	│	0525	0617	│	│	0626	0633	0717	│	│	0717	0817	│	│	0833r	0917	│	1017	│	1033r	1117	│	1217	│	1233
Herborn d.	│	│	0530	0622	│	│	0631	0640	0722	│	│	0736y	0822	│	│	0840r	0922	│	1022	│	1040r	1122	│	1222	│	1240
Wetzlar 906 d.	│	│	0547	0637	│	│	0649	0702	0737	│	│	0752	0837	│	│	0902	0937	│	1037	│	1102	1137	│	1237	│	1302
Gießen 906 a.	0534	0551	│	0646	0651	0651	0659	0714	0746	0751	0751	0801	0847	0851	0851	0914	0946	0951	1046	1051	1114	1146	1151	1246	1251	1314
Gießen d.	0536	0553	│	0655	0655	0652	0709	0722	...	0753	0753	*0808*	0855	0855	0855	0922	...	0953	1055	1055	1122	...	1153	1255	1255	1322
Bad Nauheim d.	0555	│	0611	│	│	│	0728	0739	...	│	│	*0826*	│	│	│	0939	...	│	│	│	1139	...	│	│	│	1339
Friedberg (Hess) d.	0559	0612	│	0713	0713	0712	0733	0743	...	0812	0812	*0830*	0913	0913	0913	0943	...	1012	1113	1113	1143	...	1212	1313	1313	1343
Frankfurt (Main) Hbf a.	0627	0635	0643	0738	0738	0742	0802	0809	...	0840	0837	*0858*	0939p	0941	0939	1009	...	1040	1138	1138	1209	...	1240	1338	1338	1409

	◇		◇	◇		◇		◇	◇		◇		◇	◇		◇		◇	◇		◇		◇	◇	◇	
Kassel Hbf d.	...	1223	...	1305	...	...	1423	...	1505	...	...	1623	...	1705	...	...	1823	...	1905	...	...	2023	2105	...	...	2223
Kassel Wilhelmshöhe d.	...	1229	...	1310	...	...	1429	...	1510	...	...	1629	...	1710	...	...	1829	...	1910	...	...	2029	2110	...	...	2229
Wabern d.	...	1248	...	1338	...	...	1448	...	1538	...	...	1648	...	1738	...	...	1848	...	1938	...	...	2048	2138	...	...	2252
Treysa d.	...	1305	...	1405	...	...	1505	...	1605	...	...	1705	...	1805	...	...	1905	...	2005	...	...	2106	2201	...	...	2309
Stadtallendorf d.	...	1319	...	1419	...	...	1519	...	1619	...	...	1719	...	1819	...	...	1919	...	2019	...	...	2119	2214	...	...	2323
Marburg (Lahn) d.	...	1335	...	1435	...	...	1535	...	1635	...	...	1735	...	1835	...	...	1935	...	2035	...	...	2135	2235	...	...	2340
Siegen Hbf d.	1245	│	1354	│	...	1445	│	1554	│	...	1645	│	1754	│	...	1845	│	1954	│	...	2052	│	│	2154	2310	│
Dillenburg d.	1317	│	1417	│	1433	1517	│	1617	│	1633	1717	│	1817	│	1833	1917	│	2017	│	2033	2117	│	│	2217	2334	│
Herborn d.	1322	│	1422	│	1440	1522	│	1622	│	1640	1722	│	1822	│	1840	1922	│	2022	│	2040	2122	│	│	2222	2339	│
Wetzlar 906 d.	1337	│	1437	│	1502	1537	│	1637	│	1702	1737	│	1837	│	1902	1937	│	2037	│	2102	2137	│	│	2237	2352	│
Gießen 906 a.	1346	1351	1446	1451	1514	1546	1551	1646	1651	1714	1746	1751	1846	1851	1914	1946	1951	2046	2051	2114	2147	2151	2250	2246	0001	0005
Gießen d.	...	1353	1455	1455	1522	...	1553	1655	1655	1722	...	1753	1855	1855	1922	...	1953	2054	2054	2122	...	2153	...	2255	...	0008
Bad Nauheim d.	...	│	│	│	1539	...	│	│	│	1739	...	│	│	│	1939	...	│	│	│	2139	...	│	...	│	...	0030
Friedberg (Hess) d.	...	1412	1513	1513	1543	...	1612	1713	1713	1743	...	1812	1913	1913	1943	...	2012	2113	2113	2143	...	2212	...	2313	...	0035
Frankfurt (Main) Hbf a.	...	1440	1538	1538	1615	...	1642	1738	1738	1815	...	1842	1938	1938	2009	...	2040	2138	2138	2208	...	2237	...	2338	...	0118

A – From Au (Table **807**).
D – Runs daily Frankfurt - Treysa; ⑤⑥† Frankfurt - Treysa - Kassel.
j – On ⑥ Treysa d. 0800, Stadtallendorf d. 0815.
k – ⚒ only. 0821 on ⑥.
n – 0821 on Ⓒ.
p – 0941 on †.
r – ⚒ only.
y – Arrives 0723.
⊙ – Connection from Gießen departs 1803 (Wetzlar a. 1814).
◇ – Operated by Hessische Landesbahn.

AACHEN - KÖLN - SIEGEN 807

RE / S-Bahn services

km		Ⓒ	Ⓐ 2	Ⓐ G ◇	⑥ ◇	⑥	Ⓐ	Ⓐ	Ⓒ	Ⓐ	Ⓒ	⊕														
0	**Aachen** Hbf 802 910 d.	...	...		...	...	0518	0618	...	0718	*0718*k	0818	0918	1018	1118	1218	1318	1418	1518	1618	1718	1818	1918	2018	2118	...
31	Düren 802 d.	...	...	...	...	...	0545	0645	...	0745	*0745*k	0845	0945	1045	1145	1245	1345	1445	1546	1645	1745	1845	1945	2045	2145	...
70	**Köln** Hbf 802 910 a.	...	...	...	...	...	0612	0712	...	0812	*0813*k	0912	1012	1112	1212	1312	1412	1512	1621	1712	1812	1912	2012	2112	2210	...
70	**Köln** Hbf 802 910 d.	0023	0431	...	...	0623	0623	0722	0723	0821	0821	0923	1023	1123	1221	1323	1423	1523	1623	1723	1823	1923	2023	2121	2223	2323
71	**Köln** M/D ⊡ 802 910 d.	0027	0433	...	...	0627	0627	0725	0727	0824	0824	0927	1026	1127	1226	1327	1427	1527	1627	1727	1827	1927	2027	2125	2227	2327
91	Troisdorf 802 d.	0041	0454	...	...	0641	0641	0741	0741	0841	0841	0941	1041	1141	1241	1341	1441	1541	1641	1741	1841	1941	2041	2141	2241	2341
95	Siegburg/Bonn 910 d.	0046	0459	...	...	0646	0646	0746	0746	0846	0846	0946	1046	1146	1246	1346	1446	1546	1646	1746	1846	1946	2046	2146	2246	2346
102	Hennef (Sieg) d.	0050	0505	...	...	0650	0650	0750	0750	0850	0850	0950	1050	1150	1250	1350	1450	1550	1650	1750	1850	1950	2051	2150	2250	2351
114	Eitorf d.	0059	0518	...	...	0700	0701	0759	0759	0859	0859	0959	1059	1159	1259	1359	1459	1559	1659	1759	1859	1959	2059	2159	2259	2359
136	Au (Sieg) d.	0116	0539	0556	0605	0716	0717	0816	0816	0916	0916	1016	1116	1216	1316	1416	1516	1616	1716	1816	1916	2016	2116	2216	2316	0016
142	Wissen (Sieg) d.	0124	...	0603	0612	0721	0722	0821	0821	0921	0921	1021	1121	1221	1321	1421	1521	1621	1721	1821	1921	2021	2121	2224	2323	0024
154	Betzdorf (Sieg) d.	0138	...	0618	0626	0731	0731	0831	0831	0931	0931	1031	1131	1231	1331	1431	1531	1631	1731	1831	1931	2031	2131	2238	2338	0038
171	**Siegen** Hbf a.	0200	...	0643	0651	0750	0750	0850	0850	0950	0950	1050	1150	1250	1350	1450	1550	1650	1750	1850	1950	2048	2150	2300	0001	0100

	⚒ 2	Ⓐ	Ⓐ	⑥	Ⓐ	Ⓒ	⚒																	2	2	◇
Siegen Hbf d.	...	...	0454	0458	0604	0610	0710	0710	0810	0910	1010	1110	1210	1310	1410	1510	1610	1710	1810	1910	2010	2110	2210	...	...	2311
Betzdorf (Sieg) d.	...	...	0519	0519	0624	0628	0728	0728	0828	0928	1028	1128	1228	1328	1428	1528	1628	1728	1828	1928	2028	2128	2228	...	...	2335
Wissen (Sieg) d.	...	...	0532	0532	0636	0637	0737	0737	0837	0937	1037	1137	1237	1337	1437	1537	1637	1737	1837	1937	2037	2137	2237	...	...	2347
Au (Sieg) d.	0420	...	0540	0540	0643	0643	0743	0743	0843	0943	1043	1143	1243	1343	1443	1543	1643	1743	1843	1943	2043	2143	2243	2320	...	2354
Eitorf d.	0439	...	0600	0600	0700	0700	0800	0800	0900	1000	1100	1200	1300	1400	1500	1600	1700	1800	1900	2000	2100	2200	2300	2338	...	...
Hennef (Sieg) d.	0453	...	0609	0609	0709	0709	0809	0809	0909	1009	1109	1209	1309	1409	1509	1609	1709	1809	1909	2009	2109	2209	2309	2352	0002	...
Siegburg/Bonn 910 d.	0458	...	0614	0614	0714	0714	0814	0814	0914	1014	1114	1214	1314	1414	1514	1614	1714	1814	1914	2014	2114	2214	2314	2358	0007	...
Troisdorf 802 d.	0503	...	0618	0618	0718	0718	0818	0818	0918	1018	1118	1218	1318	1418	1518	1618	1718	1818	1918	2018	2118	2218	2318	0003	0012	...
Köln M/D ⊡ 802 910 d.	0527	0534	0633	0633	0733	0733	0836	0836	0933	1033	1133	1233	1333	1433	1533	1633	1733	1833	1933	2033	2133	2233	2333	0027	0037	...
Köln Hbf 802 910 a.	0529	0537	0636	0636	0736	0736	0839	0839	0936	1036	1136	1236	1336	1436	1536	1636	1736	1836	1937	2036	2136	2236	2336	0029	0039	...
Köln Hbf 802 910 d.	...	0547	0648	...	0747	...	0848	...	0947	1047	1147	1247	1346	1447	1547	1647	1745	1847	1946	2047	2147	*2247*	2347	...	0040	...
Düren 802 d.	...	0613	0713	...	0813	...	0913	...	1013	1113	1213	1313	1413	1513	1613	1713	1813	1913	2013	2113	2213	*2314*	0013	...	0118	...
Aachen Hbf 802 910 a.	...	0640	0740	...	0840	...	0940	...	1040	1140	1240	1340	1440	1540	1640	1740	1840	1940	2040	2140	2240	*2346*	0040	...	0143	...

G – To Gießen (Table **806**).
k – ⑥ only.
⊕ – Change trains at Köln Hbf on †.
⊡ – Köln Messe/Deutz.
◇ – Operated by Hessische Landesbahn.

808 MÜNSTER - DORTMUND - SIEGEN - FRANKFURT and ESSEN - HAGEN - SIEGEN

IC services	*IC* 2221	*IC* 2223	*IC** 2223	*IC* 2225	*IC** 2225	*IC* 2227	*IC** 2229	*IC* 2321	*IC** 2323	*IC** 2325	*IC* 2327
	Ⓐ h	⚒	Ⓐ		⚒			N			
Münster (W) Hbf .... **802** d.	...	...	...	...	0619a	0829	...	1231	1419	...	1819
Hamm (Westf) ...... **802** d.	...	...	...	...	0641a	0907	...	1307	1441	...	1841
Unna ...... **802** d.	...	...	...	...	|	0917	...	1317	|	...	|
Schwerte (Ruhr) **802** d.	...	...	...	...	|	0930	...	1330	|	...	|
Dortmund Hbf ..... **802** d.	...	...	0503	...	0703	|	1101	|	1503	1703	1903
Witten Hbf .... **802** d.	...	...	0514	...	0714	|	1114	|	1514	1714	1914
Letmathe .... d.	...	...	0539	...	0739	0949	1139	1349	1539	1739	1939
Altena (Westf) .... d.	...	...	0548	...	0748	|	1148	|	1548	1748	1948
Werdohl .... d.	...	...	0557	...	0757	|	1157	|	1557	1757	1957
Finnentrop .... d.	...	...	0615	...	0815	|	1215	|	1615	1815	2015
Lennestadt ♥ .... d.	...	...	0628	...	0828	1028	1228	1428	1628	1828	2028
Kreuztal .... d.	...	...	0645	...	0845	|	1245	|	1645	1845	2045
Siegen Hbf .... a.	...	...	0655	...	0855	1055	1255	1455	1655	1855	2055
Siegen Hbf .... **806** d.	0519	0701	0701	0901	0901	1101	1301	1501	1701	1901	...
Dillenburg .... **806** d.	0546	0725	0725	0925	0925	1125	1325	1525	1725	1925	...
Wetzlar .... **806** d.	0607	0742	0742	0942	0942	1142	1342	1542	1742	1942	...
Bad Nauheim .... d.	0629	0804	0804	1004	1004	1204	1404	1604	1804	2004	...
Frankfurt (M) Hbf . **806** a.	0702	0835	0835	1035	1035	1235	1435	1635	1835	2035	...

IC services	*IC** 2328	*IC** 2326	*IC** 2326	*IC** 2324	*IC* 2322	*IC** 2320	*IC* 2228	*IC** 2226	*IC** 2224	*IC* 2222
	Ⓐ	⚒	Ⓐ S		N					
Frankfurt (Main) Hbf .. **806** d.	...	...	0526	0726r	0926	1126	1326	1526	1726	1926
Bad Nauheim .... d.	...	...	0556	0756r	0956	1156	1356	1556	1756	1956
Wetzlar .... **806** d.	...	...	0618	0818r	1018	1218	1418	1618	1818	2019
Dillenburg .... **806** d.	...	...	0636	0836r	1036	1236	1436	1636	1836	2037
Siegen Hbf .... **806** a.	...	...	0658	0858r	1058	1258	1458	1658	1858	2101
Siegen Hbf .... d.	0501	0704	0704	0904	1104	1304	1504	1704	1904	...
Kreutztal .... d.	0512	0715	0715	0915	|	1315	|	1715	1915	...
Lennestadt ♥ .... d.	0532	0733	0733	0933	1132	1333	1532	1733	1933	...
Finnentrop .... d.	0544	0746	0746	0946	|	1346	|	1746	1946	...
Werdohl .... d.	0602	0804	0804	1004	|	1404	|	1804	2004	...
Altena (Westf) .... d.	0611	0813	0813	1013	|	1413	|	1813	2013	...
Letmathe .... d.	0622	0823	0823	1023	1213	1423	1613	1823	2023	...
Witten Hbf .... **802** d.	0647	0848	0848	1048	|	1448	|	1848	2048	...
Dortmund Hbf .... **802** a.	0657	0858	0858	1057	|	1458	|	1857	2057	...
Schwerte (Ruhr) ..... **802** a.	|	...	...	|	1228	...	1628	|	...	...
Unna .... **802** a.	|	...	...	|	1238	...	1638	|	...	...
Hamm (Westf) .... **802** a.	0717	...	...	1117	1255	...	1655	1917	...	...
Münster (Westf) Hbf .. **802** a.	0738	...	...	1138	1328	...	1728	1939	...	...

Regional services DORTMUND / HAGEN - SIEGEN. See note ⊠ *for additional services Hagen - Siegen and v.v.*

km																											
		Ⓐ		Ⓐ	⚒			⚒			⚒			⚒			⚒			⚒			⚒				
	Dortmund Hbf d.	...	0525	...	...	0800	...	...	1000	...	...	1159	...	...	1359	...	...	1600	...	...	1800	...	...	2000	...	2200	...
	Witten Hbf .... d.	...	0537	...	...	0812	...	...	1012	...	...	1212	...	...	1412	...	...	1612	...	...	1812	...	...	2012	...	2212	...
0	**Hagen** Hbf .. d.	0540	|	0640	0740	|	0840	0940	|	1040	1140	|	1240	1340	|	1440	1540	|	1640	1740	|	1840	1940	|	2040	|	2315
21	Letmathe .... d.	0557	0613	0657	0757	0836	0857	0957	1036	1057	1157	1236	1257	1357	1436	1457	1557	1636	1657	1757	1836	1857	1957	2036	2057	2235	2332
30	Altena (Westf) .. d.	0605	0621	0705	0805	0844	0905	1005	1044	1105	1205	1244	1305	1405	1444	1505	1605	1644	1705	1805	1844	1905	2005	2044	2105	2243	2340
39	Werdohl .... d.	0614	0630	0714	0814	0852	0914	1014	1052	1114	1214	1252	1314	1414	1452	1514	1614	1652	1714	1814	1852	1914	2014	2052	2114	2251	2349
61	Finnentrop .... d.	0631	0650	0731	0831	0910	0931	1031	1110	1131	1231	1310	1331	1431	1510	1531	1631	1710	1731	1831	1910	1931	2031	2110	2131	2309	0007
74	Lennestadt ♥ . d.	0643	0701	0743	0843	0921	0943	1043	1121	1143	1243	1321	1343	1443	1521	1543	1643	1721	1743	1843	1921	1943	2043	2121	2143	2322	0019
96	Kreuztal .... d.	0706	0720	0806	0906	0940	1006	1106	1140	1206	1306	1340	1406	1506	1540	1606	1706	1740	1806	1906	1940	2006	2106	2140	2206	2345	0042
107	**Siegen** Hbf ..... a.	0719	0730	0819	0919	0950	1019	1119	1150	1219	1319	1350	1419	1519	1550	1619	1719	1750	1819	1919	1950	2019	2119	2150	2219	2357	0054

	Ⓐ	Ⓐ		Ⓐ	⚒			⚒			⚒			⚒			⚒			⚒			⚒				
Siegen Hbf .... d.	0400	0543	0608	0638	0743	0808	0843	0943	1008	1043	1143	1208	1243	1343	1408	1443	1543	1608	1643	1743	1808	1843	1943	2008	2035	2135	2208
Kreuztal .... d.	0412	0554	0618	0649	0754	0818	0854	0954	1018	1054	1154	1218	1254	1354	1418	1454	1554	1618	1654	1754	1818	1854	1954	2018	2046	2146	2218
Lennestadt ♥ ... d.	0435	0617	0636	0710	0817	0836	0917	1017	1036	1117	1217	1236	1317	1417	1436	1517	1617	1636	1717	1817	1836	1917	2017	2036	2109	2209	2236
Finnentrop .... d.	0448	0630	0648	0730	0830	0848	0930	1030	1048	1130	1230	1248	1330	1430	1448	1530	1630	1648	1730	1830	1848	1930	2030	2048	2122	2222	2248
Werdohl .... d.	0506	0647	0706	0747	0847	0906	0947	1047	1106	1147	1247	1306	1347	1447	1506	1547	1647	1706	1747	1847	1906	1947	2047	2106	2139	2239	2306
Altena (Westf) ... d.	0515	0655	0715	0756	0855	0915	0955	1055	1115	1155	1255	1315	1355	1455	1515	1555	1655	1715	1755	1855	1915	1955	2055	2115	2147	2247	2315
Letmathe .... d.	0523	0708	0723	0808	0908	0923	1008	1108	1123	1208	1308	1323	1408	1508	1523	1608	1708	1723	1808	1908	1923	2008	2108	2123	2158	2258	2323
Hagen Hbf .... a.	|	0724	|	0824	0924	|	1024	1124	|	1224	1324	|	1424	1524	|	1624	1724	|	1824	1924	|	2024	2124	|	2214	2314	2338
Witten Hbf .... d.	0548	...	0748	...	...	0948	...	...	1148	...	...	1348	...	...	1548	...	...	1748	...	...	1948	...	...	2148	...	...	...
Dortmund Hbf .. a.	0559	...	0759	...	...	0959	...	...	1159	...	...	1359	...	...	1559	...	...	1804	...	...	1959	...	...	2159	...	...	...

Regional services ESSEN - HAGEN - LETMATHE - ISERLOHN

	Ⓐ	Ⓐ	⚒						✣			
Essen Hbf .... d.	0634	0734	0834	0934	and	1934		0507	and	2307	0012	...
Bochum Hbf ...... d.	0647	0747	0847	0947	hourly	1947	A	0521	hourly	2321	0026	...
Witten Hbf .... d.	0657	0757	0857	0957	until	1957	L	0533	until	2333	0038	...
Hagen Hbf .... d.	0715	0815	0915	1015		2015	S	0547		2347	0052	...
Letmathe .... a.	0730	0830	0929	1030		2030	O	...		...	...	...
Iserlohn .... a.	0738	0838	0938	1038		2038		...		...	...	...

	Ⓐ	Ⓐ	⚒									
Iserlohn .... d.	0618	0722	0822	0922	and	1922		...	and	...	...	...
Letmathe .... d.	0627	0730	0830	0930	hourly	1930	A	...	hourly	...	...	...
Hagen Hbf ..... d.	0651	0751	0851	0951	until	1951	L	0516	until	2216	2319	0016
Witten Hbf ..... d.	0702	0802	0903	1002		2002	S	0531		2231	2332	0031
Bochum Hbf .. d.	0714	0814	0914	1014		2014	O	0543		2243	2343	0043
Essen Hbf .... a.	0729	0829	0929	1029		2029		0558		2258	2358	0058

N – From / to Norddeich Mole (Table **812**).
S – From Stuttgart (Table **912**).

a – Ⓐ only.
h – Also calls at Herborn (d. 0552).
r – ⚒ only.

* – Regional tickets valid Dortmund - Siegen and v.v.
✣ – Essen d. 0805 (not 0807).
♥ – Lennestadt-Altenhundem.
⊠ – Additional services Hagen - Siegen and v.v.: **From Hagen** at 0421 Ⓐ and 0715 †. **From Siegen** at 0504 ⑥.

809 PADERBORN - HAMELN - HANNOVER - HANNOVER FLUGHAFEN ✈ *S-Bahn 5*

km																									
										Ⓐ	⑥			⚒	†										
0	**Paderborn** Hbf ..... **805 811** d.	...	...	...	...	...	...	...	...	0512	...	...	...	0615	...	...	0715	...	0815	...	0915	...	1015	...	1115
17	Altenbeken .... **805 811** d.	...	...	...	...	...	...	...	...	0524	...	...	...	0627	...	...	0727	...	0827	...	0927	...	1027	...	1127
56	Bad Pyrmont .... d.	...	...	...	...	...	...	0505r	...	0602	0605	...	0635t	0702	0705	0735t	0802	...	0902	...	1002	...	1102	...	1202
75	Hameln .... a.	...	...	...	...	...	...	0519r	...	0616	0619	...	0649t	0716	0719	0749t	0816	...	0916	...	1016	...	1116	...	1216
75	Hameln .... d.	...	...	...	...	0420t	0450r	0520	0550r	0620	0620	0620	0650r	0720	0720	0750r	0820	0850r	0920	0950r	1020	1050r	1120	1150r	1220
133	**Hannover** Hbf .... a.	...	...	...	...	0503t	0533r	0603	0633r	0703	0703	0703	0733r	0803	0803	0833r	0903	0933r	1003	1033r	1103	1133r	1203	1233r	1303
133	**Hannover** Hbf .... d.	0235	0335	0411	0435	0505	0535	0605	0635	0705	0705	0705	0735	0805	0805	0835	0905	0935	1005	1035	1105	1135	1205	1235	1305
148	**Hannover** Flughafen ✈ .... a.	0253	0353	0429	0453	0523	0553	0623	0653	0723	0723	0723	0753	0823	0823	0853	0923	0953	1023	1053	1123	1153	1223	1253	1323

																								⑤⑥ j	A
Paderborn Hbf .... **805 811** d.	...	1215	...	1314	...	1415	...	1515	...	1615	...	1715	...	1815	...	1915	...	2015	...	2115	...	2215	...	2307	...
Altenbeken .... **805 811** d.	...	1227	...	1327	...	1427	...	1527	...	1627	...	1727	...	1827	...	1927	...	2027	...	2127	...	2227	...	2321	...
Bad Pyrmont .... d.	...	1302	1335t	1402	...	1502	...	1602	1635t	1702	1735t	1802	1835t	1902	...	2002	...	2102	...	2202	...	2302	...	0002	0005
Hameln .... a.	...	1316	1349t	1416	...	1516	...	1616	1649t	1716	1749t	1816	1849t	1916	...	2016	...	2116	...	2216	...	2316	...	0016	0019
Hameln .... d.	1250r	1320	1350r	1420	1450r	1520	1550	1620	1650	1720	1750	1820	1850	1920	1950	2020	2050t	2120	...	2220	...	2320	...	0020	0020
Hannover Hbf .... a.	1333r	1403	1433r	1503	1533r	1603	1633	1703	1733	1803	1833	1903	1933	2003	2033	2103	2133t	2203	...	2303	...	0003	...	0103	0103
Hannover Hbf .... d.	1335	1405	1435	1505	1535	1605	1635	1705	1735	1805	1835	1905	1935	2005	2035	2105	2135	2205	2235	2305	2335	0005	0035	0105	0105
Hannover Flughafen ✈ .... a.	1353	1423	1453	1523	1553	1623	1653	1723	1753	1823	1853	1923	1953	2023	2053	2123	2153	2223	2253	2323	2353	0023	0053	0123	0123

							⚒		Ⓐ		⚒														
Hannover Flughafen ✈ .... d.	0006	0036	0106	0136	0209	0406	0436	0436	0506	0506	0536	0536	0606	0636	0706	0736	0806	0836	0906	0936	1006	1036	1106	1136	1206
Hannover Hbf .... a.	0024	0053	0124	0154	0226	0424	0453	0453	0523	0523	0553	0553	0623	0653	0723	0753	0823	0853	0923	0953	1023	1053	1123	1153	1223
Hannover Hbf .... d.	...	...	...	...	...	...	0455	...	0525	...	0555	...	0625r	0655	0725r	0755	0825r	0855	0925r	0955	1025r	1055	1125r	1155	1225r
Hameln .... a.	...	...	...	...	...	...	0540	...	0610	...	0640	...	0710r	0740	0810r	0840	0910r	0940	1010r	1040	1110r	1140	1210r	1240	1310r
Hameln .... d.	...	...	...	...	...	...	0544	...	0614	...	0644	...	0711t	0744	...	0844	...	0944	...	1044	...	1144	...	1244	1311t
Bad Pyrmont .... d.	...	...	...	...	...	...	0600	...	0628	...	0700	...	0725t	0800	...	0900	...	1000	...	1100	...	1200	...	1300	1325t
Altenbeken .... **805 811** d.	...	...	...	...	...	...	0633	...	...	...	0733	...	...	0833	...	0933	...	1033	...	1133	...	1233	...	1333	...
Paderborn Hbf .... **805 811** a.	...	...	...	...	...	...	0646	...	...	...	0746	...	...	0846	...	0946	...	1046	...	1146	...	1246	...	1346	...

																					B	⑤⑥ j		⑤⑥	
Hannover Flughafen ✈ .... d.	1236	1306	1336	1406	1436	1506	1536	1606	1636	1706	1736	1806	1836	1906	1936	2006	2036	2106	2136	2206	2236	2236	2306	2336	2336
Hannover Hbf .... a.	1253	1323	1353	1423	1453	1523	1553	1623	1653	1723	1753	1823	1853	1923	1953	2023	2053	2123	2153	2223	2253	2253	2323	2353	2353
Hannover Hbf .... d.	1255	1325r	1355	1425r	1455	1525	1555	1625	1655	1725	1755	1825	1855	1925	1955	2025r	2055	2125t	2155	...	2255	2255	...	2355	2355
Hameln .... a.	1340	1410r	1440	1510r	1540	1610	1640	1710	1740	1810	1840	1910	1940	2010	2040	2110r	2141	2210t	2240	...	2340	2340	...	0040	0040
Hameln .... d.	1344	...	1444	...	1544	1611t	1644	1711t	1744	1811t	1844	...	1944	...	2044	...	2144	...	2244	...	2341	2344	...	0042	...
Bad Pyrmont .... d.	1400	...	1500	...	1600	1625t	1700	1725t	1800	1825t	1900	...	2000	...	2100	...	2200	...	2300	...	2355	0000	...	0056	...
Altenbeken .... **805 811** d.	1433	...	1533	...	1633	...	1733	...	1833	...	1933	...	2033	...	2133	...	2233	...	2333	...	...	0033	...	...	...
Paderborn Hbf .... **805 811** a.	1446	...	1546	...	1646	...	1746	...	1846	...	1946	...	2046	...	2146	...	2246	...	2346	...	...	0046	...	...	...

A – Mornings of ①–⑤ (also Apr. 8; not Apr. 7, May 18).
B – ⑦–④ (also Apr. 7; not Apr. 6, May 17).
j – Also Apr. 6, May 17; not Apr. 7.
k – Not Apr. 7.
r – ⚒ only.
t – Ⓐ only.

HAMM and BAD BENTHEIM - HANNOVER - BERLIN 810

Independent operator **FlixTrain** also run services Köln - Berlin (see Table **927**).

km		ICE 949	ICE 649	ICE 841	ICE 753	IC 2241	ICE 541	ICE 1041	IC 2445	ICE 843	ICE 853	ICE 1155	IC 245	IC 245	ICE 543	ICE 553	IC 2443	ICE 845	ICE 855	ICE 1545	IC 141	ICE 545	ICE 555	ICE 757
			Ⓐ	⚒	Ⓐ	⚒	⚒	†			⚒		†	⚒						⚒				
		A♥	✕	O✕	H✕	🍷	✕	✕	🍷	✕	✕	A✕	🍷	🍷	✕	K✕	🍷	✕	✕	T🍷	🍷	✕	A✕	✕
	Köln Hbf **800** d.	2315	...	...	...	...	0426	...	0510e	0525	0542	0617	...	...	0624	0648	0713	0727	0748	...	...	0828	0848	0844
	Wuppertal Hbf **800** d.	│	...	...	...	...	│	...	0543e	│	0616	│	...	...	│	0716	0744	│	0816	...	...	│	0916	│
	Düsseldorf Hbf **800** d.	2338	...	...	...	...	0450	...	│	0551	│	│	...	...	0651	│	│	0751	│	...	...	0852	│	0915
	Dortmund Hbf **800** d.	0034	...	...	...	...	0546	...	0628	0646	│	│	...	...	0748	│	0828	0848	│	0909	...	0948	│	│
0	**Hamm** (Westf) **802** d.	0051	...	...	...	...	0604	...	0645	0711	0711	│	...	...	0811	0811	0845	0911	0911	0934	...	1011	1011	│
50	Gütersloh Hbf **802** d.	0111	...	...	...	...	0627	...	0708	│	│	│	...	...	│	│	0908	│	│	0955	...	│	│	│
67	**Bielefeld** Hbf **802 811** d.	0126	...	...	...	...	0640	...	0719	0738	0738	│	...	...	0838	0838	0919	0938	0938	1006	...	1038	1038	│
81	Herford **811** d.	│	...	...	...	...	│	...	0729	│	│	│	...	...	│	│	0929	│	│	1016	...	│	│	◧
	Amsterdam C **22** d.	│	...	...	...	...	│	...	│	│	│	│	...	...	│	│	│	│	│	│	0700	│	│	│
	Bad Bentheim 🏛 **811** d.	│	...	...	...	...	│	...	│	│	│	│	...	0721	│	│	│	│	│	│	0928	│	│	│
	Rheine **811** d.	│	...	...	...	...	│	...	│	│	│	│	...	0734	│	│	│	│	│	│	0941	│	│	│
	Münster (Westf) Hbf **800** d.	│	...	...	...	0533	│	...	│	│	│	│	0733	│	│	│	│	│	│	│	│	│	│	1028
	Osnabrück Hbf **800 811** d.	│	...	...	...	0604	│	...	│	│	│	│	0803	0805	│	│	│	│	│	│	1008	│	│	1053
	Bünde (Westf) **811** d.	│	...	...	...	0627	│	...	│	│	│	│	0826	0826	│	│	│	│	│	│	│	│	│	│
97	Bad Oeynhausen **811** d.	│	...	...	...	0638	│	...	│	│	│	│	0839	0839	│	│	│	│	│	│	1037	│	│	│
112	Minden (Westf) **811** d.	0151	...	...	...	0647	│	...	0746	│	│	│	0848	0848	│	│	0946	│	│	│	1047	│	│	│
177	**Hannover** Hbf **811** a.	0223	...	...	...	0718	0728	...	0818	0828	0828	│	0918	0918	0928	0928	1018	1028	1028	1101	1118	1128	1128	1201
177	**Hannover** Hbf d.	0240	0527	0631	0703	0722	0731	0731	0835	0831	0831	│	0922	0922	0931	0931	1036	1031	1031	1104	1122	1131	1131	1204
	Magdeburg Hbf **866** a.	0402	│	│	│	│	│	│	0954	│	│	│	│	│	│	│	1154	│	│	│	│	│	│	│
	Leipzig Hbf **866** a.	│	▽	│	│	│	│	│	1117	│	│	│	│	│	│	│	1319	│	│	│	│	│	│	│
	Dresden Hbf **842** a.	│	│	│	│	│	│	│	1300	│	│	│	│	│	│	│	1446w	│	│	│	│	│	│	│
252	Wolfsburg **902** d.	│	0619	0704	0737	0754	│	0803	...	0904	0904	│	0954	0954	│	│	...	1104	1104	1136	1154	│	│	1236
327	Stendal Hbf **838** d.	│	0646	0734	0804	0827	│	0834	...	│	│	│	1026	1026	│	│	...	│	│	│	1226	│	│	│
419	**Berlin** Spandau **838 902** a.	│	0728	0811	0838	0906	0854	0906	...	0958	0958	1004	1107	1107	1054	1054	...	1158	1158	1238	1307	1254	1254	1338
435	**Berlin** Hbf **838 902** a.	0535	0747	0825	0857	0925	0915	0924	...	1015	1015	1015	1125	1125	1115	1115	...	1215	1215	1257	1325	1315	1315	1357
440	**Berlin** Ostbahnhof **838 902** a.	0548	0801	0837	0909	0936	0927	0936	...	1027	1027	...	1136	1136	1127	1127	...	1227	1227	1309	1336	1327	1327	1409

	IC 2441	ICE 847	ICE 857	ICE 759	IC 143	ICE 547	ICE 557	IC 2010	IC 2049	ICE 849	ICE 859	ICE 1157	IC 145	ICE 549	ICE 559	ICE 1055	IC 2047	ICE 941	ICE 951	IC 1916	ICE 1116	IC 147	ICE 641	ICE 651
								⑤								⑤⑦r				⑤	⑦w			
	F🍷	✕	✕	B✕	🍷	✕	✕		S🍷	✕	✕	A✕	🍷	✕	A✕	R✕	S🍷	✕	✕	S	✕	🍷	✕	A✕
Köln Hbf **800** d.	0909	0925	0948	0930	...	1028z	1048y	1048	1109	1127z	1148	1217	...	1224z	1248	1236	1309	...	1348	1346	1346	...	...	1448
Wuppertal Hbf **800** d.	│	│	1016	│	...	│	1116	1123	1143	│	1216	│	...	│	1316	│	1343	...	1416	│	│	...	...	1515
Düsseldorf Hbf **800** d.	0934	0951	│	1016	...	1052	│	│	│	1153	│	│	...	1252	│	1318	│	1352	│	1414	1414	...	1449	│
Dortmund Hbf **800** d.	1028	1048	│	1112	...	1148	│	1210	1228	1248	│	│	...	1348	│	1410	1428	1448	│	1510	1510	...	1547	│
Hamm (Westf) **802** d.	1045	1111	1111	1134	...	1211	1211	1233	1245	1311	1311	│	...	1411	1411	1434	1445	1511	1511	1533	1533	...	1611	1611
Gütersloh Hbf **802** d.	1108	│	│	1155	...	│	│	1255	1306	│	│	│	...	│	│	1455	1508	│	│	1555	1555	...	│	│
Bielefeld Hbf **802 811** d.	1119	1138	1138	1206	...	1238	1238	1306	1317	1338	1338	│	...	1438	1438	1506	1519	1538	1538	1606	1606	...	1638	1638
Herford **811** d.	1129	│	│	1216	...	│	│	1316	1329	│	│	│	...	│	│	1516	1529	│	│	1616	1616	...	│	│
Amsterdam C **22** d.	│	│	│	│	0910	│	│	│	│	│	│	│	1100	│	│	│	│	│	│	│	│	1300	│	│
Bad Bentheim 🏛 **811** d.	│	│	│	│	1128	│	│	│	│	│	│	│	1328	│	│	│	│	│	│	│	│	1528	│	│
Rheine **811** d.	│	│	│	│	1142	│	│	│	│	│	│	│	1341	│	│	│	│	│	│	│	│	1541	│	│
Münster (Westf) Hbf **800** d.	│	│	│	│	│	│	│	│	│	│	│	│	│	│	│	│	│	│	│	│	│	│	│
Osnabrück Hbf **800 811** d.	│	│	│	│	1208	│	│	│	│	│	│	│	1408	│	│	│	│	│	│	│	│	1608	│	│
Bünde (Westf) **811** d.	│	│	│	│	1228	│	│	│	│	│	│	│	│	│	│	│	│	│	│	│	1628	│	│
Bad Oeynhausen **811** d.	│	│	│	│	│	│	│	│	│	│	│	│	1437	│	│	│	│	│	│	│	│	│	│	│
Minden (Westf) **811** d.	1146	│	│	│	1247	│	│	│	1346	│	│	│	1447	│	│	│	1546	│	│	│	│	1647	│	│
Hannover Hbf **811** a.	1218	1228	1228	1301	1318	1328	1328	1401	1418	1428	1428	│	1518	1528	1528	1601	1618	1628	1628	1701	1701	1718	1728	1728
Hannover Hbf d.	1236	1231	1231	1304	1322	1331	1331	1404	1436	1431	1431	│	1522	1531	1531	1604	1636	1631	1631	1704	1704	1722	1731	1731
Magdeburg Hbf **866** a.	1354	│	│	│	│	│	│	│	1554	│	│	│	│	│	│	│	1754	│	│	│	│	│	│	│
Leipzig Hbf **866** a.	1517	│	│	│	│	│	│	│	1717	│	│	│	│	│	│	│	1917	│	│	│	│	│	│	│
Dresden Hbf **842** a.	1647	│	│	│	│	│	│	│	1846j	│	│	│	│	│	│	│	2046	│	│	│	│	│	│	│
Wolfsburg **902** d.	...	1305	1305	1336	1354	│	│	1438	...	1504	1504	│	1554	│	│	1636	...	1704	1704	1736	1739	1754	│	│
Stendal Hbf **838** d.	...	│	│	│	1426	│	│	│	...	│	│	│	1626	│	│	│	...	│	│	│	│	1826	│	│
Berlin Spandau **838 902** a.	...	1358	1358	1437	1507	1454	1454	1538	...	1557	1557	1603	1707	1654	1654	1737	...	1758	1758	1838	1838	1907	1854	1854
Berlin Hbf **838 902** a.	...	1415	1415	1448	1525	1515	1515	1557	...	1615	1615	1613	1725	1715	1715	1747	...	1815	1815	1857	1857	1925	1915	1915
Berlin Ostbahnhof **838 902** a.	...	1427	1427	...	1536	1527	1527	1609	...	1627	1627	...	1736	1727	1727	...	...	1827	1827	1908	1908	1936	1927	1927

	ICE 1059	IC 2045	ICE 943	ICE 953	ICE 1151	IC 149	ICE 643	ICE 653	ICE 1153	ICE 1159	IC 2043	ICE 945	ICE 955	IC 241	IC 241	ICE 645	ICE 655	IC 2041	ICE 947	ICE 957	IC 243	ICE 657		IC 1941
										◇		Ⓑb		Ⓑb	⑦w			†		⑤⑦	⑦w	⑤⑦		
	✕	S🍷	✕	✕	✕	🍷	✕	✕	✕	A✕	🍷	✕	✕	🍷	🍷	✕	A✕	🍷	✕	p✕	🍷	N✕		d
Köln Hbf **800** d.	1436	1509	...	1548	1537	...	...	1648	1638c	1817	1713	...	1748	...	...	...	1848	1913	1928q	1948	...	2048	...	2113
Wuppertal Hbf **800** d.	│	1543	...	1615	│	...	...	1715	│	│	1744	...	1816	...	...	...	1916	1944	│	2016	...	2116	...	2144
Düsseldorf Hbf **800** d.	1509	│	1549	│	1616	...	1649	│	1709	│	│	1751	│	...	...	1851	│	│	1952	│	...	│	...	│
Dortmund Hbf **800** d.	│	1628	1647	│	1710	...	1747	│	1806	│	1828	1848	│	...	...	1948	│	2028	2048	│	...	│	...	2226
Hamm (Westf) **802** d.	│	1645	1711	1711	1734	...	1811	1811	1833	│	1845	1911	1911	...	...	2011	2011	2045	2111	2111	...	2211	...	2245
Gütersloh Hbf **802** d.	│	1708	│	│	1755	...	│	│	1854	│	1908	│	│	...	...	│	│	2106	│	│	...	│	...	2308
Bielefeld Hbf **802 811** d.	│	1719	1738	1738	1806	...	1838	1838	1905	│	1919	1938	1938	...	...	2038	2038	2118	2138	2138	...	2238	...	2319
Herford **811** d.	◧	1729	│	│	│	...	│	│	1915	│	1929	│	│	...	...	│	│	2128	│	│	...	│	...	2329
Amsterdam C **22** d.	│	│	│	│	│	1500	│	│	│	│	│	│	│	1710	1710	│	│	│	│	│	1900	│	...	│
Bad Bentheim 🏛 **811** d.	│	│	│	│	│	1728	│	│	│	│	│	│	│	1928	1928	│	│	│	│	│	2128	│	...	│
Rheine **811** d.	│	│	│	│	│	1742	│	│	│	│	│	│	│	1941	1941	│	│	│	│	│	2141	│	...	│
Münster (Westf) Hbf **800** d.	1630	│	│	│	│	│	│	│	│	│	│	│	│	│	│	│	│	│	│	│	│	│	...	│
Osnabrück Hbf **800 811** d.	1656	│	│	│	│	1808	│	│	│	│	│	│	│	2008	2008	│	│	│	│	│	2208	│	...	│
Bünde (Westf) **811** d.	│	│	│	│	│	│	│	│	│	│	│	│	│	2028	2028	│	│	│	│	│	│	│	...	│
Bad Oeynhausen **811** d.	│	│	│	│	1824	1837	│	│	│	│	│	│	│	│	│	│	│	│	│	│	2237	│	...	│
Minden (Westf) **811** d.	│	1746	│	│	│	1847	│	│	│	│	1946	│	│	2047	2047	│	│	2146	│	│	2247	│	...	2347
Hannover Hbf **811** a.	1802	1818	1828	1828	1901	1918	1928	1928	2001	│	2018	2028	2028	2118	2118	2128	2128	2218	2228	2228	2318	2328	...	0018
Hannover Hbf d.	1805	1836	1831	1831	1904	1922	1931	1931	2004	│	2036b	2031	2031	...	2122	2131	2131	...	2231	2231	...	2331	...	...
Magdeburg Hbf **866** a.	│	1954	│	│	│	│	│	│	│	│	2154b	│	│	...	│	│	│	...	│	│	...	│	...	...
Leipzig Hbf **866** a.	│	2117	│	│	│	│	│	│	│	│	2317r	│	│	...	│	│	│	...	│	│	...	│	...	...
Dresden Hbf **842** a.	│	2246b	│	│	│	│	│	│	│	│	...	│	│	...	│	│	│	...	│	│	...	│	...	...
Wolfsburg **902** d.	1836	...	1904	1904	1936	1954	│	│	2036	│	...	2103	2103	...	2154	│	│	...	2304	2304	...	0003	...	...
Stendal Hbf **838** d.	│	...	│	│	│	2026	│	│	│	│	...	2131	2131	...	2226	│	│	...	│	│	...	│	...	...
Berlin Spandau **838 902** a.	1938	...	1958	1958	2038	2107	2054	2054	2138	2203	...	2209	2209	...	2307	2254	2254	...	2359	2359	...	0100	...	...
Berlin Hbf **838 902** a.	1957	...	2015	2015	2057	2125	2115	2115	2157	2221	...	2227	2227	...	2325	2311	2311	...	0014	0014	...	0114	...	...
Berlin Ostbahnhof **838 902** a.	2008	...	2027	2027	2109	2136	2127	2127	2209	2230	...	2238	2238	...	2336	2322	2322	...	0025	0025	...	0124	...	...

A – From Bonn (Table **800**).
B – To Ostseebad Binz (Tables **844** and **845**).
F – From Frankfurt (Table **800**).
H – From Hamburg (Table **900**).
K – From Koblenz (Table **800**).
N – ⑤⑦ (also Dec. 26; not Dec. 25). From Aachen Hbf (d. 1959) and Düren (d. 2027).
O – From Oldenburg via Bremen on Ⓐ (Table **813**).
R – To Stralsund (Table **845**).
S – From Stuttgart (Tables **800** and **912**).
T – KAROLINGER – From Aachen Hbf (d. 0707), Herzogenrath (d. 0723), Rheydt Hbf (d. 0752), Mönchengladbach Hbf (d. 0758), Viersen (d. 0806) and Krefeld Hbf (d. 0818).

b – Ⓑ (not Dec. 25).
c – Not Mar. 31.
d – Not Dec. 26. Train number **2341** on ⑦ (not Dec. 25).

e – ⚒ only.
j – ①②③④⑥⑦ to Mar. 16; daily from Mar. 18.
p – Also Dec. 24, 26; not Dec. 25.
q – ①②③④⑥ (also Dec. 25; not Dec. 24, 26).
r – ⑤⑦ (also Dec. 26; not Dec. 25).
w – ⑦ (also Dec. 26; not Dec. 25).
y – 1045 on ⑤.
z – † only.

♥ – Also calls at Braunschweig Hbf (a. 0314), Brandenburg Hbf (a. 0445), Potsdam Hbf (a. 0504), Berlin Wannsee (a. 0513) and Berlin Zoo (a. 0528).
◇ – Also calls at Berlin Zoo (a. 2214).
◧ – Via Recklinghausen (Table **800**).
▽ – Via Braunschweig Hbf (d. 0601).

810 BERLIN - HANNOVER - HAMM and BAD BENTHEIM

Independent operator **FlixTrain** also run services Berlin - Köln (see Table **927**).

km		ICE 948		IC 2040		ICE 656	ICE 646	IC 242	ICE 1158	ICE 956	ICE 946	IC 2042	ICE 654	ICE 644	IC 240	ICE 1152	ICE 954	ICE 944	IC 2044	ICE 1150	ICE 652	ICE 642	IC 148	ICE 1058
						⚒	⚒	⚒	◇		⚒			⚒	⚒									
		♥		🍷		✕	✕	🍷	A✕	✕	✕	🍷	✕	✕	🍷	✕	✕	✕	S🍷	✕	A✕	✕	🍷	✕
0	**Berlin** Ostbahnhof . **838 902** d.	0011	...	...	...	0413	0413	...	0521	0518	0518	...	0634	0634	0621	0648	0734	0734	...	0748	0834	0834	0821	0849
5	**Berlin** Hbf **838 902** d.	0022	...	...	...	0425	0425	...	0533	0529	0529	...	0646	0646	0633	0659	0746	0746	...	0759	0846	0846	0833	0900
21	**Berlin** Spandau **838 902** d.	|	...	...	...	0440	0440	...	0551	0547	0547	...	0701	0701	0650	0715	0800	0800	...	0814	0901	0901	0850	0915
113	Stendal Hbf **838** d.	|	...	...	...	0515	0515	...	|	0624	0624	...	|	|	0732	|	|	|	...	|	|	|	0932	|
188	Wolfsburg **902** d.	|	...	...	...	0547	0547	...	|	0653	0653	...	0753	0753	0801	|	0853	0853	...	0920	|	|	1001	|
	Dresden Hbf **842** d.	|	...	...	...	|	|	...	|	|	|	...	|	|	|	|	|	|	0512	|	|	|	|	|
	Leipzig Hbf **866** d.	|	...	...	...	|	|	...	|	|	|	0441g	|	|	|	|	|	|	0638	|	|	|	|	|
	Magdeburg Hbf **866** d.	0148	...	...	...	|	|	...	|	|	|	0603e	|	|	|	|	|	|	0803	|	|	|	|	|
263	**Hannover** Hbf a.	0309	...	...	...	0618	0618	...	|	0728	0728	0723e	0828	0828	0836	0853	0928	0928	0923	0953	1028	1028	1036	1053
263	**Hannover** Hbf **811** d.	0340	...	0540	...	0621	0621	0640	|	0731	0731	0740	0831	0831	0840	0856	0931	0931	0940	0956	1031	1031	1040	1056
328	Minden (Westf) **811** d.	0411	...	0612	...	0650	0650	0712	|	|	|	0813	|	|	0911	|	|	|	1013	|	|	|	1111	|
343	Bad Oeynhausen **811** d.	|	...	|	...	|	|	0722	|	|	|	|	|	|	|	|	|	|	|	|	|	|	1122	|
359	Bünde (Westf) **811** d.	|	...	|	...	|	|	|	|	|	|	|	|	|	0932	|	|	|	|	|	|	|	|	|
396	**Osnabrück** Hbf **800 811** d.	|	...	|	...	|	|	0753	|	|	|	|	|	|	0953	|	|	|	|	1106	|	|	1153	|
	Münster (Westf) Hbf **800** a.	|	...	|	...	|	|	|	|	|	|	|	|	|	|	|	|	|	|	1130	|	|	|	|
444	Rheine **811** d.	|	...	|	...	|	|	0820	|	|	|	|	|	|	1020	|	|	|	|	|	|	|	1220	|
465	Bad Bentheim 🏛 **811** a.	|	...	|	...	|	|	0834	|	|	|	|	|	|	1034	|	|	|	|	|	|	|	1234	|
647	*Amsterdam C* **22** a.	|	...	|	...	|	|	1100	|	|	|	|	|	|	1300	|	|	|	|	|	|	|	1500	|
	Herford **811** d.	|	...	0632	...	0711	0711	...	|	|	|	0832	|	|	...	0943	|	|	1032	◧	|	|	...	1143
	Bielefeld Hbf **802 811** d.	0436	...	0640	...	0721	0721	...	|	0822	0822	0840	0922	0922	...	0953	1022	1022	1040	|	1122	1122	...	1153
	Gütersloh Hbf **802** d.	0446	...	0652	...	|	|	...	|	|	|	0852	|	|	...	1003	|	|	1052	|	|	|	...	1203
	Hamm (Westf) **802** a.	0510	...	0714	...	0747	0747	...	|	0847	0847	0914	0948	0948	...	1024	1048	1048	1113	|	1148	1148	...	1224
	Dortmund Hbf **800** a.	|	...	0734	...	|	0810	...	|	|	0910	0933	|	1010	...	1048	|	1110	1133	|	|	1210	...	1249
	Düsseldorf Hbf **800** a.	|	...	|	...	|	0904	...	|	|	1002	|	|	1108	...	1142	|	1203	|	1250	|	1307	...	1344
	Wuppertal Hbf **800** a.	0607	...	0812	...	0838	...	...	|	0938	...	1012	1038	...	...	|	1138	...	1212	|	1238	...	...	|
	Köln Hbf **800** a.	0657	...	0846	...	0909	...	...	0941	1009	...	1046	1109	...	...	1212	1209	...	1246	1319	1309	...	...	1426c

	ICE 952	ICE 942	IC 2046	IC 2011	ICE 650	ICE 640	IC 146	ICE 1156	ICE 950	ICE 940	IC 2048	IC 1917	ICE 717	ICE 558	ICE 548	IC 144	ICE 1050	ICE 858	ICE 848	IC 2440	ICE 758	ICE 556	ICE 546	IC 142
				⑦w								⑦w	⑤								⑥			
	✕	✕	S🍷		✕	✕	🍷	A✕	✕	✕	S🍷	S🍷	S✕	A✕	✕	🍷	✕	✕	✕	S🍷	B✕	K✕	✕	🍷
Berlin Ostbahnhof .. **838 902** d.	0934	0934	...	0944	1034	1034	1021	...	1134	1134	...	1148	1148	1234	1234	1221	...	1334	1334	...	...	1434	1434	1421
Berlin Hbf **838 902** d.	0946	0946	...	0955	1046	1046	1033	1142	1146	1146	...	1159	1159	1246	1246	1233	1306	1346	1346	...	1353	1446	1446	1433
Berlin Spandau **838 902** d.	1000	1000	...	1014	1101	1101	1050	1152	1200	1200	...	1213	1214	1301	1301	1250	1316	1400	1400	...	1405	1501	1501	1450
Stendal Hbf **838** d.	|	|	...	|	|	|	1132	|	|	|	...	|	|	|	|	1332	|	|	|	...	1442	|	|	1532
Wolfsburg **902** d.	1053	1053	...	1120	|	|	1201	|	1253	1253	...	1321	1321	|	|	1401	|	1453	1453	...	1508	|	|	1601
Dresden Hbf **842** d.	|	|	0712e	|	|	|	|	|	|	|	0845	|	|	|	|	|	|	|	|	1045	|	|	|	|
Leipzig Hbf **866** d.	|	|	0838	|	|	|	|	|	|	|	1038	|	|	|	|	|	|	|	|	1238	|	|	|	|
Magdeburg Hbf **866** d.	|	|	1003	|	|	|	|	|	|	|	1203	|	|	|	|	|	|	|	|	1403	|	|	|	|
Hannover Hbf a.	1128	1128	1123	1153	1228	1228	1236	|	1328	1328	1323	1353	1353	1428	1428	1436	1453	1528	1528	1523	1544	1628	1628	1636
Hannover Hbf **811** d.	1131	1131	1140	1156	1231	1231	1240	|	1331	1331	1340	1356	1356	1431	1431	1440	1456	1531	1531	1540	1556	1631	1631	1640
Minden (Westf) **811** d.	|	|	1213	|	|	|	1311	|	|	|	1413	|	|	|	|	1511	|	|	|	1613	|	|	|	1711
Bad Oeynhausen **811** d.	|	|	|	|	|	|	|	|	|	|	|	|	|	|	|	1522	|	|	|	|	|	|	|	|
Bünde (Westf) **811** d.	|	|	|	|	|	|	1332	|	|	|	|	|	|	|	|	|	|	|	|	|	|	|	|	1732
Osnabrück Hbf **811** d.	|	|	|	|	|	|	1353	|	|	|	|	|	|	|	|	1553	|	|	|	|	|	|	|	1753
Münster (Westf) Hbf .. **800** a.	|	|	|	|	|	|	|	|	|	|	|	|	|	|	|	|	|	|	|	|	|	|	|	|
Rheine **811** d.	|	|	|	|	|	|	1420	|	|	|	|	|	|	|	|	1620	|	|	|	|	|	|	|	1820
Bad Bentheim 🏛 **811** a.	|	|	|	|	|	|	1434	|	|	|	|	|	|	|	|	1634	|	|	|	|	|	|	|	1834
Amsterdam C **22** a.	|	|	|	|	|	|	1649	|	|	|	|	|	|	|	|	1900	|	|	|	|	|	|	|	2100
Herford **811** d.	|	|	1232	1244	|	|	...	|	|	|	1432	1444	1444	|	|	...	1543	|	|	1632	1643	|	|	...
Bielefeld Hbf **802 811** d.	1222	1222	1240	1253	1322	1322	...	|	1422	1422	1440	1453	1453	1522	1522	...	1553	1622	1622	1640	1653	1722	1722	...
Gütersloh Hbf **802** d.	|	|	1252	1303	|	|	...	|	|	|	1452	1503	1503	|	|	...	1603	|	|	1652	1703	|	|	...
Hamm (Westf) **802** a.	1248	1248	1314	1324	1347	1347	...	|	1448	1448	1514	1525	1525	1547	1547	...	1624	1648	1648	1714	1724	1748	1748	...
Dortmund Hbf **800** a.	|	1310	1333	1349	|	1410	...	|	|	1510	1533	|	|	|	1610	...	1649	|	1710	1733	1748	|	1810	...
Düsseldorf Hbf **800** a.	|	1408	|	|	|	1508	...	|	|	1604	|	|	|	|	1707	...	1747	|	1803	|	1842	|	1907	...
Wuppertal Hbf **800** a.	1338	...	1412	1432	1438	...	...	|	1538	...	1612	1628	1628	1638	...	...	|	1738	|	1812	|	1838	...	...
Köln Hbf **800** a.	1409	...	1446	1512	1509	...	...	1541	1609	...	1646	1712	1712	1709	...	...	1819c	1809	1832p	1846	1913	1909	...	...

	ICE 1546	ICE 1595	ICE 856	ICE 846	IC 2442	ICE 754	ICE 554	ICE 544	IC 140	ICE 1154	ICE 854	ICE 844	IC 2444	ICE 750	ICE 552	ICE 542	IC 2242	ICE 872	ICE 842	ICE 1132	IC 2240	ICE 540	ICE 840	ICE 840
	⑧b	⑦w												⑤⑦				⑦w	¶	⑦w	⑦w			⑤⑥†
	G🍷	U🍷	✕	Y✕	F🍷	✕	A✕	✕	🍷	A✕	✕	✕	🍷	L✕	T✕	✕	🍷	✕	✕	R	🍷	O✕		
Berlin Ostbahnhof .. **838 902** d.	1449	1449	1534	1534	...	1547	1634	1634	1621	...	1734	1734	...	...	1834	1834	1821	1934	1934	...	2021	2034	2116	2116
Berlin Hbf **838 902** d.	1500	1500	1546	1546	...	1558	1646	1646	1633	1741	1746	1746	...	...	1846	1846	1833	1946	1946	...	2033	2046	2127	2127
Berlin Spandau **838 902** d.	1515	1515	1600	1600	...	1612	1701	1701	1650	1751	1800	1800	...	1812	1901	1901	1850	2000	2000	1954	2050	2101	2142	2142
Stendal Hbf **838** d.	1551	1551	|	|	...	1646	|	|	1732	|	|	|	...	1845	|	|	1931	|	|	2029	2132	2139	2218	2218
Wolfsburg **902** d.	1620	1620	1653	1653	...	1720	|	|	1801	|	1853	1853	...	1920	|	|	2001	2053	2053	2105	2201	2208	2248	2248
Dresden Hbf **842** d.	|	|	|	|	1312w	|	|	|	|	|	|	|	1512	|	|	|	|	|	|	|	|	|	|	|
Leipzig Hbf **866** d.	|	|	|	|	1438	|	|	|	|	|	|	|	1638	|	|	|	|	|	|	|	|	|	|	|
Magdeburg Hbf **866** d.	|	|	|	|	1603	|	|	|	|	|	|	|	1803	|	|	|	|	|	|	|	|	|	|	|
Hannover Hbf a.	1653	1653	1728	1728	1723	1753	1828	1828	1836	|	1928	1928	1923	1953	2028	2028	2036	2128	2128	2140	2236	2242	2322	2322
Hannover Hbf **811** d.	1656	...	1731	1731	1740	1756	1831	1831	1840	|	1931	1931	1940	1956	2031	2031	2040	2131	2136	...	2240	...	...	2331
Minden (Westf) **811** d.	|	...	|	|	1813	|	|	|	1911	|	|	|	2013	|	|	|	2111	|	2212	...	2311	...	...	|
Bad Oeynhausen **811** d.	1734	...	|	|	|	|	|	|	1922	|	|	|	|	|	|	|	2122	|	|	...	2322	...	...	|
Bünde (Westf) **811** d.	|	...	|	|	|	|	|	|	|	|	|	|	|	|	|	|	2135	|	|	...	2335	...	...	|
Osnabrück Hbf **811** d.	|	...	|	|	|	1905	|	|	1953	|	|	|	|	|	|	|	2201	|	|	...	2359	...	...	|
Münster (Westf) Hbf .. **800** a.	|	...	|	|	|	1930	|	|	|	|	|	|	|	|	|	|	2225	|	|	...	0025	...	...	|
Rheine **811** d.	|	...	|	|	|	|	|	|	2020	|	|	|	|	|	|	|	...	|	|	...	...	...	...	|
Bad Bentheim 🏛 **811** a.	|	...	|	|	|	|	|	|	2034	|	|	|	|	|	|	|	...	|	|	...	...	...	...	|
Amsterdam C **22** a.	|	...	|	|	|	|	|	|	2300	|	|	|	|	|	|	|	...	|	|	...	...	...	...	|
Herford **811** d.	1744	...	|	|	1832	◧	|	|	...	|	|	|	2032	2043	|	|	...	|	2232	...	...	...	...	0016
Bielefeld Hbf **802 811** d.	1753	...	1822	1822	1840	|	1922	1922	...	|	2022	2022	2040	2053	2122	2122	...	2223	2242	...	...	...	...	0027
Gütersloh Hbf **802** d.	1803	...	|	|	1852	|	|	|	...	|	|	|	2052	2103	|	|	...	|	2252	...	...	...	...	0038
Hamm (Westf) **802** a.	1824	...	1847	1847	1914	|	1948	1948	...	|	2047	2047	2114	2124	2147	2147	...	2251	2313	...	...	...	...	0059
Dortmund Hbf **800** a.	1848	...	|	1910	1933	|	|	2010	...	|	|	2110	2133	2149	|	2210	...	|	2332	...	...	...	...	0119
Düsseldorf Hbf **800** a.	...	...	|	2015	|	2115	|	2102	...	|	|	2203	|	2243	|	2302	...	|	0028	...	...	...	...	0216
Wuppertal Hbf **800** a.	...	...	1938	...	2012	...	2038	|	...	|	2138	|	2212	|	2238	|	...	2337	|	...	...	...	...	|
Köln Hbf **800** a.	...	...	2009	...	2046	...	2111	2132	...	2141	2209	2232	2246	2316	2313	2331	...	0010	0056	...	...	...	...	0244

A – To Bonn (Table **800**).
B – From Ostseebad Binz (Tables **844** and **845**).
F – To Frankfurt (Table **800**).
G – KAROLINGER – To Duisburg Hbf (a. 1926), Krefeld Hbf (a. 1941), Viersen (a. 1953), Mönchengladbach Hbf (a. 2001), Rheydt Hbf (a. 2007), Herzogenrath (a. 2037) and Aachen Hbf (a. 2052).
K – To Koblenz (Table **800**).
L – ⑤⑦ (also Dec. 26; not Dec. 25). From Stralsund (Table **845**).
O – To Oldenburg via Bremen (Table **813**).
R – From Stralsund (Table **845**).
S – To Stuttgart (Tables **800** and **912**).
T – To Bonn / Koblenz on dates in Table **800**.
U – To Stuttgart via Gießen and Frankfurt (Tables **806**, **900** and **912**).
Y – Continues to Neuss Hbf (a. 2028) and Mönchengladbach Hbf (a. 2042). On ⑦ (also Dec. 26; not Dec. 25) continues further to Aachen Hbf (a. 2133).

b – Not Dec. 25.
c – Not Mar. 31.
e – ⚒ only.
g – ① (also Dec. 27; not Dec. 26).
p – ①②③④⑥ (also Dec. 25; not Dec. 24, 26).
w – ⑦ (also Dec. 26; not Dec. 25).

◇ – Also calls at Berlin Zoo (d. 0540).
◧ – Via Recklinghausen (Table **800**).
¶ – Train number **892** on ⑦ (also Dec. 26; not Dec. 25).
♥ – Also calls at Berlin Zoo (d. 0029), Berlin Wannsee (d. 0041), Potsdam Hbf (d. 0049), Brandenburg Hbf (d. 0108) and Braunschweig Hbf (d. 0236).

Regional services BIELEFELD and HENGELO - HANNOVER and PADERBORN 811

See Table **22** for international *IC* services Amsterdam - Hengelo - Bad Bentheim - Hannover and v.v. See Table **810** for fast *ICE* / *IC* services Bielefeld / Bad Bentheim - Hannover and v.v.

km		¶	⚒‡	⚒¶	⚒§	⚒‡	¶	⚒§	‡	Ⓐ‡	¶	§	‡	⚒‡	¶	A§	A‡	B¶	A§	A‡	B¶		‡	¶
0	**Hengelo** ▷ d.	...	...	...	...	...	...	...	...	0534	...	...	...	0634	...	...	0734	...	...	0834	...	⊠	1834	...
26	Bad Bentheim 🏛 d.	...	...	...	...	...	...	...	...	0556	...	...	...	0656	...	...	0756	...	...	0856	...		1856	...
47	**Rheine** d.	...	...	...	...	0514	...	...	...	0614	0638	...	...	0714	...	...	0814	0838	...	0914	...		1914	...
69	Ibbenbüren d.	...	...	...	...	0528	...	...	...	0628	0654	...	...	0728	...	...	0828	0854	...	0928	...		1928	...
95	**Osnabrück** Hbf d.	...	0447	0517	...	0547	...	...	0647	0647	0718	...	0747	0747	...	...	0847	0917	...	0947	...	and in	1946	...
132	Bünde (Westf) d.	...	0513	0539	D	0613	...	D	0713	0713	0740	K	0813	0813	...	K	0912	0939	K	1012	...	the same	2012	...
	Bielefeld Hbf d.	0424	|	|	0600	|	0624	0700	|	|	|	0800	|	|	0824	0900	|	|	1000	|	1024		|	2024
146	Herford a.	0431	0527	|	0607	0627	0631	0707	0727	0727	|	0807	0827	0827	0831	0907	0927	|	1007	1027	1031	pattern	2027	2031
146	Herford d.	0433	0536	|	0608	0636	0633	0708	0736	0736	|	0808	0836	0836	0833	0908	0936	|	1008	1036	1033	every	2036	2033
160	**Bielefeld** Hbf a.	|	0547	|	|	0647	|	|	0747	0747	|	|	0847	0847	|	|	0947	|	|	1047	|		2047	|
	Löhne d.	0440	▬	0551	0614	...	0640	0714	...	...	0751	0814	...	...	0840	0914	...	0951	1014	...	1040	**two** hours	...	2040
	Bad Oeynhausen d.	0445	...	0557	0619	...	0645	0719	...	...	0757	0819	...	...	0845	0919	...	0957	1019	...	1045	until	...	2045
	Minden (Westf) a.	0457	...	0607	0630	...	0657	0730	...	...	0807	0830	...	...	0857	0930	...	1007	1030	...	1057		...	2057
	Minden (Westf) d.	0507	0608	0608	*0635*	...	0707	*0735*	...	...	0808	*0835*	...	...	0904	*0935*	...	1008	*1035*	...	1104		...	2104
	Hannover Hbf a.	0550	0650	0650	*0730*	...	0750	*0830*	...	...	0852	*0930*	...	...	0950	*1030*	...	1050	*1130*	...	1150		...	2150
	Hannover Hbf 866 d.	0555	0655	0655	...	...	0755	...	...	...	0855	...	...	...	0955	...	...	1055	...	...	1155		...	2155
	Peine 866 d.	0624	0724	0724	...	...	0824	...	...	...	0925	...	...	...	1024	...	...	1124	...	...	1224		...	2224
	Braunschweig Hbf 866 a.	0641	0741	0741	...	...	0841	...	...	...	0941	...	...	...	1041	...	...	1140	...	...	1241		...	2241

	§	‡	¶	§	‡	¶	§	‡	¶	‡
Hengelo ▷ d.	...	1934	...	...	2034	..	...	2134	...	2234
Bad Bentheim 🏛 d.	...	1956	...	...	2056	...	...	2156	...	2256
Rheine d.	...	2014	2038	...	2114	...	...	2214	2238	2314
Ibbenbüren d.	...	2028	2054	...	2128	...	...	2228	2254	2328
Osnabrück Hbf d.	...	2047	2117	...	2146	...	...	2247	2317	2345
Bünde (Westf) d.	K	2113	2139	K	2212	...	K	2313	2339	...
Bielefeld Hbf d.	2100	|	|	2200	|	2224	2300	|	|	...
Herford a.	2107	2127	|	2207	2227	2231	2307	2327	|	...
Herford d.	2108	2136	|	2208	2236	2233	2308	2336	|	...
Bielefeld Hbf a.	|	2147	|	|	2247	|	|	2347	|	...
Löhne d.	2114	...	2151	2214	...	2240	2315	▬	2351	...
Bad Oeynhausen d.	2119	...	2157	2219	...	2245	2320	...	2357	...
Minden (Westf) a.	2130	...	2207	2230	...	2259	2330	...	0007	...
Minden (Westf) d.	*2135*	...	2208	*2235*	...	2307	*2335*	...	...	...
Hannover Hbf a.	*2230*	...	2250	*2330*	...	2350	*0030*	¶	...	...
Hannover Hbf 866 d.	...	...	2255	...	...	0014	...	0114	...	...
Peine 866 d.	...	...	2324	...	...	0040	...	0140	...	...
Braunschweig Hbf 866 a.	...	...	2341	...	...	0059	...	0159	...	...

km		Ⓐ‡	⚒‡	Ⓐ§	⚒¶	⚒‡	‡	§	¶	‡
0	**Braunschweig** Hbf 866 d.	...	...	...	0420	...	...	...	0520	...
26	Peine 866 d.	...	...	...	0438	...	...	...	0538	...
61	**Hannover** Hbf 866 a.	...	...	...	0505	...	...	...	0605	...
61	**Hannover** Hbf d.	...	...	...	0509	...	...	*0528*r	0609	...
126	Minden (Westf) a.	...	...	...	0551	...	...	*0623*r	0654	...
126	Minden (Westf) d.	...	...	0528	0552	...	...	0628	0702	...
141	Bad Oeynhausen d.	...	...	0539	0604	...	...	0639	0714	...
147	Löhne d.	...	...	0544	0609	...	...	0644	0719	...
	Bielefeld Hbf d.	...	0511	|	|	0611	...	|	|	0712
157	Herford a.	...	0521	0549	|	0621	...	0649	0725	0723
157	Herford d.	...	0532	0550	|	0632	...	0650	0727	0732
171	**Bielefeld** Hbf a.	...	|	0557	|	|	...	0657	0739n	|
	Bünde (Westf) d.	...	0546	K	0620	0646	...	K	...	0746
	Osnabrück Hbf d.	0514	0614	...	0646	0713	...	...	...	0814
	Ibbenbüren d.	0530	0630	...	0704	0730	...	...	...	0830
	Rheine d.	0549	0649	...	0721	0749	0749	...	...	0849
	Bad Bentheim 🏛 a.	0603	0703	...	...	0803	0803	...	...	0904
	Hengelo ▷ a.	0626	0726	...	...	0826	0826	...	...	0926

	⚒§	¶	‡	A§	B¶	A‡	A§	B¶	A‡			¶	‡	§	¶	‡	§	¶	‡	§	¶	‡	¶	¶
Braunschweig Hbf 866 d.	...	0620	...	...	0720	...	...	0820	...	⊠ ✥	...	1820	...	...	1920	...	...	2020	...	...	2120	...	2220	2320
Peine 866 d.	...	0638	...	...	0738	...	...	0838	...		...	1837	...	...	1938	...	...	2038	...	...	2138	...	2238	2338
Hannover Hbf 866 a.	...	0703	...	...	0805	...	...	0905	...		...	1903	...	...	2005	...	...	2105	...	...	2205	...	2305	0004
Hannover Hbf d.	*0628*	0708	...	*0728*	0809	...	*0828*	0909	...	and in	*1828*	1905	...	*1928*	2009	...	*2028*	2109	...	*2128*	2209	...	2309	0009
Minden (Westf) a.	*0723*	0752	...	*0823*	0853	...	*0923*	0951	...	the same	*1923*	1951	...	*2023*	2053	...	*2123*	2151	...	*2223*	2253	...	2351	0052
Minden (Westf) d.	0728	0753	...	0828	0902	...	0928	0952	...	pattern	1928	1952	...	2028	2102	...	2128	2152	...	2228	2302	...	2352	...
Bad Oeynhausen d.	0739	0804	...	0839	0914	...	0939	1004	...	every	1939	2003	...	2039	2114	...	2139	2204	...	2239	2314	...	0004	...
Löhne d.	0744	0809	...	0844	0919	...	0944	1009	...	**two** hours	1944	2008	...	2044	2119	...	2144	2209	...	2244	2319	...	0009	...
Bielefeld Hbf d.	|	|	0812	|	|	0912	|	|	1012	until	|	|	2012	|	|	2112	|	|	2212	|	|	2312	|	...
Herford a.	0749	|	0823	0849	0925	0923	0949	|	1023		1949	|	2023	2049	2125	2123	2149	|	2223	2249	2325	2323	|	...
Herford d.	0750	|	0832	0850	0927	0932	0950	|	1032		1950	|	2032	2050	2127	2132	2150	|	2232	2250	2327	2332	|	...
Bielefeld Hbf a.	0757	|	|	0857	0936	|	0957	|	|		1957	|	|	2057	2136	|	2157	|	|	2257	2336	|	|	...
Bünde (Westf) d.	K	0820	0846	K	...	0946	K	1020	1046		K	2020	2046	K	...	2146	E	2220	2246	E	...	2346	0020	...
Osnabrück Hbf d.	...	0846	0914	...	...	1014	...	1046	1114		...	2046	2114	...	...	2214	...	2246	2314	...	...	0012	0041	...
Ibbenbüren d.	...	0904	0930	...	...	1030	...	1104	1130		...	2104	2130	...	...	2230	...	2304	2330	...	...	...	...	...
Rheine d.	...	0921	0949	...	...	1049	...	1121	1149		...	2121	2149	...	...	2249	...	2321	2346	...	...	...	...	...
Bad Bentheim 🏛 a.	...	...	1003	...	...	1103	...	...	1204		...	...	2203	...	...	2303	...	...	...	...	...	...	...	...
Hengelo ▷ a.	...	...	1026	...	...	1126	...	...	1226		...	...	2226	...	...	2326	...	...	...	...	...	...	...	...

BIELEFELD - PADERBORN - HOLZMINDEN - KREIENSEN ⊖ and OTTBERGEN - GÖTTINGEN ★ ⊖

km				Ⓐ	⚒	⚒	⚒																		
0	**Bielefeld** Hbf d.	...	...	0434	0534	0634	0734	0834	0934	1034	1134	1234	1334	1434	1534	...	1634	1734	1834	1934	2034	2134	...	2234	2334
44	**Paderborn** Hbf a.	...	...	0527	0627	0727	0827	0927	1027	1127	1227	1327	1427	1527	1627	...	1727	1827	1927	2027	2127	2227	...	2327	0027
	Change trains	⚒	Ⓐ	⚒	d	⚒	d								Ⓐ	Ⓒ							L		
44	**Paderborn** Hbf 805 809 d.	0453	0453	0553	0653	0753	0853	0953	1053	1153	1253	1353	1453	1553	1653	1653	1753	1853	1953	2053	2206	...	2315	...	...
61	Altenbeken 805 809 d.	0507	0507	0607	0707	0807	0907	1007	1107	1207	1307	1407	1507	1607	1707	1707	1807	1907	2007	2107	2219	...	2329	...	...
92	Ottbergen ★ a.	0532	0532	0632	0732	0832	0932	1032	1132	1232	1332	1432	1532	1632	1732	1732	1832	1932	2032	2132	2244	...	2354	...	...
92	Ottbergen d.	...	0536	0636	0736	0836	0936	1036	1136	1236	1336	1436	1536	1636	1736	1736	1836	1936	2036	2136	2245	...	2355	...	...
102	Höxter Rathaus d.	...	0545	0645	0745	0845	0945	1045	1145	1245	1345	1445	1545	1645	1745	1745	1845	1945	2045	2145	2254	...	0003	...	...
110	Holzminden a.	...	0554	0654	0754	0854	0954	1054	1154	1254	1354	1454	1554	1654	1754	1754	1854	1954	2054	2154	2302	...	0012	...	...
110	Holzminden d.	...	*0629*	*0711*t	0758	...	0958	...	1158	...	1358	...	1558	1654t	1754	1758	...	1958	...	2158	...	...	...	...	...
154	**Kreiensen** a.	...	*0703*	*0745*t	0832	...	1032	...	1232	...	1432	...	1632	1728t	1828	1832	...	2032	...	2232	...	...	...	...	...

		Ⓐ	⚒	⚒	Ⓐ	⑥											Ⓐ	Ⓒ		Ⓐ					†
Kreiensen d.	...	...	...	0627t	0709	0723	...	0754t	0923	...	1123	...	1323	...	1523	...	1652	1723	...	1828	...	1923	...	2127j	2241
Holzminden a.	...	...	...	0700t	0742	0756	...	0827t	0956	...	1156	...	1356	...	1556	...	1725	1756	...	1900	...	1956	...	2200j	2314
Holzminden d.	...	0501	0601	0701	0801	0801	0801	0902	1002	1102	1202	1301	1401	1501	1601	1702	...	1801	1801	1901	1901	2001	2101	2201	2316
Höxter Rathaus d.	...	0510	0610	0710	0810	0810	0810	0911	1011	1111	1211	1310	1410	1510	1610	1711	...	1810	1810	1910	1910	2010	2110	2210	2322
Ottbergen a.	...	0519	0619	0719	0819	0819	0819	0920	1020	1120	1220	1319	1419	1519	1619	1720	...	1819	1819	1919	1919	2019	2119	2219	2330
Ottbergen ★ d.	...	0526	0626	0726	0826	0826	0826	0926	1026	1126	1226	1326	1426	1526	1626	1726	...	1826	1826	1926	1926	2026	2126	2226	2331
Altenbeken 805 809 d.	...	0552	0652	0752	0852	0852	0852	0952	1052	1152	1252	1352	1452	1552	1652	1752	...	1852	1852	1952	1952	2052	2152	2252	2357
Paderborn Hbf 805 809 a.	...	0605	0705	0805	0905	0905	0905	1005	1105	1205	1305	1405	1505	1605	1705	1805	...	1905	1905	2005	2005	2105	2205	2305	0010
Change trains	⚒	⚒	⚒	d																					
Paderborn Hbf d.	0513	0613	0713	0813	...	...	0913	1013	1113	1213	1313	1413	1513	1613	1713	1813	...	...	1913	...	2013	2113	2213	2313	...
Bielefeld Hbf a.	0607	0707	0807	0907	...	...	1007	1107	1207	1307	1407	1507	1607	1707	1807	1907	...	...	2007	...	2107	2207	2307	0007	...

HERFORD - PADERBORN ‡

km		Ⓐ	⚒					L		⑤⑥f	
0	**Herford** d.	0530	0633	0733	and	2133	2233	2233	...	2336	...
8	Bad Salzuflen d.	0537	0640	0740		2140	2240	2240	...	2343	...
19	Lage (Lippe) d.	0549	0652	0752	hourly	2152	2252	2252	...	2355	...
28	Detmold d.	0559	0702	0802	until	2202	2258	2302	...	0002	...
57	Altenbeken 805 809 d.	0624	0727	0827		2227	...	2327	...	0027	...
74	**Paderborn** Hbf 805 809 a.	0638	0741	0841		2241	...	2341	...	0041	...

	Ⓐ	⚒					⑤⑥f
Paderborn Hbf 805 809 d.	...	0518	0621	and	2121	...	2219
Altenbeken 805 809 d.	...	0530	0633		2133	...	2233
Detmold d.	0458	0558	0701	hourly	2201	...	2301
Lage (Lippe) d.	0506	0606	0709	until	2209	...	2309
Bad Salzuflen d.	0517	0617	0720		2220	...	2320
Herford a.	0524	0624	0727		2227	...	2327

A – Train runs hourly.
B – Train runs every **two** hours.
D – From Dortmund (Table **802**).
E – To Düsseldorf (Table **802**).
K – From / to Köln via Dortmund (Table **802**).
L – ⑤⑥† (also Apr. 6, May 17).

d – Daily.
f – Also Apr. 6, 9, 30, May 17, 28.

j – 2 minutes earlier on †.
n – 0736 on Ⓒ.
r – ⚒ only.
t – Ⓐ only.

§ – Operated by National Express.
¶ – Operated by WestfalenBahn.
‡ – Operated by eurobahn.
⊖ – Operated by NordWestBahn. 2nd class only.

⊠ – Timings may vary by up to 3 minutes.
⊕ – Change trains at Hannover on Apr. 7, 9, 30, May 17, 28.
✥ – The 1220 from Braunschweig departs Hannover 1305, Bad Oeynhausen 1403, Löhne 1408.
▷ – Trains from / to Hengelo also call at Oldenzaal (7 – 9 minutes from Hengelo). German holiday dates apply.
★ – **OTTBERGEN - GÖTTINGEN** ⊖. *63 km.* Journey: 71 – 84 minutes (103 – 113 minutes for trains marked ◇). Most trains run from / to Paderborn, attached to Holzminden trains shown in the main table above.
From Ottbergen at 0534 ⚒, 0634 ⚒, 0734, 0834 ⚒, 0934, 1034 ⚒, 1134, 1234 ⑥, 1234 Ⓐ◇, 1334 Ⓒ, 1534, 1634 Ⓐ, 1734, 1834 Ⓐ, 1934 and 2034.
From Göttingen at 0601 ⚒, 0710, 0801 ⚒, 0910, 1000 ⚒, 1110, 1201 ⚒, 1310 Ⓒ, 1331 Ⓐ◇, 1400 ⑥, 1510, 1600 Ⓐ, 1710, 1800 Ⓐ, 1910, 2000 Ⓐ and 2110.

812 MÜNSTER - EMDEN - NORDDEICH

km		◇ ⚒	IC 2438 ⚒	◇ ⚒	⊡ Ⓐ	◇	⊡ Ⓐ	IC 2208 ④⑤ D	ICE 1108 ⑥h ✕	◇	⊡	◇ ●	⊡ Ⓐ	IC 2206	IC 2306 ⑥h	◇	⊡	◇	⊡ Ⓐ	IC 2204	◇ Ⓒ	◇ Ⓐ	⊡	ICE 1110 ⑥h S✕	H	◇
	Koblenz Hbf **800** d.	...	...	...	...	...	...	...	...	...	...	...	...	0641t	...	...	...	...	...	...	...	...	...	0944x	...	...
	Köln Hbf **800 802** d.	...	...	...	...	...	0521	0539	0539	...	0621r	...	0721	0746	0801	...	0821	...	0921	0938	...	...	1021	1046	...	...
	Düsseldorf Hbf **800** d.	...	...	...	...	...	|	0607	0607	...	|	...	|	0812	0829	...	|	...	|	1011	...	...	|	1117	...	...
	Hagen Hbf **802** d.	...	...	...	0522	...	0622	|	|	...	0722	...	0822	|	|	...	0922	...	1022	|	...	...	1122	|	...	...
0	**Münster** (Westf) Hbf d.	0502a	...	0602	0624	0702	0724	0731	0730	0805	0824	0903	0925	0931	0955	1005	1024	1105	1124	1131	1205	1205	1224	1230	...	1305
15	Greven d.	0513a	...	0613	0637	0713	0733	|	|	0814	0833	0912	0934	|	|	1014	1033	1114	1133	|	1214	1214	1233	|	...	1314
26	Emsdetten d.	0522a	...	0622	0646	0722	0740	|	|	0822	0840	0920	0941	|	|	1022	1040	1122	1140	|	1222	1222	1240	|	...	1322
39	**Rheine** d.	0534	...	0634	0658	0734	0751	0756	0756	0834	0851	0934	0950	0956	1025	1034	1051	1134	1151	1156	1234	1234	1251	1257	...	1334
70	Lingen (Ems) d.	0555	...	0655	▬	0755	...	0815	0815	0855	▬	0955	...	1015	|	1055	▬	1155	...	1215	1255	1255	...	|	...	1355
90	Meppen d.	0609	...	0709	...	0809	...	0830	0831	0909	...	1009	...	1030	|	1109	...	1209	...	1230	1309	1328k	...	|	...	1409
136	Papenburg (Ems) d.	0642	...	0742	H	0842	...	0857	0857	0942	H	1042	...	1057	|	1142	H	1242	...	1257	1342	1404	...	|	...	1442
153	Leer (Ostfriesl) **813** d.	0653	0715	0753	0824	0853	...	0911	0911	0953	1024	1053	...	1109	1128	1153	1224	1253	...	1309	1353	1417	...	|	1424	1453
180	**Emden** Hbf ◧ **813** a.	0709	0731	0809	0841	0909	...	0926	0927	1009	1041	1109	...	1125	1143	1209	1241	1309	...	1325	1409	1432	...	1416	1441	1509
180	**Emden** Hbf **813** d.	...	0742	...	0842	...	...	0944	0944	...	1042	...	...	1142	...	...	1242	...	...	*1342*	...	...	...	1422	1442	...
209	Norden **813** d.	...	0808	...	0906	...	...	1007	1008	...	1106	...	...	1205	...	...	1306	...	...	*1408*	...	...	...	1446	1506	...
215	**Norddeich** **813** a.	...	0814	...	0912	...	...	1013	1014	...	1112	...	...	1211	...	...	1312	...	...	*1414*	...	...	...	1452	1512	...
	Norddeich Mole ‡ **813** a.	...	0820	...	0916	...	...	1018	1019	...	1116	...	...	1216	...	...	1316	...	...	*1420*	...	...	...	1501	1516	...

	⊡ Ⓐ	IC 2322 F	◇	⊡	◇	⊡ Ⓐ	IC 2200	◇	⊡	◇	⊡ Ⓐ	IC 2014 ⑤ 🍷♦	IC 2004 ⑦–④ 🍷♦	IC 2036 Ⓑb	◇	⊡	◇	⊡ Ⓐ	IC 2002	◇	⊡	◇	◇	⊙	◇	⊙
Koblenz Hbf **800** d.	...	...	...	...	...	...	...	...	...	...	...	1444	1444x	...	...	...	...	...	...	...	...	...	...	...	...	...
Köln Hbf **800 802** d.	1121	...	...	1221	...	1321	1343f	...	1421	...	1521	1546	1546	...	...	1621	...	1721	1741	...	1821	...	...	...	...	...
Düsseldorf Hbf **800** d.	|	...	...	|	...	|	1412f	...	|	...	|	1612	1612	...	...	|	...	|	1813	...	|	...	...	...	...	...
Hagen Hbf **802** d.	1222	...	...	1322	...	1422	|	...	1522	...	1622	|	|	...	...	1722	...	1822	|	...	1922	...	...	...	...	...
Münster (Westf) Hbf d.	1324	1331	1405	1424	1505	1524	1531	1605	1624	1705	1724	1731	1731	...	1805	1824	1905	1924	1931	2005	2024	2105	2211	2313	...	0013
Greven d.	1333	|	1414	1433	1514	1533	|	1614	1633	1714	1733	|	|	...	1814	1833	1914	1933	|	2014	2033	2114	2222	2325	...	0025
Emsdetten d.	1340	|	1422	1440	1522	1540	|	1622	1640	1722	1740	|	|	...	1822	1840	1922	1940	|	2022	2040	2122	2231	2333	...	0033
Rheine d.	1351	1356	1434	1451	1534	1551	1556	1634	1651	1734	1751	1756	1756	...	1834	1851	1934	1951	1956	2034	2051	2134	2252j	2346	2356	0046
Lingen (Ems) d.	...	1415	1455	▬	1555	...	1615	1655	▬	1755	...	1815	1815	...	1855	▬	1955	...	2015	2055	▬	2155	2313	...	0017	...
Meppen d.	...	1429	1509	...	1609	...	1630	1709	...	1809	...	1830	1830	...	1909	...	2009	...	2030	2109	...	2209	2327	...	0030	...
Papenburg (Ems) d.	...	1456	1542	H	1642	...	1657	1742	H	1842	...	1857	1857	...	1942	H	2042	...	2057	2142	H	2242	0000	...	...	...
Leer (Ostfriesl) **813** d.	...	1509	1553	1624	1653	...	1709	1753	1824	1853	...	1909	1909	1922	1953	2024	2053	...	2110	2153	2224	2253	0012	...	...	...
Emden Hbf ◧ **813** a.	...	1525	1609	1641	1709	...	1725	1809	1841	1909	...	1925	1925	1938	2009	2041	2109	...	2125	2209	2241	2309	0028	...	...	...
Emden Hbf **813** d.	...	1542	...	1642	...	...	1727	...	1842	...	...	...	...	1942	...	2042	...	...	*2142*	...	2242	...	...	...	...	...
Norden **813** d.	...	1605	...	1706	...	...	1750	...	1906	...	...	...	...	2008	...	2106	...	...	*2208*	...	2306	...	...	...	...	...
Norddeich **813** a.	...	1611	...	1712	...	...	1756	...	1912	...	...	...	...	2014	...	2112	...	...	*2214*	...	2312	...	...	...	...	...
Norddeich Mole ‡ **813** a.	...	1616	...	1716	...	...	1804	...	1916	...	...	...	...	2020	...	2116	...	...	...	...	...	...	...	...	...	...

	⊙ ⚒	⊡ Ⓐ	◇ ⚒	⚒ H	◇	IC 2005 ①–⑥ 🍷♦	⊡ Ⓐ	◇ Ⓐ	◇ Ⓒ	H	◇	IC 2009	⊡ Ⓐ	◇	H	◇	IC 2321 F	⊡ Ⓐ	◇	H	◇	◇ Ⓐ	IC 2203 Ⓑb	ICE 1103 ⑥h S✕	⊡ Ⓐ	◇ Ⓐ
Norddeich Mole ‡ **813** d.	...	...	...	...	...	...	...	...	...	...	...	*0736*r	...	...	0839	...	0951	...	...	1039	...	...	1136	1136	...	...
Norddeich **813** d.	...	...	...	0445	...	*0536*b	...	...	...	0641	...	*0739*r	...	...	0841	...	0957	...	...	1041	...	...	1139	1139	...	...
Norden **813** d.	...	...	...	0451	...	*0543*b	...	...	...	0647	...	*0746*r	...	...	0847	...	1007	...	...	1047	...	...	1146	1146	...	...
Emden Hbf **813** a.	...	...	...	0517	...	*0607*b	...	...	...	0717	...	*0814*r	...	...	0917	...	1029	...	...	1117	...	...	1214	1214	...	...
Emden Hbf ◧ **813** d.	...	...	0452	0517	0552r	0634	...	0642	0652	0717	0752	0833	...	0852	0917	0952	1034	...	1052	1117	1152	1224	1234	1234	...	...
Leer (Ostfriesland) **813** d.	...	...	0509	0534	0609r	0653	...	0659	0709	0734	0809	0853	...	0909	0934	1009	1053	...	1109	1134	1209	1241	1253	1253	...	...
Papenburg (Ems) d.	...	...	0519	▬	0619r	0705	...	0709	0719	▬	0819	0905	...	0919	▬	1019	1104	...	1119	▬	1219	1251	1305	1304	...	←
Meppen d.	...	...	0550	⊡	0650	0732	...	0750j	0750	⊡	0850	0932	...	0950	⊡	1050	1131	...	1150	⊡	1250	1325	1332	1331	...	1337
Lingen (Ems) d.	...	...	0603		0703	0744	...	0804	0804		0904	0944	...	1004		1104	1144	...	1204		1303	→	1344	1344	...	1351
Rheine d.	0453	0608	0628	0708	0729	0804	0808	0829	0829	0908	0929	1004	1008	1029	1108	1129	1204	1208	1229	1308	1327	...	1404	1404	1408	1429j
Emsdetten d.	0502	0616	0636	0716	0737	|	0816	0837	0837	0916	0937	|	1016	1037	1116	1137	|	1216	1237	1316	1336	...	|	|	1416	1437
Greven d.	0510	0623	0644	0723	0745	|	0823	0845	0845	0923	0945	|	1023	1045	1123	1145	|	1223	1245	1323	1345	...	|	|	1423	1445
Münster (Westf) Hbf a.	0524	0633	0654	0733	0756	0829	0833	0856	0856	0933	0956	1029	1033	1056	1133	1156	1229	1233	1256	1333	1356	...	1429	1429	1433	1456
Hagen Hbf **802** a.	...	0737	...	0837	...	|	0937	...	...	1037	...	|	1137	...	1237	...	...	1337	...	1437	...	...	|	|	1537	...
Düsseldorf Hbf **800** a.	...	|	...	|	...	0945	|	...	...	|	...	1147	|	...	|	...	...	|	...	|	...	...	1543	1543	|	...
Köln Hbf **800 802** a.	...	0838	...	0938	...	1014	1038	...	...	1138	...	1216	1238	...	1338	...	...	1438	...	1538	...	...	1614	1614	1638	...
Koblenz Hbf **800** a.	...	...	...	...	...	1116y	...	...	...	...	...	...	...	...	...	...	...	...	...	...	...	...	...	1716x	...	...

	◇ Ⓒ	H	IC 2305 ⑥h	⊡	◇	IC 2205 ⑥h	IC 2205 Ⓑb	⊡ Ⓐ	◇	H	◇	IC 2207	⊡ Ⓐ	◇	H	◇	ICE 1107 ⑥h ✕	IC 2209 ⑤⑦ w	⊡ Ⓐ	◇	H	◇	◇	H	◇	⊙
Norddeich Mole ‡ **813** d.	...	1239	...	...	...	1336	1351	...	...	1439	...	*1537*	...	...	1639	...	1758	1758	...	...	1839	...	...	2039	...	...
Norddeich **813** d.	...	1241	...	...	...	1339	1357	...	...	1441	...	*1540*	...	...	1641	...	1801	1801	...	...	1841	...	...	2041	...	...
Norden **813** d.	...	1247	...	...	...	1347	1407	...	...	1447	...	*1547*	...	...	1647	...	1808	1808	...	...	1847	...	...	2047	...	...
Emden Hbf **813** a.	...	1317	...	...	...	1413	1429	...	...	1517	...	*1614*	...	...	1717	...	1830	1830	...	...	1917	...	...	2117	...	...
Emden Hbf ◧ **813** d.	1252	1317	1341	...	1352	1434	1434	...	1452	1517	1552	1633	...	1652	1717	1752	1834	1834	...	1852	1917	1952	2052	2117	2214	...
Leer (Ostfriesland) **813** d.	1309	1334	|	...	1409	1453	1453	...	1509	1534	1609	1653	...	1709	1734	1809	1853	1853	...	1909	1934	2009	2109	2134	2231	...
Papenburg (Ems) d.	1319	...	|	...	1419	1504	1504	...	1519	▬	1619	1704	...	1719	▬	1819	1904	1905	...	1919	...	2019	2119	▬	2240	...
Meppen d.	1350	...	|	...	1450	1531	1531	...	1550	⊡	1650	1731	...	1750	⊡	1850	1931	1932	...	1950	...	2050	2150	⊙	2313	...
Lingen (Ems) d.	1404	...	|	...	1504	1544	1544	...	1604		1704	1744	...	1804		1904	1944	1944	...	2004	...	2104	2204		2327	...
Rheine d.	1429	...	1459	1508	1529	1604	1604	1608	1629	1708	1729	1804	1808	1829	1908	1932q	2004	2004	2008	2029	...	2129	2229	2253	2349	2353
Emsdetten d.	1437	...	|	1516	1537	|	|	1616	1637	1716	1737	|	1816	1837	1916	1940	|	|	2016	2037	...	2137	2237	2302	...	0002
Greven d.	1445	...	|	1523	1545	|	|	1623	1645	1723	1745	|	1823	1845	1923	1948	|	|	2023	2046	...	2146	2245	2310	...	0010
Münster (Westf) Hbf a.	1456	...	1527	1533	1556	1629	1629	1633	1656	1733	1756	1829	1833	1856	1933	1959	2029	2029	2033	2056	...	2156	2256	2324	...	0024
Hagen Hbf **802** a.	...	...	|	1637	...	|	|	1737	...	1837	...	|	1937	...	2037	...	|	|	2137	...	...	...	...	...	...	...
Düsseldorf Hbf **800** a.	...	...	1651	|	...	1743	1743	|	...	|	...	1946	|	...	|	...	2147	2147	|	...	...	...	...	...	...	...
Köln Hbf **800 802** a.	...	...	1719	1738	...	1814	1814	1838	...	1938	...	2015	2038	...	2138	...	2215	2215	2238	...	...	...	...	...	...	...
Koblenz Hbf **800** a.	...	...	...	...	...	1916z	1916z	...	...	...	...	...	...	...	...	...	...	...	...	...	...	...	...	...	...	...

♦ – **NOTES** (LISTED BY TRAIN NUMBER)

2004 – ⑦–④ (not Dec. 25). SCHWARZWALD – 🚃12 🍷 (Konstanz - Karlsruhe ⑦**w** -) Koblenz - Emden. Does not run Konstanz - Koblenz - Köln Jan. 8 - Mar. 30.

2005 – ①–⑥ (also Dec. 25; not Dec. 26). SCHWARZWALD – 🚃12 🍷 Emden - Koblenz (- Karlsruhe - Konstanz ⑤⑥ **h**). Does not run Köln - Koblenz - Karlsruhe Jan. 6 - Mar. 31.

2014 – 🚃12 🍷 Stuttgart - Mannheim - Münster - Emden.

D – ④⑤ from Apr. 6.
F – To / from Frankfurt via Siegen (Table **808**).
H – From / to Hannover (Table **813**).
S – 🚃12 ✕ Norddeich Mole - Köln (- Stuttgart until Dec. 31) and v.v.

a – Ⓐ only.
b – Not Dec. 25.
f – On ⑤⑦ (also Dec. 26; not Dec. 25) Köln d. 1337, Düsseldorf d. 1409.
h – Also Dec. 25.
j – Arrives 9–11 minutes earlier.
k – Arrives 1307.
q – Arrives 1926.

r – ⚒ only.
t – Not Jan. 6 - Apr. 1.
w – Also Dec. 26; not Dec. 25.
x – Not Jan. 7 - Mar. 30.
y – Not Jan. 6 - Mar. 31.
z – Not Jan. 5 - Mar. 31.

● – Runs 2–4 minutes earlier Rheine - Emden on ③⑤.
⊡ – Operated by National Express.
◇ – Operated by WestfalenBahn.
⊙ – Operated by *eurobahn*.
‡ – For ⛴ to / from Juist and Norderney. See www.reederei-frisia.de for latest timings.
◧ – For train / 🚌 / ⛴ connections to / from Borkum via Emden Außenhafen (certain Emden trains may be extended to / from Emden Außenhafen to connect with sailings). See www.ag-ems.de for latest timings.

NORDDEICH - EMDEN - BREMEN - HANNOVER 813

km		RE 4447	RE 4441	ICE 841	RE 4443	IC 2033	IC 2033	RE 4405	RE 4407	ICE 533	RE 4407	IC 2035	IC 2035	RE 4409	RE 4411	ICE 535	ICE 535	RE 4411	IC 2037	RE 4413	RE 4415	ICE 537	ICE 537	RE 4415	IC 2039
		Ⓒ		Ⓐ ✕		⚒	🍷	B		⚒ ✕		⚒ 🍷	🍷	B		Ⓒ ✕	Ⓐ T ✕		🍷	B		† ✕	⚒ T ✕		🍷
	Norddeich Mole ‡ 812 d.	...	...	...	...	...	...	...	...	...	...	...	...	...	...	...	...	...	0736e	...	0839	...	...	...	0936
0	**Norddeich** 812 d.	...	...	...	...	...	...	...	0445e	...	...	0536	...	...	0641	...	...	...	0739e	...	0841	...	...	...	0939
6	Norden 812 d.	...	...	...	...	...	...	...	0451e	...	...	0543	...	...	0647	...	...	...	0746e	...	0847	...	...	...	0946
35	**Emden** Hbf ◧ 812 d.	...	...	...	...	0416	...	...	0517	...	...	0609	...	...	0717	...	...	...	0816	...	0917	...	...	...	1016
62	Leer (Ostfriesland) 812 a.	...	...	...	...	0433	...	...	0534	...	...	0626	...	...	0734	...	...	...	0833	...	0934	...	...	...	1033
62	Leer (Ostfriesland) d.	...	...	...	...	0441	...	...	0541	...	...	0634	...	...	0741	...	...	...	0841	...	0941	...	...	...	1041
101	Bad Zwischenahn d.	...	...	...	...	0513	...	...	0612	...	...	0712	...	...	0812	...	...	...	0913	...	1012	...	...	...	1113
116	**Oldenburg** (Oldb) a.	...	...	...	...	0523	...	...	0623	...	...	0723	...	...	0823	...	...	...	0923	...	1023	...	...	...	1123
116	**Oldenburg** (Oldb) d.	...	...	0440	...	0535	...	...	0635	0641j	...	0735	0735	...	0835	0843j	...	...	0935	...	1035	1041j	...	...	1135
147	Delmenhorst d.	...	...	0458	...	0554	...	...	0654	0659j	...	0754	0754	...	0854	0900j	...	...	0954	...	1054	1059j	...	...	1154
161	**Bremen** Hbf a.	...	...	0508	...	0605	...	...	0705	0709j	←	0805	0805	...	0905	0910j	...	←	1005	...	1105	1109j	...	←	1205
161	**Bremen** Hbf d.	0208	0408	0512	0517	0609	0609	0617	→	0715j	0717	0809	0809	0817	→	0915j	0915	0917	1009	1017	→	1115j	1115	1117	1209
196	Verden (Aller) d.	0239	0441	0533	0541	0630	0630	0641	...	|	0741	0830	0830	0841	...	|	|	0941	1030	1041	...	|	|	1141	1230
227	Nienburg (Weser) d.	0301	0503	|	0603	0646	0646	0703	...	|	0803	0846	0846	0903	...	|	|	1003	1046	1103	...	|	|	1203	1246
283	**Hannover** Hbf a.	0341	0538	0614	0638	0713	0713	0738	...	0814	0838	0913	0913	0938	...	1015	1015	1038	1113	1138	...	1214	1214	1238	1313
	Magdeburg Hbf **866** a.	...	...	|	...	0856	0856	...	...	|	...	1056	1056	...	...	|	|	...	1256	...	...	|	|	...	1456
	Berlin Hbf **810** a.	...	...	0825	...	|	|	...	...	|	...	|	|	...	...	|	|	...	|	...	...	|	|	...	|
	Leipzig Hbf **866** a.	...	...	...	...	1015	1015	...	...	|	...	1215	1215	...	...	|	|	...	1415	...	...	|	|	...	1615
	Nürnberg Hbf **900** a.	...	...	...	...	...	...	...	...	1125	...	...	...	...	...	1325	1325	...	...	...	...	1525	1525	...	...
	München Hbf **900** a.	...	...	...	...	...	...	...	...	1238	...	...	...	...	...	1441	1441	...	...	...	...	1641	1641	...	...

	RE 4417	ICE 1133	ICE 639	RE 4419	IC 2431	RE 4421	ICE 631	RE 4423	IC 2433	RE 4425	ICE 633	RE 4427	IC 2435	RE 4429	ICE 635	RE 4431	IC 2437	IC 2437	RE 4433	RE 4435	IC 2439	RE 4437	RE 4439	RE 4445	♣
	B	⑤T ✕	T ✕		A 🍷	B	T ✕		🍷	B	T ✕		🍷	B	T ✕			Ⓑ b 🍷	B			B			
Norddeich Mole ‡ 812 d.	...	...	...	1039	...	...	...	1239	...	...	...	1439	1537	...	...	1639	...	...	...	1839	...	...	2039	...	...
Norddeich 812 d.	...	...	...	1041	...	...	...	1241	...	...	...	1441	1540	...	...	1641	...	...	...	1841	...	...	2041	...	...
Norden 812 d.	...	...	...	1047	...	...	...	1247	...	...	...	1447	1547	...	...	1647	...	...	...	1847	...	...	2047	...	...
Emden Hbf ◧ 812 d.	...	...	...	1117	1218	...	...	1317	1417	...	...	1517	1616	...	...	1717	1813	1813	...	1917	2016	...	2117	...	...
Leer (Ostfriesland) 812 a.	...	...	...	1134	1235	...	...	1334	1434	...	...	1534	1633	...	...	1734	1833	1833	...	1934	2033	...	2134	...	...
Leer (Ostfriesland) d.	...	...	...	1141	1241	...	...	1341	1441	...	...	1541	1641	...	...	1741	1841	1841	...	1941	2041	...	2141	...	...
Bad Zwischenahn d.	...	...	...	1212	1313	...	...	1412	1513	...	...	1612	1713	...	...	1812	1913	1913	...	2012	2113	...	2212	...	2345
Oldenburg (Oldb) a.	...	...	...	1223	1323	...	...	1423	1523	...	...	1623	1723	...	...	1823	1923	1923	...	2023	2123	...	2223	...	2356
Oldenburg (Oldb) d.	...	1229	...	1235	1335	...	...	1434	1535	...	...	1635	1735	...	...	1835	1935	1935	...	2035	2135	...	2235	...	0005
Delmenhorst d.	...	1249	...	1254	1354	...	...	1454	1554	...	...	1654	1754	...	...	1854	1954	1954	...	2054	2154	...	2254	...	0030
Bremen Hbf a.	...	1300	...	1305*	1405	...	...	1505*	1605	...	...	1705*	1805	...	...	1905*	2005	2005	...	2105	2205	...	2305	...	0043
Bremen Hbf d.	1217	1305	1315	1317	1409	1417	1515	1517	1609	1617	1715	1717	1809	1817	1915	1917	...	2009	2017	2117	...	2217	2313	0013	...
Verden (Aller) d.	1241	|	|	1341	1430	1441	|	1541	1630	1641	|	1741	1830	1841	|	1941	...	2030	2041	2141	...	2241	2346	0046	...
Nienburg (Weser) d.	1303	|	|	1403	1446	1503	|	1603	1646	1703	|	1803	1846	1903	|	2003	...	2046	2103	2203	...	2303	0008	0108	...
Hannover Hbf a.	1338	1407	1414	1438	1513	1538	1614	1638	1713	1738	1814	1838	1913	1938	2014	2038	...	2113	2138	2238	...	2338	0040	0140	...
Magdeburg Hbf **866** a.	...	1536	|	...	1658	...	|	...	1858	...	|	...	2056	...	|	...	...	2302	...	...	...	...	...	...	...
Berlin Hbf **810** a.	...	|	|	...	1824	...	|	...	|	...	|	...	|	...	|	...	...	...	...	...	...	...	...	...	...
Leipzig Hbf **866** a.	...	1714	|	...	...	...	|	...	2015	...	|	...	2215	...	|	...	...	...	...	...	...	...	...	...	...
Nürnberg Hbf **900** a.	...	...	1725	...	...	...	1925	...	...	...	2125	...	...	...	2326z	...	...	...	...	...	...	...	...	...	...
München Hbf **900** a.	...	...	1839	...	...	...	2043	...	...	...	2239	...	...	...	0043q	...	...	...	...	...	...	...	...	...	...

	♣	RE 4438	RE 4446	RE 4448	RE 4400	IC 2438	RE 4402	RE 4404	IC 2436	IC 2436	RE 4406	ICE 636	RE 4408	IC 2434	RE 4410	ICE 634	RE 4412	IC 2432	RE 4414	ICE 632	RE 4416	IC 2430	RE 4418	ICE 630	RE 4420
	Ⓐ	⚒	Ⓒ	Ⓒ	Ⓐ B	⚒		B		⚒ 🍷		Ⓐ T ✕	B	🍷		①–⑥ ★✕	B	A 🍷		T ✕	B	🍷		T ✕	B
München Hbf **900** d.	...	...	...	...	...	...	...	...	...	...	...	...	...	...	...	0511	...	...	...	0718	...	...	...	0918	...
Nürnberg Hbf **900** d.	...	...	...	...	...	...	...	...	...	...	...	...	...	...	...	0632	...	...	...	0832	...	...	...	1032	...
Leipzig Hbf **866** d.	...	...	...	...	...	...	...	...	...	...	...	...	...	0542e	...	|	...	...	...	|	...	0942	...	|	...
Berlin Hbf **810** d.	...	...	...	...	...	...	...	...	...	...	...	...	...	|	...	|	...	0729	...	|	...	|	...	|	...
Magdeburg Hbf **866** d.	...	...	...	...	...	...	...	...	...	0500a	...	...	...	0700e	...	|	...	0903	...	|	...	1100	...	|	...
Hannover Hbf d.	...	...	0217	0417	0420	...	0520	0618h	...	0645	0720	0745	0820	0845	0920	0945	1020	1045	1120	1145	1220	1245	1320	1345	1420
Nienburg (Weser) d.	...	...	0258	0458	0454	...	0554	0654	...	0713	0754	|	0854	0913	0954	|	1054	1113	1154	|	1254	1313	1354	|	1454
Verden (Aller) d.	...	...	0320	0518	0515	...	0615	0715	...	0730	0815	|	0915	0930	1015	|	1115	1130	1215	|	1315	1330	1415	|	1515
Bremen Hbf a.	...	...	0351	0540	0539	...	0639	0739	...	0750	0839	0845*	0939	0950	1039	1045*	1139	1150	1239	1245*	1339	1350	1439	1445*	1539
Bremen Hbf d.	0415	...	...	...	...	0552	0653	...	0753	0753	0853	...	...	0955	1053	...	...	1155	1253	...	...	1355	1453	...	...
Delmenhorst d.	0427	...	...	...	...	0604	0703	...	0804	0804	0903	...	...	1006	1103	...	...	1206	1303	...	...	1406	1503	...	...
Oldenburg (Oldb) a.	0453	...	...	...	...	0623	0723	...	0823	0823	0923	...	...	1025	1123	...	...	1225	1323	...	...	1425	1523	...	...
Oldenburg (Oldb) d.	0458	0533	...	...	...	0626	0733	...	0833	0833	0933	...	...	1033	1133	...	...	1233	1333	...	...	1433	1533	...	...
Bad Zwischenahn d.	0511	0544	...	...	...	0637	0744	...	0844	0844	0944	...	...	1044	1144	...	...	1244	1344	...	...	1444	1544	...	...
Leer (Ostfriesland) a.	...	0613	...	...	...	0707	0813	...	0914	0914	1013	...	...	1114	1213	...	...	1314	1413	...	...	1514	1613	...	...
Leer (Ostfriesland) 812 d.	...	0624	...	...	...	0715	0824	...	0922	0922	1024	...	...	1122	1224	...	...	1322	1424	...	...	1522	1624	...	...
Emden Hbf ◧ 812 d.	...	0642	...	...	...	0742t	0842	...	0938	0938	1042	...	...	1138	1242	...	...	1342	1442	...	...	1538	1642	...	...
Norden 812 d.	...	0706	...	...	...	0808	0906	...	...	...	1106	...	...	...	1306	...	...	1408	1506	...	...	...	1706	...	...
Norddeich 812 a.	...	0712	...	...	...	0814	0912	...	...	...	1112	...	...	...	1312	...	...	1414	1512	...	...	...	1712	...	...
Norddeich Mole ‡ 812 a.	...	0716	...	...	...	0820	0916	...	...	...	1116	...	...	...	1316	...	...	1420	1516	...	...	...	1716	...	...

	IC 2038	RE 4422	ICE 538	RE 4424	IC 2036	IC 2036	RE 4426	ICE 536	RE 4428	IC 2034	IC 1934	RE 4430	ICE 776	RE 4430	RE 4432	IC 2032	IC 2032	RE 4434	RE 4434	ICE 532	RE 4442	ICE 540	RE 4444	ICE 1130	RE 4440
	🍷		T ✕	B	🍷	Ⓑ b 🍷		T ✕	B	🍷	⑦ w D ⊗		Ⓑ F ✕		B	🍷	Ⓑ b 🍷		⑥	✕				⑦ U	
München Hbf **900** d.	...	...	1118	...	...	...	...	1318	...	...	...	...	...	...	...	...	...	...	...	1717	...	...	...	...	...
Nürnberg Hbf **900** d.	...	...	1233	...	...	...	...	1434	...	...	...	...	...	...	...	...	...	...	...	1833	...	...	...	...	...
Leipzig Hbf **866** d.	1142	...	|	...	1342	1342	...	|	...	1542	1604	...	...	...	...	1740	1740	...	...	|	...	...	...	...	...
Berlin Hbf **810** d.	|	...	|	...	|	|	...	|	...	|	|	...	...	...	...	|	|	...	...	|	...	2046	...	...	...
Magdeburg Hbf **866** d.	1300	...	|	...	1500	1500	...	|	...	1700	|	...	...	...	...	1900	1900	...	...	|	...	|	...	...	...
Hannover Hbf d.	1445	1520	1545	1620	1645	1645	1720	1745	1820	1845	1900	1920	1951	...	2020	2045	2045	2120	2120	2145	2220	2245	2320	2349	0020
Nienburg (Weser) d.	1513	1554	|	1654	1713	1713	1754	|	1854	1913	1929	1954	|	...	2055	2113	2113	2154	2154	2214	2254	2314	2354	0016	0054
Verden (Aller) d.	1530	1615	|	1715	1730	1730	1815	|	1915	1930	1948	2015	|	...	2116	2130	2130	2215	2215	2234	2315	2332	0015	0034	0115
Bremen Hbf a.	1550	1639	1645	1739	1750	1750	1839	1845*	1939	1950	2009	2039	2047	←	2139	2150	2150	2239	2239	2259	2347	2351f	0047	0052	0147
Bremen Hbf d.	1555	1653	...	...	1755	1755	1853	...	...	1955	2013	→	2050	2054	...	2155	2155	2253	2253	2303	...	2353f	...	0059	...
Delmenhorst d.	1606	1703	...	...	1806	1806	1903	...	...	2006	2024	...	|	2104	...	2206	2206	2304	2304	2315	...	0005f	...	0111	...
Oldenburg (Oldb) a.	1625	1723	...	...	1825	1825	1923	...	...	2025	2040	...	2117	2123	...	2225	2225	2323	2323	2332	...	0023f	...	0128	...
Oldenburg (Oldb) d.	1633	1733	...	...	1833	1833	1933	...	...	2033	2042	...	...	2133	...	...	2233	...	2333	...	...	...	...	...	...
Bad Zwischenahn d.	1644	1744	...	...	1844	1844	1944	...	...	2044	2055	...	...	2144	...	...	2244	...	2344	...	...	...	...	...	...
Leer (Ostfriesland) a.	1714	1813	...	...	1914	1914	2013	...	...	2114	2128	...	...	2213	...	...	2314	...	0013	...	...	...	...	...	...
Leer (Ostfriesland) 812 d.	1722	1824	...	...	1922	1922	2024	...	...	2122	2136	...	...	2224	...	...	2322	...	0024	...	...	...	...	...	...
Emden Hbf ◧ 812 d.	1738	1842	...	...	1938	1942	2042	...	...	2142	2152	...	...	2242	...	...	2338	...	0041	...	...	...	...	...	...
Norden 812 d.	...	1906	...	...	...	2008	2106	...	...	2208	...	...	...	2306	...	...	...	...	...	...	...	...	...	...	...
Norddeich 812 a.	...	1912	...	...	...	2014	2112	...	...	2214	...	...	...	2312	...	...	...	...	...	...	...	...	...	...	...
Norddeich Mole ‡ 812 a.	...	1916	...	...	...	2020	2116	...	...	...	...	...	...	...	...	...	...	...	...	...	...	...	...	...	...

A – To / from Cottbus on dates in Table **837**.
B – To / from Bremerhaven (Table **815**).
D – From / to Dresden (Table **842**).
F – Ⓑ until Mar. 10 (not Dec. 25). From Frankfurt (Table **900**).
U – Until Mar. 12.
– ⑦ until Mar. 5 (also Dec. 26; not Dec. 25).

a – Ⓐ only.
b – Ⓑ (not Dec. 25).

e – ⚒ only.
f – 28–40 minutes later from Mar. 12.
h – 0620 on †.
j – 28–47 minutes **earlier** from Mar. 13.
q – Nürnberg - München on ⑤⑦ (also Dec. 26, Jan. 5).
t – Arrives 0731.
w – Also Dec. 26; not Dec. 25.
z – Not ⑥.

★ – ①–⑥ until Mar. 11 (also Dec. 25; not Dec. 26).
⊗ – From Mar. 19 terminates at Bremen Hbf (a. 2047).
* – Connects with train in previous column.
‡ – For sailings from / to Juist and Norderney (www.reederei-frisia.de).
◧ – For train / 🚌 / ⛴ connections from / to Borkum via Emden Außenhafen (www.ag-ems.de).
♣ – Operated by Nord West Bahn (2nd class only).

814 OSNABRÜCK - OLDENBURG - WILHELMSHAVEN

Nord West Bahn

km		⚒	⚒	Ⓐ						†
0	**Osnabrück** Hbf d.	...	...	0459	0601			2201	2301	2301
20	Bramsche d.	...	...	0518	0618	and		2218	2318	2318
50	Quakenbrück d.	...	...	0540	0640			2240	2341	2341
72	Cloppenburg d.	...	...	0556	0656	hourly		2256	2357	2357
113	**Oldenburg** (Oldb) a.	...	...	0629	0729			2329	0029	0029
113	**Oldenburg** (Oldb) d.	0536	0636	0636	0736	until		2336	...	0036
143	Varel (Oldb) d.	0601	0701	0701	0801			0001	...	0101
165	**Wilhelmshaven** Hbf a.	0621	0721	0721	0821			0021	...	0121

	Ⓐ	⚒		⚒	Ⓐ		❖		⑤⑥f	
Wilhelmshaven Hbf d.	...	0440	...	0540	0610	0640		2140	2310	2310
Varel (Oldb) d.	...	0458	...	0558	0628	0658	and	2158	2328	2328
Oldenburg (Oldb) a.	...	0524	...	0624	0653	0724		2224	2354	2354
Oldenburg (Oldb) d.	0403	0529	0629	0629	0659	0729	hourly	2229	2359	...
Cloppenburg d.	0435	0605	0705	0705	0735	0805		2305	0033	...
Quakenbrück d.	0450	0621	0721	0721	0751	0821	until	2321	...	...
Bramsche d.	0513	0641	0741	0741	0811	0841		2341	...	...
Osnabrück Hbf a.	0531	0658	0758	0758	0829	0858		2358	...	...

f – Not Apr. 7.

❖ – On ⑥ Wilhelmshaven d. 1328 (not 1340) and change trains at Sande (a. 1335, d. 1347).

815 OSNABRÜCK - BREMEN - BREMERHAVEN - CUXHAVEN

RE services

SERVICE UNTIL MAY 17. Warning! Services Bremen - Bremerhaven-Lehe and v.v. are subject to alteration on ⑥⑦ from March 11.

km		⚒¶	⚒	ⒶH	⚒		JH		H		H		H		A	H		H		H		H	¶		¶	
0	**Osnabrück** Hbf 800 d.	...	0417	...	0529	0629	...	0729	0829	0929	1029	1129	1229	1329	1356	1429	1529	1629	1729	1829	1929	2029	2129	2229	...	2329
53	Diepholz d.	...	0450	...	0603	0703	...	0803	0903	1003	1103	1203	1303	1403	|	1503	1603	1703	1803	1903	2003	2103	2203	2303	...	0003
122	**Bremen** Hbf 800 a.	...	0546	...	0650	0749	...	0850	0949	1050	1149	1250	1349	1450	1457	1549	1650	1749	1850	1949	2050	2149	2250	2350	...	0050
122	**Bremen** Hbf d.	0540	...	0556	0656	...	0756	0856	0956	1056	1156	1256	1356	1456	1507	1556	1656	1756	1856	1956	2056	2156	2312		0012	...
143	Osterholz-Scharmbeck d.	0556	...	0610	0710	...	0810	0910	1010	1110	1210	1310	1410	1510	1524	1610	1710	1810	1910	2010	2110	2210	2328	...	0028	...
185	**Bremerhaven** Hbf a.	0625	...	0631	0731	...	0831	0931	1031	1131	1231	1331	1431	1531	1546	1631	1731	1831	1931	2031	2131	2231	2357	...	0057	...
188	**Bremerhaven**-Lehe a.	0630	...	0635	0735	...	0835	0935	1035	1135	1235	1335	1435	1535	1553	1635	1735	1835	1935	2035	2135	2235	0002	...	0102	...

	⚒	⚒¶	⚒	ⒶH		⚒		H		H	B		H		H		H		H		H		H	¶		¶
Bremerhaven-Lehe d.	...	0407	...	0523	...	0623	...	0723	0823	0923	1004	1023	1123	1223	1323	1423	1523	1623	1723	1823	1923	2023	2123	2157	...	2257
Bremerhaven Hbf d.	...	0412	...	0528	...	0628	...	0728	0828	0928	1011	1028	1128	1228	1328	1428	1528	1628	1728	1828	1928	2028	2128	2202	...	2302
Osterholz-Scharmbeck d.	...	0444	...	0550	...	0650	...	0750	0850	0950	1035	1050	1150	1250	1350	1450	1550	1650	1750	1850	1950	2050	2150	2233	...	2333
Bremen Hbf a.	...	0503	...	0603	...	0703	...	0803	0903	1003	1051	1103	1203	1303	1403	1503	1603	1703	1803	1903	2003	2103	2203	2252	...	2350
Bremen Hbf 800 d.	0407	...	0507	...	0607	0707	0707	0807	0907	1007	1054	1107	1207	1307	1407	1507	1607	1707	1807	1907	2007	2107	2207	...	2313	...
Diepholz d.	0454	...	0554	...	0654	0754	0754	0854	0954	1054	|	1154	1254	1354	1454	1554	1654	1754	1854	1954	2054	2154	2256	...	0002	...
Osnabrück Hbf 800 a.	0526	...	0626	...	0726	0826	0826	0926	1026	1126	1151	1226	1326	1426	1526	1626	1726	1826	1926	2026	2126	2226	2328	...	0033	...

BREMERHAVEN - CUXHAVEN

km	⊡	⑥⑦c		Ⓐ	⚒					
0	**Bremerhaven** Hbf d.	0003	...	0506	0636	0736	and	2136	2236	...
3	Bremerhaven-Lehe d.	0008	...	0511	0641	0741	hourly	2141	2241	...
43	**Cuxhaven** a.	0050	...	0557	0727	0827	until	2227	2327	...

⊡	Ⓐ	⚒							
Cuxhaven d.	0509	0639	0739	and	1839	1939	2039	2139	2239
Bremerhaven-Lehe d.	0549	0719	0819	hourly	1919	2019	2119	2219	2319
Bremerhaven Hbf a.	0553	0723	0823	until	1923	2023	2123	2223	2323

A – *IC* **2202**. OSTFRIESLAND – From Koblenz / Köln (Table **800**).
B – *IC* **2201**. OSTFRIESLAND – To Köln (Table **800**).
H – From / to Hannover (Table **813**).

J – Until Mar. 11.

c – Also Apr. 10, May 1, 29.

⊡ – Operated by Eisenbahnen und Verkehrsbetriebe Elbe-Weser.
¶ – Operated by Nord West Bahn (2nd class only).

818 HAMBURG - CUXHAVEN and BREMERHAVEN

Regionalverkehre Start Deutschland; Elbe-Weser

km	❖	⑥	Ⓐ‡	Ⓐ	‡	⑥	Ⓐ	‡	†	⚒																
0	**Hamburg** Hbf ⊖ d.	...	0448	...	0528	...	0602	0628	...	0702e	0758c	0858c	1002	1102	1202	1302	1402	1502	1606r	1702	1806t	1902	2002	2102	2158	2258
12	**Hamburg** Harburg ⊖ d.	...	0503	...	0543	...	0624	0643	...	0724	0824	0924	1024	1124	1224	1324	1424	1524	1624	1724	1824	1924	2024	2124	2224	2324
33	**Buxtehude** ⊖ d.	...	0527	...	0607	...	0641	0707	...	0741	0841	0941	1041	1141	1241	1341	1441	1541	1641	1741	1841	1941	2041	2141	2241	2341
54	Stade ⊖ d.	0540	0549	0553	0629	0640	0657	0729	0740	0757	0857	0957	1057	1157	1257	1357	1457	1557	1657	1757	1857	1957	2057	2157	2257	2357
102	Otterndorf d.	0622	...	0635	...	0722	0737	...	0822	0837	0937	1037	1137	1237	1337	1437	1537	1637	1737	1837	1937	2037	2137	2237	2337	0037
116	**Cuxhaven** a.	0635	...	0648	...	0735	0750	...	0835	0850	0950	1050	1150	1250	1350	1450	1550	1650	1750	1850	1950	2050	2150	2250	2350	0050

❖	Ⓐ	⚒	Ⓐ		Ⓐ	Ⓒ																	⑤⑥j	k	‡
Cuxhaven d.	0430	0509	0549	0609	0650	0709	...	0809	0909	1009	1109	1209	1309	1409	1509	1609	1709	1809	1909	2009	2109	...	2209	2237	...
Otterndorf d.	0442	0521	0601	0621	0701	0721	...	0821	0921	1021	1121	1221	1321	1421	1521	1621	1721	1821	1921	2021	2121	...	2221	2250	...
Stade ⊖ d.	0524	0603	0643	0703	0743	0803	...	0903	1003	1103	1203	1303	1403	1503	1603	1703	1803	1903	2003	2103	2203	...	2303	2332	2334
Buxtehude ⊖ d.	0541	0621	0701	0721	0801	0821	...	0921	1021	1121	1221	1321	1421	1521	1621	1721	1821	1921	2021	2121	2221	...	2321	...	2354
Hamburg Harburg ⊖ a.	0557	0638	0717	0738	0817	0838	...	0938	1038	1138	1238	1338	1438	1538	1638	1738	1838	1938	2038	2138	2237	...	2336	...	0020
Hamburg Hbf ⊖ a.	0619	0703	0734	0803	0839	0903	...	1003	1103	1204	1303	1403	1503	1603	1703	1803	1903	2003	2104	2203	2305	...	0015	...	0035

km	△	Ⓐ	Ⓐ	Ⓐ	Ⓐ	Ⓐ	Ⓐ		Ⓐ	Ⓐ		Ⓐ	Ⓐ	Ⓐ	Ⓐ	Ⓒ	⑥	Ⓒ	Ⓒ	Ⓒ	Ⓒ		Ⓒ	Ⓒ	Ⓒ	†
	Hamburg Hbf ¶ d.		...	0448	0548	0628	0748		1248	1408		1908	2008	2108	2208		...	...	...	0648	0758		1858	1958	2058	2158*
0	**Buxtehude** d.		...	0537	0637	0717	0837	and	1337	1453	and	1953	2053	2153	2253		...	...	...	0745	0845	and	1945	2045	2145	2245
39	Bremervörde a.		...	0620	0721	0820	0920	hourly	1420	1536	hourly	2036	2136	2236	2336		...	...	...	0828	0928	hourly	2028	2128	2228	2328
39	Bremervörde d.		0538	0638	0738	0838	0938	until	1438	1538	until	2038	2138	...	...		0538	0638	0738	0838	0938	until	2038	2138	...	...
78	**Bremerhaven** Hbf a.		0620	0720	0820	0920	1020		1520	1620		2120	2220	...	...		0620	0720	0820	0920	1020		2120	2220	...	...

△	Ⓐ	Ⓐ	Ⓐ		Ⓐ	Ⓐ		Ⓐ	Ⓐ	⑤f	Ⓐ	Ⓐ	Ⓐ	Ⓒ	Ⓒ	⑥	Ⓒ		Ⓒ	†	Ⓒ	⑥z	Ⓒ	Ⓒ	Ⓒ
Bremerhaven Hbf d.		...	0536		1236	1336		1936	2036	2136	2136	2236	2354		...	0636	0736		1936	2036	2036	2136	2136	2236	2354
Bremervörde a.		...	0619	and	1319	1419	and	2019	2119	2219	2219	2320	0035		...	0719	0819	and	2019	2119	2119	2219	2219	2320	0035
Bremervörde d.		0526	0626	hourly	1326	1438	hourly	2038	2138	2238	...	...	...		0733	0733	0833	hourly	2033	2133	...	2233	...	...	...
Buxtehude a.		0609	0709	until	1409	1526	until	2126	2226	2326	...	...	...		0816	0816	0916	until	2116	2216	...	2316	...	...	...
Hamburg Hbf ¶ a.		0655	0755		1455	1615		2215	2315	0015	...	...	...		0905	0905	1005		2205	2305	...	0035	...	...	...

c – 4 minutes later on Ⓐ.
e – 0651 on ⑥.
f – Not Apr. 7.
j – Also Apr. 6, 9, 30, May 17, 28.
k – ⑦–④ (not Apr. 6, 9, 30, May 17, 28).

r – Through service on ⑤ (not Apr. 7). On other dates connection departs Hamburg Hbf 1602.
t – Through service on ①–④ (not Apr. 10, May 1, 18, 29). On other dates connection departs Hamburg Hbf 1802.
z – Also Apr. 7, 9, 30, May 28.

* – Change trains at Hamburg Harburg and Buxtehude.
‡ – Hamburg S-Bahn (2nd class only).
⊖ – Additional S-Bahn trains operate.
¶ – Connections shown are Hamburg S-Bahn services.
❖ – Operated by Regionalverkehre Start Deutschland.
△ – Operated by Eisenbahnen und Verkehrsbetriebe Elbe-Weser.

820 HAMBURG - KIEL

RE services except where shown

km					⚒				❖								ICE 1088 ⚒ G	ICE 618 F	ICE 474 D	ICE 804 E	ICE 882 M	ICE 612 F	ICE 74 Z	EC 378 P	ICE 1094 Ⓑb S	ICE 1594 ⑤ G
0	**Hamburg** Hbf 823 d.	0436	0536	0640t	0719	0737k	0822	0843	and at	2022	2043	2122	2146	2222	2343	A	0900	1017	1139	1230	1357	1617	1739	1915	2033	2050
34	Elmshorn 823 d.	0504	0604	0709t	0747	0809k	0847	0909	the same minutes	2047	2109	2147	2214	2248	0011	L	|	|	|	|	|	|	|	|	|	|
78	Neumünster 823 d.	0532	0632	0734	0814	0834	0914	0934	past each	2114	2134	2213	2240	2318	0040	S	0952	1106	1225	1325	1501	1705	1825	2004	2123	|
109	**Kiel** Hbf a.	0555	0655	0757	0834	0857	0934	0957	hour until	2134	2157	2232	2303	2338	0103	O	1009	1123	1244	1343	1519	1722	1842	2022	2141	2204

	Ⓐ			⚒			⊖										ICE 573 ⚒ S	ICE 73 ⚒ Z	EC 379 P	ICE 75 † Z	ICE 77 Z	ICE 613 F	ICE 801 E	ICE 1171 D	ICE 885 M	ICE 619 F
Kiel Hbf d.	0314	0403r	0502	0527	0602	0626	0702	0727	0802	and at	2102	2127	2205	2305	0005	A	0613	0712	0742	0912	1112	1237	1413	1512	1634	1838
Neumünster 823 d.	0334	0430	0528	0545	0628	0645	0728	0746	0828	the same minutes	2128	2146	2233	2333	0033	L	0632	0733	0759	0931	1132	1256	1432	1531	1651	1857
Elmshorn 823 d.	0400	0456r	0549	0612	0649	0711	0749	0812	0849	past each	2149	2212	2258	2358	0058	S	|	|	|	|	|	|	|	|	|	|
Hamburg Hbf 823 a.	0426	0521	0615	0637	0715	0735	0815	0837	0915	hour until	2217	2237	2325	0025	0125	O	0719	0819	0848	1020	1220	1342	1532	1620	1757	1942

D – (12) ✕ Basel - Frankfurt - Hannover - Kiel and v.v.
E – (12) ✕ München - Nürnberg - Erfurt - Berlin - Kiel and v.v.
F – (12) ✕ München - Stuttgart - Köln - Kiel and v.v.
G – (12) ✕ Frankfurt - Hannover - Kiel.
M – (12) ✕ München - Nürnberg - Hannover - Kiel and v.v.
P – (12) ✕ Praha - Dresden - Berlin - Hamburg - Kiel and v.v. Runs as *IC* **1078/1979** on ① until Feb. 13 (not Dec. 26) and does not run Praha - Dresden and v.v.

S – (12) ✕ Kiel - Frankfurt - Stuttgart and v.v.
Z – (12) ✕ Kiel - Frankfurt - Basel - Zürich and v.v.

b – Not Dec. 25.
k – On † Hamburg Hbf d. 0736, Elmshorn d. 0804.
r – On Ⓒ Kiel d. 0405, Elmshorn d. 0454.
t – On Ⓒ Hamburg Hbf d. 0636, Elmshorn d. 0704.

⊖ – On ⑦ Jan. 8 - Feb. 26 and ⑦ from Mar. 26 Neumünster d. 0735, Elmshorn d. 0756, Hamburg Hbf a. 0827.
❖ – Certain departure times are 1 minute earlier.

HAMBURG - WESTERLAND 821

See Tables **820** and **823** for connecting *RE* services Hamburg Hbf - Elmshorn and v.v. Frequent S-Bahn services operate Hamburg Hbf - Altona and v.v.

km		A		⚒		A		Ⓐ	Ⓒ	Ⓐ	Ⓒ Y		Ⓒ B		*IC*• 2214	D	Ⓒ B	① M	*IC*• 2074	Ⓒ B	D			*IC*• 2310	S	①–④ R
	Köln Hbf **800** d.	...	...	...	...	...	...	...	...	...	...	...	...	...	0507	...	...	...	...	...	...	...	...	0906	...	...
	Berlin Hbf **840** d.	...	...	...	...	...	...	...	...	...	...	...	...	...	|	...	...	...	0804	...	...	...	...	|	...	...
	Hamburg Hbf . **820** d.	...	...	...	...	...	...	...	...	...	...	...	...	...	0917	...	...	...	1009	...	...	...	...	1302	...	...
0	**Hamburg** Altona d.	...	...	...	...	...	...	0529	0629	0640	0730	0740	0830	0840	|	0940	0940	1005	|	1040	1040	1140	1240	|	1340	1340
30	Elmshorn **820** d.	...	...	...	...	...	...	0549	0649	0701	|	0801	|	0901	|	1001	1001	1032u	|	1101	1101	1201	1301	|	1401	1401
64	Itzehoe a.	...	...	...	...	...	...	0611	0713	0723	|	0823	|	0923	1003	1023	1023	|	1100	1123	1123	1223	1323	1353	1423	1423
64	Itzehoe d.	...	...	0508	...	...	...	0612	0714	0724	|	0824	|	0924	1015	1024	1024	1056u	1113	1124	1124	1224	1324	1414	1424	1424
123	Heide (Holst) a.	...	...	0548	...	...	...	0656	0758	0758	|	0858	|	0958	1050	1058	1058	1129	1149	1158	1158	1258	1358	1449	1458	1458
123	Heide (Holst) d.	...	...	0549	...	...	...	0701	0801	0801	|	0901	|	1001	1052	1100	1100	1131	1151	1201	1201	1301	1401	1451	1501	1501
157	Husum d.	0458	0558	0614	0630	0658	0730	0730	0830	0830	0905	0930	1005	1030	1118	1130	1130	1201	1218	1230	1230	1330	1430	1517	1530	1530
197	Niebüll a.	0527	0627	...	0659	0727	0759	0759	0859	0859	0929	0959	1029	1059	1145	1206	1206	1226	1244	1306	1306	1359	1459	1544	1606h	1611
197	Niebüll 🚗 d.	0531	0631	...	0701	0731	0801	0801	0901	0901	0931	1001	1031	1101	1201	1216	1231	1231	1300	1316	1331	1401	1501	1601	1616	1631
237	**Westerland** (Sylt) 🚗 a.	0605	0705	...	0735	0805	0835	0835	0937	0937	1005	1035	1107	1135	1235	1251	1305	1305	1337	1351	1405	1435	1535	1634	1651	1705

	⑤–⑦ T			*IC* 2374 ④–⑦ K 🍷								⑤⑦
Köln Hbf **800** d.	...	...	...	...	...	...	...	...	...	...	...	...
Berlin Hbf **840** d.	...	...	...	...	...	...	...	...	...	...	...	...
Hamburg Hbf ... **820** d.	1402	...	...	1533	...	...	...	...	...	...	...	...
Hamburg Altona d.	|	1440	1540	|	1640	1740	1840	1940	2040	2140	2245	2345
Elmshorn **820** d.	|	1501	1601	|	1701	1801	1901	2001	2101	2201	2306	0006
Itzehoe a.	|	1523	1623	1628	1723	1823	1925	2025	2125	2225	2330	0030
Itzehoe d.	|	1524	1624	1642	1724	1824	1926	2026	2126	2226	2331	0031
Heide (Holst) a.	1530	1558	1658	1717	1758	1858	1958	2100	2200	2310	0015	0115
Heide (Holst) d.	1532	1601	1701	1719	1801	1901	2001	2101	2201	2311	0016	0116
Husum d.	1559f	1630	1730	1743	1830	1930	2030	2130	2230	2340	0044	0144
Niebüll a.	1624	1659	1759	1808	1859	1959	2059	2159	2259	0009	...	...
Niebüll 🚗 d.	1631	1701	1801	1831	1901	2001	2101	2201	2301	0010	...	...
Westerland (Sylt). 🚗 a.	1705	1735	1835	1904	1935	2035	2135	2235	2335	0050g	...	...

	Ⓐ	Ⓐ	Ⓒ		†	⚒				*IC*• 2311
Westerland 🚗 d.	...	0419	...	0520	0620	0620	0720	0820	0907	0926
Niebüll 🚗 a.	...	0453	...	0559	0659	0659	0759	0859	0944	0959
Niebüll d.	...	0454	...	0601	0701	0701	0801	0901	1000	1013
Husum d.	0424	0524	0524j	0631	0729	0731	0831	0931	1031	1042
Heide (Holst) a.	0449	0549	0549j	0657	0752	0757	0857	0957	1057	1106
Heide (Holst) d.	0450	0550	0550	0658	0753	0802	0902	1002	1102	1108
Itzehoe a.	0533	0633	0633	0733	0836	0836	0936	1036	1136	1143
Itzehoe d.	0534	0634	0634	0734	0837	0837	0937	1037	1137	1159
Elmshorn **820** d.	0600	0700	0700	0800	0900	0900	1000	1100	1200	|
Hamburg Altona a.	0621	0721	0721	0821	0921	0921	1021	1121	1221	|
Hamburg Hbf **820** a.	...	...	...	...	...	...	...	...	...	1245
Berlin Hbf **840** a.	...	...	...	...	...	...	...	...	...	|
Köln Hbf **800** a.	...	...	...	...	...	...	...	...	...	1657

	⑤–⑦ T		*IC* 2375 ⑤–① J 🍷		⑤ E			*IC*• 2215		*IC*• 2075 🍷			⑦ N		L		⑥ Y					⑤⑥ d	⑦–④ b	△		
Westerland (Sylt). 🚗 d.	0950	1020	1053	1120	1150	1220	1307	1326	1350	1420	1520	1620	1650	1720	1750	1820	1850	1920	2020	...	2120	2120	...	...	2220	2320
Niebüll 🚗 a.	1029	1059	1129	1159	1229	1259	1344	1359	1429	1500	1559	1659	1729	1759	1829	1859	1929	1959	2059	...	2159	2159	...	...	2259	2355
Niebüll d.	1034	1101	1145	1201	1234	1301	1355	1413	1455	1513	1601	1701	1731	1801	1831	1901	1931	2001	2101	...	2201	2201	...	...	2301	0001
Husum d.	1104f	1131	1212	1231	1301	1331	1431f	1442	1531f	1545	1631	1731	1756	1831	1856	1931	1956	2031	2131	...	2229	2231	2248	...	2329	0029
Heide (Holst) a.	1126	1157	1233	1257	1323	1357	1457	1506	1557	1606	1657	1757	|	1857	|	1957	|	2057	2157	...	...	2257	2313	...	...	...
Heide (Holst) d.	1128	1202	1235	1302	1325	1402	1502	1508	1602	1608	1702	1802	|	1902	|	2002	|	2104	2204	...	...	2304	2314	...	...	...
Itzehoe a.	|	1236	1310	1336	1359	1436	1536	1543	1636	1642	1736	1836	|	1936	|	2036	|	2138	2247	...	...	2347	2354	...	...	...
Itzehoe d.	|	1237	1329	1337	1403	1437	1537	1555	1637	1658	1737	1837	|	1937	|	2037	|	2139	2248	...	...	2348	...	0002	...	...
Elmshorn **820** d.	|	1300	|	1400	1433	1500	1600	|	1700	|	1800	1900	|	2000	|	2100	|	2202	2310	...	...	0010	...	0033	...	...
Hamburg Altona a.	|	1321	|	1421	1503	1521	1621	|	1721	|	1821	1921	1928	2021	2030	2121	2128	2223	2331	...	...	0031	...	0057	...	...
Hamburg Hbf ... **820** a.	1302	...	1424	...	...	...	...	1645	...	1748	...	...	...	...	...	...	...	...	...	...	...	...	...	...	...	...
Berlin Hbf **840** a.	...	...	...	...	...	...	...	|	...	1955	...	...	...	...	...	...	...	...	...	...	...	...	...	...	...	...
Köln Hbf **800** a.	...	...	...	...	...	...	...	2057	...	...	...	...	...	...	...	...	...	...	...	...	...	...	...	...	...	...

A – Ⓐ to Mar. 24; daily from Mar. 27.
B – Ⓒ from Apr. 1.
D – Daily to Mar. 31; Ⓐ from Apr. 3.
E – ⑤ from Apr. 14 (also Apr. 6).
J – WATTENMEER – 12 🍷 Westerland - Frankfurt - Karlsruhe.
K – WATTENMEER – 12 🍷 Stuttgart Ⓐ / Karlsruhe Ⓒ - Frankfurt - Westerland and v.v.
L – ⑥ Apr. 1 – 22 (also Apr. 7, 9); ⑥⑦ from Apr. 29 (also May 18, 29).
M – ① from Apr. 3 (also Apr. 11, May 2, 30; not Apr. 10, May 1, 29).
N – ⑦ from Apr. 2 (also Apr. 10, May 1, 18, 29; not Apr. 9, 30, May 28).

R – ①–④ from Apr. 3 (not Apr. 10, May 1, 18, 29).
S – Daily to Apr. 2; ⑤⑥† from Apr. 7.
T – ⑤–⑦ from May 5 (also May 18, 29).
Y – From May 6.

b – Not Apr. 6, 9, 30, May 17, 28.
d – Also Apr. 6, 9, 30, May 17, 28.
f – Arrives 5 – 7 minutes earlier.
g – 0043 on the mornings of ⑦ (also Apr. 7, 10, May 1, 18, 29).

h – 1611 on ⑥⑦ from May 6.
j – On ⑦ Husum d. *0442*, Heide a. *0542* (by 🚌).
u – Calls to pick up only.

• – Conveys 2 to / from Dagebüll Mole on dates in Table **822**.
△ – Operated by *nordbahn*.
🚗 – Regular car-carrying shuttle services also operate between Niebüll and Westerland (18 – 28 per day in summer, 12 – 14 in winter).

SCHLESWIG-HOLSTEIN BRANCH LINES 822

NEUMÜNSTER - HEIDE - BÜSUM (operated by *nordbahn*)

km		⚒	⚒	†	⚒	⑥	Ⓐ																		
0	Neumünster d.	...	...	*0535*	...	0535	0535	...	0735	...	0935	...	1135	...	1335	...	1535	...	1735	...	1935	...	...	...	2135
63	Heide (Holst) a.	...	...	*0643*	...	0643	0710	...	0843	...	1043	...	1243	...	1443	...	1643	...	1843	...	2043	...	...	...	2243
63	Heide (Holst) d.	0449	0556	0649	0701	0701	...	0801	0901	1001	1101	1201	1301	1401	1501	1601	1701	1801	1901	2003	...	2103	2203	...	...
87	Büsum a.	0514	0621	0714	0726	0726	...	0826	0926	1026	1126	1226	1326	1426	1526	1626	1726	1826	1926	2028	...	2128	2228	...	...

	⚒	⚒	⚒	⑥		†	⚒																	
Büsum d.	...	0519	0625	0625	...	0721	0730	0830	0930	1030	1130	1230	1330	1430	1530	1630	1730	1830	1930	2032	...	...	2132	...	2232
Heide (Holst) a.	...	0545	0652	0652	...	0748	0757	0857	0957	1057	1157	1257	1357	1457	1557	1657	1757	1857	1957	2059	...	...	2159	...	2259
Heide (Holst) d.	0516	...	...	0716	0716	...	...	0916	...	1116	...	1316	...	1516	...	1716	...	1916	...	...	2116	...	...	...	2316
Neumünster a.	0624	...	...	0825	0825	...	...	1025	...	1225	...	1425	...	1625	...	1825	...	2025	...	...	2225	...	...	...	0025

HUSUM - BAD ST PETER ORDING

km		Ⓐ								
0	Husum d.	0436	0536	0636	and	1736	1836	1936	2036	2136	2236
21	Tönning d.	0501	0601	0701	hourly	1801	1901	2001	2101	2201	2301
43	Bad St Peter Ording a.	0527	0627	0727	until	1827	1927	2027	2127	2227	2327

	Ⓐ									
Bad St Peter Ording d.	0533	0633	0733	and	1833	1933	2033	2133	2233	2333
Tönning d.	0604	0704	0804	hourly	1904	2004	2104	2204	2304	0004
Husum a.	0625	0725	0825	until	1925	2025	2125	2225	2325	0025

NIEBÜLL - DAGEBÜLL MOLE *See note* ⊡

km	*Until Mar. 24*		Ⓐ		①–⑤		①–⑤					
0	Niebüll neg d.	0635	0735	0905	1010	1125	1250	1340	1440	1605	1815	1910
14	Dagebüll Mole a.	0653	0753	0923	1028	1143	1308	1358	1458	1621	1832	1928

Until Mar. 24		Ⓐ		①–⑤		①–⑤					
Dagebüll Mole d.	0700	0815	0930	1035	1145	1315	1415	1505	1625	1835	1935
Niebüll neg a.	0718	0833	0948	1053	1203	1333	1433	1523	1643	1853	1953

km	*From Mar. 25* ♥					★	★		★			
	Hamburg Hbf a.	...	...	...	...	0917	1009	...	1302	...	...	...
	Niebüll a.	...	...	...	...	1145	1244	...	1544	...	...	...
0	Niebüll neg d.	0635	0735	0905	1010	1205	1335	1435	1605	1710	1815	1910
14	Dagebüll Mole a.	0653	0753	0923	1028	1223	1353	1453	1623	1728	1832	1928

From Mar. 25 ♥		★				★	★				
Dagebüll Mole d.	0815	0930	1035	1145	1245	1340	1440	1635	1735	1835	1935
Niebüll neg a.	0833	0948	1053	1225	1303	1357	1457	1653	1753	1853	1953
Niebüll d.	...	1013n	...	...	...	1413	1513	...	...	...	...
Hamburg Hbf a.	...	1245n	...	...	...	1645	1748	...	...	...	...

n – Not Mar. 25.

★ – Conveys 2 (*IC*) from / to Hamburg and beyond (Table **821**).
♥ – **Additional journeys**: Niebüll neg → Dagebüll Mole at 1125 and 1235; Dagebüll Mole → Niebüll neg at 0700 and 1505.
⊡ – **Operator**: Norddeutsche Eisenbahngesellschaft Niebüll GmbH. ✆ +49 (0) 4661 980 880. Niebüll neg station is situated a short distance from the Niebüll DB station forecourt. Dagebüll Mole is the station for ferries to / from the islands of Föhr and Amrum (see www.faehre.de).

823 HAMBURG - NEUMÜNSTER - FLENSBURG

RE / RB services except where shown

km																											
										IC 2070			*IC* 386					*IC* 384			*EC* 174						
		D	⚒		⚒	†	⚒	†		⑥ B✕			A					A			♥ H✕						E
0	**Hamburg** Hbf **820** d.	...	...	...	0640j	...	0737	...	0843	0915	0943	1043	1053	1142	1243	1343	1443	1453	1543	1643	1714	1743	1843	1943	2043	2146	2243
34	Elmshorn **820** d.	...	...	...	0709j	...	0809	...	0909	|	1010	1109	|	1209	1309	1409	1509	|	1609	1709	|	1809	1909	2009	2109	2214	2314
78	Neumünster **820** d.	0040	0534	0646	0732	0734	0832	0834	0932	1023	1032	1132	|	1232	1332	1432	1532	|	1632	1732	1806	1832	1932	2032	2132	2237	2337
117	Rendsburg **824** d.	0107	0601	0715	0759	0759	0859	0901	0959	1046	1059	1159	1213	1259	1359	1459	1559	1618	1659	1759	1830	1859	1959	2059	2159	2304	0003
141	Schleswig **824** d.	0123	0617	0731	0815	0815	0915	0917	1015	1101	1115	1216	|	1315	1415	1515	1615	|	1715	1815	1847	1915	2015	2115	2215	2320	0021
179	**Flensburg** a.	0148	0642	0756	0840	0840	0940	0942	1040	1120	1140	1240	1248	1340	1440	1540	1640	1650	1740	1840	1907	1940	2040	2140	2240	2345	0045

									EC 175				*IC* 383					*IC* 385								
	C	Ⓐ	⚒	①-⑥ r	①-⑥ r	⑦ w			★ H✕				A					A					⑦-④ k			E
Flensburg d.	0015	0415	0415	0515	0615	0623	0715	0815	0833	0915	1015	1115	1209	1215	1315	1415	1515	1609	1615	1715	1815	1915	2015	2015	2115	2215	2315
Schleswig **824** d.	0039	0439	0439	0539	0639	0647	0739	0839	0901	0939	1039	1139	|	1239	1339	1439	1539	|	1639	1739	1839	1939	2039	2039	2139	2239	2339
Rendsburg **824** d.	0056	0456	0456	0556	0656	0704	0756	0856	0917	0956	1056	1156	1243	1256	1356	1456	1556	1643	1656	1756	1856	1956	2056	2056	2156	2256	2357
Neumünster **820** a.	0122	0522	0522	0622	0722	0730	0822	0922	0953	1022	1122	1222	|	1322	1422	1522	1622	|	1722	1822	1922	2022	2122	2122	2222	2322	0022
Elmshorn **820** a.	...	0548	...	0648	0748	...	0848	0948	|	1048	1148	1248	|	1348	1448	1548	1648	|	1748	1848	1948	2048	2148	...	...	...	...
Hamburg Hbf **820** a.	...	0613	...	0715	0815	...	0915	1015	1048	1115	1215	1313	1406	1415	1515	1615	1716	1804	1816	1916	2016	2116	2217	...	...	...	...

A – To / from Aarhus (Table **710**).
B – From Berlin (Table **840**).
C – ⑥ to Apr. 29 (also Mar. 5, 12, 19, Apr. 7, 10); Ⓒ from May 1.
D – ①-⑥ to Apr. 29 (also Mar. 5, 12, 19); daily from May 1.
E – ⑧ to Apr. 28 (also Mar. 4, 11, 18); daily from Apr. 30.

H – 12 ✕ Praha - Dresden - Berlin - Flensburg and v.v.

j – On ⑥ Hamburg d. 0636, Elmshorn 0704.
k – Not Apr. 6, 9, 30, May 17, 28.
r – Also Mar. 5, 12, 19.

w – Not Mar. 5, 12, 19.

♥ – ②-⑦ until Feb. 12; daily from Feb. 14.
★ – ①③④⑤⑥⑦ to Feb. 13; daily from Feb. 15. Runs as *IC* **1075** on ① until Feb. 13.

824 KIEL - HUSUM and FLENSBURG

RE / RB services

KIEL - HUSUM

km		⚒	D	⑦w	D					
0	**Kiel** Hbf d.	0403	0503	*0535**	0603	0703	and hourly until	2103	2203	...
40	Rendsburg **823** d.	0435	0535	0635	0635	0735		2135	2235	...
65	Schleswig **823** d.	0453	0553	0653	0653	0753		2153	2253	...
102	**Husum** a.	0525	0625	0724	0724	0825		2225	2325	...

	⚒	⑦w	D					B	B
Husum d.	0430	0530	0535	0635	and hourly until	2035	2135	2235	2335
Schleswig **823** d.	0502	0607	0607	0707		2107	2207	2307	0007
Rendsburg **823** d.	0521	0625	0626	0726		2126	2226	2329	0031
Kiel Hbf a.	0557	*0724**	0657	0757		2157	2257	2400	0113

KIEL - FLENSBURG *Temporary timetable until May 26*

km		Ⓐ	⚒							
0	**Kiel** Hbf d.	0406	0518	0608	0708	and hourly until	2008	2043	2143	2248
29	Eckernförde d.	0437	0547	0640	0740		2040	2120k	2220	2320
	Schleibrücke Süd ‡ a.	0451	0601	0655	0755		2055	2135	2235	2335
		Ⓐ	⚒							
	Schleibrücke Nord ‡ d.	0500	0610	0707	0807		2107	2147	2250	2350
50	Süderbrarup d.	0507	0631	0731	0831		2131	2201	2301	0001
81	**Flensburg** a.	0537	0657	0757	0857		2157	2246	2346	0027

	Ⓐ	⚒							
Flensburg d.	0420	0504	0604	0704	and hourly until	2004	2104	2213	2313
Süderbrarup d.	0446	0546j	0646j	0746j		2046j	2131	2239	2339
Schleibrücke Nord ‡ a.	0453	0553	0653	0753		2053	2138	2246	2346
	Ⓐ	⚒							
Schleibrücke Süd ‡ d.	0503	0605	0705	0805		2105	2147	2256	2356
Eckernförde d.	0518	0620	0720	0820		2120	2202	2321k	0021k
Kiel Hbf a.	0551	0651	0751	0851		2151	2230	2357	0057

B – ⑧ to Apr. 28 (also Mar. 4, 11, 18); daily from Apr. 30.
D – ①-⑥ (also Mar. 5, 12, 19).

j – Arrives 17 minutes earlier.
k – Arrives 11–12 minutes earlier.
w – Not Mar. 5, 12, 19.

* – By 🚌 to / from Rendsburg.
‡ – Temporary station during major upgrade work on the Schlei Bridge. Passengers must transfer on foot across the bridge (350 metres).

825 HAMBURG - LÜBECK - PUTTGARDEN and TRAVEMÜNDE

RB / RE services

HAMBURG - LÜBECK

km				Ⓒ	Ⓒ		Ⓐ		Ⓐ		⚒										ALSO	B	K	H
0	**Hamburg** Hbf d.	0006	0106	0206	0406	0506	0534	0606	0634	0706	0734	0806	0834	and at the same minutes past each hour until	2108	2134	2206	2234	2306	2334		1301	1359	2104
40	Bad Oldesloe d.	0032	0135	0232	0432	0532	0605	0632	0705	0732	0805	0832	0905		2133	2205	2232	2305	2332	0005		|	|	|
63	**Lübeck** Hbf a.	0050	0153	0250	0450	0550	0622	0650	0722	0750	0822	0850	0922		2151	2222	2250	2322	2350	0022		1338	1442	2144

			Ⓒ	Ⓒ	Ⓐ		Ⓐ		⚒											ALSO	J	A	L
Lübeck Hbf d.	0010	0110	0210	0410	0438	0510	0538	0610	0638	0710	0738	and at the same minutes past each hour until	2010	2038	2110	2138	2210	2238	2310		0816	1416	1718
Bad Oldesloe d.	0028	0128	0228	0428	0455	0528	0555	0628	0655	0728	0755		2028	2055	2128	2155	2228	2255	2328		|	|	|
Hamburg Hbf a.	0054	0157	0253	0453	0525	0553	0625	0653	0725	0753	0825		2053	2125	2153	2225	2253	2325	2353		0855	1455	1801

LÜBECK - TRAVEMÜNDE STRAND *Timings may vary by 1–2 minutes from April 1*

km										
0	**Lübeck** Hbf d.	0003	...	0503	0603	0703	and hourly until	2103	2203	2303
18	Travemünde Skandinavienkai a.	0021	...	0521	0621	0721		2121	2221	2321
21	**Travemünde** Strand a.	0026	...	0526	0626	0726		2126	2226	2326

Travemünde Strand d.	0033	...	0533	0633	0733	and hourly until	2233	2333
Travemünde Skandinavienkai d.	0038	...	0538	0638	0738		2238	2338
Lübeck Hbf a.	0056	...	0556	0656	0756		2256	2356

LÜBECK - NEUSTADT (Holst) and PUTTGARDEN

km		Ⓐ		🚌 Ⓐ		🚌		🚌 Ⓐ		🚌		🚌			🚌		🚌		🚌		🚌		🚌	
0	**Lübeck** Hbf d.	0412	0512	0512	0612	0612	0712	0712	0812	0812	0912	0912	and at the same minutes past each hour until	1912	1912	2012	2012	2112	2112	2212	2212	2312	2312	0012
30	Neustadt (Holst) a.	0446	0546	|	0650	|	0750	|	0846	|	0950	|		1950	|	2046	|	2146	|	2246	|	2346	|	0046
	Oldenburg (Holst) d.	...	...	0613	...	0713	...	0813	...	0913	...	1013		...	2013	...	2113	...	2213	...	2313	...	0013	...
	Fehmarn-Burg a.	...	...	0648	...	0748	...	0848	...	0948	...	1048		...	2048	...	2148	...	2248	...	2348	...	0048	...
	Puttgarden a.	...	...	0701	...	0801	...	0901	...	1001	...	1101		...	2101	...	2201	...	2301	...	0001	...	0101	...

			Ⓐ		🚌 Ⓐ	Ⓐ		🚌	Ⓐ		🚌 Ⓐ		🚌			🚌		🚌						
Puttgarden d.	...	...	...	...	0456	...	...	0556	...	...	0656	...	0756	and at the same minutes past each hour until	...	2156	...	2256	...	...	...	...	...	...
Fehmarn-Burg d.	...	...	...	...	0508	...	...	0608	...	...	0708	...	0808		...	2208	...	2308	...	...	...	...	...	...
Oldenburg (Holst) d.	...	...	...	...	0544	...	...	0644	...	...	0744	...	0844		...	2244	...	2344	...	...	...	...	...	...
Neustadt (Holst) d.	0115	...	0515	0615	|	0645	0715	|	0745	0815	|	0915	|		2315	|	0015	|	...	...	...	...	...	...
Lübeck Hbf a.	0148	...	0548	0648	0650	0718	0748	0750	0818	0848	0850	0948	0950		0048	2350	0048	0050	...	...	...	...	...	...

A – *ICE* **681**. To München (Table **900**).
B – *ICE* **682**. From München (Table **900**).
H – *ICE* **584**. From München (Table **900**).
J – *ICE* **585**. To München (Table **900**).
K – *IC* **2408**. From Köln (Table **800**).
L – *IC* **2409**. To Köln (Table **800**).

826 KIEL - LÜBECK

Operator: erixx

km		Ⓐ	Ⓐ	Ⓒ	Ⓐ	⑥	†	Ⓐ	⚒											
0	**Kiel** Hbf d.	0405	0443	0438	0505	0538	0538	0543	0605	0643	0705	0743	and at the same minutes past each hour until	2205	2243	2305	2343	0005	0043	0105
33	Plön d.	0445	0513	0515	0545	0615	0615	0615	0645	0715	0745	0815		2245	2315	2345	0015	0045	0115	0145
47	Eutin d.	0500	0529	0530	0600	0630	0630	0630	0700	0730	0800	0830		2300	2330	0000	0030	0100	0130	0200
80	**Lübeck** Hbf a.	0532	0555	0558	0632	0652	0658	0652	0732	0752	0832	0852		2332	2352	0032	0052	0132	0152	0232

	Ⓐ	Ⓐ	Ⓒ	Ⓐ	Ⓐ	Ⓒ	Ⓐ	⚒	Ⓒ	Ⓐ									
Lübeck Hbf d.	0351	0428	0500	0505	0528	0600	0606	0628	0706	0706	0728	0806	0828	and at the same minutes past each hour until	2306	2328	0006	0028	0106
Eutin d.	0424	0458	0530	0529	0600	0630	0629	0659	0729	0730	0759	0829	0859		2329	2359	0029	0059	0129
Plön d.	0443	0515	0545	0545	0615	0645	0644	0714	0744	0746	0814	0844	0914		2344	0014	0044	0114	0144
Kiel Hbf a.	0519	0556	0617	0617	0656	0716	0716	0756	0816	0817	0856	0916	0956		0016	0056	0116	0156	0216

LÜBECK - BÜCHEN - LÜNEBURG — 827

Operator: erixx

km		Ⓐ	Ⓐ	Ⓒ	Ⓐ	Ⓒ	Ⓐ	Ⓒ																	
0	**Lübeck** Hbf d.	0401	0501	0510	0601	0610	0705	0710	0810	0910	1010	1110	1210	1310	1410	1510	1610	1710	1810	1910	2010	2110	2210	2310	0010
9	Lübeck Flughafen ✈ ▷ d.	0410	0510	0520	0610	0620	0714	0720	0820	0920	1020	1120	1220	1320	1420	1520	1620	1720	1820	1920	2020	2120	2220	2320	0020
22	Ratzeburg d.	0420	0523	0530	0627	0630	0730	0730	0830	0930	1030	1130	1230	1330	1430	1530	1630	1730	1830	1930	2030	2130	2230	2330	0030
31	Mölln (Lauenburg) d.	0427	0530	0537	0634	0637	0737	0737	0837	0937	1037	1137	1237	1337	1437	1537	1637	1737	1837	1937	2037	2137	2237	2337	0037
50	Büchen a.	0439	0543	0550	0646	0649	0749	0749	0850	0949	1049	1149	1249	1349	1449	1549	1649	1749	1849	1949	2049	2149	2249	2349	0049
50	Büchen d.	0451	0553	0551	0655	0707	0756	0750	0907	0950	1107	1150	1307	1350	1507	1550	1707	1750	1907	1950	2107	2150	2307	2350	0050
79	**Lüneburg** a.	0515	0617	0615	0718	0730	0823	0815	0930	1015	1130	1215	1330	1415	1530	1615	1730	1815	1930	2015	2130	2215	2330	0015	0115

	Ⓐ	Ⓐ	Ⓒ	Ⓐ	Ⓒ	Ⓐ	Ⓒ																	
Lüneburg d.	0420	0524	0545	0628	0630	0744	0745	0830	0945	1030	1145	1230	1345	1430	1545	1630	1745	1830	1945	2030	2145	2230	2345	0045
Büchen a.	0442	0545	0608	0650	0652	0808	0808	0852	1008	1052	1208	1252	1408	1452	1608	1652	1808	1852	2008	2052	2208	2252	0008	0108
Büchen d.	0453	0553	0609	0657	0709	0809	0809	0909	1009	1109	1209	1309	1409	1509	1609	1709	1809	1909	2009	2109	2209	2259	0009	0114
Mölln (Lauenburg) d.	0505	0605	0622	0709	0722	0822	0822	0922	1022	1122	1222	1322	1422	1522	1622	1722	1822	1922	2022	2122	2222	2322e	0022	0126
Ratzeburg d.	0512	0612	0632	0717	0732	0832	0832	0932	1032	1132	1232	1332	1432	1532	1632	1732	1832	1932	2032	2132	2232	2332	0032	0134
Lübeck Flughafen ✈ ▷ d.	0521	0621	0640	0725	0740	0840	0840	0940	1040	1140	1240	1340	1440	1540	1640	1740	1840	1940	2040	2140	2240	2340	0040	0142
Lübeck Hbf a.	0532	0632	0652	0736	0752	0852	0852	0952	1052	1152	1252	1352	1452	1552	1652	1752	1852	1952	2052	2152	2254	2352	0052	0153

e – Arrives 2310.

▷ – Trains call at Lübeck Flughafen on request only.

HAMBURG - ROSTOCK - STRALSUND — 830

RE services except where shown

SERVICE UNTIL MARCH 3. See page 561 for service March 4 - April 14.

km		◇ S	◇ Ⓐ S		Ⓐ	◇ S	Ⓐ	Ⓐ		◇ S	ICE 1678 Ⓐ H✕		◇ S	ICE 1676 ✕♦	IC 2238 ♦		◇ S	IC 2212 🍷♦		◇ S	ICE 1672 ✕♦	◇ Ⓐ		◇ S	ICE 1074 R✕	
0	**Hamburg** Hbf d.	...	...	...	...	...	...	0511	0621	...	0742	0821	...	0943	...	1021	...	1142	1221	...	1343	...	1421	...	1543	1621
47	Büchen d.	...	...	...	0458	...	...	0552t	0658t	...	|	0858t	...	|	...	1058t	...	|	1258t	...	|	...	1458t	...	|	1658t
123	**Schwerin** Hbf 837 d.	...	...	0548	0548	...	0642	0647	0748	...	0837	0948	...	1037	1056	1148	...	1238	1348	...	1437	...	1548	...	1637	1748
140	Bad Kleinen . 836 837 d.	...	...	0603	0603	...	0659	▬	0803	...	|	1003	...	|	1109	1203	...	|	1403	...	|	...	1603	...	|	1803
181	Bützow 836 d.	...	...	0629	0629	...	0723	◇	0829	...	0910	1029	...	1110	1136	1229	...	1310	1429	...	1510	...	1629	...	1710	1829
211	**Rostock** Hbf a.	...	...	0650	0650	...	0750	Ⓐ	0850	...	0932	1050	...	1132	1156	1252	...	1332	1450	...	1532	...	1650	...	1732	1850
211	**Rostock** Hbf d.	0454	0553	...	...	0700	...	0811	...	0900	0938	...	1100	1138	...	...	1300	1338	...	1500	1538	1556	...	1700	1738c	...
240	Ribnitz-D'garten West . d.	0517	0616	...	...	0725	...	0849	...	0922	1002o	...	1122	1200	...	...	1322	1400	...	1522	1600	1623	...	1722	|	...
265	Velgast d.	0539	0638	...	...	0742	...	0903	...	0940	1015	...	1140	1215	...	...	1340	1416	...	1540	1615	1640	...	1740	1815c	...
283	**Stralsund** Hbf a.	0555	0655	...	...	0758	...	0917	...	0957	1029	...	1157	1229	...	...	1357	1429	...	1557	1630	1653	...	1757	1829c	...
	Ostseebad Binz 844 a.	...	...	...	...	...	...	...	...	...	...	...	...	...	...	...	...	1528	...	...	1720e	...	...	...	...	...

	◇ S	ICE 1578 A✕		◇ S	ICE 1576 Ⓑb A✕	ICE 1576 ⑦w A✕		◇	ICE 1574 ⑦w A		
Hamburg Hbf d.	...	1741	1821	...	1943	1943	2021	...	2143	2254	0036
Büchen d.	...	|	1858t	...	|	|	2058t	...	|	2328	0108
Schwerin Hbf 837 d.	...	1837	1948	...	2037	2037	2148	...	2237	0019	0157
Bad Kleinen .. 836 837 d.	...	1849	2003	...	2049	2049	2203	...	2249	0029	...
Bützow 836 d.	...	1913	2029	...	2113	2113	2229	...	2313	0054	...
Rostock Hbf a.	...	1933	2050	...	2133	2133	2250	...	2333	0115	...
Rostock Hbf d.	1900	1938	...	2100	...	2138	...	2300	...	...	...
Ribnitz-Damgarten West d.	1922	2000	...	2122	...	2200	...	2322	...	...	...
Velgast d.	1940	2015	...	2140	...	2215	...	2340	...	...	...
Stralsund Hbf a.	1957	2029	...	2157	...	2229	...	2357	...	...	...
Ostseebad Binz 844 a.	...	...	...	...	...	...	...	...	...	...	...

	Ⓐ	Ⓒ	Ⓐ	ICE 1599 Ⓐ		◇ Ⓐ S	ICE 1577 Ⓐ A✕	◇ S		ICE 1179 Ⓐ R✕
Ostseebad Binz 844 d.	...	...	...	...	...	...	...	...	...	...
Stralsund Hbf d.	...	...	...	...	...	0450	0521	0558	...	0727
Velgast d.	...	...	...	...	...	0506	0536	0614	...	0741
Ribnitz-Damgarten West .. d.	...	...	...	...	...	0525	0552	0632	...	|
Rostock Hbf a.	...	...	...	...	...	0548	0617	0654	...	0818
Rostock Hbf d.	...	...	...	0458	0508	...	0625	...	0708	0825
Bützow 836 d.	...	...	...	0518	0529	...	0645	...	0729	0845
Bad Kleinen 836 837 d.	...	...	...	0543	0558	...	0709	...	0758	|
Schwerin Hbf 837 d.	0350	0443	0452	0556	0611	...	0720	...	0811	0920
Büchen d.	0448	0540	0551	0634	0707t	...	|	...	0907t	|
Hamburg Hbf a.	0518	0610	0626	0704	0738	...	0816	...	0938	1016

	ICE 1579 ⑥h RA ✕	◇ S		ICE 1671 A✕	◇ S		IC 2213 🍷♦	◇		IC 2239 ♦	ICE 1021 † ✕♦	ICE 1675 F✕	◇ S		ICE 1677 Ⓑb ✕♦	◇ S		◇	E	ICE 1679 ⑦w G✕			◇ S		◇ S	
Ostseebad Binz 844 d.		...	...	0826	...	...	1043	1102	...	...	...	...	...	...	...	...	...	1603	...	...	1702	...	...	...	...	...
Stralsund Hbf d.	0727	0759	...	0926	0959	...	1136	1159	...	...	1304	1326	1359	...	1526	1559	...	1658	...	1726	1759	...	1959	...	2159	...
Velgast d.	0741	0815	...	0940	1015	...	1156	1215	...	...	1317	1340	1415	...	1540	1615	...	1711	...	1740	1815	...	2015	...	2215	...
Ribnitz-Damgarten West d.	0756	0833	...	0958	1033	...	1215	1233	...	...	|	1359	1433	...	1554o	1633	...	1737t	...	1759	1833	...	2033	...	2233	...
Rostock Hbf a.	0818	0855	...	1019	1055	...	1239	1255	...	...	1404	1419	1455	...	1619	1655	...	1801	...	1819	1855	...	2055	...	2255	...
Rostock Hbf d.	0825	...	0908	1025	...	1108	1244	...	1308	1405	1412	1425	...	1508	1625	▬	1708	...	1809	1825	...	1908	...	2108	...	2313
Bützow 836 d.	0845	...	0929	1045	...	1129	1304	...	1329	1427	1434	1445	...	1529	1645	...	1729	...	1830	1845	...	1929	...	2129	...	2334
Bad Kleinen .. 836 837 d.	|	...	0958	|	...	1158	|	...	1358	1450	|	|	...	1558	|	Ⓐ	1758	...	1903t	|	...	1958	...	2158	...	0000
Schwerin Hbf 837 d.	0920	...	1011	1120	...	1211	1339	...	1411	1459	1508	1520	...	1611	1720	1724	1811	...	1914	1920	...	2011	...	2211	...	0010
Büchen d.	|	...	1107t	|	...	1307t	|	...	1507t	...	|	|	...	1707t	|	1822	1907t	...	...	|	...	2107t	...	2303	...	...
Hamburg Hbf a.	1016	...	1138	1219	...	1338	1433	...	1538	...	1603	1616	...	1738	1816	1855	1938	...	...	2019	...	2139	...	2339	...	...

♦ – **NOTES** (LISTED BY TRAIN NUMBER)

1021 – 🚄12 ✕ Stralsund - Hamburg - Köln - Frankfurt - Nürnberg.
1672 – 🚄12 ✕ (Karlsruhe ⚒ -) Frankfurt - Hamburg - Stralsund (- Ostseebad Binz ⚒).
1676 – 🚄12 ✕ (Frankfurt ① **g** -) (Kassel Ⓐ -) (Hannover ⚒ -) Hamburg - Stralsund.
1677 – 🚄12 ✕ Stralsund - Hamburg - Hannover (- Frankfurt ⑤⑦ **w**).
2212 – RÜGEN – 🚄12 🍷 Koblenz - Köln - Hamburg - Ostseebad Binz.
2213 – RÜGEN – 🚄12 🍷 Ostseebad Binz - Hamburg - Köln.
2238 – WARNOW – 🚄12 Leipzig - Magdeburg - Stendal - Rostock - Warnemünde (a. 1214).
2239 – WARNOW – 🚄12 Warnemünde (d. 1343) - Rostock - Stendal - Magdeburg - Leipzig.

A – From / to Karlsruhe via Frankfurt, Gießen, Kassel, Hannover (Tables **806**, **900**, **912**).
E – ①②③④⑥ (not Dec. 26).
F – To Frankfurt (Tables **806** and **900**).
G – To Göttingen (Table **900**).
H – From Hannover (Table **900**).
R – To / from Greifswald on dates in Table **845**.
S – To / from Sassnitz (Table **844**).

b – Not Dec. 25.
c – Not Mar. 3.
e – ⚒ only.
g – Also Dec. 27; not Dec. 26.
h – Also Dec. 25.
o – Ribnitz-Damgarten **Ost**.
t – Arrives 6 – 7 minutes earlier.
w – Also Dec. 26; not Dec. 25.

◇ – Operated by Ostdeutsche Eisenbahn.

ROSTOCK - WARNEMÜNDE — 831

S-Bahn

ROSTOCK - WARNEMÜNDE and v.v. *13 km.* Journey time: 21 minutes. Additional services run at peak times on Ⓐ.

From Rostock Hbf at 0433, 0448 Ⓐ, 0503, 0518 Ⓐ, 0533, 0548 Ⓐ, 0603, 0618 Ⓐ, 0633, 0648 Ⓐ, 0703, 0718 Ⓐ, 0733, 0748 Ⓐ, 0803, 0818, 0833, 0848, 0903, 0918, 0933, 0948 and at 03, 18, 33 and 48 minutes past each hour until 2103, 2118, 2133, 2148; then 2203, 2233, 2303, 2333 and 0003.

From Warnemünde at 0403, 0430, 0448 Ⓐ, 0503, 0518 Ⓐ, 0533, 0548 Ⓐ, 0603, 0618 Ⓐ, 0633, 0648 Ⓐ, 0703, 0718 Ⓐ, 0733, 0748 Ⓐ, 0803, 0818 Ⓐ, 0833, 0848, 0903, 0918, 0933, 0948 and at 03, 18, 33 and 48 minutes past each hour until 2103, 2118, 2133, 2148; then 2203, 2233, 2303, 2333 and 0003.

BERLIN - KOSTRZYN — 832

Niederbarnimer Eisenbahn (2nd class only) — *Service until May 19*

km																				
0	**Berlin** Lichtenberg d.	0538**b**	0638**b**	0738**b**	0838	0938**b**	1038	1138**b**	1238	1338**b**	1438	1538**b**	1638	1738**b**	1838	1938**b**	2038	2138**b**	2237	2338**b**
26	Strausberg d.	0558	0658	0758	0858	0958	1058	1158	1258	1358	1458	1558	1658	1758	1858	1958	2058	2158	2258	2358
44	Müncheberg (Mark) ¶ .. d.	0614	0714	0814	0914	1014	1114	1214	1314	1414	1514	1614	1714	1814	1914	2014	2114	2214	2314	0014
79	Küstrin-Kietz 🏛 a.	0648	0739	0848	0939	1048	1139	1248	1339	1448	1539	1648	1739	1848	1939	2048	2139	2248	2339	0048
83	**Kostrzyn** 🏛 ... ▲ 🚌 a.	*0702*	*0753*	*0902*	*0952*	*1102*	*1152*	*1302*	*1352*	*1502*	*1552*	*1702*	*1752*	*1902*	*1952*	*2102*	*2152*	*2302*	*2352*	*0102*

Kostrzyn 🏛 ▲ 🚌 d.	*0347*	*0447*	*0547*	*0644*	*0757*	*0904*	*0957*	*1104*	*1157*	*1304*	*1357*	*1504*	*1557*	*1704*	*1757*	*1904*	*1957*	*2104*	*2157*
Küstrin-Kietz 🏛 d.	0410	0511	0611	0708	0811	0918	1011	1118	1211	1318	1411	1518	1611	1718	1811	1918	2011	2118	2211
Müncheberg (Mark) ¶ d.	0445	0549	0649	0749	0849	0949	1049	1149	1249	1349	1449	1549	1649	1749	1849	1949	2049	2149	2249
Strausberg d.	0505	0605	0705	0805	0905	1005	1105	1205	1305	1405	1505	1605	1705	1805	1905	2005	2105	2205	2305
Berlin Lichtenberg a.	0524**c**	0624**c**	0724**c**	0824	0924**c**	1024	1124**c**	1224	1324**c**	1424	1524**c**	1624	1724**c**	1824	1924**c**	2024	2124**c**	2224	2324**c**

b – From Berlin Ostkreuz (departs 5 minutes earlier).
c – To Berlin Ostkreuz (arrives 4 minutes later).
¶ – Station for Buckower Kleinbahn (operates on Ⓒ Apr. 29 - Oct. 3).
▲ – Connecting services Küstrin-Kietz - Kostrzyn and v.v. are by 🚌.

833 WISMAR - ROSTOCK

RE services

km		⚒	Ⓐ					
0	**Wismar** d.	0442	0542	0642	and		2042	2142
22	Neubukow d.	0511	0611	0711	hourly		2111	2211
41	Bad Doberan ▲ d.	0530	0630	0730	until		2130	2230
57	**Rostock** Hbf a.	0551	0651	0751			2151	2251

	Ⓐ		⚒					A
Rostock Hbf d.	0412	0506	0606	0706	and		2006	2106
Bad Doberan ▲ d.	0432	0532	0632	0732	hourly		2032	2132
Neubukow d.	0451	0551	0651	0751	until		2051	2151
Wismar a.	0515	0615	0715	0815			2115	2215

A – Daily to Mar. 25; ⑥⑦ from Apr. 1.

▲ – **BAD DOBERAN - OSTSEEBAD KÜHLUNGSBORN WEST**. All services worked by steam locomotive. 2nd class only. Journey time: 43 minutes.
Operator: Mecklenburgische Bäderbahn Molli GmbH, Am Bahnhof, 18209 Bad Doberan. ✆ +49 (0) 38293 431331. www.molli-bahn.de **Service until March 31.**
From **Bad Doberan** at 0835 Ⓐ, 1035, 1235, 1435 and 1640. From **Kühlungsborn West** at 0640 Ⓐ, 0935, 1135, 1342 and 1535.

834 STRALSUND - NEUBRANDENBURG - NEUSTRELITZ

km			Ⓐ			Ⓐ									Ⓑe			Ⓑe			Ⓑe					⑤⑥d
0	**Stralsund** Hbf d.	...	0406	...	0502	0604	...	0702	0804r	0902	1004r	1102	1204r	1302	1404	...	1502	1604	...	1702	1804	...	1902	...	2106	2106
23	Grimmen d.	...	0427	...	0523	0624	...	0723	0824r	0923	1024r	1123	1224r	1323	1424	...	1523	1624	...	1723	1824	...	1923	...	2128	2128
47	Demmin d.	...	0445	...	0546	0646	...	0746	0846r	0946	1046r	1146	1246r	1346	1446	...	1546	1646	...	1746	1846	...	1946	...	2146	2146
89	**Neubrandenburg** a.	...	0528	...	0629	0729	...	0829	0929r	1029	1129r	1229	1329r	1429	1529	...	1629	1729	...	1829	1929	...	2029	...	2229	2229
89	**Neubrandenburg** d.	0427	0529	0529	0630	0730	0730	0830	0930	1030	1130	1230	1330	1430	1530	1530	1630	1730	1730	1830	1930	1930	2030	2130	2230	2230
124	**Neustrelitz** Hbf a.	0457	0557	0557	0659	0756	0756	0859	0956	1059	1156	1259	1356	1459	1556	1556	1659	1756	1756	1859	1956	1956	2059	2156	2259	2259
	Berlin Hbf **835** a.	0609	...	...	0809	...	...	1012	...	1209	...	1409	...	1609	...	...	1809	...	...	2009	...	...	2209	...	...	0009

	Ⓐ	Ⓐ		Ⓐ									Ⓑe			Ⓑe			Ⓑe							⑤⑥d
Berlin Hbf **835** d.	...	...	...	...	...	0547	...	0747	...	0947	...	1147	...	...	1347	...	...	1547	...	...	1748	...	1947	...	2147	2347
Neustrelitz Hbf d.	...	0501	...	0602	0602	0701	0803	0901	1003	1101	1203	1301	1403	1403	1501	1603	1603	1701	1803	1803	1901	2003	2101	2203	2301	0111
Neubrandenburg a.	...	0528	...	0629	0629	0729	0829	0929	1029	1129	1229	1329	1429	1429	1529	1629	1629	1729	1829	1829	1929	2029	2129	2229	2329	0139
Neubrandenburg d.	0431	0531	0531	0631	...	0731	0831r	0931	1031r	1131	1231r	1331	1431	...	1531	1631	...	1731	1831	...	1931	...	2131	...	...	...
Demmin d.	0510	0610	0610	0710	...	0810	0910r	1010	1110r	1210	1310r	1410	1510	...	1610	1710	...	1810	1910	...	2010	...	2210	...	...	...
Grimmen d.	0529	0629	0629	0729	...	0829	0929r	1029	1129r	1229	1329r	1429	1529	...	1629	1729	...	1829	1929	...	2029	...	2229	...	...	...
Stralsund Hbf a.	0551	0651	0651	0751	...	0851	0951r	1051	1151r	1251	1351r	1451	1551	...	1651	1751	...	1851	1951	...	2051	...	2251	...	...	...

d – Also Dec. 25, Apr. 6, 9, 30, May 17, 28. e – Not Apr. 7. r – ⚒ only.

835 ROSTOCK - BERLIN - ELSTERWERDA

km		*RE* 4351		*RE* 3503	*RE* 4353	*RE* 4353	*RE* 3505	*IC* 2173	*RE* 4355	*RE* 3507	*IC* 2175	*RE* 4357	*RE* 3509	*IC* 2177	*ICE* 1630	*RE* 4359	*RE* 3511	*IC* 2179	*RE* 4361	*RE* 3513	*IC* 2271	*RE* 4363	*RE* 3515	*IC* 2273
		Ⓐ				Ⓐ		🍷			🍷			🍷	⑥ B🍴			🍷			C🍷			C🍷
	Warnemünde 831 d.	...	...	...	...	...	...	...	...	...	0756	...	...	0956	1014	...	...	1156	...	...	1352	...	...	1552
0	**Rostock** Hbf 831 d.	...	...	...	...	0434	...	0620	0634	...	0821	0834	...	1021	1036	1034	...	1220	1234	...	1421	1434	...	1621
34	Güstrow d.	...	...	...	...	0456	...	|	0656	...	|	0856	...	|	|	1056	...	|	1256	...	|	1456	...	|
85‡	Waren (Müritz) d.	...	...	...	...	0530	...	0701	0730	...	0901	0930	...	1101	|	1130	...	1301	1330	...	1501	1530	...	1701
	Stralsund Hbf **834** d.	...	...	...	...	|	0502	|	|	0702	|	|	0902	|	|	|	1102	|	|	1302	|	|	1502	|
	Neubrandenburg **834** d.	...	...	0427	...	|	0630	|	|	0830	|	|	1030	|	|	|	1230	|	|	1430	|	|	1630	|
120	**Neustrelitz** Hbf a.	...	...	0457	...	0552	0659	0717	0752	0859	0918	0952	1059	1118	|	1152	1259	1317	1352	1459	1518	1552	1659	1718
120	**Neustrelitz** Hbf d.	0349	...	0458	0600	0600	0700	0719	0800	0900	0919	1000	1100	1119	|	1200	1300	1319	1400	1500	1519	1600	1700	1719
141	Fürstenberg (Havel) d.	0401	...	0509	0612	0612	0712	|	0812	0912	|	1012	1112	|	|	1212	1312	|	1412	1512	|	1612	1712	|
162	Gransee d.	0415	...	0523	0625	0625	0723	|	0825	0923	|	1025	1123	|	|	1225	1323	|	1425	1523	|	1625	1723	|
191	Oranienburg d.	0440	...	0540	0640	0640	0740	0755	0840	0940	0955	1040	1140	1155	|	1240	1340	1355	1440	1540	1555	1640	1740	1755
223	**Berlin** Gesundbrunnen d.	0505	...	0605	0705	0705	0805	0819	0905	1008	1019	1105	1205	1219	1235	1305	1405	1419	1505	1605	1619	1705	1805	1819
227	**Berlin** Hbf a.	0509	...	0609	0709	0709	0809	0823	0909	1012	1023	1109	1209	1223	1239	1309	1409	1423	1509	1609	1623	1709	1809	1823
233	**Berlin** Südkreuz a.	0520	...	0620	0720	0720	0820	0831	0920	1029	1031	1120	1220	1231	1309	1320	1420	1431	1520	1620	1631	1720	1820	1831
	Flughafen Berlin ✈ ★ a.	...	...	...	...	...	...	0854	...	...	1053	...	...	1253	...	...	...	1454	...	...	1653	...	...	1853
	Dresden Hbf **840** a.	...	...	...	...	...	...	1033	...	...	1240	...	...	1434	...	...	...	1634	...	...	1827	...	...	2027

	RE 4365	*RE* 3517	*IC* 2275	*RE* 4367	*RE* 3519	*IC* 2277	*RE* 4369	*RE* 3521	*RE* 3525	
			🍷			L		⑤⑥ d		
Warnemünde 831 d.	...	...	1752	...	...	1956	...	...	...	...
Rostock Hbf 831 d.	1634	...	1820	1834	...	2021	2034	...	2334	...
Güstrow d.	1656	...	|	1856	...	|	2056	...	2356	...
Waren (Müritz) d.	1730	...	1901	1930	...	2101	2130	...	0030	...
Stralsund Hbf **834** d.	|	1702	|	|	1902	|	|	2106	|	...
Neubrandenburg **834** d.	|	1830	|	|	2030	|	|	2230	|	...
Neustrelitz Hbf a.	1752	1859	1917	1952	2059	2118	2152	2259	0052	...
Neustrelitz Hbf d.	1800	1900	1919	2000	2100	2119	2200	2300	...	...
Fürstenberg (Havel) d.	1812	1912	|	2012	2112	|	2212	2312	...	...
Gransee d.	1825	1923	|	2025	2123	|	2225	2323	...	...
Oranienburg d.	1840	1940	1955	2040	2140	2155	2240	2340	...	...
Berlin Gesundbrunnen d.	1905	2005	2019	2105	2205	2219	2305	0005	...	...
Berlin Hbf a.	1909	2009	2023	2109	2209	2223	2309	0009	...	...
Berlin Südkreuz a.	1920	2020	2031	2120	2220	2232	...	...	...	...
Flughafen Berlin ✈ ★ a.	...	...	2054	...	...	...	...	...	...	...
Dresden Hbf **840** a.	...	...	2240	...	...	...	...	...	...	...

	RE 4350		*RE* 3504	*IC* 94	*RE* 4352	*IC* 2274	*RE* 3506	*RE* 4354	*IC* 2272
	Ⓐ			A		🍷			C🍷
Dresden Hbf **840** d.	...	...	...	...	...	0519	...	...	0731
Flughafen Berlin ✈ ★ d.	...	...	...	...	...	0705	...	...	0905
Berlin Südkreuz d.	...	...	0536	0628	0636	0727	0736	0836	0928
Berlin Hbf d.	0447	...	0547	0636	0647	0736	0747	0847	0936
Berlin Gesundbrunnen d.	0455	...	0555	0644	0655	0744	0755	0855	0944
Oranienburg d.	0516	...	0616	0704	0716	0805	0816	0916	1004
Gransee d.	0533	...	0635	|	0733	|	0835	0933	|
Fürstenberg (Havel) d.	0547	...	0647	|	0747	|	0847	0947	|
Neustrelitz Hbf a.	0559	...	0659	0740	0759	0839	0859	0959	1040
Neustrelitz Hbf d.	0606	...	0701	0741	0806	0841	0901	1006	1041
Neubrandenburg **834** a.	|	...	0729	|	|	|	0929	|	|
Stralsund Hbf **834** a.	|	...	0851	|	|	|	1051	|	|
Waren (Müritz) d.	0630	...	...	0758	0830	0859	...	1030	1058
Güstrow d.	0701	...	...	|	0901	|	...	1101	|
Rostock Hbf 831 a.	0723	...	...	0839	0923	0937	...	1123	1137
Warnemünde 831 a.	...	...	...	0858	...	1001	...	...	1201

	RE 3508	*RE* 4356	*IC* 2270	*RE* 3510	*RE* 4358	*IC* 2178	*RE* 3512	*RE* 4360	*IC* 2176	*RE* 3514	*RE* 4362	*IC* 2174	*RE* 3516	*RE* 4364	*IC* 2172	*RE* 3518	*RE* 4366	*RE* 3520	*RE* 4368		*RE* 3522			
			C🍷			🍷			🍷			🍷			🍷						⑤⑥ d			
Dresden Hbf **840** d.	...	...	0931	...	...	1119	...	...	1319	...	...	1519	...	...	1719	...	...	...	...	...	...	...	...	...
Flughafen Berlin ✈ ★ d.	...	...	1105	...	...	1305	...	...	1505	...	...	1705	...	...	1905	...	...	...	...	...	...	...	...	...
Berlin Südkreuz d.	0936	1036	1127	1137	1236	1328	1336	1436	1528	1536	1636	1728	1736	1836	1928	1936	2036	2136	2238	...	2336	...	...	...
Berlin Hbf d.	0947	1047	1135	1147	1247	1338	1347	1448	1538	1547	1647	1738	1748	1847	1938	1947	2047	2147	2247	...	2347	...	...	...
Berlin Gesundbrunnen d.	0955	1055	1144	1155	1255	1344	1355	1455	1544	1555	1655	1744	1755	1855	1944	1955	2055	2155	2255	...	2355	...	...	...
Oranienburg d.	1016	1116	1204	1216	1316	1405	1416	1516	1604	1616	1716	1804	1816	1916	2005	2016	2116	2216	2316	...	0016	...	...	...
Gransee d.	1035	1133	|	1235	1333	|	1435	1533	|	1635	1733	|	1835	1933	|	2035	2133	2235	2333	...	0043	...	...	...
Fürstenberg (Havel) d.	1047	1147	|	1247	1347	|	1447	1547	|	1647	1747	|	1847	1947	|	2047	2147	2247	2347	...	0058	...	...	...
Neustrelitz Hbf a.	1059	1159	1240	1259	1359	1439	1459	1559	1640	1659	1759	1840	1859	1959	2039	2059	2159	2259	2359	...	0110	...	...	...
Neustrelitz Hbf d.	1101	1206	1241	1301	1406	1441	1501	1606	1641	1701	1806	1841	1901	2006	2041	2101	2206	2301	0004	...	0111	...	...	...
Neubrandenburg **834** a.	1129	|	|	1329	|	|	1529	|	|	1729	|	|	1929	|	|	2129	|	2329	|	...	0139	...	...	...
Stralsund Hbf **834** a.	1251	|	|	1451	|	|	1651	|	|	1851	|	|	2051	|	|	2251	|	...	|	...	...	...	...	...
Waren (Müritz) d.	...	1230	1258	...	1430	1459	...	1630	1658	...	1830	1858	...	2030	2059	...	2230	...	0027	...	...	...	...	...
Güstrow d.	...	1301	|	...	1501	|	...	1701	|	...	1901	|	...	2101	|	...	2301	...	0058	...	...	...	...	...
Rostock Hbf 831 a.	...	1323	1337	...	1523	1537	...	1723	1737	...	1923	1937	...	2123	2137	...	2323	...	0120	...	...	...	...	...
Warnemünde 831 a.	...	...	1405	...	...	1605	...	...	1805	...	...	2001	...	...	...	...	...	...	...	...	...	...	...	...

BERLIN - ELSTERWERDA. Operated by Ostdeutsche Eisenbahn. See also Table **840**. **SERVICE UNTIL APRIL 21.**

km											
0	**Berlin** Hbf d.	0542	0742	0943	1142	1342	1542	1742	1942	2142	...
6	**Berlin** Südkreuz d.	0554	0754	0954	1154	1354	1554	1754	1954	2154	...
120	Doberlug-Kirchhain d.	0732	0924	1124	1324	1524	1724	1924	2124	2324	...
140	**Elsterwerda** a.	0747	0939	1139	1339	1539	1739	1939	2139	2339	...

Elsterwerda d.	0412	0612	0812	1012	1212	1412	1612	1812	...	2004
Doberlug-Kirchhain d.	0428	0628	0828	1028	1228	1428	1628	1828	...	2020
Berlin Südkreuz a.	0559	0759	0959	1159	1359	1559	1759	1959	...	2158
Berlin Hbf a.	0609	0809	1009	1211	1409	1609	1809	2009	...	2207

A – From Wien via Nürnberg (Tables **849a**, **850** and **920**).
B – To Frankfurt via Erfurt (Table **850**).
C – From / to Chemnitz (Table **880**).
L – To Leipzig (Table **850**).

d – Also Dec. 25, Apr. 6, 9, 30, May 17, 28.

‡ – Rostock to Waren is 78 km direct.
★ – Flughafen Berlin Brandenburg (BER).

LÜBECK - BAD KLEINEN - PASEWALK - SZCZECIN — 836

RE services

km		Ⓐ	Ⓑ	Ⓐ																	T	⑤f			
	Lübeck Hbf ★ d.	...	...	...	...	...	0602t	...	0802	...	1002	...	1202	...	1402	...	1602	...	1802	...	...	...	2002	...	2206
0	**Bad Kleinen** 830 d.	...	...	...	...	*0603*	0705	*0803*	0904	*1003*	1102	*1203*	1304	*1403*	1504	*1603*	1705	*1803*	1904	*2003*	*2003*	*2003*	2104	*2203*	2304
41	Bützow 830 d.	...	...	...	0533	0633	0733	0833	0933	1033	1137	1233	1333	1433	1533	1633	1733	1833	1933	2033	2033	2033	2134	2233	2333
55	Güstrow a.	...	...	...	0542	0642	0742	0842	0942	1042	1146	1242	1342	1442	1542	1642	1742	1842	1942	2042	2042	2042	2143	2242	2342
55	Güstrow d.	...	...	...	0604	0704	0804	0904	1004	1104	1204	1304	1404	1504	1604	1704	1804	1904	2004	2104	2104	2104	2204	2304	...
84	Teterow d.	...	...	...	0633	0733	0833	0933	1033	1133	1233	1333	1433	1533	1633	1733	1833	1933	2033	2133	2133	2133	2233	2328	...
98	Malchin d.	...	...	0529	0644	0744	0844	0944	1044	1144	1244	1344	1444	1544	1644	1744	1844	1944	2044	2144	2144	2144	2243	2338	...
142	**Neubrandenburg** a.	...	...	0601	0721	0821	0921	1021	1121	1221	1321	1421	1521	1621	1721	1821	1921	2021	2121	2221	2221	2221	2315	0010	...
142	**Neubrandenburg** d.	0513	...	0606	0733	0833r	0933	1033	1133	1233	1333	1433	1533	1633	1733	1833	1933	2033	2133	...	2233	2233	...	...	...
195	**Pasewalk** a.	0559	...	0654	0814	0914r	1014	1114	1214	1314	1414	1514	1614	1714	1814	1914	2014	2114	2214	...	2314	2314	...	...	...
195	**Pasewalk** ▷ d.	0615	0615	0700	0815	...	1015	...	1215	...	1415	1525t	1615	...	1815	...	2015	...	...	...	...	2315	...	...	...
	Ueckermünde S¶ ▷ a.	|	|	0731	|	...	|	...	|	...	|	1556t	|	...	|	...	|	...	...	...	...	|	...	...	...
222	Grambow d.	0638	0638	...	0838	...	1038	...	1238	...	1438	...	1638	...	1838	...	2038	...	...	...	...	2338	...	...	...
232	Szczecin Gumience 🏛 d.	0648	0648	...	0848	...	1048	...	1248	...	1448	...	1648	...	1848	...	2048	...	...	...	...	2348	...	...	...
237	**Szczecin** Główny a.	0655	0655	...	0855	...	1055	...	1255	...	1455	...	1655	...	1855	...	2055	...	...	...	...	2355	...	...	...

	①g				Ⓐ		Ⓐ			Ⓐ	⚒												S		
Szczecin Główny d.	...	...	...	...	0501	...	...	...	0701	...	...	...	0901	...	1101	...	1301	...	1501	...	1701	...	1901	...	2101
Szczecin Gumience 🏛 d.	...	...	...	...	0507	...	...	...	0707	...	...	...	0907	...	1107	...	1307	...	1507	...	1707	...	1907	...	2107
Grambow d.	...	...	...	...	0518	...	...	...	0718	...	...	...	0918	...	1118	...	1318	...	1518	...	1718	...	1918	...	2118
Ueckermünde S ¶ ▷ d.	...	...	...	...	|	...	0600	...	|	0738	...	...	|	...	|	...	|	...	|	1601t	|	...	|	...	|
Pasewalk ⊙ ▷ a.	...	...	...	...	0539	...	0632	...	0739	0810	...	...	0939	...	1139	...	1339	...	1539	1632t	1739	...	1939	...	2139
Pasewalk ⊙ d.	0301	...	...	...	0541	0541	0638	...	0743	0843	0843	...	0943	1043	1143	1243	1343	1443	1543	1643	1743	1843	1943	2043	2143
Neubrandenburg a.	0339	...	...	...	0623	0623	0723	...	0826	0926	0926	...	1026	1126	1226	1326	1426	1526	1626	1726	1826	1926	2026	2126	2226
Neubrandenburg d.	0340	...	0447	0544	0641	0641	0741	0741	0841	0941	0941	0941	1041	1141	1241	1341	1441	1541	1641	1741	1841	1941	2041	2141	...
Malchin d.	0410	...	0531	0620	0713	0713	0813	0813	0913	1013	1013	1013	1113	1213	1313	1413	1513	1613	1713	1813	1913	2013	2113	2213	...
Teterow d.	0421	...	0541	0631	0730	0730	0830	0830	0930	1030	1030	1030	1130	1230	1330	1430	1530	1630	1730	1830	1930	2030	2130	2230	...
Güstrow a.	0439	...	0603	0653	0753	0753	0853	0853	0953	1053	1053	1053	1153	1253	1353	1453	1553	1653	1753	1853	1953	2053	2153	2253	...
Güstrow d.	0440	0501	0608	0708	0808	0808	0908	0908	1008	1108	1108	1108	1208	1308	1405	1508	1608	1708	1808	1908	2008	2108	2208	2308	...
Bützow 830 a.	0450	0511	0618	0718	0818	0818	0918	0918	1018	1118	1118	1118	1218	1318	1415	1518	1618	1718	1818	1918	2018	2118	2218	2318	...
Bad Kleinen 830 a.	0517	*0554*	0646	*0754*	0846	0846	*0954*	*0954*	1046	*1154*	*1154*	*1154*	1246	*1354*	1442	*1554*	1646	*1754*	1846	*1954*	2046	*2154*	2246	*2359*	...
Lübeck Hbf ★ a.	0623	...	0756	...	0956	0956	...	...	1156	...	...	...	1356	...	1556	...	1756	...	1956	...	2156	...	...	...	...

km			Ⓐ																	
0	**Lübeck** Hbf d.	0502	0602	0703	0802	0903	1002	1103	1202	1303	1402	1503	1602	1703	1802	1903	2002	2103	2206	2307
39	Grevesmühlen d.	0537	0637	0737	0837	0937	1037	1137	1237	1337	1437	1537	1637	1737	1837	1937	2037	2137	2242	2340
62	**Bad Kleinen** a.	0552	0656	0752	0854	0952	1054	1152	1254	1352	1454	1552	1656	1752	1854	1952	2054	2152	2259	2354

	Ⓐ	Ⓐ																	
Bad Kleinen d.	0434	0518	0603	0700	0803	0900	1003	1100	1203	1300	1403	1500	1603	1700	1803	1900	2003	2100	2204
Grevesmühlen d.	0448	0539	0617	0716	0817	0916	1017	1116	1217	1316	1417	1516	1617	1716	1817	1916	2017	2116	2221
Lübeck Hbf a.	0525	0623	0656	0756	0856	0956	1056	1156	1256	1356	1456	1556	1656	1756	1856	1956	2056	2156	2300

▷ – Full service **PASEWALK - UECKERMÜNDE**. *30 km*. Journey 31 – 35 minutes.
From Pasewalk at 0518 Ⓐ, 0610 ⚒, 0700 Ⓐ, 0822, 1022, 1222, 1422, 1525 Ⓐ, 1608 ‡, 1822 and 2022.
From Ueckermünde Stadthafen at 0600 Ⓐ, 0700 ⚒, 0738 Ⓐ, 0900, 1100, 1300, 1500, 1601 Ⓐ, 1700, 1900 and 2100.

S – To Schwerin Hbf (a. 2318).
T – ⑤–⑦ (also Apr. 6, 10, May 1, 17, 29).
f – Also Apr. 6, May 17; not Apr. 7, May 19.
g – Also Apr. 11, May 2, 30; not Apr. 10, May 1, 29.
r – ⚒ only.
t – Ⓐ only.
★ – See panel for full service Lübeck - Bad Kleinen and v.v.
‡ – Journey time: 45 minutes.
¶ – Ueckermünde Stadthafen.

WISMAR - BERLIN - COTTBUS — 837

km		◇	◇	◇ Ⓐ	◇	◇ ⚒	◇	◇		◇	◇		◇	▷	◇	◇		◇	◇		◇				2239 L
0	**Wismar** d.	...	...	0417	...	0522	...	...	0624	0733	...	0824	0924	and in	1724	...	1824	1924	...	2024	2125	2224	...		...
16	Bad Kleinen 830 d.	...	...	0431	...	0536	...	...	0639	0747	...	0839	0938	the same	1738	...	1839	1938	...	2039	2139	2239	...	A	1450
32	**Schwerin** Hbf 830 a.	...	...	0443	...	0548	...	...	0651	0758	...	0851	0950	pattern	1750	...	1851	1950	...	2051	2151	2251	...		1459
32	**Schwerin** Hbf d.	...	...	0500	0500	0600	...	...	0700	0800	...	0900	1000	every	1800	...	1900	2000	...	2100	2200	2300	...	L	1502
72	Ludwigslust 840 d.	...	...	0533	0533	0633	...	...	0734	0833	...	0934	1033	two hours	1833	...	1934	2033	...	2134	2233	2334	...		1526
116	Wittenberge 840 d.	0406	0506	0606v	0606v	0703v	0703	0806	...	0903v	1006	...	1103v	until	1903v	2006	...	2103v	2206	...	2307v	...	...	S	1547
207	Nauen d.	0501	0601	0701	0701	0801	0801	0901	...	1001	1101	...	1201		2001	2101	...	2201	2301	...	0003	...	...		...
229	**Berlin** Spandau 840 d.	0518	0623	0723	0723	0823	0823	0923	...	1023	1123	...	1223		2023	2123	...	2223	2323	...	0023	...	...	O	...
241	**Berlin** Zoo ‡ d.	0527	0633	0733	0733	0833	0833	0933	...	1033	1133	...	1233		2033	2133	...	2233	2333	...	0033	...	...		...
245	**Berlin** Hbf 840 ‡ d.	0532	0640	0740	0740	0840	0840	0940	...	1040	1140	...	1240		2040	2140	...	2240	2340	...	0040	...	...		...
250	**Berlin** Ostbahnhof ‡ d.	0544	0653	0753	0753	0853	0853	0953	...	1053	1153	...	1253		2053	2153	...	2253	2353	...	0053	...	...		...
252	**Berlin** Ostkreuz ‡ d.	0551	0657	0757	0757	0857	0857	0957	...	1057	1157	...	1257		2057	2157	...	2257	2357	...	0057	...	...		...
269	**Flughafen Berlin** ✈ ‡ a.	0610	0715	0815	0815	0915	0915	1015	...	1115	1215	...	1315		2115	2215	...	2315	0015	...	0115	...	...		...

		◇	◇	◇ ⚒		◇	◇	◇	2238 L		◇		◇			◇	◇		◇	◇		◇	◇	◇	◇
Flughafen Berlin ✈ ‡ d.	...	0344	0444	0444	...	0544	0644	0744	...	...	0844	...	0944	and in	...	1544	1644	...	1744	1844	...	1944	2044	2144	2244
Berlin Ostkreuz ‡ d.	...	0403	0503	0503	...	0603	0703	0803	...	...	0903	...	1003	the same	...	1603	1703	...	1803	1903	...	2003	2103	2203	2303
Berlin Ostbahnhof ‡ d.	...	0407	0507	0507	...	0607	0707	0807	...	...	0907	...	1007	pattern	...	1607	1707	...	1807	1907	...	2007	2107	2207	2307
Berlin Hbf 840 ‡ d.	...	0419	0519	0519	...	0620	0720	0820	...	...	0920	...	1020	every	...	1620	1720	...	1820	1920	...	2020	2120	2220	2319
Berlin Zoo ‡ d.	...	0425	0525	0525	...	0626	0726	0826	...	...	0926	...	1026	two hours	...	1626	1726	...	1826	1926	...	2026	2126	2226	2325
Berlin Spandau 840 d.	...	0434	0536	0536	...	0637	0737	0837	...	...	0937	...	1037	until	...	1637	1737	...	1837	1937	...	2037	2137	2237	2337
Nauen d.	...	0459	0559	0559	...	0656	0756	0856	...	...	0956	...	1056		...	1656	1756	...	1856	1956	...	2056	2156	2256	2358
Wittenberge 840 d.	...	0603v	0659	0701	...	0757	0901	0957	1011	...	1101	...	1157		...	1757	1901	...	1957	2101	...	2157	2301	2357	0056
Ludwigslust 840 d.	0457t	0628	...	0726	0826	...	0926	...	1032	1036	1126	1226	...		1826	...	1926	2026	...	2126	2256	...	2326	...	...
Schwerin Hbf a.	0529t	0658	...	0757	0858	...	0957	...	1054	1108	1157	1258	...		1858	...	1957	2104j	...	2157	2330	...	2357	...	...
Schwerin Hbf 830 d.	0539	0659	...	0806	0904	...	1006	...	1056	1109	1206	1304	...		1904	...	2006	2107	...	2206	...	...	0006	...	...
Bad Kleinen 830 d.	0601v	0711	...	0819	0917	...	1018	...	1106	1122	1218	1317	...		1917	...	2018	2119	...	2218	...	...	0032z	...	...
Wismar a.	0616	0726	...	0837	0937	...	1037	...	...	1138	1237	1337	...		1937	...	2037	2138	...	2237	...	...	0046	...	...

BERLIN - COTTBUS

km							2431 ⒷE							
0	Nauen d.	0437t	0537	0637		1737	...	1837	1937	...	2037	2208	2308	0007
22	**Berlin** Spandau d.	0505t	0605	0705	and	1805	...	1905	2005	...	2105	2233	2333	0035
34	**Berlin** Zoo d.	0517	0617	0717		1817	...	1917	2017	2040	2117	2245	2345	0047
38	**Berlin** Hbf d.	0523	0623	0723	hourly	1823	1828	1923	2023	2046	2123	2251	2351	0053
43	**Berlin** Ostbahnhof d.	0535	0635	0735		1835	1841	1935	2035	2058	2135	2302	0002	0105
45	**Berlin** Ostkreuz d.	0539	0639	0739	until	1839	1845	1939	2039	2103	2139	2307	0007	0110
76	Königs Wusterhausen d.	0603	0703	0803		1903	1909	2003	2103	2121	2203	2333	0031	0133
123	Lübben (Spreewald) d.	0626	0726	0826		1926	1933	2026	2126	2157	2226	0010	0108	0211
134	Lübbenau (Spreew) d.	0633	0733	0833		1933	1942	2033	2133	2205	2233	0017	0115	0218
163	**Cottbus** Hbf a.	0655	0755	0854		1954	2000	2055	2154	2233	2256	0040	0138	0241

				Ⓐ	2432 G									
Cottbus Hbf d.	0347	...	0501	0526	0601	0608	0703	0804		2004	2104	2203	...	2302
Lübbenau (Spreew) d.	0412	...	0527	0546	0620	0627	0727	0827	and	2027	2127	2227	...	2325
Lübben (Spreewald) d.	0418	...	0534	0553	0628	0634	0734	0834		2034	2134	2234	...	2332
Königs Wusterhausen d.	0458	...	0558	0616	0652	0658	0758	0858	hourly	2058	2158	2258	...	0010
Berlin Ostkreuz d.	0519	...	0619	0637	0712	0719	0819	0919		2119	2219	2319	...	0032
Berlin Ostbahnhof d.	0525	...	0625	0642	0718	0725	0825	0925	until	2125	2225	2325	...	0037
Berlin Hbf d.	0537	...	0637	0654	0725	0737	0837	0937		2137	2237	2337	...	0049
Berlin Zoo d.	0544	...	0644	0659	...	0744	0844	0944		2144	2244	2344	...	0054
Berlin Spandau d.	0556	...	0656	...	...	0756	0856	0956		2156	2256	2356	...	...
Nauen a.	0623	...	0723	...	...	0823	0923	1023		2223	2323	0023	...	...

E – Ⓑ (not Apr. 9, 30, May 28). *IC* **2431**. 🚃 Emden - Bremen - Hannover - Magdeburg - Berlin - Cottbus.
G – ①–⑥ (not Apr. 10, May 1, 29). *IC* **2432**. 🚃 Cottbus - Berlin - Magdeburg - Hannover - Bremen - Norddeich.
L – *IC* train. 🚃 Leipzig - Rostock - Warnemünde and v.v.

j – 2058 on ©.
t – Ⓐ only.
v – Arrives 6 – 10 minutes earlier.
z – Arrives 0017.

‡ – See also Table **847**.
◇ – Operated by Ostdeutsche Eisenbahn.
▷ – See last column for additional *IC* service.

839 MAGDEBURG - BERLIN - FRANKFURT (ODER) - COTTBUS

Ostdeutsche Eisenbahn / DB

km																									
		©			Ⓐ				Ⓐ			Ⓐ											Ⓐ¶	P¶	W♣
0	**Magdeburg** Hbf .... d.	0042	...	...	...	0419	0512	...	0554	0612c	...	0619	0712	...		1912	...	2012	2106	2206	2322		0703	1705	1856
79	**Brandenburg** Hbf ..... d.	0141	0315c	0415	0506	0520	0607	0620	0646	0706	0720	0720	0807	0820	and at	2007	2020	2107	2159	2259	0023	A	0741	1742	1946
114	Potsdam Hbf .... d.	0211	0345c	0447	0530	0550	0630	0650	0710	0730	0750	0750	0830	0850	the same	2030	2050	2130	2230	2330	0054		0802	1801	2009
123	Berlin Wannsee .... d.	0218	0352c	0454	0537	0557	0637	0657	0717	0737	0757	0757	0837	0857	minutes	2037	2057	2137	2237	2337	0101	L	0809	1810	2029
138	**Berlin** Zoo .... d.	0231	0405	0505	0550	0608	0650	0708	0730	0750	0808	0808	0850	0908	past each	2050	2108	2150	2250	2350	0115		|	|	2042
142	**Berlin** Hbf .... **1001** d.	0237	0411	0511	0556	0614	0656	0714	0736	0756	0814	0814	0856	0914	hour until	2056	2114	2156	2256	2356	0121	S	0828	1828	2048
147	**Berlin** Ostbahnhof .... d.	0249	0422	0522	0607	0625	0707	0725	0747	0807	0825	0825	0907	0925		2107	2125	2207	2307	0007	0132		0840	1841	2100
149	**Berlin** Ostkreuz .... d.	0253	0428	0528	0612	0631	0712	0731	0752	0812	0831	0831	0912	0931		2112	2131	2212	2312	0012	0136	O	...	1843b	...
194	Fürstenwalde (Spree) d.	0326	0501	0559	0645	0702	0745	0802	0822	0845	0902	0902	0945	1002		2145	2202	2245	2345	0045	0209		...	...	...
228	**Frankfurt** (Oder) **1001** a.	0354	0531	0628	0703	0731	0803	0831	0840	0903	0931	0931	1003	1031		2203	2231	2312	0012	0112	0236		...	...	...

		©		©		Ⓐ				Ⓐ						⑦z					⑤⑥		©♣	N¶	Ⓐ¶
Frankfurt (Oder) **1001** d.	0024	0024	...	...	...	...	0343	0423c	0443	0518	0526	0555		1926	1955	♣	2026	2124	2224	2324	2324		...	...	...
Fürstenwalde (Spree). d.	0052	0052	...	...	...	...	0413	0452c	0513	0536	0554	0613		1954	2013	...	2054	2152	2252	2352	2352	A	...	...	...
Berlin Ostkreuz .... d.	0125	0125	...	0252	...	...	0447	0525	0547	0607	0625	0647	and at	2025	2047	...	2125	2225	2325	0025	0025		...	0712e	...
Berlin Ostbahnhof ..... d.	0130	0130	...	0257	...	...	0452	0530	0552	0612	0630	0652	the same	2030	2052	2120	2130	2230	2330	0030	0030	L	0711	0718	1722
Berlin Hbf .... **1001** d.	0141	0141	...	0308	...	...	0503	0541	0603	0624	0641	0703	minutes	2041	2103	2131	2141	2241	2341	0041	0041		0723	0729	1733
Berlin Zoo .... d.	0146	0147	...	0314	...	...	0509	0547	0609	0630	0647	0709	past each	2047	2109	2138	2147	2247	2347	0047	0047	S	0730	|	|
Berlin Wannsee .... d.	...	0200	...	0327	...	...	0523	0600	0623	0643	0700	0723	hour until	2100	2123	2149	2200	2300	0000	0100	0100		0742	0749	1750
Potsdam Hbf .... d.	...	0209	...	0336	...	...	0531	0609	0631	0654	0709	0731		2109	2131	2157	2209	2309	0009	0109	0109	O	0753	0759	1800
Brandenburg Hbf ...... d.	...	0240	...	0408	0408	0451	0555	0640	0655	0716	0740	0755		2140	2155	2217	2241	2341	0040	0139	0141		0813	0821	1816
Magdeburg Hbf .... a.	...	...	...	0508	0508	0550	0647	...	0747	...	...	0847		...	2247	2304	2340	0034	...	...	0234		0858	0901	1854

FRANKFURT (ODER) - COTTBUS (operated by DB; certain services run to / from Leipzig as shown in Table **852**).

km											
		©	Ⓐ		Ⓐ		Ⓐ				
0	**Frankfurt (Oder)** .... d.	0031	0436	0536	0601	0636	0709	0736	and	2136	2322
23	Eisenhüttenstadt .... d.	0052	0457	0557	0619	0657	0731	0757	hourly	2157	2343
48	Guben .... d.	0113	0518	0618	0635	0718	0747	0818	until	2218	0005
86	**Cottbus** Hbf .... a.	0150	0554	0654	0659	0754	0811	0854		2254	0042

			Ⓐ					Ⓐ	
Cottbus Hbf .... d.	0402	0506	0532	0602	and	2102	...	2202	2302
Guben .... d.	0440	0540	0610	0640	hourly	2140	...	2240	2340
Eisenhüttenstadt ..... d.	0500	0600	0630	0700	until	2200	...	2300	0000
Frankfurt (Oder) .... a.	0521	0621	0651	0721		2221	...	2321	0021

N – *IC* **2432**. 12 (Cottbus ①–⑥ **e** -) Berlin - Hannover - Norddeich.
P – *IC* **2431**. 12 Emden - Hannover - Berlin (- Cottbus Ⓑ **b**).
W – ⑤⑥† (also Apr. 6, May 17).

b – Ⓑ (not Apr. 9, 30, May 28).
c – © only.
e – ①–⑥ (not Apr. 10, May 1, 29).
z – Also Apr. 10, May 1, 18, 29; not Apr. 9, 30, May 28.

♣ – *HARZ-BERLIN-EXPRESS*. 2 Berlin - Halberstadt - Thale / Ilsenburg / Goslar and v.v. (Tables **860** / **862**). Not available for local journeys Berlin - Brandenburg and v.v. Operated by Abellio Rail Mitteldeutschland. **DB tickets not valid**.
¶ – *IC* service operated by DB.

840 HAMBURG - BERLIN - DRESDEN

See Table **927** for services operated by FlixTrain

km		*EC*	*ICE*	*ICE*	*ICE*	*IC*		*EC*	*ICE*	*ICE*	*ICE*	*IC*	*EC*	*ICE*	*ICE*	*ICE*	*IC*	*EC*	*ICE*	*ICE*	*ICE*	*IC*	*EC*	*ICE*
		171	**701**	**1003**	**505**	**2173**		**253**	**703**	**93**	**507**	**2175**	**379**	**705**	**1005**	**509**	**2177**	**175**	**707**	**1707**	**1601**	**2179**	**177**	**709**
		△	Ⓐ		⚒			△		◐			△					△						
		P✕	M✕	M✕	M✕	🍷		Z✕	M✕	G✕	M✕	🍷	J✕	M✕	M✕	M✕	🍷	¶P✕	M✕	M✕	M✕	🍷	P✕	M✕
0	**Hamburg** Altona .... d.	...	0511	0532	0617	...	...	0635	0718	0749	0818	...	...	0919	0948	1017	...	...	1118	1150	1215	...	...	1319
7	**Hamburg** Hbf .... **830** d.	...	0527	0552	0634	...	...	0648	0735	0804	0834	...	0851	0936	1005	1034	...	1051	1136	1203	1234	...	...	1336
54	Büchen .... **830** d.	...	|	|	|	...	...	0715	|	|	|	...	0915	|	|	|	...	1115	|	|	|	...	...	|
122	Ludwigslust .... **837** d.	...	0613	|	|	...	...	0741	|	|	|	...	0941	|	|	|	...	1141	|	|	|	...	...	|
167	Wittenberge .... **837** d.	...	0631	|	|	...	...	0801	|	|	|	...	1001	|	|	|	...	1201	|	|	|	...	...	|
280	**Berlin** Spandau .... **837** d.	...	0712	0744	0810	...	...	0846	0912	0944	1010	...	1046	1112	1144	1210	...	1246	1312	1344	1410	...	...	1512
	Rostock Hbf **835** .... d.	...	|	|	|	0620	...	|	|	|	|	0821	|	|	|	|	1021	|	|	|	|	1220	...	|
293	**Berlin** Hbf .... **837** a.	...	0722	0755	0820	0823	...	0855	0922	0953	1020	1023	1055	1122	1155	1220	1223	1255	1322	1355	1420	1423	...	1522
293	**Berlin** Hbf .... **835** d.	0716	0734	0804	0829	0826	...	0916	0934	1004	1029	1026	1116	1134	1204	1229	1226	1316	1334	1404	1429	1426	1516	1534
299	**Berlin** Südkreuz .... **835** d.	0723	0739	0809	0834	0833	...	0923	0939	1009	1034	1033	1123	1139	1209	1234	1233	1323	1339	1409	1434	1433	1523	1539
	Flughafen Berlin ✈ ★ .... d.	|	...	...	...	0901	...	|	...	...	...	1101	|	...	...	...	1301	|	...	...	...	1501	|	...
413	Doberlug-Kirchhain .... **835** d.	|	...	...	...	0949	...	|	...	...	...	1149	|	...	...	...	1349	|	...	...	...	1549	|	...
433	Elsterwerda .... **843 835** d.	|	...	...	...	1001	...	|	...	...	...	1201	|	...	...	...	1401	|	...	...	...	1601	|	...
486	**Dresden** Neustadt .... a.	0900	...	...	...	1027	...	1100	...	...	...	1227	1300	...	...	...	1428	1500	...	...	...	1627	1700	...
490	**Dresden** Hbf .... **843** a.	0907	...	...	...	1033	...	1107	...	...	...	1240	1307	...	...	...	1434	1507	...	...	...	1634	1707	...

	ICE	*ICE*	*IC*	*ICE*	*EC*	*ICE*	*ICE*	*ICE*	*ICE*	*ICE*	*IC*	*ICE*	*ICE*	*IC*	*ICE*	*IC*	*IC*	*ICE*	*ICE*	*ICE*		*ICE*		*ICE*
	1007	**603**	**2271**	**836**	**179**	**801**	**1009**	**1605**	**1605**	**1705**	**2273**	**871**	**803**	**2075**	**1607**	**2275**	**2073**	**1743**	**699**	**609**		**805**		**907**
									Ⓑ	Ⓑ b								⑤⑦		Ⓑ b				⑤⑦
	✕M	M✕	X🍷	C✕	P✕	B✕	M✕	✕	M✕	Q✕	X🍷	✕	N✕	U	D✕	🍷		w✕	F✕	✕		✕		w✕
Hamburg Altona .... d.	1351	1418	...	1437	...	1517	1537	1616	1616	1616	...	1637	1719	...	1818	...	1835	...	1919	2017	...	2135	...	2236
Hamburg Hbf .... **830** d.	1404	1435	...	1450	...	1536	1551	1634	1634	1634	...	1651	1735	1751	1835	...	1851	...	1936	2034	...	2151	...	2252
Büchen .... **830** d.	|	|	...	1514	...	|	|	|	|	|	...	1715	|	|	|	...	1915	...	|	|	...	2215	...	2315
Ludwigslust .... **837** d.	|	|	...	1541	...	|	1646	|	|	|	...	1741	|	1843	|	...	1941	...	|	2118	...	2242	...	2342
Wittenberge .... **837** d.	|	|	...	1601	...	|	|	|	|	|	...	1801	1833	|	|	...	2001	...	|	|	...	2303	...	0002
Berlin Spandau .... **837** d.	1544	1610	...	1646	...	1712	1744	1810	1810	1810	...	1846	1912	1942s	2010	...	2044s	...	2112	2211s	...	2343s	...	0042s
Rostock Hbf **835** .... d.	|	|	1421	|	...	|	|	|	|	|	1621	|	|	|	|	1820	|	...	|	|	...	|	...	|
Berlin Hbf .... **837** a.	1555	1620	1623	1655	...	1722	1755	1820	1820	1820	1823	1855	1922	1955	2020	2023	2055	...	2122	2223	...	2353	...	0054
Berlin Hbf .... **835** d.	1604	1629	1626	1704	1716	1734	1804	...	1829	1829	1826	1915	1926	|	2029	2026	|	2116	2126	|	...	|	...	|
Berlin Südkreuz .... **835** d.	1609	1634	1633	1709	1723	1739	1809	...	1834	1834	1833	1922	1931	2022	2034	2033	2104	2123	2131	2232	...	0002	...	0103
Flughafen Berlin ✈ ★ .... d.	...	...	1701	...	|	...	...	...	...	...	1901	|	...	...	...	2101	...	|	...	...	...	...	...	...
Doberlug-Kirchhain .... **835** d.	...	...	1745	...	|	...	...	...	...	...	1945	|	...	...	...	2149	...	|	...	...	...	...	...	...
Elsterwerda .... **843 835** d.	...	...	1756	...	|	...	...	...	...	...	1956	|	...	...	...	2201	...	|	...	...	...	...	...	...
Dresden Neustadt .... a.	...	...	1821	...	1900	...	...	...	...	...	2021	2100	...	...	...	2227	...	2300	...	...	...	...	...	...
Dresden Hbf .... **843** a.	...	...	1827	...	1907	...	...	...	...	...	2027	2107	...	...	...	2240	...	2307	...	...	...	...	...	...

	ICE		*ICE*	*ICE*	*ICE*	*IC*	*IC*	*ICE*	*IC*	*ICE*	*ICE*	*IC*	*ICE*	*ICE*	*ICE*	*ICE*	*EC*	*ICE*	*ICE*	*IC*	*ICE*	*ICE*	*ICE*	*EC*
	4		**908**	**608**	**808**	**2070**	**2274**	**1606**	**2074**	**806**	**870**	**2272**	**1604**	**1704**	**1008**	**804**	**178**	**933**	**933**	**2270**	**602**	**1006**	**802**	**176**
	① g		① g	Ⓐ	⚒									⚒	r			Ⓐ	⑥					△
	R		✕	✕	✕	¶✕	🍷	L✕	U	E✕	✕	X🍷	N✕	Q✕	M✕	A✕	P✕	H✕	✕	X🍷	M✕	M✕	M✕	P✕
Dresden Hbf .... **843** d.	...	...	...	...	...	...	0519	...	...	...	0654	0731	...	...	...	...	0855	...	...	0931	...	...	...	1055
Dresden Neustadt .... d.	...	...	...	...	...	...	0526	...	...	...	0702	0737	...	...	...	...	0903	...	...	0937	...	...	...	1103
Elsterwerda .... **843 835** d.	...	...	...	...	...	...	0556	...	...	...	|	0804	...	...	...	...	|	...	...	1004	...	...	...	|
Doberlug-Kirchhain .... **835** d.	...	...	...	...	...	...	0608	...	...	...	|	0815	...	...	...	...	|	...	...	1015	...	...	...	|
Flughafen Berlin ✈ ★ .... a.	...	...	...	...	...	...	0657	...	...	...	|	0858	...	...	...	...	|	...	...	1057	...	...	...	|
Berlin Südkreuz .... **835** d.	0342	...	0457	0520	0628	0657	0727	0724	0755	0827	0839	0928	0924	0924	0948	1017t	1038	1050	1057	1127	1124	1148	1217	1236
Berlin Hbf .... **835** a.	0347	...	|	|	|	|	0732	0729	|	0832	0844	0932	0929	0929	0953	1022t	1043	1055	|	1132	1131	1153	1222	1241
Berlin Hbf .... **837** d.	0353	...	0506	0530	0638	0706	0736	0738	0804	0838	0906	0936	0938	0938	1005	1038	...	1106	1106	1135	1138	1205	1238	1303
Rostock Hbf **835** .... a.	|	...	|	|	|	|	0937	|	|	|	|	1137	|	|	|	|	...	|	|	1337	|	|	|	|
Berlin Spandau .... **837** d.	|	...	0517	0541	0648	0717	...	0748	0815	0848	0917	...	0948	0948	1015	1048	...	1117	1117	...	1148	1215	1248	1317
Wittenberge .... **837** d.	|	...	0600	0621	|	0801	...	|	|	|	1001	...	|	|	|	|	...	1201	1201	...	|	|	|	1401
Ludwigslust .... **837** d.	|	...	0618	0641	0742	0820	...	|	0913	|	1020	...	|	|	|	|	...	1220	1220	...	|	|	|	1420
Büchen .... **830** d.	|	...	0649	|	|	0850	...	|	|	|	1049	...	|	|	|	|	...	1248	1248	...	|	|	|	1449
Hamburg Hbf .... **830** a.	0537	...	0712	0725	0825	0912	...	0924	1003	1022	1115	...	1124	1124	1151	1221	...	1311	1311	...	1324	1351	1422	1511
Hamburg Altona .... a.	...	...	0726	0742	0840	...	...	0939	...	1038	1128	...	1139	1139	1203	1239	...	1324	1324	...	1340	1405	1438	1526

A – 12 ✕ (München Ⓐ -) Nürnberg - Erfurt - Berlin - Kiel.
B – 12 ✕ Kiel - Hamburg - Berlin - Halle - Erfurt - Nürnberg - München.
C – 12 ✕ Hamburg - Berlin - Erfurt - Frankfurt - Saarbrücken.
D – 12 ✕ Hamburg - Leipzig (- Erfurt Ⓑ **b**) (- München ⑤).
E – 12 ✕ (Eisenach Ⓐ -) Leipzig - Berlin - Hamburg.
F – 12 ✕ Hamburg - Berlin - Leipzig - Erfurt - Frankfurt - Stuttgart - München.
G – BEROLINA – 12 ✕ Wien - Nürnberg - Erfurt - Halle - Hamburg and v.v.
H – From Darmstadt and Frankfurt via Erfurt (Table **850**).
J – 12 ✕ Kiel - Hamburg - Berlin - Praha and v.v.
L – From Leipzig (Table **850**).
M – To / from München via Erfurt (Table **850**).

N – To / from Nürnberg via Erfurt (Table **850**).
P – To / from Praha (Tables **60**/**1100**).
Q – From / to Jena (Table **849a**).
R – From Chur via Zürich, Basel, Frankfurt and Leipzig (Tables **850**, **912**).
U – UTHLANDE – From / to Westerland (Table **821**).
X – From / to Chemnitz (Table **880**).
Z – From / to Budapest via Praha (Tables **60**/**1100**).

b – Ⓑ (not Dec. 25).
g – Also Dec. 27; not Dec. 26.
r – Not Feb. 11 - Mar. 31.

s – Arrival time. Calls to set down only.
t – 10 minutes later on †.
w – Also Dec. 26; not Dec. 25.

¶ – From / to Flensburg (Table **823**).
◐ – Train number **1993** Feb. 11 - Mar. 31.
◧ – Train number **1992** Feb. 11 - Mar. 31.
★ – Flughafen Berlin Brandenburg (BER).
△ – On ① until Feb. 13 (not Dec. 26) runs with a different train number and does not run Dresden - Praha and v.v.

HAMBURG - BERLIN - DRESDEN 840

See Table **927** for services operated by FlixTrain

	IC 2178	*ICE* 1600	*ICE* 1706	*ICE* 800	*EC* 174	*IC* 2176	*ICE* 508	*ICE* 1004	*ICE* 708	*EC* 378	*IC* 2174	*ICE* 506	*ICE* 92	*ICE* 706	*EC* 252	*IC* 2172	*ICE* 504	*ICE* 1002	*ICE* 704	*EC* 170	*ICE* 502		*ICE* 700	*ICE* 1740
					△					△			◧		△									⑤⑦
	🍷	M✕	M✕	M✕	P¶✕	🍷	M✕	M✕	M✕	J✕	🍷	M✕	G✕	M✕	Z✕	🍷	M✕	M✕	M✕	P✕	M✕		✕	w✕
Dresden Hbf .... **843** d.	1119	...	...	...	1255	1319	...	...	...	1455	1519	...	...	...	1655	1719	...	...	...	1855	...	...	...	2054
Dresden Neustadt .... d.	1126	...	...	...	1303	1326	...	...	...	1503	1526	...	...	...	1703	1726	...	...	...	1903	...	...	...	2103
Elsterwerda .... **843 835** d.	1156	...	...	...	|	1356	...	...	...	|	1556	...	...	...	|	1756	...	...	...	|	...	...	...	|
Doberlug-Kirchhain .... **835** d.	1208	...	...	...	|	1408	...	...	...	|	1608	...	...	...	|	1808	...	...	...	|	...	...	...	|
Flughafen Berlin ✈ ★ .... a.	1257	...	...	...	|	1457	...	...	...	|	1657	...	...	...	|	1857	...	...	...	|	...	...	...	|
Berlin Südkreuz .... **835** d.	1328	1324	1348	1417	1438	1528	1524	1548	1617	1638	1728	1726	1748	1817	1838	1928	1926	1948	2017	2036s	2124	...	2230	2236s
Berlin Hbf .... **835** a.	1333	1329	1353	1422	1443	1533	1529	1553	1622	1643	1734	1731	1753	1822	1843	1933	1931	1953	2022	2043	2129	...	|	2244
Berlin Hbf .... **837** d.	1338	1338	1403	1438	1506	1538	1538	1603	1638	1706	1738	1738	1805	1838	1906	1938	1938	2005	2038	...	2138	...	2238	...
Rostock Hbf **835** .... a.	1537	|	|	|	|	1737	|	|	|	|	1937	|	|	|	|	2137	|	|	|	...	|	...	|	...
Berlin Spandau .... **837** d.	...	1348	1415	1448	1517	...	1548	1615	1648	1717	...	1748	1815	1848	1917	...	1948	2015	2048	...	2148	...	2248	...
Wittenberge .... **837** d.	...	|	|	|	1601	...	|	|	|	1801	...	|	|	|	2001	...	|	|	|	...	2229	...	2329	...
Ludwigslust .... **837** d.	...	|	|	|	1620	...	|	1711	|	1820	...	|	|	|	2020	...	|	|	|	...	2249	...	2347	...
Büchen .... **830** d.	...	|	|	|	1649	...	|	|	|	1849	...	|	|	|	2049	...	|	|	|	...	|	...	|	...
Hamburg Hbf .... **830** a.	...	1524	1600	1621	1711	...	1724	1757	1822	1912	...	1924	1951	2023	2118	...	2125	2155	2222	...	2334	...	0032	...
Hamburg Altona .... a.	...	1539	1623	1638	...	...	1740	1822	1839	...	...	1940	2015	2038	2134	...	2140	2214	2238	...	2349	...	0048	...

FOR NOTES SEE PREVIOUS PAGE

MAGDEBURG - STENDAL - UELZEN and WITTENBERGE 841

RE / S-Bahn services

km																											
		⚒	Ⓐe				Ⓐe	†U			R									W	U				W	U	
0	**Magdeburg** Hbf ... d.	0351	...	0510	0552	0610	0640	0703	0710	0810	0856	0903	0910	1010	1103	1110	1210	1303	1310	1335	1403	1410	1503	1510	1535	1603	1610
58	Stendal Hbf .... a.	0436	...	0557	0632	0657	0727	0743	0757	0857	0933	0943	0957	1057	1143	1157	1257	1343	1357	1415	1443	1457	1543	1557	1615	1643	1657
58	Stendal Hbf .... d.	0440	0508	0601	0633	0701t	0730	0744	0801	0901r	0935	0944	1001	1101t	1144	1201	1301t	1344	1401	1420	1444	1501t	1544	1601	1620	1644	1701t
113	**Wittenberge** ..... a.	|	0551	0644	|	0744t	|	|	0844	0944r	1009	|	1044	1144t	|	1244	1344t	|	1444	|	|	1544t	|	1644	|	|	1744t
116	Salzwedel .... d.	0519	...	...	0714	...	0808	0814	...	...	...	1014	...	...	1214	...	...	1414	...	1456	1514	...	1614	...	1656	1714	...
167	**Uelzen** .... a.	0550	...	...	0746	...	...	0846	...	...	...	1046	...	...	1246	...	...	1446	...	1529	1546	...	1646	...	1729	1746	...

							T				
Magdeburg Hbf.... d.	1703	1710	1810	1903	1910	2010	2103	2110	2141	2210	2310
Stendal Hbf......... a.	1743	1757	1857	1943	1957	2057	2143	2157	2221	2257	2357
Stendal Hbf......... d.	1744	1801	1901t	1944	2001	2101b	2144	2201	2232b	...	...
Wittenberge ..... a.	|	1844	1944t	|	2044	2144b	|	2244	|	...	...
Salzwedel .... d.	1814	...	...	2014	...	...	2214	...	2310b	...	...
Uelzen .... a.	1846	...	...	2046	...	...	2246	...	...	...	...

		Ⓐe		⚒e			⚒		⚒⊖		†U	
Uelzen .... d.	...	...	...	...	...	...	0619	...	0700	...	0802	...
Salzwedel .... d.	...	0502	...	0525	0557	...	0652	...	0734	...	0835	...
Wittenberge .... d.	...	|	0500t	|	|	0610t	|	0710	|	0810t	|	0910
Stendal Hbf .... a.	...	0539	0541t	0556	0634	0652t	0722	0752	0813	0852t	0907	0952
Stendal Hbf .... d.	0458	0546	0557	0606	0641	0657	0723t	0757	...	0857	0910	0957
Magdeburg Hbf ..... a.	0544	0626	0644	0649	0723	0744	0802t	0844	...	0944	0950	1044

											S		U	W				U	W						Ⓑ		T
Uelzen .... d.	0902	...	...	1102	...	...	1302	...	...	1502v	...	...	1602	1624	...	1702	...	1802	1824	...	1902	...	...	2102	...	...	2302
Salzwedel .... d.	0935	...	...	1135	...	...	1335z	...	...	1535z	...	...	1635	1657	...	1735z	...	1835	1857	...	1935	...	...	2135	...	...	2336
Wittenberge ..... d.	|	1010r	1110	|	1210t	1310	|	1410t	1510	|	1549	1610t	|	|	1710	|	1810t	|	|	1910	|	2010t	2110	|	2210	2307	|
Stendal Hbf......... a.	1007	1052r	1152	1207	1252t	1352	1407	1452t	1552	1607	1620	1652t	1707	1732	1752	1807	1852t	1911	1933	1952	2007	2052t	2152	2211	2252	2347	0005
Stendal Hbf......... d.	1010	1057	1157	1210	1257	1357	1410	1457	1557	1610	1622	1657	1710	1738	1757	1810	1857	1912	1940	1957	2010	2057	2157	2223	...	2348	0007
Magdeburg Hbf.... a.	1050	1144	1244	1250	1344	1444	1450	1544	1644	1651	1656	1744	1750	1820	1844	1850	1944	1952	2020	2044	2050	2144	2243	2303	...	0033	0046

R – *IC* **2238**. [12] Leipzig - Schwerin - Rostock - Warnemünde.
S – *IC* **2239**. [12] Warnemünde - Rostock - Schwerin - Leipzig.
T – ⑤⑥† until Mar. 3.
U – Until Mar. 3.
W – From Mar. 4.

b – Not ⑥.
e – Not Jan. 6.
r – ⚒ only.
t – Ⓐ only.
v – 1504 on ⑤.

z – 2–3 minutes later from Mar. 4.

⊖ – Runs 21–23 minutes later from Mar. 4.

LEIPZIG - DRESDEN 842

	EN 40459	*EC* 459		*IC* 2249	*IC* 2449	*ICE* 1553	*IC* 2447	*ICE* 1555	*IC* 2445	*ICE* 1557	*IC* 2443	*ICE* 1559	*IC* 2441	*ICE* 1651	*IC* 2049	*ICE* 1653	*IC* 2047	*ICE* 1655	*IC* 2045	*ICE* 1657				
				⚒		⚒					⑦w				T				Ⓑb	n				
	🅁				M	E	H		K		K		K		K		K		K					
	X	Y				✕	🍷	✕	🍷	✕	🍷	✕	🍷	✕	🍷	✕	🍷	✕	🍷					
Wiesbaden Hbf **911** .... d.	...	...	...	...	...	...	...	...	...	0826	...	1026	...	1226	...	1426	...	1626	...	1826	...	...	...	...
Frankfurt (Main) Hbf **850** ...... d.	0052	0052	...	...	...	...	...	0716	...	0919	...	1119	...	1319	...	1519	...	1719	...	1919	...	...	...	...
Leipzig Hbf .... d.	0545	0545	...	0631	0731	0831	0931	1031	1131	1231	1331	1431	1531	1631	1731	1831	1931	2031	2131	2231	...	...	...	...
Riesa .... d.	0625	0625	...	0702	0802	0902	1002	1102	1202	1302	1402	1502	1602	1702	1802	1902	2002	2103	2202	2302	...	...	...	...
Dresden Neustadt .... a.	0659	0659	...	0730	0830	0930	1051	1130	1251	1330	1439	1530	1637	1730	1837	1930	2037	2130	2237	2330	...	...	...	...
Dresden Hbf .... a.	0705	0705	...	0737	0837	0938	1100	1138	1300	1338	1446	1538	1647	1738	1846	1938	2046	2138	2246	2338	...	...	...	...

	IC 2044	*ICE* 1654	*IC* 2046	*ICE* 1652	*IC* 2048	*ICE* 1650	*IC* 2440	*ICE* 1558	*IC* 2442	*ICE* 1556	*IC* 1934	*IC* 2444	*ICE* 1554	*IC* 2446	*ICE* 1552	*IC* 2448		*EN* 40458	*EC* 458				
			⚒						⑦w		⑦w					Ⓑb							
	K		K		K		K		K		G	K		H	n	H		🅁					
	🍷	✕	🍷	✕	🍷	✕	🍷	✕	🍷	✕		🍷	✕	🍷	✕			X	Y				
Dresden Hbf .... d.	0512	0610	0712	0810	0845	1010	1045	1210	1312	1410	1439	1512	1610	1712	1810	1845	...	2110	2110	...	...	...	...
Dresden Neustadt .... d.	0519	0619	0719	0819	0851	1019	1051	1219	1319	1419	1450	1519	1619	1719	1819	1851	...	2118	2118	...	...	...	...
Riesa .... d.	0547	0648	0747	0848	0947	1048	1147	1248	1347	1448	1520	1547	1648	1747	1848	1947	...	2147	2147	...	...	...	...
Leipzig Hbf .... a.	0621	0726	0821	0926	1021	1126	1221	1326	1421	1526	1554	1621	1726	1821	1926	2021	...	2219	2219	...	...	...	...
Frankfurt (Main) Hbf **850** ...... a.	...	1036	...	1236	...	1436	...	1636	...	1836	...	...	2036	...	2236	...	...	0347	0347	...	...	...	...
Wiesbaden Hbf **911** .... a.	...	1133	...	1333	...	1533	...	1733	...	1933	...	...	2133	...	...	...	...	...	...	...	...	...	...

RE services

km																							
		⚒		⚒																			
0	**Leipzig** Hbf .... d.	0400	0500	0600	0700	0800	0900		2200	...	2307	...	...	...	...	...	...	...	...	...	...	...	...
26	Wurzen .... d.	0418	0518	0618	0718	0818	0918	and	2218	...	2325	...	...	...	...	...	...	...	...	...	...	...	...
53	Oschatz .... d.	0436	0536	0636	0736	0836	0936		2236	...	2343	...	...	...	...	...	...	...	...	...	...	...	...
66	Riesa .... a.	0444	0544	0644	0744	0844	0944	hourly	2244	...	2352	...	...	...	...	...	...	...	...	...	...	...	...
66	Riesa .... d.	0455	0555	0655	0755	0855	0955		2255	...	2355	...	...	...	...	...	...	...	...	...	...	...	...
102	Coswig .... **843 856 857** d.	0525	0625	0725	0825	0925	1025	until	2325	...	0025	...	...	...	...	...	...	...	...	...	...	...	...
110	Radebeul Ost .... **857** d.	|	|	|	|	|	|		|	...	|	...	...	...	...	...	...	...	...	...	...	...	...
116	**Dresden** Neustadt ...... **856/7** a.	0534	0634	0734	0834	0934	1034		2334	...	0034	...	...	...	...	...	...	...	...	...	...	...	...
120	**Dresden** Hbf ⊡ **843 856 857** a.	0541	0641	0742	0841	0942	1041		2341	...	0041	...	...	...	...	...	...	...	...	...	...	...	...

	⚒		Ⓐ	⑥								Ⓐ	Ⓒ		Ⓐ	Ⓒ							
Dresden Hbf .... **843 856 857** d.	0409	0506	0606	0606	0706	0806	0906	1006	1106	1206	1306	1406	1406	1506	1606	1606	1706	1806	1906	2006	2106	2206	2306
Dresden Neustadt .... **856/7** d.	0416	0513	0613	0613	0713	0813	0913	1013	1113	1213	1313	1413	1413	1513	1613	1613	1713	1813	1913	2013	2113	2213	2313
Radebeul Ost .... **857** d.	0422	|	|	|	|	|	|	|	|	|	|	|	|	|	|	|	|	|	|	|	|	|	|
Coswig .... **843 856 857** d.	0429	0524	0624	0629r	0729r	0829r	0929r	1029r	1124	1229r	1324	1424	1429r	1524	1624	1629r	1724	1829r	1924	2029r	2124	2229r	2324
Riesa .... a.	0458	0554	0654	0658	0758	0858	0958	1058	1154	1258	1354	1454	1458	1554	1654	1658	1754	1858	1954	2058	2155	2258	2354
Riesa .... d.	0506	0606	0706	0706	0806	0906	1006	1106	1206	1306	1406	1506	1506	1606	1706	1706	1806	1906	2006	2106	2206	2306	0006
Oschatz .... d.	0514	0614	0714	0714	0814	0914	1014	1114	1214	1314	1414	1514	1514	1614	1714	1714	1814	1914	2014	2114	2214	2314	0014
Wurzen .... d.	0531	0631	0731	0731	0831	0931	1031	1131	1231	1331	1431	1531	1531	1631	1731	1731	1831	1931	2031	2131	2231	2331	0031
Leipzig Hbf .... a.	0550	0650	0750	0750	0850	0950	1050	1150	1250	1350	1450	1550	1550	1650	1750	1750	1850	1950	2050	2150	2250	2350	0050

E – From Eisenach (Table **850**) on ⑥.
G – [12] Dresden - Leipzig - Magdeburg - Hannover - Emden.
H – To / from Hannover (Table **866**).
K – To / from Köln via Hannover (Tables **800**, **810** and **866**).
M – From Magdeburg on Ⓐ (Table **866**).

T – ①②③④⑥⑦ to Mar. 16; daily from Mar. 18.
X – CANOPUS – 🛏 1, 2 cl. and 🛏 2 cl. Zürich - Basel - Leipzig - Dresden - Praha and v.v.
Y – CANOPUS – [2] Zürich - Basel - Leipzig - Dresden - Praha and v.v.; also conveys [1] and ✕ Leipzig - Dresden - Praha and v.v.

b – Not Dec. 25.
n – Not Dec. 24, 31.
r – Arrives 6 minutes earlier.
w – Also Dec. 26; not Dec. 25.

GERMANY

843 ELSTERWERDA - CHEMNITZ and DRESDEN; DÖBELN - LEIPZIG

RE / RB services

ELSTERWERDA - CHEMNITZ *Operated by Mitteldeutsche Regiobahn*

km																									
		Ⓐ		Ⓐ		Ⓐ		Ⓐ		Ⓐ		Ⓐ		Ⓐ		Ⓐ		Ⓐ		Ⓐ					
0	**Elsterwerda** d.	...	...	0513	...	0613	...	0713	0813	...	1013	...	1213	...	1413	1513	1613	1713	1813	1913	2013	...	...	...	2213
24	Riesa a.	...	...	0538	...	0638	...	0738	0838	...	1038	...	1238	...	1438	1538	1638	1738	1838	1938	2038	...	...	...	2238
24	Riesa d.	0449	...	0549	0549	0649	0649	0749	0849	0949	1049	1149	1249	1349	1449	1549	1649	1749	1849	1949	2049	...	2153	...	2253
50	Döbeln Hbf d.	0510	...	0610	0610	0710	0710	0810	0910	1010	1110	1210	1310	1410	1510	1610	1710	1810	1910	2010	2110	...	2218	...	2318
91	**Chemnitz** Hbf a.	0546	...	0646	0646	0746	0746	0846	0946	1046	1146	1246	1346	1446	1546	1646	1746	1846	1946	2046	2146	...	2258	...	2358

	Ⓐ			Ⓐ		Ⓐ		Ⓐ		Ⓐ		Ⓐ		Ⓐ		Ⓐ				Ⓐ			
Chemnitz Hbf d.	0409	...	0509	0509	0609	0707	0809	0909	1009	1109	1209	1309	1409	1509	1609	1709	1809	1909	2009	...	2137	2237	...	...
Döbeln Hbf d.	0447	...	0547	0547	0647	0747	0847	0947	1047	1147	1247	1347	1447	1547	1647	1747	1847	1947	2047	...	2219	2319	...	...
Riesa a.	0509	...	0609	0609	0709	0809	0909	1009	1109	1209	1309	1409	1509	1609	1709	1809	1909	2009	2109	...	2240	2340	...	...
Riesa d.	0515	...	...	0615	0715	...	0915	...	1115	...	1315	1415	1515	1615	1715	1815	1915	2015	...	...	2249	...	...	...
Elsterwerda a.	0537	...	...	0636	0737	...	0937	...	1137	...	1337	1436	1537	1636	1737	1836	1937	2036	...	...	2311	...	...	...

ELSTERWERDA - DRESDEN

km		Ⓐ		Ⓐ			
0	**Elsterwerda-Biehla** d.	0439	0539t	0639	0739	and every	2339
2	Elsterwerda d.	0443	0543	0643	0743	**two** hours	2343
41	Coswig ▷ d.	0522	0622	0722	0822	until	0022
59	**Dresden** Hbf ▷ a.	0543	0643	0743	0843		0043

		Ⓐ	ⒸA	B	ⒶA	ⒸA	B	ⒶA		⊠		
Dresden Hbf ▷ d.	0508	0608	0658	0708	0708	0858	0908	0908	1108	and every	2108	2308
Coswig ▷ d.	0531	0631	0721	0731	0742j	0921	0931	0942j	1131	**two** hours	2131	2331
Elsterwerda a.	0609	0709	0759	0809	0832	0959	1009	1032	1209	until	2209	0009
Esterwerda-Biehla a.	0613	0713	0803	0813	0836	1003	1013	1036	1213		2213	...

DÖBELN - LEIPZIG *Operated by Mitteldeutsche Regiobahn*

km		Ⓐ	Ⓐ		Ⓐ			Ⓐ		
0	**Döbeln** Hbf d.	0450	0550	0650	0750	and hourly	1850	1950	2050	...
13	Leisnig d.	0502	0602	0702	0802	on Ⓐ,	1902	2002	2102	...
28	Großbothen d.	0517	0617	0717	0817	every **two**	1917	2017	2117	...
35	Grimma ob Bf d.	0526	0626	0726	0826	hours on	1926	2026	2126	2308
66	**Leipzig** Hbf a.	0600	0700	0800	0900	Ⓒ until	2000	2100	2200	2342

	Ⓐ		Ⓐ				Ⓐ		
Leipzig Hbf d.	0506	0606	0706	and hourly	1806	1906	2006	2106	2206
Grimma ob Bf d.	0541	0641	0741	on Ⓐ,	1841	1941	2041	2139	2241
Großbothen d.	0547	0647	0747	every **two**	1847	1947	2047	...	2247
Leisnig d.	0604	0704	0804	hours on	1904	2004	2104		2301
Döbeln Hbf a.	0617	0717	0817	Ⓒ until	1917	2017	2117	...	2314

A – Until Apr. 21.
B – From Apr. 22.
j – Arrives 12 minutes earlier.
t – Ⓐ only.
⊠ – Additional service on Ⓐ: Dresden Hbf d. 1608, Coswig d. 1631, Elsterwerda a. 1709, Elsterwerda-Biehla a. 1713.
▷ – See also Tables **842**, **856**, **857**.

844 STRALSUND - OSTSEEBAD BINZ / SASSNITZ

Ostdeutsche Eisenbahn (except ICE / IC services)

km																								
														ICE 1049					*ICE* 1714				
		①–⑥ p		Ⓐ		Ⓐ	Ⓐ	Ⓐ						⑥C B					⑥ ♦				
	Rostock Hbf **830** d.	...	...	...	0454r	...	0553r	...	0700r	...	...	...	0900r	...	...	...	...	1100r	...	...	...	...	1300r	...
0	**Stralsund** Hbf d.	0000	...	0459	0559	...	0659	...	0759	...	0859	...	0959	...	1040	1059	...	1159	...	1240	1259	...	1359	...
29	Bergen auf Rügen d.	0030	...	0529	0629	...	0729	...	0829	...	0929	...	1029	...	1108	1129	...	1229	...	1305	1329	...	1429	...
39	Lietzow (Rügen) d.	0039	...	0538	0638	0641	0738	0741	0838	0841	0937	0939	1038	1041	|	1137	1139	1238	1241	|	1337	1339	1438	1441
	Ostseebad Binz a.	|	...	|	|	0655	|	0755	|	0855	0951	|	|	1055	1130	1151	|	|	1255	1328	1351	|	|	1455
51	**Sassnitz** a.	0054	...	0553	0653	...	0753	...	0853	...	...	0954	1053	...	...	...	1154	1253	...	...	...	1354	1453	...

	IC 2212	*ICE* 1043					*ICE* 1672	*ICE* 1710					*ICE* 759										
	♦	⑥ B					⚒ ♦	M					♦		Ⓐ	Ⓐ				Ⓐ	Ⓐ		
Rostock Hbf **830** d.	1338	...	...	...	1500r	...	1538	...	...	...	1700r	...	...	...	...	...	1900r	...	...	...	...	...	2100r	...
Stralsund Hbf d.	1440	1452	1459	...	1559	...	1632	1645	1659	...	1759	...	1812	...	1859	...	1959	...	...	2101	...	...	2159	...
Bergen auf Rügen d.	1506	1517	1529	...	1629	...	1656	1716	1729	...	1829	...	1838	...	1929	...	2029	...	...	2130	...	...	2229	...
Lietzow (Rügen) d.	|	|	1537	1539	1638	1641	|	|	1737	1739	1838	1841	|	...	1937	1939	2038	2041	...	2138	2140	...	2238	2241
Ostseebad Binz a.	1528	1537	1551	|	|	1655	1720	1735	1751	|	|	1855	1900	...	1951	|	|	2055	...	2153	|	...	|	2255
Sassnitz a.	...	...	...	1554	1653	...	...	...	...	1754	1853	...	...	...	...	1954	2053	...	...	...	2155	...	2253	...

km																								
												ICE 1050	*ICE* 1671			*ICE* 758			*ICE* 1711	*IC* 2213				
		Ⓐ				Ⓐ	①–⑥ p			Ⓐ	Ⓐ	B	♦			⑥ ♦			M	♦				
	Sassnitz d.	0352	...	0502	...	...	0602	...	0702	0759	...	...	...	...	0902	...	0959	...	...	...	1100	...	1159	...
0	**Ostseebad Binz** d.	|	...	|	...	0600	|	0700	|	|	0803	0819	0826	0900	|	0957	|	1003	1021	1043	|	1102	|	1203
12	Lietzow (Rügen) d.	0407	...	0517	...	0614	0617	0714	0717	0814	0818	0842	0855	0914	0917	|	1014	1018	|	|	1115	1119	1214	1218
22	Bergen auf Rügen d.	0416	...	0526	...	...	0626	...	0726	...	0827	|	|	...	0926	1018	...	1027	1042	1108	...	1128	...	1227
51	**Stralsund** Hbf a.	0446	...	0556	...	...	0656	...	0756	...	0857	0905	0921	...	0956	1047	...	1057	1109	1132	...	1158	...	1257
	Rostock Hbf **830** a.	0548r	...	0654r	...	...	...	...	0855r	...	...	...	1019	...	1055r	...	...	...	...	1239	...	1255r	...	...

	ICE 1040					*ICE* 1715																	
	⑥s B					⑥ M										Ⓐ	Ⓐ					Ⓐ	Ⓐ
Sassnitz d.	...	...	1302	1359	...	...	...	1502	1559	...	1659	...	1759	...	...	1902	1959	...	...	...	2102	...	2200	...
Ostseebad Binz d.	1219	1300	|	|	1403	1426	1500	|	|	1603	|	1702	|	1803	1900	|	|	2003	...	2100	|	...	|	2205
Lietzow (Rügen) d.	|	1314	1317	1414	1418	|	1514	1517	1614	1618	1714	1719	1814	1818	1914	1917	2014	2018	...	2114	2117	...	2215	2220
Bergen auf Rügen d.	1242	...	1326	...	1427	1449	...	1526	...	1627	...	1727	...	1827	...	1926	...	2027	...	...	2126	...	...	2229
Stralsund Hbf a.	1306	...	1356	...	1457	1514	...	1556	...	1657	...	1757	...	1857	...	1958	...	2057	...	...	2157	...	...	2258
Rostock Hbf **830** a.	...	...	1455r	...	...	...	...	1655r	...	1801r	...	1855r	...	...	...	2055r	...	...	...	...	2255r	...	...	...

♦ – NOTES (LISTED BY TRAIN NUMBER)

758/9 – [12] ✕ Ostseebad Binz - Berlin - Hannover - Köln and v.v.
1671 – Until Mar. 3. [12] ✕ Ostseebad Binz - Hamburg - Frankfurt - Karlsruhe.
1672 – ⚒ until Mar. 3. [12] ✕ Karlsruhe - Frankfurt - Hamburg - Ostseebad Binz.
1714 – POMMERSCHE BUCHT – [12] ✕ Jena - Leipzig - Berlin - Ostseebad Binz.
2212 – Until Mar. 3. RÜGEN – [12] 🍷 Koblenz - Köln - Hamburg - Ostseebad Binz.
2213 – Until Mar. 3. RÜGEN – [12] 🍷 Ostseebad Binz - Hamburg - Köln.

B – From / to Berlin (Table **845**).
C – ⑥ from Mar. 4.
M – [12] ✕ Ostseebad Binz - Berlin - Nürnberg - München and v.v.
p – Not Dec. 26, Apr. 7 – 10, May 1, 18.
r – Subject to alteration Mar. 4 - Apr. 14 (see special version of Table **830** on page 561).

844a BERGEN AUF RÜGEN - PUTBUS - LAUTERBACH and RÜGENSCHE BÄDERBAHN

Preßnitztalbahn

km		Ⓐ	Ⓐ	Ⓐ	Ⓒ						
0	**Bergen** auf Rügen d.	0640	0740	0840	0940	1040	1240	and	1740	1840	2040
10	**Putbus** a.	0649	0749	0849	0949	1049	1249	hourly	1749	1849	2049
12	**Lauterbach** Mole a.	0654	0754	0854	0954	1054	1254	until	1754	1854	...

	Ⓐ	Ⓐ	Ⓐ		Ⓒ					
Lauterbach Mole d.	0600	0700	0800	0900	1000	1100	1300	and	1800	1900
Putbus d.	0611	0711	0811	0911	1011	1111	1311	hourly	1811	1911
Bergen auf Rügen a.	0620	0720	0820	0920	1020	1120	1320	until	1820	1920

RÜGENSCHE BÄDERBAHN **SERVICE UNTIL MAY 17, 2023**. Steam train service. Please note that Binz Lokalbahn station is situated 2½ km from Ostseebad Binz DB station.

km											
0	**Lauterbach** Mole d.	...	...	...	...	...	...	...	...	...	...
2	**Putbus** a.	...	...	...	...	...	...	...	...	...	...
2	**Putbus** d.	0808	1008	1208	1408	1608	1808	...	...	...	...
14	Binz Lokalbahn d.	0840	1040	1240	1440	1640	1840	...	...	...	...
22	Sellin (Rügen) Ost d.	0909	1109	1309	1509	1709	1909	...	...	...	...
27	**Göhren** (Rügen) a.	0923	1123	1323	1523	1723	1923	...	...	...	...

Göhren (Rügen) d.	0953	1153	1353	1553	1753	1953	...	...	...	...
Sellin (Rügen) Ost d.	1011	1211	1411	1611	1811	2011	...	...	...	...
Binz Lokalbahn d.	1040	1240	1440	1640	1840	2040	...	...	...	...
Putbus a.	1106	1306	1506	1706	1906	2106	...	...	...	...
Putbus d.	...	...	...	...	...	...	...	...	...	...
Lauterbach Mole a.	...	...	...	...	...	...	...	...	...	...

RE services except where shown — BERLIN - ANGERMÜNDE - STRALSUND and SZCZECIN — 845

km			©		⚒		ICE 1179 ⚒V D	⚒		■		●			ICE 1049 ⑥U ✕		G		🚌	ICE 1714 ⑥ B✕	●		ICE 1043 ⑥ ✕	
	Berlin Südkreuz d.	0028	...	...	...	...	...	...	...	0521	...	0623	0721	...	0737	...	0824	0920	...	0924	1023	1119z	...	...
	Berlin Spandau d.	|	...	...	...	...	...	...	...	|	...	|	|	...	|	...	|	|	...	|	|	|	...	...
0	**Berlin** Hbf d.	0036	0203	...	...	...	...	...	0426	0532	...	0633	0731	...	0744	...	0833	0931	...	0942	1033	1133	1144	...
4	**Berlin** Gesundbrunnen d.	0043	0209	...	...	...	...	...	0433	0538	...	0639	0738	...	0750	0806	0839	0938	...	0950	1039	1139	1150	...
25	Bernau (b. Berlin) d.	0057	0223	...	...	...	...	...	0448	0553	...	0654	0753	...	|	0824	0854	0953	...	1005	1054	1153	1206	...
47	Eberswalde Hbf d.	0115	0243	...	...	...	...	...	0509	0609	...	0709	0809	...	0822	0839	0909	1009	...	1023	1109	1209	1223	...
73	Angermünde a.	...	...	...	...	...	...	...	0528	0629	...	0728	0829	...	0838	0854	0928	1029	...	1038	1128	1229	1240	...
	Angermünde d.	...	...	...	...	...	...	*0436**	0533	0634	*0636**	0733	0834	*0836**	0840	...	0933	1034	1036	1040	1133	1234	1242	1252
96	**Schwedt** (Oder) a.	...	...	...	...	...	...	|	|	0656	|	|	0856	|	|	...	|	1056	|	|	|	1256	|	|
	Passow d.	...	...	...	...	...	...	0510	|	▬	0710	|	...	0910	|	...	|	...	1100	|	|	▬	|	1310
113	Tantow d.	...	...	...	...	...	...	0532	|	...	0732	|	...	0932	|	...	|	...	1142	|	|	...	|	1332
132	Szczecin Gumience ▦ d.	...	...	...	...	...	...	0544	|	...	0744	|	...	0944	|	...	|	...	1207	|	|	...	|	1344
137	**Szczecin** Główny a.	...	...	...	...	...	...	0552	|	...	0752	|	...	0952	|	...	|	...	1221	|	|	...	|	1352
	Prenzlau d.	...	...	...	...	...	...	...	0601	...	...	0801	...	▬	0903	...	1001	...	▬	1104	1201	...	1305	...
	Pasewalk d.	...	...	...	0418	...	...	...	0619	...	...	0818	...	...	0919	...	1018	...	...	1120	1218	...	1321	...
	Anklam d.	...	...	...	0451	...	...	...	0650	...	...	0851	...	Ⓑ	0945	...	1051	...	Ⓑ	1146	1251	...	1347	...
	Züssow d.	...	...	...	0505	0553	...	...	0704	0747	...	0905	...	0953	0957	...	1105	...	1151	1158	1305	1348	1359	...
	Greifswald d.	...	...	0413	0523	0609	0659	...	0726j	0808j	...	0921	...	1008	1010	...	1121	...	1209	1212	1321	1402	1414	...
	Stralsund Hbf a.	...	...	0442	0545	0634	0725	...	0750	0834	...	0945	...	1038	1032	...	1145	...	1235	1234	1345	1429	1440	...
	Ostseebad Binz **844** a.	...	...	...	...	...	...	...	...	...	...	...	...	...	1130	...	...	...	...	1328	...	...	1537	...

	●			ICE 1710 J✕		●	ICE 759 K✕			●				ICE 1055 L✕	●		●		⑦–④ n●	⑤⑥ d●	⑦–④ n	⑦ w		
Berlin Südkreuz d.	1223	1319	...	1324	...	1423	...	1519	...	1623	...	1721	...	...	1823	1921k	2023	2119z	2223	2223	...	...	...	...
Berlin Spandau d.	|	|	...	|	...	|	1439	|	...	|	...	|	...	1739	|	|	|	|	|	|	...	...	...	...
Berlin Hbf d.	1233	1331	...	1341	...	1433	1514	1531	...	1633	...	1731	...	1814	1833	1941	2033	2133	2233	2233	...	...	...	2332
Berlin Gesundbrunnen d.	1239	1338	...	1348	1414	1439	1521	1538	...	1639	1721	1738	...	1821	1839	1947	2039	2139	2239	2239	...	...	...	2339
Bernau (b. Berlin) d.	1254	1353	...	1404	1436	1454	1536	1552	...	1654	1737	1753	...	1836	1854	2001	2054	2153	2253	2253	...	...	...	2354
Eberswalde Hbf d.	1309	1409	...	1419	1452	1509	1552	1609	...	1709	1752	1809	...	1852	1909	2016	2109	2214	2313	2313	...	...	...	0013
Angermünde a.	1328	1429	...	1434	1506	1528	1607	1628	...	1728	1807	1829	...	|	1928	2034	2128	2234	2332	2331	...	...	...	...
Angermünde d.	1333	1434	*1436**	1436	...	1533	1609	1634	*1636**	1733	...	1834	*1836**	|	1933	2036	2133	2236	2334	2334	2340	2340	2344	...
Schwedt (Oder) a.	|	1456	|	|	...	|	|	1656	|	|	...	1856	|	|	|	2058	|	2258	2357	|	|	|	|	...
Passow d.	|	▬	1510	|	...	|	|	▬	1710	|	...	▬	1910	|	|	▬	|	...	...	|	|	|	0002	...
Tantow d.	|	...	1532	|	...	|	|	...	1732	|	...	...	1932	|	|	...	|	...	...	|	|	|	0024	...
Szczecin Gumience ▦ d.	|	...	1544	|	...	|	|	...	1744	|	...	...	1944	|	|	...	|	...	...	|	|	|	0036	...
Szczecin Główny a.	|	...	1552	|	...	|	|	...	1752	|	...	...	1952	|	|	...	|	...	...	|	|	|	0044	...
Prenzlau d.	1401	...	▬	1500	...	1601	1632	...	...	1801	...	...	...	1930	2001	...	2201	...	...	0003	0008	0008	...	...
Pasewalk d.	1418	...	...	1517	...	1618	1649	...	...	1818	...	...	...	1947	2018	...	2218	...	...	0018	0024	0026	...	...
Anklam d.	1451	⑤	X	1546	...	1651	1716	Ⓐ	...	1851	...	...	...	2013	2051	...	2251	...	...	...	...	0057	...	...
Züssow d.	1505	1536	1547	1558	...	1705	1729	1757	...	1905	...	1952	...	|	2105	2153	2305	...	...	...	...	0111	...	...
Greifswald d.	1521	1602j	1602	1615	...	1727j	1743	1814	...	1921	...	2008	...	2036	2121	2209	2321	...	...	...	...	0126	...	...
Stralsund Hbf a.	1547	1628	1628	1639	...	1749	1806	1842	...	1945	...	2040	...	2058	2145	2236	2345	...	...	...	...	0149	...	...
Ostseebad Binz **844** a.	...	...	...	1735	...	...	1900	...	...	...	...	...	...	...	...	...	...	...	...	...	...	...	...	...

km			⚒	●	①g	Ⓐ	⚒				●		ICE 1044 ①–④ m✕		●			ICE 1050 ✕	Ⓑ	●		ICE 758 ⑥ K✕	ICE 1711 J✕	
	Ostseebad Binz **844** d.	...	...	...	...	...	...	...	...	...	...	...	...	...	...	...	...	0819	...	...	...	0957	1021	...
0	**Stralsund** Hbf d.	...	...	...	0353	...	0417	...	0519	...	...	0617	0705	0722	...	0815	...	0915	0932	...	1015	1054	1120	1123
31	Greifswald d.	...	...	...	0413	...	0439	...	0546	...	...	0639	0737r	0750	...	0839	...	0946	0957	...	1039	1115	1145	1157
49	Züssow d.	...	...	...	0427	...	0455	...	0600	...	...	0655	0753	0804	...	0855	...	1001	1010	...	1055	1128	1157	1210
66	Anklam d.	...	...	...	0438	...	0508	...	▬	...	...	0708	0807	▬	...	0908	...	1013	▬	...	1108	1139	1209	▬
109	**Pasewalk** d.	...	...	...	0505	0505	0544j	0544	...	...	...	0744j	0837	...	...	0944j	...	1039	...	...	1144j	1206	1238	...
133	Prenzlau d.	...	...	...	0522	0522	0601	0601	...	...	...	0801	0853	...	...	1001	...	1055	...	...	1201	1223	1255	🚌
	Szczecin Główny d.	...	0411	...	|	|	|	|	...	0611	...	|	|	0811	...	|	...	|	1011	...	|	|	|	1141
	Szczecin Gumience ▦ d.	...	0418	...	|	|	|	|	...	0618	...	|	|	0818	...	|	...	|	1018	...	|	|	|	1155
	Tantow d.	...	0433	...	|	|	|	|	...	0633	...	|	|	0833	...	|	...	|	1033	...	|	|	|	1220
	Passow a.	...	0454	...	|	|	|	|	...	0654	...	|	|	0854	...	|	...	|	1054	...	|	|	|	1302
	Schwedt (Oder) d.	...	|	0506	|	|	|	|	...	|	0706	|	|	|	0906	|	...	|	|	1106	|	|	|	|
170	Angermünde a.	...	*0526**	0528	0548	0548	0628	0628	...	*0726**	0728	0828	0914	*0926**	0928	1028	...	1116	1115	1129	1228	1244	1316	1326
170	Angermünde d.	0427t	...	0533	0550	0550	0633	0633	0701	...	0733	0833	0916	...	0933	1033	1101	1118	...	1133	1233	1246	1318	...
196	Eberswalde Hbf d.	0448	...	0553	0610	0610	0654	0654	0720	...	0753	0854	0933	...	0953	1054	1120	1136	...	1154	1254	1303	1335	...
218	Bernau (b. Berlin) d.	0509	...	0607	0627	0627	0708	0708	0735	...	0807	0908	|	...	1007	1108	1136	|	...	1208	1308	|	|	...
239	**Berlin** Gesundbrunnen a.	0522	...	0621	0643	0643	0722	0722	0751	...	0821	0922	0958	...	1021	1121	1152	1208	...	1221	1322	1330	1407	...
243	**Berlin** Hbf a.	0528	...	0628	0651	0651	0728	0728	...	...	0828	0928	1009	...	1028	1126	...	1217	...	1228	1328	1338	1416	...
	Berlin Spandau a.	|	...	|	|	|	|	|	...	...	|	|	|	...	|	|	...	...	...	|	|	1403	|	...
249	**Berlin** Südkreuz a.	0541	...	0639	0702	0702	0742	0742	...	...	0839	0942	1018	...	1039	1142	...	...	...	1239	1342	...	1434	...

	●		ICE 1040 ⑥s ✕	①–⑥	●		ICE 750 ⑤⑦w K✕	Ⓑ	ICE 1715 ⑥ J✕		●		ICE 1132 ⑦w A✕	⚒	●		ICE 1074 ⒷY D	①–⑥	⑦	●		①–⑥ d	⑤⑥ d	⑦ n
Ostseebad Binz **844** d.	...	...	1219	...	...	...	...	...	1426	...	...	...	...	...	...	...	...	...	...	...	...	...	...	...
Stralsund Hbf d.	...	1217c	1320	1333	...	1417	1505	1517	1521	...	...	1617	1703	1658	...	1817	1831	1927	1938	2010	2118	2217	2217	2238
Greifswald d.	...	1239	1345	1357	...	1439	1526	1550	1546	...	...	1639	1724	1727	...	1839	1850	1950	2002	2039	2147	2239	2239	2300
Züssow d.	...	1255	1358	1410	...	1455	1546	1604	1600	...	...	1655	|	1741	...	1855	▬	2004	2016	2055	2200	2255	2255	2316
Anklam d.	...	1308	1410	▬	...	1508	1558	...	1612	...	...	1708	1745	▬	...	1908	...	▬	▬	2108	▬	2308	2308	2329
Pasewalk d.	...	1344j	1437	...	...	1544j	1624	...	1638	...	...	1744j	1811	...	...	1944j	...	...	...	2144j	...	2338	2344	2359
Prenzlau d.	...	1401	1453	...	...	1601	1640	...	1655	...	...	1801	1827	...	...	2001	...	...	...	2201	...	▬	0001	...
Szczecin Główny d.	...	|	|	1411	...	|	|	...	|	1611	...	|	|	1811	...	|	...	...	2110	|	...	...	|	...
Szczecin Gumience ▦ d.	...	|	|	1418	...	|	|	...	|	1618	...	|	|	1818	...	|	...	...	2116	|	...	...	|	...
Tantow d.	...	|	|	1433	...	|	|	...	|	1633	...	|	|	1833	...	|	...	...	2130	|	...	⑤⑥	|	...
Passow a.	...	|	|	1454	...	|	|	...	|	1654	...	|	|	1854	...	|	...	●	2151	|	...	d H	|	...
Schwedt (Oder) d.	1306	|	|	|	1506	|	|	...	|	|	1706	|	|	|	1906	|	...	2106	|	|	2306	2306	|	...
Angermünde a.	1328	1428	1515	*1526**	1528	1628	1701	...	1717	*1726**	1728	1828	|	*1926**	1928	2028	...	2128	2210	2228	2328	2328	0028	...
Angermünde d.	1333	1433	1517	...	1533	1633	1703	...	1719	...	1733	1833	|	...	1933	2033	2046	2133	...	2233	2333	2333	0033	...
Eberswalde Hbf d.	1353	1454	1534	...	1553	1654	1720	...	1736	...	1753	1854	1906	...	1953	2054	2104	2153	...	2254	2353	2353	0054	...
Bernau (b. Berlin) d.	1407	1508	|	...	1607	1708	1734	...	1753	...	1808	1908	|	...	2007	2108	2118	2207	...	2313	0007	0007	0113	...
Berlin Gesundbrunnen a.	1421	1522	1601	...	1621	1722	1749	...	1807	...	1822	1921	1936	...	2021	2121	2134	2221	...	2327	0021	0021	0127	...
Berlin Hbf a.	1428	1528	1614	...	1628	1728	|	...	1816	...	1829	1927	|	...	2028	2126	...	2228	...	2332	0027	0027	0134	...
Berlin Spandau a.	|	|	|	...	|	|	1810	...	|	...	|	|	1951	...	|	|	...	|	...	|	...	|	...	...
Berlin Südkreuz a.	1439	1542	1628	...	1639	1742	...	...	1834	...	1839	1941	...	...	2039	2142z	...	2238	...	2341	...	0049	...	...

A – To Hannover (Table **810**).
B – POMMERSCHE BUCHT – (12) ✕ Nürnberg - Leipzig - Berlin - Ostseebad Binz.
D – To/from Hamburg (Table **830**).
G – From/to Lutherstadt Wittenberg (Table **851**). Starts from Halle on © (Table **848**).
H – To Halle (Table **848**).
J – (12) ✕ Ostseebad Binz - Berlin - Leipzig - München and v.v.
K – From/to Köln (Tables **800** and **810**).
L – From Köln (Tables **800** and **810**) on ⑤⑦ (also Dec. 26; not Dec. 25).
U – ⑥ from Mar. 4.
V – Until Mar. 3. Train number **1579** on ⑥.

X – ①②③④⑥.
Y – Until Mar. 2.

c – 1212 on ⑥.
d – Also Dec. 25.
g – Also Dec. 27; not Dec. 26.
j – Arrives 6–7 minutes earlier.
k – ⑥ only.
m – Also Mar. 31; not Dec. 26.
n – Not Dec. 25.

r – Arrives 0725.
s – Also Mar. 31.
t – Ⓐ only.
w – Also Dec. 26; not Dec. 25.
z – © only.

* – By 🚌 to/from Passow.
● – From/to Lutherstadt Wittenberg (Table **851**).
■ – From Jüterbog (also Falkenberg on ©). See Table **851**.

846 ZÜSSOW - ŚWINOUJŚCIE *2nd class only*

km				⊠		⊗							①–⑥	⑦
0	**Züssow** d.	...	0508		1506	1608	1708	1808	1908	2008	2108	2208	2308	2320
18	Wolgast d.	0430	0530	and	1530	1630	1730	1830	1930	2030	2130	2230	2330	2338
28	Zinnowitz ▲ d.	0449	0549	hourly	1549	1649	1749	1849	1949	2049	2149	2249	2349	2355
55	Seebad Heringsdorf a.	0525	0625		1625	1725	1825	1925	2025	2125	2225	2325	0025	0028
57	Seebad Ahlbeck a.	0534	0634	until	1634	1734	1834	*1934*	2034	*2134*	2234	...	...	...
61	**Świnoujście** Centrum a.	0539	0639		1639	1739	1839	*1939*	2039	*2139*	2239	...	...	...

			Ⓐ	Ⓒ		✣								
Świnoujście Centrum d.	...	0518	0555	0618	0718		1618	1718	1818	1918	2018	2118	2218	2318
Seebad Ahlbeck d.	...	0524	0601	0624	0724	and	1624	1724	1824	1924	2024	2124	2224	2324
Seebad Heringsdorf d.	0433	0533	0610	0633	0733	hourly	1633	1733	1833	1933	2033	2133	2233	2328
Zinnowitz ▲ d.	0511	0611	0650	0711	0811		1711	1811	1911	2011	2111	2211	2311	...
Wolgast d.	0530	0630	0726j	0726	0830	until	1730	1830	1930	2030	2130	2230	2325	...
Züssow a.	0548	0648	0744	0744	0848		1748	1848	1948	2048	2148	2248	...	...

j – Arrives 0704.

⊠ – Züssow d. 1013 / 1213 / 1413 (not xx08). On ⑥ from May 13 Züssow d. 1106 (not 1108).

⊗ – Change trains at Seebad Heringsdorf from May 13.

✣ – Wolgast d. 0926 / 1326 / 1526 (not xx30). Züssow a. 0944 / 1050 / 1250 / 1344 / 1450 / 1542 (not xx48). On ⑥ from May 13 Wolgast d. 1126 (not 1130), Züssow a. 1144 (not 1148).

▲ – **Zinnowitz - Peenemünde** (*12 km*, journey 14 minutes). **From Zinnowitz** at 0434 Ⓐ, 0513 Ⓐ, 0613, 0659 Ⓐ, 0713 Ⓒ, 0813, 0913 and hourly until 2113. **From Peenemünde** at 0453 Ⓐ, 0532 Ⓐ, 0632, 0718 Ⓐ, 0732 Ⓒ, 0832, 0932 and hourly until 2132.

847 BERLIN - DESSAU *RE services*

km		Ⓐ			Ⓐ					
0	**Berlin** Ostbahnhof d.	0402	0502		2002	2102	2202	2302	0016	...
5	**Berlin** Hbf d.	0414	0514	then hourly	2014	2114	2214	2314	0028	...
9	**Berlin** Zoo d.	0420	0520	on Ⓐ,	2020	2120	2220	2320	0034	...
24	Berlin Wannsee d.	0434	0534	every **two**	2034	2134	2234	2334	0047	...
33	Potsdam Rehbrücke d.	0443	0543	hours on Ⓒ	2043	2143	2243	2343	0056	...
76	Bad Belzig d.	0519	0619	until	2119	2219	2317	0019	0131	...
120	Roßlau (Elbe) **848** d.	0548	0648		2148	2248	...	0048	...	...
125	**Dessau** Hbf **848** a.	0553	0653		2153	2253	...	0053	...	...

	Ⓐ			Ⓐ			Ⓐ		
Dessau Hbf **848** d.	0405	0505		2005	2105	...	2205	...	2318
Roßlau (Elbe) **848** d.	0410	0510	then hourly	2010	2110	...	2210	...	2323
Bad Belzig d.	0442	0542	on Ⓐ,	2042	2142	2242	2242	...	2354
Potsdam Rehbrücke d.	0516	0616	every **two**	2116	2216	2316	2316	...	0029
Berlin Wannsee d.	0525	0625	hours on Ⓒ	2125	2225	2325	2325	...	0038
Berlin Zoo a.	0539	0639	until	2139	2239	2339	2339	...	0051
Berlin Hbf a.	0544	0644		2144	2244	2344	2344	...	0057
Berlin Ostbahnhof a.	0556	0656		2156	2256	2356	2356	...	0109

847a FLUGHAFEN BERLIN BRANDENBURG ✈ - BERLIN *RE / RB services*

	n																							②–⑦	
Flughafen Berlin ✈ **837** d.	0002	0040	0139	0240	0344	0425	0444	0458	0513	0528	0544	0558	0613	0628	0644	0658	and at	2213	2228	2244	2258	2313	2328	2344
Berlin Ostkreuz **837** a.	0018	0056	0156	0256	0401	0442	0501	0515	0529	0546	0601	0615	0629	0645	0701	0715	the same	2229	2245	2301	2315	2329	2345	2400
Berlin Ostbahnhof **837** a.	0023	0102	0202	0302	0406	|	0506	|	0534	|	0606	|	0634	|	0706	|	minutes	2234	|	2306	|	2334	|	0004
Berlin Gesundbrunnen a.	|	|	|	|	|	0455	|	0527	|	0557	|	0627	|	0656	|	0727	past each	|	2256	|	2327	|	2356	|
Berlin Hbf **837** a.	0033	0113	0213	0313	0417	0503	0517	0533	0548	0603	0618	0633	0648	0703	0718	0733	hour until	2246	2303	2317	2336	2345	0003	0015
Berlin Zoo **837** a.	0039	0120	0220	0320	0424	...	0524	...	0555	...	0625	...	0655	...	0725	...		2253	...	2324	...	2352	...	0022

															⊠							②–⑦		②–⑦
Berlin Zoo **837** d.	0141	0239	0323	...	...	0433	...	0501	...	0527	...	0604	...	0633	and at	...	2104	...	2133	...	2204	...	2305	...
Berlin Hbf **837** d.	0147	0245	0329	0351	0421	0440	0451	0507	0521	0532	0551	0610	0621	0640	the same	2051	2110	2121	2140	2154	2210	2221	2311	2321
Berlin Gesundbrunnen d.	|	|	|	0400	0429	|	0500	|	0529	|	0600	|	0629	|	minutes	2100	|	2129	|	2200	|	2229	|	2329
Berlin Ostbahnhof **837** d.	0159	0256	0340	|	|	0453	|	0518	|	0544	|	0621	|	0653	past each	|	2121	|	2153	|	2221	|	2322	|
Berlin Ostkreuz **837** d.	0203	0300	0343	0412	0441	0457	0512	0523	0541	0551	0612	0626	0641	0657	hour until	2112	2126	2141	2158	2212	2226	2241	2327	2341
Flughafen Berlin ✈ **837** a.	0221	0316	0400	0430	0500	0515	0530	0546	0600	0610	0630	0646	0700	0715		2130	2146	2200	2215	2230	2246	2300	2347	2400

n – Not ②.

⊠ – Berlin Hbf d. 1218 / 1618 / 2018 (not 1221 / 1621 / 2021).

848 MAGDEBURG - DESSAU - LEIPZIG and HALLE (SAALE) *RE / RB / S-Bahn services*

SERVICE TO JANUARY 27 AND FROM APRIL 22. See page 562 for amended service January 28 - April 21.

km		Ⓐ								
0	**Magdeburg** Hbf d.	0427	0517	0615j	0717	and	2017	2112	2202	2317
56	Roßlau (Elbe) **847** d.	0510	0605	0705	0805		2105	2153	2252	0005
61	**Dessau** Hbf **847** d.	0518	0611	0711	0811	hourly	2111	2158	2258	0009
87	Bitterfeld a.	0541	0628	0728	0828		2128	2221	2318	...
87	Bitterfeld d.	0545	0631	0731	0831	until	2131	2222	2319	...
120	**Leipzig** Hbf a.	0613	0656	0756	0856		2159	2245	2346	...

	Ⓐ			Ⓐ			◇			
Leipzig Hbf d.	...	...	0502	...	0602	0704	and	2004	*2048*	2218
Bitterfeld a.	...	...	0523	...	0625	0725		2025	*2115*	2247
Bitterfeld d.	...	0418t	0527	...	0627	0727	hourly	2027	2118	2249
Dessau Hbf **847** d.	0358	0448	0548	0627	0648	0748		2048	2148	2314
Roßlau (Elbe) **847** d.	0403	0453	0553	0632	0653	0753	until	2053	2153	2318
Magdeburg Hbf a.	0452	0542	0642	0723	0742	0842		2142	2234	0007

DESSAU / LUTHERSTADT WITTENBERG - BITTERFELD - HALLE / LEIPZIG

	ⒸB	Ⓒ			Ⓐ	Ⓒ	Ⓐ	Ⓐ		Ⓑ	⑥	Ⓐ	Ⓐ			Ⓐ	Ⓐr								
Lutherstadt Wittenberg d.	0159	...	...	...	...	0413	0413	0440	...	...	0503	0537	...	...	0603	0616	...	...	0703	0803	...	...	0903	1003	...
Dessau Hbf d.	0224	...	...	0416	...	|	0449	|	0518	...	|	|	0547	0617	|	0649	...	0719	|	|	0819	0919	|	|	1019
Bitterfeld a.	0240	...	...	0439	...	0441	0511	0508	0541	...	0540	0611	0609	0640	0643	0711	...	0742	0740	0843	0842	0942	0940	1043	1042
Bitterfeld d.	0241	0247	...	0446	0442	0445	0512	0516	0545	0546	0547	0612	0616	0646	0645	0712	0716	0745	0747	0845	0847	0945	0947	1045	1047
Leipzig Hbf a.	|	0314	...	|	0513	0513	0543	|	0613	|	|	0643	|	|	0713	0743	|	0813	|	0913	|	1013	|	1113	|
Leipzig-Stötteritz ♥ a.	|	0326	...	|	0527	0527	0557	|	0627	|	|	0657	|	|	0727	0757	|	0827	|	0927	|	1027	|	1127	|
Halle (Saale) Hbf a.	0258	...	...	0507	...	...	...	0537	...	0607	0607	...	0637	0708	...	...	0737	...	0807	...	0907	...	1007	...	1107

													Ⓐ												
Lutherstadt Wittenberg d.	...	1103	1204	...	...	1303	1403	...	...	1503	1604	...	...	...	1703	1803	...	...	1903	2017	...	...	2103	2217	...
Dessau Hbf d.	1119	|	|	1219	1319	|	|	1417	1519	|	|	1619	1649	1719	|	|	1819	1919	|	|	2019	2119	|	|	*2258*
Bitterfeld a.	1142	1140	1243	1242	1342	1340	1443	1440	1542	1540	1643	1642	1711	1742	1740	1843	1842	1942	1940	2044	2042	2142	2140	2244	*2318*
Bitterfeld d.	1145	1147	1245	1247	1345	1347	1445	1447	1545	1547	1645	1647	1712	1745	1747	1845	1847	1945	1947	2045	2047	2145	2147	2247	2324
Leipzig Hbf a.	1213	|	1313	|	1413	|	1513	|	1613	|	1713	|	1743	1813	|	1913	|	2013	|	2113	|	2213	|	|	|
Leipzig-Stötteritz ♥ a.	1227	|	1327	|	1427	|	1527	|	1627	|	1727	|	1757	1827	|	1927	|	2027	|	2127	|	2227	|	|	|
Halle (Saale) Hbf a.	...	1207	...	1307	...	1407	...	1507	...	1607	...	1707	...	...	1807	...	1907	...	2007	...	2107	...	2207	2307	2345

	Ⓒ	Ⓒ	Ⓐ		Ⓐ	Ⓐ			Ⓐ	ⒸA	Ⓐ		Ⓐ												
Halle (Saale) Hbf d.	0026	...	...	...	0355	0355	0452	...	...	0551	0553	...	...	0652	...	0752	...	0852	...	0952	...	1052	...	1152	...
Leipzig-Stötteritz ♥ d.	|	0006	0006	...	|	|	|	0434	0504	|	|	0534	0604	|	0634	|	0734	|	0834	|	0934	|	1034	|	1134
Leipzig Hbf d.	|	0020	0020	...	|	|	|	0448	0518	|	|	0548	0618	|	0648	|	0748	|	0848	|	0948	|	1048	|	1148
Bitterfeld a.	0046	0046	0047	...	0416	0416	0513	0515	0548	0614	0613	0615	0647	0713	0715	0813	0815	0913	0915	1013	1015	1113	1115	1213	1215
Bitterfeld d.	0051	0051	...	...	0418	0421	0518	0516	0550	0620	0620	0618	0648	0718	0716	0820	0818	0918	0916	1020	1018	1118	1116	1220	1218
Dessau Hbf a.	|	0114	...	...	0442	|	0542	|	0613	|	|	0642	0708	0742	|	|	0842	0942	|	|	1042	1142	|	|	1242
Lutherstadt Wittenberg a.	0120	...	...	...	...	0450	...	0550	0654	0658	0654	...	0742	...	0757	0854	...	...	0957	1054	...	...	1157	1254	...

			Ⓐ	Ⓒ						Ⓐ															
Halle (Saale) Hbf d.	1252	...	1350	1352	...	1452	...	1552	...	...	1652	...	1752	...	1852	...	1950	...	2052	...	2150	...	...	2326	...
Leipzig-Stötteritz ♥ d.	|	1234	|	|	1334	|	1434	|	1534	1604	|	1634	|	1734	|	1834	|	1934	|	2034	|	2134	2204	|	2306
Leipzig Hbf d.	|	1248	|	|	1348	|	1448	|	1548	1618	|	1648	|	1748	|	1848	|	1948	|	2048	|	2148	2218	|	2320
Bitterfeld a.	1313	1315	1410	1413	1415	1513	1515	1613	1615	1647	1713	1715	1813	1815	1913	1915	2013	2015	2113	2115	2211	2215	2247	2346	2346
Bitterfeld d.	1318	1316	1420	1420	1418	1518	1516	1620	1618	1648	1718	1716	1820	1818	1918	1916	2020	2018	2118	2116	2220	2218	2249	2351	2351
Dessau Hbf a.	1342	|	|	|	1442	1542	|	|	1642	1708	1742	|	|	1842	1942	|	|	2042	2142	|	|	2242	2312	0015	|
Lutherstadt Wittenberg a.	...	1357	1454	1454	...	...	1556	1654	...	1742	...	1756	1854	...	...	1957	2054	...	...	2157	2254	...	...	...	0020

LUTHERSTADT WITTENBERG - DESSAU

km		Ⓐ	Ⓐ	Ⓒ	Ⓐ	⚒	Ⓐ				Ⓐ			Ⓐ									
0	**Lutherstadt Wittenberg** d.	0413	0502	0516	0557	0616	0652	0716	and	1416	1452	1516	1616	1652	1716	1816	1916	2016	...	2216	...	...	...
32	Roßlau (Elbe) d.	0441	0532	0544	0626	0644	0717	0744	hourly	1444	1517	1544	1644	1717	1744	1844	1944	2044	...	2244	...	...	...
37	**Dessau** Hbf a.	0445	0536	0548	0631	0647	0721	0748	until	1448	1521	1548	1648	1721	1748	1848	1948	2048	...	2248	...	...	...

	Ⓐ		Ⓐ		⚒				Ⓐ		Ⓐ		Ⓐ		Ⓐ									
Dessau Hbf d.	0422	0509	0622	0710	0810	0910	and	1410	1435	1510	1532	1610	1635	1710	1732	1810	1910	2010	2110	...	2300	...	...	...
Roßlau (Elbe) d.	0426	0514	0626	0714	0814	0914	hourly	1414	1440	1514	1537	1614	1640	1714	1737	1814	1914	2014	2114	...	2304	...	...	...
Lutherstadt Wittenberg a.	0454	0541	0654	0742	0842	0942	until	1442	1505	1542	1602	1642	1705	1742	1802	1842	1942	2042	2142	...	2332	...	...	...

A – To Stralsund via Berlin (Tables **851** / **845**).

B – From Schwedt via Berlin (Tables **845** / **851**).

j – 0617 on Ⓒ.

r – Not Jan. 6.

t – Ⓐ only.

◇ – On ⑦ from Apr. 23 (also May 1, 29; not Apr. 30, May 28) the 1604 from Leipzig is retimed as follows: Leipzig Hbf d. 1546, Bitterfeld a. 1607, d. 1609, Dessau a. 1631, d. 1650, Roßlau d. 1654, Magdeburg a. 1742.

♥ – Trains also call at City Tunnel stations Markt, Wilhelm-Leuschner-Platz, Bayerischer Bahnhof and MDR.

Local services HALLE and LEIPZIG - EISENACH and SAALFELD 849

See Tables **849a** and **850** for faster *ICE* and *IC* trains.

HALLE / LEIPZIG - ERFURT - EISENACH (operated by Abellio Rail Mitteldeutschland). *See lower panel for other connecting services Halle - Naumburg and v.v.*

km																								
				Ⓐ		Ⓒ	Ⓐ															⊕		F	
0	**Halle** (Saale) Hbf .... d.	...	0057	0417	...	0419	0457	...	0557	...	...	...	0805	...	and in	...	1805	...	...	2005	...	...	...	...	...
	Leipzig Hbf .... d.	0021	|	|	...	|	|	0519	|	0619	0651**t**	0719	|	0819	the same	1719	|	1819	1919	|	2019	2119	2219	2219	2321
32	Weißenfels .... d.	0100	0127	0448	...	0449	0521	0558	0620	0658	0721**t**	0758	0828	0858	pattern	1758	1828	1858	1958	2028	2058	2158	2258	2258	2359
46	Naumburg (Saale) Hbf d.	0110	0138	0458	0503	0503	0532	0608	0640**r**	0708	0732	0808	0838	0908	every	1808	1838	1908	2008	2038	2108	2208	2308	2308	0010
72	Apolda .... d.	...	—	—	0525	0525	0552	0629	0700	0729	0753	0829	0857	0929	**two** hours	1829	1857	1929	2029	2057	2129	2229	2329	2329	0031
87	Weimar .... **858** d.	...	...	...	0537	0537	0603	0642	0713	0742	0804	0842	0909	0942	until	1842	1909	1942	2042	2109	2142	2242	2342	2342	0043
08	**Erfurt** Hbf .... **858** a.	...	Ⓐ	Ⓐ	0552	0552	0619	0656	0728	0758	0818	0858	0922	0958		1858	1923	1958	2058	2122	2158	2258	2358	2358	0059
08	**Erfurt** Hbf .... **865** d.	...	0423	0507	0553	0553	0625	0705	...	0800	...	0905	...	1000		1905	...	2000	2104	...	*2218*	2310	...	0008	...
36	Gotha .... **865** d.	...	0453	0535	0615	0615	0643	0727	...	0821	...	0927	...	1021		1927	...	2021	2126	...	*2240*	2333	...	0030	...
65	**Eisenach** .... a.	...	0519	0558	0636	0636	0706	0749	...	0843	...	0949	...	1043		1949	...	2043	2148	...	*2301*	2355	...	0052	...

			Ⓐ		Ⓐ				⚒															
senach .... d.	...	...	0410	...	...	0458	...	0606	0642	...	0713	...	0806	0913	...	and in	1609	1713	...	1806	1913	...	2006	2113	2215
otha ....**865** d.	...	...	0434	...	...	0522	...	0629	0706	...	0736	...	0830	0936	...	the same	1632	1736	...	1830	1936	...	2030	2135	2244
furt Hbf ....**865** a.	...	...	0456	...	...	0544	...	0649	0728	...	0758	...	0853	0958	...	pattern	1655	1758	...	1853	1958	...	2053	2158	2306
furt Hbf ....**858** d.	...	...	0458	0458	0530	0559	0630	0701	0736	0736	0801	0837	0901	1001	1037	every	1701	1801	1837	1901	2001	2036	2102	2201	2318
eimar ....**858** d.	...	...	0517	0517	0545	0617	0643	0718	0752	0752	0818	0852	0918	1018	1052	**two** hours	1718	1818	1852	1918	2018	2052	2119	2218	2335
olda .... d.	...	...	0529	0529	0555	0629	0653	0729	0803	0803	0829	0902	0929	1029	1102	until	1729	1829	1902	1929	2029	2102	2130	2229	2346
umburg (Saale) Hbf d.	0446	0446	0552	0552	0615	0652	0713	0752	0822	0822	0852	0922	0952	1052	1122		1752	1852	1922	1952	2052	2122	2152	2252	0009
eißenfels .... d.	0457	0457	0602	0602	0625	0702	0722	0802	0832	0832	0902	0932	1002	1102	1132		1802	1902	1932	2002	2102	2131	2202	2302	0020
Leipzig Hbf .... a.	|	0541	0639	0639	0704	0739	|	0839	|	|	0939	|	1039	1139	|		1839	1939	|	2039	2139	|	2239	2339	|
lle (Saale) Hbf .... a.	0528	...	...	...	...	...	0748	...	0855	0855	...	0956	...	...	1156		...	...	1956	...	...	2155	...	...	0050

HALLE / LEIPZIG - JENA - SAALFELD *See upper panel for other connecting services Leipzig - Naumburg and v.v.*

km																								
		Ⓐ	Ⓒ	◇		◇		◇		◇			◇		◇		◇		◇	**B**	◇	◇	◇	◇	**F** ◇
	Halle (Saale) Hbf .... d.	...	...	0523	...	0623	0705	0723	...	0823	and in	...	1623	1705	1723	...	1823	1905	1923	...	2023	2123	2223	2323	2323
0	**Leipzig** Hbf .... d.	...	...	|	0558	|	|	|	0809	|	the same	1609	|	|	|	1809	|	|	|	2009	|	|	|	|	|
40	Weißenfels .... d.	...	...	0552	0626	0652	0730	0752	0840	0852	pattern	1640	1652	1730	1752	1840	1852	1930	1952	2040	2052	2152	2252	2352	2352
56	Naumburg (Saale) Hbf a.	...	...	0603	0634	0703	0739	0803	0848	0903	every	1648	1703	1739	1803	1848	1903	1939	2003	2048	2103	2203	2303	0003	0003
56	Naumburg (Saale) Hbf d.	...	...	0613	0635	0713	0740	0813	0850	0913	**two** hours	1650	1713	1740	1813	1850	1913	1940	2013	2050	2113	2213	2313	0013	0013
95	**Jena** Paradies .... d.	0509	0616	0646	0708	0746	0808	0846	0917	0946	until	1717	1746	1808	1846	1917	1946	2008	2046	2117	2146	2246	2346	0045	0045
00	Jena-Göschwitz .... d.	0513	0621	0650	0713	0750	0814	0850	0922	0950		1722	1750	1814	1850	1922	1950	2014	2050	2122	2150	2250	2350	0050	0053
32	Rudolstadt (Thür) .... d.	0539	0642	0716	0740	0816	...	0916	0943	1016		1743	1816	...	1916	1943	2016	...	2116	2143	2216	2316	0016	...	0119
42	**Saalfeld** (Saale) .... a.	0548	0651	0725	0750	0825	...	0925	0951	1025		1751	1825	...	1925	1951	2025	...	2125	2151	2225	2325	0025	...	0128
	Nürnberg Hbf **875** .. a.	0848**k**	0919	...	1019	...	...	...	1219	...		2019	...	...	...	2220**c**	...	...	...	...	...	...	...	...	...

	◇	Ⓐ		◇	◇	◇		◇		◇		✣	◇		◇		◇		◇		◇		**F** ◇	**D** ◇	**F** ◇
Nürnberg Hbf **875** ... d.	...	...	...	...	...	...	0529	...	...	...	0738	and in	...	1538	...	...	...	1740	...	...	...	1938	...	...	...
alfeld (Saale) .... d.	0430	...	0523	...	0633	0733	0810	0833	...	0933	1003	the same	1733	1803	1833	...	1933	2003	2033	...	2133	2207	2233	2233	2333
dolstadt (Thür) .... d.	0439	...	0531	...	0642	0742	0820	0842	...	0942	1012	pattern	1742	1812	1842	...	1942	2012	2042	...	2142	2216	2242	2242	2342
na-Göschwitz .... d.	0505	0547	0558	0606	0708	0808	0842	0908	0944	1008	1034	every	1808	1834	1908	1944	2008	2034	2108	2144	2208	2238	2308	2308	0008
na Paradies .... d.	0511	0553	0603	0614	0714	0814	0848	0914	0950	1014	1040	**two** hours	1814	1840	1914	1950	2014	2040	2114	2150	2214	2242	2314	2314	0012
umburg (Saale) Hbf a.	0542	0624	0629	0647	0747	0847	0914	0947	1016	1047	1106	until	1847	1906	1947	2016	2047	2106	2147	2216	2247	...	2346	2347	...
umburg (Saale) Hbf d.	0556	0625	0630	0656	0756	0856	0915	0956	1017	1056	1107		1856	1907	1956	2017	2056	2107	2156	2217	2256	...	2347	...	...
eißenfels .... d.	0606	0635	0640	0706	0806	0906	0924	1006	1027	1106	1118		1906	1918	2006	2027	2106	2118	2206	2227	2306	...	2357	...	...
Leipzig Hbf .... a.	|	|	0709	|	|	|	0952	|	|	|	1152		|	1952	|	|	|	2152	|	|	|	...	0034	...	...
lle (Saale) Hbf .... a.	0635	0658	...	0735	0835	0935	...	1035	1051	1135	...		1935	...	2035	2051	2135	...	2235	2251	2335	...	...	...	...

EISENACH - BEBRA *45km.* Journey time: 35 – 48 minutes. Operated by CANTUS Verkehrsgesellschaft (2nd class only).

om Eisenach at 0436 Ⓐ, 0530 Ⓐ, 0613 ⚒, 0713 ⚒, 0813, 0902 ⚒, 1013, 1113 Ⓐ, 1213, 1302 Ⓐ, 1413, 1502 Ⓐ, 1613, 1702 Ⓐ, 1813, 1902 Ⓐ, 2013, 2116 Ⓐ and 2213 Ⓒ.

om Bebra at 0504 Ⓐ, 0559 ⚒, 0704 Ⓒ, 0716 Ⓐ, 0804 ⚒, 0904, 1004 Ⓐ, 1104, 1204 Ⓐ, 1304 Ⓒ, 1315 Ⓐ, 1404 Ⓐ, 1507, 1604 Ⓐ, 1704, 1804 Ⓐ, 1904, 2004 Ⓐ and 2104.

– To Bamberg (Table **875**).
– ⑦–④ (not Apr. 6, 9, 30, May 17, 28).
– ⑤⑥ (also Apr. 6, 9, 30, May 17, 28).

c – Ⓒ (also Jan. 6).
k – Not Jan. 6, Feb. 13 - Mar. 24.
r – Arrives 0630.
t – Ⓐ only.

⊕ – Change trains at Erfurt on ①–⑤.
✣ – The 1138 from Nürnberg is retimed as follows: Saalfeld d. 1411, Rudolstadt d. 1421, Jena-Göschwitz d. 1443, Jena Paradies d. 1448, Naumburg a. 1514, d. 1515, Weißenfels d. 1524, Leipzig a. 1552; on ⑤ (not Dec. 30, Jan. 6, Feb. 24) passengers on this service from Nürnberg must change trains at Kronach (a. 1305, d. 1309). The 1338 from Nürnberg is retimed at Naumburg (a. 1713, d. 1714) and Weißenfels (d. 1724).
◇ – Operated by Abellio Rail Mitteldeutschland.

LEIPZIG - NAUMBURG - WEIMAR - ERFURT - KASSEL and LEIPZIG - JENA - SAALFELD - NÜRNBERG 849a

	IC 95	*IC* 2156	*IC* 2156	*IC* 2068	*IC* 2152	*IC* 1956	*IC* 2150	*ICE* 1705	
		⚒	†	⚒A		⑦w	Ⓑb	Ⓑb	
	T			L		K 🍷		H ✕	
Berlin Hbf **850** .... d.	...	...	...	...	...	...	...	1829	...
ipzig Hbf .... **849 850** d.	0035	...	...	0749	...	1349	...	1952	...
Halle (Saale) Hbf... **849 850** d.	0110	...	...	|	...	|	...	|	...
eißenfels .... **849** d.	|	...	...	0821	...	1419	...	2021	...
umburg (Saale) Hbf ..... **849** d.	0143	...	...	0833	...	1430	...	2031	...
Jena Paradies...... **849 875** d.	0215	...	...	0900	...	|	...	2057	...
Jena Göschwitz.... **849 875** d.	0221	...	...	0906	...	|	...	...	...
Saalfeld (Saale) .... **849 875** d.	0249	...	...	0934	...	|	...	...	...
Kronach .... **875** d.	|	...	...	1026	...	|	...	...	...
Lichtenfels .... **875** d.	0350	...	...	1040	...	|	...	...	...
Bamberg .... **850 875** d.	0421	...	...	1059	...	|	...	...	...
Erlangen .... **850 875** d.	0443	...	...	1119	...	|	...	...	...
Nürnberg Hbf ...... **850 875** a.	0502	...	...	1133	...	|	...	...	...
olda .... **849** d.	...	...	...	...	...	1448	...	...	...
Gera Hbf .... **858** d.	...	0604	...	...	1204	|	1804	...	...
Jena Göschwitz .... **858** d.	...	0639	...	...	1239	|	1839	...	...
Jena West .... **858** d.	...	0646	...	...	1246	|	1846	...	...
eimar .... **849 858** d.	...	0704	...	...	1304	1500	1904	...	...
furt Hbf......... **849 850 858** a.	...	0716	...	...	1316	1515	1916	...	...
furt Hbf .... **849 850** d.	...	0718	0724	...	1318	1517	1918	...	...
tha .... **849 850** a.	...	0735	0741	...	1335	1535	1935	...	...
tha .... **849 850** d.	...	0748	0748	...	1348	1547	1948	...	...
senach .... **849 850** d.	...	0804	0804	...	1404	1604	2004	...	...
Frankfurt (Main) Hbf **850** ...... a.	...	|	|	...	|	1753**z**	|	...	...
bra .... **849 901** d.	...	|	|	...	|	...	2029	...	...
ssel Wilhelmshöhe ..... **901** a.	...	0900	0900	...	1500	...	2106	...	...
Dortmund Hbf **800 805** .... a.	...	1114	1114	...	1714	...	...	...	...
Düsseldorf Hbf **800** .... a.	...	1208	1208	...	1811	...	...	...	...
Köln Hbf **800** .... a.	...	1240	1240	...	...	...	...	...	...

	IC 94	*ICE* 698	*ICE* 1704	*ICE* 1714	*IC* 2151	*IC* 2155	*IC* 1957	*IC* 2161	*IC* 2157	*IC* 2157
			Ⓐ	⑥	⚒		⑤	ⒷA	⑥h	Ⓑb
	U	M ✕	H ✕	O ✕			🍷	bL		
Köln Hbf **800** .... d.	...	...	...	...	...	0918	...	...	1518	1518
Düsseldorf Hbf **800** .... d.	...	...	...	...	...	0943	...	...	1543	1543
Dortmund Hbf **800 805** .... d.	...	...	...	...	...	1044	...	...	1641	1641
Kassel Wilhelmshöhe . **901** d.	...	...	...	...	0649	1257	...	...	1859	1859
Bebra.................. **849 901** d.	...	...	...	...	0728	|	...	...	|	|
Frankfurt (Main) Hbf **850** .. d.	...	0249	...	...	|	|	1538	...	|	|
Eisenach .... **849 850** d.	...	0447	...	...	0752	1356	1754	...	1956	1956
Gotha .... **849 850** a.	...	0501	...	...	0807	1410	1819	...	2010	2010
Gotha .... **849 850** d.	...	0503	...	...	0825	1425	1821	...	2017	2025
Erfurt Hbf .... **849 850** a.	...	0518	...	...	0842	1442	1837	...	2034	2042
Erfurt Hbf ..... **849 850 858** d.	...	0522	...	...	0844	1444	1841	...	...	2044
Weimar .... **849 858** d.	...	0537	...	...	0859	1459	1857	...	...	2059
Jena West.............. **858** a.	...	|	...	...	0913	1513	|	...	...	2113
Jena Göschwitz .... **858** a.	...	|	...	...	0919	1519	|	...	...	2119
Gera Hbf .... **858** a.	...	|	...	...	0955	1555	|	...	...	2155
Apolda .... **849** d.	...	|	...	...	...	...	1909	...	...	...
Nürnberg Hbf... **850 875** d.	0026	|	...	...	...	...	|	1824	...	...
Erlangen........... **850 875** d.	0043	|	...	...	...	...	|	1840	...	...
Bamberg........... **850 875** d.	0105	|	...	...	...	...	|	1901	...	...
Lichtenfels .... **875** d.	0125	|	...	...	...	...	|	1917	...	...
Kronach.................. **875** d.	|	|	...	...	...	...	|	1933	...	...
Saalfeld (Saale). **849 875** d.	0236	|	...	...	...	...	|	2023	...	...
Jena Göschwitz **849 875** d.	0303	|	...	...	...	...	|	2054	...	...
Jena Paradies .. **849 875** d.	0311	|	0659	0659	...	...	|	2100	...	...
Naumburg (Saale) Hbf . **849** d.	0339	0605	0726	0726	...	...	1927	2127	...	...
Weißenfels.................. **849** d.	|	|	0735	0735	...	...	1937	2137	...	...
Halle (Saale) Hbf **849 850** a.	0411	0638	|	|	...	...	|	|	...	...
Leipzig Hbf .... **849 850** a.	0453	|	0804	0802	...	...	2005	2206	...	...
Berlin Hbf **850** .... a.	0632	0756	0930	0930	...	...	...	...	...	...

– Until Feb. 10.
– To / from Hamburg (Table **840**).
– To Karlsruhe (Table **912**).
– To / from Karlsruhe via Stuttgart (Tables **925/931**).
– From München via Stuttgart (Table **930**).
– To Ostseebad Binz (Tables **844** and **845**).
– To Wien via Passau (Tables **920** and **950**).
– From Wien via Passau (Tables **920** and **950**). To Warnemünde via Rostock (Table **835**).

b – Not Dec. 25.
h – Also Dec. 25.
w – Also Dec. 26; not Dec. 25.
z – Frankfurt (Main) **Süd**.

850 BERLIN - HALLE / LEIPZIG - ERFURT - FRANKFURT / NÜRNBERG

See Table **902** for other services Berlin - Frankfurt via Braunschweig. See Table **927** for services operated by FlixTrain.

Other regional services: Table **845** Berlin - Lutherstadt Wittenberg. Table **848** Lutherstadt Wittenberg - Bitterfeld - Leipzig / Halle. Table **849** Leipzig / Halle - Weimar - Erfurt - Eisenach.

km		*IC* 95 T	*IC* 1950 ①g ⊙	*IC* 1950 Ⓐ	*ICE* 1658 Ⓐ ✕	*ICE* 1656 ⚒ ✕	*ICE* 1656	*ICE* 1501 Ⓐ L✕	*ICE* 501 ⚒ ✕	*ICE* 593 M✕	*ICE* 1701 Ⓐ ✕	*ICE* 1001 r ✕	*ICE* 938 Ⓐ ✕	*ICE* 1654 ✕	*ICE* 503 ✕	*ICE* 936 Ⓐ ✕	*ICE* 595 M✕	*ICE* 701 ✕	*ICE* 1003 ✕	*ICE* 1652 ✕	*ICE* 505 ✕	*ICE* 934 Ⓒ ✕	*ICE* 597 M✕	*ICE* 703 ✕
	Hamburg Hbf **840** d.	...	...	...	...	...	...	...	...	...	...	...	...	...	...	...	...	0527t	0552	...	0634e	...	...	073
0	**Berlin** Hbf d.	...	0017c	...	...	...	...	...	0428	0526	0534	0600	0600	...	0629	0704	0726	0734	0804	...	0829	0904	0926	093
6	**Berlin** Südkreuz d.	...	0027	...	...	...	...	...	0436	0533	0540	0607	0607	...	0636	0711	0733	0741	0811	...	0836	0911	0933	094
97	Lutherstadt Wittenberg d.	...	0112	...	...	...	...	...	0511	0610	|	|	|	...	0711	|	0810	|	|	...	0911	|	1010	|
134	Bitterfeld d.	...	0131	...	...	...	...	...	|	|	0633	|	|	...	|	|	|	0833	|	...	|	|	|	103
	Halle (Saale) Hbf d.	0110z	0151	...	...	...	...	...	|	|	0652	0712	0712	...	|	0818	|	0852	0918	...	|	1018	|	105
	Dresden Hbf **842** d.	|	|	...	...	...	...	...	|	|	|	|	|	0610	|	|	|	|	|	0810	|	|	|	|
167	**Leipzig** Hbf a.	|	0213	...	...	...	...	...	0542	0642	|	|	|	0726	0742	|	0842	|	|	0926	0942	|	1042	|
167	**Leipzig** Hbf d.	0035z	0235	...	...	0533	...	...	0548	0648	|	|	|	0733	0748	|	0848	|	|	0933	0948	|	1048	|
287	**Erfurt** Hbf a.	|	0350	...	...	0616	...	...	0629	0728	0724p	0740	0740	0816	0829	0848	0928	0924p	0945	1016	1029	1048	1128	1124
287	**Erfurt** Hbf **849a** d.	|	0357	0357	0514	0618	...	...	0631	0730	0732	0745	0751	0818	0831	0850	0930	0932r	0947	1018	1031	1050	1130	113
	Coburg **875** d.	|	|	|	|	|	...	...	0704	|	|	|	|	|	|	|	|	|	|	|	|	|	|	|
	Bamberg **875** d.	0421	|	|	|	|	...	0643	0728	|	0818	|	|	|	0917	|	|	1017r	|	|	1117	|	|	121
	Erlangen **875** d.	0443	|	|	|	|	...	0709	0753	|	|	|	|	|	0938	|	|	|	|	|	1138	|	|	|
	Nürnberg Hbf **875** a.	0502	|	|	|	|	...	0725	0808	|	0852	0856	|	|	0953	|	|	1052r	1056	|	1153	|	|	125
	München Hbf **904 905** a.	...	|	|	|	|	...	0841	0917	|	1042	1002	|	|	1102	|	|	1242r	1202	|	1302	|	|	140
315	Gotha **849a** d.	...	0416	0416	0531	0634	...	...	...	|	...	...	|	0833	...	|	|	...	...	1033	...	|	|	...
344	**Eisenach** **849a** d.	...	0432	0432	0547	0648	...	...	...	0755	...	...	|	0848	...	|	0956	...	...	1048	...	|	1155	...
401	Bad Hersfeld d.	...	0506	0506	0616	0716	...	...	...	|	...	...	|	0916	...	|	|	...	...	1116	...	|	|	...
443	Fulda **900/1/2** d.	...	0538	0538	0644	0743	...	...	...	0850	...	...	|	0943	...	|	1050	...	...	1143	...	|	1250	...
524	Hanau Hbf **901** d.	...	0623	0623	|	|	...	...	...	|	...	...	|	|	...	|	|	...	...	|	...	|	|	...
547	**Frankfurt** (Main) Hbf **900/1/2** ◇ a.	...	0639	0639	0739•	0836	0842	...	...	0944	...	...	0956	1036	...	1056	1144	...	...	1236	...	1256	1344	...
558	**Frankfurt** Flughafen ✈ § ◇ a.	...	...	...	0751	0854	0854	...	...	|	...	...	...	1054	...	...	|	...	...	1254	...	...	|	...
	Stuttgart Hbf **912** a.	...	...	...	...	|	|	...	...	1108	...	...	...	|	...	...	1308	...	...	|	...	...	1508	...
586	**Mainz** Hbf ◇ a.	...	...	...	...	0915	0915	...	...	...	...	...	...	1115	...	...	...	...	...	1315	...	...	...	...
596	**Wiesbaden** Hbf ◇ a.	...	...	...	...	0933	0933	...	...	...	...	...	...	1133	...	...	...	...	...	1333	...	...	...	...

	ICE 93 △ A✕	*ICE* 1093 r ✕	*ICE* 1650 ✕	*ICE* 507 ✕	*ICE* 932 ✕	*ICE* 1219 M✕	*ICE* 705 ✕	*ICE* 1005 r ✕	*ICE* 1005 G ✕	*ICE* 1558 ✕	*ICE* 509 ✕	*ICE* 1630 ⑥h U✕	*ICE* 930 Ⓑb ✕	*IC* 1956 ⑦w D🍷	*ICE* 691 M✕	*IC* 1956 ⑦w D🍷	*ICE* 707 ✕	*ICE* 1556 ✕	*ICE* 1707 ✕	*ICE* 1601 ✕	*ICE* 1711 O✕	*ICE* 838 ✕	*ICE* 693 M✕	*ICE* 709 ✕
Hamburg Hbf **840** d.	0804	...	...	0834	...	...	0936	1005	1005	...	1034	...	...	...	...	...	1136	...	1203	1234	...	...	...	133
Berlin Hbf d.	1004	1004	...	1029	1105	1126	1134	1204	1204	...	1229	1304	1304	...	1326	...	1334	...	1404	1429	1429	1505	1526	153
Berlin Südkreuz d.	1011	1011	...	1036	1112	1133	1141	1211	1211	...	1236	1311	1311	...	1333	...	1341	...	1411	1436	1436	1512	1533	154
Lutherstadt Wittenberg d.	|	|	...	1111	|	1210	|	|	|	...	1311	|	|	...	1410	...	|	...	|	1511	1511	|	1610	|
Bitterfeld d.	|	|	...	|	|	|	1233	|	|	...	|	|	|	...	|	...	1433	...	|	|	|	|	|	163
Halle (Saale) Hbf d.	1118	1118	...	|	1218	|	1252	1318	1318	...	|	1415	1418	...	|	...	1452	...	1518	|	|	1618	|	165
Dresden Hbf **842** d.	|	|	1010	|	|	|	|	|	|	1210	|	|	|	...	|	...	|	1410	|	|	|	|	|	|
Leipzig Hbf a.	|	|	1126	1142	|	1242	|	|	|	1326	1342	|	|	...	1442	...	|	1526	|	1542	1542	|	1642	|
Leipzig Hbf d.	|	|	1133	1148	|	1248	|	|	|	1333	1348	|	|	1349	1448	...	|	1533	|	1548	1548	|	1648	|
Erfurt Hbf a.	1152	1152	1216	1229	1248	1328	1324p	1345	1351	1416	1429	1448	1448	1515	1528	...	1524p	1616	1552	1629	1629	1648	1728	1724
Erfurt Hbf **849a** d.	1154	1154	1218	1231	1250	1330	1332	1347	1353	1418	1431	1450	1450	1517	1530	...	1532	1618	1554	1631	1631	1650	1730	173
Coburg **875** d.	1229	1229	|	|	|	|	|	|	1431	|	|	|	|	|	|	...	|	|	1629	|	|	|	|	|
Bamberg **875** d.	|	|	|	1317	|	|	1417	|	...	|	1516	|	|	|	|	...	1617	|	|	|	|	|	|	181
Erlangen **875** d.	|	|	|	1338	|	|	|	|	...	|	1538	|	|	|	|	...	|	|	|	1738	1738	|	|	|
Nürnberg Hbf **875** a.	1323r	1323	|	1353	|	|	1452	1456	...	|	1552	|	|	|	|	...	1652	|	1724r	1753	1753	|	|	185
München Hbf **904 905** a.	...	1517	|	1503	|	|	1642j	1601	...	|	1701	|	|	|	|	←	1803	|	1917r	1903	1903	|	|	204
Gotha **849a** d.	...	...	1233	...	|	|	...	...	...	1433	...	|	|	1535	|	1547	...	1633	...	...	...	|	|	...
Eisenach **849a** d.	...	...	1248	...	|	1356	...	...	...	1448	...	|	|	→	1555	1604	...	1648	...	...	...	|	1755	...
Bad Hersfeld d.	...	...	1316	...	|	|	...	...	...	1516	...	|	|	...	|	1632	...	1716	...	...	...	|	|	...
Fulda **900/1/2** d.	...	...	1343	...	|	1450	...	...	...	1543	...	|	|	...	1650	1700	...	1743	...	...	...	|	1850	...
Hanau Hbf **901** d.	...	...	|	...	|	|	...	...	...	|	...	|	|	...	|	|	...	|	...	...	...	|	|	...
Frankfurt (Main) Hbf **900/1/2** ◇ a.	...	...	1436	...	1456	1544	...	...	...	1636	...	1656	1656	...	1744	1753•	...	1836	...	...	...	1856	1944	...
Frankfurt Flughafen ✈ § ◇ a.	...	...	1454	...	...	|	...	...	...	1654	...	...	...	...	|	...	...	1854	...	...	...	...	|	...
Stuttgart Hbf **912** a.	...	...	|	...	...	1708	...	...	...	|	...	...	...	...	1908	...	...	|	...	...	...	...	2108	...
Mainz Hbf ◇ a.	...	...	1515	...	...	...	...	...	...	1715	...	...	...	...	...	...	...	1915	...	...	...	...	...	...
Wiesbaden Hbf ◇ a.	...	...	1533	...	...	...	...	...	...	1733	...	...	...	...	...	...	...	1933	...	...	...	...	...	...

	ICE 1007 ✕	*ICE* 1554 ✕	*ICE* 603 ✕	*ICE* 836 S✕	*ICE* 695 M✕	*ICE* 801 K✕	*ICE* 1009 ✕	*ICE* 1552 n ✕	*ICE* 1705 Ⓑb J✕	*ICE* 1605 Ⓑ ✕	*ICE* 1715 ⑥ O✕	*ICE* 834 ✕	*ICE* 887 Ⓑb	*ICE* 1087 ⑥	*ICE* 803 ✕	*ICE* 1109 ✕	*ICE* 1550 Ⓑb ✕	*ICE* 1607 ✕	*ICE* 1607 Ⓑb ✕	*ICE* 1607 ⑤ ✕	*ICE* 699 M	*EN* 40458 N	*NJ* 408 ♣	*IC* 227 B
Hamburg Hbf **840** d.	1404	...	1435	1450	...	1536	1551	...	1634	1634	...	...	2001	2001	1735	...	...	1835	1835	1835	1936	...	...	...
Berlin Hbf d.	1604	...	1629	1704	1726	1734	1804	...	1829	1829	1829	1905	|	|	1926	2004	...	2029	2029	2029	2126	...	2051	222
Berlin Südkreuz d.	1611	...	1636	1711	1733	1741	1811	...	1836	1836	1836	1912	|	|	1933	2011	...	2036	2036	2036	2133	...	2101	223
Lutherstadt Wittenberg d.	|	...	1711	|	1810	|	|	...	1911	1911	1911	|	|	|	2009	|	...	2111	2111	2111	2212	...	|	231
Bitterfeld d.	|	...	|	|	|	1833	|	...	|	|	|	|	|	|	2025	|	...	|	|	|	2229	...	|	233
Halle (Saale) Hbf d.	1718	...	|	1818	|	1852	1918	...	|	|	|	2018	|	|	|	2118	...	|	|	|	|	...	2229	|
Dresden Hbf **842** d.	|	1610	|	|	|	|	|	1810	|	|	|	|	|	|	|	|	...	|	|	|	|	2110	|	|
Leipzig Hbf a.	|	1726	1742	|	1842	|	|	1926	1942	1942	1942	|	|	|	2044	|	...	2142	2142	2142	2248	2219	2249	235
Leipzig Hbf d.	|	1733	1748	|	1848	|	|	1933	...	1948	1948	|	|	|	2050	|	2133	...	2148	2148	2255	2346	2346	...
Erfurt Hbf a.	1745	1816	1829	1848	1928	1924	1945	2016	...	2029	2029	2048	◐	◐	2129	2145	2216	...	2229	2229	2335	0122	0122	...
Erfurt Hbf **849a** d.	1747	1818	1831	1850	1930	1932	1947r	2018	...	2031	2031	2050	|	|	2131	2147	2218	...	...	2235	2341	0124	0124	...
Coburg **875** d.	|	|	|	|	|	|	|	|	...	|	|	|	|	|	2206	|	|	...	...	|	|	|	|	...
Bamberg **875** d.	|	|	1916	|	|	2017	|	|	...	|	|	|	|	|	2230	|	|	...	...	2321	|	|	|	...
Erlangen **875** d.	|	|	1938	|	|	|	|	|	...	2137	2137	|	|	|	2252q	|	|	...	...	2342	|	|	|	...
Nürnberg Hbf **875** a.	1856	|	1952	|	|	2052	2056r	|	...	2152	2152	|	|	|	2309q	2256	|	...	...	2357	|	|	|	...
München Hbf **904 905** a.	2002	|	2103	|	|	2244j	2201r	|	...	2302	2303	|	|	|	...	0001	|	...	...	0114	|	|	|	...
Gotha **849a** d.	...	1833	...	|	|	...	...	2033	...	...	...	|	|	|	...	...	2233	...	...	...	2356	|	|	...
Eisenach **849a** d.	...	1848	...	|	1956	...	...	2048	...	...	...	|	|	|	...	...	2247	...	...	...	0012	|	|	...
Bad Hersfeld d.	...	1916	...	|	|	...	...	2116	...	...	...	|	|	|	...	...	2316	...	...	...	|	|	|	...
Fulda **900/1/2** d.	...	1943	...	|	2050	...	...	2143	...	...	...	|	2257	2308	...	...	2343	...	...	...	|	|	|	...
Hanau Hbf **901** d.	...	|	...	|	|	...	...	|	...	...	...	|	2336	2348	...	...	0020	...	...	...	|	|	|	...
Frankfurt (Main) Hbf **900/1/2** ◇ a.	...	2036	...	2056	2144	...	...	2236	...	...	...	2256	2353	0007	...	...	0040	...	...	...	0211	0347	0347	...
Frankfurt Flughafen ✈ § ◇ a.	...	2056	...	...	|	...	...	...	...	...	...	|	0026	0026	...	...	...	...	...	...	0238	...	...	...
Stuttgart Hbf **912** a.	...	|	...	...	2308	...	...	...	...	...	...	0051	|	|	...	...	...	...	...	...	0452	...	...	...
Mainz Hbf ◇ a.	...	2115	...	...	...	...	...	...	...	...	...	...	0044	0044	...	...	...	...	...	...	...	...	...	...
Wiesbaden Hbf ◇ a.	...	2133	...	...	...	...	...	...	...	...	...	...	0058	0058	...	...	...	...	...	...	...	...	...	...

A – BEROLINA – To Wien via Passau (Tables **920** and **950**).
B – From Warnemünde (Table **835**).
D – To Karlsruhe (Table **912**). Runs via Weimar (Table **849a**).
G – Feb. 11 - Mar. 31 only.
J – To Jena (Table **849a**).
K – From Kiel (Table **820**).
L – Ⓐ (not Jan. 6). From Lichtenfels (d. 0622).
M – To München via Ulm (Table **930**).
N – CANOPUS – 🛏 1, 2 cl. and ▬ 2 cl. (Ⓡ) Praha - Dresden - Leipzig - Basel - Zürich. Also conveys 🚃2 (*EC* **458**).
O – From Ostseebad Binz (Tables **844**/**845**).
S – To Saarbrücken (Table **919**).
T – To Wien via Jena and Passau (Tables **849a**, **920** and **950**).
U – From Warnemünde (Table **835**).

b – Ⓑ (not Dec. 25).
c – 0020 from Mar. 6.
e – ⚒ only.
g – Also Dec. 27; not Dec. 26.
h – Also Dec. 25.
j – 40–43 minutes earlier Feb. 11 - Mar. 31.
n – Not Dec. 24, 31.
p – Connects with train in previous column.
q – Runs Bamberg - Nürnberg daily to Jan. 8, ⑥ Feb. 11 - Mar. 25, daily from Mar. 31.
r – Not Feb. 11 - Mar. 31.
t – Ⓐ only.
w – Also Dec. 26; not Dec. 25.
z – Starts from Leipzig, then Halle (a. 0056).

⊙ – Also calls at Weimar (d. 0338).
◐ – Via Hannover (Table **900**).
♣ – To Zürich via Basel (Table **912**). Conveys 🛏 1, 2 cl. and ▬ 2 cl. (Ⓡ). Also conveys 🚃2 (*IC* **60408**).
△ – Feb. 11 - Mar. 31 runs Hamburg - Berlin Coburg only (as train *ICE* **1993**).
• – Frankfurt (Main) **Süd**.
§ – Frankfurt Flughafen Fernbahnhof ✈.
◇ – See Tables **914**, **917** and **917a** for other local services.

FRANKFURT and NÜRNBERG - ERFURT - LEIPZIG / HALLE - BERLIN 850

See Table **902** for other services Frankfurt - Berlin via Braunschweig. See Table **927** for services operated by FlixTrain.

Other regional services: Table **845** Lutherstadt Wittenberg - Berlin. Table **848** Leipzig / Halle - Bitterfeld - Lutherstadt Wittenberg. Table **849** Eisenach - Erfurt - Weimar - Leipzig / Halle.

km		*IC* 94	*NJ* 409	*EN* 40459	*ICE* 1606	*ICE* 698	*ICE* 806	*ICE* 806	*ICE* 1731	*ICE* 1714	*ICE* 1604	*ICE* 1704	*ICE* 1604	*ICE* 1553	*ICE* 1008	*ICE* 672	*ICE* 696	*ICE* 804	*ICE* 804	*ICE* 933	*ICE* 602	*ICE* 1555	*ICE* 1006	*ICE* 802
								Ⓐ	Ⓐ	⑥	⚒	⚒		⑥	r		⚒	⚒	†	Ⓐ				
		T	♣	N	✕	E✕	✕	✕	✕	O✕	✕	J✕	✕	✕	✕		L✕	K✕	K✕	♥✕	✕	✕	✕	✕
	Wiesbaden Hbf ◇ d.	...	...	...	...	...	...	...	...	...	...	...	...	...	...	0500	...	...	...	...	...	...	...	...
	Mainz Hbf ◇ d.	...	...	...	...	...	...	...	...	...	...	...	...	...	...	0512	...	...	...	...	...	...	...	...
	Stuttgart Hbf **912** d.	...	...	...	...	0011	...	...	...	...	...	...	...	...	...	|	...	...	...	...	...	...	...	...
	Frankfurt Flughafen ✈ § ◇ d.	...	...	...	...	0229	...	...	...	...	...	...	...	...	...	0532	...	...	...	...	...	...	...	...
	Frankfurt (Main) Hbf **900/1/2** ◇ d.	...	0052	0052	...	0249	...	...	...	...	...	...	...	...	...	0550	0614	...	...	0702	...	0716	...	...
	Hanau Hbf **901** d.	...	|	|	...	|	...	...	...	...	...	...	...	...	...	0607	|	...	...	|	...	|	...	...
	Fulda **900/1/2** d.	...	0150	0150	...	|	...	...	...	...	...	...	...	...	...	0647	0709	...	...	|	...	0814	...	...
	Bad Hersfeld d.	...	|	|	...	|	...	...	...	...	...	...	...	...	...	|	|	...	...	|	...	0840	...	...
	Eisenach **849a** d.	...	|	|	...	0447	...	0553	0638	...	...	...	...	0708	...	|	0801	...	...	|	...	0908	...	...
	Gotha **849a** d.	...	|	|	...	0503	...	0611u	0653	...	...	...	...	0722	...	|	|	...	...	|	...	0922	...	...
	München Hbf **904 905** d.	...	|	|	...	|	...	|	|	...	...	...	...	|	0553	|	|	0506t	...	|	0656	|	0755	0713r
0	**Nürnberg** Hbf **875** d.	0026	|	|	...	|	...	|	|	0542	0542	...	...	|	0659	|	|	0705	0705	|	0804	|	0902	0905r
24	Erlangen **875** d.	0043	|	|	...	|	...	|	|	0558	0558	...	...	|	|	|	|	|	|	|	0818	|	|	|
62	**Bamberg** **875** d.	0105	|	|	...	|	...	|	|	0622	0622	...	...	|	|	|	|	0742	0742	|	0842	|	|	0942r
	Coburg **875** d.	|	|	|	...	|	...	|	|	0644	0644	...	...	|	|	|	|	|	|	|	|	|	|	|
190	**Erfurt** Hbf **849a** a.	|	0314	0314	...	0518	...	0626	0708	0724	0724	...	...	0738	0809	◐	0826	0824p	0824	0907	0926	0938	1009	1024r
190	**Erfurt** Hbf d.	|	0316	0316	...	0522	...	0628	0710	0726	0726	...	...	0740	0811	|	0828	0832	0828	0909	0928	0940	1011	1032
	Leipzig Hbf a.	0453	0448	0448	...	|	...	0710	|	0810	0810	...	...	0824	|	|	0910	|	0910	|	1010	1024	|	|
	Leipzig Hbf d.	0507	0518	0545	0616	◧	0716	0716	|	0818	0818	0818	0818	0831	|	|	0916	|	0917	|	1016	1031	|	|
	Dresden Hbf **842** a.	|	|	0705	|	|	|	|	|	|	|	|	|	0938	|	|	|	|	|	|	|	1138	|	|
284	**Halle** (Saale) Hbf d.	0431y	0537s	...	|	0640	|	|	0744	|	|	|	|	...	0840	|	|	0906	|	0942	|	...	1040	1106
314	Bitterfeld d.	0528	0558s	...	|	0656	|	|	0801	|	|	|	|	...	|	|	|	0923	|	|	|	...	|	1123
351	Lutherstadt Wittenberg d.	0546	0619s	...	0648	|	0748	0748	|	0848	0848	0848	0848	...	|	|	0948	|	0948	|	1048	...	|	|
442	**Berlin** Südkreuz a.	0625	0713	...	0722	0748	0825	0825	0850	0922	0922	0922	0922	...	0945	|	1025	1015	1025	1048	1122	...	1145	1215
448	**Berlin** Hbf a.	0632	0720	...	0729	0756	0832	0832	0857	0929	0929	0929	0929	...	0953	|	1032	1022	1032	1055	1131	...	1153	1222
	Hamburg Hbf **840** a.	...	...	...	0924	...	1022	1022	...	...	1124	1124	1124	...	1151	0936	...	1221	1221	1311	1324	...	1351	1422

	ICE 694	*ICE* 935	*ICE* 1600	*ICE* 1710	*ICE* 1557	*ICE* 1706	*ICE* 800	*ICE* 692	*ICE* 937	*ICE* 508	*ICE* 1559	*ICE* 1004	*ICE* 1004	*ICE* 708	*ICE* 690	*ICE* 939	*ICE* 506	*ICE* 1651	*ICE* 1092	*ICE* 92	*ICE* 706	*ICE* 1218	*ICE* 831	*ICE* 504
												G	r			¶			r	△				
	✕	S✕	✕	O✕	✕	✕	✕	M✕	✕	✕	✕	✕	✕	✕	M✕	✕	✕	✕	✕	A✕	✕	M✕	✕	✕
Wiesbaden Hbf ◇ d.	...	...	...	...	0826	...	...	...	...	...	1026	...	...	...	...	...	...	1226	...	...	...	...	...	...
Mainz Hbf ◇ d.	...	...	...	...	0843	...	...	...	...	...	1043	...	...	...	...	...	...	1243	...	...	...	...	...	...
Stuttgart Hbf **912** d.	0650	...	...	...	|	...	...	0851	0903c	...	|	...	...	...	1051	...	...	|	...	...	...	1251	...	...
Frankfurt Flughafen ✈ § ◇ d.	|	...	...	...	0901	...	...	|	|	...	1101	...	...	...	|	...	...	1301	...	...	...	|	...	...
Frankfurt (Main) Hbf **900/1/2** ◇ d.	0814	0902	...	...	0919	...	...	1014	1102	...	1119	...	...	...	1214	1302	...	1319	...	...	...	1414	1502	...
Hanau Hbf **901** d.	|	|	...	...	|	...	...	|	|	...	|	...	...	...	|	|	...	|	...	...	...	|	|	...
Fulda **900/1/2** d.	0909	|	...	...	1015	...	...	1109	|	...	1215	...	...	...	1310	|	...	1416	...	...	...	1509	|	...
Bad Hersfeld d.	|	|	...	...	1040	...	...	|	|	...	1240	...	...	...	|	|	...	1441	...	...	...	|	|	...
Eisenach **849a** d.	1001	|	...	...	1108	...	...	1201	|	...	1308	...	...	...	1401	|	...	1508	...	...	...	1601	|	...
Gotha **849a** d.	|	|	...	...	1122	...	...	|	|	...	1322	...	...	...	|	|	...	1522	...	...	...	|	|	...
München Hbf **904 905** d.	|	|	0855	0855	|	0839r	0955	|	|	1055	|	...	1156	1114j	|	|	1255	|	1241	...	1354	|	|	1456
Nürnberg Hbf **875** d.	|	|	1005	1005	|	1036r	1105	|	|	1204	|	...	1301	1305	|	|	1404	|	1436	1436r	1505	|	|	1604
Erlangen **875** d.	|	|	1019	1019	|	|	|	|	|	1218	|	...	|	|	|	|	1418	|	|	|	|	|	|	1618
Bamberg **875** d.	|	|	|	|	|	|	1142	|	|	1242	|	...	|	1342	|	|	1442	|	|	|	1542	|	|	1642
Coburg **875** d.	|	|	|	|	|	1129	|	|	|	|	|	1329	|	|	|	|	|	|	1529	1529	|	|	|	|
Erfurt Hbf **849a** a.	1026p	1107	1126	1126	1138	1203	1224	1226p	1307	1326	1338	1404	1409	1424	1426p	1507	1526	1538	1602	1602	1624	1626p	1707	1726
Erfurt Hbf d.	1028	1109	1128	1128	1140	1205	1232	1228	1309	1328	1340	1406	1411	1432	1428	1509	1528	1540	1605	1605	1632	1628	1709	1728
Leipzig Hbf a.	1110	|	1210	1210	1224	|	|	1310	|	1410	1424	|	|	|	1510	|	1610	1624	|	|	|	1710	|	1810
Leipzig Hbf d.	1116	|	1216	1216	1231	|	|	1316	|	1416	1431	|	|	|	1516	|	1616	1631	|	|	|	1716	|	1816
Dresden Hbf **842** a.	|	|	|	|	1338	|	|	|	|	|	1538	|	|	|	|	|	|	1738	|	|	|	|	|	|
Halle (Saale) Hbf d.	|	1142	|	|	...	1240	1306	|	1342	|	...	1440	1440	1506	|	1542	|	...	1640	1640	1706	|	1742	|
Bitterfeld d.	|	|	|	|	...	|	1323	|	|	|	...	|	|	1523	|	|	|	...	|	|	1723	|	|	|
Lutherstadt Wittenberg d.	1148	|	1248	1248	...	|	|	1348	|	1448	...	|	|	|	1548	|	1648	...	|	|	|	1748	|	1848
Berlin Südkreuz a.	1225	1247	1322	1322	...	1345	1415	1425	1447	1522	...	1545	1545	1615	1625	1648	1723	...	1745	1745	1815	1825	1848	1923
Berlin Hbf a.	1232	1255	1329	1329	...	1353	1422	1432	1455	1529	...	1553	1553	1622	1632	1655	1731	...	1753	1753	1822	1832	1855	1931
Hamburg Hbf **840** a.	...	...	1524	...	...	1600	1621	...	...	1724	...	1757	1757	1822	...	...	1924	...	...	1951	2023	...	...	2125

	ICE 1653	*ICE* 1002	*IC* 1957	*ICE* 704	*ICE* 596	*IC* 1951	*ICE* 833	*ICE* 502	*ICE* 1655	*ICE* 1000	*ICE* 702	*ICE* 594	*ICE* 835	*ICE* 500	*ICE* 1657	*ICE* 1100	*ICE* 592	*ICE* 592	*ICE* 1500	*ICE* 1500	*ICE* 600	*ICE* 1659	*ICE* 1659	*ICE* 4
			⑤			①–④				r			Ⓑ b		n			⑤⑥ d	Ⓑ Y	①–⑤	⑦ B	Ⓑ b	⑤⑦	⑦ w
	✕	✕	🍷	✕	M✕	m	✕	✕	✕	✕	✕	M✕	✕	✕	✕	✕	M✕	M✕	✕	B✕	✕	✕	w✕	Z
Wiesbaden Hbf ◇ d.	1426	...	...	...	...	...	...	...	1626	...	...	...	...	...	1826	...	...	...	...	...	...	2026	2026	...
Mainz Hbf ◇ d.	1443	...	...	...	...	...	...	...	1643	...	...	...	...	...	1843	...	...	...	...	...	...	2043	2043	...
Stuttgart Hbf **912** d.	|	...	...	...	1451	...	...	...	|	...	...	1651	...	...	|	...	1851	1851	...	...	...	|	|	...
Frankfurt Flughafen ✈ § ◇ d.	1501	...	...	...	|	...	...	...	1701	...	...	|	...	...	1901	...	|	|	...	...	...	2101	2101	...
Frankfurt (Main) Hbf **900/1/2** ◇ d.	1519	...	1538	...	1613	1615	1702	...	1719	...	...	1814	1902	...	1919	...	2014	2014	...	...	...	2119	2119	2314
Hanau Hbf **901** d.	|	...	1557	...	|	1639	|	...	|	...	...	|	|	...	|	...	|	|	...	...	...	|	|	2330
Fulda **900/1/2** d.	1615	...	1653	...	1709	1724	|	...	1815	...	...	1909	|	...	2015	...	2109	2109	...	...	...	2215	2215	0016
Bad Hersfeld d.	1640	...	1722	...	|	1754	|	...	1840	...	...	|	|	...	2040	...	2137	2137	...	...	...	2240	2240	|
Eisenach **849a** d.	1708	...	1754	...	1801	1826	|	...	1908	...	...	2001	|	...	2108	...	2206	2206	...	...	...	2308	2308	|
Gotha **849a** d.	1722	...	1821	...	|	1844	|	...	1922	...	...	|	|	...	2122	...	2220	2220	...	...	...	2322	2322	|
München Hbf **904 905** d.	|	1556	|	1514r	|	|	|	1655	|	1754	1709j	|	|	1856	|	1956	|	|	1910	2020	2050	|	|	|
Nürnberg Hbf **875** d.	|	1701	|	1705r	|	|	|	1804	|	1900	1906	|	|	2004	|	2101	|	|	2105	2135	2159	|	|	|
Erlangen **875** d.	|	|	|	|	|	|	|	1818	|	|	|	|	|	2018	|	|	|	|	2119	2150	2214	|	|	|
Bamberg **875** d.	|	|	|	1742r	|	|	|	1842	|	|	1942	|	|	2042	|	|	|	|	2143	2215	2237	|	|	|
Coburg **875** d.	|	|	|	|	|	|	|	|	|	|	|	|	|	|	|	|	|	|	2206	|	|	|	|	|
Erfurt Hbf **849a** a.	1738	1809	1837	1824r	1826p	1900	1907	1926	1938	2009	2024	2026p	2107	2126	2138	2209	2236	2236	2238	2259	2319	2338	2338	0139
Erfurt Hbf d.	1740	1811	1841	1832	1828	...	1909	1928	1940	2011	2032	2028	2109	2128	2140	2211	...	2238	2240	2301	2321	...	2343	0141
Leipzig Hbf a.	1824	|	2005	|	1910	...	|	2010	2024	|	|	2110	|	2210	2224	|	...	2322	2326	2345	0002	...	0028	0224
Leipzig Hbf d.	1831	|	...	|	1916	...	|	2016	2031	|	|	2116	|	2216	2231	|	...	...	...	...	...	...	...	0234
Dresden Hbf **842** a.	1938	|	...	|	|	...	|	|	2138	|	|	|	|	|	2338	|	...	...	...	...	...	...	...	|
Halle (Saale) Hbf d.	...	1840	...	1906	|	...	1942	|	...	2040	2106	|	2142	|	...	2242	...	...	...	...	...	...	...	|
Bitterfeld d.	...	|	...	1923	|	...	|	|	...	|	2123	|	|	2234	...	|	...	...	...	...	...	...	...	|
Lutherstadt Wittenberg d.	...	|	...	|	1948	...	|	2048	...	|	|	2148	|	2250	...	|	...	...	...	...	...	...	...	|
Berlin Südkreuz a.	...	1946	...	2015	2025	...	2047	2122	...	2146	2215	2225	2243	2329	...	2343	...	...	...	...	...	...	...	0340
Berlin Hbf a.	...	1953	...	2022	2032	...	2054	2129	...	2153	2222	2232	2250	2336	...	2350	...	...	...	...	...	...	...	0347
Hamburg Hbf **840** a.	...	2155	...	2222	...	...	...	2334	...	...	...	...	...	...	...	...	...	...	...	...	...	...	...	0537

A – BEROLINA – From Wien via Passau (Tables **950** and **920**).
B – From Feb. 10.
E – (12) München - Stuttgart - Frankfurt - Berlin. ✕ Erfurt - Berlin.
G – Feb. 11 - Mar. 31 only.
J – From Jena (Table **849a**).
K – To Kiel (Table **820**).
L – From Karlsruhe (Table **912**) on ① (also Dec. 27).
M – From München via Ulm (Table **930**).
N – CANOPUS – 🛏 1, 2 cl. and 🛏 2 cl. (Ⓡ) Zürich - Basel - Leipzig - Dresden - Praha. Also conveys (2) (*EC* **459**).
O – To Ostseebad Binz (Tables **844/845**).
S – PFÄLZER WALD. From Saarbrücken (Table **919**).
T – From Wien via Passau and Jena (Tables **849a**, **920** and **950**). To Warnemünde via Rostock (Table **835**).

Y – Ⓑ to Feb. 9 (not Dec. 25).
Z – From Chur via Zürich (Tables **920** and **912**).

b – Not Dec. 25.
c – Ⓒ only.
d – Also Dec. 25.
j – 42–47 minutes later Feb. 11 - Mar. 31.
m – Not Dec. 26.
n – Not Dec. 24, 31.
p – Connects with train in previous column.
r – Not Feb. 11 - Mar. 31.
s – Calls to set down only.
t – Ⓐ (not Jan. 6).
u – Calls to pick up only.

w – Also Dec. 26; not Dec. 25.
y – Arrives 0411 (calls before Leipzig).

¶ – Train number **839** on Ⓒ.
◐ – Via Hannover (Table **900**).
◧ – Via Weimar (see Table **849a**).
♥ – From Darmstadt Hbf (d. 0637).
△ – Feb. 11 - Mar. 31 runs Coburg - Berlin - Hamburg only (as train *ICE* **1992**).
◇ – See Tables **914**, **917** and **917a** for other local services.
♣ – From Zürich via Basel (Table **912**). Conveys 🛏 1, 2 cl. and 🛏 2 cl. (Ⓡ). Also conveys (2) (*IC* **60409**).
§ – Frankfurt Flughafen Fernbahnhof ✈.

851 BERLIN - LUTHERSTADT WITTENBERG and FALKENBERG

RE services except where shown

km																								
		ⒸH			S		S		S		S		S		S		S		S			S	R	⊡R
0	**Berlin** Hbf .... **850** d.	0042	...	0501	0632	0701	0832	0902	1032	1101	1232	1301	1432	1501	1632	1702	1832	1902	2032	2103	2204	2231	2333	2333
6	**Berlin** Südkreuz .... **850** d.	0051	...	0514	0641	0714	0841	0914	1041	1114	1241	1314	1441	1514	1641	1714	1841	1914	2041	2115	2214	2240	2343	2343
52	Luckenwalde .... d.	0134	...	0546	0716	0746	0916	0946	1116	1146	1316	1346	1516	1545	1716	1746	1916	1946	2116	2146	2258	2326	0024	0024
65	Jüterbog .... d.	0142	...	0554	0724	0754	0924	0954	1124	1154	1324	1354	1524	1554	1724	1754	1924	1954	2124	2154	2306	2335	0032	0034
114	**Falkenberg** (Elster) .... a.	|	...	0635	|	0835	|	1035	|	1235	|	1435	|	1635	|	1835	|	2037	|	*2245*	*0003*	|	...	|
	Lutherstadt Wittenberg .. **850** a.	0158	...	...	0757	...	0957	...	1159	...	1357	...	1559	...	1757	...	1959	...	2157	...	...	0002	...	0101

km																								
		Ⓒ		S	ⒸS	R		G		R		R		R		R		R		R		J		E
0	**Lutherstadt Wittenberg** .. **850** d.	0029	...	...	...	0505	...	0659	...	0859	...	1059	...	1259	...	1459	...	1659	...	1859	...	2059	...	2259
	Falkenberg (Elster) .... d.	|	...	...	0350	|	0514	|	0714	|	0914	|	1114	|	1314	|	1514	|	1714	|	1914	|	*2114*	|
32	Jüterbog .... d.	0058	...	0432	0432	0536	0555	0736	0755	0936	0955	1136	1155	1336	1355	1536	1555	1736	1755	1936	1955	2136	2203	2336
45	Luckenwalde .... d.	0106	...	0441	0441	0545	0609	0744	0809	0944	1009	1144	1209	1344	1409	1544	1609	1744	1809	1944	2009	2144	2212	2344
91	**Berlin** Südkreuz .... **850** a.	0147	...	0519	0519	0621	0644	0822	0844	1021	1044	1221	1244	1421	1444	1621	1644	1821	1844	2021	2044	2221	2252	0026
97	**Berlin** Hbf .... **850** a.	0156	...	0528	0528	0630	0652	0831	0852	1030	1052	1230	1252	1430	1452	1630	1652	1830	1852	2030	2052	2229	2302	0034

E – To Eberswalde (Table **845**).
G – From Halle on Ⓒ (Table **848**). To Stralsund (Table **845**).
H – From Schwedt (Table **845**). To Halle (Table **848**).
J – To Schwedt on ⑦–④ / Pasewalk on ⑤⑥ (Table **845**).
R – To / from Stralsund (Table **845**).
S – To / from Schwedt (Table **845**).
⊡ – ⑤⑥ (also Apr. 6, 9, 30, May 17, 28).

852 COTTBUS - LEIPZIG

RE / *RB* services

km											
	Frankfurt (Oder) **839** d.	...	0536	0736	0936	1136	1336	1536	1736	1936	2136
0	**Cottbus** Hbf .... d.	0459	0701	0901	1101	1301	1501	1701	1901	2104	2301
24	Calau (Niederl) .... d.	0516	0719	0919	1119	1319	1519	1719	1919	2122	2322
46	Finsterwalde .... d.	0529	0733	0933	1133	1333	1533	1733	1933	2136	2337
56	Doberlug-Kirchhain ..... d.	0537	0741	0941	1141	1341	1541	1741	1941	2144	2345
79	Falkenberg (Elster) **856** d.	0557	0801	1001	1201	1401	1601	1801	2001	2159	0009
97	Torgau .... **856** d.	0610	0814	1014	1214	1414	1614	1814	2014	2211	...
124	Eilenburg .... **856** d.	0631	0831	1031	1231	1431	1631	1831	2031	2228	...
149	**Leipzig** Hbf .... **856** a.	0650	0850	1050	1250	1450	1650	1850	2050	2249	...

Leipzig Hbf .... **856** d.	0507	0712	0912	1112	1312	1512	1712	1912	2112	2333
Eilenburg .... **856** d.	0527	0731	0931	1131	1331	1531	1731	1931	2131	2352
Torgau .... **856** d.	0544	0749	0949	1149	1349	1549	1749	1949	2149	0013
Falkenberg (Elster) . **856** d.	0557	0803	1003	1203	1403	1603	1803	2003	2203	0027
Doberlug-Kirchhain ...... d.	0616	0816	1016	1216	1416	1616	1816	2016	2216	0040
Finsterwalde .... d.	0624	0825	1025	1225	1425	1625	1825	2025	2225	0048
Calau (Niederl) .... d.	0639	0839	1039	1239	1439	1639	1839	2039	2239	0102
Cottbus Hbf .... a.	0656	0855	1055	1255	1455	1655	1855	2055	2255	0119
Frankfurt (Oder) **839** . a.	0821	1021	1221	1421	1621	1821	2021	2221	0021	...

☛ Additional trains: **Cottbus** - **Falkenberg** at 0601 Ⓐ, 0801, 1001 and every **two** hours until 2201. **Falkenberg** - **Cottbus** at 0452, 0655, 0855, 1055, 1255, 1455, 1652, 1852 and 2055.

853 STEAM TRAINS IN SACHSEN

Lößnitzgrundbahn. SDG Sächsische Dampfeisenbahngesellschaft mbH, Am Bahnhof 1, 01468 Moritzburg. ✆ +49 (0) 35207 8929. SEE NOTE ⊠. www.loessnitzgrundbahn.de

km											
0	Radebeul Ost **842 857** .... d.	0851	...	1020	...	1323	...	1453	...	1750	...
8	Moritzburg .... d.	0922	...	1053	...	1354	...	1526	...	1820	...
16	Radeburg .... a.	...	...	1120	...	...	...	1552	...	...	...

Radeburg .... d.	...	...	1135	...	...	...	1607	...	...
Moritzburg .... d.	0931	...	1204	...	1403	...	1636	...	1829
Radebeul Ost **842 857** .... a.	1000	...	1234	...	1433	...	1705	...	1858

Weißeritztalbahn. SDG Sächsische Dampfeisenbahngesellschaft mbH, Am Bahnhof 1, 01468 Moritzburg. ✆ +49 (0) 35207 89290. SEE NOTE ⊠. www.weisseritztalbahn.com

km											
		△			△			△			
	Dresden Hbf .... d.	0902	...	...	1302	...	...	1634	...	...	...
0	Freital-Hainsberg .... d.	0918	0925	...	1318	1325	...	1647	1705	...	...
15	Dippoldiswalde .... d.	...	1018	...	...	1418	...	...	1750	...	...
26	Kurort Kipsdorf .... a.	...	1051	...	...	1451	...	...	...	...	...

		△			△			△	
Kurort Kipsdorf .... d.	1111	...	...	1511	...	...	...	...	...
Dippoldiswalde .... d.	1145	...	...	1545	...	...	1802	...	...
Freital-Hainsberg .... a.	1230	1238	...	1630	1638	...	1847	1908	...
Dresden Hbf .... a.	...	1252	...	...	1652	...	...	1923	...

Zittauer Schmalspurbahn. SOEG - Sächisch Oberlausitzer Eisenbahngesellschaft mbH, Bahnhofstraße 41, 02763 Zittau. ✆ +49 (0) 3583 540540. www.soeg-zittau.de

km																										
				🍷			🍷			🍷			🍷				⊙	⊙			🍷	🍷	🍷	🍷	🍷	🍷
0	Zittau .... d.	High	0847	0909	...	...	1109	...	...	1309	...	...	1509	...	...	...	1709	...	...	Low	0907	...	...	1307	...	...
9	Bertsdorf .... d.	season	0946r	0946t	...	1055	1146t	1146	1255	1346t	1346	1455	1546t	1546	1655	...	1741	1835	...	season	0938	1039	1135	1338	1439	1535
12	Kurort Oybin a.	♥	|	0956	...	1106	1156	|	1306	1356	|	1506	1556	|	1706	...	|	1846	...	♣	0949	|	1146	1349	|	1546
13	Kurort Jonsdorf a.	→	0959	...	...	...	...	1159	...	...	1359	...	...	1559	...	...	1754	...	...	→	...	1051	...	...	1451	...

			🍷				🍷			🍷			🍷			⊙	⊙			🍷	🍷	🍷	🍷	🍷	🍷
Kurort Jonsdorf .... d.	High	1008	...	...	...	1208	...	...	1408	...	...	1608	...	...	...	1803	...	...	Low	...	1101	...	...	1501	...
Kurort Oybin .... d.	season	|	1007	...	1115	|	1207	1315	|	1407	1515	|	1607	1728	...	|	1855	...	season	0959	|	1156	1359	|	1556
Bertsdorf .... d.	♥	1019	1020	...	1126	1219	1220	1326	1419	1420	1526	1619	1620	1741	...	1814	1907	...	♣	1010	1112	1208	1410	1512	1608
Zittau .... a.	→	...	1049	...	...	...	1249	...	...	1449	...	...	1649	1811	...	...	1936	...	→	...	...	1237	...	...	1637

r – Arrives 0916.
t – Arrives 6 minutes earlier.
♣ – Dec. 11–21, Jan. 2–27, Feb. 27 - Mar. 31.
♥ – Dec. 22 - Jan. 1, Jan. 28 - Feb. 26 and from Apr. 1.
⊙ – From Apr. 1.
△ – Suggested main-line connecting service.
⊠ – No service Mar. 6–24.

854 FORST - COTTBUS - GÖRLITZ - ZITTAU

Ostdeutsche Eisenbahn (ODEG); 2nd class only

km																
		⑥⑦c		Ⓐ	Ⓐ	⚒	⚒		⚒							
0	**Cottbus** Hbf .... d.	0048	...	...	0504	...	0604	0704	0804	...	0904		2104	2204	2304	...
24	Spremberg .... d.	0106	...	...	0522	...	0622	0722	0822	...	0922	and	2122	2222	2322	...
42	Weißwasser .... d.	0121	...	0430	0535	...	0635	0735	0835	...	0935		2135	2235	2336	...
72	Horka .... d.	0142	...	0453	0559	...	0659	0759	0859	...	0959	hourly	2159	2259	2359	...
93	**Görlitz** .... a.	0157	...	0508	0614	...	0714	0814	0914	...	1014		2214	2314	0014	...
93	**Görlitz** .... d.	...	...	*0511*	...	0617	*0717*	0817	...	0917	1017	until	2217	...	...	...
103	Hagenwerda .... a.	...	...	*0520*	...	0626	*0726*	0826	...	0926	1026		2226	...	...	...
127	**Zittau** .... a.	...	...	*0556**	...	*0702**	*0802**	*0902**	...	*1002**	*1102**		*2302**	...	...	...

	Ⓐ	⚒	⚒		Ⓐ	⚒		⚒						A	⑤⑥f	
Zittau .... d.	...	...	*0448**	...	*0554**	...	*0654**	*0754**	...	*0854**		*2054**	*2154**	...	...	...
Hagenwerda .... d.	...	...	0524	...	0630	...	0730	0830	...	0930	and	2130	2230	...	...	...
Görlitz .... a.	...	...	0532	...	0639	...	0739	0839	...	0939		2139	2239	...	...	...
Görlitz .... d.	0344	0437	...	0543	...	0643	0743	...	0843	0943	hourly	2143	...	2243	2243	...
Horka .... d.	0358	0453	...	0559	...	0659	0759	...	0859	0959		2159	...	2259	2259	...
Weißwasser .... d.	0420	0520	...	0620	...	0720	0820	...	0920	1020	until	2220	...	2319	2320	...
Spremberg .... d.	0434	0538	...	0638	...	0738	0838	...	0938	1038		2238	...	...	2338	...
Cottbus Hbf .... a.	0452	0556	...	0656	...	0756	0856	...	0956	1056		2256	...	...	2356	...

FORST (Lausitz) - **COTTBUS** and v.v. *22 km*.
Journey time: 18 minutes.
From Forst at 0431 Ⓐ, 0533, 0633 and hourly until 2133.
From Cottbus Hbf at 0507 Ⓐ, 0607, 0707 and hourly until 2107; then 2307.

A – ⑦–④ (not Apr. 9, 30, May 28).
c – Also Apr. 10, May 1, 29; not Apr. 8, 29, May 27.
f – Also Apr. 9, 30, May 28; not Apr. 7, 28, May 26.
* – By 🚌 Hagenwerda - Zittau and v.v.

855 DRESDEN - BISCHOFSWERDA - GÖRLITZ and ZITTAU

Trilex (2nd class only)

DRESDEN - GÖRLITZ (- ZGORZELEC)

km																										
		⚒	Ⓐ¶			⚒			⚒⊙			⚒		⊖		◇					⚒‡					
0	**Dresden** Hbf .... ● d.	0356	0525	0629	0656	0729	0829	0859	0929	1029	1059	*1129*	1229	1329	1429	1529	1629	1729	1829	1859	1929	2029	2059	2129	2229	*2328*
4	Dresden Neustadt . ● d.	0402	0531	0635	0706	0735	0835	0906	0935	1035	1106	*1135*	1235	1335	1435	1535	1635	1735	1835	1906	1935	2035	2106	2135	2235	*2335*
41	Bischofswerda .... ● d.	0437	0605	0705	0741	0808	0905	0941	1008	1105	1141	1208	1305	1408	1505	1608	1705	1808	1905	1941	2008	2105	2141	2208	2305	0015
60	Bautzen .... d.	0452	0617	0717	0755	0820	0917	0955	1020	1117	1155	1220	1317	1420	1517	1620	1717	1820	1917	1955	2020	2117	2155	2223	2317	0029
82	Löbau (Sachs) .... d.	0510	0631	0731	0813	0833	0931	1013	1033	1131	1213	1233	1331	1433	1531	1633	1731	1833	1931	2013	2033	2131	2213	2240	2331	0047
105	**Görlitz** .... **1085** a.	0530	0646	0746	0833	0848	0946	1033	1048	1146	1233	1248	1346	1448	1546	1648	1746	1848	1946	2033	2048	2146	2233	2300	2346	0107
106	Zgorzelec 🏛 .... **1085** a.	...	0655	0754	...	...	...	...	...	1154	...	1254	1354	1454	1554	1654	...	1854	1954	...	...	...	...	...	...	...

	Ⓐ	Ⓒ	Ⓐ		Ⓐ															⚒					
Zgorzelec 🏛 ...... **1085** d.	...	...	...	...	...	0712t	0800	...	...	...	1200	1300	...	1400	1500	...	1600	1700	...	...	1900	*1900*	2000	...	...	...
Görlitz .... **1085** d.	0351	0526	0539	0611	0652	0722	0811	0926	1011	1126	1211	1309	1322	1411	1509	1522	1611	1709	1726	1811	1909	1926	2011	2119	2219	2319
Löbau (Sachs) .... d.	0411	0546	0554	0626	0708	0742	0826	0946	1026	1146	1226	1324	1342	1426	1524	1542	1626	1724	1746	1826	1924	1946	2026	2139	2239	2337
Bautzen .... d.	0428	0603	0607	0640	0722	0800	0840	1003	1040	1203	1240	1337	1400	1440	1537	1600	1640	1737	1803	1840	1937	2003	2040	2156	2256	2353
Bischofswerda .... d.	0443	0620	0620	0654	0735	0820	0854	1020	1054	1220	1254	1349	1420	1454	1549	1620	1654	1749	1820	1854	1949	2020	2054	2212	2312	0014
Dresden Neustadt ...... a.	0516	0652	0652	0722	0803	0852	0920	1052	1120	1252	1320	*1421*	1452	1520	*1621*	1652	1720	*1821*	1852	1920	*2021*	2052	2120	2245	2345	0046
Dresden Hbf .... a.	0523	0659	0659	0728	0810	0859	0927	1059	1127	1259	1327	*1427*	1459	1527	*1627*	1659	1727	*1827*	1859	1927	*2027*	2059	2127	2251	2351	0052

FOR NOTES AND DRESDEN - ZITTAU TIMINGS, SEE NEXT PAGE →

rilex (2nd class only) **DRESDEN - BISCHOFSWERDA - GÖRLITZ and ZITTAU** **855**

DRESDEN - ZITTAU (- LIBEREC)

km																										
			Ⓐ																							
0	**Dresden** Hbf ● d.	0356	...	...	0525	0556	0729	0756	0929	0956	1129	1156	1329	1356	1529	1556	1729	1756	1929	1956	2129	2207	...	2328	...	...
4	Dresden Neustadt ● d.	0402	...	...	0531	0602	0735	0802	0935	1002	1135	1202	1335	1402	1535	1602	1735	1802	1935	2002	2135	2213	...	2335	...	...
41	Bischofswerda ● d.	0435	0440	...	0601	0637	0805	0837	1005	1037	1205	1237	1405	1437	1605	1637	1805	1837	2005	2037	2205	2248	...	0012	...	...
79	Ebersbach (Sachs) d.	...	0522	...	0633	0725	0834	0925	1034	1125	1234	1325	1434	1525	1634	1725	1834	1925	2034	2127	2234	2327	...	0047	...	...
83	Neugersdorf d.	...	0526	...	0637	0729	0838	0929	1038	1129	1238	1329	1438	1529	1638	1729	1838	1929	2038	2131	2238	2331	...	0051	...	...
05	**Zittau** a.	...	0547	...	0655	0749	0856	0949	1056	1149	1256	1349	1456	1549	1656	1749	1856	1949	2056	2152	2256	2352	...	0112	...	...
	Zittau 🚌 **1117** d.	...	...	...	0715c	...	0901	...	1101	...	1301c	...	1501c	...	1701	...	1901	...	2101c	...	...	...	...	...	...	...
32	Liberec 🚌 **1117** a.	...	...	...	0754c	...	0929	...	1129	...	1329c	...	1529c	...	1729	...	1929	...	2131c	...	...	...	...	...	...	...

	Ⓐ		Ⓐ	⊕																					
berec 🚌 **1117** d.	...	...	...	...	0628	...	0828	...	1028	...	1228c	1332e	1428c	...	1628	...	1828	...	2028c	...	...	...	...	...	...
ttau 🚌 **1117** a.	...	...	...	...	0658	...	0856	...	1056	...	1256c	1404e	1456c	...	1659	...	1856	...	2056c	...	...	...	...	...	...
ttau d.	0414	0459	0531	0606	0702	0806	0902	1006	1102	1206	1302	1406	1502	1606	1702	1806	1902	2006	2101	...	...	2301	...	...	...
eugersdorf d.	0436	0517	0553	0627	0720	0827	0920	1027	1120	1227	1320	1427	1520	1627	1720	1827	1920	2027	2123	...	...	2323	...	...	...
ersbach (Sachs) d.	0441	0523	0557	0636	0724	0836	0924	1036	1124	1236	1324	1436	1524	1636	1724	1836	1924	2036	2126	...	...	2326	...	...	...
schofswerda d.	0520	0554	0634	0720	0754	0920	0954	1120	1154	1320	1354	1520	1554	1720	1754	1920	1954	2120	2201	2212	...	0001	0014	...	...
esden Neustadt a.	0552	0621	0704	0752	0821	0952	1021	1152	1221	1352	1421	1552	1621	1752	1821	1952	2021	2152	...	2245	...	...	0046	...	...
esden Hbf a.	0559	0627	0711	0759	0827	0959	1027	1159	1227	1359	1427	1559	1627	1759	1827	1959	2027	2159	...	2251	...	...	0052	...	...

- ⑥⑦ (also Apr. 7, 10, May 1, 8).
- ①–⑤ (not Apr. 7, 10, May 1, 8).
- Ⓐ only.

– Change trains at Bischofswerda on Ⓐ.
– Change trains at Bischofswerda on ⑥.

◇ – Change trains at Bischofswerda on ✝.
⊖ – Change trains at Bischofswerda on ⑥⑦ (also Apr. 7, 10, May 1, 8).
¶ – Change trains at Bischofswerda on May 8.
‡ – Change trains at Bischofswerda on ⑥ (also May 8).
● – Certain trains between Dresden and Bischofswerda convey portions for two separate destinations. Please take care to join the correct portion for your destination.

RE / RB services **DRESDEN and LEIPZIG - RUHLAND - COTTBUS and HOYERSWERDA** **856**

See Tables **842**, **843** and **857** for other services Dresden - Coswig. See Table **852** for other direct services Leipzig - Falkenberg - Cottbus.

km																									
			Ⓐ					Ⓐ						Ⓐ						Ⓐ					
0	**Dresden** Hbf d.	...	...	0551	...	...	0651	...	0751	...	...	0851	...	0951	...		...	1851	...	1951	...	...	2051	...	2151
4	**Dresden** Neustadt d.	...	...	0558	...	...	0658	...	0758	...	...	0858	...	0958	...		...	1858	...	1958	...	...	2058	...	2158
18	Coswig d.	...	...	0607	...	...	0707	...	0807	...	...	0907	...	1007	...		...	1907	...	2007	...	...	2107	...	2207
	Leipzig Hbf d.	...	...	|	0507	...	|	...	|	0712	...	|	...	|	0912	and in	...	|	...	|	1912	...	|	...	|
	Eilenburg d.	...	...	|	0527	...	|	...	|	0731	...	|	...	|	0931	the same	...	|	...	|	1931	...	|	...	|
	Torgau d.	...	...	|	0544	...	|	...	|	0749	...	|	...	|	0949		...	|	...	|	1949	...	|	...	|
	Falkenberg (Elster) a.	...	...	|	0555	...	|	...	|	0801	...	|	...	|	1001	pattern	...	|	...	|	2001	...	|	...	|
	Falkenberg (Elster) d.	0514	...	|	0613	0715	|	...	|	0813	0915	|	...	|	1013	every **two**	1915	|	...	|	2013	2115	|	2215	|
	Elsterwerda d.	|	0602	|	|	|	|	0802	|	|	|	|	1002	|	|		|	|	2002	|	|	|	|	|	|
	Elsterwerda-Biehla d.	0534	0606	|	0634	0734	|	0806	|	0834	0934	|	1006	|	1034	hours until	1934	|	2006	|	2034	2134	|	2234	|
73	Ruhland a.	0555	0626	0656	0655*	0755	0756*	0826	0856	0855*	0955	0956*	1026	1056	1055*		1955	1956*	2026	2056	2055*	2155	2156*	2255	2256*
73	Ruhland d.	0559	0627	0700	0702	0759	0802	0827	0900	0902	0959	1002	1027	1100	1102		1959	2002	2027	2100	2102	2159	2202	2259	2302
	Hoyerswerda a.	|	|	|	0725	|	0825	|	|	0925	|	1025	|	|	1125		|	2025	|	|	2125	|	2225	|	2325
86	Senftenberg d.	0610	0637	0711	...	0810	...	0837	0910	...	1010	...	1037	1110	...		2010	...	2037	2110	...	2210	...	2310	...
20	**Cottbus** Hbf a.	0643	0703	0744	...	0843	...	0903	0942	...	1040	...	1103	1138	...		2040	...	2103	2138	...	2240	...	2340	...

km																									
					Ⓐ			Ⓐ					Ⓐ						Ⓐ						
	Cottbus Hbf d.	...	0414	...	0516	...	0614	0651	...	0716	...	0818	0851	⊠	...	1714	...	1816	1851	...	1914	...	2016	2116	2216
	Senftenberg d.	...	0446	...	0547	...	0646	0718	...	0747	...	0846	0918		...	1747	...	1846	1918	...	1947	...	2047	2147	2247
0	**Hoyerswerda** d.	0433	|	0533	|	0633	|	|	0733	|	0833	|	|		1733	|	1833	|	|	1933	|	2033	|	|	|
25	Ruhland a.	0455	0456*	0555	0558*	0655	0656*	0727	0755	0758*	0855	0856*	0927	and in	1755	1758*	1855	1856*	1927	1955	1958*	2055	2059*	2158	2258
25	Ruhland d.	0502	0502	0602	0605	0702	0702	0728	0802	0805	0902	0902	0928	the same	1802	1805	1902	1902	1928	2002	2005	2102	2105	2205	...
51	Elsterwerda-Biehla d.	0524	|	|	0627	0724	|	0751	|	0827	0924	|	0951		|	1827	1924	|	1951	|	2027	|	2127	2227	...
	Elsterwerda a.	|	|	|	|	|	|	0754	|	|	|	|	0954	pattern	|	|	|	|	1954	|	|	|	|	|	...
75	Falkenberg (Elster) a.	0546	|	|	0646	0746	|	...	|	0846	0946	|	...	every **two**	|	1846	1946	|	...	|	2046	|	2146	2246	...
75	Falkenberg (Elster) d.	0557	|	|	...	0801	|	...	|	...	1001	|	...		|	...	2001	|	...	|	...	|	...	...	...
93	Torgau d.	0610	|	|	...	0814	|	...	|	...	1014	|	...	hours until	|	...	2014	|	...	|	...	|	...	...	...
20	Eilenburg d.	0631	|	|	...	0831	|	...	|	...	1031	|	...		|	...	2031	|	...	|	...	|	...	...	...
45	**Leipzig** Hbf a.	0650	|	|	...	0850	|	...	|	...	1050	|	...		|	...	2050	|	...	|	...	|	...	...	...
	Coswig d.	...	0547	0647	...	...	0747	...	0847	...	...	0947	...		1847	...	...	1947	...	2047	...	2147	...	...	...
	Dresden Neustadt a.	...	0555	0655	...	...	0755	...	0855	...	...	0955	...		1855	...	...	1955	...	2055	...	2155	...	...	...
	Dresden Hbf a.	...	0602	0702	...	...	0802	...	0902	...	...	1002	...		1902	...	...	2002	...	2102	...	2202	...	...	...

YERSWERDA - GÖRLITZ. *72 km*. Journey time: 52–53 minutes.
om Hoyerswerda at 0532 Ⓐ, 0632 ⚒, 0732 Ⓐ, 0832, 1032, 1232, 1432, 1532 Ⓐ, 1632, 1832, 2032 and 2232 ⑥.
om Görlitz at 0535 Ⓐ, 0633 ⚒, 0733 Ⓐ, 0833, 1033, 1233, 1433, 1533 Ⓐ, 1633, 1833, 2033 and 2233 ⑥.

- Connects with train in preceding column.

⊠ – Cottbus departure variations: 1416 (not 1418), 1514 (not 1516), 1616 (not 1618).

S-Bahn **BAD SCHANDAU - DRESDEN - MEISSEN** **857**

km																						
				Ⓐ			⚒															
0	**Bad Schandau** ⊡ **1100** ▷ d.	...	...	0443	...	0509	0543	...	0609	0643		1909	1943	2009	2043	2109	2143	2209	2243	2314	...	0014
23	Pirna d.	...	0434	0507	0507	0537	0607	0607	0637	0707	and at	1937	2007	2037	2107	2137	2207	2237	2307	2337	0007	0037
40	**Dresden** Hbf **842 843 856 1100** d.	0430	0456	0530	0530	0600	0630	0630	0700	0730	the same	2000	2030	2100	2130	2200	2230	2300	2330	0000	0028	0058
44	**Dresden** Neustadt **842 856** d.	0437	0503	0537	0537	0607	0637	0637	0707	0737	minutes	2007	2037	2107	2137	2207	2237	2307	2337	0007	...	...
50	Radebeul Ost d.	0446	0512	0546	0546	0616	0646	0646	0716	0746	past each	2016	2046	2116	2146	2216	2246	2316	2346	0016	...	...
58	Coswig **842 843 856** d.	0456	0526	0556	0556	0626	0656	0656	0726	0756	hour until	2026	2056	2126	2156	2226	2256	2326	2356	0029	...	...
68	**Meißen** a.	0504	0534	0604	0604	0634	0704	0704	0734	0804		2034	2104	2134	2204	2234	2304	2334	0005	0037	...	...

		Ⓐ			⚒																
eißen d.	...	...	0421	0451	0451	0521	0551	0621	0651		2021	2051	2121	2151	2221	2251	2321	...	0021	...	...	...
swig **842 843 856** d.	...	...	0430	0500	0500	0530	0600	0630	0700	and at	2030	2100	2130	2200	2230	2300	2330	...	0030	...	...	...
adebeul Ost d.	...	...	0440	0510	0510	0540	0610	0640	0710	the same	2040	2110	2140	2210	2240	2310	2340	...	0040	...	...	...
resden Neustadt **842 856** d.	...	...	0450	0520	0520	0550	0620	0650	0720	minutes	2050	2120	2150	2220	2250	2320	2350	...	0050	...	...	...
resden Hbf **842 843 856 1100** d.	0429	0429	0459	0529	0529	0559	0629	0659	0729	past each	2059	2129	2159	2229	2259	2329	0012f	...	0057	0100	...	...
rna ⊠ d.	0450	0451	0526	0550	0552	0626	0652	0726	0752	hour until	2126	2152	2226	2256	2321	2350	0034	...	...	0121	...	...
ad Schandau ⊡ **1100** ⊠ a.	...	0514	0548	...	0614	0648	0714	0748	0814		2148	2214	2248	2320	2343	...	0059	...	...	...	...	...

- Arrives 2357.

▷ – Bad Schandau departures may be up to 5 minutes later from Feb. 19.
⊠ – Pirna and Bad Schandau timings may be up to 5 minutes earlier from Feb. 19.
⊡ – A frequent ferry services links the railway station with Bad Schandau town centre.
Operator: Oberelbische Verkehrsgesellschaft Pirna - Sebnitz mbH. ✆ +49 (0) 3501 7920. www.ovps.de

S-Bahn **DRESDEN - DRESDEN FLUGHAFEN ✈** **857a**

km									
0	**Dresden** Hbf d.	0418	0448	and every	2218	2248	2318	...	...
4	**Dresden** Neustadt d.	0425	0455	30 minutes	2225	2255	2325	...	...
15	**Dresden** Flughafen ✈ a.	0439	0509	until	2239	2309	2339	...	...

Dresden Flughafen ✈ d.	0448	0518	and every	2248	2318	2348	...	...
Dresden Neustadt a.	0500	0530	30 minutes	2300	2330	2400	...	...
Dresden Hbf a.	0508	0538	until	2308	2338	0008	...	...

858 GLAUCHAU - GERA - ERFURT *RE services*

km		Ⓐ ◧	Ⓒ ◧	⚒		①–⑥ e★	⑦ s						★						⑥k	Ⓑb ★				◧	◧	
0	**Glauchau** (Sachs) d.	...	...	...	...	...	...	0607r	...	0807	...	1007	...	1207	...	1407	...	1607	...	...	1807	...	2007	...	...	...
16	Gößnitz a.	...	...	...	...	...	...	0621r	...	0821	...	1021	...	1221	...	1421	...	1621	...	...	1821	...	2021	...	...	...
16	Gößnitz d.	...	...	...	...	...	...	0630	...	0830	...	1030	...	1230	...	1430	...	1630	...	...	1830	...	2030	...	...	...
51	**Gera** Hbf a.	...	...	...	...	...	...	0659	...	0859	...	1059	...	1259	...	1459	...	1659	...	...	1859	...	2059	...	...	...
51	**Gera** Hbf d.	...	...	0503	0555	0604	0617	0705	0805	0905	1005	1105	1204	1305	1405	1505	1605	1705	1805	1804	1905	2005	2106	2213	2341	...
91	Jena-Göschwitz d.	0412	0416	0532	0623	0639	0644	0732	0832	0932	1032	1132	1239	1332	1432	1532	1632	1732	1832	1839	1932	2032	2133	2243	0014	...
96	**Jena** West d.	0418	0421	0538	0629	0646	0650	0738	0838	0938	1038	1138	1246	1338	1438	1538	1638	1738	1838	1846	1938	2038	2139	2248	0019	...
119	Weimar **849 850** d.	0438	0438	0554	0646	0704	0706	0754	0854	0954	1054	1154	1304	1354	1454	1554	1654	1754	1854	1904	1954	2054	2155	2305	0038	004
140	**Erfurt** Hbf **849 850** a.	0455	0452	0607	0701	0716	0721	0807	0909	1007	1109	1207	1316	1407	1509	1607	1709	1807	1909	1916	2007	2108	2208	2318	...	005
	Göttingen **865** a.	...	...	0751	...	...	...	0951	...	1151	...	1351	...	1551	...	1751	...	1951	...	...	2150	2250	...	...	...	...

	◧	†	⚒	Ⓐ				①–⑥ e★	⑦ s						★						Ⓑ	Ⓑb ★	⑥k			◧
Göttingen **865** d.	...	...	...	...	...	...	0604	...	...	0808	...	1008	...	1208	...	1408	...	1608	...	1808	1808	...	...	2008	2108	...
Erfurt Hbf **849 850** d.	0038	0437	0437	0544	...	0652	0752	0844	0850	0952	1050	1152	1250	1352	1444	1552	1650	1752	1850	1952	1952	2044	2050	2152	2301	234
Weimar **849 850** d.	0055	0451	0451	0558	...	0706	0806	0859	0904	1006	1104	1206	1304	1406	1459	1606	1704	1806	1904	2006	2006	2059	2104	2206	2316	000
Jena West d.	0114	0505	0505	0612	...	0722	0822	0915	0920	1022	1120	1222	1320	1422	1515	1622	1720	1822	1920	2022	2022	2115	2120	2222	2332	002
Jena-Göschwitz d.	0120	0513	0516j	0625j	...	0727	0827	0921	0925	1027	1125	1227	1325	1427	1521	1627	1725	1827	1925	2027	2027	2121	2125	2227	2337	002
Gera Hbf a.	0151z	0541	0544	0654	...	0755	0855	0955	0953	1055	1153	1255	1353	1455	1555	1655	1753	1855	1953	2055	2055	2155	2153	2255	0005	010
Gera Hbf d.	...	0547	...	0658	0658	...	0858	...	...	1058	...	1258	...	1458	...	1658	...	1858	...	...	2058	...	...	...	...	...
Gößnitz a.	...	0623	...	0729	0729	...	0929	...	...	1129	...	1329	...	1529	...	1729	...	1929	...	...	2129	...	...	...	...	...
Gößnitz d.	...	...	...	0735	0735	...	0935	...	...	1135	...	1335	...	1535	...	1735	...	1935	...	...	2135	...	...	...	...	...
Glauchau (Sachs) a.	...	...	...	0750	0750	...	0950	...	...	1150	...	1350	...	1550	...	1750	...	1950	...	...	2150	...	...	...	...	...

b – Not Apr. 7, 9, 30.
e – Not Apr. 8, 10, May 1.
j – Arrives 7–9 minutes earlier.
k – Also Apr. 7, 9, 30.
r – ⚒ only.
s – Also Apr. 8, 10, May 1.
z – Ⓒ only.
★ – *IC* service (see Table **849a**). Regional tickets are valid Gera - Erfurt and v.v.
◧ – Operated by Erfurter Bahn.

859 BRAUNSCHWEIG - BAD HARZBURG, GOSLAR and HERZBERG *DB (RB services); erix*

BRAUNSCHWEIG - GOSLAR and BAD HARZBURG ⊠

km		⚒	Ⓐ	⚒	⚒					
0	**Braunschweig** Hbf d.	0524	0524	0624	0624	0724	0724	and	2324	2324
12	Wolfenbüttel d.	0533	0533	0633	0633	0733	0733	hourly	2333	2333
39	Vienenburg **860** d.	0601	0602	0700	0702	0800	0802		0000	0002
47	**Bad Harzburg 860** a.	|	0611	|	0711	|	0811	until	|	0011
52	**Goslar 860** a.	0616	...	0712	...	0812	...		0012	...

	⚒	⚒	⚒	Ⓐ		Ⓒ					
Goslar 860 d.	0445	...	0545	...	0645	...	...	0745	and	...	224
Bad Harzburg 860 d.	|	0545	|	0626	|	0645	0745	|	hourly	2245	|
Vienenburg **860** d.	0503	0603	0603	0635	0700h	0703	0803	0803		2303	230
Wolfenbüttel d.	0526	0626	0626	0659	0726	0726	0826	0826	until	2326	232
Braunschweig Hbf a.	0535	0635	0635	0709	0735	0735	0835	0835		2335	233

BRAUNSCHWEIG - HERZBERG

km		CB		Ⓐ		⚒				D
0	**Braunschweig** Hbf d.	0005	...	0505	0605	0605	0705	and	2205	2305
31	Salzgitter-Ringelheim d.	0029	...	0529	0629	0629	0729	hourly	2229	2329
52	Seesen d.	0043	...	0544	0643	0644	0744		2244	2343
71	Osterode (Harz) Mitte d.	...	...	0606	...	0706	0806	until	2306	...
83	**Herzberg** (Harz) a.	...	...	0620	...	0720	0820		2320	...

	L		ⒶB	⑥B	Ⓐ			⚒			
Herzberg (Harz) d.	...	...	...	...	0534	...	...	0634	0734	and	223
Osterode (Harz) Mitte d.	...	...	...	...	0548	...	...	0648	0748	hourly	224
Seesen d.	0011	...	0511	0611	0611	...	0711	0711	0811		231
Salzgitter-Ringelheim d.	0028	...	0528	0628	0628	...	0728	0728	0828	until	232
Braunschweig Hbf a.	0050	...	0550	0650	0650	...	0750	0750	0850		235

BAD HARZBURG - KREIENSEN - GÖTTINGEN

km		CB	Ⓐ	⚒	Ⓒ	Ⓐ			Ⓐ	Ⓒ															HB
0	**Bad Harzburg 860** d.	...	...	0548	...	0628	0735	0748	...	0822	0935	1022	1135	1222	1335	1422	1535	1622	1735	1822	1935	2022	2135	2222	...
11	Goslar **860** d.	...	0544	0600	0636	0641	0757	0800	0836	0836	0957	1036	1157	1236	1357	1436	1557	1636	1757	1836	1957	2036	2157	2236	...
34	Seesen d.	0044	0603	...	0655	0700	0816	...	0855	0855	1016	1055	1216	1255	1416	1455	1616	1655	1816	1855	2016	2055	2216	2255	234
48	Bad Gandersheim d.	0054	0613	...	0705	0711	0826	...	0905	0905	1026	1105	1226	1305	1426	1505	1626	1705	1826	1905	2026	2105	2226	2305	235
54	**Kreiensen** a.	0100	0618	...	0711	0716	0831	...	0911	0911	1031	1111	1231	1311	1431	1511	1631	1711	1831	1911	2031	2111	2231	2311	240
54	**Kreiensen 903** d.	...	*0624*	...	*0719*	*0723*	0839	...	*0919*	*0919*	1039	*1119*	1239	*1319*	1439	*1519*	1639	*1719*	1839	*1919*	2039	*2119*	2239	*2322*	*002*
73	Northeim (Han) **903** d.	...	*0637*	...	*0733*	*0736*	0855	...	*0933*	*0933*	1055	*1133*	1255	*1333*	1455	*1533*	1655	*1733*	1855	*1933*	2055	*2133*	2255	*2336*	*003*
93	**Göttingen 903** a.	...	*0650*	...	*0746*	*0749*	0909	...	*0946*	*0946*	1109	*1146*	1309	*1346*	1509	*1546*	1709	*1746*	1909	*1946*	2109	*2146*	2309	*2349*	*004*

	ⒶB	Ⓐ	⑥B		Ⓐ	Ⓒ	Ⓒ	Ⓐ																	
Göttingen 903 d.	*0408*	*0504*	*0504*	0604	...	...	0648	0719	...	*0809*	0848	*1009*	1048	*1209*	1248	*1407*k	1448	*1609*	1648	*1809*	1848	*2009*	2048	*2209*	...
Northeim (Han) **903** d.	*0421*	*0517*	*0517*	0617	...	...	0702	0734	...	*0823*	0902	*1023*	1102	*1223*	1302	*1421*k	1502	*1623*	1702	*1823*	1902	*2023*	2102	*2223*	...
Kreiensen 903 a.	*0434*	*0530*	*0530*	0631	...	...	0718	0750	...	*0836*	0918	*1036*	1118	*1236*	1318	*1434*k	1518	*1636*	1718	*1836*	1918	*2036*	2118	*2236*	...
Kreiensen d.	0456	0535	0556	...	0640	0642	0724	0750	...	0842	0924	1042	1124	1242	1324	1442	1524	1642	1724	1842	1924	2042	2124	2242	...
Bad Gandersheim d.	0501	0540	0601	...	0645	0647	0729	0756	...	0847	0929	1047	1129	1247	1329	1447	1529	1647	1729	1847	1929	2047	2129	2247	...
Seesen d.	0511	0551	0611	...	0656	0658	0739	0806	...	0858	0939	1058	1139	1258	1339	1458	1539	1658	1739	1858	1939	2058	2139	2258	...
Goslar **860** d.	...	0610	...	...	0718	0718	0800	0826	0856	0918	1000	1118	1200	1318	1400	1518	1600	1718	1800	1918	2000	2118	2200	2316	235
Bad Harzburg 860 a.	...	0623	...	...	0730	0730	0814	...	0907	0930	1014	1130	1214	1330	1414	1530	1614	1730	1814	1930	2014	2130	2214	...	000

B – 12 Braunschweig - Seesen - Kreiensen and v.v.
C – ⑥⑦ (also Apr. 10, May 1, 18, 19).
D – To Kreisensen on dates in note **H** (see lower panel).
H – ①–④ (not Apr. 10, May 1, 17, 18).
L – ①⑥⑦ (also Apr. 11, May 2, 18, 19).
h – 0703 on Ⓒ.
k – 2 minutes later on Ⓒ.
⊠ – Operated by *erixx*.

860 HANNOVER - BAD HARZBURG and GOSLAR - HALLE *erixx; Abelli*

HANNOVER - BAD HARZBURG ⊠

km		Ⓐ	⚒							
0	**Hannover** Hbf d.	0448	0548	0648	0746	0848		2248	2348	...
36	**Hildesheim** Hbf d.	0515	0614	0714	0814	0914	and	2314	0015	...
70	Salzgitter-Ringelheim d.	0542	0641	0741	0841	0941	hourly	2341	0042	...
89	Goslar **859** d.	0556	0656	0756	0856	0956	until	2356	0057	...
100	**Bad Harzburg 859** a.	0607	0707	0807	0907	1007		0007	0108	...

	Ⓐ	Ⓐ	⚒	⚒		Ⓐ				⚒	†
Bad Harzburg 859 d.	...	0448	...	0548	...	...	0648		2148	2248	224
Goslar **859** d.	0403	0503	0503	0603	0603	0635	0703	and	2203	2303	230
Salzgitter-Ringelheim d.	0416	0516	0516	0616	0616	0648	0716	hourly	2216	2316	231
Hildesheim Hbf d.	0444	0544	0544	0644	0644	0717	0744	until	2244	2344	234
Hannover Hbf a.	0510	0610	0610	0710	0710	0744	0810		2310	0010	001

GOSLAR - HALBERSTADT - HALLE ◇

km				Ⓐt	Ⓒz	Ⓐt			Ⓒ	⑥	Ⓐ														
0	**Goslar 859** d.	...	...	...	...	...	...	...	...	0606	0606	0705	...	0806	0904	...	1006	1105	...	1206	1305	...	1406	1505	...
13	Vienenburg **859** d.	...	...	...	...	...	...	...	...	0616	0616	0715	...	0816	0915	...	1016	1115	...	1216	1315	...	1416	1515	...
29	Ilsenburg d.	...	...	0411	...	...	0529	...	0629	0629	0629	0731	...	0831	0931	...	1031	1131	...	1231	1331	...	1431	1531	...
38	Wernigerode d.	...	...	0422	...	...	0540	...	0640	0640	0640	0742	...	0840	0942	...	1040	1142	...	1240	1342	...	1440	1542	...
62	**Halberstadt** a.	...	...	0438	...	...	0555	...	0656	0656	0656	0755	...	0856	0955	...	1056	1155	...	1256	1355	...	1456	1555	...
62	**Halberstadt** d.	0339	...	0446	0446	0528	0602	0607	0657	0657	0701	0801	0802	0901	1001	1002	1101	1201	1202	1301	1401	1402	1501	1601	160
	Magdeburg Hbf **862** a.	|	...	|	|	|	0646	|	|	|	|	0846	|	|	1046	|	|	1246	|	|	1446	|	|	1646	|
	Berlin Hbf **839** a.	|	...	|	|	|	...	|	|	|	|	...	|	|	...	|	|	...	|	|	...	|	|	...	|
94	Aschersleben d.	0404	...	0520	0520	0557	...	0641	0726	0726	0726	...	0824	0926	...	1024	1126	...	1224	1326	...	1424	1526	...	162
105	Sandersleben (Anh) d.	0419	...	0537	0537	0606	...	0656	0737	0737	0737	...	0837	0937	...	1037	1137	...	1237	1337	...	1437	1537	...	163
122	Könnern d.	0433	...	0550	0550	0620	...	0710	0750	0750	0750	...	0850	0950	...	1050	1150	...	1250	1350	...	1450	1550	...	165
152	**Halle** (Saale) Hbf a.	0459	...	0608	0619	0637	...	0737	0811	0811	0811	...	0911	1011	...	1111	1211	...	1311	1411	...	1511	1611	...	171

B – Mornings of ①③④⑤⑥⑦ (also Jan. 3, 10. 17, 24, 31, Feb. 7, Apr. 11, May 2; not Apr. 12, May 3, 20).
D – ⑤⑥† (not Dec. 24).
c – Arrives 0618.
e – Arrives 2239.
j – Also Dec. 26; not Dec. 25.
t – Not Jan. 6.
z – Also Jan. 6.
⊠ – Operated by *erixx*.
◇ – Operated by Abellio Rail Mitteldeutschland.
¶ – *HARZ-BERLIN-EXPRESS*.

TIMINGS CONTINUE ON NEXT PAGE →

rixx ; Abellio — HANNOVER - BAD HARZBURG and GOSLAR - HALLE — 860

			D¶									
oslar 859 d.	1606	1705	1705	...	1806	1905	...	2006	2105	2206	2305	...
enenburg **859** d.	1616	1715	1715	...	1816	1915	...	2016	2115	2216	2315	...
enburg d.	1631	1731	1731	...	1831	1931	...	2031	2131	2232	2331	...
ernigerode d.	1640	1742	1742	...	1840	1942	...	2040	2142	2243	2342	...
alberstadt a.	1656	1755	1755	...	1856	1955	...	2056	2155	2258	2355	...
alberstadt d.	1701	1801	1801	1802	1901	2001	2002	2101	2202	2305	...	...
Magdeburg Hbf **862** a.	|	1846	1846	|	|	2056	|	|	2257	|	...	...
Berlin Hbf **839** a.	|	...	2048	|	|	...	|	|	...	|	...	...
schersleben d.	1726	...	...	1824	1926	...	2024	2126	...	2333	...	...
ndersleben (Anh) d.	1737	...	...	1837	1937	...	2037	2137	...	2347	...	...
nnern d.	1750	...	...	1850	1950	...	2050	2150	...	0000	...	...
alle (Saale) Hbf a.	1811	...	...	1911	2011	...	2111	2208	...	0028	...	...

	⚒	Ⓐ						
Halle (Saale) Hbf d.	...	0345	...	0525	0638	...	0749	0849
Könnern d.	...	0405	...	0551	0710	...	0810	0910
Sandersleben (Anh) d.	...	0418	...	0606	0724	...	0823	0923
Aschersleben d.	...	0429	...	0627c	0737	...	0835	0937
Berlin Hbf **839** d.	...	|	...	|	|	...	|	|
Magdeburg Hbf **862** d.	...	|	...	|	|	0707	|	|
Halberstadt a.	...	0458	...	0657	0757	0758	0900	0957
Halberstadt d.	0459	0459	0559	0702	...	0804	0904	...
Wernigerode d.	0516	0516	0616	0719	...	0818	0921	...
Ilsenburg d.	0530	0530	0630	0730	...	0829	0930	...
Vienenburg **859** d.	0541	0541	0643	0741	...	0842	0941	...
Goslar 859 a.	0552	0552	0654	0752	...	0853	0952	...

		©¶																			Ⓐt		B	⑦j¶	
alle (Saale) Hbf d.	...	...	0949	1049	...	1149	1249	...	1349	1449	...	1549	1649	...	1749	1849	...	1949	2049	...	2207	2309	...	...	2325
önnern d.	...	...	1010	1110	...	1210	1310	...	1410	1510	...	1610	1710	...	1810	1910	...	2010	2110	...	2246e	2329	...	...	2358
andersleben (Anh) d.	...	...	1023	1123	...	1223	1323	...	1423	1523	...	1623	1723	...	1823	1923	...	2023	2123	...	2300	2347	...	...	|
schersleben d.	...	...	1035	1137	...	1235	1337	...	1435	1537	...	1635	1737	...	1835	1937	...	2035	2137	...	2309	0001	...	...	0047
Berlin Hbf **839** d.	...	0723	|	|	...	|	|	...	|	|	...	|	|	...	|	|	...	|	|	...	|	|	...	2131	|
Magdeburg Hbf **862** d.	0908	0908	|	|	1108	|	|	1308	|	|	1508	|	|	1707	|	|	1908	|	|	2108	|	|	...	2319	|
alberstadt a.	0958	0958	1100	1157	1158	1300	1357	1358	1500	1557	1558	1700	1757	1758	1900	1957	1958	2102	2158	2159	2338	0028	...	0009	0115
alberstadt d.	1004	1004	1104	...	1204	1304	...	1404	1504	...	1604	1704	...	1804	1904	...	2004	2105	...	2205	...	...	0035	0035	...
ernigerode d.	1018	1018	1121	...	1218	1321	...	1418	1521	...	1618	1721	...	1818	1921	...	2018	2121	...	2219	...	...	0051	0051	...
enburg d.	1029	1029	1130	...	1229	1330	...	1429	1530	...	1629	1730	...	1829	1930	...	2029	2129	...	2230	...	...	0101	0101	...
enenburg **859** d.	1042	1042	1141	...	1242	1341	...	1442	1541	...	1642	1741	...	1842	1941	...	2042	2141	...	2242	...	...	...	...	...
oslar 859 a.	1053	1053	1152	...	1253	1352	...	1453	1552	...	1653	1752	...	1853	1952	...	2053	2152	...	2253	...	...	...	...	...

- **FOR NOTES SEE BOTTOM OF PREVIOUS PAGE**

MAGDEBURG - SANGERHAUSEN - ERFURT and DESSAU - ASCHERSLEBEN — 861

Operated by Abellio Rail Mitteldeutschland

Magdeburg - Erfurt and Aschersleben

km																									
		©	Ⓐ	Ⓐt		Ⓐt	©z								Ⓐt	©z	Ⓐt		Ⓐt						
0	**Magdeburg** Hbf d.	0051	0437	0511	0608	0712	0712	0826	0911	1026	1111	1226	1311	1426	1457	1511	1529	1626	1711	1711	1826	1911	2026	2111	2226	2255
17	Schönebeck (Elbe) d.	0106	0450	0526	0623	0726	0726	0839	0926	1039	1126	1239	1326	1439	1510	1526	1542	1639	1726	1726	1839	1926	2039	2126	2239	2316
37	Staßfurt d.	0130	0509	0550	0649	0750	0747	0853	0950	1053	1150	1253	1350	1453	1534	1550	1608	1653	1750	1750	1853	1950	2053	2150	2253	2337
44	Güsten d.	0137	0514	0558	0657	0758	0754	0859	0958	1059	1158	1259	1358	1459	1541	1558	1615	1659	1803	1759	1859	1958	2059	2158	2259	2344
	Aschersleben a.	0149	|	0610	|	0810	*0816*	|	1010	|	1210	|	1410	|	|	1610	1627	|	|	1810	|	2010	|	2210	|	2356
60	Sandersleben d.	▬	0546k	▬	0712	...	▬	0912	▬	1112	▬	1312	▬	1512	1555	▬	▬	1712	1816	▬	1912	▬	2112	...	2312	...
66	Hettstedt d.	...	0554	...	0719	...	...	0919	...	1119	...	1319	...	1519	1602	...	...	1719	1822	...	1919	...	2119	...	2319	...
75	Klostermansfeld d.	...	0603	...	0728	...	...	0928	...	1128	...	1328	...	1528	1611	©	Ⓐ	1728	1831	...	1928	...	2128	...	2328	...
97	**Sangerhausen** d.	0547	0623	0641	0748	...	0852	0948	1052	1148	1252	1348	1452	1548	1636	1652	1652	1748	1854	1905	1956j	2100	2159n	...	2345	...
42	Sömmerda d.	0633	0700	0731	0829	...	0931	1029	1131	1229	1331	1429	1531	1629	...	1731	1736	1829	...	1953	2037	2142	2244	...	...	...
67	**Erfurt** Hbf a.	0654	0720	0751	0850	...	0951	1050	1151	1250	1351	1451	1551	1650	...	1751	1756	1849	...	2014	2058	2202	2305	...	...	...

	Ⓐt	Ⓐt	©z	Ⓐt	Ⓐt			Ⓐ																	
rfurt Hbf d.	...	...	...	...	...	0503	...	0613	0704	0809	0910	1009	1110	1209	1310	1409	1509	1609	1710	1809	1906	...	2018	2136	2327
ömmerda d.	...	...	...	...	...	0523	...	0633	0730	0829	0932	1029	1132	1229	1332	1429	1532	1629	1732	1829	1928	...	2038	2155	2347
angerhausen d.	...	...	...	0511	...	0618j	...	0723	0818	0909	1018	1109	1218	1309	1418	1509	1618	1709	1818	1909	2018	...	2123	2243	0032
ostermansfeld d.	...	...	...	0529	...	0637	...	...	0837	▬	1037	▬	1237	▬	1437	▬	1637	▬	1837	▬	2037	...	...	...	...
ettstedt d.	...	...	...	0538	...	0645	...	...	0845	...	1045	...	1245	...	1445	...	1645	...	1845	...	2045	...	...	...	...
andersleben d.	...	...	...	0545	...	0653	...	...	0853	...	1053	...	1253	...	1453	...	1653	...	1853	...	2053	...	...	...	...
Aschersleben d.	0448	0530	0544	|	0623	|	0746	...	|	0946	|	1146	|	1346	|	1546	|	1746	|	1946	|	*2145*	...	...	...
üsten d.	0501	0541	0556	0559	0635	0708	0758	...	0908	0958	1108	1158	1308	1358	1508	1558	1708	1758	1908	1958	2108	2159	...	...	...
aßfurt d.	0509	0553	0604	0612	0644	0715	0808	...	0915	1008	1115	1208	1315	1408	1515	1608	1715	1808	1915	2008	2115	2208	...	...	...
chönebeck (Elbe) d.	0529	0615	0626	0629	0704	0730	0829	...	0930	1029	1130	1229	1330	1429	1530	1629	1730	1829	1930	2029	2130	2230	...	...	...
agdeburg Hbf a.	0543	0627	0640	0643	0717	0742	0842	...	0942	1042	1142	1242	1343	1442	1542	1642	1742	1842	1942	2042	2142	2249	...	...	...

Dessau - Aschersleben (- Halberstadt)

km																										
		Ⓐt	©z	Ⓐt		Ⓐt	©z	Ⓐt								Ⓐt	©z									
0	**Dessau** Hbf d.	0428	0454	0515	0553v	0643	0712	0730	0802	0902	1002	1102	1202	1302	1402	1502	1502	1602	1702	1802	1902	2002	2102	2212	2329	...
21	Köthen a.	0448	0515	0536	0620	0707	0732	0754	0822	0922	1022	1122	1222	1322	1422	1522	1522	1622	1722	1822	1922	2022	2122	2231	2349	...
21	Köthen d.	0451	0517	0539	0632	0723	0733	0754	0832	0923	1032	1123	1232	1323	1432	1523	1523	1632	1723	1832	1923	2032	2123	2232	2351	...
42	Bernburg Hbf d.	0512	0539	0558	0651	0743	0754	0813	0853	0942	1053	1142	1253	1342	1453	1542	1542	1653	1742	1853	1942	2053	2142	2253	0012	0023
54	Güsten d.	0524	0550	0610	0703	0754	0805	0824	0904	0954	1104	1154	1304	1354	1504	1553	1554	1704	1754	1904	1954	2104	2153	2304	...	0034
66	**Aschersleben** ... **860** a.	0535	0602	0621	0715	*0810*	0816	0832	0915	*1010*	1115	*1210*	1315	*1410*	1515	1604	*1610*	1715	*1810*	1915	*2010*	2115	*2210*	2315	...	0046
	Halberstadt .... **860** a.	...	...	...	...	...	...	...	0951	...	...	...	1351	...	1551	...	...	1751	...	...	...	...	...	...	...	0115

		Ⓐt											Ⓐt	©z											
alberstadt .... **860** d.	...	...	...	...	...	...	...	1011	...	...	...	1411	...	...	1611	...	...	...	...	...	...	...	...	...	...
schersleben .... **860** d.	0421	0516	0557	0649	*0746*	0849	*0946*	1049	*1146*	1249	*1346*	1449	1537	*1546*	1649	*1746*	1849	*1946*	2049	2145	...	...	...	...	...
üsten d.	0433	0527	0607	0701	0801	0902	1001	1102	1201	1302	1401	1502	1549	1601	1702	1801	1902	2001	2102	2202r	...	...	...	...	...
ernburg Hbf d.	0454j	0538	0617	0713	0813	0913	1013	1113	1213	1313	1413	1513	1600	1613	1713	1813	1913	2013	2113	2214	...	...	...	...	...
öthen a.	0516	0600	0638	0735	0834	0935	1034	1135	1234	1335	1434	1535	1622	1634	1735	1834	1935	2034	2135	2234	...	...	...	...	...
öthen d.	0518	0603	0640	0737	0835	0937	1035	1137	1235	1337	1435	1537	1635	1635	1737	1835	1937	2035	2137	2235	...	...	...	...	...
essau Hbf a.	0542	0622	0700	0756	0854	0956	1054	1156	1254	1356	1454	1556	1654	1654	1756	1854	1956	2054	2156	2254	...	...	...	...	...

- Arrives 11 minutes earlier. **k** – Arrives 0529. **n** – Arrives 2145. **r** – Arrives 2156. **t** – Not Jan. 6. **v** – 0559 on © (also Jan. 6). **z** – Also Jan. 6.

bellio Rail Mitteldeutschland — MAGDEBURG - HALBERSTADT - THALE — 862

km																									
			Ⓐ t			◧		◧	© ▲		◧		◧		◧		◧			◧		◧			⑦ ▲
	Berlin Hbf **839** d.	...	...	...	...	...	...	...	0723	...	...	...	...	...	...	...	...	...	...	...	...	...	...	...	2131
0	**Magdeburg** Hbf d.	...	0425	...	0544	0707	0807	0908	0908	1007	1108	1207	1308	1407	1508	1607	1707	1808	1846	1908	2007	2108	2208	2319	2319
39	Oschersleben (Bode) d.	...	0502	...	0624	0742	0842	0942	0942	1042	1142	1242	1342	1442	1542	1642	1742	1842	1924	1942	2045	2145	2247	2355	2355
59	**Halberstadt** a.	...	0516	...	0640	0758	0857	0958	0958	1057	1158	1257	1358	1457	1558	1657	1758	1857	1940	1958	2100	2159	2302	0009	0009
59	**Halberstadt** d.	0517	0517	0610	0708	0808	0908	1008	1008	1108	1208	1308	1408	1508	1608	1708	1808	1908	...	2008	2109	2202	...	0029	0029
77	Quedlinburg a.	0532	0532	0625	0723	0823	0923	1023	1023	1123	1223	1323	1423	1523	1623	1723	1823	1923	...	2023	2124	2217	...	0043	0043
77	Quedlinburg d.	0536	0536	0630	0730	0830	0930	1030	1030	1130	1230	1330	1430	1530	1630	1730	1830	1930	...	2030	2130	2218	...	0044	0044
87	**Thale** Hbf a.	0548	0548	0642	0742	0842	0942	1042	1042	1142	1242	1342	1442	1542	1642	1742	1842	1942	...	2042	2142	2228	...	0054	0054

	Ⓐ t			◐		◧		◧		◧		◧		◧		◧	⑤⑥† ▲		◧		◧			
hale Hbf d.	...	...	...	0522	0617	0717	0817	0917	1017	1117	1217	1317	1417	1517	1617	1717	1717	1817	1917	2017	2117	...	2230	2342
uedlinburg a.	...	...	...	0533	0628	0728	0828	0928	1028	1128	1228	1328	1428	1528	1628	1728	1728	1828	1928	2028	2128	...	2240	2352
uedlinburg d.	...	...	...	0535	0633	0733	0833	0932	1033	1133	1233	1336	1433	1532	1633	1733	1733	1833	1936	2033	2133	...	2241	2353
alberstadt a.	...	...	...	0551	0649	0749	0849	0948	1049	1149	1249	1351	1449	1548	1649	1749	1749	1849	1951	2049	2149	...	2257	0009
alberstadt d.	0359	0442	...	0602	0701	0801	0901	1001	1101	1201	1301	1401	1501	1601	1701	1801	1801	1901	2001	2103	2202	...	...	...
schersleben (Bode) d.	0414	0458	...	0617	0717	0817	0917	1017	1117	1217	1317	1417	1517	1617	1717	1817	1817	1917	2017	2119	2218	...	...	...
agdeburg Hbf a.	0453	0535	...	0646	0746	0846	0946	1046	1146	1246	1347	1446	1546	1646	1746	1846	1846	1946	2056	2152	2257	...	...	...
Berlin Hbf **839** a.	...	...	...	...	...	...	...	...	...	...	...	...	...	...	...	...	2048	...	...	...	...	...	...	...

- Not Jan. 6.

◧ – Conveys (12) Magdeburg - Halberstadt - Goslar and v.v. (Table **860**).
◐ – Conveys (12) Ilsenburg - Halberstadt - Magdeburg (Table **860**).
▲ – *HARZ-BERLIN-EXPRESS*. DB tickets not valid for journeys from / to Berlin. Conveys (2) Berlin - Halberstadt - Ilsenburg / Goslar and v.v. (Table **860**).

863 WOLFSBURG - HILDESHEIM - HAMELN - LÖHNE

Regionalverkehre Start Deutschland ◇; enno ⊠

km		Ⓐ	Ⓐ	⑥	Ⓐ	Ⓒ	⑥																
0	**Hildesheim** Hbf .... d.	...	0537	0527	0634	...	0634	0737	0834	0937	1034	1137	1234	1337	1434	1537	1634	1737	1834	1937	2034	...	2137	...	223
18	Elze .... a.	...	0553	0553	0650	...	0650	0753	0850	0953	1050	1153	1250	1353	1450	1553	1650	1753	1850	1953	2050	...	2153	...	225
18	Elze .... d.	...	0602	0602	0702	...	0702	0802	0902	1002	1102	1202	1302	1402	1502	1602	1702	1802	1902	2002	2102	...	2202	...	230
47	**Hameln** .... d.	0529	0629	0629	0729	0729	0729	0829	0929	1029	1129	1229	1329	1429	1529	1629	1729	1829	1929	2029	2129	...	2229	...	233
71	Rinteln .... d.	0546	0646	0646	0746	0746	0746	0846	0946	1046	1146	1246	1346	1446	1546	1646	1746	1846	1946	2046	2146	...	2246	...	
88	Vlotho .... d.	0600	0700	0700	0800	0800	0800	0900	1000	1100	1200	1300	1400	1500	1600	1700	1800	1900	2000	2100	2200	...	2300	...	
100	Löhne (Westf) ...... **811** a.	0613	0713	0713	0813	0813	0813	0913	1013	1113	1213	1313	1413	1513	1613	1713	1813	1913	2013	2113	2213	...	2313	...	
	Bünde (Westf) ... **811** a.	0625	0725	|	0825	|	|	|	1025t	|	1225t	1325t	1425t	|	1625t	1725t	1825t	|	|	|	|	...	...	...	
	Herford .... **811** a.	...	...	0724	...	0824	0824	0924z	1024z	1124z	1224z	1324z	1424z	1524z	1624z	1724z	1824z	1924z	2024z	2124z	2224z	...	...	...	

	Ⓐ	⚒	Ⓐ	⚒	⚒		Ⓐt	⑥					Ⓒ	ⒶD	Ⓐe									
Herford .... **811** d.	...	...	...	...	...	...	...	0736	0836z	0936z	1036z	1136z	1236	...	...	1336z	1436z	1536z	1636z	1736z	1836z	1936z	2036z	213
Bünde (Westf) .... **811** d.	...	...	...	...	0632t	...	0732	|	0832t	|	1032t	|	|	1232	1232	1332t	1432t	|	1632t	1732t	1832t	|	|	|
Löhne (Westf) .... **811** d.	0446	...	0546	...	0646	...	0746	0746	0846	0946	1046	1146	1246	1246	1246	1346	1446	1546	1646	1746	1846	1946	2046	214
Vlotho .... d.	0459	...	0559	...	0659	...	0759	0759	0859	0959	1059	1159	1259	1259	1259	1359	1459	1559	1659	1759	1859	1959	2059	215
Rinteln .... d.	0510	...	0610	...	0710	...	0810	0810	0910	1010	1110	1210	1310	1310	1310	1410	1510	1610	1710	1810	1910	2010	2110	221
Hameln .... d.	0528	0528	0628	0628	0728	0728	0828	0828	0928	1028	1128	1228	1328	1328	1335r	1428	1528	1628	1728	1828	1928	2028	2128	222
Elze .... a.	0553	0553	0652	0653	0753	0753	0852	0852	0953	1052	1153	1252	1353	1353	1400	1452	1553	1652	1753	1852	1953	2052	2153	225
Elze .... d.	0602	0602	0702	0702	0802	0802	0907	0907	1002	1107	1202	1307	1402	1402	1402	1507	1602	1707	1802	1907	2002	2107	2202	230
Hildesheim Hbf .... a.	0620	0620	0720	0720	0820	0820	0925	0925	1020	1125	1220	1325	1420	1420	1423	1525	1620	1725	1820	1925	2020	2125	2220	232

Regional trains **WOLFSBURG - BRAUNSCHWEIG - HILDESHEIM** ⊠

km		Ⓐ	⚒	Ⓐ					
0	**Wolfsburg** Hbf .... d.	0514	0614	0643	0714	and	2314	0014	...
32	**Braunschweig** Hbf ..... d.	0535	0635	0704	0735	hourly	2335	0033	...
75	**Hildesheim** Hbf .... a.	0602	0702	...	0802	until	0002	...	...

	Ⓐ	⚒	Ⓐ	⚒		Ⓐ		⊡		
Hildesheim Hbf .... d.	0455	...	...	0555	...	...	0655	and	2255	...
Braunschweig Hbf .. d.	0526	0526	0551	0626	0626	0656	0726	hourly	2326	004
Wolfsburg Hbf .... a.	0545	0545	0612	0645	0645	0719	0745	until	2345	010

D – Dec. 23 - Jan. 6 and Mar. 27 - Apr. 11 (also Jan. 30, 31, May 19).
e – Not Dec. 23 - Jan. 6, Jan. 30, 31, Mar. 27 - Apr. 11, May 19.
r – Arrives 1326.
t – Ⓐ only.
z – Ⓒ only.
⊡ – Braunschweig d. 0925 / 1325 (not 0926 / 1326).
◇ – Bünde - Hildesheim operated by Regionalverkehre Start Deutschland.
⊠ – Wolfsburg - Hildesheim operated by *enno*. See Table **902** for *ICE* trains operated by D

865 ERFURT and HALLE - LEINEFELDE - KASSEL and GÖTTINGEN

DB (*RE* / *RB* services); Abelli

km		Ⓐ △	Ⓐ	Ⓐ △	Ⓐ		Ⓐ	△	G	Ⓐ △			△	A	⚒ △			△	A	△			△	A	△
0	**Erfurt** Hbf .... **849 850** d.	...	...	...	...	0423	0502	...	0609	...	0622	0707	...	0809	...	0833	0907	...	1009	...	1033	1107	...	1209	...
27	Gotha .... **849 850** d.	...	...	...	...	0458	◇	...	0634	...	|	◇	...	0835	...	|	◇	...	1035	...	|	◇	...	1235	...
48	Bad Langensalza .... d.	...	...	...	0446	0509	0555	...	0646	...	0710	0800	...	0847	...	0914	1000	...	1047	...	1114	1200	...	1247	...
67	Mühlhausen (Thür) .... d.	...	...	...	0503	0524	0611	...	0700	...	0726	0815	...	0900	...	0926	1015	...	1100	...	1126	1215	...	1300	...
	Halle (Saale) Hbf .... d.	...	...	...	|	|	|	0453	|	0527	|	|	0702	|	0758	|	|	0902	|	0958	|	|	1102	|	115
	Röblingen am See .... d.	...	...	...	|	|	|	0517	|	0601	|	|	0721	|	0819	|	|	0921	|	1019	|	|	1121	|	121
	Lutherstadt Eisleben .... d.	...	...	...	|	|	|	0526	|	0610	|	|	0730	|	0827	|	|	0930	|	1027	|	|	1130	|	122
	Sangerhausen .... d.	...	...	0413	|	|	|	0545	|	0632	|	|	0753	|	0848e	|	|	0953	|	1048e	|	|	1153	|	124
	Nordhausen .... d.	...	...	0449	|	|	|	0619	|	0705	|	|	0826	|	0917	|	|	1026	|	1117	|	|	1226	|	131
94	**Leinefelde** .... d.	0423	0502	0529	0533	0544	0634	0655	0718	0745	0751	0840	0858	0918	0948	0953	1040	1058	1118	1148	1153	1240	1258	1318	134
110	Heilbad Heiligenstadt .... d.	0438	0513	...	0547	0556	...	0705	0729	...	0801	...	0908	0929	...	1004	...	1108	1129	...	1204	...	1308	1329	...
144	**Göttingen** .... a.	|	0539	...	|	0625	...	|	0751	...	|	...	|	0951	...	|	...	|	1151	...	|	...	|	1351	...
125	Eichenberg .... **865a** d.	0501f	...	...	0602	...	...	0719	...	...	0816	...	0919	...	...	1018	...	1119	...	...	1218	...	1319	...	...
148	Hann Münden .... **865a** d.	0520	...	...	0622	...	...	0736	...	...	0833	...	0936	...	...	1035	...	1136	...	...	1235	...	1336	...	...
172	**Kassel** Hbf .... **865a** a.	0540	...	...	0643	...	...	|	...	...	|	...	|	...	...	|	...	|	...	...	|	...	|	...	...
176	**Kassel** Wilhelmshöhe .... a.	...	...	...	0656	...	...	0753	...	...	0852	...	0953	...	...	1054	...	1153	...	...	1254	...	1356	...	...

			△	A	△			△	A	△			△	A	△			△	A		△	G		△	△
Erfurt Hbf .... **849 850** d.	1233	1307	...	1409	...	1433	1507	...	1609	...	1633	1707	...	1809	...	1833	1907	...	2009	2033	...	2111	2253	...	...
Gotha .... **849 850** d.	|	◇	...	1435	...	|	◇	...	1636	...	|	◇	...	1835	...	|	◇	...	2035	|	...	2135	2326k	...	...
Bad Langensalza .... d.	1314	1400	...	1447	...	1514	1600	...	1647	...	1714	1800	...	1847	...	1914	2000	...	2047	2112	...	2147	2339	...	...
Mühlhausen (Thür) .... d.	1326	1415	...	1500	...	1526	1615	...	1700	...	1726	1815	...	1900	...	1926	2016	...	2100	2127	...	2158	2353	...	...
Halle (Saale) Hbf .... d.	|	|	1302	|	1358	|	|	1502	|	1558	|	|	1702	|	1758	|	...	1902	|	|	1958	|	|	2109	232
Röblingen am See .... d.	|	|	1321	|	1419	|	|	1521	|	1619	|	|	1721	|	1819	|	...	1921	|	|	2019	|	|	2128	234
Lutherstadt Eisleben .... d.	|	|	1330	|	1427	|	|	1530	|	1627	|	|	1730	|	1827	|	...	1930	|	|	2027	|	|	2137	234
Sangerhausen .... d.	|	|	1353	|	1448e	|	|	1553	|	1648e	|	|	1753	|	1848e	|	...	1953	|	|	2048e	|	|	2156	000
Nordhausen .... d.	|	|	1426	|	1517	|	|	1626	|	1717	|	|	1826	|	1917	|	...	2026	|	|	2123f	|	|	2228	004
Leinefelde .... d.	1353	1440	1456	1518	1548	1553	1640	1658	1718	1748	1753	1840	1858	1918	1948	1953	...	2058	2118	2147	2204	2217	0010	...	...
Heilbad Heiligenstadt .... d.	1404	...	1507	1529	...	1604	...	1708	1729	...	1804	...	1908	1929	...	2004	...	2108	2129	2158	▬	2228	...	...	...
Göttingen .... a.	|	...	|	1551	...	|	...	|	1751	...	|	...	|	1951	...	|	...	|	2150	|		2250	...	...	...
Eichenberg .... **865a** d.	1418	...	1519	...	...	1618	...	1719	...	...	1818	...	1919	...	...	2018	...	2119	...	2212	2233	...	...	...	...
Hann Münden .... **865a** d.	1435	...	1536	...	...	1635	...	1736	...	...	1835	...	1936	...	...	2035	...	2136	...	...	2253	...	...	...	...
Kassel Hbf .... **865a** a.	|	...	|	...	...	|	...	|	...	...	|	...	|	...	...	|	...	2154	...	...	2313	...	...	...	...
Kassel Wilhelmshöhe .... a.	1454	...	1553	...	...	1655	...	1756	...	...	1854	...	1953	...	...	2054	...	...	...	...	...	...	...	...	...

km		△		Ⓐ △	Ⓐ	⚒ △	A	Ⓐ △	Ⓒ △		Ⓐ		△	A	△			△	A	△			△	A	△
0	**Kassel** Wilhelmshöhe .... d.	...	...	...	...	...	...	...	...	...	0706	...	...	...	0805	...	0906	...	...	1006	...	1106	...	...	120
	Kassel Hbf .... **865a** d.	...	...	0416	...	...	...	0546	0606	...	|	...	...	...	|	...	|	...	...	|	...	|	...	...	|
23	Hann Münden .... **865a** d.	...	...	0436	...	...	...	0605	0623	...	0722	...	...	...	0823	...	0922	...	...	1023	...	1122	...	...	122
46	Eichenberg .... **865a** d.	...	...	0457	...	...	...	0633f	0640	...	0741	...	...	...	0840	...	0941	...	...	1040	...	1141	...	...	124
	Göttingen .... d.	...	...	|	...	...	0604	|	|	...	|	...	...	0808	|	...	|	...	1008	|	...	|	...	1208	|
61	Heilbad Heiligenstadt .... d.	...	0444t	0510	...	...	0627	0647	0652	...	0755	...	...	0831	0852	...	0955	...	1031	1052	...	1155	...	1231	125
77	**Leinefelde** .... d.	0440t	0502	0524	0547	0551b	0640	0703	0703	0719t	0807	0807	0810t	0843	0903	0919	1007	1009r	1043	1103	1119	1207	1209	1243	130
119	**Nordhausen** .... d.	0532k	|	0558	|	0639f	|	0735	0735	|	|	|	0843t	|	0935	|	|	1043r	|	1135	|	|	1243	|	133
157	Sangerhausen .... d.	0611	|	0634	|	0717	|	0812	0812	|	|	|	0918	|	1012	|	|	1118	|	1212	|	|	1318	|	141
179	Lutherstadt Eisleben .... d.	0629	|	0652	|	0735	|	0833	0833	|	|	|	0935	|	1033	|	|	1135	|	1233	|	|	1335	|	143
190	Röblingen am See .... a.	0637	|	0702	|	0743	|	0841	0841	|	|	|	0943	|	1041	|	|	1143	|	1241	|	|	1343	|	144
217	**Halle** (Saale) Hbf .... a.	0658	|	0734	|	0803	|	0859	0859	|	|	|	1003	|	1059	|	|	1203	|	1259	|	|	1403	|	145
—	Mühlhausen (Thür) .... d.	...	0522	...	0612	...	0658	...	...	0742	0832	0832	...	0859	...	0942	1032	...	1059	...	1142	1232	...	1259	...
0	Bad Langensalza .... d.	...	0535	...	0630	...	0710	...	...	0759	0844	0844	...	0910	...	0959	1044	...	1110	...	1159	1244	...	1310	...
	Gotha .... **849 850** a.	...	0551	...	⊙	...	0722	...	...	⊙	|	|	...	0922	...	⊙	|	...	1122	...	⊙	|	...	1322	...
38	**Erfurt** Hbf .... **849 850** a.	...	0615	...	0720	...	0746	...	...	0846	0921	0921	...	0946	...	1046	1121	...	1146	...	1246	1321	...	1346	...

			△	A	△			△	A	△			△	A	△			△	G	△	G		△		
Kassel Wilhelmshöhe .... d.	...	1306	...	...	1406	...	1506	...	...	1606	...	1706	...	...	1805	...	1905	...	...	2004	...	2106	...		...
Kassel Hbf .... **865a** d.	...	|	...	...	|	...	|	...	...	|	...	|	...	...	|	...	|	...	...	|	...	|	...	*2146*	...
Hann Münden .... **865a** d.	...	1322	...	...	1423	...	1523	...	...	1623	...	1722	...	...	1823	...	1922	...	...	2023	...	2122	...	*2206*	...
Eichenberg .... **865a** d.	...	1341	...	...	1440	...	1541	...	...	1640	...	1741	...	...	1840	...	1941	...	...	2040	...	2141	...	*2242*	...
Göttingen .... d.	...	|	...	1408	|	...	|	...	1608	|	...	|	...	1808	|	...	|	...	2008	|	2108	|	...	|	230
Heilbad Heiligenstadt .... d.	...	1355	...	1431	1452	...	1555	...	1631	1652	...	1755	...	1831	1852	...	1955	...	2031	2052	2132	2155	...	2254	233
Leinefelde .... d.	1319	1407	1409	1443	1503	1519	1607	1609	1643	1703	1719	1807	1809	1843	1903	1919	2007	2013	2043	2103	2148	2220k	2223	2304	234
Nordhausen .... d.	|	|	1443	|	1535	|	|	1643	|	1735	|	|	1843	|	1935	|	|	2054e	|	2137	|	|	2303	...	...
Sangerhausen .... d.	|	|	1518	|	1612	|	|	1718	|	1812	|	|	1918	|	2012	|	|	2132	|	2215	|	|	2339	...	...
Lutherstadt Eisleben .... d.	|	|	1535	|	1633	|	|	1735	|	1833	|	|	1935	|	2033	|	|	2150	|	2235	|	|	2358	...	...
Röblingen am See .... a.	|	|	1543	|	1641	|	|	1743	|	1841	|	|	1943	|	2041	|	|	2159	|	2243	|	|	0008	...	...
Halle (Saale) Hbf .... a.	|	|	1603	|	1659	|	|	1803	|	1859	|	|	2003	|	2059	|	|	2234	|	2301	|	|	0040	...	...
Mühlhausen (Thür) .... d.	1342	1432	...	1459	...	1542	1632	...	1659	...	1742	1832	...	1859	...	1942	2027	...	2059	...	2212	2239	...	...	...
Bad Langensalza .... d.	1359	1444	...	1510	...	1559	1644	...	1710	...	1759	1844	...	1910	...	1959	2042	...	2110	...	2222	2255	...	...	...
Gotha .... **849 850** a.	⊙	|	...	1522	...	⊙	|	...	1722	...	⊙	|	...	1922	...	⊙	|	...	2122	...	2235	|	...	...	...
Erfurt Hbf .... **849 850** a.	1446	1521	...	1546	...	1646	1721	...	1746	...	1846	1921	...	1946	...	2051	2121	...	2149	...	2258	2334	...	...	...

FOR NOTES SEE UNDER TABLE 865a ON NEXT PAGE →

GÖTTINGEN - KASSEL local services 865a

CANTUS Verkehrsgesellschaft (2nd class only)

km																										
		Ⓒ	Ⓐ	⚒	⚒	Ⓒ	Ⓐ	Ⓐ						Ⓒ	Ⓐ			Ⓐ								
0	**Göttingen** .... **908** d.	0026	0414	0514	0614	0714	0718	0748	0814	0914	1014	1114	1214	1314	1325	1414	1514	1543	1614	1714	1814	1914	2014	2114	2214	2314
20	Eichenberg......... **908** a.	0040	0428	0528	0628	0728	0732	0802	0828	0928	1028	1128	1228	1328	1339	1428	1528	1557	1628	1728	1828	1928	2028	2128	2228	2328
20	Eichenberg......... **865** d.	0041	0433	0533	0633	0733	0733	0803	0833	0933	1033	1133	1233	1333	1342	1433	1533	1603	1633	1733	1833	1933	2033	2133	2233	2333
43	Hann Münden .... **865** d.	0101	0453	0553	0653	0753	0753	0823	0853	0953	1053	1153	1253	1353	1402	1453	1553	1623	1653	1753	1853	1953	2053	2153	2253	2353
67	**Kassel** Hbf ⊡.... **865** a.	0121	0513	0613	0713	0813	0813	0843	0913	1013	1113	1213	1313	1413	1426	1513	1613	1643	1713	1813	1913	2013	2113	2213	2313	0013

	Ⓒ	Ⓐ	Ⓐ	⑥	Ⓐ								Ⓐ					Ⓐ		Ⓐ						
Kassel Hbf ⊡......**865** d.	0115	0416	0518	0546	0616	0646	0746	0846	0946	1046	1146	1246	1316	1346	1446	1546	1616	1646	1716	1746	1846	1946	2046	2146	2246	2346
Hann Münden......**865** d.	0135	0436	0537	0606	0636	0706	0806	0906	1006	1106	1206	1306	1336	1406	1506	1606	1636	1706	1736	1806	1906	2006	2106	2206	2306	0006
Eichenberg ....**865** a.	0154	0456	0557	0626	0656	0726	0826	0926	1026	1126	1226	1326	1356	1426	1526	1626	1656	1726	1756	1826	1926	2026	2126	2225	2326	0026
Eichenberg ....**908** d.	0155	*0502*	0605	0631	0704	0731	0831	0931	1031	1131	1231	1331	1357	1431	1531	1631	1659	1731	1806	1831	1931	2031	2131	2229	2331	0027
Göttingen ....**908** a.	0209	*0515*	0619	0645	0717	0745	0845	0945	1045	1145	1245	1345	1411	1445	1545	1645	1713	1745	1820	1845	1945	2045	2145	2243	2345	0041

NOTES FOR TABLES 865 AND 865a

A – From / to Glauchau (Table **858**).
G – From / to Gera (Table **858**).

b – 0558 on ⑥.
e – Arrives 5 minutes earlier.

f – Arrives 7 – 9 minutes earlier.
k – Arrives 12 – 14 minutes earlier..
r – ⚒ only.
t – Ⓐ only.

△ – Operated by Abellio Rail Mitteldeutschland.
◇ – Connecting trains Gotha - Bad Langensalza (journey time: 18 – 21 minutes). **From Gotha** at 0529 Ⓐ, 0737, 0937, 1137, 1337, 1537, 1737 and 1937.
⊙ – Connecting trains Bad Langensalza - Gotha (journey time: 19 minutes). **From Bad Langensalza** at 0650 Ⓐ, 0801, 1001, 1201, 1401, 1601, 1801 and 2001.
⊡ – See Tables **806** and **901** for connecting trains to / from Kassel Wilhelmshöhe.

HANNOVER - MAGDEBURG - LEIPZIG 866

See panels below main table for regional trains Braunschweig - Magdeburg - Halle (Saale) and v.v. See Table **848** for other regional trains between Magdeburg and Leipzig via Dessau.

km		*IC* 2449	*IC* 2031	*IC* 2031	*IC* 2447	*IC* 2033	*IC* 2445	*IC* 2035	*IC* 2443	*IC* 2037	*IC* 2441	*IC* 2039	*ICE* 1133	*IC* 2049	*IC* 2431	*IC* 2239	*IC* 2047	*IC* 2433	*IC* 2045	*IC* 2435	*IC* 2043	*IC* 2043	*RE* 16339	*IC* 2437	*RE* 16341
		Ⓐ	⚒	Ⓐ	⚒								⑤								Ⓑ	⑤⑦		Ⓑ	
															C	A					b	r		b	
			🍷	🍷	🍷	🍷	🍷	🍷	🍷	🍷	F 🍷	🍷	✕	S 🍷	🍷		S 🍷	🍷	S 🍷	🍷					
	Köln Hbf **800** ....d.	...	...	...	...	...	0510e	...	0713	...	0909	...	...	1109	...	...	1309	...	1509	...	1713	1713	...	...	...
	Dortmund Hbf **800** ....d.	...	...	...	...	...	0628	...	0828	...	1028	...	...	1228	...	...	1428	...	1628	...	1828	1828	...	...	...
	Bielefeld Hbf **810** ....d.	...	...	...	...	...	0719	...	0919	...	1119	...	...	1317	...	...	1519	...	1719	...	1919	1919	...	...	...
	Norddeich **813**..............d.	...	...	...	...	...	|	0536e	|	0739e	|	0939	...	|	...	...	|	...	|	1540	|	|	...	...	...
	Emden Hbf **813**............d.	...	...	...	...	0416e	|	0609e	|	0816	|	1016	...	|	1218	...	|	1417	|	1616	|	|	...	1813	...
	Oldenburg (Oldb) **813** ...d.	...	...	...	...	0535e	|	0735	|	0935	|	1135	1229h	|	1335	...	|	1535	|	1735	|	|	...	1935	...
	Bremen Hbf **813**............d.	...	...	...	...	0609	|	0809	|	1009	|	1209	1305h	|	1409	...	|	1609	|	1809	|	|	...	2009	...
0	**Hannover** Hbf............. **811** d.	...	...	0534	0636	0735	0835	0936	1036	1136	1236	1336	1411	1436	1536	...	1636	1736	1836	1936	2036	2036	...	2136	...
35	Peine .... **811** d.	...	...	0555	|	|	|	|	|	|	|	|	|	|	|	...	|	|	|	|	|	|	...	2157	...
61	**Braunschweig** Hbf...... **811** d.	...	...	0610	0710	0810	0910	1010	1110	1210	1310	1410	1448	1511	1610	...	1710	1810	1910	2010	2110	2110	...	2213	...
97	Helmstedt ....d.	...	...	0631	|	0831	|	1031	|	1231	|	1431	|	|	1631	...	|	1831	|	2031	|	|	...	2234	...
145	**Magdeburg** Hbf.................a.	...	...	0656	0754	0856	0954	1056	1154	1256	1354	1456	1536	1554	1658	...	1754	1858	1954	2056	2154	2154	...	2302	...
145	**Magdeburg** Hbf.................d.	0600	0704	0704	0800	0905	1000	1104	1200	1304	1400	1504	1542	1600	1705	1704	1800	1904	2000	2104	...	2200	2208	...	2308
	Berlin Hbf **839** ....a.	|	|	|	|	|	|	|	|	|	|	|	|	|	1824	|	|	|	|	|	...	|	|	...	|
195	Köthen ....d.	0629	0733	0733	0829	0933	1029	1133	1229	1333	1429	1533	1621	1629	...	1733	1829	1933	2029	2133	...	2229	2247	...	2347
231	**Halle** (Saale) Hbf ....a.	0647	0753	0753	0847	0953	1047	1153	1247	1353	1447	1553	1644	1647	...	1753	1847	1953	2047	2153	...	2247	2314	...	0014
231	**Halle** (Saale) Hbf .... ⊡ d.	0655	0755	0755	0855	0955	1055	1155	1255	1355	1455	1555	1646	1655	...	1755	1855	1955	2055	2155	...	2255	*2325*	...	*0025*
249	Leipzig/Halle Flughafen ✈ ⊡ a.	0705	|	|	0905	|	1105	|	1305	|	1505	|	|	1708	...	|	1905	|	2105	|	...	2305	|	...	|
268	**Leipzig** Hbf..................... ⊡ a.	0717	0815	0815	0917	1015	1117	1215	1319	1415	1517	1615	1714	1717	...	1815q	1917	2015	2117	2215	...	2317	*0002*	...	*0102*
	Dresden Hbf **842** ....a.	0837	...	...	1100	...	1300	...	1446w	...	1647	...	...	1846p	...	...	2046	...	2246b	...	...	...	...	...	...

	IC 2436		*RE* 16302	*RE* 16302	*IC* 2042	*IC* 2042		*IC* 2434	*IC* 2044	*IC* 2238	*IC* 2432	*IC* 2046	*IC* 2430	*IC* 2048	*IC* 2038	*IC* 2440	*IC* 2036	*IC* 2442	*IC* 2034	*IC* 1934	*IC* 2444	*IC* 2032	*IC* 2446	*IC* 2030	*IC* 2448
	Ⓐ			Ⓐ	①	⚒		⚒												⑦				⑤	Ⓑ
				t	g					A	C									w					b
								🍷	S 🍷		🍷	S 🍷	🍷	S 🍷	🍷	S 🍷	🍷	F 🍷	🍷		🍷	🍷	🍷		🍷
Dresden Hbf **842** ....d.	...	...	...	...	...	...	...	...	0512	...	...	0712e	...	0845	...	1045	...	1312w	...	1439	1512	...	1712	...	1845
Leipzig Hbf .... ⊡ d.	...	...	...	*0358*	0441	...	...	0542	0638	0742	...	0838	0942	1038	1142	1238	1342	1438	1542	1604	1638	1740	1838	1942	2038
Leipzig/Halle Flughafen ✈ ⊡ d.	...	...	...	*0412*	0455	...	...	|	0650	|	...	0850	|	1050	|	1250	|	1450	|	|	1650	|	1850	|	2050
Halle (Saale) Hbf............. ⊡ a.	...	...	...	*0422*	0507	...	...	0602	0701	0800	...	0901	1000	1101	1200	1301	1400	1501	1600	1622	1701	1758	1901	2000	2101
Halle (Saale) Hbf..................d.	...	...	...	0442	0509	...	...	0606	0709	0806	...	0909	1006	1109	1206	1309	1406	1509	1606	1627	1709	1806	1909	2006	2109
Köthen..................................d.	...	...	0510	0510	0528	...	...	0627	0727	0827	...	0927	1027	1127	1227	1327	1427	1527	1627	1650	1727	1827	1927	2027	2127
Berlin Hbf **839** ....d.	...	...	|	|	|	...	...	|	|	|	0729	|	|	|	|	|	|	|	|	|	|	|	|	|	|
Magdeburg Hbf.....................a.	...	...	0549	0549	0556	...	...	0653	0756	0853	0901	0956	1053	1156	1253	1356	1453	1556	1653	|	1756	1854	1956	2053	2156
Magdeburg Hbf.....................d.	0500	...	...	...	0603	0603	...	0700	0803	...	0903	1003	1100	1203	1300	1403	1500	1603	1700	|	1803	1900	2003	2100	2203
Helmstedt ....d.	0526	...	...	...	0628	0628	...	0726	|	...	0928	|	1126	|	1326	|	1526	|	1726	|	|	1926	|	2126	|
Braunschweig Hbf....... **811** d.	0549	...	...	...	0649	0649	...	0749	0849	...	0951	1049	1149	1249	1349	1449	1549	1649	1749	1814	1849	1949	2049	2149	2250
Peine.............................. **811** d.	0606	...	...	...	|	|	...	|	|	...	|	|	|	|	|	|	|	|	|	|	|	|	|	|	|
Hannover Hbf .... **811** a.	0626	...	...	...	0723	0723	...	0823	0923	...	1025	1123	1223	1323	1423	1523	1623	1723	1823	1851	1923	2023	2123	2223	2326
Bremen Hbf **813**............ a.	0750	...	...	...	|	|	...	0950	|	...	1150	|	1350	|	1550	|	1750	|	1950	2009j	|	2150	...	...	...
Oldenburg (Oldb) **813** .... a.	0823	...	...	...	|	|	...	1025	|	...	1225	|	1425	|	1625	|	1825	|	2025	2040k	|	2225	...	...	...
Emden Hbf **813**............. a.	0938	...	...	...	|	|	...	1138	|	...	1338	|	1538	|	1738	|	1938	|	2138	2152k	|	2338b	...	...	...
Norddeich **813** .... a.	...	...	...	...	|	|	...	...	|	...	1414	|	...	|	...	|	2014b	|	2214	...	|	...	...	...	...
Bielefeld Hbf **810**............. a.	...	...	...	...	0839	0839	...	...	1039	...	...	1239	...	1439	...	1639	...	1839	...	...	2039	...	...	...	...
Dortmund Hbf **800** .... a.	...	...	...	...	0933	0933	...	...	1133	...	...	1333	...	1533	...	1733	...	1933	...	...	2133	...	...	...	...
Köln Hbf **800** .... a.	...	...	...	...	1046	1046	...	...	1246	...	...	1446	...	1646	...	1846	...	2046	...	...	2246	...	...	...	...

Other regional stopping trains **BRAUNSCHWEIG - MAGDEBURG**

	†z		Ⓐ	Ⓒ	⚒	Ⓐ		Ⓐ		Ⓐ		Ⓐ	Ⓒz	Ⓐt	Ⓐ		Ⓐ		Ⓐ			Ⓑ	⑥	Ⓑ	
Braunschweig Hbf.............. d.	0107	...	*0529*	0542	...	0617	0717	0817	0917	1017	1117	1217	1317	1320	1417	1517	1617	1717	1817	1917	2017	2117	2147	2217	2347
Helmstedt .... d.	0136	0405	0606	0610	0646	0646	0746	0846	0946	1046	1146	1246	1346	1348	1446	1546	1646	1746	1846	1946	2046	2146	2216	2246	0017
Magdeburg Hbf..................... a.	0218	0447	0652	0652	0729	0729	0829	0929	1029	1129	1229	1329	1429	1429	1529	1629	1729	1829	1929	2028	2129	2229	2259	2329	...

	⑥	Ⓐ	Ⓒ	Ⓐ				Ⓐ			Ⓐ		Ⓐ		Ⓐ			Ⓐ			Ⓐ				
Magdeburg Hbf.................... d.	0253	0433	0533	*0530*	0633	0733	...	0833	0933	...	1033	1133	1233	1333	1433	1532	...	1633	1733	...	1833	1933	2033	2205	2314
Helmstedt .... d.	0333	0513	0613	0615	0713	0813	0913	0913	1013	1113	1113	1213	1313	1413	1513	1613	1713	1713	1813	1913	1913	2013	2113	2245	2354
Braunschweig Hbf.............. a.	0402	0541	0641	0645	0741	0841	0941	0941	1041	1141	1141	1241	1341	1441	1541	1641	1741	1741	1841	1941	1941	2041	2141	2313	...

Other regional trains **MAGDEBURG - HALLE**

		Ⓐt						
Magdeburg Hbf................... d.	0414	0500	0535	0635	and hourly until	2035	2208	2308
Schönebeck (Elbe) .... d.	0423	0512	0546	0646		2046	2219	2319
Köthen.................................... d.	0447	0536	0614	0714		2114	2247	2347
Halle (Saale) Hbf.................. a.	0514	0600	0642	0741		2141	2314	0014

	Ⓐt			Ⓐt					
Halle (Saale) Hbf.............. d.	0442	...	0542	0614	0714	and hourly until	2014	2124	2259
Köthen.................................. d.	0510	0510	0610	0643	0742		2042	2152	2327
Schönebeck (Elbe) .... d.	0537	0537	0637	0709	0809		2109	2219	2353
Magdeburg Hbf.................. a.	0549	0549	0649	0723	0822		2122	2230	0005

A – To / from Warnemünde via Schwerin and Rostock (see Tables **830**, **837** and **841**).
C – To / from Cottbus on dates in Table **837**.
F – From / to Frankfurt (Table **800**).
S – From / to Stuttgart (Tables **800** and **912**).

b – Ⓑ (not Dec. 25).
e – ⚒ only.
g – ① (also Dec. 27; not Dec. 26).
h – Until Mar. 10.
j – 2047 from Mar. 19.

k – Until Mar. 12.
p – ①②③④⑥⑦ to Mar. 16; daily from Mar. 18.
q – 1820 on ⑤.
r – Also Dec. 26; not Dec. 25.
t – Not Jan. 6.
w – ⑦ (also Dec. 26; not Dec. 25).
z – Also Jan. 6.

⊡ – See Table **881** for other S-Bahn services.

867 HARZER SCHMALSPURBAHNEN

2nd class only

Nordhausen - Wernigerode: *Die Harzquerbahn*; Eisfelder Talmühle - Stiege - Alexisbad - Quedlinburg: *Die Selketalbahn*; Drei Annen Hohne - Brocken: *Die Brockenbahn*

WINTER SERVICE VALID UNTIL MARCH 31, 2023 (SEE NOTE ⊠). The origin / destination of certain trains may vary on Dec. 24, 31, Jan. 1.

km		v	A 🚂	🚂	🚂	🚂	B 🚂	r 🚂	r 🚂	r 🚂	r 🚂	n
0	**Wernigerode** § ¶ d.	0825	0855	0940	1025	1158	...	...	...	1455	B	1725
15	Drei Annen Hohne ¶ a.	0902	0932	1017	1102	1237	...	...	...	1534	...	1802
15	Drei Annen Hohne ¶ d.	0903	0945	1030	1115	1248	1250	1339	1506	1552	1548	1803
20	Schierke ¶ d.	|	1005	1050	1135	|	1313	1358	1539	1621	|	|
34	**Brocken** ¶ a.	|	1036	1121	1206	|	1344	1428	1609	1652	|	|
19	Elend d.	0915	...	...	...	1300	▬	...	...	...	1600	1818
28	Sorge d.	0934	...	...	...	1319	...	...	...	...	1619	1837
31	Benneckenstein d.	0948	...	...	...	1328	...	...	...	...	1628	1846
44	Eisfelder Talmühle a.	1016	...	...	...	1356	...	...	...	...	1657	1914
44	Eisfelder Talmühle d.	1017	...	...	...	...	1402	...	...	...	1714	1915
50	Ilfeld d.	1032	...	...	...	...	1417	...	...	...	1729	1929
61	**Nordhausen** Nord § a.	1053	...	...	...	...	1439‡	...	...	...	1751	1952

	v	B 🚂	🚂	🚂	A 🚂	🚂	r	r 🚂	r 🚂	r 🚂	n
Nordhausen Nord § d.	0833	1033	...	...	...	...	1304	...	...	...	1626
Ilfeld d.	0900	1059	...	...	...	...	1329	...	...	...	1648
Eisfelder Talmühle a.	0914	1113	...	...	...	...	1342	...	...	...	1702
Eisfelder Talmühle d.	0915	1120	...	...	...	...	▬	1411	...	...	1712
Benneckenstein d.	0947	1150	...	...	...	...	...	1441	...	...	1742
Sorge d.	0955	1158	...	...	...	...	🚂	1449	...	...	1750
Elend d.	1014	1217	...	...	...	...	r B	1508	...	...	1819
Brocken ¶ d.	|	|	1136	1221	1314	1359	1451	|	1622	1707	|
Schierke ¶ d.	|	|	1231	1312	1355	1439	1522	|	1703	1747	|
Drei Annen Hohne ¶ a.	1025	1228	1243	1324	1407	1451	1533	1519	1714	1759	1830
Drei Annen Hohne ¶ d.	1041	...	1253	...	1423	...	...	1553	1721	1808	1831
Wernigerode § ¶ a.	1121	...	1333	...	1503	...	...	1633	1802	1845	1908

km	SEE NOTE ⊠	v 🚂		🚂	🚂	n 🚂	n 🚂	r 🚂	r	n	n 🚂	n
0	**Quedlinburg** § d.	...	0830v	1030	1256	*1341*	...	...	1530	1728	1941	2030
8	**Gernrode** a.	...	0845v	1045	1312	*1357*	...	...	1545	1743	1956	2045
8	**Gernrode** d.	0736	0846	1046	▬	1413	...	...	1546	1744	...	...
18	Mägdesprung d.	0806	0919	1117	...	1443	...	...	1624	1815	...	...
	Harzgerode d.	|	|	|	1216	|	...	...	|	|	...	...
23	Alexisbad a.	0820	0933	1131	1226	1457	...	...	1638	1829	...	...
23	Alexisbad d.	0827	0940	*1147*	1237	1504	...	...	1645	1830	...	...
26	**Harzgerode** a.	0837	|	*1156*	|	|	...	...	|	1839	...	...
26	Silberhütte d.	...	0943	▬	1246	1513	...	...	1655	▬	...	...
30	Straßberg (Harz) d.	...	0955	...	1257	1525	...	...	1707	...	...	...
35	Güntersberge d.	...	1004	...	1307	1535	...	...	1718	r	...	...
	Hasselfelde d.	...	|	1038	|	|	1615	...	|	1758	...	...
44	Stiege a.	...	1020	1051	1323	1551	1628	...	1734	1811	...	...
44	Stiege d.	...	1021	1052	1329	1552	1629	...	1736	1812	...	...
48	**Hasselfelde** a.	...	1034	|	|	1605	|	...	1749	|	...	...
53	Eisfelder Talmühle d.	...	...	1112	1402f	...	1649	1714	...	1833	...	...
59	Ilfeld d.	...	...	|	1417	...	...	1729	...	1850	...	...
70	**Nordhausen** Nord § a.	...	...	*1151**	1439	...	...	1751	...	1913	...	...

SEE NOTE ⊠	v			🚂	🚂		r	r	n 🚂	r	n
Nordhausen Nord § d.	...	...	0933	...	1033	...	1304	...	*1626*	...	...
Ilfeld d.	...	...	1000	...	1059	...	1329	...	*1648*	...	...
Eisfelder Talmühle d.	...	...	1018	...	1113	1118	1401e	...	1704	...	...
Hasselfelde d.	...	1038	|	...	▬	|	|	1444	|	...	...
Stiege a.	...	1051	1038	...	...	1138	1421	1457	1724	...	...
Stiege d.	...	▬	1053	...	...	1139	1422	1458	1734	1736	...
Hasselfelde a.	...	...	|	...	...	|	1435	|	|	1749	...
Güntersberge d.	...	...	1111	...	...	1157	▬	1514	1750	▬	...
Straßberg (Harz) d.	...	...	1120	...	...	1206	...	1526	1759	...	...
Silberhütte d.	...	v 🚂	1132	...	...	1218	...	1538	1810	...	...
Harzgerode d.	...	0847	|	...	1216	|	...	|	|	...	1910
Alexisbad a.	...	0857	1141	...	1226	1227	...	1547	1820	n	1920
Alexisbad d.	...	0904	1147	1146	...	1229	...	1603	1831	1830	1923
Harzgerode a.	...	|	1156	|	...	|	...	|	|	1839	|
Mägdesprung d.	...	0918	...	1200	...	1243	...	1623	1845	...	1937
Gernrode a.	...	0949	...	1230	...	1313	r	1653	1915	...	2008
Gernrode d.	0800	0959	...	1231	...	1316	1459	1655	1916	...	2010
Quedlinburg § a.	0815	1015	...	1246	...	1331	1515	1710	1931	...	2025

A – Dec. 21 - Jan. 8 and Jan. 28 - Feb. 19.
B – (2) Brocken - Nordhausen and v.v.

e – Arrives 1342.
f – Arrives 1350.
n – Not Dec. 24, 31.
r – Not Dec. 24.
v – Not Jan. 1.

* – By 🚌 from Eisfelder Talmühle.
⊠ – Selketalbahn services are subject to alteration until Dec. 16 (please check before travelling).
¶ – Additional journeys Dec. 25 - Jan. 8, Feb. 1 – 4, 8 – 11, 15 – 19.
🚂: Wernigerode d. 1325 → Drei Annen Hohne d. 1415 → Brocken a. 1530.
🚂: Brocken d. 1540 → Drei Annen Hohne a. 1632 → Wernigerode a. 1721.
🚂 – Normally operated by Steam train.
§ – Adjacent to DB station.

Operator: Harzer Schmalspurbahnen.
Friedrichstrasse 151, 38855 Wernigerode.
✆ + 49 (0) 3943 558 0. www.hsb-wr.de

868 ERFURT - NORDHAUSEN

RE / *RB* services

km		Ⓐ																	
0	**Erfurt** Hbf d.	0448	0559	0700	0802	0902	1002	1102	1202	1302	1402	1502	1602	1702	1802	1902	2016	...	2213
27	Straußfurt d.	0514	0624	0724	0828	0924	1028	1124	1228	1324	1428	1524	1628	1724	1828	1924	2045	...	2245
60	Sondershausen d.	0547	0657	0757	0857	0957	1057	1157	1257	1357	1457	1557	1657	1757	1857	1957	2113	...	2317
80	**Nordhausen** a.	0610	0714	0820	0914	1020	1114	1220	1314	1420	1514	1620	1714	1820	1914	2020	2130	...	2339

	Ⓐ	Ⓐ																
Nordhausen d.	0420	0521	0623	0729	0834	0929	1034	1129	1234	1329	1434	1529	1634	1729	1834	1929	...	2137
Sondershausen d.	0443	0550	0640	0757	0857	0957	1057	1157	1257	1357	1457	1557	1657	1757	1857	1957	...	2158
Straußfurt d.	0515	0626	0709	0830	0924	1030	1124	1230	1324	1430	1524	1630	1724	1830	1924	2030	...	2230
Erfurt Hbf a.	0541	0651	0738	0856	0950	1056	1150	1256	1350	1456	1550	1656	1750	1856	1950	2056	...	2256

869 NORDHAUSEN - GÖTTINGEN

RB services

km		Ⓐ	⚒																	
0	**Nordhausen** d.	...	0539	0639	0739	0839	0939	1039	1139	1239	1339	1439	1539	1639	1739	1839	1939	2039	2139	...
20	Walkenried d.	0503	0603	0703	0803	0903	1003	1103	1203	1303	1403	1503	1603	1703	1803	1903	2003	2103	2203	...
23	Bad Sachsa d.	0508	0608	0708	0808	0908	1008	1108	1208	1308	1408	1508	1608	1708	1808	1908	2008	2108	2208	...
37	Bad Lauterberg ⊡ d.	0519	0619	0719	0819	0919	1019	1119	1219	1319	1419	1519	1619	1719	1819	1919	2019	2119	2219	...
43	Herzberg (Harz) d.	0526	0626	0726	0826	0926	1026	1126	1226	1326	1426	1526	1626	1726	1826	1926	2026	2126	2226	2326
70	Northeim **859 903** a.	0550	0650	0750	0850	0950	1050	1150	1250	1350	1450	1550	1650	1750	1850	1950	2050	2150	2250	2350
90	**Göttingen** **859 903** a.	0608	0710	0808	*0909*	1008	*1109*	1209	*1309*	1408	*1509*	1608	*1709*	1808	*1909*	2008	*2109*	2209	*2309*	0008

	Ⓐ	⚒	Ⓒ	Ⓐ															⑤⑥f	
Göttingen **859 903** d.	*0408*	0549	*0648*	0649	0749	*0848*	0949	*1048*	1149	*1248*	1349	*1448*	1549	*1648*	1749	*1848*	1949	*2048*	2149	2249
Northeim **859 903** d.	0506	0606	0706	0706	0806	0906	1006	1106	1206	1306	1406	1506	1606	1706	1806	1906	2006	2106	2206	2306
Herzberg (Harz) d.	0530	0630	0730	0730	0830	0930	1030	1130	1230	1330	1430	1530	1630	1730	1830	1930	2030	2130	2230	2330
Bad Lauterberg ⊡ d.	0536	0636	0736	0736	0836	0936	1036	1136	1236	1336	1436	1536	1636	1736	1836	1936	2036	2136	2236	...
Bad Sachsa d.	0547	0647	0747	0747	0847	0947	1047	1147	1247	1347	1447	1547	1647	1747	1847	1947	2047	2147	2247	...
Walkenried d.	0551	0651	0751	0751	0851	0951	1051	1151	1251	1351	1451	1551	1651	1751	1852	1951	2051	2151	2251	...
Nordhausen a.	0615	0715	0815	0815	0915	1015	1115	1215	1315	1415	1515	1615	1715	1815	1915	2015	2115	2215	2315	...

f – Runs daily Göttingen - Herzberg.

⊡ – Bad Lauterberg im Harz Barbis.

870 ERFURT - MEININGEN

DB (*RE* services); *STB* ▽

km			H	⚒		Ⓐ			E				E	Ⓐ			E						
0	**Erfurt** Hbf **872** d.	0500	...	0602	...	0701	0735	...	0805	and in	1535	...	1605	1702	1735	...	1805	1935	...	2005	2116	2250	0003
23	Arnstadt Hbf **872** d.	0516	...	0620	...	0718	0751	...	0823	the same	1551	...	1623	1719	1751	...	1823	1951	...	2026	2134	2308	0024
31	Plaue (Thür) d.	0523	...	0628	...	0726	0758	...	0830	pattern	1558	...	1630	1727	1758	...	1830	1958	...	2034	2143	2317	0033
37	Gräfenroda d.	0528	...	0633	...	0731	|	...	0835	every	|	...	1635	1732	|	...	1835	2003	...	2039	2148	2322	0038
58	Zella-Mehlis d.	0543	...	0652	...	0750	0816	...	0857	two hours	1616	...	1657	1751	1816	...	1857	2018	...	2101	2205	2339	0058
64	Suhl d.	0549	...	0658	...	0756	0822	...	0903	until	1622	...	1703	1758	1822	...	1903	2024	...	2107	2211	2345	0104
84	Grimmenthal **873** a.	0559	0603	0714	0718	0812	0832	0842	0918		1632	1642	1718	1811	1832	1842	1918	2035	2043	2123	2228	2357	0120
	Schweinfurt Hbf **870a** a.	0713	|	0842b	|	|	0926	|	|		1725	|	|	|	1926	|	|	2126	|	|	|	|	|
	Würzburg Hbf **870a** a.	0745	|	...	|	|	0955	|	|		1755	|	|	|	1955	|	|	2157	|	|	|	|	|
92	**Meiningen** **873** a.	...	0609	...	0724	0819	...	0849	0933		...	1649	1733	1818	...	1849	1934	...	2050	2136	2241	0003	0128

	Ⓐ	Ⓐ	E			⚒	⚒E	E				E			Ⓐ	E			E				⑤⑥r
Meiningen **873** d.	0403	0504	0524	0609	...	...	0710	0820	0901	...	and in	1620	1701	...	1736	1820	1901	...	2020	2110	...	...	2321
Würzburg Hbf **870a** d.	|	|	|	|	...	...	|	|	|	0801	the same	|	|	1601	|	|	|	1801	|	|	2001	...	|
Schweinfurt Hbf **870a** d.	|	|	|	|	0530	...	|	|	|	0830	pattern	|	|	1630	|	|	|	1830	|	|	2030	...	|
Grimmenthal **873** d.	0415	0511	0532	0616	0621	0628	0717	0834j	0908	0920	every	1634j	1708	1720	1744	1834j	1908	1920	2037k	2117	2128	...	2335j
Suhl d.	0432	0524	0549	...	0633	0646	0730	0850	...	0932	two hours	1650	...	1732	1759	1850	...	1932	2053	...	2145	...	2356
Zella-Mehlis d.	0439	0531	0555	...	0639	0656	0736	0900	...	0938	until	1700	...	1738	1805	1900	...	1938	2100	...	2151	...	0002
Gräfenroda d.	0456	0548	0613	...	0654	0714	0753	0918	...	|		1718	...	|	1822	1918	...	|	2118	...	2205	...	0018
Plaue (Thür) d.	0506	0553	0626j	...	0700	0719	|	0923	...	0958		1723	...	1758	1828	1923	...	1958	2123	...	2210	...	0028
Arnstadt Hbf **872** d.	0514	0604	0634	...	0707	0728	0804	0933	...	1006		1733	...	1806	1838	1933	...	2006	2133	...	2217	...	0036
Erfurt Hbf **872** a.	0535	0621	0654	...	0721	0749	0821	0951	...	1021		1751	...	1821	1856	1951	...	2021	2153	...	2232	...	0053

E – To / from Eisenach (Table **873**).
H – 20 minutes later on Ⓒ.
b – Not ⑥.
j – Arrives 7 minutes earlier.
k – Arrives 2027.
r – Also Apr. 6, 9, 30, May 17.
▽ – Most services to / from Meiningen are operated by Süd Thüringen Bahn (2nd class only).

MEININGEN - SCHWEINFURT - WÜRZBURG 870a

DB (*RE* services); *EB* ◇

km					⚒r	Ⓐt	⚒	Ⓐ	Ⓒ																
0	**Meiningen** 873 d.	0521	0548	...	...	0642	0710	...	0719	◧	0924	◧	1124	◧	1324	◧	1539	◧	1724	◧	1924	◧	2124	2226	...
	Erfurt Hbf 870 d.	|	|	0500	...	|	|	0602	|	0735	|	0935	|	1135	|	1335	|	1535	|	1735	|	1935	|	|	...
	Grimmenthal 873 d.	|	0555	0604	...	|	0716	0726	|	0835	|	1035	|	1235	|	1435	|	1635	|	1835	|	2035	|	2233	2238
25	Mellrichstadt d.	0548	...	0623	0709	0709	...	0747	0747	0849	0948	1049	1148	1249	1348	1449	1603	1649	1748	1849	1948	2049	2148	...	2256
39	Bad Neustadt (Saale) d.	0559	...	0633	0718	0718	...	0759	0759	0857	0959	1057	1159	1257	1358	1457	1611	1657	1759	1857	1959	2057	2159	...	2305
49	Münnerstadt d.	0607	...	0642	0726	0726	...	0807	0807	0903	1007	1103	1207	1304	1406	1504	1619	1703	1807	1903	2007	2103	2207	...	2313
64	Ebenhausen (Unterfr) a.	0618	...	0653	0736	0736	...	0818	0818	0912	1018	1112	1218	1312	1417	1512	1630	1712	1818	1912	2018	2112	2218	...	2324
	Ebenhausen (Unterfr) d.	0625	...	0657	0742	0742	...	0826	0826	0917	1025	1117	1225	1317	1425	1517	1639	1717	1825	1917	2025	2117	2225	...	2328
78	**Schweinfurt** Hbf 875 a.	0637	...	0713	0753	0753	...	0842	0842	0926	1042	1126	1241	1326	1440	1525	1652	1725	1841	1926	2042	2126	2236	...	2339
121	**Würzburg** Hbf 875 a.	*0721*	...	0745	*0821*	*0821*	...	*0920*	*0920*	0955	*1120*	1155	*1320*	1355	*1521*	1555	*1721*	1755	*1921*	1955	*2121*	2157	...	...	*0016*

km				⚒r	Ⓐt	Ⓒz						Ⓐt	Ⓒz											e	⑤⑥f
	Würzburg Hbf 876 d.	*0454r*	...	...	*0622*	*0603*	0801	*0835*	1001	*1035*	1201	*1208*	*1235*	1401	*1435*	1601	*1637*	1801	*1836*	2001	...	*2035*	...	*2139*	*2139*
	Schweinfurt Hbf 876 d.	0530	...	0610	0700	0718	0830	0912	1030	1112	1230	1242	1312	1430	1512	1630	1712	1830	1912	2030	...	2113	...	2224	2224
	Ebenhausen (Unterf) a.	0539	...	0622	0712	0731	0838	0928	1038	1128	1238	1252	1328	1439	1528	1638	1728	1838	1928	2038	...	2128	...	2239	2239
	Ebenhausen (Unterf) d.	0541	...	0629	0714	0738	0840	0932	1040	1132	1240	1252	1332	1441	1532	1640	1732	1840	1932	2040	...	2132	...	2242	2242
	Münnerstadt d.	0550	...	0646	0726	0749	0849	0944	1049	1144	1249	1308	1344	1450	1544	1649	1744	1849	1944	2049	...	2144	...	2253	2253
	Bad Neustadt (Saale) d.	0557	...	0654	0737	0758	0857	0958	1057	1158	1257	1319	1358	1457	1553	1657	1758	1857	1958	2057	...	2157	...	2305	2305
0	Mellrichstadt d.	0605	...	0707	0746	0807	0906	1007	1106	1207	1306	1328	1407	1506	1607	1706	1807	1906	2007	2106	...	2206	...	2313	2313
21	Grimmenthal 873 a.	0619	0623	|	|	|	0919	|	1119	|	1319	|	|	1519	|	1719	|	1919	|	2121	2130	2224	2234	|	2331
	Erfurt Hbf 870 a.	0721	|	|	|	|	1021	|	1221	|	1421	|	|	1621	|	1821	|	2021	|	2232	|	...	|	|	|
	Meiningen 873 a.	...	0629	0731t	0810	0831	◧	1031	◧	1231	◧	1358	1431	◧	1631	◧	1831	◧	2031	...	2136	...	2241	2338	2342

e – ⑦–④ (not Apr. 6, 9, 30, May 17, 28).
f – ⑤⑥ (also Apr. 6, 9, 30, May 17, 28).
r – ⚒ (not Jan. 6).
t – Ⓐ (not Jan. 6).
◧ – Other local connections Meiningen - Grimmenthal and v.v. (journey 7 minutes):
From Meiningen at 0820, 1020 and every **two** hours until 2020.
From Grimmenthal at 0926, 1126 and every **two** hours until 1726; then 1928.
◇ – Erfurter Bahn (2nd class only).

LEIPZIG - GERA - SAALFELD 871

Erfurter Bahn; 2nd class only

km		Ⓐ	Ⓐ	Ⓒ		Ⓐ	Ⓐ		Ⓒ	⑥	⚒														
0	**Leipzig** Hbf d.	...	...	...	...	0508	0609	0609	...	0654	0654	...	0754	0854	0854	and in	1554	1654	1654	1754	1854	1957	2057	2157	2309
45	Zeitz d.	0430	...	...	...	0550	0654	0654	...	0735	0735	...	0835	0935	0935	the same	1635	1735	1735	1835	1935	2037	2137	2236	2350
72	**Gera** Hbf a.	0452	...	...	...	0619	0723	0723	...	0800	0800	...	0858	0959	0959		1658	1759	1759	1858	1959	2101	2204	2300	0013
72	**Gera** Hbf d.	0453	0519	0555	0555	0628	0747	...	0802	0802	0802	0802	0902	1002	1002	pattern	1702	1802	1802	1902	2002	2103	*2209*	2308	...
84	Weida d.	0505	0530	0608	0611	0640	0759	...	0815	0815	0817	0817	0914	1015	1017		1714	1815	1817	1914	2015	2115	*2221*	2320	...
156	**Hof** Hbf a.	|	|	|	0726	|	|	...	|	|	0926	0926	|	|	1126	every	|	|	1926	|	|	|	...	|	...
99	Triptis d.	0517	0541	0620	...	0654	0811	...	0827	0827	...	...	0930	1027	...	two hours	1730	1827	...	1930	2027	2129	...	2333	...
108	Neustadt (Orla) d.	0523	0550	0626	...	0700	0821	...	0833	0833	...	...	0936	1033	...	until	1736	1833	...	1936	2037	2135	...	2339	...
139	**Saalfeld** (Saale) a.	0552	0625	0653	...	0727	0848	...	0900	0900	...	...	0958	1100	...		1759	1900	...	1958	2105	2202	...	0006	...

	Ⓐ		⚒	⚒		Ⓐ		Ⓒ	Ⓐ					⊠											⑤⑥f
Saalfeld (Saale) d.	...	...	...	0515	...	0553	...	0651	0651	0758	0855	...	0958	and in	1557	1655	...	1758	1856	...	2009	...	2057	2211	2211
Neustadt (Orla) d.	...	...	...	0550	...	0619	...	0718	0724	0819	0922	...	1019	the same	1620	1722	...	1819	1923	...	2036	...	2121	2237	2237
Triptis d.	...	...	...	0556	...	0626	...	0725	0731	0828	0929	...	1028		1628	1729	...	1828	1929	...	2043	...	2128	2243	2243
Hof Hbf d.	...	...	...	|	...	|	...	|	|	|	|	0834	|	pattern	|	|	1634	|	|	1834	|	2034	|	|	|
Weida d.	...	...	0530t	0608	...	0641	...	0745	0742	0843	0946	0946	1041	every	1641	1746	1746	1841	1946	1946	2055	2137	2140	2256	2256
Gera Hbf a.	...	...	0541t	0621	...	0653	...	0756	0755	0855	0957	0957	1053		1653	1757	1757	1853	1957	1957	2108	...	2150	2307	2307
Gera Hbf d.	0348	0454	0545	0628	0628	0659	0659	0801	0801	0901	1001	1001	1101	two hours	1700	1801	1801	1901	2001	2001	...	...	2151	...	2311
Zeitz d.	0412	0520	0609	0654	0654	0725	0725	0825	0825	0925	1025	1025	1125	until	1725	1825	1825	1925	2025	2025	...	...	2215	...	2338
Leipzig Hbf a.	0452	0600	0649	0734	0734	0808	0808	0905	0905	1005	1105	1105	1205		1805	1905	1905	2008	2105	2105	...	...	2253	...	0022

f – Also Apr. 6, 9, 30, May 17, 25, 28.
t – Ⓐ only.
⊠ – Timings may vary by 1–2 minutes.

ERFURT - SAALFELD and ROTTENBACH - KATZHÜTTE 872

DB; Erfurter Bahn; 2nd class only

km		Ⓐ	Ⓐ							
0	**Erfurt** Hbf 870 d.	0431	0525	0638		2038	2145	...	2250	...
23	Arnstadt Hbf 870 d.	0453	0548	0700	and	2100	2205	2209	2307	2313
38	Stadtilm d.	0506	0601	0713	hourly	2113	...	2222	...	2326
54	Rottenbach d.	0520	0613	0727	until	2127	...	2236	...	2340
62	Bad Blankenburg d.	0528	0621	0735		2135	...	2244	...	2347
70	**Saalfeld** (Saale) a.	0535	0629	0742		2142	...	2252	...	2355

	Ⓐ								
Saalfeld (Saale) d.	0504	0612	0712		2012	2112	...	...	2221
Bad Blankenburg d.	0511	0622	0719	and	2019	2119	...	...	2228
Rottenbach d.	0519	0629	0727	hourly	2027	2127	...	...	2237
Stadtilm d.	0533	0642	0740	until	2040	2140	...	...	2249
Arnstadt Hbf 870 d.	0550	0659	0756		2056	2153	2157	...	2304
Erfurt Hbf 870 a.	0610	0716	0817		2117	...	2218	...	2319

km		Ⓐ						⑤⑦v		
0	Rottenbach d.	0535	...	0641	and	1941	...	2041	...	...
15	Obstfelderschmiede a.	0558	...	0705	hourly	2005	...	2105	...	...
25	Katzhütte a.	0614	...	0722	until	2022	...	2122	...	...

	Ⓐ						⑤⑦v		
Katzhütte d.	0529	...	0636	and	1936	...	2036	...	...
Obstfelderschmiede d.	0546	...	0653	hourly	1953	...	2053	...	...
Rottenbach a.	0609	...	0716	until	2016	...	2116	...	...

v – Also Apr. 10, May 1, 29; not Apr. 7, 9, 30, May 28.

☛ **Thüringer Bergbahn**. Obstfelderschmiede - Lichtenhain - Cursdorf. www.thueringerbergbahn.com. Journey: 28–44 minutes.
From Obstfelderschmiede at 0630, 0700, 0730 and every 30 minutes until 1730; then 1808, 1830, 1908, 1930.
From Cursdorf at 0614, 0640, 0706, 0734, 0814, 0844 and every 30 minutes until 1944.

EISENACH - MEININGEN - SONNEBERG 873

Süd Thüringen Bahn (2nd class)

km				ⒶE		E	E		E		E				E				E		E		E			E
0	**Eisenach** d.	...	...	0418	0500t	0603	0716	0816	0916	1016	1116	...	...	1216	1316	...	...	1416	1516	1616	1716	1816	1916	2016	2121	2216
27	Bad Salzungen d.	...	...	0444	0531t	0632	0742	0842	0942	1042	1142	...	...	1242	1342	...	...	1442	1542	1642	1742	1842	1942	2042	2152	2242
41	Wernshausen d.	...	...	0500	0547t	0649	0758	0858	0958	1058	1158	...	...	1258	1358	...	...	1458	1558	1658	1758	1858	1958	2058	2208	2301
61	**Meiningen** a.	...	...	0517	0604t	0706	0815	0915	1015	1115	1215	...	...	1315	1415	...	...	1515	1615	1715	1815	1915	2015	2115	2224	2317
		Ⓐ	Ⓐ		|	▽	▽	|	▽	|		Ⓒ	Ⓐ	|		Ⓒ	Ⓐ	|	▽	|	▽	▽	▽		|	
61	**Meiningen** 870 d.	0403	0455	...	0609	0725	0834	0918	1034	1118	...	1234	1234	1318	...	1434	1434	1518	1634	1718	1834	1920	2035	...	2226	...
68	Grimmenthal 870 d.	0412	0506	...	0623j	0734	0842	0930	1042	1130	...	1242	1242	1330	...	1442	1442	1530	1642	1730	1842	1930	2045	...	2234	...
82	Themar d.	0425	0519	...	0636	0747	0900j	0943	1100j	1143	...	1300j	1300j	1343	...	1500j	1500j	1543	1700j	1743	1900j	1943	2058	...	2247	...
94	Hildburghausen d.	0437	0535	...	0652j	0801	0912	1001j	1112	1201j	...	1312	1320j	1401j	...	1512	1528k	1601j	1712	1801j	1912	2004f	2114j	...	2302	...
109	**Eisfeld** d.	0452	0550	...	0707	0816	0927	1016	1127	1216	...	1327	1335	1416	...	1527	1543	1616	1727	1816	1927	2019	2129	...	2317	...
141	**Sonneberg** (Thür) Hbf a.	0536	0638	...	...	0900	...	1100	...	1300	...	...	...	1500	...	...	...	1700	...	1900	...	2103	...	...	...	...

		Ⓐ		Ⓐ																
Sonneberg (Thür) Hbf d.	...	...	...	...	...	0546t	0702	...	0902	...	1102	...	1302	...	1502	...	1702	...	1902	2012
Eisfeld d.	...	0418	...	0518	...	0632	0746	0831	0946	1031	1146	1231	1346	1431	1546	1631	1746	1831	1949	2059
Hildburghausen d.	...	0440j	...	0534	...	0649	0801	0847	1001	1047	1201	1247	1401	1447	1601	1647	1801	1847	2004	2114
Themar d.	...	0452	...	0545	...	0659	0812	0858	1012	1058	1212	1258	1412	1458	1612	1658	1812	1858	2015	2125
Grimmenthal 870 d.	...	0511j	...	0603j	0623	0718j	0828	0911	1028	1111	1228	1311	1428	1511	1628	1711	1828	1911	2028	2138
Meiningen 870 a.	...	0518	...	0609	0629	0724	0833	0917	1033	1117	1233	1317	1433	1517	1633	1717	1833	1917	2034	2145
	Ⓐ	|			|	|	|	▽E	|	▽E	|	▽E	|	▽E	|	▽E	|	▽E	|	▽
Meiningen d.	0441	0523	0523	...	0630	0738	0838	0938	1038	1138	1238	1338	1438	1538	1638	1738	1838	1938	2038	2150
Wernshausen d.	0500	0548j	0548j	...	0649	0758	0858	0958	1058	1158	1258	1358	1458	1558	1658	1758	1858	1958	2058	2210
Bad Salzungen d.	0514	0602	0602	...	0712f	0812	0912	1012	1112	1212	1312	1412	1512	1612	1712	1812	1912	2012	2112	2224
Eisenach a.	0542	0629	0628	...	0743	0843	0943	1043	1143	1243	1343	1443	1543	1643	1743	1843	1943	2043	2138	2255

E – To / from Erfurt (Table 870).
f – Arrives 10–11 minutes earlier.
j – Arrives 6–9 minutes earlier.
k – Arrives 1511.
t – Ⓐ only.
▽ – Change trains.

LEIPZIG - CHEMNITZ 874

Mitteldeutsche Regiobahn

km			⚒				
0	**Leipzig** Hbf d.	0518	0622	0722		2222	2337
33	Bad Lausick d.	0547	0647	0747	and	2247	0000
44	Geithain d.	0556	0656	0756	hourly	2256	0009
66	Burgstädt d.	0613	0713	0813	until	2313	0026
81	**Chemnitz** Hbf a.	0625	0725	0825		2325	0039

		⚒				
Chemnitz Hbf d.	0421	0531	0631		2131	2231
Burgstädt d.	0433	0543	0643	and	2143	2243
Geithain d.	0451	0600	0700	hourly	2200	2300
Bad Lausick d.	0500	0609	0709	until	2209	2309
Leipzig Hbf a.	0526	0631	0730		2230	2333

875 NÜRNBERG - BAMBERG - SONNEBERG, SAALFELD and WÜRZBURG *RE / RB services*

km		¶		Ⓒz	Ⓐt¶	¶			Ⓒz¶		Ⓐt¶	k		⊖¶		Ⓐt¶	Ⓐt	⊖¶		¶		Ⓐt¶				b
0	**Nürnberg** Hbf ... 850 d.	0607	...	0636	0710	0810	0838	0938	1010	1040	1110	1210	1238	1410	1441	1510	...	1610	1638	1810	1838	1910	1938	...	2140	2246
8	Fürth (Bay) Hbf ... d.	0613	...	0644	0716	0816	0844	0944	1016	1046	1116	1216	1244	1416	1447	1516	...	1616	1644	1816	1844	1917	1944	...	2146	2252
24	Erlangen ... 850 d.	0623	...	0654	0727	0827	0854	0954	1027	1056	1127	1227	1254	1427	1457	1527	...	1627	1655	1827	1854	1927	1954	...	2156	2302
39	Forchheim (Oberfr) ... d.	0632	...	0703	0735	0835	0902	1002	1035	1104	1135	1235	1302	1435	1505	1535	...	1635	1703	1835	1902	1935	2002	...	2204	2311
62	**Bamberg** ... 850 a.	0652	...	0720	0752	0852	0920	1020	1053	1120	1152	1252	1320	1452	1520	1552	...	1652	1720	1852	1920	1952	2020	...	2222	2328
62	**Bamberg** ... 876 d.	0654	...	0723	0805	0854	0922	1022	1055	1122	1154	1254	1322	1455	1522	1554	1605	1654	1722	1854	1922	1954	2022	...	2241	2340
94	Lichtenfels ... 876 a.	|	...	0741	|	|	0940	1044	|	1140	|	|	1343	|	1540	1622	|	|	1742	|	1945	|	2044	...	2306	0005
94	Lichtenfels ... d.	|	0701	0757	|	|	0944	1102	|	1159	|	|	1401	|	1544	1624	|	|	1802	|	2001	|	2049	2103z	2316	0006
114	**Coburg** ... 850 a.	0720	0724	0822	0828	0920	1001	1122	1118	1224	1218	1317	1425	1519	1600	1646	1628	1720	1823	1918	2025	2018	2108	2121z	2335	0025
114	**Coburg** ... d.	0731z	0729t	0831	0831	0931	1031	1134t	1134	1232	1232	1331	1433	1534	1633	1707	1633	1731	1831	1931	2031z	2039	...	2126	2336	...
135	**Sonneberg** (Thür) Hbf a.	0753z	0754t	0853	0853	0953	1053	1155t	1153	1254	1254	1353	1455	1555	1655	1735	1655	1753	1853	1953	2053z	2101	...	2148	2358	...

		Ⓐt¶			Ⓐt¶	Ⓐt	Ⓒz	Ⓒz¶		Ⓐt¶		¶		⊖¶		¶	Ⓐt¶		⊖¶	Ⓐt¶		Ⓒz¶	Ⓐt		Ⓐt	Ⓒz
Sonneberg (Thür) Hbf d.	...	0445	0539	0610t	...	0706	0705	0806	0806t	0906	0906z	1006	1104	1203	1306	1406	...	1505	1603	...	1706	1806	1806	1906	2005	2005
Coburg ... a.	...	0507	0600	0631t	...	0727p	0726	0827	0827t	0927	0927z	1027	1125	1223	1327	1427	...	1526p	1624	...	1727p	1827	1827	1927	2026	2026
Coburg ... 850 d.	0446	0508	0611	0635t	0732	0728	0753	0838e	0832r	0939	0954	1038	1154	1238	1332	1436	1530	1554	1638	1739	1731	1838	1832	1929	2029	2029
Lichtenfels ... a.	0506	0529	|	0655t	|	0759	0811	|	0855r	|	1011	|	1211	|	1355	|	|	1611	|	|	1753	|	1855	1953	2047	2047
Lichtenfels ... 876 d.	0509	0530	|	0709	|	0818	0818	|	0912	|	1018	|	1218	|	1418	|	|	1618	|	|	1818	|	1912	2018	2114	2112
Bamberg ... 876 a.	0535	0556	0634	0735	0756	0836	0836	0901e	0935	1003	1036	1102	1236	1302	1436	1502	1554	1635	1702	1803	1836	1903	1935	2036	2138	2136
Bamberg ... 850 d.	0538	0604	0638	0739	0804	0838	0838	0904	0939	1005	1038	1104	1238	1304	1438	1504	1603	1638	1704	1805	1838	1905	1939	2038	2140	2140
Forchheim (Oberfr) ... d.	0552	0620	0652	0754	0820	0852	0852	0920	0954	1020	1052	1120	1252	1320	1452	1520	1619	1652	1720	1821	1852	1920	1954	2052	2154	2154
Erlangen ... 850 d.	0601	0629	0701	0803	0830	0901	0901	0929	1003	1029	1101	1129	1301	1329	1501	1529	1629	1701	1729	1830	1901	1929	2003	2101	2203	2203
Fürth (Bay) Hbf ... d.	0612	0641	0712	0813	0841	0912	0912	0941	1012	1041	1112	1141	1312	1341	1512	1541	1642	1712	1743	1841	1912	1941	2012	2112	2214	2214
Nürnberg Hbf ... 850 a.	0619	0648	0719	0819	0848	0919	0919	0948	1019	1048	1119	1148	1319	1348	1519	1548	1649	1719	1749	1848	1919	1948	2019	2119	2220	2220

km		Ⓐt	◧	Ⓐt	Ⓒz	Ⓐt¶	◧		◧		⊗◧	Ⓒz	Ⓐt	◧		◧		Ⓐt¶	◧		◧			c	2
0	**Nürnberg** Hbf ... 849a 850 d.	...	0529	0628	0636	0710	0738	0838	0938	1040	1138	1238	1238	1338	1441	1538	1638	1710	1740	1838	1938	2038	2140	2346	0049
8	Fürth (Bay) Hbf ... d.	...	0537	0635	0644	0716	0744	0844	0944	1046	1144	1244	1244	1344	1447	1544	1644	1716	1746	1844	1944	2044	2146	2352	0057
24	Erlangen ... 849a 850 d.	...	0547	0647	0654	0727	0754	0854	0954	1055	1154	1254	1254	1354	1457	1554	1655	1727	1756	1854	1954	2055	2156	0002	0114
39	Forchheim (Oberfr) ... d.	...	0557	0657	0703	0735	0802	0902	1002	1104	1202	1302	1302	1402	1505	1602	1703	1735	1804	1902	2002	2103	2204	0011	0129
62	**Bamberg** ... 849a 850 d.	0507	0627f	0723	0723	0754	0822	0922	1022	1122	1222	1322	1322	1422	1522	1622	1722	1804f	1822	1922	2022	2136j	2241j	0034	0149
94	Lichtenfels ... 849a d.	0535	0653	0741	0743	0820	0845	0942	1045	1142	1245	1343	1345	1445	1542	1645	1744	1830	1845	1947	2045	2203	2309	0100	...
118	Kronach ... 849a d.	0557	0713	0758	0757	...	0905	0957	1105	1157	1309	1357	1359	1505	1557	1705	1758	...	1905	2007	2107	2223	2329	...	...
181	**Saalfeld** (Saale) ... 849a a.	0654	0809	0852	0851	...	1002	1051	1202	1251	1410	1451	1454	1602	1651	1802	1853	...	2002	2103	2204	...	...	...	...
	Jena Paradies 849 ... a.	...	0846	...	...	...	1038	...	1238	...	1446	...	...	1638	...	1838	...	...	2038	...	2242	...	...	...	...
	Leipzig Hbf 849 ... a.	...	0952	...	...	...	1152	...	1352	...	1552	...	...	1752	...	1952	...	...	2152	...	...	...	...	...	...

	Ⓐt	Ⓐt¶	◧	Ⓐt¶	Ⓒz	Ⓐt	◧		◧		◧		◧		◧		◧			Ⓒz◧	Ⓐt	b		Ⓒz2	Ⓐt2
Leipzig Hbf 849 ... d.	◇	...	...	...	...	...	0558	...	0809	...	1009	...	1209	...	1409	...	1609	...	1809	1809	...	...	2009	...	...
Jena Paradies 849 ... d.	...	...	...	0509	0616n	...	0708	...	0917	...	1117	...	1317	...	1517	...	1717	...	1917	1917	...	...	2117	...	...
Saalfeld (Saale) ... 849a d.	...	...	...	0610	0658	0701	0752	0905	0952	1105	1152	1305	1352	1505	1552	1705	1752	1905	1952	1952	...	...	2152	...	...
Kronach ... 849a d.	...	0610	0647	0715	0753	0757	0852	0959	1052	1159	1252	1359	1452	1559	1652	1759	1852	1959	2052	2052	...	...	2252	...	...
Lichtenfels ... 849a d.	0622	0635	0709	0735	0818	0818	0912	1018	1112	1218	1312	1418	1512	1618	1712	1818	1912	2018	2111	2112	2114	2212	2316	...	...
Bamberg ... 849a 850 d.	0643	0706f	0739	0804	0838	0838	0939	1038	1139	1238	1339	1438	1539	1638	1739	1838	1939	2038	...	2140	2140	2239	2342	0008	0034
Forchheim (Oberfr) ... d.	|	0721	0754	0820	0852	0852	0954	1052	1154	1252	1354	1452	1554	1652	1754	1852	1954	2052	...	2154	2154	2254	...	0028	0054
Erlangen ... 849a 850 d.	0709	0730	0803	0830	0901	0901	1003	1101	1203	1301	1403	1501	1603	1701	1803	1901	2003	2101	...	2203	2203	2303	...	0042	0108
Fürth (Bay) Hbf ... d.	|	0742	0813	0841	0912	0912	1012	1112	1212	1312	1412	1512	1612	1712	1812	1912	2012	2112	...	2214	2214	2313	...	0100	0125
Nürnberg Hbf ... 849a 850 a.	0725	0749	0819	0848	0919	0919	1019	1119	1219	1319	1419	1519	1619	1719	1819	1919	2019	2119	...	2220	2220	2319	...	0108	0133

km		Ⓐt	Ⓒz	Ⓐt		⊙			⊙			⊙		⊙		⊙		⊙		⊙					
	Nürnberg Hbf ⊡ ... d.	...	...	...	0529	...	0738	...	...	...	0938	...	1138	...	1338	...	1538	...	1740	...	1938	...	...	...	...
0	**Bamberg** ... d.	0445	0445	0526	0625	0726	0827	0841	0926	0941	1027	1126	1227	1326	1427	1526	1627	1726	1827	1926	2027	2042	2141	2304	0036
32	Haßfurt ... d.	0506	0506	0548	0641	0742	0843	0902	0942	1002	1043	1142	1243	1342	1443	1542	1643	1742	1843	1942	2043	2102	2202	2326	0058
57	Schweinfurt Hbf ... 870 d.	0526	0526	0610	0656	0756	0856	0919	0956	1019	1056	1156	1256	1356	1456	1556	1656	1756	1857	1956	2056	2119	2220	2345	0116
100	**Würzburg** Hbf ... 870 a.	0548	0557	0648	0721	0821	0920	0951	1021	1051	1120	1221	1320	1421	1521	1621	1721	1821	1921	2021	2121	2150	2251	0016	...

	⚒r		Ⓐt	⊙			⊙			⊙		⊙		⊙					⊙			⊙			
Würzburg Hbf ... 870 d.	0454	0603	0635	0739	0835	0907	0939	1008	1035	1139	1235	1339	1435	1539	1637	1739	1808	1836	1939	2008	2035	2139	2236	2307	0036
Schweinfurt Hbf ... 870 d.	0543j	0634	0701	0803	0900	0938	1003	1038	1101	1203	1301	1403	1501	1603	1701	1803	1838	1901	2003	2038	2101	2203	2301	2345	0106
Haßfurt ... d.	0600	0652	0714	0816	0912	0955	1016	1055	1114	1216	1314	1416	1514	1616	1714	1816	1855	1914	2016	2055	2114	2216	2314	0004	...
Bamberg ... a.	0621	0715	0733	0832	0930	1016	1032	1116	1130	1232	1330	1432	1530	1632	1730	1832	1916	1930	2032	2116	2130	2232	2332	0028	...
Nürnberg Hbf ⊡ ... a.	...	...	0819	...	1019	...	...	...	1219	...	1419	...	1619	...	1819	...	...	2019	...	...	2220z	...	...	...	...

b – Not Feb. 10 - Mar. 23.
c – Not Feb. 10 - Mar. 24.
e – Feb. 11 - Mar. 19 Coburg d. 0828, Bamberg a. 0853.
f – Arrives 9 – 11 minutes earlier.
j – Arrives 16 – 19 minutes earlier.
k – Not Feb. 11 - Mar. 31.
n – Not Jan. 6.

p – Connects with train in previous column.
r – ⚒ (not Jan. 6).
t – Ⓐ (not Jan. 6).
z – Ⓒ (also Jan. 6).

⊙ – From / to Frankfurt (Table **921**).

¶ – Does not run Nürnberg - Bamberg and v.v. Feb. 11 - Mar. 24.
⊖ – Change trains at Coburg on Ⓐ (not Jan. 6).
⊗ – Change trains at Kronach on ⑤ (not Dec. 30, Jan. 6, Feb. 24).
◧ – Conveys 🚲 Nürnberg - Bamberg - Würzburg and v.v. (see lower panel).
⊡ – See Nürnberg - Saalfeld panel for intermediate calling points.
◇ – *ICE* **1501**. To München (Table **904**).

876 BAMBERG - HOF and BAYREUTH *RE services*

km				Ⓒz		Ⓐt								N				N				N				N
0	**Bamberg** ... 875 d.	...	...	...	...	...	...	...	0838	0838	...	...	1046	1046	...	...	1246	1246	...	...	1446	1446	...	...	1646	1646
32	Lichtenfels ... 875 d.	0546z	0549t	0658	0658z	0658	0801	0801	0859	0859	1003	1003	1104	1104	1203	1203	1304	1304	1403	1403	1504	1504	1603	1603	1704	1704
62	Kulmbach ... d.	0608z	0613t	0717	0717z	0720	0822	0822	0917	0917	1022	1022	1123	1123	1222	1222	1323	1323	1422	1422	1523	1523	1622	1622	1723	1723
74	Neuenmarkt-Wirsberg a.	0620z	0624t	0727	0727z	0728p	0830	0830	0927	0927	1032	1032	1131	1131	1232	1232	1331	1331	1432	1432	1531	1531	1632	1632	1731	1731
74	Neuenmarkt-Wirsberg d.	0634	0625	0729	0732	0729	0832	0835	0929	0932	1033	1035	1132	1135	1233	1235	1332	1335	1433	1435	1532	1535	1633	1635	1732	1735
96	**Bayreuth** Hbf ... a.	0658	|	|	0757	|	|	0857	|	0956	|	1057	|	1156	|	1257	|	1356	|	1457	|	1556	|	1657	|	1756
103	Münchberg ... 880 d.	...	0649	0755	...	0755	0859	...	0955	...	1100	...	1155	...	1300	...	1356	...	1500	...	1556	...	1700	...	1755	...
116	Schwarzenbach ... d.	...	0704	0806	...	0806	0911	...	1007	...	1112	...	1205	...	1312	...	1406	...	1512	...	1606	...	1712	...	1805	...
127	**Hof** Hbf ... 880 a.	...	0717	0818	...	0818	0921	...	1019	...	1123	...	1214	...	1323	...	1416	...	1523	...	1614	...	1724	...	1814	...

				N					◐	B◐		T
Bamberg ... 875 d.	...	...	1846	1846	...	...	2046	2046	...		2244h	2244h
Lichtenfels ... 875 d.	1804	1804	1904	1904	2003	2003	2106	2106	2236	...	2313	2313
Kulmbach ... d.	1824	1824	1923	1923	2022	2022	2128	2128	2300	...	2338	2338
Neuenmarkt-Wirsberg a.	1834	1834	1931	1931	2032	2032	2138	2138	2311	...	2350	2350
Neuenmarkt-Wirsberg d.	1835	1837	1932	1935	2033	2036	2139	2141	2312	2314	2350	2350
Bayreuth Hbf ... a.	|	1857	|	1956	|	2058	|	2200	2332	|	0016	|
Münchberg ... 880 d.	1902	...	1955	...	2100	...	2206	...	...	2341	...	0038
Schwarzenbach ... d.	1916	...	2006	...	2112	...	2217	...	...	2354	...	0047
Hof Hbf ... 880 a.	1928	...	2020	...	2123	...	2230	...	...	0008	...	0058

		Ⓒz	Ⓐt			N			
Hof Hbf ... 880 d.	...	0523	0526	...	0635	...	0744	...	0835
Schwarzenbach ... d.	...	0534	0536	...	0645	...	0752	...	0845
Münchberg ... 880 d.	...	0545	0545	...	0657	...	0802	...	0856
Bayreuth Hbf ... d.	0545	|	|	0701	|	0802	|	0902	|
Neuenmarkt-Wirsberg ... a.	0608	0613	0615	0720	0725	0820	0824	0920	0925
Neuenmarkt-Wirsberg ... d.	0615z	0615	0616	0727	0727	0827	0827	0927	0927
Kulmbach ... d.	0625z	0625	0626	0737	0737	0835	0835	0937	0937
Lichtenfels ... 875 a.	0648z	0648	0647	0756	0756	0853	0853	0957	0957
Bamberg ... 875 a.	...	...	...	0820	0820	0912	0912	...	...

	N				N				N				N												R⊖	⊖
Hof Hbf ... 880 d.	...	0944	...	1036	...	1144	...	1236	...	1344	...	1436	...	1544	...	1636	...	1743	...	1836	1935	...	...	2035	2135	
Schwarzenbach ... d.	...	0952	...	1045	...	1152	...	1245	...	1352	...	1445	...	1552	...	1645	...	1753	...	1845	1943	...	...	2046	2143	...
Münchberg ... 880 d.	...	1002	...	1056	...	1202	...	1256	...	1402	...	1456	...	1602	...	1656	...	1804	...	1856	1954	...	...	2058	2154	...
Bayreuth Hbf ... d.	1002	|	1102	|	1202	|	1301	|	1402	|	1502	|	1602	|	1702	|	1803	|	1902	|	|	2003	2103	|	|	2205
Neuenmarkt-Wirsberg a.	1020	1024	1120	1125	1221	1225	1321	1325	1421	1425	1520	1525	1621	1625	1720	1725	1825	1830	1920	1925	2022	2026	2121	2126	2231	2231
Neuenmarkt-Wirsberg d.	1027	1027	1127	1127	1227	1227	1328	1328	1427	1427	1527	1527	1627	1627	1727	1727	1832	1832	1927	1927	...	2027	2128	2128	2232	2232
Kulmbach ... d.	1035	1035	1137	1137	1235	1235	1337	1337	1435	1435	1537	1537	1635	1635	1737	1737	1841	1841	1936	1936	...	2036	2138	2138	2244	2244
Lichtenfels ... 875 a.	1053	1053	1156	1156	1254	1254	1358	1358	1453	1453	1557	1557	1653	1653	1756	1756	1901	1901	1956	1956	...	2056	2200	2200	2307	2307
Bamberg ... 875 a.	1112	1112	...	...	1313	1313	...	...	1511	1511	...	...	1712	1712	...	...	1922	1922	...	...	...	2120h	...	...	...	...

B – From Bayreuth (d. 2250).
N – To / from Nürnberg via Pegnitz (Table **880**).
R – Change trains at Trebgast (a. 2215, d. 2225).
T – Change trains at Trebgast (a. 2355, d. 0011).

h – ⑤-⑦ (also Dec. 26).
p – Connects with train in previous column.
t – Ⓐ (not Jan. 6).
z – Ⓒ (also Jan. 6).

⊖ – Not Jan. 5, 31.
◐ – Operated by *agilis* (2nd class only).

LANDSHUT - MÜHLDORF - SALZBURG 877

RB services

km					◇					⊡	
0	**Landshut** (Bay) Hbf... d.	0608f	0738	0837	0936	1037	1136	1237	⊠	2037	2137
55	Mühldorf (Oberbay).... a.	0712f	0825	0928	1025	1128	1225	1329	and	2128	2228
55	Mühldorf (Oberbay).... d.	0741	0843	0943	1043	1143	1243	1342	hourly	2146	2250
120	Freilassing ...... 890/1 a.	0834	0944	1043	1143	1243	1343	1443	until	2239	2344
126	**Salzburg** Hbf.. 890/1 a.	0855	0955	1055	1155	1255n	1355	1455		2254	0017

	⊙	⊙			⊖						
Salzburg Hbf 890/1 d.	0615	0742	0908	1008	1108	1208	1313	1408	1508	⊠	2108
Freilassing .... 890/1 d.	0628	0813	0924	1024	1124	1224	1324	1424	1524	and	2124
Mühldorf (Oberbay). a.	0723	0915	1015	1115	1215	1315	1415	1515	1615	hourly	2222
Mühldorf (Oberbay). d.	0730	0933	1030	1132	1230	1332	1430	1532	1630	until	2240
Landshut (Bay) Hbf a.	0821	1021	1121	1221	1321	1421	1521	1620	1721		2328

f – On Ⓒ (also Jan. 6) Landshut d. 0637, Mühldorf a. 0726.
n – *1317* on Ⓐ (not Jan. 6).
⊡ – Change trains at Mühldorf and Freilassing.
⊙ – Change trains at Freilassing and Mühldorf.
⊖ – Change trains at Mühldorf on †.
◇ – Change trains at Mühldorf and Freilassing on Ⓐ (not Jan. 6).
⊠ – Timings may vary by up to 4 minutes. Certain services require a change of trains at Mühldorf.

MÜNCHEN - REGENSBURG 878

DB (RE services); ALX

See Table **892** for services Regensburg - Landshut - Freising - München Flughafen ✈ and v.v.

km		ALX		ALX		ALX		ALX		ALX		ALX		ALX	ALX	ALX			ALX		ALX	ALX		ALX	ALX
		⚒rP	N	P	N	P	N	P	N	P	N	P	N	⑦w	R	P	Ⓐt	N		N		⑦w			
0	**München** Hbf ...... 944 d.	0444	0544	0644	0744	0843	0944	1043	1144	1243	1344	1443	1544	1604	1604	1643	1700	1744	1843	1944	2043	2043	2144	2244	0004
42	Freising .... 944 d.	0508	0608	0708	0808	0908	1008	1108	1208	1308	1408	1508	1608	1628	1628	1708	1733	1808	1908	2008	2108	2108	2208	2308	0028
76	Landshut (Bay) Hbf 944 d.	0529	0631	0729	0830	0929	1030	1129	1230	1329	1430	1529	1630	1649	1649	1729	1800	1830	1929	2030	2129	2129	2230	2334	0050
99	Neufahrn (Niederbay) .. d.	0543	0648	0744	0848	0943	1048	1143	1248	1343	1448	1543	1648	|	|	1743	1818	1848	1946	2048	2146	2146	2248	2351	0107
138	**Regensburg** Hbf .... a.	0607	0716	0807	0915	1006	1115	1206	1315	1406	1515	1607	1715	1726	1726	1806	1846	1915	2009	2115	2208	2208	2321	0017	0131
	Schwandorf 879 885 a.	0646	...	0842	...	1042	...	1242	...	1442	...	1642	...	1758	1802	1842	...	...	2105	...	2252	2252	...	0109	...
	Hof Hbf 879 .... a.	...	...	1018	...	1218	...	1420	...	1618	...	1818	...	m	1932	2017	...	...	m	...	...	0028	...	...	...

	ALX	ALX		ALX	ALX		ALX			ALX		ALX		ALX		ALX		ALX		ALX		ALX	ALX	ALX	
	⚒r		Ⓐt	Ⓒz	Ⓐt	ⒶtN		Ⓐt	N	P	N	P	N	P	N	P	N	P	N	P	QN	⑦w		P	N
Hof Hbf 879 .... d.	...	...	...	m	m	...	0531r	...	...	0739	...	0939	...	1139	...	1339	...	1539	...	1739	...	m	...	1940c	...
Schwandorf 879 885. d.	0400t	0502r	...	0603	0609	...	0707	...	...	0917	...	1117	...	1317	...	1517	...	1717	...	1917	...	2013	...	2117	...
Regensburg Hbf .... d.	0442	0546	0624	0646	0649	0702	0753	0826	0846	0953	1046	1153	1246	1353	1446	1553	1646	1753	1846	1953	2040	2053	2053	2157	2247
Neufahrn (Niederbay) ... d.	0508	0610	0652	0711	|	0728	0816	|	0912	1016	1112	1216	1312	1416	1512	1616	1712	1816	1912	2016	2108	2116	2116	2222	2313
Landshut (Bay) Hbf 944 d.	0527	0628	0710	0729	0733	0747	0832	0904	0929	1032	1129	1232	1329	1432	1529	1632	1729	1832	1929	2032	2126	2132	2132	2237	2335
Freising .... 944 d.	0548	0649	0732	0751	|	0810	0852	0931	0950	1051	1150	1251	1350	1451	1550	1651	1750	1851	1950	2051	...	2151	2151	2256	2356
München Hbf .... 944 a.	0616	0716	0757	0817	0821	0836	0919	1001	1018	1118	1216	1318	1416	1518	1616	1718	1816	1918	2016	2118	...	2217	2217	2321	0020

NOTES FOR TABLES 878 and 879

N – To / from Nürnberg (Table **921**).
P – Also conveys [12] München - Schwandorf - Praha and v.v. See Tables **76** and **885**.
Q – ⑤⑥ (also Dec. 25, Jan. 5, Apr. 6, 9, 30, May 17).
R – ①–⑥ (also Dec. 25, Apr. 9, 30; not Dec. 26, Apr. 10, May 1).
c – Change trains at Schwandorf on ①–⑤ (not Dec. 26, Jan. 5, Apr. 6, 10, May 1, 17).
d – Also Dec. 26, Apr. 10, May 1.
j – Arrives 2154.
m – To / from Marktredwitz (Table **879**).
r – ⚒ (not Jan. 6).
t – Ⓐ (not Jan. 6).
v – Not Jan. 6.
w – Also Dec. 26, Apr. 10, May 1; not Dec. 25, Apr. 9, 30.
z – Also Jan. 6.
ALX – *alex* train. Operated by Die Länderbahn.

REGENSBURG - HOF 879

ALX; Oberpfalzbahn

km		2	ALX	2	ALX	2	ALX	2	ALX	2	ALX	2		ALX	2	ALX	ALX	ALX	2	2	ALX	2	ALX	ALX	2	2
		Ⓐt	⚒r										⑤v			⑦w	R							⑦w		
	München Hbf 878 .. d.	...	0444	...	0644	...	0843	...	1043	...	1243	...	...	1443	...	1604	1604	1643	...	...	1843	...	2043	2043	...	...
0	**Regensburg** Hbf 885 d.	...	0615	0707	0815	0857	1014	1057	1214	1257	1414	1457	1529	1615	1657	1734	1734	1814	1857	1957	2037	2138	2220	2220	...	2336
42	Schwandorf .... 885 a.	...	0646	0734	0842	0925	1042	1125	1242	1325	1442	1525	1558	1642	1727	1758	1802	1842	1925	2026	2105	2207	2252	2252	...	0006
42	Schwandorf .... d.	0502	0651	0735	0846	0926	1046	1126	1246	1326	1446	1526	1603	1646	1728	1759	1803	1846	1926	2027	2107	2209	...	2257	2315	0007
86	Weiden (Oberpf) .... d.	0539	0718	0814	0914	1002	1114	1202	1314	1402	1514	1602	1626	1714	1804	1825	1830	1916	2002	2102	2132	2248	...	2323	2350	0042
137	Marktredwitz ...... 880 a.	0621	0752	0855	0949	1044	1149	1244	1350	1442	1549	1644	1657	1749	1844	1859	1906	1950	2044	2143	2213	2327	...	2359	...	...
179	**Hof** Hbf............... 880 a.	0702	0820	0924	1018	1115	1218	1315	1420	1515	1618	1715	1720	1818	1915r	1924	1932	2017	2126	...	2242	0006	...	0028	...	...

	ALX	ALX	ALX	ALX	ALX	2	2	ALX	2	ALX	2	ALX	2	ALX	2	ALX	2	2	2	ALX	2	ALX	ALX		2	2
	⚒r	⑥	Ⓒz	Ⓐt		Ⓒz	Ⓐt											⑦d				⑦w	c			
Hof Hbf .... 880 d.	...	...	...	0420	0531r	0629	0629	0739	0843	0939	1043	1139	1243	1339	1443	1539	...	1643	1643r	1739	...	1843	1940	2043	...	2237
Marktredwitz .... 880 d.	...	0502	...	0506	0559	0704	0706	0806	0915	1006	1115	1206	1315	1406	1515	1606	1615	1707	1715r	1806	1815	1912	2006	2104	2115	2335
Weiden (Oberpf) .... d.	0414t	0539	...	0543	0639	0742	0745	0841	0955	1041	1155	1241	1356	1441	1555	1641	1656	1744	1755	1841	1856	1946	2041	...	2222j	0014
Schwandorf .... a.	0451t	0602	...	0606	0703	0807	0809	0906	1031	1106	1230	1306	1431	1506	1630	1706	1731	1809	1830	1906	1931	2010	2106	...	2257	...
Schwandorf .... 885 d.	0502	0603	0603	0609	0707	0808	0810	0917	1032	1117	1232	1317	1432	1517	1632	1717	1732	1810	1832	1917	1932	2013	2117	...	2313	...
Regensburg Hbf . 885 a.	0536	0636	0636	0640	0741	0837	0837	0945	1104	1145	1304	1345	1504	1545	1704	1745	1804	1838	1904	1945	2004	2045	2149	...	2341	...
München Hbf 878 ... a.	0716	0817	0817	0821	0919	...	...	1118	...	1318	...	1518	...	1718	...	1918	...	...	...	2118	...	2217	2321	...	...	...

FOR NOTES SEE TABLE 878 ABOVE

NÜRNBERG - HOF - DRESDEN 880

RE / RB services

NÜRNBERG - HOF

km				Ⓒz	Ⓒz	Ⓐt	Ⓐt	B			Ⓐt		B			Ⓐt			B			Ⓐt			B
0	**Nürnberg** Hbf .... ● d.	0535j	0535j	0631	0631	0637	0637	0656	0738	0738	0805	0837	0905	0938	0938	1005	1037	1037	1105	1138	1138	1205	1237	1237	1305
28	Hersbruck (r Pegnitz)....... ● d.	0556	0556	0652	0652	|	|	0715	0754	0754	0820	|	0920	|	|	1020	|	|	1120	|	|	1220	|	|	1320
67	Pegnitz .... ● a.	0617	0617	0714	0714	0714	0714	0738	0822	0822	0841	0914	0941	1015	1015	1041	1114	1114	1141	1215	1215	1241	1314	1314	1341
67	Pegnitz .... d.	0628	0619	0716	0720	0716	0720	0739	0824	0828	0842	0916	0942	1017	1021	1042	1116	1120	1142	1217	1221	1242	1316	1320	1342
	Bayreuth Hbf .... d.	|	0641	0732	|	0732	|	0758	0847	|	0857	0932	1000	1042	|	1057	1132	|	1200	1242	|	1257	1332	|	1400
	Münchberg .... 876 d.	|	▬	0805	|	0805	|	...	...	|	▬	1004	...	...	|	▬	1205	|	...	...	|	▬	1405	|	...
94	Kirchenlaibach .... d.	0643	⊖	|	0734	|	0734	...	...	0845	⊖	|	...	...	1035	⊖	|	1134	...	...	1235	⊖	|	1334	...
125	Marktredwitz .... 879 d.	0700	0712	|	0759r	|	0759r	...	...	0901	0908	|	...	...	1053	1108	|	1159r	...	...	1253	1308	|	1359r	...
	Cheb .... a.	|	0737	|	0822	|	0822	...	...	|	0933	|	...	...	|	1133	|	1222	...	...	|	1333	|	1422	...
167	**Hof** Hbf................ 876 879 a.	0723	...	0824	...	0824	...	...	...	0924	...	1022	...	...	1115	...	1222	...	...	...	1315	...	1424	...	...

			Ⓐt			B			Ⓐt						Ⓐt										
Nürnberg Hbf .... ● d.	1338	1338	1405	1437	1437	1505	1537	1537	1605	1637	1637	1705	1738	1738	1805	1837	1837	1905	1938	1938	2055	2055	2206	2206	2257
Hersbruck (r Pegnitz)....... ● d.	|	|	1420	|	|	1520	|	|	1620	|	|	1720	|	|	1820	|	|	1920	1954	1954	2112	2112	2223	2223	2313
Pegnitz .... ● a.	1415	1415	1442	1514	1514	1542	1615	1615	1642	1714	1714	1742	1815	1815	1842	1914	1914	1942	2021	2021	2137	2137	2248	2248	2337
Pegnitz .... d.	1417	1421	1443	1516	1520	1543	1617	1621	1643	1716	1720	1743	1817	1821	1843	1916	1920	1943	2023	2027	2139	2144	2250	2255	2338
Bayreuth Hbf .... d.	1442	|	1458	1532	|	1600	1642	|	1658	1732	|	1800	1842	|	1859	1932	|	2000	2048	|	2158	|	2310	|	2357
Münchberg .... 876 d.	...	|	▬	1605	|	...	...	|	▬	1805	|	...	...	|	▬	2005	|	...	...	|	...	|	▬	|	0038
Kirchenlaibach .... d.	...	1435	⊖	|	1534	...	...	1635	⊖	|	1734	...	...	1835	⊖	|	1935	...	...	2044	...	2158	⊖	2309	|
Marktredwitz .... 879 d.	...	1453	1508	|	1559r	...	...	1653	1708	|	1759r	...	...	1853k	1911	|	2001	...	...	2101	...	2216	2218	2333	|
Cheb .... a.	...	|	1533	|	1622	...	...	|	1733	|	1822	...	...	|	1936	|	...	...	...	|	...	|	2243	|	|
Hof Hbf................ 876 879 a.	...	1515	...	1623	...	...	...	1715	...	1823	...	...	...	1915k	...	2022	...	...	...	2126	...	2242	...	0006	0058

HOF - DRESDEN ⊠

km					★					★												◇		◇
0	**Hof** Hbf .... 881 d.	...	...	0428	...	...	0528	...	0628	...	...	0728	...		1828	...	1937	...	2028	...	...	...	...	2248
48	Plauen (Vogtl) ob Bf ..... 881 d.	...	...	0459	...	...	0559	...	0659	...	...	0800	...	and at	1859	...	2009	...	2059	...	...	2158	...	2328
73	Reichenbach (Vogtl) ob Bf 881 d.	...	...	0516	...	...	0616	...	0716	...	...	0817	...	the same	1916	...	2026	...	2116	...	...	2221	...	2351
96	**Zwickau** (Sachs) Hbf.... 881 d.	...	0439	0532	...	0539	0632	0639	0732	...	0739	0832	0839	minutes	1932	1939	2042	...	2132	2139	2239	2250	2343	0016
112	Glauchau (Sachs) .... 858 d.	...	0455	0541	...	0555	0641	0655	0741	...	0755	0841	0855	past each	1941	1955	2051	2055	2141	2155	2255	...	2359	...
144	**Chemnitz** Hbf .... 858 d.	0504	0530r	0604	0626	0630r	0704	0730r	0804	0826	0830r	0904	0930r	hour until	2004	2030r	2114	2130	2203	2230r	2330r	...	0029	...
157	Flöha .... d.	0514	0543	0614	|	0643	0714	0743	0814	|	0843	0914	0943		2014	2043	2124	2143	...	2243	2343	...	...	...
183	Freiberg (Sachs) .... d.	0531	0607	0631	0655	0707	0731	0807	0831	0855	0907	0931	1007		2031	2107	2141	2207	...	2307	0007	...	...	...
223	**Dresden** Hbf .... a.	0606	0652	0706	0726	0752	0806	0852	0906	0926	0952	1006	1052		2106	2152	2216	2252	...	2352	0052	...	...	...

B – To Bamberg (Table **876**).
j – 0538 on Ⓐ (not Jan. 6).
k – On †z: Marktredwitz a. 1852, d. 1902, Hof a. 1924.
r – Arrives 5–6 minutes earlier.
t – Not Jan. 6.
z – Also Jan. 6.
⊖ – Operated by Oberpfalzbahn.
◇ – Operated by Vogtlandbahn.
⊠ – Operated by Mitteldeutsche Regiobahn (2nd class only).
★ – *IC* service to Warnemünde via Berlin and Rostock (Tables **835** and **840**). Operated by DB.
● – Certain trains between Nürnberg and Pegnitz convey portions for two separate destinations. Passengers should take care to join the correct portion for their destination.

880 DRESDEN - HOF - NÜRNBERG *RE / RB services*

DRESDEN - HOF ⊠

	Ⓐ◇												★					★		◇				
Dresden Hbf d.	...	...	...	0448	0504	0551	0602	0651	and at the same minutes past each hour until	1702	1751	1802	1832	1851	1902	1951	2002	2032	...	...	2102	2152	2202	2302
Freiberg (Sachs) d.	...	...	...	0524	0551	0624	0651	0724		1751	1824	1851	1906	1924	1951	2024	2051	2106	...	...	2151	2224	2251	2351
Flöha d.	...	...	...	0542	0614	0642	0714	0742		1814	1842	1914	|	1942	2014	2042	2114	|	←	...	2214	2242	2314	0014
Chemnitz Hbf 858 d.	...	...	0409	0552	0630f	0652	0730f	0752		1830f	1852	1930f	1931	1952	2030f	2052	2125	2131	2136	...	2230f	2252	2330f	0025
Glauchau (Sachs) 858 d.	...	...	0441	0616	0702	0716	0802	0816		1902	1916	2002	...	2016	2102	2116	→	...	2208	...	2302	2316	0002	...
Zwickau (Sachs) Hbf 881 d.	*0349*h	...	0512c	0626	0717	0726	0817	0826		1917	1926	2017	...	2026	2117	2126	...	...	2223	2248	2317	2327	0017	...
Reichenbach (Vogtl) ob Bf 881 d.	0416	...	0528	0641	...	0741	...	0841		...	1941	...	...	2041	...	2141	...	...	...	2314	...	...	...	...
Plauen (Vogtl) ob Bf 881 d.	0439	...	0547	0700	...	0800	...	0900		...	2000	...	...	2100	...	2200	...	...	...	2337	...	...	...	...
Hof Hbf 881 a.	0518	...	0621	0732	...	0832	...	0932		...	2032	...	...	2132	...	2232	...	...	...	...	...	...	...	...

HOF - NÜRNBERG

km			Ⓐt	Ⓐt	Ⓒz	Ⓒz	Ⓐt	Ⓐt	⊖				⚒t	⊖						⊖			B		⊖
0	**Hof** Hbf 876 879 d.	...	0420	...	...	*0518*k	*0531*	0526	...	0629	...	...	0735	...	0843	...	...	...	0935	...	1043	...	...	1135	...
	Cheb d.	...	|	...	...	|	|	|	0629	|	...	...	|	0829	|	...	...	0936	|	1025	|	...	...	|	1225
	Marktredwitz 879 d.	...	0442	...	...	0601	0601	|	0654	0657	...	...	|	0855	0905	...	...	1009r	|	1050	1105	...	...	|	1250
	Kirchenlaibach d.	...	0507	...	...	0616	0620f	|	▬	0713	...	...	|	▬	0923	...	...	1024	|	▬	1123	...	...	|	▬
24	Münchberg 876 d.	...	|	...	...	|	|	0545	Ⓐt	|	...	...	0752	Ⓐt	|	...	...	|	0952	Ⓐt	|	...	...	1152	Ⓐt
72	**Bayreuth** Hbf d.	0500	|	0551	0605	|	|	0624	0703	|	0712	0800	0829	0903	|	0915	1001	|	1029	1103	|	1115	1201	1229	1303
99	Pegnitz a.	0521	0525	0611	0624	0631	0634	0639	0717	0731	0735	0817	0844	0918	0937	0941	1018	1038	1043	1118	1137	1141	1218	1244	1318
99	Pegnitz d.	0529j	0529	0612	0634	0634	0641	0641	0718	0738	0738	0818	0845	0919	0944	0944	1019	1046	1046	1119	1144	1144	1219	1245	1319
138	Hersbruck (r Pegnitz) d.	0552j	0552	0634	0657	0657	0702	0702	0742	0802	0802	0841	|	0939	|	|	1039	|	|	1139	|	|	1239	|	|
166	**Nürnberg** Hbf a.	0607j	0607	0651	0713	0713	0719	0719	0757	0819	0819	0857	0922	0955	1020	1020	1056	1122	1122	1155	1220	1220	1256	1322	1355

		B				⊖			B			⊖			B			⊖		B			⊖		
Hof Hbf 876 879 d.	1243	...	...	...	1335	...	1443	...	...	...	1535	...	1643	...	...	...	1735	...	1843	...	...	1935	...	2043	2135
Cheb d.	|	...	...	1336	|	1425	|	...	...	1536	|	1625	|	...	...	1736	|	1825	|	...	1937	|	2025	|	|
Marktredwitz 879 d.	1306	...	...	1409r	|	1450	1506	...	...	1609r	|	1650	1705	...	...	1809r	|	1850	1906	...	2009r	|	2050	2105	|
Kirchenlaibach d.	1323	...	...	1424	|	▬	1523	...	...	1624	|	▬	1723	...	...	1824	|	▬	1923	...	2025	|	▬	2122	|
Münchberg 876 d.	|	...	...	|	1352	Ⓐt	|	...	...	|	1552	Ⓐt	|	...	...	|	1754	...	|	...	|	1954	...	|	2154
Bayreuth Hbf d.	|	1315	1401	|	1429	1503	|	1515	1601	|	1629	1703	|	1715	1801	|	1829	1915	|	2001	|	2029	2113	|	2227
Pegnitz a.	1337	1341	1418	1438	1444	1518	1537	1541	1618	1638	1643	1718	1737	1741	1818	1838	1843	1941	1937	2018	2039	2044	2133	2137	2246
Pegnitz d.	1344	1344	1419	1446	1446	1519	1544	1544	1619	1646	1646	1719	1744	1744	1819	1846	1846	1944	1944	2019	2046	2046	2140	2140	2247
Hersbruck (r Pegnitz) d.	1405	1405	1439	|	|	1539	|	|	1639	|	|	1739	|	|	1839	|	|	2007	2007	2039	|	|	2206	2206	2314
Nürnberg Hbf a.	1420	1420	1456	1522	1522	1555	1620	1620	1656	1722	1722	1755	1820	1820	1856	1922	1922	2022	2022	2056	2121	2121	2222	2222	2329

B – From Bamberg (Table **876**).
c – Arrives 0457.
f – Arrives 5 minutes earlier.
h – Change trains at Werdau (a. *0359*, d. 0403).
j – 7–8 minutes **earlier** on Ⓒ (also Jan. 6).
k – *0531* on ⑥.
r – Arrives 10 minutes earlier.
t – Not Jan. 6.
z – Also Jan. 6.
★ – *IC* service from Warnemünde via Rostock and Berlin (Tables **835** and **840**). Operated by DB.
⊖ – Operated by Oberpfalzbahn.
◇ – Operated by Vogtlandbahn.
⊠ – Operated by Mitteldeutsche Regiobahn (2nd class only).

881 ZWICKAU - LEIPZIG - HALLE *S-Bahn 5*

km																						
0	**Zwickau** (Sachs) Hbf 858 d.	0349	...	0504t	0520	0604	...	0704t	0720	0804	...	0904	and in the same pattern every **two** hours until	1720	1804	...	1904	1920	2004	...	2104t	2120	2230
9	Werdau 858 d.	0400	...	0513t	0531	0613	...	0713t	0731	0813	...	0913		1731	1813	...	1913	1931	2013	...	2113t	2131	2241
29	Gößnitz 858 d.	0418	...	0528t	0549	0628	...	0728t	0749	0828	...	0928		1749	1828	...	1928	1949	2028	...	2128t	2149	2259
44	Altenburg d.	0431	0502	0538	0602	0638	0702	0738	0802	0838	0902	0938		1802	1838	1902	1938	2002	2038	2102	2138	2202	2312
80	Leipzig-Connewitz ★ d.	0511	0541	0611	0641	0711	0741	0811	0841	0911	0941	1011		1841	1911	1941	2011	2041	2111	2141	2211	2243	2351
85	**Leipzig** Hbf ★ 866 d.	0523	0553	0623	0653	0723	0753	0823	0853	0923	0953	1023		1853	1923	1953	2023	2053	2123	2153	2223	2253	0002
104	Leipzig/Halle Flughafen ✈ 866 d.	0536	0606	0636	0706	0736	0806	0836	0906	0936	1006	1036		1906	1936	2006	2036	2105	2136	2205	2236	*2321*	*0026*
122	**Halle** (Saale) Hbf 866 a.	0546	0618t	0645	0718	0745	0818	0845	0918	0945	1018	1045		1918	1945	2018	2045	...	2145	...	2245	...	*0036*

	Ⓐd										⊠												
Halle (Saale) Hbf 866 d.	0410	...	0515	0540t	0615	0640t	0715	0740	0815	0840	and in the same pattern every **two** hours until	1915	1940	2015	2040	2115	...	2215	...	...	...	2359	0059
Leipzig/Halle Flughafen ✈ 866 d.	0421	0456	0526	0552	0626	0652	0726	0752	0826	0852		1926	1952	2026	2052	2126	2152	2226	2245	2328	2344	0010	0110
Leipzig Hbf ★ 866 d.	0435	0510	0540	0610	0640	0710	0740	0810	0840	0910		1940	2010	2040	2110	2140	2210	2240	2307k	2341	2357	0026	0123
Leipzig-Connewitz ★ d.	0445	0520	0550	0620	0650	0720	0750	0820	0850	0920		1950	2020	2050	2120	2150	2220	2250	2317	2351	...	...	...
Altenburg d.	0517	0556	0617	0655	0717	0756	0817	0855	0917	0956		2017	2055	2117	2156	2223	2255	...	2358	...	...	...	...
Gößnitz 858 d.	0532	0609	0632t	...	0732	0809	0832	...	0932	1009		2032	...	2132	2209	2234	...	...	0009	...	...	...	...
Werdau 858 d.	0548	0633	0648t	...	0748	0833	0848	...	0948	1033		2048	...	2148	2233	2249	...	...	0027	...	...	...	...
Zwickau (Sachs) Hbf 858 a.	0556	0645	0656t	...	0756	0845	0856	...	0956	1045		2056	...	2156	2245	2257	...	...	0039	...	...	...	...

PLAUEN - WERDAU ◇

km		Ⓐ	⚒							
	Plauen (Vogt) ob Bf 880 d.	0433	0528	0633	0728	and in the same pattern every **two** hours until	1928	2033	2158	2328
0	Reichenbach (Vogt) ¶ 880 d.	0455	0550	0655	0750		1950	2055	2221	2351
17	**Werdau** a.	0507	0602	0707	0802		2002	2107	2233	0003
	Zwickau (Sachs) Hbf 880 a.	0522	0615	0722	0815		2015	2122	2250	0016

	Ⓐ	⚒						
Zwickau (Sachs) Hbf 880 d.	0544	0636	0744	0836	and in the same pattern every **two** hours until	2036	2144	2248
Werdau d.	0557	0651	0757	0851		2051	2157	2301
Reichenbach (Vogt) ¶ 880 d.	0610	0704	0810	0904		2104	2210	2314
Plauen (Vogt) ob Bf 880 a.	0632	0726	0832	0926		2126	2233	2337

d – Runs daily Halle - Leipzig-Connewitz.
k – Arrives 2257.
t – Ⓐ only.
¶ – Reichenbach (Vogtl) ob Bf.
⊠ – The 1840 from Halle departs Werdau 2037 (not 2033), arrives Zwickau 2050 (not 2045).
◇ – Operated by Vogtlandbahn (2nd class only). Certain services run from / to Cheb (see Table **1122**).
★ – All trains also call at Leipzig MDR, Bayerischer Bahnhof, Wilhelm-Leuschner-Platz and Markt.

882 CHEMNITZ - CRANZAHL - VEJPRTY - CHOMUTOV DB (*RB* services)

km												
0	**Chemnitz** Hbf 880 d.	0636	0836	0936	1136	1236	1336	1436	1636	1836	2036	2236
13	Flöha 880 d.	0647	0847	0947	1147	1247	1347	1447	1647	1847	2047	2247
31	Zschopau d.	0708	0908	1008	1208	1309	1410	1509	1708	1910	2108	2308
57	Annaberg-Buchholz ¶ d.	0743	0943	1049	1243	1349	1445	1544	1743	1945	2143	2343
64	Cranzahl ⊖ a.	...	0955	1101	1255	1402	1501	1556z	1755	...	...	...
			C⊙			C⊙			C⊙			
64	Cranzahl d.	...	1007	...	...	1407	...	...	1807	...	...	...
75	Vejprty ▦ d.	...	1026	...	...	1426	...	...	1826	...	...	...
133	**Chomutov** a.	...	1145	...	...	1545	...	...	1945	...	...	...

			C⊙			C⊙			C⊙	
Chomutov d.	...	...	0810	...	...	1210	...	...	1610	...
Vejprty ▦ a.	...	...	0930	...	...	1330	...	...	1730	...
Cranzahl a.	...	...	0948	...	...	1358	...	...	1748	...
			d			d			d	
Cranzahl ⊖ d.	...	...	1001	1155	1301	1445	1558	1655z	1801	...
Annaberg-Buchholz ¶ d.	0607	0807	1013	1207	1313	1508	1610	1707	1813	2007
Zschopau d.	0644	0844	1047	1245	1347	1545	1645	1744	1847	2045
Flöha 880 a.	0708	0908	1108	1308	1408	1608	1708	1808	1908	2108
Chemnitz Hbf 880 a.	0720	0920	1120	1320	1420	1620	1720	1820	1920	2120

⊖ – **Cranzahl - Kurort Oberwiesenthal** *Fichtelbergbahn* (17 km, narrow gauge steam). Journey: ± 60 minutes. **No service Mar. 6–24.**
Operator: SDG Sächsische Dampfeisenbahngesellschaft GmbH, Bahnhofstraße 7, 09484 Kurort Oberwiesenthal. ✆ + 49 (0) 37348 151 0.
From Cranzahl at 1004, 1310, 1620 and 1905. **From Kurort Oberwiesenthal** at 0845, 1152, 1456 and 1755.

C – ⑥⑦ from Apr. 29 (also May 1, 8).
d – Daily.
z – Ⓒ only.
¶ – Annaberg-Buchholz unterer Bf.
⊙ – Operated by Die Länderbahn CZ. **Cranzahl timings are subject to confirmation.**

883 CHEMNITZ - AUE *City-Bahn Chemnitz*

km		⚒								
0	**Chemnitz** Hbf d.	0551	0651	and hourly until	2051	...	2202	...	...	...
27	Thalheim d.	0646	0746		2146	...	2302	...	...	...
36	Zwönitz d.	0658	0758		2158	...	2313	...	...	...
51	**Aue** (Sachs) a.	0716	0816		2216	...	2330	...	...	...

	Ⓐ								
Aue (Sachs) d.	0359	0439	and hourly until	2039	...	2221	...	...	...
Zwönitz d.	0417	0458		2058	...	2239	...	...	...
Thalheim d.	0428	0509		2109	...	2250	...	...	...
Chemnitz Hbf a.	0523	0603		2203	...	2346	...	...	...

ZWICKAU - JOHANNGEORGENSTADT - KARLOVY VARY 884

DB; ČD (2nd class only)

km		Ⓐ								⑤⑥p
0	**Zwickau** (Sachs) Hbf . d.	0503	...	0603	and	1903	2003	2103	2203	2303
27	Aue (Sachs) .... d.	0540	0540	0640	hourly	1940	2040	2140	2235	2340
37	Schwarzenberg (Erzg) . d.	0555	0555	0655	until	1955	2055	2153	...	2353
56	**Johanngeorgenstadt**. a.	0620	0620	0720		2020	2120	...	...	...

	Ⓐ	Ⓐ							
Johanngeorgenstadt...... d.	...	0429	...	0529	and	1829	1929	2029	2129
Schwarzenberg (Erzg) ...... d.	0355	0455	0455	0555	hourly	1855	1955	2055	2155
Aue (Sachs) .... d.	0408	0508	0508	0608	until	1908	2008	2108	2208
Zwickau (Sachs) Hbf .... a.	0440	0540	0540	0640		1940	2040	2140	2240p

km	SEE NOTE ▶		Ⓐ	⊗						Ⓒ	
0	**Johanngeorgenstadt**. d.	...	...	0729	0930	1230	1451	1633	2054	2054	...
1	Potučky ⊞ .... d.	0434	0558	0732	0933	1233	1454	1636	2057	2057	...
28	Nejdek .... d.	0519	0700	0817	1015	1315	1540	1717	2137	2138	2226
44	**Karlovy Vary**............ a.	0545	0727	0844	1042	1342	1606	1744	...	2206	2251
47	**Karlovy Vary** dolní ... a.	0551	0734	0852	1052	1347	1612	1752	...	...	...

SEE NOTE ▶					Ⓐ	Ⓒ	Ⓐ	Ⓒ		
Karlovy Vary dolní .... d.	0541t	0746	1003	1303	1403	1440	1703	1803	2103	...
Karlovy Vary.................... d.	0548	0752	1011	1311	1411	1449	1711	1811	2111	...
Nejdek .... d.	0616	0818	1038	1338	1441	1515	1741	1841	2137	2221
Potučky ⊞ .... d.	0704	0900	1121	1421	1524	1558	1824	1924	...	2303
Johanngeorgenstadt...... a.	0706	0902	1123	1423	1526	1600	1826	1926	...	...

p – ⑤⑥ (also Apr. 6, 9, May 28).
t – Ⓐ only.
⊗ – Change trains at Nejdek on Ⓐ.
▶ – Czech holiday dates apply (see page 4).

REGENSBURG - SCHWANDORF - FURTH IM WALD - PLZEŇ 885

km		Ⓒ	Ⓐ	◇ Ⓐt	◇ ⚒r	351 ‡🍷	◇	353 ‡x🍷	◇	355 ‡🍷	◇	357 ‡🍷	◇ Ⓒz	◇	359 ‡🍷	◇	◇	361 ‡🍷	◇	DN	363 ‡🍷	◇	N	◇
	München Hbf 878 .... d.	...	...	...	...	0444r	...	0644	...	0843	...	1043	...	...	1243	...	...	1443	...	...	1643	...	...	...
0	**Regensburg** Hbf .... **879** d.	...	...	...	...	0615	...	0815	...	1014	...	1214	...	...	1414	...	...	1615	...	...	1814	...	...	...
42	**Schwandorf**................. **879** d.	...	...	0544	0623	0654	0801	0852	1001	1052	1202	1252	1309	1403	1452	1509	1601	1652	1709	1737	1852	2003	2110	2317
90	Cham (Oberpf) .... d.	...	...	0621	0707	0725	0839	0924	1040	1124	1237	1324	1346	1437	1524	1546	1641	1724	1743	1815	1924	2037	2143	2351
109	**Furth im Wald** ⊞ .... d.	...	...	0637	0724	0740	0900	0940	1056	1140	1254	1340	1402	1454	1540	1602	1658	1740	1800	1832	1940	2053	2201	0008
131	Domažlice .... ☒ d.	0635	0651	...	...	0801	0922c	1001	...	1201	...	1401	...	...	1601	...	...	1801	1823c	...	2001	...	...	...
190	**Plzeň** hl.n. .... ☒ a.	0740	0749	...	...	0847	...	1047	...	1247	...	1447	...	...	1647	...	...	1847	...	...	2047	...	...	...
	Praha hl.n. **1120** .... a.	...	...	...	...	1017	...	1217	...	1417	...	1617	...	...	1817	...	...	2017	...	...	2217	...	...	...

	Ⓐ t N	N	◇	◇	362 ‡🍷	◇	360 ‡🍷	◇	◇ Ⓐt	358 ‡🍷	◇	◇ Ⓒz	◇ Ⓐt	356 ‡🍷	◇	354 ‡🍷	◇	◇	352 ‡🍷		350 ‡y🍷	◇		
Praha hl.n. **1120** .... d.	...	...	...	...	0543	...	0743	...	...	0943	...	...	...	1143	...	1343	...	...	1543	...	1743	...	...	...
Plzeň hl.n. .... ☒ d.	...	...	...	...	0711	...	0911	...	...	1111	...	...	...	1311	...	1511	...	...	1711	...	1911	...	2120	2247
Domažlice .... ☒ d.	...	...	...	...	0801	...	1001	1036c	...	1201	...	...	...	1401	...	1601	...	...	1801	1836c	2001	...	2222	2347
Furth im Wald ⊞ .... d.	0443	0558	0659	0753	0823	0904	1022	1104	1150	1222	1304	1350	1354	1422	1502	1622	1704	1748	1822	1904	2022	2103	...	...
Cham (Oberpf) .... d.	0459	0618	0724	0813	0837	0924	1037	1124	1213	1237	1324	1413	1413	1437	1524	1637	1724	1814	1837	1924	2037	2122	...	...
Schwandorf.................. **879** a.	0531	0653	0756	0851	0904	0956	1104	1155	1250	1304	1356	1450	1450	1504	1556	1704	1756	1850	1904	1956	2105	2156	...	...
Regensburg Hbf .... **879** a.	...	...	...	...	0945	...	1145	...	...	1345	...	...	...	1545	...	1745	...	...	1945	...	2149	...	...	...
München Hbf **878** .... a.	...	...	...	...	1118	...	1318	...	...	1518	...	...	...	1718	...	1918	...	...	2118	...	2321	...	...	...

D – ①–④ (not Apr. 10, May 1, 18, 29).
N – From / to Nürnberg (Table **886**).
c – ⑥⑦ only.
r – ⚒ (not Jan. 6).
t – Not Jan. 6.
x – Change trains at Schwandorf on † (also Jan. 6).
y – Change trains at Schwandorf on ⑥ (also Apr. 6, 9, 30, May 17, 28).
z – Also Jan. 6.
◇ – Operated by Oberpfalzbahn (2nd class only).
‡ – ZÁPADNÍ EXPRES. *ALX* train in Germany (operated by Die Länderbahn).
☒ – Other local trains Domažlice - Plzeň and v.v. (journey 60 – 78 minutes): **From Domažlice** at 0345, 0430 Ⓐ, 0530, 0612 Ⓐ, 0726 Ⓐ, 0835, 1035, 1235, 1326 Ⓐ, 1434, 1528 Ⓐ, 1634 Ⓒ, 1636 Ⓐ, 1738 Ⓐ, 1834 Ⓒ, 1925 Ⓐ and 2034 Ⓒ. **From Plzeň hl.n.** at 0505 Ⓐ, 0605 Ⓐ, 0620 Ⓒ, 0820, 1020, 1220, 1320 Ⓐ, 1418, 1518 Ⓐ, 1620, 1720 Ⓐ, 1820, 1920 Ⓐ and 2020 Ⓒ.

NÜRNBERG - SCHWANDORF and WEIDEN 886

RE services

km			Ⓐt		Ⓐt	Ⓒz	Ⓐt										Ⓐ t F		D		D		F			
0	**Nürnberg** Hbf........ ◧d.	0032	0430	0535	0559	0631	0631	0738	0843	0943	1043	1143	1243	1343	1443	1543	1605	1643	1705	1743	1805	1843	1938	2055	2206	2257
28	Hersbruck (r Pegnitz) ◧d.	0048	0445	0551	0621	0648	0648	0757	0858	0958	1058	1158	1258	1358	1458	1558	1625	1658	1725	1758	1825	1858	1958	2117	2227	2316
56	Sulzbach-Rosenberg . d.	0114	0506	0619	0647	0722	0726	0826	0925	1025	1126	1225	1326	1425	1525	1625	1649	1726	1751	1825	1852	1926	2026	2142	2251	2341
68	Amberg .... d.	0122	0517	0627	0704	0731	0735	0833	0935	1033	1133	1233	1333	1433	1533	1632	1701	1736	1803	1833	1901	1933	2036	2150	2259	2348
94	**Schwandorf** .... a.	0136z	0531	0643	0727	0744	0756	0847	0948	1046	1148	1246	1350	1446	1548	1647	1724	1751	1824	1846	1927	1947	2051	2204	2312	0002

		Ⓐt	Ⓐt	Ⓒz	Ⓐt	Ⓐ t F	Ⓒz	Ⓐt	F	Ⓐt															
Schwandorf......................... d.	0010	0407	0458	0516	0544	0607	0609	0644	0707	0739	0808	0908	1007	1107	1207	1307	1407	1507	1607	1707	1807	1908	2007	2111	2212
Amberg .... d.	0026	0423	0526	0532	0559	0624	0626	0700	0725	0755	0822	0921	1021	1121	1221	1321	1421	1521	1621	1721	1821	1922	2021	2125	2226
Sulzbach-Rosenberg............ d.	0032z	0432	0535	0541	0607	0635	0634	0707	0732	0807	0829	0929	1029	1129	1229	1329	1429	1529	1629	1729	1829	1929	2029	2133	2234
Hersbruck (r pegnitz) .... d.	...	0503	0607	0607	|	0707	0707	|	0757	0841	0900	0959	1100	1159	1300	1359	1500	1600	1700	1759	1900	1959	2100	2206	2314
Nürnberg Hbf...................... a.	...	0518	0621	0622	0651	0723	0723	0751	0814	0857	0915	1014	1115	1214	1315	1414	1515	1615	1715	1814	1916	2014	2116	2222	2329

km												
0	**Nürnberg** Hbf........ ◧d.	0535	0631	0738	0843	and	1743	1843	1938	2055	2206	2257
28	Hersbruck (r Pegnitz) ◧d.	0551	0648	0757	0858	hourly	1758	1858	1958	2117	2227	2316
97	**Weiden** (Oberpf) .... a.	0646	0749	0852	0950	until	1850	1952	2051	2214	2321	0008

Weiden (Oberpf)..... d.	0610	0657	0806	and	1604	1704	1804	1906	2006	2215
Hersbruck (r Pegnitz) a.	0706	0756	0859	hourly	1659	1758	1859	1958	2059	2306
Nürnberg Hbf .... a.	0723	0814	0915	until	1715	1814	1916	2014	2116	2329

D – ①–④ (not Apr. 10, May 1, 18, 29).
F – To / from Furth im Wald (Table **885**).
t – Not Jan. 6.
z – Ⓒ (also Jan. 6).
◧ – Certain trains from Nürnberg and Hersbruck convey portions for two separate destinations. Passengers should take care to join the correct portion for their destination.

BAYREUTH - WEIDEN 887

Operated by *agilis* (2nd class only)

km				Ⓐt					Ⓒz	Ⓐt												
0	**Bayreuth** Hbf.. d.	0002	...	0442	0617	0718	0805	0901	1001	1004	1101	1201	1300	1401	1501	1601	1701	1801	1901	2005	2023	2203
19	Kirchenlaibach d.	0018	...	0504	0652b	0740	0826	0920	1020	1020	1120	1220	1320	1420	1520	1620	1720	1820	1920	2021	2048c	2224
59	**Weiden**........... a.	...	...	0532	0726	...	0855	0950	1050	1050	1150	1249	1352	1449	1549	1649	1749	1849	1948	...	2117	2252

	Ⓐt	Ⓐt			Ⓐt							Ⓒz	Ⓐt									
Weiden ....d.	...	0549	...	...	0638	*0734*	...	0907	1007	1107	1207	1307	1323	1407	1507	1607	1707	1807	1907	2007	2134	...
Kirchenlaibach ..d.	0509	0618	0657	0720	0720	0807	0840	0941	1042	1142	1241	1342	1355	1442	1542	1642	1742	1842	1941	2045	2204	2337
Bayreuth Hbf ...a.	0525	0634	0716	0735	0735	0823	0856	0957	1056	1157	1257	1357	1415	1457	1557	1657	1757	1856	1957	2100	2220	2353

b – Arrives 0638.
c – Arrives 2039.
t – Not Jan. 6.
z – Also Jan. 6.

KEMPTEN - REUTTE IN TIROL - GARMISCH-PARTENKIRCHEN 888

RB services

km		Ⓐt	Ⓒz		✣		Ⓒz	Ⓐt				
0	**Kempten** (Allgäu) Hbf d.	0614	0630	0731		1131	1231	1300	1335		2035	2258
18	Oy-Mittelberg .... d.	0700r	0658	0800	and	1200	1300	1331	1403	and	2103	2329
24	Nesselwang .... d.	0711	0709	0811	hourly	1211	1311	1348	1414	hourly	2114	2340
31	Pfronten-Ried .... d.	0721	0719	0821	until	1224	1321	1357	1424	until	2124	2350
33	**Pfronten-Steinach** ... a.	0725	0723	0825		1227	1325	1401	1428		2128	2354

Pfronten-Steinach........... d.	0633	0734		1234	1334	1436		1936	2136
Pfronten-Ried .... d.	0637	0738	and	1238	1338	1440	and	1940	2140
Nesselwang .... d.	0646	0747	hourly	1247	1347	1449	hourly	1949	2149
Oy-Mittelberg...................... d.	0657	0759	until	1259	1403	1503	until	2003	2203
Kempten (Allgäu) Hbf .... a.	0725	0825		1329	1429	1529		2029	2229

km		v		a	⑥						c							
0	**Pfronten-Steinach** ... d.	...	0636	...	...	0837c	0936	1036	1133j	1236	1336	1436	1536	1636	1736	1836	2036	2136
5	**Vils** Stadt ⊗ .... ‡d.	...	0643	...	...	0845	0943	1043	1140j	1243	1343	1443	1543	1643	1743	1843	2043	2143
15	**Reutte in Tirol** .... ‡d.	0513	0701	0750	0801	0901	0958	1101	1158j	1301	1401	1501	1601	1701	1801	1901	2101	2158
35	Lermoos.................. ‡d.	0537	0725	0825	0825	0925	...	1125	1225	1325	1425	1525	1625	1725	1825	1925	2125	...
38	Ehrwald Zugspitzbahn ‡d.	0543	0731	0831	0831	0931	...	1131	1231	1331	1431	1531	1631	1731	1831	1931	2131	...
60	**Garmisch**-Partenk. ... a.	0612	0757	0857	0901	0957	...	1157	1257	1357	1457	1557	1659	1757	1857	1957	2157	...
	München Hbf **895** .. a.	...	...	...	...	...	...	...	...	...	...	...	...	...	...	...	...	...

		v	c	a			a		c				c				Ⓑw	
München Hbf **895** ... d.	...	...	...	...	...	...	...	...	...	...	...	...	...	...	...	...	...	...
Garmisch-Partenk. .... d.	...	0637	0704	0722	0804	...	0904	1004	1104	1204	1304	1404	1504	1604	1704	1804	1904	2004
Ehrwald Zugspitzbahn ‡d.	...	0702	0731	0752	0831	...	0931	1031	1131	1231	1331	1431	1531	1631	1731	1831	1931	2031
Lermoos .... ‡d.	...	0706	0735	0756	0835	...	0935	1035	1135	1235	1335	1435	1535	1635	1735	1835	1935	2035
Reutte in Tirol .... ‡d.	0602	0736	0802	0823	0902	1004	1004	1102	1202	1302	1402	1502	1602	1702	1802	1902	2002	2102
Vils Stadt ⊗ .... ‡d.	0617	...	0817	0838	0917	1019	1019	1117	1217	1317	1417	1517	1617	1717	1817	1917	2017	2117
Pfronten-Steinach .... a.	0624	...	0824	...	0924	1026	1026	1124	1224	1324	1424	1524	1624	1724	1824	1924	2024	2124

a – ①–⑤ (not Dec 26, Jan. 6).
c – ⑥⑦ (also Dec. 26, Jan. 6).
j – 3 minutes later on ⑥⑦ (also Dec. 26, Jan. 6).
r – Arrives 0641.
t – Not Jan. 6.
v – ①–⑥ (not Dec. 26, Jan. 6).
w – Not Dec. 25, Jan. 5.
z – Also Jan. 6.

✣ – The 0831 from Kempten runs 1 – 2 minutes earlier Oy-Mittelberg - Pfronten-Steinach.
⊗ – Most services call on request.
‡ – Station is in Austria.

890 MÜNCHEN - SALZBURG

Bayerische Oberlandbahn; DB

km		◇	WB 961 Ⓐt ①–⑥ n⊙🍷	◇	RJX 265 ✕	◇	RJX 61 B✕	WB 963 ⊙ 🍷	◇	RJ 111 ✕◆	◇	RJX 63 B✕	◇	EC 217 🍷◆	◇	RJX 65 B✕	WB 967 ⊙ 🍷	◇	EC 113 ✕◆	◇	RJX 67 B✕	WB 969 ⊙ 🍷	◇	IC 2083 🍷◆	EC 115 🍷◆
	Frankfurt (Main) Hbf 912 d.	...	...	...	...	...	...	...	...	...	...	...	...	...	...	...	...	...	0820	...	...	...	...	...	...
	Stuttgart Hbf 930 d.	...	...	...	...	...	...	...	...	...	...	...	...	0758	...	...	...	...	0958	...	...	...	...	...	1158
0	**München** Hbf 951 d.	...	0548	0555	0623	0655	0723	0748	0756	0816	0856	0929	0955	1016	1055	1128	1148	1155	1217	1255	1329	1348	1355	...	1416
10	München Ost 951 d.	...	0558	0603	0633	0704	|	0758	0804	0826	0904	|	1004	1025	1104	|	1158	1204	1227	1304	|	1358	1404	1413	1425
65	Rosenheim 951 d.	0532	0630	0639	0704	0735	0803	0830	0835	0855	0935	|	1035	1054	1135	|	1230	1235	1254	1335	|	1430	1435	1442	1454
82	Bad Endorf d.	0543	|	0650	|	0746	|	|	0846	|	0946	|	1046	|	1146	|	|	1246	|	1346	|	|	1446	1455	|
90	Prien am Chiemsee d.	0549	|	0657	|	0752	|	|	0852	0913	0952	|	1052	1111	1152	|	|	1252	1311	1352	|	|	1452	1503	1511
118	Traunstein d.	0612	|	0720	|	0816	|	|	0916	0932	1016	|	1116	1131	1216	|	|	1316	1331	1416	|	|	1516	1525	1532
147	Freilassing 891 d.	0633	|	0742	|	0835	|	|	0935	0952	1035	|	1135	1152	1235	|	|	1335	1352	1435	|	|	1535	1542	1552
153	**Salzburg** Hbf 🛃 891 a.	0640	0721	0752	0758	0842	0858	0921	0942	0959	1042	1058	1142	1159	1242	1258	1321	1342	1359	1442	1458	1521	1542	...	1559
	Wien Westbahnhof 950 a.	...	0952	...	|	...	|	1152	...	...	...	|	...	...	...	|	1552	...	...	...	|	1752	...	...	...
	Wien Hbf 950 a.	...	...	...	1032	...	1132	...	...	...	...	1332	...	...	...	1532	...	...	...	...	1732	...	...	...	...

	◇	RJX 69 ✕	WB 971 ⊙ 🍷	◇	EC 219 🍷◆	◇ Ⓐt	◇	◇ Ⓐt	RJX 261 B✕	WB 973 ⊙ 🍷	◇	EC 117 🍷◆	◇	RJ 1299 Ⓑb	◇	NJ 295 🅁 ◆	IC 1291 Ⓑb 🍷	◇	◇	◇		EN 50237 🅁 K	EN 40237 🅁 ◆	NJ 237 🅁 ◆	◇
Frankfurt (Main) Hbf 912 d.	...	...	...	...	1220	...	...	...	...	...	...	1420	...	...	...	...	1620	...	...	...	...	...	...	...	...
Stuttgart Hbf 930 d.	...	...	...	...	1358	...	...	...	...	...	...	1559	...	...	...	...	1758	...	...	...	...	2029	2029	2029	...
München Hbf 951 d.	1455	1529	1548	1555	1616	1636	1655	1722	1730	1748	1755	1817	1855	1917	1955	2009	2017	2043	2143	2243	2328	|	|	|	2351
München Ost 951 d.	1504	|	1558	1604	1625	1645	1704	1735	|	1758	1804	1826	1904	1928	2004	2020u	2028	2052	2152	2252	2336	2354	2354	2354	0002
Rosenheim 951 d.	1535	|	1630	1635	1654	1714	1735	1815	|	1830	1835	1854	1935	1957	2035	2050u	2055	2131	2231	2331	...	0033	0033	0033	0038
Bad Endorf d.	1546	|	|	1646	|	1726	1746	1827	|	|	1846	|	1946	2009	2046	|	2108	2142	2242	2342	...	|	|	|	0049
Prien am Chiemsee d.	1552	|	|	1652	1711	1732	1752	1833	|	|	1852	1912	1952	2016	2052	|	2116	2148	2248	2348	...	|	|	|	0056
Traunstein d.	1616	|	|	1716	1731	1756	1816	1856	|	|	1916	1932	2016	2035	2116	|	2136	2211	2311	0011	...	|	|	|	0120
Freilassing 891 d.	1635	|	|	1735	1752	...	1835	...	|	|	1935	1952	2035	2054	2135	|	2155	2230	2330	0030	...	|	|	|	0139
Salzburg Hbf 🛃 891 a.	1642	1658	1721	1742	1759	...	1842	...	1858	1921	1942	1959	2042	2100	2142	2152	2202	2237	2337	0037	...	0128	0128	0128	0146
Wien Westbahnhof 950 a.	...	|	1952	...	...	...	...	...	|	2152	...	...	...	...	...	...	...	...	...	...	...	|	...	...	...
Wien Hbf 950 a.	...	1932	...	...	...	...	...	...	2132	...	...	...	...	...	...	...	...	...	...	...	...	0634	...	...	...

	◇ Ⓐt	NJ 236 🅁 ◆	EN 414 🅁 ◆	EN 50462 🅁 K		◇	IC 1296 ⚒	◇ Ⓐt	◇	RJ 1298 ⚒	◇ Ⓐt	NJ 294 🅁 ◆	◇	◇ Ⓒz	IC 1290 🍷	◇	WB 960 ①–⑥ n⊙🍷	RJX 260 ✕	◇	IC 2082 🍷◆	EC 218 🍷◆	◇	WB 962 ⊙ 🍷	RJX 262 ✕	◇
Wien Hbf 950 d.	...	...	...	2327	...	...	...	...	...	...	...	...	...	...	...	...	...	0628	...	...	...	...	...	0828	...
Wien Westbahnhof 950 d.	...	...	...	|	...	...	...	...	...	...	...	...	...	...	...	...	0608	|	...	...	...	...	0808	|	...
Salzburg Hbf 🛃 891 d.	0354	0405	0405	0405	...	0515	0543	0600	0615	0640	0646	0701	...	0715	0800	0815	0839	0900	0915	...	1000	1015	1039	1100	1115
Freilassing 891 d.	0403	|	|	|	...	0524	0551	0608	0624	0648	0654	|	0724	0724	0808	0824	|	|	0924	0947	1008	1024	|	|	1124
Traunstein d.	0422	|	|	|	...	0544	0609	0627	0644	0705	0714	|	0744	0744	0825	0844	|	|	0944	1006	1025	1044	|	|	1144
Prien am Chiemsee d.	0444	|	|	|	...	0606	0627	0650	0706	0725	0741	|	0806	0806	0844	0906	|	|	1006	1027	1044	1106	|	|	1206
Bad Endorf d.	0451	|	|	|	...	0613	0635	0656	0713	0733	0748	|	0813	0813	|	0913	|	|	1013	1035	|	1113	|	|	1213
Rosenheim 951 d.	0504	0517s	0517s	0517s	...	0629	0649	0711	0729	0748	0806	0834s	0829	0829	0902	0929	0930	|	1029	1047	1102	1129	1130	|	1229
München Ost 951 a.	0531	0550	0550	0550	0557	0656	0717	0738	0756	0818	0840	|	0856	0856	0931	0955	1000	|	1056	1115	1131	1155	1200	|	1256
München Hbf 951 a.	0541	|	|	|	0605	0706	0730	0747	0806	0830	0850	0922	0906	0906	0941	1006	1013	1033	1106	...	1141	1205	1213	1232	1306
Stuttgart Hbf 930 a.	...	0837	0837	0837	...	...	0959	...	...	...	...	...	...	...	1159	...	...	...	...	...	1359	...	...	...	...
Frankfurt (Main) Hbf 912 a.	...	...	...	...	...	...	1140	...	...	...	...	...	...	...	1340	...	...	...	...	...	1540	...	...	...	...

	EC 114 🍷◆	◇	WB 964 ⊙ 🍷	RJX 60 B✕	◇	EC 112 ✕◆	◇	WB 966 ⊙ 🍷	RJX 62 B✕	◇	EC 216 🍷◆	◇	RJX 64 B✕	◇	◇	WB 970 ⊙ 🍷	RJX 66 B✕	◇	RJ 110 ✕◆	◇	WB 972 ⊙ 🍷	RJX 68 B✕	◇	◇	◇
Wien Hbf 950 d.	...	...	...	1028	...	...	...	...	1228	...	...	...	1428	...	...	...	1628	...	...	...	...	1828	...	...	...
Wien Westbahnhof 950 d.	...	...	1008	|	...	...	...	1208	|	...	...	...	|	...	...	1608	|	...	...	...	1808	|	...	...	...
Salzburg Hbf 🛃 891 d.	1200	1215	1239	1300	1313	1400	1415	1439	1500	1515	1600	1615	1700	1715	1815	1839	1900	1915	2000	2015	2039	2100	2115	2215	2300
Freilassing 891 d.	1208	1224	|	|	1324	1408	1424	|	|	1524	1608	1624	|	1724	1824	|	|	1926	2008	2024	|	|	2129	2224	2310
Traunstein d.	1225	1244	|	|	1344	1425	1444	|	|	1544	1625	1644	|	1744	1844	|	|	1946	2025	2044	|	|	2149	2244	2329
Prien am Chiemsee d.	1244	1306	|	|	1406	1444	1506	|	|	1606	1644	1706	|	1806	1906	|	|	2008	2044	2106	|	|	2211	2306	2351
Bad Endorf d.	|	1313	|	|	1413	|	1513	|	|	1613	|	1713	|	1813	1913	|	|	2015	|	2114	|	|	2218	2313	2357
Rosenheim 951 d.	1302	1329	1330	|	1429	1502	1529	1530	|	1629	1702	1729	|	1829	1929	1930	|	2032	2102	2135j	2130	2156	2232	2332	0012
München Ost 951 a.	1331	1355	1400	|	1456	1530	1556	1600	|	1656	1731	1756	|	1855	1956	2000	|	2106	2131	2209	2155	|	2306	0007	0048
München Hbf 951 a.	1341	1405	1413	1432	1505	1541	1606	1613	1632	1706	1741	1806	1831	1906	2006	2013	2031	2116	2141	2218	2207	2231	2316	0016	0058
Stuttgart Hbf 930 a.	1559	...	...	...	...	1759	...	...	...	...	1959	...	...	...	...	...	...	...	...	...	...	...	...	...	...
Frankfurt (Main) Hbf 912 a.	...	...	...	...	...	1940	...	...	...	...	...	...	...	...	...	...	...	...	...	...	...	...	...	...	...

◆ – NOTES (LISTED BY TRAIN NUMBER)

110/1 – HOHE TAUERN – (12) ✕ Klagenfurt - Villach - München and v.v.
112/3 – BLAUER ENZIAN – (12) ✕ Klagenfurt - Villach - München - Frankfurt and v.v.; (12) Zagreb (212/3) - Ljubljana - Jesenice 🛃 - Villach - München - Frankfurt and v.v.
114 – WÖRTHERSEE – (12) 🍷 Klagenfurt - München - Mannheim - Köln - Dortmund.
115 – WÖRTHERSEE – (12) 🍷 Münster - Köln - Mannheim - München - Klagenfurt.
117 – SALZACH – (12) 🍷 Frankfurt - Villach - Klagenfurt.
216/7 – DACHSTEIN – (12) 🍷 Graz - Salzburg - Mannheim - Saarbrücken and v.v.
218/9 – CHIEMGAU – (12) 🍷 Graz - Bischofshofen - Salzburg - Frankfurt and v.v.
236/7 – 🛏 1,2 cl., ▬ 2 cl. and (2) Venezia - Villach - München - Stuttgart and v.v.
294/5 – 🛏 1,2 cl., ▬ 2 cl. and (2) Roma - Firenze - Bologna - München and v.v.; 🛏 1,2 cl., ▬ 2 cl. and (2) La Spezia (40235/40295) - Genova - Milano - München and v.v.
414 – LISINSKI – 🛏 1,2 cl., ▬ 2 cl. and (12) Zagreb - Ljubljana - Jesenice 🛃 - Villach - München - Stuttgart; conveys Dec. 11 - Jan. 8 and Mar. 30 - Apr. 16 (from Rijeka) 🛏 1,2 cl. and ▬ 2 cl. (480) Rijeka - Ljubljana - Stuttgart.
2082/3 – KÖNIGSSEE – (12) 🍷 Berchtesgaden - Augsburg - Hamburg and v.v.
40237 – LISINSKI – 🛏 1,2 cl., ▬ 2 cl. and (2) Stuttgart - München - Villach - Jesenice 🛃 - Ljubljana - Zagreb; conveys Dec. 12 - Jan. 9 and Mar. 31 - Apr. 17 🛏 1,2 cl. and ▬ 2 cl. (60237) Stuttgart - Ljubljana - Rijeka.

B – To / from Budapest (Table 1250).
K – KÁLMÁN IMRE – 🛏 1,2 cl., ▬ 2 cl., (2) and 🍷 Budapest - München - Stuttgart and v.v.

b – Not Dec. 25.
j – Arrives 2124.
n – Not Jan. 6, Apr. 10, May 1, 18, 29.
s – Calls to set down only.
t – Not Jan. 6.
u – Calls to pick up only.
z – Also Jan. 6.

◇ – *Meridian* regional service (operated by Bayerische Regiobahn; German holiday dates apply).
⊙ – Operated by *Westbahn* (special fares).

891 SALZBURG - FREILASSING - BERCHTESGADEN

Berchtesgadener Land Bahn *

km		◇	Ⓐt	Ⓒz												A									
0	**Salzburg** Hbf 890 d.	0615	0657	0715	0815	0842	0915	0942	and at	1313	1342	1415	1442	1515	1542	...	1615	1642	1715	1742	1815	1915	2042	2142	2229
6	Freilassing 890 a.	0622	0710	0722	0822	0854	0922	0954	the same	1320	1354	1422	1454	1522	1554	...	1622	1654	1722	1754	1822	1922	2054	2154	2241
6	Freilassing d.	0634	0718	0740	0840	0859	0939	0958	minutes	1339	1358	1439	1458	1539	1558	1618	1639	1658	1739	1758	1839	1939	2100	2201	2246
21	Bad Reichenhall d.	0655	0741	0759	0901	0920	1001	1020	past each	1401	1420	1501	1520	1601	1620	1631	1701	1720	1801	1820	1901	2001	2122	2219	2306
39	**Berchtesgaden** Hbf a.	0726	0810	0826	0928	...	1028	...	hour until	1428	...	1528	...	1628	...	1707	1728	...	1828	...	1928	2028	2150	2247	2334

	Ⓐt	①m	Ⓐt			Ⓐt		A												◇						
Berchtesgaden Hbf d.	...	0526	...	0621	0706	...	...	0827	...	...	0932	...	and at	1532	...	1632	...	1732	1750	...	1832	...	1932	2032	2210
Bad Reichenhall d.	0526	0556	0556	0654	0740	0800	0837	0900	...	0937	1000	1037	the same	1600	1637	1700	1737	1800	1826	1837	1900	1937	2000	2100	2245
Freilassing a.	0544	0613	0613	0712	0757	0821	0858	0919	...	0957	1018	1057	minutes	1618	1657	1718	1757	1818	1838	1857	1918	1957	2018	2118	2303
Freilassing 890 d.	0547	0616	0616	0722	0807	0835	0907	...	0935	1007	1035	1107	past each	1635	1707	1735	1807	1835	1846	1907	1935	2007	2035	2135	2307
Salzburg Hbf 890 a.	0558	0627	0627	0733	0817	0842	0917	...	0942	1017	1042	1117	hour until	1642	1717	1742	1817	1842	1855	1917	1942	2017	2042	2142	2317

A – *IC* 2082/3: KÖNIGSSEE – (12) 🍷 Berchtesgaden - Hamburg and v.v. Train category *RE* Berchtesgaden - Freilassing and v.v. Operated by DB.

m – Not Apr. 10, May 1, 29.

t – Not Jan. 6
z – Also Jan. 6.

* – Services to / from Bad Reichenhall or Berchtesgaden are operated by Berchtesgadener Land Bahn. 2nd class only. Other trains are operated by either DB or ÖBB. German holiday dates apply.
◇ – Operated by DB.

MÜNCHEN FLUGHAFEN ✈ 892

S-Bahn services S1 and S8 from / to München (2nd class only). Services on both routes run approximately every 20 minutes.

S1 München Hbf (low level) - Freising - München Flughafen Terminal ✈ (41 km). **From München Hbf** 0503 to 2323. **From München Flughafen** 0531 to 0011. Journey: ± 45 minutes. **S1** trains from München Hbf are often combined with a Freising service - travel in the rear portion for the Airport.

S8 München Pasing - München Hbf (low level) - München Ost - München Flughafen Terminal ✈ (44 km). **From München Pasing** 0305 to 0005 (10 minutes later from München Hbf, 19 minutes later from München Ost). **From München Flughafen** 0404 to 0004. Journey: 50 minutes from / to Pasing, 40 minutes from / to Hbf, 31 minutes from / to Ost.

Direct *RE* services Regensburg - Landshut - Freising - München Flughafen

						Ⓒz	Ⓐt				
Regensburg Hbf	878 d.	0319	0417	0528	0614	0720	0730	0814	0919	and	2219
Landshut (Bay) Hbf	878 d.	0405	0505	0617	0704	0806	0819	0859	1005	hourly	2305
Freising	878 d.	0428	0528	0640	0728	0828	0840	0920	1028	until	2328
München Flughafen ⊡ ✈	a.	0441	0541	0652	0741	0841	0852	0932	1041		2341

				Ⓐt	Ⓒz	Ⓐt	Ⓒz		⊠		
München Flughafen ⊡ ✈	d.	0428	0528	0607	0628	0708	0716	0816	and	2316	0025
Freising	878 d.	0439	0539	0620	0639	0719	0728	0828	hourly	2328	0037
Landshut (Bay) Hbf	878 d.	0505	0614f	0646	0702	0745	0753	0853	until	2353	0101
Regensburg Hbf	878 a.	0552t	0700	0734	0746	0832	0842	0942		0044	0151

f – Arrives 0601.
t – Ⓐ (not Jan. 6).
z – Also Jan. 6.
⊠ – München Flughafen Terminal d. 1628 / 1928 (not 1616 / 1916; then Freising d. 1639 / 1939, Landshut d. 1702 / 2002, Regensburg a. 1746 / 2046).
⊡ – München Flughafen Terminal.

MÜNCHEN - MÜHLDORF - SIMBACH 893

On Jan. 6 services run as on ⑦

km		Ⓐ	Ⓒ	⊙								Ⓐ		Ⓐ	Ⓒ	Ⓐ	Ⓒ	Ⓐ		Ⓐ		Ⓐ		⊗		
0	**München** Hbf d.	0606	0606	0707	0807c	0907	1007	1107	1207	1307	1406	1425	1506	1521	1607	1626	1707	1726	1807	1831	1907	1948	2027	2127	2228	2328
10	**München** Ost d.	0615	0617	0716	0816	0917	1017	1117	1217	1317	1417	1439	1515	1533	1617	1638	1717	1738	1818	1840	1917	1957	2038	2138	2238	2337
85	**Mühldorf** (Oberbay) a.	0721	0722	0819	0919	1017	1117	1217	1317	1417	1517	1535	1619	1630	1717	1731	1816	1830	1919	1931	2020	2102	2140	2235	2335	0038
		Ⓐ	|	|							Ⓒ	|	Ⓒ	|		d	Ⓒ	|		d				|		
85	**Mühldorf** (Oberbay) d.	0737	0737	0837	0937	1037	1137	1227f	1337	1437	1538	1538	1637	1634	...	1737	1837	1834	...	1937	2037	...	2147	2247	2342	...
124	**Simbach** (Inn) 962 a.	0813	0813	0913	1013	1113	1213	1258f	1413	1513	1613	1613	1713	1708	...	1813	1913	1907	...	2013	2113	...	2219	2319	0014	...

			Ⓐ	⑥	Ⓐ	Ⓐ	Ⓒ	⊙										Ⓐ	Ⓒ		Ⓐ	Ⓒ	⊖			
Simbach (Inn) 962 d.	...	...	0507	0540	0554	0648	0648	0749	0849	0949	1049	1149	1249e	1349	1449	1549	...	1641	1649	1749	1841	1849	1949	2049	2154	2254
Mühldorf (Oberbay) a.	...	...	0540	0611	0628	0722	0722	0822	0922	1022	1122	1222	1322e	1422	1523	1622	...	1718	1722	1822	1917	1922	2022	2125	2229	2329
		⚒	Ⓐ	Ⓒ	|	|	Ⓒ	|								Ⓒ	Ⓐ		d			d	|	|	|	
Mühldorf (Oberbay) d.	0429	0519	0546	0623	0637	0732	0732	0832	0937	1030	1138	1231	1340	1430	1538	1630	1634	...	1737	1843	...	1940	2034	2146	2246	...
München Ost a.	0524	0622	0640	0724	0722	0823	0826	0926	1045	1127	1244	1326	1444	1524	1643	1725	1744	...	1844	1943	...	2044	2143	2246	2349	...
München Hbf a.	0533	0633	0650	0735	0733	0835	0837	0936	1055	1137	1254	1337	1454	1534	1653	1737	1755	...	1854	1955	...	2055	2155	2258	0002	...

c – Ⓒ only.
d – Daily from Mühldorf.
e – 10 minutes later on Ⓐ.
f – On Ⓒ Mühldorf d. 1237, Simbach a. 1313.
⊗ – Change trains at Mühldorf on †.
⊙ – Change trains at Mühldorf on ⚒.
⊖ – Change trains at Mühldorf on ⑤⑥†.

MÜNCHEN - GARMISCH - INNSBRUCK 895

DB; ÖBB (2nd class only in Austria)

km		Ⓐ t		Ⓒ z			Ⓒ z		Ⓒ z		Ⓒ z							*ICE* 529 ⑥ D				*ICE* 1207 ⑥ A			Ⓐ t	
0	**München** Hbf d.	0447	...	0532	0632	...	0713	0732	0813	0832	0913	0932	1032	...	1132	...	1232	1313	1332	1432	...	1505	1532	...	1613	1632
7	München Pasing d.	0453	...	0538	0638	...	0720	0738	0820	0839	0920	0937	1038	...	1138	...	1238	|	1338	1438	...	|	1538	...	1620	1638
40	Tutzing d.	0516	...	0601	0701	...	|	0801	|	0901	|	1000	1101	...	1201	...	1301	1343	1401	1501	...	1538	1601	...	|	1700
54	Weilheim (Oberbay) d.	0528	...	0612	0712	...	0748	0814	0848	0912	0948	1011	1112	...	1212	...	1312	1359	1412	1512	...	1549	1612	...	1648	1712
75	Murnau d.	0547	...	0628	0728	...	0801	0832	0901	0928	1001	1027	1128	...	1228	...	1328	1414	1428	1528	...	1610	1628	...	1701	1728
101	**Garmisch**-Partenk. ¶ a.	0613	...	0654	0759j	...	0822	0856	0923	0955	1022	1055	1154	...	1255	...	1355	1441	1455	1554	...	1634	1655	...	1724	1755
101	**Garmisch**-Partenk. ¶ d.	...	0617	...	▬	0812	0830	*0902*	0942	*1012*	1027	*1102*	▬	1212	*1302*	...	*1412*	...	*1502*	▬	1609	1636	*1702*	...	1742	*1812*
118	**Mittenwald** a.	...	0644	...	...	0846	0902	*0929*	1008	*1046*	1059	*1128*	...	1246	*1328*	...	*1446*	...	*1529*	...	1646	1707	*1729*	...	1808	*1846*
118	**Mittenwald** 🏛 d.	...	0648	...	...	0848	...	*0936*	▬	*1048*	...	*1136*c	...	1248	*1336*c	...	*1448*	...	*1536*	...	1648	1715	*1736*c	...	...	*1848*
125	Scharnitz 🏛 ⊡ d.	...	0657	...	0803	0903	...	*0944*	...	*1103*k	...	*1144*c	1203a	1303r	*1343*c	1403a	*1503*	...	*1544*	...	1703	|	*1744*c	1803a	...	*1903*
135	Seefeld in Tirol ⊡ d.	...	0716	...	0816	0916	...	*0956*	1016	*1116*	...	*1156*c	1216	1316	*1355*c	1416	*1516*	...	*1556*	1616	1716	1746	*1756*c	1816	...	*1916*
160	**Innsbruck** Hbf ⊡ a.	...	0753	...	0853	0953	...	...	1053	*1153*	...	...	1253	1353	...	1453	*1553*	...	...	1653	1753	1822	...	1853	...	*1953*

	Ⓐ t		Ⓐ t				*ICE* 1205 ⑤E A					
München Hbf d.	1710	1732	1813	1832	1932	...	2013	...	2032	2132	2232	2332
München Pasing d.	1716	1738	1820	1838	1938	...	|	...	2038	2138	2238	2338
Tutzing d.	|	1801	|	1901	2001	...	2043	...	2101	2201	2301	0001
Weilheim (Oberbay) d.	1748	1812	1849	1912	2012	...	2058	...	2112	2212	2312	0012
Murnau d.	1801	1828	1901	1928	2028	...	2112	...	2128	2228	2328	0028
Garmisch-Partenk. ¶ a.	1823	1855	1924	1954	2055	...	2135	...	2155	2255	2355	0054
Garmisch-Partenk. ¶ d.	1829	*1902*	1942	*2012*	*2102*	...	2139	...	*2202*	*2305*	*0006*	▬
Mittenwald a.	1901	*1928*	2008	*2046*	*2128*	...	2210	...	*2229*	*2332*	*0033*	...
Mittenwald 🏛 d.	...	*1936*	▬	*2048*	...	...	2212	...	...	...	...	...
Scharnitz 🏛 ⊡ d.	...	*1945*	...	*2103*	...	2203	|	2303	...	...	...	0003
Seefeld in Tirol ⊡ d.	...	*1956*	2016	*2116*	...	2216	2233	2316	...	...	...	0016
Innsbruck Hbf ⊡ a.	...	...	2053	*2153*	...	2253	2312	2353	...	...	...	0053

	⚒ t	Ⓐ t	Ⓒ z	Ⓐ t	Ⓐ t	Ⓒ z	Ⓐ t			
Innsbruck Hbf ⊡ d.	...	...	...	...	...	...	...	0635	0708	...
Seefeld in Tirol ⊡ d.	...	...	...	...	...	...	...	0712	0745	...
Scharnitz 🏛 ⊡ d.	...	...	...	...	...	...	...	0725	0757	...
Mittenwald 🏛 a.	...	...	...	...	...	...	...	0732	▬	...
Mittenwald d.	...	*0520*	*0520*	0542	*0623*	*0623*	*0651*	0733	...	*0827*
Garmisch-P ¶ a.	...	*0547*	*0547*	0613	*0654*	*0654*	*0719*	0801	...	*0855*
Garmisch-P ¶ d.	0500	0556	0607	0635	0659	0707	0732	...	0805e	0905e
Murnau d.	0524	0623	0632	0654	0728	0732	0757	...	0832	0932
Weilheim (Oberbay) d.	0541	0645	0649	0711	0746	0749	0812	...	0849	0949
Tutzing d.	0553f	0700	0700	|	0800	0800	|	...	0900	1000
München Pasing a.	0611f	0719	0719	0741	0819	0819	0839	...	0919	1019
München Hbf a.	0619f	0726	0726	0748	0826	0826	0846	...	0926	1026

				ICE 1206 ⑥ A					*ICE* 1204 ⑦ A			*ICE* 528 ⑥ D	Ⓒ E				Ⓒ z									
Innsbruck Hbf ⊡ d.	*0808*	0908	...	1023	1008	1108	...	*1208*	1224	1308	...	...	...	1408	1508	...	...	*1608*	1708	...	1808	1908	...	*2008*	...	2108
Seefeld in Tirol ⊡ d.	*0845*	0944	*1004*	1104	1045	1145	*1204*c	*1245*	1304	1345	*1404*c	...	...	1445	1544	*1604*	...	*1645*	1745	*1804*c	1845	1944	*2004*	*2045*	...	2145
Scharnitz 🏛 ⊡ d.	*0858*	...	*1016*	|	1058	1157a	*1216*c	*1258*	|	1357a	*1416*c	...	...	1458	▬	*1616*	...	*1658*	1757a	*1816*c	1858	▬	*2016*	*2058*	...	2157
Mittenwald 🏛 a.	*0905*	...	*1025*	1128	1105	▬	*1225*c	*1305*	1328	...	*1425*c	...	...	1505	...	*1625*	...	*1705*	...	*1825*c	1905	...	*2025*	*2105*	...	...
Mittenwald d.	*0908*	...	*1026*	1129	1108	...	*1227*	*1308*	1329	...	*1427*	...	1453	1508	...	*1627*	1647	*1708*	...	*1827*	1908	...	*2027*	*2108*	2235	...
Garmisch-Partenk. ¶ a.	*0940*	...	*1053*	1155	1142	...	*1253*	*1340*	1354	...	*1454*	...	1524	1540	...	*1653*q	1725	*1740*	...	*1854*h	1940	...	*2054*	*2139*	*2302*	...
Garmisch-Partenk. ¶ d.	1005	...	1106	1157	...	1207	1307	1406	1359	...	1506	1515	1525	...	1605	1705	1735	1805	...	1905	...	2005	2106	2206	2307	...
Murnau d.	1032	...	1132	1217	...	1231	1332	1432	1427	...	1532	1543	1549	...	1631	1732	1758	1832	...	1932	...	2031	2132	2232	2332	...
Weilheim (Oberbay) d.	1049	...	1149	1235	...	1249	1349	1449	1442	...	1549	|	1612	...	1649	1749	1812	1849	...	1949	...	2049	2149	2249	2349	...
Tutzing d.	1100	...	1200	1251	...	1259	1400	1500	1453	...	1600	1616	|	...	1700	1800	|	1900	...	2000	...	2100	2200	2300	0000	...
München Pasing a.	1119	...	1219	|	...	1318	1419	1519	|	...	1619	|	1641	...	1719	1819	1840	1919	...	2019	...	2119	2219	2319	0019	...
München Hbf a.	1126	...	1226	1335	...	1326	1426	1526	1535	...	1626	1643	1648	...	1726	1826	1847	1926	...	2026	...	2126	2226	2326	0026	...

A – [12] ✕ Innsbruck - Garmisch - München - Hamburg and v.v.
D – [12] ✕ Garmisch - Nürnberg - Frankfurt - Dortmund and v.v.
E – Until Mar. 24.

a – ①-⑤ (not Dec. 26, Jan. 6).
c – ⑥⑦ (also Dec. 26, Jan. 6).
e – 2 minutes later on Ⓐ (not Jan. 6).
f – 3-5 minutes later on ⑥.

h – *1859* on ⑥ from Jan. 21.
j – 0754 on Ⓒ (also Jan. 6).
k – *1058* on ⑥.
q – *1657* on ⑥.
r – 1258 on ⑦.
t – Not Jan. 6.
z – Also Jan. 6.

⊡ – Other local trains Scharnitz - Innsbruck and v.v. (Austrian holiday dates apply). **From Scharnitz** at 0630, 0733 ⚒, 0833, 1033, 1233, 1433, 1633 and 2133. **From Innsbruck** at 0838, 1038, 1238, 1438, 1638, 1838, 2038, 2208 and 2308.

¶ – Bayerische Zugspitzbahn (rack railway) operates Garmisch - Zugspitzplatt: Departures at 0815 and hourly to 1415, returning from Zugspitzplatt at 0930 and hourly to 1630.

MURNAU - OBERAMMERGAU 897

RB services

km		Ⓐ	⑥🚌	🚌		🚌		🚌		🚌		🚌		🚌		🚌		🚌		🚌	🚌
0	**Murnau** d.	0531	0548	0648	0735	0842	0937	1042	1137	1234	1337	1442	1537	1642	1737	1842	1937	2042	2137	2242	2334
12	Bad Kohlgrub d.	0554	0609	0709	0758	0903	1000	1103	1200	1255	1400	1503	1600	1703	1800	1903	2000	2103	2200	2303	2355
24	**Oberammergau** ♥ a.	0620	0630	0730	0823	0924	1025	1124	1225	1316	1425	1524	1625	1724	1825	1924	2025	2124	2225	2324	0016

	Ⓐ🚌	⑥🚌	Ⓐ🚌		🚌		🚌		🚌		🚌		🚌		🚌		🚌		🚌		🚌
Oberammergau ♥ d.	0500	0543	0554	0630	0735	0834	0935	1034	1135	1234	1326	1434	1535	1634	1735	1834	1935	2034	2135	2234	2326
Bad Kohlgrub d.	0521	0604	0615	0658	0756	0901	0956	1101	1156	1301	1347	1501	1556	1701	1756	1901	1956	2101	2156	2301	2347
Murnau a.	0542	0625	0636	0721	0817	0923	1017	1123	1217	1323	1408	1523	1617	1723	1817	1923	2017	2123	2217	2323	0008

♥ – Services also call at Unterammergau (*km 20*) 4-7 minutes from Oberammergau.

☛ On Jan. 6 services run as on ⑦.

900 NÜRNBERG and FRANKFURT - HAMBURG

km		ICE 990 ①g	ICE 1688	ICE 1678 Ⓐ T	NJ 470 ♦		ICE 1686 Ⓐ ✕	ICE 1686 ①m ✕	NJ 40420 Ⓡ B	NJ 490 Ⓡ ♦		ICE 1088 ⚒ K✕	ICE 1676 Ⓐ T✕	ICE 1676 ⚒ T✕	ICE 672 Y✕	ICE 888 Ⓐ ✕		ICE 774 ✕	ICE 684 ✕	ICE 634 ①–⑥ ★✕	ICE 1674 ⚒ ✕	ICE 474 K✕	ICE 886 ✕
	Basel SBB **912** ▦ d.	...	...	...	2213	...	...	...	...	...	...	...	...	...	...	...	...	...	...	...	...	0508‡	...
	Karlsruhe Hbf **912** d.	...	...	...	0019	...	...	...	...	...	...	...	...	...	...	...	...	...	...	...	...	0651	...
	Stuttgart Hbf **912** d.	2251p	...	...	|	...	...	...	...	...	...	...	...	...	...	...	...	0502	...	...	...	|	...
	Mannheim Hbf **912** d.	2332p	...	...	|	...	...	...	...	...	...	...	...	...	...	...	...	0604	...	...	...	0716	...
	Frankfurt Flughafen Fernbf ✈ **912** d.	|	...	...	|	...	...	...	...	...	...	...	...	...	0532	...	...	0641	...	...	...	|	...
	Frankfurt (Main) Hbf **850 901 902** d.	0017	...	...	0214x	...	...	...	...	...	...	0506	0344g	...	0550	...	...	0658	...	...	0649	0758	...
	Hanau Hbf **850 901 902** d.	0034	...	...	0231	...	...	...	...	...	...	0521	|	...	0607	...	...	|	...	...	|	|	...
	München Hbf **904 905** d.	|	2300	...	|	...	...	...	2252	...	...	|	|	...	|	0413	...	|	0511	0511	|	|	0614
	Augsburg Hbf **905** d.	|	|	...	|	...	...	...	2325	...	...	|	◧	...	|	|	...	|	|	|	◧	|	|
0	**Nürnberg** Hbf **905 920 921** d.	|	0017	...	|	...	...	...	0142	0142	...	|	|	...	|	0532	...	|	0632	0632	|	|	0733
102	**Würzburg** Hbf **920 921** d.	|	0120	...	|	...	...	...	0235	0235	...	|	|	...	|	0628	...	|	0730	0730	|	|	0828
195	Fulda **850 901 902** d.	0117	|	...	|	...	...	...	|	|	...	0604	|	...	0647	0704	...	|	0805	0805	|	|	0904
285	**Kassel** Wilhelmshöhe **901 902** d.	|	|	...	|	...	...	...	|	|	...	0636	0623	...	0724	0736	...	0821	0838	0838	0856	0921	0936
330	Göttingen **902 903** d.	0245	0405	...	0433	...	0546	0546	0553	0553	...	0655	0645	...	0744	0755	...	0840	0857	0857	0917	0940	0955
430	**Hannover** Hbf **903** a.	0341	0506	...	0529	...	0657	0657	0649	0649	...	0732	0756	...	0819	0832	...	0917	0932	0932	0957	1017	1032
430	**Hannover** Hbf **903** d.	0344	0511	0554	0532	...	0701	0701	0705	0705	...	0736	0759	0759	0822	0836	...	0920	0936	0945	1000	1020	1036
	Bremen Hbf **813** a.	|	|	|	0643q	...	|	|	|	|	...	|	|	|	|	|	...	|	|	1045	|	|	|
471	Celle **903** d.	0405	0531	0617	|	...	0720	0720	|	|	...	|	0818	0818	|	|	...	|	|	...	1019	|	|
523	Uelzen **903** d.	0429	0555	0642	|	...	0742	0742	|	|	...	|	0842	0842	|	|	...	|	|	...	1043	|	|
559	Lüneburg **903** d.	0451	0613	0659	|	...	0756	0758	|	|	...	|	0902	0902	|	|	...	|	|	...	1059	|	1127
596	**Hamburg** Harburg **903** a.	0514	0629	0716	0736	...	...	0816	0830	0830	...	0843	0919	0919	|	|	...	|	|	...	1117	|	1144
608	**Hamburg** Hbf **903** a.	0528	0642	0730	0754	...	...	0829	0847	0847	...	0857	0932	0932	0936	0954	...	1036	1055	...	1130	1136	1158
615	**Hamburg** Altona a.	0542	0659	...	0810	...	...	0846	0905	0905	...	...	...	...	0952	1011	...	1052	1112	...	1145	...	1214

	ICE 772 ✕	ICE 682 L✕	ICE 632 ✕	ICE 1672 ✕♦	ICE 78 Z✕	ICE 882 K✕	ICE 1586 Ⓑb ✕	ICE 1176 ⑥ ✕	ICE 770 ✕	ICE 680 ✕	ICE 630 J ✕	IC 2374 Ⓐ ♣🍷	IC 2374 Ⓒ ♣🍷	ICE 76 Z✕	ICE 880 ✕		ICE 1224 ✕♦	ICE 578 ✕	ICE 588 ✕	ICE 538 J ✕	ICE 1578 T✕	ICE 74 ✕♦	ICE 788 ✕
Basel SBB **912** ▦ d.	...	...	...	...	0706	...	...	...	...	...	...	...	...	0906	...	...	...	...	...	...	...	1106	...
Karlsruhe Hbf **912** d.	...	...	...	0702e	0851	...	...	...	...	...	...	...	0910	1051	...	...	...	...	...	...	1110	1251	...
Stuttgart Hbf **912** d.	0725	...	...	|	|	...	...	...	0923	...	...	0855	|	|	...	...	...	1123	...	...	|	|	...
Mannheim Hbf **912** d.	0805	...	...	|	0916	...	...	...	1004	...	...	|	|	1116	...	...	...	1204	...	...	|	1316	...
Frankfurt Flughafen Fernbf ✈ **912** d.	0841	...	...	|	|	...	...	...	1041	...	...	|	|	|	...	...	...	1241	...	...	|	|	...
Frankfurt (Main) Hbf **850 901 902** d.	0858	...	...	0851	0958	...	...	1018	1058	...	...	1051	1051	1158	...	...	...	1258	...	...	1251	1358	...
Hanau Hbf **850 901 902** d.	|	...	...	|	|	...	...	1038	|	...	...	|	|	|	...	...	...	|	...	...	|	|	...
München Hbf **904 905** d.	|	0718	0718	|	|	0820	0816	|	|	0918	0918	|	|	|	1021	...	1051	|	1118	1118	|	|	1221
Augsburg Hbf **905** d.	|	|	|	◧	|	|	0847	|	|	|	|	◧	◧	|	|	...	|	|	|	|	◧	|	|
Nürnberg Hbf **905 920 921** d.	|	0832	0832	|	|	0933	|	|	|	1032	1032	|	|	|	1133	...	1159	|	1233	1233	|	|	1333
Würzburg Hbf **920 921** d.	|	0928	0928	|	|	1028	1040	|	|	1129	1129	|	|	|	1228	...	1301t	|	1328	1328	|	|	1428
Fulda **850 901 902** d.	|	1004	1004	|	|	1104	1122	1122	|	1204	1204	|	|	|	1304	...	1333	|	1404	1404	|	|	1504
Kassel Wilhelmshöhe **901 902** d.	1021	1036	1036	1056	1121	1136	1156	1157	1221	1236	1236	1256	1256	1321	1336	...	1401	1421	1436	1436	1456	1521	1537
Göttingen **902 903** d.	1040	1055	1055	1116	1140	1155	1219	1219	1240	1255	1255	1317	1317	1340	1355	...	...	1440	1455	1455	1516	1540	1556
Hannover Hbf **903** a.	1117	1132	1132	1156	1217	1232	1258	1258	1317	1332	1332	1356	1356	1417	1432	...	...	1517	1532	1532	1556	1617	1632
Hannover Hbf **903** d.	1120	1136	1145	1159	1220	1236	1301	1301	1320	1336	1345	1359	1359	1420	1436	...	...	1520	1536	1545	1559	1620	1636
Bremen Hbf **813** a.	|	|	1245	|	|	|	|	|	|	|	1445	|	|	|	|	...	...	|	|	1645	|	|	|
Celle **903** d.	|	|	...	1218	|	|	1319	1319	|	|	...	1418	1418	|	|	...	...	|	|	...	1618	|	|
Uelzen **903** d.	|	|	...	1242	|	|	1342	1342	|	|	...	1442	1442	|	|	...	...	|	|	...	1642	|	|
Lüneburg **903** d.	|	|	...	1259	|	|	1358	1358	|	|	...	1459	1459	|	|	...	...	|	|	...	1702	|	|
Hamburg Harburg **903** a.	|	1241	...	1316	|	|	1416	1416	|	|	...	1517	1517	|	1540	...	...	|	|	...	1719	|	1741
Hamburg Hbf **903** a.	1236	1255	...	1330	1336	1354	1429	1429	1436	1455	...	1530	1530	1536	1555	...	...	1636	1655	...	1732	1736	1755
Hamburg Altona a.	1252	...	...	...	1351	...	1444	1444	1452	1511	...	...	...	1551	1611	...	...	1652	1711	...	...	...	1811

	IC 2082 D 🍷	ICE 576 ✕	ICE 586 ✕	ICE 536 J ✕	ICE 1576 ⑥h ✕	ICE 1576 Ⓑb U✕	ICE 72 ✕♦	ICE 786 ✕	ICE 1206 ⑥ R✕	ICE 1284 ⑤† S✕	ICE 1594 ⑦w ✕	ICE 1594 ⑤ K✕	ICE 1094 Ⓑb K✕	ICE 1594 ⑦w ✕	ICE 1594 ⑤ K✕	ICE 574 ⑥k ✕	ICE 584 L✕	ICE 984 ⑤⑦ w✕	ICE 776 Ⓑb N✕	ICE 1574 G ✕	ICE 1574 ⑦H ✕		ICE 70 ✕♦
Basel SBB **912** ▦ d.	...	...	...	...	...	...	1306	...	...	...	...	...	...	...	...	...	...	...	...	...	...	...	1506
Karlsruhe Hbf **912** d.	...	...	...	...	1310	1310	1451	...	...	...	...	...	...	...	...	...	...	...	...	1510	1510	...	1651
Stuttgart Hbf **912** d.	...	1323	...	...	|	|	|	...	...	...	...	...	1523	...	...	1523	...	...	...	|	|	...	|
Mannheim Hbf **912** d.	...	1404	...	...	|	|	1516	...	...	...	...	...	1604	...	...	1604	...	...	...	|	|	...	1716
Frankfurt Flughafen Fernbf ✈ **912** d.	...	1441	...	...	|	|	|	...	...	...	...	...	1641	...	...	1641	...	...	...	|	|	...	|
Frankfurt (Main) Hbf **850 901 902** d.	...	1458	...	...	1448	1448	1558	...	...	...	1614	1614	1658	...	...	1658	...	...	1701	1648	1648	...	1758
Hanau Hbf **850 901 902** d.	...	|	...	...	|	|	|	...	...	...	1640	1640	|	...	...	|	...	...	1737	|	|	...	|
München Hbf **904 905** d.	1117o	|	1318	1318	|	|	|	1421	1356	1357	|	|	|	...	...	|	1518	1518	|	|	|	...	|
Augsburg Hbf **905** d.	1230	|	|	|	◧	◧	|	|	1425	1425	|	|	|	...	...	|	|	|	|	◧	◧	...	|
Nürnberg Hbf **905 920 921** d.	|	|	1434	1434	|	|	|	1534	|	|	|	|	|	...	...	|	1633	1633	|	|	|	...	|
Würzburg Hbf **920 921** d.	1440	|	1529	1529	|	|	|	1628	1634	1634	|	|	|	...	...	|	1728	1728	|	|	|	...	|
Fulda **850 901 902** d.	1518	|	1604	1604	|	|	|	1704	1720	1720	1724	1724	|	...	...	|	1804	1804	1819	|	|	...	|
Kassel Wilhelmshöhe **901 902** d.	1555	1621	1636	1636	1656	1656	1721	1736	1758	1757	1801	1801	|	...	...	1821	1836	1836	1852	1856	1856	...	1921
Göttingen **902 903** d.	1615	1640	1655	1655	1716	1716	1740	1755	1820	1820	1823	1823	|	...	...	1840	1855	1855	1912	1917	1917	...	1940
Hannover Hbf **903** a.	1654	1717	1732	1732	1756	1756	1817	1832	1858	1858	1902	1902	1912	←	←	1917	1932	1932	1948	1956	1956	...	2017
Hannover Hbf **903** d.	1657	1720	1736	1745	1759	1759	1820	1836	1901	1901	→	→	1915	1918	1918	1920	1936	1936	1951	1959	1959	...	2020
Bremen Hbf **813** a.	|	|	|	1845	|	|	|	|	|	|	...	...	|	|	|	|	|	|	2047	|	|	...	|
Celle **903** d.	1717	|	|	...	1818	1818	|	|	1920	1922	...	...	|	1938	1938	|	|	|	...	2018	2018	...	|
Uelzen **903** d.	1742	|	|	...	1842	1842	|	|	1943	1945	...	...	|	|	|	|	|	|	...	2042	2042	...	|
Lüneburg **903** d.	1758	|	|	...	1858	1858	|	|	1959	2006j	...	...	|	2015	2015	2013	2028	2028	...	2058	2058	...	|
Hamburg Harburg **903** a.	1815	|	|	...	1916	1916	|	1941	2016	2024j	...	...	|	2033	2033	|	2044	2044	...	2116	2116	...	2126
Hamburg Hbf **903** a.	1829	1836	1855	...	1929	1929	1936	1955	2030	2038j	...	...	2030	2047	2047	2040	2059	2059	...	2129	2129	...	2139
Hamburg Altona a.	1845	1852	1911	...	1945	...	1951	2011	2046	2052j	...	...	...	2103	...	2059	...	2116	...	2147	...	...	2154

♦ – **NOTES** (LISTED BY TRAIN NUMBER)

70/2 – 🚃12 ✕ Chur - Zürich - Basel - Hamburg.
74 – 🚃12 ✕ Zürich - Basel - Hamburg - Kiel.
470 – 🛏 1, 2 cl. and ▬ 2 cl. Zürich (d. 2059) - Basel - Hamburg. Also conveys 🚃2 (*IC* **60470**).
490 – 🛏 1, 2 cl., ▬ 2 cl. and 🚃2 Wien - Passau - Nürnberg - Hamburg.
1224 – 🚃12 ✕ München - Paderborn - Hamm - Oberhausen.
1672 – 🚃12 ✕ (Karlsruhe ⚒ -) Frankfurt - Hamburg - Rostock - Stralsund (- Ostseebad Binz ⚒). Terminates at Rostock from Mar. 4.

B – 🛏 1, 2 cl., ▬ 2 cl. and 🚃2 Innsbruck - Hamburg (Table **53**).
D – KÖNIGSSEE – 🚃12 🍷 Berchtesgaden - München Ost - Hamburg; 🚃12 Oberstdorf (**2084**) - Augsburg (**2082**) - Hamburg.
G – ①–⑥ to Feb. 25 (also Dec. 25; not Dec. 26); daily from Feb. 27.
H – ⑦ to Feb. 26 (also Dec. 26; not Dec. 25). To Rostock (Table **830**).
J – Until Mar. 12.
K – To Kiel (Table **820**).
L – To Lübeck (Table **825**).
N – To Oldenburg (Table **813**). Terminates at Hannover from Mar. 12.
R – From Innsbruck via Garmisch (Table **895**).
S – From Schwarzach-St Veit (Table **960**) on ⑦ (not Dec. 25).
T – To Stralsund via Rostock (Table **830**).
U – To Rostock (Table **830**), also Stralsund on ⑦ to Feb. 26 (also Dec. 26; not Dec. 25).
Y – From Wiesbaden (Table **850**).
Z – From Zürich (Table **510**).

b – Not Dec. 25.
e – ⚒ only.
g – ① (also Dec. 27; not Dec. 26).
h – Also Dec. 25.
j – 5–7 minutes earlier on Dec. 25.
k – Also Dec. 25.
m – Not Dec. 26.
o – München **Ost**.
p – Previous day.
q – Until Mar. 12.
t – Arrives 1251.
w – Also Dec. 26; not Dec. 25.
x – Frankfurt (Main) **Süd**.

‡ – Basel **Badischer Bahnhof**.
★ – ①–⑥ until Mar. 11 (also Dec. 25; not Dec. 26).
♣ – WATTENMEER – To Westerland on dates in Table **821**.
◧ – Via Gießen (Table **806**).

NÜRNBERG and FRANKFURT - HAMBURG 900

	ICE 90	ICE 1204	ICE 1204	ICE 572	ICE 582	ICE 532	ICE 1572	ICE 1572	ICE 376	ICE 782		ICE 570	ICE 580	ICE 580	ICE 292	ICE 580	ICE 272	ICE 272	ICE 1570		ICE 780		ICE 926
		⑦	Ⓐ				⑤–⑦	n	Ⓑ b			⑦ w	Ⓑ	⑦ w	⑦ w	⑦ w	⑥ h	Ⓐ	⑦ w		⑦ w		⑦ w
	✕♦	R✕	✕	✕	✕	M✕	u✕	✕	✕♦	✕		✕	✕	✕	✕♦		C✕	Z✕			✕		
Basel SBB **912** 🚌 ... d.	...	...	...	...	...	...	...	...	1707	...	...	...	...	...	1813	...	1813	1813	...	...	...	...	...
Karlsruhe Hbf **912** ... d.	...	...	...	...	...	...	1710	1710	1851	...	...	...	...	...	2000	...	2000	2000	1910	...	...	...	...
Stuttgart Hbf **912** ... d.	...	...	...	1723	...	...	|	|	|	...	...	1923	...	...	|	...	|	|	|	...	...	...	...
Mannheim Hbf **912** ... d.	...	...	...	1804	...	...	|	|	1916	...	...	2005	...	...	2032	...	2032	2032	|	...	...	...	...
Frankfurt Flughafen Fernbf ✈ **912** .. d.	...	...	...	1841	...	...	|	|	|	...	...	2041	...	...	|	...	|	|	|	...	...	...	...
Frankfurt (Main) Hbf ... **850 901 902** d.	...	...	...	1858	...	...	1848	1848	1958	...	...	2058	...	...	2114	...	2114	2114	2051	...	...	...	...
Hanau Hbf ... **850 901 902** d.	...	...	...	1914	...	...	|	|	|	...	...	2114	...	...	2130	...	2130	2130	|	...	...	...	...
München Hbf **904 905** ... d.	...	1552	1618	|	1717	1717	|	|	|	1819	...	|	1919	1919	|	...	|	|	|	...	2021	...	2154
Augsburg Hbf ... **905** d.	...	1624	|	|	|	|	◧	◧	|	|	...	|	|	|	|	...	|	|	◧	...	|	...	|
Nürnberg Hbf ... **905 920 921** d.	1732	|	1736	|	1833	1833	|	|	|	1934	...	|	2032	2032	|	...	|	|	|	...	2134	...	2304
Würzburg Hbf ... **920 921** d.	1826	1834	1834	|	1928	1928	|	|	|	2028	...	|	2128	2128	|	...	|	|	|	...	2228	...	2357
Fulda ... **850 901 902** d.	1904	1920	1920	|	2004	2004	|	|	|	2104	...	|	2204	2204	2212	...	2212	2212	|	...	2304	...	...
Kassel Wilhelmshöhe ... **901 902** d.	1938	1956	1956	2025	2036	2036	2056	2056	2121	2137	...	2225	2234	2236	2245	←	2245	2245	2258	...	2335	...	...
Göttingen ... **902 903** d.	1958	2016	2016	2046	2055	2055	2117	2117	2140	2157	...	2245	...	2255	2303	2307	2306	2306	2318	...	...	...	...
Hannover Hbf ... **903** a.	2033	2053	2053	2119	2132	2132	2156	2156	2217	2232	...	2318	...	→	...	2341	2341	0002	0010	...	...	...	...
Hannover Hbf ... **903** d.	2036	2058	2058	2122	2136	2145	2159	...	2220	2236	...	2321	...	...	...	2345	2344	0005	...	...	...	...	...
Bremen Hbf **813** ... a.	|	|	|	|	|	2259	|	...	|	|	...	|	...	...	...	|	|	|	...	...	...	...	...
Celle ... **903** d.	|	2118	2118	|	|	...	2218	...	|	2256	...	|	...	...	...	0005	|	0026	...	...	...	...	...
Uelzen ... **903** d.	|	2143	2143	|	|	...	2242	...	|	2318	...	|	...	...	...	0027	0024	0050	...	...	...	...	...
Lüneburg ... **903** d.	|	2200	2200	2214	|	...	2259	...	|	2335	...	0014	...	...	...	0044	0041	0106	...	...	...	...	...
Hamburg Harburg ... **903** a.	2141	2216	2216	2232	2241	...	2315	...	|	2352	...	0030	...	...	...	0102	0101	0123	...	...	...	...	...
Hamburg Hbf ... **903** a.	2155	2229	2229	2246	2255	...	2329	...	2342	0006	...	0044	...	...	...	0116	0115	0137	...	...	...	...	...
Hamburg Altona ... a.	2209	2245	2245	2301	2311	...	2346	...	2400	0022	...	0101	...	...	...	0132	0130	0201	...	...	...	...	...

	ICE 1271		ICE 591	ICE 781	ICE 781		ICE 1573		ICE 581	ICE 571	ICE 753	ICE 1097	ICE 783	ICE 783		ICE 71	ICE 1575	ICE 533	ICE 583		ICE 573	ICE 573	IC 2083
	① g		①–⑥	① g	⚒		Ⓐ		①–⑥		Ⓐ	Ⓐ	①–⑤	⑥⑦			⚒	⚒			⚒	†	D
	C		N✕	✕	✕		✕		e✕	✕	✕	✕	✕	✕		C✕	✕	M✕	✕		K✕	✕	🍷
Hamburg Altona ... d.	0028	...	0302	0332	...	...	...	...	0436	0458	0503	0551	0537	0537	...	0604y	0607	...	0644	...	...	0705	0712
Hamburg Hbf ... **903** d.	0045	...	0319	0349	...	...	...	...	0454	0515	0523	0606	0554	0554	...	0618	0624	...	0701	...	0723	0723	0728
Hamburg Harburg ... **903** d.	0057	...	0331	0402	...	...	...	...	0506	0528	0535	|	0606	0606	...	0630	0636	...	0713	...	|	|	0741
Lüneburg ... **903** d.	|	...	0350	0421	...	...	...	...	0526	0547	0554	|	0624	0624	...	0648	0655	...	|	...	|	|	0801
Uelzen ... **903** d.	|	...	0408	0438	...	...	...	...	0542	|	0614	|	|	0641	...	|	0715	...	|	...	|	|	0817
Celle ... **903** d.	|	...	0437	0501	...	...	...	...	0604	|	0637	|	|	0704	...	|	0738	...	|	...	|	|	0839
Bremen Hbf **813** ... d.	|	...	|	|	...	...	...	...	|	|	|	|	|	|	...	|	|	0715j	|	...	|	|	|
Hannover Hbf ... **903** a.	0207	...	0456	0520	...	...	...	...	0623	0638	0657	0719	0723	0723	...	0738	0758	0814	0822	...	0838	0838	0859
Hannover Hbf ... **903** d.	0210	...	0519	0526	...	...	0557	...	0626	0641	▽	0722	0726	0726	...	0741	0801	0826	0826	...	0841	0841	0903
Göttingen ... **902 903** d.	0307	...	0554	0602	...	...	0636	...	0702	0716	...	|	0802	0802	...	0816	0839	0902	0902	...	0916	0916	0944
Kassel Wilhelmshöhe ... **901 902** d.	|	...	0615	0623	0623	...	0701	...	0723	0737	...	|	0823	0823	...	0837	0903	0923	0923	...	0937	0937	1007
Fulda ... **850 901 902** d.	0431	...	0648	0656	0656	...	|	...	0756	|	...	|	0856	0856	...	|	|	0956	0956	...	|	|	1043
Würzburg Hbf ... **920 921** d.	|	...	|	0730	0730	...	|	...	0832	|	...	|	0931	0931	...	|	|	1032	1032	...	|	|	1124
Nürnberg Hbf ... **905 920 921** a.	|	...	|	0824	0824	...	◧	...	0925	|	...	|	1024	1023	...	|	◧	1125	1125	...	|	|	|
Augsburg Hbf ... **905** a.	|	...	|	|	|	...	|	...	|	|	...	|	|	|	...	|	|	|	|	...	|	|	1330
München Hbf **904 905** ... a.	|	...	|	0939	0939	...	|	...	1043	|	...	|	1141	1141	...	|	|	1238	1238	...	|	|	1411o
Hanau Hbf ... **850 901 902** d.	0519	...	0728	...	...	...	|	...	...	|	...	|	...	...	...	|	|	...	...	...	|	|	...
Frankfurt (Main) Hbf ... **850 901 902** a.	0537	...	0744	...	...	...	0910	...	...	0900	...	0928	...	...	...	1000	1110	...	...	...	1100	1100	...
Frankfurt Flughafen Fernbf ✈ **912** a.	|	...	|	...	...	...	|	...	...	0918	...	0951	...	...	...	|	|	...	...	...	1118	1118	...
Mannheim Hbf **912** ... a.	0627	...	0827	...	...	...	|	...	...	0956	...	...	...	...	...	1044	|	...	...	...	1156	1156	...
Stuttgart Hbf **912** ... a.	|	...	0908	...	...	...	|	...	...	1038	...	...	...	...	...	|	|	...	...	...	1238	1238	...
Karlsruhe Hbf **912** ... a.	0656	...	...	...	...	...	1050	...	...	...	...	...	...	...	...	1109	1250	...	...	...	...	...	...
Basel SBB **912** ... a.	0847	...	...	...	...	...	...	...	...	...	...	...	...	...	...	1255	...	...	...	...	...	...	...

	ICE 91	ICE 73	ICE 73	ICE 1577	ICE 1577	ICE 1207	ICE 535	ICE 585	ICE 575	ICE 1223		ICE 787	ICE 75	ICE 75	ICE 1579	ICE 1579	ICE 537	ICE 587	ICE 577	ICE 1285	ICE 1285		ICE 789
		⚒	†	Ⓐ	Ⓒ	⑥	G						⚒	†	Ⓑ b	⑥ h	H			Ⓑ	⑥		
	✕♦	✕♦	✕♦	T✕	✕	R✕	M✕	L✕	✕	✕♦		✕	C✕	B✕	✕	T✕	M✕	✕	✕	S✕	✕		✕
Hamburg Altona ... d.	0744	...	0806	...	0810	...	...	...	0905	...	...	0944	1007	...	1012	...	...	1044	1105	1111	1111	...	1144
Hamburg Hbf ... **903** d.	0801	0824	0824	0828	0828	0828	...	0901	0924	...	...	1001	1024	1024	1028	1028	...	1101	1124	1128	1128	...	1201
Hamburg Harburg ... **903** d.	0813	|	|	0841	0841	0841	...	0914	|	...	...	1013	|	|	1041	1041	...	1113	|	|	|	...	1213
Lüneburg ... **903** d.	|	|	|	0859	0859	0859	...	|	|	...	...	|	|	|	1059	1059	...	|	|	1155	1155	...	|
Uelzen ... **903** d.	|	|	|	0916	0916	0916	...	|	|	...	...	|	|	|	1115	1115	...	|	|	|	|	...	|
Celle ... **903** d.	|	|	|	0938	0938	0938	...	|	|	...	...	|	|	|	1138	1138	...	|	|	|	|	...	|
Bremen Hbf **813** ... d.	|	|	|	|	|	|	0915j	|	|	...	...	|	|	|	|	|	1115	|	|	|	|	...	|
Hannover Hbf ... **903** a.	0921	0938	0938	0958	0958	0958	1015	1022	1038	...	...	1120	1138	1138	1158	1158	1214	1222	1238	1246	1246	...	1320
Hannover Hbf ... **903** d.	0926	0941	0941	1001	1001	1001	1026	1026	1041	...	...	1126	1141	1141	1201	1201	1226	1226	1241	1255	1255	...	1326
Göttingen ... **902 903** d.	1003	1016	1016	1037	1037	1037	1102	1102	1116	...	...	1202	1216	1216	1239	1239	1302	1302	1316	1333	1333	...	1402
Kassel Wilhelmshöhe ... **901 902** d.	1025	1037	1037	1104	1104	1107	1123	1123	1137	1158	...	1223	1237	1237	1303	1303	1323	1323	1337	1354	1354	...	1423
Fulda ... **850 901 902** d.	1057	|	|	|	|	1142	1156	1156	|	1228	...	1256	|	|	|	|	1356	1356	|	1432	1432	...	1456
Würzburg Hbf ... **920 921** d.	1134	|	|	|	|	1219	1232	1232	|	1313r	...	1330	|	|	|	|	1432	1432	|	1511	|	...	1530
Nürnberg Hbf ... **905 920 921** a.	1227	|	|	◧	◧	|	1325	1325	|	1404	...	1424	|	|	◧	◧	1525	1525	|	|	|	...	1624
Augsburg Hbf ... **905** a.	...	|	|	|	|	1409	|	|	|	|	...	|	|	|	|	|	|	|	|	1731	|	...	|
München Hbf **904 905** ... a.	...	|	|	|	|	1445	1441	1441	|	1509	...	1541	|	|	|	|	1641	1641	|	1804	|	...	1739
Hanau Hbf ... **850 901 902** d.	...	|	|	|	|	...	...	...	|	...	...	...	|	|	|	|	...	...	|	...	1515	...	...
Frankfurt (Main) Hbf ... **850 901 902** a.	...	1200	1200	1309	1309	...	...	...	1300	...	...	...	1400	1400	1509	1509	...	...	1500	...	1540	...	...
Frankfurt Flughafen Fernbf ✈ **912** a.	...	|	|	|	|	...	...	...	1318	...	...	...	|	|	|	|	...	...	1518	...	...	...	...
Mannheim Hbf **912** ... a.	...	1244	1244	|	|	...	...	...	1356	...	...	...	1444	1444	|	|	...	...	1556	...	...	...	...
Stuttgart Hbf **912** ... a.	...	|	|	|	|	...	...	...	1438	...	...	...	|	|	|	|	...	...	1638	...	...	...	...
Karlsruhe Hbf **912** ... a.	...	1309	1309	1450	1450	...	...	...	...	...	...	...	1509	1509	1650	1650	...	...	...	...	...	...	...
Basel SBB **912** ... a.	...	1455	1455	...	...	...	...	...	...	...	...	...	1655	1655	...	...	...	...	...	...	...	...	...

♦ – **NOTES** (LISTED BY TRAIN NUMBER)

73 – 12 ✕ (Kiel ⚒ -) Hamburg - Basel - Zürich.

90/1 – DONAUWALZER – 12 ✕ Wien - Linz - Passau - Regensburg - Hamburg and v.v.

292 – 12 ✕ Chur - Zürich - Basel - Berlin.

376 – 12 ✕ Interlaken - Bern - Basel - Hamburg.

1223 – On Ⓐ: 12 ✕ Köln - Hamm - Paderborn - Kassel - München.
On Ⓒ: 12 ✕ Oberhausen - Hamm - Paderborn - Kassel - München.

B – 12 Kiel - Hamburg - Basel - Zürich - Chur.
C – 12 Hamburg - Basel - Zürich - Chur and v.v.
D – KÖNIGSSEE – 12 🍷 Hamburg - München Ost - Berchtesgaden; 12 Hamburg - Augsburg (**2085**) - Oberstdorf.
G – Daily until Mar. 12; ⑥⑦ from Mar. 18.
H – Daily to Mar. 12; ⑦ from Mar. 19.
K – From Kiel (Table **820**).
L – From Lübeck (Table **825**).
M – To / from Oldenburg on dates in Table **813**.
N – To München (Table **930**).
R – From / to Innsbruck via Garmisch (Table **895**).
S – To Schwarzach (Table **960**) on ⑤ (not Dec. 23, Mar. 31).
T – From Stralsund via Rostock (Table **830**).
Z – From Zürich (Table **510**).

b – Not Dec. 25.
e – Also Dec. 25; not Dec. 26.
g – Also Dec. 27; not Dec. 26.
h – Also Dec. 25.
j – 29 – 34 minutes **earlier** from Mar. 13.
n – Not Dec. 24.
o – München **Ost**.
r – Arrives 1300.
u – Also Dec. 26; not Dec. 24.
w – Also Dec. 26; not Dec. 25.
y – 0555 on Ⓒ.

▽ – Continues to Berlin (Table **810**).
◧ – Via Gießen (Table **806**).

900 HAMBURG - FRANKFURT and NÜRNBERG

	ICE	ICE	ICE	ICE	ICE	ICE	ICE		ICE	ICE	ICE	ICE	IC	ICE	ICE	ICE	ICE	ICE	ICE	ICE	ICE	ICE	ICE
	77	1671	639	689	579	1205	1597		881	79	1091	1091	2375	631	681	771	1595	1585	1585	1585	883	1171	1675
			J			Ⓑb	⑦w				⑤	⑦w		J			⑦w	⑤	①m	①–④			
	E✕	T✕	✕	✕	✕	S✕	✕		✕	Z✕	R✕	R✕	M🍷	✕	L✕	✕	B🍷	✕	✕	m✕	✕	K✕	T✕
Hamburg Altona d.	...	...	...	1244	1306	1311	1311	...	1344	1406	...	...	...	...	...	1505	...	...	1511	...	1544	...	...
Hamburg Hbf **903** d.	1224	1228	...	1301	1324	1328	1328	...	1401	1424	...	...	1427	...	1501	1524	...	...	1528	...	1601	1624	1628
Hamburg Harburg **903** d.	|	1241	...	1313	|	1340	1340	...	1413	|	...	...	1439	...	1514	|	...	...	1540	...	1613	|	1640
Lüneburg **903** d.	|	1259	...	|	|	1359	1359	...	|	|	...	...	1458	...	|	|	...	1558	1558	1558	|	|	1659
Uelzen **903** d.	|	1315	...	|	|	1415	1415	...	|	|	...	...	1515	...	|	|	...	1619	1619	1619	|	|	1715
Celle **903** d.	|	1338	...	|	|	|	|	...	|	|	...	...	1538	...	|	|	...	1640	1640	1640	|	|	1737
Bremen Hbf **813** d.	|	|	1315	|	|	|	|	...	|	|	...	...	|	1515	|	|	...	|	|	|	|	|	|
Hannover Hbf **903** a.	1338	1358	1414	1422	1438	1451	1451	...	1520	1538	...	...	1558	1614	1622	1638	...	1700	1700	1700	1720	1738	1757
Hannover Hbf **903** d.	1341	1401	1426	1426	1441	1454	1454	...	1526	1541	1551	1551	1601	1626	1626	1641	1702	1707	1703	1703	1726	1741	1801
Göttingen **902 903** d.	1416	1439	1502	1502	1516	1535	1535	...	1602	1616	1631	1631	1640	1702	1702	1716	1743	1746	1814	1814	1802	1816	1839
Kassel Wilhelmshöhe **901 902** d.	1437	1503	1523	1523	1537	1558	1558	...	1623	1637	1654	1654	1703	1723	1723	1737	1811	1810	...	...	1823	1837	1903
Fulda **850 901 902** d.	|	|	1556	1556	|	1634	1638	...	1656	|	1729	1729	|	1756	1756	|	|	1843	...	...	1856	|	|
Würzburg Hbf **920 921** d.	|	|	1632	1632	|	1712	|	...	1731	|	|	|	|	1832	1832	|	|	|	...	...	1930	|	|
Nürnberg Hbf **905 920 921** a.	|	◧	1725	1725	|	|	|	...	1824	|	|	|	◧	1925	1925	|	◧	|	...	...	2024	|	◧
Augsburg Hbf **905** a.	|	|	|	|	|	1930	|	...	|	|	|	|	|	|	|	|	|	|	...	...	|	|	|
München Hbf **904 905** a.	|	|	1839	1839	|	2002	|	...	1941	|	|	|	|	2043	2043	|	|	|	...	...	2141	|	|
Hanau Hbf **850 901 902** d.	|	|	...	...	|	...	|	...	...	|	|	|	|	...	...	|	|	1937	...	...	...	|	|
Frankfurt (Main) Hbf ... **850 901 902** a.	1600	1709	...	...	1700	...	1740	...	...	1800	1831	1831	1909	...	...	1900	2014	1956	...	...	...	2000	2109
Frankfurt Flughafen Fernbf ✈ **912** a.	|	|	...	...	1718	...	...	...	...	|	...	|	|	...	...	1918	|	|	...	...	...	|	...
Mannheim Hbf **912** a.	1644	|	...	...	1755	...	...	...	...	1844	...	1916	|	...	...	1955	|	|	...	...	...	2044	...
Stuttgart Hbf **912** a.	|	|	...	...	1838	...	...	...	...	|	...	1958	|	...	...	2038	2155	2156	...	...	...	|	...
Karlsruhe Hbf **912** a.	1709	1852	...	...	...	...	...	...	...	1909	...	...	2053	...	...	...	...	...	...	...	...	2109	...
Basel SBB **912** a.	1855	...	...	...	...	...	...	...	...	2055	...	...	...	...	...	...	...	...	...	...	...	2304	...

	ICE	ICE	ICE	ICE	ICE	ICE	ICE	ICE	ICE	ICE	ICE	ICE	ICE	ICE	ICE	ICE	ICE	ICE	NJ	NJ		NJ	ICE
	633	683	773	1687	1687	885	273	273	1677	1677	635	685	635	685	775	887	1087	1679	491	40491		471	1689
	J			⑦b	⑦–④			⑤⑥	Ⓑb	⑤⑦	Ⓑ		⑤⑦	⑤–⑦	Ⓑb	Ⓑb	⑥	⑦w	Ⓡ	Ⓡ			
	✕	✕	✕	✕	b✕	K✕	✕	h✕	T✕	wT ✕	J✕	✕	U✕	Y✕	✕	N✕	N✕	T✕	H	A		D	
Hamburg Altona d.	...	1644	1706	1711	...	...	1806	1806	...		...	1844t	...	1844	1906	1944	1944	...	1958	1958	...	2152	2211
Hamburg Hbf **903** d.	...	1701	1724	1728	...	1801	1824	1824	1828	1828	...	1901t	...	1901	1924	2001	2001	2024	2024	2024	...	2207	2228
Hamburg Harburg **903** d.	...	1713	|	1740	...	1813	|	|	1840	1840	...	1913	...	1913	|	|	|	|	|	|	...	2220	|
Lüneburg **903** d.	...	|	|	1758	...	|	|	|	1859	1859	...	|	...	|	|	2028	2028	2051	|	|	...	|	2259
Uelzen **903** d.	...	|	|	1819	...	|	|	|	1915	1915	...	|	...	|	|	2044	2044	2108	|	|	...	|	2315
Celle **903** d.	...	|	|	1840	...	|	|	|	1938	1938	...	|	...	|	|	|	|	2140	|	|	...	|	2340
Bremen Hbf **813** d.	1715	|	|	|	...	|	|	|	|	|	1915	|	1915	|	|	|	|	|	|	|	...	2311	|
Hannover Hbf **903** a.	1814	1822	1838	1905	...	1920	1938	1938	1958	1958	2014	2022	2014	2022	2038	2123	2123	2159	2154	2154	...	0026	2400
Hannover Hbf **903** d.	1826	1826	1841	1909	1909	1926	1941	1941	...	2001	2026	2026	2026	2026	2041	2126	2137	2202	2157	2157	...	0030	0003
Göttingen **902 903** d.	1902	1902	1916	1946	1946	2002	2016	2016	...	2040	2102	2102	2102	2102	2116	2202	2213	2242	2259	2259	...	0132	0113
Kassel Wilhelmshöhe **901 902** d.	1923	1923	1937	2009	2009	2023	2037	2037	...	2103	2123	2123	2123	2123	2137	2223	2235	...	|	|	...	|	|
Fulda **850 901 902** d.	1956	1956	|	...	...	2056	|	|	...	|	2156	2156	2156	2156	|	2257	2308	...	|	|	...	|	|
Würzburg Hbf **920 921** d.	2031	2031	|	...	...	2130	|	|	...	|	2231	2231	2231	2231	|	|	|	...	0145	0145	...	|	0354
Nürnberg Hbf **905 920 921** a.	2125	2125	|	...	...	2225	|	|	...	◧	2326	2326	2326	2326	|	|	|	...	0324	0324	...	|	0447
Augsburg Hbf **905** a.	|	|	|	...	...	|	|	|	...	|	...	...	|	|	|	|	|	...	...	0624	...	|	|
München Hbf **904 905** a.	2239	2239	|	...	...	2340	|	|	...	|	...	...	0043	0043	|	|	|	...	...	0706	...	|	0604
Hanau Hbf **850 901 902** d.	...	...	|	...	...	...	|	|	...	|	...	...	...	...	|	2336	2348	...	...	...	...	0417	...
Frankfurt (Main) Hbf ... **850 901 902** a.	...	...	2100	...	...	...	2200	2200	...	2309	...	...	...	...	2300	2353	0007	...	...	...	...	0428x	...
Frankfurt Flughafen Fernbf ✈ **912** a.	...	...	2118	...	...	...	|	|	...	...	...	...	...	...	2318	0026	0026	...	...	...	...	|	...
Mannheim Hbf **912** a.	...	...	2155	...	...	...	2244	2244	...	...	...	...	...	...	0005	...	...	...	...	...	...	|	...
Stuttgart Hbf **912** a.	...	...	2255	...	...	...	|	|	...	...	...	...	...	...	|	...	...	...	...	...	...	|	...
Karlsruhe Hbf **912** a.	...	...	...	...	...	...	2309	2309	...	...	...	...	...	...	0037	...	...	...	...	...	...	0602	...
Basel SBB **912** a.	...	...	...	...	...	...	...	0105	...	...	...	...	...	...	...	...	...	...	...	...	...	0810	...

A – 🛏 1, 2 cl., 🛌 2 cl. and 🚃(2) Hamburg - München - Innsbruck (Table **53**).
B – From Berlin (Table **810**).
D – 🛏 1, 2 cl. and 🛌 2 cl. (Ⓡ) Hamburg - Basel - Zürich (a. 1005). Also conveys 🚃(2) (*IC* **60471**).
E – 🚃(12) ✕ Kiel - Hamburg - Basel - Zürich.
H – 🛏 1, 2 cl., 🛌 2 cl. and 🚃(2) Hamburg - Passau - Wien.
J – Until Mar. 12.
K – From Kiel (Table **820**).
L – From Lübeck (Table **825**).
M – WATTENMEER – 🚃(12) 🍷 (Westerland ⑤–① -) Hamburg - Hannover Frankfurt - Karlsruhe.
N – To Wiesbaden (Table **850**).
R – From Berlin (Table **902**).
S – On ⑤ until Mar. 24 continues to Innsbruck via Garmisch (Table **895**).
T – From Stralsund via Rostock (Table **830**).

U – ⑤⑦ to Mar. 12 (also Dec. 26, Jan. 5).
Y – ⑤–⑦ (also Dec. 26, Jan. 5).
Z – To Zürich (Table **510**).

b – Not Dec. 25.
h – Also Dec. 25.
m – Not Dec. 26.
r – Also Dec. 26, Jan. 5.
t – ②⑤⑥⑦ only.
w – Also Dec. 26; not Dec. 25.
x – Frankfurt (Main) **Süd**.

◧ – Via Gießen (Table **806**).

901 Local services FRANKFURT - FULDA - KASSEL

RE / *RB* services

Other *ICE* / *IC* services: Table **850** for Bebra - Kassel Wilhelmshöhe and v.v., also Frankfurt - Fulda - Bad Hersfeld and v.v. Tables **900** / **902** for Frankfurt - Fulda - Kassel Wilhelmshöhe and v.v.

km		⚒	†					A	
0	**Frankfurt** (Main) Hbf **921** d.	0519	0524	0626	0726		2126	2226	2326
4	**Frankfurt** (Main) Süd **921** d.	0524	0529	0633	0733	and	2133	2233	2333
10	Offenbach (Main) Hbf **921** d.	0529	0534	0638	0738	hourly	2138	2238	2338
23	Hanau Hbf **921** d.	0540	0544	0648	0748	until	2148	2248	2348
104	**Fulda** a.	0641	0644	0749	0849		2249	2349	0049

	ⒶB	†	⚒	ⒶB			❖			
Fulda d.	0400	0437	0507	0515	0600	0607	0707		2107	2207	2311
Hanau Hbf **921** d.	0500	0539	0609	0616	0655	0709	0809	and	2209	2309	0012
Offenbach (Main) Hbf **921** d.	0509	0548	0617	0624	|	0719	0817	hourly	2217	2317	0020
Frankfurt Main) Süd **921** d.	0515	0553	0623	0630	0710	0723	0823	until	2223	2323	0026
Frankfurt (Main) Hbf **921** a.	0520	0559	0628	0636	0716	0728	0828		2228	2328	0031

FULDA - KASSEL. Operated by CANTUS Verkehrsgesellschaft (except trains marked with note **B** and **E**). 2nd class only. Additional trains run Bad Hersfeld - Kassel and v.v.

km		Ⓐ		Ⓐ		Ⓐ												D	⑤⑦						E
0	**Fulda** d.	...	...	0548	0616	0644	0720	0820	0920	1020	1120	1220	1320	1420	1520	1620	1720	1820	1820	1920	2020	2122	2221	2309	2356
42	Bad Hersfeld d.	0505	...	0615	0644	0713	0748	0848	0948	1048	1148	1248	1348	1448	1548	1648	1748	1848	1848	1948	2048	2149	2249	2335	0027
56	Bebra a.	0515	....	0626	0654	0722	0758	0858	0959	1058	1158	1258	1358	1458	1558	1658	1758	1858	1858	1958	2058	2159	2258	2345	0041
56	Bebra d.	0518	0559	0627	0659	0727	0759	0859	1000	1059	1159	1259	1359	1459	1559	1659	1759	1859	1906	1959	2059	2200	2302	2348	...
62	Rotenburg (Fulda) d.	0524	0605	0633	0705	0733	0805	0905	1006	1105	1205	1305	1405	1505	1605	1705	1805	1905	1912	2005	2105	2206	2308	2354	...
84	Melsungen d.	0543	0624	0652	0724	0752	0824	0924	1024	1124	1224	1324	1424	1524	1624	1724	1824	1924	1930	2024	2124	2224	2326	0012	...
110	**Kassel** Wilhelmshöhe **804/6** d.	0609	0643	0713	0743	0814	0843	0943	1043	1143	1243	1343	1443	1543	1643	1743	1843	1943	1948	2043	2144	2252	2352	0037	...
114	**Kassel** Hbf **804/6** a.	0616	0647	0717	0748	0818	0847	0947	1047	1148	1248	1347	1447	1547	1647	1747	1848	1947	1954	2048	2148	2256	2356	0042	...

		ⒶB	Ⓐ	ⒶB	⚒◐	Ⓒ	Ⓐ																⑤⑥	
Kassel Hbf **804/6** d.	...	...	0355	...	0506	0606	0611	0711	0811v	0911	1011	1111	1211	1311	1411	1511	1611	1710	1811	1911	2011	2111	2211	2211	2311
Kassel Wilhelmshöhe **804/6** d.	...	...	0359	...	0510	0615	0618	0715	0815	0915	1015	1115	1215	1315	1415	1515	1615	1715	1815	1915	2015	2115	2216	2216	2316
Melsungen d.	...	...	0418	...	0528	0634	0635	0734	0834	0934	1034	1134	1234	1334	1434	1534	1634	1734	1834	1934	2034	2134	2234	2234	2334
Rotenburg (Fulda) d.	...	...	0437	...	0547	0653	0653	0753	0853	0953	1053	1153	1253	1353	1453	1553	1653	1753	1853	1953	2053	2153	2253	2253	2353
Bebra a.	...	...	0443	...	0554	0658	0659	0758	0859	0958	1058	1158	1258	1358	1459	1558	1658	1758	1858	1958	2058	2158	2258	2258	2358
Bebra d.	0314	0359	0446	0522	0559	0659	0701	0759	0859	0959	1059	1159	1259	1359	1459	1559	1659	1759	1859	1959	2059	2159	2259	2259	2359
Bad Hersfeld d.	0324	0409	0456	0531	0609	0709	0725b	0809	0909	1009	1109	1209	1309	1409	1509	1609	1709	1809	1909	2009	2109	2209	2309	2310	0011
Fulda a.	0353	0436	...	0558	0637	0737	0753	0837	0937	1037	1137	1237	1337	1437	1537	1637	1737	1837	1937	2037	2137	2237	...	2338	...

A – Continues to Bebra on ⑦–④; see lower panel.
B – 🚃(12) Bebra - Fulda - Frankfurt.
D – ①②③④⑥.
E – Starts from Frankfurt on ⑦–④; see upper panel.

b – Arrives 0711.
v – 0806 on †.

❖ – On Ⓐ the 0807 from Fulda runs 4 minutes later Offenbach - Frankfurt.
◐ – Runs daily Bebra - Fulda.

FRANKFURT - BRAUNSCHWEIG - BERLIN — 902

See Table **850** for additional services Frankfurt - Berlin and v.v. Independent operator **FlixTrain** also run services Stuttgart - Berlin and v.v. (see Table **927**).

km		ICE 649		ICE 1088	ICE 876	ICE 1598	ICE 998	ICE 270	ICE 1590	ICE 374	ICE 992	ICE 372	ICE 798	ICE 370	ICE 796	ICE 278	ICE 794	ICE 276	ICE 792	ICE 274		ICE 1690	ICE 292
		Ⓐ ✕		⚒ ✕	✕	Ⓐ ✕	①g ✕	✕	✕	✕	✕	L✕	✕	✕	✕	L✕	✕	✕	✕	✕		⊖ ✕	⑦w Z✕
	Basel SBB **912** d.	...	...	...	...	...	...	0412g	...	0606	...	0813	...	1013	...	1213	...	1413	...	1613	...		1813
	Karlsruhe Hbf **912** d.	...	...	...	...	...	...	0558	...	0800	...	1000	...	1200	...	1400	...	1600	...	1800	...		2000
	Stuttgart Hbf **912** d.	...	...	...	...	...	...	|	...	|	...	|	...	|	...	|	...	|	...	|	...	...	|
	Mannheim Hbf **912** d.	...	...	...	...	...	...	0632	...	0832	...	1032	...	1232	...	1432	...	1632	...	1832	...	...	2032
	Frankfurt Flughafen Fernbf ✈ d.	...	...	...	...	...	...	|	0809	|	1009	|	1209	|	1409	|	1609	|	1809	|	...	2009	|
0	**Frankfurt** (Main) Hbf **850 900** d.	...	...	0506	...	0558	...	0714	|	0914	|	1114	|	1314	|	1514	|	1714	|	1914	...	|	2114
4	**Frankfurt** (Main) Süd d.	...	...	|	...	|	...	|	0820	|	1020	|	1220	|	1420	|	1620	|	1820	|	...	2020	|
23	Hanau Hbf **850 900** d.	...	...	0521	...	|	...	0730	|	0930	1033	1130	1233	1330	1433	1530	1633	1730	1834	1930	...	2033	2130
104	Fulda **850 900** d.	...	...	0604	...	|	...	0812	0914	1012	1116	1212	1316	1412	1516	1612	1716	1812	1916	2012	...	2117	2212
194	**Kassel** Wilhelmshöhe **900** d.	...	...	0636	0643	|	0747	0845	0948	1045	1149	1245	1349	1445	1549	1645	1749	1845	1949	2045	...	2151	2245
239	Göttingen **900** d.	...	...	0654	0706	|	0809	0906	1008	1106	1209	1306	1409	1506	1609	1706	1809	1906	2009	2106	...	2210	2304
317	Hildesheim Hbf **863** d.	...	...	...	0736	|	0837	0936	1037	1136	1237	1336	1437	1536	1637	1736	1837	1936	2037	2136	...	2242	2333
360	**Braunschweig** Hbf **863** d.	0601	...	...	0801	|	0902	1001	1102	1201	1303	1401	1503	1601	1703	1801	1903	2001	2103	2201	...	2304	0001
392	Wolfsburg **810 863** d.	0619	...	...	0819	|	0919	1019	|	1219	|	1419	|	1619	|	1819	|	2019	2121	2219	...	2323	0018
559	**Berlin** Spandau **810** a.	0728	...	...	0914	0939	1014	1114	1214	1314	1414	1514	1614	1714	1814	1914	2014	2114	2217	2314	...	0029	0113
575	**Berlin** Hbf **850 810** a.	0747	...	...	0929	0957	1029	1129	1229	1329	1429	1529	1629	1729	1829	1929	2029	2129	2231	2329	...	0044	0127
580	**Berlin** Ostbahnhof **810** a.	0801	...	...	0940	1008	1039	1139	1240	1339	1439	1540	1639	1740	1839	1940	2039	2139	2241	2339t	...	0054	0138

	ICE 275		ICE 277	ICE 791	ICE 279	ICE 793	ICE 371	ICE 795	ICE 373	ICE 797	ICE 1091	ICE 1091	ICE 375	ICE 1699	ICE 377	ICE 995	ICE 877	ICE 877	ICE 997	ICE 887	ICE 1087		ICE 879
	Ⓐ L✕		✕	✕	✕	✕	L✕	✕	L✕	✕	⑤ ✕	⑦w ✕	✕	✕	✕	✕	✕	⑥k ✕	✕	⑧b J✕	⑥ J✕		⑦w ✕
Berlin Ostbahnhof **810** d.	0414	...	0614	0718	0814	0917	1017	1115	1214	1317	1345	1345	1414	1514	1614	1714	1814	1814	1917	...	...	...	2017
Berlin Hbf **850 810** d.	0429	...	0629	0733	0829	0931	1029	1130	1229	1329	1359	1359	1429	1529	1629	1729	1829	1829	1931	...	...	...	2029
Berlin Spandau **810** d.	0444	...	0644	0748	0844	0947	1044	1144	1244	1347	1413	1413	1444	1545	1644	1746	1844	1844	1946	...	...	...	2044
Wolfsburg **810 863** d.	0538	...	0738	|	0938	|	1138	|	1338	|	1510	1510	1538	|	1738	|	1938	1938	2042	...	...	...	2138
Braunschweig Hbf **863** d.	0557	...	0757	0859	0957	1059	1157	1259	1357	1459	⊙	⊙	1557	1659	1757	1859	1957	1957	2059	...	...	...	2157
Hildesheim Hbf **863** d.	0619	...	0819	0921	1019	1121	1219	1321	1419	1521	|	|	1619	1721	1819	1921	2019	2019	2121	...	...	...	2219
Göttingen **900** d.	0652	...	0852	0952	1052	1152	1252	1352	1452	1552	1631	1631	1652	1754	1852	1952	2052	2052	2152	2202	2213	...	2252
Kassel Wilhelmshöhe **900** d.	0714	...	0914	1014	1114	1214	1314	1414	1514	1614	1654	1654	1714	1816	1914	2015	2114	2114	2212	2223	2235	...	2314
Fulda **850 900** d.	0747	...	0947	1046	1147	1246	1347	1446	1547	1646	1729	1729	1747	1847	1947	2047	2147	2147	...	2257	2308	...	2347
Hanau Hbf **850 900** d.	0828	...	1027	1124	1227	1325	1427	1525	1627	1724	|	|	1827	|	2027	|	2227	2227	...	2336	2348	...	0028
Frankfurt (Main) Süd a.	|	...	|	1139	|	1339	|	1539	|	1739	|	|	|	1939	|	|	|	|	...	|	|	...	|
Frankfurt (Main) Hbf **850 900** a.	0844	...	1044	|	1244	|	1444	|	1644	|	1831	1831	1844	|	2044	2140	2244	2244	...	2353	0007	...	0044
Frankfurt Flughafen Fernbf ✈ a.	|	...	|	1151	|	1351	|	1551	|	1751	...	|	|	1951	|	...	...	2318	...	0026	0026	...	|
Mannheim Hbf **912** a.	0927	...	1127	...	1327	...	1527	...	1727	...	...	1916	1927	...	2127	...	...	0006	...	...	...	...	0127
Stuttgart Hbf **912** a.	|	...	|	...	|	...	|	...	|	...	...	1958	|	...	|	...	...	|	...	...	...	...	|
Karlsruhe Hbf **912** a.	0958	...	1158	...	1358	...	1558	...	1758	...	...	...	1959	...	2158	...	...	0037	...	...	...	...	0155
Basel SBB **912** a.	1147	...	1347	...	1547	...	1747	...	1947	...	...	...	2149	...	2359	...	...	...	...	...	...	...	...

J – To Wiesbaden (Table **850**).
L – From/to Interlaken via Bern (Table **560**).
Z – From Chur via Zürich (Tables **520** and **510**).

b – Not Dec. 25.
g – ① (also Dec. 27; not Dec. 26). Basel **Badischer Bahnhof**.

k – Also Dec. 25.
t – ③–⑦.
w – Also Dec. 26; not Dec. 25.

⊖ – Also calls at Stendal (a. 2352).
⊙ – Via Hannover Hbf (a. 1544, d. 1551).

metronom

Local services GÖTTINGEN - HANNOVER - UELZEN - HAMBURG — 903

Services below are operated by ***metronom*** (except trains **A**, **B** and **C**). For faster *ICE* and *IC* services see Table **900**.

km																											
			⚒		⊖	Ⓐ A✕		Ⓐ B✕	Ⓒ	Ⓐ																	
0	**Göttingen** d.	...	0408	...	0504	0546	0604	0645	0704	0707	0809	0904	1009	1104	1209	1304	1407r	1504	1609	1704	1809	1904	...	2009	2104	2209	2311t
20	Northeim (Han) d.	...	0421	...	0517	0600	0617	0658	0717	0720	0823	0917	1023	1117	1223	1317	1421r	1517	1623	1717	1823	1917	...	2023	2117	2223	2324t
39	Kreiensen d.	...	0435	...	0531	0616	0631	0712	0731	0733	0837	0931	1037	1131	1237	1331	1437	1531	1637	1733q	1837	1931	...	2037	2131	2237	2338
58	Alfeld (Leine) d.	...	0448	...	0544	0629	0644	0725	0744	0746	0850	0944	1050	1144	1250	1344	1450	1544	1650	1746q	1850	1944	...	2050	2144	2250	2351
75	Elze (Han) d.	...	0503	...	0558	0640	0659	0736	0759	0759	0903	0959	1103	1159	1303	1359	1503	1559	1703	1759	1903	1959	...	2103	2159	2303	0003
108	**Hannover** Hbf. a.	...	0526	...	0624	0657	0723	0756	0823	0823	0926	1023	1126	1223	1326	1423	1526	1623	1726	1823	1926	2023	...	2126	2223	2326	0027
			▽		|	|	▽	|	|	|	▽	|	▽	|	▽	|	▽	|	▽	|	▽	|		▽	|	▽ ⊙	|
			Ⓐ	⑥																							
108	**Hannover** Hbf. d.	...	0540	0540	0640	0701	0740	0759	0840	0840	0940	1040	1140	1240	1340	1440	1540	1640	1740	1840	1940	2040	...	2140	2248	2340	0040
149	Celle d.	...	0608	0608	0708	0720	0808	0818	0908	0908	1008	1108	1208	1308	1408	1508	1608	1708	1808	1908	2008	2108	...	2208	2316	0008	0106
201	**Uelzen** a.	...	0639	0639	0739	0740	0839	0840	0939	0939	1039	1139	1239	1338	1439	1539	1639	1738	1839	1939	2039	2139	...	2239	2347	0039	0138
			|	|	▬	|	▬	|	▬	▽	|	▽	|	▽	|	▽	|	▽	|	▽	|	▽		|	▽		
																						⚒	†		D		
201	**Uelzen** d.	0605	0647	0704	0704	0742	0801	0842	0901	1001	1101	1201	1301	1401	1501	1601	1701	1801	1901	2001	2101	2201	2201	2306	2359	...	...
214	Bad Bevensen d.	0614	0655	0713	0713	|	0809	0849	0910	1009	1109	1209	1309	1409	1509	1609	1709	1809	1909	2009	2109	2209	2209	2314	0007	...	...
237	Lüneburg d.	0629	0709	0727	0727	0758	0828	0902	0928	1028	1130j	1228	1328	1428	1528	1628	1728	1828	1928	2031j	2128	2228	2232j	2338k	0021	...	...
256	Winsen (Luhe) d.	0640	0720	0739	0739	|	0839	|	0939	1039	1141	1239	1339	1439	1539	1639	1739	1839	1939	2042	2139	2239	2248	2354	0036	...	...
274	Hamburg Har ¶ a.	0651	0730	0752	0752	0816g	0850	0921	0951	1051	1152	1251	1351	1451	1551	1651	1751	1852	1951	2053	2151	2250	2309	0016	0057	...	...
286	**Hamburg** Hbf a.	0703	...	0803	0803	0829g	0903	0932	1003	1103	1204	1303	1403	1503	1603	1703	1803	1903	2003	2104	2203	2302	2321	0027	0109	...	...

					Ⓐ	Ⓐ	Ⓒ									①–④ C✕										⑤⑥ f	
Hamburg Hbf d.	...	...	...	...	0433	0542	0558	0651	0757	0857	0957	1057	1157	1257	1357	1511g	1457	1557	1657	1757	1857	1957	2057	2157	2234	2234	2333
Hamburg Har ¶ d.	...	...	...	...	0445	0553	0611	0702	0808	0908	1008	1108	1208	1308	1409	1528g	1508	1608	1708	1808	1908	2008	2107	2212	2245	2245	2345
Winsen (Luhe) d.	...	...	...	...	0506	0604	0623	0713	0820	0920	1020	1120	1220	1320	1421	1540g	1520	1620	1720	1820	1920	2020	2119	2223	2306	2306	0006
Lüneburg d.	...	...	...	...	0532k	0615	0634	0724	0834	0934	1034	1134	1234	1332	1434	1558	1534	1634	1734	1834	1934	2034	2130	2234	2324	2324	0023
Bad Bevensen d.	...	...	...	...	0549	0630	0648	0742	0848	0948	1048	1148	1248	1347	1448b	1609	1548	1648	1748	1848	1948	2048	2145	2249	2338	2338	0037
Uelzen a.	...	...	...	...	0559	0638	0656	0750	0856	0956	1056	1156	1256	1355	1456b	1617	1556	1656	1756	1856	1956	2056	2153	2256	2346	2346	0045
					▽	▽	▽	|	▽	|	▽	|	▽	|	▽	|		▽	|	▽	|	▽	|	▽	▬	|	
		Ⓐ	Ⓒ	Ⓐ	d	Ⓐ	Ⓒ																	⑤⑥ f			
Uelzen d.	...	0412	0513	0513	0609	0651	0709	0809	0909	1009	1109	1209	1309	1409	1509	1619	1609	1709	1809	1909	2009	2114	2209	2309	2309	2351	...
Celle d.	...	0446	0547	0547	0647	0747v	0747	0848	0947	1048	1147	1247	1347	1447	1547	1640	1647	1747	1847	1947	2048	2147	2247	2349	2349	0028	...
Hannover Hbf a.	...	0514	0615	0615	0715	0815	0815	0915	1015	1115	1215	1315	1415	1515	1615	1700	1715	1815	1915	2015	2115	2215	2315	0017	0017	0057	...
		▽	|	|	▽	|	|	▽	|	▽	|	▽	|	▽	|	|	▽ ⊡	|	▽	|	▽	|	▽	|			
	Ⓐ	⚒																									
Hannover Hbf d.	0432	0536	0633	0634	0736	0833	0833	0936	1033	1136	1233	1336	1433	1536	1633	1703	1736	1833	1936	2033	2136p	2236	2336	0038	...	...	...
Elze (Han) d.	0455	0558	0655	0658	0800	0855	0855	1000	1055	1200	1255	1400	1455	1600	1655	1722	1758	1855	2000	2055	2200	2258	2358	0100	...	...	...
Alfeld (Leine) d.	0507	0610	0706	0710	0812	0906	0906	1012	1106	1212	1306	1412	1506	1612	1706	1733	1810	1906	2012	2106	2212	2309	0010	0112	...	...	...
Kreiensen d.	0520	0624	0719	0723	0825	0919	0919	1025	1119	1225	1319	1425	1519	1625	1719	1746	1823	1919	2025	2119	2225	2322	0023	0125	...	...	...
Northeim (Han) d.	0533	0637	0733	0736	0838	0933	0933	1038	1133	1238	1333	1438	1533	1638	1733	1759	1836	1933	2038	2133	2238	2336	0036	0138	...	...	...
Göttingen a.	0546	0650	0746	0749	0851	0946	0946	1051	1146	1251	1346	1451	1546	1651	1746	1814	1849	1946	2051	2146	2251	2349	0049	0153	...	...	...

A – *ICE* **1686**. Operated by DB. Subject to alteration from Apr. 1.
B – *ICE* **1676**. Operated by DB. 12 (Frankfurt ① **m** -) Kassel - Hamburg - Rostock - Stralsund. Subject to alteration from Apr. 1.
C – ①–④ (not Dec. 26). *ICE* **1585**. Operated by DB. Subject to alteration from Apr. 1.
D – ①–⑥ (also Apr. 9, 30, May 28; not Apr. 10, May 1, 18, 29).

b – 3 minutes later on ⑤ (also Apr. 6, May 17; not Apr. 7, May 19).
d – Daily.

f – Also Apr. 6, 9, 30, May 17, 28.
g – ① only.
j – Arrives 6–8 minutes earlier.
k – Arrives 9–11 minutes earlier.
m – Also Dec. 27; not Dec. 26.
p – 2134 on ⑥.
q – 2 minutes **earlier** on ©.
r – 2 minutes later on ©.

t – 2 minutes **earlier** on †.
v – Arrives 0728.

¶ – Hamburg **Harburg**.
⊖ – Timings Göttingen - Elze are 2–4 minutes later on †.
⊡ – Timings Elze - Göttingen are 2 minutes later on ©.
⊙ – Runs 8 minutes later on ©.
▽ – Change trains.

904 MÜNCHEN - INGOLSTADT - NÜRNBERG

km	Most *ICE* trains convey ✕	*ICE* 888	*ICE* 822	*ICE* 684	*ICE* 1008	*ICE* 820	*ICE* 886	*ICE* 728	*ICE* 602	*ICE* 682	*ICE* 726	*ICE* 1006	*ICE* 882	*ICE* 724	*ICE* 1600	*ICE* 680	*ICE* 722	*ICE* 800	*ICE* 880	*ICE* 720	*ICE* 508	*ICE* 588	*ICE* 628	*ICE* 1004	*ICE* 788	*ICE* 626	*ICE* 506
		Ⓐ	⚒		r	①–⑥																		r			
			K			BK		K		D	K		L	K			K			K			K			K	
0	**München** Hbf ... d.	0413	0449	0511	0553	0553	0614	0648	0656	0718	0747	0755	0820	0848	0855	0918	0951	0955	1021	1051	1055	1118	1151	1156	1221	1250	1255
81	**Ingolstadt** Hbf ... d.	0451	0527	0557	|	|	0654	0726	|	0758	0825	|	0900	0925	|	0958	|	1032	1100	|	|	1158	|	|	1300	|	|
171	**Nürnberg** Hbf ... a.	0522	0557	0629	0655	0656	0725	0756	0801	0829	0854	0859	0930	0955	1002	1029	1055	1102	1130	1155	1201	1230	1254	1258	1330	1354	1400
	Würzburg Hbf **900 920** . a.	0625	0652	0724	|	0753	0825	0852	|	0925	0952	|	1025	1052	|	1125	1152	|	1225	1251	|	1325	1352	|	1425	1452	|
	Frankfurt (Main) Hbf **920** a.	|	0804	|	|	0904	|	1004	|	|	1104	|	|	1204	|	|	1304	|	|	1404	|	|	1504	|	|	1604	|
	Leipzig Hbf **850** ... a.	|	...	|	|	...	|	...	1010	|	...	|	|	...	1210	|	...	|	|	...	1410	|	...	|	|	...	1610
	Berlin Hbf **850** ... a.	|	...	|	0953	...	|	...	1131	|	...	1153	|	...	1329	|	...	1422	|	...	1529	|	...	1553	|	...	1731
	Hamburg Hbf **840 900** .. a.	0954	...	1055	1151	...	1158	...	1324	1255	...	1351	1354	...	1524	1455	...	1621	1555	...	1724	1655	...	1757	1755	...	1924

Most *ICE* trains convey ✕	*ICE* 586	*ICE* 624	*ICE* 706	*ICE* 786	*ICE* 622	*ICE* 504	*ICE* 584	*ICE* 620	*ICE* 1002	*ICE* 1222	*ICE* 1204	*ICE* 528	*ICE* 502	*ICE* 582	*ICE* 526	*ICE* 1000	*ICE* 782	*ICE* 524	*ICE* 500	*ICE* 580	*ICE* 580	*ICE* 522	*ICE* 1100	*ICE* 780	*ICE* 520	*ICE* 926	*ICE* 1688
											Ⓐ				B	r				Ⓑ	⑦w			⑦w		⑦w	
		K			K		D	K		K		GK			K			K		R		K		R			
München Hbf ... d.	1318	1351	1354	1421	1451	1456	1518	1551	1556	1618	1618	1649	1655	1717	1752	1754	1819	1851	1856	1919	1919	1948	1956	2021	2054	2154	2300
Ingolstadt Hbf ... d.	1358	|	1431	1500	|	|	1558	|	|	1700	1700	1726	|	1757	|	|	1900	|	|	1958	1958	2025	|	2100	2131	2233	2337
Nürnberg Hbf ... a.	1431	1455	1502	1531	1555	1601	1630	1654	1658	1733	1733	1756	1801	1829	1856	1856	1931	1955	2001	2029	2029	2054	2058	2131	2200	2301	0013
Würzburg Hbf **900 920** .. a.	1525	1552	|	1625	1652	|	1726	1752	|	1827	1827	1852	|	1925	1953	|	2025	2052	|	2124	2124	2152	|	2225	2255	2357	0116
Frankfurt (Main) Hbf **920**. a.	|	1704	|	|	1804	|	|	1904	|	1936	|	2004	|	|	2104	|	|	2204	|	...	|	2304	|	...	0004	...	|
Leipzig Hbf **850** ... a.	|	...	|	|	...	1810	|	...	|	...	|	...	2010	|	...	|	|	...	2210	...	|	...	|	...	...	...	|
Berlin Hbf **850** ... a.	|	...	1822	|	...	1931	|	...	1953	...	|	...	2129	|	...	2153	|	...	2336	...	|	...	2350	...	...	...	|
Hamburg Hbf **840 900** ... a.	1855	...	2023	1955	...	2125	2059	...	2155	...	2229	...	2334	2255	...	...	0006	...	...	...	0116	...	...	...	...	...	0642

Most *ICE* trains convey ✕	*ICE* 1689	*ICE* 825	*ICE* 985	*ICE* 827	*ICE* 1501	*ICE* 521	*ICE* 501	*ICE* 781	*ICE* 1001	*ICE* 523	*ICE* 581	*ICE* 503	*ICE* 525	*ICE* 783	*ICE* 1003	*ICE* 527	*ICE* 583	*ICE* 505	*ICE* 529	*ICE* 1621	*ICE* 703	*ICE* 621	*ICE* 585	*ICE* 507	*ICE* 623	*ICE* 787	*ICE* 1005
		①–⑤	Ⓐ	⚒	Ⓐt		⚒	⚒	r		①–⑥								u								r
		m	t	K	E	K		N		K	p		K			K			KG	K		K	D		K		
Hamburg Hbf **840 900** ... d.	2228	...	...	...	...	...	...	0349g	...	...	0454	...	...	0554	0552	...	0701	0634e	...	...	0735	...	0901	0834	...	1001	1005
Berlin Hbf **850** ... d.	|	...	...	...	...	...	0428	|	0600	...	|	0629	...	|	0804	...	|	0829	...	...	0934	...	|	1029	...	|	1204
Leipzig Hbf **850** ... d.	|	...	...	...	...	...	0548	|	|	...	|	0748	...	|	|	...	|	0948	...	...	|	...	|	1148	...	|	|
Frankfurt (Main) Hbf **920**. d.	|	...	...	0453	...	0553	|	|	|	0653	|	|	0753	|	|	0853	|	|	0953	1022	|	1053	|	|	1153	|	|
Würzburg Hbf **900 920** .. d.	0354	...	...	0604	...	0705	|	0730	|	0804	0832	|	0904	0931	|	1004	1032	|	1104	1131	|	1204	1232	|	1313	1330	|
Nürnberg Hbf ... d.	0452	0556	0630	0701	0728	0802	0812	0827	0859	0904	0930‡	0956	1002	1027	1059	1104	1128	1156	1202	1227	1253	1302	1328	1356	1407	1427	1459
Ingolstadt Hbf ... d.	0525	0626	0703	0729	0803	|	|	0901	|	|	1005‡	|	1032	1101	|	|	1201	|	|	1301	1324	|	1401	|	|	1501	|
München Hbf ... a.	0604	0704	0740	0806	0841	0906	0917	0939	1002	1006	1043	1102	1110	1141	1202	1206	1238	1302	1306	1338	1402	1406	1441	1503	1509	1541	1601

Most *ICE* trains convey ✕	*ICE* 625	*ICE* 587	*ICE* 509	*ICE* 627	*ICE* 789	*ICE* 707	*ICE* 629	*ICE* 689	*ICE* 1601	*ICE* 721	*ICE* 881	*ICE* 1007	*ICE* 723	*ICE* 681	*ICE* 603	*ICE* 725	*ICE* 883	*ICE* 1009	*ICE* 727	*ICE* 683	*ICE* 1605 1715	*ICE* 729	*ICE* 885	*ICE* 1109	*ICE* 821	*ICE* 685	*ICE* 1607
																		r								⑤–⑦	⑤
	K			K			K			K			K	D		K			K		O	K	L		K	y	
Hamburg Hbf **840 900** ... d.	...	1101	1034	...	1201	1136	...	1301	1234	...	1401	1404	...	1501	1435	...	1601	1551	...	1701	1634h	...	1801	...	...	1901	1835
Berlin Hbf **850** ... d.	...	|	1229	...	|	1334	...	|	1429	...	|	1604	...	|	1629	...	|	1804	...	|	1829	...	|	2004	...	|	2029
Leipzig Hbf **850** ... d.	...	|	1348	...	|	|	...	|	1548	...	|	|	...	|	1748	...	|	|	...	|	1948	...	|	|	...	|	2148
Frankfurt (Main) Hbf **920**. d.	1253	|	|	1353	|	|	1453	|	|	1553	|	|	1653	|	|	1753	|	|	1853	|	|	1953	|	|	2053	|	|
Würzburg Hbf **900 920** .. d.	1404	1432	|	1504	1530	|	1604	1632	|	1704	1731	|	1804	1832	|	1904	1930	|	2004	2031	|	2104	2130	|	2204	2231	|
Nürnberg Hbf ... d.	1504	1528	1555	1602	1627	1655	1702	1728	1756	1802	1827	1859	1903	1925	1955	2002	2027	2059	2104	2128	2155	2203	2228	2259	2313	2331	0001
Ingolstadt Hbf ... d.	|	1601	|	|	1701	1726	|	1802	|	1833	1902	|	|	2003	|	2032	2101	|	|	2201	|	2233	2301	|	2341	0004	0034
München Hbf ... a.	1606	1641	1701	1706	1739	1803	1807	1839	1903	1911	1941	2002	2007	2043	2103	2111	2141	2201	2206	2239	2303	2311	2340	0001	0019	0043	0114

RE services via the high-speed line

km																												
			⑥		Ⓐt	Ⓒz		Ⓒz	Ⓐt		Ⓐt	Ⓒz			S		S	Y	Ⓒz	Ⓐt	T	⑤⑥t		T	⑤⑥t		⑤⑥t	T
0	**München** Hbf ... d.	0501	...	0704	0803	0804	0904	1003	1003	1103	1201	1204	1304	1404	1404	1504	1604	1622	1704	1711	*1801*	1805	1905	*2003*	2005	2105	2227	*2227*
50	Pfaffenhofen (Ilm) ... d.	0531	...	0732	0832	0831	0931	1031	1031	1131	1232	1232	1331	1432	1432	1531	1632	1646	1731	1743	*1831*	1832	1932	*2034*	2032	2132	2301	*2301*
81	**Ingolstadt** Hbf ... a.	0551	...	0752	0852	0851	0951	1051	1053	1151	1252	1251	1351	1451	1451	1551	1651	1705	1751	1802	*1852*	1852	1951	*2055*	2052	2151	2322	*2322*
81	**Ingolstadt** Hbf ... d.	0601	0704	0802	...	0904	1004	1104	...	1204	...	1304	1404	...	1504	1604	1704	1707	1802	1803	1904	1904	2001	2104	2104	2157	2324	2330
112	Kinding ... d.	0622	0720	0818	...	0920	1020	1120	...	1220	...	1320	1420	...	1520	1620	1720	1723	1823	1823	1920	1920	2018	2120	2120	2213	2340	2351
146	Allersberg ... d.	0637	0735	0833	...	0935	1035	1135	...	1235	...	1335	1435	...	1535	1635	1735	1738	1838	1838	1935	1935	2033	2135	2135	2228	2355	0007
171	**Nürnberg Hbf** ... a.	0651	0749	0847	...	0949	1049	1149	...	1249	...	1349	1449	...	1549	1649	1749	1752	1853	1853	1949	1949	2047	2149	2149	2241	0008	0021

	Ⓐt	Ⓐt	†v	⑥	Ⓒz	Ⓐt	⑥	Ⓒz	Ⓐt	Ⓒz		Ⓒz		Ⓒz		S		⑥	⑤t	†v	Y		⑤⑥t	T		⑤⑥t	T	⑤⑥f
Nürnberg Hbf ... d.	0508	0608	0607	0607	0711	0732	0816	0909	0909	1009	1108	1207	1309	1400	1509	1609	1710	1806	1808	1806	1808	1908	2006	2006	2108	2233	2233	2337
Allersberg ... d.	0522	0621	0620	0620	0724	0745	0829	0923	0923	1022	1122	1220	1323	1417	1522	1622	1724	1819	1821	1819	1821	1922	2019	2019	2121	2246	2246	2350
Kinding ... d.	0538	0636	0636	0636	0740	0801	0849	0938	0939	1038	1137	1236	1338	1433	1538	1638	1739	1835	1837	1835	1837	1938	2035	2035	2137	2301	2301	0005
Ingolstadt Hbf ... a.	0555	0654	0654	0654	0758	0817	0907	0956	1000	1055	1155	1253	1356	1451	1556	1657	1757	1852	1857	1852	1857	2000	2052	2054	2155	2319	2319	0023
Ingolstadt Hbf ... d.	0600	0656	0701	*0705*	0806	0819	0908	1004	1008	1105	1205	1305	1404	1505	1605	1705	1805	1906	1906	*1907*	*1907*	2008	2105	*2105*	2205	2336	*2334*	0024
Pfaffenhofen (Ilm) ... d.	0619	0711	0720	*0726*	0828	0837	0927	1025	1029	1126	1226	1326	1426	1526	1626	1726	1826	1927	1927	*1928*	*1928*	2029	2126	*2127*	2226	0004	*0004*	0042
München Hbf ... a.	0647	0735	0748	*0754*	0852	0902	0953	1054	1058	1154	1254	1356	1454	1554	1655	1754	1854	1955	1955	*1958*	*1958*	2057	2153	*2158*	2254	0039	*0040*	0110

RE services via EICHSTÄTT and TREUCHTLINGEN

km																												
		Ⓒz	⑥	Ⓐt	Ⓐt		Ⓐt														Ⓐ	Ⓒ		T	⑤⑥t		
0	**München** Hbf ... d.	...	...	...	0519	...	0600	0618	0725	0825	0927	1027	1127	1226	1324	1426	1527	1627	1722	1827	1924	2022j	2027	2131	2227	2227	2325	0030
50	Pfaffenhofen (Ilm) ... d.	...	0500	0500	0601	...	0628	0653	0801	0900	1003	1102	1202	1302	1359	1501	1601	1702	1802	1902	1959	2101j	2102	2206	2301	2301	0002	0106
81	**Ingolstadt** Hbf ... a.	...	0523	0521	0624	...	0647	0716	0822	0921	1025	1125	1224	1324	1422	1523	1623	1723	1824	1924	2020	2124j	2124	2227	2322	2322	0026	0127
81	**Ingolstadt** Hbf ... d.	0524	0524	0523	0627	0627	0650	0730	0830	0930	1027	1129	1226	1326	1429	1526	1628	1727	1826	1926	2030	2130	2130	2230	2323	*2344*	...	...
108	Eichstätt Bahnhof ♥ d.	0556	0556	0556	0656	0656	0710	0758	0857	0957	1056	1157	1256	1356	1457	1557	1657	1757	1857	1953	2057	2156	2156	2257	2349	*0010*	...	...
137	Treuchtlingen ... a.	0620	0620	0620	0719	0719	...	0820	0919	1020	1119	1220	1319	1420	1519	1620	1720	1821	1919	2016	2119	2219	2219	2320	0012	*0034*	...	...
137	Treuchtlingen ... **905** d.	0626v	*0626*	0638	0725	0725	...	*0828*	0925	*1028*	1125	*1228*c	1325	*1428*	1525	*1628*	1728	*1829*	1925	*2029*	2125	*2225*	*2225*	2325	...	...	...	...
146	Weißenburg ... **905** d.	0632v	*0633*	0644	0731	0731	...	*0834*	0931	*1034*	1131	*1234*c	1331	*1434*	1531	*1635*	1734	*1835*	1931	*2036*	2131	*2231*	*2231*	2331	...	...	...	...
199	**Nürnberg** Hbf.. **905** a.	0715v	*0715*	0724	0815	0815	...	*0916*	1015	*1116*	1215	*1316*c	1416	*1516*	1615	*1717*	1816	*1918*	2015	*2118*	2214	*2313*	*2313*	0015	...	...	...	...

	Ⓐt	Ⓒz	⚒t	†v	Ⓐt	Ⓒz	Ⓐt	Ⓒ	Ⓐt					Ⓒz	Ⓐt										T	⑤⑥t		
Nürnberg Hbf... **905** d.	...	...	*0433*	0436	0526	0539	...	*0636*	0630	0738	*0838*	0939	*1039*	1139	1139	*1238*	1339	*1438*	1539	*1639*	1739	*1838*	1937	*2039*	2138	2138	2245	2344
Weißenburg ... **905** d.	...	...	*0518*	0523	0608	0621	...	*0718*	0712	0821	*0920*	1021	*1120*	1221	1221	*1320*	1421	*1520*	1621	*1720*	1821	*1920*	2019	*2120*	2221	2221	2327	0025
Treuchtlingen ... **905** a.	...	...	*0525*	0530	0616	0628	...	*0723*	0720	0827	*0927*	1027	*1127*	1227	1227	*1327*	1427	*1527*	1627	*1727*	1830	*1927*	2025	*2127*	2230	2230	2334	0031
Treuchtlingen ... d.	0443	...	0532	0532	0632	0632	...	0735	0735	0835	0935	1035	1135	1235	1240	1336	1435	1535	1635	1735	1835	1935	2035	2135	2235	2235	2337	...
Eichstätt Bahnhof ♥. d.	0507	...	0556	0556	0655	0655	0720	0759	0759	0900	0959	1058	1159	1258	1303	1400	1458	1559	1658	1759	1858	1959	2058	2159	2258	2258	2359	...
Ingolstadt Hbf ... a.	0532	...	0621	0621	0721	0721	0745	0825	0825	0935	1035	1135	1235	1328	1335	1430	1535	1634	1735	1837	1930	2035	2135	2224	2329	2329	0027	...
Ingolstadt Hbf ... d.	0534	0538	0630	0630	0734	0734	0749	0831	0831	0937	1036	1137	1237	1334	1338	1436	1537	1635	1736	1838	1934	2036	2137	2237	2334	*2336*	...	...
Pfaffenhofen (Ilm) ... d.	0555	0559	0654	0654	0758	0758	0810	0854*	0900	1002	1059	1157	1258	1357	1401	1500	1600	1658	1759	1901	2003	2100	2158	2300	0004	*0004*	...	...
München Hbf ... a.	0630	0634	0731x	0734	0833	0834	0837	0933*	0935	1038	1135	1233	1334	1433	1437	1535	1636	1734	1834	1936	2039	2137	2234	2336	0040	*0039*	...	...

B – From Feb. 11.
D – To/from Lübeck (Table **825**).
E – From Lichtenfels (Table **850/875**).
G – From/to Garmisch on ⑥ (Table **895**).
K – To/from Köln, Essen or Dortmund (Table **910**).
L – To/from Kiel (Table **820**).
N – From Kassel (also Hamburg on ① g). See Table **900**.
O – From Ostseebad Binz on ⑥ (Tables **844** and **845**).
R – To Kassel (Table **900**).
S – ⑤⑥†.
T – ⑦–④ (also Jan. 6).
Y – ①–④ (not Dec. 26).

c – On Ⓐ (not Jan. 6) Treuchtlingen d. *1238*, Weißenburg d. *1245*, Nürnberg a. *1329*.
e – ⚒ only.
f – Also Dec. 25, Jan. 5.
g – ① (also Dec. 27; not Dec. 26).
j – Feb. 10 - Mar. 30 departs München 2025, Pfaffenhofen 2107, arrives Ingolstadt 2128.
m – Not Dec. 26 - Jan. 6.
p – Also Dec. 25; not Dec. 26.
r – Not Feb. 11 - Mar. 31.
t – Not Jan. 6.
u – Not Dec. 25.

v – † (also Jan. 6).
w – Also Dec. 26; not Dec. 25.
x – 0734 on ⑥.
y – Also Dec. 26, Jan. 5.
z – Also Jan. 6.

* – On ⑥ Pfaffenhofen d. 0900, München a. 0935.
‡ – On ⑥ (also Dec. 25) Nürnberg d. 0928, Ingolstadt d. 1001.
♥ – Connecting trains run Eichstätt Bahnhof - Eichstätt Stadt (*5 km*; operated by Bayerische Regiobahn).

MÜNCHEN - AUGSBURG - NÜRNBERG and WÜRZBURG 905

ICE / IC services. See Table **904** for services via Ingolstadt. See Table **905a** for local trains Treuchtlingen - Würzburg.

	ICE		ICE	ICE	ICE	ICE		ICE	ICE	ICE	IC	ICE	ICE	ICE	ICE	ICE	ICE	ICE	ICE	IC	ICE	ICE	ICE	ICE
	804		**802**	**1908**	**1586**	**1706**		**708**	**1906**	**708**	**2082**	**1092**	**1206**	**1284**	**1904**	**704**	**1204**	**1502**	**702**	**1902**	**702**	**1500**	**1500**	**600**
	Ⓐ				Ⓑ								⑥	⑤†			⑦	①-④				Ⓑ	①-⑤	⑦
	t		d	R	b	d		d	R	R	K	d	G⊙	F⊙	R	d	G	m	d	R	R	QL	PL	PL
	✕		✕		✕	✕		✕		✕	🍷	✕	✕	✕		✕	✕	✕	✕		✕	✕	✕	✕
München Ost ... d.	...	...	...	...	...	...	...	...	...	...	1117	...	...	1338c	...	...	...	...	...	...	...	...	...	...
München Hbf ... 930 d.	0506	...	0713	0713	0816	0839	...	1114	1114	1156	|	1241	1356	1357	1513	1514	1552	1608	1709	1709	1756	1910	2020	2050
München Pasing ... 930 d.	0515	...	0722	0722	|	0848	...	1123	1123	|	1130	|	|	|	1522	1523	1601	1617	1718	1718	|	1919	|	|
Augsburg Hbf ... 900 930 d.	0538	...	0746	0748	0847	0913	...	1146	1147	|	1230h	1312	1425	1425	1546	1546	1624	1643	1741	1742	|	1943	|	|
Donauwörth ... d.	0602	...	0808	0808	|	0933	...	1208	1208	|	1251	1331	1444	1445	1608	1608	1646	1704	1803	1804	|	2007	|	|
Treuchtlingen ... 905a d.	0622	...	|	|	|	|	...	|	|	|	1312	|	1505	1507	|	|	1707	1725	1824	1825	|	2026	|	|
Nürnberg Hbf ... 900 920 a.	0657	...	0859	0859	|	1026	...	1258	1300	1302	|	1421	|	|	1702	1659	|	1759	1859	1904	1903	2059	2131	2155
Berlin Hbf **850** ... a.	1022	...	1222	...	|	1353	...	1622	...	1622	|	1753	|	|	...	2022	|	...	2222	...	2222	...	...	...
Ansbach ... 905a d.	|	...	|	...	0948	|	...	|	...	|	1344	...	1534	1534	...	|	1741	...	...	...	...	...	...	...
Steinach (b. Rothenb) ... 905a d.	|	...	|	...	|	|	...	|	...	|	1403	...	|	|	...	|	|	...	...	...	...	...	...	...
Würzburg Hbf . 900 905a 920 a.	|	...	|	...	1038	|	...	|	...	|	1437	...	1629	1629	...	|	1831	...	...	...	...	...	...	...
Hamburg Hbf **840 900** ... a.	1221	...	1422	...	1429	1600	...	1822	...	1822	1829	...	2030	2038	...	2222	2229	...	...	...	...	...	...	...

	ICE	ICE	ICE		ICE		ICE	ICE	IC	ICE	IC	ICE		ICE	ICE	ICE	ICE	ICE	ICE	ICE	ICE		ICE	ICE
	981	**987**	**989**		**1701**		**1901**	**701**	**2083**	**1207**	**1903**	**1093**		**705**	**705**	**1285**	**1907**	**1707**	**1587**	**1909**	**709**		**801**	**801**
	Ⓐ	Ⓐ	Ⓐ		Ⓐ					⑥						Ⓑ			Ⓑ					
	s	t	t				R	d	K	G	R	d		R	d	E	R	d	b	R	d		R	d
	✕	✕	✕		✕			✕	🍷	✕		✕		✕	✕	✕		✕	J✕		✕		✕	✕
Hamburg Hbf **840 900** ... d.	...	...	...	...	...	...	...	0527a	0728	0828	...	...	...	0936	0936	1128	...	1203	1328	...	1336	...	1536	1536
Würzburg Hbf . 900 905a 920 d.	...	...	...	...	...	...	...	|	1124	1219	...	...	...	|	|	1511	...	|	1712	...	|	...	|	|
Steinach (b. Rothenb) ... 905a d.	...	...	...	...	...	...	...	|	1158	|	...	...	...	|	|	|	...	|	|	...	|	...	|	|
Ansbach ... 905a d.	...	...	...	...	...	...	...	|	1219	|	...	...	...	|	|	1608	...	|	1813	...	|	...	|	|
Berlin Hbf **850** ... d.	...	...	...	...	0534	...	...	0734	|	|	...	1004	...	1134	1134	|	...	1404	|	...	1534	...	1734	1734
Nürnberg Hbf ... 900 920 d.	...	...	0615	...	0900	...	1057	1059	|	|	1330	1330	...	1456	1459	|	1728	1732	|	1857	1859	...	2056	2100
Treuchtlingen ... 905a d.	...	0621	0651	...	|	...	|	|	1247	|	|	|	...	|	|	1642	|	|	1845	|	|	...	|	|
Donauwörth ... d.	0557	0642	0711	...	0950	...	1150	1150	1309	|	1421	1421	...	|	1550	1707	1826	1826	1907	1950	1950	...	|	2151
Augsburg Hbf ... 900 930 a.	0618	0705	0732	...	1009	...	1208	1208	1330	1409	1442	1443	...	|	1609	1731	1846	1846	1930	2009	2009	...	|	2210
München Pasing ... 930 a.	0641	0729	0758	...	1032	...	1232	1232	1358	|	|	|	...	|	1632	|	|	|	1953	2032	2032	...	|	2233
München Hbf ... 930 a.	0650	0738	0808	...	1042	...	1242	1242	|	1445	1517	1517	...	1602	1642	1804	1917	1917	2002	2043	2043	...	2201	2244
München Ost ... a.	...	...	...	...	...	...	...	...	1411	...	...	...	...	...	...	...	...	...	...	...	...	...	...	...

RE services. See Table **930** for other connecting trains München - Augsburg and v.v.

km																											
		Ⓒ		Ⓒ	⚒							Ⓒ	Ⓐ														
		z		z	t	W		W¶	H		W¶	z	t	W¶		W¶		W¶		B	H		A¶			N	
		◇	...			◇		◇			◇			◇		◇		◇		◇			◇		◇	◇	◇
0	**München** Hbf ... 930 d.	0006	...	0159	...	0528	...	0735	...	...	0935	...	...	1135	...	1335	...	1535	...	1735	...	...	1935	...	2057	2159	2257
7	München Pasing 930 d.	0014	...	0207	...	0536	...	0743	...	...	0943	...	...	1143	...	1343	...	1543	...	1743	...	...	1943	...	2105	2207	2305
62	**Augsburg** Hbf .. 930 a.	0053	...	0248	...	0620	...	0818	...	...	1018	...	...	1219	...	1419	...	1619	...	1819	...	...	2019	...	2146	2246	2346
62	**Augsburg** Hbf ... d.	0057	...	0319	0517	0628	0719	0828	0926	0932	1028	1127	1127	1225	1325	1428	1527	1628	1726	1828	1918	1927	2028	2129	2154	2254	0001
103	Donauwörth ... d.	0139	...	0359	0555f	0659	0759	0859	0949	1000	1059	1159	1159	1259	1359	1459	1559	1659	1758	1859	1945	1959	2059	2159	2239	2334	0040
137	Treuchtlingen ... a.	...	0418	0417	0616	0720	0820	0920	1006	1020	1120	1220	1220	1320	1420	1520	1620	1720	1818	1920	2003	2020	2120	2220	2301	...	...
137	Treuchtlingen ... 904 d.	...	0424	0418	0626	0725	0828	0925	1008	1028	1125	1228	1238	1325	1428	1525	1628	1728	1829	1925	2004	2029	2125	2225	2325	...	...
146	Weißenburg (Bay) 904 d.	...	0507	0424	0633	0731	0834	0931	|	1034	1131	1234	1245	1331	1434	1531	1635	1734	1835	1931	|	2036	2131	2231	2331	...	...
199	**Nürnberg** Hbf ... 904 a.	...		0507	0715	0815	0916	1015	1045	1116	1215	1316	1329	1416	1516	1615	1717	1816	1918	2015	2036	2118	2214	2313	0015	...	...

	Ⓒ	Ⓒ	Ⓐ	⑥	Ⓐ	Ⓐ	Ⓒ		Ⓒ	Ⓐ																
	z	z	t		t	t	z	C	z	t	H	W¶		W¶		W¶		W¶		W¶		H	W¶		W¶		W
		◇	◇					◇				◇		◇		◇		◇		◇			◇		◇		◇
Nürnberg Hbf ... 904 d.	0053	...	...	0433	0433	0526	0539	...	0636	0649	0716	0738	0838	0939	1039	1139	1238	1339	1438	1539	1639	1713	1739	1838	1937	2039	2138
Weißenburg (Bay) 904 d.	0132	...	...	0518	0518	0608	0621	...	0718	0724	|	0821	0920	1021	1120	1221	1320	1421	1520	1621	1720	|	1821	1920	2019	2120	2221
Treuchtlingen ... 904 a.	0139	...	...	0525	0525	0616	0628	...	0723	0730	0748	0827	0927	1027	1127	1227	1327	1427	1527	1627	1727	1745	1830	1927	2025	2127	2230
Treuchtlingen ... d.	0142	...	...	0528	0528	...	...	0634	0725	0731	0749	0834	0934	1034	1134	1234	1334	1434	1534	1634	1734	1746	1834	1935	2034	2135	2234
Donauwörth ... d.	0203	0523	0523	0549	0604j	...	...	0659	0754f	0754	0807	0859	0958	1059	1158	1259	1358	1459	1558	1658	1758	1806	1859	1958	2059	2158	2259
Augsburg Hbf ... a.	0226	0608	0608	0620	0636	...	...	0728	0825	0825	0828	0928	1029	1128	1228	1328	1428	1528	1628	1728	1827	1829	1928	2029	2128	2228	2341
Augsburg Hbf ... 930 d.	...	0613	0619	...	0653	...	...	0737	...	...	...	0938	...	1138	...	1338	...	1538	...	1738	...	...	1938	...	2139	...	...
München Pasing 930 a.	...	0653	0653	...	0737	...	...	0811	...	...	...	1012	...	1212	...	1412	...	1612	...	1812	...	...	2012	...	2223	...	...
München Hbf ... 930 a.	...	0701	0702	...	0745	...	...	0819	...	...	...	1020	...	1220	...	1420	...	1620	...	1821	...	...	2020	...	2231	...	...

- **A** – To Ansbach (Table **905a**).
- **B** – To Ansbach on Ⓐ. To Würzburg on Ⓒ. See Table **905a**. On Ⓒ conveys [12] München - Donauwörth - Aalen (Table **926**).
- **C** – From Ansbach on Ⓐ. From Würzburg on ⑥. See Table **905a**.
- **E** – To Schwarzach St-Veit (Table **960**) on ⑤ (not Dec. 23, Mar. 31).
- **F** – From Schwarzach St-Veit (Table **960**) on ⑦ (not Dec. 25).
- **G** – From / to Innsbruck via Garmisch (Table **895**).
- **H** – From / to Lindau and Oberstdorf (Table **935**).
- **J** – On ⑤ until Mar. 24 continues to Innsbruck via Garmisch (Table **895**).
- **K** – KÖNIGSSEE – [12] 🍷 Berchtesgaden - München Ost - Augsburg - Hamburg and v.v.; conveys [12] Oberstdorf (**2084/5**) - Augsburg - Hamburg and v.v.
- **L** – To Leipzig (Table **850**).
- **N** – To Aalen (Table **926**).
- **P** – From Feb. 10.
- **Q** – Ⓑ to Feb. 9 (not Dec. 25).
- **R** – Feb. 11 - Mar. 31 only.

- **W** – To / from Würzburg (Table **905a**).

- **a** – Ⓐ only.
- **b** – Not Dec. 25.
- **c** – ⑦ (not Dec. 25).
- **d** – Not Feb. 11 - Mar. 31.
- **f** – Arrives 8 minutes earlier.
- **h** – Arrives 1159.
- **j** – Arrives 0550.
- **m** – Not Dec. 26.
- **s** – Not Dec. 26 - Jan. 6.
- **t** – Not Jan. 6.
- **z** – Ⓒ (also Jan. 6).

- ◇ – Operated by Go-Ahead Bayern.
- ¶ – Conveys [12] München - Donauwörth - Aalen and v.v. (Table **926**).

TREUCHTLINGEN - WÜRZBURG 905a

Operator: Go-Ahead Bayern

km																										
		⚒t	Ⓐt	Ⓒz	Ⓐt	Ⓐt	Ⓐt	Ⓒz													Ⓐt	Ⓒz				
	München Hbf **905** .. d.	...	...	...	...	...	...	...	0528	...	0735	...	0935	...	1135	...	1335	...	1535	...	1735	1735	...	...	1935	...
	Augsburg Hbf **905** .. d.	...	...	...	...	...	...	...	0628	...	0828	...	1028	...	1225	...	1428	...	1628	...	1828	1828	...	...	2028	...
0	**Treuchtlingen** ... 905 d.	...	...	0502	0512	0549	0616	0625	0725	0825	0928	1025	1128	1225	1328	1425	1528	1625	1728	1826	1928	1928	...	2024	2128	2225
24	Gunzenhausen ... d.	...	...	0516	0526	0603	0630	0639	0739	0838	0942	1039	1142	1239	1342	1439	1542	1639	1742	1840	1942	1942	...	2039	2142	2239
51	Ansbach ... 905 a.	...	...	0536	0546	0623	0650	0658	0759	0858	1002	1059	1201	1259	1401	1459	1602	1659	1801	1900	2001	2001	...	2059	2202	2259
51	Ansbach ... 905 d.	0440	0524	0537	0601	0631	0659	0711	0811	0910	1010	1111	1211	1311	1410	1511	1611	1711	1810	1911	...	2011	2011	2111	...	2311
83	Steinach (b. Rothenb) d.	0503	0547	0601	0624	0653	0722	0733	0833	0932	1031	1133	1233	1333	1431	1533	1633	1733	1831	1933	...	2033	2033	2133	...	2333
140	**Würzburg** Hbf ... 905 a.	0547	0631	0644	0708	0736	0805	0817	0918	1017	1119	1217	1317	1417	1519	1616	1717	1816	1919	2017	...	2117	2117	2217	...	0017

	⚒t	⑥	Ⓐt	Ⓐt	Ⓒz	Ⓐt	⊕					Ⓒz	Ⓐt											⚒t	
Würzburg Hbf ... 905 d.	0430	0430	...	0523	0523	0555	0641	0741	0843	0941	1041	1140	1140	1243	1340	1441	1541	1643	1741	1841	1941	2041	2141	2304	2304
Steinach (b. Rothenburg) ... d.	0513	0513	...	0606	0606	0637	0724	0824	0925	1024	1124	1224	1224	1326	1424	1524	1625	1725	1825	1924	2024	2124	2224	2347	2347
Ansbach ... 905 a.	0535	0535	...	0627	0627	0700	0747	0845	0947	1045	1145	1245	1245	1347	1445	1545	1646	1747	1846	1945	2045	2145	2245	0009	0009
Ansbach ... 905 d.	0537	0537	0601	0628	0654	0710	0754	0854	0954	1054	1154	1254	1316	1354	1454	1554	1654	1754	1854	1954	2054	2154	2254	0010	...
Gunzenhausen ... d.	0556	0556	0620	0648	0715	0730	0815	0913	1015	1115	1214	1313	1336	1415	1513	1615	1713	1815	1913	2014	2113	2215	2313	0029	...
Treuchtlingen ... 905 a.	0609	0609	0633	0701	0729	0744	0829	0927	1029	1128	1229	1327	1351	1429	1527	1629	1727	1830	1927	2029	2127	2229	2327	0044	...
Augsburg Hbf **905** ... a.	...	0728	0728	...	...	...	0928	...	1128	...	1328	...	...	1528	...	1728	...	1928	...	2128	...	2341	...	...	...
München Hbf **905** ... a.	...	0819	0819	...	...	...	1020	...	1220	...	1420	...	...	1620	...	1821	...	2020	...	2231	...	...	...	...	...

Local trains **STEINACH** (b. Rothenburg) - **ROTHENBURG OB DER TAUBER** and v.v. 2nd class only. *12 km*. Journey time: 15 minutes. Operated by DB.

From Steinach at 0422 ⚒ **t**, 0517, 0627, 0727 Ⓐ **t**, 0736 Ⓒ **z**, 0836, 0936, 1036, 1136, 1236, 1336, 1436, 1536, 1636, 1737, 1836 Ⓒ **z**, 1845 Ⓐ **t**, 1936, 2036 and 2236.

From Rothenburg ob der Tauber at 0444 ⚒ **t**, 0540 Ⓒ **z**, 0547 Ⓐ **t**, 0658 Ⓐ **t**, 0705 Ⓒ **z**, 0805, 0905, 1005, 1105, 1205, 1309, 1405, 1505, 1605, 1705, 1805, 1905, 2005, 2205 and 2305.

- **t** – Not Jan. 6.
- **z** – Also Jan. 6.

⊕ – Change trains at Treuchtlingen on † (also Jan. 6).

906 GIESSEN - KOBLENZ; LIMBURG - FRANKFURT and WIESBADEN

DB (*RE* services); HLB★

GIESSEN - KOBLENZ (additional stopping trains operate).

km												
				⚒								
0	**Gießen** 807 d.	...	0618	0716	0916	1116	1316	1516	1716	1916	2116	2122	2222
13	Wetzlar 807 d.	...	0631	0726	0926	1126	1326	1526	1726	1926	2126	2136	2236
36	Weilburg d.	...	0655	0743	0943	1143	1343	1543	1743	1943	2143	2200	2300
65	**Limburg** (Lahn) a.	...	0733	0808	1008	1208	1408	1608	1808	2008	2208	2237	2337
			◧	|	|	|	|	|	|	|	|	◧ ⑥⑦	◧ ⑤⑥
65	**Limburg** (Lahn) d.	0646	0746	0809	1009	1209	1409	1609	1809	2009	2209	2246	2346
68	Diez d.	0651	0751	0813	1013	1213	1413	1613	1813	2013	2213	2251	2351
91	Nassau (Lahn) d.	0716	0816	0833	1033	1233	1433	1633	1833	2033	2233	2316	0016
99	Bad Ems d.	0725	0825	0840	1040	1240	1440	1640	1840	2040	2240	2325	0025
112	Niederlahnstein d.	0742	0842	0853	1053	1253	1453	1653	1853	2053	2253	2342	0042
117	**Koblenz** Hbf a.	0750	0850	0900	1100	1300	1500	1700	1900	2100	2300	2351	0050

	Ⓐ										©
Koblenz Hbf d.	0509	0657	0857	1057	1257	1457	1657	1857	2009	2109	2209
Niederlahnstein d.	0516	0704	0904	1104	1304	1504	1704	1904	2016	2116	2216
Bad Ems d.	0532	0716	0916	1116	1316	1516	1716	1916	2032	2132	2232
Nassau (Lahn) d.	0544	0726	0926	1126	1326	1526	1726	1926	2044	2144	2244
Diez d.	0610	0746	0946	1146	1346	1546	1746	1946	2110	2210	2310
Limburg (Lahn) a.	0614	0750	0950	1150	1350	1550	1750	1950	2114	2214	2314
	◧ d	|	|	|	|	|	|	|	◧	◧	
Limburg (Lahn) d.	0618	0751	0951	1151	1351	1551	1751	1951	2123	2223	...
Weilburg d.	0655	0816	1016	1216	1416	1616	1816	2016	2200	2300	...
Wetzlar 807 d.	0720	0832	1032	1232	1432	1632	1832	2032	2227	2327	...
Gießen 807 a.	0731	0842	1042	1242	1442	1642	1842	2042	2238	2338	...

LIMBURG - NIEDERNHAUSEN - FRANKFURT and WIESBADEN

km																									
		©	©		⚒	Ⓐ	Ⓐ			Ⓐ	Ⓐ	Ⓐ	Ⓐ	©	Ⓐ	Ⓐ	Ⓐ	Ⓐ			Ⓐ	Ⓐ			
0	**Limburg** (Lahn) d.	0019	...	0419	...	0449	...	0519	...	0556	...	0612	0626	0632	0633	0640	0656	...	0719	...	0756	...	0819	...	and at
21	Bad Camberg d.	0042	...	0443	...	0513	...	0543	...	0615	...	0636	0645	0656	0657	0704	0715	...	0743	...	0815	...	0843	...	the same
30	Idstein d.	0050	...	0452	...	0522	...	0552	...	0622	...	0646	0652	0705	0706	0715	0722	...	0752	...	0822	...	0852	...	minutes
38	Niedernhausen ‡ d.	0057	0105	0459	0505	0529	0535	0559	0605	0629	0635	0653	0659	0712	0714	0723	0729	0735	0759	0805	0829	0835	0859	0905	past each
58	**Wiesbaden** Hbf a.	|	0128	|	0527	|	0559	|	0628	|	0659	0715	|	|	|	0745	|	0759	|	0828	|	0859	|	0928	hour until
70	**Frankfurt** (Main) Hbf ‡ a.	0135	...	0531	...	0601	...	0631	...	0701	...	...	0731	0744	0743	...	0759	...	0831	...	0859	...	0931	...	

			Ⓐ			Ⓐ	Ⓐ				Ⓐ	Ⓐ			Ⓐ										
Limburg (Lahn) d.	1219	...	1250	1319	...	1356	...	and at	1716	...	1756	...	1819	...	1849	1919	...	2019	...	2119	...	2219	...	2316	...
Bad Camberg d.	1243	...	1314	1343	...	1415	...	the same	1743	...	1815	...	1843	...	1913	1943	...	2043	...	2143	...	2243	...	2343	...
Idstein d.	1252	...	1324	1352	...	1422	...	minutes	1752	...	1822	...	1852	...	1923	1952	...	2052	...	2152	...	2252	...	2352	...
Niedernhausen ‡ d.	1259	1305	1335	1359	1405	1429	1435	past each	1759	1805	1829	1835	1859	1905	1935	1959	2005	2059	2105	2159	2205	2259	2305	2359	0005
Wiesbaden Hbf a.	|	1328	1356	|	1428	|	1459	hour until	|	1828	|	1859	|	1928	1959	|	2028	|	2128	|	2228	|	2328	|	0028
Frankfurt (Main) Hbf ‡ a.	1331	...	...	1431	...	1501	...		1831	...	1901	...	1931	...	...	2031	...	2131	...	2229	...	2331	...	0033	...

			⚒		Ⓐ	Ⓐ	©	©	Ⓐ	Ⓐ	Ⓐ	©		Ⓐ			⊠			Ⓐ	Ⓐ			Ⓐ	Ⓐ
Frankfurt (Main) Hbf ‡ d.	...	0029	...	0526	...	0559	...	0629	...	0659	...	...	0728	...	...	0829	and at	...	1329	...	1359	...	1429	...	1459
Wiesbaden Hbf d.	0036	|	0536	|	0606	|	0636	|	0653	|	0723	0736	|	0806	0836	|	the same	1336	|	1406	|	1436	|	1506	|
Niedernhausen ‡ d.	0058	0101	0558	0601	0628	0631	0658	0701	0718	0731	0758	0758	0801	0831	0858	0901	minutes	1358	1401	1428	1431	1458	1501	1528	1531
Idstein d.	...	0108	...	0607	...	0637	...	0707	...	0737	...	...	0807	0838	...	0907	past each	...	1407	...	1437	...	1507	...	1537
Bad Camberg d.	...	0117	...	0616	...	0646	...	0716	...	0744	...	...	0816	0847	...	0916	hour until	...	1416	...	1444	...	1516	...	1544
Limburg (Lahn) a.	...	0142	...	0639	...	0709	...	0739	...	0803	...	...	0841	0911	...	0941		...	1441	...	1503	...	1541	...	1603

	©	©	Ⓐ	Ⓐ	Ⓐ	©	©	Ⓐ	Ⓐ	Ⓐ	Ⓐ		©	Ⓐ	Ⓐ	Ⓐ			Ⓐ	Ⓐ					
Frankfurt (Main) Hbf ‡ d.	...	1529	...	...	1559	...	1629	...	1643	...	1657	...	1729	1743	...	1759	...	1829	...	1859	...	1929	and at	...	2329
Wiesbaden Hbf d.	1536	|	1536	1606	|	1636	|	1636	|	1706	|	1736	|	|	1806	|	1836	|	1906	|	1936	|	the same	2336	|
Niedernhausen ‡ d.	1558	1601	1601	1628	1631	1658	1701	1701	1716	1728	1731	1758	1801	1816	1828	1831	1858	1901	1928	1931	1958	2001	minutes	2358	0001
Idstein d.	...	1607	1608	...	1637	...	1707	1708	1722	...	1737	...	1807	1822	...	1837	...	1907	...	1937	...	2007	past each	...	0007
Bad Camberg d.	...	1616	1617	...	1644	...	1716	1717	1731	...	1744	...	1816	1831	...	1844	...	1916	...	1944	...	2016	hour until	...	0016
Limburg (Lahn) a.	...	1641	1641	...	1703	...	1741	1741	1755	...	1803	...	1841	1853	...	1903	...	1941	...	2003	...	2041		...	0041

d – Daily. Runs 5–7 minutes later on ©.

◧ – Change trains at Limburg.

★ – Hessische Landesbahn.

⊠ – Frankfurt (Main) Hbf d. 0926 (not 0929).

‡ – Frequent S-Bahn *S2* services also run Frankfurt - Niedernhausen and v.v.

907 GIESSEN - FULDA

Hessische Landesbahn

km																										
		Ⓐ	Ⓐ	Ⓐ	⑥	Ⓐ	⚒	Ⓐ	©	Ⓐ					Ⓐ	©										
0	**Gießen** d.	...	...	0524	...	...	...	0615	0744	0747	0844	0947	1044	1147	1241	1244	1347	1444t	1547	1644t	1747	1844t	1947	2111	2211	2311
23	Grünberg (Oberhess) d.	...	...	0550	...	0615	...	0709j	0811	0816	0911	1013	1111	1213	1311	1311	1411v	1511	1611v	1711	1811v	1911	2015	2135	2239	2336
60	Alsfeld (Oberhess) d.	0515	0557	0635j	0650	0723r	0750	0750	0850	0850	0950	1050	1150	1250	1350	1350	1450	1550	1650	1750	1850	1950	2056j	2219j	2319	0010
79	Lauterbach (Hess) d.	0529	0611	0649	0704	0738	0804	0804	0904	0904	1004	1104	1204	1304	1404	1404	1504	1604	1704	1804	1904	2008	2109	2237	...	...
106	**Fulda** a.	0602	0637	0719	0730	0804	0830	0830	0930	0930	1030	1130	1230	1330	1430	1430	1530	1630	1730	1830	1930	2039	2139	2301	...	...

	Ⓐ	Ⓐ	Ⓐ	⑥	Ⓐ	©	Ⓐ	Ⓐ	©	⑥															⑤⑥f	
Fulda d.	...	...	...	...	0535	...	0610	0653	...	0733	0833	0933	1033	1133	1233	1333	1433	1533	1633	1733	1833	2010	2101	2209	2209	2309
Lauterbach (Hess) d.	...	...	...	...	0612k	...	0651k	0723	...	0805	0905	1005	1105	1205	1305	1405	1505	1605	1705	1805	1905	2037	2127	2236	2236	2336
Alsfeld (Oberhess) d.	0419	0532	0556	0612	0631	0712	0719k	0757k	0819	0819	0919	1019	1119	1219	1319	1419	1519	1619	1719	1819	1919	2058j	2141	2249	2251	2349
Grünberg (Oberhess) d.	0453	0613	0639	0647	0705	0747	0753	0838	0851	0851	0953	1051	1153	1251t	1353	1451t	1553	1651t	1753	1851t	1953	2137	2217	...	2337	...
Gießen a.	0518	0639	0704	0711	0730	0816	0818	0906	0916	0916	1018	1116	1218	1316	1416v	1516	1616v	1716	1816v	1916	2018	2202	2242	...	0002	...

f – Also Apr. 6, 9, 30, May 17, 28.

j – Arrives 7–8 minutes earlier.

k – Arrives 10–14 minutes earlier.

r – Arrives 0702.

t – 2–3 minutes later on Ⓐ.

v – 2 minutes later on ©.

908 GÖTTINGEN - BEBRA

CANTUS Verkehrsgesellschaft (2nd class only)

km											
		Ⓐ	⚒	⚒	Ⓐ	©d					
0	**Göttingen** 864 d.	0414	0514	0614	0646	0714	0814	and	2114	2214	2314
20	Eichenberg 864 d.	0430	0530	0630	0701	0730	0830	hourly	2130	2230	2330
35	Bad Sooden-Allendorf d.	0440	0540	0640	0710	0740	0840	until	2140	2240	2340
49	Eschwege a.	0451	0551	0651	0721	0751	0851		2151	2251	2351
49	Eschwege d.	0521	0621	0725	|	0821	0921		2221	2313	2357
87	**Bebra** a.	0550	0650	0754	*0754e*	0850	0950		2250	2342	0027

	Ⓐ	⚒						
Bebra d.	0400	0530	0631	0708	and	2008	2108	2208
Eschwege a.	0428	0558	0659	0737	hourly	2036	2136	2236
Eschwege d.	0434	0605	0705	0805	until	2105	2205	2305
Bad Sooden-Allendorf d.	0445	0616	0716	0816		2116	2216	2316
Eichenberg 864 d.	0502	0631	0731	0831		2131	2229	2331
Göttingen 864 a.	0515	0645	0745	0845		2145	2243	2345

d – Runs daily Eschwege - Bebra.

e – Change trains at Eschwege-Niederhone (a. 0718, d. *0728*).

909 WÜRZBURG - BAD KISSINGEN - GEMÜNDEN

DB (*RE* services); EB★

On Jan. 6 services run as on ⑦.

km																									
								©	Ⓐ		Ⓐ														
0	**Würzburg** Hbf 870 876 ‡ d.	...		0801	...		1001	...	...	1201	...	...	1401	...	...	1601	...	...	1801	...	...	2001	...	...	...
43	**Schweinfurt** Hbf. 870 876 ‡ d.	0610	0812	0830	0912	1012	1030	1205	1205	1230	1302	1412	1430	1512	1612	1630	1712	1812	1830	1912	2012	2030	2113	2224	2351
57	Ebenhausen (Unterf) 870 ‡ d.	0624	0825	0843	0929	1025	1043	1226	1226	1243	1316	1425	1443	1529	1625	1643	1729	1825	1843	1929	2025	2043	2129	2240	0005
66	**Bad Kissingen** a.	0633	0834	0853	0938	1034	1053	1235	1235	1253	1325	1434	1453	1538	1634	1653	1738	1834	1853	1938	2034	2053	2138	2249	0014
66	**Bad Kissingen** d.	0637	0841	...	...	1041	...	1241	1241	...	1343	1441	...	1543t	1641	...	1743t	1841	...	1943	2043	...	2142	...	...
85	Hammelburg d.	0659	0908	...	...	1105	...	1306	1313	...	1406	1506	...	1606t	1706	...	1807t	1906	...	2006	2107	...	2207	...	...
113	**Gemünden** (Main) a.	0737	0941	...	...	1140	...	1340	1350	...	1441	1540	...	1641t	1741	...	1841t	1941	...	2039	2143	...	...	...	...

	Ⓐ		©	Ⓐ							©	Ⓐ	Ⓐ												
Gemünden (Main) d.	...	...	...	*0614*	0707r	...	0811	...	1011	...	1211	1211	1320	...	1411	1510t	...	1610	1710t	...	1810	1910t	...	2113	2211
Hammelburg d.	0545	*0612*t	0636	*0700*	0748r	...	0844	...	1044	...	1244	1244	1407e	...	1444	1543t	...	1644	1743t	...	1845	1943t	...	2146	2248
Bad Kissingen a.	0607	*0636*t	0702	*0722*	0810r	...	0907	...	1107	...	1307	1307	1429	...	1507	1609t	...	1707	1808t	...	1907	2008t	...	2208	2309
Bad Kissingen d.	0612	0641	0706	0730	0814	0900	0918	1100	1118	1300	1318	1326	...	1500	1518	1614	1700	1718	1813	1900	1918	2013	2100	2213	2313
Ebenhausen (Unterf) 870 a.	0621	0650	0715	0739	0823	0909	0927	1109	1127	1309	1327	1335	...	1509	1527	1623	1709	1727	1822	1909	1927	2022	2109	2222	2321
Schweinfurt Hbf 870 876 a.	0637	0713	0730	0753	0842	0926	0942	1126	1144	1326	1342	1356	...	1525	1542	1641	1725	1743	1841	1926	1942	2042	2126	2236	2339
Würzburg Hbf 870 876 a.	...	0745	...	...	...	0955	...	1155	...	1355	...	...	...	1555	...	...	1755	...	...	1955	...	...	2157	...	...

e – Arrives 1353.

t – Ⓐ only.

r – ⚒ only.

★ – Erfurter Bahn (2nd class only).

‡ – Trains between Würzburg, Schweinfurt and Ebenhausen are often combined with a service to Meiningen or Erfurt. Passengers should take care to join the correct portion for their destination.

AACHEN - KÖLN - FRANKFURT via high-speed line 910

See panel below main table for services Mainz - Wiesbaden - Köln. See Tables **800**/**911** for services via Bonn and Koblenz. See Table **20** for other services Brussels - Aachen - Köln.

km	km		ICE 827 Y	ICE 521	ICE 523 ⚒ ✖	ICE 511 ✖	ICE 811 Ⓐ ✖	ICE 1121 Ⓐ ✖	ICE 525 ✖	ICE 101 ⚒ ✖	ICE 101 ✖	ICE 913 ⚒ ✖	ICE 813 Ⓐ ✖	ICE 813 ✖	ICE 527 ✖	ICE 513 M✖	ICE 11 ✖	ICE 815 Ⓐ ✖	ICE 529 b G✖	ICE 103 ✖	ICE 915 ✖	ICE 121 ⊠ ✖	ICE 621 ✖	ICE 515 ✖
		Hamburg Hbf **800** d.	...	...	...	...	...	...	...	...	...	...	...	...	...	...	...	...	...	...	...	...	...	0545
		Dortmund Hbf **800** d.	...	...	0401	...	...	...	0522	0528	...	0547	0558	...	0622	0636	...	0649	0722	...	0756	...	...	0835
		Essen Hbf **800** d.	...	...	0427	...	...	...	0549	|	...	0615	|	...	0651	0700	...	0715	0750	...	0815	...	0839	|
		Amsterdam Centraal **28** ⊠ d.	...	...	|	...	...	...	|	|	...	|	|	...	|	|	...	|	|	...	|	0638	|	|
		Düsseldorf Hbf **800** d.	...	...	0454	...	...	0605	0617	◐	...	0645	◐	...	0718	0724	...	0745	0818	...	0843	0851	0910	◐
		Brussels Midi/Zuid **21** d.	...	...	|	...	...	|	|	|	...	|	|	...	|	|	0623	|	|	...	|	|	|	|
		Aachen Hbf **802 807** d.	...	...	|	...	...	|	|	|	...	|	|	...	|	|	0739	|	|	...	|	|	|	|
		Köln Hbf **800 802 807** a.	...	...	|	...	...	|	|	0646	...	|	0708	...	|	0749	0816	|	|	...	|	0919	|	0949
0	0	**Köln** Hbf **802 807** d.	0321	0422	|	0549	0600	|	|	0655	0655	|	0719	0719	|	0755	0825	|	|	0855	|	0928	|	0955
1	1	**Köln** Messe/Deutz **802** d.	|	|	0520	|	|	0629	0644	|	|	0711	|	|	0744	|	|	0811	0844	|	0911	|	0944	|
	15	Köln/Bonn Flughafen ✈ **802** d.	0334	|	0531	|	|	|	|	|	|	|	|	|	|	|	|	0822	|	|	|	|	|	|
25	31	Siegburg/Bonn 🚋 **807** d.	0343	0436	0541	0604	0615	|	|	|	|	0725	0735	0735	|	|	|	0831	|	|	0925	|	|	|
88		Montabaur d.	0403	0456	0603	|	0635	|	|	|	|	|	0756	0756	|	|	|	0857	|	|	|	|	|	|
110		Limburg Süd d.	0414	0507	0614	|	0646	|	|	|	|	|	0807	0807	|	|	|	0907	|	|	|	|	|	|
169		**Frankfurt** Flughafen Fernbf ✈ a.	0434	0526	0634	0650	0708	0717	0733	0750	0750	0807	0826	0826	0833	0850	0917	0926	0933	0950	1007	1017	1033	1050
180		**Frankfurt** (Main) Hbf a.	0448	0540	0648	|	0723	|	0748	|	|	|	0841	0841	0848	|	0931	0941	0948	|	|	1031	1048	|
		Nürnberg Hbf **920** a.	0658e	0759	0900	|	...	0915	0958	|	|	|	...	...	1100	|	...	...	1158	|	|	...	1259	|
		Mannheim Hbf **912** a.	|	|	|	0723	...	|	|	0823	0823	0840	...	...	|	0923	...	...	|	1023	1039	...	|	1123
		Karlsruhe Hbf **912** a.	|	|	|	|	...	|	|	0858	0858	|	...	...	|	|	...	...	|	1058	|	...	|	|
		Basel SBB **912** a.	|	|	|	|	...	|	|	1047	1047	|	...	...	|	|	...	...	|	1247	|	...	|	|
		Stuttgart Hbf **912** a.	|	|	|	0808	...	|	|	...	...	0922	...	...	|	1008	...	...	|	...	1122	...	|	1208
		München Hbf **904 930** a.	0806e	0906	1006	1026	...	1020	1110	...	...	1126	...	...	1206	1226	...	...	1306	...	1326	...	1406	1426

	ICE 817 ✖	ICE 13 ✖	ICE 623 ✖	ICE 105 ⊠ ✖	ICE 917 ✖	ICE 625 ✖	ICE 517 ✖	ICE 819 ✖	ICE 15 ✖	ICE 627 ✖	ICE 107 ✖	ICE 123 ⊠ ✖	ICE 629 ✖	ICE 519 ✖	ICE 901 ✖	ICE 315 ✖	ICE 721 ✖	ICE 109 ✖	ICE 1011 ✖	ICE 125 ⊠ ✖	ICE 723 ✖	ICE 611 ✖	ICE 903 ✖	ICE 17 ✖
Hamburg Hbf **800** d.	...	...	...	...	...	...	0745	...	...	...	0845	...	...	0945	...	...	...	1045	...	...	...	1145	...	...
Dortmund Hbf **800** d.	...	...	0912y	...	...	...	1035	...	...	1122y	|	...	...	1236	...	...	...	|	1349q	...	...	1435	...	...
Essen Hbf **800** d.	...	...	0941	...	...	1051	|	...	...	1150	1157	...	1251	1300	...	...	1351	1357	1415q	...	1451	|	...	...
Amsterdam Centraal **28** ⊠ d.	...	...	|	0808	...	|	|	...	...	|	|	1038	|	|	...	...	|	|	|	1238	|	|	...	...
Düsseldorf Hbf **800** d.	...	...	1010	1019	1051	1118	◐	...	...	1217	1223	1248	1318	1324	...	...	1418	1423	1445	1450	1518	◐	...	...
Brussels Midi/Zuid **21** d.	...	0823j	|	|	|	|	|	...	1025	|	|	|	|	|	...	1225	|	|	|	|	|	|	...	1425
Aachen Hbf **802 807** d.	...	0939	|	|	|	|	|	...	1139	|	|	|	|	|	...	1339	|	|	|	|	|	|	...	1539
Köln Hbf **800 802 807** a.	...	1015	|	1045	|	|	1146	...	1215	|	1249	1315	|	1349	...	1415	|	1449	|	1519	|	1546	...	1615
Köln Hbf **802 807** d.	0959	1018	|	1055	|	|	1155	1159	1218x	|	1255	1321	|	1355	1359	1427	|	1455	|	1528	|	1555	...	1620
Köln Messe/Deutz **802** d.	|	|	1034	|	1116	1145	|	|	|	1244	|	|	1344	|	|	|	1444	|	1511	|	1545	|	1600	|
Köln/Bonn Flughafen ✈ **802** d.	|	|	1045	|	|	|	|	|	|	|	|	|	|	|	|	|	|	|	|	|	|	|	|	|
Siegburg/Bonn 🚋 **807** d.	1017	1032	|	1110	|	|	|	1217	1232x	|	|	1337	|	|	1417	|	|	|	1525	|	|	|	1617	|
Montabaur d.	1038	|	|	|	|	|	|	1238	|	|	|	|	|	|	1438	|	|	|	|	|	|	|	1638	|
Limburg Süd d.	1049	|	|	|	|	|	|	1249	|	|	|	|	|	|	1449	|	|	|	|	|	|	|	1649	|
Frankfurt Flughafen Fernbf ✈ a.	1108	1117	1133	1150	1207	1233	1250	1308	1317	1333	1350	1417	1433	1450	1508	1517	1533	1550	1607	1617	1633	1650	1708	1725p
Frankfurt (Main) Hbf a.	1123	1131	1148	|	|	1248	|	1323	1331	1348	|	1431	1448	|	1523	1531	1548	|	|	1631	1648	|	1723	1740p
Nürnberg Hbf **920** a.	...	...	1404	|	|	1500	|	...	...	1559	|	...	1658	|	...	...	1759	|	|	...	1859	|	...	...
Mannheim Hbf **912** a.	...	...	|	1223	1239	|	1323	...	...	|	1423	...	|	1523	...	...	|	1623	1639	...	|	1723	...	...
Karlsruhe Hbf **912** a.	...	...	|	1258	|	|	|	...	...	|	1458	...	|	|	...	...	|	1658	|	...	|	|	...	...
Basel SBB **912** a.	...	...	|	1447	|	|	|	...	...	|	1647	...	|	|	...	...	|	1847	|	...	|	|	...	...
Stuttgart Hbf **912** a.	...	...	|	...	1320	|	1408	...	...	|	...	...	|	1608	...	...	|	...	1721	...	|	1808	...	...
München Hbf **904 930** a.	...	...	1509	...	1527	1606	1626	...	...	1706	...	...	1807	1826	...	...	1911	...	1927	...	2007	2026	...	...

	ICE 1123 Ⓑ b ✖	ICE 725 ✖	ICE 201 ✖	ICE 1013 ✖	ICE 127 ⊠ ✖	ICE 727 ✖	ICE 613 K✖	ICE 317 ✖	ICE 729 ✖	ICE 905 ✖	ICE 203 ✖	ICE 1015 Ⓑ ✖	ICE 129 ⊠ ✖	ICE 821 ✖	ICE 615 ✖	ICE 19 ✖	ICE 823 ✖	ICE 205 ✖	ICE 221 ⊠ ✖	ICE 617 ✖		ICE 319 ⑦ w ✖		ICE 619 U K
Hamburg Hbf **800** d.	...	...	1245	...	...	...	1345	...	...	...	...	...	...	...	1545	...	...	1645	...	1745	...	...	...	1945
Dortmund Hbf **800** d.	...	...	|	1549	...	...	1635	...	...	...	...	1750	...	...	1835	...	...	|	...	2036	...	...	...	2236
Essen Hbf **800** d.	...	1549	1556	1615	...	1649	|	...	1749	...	...	1815	...	1837	|	...	1941	1955	...	2100	...	...	...	2300
Amsterdam Centraal **28** ⊠ d.	...	|	|	|	1438	|	|	...	|	...	...	|	1638	|	|	...	|	|	1838	|	...	...	...	|
Düsseldorf Hbf **800** d.	1604	1618	1623	1644	1650	1718	◐	...	1818	...	...	1844	1849	1905	◐	...	2008	2022	2048	2123	...	...	...	2324
Brussels Midi/Zuid **21** d.	|	|	|	|	|	|	|	1622t	|	...	...	|	|	|	|	1825	|	|	|	|	...	2025	...	|
Aachen Hbf **802 807** d.	|	|	|	|	|	|	|	1739	|	...	...	|	|	|	|	1939	|	|	|	|	...	2140	...	|
Köln Hbf **800 802 807** a.	|	|	1649	|	1716	|	1746	1815	|	...	...	|	1915	|	1947	2015	|	2049	2115	2149	...	2213c	...	2349
Köln Hbf **802 807** d.	|	|	1655	|	1728	|	1755	1818	|	1827	1855	|	1921	|	1955	2017x	|	2055	2128	2155	...	...	...	2355
Köln Messe/Deutz **802** d.	1629	1644	|	1710	|	1744	|	|	1844	|	|	1911	|	1933	|	|	2033	|	|	|	...	...	...	|
Köln/Bonn Flughafen ✈ **802** d.	|	|	|	|	|	|	|	|	|	|	|	|	|	|	|	|	|	|	|	|	...	...	...	|
Siegburg/Bonn 🚋 **807** d.	|	|	|	1725	|	|	|	1832	|	1842	|	1925	1937	|	|	2032x	|	|	|	2209	...	...	...	0009
Montabaur d.	|	|	|	|	|	|	|	|	|	1903	|	|	|	2005	|	|	2103	|	|	|	...	...	...	|
Limburg Süd d.	|	|	|	|	|	|	|	|	|	1920f	|	|	|	2015	|	|	2114	|	|	|	...	...	...	|
Frankfurt Flughafen Fernbf ✈ a.	1717	1733	1750	1807	1817	1833	1850	1917	1933	1938	1950	2007	2017	2034	2050	2117	2134	2150	2217	2254	...	...	...	0054
Frankfurt (Main) Hbf a.	|	1748	|	|	1831	1848	|	1931	1948	1955	|	|	2031	2048	|	2131	2148	|	2231	|	...	...	...	0110
Nürnberg Hbf **920** a.	1915	1959	|	|	...	2100	|	...	2159	...	|	|	...	2259	|	...	...	|	...	|	...	...	...	|
Mannheim Hbf **912** a.	|	|	1823	1839	...	|	1923	...	|	...	2023	2039	...	|	2124	...	...	2223	...	2327	...	...	...	0202
Karlsruhe Hbf **912** a.	|	|	1858	|	...	|	|	...	|	...	2058	|	...	|	|	...	...	2259	...	|	...	...	...	|
Basel SBB **912** a.	|	|	2047	|	...	|	|	...	|	...	2255	|	...	|	|	...	...	0059	...	|	...	...	...	|
Stuttgart Hbf **912** a.	|	|	...	1922	...	|	2008	...	|	...	...	2122	...	|	2208	...	...	...	...	0008	...	...	...	0333
München Hbf **904 930** a.	2020	2111	...	2126	...	2206	2226	...	2311	...	...	2326	...	0019	0028	...	...	...	...	...	...	...	...	0603

KÖLN - WIESBADEN - MAINZ

km		ICE 711 Ⓐ ✖		ICE 713 Ⓑ b✖
0	**Köln** Hbf d.	0559	...	1731
	Köln/Bonn Flughafen ✈ d.	|	...	|
25	Siegburg/Bonn 🚋 d.	0624	...	1746
88	Montabaur d.	0644	...	1805
110	Limburg Süd d.	0654	...	1820
165	**Wiesbaden** Hbf a.	0720	...	1840
175	**Mainz** Hbf a.	0744	...	1855
	Stuttgart Hbf **912** a.	0918	...	...

Amended Amsterdam service on Feb. 11 – 24

	ICE 255 ①–⑤ ✖	ICE 255 ⑥⑦ ✖	ICE 153 ⑦ ✖	ICE 153 ①–⑥ ✖	ICE 155 ✖	ICE 157 ✖	ICE 159 ✖	ICE 251 Ⓑ ✖	ICE 251 ⑥ ✖
Amsterdam Centraal d.	0738	0746	0907	0908	1208	1408	1708	1838	1838
Utrecht Centraal d.	0808	0816	0936	0938	1238	1438	1738	1908	1908
's-Hertogenbosch d.	0839	0844	1003	1009	1309	1509	1809	1939	1939
Mönchengladbach Hbf a.	1003	1003	1130	1130	1430	1631	1930	2102	2102
Köln Hbf a.	1048	1048	1222	1222	1522	1721	2022	2153	2153
Frankfurt Flughafen Fernbf ✈ a.	1150	1150	1317	1317	1617	1817	2117	2308	...
Frankfurt (Main) Hbf a.	|	|	1331	1331	1631	1831	2131	2324	...
Basel SBB **912** a.	1447	1447	...	...	...	...	...	...	...

G – To Garmisch on ⑥ (Table **895**).
K – From Kiel (Table **820**).
M – From Münster (Table **800**).
U – Daily until Jan. 8; ⑤⑥ from Jan. 13.
Y – Daily to Jan. 9; ⑥⑦ from Jan. 14.

b – Not Dec. 25.
c – 2222 on Dec. 26.
e – ⚒ only.
f – Arrives 1913.
j – 0825 on ⑥⑦.

p – 8 – 9 minutes earlier on ⑥ (also Dec. 25).
q – ①②③④⑥ (also Dec. 25; not Dec. 26).
t – 1625 on ⑥⑦.
w – Also Dec. 26; not Dec. 25.
x – Feb. 11 – 24 departs Köln Hbf 9 – 10 minutes later and does not call at Siegburg/Bonn.
y – † only.

◐ – Via Wuppertal (Table **800**).
⊠ – Subject to alteration Feb. 11 – 24 (see panel below).
🚋 – Frequent light-rail services operate from / to Bonn Hbf.

910 FRANKFURT - KÖLN - AACHEN via high-speed line

See panel below main table for services Köln - Wiesbaden - Mainz. See Tables **800**/**911** for services via Koblenz and Bonn. See Table **20** for other services Köln - Aachen - Brussels.

	ICE 618	ICE 222	ICE 826	ICE 18	ICE 616	ICE 824	ICE 1223	ICE 220	ICE 1014	ICE 206	ICE 822	ICE 316	ICE 1122	ICE 614	ICE 820	ICE 128	ICE 1012	ICE 1012	ICE 202	ICE 728	ICE 16	ICE 904	ICE 612	ICE 726
		Ⓐ				⚒	Ⓐ	⊠	⚒				Ⓐ		⚒	⊠	⑥	Ⓐ						
	K✕	✕	✕	✕	✕	A✕	D✕	✕	✕	✕	✕	✕	✕	✕	✕	✕	✕	✕	✕	✕	✕	✕	K✕	✕
München Hbf **904 930** d.	0001	...	...	...	0332	...	...	...	...	...	0449e	...	0534	0533	0553z	...	0626	0626	...	0648	...	...	0728	0747
Stuttgart Hbf **912** d.	0222	...	...	...	0551	...	...	...	0636	...	|	...	|	0751	|	...	0839	0839	...	|	...	...	0951	|
Basel SBB **912** d.	|	...	...	...	|	...	...	...	|	0513	|	...	|	|	|	...	|	|	0713	|	...	...	|	|
Karlsruhe Hbf **912** d.	|	...	...	...	|	...	...	...	|	0700	|	...	|	|	|	...	|	|	0900	|	...	...	|	|
Mannheim Hbf **912** d.	0401	...	...	...	0636	...	...	...	0721	0736	|	...	|	0836	|	...	0921	0921	0936	|	...	...	1036	|
Nürnberg Hbf **920** d.	|	...	...	...	|	...	...	...	|	|	0600e	...	0639	|	0702	...	|	|	|	0800	...	...	|	0859
Frankfurt (Main) Hbf d.	0446	0526	0540	0628	|	0709	...	0728	|	|	0809	0816	|	|	0909	0926	|	|	|	1009	1026	1032	|	1109
Frankfurt Flughafen Fernbf ✈ d.	0500	0539	0551	0642	0706	0721	0710	0742	0753	0807	0821	0831	0841	0907	0922	0942	0953	0953	1007	1021	1042	1049	1107	1121
Limburg Süd d.	|	|	0611	|	|	|	0732	|	|	|	|	0850	|	|	|	|	|	|	|	|	|	1109	|	|
Montabaur d.	|	|	0622	|	|	|	0748	|	|	|	|	0901	|	|	|	|	|	|	|	|	|	1120	|	|
Siegburg/Bonn 🚋 **807** d.	0547	0616	0643	|	|	|	0808	|	0831	|	0901	|	|	|	1001	|	|	1031	|	|	|	1140	|	1201
Köln/Bonn Flughafen ✈ **802** a.	|	|	|	|	|	|	|	|	|	|	|	|	|	|	|	|	|	|	|	|	|	|	|	|
Köln Messe/Deutz **802** a.	|	|	|	|	|	0813	0822	|	0848	|	0915	|	0936	|	1016	|	1041	1048	|	1115	|	1155	|	1215
Köln Hbf **802 807** a.	0603	0632	0704	0733	0804	|	|	0833	|	0904	|	0932	|	1004	|	1033	|	|	1104	|	1132	1201	1205	|
Köln Hbf **800 802 807** d.	0609	0640	0713	0742	0811	|	|	0841	|	0910	|	0942	|	1011	|	1041	|	|	1111	|	1142	...	1211	|
Aachen Hbf **802 807** a.	|	|	|	0817	|	|	|	|	|	|	|	1014	|	|	|	|	|	|	|	|	1216	...	|	|
Brussels Midi/Zuid **21** a.	|	|	|	0935	|	|	|	|	|	|	|	1135	|	|	|	|	|	|	|	|	1335	...	|	|
Düsseldorf Hbf **800** a.	0631	0705	0735	...	0832	0840	0845	0905	0915	◐	0936	...	1006	◐	1037	1105	1109	1110	1132	1136	...	...	◐	1239
Amsterdam Centraal **28** a.	|	0929	|	...	|	|	|	1129	...	|	|	...	...	|	|	1329	|	|	|	|	...	...	|	|
Essen Hbf **800** a.	0658	...	0805	...	0858	0905	0915	...	...	|	1005	...	...	|	1104	...	1140	1140q	1158	1203	...	...	|	1306
Dortmund Hbf **800** a.	0722	...	...	...	0922	...	0940	...	...	1021	...	...	...	1121	...	...	1205	1205q	1222	...	...	...	1321	...
Hamburg Hbf **800** a.	1014	...	...	...	1214	...	...	...	...	1314	...	...	...	1414	...	...	...	...	1514	...	...	...	1614	...

	ICE 126	ICE 1010	ICE 200	ICE 724	ICE 314	ICE 902	ICE 610	ICE 722	ICE 124	ICE 918	ICE 108	ICE 720	ICE 14	ICE 900	ICE 518	ICE 628	ICE 818	ICE 106	ICE 626	ICE 816	ICE 12	ICE 122	ICE 516	ICE 624
	⊠								⊠											⑥P		⊠		
	✕	✕	✕	✕	✕	✕	✕	✕	✕	✕	✕	✕	✕	✕	✕	✕	✕	✕	✕	✕	✕	✕	✕	✕
München Hbf **904 930** d.	...	0828	...	0848	...	...	0928	0951	...	1028y	...	1051	...	...	1128	1151	...	...	1250	...	...	...	1328	1351
Stuttgart Hbf **912** d.	...	1037	...	|	...	...	1151	|	...	1238	...	|	...	...	1351	|	...	...	|	...	...	...	1551	|
Basel SBB **912** d.	...	|	0913	|	...	...	|	|	...	|	1113	|	...	...	|	|	...	1313	|	...	...	...	|	|
Karlsruhe Hbf **912** d.	...	|	1100	|	...	...	|	|	...	|	1300	|	...	...	|	|	...	1500	|	...	...	...	|	|
Mannheim Hbf **912** d.	...	1121	1136	|	...	...	1236	|	...	1321	1336	|	...	...	1436	|	...	1536	|	...	...	...	1636	|
Nürnberg Hbf **920** d.	...	|	|	1000	...	...	|	1100	...	|	|	1159	...	...	|	1257	...	|	1400	...	...	...	|	1500
Frankfurt (Main) Hbf d.	1126	|	|	1209	1226	1232	|	1309	1326	|	|	1409	1426	1432	|	1509	1516	|	1609	1616	1628	1628	|	1709
Frankfurt Flughafen Fernbf ✈ d.	1142	1153	1207	1223	1242	1249	1307	1321	1342	1353	1407	1421	1442	1449	1507	1521	1528	1607	1621	1631	1642	1642	1707	1721
Limburg Süd d.	|	|	|	|	|	1309	|	|	|	|	|	|	|	1509	|	|	1547	|	|	1650	|	|	|	|
Montabaur d.	|	|	|	|	|	1320	|	|	|	|	|	|	|	1520	|	|	1558	|	|	1706f	|	|	|	|
Siegburg/Bonn 🚋 **807** d.	|	1231	|	|	|	1340	|	1401	|	1431	|	|	|	1540	|	|	1618	|	|	1727	|	|	|	|
Köln/Bonn Flughafen ✈ **802** a.	|	|	|	|	|	|	|	|	|	|	|	|	|	|	|	|	|	|	|	|	|	|	|	|
Köln Messe/Deutz **802** a.	|	1248	|	1315	|	1355	|	1415	|	1448	|	1515	|	|	|	1614	|	|	1713	|	|	|	|	1814
Köln Hbf **802 807** a.	1233	|	1304	|	1333	...	1404	|	1432	|	1504	|	1533	1556	1605	|	1639	1704	|	1743	1733	1733	1804	|
Köln Hbf **800 802 807** d.	1241	|	1311	|	1342	...	1411	|	1441	|	1510	|	1540	...	1611	|	...	...	|	...	1741	1746	1811	|
Aachen Hbf **802 807** a.	|	|	|	|	1416	...	|	|	|	|	|	|	1616	...	|	|	...	...	|	...	1816	|	|	|
Brussels Midi/Zuid **21** a.	|	|	|	|	1535	...	|	|	|	|	|	|	1735	...	|	|	...	...	|	...	1935	|	|	|
Düsseldorf Hbf **800** a.	1305	1310	1332	1336	...	...	◐	1436	1509	1514	1532	1536	...	...	1632	1639	...	...	1736	...	...	1809	◐	1840
Amsterdam Centraal **28** a.	1529	|	|	|	...	...	|	|	1729	|	|	|	...	...	|	|	...	...	|	...	...	2028	|	|
Essen Hbf **800** a.	...	1340v	1358	1403	...	...	|	1503	...	1542	1558	1603	...	...	1658	1706	...	...	1803	...	...	...	|	1914
Dortmund Hbf **800** a.	...	1404v	1422	...	...	...	1521	...	...	1606	1622	...	...	...	1722	...	...	...	1841	...	...	...	1921	1939
Hamburg Hbf **800** a.	...	...	1714	...	...	...	1814	...	...	...	1914	...	...	...	2014	...	...	...	...	...	...	...	2214	...

	ICE 814	ICE 914	ICE 204	ICE 104	ICE 622	ICE 812	ICE 812	ICE 10	ICE 514	ICE 620	ICE 120	ICE 912	ICE 102	ICE 528	ICE 1120	ICE 318	ICE 810	ICE 512	ICE 526	ICE 910	ICE 100	ICE 524	ICE 510	ICE 522
			Ⓐ	⊠		①–④	⑤⑦				⊖				⑧b	⑦w	⚒			⑧b				
	✕	✕	✕	✕	✕	m✕	w✕	✕	✕	✕	✕	✕	✕	G✕	✕	✕	✕	M✕	✕	✕	✕	✕	U	
München Hbf **904 930** d.	...	1428	...	...	1451	...	...	...	1528	1551	...	1627	...	1649	1735	...	...	1728	1752z	1828	...	1851	1928	1948
Stuttgart Hbf **912** d.	...	1637	...	...	|	...	...	...	1751	|	...	1838	...	|	|	...	...	1951	|	2038	...	|	2151	|
Basel SBB **912** d.	...	|	1513	1513	|	...	...	...	|	|	...	|	1713	|	|	...	...	|	|	|	1913	|	|	|
Karlsruhe Hbf **912** d.	...	|	1700	1700	|	...	...	...	|	|	...	|	1900	|	|	...	...	|	|	|	2100	|	|	|
Mannheim Hbf **912** d.	...	1721	1736	1736	|	...	...	...	1836	|	...	1921	1936	|	|	...	...	2036	|	2121	2136	|	2236	|
Nürnberg Hbf **920** d.	...	|	|	|	1600	...	...	...	|	1657	...	|	|	1800	1841	...	...	|	1903	|	|	2000	|	2057
Frankfurt (Main) Hbf d.	1716	|	|	|	1809	1816	1816	1828	|	1909	1928	|	|	2009	|	2016	2032	|	2109	|	|	2209	|	2309
Frankfurt Flughafen Fernbf ✈ d.	1728	1753	1807	1807	1821	1831	1831	1842	1907	1921	1942	1953	2007	2023	2041	2029	2049	2106	2121	2155	2207	2221	2306	2322
Limburg Süd d.	1747	|	|	|	|	1850	1850	|	|	1940	|	|	|	|	|	2047	2109	|	|	|	|	2240	|	2341¦
Montabaur d.	1758	|	|	|	|	1906f	1906f	|	|	1951	|	|	|	|	|	2105	2120	|	|	|	|	2251	|	2352¦
Siegburg/Bonn 🚋 **807** d.	1818	1831	1848	1848	1902	1927	1927	|	|	2011	|	2031	|	|	|	|	2140	2151	|	2234	2251	2311	2351	0012¦
Köln/Bonn Flughafen ✈ **802** a.	1828	|	|	|	|	1937	1937	|	|	|	|	|	|	|	|	|	|	|	|	|	|	2325	|	|
Köln Messe/Deutz **802** a.	1840	1848	|	|	1915	1949	|	|	|	2025	|	2048	|	2114	2130	|	2154	|	2215	|	|	2336	|	|
Köln Hbf **802 807** a.	...	|	1904	1904	|	|	1955	1931	2004	|	2033	|	2104	|	|	2140	2202	2206	|	2251	2307	|	0007	0029¦
Köln Hbf **800 802 807** d.	...	|	1911	1914	|	|	...	1940	2011	|	2041	|	...	|	|	2142	...	2212	|	...	2313r	|	...	...
Aachen Hbf **802 807** a.	...	|	|	|	|	|	...	2016	|	|	|	|	...	|	|	2215	...	|	|	...	|	|	...	...
Brussels Midi/Zuid **21** a.	...	|	|	|	|	|	...	2135	|	|	|	|	...	|	|	2335	...	|	|	...	|	|	...	...
Düsseldorf Hbf **800** a.	...	1912	◐	1935	1944	◐	...	...	◐	2047	2105	2110	...	2135	2151	...	...	2233	2237	...	◐	2357	...	...
Amsterdam Centraal **28** a.	...	|	|	2159	|	|	...	...	|	|	2329	|	...	|	...	...	...	|	|	...	|	|	...	...
Essen Hbf **800** a.	...	1940	|	...	2015	|	...	...	|	2115	...	2141	...	2202	...	...	...	2300	2302	...	|	0024	...	...
Dortmund Hbf **800** a.	...	2005	2021	...	2042	2107	...	...	2121	2140	...	2205	...	2227	...	...	...	...	2326	...	0024r	0048	...	...
Hamburg Hbf **800** a.	...	...	...	...	...	...	...	...	0015	...	...	...	...	...	...	...	...	...	...	...	...	...	...	...

MAINZ - WIESBADEN - KÖLN

	ICE 712		ICE 710
	Ⓐ		Ⓐ
			✕
Stuttgart Hbf **912** d.	...	...	1435
Mainz Hbf d.	0606	...	1622
Wiesbaden Hbf d.	0622	...	1645
Limburg Süd d.	0643	...	1708
Montabaur d.	0654	...	1718
Siegburg/Bonn 🚋 d.	|	...	1739
Köln/Bonn Flughafen ✈ a.	|	...	1747
Köln Hbf a.	0727	...	1801

Amended Amsterdam service on Feb. 11 – 24

	ICE 250	ICE 250	ICE 158	ICE 156	ICE 154	ICE 152	ICE 152	ICE 254	ICE 254
	⑦	①–⑥				①–⑥	⑦	①–⑥	⑦
	✕	✕	✕	✕	✕	✕	✕	✕	✕
Basel SBB **912** d.	...	...	...	...	...	...	...	1513	1513
Frankfurt (Main) Hbf d.	...	0628	0816	1126	1326	1628	1628	|	|
Frankfurt Flughafen Fernbf ✈ d.	...	0642	0831	1142	1342	1642	1642	1807	1807
Köln Hbf d.	0739	0739	0939	1239	1439	1748	1748	1910	1910
Mönchengladbach Hbf d.	0830	0830	1030	1330	1530	1831	1831	2003	2003
's-Hertogenbosch a.	0947	0952	1152	1452	1652	1947	1952	2136	2140
Utrecht Centraal a.	1015	1021	1221	1521	1721	2015	2021	2204	2208
Amsterdam Centraal a.	1044	1053	1253	1553	1753	2044	2053	2230	2244

A – From Würzburg on Ⓐ (Table **920**).
D – 🚌12 ✕ Darmstadt Hbf (d. 0647) - Köln - Paderborn - Kassel.
G – From Garmisch on ⑥ (Table **895**).
K – To Kiel (Table **820**).
M – To Münster (Table **800**).
P – Until Mar. 11.
U – Daily until Jan. 8; ⑤⑥ from Jan. 13.

b – Not Dec. 25.
e – ⚒ only.
f – Arrives 7 minutes earlier.
m – Not Dec. 26.
q – Not ⑤.

r – Köln - Dortmund on ⑧ (not Dec. 25).
v – ①–⑥ (also Dec. 25; not Dec. 26).
w – Also Dec. 26; not Dec. 25.
y – 1030 on ⑥⑦.
z – From Feb. 11.

¦ – On ⑦–④ Jan. 9 - Mar. 30 service is diverted via Mainz Hbf (a. 2348), Koblenz Hbf (a. 0041), Bonn Hbf (a. 0120) and arrives Köln Hbf 0150 (not calling at Limburg Süd, Montabaur or Siegburg/Bonn).
⊖ – Does not run Köln - Amsterdam Feb. 10 – 23.
⊠ – Subject to alteration Feb. 11 – 24 (see panel below).
◐ – Via Wuppertal (Table **800**).
🚋 – Frequent light-rail services operate from / to Bonn Hbf.

STRASBOURG - OFFENBURG 911

Südwestdeutsche Landesverkehrs / SNCF (2nd class only)

On Apr. 7, 10, May 1, 18, 29 services run as on ⑦.

km		b			①–⑤		①–⑤	①–⑤		①–⑤					①–⑤		①–⑤		①–⑤			①–⑤	①–⑤				
0	**Strasbourg** d.	0005	...	0620	0720	0749	0820	0850	0920	0950	1051	...	1250	1320	1420	1450	1520	1620	1651	1721	1750	1820	1850	1922	2020	2150	2250
21	Kehl 🏛 d.	0016	...	0633	0733	0803	0831	0903	0933	1003	1103	...	1303	1333	1433	1503	1533	1633	1703	1733	1803	1833	1903	1933	2033	2203	2303
29	**Offenburg** a.	0034	...	0652	0751	0822	0849	0922	0952	1022	1122	...	1322	1353	1452	1522	1552	1652	1722	1752	1822	1852	1922	1952	2052	2222	2322

		①–⑤		①–⑤		①–⑤	①–⑤	⑥⑦	①–⑤	⑥⑦		①–⑤	①–⑤	⑥⑦	①–⑤			①–⑤		①–⑤	①–⑤		①–⑤				c
Offenburg d.	0632	0705	0735	0805	0842	0905	0935	1005	1035	1205	1235	1305	1335	1405	1435	1505	1605	1635	1705	1733	1805	1835	1905	2005	2105	2205	2325
Kehl 🏛 d.	0654	0724	0754	0826	0900	0924	0954	1022	1054	1224	1254	1323	1355	1424	1454	1524	1624	1654	1724	1753	1824	1854	1924	2024	2124	2224	2346
Strasbourg a.	0706	0736	0806	0836	0910	0936	1006	1033	1106	1236	1306	1334	1406	1436	1506	1536	1636	1706	1736	1806	1836	1906	1935	2036	2136	2236	2358

b – Not Mar. 7 – 11, 28 – 31, Apr. 1, 4 – 7.

c – Not Mar. 6 – 10, 27 – 31, Apr. 3 – 6.

Local services MAINZ - MANNHEIM and MAINZ - SPEYER - KARLSUHE 911a

RE / S-Bahn services

km		Ⓐ	⚒	Ⓐ	Ⓐ		Ⓐ																	Ⓒ	Ⓐ	Ⓒ
	Frankfurt (Main) Hbf ‡ d.	...	...	...	...	...	0608	...	...	...	...	...	0838	...	...	1038	...	...	1238	...	...	1438	...	...	1538	1638
0	**Mainz** Hbf .... **912** ‡ d.	0456	0515	0545	...	0552t	0647	0622	0656	0722	0813	...	0913	1013	...	1117	1213	...	1317	1413	...	1517	1613	...	1617	1717
46	Worms Hbf a.	0540	0556	0614	...	0634t	0714	0706	0739	0806	0839	...	0940	1039	...	1144	1239	...	1344	1439	...	1544	1639	...	1652	1744
46	Worms Hbf d.	0541	0556	0615	...	0635	0715	0717	0746	0816	0840	0848	0941	1040	1048	1145	1240	1249	1345	1440	1448	1545	1640	1648	1653	1745
67	Ludwigshafen Hbf **918** d.	0600	0616	0637	0654	0653	0731	0735	0804	0836	0857	0909		1057	1109		1257	1309		1457	1509		1655	1709	1708	
87	Speyer Hbf ..... **918** d.				0713						0913			1113			1313			1513			1713			
101	Germersheim.. **918** d.				0723						0923			1123			1323			1523			1723			
138	**Karlsruhe** Hbf a.				0753						0953			1153			1353			1553			1753			
68	Ludwigshafen Mitte ... d.	0602	0619		...	0655	0734	0738	0809	0838	...	0912	1000	...	1111	1204	...	1311	1402	...	1511	1603	...	1711	1711	1806
70	**Mannheim** Hbf .. **912** a.	0604	0621	0641	...	0658	0737	0741	0813	0841	...	0915	1003	...	1115	1207	...	1314	1405	...	1514	1606	...	1714	1715	1810

	Ⓐ											
Frankfurt (Main) Hbf ‡ d.	1638	...	...	...	1838	...	...	...	...	2038	...	...
Mainz Hbf .... **912** ‡ d.	1717	...	1813	...	1917	1925	2013	...	2052	2117	2206	2308
Worms Hbf a.	1744	...	1839	...	1944	2008	2039	...	2136	2155	2251	2351
Worms Hbf d.	1745	1749	1840	1848	1945	2018	2040	2048	2148	2156	2251	2351
Ludwigshafen Hbf.. **918** d.	1800	1809	1857	1909		2037	2057	2109	2208	2215	2309	0009
Speyer Hbf .... **918** d.	1819		1913				2113					
Germersheim ... **918** d.	1828		1923				2123					
Karlsruhe Hbf a.	...		1953				2153					
Ludwigshafen Mitte .... d.	...	1811	...	1913	2005	2039	...	2111	2211	2218	2311	0012
Mannheim Hbf .... **912** a.	...	1814	...	1916	2007	2042	...	2114	2214	2221	2314	0014

		Ⓒ	⑥k	Ⓐn	Ⓐ	⚒	Ⓐ	Ⓐ	
Mannheim Hbf .... **912** d.	0018	0018	0424	0425	0459	0530	0540	...	0650
Ludwigshafen Mitte .... d.	0020	0020	0427	0428	0501	0533	0542	...	0653
Karlsruhe Hbf d.								...	
Germersheim .... **918** d.								0619	
Speyer Hbf .... **918** d.								0632	
Ludwigshafen Hbf...... **918** d.	0023	0023	0433	0433	0504	0535	0546	0656	0659
Worms Hbf a.	0039	0039	0451	0451	0522	0553	0607	0712	0718
Worms Hbf d.	...	0040	0452	0452	0523	0555	0607	0713	0725
Mainz Hbf .... **912** ‡ a.	...	0122	0538	0538	0608	0638	0641	0747	0808
Frankfurt (Main) Hbf ...... ‡ a.	...	...	...	...	...	...	0722	0822	...

	Ⓐ	Ⓒ	Ⓐ																							
Mannheim Hbf .... **912** d.	...	0751	0749	0844	...	0915	0958	1044	...	1152	1244	...	1352	1445	...	1549	1644	...	1752	1844	...	1951	2044	...	2144	2247
Ludwigshafen Mitte .... d.	...	0753	0751	0847	...	0917	1000	1047	...	1154	1248	...	1354	1448	...	1552	1646	...	1754	1847	...	1954	2047	...	2146	2249
Karlsruhe Hbf d.	0655				0808				1008			1208			1408			1608			1808			2008		
Germersheim ... **918** d.	0724				0838				1038			1238			1438			1638			1838			2038		
Speyer Hbf .... **918** d.	0733				0847				1047			1247			1447			1647			1847			2047		
Ludwigshafen Hbf **918** d.	0751		0755	0850	0904	0920		1050	1104		1250	1304		1451	1504		1649	1704		1850	1904		2050	2104	2150	2252
Worms Hbf a.	0804	0816	0814	0914	0919	0938	1019	1111	1119	1216	1311	1319	1416	1514	1519	1616	1714	1719	1816	1913	1919	2016	2114	2119	2213	2309
Worms Hbf d.	0809	0817	0825	...	0920	0955	1020	...	1120	1217	...	1320	1417	...	1520	1617	...	1720	1817	...	1920	2017	...	2120	2218	2310
Mainz Hbf .... **912** a.	0836	0843	0908	...	0947	1036	1046	...	1147	1243	...	1347	1443	...	1547	1643	...	1747	1843	...	1947	2043	...	2147	2301	2353
Frankfurt (Main) Hbf ‡ a.	*0922*	0922	...	...	1022	...	1122	...	1222	1322	...	1422	1523	...	1623	...	...	...	1922j	...	2022	2122	...	2222	...	...

j – Change trains at Mainz on Ⓐ.
k – Also Jan. 6.
n – Not Jan. 6.
t – Ⓐ only.
‡ – See Tables **800**, **914**, **917** and **917a** for other services Frankfurt - Mainz and v.v.

FRANKFURT - BASEL and STUTTGART 912

See Table **927** for services operated by FlixTrain

km	km		*ICE* **879** ①g	*ICE* **619** U K	*ICE* **1119** ①–⑤ Y	*ICE* **699** ♦		*NJ* **403** ♦	*NJ* **408** ♦	*ICE* **3** Ⓐ ✕	*NJ* **471** ♦		*IC* **2381** Ⓐ R	*ICE* **991** W	*ICE* **271** ②–⑦ dH ✕	*ICE* **1271** ①g H✕	*TGV* **9578** ①–⑥ ♦🅁	*RJ* **897** ✕♦	*ICE* **911** ⚒ ✕	*EC* **217** 🍷♦	*ICE* **511** ✕	*ICE* **5** ⚒ ✕	*ICE* **9568** ⒷQ 🅁✕	*ICE* **1511** Ⓐ
		Hamburg Hbf **800 900** d.	...	1945p	...	1936	...	...	...	...	2207	...	...	...		0045	...	...	...	...	...	...	...	...
		Berlin Hbf **810 850 902** d.	2029p		...	2126	...	...	2051	...		...	...	...	...		...	...	...	...	...	...	...	...
		Hannover Hbf **810 900** d.			...		...	...		...	0030	...	...	...	...	0210	...	...	...	...	...	...	...	...
		Dortmund Hbf **800** d.		2236p	...		...	...		...		...	...	...	...		...	...	...	...	...	...	...	...
		Köln Hbf **800 910** d.		2355p	...		...	2353j		...		...	...	...	...		...	...	...	...	0549	...	...	...
		Koblenz Hbf **800** d.			...		...	0049		...		...	...	...	...		...	...	...	...		...	...	...
		Wiesbaden Hbf ... **917a 918a** d.			...		...			...		...	...	0526	...		...	...	...	...		...	...	...
		Mainz Hbf .... **917a 918a** d.			...		...	0142		...		...	...	0540	...		...	...	...	...		...	...	...
0	0	**Frankfurt** (Main) Hbf ... **913** d.	0050	0117	0117	0225	...	0245	0400	...	0432x	...	0519		0550	0550	...	0554	0603	...		0648	0656	0706
		Frankfurt Flughafen ✈ ◧ .. d.		0056*		0246	...	0209*		...		...					...			...	0651			
78		**Mannheim** Hbf .... **913** a.	0127	0202	0202	0323	...	0331	0439	...		...		0623	0627	0627	...			...	0723	0727	0736	0748
78		**Mannheim** Hbf .... **913** d.	0130	0204	0204	0325	...	0333	0441	...		...		0629	0633	0633	...			0711	0731	0735	0738	0752
	28	Darmstadt Hbf ... **913 918a** d.					...			...	0450	...	0536				...	0613						
	50	Bensheim .... **913** d.					...			...		...	0550				...	0625						
	64	Weinheim .... **913** d.					...			...		...	0600				...	0636						
	87	**Heidelberg** Hbf ... **913 931** d.		0219	0219	0340	...			...	0534	...	0615				...	0652						0805
	120	Bruchsal .... **913 931** d.					...			...		...					...							
		Vaihingen (Enz) .... **931** d.					...			...		...					...							
		Stuttgart Hbf .... **931** a.		0333	0333	0452	...			...		...	0702	0708			...	0737	0720	0753	0808			0849
		München Hbf **930** a.		0603	0603	0728	...			...		...	...	0918			...	...	0928	1010	1026			...
138	141	**Karlsruhe** Hbf .... **913 916** ☆ d.	0155	...	...	...	...	0403	0509	0556	0604	...	...	...	0658	0658	0732	...	...	...	...	0800	0806	...
167	172	Baden-Baden .... **916** ☆ d.	...	...	...	...	...	0427	0528	0613		...	...	...	0717	0717		...	...	...	...			...
207		Offenburg .... **911 916** ☆ d.	...	...	...	...	...	0452	0547	0630	0643	...	...	...	0733	0733		...	...	...	...	0832		...
	225	**Strasbourg** ⊖ .... **911** a.	...	...	...	...	...					...	...	...			0813	...	...	...	...		0847	...
270		**Freiburg** (Brsg) Hbf .... ☆ d.	...	...	...	...	...	0528	0619	0702	0723	...	...	...	0804	0804	...	...	...	...	...	0902	...	...
327		**Basel** Bad Bf 🏛 .... ☆ a.	...	...	...	...	...	0611	0656	0736	0759	...	...	...	0837	0837	...	...	...	...	...	0936	...	...
332		**Basel** SBB .... ☆ a.	...	...	...	...	...	0620	0720	0747	0810	...	...	...	0847	0847	...	...	...	...	...	0947	...	...
		Zürich HB **510** a.	...	...	...	...	...	0805	0905	0900	1005	...	...	...	1000	1000	...	...	...	...	...	...	...	...

♦ – **NOTES** (LISTED BY TRAIN NUMBER)

217 – DACHSTEIN – 🚃12 🍷 Saarbrücken - München - Salzburg - Graz.
403 – 🛏 1, 2 cl. and 🛌 2 cl. (🅁) Amsterdam - Utrecht - Basel - Zürich. Also conveys 🚃2 (*IC* **60403**).
408 – 🛏 1, 2 cl. and 🛌 2 cl. (🅁) Berlin - Leipzig - Basel - Zürich. Also conveys 🚃2 (*IC* **60408**).
🛏 1, 2 cl. and 🛌 2 cl. (*EN* **40458** 🅁) and 🚃2 (*EC* **458**) Praha - Dresden - Leipzig - Basel - Zürich.
471 – 🛏 1, 2 cl. and 🛌 2 cl. (🅁) Hamburg - Basel - Zürich (a. 0905). Also conveys 🚃2 (*IC* **60471**).
699 – 🚃12 Hamburg - Berlin - Leipzig - Erfurt - Frankfurt - München.
897 – 🚃12 ✕ Frankfurt - Ulm - Lindau - Bregenz (**867**) - Innsbruck - Wien.
9578 – 🚃12 🍷 Stuttgart - Karlsruhe - Paris (Table **32**).

H – To Chur (Table **520**).
K – From Kiel (Table **820**).
Q – To Paris (Table **30**).
R – To Radolfzell (Table **940**).
U – Daily until Jan. 9; ⑥⑦ from Jan. 14.

W – Also calls at Worms Hbf (d. 0608).
Y – ①–⑤ from Jan. 10.

d – Also Dec. 26; not Dec. 27.
g – Also Dec. 27; not Dec. 26.
j – 2342 Feb. 10 – 23.
p – Previous day.
x – Frankfurt (Main) **Süd**.

* – Calls at Frankfurt Flughafen before Frankfurt (Main) Hbf.
☆ – See also panel on page 423 for other local services.
⊖ – 🏛 is at Kehl (8 km from Strasbourg). See Table **911** for local journeys Offenburg - Strasbourg.
◧ – Frankfurt Flughafen Fernbahnhof.

912 FRANKFURT - BASEL and STUTTGART

	ICE 1571 Ⓐ Y✕		ICE 1178 Ⓐ ✕	ICE 711 Ⓐ ✕	IC 1913 ⑥	ICE 591 ✕	ICE 101 ✕	ICE 913 ⚒ ✕	ECE 151 ✕◆	TGV 9576 H Ⓡ🍸	EC 113 ✕◆	ICE 1548 M✕	ICE 513 M✕	ICE 275 © N✕	ICE 275 Ⓐ N✕	ICE 9566 ⑥Q Ⓡ✕	ICE 571 ✕	ICE 1573 ✕◆	ICE 563 S✕	ICE 593 ✕	ICE 103 ✕	ICE 915 ✕	ICE 71 C✕	ICE 9574 P Ⓡ✕
Hamburg Hbf **800 900** d.						0319r											0515						0618	
Berlin Hbf **810 850 902** d.															0429					0526				
Hannover Hbf **810 900** d.						0519r											0641	0557a					0741	
Dortmund Hbf **800** d.							0528e	0547				0536	0636									0756		
Köln Hbf **800 910** d.				0559			0655	0711•				0653	0755								0855	0911•		
Koblenz Hbf **800** d.												0748												
Wiesbaden Hbf **917a 918a** d.				0732	0731																			
Mainz Hbf **917a 918a** d.				0746	0746							0842												
Frankfurt (Main) Hbf **913** d.	0714					0750			0806		0820			0849	0850	0856	0906	0920		0950			1006	
Frankfurt Flughafen ✈ ◧ d.							0751	0809					0851				0924				0951	1009		
Mannheim Hbf **913** a.				0824	0824	0827	0823	0840	0844			0921	0923	0927	0927	0937	0956			1027	1023	1039	1044	
Mannheim Hbf **913** d.			0818	0826	0826	0830	0835	0843	0847			0923	0931	0935	0935	0939	0959		1002	1030	1035	1043	1046	
Darmstadt Hbf **913 918a** d.	0731										0838							0937						
Bensheim **913** d.	0746										0849							0950						
Weinheim **913** d.	0758										0859							1000						
Heidelberg Hbf **913 931** d.	0814			0839	0839						0913	0935						1015						
Bruchsal **913 931** d.	0835																	1035						
Vaihingen (Enz) **931** d.			0848									1005												
Stuttgart Hbf **931** a.			0905	0918	0919	0908		0922			0952	1024	1008				1038		1045	1108		1122		
München Hbf **930** a.						1114		1126			1210	...	1226						1257	1313		1326		
Karlsruhe Hbf **913 916** ☆ d.	0850						0900		0911	0953				1000	1000	1006		1050			1100		1111	1131
Baden-Baden **916** ☆ d.							0917																1127	
Offenburg **911 916** ☆ d.							0935							1032	1032						1133			
Strasbourg ⊖ **911** a.										1037						1047								1213
Freiburg (Brsg) Hbf ☆ d.							1005		1014					1102	1102						1202		1214	
Basel Bad Bf 🏛 ☆ a.							1038		1045					1136	1136						1236		1246	
Basel SBB ☆ a.							1047		1054					1147	1147						1247		1255	
Zürich HB **510** a.																							1400	

	ICE 999 ✕	EC 115 🍸◆	EC 7 N✕	ICE 515 ✕	ICE 277 ✕	IC 119 ◆	ICE 573 K✕	ICE 1575 ✕		ICE 595 ✕	ICE 105 ✕◆	ICE 917 D✕	ICE 73 K✕	EC 219 🍸◆	IC 2005 ⑤⑥ 🍸◆	EC 9 ✕	ICE 517 ✕	ICE 279 ✕	IC 2013 🍸◆	ICE 575 ✕	ICE 1577 T✕		ICE 597 ✕	ICE 107 ✕
Hamburg Hbf **800 900** d.			0437	0545			0723	0624e					0824			0645	0745			0924	0828			0845
Berlin Hbf **810 850 902** d.					0629					0726								0829					0926	
Hannover Hbf **810 900** d.							0841	0801e					0941							1041	1001			
Dortmund Hbf **800** d.				0835		0751											1035		0949					
Köln Hbf **800 910** d.		0817	0853	0955		0917					1055	1116•			1017	1053	1155		1117					1255
Koblenz Hbf **800** d.		0918	0948			1018									1118	1148			1218					
Wiesbaden Hbf **917a 918a** d.																								
Mainz Hbf **917a 918a** d.		1017	1042			1113									1217	1242			1313					
Frankfurt (Main) Hbf **913** d.	1020				1050		1106	1120		1150			1206	1220				1250		1306	1320		1350	
Frankfurt Flughafen ✈ ◧ d.				1051			1124				1151	1209					1251			1324				1351
Mannheim Hbf **913** a.		1100	1121	1123	1127	1152	1156			1227	1223	1239	1244		1306	1321	1323	1327	1352	1356			1427	1423
Mannheim Hbf **913** d.		1102	1123	1131	1135	1154	1159			1230	1235	1243	1246		1308	1323	1331	1335	1354	1359			1430	1435
Darmstadt Hbf **913 918a** d.	1037							1137						1237							1337			
Bensheim **913** d.								1150						1249							1350			
Weinheim **913** d.	1056							1200						1259							1400			
Heidelberg Hbf **913 931** d.	1111					1206		1215						1313					1406		1415			
Bruchsal **913 931** d.								1235													1435			
Vaihingen (Enz) **931** d.		1137																						
Stuttgart Hbf **931** a.	1151	1153		1208		1248	1238			1308		1320		1353			1408		1450	1438			1508	
München Hbf **930** a.		1410		1426						1513		1527		1610			1626						1716	
Karlsruhe Hbf **913 916** ☆ d.			1149		1200			1250			1300		1311		1336	1349		1400			1450			1500
Baden-Baden **916** ☆ d.					1216								1327		1354	1407								
Offenburg **911 916** ☆ d.					1231						1333				1413			1432						1533
Strasbourg ⊖ **911** a.																								
Freiburg (Brsg) Hbf ☆ d.			1250		1303						1402		1414			1455		1501						1602
Basel Bad Bf 🏛 ☆ a.			1322		1337						1436		1446			1528		1536						1636
Basel SBB ☆ a.			1333		1347						1447		1455			1536		1547						1647
Zürich HB **510** a.													1600			1700								

◆ – **NOTES** for pages 422 and 423 (LISTED BY TRAIN NUMBER)

75 – 🚃12 ✕ (Kiel ✝ -) Hamburg - Zürich - Chur.
105 – 🚃12 ✕ Amsterdam - Basel. Subject to alteration Feb. 11 – 24.
113 – BLAUER ENZIAN – 🚃12 ✕ Frankfurt - Salzburg - Villach - Klagenfurt; 🚃12 Frankfurt - Villach (**213**) - Ljubljana - Zagreb.
115 – WÖRTHERSEE – 🚃12 🍸 Münster - München - Salzburg - Villach - Klagenfurt. Also calls at Worms Hbf (d. 1045).
117 – SALZACH – 🚃12 🍸 Frankfurt - München - Salzburg - Klagenfurt.
119 – BODENSEE – 🚃12 Dortmund - Stuttgart - Ulm - Lindau - Bregenz - Innsbruck.
151 – 🚃12 ✕ Frankfurt - Basel - Luzern - Chiasso - Milano.
219 – CHIEMGAU – 🚃12 🍸 Frankfurt - München - Salzburg - Bischofshofen - Graz.
266 – BADEN-KURIER – 🚃12 ✕ München - Stuttgart - Basel.
1103 – ⑥ (also Dec. 25; not Jan. 7 - Mar. 25). NORDERNEY – 🚃12 ✕ Norddeich Mole - Münster - Stuttgart. Also calls at Worms Hbf (d. 1845).
1219 – 🚃12 ✕ Berlin - Frankfurt - München (- Innsbruck ⑤⑥).
1291 – 🚃12 🍸 Frankfurt - München (- Salzburg Ⓑ **b**).
1573 – 🚃12 ✕ (Hannover Ⓐ -) (Kassel - Gießen ⚒ -) Frankfurt - Karlsruhe.
2005 – ⑤⑥ (also Dec. 25; not Jan. 6 - Mar. 31). SCHWARZWALD – 🚃12 🍸 Emden - Münster - Karlsruhe - Konstanz. Also calls at Worms Hbf (d. 1245).
2013 – Not Jan. 5 - Mar. 31. ALLGÄU – 🚃12 🍸 Dortmund - Stuttgart - Ulm - Oberstdorf.
2375 – WATTENMEER – 🚃12 🍸 (Westerland ⑤–① -) Hamburg - Hannover - Gießen - Frankfurt - Karlsruhe.
9580 – 🚃12 🍸 Frankfurt - Strasbourg - Mulhouse - Lyon - Marseille.

A – From Stralsund via Rostock (Table **830**).
B – From Leipzig (Tables **849a**/**850**).
C – To Chur (Table **520**).
D – From Düsseldorf (Table **910**).
E – From Stuttgart (Table **931**). Also calls at Rastatt (a. 1744).
G – Runs as *TGV* **9592** on ⑥. *ICE* ✕, *TGV* 🍸.
H – 🚃12 🍸 München - Stuttgart - Paris (Table **32**).
K – From Kiel (Table **820**).
L – ①②③④⑥ (also Dec. 25; not Dec. 26).
M – From Münster (Table **800**).
N – To Interlaken via Bern (Table **560**).
P – 🚃12 Stuttgart - Karlsruhe - Paris (Table **32**).
Q – To Paris (Table **30**).
R – From Dresden via Leipzig (Table **866**).
S – From Saarbrücken (Table **919**).
T – From Stralsund via Rostock on dates in Table **830**.
Y – From Kassel (Table **806**).

a – Ⓐ only.
b – Ⓑ (not Dec. 25).
d – Not Jan. 6 - Mar. 31.
e – ⚒ only.
h – Also Dec. 25.
m – Not Dec. 26.
q – ①②③④⑥ (also Dec. 25; not Dec. 26).
r – ①–⑥ only.
u – Also Apr. 6, 10, May 1.
w – ⑦ (also Dec. 26; not Dec. 25).
y – Not Dec. 25.

* – On © arrives 4 – 5 minutes later (change trains at Basel Bad Bf).
♠ – Until Jan. 4. LORELEY. To Tübingen on dates in Table **936**.
❖ – Offenburg - Basel Bad Bf daily; Basel Bad Bf - Basel SBB on Ⓐ.
¦ – Frankfurt (Main) **Süd**.
• – Köln **Messe/Deutz**.
☆ – See panel on page 423 for other local services.
⊖ – 🏛 is at Kehl (8 km from Strasbourg). See Table **911** for local journeys Offenburg - Strasbourg.
◧ – Frankfurt Flughafen Fernbahnhof.

FRANKFURT - BASEL and STUTTGART — 912

	TGV 9580	ICE 75	TGV 9580	ICE 9572	EC 117	IC 2044	ICE 519	ICE 371	IC 2015	IC 1915	ICE 577	ICE 1579	ICE 1219	ICE 109	ICE 1011	ICE 77	IC 2044	IC 1291	IC 2046	ICE 611	ICE 373	TGV 9560	IC 1177	IC 1995
	🅁		🅁	G P 🅁					⑤d	⑦w							Ⓐ					Q	⑤	①–④
	🍷♦	🍴♦	🍷♦		🍷♦	R🍷	🍴	N🍴	🍷	🍷	🍴	T🍴	🍴♦	🍴	🍴	K🍴	E🍷	🍷♦	R🍷	🍴	N🍴	🅁🍷	🍷	m
Hamburg Hbf 800 900 d.	...	1024	...	...	...	...	0945	...	...	...	1124	1028	...	1045	...	1224	...	...	...	1145	...	...	...	...
Berlin Hbf 810 850 902 d.	...	│	...	...	...	...	│	1029	...	...	│	│	1126	│	...	│	...	...	...	│	1229	...	...	...
Hannover Hbf 810 900 d.	...	1141	...	...	...	0940	│	│	...	...	1241	1201	│	│	...	1341	...	...	1140	│	│	...	...	...
Dortmund Hbf 800 d.	...	│	...	...	...	1135	1236	│	1151	1149	│	│	│	│	1349q	│	...	...	1336	1435	│	...	...	...
Köln Hbf 800 910 d.	...	│	...	...	...	1253	1355	│	1317	1317	│	│	│	1455	1511●	│	...	...	1453	1555	│	...	...	...
Koblenz Hbf 800 d.	...	│	...	...	...	1348	│	│	1418	1418	│	│	│	│	│	│	...	...	1548	│	│	...	...	...
Wiesbaden Hbf 917a 918a d.	...	│	...	...	...	│	│	│	│	│	│	│	│	│	│	│	...	...	│	│	│	...	...	...
Mainz Hbf 917a 918a d.	...	│	...	...	...	1442	│	│	1513	1513	│	│	│	│	│	│	...	...	1642	│	│	...	...	...
Frankfurt (Main) Hbf 913 d.	1356	1406	...	...	1420	│	│	1450	│	│	1506	1520	1550	│	│	1606	...	1620	│	│	1650	1656	1646	1651
Frankfurt Flughafen ✈ d.	│	│	...	...	│	│	1451	│	│	│	1524	│	│	1551	1609	│	...	│	│	1651	│	│	│	│
Mannheim Hbf 913 a.	1437	1444	...	...	│	1521	1523	1527	1552	1552	1556	│	1627	1623	1639	1644	...	│	1721	1723	1727	1736	│	│
Mannheim Hbf 913 d.	1439	1446	...	...	│	1523	1531	1535	1554	1554	1559	│	1630	1635	1643	1646	...	│	1723	1731	1735	1738	│	│
Darmstadt Hbf 913 918a d.	│	│	...	...	1437	│	│	│	│	│	│	1537	│	│	│	│	...	1637	│	│	│	│	1704	1715
Bensheim 913 d.	│	│	...	...	1449	│	│	│	│	│	│	1550	│	│	│	│	...	1649	│	│	│	│	│	│
Weinheim 913 d.	│	│	...	...	1459	│	│	│	│	│	│	1600	│	│	│	│	...	1659	│	│	│	│	1728	│
Heidelberg Hbf 913 931 d.	│	│	...	...	1513	1535	│	│	1606	1607	│	1615	│	│	│	│	...	1713	1735	│	│	│	1744	│
Bruchsal 913 931 d.	│	│	...	...	│	│	│	│	│	│	│	1635	│	│	│	│	...	│	│	│	│	│	│	│
Vaihingen (Enz) 931 d.	│	│	...	...	│	1604	│	│	│	1639	│	│	│	│	│	│	...	│	1810	│	│	│	│	│
Stuttgart Hbf 931 a.	│	│	...	...	1553	1622	1608	│	1649	1656	1638	│	1708	│	1721	│	...	1753	1827	1808	│	│	│	1830
München Hbf 930 a.	│	│	←	...	1810	...	1826	│	...	...	...	│	1913	│	1927	│	...	2010	...	2026	│	│	│	...
Karlsruhe Hbf 913 916 ☆ d.	1505	1511	1512	1532	...	...	...	1600	...	...	...	1650	...	1700	...	1711	1732	...	...	...	1800	1805	1827	...
Baden-Baden 916 ☆ d.	→	1527	1535	│	...	...	...	│	...	...	...	...	...	│	...	1727	1754	...	...	...	│	│	1845	...
Offenburg 911 916 ☆ d.	...	│	│	│	...	...	...	1632	...	...	...	...	...	1733	...	│	1811	...	...	...	1832	│	1904	...
Strasbourg ⊖ 911 a.	...	│	1602	1613	...	...	...	│	...	...	...	...	...	│	...	│	...	...	...	...	│	1848	│	...
Freiburg (Brsg) Hbf ☆ d.	...	1614	...	...	...	...	...	1702	...	...	...	...	...	1802	...	1814	...	...	...	...	1901	...	1940	...
Basel Bad Bf 🏛 ☆ a.	...	1646	...	...	...	...	...	1736	...	...	...	...	...	1836	...	1846	...	...	...	...	1936	...	2019	...
Basel SBB ☆ a.	...	1655	...	...	...	...	...	1747	...	...	...	...	...	1847	...	1855	...	...	...	...	1947	...	2030	...
Zürich HB 510 a.	...	1800	...	...	...	...	...	...	...	...	...	...	...	...	...	2000	...	...	...	...	...	...	...	...

	ICE 579	IC 2011	IC 2011	ICE 1671	IC 2183	ICE 691	ICE 201	ICE 1013	ICE 79	TGV 9570	IC 1956	ICE 1099	ICE 1103	ICE 1091	IC 2048	ICE 613	ICE 266	ICE 375	ICE 266	IC 1917	ICE 717		ICE 771	IC 2375
		Ⓐ	⑦		①–④					P	⑦w		⑥	⑦w			Ⓑb		Ⓑb	⑦w	⑤			
	🍴	♠	♠	A🍴	m	🍴	🍴	🍴	🍴	🅁🍷	B🍷	🍴	🍴♦	🍴	R🍷	K🍴	🍴♦	🍴	♦	🍷	🍴		🍴	🍷♦
Hamburg Hbf 800 900 d.	1324	...	...	1228	...	...	1245	...	1424	...	...	...	...	...	...	1345	...	...	...	...	...	...	1524	1427
Berlin Hbf 810 850 902 d.	│	...	0955	│	...	1326	│	...	│	...	...	...	...	1359	...	│	...	1429	...	1159	1159	...	│	│
Hannover Hbf 810 900 d.	1441	...	1156	1401	...	│	│	...	1541	...	...	...	...	1551	1340	│	...	│	...	1356	1356	...	1641	1601
Dortmund Hbf 800 d.	│	...	1351	│	...	│	│	1549	│	...	...	...	...	│	1536	1635	...	│	...	│	│	...	│	│
Köln Hbf 800 910 d.	│	1517	1517	│	...	│	1655	1710●	│	...	...	...	1617	│	1653	1755	...	│	...	1717	1717	...	│	│
Koblenz Hbf 800 d.	│	1618	1618	│	...	│	│	│	│	...	...	...	1718	│	1748	│	...	│	...	1818	1818	...	│	│
Wiesbaden Hbf 917a 918a d.	│	│	│	│	...	│	│	│	│	...	...	...	│	│	│	│	...	│	...	│	│	...	│	│
Mainz Hbf 917a 918a d.	│	1713	1713	│	...	│	│	│	│	...	...	...	1817	│	1842	│	...	│	...	1913	1913	...	│	│
Frankfurt (Main) Hbf 913 d.	1706	│	│	1720	1746	1750	│	│	1806	...	1755⁝	1819	│	1838	│	│	...	1850	...	│	│	...	1906	1920
Frankfurt Flughafen ✈ d.	1724	│	│	│	│	│	1751	1809	│	...	│	│	│	│	│	1851	...	│	...	│	│	...	1924	│
Mannheim Hbf 913 a.	1755	1752	1752	│	│	1827	1823	1839	1844	...	│	│	1901	1916	1921	1923	...	1927	...	1952	1952	...	1955	│
Mannheim Hbf 913 d.	1759	1754	1754	│	│	1830	1835	1842	1846	...	│	│	1903	1918	1923	1931	...	1935	...	1954	1954	...	1959	│
Darmstadt Hbf 913 918a d.	│	│	│	1737	1803	│	│	│	│	...	1813	1837	│	│	│	│	...	│	...	│	│	...	│	1937
Bensheim 913 d.	│	│	│	1750	1817	│	│	│	│	...	1825	1849	│	│	│	│	...	│	...	│	│	...	│	1950
Weinheim 913 d.	│	│	│	1800	1828	│	│	│	│	...	1839	1859	│	│	│	│	...	│	...	│	│	...	│	2000
Heidelberg Hbf 913 931 d.	│	1806	1806	1815	1843	│	│	│	│	...	1902	1913	│	│	1935	│	...	│	...	2006	2006	...	│	2015
Bruchsal 913 931 d.	│	│	│	1835	1902	│	│	│	│	...	1926	│	│	│	│	│	...	│	...	│	│	...	│	2035
Vaihingen (Enz) 931 d.	│	│	│	│	│	│	│	│	│	...	│	│	│	│	2005	│	...	│	...	│	│	...	│	│
Stuttgart Hbf 931 a.	1838	1846	1846	│	│	1908	│	1922	│	...	│	1953	1946	1958	2023	2008	...	│	...	2047	2048	...	2038	│
München Hbf 930 a.	...	...	...	│	│	2113	│	2126	│	...	│	2213b	...	...	...	2226	...	│	...	...	...	...	...	│
Karlsruhe Hbf 913 916 ☆ d.	...	...	...	1852	1916	...	1900	...	1911	1932	1941	...	...	...	...	...	1955	2001	...	...	...	...	...	2053
Baden-Baden 916 ☆ d.	...	...	...	...	...	...	│	...	1927	│	...	...	...	...	...	...	2012	2018	...	...	...	...	...	...
Offenburg 911 916 ☆ d.	...	...	...	...	...	...	1933	...	│	│	...	...	...	...	...	...	2029	2036	...	...	...	...	...	...
Strasbourg ⊖ 911 a.	...	...	...	...	...	...	│	...	│	2013	...	...	...	...	...	...	│	│	←	...	...	...	...	...
Freiburg (Brsg) Hbf ☆ d.	...	...	...	...	...	...	2002	...	2014	...	...	...	...	...	...	...	2101	2107	2111	...	...	...	...	...
Basel Bad Bf 🏛 ☆ a.	...	...	...	...	...	...	2036	...	2046	...	...	...	...	...	...	...	→	2140	2147	...	...	...	...	...
Basel SBB ☆ a.	...	...	...	...	...	...	2047	...	2055	...	...	...	...	...	...	...	...	2149	2156	...	...	...	...	...
Zürich HB 510 a.	...	...	...	...	...	...	...	...	2200	...	...	...	...	...	...	...	...	...	...	...	...	...	...	...

	ICE 693	ICE 203	ICE 1015	ICE 1171	ICE 1595	ICE 1585	IC 2299	IC 2440	ICE 615	ICE 377	ICE 773	ICE 695	ICE 695	ICE 205	ICE 205	IC 1997	ICE 273	ICE 273	ICE 205		ICE 617	ICE 775	ICE 877	ICE 834
			Ⓑ		⑦w	⑤	L						Ⓒ	⑦–④	⑤⑥	⑦w		⑤⑥	⑦–④			Ⓑb	⑥h	
	🍴	🍴	🍴	K	🍷	🍴	🍴	R🍷	🍴	🍴	🍴	🍴	🍴	y🍴	h🍴	🍷	🍴	h🍴	y		🍴			
Hamburg Hbf 800 900 d.	...	...	...	1624	...	...	...	...	1545	...	1724	...	...	1645	1645	...	1824	1824	...	...	1745	1924	...	...
Berlin Hbf 810 850 902 d.	1526	...	...	│	1500	...	...	...	│	1629	│	1726	1726	│	│	...	│	│	...	...	│	│	1829	1905
Hannover Hbf 810 900 d.	│	...	...	1741	1702	1707	...	1540	│	│	1841	│	│	│	│	...	1941	1941	...	...	│	2041	│	│
Dortmund Hbf 800 d.	│	...	1750	│	│	│	...	1736	1835	│	│	│	│	│	│	...	│	│	...	...	2036	│	│	│
Köln Hbf 800 910 d.	│	1855	1911●	│	│	│	...	1853	1955	│	│	│	│	2055	2055	...	│	│	...	...	2155	│	│	│
Koblenz Hbf 800 d.	│	│	│	│	│	│	...	1948	│	│	│	│	│	│	│	...	│	│	...	...	│	│	│	│
Wiesbaden Hbf 917a 918a d.	│	│	│	│	│	│	...	│	│	│	│	│	│	│	│	...	│	│	...	...	│	│	│	│
Mainz Hbf 917a 918a d.	│	│	│	│	│	│	...	2042	│	│	│	│	│	│	│	...	│	│	...	...	│	│	│	│
Frankfurt (Main) Hbf 913 d.	1950	│	│	2006	2020	2020	2020	│	│	2050	2106	2150	2150	│	│	2155	2206	2206	...	...	│	2306	2306	2308
Frankfurt Flughafen ✈ d.	│	1951	2009	│	│	│	│	│	2051	│	2124	│	│	2151	2151	│	│	│	...	...	2255	2324	2324	│
Mannheim Hbf 913 a.	2027	2023	2039	2044	│	│	│	2121	2124	2127	2155	2227	2227	2223	2223	│	2244	2244	...	...	2327	0005	0006	│
Mannheim Hbf 913 d.	2030	2035	2043	2046	│	│	│	2123	2131	2135	2158	2230	2230	2235	2235	│	2246	2246	...	...	2330	0012	0012	│
Darmstadt Hbf 913 918a d.	│	│	│	│	2037	2037	2037	│	│	│	│	│	│	│	│	2212	│	│	...	...	│	│	│	2326
Bensheim 913 d.	│	│	│	│	2049	2050	2049	│	│	│	│	│	│	│	│	2224	│	│	...	...	│	│	│	2339
Weinheim 913 d.	│	│	│	│	2100	2100	2059	│	│	│	│	│	│	│	│	2234	│	│	...	...	│	│	│	2350
Heidelberg Hbf 913 931 d.	│	│	│	│	2114	2115	2114	2135	│	│	2211	│	│	│	│	2249	│	│	...	...	│	│	│	0006
Bruchsal 913 931 d.	│	│	│	│	│	│	│	│	│	│	│	│	│	│	│	│	│	│	...	...	│	│	│	│
Vaihingen (Enz) 931 d.	│	│	│	│	│	│	│	2205	│	│	│	│	│	│	│	2321	│	│	...	...	│	│	│	0034
Stuttgart Hbf 931 a.	2108	│	2122	│	2155	2156	2156	2223	2208	│	2255	2308	2308	│	│	2337	│	│	...	...	0008	│	│	0051
München Hbf 930 a.	2313b	│	2326	│	...	...	...	...	0028	│	...	...	0118	│	│	...	│	│	←	...	...	│	│	...
Karlsruhe Hbf 913 916 ☆ d.	...	2103	...	2112	...	...	...	...	...	2200	...	...	...	2259	2302	...	2309	2312	2312	...	...	0037	0037	...
Baden-Baden 916 ☆ d.	...	2120	...	2129	...	...	...	...	...	2217	...	...	...	→	2320	...	...	2329	2330	...	...	...	...	...
Offenburg 911 916 ☆ d.	...	2138	...	2147	...	...	...	...	...	2235	...	...	...	...	2338	...	...	2347	2348	...	...	...	...	...
Strasbourg ⊖ 911 a.	...	│	...	│	...	...	...	...	...	│	...	...	...	...	│	...	...	│	│	...	...	...	...	...
Freiburg (Brsg) Hbf ☆ d.	...	2208	...	2217	...	...	...	...	...	2309	...	...	...	...	0014	...	...	0020	0017	...	...	...	...	...
Basel Bad Bf 🏛 ☆ a.	...	2242	...	2251	...	...	...	...	...	2346	...	...	...	...	0050	...	...	0055	0050	...	...	...	...	...
Basel SBB ☆ a.	...	2255	...	2304	...	...	...	...	...	2359	...	...	...	...	0059	...	...	0105	0059	...	...	...	...	...
Zürich HB 510 a.	...	...	...	...	...	...	...	...	...	...	...	...	...	...	...	...	...	...	...	...	...	...	...	...

Selected regional trains **KARLSRUHE - OFFENBURG - BASEL** (German holiday dates apply; on Jan. 6 services between Karlsruhe and Basel Bad Bf run as on ⑦).

	Ⓒ	Ⓐ		Ⓐ	❖															❖	⚒				
Karlsruhe Hbf 916 d.	...	...	...	...	...	...	...	0733	...	...	...	...	1239	...	1439	1539	1639	1739	1839	...	...	...	...	...	2308
Baden-Baden 916 d.	...	...	...	...	...	...	...	0755	...	...	...	...	1259	...	1459	1600	1659	1759	1859	...	...	...	...	...	2335
Offenburg 916 d.	0107	0423	...	0511	0552	0634	0742	0836	0946	1035	1148	1226	1347	1436	1547	1635	1747	1836	1937	2046	...	2141	2246	2317	0007
Freiburg (Brsg) Hbf a.	0150	0522	...	0607	0644	0716	0829	0914	1031	1115	1230	1315	1430	1515	1630	1715	1830	1915	2032	2130	...	2231	2336	0011	0051
Freiburg (Brsg) Hbf d.	0152	0532	0600	0627	0646	0718	0832	0918	1034	1118	1238	1317	1432	1518	1632	1718	1832	1918	2033	2132	...	2234	2343	0027	...
Müllheim (Baden) d.	0212	0553	0625	0649	0711	0737	0852	0937	1053	1137	1258	1338	1451	1537	1651	1737	1851	1937	2052	2151	...	2253	0008	0052	...
Basel Bad Bf 🏛 a.	0244	0623	0701	0721	0746	0803	0929	1002	1130	1201	1330	1402	1523	1602	1723	1804	1923	2001	2129	2223	2245	2323	0043	0128	...
Basel SBB a.	...	*0650*	*0723*	0730	0801	*0823*	*0950*e	*1023*	*1150*e	1218*	*1350*e	*1423*	*1550*e	1619*	*1750*e	1819*	*1950*e	*2023*	*2150*e	2231	2250	...	...	...	...

← FOR NOTES SEE PAGE 422

912 BASEL and STUTTGART - FRANKFURT

km	km		ICE 618 K	IC 2326 Ⓐ ◆		ICE 696 ①g ✕	ICE 774 ✕	ICE 270 ①g ✕	ICE 270 ✕	ICE 616 ✕	IC 2372 ①–④ m🍷	IC 2049 Ⓐ F🍷	ICE 474 K✕	IC 2298 Ⓐ ✕	ICE 1014 ⚒ D✕	ICE 206 ✕	ICE 1118 Ⓐ	ICE 694 ✕	ICE 1672 ⚒ A✕	ICE 1178 Ⓐ ✕	ICE 772 ✕	ICE 1110 ⑥ ✕◆	IC 2010 Ⓐ ♠	IC 2286 ①–④ U
		Zürich HB **510** d.	...	...	...	...	...	...	...	...	...	...	...	...	...	...	...	...	...	...	...	...	...	...
		Basel SBB ☆ d.	...	...	...	...	...	...	...	...	...	...	...	...	...	0513	...	...	...	0537	...	...	...	...
		Basel Bad Bf ☆ d.	...	...	...	...	...	0412	...	...	...	...	0508	...	...	0521	...	...	...	0546	...	...	...	...
		Freiburg (Brsg) Hbf ☆ d.	...	...	...	...	...	0446	...	...	...	...	0543	...	...	0552	...	...	...	0620	...	...	...	...
	0	**Strasbourg** ⊖ **911** d.	...	...	...	...	...	|	...	...	...	...	|	...	...	|	...	...	...	|	...	...	...	...
	29	Offenburg **911 916** ☆ d.	...	...	...	...	...	0519	...	...	...	0555	|	...	...	0625	...	...	...	0656	...	...	...	...
	——	Baden-Baden **916** ☆ d.	...	...	...	...	...	0535	...	...	...	0615	0632	...	...	0642	...	...	...	0714	...	...	...	...
		Karlsruhe Hbf **913 916** ☆ d.	...	0335	...	0500	...	0558	0558	...	0612	0635	0651	...	...	0700	...	...	0702	0736	...	...	...	...
		München Hbf **930** d.	0001	|	...	|	...	|	|	0332	|	...	|	...	...	|	...	...	|	|	...	...	...	...
0	0	**Stuttgart** Hbf **931** d.	0222	0226	...	|	0502	|	|	0551	|	...	|	0602	0636	|	0626	0650	|	|	0725	0713	0714	0727
29	29	Vaihingen (Enz) **931** d.	|	|	...	|	0519	|	|	|	|	...	|	0625	|	|	0643	|	|	|	|	|	|	|
		Bruchsal **913 931** d.	|	0347	...	|	|	|	|	|	0630	...	|	|	|	|	|	|	0722	|	|	|	|	|
	92	**Heidelberg** Hbf **913 931** d.	0343	0410	...	|	0547	|	|	|	0655	...	|	0659	|	|	0720	|	0746	|	|	0755	0755	|
		Weinheim **913** d.	|	|	...	|	|	|	|	|	|	...	|	0714	|	|	|	|	0800	|	|	|	|	0823
		Bensheim **913** d.	|	|	...	|	|	|	|	|	|	...	|	0728	|	|	|	|	0809	|	|	|	|	0833
		Darmstadt Hbf **913 918a** d.	|	|	...	|	|	|	|	|	|	...	|	0742	|	|	|	|	0824	|	|	|	|	0847
107	109	**Mannheim** Hbf **913** a.	0355	0421	...	0525	0559	0624	0624	0628	0707	...	0714	|	0718	0724	0732	0729	|	0800	0802	0806	0806	|
107		**Mannheim** Hbf **913** d.	0401	0427	...	0528	0604	0632	0632	0636	0711	...	0716	|	0721	0736	0734	0732	|	...	0805	0808	0808	|
179		**Frankfurt** Flughafen ✈ a.	0457§	0501	...	|	0635	|	|	0706	|	...	|	|	0751	0806	|	|	|	...	0835	|	|	|
		Frankfurt (Main) Hbf **913** a.	0439	0519	...	0608	0652	0708	0708	|	0756	...	0752	0800	|	|	|	0808	0840	...	0852	|	|	0910
		Mainz Hbf **917a 918a** a.	|	|	...	|	|	|	|	|	...	...	|	...	|	|	0815	|	|	...	|	0847	0847	...
		Wiesbaden Hbf **917a 918a** a.	|	|	...	|	|	|	|	|	...	...	|	...	|	|	0833	|	|	...	|	|	|	...
		Koblenz Hbf **800** a.	|	|	...	|	|	|	|	|	...	...	|	...	|	|	...	|	|	...	|	0942	0942	...
		Köln Hbf **800 910** a.	0603	|	...	|	|	|	|	0804	...	...	|	...	0848•	0904	...	|	|	...	|	1043	1043	...
		Dortmund Hbf **800** a.	0722	0858	...	|	|	|	|	0922	...	...	|	...	...	1021	...	|	|	...	|	...	1203f	...
		Hannover Hbf **810 900** a.	|	...	...	|	0917	|	|	|	...	...	1017	...	...	|	...	|	1156	...	1117	...	1401f	...
		Berlin Hbf **810 850 902** a.	|	...	...	1032	|	1129	1129	|	...	...	|	...	...	|	...	1232	|	...	|	...	1557f	...
		Hamburg Hbf **800 900** a.	1014	...	...	...	1036	...	...	1214	...	...	1136	...	...	1314	...	...	1330	...	1236	...	...	...

	ICE 267 ⚒ ✕◆	ICE 374 ✕	ICE 614 ✕	IC 2049 R🍷	ICE 1098 ⚒ ✕	ICE 78 ✕	ICE 1012 ⚒ ✕	ICE 202 ✕	ICE 692 ✕	IC 2374 © ♣🍷	IC 2374 Ⓐ ♣🍷	ICE 937 © ✕	ICE 770 ✕	ICE 9571 P [R]✕	TGV 9561 ①–⑥ E[R] 🍷	ICE 372 N✕	ICE 612 K✕	IC 2047 R🍷	ICE 1166 ⑦w	IC 1296 ①–⑥ eG 🍷	IC 1916 ⑤ ⊗	ICE 1116 ⑦y ⊗✕	ICE 76 ✕	ICE 1010 ✕
Zürich HB **510** d.	...	...	...	...	...	0559	...	...	...	...	...	...	...	...		...	...	...	...		...	...	0759	...
Basel SBB ☆ d.	0551	0606	...	...	...	0706	...	0713	...	...	...	...	...	...	...	0813	...	...	...	...	...	...	0906	...
Basel Bad Bf ☆ d.	0600	0616	...	...	...	0714	...	0721	...	...	...	...	...	...	...	0822	...	...	...	...	...	...	0914	...
Freiburg (Brsg) Hbf ☆ d.	0643	0650	...	...	...	0748	...	0753	...	...	...	...	...	...	...	0855	...	...	...	...	...	...	0948	...
Strasbourg ⊖ **911** d.	|	|	...	...	...	|	...	|	...	...	...	...	...	0846	0912	|	...	...	...	...	...	...	|	...
Offenburg **911 916** ☆ d.	0730	0723	...	...	...	|	...	0824	...	...	...	...	...	|	|	0927	...	...	...	...	...	...	|	...
Baden-Baden **916** ☆ d.	0746	0740	...	...	...	0832	...	0841	...	...	...	...	...	|	|	|	...	...	...	...	...	...	1032	...
Karlsruhe Hbf **913 916** ☆ d.	0803	0800	...	...	...	0851	...	0900	...	0910	...	...	...	0926	0955	1000	...	...	...	...	...	...	1051	...
München Hbf **930** d.	...	|	0533	...	0544	|	0626	|	0642	|	...	...	...	...	|	|	0728	...	...	0746	...	...	|	0828
Stuttgart Hbf **931** d.	...	|	0751	0736	0805	|	0839	|	0851	|	0855	0903	0923	...	|	|	0951	0937	1005	1005	1008	1008	|	1037
Vaihingen (Enz) **931** d.	...	|	|	0754	|	|	|	|	|	|	|	0927	|	...	|	|	|	0954	|	|	|	|	|	|
Bruchsal **913 931** d.	...	|	|	|	|	|	|	|	|	0922	|	|	|	...	|	|	|	|	|	|	|	|	|	|
Heidelberg Hbf **913 931** d.	...	|	|	0824	0846	|	|	|	|	0946	0946	0956	|	...	|	|	|	1024	1046	1046	|	|	|	|
Weinheim **913** d.	...	|	|	|	0900	|	|	|	|	1000	1000	1012	|	...	|	|	|	|	1100	1100	|	|	|	|
Bensheim **913** d.	...	|	|	|	0909	|	|	|	|	1009	1009	1022	|	...	|	|	|	|	1109	1109	|	|	|	|
Darmstadt Hbf **913 918a** d.	...	|	|	|	0924	|	|	|	|	1024	1024	1040	|	...	|	|	|	|	1124	1124	|	|	|	|
Mannheim Hbf **913** a.	...	0824	0828	0837	|	0914	0918	0924	0929	|	|	|	1001	...	1018	1024	1028	1037	|	|	1050	1050	1114	1118
Mannheim Hbf **913** d.	...	0832	0836	0839	|	0916	0921	0936	0932	|	|	|	1004	...	1021	1032	1036	1039	|	|	1052	1052	1116	1121
Frankfurt Flughafen ✈ a.	...	|	0906	|	|	|	0951	1006	|	|	|	|	1035	...	|	|	1106	|	|	|	|	|	|	1151
Frankfurt (Main) Hbf **913** a.	...	0908	|	|	0940	0952	|	|	1008	1040	1040	1056	1052	...	1059	1108	|	|	1140	1140	|	|	1152	|
Mainz Hbf **917a 918a** a.	...	|	|	0918	...	|	|	|	|	|	|	|	|	...	...	|	|	1118	...	...	1142	1142	|	|
Wiesbaden Hbf **917a 918a** a.	...	|	|	|	...	|	|	|	|	|	|	|	|	...	...	|	|	|	...	...	|	|	|	|
Koblenz Hbf **800** a.	...	|	|	1011	...	|	|	|	|	|	|	|	|	...	...	|	|	1211	...	...	1242	1242	|	|
Köln Hbf **800 910** a.	...	|	1004	1106	...	|	1048x	1104	|	|	|	|	|	...	...	|	1205	1305	...	...	1343	1343	|	1248•
Dortmund Hbf **800** a.	...	|	1121	1221	...	|	1205q	1222	|	|	|	|	|	...	...	|	1321	1421	...	...	1508	1508	|	1404e
Hannover Hbf **810 900** a.	...	|	|	1418	...	1217	...	|	|	1356	1356	|	1317	...	...	|	|	1618	...	...	1701	1701	1417	...
Berlin Hbf **810 850 902** a.	...	1329	|	...	...	|	...	|	1432	|	|	1455	|	...	...	1529	|	...	...	...	1857	1857	|	...
Hamburg Hbf **800 900** a.	...	...	1414	...	...	1336	...	1514	...	1530	1530	...	1436	...	...	...	1614	...	...	...	...	...	1536	...

	ICE 200 ✕	ICE 690 ✕	ICE 1578 A✕	ICE 578 ✕	ICE 370 ✕	ICE 610 ✕	IC 2045 R🍷		IC 1290 G🍷	IC 2006 ⑥ 🍷◆	IC 2004 ⑦w 🍷◆	IC 2014 ⑤ 🍷◆	ICE 74 K✕	ICE 918 ✕	ICE 108 ✕	ICE 1218 ✕◆	ICE 1576 ✕◆	IC 2012 🍷◆	ICE 576 ✕	ICE 9573 Q P[R]	ICE 278 N✕	ICE 518 ✕	EC 8 ✕	EC 218 🍷◆
Zürich HB **510** d.	...	...	...	...	...	...	...	...	...	...	...	...	0959	...	...	...	...	...	...	...	...	...	1059	...
Basel SBB ☆ d.	0913	...	...	...	1013	...	...	...	...	...	...	...	1106	...	1113	...	...	...	...	...	1213	...	1220	...
Basel Bad Bf ☆ d.	0922	...	...	...	1022	...	...	...	...	...	...	...	1114	...	1122	...	...	...	...	...	1222	...	1228	...
Freiburg (Brsg) Hbf ☆ d.	0955	...	...	...	1055	...	...	...	...	...	...	...	1148	...	1155	...	...	...	...	...	1255	...	1304	...
Strasbourg ⊖ **911** d.	|	...	...	...	|	...	...	...	...	...	...	...	|	...	|	...	...	...	...	1246	|	...	|	...
Offenburg **911 916** ☆ d.	1028	...	...	...	1127	...	...	...	...	1139	1139	...	|	...	1228	...	...	...	...	|	1328	...	|	...
Baden-Baden **916** ☆ d.	|	...	...	...	|	...	...	...	...	1204	1204	...	1232	...	|	...	...	...	...	|	|	...	1352	...
Karlsruhe Hbf **913 916** ☆ d.	1100	...	1110	...	1200	...	...	...	...	1223	1223	...	1251	...	1300	...	1310	...	...	1326	1400	...	1412	...
München Hbf **930** d.	|	0846	|	...	|	0928	...	...	0947	|	|	...	|	1028d	|	1047	|	...	...	...	|	1128	|	1147
Stuttgart Hbf **931** d.	|	1051	|	1123	|	1151	1137	...	1204	|	|	1208	|	1238	|	1251	|	1312	1323	...	|	1351	|	1405
Vaihingen (Enz) **931** d.	|	|	|	|	|	|	1154	...	|	|	|	|	|	|	|	|	|	|	|	...	|	|	|	|
Bruchsal **913 931** d.	|	|	1122	|	|	|	|	...	|	|	|	|	|	|	|	|	1322	|	|	...	|	|	|	|
Heidelberg Hbf **913 931** d.	|	|	1146	|	|	|	1224	...	1246	|	|	|	|	|	|	|	1346	1355	|	...	|	|	|	1446
Weinheim **913** d.	|	|	1200	|	|	|	|	...	1300	|	|	|	|	|	|	|	1400	|	|	...	|	|	|	1500
Bensheim **913** d.	|	|	1209	|	|	|	|	...	1309	|	|	|	|	|	|	|	1409	|	|	...	|	|	|	1509
Darmstadt Hbf **913 918a** d.	|	|	1224	|	|	|	|	...	1324	|	|	|	|	|	|	|	1424	|	|	...	|	|	|	1524
Mannheim Hbf **913** a.	1124	1129	|	1201	1224	1228	1237	...	|	1250	1250	1256	1314	1318	1324	1329	|	1406	1401	...	1424	1428	1437	|
Mannheim Hbf **913** d.	1136	1132	|	1204	1232	1236	1239	...	|	1258	1258	1258	1316	1321	1336	1332	|	1408	1404	...	1432	1436	1439	|
Frankfurt Flughafen ✈ a.	1206	|	|	1235	|	1306	|	...	|	|	|	|	|	1351	1406	|	|	|	1435	...	|	1506	|	|
Frankfurt (Main) Hbf **913** a.	|	1208	1240	1252	1308	|	|	...	1340	|	|	|	1352	|	|	1408	1440	|	1452	...	1508	|	|	1540
Mainz Hbf **917a 918a** a.	|	|	|	|	|	|	1318	...	...	1342	1342	1342	|	|	|	|	|	1447	|	...	|	|	1518	...
Wiesbaden Hbf **917a 918a** a.	|	|	|	|	|	|	|	...	...	|	|	|	|	|	|	|	|	|	|	...	|	|	|	...
Koblenz Hbf **800** a.	|	|	|	|	|	|	1411	...	...	1442	1442	1442	|	|	|	|	|	1542	|	...	|	|	1611	...
Köln Hbf **800 910** a.	1304	|	|	|	|	1404	1505	...	...	1543	1543	1543	|	1448•	1504	|	|	1643	|	...	|	1605	1705	...
Dortmund Hbf **800** a.	1422	|	|	|	|	1521	1621	...	...	1708	...	...	|	1606	1622	|	|	...	|	...	|	1722	|	...
Hannover Hbf **810 900** a.	|	|	1556	1517	|	|	1818	...	...	...	...	...	1617	...	|	|	1756	...	1717	...	|	|	|	...
Berlin Hbf **810 850 902** a.	|	1632	|	|	1729	|	...	...	...	...	...	...	|	...	|	1832	|	...	|	...	1929	|	|	...
Hamburg Hbf **800 900** a.	1714	...	1732	1636	...	1814	...	...	...	...	...	...	1736	...	1914	...	1929	...	1836	...	...	2014	2114	...

Selected regional trains **BASEL - OFFENBURG - KARLSRUHE** (German holiday dates apply; on Jan. 6 services between Basel Bad Bf and Offenburg run as on ⑦).

		⚒		Ⓐ			❖			⚒	†		❖				❖		❖					❖	
Basel SBB d.	...	...	...	*0501*	*0603*t	0736	0737	*0804*t	*0936*	*1006*	...	*1134*	1225	*1336*	*1406*t	*1534*	1628	*1734*	1828	*1936*	*2006*t	*2136*	2250	2259	...
Basel Bad Bf d.	0406	...	...	0537	0636	0740	0758	0828	0958	1028	1028	1158	1233	1358	1427	1557	1638	1758	1838	1958	2028	2158	2255	2308	2353
Müllheim (Baden) d.	0444	...	...	0607	0705	...	0821	0904	1022	1104	1102	1222	1306	1422	1501	1620	1707	1822	1907	2021	2104	2222	...	2337	0027
Freiburg (Brsg) Hbf a.	0510	...	...	0630	0724	...	0839	0924	1040	1124	1121	1240	1325	1440	1523	1638	1726	1840	1926	2040	2124	2240	...	2357	0053
Freiburg (Brsg) Hbf d.	...	0522	0626	...	0726	...	0843	0927	1042	1126	1129	1245	1327	1443	1527	1642	1729	1843	1929	2042	2127	2242	...	0010	...
Offenburg **916** a.	...	0614	0712	...	0812	...	0924	1013	1121	1211	1214	1325	1412	1530	1613	1722	1814	1923	2014	2121	2213	2321	...	0106	...
Baden-Baden **916** a.	...	0652	0800	...	...	...	...	...	...	...	...	1400	1500	1600	1700	1800	...	...	...	2200	...	2400	...	...	...
Karlsruhe Hbf **916** a.	...	0714	0821	...	...	...	...	...	...	...	...	1421	1522	1621	1721	1821	...	...	...	2221	...	0021	...	...	...

FOR NOTES SEE PAGE 425 →

BASEL and STUTTGART - FRANKFURT 912

	TGV 9583 Ⓡ 🍷♦	ICE 72 H✕	TGV 9583 Ⓡ 🍷♦	ICE 106 ✕	ICE 596 ✕	ICE 710 Ⓐ ✕	ICE 1574 T✕	IC 118 ♦	ICE 1094 Ⓑb K✕	ICE 574 ⑥h ✕	ICE 276 ✕	ICE 516 ✕	EC 6 N✕		ICE 1168 ✕	EC 114 🍷♦	TGV 9575 P Ⓡ🍷	ICE 70 H✕	ICE 914 ✕		ICE 104 ✕♦	ICE 204 Ⓐ ✕	ICE 594 ✕	ICE 1512 Ⓐ ■	ICE 562 S✕
Zürich HB **510** d.	...	1159	...	...	...	...	...	...	...	...	...	...	...	...	...	...	...	1359	...	...	...	...	...	...	...
Basel SBB ☆ d.	...	1306	...	1313	...	...	...	...	...	...	1413	...	1427	...	...	...	...	1506	...	...	1513	1513	...	...	...
Basel Bad Bf 🏛 ☆ d.	...	1314	...	1322	...	...	...	...	...	...	1422	...	1435	...	...	...	...	1514	...	...	1522	1522	...	...	...
Freiburg (Brsg) Hbf ☆ d.	...	1348	...	1355	...	...	...	...	...	...	1455	...	1507	...	...	...	...	1548	...	...	1555	1555	...	...	...
Strasbourg ⊖ **911** d.	1355	|	...	|	...	...	...	...	...	...	|	...	|	...	...	...	1546	|	...	...	|	|	...	...	...
Offenburg **911 916** ☆ d.	|	|	...	1428	...	...	...	...	...	...	1527	...	|	...	...	...	|	|	...	...	1628	1628	...	...	...
Baden-Baden **916** ☆ d.	1425	1432	←	|	...	...	...	...	...	...	|	...	|	...	...	...	|	1632	...	...	|	|	...	...	...
Karlsruhe Hbf **913 916** ☆ d.	1446	1451	1454	1500	...	...	1510	...	...	...	1600	...	1613	...	...	...	1625	1651	...	...	1700	1700	...	...	...
München Hbf **930** d.	→	|	|	|	1245	...	|	...	...	...	|	1328	|	...	...	1347	...	|	1428	...	|	|	1447	...	1502
Stuttgart Hbf **931** d.	...	|	|	|	1451	1435	|	1512	1523	1523	|	1551	|	...	1559	1607	...	|	1637	...	|	|	1651	1622	1708
Vaihingen (Enz) **931** d.	...	|	|	|	|	1454	|	|	|	|	|	|	|	...	|	1625	...	|	|	...	|	|	|	|	|
Bruchsal **913 931** d.	...	|	|	|	|	|	1522	|	|	|	|	|	|	...	|	|	...	|	|	...	|	|	|	|	|
Heidelberg Hbf **913 931** d.	...	|	|	|	|	1520	1546	1555	|	|	|	|	|	...	1646	|	...	|	|	...	|	|	|	1720	|
Weinheim **913** d.	...	|	|	|	|	|	1600	|	|	|	|	|	|	...	1700	|	...	|	|	...	|	|	|	|	|
Bensheim **913** d.	...	|	|	|	|	|	1609	|	|	|	|	|	|	...	1709	|	...	|	|	...	|	|	|	|	|
Darmstadt Hbf **913 918a** d.	...	|	|	|	|	|	1624	|	|	|	|	|	|	...	1724	|	...	|	|	...	|	|	|	|	|
Mannheim Hbf **913** a.	...	1514	1518	1524	1529	1531	|	1606	1601	1601	1624	1628	1637	...	|	1655	...	1714	1718	...	1724	1724	1729	1736	1746
Mannheim Hbf **913** d.	...	1516	1521	1536	1532	1533	|	1608	1604	1604	1632	1636	1639	...	|	1657	...	1716	1721	...	1736	1736	1732	1738	...
Frankfurt Flughafen ✈ ◧ a.	...	|	|	1606	|	|	|	|	1635	1635	|	1706	|	...	|	|	...	|	1751	...	1806	1806	|	|	...
Frankfurt (Main) Hbf **913** a.	...	1552	1559	|	1608	|	1640	|	1652	1652	1708	|	|	...	1740	|	...	1752	|	...	|	|	1808	|	...
Mainz Hbf **917a 918a** a.	...	|	...	|	|	1615	|	1647	|	|	|	|	1718	...	...	1740	...	|	|	...	|	|	|	1815	...
Wiesbaden Hbf **917a 918a** a.	...	|	...	|	|	1633	|	|	|	|	|	|	|	...	...	|	...	|	|	...	|	|	|	1833	...
Koblenz Hbf **800** a.	...	|	...	|	|	|	|	1742	|	|	|	|	1811	...	...	1842	...	|	|	...	|	|	|	...	...
Köln Hbf **800 910** a.	...	|	...	1704	|	1801	|	1842	|	|	|	1804	1905	...	...	1943	...	|	1848•	...	1904	1904	|	...	...
Dortmund Hbf **800** a.	...	|	...	...	|	...	|	...	|	|	|	1921	2022	...	...	2104	...	|	2005	...	...	2021	|	...	...
Hannover Hbf **810 900** a.	...	1817	...	...	|	...	1956	...	1912	1917	|	|	|	...	...	...	...	2017	...	...	...	...	|	...	...
Berlin Hbf **810 850 902** a.	...	|	...	...	2032	...	|	...	|	|	2129	|	|	...	...	...	...	|	...	...	...	...	2232	...	...
Hamburg Hbf **800 900** a.	...	1936	...	...	...	...	2129	...	2030	2040	...	2214	2316	...	...	...	...	2139	...	...	...	...	...	...	...

	ICE 1572 ✕	ECE 52 ✕♦	ICE 572 ✕	ICE 9563 E Ⓡ✕	ICE 274 ✕	ICE 514 ✕	ICE 1549 ✕		EC 112 ✕♦	TGV 9577 Ⓑ Ⓡ♦ 🍷	ICE 376 Ⓑb N✕	ICE 376 ⑥h N✕	ICE 912 ✕	ICE 102 ✕	ICE 592 L✕		ICE 1570 ✕♦	ICE 1570 ⑦w ✕♦	ICE 570 ✕	ICE 570 ⑦w ✕	IC 1910 ⑦z 🍷		ICE 272 ⑥h H✕	ICE 272 Ⓐ ✕	ICE 292 ⑦w H✕
Zürich HB **510** d.	...	...	...	...	...	...	...	...	...	...	...	...	...	...	...	...	...	...	...	...	...	...	1659	1659	1659
Basel SBB ☆ d.	...	1538	...	...	1613	...	...	...	...	...	1707	1707	...	1713	...	...	...	...	...	...	...	...	1813	1813	1813
Basel Bad Bf 🏛 ☆ d.	...	1552	...	...	1622	...	...	...	...	...	1715	1715	...	1721	...	...	...	...	...	...	...	...	1822	1822	1822
Freiburg (Brsg) Hbf ☆ d.	...	1624	...	...	1655	...	...	...	...	...	1748	1748	...	1753	...	...	...	...	...	...	...	...	1855	1855	1855
Strasbourg ⊖ **911** d.	...	|	...	1713	|	...	...	...	...	1746	|	|	...	|	...	...	...	...	...	...	...	...	|	|	|
Offenburg **911 916** ☆ d.	...	|	...	|	1727	...	...	...	...	|	|	|	...	1826	...	...	...	...	...	...	...	...	1927	1927	1927
Baden-Baden **916** ☆ d.	...	|	...	|	|	...	...	...	...	|	1832	1832	...	1841	...	...	...	...	...	...	...	...	|	|	|
Karlsruhe Hbf **913 916** ☆ d.	1710	1729	...	1755	1800	...	...	...	...	1824	1851	1851	...	1900	...	...	1910	1910	...	...	...	...	2000	2000	2000
München Hbf **930** d.	|	|	...	|	|	1528	...	...	1547	...	|	|	1627	|	1645	...	|	|	...	...	1614	...	|	|	|
Stuttgart Hbf **931** d.	|	|	1723	|	|	1751	1737	...	1804	...	|	|	1838	|	1851	...	|	|	1923	1923	1905	...	|	|	|
Vaihingen (Enz) **931** d.	|	|	|	|	|	|	|	...	|	...	|	|	|	|	|	...	|	|	|	|	|	...	|	|	|
Bruchsal **913 931** d.	1722	|	|	|	|	|	|	...	|	...	|	|	|	|	|	...	1922	1922	|	|	|	...	|	|	|
Heidelberg Hbf **913 931** d.	1746	|	|	|	|	|	1824	...	1846	...	|	|	|	|	|	...	1946	1946	|	|	1955	...	|	|	|
Weinheim **913** d.	1800	|	|	|	|	|	|	...	1900	...	|	|	|	|	|	...	2000	2000	|	|	|	...	|	|	|
Bensheim **913** d.	1809	|	|	|	|	|	|	...	1909	...	|	|	|	|	|	...	2009	2009	|	|	|	...	|	|	|
Darmstadt Hbf **913 918a** d.	1824	|	|	|	|	|	|	...	1924	...	|	|	|	|	|	...	2024	2024	|	|	|	...	|	|	|
Mannheim Hbf **913** a.	|	1758	1801	1818	1824	1828	1837	...	|	...	1914	1914	1918	1924	1929	...	|	|	2002	2002	2006	...	2024	2024	2024
Mannheim Hbf **913** d.	|	1800	1804	1821	1832	1836	1839	...	|	...	1916	1916	1921	1936	1932	...	|	|	2005	2005	2008	...	2032	2032	2032
Frankfurt Flughafen ✈ ◧ a.	|	|	1835	|	|	1906	|	...	|	...	|	|	1951	2006	|	...	|	|	2035	2035	|	...	|	|	|
Frankfurt (Main) Hbf **913** a.	1840	1844	1852	1859	1908	|	|	...	1940	...	1952	1954	|	|	2008	...	2040	2040	2052	2052	|	...	2108	2108	2108
Mainz Hbf **917a 918a** a.	|	...	|	...	|	|	1918	...	...	...	|	...	|	|	...	...	...	|	...	|	2047	...	|	|	|
Wiesbaden Hbf **917a 918a** a.	|	...	|	...	|	|	|	...	...	...	|	...	|	|	...	...	...	|	...	|	|	...	|	|	|
Koblenz Hbf **800** a.	|	...	|	...	|	|	2011	...	...	...	|	...	|	|	...	...	...	|	...	|	2142	...	|	|	|
Köln Hbf **800 910** a.	|	...	|	...	|	2004	2105	...	...	...	|	...	2048•	2104	...	...	...	|	...	|	2243	...	|	|	|
Dortmund Hbf **800** a.	|	...	|	...	|	2121	2222	...	...	...	|	...	2205	...	...	...	...	|	...	|	0002	...	|	|	|
Hannover Hbf **810 900** a.	2156j	...	2119	...	|	|	...	...	...	...	2217	...	...	...	...	...	...	0010	...	2318	...	...	2341	0002	|
Berlin Hbf **810 850 902** a.	|	...	|	...	2329	|	...	...	...	...	|	...	...	...	...	...	...	...	...	|	...	...	|	|	0127
Hamburg Hbf **800 900** a.	2329r	...	2246	...	...	0015	...	...	...	...	2342	...	...	...	...	...	...	...	...	0044	...	...	0115	0137	...

♦ – **NOTES** for pages 424 and 425 (LISTED BY TRAIN NUMBER)

52 – [12] ✕ Milano - Brig - Bern - Basel - Frankfurt.
104 – [12] ✕ Basel - Amsterdam. Subject to alteration Feb. 11–24.
112 – BLAUER ENZIAN – [12] ✕ Klagenfurt - Villach - Salzburg - Frankfurt; [12] Zagreb (**212**) - Ljubljana - Villach (**112**) - Frankfurt.
114 – WÖRTHERSEE – [12] 🍷 Klagenfurt - Salzburg - München - Dortmund. Also calls at Worms Hbf (d. 1714).
118 – BODENSEE – [12] Innsbruck - Bregenz - Lindau - Ulm - Stuttgart - Bochum.
218 – CHIEMGAU – [12] 🍷 Graz - Bischofshofen - Salzburg - München - Frankfurt.
267 – BADEN-KURIER – [12] ✕ Basel - Stuttgart - München.
1110 – ⑥ (also Dec. 25; not Jan. 7 - Mar. 25). LORELEY – [12] ✕ Stuttgart - Köln - Münster - Norddeich Mole.
1218 – [12] ✕ (Innsbruck ⑥⑦ -) München - Frankfurt - Berlin.
1570 – [12] ✕ Karlsruhe - Frankfurt (- Gießen - Kassel Ⓑ **b**) (- Hannover ⑦ **w**).
1576 – [12] ✕ Karlsruhe - Frankfurt - Gießen - Hamburg (- Rostock Ⓑ **b**) (- Stralsund ⑦ **w**).
2004 – ⑦ (also Dec. 26; not Dec. 25, Jan. 8 - Mar. 26). SCHWARZWALD – [12] 🍷 Konstanz - Karlsruhe - Münster - Emden. Also calls at Worms Hbf (d. 1315).
2006 – ⑥ (also Dec. 25; not Jan. 7 - Apr. 1). SCHWARZWALD – [12] 🍷 Konstanz - Karlsruhe - Dortmund. Also calls at Worms Hbf (d. 1315).
2012 – Not Jan. 6 - Apr. 1. ALLGÄU – [12] 🍷 Oberstdorf - Ulm - Stuttgart - Köln - Bochum.
2014 – [12] 🍷 Stuttgart - Münster - Emden. Also calls at Worms Hbf (d. 1315).
2326 – [12] Stuttgart - Karlsruhe - Frankfurt - Siegen - Dortmund. See Table **808** for timings Frankfurt - Dortmund.
9577 – [12] 🍷 Paris - Strasbourg - München.
9583 – [12] 🍷 Marseille - Lyon - Mulhouse - Strasbourg - Frankfurt.

A – To Stralsund via Rostock (Table **830**).
D – To Düsseldorf (Table **910**).
E – From Paris (Table **30**).
F – To Stuttgart (Table **931**). Also calls at Rastatt (d. 0623).
G – From Salzburg (Table **890**).
H – From Chur (Table **520**).
K – To Kiel (Table **820**).
L – To Leipzig via Erfurt (Table **850**).
N – From Interlaken via Bern (Table **560**).
P – [12] Paris - Karlsruhe - Stuttgart (Table **32**).
Q – Runs as *TGV* **9593** on ⑥. *ICE* ✕, *TGV* 🍷.
R – To Dresden via Leipzig (Table **866**).
S – To Saarbrücken (Table **919**).
T – To Rostock on dates in Table **830**.
U – ①–④ (not Dec. 26). From Rottweil (Table **940**).

b – Ⓑ (not Dec. 25).
d – 1030 on ⑥⑦.
e – ①–⑥ (also Dec. 25; not Dec. 26).
f – ⑤ only.
g – Also Dec. 27; not Dec. 26.
h – Also Dec. 25.
j – Not Dec. 24.
m – Not Dec. 26.
q – Not ⑤.
r – ⑤–⑦ (also Dec. 26; not Dec. 24).
t – ⚒ only.
w – ⑦ (also Dec. 26; not Dec. 25).
x – Köln **Messe/Deutz**. Arrives 1041 on ⑥.
y – ⑦ (also Dec. 26; not Dec. 25, Jan. 8 - Mar. 26).
z – ⑦ (also Dec. 26; not Dec. 25, Jan. 8 - Apr. 2).

✣ – Basel SBB - Basel Bad Bf on Ⓐ; Basel Bad Bf - Offenburg daily.
⊗ – Also calls at Worms Hbf (d. 1115).
■ – Runs as *ICE* **1114** on ⑤.
♣ – WATTENMEER – To Westerland on dates in Table **821**.
♠ – Ⓐ to Jan. 5. LORELEY. From Tübingen (Table **936**).
• – Köln **Messe/Deutz**.
☆ – See panel on page 424 for other local services.
⊖ – 🏛 is at Kehl (8 km from Strasbourg). See Table **911** for local journeys Strasbourg - Offenburg.
§ – Calls at Frankfurt Flughafen after Frankfurt (Main) Hbf.
◧ – Frankfurt Flughafen Fernbahnhof.

912 BASEL and STUTTGART - FRANKFURT

See Table 927 for services operated by FlixTrain

	ICE 512	IC 2343	IC 2343	EC 216	RJ 890		ICE 910	TGV 9579	ICE 100	ICE 590	ICE 4	ICE 4	ICE 510	IC 2290		ICE 990	ICE 990		NJ 409		IC 1998		NJ 470	ICE 698	NJ 402
		①-④	⑤-⑦				Ⓑ b	P				⑦ w		⑤		⑦ w					⑤⑥				
	M ✕	m 🍷	v 🍷	🍷 ♦	✕ ♦		✕	(R) 🍷	✕	✕	C ✕	C ✕	✕			✕	✕		♦		h		♦		♦
Zürich HB **510** d.	...	...	...	...	...	...	...	...	...	...	1859	1859	...	...	...	...	...	...	1959	...	...	...	2059	...	2159
Basel SBB ☆ d.	...	...	...	...	...	...	...	...	1913	...	2013	2013	...	...	...	...	...	...	2113	...	...	...	2213	...	2313
Basel Bad Bf ☆ d.	...	...	...	...	...	...	...	...	1921	...	2022	2022	...	...	...	...	...	...	2122	...	...	...	2222	...	2323
Freiburg (Brsg) Hbf ☆ d.	...	...	...	...	...	...	...	...	1954	...	2054	2054	...	...	...	...	...	...	2158	...	...	...	2258	...	0005
Strasbourg ⊖ **911** d.	...	...	...	...	...	...	...	1946	|	...	|	|	...	...	...	...	...	...	|	...	...	...	|	...	|
Offenburg **911 916** ☆ d.	...	...	...	...	...	...	...	|	2025	...	2126	2126	...	...	...	...	...	...	2231	...	...	...	2333	...	0041
Baden-Baden **916** ☆ d.	...	...	...	...	...	...	...	|	2041	...	2144	2144	...	...	...	...	...	...	|	...	...	...	2354	...	0102
Karlsruhe Hbf **913 916** ☆ d.	...	...	...	...	...	...	...	2025	2100	...	2202	2202	...	...	...	...	...	...	2307	...	...	...	0019	...	0120
München Hbf **930** d.	1728	...	...	1747	...	...	1828	...	|	1847	|	|	1928	...	...	2044	2044	...	|	...	...	...	|	2151	|
Stuttgart Hbf **931** d.	1951	1915	1937	2004	2012	...	2038	...	|	2051	|	|	2151	2204	...	2251	2251	...	|	...	2309	...	|	0011	|
Vaihingen (Enz) **931** d.	|	|	1954	|	|	...	|	...	|	|	|	|	|	|	...	|	|	...	|	...	2326	...	|	|	|
Bruchsal **913 931** d.	|	|	|	|	|	...	|	...	|	|	|	|	|	|	...	|	|	...	|	...	|	...	0038	|	|
Heidelberg Hbf **913 931** d.	|	2025t	2025	|	2055	...	|	...	|	|	|	|	|	2247	...	|	|	...	|	...	0002	...	0108	0127	|
Weinheim **913** d.	|	|	|	|	2109	...	|	...	|	|	|	|	|	2302	...	|	|	...	|	...	0018	...	|	|	|
Bensheim **913** d.	|	|	|	|	2119	...	|	...	|	|	|	|	|	2313	...	|	|	...	|	...	0028	...	|	|	|
Darmstadt Hbf **913 918a** d.	|	|	|	|	2133	...	|	...	|	|	|	|	|	2327	...	|	|	...	|	...	0051	...	0153	|	|
Mannheim Hbf **913** a.	2028	2037	2037	2047	|	...	2118	...	2124	2129	2224	2224	2228	|	...	2329	2329	...	2340	...	|	...	|	0142	0149
Mannheim Hbf **913** d.	2036	2039	2039	...	|	...	2121	...	2136	2132	2233	2233	2236	|	...	2332	2332	...	2342	...	|	...	|	0144	0152
Frankfurt Flughafen ✈ ◧ a.	2106	|	|	...	|	...	2151	...	2206	|	|	|	2306	|	...	|	|	...	|	...	|	...	|	0219	0325*
Frankfurt (Main) Hbf **913** a.	|	|	|	...	2152	...	|	...	|	2208	2308	2308	|	2343	...	0008	0008	...	0027	...	0106	...	0210x	0240	0245
Mainz Hbf **917a 918a** a.	|	2118	2118	...	...	...	|	...	|	...	...	|	|	...	...	|	...	...	|	...	...	...	|	|	0346
Wiesbaden Hbf **917a 918a** a.	|	|	|	...	...	...	|	...	|	...	...	|	|	...	...	|	...	...	|	...	...	...	|	|	|
Koblenz Hbf **800** a.	|	2211	2211	...	...	...	|	...	|	...	...	|	|	...	...	|	...	...	|	...	...	...	|	|	0441
Köln Hbf **800 910** a.	2206	2305	2305	...	...	...	2251	...	2307	...	...	|	0007y	...	...	|	...	...	|	...	...	...	|	|	0553
Dortmund Hbf **800** a.	...	...	...	...	...	...	...	...	0024z	...	...	|	...	...	...	|	...	...	|	...	...	...	|	|	...
Hannover Hbf **810 900** a.	...	...	...	...	...	...	...	...	...	...	...	|	...	...	...	0341	...	...	|	...	...	...	0529	|	...
Berlin Hbf **810 850 902** a.	...	...	...	...	...	...	...	...	...	...	...	0347	...	...	...	|	...	...	0720	...	...	...	|	0756	...
Hamburg Hbf **800 900** a.	...	...	...	...	...	...	...	...	...	...	...	0537	...	...	...	0528	...	...	...	...	...	...	0754	...	...

♦ – **NOTES** (LISTED BY TRAIN NUMBER)

216 – DACHSTEIN – (12) 🍷 Graz - Bischofshofen - Salzburg - München - Saarbrücken.
402 – 1, 2 cl. and 2 cl. ((R)) Zürich - Basel - Amsterdam. Also conveys (2) (*IC* **60402**).
409 – 1, 2 cl. and 2 cl. ((R)) Zürich - Basel - Leipzig - Berlin. Also conveys (2) (*IC* **60409**).
1, 2 cl. and 2 cl. (*EN* **40459** (R)) and (2) (*EC* **459**) Zürich - Basel - Leipzig - Dresden - Praha.
470 – 1, 2 cl. and 2 cl. ((R)) Zürich - Basel - Hannover - Hamburg. Also conveys (2) (*IC* **60470**).
890 – (12) ✕ Wien (**860**) - Innsbruck - Bregenz (**890**) - Lindau - Ulm - Frankfurt.

C – From Chur on dates in Table **520**.
M – To Münster (Table **800**).
P – (12) 🍷 Paris - Strasbourg - Stuttgart (- München ⑥).

b – Not Dec. 25.
h – Also Dec. 25.
m – Not Dec. 26.
t – Arrives 2005.
v – Also Dec. 26.
w – ⑦ (also Dec. 26; not Dec. 25).
x – Frankfurt (Main) **Süd**.
y – Frankfurt Flughafen - Köln daily until Jan. 8, ⑤⑥ from Jan. 13.
z – Köln - Dortmund on Ⓑ (not Dec. 25).

* – Calls at Frankfurt Flughafen after Frankfurt (Main) Hbf.
☆ – See panel on page 424 for other local services.
⊖ – is at Kehl (8 km from Strasbourg). See Table **911** for local journeys Strasbourg - Offenburg.
◧ – Frankfurt Flughafen Fernbahnhof.

913 Local trains FRANKFURT - HEIDELBERG - KARLSRUHE

RE | *RB* | *S-Bahn* services

FRANKFURT - DARMSTADT - HEIDELBERG and MANNHEIM

			Ⓒ			Ⓐ			Ⓒ	Ⓐ		Ⓒ	Ⓐ			Ⓐ									
Frankfurt (Main) Hbf d.	0006	...	0206	...	0406	0406	...	0506	0506	0533	0606	0606	0632	0706	...	0736	0806	0834	0906	0938	1006	1034	1106	1131	1206
Darmstadt Hbf d.	0030	...	0226	...	0433	0433	...	0530	0530	0553	0630	0630	0653	0734	...	0758	0830	0853	0930	0956	1030	1053	1130	1150	1230
Bensheim d.	0054	...	0254	...	0457	0457	...	0557	0557	0610	0655	0655	0710	0758	...	0813	0857	0910	0957	1011	1057	1110	1158	1211	1257
Weinheim (Bergstr) d.	0109	...	0309	...	0512	0512	...	0612	0612	0622	0711	0711	0722	0813	...	0826	0913	0922	1014	1023	1113	1122	1213	1223	1313
Neu-Edingen / Friedrichsfeld a.	0123	...	0321	...	0524	0524	...	0625	0625	0631	0724	0724	0731	0825	0835	0835	0925	0933	1026	1032	1126	1132	1225	1233	1326
Mannheim Hbf a.	|	...	|	...	|	0546	...	|	0645	0646	|	0746	0743	|	0847	0847	|	0945	|	1046	|	1145	|	1246	|
Heidelberg Hbf a.	0134	...	0331	...	0539	...	...	0637	...	...	0736	...	...	0842	...	...	0939	...	1039	...	1139	...	1238	...	1339

											Ⓒ	Ⓐ												Ⓒ	
Frankfurt (Main) Hbf d.	1234	1306	1331	1406	1434	1506	1534	1606	1634	1706	1731	1734	1806	1834	1906	1906	1931	2006	2034	2106	2106	2206	2206	2234	2312
Darmstadt Hbf d.	1253	1330	1350	1430	1453	1530	1553	1630	1653	1730	1750	1754	1830	1853	1930	1930	1951	2030	2053	2130	2130	2230	2230	2253	2333
Bensheim d.	1310	1357	1411	1457	1510	1558	1611	1657	1710	1757	1810	1831	1859	1910	1957	1957	2011	2057	2110	2155	2155	2255	2255	2310	2355
Weinheim (Bergstr) d.	1322	1413	1423	1513	1522	1613	1624	1713	1722	1813	1822	1844	1915	1922	2012	2012	2023	2113	2122	2210	2210	2310	2310	2322	0010
Neu-Edingen / Friedrichsfeld a.	1332	1425	1433	1525	1532	1625	1633	1725	1732	1825	1832	1853	1927	1932	2025	2025	2032	2125	2132	2222	2222	2322	2322	2330	0023
Mannheim Hbf a.	1344	|	1446	|	1545	|	1645	|	1745	|	1845	1905	|	1945	|	2041	2045	|	2142	|	2243	|	2344	2341	|
Heidelberg Hbf a.	...	1439	...	1540	...	1641	...	1739	...	1836	...	...	1939	...	2039	...	...	2142	...	2237	...	2337	...	...	0034

	Ⓒ	Ⓒ	Ⓒ	Ⓐ	Ⓐ			Ⓐ			Ⓐ	Ⓐ	Ⓒ	Ⓒ	Ⓐ										
Heidelberg Hbf d.	0020	...	0225	0423	...	...	0520	...	...	0622	...	...	...	0723	0724	...	0820	...	0920	...	1020	...	1120	...	1220
Mannheim Hbf d.	|	0017	|	|	0445	0514	|	0606	0617	|	0650	0715	0715	|	|	0815	|	0915	|	1015	|	1115	|	1215	|
Neu-Edingen / Friedrichsfeld d.	0033	0033	0235	0433	0504	0533	0533	0616	0633	0633	0707	0728	0736	0736	0736	0828	0833	0925	0933	1028	1033	1128	1133	1228	1233
Weinheim (Bergstr) d.	0046	0046	0251	0451	0518	0546	0546	0626	0647	0647	0720	0739	0748	0748	0748	0839	0846	0936	0946	1039	1046	1139	1146	1239	1246
Bensheim d.	0104	0104	0307	0506	0534	0603	0603	0640	0702	0702	0735	0752	0802	0802	0802	0851	0901	0948	1001	1051	1101	1151	1201	1251	1301
Darmstadt Hbf d.	0128	0128	0330	0530	0600	0630	0630	0658	0730	0730	0757	0810	0830	0830	0830	0907	0930	1005	1030	1107	1130	1207	1230	1307	1330
Frankfurt (Main) Hbf a.	0149	0149	0349	0548	0620	0648	0648	0716	0748	0748	0816	0832	0848	0848	0848	0924	0948	1024	1048	1124	1148	1224	1248	1324	1348

						Ⓒ	Ⓐ													Ⓒ	Ⓒ	Ⓐ	Ⓐ		
Heidelberg Hbf d.	...	1320	...	1420	...	1520	1523	...	1620	...	1717	...	1820	...	1920	...	2020	...	2120	...	2220	2220	...	...	2320
Mannheim Hbf d.	1315	|	1415	|	1515	|	|	1615	|	1715	|	1815	|	1915	|	2015	|	2117	|	2214	|	|	2216	2316	|
Neu-Edingen / Friedrichsfeld d.	1326	1333	1428	1433	1528	1535	1535	1628	1633	1728	1734	1828	1833	1928	1933	2028	2033	2133	2133	2226	2233	2233	2233	2333	2333
Weinheim (Bergstr) d.	1337	1346	1439	1446	1539	1548	1548	1639	1646	1739	1746	1839	1846	1939	1946	2039	2046	2146	2146	2239	2246	2246	2246	2346	2346
Bensheim d.	1348	1401	1451	1501	1551	1602	1602	1651	1701	1751	1801	1851	1901	1951	2001	2051	2102	2203	2203	2251	2301	2301	2301	0003	0003
Darmstadt Hbf d.	1407	1430	1507	1530	1607	1630	1630	1707	1730	1807	1830	1907	1930	2007	2030	2107	2130	2230	2230	2307	2330	2331	2331	0030	0030
Frankfurt (Main) Hbf a.	1424	1448	1524	1548	1624	1648	1648	1724	1748	1824	1848	1924	1948	2024	2048	2124	2148	2248	2248	2324	2348	2348	2348	0048	0048

MANNHEIM - HEIDELBERG - KARLSUHE ⊠

	Ⓐt	Ⓐt	Ⓒz		Ⓒz	Ⓐt			†z											◧		⚒t	†z			
Mannheim Hbf ⊡ d.	...	0454	0504	0554	*0635*	0646	...	*0748*k	0812	*0837*	*0938*	*1038*	*1138*	*1238*	*1338*	*1438*	*1538*	*1638*	*1738*	*1838*	*1938*	*2038*	2055	2202	2258	0021
Heidelberg Hbf ⊡ a.	...	0505	0515	0605	*0647*	0704	...	*0801*k	0828	*0853*	*0954*	*1055*	*1154*	*1254*	*1354*	*1454*	*1554*	*1654*	*1754*	*1855*	*1954*	*2054*	2106	2213	2309	0037
Heidelberg Hbf d.	0420	0510	0516	0610	0705	0707	0722	0810	0829	0907	1010	1105	1210	1307	1410	1507	1610	1707	1810	1903	2010	2107	2107	2215	2310	0044
Bruchsal d.	0449	0530	0542	0633	0733	0734	0744	0830	0849	0930	1030	1130	1230	1330	1430	1530	1630	1730	1830	1930	2030	2130	2130	2235	2330	0113
Karlsruhe Hbf a.	0503	0544	0557	0647	0751	0751	0758	0844	0901	0944	1044	1144	1244	1344	1444	1544	1644	1744	1844	1944	2044	2144	2144	2249	2344	0131

	Ⓐt	Ⓐt			Ⓐt	†z	⑥	Ⓐt												†z	⚒t					
Karlsruhe Hbf d.	0420	0512	0516	0610	0648	0715	0715	0717	0817	0913	1015	1113	1215	1313	1415	1513	1613	1713	1813	1917	1917	2013	2115	2218	2318	0011
Bruchsal d.	0437	0530	0534	0623	0703	0728	0728	0732	0833	0930	1032	1130	1232	1330	1432	1530	1632	1730	1830	1930	1930	2026	2130	2230	2331	0027
Heidelberg a.	0505	0549	0601	0642	0731	0748	0748	0749	0900	0949	1051	1151	1252	1349	1452	1549	1652	1751	1852	1949	1949	2046	2149	2249	2349	0055
Heidelberg Hbf ⊡ d.	0506	*0559*	0602	*0650*h	0731	0750	*0804*	*0804*	*0910*	*1003*	*1103*	*1203*	*1303*	*1403*	*1503*	*1603*	*1703*	*1803*	*1903*	1950	*2003*	2050	2152	2252	2350	0056
Mannheim Hbf ⊡ a.	0522	*0615*	0621	*0706*h	0748	0803	*0819*	*0819*	*0924*	*1019*	*1119*	*1219*	*1319*	*1419*	*1520*	*1619*	*1719*	*1819*	*1920*	2004	*2019*	2106	2203	2305	0006	0114

h – On Ⓒ (also Jan. 6) Heidelberg Hbf d. *0703*, Mannheim Hbf a. *0720*.
k – On Ⓒ (also Jan. 6) Mannheim Hbf d. *0738*, Heidelberg Hbf a. *0753*.
t – Not Jan. 6.
z – Also Jan. 6.

◧ – On † (also Jan. 6) Heidelberg Hbf d. 1909, Bruchsal d. 1934, Karlsruhe Hbf a. 1950.
⊠ – Most services shown are limited stop *RE* services. Additional stopping S-Bahn services operate.
⊡ – See also Tables **918**, **919**, **923**, **924**.

Local trains KOBLENZ - FRANKFURT 914

Koblenz - Bingen - Mainz - Frankfurt *(Linke Rheinstrecke)* ⊠

km			Ⓐ	Ⓐ	Ⓐ	Ⓒ	K		K		K		K		K		K				⚒d		❖			
0	**Koblenz** Hbf d.	0507	0606	0617	0652	0707	0803	0904	1003	1104	1203	1304	1403	1504	1603	1704	1803	1902	2104		0552	0730		1930	2030	2152
19	Boppard Hbf d.	0519	0618	0632	0704	0719	0815	0916	1015	1116	1215	1316	1415	1516	1615	1716	1815	1916	2116		0607	0744		1944	2044	2207
24	Boppard-Bad Salzig d.	|	|	0636	|	|	|	|	|	|	|	|	|	|	|	|	|	|	|		0611	0748		1948	2048	2211
34	St Goar d.	|	|	0645	|	|	|	|	|	|	|	|	|	|	|	|	|	|	|	A	0619	0756	and	1956	2056	2219
41	Oberwesel d.	0533	0633	0651	0718	0733	0829	0930	1029	1130	1229	1330	1429	1530	1629	1730	1829	1930	2130	L	0625	0801		2001	2101	2225
47	Bacharach d.	0537	|	0656	0723	0737	|	0936	|	1136	|	1336	|	1536	|	1736	|	1936	2136	S	0629	0806	hourly	2006	2106	2229
61	Bingen (Rhein) Hbf a.	0546	0646	0709	0733	0746	0842	0946	1042	1146	1242	1346	1442	1546	1642	1746	1842	1946	2146	O	0643	0819		2019	2119	2243
61	Bingen (Rhein) Hbf d.	0547	0647	0713	0734	0747	*0854*t	0947	*1056*t	1147	*1256*t	1347	*1456*t	1547	*1656*t	1747	*1856*t	1947	2147		0654	0824	until	2024	2127	2254
62	Bingen (Rhein) Stadt d.	|	|	0716	|	|	*0857*t	|	*1059*t	|	*1259*t	|	*1459*t	|	*1659*t	|	*1859*t	|	|	⊡	0657	0827		2027	2129	2257
73	Ingelheim d.	0556	0655	0722	0745	0755	*0907*t	0955	*1109*t	1155	*1309*t	1355	*1509*t	1555	*1709*t	1755	*1909*t	1955	2155		0707	0837		2037	2139	2307
91	**Mainz** Hbf a.	0608	0708	0736	0757	0808	*0926*t	1008	*1126*t	1208	*1326*t	1408	*1526*t	1608	*1726*t	1808	*1926*t	2008	2208		0728	0900		2058	2156	2325
119	Frankfurt Flughafen ◧ a.	0634	0734	0804	0819	0834	...	1034	...	1234	...	1434	...	1634	...	1834	...	2034	*2234*		...	...		...	...	...
130	**Frankfurt** (Main) Hbf a.	0648	0748	0825	0836	0848	...	1048	...	1248	...	1448	...	1648	...	1851	...	2051	*2248*		...	...		...	...	...

	Ⓐ		K		K		K		K		K	Ⓐ		ⒸK	Ⓐ				Ⓐ							
Frankfurt (Main) Hbf d.	0456	0659	...	0908	...	1108	...	1308	...	1508	...	1625	1708	...	1825	1908	2108		...	...	...	...		...	...	...
Frankfurt Flughafen ◧ d.	0507	0709	...	0924	...	1123	...	1323	...	1524	...	1637	1724	...	1837	1923	2123		...	...	...	...		...	...	...
Mainz Hbf d.	0532	0732	*0832*t	0951	*1032*t	1151	...	1351	*1432*t	1551	*1632*t	1700	1751	...	1900	1951	2151		...	0547	0701	0803		2103	2203	2303
Ingelheim d.	0547	0747	*0850*t	1002	*1050*t	1202	...	1402	*1450*t	1602	*1650*t	1711	1802	...	1911	2002	2202	A	...	0605	0719	0821	and	2121	2221	2321
Bingen (Rhein) Stadt d.	|	|	*0900*t	|	*1100*t	|	...	|	*1500*t	|	*1700*t	|	|	...	|	|	|	L	...	0615	0734	0831		2131	2231	2331
Bingen (Rhein) Hbf a.	0555	0755	*0903*t	1011	*1103*t	1211	...	1411	*1503*t	1611	*1703*t	1721	1811	...	1921	2011	2211	S	...	0618	0738	0834	hourly	2134	2234	2334
Bingen (Rhein) Hbf d.	0556	0756	0913	1013	1113	1213	1313	1413	1513	1613	1713	1722	1813	1913	1922	2013	2216	O	0517	0626	0739	0839		2139	...	2335
Bacharach d.	0604	0804	|	1021	|	1221	|	1421	|	1621	|	1734	1821	|	1930	2021	2228		0529	0638	0750	0850	until	2150	...	2346
Oberwesel d.	0609	0809	0926	1026	1125	1226	1325	1426	1525	1626	1726	1739	1826	1925	1935	2026	2232	⊡	0533	0649	0754	0854		2154	...	2350
St Goar d.	|	|	|	|	|	|	|	|	|	|	|	1745	|	|	|	|	2238		0539	0655	0800	0900		2200	...	2356
Boppard-Bad Salzig d.	|	|	|	|	|	|	|	|	|	|	|	|	|	|	|	|	2247		0547	0703	0808	0908		2208	...	0004
Boppard Hbf d.	0623	0823	0940	1040	1139	1240	1339	1440	1539	1640	1740	1754	1840	1939	1949	2040	2251		0551	0707	0812	0912		2212	...	0008
Koblenz Hbf a.	0638	0838	0954	1054	1153	1254	1353	1454	1553	1654	1754	1809	1856	1953	2004	2054	2309		0610	0723	0827	0927		2227	...	0023

Neuwied - Koblenz - St Goarshausen - Wiesbaden - Frankfurt *(Rechte Rheinstrecke; operated by VIAS)*

km		Ⓐ	Ⓐ	Ⓐ	Ⓒ	Ⓐ	Ⓐ		Ⓐ					Ⓐ			Ⓐ		Ⓐ					⑤⑥f		⑤⑥f
0	**Neuwied** 802 d.	...	...	0437	...	...	0537	...	...	0637z	0737		1237	...	1337	1437	...	1537	...	1637		2037	2137	2137	2237	2237
15	**Koblenz** Hbf 802 906 d.	...	...	0452	...	...	0552	...	...	0652	0752		1252	1322	1352	1452	...	1552	1622	1652		2052	2152	2152	2252	2252
20	Niederlahnstein 906 d.	...	...	0459	...	...	0559	...	...	0659	0759		1259	1329	1359	1459	...	1559	1629	1659		2059	2159	2159	2259	2259
26	Braubach d.	...	...	0506	...	...	0606	...	...	0706	0806	and	1306	1336	1406	1506	...	1606	1636	1706	and	2106	2206	2206	2306	2306
38	Kamp-Bornhofen d.	...	...	0516	...	...	0616	...	...	0716	0816		1316	1346	1416	1516	...	1616	1646	1716		2116	2216	2216	2316	2316
50	St Goarshausen d.	...	...	0526	...	...	0626	...	...	0726	0826	hourly	1327	1357	1427	1527	...	1627	1657	1727	hourly	2127	2227	2227	2327	2327
61	Kaub d.	...	0506	0536	...	0606	0636	0636	0706	0736	0836		1336	1406	1436	1536	1606	1636	1706	1736		2136	2236	2236	2335	2336
67	Lorch (Rhein) d.	...	0512	0542	...	0612	0642	0642	0712	0742	0842	until	1342	1412	1442	1542	1612	1642	1712	1742	until	2142	2242	2242	...	2342
79	Rüdesheim (Rhein) d.	0453	0523	0553	0553h	0623	0653	0653	0723	0753	0853		1353	1423	1453	1553	1623	1653	1723	1753		2153	2253	2253	...	2353
109	**Wiesbaden** Hbf a.	0525	0555	0625	0625h	0655	0725	0725	0755	0825	0925		1425	1455	1525	1625	1655	1725	1755	1825		2225	2325	2325	...	0025
109	**Wiesbaden** Hbf d.	0532	0602	0632	0632	0702	0732	0732	0802	0832	0932		1432	1502	1532	1632	1702	1732	1802	1832		2232	...	2332	...	0032
117	**Mainz** Kastel d.	0539	0609	0639	0639	0709	0739	0739	0809	0839	0939		1439	1509	1539	1639	1709	1739	1809	1839		2239	...	2339	...	0039
150	**Frankfurt** (Main) Hbf a.	0605	0635	0705	0705	0735	0805	0805	0835	0905	1005		1505	1535	1605	1705	1735	1805	1834	1905		2305	...	0005	...	0105

	Ⓐ	Ⓐ		⚒						Ⓐ		Ⓐ		Ⓐ		Ⓐ		Ⓐ		Ⓐ				⑤⑥f		L
Frankfurt (Main) Hbf d.	...	...	...	0553t	0654	0754	0853		1353	1423	1453	1523	1553	1623	1654	1723	1754	1822	1853	1923	1953	2053	2153	2153	2253	2253
Mainz Kastel d.	...	...	...	0619t	0719	0819	0919		1419	1449	1519	1549	1619	1649	1720	1749	1819	1849	1919	1949	2019	2119	2219	2219	2319	2319
Wiesbaden Hbf a.	...	...	...	0628t	0728	0828	0928		1428	1458	1528	1558	1628	1658	1728	1758	1828	1858	1928	1958	2028	2128	2228	2228	2328	2328
Wiesbaden Hbf d.	...	...	0533t	0633	0733	0833	0933	and	1433	1503	1533	1603	1633	1703	1733	1803	1833	1903	1933	2003	2033	2133	2233	2233	2333	2333
Rüdesheim (Rhein) d.	...	0536	0606t	0706	0806	0906	1006		1506	1536	1606	1636	1706	1736	1806	1836	1906	1936	2006	2035	2106	2206	2306	2306	0005	0006
Lorch (Rhein) d.	...	0545	0615t	0715	0816	0915	1015	hourly	1515	1546	1615	1646	1715	1745	1815	1845	1915	1945	2015	...	2115	2215	2315	2315	...	0015
Kaub d.	0453	0553	0623	0723	0823	0923	1023		1523	1552	1623	1653	1723	1753	1823	1853	1923	1953	2023	...	2123	2223	2322	2323	...	0022
St Goarshausen d.	0501	0601	0631	0731	0831	0931	1031	until	1531	...	1631	1702	1731	1801	1831	1901	1931	2001	2031	...	2131	2231	...	2331	...	...
Kamp-Bornhofen d.	0512	0612	0642	0742	0842	0942	1042		1542	...	1642	1713	1742	1812	1842	1912	1942	2012	2042	...	2142	2242	...	2342	...	...
Braubach d.	0523	0623	0653	0753	0853	0953	1053		1553	...	1653	1723	1753	1823	1853	1923	1953	2023	2053	...	2153	2253	...	2353	...	...
Niederlahnstein 906 d.	0529	0629	0659	0759	0859	0959	1059		1559	...	1659	1729	1759	1829	1859	1929	1959	2029	2059	...	2159	2259	...	2359	...	...
Koblenz Hbf 802 906 a.	0537	0636	0706	0806	0906	1006	1106		1606	...	1706	1736	1806	1836	1906	1936	2006	2036	2106	...	2206	2306	...	0006	...	...
Neuwied 802 a.	0556	...	0726	0826	0926	1026	1126		1626	...	1726	...	1826	...	1926	...	2026	...	2126	...	2226	2326	...	...	...	...

K – To/from Kaiserslautern (Table **918**). Operated by Vlexx.
– ⑤–⑦ (also Dec. 26; not Dec. 25).
– Runs daily Bingen (Rhein) Hbf - Mainz.

f – Also Dec. 25.
h – ⑥ only.
t – Ⓐ only.
z – Ⓒ only.

◧ – Frankfurt Flughafen Regionalbahnhof ✈.
⊡ – Stopping services (operated by Mittelrheinbahn).
❖ – Timings Bingen (Rhein) Hbf - Mainz may vary by up to 5 minutes.
⊠ – See Table **800** for long-distance *ICE / IC* services. See Table **917** for other services Ingelheim - Mainz - Frankfurt and v.v. See Table **917a** for S-Bahn services Mainz - Frankfurt Flughafen ✈ - Frankfurt (Main) Hbf and v.v.

Köln Düsseldorfer Deutsche Rheinschiffahrt — KÖLN - KOBLENZ - MAINZ *2023 service* 914a

◐		A	A	B⛴	E	A	E	A	B	B	B	E
750	**Köln** (Rheingarten) d.	...	...	...	...	...	...	...	...	0930	...	...
600	**Bonn** d.	...	...	...	...	...	...	...	1030	1230	1430	...
900	Königswinter Fähre d.	...	...	...	...	...	...	...	1130	1330	1530	...
750	Bad Honnef (Rhein) d.	...	...	...	...	...	...	...	1150	1350	1550	...
400	Remagen d.	...	...	...	...	...	...	...	1220	1420	1620	...
750	Linz am Rhein d.	...	...	...	...	...	...	...	1250	1450	1650	...
500	Bad Breisig d.	...	...	...	...	...	...	...	▬	...	...	...
400	Bad Hönningen d.	...	...	...	...	...	...	...	...	...	...	...
200	Andernach d.	...	...	...	...	...	...	...	...	...	...	...
2200	**Koblenz** ⊙ d.	...	...	0900	...	...	1200	...	...	...	...	1750
150	Oberlahnstein d.	...	...	0940	...	...	1240	...	...	...	...	1830
450	Braubach d.	...	...	1005	...	...	1305	...	A	...	...	1855
400	**Boppard** d.	...	1000	1100	...	1300	1400	...	1600	...	...	1945
400	Kamp-Bornhofen d.	...	1010	1110	...	1310	1410	...	1610	...	...	...
300	Bad Salzig d.	...	1025	1125	...	1325	1425	...	1625	...	...	...
450	**St Goarshausen** ★ d.	1045	|	1210	1300	|	|	1600	|	...	...	...
250	**St Goar** ★ d.	1055	1120	1220	1315	1420	1520	1610	1720	...	...	...
450	Oberwesel d.	1125	...	1250	1350	...	...	1640	...	...	...	...
900	Kaub d.	1140	...	1305	1405	...	...	1655	...	...	...	...
600	Bacharach d.	1205	...	1330	1430	...	...	1720	...	...	...	...
400	**Bingen** (Rhein) ♥ d.	1335	...	1500	1600	...	...	1850	...	...	...	...
900	**Rüdesheim** ♥ a.	1350	...	1515	1620	...	...	1900	...	...	...	...
500	Wiesbaden-Biebrich a.	...	...	...	1810t	...	...	...	...	...	...	...
600	**Mainz** a.	...	...	...	1840t	...	...	...	...	...	...	...

	A	E	B	A	E	A	E	A	A	B⛴
Mainz d.	...	...	...	...	0915t	...	...	...	...	...
Wiesbaden-Biebrich d.	...	...	...	...	0930t	...	...	...	...	...
Rüdesheim ♥ d.	0900	...	...	...	1100	...	...	1415	...	1615
Bingen (Rhein) ♥ d.	0915	...	...	...	1115	...	...	1430	...	1630
Bacharach d.	1000	...	...	...	1200	...	...	1515	...	1715
Kaub d.	1010	...	...	...	1210	...	...	1525	...	1725
Oberwesel d.	1020	...	...	...	1220	...	...	1535	...	1735
St Goar ★ d.	|	...	...	1130	|	1430	1530	|	1730	1755
St Goarshausen ★ d.	1045	...	...	1140	1250	1440	1540	1600	1740	1805
Bad Salzig d.	...	...	...	1205	▬	1505	1605	...	1805	1830
Kamp-Bornhofen d.	...	...	...	1215	...	1515	1615	...	1815	1840
Boppard d.	...	1015	...	1230	...	1530	1630	...	1830	1850
Braubach d.	...	1045	...	▬	...	▬	1700	...	...	1915
Oberlahnstein d.	...	1100	...	...	...	...	1715	...	...	1930
Koblenz ⊙ d.	...	1145	...	...	...	...	1740	...	...	2000
Andernach d.	...	...	...	...	...	...	...	...	...	...
Bad Hönningen d.	...	...	...	...	...	...	...	...	...	...
Bad Breisig d.	...	...	...	D	C	B	...	...	...	...
Linz am Rhein d.	...	...	1250	1450	1550	1650	...	...	...	...
Remagen d.	...	...	1300	1500	1600	1700	...	...	...	...
Bad Honnef (Rhein) d.	...	...	1325	1525	1625	1725	...	...	...	...
Königswinter Fähre d.	...	...	1340	1540	1640	1740	...	...	...	...
Bonn d.	...	...	1415	1615	1715	1815	...	...	...	...
Köln (Rheingarten) a.	...	...	...	1800	1900	...	...	...	...	...

– Apr. 1 - Oct. 22.
– ②–⑦ Apr. 29 - Oct. 3.
– ②③④⑦ Apr. 30 - Oct. 3.
– ⑤⑥ Apr. 29 - Sept. 30.
– Apr. 29 - Oct. 22.

t – Not Oct. 4 – 22.

⊙ – Koblenz (Konrad-Adenauer-Ufer).
◐ – Distance in metres from rail station to river landing stage.
⛴ – Operated by paddlesteamer *Goethe*.

★ – A frequent ferry service sails between St Goar and St Goarshausen operated by Rheinschifffahrt Goar. ✆ + 49 (0) 6771 26 20. www.faehre-loreley.de
♥ – A frequent ferry service sails between Bingen and Rüdesheim operated by Bingen-Rüdesheimer Fähr- und Schiffahrtsgesellschaft. ✆ + 49 (0) 6721 30808. www.bingen-ruedesheimer.de

Operator: Köln Düsseldorfer Deutsche Rheinschiffahrt, Frankenwerft 35, D-50667 Köln. ✆ +49 (0) 221 20 88 318. www.k-d.com

915 KOBLENZ - TRIER - LUXEMBOURG and SAARBRÜCKEN

RE services except where shown

Many Saarbrücken services continue to / start from stations in Table **919**. **Warning!** Journeys to / from Luxembourg are subject to alteration on ⑥⑦ Mar. 4 - Apr. 2 and on Apr. 15, 16.

km		Ⓐ	†	Ⓐ				⚒	⚒			⑥				⊠					D				
0	**Koblenz** Hbf d.	...	...	...	...	...	...	0603	0603	...	0706	0706	...	0806	0806	and at	1406	1406	1506	1506	1520	1606	1606	1706	1706
47	Cochem (Mosel) d.	...	...	0502	...	...	...	0638	0638	...	0741	0741	...	0841	0841		1441	1441	1541	1541	1555	1641	1641	1741	1741
59	Bullay d.	...	...	0513	...	...	...	0648	0648	...	0751	0751	...	0851	0851	the same	1451	1451	1551	1551	1603	1651	1651	1751	1751
76	Wittlich Hbf d.	...	...	0529	...	...	...	0700	0700	...	0803	0803	...	0903	0903		1503	1503	1603	1603	1616	1703	1703	1803	1803
112	**Trier** Hbf a.	...	...	0604	...	...	...	0731	0731	...	0830	0830	...	0930	0930	minutes	1530	1530	1630	1630	1643	1730	1730	1830	1830
112	**Trier** Hbf d.	0456	0533	...	0633	0637	0733	0733	0737	0737	0833	0837	0837	0933	0937		1533	1537	1633	1637	1646	1733	1737	1833	1837
163	**Luxembourg** a.	|	|	...	|	0723	|	|	0823	0823	|	0923	0923	|	1023	past each	|	1623	|	1723	1748	|	1823	|	1923
135	Saarburg d.	0514	0551	...	0651	...	0751	0751	...	...	0851	...	...	0951	...		1551	...	1651	...	...	1751	...	1851	...
161	Merzig (Saar) d.	0534	0610	...	0710	...	0810	0810	...	...	0910	...	...	1010	...	hour until	1610	...	1710	...	...	1810	...	1910	...
173	Dillingen (Saar) d.	0543	0619	...	0720	...	0820	0820	...	...	0920	...	...	1020	...		1620	...	1720	...	...	1820	...	1920	...
177	Saarlouis Hbf d.	0547	0623	...	0724	...	0824	0824	...	...	0924	...	...	1024	...		1624	...	1724	...	...	1824	...	1924	...
190	Völklingen d.	0557	0632	...	0732	...	0832	0832	...	...	0932	...	...	1032	...		1632	...	1732	...	...	1832	...	1932	...
200	**Saarbrücken** Hbf a.	0606	0641	...	0741	...	0841	0841	...	...	0941	...	...	1041	...		1641	...	1741	...	...	1841	...	1941	...

								©				
Koblenz Hbf d.	1806	1806	1902**b**	1919	2019	2019	2119	2119	...	2219	2219	2321
Cochem (Mosel) d.	1841	1841	1938	1954	2054	2054	2154	2154	...	2254	2254	2356
Bullay d.	1851	1851	1948	2002	2102	2102	2202	2202	...	2302	2302	0004
Wittlich Hbf d.	1903	1903	2001	2014	2114	2114	2214	2214	...	2314	2314	0016
Trier Hbf a.	1930	1930	2030	2041	2140	2140	2240	2240	...	2340	2340	0042
Trier Hbf d.	1933	1937	2033	2043	2143	2149	2249	2243	2243	2345	2349	...
Luxembourg a.	|	2023	|	2129	2229	|	|	2329	2329	|	0034	...
Saarburg d.	1951	...	2051	...	...	2210	2310	...	...	0010	...	...
Merzig (Saar) d.	2010	...	2110	...	...	2230	2330	...	...	0036	...	...
Dillingen (Saar) d.	2020	...	2120	...	...	2240	2340	...	...	0046	...	...
Saarlouis Hbf d.	2024	...	2124	...	...	2244	2344	...	...	0050	...	...
Völklingen d.	2032	...	2132	...	...	2252	2352	...	...	0101	...	...
Saarbrücken Hbf a.	2041	...	2141	...	...	2301	0001	...	...	0114	...	...

	Ⓐ		Ⓐ	©	†	Ⓐ	Ⓐ	⚒		D
Saarbrücken Hbf d.	...	...	...	...	...	...	0458	...	0516	...
Völklingen d.	...	...	...	...	...	...	0506	...	0528	...
Saarlouis Hbf d.	...	...	...	...	...	...	0514	...	0539	...
Dillingen (Saar) d.	...	...	...	...	...	...	0518	...	0542	...
Merzig (Saar) d.	...	...	...	...	...	...	0527	...	0553	...
Saarburg d.	...	...	...	...	...	...	0547	...	0619	...
Luxembourg d.	...	...	...	...	...	0510	|	...	|	0618
Trier Hbf a.	...	...	...	...	...	0602	0606	...	0646	0707
Trier Hbf d.	0410	...	0510	...	0525	0610	0610	0610	...	0710
Wittlich Hbf d.	0436	...	0536	...	0551	0636	0636	0636	...	0736
Bullay d.	0449	...	0549	...	0605	0649	0649	0649	...	0749
Cochem (Mosel) d.	0458	...	0558	0627	0627**h**	0658	0658	0658	...	0758
Koblenz Hbf a.	0536	...	0636	0718	0718	0736	0736	0736	...	0836

																		⑤	⑥						
Saarbrücken Hbf d.	0619	...	0719	and at	...	1619	...	1719	...	1819	...	1919	...	2019	...	2119	...	...	2222	2222	2232	...	2335	0034	0120
Völklingen d.	0627	...	0727		...	1627	...	1727	...	1827	...	1927	...	2027	...	2127	...	...	2231	2231	2244	...	2347	0045	0131
Saarlouis Hbf d.	0636	...	0736	the same	...	1636	...	1736	...	1836	...	1936	...	2036	...	2136	...	...	2239	2239	2255	...	2358	0056	0141
Dillingen (Saar) d.	0640	...	0740		...	1640	...	1740	...	1840	...	1940	...	2040	...	2140	...	...	2242	2242	2258	...	0001	0059	0145
Merzig (Saar) d.	0648	...	0748	minutes	...	1648	...	1748	...	1848	...	1948	...	2048	...	2148	...	...	2250	2250	2309	...	0012	0111	0156
Saarburg d.	0708	...	0808		...	1708	...	1808	...	1908	...	2008	...	2108	...	2208	...	...	2309	2309	2335	...	0038	...	...
Luxembourg d.	|	0733	|	past each	1633	|	1733	|	1833	|	1933	|	2033	|	2133	|	2233	2233	|	|	|	2333	|	...	...
Trier Hbf a.	0727	0824	0827		1724	1727	1823	1828	1924	1927	2024	2027	2124	2127	2224	2227	2324	2324	2328	2328	0001	0024	0105	...	...
Trier Hbf d.	0731	0831	0831	hour until	1731	1731	1831	1831	1931	1931	2031	2031	2131	2131	...	2231	...	2331	2331	...	...	...	...	...	...
Wittlich Hbf d.	0756	0856	0856		1756	1756	1856	1856	1956	1956	2056	2056	2156	2156	...	2256	...	2356	2356	...	...	...	...	...	...
Bullay d.	0809	0909	0909		1809	1809	1909	1909	2009	2009	2109	2109	2209	2209	...	2309	...	0009	0009	...	...	...	...	...	...
Cochem (Mosel) d.	0818	0918	0918		1818	1818	1918	1918	2018	2018	2118	2118	2218	2218	...	2318	...	0018	0018	...	...	...	...	...	...
Koblenz Hbf a.	0856	0956	0956		1856	1856	1956	1956	2056	2056	2156	2156	2256	2256	...	2356	...	0056	0056	...	...	...	...	...	...

D – To / from Düsseldorf (Table **800**). Train classification is *IC* Koblenz - Düsseldorf and v.v.

b – 1900 on ⑦.
c – 2117 on ⑥.
e – 3–4 minutes earlier on Apr. 7, 10.
h – Arrives 0614.
j – Also Apr. 7, 10.

⊠ – The 0906 from Koblenz to Luxembourg requires a change of trains at Trier.

BULLAY - TRABEN-TRARBACH

13 km Journey time: 18 minutes

Operated by Rhenus Veniro.
From Bullay at 0600 ⚒, 0658, 0838, 0938 and hourly until 2138.
From Traben-Trarbach at 0625 ⚒, 0741, 0901, 1001 and hourly until 2201.

TRIER - PERL - METZ

km		⑥⑦j		⑥⑦j			⑥⑦j		⑥⑦j	
0	**Trier** Hbf d.	1042	...	1942	...	**Metz** d.	0842	...	1742	...
49	Perl 🏛 d.	1120	...	2020	...	Thionville d.	0907	...	1808**e**	...
70	Thionville a.	1153	...	2053	...	Perl 🏛 d.	0945	...	1845	...
100	**Metz** a.	1215	...	2123**c**	...	**Trier** Hbf a.	1018	...	1918	...

Local *RB* services **Trier** - **Perl** and v.v. Journey time: 47–54 minutes.
From Trier Hbf at 0506 Ⓐ, 0614 Ⓐ, 0706 ⚒, 0750, 0850, 0950, 1050, 1150, 1250, 1325 Ⓐ, 1350 ©, 1450, 1605, 1706, 1750, 1850, 1950, 2107 and 2221.
From Perl at 0505 Ⓐ, 0612 ⚒, 0649 Ⓐ, 0715 ⚒, 0815, 0915, 1015, 1115, 1215, 1317, 1415, 1515, 1613, 1715, 1815, 1915, 2015 and 2115.

915a KÖLN - KALL - GEROLSTEIN - TRIER

Temporary service until further notice. All services Kall - Gerolstein - Kyllburg and v.v. are currently operated by 🚌. Services Köln - Kall and Kyllburg - Trier are by train.

By Train	Ⓐ	⑥	Ⓐ	⑥	Ⓐ	Ⓐ	©																
Köln Hbf d.	...	...	0512	...	0546	0612	0621	0646	0721	0746	and at the	1721	1745	1821	1846	1921	1944	2021	2046	2121	2148	2221	2246
Euskirchen d.	0430	0500	0556	0600	0630	0658	0700	0730	0800	0830	same minutes	1800	1830	1901	1930	2000	2030	2100	2130	2200	2231	2300	2330
Mechernich d.	0439	0509	0608	0609	0642	0708	0709	0742	0809	0842	past each	1809	1842	1910	1942	2009	2042	2109	2142	2209	2243	2309	2342
Kall a.	0447	0517	0617	0617	0651	0717	0717	0751	0817	0851	hour until	1817	1851	1918	1951	2017	2051	2117	2151	2217	2252	2317	2351

By Train		©		Ⓐ	Ⓐ	⑥	Ⓐ	Ⓐ	⚒	Ⓐ	⑥	Ⓐ	Ⓐ										
Kall d.	0005	0005	...	0505	0529	0538	0559	0613	0642	0659	0705	0710	0727	0742	0805	0842	and at the	2105	2142	2205	2242	2305	2342
Mechernich d.	0014	0014	...	0514	0538	0547	0608	0622	0649	0708	0714	0717	0736	0749	0814	0849	same minutes	2114	2149	2214	2249	2314	2349
Euskirchen d.	0026	0030	...	0530	0556	0603	0626	0639	0703	0722	0730	0730	0750	0803	0830	0903	past each	2130	2203	2230	2303	2330	2359
Köln Hbf a.	...	0112	...	0612	0639	0639	0712	0715	0739	0758	0812	0812	0834	0839	0912	0939	hour until	2212	2239	2314	2339	0012	...

By 🚌	©		⚒						Ⓐ	Ⓐ	Ⓐ	Ⓐ	Ⓐ	Ⓐ	Ⓐ	Ⓐ								
Kall d.	0025	...	0525	0625	and	2325	...	A	0625	0825	1025	1225	1425	1625	1825	2025	...	...	...	...	...	...	...	...
Blankenheim d.	0059	...	0544	0644	hourly	2344	...	L	|	|	|	|	|	|	|	|	...	...	...	...	...	...	...	...
Jünkerath d.	0130	...	0611	0711		0011	...	S	|	|	|	|	|	|	|	|	...	...	...	...	...	...	...	...
Gerolstein d.	0200	...	0641	0741	until	0041	...	O	|	|	|	|	|	|	|	|	...	...	...	...	...	...	...	...
Trier Hbf a.	...	...	...	...		...	...		0820	1020	1220	1420	1620	1820	2020	2220	...	...	...	...	...	...	...	...

By 🚌	Ⓐ	⚒							Ⓐ	Ⓐ	Ⓐ	Ⓐ	Ⓐ	Ⓐ	Ⓐ	Ⓐ								
Trier Hbf d.	...	...	...	and	...	...	...	A	0539	0739	0939	1139	1339	1539	1739	1939	...	...	...	...	...	...	...	...
Gerolstein d.	0404	0517	0617	hourly	2117	2159	...	L	|	|	|	|	|	|	|	|	...	...	...	...	...	...	...	...
Jünkerath d.	0434	0547	0647		2147	2229	...	S	|	|	|	|	|	|	|	|	...	...	...	...	...	...	...	...
Blankenheim d.	0501	0614	0714	until	2214	2300	...	O	|	|	|	|	|	|	|	|	...	...	...	...	...	...	...	...
Kall d.	0521	0634	0734		2234	2334	...		0734	0934	1134	1334	1534	1734	1934	2134	...	...	...	...	...	...	...	...

By train / 🚌	⚒						🚌	🚌	
Gerolstein d.	*0450**	*0550**	and	*1950**	*2050**	...	2113	2213	...
Kyllburg d.	0534	0634	hourly	2034	2134	...	2150	2250	...
Bitburg-Erdorf d.	0540	0640	until	2040	2140	...	2200	2300	...
Trier Hbf a.	0627	0727		2127	2227	...	2351	0051	...

By train / 🚌	⚒🚌	†🚌	⚒					🚌	🚌
Trier Hbf d.	0323	0423	0435	0535	and	2035	...	2110	2210
Bitburg-Erdorf d.	0420	0520	0519	0619	hourly	2119	...	2301	0001
Kyllburg a.	0433	0533	0525	0625	until	2125	...	2311	0011
Gerolstein a.	0509	0609	*0609**	*0709**		*2209**	...	2348	0048

* – By 🚌 to / from Kyllburg.

KARLSRUHE - OFFENBURG - KONSTANZ — 916

RE services except where shown

km		⚒ t		Ⓐ t	Ⓒ z									*IC* 2005 ⑤⑥ F 🍷									Ⓑ	⑥	Ⓑ H
0	**Karlsruhe** Hbf 912 943 d.	...	...	...	0456	0606	0702	0809g	0907	1007	1107	1207	1307	1336	1407	1507	1607	1707	1809	1907	2009	2109	2109	2209	2209
21	Rastatt 943 d.	...	...	...	0510	0620	0718	0823	0923	1025	1123	1223	1323	|	1423	1523	1623	1723	1823	1923	2023	2125	2125	2229	2229
29	Baden-Baden 912 d.	...	...	...	0516	0627	0726	0831	0931	1031	1131	1231	1331	1354	1431	1531	1631	1731	1831	1931	2031	2132	2132	2237	2237
69	**Offenburg** 912 a.	...	...	...	0540	0653	0755	0856	0956	1056	1156	1256	1356	1413	1456	1556	1656	1756	1856	1956	2056	2156	2156	2306	2306
69	**Offenburg** 942 d.	...	...	0510	0544	0657	0759	0859	0959	1059	1159	1259	1359	1415	1459	1559	1659	1759	1859	1959	2059	2159	2159	2328	2328
102	Hausach 942 d.	...	...	0534	0611	0722	0821	0922	1022	1122	1222	1322	1422	1436	1522	1622	1722	1822	1922	2022	2124	2223	2223	2352	2353
112	Hornberg (Schwarzw) d.	...	...	0542	0619	0730	0829	0929	1029	1129	1229	1329	1429	1445	1529	1629	1729	1829	1929	2029	2132	2231	2231	...	0001
125	Triberg d.	...	...	0557	0636	0743	0843	0943	1043	1143	1243	1343	1443	1500	1543	1643	1743	1843	1943	2043	2146	2244	2244	...	0015
140	St Georgen (Schwarzw) d.	...	...	0625h	0657k	0757	0857	0957	1057	1157	1257	1357	1457	1517	1557	1657	1757	1857	1957	2057	2200	2259	2259	...	0029
155	Villingen (Schwarzw) 938 d.	...	0551	0639k	0706	0806	0906	1006	1106	1206	1306	1406	1506	1528	1606	1706	1806	1906	2006	2106	2209	2307	2308	...	0037
169	Donaueschingen 938 d.	...	0602	0654k	0716	0816	0916	1016	1116	1216	1316	1416	1516	1542	1616	1716	1816	1916	2016	2116	2219	...	2317	...	...
188	Immendingen 938 d.	...	0619	0706	0728	0828	0928	1028	1128	1228	1328	1428	1528	1554	1628	1728	1828	1928	2028	2128	2232	...	2330	...	...
204	Engen 940 d.	0530	0633	0719	0740	0840	0940	1040	1140	1240	1340	1440	1540	|	1640	1740	1840	1940	2040	2140	2245	...	|	...	...
218	**Singen** 939 940 d.	0557	0654j	0735	0752	0852	0952	1052	1152	1252	1352	1452	1552	1621	1652	1752	1852	1952	2052	2152	2259	...	2352	...	...
228	Radolfzell 939 940 d.	0610	0705	0746	0800	0900	1000	1100	1200	1300	1400	1500	1600	1630	1700	1800	1900	2000	2100	2200	2307	...	0000	...	...
248	**Konstanz** 940 a.	0633	0727	0810	0816	0916	1016	1116	1216	1316	1416	1516	1616	1645	1716	1816	1916	2016	2116	2216	2322	...	0014	...	...

		①–⑤	⑥						*IC* 2006 ⑥ D 🍷	*IC* 2004 ⑦ E 🍷							H								
Konstanz 940 d.	...	0451	0451	...	0520	0640	0736	0839	0907	0907	0939	1039	1139	1239	1339	1439	1539	1639	1739	1839	1939	2039	2158	2223	2323
Radolfzell 939 940 d.	...	0505	0505	...	0534	0656	0753	0856	0920	0920	0956	1056	1156	1256	1356	1456	1556	1656	1756	1856	1956	2056	2222	2249	2346
Singen 939 940 d.	...	0512	0512	...	0546	0706	0807k	0907	0929	0929	1007	1107	1207	1307	1407	1507	1607	1707	1807	1907	2007	2106	2234	2259	0000
Engen 940 d.	...	0523	0523	...	0555	0715	0816	0916	|	|	1016	1116	1216	1316	1416	1516	1616	1716	1816	1916	2016	2115	2250	...	0012
Immendingen 938 d.	...	0536	0536	...	0612	0728	0830	0930	|	|	1030	1130	1230	1330	1430	1530	1630	1730	1830	1930	2030	2128	2307	...	...
Donaueschingen 938 d.	*0502*	0551	0551	...	0624	0740	0840	0940	1001	1001	1040	1140	1240	1340	1440	1540	1640	1740	1840	1940	2040	2140	2319	...	...
Villingen (Schwarzw) 938 d.	0535	0600	0600	...	0635	0750	0850	0950	1013	1013	1050	1150	1250	1350	1450	1550	1650	1750	1850	1950	2050	2150	2328	...	...
St Georgen (Schwarzw) d.	0544	0610	0610	...	0644r	0759	0859	0959	1023	1023	1059	1159	1259	1359	1459	1559	1659	1759	1859	1959	2059	2159	...	...	...
Triberg d.	0558	0625	0633	...	0659r	0815	0914	1014	1039	1039	1114	1214	1314	1414	1514	1614	1714	1814	1914	2014	2114	2214	...	...	...
Hornberg (Schwarzw) d.	0612	0639	0647	...	0712r	0826	0926	1026	|	|	1126	1226	1326	1426	1526	1626	1726	1826	1926	2026	2128	2227	...	...	...
Hausach 942 d.	0621	0649	0656	...	0720r	0837	0937	1037	1059	1059	1137	1237	1337	1437	1537	1637	1737	1837	1937	2037	2137	2235	...	...	...
Offenburg 942 a.	0645	0721	0724	...	0744r	0859	0959	1059	1118	1118	1159	1259	1359	1459	1559	1659	1759	1859	1959	2059	2159	2258	...	...	...
Offenburg 912 d.	0658	...	...	0734	0753	0902	1002	1102	1139	1139	1202	1302	1402	1502	1602	1702	1802	1902	2002	2102	2202	*2302*	...	...	...
Baden-Baden 912 a.	0724	...	...	0800	0818	0927	1027	1127	1202	1202	1227	1327	1427	1527	1627	1727	1827	1927	2027	2127	2227	*2327*	...	...	...
Rastatt 943 a.	0731	...	...	0807	0826	0934	1034	1134	|	|	1234	1334	1434	1534	1634	1734	1834	1934	2034	2134	2234	*2333*	...	...	...
Karlsruhe Hbf 912 943 a.	0749	...	...	0821	0839	0949	1049	1149	1221	1221	1249	1349	1449	1549	1649	1749	1849	1949	2049	2149	2249	*2349*	...	...	...

D – ⑥ (also Dec. 25; not Jan. 7 - Apr. 1). SCHWARZWALD – [12] 🍷 Konstanz - Mannheim - Köln - Dortmund.
E – ⑦ (also Dec. 26; not Dec. 25, Jan. 8 - Mar. 26). SCHWARZWALD – [12] 🍷 Konstanz - Mannheim - Köln - Emden.
F – ⑤⑥ (also Dec. 25; not Jan. 6 - Mar. 31). SCHWARZWALD – [12] 🍷 Emden - Köln - Mannheim - Konstanz.
H – Change trains at Offenburg on Ⓐ (not Jan. 6).

g – 0811 on † (also Jan. 6).

h – Arrives 0612.
j – Arrives 0645.
k – Arrives 5–7 minutes earlier.
r – 7 minutes later on Ⓒ (also Jan. 6).
t – Not Jan. 6.
z – Also Jan. 6.

FRANKFURT - MAINZ - IDAR OBERSTEIN - SAARBRÜCKEN — 917

Vlexx

km			Ⓐ		⚒												Ⓒ	Ⓐ		Ⓒ	Ⓐ			
0	**Frankfurt** (Main) Hbf 914 ‡ d.	...	...	...	*0456*t	0608t	0708	0808	*0908*	1008	*1108*	1202k	*1308*	1408	*1508*	1608	*1708*	1726	1808	*1908*	1925	2008	*2108*	2208r
11	Frankfurt Flughafen ✈ § 914 ‡ d.	...	...	...	*0507*t	0624t	0724	0824	*0924*	1023	*1123*	1223	*1323*	1423	*1524*	1624	*1724*	1737	1824	*1923*	1937	2023	*2123*	2223r
39	**Mainz** Hbf 914 ‡ a.	...	...	..	*0530*t	0649t	0749	0848	*0949*	1049	*1149*	1249	*1349*	1449	*1549*	1648	*1749*	1758	1849	*1949*	1958	2049	*2149*	2249r
39	**Mainz** Hbf 914 d.	...	0408	...	0542	0655	0751	0852	0956	1053	1156	1254	1356	1453	1556	1652	1756	1800	1853	1956	2000	2053	2156	2253
57	Ingelheim 914 d.	...	0423	...	0555	0710	0805	0907	1010	1105	1210	1306	1410	1505	1610	1707	1810	1811	1905	2010	2011	2105	2210	2305
80	Bad Kreuznach d.	...	0503g	...	0611	0724	0822	0922	1024	1122	1224	1322	1424	1522	1624	1722	1824	1829	1922	2024	2026	2122	2224	2322
102	Bad Sobernheim d.	...	0526	...	0634	0744	0843	0943	1045	1143	1244	1343	1444	1543	1644	1743	1844	1849	1943	2044	2046	2143	2244	2343
117	Kirn d.	...	0540	...	0645	0754	0853	0953	1055	1153	1254	1353	1454	1553	1654	1753	1854	1859	1953	2054	2056	2153	2254	2353
131	Idar-Oberstein d.	...	0602h	...	0657	0805	0905	1005	1106	1205	1305	1405	1505	1605	1705	1805	1905	1910	2005	2105	2107	2205	2305	0005
170	St Wendel d.	0557	0651	0659	0735	0836	0936	1036	1137	1236	1336	1436	1536	1636	1736	1836	1936	1941	2036	2136	2138	2236	2336	0036
179	Ottweiler (Saar) d.	0606	0658	0708	0742	0842	0942	1042	1143	1242	1342	1442	1542	1642	1742	1842	1942	1947	2042	2142	2144	2242	2342	0042
184	Neunkirchen (Saar) d.	0613	0705	0717	0751	0851	0951	1051	1151	1251	1351	1451	1551	1651	1751	1851	1951	1954	2051	2151	2151	2251	2351	0051
205	**Saarbrücken** Hbf a.	0638	0723	0744	0810	0910	1010	1110	1210	1310	1410	1510	1610	1710	1810	1910	2010	2013	2110	2210	2210	2310	0010	0110

			Ⓐ	Ⓒ																				
Saarbrücken Hbf d.	0342	0442	0545	0551	0651	0751	0851	0951	1051	1151	1251	1351	...	1451	1551	...	1651	1751	1851	1951	2035	2151	2235	2351
Neunkirchen (Saar) d.	0400	0500	0603	0610	0711	0810	0911	1010	1111	1210	1311	1410	...	1511	1609	...	1711	1810	1911	2010	2100	2214	2323e	0016
Ottweiler (Saar) d.	0406	0506	0609	0615	0716	0815	0916	1015	1116	1215	1316	1415	...	1516	1614	...	1716	1815	1916	2015	2107	2219	2330	0023
St Wendel d.	0413	0513	0616	0622	0723	0822	0923	1022	1123	1222	1323	1422	...	1523	1621	...	1723	1822	1923	2022	2117	2226	2339	0033
Idar-Oberstein d.	0445	0545	0648	0652	0754	0852	0954	1052	1154	1252	1354	1453	...	1554	1653	...	1754	1852	1954	2052	...	2259	...	...
Kirn d.	0456	0556	0659	0703	0806	0903	1006	1103	1206	1303	1406	1504	...	1606	1704	...	1806	1903	2006	2103	...	2310	...	...
Bad Sobernheim d.	0506	0606	0709	0712	0816	0912	1016	1112	1216	1312	1416	1513	...	1616	1713	...	1816	1912	2016	2112	...	2319	...	...
Bad Kreuznach d.	0527	0627	0737h	0733	0839	0933	1039	1133	1239	1331	1439	1533	...	1639	1733	...	1839	1933	2039	2133	...	2341	...	...
Ingelheim 914 d.	0544	0644	0754	0747	0854	0947	1054	1147	1254	1347	1454	1547	...	1654	1747	...	1854	1947	2054	2147	...	0001	...	...
Mainz Hbf 914 a.	0556	0656	0806	0759	0906	0959	1106	1159	1306	1359	1506	1557	...	1706	1757	...	1906	1959	2106	2159	...	0019	...	...
Mainz Hbf 914 ‡ d.	0558	0658	0810	*0810*	0910	*1010*	1110	*1210*	1310	*1410*	1510	1559t	1610	1710	1759t	1810	1910	*2010*	2110	2214	...	...	...	...
Frankfurt Flughafen ✈ § 914 ‡ a.	0619	0719	0833	*0834*	0933	*1034*	1134	*1234*	1334	*1434*	1534	1619t	1634	1733	1819t	1834	1933	*2034*	2134	2234	...	...	...	...
Frankfurt (Main) Hbf 914 ‡ a.	0633	0733	0848	*0848*	0948	*1048*	1148	*1248*	1348	*1448*	1548	1636t	1648	1748	1836t	1851	1948	*2051*	2148	2248	...	...	...	...

e – Arrives 2259.
g – Arrives 0445.
h – Arrives 6–7 minutes earlier.
k – 1208 on Ⓒ.
r – From Mar. 31 Frankfurt (Main) Hbf d. 2211, Mainz a. 2245 (not calling at Frankfurt Flughafen).

t – Ⓐ only.

‡ – See also Tables **800** and **917a**.
§ – Frankfurt Flughafen Regionalbahnhof.

FRANKFURT - FRANKFURT FLUGHAFEN ✈ - MAINZ - WIESBADEN — 917a

S-Bahn 8/9

Subject to alteration from March 31

			v	v																					
Frankfurt (Main) Hbf d.	0002	0017n	0047	0117	0217	0317	0417	0447	0502	0517	0532	0547	and at	2102	2117	2132	2147	2202	2217	2232	2247	2302	2317	2332	2347
Frankfurt Flughafen ★ d.	0015	0030	0100	0130	0230	0330	0430	0500	0515	0530	0545	0600	the same	2115	2130	2145	2200	2215	2230	2245	2300	2315	2330	2345	0000
Mainz Hbf d.	|	0059	0129	0159	0259	0359	0459	0529	|	0559	|	0629	minutes	|	2159	|	2229	|	2259	|	2329	|	2359	|	0029
Mainz-Kastel d.	0040	|	|	|	|	|	|	|	0540	|	0610	|	past each	2140	|	2210	|	2240	|	2310	|	2340	|	0010	|
Wiesbaden Hbf a.	0049	0114	0144	0214	0314	0414	0514	0544	0549	0614	0619	0644	hour until	2149	2214	2219	2244	2249	2314	2319	2344	2349	0014	0019	0044

Wiesbaden Hbf d.	0018	...	0148	0248	0348	0409	0418	0439	0448	0509	0518	0539	0548	and at	2109	2118	2139	2148	2209	2218	2239	2248	2309	2318	2348
Mainz-Kastel d.	|	...	|	|	|	0417	|	0447	|	0517	|	0547	|	the same	2117	|	2147	|	2217	|	2247	|	2317	|	|
Mainz Hbf d.	0032	...	0202	0302	0402	|	0432	|	0502	|	0532	|	0602	minutes	|	2132	|	2202	|	2232	|	2302	|	2332	0002
Frankfurt Flughafen ★ d.	0100	...	0230	0330	0430	0445	0500	0515	0530	0545	0600	0615	0630	past each	2145	2200	2215	2230	2245	2300	2315	2330	2345	0000	0030
Frankfurt (Main) Hbf a.	0113	...	0243	0343	0443	0458	0513	0528	0543	0558	0613	0628	0643	hour until	2158	2213	2228	2243	2258	2313	2328	2343	2358	0013z	0043

n – 0015 on ① from Jan. 2.
v – Runs 5–8 minutes later on ① from Jan. 2.
z – 0017 on the mornings of ① from Jan. 2.

★ – Frankfurt Flughafen Regionalbahnhof ✈.

918 RHEINLAND-PFALZ LOCAL SERVICES

RB / S-Bahn services

PIRMASENS - SAARBRÜCKEN

km		Ⓐ	⚒	Ⓐ	⚒					
0	**Pirmasens** Hbf d.	0515	0552	0622	*0732*	0832	and	1832	1932	2032
7	Pirmasens Nord d.	0522	0559	0641	0743	0843	hourly	1843	1943	2043
31	Zweibrücken Hbf d.	0552	0640	0713	0813	0913	until	1913	2013	2113
67	**Saarbrücken** Hbf a.	0632	0724	0752	0852	0952		1952	2051	2152

	Ⓐ	⑥	Ⓐ						
Saarbrücken Hbf d.	0602	0602	0633	0705	0807	and	1907	2007	2107
Zweibrücken Hbf d.	0643	0643	0713	0745	0845	hourly	1945	2045	2145
Pirmasens Nord a.	0715	0715	0741	0815	0915	until	2015	2115	2215
Pirmasens Hbf a.	*0728*	*0757*	0753	0826	0926		2026	2126	2226

PIRMASENS - LANDAU (Pfalz)

km		Ⓐ	⑥	Ⓐ	Ⓐ					
0	**Pirmasens** Hbf d.	0438	0542	0544	*0622*	0702q	0802	and	1902	2002
7	Pirmasens Nord d.	0450	0555	0609	0636	0718	0818	hourly	1918	2018
55	**Landau** (Pfalz) Hbf a.	0546	0658	0708	0734	0818	0918	until	2018	2118

	ⒶN	Ⓐ	⑥						
Landau (Pfalz) Hbf d.	0527	0608	0641	...	0741	and	1841	1941	2041
Pirmasens Nord a.	0632	0715	0740	...	0840	hourly	1940	2040	2140
Pirmasens Hbf a.	0657	0728	0757	...	0857	until	1957	2057	2157

BINGEN - KAISERSLAUTERN - PIRMASENS

km			Ⓐ	⚒			◇			✣		◇		Ⓒ	Ⓐ	◇		m		⑤⑥f		◇	◇	◇
	Koblenz Hbf **914** d.	...	...	...	...	...	0803	...	...		...	1603	...	...	...	1803	...	...	...	...		1003	1203	1403
0	**Bingen** (Rhein) Hbf d.	...	...	0546t	0651r	0756	0843	0856	0956	and at	1556	1643	1656	1756	1756	1843	1856	1956	2056	2256	A	1043	1243	1443
16	Bad Kreuznach a.	...	...	0606t	0711r	0816	0855	0916	1016	the same	1616	1655	1716	1816	1816	1855	1916	2016	2116	2316	L	1055	1255	1455
16	Bad Kreuznach d.	...	0507	0607	0712	0827	0857	0927k	1018	minutes	1618	1657	1727	1818	1834	1857	1927	2032	2127	2334	S	1057	1257	1457
43	Rockenhausen d.	...	0535	0635	0740	0856	0926	0956	1056	past each	1656	1726	1756	1856	1901	1926	1956	2059	2154	0001	O	1126	1326	1526
79	**Kaiserslautern** Hbf a.	...	0611	0712	0811	0926h	0954	1027	1126	hour until	1726	1754	1827	1926	1938	1954	2026	2130	2224	0033		1154	1354	1554
	Change trains	Ⓐ	⚒	d										d						|				
79	**Kaiserslautern** Hbf d.	0514	0616	0735	0835	0935	...	1035	1135		1735	...	1835	1935	...	...	2035	...	2300	0053		...	...	...
108	Pirmasens Nord a.	0554	0702	0809	0909	1009	...	1109	1209		1809	...	1909	2009	...	...	2109	...	2332	0125		...	...	...
115	**Pirmasens** Hbf a.	0608	0719	0818	0918	1018	...	1118	1218		1818	...	1918	2018	...	...	2118	...	2341	0134		...	...	...

			Ⓐ	⊖		⚒	†		⊠														
Pirmasens Hbf d.	...	...	0528	0637	...	0732	0741	0841		1441	...	1541	1641	...	...	1741	1841	1941	2041		...	...	...
Pirmasens Nord d.	...	...	0535	0645	...	0750	0750	0850	and at	1450	...	1550	1650	...	...	1750	1850	1950	2050		...	...	...
Kaiserslautern Hbf a.	...	...	0607	0722	...	0826	0826	0926	the same	1526	...	1626	1726	...	...	1826	1926	2026	2126		...	...	...
Change trains	Ⓐ	⑥	⚒		◇		d		minutes		◇		Ⓒ	Ⓐ	◇						◇	◇	◇
Kaiserslautern Hbf d.	0520	0520	0620	0736	0801	...	0831	0931	past each	1531	1603	1634	1731	1736	1803	1834	1931	2032	2150		1003	1203	1403
Rockenhausen d.	0551	0551	0651	0805	0830	...	0900	1000	hour until	1600	1629	1703	1800	1809	1829	1903	2000	2101	2223	A	1029	1229	1429
Bad Kreuznach a.	0620	0621	0720	0842	0859	...	0929	1029		1629	1651	1738	1842	1842	1859	1938	2030	2137	2253	L	1059	1259	1451
Bad Kreuznach d.	0621	0641	0721	0843	0900	...	0941	1041		1641	1701	1741	1843	1843	1900	1941	2041	2141	...	S	1100	1300	1501
Bingen (Rhein) Hbf a.	0642	0702	0742	0904	0912	...	1002	1102		1702	1712	1802	1904	1904	1912	2002	2102	2202	...	O	1112	1312	1512
Koblenz Hbf **914** a.	...	...	...	...	0954	...	...	...		...	1754	...	...	...	1953z	...	...	...	...		1153	1353	1553

(KAISERSLAUTERN -) NEUSTADT - KARLSRUHE and WISSEMBOURG

km		Ⓐ	Ⓐ	Ⓐ	Ⓐ	⚒	⚒	Ⓐ	Ⓐ	†	⑥		⑥	Ⓑ					D	†E		D	†E	
	Kaiserslautern Hbf **919** d.	...	...	...	...	...	...	...	0629	...	0629	...	...	...	...	0841v	...	0941	...	...	...	...	...	1141
0	**Neustadt** (Weinstr) Hbf **919** d.	0427	...	*0504*	...	0529	0608	0636	0659	0700	0709	0736	0805	0809	0836	0909	0936	1009	1036	1045	1109	1136	1145	1209
18	Landau (Pfalz) Hbf d.	0449	...	0535	...	0555	0634	0658	0713	0722	0722	0758	0822	0822	0858	0922	0958	1022	1058	1058	1122	1158	1158	1222
31	Winden (Pfalz) d.	0503	0505	0550	0555	0603	0650	0708	0722	0731	0731	0809	0831	0831	0909	0931	1009	1031	1109	1109	1131	1209	1209	1231
47	**Wissembourg** ▦ ◐ a.	|	0521	|	0615	|	|	0726	|	|	|	0827	|	|	0927	|	1028	|	1127	1127	|	1227	1227	|
44	Wörth (Rhein) d.	0520	...	0607	...	0616	0708	...	0735	0744	0744	...	0844	0844	...	0944	...	1044	...	...	1144	...	...	1244
58	**Karlsruhe** Hbf a.	0534	...	0619	...	0636	0725	...	0753	0754	0754	...	0854	0854	...	0954	...	1054	...	...	1154	...	...	1254

		Ⓐ	Ⓒ														†E							⑥
Kaiserslautern Hbf **919** d.	...	...	...	...	...	...	...	...	1541z	...	...	...	...	...	...	...	...	...	...	...	...	...	...	...
Neustadt (Weinstr) Hbf **919** d.	1236	1305	1309	1336	1409	1436	1509	1536	1609	1636	1709	1736	1809	1836	1909	1936	1952	2009	2104	2136	...	2230	2336	2336
Landau (Pfalz) Hbf d.	1258	1319	1322	1358	1422	1458	1522	1558	1622	1658	1722	1758	1822	1858	1922	1958	2008	2022	2122	2158	...	2252	2358	2359
Winden (Pfalz) d.	1309	1331	1331	1409	1431	1509	1531	1609	1631	1709	1731	1808	1831	1908	1931	2008	|	2031	2131	2213	2231	2306	...	0023e
Wissembourg ▦ ◐ a.	1327	|	|	1427	|	1527	|	1627	|	1727	|	1826	|	1926	|	2026	|	|	|	...	|	|	...	|
Wörth (Rhein) d.	...	1344	1344	...	1444	...	1544	...	1644	...	1744	...	1844	...	1944	...	2030	2044	2144	...	2244	2320	...	0038
Karlsruhe Hbf a.	...	1354	1354	...	1454	...	1554	...	1654	...	1754	...	1854	...	1954	...	2041	2054	2154	...	2254	2337	...	0049

	Ⓐ	Ⓐ	⑥	Ⓐ	Ⓐ	⑥	Ⓐ	Ⓒ	Ⓐ		Ⓐ	D	†E	Ⓑ	⑥									Ⓐ
Karlsruhe Hbf d.	0430	...	0528	0557	...	0611	0642	0705	0717	...	...	0805	0806	...	...	0905	...	1005	...	1105	...	1205	...	1305
Wörth (Rhein) d.	0447	...	0546	0616	...	0628	0652	0715	0736	...	...	0816	0816	...	...	0916	...	1016	...	1116	...	1216	...	1316
Wissembourg ▦ ◐ d.	|	0527	|	|	0626	|	|	|	|	...	0733	|	|	0832	0833	|	0933	|	1033	|	1133	|	1233	|
Winden (Pfalz) d.	0502	0547	0600	0631	0647	0641	0706	0727	0749	...	0758	0829	0829	0853	0853	0929	0953	1029	1053	1129	1153	1229	1253	1330
Landau (Pfalz) Hbf d.	0518	0601	0615	0645	0701	0703e	0721	0736	0758	0807	0807	0838	0838	0903	0903	0938	1003	1038	1103	1138	1203	1238	1303	1339
Neustadt (Weinstr) Hbf **919** a.	0540	0622	0637	0704	0722	0724	0744	0751	0812	0826	0826	0851	0851	0924	0924	0951	1024	1051	1124	1151	1224	1251	1324	1351
Kaiserslautern Hbf **919** a.	...	...	...	...	...	...	0818	0818	...	...	...	...	...	...	...	1016	...	...	...	...	...	...	...	...

	Ⓒ						Ⓐ	Ⓒ	†E	D		†E	D							Ⓑ	⑥			
Karlsruhe Hbf d.	1306	...	1405	...	1505	...	1601	1605	...	...	1705	...	...	1805	...	1905	...	2005	...	...	...	2106	2206	2318
Wörth (Rhein) d.	1316	...	1416	...	1516	...	1616	1616	...	...	1716	...	...	1816	...	1916	...	2016	...	...	...	2116	2216	2331
Wissembourg ▦ ◐ d.	|	1333	|	1433	|	1533	|	|	1633	1633	|	1733	1733	|	1833	|	1933	|	...	2033	2103	|	|	|
Winden (Pfalz) d.	1329	1353	1429	1453	1529	1553	1629	1629	1653	1653	1729	1753	1753	1829	1853	1929	1953	2029	...	2053	2123	2131	2229	2344
Landau (Pfalz) Hbf d.	1338	1403	1438	1503	1538	1603	1638	1638	1701	1703	1738	1801	1803	1838	1903	1938	2003	2038	2103	2103	2131	2140	2238	2353
Neustadt (Weinstr) Hbf **919** a.	1351	1424	1451	1524	1551	1624	1651	1651	1712	1724	1751	1815	1824	1851	1924	1951	2024	2051	2124	2124	...	2201	2256	0012
Kaiserslautern Hbf **919** a.	1416	...	...	...	...	...	...	...	...	...	...	...	...	1919	...	...	...	...	...	...	...	2226b	...	...

GERMERSHEIM - SPEYER - MANNHEIM - HEIDELBERG

km		Ⓐ	Ⓒ	Ⓐ	Ⓐ	⑥	Ⓐ	Ⓒ	Ⓐ				▲										
0	**Germersheim** **911a** d.	0409	0409	0514	0559	0622	0704	0703	0727	0749	0812	0849	and at	1912	1949	2014	2049	2114	2211	2257	2322	0008	...
14	Speyer Hbf **911a** d.	0423	0423	0527	0613	0635	0713	0716	0740	0802	0825	0902	the same	1925	2002	2027	2102	2127	2224	2310	2335	0020	...
23	Schifferstadt **919** d.	0433	0433	0537	0627	0647	|	0729	0751	0811	0835	0911	minutes	1935	2011	2046	2119e	2148e	2238	2320	2351	0031	...
34	Ludwigshafen Hbf. **911a 919** d.	0451	0455	0545	0640	0659	0726	0742	0805	0820	0847	0921	past each	1948	2022	2057	2131	2201	2250	2331	0002	0042	0111
35	Ludwigshafen Mitte **919** d.	0453	0457	0548	0643	0702	0729	0745	0808	0823	0850	0923	hour until	1950	2024	2059	2133	2203	2254	2333	0006	...	0113
37	**Mannheim** Hbf **919** ⊡ a.	0456	0500	0552	0646	0705	0733	0748	0810	0826	0853	0926		1953	2027	2102	2136	2205	2258	2336	0009	...	0116
54	**Heidelberg** Hbf **919** ⊡ a.	0515	*0552*	*0622*	0704	0723	0753	*0816*	...	0844	0916	0945		2017	2046	2123	2154	2223	2322	2354	0037	...	0140

	Ⓐ	Ⓒ	Ⓒ	Ⓐ	Ⓐ	Ⓐ	Ⓒ	Ⓐ	⚒	Ⓒ	Ⓐ			▲									
Heidelberg Hbf **919** ⊡ d.	0506	0534	...	0602	0616	...	*0602*	0643	0712	*0734*	0743	0813	0843	and at	1913	1943	2013	*2033*	2113	2144	2214	2244	2314
Mannheim Hbf **919** ⊡ d.	0526	0554	...	0622	0641	0647	0656	0705	0731	0804	0804	0831	0904	the same	1931	2004	2031	2056	2137	2206	2243	2309	2338
Ludwigshafen Mitte **919** d.	0528	0556	...	0625	0646	0650	0658	0707	0733	0806	0806	0833	0907	minutes	1933	2007	2033	2058	2139	2209	2246	2311	2340
Ludwigshafen Hbf.. **911a 919** d.	0531	0600	0610	0637e	0649	0654	0702	0710	0736	0810	0810	0836	0910	past each	1936	2009	2038	2103	2142	2214	2248	2315	2343
Schifferstadt **919** d.	0545	0611	0623	0650	0657	0706	0717	0725	0750	0824	0824	0847	0924	hour until	1947	2024	2047	2120	2159	2234	2302	2326	2358
Speyer Hbf **911a** d.	0555	...	0632	0700	...	0713	0726	0733	0759	0832	0832	0856	0932		1956	2032	2056	2129	2208	2243	2311	2336	0007
Germersheim **911a** a.	0609	...	0645	0712	...	0722	0740	0745	0812	0845	0845	0909	0945		2009	2045	2109	2142	2221	2256	2323	2349	0020

D – Daily to Apr. 1; ⚒ from Apr. 3.
E – † from Apr. 2.
N – From Neustadt (Weinstr) Hbf, d. 0504.

b – Not ⑥.
d – Daily.
e – Arrives 8 – 11 minutes earlier.
f – Not Apr. 7.

h – 0929 on †.
k – 0918 on †.
m – Change trains at Bad Kreuznach on Ⓐ.
q – Change trains at Pirmasens Nord on Ⓐ.
r – ⚒ only.
t – Ⓐ only.
v – † only.
z – Ⓒ only.

◇ – Operated by Vlexx.
✣ – The 1056, 1256 and 1456 from Bingen depart Bad Kreuznach at 1127, 1327 and 1527 respectively (other timings follow the regular pattern).
⊠ – The 1231 from Kaiserslautern arrives Bad Kreuznach 1338 (other timings follow the regular pattern).
⊖ – On † Pirmasens Hbf d. 0641, Pirmasens Nord d. 0652, Kaiserslautern a. 0724.
▲ – Timings may vary by 1 – 2 minutes.
◐ – For Strasbourg connections see Table **396**.
⊡ – See also Tables **913**, **923** and **924**.

WIESBADEN - MAINZ - DARMSTADT - ASCHAFFENBURG 918a

Hessische Landesbahn

km														
		©	⚒	Ⓐ	⚒		†	⚒						
0	**Wiesbaden** Hbf .... d.	0036	...	0436	0536	0536	0637	0637	0736		2036	2136	2236	2336
10	**Mainz** Hbf .... a.	0048	...	0447	0548	0548	0648	0648	0748	and	2048	2148	2248	2348
10	**Mainz** Hbf .... d.	0049	...	0449	0549	0549	0649	0649	0749	hourly	2049	2149	2249	2349
43	Darmstadt Hbf .... a.	0121	...	0521	0621	0621	0721	0721	0821	until	2121	2221	2321	0021
43	Darmstadt Hbf .... d.	...	0530	0530	0630	...	0731	0735	0831		2131	2231	2331	...
87	**Aschaffenburg** Hbf .... a.	...	0615	0615	0712	...	0812	0815	0912		2212	2312	0012	...

	Ⓐ		Ⓐ											⑤⑥f
Aschaffenburg Hbf ..... d.	...	...	0443	0540r	0643r	0747		1747	1847	1947	2047	2147	2247	2347
Darmstadt Hbf .... a.	...	...	0527	0626r	0730r	0827	and	1827	1927	2027	2127	2227	2327	0027
Darmstadt Hbf .... d.	0438	0538	0538	0638	0738	0838	hourly	1838	1938	2038	2138	2238	2338	0038
Mainz Hbf .... a.	0510	0611	0611	0711	0811	0911	until	1911	2011	2111	2211	2312	0012	0111
Mainz Hbf .... d.	0512	0613	0613	0713	0814	0913		1913	2013	2113	2213	2313	0013	0113
Wiesbaden Hbf .... a.	0527	0625	0625	0727	0827	0927		1927	2028	2127	2227	2327	0027	0127

f – ⑤⑥ (also Dec. 25); runs daily Aschaffenburg - Darmstadt.
r – ⚒ only.

☛ Additional services run Wiesbaden - Darmstadt and v.v. on ⚒, Darmstadt - Aschaffenburg and v.v. on Ⓐ.

SAARBRÜCKEN - MANNHEIM - FRANKFURT and STUTTGART 919

Additional S-Bahn services run Kaiserslautern - Mannheim - Heidelberg and v.v.

km																								
						EC 217					*ICE* 935							*ICE* 563				*TGV* 9551		
		©	©	Ⓐ	⚒	G🍷			Ⓐ		A✕	†				Ⓐ	†	M✕				P🍷		
	Trier Hbf **915** .... d.	...	...	...	...	...	...	...	0456	...	...	0533	...	0633	...	0733	0733	...	...	0833	...	...	...	1033
0	**Saarbrücken** Hbf .... d.	...	...	0444	...	0537	...	0550	0608	...	0628	0647	*0700*	0747	*0801*	0847	0847	0827	*0902*	0947	*1002*	1058	*1102*	1147
31	Homburg (Saar) Hbf .... d.	...	...	0505	0538	0558	...	0620	0632	...	0650	0709	*0727*	0809	*0828*	0909	0909	0849	*0928*	1009	*1028*	|	*1128*	1209
67	**Kaiserslautern** Hbf .... a.	...	...	0527	0607	0621	...	0650	0653	...	0712	0729	*0754*	0829	*0855*	0929	0936	0909	*0954*	1029	*1054*	1134	*1154*	1229
67	**Kaiserslautern** Hbf .... d.	0009	0511	0528	0611	0623	←	...	0654	0702	0714	0730	0758	0834	0858	...	0937	0911	0958	1034	1058	1136	1158	1234
100	Neustadt (Weinstr) Hbf .... d.	0042	0544	0551	0641	0647	0650	...	0717	0732	0740	0759	0830	0859	0930	...	1000	0937	1031j	1059	1130	|	1230j	1259
117	Schifferstadt .... **918** d.	0057	0559	|	→	|	0707	...	|	0747	|	|	0845	|	0945	...	|	|	1045	|	1145	|	1245	|
128	Ludwigshafen Hbf .... **918** d.	0111	0612	0609	...	0705	0719	...	0737	0800	|	|	0857	|	0957	...	|	|	1057	|	1158	|	1257	|
129	Ludwigshafen Mitte .... **918** d.	0113	0614	|	...	|	0722	...	|	0803	|	0817	0900	0917	1000	...	1017	|	1100	1117	1200	|	1300	1317
131	**Mannheim** Hbf .... **918** a.	0116	0617	0616	...	0709	0725	...	0745	0805	0800	0821	0903	0921	1003	...	1021	0957	1103	1121	1203	1217	1303	1320
131	**Mannheim** Hbf ... **912 918** ▽ d.	0121	0628	*0629*	...	0711	0729	...	0748	0807	0802	*0830*	0907	*0930*	1007	...	*1030*	1002	1107	*1130*	1207	1219	1308	*1330*
	Heidelberg Hbf ... **912 918** a.	0140	0645	*0642*	...	|	0744	...	0801	0823	|	*0844*	0923	*0945*	1023	...	*1045*	|	1123	*1144*	1223	|	1323	*1345*
	Stuttgart Hbf .... **912** a.	...	...	...	...	0753	...	...	...	...	|	...	...	...	...	...	...	1045	...	...	...	|	...	...
	Bensheim .... ▽ a.	...	...	...	...	...	...	...	...	...	0825	...	...	...	...	...	...	...	...	...	...	|	...	...
191	Darmstadt Hbf .... ▽ a.	...	...	...	...	...	...	...	...	...	0838	...	...	...	...	...	...	...	...	...	...	|	...	...
219▲	**Frankfurt** (Main) Hbf .... ▽ a.	...	...	...	...	...	...	...	...	...	0856	...	...	...	...	...	...	...	...	...	...	1259	...	...

					ICE 9553									*ICE* 9555					*ICE* 9557				
													⑥	Ⓑ				Ⓑ	⊡			†	⚒
					P✕									P✕					P✕				
Trier Hbf **915** .... d.	...	1133	...	1233	...	...	...	1433	...	1533	...	1633	...	1733	...	...	1833	...	1933	...	...	2033	...	...
Saarbrücken Hbf .... d.	*1202*	1247	*1302*	1347	*1402*	1459	*1503*	1547	*1601*	1647	*1702*	1747	*1802*	1847	1859	*1903*	1947	*2002*	2047	2059	...	2147	...	*2202*
Homburg (Saar) Hbf .... d.	*1228*	1309	*1328*	1409	*1428*	|	*1528*	1609	*1628*	1709	*1728*	1809	*1828*	1909	|	*1928*	2009	*2028*	2109	|	...	2209	...	*2228*
Kaiserslautern Hbf .... a.	*1254*	1329	*1354*	1429	*1454*	1535	*1554*	1629	*1654*	1729	*1754*	1829	*1854*	1929	1935	*1954*	2029	*2054*	2130	2135	...	2229	...	*2257*
Kaiserslautern Hbf .... d.	1258	1334	1358	1434	1458	1537	1558	1634	1658	1734	1758	1834	1858	1934	1937	1959	2034	2058	...	2136	2145	2230	2300	2301
Neustadt (Weinstr) Hbf .... d.	1330	1359	1430	1459	1530j	|	1630	1659	1730	1759	1830	1859	1930	1959	|	2030	2059	2130	...	|	2214	2302n	2332	2330
Schifferstadt .... **918** d.	1345	|	1445	|	1545	|	1645	|	1745	|	1845	|	1945	|	|	2046	|	2148	...	|	2238k	2315	2351	2351
Ludwigshafen Hbf .... **918** d.	1357	|	1457	|	1557	|	1657	|	1757	|	1857	|	1957	|	|	2057	|	2201	...	|	2250	|	0002	0002
Ludwigshafen Mitte .... **918** d.	1400	1417	1500	1517	1600	|	1700	1717	1800	1817	1900	1917	2000	2017	|	2059	2117	2203	...	|	2254	2326	0006	0006
Mannheim Hbf .... **918** a.	1403	1421	1503	1521	1602	1617	1703	1721	1803	1821	1903	1921	2003	2021	2017	2102	2121	2205	...	2217	2258	2330	0009	0009
Mannheim Hbf .... **912 918** ▽ d.	1407	*1430*	1507	*1530*	1607	1619	1707	*1730*	1807	*1830*	1907	*1930*	2007	*2030*	2019	2107	*2137*	2207	...	2219	2304	*2336*	0021	0021
Heidelberg Hbf .... **912 918** a.	1423	*1443*	1523	*1546*	1623	|	1723	*1745*	1823	*1845*	1923	*1945*	2023	*2046*	|	2123	*2154*	2223	...	|	2322	*2354*	0037	0037
Stuttgart Hbf .... **912** a.	...	...	...	...	...	|	...	...	...	...	...	...	...	...	|	...	...	...	...	|	...	...	...	...
Frankfurt (Main) Hbf .... ▽ a.	...	...	...	...	...	1659	...	...	...	...	...	...	...	...	2059	...	...	...	...	2259	...	...	...	...

						ICE 9558						*ICE* 9586					*ICE* 9556						*ICE* 9554	
	⚒	①–⑤	©	Ⓐ	Ⓐ	①–⑤	Ⓐ	⑥		Ⓑ	⑥	⑥	Ⓑ				①–⑤		⑥⑦				⑥⑦	①–⑤
						P✕						P✕					P✕						P✕	
Frankfurt (Main) Hbf .... ▽ d.	...	...	...	...	...	0556	...	...	...	...	...	0656	...	...	...	...	0856	...	...	...	...	...	1056	...
Stuttgart Hbf .... **912** d.	...	...	...	...	...	|	...	...	...	...	...	|	...	...	...	...	|	...	...	...	...	...	|	...
Heidelberg Hbf .... **912 918** d.	...	...	0534	0536	*0602*	|	...	...	0631t	...	...	|	*0712*	0734	0817v	0834	|	...	*0913*	0933	*1013*	1033	|	*1113*
Mannheim Hbf .... **912 918** ▽ a.	...	...	0553	0552	*0621*	0639	...	...	0650t	...	...	0738	*0729*	0753	0836v	0851	0939	...	*0929*	0951	*1029*	1051	1139	*1130*
Mannheim Hbf .... **918** d.	...	...	0554	0554	0628	0640	...	...	0656	...	0719	0740	0738	0756	0839	0856	0940	...	0939	0954	1036	1056	1140	1139
Ludwigshafen Mitte .... **918** d.	...	...	0556	0556	0631	|	...	...	0658	...	0722	|	0741	0758	0842	0858	|	...	0942	0956	1040	1058	|	1142
Ludwigshafen Hbf .... **918** d.	...	...	0600	0600	|	|	...	...	0702	...	|	|	0744	0804	|	0903	|	...	|	1002	|	1103	|	|
Schifferstadt .... **918** d.	...	...	0613	0611	|	|	...	...	0713	...	|	|	|	0815	|	0915	|	...	|	1015	|	1115	|	|
Neustadt (Weinstr) Hbf .... d.	...	...	0631	0631	0648	|	←	...	0731	...	0739	|	0800	0832	0900	0932	|	...	1000	1032	1100	1132	|	1200
Kaiserslautern Hbf .... a.	...	...	0658	0658	0716	0721	0716	...	0759	...	0802	0821	0824	0859	0924	0959	1021	...	1024	1059	1124	1159	1223	1224
Kaiserslautern Hbf .... d.	0425	0623	...	...	→	0722	0731	0731	...	0803	0803	0822	0831	*0903*	0931	*1003*	1022	1031	1031	*1103*	1131	*1203*	1224	1231
Homburg (Saar) Hbf .... d.	0501	0653	...	...	...	|	0752	0752	...	0832	0831	|	0852	*0930*	0952	*1030*	|	1052	1052	*1130*	1152	*1230*	|	1252
Saarbrücken Hbf .... a.	0535	0716	...	...	...	0800	0816	0816	...	0858	0858	0900	0915	*0956*	1015	*1056*	1100	1115	1115	*1156*	1215	*1256*	1301	1315
Trier Hbf **915** .... a.	...	0827	...	...	...	...	0927	0927	...	...	1027	...	1027	...	1127	...	...	1227	1227	...	1327	...	...	1427

				TGV 9552									*ICE* 562				*ICE* 9550			*EC* 216		*ICE* 836		
																	Ⓑ	⑥						
				P🍷									M✕				P✕			G🍷		B✕		
Frankfurt (Main) Hbf .... ▽ d.	...	...	...	1256	...	...	...	...	...	...	...	...	...	...	...	...	1856	...	...	...	...	2102	...	...
Darmstadt Hbf .... ▽ d.	...	...	...	|	...	...	...	...	...	...	...	...	...	...	...	...	|	...	...	...	...	2119	...	...
Bensheim .... ▽ d.	...	...	...	|	...	...	...	...	...	...	...	...	...	...	...	...	|	...	...	...	...	2132	...	...
Stuttgart Hbf .... **912** d.	...	...	...	|	...	...	...	...	...	...	...	...	1708	...	...	...	|	...	...	2004	...	|	...	...
Heidelberg Hbf .... **912 918** d.	1133	*1213*	1233	|	1335	*1413*	1433	*1513*	1533	*1613*	1633	*1713*	|	1733	*1813*	1833	|	*1913*	1933	|	2033	|	*2214*	2314
Mannheim Hbf .... **912 918** ▽ a.	1151	*1229*	1251	1338	1351	*1429*	1451	*1529*	1549	*1629*	1649	*1729*	1746	1751	*1829*	1851	1939	*1929*	1950	2047	2051	2155	*2230*	2330
Mannheim Hbf .... **918** d.	1156	1236	1256	1342	1356	1439	1456	1539	1556	1636	1656	1735	1748	1756	1836	1856	1940	1939	1956	2049	2056	2157	2239	2338
Ludwigshafen Mitte .... **918** d.	1158	1240	1258	|	1358	1442	1458	|	1558	|	1658	1739	|	1758	1840	1858	|	1942	1958	|	2058	|	2242	2340
Ludwigshafen Hbf .... **918** d.	1203	|	1303	|	1403	|	1503	1544	1603	1644	1703	|	|	1805	|	1903	|	|	2002	|	2103	|	|	2343
Schifferstadt .... **918** d.	1215	|	1315	|	1415	|	1515	|	1616	|	1715	|	|	1816	|	1915	|	|	2015	|	2115	|	|	2355
Neustadt (Weinstr) Hbf .... d.	1232	1300	1332	|	1432	1500	1532	1600	1632	1700	1732	1800	1811	1832	1900	1932	|	2000	2032	2111	2132	2219	2302	*0019*
Kaiserslautern Hbf .... a.	1259	1324	1359	1423	1459	1524	1559	1624	1659	1724	1759	1824	1833	1859	1924	1959	2021	2024	2059	2132	2159	2243	2327	*0047*
Kaiserslautern Hbf .... d.	*1303*	1331	*1403*	1424	*1503*	1531	*1603*	1631	*1703*	1731	*1803*	1830	1835	*1903*	1931	*2003*	2022	2031	*2105*	2134	*2205*	2245	2329	...
Homburg (Saar) Hbf .... d.	*1330*	1352	*1430*	|	*1530*	1552	*1631*	1652	*1730*	1752	*1830*	1850	1856	*1930*	1952	*2030*	|	2052	*2133*	2155	*2233*	2305	2356	...
Saarbrücken Hbf .... a.	*1356*	1415	*1456*	1502	*1558*	1615	*1659*	1715	*1758*	1815	*1856*	1912	1917	*1956*	2015	*2056*	2100	2115	*2159*	2216	*2259*	2329	0019	...
Trier Hbf **915** .... a.	...	1527	...	...	...	1727	...	1828	...	1927	...	2027	...	...	2127	...	...	2227	...	...	...	...	...	...

A – PFÄLZER WALD. 🚃12 ✕ Saarbrücken - Frankfurt - Erfurt - Halle - Berlin.
B – 🚃12 ✕ Hamburg - Berlin - Halle - Erfurt - Frankfurt - Saarbrücken.
G – DACHSTEIN – 🚃12 🍷 Graz - Salzburg - München - Saarbrücken and v.v.
M – From / to München (Table **930**).
P – From / to Paris (Table **390**). 🅁 for international journeys.

j – Arrives 5–6 minutes earlier.
k – Arrives 2229.
n – 2300 on ⑦.
t – Ⓐ only.
v – On © Heidelberg d. *0813*, Mannheim a. *0829* (change trains at Mannheim).

⊡ – On ⑥ runs as *TGV* **9559** (🍷).
▽ – See also Table **912** (*ICE* trains) and Table **913** (local trains).
▲ – *209 km* for trains running non-stop Mannheim - Frankfurt.

920 FRANKFURT - NÜRNBERG - PASSAU (- WIEN)

See Table **921** for other regional trains

km		NJ 491	NJ 40491	NJ 421	NJ 40421		IC 95		ICE 827	ICE 521	ICE 21	ICE 523	ICE 523	ICE 1121	ICE 525	ICE 23	ICE 527	ICE 529	ICE 1621	ICE 91	ICE 621	ICE 93	ICE 623	ICE 27
		R	R	R	R				⚒				⚒	Ⓐ				b						
		N	NL	A	J		R		✕	✕	✕	✕	✕	✕	✕	⊙✕	✕	G✕	✕	✕	✕	B✕	✕	✕
	Hamburg Hbf **800 900** d.	2024	2024	...	...	...	...	...	...	...	...	...	...	...	...	...	...	...	...	0801	...	...	...	...
	Dortmund Hbf **800** d.	|	|	...	...	...	...	...	...	...	...	...	0401	...	0522	0431	0622	0722	0629	|	...	...	0912v	0829
	Essen Hbf **800** d.	|	|	...	...	...	...	...	...	...	...	...	0427	...	0549	0457	0651	0750	|	|	0839	...	0941	0900
	Düsseldorf Hbf **800** d.	|	|	2144y	2144y	...	...	...	...	...	...	...	0454	0605	0617	0524	0718	0818	|	|	0910	...	1010	0924
	Köln Hbf **800 910** d.	|	|	2216y	2216y	...	...	...	0321q	0422	...	...	|	|	|	0553	|	|	0753	|	|	...	|	0953
	Köln Messe/Deutz **910** d.	|	|	|	|	...	...	...	|	|	...	...	0520	0629	0644	|	0744	0844	|	|	0944	...	1034	|
	Bonn Hbf **800** d.	|	|	2311	2311	...	...	...	|	|	...	...	|	|	|	0614	|	|	0814	|	|	...	|	1014
	Koblenz Hbf **800** d.	|	|	2346	2346	...	...	...	|	|	...	...	|	|	|	0648	|	|	0848	|	|	...	|	1048
	Mainz Hbf **800** d.	|	|	0041	0041	...	...	...	|	|	...	...	|	|	|	0740	|	|	0942	|	|	...	|	1142
0	**Frankfurt** Flughafen ✈ § d.	|	|	0103	0103	...	...	...	0434	0526	...	...	0634	0719	0734	0801	0834	0934	1001	|	1034	...	1134	1201
11	**Frankfurt** (Main) Hbf d.	|	|	0117f	0117f	...	...	...	0453	0553	0621	0654	0653	|	0753	0822	0853	0953	1022	|	1053	...	1153	1222
35	Hanau Hbf d.	|	|	|	|	...	...	...	|	0610	0637	|	|	|	|	0838	|	|	1037	|	|	...	|	1238
57	Aschaffenburg Hbf d.	|	|	|	|	...	...	...	0523	0624	0652	0723	0723	|	0823	|	0923	1023	|	|	1123	...	1223	|
136	**Würzburg** Hbf **900** d.	0145	0145	0237	0237	...	...	...	0604	0705	0735	0804	0804	|	0904	0934	1004	1104	1131	1134	1204	...	1313j	1335
238	**Nürnberg** Hbf **900** a.	0324	0324	0336	0336	...	...	...	0658	0759	0827	0900	0900	0915	0958	1028	1100	1158	1224	1227	1259	...	1404	1427
238	**Nürnberg** Hbf d.	0408	0436	0436	0408	...	0600	...	0701	0802	0831	0904	0904	0917	1002	1031	1104	1202	1227	1231	1302	1332	1407	1431
	Augsburg Hbf **905** a.	|	0624	0624	|	...	|	...	|	|	|	|	|	|	|	|	|	|	|	|	|	|	|	|
	München Hbf **904** a.	|	0706	0706	|	...	|	...	0806	0906	|	1006	1006	1020	1110	|	1206	1306	1338	|	1406	|	1509	|
335	**Regensburg** Hbf d.	0509	...	...	0509	...	0711	...	...	...	0926	...	...	...	...	1126	...	...	...	1326	...	1426	...	1526
375	Straubing d.	|	...	...	|	...	0734	...	...	...	|	...	...	...	...	|	...	...	...	|	...	1449	...	|
400	Plattling **944** d.	|	...	...	|	...	0753c	...	...	...	0958	...	...	...	...	1159	...	...	...	1359	...	|	...	1559
452	**Passau** Hbf 🏛 **944** a.	0613	...	...	0613	...	0822	...	...	...	1023	...	...	...	...	1225	...	...	...	1425	...	1526	...	1625
	Linz Hbf **950** a.	0744	...	...	0744	...	0925	...	...	...	1126	...	...	...	...	1326	...	...	...	1526	...	1626	...	1726
	Wien Hbf **950** a.	0914	...	...	0914	...	1047	...	...	...	1247	...	...	...	...	1447	...	...	...	1647	...	1747	...	1847

	ICE 625	ICE 627	ICE 29	ICE 629	ICE 721	ICE 229	ICE 723	ICE 1123	ICE 725	ICE 927	ICE 727	ICE 729	ICE 929		ICE 821	RE 59499		ICE 1021
								Ⓑb										
	✕	✕	✕	✕	✕	✕	✕	✕	✕	✕	✕	✕	✕		✕			
Hamburg Hbf **800 900** d.	...	...	...	...	...	...	...	...	...	1153	...	...	...	...	...	...	...	1610
Dortmund Hbf **800** d.	...	1122v	1029	...	...	1229	...	...	...	|	...	...	1629	...	...	...	...	|
Essen Hbf **800** d.	1051	1150	1100	1251	1351	|	1451	...	1549	|	1649	1749	1700	...	1837	...	...	1854
Düsseldorf Hbf **800** d.	1118	1217	1124	1318	1418	|	1518	1604	1618	1524	1718	1818	1724	...	1905	...	...	1923
Köln Hbf **800 910** d.	|	|	1153	|	|	1353	|	|	|	1553	|	|	1753	...	|	...	...	1953
Köln Messe/Deutz **910** d.	1145	1244	|	1344	1444	|	1545	1629	1644	|	1744	1844	|	...	1933	...	...	|
Bonn Hbf **800** d.	|	|	1214	|	|	1414	|	|	|	1614	|	|	1814	...	|	...	...	2014
Koblenz Hbf **800** d.	|	|	1248	|	|	1448	|	|	|	1648	|	|	1848	...	|	...	...	2048
Mainz Hbf **800** d.	|	|	1342	|	|	1542	|	|	|	1742	|	|	1942	...	|	...	...	2144
Frankfurt Flughafen ✈ § d.	1234	1334	1401	1434	1534	1601	1634	1719	1734	1802	1834	1934	2001	...	2034	...	...	2201
Frankfurt (Main) Hbf d.	1253	1353	1421	1453	1553	1621	1653	|	1753	1821	1853	1953	2022	...	2053	...	...	2222
Hanau Hbf d.	|	|	1438	|	|	1637	|	|	|	1837	|	|	2037	...	|	...	...	2238
Aschaffenburg Hbf d.	1323	1423	|	1523	1623	1652	1723	|	1823	1851	1923	2023	2052	...	2123	...	...	2252
Würzburg Hbf **900** d.	1404	1504	1535	1604	1704	1735	1804	|	1904	1934	2004	2104	2134	...	2204	...	...	2346
Nürnberg Hbf **900** a.	1500	1559	1627	1658	1759	1827	1859	1915	1959	2028	2100	2159	2228	...	2259	...	...	0042
Nürnberg Hbf d.	1504	1602	1631	1702	1802	1831	1903	1917	2002	2031	2104	2203	2237	...	2313	2316	...	...
Augsburg Hbf **905** a.	|	|	|	|	|	|	|	|	|	|	|	|	|	...	|	|	...	...
München Hbf **904** a.	1606	1706	|	1807	1911	|	2007	2020	2111	|	2206	2311	|	...	0019	|	...	...
Regensburg Hbf d.	...	...	1726	...	...	1926	...	...	...	2133	...	...	2340	...	...	0028	...	...
Straubing d.	...	...	|	...	...	|	...	...	...	|	...	...	|	...	...	...	...	...
Plattling **944** d.	...	...	1759	...	...	1959	...	...	...	2208	...	...	0017	...	...	...	...	...
Passau Hbf 🏛 **944** a.	...	...	1826	...	...	2026	...	...	...	2242	...	...	0050	...	...	...	...	...
Linz Hbf **950** a.	...	...	1926	...	...	2134	...	...	...	...	...	...	...	...	...	...	...	...
Wien Hbf **950** a.	...	...	2047	...	...	2305	...	...	...	...	...	...	...	...	...	...	...	...

	ICE 824	ICE 1022	RE 59490	ICE 822	ICE 1122	RE 59496	RE 59492	ICE 820		ICE 1020		ICE 728		ICE 726	ICE 928	ICE 724		ICE 722	ICE 228	ICE 720		ICE 628	ICE 28	ICE 626
	Ⓐ		Ⓐ	⚒	Ⓐ	Ⓒ	Ⓐ	⚒																
	✕	✕	t	✕	✕	z	t	✕		✕		✕		✕	✕	✕		✕	✕	✕		✕	✕	✕
Wien Hbf **950** d.	...	...	...	...	...	...	...	...	...	...	...	...	...	...	...	...	...	...	0651	...	...	...	0913	...
Linz Hbf **950** d.	...	...	...	...	...	...	...	...	...	...	...	...	...	...	...	...	...	...	0817	...	...	...	1034	...
Passau Hbf 🏛 **944** d.	...	...	...	...	...	...	...	...	...	0511	...	...	...	...	0717	...	...	...	0934	...	...	...	1134	...
Plattling **944** d.	...	...	...	...	...	...	...	...	...	0543	...	...	...	...	0751	...	...	...	1001	...	...	...	1201	...
Straubing d.	...	...	...	...	...	...	...	...	...	0557	...	...	...	...	0805	...	...	...	|	...	...	...	|	...
Regensburg Hbf d.	...	...	0421	...	...	0530	0530	...	...	0622	...	...	...	...	0827	...	...	...	1032	...	...	...	1235	...
München Hbf **904** d.	...	...	|	0449	0534	|	|	0553r	...	|	...	0648	...	0747	|	0848	...	0951	|	1051	...	1151	|	1250
Augsburg Hbf **905** d.	...	...	|	|	|	|	|	|	...	|	...	|	...	|	|	|	...	|	|	|	...	|	|	|
Nürnberg Hbf a.	...	...	0545	0557	0637	0640	0642	0656r	...	0721	...	0756	...	0854	0926	0955	...	1055	1127	1155	...	1254	1327	1354
Nürnberg Hbf **900** d.	...	0528	...	0600	0639	...	...	0702	...	0730	...	0800	...	0859	0930	1000	...	1100	1130	1159	...	1257	1330	1400
Würzburg Hbf **900** d.	0555	0624	...	0655	|	...	...	0755	...	0824	...	0855	...	0955	1024	1055	...	1155	1224	1255	...	1355	1424	1455
Aschaffenburg Hbf d.	0633	0705	...	0733	|	...	...	0833	...	|	...	0933	...	1033	|	1133	...	1233	|	1333	...	1433	|	1533
Hanau Hbf d.	|	|	...	|	|	...	...	|	...	0915	...	|	...	|	1116	|	...	|	1316	|	...	|	1516	|
Frankfurt (Main) Hbf a.	0704	0736	...	0804	|	...	...	0904	...	0936	...	1004	...	1104	1136	1204	...	1304	1336	1404	...	1504	1536	1604
Frankfurt Flughafen ✈ § a.	0720	0755	...	0820	0839	...	...	0921	...	0955	...	1020	...	1120	1155	1222	...	1320	1355	1420	...	1520	1555	1620
Mainz Hbf **800** a.	|	0818	...	|	|	...	...	|	...	1018	...	|	...	|	1218	|	...	|	1418	|	...	|	1618	|
Koblenz Hbf **800** a.	|	0911	...	|	|	...	...	|	...	1111	...	|	...	|	1311	|	...	|	1511	|	...	|	1711	|
Bonn Hbf **800** a.	|	0943	...	|	|	...	...	|	...	1143	...	|	...	|	1343	|	...	|	1543	|	...	|	1743	|
Köln Messe/Deutz **910** a.	0813	|	...	0915	0936	...	...	1016	...	|	...	1115	...	1215	|	1315	...	1415	|	1515	...	1614	|	1713
Köln Hbf **800 910** a.	|	1005	...	|	|	...	...	|	...	1205	...	|	...	|	1405	|	...	|	1605	|	...	|	1805	|
Düsseldorf Hbf **800** a.	0840	1031	...	0936	1006	...	...	1037	...	1231	...	1136	...	1239	1431	1336	...	1436	|	1536	...	1639	1832	1736
Essen Hbf **800** a.	0905	1058	...	1005	...	...	...	1104	...	1258	...	1203	...	1306	1458	1403	...	1503	|	1603	...	1706	1858	1803
Dortmund Hbf **800** a.	...	1121	...	...	...	...	...	...	...	|	...	...	...	...	|	...	...	...	1721	...	...	...	1922	1841
Hamburg Hbf **800 900** a.	...	...	...	...	...	...	...	...	...	1550	...	...	...	...	1753	...	...	...	...	...	...	...	...	...

A – 🛏 1,2 cl., ▬ 2 cl. and (2) Amsterdam - Innsbruck and v.v. (Table **53**).
B – BEROLINA – From/to Berlin on dates in Table **850**.
E – To Wiesbaden Hbf (a. 2105).
G – To/from Garmisch on ⑥ (Table **895**).
J – 🛏 1,2 cl., ▬ 2 cl. and (2) Amsterdam - Wien (Table **53**); on ①③⑤ conveys 🛏 1,2 cl., ▬ 2 cl. and (2) (*NJ* **50425**) Brussels - Bonn - Wien (Table **53**).
K – 🛏 1,2 cl., ▬ 2 cl. and (2) Wien - Amsterdam (Table **53**); on ②④⑦ conveys 🛏 1,2 cl., ▬ 2 cl. and (2) (*NJ* **50490**) Wien - Bonn - Brussels (Table **53**).
L – To/from Innsbruck (Table **53**).
N – Conveys 🛏 1,2 cl., ▬ 2 cl. and (2).
R – From Leipzig (Tables **849a** and **850**).
S – To Warnemünde via Jena and Berlin (Tables **835**, **849a**, **850**).
T – ⑦-④ Jan. 9 - Mar. 30.
Y – Daily to Jan. 8; ⑤⑥ from Jan. 13.

b – Not Dec. 25.
c – Arrives 0748.
f – Frankfurt (Main) **Süd**.
j – Arrives 1305.
q – ⚒ to Jan. 9; ⑥ from Jan. 14.
r – From Feb. 11.
t – Not Jan. 6.
v – † only.
x – Not mornings Feb. 11 - 24.
y – Not Feb. 10 - 23.
z – Also Jan. 6.

⊗ – Does not run Frankfurt - Dortmund on Dec. 24, 25, 31.
⊙ – Does not run Dortmund - Frankfurt on Dec. 25, 26, Jan. 1.
§ – Frankfurt Flughafen Fernbahnhof.
◐ – Operated by *agilis*.

(WIEN -) PASSAU - NÜRNBERG - FRANKFURT — 920

See Table **921** for other regional trains.

	ICE 92 B✕	ICE 624 ✕	ICE 26 ✕	ICE 622 ✕	ICE 620 ✕	ICE 1222 ✕	ICE 90 ✕	ICE 528 G✕	ICE 1128 Ⓐ E✕	ICE 1120 Ⓑb ✕	ICE 526 ✕	ICE 22 ⊗✕	ICE 524 ✕	ICE 522 Y ✕	ICE 522 ⑦–④ T✕	ICE 20 ✕	ICE 520		IC 94 S		NJ 490 Ⓡ N	NJ 40420 Ⓡ NL	NJ 420 Ⓡ A	NJ 40490 Ⓡ K
Wien Hbf **950** d.	1013	...	1113	...	...	...	1313	...	...	...	...	1513	...	...	...	1713	...	...	1913	...	2011	...	...	2011
Linz Hbf **950** d.	1134	...	1234	...	...	...	1434	...	...	...	...	1634	...	...	...	1834	...	...	2034	...	2134	...	...	2134
Passau Hbf 🚌 **944** d.	1233	...	1337	...	...	...	1537	...	...	...	...	1737	...	...	...	1937	...	...	2147	...	2253	...	...	2253
Plattling **944** d.	|	...	1404	...	...	...	1604	...	...	...	...	1804	...	...	...	2004	...	...	2217	...	|	...	...	|
Straubing d.	1312	...	|	...	...	...	|	...	...	...	...	|	...	...	...	|	...	...	2237	...	|	...	...	|
Regensburg Hbf d.	1333	...	1435	...	...	...	1635	...	...	...	...	1835	...	...	...	2035	...	...	2259	...	2356	...	...	2356
München Hbf **904** d.	|	1351	|	1451	1551	1618	|	1649	1649	1735	1752r	|	1851	1948	1948	|	2054	...	|	...	|	2252	2252	|
Augsburg Hbf **905** d.	|	|	|	|	|	|	|	|	|	|	|	|	|	|	|	|	|	...	|	...	|	2325	2325	|
Nürnberg Hbf a.	1428	1455	1528	1555	1654	1733	1729	1756	1756	1839	1856r	1928	1955	2054	2054	2128	2200	...	2400	...	0057	0054	0054	0057
Nürnberg Hbf **900** d.	...	1500	1531	1600	1657	1736	1732	1800	1800	1841	1903	1931	2000	2057	2057	2131	2204	...	...	...	0142	0142	0139	0139
Würzburg Hbf **900** d.	...	1555	1624	1655	1755	1831	1826	1855	1855	|	1955	2024	2055	2155	2155	2224	2257	...	...	...	0235	0235	|	|
Aschaffenburg Hbf d.	...	1633	|	1733	1833	|	|	1933	1933	|	2033	|	2133	2233	2233	2305	2335	...	...	...	|	|	|	|
Hanau Hbf d.	...	|	1716	|	|	1919	|	|	|	|	|	2116	|	2247	2247	2320	|	...	...	...	|	|	|	|
Frankfurt (Main) Hbf a.	...	1704	1736	1804	1904	1936	|	2004	2004	|	2104	2136	2204	2304	2304	2337	0004	...	...	...	|	|	0344f	0344f
Frankfurt Flughafen ✈ § a.	...	1720	1755	1820	1920	1955	|	2020	2020	2039	2120	2156	2220	2321	2321	...	...	...	...	...	|	|	0356	0356
Mainz Hbf **800** a.	...	|	1818	|	|	2018	|	|	2052	|	|	2218	|	|	2348	...	...	...	...	...	|	|	0416	0416
Koblenz Hbf **800** a.	...	|	1911	|	|	2111	|	|	...	|	|	2311	|	|	0041	...	...	...	...	...	|	|	0511	0511
Bonn Hbf **800** a.	...	|	1943	|	|	2143	|	|	...	|	|	2343	|	|	0120	...	...	...	...	...	|	|	0558	0558
Köln Messe/Deutz **910** a.	...	1814	|	1915	2025	|	|	2114	...	2130	2215	|	2336	|	|	...	...	...	...	...	|	|	|	|
Köln Hbf **800 910** a.	...	|	2005	|	|	2205	|	|	...	|	|	0005	|	0029	0150	...	...	...	...	...	|	|	0651x	0651x
Düsseldorf Hbf **800** a.	...	1840	2031	1944	2047	|	|	2135	...	2151	2237	0034	2357	...	...	...	...	...	...	...	|	|	0723x	0723x
Essen Hbf **800** a.	...	1914	2057	2015	2115	|	|	2202	...	...	2302	0100	0024	...	...	...	...	...	...	...	|	|	...	...
Dortmund Hbf **800** a.	...	1939	2121	2042	2140	2321	|	2227	...	...	2326	0125	0048	...	...	...	...	...	...	...	|	|	...	...
Hamburg Hbf **800 900** a.	...	...	...	...	...	...	2155	...	...	...	...	...	...	...	...	...	...	...	...	...	0847	0847	...	...

← FOR NOTES SEE PREVIOUS PAGE

RE services — Regional trains FRANKFURT - WÜRZBURG - NÜRNBERG - REGENSBURG - PASSAU — 921

See Table **920** for faster *ICE* / *IC* trains

km			Ⓒ	Ⓐ										Ⓒ	Ⓐ		Ⓒ	Ⓐ							⑤⑥f	
0	**Frankfurt** (Main) Hbf d.	...	0450k	0524	0634	0730	0834	0930	1034	1130	1234	1330	1434	1530	1534	1634	1730	1734	1834	1930	2034	2130	2230	2330	2330	0030
4	**Frankfurt** (Main) Süd d.	...	0457k	0530	0640	0736	0840	0936	1040	1136	1240	1336	1440	1536	1540	1640	1736	1740	1840	1936	2040	2136	2236	2336	2336	0036
10	Offenbach (Main) Hbf d.	...	|	0535	0645	|	0845	|	1045	|	1245	|	1445	|	1545	1645	|	1745	1845	|	2045	|	|	|	|	|
24	Hanau Hbf d.	...	0521k	0545	0657	0758	0857	0958	1057	1158	1257	1358	1457	1558	1557	1657	1758	1757	1857	1958	2057	2158	2259	2359	2359	0100
46	Aschaffenburg Hbf d.	0501	0612	0612j	0716	0816	0916	1016	1116	1216	1316	1416	1516	1616	1616	1716	1816	1816	1916	2016	2116	2218	2322	0022	0022	0122
84	Lohr Bahnhof d.	0530	0640	0640	0741	0841	0941	1041	1141	1241	1341	1441	1541	1641	1641	1741	1841	1841	1941	2041	2141	2247	2350	0051	0051	...
96	Gemünden (Main) d.	0542	0654	0654	0752	0852	0952	1052	1152	1252	1356	1452	1552	1652	1652	1752	1852	1852	1952	2053	2152	2300	0002	0102	0103	...
109	Karlstadt (Main) d.	0554	0703	0703	0800	0900	1000	1100	1200	1300	1404	1500	1600	1700	1700	1800	1900	1900	2000	2101	2200	2309	0012	...	0112	...
134	**Würzburg** Hbf a.	0616	0721	0721	0821	0921	1021	1121	1221	1321	1421	1521	1621	1721	1721	1821	1921	1921	2021	2121	2221	2334	0027	...	0128	...
	Bamberg **875** a.	...	0832	0832	...	1032	...	1232	...	1432	...	1632	...	1832	1832	...	2032	2032	...	2232	...	...	...	...	...	...

		Ⓒz			Ⓐ	Ⓒ		Ⓐ	Ⓒ																	
Bamberg **875** d.	...	...	...	...	...	...	...	...	...	...	0726	...	0926	...	1126	...	1326	...	1526	...	1726	...	1926	...	...	...
Würzburg Hbf d.	0044	0044	...	...	0419	...	0515	0637	0637	0737	0837	0937	1037	1137	1237	1337	1437	1537	1637	1737	1837	1937	2037	2135	2236	2340
Karlstadt (Main) d.	0110	0110	...	...	0443	...	0538	0654	0654	0755	0855	0955	1055	1155	1255	1355	1455	1555	1655	1755	1855	1955	2055	2156	2258	0003
Gemünden (Main) d.	0121	0122	...	...	0453	...	0548	0705	0705	0805	0905	1005	1105	1205	1305	1405	1505	1605	1705	1805	1905	2005	2105	2207	2309	0013
Lohr Bahnhof d.	...	0131	...	...	0504	...	0559	0715	0715	0816	0915	1015	1115	1215	1315	1415	1515	1615	1715	1816	1915	2015	2115	2217	2319	0023
Aschaffenburg Hbf d.	...	0202	...	0428	0536	0536	0637j	0743	0743	0843	0943	1043	1143	1243	1343	1443	1543	1643	1743	1843	1943	2043	2151j	2251	2352	0055
Hanau Hbf d.	...	...	...	0454	0600	0600	0702	0801	0802	0902	1002	1102	1201	1302	1403	1501	1601	1701	1803	1902	2002	2102	2215	2315	0017	...
Offenbach (Main) Hbf d.	...	...	...	|	0611	|	0711	0811	|	0912	|	1112	|	1312	|	1512	|	1712	|	1912	|	2112	|	|	|	...
Frankfurt (Main) Süd a.	...	...	...	0516	0615	0624	0716	0816	0824	0916	1025	1116	1224	1316	1425	1516	1624	1716	1825	1917	2025	2116	2238	2338	0040	...
Frankfurt (Main) Hbf a.	...	...	...	0524	0624	0632	0724	0828	0832	0924	1032	1124	1232	1326	1432	1524	1632	1726	1832e	1926	2032e	2124	2246	2346	0050	...

WÜRZBURG - NÜRNBERG

km		Ⓐt	⚒r	Ⓐt			⊠			
0	**Würzburg** Hbf d.	0438	0536	0608	0636	0741		2041	2148	2304
23	Kitzingen d.	0456	0554	0623	0655	0801	and	2101	2208	2323
61	Neustadt (Aisch) Bf d.	0518	0616	0647	0718	0826	hourly	2126	2240j	2346
94	Fürth (Bay) Hbf d.	0547	0644	0714	0740	0847	until	2147	2309	0015
102	**Nürnberg** Hbf a.	0553	0652	0721	0749	0853		2154	2316	0024

	⚒r						⊠			
Nürnberg Hbf d.	0428	0604	0703	0805	0905	1005		2105	2206	2335
Fürth (Bay) Hbf d.	0436	0611	0711	0811	0912	1011	and	2111	2212	2344
Neustadt (Aisch) Bf d.	0506	0634	0734	0834	0934	1034	hourly	2134	2234	0013
Kitzingen d.	0528	0657	0758	0857	0958	1057	until	2157	2257	0035
Würzburg Hbf a.	0548	0715	0817	0916	1016	1116		2219	2316	0052

NÜRNBERG - REGENSBURG - PASSAU ◇

	⚒r	†w	Ⓐt	Ⓐt	Ⓒz	Ⓐt	Ⓐt		ⒸD		¶	Ⓐt	Ⓒz¶		¶			¶			¶			¶	Ⓐt	
Nürnberg Hbf d.	...	...	0501	...	...	0551	0615	...	0705	0735	...	...	...	0936	...	...	1136	...	...	1336	...	...	1536	...	1636	...
Neumarkt (Oberpf) d.	0447	...	0534	0549	...	0619	0638	...	0726	0759	...	0910	...	0959	...	1110	1159	...	1316	1359	...	1510	1559	...	1657	1710
Ingolstadt Hbf **945** d.	|	...	...	|	0601	|	|	0705	|	|	0805	|	0905	|	1005	|	|	1205	|	|	1405	|	|	1605	|	|
Regensburg Hbf a.	0539	...	...	0642	0707	0700	0726	0808h	0810	0840	0908	1003	0958	1039	1108	1203	1239	1308	1407	1439	1508	1603	1643	1708	1745	1803
Regensburg Hbf d.	0541	0609	...	0653	0715	0702	...	0810	0818	0846	0910	1010	1010	1046	1110	1210	1246	1310	1410	1446	1510	1610	1646	1710	...	1810
München Hbf **878** a.	|	|	...	|	|	0836	...	|	|	1018	|	|	|	1216	|	|	1416	|	|	1616	|	|	1816	|	...	|
Straubing d.	0608	0636	...	0724	0742	...	...	0837	0844	...	0937	1037	1037	▬	1137	1237	...	1337	1437	...	1537	1637	...	1737	...	1837
Plattling a.	0623	0651	...	0738	0756	...	...	0852	0856	...	0952	1052	1052	...	1152	1252	...	1352	1452	...	1552	1652	...	1752	...	1852
Plattling **944** d.	0642	...	...	0800	0802	...	...	0902	0858	...	1004	...	1054D	1102	1204	1302	...	1404	1504	...	1604	1702	...	1804	...	1902
Passau Hbf **944** a.	0716	...	...	0835	0837	...	...	0937	0930	...	1039	...	1129D	1137	1239	1337	...	1439	1539	...	1639	1737	...	1839	...	1937

		¶		L	¶			¶	¶	
Nürnberg Hbf d.	1736	...		1936	...	...	2136	...	...	2316
Neumarkt (Oberpf) d.	1759	...	1910	1959	...	2110	2159	...	...	2338
Ingolstadt Hbf **945** d.	|	1804	|	|	2005	|	|	2205	2305	|
Regensburg Hbf a.	1842	1908	2003	2039	2108	2203	2239	2308	0008	0028
Regensburg Hbf d.	1846	1910	2010	...	2110	2210	2247	2310	0010	...
München Hbf **878** a.	2016	|	|	...	|	|	0020	|	|	...
Straubing d.	...	1937	2037	...	2137	2237	...	2337	0037	...
Plattling a.	...	1952	2052	...	2152	2252	...	2351	0051	...
Plattling **944** d.	...	2004	2102	...	2202	2306	...	...	0055	...
Passau Hbf **944** a.	...	2039	2137	...	2237	2341	...	...	0130	...

	Ⓐt	Ⓒz¶	Ⓒz	Ⓐt	Ⓐt	¶		Ⓐt	Ⓒz		¶
Passau Hbf **944** d.	...	...	...	...	0440	0523	...	0600	0627	...	0726
Plattling **944** a.	...	...	...	...	0513	0558	...	0636	0701	...	0800
Plattling d.	...	0441	...	...	0516	0604	...	...	...	0708	0808
Straubing d.	...	0456	...	...	0531	0618	...	...	...	0723	0823
München Hbf **878** d.	...	|	...	...	|	|	0544	...	...	|	|
Regensburg Hbf a.	...	0523	...	...	0559	0647	0716	...	...	0750	0850
Regensburg Hbf d.	0421	0543	0530	0530	0626	0652	0718	...	...	0753	0853
Ingolstadt Hbf **945** a.	|	0645	|	|	|	0754	|	...	...	|	0954
Neumarkt (Oberpf) d.	0520	...	0618	0620	0720	...	0800	...	...	0847	...
Nürnberg Hbf a.	0545	...	0640	0642	...	...	0823	...	...	...	...

			¶			¶			¶			¶		ⒸD¶	Ⓒz¶	Ⓐt	¶		ⒸD		¶		¶			
Passau Hbf **944** d.	...	0826	0919	...	1026	1119	...	1219	1319	...	1426	1519	...	1620	1626	1626	1719	...	1820	1826	1919	...	2026	2126	...	...
Plattling **944** a.	...	0900	0953	...	1100	1153	...	1253	1353	...	1500	1553	...	1655	1700	1700	1753	...	1855	1900	1953	...	2100	2200	...	...
Plattling d.	...	0908	1008	...	1106	1208	...	1308	1408	...	1508	1608	...	1708	1708	1708	1808	...	1900	1908	2008	...	2108	2208	...	2306
Straubing d.	...	0923	1023	...	1121	1223	...	1323	1423	...	1523	1623	...	1723	1723	1723	1823	...	1913	1923	2023	...	2123	2223	...	2321
München Hbf **878** d.	0744	|	|	0944	|	|	1144	|	|	1344	|	|	1544	|	|	|	|	1744	|	|	|	1944	|	|	...	|
Regensburg Hbf a.	0915	0950	1050	1115	1148	1250	1315	1350	1450	1515	1550	1650	1715	1750	1750	1750	1850	1915	1934	1950	2050	2115	2152	2250	...	2350
Regensburg Hbf d.	0918	0953z	1053	1118	1153	1253	1318	1353	1453	1518	1553	1653	1717	1755	1755	1757	1853	1918	1937	2004	2053	2118	2157z	2253	2328	...
Ingolstadt Hbf **945** a.	|	|	1154	|	|	1354	|	|	1554	|	|	1754	|	1855	1855	|	1954	|	|	|	2153	|	2254z	2353	|	...
Neumarkt (Oberpf) d.	1000	1047z	...	1200	1250	...	1400	1447	...	1600	1647	...	1801	...	...	1851	...	2000	2023	2059	...	2200	...	...	0023	...
Nürnberg Hbf a.	1023	...	...	1222	...	...	1423	...	...	1623	...	...	1824	...	...	...	...	2022	2043	...	...	2223	...	...	0045	...

D – Ⓒ from Apr. 1.
L – To Landshut on dates in Table **878**.
e – 8 minutes later on ⑤⑦.
f – Also Apr. 6, 9, 30, May 17, 28.
h – 0757 on Ⓒ (also Jan. 6).
j – Arrives 9 – 10 minutes earlier.
k – ⑥ only.
r – Not Jan. 6.
t – Ⓐ (not Jan. 6).
w – Also Jan. 6.
z – Ⓒ (also Jan. 6).
◇ – Plattling - Regensburg - Neumarkt / Ingolstadt trains are operated by *agilis*.
⊠ – Timings may vary by 1 – 2 minutes.
¶ – To / from Ulm on Ⓒ (Table **945**).

922 WÜRZBURG - HEILBRONN - STUTTGART

On Jan. 6 services run as on ⑦. Operators: Go-Ahead Baden-Württemberg and SWEG Bahn.

km		Ⓐ	Ⓐ	Ⓒ	Ⓐ	Ⓐ																				
0	**Würzburg** Hbf d.	...	...	...	0506	...	0630t	0736	0837	0937	1037	1137	1237	1337	1437	1537	1637	1737	1837	1937	2038	2137		...		...
43	Lauda d.	...	0458	0537	0550	0609	0708	0809	0909	1009	1109	1209	1309	1409	1509	1609	1709	1809	1909	2009	2109	2209		...		...
78	Osterburken d.	0500	0526	0605	0617	0631	0730	0831	0931	1031	1131	1231	1331	1431	1531	1631	1731	1831	1931	2031	2131	2231		0836		2036
94	Möckmühl d.	0516	0540	0621	...	0643	0743	0843	0943	1043	1143	1243	1343	1443	1543	1643	1743	1843	1943	2043	2143	2243	A	0851	and	2051
116	Bad Friedrichshall Hbf d.	0539	0558	0644	...	0702	0801	0901	1001	1101	1201	1301	1401	1501	1601	1701	1801	1901	2001	2101	2201	2301	L	0916		2116
127	**Heilbronn** Hbf ★d.	0557	0612	0657	...	0720	0814	0912	1012	1112	1212	1312	1412	1512	1612	1712	1812	1912	2012	2112	2212	2312	S	0930	hourly	2130
140	Lauffen (Neckar) ★d.	0607	|	0706	...	|	|	|	|	|	|	|	|	|	|	|	|	|	|	|	|	|	O	0940		2140
157	Bietigheim-Bissingen ★d.	0624	0632	0725	...	0740	0833	0932	1032	1132	1232	1332	1432	1532	1632	1732	1832	1932	2032	2132	2232	2334		0957	until	2157
180	**Stuttgart** Hbf ★a.	0642	0653	0742	...	0758	0853	0956	1053	1156	1253	1351	1453	1550	1653	1756	1853	1951	2053	2152	2256	2353		1015		2215

	Ⓐ	Ⓐ	Ⓒ															⚒	†	⚒	†					
Stuttgart Hbf ★d.	0453	0546	0603	0708	0808	0908	1012	1108	1211	1306	1408	1506	1611	1711	1811	1909	2008	2108	2115	2212	2215		0943		2042	2143
Bietigheim-Bissingen ★d.	0512	0603	0622	0729	0829	0929	1029	1129	1229	1329	1429	1529	1629	1729	1829	1929	2029	2129	2134	2229	2234		1000	and	2100	2200
Lauffen (Neckar) ★d.	|	0617	0637	|	|	|	|	|	|	|	|	|	|	|	|	|	|	|	2149	|	2249	A	1016		2116	2216
Heilbronn Hbf ★d.	0530	0629	0648	0748	0848	0948	1048	1148	1248	1348	1448	1548	1648	1748	1848	1948	2048	2148	2202	2248	2302	L	1028	hourly	2128	2228
Bad Friedrichshall Hbf d.	0543	0642	0658	0758	0858	0958	1058	1157	1258	1358	1458	1558	1658	1758	1858	1958	2058	2200	2212	2258	2312	S	1043		2140	2243
Möckmühl d.	0601	0705	0715	0815	0915	1015	1115	1215	1314	1415	1515	1615	1715	1815	1915	2015	2115	2217	2229	2321	2335	O	1105	until	2202	2305
Osterburken d.	0614	0727	0727	0827	0927	1027	1127	1227	1327	1427	1527	1627	1727	1827	1927	2027	2127	2228	2242	2337	2351		1121		2218	2321
Lauda d.	0639	0750	0750	0850	0950	1050	1150	1250	1350	1450	1550	1650	1750	1850	1950	2050	2150	2250	2306	0006	0020		...		...	...
Würzburg Hbf a.	0721	0820	0820	0921	1020	1122	1221	1321	1420	1522	1619	1720	1821	1922	2020	2121	2221	2324	2334	...	...		...		...	...

Additional trains Heilbronn - Stuttgart and v.v.

	Ⓒ		Ⓒ		Ⓐ	Ⓐ	Ⓒ	Ⓐ	Ⓒ		Ⓐ	Ⓐ¶	Ⓐ¶	Ⓒ	Ⓐ	¶					⚒	⚒		Ⓐ		Ⓐ
Heilbronn Hbf d.	0111	...	0311	...	0429	0452	0455	0533	0557	0630	0637	0653	0730	0730	0757	0830	0857	and	1857	1957	2057	2157	2229	2257	2330	2357
Lauffen (Neckar) d.	0121	...	0321	...	0439	0502	0505	0542	0607	0640	0647	0703	0740	0740	0807	0840	0907	hourly	1907	2007	2107	2207	2239	2307	2340	0007
Bietigheim-Bissingen d.	0138	...	0337	...	0457	0519	0522	0559	0624	0657	0703	0719	0757	0757	0825	0857	0925	until	1925	2025	2125	2225	2256	2325	2357	0027
Stuttgart Hbf a.	0156	...	0355	...	0515	0539	0540	0617	0642	0715	0723	0740	0815	0816	0842	0915	0942		1942	2044	2146	2245	2314	2342	0015	0044

		Ⓒ		Ⓒ	Ⓐ	Ⓐ	Ⓐ¶		Ⓐ		Ⓐ					¶	¶	¶			⚒	⚒		†	⚒	⚒
Stuttgart Hbf d.	0019	0210	...	0410	0443	0510	0612	0644	0721	0744	0816	0845	0919	and	1519	1619	1719	1819	1919	2016	2120	2219	2243	2317	2319	2342
Bietigheim-Bissingen d.	0036	0227	...	0427	0501	0527	0630	0701	0738	0801	0836	0902	0936	hourly	1536	1636	1736	1836	1936	2036	2138	2236	2300	2336	2336	0000
Lauffen (Neckar) d.	0051	0242	...	0441	0516	0542	0645	0716	0753	0816	0851	0917	0951	until	1551	1651	1751	1851	1951	2051	2153	2251	2316	2351	2351	0016
Heilbronn Hbf a.	0101	0252	...	0452	0526	0552	0655	0726	0802	0826	0901	0926	1001		1601	1701	1801	1901	2001	2101	2202	2301	2326	0001	0001	0026

t – Ⓐ only. ¶ – From/to stations in Table **924** on Ⓐ. ★ – See also panel below main table.

923 MANNHEIM - EBERBACH - OSTERBURKEN S-Bahn

On Jan. 6 services run as on ⑦.

km		Ⓒ	Ⓐ		Ⓒ	Ⓐ	Ⓐ		Ⓐ															
0	**Mannheim** Hbf 924 ▷ d.	0211	0419	0535	0628	0634	*0646*	0738	0807	0837	0907	0938	and at	1907	1938	2007	2038	2107	2143	...	...	2207	2304	0021
17	**Heidelberg** Hbf 924 ▷ d.	0240	0442	0555	0655	0655	0727	0754	0825	0854	0925	0955		1925	1955	2026	2055	2127	2157	...	2201	2235	2329	0038
28	Neckargemünd 924 d.	0255	0456	0609	0709	0709	0741	0809	0839	0909	0939	1009	the same	1939	2009	2040	2109	2141	2207	...	2216	2249	2343	0053
34	Neckarsteinach d.	0301	0502	0616	0715	0715	0747	0815	0845	0915	0945	1015	minutes	1945	2015	2046	2115	2147	|	...	2222	2255	2349	0059
41	Hirschhorn (Neckar) d.	0308	0509	0622	0722	0722	0754	0822	0852	0922	0952	1022		1952	2022	2053	2122	2154	|	...	2229	2302	2356	0106
50	Eberbach 924 d.	0315	0516	0629	0729	0729	0801	0829	0859	0929	0959	1029	past each	1959	2029	2100	2129	2201	2224	...	2235	2309	0002	0113
69	Mosbach-Neckarelz 924 d.	0333	0535	0648	0748	0748	0820	0848	0918	0948	1018	1048	hour until	2018	2048	2119	2148	2219	2237	2243	2254	2329	0021	0132
72	Mosbach (Baden) d.	0338	0540	0653	0753	0753	0824	0853	0923	0953	1023	1053		2023	2053	2123	2153	...	...	2248	...	2333	0026	0137
101	**Osterburken** a.	...	0610	0723	0823	0823	...	0923	...	1023	...	1123		...	2123	...	2223	...	...	2320	...	...	0056	...

	Ⓐ	Ⓒ	Ⓐ	Ⓐ	Ⓐ	Ⓒ	Ⓐ	Ⓐ	Ⓒ		Ⓐ		⚒											
Osterburken d.	...	...	...	0508	0534	0536	0557	...	0636	...	0640	...	0702t	0733	...	0836	and at	...	1836	...	1938	2038	2138	2238
Mosbach (Baden) d.	0432	0454	0508	0537	0603	0605	0628	...	0705	0705	0718	...	0731t	0802	0835	0905		1835	1905	1935	2007	2107	2207	2307
Mosbach-Neckarelz 924 d.	0437	0459	0521v	0546	0608	0610	0633	0638	0710	0710	0724	0728	0740	0810	0840	0910	the same	1840	1910	1940	2012	2112	2212	2312
Eberbach 924 d.	0456	0518	0541	0605	0627	0629	0647	0656	0729	0729	...	0742	0759	0829	0859	0929	minutes	1859	1929	1959	2031	2131	2231	2331
Hirschhorn (Neckar) d.	0503	0525	0548	0612	0634	0636	|	0703	0736	0736	...	|	0806	0836	0906	0936		1906	1936	2006	2038	2138	2238	2338
Neckarsteinach d.	0509	0532	0555	0618	0640	0642	0659	0711	0742	0742	...	|	0812	0842	0912	0942	past each	1912	1942	2012	2045	2144	2244	2344
Neckargemünd 924 d.	0516	0538	0601	0625	0647	0649	0704	0717	0749	0749	...	0758	0819	0849	0919	0949	hour until	1919	1949	2019	2051	2151	2251	2351
Heidelberg Hbf 924 ▷ a.	0530	0551	0614	0639	0701	0702	0716	0733	0802	0802	...	0809	0832	0902	0932	1002		1932	2002	2032	2105	2205	2305	0005
Mannheim Hbf 924 ▷ a.	0552	0609	0634	0700	0719	0720	*0746*	0753	0819	0819	...	0824	0851	0920	0951	1019		1950	2019	2051	2129	2230	2330	0030

t – Ⓐ only. v – Arrives 0512. ▷ – See also Tables **913**, **918**, **919**.

924 MANNHEIM - HEIDELBERG - HEILBRONN

On Jan. 6 services run as on ⑦. Additional S-Bahn trains run Heidelberg - Sinsheim and Mosbach-Neckarelz / Sinsheim - Heilbronn.
Mannheim - Heilbronn operated by SWEG Bahn. S-Bahn Heidelberg - Sinsheim operated by DB. S-Bahn Mosbach-Neckarelz / Sinsheim - Heilbronn operated by Albtal-Verkehrs-Gesellschaft

km		Ⓒ2	Ⓐ2	Ⓐ	Ⓐ	Ⓒ2	Ⓐ	Ⓒ	Ⓐ2	Ⓒ2	Ⓐ	Ⓐ	2	2										
0	**Mannheim** Hbf 923 ▷ d.	...	...	...	...	...	0629	0635	0719	...	...	0735	*0738*	...	0834	0935	1035	1135	1235	1335	1435	1535	1635	1735
17	**Heidelberg** Hbf 923 ▷ d.	...	...	...	...	...	0645	0649	0731	...	...	0749	0804	...	0849	0949	1049	1149	1249	1349	1449	1549	1649	1749
28	Neckargemünd 923 d.	...	...	...	...	...	0655	0659	0745	...	...	0759	0818	...	0859	0959	1059	1159	1259	1359	1459	1559	1659	1759
50	Eberbach 923 d.	...	...	...	...	...	|	|	|	...	...	0815	|	...	|	1015	|	1215	|	1415	|	1615	|	1815
69	Mosbach-Neckarelz 923 d.	...	...	0619	0650	0650	|	|	|	0750	0752	0829	|	0850	|	1029	|	1229	|	1429	|	1629	|	1829
	Sinsheim (Elsenz) Hbf d.	0542	0540	|	|	|	0710	0714	0808	|	|	|	0838	|	0914	|	1114	|	1314	|	1514	|	1714	|
	Bad Rappenau d.	0600	0603	|	|	|	0727	0727	...	|	|	|	...	|	0927	|	1127	|	1327	|	1527	|	1727	|
	Bad Wimpfen d.	0608	0612	|	|	|	0732	0732	...	|	|	|	...	|	0932	|	1132	|	1332	|	1532	|	1732	|
87	Bad Friedrichshall Hbf 922 d.	0614	0619	0637	0708	0708	0741	0738	...	0808	0811	0843	...	0908	0938	1042	1138	1242	1338	1442	1538	1642	1738	1842
98	**Heilbronn** Hbf 922 a.	0643	0648	0649	0721	0737	0753	0749	...	0837	0822	0853	...	0937	0949	1051	1149	1251	1349	1451	1549	1651	1749	1851
	Stuttgart Hbf 922 a.	...	...	0740	0815	...	...	...	...	...	0915	...	...	...	...	...	...	...	...	...	...	...	...	...

							2	
Mannheim Hbf 923 ▷ d.	1835	1935	2035	2143	2240	0013	*0021*	...
Heidelberg Hbf 923 ▷ d.	1849	1949	2050	2157	2259	0025	0045	...
Neckargemünd 923 d.	1859	1959	2100	2207	2309	0035	0059	...
Eberbach 923 d.	|	2015	|	2224	|	0050	|	...
Mosbach-Neckarelz 923 d.	|	2029	|	2238	|	0104	|	...
Sinsheim (Elsenz) Hbf d.	1914	|	2114	|	2325	|	0120	...
Bad Rappenau d.	1927	|	2127	|	2339	|	...	...
Bad Wimpfen d.	1932	|	2132	|	2344	|	...	...
Bad Friedrichshall Hbf 922 d.	1938	2042	2138	2251	2350	0116	...	...
Heilbronn Hbf 922 a.	1949	2051	2149	2300	2359	0125	...	...
Stuttgart Hbf 922 a.	...	...	...	...	...	...	...	...

km		Ⓐ2		Ⓐ	Ⓒ2	Ⓒ2	Ⓒ2	Ⓐ	Ⓐ	Ⓒ	2
	Stuttgart Hbf 922 d.	...	...	...	...	...	...	...	0612	...	...
	Heilbronn Hbf 922 d.	...	0455	0542	0543	...	0618	0636	0700	0706	...
0	Bad Friedrichshall Hbf 922 d.	...	0504	0553	0614	...	0648	0647	0710	0716	...
3	Bad Wimpfen d.	...	|	0556	0620	...	|	|	|	|	...
9	Bad Rappenau d.	...	|	0604	0628	...	|	|	|	|	...
26	Sinsheim (Elsenz) Hbf d.	0449	|	0620	0645	0649	|	|	|	|	0749
	Mosbach-Neckarelz 923 d.	|	0517	|	...	|	0707	0706	0728	0728	|
	Eberbach 923 d.	|	0531	|	...	|	...	...	0742	0742	|
47	Neckargemünd 923 d.	0510	0547	0637	...	0712	...	...	0758	0758	0812
58	**Heidelberg** Hbf 923 ▷ a.	0526	0558	0648	...	0728	...	...	0809	0809	0828
75	**Mannheim** Hbf 923 ▷ a.	*0552*	0615	0706	...	*0753*	...	...	0824	0824	*0851*

	2											Ⓐ		Ⓐ		Ⓐ				2	2	2	2	2
Stuttgart Hbf 922 d.	...	...	...	...	...	...	...	...	...	...	...	1619	...	1719	...	1819	...	...	...	...	...	...	...	...
Heilbronn Hbf 922 d.	0703	0806	0906	1006	1106	1206	1306	1406	1504	1607	1706	1709	1807	1812	1906	1912	2006	2106	2206	2218	2256	2318	2350	0018
Bad Friedrichshall Hbf 922 d.	0737	0819	0916	1019	1116	1219	1316	1419	1516	1619	1716	1724	1819	1824	1916	1924	2019	2116	2219	2248	2326	2348	0019	0048
Bad Wimpfen d.	0742	0822	|	1022	|	1222	|	1422	|	1622	|	|	1822	|	|	|	2022	|	2223	|	2330	|	0023	|
Bad Rappenau d.	0749	0827	|	1027	|	1227	|	1427	|	1627	|	|	1827	|	|	|	2027	|	2230	|	2341	|	0031	|
Sinsheim (Elsenz) Hbf d.	0810	0843	|	1043	|	1243	|	1443	|	1643	|	|	1843	|	|	|	2043	|	2245	|	2359	|	0048	|
Mosbach-Neckarelz 923 d.	...	|	0929	|	1129	|	1329	|	1529	|	1729	1743	|	1843	1929	1943	|	2129	|	2307	...	0007	...	0107
Eberbach 923 d.	...	|	0942	|	1142	|	1342	|	1542	|	1742	...	|	...	1942	...	|	2142	|	...	...	...	...	...
Neckargemünd 923 d.	...	0858	0958	1058	1158	1258	1358	1458	1558	1658	1758	...	1858	...	1958	...	2058	2158	2259	...	...	...	...	...
Heidelberg Hbf 923 ▷ a.	...	0909	1009	1109	1209	1309	1409	1509	1609	1709	1809	...	1909	...	2009	...	2109	2209	2308	...	...	...	...	...
Mannheim Hbf 923 ▷ a.	...	0924	1024	1124	1224	1323	1424	1524	1624	1723	1824	...	1924	...	2024	...	2124	2224	2324	...	...	...	...	...

▷ – See also Tables **913**, **918** and **919**.

STUTTGART - BACKNANG / AALEN - NÜRNBERG 925

km				*IC* 2061			*IC* 2063				*IC* 2065				*IC* 2067				*IC* 2069				*IC* 2161			
		◇	◇	Ⓐt	◇	◇		◇	◇			◇	◇			◇	◇			◇	◇	◇	A	◇	◇	
	Karlsruhe Hbf **931** .. d.	...	...	...	...	...	0707	...	...	...	0906	...	...	...	1106	...	...	...	1306	...	...	...	1506	...	...	...
0	**Stuttgart** Hbf .... ‡ d.	0438	0513	0605	0618	0653	0808	0820	0857	0955	1009	1020	1057	1155	1209	1220	1300	1354	1409	1420	1456	1555	1609	1620	1657	1755
31	Backnang .... d.	0506	0541	|	|	0724	|	|	0924	1024	|	|	1124	1224	|	|	1324	1425	|	|	1524	1624	|	|	1724	1825
73	Schwäbisch H-H ⊡ a.	0543	0623	|	|	0759	|	|	0959	1056	|	|	1158	1256	|	|	1358	1458	|	|	1559	1656	|	|	1758	1857
73	Schwäbisch H-H ⊡ d.	0543	0624	|	|	0800	|	|	1000	*1100*	|	|	1200	*1300*	|	|	1400	*1501*	|	|	1600	*1700*	|	|	1800	*1900*
	Schwäbisch Gmünd ‡ d.	|	|	0642	0702	|	0842	0902	|	|	1041	1102	|	|	1241	1302	|	|	1441	1502	|	|	1641	1702	|	|
	Aalen Hbf .... ‡ a.	|	|	0657	0720	|	0857	0920	|	|	1057	1120	|	|	1257	1320	|	|	1457	1520	|	|	1657	1720	|	|
	Aalen Hbf .... d.	|	|	0659	0728	|	0859	0928	|	|	1058	1128	|	|	1258	1328	|	|	1458	1528	|	|	1658	1728	|	|
	Ellwangen .... d.	|	|	0710	0748	|	0910	0948	|	|	1109	1148	|	|	1309	1348	|	|	1509	1548	|	|	1709	1748	|	|
100	Crailsheim .... d.	0610**k**	0641	0726	0812	0820	0926	1012	1020	*1120*	1125	1212	1220	*1320*	1325	1412	1420	*1521*	1525	1612	1620	*1720*	1725	1812	1820	*1920*
146	Ansbach .... d.	0641	...	0751	...	0850	0951	...	1050	...	1150	...	1250	...	1351	...	1450	...	1550	...	1650	...	1750	...	1850	...
190	**Nürnberg** Hbf .... a.	0717	...	0818	...	0920	1018	...	1120	...	1218	...	1320	...	1418	...	1520	...	1618	...	1720	...	1818	...	1920	...

	IC 2163			*IC* 2165				*IC* 2167		
				Ⓑ				⑦		
		◇	◇	b	◇	◇	◇	w	◇	◇
Karlsruhe Hbf **931** .. d.	1706	...	...	1906	...	...	...	2106	...	...
Stuttgart Hbf .... ‡ d.	1809	1820	1854	2009	2020	2057	2153	2209	2220	2327
Backnang .... d.	|	|	1924	|	|	2124	2224	|	|	2356
Schwäbisch H-H ⊡. a.	|	|	1959	|	|	2159	2258	|	|	0029
Schwäbisch H-H ⊡. d.	|	|	2000	|	|	2200	*2301*	|	|	0030
Schwäbisch Gmünd . ‡ d.	1841	1902	|	2041	2102	|	|	2240	2302	|
Aalen Hbf .... ‡ a.	1857	1920	|	2057	2120	|	|	2256	2320	|
Aalen Hbf .... d.	1858	1928	|	2058	2128	|	|	2257	2335	|
Ellwangen .... d.	1909	1948	|	2109	2148	|	|	2308	2352	|
Crailsheim .... d.	1925	2012	2020	2125	2212	2220	*2321*	2325	0009	0047
Ansbach .... d.	1950	...	2050	2150	...	2250	...	2350	...	...
Nürnberg Hbf .... a.	2018	...	2120	2218	...	2320	...	0018	...	...

km					*IC* 2164					*IC* 2162		
			Ⓐt	Ⓐt	Ⓐt							
		◇				◇	◇	◇	◇			◇
0	**Nürnberg** Hbf .... d.	...	...	...	0538	...	...	0637	...	0741	...	0837
44	Ansbach .... d.	...	...	...	0603	...	...	0705	...	0807	...	0907
90	Crailsheim .... d.	0456	*0509*	0540	0631	0635	0648	0742**k**	*0752*	0835	*0838*	0942
111	Ellwangen .... d.	|	*0527*	|	0647	|	0711	|	*0811*	0850	|	|
127	**Aalen** Hbf .... a.	|	*0544*	|	0658	|	0728	|	*0828*	0900	|	|
127	**Aalen** Hbf .... ‡ d.	|	0600	|	0700	|	0735	|	0837	0902	|	|
152	Schwäbisch Gmünd ‡ d.	|	0615	|	0718	|	0754	|	0856	0918	|	|
	Schwäbisch H-H ⊡ a.	0512	|	0556	|	0652	|	0758	|	|	*0859*	0958
	Schwäbisch H-H ⊡ d.	0520	|	0559	|	0700	|	0800	|	|	0903	1000
	Backnang .... d.	0605	|	0635	|	0737	|	0838	|	|	0937	1038
203	**Stuttgart** Hbf .... ‡ a.	0631	0650	0700	0753	0804	0840	0905	0939	0953	1004	1105
	Karlsruhe Hbf **931** . a.	...	0753	...	0853	...	...	...	...	1053	...	...

		IC 2160				*IC* 2068				*IC* 2066				*IC* 2064				*IC* 2062				*IC* 2060				
																						Ⓑ				
	◇			◇	◇	A		◇	◇			◇	◇			◇	◇			◇	e ◇	b	◇	◇	◇	◇
Nürnberg Hbf .... d.	...	0942	...	1038	...	1142	...	1238	...	1341	...	1438	...	1541	...	1638	...	1742	...	1838	...	1942	2038	...	...	2238
Ansbach .... d.	...	1007	...	1107	...	1207	...	1310	...	1407	...	1507	...	1607	...	1707	...	1807	...	1907	...	2007	2107	...	...	2307
Crailsheim .... d.	0952	1035	*1038*	1142	1152	1235	*1238*	1342	1352	1435	*1438*	1542	1552	1635	*1638*	1742	1752	1835	*1838*	1942	1952	2035	2142	2152	*2240*	2342
Ellwangen .... d.	1011	1050	|	|	1211	1250	|	|	1411	1450	|	|	1611	1650	|	|	1811	1850	|	|	2011	2050	|	2211	|	|
Aalen Hbf .... a.	1028	1100	|	|	1230	1300	|	|	1428	1500	|	|	1628	1700	|	|	1828	1900	|	|	2028	2100	|	2228	|	|
Aalen Hbf .... ‡ d.	1037	1102	|	|	1237	1302	|	|	1437	1502	|	|	1637	1702	|	|	1837	1902	|	|	2037	2102	|	2237	|	|
Schwäbisch Gmünd . ‡ d.	1056	1118	|	|	1256	1318	|	|	1456	1518	|	|	1656	1718	|	|	1856	1918	|	|	2056	2118	|	2256	|	|
Schwäbisch H-H ⊡. a.	|	|	*1059*	1158	|	|	*1259*	1358	|	|	*1459*	1558	|	|	*1659*	1758	|	|	*1859*	1958	|	|	2158	|	*2258*	2358
Schwäbisch H-H ⊡. d.	|	|	1103	1200	|	|	1303	1400	|	|	1503	1600	|	|	1703	1800	|	|	1903	1959	|	|	2200	|	2312	0000
Backnang .... d.	|	|	1137	1238	|	|	1337	1438	|	|	1537	1638	|	|	1737	1838	|	|	1937	2038	|	|	2238	|	2353	0039
Stuttgart Hbf .... ‡ a.	1139	1153	1204	1307	1339	1352	1404	1505	1539	1552	1604	1702	1739	1753	1803	1905	1939	1953	2003	2106	2139	2153	2304	2339	0023	0107
Karlsruhe Hbf **931** .. a.	...	1253	...	...	...	1453	...	...	...	1652	...	...	...	1853	...	...	...	2053	...	...	...	2300	...	...	...	...

A – To / from Leipzig (Table **849a**).
b – Not Dec. 25.
e – On ⑤ (not Jan. 6) Crailsheim d. 1951 and change trains at Aalen.
k – Arrives 7 – 9 minutes earlier.
r – Not Jan. 6.
t – Ⓐ (not Jan. 6).

w – Also Dec. 26; not Dec. 25.
z – Also Jan. 6.
***** – Journey time 48 – 49 minutes.
⊡ – Schwäbisch Hall-Hessental.
◇ – Operated by Go-Ahead Baden-Württemberg.

‡ – Other regional services (◇) Stuttgart - Schwäbisch Gmünd - Aalen and v.v. (journey 60 – 66 minutes).
From Stuttgart Hbf at 0020, 0120 Ⓒ**z**, 0320 Ⓒ**z**, 0447 Ⓐ**t**, 0519 Ⓐ**t**, 0549 Ⓐ**t**, 0647 Ⓐ**t**, 0708 Ⓐ**t***, 0720, 0747 Ⓐ**t**, 0847 Ⓐ**t**, 0908*, 0920, 0947, 1047, 1108*, 1118, 1147, 1247, 1308*, 1321, 1347, 1446, 1508*, 1520, 1547, 1647, 1708*, 1720, 1747, 1846, 1908*, 1918, 1947, 2047 ⚒**r**, 2108*, 2120, 2147 ⚒**r**, 2238*, 2247 ⚒**r**, 2320 and 2347 ⚒**r**.
From Aalen at 0037, 0237 Ⓒ**z**, 0435 Ⓐ**t**, 0505 Ⓐ**t**, 0535, 0635, 0705 Ⓐ**t**, 0802*, 0806 Ⓐ**t**, 0907, 0937, 1002*, 1007, 1107, 1137, 1202*, 1207, 1307, 1337, 1402*, 1407, 1507, 1537, 1602*, 1607, 1707, 1737, 1802*, 1807, 1907, 1937, 2002*, 2007 ⚒**r**, 2107 ⚒**r**, 2137, 2202*, 2207 ⚒**r**, 2307 ⚒**r** and 2337.

RE / RB services HEILBRONN / ASCHAFFENBURG - CRAILSHEIM and AALEN - DONAUWÖRTH / ULM 926

ASCHAFFENBURG - LAUDA - CRAILSHEIM

2nd class only

km		Ⓒz	Ⓐt	Ⓐt							
0	**Aschaffenburg** Hbf .. d.	...	...	0541	0719**k**	0926	1126	1326	1526	1726	1926
38	Miltenberg .... d.	...	0551	0653**f**	0753**k**	1000	1200	1400	1600	1800	2000**j**
69	Wertheim .... d.	0626	0639	0735	0834	1034	1234	1434	1634	1834	2034**j**
93	Tauberbischofsheim .. d.	0652	0705	0800	0900	1100	1300	1500	1700	1900	2102
100	**Lauda** .... a.	0700	0712	0806	0906	1106	1306	1506	1706	1906	2111
100	**Lauda** .... d.	0717	0715	0812	0912	1112	1312	1512	1712	1912	2116
110	Bad Mergentheim ...... d.	0730	0728	0823	0922	1122	1322	1522	1722	1922	2137**n**
169	**Crailsheim** .... a.	0827	0827	0926	1026	1226	1426	1626	1826	2026	2237

	Ⓐt	Ⓒz	Ⓐt						Ⓒz	Ⓐt	
Crailsheim .... d.	...	...	0626	0733	0933	1133	1333	1533	1733	1733	1933
Bad Mergentheim ... d.	0545	0629	0735	0837	1037	1236	1437	1637	1837	1837	2036
Lauda .... a.	0555	0639	0746	0846	1046	1246	1446	1646	1846	1846	2046
Lauda .... d.	0601	0640	0752	0852	1052	1252	1452	1652	1852	1852	2052
Tauberbischofsheim d.	0610	0700**n**	0800	0900	1100	1300	1500	1700	1900	1900	2106
Wertheim .... d.	0700**r**	0726	0827	0926	1126	1326	1526	1726	1926	1935**n**	2135
Miltenberg .... d.	0741	0800	0900	1000	1200	1359	1600	1800	2000	2017**n**	2215**v**
Aschaffenburg Hbf. a.	0835	0835	0935	1032	1232	1435	1632	1832	2032	2104	2259

HEILBRONN - CRAILSHEIM

2nd class only

km		Ⓐt							
0	**Heilbronn** Hbf .... d.	0702	0806	0906	and in the same pattern every **two** hours until	2006	2106	2206	2306
27	Öhringen .... d.	0726	0828	0926		2028	2126	2228	2326
54	Schwäbisch Hall .... d.	0749	0851	0949		2051	2149	2251	2349
61	Schwäbisch H-H ⊡ ... a.	0756	0858	0956		2058	2156	2258	2356
88	**Crailsheim** .... a.	*0817*	0920	*1017*		2120	*2217*	2321	*0047*

	Ⓐt	Ⓐt	Ⓒz						
Crailsheim .... d.	0520	*0635*	*0635*	*0742*	0838	and in the same pattern every **two** hours until	2038	*2142*	2240
Schwäbisch H-H ⊡ d.	0540	0655	0701	0803	0901		2101	2203	2302
Schwäbisch Hall ..... d.	0546	0701	0707	0809	0907		2107	2209	2308
Öhringen .... d.	0610	0731	0731	0832	0931		2131	2232	2332
Heilbronn Hbf .... a.	0635	0752	0752	0852	0952		2152	2252	2353

AALEN - DONAUWÖRTH (- MÜNCHEN) ◇

km		Ⓐt	Ⓐt		Ⓐt	Ⓐt	Ⓒz	Ⓐt										Ⓐt				Ⓒz	Ⓐt				
0	**Aalen** Hbf .... d.	...	...	...	0537	0608	0631	0631	0734	0834	0934	1034	1134	1234	1334	1434	1534	...	1634	1734	1834	1934	1944	2034	2134	2234	2331
39	Nördlingen ...... d.	0525	0557	0623	0623	0640	0708	0708	0821**v**	0915	1021**v**	1114	1221**v**	1321**v**	1421**v**	1521**v**	1621**v**	1703	1721**v**	1821**v**	1921**v**	2025**n**	2025	2114	2221**v**	2310	0008
68	**Donauwörth** ... a.	0551	0630	0651	0651	0706	0734	0737	0851	0947	1051	1145	1251	1351	1449	1551	1651	1734	1751	1851	1951	2051	2051	2146	2252	...	...
	Augsburg Hbf .. a.	...	0710	...	...	0800	...	0821	0928	...	1128	...	1328	...	1528	...	1728	...	...	1928	...	2128	2128	...	...	...	...
	München Hbf . a.	...	0802	...	...	0850	...	...	1020	...	1220	...	1420	...	1620	...	1821	...	...	2020	...	2231	2231	...	...	...	...

	Ⓐt	Ⓐt	Ⓒz	Ⓐt											Ⓐt		Ⓐt		Ⓐt	Ⓐt	Ⓐt	Ⓒz				⚒t	†z
München Hbf ... d.	...	...	...	...	...	...	0735	...	0935	...	1135	...	1335	...	...	1535	...	1641	...	...	...	1735	...	1935	...	2159	*2159*
Augsburg Hbf .... d.	...	...	...	0522	...	...	0828	...	1028	...	1225	...	1428	...	...	1628	...	1733	...	...	...	1828	...	2028	...	2254	*2254*
Donauwörth ..... d.	...	...	0607	0607	0710	0812	0906	1012	1107	1212	1312	1405	1512	1611	1626	1712	1754	1812	1826	1900	1912	1912	2009	2105	2212	2339	2339
Nördlingen .... d.	0441	0534	0641	0641	0742	0842	0942**n**	1042	1142**v**	1242	1342	1442	1542	1642	1657	1742	1820	1842	1859	1921	1939	1942	2050**n**	2142**n**	2242	0012	0012
Aalen Hbf .... a.	0519	0613	0722	0723	0824	0924	1024	1124	1224	1324	1424	1524	1624	1724	...	1824	...	1924	...	1950	2016	2024	2126	2224	2324	0048	0048

AALEN - ULM ⊖

km		Ⓐt	Ⓒz2	Ⓐt	2	2		2	2		2	2		2	2		2	2		2	2		2	2		2	2
0	**Aalen** Hbf .... d.	0553	0630	0703	0734	0834	0907	0934	1034	1107	1134	1234	1307	1334	1434	1507	1534	1634	1707	1734	1834	1907	1934	2034	2107	2134	2234
23	Heidenheim ..... d.	0612	0654	0726	0800	0900	0924	1000	1100	1124	1200	1300	1324	1400	1500	1524	1600	1700	1724	1800	1900	1924	2000	2100	2124	2200	2300
73	**Ulm** Hbf .... a.	0658	0742	0758	0847	0947	0956	1047	1147	1156	1247	1347	1356	1447	1547	1556	1647	1747	1756	1847	1947	1956	2047	2147	2156	2251	2351

	Ⓐt	Ⓐt	2	Ⓐt2	Ⓒz2		2	2		2	2		2	2		2	2		2	2		2	2		2	2	2
Ulm Hbf .... d.	0425	0538	0555**c**	0644	0705	0804	0811	0911	1002	1011	1111	1202	1211	1311	1402	1411	1511	1602	1609	1711	1802	1809	1911	2002	2011	2111	2211
Heidenheim ...... d.	0516	0626	0658	0800	0800	0835	0900	1000	1034	1100	1200	1234	1300	1400	1434	1500	1600	1634	1700	1800	1834	1900	2000	2034	2100	2200	2300
Aalen Hbf .... a.	0545	0650	0724	0824	0824	0852	0924	1024	1051	1124	1224	1251	1324	1424	1451	1524	1624	1651	1724	1824	1851	1924	2024	2051	2124	2224	2324

c – 0606 on Ⓒ (also Jan. 6).
f – Arrives 0635.
j – On Ⓐ**t**: Miltenberg a. 1958, d. 2008, Wertheim d. 2041.
k – On Ⓒ**z**: Aschaffenburg d. 0718, Miltenberg d. 0800.
n – Arrives 10 – 12 minutes earlier.

r – Arrives 0637.
t – Not Jan. 6.
v – Arrives 7 – 8 minutes earlier.
z – Also Jan. 6.

◇ – Operated by Go-Ahead Bayern. See Table **905** for other services Donauwörth - Augsburg - München.
⊖ – Operated by Südwestdeutsche Landesverkehrs (2nd class only trains) or DB.
⊡ – Schwäbisch Hall-Hessental.

927 FLIXTRAIN service summary

Special fares (**DB tickets not valid**). Engineering work may affect timings; **subject to alteration on and around public holidays** (please check when booking). Website: www.flixtrain.de

Routes *FLX* 10/11/15		1249 M	1240	1244 ⑤–①	1246 D	1246 ⑥⑦	1808 ④–⑦
Stuttgart Hbf	d.	...	0717	...	1516	1529	1554
Basel Bad Bf	d.	...	|	0917	|	|	|
Freiburg (Brsg) Hbf	d.	...	|	0959	|	|	|
Offenburg	d.	...	|	1043	|	|	|
Baden Baden	d.	...	|	1105	|	|	|
Karlsruhe Hbf	d.	...	|	1125	|	|	|
Heidelberg Hbf	d.	...	0807	1206	1606	1617	1706
Darmstadt Hbf	d.	...	0853	1252	1651	1651	1741
Wiesbaden Hbf	d.	0529	|	|	|	|	|
Mainz Hbf	d.	0544	|	|	|	|	|
Frankfurt Flug ✈ ⊡	d.	0605	|	|	|	|	|
Frankfurt (Main) Süd	d.	0628	0912	1312	1713	1713	1809
Hanau Hbf	d.	0643	|	|	|	|	|
Fulda	d.	0733	1007	|	1808	1808	1923
Bad Hersfeld	d.	|	|	1433	|	|	|
Eisenach	d.	|	|	|	1858	1858	|
Gotha	d.	|	1107	|	|	|	|
Erfurt Hbf	d.	|	1122	1522	1923	1923	|
Halle (Saale) Hbf	d.	|	1201	1601	2001	2001	|
Kassel Wilhelmshöhe	d.	0811	|	|	|	|	2000
Göttingen	d.	0832	|	|	|	|	2022
Hannover Hbf	d.	|	|	|	|	|	2108
Lüneburg	d.	|	|	|	|	|	2207
Hamburg Hbf	a.	|	|	|	|	|	2233
Hildesheim Hbf	d.	0905	|	|	|	|	...
Braunschweig Hbf	d.	0929	|	|	|	|	...
Wolfsburg Hbf	d.	0947	|	|	|	|	...
Berlin Spandau	a.	1100	|	|	|	|	...
Berlin Südkreuz	a.	|	|	1712z	2107	2107	...
Berlin Hbf	a.	1113	1316	1719	2116	2116	...

Routes *FLX* 10/11/15		1241 ④–①	1803 ⑤–①	1243 ④–⑦	1247	1248 K
Berlin Hbf	d.	0728	...	1129	1527	1730
Berlin Südkreuz	d.	0737	...	1136z	|	|
Berlin Spandau	d.	|	...	|	|	1739
Wolfsburg Hbf	d.	|	...	|	|	1850
Braunschweig Hbf	d.	|	...	|	|	1909
Hildesheim Hbf	d.	|	...	|	|	1932
Hamburg Hbf	d.	|	0811	|	|	|
Lüneburg	d.	|	0841	|	|	|
Hannover Hbf	d.	|	0945	|	|	|
Göttingen	d.	|	1026	|	|	2009
Kassel Wilhelmshöhe	d.	|	1049	|	|	2030
Halle (Saale) Hbf	d.	0844	|	1244	1644	|
Erfurt Hbf	d.	0920	|	1321	1720	|
Gotha	d.	|	|	|	1739	|
Eisenach	d.	0951	|	|	|	|
Bad Hersfeld	d.	|	|	1417	|	|
Fulda	d.	1043	1125	|	1843	|
Hanau Hbf	d.	|	|	|	|	2151
Frankfurt (Main) Süd	d.	1136	1230	1535	1936	2208
Frankfurt Flug ✈ ⊡	d.	|	|	|	|	2238
Mainz Hbf	d.	|	|	|	|	2300
Wiesbaden Hbf	a.	|	|	|	|	2318
Darmstadt Hbf	d.	1154	1248	1557	1954	...
Heidelberg Hbf	d.	1236	1345	1638	2035	...
Karlsruhe Hbf	d.	|	|	1727	|	...
Baden Baden	d.	|	|	1748	|	...
Offenburg	d.	|	|	1804	|	...
Freiburg (Brsg) Hbf	d.	|	|	1839	|	...
Basel Bad Bf	a.	|	|	1914	|	...
Stuttgart Hbf	a.	1330	1429	...	2119	...

Routes *FLX* 30/35		1326 C	1230 ⑦	1230 ⑤	1230 ①⑥	1358 ⑦	1236 D	1236 ②③	1236 ⑦
Leipzig Hbf	d.	0641	...	...	...	...	1442	...	...
Lutherstadt Wittenberg	d.	|	...	...	...	...	1515	...	...
Dresden Hbf	d.	|	...	0622	0622	...	|	...	...
Dresden Neustadt	d.	|	...	0629	0629	...	|	...	...
Berlin Südkreuz	d.	0810	...	0812	0812	...	1611	1611	...
Berlin Hbf	a.	0817	...	0817	0817	...	1616	|	...
Berlin Hbf	d.	0822	0824	0830	0830	1207	1627	1627	1625
Berlin Spandau	d.	|	0840	0840	0840	|	1639	1639	1639
Wittenberge	d.	|	|	|	|	|	|	|	|
Ludwigslust	d.	|	|	|	|	|	|	|	|
Büchen	d.	|	|	|	|	|	|	|	|
Hamburg Hbf	a.	1050	|	|	|	1410	|	|	|
Stendal Hbf	d.	...	0916	0916	0916	...	1720	1720	1720
Hannover Hbf	d.	...	1023	1023	1023	...	1823	1823	1823
Herford	d.	...	|	|	|	...	|	|	|
Bielefeld Hbf	d.	...	1116	1116	1116	...	1916	1916	1916
Gütersloh Hbf	d.	...	1132	1132	1132	...	1932	1932	1932
Hamm (Westf)	d.	...	1202	1202	1202	...	2006	2006	2006
Dortmund Hbf	d.	...	1221	1221	1221	...	2025	2025	2025
Bochum Hbf	d.	...	|	|	|	...	2039	2039	2039
Essen Hbf	d.	...	1242	1242	1242	...	2050	2050	2050
Duisburg Hbf	d.	...	1258	1258	1258	...	2104	2104	2104
Düsseldorf Hbf	d.	...	1313	1313	1313	...	2122	2122	2122
Köln Hbf	a.	...	1345	1345	1345	...	2155	2155	2155
Aachen Hbf	a.	...	1424	1424	...	...	...	...	...

Routes *FLX* 30/35		1233 D	1233 E	1235 ⑦	1365 ⑥	1361 D	1361 ⑦	1239 ④	1239 ⑤⑦
Aachen Hbf	d.	...	...	...	...	...	...	...	1526
Köln Hbf	d.	0645	0645	0814	...	...	...	1614	1614
Düsseldorf Hbf	d.	0714	0714	0838	...	...	...	1637	1637
Duisburg Hbf	d.	0731	0731	0852	...	...	...	1651	1651
Essen Hbf	d.	0744	0744	0904	...	...	...	1704	1704
Bochum Hbf	d.	0754	0754	0915	...	...	...	1715	1715
Dortmund Hbf	d.	0808	0808	0932	...	...	...	1732	1732
Hamm (Westf)	d.	0834	0834	0952	...	...	...	1752	1752
Gütersloh Hbf	d.	0855	0855	1023	...	...	...	1823	1823
Bielefeld Hbf	d.	0906	0906	1042	...	...	...	1842	1842
Herford	d.	|	|	|	...	...	...	1853	1853
Hannover Hbf	d.	1007	1007	1144	...	...	...	1944	1944
Stendal Hbf	d.	1104	1108	1244	...	...	...	2043	2043
Hamburg Hbf	d.	|	|	|	1252	1734	1745	|	|
Büchen	d.	|	|	|	|	|	|	|	|
Ludwigslust	d.	|	|	|	|	|	|	|	|
Wittenberge	d.	|	|	|	|	|	|	|	|
Berlin Spandau	d.	1140	|	1334	1446	|	|	|	|
Berlin Hbf	a.	1149	1157	1350	1453	1948	1948	2127	2127
Berlin Hbf	d.	1154	...	|	|	1953	1953	2134	2134
Berlin Südkreuz	a.	1159	...	1403	1503	1957	1957	2138	2138
Dresden Neustadt	a.	|	...	...	...	|	|	2317	2317
Dresden Hbf	a.	|	...	...	...	|	|	2324	2324
Lutherstadt Wittenberg	d.	1238	...	...	...	|	|	...	...
Leipzig Hbf	a.	1315	...	...	...	2117	2117	...	...

Route *FLX* 20		1345 ⑤–①	1351
Hamburg Hbf	d.	0849	1449
Bremen Hbf	d.	|	|
Osnabrück Hbf	d.	1044	1644
Münster (Westf) Hbf	d.	1109	1709
Gelsenkirchen Hbf	d.	1148	1749
Essen Hbf	d.	1203	1803
Duisburg Hbf	d.	1215	1816
Düsseldorf Hbf	d.	1230	1830
Köln Hbf	a.	1256	1857

Route *FLX* 20		1340	1348 ④–⑦
Köln Hbf	d.	0701	1501
Düsseldorf Hbf	d.	0729	1527
Duisburg Hbf	d.	0745	1542
Essen Hbf	d.	0757	1556
Gelsenkirchen Hbf	d.	0807	1606
Münster (Westf) Hbf	d.	0848	1648
Osnabrück Hbf	d.	0915	1715
Bremen Hbf	d.	|	|
Hamburg Hbf	a.	1108	1907

C – ①④⑤⑥.
D – ①④⑤.
E – ②③⑥.
K – ④⑤⑦.
M – ①⑤⑥.

z – ⑥⑦.

⊡ – Frankfurt Flughafen Regionalbahnhof.

Bayerische Regiobahn — MÜNCHEN - BAYRISCHZELL, LENGGRIES and TEGERNSEE — 928

Most trains run with multiple portions from München (make sure you join the correct portion for your journey). On Jan. 6 services run as on ⑦.

km			Ⓐ		Ⓐ	Ⓐ	Ⓐ	Ⓐ		Ⓐ	Ⓐ	Ⓐ	Ⓐ	Ⓐ			Ⓒ		†	Ⓒ ⊡⊙		Ⓒ	Ⓒ	Ⓒ	†	Ⓒ	Ⓒ	Ⓒ
0	**München** Hbf. d.	Ⓐ	0010	...	0629	0703	0804	0904	and	1904	2004	2104	2204	2310	...	Ⓒ	0010	...	0530	0630	and	1830	1930	2003	2030	2103	2204	2310
37	Holzkirchen .... d.		0037	...	0701	0732	0832	0932	hourly	1932	2032	2132	2232	2337	...		0037	...	0600	0700	hourly	1900	2000	2030	2100	2130	2232	2337
61	Schliersee ...... d.		0106	...	0727	0802	0902	1001	until	2001	2102	2202	2302	0006	...		0106	...	0632	0732	until	1932	2025	2102	2126	2202	2302	0006
78	**Bayrischzell** .. a.		0130	...	...	0825	0925	1025		2025	2125	2225	2325	0030	...		0130	...	0656	0756		1956	...	2125	...	2225	2325	0030

km			Ⓐ		Ⓐ	Ⓐ	Ⓐ	Ⓐ	⊖	Ⓐ	Ⓐ			Ⓒ		Ⓒ	Ⓒ	Ⓒ	◇⊡	Ⓒ	Ⓒ	Ⓒ	†	Ⓒ	Ⓒ	Ⓒ
0	**München** Hbf. d.	Ⓐ	0010	...	0604	0629	0703	0804	and	2204	2310	...	Ⓒ	0010	...	0604	0704	0730	and at the	1904	1930	2003	2030	2103	2204	2310
37	Holzkirchen .... d.		0040	...	0635	0705	0735	0835	hourly	2235	2340	...		0040	...	0635	0735	0802	same minutes	1935	2002	2035	2102	2135	2235	2340
47	Schaftlach ...... d.		0053	...	0648	0718	0748	0848	until	2248	2353	...		0053	...	0648	0748	0818	past each	1948	2018	2048	2118	2148	2248	2353
57	Bad Tölz .... d.		0105	...	0700	0730	0800	0900		2300	0005	...		0105	...	0700	0800	0830	hour until	2000	2030	2100	2130	2200	2300	0005
67	**Lenggries** ...... a.		0116	...	0711	0741	0811	0911		2311	0016	...		0116	...	0711	0811	0841		2011	2041	2111	2141	2211	2311	0016

km			Ⓐ		Ⓐ	Ⓐ	Ⓐ	Ⓐ	⊖	Ⓐ	Ⓐ			Ⓒ		Ⓒ	Ⓒ	Ⓒ	◇⊡	Ⓒ	Ⓒ	Ⓒ	†	Ⓒ	Ⓒ	Ⓒ
	München Hbf d.	Ⓐ	0010	...	0604	0629	0703	0804	and	2204	*2310*	...	Ⓒ	0010	...	0604	0704	0730	and at the same	1904	1930	2003	2030	2103	2204	2310
0	Schaftlach ...... d.		0053	...	0648	0718	0748	0848	hourly	2248	2353	...		0053	...	0648	0748	0818	minutes past	1948	2018	2048	2118	2148	2248	2353
12	**Tegernsee** ..... a.		0113	...	0709	0739	0809	0909	until	2309	0013	...		0113	...	0709	0809	0839	each hour until	2009	2039	2109	2139	2209	2309	0013

		Ⓐ	Ⓐ	Ⓐ	Ⓐ	Ⓐ	Ⓐ	Ⓐ	Ⓐ	Ⓐ	Ⓐ	Ⓐ	Ⓐ	Ⓐ	Ⓐ	Ⓐ	Ⓐ		Ⓐ			Ⓒ	Ⓒ		Ⓒ	Ⓒ	Ⓒ	Ⓒ
Bayrischzell.... d.	Ⓐ	0449	0532	0607	0634	0705	0732	0832	0932	1032	1132	1232	...	1432	1532	1632	1732	and	2232	...	Ⓒ	0503	0603	and	2003	2032	2132	2232
Schliersee........ d.		0516	0559	0635	0702	0734	0759	0900	0959	1059	1159	1304	1359	1459	1559	1704	1759	hourly	2259	...		0530	0630	hourly	2031	2101	2201	2259
Holzkirchen........ d.		0544	0629	0705	0732	0803	0831	0931	1030	1129	1231	1332	1429	1531	1631	1732	1829	until	2329	...		0604	0704	until	2104	2132	2231	2331
München Hbf .. a.		0612	0655	0735	0758	0832	0857	0957	1056	1155	1257	1359	1455	1557	1657	1758	1855		2355	...		0632	0732		2132	2158	2257	2357

		Ⓐ	Ⓐ	Ⓐ	Ⓐ	Ⓐ	Ⓐ	Ⓐ	Ⓐ	Ⓐ	△	Ⓐ			⑥	Ⓒ	Ⓒ	Ⓒ	⊗	Ⓒ	Ⓒ	Ⓒ	Ⓒ		Ⓒ	Ⓒ
Lenggries .... d.	Ⓐ	0506	0547	0617	0647	0717	0747	0817	0847	0947	and	2247	...	Ⓒ	0447	0517	0617	0647	and at the	1917	1947	2017	2047	...	2147	2247
Bad Tölz.......... d.		0518	0600	0630	0700	0730	0800	0830	0900	1000	hourly	2300	...		0500	0530	0630	0700	same minutes	1930	2000	2030	2100	...	2200	2300
Schaftlach........ d.		0531	0617	0647	0717	0747	0817	0847	0917	1017	until	2317	...		0517	0549	0649	0717	past each	1949	2017	2049	2117	...	2217	2317
Holzkirchen........ d.		0544	0629	0701	0732	0803	0831	0903	0931	1030		2329	...		0531	0604	0704	0729	hour until	2004	2029	2104	2132	...	2231	2331
München Hbf .. a.		0612	0655	0730	0758	0832	0857	0932	0957	1056		2355	...		0557	0632	0732	0755		2032	2055	2132	2158	...	2257	2357

		Ⓐ	Ⓐ	Ⓐ	Ⓐ	Ⓐ	Ⓐ	Ⓐ	Ⓐ	Ⓐ	△	Ⓐ			⑥	Ⓒ	Ⓒ	Ⓒ	⊗	Ⓒ	Ⓒ	Ⓒ	Ⓒ		Ⓒ	Ⓒ
Tegernsee ...... d.	Ⓐ	0505	0552	0622	0652	0722	0752	0822	0852	0952	and	2252	...	Ⓒ	0452	0522	0622	0652	and at the same	1922	1952	2022	2052	...	2152	2252
Schaftlach........ a.		0525	0613	0643	0713	0743	0813	0843	0913	1013	hourly	2313	...		0513	0543	0643	0713	minutes past	1943	2013	2043	2113	...	2213	2313
München Hbf a.		0612	0655	0730	0758	0832	0857	0932	0957	1056	until	2355	...		0557	0632	0732	0755	each hour until	2032	2055	2132	2158	...	2257	2357

⊡ – München Hbf d. 1528, 1628, 1728 (not 1530, 1630, 1730).
⊙ – Holzkirchen d. 1558, 1658, 1758 (not 1600, 1700, 1800).
◇ – München Hbf d. 0803, 0903, 1003 (not 0804, 0904, 1004). No service from München (to Lenggries / Tegernsee) at 1230 or 1330.

△ – Holzkirchen and München timings may vary by up to 3 minutes. Extra trains on Ⓐ: from Lenggries to München at 1217, 1317, 1517, 1617 and 1817; from Tegernsee to München at 1222, 1322, 1522, 1622 and 1822.

⊖ – Extra trains on Ⓐ from München (to Lenggries / Tegernsee) at 0926, 1130, 1229, 1526, 1627, 1726, 1826 and 1926.
⊗ – Timings may vary by 1 – 2 minutes. No service from Tegernsee (to München) at 1322 or 1422. No service from Lenggries (to München) at 1417.

Waldbahn ⊠; ČD; 2nd class only — PLATTLING - BAYERISCH EISENSTEIN - PLZEŇ — 929

km		753		755	757	759				761			763			767			771				775		
		◇¶	Ⓐ	◇	◇	◇	Ⓐt	Ⓐt		◇			◇			◇			◇		B		◇		ⒸE
0	**Plattling** .... d.	...	...	...	...	...	0519	0629	0659	...	0806	0906	...	1006	1106	...	1206	1306	...	1406	...	1506	...	1606	...
9	Deggendorf Hbf........ d.	...	...	...	...	...	0531	0638	0709	...	0816	0916	...	1016	1116	...	1216	1316	...	1416	...	1516	...	1616	...
33	Gotteszell........ d.	...	...	...	...	...	0554	0657	0733	...	0835	0935	...	1035	1135	...	1235	1335	...	1435	...	1535	...	1635	...
48	Regen........ d.	...	...	...	...	...	0609	0711	0748	...	0848	0948	...	1048	1148	...	1248	1348	...	1448	...	1548	...	1648	...
58	Zwiesel (Bay)........ d.	...	...	...	...	...	0623	0725	0800	...	0900	1000	...	1100	1200	...	1300	1400	...	1500	...	1600	...	1700	...
72	**Bayerisch Eisenstein** ☆ 🏛 a.	...	...	...	...	...	0636	0738	0813	...	0913	1013	...	1113	1213	...	1313	1413	...	1513	...	1613	...	1713	...
72	**Železná Ruda-Alžbětín** ☆ 🏛 d.	...	0417	...	...	*0617*	▬	...	...	*0816*	▬	...	1017	▬	...	*1217*	▬	...	*1416*	▬	1553	...	1617	▬	1740
75	Železná Ruda centrum........ d.	...	0421	...	...	*0621*	...	...	...	*0820*	...	...	1021	...	...	*1221*	...	...	*1420*	...	1557	...	1621	...	1744
79	Špičák........ d.	...	0429	...	...	*0629*	...	...	...	*0827*	...	...	1029	**765**	...	*1229*	**769**	...	*1427*	**773**	1606	...	1629	**777**	1752
131	**Klatovy** .... a.	...	0517	...	...	*0716*	◇	...	...	*0916*	◇	...	1116	◇	...	*1316*	◇	...	*1516*	◇	1704	...	1716	◇	1834
131	**Klatovy** .... d.	0428	...	0528	0630	0730	0828	...	...	0930	1028	...	1130	1228	...	1330	1428	...	1530	1628	1708	...	1730	1828	1845
141	Švihov u Klatov........ d.	0437	...	0537	0639	0740	0837	...	...	0940	1037	...	1140	1237	...	1340	1437	...	1540	1637	|	...	1740	1837	|
170	**Plzeň** hl.n. .... a.	0519	...	0619	0719	0819	0919	...	...	1019	1119	...	1219	1319	...	1419	1519	...	1619	1719	1757	...	1819	1919	1935
	Praha hl.n. **1120** .... a.	0647	...	0747	0848	0947	...	...	...	1147	...	...	1347	1447	...	1547	1647	...	1747	1847	...	...	1947	2047	...

		779								
		◇								
Plattling .... d.	1707	...	1806	...	1906	2006	2106	2213	2308	0101
Deggendorf Hbf .... d.	1716	...	1816	...	1916	2016	2116	2222	2319	0110
Gotteszell .... d.	1735	...	1835	...	1935	2035	2135	2241	2338	0129
Regen........ d.	1748	...	1848	...	1948	2048	2148	2254	2350	0143
Zwiesel (Bay) .... d.	1800	...	1900	...	2000	2100	2158	2304	0001	0153
Bayerisch Eisenstein ☆ 🏛. a.	1813	...	1913	...	2013	2113	...	...	...	...
Železná Ruda-Alžbětín ☆ 🏛. d.	...	*1817*	...	1953	...	...	...	...	...	...
Železná Ruda centrum........ d.	...	*1821*	...	1957	...	...	...	...	...	...
Špičák .... d.	...	*1829*	...	2005	...	...	...	...	...	...
Klatovy .... a.	...	*1918*	...	2057	...	...	...	...	...	...
Klatovy .... d.	...	1930	...	2059	...	...	...	...	...	...
Švihov u Klatov........ d.	...	1940	...	2110	...	...	...	...	...	...
Plzeň hl.n. .... a.	...	2019	...	2153	...	...	...	...	...	...
Praha hl.n. **1120** .... a.	...	2147	...	...	...	...	...	...	...	...

								778	778
	Ⓐt	Ⓐt	Ⓒz	Ⓐt	Ⓒz	Ⓐt		◇	Ⓐ◇
Praha hl.n. **1120** .... d.	...	...	...	...	...	...	...	...	0513
Plzeň hl.n. .... d.	...	...	...	...	...	...	0540	0640	0640
Švihov u Klatov........ d.	...	...	...	...	...	...	0619	0719	0719
Klatovy .... a.	...	...	...	...	...	...	0629	0729	0729
Klatovy .... d.	...	...	...	...	...	...	*0640*	▬	▬
Špičák .... d.	...	...	...	...	...	...	*0728*	...	...
Železná Ruda centrum........ d.	...	...	...	...	...	...	*0734*	...	...
Železná Ruda-Alžbětín ☆ 🏛 ..... a.	...	...	...	...	...	...	*0738*	Ⓐt	...
Bayerisch Eisenstein ☆ 🏛 ..... d.	...	...	...	...	...	0705	...	0744	...
Zwiesel (Bay) .... d.	0414	0529	0559	0621	0652	0722	...	0759	0759
Regen........ d.	0424	0539	0609	0631	0702	0732	...	0809	0809
Gotteszell........ d.	0438	0555	0622	0644	0715	0751	...	0822	0822
Deggendorf Hbf........ d.	0459	0614	0645	0709	0738	0815	...	0845	0845
Plattling .... a.	0508	0623	0654	0718	0747	0825	...	0854	0854

			776		774	772			770			768	766			764		762	760		758	756		752	
		C	◇		◇	◇		◇	◇	D	◇	◇	◇	Ⓐ		◇		◇	◇		◇	◇		◇	
Praha hl.n. **1120** .... d.	...	...	0613	...	0713	0813	...	...	1013	...	...	1213	1313	...	...	1413	...	1513	1613	...	1713	1813	...	2113	...
Plzeň hl.n. .... d.	...	0700	0740	...	0840	0940	...	1040	1140	...	1240	1340	1440	...	...	1540	...	1640	1740	...	1840	1940	2111	2240	...
Švihov u Klatov........ d.	...	|	0818	...	0919	1018	...	1119	1218	...	1319	1418	1519	...	...	1618	...	1719	1818	...	1919	2019	2156	2319	...
Klatovy .... a.	...	0751	0827	...	0929	1027	...	1129	1227	...	1329	1427	1529	...	...	1627	...	1729	1827	...	1929	2029	2208	2329	...
Klatovy .... d.	...	0803	0840	...	▬	*1040*	...	▬	*1240*	...	▬	1440	▬	1535	...	*1640*	...	▬	*1840*	...	▬	*2035*	▬	▬	...
Špičák .... d.	...	0849	0929	...	...	*1128*	...	...	*1328*	...	...	1529	...	1629	...	*1728*	...	...	*1928*	...	...	*2122*	...	...	...
Železná Ruda centrum........ d.	...	0856	0936	...	...	*1134*	...	...	*1334*	...	...	1536	...	1636	...	*1734*	...	...	*1934*	...	...	*2129*	...	...	...
Železná Ruda-Alžbětín ☆ 🏛. a.	...	0900	0940	...	...	*1138*	...	...	*1338*	...	...	1540	...	1640	...	*1738*	...	...	*1938*	...	...	*2133*	...	...	...
Bayerisch Eisenstein ☆ 🏛. d.	0841	...	...	0944	1041	...	1144	1241	...	1344	1444	...	1544	...	1644	...	1744	1841	...	1944	2041	...	2141	...	...
Zwiesel (Bay) .... d.	0859	...	...	0959	1059	...	1159	1259	...	1359	1459	...	1559	...	1659	...	1759	1859	...	1959	2059	...	2204j	...	...
Regen........ d.	0909	...	...	1009	1109	...	1209	1309	...	1409	1509	...	1609	...	1709	...	1809	1909	...	2009	2109	...	2214	...	...
Gotteszell .... d.	0922	...	...	1022	1122	...	1222	1322	...	1422	1522	...	1622	...	1722	...	1822	1922	...	2022	2122	...	2228	...	...
Deggendorf Hbf .... d.	0945	...	...	1045	1145	...	1245	1345	...	1445	1545	...	1645	...	1745	...	1845	1945	...	2045	2145	...	2251	2329	0038
Plattling .... a.	0954	...	...	1054	1154	...	1254	1354	...	1454	1554	...	1654	...	1754	...	1854	1954	...	2054	2154	...	2300	2339	0049

BRANCH LINE SERVICES ⊠

ZWIESEL - GRAFENAU *32 km.* Journey time: 47 minutes.
From Zwiesel (Bay) at 0622 Ⓐ **t**, 0802, 0902 and hourly until 2102.
From Grafenau at 0628 Ⓐ **t**, 0808, 0908 and hourly until 2108.

ZWIESEL - BODENMAIS *15 km.* Journey time: 20 minutes.
From Zwiesel at 0624 Ⓐ **t**, 0802 Ⓐ **t**, 0902, 1002 and hourly until 2002; then 2202.
From Bodenmais at 0558 Ⓐ **t**, 0649 Ⓐ **t**, 0829, 0929 and hourly until 2029.

GOTTESZELL - VIECHTACH *25 km.* Journey time: 40 – 47 minutes.
From Gotteszell at 0450 Ⓐ **t**, 0601 Ⓐ **t**, 0658 Ⓐ **t**, 0739 ⑥, 0751 Ⓐ **t**, 0939, 1039 ⚒ **t**, 1139, 1239 ⚒ **t**, 1336 Ⓐ **t**, 1339 Ⓒ **z**, 1439, 1539, 1639, 1739, 1839, 1939, 2039 and 2245.
From Viechtach at 0351 Ⓐ **t**, 0451 Ⓐ **t**, 0600 Ⓐ **t**, 0629 ⑥, 0656 Ⓐ **t**, 0837, 0937 ⚒ **t**, 1037, 1137 ⚒ **t**, 1237, 1328 Ⓐ **t**, 1337 Ⓒ **z**, 1437, 1537, 1637, 1737, 1837, 1937 and 2137.

B – Ⓒ to Apr. 23 (also Apr. 6); runs daily Dec. 23 - Feb. 5, Feb. 11 – 19, Mar. 4 – 12.
C – Ⓒ (also Apr. 6); runs daily Dec. 23 - Feb. 5, Feb. 11 – 19, Mar. 4 – 12.
D – Change trains at Zwiesel on Ⓐ (not Jan. 6).
E – Ⓒ from Apr. 29.

j – Arrives 2154.
t – Not Jan. 6.
z – Also Jan. 6.

◇ – Also conveys 🚃.
¶ – Train number **743** on Ⓒ.
⊠ – *Waldbahn* services are operated by Die Länderbahn.
☆ – Bayerisch Eisenstein (German) / Železná Ruda-Alžbětín (Czech) is the same station.

930 STUTTGART - MÜNCHEN

Regional journeys Stuttgart - Ulm are also possible via Wendlingen (see Table **936**).

km		ICE 619	ICE 1119		ICE 699	ICE 1061	RE 4243	ICE 1561	ICE 1561	ICE 561	RE 4205	ICE 991	ICE 911	RE 4207	RJ 897	EC 217	ICE 511	ICE 267	RE 4209	ICE 591	ICE 913	RE 4211	EC 113	ICE 513	ICE 563
		U H	①–⑤ Y		✕♦	Ⓐ ✕	Ⓐt	Ⓐd	①g	Ⓐ ✕	Ⓐt	A✕	⚒ ✕		✕♦	🍷♦	✕	✕♦		G✕	⚒ ✕		✕♦	M✕	S✕
	Dortmund Hbf **800** d.	2236**p**	...	...	...	...	...	...	...	...	...	...	...	...	...	...	...	...	...	...	0547	...	...	0636	...
	Köln Hbf **800 910** d.	2355**p**	...	...	...	...	...	...	...	...	...	...	...	...	...	...	0549	...	...	...	0711•	...	...	0755	...
	Frankfurt (Main) Hbf **912** d.	0117	0117	...	0225	...	...	...	...	...	...	...	0603	...	0554	...	|	...	...	0750	|	...	0820	|	...
	Frankfurt Flughafen + **912** d.	0056*	|	...	0246	...	...	...	...	...	...	...	|	...	|	...	0651	...	...	|	0809	...	|	0851	...
	Mannheim Hbf **912** d.	0204	0204	...	0325	...	...	...	...	...	...	0629	|	...	|	0711	0731	...	...	0830	0843	...	|	0931	1002
	Heidelberg Hbf **912** d.	0219	0219	...	0340	...	...	...	...	...	...	|	|	...	0652	|	|	...	...	|	|	...	0913	|	|
	Karlsruhe Hbf **931** d.	|	|	...	|	0453	...	...	...	0600	...	|	|	...	|	|	|	0805	...	|	|	...	|	|	|
0	**Stuttgart** Hbf **936** d.	0339	0339	...	0512	0552	0539	...	0558	0650	0639	0715	0728	0736	0744	0758	0814	0851	0839	0915	0928	0937	0958	1014	1051
22	Plochingen **936** d.	|	|	...	|	|	0556	...	0613	|	0656	|	|	0754	|	|	|	|	0856	|	|	0956	|	|	|
42	Göppingen d.	|	|	...	|	⊙	0607	...	|	⊙	0707	⊙	⊙	0807	|	|	|	⊙	0907	⊙	⊙	1007	|	|	⊙
61	Geislingen (Steige) d.	|	|	...	|	|	0619	...	|	|	0719	|	|	0819	|	|	|	|	0919	|	|	1019	|	|	|
94	**Ulm** Hbf **945** d.	0440	0440	...	0608	0638	0644	0705	0705	0736	0747**r**	0801	0812	0847**r**	0902	0855	0912	0936	0947**r**	1000	1012	1047**r**	1056	1112	1136
	Friedrichshafen Stadt **933** a.	|	|	...	|	|	0755	|	|	|	0852	|	|	0952	1003	|	|	|	1052	|	|	1152	|	|	|
118	Günzburg **945** d.	0455	0455	...	0623	0652	...	0724	0724	|	...	0816	|	...	...	0910	|	|	...	|	|	...	1110	|	|
180	**Augsburg** Hbf **905** d.	0532	0532	...	0655	0723	...	0755	0755	0824	...	0848	0855	...	...	0941	0955	1024	...	1043	1055	...	1141	1155	1224
235	München Pasing **905** a.	0553	0553	...	0717	0743	...	0817	0817	0847	...	0908	0919	...	...	|	1017	1047	...	1104	1117	...	|	1217	1247
242	**München** Hbf **905** a.	0603	0603	...	0728	0754	...	0826	0826	0858	...	0918	0928	...	...	1010	1026	1056	...	1114	1126	...	1210	1226	1257
	Salzburg Hbf **890** a.	...	...	...	...	...	...	...	...	...	...	...	...	...	...	1159	...	...	...	...	...	...	1359	...	...

	RE 4213	ICE 593	ICE 915	RE 4215	EC 115	ICE 515	ICE 565	RE 4217	IC 119	ICE 595	ICE 917	RE 4219	EC 219	ICE 517	ICE 567	RE 4221	IC 2013	ICE 597	ICE 919	RE 4223	EC 117	ICE 519	ICE 569	RE 4225	ICE 1219
		B✕	✕		🍷♦	H✕	✕		♦	B✕	D✕		🍷♦	H✕	✕		🍷♦	B✕	✕		🍷♦	H✕	✕		✕♦
Dortmund Hbf **800** d.	...	...	0756	...	...	0835	...	...	0751	...	...	...	...	1035	...	...	0949	...	...	...	...	1236	...	...	...
Köln Hbf **800 910** d.	...	...	0911•	...	0817	0955	...	...	0917	...	1116•	...	...	1155	...	...	1117	...	...	...	...	1355	...	...	...
Frankfurt (Main) Hbf **912** d.	...	0950	|	...	|	|	...	...	|	1150	|	...	1220	|	...	...	|	1350	...	...	1420	|	...	...	1550
Frankfurt Flughafen + **912** d.	...	|	1009	...	|	1051	...	...	|	|	1209	...	|	1251	...	...	|	|	...	...	|	1451	...	...	|
Mannheim Hbf **912** d.	...	1030	1043	...	1102	1131	...	...	1154	1230	1243	...	|	1331	...	...	1354	1430	...	...	|	1531	...	...	1630
Heidelberg Hbf **912** d.	...	|	|	...	|	|	...	...	1206	|	|	...	1313	|	...	...	1406	|	...	...	1513	|	...	...	|
Karlsruhe Hbf **931** d.	...	|	|	...	|	|	1205	...	|	|	|	...	|	|	1405	...	|	|	...	...	|	|	1605	...	|
Stuttgart Hbf **936** d.	1039	1115	1128	1139	1158	1214	1251	1237	1257	1315	1328	1339	1358	1414	1451	1439	1459	1515	1528	1537	1559	1614	1651	1639	1715
Plochingen **936** d.	1056	|	|	1156	|	|	|	1256	|	|	|	1356	|	|	|	1456	1519	|	|	1556	|	|	|	1656	|
Göppingen d.	1107	⊙	⊙	1207	|	|	⊙	1307	1325	⊙	⊙	1407	|	|	⊙	1507	1533	⊙	⊙	1607	|	|	⊙	1707	⊙
Geislingen (Steige) d.	1119	|	|	1219	|	|	|	1319	|	|	|	1419	|	|	|	1519	|	|	|	1619	|	|	|	1719	|
Ulm Hbf **945** d.	1147**r**	1200	1212	1247**r**	1256	1312	1336	1347**r**	1411**j**	1400	1412	1447**r**	1456	1512	1536	1547**r**	1614	1600	1612	1647**r**	1656	1712	1736	1747**r**	1800
Friedrichshafen Stadt **933** a.	1252	|	|	1352	|	|	|	1452	1516**k**	|	|	1552	|	|	|	1652	...	|	|	1752	|	|	|	1852	|
Günzburg **945** d.	...	|	|	...	1311	|	|	...	...	|	|	...	1510	|	|	...	...	|	|	...	1710	|	|	...	|
Augsburg Hbf **905** d.	...	1243	1255	...	1341	1355	1424	...	...	1443	1455	...	1541	1555	1624	...	...	1643	1655	...	1741	1755	1824	...	1843
München Pasing **905** a.	...	1304	1317	...	|	1417	1447	...	...	1504	1518	...	|	1617	1647	...	...	1704	1717	...	|	1817	1847	...	1904
München Hbf **905** a.	...	1313	1326	...	1410	1426	1458	...	...	1513	1527	...	1610	1626	1656	...	...	1716	1726	...	1810	1826	1856	...	1913
Salzburg Hbf **890** a.	...	...	...	...	1559	...	...	...	...	...	...	...	1759	...	...	...	...	...	...	...	1959	...	...	...	...

	ICE 1011	RE 4227	IC 1291	ICE 611	ICE 1069	RE 4229	ICE 691	ICE 1013	TGV 9577	RE 4231	ICE 1099	ICE 613	RE 4233	NJ 237	ICE 693	TGV 9579	ICE 1015	RE 4235	IC 182	ICE 615	RE 4237	ICE 695	ICE 895		RE 4239
	✕		🍷	H✕	✕		B✕	✕	Ⓑ P🍷		Ⓑb ✕	H✕	L	Ⓡ ♦	Ⓑb B✕	⑥ P🍷	Ⓑ ✕		Ⓑb T	H		Ⓒ B	⑤		
Dortmund Hbf **800** d.	1349**q**	...	...	1435	...	...	...	1549	...	...	...	1635	...	...	...	...	1750	...	...	1835	...	...	...	...	...
Köln Hbf **800 910** d.	1511•	...	...	1555	...	...	...	1710•	...	...	...	1755	...	...	...	...	1911•	...	...	1955	...	...	...	...	...
Frankfurt (Main) Hbf **912** d.	|	...	1620	|	...	...	1750	|	...	...	1819	|	...	...	1950	...	|	...	...	|	...	2150	...	...	...
Frankfurt Flughafen + **912** d.	1609	...	|	1651	...	...	|	1809	...	...	|	1851	...	...	|	...	2009	...	...	2051	...	|	...	...	...
Mannheim Hbf **912** d.	1643	...	|	1731	...	...	1830	1842	...	...	|	1931	...	...	2030	...	2043	...	...	2131	...	2230	...	...	...
Heidelberg Hbf **912** d.	|	...	1713	|	...	...	|	|	...	...	1913	|	...	...	|	...	|	...	...	|	...	|	...	...	...
Karlsruhe Hbf **931** d.	|	...	|	|	1805	...	|	|	1827	...	|	|	...	...	|	2028	|	...	...	|	...	|	...	...	...
Stuttgart Hbf **936** d.	1728	1739	1758	1814	1857	1839	1915	1928	1920	1937	1958	2014	2039	2029	2115	2114	2128	2139	2143	2214	2239	2315	2315	...	2339
Plochingen **936** d.	|	1757	|	|	|	1856	|	|	|	1956	|	|	2056	|	|	|	|	2156	|	|	2256	|	|	...	2356
Göppingen d.	⊙	1808	|	|	⊙	1907	⊙	⊙	|	2007	|	|	2107	2113	⊙	|	⊙	2207	|	|	2307	⊙	|	...	0007
Geislingen (Steige) d.	|	1820	|	|	|	1919	|	|	|	2019	|	|	2119	|	|	|	|	2219	|	|	2319	|	|	...	0019
Ulm Hbf **945** d.	1812	1847**r**	1856	1912	1939	1947**r**	2000	2012	2023	2047**r**	2056	2112	2145	2153	2200	2212	2212	2242	2300	2312	2344	0000	0017	...	0042
Friedrichshafen Stadt **933** a.	|	1952	|	|	|	2052	|	|	|	2152	|	|	2251	|	|	|	|	...	|	|	...	|	|	...	...
Günzburg **945** d.	|	...	1910	|	|	...	|	|	|	...	2110	|	...	|	|	|	|	...	|	|	...	0016	0033	...	...
Augsburg Hbf **905** d.	1855	...	1941	1955	2024	...	2043	2055	2107	...	2142	2155	...	2302	2243	2258	2255	...	2344	2355	...	0048	0105	...	...
München Pasing **905** a.	1918	...	|	2017	2047	...	2104	2117	|	...	2204	2217	...	|	2304	|	2317	...	0005	0018	...	0109	0127	...	...
München Hbf **905** a.	1927	...	2010	2026	2056	...	2113	2126	2136	...	2213	2226	...	|	2313	2326	2326	...	0015	0028	...	0118	0135	...	...
Salzburg Hbf **890** a.	...	...	2202**b**	...	...	...	...	...	...	...	...	...	...	0128	...	...	...	...	...	...	...	...	...	...	...

Regional trains **ULM - MÜNCHEN** ⊡

	Ⓐt		Ⓐt	⊖	Ⓐt																				
Ulm Hbf d.	0447	0518	0546	0611	0646	0716	...	0819	0916	1018	1116	1219	1319	1419	1519	1619	1718	1818	1919	2018	2119	2219	...	2324	...
Günzburg d.	0507	0538	0607	0630	0706	0735	...	0839	0934	1038	1134	1239	1338	1439	1537	1639	1737	1839	1937	2041	2139	2241	...	2342	...
Augsburg Hbf a.	0604	0635	0704	0723	0804	0834	...	0933	1033	1133	1233	1333	1434	1533	1634	1733	1837	1933	2034	2133	2234	2336	...	...	...
Augsburg Hbf **905** d.	0608	0638	0708	0737	0808	0838	...	*0938*	1038	*1138*	1238	*1338*	1438	*1538*	1638	*1738*	1838	*1938*	2035	*2139*	2237	2349	...	...	...
München Pasing **905** a.	0648	0713	0750	0812	0842	0915	...	*1013*	1112	*1213*	1313	*1412*	1514	*1613*	1713	*1812*	1914	*2012*	2113	*2224*	2313	0030	...	...	...
München Hbf **905** a.	0656	0720	0758	0819	0850	0923	...	*1020*	1121	*1220*	1320	*1420*	1521	*1620*	1722	*1821*	1921	*2020*	2120	*2231*	2320	0037	...	...	...

Local *RB* trains **AUGSBURG - INGOLSTADT**. 2nd class only. *67 km*. Journey time: 60–69 minutes. Operator Bayerische Regiobahn.
From Augsburg Hbf at 0537, 0644, 0745, 0843, 0945, 1046, 1145, 1246, 1345, 1442, 1545, 1646, 1745, 1838, 1946, 2046, 2145, 2245 and 2359.

♦ – **NOTES** (LISTED BY TRAIN NUMBER)

113 – BLAUER ENZIAN – [12] ✕ Frankfurt - Salzburg - Villach - Klagenfurt; [12] Frankfurt - Villach (**213**) - Ljubljana - Zagreb.
115 – WÖRTHERSEE – [12] 🍷 Münster - Köln - Koblenz - Salzburg - Villach - Klagenfurt.
117 – SALZACH – [12] 🍷 Frankfurt - Salzburg - Villach - Klagenfurt.
119 – BODENSEE – [12] Dortmund - Köln - Koblenz - Ulm - Lindau - Bregenz - Innsbruck.
217 – DACHSTEIN – [12] 🍷 Saarbrücken - München - Salzburg - Bischofshofen - Selzthal - Graz.
219 – CHIEMGAU – [12] 🍷 Frankfurt - München - Salzburg - Bischofshofen - Selzthal - Graz.
237 – 🛏 1, 2 cl., ▬ 2 cl. and [2] Stuttgart - München - Villach - Venezia. Conveys 🛏 1, 2 cl., ▬ 2 cl. and [2] (*EN* **50237** – KÁLMÁN IMRE) Stuttgart - Wien - Budapest; 🛏 1, 2 cl., ▬ 2 cl. and [2] (*EN* **40237** – LISINSKI) Stuttgart - Villach - Jesenice 🏛 - Ljubljana - Zagreb.
267 – BADEN-KURIER – [12] ✕ (Basel ⚒ -) Karlsruhe - München.
699 – [12] Hamburg - Berlin - Leipzig - Erfurt - Frankfurt - München. ✕ Stuttgart - München.
897 – [12] ✕ Frankfurt - Ulm - Lindau - Bregenz (**867**) - Innsbruck - Wien.
1219 – [12] ✕ Berlin - Frankfurt - München (- Innsbruck ⑤⑥).
2013 – ALLGÄU – [12] and 🍷 Dortmund - Köln - Koblenz - Ulm - Kempten - Oberstdorf. Does not run Dortmund - Stuttgart Jan. 5 - Mar. 31.

A – From Wiesbaden (Table **912**).
B – From Berlin via Leipzig and Erfurt (Table **850**).
D – From Düsseldorf (Table **910**).
G – From Hamburg (Table **900**).
H – From Hamburg (Table **800**).
L – To Lindau (Table **933**).
M – From Münster (Table **800**).
P – [12] and 🍷 Paris - Strasbourg - München. Ⓡ for international journeys.
S – From Saarbrücken (Table **919**).
T – From Zürich via Singen (Table **940**).
U – Daily until Jan. 9; ⑥⑦ from Jan. 14.
Y – ①–⑤ from Jan. 10.

b – Ⓑ (not Dec. 25).
d – Not Dec. 28–30, Jan. 3–6.
g – ① (also Dec. 27; not Dec. 26).
j – Arrives 1404.
k – Not Jan. 9–20, Feb. 13 - Mar. 10.
p – Previous day.
q – ①②③④⑥ (also Dec. 25; not Dec. 26).
r – Arrives 4–5 minutes earlier.
t – Not Jan. 6.

* – Calls at Frankfurt Flughafen before Frankfurt (Main) Hbf.
• – Köln **Messe/Deutz**.
⊡ – Operated by Go-Ahead Bayern.
⊖ – Change trains at Augsburg on † (also Jan. 6).
⊙ – Via high-speed line.

MÜNCHEN - STUTTGART 930

Regional journeys Ulm - Stuttgart are also possible via Wendlingen (see Table **936**).

km ⊙		*ICE* 618		*IC* 2460		*ICE* 616	*RE* 4200		*RE* 4202	*ICE* 1068	*ICE* 614	*ICE* 1098	*RE* 4204	*NJ* 236	*ICE* 1012	*ICE* 692	*TGV* 9576	*RE* 4206		*ICE* 612	*IC* 1296	*RE* 4208	*ICE* 1010	*ICE* 690	*RE* 4210
				①–⑥			Ⓐt		Ⓐt	⚒		⚒		Ⓡ	⚒						①–⑥				
		H		n		H				✕	H✕	✕	L	♦	✕	B✕	P🍷			H✕	e🍷		✕	B✕	
	Salzburg Hbf **890** d.	...	...	...	...	...	...	...	...	...	...	...	...	0405	...	...	...	...	...	...	0543b	...	...	...	...
0	**München** Hbf **905** d.	0001	...	0237	...	0332	...	...	...	0500	0533	0544	...	|	0626	0642	0651	...	...	0728	0746	...	0828	0846	...
7	München Pasing **905** d.	0008	...	0246	...	0340	...	...	...	0508	0541	0553	...	|	0635	0651	|	...	...	0736	|	...	0837	0855	...
62	**Augsburg** Hbf **905** d.	0032	...	0313	...	0404	...	...	...	0535	0604	0616	...	0648	0700	0713	0721	...	...	0801	0815	...	0901	0918	...
124	Günzburg **945** d.	0103	...	|	...	|	...	...	...	|	|	0648	...	|	|	|	|	...	...	|	0848	...	|	|	...
	Friedrichshafen Stadt **933** d.	|	...	|	...	|	...	...	0449	|	|	|	0604	|	|	|	|	0704	...	|	|	0806	|	|	0905
148	**Ulm** Hbf **945** d.	0117	...	0354	...	0447	0503	...	0602	0619	0647	0703	0715	0738	0746	0758	0805	0815	...	0847	0902	0915	0946	1001	1015
	Geislingen (Steige) d.	|	...	|	...	|	0533	...	0629	|	|	|	0738	|	|	|	|	0838	...	|	|	0938	|	|	1038
	Göppingen d.	|	...	|	...	|	0548	...	0647	⊙	|	|	0751	0814	⊙	⊙	|	0851	...	|	|	0951	⊙	⊙	1051
	Plochingen **936** d.	|	...	|	...	|	0602	...	0703	|	|	|	0804	|	|	|	|	0903	...	|	|	1003	|	|	1103
237	**Stuttgart** Hbf **936** a.	0216	...	0507	...	0545	0620	...	0720	0704	0745	0759	0821	0837	0832	0844	0901	0920	...	0945	0959	1020	1031	1043	1120
	Karlsruhe Hbf **931** a.	|	...	...	...	|	...	...	...	0753	|	|	...	...	|	|	0951	...	...	|	|	...	|	|	...
	Heidelberg Hbf **912** a.	0335	...	...	...	|	...	...	...	...	|	0844	...	...	|	|	...	...	...	|	1044	...	|	|	...
	Mannheim Hbf **912** a.	0355	...	...	...	0628	...	...	...	...	0828	|	...	...	0918	0929	...	...	...	1028	|	...	1118	1129	...
	Frankfurt Flughafen ✈ **912** a.	0457*	...	...	...	0706	...	...	...	...	0906	|	...	...	0951	|	...	...	...	1106	|	...	1151	|	...
	Frankfurt (Main) Hbf **912** a.	0439	...	...	...	|	...	...	...	...	|	0940	...	...	|	1008	...	...	...	|	1140	...	|	1208	...
	Köln Hbf **800 910** a.	0603	...	...	...	0804	...	...	...	...	1004	...	...	...	1048x	...	...	...	...	1205	...	...	1248•	...	...
	Dortmund Hbf **800** a.	0722	...	...	...	0922	...	...	...	...	1121	...	...	...	1205h	...	...	...	...	1321	...	...	1404e	...	...

	ICE 568	*ICE* 610	*IC* 1290	*RE* 4212	*ICE* 918	*ICE* 1218	*IC* 2012	*RE* 4214	*ICE* 566	*ICE* 518	*EC* 218	*RE* 4216 4242	*ICE* 916	*ICE* 596	*IC* 118	*RE* 4218	*ICE* 564	*ICE* 516	*EC* 114	*RE* 4220	*ICE* 914	*ICE* 594	*RE* 4222	*ICE* 562	*ICE* 514
	✕	H✕	🍷		✕	✕♦	🍷♦		✕	H✕	🍷♦		✕	B✕	♦		✕	H✕	🍷♦		✕	B✕		S✕	H✕
Salzburg Hbf **890** d.	...	...	0800	...	...	...	...	...	...	...	1000	...	...	...	...	...	...	...	1200	...	...	...	...	...	...
München Hbf **905** d.	0903	0928	0947	...	1028j	1047	...	...	1102	1128	1147	...	1228	1245	...	...	1303	1328	1347	...	1428	1447	...	1502	1528
München Pasing **905** d.	0911	0936	|	...	1037j	1056	...	...	1110	1136	|	...	1237	1254	...	...	1311	1336	|	...	1437	1456	...	1511	1536
Augsburg Hbf **905** d.	0935	1001	1015	...	1101	1118	...	...	1135	1201	1215	...	1301	1318	...	...	1335	1401	1415	...	1501	1518	...	1535	1601
Günzburg **945** d.	|	|	1048	...	|	|	...	...	|	|	1248	...	|	|	...	...	|	|	1448	...	|	|	...	|	|
Friedrichshafen Stadt **933** d.	|	|	|	1005	|	|	...	1105	|	|	|	1203r	|	|	1235k	1305	|	|	|	1405	|	|	1505	|	|
Ulm Hbf **945** d.	1019	1047	1103	1115	1146	1201	1157	1215	1219	1247	1303	1315	1346	1401	1354	1415	1419	1447	1503	1515	1546	1601	1615	1619	1647
Geislingen (Steige) d.	|	|	|	1138	|	|	|	1238	|	|	|	1338	|	|	|	1438	|	|	|	1538	|	|	1638	|	|
Göppingen d.	⊙	|	|	1151	⊙	⊙	|	1251	⊙	|	|	1351	⊙	⊙	1433	1452	⊙	|	|	1551	⊙	⊙	1651	⊙	|
Plochingen **936** d.	|	|	|	1203	|	|	|	1303	|	|	|	1403	|	|	|	1503	|	|	|	1604	|	|	1703	|	|
Stuttgart Hbf **936** a.	1102	1145	1159	1220	1232	1243	1259	1320	1302	1345	1359	1422	1432	1443	1459	1520	1502	1545	1559	1622	1631	1643	1720	1702	1745
Karlsruhe Hbf **931** a.	1152	|	|	...	|	|	|	...	1352	|	|	...	...	|	|	...	1552	|	|	...	|	|	...	|	|
Heidelberg Hbf **912** a.	...	|	1244	...	|	|	1353	...	...	|	1444	...	...	|	1553	...	...	|	|	...	|	|	...	|	|
Mannheim Hbf **912** a.	...	1228	|	...	1318	1329	1406	...	...	1428	|	...	...	1529	1606	...	...	1628	1655	...	1718	1729	...	1746	1828
Frankfurt Flughafen ✈ **912** a.	...	1306	|	...	1351	|	|	...	...	1506	|	...	...	|	|	...	...	1706	|	...	1751	|	...	...	1906
Frankfurt (Main) Hbf **912** a.	...	|	1340	...	|	1408	|	...	...	|	1540	...	...	1608	|	...	...	|	|	...	|	1808	...	...	|
Köln Hbf **800 910** a.	...	1404	...	...	1448•	...	1643	...	...	1605	...	...	...	...	1842	...	...	1804	1943	...	1848•	...	...	...	2004
Dortmund Hbf **800** a.	...	1521	...	...	1606	...	...	...	...	1722	...	...	...	...	...	...	...	1921	2104	...	2005	...	...	...	2121

	EC 112	*RE* 4224	*IC* 1910	*ICE* 912	*ICE* 592	*IC* 1910	*RE* 4226 4238	*ICE* 266	*ICE* 1560	*ICE* 512	*EC* 216	*RJ* 890	*RE* 4228	*ICE* 910	*ICE* 590	*RE* 4230	*ICE* 560	*ICE* 510	*RE* 4232		*ICE* 990	*RE* 4234		*ICE* 698	*RE* 4236
			⑦w			⑦w			①–④					Ⓑb			Ⓑd								
	✕♦		🍷	✕	A✕	🍷		✕♦	u✕	M✕	🍷♦	✕♦		✕	✕		✕	✕			✕			♦	
Salzburg Hbf **890** d.	1400	...	...	...	...	...	...	...	...	...	1600	...	...	...	...	...	...	...	...	...	...	...	...	...	...
München Hbf **905** d.	1547	...	1614	1627	1645	...	...	1658	1703o	1728	1747	...	...	1828	1847	...	1901	1928	...	...	2044	...	...	2151	...
München Pasing **905** d.	|	...	1623	1636	1654	...	...	1706	1725	1736	|	...	...	1837	1856	...	1909	1936	...	...	2053	...	...	|	...
Augsburg Hbf **905** d.	1615	...	1651	1701	1718	...	...	1733	1749	1801	1815	...	...	1901	1918	...	1933	2001	...	...	2115	...	...	2218	...
Günzburg **945** d.	1648	...	1724	|	|	...	...	|	1819	|	1848	...	...	|	|	...	2005	|	...	...	2145	...	...	2249	...
Friedrichshafen Stadt **933** d.	|	1605	|	|	|	...	1703r	|	|	|	|	1802	1808	|	|	1905	|	|	2005	...	|	2105	...	|	2205
Ulm Hbf **945** d.	1703	1715	1740	1746	1801	...	1815	1818	1836	1847	1903	1910	1915	1946	2001	2015	2019	2047	2115	...	2201	2215	...	2303	2315
Geislingen (Steige) d.	|	1738	1809	|	|	←	1838	|	...	|	|	|	1938	|	|	2038	|	|	2138	...	|	2238	...	|	2338
Göppingen d.	|	1751	1823	⊙	⊙	1827	1851	⊙	...	|	|	|	1951	⊙	⊙	2051	⊙	|	2151	...	⊙	2251	...	|	2351
Plochingen **936** d.	|	1803	→	|	|	|	1904	|	...	|	|	|	2005	|	|	2103	|	|	2203	...	|	2303	...	|	0003
Stuttgart Hbf **936** a.	1759	1820	...	1832	1843	1859	1921	1902	...	1945	1959	2005	2023	2032	2043	2120	2103	2145	2220	...	2243	2320	...	0001	0020
Karlsruhe Hbf **931** a.	|	...	...	|	|	|	...	1952	...	|	|	|	...	|	|	...	2152	|	...	...	|	...	...	|	...
Heidelberg Hbf **912** a.	1844	...	...	|	|	1953	...	...	...	|	|	2053	...	|	|	...	...	|	...	...	|	...	...	0123	...
Mannheim Hbf **912** a.	|	...	...	1918	1929	2006	...	...	...	2028	2047	|	...	2118	2129	...	...	2228	...	...	2329	...	...	0142	...
Frankfurt Flughafen ✈ **912** a.	|	...	...	1951	|	|	...	...	...	2106	...	|	...	2151	|	...	...	2306	...	...	|	...	...	0219	...
Frankfurt (Main) Hbf **912** a.	1940	...	...	|	2008	|	...	...	...	|	...	2152	...	|	2208	...	...	|	...	...	0008	...	...	0240	...
Köln Hbf **800 910** a.	...	...	...	2048•	...	2243	...	...	...	2206	...	...	...	2251	...	...	...	0007v	...	...	...	...	...	...	...
Dortmund Hbf **800** a.	...	...	...	2205	...	0002	...	...	...	...	...	...	...	...	...	...	...	...	...	...	...	...	...	...	...

Regional trains **MÜNCHEN - ULM** ⊡

		Ⓒz					⊖								†z	⚒t	Ⓐt		⊖			Ⓒz			
München Hbf d.	0006	0006	...	...	...	0633	0735	0834	*0935*	1035	*1135*	1235	*1335*	1435	*1535*	*1535*	1603	1633	1735	1835	*1935*	2035	2057	2159	2257
München Pasing d.	0014	0014	...	...	...	0641	0743	0842	*0943*	1043	*1143*	1243	*1343*	1443	*1543*	*1543*	1611	1641	1743	1843	*1943*	2043	2105	2207	2305
Augsburg Hbf a.	0053	0053	...	...	...	0719	0818	0918	*1018*	1118	*1219*	1319	*1419*	1518	*1619*	*1619*	1646	1717	1819	1918	*2019*	2118	2146	2246	2346
Augsburg Hbf d.	...	0054	...	0522	0622	0725	0825	0924	1025	1122	1222	1322	1425	1522	1622	1625	1649	1722	1825	1923	2025	2125	2149	2249	2351
Günzburg d.	...	0149	...	0622	0721	0821	0920	1022	1121	1222	1321	1422	1521	1623	1714	1720	1755	1836c	1921	2023	2121	2221	2257q	2350c	0047
Ulm Hbf a.	...	0208	...	0641	0740	0840	0939	1041	1140	1241	1340	1441	1540	1642	1733	1739	1814	1855	1940	2042	2140	2240	2316	0011	0106

Local *RB* trains **INGOLSTADT - AUGSBURG**. 2nd class only. *67 km*. Journey time: 57–67 minutes. Operator Bayerische Regiobahn.
From Ingolstadt Hbf at 0453 Ⓐ**t**, 0502 Ⓒ**z**, 0605, 0709, 0806, 0908 and hourly until 1608; then 1709 Ⓒ**z**, 1710 Ⓐ**t**, 1810, 1908, 2008 Ⓒ**z**, 2009 Ⓐ**t**, 2108 Ⓒ**z**, 2109 Ⓐ**t**, 2208 and 2308.

♦ – **NOTES** (LISTED BY TRAIN NUMBER)

112 – BLAUER ENZIAN – [12] ✕ Klagenfurt - Villach - Salzburg - Frankfurt; [12] Zagreb (**212**) - Ljubljana - Villach (**112**) - Frankfurt.
114 – WÖRTHERSEE – [12] 🍷 Klagenfurt - Villach - Salzburg - Mannheim - Koblenz - Köln - Dortmund.
118 – BODENSEE – [12] Innsbruck - Bregenz - Lindau - Ulm - Koblenz - Köln - Bochum.
216 – DACHSTEIN – [12] 🍷 Graz - Selzthal - Bischofshofen - Salzburg - München - Saarbrücken.
218 – CHIEMGAU – [12] 🍷 Graz - Selzthal - Bischofshofen - Salzburg - München - Frankfurt.
236 – 🛏 1, 2 cl., ▬ 2 cl. and [2] Venezia - Villach - München - Stuttgart. Conveys 🛏 1, 2 cl., ▬ 2 cl. and [2] (*EN* **50462** – KÁLMÁN IMRE) Budapest - Wien - Stuttgart; 🛏 1, 2 cl., ▬ 2 cl. and [2] (*EN* **414** – LISINSKI) Zagreb - Ljubljana - Jesenice ▦ - Villach - Stuttgart.
266 – BADEN-KURIER – [12] ✕ München - Karlsruhe (- Basel Ⓑ **b**).
698 – [12] München - Stuttgart - Frankfurt - Erfurt - Weimar - Halle - Berlin.
890 – [12] ✕ Wien (**860**) - Innsbruck - Bregenz (**890**) - Lindau - Ulm - Frankfurt.
1218 – [12] ✕ (Innsbruck ⑥⑦ -) München - Frankfurt - Berlin.
2012 – ALLGÄU – [12] and 🍷 Oberstdorf - Ulm - Stuttgart - Köln - Bochum. Does not run Stuttgart - Bochum Jan. 6 - Apr. 1.

A – To Leipzig via Erfurt (Table **850**).
B – To Berlin via Erfurt and Leipzig (Table **850**).
H – To Hamburg (Table **800**).
L – From Lindau on Ⓐ**t** (Table **933**).
M – To Münster (Table **800**).
P – [12] and 🍷 München - Strasbourg - Paris. Ⓡ for international journeys.
S – To Saarbrücken (Table **919**).

b – Not Dec. 25.
c – Arrives 5–6 minutes earlier.
d – Also Dec. 24; not Dec. 25.
e – ①–⑥ (also Dec. 25; not Dec. 26).
h – Not ⑤.
j – On ⑥⑦ departs München Hbf 1030 and does not call at München Pasing.
k – Not Jan. 9–20, Feb. 13 - Mar. 10.
n – Not Mar. 27.
o – München **Ost**.
q – Arrives 2244.
r – 2 minutes later on Ⓒ (also Jan. 6).
t – Not Jan. 6.
u – Not Dec. 23 - Jan. 6.
v – Frankfurt Flughafen - Köln daily until Jan. 8, ⑤⑥ from Jan. 13.
w – Also Dec. 26; not Dec. 25, Jan. 8 - Apr. 2.
x – Köln **Messe/Deutz**. Arrives 1041 on ⑥.
z – Also Jan. 6.

* – Calls at Frankfurt Flughafen after Frankfurt (Main) Hbf.
• – Köln **Messe/Deutz**.
⊖ – Change trains at Augsburg on Ⓒ (also Jan. 6).
⊡ – Operated by Go-Ahead Bayern.
⊙ – Via high-speed line.

931 KARLSRUHE - STUTTGART

See Table **32** for full details of international *TGV* services from / to Paris. See note ▷ for connecting regional trains Bruchsal - Mühlacker and v.v.

km ◧		*ICE* **1061** Ⓐ	◇ Ⓐt	*ICE* **561** Ⓐ ✕	*IC* **1961** ⑥	◇	◇ Ⓐ t	*IC* **2216** Ⓐ O🍷	*ICE* **1063** Ⓐ	*IC* **2063**	◇	*ICE* **267** B✕	◇	◇	*IC* **2065**	◇	*ICE* **1065**	◇	◇	*IC* **2067**	◇	*ICE* **565** ✕	◇	◇	*IC* **2069**	◇
0	**Karlsruhe** Hbf .... d.	0453	0531	0600	0554	0602	0631	0637	0658	0707	0731	0805	0806	0831	0906	0933	1005	1006	1031	1106	1131	1205	1206	1231	1306	1332
	Pforzheim .... d.	|	0554	|	|	0624	0655	|	|	0726	0754	|	0828	0854	0926	0955	|	1028	1054	1126	1154	|	1228	1254	1326	1355
21	Bruchsal .... ▷ d.	0509	|	0616	0617	|	|	0655	0719	|	|	0817	|	|	|	|	1019	|	|	|	|	1217	|	|	|	|
	Mühlacker .... ▷ d.	|	0602	|	|	0633	0703	|	|	0737	0802	|	0836	0902	0937	1003	|	1036	1102	1137	1202	|	1236	1302	1337	1403
58	Vaihingen (Enz) .... d.	0526	0608	|	|	0639	0712	|	|	0746	0808	|	0842	0910	|	1010	|	1042	1108	1144	1208	|	1242	1310	|	1408
87	**Stuttgart** Hbf .... a.	0545	0625	0644	0649	0655	0733	0727	0748	0802	0826	0845	0900	0928	1002	1027	1049	1100	1125	1202	1225	1245	1300	1328	1358	1425
	Nürnberg Hbf **925** .. a.	|	...	|	...	...	...	...	...	1018	...	|	...	...	1218	...	...	...	...	1418	...	|	...	...	1618	...
	München Hbf **930** .. a.	0754	...	0858	...	...	...	...	...	...	...	1056	...	...	...	...	...	...	...	...	...	1458	...	...	...	...

	ICE **567** ✕	◇	◇	*IC* **2161** L	◇	*ICE* **569** ✕	◇	◇	*IC* **2163**	◇	*ICE* **1069** ✕	◇	*TGV* **9577** Ⓑ P🍷	◇	*IC* **2165**	◇	*IC* **2369** ①-④ m	*IC* **2169** ⑦w	◇	*TGV* **9579** ⑥ P🍷	◇	*IC* **2167**	◇	◇	◇	◇
Karlsruhe Hbf .... d.	1405	1406	1431	1506	1531	1605	1606	1633	1706	1731	1805	1806	1827	1832	1906	1931	2005	2006	2006	2028	2033	2106	2133	2205	2231	2312
Pforzheim .... d.	|	1428	1455	1526	1554	|	1628	1655	1726	1754	|	1828	|	1855	1926	1954	|	|	2029	|	2055	2126	2154	2228	2254	2338
Bruchsal .... ▷ d.	1417	|	|	|	|	1617	|	|	|	|	1817	|	|	|	|	|	2018	2019	|	|	|	|	|	|	|	|
Mühlacker .... ▷ d.	|	1436	1502	1537	1603	|	1636	1703	1737	1802	|	1836	|	1903	1937	2002	|	|	2037	|	2103	2137	2202	2236	2302	2346
Vaihingen (Enz) .... d.	|	1442	1508	1544	1610	|	1642	1709	1745	1808	|	1842	|	1909	1945	2010	|	|	2042	|	2109	2145	2210	2245	2308	2352
Stuttgart Hbf .... a.	1445	1500	1525	1602	1625	1645	1700	1727	1803	1824	1851	1900	1904	1925	2003	2027	2047	2056	2059	2104	2125	2202	2225	2300	2325	0021
Nürnberg Hbf **925** ... a.	|	...	...	1818	...	|	...	...	2018	...	|	...	|	...	2218**b**	...	...	...	...	|	...	0018‡	...	...	...	...
München Hbf **930** ... a.	1656	...	...	...	...	1856	...	...	...	...	2056	...	2136	...	...	...	...	...	...	2326	...	...	...	...	...	...

km ◐		*IC* **2326** Ⓐ D	◇ Ⓐ t	◇ Ⓒ z	*IC* **2368** Ⓐt	◇ Ⓐ t	◇ A	*ICE* **1068** ⚒ ✕	◇	*IC* **2164**	◇	◇	*TGV* **9576** P🍷	◇	*IC* **2162**	◇	◇	*ICE* **568** ✕	◇	*IC* **2160**	◇	◇	*ICE* **566** ✕	◇	*IC* **2068** L	◇
	München Hbf **930** .. d.	...	...	...	...	...	...	0500	...	...	...	...	0651	...	...	...	...	0903	...	...	...	...	1102	...	...	...
	Nürnberg Hbf **925** .. d.	...	...	...	...	...	...	|	...	0538t	...	...	|	...	0741	...	...	|	...	0942	...	...	|	...	1142	...
0	**Stuttgart** Hbf .... d.	0226	0529	0559	0602	0632	0659	0710	0732	0759	0831	0900	0911	0932	0959	1032	1100	1112	1132	1159	1232	1300	1309	1332	1358	1430
39	Vaihingen (Enz) .... d.	|	0548	0616	|	0648	0716	|	0748	0816	0848	0916	|	0948	1016	1048	1116	|	1148	1216	1248	1316	|	1348	1416	1446
47	Mühlacker .... ▷ d.	|	0554	0622	|	0654	0722	|	0754	0824	0854	0922	|	0954	1023	1054	1122	|	1154	1223	1254	1322	|	1354	1423	1454
79	Bruchsal .... ▷ d.	|	|	|	0640	|	|	0739	|	|	|	|	|	|	|	|	|	1140	|	|	|	|	1340	|	|	|
60	Pforzheim .... d.	0306	0603	0631	|	0703	0731	|	0803	0833	0903	0931	|	1003	1032	1103	1131	|	1203	1232	1303	1331	|	1403	1432	1503
86	**Karlsruhe** Hbf .... a.	0327	0627	0653	0651	0725	0753	0753	0825	0853	0926	0953	0951	1025	1053	1125	1153	1152	1225	1253	1327	1353	1352	1425	1453	1526

	◇	*ICE* **564** ✕	◇	*IC* **2066**	◇	*IC* **2044** Ⓐ O🍷	◇	*ICE* **1064**	*ICE* **1062** ①-④ m	◇	*IC* **2064**	◇	◇	*ICE* **266** B✕	◇	*IC* **2062**	◇	◇	*ICE* **560** Ⓑ d ✕	◇	*IC* **2060**	◇	*ICE* **1060** ⑦-④ k	◇		◇
München Hbf **930** ... d.	...	1303	...	...	...	...	...	...	...	...	...	...	...	1658	...	...	...	...	1901	...	...	...	...	...	...	...
Nürnberg Hbf **925** ... d.	...	|	...	1341	...	...	...	...	...	...	1541	...	...	|	...	1742	...	...	|	...	1942**b**	...	...	...	...	...
Stuttgart Hbf .... d.	1500	1509	1533	1558	1632	1640	1700	1701	1734	1727	1759	1832	1900	1912	1932	1959	2032	2100	2111	2132	2159	2232	2309	2313	...	0016
Vaihingen (Enz) .... d.	1516	|	1548	1616	1648	|	1716	|	|	1748	1817	1848	1916	|	1949	2016	2048	2116	|	2148	2216	2248	|	2331	...	0042
Mühlacker .... ▷ d.	1522	|	1554	1623	1654	|	1722	|	|	1754	1824	1854	1922	|	1954	2023	2054	2122	|	2154	2224	2254	|	2340	...	0048
Bruchsal .... ▷ d.	|	1540	|	|	|	1710	|	1736	1802	|	|	|	|	1940	|	|	|	|	2140	|	|	|	2339	|	...	|
Pforzheim .... d.	1531	|	1603	1632	1703	|	1731	|	|	1803	1833	1903	1931	|	2003	2032	2103	2131	|	2203	2233	2303	|	2348	...	0057
Karlsruhe Hbf .... a.	1553	1552	1626	1652	1727	1730	1753	1753	1820	1825	1853	1925	1953	1952	2026	2053	2125	2153	2152	2226	2300	2325	2352	0011	...	0119

A – From Aalen (Table **925**) on Ⓐ t.
B – BADEN-KURIER. From / to Basel on dates in Table **912**.
D – To Dortmund via Frankfurt and Siegen (Tables **808** and **912**).
L – To / from Leipzig on dates in Table **849a**.
O – To / from Offenburg (Table **912**).
P – 🚃12 and 🍷 München - Stuttgart - Paris and v.v. Ⓡ for international journeys.

b – Ⓑ (not Dec. 25).
d – Also Dec. 24; not Dec. 25.
k – Not Dec. 25.
m – Not Dec. 26.
t – Ⓐ (not Jan. 6).
w – Also Dec. 26; not Dec. 25.
z – Also Jan. 6.

‡ – Stuttgart - Nürnberg on ⑦ (also Dec. 26; not Dec. 25).
◧ – Distance via high-speed line.
◐ – Distance via classic route.
◇ – Regional service operated by Go-Ahead Baden-Württemberg.
▷ – Fast *RE* connecting trains (operated by SWEG Bahn) operate Bruchsal - Mühlacker and v.v. Journey time: 24 – 26 minutes.
From Bruchsal at 0930, 1128, 1330, 1530, 1730, 1930 and 2130.
From Mühlacker at 0803, 1001, 1203, 1403, 1602, 1802 and 2002.

933 ULM - FRIEDRICHSHAFEN - LINDAU

IRE / RE services

km		Ⓐt	Ⓒz		Ⓒz	Ⓐt					*RJ* **897** G	⊡				⊠			*IC* **119** D						⊙	
	Stuttgart Hbf **930** ... d.	...	...	...	...	0539	...	0639t	...	0736	0744	...	0839	...	0937	and at the same minutes past each hour until	...	1237	1257	1339	...	1439	...	1537	...	1639
0	**Ulm** Hbf .... d.	0500	0507	0610	0647	0644	0717	0747	0819	0847	0902	0919	0947	1019	1047		1319	1347	1411	1447	1519	1547	1618	1647	1718	1747
37	Biberach (Riß) .... d.	0525	0531	0632	0708	0710	0740	0808	0841	0908	0924	0941	1008	1041	1108		1341	1408	1433	1508	1541	1608	1640	1708	1740	1808
62	Aulendorf .... d.	0545	0549	0650	0724	0728	0759	0824	0859	0924	0939	0959	1024	1059	1124		1359	1424	1451	1524	1559	1624	1659	1724	1759	1824
84	Ravensburg .... d.	0559	0602	0702	0737	0741	0812	0837	0912	0937	0952	1012	1037	1112	1137		1412	1437	1505	1537	1612	1637	1712	1737	1812	1837
95	Meckenbeuren .... d.	0606	0609	0709	0744	0748	|	0844	|	0944	|	|	1044	|	1144		|	1444	|	1544	|	1644	|	1744	|	1844
103	Friedrichshafen Stadt a.	0614	0617	0719	0752	0755	0825	0852	0925	0952	1003	1025	1052	1124	1152		1425	1452	1516k	1552	1625	1652	1725	1752	1825	1852
103	Friedrichshafen Stadt d.	*0627*	*0658*	0728t	*0810*	*0810*	0832	*0907*	0931	*0957*	1010	1031	*1107*	1131	*1205*		1431	*1507*	1532k	*1607*	1631	*1700*	1731	*1806*	1831	*1907*
	Lindau Insel .... a.	|	*0730*	|	*0843*	*0843*	|	*0941*	|	*1026*	|	|	*1141*	|	*1241*		|	*1541*	|	*1641*	|	*1733*	|	*1841*	|	*1941*
127	**Lindau** Reutin .... a.	*0655*	...	0755t	...	...	0855	...	0955	...	1028	1055	...	1155	...		1455	...	1556	...	1655	...	1755	...	1855	...

			⊡								
Stuttgart Hbf **930** ... d.	...	1739	...	1839	...	1937	...	2039	...	...	...
Ulm Hbf .... d.	1819	1847	1919	1947	2019	2047	2119	2145	2219	2247	0008
Biberach (Riß) .... d.	1841	1908	1941	2008	2041	2108	2141	2208	2241	2308	0032
Aulendorf .... d.	1859	1924	1959	2024	2059	2124	2201	2224	2259	2324	0050
Ravensburg .... d.	1912	1937	2012	2037	2112	2137	2214	2237	2312	2337	0103
Meckenbeuren .... d.	|	1944	|	2044	|	2144	|	2244	|	2344	0110
Friedrichshafen Stadt. a.	1925	1952	2025	2052	2125	2152	2225	2251	2325	2352	0118
Friedrichshafen Stadt. d.	1931	*2007*	2031	...	2131	...	2231	2258	2332	...	...
Lindau Insel .... a.	|	*2041*	|	...	|	...	|	|	2356	...	...
Lindau Reutin .... a.	1955	...	2055	...	2157	...	2252	2325	0005	...	...

	Ⓐt			Ⓐt	Ⓒz		Ⓒz	Ⓐt			
Lindau Reutin .... d.	...	...	0528t	...	...	...	0650	0702	*0650*t	0806	...
Lindau Insel .... d.	...	*0454*t	|	...	*0604*	*0615*t	0706	|	*0707*t	|	*0822*
Friedrichshafen Stadt ...... a.	...	*0521*t	0557t	...	*0627*	*0643*t	0727	0726	*0740*t	0828	*0854*
Friedrichshafen Stadt ...... d.	0449	0530	0604	0630	0634	0704	0734	0732	0806	0835	0905
Meckenbeuren .... d.	0455	|	0610	0637	|	0711	|	|	0812	|	0912
Ravensburg .... d.	0502	0542	0617	0644	0646	0718	0746	0745	0819	0846	0919
Aulendorf .... d.	0516	0557	0631	0659	0701	0732	0801	0759	0833	0901	0932
Biberach (Riß) .... d.	0532	0616	0647	0718	0718	0748	0818	08***18***	0848	0918	0948
Ulm Hbf .... a.	0558	0640	0711	0740	0740	0811	0840	***0840***	0911	0940	1011
Stuttgart Hbf **930** .... a.	0727	...	0821	...	...	0920	...	...	1020	...	1120

							IC **118** B			✥					*RJ* **890** G								⊙			
Lindau Reutin .... d.	0905	...	*1003*	...	1105	...	1200	...	1305	and at the same minutes past each hour until	...	1605	...	1703	1731	...	*1805*	...	1905	...	2005	...	2103	...	2202	...
Lindau Insel .... d.	|	*0920*	|	*1031*	|	*1120*	|	*1220*	|		*1520*	|	*1620*	|	|	*1722*	|	*1820*	|	*1920*	|	*2020*	|	...	|	...
Friedrichshafen Stadt a.	0927	*0950*	*1027*	*1058*	1127	*1150*	1219k	*1257*	1327		*1550*	1627	*1650*	1727	1754	*1749*	*1827*	*1850*	1927	*1950*	2027	*2050*	2128	...	2228	...
Friedrichshafen Stadt d.	0934	1005	1034	1105	1134	1203r	1235k	1305	1334		1605	1634	1703r	1734	1802	1808	1835	1905	1934	2005	2034	2105	2134	2205	2234	2337
Meckenbeuren .... d.	|	1012	|	1112	|	1210r	|	1312	|		1612	|	1712	|	|	1815	|	1912	|	2012	|	2112	|	2212	|	2343
Ravensburg .... d.	0946	1019	1046	1119	1146	1217r	1249	1319	1346		1619	1647	1719	1746	1816	1822	1847	1919	1946	2019	2046	2119	2146	2219	2246	2351
Aulendorf .... d.	1001	1032	1101	1132	1201	1230r	1304	1332	1401		1632	1701	1732	1801	1830	1835	1901	1932	2001	2032	2101	2132	2201	2232	2301	0008
Biberach (Riß) .... d.	1018	1048	1118	1148	1218	1248	1321	1348	1418		1648	1718	1748	1818	1845	1851	1918	1948	2018	2048	2118	2148	2218	2248	2318	0024
Ulm Hbf .... a.	1040	1111	1140	1211	1240	1311	1346	1410	1440		1711	1740	1813	1840	1907	1913	1940	2011	2040	2111	2140	2211	2240	2311	2340	0051
Stuttgart Hbf **930** ... a.	...	1220	...	1320	...	1420	1459	1520	...		1820	...	1921	...	2005	2023	...	2120	...	2220	...	2320	...	0020	...	...

B – BODENSEE – 🚃12 Innsbruck - Bregenz - Lindau - Bochum.
D – BODENSEE – 🚃12 Dortmund - Lindau - Bregenz - Innsbruck.
G – 🚃12 ✕ Wien - Innsbruck - Bregenz - Stuttgart - Frankfurt and v.v.

k – Not Jan. 9 – 20, Feb. 13 - Mar. 10.
r – 2 minutes later on Ⓒ (also Jan. 6).
t – Ⓐ (not Jan. 6).
z – Ⓒ (also Jan. 6).

⊡ – Change trains at Friedrichshafen on Ⓒ (also Jan. 6).
⊙ – Change trains at Friedrichshafen on Ⓐ (not Jan. 6).
✥ – The *1320* and *1420* connecting trains from Lindau Insel arrive Friedrichshafen Stadt *1350 / 1450* (not *1357 / 1457*). The 1505 from Friedrichshafen Stadt arrives Ulm Hbf 1613 (not 1610).
⊠ – Timings may vary by 1 – 2 minutes.

RE/*RB* services except where shown — MÜNCHEN and AUGSBURG - MEMMINGEN - LINDAU — 934

See Table **935** for services via Kempten (also for connecting services from/to Augsburg).

km		⊖ Ⓐt	Ⓐt	⊖ Ⓐt	Ⓐt	Ⓒz	⊖	⊖	*ECE* **198** ✕				⊖	⊖	*ECE* **196** ✕				⊖	⊖				⊖	⊖	*ECE* **192** ✕	
0	**München** Hbf ⊡ d.	...	0439	...	...	...	...	0620	0655	0720	...	...	0754	0820	0855	0920	...	...	0954	1020	1120	...	...	1154	1220	1255	1320
7	München Pasing d.	...	0447	...	...	...	...	0627	|	0727	...	...	0801	0827	|	0927	...	...	1001	1027	1127	...	...	1201	1227	|	1327
42	Geltendorf d.	...	0507	...	...	...	...	0648	|	0748	...	...	|	0849	|	0948	...	...	|	1048	1148	...	...	|	1248	|	1348
56	Kaufering d.	...	0515	...	...	...	...	0656	|	0757	...	...	|	0857	|	0957	...	...	|	1056	1157	...	...	|	1256	|	1357
	Augsburg Hbf d.	...	|	...	0522	0532	...	|	|	|	0737k	0737k	|	|	|	|	0941	0941	|	|	|	1141	1141	|	|	|	|
68	Buchloe a.	...	0522	...	0555	0603	...	0703	0733	0805	0804	0804	0832	0903	0933	1005	1004	1004	1032	1103	1205	1204	1204	1232	1303	1333	1405
68	Buchloe d.	...	▬	0543	0558	0606	...	0712	0736	▬	0809	0809	0833	0912	0936	▬	1009	1009	1033	1112	▬	1209	1209	1233	1312	1336	▬
76	Türkheim (Bay) ♠ d.	...	...	0549	0616j	0619f	...	0720	|	...	0817	0820	0839	0920	|	...	1017	1020	1039	1120	...	1217	1220	1239	1320	|	...
81	Bad Wörishofen ♠ a.	...	...	|	|	|	...	|	|	...	0823	|	|	|	|	...	1023	|	|	|	...	1223	|	|	|	|	...
87	Mindelheim d.	...	⊖	0559	0630	0630	...	0729	|	⊖	...	0831	0846	0929	|	⊖	...	1031	1046	1129	⊖	...	1232	1246	1329	|	⊖
114	**Memmingen** a.	...	Ⓒz	0621	0657	0651	...	0748	0758		...	0851	0859	0948	0958		...	1051	1059	1148		...	1252	1259	1348	1358	
114	**Memmingen** d.	0455	0606	0624	...	...	0706	...	0801	0806	...	...	0901	...	1001	1006	...	...	1101	...	1206	...	...	1301	...	1401	1406
146	Leutkirch 937 d.	0523	0636f	0703	...	...	0736f	...	|	0836f	...	...	0923	...	|	1036f	...	...	1123	...	1236f	...	...	1323	...	|	1436f
157	Kißlegg 937 a.	0531	0643	0711	...	...	0743	...	|	0843	...	...	0931	...	|	1043	...	...	1131	...	1243	...	...	1331	...	|	1443
157	Kißlegg 937 d.	0537	0644	0718	...	...	0744	...	|	0844	...	...	0939	...	|	1044	...	...	1139	...	1244	...	...	1339	...	|	1444
170	Wangen (Allgäu) 937 d.	0546	0653	0729	...	...	0753	...	|	0853	...	...	0952	...	|	1053	...	...	1152	...	1253	...	...	1352	...	|	1453
176	Hergatz d.	0550	0657	0735	...	...	0758	...	|	0858	...	...	0956	...	|	1059	...	...	1159	...	1259	...	...	1356	...	|	1459
199	**Lindau** Insel a.	0607	0715	0751	...	...	0816	...	|	0916	...	...	1015	...	|	1116	...	...	1216	...	1316	...	...	1416	...	|	1516
	Lindau Reutin a.	*0624*	*0728*	*0758*	...	...	*0826*	...	0850	*0928*	...	...	*1024*	...	1050	*1128*	...	...	*1226*	...	*1328*	...	...	*1426*	...	1450	*1528*
	Zürich HB **75** a.	...	...	...	...	...	...	...	1027	...	...	...	...	...	1227	...	...	...	...	...	...	...	...	...	...	1627	...

			⊖	⊖	*ECE* **190** ✕				⊖	⊖	*ECE* **98** ✕				⊖	⊖	*ECE* **96** ✕				⊖	⊖			⊖		
München Hbf ⊡ d.	...	...	1354	1420	1455	1520	...	...	1552	1620	1652	1720	...	...	1751e	1820	1852	1920	...	...	1954	2020	2120	...	2220	2320	...
München Pasing d.	...	...	1401	1427	|	1527	...	...	1559	1627	|	1727	...	...	1759e	1827	|	1927	...	...	2001	2027	2127	...	2227	2327	...
Geltendorf d.	...	...	|	1448	|	1548z	...	...	|	1648	|	1748z	...	...	|	1848	|	1948	...	...	|	2048	2148	...	2248	2348	...
Kaufering d.	...	...	|	1456	|	1557	...	...	|	1656	|	1757	...	...	|	1856	|	1957	...	...	|	2056	2157	...	2256	2357	...
Augsburg Hbf d.	1325b	1325b	|	|	|	|	1541	1541	|	|	|	|	1741	1741	|	|	|	|	1941	1941	|	|	|	2133	|	|	2333
Buchloe a.	1404	1404	1432	1503	1533	1605	1603	1603	1632	1703	1733	1805	1804	1804	1832	1903	1933	2005	2004	2004	2032	2103	2205	2204	2303	0004	0004
Buchloe d.	1409	1409	1433	1512	1536	▬	1609	1609	1633	1712	1736	▬	1809	1809	1833	1912	1936	▬	2009	2009	2033	2112	...	2209	2312	...	0009
Türkheim (Bay) ♠ d.	1417	1420	1439	1520	|	...	1617	1620	1639	1720	|	...	1817	1820	1839	1920	|	...	2017	2020	2039	2120	...	2220f	2320	...	0020
Bad Wörishofen ♠ a.	1423	|	|	|	|	...	1623	|	|	|	|	...	1823	|	|	|	|	...	2023	|	|	|	...	|	|	...	|
Mindelheim d.	...	1431	1446	1529	|	⊖	...	1631	1646	1729	|	⊖	...	1831	1846	1929	|	⊖	...	2031	2046	2129	...	2231	2329	...	0031
Memmingen a.	...	1451	1459	1548	1558		...	1651	1659	1748	1758		...	1851	1859	1948	1958		...	2051	2059	2148	...	2251	2348	...	0053
Memmingen d.	...	...	1501	...	1601	1606	...	...	1701	...	1801	1806	...	...	1901	...	2001	2006	...	...	2101	*2206*	...	*2306*	...	...	...
Leutkirch 937 d.	...	...	1523	...	|	1636f	...	...	1723	...	|	1836f	...	...	1923	...	|	2036f	...	...	2123	*2236*	...	*2329*	...	...	...
Kißlegg 937 a.	...	...	1531	...	|	1643	...	...	1731	...	|	1843	...	...	1931	...	|	2043	...	...	2131	*2243*	...	*2336*	...	...	...
Kißlegg 937 d.	...	...	1539	...	|	1644	...	...	1739	...	|	1844	...	...	1939	...	|	2044	...	...	2139	*2244*	...	*2339*	...	...	...
Wangen (Allgäu) 937 d.	...	...	1552	...	|	1653	...	...	1752	...	|	1853	...	...	1952	...	|	2053	...	...	2152	*2253*	...	*2349*	...	...	...
Hergatz d.	...	...	1556	...	|	1659	...	...	1756	...	|	1859	...	...	1956	...	|	2058	...	...	2156	...	...	*2353*	...	...	...
Lindau Insel a.	...	...	1616	...	|	1716	...	...	1815	...	|	1916	...	...	2016	...	|	2116	...	...	2216	...	...	*0012*	...	...	...
Lindau Reutin a.	...	...	*1628*	...	1650	*1725*	...	...	*1826*	...	1850	*1928*	...	...	*2032*	...	2050	*2130*	...	...	*2228*	...	...	...	...	...	...
Zürich HB **75** a.	...	...	...	...	1827	...	...	...	...	...	2027	...	...	...	...	...	2227	...	...	...	...	...	...	...	...	...	...

	⊖ Ⓐt	⚒r	⊖ Ⓐt	⊖	⊖ Ⓐt	⊖ Ⓐt				⊖ Ⓐt	⊖	⊖			⊖	*ECE* **97** ✕	⊖	⊖			⊖	*ECE* **99** ✕	⊖	⊖			⊖
Zürich HB **75** d.	...	...	...	...	...	...	...	...	...	...	...	...	...	...	...	0733	...	...	...	...	...	0933	...	...	...	...	...
Lindau Reutin d.	...	...	...	...	...	...	...	...	...	...	...	*0729*	...	...	*0829*	0910	...	*0930*	...	...	*1029*	1110	...	*1127*	...	...	*1229*
Lindau Insel d.	...	...	...	...	...	0548	...	...	...	0646	0646z	0746	...	...	0835	|	...	0946	...	...	1035	|	...	1146	...	...	1235
Hergatz d.	...	...	...	...	...	0606	...	...	...	0703	0703z	0804	...	...	0900f	|	...	1004	...	...	1100f	|	...	1204	...	...	1300f
Wangen (Allgäu) 937 d.	...	...	...	0526t	...	0612	*0608z*	...	...	0707	0707z	0808	...	...	0904	|	...	1008	...	...	1104	|	...	1208	...	...	1304
Kißlegg 937 a.	...	...	...	0535t	...	0621	*0618z*	...	...	0716	0716z	0818	...	...	0913	|	...	1018	...	...	1113	|	...	1218	...	...	1313
Kißlegg 937 d.	...	...	0501	0536t	...	0623	*0628z*	...	...	0723	0723z	0828	...	...	0914	|	...	1028	...	...	1114	|	...	1228	...	...	1314
Leutkirch 937 d.	...	...	0509	0544t	...	0630	*0635z*	...	...	0731	0731z	0835	...	...	0928f	|	...	1035	...	...	1128f	|	...	1235	...	...	1328f
Memmingen a.	...	...	0533	0607t	...	0657	*0658z*	...	...	0753	0753z	0858	...	...	0954	0959	...	1058	...	...	1153	1159	...	1258	...	...	1354
Memmingen d.	0450	0504	0541	0611	0640	...	0706	...	...	0800	0811	0900	0908	...	▬	1001	1011	1100	1108	...	▬	1201	1208	1300	1308	...	▬
Mindelheim d.	0508	0524	0558	0630	0658	...	0729	...	...	0813	0831	0913	0929	...	...	|	1031	1113	1129	...	...	|	1231	1313	1329	...	...
Bad Wörishofen ♠ d.	|	|	|	|	|	...	|	0735	...	|	|	|	|	0935	...	|	|	|	|	1135	...	|	|	|	|	1335	...
Türkheim (Bay) ♠ d.	0515	0535	0605	0641	0705	...	0744	0744	...	0820	0841	0920	0944	0944	...	|	1041	1120	1144	1144	...	|	1241	1320	1344	1344	...
Buchloe a.	0520	0541	0611	0649	0711	...	0750	0750	...	0826	0847	0926	0950	0950	...	1023	1047	1126	1150	1150	...	1223	1247	1326	1350	1350	...
Buchloe d.	0522	0552	0616	0656	0716	...	0756	0756	0755	0827	0856	0927	0956	0956	0955	1025	1056	1127	1156	1156	1155	1225	1256	1327	1356	1356	1355
Augsburg Hbf a.	|	0624	|	|	|	...	0819	0819	|	|	|	|	1018	1018	|	|	|	|	1219	1219	|	|	|	|	1418	1418	|
Kaufering d.	0529	...	0623	0703	0723	...	...	...	0803	|	0903	|	...	...	1003	|	1103	|	...	...	1203	|	1303	|	...	...	1403
Geltendorf d.	0538	...	0631	0711	0731	...	...	...	0811z	|	0911	|	...	...	1011	|	1111	|	...	...	1211	|	1311	|	...	...	1411
München Pasing a.	0558	...	0652	0735	0757	...	...	...	0832	0857	0932	0957	...	...	1032	|	1132	1157	...	...	1232	|	1332	1357	...	...	1432
München Hbf ⊡ a.	0606	...	0659	0742	0804	...	...	...	0839	0904	0940	1004	...	...	1041	1104	1141	1204	...	...	1241	1304	1339	1405	...	...	1439

	ECE **191** ✕	⊖	⊖			⊖	*ECE* **193** ✕	⊖	⊖			⊖	⊖	⊖			⊖	*ECE* **197** ✕	⊖	⊖	⊖ †w		⊖	*ECE* **199** ✕	⊖		
Zürich HB **75** d.	1133	...	...	...	...	...	1333	...	...	...	...	...	...	...	...	...	...	1733	...	...	...	...	...	1933	...	...	...
Lindau Reutin d.	1310	...	*1330*	...	...	*1429*	1510	...	*1530*	...	...	*1629*	...	*1726*	...	...	*1829*	1910	...	*1930*	*1930*	...	*2029*	2110	...	*2119*	...
Lindau Insel d.	|	...	1346	...	...	1435	|	...	1546	...	...	1635	...	1746	...	...	1835	|	...	1946	1946	...	2035	|	...	*2146*	...
Hergatz d.	|	...	1404	...	...	1500f	|	...	1604	...	...	1700f	...	1804	...	...	1900f	|	...	2004	2004	...	2100f	|	...	*2204*	...
Wangen (Allgäu) 937 d.	|	...	1408	...	...	1504	|	...	1608	...	...	1704	...	1808	...	...	1904	|	...	2008	2008	...	2104	|	...	*2208*	...
Kißlegg 937 a.	|	...	1418	...	...	1513	|	...	1618	...	...	1713	...	1818	...	...	1913	|	...	2018	2018	...	2113	|	...	*2218*	...
Kißlegg 937 d.	|	...	1428	...	...	1514	|	...	1628	...	...	1714	...	1828	...	...	1914	|	...	2028	2028	...	2114	|	...	*2228*	...
Leutkirch 937 d.	|	...	1435	...	...	1528f	|	...	1635	...	...	1728f	...	1835	...	...	1928f	|	...	2035	2035	...	2128f	|	...	*2235*	...
Memmingen a.	1359	...	1458	...	...	1554	1558	...	1658	...	...	1754	...	1858	...	...	1954	1959	...	2058	2058	...	2154	2159	...	*2258*	...
Memmingen d.	1401	1411	1500	1508	...	▬	1601	1612	1700	1708	...	▬	1811	1900	1908	...	▬	2001	2011	...	2100	2108	▬	2201	2211	2308	...
Mindelheim d.	|	1431	1513	1529	...	...	|	1631	1713	1729	...	...	1831	1913	1929	...	...	|	2031	...	2113	2129	...	|	2231	2329	...
Bad Wörishofen ♠ d.	|	|	|	|	1535	...	|	|	|	|	1735	...	|	|	|	1935	...	|	|	...	|	|	...	|	|	|	...
Türkheim (Bay) ♠ d.	|	1441	1520	1544	1544	...	|	1641	1720	1744	1744	...	1841	1920	1944	1944	...	|	2041	...	2120	2144	...	|	2241	2344	...
Buchloe a.	1423	1447	1526	1550	1550	...	1622	1647	1726	1750	1750	...	1847	1926	1950	1950	...	2022	2047	...	2126	2150	...	2223	2247	2350	...
Buchloe d.	1425	1456	1527	1556	1556	1555	1625	1656	1727	1756	1756	1755	1856	1927	1956	1956	1955	2025	2056	...	2127	2158	2155	2225	2257	0010	2355
Augsburg Hbf a.	|	|	|	1618	1618	|	|	|	|	1818	1818	|	|	|	2019	2019	|	|	|	...	|	2226	|	|	|	0046	|
Kaufering d.	|	1503	|	...	...	1603	|	1703	|	...	...	1803	1903	|	...	...	2003	|	2103	...	|	...	2203	|	2303	...	0003
Geltendorf d.	|	1511	|	...	...	1611	|	1711	|	...	...	1811	1911	|	...	...	2011	|	2111	...	|	...	2211	|	2311	...	0011
München Pasing a.	|	1533	1557	...	...	1632	|	1732	1757	...	...	1832	1934	1957	...	...	2032	|	2132	...	2157	...	2232	|	2333	...	0032
München Hbf ⊡ a.	1504	1542	1605	...	...	1639	1704	1741	1804	...	...	1841	1942	2005	...	...	2041	2104	2141	...	2204	...	2241	2304	2342	...	0041

b – 1341 on Ⓒ (also Jan. 6).
e – On Ⓒ (also Jan. 6) departs München Hbf 1754, München Pasing 1801.
f – Arrives 6–8 minutes earlier.
j – Arrives 0605.
k – 0741 on Ⓒ (also Jan. 6).
r – ⚒ (not Jan. 6).
t – Ⓐ (not Jan. 6).
w – † (also Jan. 6).
z – Ⓒ (also Jan. 6).

¶ – From Buchloe (departs 6–8 minutes earlier).
‡ – From Buchloe (d. 0732).

§ – To Buchloe (a. 0821).
◧ – To Buchloe (a. 0044).
⊖ – Operated by Go Ahead Bayern.
⊡ – Most trains in Table **934** use platforms 27–36 at München Hbf (minimum connecting time with other services is 10 minutes).
♠ – Other journeys Türkheim - Bad Wörishofen and v.v. (journey time: 6–7 minutes).
From Türkheim at 0435 Ⓐt¶, 0510 Ⓐt, 0510 ⑥¶, 0543 ⚒r, 0549 †w¶, 0617, 0643, 0722, 0747 Ⓐt‡, 0843, 0922, 1043, 1122, 1243, 1322, 1443, 1522, 1643, 1722, 1843, 1922, 2043, 2122, 2217, 2247, 2322 and 0018.
From Bad Wörishofen at 0448 Ⓐt, 0525 ⚒r, 0555 Ⓐt, 0602 Ⓒz, 0629, 0655 Ⓐt, 0702 Ⓒz, 0806 Ⓐt§, 0829, 0908, 1029, 1108, 1229, 1308, 1429, 1508, 1629, 1708, 1829, 1908, 2029, 2108, 2134, 2229, 2301, 2334 and 0030◧.

935 MÜNCHEN, AUGSBURG and ULM - KEMPTEN - LINDAU

RE | RB services except where shown

See Table **934** for other services München - Buchloe - Memmingen - Lindau.

km																											
		⚒r	Ⓐt	Ⓐt	◇ Ⓐt	Ⓐt	Ⓒz	⚒r	◇ Ⓒz			◇ Ⓐt	⊖			◇ Ⓒz	◇ Ⓐt		Ⓐt	Ⓒz				◇			◇ Ⓒz
0	**München** Hbf ⊡ d.	...	0439	...	...	...	...	0520	...	0539	...	...	0620	...	...	...	...	0639	...	...	...	0720	0739	...	...	...	0807
7	München Pasing d.	...	0447	...	...	...	...	0527	...	0547	...	...	0627	...	...	...	...	0647	...	...	...	0727	0746	...	...	...	0815
42	Geltendorf d.	...	0507	...	...	...	...	0548	...	0607	...	...	0648	...	...	...	...	0707	...	...	...	0748	0807	...	...	...	|
56	Kaufering d.	...	0515	...	...	...	...	0556	...	0615	...	...	0656	...	...	...	...	0715	...	...	...	0757	0815	...	...	...	|
	Nürnberg Hbf **905** d.	...	|	...	...	...	...	|	...	|	...	...	|	...	...	...	...	|	...	...	...	|	|	...	...	...	|
	Augsburg Hbf d.	...	|	0450	...	0522	0532	|	...	|	0610t	0617	|	0632	0632	...	...	|	0710	...	0737q	|	|	0747	0810	...	|
68	Buchloe a.	...	0522	0522	...	0555	0603	0603	...	0622	0638t	0651	0703	0658p	0658p	...	...	0722	0738	...	0804	0805	0822	0819	0838	...	0853
68	Buchloe d.	...	▬	0529	0557	▬	▬	0606	...	▬	0639	0655	▬	0706	0706	...	←	▬	0739	0739	▬	0807	▬	0831	0839	...	0858
88	Kaufbeuren d.	...	...	0546	0612	...	...	0616	0621	...	0651	0708	...	0717	0717	0721	0728	...	0751	0751	...	0818	...	0845	0851	...	0910
94	Biessenhofen d.	...	...	0550	0618	...	...	|	0626	...	0656	→	...	|	|	0727	0734	...	0758	0758	...	|	...	0850	0856	...	|
100	Marktoberdorf d.	...	...	|	0639k	...	...	|	0635	...	|	▬	...	|	|	0736	0745	...	|	|	...	|	...	0859	|	...	0927
131	**Füssen** a.	...	...	|	0721	...	Ⓒz	|	0716	...	|	Ⓐt	Ⓒz	|	|	0816	0837	Ⓒz	|	|	Ⓐt	|	...	0939	|	...	1007
	Ulm Hbf d.	...	...	|	...	...	0510	|	▬	...	|	0548	0614	|	|	...	...	0719	|	|	0658	|	...	...	|	0817	...
	Memmingen a.	...	...	|	...	Ⓐt	0553	|	...	...	|	0641	0701	|	|	...	...	0751	|	|	0747	|	...	...	|	0855	...
	Memmingen d.	...	...	|	...	0555	0601	|	...	...	|	0642	0703	|	|	...	...	0758	|	|	0758	|	...	...	|	0904	...
131	**Kempten** Hbf a.	...	⚒r	0616	...	0623	0625	0640	...	...	0722	0709	0727	0742	0742	...	...	0818	0822	0822	0825	0841	...	...	0922	0925	...
131	**Kempten** Hbf d.	0543	0543	...	...	0627	...	0641	0641	...	...	0727	0730	0744	0744	...	...	0819	...	0830	0830	0843	...	...	...	0930	...
152	Immenstadt a.	0555	0555	...	...	0643	...	0655	0655	◐	...	0742	0745	0756	0756	...	...	0833	...	0845	0845	0855	◄	...	...	0945	...
152	Immenstadt d.	0557	0612	...	...	0649	...	0657	0657	0710	...	0751	0751	0758	0812	...	...	0839	...	0851	0851	0857	0912	...	...	0951	...
	Sonthofen d.	|	0621	...	...	0704	...	|	|	0719	...	0800	0800	|	0823	...	...	0848	...	0900	0900	|	0923	...	...	1000	...
	Oberstdorf a.	|	0645	...	...	0723	...	|	|	0739	...	0819	0819	|	0840	...	...	0912	...	0919	0919	|	0940	...	...	1022	...
197	Hergatz d.	0628	...	...	...	...	...	0729	0729	...	...	...	...	0829	...	...	...	...	...	...	...	0929	...	...	...	...	...
220	**Lindau** Insel a.	|	...	...	...	...	...	|	|	...	...	...	...	|	...	...	...	...	...	...	...	|	...	...	...	...	...
	Lindau Reutin a.	0645	...	...	...	...	...	0745	0745	...	...	...	...	0845	...	...	...	...	...	...	...	0945	...	...	...	...	...

	⊖			◇				◇	◇		⊖			◇						◇ Ⓒz	◇ Ⓐt		⊖			◇	
München Hbf ⊡ d.	0820	...	0840	...	...	...	0920	...	0941	...	1020	...	1039	...	...	...	...	1120	1139	...	...	...	1220	...	1239	...	...
München Pasing d.	0827	...	0847	...	...	...	0927	...	0947	...	1027	...	1047	...	...	...	...	1127	1147	...	...	...	1227	...	1247	...	...
Geltendorf d.	0849	...	0907	...	...	...	0948	...	1007	...	1048	...	1107	...	...	...	...	1148	1207	...	...	...	1248	...	1307	...	...
Kaufering d.	0857	...	0915	...	...	...	0957	...	1015	...	1056	...	1115	...	...	...	...	1157	1215	...	...	...	1256	...	1315	...	...
Nürnberg Hbf **905** d.	|	0716	|	...	...	...	|	...	|	...	|	...	|	...	...	...	...	|	|	...	...	...	|	...	|	...	...
Augsburg Hbf d.	|	0842	|	0847	0910t	0941	|	0947	|	1010	|	1042	|	1047	1110t	...	1141	|	|	1147	1147	1212	|	1242	|	1248	...
Buchloe a.	0903	0905	0922	0922	0939t	1004	1005	1022	1022	1039	1103	1105	1122	1122	1139t	...	1204	1205	1222	1220	1220	1238	1303	1305	1322	1322	...
Buchloe d.	...	0907	▬	0931	0940	▬	1007	▬	1029	1040	▬	1107	▬	1129	1142	...	▬	1207	▬	1229	1229	1239	▬	1307	▬	1329	1339
Kaufbeuren d.	...	0919	...	0945	0951	...	1019	...	1045	1051	...	1119	...	1145	1153	...	...	1219	...	1245	1245	1251	...	1320	...	1345	1351
Biessenhofen d.	...	|	...	0950	0956	...	|	...	1051	1056	...	|	...	1150	1157	...	...	|	...	1251	1250	1256	...	|	...	1350	1356
Marktoberdorf d.	...	|	...	0959	|	...	|	...	1101	|	...	|	...	1200	|	...	...	|	...	1302	1306f	|	...	|	...	1406f	|
Füssen a.	...	|	...	1041	|	...	|	...	1141	|	...	|	...	1241	|	...	Ⓐt	|	...	1343	1346	|	...	|	...	1445	|
Ulm Hbf d.	...	|	...	...	|	0917	|	...	...	|	1017	|	...	...	|	1117	1117	|	...	▬	...	|	1217	|	...	...	|
Memmingen a.	...	|	...	...	|	0954	|	...	...	|	1054	|	...	...	|	1200	1200	|	...	...	...	|	1255	|	...	...	|
Memmingen d.	...	|	...	...	|	1000	|	...	...	|	1104	|	...	...	|	1201	1201	|	...	...	...	|	1304	|	...	...	|
Kempten Hbf a.	...	0941	...	...	1022	1025	1041	...	...	1122	1125	1141	...	...	1222	1226	1226	1241	...	...	...	1322	1325	1341	...	...	1422
Kempten Hbf d.	...	0943	...	...	...	1030	1043	...	...	...	1130	1143	...	...	...	...	1230	1243	Ⓒz	Ⓐt	...	...	1329	1343	...	...	...
Immenstadt a.	...	0955	◄	...	...	1045	1055	◄	...	...	1145	1155	◄	...	...	...	1245	1255	◄	◄	...	...	1345	1355	◄	...	...
Immenstadt d.	...	0957	1021	...	...	1051	1057	1112	...	...	1151	1157	1212	...	...	...	1251	1257	1312	1315	...	...	1351	1357	1412	...	...
Sonthofen d.	...	|	1030	...	...	1100	|	1122	...	...	1201	|	1223	...	...	...	1300	|	1321	1328	...	...	1400	|	1421	...	...
Oberstdorf a.	...	|	1059	...	...	1119	|	1140	...	...	1219	|	1242	...	...	...	1319	|	1340	1351	...	...	1418	|	1440	...	...
Hergatz d.	...	1029	...	...	...	...	1129	...	...	...	...	1229	...	...	...	...	...	1329	...	...	...	...	...	1429	...	...	...
Lindau Insel a.	...	|	...	...	...	...	|	...	...	...	...	|	...	...	...	...	...	|	...	...	...	...	...	|	...	...	...
Lindau Reutin a.	...	1045	...	...	...	...	1145	...	...	...	...	1245	...	...	...	...	...	1345	...	...	...	...	...	1445	...	...	...

	Ⓐt	Ⓒz			*IC* 2085 H		◇		⊖		◇	◇					*RE* 2013 A🍷		◇		Ⓐt	⊖			◇		
München Hbf ⊡ d.	...	...	1320	1320	...	1340	...	...	1420	...	...	1440	...	...	1520	1520	...	1536q	...	...	...	1620	...	1639	...	...	...
München Pasing d.	...	...	1327	1327	...	1347	...	...	1427	...	...	1447	...	...	1527	1527	...	1543q	...	...	...	1627	...	1647	...	...	...
Geltendorf d.	...	...	1348	1348	...	1407	...	...	1448	...	...	1507	...	...	1548z	1548z	...	1607	...	...	...	1648	...	1707	...	...	...
Kaufering d.	...	...	1357	1357	...	1415	...	...	1456	...	...	1515	...	...	1557	1557	...	1615	...	...	...	1656	...	1715	...	...	...
Nürnberg Hbf **905** d.	...	...	|	|	...	|	...	...	|	...	...	|	...	...	|	|	...	|	...	...	...	|	...	|	...	...	...
Augsburg Hbf d.	1325	1341	|	|	1355	|	1347	1410	|	1443	1447	|	...	1541	|	|	...	|	1547	1610	1610	|	1641	|	1645	1710t	1741
Buchloe a.	1404	1404	1405	1405	1423	1422	1430	1438	1503	1505	1519	1522	...	1603	1605	1605	...	1622	1622	1637	1637	1703	1705	1722	1720	1738t	1804
Buchloe d.	▬	▬	1407	1407	1424	...	1431	1439	▬	1507	▬	1529	1539	▬	1607	1607	...	...	1627	1639	1639	▬	1707	▬	1731	1739	▬
Kaufbeuren d.	...	...	1420	1420	1439	...	1445	1451	...	1520	...	1545	1551	...	1620	1620	...	...	1645	1651	1651	...	1720	...	1745	1751	...
Biessenhofen d.	...	...	|	|	|	...	1450	1456	...	|	...	1550	1556	...	|	|	...	...	1650	1656	1656	...	|	...	1750	1756	...
Marktoberdorf d.	...	...	|	|	|	...	1506f	|	...	|	...	1607f	|	...	|	|	...	...	1712n	|	|	...	|	...	1759	|	...
Füssen a.	...	Ⓐt	|	|	|	...	1546	|	...	|	...	1645	|	...	|	|	...	...	1754	|	|	Ⓒz	|	...	1841	|	...
Ulm Hbf d.	1317	1317	|	|	|	...	...	|	1417	|	...	...	|	1517	|	|	1616	...	...	|	|	1620	|	...	...	|	1717
Memmingen a.	1354	1354	|	|	|	...	...	|	1455	|	...	...	|	1554	|	|	1644	...	...	|	|	1703	|	...	...	|	1755
Memmingen d.	1400	1400	|	|	|	...	...	|	1504	|	...	...	|	1600	|	|	1645	...	...	|	|	1704	|	...	...	|	1800
Kempten Hbf a.	1425	1425	1442	1442	1509	...	...	1522	1525	1541	...	...	1622	1625	1641	1641	1708	...	...	1721	1721	1729	1741	...	...	1822	1825
Kempten Hbf d.	...	1429	1443	1443	1510	...	...	...	1530	1543	...	...	...	1629	1643	1643	1709	...	...	...	1730	1730	1743	...	...	...	1829
Immenstadt a.	...	1445	1455	1455	1527	...	...	...	1545	1555	◄	...	...	1645	1655	1655	1725	...	...	...	1745	1745	1755	◄	...	...	1845
Immenstadt d.	...	1451	1457	1512	1542	...	...	...	1551	1557	1612	...	...	1651	1657	1712	1743	...	...	...	1751	1751	1757	1812	...	...	1851
Sonthofen d.	...	1501	|	1523	1552	...	...	...	1601	|	1621	...	...	1701	|	1721	1752	...	...	...	1801	1801	|	1821	...	...	1900
Oberstdorf a.	...	1519	|	1539p	1611	...	...	...	1619	|	1640	...	...	1724	|	1738	1813	...	...	...	1819	1819	|	1840	...	...	1919
Hergatz d.	...	...	1529	...	...	...	...	...	...	1629	...	...	...	...	1729	...	...	...	...	...	...	...	1829	...	...	...	...
Lindau Insel a.	...	...	|	...	...	...	...	...	...	|	...	...	...	...	|	...	...	...	...	...	...	...	|	...	...	...	...
Lindau Reutin a.	...	...	1545	...	...	...	...	...	...	1645	...	...	...	...	1745	...	...	...	...	...	...	...	1845	...	...	...	...

			◇		⊖			◇				◇	◇		⊖		⊗	◇				◇	⊖		◇		
München Hbf ⊡ d.	1720	1736q	...	...	1820	...	1839	...	...	...	1920	...	1939	*1954*	2020	...	...	...	2039	...	2120	...	2220	...	...	...	2320
München Pasing d.	1727	1743q	...	...	1827	...	1847	...	...	...	1927	...	1947	*2001*	2027	...	...	...	2047	...	2127	...	2227	...	...	...	2327
Geltendorf d.	1748z	1807	...	...	1848	...	1907	...	...	...	1948	...	2007	|	2048	...	...	...	2107	...	2148	...	2248	...	...	...	2348
Kaufering d.	1757	1815	...	...	1856	...	1915	...	...	...	1957	...	2015	|	2056	...	...	...	2115	...	2157	...	2256	...	...	...	2357
Nürnberg Hbf **905** d.	|	|	...	...	|	1713	|	...	...	...	|	...	|	|	|	...	...	...	|	...	|	...	|	...	...	...	|
Augsburg Hbf d.	|	|	1747	1810	|	1842	|	1847	1910t	1941	|	1947	|	|	|	2032	2032	...	|	2133	|	...	|	2232	...	2333	|
Buchloe a.	1805	1822	1822	1839	1903	1905	1922	1922	1939t	2004	2005	2019	2023	*2032*	2103	2105	2105	...	2122	2204	2205	...	2303	2304	...	0004	0004
Buchloe d.	1807	▬	1828	1840	▬	1907	▬	1929	1940	▬	2007	▬	2027	2039	▬	2107	2107	...	...	▬	2207	...	▬	2307	...	▬	0007
Kaufbeuren d.	1818	...	1845	1851	...	1919	...	1945	1951	...	2020	...	2045f	2051	...	2118	2118	2122	...	...	2218	2226	...	2318	2330	...	0018
Biessenhofen d.	|	...	1850	1856	...	|	...	1950	1956	...	|	...	2050	2056	...	2123	2123	2127	...	...	2222	2231	...	2323	2339	...	0022
Marktoberdorf d.	|	...	1900	|	...	|	...	2006f	|	...	|	...	2105f	|	...	|	|	2136	...	...	|	2240	...	|	2349	...	|
Füssen a.	|	...	1942	|	...	|	...	2045	|	...	|	...	2147	|	...	|	|	2218	...	...	|	2321	...	|	0029	...	|
Ulm Hbf d.	|	...	▬	|	1817	|	...	...	|	1917	|	...	...	|	2017	|	|	...	...	2119	|	▬	2219	|	▬	2319	|
Memmingen a.	|	...	...	|	1855	|	...	...	|	1954	|	...	...	|	2055	|	|	...	...	2154	|	...	2257	|	...	0006	|
Memmingen d.	|	...	...	|	1904	|	...	...	|	2004	|	...	...	|	2100	|	|	...	...	2204	|	...	2301	|	...	0007	|
Kempten Hbf a.	1841	...	Ⓐt	1922	1925	1941	...	...	2022	2030	2041	...	...	2121	2125	2143	2143	...	...	2229	2243	...	2326	2343	...	0032	0044
Kempten Hbf d.	1843	...	1916	...	1929	1943	...	...	...	...	2043	...	...	...	...	2145	2145	...	...	...	2245	...	...	2345	...	...	...
Immenstadt a.	1855	◄	1931	...	1945	1955	◄	...	...	...	2056	◄	...	...	...	2201	2201	...	...	...	2300	...	...	0001	...	...	...
Immenstadt d.	1857	1912	1932	...	1951	1957	2012	...	...	...	2058	2112	...	...	...	2202	2212	...	...	...	2302	2312	...	0003	0012	...	...
Sonthofen d.	|	1921	|	...	2001	|	2021	...	...	...	|	2121	...	...	...	|	2221	...	...	...	|	2321	...	|	0021	...	...
Oberstdorf a.	|	1941	|	...	2019	|	2043	...	...	...	|	2143	...	...	...	|	2243	...	...	...	|	2343	...	|	0040	...	...
Hergatz d.	1929	...	2012	...	...	2029	...	...	...	...	2129	...	...	...	...	2233	...	...	...	...	2333	...	...	0035	...	...	...
Lindau Insel a.	|	...	2029	...	...	|	...	...	...	...	|	...	...	...	...	|	...	...	...	...	0008*	...	...	0050	...	...	...
Lindau Reutin a.	1945	...	...	...	...	2045	...	...	...	...	2145	...	...	...	...	2250	...	...	...	...	2350	...	...	...	...	...	...

FOR NOTES SEE NEXT PAGE →

RE / RB services except where shown

LINDAU - KEMPTEN - ULM, AUGSBURG and MÜNCHEN 935

See Table **934** for other services Lindau - Memmingen - Buchloe - München.

km																											
			⊖						◇				⊖	◇				◇						◇			
		Ⓐt	Ⓐt	Ⓐt	⑥	Ⓐt		Ⓐt		Ⓐt	Ⓐt			Ⓐt	Ⓐt	Ⓐt	Ⓒz	Ⓒz				Ⓐt		Ⓐt	Ⓐt	Ⓒz	
	Lindau Reutin d.	...	...	...	...	...	...	...	...	...	...	...	...	...	...	...	...	...	...	...	...	...	...	...	...	...	0715
	Lindau Insel d.	...	...	...	...	...	0412t	...	...	...	0505	...	...	...	...	...	...	...	...	0608	...	...	...	...	...	...	|
	Hergatz d.	...	...	...	...	...	0429t	...	...	...	0519	...	...	...	...	...	...	...	...	0623	...	...	...	...	...	...	0730
0	**Oberstdorf** d.	...	...	...	...	0438	|	...	...	0521	|	...	...	...	0535	...	...	...	0614	|	...	0630	...	...	0700	0719	|
13	Sonthofen d.	...	...	...	...	0456	|	...	...	0539	|	...	...	...	0555	...	...	...	0632	|	...	0654	...	...	0728	0741	|
21	Immenstadt a.	...	...	...	...	0504	0507t	...	...	0548	0554	...	...	...	0604	...	...	...	0642	0658	...	0706	...	...	0737	0750	0803
21	Immenstadt d.	...	...	...	...	▬	0509t	...	...	▶	0557	...	...	...	0610	...	...	...	▶	0701	...	0713	...	...	▶	▶	0806
42	**Kempten** Hbf a.	...	...	...	...	...	0524t	...	...	▬	0611	...	...	...	0626	...	...	...	▬	0714	...	0728	...	...	▬	▬	0818
42	**Kempten** Hbf d.	0433	...	0506	0512	...	0529	0533	...	...	0616	0616	...	...	0630	0633	0631	...	...	0718	0732	0732	0737	...	...	...	0819
77	Memmingen a.	|	...	|	|	...	0554	|	...	...	|	|	...	...	0701	|	0656	...	...	|	0757	0757	|	...	...	...	|
77	Memmingen d.	|	...	|	|	◇	0555	|	...	...	|	|	...	...	0708	|	0703	...	...	|	0804	0804	|	...	◇	...	|
129	**Ulm** Hbf a.	|	...	|	|	Ⓐt	0642	|	...	...	|	|	...	...	0743	|	0741	...	...	|	0838	0838	|	...	Ⓒz	...	|
—	**Füssen** d.	|	...	|	|	0450	▬	|	0517z	...	|	|	...	0550	...	|	▬	0623	...	|	▬	...	|	0659	0726	...	|
	Marktoberdorf d.	|	...	|	|	0532	...	|	0600	...	|	|	...	0632	...	|	...	0707	...	|	...	...	|	0747f	0808	...	|
	Biessenhofen d.	0457	...	0530	0535	0540	...	0557	0607	...	|	|	...	0640	...	0657	...	0715	...	|	...	...	0801	0756	0816	...	|
	Kaufbeuren d.	0502	...	0537	0540	0548	⊖	0602	0619	...	0640	0640	...	0648	...	0702	⊖	0720	...	0742	...	...	0806	0819g	0820	◇	0842
	Buchloe a.	0513	...	0548	0551	0601	Ⓐt	0613c	0631	...	0650	0650	...	0701	...	0713	Ⓐt	0731	Ⓒz	0753	...	...	0818	0830	0830		0853
0	Buchloe d.	0523	0522	0555	0555	0606	0616	0623	0638	0636	0652	0652	0656	0706	...	0723	0716	0738	0736	0755	0756	...	0823t	0835	0835	0838	0855
40	**Augsburg** Hbf a.	0557	|	|	|	0640	|	0650	0710	|	0716	0716	|	0742	...	0749	|	0810	|	|	0819	...	0850t	|	|	0911	0915
	Nürnberg Hbf **905** a.	...	|	|	|	...	|	...	...	|	...	...	|	...	...	...	|	...	|	|	...	...	...	|	|	...	1045
	Kaufering d.	...	0529	0603	0603	...	0623	...	...	0644	...	...	0703	...	...	...	0723	...	0744	0803	...	...	...	0844	0844	...	...
	Geltendorf d.	...	0538	|	0611	...	0631	...	...	0651	...	...	0711	...	...	...	0731	...	0751	0811z	...	...	...	0852	0852	...	...
	München Pasing a.	...	0558	0632	0632	...	0652	...	...	0712	...	...	0735	...	...	...	0757	...	0812	0832	...	...	...	0912	0912	...	...
	München Hbf ⊡ a.	...	0606	0641	0641	...	0659	...	...	0719	...	...	0742	...	...	...	0804	...	0819	0839	...	...	...	0919	0919	...	...

													IC **2084**	◇	*IC* **2012**					◇					◇		
			Ⓐt	Ⓒz				Ⓒz	Ⓐt				N		B												
Lindau Reutin d.	...	...	...	...	0815	...	...	...	...	0915	...	...	...	...	...	...	1015	...	...	...	...	1115	...	...	...	...	1215
Lindau Insel d.	...	...	...	...	|	...	...	...	...	|	...	...	...	...	...	...	|	...	...	...	...	|	...	...	...	...	|
Hergatz d.	...	...	...	...	0830	...	...	...	...	0930	...	...	...	...	...	...	1030	...	...	...	...	1130	...	...	...	...	1230
Oberstdorf d.	0741	...	0820	0826	|	0841	...	0859	0905	|	...	...	0938	...	0950	1023	|	1041	...	...	1120	|	1141	...	...	1220	|
Sonthofen d.	0801	...	0840	0848	|	0901	...	0931	0926	|	...	...	1000	...	1011	1041	|	1101	...	...	1140	|	1201	...	...	1241	|
Immenstadt a.	0811	...	0850	0900	0903	0911	...	0940	0935	1003	...	...	1010	...	1019	1050	1103	1111	...	...	1150	1203	1211	...	...	1251	1303
Immenstadt d.	0817	...	▶	▶	0906	0917	...	▶	▶	1006	...	...	1027	...	1038	1106	1106	1117	...	...	▶	1206	1217	...	...	▶	1306
Kempten Hbf a.	0832	...	▬	▬	0918	0932	...	▬	▬	1018	...	...	1043	...	1052	1118	1118	1132	...	...	▬	1218	1232	...	...	▬	1318
Kempten Hbf d.	0834	0837	...	...	0919	0934	0937	...	...	1019	1032	1037	1044	...	1054	1119	1119	1132	1137	...	...	1219	1234	1237	...	...	1319
Memmingen a.	0855	|	...	...	|	0959	|	...	...	|	1055	|	|	...	1121	|	|	1157	|	...	...	|	1255	|	...	...	|
Memmingen d.	0904	|	◇	...	|	1004	|	◇	...	|	1101	|	|	...	1124	|	|	1204	|	...	...	|	1304	|	...	...	|
Ulm Hbf a.	0938	|		...	|	1038	|		...	|	1143	|	|	...	1155	|	|	1238	|	...	...	|	1340	|	...	...	|
Füssen d.	▬	|	0815	...	|	▬	|	0915	...	|	▬	|	|	1016	▬	|	|	▬	|	1116	...	|	▬	|	1217	...	|
Marktoberdorf d.	...	|	0901	...	|	...	|	1001	...	|	...	|	|	1104f	...	|	|	...	|	1202f	...	|	...	|	1304	...	|
Biessenhofen d.	...	0901	0909	...	|	...	1001	1009	...	|	...	1101	|	1113	...	|	|	...	1201	1210	...	|	...	1301	1312	...	|
Kaufbeuren d.	⊖	0906	0918	...	0942	...	1006	1019	...	1042	⊖	1106	1114	1121	...	1142	1142	...	1206	1219	...	1242	⊖	1306	1320	◇	1342
Buchloe a.		0918	0931	...	0953	...	1018	1030	...	1053		1118	1129	1132	...	1153	1153	...	1218	1230	...	1253		1318	1331		1353
Buchloe d.	0856	0923	0938	0936	0955	0956	1023t	1038	1036	1054	1056	1123	1134	1142	1136	1155	1155	1156	...	1238	1236	1254	1256	1323	1335	1338	1355
Augsburg Hbf a.	|	0949	1010	|	|	1018	1049t	1110	|	1116	|	1150	1200	1211	|	|	|	1219	...	1310	|	1315	|	1350	|	1410	|
Nürnberg Hbf **905** a.	|	...	...	|	|	...	...	...	|	...	|	...	...	...	|	|	|	...	...	...	|	...	|	...	|	...	|
Kaufering d.	0903	...	...	0944	1003	...	...	...	1044	...	1103	...	...	...	1144	1203	1203	...	...	...	1244	...	1303	...	1344	...	1403
Geltendorf d.	0911	...	...	0951	1011	...	...	...	1051	...	1111	...	...	...	1151	1211	1211	...	...	...	1251	...	1311	...	1352	...	1411
München Pasing a.	0932	...	...	1012	1032	...	...	...	1112	...	1132	...	...	...	1212	1232	1232	...	...	...	1312	...	1332	...	1413	...	1432
München Hbf ⊡ a.	0940	...	...	1019	1041	...	...	...	1119	...	1141	...	...	...	1219	1241	1241	...	...	...	1319	...	1339	...	1420	...	1439

			◇					◇						◇					◇					◇			
Lindau Reutin d.	...	...	...	...	1315	...	...	...	...	...	1414	...	...	...	...	1515	...	...	...	...	1615	...	...	...	...	1715	...
Lindau Insel d.	...	...	...	...	|	...	...	...	...	...	|	...	...	...	...	|	...	...	...	...	|	...	...	...	...	|	...
Hergatz d.	...	...	...	...	1330	...	...	...	...	...	1429	...	...	...	...	1530	...	...	...	...	1630	...	...	...	...	1730	...
Oberstdorf d.	1241t	...	...	1319	|	1337q	...	...	...	1419	|	1441	...	...	1505	|	1540v	...	...	1623	|	1641t	...	...	1705	|	1739
Sonthofen d.	1301t	...	...	1341	|	1401	...	...	...	1441	|	1501	...	...	1531	|	1601	...	...	1641	|	1701t	...	...	1731	|	1801
Immenstadt a.	1311t	...	...	1350	1403	1411	...	...	...	1450	1502	1511	...	...	1540	1603	1611	...	...	1650	1703	1711t	...	...	1740	1803	1811
Immenstadt d.	1317t	...	...	▶	1406	1417	...	...	...	1505	1505	1517	...	...	▶	1606	1617	...	...	▶	1706	1717t	...	...	▶	1806	1817
Kempten Hbf a.	1331t	...	...	▬	1418	1432	...	...	...	1518	1518	1532	...	...	▬	1618	1632	...	...	▬	1718	1732t	...	...	▬	1818	1832
Kempten Hbf d.	1334	1337	...	...	1419	1434	1437	...	...	1519	1519	1534	1537	...	...	1619	1635	1637	...	...	1719	1734	1737	...	...	1819	1834
Memmingen a.	1359	|	...	...	|	1455	|	...	...	|	|	1559	|	...	...	|	1704	|	...	...	|	1759	|	...	...	|	1855
Memmingen d.	1404	|	...	...	|	1504	|	...	...	|	|	1603	|	...	...	|	1706	|	...	...	|	1804	|	...	...	|	1904
Ulm Hbf a.	1439	|	...	...	|	1538	|	...	...	|	|	1641	|	...	...	|	1739	|	...	...	|	1839	|	...	...	|	1938
Füssen d.	▬	|	1320	...	|	▬	|	1423	...	|	|	▬	|	1523	...	|	▬	|	1623	...	|	▬	|	1705	...	|	▬
Marktoberdorf d.	...	|	1404	...	|	...	|	1504	...	|	|	...	|	1605	...	|	...	|	1704	...	|	...	|	1801b	...	|	...
Biessenhofen d.	...	1401	1412	...	|	...	1501	1512	...	|	|	...	1601	1613	...	|	...	1701	1712	...	|	...	1801	1809	...	|	...
Kaufbeuren d.	...	1406	1419	...	1442	⊖	1506	1519	...	1542	1542	...	1606	1619	...	1642	⊖	1706	1719	...	1742	...	1806	1819	◇	1842	⊖
Buchloe a.	...	1418	1430	...	1453		1518	1531	...	1552	1552	...	1618	1630	...	1653		1718	1731	...	1753	...	1818	1830		1853	
Buchloe d.	1356	...	1438	1436	1454	1456	1523	1538	1536	1555	1555	1556	1623t	1638	1636	1656	1656	1723	1738	1736	1755	1756	1823t	1835	1838	1856	1856
Augsburg Hbf a.	1418	...	1510	|	1515	|	1550	1610	|	|	|	1618	1649t	1710	|	1717	|	1750	1810	|	|	1818	1850t	|	1910	1916	|
Nürnberg Hbf **905** a.	...	...	...	|	...	|	...	...	|	|	|	...	...	...	|	...	|	...	...	|	|	...	...	|	...	2036	|
Kaufering d.	...	...	...	1444	...	1503	...	...	1544	1603	1603	...	...	...	1644	...	1703	...	...	1744	1803	...	...	1844	...	...	1903
Geltendorf d.	...	...	...	1451	...	1511	...	...	1551	1611	1611	...	...	...	1651	...	1711	...	...	1751	1811	...	...	1852	...	...	1911
München Pasing a.	...	...	...	1512	...	1533	...	...	1612	1632	1632	...	...	...	1712	...	1732	...	...	1812	1832	...	...	1912	...	...	1934
München Hbf ⊡ a.	...	...	...	1519	...	1542	...	...	1619	1639	1639	...	...	...	1719	...	1741	...	...	1819	1841	...	...	1919	...	...	1942

NOTES for Table 935 (pages 442–444)

A – ALLGÄU – (12) 🍷 Dortmund (*IC* **2013**) - Köln - Stuttgart - Ulm (*RE* **2013**) - Oberstdorf. Does not run Dortmund - Stuttgart Jan. 5 - Mar. 31.

B – ALLGÄU – (12) 🍷 Oberstdorf - Ulm - Stuttgart - Bochum. Does not run Stuttgart - Bochum Jan. 6 - Apr. 1.

H – NEBELHORN – (12) Hamburg (**2083**) - Augsburg (**2085**) - Oberstdorf.

N – NEBELHORN – (12) Oberstdorf - Augsburg (**2082**) - Hamburg.

b – Arrives 1746.

c – Connects with train in previous column.

f – Arrives 6–10 minutes earlier.

g – Arrives 0801. Connects with train in previous column.

k – Arrives 0625.

n – Arrives 1657.

p – 5–6 minutes later on Ⓒ (also Jan. 6).

q – 3–4 minutes later on Ⓒ (also Jan. 6).

r – Not Jan. 6.

t – Ⓐ (not Jan. 6).

v – 1531 on Ⓒ (also Jan. 6).

z – Ⓒ (also Jan. 6).

⊗ – Change trains at Immenstadt on Ⓒ (also Jan. 6).

◐ – On Ⓒ (also Jan. 6) runs 1–2 minutes later and is detached from train in preceding column

* – Calls at Lindau Insel after Lindau Reutin.

◀ – Detached from train at Immenstadt in preceding column.

▶ – Attached to train at Immenstadt in following column.

◇ – Operated by Bayerische Regiobahn.

⊖ – Operated by Go Ahead Bayern.

⊡ – Most trains in Table **935** use platforms 27–36 at München Hbf (minimum connecting time with other services is 10 minutes).

935 LINDAU and OBERSTDORF - ULM, AUGSBURG and MÜNCHEN

RE/RB services except where shown

See Table **934** for other services Lindau - Memmingen - Buchloe - München.

		◇				◇					◇	◇				◇										
						Ⓒz	Ⓐt	Ⓒz		Ⓒz	Ⓐt	Ⓒz														
Lindau Reutin d.	...	...	...	1815	...	...	...	...	...	...	...	...	...	1915	...	...	...	2011	...	...	2115	...	...	2206	...	2311
Lindau Insel d.	...	...	...	|	...	...	...	...	...	...	...	...	...	|	...	...	...	|	...	...	|	...	...	|	...	|
Hergatz d.	...	...	...	1830	...	...	...	...	...	...	...	...	...	1930	...	...	...	2026	...	...	2130	...	...	2221	...	2326
Oberstdorf d.	...	...	1823	|	...	...	1841	1841	...	1847	...	...	1923	|	...	...	2023	|	...	2123	|	...	2223	|	2323	|
Sonthofen d.	...	...	1841	|	...	...	1901	1901	...	1909	...	...	1941	|	...	...	2041	|	...	2141	|	...	2241	|	2341	|
Immenstadt a.	...	...	1850	1903	...	...	1911	1911	...	1922	...	...	1950	2003	...	...	2050	2059	...	2150	2203	...	2250	2255	2350	2400
Immenstadt d.	...	...	▶	1906	...	...	1917	1917	...	1928	...	...	▶	2006	...	...	▶	2104	...	▬	2204	...	▬	2300	▬	0001
Kempten Hbf a.	...	...	▬	1918	...	...	1932	1932	...	1942	...	...	▬	2018	...	...	▬	2117	...	...	2218	...	...	2314	...	0015
Kempten Hbf d.	1837	...	...	1919	...	...	1934	1937	1937	1943	...	...	...	2019	2034	...	...	2118	2132	...	2218	2235	...	2317	2335	...
Memmingen a.	|	...	...	|	...	...	1959	|	|	2003	...	...	...	|	2058	...	...	|	2158	...	|	2301	...	|	2400	...
Memmingen d.	|	...	...	|	...	...	2004	|	|	2004	...	...	...	|	2102	...	◇	|	2204	◇	|	2304	◇	|	0007	...
Ulm Hbf a.	|	...	...	|	...	...	2038	|	|	2038	...	...	...	|	2140	...	Ⓒz	|	2239		|	2353		|	0055	...
Füssen d.	|	1817	...	|	...	1853	...	|	|	▬	1920	1920	...	|	▬	2023	2023	|	▬	2126	|	▬	2230	|	▬	...
Marktoberdorf d.	|	1902f	...	|	...	1936f	...	|	|	...	2004	2004	...	|	...	2103	2103	|	...	2208	|	...	2312	|	...	...
Biessenhofen d.	1901	1910	...	|	...	|	...	2001	2001	...	2011	2011	...	|	...	2111	2111	2138	...	2216	|	...	2320	2338	...	...
Kaufbeuren d.	1906	1919	...	1942	...	1948	...	2006	2006	...	2019	2019	◇	2042	⊖	2116	2119	2142	...	2221	2242	⊖	2325	2342	...	...
Buchloe a.	1918	1931	...	1953	...	1959	...	2018	2018	Ⓒz	2030	2030	Ⓐt	2053		...	2130	2154	...	...	2254		...	2353	...	...
Buchloe d.	1923	1938	1936	1955	1956	2001	...	...	...	2036	2036	2038	2038	2054	2056	...	2138	2155	2158	...	2258	2257	...	2355	0010	...
Augsburg Hbf a.	1950	2010	|	|	2019	|	...	...	...	|	|	2110	2110	2121	|	...	2210	|	2226	...	2326	|	...	|	0046	...
Nürnberg Hbf **905** a.	...	...	|	|	...	|	...	...	...	|	|	...	...	...	|	...	...	|	...	...	...	|	...	|	...	...
Kaufering d.	...	...	1944	2003	...	|	...	...	...	2044	2044	...	...	...	2103	...	...	2203	...	...	...	2303	...	0003	...	...
Geltendorf d.	...	...	1951	2011	...	|	...	...	...	2051	2053	...	...	...	2111	...	...	2211	...	...	...	2311	...	0011	...	...
München Pasing a.	...	...	2012	2032	...	2037	...	...	...	2112	2113	...	...	...	2132	...	...	2232	...	...	...	2333	...	0032	...	...
München Hbf ⊡ a.	...	...	2019	2041	...	2045	...	...	...	2119	2120	...	...	...	2141	...	...	2241	...	...	...	2342	...	0041	...	...

← FOR NOTES SEE PREVIOUS PAGE

936 STUTTGART - TÜBINGEN - AULENDORF

IRE/RB services

Operated by DB except local services Stuttgart - Tübingen (SWEG ⊖) and local services Tübingen - Sigmaringen (HzL ◇). On Jan. 6 regional services run as on ⑦.

km																											
		Ⓐ2	2		2	2		2	2		2	2		2	2		2	2		2	2		2	2			⊙
0	**Stuttgart** Hbf ☆ d.	...	...	0607	...	...	0817	...	...	1017	...	...	1217	...	...	1417	...	...	1617	...	...	1817	...	...	2017	...	2217
57	Reutlingen ☆ d.	...	...	0645	...	...	0850	...	...	1050	...	...	1250	...	...	1450	...	...	1650	...	...	1850	...	...	2050	...	2250
71	**Tübingen** Hbf ☆ d.	...	...	0658	...	0729	0900	...	0929	1100	...	1129	1300	...	1329	1500	...	1529	1700	...	1729	1900	...	1929	2100	...	2310
96	Hechingen d.	...	...	0719	...	0801	0920	...	1000	1120	...	1200	1320	...	1400	1520	...	1600	1720	...	1800	1920	...	2000	2120	...	2329
113	Balingen (Württ) d.	...	...	0734	...	0823	0936	...	1023f	1136	...	1223f	1336	...	1423f	1536	...	1623f	1736	...	1823f	1936	...	2023f	2136	...	2342
131	Albstadt-Ebingen d.	...	0625r	0747	...	0845	0948	...	1045	1148	...	1245	1348	...	1445	1548	...	1645	1748	...	1845	1948	...	2045	2148	...	2355
158	**Sigmaringen** **938** d.	0558	0655	0813	0906	0914	1013	1106	1114	1213	1306	1314	1413	1506	1514	1613	1706	1714	1813	1906	1914	2013	2106	2114	2213	2311	0017
175	Herbertingen **938** d.	0618	0714	0831	0931	...	1031	1131	...	1231	1331	...	1431	1531	...	1631	1731	...	1831	1931	...	2031	2131	...	2231	2335	...
184	Bad Saulgau d.	0628	0730f	0840	0940	...	1040	1140	...	1240	1340	...	1440	1540	...	1640	1740	...	1840	1940	...	2040	2140	...	2240	2344	...
203	**Aulendorf** a.	0644	0745	0856	0956	...	1056	1156	...	1256	1356	...	1456	1556	...	1656	1756	...	1856	1955	...	2056	2156	...	2256	2400	...

	Ⓐ	Ⓒ	Ⓐ2		2	2		2	2		2	2		2	2		2	2		2	2		2	2	2	2	
Aulendorf d.	...	...	0542	0704	...	0806	0906	...	1006	1106	...	1206	1306	...	1406	1506	...	1606	1706	...	1806	1906	...	2006	2106	2206	2306
Bad Saulgau d.	...	...	0557	0723	...	0821	0921	...	1021	1121	...	1221	1321	...	1421	1521	...	1621	1721	...	1821	1921	...	2021	2121	2221	2321
Herbertingen **938** d.	...	...	0606	0732	...	0829	0929	...	1029	1129	...	1229	1329	...	1429	1529	...	1629	1729	...	1829	1929	...	2029	2129	2231	2332
Sigmaringen **938** d.	0538	0544	0621	0750	0847	0850	0950	1047	1050	1150	1247	1250	1350	1447	1450	1550	1647	1650	1750	1847	1850	1950	2047	2050	2149	2251	2348
Albstadt-Ebingen d.	0601	0612	...	0811	0915	...	1010	1115	...	1210	1315	...	1410	1515	...	1610	1715	...	1810	1915	...	2010	2115	...	2213	2315	...
Balingen (Württ) d.	0615	0625	...	0825	0943f	...	1025	1143f	...	1225	1343f	...	1425	1543f	...	1625	1743f	...	1825	1943f	...	2025	2143f	...	2232	...	...
Hechingen d.	0631	0639	...	0839	1001	...	1039	1201	...	1239	1401	...	1439	1601	...	1639	1801	...	1839	2001	...	2039	2201	...	2244	...	...
Tübingen Hbf ☆ a.	0652	0657	...	0857	1028	...	1057	1228	...	1257	1428	...	1457	1628	...	1657	1828	...	1857	2028	...	2057	2227	...	2302	...	...
Reutlingen ☆ a.	0707	0708	...	0908	...	...	1108	...	...	1308	...	...	1508	...	...	1708	...	...	1908	...	...	2108	...	...	...	...	...
Stuttgart Hbf ☆ a.	0743	0743	...	0943	...	...	1143	...	...	1343	...	...	1543	...	...	1743	...	...	1943	...	...	2143	...	...	...	...	...

OTHER SERVICES STUTTGART - TÜBINGEN

km																
			Ⓐ					Ⓐ			⊠					♥
0	**Stuttgart** Hbf **930** d.	0546	0622	0656	0723	0752	0823	0854	0923	0952	and at	2223	2252	2323		1851
22	Plochingen **930** d.	0605	0644	0715	0745	0812	0845	0912	0945	1012	the same	2245	2312	2345	A	|
29	Wendlingen ▷ d.	0613	0650	0722	0751	0818	0851	0918	0951	1018	minutes	2251	2318	2351	L	|
35	Nürtingen d.	0620	0655	0728	0757	0824	0856	0924	0956	1024	past each	2256	2324	2357	S	1915
57	Reutlingen Hbf d.	0638	0710	0744	0814	0842	0912	0942	1012	1042	hour until	2312	2342	0014	O	1937
71	**Tübingen** Hbf a.	0649	0723	0754	0824	0853	0922	0953	1022	1053		2322	2353	0024		1947

	Ⓐ			Ⓐ♠		Ⓐ		Ⓐ					❖			
Tübingen Hbf d.	0414	0532	0551	0610	0633	0703	0733	0805	0831	0905	0933	1005	and at	2233	2305	2333
Reutlingen Hbf d.	0426	0543	0601	0623	0643	0717	0743	0816	0841	0916	0943	1016	the same	2243	2316	2343
Nürtingen d.	0445	0559	0617	0642	0700	0734	0759	0833	0858	0933	0958	1033	minutes	2259	2333	2359
Wendlingen ▷ d.	0451	0606	|	|	0707	0741	0806	0841	0905	0941	1005	1041	past each	2306	2341	0006
Plochingen **930** d.	0501	0616	0628	0655	0717	0750	0813	0848	0912	0949	1012	1048	hour until	2314	2349	0014
Stuttgart Hbf **930** a.	0519	0635	0643	0709	0735	0808	0829	0908	0928	1006	1028	1108		2332	0006	0032

⊠ – Timings may vary by 1 – 2 minutes.
❖ – Tübingen d. 1030 (not 1033), Reutlingen d. 1040 (not 1043), Nürtingen d. 1055 (not 1058).
⊙ – Change trains at Tübingen on Ⓐ.
☆ – See panel below main table for other services.
⊖ – Südwestdeutsche Landesverkehrs.
◇ – Hohenzollerische Landesbahn.
▷ – Regional *IRE* connections **Wendlingen - Ulm**. Operates via the high-speed line.
From Wendlingen at 0724 and hourly until 2324. Journey time Wendlingen - Ulm: 27 minutes (all trains call at Merklingen, 15 minutes from Wendlingen);
From Ulm Hbf at 0529 Ⓐ, 0629 and hourly until 2229. Journey time Ulm - Wendlingen: 30 minutes (all trains call at Merklingen, 10 minutes from Ulm).

f – Arrives 8 minutes earlier.
r – 0630 on Ⓒ.

♥ – ⑦–④ to Jan. 4 (not Dec. 25). *IC* **2011**. See also Tables **800** and **912**.
♠ – Ⓐ to Jan. 5. *IC* **2010**. See also Tables **800** and **912**.

936a STUTTGART - STUTTGART FLUGHAFEN / MESSE ✈

S-Bahn 2/3

20 km. Journey time: 27 minutes. On Jan. 6 services run as on ⑦.

***Warning!** Timings of late evening services (2200 to 0100 the following morning) may vary on Dec. 12, Jan. 9, 16, 23, Feb. 6, 13, 27, Mar. 6, 20, 27, Apr. 3, May 8, 22.*

From Stuttgart Hbf: On Ⓐ at 0025, 0055, 0430, 0455, 0515, 0525, 0540, 0555, 0610, 0625, 0640, 0655 and every 15 minutes until 2010, 2025, 2040, 2055; then 2115, 2125, 2145, 2155, 2215, 2225, 2245, 2255, 2315, 2325 and 2355. On ⑥ at 0025, 0055, 0125, 0225, 0325, 0345, 0425, 0525, 0555, 0625, 0655, 0725, 0740, 0755, 0810, 0825, 0840, 0855 and and every 15 minutes until 2010, 2025, 2040, 2055; then 2125, 2155, 2225, 2255, 2325 and 2355. On † at 0025, 0055, 0125, 0225, 0325, 0345, 0425, 0525, 0545, 0625, 0645, 0725, 0745, 0755, 0815, 0825, 0845, 085[illegible] and at 15, 25, 45 and 55 minutes past each hour until 1815, 1825, 1845, 1855; then 1925, 1955 and every 30 minutes until 2325, 2355.

From Stuttgart Flughafen ✈: On Ⓐ at 0008, 0038, 0508, 0518, 0538, 0548, 0608, 0623, 0638, 0653 and every 15 minutes until 1953, 2008, 2023, 2038; then 2048, 2108, 2118, 2138, 2148, 2208, 2218, 2238, 2248, 2308, 2318, 2338, 2348. On ⑥ at 0008, 0038, 0108, 0208, 0308, 0408, 0508, 0538, 0608, 0638, 0708, 0738, 0808, 0823, 0838, 0853 and every 15 minutes until 1953, 2008, 2023, 2038; then 2108, 2138, 2208, 2238, 2308 and 2338. On † at 0008, 0038, 0108, 0208, 0308, 0408, 0508, 0548, 0608, 0648, 0708, 0748, 0808, 0818, 0838, 0848 and at 08, 18, 38 and 48 minutes past each hour until 1808, 1818, 1838, 1848; then 1908, 1918, 1938, 2008, 2038 and every 30 minutes until 2308, 2338.

937 AULENDORF - KISSLEGG - LEUTKIRCH and WANGEN

RB services; 2nd class only

km																					
		Ⓐt	Ⓐt																		
0	**Aulendorf** d.	0507	0547	0651	0803	0907	1003	1107	1203	1307	1403	1507	1603	1707	1803	1907	2003	2107	2205	2310	...
10	Bad Waldsee d.	0514	0555	0658	0811	0915	1011	1115	1211	1315	1411	1515	1611	1715	1811	1915	2011	2115	2213	2318	...
30	Kißlegg a.	0531	0612	0715	0825	0933	1025	1133	1225	1333	1425	1533	1625	1733	1825	1933	2025	2133	2227	2335	...
	Kißlegg **934** d.	*0536*	0623	*0723*	0832	0943	1032	1143	1232	1343	1432	1543	1632	1743	1832	1943	2032	2143	*2244*	2338	2339
	Wangen (Allgäu) **934** a.	|	0633	|	0842	|	1042	|	1242	|	1442	|	1642	|	1842	|	2042	|	*2253*	|	2348
	Leutkirch **934** a.	*0543*	...	*0730*	...	0951	...	1151	...	1351	...	1551	...	1751	...	1951	...	2151	...	2346	...

	Ⓐt	Ⓐt		Ⓒz		Ⓐt															
Leutkirch **934** d.	0453	...	...	0714	...	0806	...	1006	...	1206	...	1406	...	1606	...	1806	...	2006	...	2206	*2329*
Wangen (Allgäu) **934** d.	|	*0526*	*0707*	|	*0808*	|	0915	|	1115	|	1315	|	1515	|	1715	|	1915	|	2115	|	|
Kißlegg **934** a.	0500	*0535*	*0716*	0722	*0818*	0814	0925	1014	1125	1214	1325	1414	1525	1614	1725	1814	1925	2014	2125	2214	*2336*
Kißlegg d.	0506	0546	0725	0725	0827	0827	0934	1027	1134	1227	1334	1427	1534	1627	1734	1827	1934	2027	2134	2228	2341
Bad Waldsee d.	0528	0608	0741	0741	0846	0846	0948	1046	1148	1246	1348	1446	1548	1646	1748	1843	1948	2043	2149	2245	2357
Aulendorf a.	0535	0616	0749	0749	0854	0854	0955	1054	1155	1254	1355	1454	1555	1654	1755	1851	1955	2051	2157	2253	0005

t – Not Jan. 6.
z – Also Jan. 6.

ULM and ROTTWEIL - DONAUESCHINGEN - NEUSTADT - FREIBURG — 938

DB (*RE* / *S-Bahn* services)

ULM - DONAUESCHINGEN - VILLINGEN. On Jan. 6 services run as on ⑦.

km		Ⓐ	Ⓒ	Ⓒ	Ⓐ			Ⓐ					Ⓐ			Ⓐ									
0	**Ulm** Hbf d.	0602	0602	0644	0702	0817	0917	0917	1017	1117	1217	1317	1317	1417	1517	1517	1617	1717	1817	1917	2017	...	2117	2217	2326
16	Blaubeuren d.	0614	0618	0702	0714	0829	0929	0929	1029	1129	1229	1329	1329	1429	1529	1529	1629	1729	1829	1929	2029	...	2130	2231	2344
34	Ehingen (Donau) d.	0636	0636	0725	0737	0842	0942	0942	1042	1142	1242	1342	1342	1442	1542	1542	1642	1742	1842	1942	2042	...	2143	2243	0001
76	Herbertingen 937 d.	0712	0713	0758	0814	0915	1015	1015	1115	1215	1316	1415	1415	1515	1615	1615	1716	1815	1916	2015	2116	...	2218	2320	0032
93	**Sigmaringen** 937 d.	0730	0728	0812	0829	0932	1029	1032	1132	1229	1332	1429	1432	1532	1629	1632	1732	1832	1932	2030	2130	2134	2232	2335	0046
135	Tuttlingen d.	0813	0813	...	...	1013	...	1113	1213	...	1413	...	1513	1613	...	1713	1813	1913	2013	...	...	2216	...	...	...
145	Immendingen 916 d.	0821	0821	...	...	1021	...	1121	1221	...	1421	...	1521	1621	...	1721	1821	1921	2021	...	...	2224	...	...	...
164	**Donaueschingen** 916 a.	0835	0835	...	...	1035	...	1135	1235	...	1435	...	1535	1635	...	1735	1835	1935	2035	...	...	2236	...	...	...
178	**Villingen** (Schwarwz) 916 a.	...	...	...	...	...	...	...	...	...	...	...	...	...	...	...	...	1945	2045	...	...	2305	...	...	...

	Ⓐ	Ⓒ	Ⓐ			Ⓐ	Ⓒ								Ⓐ			Ⓐ	Ⓐ	Ⓒ		Ⓐ			
Villingen (Schwarzw) 916 d.	...	...	0504	...	...	0705	0711	0812	...	...	...	...	...	...	...	...	...	...	...	...	...	...	...	...	2059
Donaueschingen 916 d.	...	...	0514	...	...	0717	0721	0821	0921	...	1121	...	1321	...	1421	1521	...	1604	1721	1721	...	1821	1921	...	2121
Immendingen 916 d.	...	...	0528	...	...	0733	0735	0835	0935	...	1135	...	1335	...	1435	1535	...	1621	1735	1736	...	1835	1935	...	2135
Tuttlingen d.	...	...	0536	...	...	0750j	0746	0844	0944	...	1144	...	1344	...	1444	1544	...	1637f	1744	1744	...	1844	1944	...	2147
Sigmaringen 937 d.	0520	0522	0619	0627	0728	0830	0830f	0931	1030	1131	1230	1331	1430	1531	1531	1630	1731	1731	1830	1830	1931	1931	2031	2131	2233
Herbertingen 937 d.	0534	0536	...	0640	0742	0843	0843	0944	1043	1144	1243	1344	1443	1544	1544	1643	1744	1744	1843	1843	1944	1944	2045	2147	2246
Ehingen (Donau) d.	0606	0605	...	0712	0814	0913	0913	1013	1113	1213	1313	1413	1513	1613	1613	1713	1813	1813	1914	1913	2013	2013	2114	2217	2317
Blaubeuren d.	0625	0621	...	0729	0829	0929	0929	1029	1129	1229	1329	1429	1529	1629	1629	1729	1829	1829	1929	1929	2029	2029	2131	2230	2332
Ulm Hbf a.	0637	0638	...	0741	0842	0941	0941	1041	1141	1241	1341	1441	1541	1641	1641	1741	1841	1841	1942	1941	2041	2041	2143	2242	2351

VILLINGEN / SEEBRUGG - FREIBURG (BREISGAU). On Jan. 6 services run as on ⑦.

km		⚒	⚒	⚒	Ⓐ	⚒	⚒	⚒	⚒	⚒	⚒		⚒	⚒	⚒	⚒	⚒	⚒	⚒	⚒	🚌	⚒	🚌	⚒
	Villingen (Schwarzw) d.	...	...	0521	...	...	...	0618	...	...	0737	and at the same minutes past each hour until	...	...	1837	...	...	1937	...	2037	...	2137	...	2237
	Donaueschingen d.	...	...	0540	0611	...	...	0639	...	...	0748		...	...	1848	...	...	1948	...	2048	...	2148	...	2248
0	**Neustadt** (Schwarzw) d.	0550	...	0623	0651	0656	...	0728	0802	...	0828		1902	...	1928	2002	...	2028	...	2128	...	2228	...	2328
	Seebrugg d.	│	0600	│	...	│	0701	│	│	0801	│		│	1901	│	│	2001	│	2101	│	2200	│	2300	│
5	Titisee a.	0556	0626	0629	...	0702	0727	0734	0808	0827	0834		1908	1927	1934	2008	2027	2034	2127	2134	2233	2234	2333	2334
	Titisee d.	0600	0633	0633	...	0705	0737	0737	0809	0838	0838		1909	1938	1938	2009	2038	2038	...	2138	...	2238	...	2338
36	**Freiburg** (Brsg) Hbf a.	0638	0715	0715	...	0743	0818	0818	0848	0918	0918		1948	2018	2018	2048	2118	2118	...	2218	...	2318	...	0018

	†	†	†	†	†	†	†	†	❖	†	†	†	†	†	†	†	†	†	†	†	🚌	†	🚌	†
Villingen (Schwarzw) d.	...	...	...	...	...	...	0737	...	and at the same minutes past each hour until	...	1737	...	1837	...	...	1937	...	...	2037	...	...	2137	...	2237
Donaueschingen d.	...	...	...	...	...	...	0748	...		...	1748	...	1848	...	...	1948	...	...	2048	...	...	2148	...	2248
Neustadt (Schwarzw) d.	...	0623	0728	...	0758	...	0836f	0858		...	1834f	1858	1928	...	1958	2028	...	2059	2128	2158	...	2228	...	2328
Seebrugg d.	0600	│	│	0728	│	0810	│	│		1810	│	│	│	1931	│	│	2036	│	│	│	2200	│	2300	│
Titisee a.	0626	0629	0734	0755	0804	0838	0842	0904		1838	1840	1904	1934	1957	2004	2034	2102	2105	2134	2204	2233	2234	2333	2334
Titisee d.	0633	0633	0736	0807	0807	0845	0845	0905		1845	1845	1905	1938	2008	2008	2038	2108	2108	2138	2205	...	2238	...	2338
Freiburg (Brsg) Hbf a.	0715	0715	0815	0843	0843	0924	0924	0944		1931	1931	1944	2015	2045	2045	2115	2145	2145	2215	2244	...	2315	...	0018

km		⚒	⚒	Ⓐ	Ⓐ	⚒	Ⓐ	Ⓐ	⚒	⚒	⚒		⚒	⚒	⚒	⚒	⚒	⚒	⚒	🚌	⚒	🚌	⚒	⚒
0	**Freiburg** (Brsg) Hbf d.	0536	0536	0608	...	0642	0642	0713	0740	0740	0810	and at the same minutes past each hour until	1840	1840	1910	1940	1940	2010	2040	...	2140	...	2240	2340
31	Titisee a.	0610	0610	0643	...	0715	0715	0746	0819	0819	0848		1919	1919	1948	2019	2019	2048	2119	...	2219	...	2319	0019
	Titisee ⊡ d.	0613	0630	0644	...	0717	0729	0747	0820	0829	0849		1920	1929	1949	2020	2029	2049	2120	2123	2220	2223	2320	0020
50	**Seebrugg** ⊡ a.	│	0655	│	...	│	0755	│	│	0855	│		│	1955	│	│	2055	│	│	2159	│	2259	│	│
	Neustadt (Schwarzw) d.	0623	...	0650	0657	0730f	...	0753	0830	...	0855		1930	...	1955	2030	...	2055	2130	...	2230	...	2330	0026
	Donaueschingen d.	0703	...	...	0737	0810	...	...	0910	...	...		2010	...	...	2110	...	...	2210	...	2310	...	0010	...
	Villingen (Schwarzw) a.	0718	...	...	...	0820	...	...	0920	...	...		2020	...	...	2120	...	...	2220	...	2320	...	0020	...

	†	†	†	†	†	†	†		†	†	†	†	†	†	†	†	†🚌	†	†	🚌	†	🚌	†	†
Freiburg (Brsg) Hbf d.	0642	0642	0745	0745	0837	0837	0857	and at the same minutes past each hour until	1737	1737	1757	1817	1846	1905	1905	1940	...	2016	2046	...	2146	...	2246	2346
Titisee a.	0715	0715	0818	0818	0915	0915	0935		1815	1815	1835	1855	1918	1948	1948	2019	...	2048	2118	...	2218	...	2318	0018
Titisee ⊡ d.	0717	0719	0819	0821	0917	0920	0942		1817	1820	1842	1905	1920	1950	1958	2020	2023	2050	2119	2123	2220	2223	2320	0020
Seebrugg ⊡ a.	│	0745	│	0948	│	0948	│		│	1848	│	│	│	│	2025	│	2059	│	│	2159	│	2259	│	│
Neustadt (Schwarzw) d.	0730f	...	0830	...	0930f	...	0948		1830f	...	1848	1910	1930	1956	...	2030	...	2056	2130	...	2226	...	2330	0026
Donaueschingen d.	0810	...	0910	...	1010	...	...		1910	...	...	...	2010	...	...	2110	...	...	2210	...	...	...	0010	...
Villingen (Schwarzw) a.	0820	...	0920	...	1020	...	...		1920	...	...	...	2020	...	...	2120	...	...	2220	...	...	...	0025	...

ROTTWEIL - DONAUESCHINGEN. ◇ On Jan. 6 services run as on ⑦.

km		Ⓐ				⊠				
0	**Rottweil** d.	0514	...	0643	0749	and	1949	2049	2149	2249
12	Trossingen Bf ▲ d.	0529	...	0655	0800	hourly	2000	2100	2200	2300
27	Villingen (Schwarzw) d.	0548	0551	0720f	0823	until	2023	2123	2223	2318
41	**Donaueschingen** a.	...	0601	0738	0840		2040	2140	2240	*2340*

		Ⓐ		Ⓐ		Ⓒ				k	
Donaueschingen d.	0502	0537	*0624*	*0703*	...	0714	0816	and	2016	2116	*2319*
Villingen (Schwarzw) d.	0525	0606j	0638	0722	...	0735	0840	hourly	2040	2140	2333
Trossingen Bf ▲ d.	0547	0625	0656	0739	0801	0801	0901	until	2101	2201	2346
Rottweil a.	0558	0635	0707	...	0811	0811	0911		2111	2212	2355

f – Arrives 7 – 9 minutes earlier.
j – Arrives 10 – 11 minutes earlier.
k – Change trains at Villingen on Ⓑ.

❖ – The 1037 and subsequent xx37 departures from Villingen run 2 minutes earlier Neustadt - Titisee.
⊠ – The 1449 from Rottweil departs Villingen 1522, arrives Donaueschingen 1537.
◇ – Operated by Südwestdeutsche Landesverkehrs (SWEG).
⊡ – Other daily 🚌 connections Titisee - Seebrugg. (journey 36 minutes): **From Titisee** at 2323 and 0023.
▲ – Connecting services run to / from Trossingen Stadt (operated by SWEG ◇). Journey time: 5 minutes.

FRIEDRICHSHAFEN - SINGEN - BASEL — 939

IRE / *RB* services (some 2nd class only)

km		Ⓐ	Ⓐt	Ⓐt	Ⓒz	Ⓐt	Ⓒz	Ⓐt	Ⓒz	Ⓐt			⊙													
0	**Friedrichshafen** Stadt d.	0418t	0524	0619	0645	0651	0705	0734	0800	0800	0845	0902	1045	1105	1245	1305	1445	1502	1645	1702	1845	1902	2045	2105	2202	2305
34	Überlingen d.	0500t	0555	0653	0710	0730	0742	0809	0842	0842	0910	0942	1110	1142	1310	1342	1510	1542	1710	1742	1910	1942	2110	2142	2242	2342
59	Radolfzell a.	0527t	0621	0719	0731	0755	0809	0839	0909	0909	0930	1009	1130	1209	1330	1409	1530	1609	1730	1809	1930	2009	2130	2209	2309	0007
59	Radolfzell 916 d.	0528t	*0632*	0722	0732	*0816*	*0816*	*0846*	*0914*	*0916*	0932	*1016*	1132	*1216*	1332	*1416*	1532	*1616*	1732	*1816*	1932	*2016*	2132	*2222*	*2346*	...
69	**Singen** 916 a.	0536t	*0642*	0730	0740	*0826*	*0826*	*0856*	*0923*	*0926*	0940	*1026*	1140	*1226*	1340	*1426*	1540	*1626*	1740	*1826*	1940	*2026*	2140	*2233*	*2356*	...
			d				d	d																		
69	**Singen** ▣ 940 d.	0545	0645	0745	0745	...	0845	0906	...	...	0945	1045	1145	1245	1345	1445	1545	1645	1745	1845	1945	2045	2145	2236	0006	...
88	**Schaffhausen** ▣ 940 d.	0600	0700	0800	0800	...	0900	0924	...	...	1000	1100	1200	1300	1400	1500	1600	1700	1800	1900	2000	2100	2200	2254	0024	...
107	Erzingen (Baden) ▣ d.	0613	0714	0815	0815	...	0915	...	...	...	1015	1115	1215	1314	1415	1515	1615	1715	1815	1915	2015	2115	2215	...	...	...
127	Waldshut d.	0636f	0731	0834f	0834f	...	0934f	...	...	...	1034f	1134f	1234f	1334f	1434f	1534f	1634f	1734f	1834f	1934f	2034f	2131	2231	...	...	...
150	Bad Säckingen d.	0653	0750	0849	0849	...	0949	...	...	...	1049	1149	1249	1349	1449	1549	1649	1749	1849	1949	2049	2153	2254	...	...	...
167	Rheinfelden (Baden) d.	0705	0801	0901	0901	...	1001	...	...	...	1101	1201	1301	1401	1501	1601	1701	1801	1901	2001	2101	2209	2304	...	...	...
182	**Basel** Bad Bf a.	0715	0812	0912	0912	...	1012	...	...	...	1112	1212	1312	1412	1512	1612	1712	1812	1912	2012	2112	2224	2317	...	...	...

						Ⓐ		Ⓐt	Ⓒz	Ⓐt																
Basel Bad Bf d.	...	...	...	...	...	0458	...	0534	0633	0638	0749	0849	0949	1049	1149	1249	1349	1449	1549	1649	1749	1849	1949	2049	2152	2253
Rheinfelden (Baden) d.	...	...	...	...	...	0513	...	0549	0648	0649	0759	0859	0959	1059	1159	1259	1359	1459	1559	1659	1759	1859	1959	2059	2206	2307
Bad Säckingen d.	...	...	...	...	...	0529	...	0605	0704	0701	0809	0909	1009	1109	1209	1309	1409	1511	1609	1709	1809	1909	2009	2109	2223	2324
Waldshut d.	...	...	...	...	...	0553	...	0629	0729	0729	0829	0929	1029	1129	1229	1329	1429	1529	1629	1729	1829	1929	2029	2129	2246	2346
Erzingen (Baden) ▣ d.	...	...	...	...	...	0614	...	0644	0744	0744	0844	0944	1044	1144	1244	1344	1444	1544	1644	1744	1844	1944	2044	2144	2303	...
Schaffhausen ▣ 940 d.	...	...	...	0521	0607	0628	0632	0700	0800	0800	0900	1000	1100	1200	1300	1400	1500	1600	1700	1800	1900	2000	2100	2200	2318	...
Singen ▣ 940 a.	...	...	...	0539	0625	0641	0651	0719	0814	0814	0914	1014	1114	1214	1314	1414	1514	1614	1714	1814	1914	2014	2114	2214	2332	...
	Ⓐt	Ⓐt	Ⓒz	Ⓐt	Ⓒz	Ⓐt	Ⓒz			d																
Singen 916 d.	0412	0503	0539	*0557*	0637	*0654*	0716	0721	...	*0832*	0916	*1032*	1116	*1232*	1316	*1432*	1516	*1632*	1716	*1832*	1916	*2032*	2116	...	*2336*	...
Radolfzell 916 a.	0419	0511	0546	*0606*	0646	*0704*	0723	0729	...	*0841*	0923	*1041*	1123	*1241*	1323	*1441*	1523	*1641*	1723	*1841*	1923	*2041*	2123	...	*2345*	...
Radolfzell d.	0420	0516	0547	0610	0647	0708	0725	0730	...	0847	0925	1047	1125	1247	1325	1447	1525	1647	1725	1847	1925	2047	2125	...	2356	...
Überlingen d.	0443	0540	0615	0639	0715	0735	0747	0756	...	0915	0948	1115	1148	1315	1348	1515	1548	1715	1748	1915	1948	2115	2148	...	0021	...
Friedrichshafen Stadt. a.	0523	0618	0655	0721	0752	0813	0813	0828	...	0955	1013	1152	1213	1355	1413	1555	1613	1755	1813	1952	2013	2152	2213	...	0058	...

d – Daily. f – Arrives 6 – 8 minutes earlier. t – Not Jan. 6. z – Also Jan. 6. ⊙ – Change trains at Singen on Ⓐ (not Jan. 6).

940 STUTTGART - SINGEN - ZÜRICH and KONSTANZ

Regional tickets are valid on *IC* trains in this table. German holiday dates apply.

km		*IC* 1181 Ⓐ	*RE* 17611 Ⓐ	*IC* 1081 ⑥⑦ c	*IC* 181 ①–⑤ a‡	*RE* 4775 ©	*IC* 2381 Ⓐ F	*IC* 481	*IC* 183 ⚒u ‡	*IC* 483	*IC* 185	*IC* 2385	*IC* 187	*IC* 2387	*IC* 189	*IC* 2389	*IC* 489	*IC* 281	*IC* 2281	*IC* 283	*IC* 2289	*IC* 285 Ⓑq	*IC* 2285 Ⓑq	*RE* 4779 ⑥	*RB* 17677	*IC* 2287 ¶
0	**Stuttgart** Hbf ..... **942** d.	...	0458	0616	0616	0715	0716	...	0826	0916	1028	1116	1229	1316	1429	1516	...	1624	1715	1826	1916	2028	2116	2117	2217	2324
26	Böblingen .... **942** d.	...	0522	0638	0638	0738	0738	...	0850	0938	1050	1138	1250	1338	1450	1538	...	1650	1738	1850	1938	2048	2138	2139	2239	2347
42	Herrenberg .... **942** d.	...	0535	0647	0648	0747	0747	...	|	0947	|	1147	|	1347	|	1547	...	|	1747	|	1947	|	2147	2148	2248	2356
51	Bondorf .... **942** d.	...	0542	0655	0656	0755	0755	...	|	0955	|	1155	|	1355	|	1555	...	|	1755	|	1955	|	2155	2156	2256	0004
67	Horb .... d.	...	0557	0711	0710	0806	0807	...	0914	1007	1114	1207	1314	1407	1514	1607	...	1714	1807	1914	2007	2113	2207	2208	2320	0023
110	Rottweil .... d.	...	0639	0743	0743	0842	0842	...	0944	1042	1144	1242	1344	1442	1544	1642	...	1744	1842	1944	2042	2145	2242	2243	2353	0056
138	Tuttlingen .... d.	...	0719	0801	0801	0859	0859	...	1001	1059	1201	1259	1401	1459	1601	1659	...	1801	1859	2001	2059	2203	2259	2300	...	...
157	Engen .... **916** d.	...	*0740*	|	|	0913	0913	...	|	1113	|	1313	|	1513	|	1713	...	|	1913	|	2113	|	2313	2314	...	...
172	**Singen** .... **916** a.	...	*0751*	0825	0825	0922	0925	...	1025	1125	1225	1325	1425	1525	1625	1725	...	1825	1925	2025	*2125*	2225	2325	2326	...	...
172	**Singen** ....**916 939** d.	0732	...	0827	0832	0924	...	0932	1032	1132	1232	*1332*	1432	*1532*	1632	1727	1732	1832	*1932*	2032	*2132*	2232	2327	2328	...	...
	Radolfzell .... **916** d.	|	...	0833	|	0932	...	|	|	|	|	|	|	|	|	1736	|	|	|	|	|	|	2334	2336	...	...
	Konstanz .... **916** a.	|	...	...	|	0948	...	|	|	|	|	|	|	|	|	1748a	|	|	|	|	|	|	2346	2352	...	...
191	**Schaffhausen** 🏛 **939** a.	0745	...	...	0845	...	...	0945	1045	1145	1245	*1345*	1445	*1545*	1645	...	1745	1845	*1945*	2045	*2145*	2245	...	...	...	...
239	**Zürich** HB .... a.	0823	...	...	0923	...	...	1023	1123	1223	1323	*1423*	1523	*1623*	1723	...	1823	1923	*2023*	2123	*2223*	2323	...	...	...	...

	RE 17604 Ⓐ	*RE* 17608	*IC* 2286 Ⓐ F	*RE* 17618 ⚒	*RE* 17620 †	*IC* 1184 Ⓐ	*IC* 2284 ①–⑥ e	*RE* 4774 ⑦	*IC* 284 ①–⑥ e	*IC* 2288	*IC* 282	*IC* 2280	*IC* 280	*IC* 488	*IC* 188	*IC* 2386	*IC* 186	*IC* 2384	*RE* 4778 ©	*IC* 184	*IC* 482	*IC* 2382	*IC* 182 Ⓑq M	*IC* 182	*IC* 2380	*IC* 180
Zürich HB .... d.	...	...	...	...	...	...	...	...	0637	*0737*	0837	*0937*	1037	1137	1237	*1337*	1437	*1537*	...	1637	1737	...	1837	1837	*1937*	2037
Schaffhausen 🏛 **939** d.	...	...	...	...	...	0530	...	...	0716	*0816*	0916	*1016*	1116	1216	1316	*1416*	1516	*1616*	...	1716	1816	...	1916	1916	*2016*	2116
Konstanz ....**916** d.	...	...	...	...	...	|	0604	0603	|	|	|	|	|	|	|	|	|	|	1648	|	|	1806a	|	|	|	|
Radolfzell ....**916** d.	...	...	...	...	...	|	0620	0620	|	|	|	|	|	|	|	|	|	|	1704	|	|	1825	|	|	|	|
Singen ....**916 939** a.	...	...	...	...	...	0544	0627	0627	0730	*0830*	0930	*1030*	1130	1229	1330	*1430*	1530	*1630*	1710	1730	1830	1833	1930	1930	*2030*	2130
Singen ....**916** d.	...	...	...	...	...	0551	0629	0629	0737	0835	0937	1035	1137	1235	1337	1435	1537	1635	1712	1737	...	1835	1937	...	2035	...
Engen ....**916** d.	...	...	...	...	...	0600	0638	0638	|	0844	|	1044	|	1244	|	1444	|	1644	|	|	...	1844	|	...	2044	...
Tuttlingen .... d.	...	...	...	...	...	0615	0652	0652	0800	0859	1000	1059	1200	1259	1400	1459	1600	1659	1735	1800	...	*1859*	2000	...	2059	...
Rottweil .... d.	...	0511t	0537	0604	0614	0639	0711	0711	0816	0917	1016	1117	1216	1317	1416	1517	1616	*1717*	*1756*	1816	...	*1917*	2016	...	2117	...
Horb .... d.	0447	0547	0610	0638	0645	0711	0751	0751	0845	0951	1045	1151	1245	1351	1445	1551	*1645*	1751	1828	1845	...	1951	2045	...	2151	...
Bondorf ....**942** d.	0502	0602	0630	0702	0702	|	0802	0803	|	1003	|	1203	|	1403	|	1603	|	1803	|	|	...	2003	|	...	2203	...
Herrenberg ....**942** d.	0511	0611	0640	0711	0711	0726	0810	0811	|	1011	|	1211	|	1411	|	1611	|	1811	1843	|	...	2011	|	...	2211	...
Böblingen ....**942** d.	0521	0621	0650	0721	0721	0736	0821	0822	0911	1022	1111	1222	1311	1422	1511	1622	1711	1822	1853	1911	...	2022	2111	...	2222	...
Stuttgart Hbf ....**942** a.	0544	0642	0711	0742	0742	0759	0843	0843	0932	1043	1132	1243	1332	1443	1536	1643	1733	1843	1916	1933	...	2043	2132	...	2243	...

SCHAFFHAUSEN - ZÜRICH (operated by SBB)

km										
0	**Schaffhausen** .... d.	0547	0617	and at the same	2117	2147	2157	2247	2327
28	Bülach .... d.	|	0637	minutes past	2137	|	2228	|	2358
48	**Zürich** HB .... a.	0623	0655	each hour until	2155	2223	2253	2323	0023

Zürich HB .... d.	0507	0605	0637	and at the same	2037	2105	2205	2305	0005
Bülach .... d.	0532	0623	|	minutes past	|	2123	2223	2323	0023
Schaffhausen .... a.	0604	0643	0713	each hour until	2113	2143	2243	2344	0044

F – From/to Frankfurt (Table **912**).
M – To München (Table **930**).
a – ①–⑤ (not Apr. 7, 10, May 1, 29).
c – Also Apr. 7, 10, May 1, 29.
e – Not Apr. 10, May 1, 29.
q – Not Apr. 9, 30, May 28.
t – Ⓐ only.
u – Also Apr. 7.
¶ – On ⑤⑥ (also Apr. 6, 9, 30, May 17, 28) runs as *RE* **17685** and departs Stuttgart 2326.
‡ – Runs daily Singen - Zürich.

941 TÜBINGEN - HORB - PFORZHEIM

km		Ⓐ	Ⓐ	Ⓐ	©⊖	Ⓐ			⊖		⊖		Ⓐ	Ⓐ⊖	©				Ⓐ			⊖		⊖		
0	**Tübingen** Hbf .... d.	0524	0600	0628	0723	0725	...	0834	0929	1034	1129	1234	1303	1330	1330	1433	1530	1634	1703	1728	1834	1929	2034	2129	...	2234
32	**Horb** .... a.	0553	0633	0705	0752	0755	...	0910	0957	1110	1157	1310	1336	1358	1358	1510	1558	1710	1736	1757	1910	1957	2110	2157	...	2310

km		Ⓐ	Ⓐ	⑥	Ⓐ	Ⓐ	©	©⊖	Ⓐ		⊖		Ⓐ	⊖		Ⓐ⊖	©				©	Ⓐ			⊖	⊖
0	**Horb** .... d.	0424	...	0557	0616	0647	0649	0756	0804	0853	1004	1056	1125	1204	1256	1404	1404	1456	1604	...	1656	1725	1804	1856	2007	2204
15	Hochdorf (b. Horb) ..... d.	0437	0602	0610	0627	0659	0702	0820c	0820	0917c	1020	1117c	1149c	1220	1317c	1420	1420	1517c	1620	1717	1717c	1749c	1820	1917c	2020	2220
25	Nagold .... d.	0455c	0614	0621	0638	0712	0712	0831	0831	0931	1031	1131	1201	1231	1331	1431	1431	1531	1631	1731	1731	1801	1831	1931	2031	2231
34	Wildberg (Württ) .... d.	0503	0621	0629	0646	0720	0720	0839	0839	0939	1039	1139	1209	1239	1339	1439	1439	1539	1639	1739	1739	1809	1839	1939	2039	2239
45	Calw .... d.	0518	0631	0639	0657	0730	0730	0850	0850	0950	1050	1150	1220	1250	1350	1450	1450	1550	1650	1750	1750	1820	1850	1950	2050	2250
52	Bad Liebenzell .... d.	0526	0639	0647	0705	0738	0738	0901	0901	1001	1101	1201	1231	1301	1401	1501	1501	1601	1701	1801	1801	1831	1901	2001	2101	2308c
71	**Pforzheim** Hbf .... a.	0548	0659	0708	0726	0759	0759	0922	0922	1022	1122	1222	1253	1322	1422	1522	1522	1622	1722	1822	1822	1852	1922	2022	2122	2329

	Ⓐ		Ⓐ	©⊖	Ⓐ	⚒	⊖		⊖		Ⓐ	©⊖				Ⓐ		Ⓐ		⊖	Ⓐ		⊖			⑤⑥f
Pforzheim Hbf .... d.	0439	...	0618	0638	0641	0741	0836	0936	1036	1136	1236	1236	1336	1436	1536	1606	1636	1706	1736	1836	1906	1936	2036	...	2246	2352
Bad Liebenzell .... d.	0459	...	0641	0702	0710	0805	0900	1000	1100	1200	1300	1300	1400	1500	1600	1630	1700	1730	1800	1900	1930	2000	2100	...	2307	0012
Calw .... d.	0506	...	0648	0709	0716	0812	0907	1007	1107	1207	1307	1307	1407	1507	1607	1637	1707	1737	1807	1907	1937	2007	2107	...	2314	0019
Wildberg (Württ) .... d.	0516	...	0703	0721	0731	0822	0921	1021	1121	1221	1321	1321	1421	1521	1621	1651	1721	1751	1821	1921	1951	2021	2121	...	2324	0029
Nagold .... d.	0523	...	0716	0728	0739	0834	0929	1032	1129	1232	1329	1329	1432	1529	1632	1701	1729	1801	1832	1929	2001	2032	2129	...	2332	0035
Hochdorf (b. Horb) ...... d.	0535	...	0728	0740	0750	0851c	0940	1052c	1140	1252c	1340	1340	1452c	1540	1652c	1712	1740	1821c	1850c	1940	2021c	2052c	2140	...	2344	...
Horb .... a.	...	...	0741	0753	0801	0904	0956	1105	1156	1305	1356	1356	1505	1553	1705	...	1756	1834	1903	1953	2033	2105	2154	...	2358	...

	Ⓐ	Ⓐ		©	Ⓐ	Ⓐ	©⊖	©	⊖		⊖		Ⓐ	©⊖				Ⓐ		Ⓐ			⊖		⊖	
Horb .... d.	0452	0613	0644	0652	0725	0759	0759	0852	0959	1052	1159	1252	1400	1400	1452	1600	1652	1716	1801	1820	1852	...	1959	2052	2159	2252
Tübingen Hbf .... a.	0522	0651	0724	0723	0801	0829	0829	0923	1029	1123	1229	1323	1429	1429	1523	1629	1723	1752	1829	1854	1923	...	2029	2124	2229	2326

c – Arrives 8–12 minutes earlier.
f – Also Dec. 25, Jan. 5.
⊖ – Through service Tübingen - Horb - Pforzheim and v.v.

942 STUTTGART - FREUDENSTADT - OFFENBURG

km			Ⓐ					†	†	⚒															
0	**Stuttgart** Hbf....... **940** d.	0535•	...	0616	...	...	...	0818	...	0818	...	1018	...	1217	...	1418	...	1616	...	1816	...	2018	...	2217	...
26	Böblingen .... **940** d.	0559	...	0638	...	...	...	0838	...	0839	...	1039	...	1239	...	1439	...	1639	...	1839	...	2039	...	2239	...
42	Herrenberg .... **940** d.	0614	0620	0647	...	...	...	0847	...	0848	...	1048	...	1248	...	1448	...	1648	...	1848	...	2048	...	2248	...
51	Bondorf................ **940** d.	...	0627	0655	...	...	0802	0854	...	0856	1002	1056	1202	1256	1402	1456	1602	1656	1802	1856	2002	2056	2202	2256	...
57	Eutingen im Gäu.........d.	...	0636	0702	0708	...	0809	0900	0908	0908	1009	1108	1209	1308	1409	1508	1609	1708	1809	1908	2009	2108	2209	2303	2309
62	Hochdorf (b. Horb) ......d.	...	0642	...	0713	...	0814	...	0913	0913	1014	1113	1214	1313	1414	1513	1614	1713	1814	1913	2014	2114	2214	...	2315
87	**Freudenstadt** Hbf ......a.	...	0710	...	0744	...	0843	...	0944	0944	1043	1144	1243	1344	1443	1543	1643	1744	1843	1944	2043	2146	2243	...	2343

	Ⓐ		⚒	†		⚒	†										⚒	†		†	⚒			¶	
Freudenstadt Hbf ....d.	0513	...	0611	*0616*	0715	0813	*0813*	0915	1013	1115	1213	1315	1413	1515	1614	1715	1813	*1813*	1915	*2013*	2015	2115	2215	...	...
Hochdorf (b. Horb)........d.	0541	...	0643	*0646*	0745	0845	*0845*	0945	1045	1145	1245	1345	1445	1545	1646	1745	1845	*1845*	1945	*2045*	2045	2145	2245	...	...
Eutingen im Gäu..........d.	0548	0556	0656	0656	0751	0856	0856	0951	1056	1151	1256	1351	1456	1551	1656	1751	1856	1856	1951	2056	2056	2151	2250	2256	...
Bondorf................. **940** a.	0555	0602	0702	0702	0757	0902	0902	0957	1102	1157	1302	1357	1502	1557	1702	1757	1902	1902	1957	2102	2102	2157	...	2303	...
Herrenberg .... **940** a.	0604	0610	0710	0710	...	0910	0910	...	1110	...	1310	...	1510	...	1710	...	1910	1910	...	2110	2110	...	...	2311	2316
Böblingen .... **940** a.	...	0620	0720	0720	...	0920	0920	...	1120	...	1320	...	1520	...	1720	...	1920	1920	...	2120	2120	...	...	...	2330
Stuttgart Hbf........ **940** a.	...	0642	0742	0742	...	0942	0942	...	1143	...	1342	...	1543	...	1742	...	1942	1942	...	2142	2142	...	...	...	2355•

FREUDENSTADT - OFFENBURG (operated by Südwestdeutsche Landesverkehrs; 2nd class only).

km		Ⓐ	⚒◇				✣		
0	**Freudenstadt** Hbf ......d.	0531	0636	0720	0821	0900	and	2100	2200
16	Alpirsbach....................d.	0551	0659	0737	0838	0916	hourly	2116	2216
25	Schiltach......................d.	0602	0710	0750	0850	0930	until	2130	2230
35	Wolfach ....d.	0614	0720	0801	0902	0941		2141	2241
39	Hausach .... **916** a.	0618	0725	0805	0906	0945		2145	2245
72	**Offenburg** .... **916** a.	0659	0755	0834	0935	1014		2214	2314

	Ⓐ	⑥	Ⓐ							
Offenburg .... **916** d.	0453	*0544*	0558	0702	0740	0841	and	2041	...	2241
Hausach .... **916** d.	0522	0626	0626	0730	0810	0910	hourly	2110	...	2310
Wolfach ....d.	0527	0631	0631	0734	0815	0915	until	2115	...	2315
Schiltach ....d.	0537	0642	0642	0749	0826	0929		2129	...	2329
Alpirsbach..................d.	0551	0654	0654	0800	0840	0940		2140	...	2340
Freudenstadt Hbf....a.	0607	0711	0711	0816	0856	0956		2156	...	2356

✣ – The 1200 from Freudenstadt runs on © only. On Ⓐ service is retimed as follows: Freudenstadt d. 1221, Alpirsbach d. 1242, Schiltach d. 1255, Wolfach d. 1307, Hausach a. 1311, Offenburg a. 1342.
¶ – Not Apr. 6, 9, 30, May 17, 28.
• – Underground platforms.
◇ – On ⑥ runs 5–8 minutes earlier Alpirsbach - Offenburg.

S-Bahn (2nd class only)

KARLSRUHE - FREUDENSTADT 943

km		Ⓐt	Ⓐt	⑥	Ⓐt	Ⓒz		Ⓐt	†w									⑤⑥f						
	Karlsruhe Bahnhofsvorplatz d.	0431	0505	0511	...	0611	0711z	...	...	0811	0911	...	1011	1111		2111	2211	2311						
0	**Karlsruhe** Hbf .... **916** d.	|	|	|	0610	|	0707t	0745	0807	|	|	1010	|	|		|	|	|		...	...	...	...	...
24	Rastatt .... **916** d.	0503	0533	0538	0633	0638	0738	0808	0829	0838	0938	1029	1038	1138	and	2138	2238	2338	A	1210	1410	1610	1810	2007
40	Gernsbach Bf .... d.	0525	0556	0600	0656	0700	0800	0830	0844	0900	1000	1044	1100	1200		2200	2300	0000	L	1229	1429	1629	1829	2029
51	Forbach (Schwarzw) .... d.	0544	0613	0618	0717	0717	0817	0850	0900	0917	1017	1100	1117	1217	hourly	2217	2317	0017		1244	1444	1644	1844	2044
61	Schönmünzach .... d.	0556	0624	0631	0729	0729	0829	0901	0911	0929	1029	1111	1129	1229		2229	2329	0029	S	1300	1500	1700	1900	2100
74	Baiersbronn Bf .... d.	0612	0642	0649	0750	0749	0849	0923	0922	0949	1049	1122	1149	1249	until	2249	2346	0046		1311	1511	1711	1911	2111
79	**Freudenstadt** Stadt .... a.	0620	0650	0657	0758	0757	0857	0931	0930	0957	1057	1130	1157	1257		2257	2354	0054	O	1322	1522	1722	1922	2122
82	**Freudenstadt** Hbf .... a.	0625	0705	0707	0807	0807	0907	0937	0937	1007	1112k	1137	1210n	1307		2307	2400	0100		1330	1530	1730	1930	2130
																				1337	1537	1737	1937	2137

	Ⓒz	Ⓐt	Ⓐt	⑥	Ⓐt	⑥	Ⓐt	Ⓒz	Ⓐt	Ⓐt	Ⓒz														Ⓒz
reudenstadt Hbf .... d.	0015	0437	0524	0555	0614	0621	0648	0653	0720	0748	0753	0823	0853		1953	2053	2153	2253		1021	1223	1423	1623	1823
reudenstadt Stadt .... d.	0025	0443	0530	0607	0620	0630	0654	0703	0730	0803	0803	0830	0903		2003	2103	2203	2303	A	1030	1230	1430	1630	1830
aiersbronn Bf .... d.	0032	0453	0539	0616	0628	0638	0702	0711	0738	0811	0811	0838	0911	and	2011	2111	2211	2311		1038	1238	1438	1638	1838
chönmünzach .... d.	0049	0508	0556	0631	0645	0649	0728e	0728	0749	0828	0828	0849	0928		2028	2128	2228	2328	L	1049	1249	1449	1649	1849
orbach (Schwarzw) .... d.	0100	0525	0613	0643	0701	0701	0742	0742	0801	0842	0842	0901	0942	hourly	2042	2153v	2254v	2341		1101	1301	1501	1701	1901
ernsbach Bf .... d.	0117	0541	0631	0659	0728	0715	0800	0800	0815	0900	0900	0915	1000		2100	2211	2311	0000	S	1115	1315	1515	1715	1915
astatt .... **916** d.	0140	0557	0706v	0722	0754	0738e	0822	0822	0830	0922	0922	0931	1022	until	2122	2232	2332	0022		1131	1331	1531	1731	1931
Karlsruhe Hbf .... **916** a.	|	0614	0728	|	0816	0750	|	|	0843	|	|	0949	|		|	|	|	|	O	1149	1349	1549	1749	1949
arlsruhe Bahnhofsvorplatz a.	0204	...	...	0746	...	...	0846	0846	...	0946	0946	...	1046		2146	2256	2356	0046		...	...	...	...	...

– Arrives 8–9 minutes earlier.
– Also Dec. 25, Jan. 5, Apr. 6, 9, 30, May 17, 28.
k – 1107 on Ⓒ (also Jan. 6).
n – 1207 on Ⓒ (also Jan. 6).
t – Ⓐ (not Jan. 6).
v – Arrives 13–15 minutes earlier.
w – Also Jan. 6.
z – Ⓒ (also Jan. 6).

RE services

MÜNCHEN - PASSAU 944

km		Ⓐt	⚒t	⚒t	Ⓐt	Ⓐt	Ⓒz																	
0	**München** Hbf .... **878** d.	...	0444	...	0524	0604	0624	0724	0824	0924	1024	1124	1224	1324	1424	1524	1623	1724	1824	1924	2024	2124	...	2324
42	Freising .... **878** d.	...	0508	...	0549	0628	0649	0749	0849	0949	1049	1149	1249	1349	1449	1549	1650	1749	1849	1949	2049	2149	...	2349
76	Landshut (Bay) Hbf .... **878** d.	...	0527	0543	0614	0701n	0715	0815	0915	1015	1115	1215	1315	1416	1515	1615	1715	1815	1915	2015	2115	2215	...	0013
121	Landau (Isar) .... d.	...	...	0624	0701v	0737	0748	0848	0948	1048	1148	1248	1348	1448	1548	1648	1748	1848	1948	2048	2148	2248	...	0042
139	Plattling .... a.	...	...	0636	0714	0750	0800	0900	1000	1100	1200	1300	1400	1500	1600	1700	1800	1900	2000	2100	2200	2300	...	0054
139	Plattling .... **920** d.	0559	...	0642	0725	0800	0802	0902	1004	1102	1204	1302	1404	1504	1604	1702	1804	1902	2004	2102	2202	2306	...	0055
191	**Passau** Hbf .... **920** a.	0634	...	0716	0800	0835	0837	0937	1039	1137	1239	1337	1439	1539	1639	1737	1839	1937	2039	2137	2237	2341	...	0130

	⚒t		Ⓐt	Ⓒz	Ⓐt																		
assau Hbf .... **920** d.	0440	0523	0600	0627	0646	0726	0826	0919	1026	1119	1219	1319	1426	1519	1626	1719	1826	1919	2026	2126	...	2319	...
attling .... **920** a.	0513	0558	0636	0701	0720	0800	0900	0953	1100	1153	1253	1353	1500	1553	1700	1753	1900	1953	2100	2200	...	2353	...
attling .... d.	0520	0600	0639	0702	0723	0802	0902	1002	1102	1202	1302	1402	1502	1602	1702	1802	1902	2002	2102	2202	...	2357	...
andau (Isar) .... d.	0532	0613	0653	0714	0736	0814	0914	1014	1114	1214	1314	1414	1514	1614	1714	1814	1914	2014	2114	2214	...	0008	...
andshut (Bay) Hbf .... **878** d.	0608	0644	0728	0747	0806	0848	0948	1048	1148	1248	1348	1448	1548	1648	1748	1848	1948	2048	2148	2248	...	0038	...
reising .... **878** a.	0629	0709	0749	0810	0829	0910	1010	1110	1210	1310	1410	1510	1610	1710	1810	1910	2010	2110	2210	2310	...	...	...
ünchen Hbf .... **878** a.	0656	0736	0817	0836	0856	0937	1036	1137	1236	1337	1436	1537	1637	1737	1836	1937	2036	2137	2237	2337	...	...	...

– Arrives 0651.
t – Not Jan. 6.
v – Arrives 0649.
z – Also Jan. 6.

gilis

REGENSBURG - INGOLSTADT - DONAUWÖRTH - ULM 945

On Jan. 6 services run as on ⑦. Certain services run from / to Plattling (see Table **921**). **Warning!** Timings Donauwörth - Ulm and v.v. may vary by up to 3 minutes from Mar. 5.

km			Ⓐ	Ⓐ	Ⓐ	Ⓐ	Ⓐ	Ⓐ	Ⓐ	Ⓐ	Ⓐ	Ⓐ	Ⓐ	Ⓐ	Ⓐ	Ⓐ	Ⓐ	Ⓐ	Ⓐ	Ⓐ	Ⓐ	Ⓐ	Ⓐ	Ⓐ	Ⓐ
0	**Regensburg** Hbf .... d.	Ⓐ	...	...	*0418*	*0514*	...	0550	*0652*	*0742*	*0853*	*0947*	*1053*	*1147*	*1253*	*1342*	*1453*	*1545*	*1614*	*1653*	...	*1746*	...	*1853*	*1947*
46	Neustadt (Donau) .... d.		...	...	*0457*	*0551*	...	0651	*0732*	*0829*	*0932*	*1029*	*1132*	*1229*	*1332*	*1429*	*1532*	*1627*	*1703*	*1734*	...	*1829*	...	*1932*	*2029*
74	**Ingolstadt** Hbf .... a.		...	...	*0523*	*0618*	...	0719	*0754*	*0853*	*0953*	*1053*	*1153*	*1253*	*1353*	*1454*	*1553*	*1654*	*1730*	*1754*	...	*1854*	...	*1954*	*2051*
74	**Ingolstadt** Hbf .... d.		...	0505	0557	0627	0701	...	0810	0905	1011	1111	1211	1311	1411	1511	1611	1706	1734	1806	1835	1911	...	2011	2111
95	Neuburg (Donau) .... d.		...	0527	0619	0651	0719	...	0829	0928	1029	1129	1229	1329	1429	1529	1629	1728	1759	1828	1859	1929	...	2029	2129
127	**Donauwörth** .... a.		...	0552	0650	0725	0752	...	0853	0953	1053	1153	1253	1353	1453	1553	1653	1753	1837	1853	1936	1953	...	2053	2153
127	**Donauwörth** .... d.		0447	0555	0702	0734	0818	...	0902	1016	1102	1216	1302	1416	1502	1616	1708	1816	...	1902	...	1957	2016	2102	2216
153	Dillingen (Donau) .... d.		0508	0616	0730	0755	0839	...	0928	1037	1128	1237	1328	1437	1528	1637	1733	1837	...	1928	...	2023	2037	2123	2237
176	Günzburg .... **930** a.		0528	0638	0749	0812	0855	...	0945	1054	1145	1254	1345	1454	1545	1654	1751	1855	...	1945	...	2040	2054	2141	2253
200	**Ulm** Hbf .... **930** a.		0546	0657	0811	0832	0915	...	1008	1115	1209	1315	1408	1515	1608	1715	1810	1915	...	2008	...	...	2115	2208	2312e

	Ⓐ	Ⓐ	Ⓐ		Ⓒ	⑥	Ⓒ	Ⓒ	Ⓒ	Ⓒ	Ⓒ	Ⓒ	Ⓒ	Ⓒ	Ⓒ	Ⓒ	Ⓒ	Ⓒ	Ⓒ	Ⓒ	Ⓒ	Ⓒ	Ⓒ	Ⓒ¶	Ⓒ
egensburg Hbf .... d.	*2053*	*2147*	2253	Ⓒ	...	...	...	0543	0653	0758	0853	0957	1053	1157	1253	1357	1453	1557	1653	1755	1853	1957	2053	2157	2253
eustadt (Donau) .... d.	*2132*	*2229*	2332		...	...	...	0623	0733	0837	0933	1037	1133	1237	1333	1437	1533	1637	1733	1837	1933	2037	2133	2237	2332
golstadt Hbf .... a.	*2153*	*2253*	2353		...	...	...	0645	0754	0854	0954	1054	1154	1254	1354	1454	1554	1654	1754	1855	1954	2054	2153	2254	2353
golstadt Hbf .... d.	2211	2311	*0038*		...	...	0612	0711	0810	0911	1011	1111	1211	1311	1411	1511	1611	1711	1808	1911	2011	2111	2211	2311	*0038*
euburg (Donau) .... d.	2229	2329	*0054*		...	...	0629	0729	0829	0929	1029	1129	1229	1329	1429	1529	1629	1729	1828	1929	2029	2129	2229	2329	*0054*
onauwörth .... a.	2253	2355	*0120*		...	...	0653	0753	0853	0953	1053	1153	1253	1353	1454	1553	1653	1753	1853	1953	2053	2153	2253	2355	*0120*
onauwörth .... d.	...	0000	...		0513	0616	0702	0816	0902	1016	1102	1216	1302	1416	1502	1616	1702	1816	1902	2016	2102	2216	2302	0000	...
illingen (Donau) .... d.	...	0022	...		0534	0637	0730	0837	0928	1037	1128	1237	1328	1437	1528	1637	1728	1837	1928	2037	2123	2237	2329	0022	...
ünzburg .... **930** a.	...	0038	...		0550	0653	0749	0854	0945	1054	1145	1254	1345	1454	1545	1654	1745	1854	1945	2054	2141	2253	2346	0038	...
m Hbf .... **930** a.	...	0057	...		0609	0712	0811	0915	1008	1115	1209	1315	1408	1515	1608	1715	1808	1915	2008	2115	2208	2312e	0005	0057	...

		Ⓐ	Ⓐ	Ⓐ	Ⓐ	Ⓐ	Ⓐ	Ⓐ	Ⓐ	Ⓐ	Ⓐ	Ⓐ	Ⓐ	Ⓐ	Ⓐ	Ⓐ	Ⓐ	Ⓐ	Ⓐ	Ⓐ	ⒶB	ⒶA	Ⓐ	Ⓐ	Ⓐ
m Hbf .... **930** d.	Ⓐ	...	...	...	...	0453	0531	0552	0626	...	...	0747	0847	0947	1047	1147	1247	1347	1447	1547	1638	1647	1747	1847	1947
ünzburg .... **930** d.		...	...	...	...	0511	0555	0611	0644	...	0740	0806	0905	1006	1105	1206	1305	1406	1505	1606	1659	1705	1806	1905	2006
illingen (Donau) .... d.		...	...	...	...	0528	0616	0633	0701	...	0803	0823	0923	1023	1123	1223	1328	1423	1523	1623	1714	1722	1823	1923	2023
onauwörth .... a.		...	...	...	...	0549	0637	0700f	0726	...	0829	0850f	0944	1048f	1144	1248f	1349	1448f	1544	1648f	1735	1749	1848f	1944	2048f
onauwörth .... d.		...	0433	...	0529	0554	0640	0702	0728	...	0831	0901	1002	1102	1202	1302	1402	1502	1601	1702	1802	1802	1901	2001	2102
euburg (Donau) .... d.		...	0457	...	0600	0630	0706	0731	0758	...	0900	0926	1031	1131	1231	1331	1431	1530	1631	1728	1828	1828	1931	2031	2131
golstadt Hbf .... a.		...	0514	...	0617	0649	0727	0749	0817	...	0923	0942	1047	1147	1247	1349	1447	1547	1647	1748	1849	1849	1947	2047	2147
golstadt Hbf .... d.		0452	...	0606	*0625*	*0705*	...	*0807*	...	0905	...	*1005*	*1105*	*1205*	*1318*	*1405*	*1505*	*1605*	*1718*	*1804*	*1905*	*1905*	*2006*	*2105*	*2205*
eustadt (Donau) .... d.		0518	...	0627	*0652*	*0730*	...	*0827*	...	0930	...	*1027*	*1130*	*1227*	*1343*	*1427*	*1530*	*1627*	*1746*	*1827*	*1930*	*1930*	*2027*	*2130*	*2227*
egensburg Hbf .... a.		0607	...	0707	*0740*	*0808*	...	*0908*	...	1013	...	*1108*	*1213*	*1308*	*1422*	*1508*	*1613*	*1708*	*1838*	*1908*	*2013*	*2013*	*2108*	*2213*	*2308*

	Ⓐ	Ⓐ	Ⓐ		Ⓒ	⑥	Ⓒ	Ⓒ	Ⓒ	Ⓒ	Ⓒ	Ⓒ	Ⓒ	Ⓒ	Ⓒ	Ⓒ	Ⓒ	Ⓒ	Ⓒ	Ⓒ	Ⓒ	Ⓒ	Ⓒ	Ⓒ	Ⓒ
m Hbf .... **930** d.	2047	2147	2247	Ⓒ	...	...	...	0547	0642	0747	0847	0947	1047	1147	1247	1347	1447	1547	1647	1747	1847	1947	2047	2147	2247
ünzburg .... **930** d.	2105	2206	2305		...	...	...	0606	0702	0806	0905	1006	1105	1206	1305	1406	1505	1606	1705	1806	1905	2006	2105	2206	2305
illingen (Donau) .... d.	2123	2223	2323		...	...	...	0623	0724	0823	0923	1023	1123	1223	1323	1423	1523	1623	1723	1823	1923	2023	2123	2223	2323
nauwörth .... a.	2144	2248f	2345		...	...	...	0648f	0745	0850f	0944	1048f	1144	1248f	1344	1448f	1544	1648f	1744	1848f	1944	2048f	2144	2248f	2345
nauwörth .... d.	2202	2302	...		...	0507	0554	0702	0802	0901	1002	1102	1202	1302	1402	1502	1601	1702	1802	1901	2001	2102	2202	2302	...
uburg (Donau) .... d.	2231	2331	...		...	0532	0631	0731	0831	0931	1031	1131	1231	1331	1431	1531	1631	1731	1828	1931	2031	2131	2231	2331	...
olstadt Hbf .... a.	2249	2348	...		...	0547	0648	0748	0847	0947	1047	1147	1247	1347	1447	1547	1647	1747	1849	1948	2047	2147	2249	2348	...
olstadt Hbf .... d.	*2305*	...	...		0601	0601	0705	0805	0905	1005	1105	1205	1305	1405	1505	1605	1705	1804	1905	2005	2105	2205	2305	...	...
ustadt (Donau) .... d.	*2331*	...	...		0625	0625	0722	0827	0922	1027	1122	1227	1322	1427	1522	1627	1722	1827	1922	2027	2122	2227	2331	...	...
gensburg Hbf .... a.	*0008*	...	...		0707	0707	0757	0908	0958	1108	1158	1308	1358	1508	1559	1708	1758	1908	1958	2108	2159	2308	0008	...	...

– Until Mar. 3.
B – From Mar. 6.
e – 2321 from Mar. 5.
f – 5–8 minutes earlier from Mar. 5.
¶ – Change trains at Donauwörth on †.

Bahn 6; on Jan. 6 services run as on ⑦

PFORZHEIM - BAD WILDBAD 946

m		Ⓐ	⑥	Ⓐ	Ⓐ	Ⓒ	Ⓐ	Ⓐ				Ⓒ	Ⓐ				Ⓐ			Ⓐ				
0	**Pforzheim** Hbf .... d.	0507	0557	0607	0645	0657	0717	0747	0817	and	1117	1217	1224	1317	1417	1517	1547	and at the same	1817	1847	1917	and	2317	2357
3	**Bad Wildbad** Bf .... a.	0537	0628	0638	0718	0728	0748	0818	0848	hourly	1148	1248	1255	1348	1448	1548	1618	minutes past	1848	1918	1948	hourly	2348	0028
5	**Bad Wildbad** Kurpark a.	0540	0632	0642	0722	0732	0752	0822	0852	until	1152	1252	1259	1352	1452	1552	1622	each hour until	1852	1922	1952	until	2352	0032

	Ⓐ	Ⓐ	Ⓐ	⑥	Ⓐ	Ⓐ	†	⚒				Ⓒ	Ⓐ		Ⓐ			Ⓐ		Ⓐ		Ⓐ				
Wildbad Kurpark d.	0459	0559	0635	0647	0705	0735	0747	0805	0905	1005	1105	1205	1216	1305	1335	1405	1505	1535	1605	1635	1705	1735	1805	and	2305	0015
Wildbad Bf .... d.	0502	0602	0639	0651	0709	0739	0751	0809	0909	1009	1109	1209	1219	1309	1339	1409	1509	1539	1609	1639	1709	1739	1809	hourly	2309	0019
rzheim Hbf .... a.	0533	0633	0710	0722	0740	0810	0822	0840	0940	1040	1140	1240	1250	1340	1410	1440	1540	1610	1640	1710	1740	1810	1840	until	2340	0049

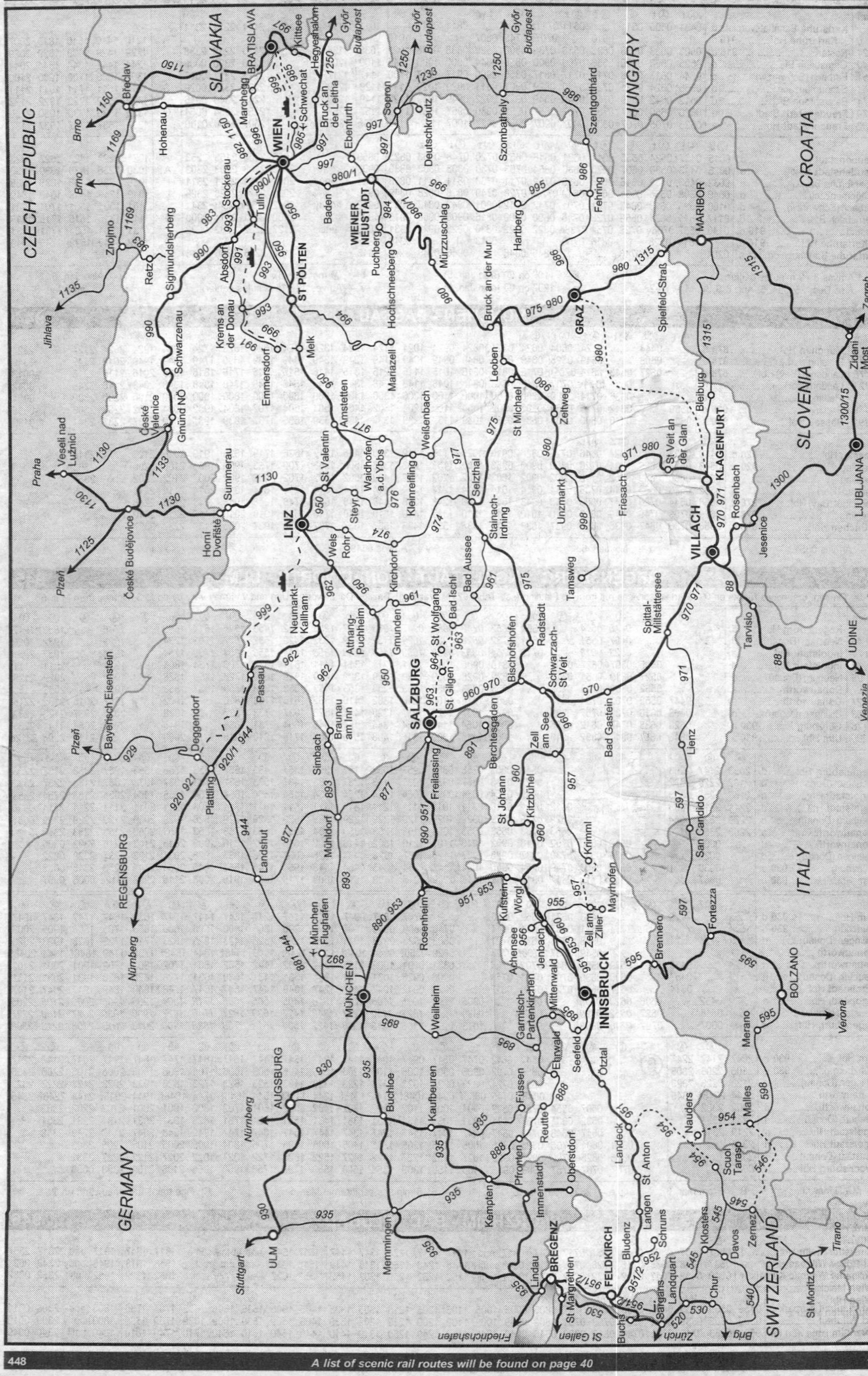

A list of scenic rail routes will be found on page 40

AUSTRIA

Operator: Except where otherwise stated, rail services are operated by Österreichische Bundesbahnen (**ÖBB**) www.oebb.at

Timings: Valid **until December 9, 2023** unless stated otherwise in individual tables. See page 4 for public holiday dates.

Services: Trains convey both first and second class seating unless footnotes show otherwise or there is a '2' in the train column. Overnight sleeping car (🛏) or couchette (▬) trains do not necessarily convey seating accommodation - refer to individual footnotes for details. Descriptions of sleeping and couchette cars appear on page 10.

Train categories:

RJX or *RJ*	**Railjet xpress** **Railjet**	Austrian high-speed train. Conveys first and economy (2nd) class. *Business class* also available to first class ticket holders (supplement payable).	*D*	**Schnellzug**	Ordinary fast train.
ICE	**InterCity Express**	German high-speed train.	*NJ*	**ÖBB nightjet**	Quality overnight express train - see page 10.
EC	**EuroCity**	International express train.	*EN*	**EuroNight**	Other international overnight express train - see page 10.
IC	**InterCity**	Internal or international express train.	*WB*	**Westbahn**	Wien - Salzburg private operator (special fares payable).
			REX	**Regional Express**	Semi-fast regional train (train number not usually shown).
			CJX	**Cityjet xpress**	Similar to *REX* but using dedicated modern rolling stock.
				Regional / S-Bahn	Local stopping trains – no category or train number shown.

Reservations: Seats may be reserved on all long-distance express trains (*RJX, RJ, ICE, EC, IC, NJ, D*).

Catering: Three types of catering are indicated in the tables: ✕ – Restaurant car; ⊗ – Bordbistro; 🍷 – At seat trolley service.

WIEN - LINZ - SALZBURG — 950

km		*RJ* 848	*RJX* 368	*RJ* 540	*RJX* 660	*RJX* 260	*ICE* 228	*RJ* 542	*RJX* 160	*RJX* 560	*RJX* 1162	*RJ* 544	*RJX* 662	*RJX* 262	*IC* 1018	*RJ* 596	*ICE* 28	*RJX* 162	*RJX* 562	*RJX* 1262	*RJ* 860	*ICE* 92	*RJX* 60	*RJ* 640	*ICE* 26	*RJX* 766
		Ⓐ♠		♡						e	⑥h									⑥m						
		✕	✕	✕	✕	✕	R✕	✕	L✕	F✕	G✕	✕	✕	✕	S	K✕	R✕	B✕	F✕	G✕	V✕	P✕	B✕	✕	R✕	✕
0	**Flughafen Wien** ✈ d.	...	...	...	...	...	...	...	...	0703	...	0733	0803	...	...	0833	...	...	0903	...	...	...	...	1033	...	1103
17	**Wien** Hbf d.	0455	0528	0555	0628	0628	0649	0655	0728	0728	0750	0755	0828	0828	0837	0855	0913	0928	0928	0950	0955	1013	1028	1055	1113	1128
21	**Wien** Meidling d.	0502	0535	0602	0635	0635	0656	0702	0735	0735	0758	0802	0835	0835	0844	0902	0920	0935	0935	0958	1002	1020	1035	1102	1120	1135
52	Tullnerfeld **993** d.	0516	|	0616	|	|	|	0716	|	|	|	0816	|	|	|	0916	|	|	|	|	1016	|	|	1116	|	|
82	**St Pölten** Hbf **993** d.	0530	0559	0630	0659	0659	0722	0730	0759	0759	0823	0830	0859	0859	0911	0930	0946	0959	0959	1023	1030	1046	1059	1130	1146	1159
142	Amstetten d.	0600p	|	0655	|	|	0749	0755	|	|	|	0855	|	|	|	1000p	|	|	|	|	1055	|	|	1155	|	|
179	St Valentin **976** d.	0615	|	0714	|	|	|	0814	|	|	|	0914	|	|	|	1015	|	|	|	|	1114	|	|	1214	|	|
204	**Linz** Hbf **976** a.	0628	0643	0728	0743	0743	0815	0828	0843	0843	0913	0928	0943	0943	0958	1028	1032	1043	1043	1113	1128	1132	1143	1228	1232	1243
204	**Linz** Hbf **962** d.	0630	0645	0730	0745	0745	0817	0830	0845	0845	0915	0930	0945	0945	1004	1030	1034	1045	1045	1115	1130	1134	1145	1230	1234	1245
229	**Wels** Hbf **962** d.	0646	|	0746	|	|	0833	0846	|	|	|	0946	|	|	|	1046	|	|	|	|	1146	|	|	1246	|	|
	Passau Hbf **962** 🏛 a.	|	|	|	|	|	0922	|	|	|	|	|	|	|	|	|	1131	|	|	|	|	1231	|	|	1331	|
259	Attnang-Puchheim d.	0701	|	0801	|	|	...	0901	|	|	|	1001	|	|	1035	1101	...	|	|	|	1201	...	|	1301	...	|
264	Vöcklabruck d.	0707	|	0807	|	|	...	0907	|	|	|	1007	|	|	...	|	...	|	|	|	1207	...	|	1307	...	|
329	**Salzburg** Hbf a.	0749	0753	0849	0853	0853	...	0949	0953	0953	1030	1049	1053	1053	...	1149	...	1153	1153	1230	1249	...	1253	1349	...	1353
	München Hbf **890** a.	...	|	...	|	1033	...	...	|	|	...	...	|	1231	...	...	...	|	|	...	|	...	1432	...	...	|
	Innsbruck Hbf **951** a.	...	0944	...	1044	...	...	...	1144	1144	...	...	1244	...	...	...	...	1344	1344	...	1444	...	...	...	...	1544
	Zürich HB **520** a.	...	1320	...	|	...	...	...	1520	...	...	...	|	...	...	...	...	1720	...	...	|	...	...	...	...	...
	Bregenz **951** a.	...	...	...	1317	...	...	...	...	...	...	...	1517	...	...	...	...	...	...	...	1717	...	...	...	...	...

	RJ 642	*RJX* 62	*RJX* 862	*RJ* 644	*ICE* 90	*RJX* 166	*RJX* 566	*RJ* 646	*RJX* 64	*RJX* 864	*RJ* 698	*ICE* 22	*RJX* 168	*RJ* 740	*RJX* 66	*RJX* 866	*RJ* 742	*ICE* 20	*RJX* 760	*RJX* 1260	*RJ* 744	*RJX* 68	*RJX* 868	*RJ* 746	*IC* 94	*RJX* 762
																				⑤★						
	✕	B✕	✕	✕	E✕	✕	F✕	✕	B✕	✕	K✕	R✕	Y✕	✕	B✕	✕	✕	Q✕	✕	G✕	✕	B✕	✕	✕	U🍷	✕
Flughafen Wien ✈ d.	...	...	1203	1233	...	...	1303	...	...	1403	1433	...	1503	1533	...	1603	1633	...	1703	...	...	...	1803	1833	...	1903
Wien Hbf d.	1155	1228	1228	1255	1313	1328	1328	1355	1428	1428	1455	1513	1528	1555	1628	1628	1655	1713	1728	1728	1755	1828	1828	1855	1913	1928
Wien Meidling d.	1202	1235	1235	1302	1320	1335	1335	1402	1435	1435	1502	1520	1535	1602	1635	1635	1702	1720	1735	1735	1802	1835	1835	1902	1920	1935
Tullnerfeld **993** d.	1216	|	|	1316	|	|	|	1416	|	|	1516	|	|	1616	|	|	1716	|	|	|	1816	|	|	1916	|	|
St Pölten Hbf **993** d.	1230	1259	1259	1330	1346	1359	1359	1430	1459	1459	1530	1546	1559	1630	1659	1659	1730	1746	1759	1759	1830	1859	1859	1930	1946	1959
Amstetten d.	1255	|	|	1400p	|	|	|	1455	|	|	1555	|	|	1655	|	|	1755	|	|	|	1855	|	|	1955	|	|
St Valentin **976** d.	1314	|	|	1415	|	|	|	1514	|	|	1614	|	|	1714	|	|	1814	|	|	|	1914	|	|	2014	|	|
Linz Hbf **976** a.	1328	1343	1343	1428	1432	1443	1443	1528	1543	1543	1628	1632	1643	1728	1743	1743	1828	1832	1843	1843	1928	1943	1943	2028	2032	2043
Linz Hbf **962** d.	1330	1345	1345	1430	1434	1445	1445	1530	1545	1545	1630	1634	1645	1730	1745	1745	1830	1834	1845	1845	1930	1945	1945	2030	2034	2045
Wels Hbf **962** d.	1346	|	|	1446	|	|	|	1546	|	|	1646	|	|	1746	|	|	1846	1850	|	|	1946	|	|	2046	2050	|
Passau Hbf **962** 🏛 a.	|	|	|	|	1531	|	|	|	|	|	|	1731	|	|	|	|	|	1934	|	|	|	|	|	|	2137	|
Attnang-Puchheim d.	1401	|	|	1501	...	|	|	1601	|	|	1701	...	|	1801	|	|	1901	...	|	|	2001	|	|	2101	...	|
Vöcklabruck d.	1407	|	|	1507	...	|	|	1607	|	|	1707	...	|	1807	|	|	1907	...	|	|	2007	|	|	2107	...	|
Salzburg Hbf a.	1449	1453	1453	1549	...	1553	1553	1649	1653	1653	1749	...	1753	1849	1853	1853	1949	...	1953	1953	2049	2053	2053	2149	...	2153
München Hbf **890** a.	...	1632	|	...	...	|	|	...	1831	|	...	...	|	...	2031	|	...	...	|	...	...	2231	|	...	...	|
Innsbruck Hbf **951** a.	...	...	1644	...	...	1744	1744	...	...	1844	...	...	1944	...	...	2044	...	...	2144	...	...	...	2248	...	...	2348
Zürich HB **520** a.	...	...	|	...	...	2120	...	...	...	|	...	...	2322n	...	...	|	...	...	|	...	...	...	...	...	...	...
Bregenz **951** a.	...	...	1917	...	...	...	...	...	...	2117	...	...	...	...	...	2317	...	...	0017	...	...	...	...	...	...	...

	RJ 748	*NJ* 490	*RJX* 42	*RJ* 840	*NJ* 466	*IC* 460	*RJX* 764	*NJ* 446	*EN* 70462	*EN* 40462
			⊡							
	✕	H♣	✕	✕	A	C	✕	♥	D♣	⊙
Flughafen Wien ✈ d.	1933	...	2003b	2033	...	...	2203	*2233*	...	...
Wien Hbf d.	1955	2011	2028	2055	2127	2155	2228	2255	2327	2327
Wien Meidling d.	2002	2019	2035	2102	2135	2202	2235	2303	2335	2335
Tullnerfeld **993** d.	2016	|	|	2116	|	2216	|	2321	|	|
St Pölten Hbf **993** d.	2030	2045	2059	2130	2201	2230	2259	2338	0001	0001
Amstetten d.	2055	|	|	2200p	2227	2300	|	0007	|	|
St Valentin **976** d.	2114	|	|	2215	|	2315	|	0026	|	|
Linz Hbf **976** a.	2128	2132	2143	2228	2254	2328	2343	0040	0048	0048
Linz Hbf **962** d.	2130	2134	2145	2230	2256	2330	2345	0042	0059	0059
Wels Hbf **962** d.	2146	2151	2202	2246	2315	2346	0002	0059	0116	0116
Passau Hbf **962** 🏛 a.	|	2235	|	|	|	|	|	|	|	|
Attnang-Puchheim d.	2201	...	2218	2301	2333	0001	0018	0117	|	|
Vöcklabruck d.	2207	...	|	2307	|	0005	|	0123	|	|
Salzburg Hbf a.	2249	...	2259	2349	0016	0049	0059	0203	0212	0212
München Hbf **890** a.	...	...	...	...	|	0231	...	|	0550d	|
Innsbruck Hbf **951** a.	...	...	...	...	0423z	...	...	0519	...	0423z
Zürich HB **520** a.	...	...	...	...	0820z	...	...	|	...	0820z
Bregenz **951** a.	...	...	...	...	...	...	...	0829	...	...

	RJ 825	*IC* 461	*NJ* 447	*EN* 40467	*EN* 463	*RJ* 821	*RJX* 823	*NJ* 467	*RJ* 541	*RJX* 761	*RJ* 543	*NJ* 491
	Ⓐ	⚒v										
	✕	🍷	♥	⊖	D♣	✕	✕	A	✕☆	✕	✕	H♣
Bregenz **951** d.	...	...	2140	...	...	...	...	...	...	...	...	...
Zürich HB **520** d.	...	...	|	2140	...	...	...	2140	...	...	...	...
Innsbruck Hbf **951** d.	...	...	0044	0128	...	...	...	0128	...	...	...	...
München Hbf **890** d.	...	...	|	|	2320	...	...	|	...	...	...	...
Salzburg Hbf d.	...	0311	0319	0345	0345	...	0501a	0432	0511	0601	0611	...
Vöcklabruck d.	...	0354	0401	|	|	...	|	|	0554	|	0654	...
Attnang-Puchheim d.	...	0400	0407	|	|	...	0545a	0520	0600	0645	0700	...
Passau Hbf **962** 🏛 d.	...	|	|	|	|	...	|	|	|	|	|	0615
Wels Hbf **962** d.	0354	0416	0426	|	|	...	0601a	0541	0616	0701	0716	0716
Linz Hbf **962** a.	0408	0430	0443	0452	0452	...	0615a	0558	0630	0715	0730	0744
Linz Hbf **976** d.	0410	0432	0448	0510	0510	0532	0617	0610	0632	0717	0732	0746
St Valentin **976** d.	|	0447	0506	|	|	0545	|	|	0645	|	0750	|
Amstetten d.	0437	0505	0526	|	|	0607p	|	0637	0707	|	0807	0813
St Pölten Hbf **993** d.	0502	0530	0610	0602	0602	0632	0703	0710	0732	0803	0832	0840
Tullnerfeld **993** a.	0514	0542	|	|	|	0643	|	|	0743	|	0843	|
Wien Meidling a.	0532	0558	0648	0626	0626	0658	0725	0751	0758	0825	0858	0905
Wien Hbf a.	0539	0605	0658	0634	0634	0705	0732	0758	0805	0832	0905	0914
Flughafen Wien ✈ a.	0557	...	...	...	...	0727	0757	...	0827	0857	0927	...

	RJX 669	*RJ* 545	*RJX* 763	*RJX* 265	*IC* 95	*RJ* 547	*RJX* 861	*RJX* 61	*RJ* 549	*RJX* 765	*ICE* 21	*RJ* 691	*RJX* 863	*RJ* 63	*RJ* 643	*RJX* 161	*ICE* 23	*RJ* 645	*RJX* 1265	*RJ* 65	*RJ* 865	*RJX* 563	*ICE* 91	*RJ* 649	*RJX* 897	*RJX* 67
																			⊕							
	N✕	✕	✕	✕	M🍷	✕	✕	B✕	✕	✕	Q✕	K✕	✕	B✕	✕	X✕	R✕	✕	G✕	B✕	✕	✕	E✕	✕	W✕	B✕
Bregenz **951** d.	...	...	...	...	...	...	0437a	...	...	0548	...	...	0639	...	...	...	...	...	...	...	0840	...	...	...	1040	...
Zürich HB **520** d.	...	...	...	...	...	...	|	...	...	|	...	...	|	...	...	0640	...	...	...	...	|	...	...	...	|	...
Innsbruck Hbf **951** d.	0510	...	0610	...	...	...	0713	...	...	0817	...	...	0914	...	...	1017	...	...	...	...	1114	1217	...	...	1314	...
München Hbf **890** d.	|	...	|	0623	...	...	|	0723	...	|	...	...	|	0929	...	|	...	...	...	1128	|	|	...	...	|	1329
Salzburg Hbf d.	0707	0711	0807	0807	...	0811	0907	0907	0911	1007	...	1011	1107	1107	1111	1207	...	1211	1307	1307	1311	1407	...	1411	1507	1507
Vöcklabruck d.	|	0754	|	|	...	0854	|	|	0954	|	...	1054	|	|	1154	|	...	1254	|	|	1354	|	...	1454	|	|
Attnang-Puchheim d.	|	0800	|	|	...	0900	|	|	1000	|	...	1100	|	|	1200	|	...	1300	|	|	1400	|	...	1500	|	|
Passau Hbf **962** 🏛 d.	|	|	|	|	0824	|	|	|	|	|	1026	|	|	|	|	|	1229	|	|	|	|	|	1429	|	|	|
Wels Hbf **962** d.	|	0816	|	|	0911	0916	|	|	1016	|	1112	1116	|	|	1216	|	|	1316	|	|	1416	|	|	1516	|	|
Linz Hbf **962** a.	0815	0830	0915	0915	0925	0930	1015	1015	1030	1115	1126	1130	1215	1215	1230	1315	1326	1330	1415	1415	1430	1515	1526	1530	1615	1615
Linz Hbf **976** d.	0817	0832	0917	0917	0927	0932	1017	1017	1032	1117	1128	1132	1217	1217	1232	1317	1328	1332	1417	1417	1432	1517	1528	1532	1617	1617
St Valentin **976** d.	|	0850	|	|	|	0950	|	|	1050	|	|	1145	|	|	1250	|	|	1350	|	|	1450	|	|	1550	|	|
Amstetten d.	|	0907	|	|	|	1007	|	|	1107	|	|	1207p	|	|	1307	|	|	1407	|	|	1507	|	|	1607	|	|
St Pölten Hbf **993** d.	0903	0932	1003	1003	1016	1032	1103	1103	1132	1203	1216	1232	1303	1303	1332	1403	1416	1432	1503	1503	1532	1603	1616	1632	1703	1703
Tullnerfeld **993** a.	|	0943	|	|	|	1043	|	|	1143	|	|	1243	|	|	1343	|	|	1443	|	|	1543	|	|	1643	|	|
Wien Meidling a.	0925	0958	1025	1025	1039	1058	1125	1125	1158	1225	1240	1258	1325	1325	1358	1425	1440	1458	1525	1525	1558	1625	1640	1658	1725	1725
Wien Hbf a.	0932	1005	1032	1032	1047	1105	1132	1132	1205	1232	1247	1305	1332	1332	1405	1432	1447	1505	1532	1532	1605	1632	1647	1705	1732	1732
Flughafen Wien ✈ a.	0957	*1027*	1057	...	...	1127	1157	...	*1227*	1257	...	1327	1357	...	1427	1457	...	1527	1557	...	*1627*	1657	...	1727	1757	...

☛ See page 450 for regional trains Wien Westbf - St Pölten - Melk - Amstetten - Linz, also services Wien - Linz - Salzburg operated by *Westbahn*.

FOR NOTES SEE PAGE 450 →

950 SALZBURG - LINZ - WIEN

	ICE	RJ	RJX	RJX	ICE	RJ	RJX	RJX	RJ	RJX	RJX	ICE	RJ	RJ	IC	RJX	RJX	RJX	RJ	RJX	RJ	ICE	RJX	RJ	RJX	RJ
	93	741	565	165	27	743	869	69	745	167	567	29	797	1267	1019	661	1261	261	769	169	841	229	663	843	367	845
											⑦–④			⑦k		⑦x	⑥q		¶							
	P✕	✕	F✕	B✕	R✕	✕	✕	✕	✕	L✕	F✕	R✕	K✕	G✕	S	✕	G✕	B✕	✕	✕	✕	R✕	✕	✕	✕	✕
Bregenz 951 ... d.	...	...	...	...	...	...	1240	...	...	...	...	...	...	...	...	1440	...	...	1440f	...	...	...	...	...	...	...
Zürich HB 520 ... d.	...	...	...	1040	...	...	|	...	...	1240	...	...	...	...	...	|	...	...	|	1440	...	...	...	...	1640	...
Innsbruck Hbf 951 .. d.	...	...	1417	1417	...	...	1514	...	...	1617	1617	...	...	...	...	1714	...	...	1714f	1817	...	...	1914	...	2017	...
München Hbf 890 ... d.	...	...	|	|	...	...	|	1529	...	|	|	...	...	...	...	|	...	1730	|	|	...	...	|	...	|	...
Salzburg Hbf ... d.	...	1511	1607	1607	...	1611	1707	1707	1711	1807	1807	...	1812	1830	...	1907	1907	1907	1911	2007	2011	...	2107	2111	2207	2211
Vöcklabruck ... d.	...	1554	|	|	...	1654	|	|	1754	|	|	...	1854	|	...	|	|	|	1954	|	2054	...	|	2154	|	2254
Attnang-Puchheim ... d.	...	1600	|	|	...	1700	|	|	1800	|	|	...	1900	|	1925	|	|	|	2000	|	2100	...	|	2200	|	2300
Passau Hbf 962 ... d.	1529	|	|	|	1629	|	|	|	|	|	|	1829	|	|	|	|	|	|	|	|	|	2031	|	|	|	|
Wels Hbf ... 962 d.	|	1616	|	|	|	1716	|	|	1816	|	|	|	1916	|	|	|	|	|	2016	|	2116	2119	|	2216	2304	2316
Linz Hbf ... 962 a.	1626	1630	1715	1715	1726	1730	1815	1815	1830	1915	1915	1926	1930	1946	1959	2015	2015	2015	2030	2115	2130	2134	2215	2230	2318	2330
Linz Hbf ... 976 d.	1628	1632	1717	1717	1728	1732	1817	1817	1832	1917	1917	1928	1932	1948	2001	2017	2017	2017	2032	2117	...	2136	2217	2232	2320	...
St Valentin ... 976 d.	|	1650	|	|	|	1750	|	|	1850	|	|	|	1950	|	|	|	|	|	2050	|	...	|	|	2245	|	...
Amstetten ... d.	|	1707	|	|	|	1807	|	|	1907	|	|	|	2007	|	|	|	|	|	2107	|	...	2207p	|	2307p	|	...
St Pölten Hbf ... 993 d.	1716	1732	1803	1803	1816	1832	1903	1903	1932	2003	2003	2016	2032	2038	2048	2103	2103	2103	2132	2203	...	2232	2303	2332	0006	...
Tullnerfeld ... 993 a.	|	1743	|	|	|	1843	|	|	1943	|	|	|	2043	|	|	|	|	|	2145	|	...	2243	|	2343	|	...
Wien Meidling ... a.	1740	1758	1825	1825	1840	1858	1925	1925	1958	2025	2025	2040	2058	2103	2112	2125	2125	2125	2158	2225	...	2258	2325	2358	0028	...
Wien Hbf ... a.	1747	1805	1832	1832	1847	1905	1932	1932	2005	2032	2032	2047	2105	2111	2120	2132	2132	2132	2205	2232	...	2305	2332	0005	0035	...
Flughafen Wien ✈ ❦ a.	...	1827	1857	...	...	1927	1957	...	2027	...	2057	...	2127	...	...	2157	2157	...	2227	...	...	...	...	...	...	...

Regional ÖBB trains WIEN - MELK - AMSTETTEN - ST VALENTIN (2nd class only; most from/to Wien are classified *CJX*)

km‡																									
		⚒		Ⓐ								Ⓐ	◧	Ⓐ		Ⓐ	◇		Ⓐ						
0	**Wien** Westbahnhof ... d.	...	0518	0548	0618	0718	0748a	0818		1418	1518	1548	1618	1648	1718	1748	1818	...	1848	1918	2018	2118	2218	2318	0018
6	**Wien** Hütteldorf ... d.	...	0526	0555	0626	0726	0755a	0826		1426	1526	1555	1626	1655	1726	1755	1826	...	1855	1926	2026	2126	2226	2326	0026
	Tullnerfeld ... d.	...	0540	0608	0640	0740	0810a	0840	and	1440	1540	1608	1640	1708	1740	1808	1840	...	1908	1940	2040	2140	2240	2340	0040
61	**St Pölten** Hbf ... a.	...	0554	0622	0654	0754	0824a	0854		1454	1554	1622	1654	1722	1754	1822	1854	...	1922	1954	2054	2154	2254	2354	0054
61	**St Pölten** Hbf ... d.	0447	0603	0624	0703	0803	0839	0903	hourly	1503	1603	1624	1703	1724	1803	1824	1903	...	1924	2003	2103	2205	2305	0005	0109
85	Melk ... d.	0506	0619	0644	0721	0819	0858	0921		1519	1619	1639	1719	1739	1819	1839	1921	...	1939	2019	2119	2221	2321	0021	0125
94	Pöchlarn ... d.	0512	0628	0656	0728	0828	0905	0928	until	1528	1628	1646	1728	1746	1828	1846	1928	...	1946	2028	2128	2228	2328	0028	0132
107	Ybbs an der Donau ... d.	0523	0637	0707	0737	0837	...	0937		1537	1637	1654	1737	1754	1837	1854	1937	...	1954	2037	2137	2237	2337	0037	0141
124	Amstetten ... a.	0536	0650	0720	0750	0850	...	0950		1550	1650	1709	1750	1809	1850	1909	1950	...	2013	2050	2150	2250	2350	0050	0154
124	Amstetten ... d.	0537	0708	...	0808	0908	...	1008		1608	1708	...	1808	...	1908	...	2008	...	...	2108	2208	2308	0013	...	0432
163	**St Valentin** ... a.	0606	0737	...	0837	0937	...	1037		1637	1737	...	1837	...	1937	...	2037	...	...	2137	2237	2337	0041	...	0500

		Ⓐ		Ⓐ	Ⓐ	Ⓐ		Ⓐ	Ⓐ	Ⓐ							Ⓐ		①–④					⑦–④	⑤⑥
St Valentin ... d.	...	0400	...	0430	...	0454	0523	...	...	0559	0623	...	0723	0823		1623	...	1723	1751	1823	1923	2023	2123	2223	2223
Amstetten ... a.	...	0429	...	0459	...	0523	0552	...	...	0628	0652	...	0752	0852		1652	...	1752	1822	1852	1953	2052	2153	2252	2252
Amstetten ... d.	0407	0442	0503	0517	0531	0547	0604	0617	0631	0646	0710	0730a	0810	0910	and	1710	1746	1810	...	1910	2010	2110	2210	...	2310
Ybbs an der Donau ... d.	0420	0455	0516	0527	0544	0557	0617	0627	0644	0657	0723	0743a	0823	0923		1723	1759	1823	...	1923	2023	2123	2223	...	2323
Pöchlarn ... d.	0431	0504	0528	0535	0556	0605	0628	0635	0656	0705	0734	0755	0834	0934	hourly	1734	1810	1834	...	1934	2034	2134	2234	...	2334
Melk ... d.	0437	0510	0533	0541	0602	0611	0634	0641	0702	0711	0740	0801	0840	0940		1740	1816	1840	...	1940	2040	2140	2240	...	2340
St Pölten Hbf ... a.	0457	0527	0554	0557	0624	0627	0653	0658	0724	0727	0758	0821	0858	0958	until	1758	1834	1858	...	1958	2058	2158	2258	...	2358
St Pölten Hbf ... d.	0505	0535	0606	0606	0636	0636	0706	0706	0736	0736	0806	0844a	0906	1006		1806	1838	1906	...	2006	2106	2206	2306	...	0009
Tullnerfeld ... a.	0518	0548	0619	0619	0649	0649	0719	0719	0749	0749	0819	0857a	0919	1019		1819	1851	1919	...	2019	2119	2219	2319	...	0022
Wien Hütteldorf ... a.	0531	0601	0634	0634	0704	0704	0734	0734	0804	0804	0834	0911a	0934	1034		1834	1905	1934	...	2034	2134	2234	2334	...	0036
Wien Westbahnhof ... a.	0538	0608	0642	0642	0712	0712	0742	0742	0812	0812	0842	0918a	0942	1042		1842	1912	1942	...	2042	2142	2242	2342	...	0043

Services operated by *WESTbahn* WIEN - LINZ - SALZBURG. Special fares payable (ÖBB tickets not valid). All trains convey 🍸. **Warning!** Subject to alteration.

km		WB	WB	WB	WB	WB	WB	WB	WB	WB	WB	WB	WB	WB	WB	WB	WB	WB	WB	WB	WB	WB	WB	WB	WB	WB	WB	WB	WB
		900	960	902	410	904	962	906	908	964	910	412	912	966	914	916	968	918	988	920	970	922	416	924	972	926	992	928	930
		⚒	⚒J		Z		J			J		Z		J							J		Z		J				
0	**Wien** Westbahnhof d.	0538	0608	0638	0708	0738	0808	0838	0938	1008	1038	1108	1138	1208	1238	1338	1408	1438	1508	1538	1608	1638	1708	1738	1808	1838	1908	1938	2038
6	**Wien** Hütteldorf ... d.	0545	0615	0645	0715	0745	0815	0845	0945	1015	1045	1115	1145	1215	1245	1345	1415	1445	1515	1545	1615	1645	1715	1745	1815	1845	1915	1945	2045
60	**St Pölten** Hbf ... d.	0606	0636	0706	0736	0806	0836	0906	1006	1036	1106	1136	1206	1236	1306	1406	1438	1506	1536	1606	1636	1706	1736	1806	1836	1906	1936	2006	2106
120	Amstetten ... d.	0630	0700	0730	0800	0830	0900	0930	1030	1100	1130	1200	1230	1300	1330	1430	1500	1530	1600	1630	1700	1730	1800	1830	1900	1930	2000	2030	2130
182	**Linz** Hbf ... d.	0656	0726	0756	0826	0856	0926	0956	1056	1126	1156	1226	1256	1326	1356	1456	1526	1556	1626	1656	1726	1756	1826	1856	1926	1956	2026	2056	2156
207	Wels Hbf ... d.	0711	0741	0811	0841	0911	0941	1011	1111	1141	1211	1241	1311	1341	1411	1511	1541	1611	1641	1711	1741	1811	1841	1911	1941	2011	2041r	2111	2211
237	Attnang-Puchheim ... d.	0725	0755	0825	0855	0925	0955	1025	1125	1155	1225	1255	1325	1355	1425	1525	1555	1625	1655	1725	1755	1825	1855	1925	1955	2025	2055r	2125	2225
242	Vöcklabruck ... d.	0730	0800	0830	0900	0930	1000	1030	1130	1200	1230	1300	1330	1400	1430	1530	1600	1630	1700	1730	1800	1830	1900	1930	2000	2030	2100r	2130	...
307	**Salzburg** Hbf ... a.	0814	0838	0908	0938	1008	1038	1108	1208	1238	1308	1338	1408	1438	1508	1608	...	1708	1738	1808	1838	1908	1938	2008	2038	2108	2138r	2208	...

	WB	WB	WB	WB	WB	WB	WB	WB	WB	WB	WB	WB	WB	WB	WB	WB	WB	WB	WB	WB	WB	WB	WB	WB	WB	WB	WB	WB	WB
	901	959	903	979	905	961	907	411	909	963	911	913	965	915	917	967	919	413	921	969	923	989	925	917	927	417	929	973	931
	⚒	⚒				O		Z		J						J		Z		J				J		Z		J	
Salzburg Hbf ... d.	...	...	0552t	0622t	0652	0722	0752	0822	0852	0922	0952	1052	1122	1152	1252	1322	1352	1422	1452	1522	1546	...	1646	1722	1746	1822	1852	1922	1952
Vöcklabruck ... d.	...	...	0631t	0701t	0731	0801	0831	0901	0931	1001	1031	1131	1201	1231	1331	1401	1431	1501	1531	1601	1631	1701	1731	1801	1831	1901	1931	2001	2031
Attnang-Puchheim ... d.	...	0606	0636t	0706	0736	0806	0836	0906	0936	1006	1036	1136	1206	1236	1336	1406	1436	1506	1536	1606	1636	1706	1736	1806	1836	1906	1936	2006	2036
Wels Hbf ... d.	...	0620	0650t	0720	0750	0820	0850	0920	0950	1020	1050	1150	1220	1250	1350	1420	1450	1520	1550	1620	1650	1720	1750	1820	1850	1920	1950	2020	2050
Linz Hbf ... d.	0606	0636	0706	0736	0806	0836	0906	0936	1006	1036	1106	1206	1236	1306	1406	1436	1506	1536	1606	1636	1706	1736	1806	1836	1906	1936	2006	2036	2106
Amstetten ... d.	0631	0701	0731	0801	0831	0901	0931	1001	1031	1101	1131	1231	1301	1331	1431	1501	1531	1601	1631	1701	1731	1801	1831	1901	1931	2001	2031	2101	2131
St Pölten Hbf ... d.	0655	0725	0755	0825	0855	0925	0955	1025	1055	1125	1155	1255	1325	1355	1455	1525	1555	1625	1655	1725	1755	1825	1855	1925	1955	2025	2055	2125	2155
Wien Hütteldorf ... a.	0714	0744	0814	0844	0914	0944	1014	1044	1114	1144	1214	1314	1344	1414	1514	1544	1614	1644	1714	1744	1814	1844	1914	1944	2014	2044	2114	2144	2214
Wien Westbf ... a.	0722	0752	0822	0852	0922	0952	1022	1052	1122	1152	1222	1322	1352	1422	1522	1552	1622	1652	1722	1752	1822	1852	1922	1952	2022	2052	2122	2152	2222

A – 🛏 1, 2 cl., ▬ 2 cl. and (2) Wien - Zürich and v.v.; conveys 🛏 1, 2 cl., ▬ 2 cl. and (2) (*NJ* **40466** / *NJ* **40236**) Wien - Salzburg - Villach - Tarvisio 🏛 - Venezia and v.v.
B – From / to Budapest (Table **1250**).
C – Wien - Linz daily (runs as train *RJ* **822** on ⑥ until May 27); Wien - Salzburg on Ⓑ until May 26, then daily from May 28. Runs Wien - München - Stuttgart from June 10 (Tables **890** and **930**).
D – KÁLMÁN IMRE – 🛏 1, 2 cl., ▬ 2 cl. and (2) Budapest - Wien - München - Stuttgart and v.v.
E – (12) and ✕ Hamburg - Hannover - Nürnberg - Regensburg - Passau - Wien and v.v.
F – To / from Feldkirch on dates in Table **951**.
G – To / from Wörgl via Zell am See (Table **960**).
H – 🛏 1, 2 cl., ▬ 2 cl. and (2) Wien - Hannover - Hamburg and v.v.; 🛏 1, 2 cl., ▬ 2 cl. and (2) (**40490** / **50490**) Wien - Köln - Brussels / Amsterdam and v.v. (see Table **53**).
J – To / from München (Table **890**).
K – To / from Klagenfurt (Table **970**).
L – From / to Bratislava (Table **86**).
M – (12) Leipzig - Nürnberg - Wien.
N – Also conveys on ⚒ (12) (*RJX* **269**) Salzburg - Budapest (Table **1250**).
O – From München on ⚒ (Table **890**).
P – (12) and ✕ Hamburg - Berlin - Erfurt - Nürnberg - Regensburg - Passau 🏛 - Wien and v.v.
Q – (12) and ✕ Frankfurt - Nürnberg - Regensburg - Passau 🏛 - Wien and v.v.
R – (12) and ✕ Dortmund - Frankfurt - Nürnberg - Regensburg - Passau 🏛 - Wien and v.v.
S – SALZKAMMERGUT – (12) Wien - Attnang-Puchheim - Stainach-Irdning and v.v. (Table **961**).
U – (12) Wien - Nürnberg - Leipzig - Berlin - Rostock.
V – Conveys (12) Wien - Bregenz (*RJ* **890**) - Ulm - Stuttgart - Frankfurt (Tables **912** and **933**).
W – Conveys (12) Frankfurt - Stuttgart - Ulm - Bregenz (*RJ* **867**) - Wien (Tables **912** and **933**).
X – Conveys (12) (*RJX* **184**) Bolzano - Innsbruck - Wien Hbf and v.v. (Tables **86/595**).
Y – Conveys (12) (*RJX* **185**) Wien Hbf - Innsbruck - Bolzano and v.v. (Tables **86/595**).
Z – To / from Innsbruck (Table **951**).

a – Ⓐ only.
b – ④⑥⑦ (also Apr. 10, May 1, 16, 29, June 6, Aug. 15, Oct. 24, Dec. 6; not May 18, June 8, Aug. 13, Oct. 26). Train number **664** from Wien Flughafen.
d – München **Ost**.

e – ①–⑥ (also Apr. 9, 30, May 18, 28, June 8, Aug. 13, Oct. 26, Nov. 1, Dec. 8).
f – ①–⑥ (also Apr. 9, 30, May 28, Aug. 13; not Apr. 10, May 1, 29, Aug. 15).
h – ⑥ Dec. 24 - Apr. 8.
k – ⑦ Jan. 1 - Apr. 2 (also Apr. 10); ⑦ July 2 - Sept. 10 (not Aug 13).
m – ⑥ July 1 - Sept. 9.
n – Arrives 0012 on Ⓑ Oct. 30 - Dec. 8.
p – Arrives 7 minutes earlier.
q – ⑥ Dec. 24 - Apr. 8.
r – ⑤⑥ only.
t – ⚒ only.
x – ⑦ (also Apr. 10, May 1, 29, Aug. 15; not Apr. 9, 30, May 28, Aug. 13).
z – Arrives Innsbruck 0546 and Zürich 1020 on the mornings Feb. 18–20, 25–27, Mar. 11–17, 19, 26, 27, Apr. 1–7.

★ – ⑤ (also May 17, June 7, Oct. 25, Dec. 12; not May 19, June 9, Oct. 27, Dec. 8).
⊕ – ⑥ Dec. 24 - Apr. 8; ⑥ July 1 - Sept. 9.
♠ – Runs daily Linz - Salzburg.
◧ – Change trains at Amstetten on Ⓐ.
◇ – Change trains at Amstetten on Ⓒ.
¶ – Train number **749** on dates in note **x**.
⊡ – From Budapest (Table **1250**) on Ⓑ (not Apr. 9, 30, May 28). Train number **664** on ⑥ (also Apr. 9, 30, May 28).
⊙ – 🛏 1, 2 cl., ▬ 2 cl. and (2) Budapest (**462**) - Salzburg (**466**) - Zürich.
⊖ – 🛏 1, 2 cl., ▬ 2 cl. and (2) Zürich (**467**) - Salzburg (**463**) - Budapest.
♥ – Conveys 🛏 1, 2 cl., ▬ 2 cl. and (2).
❦ – See Table **985** for full service from / to Wien Flughafen ✈.
♣ – 🄡 for journeys to / from Germany.
‡ – Distance via the classic route. Trains calling at Tullnerfeld use the high-speed line between Wien and St Pölten.
♡ – Train number *RJ* **1240** on †.
☆ – Train number *RJ* **1241** on †.

SALZBURG - INNSBRUCK - FELDKIRCH - BREGENZ - LINDAU 951

km		NJ 466 △ N	EN 40462 △ ⊙	2	NJ 464 ♦	2	NJ 446 N	Ⓐ 2	RJ 666 ✕	Ⓒ 2	⚒ 2	RJX 366 ✕	RJ 668 ✕	IC 118 🍷♦	RJX 368 ✕	2	2	RJX 660 ✕	2	WB 410 🍷	RJX 160 D R✕	2	2	RJ 662 F✕	2	RJX 162 U B✕
	Wien Hbf **950** d.	2127	2327	...	...	...	2255	...	...	...	...	...	...	...	0528	...	...	0628	...	...	0728	...	...	0828	...	0928
	Wien Westbahnhof **950** d.	|	|	...	...	...	|	...	...	...	...	...	...	...	|	...	...	|	...	0708	|	...	...	|	...	|
	Linz Hbf **950** d.	2256	0059	...	...	...	0042	...	...	...	...	...	...	...	0645	...	...	0745	...	0826	0845	...	...	0945	...	1045
0	**Salzburg** Hbf d.	0230	0230	...	...	...	0306	...	...	...	...	0556	0656	...	0756	...	...	0856	...	0939	0956	...	...	1056	...	1156
120	Kufstein 🏛 d.	|	|	...	...	...	|	0539	...	0539	0636	0709	|	...	0909	...	0934	|	...	1051	1109	...	1134	|	...	1309
134	Wörgl Hbf **960** d.	|	|	...	...	...	|	0553	...	0559	0649	0719	0817	...	0919	...	0947	1015	...	1100	1119	...	1147	1215	...	1319
159	Jenbach **960** d.	|	|	...	...	...	|	0613	...	0621	0709	|	0831	...	|	...	1000	1029	...	|	|	...	1200	1229	...	|
193	**Innsbruck** Hbf **960** a.	0423	0423	...	...	...	0519	0639	...	0655	0740	0744	0846	...	0944	...	1020	1044	...	1129	1144	...	1220	1244	...	1344
193	**Innsbruck** Hbf d.	0431	0431	...	0453	...	0523	...	0641	0659	...	0747	▬	0854	0947	0952	...	1047	1052	...	1147	1152	...	1247	1252	1347
239	Ötztal d.	|	|	...	|	...	0551	...	0706	0750	...	0812	...	0928	1012	1030	...	|	1127	...	1212	1230	...	|	1327	1412
248	Imst-Pitztal d.	|	|	...	|	...	0602	...	0716	0800	...	|	...	0939	|	1041	...	1119	1139	...	|	1241	...	1319	1339	|
265	Landeck - Zams d.	0520	0520	...	0545	...	0622	...	0730	0815	...	0833	...	0954	1033	1056	...	1133	1154	...	1233	1256	...	1333	1354	1433
293	St Anton am Arlberg d.	|	|	...	0616	...	0648	...	0754	...	...	0857	...	1022	1057	▬	...	|	...	...	1257	▬	...	|	...	1457
304	Langen am Arlberg d.	|	|	...	0626	...	0659	...	0804	...	...	|	...	1032	|	...	...	1204	...	...	|	...	...	1404	...	|
329	Bludenz **952** d.	0625	0625	0630	0706	...	0735	...	0831	...	...	0931	...	1102	1131	...	...	1231	...	...	1331	...	...	1431	...	1531
350	**Feldkirch** **952** a.	0637	0637	0645	0721	...	0749	...	0842	...	...	0942	2	1113	1142	2	...	1242	...	...	1342	2	...	1442	...	1542
350	**Feldkirch** **952** d.	0640	0640	0647	0739	0747	0754	...	0847	...	...	0944	0947	1117	1148	1147	...	1247	...	...	1348	1347	...	1447	...	1548
369	**Buchs** 🏛 **952** a.	0656	0656	|	0753	|	|	...	|	...	...	0959	|	|	1206	|	...	|	...	...	1406	|	...	|	...	1606
	Zürich HB **520** a.	0820	0820	|	0920	|	|	...	|	...	...	1120	|	|	1320	|	...	|	...	...	1520	|	...	|	...	1720
375	Dornbirn **952** d.	...	...	0709	...	0809	0821	...	0909	...	...	...	1009	1142	...	1209	...	1309	...	...	...	1409	...	1509	...	...
387	**Bregenz** 🏛 **952** a.	...	...	0718	...	0818	0829	...	0917	...	...	...	1018	1149	...	1218	...	1317	...	...	...	1418	...	1517	...	...
	Lindau Reutin 🏛 **952** a.	...	...	0728	...	0828	*0858*	...	*0929*	...	...	...	1028	1158	...	1228	...	*1329*	...	...	...	1428	...	*1529*	...	...
397	**Lindau**-Insel 🏛 **952** a.	...	...	0733	...	0832	*0903*	...	*0934*	...	...	...	1032	...	...	1232	...	*1334*	...	...	...	1432	...	*1534*	...	...

	2◧	2	RJX 860 T ✕	2	WB 412 🍷	RJX 564 F✕	EC 164 ✕♦	2	2	RJ 1287 ⑥E ✕	RJX 862 F✕	RJ 1287 ⑥E ✕	2	RJX 166 V ✕	2	2	RJX 864 F✕	2	RJX 168 F Y✕	2	RJX 866 F✕	WB 416 🍷	RJX 760 F✕	2	RJX 868 F✕	RJX 762 F✕
Wien Hbf **950** d.	...	...	0955	...	...	1128	...	...	...	...	1228	...	...	1328	...	...	1428	...	1528	...	1628	...	1728	...	1828	1928
Wien Westbahnhof **950** d.	...	...	|	...	1108	|	...	...	...	...	|	...	...	|	...	...	|	...	|	...	|	1708	|	...	|	|
Linz Hbf **950** d.	...	...	1130	...	1226	1245	...	...	...	...	1345	...	...	1445	...	...	1545	...	1645	...	1745	1826	1845	...	1945	2045
Salzburg Hbf d.	...	...	1256	...	1339	1356	...	...	...	...	1456	...	...	1556	...	...	1656	...	1756	...	1856	1939	1956	...	2056	2156
Kufstein 🏛 d.	...	1334	|	...	1451	1509	...	...	1534	...	|	...	...	1709	...	1734	|	...	1909	1934	|	2051	2109	2136	2209	2309
Wörgl Hbf **960** d.	...	1347	1415	...	1500	1519	1503	...	1547	...	1615	...	...	1719	...	1747	1815	...	1919	1947	2015	2100	2119	2154	2219	2319
Jenbach **960** d.	...	1400	1429	...	|	|	1518	...	1600	...	1629	...	...	|	...	1800	1829	...	|	2000	2029	|	|	2214	2233	2333
Innsbruck Hbf **960** a.	...	1420	1444	...	1529	1544	1540	...	1620	...	1644	...	...	1744	...	1820	1844	...	1944	2020	2044	2129	2144	2240	2248	2348
Innsbruck Hbf d.	1352	...	1447	1452	...	...	1547	1552	...	1620	1647	...	1652	1747	1752	...	1847	1852	1947	▬	2047	...	2147	2258	...	...
Ötztal d.	1430	...	|	1527	...	...	1612	1630	...	1652	|	...	1727	1812	1830	...	|	1927	2012	...	|	...	2212	2342	...	...
Imst-Pitztal d.	1441	...	1519	1539	...	...	|	1641	...	1702	1719	...	1739	|	1841	...	1919	1939	2022	...	2119	...	2222	2357	...	...
Landeck - Zams d.	1456	...	1533	1554	...	...	1633	1656	...	1726c	1733	←	1754	1833	1856	...	1933	1954	2036	...	2133	...	2236	0013	...	...
St Anton am Arlberg d.	▬	...	|	...	...	...	1657	▬	...	1804	|	1806	...	1857	▬	...	|	...	2100	...	|	...	2300	...	...	...
Langen am Arlberg d.	...	...	1604	...	...	...	|	...	...	→	1804	1816	...	|	...	...	2004	...	|	...	2204	...	2310	...	...	...
Bludenz **952** d.	...	...	1631	...	...	...	1731	...	...	...	1831	1854	...	1931	...	...	2031	...	2134	...	2231	...	2337	...	...	...
Feldkirch **952** a.	2	...	1642	...	...	...	1742	2	...	...	1842	1905	...	1942	2	...	2042	...	2145	2	2242	...	2348	...	...	...
Feldkirch **952** d.	1547	...	1647	...	...	...	1744	1747	...	...	1847	...	...	1948	1947	...	2047	...	2148	2150	2247	...	2350	...	...	...
Buchs 🏛 **952** a.	|	...	|	...	...	...	1759	|	...	...	|	...	...	2006	|	...	|	...	2203	|	|	...	|	...	...	...
Zürich HB **520** a.	|	...	|	...	...	...	1920	|	...	...	|	...	...	2120	|	...	|	...	2322f	|	|	...	|	...	...	...
Dornbirn **952** d.	1609	...	1709	...	...	...	...	1809	...	...	1909	...	...	...	2009	...	2109	...	...	2212	2309	...	0009	...	...	...
Bregenz 🏛 **952** a.	1618	...	1717	...	...	...	...	1818	...	...	1917	...	...	...	2018	...	2117	...	...	2221	2317	...	0017	...	...	...
Lindau Reutin 🏛 **952** a.	1628	...	1728	...	...	...	...	1828	...	...	*1929*	...	...	...	2028	...	*2130*	...	...	2231	*2329*	...	...	...	...	...
Lindau-Insel 🏛 **952** a.	1632	...	...	...	...	...	...	1832	...	...	*1934*	...	...	...	2032	...	*2135*	...	...	2236	*2335*	...	...	...	...	...

	RJX 269 F✕	RJX 763 F✕	2	WB 411 🍷	RJX 861 Ⓐ F✕	RJX 861 F✕	RJX 765 F✕	RJX 863 F✕	2	2	RJX 161 F X✕	2	RJ 1286 ⑥E ✕	RJ 865 ✕	RJ 1286 ⑥E ✕	2	2	EC 163 ✕♦	RJX 563 F✕	WB 413 🍷	2	RJX 897 Z F✕	2	2	RJX 165 W B✕	2
Lindau-Insel 🏛 **952** d.	...	...	...	...	...	...	...	*0621*	...	0725	...	...	...	*0823*	...	...	0925	...	...	...	...	*1021*	...	1125	...	...
Lindau Reutin 🏛 **952** d.	...	...	...	...	...	...	...	*0626*	...	0729	...	...	...	*0827*	...	...	0929	...	...	...	...	1031	...	1129	...	...
Bregenz 🏛 **952** d.	...	...	...	...	0437	...	0548	0639	...	0741	...	...	...	0840	...	...	0941	...	...	...	...	1040	...	1141	...	...
Dornbirn **952** d.	...	...	...	...	0446	...	0557	0652	...	0752	...	...	...	0851	...	...	0952	...	...	...	...	1051	...	1152	...	...
Zürich HB **520** d.	...	...	...	...	|	...	|	|	...	|	0640	...	...	|	...	...	|	0840	...	...	...	|	...	|	1040	...
Buchs 🏛 **952** d.	...	...	...	...	|	...	|	|	...	|	0754	...	...	|	...	...	|	1000	...	...	...	|	...	|	1154	...
Feldkirch **952** a.	...	...	...	...	0500	...	0611	0712	...	0812	0812	...	...	0912	...	...	1012	1015	...	...	...	1112	...	1212	1209	...
Feldkirch **952** d.	...	...	...	...	0502	...	0613	0717	...	▬	0817	...	0850	0917	...	...	▬	1017	...	...	...	1117	...	▬	1217	...
Bludenz **952** d.	...	...	...	...	0515	...	0626	0730	...	...	0830	...	0905	0930	...	...	...	1030	...	...	...	1130	...	...	1230	...
Langen am Arlberg d.	...	...	...	...	|	...	0652	0756	...	...	|	...	0937	0956	...	...	...	|	...	...	...	1156	...	...	|	...
St Anton am Arlberg d.	...	...	...	...	0548	...	0703	|	...	2	0903	...	0948	|	...	...	2	1103	...	...	...	|	...	2	1303	...
Landeck - Zams d.	...	...	0503	...	0612	...	0727	0827	...	0901	0927	1001	1017	1027	←	...	1101	1127	...	...	1201	1227	...	1301	1327	1401
Imst-Pitztal d.	...	...	0519	...	0627	...	0740	0840	...	0917	|	1020	1033	1040	1048	...	1118	|	...	...	1220	1240	...	1318	|	1420
Ötztal d.	...	...	0529	...	0638	...	0751	|	...	0931	0948	1031	→	|	1107	...	1131	1148	...	...	1231	|	...	1331	1348	1431
Innsbruck Hbf a.	...	...	0610	...	0706	...	0814	0911	...	1006	1011	1106	...	1111	1136	...	1206	1211	...	...	1306	1311	...	1406	1411	1506
Innsbruck Hbf **960** d.	0510	0610	0620	0631	0713	0713	0817	0914	0940	...	1017	...	...	1114	...	1140	...	1221	1217	1231	...	1314	1340	...	1417	...
Jenbach **960** d.	0527	0627	0649	|	0730	0730	|	0931	1001	...	|	...	...	1131	...	1201	...	1243	|	|	...	1331	1401	...	|	...
Wörgl Hbf **960** d.	0541	0641	0709	0701	0745	0745	0843	0945	1017	...	1043	...	...	1145	...	1217	...	1256	1243	1301	...	1345	1417	...	1443	...
Kufstein 🏛 d.	0551	0651	0722	0710	|	|	0853	|	1026	...	1053	...	...	|	...	1226	...	...	1253	1310	...	|	1426	...	1453	...
Salzburg Hbf a.	0702	0802	...	0821	0902	0902	1003	1102	...	...	1203	...	...	1302	...	...	...	...	1403	1421	...	1502	...	...	1603	...
Linz Hbf **950** a.	0815	0915	...	0934	1015	1015	1115	1215	...	...	1315	...	...	1430	...	...	...	...	1514	1534	...	1615	...	...	1715	...
Wien Westbahnhof **950** a.	|	|	...	1052	|	|	|	|	...	...	|	...	...	|	...	...	...	...	|	1652	...	|	...	...	|	...
Wien Hbf **950** a.	0932	1032	...	...	1132	1132	1232	1332	...	...	1432	...	...	1605	...	...	...	...	1630	...	...	1732	...	...	1832	...

♦ – **NOTES** (LISTED BY TRAIN NUMBER)

118 – BODENSEE – (12) Innsbruck - Lindau - Stuttgart - Köln - Dortmund.

163/4 – TRANSALPIN – (12) and ✕ Zürich - Kitzbühel - Schwarzach - Graz and v.v.

464 – 🛏 1, 2 cl., ▬ 2 cl. and (2) Graz - Schwarzach - Zürich; 🛏 1, 2 cl., ▬ 2 cl. and (2) (*EN* **40414**) Zagreb - Ljubljana - Villach - Schwarzach - Zürich.

X – Conveys (12) (*RJX* 184) Bolzano - Innsbruck - Wien Hbf (Tables **86** and **595**).

Y – Conveys (12) (*RJX* 185) Wien Hbf - Innsbruck - Bolzano (Tables **86** and **595**).

Z – Conveys (12) Frankfurt - Stuttgart - Ulm - Bregenz (*RJ* **867**) - Wien (Tables **912** and **933**).

B – From/to Budapest (Table **1250**).

D – On ①–⑥ (also Apr. 9, 30, May 28, Aug. 13; not Apr. 10, May 1, 29, Aug. 15) conveys (12) (*RJ* **560**) Flughafen Wien - Wien Hbf - Innsbruck (- Feldkirch ⑤⑥ **v**).

E – ⑥ Dec. 31 - Apr. 15, June 24 - Sep. 30. To/from München Hbf (Table **953**).

F – From/to Flughafen Wien ✈ (Table **950**).

N – Conveys 🛏 1, 2 cl., ▬ 2 cl. and (2).

R – From Bratislava (Table **86**).

T – Conveys (12) Wien - Bregenz (*RJ* **890**) - Ulm - Stuttgart - Frankfurt (Tables **912** and **933**).

U – Conveys (12) (*RJX* **562**) Flughafen Wien - Wien Hbf - Innsbruck (- Feldkirch ⑤–⑦ **z**).

V – Conveys (12) (*RJX* **566**) Flughafen Wien - Wien Hbf - Innsbruck (- Feldkirch Ⓑ **t**).

W – Conveys (12) (*RJX* **565**) (Feldkirch ⑥⑦ **r** -) Innsbruck - Wien Hbf - Flughafen Wien.

c – Arrives 1715.

f – Arrives 0012 on Ⓑ Oct. 30 - Dec. 8.

r – Also Dec. 26, Apr. 10, May 1, 29, Aug. 15; not Dec. 25, Apr. 9, 30, May 28, Aug. 13.

t – Not Dec. 25, Apr. 9, 30, May 28.

v – Also June 7, 8, Oct. 25, 26, Dec. 7; not June 9, 10, Oct. 27, 28, Dec. 9.

z – Also Dec. 26, Apr. 10, May 1, 17, 18, 29, June 7, 8, Aug. 15, Oct. 25, 26, Nov. 1, Dec. 7; not Dec. 25, Apr. 9, 30, May 19, 20, 28, June 9, 10, Aug. 13, Oct. 27, 28, Dec. 9.

△ – On the mornings Feb. 18 – 20, 25 – 27, Mar. 11 – 17, 19, 26, 27, Apr. 1 – 7 Innsbruck a. 0546, d. 0552, Landeck d. 0657, Bludenz d. 0753, Feldkirch a. 0805, d. 0812, Buchs a. 0834, Zürich a. 1020.

⊙ – 🛏 1, 2 cl., ▬ 2 cl. and (2) Budapest (**462**) - Salzburg (**466**) - Zürich. Also conveys through cars from Praha (see Table **52**).

951 LINDAU - BREGENZ - FELDKIRCH - INNSBRUCK - MÜNCHEN and SALZBURG

	RJX 869			RJX 167 E	WB 417		RJX 661 ⑦	RJ 769 ①–⑥			RJX 169	IC 119	RJX 663		RJX 367			RJX 667		RJX 369			NJ 447	NJ 465		EN 40467	NJ 467
	F✕	2	2	R✕	🍷	2	t✕	w✕	2	2	✕	🍷♦	✕	2	✕	2Ⓐ	2	✕	2	✕	2	2	N	♦	2	⊙	N
Lidau-Insel 🏛 ... 952 d.	1155	...	1325	...	...	...	1423	1423	...	1525	...	...	...	1722	...	...	...	1823	1925	...	...	...	2056	...	2225	...	...
Lindau Reutin 🏛 ... 952 d.	1159	...	1329	...	...	...	1427	1427	...	1529	...	1558	...	1729	...	...	...	1827	1929	...	...	...	2103	...	2229	...	...
Bregenz 🏛 ... 952 d.	1240	...	1341	...	...	...	1440	1440	...	1541	...	1606	...	1741	...	...	...	1840	1941	...	...	...	2140	...	2241	...	...
Dornbirn ... 952 d.	1251	...	1352	...	...	...	1451	1451	...	1552	...	1617	...	1752	...	...	...	1851	1952	...	...	...	2151	...	2252	...	...
Zürich HB **520** ... d.	|	...	|	1240	...	...	|	|	...	|	1440	|	...	|	1640	...	...	|	|	1840	...	...	|	2040	|	2140	2140
Buchs 🏛 ... 952 d.	|	...	|	1354	...	...	|	|	...	|	1554	|	...	|	1800	...	...	|	|	1954	...	...	|	2205	|	2305	2305
Feldkirch ... 952 a.	1312	...	1412	1409	...	...	1512	1511	...	1612	1609	1634	...	1812	1815	...	...	1912	2012	2009	...	...	2216	2220	2314	2321	2321
Feldkirch ... 952 d.	1317	...	▬	1417	...	...	1517	1517	...	▬	1617	1637	...	▬	1817	...	...	1917	▬	2017	...	...	2227	2245	2329	2324	2324
Bludenz ... 952 d.	1330	...	...	1430	...	...	1530	1530	...	...	1630	1656	...	...	1830	...	...	1930	...	2030	...	...	2242	2301	...	2340	2340
Langen am Arlberg ... d.	1356	...	...	|	...	...	1556	1556	...	...	|	1728	...	...	|	...	...	1956	...	|	...	...	2310	2335	...	|	|
St Anton am Arlberg ... d.	|	...	2	1503	...	...	|	|	...	2	1703	1738	...	2Ⓐ	1903	...	...	2007	...	2103	...	...	2320	2345	...	|	|
Landeck-Zams ... d.	1427	...	1501	1527	...	1601	1627	1627	...	1701	1727	1805	...	1901	1927	...	2001	2031	...	2127	...	2201	2344	0009	...	0036	0036
Imst-Pitztal ... d.	1440	...	1518	|	...	1620	1640	1640	...	1718	|	1821	...	1918	1940	...	2020	2044	...	2140	...	2221	2358	|	...	|	|
Ötztal ... d.	|	...	1531	1548	...	1631	|	|	...	1731	1748	1833	...	1931	1951	...	2031	2055	...	2151	...	2231	0009	|	...	|	|
Innsbruck Hbf ... a.	1511	...	1606	1611	...	1706	1711	1711	...	1806	1811	1905	...	2006	2014	←	2106	2118	2	2214	...	2306	0035	0054	...	0120	0120
Innsbruck Hbf ... 960 d.	1514	1540	...	1617	1631	...	1714	1714	1740	...	1817	...	1914	→	2017	2021	...	...	2121	2217	2221	...	0044	...	...	0128	0128
Jenbach ... 960 d.	1531	1601	...	|	|	...	1731	1731	1801	...	|	...	1931	...	|	2048	...	...	2148	|	2248	...	|	...	...	|	|
Wörgl Hbf ... 960 d.	1545	1617	...	1643	1701	...	1745	1745	1817	...	1843	...	1945	...	2043	2108	...	...	2218	2243	2317	...	|	...	...	|	|
Kufstein 🏛 ... d.	|	1626	...	1653	1710	...	|	|	1826	...	1853	...	|	...	2053	2121	...	...	2228	2253	2327	...	|	...	...	|	|
Salzburg Hbf ... a.	1702	...	...	1802	1821	...	1902	1902	...	...	2003	...	2104	...	2205	...	...	...	...	0003	...	...	0255	...	...	0322	0322
Linz Hbf **950** ... a.	1815	...	...	1915	1934	...	2015	2032	...	...	2115	...	2215	...	2318	...	...	...	...	...	...	...	0443	...	...	0452	0558
Wien Westbahnhof **950** . a.	|	...	...	|	2052	...	|	|	...	...	|	...	|	...	|	...	...	...	...	...	...	...	|	...	...	|	|
Wien Hbf **950** ... a.	1932	...	...	2032	...	...	2132	2205	...	...	2232	...	2332	...	0035	...	...	...	...	...	...	...	0658	...	...	0634	0758

♦ – **NOTES** (LISTED BY TRAIN NUMBER)

119 – BODENSEE – 12 Dortmund - Köln - Stuttgart - Lindau - Innsbruck.

465 – 🛏 1, 2 cl., ▬ 2 cl. and 2 Zürich - Schwarzach - Graz; 🛏 1, 2 cl., ▬ 2 cl. and 2 (*EN* **40465**) Zürich - Schwarzach - Villach - Ljubljana - Zagreb.

E – On ①②③④⑦ conveys 12 (*RJX* **567**) (Feldkirch ⑦**t** -) Innsbruck - Wien Hbf - Flughafen Wien.

F – To Flughafen Wien ✈ (Table **950**).

N – Conveys 🛏 1, 2 cl., ▬ 2 cl. and 2.

R – To Bratislava (Table **86**).

t – Also Dec. 26, Apr. 10, May 1, 29, Aug. 15; not Dec. 25, Apr. 9, 30, May 28, Aug. 13.

w – Also Dec. 25, Apr. 9, 30, May 28, Aug. 13; not Dec. 26, Apr. 10, May 1, 29, Aug. 15.

⊙ – 🛏 1, 2 cl., ▬ 2 cl. and 2 Zürich (**467**) - Salzburg (**463**) - Budapest. Also conveys through cars to Praha (see Table **52**).

‡ – Additional local services run München - Rosenheim - Kufstein and v.v. (branded *Meridian*, operated by Bayerische Oberlandbahn). Journey time: 73 – 80 minutes.
From München at 0640, 0743, 0843 and hourly until 2043 (also Rosenheim to Kufstein at 0039, 2235 and 2335).
From Kufstein at 0600, 0702, 0801 and hourly until 1902 (also Kufstein to Rosenheim at 1959, 2058, 2158 and 2258).

952 VORARLBERG LOCAL SERVICES

2nd class only (except where shown)

BLUDENZ - BREGENZ - LINDAU ⊖ △

																											Ⓒ
Bludenz ... d.	0439	0600	0656	0730	0800	0809	0900	1000	1009	1200	1209	1300	1400	1409	1500	1600	1609	1700	1800	1809	1900	2000	2039	2139	2209	2309	0039
Feldkirch ... d.	0500	0617	0715	0747	0817	0830	0917	1017	1030	1217	1230	1317	1417	1430	1517	1617	1630	1717	1817	1830	1917	2017	2100	2200	2230	2330	0100
Dornbirn ... d.	0529	0639	0739	0809	0839	0859	0939	1039	1059	1239	1259	1339	1439	1459	1539	1639	1659	1739	1839	1859	1939	2039	2129	2229	2259	2359	0129
Bregenz 🏛 ... d.	0545	0649	0750	0819	0849	0920c	0949	1049	1115	1249	1320c	1349	1449	1520c	1549	1649	1715	1749	1849	1920c	1949	2049	2149c	2249c	2320c	0014	0144
Lindau Reutin 🏛 a.	0554	0658	0759	0828	0858	0929	0958	1058	1125	1258	1329	1358	1458	1529	1558	1658	1724	1758	1858	1929	1958	2058	2158	2258	2329	...	...
Lindau Insel 🏛 a.	0600	0703	0804	0832	0903	0934	1003	1103	1131	1303	1334	1403	1503	1534	1605	1703	1730	1803	1903	1934	2003	2104	2204	2304	2335	...	...

Lindau Insel 🏛 d.	0552	0621	0655	0755	0823	0855	0955	1021	1055	1155	1223	1255	1355	1423	1455	1557	1625	1655	1755	1823	1855	1955	2029	2127	2225	2256	2327
Lindau Reutin 🏛 d.	0559	0626	0659	0800	0827	0859	0959	1024	1059	1159	1227	1259	1359	1427	1459	1603	1629	1659	1759	1827	1859	1959	2033	2133	2229	2303	2333
Bregenz 🏛 ... d.	0611	0644e	0711	0811	0844e	0911	1011	1044f	1111	1211	1244e	1311	1411	1444e	1511	1614	1641	1711	1811	1844e	1911	2011	2044	2144	2241	2314	2344
Dornbirn ... d.	0622	0700	0722	0822	0900	0922	1022	1100	1122	1222	1300	1322	1422	1500	1522	1630	1652	1722	1822	1900	1922	2022	2100	2200	2252	2330	0000
Feldkirch ... d.	0644	0731	0744	0844	0931	0944	1044	1131	1144	1244	1331	1344	1444	1531	1544	1701	1714	1744	1844	1931	1944	2044	2131	2231	2314	0001	0031
Bludenz ... a.	0659	0751	0759	0859	0951	0959	1059	1151	1159	1259	1351	1359	1459	1551	1559	1721	1729	1802	1859	1951	1959	2059	2151	2251	2329	0021	0051

ST MARGRETHEN - BREGENZ - LINDAU △

km							EC 97				EC 99				EC 191				EC 193						
					Ⓐ		♥		Ⓐ		♥		Ⓐ		♥		Ⓐ		♥		Ⓐ		Ⓐ		Ⓐ
0	St Margrethen 🏛 ... d.	0550	0625	0655	0725	0755	0851	0855	0925	0955	1051	1055	1125	1155	1251	1255	1325	1355	1451	1455	1525	1555	1625	1655	1725	1755
12	**Bregenz** 🏛 ... a.	0610	0640	0710	0740	0810	0900	0910	0940	1010	1102	1110	1140	1210	1300	1310	1340	1410	1500	1510	1540	1610	1640	1710	1740	1810
20	Lindau Reutin 🏛 ... a.	0624	0658	0728	0759	0828	0908	0929	0958	1028	1108	1125	...	1228	1308	1329	1358	1428	1508	1529	1558	1628	1658	1724	1758	1828
22	**Lindau** Insel 🏛 ... a.	0629	0703	0733	0804	0832	0934	0934	1003	1032	1131	1131	...	1232	1334	1334	1403	1432	1534	1534	1605	1632	1703	1730	1803	1832

		EC 197				EC 199					
	Ⓐ	♥		Ⓐ		♥					
St Margrethen 🏛 ... d.	1825	...	1855	1925	1955	2051	2055	2155	2255	2355	0025
Bregenz 🏛 ... a.	1840	1902	1910	1940	2010	2100	2113	2210	2310	0010	0040
Lindau Reutin 🏛 ... a.	1858	1908	1929	1958	2028	2108	2130	2231	2329	...	...
Lindau Insel 🏛 ... a.	1903	1934	1934	2003	2032	2135	2135	2236	2335	...	...

									EC 198		
					Ⓐ		Ⓐ		♥		Ⓐ
Lindau Insel 🏛 ... d.	...	...	0552	0621	0655	0725	0755	0823	0823	0925	0955
Lindau Reutin 🏛 ... d.	...	...	0559	0626	0659	0729	0759	0827	0852	0929	0959
Bregenz 🏛 ... d.	0517	0542	0617	0647	0717	0747	0817	0847	0900	0947	1017
St Margrethen 🏛 ... a.	0534	0559	0634	0704	0734	0804	0834	0904	0909	1004	1034

		EC 196								EC 192				EC 190						EC 98				EC 96			
		♥		Ⓐ		Ⓐ		Ⓐ		♥		Ⓐ		♥	Ⓐ		Ⓐ		♥	Ⓐ			♥			
Lindau Insel 🏛 ... d.	1021	1021	1125	1155	1223	1255	1325	1355	1423	1423	1525	1557	1625	1625	1655	1722	1755	1823	1823	1855	1925	2029	2029	2127	2225	2327
Lindau Reutin 🏛 ... d.	1024	1052	1129	1159	1227	1259	1329	1359	1427	1452	1529	1603	1629	1652	1659	1729	1759	1827	1852	1859	1929	2033	2052	2133	2229	2333
Bregenz 🏛 ... d.	1047	1100	1147	1217	1247	1317	1347	1417	1447	1500	1547	1617	1647	1700	1717	1747	1817	1847	1900	1917	1947	2047	2100	2147	2247	2347
St Margrethen 🏛 ... a.	1104	1109	1204	1234	1304	1334	1404	1434	1504	1509	1604	1634	1704	1709	1734	1804	1834	1904	1909	1934	2004	2104	2109	2204	2304	0004

FELDKIRCH - BUCHS ⊖

km		A	A	AB	A	A	A	A	A	A	A	A
0	**Feldkirch** ... d.	0535	0648	0709	0747	0847	1520	1615	1645	1715	1815	1845
16	Schaan-Vaduz d.	0554	0707	0731	0809	0906	1539	1634	1704	1734	1834	1904
19	**Buchs** 🏛 ... a.	0557	0710	0734	0812	0909	1542	1637	1707	1737	1837	1907

	A	A	A	A	A	A	A	A	A	A	A
Buchs 🏛 ... d.	0617	0716	0819	0919	1233	1619	1649	1719	1819	1849	1919
Schaan-Vaduz ... d.	0620	0719	0822	0922	1236	1622	1652	1722	1822	1852	1922
Feldkirch ... a.	0639	0738	0841	0941	1255	1641	1711	1741	1841	1911	1941

BLUDENZ - SCHRUNS ⊡

Operated by Montafonerbahn.

km		Ⓒ	Ⓐ												Ⓐ						
0	**Bludenz** ... d.	0053	0535	...	0602	...	0632	...	0702	0735	0805	and at the same	1805	1835	1905	1935	2035	2135	...	2245	2353
6	St. Anton im Montafon ... d.	0102	0544	...	0611	...	0641	...	0711	0744	0814	minutes past	1814	1844	1914	1944	2044	2144	...	2254	0002
12	**Schruns** ... a.	0112	0554	...	0621	...	0651	...	0721	0754	0824	each hour until	1824	1854	1924	1954	2054	2154	...	2304	0012

	Ⓒ		Ⓐ																		
Schruns ... d.	0018	...	0504	...	0534	0601	...	0631	0701	0734	0804	and at the same	1834	1904	2004	...	2104	...	2204	...	2312
St. Anton im Montafon ... d.	0028	...	0514	...	0544	0611	...	0641	0711	0744	0814	minutes past	1844	1914	2014	...	2114	...	2214	...	2322x
Bludenz ... a.	0037	...	0523	...	0553	0620	...	0650	0720	0753	0823	each hour until	1853	1923	2023	...	2123	...	2223	...	2331

A – ①–⑤ (not Dec. 26, Apr. 10, May 1, 18, 29, June 8, Aug. 15, Nov 1).

B – From Bludenz (d. 0646).

c – Arrives 5 – 6 minutes earlier.

e – Arrives 7 – 8 minutes earlier.

f – Arrives 10 minutes earlier.

x – Calls on request.

♥ – 12 and ✕ Zürich - München and v.v. See Table **75**.

⊖ – Selected local trains. See also Table **951**.

△ – Austrian holiday dates apply.

⊡ – Certain services run as through trains from / to Bregenz or Lindau.

MÜNCHEN - INNSBRUCK 953

km		NJ 421 R ◆	EC 81 ⊕ A🍷	EC 83 A🍷	EC 85 A🍷	EC 87 A🍷	RJ 1287 ⑥E ✕	ICE 1283 ⑥C ✕S	EC 89 A🍷	EC 287 ✕	EC 289 🍷T	EC 1289 ⑤⑥ 🍷
0	**München** Hbf..890 ‡ d.	0728	0734	0934	1132	1334	1427	1520	1534	1734	1934	2134
10	**München** Ost..890 ‡ d.	|	0744	0944	1144	1344	1437	|	1544	1744	1944	2144
65	Rosenheim......890 ‡ d.	0806	0813	1013	1213	1413	1507	1601	1613	1813	2013	2213
99	Kufstein 🏛 ....‡ d.	0828	0836	1036	1236	1436	1528	1622	1636	1836	2036	2236
113	Wörgl Hbf..........960 d.	0839	0846	1046	1246	1446	1539	1630	1646	1846	2046	2246
138	Jenbach ....960 d.	0855	0900	1100	1300	1500	1555	...	1700	1900	2100	2300
172	**Innsbruck** Hbf ..960 a.	0914	0918	1118	1318	1518	1615	...	1718	1918	2118	2318

	EC 288 🍷	ICE 1218 ⑥⑦ ◆	ICE 1282 ⑥C S✕	EC 286 ✕	RJ 1286 ⑥E ✕	EC 88 A🍷	EC 86 A🍷	EC 84 A🍷	EC 86 A🍷	EC 80 ◧ A🍷	NJ 420 R ◆
Innsbruck Hbf 960 d.	0717	0840	...	1040	1146	1240	1440	1640	1840	2040	2044
Jenbach ....960 d.	0735	0902	...	1102	1206	1302	1502	1702	1902	2102	2106
Wörgl Hbf........960 d.	0749	0916	1027	1116	1222	1316	1516	1716	1916	2116	2123
Kufstein 🏛 ....‡ d.	0759	0926	1037	1126	1232	1326	1526	1726	1926	2126	2135
Rosenheim....890 ‡ a.	0818	0948	1057	1145	|	1345	1545	1745	1945	2145	2157
München Ost.890 ‡ a.	0849	1017	|	1217	1323	1416	1616	1816	2014	2216	|
München Hbf.890 ‡ a.	0902	1029	1134	1227	1333	1427	1627	1827	2026	2227	2236

◆ – NOTES (LISTED BY TRAIN NUMBER)

421 – 🛏 1, 2 cl., couchette 2 cl. and [2] Amsterdam / Brussels / Düsseldorf - Innsbruck;
🛏 1, 2 cl., couchette 2 cl. and [2] (**40491**) Hamburg - Innsbruck.

420 – 🛏 1, 2 cl., couchette 2 cl. and [2] Innsbruck - Frankfurt - Düsseldorf - Amsterdam;
🛏 1, 2 cl., couchette 2 cl. and [2] (**40420**) Innsbruck - Hamburg.

1218 – [12] and ✕ Innsbruck - Frankfurt (- Berlin until Mar. 26) / (- Hamburg from Apr. 1).

A – To Verona, Bologna or Venezia via Brennero (Table **70**).

C – ⑥ Dec. 17 - Mar. 25 (not Dec. 24).

E – ⑥ Dec. 31 - Apr. 15, June 24 - Sep. 30. To / from Feldkirch (Table **951**).

S – To / from Schwarzach (Table **960**).

T – Also conveys [12] and ✕ (**1219**) on ⑤⑥ (Berlin until Mar. 26 -) / (Hamburg from Apr. 1 -) Frankfurt - Innsbruck.

‡ – See note on page 452 for other regional services Kufstein - München and v.v.

◧ – Train number **1280** on ⑥⑦.

⊕ – Train number **1281** on ⑥⑦.

🚌 LANDECK - NAUDERS - SCUOL and MALLES 954

Landeck - Nauders and Martina

Route **210**												Ⓐ											
Landeck - Zams Bahnhof ....d.	0650	0800	0855	1000	1055	1212	1255	1400	1455	1600	1647	1702	1805	1905	...	...	...	...	...	...	...	...	...
Ried im Oberinntal (Gemeindeamt) .. d.	0718	0828	0923	1028	1123	1240	1323	1428	1523	1628	1715	1730	1833	1933	...	...	...	...	...	...	...	...	...
Martina cunfin 🏛 ....a.	|	|	0956	|	1156	|	1356	|	1556	|	1756	|	|	|	...	...	...	...	...	...	...	...	...
Nauders Mühle ....a.	0800	0910	*1016*	1110	*1216*	1322	*1416*	1510	*1616*	1710	*1816*	1812	1915	2015	...	...	...	...	...	...	...	...	...

		Ⓐ																					
Nauders Mühle ....d.	0607	0622	0640	...	0847	*0938*	1047	*1138*	1247	*1338*	1447	*1538*	1647	*1738*	1847	...	...	...	...	...	...	...	...
Martina cunfin 🏛 ....d.	|	|	|	...	|	1000	|	1200	|	1400	|	1600	|	1800	|	...	...	...	...	...	...	...	...
Ried im Oberinntal (Gemeindeamt) .. d.	0647	|	0727	...	0927	1032	1127	1232	1327	1432	1527	1632	1727	1832	1927	...	...	...	...	...	...	...	...
Landeck - Zams Bahnhof ....a.	0712	0713	0752	...	0952	1057	1152	1257	1352	1457	1552	1657	1752	1857	1952	...	...	...	...	...	...	...	...

Scuol Tarasp - Nauders - Malles

Routes **273 / 921**													
Scuol Tarasp Staziun ....d.	0630	...	0730	...	and at	...	1830	...	1930	...	2030	...
Martina cunfin 🏛 ....d.	0657	0705	0757	0805	the same	1805	1857	1910	*2003*	2010	2100	2110
Nauders Mühle 🏛 ....d.	...	0716	...	0816	minutes	1816	...	1921	...	2021	...	2121
Reschenpass / Passo di Resia 🏛 ......d.	...	0720	...	0820	past each	1820	...	1925	...	2025	...	2125
Resia ....d.	...	0723	...	0823	hour until	1823	...	1928	...	2028	...	2128
Malles Stazione **597** ....a.	...	0753	...	0853		1853	...	1958	...	2058	...	2158

Malles Stazione **597** ....d.	0601	...	0701	...	and at	1801	...	1901	...	2001	...	...
Resia ....d.	0631	...	0731	...	the same	1831	...	1931	...	2031	...	...
Passo di Resia / Reschenpass 🏛 .....d.	0634	...	0734	...	minutes	1834	...	1934	...	2034	...	...
Nauders Mühle 🏛 ....d.	0638	...	0738	...	past each	1838	...	1938	...	2038	...	...
Martina cunfin 🏛 ....d.	0649	0701	0749	0801	hour until	1849	1901	1949	1954	2049	2101	...
Scuol Tarasp Staziun ....a.	...	0727	...	0827		...	1927	...	*2027*	...	2133	...

Operators

Landeck - Nauders: Tioler Linien Bus GmbH, Nauders. ✆ +43 (0)664 384 1360.

Scuol Tarasp - Martina: Auto Da Posta, Svizra. CH - 7550 Scuol. ✆ +41 (0) 58 453 28 28.

Martina - Nauders - Malles: Servizi Autobus Dolomiti (SAD). Corso Italia 13N, I - 39100 Bolzano. ✆ +39 0471 450 111.

JENBACH - MAYRHOFEN 955

2nd class only Narrow gauge Zillertalbahn *

km																	🚂 A
0	**Jenbach** Zillertalbahnhof § ... d.	0630	0652	0748	0811	0841	0911	0941	and at	1711	1741	1811	1841	1858	2007		1044
11	Fügen-Hart..........d.	0646	0709	0806	0826	0856	0926	0956	the same	1726	1756	1826	1856	1913	2022		1114
17	Kaltenbach-Stumm..........d.	0656	0720	0817	0837	0907	0937	1007	minutes	1737	1807	1837	1907	1924	2033	also	1131
21	Aschau im Zillertal..........d.	0703	0727	0823	0843	0913	0943	1013	past each	1743	1813	1843	1913	1930	2039		1146
25	**Zell am Ziller** ....d.	0710	0735	0830	0850	0920	0950	1020	hour until	1750	1820	1850	1920	1937	2046		1157
32	**Mayrhofen** ....a.	0722	0747	0841	0901	0931	1001	1031		1801	1831	1901	1931	1948	2057		1216

	Ⓒ	Ⓐ															🚂 A
Mayrhofen ....d.	0546	0552	0610	0635	0734	0819	0849	and at	1619	1649	1719	1749	1819	1909	1949		1335
Zell am Ziller ....d.	0557	0601x	0621	0647	0744	0831	0901	the same	1631	1701	1731	1801	1831	1921	2001		1352
Aschau im Zillertal ....d.	0603	0606x	0627	0653	0750	0837	0907	minutes	1637	1707	1737	1807	1837	1926	2006	also	1409
Kaltenbach-Stumm..........d.	0610	0611x	0634	0659	0757	0843	0913	past each	1643	1713	1743	1813	1843	1933	2013		1419
Fügen-Hart ....d.	0620	0621x	0646	0710	0807	0854	0925	hour until	1654	1725	1754	1825	1854	1944	2023		1441
Jenbach Zillertalbahnhof § .. a.	0637	0636	0704	0727	0823	0910	0940		1710	1740	1810	1840	1910	1959	2038		1504

A – ⑥⑦ May 6–28; ②–⑥ May 30 - Aug. 26; ②–⑦ Aug. 29 - Oct. 1.

x – Trains call on request.

🚂 – Steam train. Special fares apply.

§ – Adjacent to ÖBB station.

* – Zillertaler Vehrkehrsbetriebe, Austraße 1, A - 6200 Jenbach. ✆ +43 (0) 5244 606 0.

JENBACH - ACHENSEE 956

2nd class only *Achenseebahn*

Narrow gauge rack railway operated by steam locomotives (special fares apply). *7 km.* Journey time 42–50 minutes. **Service shown is for 2022 (awaiting confirmation for 2023).**
Operator: Achenseebahn AG, A - 6200 Jenbach: ✆ +43 (0) 5244 62243, Fax +43 (0) 5244 622435. Jenbach Achensee Bf is adjacent to the ÖBB station.

⑥⑦ Apr. 30 - June 5 (also May 26, 27, June 6, 7); daily except ② June 9–24; daily except ② Sept. 19 - Oct. 3; Ⓒ Oct. 8–30:
From Jenbach Achensee Bf at 1100, 1315, 1530. **From Achnsee Seespitz Bahnstation** at: 1210, 1425, 1635.

Daily except ② June 25–Sept. 18: **From Jenbach Achensee Bf** at 0955, 1053, 1210, 1410, 1529. **From Achnsee Seespitz Bahnstation** at: 1113, 1308, 1430, 1549, 1638.

ZELL AM SEE - KRIMML and 🚌 KRIMML - MAYRHOFEN 957

2nd class only

ZELL AM SEE - KRIMML ⊡

						Ⓐ				Ⓐ	Ⓒ			T 🚂		
0	**Zell am See** Lokalbahn........d.	0557	0800	and	1600	1650	1700	1800	1900	2000	2050	...		0918	...	...
29	Mittersill ....d.	0636	0848	hourly	1648	1727	1748	1848	1948	2048	2134	...	also	1108j	...	...
39	Bramberg..........d.	0650	0903	until	1703	1739	1803	1903	2003	2103	2147	...		1131	...	...
53	**Krimml** ....a.	0756	0923		1723	1756	1823	1923	2023	2123	2205	...		1202	...	...

		Ⓐ	Ⓐ											T 🚂		
Krimml..........d.	0533	0603	0628	0640	0733	and	1533	1633	1733	1833	...	also	1355	...	...
Bramberg..........d.	0552	0622	0644	0658	0752	hourly	1552	1652	1752	1852	...		1420	...	...
Mittersill ....d.	0608	0638	0656	0720	0808	until	1608	1708	1808	1908	...		1520k	...	...
Zell am See Lokalbahn..........a.	0655	0725	0738	0807	0855		1655	1755	1855	1955	...		1637	...	...

🚌 Krimml Bahnhof - Krimml Wasserfälle and v.v. Route **670**. *3 km.* Journey time: 6–9 minutes.

From Krimml Bahnhof at 0753, 0829Ⓐ, 0921 and hourly until 1721, 1744Ⓐ, 1844, 1939Ⓐ, 2202Ⓐ.

From Krimml Wasserfälle at 0537Ⓐ, 0620, 0828, 0900Ⓐ, 1028 and hourly until 1828, 1928Ⓐ.

Additional buses also run at irregular intervals.

🚌 routes **673** and **4094**: KRIMML - KÖNIGSLEITEN - MAYRHOFEN *Winter service December 11, 2022 - April 16, 2023.*

km			Z			V			Z	V	
0	**Krimml** Bahnhof.......... d.	...	0837	...	*1037*	*1107*	...	...	1527	...	*1630*
3	Krimml Wasserfälle.......... d.	...	|	...	|	|	...	...	|	...	|
16	Almdorf (Königsleiten)....... d.	...	0915	1000	1123	1303	1428	1513	1600	...	1703
25	**Gerlos** Gasthaus Oberwirt d.	0701	...	1011	1141	1321	1446	1531	...	1621	1721
45	Zell am Ziller Bahnhof.**955** a.	0735	...	1047	1217	1357	1522	1607	...	1657	1757
53	**Mayrhofen** Bahnhof ...**955** a.	0746	...	...	...	1406	...	...	...	1708	1806

	V		Z				V			
Mayrhofen Bahnhof .. **955** d.	0805	0845	...	0945	...	...	1445	...	...	1845
Zell am Ziller Bahnhof **955** d.	0820	0900	...	1000	1105	1325	1500	1600	1700	1900
Gerlos Gasthaus Oberwirt d.	0851	0931	...	1031	1141	1401	1536	1636	1736	1929
Königsleiten Almdorf .... d.	...	0951	1028	1051	1201	*1420*	...	1647	...	...
Krimml Wasserfälle.......... a.	...	...	|	...	|	...	...	|	...	...
Krimml Bahnhof.......... a.	...	...	1054	...	*1330*	...	...	*1800*	...	...

T – ④ May 20 - Sept. 23 (also Sept. 11).

V – Dec. 23 - Apr. 4.

Z – Dec. 17 - Apr. 16.

j – Arrives 1038.

k – Arrives 1440.

🚂 – Steam train with special fares. A Christmas and New Year service also operates.

⊡ – Narrow gauge railway. **Operator**: Pinzgauer Lokalbahn. Trains call at Mittersill and Bramberg on request only. **Warning!** Following flood damage, rail services are replaced by 🚌 Niedernsill (km15) - Krimml and v.v. until further notice (in similar timings).

960 SALZBURG - SCHWARZACH - INNSBRUCK

km		NJ 464										IC 894			ICE 1282	ICE 1216		IC 898				RJ 111			
		A	2	Ⓐ 2	⚒ 2	⚒ 2	2	Ⓒ 2	Ⓒ 2	Ⓐ 2	Ⓐ 2	🍷⊖	2	2	⑥K ✕	P ✕	2	🍷⊖	2	2	2	✕⊖	2	2	2
	Wien Hbf 950 d.	...	...	...	...	...	...	...	...	...	...	...	...	...	...	...	...	...	...	...	...	...	...	...	...
0	**Salzburg** Hbf. 951 970 975 ‡ d.	...	...	...	...	...	...	0411	...	0430	...	0612	...	...	...	...	0708	0812	...	...	0908	1012	...	...	1108
29	Golling-Abtenau 970 ‡ d.	...	...	...	...	...	...	0449	...	0454	...	0633	...	...	...	...	0734	0833	...	...	0934	1033	...	...	1134
53	**Bischofshofen** 970 975 ‡ d.	0158	...	...	...	...	...	0513	...	0518	...	0654	...	...	...	...	0756	0854	...	...	0956	1054	...	...	1156
61	St Johann im Pongau 970 ‡ d.	|	...	...	...	...	...	0523	...	0528	...	0703	...	...	...	...	0804	0903	...	...	1004	1103	...	...	1204
67	**Schwarzach - St Veit** 970 ‡ a.	0211	...	...	...	...	...	0529	...	0534	...	0709	...	...	...	...	0810	0909	...	...	1010	1109	...	...	1210
67	**Schwarzach - St Veit** d.	0232	...	...	...	...	...	0531	...	0536	...	▬	0712	...	0800	0800	0812	▬	0912	...	1012	▬	1112	...	1212
99	**Zell am See** d.	|		...	...	...	...	0607	...	0612	...	2	0745	...	0832	0832	0845	...	0945	...	1045	...	1145	...	1245
113	Saalfelden d.	|	0401	0451	0516	...	0536	0619	0625	0625	0644	0716c	0755	...	0843	0843	0855	2	0955	...	1055	2	1155	...	1255
131	Hochfilzen d.	|	0418	0509	0533	...	0554	▬	0643	0643	0702	0734c	0813	0834	0859	0859	0913	0934	1013	1034	1113	1134	1213	1234	1313
148	St Johann in Tirol d.	|	0434	0527	0549	...	0612	...	0700	0700	0720	0752	0828	0852	0917	0917	0928	0956	1028	1052	1128	1152	1228	1252	1328
157	**Kitzbühel** d.	|	0442	0536	0557	...	0621	...	0708	0708	0729	0801	0835	0901	0926	0926	0935	1001	1035	1101	1135	1201	1235	1301	1335
166	Kirchberg in Tirol d.	|	0451	0546	0607	...	0631	...	0717	0717	0739	0811	0844	0911	0938	0938	0943	1011	1044	1111	1143	1211	1244	1311	1343
192	Wörgl Hbf a.	|	0518	0615	0633	...	0700	2 Ⓐ	0742	0742	0808	0840	0909	0940	1002	1002	1008	1040	1109	1140	1208	1240	1309	1340	1408
192	Wörgl Hbf 951 d.	|	0519	0617	0640a	0649	0719	0709	0747	0747	0817	0846	0919	0947	1027	1027	1015	1046	1119	1147	1215	1246	1319	1347	1415
	München Hbf 951 a.		|	|	|	|	|	|	|	|	|	|	|	|	1134	1138	|	|	|	|	|	|	|	|	|
217	Jenbach 951 a.	|	0538	0638	0657a	0708	|	0727	0759	0759	0829	0858	|	0959	...	...	1027	1058	|	1159	1227	1258	|	1359	1427
251	**Innsbruck** Hbf 951 a.	0449	0607	0713	0717a	0740	0744	0748	0820	0820	0846	0918	0944	1020	...	...	1044	1118	1144	1220	1244	1318	1344	1420	1444

		RJ 596	EC 164 Z		RJX 1262 ⑥H		EC 113					IC 518 G	EC 115					RJ 698					EC 117	RJ 1260 ⑤J	
	2	✕⊖	✕	2	✕	2	🍷⊖	2	2	2	2	🍷	🍷⊖	2	2	2	Ⓐ 2	✕⊖	2	2	2	2	🍷⊖	✕	2
Wien Hbf 950 d.	...	0855	...	...	0950	...	...	...	...	...	...	...	...	...	...	...	...	1455	...	...	...	...	...	1728	...
Salzburg Hbf 951 970 975 ‡ d.	...	1212	...	...	1244	1308	1412	...	...	1508	...	...	1612	...	1708	...	1743	1812	...	...	1908	...	2012	2008	2215
Golling-Abtenau 970 ‡ d.	...	1233	...	...	1309	1334	1433	...	...	1534	...	...	1633	...	1734	...	1812	1833	...	...	1934	...	2033	2045	2242
Bischofshofen 970 975 ‡ d.	...	1254	1250	...	1330	1356	1454	...	...	1556	...	1650	1654	...	1756	...	1837	1854	...	...	1956	...	2054	2107	2305
St Johann im Pongau 970 ‡ d.	...	1303	1259	...	1340	1404	1503	...	...	1604	...	1659	1703	...	1804	...	1847	1903	...	...	2004	...	2103	2117	2314
Schwarzach - St Veit 970 ‡ a.	...	1309	1305	...	1346	1410	1509	...	...	1610	...	1705	1709	...	1810	...	1852	1909	...	...	2010	...	2109	2122	2319
Schwarzach - St Veit d.	...	▬	1313	...	1352	1412	▬	1512	...	1612	...	1713	...	...	1813	...	1853	...	1912	...	2012	...	▬	2124	2321
Zell am See d.	...	...	1344	...	1424	1445	...	1545	...	1645	...	1744	...	...	1846	...	1929	...	1946	...	2046	...	2	2156	2356
Saalfelden d.	...	...	1355	1416a	1435	1455	2	1555	...	1655	...	1754	...	...	1856	...	1941	...	1957	...	2057	...	2148	2208	0005
Hochfilzen d.	1334	...	|	1434	|	1513	1534	1613	1634	1713	1734	|	...	1834	1914	1934	...	...	2016	2034	2116	2134	2206	|	...
St Johann in Tirol d.	1352	...	1423	1452	1506	1528	1552	1628	1652	1728	1752	1822	...	1852	1929	1952	...	...	2030	2052	2130	2152	2224	2240	...
Kitzbühel d.	1401	...	1431	1501	1515	1535	1601	1635	1701	1735	1801	1830	...	1901	1936	2001	...	...	2038	2101	2138	2201	2233	2249	...
Kirchberg in Tirol d.	1411	Ⓐ	1439	1511	1524	1543	1611	1644	1711	1743	1811	1838	...	1911	1944	2011	...	...	2047	2111	2147	2211	2243	2258	...
Wörgl Hbf a.	1440	2	1501	1540	1548	1608	1640	1709	1740	1808	1840	1900	...	1940	2009	2040	...	...	2112	2140	2212	2240	2312	2322	...
Wörgl Hbf 951 d.	1446	1449	1503	1547	...	1615	1646	1719	1747	1815	1846	1902	...	1947	2015	2046	...	...	2119	2154	2219	...	2319	2329	...
München Hbf 951 a.	|	|	|	|	...	|	|	|	|	|	|	|	...	|	|	|	...	...	|	|	|	...	|	|	...
Jenbach 951 a.	1458	1508	1516	1559	...	1627	1658	|	1759	1827	1858	1916	...	1959	2027	2058	...	...	|	2213	2231	...	2331	2350	...
Innsbruck Hbf 951 a.	1518	1535	1540	1620	...	1644	1718	1744	1820	1844	1918	1940	...	2020	2044	2118	...	...	2144	2240	2248	...	2348	0025	...

	NJ 465							RJ 691				IC 515 G	EC 114	RJX 1265 ⑥Q				EC 112				EC 163 Z	IC 793		
	A	⚒ 2	2	⚒f 2	2	2	2	✕⊖	2	2	2	🍷	⊗⊖	✕	2	2	2	✕⊖	2	2	2	✕	⊖	2	2
Innsbruck Hbf 951 d.	0056	...	...	0510	0514a	...	0610	...	0620r	0717	0721	0821	...	0850	0914	0940	1017	...	1040	1114	1140	1221	...	1240	1314
Jenbach 951 d.	|	...	...	0527	0541a	...	0627	...	0649r	0735	0750	0844	...	0917	0931	1001	|	...	1101	1131	1201	1243	...	1301	1331
München Hbf 951 d.	|	...	...	|	|	...	|	...	|	|	|	|	...	|	|	|	|	...	|	|	|	|	...	|	|
Wörgl Hbf 951 a.	|	...	...	0539	0600a	...	0639	...	0708r	0747	0809	0857	...	0936	0943	1013	1041	...	1114	1143	1213	1256	...	1314	1343
Wörgl Hbf d.	|	...	...	0542	0605	...	0649	...	0722	0750	0822	0859	...	0941	0952	1022	1050	...	1122	1152	1222	1258	...	1322	1352
Kirchberg in Tirol d.	|	...	...	0609	0634	...	0714	...	0751	0816	0851	0920	...	1007	1017	1051	1116	...	1151	1217	1251	1319	...	1351	1417
Kitzbühel d.	|	...	...	0620	0645	...	0725	...	0802	0825	0902	0929	...	1016	1025	1102	1125	...	1202	1225	1302	1328	...	1402	1425
St Johann in Tirol d.	|	...	...	0629	0654	...	0732	...	0811	0832	0911	0937	...	1025	1032	1111	1132	...	1211	1232	1311	1336	...	1411	1432
Hochfilzen d.	|	...	...	0646	0714	...	0747	...	0828	0847	0928	|	...	|	1047	1128	1147	...	1228	1247	1328	|	...	1429	1447
Saalfelden d.	|	0458	0551	0705	0731b	0734r	0805	...	...	0905	...	1005	...	1057	1105	...	1205	...	...	1305	...	1405	...	1446a	1505
Zell am See d.	|	0508	0602	0715	...	0747r	0815	...	...	0915	...	1016	...	1109	1115	...	1215	...	...	1315	...	1416	...	...	1515
Schwarzach - St Veit a.	0317	0541	0637	0748	...	0822r	0848	...	...	0948	...	1046	...	1139	1148	...	1248	...	...	1348	...	1446	...	...	1548
Schwarzach - St Veit 970 ‡ d.	0324	0542	0639	0749	...	0824	...	0852	...	0949	...	1056	1052	1143	1149	...	...	1252	...	1349	...	1456	1452	...	1549
St Johann im Pongau 970 ‡ d.	|	0548	0646	0755	...	0829	...	0858	...	0955	...	1102	1058	1150	1155	...	...	1258	...	1355	...	1502	1458	...	1555
Bischofshofen 970 975 ‡ d.	0336	0558	0655	0804	...	0840	...	0907	...	1004	...	1110	1107	1200	1204	...	...	1307	...	1404	...	1510	1507	...	1604
Golling-Abtenau 970 ‡ d.	...	0620	0718	0825	...	0904	...	0928	...	1025	...	...	1128	1221	1225	...	...	1328	...	1425	...	...	1528	...	1625
Salzburg Hbf 951 970 975 ‡ a.	...	0645	0744	0851	...	0940	...	0948	...	1051	...	...	1148	1245	1251	...	...	1348	...	1451	...	...	1548	...	1651
Wien Hbf 950 a.	...	...	...	...	...	...	...	1305	...	...	...	...	...	1532	...	...	...	...	...	...	...	...	...	...	...

			RJ 797	RJ 1267 ⑦L		RJX 1261 ⑥R			ICE 1283 ⑥K		RJ 110			ICE 585 B			IC 895								
	2	2	✕⊖	✕	2	✕	2	2	✕	2	✕⊖	2	2	✕	2	2	🍷⊖	2	2	2	2	2	2	2	2
Innsbruck Hbf 951 d.	1320	1417	...	...	1440	...	1514	1540	...	1600a	...	1640	1714	...	1740	1817	...	1840	1914	1920	2017	2121	2135	2335	0105
Jenbach 951 d.	1347	|	...	...	1501	...	1531	1601	...	1625a	...	1701	1731	...	1801	|	...	1901	1931	1947	|	2148	2209	0009	0139
München Hbf 951 d.	|	|	...	...	|	...	|	|	1520	|	...	|	|	1611	|	|	...	|	|	|	|	|	|	|	|
Wörgl Hbf 951 a.	1406	1441	...	...	1514	...	1543	1613	1630	1647a	...	1714	1743	1738	1816	1841	...	1914	1943	2006	2041	2207	2231	0031	0204
Wörgl Hbf d.	1422	1450	...	1516	1522	1541	1552	1622	1638	1650	...	1722	1752	1758	1822	1850	...	1922	1952	2022	2052	2222	▬	0037	0210
Kirchberg in Tirol d.	1451	1516	...	1542	1551	1607	1617	1651	1704	1716	...	1751	1817	1824	1851	1916	...	1951	2017	2051	2117	2251	...	0106	0239
Kitzbühel d.	1502	1525	...	1551	1602	1616	1625	1702	1716	1725	...	1802	1825	1836	1902	1925	...	2002	2026	2102	2125	2302	...	0117	0250
St Johann in Tirol d.	1511	1532	...	1600	1611	1625	1632	1711	1725	1732	...	1811	1832	1845	1911	1932	...	2011	2034	2111	2132	2311	...	0126	0259
Hochfilzen d.	1528	1547	...	|	1628	|	1647	1728	1742	1747	...	1828	1847	1902	1928	1947	...	2028	2050	2128	2147	2329	D	0144	0317
Saalfelden d.	...	1605	...	1632	...	1657	1705	...	1759	1805	...	...	1905	1919	...	2005	...	...	2107	...	2205	2346	899	0201	0334
Zell am See d.	...	1615	...	1644	...	1709	1715	...	1810	1815	...	...	1915	1930	...	2015	...	...	...	...	2215	...		...	...
Schwarzach - St Veit a.	...	1648	...	1714	...	1739	1748	...	1840	1848	...	...	1948	2000	...	2048	...	...	...	...	2248	...	2	...	...
Schwarzach - St Veit 970 ‡ d.	...	...	1652	1717	...	1743	1749	...	...	...	1852	...	1949	...	...	...	2052	...	...	...	...	...	2252	...	...
St Johann im Pongau 970 ‡ d.	...	...	1658	1724	...	1750	1755	...	...	...	1858	...	1955	...	...	...	2058	...	...	...	...	...	2258	...	...
Bischofshofen 970 975 ‡ d.	...	...	1707	1734	...	1800	1804	...	...	...	1907	...	2004	...	...	...	2107	...	...	...	...	...	2307	...	...
Golling-Abtenau 970 ‡ d.	...	...	1728	1756	...	1821	1825	...	...	...	1928	...	2025	...	...	...	2128	...	...	...	...	...	2328	...	...
Salzburg Hbf 951 970 975 ‡ a.	...	...	1748	1817	...	1845	1851	...	...	...	1948	...	2051	...	...	...	2148	...	...	...	...	...	2348	...	...
Wien Hbf 950 a.	...	...	2105	2111	...	2132	...	...	...	...	...	...	...	...	...	...	...	...	...	...	...	...	...	...	...

A – 🛏 1,2 cl., 🛏 2 cl. and (2) Graz - Feldkirch - Buchs 🏛 - Zürich and v.v. Conveys from / to Schwarzach 🛏 1,2 cl., 🛏 2 cl. and (2) (*EN* **40414/40465**) Zagreb - Ljubljana - Villach - Zürich and v.v.
B – ⑤⑥ May 27 - Sept. 9. From Lübeck (Table **825** and **900**).
G – From / to Graz (Table **975**).
H – ⑥ July 1 - Sept. 9.
J – ⑤ Dec. 23 - Apr. 7; ⑤ June 30 - Sept. 8.
K – ⑥ Dec. 17 - Mar 25.
L – ⑦ Jan. 1 - Apr. 2 (also Apr. 10); ⑦ July 2 - Sept. 10.
P – ⑥⑦ May 28 - Sept. 10. To Bremen (Table **900**).
Q – ⑥ Dec. 24 - Apr. 8; ⑥ 1 July - Sept. 9. To Flughafen Wien (Table **950**).
R – ⑥ Dec. 24 - Apr. 8.
Z – TRANSALPIN – (12) and ✕ Graz - Bischofshofen - Innsbruck - Buchs 🏛 - Zürich and v.v.

a – Ⓐ only.
b – Ⓑ only.
c – Ⓒ only.
f – Runs daily Saalfelden - Salzburg.
r – ⚒ only.

⊖ – See Table **970** for further details.
‡ – See panel below main table for additional S-Bahn services (calling at all stations).

Freilassing 890 d.	0607		2307
Salzburg Hbf 890 d.	0621	and	2321
Golling-Abtenau d.	0659	hourly	2359
Bischofshofen d.	0724	until	0024
St Johann im Pongau d.	0734		0034
Schwarzach - St Veit a.	0739		0039

Schwarzach - St Veit d.	0524		2224
St Johann im Pongau d.	0529	and	2229
Bischofshofen d.	0540	hourly	2240
Golling-Abtenau d.	0604	until	2304
Salzburg Hbf 890 a.	0640		2340
Freilassing 890 a.	0653		2354

ATTNANG-PUCHHEIM - STAINACH-IRDNING — 961

2nd class only (except trains A and B)

km																							
		⚒	Ⓐ		Ⓒ	Ⓐ					🍷A			⑤E									
	Wien Hbf **950** d.	...	...	...	...	...	...	...	...	...	0837	...	...	...	...	...	...	...	...	...	...	...	...
0	**Attnang-Puchheim** d.	...	0446	...	0604	0604	0716	0808	0908	1008	1037	1108	1208	1236	1308	1408	1508	1608	1708	1808	1908	2008	2108
12	**Gmunden** d.	...	0456	...	0621	0621	0736	0824	0924	1024	1052	1124	1224	1252	1324	1424	1524	1624	1724	1824	1924	2024	2124
17	Altmünster am Traunsee d.	...	0501	...	0626	0626	0742	0830	0930	1030	1059	1130	1230	1257	1330	1430	1530	1630	1730	1830	1930	2030	2130
22	Traunkirchen d.	...	0509	...	0633	0633	0748	0836	0937	1036	|	1137	1236	1303	1337	1436	1537	1636	1737	1836	1937	2036	2137
27	Ebensee Landungsplatz d.	...	0517	...	0640	0640	0756	0843	0944	1043	|	1144	1243	1309	1344	1443	1544	1643	1744	1843	1944	2043	2144
28	Ebensee d.	...	0519	...	0643	0643	0759	0846	0947	1046	1112	1147	1246	1312	1347	1446	1547	1646	1747	1846	1947	2046	2147
44	**Bad Ischl** d.	...	0536	...	0704	0705	0819	0903	1010	1103	1128	1210	1303	1330	1410	1503	1610	1703	1810	1903	2010	2103	2205
54	Bad Goisern d.	...	...	...	0713	0717	0832	0913	1025	1113	1142	1225	1313	...	1425	1513	1625	1713	1825	1913	2025	2113	|
64	Hallstatt ⊡ d.	...	...	...	0725	0730	0848	0925	1048	1125	1156	1248	1325	...	1448	1525	1648	1725	1848	|	|	|	2218
67	Obertraun-Dachsteinhöhlen d.	...	...	...	0728	0734	0851	0928	1051	1128	1201	1251	1328	...	1451	1528	1651	1728	1851	1928	2050	2128	2233
78	**Bad Aussee** d.	0502	...	0630	0742	0749	...	0942	...	1142	1216	...	1342	...	...	1542	...	1742	...	1942	...	2142	2245
93	Bad Mitterndorf d.	0520	...	0648	0759	0804	...	0959	...	1159	1235	...	1359	...	...	1559	...	1759	...	1959	...	2159	...
108	**Stainach-Irdning** a.	0537	...	0705	0815	0818	...	1015	...	1215	1251	...	1415	...	...	1615	...	1815	...	2015	...	2215	...

			Ⓐ	⚒	⚒		Ⓐ	Ⓒ						E					🍷B				
Stainach-Irdning d.	...	...	...	...	0609	...	0713	0740	...	0940	...	1140	...	...	1340	...	1540	...	1704	1740	...	1940	2140
Bad Mitterndorf d.	...	...	...	...	0627	...	0730	0759	...	0959	...	1159	...	...	1359	...	1559	...	1721	1759	...	1959	2159
Bad Aussee d.	...	0459	...	0612	0651	0651	0810f	0816	...	1016	...	1216	...	...	1416	...	1616	...	1742	1816	...	2016	2215
Obertraun-Dachsteinhöhlen d.	...	0511	...	0624	0703	0703	0823	0828	0903	1028	1103	1228	1303	...	1428	1503	1628	1703	1755	1828	1903	2028	...
Hallstatt ⊡ d.	...	|	...	|	0707	0707	0828	0832	0907	1032	1107	1232	1307	...	1432	1507	1632	1707	1800	1832	|	|	...
Bad Goisern d.	...	0526	...	0639	0725	0725	0843	0843	0934	1043	1134	1243	1334	...	1443	1534	1643	1734	1814	1843	1934	2043	...
Bad Ischl d.	0440	0540	0554	0652	0740	0740	0853	0853	0953	1053	1153	1253	1353	1428	1453	1553	1653	1753	1831	1853	1953	2053	...
Ebensee d.	0459	0559	0611	0712	0800	0800	0912	0912	1013	1112	1213	1312	1413	1445	1512	1613	1712	1813	1847	1912	2013	2112	...
Ebensee Landungsplatz d.	0501	0601	0613	0714	0803	0803	0914	0914	1015	1114	1215	1314	1415	1448	1514	1615	1714	1815	|	1914	2015	2114	...
Traunkirchen d.	0509	0609	0620	0722	0811	0811	0922	0922	1023	1122	1223	1322	1423	1454	1522	1623	1722	1823	|	1922	2023	2122	...
Altmünster am Traunsee d.	0514	0614	0630	0727	0817	0817	0930	0930	1030	1130	1230	1330	1430	1501	1530	1630	1730	1830	1859	1930	2030	2130	...
Gmunden d.	0521	0621	0636	0736	0836r	0836r	0936	0936	1036	1136	1236	1336	1436	1506	1536	1636	1736	1836	1906	1936	2036	2136	...
Attnang-Puchheim a.	0538	0638	0652	0752	0852	0852	0951	0951	1052	1151	1252	1351	1452	1524	1551	1652	1751	1852	1923	1951	2052	2151	...
Wien Hbf **950** a.	...	...	...	...	...	...	...	...	...	...	...	...	...	...	...	...	...	...	2120	...	...	...	...

A – *IC* **1018**. SALZKAMMERGUT – (12) Wien - Attnang-Puchheim - Stainach-Irdning.
B – *IC* **1019**. SALZKAMMERGUT – (12) Stainach-Irdning - Attnang-Puchheim - Wien.
E – ⑤ Dec. 16 - June 30 (not Dec. 30, Jan. 6, Feb. 24, Apr. 7); ⑤ Sept. 15 - Dec. 1 (not Oct. 27).

f – Arrives 0748.
r – Arrives 0822.

⊡ – ⛴ services operate Hallstatt Bahnhof - Hallstatt Markt. Journey: 8 minutes.
Operator: Hallstättersee-Schifffahrt Hemetsberger KG ✆ +43 (0) 6134 8228.
From Hallstatt Bahnhof at 0707⚒, 0735⚒, 0830⚒, 0900, 0930, 1035, 1100, 1130, 1235, 1300, 1330, 1435, 1500, 1530, 1635, 1700, 1730 and 1850.
From Hallstatt Markt at 0650⚒, 0715⚒, 0810⚒, 0845, 0915, 1015, 1045, 1215, 1245, 1415, 1445, 1615, 1645, 1715 and 1815.

LINZ - PASSAU and SIMBACH — 962

km																										
										ICE 228					*ICE* 28			*ICE* 92				*ICE* 26				
		Ⓐ		⚒	Ⓐ									Ⓐ						⚒	Ⓐ					⚒
		2	2	2	2	G2	2	2	2	D✕	2	2	2	2	D✕	2	2	B✕	2	2	2	D✕	2	2	2	2
	Wien Hbf **950** d.	...	...	...	...	...	...	...	...	0649	...	...	...	...	0913	...	...	1013	...	...	...	1113	...	...	...	...
0	**Linz** Hbf **950** d.	...	...	0452	...	0540	0552	0650	...	0817	0850	...	0950	...	1034	1050	...	1134	1150	...	...	1234	1250	...	1350	...
25	**Wels** Hbf **950** d.	0444	...	0516	...	0613j	0620	0709	...	0833	0909	...	1009	...	|	1109	...	|	1209	...	...	|	1309	...	1409	...
54	Neumarkt-Kallham d.	0508	...	0543	0553	0641	0646	0736	0740	|	0936	0940	1032	1040	|	1140t	1140	|	1232	1240	1301	|	1336	1340	1432	1440
	Ried im Innkreis d.	0529	...	|	0614	|	0710	|	0801	|	|	1001	|	1101	|	1201	|	|	|	1301	1323	|	|	1401	|	1501
	Braunau am Inn a.	0604	0642	|	...	|	0740	|	0841	|	|	1041	|	1141	|	1241	|	|	|	1341	...	|	|	1441	|	1541
	Simbach (Inn) 🏛 **893** a.	...	0645	|	...	|	0745	|	0845	|	|	1045	|	1145	|	1245	|	|	|	1345	...	|	|	1445	|	1545
92	Schärding d.	...	...	0615	...	0714	...	0809	...	0911	1009	...	1057	...	|	...	1211	|	1257	...	...	|	1409	...	1457	...
106	**Passau** Hbf a.	...	...	0628	...	0727	...	0822	...	0922	1022	...	1112	...	1131	...	1224	1231	1312	...	...	1331	1422	...	1512	...
	Nürnberg Hbf **920** a.	...	...	...	...	...	...	...	...	1127	...	...	...	...	1327	...	...	1430	...	...	...	1527	...	...	...	...
	Frankfurt (Main) Hbf **920** a	...	...	...	...	...	...	...	...	1336v	...	...	...	...	1536v	...	...	...	...	...	...	1736v	...	...	...	...

	ICE 90							*ICE* 22							*ICE* 20					*IC* 94		*NJ* 490	*RJX* 42		*RJ* 840	
				Ⓐ			Ⓐ		Ⓐ			Ⓐ		Ⓐ												
	H✕	2	2	2	2	2	2	D✕	2	2	2	2	2	2	✕	2	2	2	2	W🍷	2	⊡	✕	2	✕	2
Wien Hbf **950** d.	1313	...	...	...	...	...	...	1513	...	...	...	...	...	...	1713	...	...	...	...	1913	...	2011	2028	...	2055	...
Linz Hbf **950** d.	1434	1450	...	*1534*	1550	...	1614	1634	1640	1650	...	1714	1750	1814	1834	1850	...	1950	...	2034	2050	2134	2145	...	2230	...
Wels Hbf **950** d.	|	1509	...	*1551*	1609	...	1631	|	1655	1709	...	1731	1809	1831	1850	1909	...	2009	...	2050	2109	2151	2200	2209	2244	2249
Neumarkt-Kallham d.	|	1540t	1540	1620	1632	1640d	1652	|	1720	1736	1740	1758	1840t	1852	|	1936	1940a	2036	2040	|	2136	|	...	2237	...	2316
Ried im Innkreis d.	|	1601	|	1637	|	1701d	|	|	1737	|	1801	|	1901	|	|	|	2001a	|	2101	|	|	|	...	2257	...	|
Braunau am Inn a.	|	1641	|	1707	|	1741	|	|	1808	|	1841	|	1941	|	|	|	2041	|	2141	|	|	|	...	2331	...	|
Simbach (Inn) 🏛 **893** a.	|	1645	|	1711	|	1745	|	|	...	|	1845c	|	1945	|	|	|	2045	|	2145	|	|	|	...	...	...	|
Schärding d.	|	...	1611	...	1657	...	1717	|	...	1809	...	1831	...	1918	|	2009	...	2109	...	2125	2209	|	...	...	...	2348
Passau Hbf a.	1531	...	1624	...	1712	...	...	1731	...	1822	...	1844	...	1930	1934	2022	...	2122	...	2137	2222	2235	...	...	...	...
Nürnberg Hbf **920** a.	1729	...	...	...	...	...	...	1928	...	...	...	...	...	...	2128	...	...	...	...	2400	...	0057	...	...	...	...
Frankfurt (Main) Hbf **920** a.	...	...	...	...	...	...	...	2136v	...	...	...	...	...	...	2337v	...	...	...	...	...	...	...	...	...	...	...

km																										
									NJ 491							*IC* 95				*ICE* 21					*ICE* 23	
		⚒	Ⓐ		⚒	†		⚒		Ⓐ	Ⓐ										Ⓐ					Ⓐ
		2	2	2	2	2	2	2	⊡	2	2	2	2	2	2	E🍷	2	2	2	✕	2	2	2	2	D✕	2
	Frankfurt (Main) Hbf **920** d.	...	...	...	...	...	...	...	...	...	...	...	...	...	...	...	...	...	...	0621v	...	...	...	...	0822v	...
	Nürnberg Hbf **920** d.	...	...	...	...	...	...	...	0408	...	...	...	...	...	...	0600	...	...	...	0831	...	...	...	...	1031	...
	Passau Hbf d.	...	0411	0420c	...	...	0539	0604	0615	...	0625	...	0650	0740	...	0824	...	0840	...	1026	...	1048	...	1140	1229	...
	Schärding d.	0358	0423	0432	...	...	0552	0616	|	...	0637	...	0703	0752	...	|	...	0852	...	|	...	1102	...	1152	|	...
0	**Simbach** (Inn) 🏛 **893** d.	|	|	|	...	...	|	|	|	...	|	...	|	|	0718	|	...	|	0918	|	1018	|	1118	|	|	1218
2	**Braunau** am Inn d.	|	|	|	0514	0526	|	|	|	0610	|	0629	|	|	0723	|	0824	|	0924	|	1024	|	1124	|	|	1224
39	Ried im Innkreis d.	|	|	|	0552	0601	|	|	|	0643	|	0710	|	|	0801	|	0901	|	1001	|	1101	|	1201	|	|	1301
61	Neumarkt-Kallham d.	0429	0451	0504	0613	0619	0624	0642	|	0709r	0706	0728	0736	0820	0824	|	0919	0924	1024t	|	1119	1128	1219	1224	|	1319
90	**Wels** Hbf **950** d.	0456	0515	0531	0637	...	0652	0710	0716	0737	0730	...	0806	...	0853	0911	...	0953	1053	1112	...	1153	...	1253	|	...
115	**Linz** Hbf **950** a.	0519	0532	0554	0652	...	0708	0740	0746	...	0747	...	0824	...	0910	0925	...	1010	1110	1126	...	1210	...	1310	1326	...
	Wien Hbf **950** a.	...	...	...	...	...	...	...	0914	...	...	...	...	...	...	1047	...	...	...	1247	...	...	...	...	1447	...

					ICE 91				*ICE* 93		*ICE* 27					*ICE* 29			*RJ* 749 769		*ICE* 229			*RJ* 843		*RJX* 367
		Ⓐ				⚒						⚒										Ⓐ				
	2	2	2	2	H✕	2	2	2	B✕	2	D✕	2	2	2	2	D✕	2	2	✕	2	D✕	2	2	✕	2	✕
Frankfurt (Main) Hbf **920** d.	...	...	...	...	...	...	...	...	...	...	1222v	...	...	...	...	1422v	...	...	...	...	1621v	...	...	...	...	...
Nürnberg Hbf **920** d.	...	...	...	...	1231	...	...	...	1332	...	1431	...	...	...	...	1631	...	...	...	...	1831	...	...	...	...	...
Passau Hbf d.	1248	...	1336	...	1429	...	1448	...	1529	1540	1629	...	1648	1736	...	1829	...	1840	...	...	2031	...	2040	...	...	...
Schärding d.	1302	...	1349	...	|	...	1502	...	|	1552	|	...	1702	1749	...	|	...	1852	...	...	2043	...	2052	...	...	...
Simbach (Inn) 🏛 **893** d.	|	...	|	1318	|	1418	|	1518	|	|	|	1618	|	|	1718	|	1818	|	...	1918	|	*2018*	|	...	2118	...
Braunau am Inn d.	|	...	|	1324	|	1424	|	1524	|	|	|	1624	|	|	1724	|	1824	|	...	1924	|	2024	|	...	2124	...
Ried im Innkreis d.	|	1337	|	1401	|	1501	|	1601	|	|	|	1701	|	|	1801	|	1901	|	...	2001	|	2101	|	...	2201	...
Neumarkt-Kallham d.	1328	1357	1420	1424t	|	1519	1528	1619	|	1624	|	1719	1728	1820	1824t	|	1919	1924	...	2024t	|	2119	2124	...	2224	...
Wels Hbf **950** d.	1353	...	...	1453	|	...	1553	...	|	1653	|	...	1753	...	1853	|	...	1953	2016	2053	2119	...	2151	2216	2251	2304
Linz Hbf **950** a.	1410	...	...	1510	1526	...	1610	...	1626	1710	1726	...	1810	...	1910	1926	...	2010c	2030	2110	2134	...	...	2230	...	2318
Wien Hbf **950** a.	...	...	...	...	1647	...	...	...	1747	...	1847	...	...	...	...	2047	...	...	2205	...	2305	...	...	0005	...	0035

B – To / from Berlin and Hamburg (Table **850**).
D – To / from Dortmund (Table **800**).
E – From Leipzig (Table **849a**).
G – From Garsten (Table **976**).
H – To / from Hamburg (Table **900**).
W – From Warnemünde via Berlin (Tables **835** and **849a**).

a – Ⓐ only.
c – Ⓒ only.
d – ⚒ only.
j – Arrives 0603.
r – Arrives 0702.
t – Arrives 5 minutes earlier.

v – Subject to alteration from May 26.

⊡ – 🛏 1, 2 cl., 🛏 2 cl. and (2) Wien - Nürnberg - Hamburg and v.v.;
🛏 1, 2 cl., 🛏 2 cl. and (2) (**40490**/**40421**/**50490**/**50425**) Wien - Frankfurt - Köln - Amsterdam / Brussels and v.v. 🅁 for journeys to / from Germany.

963 SALZBURG and ST WOLFGANG - STROBL - BAD ISCHL

Routes 150, 546

km	Route 150	⚒	Ⓐ	Ⓒ		Ⓐ																	⚒	
0	**Salzburg** Hbf △ .... d.	0526	0556	0615	...	0615	0645	0715	0745	and every	1615	1645	1715	1745	...	1815	1845	1915	1945	2015	...	2115	2215	2315
32	St Gilgen (Busbahnhof) d.	0610	0645	0659	...	0704	0738	0808	0838	30 minutes	1708	1738	1808	1834	...	1904	1934	2004	2029	2059	...	2159	2259	2359
45	Strobl (Busbahnhof) ..... d.	0624	0702	0713	...	0721	0756	0826	0856	until	1726	1756	1826	1851	...	1921	1951	2021	2043	2113	...	2213	2313	0013
57	**Bad Ischl** Bahnhof ...... a.	0640	0719	0729	...	0738	0815	0845	0915		1745	1815	1845	1908	...	1938	2008	2038	2059	2129	...	2229	2329	0029

Route 150	⚒	Ⓐ	⑥	Ⓐ	Ⓐ	Ⓒ	Ⓐ	⑥	Ⓑ	⚒	Ⓑ											Ⓒ		⑥
Bad Ischl Bahnhof ...... d.	0457	0525	0541	0541	0557	0624	0646	0654	0724	0754	0824	0854	0924	and every	1724	1754	1824	1854	1924	1954	2024	2054	2124	2224
Strobl (Busbahnhof) ..... d.	0513	0542	0557	0600	0616	0640	0705	0715	0745	0815	0845	0915	0945	30 minutes	1745	1811	1841	1911	1941	2010	2040	2110	2140	2240
St Gilgen (Busbahnhof) d.	0528	0558	0612	0615	0631	0655	0721	0734	0804	0834	0904	0934	1004	until	1804	1827	1857	1927	1957	2025	2055	2125	2155	2255
Salzburg Hbf △ .... a.	0613	0645	0656	0700	0716j	0739	0812	0826	0856	0926	0956	1026	1056		1856	1914	1944	2014	2044	2109	2139	2209	2239	2339

km	Route 546	Ⓐ	⚒	⚒	Ⓒ	Ⓐ	Ⓐ	Ⓐ			Ⓐ	Ⓒ		Ⓒ	Ⓐ			Ⓐ			Ⓐ		Ⓒ		
0	**St Wolfgang** ⊡ ‡....... d.	0500	0600	0649	0732	0740	0813	0900	0913	1013	1100	1113	1213	1313	1323	1413	1513	1513	1613	1713	1713	1813	1828	1908	1956
7	Strobl (Busbahnhof) .... d.	0512	0613	0702	0745	|	0824	|	0924	1026	|	1124	1226	1324	1336	1426	1526	1526	1626	1724	1726	1826	1839	1919	2007
19	**Bad Ischl** Bahnhof ...... a.	0531	0639	0728	0811	0811	...	0931	...	1047	1131	...	1247	...	1402	1447	...	1552	1647	...	1752	1847	...	...	...

Route 546	Ⓐ	⚒	Ⓐ				Ⓒ	Ⓐ		Ⓑ	⚒	Ⓒ	Ⓐ	Ⓒ	Ⓐ				Ⓐ		Ⓒ	Ⓐ			
Bad Ischl Bahnhof ...... d.	0606	0642	...	0823	0913	...	...	1023	1113	...	1223	1323	1336	...	1423	...	1513	...	1623	1713	...	1823	...	1913	...
Strobl (Busbahnhof) ..... d.	0630	0706	0825	0845	0935	...	1045	1045	1135	1245	1245	1345	1358	1445	1445	...	1535	1645	1645	1735	1845	1845	1925	|	2045
St Wolfgang ⊡ ‡........ a.	0642	0718	0837	0857	0947	...	1057	1057	1147	1257	1257	1357	1410	1457	1457	...	1547	1657	1657	1747	1857	1857	1937	1940	2057

j – 0723 on school days.

△ – All services also call at Mirabellplatz.

⊡ – St Wolfgang Schafbergbahnhof. All services also call at St Wolfgang Markt.

‡ – **Schafbergbahn** narrow-gauge steam rack railway operates St Wolfgang - Schafbergspitze (*6 km*). Services operate subject to demand and weather conditions **April 29 - Oct. 8**, 2023. 2nd class only. Special fares payable. Journey time: 35 minutes each way. ✆ +43 (0) 6138 2232 0.

964 STROBL - ST GILGEN (WOLFGANGSEE)

Planned service April 29 - June 16, 2023 (on May 1, 18, 19, 29, June 8, 9 services run as on Ⓒ). A limited service is also planned Apr. 1, 2, 6 – 10, 15, 16, 22 – 28 (please check locally).

	Ⓒ	Ⓒ	Ⓐ	Ⓒ		Ⓒ	Ⓐ	Ⓒ		Ⓒ	Ⓐ	Ⓒ		Ⓒ	Ⓐ	Ⓒ		
Strobl Schiffstation ⊡ .... d.	...	0845	...	0925	1025	1125	1155	1225	1325	1425	1455	1525	1625	1725	1750	1820	...	...
St Wolfgang Markt .... d.	...	|	...	|	|	1200	1230	1300	1400	1500	1530	1600	1700	1752s	1815s	1832s	...	...
St Wolfgang Schafbergbahnhof ‡ .. d.	0830	0910	0925	0955	1055	1208	1238	1308	1408	1508	1538	1608	1708	1800	1823	1840	...	...
St Wolfgang Markt .... d.	|	0918	0932	1005	1105	|	|	|	|	|	|	|	|	...	...	...	...	...
St Gilgen Schiffstation ● .... a.	0855	0955	1005	1045	1145	1245	1315	1345	1445	1545	1615	1645	1745	...	...	...	...	...

	Ⓒ	Ⓒ	Ⓒ	Ⓐ	Ⓒ	Ⓐ	Ⓒ	Ⓐ	Ⓒ	Ⓒ	Ⓐ	Ⓒ	Ⓐ	Ⓒ	Ⓒ	Ⓐ	Ⓒ	
St Gilgen Schiffstation ● .... d.	...	...	0900	0920	1000	1020	1100	1200	1200	1300	1330	1400	1500	1500	1600	1630	1700	1800
St Wolfgang Markt .... d.	...	...	|	|	|	|	|	|	|	|	|	|	|	|	|	|	|	|
St Wolfgang Schafbergbahnhof ‡ .... d.	0825	0855	0937	0952	1037	1100	1137	1235	1237	1337	1405	1437	1535	1537	1637	1705	1737	1837s
St Wolfgang Markt .... d.	|	0905	0950	1000	1050	1115	1150	1245	1250	1350	1415	1450	1545	1550	1650	1715	1750	1845
Strobl Schiffstation ⊡ .... a.	0840	0920	1015	1015	1115	1140	1215	1310	1315	1415	1440	1515	1610	1615	1715	1740	1815	...

s – Set down only.

‡ – See note under Table **963**.

⊡ – Approximately 400 metres from Strobl Busbahnhof.

● – Approximately 500 metres from St Gilgen Busbahnhof.

969 TAUERN TUNNEL CAR - CARRYING TRAINS

BÖCKSTEIN - MALLNITZ-OBERVELLACH *11 km.* Transit time: 11 minutes. Passengers without cars are also conveyed. ✆ 05-1717. E-mail: autoschleuse.tauernbahn@pv.oebb.at

From Böckstein at 0620, 0720 and hourly until 2320. **From Mallnitz-Obervellach** at 0550, 0650 and hourly until 2250.

970 SALZBURG - VILLACH - KLAGENFURT

km		*NJ* 40237 R ♦	*NJ* 237 R ♦	*NJ* 40466 R ♦	⚒ 2	*NJ* 40237 R ♦	*EN* 40465 R ♦	2	Ⓐ 2	Ⓐ 2	2	*IC* 894 ✕	*IC* 898 🍷	*RJ* 111 ✕	*RJ* 596 ✕	*EC* 113 ✕♦	*EC* 115 ✕♦	Ⓐ 2	2	*RJ* 698 ✕	*EC* 117 ✕♦	*IC* 794 🍷	*NJ* 295 R ♦
	Wien Hbf **950** .... d.	...	...	2127	...	...	...	...	...	...	...	...	...	...	0855	...	...	...	...	1455	...	...	...
	München Hbf **890** .... d.	2354t	2354t	|	...	...	...	...	...	...	...	...	...	0816	|	1217	1416	...	...	|	1817	...	2009
0	**Salzburg** Hbf .... **960 975** d.	0210	0230	0230	...	...	...	...	...	...	...	0612	0812	1012	1212	1412	1612	...	...	1812	2012	2112	2202
29	Golling-Abtenau .... **960** d.	|	|	|	...	...	...	...	...	...	...	0633	0833	1033	1233	1433	1633	...	...	1833	2033	2138	|
53	**Bischofshofen** .... **960 975** d.	|	0311	0311	...	...	...	...	...	...	...	0654	0854	1054	1254	1454	1654	...	...	1854	2054	2200	|
61	St Johann im Pongau .... **960** d.	|	|	|	...	←	...	...	...	...	...	0703	0903	1103	1303	1503	1703	...	...	1903	2103	2209	|
67	**Schwarzach - St Veit** .... **960** d.	0300	|	|	...	0425	0425	...	...	...	...	0711	0911	1111	1311	1511	1711	...	...	1911	2111	2216	2254
86	Bad Hofgastein .... d.	→	|	|	...	0444	0444	...	...	...	...	0729	0929	1129	1329	1529	1729	...	...	1929	2129	2233	|
97	Bad Gastein .... d.	...	|	|	...	0458	0458	...	...	...	...	0742	0942	1142	1342	1542	1742	...	...	1942	2142	2245	|
113	Mallnitz-Obervellach .... d.	...	|	|	...	0515	0515	...	...	0650	...	0756	0956	1156	1356	1556	1756	1800	...	1956	2156	2259	|
146	Spittal-Millstättersee .... **971** d.	...	|	|	...	0540	0540	...	0630	0717	0729	0820	1020	1220	1420	1620	1820	1827	1832	2020	2220	2322	|
182	**Villach** Hbf .... **971** a.	...	0442	0442	...	0604	0604	...	0656	...	0753	0843	1043	1243	1443	1643	1843	...	1904	2043	2243	2344	0019
182	**Villach** Hbf .... **971** d.	...	...	...	0450	...	...	0620	0659	...	0756	0847	1047	1247	1447	1648	1847	...	1920	2047	2247	2347	...
198	Velden am Wörthersee .... **971** d.	...	...	...	0505	...	...	0634	0711	...	0806	0858	1058	1258	1458	1659	1858	...	1934	2058	2258	2358	...
207	Pörtschach am Wörthersee ...... **971** d.	...	...	...	0513	...	...	0642	|	...	|	0904	1104	1304	1504	1705	1904	...	1942	2104	2304	0004	...
220	**Klagenfurt** Hbf .... **971** a.	...	...	...	0529	...	...	0656	0727	...	0822	0913	1113	1316	1513	1717	1916	...	1956	2116	2316	0013	...

	2	*EN* 40414 R ♦	*EN* 414 R ♦	*NJ* 236 R ♦	*NJ* 40236 R ♦	*NJ* 294 R ♦	*IC* 597 🍷	Ⓐ 2		*RJ* 691 ✕	Ⓐ 2	*EC* 114 ✕♦		*EC* 112 ✕♦	*IC* 793 🍷		*RJ* 797 ✕	Ⓐ 2	Ⓐ 2	*RJ* 110 ✕		*IC* 895 ✕	*D* 899 2
Klagenfurt Hbf .... **971** d.	2232	...	...	...	...	...	0442	...	...	0645	0744	0842	...	1027	1245	...	1445	1532	...	1642	...	1845	2045
Pörtschach am Wörthersee ...... **971** d.	2247	...	...	...	...	...	0455	...	...	0655	0757	0855	...	1040	1255	...	1455	1547	...	1655	...	1855	2055
Velden am Wörthersee .... **971** d.	2254	...	...	...	...	...	0502	...	...	0702	0804	0902	...	1047	1302	...	1502	1554	...	1702	...	1902	2102
Villach Hbf .... **971** a.	2309	...	...	...	...	...	0513	...	...	0713	0820	0913	...	1058	1313	...	1513	1609	...	1713	...	1913	2113
Villach Hbf .... **971** d.	...	0013	0013	0045	0045	0429	0516	0529	...	0716	...	0916	...	1116	1316	...	1516	1610	...	1716	...	1916	2116
Spittal-Millstättersee .... **971** d.	...	0037	0037	|	|	|	0540	0605	...	0740	...	0940	...	1140	1340	...	1540	1634	1644	1740	...	1940	2140
Mallnitz-Obervellach .... d.	...	0102	0102	|	|	|	0604	0633	...	0804	...	1004	...	1204	1404	...	1604	...	1712	1804	...	2004	2204
Bad Gastein .... d.	...	0116	0116	|	|	|	0617	...	...	0817	...	1017	...	1217	1417	...	1617	...	...	1817	...	2017	2217
Bad Hofgastein .... d.	...	0129	0129	|	|	|	0630	...	...	0830	...	1030	...	1230	1430	...	1630	...	...	1830	...	2030	2230
Schwarzach - St Veit .... **960** d.	...	0157	0157	|	|	0549	0652	...	...	0852	...	1052	...	1252	1452	...	1652	...	...	1852	...	2052	2252
St Johann im Pongau .... **960** a.	...	...	|	|	|	|	0657	...	...	0857	...	1057	...	1257	1457	...	1657	...	...	1857	...	2057	2257
Bischofshofen .... **960 975** a.	...	...	|	0220	0220	|	0705	...	...	0905	...	1105	...	1305	1505	...	1705	...	...	1905	...	2105	2305
Golling-Abtenau .... **960** a.	...	...	|	|	|	|	|	...	...	0927	...	1127	...	1327	1527	...	1727	...	...	1927	...	2127	2327
Salzburg Hbf .... **960 975** a.	...	...	0245	0300	0404	0649	0748	...	...	0948	...	1148	...	1348	1548	...	1748	...	...	1948	...	2148	2348
München Hbf **890** .... a.	...	...	0550t	0550t	|	0922	...	...	...	|	...	1341	...	1541	...	...	|	...	...	2141	...	...	...
Wien Hbf **950** .... a.	...	...	...	...	0758	...	...	...	...	1305	...	...	...	...	...	...	2105	...	...	...	...	...	...

♦ – **NOTES** (LISTED BY TRAIN NUMBER)

112 – BLAUER ENZIAN – [12] and ✕ Klagenfurt - München - Stuttgart - Frankfurt; also conveys [12] Zagreb (**212**) - Ljubljana - Villach (**112**) - Frankfurt.

113 – BLAUER ENZIAN – [12] and ✕ Frankfurt - Stuttgart - München - Klagenfurt; also conveys [12] Frankfurt - Villach (**213**) - Ljubljana - Zagreb.

114 – WÖRTHERSEE – [12] and ✕ Klagenfurt - München - Stuttgart - Köln - Dortmund.

115 – WÖRTHERSEE – [12] and ✕ Münster - Köln - Stuttgart - München - Klagenfurt.

117 – SALZACH – [12] and ✕ Frankfurt - Stuttgart - München - Salzburg - Klagenfurt.

236/7 – 🛏 1, 2 cl., ▬ 2 cl. and [2] Venezia - Tarvisio 🏛 - Villach - Salzburg - München - Stuttgart and v.v.

294/5 – 🛏 1, 2 cl., ▬ 2 cl. and [2] Roma - Firenze - Bologna - München and v.v.; 🛏 1, 2 cl., ▬ 2 cl. and [2] (**40235/40295**) La Spezia - Milano - Verona - München and v.v.

414 – LISINSKI 🛏 1, 2 cl., ▬ 2 cl. and [2] Zagreb - Ljubljana - Villach - Schwarzach - Salzburg - München - Stuttgart; conveys on dates in Table **62** 🛏 1, 2 cl. and ▬ 2 cl. (**480**) Rijeka - Ljubljana - München - Stuttgart.

40236 – 🛏 1, 2 cl., ▬ 2 cl. and [2] Venezia - Tarvisio 🏛 - Villach - Salzburg - Wien.

40237 – LISINSKI 🛏 1, 2 cl., ▬ 2 cl. and [2] Stuttgart - München - Villach - Jesenice 🏛 - Ljubljana - Zagreb; conveys on dates in Table **62** 🛏 1, 2 cl. and ▬ 2 cl. (**60237**) Stuttgart - München - Ljubljana - Rijeka.

40414 – 🛏 1, 2 cl., ▬ 2 cl. and [2] Zagreb - Ljubljana - Villach - Schwarzach - Innsbruck - Feldkirch - Zürich.

40465 – 🛏 1, 2 cl., ▬ 2 cl. and [2] Zürich - Feldkirch - Innsbruck - Schwarzach - Villach - Ljubljana - Zagreb.

40466 – 🛏 1, 2 cl., ▬ 2 cl. and [2] Wien - Salzburg - Villach - Tarvisio 🏛 - Venezia.

R – 🄡 for international journeys.

t – München **Ost**.

v – Arrives 1646.

LIENZ - VILLACH - KLAGENFURT - FRIESACH (- WIEN) 971

km		NJ 235		RJ 530			IC 730			RJ 532				IC 894	RJ 534			IC 898	RJ 536			RJ 111	RJ 132		D 738
		★	⚒																						⑦w
		2	2	✕	U 2	2	🍷	2	2	✕	2	2	2	◐✕	✕	2	2	◐🍷	✕	2	2	◐✕	V✕	2	2
0	**Lienz** d.	...	...	...	...	...	...	...	0524	...	...	0629	...	...	0753a	0719	*0824*	...	...	0924	1024	...	...	1124	1253
68	Spittal-Millstättersee a.	...	...	...	...	...	...	...	0627	...	...	0726	...	...	0842a	0822	*0922*	...	...	1022	1122	...	...	1222	1343
68	Spittal-Millstättersee 970 d.	...	...	...	0448r	0530a	...	...	0630	...	0635a	0729	0732	0820	0846a	0832	0932	1020	...	1032	1132	1220	...	1232	1346
104	**Villach** Hbf 970 a.	...	...	...	0520r	0558a	...	...	0656	...	0708a	0753	0804	0843	0909a	0904p	1004	1043	...	1104p	1204	1243	...	1304p	1409
104	**Villach** Hbf 970 d.	0417	0450	0525	0529	0604	0613	0620	0659a	0714	0720	0756	0820	0847	0914	0920	1020	1047	1114	1120	1220	1247	1314	1320	1413
120	Velden am Wörthersee 970 d.	|	0505	|	0543	|	0624	0634	0711a	0725	0734	0806	0834	0858	|	0934	1034	1058	1125	1134	1234	1258	|	1334	1424
129	Pörtschach am W ⊡ 970 d.	|	0513	|	0551	|	0630	0642	|	|	0742	|	0842	0904	0929	0942	1042	1104	|	1142	1242	1304	1329	1342	1430
135	Krumpendorf d.	|	0520	|	0557	|	|	0648	|	|	0748	|	0848	|	|	0948	1048	|	|	1148	1248	1310	|	1348	|
142	**Klagenfurt** Hbf 970 a.	0438	0529	0546	0605	0625	0638	0656	0727a	0737	0756	0822	0856	0913	0937	0956	1056	1113	1137	1156	1256	1316	1337	1356	1438
142	**Klagenfurt** Hbf 980 d.	0440	...	0548	0607	0626	0639	0704	...	0739	0804	0824	0904	...	0939	1004	1104	...	1139	1204	1304	...	1339	1404	1439
162	St Veit an der Glan 980 d.	|	...	0601	0627	0639	0652	0724	...	0753	0824	0838	0924	...	0953	1024	1124	...	1153	1224	1324	...	1353	1424	1452
195	**Friesach** 980 a.	|	...	|	0658	0703	0716	0756	...	|	0856	...	0956	...	1015	1056	1156	...	|	1256	1356	...	1415	1456	1516
	Wien Hbf 980 a.	0852	...	0942	...	...	1042	...	...	1142	...	...	...	...	1342	...	...	...	1542	...	...	...	1742	...	1842

		RJ 596	RJ 630			IC 830		EC 113		IC 632				D 832		EC 115	RJ 130			RJ 698			EC 117	IC 794	
												Ⓐ		⑦w							◇				
	2	◐✕	✕	2	2	🍷	2	◐✕	2	✕	2	2	2	2	2	◐🍷	V✕	2	2	◐✕	2	2	◐✕	◐	2
Lienz d.	1224	...	...	1324	1424	...	...	...	1524	1553	...	...	1624	...	...	...	...	1724	1824	...	1924	2024	...	...	...
Spittal-Millstättersee a.	1322	...	...	1422	1522	...	...	...	1622	1642	...	...	1722	...	...	...	...	1822	1922	...	2022	2122	...	...	...
Spittal-Millstättersee 970 d.	1332	1420	...	1432	1532	...	...	1620	1632	1646	...	...	1732	...	...	1820	...	1832	1932	2020	2032	2132	2220	2322	...
Villach Hbf 970 a.	1404p	1443	...	1504p	1604	...	←	1643	1704	1709	←	...	1804	...	←	1843	...	1904p	2004	2043	2104	2204	2243	2344	...
Villach Hbf 970 d.	1420	1447	1514	1520	1620	1613	1620	1648	1720	1714	1720	1750	1820	1813	1820	1847	1914	1920	2020	2047	2120	2220	2247	2347	2350
Velden am Wörthersee 970 d.	1434	1458	1525	1534	→	1624	1634	1659	→	|	1734	1804	→	1824	1834	1858	1925	1934	2034	2058	2134	2234	2258	2358	0004
Pörtschach am W ⊡ 970 d.	1442	1504	|	1542	...	1630	1642	1705	...	1729	1742	1812	...	1830	1842	1904	|	1942	2042	2104	2142	2242	2304	0004	0012
Krumpendorf d.	1448	|	|	1548	...	|	1648	1711	...	|	1748	1818	...	|	1848	1910	|	1948	2048	2110	2148	2248	2310	|	0018
Klagenfurt Hbf 970 a.	1456	1513	1537	1556	...	1638	1656	1717	...	1737	1756	1826	...	1838	1856	1916	1937	1956	2056	2116	2156	2256	2316	0013	0026
Klagenfurt Hbf 980 d.	1504	...	1539	1604	...	1639	1704	...	...	1739	1804	1828	...	1839	1904	...	1939	2004	2104	...	2204	2304	...	...	0028
St Veit an der Glan 980 d.	1524	...	1553	1624	...	1652	1724	...	...	1753	1824	1847	...	1852	1924	...	1953	2024	2124	...	2224	2324	...	...	0047
Friesach 980 a.	1556	...	|	1656	...	1716	1756	...	...	1815	1856	...	...	1916	1956	...	|	2056	2156	...	2256	2356	...	...	...
Wien Hbf 980 a.	...	...	1942	...	...	2042	...	...	...	2142	...	...	...	2242	...	...	2342	...	...	...	...	...	...	...	...

	IC 597				RJ 691				RJ 639	EC 114			RJ 131	EC 112			IC 533		IC 793		IC 735		RJ 535	RJ 797	
		⚒		⚒			⚒⊕	◇																	
	◐	2	2	2	◐✕	2	U 2	2	G✕	◐✕	2	2	V✕	◐✕	2	2	✕	2	◐🍷	2	🍷	2	✕	◐✕	2
Wien Hbf 980 d.	...	...	...	...	...	...	...	...	...	...	...	...	0618	...	...	...	0818	...	...	...	0918	...	1018	...	...
Friesach 980 d.	...	...	0508	0546	...	0608	0643	0708	0741	...	0808	0908	|	...	1008	1108	1144	...	...	1208	1242	1308	|	...	1408
St Veit an der Glan 980 d.	...	0512	0542	0617	...	0642	0718	0742	0808	...	0842	0942	1008	...	1042	1142	1208	...	...	1242	1308	1342	1408	...	1442
Klagenfurt Hbf 980 a.	...	0530	0600	0631	...	0700	0738	0800	0820	...	0900	1000	1020	...	1100	1200	1220	...	...	1300	1319	1400	1420	...	1500
Klagenfurt Hbf 970 d.	0442	0532	0602	0633	0645	0702	0744	0802	0822	0842	0902	1002	1022	1027	1102	1202	1222	...	1245	1302	1321	1402	1422	1445	1502
Krumpendorf d.	0448	0540	0610	0642	|	0710	0752	0810	|	0848	0910	1010	|	1033	1110	1210	|	...	|	1310	|	1410	|	|	1510
Pörtschach am W ⊡ 970 d.	0455	0547	0617	0647	0655	0717	0757	0817	0832	0855	0917	1017	|	1040	1117	1217	1232	...	1255	1317	1331	1417	|	1455	1517
Velden am Wörthersee 970 d.	0502	0554	0624	0654	0702	0724	0804	0824	|	0902	0924	1024	1036	1047	1124	1224	|	...	1302	1324	1338	1424	1436	1502	1524
Villach Hbf 970 a.	0513	0609	0639	0710	0713	0739	0820	0839	0846p	0913	0939	1039	1046p	1058	1139	1239	1246	←	1313	1339	1348p	1439	1446p	1513	1539
Villach Hbf 970 d.	0516	0619a	0654	...	0716	0754	...	0854	...	0916	0954	1054	...	1116	1154	1254	1250	1254	1316	1354	...	1454	...	1516	1554
Spittal-Millstättersee 970 a.	0538	0652a	0726	...	0738	0826	...	0926	...	0938	1026	1126	...	1138	1226	→	1314	1326	1338	1426	...	1526	...	1538	1626
Spittal-Millstättersee d.	...	...	0737	...	...	0837	...	0937	...	...	1037	1137	...	...	1237	...	1316	1337	...	1437	...	1537	...	...	*1637*
Lienz a.	...	...	0837	...	...	0937	...	1037	...	...	1137	1237	...	...	1337	...	1406	1437	...	1537	...	1637	...	...	*1647*

			RJ 133		RJ 110		D 739				RJ 539		IC 895		IC 831			RJ 631	D 899			RJ 633		NJ 233	
	Ⓐ			Ⓐ			⑤y		Ⓐ								⊖							★	
	2	2	V✕	2	◐✕	2	2	2	2	2	✕	2	◐✕	2	🍷	2	2	✕	◐2	2	2	✕	2	2	2
Wien Hbf 980 d.	...	...	1218	...	...	...	1318	...	...	...	1418	...	...	...	1518	...	...	1618	...	...	...	1818	...	1918	...
Friesach 980 d.	...	1508	1544	...	...	1608	1642	...	...	1708	|	...	...	1808	1842	...	1908	1944	...	2008	2108	|	...	|	...
St Veit an der Glan 980 d.	1512	1542	1608	1612	...	1642	1708	...	1712	1742	1808	...	...	1842	1908	...	1942	2008	...	2042	2142	2208	...	2322	...
Klagenfurt Hbf 980 a.	1530	1600	1620	1630	...	1700	1719	...	1730	1800	1820	...	...	1900	1919	...	2000	2020	...	2100	2200	2220	←	2334	...
Klagenfurt Hbf 970 d.	1532	1602	1622	1632	1642	1702	1721	...	1732	1802	1822	...	1845	1902	1921	...	2002	2022	2045	2102	2232	2222	2232	2336	2340
Krumpendorf d.	1540	1610	|	1640	1648	1710	|	...	1740	1810	|	...	|	1910	|	...	2010	|	|	2110	→	|	2240	|	2349
Pörtschach am W ⊡ 970 d.	1547	1617	1632	1647	1655	1717	1731	...	1747	1817	|	...	1855	1917	1931	...	2017	2032	2055	2117	...	|	2247	|	2356
Velden am Wörthersee 970 d.	1554	1624	|	1654	1702	1724	1738	...	1754	1824	1836	...	1902	1924	1938	...	2024	|	2102	2124	...	2236	2254	|	0003
Villach Hbf 970 a.	1609	1639	1646p	1709	1713	1739	1748	←	1809	1839	1846	←	1913	1939	1948	←	2039	2046p	2113	2139	...	2246	2309	0000	0019
Villach Hbf 970 d.	1610	1654	...	1710	1716	1754	1750	1754	1810	1854	1850z	1854	1916	1954	...	1954	2054	2050v	2116	2154	...	*2254*	...	*0013*	...
Spittal-Millstättersee 970 a.	1634	1726	...	1734	1738	→	1814	1826	1834	→	1914z	1926	1938	→	...	2026	2126	2114v	2138	2226	...	*2326*	...	*0035*	...
Spittal-Millstättersee d.	1637	1737	...	...	...	...	1816	1837	...	...	1916z	1937	...	...	...	*2037*	2143	2116v	...	...	...	...	...	...	...
Lienz a.	1737	1837	...	...	...	...	1906	1937	...	...	2006z	2037	...	...	...	*2136*	2241	2206v	...	...	...	...	...	...	...

G – From Graz (Table **980**).
U – To / from Unzmarkt (Table **980**).
V – From / to Venezia (Table **88**).

a – Ⓐ only.
p – Connects with train in previous column.

r – ⚒ only.
v – ⑤ (also Jan. 5, May 17, June 7, Oct. 25, Dec. 7).
w – ⑦ (also Dec. 26, Apr. 10, May 1, 29, June 6, Aug. 15; not Dec. 25, Apr. 9, 30, May 28, June 5, Aug. 13).
y – ⑤ (also Jan. 5, May 17, June 7, Oct. 25, Dec. 7; not Jan. 6, May 19, June 9, Oct. 27, Dec 8).
z – ①②③④⑦ only.

⊕ – Change trains at Klagenfurt on Ⓐ.
◇ – Change trains at Spittal-Millstättersee on Ⓐ.
⊖ – Change trains at Spittal-Millstättersee on Ⓑ.
★ – See Table **980** for through cars to / from Roma and Milano.
◐ – See Table **970** for further details.
⊡ – Pörtschach am Wörthersee.

LINZ - SELZTHAL 974

2nd class only (except *IC* trains)

km					IC 501			IC 503				IC 507									IC 603						
		⚒	Ⓐ		⚒🍷f			🍷				🍷		Ⓐ	Ⓐ			Ⓐ			🍷						
0	**Linz** Hbf d.	0457	0506	0536	0557	0657	0736	0757	0857	1057	1136	1157	1257	1357	1406	1457	1536	1557	1657	1736	1757	1857	1936	2057	2136	2236	2336
28	Rohr - Bad Hall d.	0519	0540	0610	0619	0719	0810	0819	0919	1119	1209	1219	1319	1419	1440	1519	1609	1619	1719	1810	1819	1919	2010	2119	2210	2310	0010
32	Kremsmünster d.	0524	0546	0616	0624	0724	0816	0824	0924	1124	1215	1224	1324	1424	1446	1524	1615	1624	1724	1815	1824	1924	2016	2124	2215	2315	0015
51	Kirchdorf a. d. Krems d.	0537	0603	0633	0639	0737	0833	0839	0939	1139	1233	1239	1339	1437	1503	1539	1633	1637	1739	1833	1839	1939	2033	2139	2233	2334	0033
68	Hinterstoder d.	0601	...	...	0700	0801	...	0900	1001	1201	...	1300	1401	1501	...	1601	...	1659	1801	...	1900	2001	...	2201	...	2355	...
82	Windischgarsten d.	0615	...	...	0713	0815	...	0913	1015	1215	...	1313	1415	1515	...	1615	...	1713	1815	...	1913	2015	...	2215	...	0010	...
87	Spital am Pyhrn d.	0621	...	...	|	0821	...	|	1021	1221	...	|	1421	1520	...	1621	...	1719	1821	...	|	2021	...	2221	...	0016	...
104	**Selzthal** a.	0639	...	...	0733	0840	...	0933	1040	1240	...	1335	1440	...	...	1640	...	1734	1840	...	1933	2040	...	2240	...	0032	...
	Liezen 975 a.	0700	...	...	|	0851a	...	|	...	1251a	...	|	1451a	...	...	1648a	...	...	...	...	|	...	...	...	...	...	...
	Graz Hbf 975 a.	...	...	...	0903	...	...	1103	...	...	...	1503	...	...	...	...	...	...	...	...	2103	...	...	...	...	...	...

											IC 500						IC 506						IC 600		IC 602		
		Ⓐ		⚒	⚒	Ⓐ	Ⓐ	Ⓒ			🍷						🍷		Ⓐ				🍷		Ⓑ🍷		
Graz Hbf 975 d.	...	...	...	...	...	...	...	...	...	...	0656	...	...	...	...	...	1256	...	...	...	...	...	1656	...	1856	...	...
Liezen 975 d.	...	...	...	...	...	...	...	...	0706r	...	|	...	0906a	...	...	1306a	|	1506a	...	...	1706a	...	|	...	|	...	...
Selzthal d.	...	0420	...	...	0520	...	0615	0615	0720	...	0826	...	0920	1120	...	1320	1426	1520	...	...	1720	...	1826	1920	2026	...	2120
Spital am Pyhrn d.	...	0438	...	...	0538	...	0638	0638	0738	...	|	...	0938	1138	...	1338	|	1538	...	1637	1738	...	|	1938	|	...	2138
Windischgarsten d.	...	0444	...	...	0544	...	0644	0644	0744	...	0846	...	0944	1144	...	1344	1446	1544	...	1643	1744	...	1846	1944	2046	...	2144
Hinterstoder d.	...	0500	...	...	0600	...	0700	0700	0800	...	0900	...	1000	1200	...	1400	1500	1600	...	1700	1800	...	1900	2000	2100	...	2200
Kirchdorf a. d. Krems d.	0425	0521	0525	0555	0621	0648	0721	0725	0821	0825	0918	0925	1021	1221	1325	1421	1518	1621	1650	1725	1821	1825	1918	2021	2118	2125	2221
Kremsmünster d.	0445	0535	0545	0615	0635	0703	0735	0745	0835	0845	0935	0945	1035	1235	1345	1435	1535	1635	1715	1745	1835	1845	1935	2035	2135	2145	2235
Rohr - Bad Hall d.	0449	0540	0549	0619	0640	0709	0740	0749	0840	0849	0940	0949	1040	1240	1349	1440	1540	1640	1719	1749	1840	1849	1940	2040	2140	2149	2240
Linz Hbf a.	0524	0604	0624	0654	0704	0738	0804	0824	0904	0924	1004	1024	1104	1304	1424	1504	1604	1704	1754	1824	1904	1924	2004	2104	2204	2224	2304

a – Ⓐ only.
f – Not Dec. 26, Apr. 10, May 29.
r – ⚒ only.

☛ Additional trains run Linz - Kirchdorf and v.v.:
From **Linz** at 0636, 0836 Ⓑ, 0936, 1036, 1236, 1336, 1436, 1636, 1836, 2036.
From **Kirchdorf** at 0455 Ⓐ, 0625, 1025, 1125, 1225, 1425, 1525, 1625, 1925, 2025.

975 SALZBURG - BISCHOFSHOFEN - SELZTHAL - GRAZ

km			NJ 465		D 619	IC 501				IC 719	IC 503				IC 513	RJ 111	IC 515		IC 507		EC 217		EC 113	EC 163		
		⚒ 2	A 🍷	⚒ 2	2 🍷	⚒g	⚒ 2L	Ⓐ 2	2	✕	🍷	Ⓐ 2L	2	⚒ 2	🍷		🍷	Ⓐ 2L	🍷	2	G✕	Ⓐ 2L		Z✕	Ⓐ 2L	2
0	**Salzburg** Hbf 960 970 d.	...	...	...	...	...	...	...	...	0616	...	...	...	*0621*	0816	1012	...	...	...	...	1216	...	1412	...	...	...
	Innsbruck Hbf 960 d.	...	0056	...	...	...	...	...	...	|	...	...	...	|	|	|	0821	...	...	...	|	...	|	1221	...	...
	Schwarzach ⊖ 960 970 d.	...	0324	...	0446	...	...	...	...	|	...	...	...	|	|	|	1056	...	...	...	|	...	|	1456	...	...
53	**Bischofshofen** 960 970 a.	...	0336	...	0500	...	...	...	...	0702	...	...	...	*0722*	0902	1052	1110	...	...	...	1302	...	1452	1510	...	...
53	**Bischofshofen** d.	...	0338	...	0502	...	...	...	...	0712	...	...	...	0741	0912	▬	1112	...	...	...	1312	...	▬	1512	...	...
77	Radstadt d.	...	|	...	0527	...	...	...	0603	0735	...	...	0809	0809	0935	2	1135	...	...	...	1335	...	2	1535	...	...
94	Schladming d.	...	0416	0459	0544	...	...	...	0626	0752	...	...	0831	0831	0952	1031	1152	...	...	1231	1352	...	1431	1552	...	1631
133	**Stainach-Irdning** d.	0415	0446	0540	0619	...	...	...	0708	0822	...	...	0912	0912	1022	1112	1222	...	...	1312	1422	...	1512	1622	...	1712
145	Liezen d.	0427	0457	0552	0629	...	0706	...	0726	0832	...	0906	0926	0926	1032	1126	1232	1306	...	1326	1432	1506	1526	1632	1706	1726
	Linz Hbf 974 d.	|	|	|	|	0557	|	...	|	|	0757	|	|	|	|	|	|	|	1157	|	|	|	|	|	|	|
152	**Selzthal** a.	0433	0504	0558	0636	0733	0712	...	0732	0839	0933	0912	0932	0932	1039	1132	1239	1312	1333	1332	1439	1512	1532	1639	1712	1732
152	**Selzthal** d.	0440	0513	0606	0644	0735	...	0716	0739	0848	0935	...	0939	0939	1048	1139	1248	...	1335	1339	1446	...	1539	1648	...	1739
158	Stadt Rottenmann d.	0447	|	0613	0652	0742	...	0722	0745	|	0942	...	0945	0945	|	1145	|	...	1342	1345	|	...	1545	|	...	1745
169	Trieben d.	0455	|	0621	|	|	...	0729	0753	|	|	...	0953	0953	|	1153	|	...	|	1353	|	...	1553	|	...	1753
215	St Michael 975 980 a.	0530	0550	0655	0721	|	...	0802	0828	0921	|	...	1028	1028	1121	1228	1321	...	|	1428	1521	...	1628	1721	...	1828
225	Leoben Hbf 975 980 a.	0538	0557	0708	0728	0717	...	0811	*0841*	0928	1017	...	*1041*	*1041*	1128	*1241*	1328	...	1417	*1441*	1528	...	*1641*	1728	...	*1841*
	Bruck a. d. Mur 975 980 a.	|	0610	|	|	|	...	0826	*0854*	|	|	...	*1054*	*1054*	|	*1254*	|	...	|	*1454*	|	...	*1654*	|	...	*1854*
293	**Graz** Hbf 975 980 a.	0635	0658	0801	0817	0903	...	*0925*	...	1014	1103	...	...	...	1214	...	1414	...	1503	...	1614	...	...	1814	...	...

	IC 611	IC 603			EC 219	EC 117	IC 615	
	🍷	🍷	2	Ⓐ 2	F✕		🍷	Ⓑ 2
Salzburg Hbf 960 970 d.	1616	...	...	*1643*	1816	2012	2016	...
Innsbruck Hbf 960 d.	|	...	...	|	|	|	|	...
Schwarzach ⊖ 960 970 d.	|	...	...	|	|	|	|	...
Bischofshofen 960 970 a.	1702	...	...	*1735*	1902	2052	2102	...
Bischofshofen d.	1712	...	...	1740	1912	...	2112	2213
Radstadt d.	1735	...	...	1808	1935	...	2135	2243
Schladming d.	1752	...	1833	...	1952	...	2152	2301
Stainach-Irdning d.	1822	...	1912	...	2022	...	2222	2340
Liezen d.	1832	...	1926	...	2032	...	2232	...
Linz Hbf 974 d.	|	1757	|	...	|	...	|	...
Selzthal a.	1839	1933	1932	...	2039	...	2239	...
Selzthal d.	1848	1935	1939	...	2048	...	2246	...
Stadt Rottenmann d.	|	1942	1945	...	|	...	2253	...
Trieben d.	|	|	1953	...	|	...	|	...
St Michael 975 980 a.	1921	|	2028	...	2121	...	2321	...
Leoben Hbf 975 980 a.	1928	2017	*2041*	...	2128	...	2328	...
Bruck a. d. Mur 975 980 a.	|	|	*2054*	...	|	...	|	...
Graz Hbf 975 980 a.	2014	2103	...	...	2214	...	0014	...

			D 618			EC 218		IC 500		IC 512		EC 164
	⚒ 2	⚒ 2	2	⚒ 2	Ⓐ 2	F✕	2		Ⓐ 2L	🍷	2	Z✕
Graz Hbf 975 980 d.	...	...	...	...	...	0545	...	0656	...	0745	...	0945
Bruck a. d. Mur 975 980 d.	...	...	...	...	*0536*	|	*0706*	|	...	|	*0906*	|
Leoben Hbf 975 980 d.	...	...	...	...	*0549*	0630	*0719*	0741	...	0830	*0919*	1030
St Michael 975 980 d.	...	...	...	...	0600	0638	0731	|	...	0838	0931	1038
Trieben d.	...	...	...	...	0636	|	0805	|	...	|	1005	|
Stadt Rottenmann d.	...	...	...	...	0644	0708	0812	0818	...	|	1012	|
Selzthal a.	...	...	...	...	0650	0713	0818	0823	...	0911	1018	1111
Selzthal d.	...	...	...	0543	...	0719	0826	0826	0844	0919	1026	1119
Linz Hbf 974 a.	...	...	...	|	...	|	|	1004	|	|	|	|
Liezen d.	...	...	...	0551	...	0727	0832	...	0851	0927	1032	1127
Stainach-Irdning d.	...	...	...	0603	...	0738	0845	...	...	0938	1045	1138
Schladming d.	0506	...	0545	0645	...	0810	0928	...	...	1010	1128	1210
Radstadt d.	0526	...	0602	0704	...	0826	...	...	...	1026	...	1226
Bischofshofen a.	0554	...	0628	0735	...	0848	...	...	...	1048	...	1248
Bischofshofen 960 970 d.	0557	0558	0635	*0740*	...	0857	...	...	...	1057	...	1250
Schwarzach ⊖ 960 970 a.	0612	|	|	|	...	|	...	...	...	|	...	1305
Innsbruck Hbf 960 a.	...	|	|	|	...	|	...	...	...	|	...	1540
Salzburg Hbf 960 970 a.	...	0645	0719	*0840*	...	0944	...	...	...	1144	...	...

	EC 112			EC 216		IC 506		IC 518	RJ 797				IC 610				IC 600		IC 718		IC 602	D 614	D 899	D 616	NJ 464
	✕	2	Ⓐ 2L	G	2	🍷	Ⓐ 2L	🍷	✕	2	Ⓐ 2L	Ⓐ 2	🍷	Ⓐ 2		2	🍷	⚒ 2	✕	2	🍷	2	2	2	A
Graz Hbf 975 980 d.	...	...	...	1145	...	1256	...	1345	...	...	...	1501	1545	...	...	...	1656	1701f	1745	...	1856	1945	...	2145	2225
Bruck a. d. Mur 975 980 d.	...	*1106*	...	|	*1306*	|	...	|	...	*1506*	...	|	|	...	...	*1706*	|	|	|	*1906*	|	|	...	|	2317
Leoben Hbf 975 980 d.	...	*1119*	...	1230	*1319*	1341	...	1430	...	*1519*	...	1557	1630	...	...	*1719*	1741	1801	1830	*1919*	1941	2030	...	2230	2330
St Michael 975 980 d.	...	1131	...	1238	1331	|	...	1438	...	1531	...	1608	1638	...	...	1731	|	1810	1838	1931	|	2038	...	2238	2340
Trieben d.	...	1205	...	|	1405	|	...	|	...	1605	...	1644	|	...	...	1805	|	1846	|	2005	|	|	...	|	|
Stadt Rottenmann d.	...	1212	...	|	1412	1418	...	|	...	1612	...	1652	|	...	...	1812	1818	1854	|	2012	2018	2108	...	2310	|
Selzthal a.	...	1218	...	1311	1418	1423	...	1511	...	1618	...	1658	1711	...	...	1818	1823	1900	1911	2018	2023	2113	...	2315	0017
Selzthal d.	...	1226	1244	1319	1426	1426	1444	1519	...	1626	1641	...	1719	1746	...	1826	1826	...	1919	2026	2026	2120	...	2321	0028
Linz Hbf 974 a.	...	|	|	|	|	1604	|	|	...	|	|	...	|	|	...	|	2004	...	|	|	2204	|	...	|	|
Liezen d.	...	1232	1251	1327	1432	...	1451	1527	...	1632	1648	...	1727	1753	...	1832	...	...	1927	2032	...	2127	...	2329	0036
Stainach-Irdning d.	...	1245	...	1338	1445	...	...	1538	...	1645	...	...	1738	1806	...	1845	...	...	1937	2045	...	2137	...	2341	0046
Schladming d.	...	1328	...	1410	1528	...	...	1610	...	1728	...	...	1810	1849	...	1928	...	...	2010	2126	...	2210	...	0024	0118
Radstadt d.	...	...	...	1426	...	...	...	1626	...	...	...	...	1826	...	...	1952	...	...	2026	...	...	2226	...	...	|
Bischofshofen a.	...	...	...	1448	...	...	...	1648	...	...	...	...	1848	...	...	...	...	...	2048	...	...	2251	...	...	0156
Bischofshofen 960 970 d.	1307	...	...	1457	...	...	...	1650	1707	...	...	...	1857	...	...	...	...	...	2057	...	...	2253	2307	...	0158
Schwarzach ⊖ 960 970 a.	|	...	...	|	...	...	...	1705	|	...	...	...	|	...	...	...	...	...	|	...	...	2308	|	...	0211
Innsbruck Hbf 960 a.	|	...	...	|	...	...	...	1940	|	...	...	...	|	...	...	...	...	...	|	...	...	...	|	...	0449
Salzburg Hbf 960 970 a.	1348	...	...	1544	...	...	...	...	1748	...	...	...	1944	...	...	...	...	...	2144	...	...	...	2348	...	...

A – 🛏 1, 2 cl., ▬ 2 cl. and (2) Graz - Innsbruck - Buchs 🏛 - Zürich and v.v.
F – CHIEMGAU – (12) and ⊗ Graz - München - Stuttgart - Frankfurt and v.v.
G – DACHSTEIN – (12) Graz - München - Stuttgart - Saarbrücken and v.v.
L – To / from Linz (Table **974**).
Z – TRANSALPIN – (12) and ✕ Zürich - Graz and v.v.

f – On ⑥ change at Leoben.
g – Not Dec. 26, Apr. 10, May 29.

⊖ – Schwarzach-St Veit.

976 LINZ - STEYR - KLEINREIFLING - WEISSENBACH

2nd class only

km		⚒	Ⓐ		Ⓐ	Ⓒ		Ⓒ	Ⓐ			Ⓒ	Ⓐ			Ⓒ	Ⓐ		Ⓐ		Ⓒ	Ⓐ		Ⓐ		Ⓒ
0	**Linz** Hbf 950 992 d.	0425	0514	0621	0649	0649	0753	0753	0823	0853	0953	0953	*1030*	1053	1153	1153	1223	1253	1253	1353	1353	1423	1453	1523	1553	1553
17	Enns 992 d.	0442	0532	0638	0707	0707	0811	0811	0841	0911	1011	1011	|	1111	1211	1211	1241	1311	1311	1411	1411	1441	1511	1541	1611	1611
25	St Valentin 950 d.	0509v	0540	0649	0721t	0721t	0821	0821	0851	0921	1021	1021	1051	1121	1221	1221	1251	1321	1321	1421	1421	1451	1521	1551	1621	1621
45	**Steyr** d.	0532	0605	0714	0754t	0754t	0846	0846	0912	0946	1046	1046	1112	1146	1246	1246	1312	1346	1346	1446	1446	1512	1546	1612	1646	1646
47	Garsten d.	0536	0608	0717	0758	0758	0849	0850	0916	0949	1049	1050	1116	1149	1249	1250	1316	1349	1350	1449	1450	1516	1549	1616	1649	1650
67	Losenstein d.	0601	...	...	0822	0822	...	0917	0937	...	...	1117	1137	...	...	1317	1337	...	1423	...	1517	1537	...	1640	...	1717
89	Kastenreith 977 a.	0628	...	...	0848	0852	...	0941	1004	...	...	1141	1204	...	...	1341	1404	...	1447	...	1541	1604	...	1704	...	1741
92	**Kleinreifling** 977 a.	0633	...	...	0852	0856	...	0946	1008	...	...	1146	1208	...	...	1346	1408	...	1451	...	1546	1608	...	1708	...	1746
106	Weißenbach ⊡ 977 a.	0648a	...	...	0907	*0916*	...	...	...	...	...	*1216*	...	...	...	*1416*	...	...	...	...	...	1623	...	1723	...	*1816*k

	Ⓐ		Ⓐ		Ⓒ	Ⓐ					
Linz Hbf 950 992 d.	1623	1653	1723	1753	1753	1823	*1853*	1953	*2053*	2153	2253
Enns 992 d.	1641	1711	1741	1811	1811	1841	*1911*	2011	*2111*	2211	2311
St Valentin 950 d.	1651	1721	1751	1821	1821	1851	1921	2021	2121	2221	2321
Steyr d.	1712	1746	1812	1846	1846	1912	1946	2045	2146	2246	2346
Garsten d.	1716	1749	1816	1849	1850	1916	1949	2048	2149	2249	2349
Losenstein d.	1737	...	1841	...	1917	1937	...	2111	...	...	...
Kastenreith 977 a.	1804	...	1905	...	1941	2005	...	2135	...	...	...
Kleinreifling 977 a.	1808	...	1910	...	1946	2009	...	2139	...	...	...
Weißenbach ⊡ 977 a.	1823	...	1924	...	...	...	...	...	...	...	...

	P	Ⓐ	⚒		Ⓐ			Ⓐ	Ⓐ		Ⓒ
Weißenbach ⊡ 977 d.	...	...	...	...	...	0603a	...	0706	...	...	...
Kleinreifling 977 d.	...	0437	0513	...	...	0618	...	0721	0754	...	0812
Kastenreith 977 d.	...	0441	0517	...	...	0622	...	0724	0758	...	0816
Losenstein d.	...	0505	0540	...	...	0647	...	...	0822	...	0843
Garsten d.	0442	0527	0601	0609	0637	0709	0809	...	0843	0909	0909
Steyr d.	0446	0532	0606	0614	0642	0714	0814	...	0847	0914	0914
St Valentin 950 d.	0511	0556	0623	0641	0711	0741	0841	...	0907	0941	0941
Enns 992 d.	0518	0602	0628	0646	0718	0748	0848	...	|	0948	0948
Linz Hbf 950 992 a.	0534	0617	0639	0701	0735	0804	0904	...	*0928*	1004	1004

		Ⓐ		Ⓒ		Ⓐ		Ⓒ		Ⓐ		Ⓒ	Ⓐ		Ⓐ		Ⓒ	Ⓐ		Ⓐ	Ⓐ		Ⓒ			
Weißenbach ⊡ 977 d.	...	0940	...	...	...	...	...	*1144*	...	1338	...	*1341*	...	...	...	...	*1541*	...	...	1639	1738	...	*1744*	...	*1941*	...
Kleinreifling 977 d.	...	0954	...	1015	...	1154	...	1215	...	1354	...	1415	...	...	1554	...	1615	...	...	1654	1753	...	1815	...	2021	...
Kastenreith 977 d.	...	0958	...	1019	...	1158	...	1219	...	1358	...	1419	...	...	1558	...	1619	...	...	1658	1757	...	1819	...	2025	...
Losenstein d.	...	1022	...	1044	...	1222	...	1244	...	1422	...	1444	...	...	1621	...	1644	...	...	1744v	1821	...	1844	...	2050	...
Garsten d.	1009	1043	1109	1109	1209	1243	1309	1309	1409	1443	1509	1509	1543	1609	1643	1709	1709	1743	1809	1809	1843	1909	1909	2009	2113	2209
Steyr d.	1014	1047	1114	1114	1214	1247	1314	1314	1414	1447	1514	1514	1547	1614	1647	1714	1714	1747	1814	1814	1847	1914	1914	2014	2116	2214
St Valentin 950 d.	1041	1111	1141	1141	1241	1311	1341	1341	1441	1511	1541	1541	1607	1641	1711	1741	1741	1807	1841	1841	1907	1941	1941	2041	2141	2241
Enns 992 d.	1048	1118	1148	1148	1248	1318	1348	1348	1448	1518	1548	1548	|	1648	1718	1748	1748	|	1848	1848	|	1948	1948	2048	2148	2248
Linz Hbf 950 992 a.	1104	1139	1204	1204	1304	1339	1404	1404	1504	1539	1604	1604	*1628*	1704	1739	1804	1804	*1828*	1904	1904	*1928*	2004	2004	2104	2204	2304

P – To Passau (Table **962**). a – Ⓐ only. k – ⑥ only. t – Arrives 8–9 minutes earlier. v – Arrives 19 minutes earlier. ⊡ – Weißenbach-St Gallen.

AMSTETTEN - KLEINREIFLING - SELZTHAL 977

2nd class only

km		⚒	⚒		†		Ⓒ	Ⓒ	Ⓐ		Ⓒ	Ⓐ		Ⓐ	Ⓒ	Ⓐ	Ⓐ		Ⓒ	Ⓒ	Ⓐ		Ⓐ	†	⑥
	Wien Westbahnhof **950** d.	...	0424a	...	...	...	0648	...	...	...	...	...	...	...	1118	...	...	...	1218	...	...	...	...	1518	...
0	**Amstetten** d.	0451	0621	0705	0705	0805	0805	0905	0905	1005	1105	1104	1205	1205	1305	1305	1323	1405	1405	1505	1505	1605	1605	1704	1705
23	Waidhofen a. d. Ybbs d.	0548h	0710j	0732	0732	0829	0830	0930	0930	1029	1130	1131	1232	1232	1330	1330	1351	1430	1430	1530	1530	1632	1632	1731	1730
41	Weyer d.	0608	0729	...	0748	...	0852	0948	0948	...	1148	1148	...	1248	1348	1348	...	1448	1448	1548	1548	...	1648	1748	1748
44	Kastenreith **976** d.	0611	0733	...	0752	...	0856	0952	0952	...	1152	1152	...	1252	1352	1352	...	1452	1452	1552	1552	...	1651	1752	1752
47	**Kleinreifling** **976** a.	0615	0737	...	0756	...	0859	0956	*1008*	...	1156	*1208*	...	1256	1356	*1408*	...	1456	1456	1556	*1608*	...	*1708*	1756	1756
61	Weißenbach-St Gallen . **976** a.	*0648*a	...	...	...	...	0916	...	...	...	1216	...	...	...	1416	...	...	...	1516	...	*1623*	...	*1723*	...	1816
119	**Selzthal** a.	...	...	...	...	...	1015	...	...	...	...	...	...	...	...	...	...	...	1615	...	...	...	...	...	...

	Ⓐ		Ⓐ	†			e				
Wien Westbahnhof **950** d.	...	...	...	...	...	...	...	1918v	...	...	...
mstetten d.	1705	1805	1805	1805	1905	2005	2005	2105	2205	2305	0010
/aidhofen a. d. Ybbs d.	1730	1829	1830	1830	1930	2029	2034	2129	2229	2329	0036
/eyer d.	1748	...	1848	1848	1948	...	2051	...	...	...	...
astenreith **976** d.	1751	...	1852	1852	1952	...	2056	...	...	...	...
leinreifling **976** a.	*1808*	...	1956	1856	1956	...	2059	...	...	...	...
/eißenbach-St Gallen ... **976** a.	*1823*	...	...	1911	...	...	...	...	...	...	...
elzthal a.	...	...	...	...	...	...	...	...	...	...	...

	⚒	Ⓐ		Ⓐ	Ⓐ		⚒		Ⓐ
Selzthal d.	...	...	...	...	...	...	...	...	...
Weißenbach-St Gallen .. **976** d.	...	...	...	...	...	...	*0603*a	...	0706
Kleinreifling **976** d.	...	...	...	0504	...	0600	0623	...	0721
Kastenreith **976** d.	...	...	...	0508	...	0604	0632	...	0725
Weyer d.	...	...	...	0511	...	0609	0635	...	0728
Waidhofen a. d. Ybbs d.	0430	0459	0530	0530	0550	0628	0651	0734	...
Amstetten a.	0455	0526	0555	0555	0615	0655	0720	0755	...
Wien Westbahnhof **950** .. a.	0642a	0712	0742	0742	0812	...	...	0942	...

			Ⓐ	Ⓒ		Ⓐ	Ⓒ	Ⓒ	Ⓐ	Ⓐ	Ⓒ		Ⓐ	Ⓐ	Ⓒ		Ⓐ	Ⓐ	Ⓒ		†				
elzthal d.	...	...	...	...	...	...	1045	...	...	...	...	...	...	...	...	...	...	...	1645	...	...	...	...	...	...
/eißenbach-St Gallen ... **976** d.	...	...	*0940*	...	...	...	1144	...	...	*1338*	1341	...	...	...	*1541*	...	*1639*	*1738*	1744	...	...	1941	...	...	...
leinreifling **976** d.	0804	...	*0954*	1004	...	*1154*	1204	...	1304	*1354*	1404	...	1504	*1554*	1604	...	*1654*	*1753*	1804	...	1904	1955	2004	...	...
astenreith **976** d.	0808	...	1008	1008	...	1208	1208	...	1308	1408	1408	...	1508	1608	1608	...	1708	1808	1808	...	1908	...	2008	...	...
/eyer d.	0811	...	1011	1011	...	1211	1211	...	1311	1411	1411	...	1511	1611	1611	...	1711	1811	1811	...	1911	...	2011	...	...
/aidhofen a. d. Ybbs d.	0830	0930	1030	1030	1130	1230	1230	1330	1330	1430	1430	1530	1530	1630	1630	1730	1730	1830	1830	1930	1930	...	2030	2130	2230
mstetten a.	0855	0955	1055	1055	1155	1255	1255	1355	1355	1455	1455	1555	1555	1655	1655	1755	1755	1855	1855	1955	1955	...	2055	2155	2255
Wien Westbahnhof **950** a.	...	...	...	...	...	...	1442	1542	...	...	...	...	...	...	...	...	...	...	2012	...	...	...	...	...	...

– Ⓐ only. **e** – ①②③④⑦. **h** – Arrives 0525. **j** – Arrives 0652. **v** – † only.

WIEN - GRAZ and KLAGENFURT 980

km				RJ 639		RJ 72				RJ 551		RJ 131		RJ 553		EC 151		IC 533	RJ 71		IC 735		RJ 559		RJ 535		RJ 73	
		Ⓐ	⚒		Ⓐ		†	⚒	†								Ⓐ											
		2	2	✕	2	✕	2	2	2	✕	2	V✕	2	✕	2	E✕	2	L✕	P✕	2	🍷	2	✕	2	✕	2	P✕	2
	Flughafen Wien ✈ **985** d.	...	...	...	...	...	...	...	...	...	...	...	...	0633	...	...	...	...	...	...	...	...	0933	...	...	...	...	...
0	**Wien** Hbf **981 985** d.	...	...	...	...	...	...	...	...	0558	...	0618	...	0658	...	0758	...	0818	0858	...	0918	...	0958	...	1018	...	1058	...
4	**Wien** Meidling **981** d.	...	...	...	...	...	...	...	...	0605	...	0625	...	0705	...	0805	...	0825	0905	...	0925	...	1005	...	1025	...	1105	...
49	**Wiener Neustadt** Hbf **981** a.	...	...	...	...	...	...	...	...	0628	...	0650	...	0728	...	0828	...	0850	0928	...	0950	...	1028	...	1050	...	1128	...
	Wiener Neustadt Hbf **981** d.	...	...	...	...	...	...	...	...	0632	...	0652	...	0732	...	0832	...	0852	0932	...	0952	...	1032	...	1052	...	1132	...
104	Semmering **981** d.	...	...	...	...	...	...	...	...	|	...	|	...	|	...	0916	...	|	1016	...	|	...	1116	...	|	...	1216	...
118	Mürzzuschlag **981** d.	...	0520	...	...	...	0621	0621	...	0730	...	|	...	0830	...	0930	...	|	1030	...	|	...	1130	...	|	...	1230	...
	Graz Hbf **975** ▷ d.	...	|	0519	...	0625	|	|	0611	|	*0725*	|	...	|	*0825*	|	*0925*	|	|	*1025*	|	...	|	*1125*	|	...	|	*1225*
158	**Bruck** an der Mur a.	...	0600	0557	...	0700	0701	0701	0657	0757	*0800*	0813	...	0857	*0900*	0957	*1000*	1013	1057	*1100*	1113	...	1157	*1200*	1213	...	1257	*1300*
158	**Bruck** an der Mur . **975** ⊙ d.	0436	0608	0609	0636	...	0708	0706	0706	0759	0806	0815	...	0859	0906	0959	1006	1015	1059	1106	1115	...	1159	1206	1215	...	1259	1306
212	**Graz** Hbf ⊙ a.	|	0655	|	|	...	0755	|	|	0834	|	|	...	0934	|	1034	|	|	1134	|	|	...	1234	|	|	...	1334	|
174	Leoben Hbf **975** d.	0451	▬	0622	0650	...	...	0721	0721	▬	0821	0827	...	...	0921	▬	1021	1027	...	1121	1127	...	▬	1221	1227	...	...	1321
◧	St Michael **975** a.	0458	...	|	0657	...	...	0728	0728	...	0828	|	←	...	0928	...	1028	|	...	1128	|	←	...	1228	|	←	...	1328
◧	St Michael d.	0507	...	|	0702	...	...	0734	0734	...	0834	|	0834	...	0934	...	1034	|	...	1134	|	1134	...	1234	|	1234	...	1334
205	Knittelfeld d.	0525	...	0642	0720	...	...	0752	0752	...	→	0847	0852	...	0952	...	1052	1047	...	→	1147	1152	...	→	1247	1252	...	1352
213	Zeltweg d.	0531	⚒	|	0727	...	...	0758	0758	...	...	|	0858	...	0958	...	1058	|	...	...	|	1158	...	...	|	1258	...	1358
220	Judenburg d.	0539	2	0655	0734	...	...	0806	0806	...	...	0859	0906	...	1006	...	1106	1059	...	...	1159	1206	...	...	1259	1306	...	1406
239	Unzmarkt d.	0554	0608	0709	0750	...	...	0822	0822	2L	...	0913	0921	...	1022	2L	1121	1113	...	...	|	1222	2L	...	1313	1321	...	1422
276	Friesach **971** a.	...	0642	0739	...	...	...	0855	0855	0908	...	|	...	...	1055	1108	...	1143	...	...	1241	1255	1308	...	|	...	...	1455
309	St Veit an der Glan **971** a.	...	0716	0806	...	...	...	...	...	0940	...	1006	...	...	...	1140	...	1206	...	...	1307	...	1340	...	1406	...	...	...
329	**Klagenfurt** Hbf **971** ▷ a.	...	0738	0820	...	...	...	...	...	1000	...	1020	...	...	...	1200	...	1220	...	...	1319	...	1400	...	1420	...	...	...
	Villach Hbf **971** a.	...	0820t	0846	...	...	...	...	...	1039	...	1046	...	...	...	1239	...	1246	...	...	1348	...	1439	...	1446	...	...	...

	RJ 653		RJ 133	RJ 75		IC 737		RJ 657		RJ 539	RJ 259		IC 831				EC 159		RJ 631		RJ 79			D 859	RJ 755		RJ 633	
		Ⓐ				⑤f		‡	Ⓐ		❖				⚒		¶						Ⓐ	a	§			
	✕	2	V✕	P✕	2	L	2L	✕	2	L✕	N✕	2	L🍷	2	2	2L	F✕	2	✕	2	P✕	2	2	2	✕	2	✕	2
lughafen Wien ✈ **985** d.	1133	...	...	...	...	...	...	1333	...	...	...	...	...	...	...	...	...	...	...	...	...	...	...	...	1733	...	...	...
/ien Hbf **981 985** d.	1158	...	1218	1258	...	1318	...	1358	...	1418	1458	...	1518	...	...	...	1558	...	1618	...	1658	...	...	1718	1758	...	1818	...
/ien Meidling **981** d.	1205	...	1225	1305	...	1325	...	1405	...	1425	1505	...	1525	...	...	...	1605	...	1625	...	1705	...	...	1725	1805	...	1825	...
/iener Neustadt Hbf. **981** a.	1228	...	1250	1328	...	1350	...	1430	...	1450	1530	...	1550	...	...	...	1628	...	1650	...	1730	...	...	1750	1830	...	1850	...
/iener Neustadt Hbf. **981** d.	1232	...	1252	1332	...	1352	...	1432	...	1452	1532	...	1552	...	...	...	1632	...	1652	...	1732	...	...	1752	1832	...	1852	...
emmering **981** d.	1316	...	|	|	...	|	...	1516	...	|	|	...	|	...	...	...	1716	...	|	...	|	...	...	1842	1916	...	|	...
lürzzuschlag **981** d.	1330	...	|	1430	...	|	...	1530	...	|	1630	...	|	...	...	...	1730	...	|	...	1830	...	...	1906j	1930	...	|	...
Graz Hbf **975** ▷ d.	|	*1325*	|	|	*1425*	|	...	|	*1525*	|	|	*1625*	|	...	1701	...	|	*1725*	|	...	|	*1825*	1901	|	|	*1925*	|	...
ruck an der Mur a.	1357	*1400*	1413	1457	*1500*	1513	...	1557	*1600*	1613	1657	*1700*	1713	...	|	...	1757	*1800*	1813	...	1857	*1900*	|	1937	1957	*2000*	2013	...
ruck an der Mur ... **975** ⊙ d.	1359	1406	1415	1459	1506	1515	...	1559	1606	1615	1659	1706	1715	...	|	...	1759	1806	1815	...	1859	1906	|	1945	1959	2006	2015	...
Graz Hbf ⊙ a.	1434	|	|	1534	|	|	...	1634	|	|	1734	|	|	...	|	...	1834	|	|	...	1934	|	|	|	2034	|	|	...
eoben Hbf **975** d.	▬	1421	1427	...	1521	1527	...	...	1621	1627	...	1721	1727	...	1758	...	...	1821	1827	...	...	1921	1956	2000	...	2021	2027	...
St Michael **975** a.	...	1428	|	...	1528	|	...	...	1628	|	...	1728	|	←	|	...	...	1828	|	←	...	1928	2003	|	...	2028	|	←
St Michael d.	...	1434	|	...	1534	|	...	...	1634	|	...	1734	|	1734	|	...	...	1834	|	1834	...	1934	2009	|	...	2034	|	2034
nittelfeld d.	...	1452	1447	...	1552	1546	...	...	1652	1647	...	→	1746	1752	1820	...	...	→	1847	1852	...	1952	2027	2020	...	→	2047	2052
eltweg d.	...	1458	|	...	1558	|	...	...	1658	|	...	...	|	1758	1827	...	...	...	|	1858	...	1958	2034	|	...	...	|	2058
udenburg d.	...	1506	1459	...	1606	1559	...	...	1706	1659	...	...	1759	1806	1834	...	...	...	1859	1906	...	2006	2041	2033	...	...	2059	2106
nzmarkt d.	2L	1521	1513	...	1622	|	...	...	1721	1713	...	...	|	1822	1850	...	...	...	1913	1921	...	2021	2057	2048	...	...	2113	2121
riesach **971** a.	1508	...	1543	...	1655	1641	1708	...	...	|	...	...	1841	1855	...	1908	...	...	1943	...	...	...	...	2119	...	...	|	...
t Veit an der Glan **971** a.	1540	...	1606	...	...	1707	1740	...	...	1806	...	...	1907	...	...	1940	...	...	2006	...	...	...	...	2147	...	...	2206	...
lagenfurt Hbf **971** ▷ a.	1600	...	1620	...	...	1719	1800	...	...	1820	...	...	1919	...	...	2000	...	...	2020	...	...	...	...	2203	...	...	2220	...
Villach Hbf **971** a.	1639	...	1646	...	...	1748	1839	...	...	1846	...	...	1948	...	...	2039	...	...	2046	...	...	...	...	2232	...	...	2246	...

– EMONA – [12] and ✕ Wien - Graz - Spielfeld-Straß 🏛 - Maribor - Ljubljana - Trieste (Table **91**).
– CROATIA – [12] and ✕ Wien - Graz - Spielfeld-Straß 🏛 - Maribor - Zagreb (Table **91**).
– To Lienz (Table **971**).
– [12] and ✕ Decin - Praha - Břeclav 🏛 - Wien - Graz (Table **60**).
– [12] and ✕ Praha - Břeclav 🏛 - Wien - Graz (Table **60**).
– [12] and ✕ Wien - Tarvisio 🏛 - Udine - Venezia (Table **88**).

– Dec. 22, 23, Feb. 3, Mar. 31, Apr. 6, 7, 28, May 17, 26, June 7, Aug. 11, Oct. 25, Dec. 7.
– ⑤ (also Jan. 5, May 17, June 7, Oct. 25, Dec. 7; not Jan. 6, May 19, June 9, Oct. 27, Dec. 8).
– Arrives 1856.
– ⚒ only.

t – Change trains at Klagenfurt on Ⓐ.

◧ – Leoben - St Michael is *10 km*. St Michael - Knittelfeld is *22 km*.
¶ – Train number **1259** on Ⓒ.
§ – Train number **1255** on Ⓒ.
‡ – Train number **1057** on ⑤ (also Jan. 5, May 17, June 7, Oct. 25, Dec. 7; not Jan. 6, May 19, June 9, Oct. 27, Dec. 8).
❖ – Train number **257** from July 1.
⊙ – For other local journeys see panel below main table on page 460.
▷ – For fast **ÖBB** *Intercitybus* services Graz - Klagenfurt and v.v., see panel below main table on page 460.

980 WIEN - GRAZ and KLAGENFURT

	RJ 371		NJ 233	EC 105			RJ 373	RJ 853	D 855 Ⓐ
	P✕	2	AR	Q✕	2		P✕	✕	b2
Flughafen Wien ✈ ...... **985** d.	...	...	...	...	...	...	...	...	...
Wien Hbf .... **981 985** d.	1858	...	1918	1958	...	...	2058	2158	2258
Wien Meidling .... **981** d.	1905	...	1925	2005	...	...	2105	2205	2305
Wiener Neustadt Hbf ... **981** a.	1930	...	1950	2028	...	...	2128	2228	2330
Wiener Neustadt Hbf ... **981** d.	1932	...	1952	2032	...	...	2132	2232	2332
Semmering .... **981** d.	|	...	|	|	...	...	2216	|	0016
Mürzzuschlag .... **981** d.	2030	...	|	2130	...	...	2230	2330	0030
Graz Hbf .... **975** ▷ d.	|	2025	|	|	2125	...	|	|	|
Bruck an der Mur .... a.	2057	2100	2118	2157	2200	...	2257	2357	0057
Bruck an der Mur ..... **975** ⊙ d.	2059	2106	2121	2159	2206	...	2259	2359	0059
Graz Hbf .... ⊙ a.	2134	|	|	2234	|	...	2334	0034	0134
Leoben Hbf .... **975** d.	...	2121	2136	...	2220	...	...	...	...
St Michael .... **975** a.	...	2128	|	...	|	...	...	...	...
St Michael .... d.	...	2134	|	...	|	...	...	...	...
Knittelfeld .... d.	...	2152	2203	...	2243	...	...	...	...
Zeltweg .... d.	...	2158	|	...	2249	...	...	...	...
Judenburg .... d.	...	2206	|	...	2256	...	...	...	...
Unzmarkt .... d.	...	2221	|	...	2311	...	...	...	...
Friesach .... **971** a.	...	...	|	...	...	...	...	...	...
St Veit an der Glan .... **971** a.	...	...	2320	...	...	...	...	...	...
Klagenfurt Hbf .... **971** ▷ a.	...	...	2334	...	...	...	...	...	...
Villach Hbf **971** .... a.	...	...	0001	...	...	...	...	...	...

	D 858					EC 104	NJ 235				
	Ⓐ 2	⚒ 2	⚒ 2	⚒ 2	⚒ 2	Q✕	AR	Ⓐ 2	Ⓒ 2	⚒ 2	Ⓐ 2
Villach Hbf **971** .... d.	...	...	...	...	...	...	0417	...	...	...	...
Klagenfurt Hbf ..... **971** ▷ d.	...	...	...	...	...	...	0440	...	...	...	...
St Veit an der Glan .... **971** d.	...	...	...	...	...	...	|	...	...	0501	...
Friesach .... **971** d.	...	...	...	...	...	...	|	...	...	0527	...
Unzmarkt .... d.	...	...	0438	...	...	...	|	0548	0548	0601	060
Judenburg .... d.	...	...	0455	...	...	...	|	0605	0605	▬	062
Zeltweg .... d.	...	...	0502	...	...	...	|	0612	0612	...	063
Knittelfeld .... d.	...	...	0509	...	...	...	|	0619	0619	RJ	063
St Michael .... a.	...	...	0526	...	←	...	|	|	|	**72**	065
St Michael .... **975** d.	...	...	0535	0531	0535	...	|	|	|		070
Leoben Hbf .... **975** d.	...	...	→	0539	0543	...	0627	0641	0641	P✕	071
Graz Hbf .... ⊙ d.	0414	0422	...	|	|	0525	|	|	|	0625	|
Bruck an der Mur . **975** ⊙ a.	0452	0508	...	|	0557	0600	0639	0655	0655	0700	072
Bruck an der Mur .... d.	0454	0517	...	|	0608	0602	0641	0708	0719	0702	...
Graz Hbf .... **975** ▷ a.	|	|	...	0634	0655	|	|	0755	|	|	...
Mürzzuschlag .... **981** d.	0525	0606f	...	...	...	0632	|	...	0800	0732	...
Semmering .... **981** d.	0538	0621a	...	...	...	|	|	...	...	0746	...
Wiener Neustadt Hbf .. **981** a.	0626	...	...	...	...	0728	0802	...	...	0828	...
Wiener Neustadt Hbf .. **981** d.	0630	...	...	...	...	0730	0804	...	...	0832	...
Wien Meidling .... **981** a.	0655	...	...	...	...	0755	0845	...	...	0855	...
Wien Hbf .... **981 985** a.	0702	...	...	...	...	0802	0852	...	...	0902	...
Flughafen Wien ✈ ... **985** a.	...	...	...	...	...	...	...	...	...	...	...

			RJ 530	RJ 551		IC 730		RJ 74	RJ 532				RJ 258 c	RJ 534		EC 158			RJ 78	RJ 536				RJ 370	RJ 132
	⚒ 2	2	✕	✕	2	🍷	2	P✕	✕	2	2	2	N✕	✕	Ⓐ 2	F✕	2L	2	P✕	✕	Ⓐ 2	2L	2	P✕	V✕
Villach Hbf **971** .... d.	...	...	0525	...	0529	0613	...	...	0714	...	0720	...	...	0914	...	...	0920	...	...	1114	...	1120	...	...	131
Klagenfurt Hbf .... **971** ▷ d.	...	...	0548	...	0607	0639	...	...	0739	...	0804	...	...	0939	...	...	1004	...	...	1139	...	1204	...	...	133
St Veit an der Glan .... **971** d.	...	...	0601	...	0627	0652	...	...	0753	...	0824	...	...	0953	...	...	1024	...	...	1153	...	1224	...	...	135
Friesach .... **971** d.	...	...	|	...	0659	0718	...	...	|	...	0856	0904	...	1016	...	...	1056	1104	...	|	...	1256	1304	...	141
Unzmarkt .... d.	...	0632	|	...	0733	|	0738	...	0848	0838	▬	0938	...	1048	1038	...	...	1138	...	1248	1238	▬	1338	...	144
Judenburg .... d.	...	0649	|	...	▬	0802	0754	...	0902	0854	...	0954	...	1102	1054	...	...	1154	...	1302	1254	...	1354	...	150
Zeltweg .... d.	...	0656	|	...	...	|	0802	...	|	0902	...	1002	...	|	1102	...	...	1202	...	|	1302	...	1402	...	|
Knittelfeld .... d.	...	0703	|	...	RJ	0814	0808	...	0914	0908	RJ	1008	...	1114	1108	...	...	1208	...	1314	1308	RJ	1405	...	151
St Michael .... a.	...	|	|	...	**554**	|	0825	...	|	0925	**558**	1025	...	|	1125	...	...	1225	...	|	1325	**656**	1425	...	|
St Michael .... **975** d.	0701	|	|	...		|	0832	...	|	0932		1032	...	|	1132	...	...	1232	...	|	1332		1432	...	|
Leoben Hbf .... **975** d.	0709	0725	0733	...	✕	0833	0841	...	0933	0941	✕	1041	...	1133	1141	...	...	1241	...	1333	1341	✕	1441	...	153
Graz Hbf .... ⊙ d.	|	|	|	...	0725	|	|	0825	|	|	0925	|	1025	|	|	1125	...	|	1225	|	|	1325	|	1425	|
Bruck an der Mur ..... **975** ⊙ a.	|	0735	0743	...	0800	0843	0854	0900	0943	0954	1000	1054	1100	1143	1154	1200	...	1254	1300	1343	1354	1400	1454	1500	154
Bruck an der Mur .... d.	|	0743r	0745	0759	0802	0845	0859	0902	0945	0959	1002	1059	1102	1145	159	1202	...	1259	1302	1345	1358	1402	1459	1502	154
Graz Hbf .... **975** ▷ a.	0801	0829r	|	0834	|	|	0934	|	|	1034	|	1134	|	|	1234	|	...	1334	|	|	1433	|	1534	|	|
Mürzzuschlag .... **981** d.	...	...	|	...	0832	|	...	0932	|	...	1032	...	1132	|	...	1232	...	...	1332	|	...	1432	...	1532	|
Semmering .... **981** d.	...	...	|	...	0846	|	...	0946	|	...	|	...	1146	|	...	|	...	...	1346	|	...	|	...	1546	|
Wiener Neustadt Hbf ... **981** a.	...	...	0906	...	0928	1006	...	1028	1106	...	1128	...	1228	1306	...	1328	...	...	1428	1506	...	1528	...	1628	1706
Wiener Neustadt Hbf ... **981** d.	...	...	0908	...	0932	1008	...	1032	1108	...	1132	...	1232	1308	...	1332	...	...	1432	1508	...	1532	...	1632	1708
Wien Meidling .... **981** a.	...	...	0935	...	0955	1035	...	1055	1135	...	1155	...	1255	1335	...	1355	...	...	1455	1535	...	1555	...	1655	1735
Wien Hbf .... **981 985** a.	...	...	0942	...	1002	1042	...	1102	1142	...	1202	...	1302	1342	...	1402	...	...	1502	1542	...	1602	...	1702	1742
Flughafen Wien ✈ ...... **985** a.	...	...	...	...	1027	...	...	...	...	...	1227	...	...	...	...	...	...	...	...	...	...	1627	...	...	...

				D 738 ⑦w	RJ 372		RJ 630				IC 830	RJ 374		IC 632		⑦z			D 832 ⑦w	RJ 850	RJ 130	EC 105	D 852	⑤⑥†	⚒
	Ⓐ 2	2L	2	2L	P✕	2	✕	2	2L	2	🍷	S✕	2	L✕	2	2	2L	2	2	✕	V✕	✕	2	2	2
Villach Hbf **971** .... d.	...	1320	...	1413	...	...	1514	...	1520	...	1613	...	...	1714	...	...	1720	...	1813	...	1914	...	...	...	...
Klagenfurt Hbf .... **971** ▷ d.	...	1404	...	1439	...	...	1539	...	1604	...	1639	...	...	1739	...	...	1804	...	1839	...	1939	...	...	...	...
St Veit an der Glan .... **971** d.	...	1424	...	1552	...	...	1553	...	1624	...	1652	...	...	1753	...	...	1824	...	1852	...	1953	...	...	...	...
Friesach .... **971** d.	...	1456	1504	1518	...	...	|	...	1656	1704	1718	...	...	1816	...	...	1856	1904	1918	...	|	...	...	...	...
Unzmarkt .... d.	1438	▬	1538	|	...	1638	1648	...	▬	1738	|	...	1838	1848	...	1906	▬	1938	|	...	2048	...	...	2138	...
Judenburg .... d.	1454	...	1554	1602	...	1654	1702	...	...	1754	1802	...	1854	1902	...	1919	...	1954	2002	...	2102	...	...	2154	...
Zeltweg .... d.	1502	...	1602	|	...	1702	|	...	...	1802	|	...	1902	|	...	1927	...	2002	|	...	|	...	...	2202	...
Knittelfeld .... d.	1508	RJ	1608	1614	...	1708	1714	...	RJ	1808	1814	...	1908	1914	...	1933	EC	2008	2014	...	2114	...	...	2208	...
St Michael .... a.	1525	**750**	1625	|	...	1725	|	←	**754**	1825	|	...	1925	|	←	|	**150**	2025	|	...	|	...	...	2225	...
St Michael .... **975** d.	1532		1632	|	...	1732	|	1732		1832	|	...	1932	|	1932	|		2032	|	...	|	...	...	2232	...
Leoben Hbf .... **975** d.	1541	✕	1641	1633	...	→	1733	1741	✕	1841	1833	...	→	1933	1941	1954	E✕	2041	2033	...	2133	...	...	2241	...
Graz Hbf .... ⊙ d.	|	1525	|	|	1625	...	|	|	1725	|	|	1825	...	|	|	|	1925	|	|	2025	|	...	2125	|	2205
Bruck an der Mur ..... **975** ⊙ a.	1554	1600	1654	1643	1700	...	1743	1754	1800	1854	1843	1900	...	1943	1954	|	2000	2054	2043	2100	2143	...	2200	2254	2251
Bruck an der Mur .... d.	1558	1602	1659	1645	1702	...	1745	1759	1802	1859	1845	1902	...	1945	1959	|	2002	2059	2045	2102	2145	2159	2202	2259	2311
Graz Hbf .... **975** ▷ a.	1633	|	1734	|	|	...	|	1834	|	1934	|	|	...	|	2034	2038	|	2134	|	|	|	2234	|	2334	|
Mürzzuschlag .... **981** d.	...	1632	...	|	1732	...	|	...	1832	...	|	1932	...	|	...	...	2032	...	|	2132	|	...	2232	...	2351
Semmering .... **981** d.	...	|	...	|	1746	...	|	...	1846	...	|	|	...	|	...	...	|	...	|	|	|	...	2246	...	...
Wiener Neustadt Hbf ... **981** a.	...	1728	...	1806	1828	...	1906	...	1928	...	2006	2028	...	2106	...	...	2128	...	2206	2228	2306	...	2328	...	...
Wiener Neustadt Hbf ... **981** d.	...	1732	...	1808	1832	...	1908	...	1932	...	2008	2032	...	2108	...	...	2132	...	2208	2232	2308	...	2332	...	...
Wien Meidling .... **981** a.	...	1755	...	1835	1855	...	1935	...	1955	...	2035	2055	...	2135	...	...	2155	...	2235	2255	2335	...	2355	...	...
Wien Hbf .... **981 985** a.	...	1802	...	1842	1902	...	1942	...	2002	...	2042	2102	...	2142	...	...	2202	...	2242	2302	2342	...	0002	...	...
Flughafen Wien ✈ ...... **985** a.	...	1827	...	...	...	...	...	...	2027	...	...	...	...	...	...	...	...	...	...	...	...	...	...	...	...

Local stopping trains **BRUCK AN DER MUR - GRAZ - SPIELFELD-STRASS** (for international services Graz - Spielfeld Straß - Maribor - Ljubljana / Zagreb see Table **1315**).

km			⚒	Ⓐ							
	Bruck a. d. Mur .... d.	0457	0608	0651	0708	and hourly until	1808	1908	2008r	2108	2210
	Graz Hbf .... a.	0544	0655	0730	0755		1855	1955	2055r	2155	2257
0	**Graz** Hbf .... **1315** d.	0610	0710a	0740	0810		1910	2010	2110	2210	2310
9	Flughafen Graz ✈ ..... d.	0621	0721a	0751	0821		1921	2021	2121	2221	2321
35	Leibnitz .... d.	0649	0749a	0819	0849		1949	2049	2149	2249	2349
47	**Spielfeld-Straß 1315** a.	0659	0759a	0829	0859		1959	2059	2159	2259	2359

	Ⓐ			⚒	Ⓐ		❖				⚒
Spielfeld-Straß 1315 d.	0400	0430	0500	0525	0614	0700	and hourly until	1854	2000	2100	...
Leibnitz .... d.	0410	0440	0510	0535	0624	0710		1910	2010	2110	...
Flughafen Graz ✈ .. d.	0438	0508	0538	0603	0651	0738		1938	2038	2138	...
Graz Hbf .... **1315** a.	0450	0520	0550	0615	0703	0750		1950	2050	2150	...
Graz Hbf .... d.	...	...	0604a	0640a	0725	0805		2005	2105r	2205	2305
Bruck a. d. Mur ...... a.	...	...	0644a	0729a	0800	0851		2051	2151r	2251	2351

ÖBB *Intercitybus* services **GRAZ - KLAGENFURT**. Rail tickets valid. 1st and 2nd class. 🍷 in 1st class. Number of seats limited so reservation is recommended.

	🚌 Ⓐ	🚌	🚌		🚌	🚌	🚌	🚌	🚌	
Graz Hbf .... d.	0550	0750	0950	...	1150	1350	1550	1750	1950	...
Klagenfurt Hbf .... a.	0750	0950	1150	...	1350	1550	1750	1950	2150	...

	🚌 Ⓐ	🚌	🚌		🚌	🚌	🚌		🚌	🚌	
Klagenfurt Hbf ...... d.	0610	0810	1010	...	1210	1410	1610	...	1810	2010	...
Graz Hbf .... a.	0810	1010	1210	...	1410	1610	1810	...	2010	2210	...

A – 🛏 1, 2 cl., 🛌 2 cl. and (2) La Spezia - Milano - Wien and v.v.; 🛏 1, 2 cl., 🛌 2 cl. and (2) (**40294/40233**) Roma - Bologna - Venezia - Wien and v.v.
E – EMONA – (12) and ✕ Trieste - Ljubljana - Maribor - Spielfeld-Straß 🏛 - Graz - Wien (Table **91**).
F – CROATIA – (12) and ✕ Zagreb - Maribor - Spielfeld-Straß 🏛 - Graz - Wien (Table **91**).
L – From Lienz (Table **971**).
N – (12) and ✕ Graz - Wien - Břeclav 🏛 - Praha - Decin (Table **60**).
P – (12) and ✕ Graz - Wien - Břeclav 🏛 - Praha and v.v. (Table **60**).
Q – PORTA MORAVICA – (12) and ✕ Przemyśl - Kraków - Katowice - Wien - Graz and v.v. (Table **99**).
R – 🅁 for journeys from / to Italy.
S – (12) and ✕ Graz - Wien - Břeclav 🏛 - Brno (Table **60**).
V – (12) and ✕ Venezia - Udine - Tarvisio 🏛 - Wien (Table **88**).

a – Ⓐ only.
b – Also calls at Baden (d. 2318).
c – Train number **256** from July 1.
f – Arrives 0557.
r – ⚒ only.
w – ⑦ (also Dec. 26, Apr. 10, May 1, 29, June 6, Aug. 15; not Dec. 25, Apr. 9, 30, May 28, June 5, Aug. 13).
z – Also Dec. 26, Apr. 10, May, 1, 29; not Dec. 25, Apr. 9, 30, May 28.

❖ – Spielfeld-Straß d. 1053 (not 1100).
⊙ – For other local journeys see panel below main table.
▷ – For fast **ÖBB** *Intercitybus* services Graz - Klagenfurt and v.v., see panel below main table.

2nd class only — Local trains WIEN - WIENER NEUSTADT - MÜRZZUSCHLAG — 981

WIEN - WIENER NEUSTADT ⊡

km		⚒	Ⓐ						
0	**Wien** Floridsdorf .... d.	0409	0439	0509	0539		2309	2339	0009
5	**Wien** Praterstern....... d.	0418	0448	0518	0548	and at	2318	2348	0018
7	**Wien** Mitte .... d.	0422	0452	0522	0552	the same	2322	2352	0022
10	**Wien** Hbf .... d.	0429	0459	0529	0559	minutes	2329	2359	0029
14	**Wien** Meidling........... d.	0437	0507	0537	0607	past each	2337	0007	0037
26	Mödling .... d.	0449	0519	0549	0619	hour until	2349	0019	0049
37	Baden .... d.	0457	0527	0557	0627		2357	0027	0057
59	**Wiener Neustadt** Hbf a.	0521	0547	0621	0647		0021	0047	0121

			A							
Wiener Neustadt Hbf d.	0503		0733	0811	0838		2211	2238	2311	0011
Baden..........................d.	0523		0753	0833	0903	and at	2233	2303	2333	0033
Mödling.........................d.	0530	and every	0800	0840	0910	the same	2240	2310	2340	0040
Wien Meidling ....a.	0542	30 minutes	0812	0853	0923	minutes	2253	2323	2353	0053
Wien Hbf...................a.	0549	until	0819	0859	0929	past each	2259	2329	2359	0059
Wien Mitte.................a.	0556		0826	0906	0936	hour until	2306	2336	0006	0106
Wien Praterstern .....a.	0600		0830	0910	0940		2310	2340	0010	0110
Wien Floridsdorf......a.	0609		0839	0919	0949		2319	2349	0019	0119

(WIEN -) WIENER NEUSTADT - PAYERBACH-REICHENAU - MÜRZZUSCHLAG ⊡

km		Ⓒ	Ⓐ		Ⓒ B	Ⓐ									Ⓒ	Ⓐ		Ⓐ	Ⓒ	Ⓐ		Ⓒ	Ⓐ			Ⓒ
	Wien Hbf .... d.	0529	0538	...	0725	0759	...	0929	...	1129	...	1329	...	...	1529	1538	...	1718	1729	1808	...	1829	1852	2029	...	2225
	Wien Meidling........... d.	0537	0545	...	0731	0807	...	0937	...	1137	...	1337	...	...	1537	1545	...	1725	1737	1815	...	1837	1900	2037	...	2231
	Baden .... d.	0557	0606	...	|	|	...	0957	...	1157	...	1357	...	...	1557	1606	...	|	1757	1836	...	1857	|	2057	...	2245
	Wiener Neustadt Hbf a.	0621	0624	...	0755	0847	...	1021	...	1221	...	1421	...	...	1621	1624	...	1750	1821	1854	...	1921	1927	2121	...	2257
0	**Wiener Neustadt** Hbf d.	0635	0635	...	0758	0902	...	1035	...	1235	...	1435	...	...	1635	1635	...	1752	1835	1902	...	1935	1935	2135	...	2335
14	Neunkirchen NÖ .... d.	0648	0648	...	0810	0915	...	1048	...	1248	...	1448	...	...	1648	1648	...	|	1848	1915	...	1948	1948	2148	...	2348
27	Gloggnitz .... d.	0700	0700	...	0818	0926	...	1100	...	1300	...	1500	...	...	1700	1700	...	1810	1900	1926	...	2000	2000	2200	...	0000
34	Payerbach-Reichenau d.	0709	0709	0739	0827	0936	0939	1109	1139	1309	1339	1509	1539	...	1709	1709	1739	1818	1909	1936	1939	2009	2009	2209	2212	0010
55	Semmering .... a.	...	...	0807	0854	...	1007	...	1207	...	1407	...	1607	...	...	...	1807	1841	...	...	2007	...	...	...	2240	0039
69	**Mürzzuschlag** .... a.	...	...	0823	0912	...	1023	...	1223	...	1423	...	1623	...	...	...	1823	1856	...	...	2023	...	...	...	2256	0055

	Ⓐ	Ⓐ	Ⓒ	G	Ⓐ G		Ⓒ	Ⓐ	⑥									Ⓐ		Ⓒ B	Ⓐ	Ⓒ				
Mürzzuschlag........... d.	0345	...	...	0525v	0606	...	0636	...	...	0836	...	1036	...	1236	...	1436	...	1636	...	1650	...	...	1836	...	2100	...
Semmering .... d.	0400	...	...	0536	0621	...	0651	...	...	0851	...	1051	...	1251	...	1451	...	1651	...	1707	...	...	1851	...	2115	...
Payerbach-Reichenau d.	0427	0525	0525	0602	0650	0654	0723	0727	0753	0923	0953	1123	1153	1323	1353	1523	1553	1723	1723	1734	1753	1753	1923	1953	2143	2153
Gloggnitz .... d.	0436	0534	0534	0610	...	0703	...	0736	0802	...	1002	...	1202	...	1402	...	1602	...	1732	1741	1802	1802	...	2002	...	2202
Neunkirchen NÖ .... d.	0446	0546	0546	|	...	0714	...	0747	0813	...	1013	...	1213	...	1413	...	1613	...	1743	1749	1813	1813	...	2013	...	2213
Wiener Neustadt Hbf a.	0458	0558	0558	0626	...	0725	...	0759	0825	...	1025	...	1225	...	1425	...	1625	...	1755	1758	1825	1825	...	2025	...	2225
Wiener Neustadt Hbf d.	0500	0600	0603	0630	...	0733	...	0802	0838	...	1038	...	1238	...	1438	...	1635	...	1807	1759	1835	1838	...	2035	...	2238
Baden.......................... d.	|	0614	0623	|	...	0753	...	|	0903	...	1103	...	1303	...	1503	...	1653r	...	|	|	1853	1903	...	2053t	...	2303
Wien Meidling............ a.	0529	0629	0642	0655	...	0812	...	0829	0923	...	1123	...	1323	...	1523	...	1713r	...	1835	1829	1913	1923	...	2113t	...	2323
Wien Hbf.................... a.	0536	0638	0649	0702	...	0819	...	0836	0929	...	1129	...	1329	...	1529	...	1719r	...	1842	1836	1919	1929	...	2119t	...	2329

B – From / to Bratislava-Petržalka (Table **997**).
G – From Graz on Ⓐ (Table **980**).

r – 10 minutes later on Ⓒ.
t – 10 minutes later on †.
v – 0521 on Ⓒ.

⊡ – Only selected services are shown Wien Floridsdorf - Wiener Neustadt - Payerbach-Reichenau and v.v. Some services may only run on certain dates - please check locally. Additional journeys Wien Floridsdorf - Wiener Neustadt are shown in Tables **982** and **983**. See Table **980** for long-distance services.

2nd class only; Austrian Holiday dates apply — Local trains WIEN - BŘECLAV — 982

See Table **1150** for other fast international services

km				Ⓐ		E		E		E	Ⓐ		E	Ⓐ		Ⓐ	E	Ⓐ		Ⓐ	E				
	Wiener Neustadt Hbf. 980/1 d.	....	0515a	0615	0715a	0811	0911	1011	1111	1211	1238	1311	1411	1438	1511	1538	1611	1638	1711	1738	1811	1911	2011	2111	2211
	Baden .... 981 d.	...	0538a	0638	0738a	0833	0933	1033	1133	1233	1303	1333	1433	1503	1533	1603	1633	1703	1733	1803	1833	1933	2033	2133	2233
0	**Wien** Meidling........... 980/1 d.	0457	0557	0700	0800	0854	0954	1054	1154	1254	1324	1354	1454	1524	1554	1624	1654	1724	1754	1824	1854	1954	2054	2154	2254
4	**Wien** Hbf .... 980/1 d.	0503	0603	0706	0806	0900	1000	1100	1200	1300	1330	1400	1500	1530	1600	1630	1700	1730	1800	1830	1900	2000	2100	2200	2300
7	**Wien** Mitte .... 981 d.	0510	0610	0713	0813	0907	1007	1107	1207	1307	1337	1407	1507	1537	1607	1637	1707	1737	1807	1837	1907	2007	2107	2207	2307
9	**Wien** Praterstern.......... 981 d.	0514	0614	0717	0817	0911	1011	1111	1211	1311	1341	1411	1511	1541	1611	1641	1711	1741	1811	1841	1911	2011	2111	2211	2311
14	**Wien** Floridsdorf .... 981 d.	0523	0623	0726	0826	0920	1020	1120	1220	1320	1350	1420	1520	1550	1620	1650	1720	1750	1820	1850	1920	2020	2120	2220	2320
40	Gänserndorf.......................d.	0545	0645	0748	0848	0942	1042	1142	1242	1342	1412	1442	1542	1612	1642	1712	1742	1812	1842	1913	1942	2042	2142	2242	2342
74	Hohenau 🛃 ....a.	0617	0718	0820	0920	1014	1114	1214	1314	1414	1444	1514	1614	1644	1714	1736	1814	1836	1914	1936	2014	2114	2214	2314	0014
92	**Břeclav** 🛃 ....a.	0632	0746	0835	0935	1029	1129	1229	1329	1429	...	1529	1629	...	1729	...	1829	...	1929	...	2029	2129	...	...	0029

	Ⓐ	Ⓐ		Ⓐ		Ⓒ	Ⓐ			D		D		D		Ⓐ	D		Ⓐ	D		D		Ⓐ	
Břeclav 🛃........................... d.	0427	...	...	0557	...	0627	0657	0727	0827	0927	1027	1127	1227	1327	1427	...	1527	1627	...	1727	1827	1927	2027	2127	2227
Hohenau 🛃 .... d.	0442	0503	0533	0612	0642	0642	0712	0742	0842	0942	1042	1142	1242	1342	1442	1512	1542	1642	1716	1742	1842	1942	2042	2142	2242
Gänserndorf.......................... d.	0515	0545	0615	0645	0715	0715	0745	0815	0915	1015	1115	1215	1315	1415	1515	1545	1615	1715	1741	1815	1915	2015	2115	2215	2315
Wien Floridsdorf .... 981 a.	0538	0608	0638	0708	0738	0738	0808	0838	0938	1038	1138	1238	1338	1438	1538	1608	1638	1738	1808	1838	1938	2038	2138	2238	2338
Wien Praterstern .... 981 a.	0546	0616	0646	0716	0746	0746	0816	0846	0946	1046	1146	1246	1346	1446	1546	1616	1646	1746	1816	1846	1946	2046	2146	2246	2346
Wien Mitte..................... 981 a.	0550	0620	0650	0720	0750	0750	0820	0850	0950	1050	1150	1250	1350	1450	1550	1620	1650	1750	1820	1850	1950	2050	2150	2250	2350
Wien Hbf.................... 980/1 a.	0559	0629	0659	0729	0759	0759	0829	0859	0959	1059	1159	1259	1359	1459	1559	1629	1659	1759	1829	1859	1959	2059	2159	2259	2359
Wien Meidling............ 980/1 a.	0604	0634	0704	0734	0804	0804	0834	0904	1004	1104	1204	1304	1404	1504	1604	1634	1704	1804	1834	1904	2004	2104	2204	2304	0004
Baden........................... 981 a.	0627	0657	0727	0757	0827	0827	0857	0927	1027	1127	1227	1327	1427	1527	1627	1657	1727	1827	1857	1927	2027	2127	2227	2327	0027
Wiener Neustadt Hbf 980/1 a.	0649	0721	0749	0821	0849	0849	0921	0949	1049	1149	1249	1349	1449	1549	1649	1721	1749	1849	1921	1949	2049	2149	2249	2349	0049

D – Břeclav - Gänserndorf on Ⓐ only; Gänserndorf - Wiener Neustadt daily.
E – Wiener Neustadt - Gänserndorf daily; Gänserndorf - Břeclav on Ⓐ only.

a – Ⓐ only.

2nd class only; Austrian holiday dates apply — WIEN - RETZ - ZNOJMO — 983

km		⚒											Ⓐ		Ⓐ		Ⓐ		Ⓐ						
	Wiener Neustadt Hbf 980/1 d.	...	0503	0603	0703	0808r	0908a	...	...	...	...	...	...	1508a	1535	1608a	1635	1708a	1735	1808a	1908a	2008a	...	...	...
	Baden .... 981 d.	...	0523	0623	0723	0823r	0923a	...	...	...	...	...	...	1523a	1553	1623a	1653	1723a	1753	1823a	1923a	2023a	...	...	...
0	**Wien** Meidling........... 980/1 d.	...	0544	0644	0744	0844	0944	1044	1144	1244	1344	1444	1514	1544	1614	1644	1714	1744	1814	1844	1944	2044	2144	2244	2344
4	**Wien** Hbf .... 980/1 d.	...	0550	0650	0750	0850	0950	1050	1150	1250	1350	1450	1520	1550	1620	1650	1720	1750	1820	1850	1950	2050	2150	2250	2350
7	**Wien** Mitte .... 981 d.	...	0557	0657	0757	0857	0957	1057	1157	1257	1357	1457	1527	1557	1627	1657	1727	1757	1827	1857	1957	2057	2157	2257	2357
9	**Wien** Praterstern.......... 981 d.	...	0601	0701	0801	0901	1001	1101	1201	1301	1401	1501	1531	1601	1631	1701	1731	1801	1831	1901	2001	2101	2201	2301	0001
14	**Wien** Floridsdorf .... 981 d.	...	0611	0711	0811	0911	1011	1111	1211	1311	1411	1511	1541	1611	1641	1711	1741	1811	1841	1911	2011	2111	2211	2311	0011
34	Stockerau ....d.	...	0628	0728	0828	0928	1028	1128	1228	1328	1428	1528	1601	1628	1701	1728	1801	1828	1901	1928	2028	2128	2228	2328	0028
60	Hollabrunn ....d.	...	0645	0745	0845	0945	1045	1145	1245	1345	1445	1545	1623	1645	1723	1745	1823	1845	1923	1945	2045	2145	2245	2354	0054
90	**Retz**..................................a.	...	0712	0812	0912	1012	1112	1212	1312	1412	1512	1612	1652	1712	1752	1812	1852	1912	1952	2012	2112	2212	2312	0020	0120
90	**Retz** 🛃 ....d.	0620	...	0817	...	1017	...	1217	...	1417	...	1617	...	...	...	1817	...	...	...	2017	...	...	...	...	...
96	Šatov 🛃 ....d.	0628	...	0825	...	1025	...	1225	...	1425	...	1625	...	...	...	1825	...	...	...	2025	...	...	...	...	...
107	**Znojmo** ....a.	0638	...	0836	...	1036	...	1236	...	1436	...	1636	...	...	...	1836	...	...	...	2036	...	...	...	...	...

	Ⓐ	Ⓐ	Ⓐ	⚒	Ⓒ	Ⓐ	Ⓐ	Ⓒ		⚒															
Znojmo .... d.	...	...	...	...	...	...	0555	...	...	0655	...	0857	...	1057	...	1257	...	1457	...	1657	...	1857	...	2057	...
Šatov 🛃 .... d.	...	...	...	...	...	...	0606	...	...	0706	...	0906	...	1106	...	1306	...	1506	...	1706	...	1906	...	2106	...
Retz 🛃 .... a.	...	...	...	...	...	...	0614	...	...	0714	...	0914	...	1114	...	1314	...	1514	...	1714	...	1914	...	2114	...
Retz .... d.	0402	0434	0510	0510	0514h	0530	0616	0616	0716	0716	0816	0916	1016	1116	1216	1316	1416	1516	1616	1716	1816	1916	2016	2116	2216
Hollabrunn .... d.	0430	0502	0539	0539	0543	0558	0645	0645	0745	0745	0845	0945	1045	1145	1245	1345	1445	1545	1645	1745	1845	1945	2045	2145	2245
Stockerau .... d.	0447	0527	0556	0556	0614	0625	0702	0702	0802	0802	0902	1002	1102	1202	1302	1402	1502	1602	1702	1802	1902	2002	2102	2202	2302
Wien Floridsdorf .... 981 a.	0502	0547	0617	0617	0641	0647	0717	0717	0817	0817	0917	1017	1117	1217	1317	1417	1517	1617	1717	1817	1917	2017	2117	2217	2317
Wien Praterstern .... 981 a.	0510	0556	0626	...	0649	0656	0726	0726	0826	0826	0926	1026	1126	1226	1326	1426	1526	1626	1726	1826	1926	2026	2126	2226	2326
Wien Mitte..................... 981 a.	0514	0600	0630	...	0653	0700	0730	0730	0830	0830	0930	1030	1130	1230	1330	1430	1530	1630	1730	1830	1930	2030	2130	2230	2330
Wien Hbf.................... 980/1 a.	0522	0607	0637	...	0701	0707	0737	0737	0837	0837	0937	1037	1137	1237	1337	1437	1537	1637	1737	1837	1937	2037	2137	2237	2337
Wien Meidling............ 980/1 a.	0528	0614	0644	...	0707	0714	0744	0744	0844	0844	0944	1044	1144	1244	1344	1444	1544	1644	1744	1844	1944	2044	2144	2244	2344
Baden........................... 981 a.	|	0636	0706	...	...	0736	0806	0806k	...	...	...	...	...	...	...	1506a	1606a	1706a	1806a	1906a	2006a	...	...	...	...
Wiener Neustadt Hbf 980/1 a.	0559	0652	0724	...	...	0752	0824	0824k	...	...	...	...	...	...	...	1524a	1624a	1724a	1824a	1924a	2024a	...	...	...	...

a – Ⓐ only. h – † only. k – ⑥ only. r – ⚒ only.

984 WIENER NEUSTADT - PUCHBERG am Schneeberg - HOCHSCHNEEBERG — 2nd class only

WIENER NEUSTADT - **PUCHBERG** am Schneeberg *28 km.* Journey time: 45 – 48 minutes.

From Wiener Neustadt at 0039 Ⓒ, 0637 Ⓒ, 0737, 0837, 0937 Ⓒ, 1037 and hourly until 2237; then 2339 ⑦–④.

From Puchberg at 0406 Ⓐ, 0452 Ⓐ, 0522 Ⓐ, 0536 Ⓒ, 0552 Ⓐ, 0622 Ⓐ, 0636 Ⓒ, 0645 Ⓐ, 0736, 0836 and hourly until 2136.

PUCHBERG am Schneeberg - **HOCHSCHNEEBERG** *Schneebergbahn* (narrow-gauge rack railway). *9 km.* Journey time: ± 40 minutes. **Service shown is for 2022 - 2023 service to be advised.** Services operate April 30 - Nov. 13, **subject to demand and weather conditions.** Operator**: NÖ Schneebergbahn GmbH, Bahnhofplatz 1, A-2734 Puchberg.** ✆ +43 (0) 2636 3661 20.

From Puchberg at 0900, 1030, 1200, 1430. **From Hochschneeberg** at 0945, 1115, 1345, 1515. Additional trains operate during July and August, also at other times when there is sufficient demand. A steam service operates on † July 3 - August 28: also Aug. 15. Departs Puchberg 1053, departs Hochschneeberg 1517 (extended journey time; special fares apply).

985 FLUGHAFEN WIEN ✈ Schwechat — *CAT* ★; S-Bahn (2nd class only)

km						★		★		★			★		★		★						
0	**Wien** Floridsdorf d.	0406	0436	...	0506	...	0536	...	0606	...	0636	and at the same	...	2206	...	2236	...	2306	...	2336	0006	...	0036
5	**Wien** Praterstern d.	0415	0445	...	0515	...	0545	...	0615	...	0645	minutes past	...	2215	...	2245	...	2315	...	2345	0015	...	0045
7	**Wien** Mitte d.	0419	0449	...	0519	0537	0549	0607	0619	0637	0649	each hour until	2207	2219	2237	2249	2307	2319	...	2349	0019	...	0049
26	**Flughafen Wien** ✈ a.	0441	0511	...	0541	0553	0611	0623	0641	0653	0711		2223	2241	2253	2311	2323	2341	...	0011	0041	...	0111

				★		★		★		★		★		★			★		★		★		
Flughafen Wien ✈ d.	0449	0519	0549	0608	0619	0638	0646	0708	0719	0738	0746	0808	0819	0838	0849	and at the same	2238	2319	2308	2349	2338	0019	0049
Wien Mitte d.	0513	0543	0613	0624	0643	0654	0710	0724	0743	0754	0810	0824	0843	0854	0913	minutes past	2254	2343	2324	0013	2354	0043	0113
Wien Praterstern d.	0517	0547	0617	...	0647	...	0714	...	0747	...	0814	...	0847	...	0917	each hour until	...	2347	...	0017	...	0047	0117
Wien Floridsdorf a.	0525	0555	0625	...	0655	...	0722	...	0755	...	0822	...	0855	...	0925		...	2355	...	0025	...	0055	0125

★ – *City Airport Train (CAT).* Non-stop service with special fares.

RJ trains **Wien Hbf** - **Flughafen Wien** ✈ and v.v. Journey time: 15 – 17 minutes. Most trains run from / to Salzburg, Linz and St Pölten (Table **950**) or Graz (Table **980**).

From Wien Hbf at 0528, 0542, 0612, 0642, 0712, 0742, 0812, 0840, 0912, 0942, 1012, 1040, 1112, 1142, 1212, 1240, 1312, 1328, 1342, 1412, 1440, 1512, 1540, 1612, 1640, 1712, 1742, 1812, 1840, 1912, 1940, 2012, 2028, 2040, 2112, 2142 and 2212. **From Flughafen Wien** ✈ at 0615, 0633, 0703, 0733 and at 03 and 33 minutes past each hour until until 2203, 2233, 2303.

🚌 *Vienna Airport Lines*: Wien Westbahnhof (Europaplatz) – Flughafen Wien ✈ and v.v. Journey time: 40 minutes.

🚌 From **Wien Westbahnhof**: 0030, 0130, 0230, 0300, 0330, 0400, 0430 and hourly until 2230. 🚌 From **Flughafen Wien** ✈: 0015, 0115, 0215, 0615 and hourly until 2315.

🚌 Slovak Lines: **Bratislava**, AS Mlynské nivy (bus station) – **Flughafen Wien** ✈ and v.v. Journey time: 60 minutes.
Reservation recommended ✆ +43 (0) 810 222333-6 or +421 2 55422734. Please note that a much reduced service operates on Dec. 24, 25, 26, 31, Jan. 1.

🚌 From **Bratislava** AS Mlynské nivy at 0300, 0400, 0600, 0700, 0800 and hourly 1600, 1800, 1900, 2000.

🚌 From **Flughafen Wien** ✈ at 0355, 0530, 0830, 0930, 1030 and hourly until 1830, 2030, 2130, 2250.

986 GRAZ - SZENTGOTTHÁRD - SZOMBATHELY — ÖBB, GySEV •; 2nd class only

km			W		A ✗	W						⊖		Ⓐ		Ⓐ	N	Ⓐ				Ⓐ		⚒		⚒	
0	**Graz** Hbf d.	0607	0707	0807	0837	0907	1008	1107	1207	1307	1407	1437	1507	1537	1607	1637	1707	1738	1807	1837	1907	1937	2007	2107	2207	2307	0007
29	Gleisdorf d.	0650	0749	0850	0914	0950	1050	1150	1250	1350	1450	1513	1550	1613	1650	1713	1750	1813	1850	1913	1950	2013	2050	2150	2249	2345	0045
53	Feldbach d.	0714	0814	0914	0929	1014	1114	1214	1314	1414	1514	1530	1614	1630	1714	1730	1814	1830	1914	1930	2014	2033	2114	2214	2310	0006	0106
62	Fehring d.	0727	0822	0924	0936	1022	1124	1227z	1326	1431j	1524	1538	1622	1637	1724	1737	1822	1842	1924	1942v	2022	2042	2130t	2222	2318	0015	0115
82	**Szentgotthárd** 🏛 a.	0748	...	0945	0956	...	1145	1248	1347	1452a	1545c	1556	...	*1703*	1745c	*1803*	...	...	1945c	2003a	...	2103	2151	...	...	...	...

	Ⓐ	Ⓑ	Ⓐ	Ⓐ	⑥	†	Ⓐ	⚒	Ⓐ H			N		N	⊖		Ⓐ	Ⓒ					Wg	B ✗	Ⓐ		
Szentgotthárd 🏛 d.	...	*0450*	0450a	*0534*	...	...	0618	*0620*	0642k	...	...	0818	...	1018	...	1206	1304	1409	1418	*1509*a	1618	1718a	1818	...	2006	...	2108
Fehring d.	0406	0514	0541	0558	0616	0618	0641	0644	0704	0733	0741	0841	0941	1041	1141	1226	1326z	1432	1441	1541	1641	1741	1841	1941	2025	2041	2141h
Feldbach d.	0416	0523	0550	0606	0626	0627	0650	0654	0715	0741	0750	0850	0950	1050	1150	1234	1350r	1450t	1450	1550	1650	1750	1850	1950	2034	2050	2153
Gleisdorf d.	0439	0542	0613	0626	0650	0655	0713	0714	0738	0802	0813	0914	1013	1113	1213	1250	1413	1513	1513	1613	1713	1813	1913	2013	2050	2113	2213
Graz Hbf a.	0515	0615	0653	0704	0724	0734	0753	0748	0816	0836	0853	0953	1053	1153	1253	1320	1453	1553	1553	1653	1753	1853	1953	2053	2120	2153	2253

SZENTGOTTHÁRD - SZOMBATHELY •

km				⊖		Ⓐ			A ✗				Ⓐ		Ⓐ		Ⓐ	⊖	Ⓐ							
0	**Szentgotthárd** 🏛 d.	0401	0431	0501	0606	0636	0706	0806	1006	1206	...	1306	1336	1406	1436	1506	1536	1606	1636	1706	1806	1906	...	2006	2106	2236
28	Körmend d.	0425	0455	0525	0630	0700	0730	0830	1030	1230	...	1330	1400	1430	1500	1530	1600	1630	1700	1730	1830	1930	...	2030	2130	2300
64	**Szombathely** a.	0448	0518	0547	0653	0723	0753	0853	1053	1253	...	1353	1423	1453	1523	1553	1623	1653	1723	1753	1853	1953	...	2053	2153	2323
	Sopron **1233** a.	0556	...	...	...	...	0851	0951	...	1351	...	1451	...	1551	...	1651	...	...	...	1851	1951	2051	...	2151	...	...

				Ⓐ				⊖	Ⓐ		Ⓐ		Ⓐ		Ⓐ			Ⓐ			B ✗				⊖	
Sopron **1233** d.	...	0408	0450	...	0556	...	0808	...	...	1208	...	1308	...	1408	...	...	1508	...	1608	1706	...	...	1906	...	...	...
Szombathely d.	0431	0501	0606	0636	0706	...	0906	1106	1236	1306	1336	1406	1436	1506	1536	...	1606	1636	1706	1806	1906	...	2006	2036	2106	2236
Körmend d.	0455	0525	0630	0700	0730	...	0930	1130	1300	1330	1400	1430	1500	1530	1600	...	1630	1700	1730	1830	1930	...	2030	2100	2130	2300
Szentgotthárd 🏛 a.	0519	0549	0654	0724	0754	...	0954	1154	1324	1354	1424	1454	1524	1554	1624	...	1654	1724	1754	1854	1954	...	2054	2124	2154	2324

A – 🚃12 and 🍷 Ljubljana (*IC* **311**) - Graz - Szentgotthárd - Budapest.
B – 🚃12 and 🍷 Budapest (*IC* **310**) - Szentgotthárd - Graz - Ljubljana.
H – From Hartberg (Table **995**).
N – To / from Wiener Neustadt on dates shown in Table **995**.
W – To / from Wiener Neustadt (Table **995**).

a – Ⓐ only.
c – Ⓒ only.
g – ⑤⑥†.
h – Arrives 2129.
j – Arrives 1422.
k – ⑥ only.
r – Arrives 1335 on Ⓐ.
t – Arrives 8 minutes earlier.
v – Arrives 1937.
z – Arrives 1325; departs 1341 on Ⓒ.
◇ – Change trains at Fehring on ⑤ (Fehring d. *1546*, Szentgotthárd a. *1607*)
⊖ – *IC* train to / from Budapest (Tables **1250/2**). 🅁 and supplement payable.
✗ – 🅁 and supplement payable in Hungary.
• – Szentgotthárd - Szombathely operated by Győr-Sopron-Ebenfurti Vasút.

990 WIEN - GMÜND - ČESKÉ VELENICE — 2nd class only

km					A							ⒸA		Ⓐ		Ⓒ	Ⓐ		Ⓐ		Ⓒ	Ⓐ				
0	**Wien** Franz-Josefs-Bf **991/3** d.	0628	0732	0828	0900	0932	1028	1132	1228	1328	1428	1500	1528	1616	1628	1628	1658	1728	1816	1828	1828	1859	1928	2028	2128	2228
1	Wien Spittelau ● **991/3** d.	0631	0735	0831	0903	0935	1031	1135	1231	1331	1431	1503	1531	1619	1631	1631	1701	1731	1818	1831	1831	1902	1931	2031	2131	2231
3	Wien Heiligenstadt △ **991/3** d.	0634	0738	0834	0906	0938	1034	1138	1234	1334	1434	1506	1534	1622	1634	1634	1705	1734	1821	1834	1834	1906	1934	2034	2134	2234
33	Tulln a. d. Donau **991/3** d.	0657	0759	0857	0930	0959	1057	1159	1257	1357	1457	1527	1557	|	1657	1657	1728	1757	1844	1857	1857	1927	1957	2057	2157	2257
44	Absdorf-Hippersdorf **991** d.	0705	0808	0905	|	1008	1105	1208	1305	1405	1505	|	1605	|	1705	1705	|	1806	|	1905	1905	|	2006	2105	2205	2305
79	Eggenburg d.	0734	0838	0934	1003	1038	1134	1238	1334	1438	1534	1601	1637	1715	1734	1734	1802	1837	1913	1934	1934	2002	2037	2134	2234	2334
89	Sigmundsherberg d.	0742	0846	0942	1014	1046	1142	1246	1342	1446	1542	1614	1646	1723	1741	1742	1813	1846	1922	1941	1942	2014	2046	2144	2242	2342
121	Göpfritz an der Wild d.	0807	0907c	1007	1036	...	1207	...	1407	...	1607	1635	1711a	1748	...	1806	1837	1911a	1947	...	2006	2037f	2110a	2209	2307a	0007r
138	Schwarzenau d.	0820	0919c	1020	1049	...	1220	...	1420	...	1620	1648	1729a	1801	...	1821	1849	1933a	2001	...	2021	2050f	2123a	2222	2321a	0020r
162	**Gmünd** NÖ a.	0842	0938c	1042	1109	...	1242	...	1442	...	1642	1706	1751a	1822	...	1842	1911	1956a	2022	...	2042	2112f	2145a	2244	2344a	0042r
162	**Gmünd** NÖ 🏛 ⊡ d.	0845	...	1046	1112	...	1245	...	1445	...	1645	1709	...	1825	...	1845	...	...	2025	...	2045	...	...	...	...	...
164	**České Velenice** 🏛 ⊡ a.	0849	...	1050	1116	...	1249	...	1449	...	1649	1713	...	1829	...	1849	...	...	2029	...	2049	...	...	...	...	...

	Ⓐ	⚒		Ⓐ	Ⓐ		Ⓐ						ⒸA						Ⓐ	Ⓒ		Ⓒ	Ⓐ	Ⓒ		A
České Velenice 🏛 ⊡ d.	...	...	...	...	...	...	...	0602	0707	...	0907	...	1039	1107	...	1307	...	1507	...	...	1701	...	...	...	1905	2039
Gmünd NÖ 🏛 ⊡ a.	...	...	...	...	...	...	...	0606	0711	...	0911	...	1042	1111	...	1311	...	1511	...	...	1705	...	...	...	1909	2042
Gmünd NÖ d.	...	0351	...	0430	...	0511	0546	0609	0714	...	0914	...	1045	1114	...	1314	...	1514	...	...	1708	1802	...	...	1912	2045
Schwarzenau d.	...	0412	...	0450	...	0534	0605	0631	0735	...	0935	...	1105	1135	...	1335	...	1535	...	...	1733	1821	...	...	1933	2108
Göpfritz an der Wild d.	...	0426	...	0502	...	0548	0617	0645	0749	...	0949	...	1120	1149	...	1349	...	1549	...	...	1748	1834	...	...	1948	2122
Sigmundsherberg d.	0409	0449	0509	0522	0539	0614	0639	0710	0814	0909	1014	1109	1143	1214	1309	1414	1509	1614	1655	1709	1813	1855	1855	1909	2014	2144
Eggenburg d.	0419	0457	0518	0530	0548	0622	0648	0718	0822	0918	1022	1118	1154	1222	1318	1422	1518	1622	1718	1718	1822	1903	1918t	1918	2022	2155
Absdorf-Hippersdorf **991** d.	0449	|	0546	|	0616	0651	0718	0748	0852	0948	1052	1148	|	1252	1348	1455	1548	1652	1748	1748	1852	|	1948	1948	2052	2227
Tulln a. d. Donau **991/3** d.	0458	|	0554	|	0624	0659	0727	0757	0901	0958	1101	1158	1227	1301	1358	1504	1558	1701	1758	1758	1901	|	1958	1958	2101	|
Wien Heiligenstadt △ **991/3** d.	0520	0554	0620	0624	0620	0724	0749	0820	0923	1020	1123	1220	1249	1323	1420	1526	1620	1723	1820	1820	1923	1956	2020	2020	2123	2249
Wien Spittelau ● **991/3** d.	0523	0557	0623	0627	0653	0727	0753	0823	0926	1023	1126	1223	1252	1326	1423	1529	1623	1726	1823	1823	1926	2000	2023	2023	2126	2252
Wien Franz-Josefs-Bf **991/3** a.	0525	0559	0625	0629	0655	0729	0755	0825	0928	1025	1128	1225	1254	1328	1425	1531	1625	1728	1825	1825	1928	2002	2025	2025	2128	2254

A – To / from Praha (Table **1130**).

a – Ⓐ only.
b – Not Jan. 6.
c – Ⓒ only.
f – Not ⑤.
r – ⑤⑥⑦ mornings.
t – Arrives 1904.

⊡ – Additional trains Gmünd - České Velenice and v.v.: **From Gmünd** at 0522, 0635 and 1112. **From České Velenice** at 2034 Ⓐ.
△ – S-Bahn (Line **S45**) trains run every 10 – 15 minutes from / to Wien Hütteldorf (journey: 21 – 23 minutes).
● – Direct U-Bahn links: Line **U4** – Wien Mitte - Spittelau. Line **U6** – Wien Meidling - Westbahnhof - Spittelau - Floridsdorf.

WIEN - KREMS an der Donau - EMMERSDORF 991

nd class only

km		Ⓐ						⑤g		Ⓐ		Ⓐ	Ⓐ	Ⓒ	Ⓐ		Ⓐ	Ⓐ	Ⓒ	Ⓐ		Ⓑb				
0	**Wien** Franz-Josefs-Bf **990/3** d.	0505	0605	0705	0805	and	1305	1333	1405	1433	1505	1533	1601	1605	1633	1705	1733	1801	1805	1833	1905	1933	2005	and	2305	0005
1	Wien Spittelau ...... ● **990/3** d.	0507	0607	0707	0807	hourly	1307	1336	1407	1436	1507	1536	1604	1607	1636	1707	1736	1804	1807	1836	1907	1936	2007	hourly	2307	0007
3	Wien Heiligenstadt △ **990/3** d.	0510	0610	0710	0810	until	1310	1339	1410	1439	1510	1539	1608	1610	1639	1710	1739	1808	1810	1839	1910	1939	2010	until	2310	0010
33	Tulln a. d. Donau .... **990/3** d.	0533	0633	0733	0833		1333	1401	1433	1501	1533	1601	1633	1633	1701	1733	1801	1833	1833	1901	1933	2001	2033		2333	0033
44	Absdorf-Hippersdorf...... **990** d.	0541	0641	0741	0841		1341	1409	1441	1509	1541	1609	1641	1641	1709	1741	1809	1841	1841	1909	1941	2009	2041		2341	0041
76	**Krems** a. d. Donau.............. a.	0614	0716	0814	0914		1414	1436	1514	1536	1614	1636	1714	1714	1736	1814	1836	1914	1914	1936	2014	2036	2114		0014	0114

	Ⓐ		Ⓐ		Ⓐ	Ⓐ			Ⓐ		Ⓐ							Ⓐc	Ⓒd							
rems a. d. Donau .... d.	0429	0451	0529	0551	0616	0629	0651	0729	0751	...	0829	0851	0951	1051	1151	1251	...	1343	1351	1451	1551	1651	1751	and	2151	2251
bsdorf-Hippersdorf...... **990** d.	0454	0523	0555	0625	0642	0655	0723	0754	0823	...	0856	0923	1023	1123	1223	1323	...	1423	1423	1523	1623	1723	1823	hourly	2223	2323
ulln a. d. Donau .... **990/3** d.	0503	0532	0603	0633	0653	0703	0734	0803	0831	...	0905	0931	1031	1131	1231	1331	...	1431	1431	1531	1631	1731	1831	until	2231	2331
ien Heiligenstadt . △ **990/3** d.	0524	0558	0628	0658	0720	0728	0755	0824	0852	...	0927	0952	1052	1152	1252	1352	...	1452	1452	1552	1652	1752	1852		2252	2352
ien Spittelau .... ● **990/3** d.	0528	0601	0631	0701	0723	0731	0758	0828	0856	...	0930	0956	1056	1156	1256	1356	...	1456	1456	1556	1656	1756	1856		2256	2356
ien Franz-Josefs-Bf **990/3** a.	0530	0603	0633	0703	0725	0733	0800	0830	0858	...	0932	0958	1058	1158	1258	1358	...	1458	1458	1558	1658	1758	1858		2258	2358

KREMS - EMMERSDORF ⊠

km		R		R		R		R		
0	**Krems** an der Donau............d.	0920	...	1120	...	1320	...	1620	...	...
18	**Spitz** an der Donau ....d.	0951	...	1151	...	1351	...	1650	...	...
34	**Emmersdorf** an der Donau ..a.	1010	...	1210	...	1410	...	1705	...	...

	R		R		R		R		
Emmersdorf an der Donau d.	1020	...	1220	...	1450	...	1750	...	...
Spitz an der Donau ....d.	1040	...	1240	...	1510	...	1810	...	...
Krems an der Donau.........a.	1110	...	1310	...	1540	...	1840	...	...

– Ⓒ to May 21; daily May 27 - Nov. 1. Special fares apply.

b – Not Dec. 25, Apr. 9, 30, May 28.
c – Ⓐ to June 30 and from Sept. 4.
d – Ⓒ (daily July 1 - Sept. 3).
g – Not Jan. 6.

● – Direct U-bahn links: Line **U4** – Wien Mitte - Spittelau. Line **U6** – Wien Meidling - Westbahnhof - Spittelau - Floridsdorf.
△ – S-Bahn trains run every 10 – 15 minutes from / to Wien Hütteldorf (journey: 21 – 23 minutes).
⊠ – Operated by NÖVOG (Wachaubahn). ✆ +43 (0) 2742 360 990-99. www.wachaubahn.at

ST PÖLTEN - KREMS and TULLN 993

2nd class only

ST PÖLTEN - KREMS

km					Ⓐ		Ⓐ				Ⓐ		Ⓐ		Ⓐ		Ⓐ		Ⓐ		Ⓐ		Ⓐ			
0	**St Pölten** Hbf .... d.	0009	...	0506	0538	0606	0638	0706	and	1206	1238	1306	1338	1406	1438	1506	1538	1606	1638	1706	1738	1806	1838	1906	and	2306
10	Herzogenburg .... d.	0018	...	0514	0546	0614	0646	0714	hourly	1214	1247	1314	1347	1414	1447	1514	1547	1614	1647	1714	1747	1814	1847	1914	hourly	2314
30	**Krems** a. d. Donau .... a.	0045	...	0541	0627	0641	0727	0741	until	1241	1316	1341	1416	1442	1516	1541	1612	1641	1712	1741	1812	1841	1912	1941	until	2341

	Ⓒ	Ⓐ	Ⓐ		⚒		Ⓐ		Ⓐ								Ⓐ	Ⓒ	Ⓐ							
rems a. d. Donau ..... d.	0023	0419	0446	0519	0546	0618	0646	0718	0746	0819	0919	1019	1119	...	1219	1319	1342	1419	1421	1519	1619	and	2019	2119	2219	2319
erzogenburg .... d.	0047	0446	0513	0546	0613	0646	0714	0746	0814	0846	0946	1046	1146	...	1246	1346	1414	1446	1446	1546	1646	hourly	2046	2146	2246	2346
t Pölten Hbf............. a.	0059	0454	0522	0554	0622	0654	0723	0754	0822	0854	0954	1054	1154	...	1254	1354	1422	1454	1454	1554	1654	until	2054	2154	2254	2354

ST PÖLTEN - TULLN - WIEN

km		⚒	⚒		⚒			⚒																	
0	**St Pölten** Hbf .... **950** d.	0404	0445a	0512	0545a	...	0612	0656a	...	0713	0812	0912		1412	1512	...	1612	...	1712	...	1812	1912	2012	2112	2212
10	Herzogenburg ....d.	0417	0503a	0528	0602a	...	0629	0708a	...	0730	0833	0929		1429	1529	...	1629	...	1731	...	1829	1929	2029	2129	2229
40	Tullnerfeld...................... **950** a.	0449	0538a	0607	0638a	...	0708	0737a	...	0811	0911	1011		1511	1611	...	1711	...	1811	...	1911	2011	2111	2211	2311
40	Tullnerfeld..............................d.	0450	0554	0624	0654	0648	0724	0754	0749	0825	0925	1025	and	1525	1625	1648	1725	1748	1825	1848	1925	2025	2125	2225	2325
46	**Tulln** Stadt ....d.	0456	0600	0630	0700	0653	0730	0801	0754	0830	0930	1030		1530	1630	1653	1730	1753	1830	1853	1930	2030	2130	2230	2330
	Absdorf-Hippersdorf..... ▷ a.	|	|	|	|	0701	|	|	0802	|	|	|	hourly	|	|	1701	|	1801	|	1901	|	|	|	|	|
	Stockerau......................▷ a.	|	|	|	|	0724	|	|	0826	|	|	|		|	|	1726	|	1826	|	1926	|	|	|	|	|
47	**Tulln** a. d. Donau....... **990/1** a.	0458	0602	0632	0702	...	0732	0802	...	0832	0932	1032	until	1532	1632	...	1732	...	1832	...	1932	2032	2132	2232	2332
77	Wien Heiligenstadt .... **990/1** a.	0551	0647	0717	0747	...	0817	0847	...	0915	1015	1115		1615	1715	...	1815	...	1915	...	2015	2115	2215	2315	0015

	Ⓐ			⚒			⚒																		
Vien Heiligenstadt..... **990/1** d.	...	...	...	0515	0545	...	0613	0643	...	0743	0843	0943	1043		1443	1543	...	1643	...	1743	1843	1943	2043	2143	2243
ulln a. d. Donau .... **990/1** d.	0441	0527	...	0557	0627	...	0658	0727	...	0827	0927	1027	1127	and	1527	1627	...	1727	...	1827	1927	2027	2127	2227	2327
Stockerau....................▷ d.	|	|	0531	|	|	0631	|	|	0731	|	|	|	|		|	|	1631	|	1731	|	|	|	|	|	|
Absdorf-Hippersdorf...... ▷ d.	|	|	0558	|	|	0658	|	|	0758	|	|	|	|	hourly	|	|	1700	|	1800	|	|	|	|	|	|
ulln Stadt ....d.	0445	0530	0606	0600	0630	0706	0701	0730	0806	0830	0930	1030	1130		1530	1630	1708	1730	1808	1830	1930	2030	2130	2230	2330
ullnerfeld............................a.	0450	0535	0610	0605	0635	0710	0706	0735	0810	0835	0935	1035	1135	until	1535	1635	1713	1735	1813	1835	1935	2035	2135	2235	2335
ullnerfeld...................... **950** d.	0451	0548	...	0617	0648	...	0718	0748	...	0848	0948	1048	1148		1548	1648	...	1748	...	1848	1948	2048	2148	2248	...
erzogenburg.........................d.	0524	0630	...	0652	0730	...	0752	0830	...	0930	1030	1130	1230		1630	1732	...	1830	...	1930	2030	2130	2230	2330	...
t Pölten Hbf.............. **950** a.	0537	0649	...	0704	0744	...	0804	0844	...	0944	1044	1144	1249		1649	1749	...	1849	...	1944	2044	2144	2244	2344	...

– Ⓐ only.

▷ – Additional local trains run Absdorf-Hippersdorf - Stockerau and v.v.

ST PÖLTEN - MARIAZELL 994

Narrow gauge — 2nd class only

km				★	CⓇ	SⓇ						
0	**St Pölten** Hbf ...... d.	0635	0735	0837	0842	0902	0937	1037	1237	1437	1637	1837
12	Ober Grafendorf... d.	0654	0754	0854	0904	0924	0954	1054	1254	1454	1654	1854
31	Kirchberg .... d.	0723	0823	0923	0938	1003	1023	1123	1323	1523	1723	1923
43	Frankenfels ...... ⊗ d.	0741	0841	0941	0958	1029	1041	1141	1341	1541	1741	1941
48	Laubenbachmühle d.	0751	0851	0951	1011	1056f	1051	1151	1351	1551	1751	1949
67	Gösing .... ⊗ d.	0819	0919t	1019	1047	1142	1119z	1219	1419	1619	1819	...
80	Mitterbach .... ⊗ d.	0846	0946t	1046	1116	1216	1146z	1246	1446	1646	1846	...
84	**Mariazell**............ a.	0854	0954t	1054	1124	1224	1154z	1254	1454	1654	1854	...

						CⓇ	SⓇ	★			
Mariazell............. d.	...	0905	1105	1305	1505	1520	1540	1605v	1705	1805z	1905
Mitterbach .... ⊗ d.	...	0911	1111	1311	1511	1526	1547	1611v	1711	1811z	1911
Gösing .... ⊗ d.	...	0938	1138	1338	1538	1558	1620	1638v	1738	1838z	1938
Laubenbachmühle d.	0609	1009	1209	1409	1609	1633	1713r	1709	1809	1909	2009
Frankenfels....... ⊗ d.	0617	1017	1217	1417	1617	1642	1723	1717	1817	1917	2017
Kirchberg .... d.	0635	1036	1236	1436	1636	1702	1748	1736	1836	1936	2036
Ober Grafendorf...... d.	0704	1104	1304	1504	1704	1734	1824	1804	1904	2004	2104
St Pölten Hbf........ a.	0722	1122	1322	1522	1722	1757	1847	1822	1922	2022	2122

– Ⓒ May 18 - Nov. 1 (also Nov. 25, Dec. 2, 9; not June 11, July 9, Aug. 13, Sept. 10, Oct, 8). ÖTSCHERBÄR – Traditional loco-hauled electric train. Conveys (12) and 🍸.
– Runs on June 11, July 9, Aug. 13, Sept. 10, Oct. 8, Nov. 26, Dec. 3, 8. Steam train with special fares. Conveys (12) and 🍸.
– Arrives 1039.
– Arrives 1654.

t – Feb. 4 – 12, May 18 - Nov. 1 and from Nov. 25.
v – May 18 - Nov. 1 and from Nov. 25.
z – Ⓒ May 18 - Dec. 9 (not Nov. 4 – 19).
★ – On Ⓒ May 18 - Dec. 9 (not Nov. 4 – 19) conveys first class panorama cars (Ⓡ and special fares payable for travel in the panorama car which includes drinks and meals served at your seat).

⊗ – Trains call on request only.

Operator: NÖVOG. ✆ +43 (0) 2742 360 990 99 www.noevog.at/mariazellerbahn
Additional trains run between St Pölten and Laubenbachmühle.

(WIEN -) WIENER NEUSTADT - FEHRING 995

2nd class only

km		⚒	Ⓐ			Ⓐ			B	Ⓐ		Ⓐ	Ⓐ		Ⓑ	Ⓐ			
	Wien Hbf.................. **980/1** d.	...	...	0825c	...	...	...	...	...	...	...	...	...	...	...	...	...	...	...
0	**Wien** Meidling .... **980/1** d.	...	...	0832c	...	...	...	...	...	...	...	1735	...	...	...	...	...	...	...
44	**Wiener Neustadt** Hbf. **980/1** d.	...	0639	0903	1103	...	1303	1503	1503	1633	1703	1801	1833	1903	2003	2003	2103	2139	2239
99	Friedberg.............................d.	...	0802	1002	1202	...	1402	1602	1602	1738	1802	1857	1932	2003	2057	2058	2158	2245	2345
126	Hartberg ....d.	0621	0836	1036	1235	1328	1436	1635	1636	1814	1836	1929	...	2038	...	2132	2232b	...	...
157	Fürstenfeld ....d.	0655	0910	1110	...	1359	1510	...	1710	...	1910	...	...	2110	...	...	...	...	...
177	**Fehring**...............................a.	0722	0937	1137	...	1426	1537	...	1737	...	1937	...	...	2137	...	...	...	...	...
	Graz Hbf **986** ....a.	0836a	1053	1253a	...	...	...	...	...	...	2053d	...	...	...	...	...	...	...	...

	Ⓐ	Ⓐ	Ⓐ	⚒	†	Ⓐ						Ⓐ	Ⓒ			Ⓒ	B		
Graz Hbf **986** ....d.	...	...	...	...	...	...	...	...	0707	0907	...	...	...	...	...	...	...	...	1708a
ehring.................................d.	...	...	...	...	...	0501	...	0627	0827	1027	...	1227	1427	1427	...	1627	1627	...	1827
ürstenfeld ....d.	...	...	...	...	...	0528	...	0654	0854	1054	...	1254	1454	1454	...	1654	1654	...	1854
lartberg ....d.	...	...	0435	0533	...	0601	...	0727	0927	1127	1327	1327	1527	1527	1727	1727	1727	...	1930
riedberg...............................d.	0347	0428	0509	0607	0632	0636	0700	0802	1002	1202	1402	1402	1602	1602	1802	1802	1802	...	2004
Viener Neustadt Hbf.. **980/1** a.	0454	0529	0611	0711f	0732	0735	0757	0857	1057	1257	1457	1457	1657	1657	1857	1857	1857	...	2057
Vien Meidling.............. **980/1** a.	...	0559	0643	0743a	...	...	...	...	...	...	...	...	1732	...	...	1933	...	...	...
Vien Hbf..................... **980/1** a.	...	0606	0651	...	...	...	...	...	...	...	...	...	1740	...	...	1940	...	...	...

B – ⑤⑥† (also May 17, June 7; not May 19, June 9).

a – Ⓐ only.
b – Not ⑥.
c – Ⓒ only.
d – ⑤⑥† only.
f – 0715 on ⑥.

996 WIEN - BRATISLAVA via Marchegg

2nd class only; Austrian holiday dates apply

km															A	C
0	**Wien** Hbf	d.	0517	0617	0717	0817	0917		2017	2117	2217	2317	0017	A	1442	2042
4	**Wien** Simmering ⊖	d.	0523	0623	0723	0823	0923	and	2023	2123	2223	2323	0023	L	|	|
47	Marchegg 🏛	d.	0603	0703	0803	0903	1003	hourly	2103	2200	2303	2400	0100	S	⊠	⊠
53	Devínska Nová Ves 🏛	d.	0611	0711	0811	0911	1011	until	2111	...	2311	...	...	O	|	|
66	**Bratislava** hl. st.	a.	0623	0723	0823	0923	1023		2123	...	2323	...	...		1601	2151

												D		B	
Bratislava hl. st.	d.	...	0538	0638		2038	...	2238	...	...	A	0610	...	1156	...
Devínska Nová Ves 🏛	d.	...	0551	0651	and	2051	...	2251	...	...	L	|	...	|	...
Marchegg 🏛	d.	0501	0601	0701	hourly	2101	2201	2301	0001	...	S	⊠	...	⊠	...
Wien Simmering ⊖	a.	0537	0637	0737	until	2137	2237	2337	0037	...	O	|	...	|	...
Wien Hbf	a.	0544	0644	0744		2144	2244	2344	0044	...		0718	...	1324	...

A – *IC* **45** – (12) ✕ Wien - Bratislava - Košice (Table **1180**). R Bratislava - Košice.
B – *IC* **44** – (12) ✕ Košice - Bratislava - Wien (Table **1180**). R Košice - Bratislava.
C – *RJX* **167** – (12) ✕ Zürich - Bratislava.
D – *RJX* **160** – (12) ✕ Bratislava - Zürich.

⊠ – Via Bratislava - Petržalka
⊖ – For U-Bahn connections (line U3) from / to Wien Mitte and Wien Westbahnhof.

997 BRATISLAVA - WIEN - SOPRON - DEUTSCHKREUTZ

2nd class only; Austrian holiday dates apply

km	△			Ⓐ		Ⓐ	©M	Ⓐ		Ⓐ	♣			Ⓐ	♣	Ⓐ	♣	Ⓐ	♣	♣	♣	♣	♣	©	
0	**Bratislava**-Petržalka 🏛 ☆	d.	0415a	0446	0515	0546	0611	0611	...	0646	0715		1415	...	1515	...	1615	...	1715	1815	1915	2015	2115	2215	2315
5	Kittsee 🏛	d.	0421a	0452	0521	0552	0617	0617	...	0652	0721		1421	...	1521	...	1621	...	1721	1821	1921	2021	2121	2221	2321
33	Bruck an der Leitha	d.	0446a	0418	0546	0618	0646	0646	...	0718	0746	and	1446	...	1546	...	1646	...	1746	1846	1946	2046	2146	2246	2346
74	**Wien** Hbf	a.	0516a	0547	0615	0646	0715	0715	...	0746	0815		1515	...	1615	...	1715	...	1815	1915	2015	2115	2215	2315	0015
74	**Wien** Hbf	d.	0517	...	0617	...	0725	0723	0723	...	0823	hourly	1523	1546	1623	1646	1723	1746	1823	1923	2023	2123	2223	...	...
78	**Wien** Meidling	d.	0524	...	0624	...	0730	0730	0730	...	0830		1530	1553	1630	1653	1730	1753	1830	1930	2030	2130	2230	...	...
116	Ebenfurth	d.	0602	...	0702	...	...	0802	0802	...	0902	until	1602	1636	1702	1736	1802	1836	1902	2002	2102	2202	2302	...	...
148	**Sopron** 🏛	a.	0637	...	0737	...	...	0837	0837	...	0937		1637	1710	1737	1810	1837	1910	1937	2037	2137	2237	2337	...	...
157	**Deutschkreutz**	a.	0658	...	0759	...	...	0847	0847	...	0947		1647	1722	1747	1822	1847	1922	1947	2047	2147	2247	2347	...	...

△					Ⓐ	†	Ⓐ	♣	Ⓐ	♣	Ⓐ	♣	Ⓐ	♣		♣			©M	♣		♣	♣		
Deutschkreutz	d.	...	...	...	0413	...	0435	0513	0535	0613	0635	0713	0735	0813		1613	1713	...	...	1813	...	1913	2013	...	...
Sopron 🏛	d.	...	...	...	0423	...	0446	0523	0546	0623	0646	0723	0746	0823		1623	1723	...	...	1823	...	1926	2023	...	...
Ebenfurth	d.	...	...	...	0504	...	0526	0604	0626	0704	0726	0804	0826	0904	and	1704	1804	...	...	1904	...	2005	2104	...	...
Wien Meidling	d.	...	...	...	0531	...	0557	0632	0657	0732	0757	0832	0857	0932		1732	1832	...	1831	1932	...	2032	2132	...	...
Wien Hbf	a.	...	...	...	0537	...	0603	0637	0703	0737	0803	0837	0903	0937	hourly	1737	1837	...	1836	1937	...	2037	2137	...	...
Wien Hbf	d.	0050	...	0445	0538	0538	...	0645	...	0745	...	0845	...	0945		1745	...	1845	1845	1945	2042	2045	2145	2245	2345
Bruck an der Leitha	d.	0129	...	0513	0607	0607	...	0713	...	0813	...	0913	...	1013	until	1813	...	1913	1913	2013	|	2113	2213	2313	0013
Kittsee 🏛	a.	0153	...	0538	0634	0634	...	0738	...	0838	...	0938	...	1038		1838	...	1938	1938	2038	|	2138	2238	2338	0038
Bratislava-Petržalka 🏛 ☆	a.	0159	...	0544	0641	0641	...	0744	...	0844	...	0944	...	1044		1844	...	1944	1944	2044	2126	2144	2244	2344	0044

km	▽		Ⓐ							Ⓐ	Ⓐ	©	Ⓐ	Ⓐ		Ⓐ	Ⓐ	©	Ⓐ	Ⓐ	©	Ⓐ	Ⓐ	©	Ⓐ	Ⓐ
	Wien Meidling **980 981**	d.	...	...	...	...	...		...	...	...	...	...	...	...	...	...	...	...	1600	...	...	1700	...	...	1800
0	**Wiener Neustadt** Hbf	d.	0503	0603	0703	0739	0837	and	1237	1301	1331	1337	1401	1431	1437	1501	1531	1537	1601	1631	1637	1701	1731	1737	1801	1831
16	Mattersburg	d.	0526	0626	0726	0803	0902	hourly	1302	1321	1344	1402	1421	1444	1502	1521	1544	1602	1621	1644	1702	1721	1744	1802	1821	1844
33	**Sopron** 🏛	a.	0541	0641	0741	0818	0917	until	1317	1336	1400	1417	1436	1500	1517	1536	1600	1617	1636	1700	1717	1736	1800	1817	1836	1900
42	**Deutschkreutz**	a.	...	...	...	...	...		...	...	1410	...	...	1510	...	...	1610	...	...	1710	...	...	1810	...	...	1910

▽		©	Ⓐ	Ⓐ					
Wien Meidling **980 981**	d.	...	...	...	...	...	...	...	...
Wiener Neustadt Hbf	d.	1837	1901	1931	1937	2037	2137	2237	2337
Mattersburg	d.	1902	1921	1944	2002	2102	2202	2302	0002
Sopron 🏛	a.	1917	1936	2000	2017	2117	2217	2317	0017
Deutschkreutz	a.	...	...	2010	...	...	...	...	...

▽		Ⓐ	⚒	Ⓐ		Ⓐ		⑥	Ⓐ				
Deutschkreutz	d.	...	...	0459	...	0559	...	0635	0659	...			
Sopron 🏛	d.	0417	0447	0509	0547	0609	0647	0647	0709	0747	0844	and	2244
Mattersburg	d.	0435	0503	0527	0603	0627	0703	0703	0727	0803	0902	hourly	2302
Wiener Neustadt Hbf	a.	0453	0525	0539	0625	0639	0725	0725	0739	0825	0925	until	2325
Wien Meidling **980 981**	a.	...	...	0613	...	0713	...	...	0813	...	...		...

M – To / from Mürzzuschlag (Table **981**).
♣ – Change at Wien Hbf.
☆ – Bus 93 links Petržalka station with Bratislava hlavná every 5 – 10 minutes (journey time ± 12 minutes).
△ – Operated by GySEV Györ-Sopron-Ebenfurti Vasút (in German Raab-Oedenburg-Ebenfurter Eisenbahn – ROeEE).
▽ – Operated by ÖBB.

998 UNZMARKT - TAMSWEG

2nd class only; narrow gauge

km			Ⓐ	Ⓐ	⑥ 🚌		④B 🚂	©	Ⓐ	②A 🚂		⑦C 🚂				🚌		🚌
0	**Unzmarkt**	d.	...	0719	0722	0922	...	*1118**	1122	...	1322	...	1522	...	1722	...	1917	2125
27	Murau-Stolzalpe	d.	0623	0800	0800	1000	1015	1200	1200	1250	1400	1410	1600	...	1758	1805	1951	2202
34	St Lorenzen	d.	0636	0813	0812	1013	1035	1213	1213	1310	1413	1430	1613	...	...	1816s	2000	2208s
44	Stadl an der Mur	d.	0653	0827	0825	1027	1105	1227	1227	1343	1427	1450	1627	...	...	1827s	2013	2219s
65	**Tamsweg**	a.	0727	0857	0852	1057	1153	1257	1257	1431	1457	...	1657	...	...	1855	2039	2240

		Ⓐ	Ⓐ	©	Ⓐ	© 🚌				④B 🚂	⑦C 🚂			②A 🚂		Ⓐ 🚌	Ⓐ 🚌	© 🚌
Tamsweg	d.	*0535**	0650	0703	0903	0910	1103	...	1303	1335	...	1503	...	1615	1703	1820	...	1910
Stadl an der Mur	d.	*0601**	0718	0731	0931	0929	1131	...	1331	1425	1515	1531	...	1710	1731	1840	...	1929
St Lorenzen	d.	*0615**	0732	0745	0945	0943	1145	...	1345	1446	1535	1545	...	1732	1745	1853	...	1943
Murau-Stolzalpe	d.	0630	0802	0800	1000	1000	1200	...	1400	1500	1550	1600	...	1745	1800	1905	2000	2000
Unzmarkt	a.	0710	0840	0836	1036	1040	1236	...	1436	...	...	1636	...	...	1842	...	2040	2040

A – June 14 - Sept. 6.
B – June 16 - Sept. 22.
C – July 24 - Aug. 28.

s – Stops to set down only.

* – By 🚌.
🚂 – Steam train. Special fares payable.
2023 schedules not yet confirmed (2022 timings/running dates shown).

Operator: Steiermärkische Landesbahnen.

999 Danube shipping

2023 service

Catamaran services. 🍸		W R♠		Z R♠		W R♠		W R♠		
Wien Schwedenplatz ▲	d.	0830	...	0900	...	1230	...	1630	...	...
Bratislava	a.	0945	...	1015	...	1345	...	1745	...	...

Catamaran services. 🍸		W R♠		W R♠		Z R♠			W R♠	
Bratislava	d.	1030	...	1430	...	1600	...	...	1830	...
Wien Schwedenplatz ▲	a.	1200	...	1600	...	1730	...	...	2000	...

All sailings convey ✕		C ⊡	B ◐		E ◐	⑦J ◐ R	E ⊡	E ◐	E ◐	
Wien Reichsbrücke ▲	d.	...	...	...	...	0830	...	...	...	...
Tulln	d.	...	...	...	...	1120	...	...	...	...
Krems an der Donau	d.	1005	1015	...	1310	1400	1540	1545	...	...
Dürnstein	d.	1040	1050	...	1340	1430	1610	1620	...	...
Spitz an der Donau	d.	1135	1145	...	1445	...	1700	1720	1730	...
Melk	a.	1255	1320	...	1605	...	*1730**	...	1850	...

All sailings convey ✕		E ◐		C ⊡	B ◐		⑦J ◐ R	E ⊡	E ◐	E ◐
Melk	d.	1100	...	1345	1350	...	...	...	1625	...
Spitz an der Donau	d.	1200‡	...	1430	1440	...	...	1705	1710	1725
Dürnstein	d.	1230	...	1500	1510	...	1640	1730	...	1750
Krems an der Donau	d.	1250	...	1525	1530	...	1700	1755	...	1810
Tulln	d.	...	...	...	...	...	1900	...	...	...
Wien Reichsbrücke ▲	a.	...	...	...	...	...	2100	...	...	...

All sailings convey ✕		⊖A	⊖F	
Linz Lentos	d.	...	1420	...
Schlögen	d.	...	1800	...
Engelhartszell	d.	1400	1845	...
Passau Liegestelle 11 🏛	d.	1630	2050	...
Deggendorf	a.	...	...	...

All sailings convey ✕		⊖F	⊖A	
Deggendorf	d.	...	...	...
Passau Liegestelle 11 🏛	d.	0900	1230	...
Engelhartszell	d.	1030	1400	...
Schlögen	a.	1110	...	...
Linz Lentos	a.	1410	...	...

A – May 13 - Oct. 3.
B – Apr. 1 - Oct. 29.
C – Apr. 15 - Oct. 26.
E – May 6 - Oct. 8.
F – ⑤⑥ Aug. 11 - Sept. 30.
J – ⑦ Apr. 2 - Oct. 29; ⑤ May 5 - Sept. 22.
W – May 1 - Oct. 1; ⑤⑥† Mar. 31 - Apr. 30, Oct. 3 - Nov. 11.
Z – ①-④ Mar. 31 - Apr. 30, Oct. 2 - Nov. 5.

a – May 6 - Oct. 8.
b – From Mar. 1.

* – By 🚌 from Spitz.
‡ – Arrives 1140.

▲ – DDSG operates Wien sightseeing cruises Schwedenplatz - Reichsbrücke and v.v. Daily Apr. 1 - Oct. 29.
From Schwedenplatz (duration 1 h 55 m via Schleuse Freudenau) at 1350.
From Reichsbrücke (duration 1 h 20 m via Schleuse Nussdorf) at 1225, 1555.
Also shorter *City Cruise* available daily throughout the year from Schwedenplatz at 1100, 1300, 1430, 1600 **b** and 1900 **a** (duration 1 h 15 m).

Operators:
⊡ – Brandner Schiffahrt, Ufer 15, A-3313 Wallsee. ✆ +43 (0)7433 25 90 21. www.brandner.at
◐ – DDSG Blue Danube Schiffahrt, Handelskai 265, A-1020 Wien. ✆ +43 (0)1 588 80. www.ddsg-blue-danube.at
⊖ – Wurm und Köck, Höllgasse 26, D-94032 Passau. ✆ +49 (0)851 92 92 92. www.donauschiffahrt.de
♠ – *Twin City Liner*. DDSG Blue Danube, Handelskai 265, A-1020 Wien. Check-in 30 minutes before departure. Austrian holiday dates apply. ✆ +43 (0)1 904 88 80. Internet booking: www.twincityliner.com

POLAND

Operators: Express services are operated by PKP Intercity www.intercity.pl. Most local trains are operated by Przewozy Regionalne (PR) www.przewozyregionalne.pl. Certain local services are operated by regional companies owned by local government: e.g. Koleje Dolnośląskie, Koleje Mazowieckie, Koleje Śląskie and Koleje Wielkopolskie.

Services: **PKP InterCity** : Note reservation is compulsory (Ⓡ) on all services operated by PKP InterCity (*EC, EIC, EIP, EN, IC, MP, TLK*). *EC, EIC* and *EIP* trains are fast premium-rate trains on long-distance routes (*EC* or *EuroCity* trains run on international routes) - first and second class seats, higher rate of fares apply and a supplement is payable for pass holders. *EC, EIC* and *EIP* trains normally convey ✕ or 🍷 for at least part of the route. *IC* and *TLK* trains are lower-cost long distance trains with first and second class seats (also sleepers and couchettes on nights routes as shown in the tables). *TLK* is short for *Twoje Linie Kolejowe* (Your Railway Lines). *IRE* is an Interregio-Express. Certain trains convey 🍷 but it is not possible to identify these in the tables. *MP* is the classification (within Poland) for other international trains; *TLK* fares apply within Poland. *EN* trains are *EuroNight* services with 'global' fares which include the sleeping accommodation. Descriptions of sleeping (🛏) and couchette (▬) cars appear on page 10.

Przewozy Regionalne and other local operators : *IR (InterRegio)* and *RE* (*Regional Express*) trains are semi-fast trains operated by Przewozy Regionalne on longer distance routes, with second class seats. Fares are cheaper than *TLK* services but slightly higher than local *Regio* trains. All other trains are local *R* (*Regio*) trains, second class only, calling at all or most stations en route. No train category is shown in our tables for these trains. They are operated by Przewozy Regionalne unless otherwise shown in the table heading or by a footnote. Fares on *Regio* trains are the cheapest available.

Timings: Valid from **December 11, 2022**, but subject to confirmation from **March 12, 2023**. *However, alterations and amendments are possible at any time (particularly on and around public holidays) and readers are advised to check specific dates locally before travelling.* Engineering work can often affect schedules; major changes are shown in the tables where possible but other changes may occur at short notice. A number of long-distance trains running only in high summer (particularly to coastal resorts) are not shown owing to lack of space. Note that train numbers often change en route by one or two digits. In station names, Gł. is short for Główny or Główna, meaning main station.

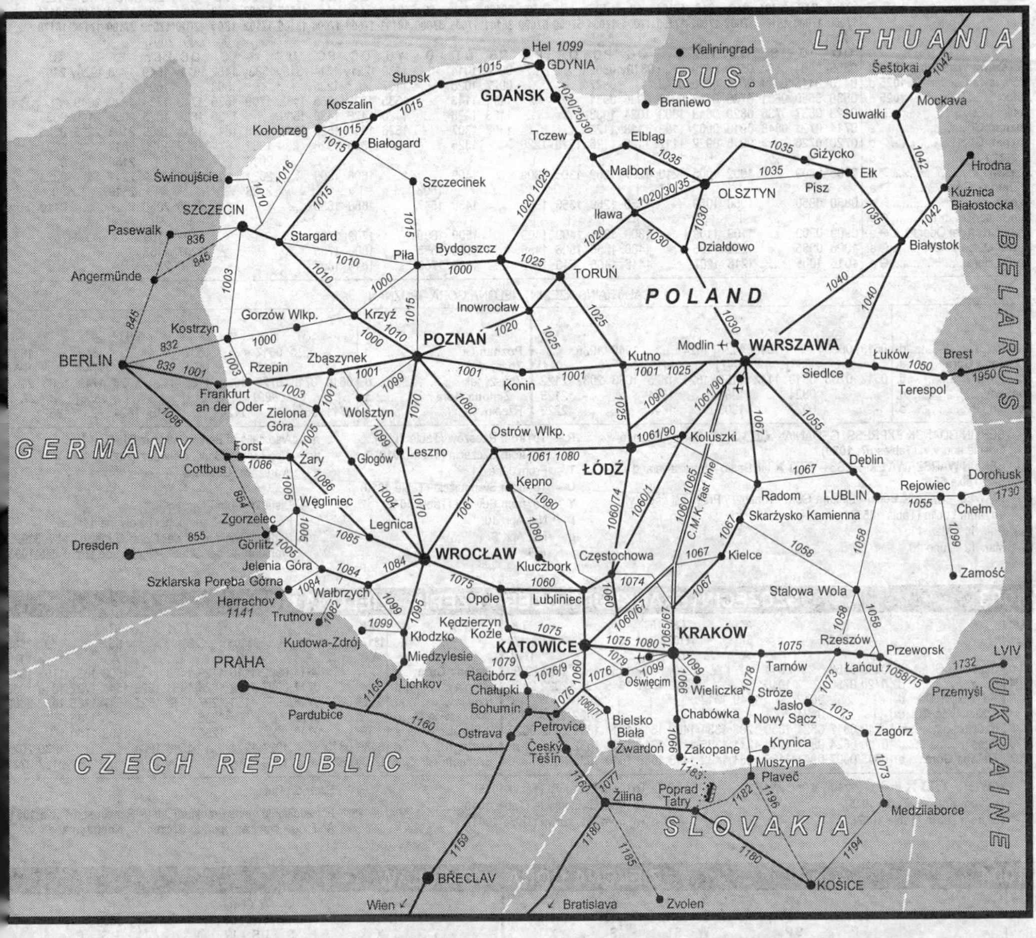

KOSTRZYN - KRZYŻ - POZNAŃ and BYDGOSZCZ — 1000

km		*IC* 81110 W	Ⓐ					*IC* 80104 2	*IC* 82104 BK		⚒		Ⓑ		*TLK* 82100 A	Ⓐ			Ⓐ	*TLK* 85110 2G			Ⓐ			Ⓑ	
0	**Kostrzyn** d.	...	...	...	0540	0646	...	...	...	0844	...	1031	...	...	...	1241	...	1356	1446	1519	1604	...	1709	1754	2039	...	2200
43	Gorzów Wlkp. d.	...	...	...	0621	0726	...	0906	...	0926	...	1115	...	...	...	1320	...	1437	1526	1558	1647	...	1749	1836	2119	...	2241
103	Krzyż 1010 a.	...	...	...	0715	0818	...	1000	...	1020	...	1208	...	...	...	1413	...	1531	1619	1651	1741	...	1841	1930	2212	...	2336
103	Krzyż 1010 d.	...	0540	0630	0718	...	0836	1001	...	1023	1049	▬	1250	1338	...	...	1448	▬	...	1652	1746	1748	▬	▬	...	2217	...
186	**Poznań** 1010 a.	...	|	|	0838	...	|	|	...	1141	|	...	|	|	...	...	|	Ⓑ	...	|	1918	|	...	...	...	|	...
163	Piła Gł. d.	0505	0629	0720	...	...	0926	1051	1115	...	1138	1146	1339	1428	1459	...	1537	1610	...	1742	...	1838	1847	2026	...	2306	...
248	**Bydgoszcz** a.	0613	...	...	...	...	...	...	1225	...	...	1307	...	...	1608	...	...	1732	...	...	...	...	2008	2146	...	...	...

	Ⓐ		⚒	⚒						Ⓐ	*TLK* 58111 2G		*TLK* 28101 A	⚒	Ⓐ		Ⓑ	Ⓑ			*IC* 28105 BK	*IC* 88105 2					*IC* 18111 W
Bydgoszcz d.	...	...	...	0545	...	0742	...	...	...	...	...	...	1138	...	...	...	1438	...	1551	...	1613	...	1745	...	...	2024	2109
Piła Gł. d.	...	...	0521	0706	0728	0901	0915	...	1123	...	1159	...	1245	1328	...	1447	1559	1604	1709	1728	1723	1751	1905	2023	...	2143	2217
Poznań 1010 d.	...	...	|	▬	|	▬	|	0847	|	...	|	1151	...	|	...	|	▬	|	▬	|	...	|	▬	|	2002	...	...
Krzyż 1010 a.	...	...	0611	...	0819	...	1005	1006	1213	...	1250	1309	...	1419	...	1539	...	1655	Ⓒ	1819	...	1842	...	2114	2131	...	...
Krzyż 1010 d.	...	0519	...	0630	...	0830	...	1020	...	1225	1251	1318	...	...	1426	...	1544	...	1730	...	...	1843	1952	...	2135	...	...
Gorzów Wlkp. d.	0517	0614	...	0725	...	0923	...	1114	...	1320	1404	1423	...	...	1519	...	1639	...	1824	...	...	1937	2048	...	2234	...	...
Kostrzyn a.	0555	0652	...	0803	...	0959	...	1151	...	1357	1441	1502	...	...	1557	...	1717	...	1901	...	...	...	2126	...	2311	...	...

A – (12) Szczecin - Piła - Bydgoszcz - Warszawa - Lublin and v.v.
B – To/from Lublin (Table **1055**).
G – To/from Gdynia (Table **1025**).
K – To/from Kołobrzeg (Table **1015**).
W – To/from Warszawa (Table **1025**).

1001 BERLIN - POZNAŃ - WARSZAWA

km		*TLK*	*IC*	*EIC*	*IC*	*EC*	*EC*	*IC*	*IC*	*EC*	*EC*	*IC*	*EC*	*EC*	*IC*	*EC*	*EC*	*EC*	*EC*	*IC*	*EC*	*EC*	*IC*	*EC*	*EC*
		81170	**71105**	**8100**	**72101**	**41**	**41**	**71102**	**81106**	**45**	**45**	**81102**	**57**	**47**	**83100**	**59**	**59**	**49**	**49**	**71100**	**247**	**247**	**81100**	**249**	**249**
		81171	**71104**	**8101**	**72100**	**71010**	**71010**	**71103**	**81107**	**71008**	**71008**	**81103**	**73000**	**71006**	**83101**	**75000**	**75000**	**71004**	**71004**	**71101**	**71002**	**71002**	**81101**	**71000**	**71000**
				⚒		⚒ w	⚒																	Ⓑ	Ⓑ
		U		**S**	**E**	**PCf**	**QC**		**U**	**PC**	**QC**	**UY**	**D**	**QT**	**SR**	**PA**	**QA**	**PC**	**QC**		**PC**	**QC**	**S**	**PC**	**QC**
0	**Berlin** Hbf ⊖ d.	...	...	...	...	0552	0543	...	...	0951	0937	...	1052	1152	...	1252	1237	1351	1342	...	1552	1543	...	1752	1743
5	**Berlin** Ostbahnhof ⊖ d.	...	...	...	...	0601	0555	...	...	1003	0951	...	1103	1203	...	1303	1253	1403	1353	...	1603	1553	...	1803	1753
87	Frankfurt an der Oder 🏛 ⊖ d.	...	...	...	...	0649	0649	...	...	1049	1049	...	1149	1249	...	1349	1349	1449	1449	...	1649	1649	...	1849	1849
98	Kunowice 🏛 ⊖ d.	...	...	...	...	|	|	...	...	|	|	...	|	|	...	|	|	|	|	...	|	|	...	|	|
110	Rzepin ▷ d.	0025	...	...	...	0710	0710	...	...	1110	1110	...	1212	1310	...	1410	1410	1510	1510	...	1710	1710	...	1910	1910
•58	**Zielona Góra** ▷ d.	|	...	...	0455	|	|	0632	...	|	|	...	1254	|	...	|	|	|	|	1501	|	|	...	|	|
185	Zbąszynek ▷ d.	0113	...	...	0617	0748	0749	0755	...	1148	1150	...	...	1348	...	1448	1449	1548	1549	1623	1748	1750	...	1948	1951
191	Zbąszyń ▷ d.	0123	...	...	0624	|	|	0802	...	|	|	...	...	|	...	|	|	|	|	1630	|	|	...	|	|
266	**Poznań** Gł. ▷ a.	0216	...	...	0711	0832	0836	0845	...	1232	1246	...	...	1432	...	1532	1547	1632	1636	1713	1832	1837	...	2034	2037
266	**Poznań** Gł. d.	0231	0540	0709	0727	0837	0846	0855	1123	1236	1251	1306	...	1436	1533	...	...	1642	1647	1738	1837	1842	1933	2037	2047
366	Konin d.	0343	0644	0803	0833	0922	0936	|	1233	1322	1341	1415	...	1522	1633	...	...	1727	1739	1837	1922	1932	2043	2123	2139
445	Kutno **1025** d.	0437	0731	0845	0921	1005	1027	1119	1317	1403	1437	1500	...	1603	1717	...	...	1820	1829	1924	2006	2023	2131	2206	2227
572	**Warszawa** Centralna **1025** a.	|	0902	1009	|	1139	|	1300	|	1533	|	1632	...	1722	1908	...	...	1942	|	|	2129	|	2300	|	|
577	**Warszawa** Wschodnia **1025** a.	0625**y**	0916	1021	1101	1201	1148**y**	1311	1450**y**	1551	1554**y**	1641	...	1746	1921	...	...	1956	1948**y**	2051**y**	2138	2145**y**	2316	2342	2349**y**

	EC	*EC*	*IC*	*EC*	*EC*	*IC*	*EC*	*EC*	*EC*	*EC*	*IC*	*EC*	*EC*	*IC*	*EC*	*EC*	*IC*	*IC*	*EIC*	*EC*	*EC*	*IC*	*IC*	*TLK*	
	248	**248**	**18101**	**246**	**246**	**17101**	**48**	**48**	**58**	**58**	**38100**	**46**	**56**	**18102**	**44**	**44**	**18107**	**17103**	**1800**	**40**	**40**	**27101**	**17105**	**18171**	
	17000	**17000**	**18100**	**17002**	**17002**	**17100**	**17004**	**17004**	**57000**	**57000**	**38101**	**17006**	**37000**	**18103**	**17008**	**17008**	**18106**	**17102**	**1801**	**17010**	**17010**	**27100**	**17104**	**18170**	
	⚒	⚒																	Ⓑ	Ⓑ	Ⓑ g				
	QC	**PC**	**S**	**QC**	**PC**		**QC**	**PC**	**QA**	**PA**	**RS**	**QT**	**D**	**YU**	**QC**	**PC**	**U**		**S**	**QC**	**PCm**	**E**		**U**	
Warszawa Wschodnia. **1025** d.	0359	0404	0504	0550	0539	0729	0819**y**	0809	...	...	0914	1014	...	1139	1221**y**	1214	1316**y**	1533**y**	1452	1614**y**	1549	1728	1920**y**	2107	...
Warszawa Centralna... **1025** d.	0410	0415	0514	0611	0556	0742	|	0827	...	...	0927	1025	...	1157	|	1225	|	|	1503	|	1604	|	|	|	...
Kutno **1025** d.	0538	0550	0651	0735	0728	0918	0936	0951	...	...	1111	1143	...	1335	1339	1355	1452	1709	1636	1740	1736	1920	2049	|	...
Konin d.	0623	0637	0736	0820	0818	1003	1024	1038	...	...	1158	1223	...	1420	1426	1438	1539	|	1720	1826	1825	2005	2140	0059	...
Poznań Gł. a.	0714	0721	0848	0910	0902	1103	1113	1122	...	...	1308	1307	...	1526	1515	1525	1649	1928	1813	1915	1909	2103	2239	0205	...
Poznań Gł. ▷ d.	0720	0726	...	0916	0922	1112	1120	1126	1220	1226	...	1325	...	...	1520	1526	...	1932	...	1920	1926	2012	...	0221	...
Zbąszyń ▷ d.	|	|	...	|	|	1105	|	|	|	|	...	|	...	...	|	|	...	2014	...	|	|	2150	...	0314	...
Zbąszynek ▷ d.	0806	0809	...	1002	1005	1210	1207	1209	1306	1309	...	1409	...	...	1606	1609	...	2031	...	2008	2009	2211	...	0323	...
Zielona Góra ▷ a.	|	|	...	|	|	1317	|	|	|	|	...	|	1503	...	|	|	...	2138	...	|	|	2318	...	|	...
Rzepin ▷ d.	0850	0850	...	1050	1050	...	1250	1250	1350	1350	...	1450	1547	...	1650	1650	...	...	...	2050	2050	...	...	0410	...
Kunowice 🏛 ⊖ d.	|	|	...	|	|	...	|	|	|	|	...	|	|	...	|	|	...	...	...	|	|	...	...	...	...
Frankfurt an der Oder 🏛 ⊖ a.	0909	0909	...	1109	1109	...	1309	1309	1409	1409	...	1509	1609	...	1709	1709	...	...	...	2109	2109	...	...	...	...
Berlin Ostbahnhof ⊖ a.	1006	0955	...	1206	1155	...	1406	1355	1506	1455	...	1555	1655	...	1806	1755	...	...	...	2207	2157	...	...	...	...
Berlin Hbf ⊖ a.	1016	1005	...	1216	1207	...	1416	1405	1516	1505	...	1605	1705	...	1816	1807	...	...	...	2216	2205	...	...	...	...

LOCAL TRAINS RZEPIN / ZIELONA GORA - POZNAŃ

		Ⓐ		⚒		Ⓐ				
Rzepin d.	0515	0635	...	1045	...	1424	...	1540	1935	...
Zielona Góra d.	|	|	*0658*j	|	*1047*j	|	*1419*j	|	|	*2014*j
Zbąszynek d.	0612	0738	0818	1142	1155	1521	1525	1638	2032	2122
Zbąszyń d.	...	...	0824	...	1200	...	1531	...	...	2128
Poznań Gł. a.	...	...	0927	...	1303	...	1640	...	...	2229

		Ⓐ		⚒			Ⓐ			
Poznań Gł. d.	...	...	0617	...	1001	...	...	1643	...	1887
Zbąszyń d.	...	...	0717	...	1101	...	...	1744	...	1957
Zbąszynek d.	0610	0718	0722	1028	1106	1420	1528	1749	1803	2002
Zielona Góra a.	|	|	*0829*j	|	*1213*j	|	|	*1856*j	|	*2135*
Rzepin a.	0711	0814	...	1124	...	1515	1624	...	1859	...

A – BERLIN GDANSK EXPRESS / GEDANIA – (12) ✕ Ⓡ, Berlin - Poznań - Gdynia and v.v. (Tables **57**, **1020**).
C – BERLIN WARSZAWA EXPRESS – (12) ✕ Ⓡ, Berlin - Warszawa and v.v. See Table **56**.
D – WAWEL – (12) ✕ Berlin - Zielona Góra - Krakow - Przemyśl and v.v.
E – To / from Lublin (Table **1055**).
P – Dec. 11 - Mar. 11.
Q – Mar. 12 - June 10.

R – To / from Rzeszów (Table **1058**).
S – To / from Szczecin (Table **1010**).
T – From June 11.
U – To / from Świnoujście (Table **1010**).
Y – To / from Suwałki (Table **1042**).
f – Not Apr. 10.
g – Not Apr. 9.
j – 🚌.

m – Also calls at Berlin Ostkreuz 2151.
w – Also calls at Berlin Ostkreuz 0606.
y – Warszawa **Gdańska**.

• – Distance from Zbąszynek.
▷ – For local trains see panel below main table.
⊖ – Berlin - Frankfurt an der Oder: see also Table **839**. Frankfurt an der Oder - Rzepin: see also Table **1003**

1003 SZCZECIN \ FRANKFURT ODER - RZEPIN - ZIELONA GÓRA

km			*IC*			*IC*		*TLK*	*IC*				*TLK*
			8304			**57**		**82102**	**83104**	Ⓐ			**81170**
			P			**A**		**L**	**K**				**UW**
0	**Szczecin** Gł. d.	0533	0553	...	0814	...	...	1220**y**	1436**y**	1453	...	1821	2239**y**
104	Kostrzyn d.	0720	0756	...	1010	...	...	1340	1551	1645	...	2022	2355
	Frankfurt / Oder d.	|	|	0812	|	1149	1312	|	|	|	1810	|	|
	Kunowice 🏛 d.	|	|	0824	|	|	1324	|	|	|	1822	|	|
136	Rzepin a.	0749	0817	0824	1039	1208	1334	1402	1613	1714	1831	2052	0020
136	Rzepin d.	0750	0824	0844	1040	1211	1335	1403	1614	1724	1832	...	...
207	**Zielona Góra** a.	0845	0907	0941	1135	1254	1432	1446	1658	1819	1930	...	...

	TLK				*IC*		*TLK*		*IC*			*IC*
	18171				**38105**		**28103**		**56**		Ⓑ	**3805**
	WU				**K**		**L**		**A**			**P**
Zielona Góra d.	...	...	0614	0902	1110	1129	1408	1432	1503	1625	1753	1913
Rzepin a.	...	...	0711	0957	1152	1226	1451	1526	1544	1722	1848	1956
Rzepin d.	0411	0539	0716	0958	1153	1227	1452	1527	1547	1725	1857	2002
Kunowice 🏛 d.	|	|	0726	|	|	1236	|	|	|	1735	|	|
Frankfurt / Oder a.	|	|	0740	|	|	1250	|	|	1609	1750	|	|
Kostrzyn d.	0439	0610	...	1027	1221	...	1513	1604	...	...	1930	2025
Szczecin Gł. a.	1220**y**	0801	...	1215	1350**y**	...	1639**y**	1800	...	...	2122	2221

A – WAWEL – (12) ✕ Berlin - Przemyśl and v.v.
K – To / from Kraków (Table **1075**).
L – To / from Lublin (Table **1067**).

P – To / from Przemyśl (Table **1075**).
U – To / from Świnoujście (Table **1010**).
W – To / from Warszawa (Table **1001**).

y – Szczecin Dąbie.

☛ For additional trains Frankfurt/Oder - Rzepin see Table **1001**. Additional services operate **Szczecin - Kostrzyn** and v.v.

1004 ZIELONA GÓRA - WROCŁAW

km			*IC*		*IC*			*IC*	*TLK*		*IC*		*NJ*	
		⚒	**73104**		**8304**			**57**	**82102**		**83104**		**74010**	
			P		**SP**			**W**	**SL**		**S**		**X**	
0	**Zielona Góra** d.	0522	0635	0759	0909	0924	1152	1256	1448	1553	1659	2005	2057	...
23	Nowa Sól d.	0541	0652	0826	0927	0943	1212	|	1506	1614	1717	2025	|	...
54	Glogów d.	0625	0724	0855	0952	1013	1243	1334	1538	1651	1742	2055	2135	...
154	**Wrocław** Gł a.	0813	0847	1041	1125	1207	1431	1454	1718	1837	1908	2240	2257	...
	Kraków **1075** a.	...	1250	...	1517	...	...	1759	...	...	2317	...	...	...

	NJ			*IC*	*TLK*	*IC*				*IC*	*IC*		
	47010			**38105**	**28103**	**56**				**3805**	**37105**		
	X			**S**	**LS**	**W**	Ⓑ			**PS**	**P**		
Kraków **1075** d.	...	...	...	0514	...	0952	...	...	...	1312	1520	...	...
Wrocław Gł. d.	0520	0551	0758	0905	1137	1255	1350	1457	1652	1710	1922	1955	...
Glogów d.	0650	0723	0936	1028	1311	1420	1521	1363	1842	1833	2054	2134	...
Nowa Sól d.	|	0753	1005	1054	1337	|	1552	1704	1911	1858	2118	2203	...
Zielona Góra a.	0726	0817	1029	1109	1352	1455	1616	1737	1934	1912	2138	2227	...

L – To / from Lublin (Table **1067**).
P – To / from Przemyśl (Table **1075**).

S – To / from Szczecin (Table **1003**).
W – WAWEL – (12) ✕ Berlin - Przemyśl and v.v.

X – *ÖBB nightjet* METROPOL – 🛏 1,2 cl., ▬ 2 cl., (2) Berlin - Graz / Budapest and v.v. See Table **77**.

1005 ZIELONA GÓRA - WEGLINIEC - JELENIA GÓRA

km		⊖		⊖		⊖			⊖		⊖	
			Ⓒ									
0	**Zielona Góra** d.	...	0625	...	0747	...	1052	1336	...	1536	...	1919
54	Zary **1086** d.	...	0739	...	0853	...	1158	1442	...	1642	...	2025
94	Wegliniec **1085** d.	...	0839	...	0951	...	1335	1543	...	1748	...	2146
118	Zgorzelec Miasto d.	...	|	...	1012	...	1356	1603	...	1809	...	2207
	Görlitz **1085** d.	0539	|	0939	|	1339	|	|	1739	|	1939	|
120	Zgorzelec **1085** d.	0544	|	0944	1017	1344	1406	1607	1744	1814	1944	2212
	Görlitz **1085** a.	|	|	|	1024	|	1410	1611	|	1820	|	2218
144	Lubań Śląski d.	0613	0906	1013	...	1413	...	...	1815	...	2016	...
196	**Jelenia Góra** a.	0715	1013	1115	...	1515	...	...	1915	...	2118	...

	⊖			⊖		⊖		⊖			⊖
										Ⓒ	
Jelenia Góra d.	0545	...	...	0945	...	1345	...	1545	...	1917	1945
Lubań Śląski d.	0653	...	...	1053	...	1453	...	1653	...	2019	2054
Görlitz **1085** d.	|	0908	1051	|	1508	|	1708	|	1905	|	|
Zgorzelec **1085** d.	0723	0913	1056	1123	1513	1523	1713	1723	1909	|	2123
Görlitz **1085** a.	0727	|	|	1127	|	1527	|	1727	|	|	2127
Zgorzelec Miasto d.	...	0916	1059	...	1515	...	1716	...	1912	|	...
Wegliniec **1085** d.	...	0947	1129	...	1555	...	1746	...	1945	2055	...
Zary **1086** d.	...	1059	1221	...	1706	...	1923	...	2038	2153	...
Zielona Góra a.	...	1211	1326	...	1810	...	2036	...	...	2257	...

⊖ – Operator: Koleje Dolnośląskie.

☛ 🚌 Görlitz Bahnhof - Zgorzelec Miasto and v.v. every 30 minutes (journey 22 minutes).

SZCZECIN - POZNAŃ 1010

km		EIC 8100 8101 ⚒	K	IC 83102 83103	Ⓐ	Ⓒ		IC 81106 81107	K	IC 81103 81102 Y		IC 83100 83101 R			K	IC 81100 81101			IC 83173 83172 P		TLK 81170 81171		
	Świnoujście d.	...	...	...	...	...	...	0614	...	0801	...	...	...	1215	...	...	...	...	1705	...	2103	...	...
0	**Szczecin** Gł. **1015** d.	0349	...	0525	0527	...	...	0750	...	0930	1011	1156	1240	1405	...	1602	1635	1810	1840	...	2238	...	...
15	Szczecin Dąbie **1015** d.	0401	...	0538	0542	...	...	0803	...	0942	1025	1209	1256	1419	...	1614	1648	1826	1854	...	|	...	...
40	Stargard **1015** d.	0420	...	0601	0607	...	...	0822	...	1002	1048	1228	1321	1442	...	1635	1719	1854	1914	...	|	...	...
130	Krzyż **1000** d.	0604	0718	0748	0803	0803	...	1015	1023	1154	1311	1422	1509	1700	1746	1820	1912	2059	2108	...	|	...	...
213	**Poznań** Gł. **1000** a.	0706	0838	0855	0921	0921	...	1120	1141	1300	1423	1529	1629	1812	1914	1925	2042	2214	2221	...	0216	...	...
	Warszawa Cent. **1001** a.	1009	...	|	...	...	...	1450y	...	1632	...	1908	...	...	...	2300	...	...	|	...	0625y	...	...
	Katowice **1075 1080** a.	...	...	1302	...	...	...	...	...	...	...	...	...	...	...	...	...	...	0436	...	...	...	...
	Kraków Gł **1075 1080** a.	...	...	1412	...	...	...	...	...	...	...	...	...	...	...	...	...	...	0612	...	...	...	...

	Ⓐ	⚒	IC 38173 38172 P		K	IC 18101 18100			K		IC 38100 38101 R		IC 18103 18102 Y		IC 18107 18106	EIC 1800 1801 Ⓑ	⑤⑦	IC 38103 38102	K	TLK 18171 18170		
Kraków Gł. **1075 1080** d.	...	...	2138	...	...	...	...	...	...	...	...	...	...	...	...	...	...	1400	...	...	...	...
Katowice **1075 1080** d.	...	...	2303	...	...	...	...	...	...	...	...	...	...	...	...	...	...	1519	...	...	...	...
Warszawa Cent. **1001** d.	...	...	|	...	...	0514	...	...	...	...	0927	...	1157	...	1316y	1503	...	|	...	2107j	...	...
Poznań Gł. **1000** d.	...	...	0500	0621	0847	0908	0915	...	1151	1211	1313	...	1536	1602	1707	1822	1830	1934	2002r	0221	...	...
Krzyż **1000** d.	0446	0516	0629	0804	1006	1025	1101	...	1309	1334	1425	...	1647	1734	1822	1933	2000	2109	2131	|	...	...
Stargard **1015** d.	0645	0731	0822	0950	...	1220	1307	...	...	1526	1619	...	1850	1953	2036	2123	2207	2253	...	|	...	...
Szczecin Dąbie **1015** d.	0707	0754	0840	1012	...	1241	1328	...	...	1548	1637	...	1907	2015	2057	2140	2226	2311	...	|	...	...
Szczecin Gł. **1015** a.	0722	0809	0854	1026	...	1253	1342	...	...	1603	1708	...	1920	2045	2110	2153	2240	2323	...	0559	...	...
Świnoujście a.	...	...	1028	1206	...	...	...	...	...	...	...	...	2101	...	2236	...	...	...	...	0733	...	...

km		Ⓐ	Ⓒ	Ⓐ								Ⓑ
0	**Świnoujście** d.	0432	0526	0622	0819	1016	1215	...	1536	...	1802	1943
99	Szczecin Dąbie a.	0553	0651	0746	0943	1140	1337	...	1701	...	1927	2114
111	**Szczecin** Gł. a.	0608	0707	0807	0958	1156	1355	...	1716	...	1945	2129

	Ⓐ	Ⓒ							Ⓑ	
Szczecin Gł. d.	0511	0515	0732	...	1029	...	1337	1538	1741	1953
Szczecin Dąbie d.	0525	0529	0748	...	1042	...	1356	1551	1757	2010
Świnoujście a.	0700	0700	0911	...	1206	...	1521	1718	1923	2134

km		⚒					82100 §M		Ⓑ	⑦	⑤	
0	**Szczecin** Gł. d.	...	...	0700	...	0853	1130	...	1706	1920	...	...
12	Szczecin Dąbie d.	...	...	0713	...	0907	1145	...	1720	1935	...	...
37	Stargard d.	0442	...	0739	...	0946	1209	...	1743	2003	2003	...
102	Kalisz Pomorski d.	0553	...	0849	...	1048	1311	...	1853	2118	2118	...
146	Wałcz d.	0640	...	0934	...	1136	1359	...	1948	2204	2204	...
176	**Piła** Główna a.	0709	...	1003	...	1206	1430	...	2017	...	...	...

	①⑥	⚒	⚒			28101 §M	⚒	†		
Piła Główna d.	...	0606	0735	1102	...	1323	1528	1528	...	1917
Wałcz d.	0349	0641	0803	1137	...	1358	1556	1556	...	1945
Kalisz Pomorski d.	0435	0725	0848	1221	...	1440	1642	1642	...	2030
Stargard d.	0558	0834	0953	1328	...	1544	1744	1745	...	2133
Szczecin Dąbie d.	0625	0857	1019	1353	...	1606	...	1805	...	2158
Szczecin Gł. a.	0640	0911	1034	1410	...	1621	...	1820	...	2216

K – To / from Kostrzyn (Table **1000**).
M – To / from Lublin (Table **1055**).
P – To / from Przemyśl (Table **1075**).
R – To / from Rzeszów (Table **1058**).
Y – To / from Suwałki (Table **1042**).
j – Warszawa **Wschodnia**.
r – 1949 Jan. 29 - Feb. 11.
y – Warszawa **Gdańska**.
§ – *TLK* service.

SZCZECIN - KOSZALIN - GDYNIA - GDAŃSK 1015

km		EIP 8300 8301 K	IC 85108 85109 O	IC 78172 78173 P	IC 85106 85107 O			IC 81114 81115 L		IC 48101 48100 S	IC 81104 81105 Y		IC 3807 J	IC 85104 85105 O	Ⓐ	IC 48103 48102 A	IC 85102 85103 O			IC 82105 B	IC 85100		IC 68103 68102 A	TLK 83170 K	
0	**Szczecin** Gł. **1010** d.	...	0505	...	0713	0738	...	...	...	...	1110	1203	...	1317	1345	...	1520	1532	...	...	1804	...	...	...	2009
15	Szczecin Dąbie **1010** d.	...	0518	...	0726	0753	...	...	...	...	1123	1217	...	1329	1359	...	1533	1546	...	...	1816	...	...	...	2023
40	Stargard **1010** d.	...	0538	...	0747	0815	...	...	...	...	1143	1243	...	1349	1421	...	1552	1609	...	...	1836	...	...	...	2046
*231	**Poznań** Gł. d.	...	|	0523	|	|	0537	...	0829	0935	|	|	1144	|	|	1341	|	|	1440	...	|	1647	1732	...	|
*135	Piła Gł. d.	...	|	0639	|	|	0725	...	1008	1044	|	|	1254	|	|	1455	|	|	1617	1747	|	1824	1843	...	|
*64	Szczecinek d.	...	|	0739	|	|	0832	...	1116	1138	|	|	1348	|	|	1550	|	|	1721	1844	|	1928	1954	...	|
151	Białogard a.	...	0652	0833	0905	0939	0938	...	1218	1234	1304	1420	1445	1505	1551	1656	1705	1741	1826	1948	1959	2031t	2106	...	2214
151	Białogard d.	...	0653	0836	0906	0943	0944	...	1218	1235	1309	1422	1448	1507	1552	1657	1710	1743	1827	1952	2000	2036t	2113	...	2224
187	Kołobrzeg a.	...	|	|	|	|	1017	...	|	|	|	|	1518	|	|	|	|	|	1904	2022	|	|	|	...	|
**43	Kołobrzeg d.	0615	|	|	|	|	...	1039	|	|	|	|	...	|	|	|	|	|	...	...	|	|	|	2019	|
175	**Koszalin** d.	0650	0715	0900	0922	1005	...	1121	1238	1251	1325	1510	...	1531	1628	1714	1726	1807	...	...	2016	2111t	2131	2110	2241
242	Słupsk d.	0728	0755	0941	1002	1112	...	1206	...	1332	1405	1602	...	1613	1722	1753	1807	1914	...	...	2107	...	2212	2155	...
294	Lębork d.	0800	0827	...	1034	...	...	1239	...	...	1437	...	...	1652	...	...	1840	...	...	...	2138	...	...	2228	...
353	**Gdynia** Gł. a.	0835	0906	...	1115	...	...	1322	...	...	1518	...	...	1733	...	...	1929	...	...	...	2220	...	...	2311	...
353	**Gdynia** Gł. ▷ d.	0838	0912	...	1118	...	...	1342	...	...	1522	...	...	1744	...	...	1945	...	...	...	2222	...	...	2336	...
362	Sopot ▷ d.	0846	0921	...	1126	...	...	1351	...	...	1531	...	...	1752	...	...	1954	...	...	...	2230	...	...	2346	...
374	**Gdańsk** Gł. ▷ a.	0901	0934	...	1140	...	...	1406	...	...	1545	...	...	1806	...	...	2008	...	...	...	2244	...	...	0003	...
	Warszawa C. **1025/30** a.	1135	...	...	...	...	...	1725	...	...	...	...	...	...	...	...	...	...	...	...	...	...	...	0338f	...

				IC 86103 86102 A	IC 58101		IC 82104 83105 B	TLK 38171 38170 K	Ⓐ	IC 84103 84102 A	IC 58103 58102 O		TLK 58105 O	IC 8306 J		IC 84101 84100 S	IC 18105 18104 Y			IC 18115 18114 L	IC 58107 58106 O	IC 87173 87172 P	Ⓑ	IC 58109 58108 O	EIP 3801 3800 K
Warszawa C. **1025/30** d.	...	...	...	...	...	...	...	0213f	...	...	...	...	...	...	...	...	...	...	...	1045g	...	...	...	...	1633f
Gdańsk Gł. ▷ d.	...	...	...	...	0515	...	...	0554	...	...	0823	...	1020	...	...	...	1215	...	...	1350	1610	...	...	1819	1857
Sopot ▷ d.	...	...	...	...	0529	...	...	0610	...	...	0838	...	1034	...	...	...	1230	...	...	1407	1624	...	...	1833	1911
Gdynia Gł. ▷ a.	...	...	...	...	0537	...	...	0619	...	...	0847	...	1043	...	...	...	1240	...	...	1417	1632	...	...	1841	1919
Gdynia Gł. d.	...	...	...	...	0541	...	...	0639	...	...	0908	...	1048	...	...	...	1243	...	...	1438	1635	...	...	1847	1922
Lębork d.	...	...	...	...	0634	...	...	0731	...	...	0954	...	1131	...	...	...	1333	...	...	1529	1736	...	...	1933	1959
Słupsk d.	...	...	0500k	0551	0710	...	...	0825	0943	1010	1031	...	1205	...	...	1415	1406	1440	...	1613	1807	1818	1826	2008	2030
Koszalin d.	0412	...	0548	0654	0804	...	...	0922	1038	1055	1114	1155	1252	...	1421	1509	1448	1555	...	1703	1853	1906	1917	2056	2109
Kołobrzeg a.	|	...	|	|	|	...	...	1009	|	|	|	|	|	...	|	|	|	|	...	1749	|	|	|	|	2143
Kołobrzeg d.	|	0447j	|	|	|	0721	0830		|	|	|	|	|	1233	|	|	|	|	1729	...	|	|	|	|	...
Białogard a.	0427	0521j	0605	0711	0820	0832	0859	IC	1053	1110	1129	1216	1307	1304	1443	1525	1504	1614	1801	...	1909	1921	1933	2111	...
Białogard d.	0428	0524j	0607	0712	0822	0835	0900	**83106**	1054	1111	1130	1239	1309	1312	1447	1526	1508	1617	1802	...	1912	1922	1934	2112	...
Szczecinek d.	|	0622	|	0813	|	0938	0955	2 **K**	|	1216	|	|	|	1414	1549	1622	|	|	1907	...	|	2021	|	|	...
Piła Gł. d.	|	0729	|	0909	|	1045	1053	1121	|	1322	|	|	|	1522	1655	1719	|	|	2029	...	|	2103	|	|	...
Poznań Gł. a.	|	0912	|	1024	|	1223	...	1234	|	1431	|	|	|	1636	1836	1843	|	|	2207	...	|	2228	|	|	...
Stargard **1010** d.	0612	...	0746	...	0941	...	...	...	1211	...	1243	1407	1425	...	...	...	1624	1752	...	...	2026	...	2101	2225	...
Szczecin Dąbie **1010** a.	0635	...	0809	...	1000	...	...	...	1233	...	1301	1434	1444	...	...	...	1644	1815	...	...	2045	...	2123	2244	...
Szczecin Gł. **1010** a.	0652	...	0824	...	1013	...	...	...	1247	...	1314	1447	1458	...	...	...	1659	1830	...	...	2059	...	2137	2257	...

A – To / from Wrocław (Table **1070**).
B – To / from Lublin and Zamość (Table **1055**).
J – To / from Kraków (Tables **1070**, **1075**).
K – To / from Kraków (Tables **1065**, **1067**).
L – To / from Łódź (Table **1090**).
O – To / from Olsztyn (Table **1035**).
P – To / from Przemyśl (Table **1075**).
S – To / from Katowice (Tables **1070**, **1075**).
Y – To / from Białystok (Table **1035**).
f – Warszawa **Wschodnia**.
g – Warszawa **Gdańska**.
j – Not ⑦.
k – Ⓐ.
t – Not ⑥.
***** – Distance from Białogard.
****** – Distance from Koszalin.
▷ – Frequent local trains run between Gdynia and Gdansk.

1016 SZCZECIN - KOŁOBRZEG

km											
		Ⓐ	⚒	Ⓒ		Ⓐ		Ⓐ	Ⓑ		⑤
0	**Szczecin** Gł. d.	0547	0637	0907	1038	1323	1500	1609	1816	2033	2217
35	Goleniów ✈ d.	0620	0714	0940	1110	1401	1534	1646	1900	2112	2255
141	Kołobrzeg a.	0757	0902	1123	1258	1539	1722	1828	2101	2255	0025

	⚒		Ⓑ	⚒	Ⓐ	Ⓑ		⑦		
Kołobrzeg d.	0402	0624	0803	1023	1202	1337	1550	1724	1832	...
Goleniów ✈ d.	0542	0829	1002	1212	1403	1523	1734	1849	2022	...
Szczecin Gł. a.	0614	0906	1036	1252	1445	1601	1819	1929	2056	...

1020 GDYNIA - GDAŃSK - BYDGOSZCZ - POZNAŃ

km		*IC*		*IC*	*IC*	*IC*		*IC*	*IC*	*IC*	*IC*		*IC*		*IC*	*IC*	*IC*		*IC*	*IC*	*IC*		*TLK*	
		54150		**5600**	**56100**	**57108**		**5312**	**58**	**57100**	**5314**		**5602**		**57104**	**56102**	**5604**		**57106**	**57102**	**5700**		**53172**	
		53150		**5601**	**56101**	**57109**		**5313**	**57000**	**57101**	**5315**		**5603**		**57105**	**56103**	**5605**		**56151**	**57103**	**5701**		**53173**	
			Ⓐ											Ⓐ										
						F		**J**	**B**	**F**	**P**				**F**	**G**							**A**	
0	**Gdynia** Gł. ▷ d.	...	...	0444	...	0557	...	0740	0906	...	0953	...	1144	...	1349	...	1547	...	1749	...	1906	...	2240	...
9	Sopot ▷ d.	...	...	0453	...	0606	...	0750	0915	...	1003	...	1154	...	1358	...	1557	...	1759	...	1915	...	2249	...
21	**Gdańsk** Gł. ▷ d.	...	...	0512	...	0622	...	0809	0931	...	1022	...	1214	...	1415	...	1615	...	1818	...	1932	...	2310	...
53	Tczew ▷ d.	...	...	0532	...	0645	...	0829	0947	...	1040	...	1234	...	1435	...	1634	...	1839	...	1951	...	2331	...
181	**Bydgoszcz** Gł. ▷ a.	...	...	0645	...	0757	...	0943	1050	...	1150	...	1345	...	1549	...	1746	...	1953	...	2100	...	0047	...
181	**Bydgoszcz** Gł. d.	0448	...	0650	...	0800	...	0946	1053	...	1153	...	1348	...	1556	...	1749	...	1956	...	2103	...	0050	...
	Olsztyn Gł. d.	|	...	|	0545	|	...	|	|	0919	|	...	|	...	|	1432	|	...	|	1802	|	...	|	...
	Iława d.	|	...	|	0640	|	...	|	|	1015	|	...	|	...	|	1526	|	...	|	1900	|	...	|	...
	Toruń Gł. d.	|	...	|	0753	|	...	|	|	1127	|	...	|	1434	|	1636	|	...	|	2013	|	...	|	...
227	Inowrocław d.	0518	0703	0718	0815	0828	...	1016	1122	1149	1221	...	1416	1503	1624	1659	1818	...	2025	2036	2130	...	0120	...
283	Gniezno d.	0558	0804	0755	0853	0906	...	1056	1154	1231	1259	...	1456	1600	1702	1746	1853	...	2105	2113	2205	...	0210	...
334	**Poznań** Gł. a.	0628	0851	0824	0923	0936	...	1127	1221	1301	1327	...	1526	1647	1732	1817	1921	...	2137	2144	2235	...	0251	...
	Wrocław **1070** a.	0823	...	1017	1128	...	...	1319	...	...	1522	...	1703	...	...	2008	2120	...	...	...	...	...	0451	...

km		*TLK*		*IC*	*IC*	*IC*		*IC*		*IC*	*IC*		*IC*	*IC*	*IC*	*IC*	*IC*		*IC*	*IC*	*IC*		*IC*	
		35173		**7501**	**75106**	**75103**		**6505**		**65103**	**75104**		**6503**	**3515**	**75101**	**59**	**3512**		**75108**	**65101**	**6501**		**45151**	
		35172		**7500**	**65150**	**75102**		**6504**		**65102**	**75105**		**6502**	**3514**	**75100**	**75000**	**3513**		**75109**	**65100**	**6500**		**35151**	
			Ⓐ				Ⓐ																	
		A								**G**	**F**			**P**	**F**	**B**			**F**					
	Wrocław **1070** d.	2353	...	...	...	...	...	0645	...	0842	...	...	1056	1236	...	...	1450	...	...	1634	1756	...	2014	...
	Poznań Gł. d.	0207	0425	0528	0619	0646	0652	0833	...	1037	1045	...	1232	1421	1450	1537	1638	...	1850	1825	1942	...	2205	...
	Gniezno d.	0244	0517	0558	0658	0720	0800	0907	...	1110	1118	...	1304	1455	1525	1606	1711	...	1922	1903	2014	...	2238	...
0	Inowrocław d.	0327	0600	0631	0738	0757	0847	0938	...	1145	1155	...	1341	1533	1559	1637	1750	...	1959	1941	2049	...	2319	...
35	**Toruń** Gł. d.	|	...	|	|	0820	0917	|	...	1215	|	...	|	|	1628	|	|	...	|	2005	|	...	|	...
129	Iława d.	|	...	|	|	0931	...	|	...	1330	|	...	|	|	1736	|	|	...	|	2117	|	...	|	...
198	**Olsztyn** Gł. a.	|	...	|	|	1023	...	|	...	1427	|	...	|	|	1842	|	|	...	|	2209	|	...	|	...
	Bydgoszcz Gł. a.	0355	...	0657	0806	...	...	1007	...	...	1222	...	1407	1559	...	1702	1819	...	2027	...	2116	...	0001	...
	Bydgoszcz Gł. ▷ d.	0358	...	0700	0809	...	...	1010	...	...	1225	...	1410	1605	...	1705	1822	...	2032	...	2121	...	...	...
	Tczew ▷ d.	0519	...	0811	0929	...	...	1121	...	...	1341	...	1526	1718	...	1811	1941	...	2155	...	2240	...	...	...
	Gdańsk Gł. ▷ a.	0538	...	0828	0948	...	...	1137	...	...	1359	...	1542	1734	...	1827	1959	...	2215	...	2256	...	...	...
	Sopot ▷ a.	0559	...	0846	1009	...	...	1154	...	...	1415	...	1601	1754	...	1844	2017	...	2232	...	2314	...	...	...
	Gdynia Gł. ▷ a.	0608	...	0854	1018	...	...	1203	...	...	1423	...	1610	1803	...	1852	2025	...	2240	...	2322	...	...	...

A – ROZEWIE – 1, 2 cl., 2 cl., (2) Gdynia - Wrocław - Kraków and v.v.
B – BERLIN GDANSK EXPRESS / GEDANIA – (12) ✕ Ⓡ Berlin - Poznań - Gdynia and v.v. (Table **57**).
F – To / from Zielona Góra (Table **1001**).
G – To / from Giżycko (Table **1035**).
J – To / from Kraków (Table **1075**).
P – To / from Przemyśl (Table **1075**).
▷ – See also Table **1025**. Frequent local services run between Gdynia and Gdansk (see Table **1035**).

1025 GDYNIA - GDAŃSK - BYDGOSZCZ - WARSZAWA / ŁODŹ

km		*IC*	*IC*		*IC*		*IC*	*TLK*	*TLK*	*IC*	*IC*	*TLK*	*IC*		*IC*	*IC*	*TLK*	*IC*		*IC*	*IC*		
		5332	**5130**		**81110**		**52100**	**54100**	**58110**	**5128**	**82104**	**54102**	**5360**		**5126**	**7322**	**82100**	**5420**		**5132**	**5124**		
		5333	**5131**				**52101**	**54101**	**58111**	**5129**	**82105**	**54103**	**5361**		**5127**	**7323**	**82101**	**5421**		**5133**	**5125**		
					2				2														
		R			**L**		**C**		**K**		**T D**						**T S**	**M**					
0	**Gdynia** Gł. ▷ d.	...	...	...	...	...	...	0643	0807	...	...	0924	1047	...	...	...	...	1445	...	1658	...	...	...
9	Sopot ▷ d.	...	...	...	...	...	...	0653	0817	...	...	0933	1056	...	...	...	...	1454	...	1707	...	...	...
21	**Gdańsk** Gł. ▷ d.	...	...	...	...	...	...	0709	0835	...	...	0948	1117	...	...	...	...	1511	...	1724	...	...	...
53	Tczew ▷ d.	...	...	...	...	...	...	0732	0900	...	...	1011	1136	...	...	...	...	1532	...	1746	...	...	...
181	**Bydgoszcz** Gł. ▷ a.	...	...	...	...	...	...	0846	...	...	...	|	1244	...	...	...	...	1640	...	1856	...	...	...
181	**Bydgoszcz** Gł. d.	0400	0535	...	0633	...	0824	0906	...	1028	1228	|	1254	...	1423	...	1611	1650	...	1911	1900	...	...
232	**Toruń** Gł. d.	0439	0614	...	0714	...	0904	0950	...	1107	1306	|	1333	...	1502	...	1649	1729	...	1952	1939	...	...
287	Włocławek d.	0514	|	...	0749	...	0939	1026	...	|	1341	|	1411	...	|	...	1723	1804	...	2027	2014	...	...
342	Kutno d.	0556	|	...	0826	...	1017	1109	...	|	1426	1518	1455	...	|	1753	1759	1846	...	2116	2052	...	...
	Warszawa Wschodnia a.	|	0922		|	...	|	|	...	1407	|	|	|	...	1814	|	|	|	...	|	|	...	...
469	**Warszawa** Centralna a.	0726y	0930	...	0952y	...	1149y	|	...	1415	1555y	|	|	...	1824	|	1935	|	...	|	2219y	...	...
474	**Warszawa** Wschodnia a.	0739	...	...	1013	...	1201	|	...	...	...	|	|	...	...	|	1946	|	...	|	2235	...	...
413	**Łódź** Widzew a.	...	...	...	...	...	...	1228	...	...	...	1635	1625	...	...	1917	...	2006	...	2234	...	...	...
	Katowice **1060** a.	...	...	...	...	...	...	1508	...	...	...	1932	|	...	...	|	...	2246	...	...	...	...	...
	Kraków **1065** a.	...	...	...	...	...	...	...	...	...	...	...	1928	...	...	2210	...	...	...	...	...	...	...

		IC	*IC*		*IC*	*TLK*	*IC*	*IC*		*TLK*	*IC*	*IC*		*IC*	*TLK*	*TLK*	*IC*	*IC*	*IC*		*IC*		
		1533	**1525**		**4521**	**28100**	**3722**	**1527**		**45103**	**3561**	**28104**		**1529**	**85110**	**45100**	**25101**	**18111**	**1530**		**3533**		
		1532	**1524**		**4520**	**28101**	**3723**				**3560**	**28105**		**1528**	**85111**	**45101**	**25100**	**18110**	**1531**		**3532**		
															2			2					
					M	**S T**						**T D**			**K**		**C**	**L**			**R**		
Kraków **1065** d.	...	...	...	...	...	...	0635	...	...	...	0920	...	...	...	...	...	...	...	...	...	...	...	...
Katowice **1060** d.	...	...	...	...	0541	...	|	...	...	0913	|	...	...	...	...	1319	...	...	...	...	...	...	...
Łódź Widzew d.	...	0551	...	...	0820	...	0920	...	...	1152	1210	...	...	...	...	1609	...	...	...	...	...	...	...
Warszawa Wschodnia d.	...	|	...	...	|	...	|	...	...	|	|	1209	...	1429	...	|	1628	1721	...	...	2013	...	...
Warszawa Centralna d.	...	|	0540	...	|	0816y	|	1007t	...	|	|	1236	...	1448	...	|	1639y	1750y	1859	...	2022	...	...
Warszawa Wschodnia d.	...	|	0548	...	|	|	|	|	...	|	|	|	...	|	...	|	|	|	1907	...	|	...	...
Kutno d.	...	0720	|	...	0935	0944	1046	1146	...	1310	1328	1421	...	1623	...	1728	1816	1902	|	...	2203	...	...
Włocławek d.	...	0756	|	...	1013	1022	...	1223	...	|	1403	1457	...	1704	...	1810	1853	1938	|	...	2239	...	...
Toruń Gł. d.	...	0834	0853	...	1050	1059	...	1300	...	|	1452	1533	...	1741	...	1848	1929	2017	2212	...	2315	...	...
Bydgoszcz Gł a.	...	0911	0931	...	1128	1135	...	1338	...	|	1530	1610	...	1821	...	1926	2007	2054	2252	...	2353	...	...
Bydgoszcz Gł. ▷ d.	...	0922	...	...	1138	...	...	...	...	|	1540	...	...	...	...	1946	...	...	...	...	...	...	...
Tczew ▷ d.	...	1036	...	...	1253	...	...	...	...	1846	1657	...	...	...	2051	2102	...	...	...	...	...	...	...
Gdańsk Gł. ▷ a.	...	1056	...	...	1312	...	...	...	...	1907	1714	...	...	...	2116	2123	...	...	...	...	...	...	...
Sopot ▷ a.	...	1112	...	...	1331	...	...	...	...	1924	1733	...	...	...	2133	2140	...	...	...	...	...	...	...
Gdynia Gł. ▷ a.	...	1121	...	...	1339	...	...	...	...	1932	1741	...	...	...	2144	2149	...	...	...	...	...	...	...

C – To / from Chełm (Table **1055**).
D – To / from Kołobrzeg (Table **1015**).
K – To / from Kostrzyn (Table **1000**).
L – To / from Piła (Table **1000**).
M – To / from Bielsko Biała (Table **1060**).
R – To / from Rzeszów (Table **1058**).
S – To / from Szczecin (Table **1010**).
T – To / from Lublin (Table **1055**).
t – Warszawa **Główna**.
y – Warszawa **Gdańska**.
▷ – See also Table **1020**. Frequent local services run between Gdynia and Gdansk.

GDYNIA - GDAŃSK - (OLSZTYN -) WARSZAWA 1030

km		IC	TLK	EIP	EIP	IC	EIP	IC	EIP	IC	TLK	IC	EIP	EIP	IC	EIP	TLK	EIP	IC	EIP	EIP	IC	IC	EIP	TLK	EIP	IC	EIP	TLK
		5326	**53104**	**5300**	**5302**	**5424**	**5400**	**5112**	**8300**	**5324**	**53102**	**54000**	**5304**	**5306**	**5320**	**5404**	**81114**	**5308**	**5422**	**5406**	**5104**	**5122**	**5110**	**5310**	**53170**	**5102**	**5328**	**5100**	**83170**
		5327	**53105**	**5301**	**5303**	**5461**	**5401**		**8301**	**5325**	**83152**	**107**	**5305**	**5307**	**5321**	**5405**	**81115**	**5309**	**5423**	**5407**		**5123**		**5311**	**53171**		**5329**		**83171**
							Ⓑ																Ⓐ						
		K	Z	K	K	T	T		K	K	K	X	K	K	K	T	L	R	B	T		L		K	Z		K		K
	Kołobrzeg **1015** ..d.	...	...	...	...	...	...	...	0615	...	0644t	...	...	...	...	...	1039	...	...	...	...	...	...	...	...	...	...	...	2019
0	**Gdynia** Gł. ▶ d.	...	0437	0534	0637	...	0734	0748	0838	...	0942	1021	1031	1232	...	1331	1342	1434	...	1531	1634	...	1646	1738	1825	1843	...	1955	2336
9	Sopot ▶ d.	...	0446	0542	0645	...	0742	0757	0846	...	0951	1030	1039	1240	...	1339	1351	1442	...	1539	1642	...	1655	1746	1834	1851	...	2003	2346
21	**Gdańsk** Gł. ▶ d.	...	0504	0559	0702	...	0759	0816	0903	...	1010	1048	1058	1257	...	1357	1410	1459	...	1556	1659	...	1710	1803	1852	1908	...	2020	0008
53	Tczew ▶ d.	...	0521	0614	|	...	0814	0833	|	...	1028	1106	1113	1311	...	1412	1428	1514	...	1611	1714	...	1726	|	1911	1923	...	2035	0028
72	Malbork ▶ d.	...	0534	0625	|	...	0825	0845	|	...	1042	1128	1124	1322	...	1423	1441	1525	...	1622	1725	...	1728	|	1925	1935	...	2046	0043
•	**Olsztyn** ▶ d.	0502	|	|	|	0803	|	|	|	1001	|	|	|	|	1353	|	|	|	1601	|	|	1755	|	|	|	|	1937	|	|
141	Iława Gł. ▶ d.	|	0614	0658	|	|	0858	0924	|	|	1125	1207	1158	1355	|	1456	1521	1558	|	1656	1758	|	1817	|	2013	2009	2030	2119	0128
201	Działdowo d.	0602	0646	|	|	0903	|	0956	|	1100	1158	1239	|	|	1453	1527	1554	|	1701	|	|	1855	1848	|	2046	|	2101	|	0204
251	Ciechanów d.	0627	0713	|	|	0928	|	1023	|	1126	1227	|	|	|	1519	|	1622	|	1726	1745	|	1922	1915	|	2117	|	2127	|	0237
305	Modlin ✈ d.	|	|	|	|	|	|	|	|	|	|	|	|	|	|	|	|	|	|	|	|	|	|	|	|	|	|	|	|
345	**Warszawa** Wsch. ..a.	0721	0809	0829	0929	1020	1029	1116	1129	1217	1323	1413j	1329	1526	1611	1629	1717	1729	1818	1829	1927	2016	2006	2029	2214	2140	2219	2254	0338
350	**Warszawa** Cent. ...a.	0733y	0820	0837	0937	1028	1037	1125	1136	1228y	1330	...	1336	1534	1628y	1637	1725	1737	1828	1837	1935	2024	...	2036	2222	2148	2226	2301	...

	TLK	TLK	IC	EIP	EIP	IC	EIC	IC	EIP	EIP	IC	EIP	IC	EIP	IC	EIP	IC	EIP	TLK	EIP	IC	EIP	IC	EIP	IC	EIP	TLK	EIP	IC
	38171	**35170**	**1521**	**1501**	**1503**	**1522**	**4550**	**1511**	**3510**	**4508**	**4523**	**3508**	**18115**	**4506**	**3520**	**3506**	**106**	**3504**	**38153**	**4504**	**3524**	**3801**	**1513**	**4502**	**4560**	**3502**	**35105**	**3500**	**3526**
	38170	**35171**				**1523**	**4551**		**3511**	**4509**	**4522**	**3509**	**18114**	**4507**	**3521**	**3507**	**45000**	**3505**	**35102**	**4505**	**3525**	**3800**		**4503**	**4524**	**3503**	**35104**	**3501**	**3527**
							⑥	Ⓐ																Ⓑ					
	K	Z				L	T		K	T	T	R	L	T	K	K	X	K	K	T	K	K		T	T	K	Z	T	K
Warszawa Cent. ....d.	...	0430	0530	0557	0720	0729	0820	0825	0830	0920	...	1025	...	1125	1135y	1225	...	1425	...	1529	1535y	1625	1617	1730	1735	1830	1840	1930	1940y
Warszawa Wsch. ...d.	0213	0444	0538	0608	0728	0744	0829	0844	0838	0928	0958j	1033	1045j	1133	1145	1233	1334j	1433	1445j	1537	1544	1633	1643	1738	1744	1838	1849	1938	1948
Modlin ✈ d.	|	|	|	|	|	|	|	|	|	|	|	|	|	|	|	|	|	|	|	|	|	|	|	|	|	|	|	|	|
Ciechanów d.	0318	0545	0633	|	|	0837	|	0939	|	|	1048	|	1139	1216	1237	|	|	|	1540	|	1638	|	1735	|	1838	|	1944	|	2042
Działdowo d.	0352	0617	0659	|	|	0904	|	1008	|	|	1114	|	1209	|	1303	|	1449	|	1609	|	1705	|	1802	|	1906	|	2012	|	2109
Iława Gł. ▶ d.	0430	0651	0731	0741	0900	|	|	1041	|	1059	|	1204	1242	1307	|	1405	1524	1604	1642	1708	|	|	1833	1909	|	|	2046	2108	|
Olsztyn ▶ a.	|	|	0825	|	|	1005	|	|	|	|	1223	|	|	|	1402	|	|	|	|	|	1804	|	|	|	2005	|	|	|	2208
Malbork ▶ d.	0515	0731	...	0813	0932	...	|	1118	|	1132	...	1236	1320	1340	...	1428	1600	1636	1722	1740	...	|	1909	1941	...	|	2126	2141	...
Tczew ▶ d.	0531	0744	...	0824	0943	...	|	1131	|	1142	...	1247	1332	1350	...	1448	1613	1647	1727	1751	...	|	1921	1952	...	|	2139	2251	...
Gdańsk Gł. ▶ a.	0549	0802	...	0838	0956	...	1113	1146	1101	1156	...	1300	1347	1404	...	1502	1630	1700	1754	1804	...	1856	1936	2005	...	2101	2154	2205	...
Sopot ▶ a.	0610	0824	...	0855	1015	...	1132	1205	1118	1213	...	1317	1407	1421	...	1519	1650	1716	1812	1823	...	1911	1955	2022	...	2117	2212	2222	...
Gdynia Gł. ▶ a.	0619	0833	...	0903	1023	...	1139	1213	1126	1221	...	1325	1417	1429	...	1527	1658	1724	1821	1831	...	1919	2003	2030	...	2125	2221	2230	...
Kołobrzeg **1015** ...a.	1009	...	...	...	...	...	...	...	...	...	...	...	1749	...	...	...	...	...	...	...	...	2143	...	...	...	...	...	...	...

B – To / from Bielsko Biała (Table **1060**).
K – To / from Kraków (Tables **1065/1067**).
L – To / from Łódź (Table **1090**).
R – To / from Rzeszów (Table **1075**).
T – To / from Katowice (Table **1060**).

X – SOBIESKI – (12) ✕ Gdynia - Warszawa - Katowice - Wien and v.v.
Z – To / from Zakopane (Table **1066**).

j – Warszawa **Gdańska**.
t – ⑥ only.

y – Warszawa **Śródmieście**.

• – Olsztyn - Działdowo : *84 km.*
▶ – For additional trains Gdynia - Gdańsk - Iława (- Olsztyn) see Table **1035**. Frequent local trains (every 10 - 30 mins.) run between Gdynia and Gdańsk operated by *SKM*.

GDYNIA - GDAŃSK - EŁBLAG - OLSZTYN - BIAŁYSTOK 1035

Olsztyn - Ełblag - Malbork and v.v. subject to alteration February 18 - March 11.

km		IC	IC	TLK	IC	IC	IC		IC	IC	IC	
		5620	**50105**	**51102**	**85108**	**85106**	**65103**		**81104**	**85104**	**85102**	
		5621	**50104**	**51103**	**85109**	**85107**	**65102**		**81105**	**85105**	**85103**	
		B		A			C	Ⓑ				
	Szczecin Gł. **1015**.. d.	...	...	...	0505	0713	...	...	1110	1317	1520	...
0	**Gdynia** Gł. ▶ d.	...	0522	0800	0912	1118	...	1452	1522	1744	1945	2140
9	Sopot ▶ d.	...	0530	0810	0921	1126	...	1500	1531	1752	1954	2149
21	**Gdańsk** Gł. ▶ d.	...	0546	0829	0938	1144	...	1515	1547	1807	2011	2201
53	Tczew ▶ d.	...	0606	0847	0958	1203	...	1545	1614	1827	2038	2232
72	Malbork ▶ d.	...	0620	0902	1011	1216	...	1606	1630	1840	2051	2250
101	**Ełblag** d.	...	0644	0923	1036	1236	...	1631	1651	|	2112	2315
	Iława Gł. ▶ a.	...	|	|	|	|	...	...	|	1922	|	...
	Iława Gł. d.	...	|	|	|	|	1330	...	|	1944	|	...
*200	**Olsztyn** a.	...	0811	1103	1202	1402	1427	...	1850	2041	2237	...
200	**Olsztyn** d.	...	0814	1128	...	...	1432	...	1912	...	...	...
319	Giżycko d.	...	1022	|	...	...	1638	...	|	...	...	...
366	Ełk a.	...	...	1334	...	...	...	...	2131	...	...	...
366	Ełk d.	0557	...	1359	...	...	...	...	2156	...	...	...
470	**Białystok** a.	0723	...	1532	...	...	...	...	2325	...	...	...

			IC	IC	IC	IC	IC	IC	TLK	IC	IC
			58103	**58105**	**18105**	**58107**	**56103**	**58109**	**15103**	**55105**	**6521**
			58102	**58104**	**18104**	**58106**	**56102**	**58108**	**15102**	**55104**	**6520**
		⚒					C		A		B
Białystok d.	...	...	...	...	0510	...	...	...	1253	...	2117
Ełk a.	...	...	...	...	0636	...	...	...	1429	...	2237
Ełk d.	...	...	...	...	0701	...	...	...	1457	...	...
Giżycko d.	...	...	...	...	|	...	1230	...	|	1805	...
Olsztyn a.	...	...	...	...	0914	...	1430	...	1708	2013	...
Olsztyn d.	...	...	0551	0744	0944	1343	1432	1542	1733	2016	...
Iława Gł. a.	...	...	|	0840	|	|	1525	|	|	|	...
Iława Gł. ▶ d.	...	...	|	0904	|	|	...	|	|	|	...
Ełblag d.	0429	0618	0723	|	1117	1516	...	1712	1908	2154	...
Malbork ▶ d.	0455	0646	0749	0945	1139	1537	...	1733	1931	2215	...
Tczew ▶ d.	0513	0709	0802	0959	1153	1550	...	1756	1955	2229	...
Gdańsk Gł. ▶ a.	0544	0733	0820	1017	1212	1608	...	1816	2013	2247	...
Sopot ▶ a.	0604	0748	0838	1034	1232	1624	...	1833	2030	2305	...
Gdynia Gł. ▶ a.	0613	0758	0847	1043	1240	1632	...	1841	2038	2314	...
Szczecin Gł. **1015** a.	...	...	1314	1458	1659	2059	...	2257	...	...	...

LOCAL SERVICES OLSZTYN - EŁK - BIAŁYSTOK

km		⚒	Ⓑ	🚌			🚌		Ⓑ	Ⓐ	🚌			P Ⓑ
0	**Olsztyn** d.	...	...	0905	0933	...	1345	1419	...	1617	1648	...	1809	2059
45	Szczytno d.	...	...	|	1014	...	|	1503	...	1703	|	...	1852	|
102	Pisz d.	...	...	|	1105	...	|	1553	...	1802	|	...	1942	|
	Giżycko d.	...	...	1102	|	...	1541	|	...	|	1845	...	|	2256
157	Ełk d.	0456	0736	1211	1202	1445	1650	1653	1714	1901	1954	...	2041	0023
261	**Białystok** a.	0646	0908	...	...	1637	...	...	1852	...	...	...	...	...

	P ⚒		Ⓐ	🚌		🚌		🚌	Ⓑ			Ⓐ	
Białystok d.	...	...	0539	...	1035	...	...	...	1453	...	1754	...	...
Ełk d.	0424	0434	0725	0730	1211	1216	1235	1528	1636	1703	1928	1936	...
Giżycko d.	0545	|	...	0851	...	1337	|	1649	...	|	...	|	...
Pisz d.	|	0530	...	|	...	|	1339	|	...	1801	...	2039	...
Szczytno d.	|	0621	...	|	...	|	1430	|	...	1854	...	2130	...
Olsztyn a.	0739	0703	...	1049	...	1531	1511	1848	...	1944	...	2212	...

A – To / from Warszawa via Siedlce (Table **1040**).
B – To / from Wrocław (Table **1061**).
C – To / from Wrocław (Table **1020**).

P – 🚌.
* – *210 km* via Iława.

▶ – For additional trains Gdynia - Gdansk - Iława (- Warszawa) see Table **1030**. Frequent local trains run between Gdynia and Gdańsk operated by *SKM* (every 10 – 30 minutes).

WARSZAWA - BIAŁYSTOK 1040

km			IC		TLK		IC		IC		IC		IC		IC		IC						
			31000		**15103**		**61103**		**61105**		**4123**		**81103**		**6521**		**1003**						
					15102		**61102**		**61104**		**4122**		**81102**		**6520**								
			V		G		C		C		A		P T		C E								
0	**Warszawa** Cent d.	...	0735	...	...	...	0950	...	1117	...	1347	...	1635	...	1835	...	2035	...	...	...	...	...	...
5	**Warszawa** Wsch d.	...	0745	...	0843	...	0959	...	1125	...	1356	...	1644	...	1844	...	2043	...	...	...	...	...	...
95	Małkinia d.	...	0847	...	|	...	1105	...	1233	...	1456	...	1743	...	1943	...	2144	...	...	...	...	...	...
184	**Białystok** a.	...	1021	...	1225	...	1244	...	1402	...	1624	...	1905	...	2108	...	2300	...	...	...	...	...	...

		IC		IC		IC		IC		IC		TLK		TLK		IC							
		1102		**5620**		**18102**		**16104**		**16102**		**51102**		**13000**		**1100**							
				5621		**18103**		**16105**		**16103**		**51103**											
				E C		P T		C		C		G		V		L							
Białystok d.	...	0500	...	0734	...	0920	...	1410	...	1520	...	1557	...	1741	...	2015	...	...	...	...	...	...	...
Małkinia d.	...	0619	...	0855	...	1042	...	1535	...	1705	...	|	...	1901	...	2139	...	...	...	...	...	...	...
Warszawa Wsch a.	...	0717	...	0953	...	1138	...	1636	...	1811	...	1945	...	2003	...	2233	...	...	...	...	...	...	...
Warszawa Cent a.	...	0730	...	1000	...	1147	...	1645	...	1820	...	...	...	2013	...	2240	...	...	...	...	...	...	...

A – From / to Katowice (Table **1060**).
C – To / from Wrocław (Table **1061**).
E – To / from Ełk (Table **1035**).
G – From / to Gdynia (Table **1035**).

L – To Łódź (Table **1090**).
P – To / from Suwałki (Table **1042**).
T – To / from Świnoujście (Table **1010**).

V – HAŃCZA – (12) Kraków - Warszawa - Białystok - Mockava and v.v.

1042 BIAŁYSTOK - VILNIUS and HRODNA

PKP, BCh, LG

km			*IC* 31000 144 H	24	①–⑤		*IC* 4123	Ⓑ		*IC* 81103 S
0	*Warszawa Cent* **1040** d.	...	0735	...	...	...	1347	...	...	1635
5	*Warszawa Wsch* **1040** d.	...	0745	...	...	...	1356	...	...	1644
184	**Białystok** a.	...	1021	...	...	...	1624	...	...	1905
184	**Białystok** d.	0610	1045	...	1325	1540	...	1659	1845	1930
225	Sokółka d.	0647	1120	...	1407	1617	...	1751	1931	2005
324	**Suwałki** d.	|	1256	...	|	|	...	|	|	2115
	Mockava ▦ ◐ § a.	|	1441	1505	|	|	...	|	|	...
377	Šeštokai § a.	|	...	|	|	|	...	|	|	...
471	**Kaunas** **1811** § a.	|	...	1626	|	|	...	|	|	...
575	**Vilnius** **1811** § a.	|	...	1734	|	|	...	|	|	...
241	Kuźnica Białostocka ▦ a.	0703	...	...	1423	1633	...	1807	1947	...
241	Kuźnica Białostocka ▦ d.	...	...	...	...	...	...	...	...	...
268	**Hrodna** ▦ ‡ a.	...	...	...	...	...	...	...	...	...

			IC 18102 S			23	*IC* 143 H 13000	Ⓑ	*IC* 1100 1101
Hrodna ▦ ‡ d.	...	...	...	...	...	...	...	...	...
Kuźnica Białostocka ▦ a.	...	...	...	...	...	...	...	...	...
Kuźnica Białostocka ▦ d.	0504	0719	...	1457	1643	...	...	1911	...
Vilnius **1811** § d.	|	|	...	|	|	1210	...	|	...
Kaunas **1811** § d.	|	|	...	|	|	1320	...	|	...
Šeštokai § d.	|	|	...	|	|	|	...	|	...
Mockava ▦ ◐ d.	|	|	...	|	|	1441	1514	|	...
Suwałki d.	|	|	0709	|	|	...	1527	|	...
Sokółka d.	0520	0735	0820	1523	1658	...	1640	1928	...
Białystok a.	0557	0812	0855	1606	1736	...	1716	2010	...
Białystok d.	...	...	0921	...	...	...	1741	...	2015
Warszawa Wsch **1040** a.	...	...	1137	...	...	...	2003	...	2233
Warszawa Cent **1040** a.	...	...	1145	...	...	...	2013	...	2240

H – HAŃCZA – (12) Kraków - Warszawa - Mockava and v.v.
S – From/to Świnoujście (Table **1010**).
§ – Lithuanian time.
‡ – Belarus time.
◐ – ▦ = Trakiszki (Poland) / Mockava (Lithuania); ticketing point is Mockava.

1050 WARSZAWA - TERESPOL - BREST

km				*IC* 11101			*IC* 11103		*IC* 11105		*IC* 41004 130 B	*IC* 11107 Ⓑ
0	**Warszawa** Cent. d.	...	...	...	...	...	...	...	...	...	1949j	...
5	**Warszawa** Wsch. d.	...	...	0738	...	...	1347	...	1618	...	|	2050
93	Siedlce d.	...	...	0839	0931	1232	1447	1650	1722	...	2050	2149
121	Łuków d.	0535	0752	0856	0958	1300	1504	1717	1744	1928	2104	2206
173	Biała Podlaska d.	0618	0834	0928	1042	1343	1536	1801	1816	2017	2133	2238
210	Terespol ▦ a.	0651	0907	0957	1115	1415	1606	1834	1844	2051	2206	2307
217	**Brest** Tsentralny ▦ ‡ a.	...	...	...	...	...	...	...	...	...	...	...

	IC 11116 ①–⑥		*IC* 131 14004 B		*IC* 11114		*IC* 11110	Ⓐ		*IC* 11112	
Brest Tsentralny ▦ ‡ d.	...	...	...	...	...	...	...	...	...	...	...
Terespol ▦ d.	0518	0549	0617	0829	0953	1142	1337	1440	1613	1839	1914
Biała Podlaska d.	0549	0622	0643	0902	1023	1215	1409	1513	1647	1910	1947
Łuków d.	0621	0716	0711	0947	1055	1258	1442	1603	1730	1942	2031
Siedlce d.	0638	0743	0726	1013	1110	...	1500	1630	...	1959	...
Warszawa Wsch. a.	0737	...	|	...	1212	...	1600	...	...	2100	...
Warszawa Cent. a.	...	...	0825j	...	...	...	...	...	...	...	...

B – BÁTHORY – (12) ✕ Budapest - Warszawa - Terespol and v.v.

j – Warszawa **Gdańska**.

‡ – Belarus time.

TERESPOL - BREST and v.v. local services

Terespol d.	...	...	...	Brest ‡ d.	...	...	...
Brest ‡ a.	...	...	...	Terespol a.	...	...	...

1055 WARSZAWA - LUBLIN - CHEŁM - DOROHUSK

km		Ⓐ			⚒	*IC* 12101		*IC* 1200 1201 L			*IC* 72101 72100 T	*IC* 52100 52101 K		*IC* 6220 6221 C	Ⓐ	Ⓑ	Ⓐ	*IC* 82104 82105 2JY	*IC* 1206 1207 L		*MP* 12011 68*LJ* A	Ⓑ Z	*IC* 83100 83101 SR	Ⓐ		*TLK* 82100 82101 S
0	**Warszawa** Cent d.	...	...	...	...	...	...	0830y	...	...	1054y	1153y	...	1320	...	...	...	1600y	1627y	...	...	...	1915	...	...	1940
5	**Warszawa** Wsch d.	...	...	...	...	0655	...	0851	...	...	1121	1221	...	1331	...	...	...	|	1651	...	1754	...	1923	...	...	1949
104	Dęblin d.	0405	0501	0601	0720	0804	...	0956	1020	1209	1224	1324	1408	1437	1521	1705	...	1722	1803	1810	1904	...	2033	2008	...	2100
125	Puławy Miasto d.	0425	0522	0623	0741	0817	...	1010	1040	1229	1237	1338	1428	1451	1541	1726	...	1735	1818	1831	1917	...	2047	2028	...	2114
175	**Lublin** a.	0511	0609	0715	0828	0852	...	1044	1127	1324	1313	1412	1517	1526	1635	1820	...	1810	1852	1918	1949	...	2121	2115	...	2153
		|	|	⚒		|	Z		|	Z		|	Ⓐ		Z						|		⑥			
175	**Lublin** d.	0518	0619	0720	...	0855	0930	...	1128	1341	...	1415	1525	1555	1700	...	1755	...	1858	...	2019	1955	1955	2137	2240	...
228	Rejowiec d.	0610	0708	0811	...	0932	1022	1027	1219	1430	1435	1452	1619	1649	1757	...	1844	...	1949	...	2102	2046	2044	2228	2331	...
249	Chełm a.	0625	0724	0826	...	0946	...	1043	1235	...	1451	1507	1636	1706	...	...	1859	...	2004	...	2116	...	2100	2248	2346	...
270	**Dorohusk** ▦ a.	...	...	...	...	...	...	...	...	...	...	...	...	...	...	...	...	...	...	...	2139	...	...	...	...	...

	Ⓐ			Ⓐ	*IC* 38101 38100 RS	⚒ Z	*MP* 67*KJ* 21010 A	Ⓐ		*TLK* 28104 28105 2JV		Z	⚒	*IC* 2620 2621 C		*IC* 25101 25100 K	Z	*IC* 27100 27101 T	Ⓐ	B	*IC* 2100 2101 M		Z	*IC* 21100		
Dorohusk ▦ d.	...	...	...	...	...	...	0633	...	...	...	...	...	...	...	...	...	...	...	...	...	...	...	...	...	...	...
Chełm d.	0402	0454	...	0554	...	...	0707	0710	0817	...	0937	...	1054	...	1210	1302	...	...	1424	1501	...	1624	...	1808	1819	2011
Rejowiec d.	0418	0509	...	0609	...	0638	0723	0727	0835	...	0953	0958	1109	...	1225	1318	1335	...	1439	1516	...	1639	1732	1824	1836	2027
Lublin a.	0510	0600	...	0700	...	0730	0804	0821	0928	...	...	1049	1200	...	1316	1356	1425	...	1530	1607	...	1730	1823	1901	1930	2119
	|	*TLK* 28100/1 S					|									|	Ⓐ						Ⓐ	|		Ⓐ
Lublin d.	0515	0605	0620	...	0705	0735	0823	...	...	1005	...	1054	...	1205	1335	1405	1432	1505	1535	1632	1705	...	1836	1905	1937	2236
Puławy Miasto d.	0600	0640	0707	...	0740	0822	0853	...	...	1040	...	1141	...	1240	1421	1440	1520	1520	1626	1719	1740	...	1923	1940	2024	2323
Dęblin d.	0620	0654	0728	...	0754	0843	0905	...	...	1054	...	1202	...	1154	1441	1454	1540	1554	1648	1740	1754	...	1944	1954	2045	2344
Warszawa Wsch a.	...	|	...	...	0905	...	1012	...	...	1207	...	...	...	1409	...	1608	...	1708	...	...	1911	...	...	2104	...	...
Warszawa Cent a.	...	0812y	...	...	0920	...	...	...	...	1215	...	...	...	1420	...	1636y	...	1736y	...	...	1935y	...	...	...	...	...

A – KYIV EKSPRES / KIEV EXPRESS – 🛏 1, 2 cl. Kyiv - Warszawa and v.v. (Table **1730**). International journeys only.
B – Runs 20 minutes later on Ⓐ.
C – To/from Wrocław (Table **1061**).
J – To/from Kołobrzeg (Table **1015**).
K – To/from Bydgoszcz (Table **1025**).
L – From Łódź (Table **1090**).
R – To/from Rzeszów (Table **1058**).
S – To/from Szczecin (Table **1010**).
T – To/from Zielona Góra (Table **1001**).
V – From Zamość (depart 0737).
Y – To Zamość (arrive 2032).
Z – To/from Zamość (Table **1099**).
y – Warszawa **Gdańska**.

1058 LUBLIN - RZESZÓW - PRZEMYŚL

km			Ⓐ	*IC* 2701	Ⓒ	*IC* 13105 2		*TLK* 24001 310 C2		*IC* 13107 13106		*IC* 83101 83100 S
	Warszawa Cent. **1055** d.	...	...	...	...	...	...	...	...	...	...	1915
	Warszawa Wsch. **1055** d.	...	...	...	...	0630	...	...	...	1719	...	1929
0	**Lublin** d.	...	0545	0704	0743	◧	1225	1430	1655	◧	...	2152
103	Stalowa Wola Rozwadów d.	0503	0738	0839	0934	1047	1420	1544	1850	2157	...	|
132	Tanobrzeg d.	0555	0806	|	1002	|	1458	|	1918	|	...	2324
204	**Rzeszów** a.	0718	0926	1021	1126	|	1624	1721	2043	|	...	0019
204	**Rzeszów** **1075** d.	0748	...	1102	1249	|	1712	1924	...	|	2225	...
178	Przeworsk **1075** d.	0823	...	1137	1324	1200	1754	1959	...	2304	2308	...
193	Jarosław **1075** d.	0834	...	1150	1342	1210	1807	2010	...	2315	2320	...
228	**Przemyśl** **1075** a.	0913	...	1228	1419	1243	1846	2049	...	2350	0006	...

	IC 38100 38101 S	*IC* 31106 31107			*TLK* 42000 311 C2	⚒		*IC* 31104 2			*IC* 7200
Przemyśl **1075** d.	...	0436	...	0442	...	0954	1142	1512	1427	...	1537
Jarosław **1075** d.	...	0506	...	0518	...	1029	1221	1540	1515	...	1614
Przeworsk **1075** d.	...	0520	...	0529	...	1049	1232	1552	1526	...	1625
Rzeszów **1075** a.	...	|	...	0604	...	1123	1317	|	1606	...	1659
Rzeszów d.	0402	|	0516	...	0903	1154	...	|	...	1634	1744
Tanobrzeg d.	0505	|	0653	...	|	1323	...	|	...	1800	|
Stalowa Wola Rozwadów d.	|	0632	0732	...	1040	1405	...	1701	...	1844	1935
Lublin a.	0640	◧	0910	...	1150	1548	...	◧	...	2023	2044
Warszawa Wsch. **1055** a.	0910	1053	...	...	...	...	...	2131	...	...	...
Warszawa Cent. **1055** a.	0920	...	...	...	...	...	...	...	...	...	...

C – To/from Bohumín (Table **1076**).
S – To/from Szczecin (Tables **1010**).
◧ – Via Radom (Table **1067**).

WARSZAWA / ŁÓDŹ - KATOWICE and BIELSKO BIAŁA 1060

km																								
km		*IC*	*IC*	*IC*	*IC*	*EIP*	*TLK*	*IC*		*IC*	*EIP*	*TLK*	*IC*	*IC*	*IC*	*EIC*	*EIP*	*TLK*	*IC*	*IC*	*EIP*		*TLK*	
		14000	**14002**	**1420**	**1460**	**1400**	**14101**	**14004**		**5424**	**5400**	**54101**	**14006**	**54000**	**1422**	**1410**	**5404**	**54103**	**14008**	**5422**	**5406**		**53170**	
		116	**103**	**1421**	**1461**	**1401**	**14100**	**131**		**5460**	**5401**	**54100**	**112**	**107**	**1423**	**1411**	**5405**	**54102**	**110**	**5423**	**5407**		**53171**	
				Ⓐ	Ⓒ						Ⓑ					Ⓐ								
		Z	P	B				V		O	G	G	M	S	B		G	G	Q	O	G		E	
0	**Warszawa** Wschodnia d.	0456	0532	0529	0529	0624	...	...	...	1022	1030	...	1251	...	1434	1539	1629	...	1649	1819	1830	...	2216	...
5	**Warszawa** Centralna d.	0507	0543	0542	0542	0633	...	0827j	...	1033y	1041	...	1302	1413j	1458	1551	1640	...	1659	1829	1841	...	2227	...
	Łódź Widzew d.	|	|	|	|	|	0736	|	...	|	|	1230	|	|	|	|	|	1638	|	|	|	...	|	...
	Koluszki d.	|	|	0656	0656	|	|	|	...	1200	|	|	|	|	1611	|	|	|	|	1947	|	...	2358	...
	Piotrków Trybunalski d.	|	|	0720	0720	|	0814	|	...	1223	|	1306	|	|	1638	|	|	1720	|	2011	|	...	0026	...
	Częstochowa d.	|	|	0813	0813	|	0917	|	...	1320	|	1402	|	|	1736	|	|	1823	|	2105	|	...	0120	...
259	Zawiercie **1067** d.	0734	0824	0849	0849	|	0948	1042	...	1349	|	1432	1543	1628	1806	1800	1842	1853	1926	2135	|	...	...	...
294	Sosnowiec Gł. **1067** d.	0801	0848	0919	0919	0902	1015	1108	...	1417	1301	1459	1609	1650	1833	1824	1909	1923	1955	2205	2109	...	...	...
302	**Katowice** **1067** a.	0811	0859	0929	0929	0911	1024	1119	...	1428	1310	1508	1619	1701	1844	1834	1920	1932	2004	2216	2118	...	...	...

km																							
km		*EIC*	*IC*	*EIP*	*IC*	*EIP*	*TLK*	*IC*	*IC*	*IC*	*EIP*	*TLK*	*IC*	*EIP*	*IC*	*TLK*	*IC*	*IC*	*IC*	*IC*		*TLK*	
		4550	**4110**	**4508**	**111**	**4506**	**45102**	**4122**	**106**	**113**	**4504**	**45100**	**4560**	**4502**	**130**	**41100**	**4160**	**4120**	**102**	**117**		**35170**	
		4551	**4111**	**4509**	**41008**	**4507**		**4123**	**45000**	**41006**	**4505**	**45101**	**4524**	**4503**	**41004**	**41101**	**4161**	**4121**	**41002**	**41000**		**35171**	
		⑥	Ⓐ											Ⓑ			Ⓒ	Ⓐ					
		G		G	Q	BG	G	L	S	M	BG	G	O	G	V			B	P	Z		E	
	Katowice d.	0536	0536	0650	0743	0859	0913	1002	1057	1135	1257	1319	1355	1457	1638	1718	1934	1934	1851	1946	...	...	...
	Sosnowiec Gł. **1067** d.	0546	0546	0659	0754	0908	0922	1014	1107	1146	1307	1329	1404	1507	1649	|	1943	1943	1903	2000	...	...	...
0	Zawiercie **1067** d.	0611	0611	0722	0819	|	0950	1041	1131	1210	1329	1356	1430	|	1719	1805	2009	2009	1925	2026	...	...	...
43	**Częstochowa** d.	|	|	|	|	|	1024	1113	|	|	|	1432	1501	|	|	1839	2041	2041	|	|	...	0149	...
129	Piotrków Trybunalski d.	|	|	|	|	|	1115	1205	|	|	|	1526	1551	|	|	1930	2132	2132	|	|	...	0243	...
168	Koluszki d.	|	|	|	|	|	|	1229	|	|	|	|	1614	|	|	|	2159	2159	|	|	...	0309	...
	Łódź Widzew a.	|	|	|	|	|	1150	|	|	|	|	1603	|	|	|	2006	|	|	|	|	...	|	...
273	**Warszawa** Centralna a.	0814	0814	0915	1038j	1121	...	1333	1334j	1429	1524	...	1717	1727	1951	...	2308j	2308	2147	2243j	...	0420	...
278	**Warszawa** Wschodnia a.	0826	0826	0926	...	1131	...	1353	...	1441	1535	...	1742	1737	2001	...	2322	2317	2156	2259	...	0441	...

Services between Katowice and Bielsko Biała are subject to alteration from February 25. 🚌 between Katowice and Bielsko Biała.

km																								
km		*IC*	*LE*		*IC*	*IC*	*EIP*	*IC*		*IC*	*IC*		*IC*	*IC*	*TLK*	*IC*	*IC*	*IC*	*IC*		*IC*			
		40001	**412**		**14000**	**14002**	**1401**	**1420**		**14004**	**34000**		**5425**	**34002**	**34004**	**14006**	**54000**	**1422**	**14008**		**5420**			
		101	🍷		**116**	**103**	**1400**	**1421**		**131**	**114**		**5424**	**105**	**212**	**112**	**107**	**1423**	**110**		**5421**			
								Ⓐ					Ⓐ					Ⓐ						
		R	J		Z	P				V	H		G	C	K	M	S		Q		G			
0	**Katowice** **1075** d.	0451	0706	...	0814	0909	0914	0937	...	1127	1141	...	1436	1502	1542	1622	1704	1849	2022	...	2254	...	...	...
	Tychy ▷ d.	|	0721	...	0830	0923	0932	0951	...	|	1156	...	1541	|	|	1637	1720	1911	2038	...	2309	...	...	...
45	Rybnik ▷ a.	|	...	...	0858	...	|	|	...	|	1232	...	|	1551	|	1706	1749	|	2108	...	|	...	...	...
	Gliwice **1075** a.	0514	...	...	...	...	|	|	...	1151	...	...	|	...	1605	...	...	|	...	...	|	...	...	...
	Bielsko Biała ▷ a.	...	...	...	...	...	1026	1041	...	...	...	...	1546	...	...	...	...	2007	...	...	0001	...	...	...

km																								
km		*IC*		*IC*		*IC*	*IC*	*IC*	*TLK*	*IC*	*EIP*		*IC*	*IC*		*IC*	*IC*	*IC*	*LE*		*IC*			
		4520		**111**		**4122**	**106**	**113**	**213**	**104**	**4504**		**115**	**130**		**102**	**4120**	**117**	**413**		**100**			
		4521		**41008**		**4123**	**45000**	**41006**	**43004**	**43002**	**4505**		**43000**	**41004**		**41002**	**4121**	**41000**	🍷		**44000**			
		G		Q			S	M	K	C	G		H	V		P	Ⓐ	Z	A		R			
0	**Bielsko Biała** ▷ d.	0412	...	...	...	0830	...	...	...	...	1145	...	...	...	...	...	1805	...	...	...	...	...	...	...
	Gliwice **1075** d.	|	...	...	...	|	...	...	1136	...	|	...	...	1604	...	...	|	...	...	...	2236	...	...	...
	Rybnik ▷ d.	|	...	0652	...	|	1007	1049	|	1207	|	...	1526	|	...	...	|	1859	...	...	|	...	...	...
39	Tychy ▷ d.	0518	...	0724	...	0937	1039	1118	|	|	1240	...	1556	|	...	1834	1910	1929	2021	...	|	...	...	...
55	**Katowice** **1075** a.	0531	...	0740	...	0950	1054	1132	1203	1248	1254	...	1610	1632	...	1848	1923	1943	2036	...	2259	...	...	...

A – ⑤⑦: LEO EXPRESS – [12] 🍷 Praha - Bohumín - Katowice - Kraków.
B – To / from Bielsko Biała.
C – PORTA MORAVIA – [12] ✕ Przemyśl - Katowice - Wien - Graz and v.v.
E – 🛏 1, 2 cl., [12] Gdynia Gł. - Warszawa - Kraków - Zakopane and v.v. (Tables **1030 / 1066**).
G – To / from Gdynia (Tables **1025 / 30**).
H – CRACOVIA – [12] 🍷 Przemyśl - Katowice - Bohumín - Praha and v.v.
J – ①⑥: LEO EXPRESS – [12] 🍷 Kraków - Katowice - Bohumín - Praha.
K – GALICJA – [12] Kraków - Katowice - Ostrava - Praha and v.v.
L – To Białystok (Table **1040**).
M – [12] ✕ Warszawa - Praha and v.v.
O – From / to Olsztyn (Table **1030**).

P – POLONIA – [12] ✕ Warszawa - Wien and v.v.
Q – SILESIA – [12] ✕ Warszawa - Ostrava and v.v.
R – MORAVIA – [12] ✕ Katowice - Ostrava - Wien and v.v.
S – SOBIESKI – [12] ✕ Gdynia - Warszawa - Wien and v.v.
V – BÁTHORY – [12] ✕ Terespol - Warszawa - Bohumín - Budapest and v.v.
Z – SILESIA – [12] ✕ Warszawa - Praha and v.v.

j – Warszawa **Gdańska**.
y – Warszawa **Śródmieście**.

▷ – For local trains Katowice - Bielsko Biała and Rybnik – see Tables **1077/79**.

WARSZAWA - ŁÓDŹ / CZESTOCHOWA - WROCŁAW 1061

km																									
km		*IC*	*IC*	*EIC*	*IC*	*IC*		*TLK*	*IC*	*EIC*		*IC*		*IC*		*IC*	*IC*	*EIP*		*IC*		*IC*			
		18109	**1620**	**1600**	**1650**	**1622**		**16101**	**5620**	**1601**		**1625**		**2620**		**1626**	**16104**	**1603**		**16102**		**1629**			
		18108	**1621**	**1601**	**1651**	**2622**		**16100**	**5621**			**1624**		**2621**		**1627**	**16105**	**1602**		**16103**		**1628**			
				Ⓐ	Ⓒ			2		Ⓒ						Ⓑ						Ⓑ			
		P						J	E					L		Z	Y			Y					
0	**Warszawa** Wschodnia d.	...	0429	0614	0614	0714	...	0835	0954	1017	...	1134	...	1413	...	1555	1639	1724	...	1814	...	1939	...	...	...
4	**Warszawa** Centralna d.	...	0441	0626	0626	0729	...	0845	1022	1029	...	1152	...	1437	...	1610j	1653	1734	...	1850	...	1953	...	...	...
122	Koluszki d.	...	0558	|	|	0845	...	1004	1131	|	...	1303	...	1558	...	1713	1812	|	...	2019	...	2106	...	...	...
160	Piotrków Trybunalski d.	...	|	|	|	|	...	1028	|	|	...	1327	...	|	...	|	1835	|	...	|	...	2130	...	...	...
•	Częstochowa d.	...	|	|	|	|	...	1120	|	|	...	1419	...	|	...	|	1927	|	...	|	...	2222	...	...	...
	Częstochowa Stradom d.	...	|	0849	0849	|	...	1126	|	1247	...	1424	...	|	...	|	1933	1952	...	|	...	2227	...	...	...
130	**Łódź** Widzew ▷ d.	0534	0620	|	|	0903	...	|	1146	|	...	|	...	1618	...	1739	|	|	...	2038	...	|	...	...	...
257	Kalisz ▷ d.	0712	0749	|	|	1035	...	|	1312	|	...	|	...	1744	...	1910	|	|	...	2210	...	|	...	...	...
281	Ostrów Wlkp ▷ d.	...	0808	|	|	1052	...	|	1328	|	...	|	...	1801	...	1926	|	|	...	2227	...	|	...	...	...
	Opole Gł. d.	...	|	0948	0948	|	...	1231	|	1342	...	1519	...	|	...	|	2030	2047	...	|	...	2327	...	...	...
	Brzeg d.	...	|	|	1011	|	...	1257	|	|	...	1543	...	|	...	|	2103	2110	...	|	...	2350	...	...	...
382*	**Wrocław** Gł. ▷ a.	...	0928	1031	1034	1209	...	1326	1444	1425	...	1610	...	1925	...	2100	2138	2133	...	0009	...	0015	...	...	...

	IC		*IC*		*EIP*	*IC*	*IC*		*IC*		*IC*		*IC*		*TLK*	*EIC*	*IC*	*IC*	*IC*	*IC*			
	6128		**61103**		**6102**	**6126**	**61104**		**6221**		**6124**		**6521**		**61100**	**6100**	**6123**	**6150**	**6121**	**81108**			
	6129		**61102**		**6103**	**6127**	**61105**		**6220**				**6520**				**6122**		**6120**	**81109**			
	①–⑥					①–⑥									2			Ⓒ					
			Y			Z	Y		L				E		J					P			
Wrocław Gł. ▷ d.	0320	...	0417	...	0554	0557	0636	...	0836	...	1108	...	1331	...	1528	1634	1703	1837	1919	...	...	...	...
Brzeg d.	0346	...	|	...	0617	|	0716	...	|	...	1136	...	|	...	1559	|	|	1902	|	...	...	...	...
Opole Gł. d.	0410	...	|	...	0641	|	0746	...	|	...	1201	...	|	...	1628	1724	|	1931	|	...	...	...	...
Ostrów Wlkp. ▷ d.	|	...	0558	...	|	0807	|	...	0956	...	|	...	1458	...	|	|	1825	|	2038	...	...	...	...
Kalisz ▷ d.	|	...	0615	...	|	0823	|	...	1012	...	|	...	1515	...	|	|	1842	|	2055	2118	...	...	...
Łódź Widzew ▷ d.	|	...	0753	...	|	0959	|	...	1142	...	|	...	1644	...	|	|	2017	|	2239	2256	...	...	...
Częstochowa Stradom d.	0505	...	|	...	0734	|	0841	...	|	...	1256	...	|	...	1724	1822	|	2039	|	...	...	...	...
Częstochowa d.	0511	...	|	...	|	|	0848	...	|	...	1303	...	|	...	1731	|	|	|	|	...	...	...	...
Piotrków Trybunalski d.	0602	...	|	...	|	|	0939	...	|	...	1354	...	|	...	1822	|	|	|	|	...	...	...	...
Koluszki d.	0630	...	0811	...	|	1015	1001	...	1157	...	1419	...	1659	...	1846	|	2035	|	2255	...	...	...	...
Warszawa Centralna a.	0731j	...	0923	...	0944	|	1112	...	1309	...	|	...	1814	...	|	2044	2134j	|	2400j	...	...	...	...
Warszawa Wschodnia a.	...	...	0956	...	1001	1133	1123	...	1326	...	1553	...	1841	...	1957	2056	2154	2316	...	...	...	...	...

E – To / from Ełk (Table **1035**).
J – To / from Jelenia Góra (Table **1084**).
L – To / from Lublin (Table **1055**).
P – To / from Poznań (arr. 0856; depart 1943).
Y – To / from Białystok (Table **1040**).
Z – To / from Zgorzelec (Table **1085**).
j – Warszawa **Gdańska**.
▷ – For local trains see Table **1080**.
* – *406 km* via CMK.
• – Częstochowa - Opole Gł: *91 km*.

1065 WARSZAWA - KRAKÓW

km		IC	EIP	EIP	TLK	EIP	EIP		EIP	EIP	TLK	EIP	EIP	EIP	IC	EIP	EIP	EIP		IC	EIP	IC		
		13100	1300	1302	53104	5300	5302		8300	1306	53102	5304	1308	5306	13103	1310	5308	1312		13000	5310	5328		
		13101	1301	1303	53105	5301	5303		8301	1307	83152	5305	1309	5307	13102	1311	5309	1313		143	5311	5329		
		P			GZ	G	G		S		G	G		G			GR	G		C	G	O		
			Ⓐ										Ⓑ		Ⓑ	Ⓑ		Ⓑ						
0	**Warszawa** Wsch .... d.	0417	0441	0624	0814	0830	0931	...	1129	1224	1324	1329	1354	1526	1607	...	1729	1836	...	2005	2029	2220	...	...
4	**Warszawa** Cent.......... d.	0428	0454	0633	0834	0841	0945	...	1142	1234	1346	1339	1424	1537	1621**g**	1642**g**	1748	1846	...	2016	2042	2231	...	...
246	**Kraków** Gł.......... a.	0722	0727	0908	1215	1120	1221	...	1420	1506	1653	1612	1713	1815	1941	1909	2031	2125	...	2339	2323	0134	...	...

	IC	EIP	EIP		EIP	IC		EIP	EIP	TLK	EIP	EIP	EIP	TLK	EIP	EIP	EIP	EIP	EIC	IC	EIP	IC		
	31000	3510	3112		3508	31102		3110	3506	35102	3504	3108	3800	35105	3106	3502	3500	3104	3151	3102	3100	31100		
	144	3511	3113		3509	31103		3111	3507	38153	3505	3109	3801	35104	3107	3503	3501	3105	3150	3103	3101	31101		
	C	G			RG				G	G	G		S	GZ		G	G					P		
			⚒			⚒		Ⓐ										Ⓑ			Ⓑ			
Kraków Gł. .... d.	0401	0556	0709	...	0748	0811	...	0858	0953	1133	1154	1252	1347	1440	1514	1558	1655	1804	1829	1906	1958	2056	...	...
Warszawa Centralna .... a.	0710	0823	0937**g**	...	1018	1142**g**	...	1130	1224	1432**g**	1420	1516**g**	1621	1834	1743**g**	1825	1923	2031**g**	2120	2138	2228	2338**g**	...	...
Warszawa Wschodnia .... a.	0741	0836	...	...	1031	...	...	1141	1233	...	1431	...	1631	1847	1802	1836	1936	...	2131	2151	2241	2350	...	...

C – HAŃCZA – (12) Kraków - Warszawa - Białystok - Mockava and v.v. (Table **1042**).
G – From / to Gdynia (Table **1030**).
O – From Olsztyn (Table **1030**).
P – To / from Przemyśl (Table **1075**).
R – To / from Rzeszów (Table **1075**).
S – From / to Kołobrzeg (Table **1015**).
Z – To / from Zakopane (Table **1066**).
g – Warszawa **Gdańska**.

1066 KRAKÓW - ZAKOPANE

km			TLK				TLK			IC
			53171				53105			5360
		🚌	G	🚌		🚌	G		🚌	H
	Warszawa Cent. **1065** .... d.	...	2227	...	...	...	0834	...	...	...
0	**Kraków** Gł. .... d.	...	0346	0747	...	1241	1230	...	1743	1948
62	Sucha Beskidzka Zamek .... d.	0452**c**	0446	0940**c**	...	1410**c**	1346	...	1909**c**	2049
95	Chabówka .... a.	0602	0529	1050	...	1520	1436	...	2019	2135
95	Chabówka .... d.	0603	0547	1051	...	1520	1506	...	2019	2145
121	Nowy Targ .... d.	0651	0620	1139	...	1608	1549	...	2107	2216
142	**Zakopane** .... a.	0728	0648	1217	...	1646	1613	...	2145	2246

		IC		TLK					TLK
		3560		35105					35170
	🚌	H	🚌	G		🚌	🚌		G
Zakopane .... d.	0353	0630	0813	1050	...	1412	1635	...	2040
Nowy Targ .... d.	0431	0654	0851	1119	...	1450	1714	...	2105
Chabówka .... a.	0518	0724	0939	1150	...	1538	1801	...	2136
Chabówka .... d.	0519	0734	0939	1207	...	1538	1802	...	2154
Sucha Beskidzka Zamek .... d.	0638**c**	0817	1057**c**	1250	...	1658**c**	1920**c**	...	2238
Kraków Gł. .... a.	0806	0915	1232	1412	...	1818	2048	...	2337
Warszawa Cent. **1065** .... a.	...	...	...	1834	...	...	...	...	0420

G – To / from Gdynia (Tables **1030**/**1065**).
H – To / from Gdynia (Table **1025**).
c – Sucha Beskidzka.

1067 WARSZAWA and LUBLIN - KIELCE - KATOWICE and KRAKÓW

km	*For fast trains to Kraków see Table* **1065**		TLK		TLK		IC	IC	IC		IC		IC		IC	IC	IC		TLK	IC		TLK		
			83170		28103		13105	24101	5326		26101		5324		5322	26103	5320		13107	23100		12111		
			83171		28102				5327				5325		5323	26102	5321		13106	23101		12110		
				Ⓐ			2											Ⓐ			Ⓐ	Ⓑ		
			Y		S		P		O		W		O		O	W	O		P					
0	**Warszawa** Wschodnia .... d.	...	0403	...	...	...	0630	...	0724	...	...	...	1219	...	1419	...	1619	...	1719	...	...	2019	...	...
4	**Warszawa** Centralna .... d.	...	|	...	...	...	|	...	0733**y**	...	...	...	1228**y**	...	1428**y**	...	1628**y**	...	1728**y**	...	...	2028**y**	...	...
	Warszawa Wschodnia .... d.	...	|	...	...	...	|	...	|	...	...	...	|	...	|	...	|	...	|	...	...	|	...	...
	Lublin .... d.	...	|	...	0500	...	|	0716	|	...	1135	...	|	...	|	1619	|	...	|	1830	...	|	...	...
•	Dęblin .... d.	0408	0509	0449	|	0706	0731	|	|	1014	|	1228	|	1458	|	|	|	1815	1838	|	1918	|	2059	...
107*	Radom .... d.	0458	0548	0539	0625	0756	0809	0835	0858	1105	1253	1317	1354	1548	1553	1737	1754	1908	1857	1953	2008	2159	2149	...
148	Skarżysko Kamienna .... d.	...	0616	...	0658	...	0838**k**	0901	0926	1141	1320	1356	1421	...	1621	1803	1824	1944	1940**k**	2020	2046	2225	...	...
192	Kielce .... d.	...	0656	...	0727	...	...	0956	1007	...	1406	...	1506	...	1700	1837	1903	...	...	2058	...	2301	...	...
	Zawiercie .... **1060** d.	...	|	...	...	...	...	1112	|	...	1522	...	|	...	|	...	|	...	...	|	...	...	...	...
	Sosnowiec Gł. .... **1060** d.	...	|	...	...	...	...	1139	|	...	1547	...	|	...	|	...	|	...	...	|	...	...	...	...
	Katowice .... **1060** a.	...	|	...	...	...	...	1147	|	...	1556	...	|	...	|	...	|	...	...	|	...	...	...	...
324	**Kraków** Gł. .... a.	...	0831	...	...	...	...	...	1138	...	...	...	1640	...	1829	...	2033	...	...	2229	...	...	...	...

km				TLK		IC	TLK		IC	IC		IC		IC		IC		IC	IC	IC		TLK		TLK
				21110		32100	31106		3520	62103		3522		3524		62100		3526	42100	31104		82102		38170
				21111			31107		3521	62102		3523		3525		62101		3527						38171
																				2				
			Ⓐ	①–⑥			P		O	W		O		O		W	Ⓐ	O		P		S		Y
	Kraków Gł. .... d.	...	...	...	...	0550	...	...	0730	...	...	0935	...	1125	...	...	...	1527	...	...	...	...	...	2102
0	**Katowice** .... **1060** d.	...	...	...	...	|	...	...	|	...	...	|	...	|	...	1146	...	|	1557	...	...	...	...	|
9	Sosnowiec Gł. .... **1060** d.	...	...	...	...	|	...	...	|	...	...	|	...	|	...	1156	...	|	1607	...	...	...	...	|
44	Zawiercie .... **1060** d.	...	...	...	...	|	...	...	|	...	...	|	...	|	...	1224	...	|	1633	...	...	...	...	|
161	Kielce .... d.	...	...	0501	...	0720	...	...	0900	1007	...	1107	...	1301	...	1350	...	1701	1811	...	...	2132	...	2235
	Skarżysko Kamienna .... d.	...	...	0538	...	0758	0846**k**	0917	0942	1046	...	1146	1235	1341	1407	1430	...	1746	1853	1913**k**	...	2213	...	2321
	Radom .... d.	0401	0519	0609	0615	0827	0919	0958	1012	1116	1158	1216	1314	1411	1447	1502	1604	1816	1922	1950	1958	2244	2254	2351
	Dęblin .... d.	0452	0610	|	0706	|	|	1048	|	|	1249	|	1405	|	1537	|	1655	|	|	2028	2049	|	2345	0029
	Lublin .... a.	...	...	|	...	0948	|	...	|	1233	...	|	...	|	...	1623	...	|	2041	|	...	0005	...	|
	Warszawa Wschodnia .... a.	...	...	|	...	...	|	...	|	...	...	|	...	|	...	...	...	|	...	|	...	...	...	|
	Warszawa Centralna .... a.	...	...	0734**y**	...	...	1044**y**	...	1133**y**	...	...	1338**y**	...	1533**y**	...	...	...	1938**y**	...	|	...	...	...	|
	Warszawa Wschodnia .... a.	...	...	0743	...	...	1053	...	1142	...	...	1346	...	1542	...	...	...	1946	...	2131	...	...	...	0142

O – To / from Olsztyn (Table **1030**).
P – To / from Przemyśl (Table **1058**).
S – To / from Szczecin (Table **1003**).
W – To / from Wrocław (Tables **1075**).
Y – To / from Kołobrzeg (Table **1030**).
k – Skarżysko Kościelne.
y – Warszawa **Śródmieście**.
• – Lublin - Radom: *121 km*.
***** – *161 km* via Dęblin

1070 POZNAŃ - WROCŁAW

km			IC	IC			IC		IC	IC		IC		IC	IC	IC		IC	IC	IC		IC	IC	
			7300	54151			5601		56100	86102		5312		5315	84102	5603		8306	56103	84100		5605	83172	
			7301	53151			5600		56101	86103		5313		5314	84103	5602		8307	56102	84101		5604	83173	
			P	A	S		G		O	D		GH		GP	D	G		EH	Q	DB		G	UP	
0	**Poznań** Gł. .... d.	0515	0534	0636	0655	...	0840	0844	0941	1039	1043	1132	1229	1340	1440	1540	1640	1654	1820	1850	1854	1942	2253	...
69	Leszno .... d.	0625	0618	0720	0747	...	0921	0948	1025	1123	1146	1216	1340	1420	1524	1615	1752	1735	1904	1933	1955	2022	2342	...
165	**Wrocław** Gł. .... a.	0746	0720	0823	0852	...	1017	1108	1128	1228	1309	1319	1511	1522	1632	1703	1912	1833	2008	2036	2115	2120	0053	...

	IC		IC	IC		IC		IC	IC	IC			IC		IC	IC		IC	TLK		IC	IC		
	6505		48101	65103		3806		6503	48103	3515			3512		68103	65101		6501	45151		3701	38172		
	6504		48100	65102		3807		6502	48102	3514			3513		68102	65100		6500	35151		3700	38173		
																				Ⓒ				
	G		BD	Q		EH		G	D	PG			HG		D	O	T	G	A	S	P	PU		
Wrocław Gł .... d.	0645	0656	0735	0842	0900	0941	1025	1056	1145	1236	1242	...	1450	1455	1536	1634	1639	1756	2014	1914	2054	0245	...	...
Leszno .... d.	0744	0816	0840	0948	1030	1041	1158	1144	1252	1336	1408	...	1552	1616	1640	1739	1807	1853	2119	2026	2158	0357	...	...
Poznań Gł .... a.	0823	0919	0923	1032	1150	1120	1300	1222	1336	1416	1511	...	1635	1718	1725	1820	1915	1932	2200	2117	2241	0442	...	...

A – To / from Bydgoszcz (Table **1020**).
B – To / from Katowice (Table **1075**).
D – To / from Słupsk (Table **1015**).
E – To / from Kołobrzeg (Table **1015**).
G – To / from Gdynia (Tables **1015/20**).
H – To / from Kraków (Table **1075**).
O – To / from Olsztyn (Table **1020**).
P – To / from Przemyśl (Table **1075**).
Q – To / from Giżycko (Table **1035**).
S – To / from Szklarska Poreba Górna (Table **1084**).
T – On Ⓐ from Szklarska Poreba Górna (Table **1084**)
U – To / from Świnoujście (Table **1010**).

RZESZÓW - JASŁO - ZAGÓRZ - MEDZILABORCE 1073

km					TLK							TLK
					30113							30111
												63111
		Ⓐ			R	Ⓐ	Ⓐ	⚒		Ⓐ		P 2
					2							
0	**Rzeszów** Gł ..... d.	...	0445	0724	...	1147	...	1444	1540	1655	1922	...
9	Boguchwała ...... d.	...	0505	0742	...	1205	...	1502	1600	1713	1942	...
48	Frysztak .... d.	...	0601	0825	...	1251	...	1545	1644	1800	2027	...
52	Przybówka .... d.	...	0605	0830	...	1255	...	1550	1648	1805	2031	...
70	**Jasło** .... d.	0450	0625	0625	1145	1315	1345	1609	1707	1836	2050	2217
94	Krosno .... d.	0520	...	...	1213	...	1415	...	...	1906f	...	2245
133	Sanok .... d.	0622	...	...	1304	...	1510	...	...	2000f	...	2336
139	Nowy Zagórz .... d.	...	...	...	|	...	...	...	...	...	...	|
140	**Zagórz** .... d.	...	...	...	1313	...	...	...	...	...	...	2345
188	Łupków .... 🏛 a.	...	...	...	...	...	...	...	...	...	...	...
204	**Medzilaborce** mesto a.	...	...	...	...	...	...	...	...	...	...	...
206	Medzilaborce .... a.	...	...	...	...	...	...	...	...	...	...	...

			TLK							TLK	
			33110							33112	
	Ⓐ		36110		Ⓐ		Ⓐ		Ⓐ	S	
			Q 2							2	
Medzilaborce . d.	...	...	...	...	...	...	...	...	...	...	...
Medzilaborce mesto d.	...	...	...	...	...	...	...	...	...	...	...
Łupków ..... 🏛 d.	...	...	...	...	...	...	...	...	...	...	...
Zagórz .... d.	...	...	0443	...	...	...	...	...	...	1550	...
Nowy Zagórz . d.	...	...	|	...	...	...	...	...	...	|	...
Sanok .... d.	...	...	0453	...	0640	...	...	1454t	1523	1600	...
Krosno .... d.	...	...	0544	...	0735	...	...	1548t	1618	1651	...
Jasło .... d.	0428	0535	0611	0724	0806	0908	1418	1628	1649	1718	2000
Przybówka ..... d.	0446	0553	...	0743	...	0927	1437	1651	...	...	2019
Frysztak .... d.	0451	0558	...	0747	...	0931	1442	1655	...	...	2029
Boguchwała ... d.	0503	0645	...	0843	...	1018	1535	1747	...	...	2121
Rzeszów Gł ... a.	0519	0701	...	0859	...	1034	1551	1802	...	...	2137

P – From Kraków, depart 1932. **Q** – To Kraków, arrive 0910. **R** – From Kraków, depart 0900. **S** – To Kraków, arrive 2019. **f** – ⑤ only. **t** – ⑦ only.

ŁÓDŹ - CZESTOCHOWA - KRAKÓW / KATOWICE 1074

km		IC		TLK		TLK		TLK		IC
		13109		14101		54101		54103		5421
				14100		54100		54102		5420
						G		G		G
	Łódź Kaliska .... d.	...	...	0712	0949	1212	...	1619	1755	1949
0	**Łódź** Fabryczna .... d.	0523	...	|	1033	|	1548	|	1845	|
	Koluszki .... **1060** d.	|	...	|	|	|	|	|	|	|
15	**Łódź** Widzew .... **1060** d.	0532	0535	0736	1040	1212	1555	1638	1852	2008
	Koluszki .... **1060** d.	|	0608	|	1113	|	1628	|	1926	|
67	Piotrków Trybunalski .... **1060** d.	0610	0641	0814	1146	1306	1701	1720	1959	2046
153	**Częstochowa** .... **1060** d.	0703	0756	0917	1300	1402	1824	1823	2122	2137
	Katowice .... **1060** a.	|	...	1024	...	1508	...	1932	...	2246
299*	**Kraków** Gł. .... a.	0838	...	...	...	...	...	...	...	...

		IC	TLK		TLK		TLK		IC
		4520	45102		45100		41100		31108
		4521	45103		45101		41101		
		G	G		G				
Kraków Gł. .... d.	...	...	...	...	...	...	...	...	1914
Katowice .... **1060** d.	...	0541	0913	...	1319	...	1718	...	|
Częstochowa .... **1060** d.	0457	0647	1024	1242	1432	1550	1839	1915	2054
Piotrków Trybunalski . **1060** d.	0618	0743	1115	1405	1526	1705	1930	2029	2147
Koluszki .... **1060** d.	0700	|	|	1447	|	1748	|	2112	|
Łódź Widzew .... **1060** a.	0724	0819	1150	1510	1603	1811	2006	2136	2222
Koluszki .... **1060** a.	|	|	|	|	|	|	|	|	|
Łódź Fabryczna .... a.	0732	|	|	1518	|	1819	|	2144	2230
Łódź Kaliska .... a.	0823	0835	1208	...	1624	1906	2034	2250	...

G – To / from Gdynia (Table **1025**). * – *274 km* via CMK.

WROCŁAW - KATOWICE - KRAKÓW - PRZEMYŚL 1075

For other trains Poznań - Katowice / Kraków see Tables **1080** (via Ostrów Wlkp) and **1025** (via Łódź)

km		RJ	TLK	IC	TLK	IC	IC	IC	IC	IC	IC	TLK	IC	IC	IC	IC	IC	IC	IC	EIP	TLK	IC	IC	IC	IC	IC	
		1023	42000	13100	53172	62102	6300	7300	63104	73104	62100	213	104	8304	7201	5312	115	73000	5314	5309	82102	6305	8306	83104	84100	83172	
			311	13101	53173	62103	6301	7301	63105	73105	62101	43004	43002	8305	7200	5313	43000	57	5315	5308	82103	6304	8307		84101	83173	
		A	UN	W		L				Z	L	G	H	K	L	Q	S	B	Q	P	KL		M	K	X	T	
0	**Wrocław** Gł. .... **1061** d.	...	...	...	0512	0617	0649	0725	0846	0907	0924	...	...	1135	1248	1333	...	1504	1538	...	1735	1757	1847	1915	2047	0120	...
42	Brzeg .... **1061** d.	...	...	...	0541	0645	|	0755	|	0939	0952	...	...	1204	|	1403	...	|	1608	...	1807	1830	|	1945	2117	|	...
82	Opole Gł. .... **1061** d.	...	...	...	0611	0717	0738	0824	0932	1011	1019	...	...	1231	1335	1434	...	1550	1637	...	1845	1901	1937	2015	2148	|	...
162	Gliwice .... **1060** d.	...	0520	...	0709	|	0827	0916	1025	|	1111	1136	...	1344	1424	1529	...	1639	1733	...	|	1958	2032	2133	2246	0409	...
190	**Katowice** .... **1060** a.	...	0543	...	0733	|	0852	0943	1051	|	1136	1203	...	1407	1448	1553	...	1702	1802	...	|	2026	2100	2157	2311	0436	...
190	**Katowice** .... d.	0413	0547	...	0739	|	0856	0947	1103	|	...	1208	1251	1415	1452	1557	1613	1710	1812	...	|	2030	2105	2203	...	0458	...
•	Częstochowa Stradom .. d.	|	|	...	|	0813	|	|	|	1109	...	|	|	|	|	|	|	|	|	...	1943	|	|	|	...	|	...
268	**Kraków** Gł. .... a.	0509	0649	...	0843	...	0948	1052	1156	1250	...	1311	1349	1517	1545	1702	1707	1759	1916	...	...	2132	2200	2317	...	0612	...
268	**Kraków** Gł. .... **1078** d.	0521	0712	0747	...	...	0959	1105	1206	1305	...	...	1404	1528	1603	...	1712	1813	1924	2034	...	2142	...	...	...	0627	...
273	Kraków Płaszów ...... **1078** d.	|	0720	0755	...	...	1007	1112	1213	1312	...	...	1412	1536	1611	...	1720	1821	1932	2042	...	2150	...	...	...	0635	...
346	Tarnów .... **1078** d.	0611	0808	0843	...	...	1050	1204	1255	1406	...	...	1458	1624	1652	...	1807	1900	2018	2121	...	2238	...	...	...	0733	...
379	Dębica .... d.	|	0827	0900	...	...	1108	1224	1311	1427	...	...	1517	1643	1710	...	1826	1917	2035	2137	...	2257	...	...	...	0754	...
426	**Rzeszów** .... **1058** d.	0707	0900	0936	...	...	1145	1301	1339	1516	...	...	1556	1719	1736	...	1902	1954	2111	2202	...	2334	...	...	...	0828	...
463	Przeworsk .... **1058** d.	|	...	1006	...	...	1213	1329	1407	1546	...	...	1623	1750	...	...	1930	2020	2140	...	...	0003	...	...	...	0901	...
478	Jarosław .... **1058** d.	|	...	1017	...	...	1224	1339	1417	1557	...	...	1633	1801	...	...	1940	2030	2151	...	...	0013	...	...	...	0913	...
513	**Przemyśl** .... **1058** a.	0817	...	1052	...	...	1256	1414	1459	1632	...	...	1712	1840	...	...	2018	2058	2227	...	...	0047	...	...	...	0945	...

	IC	IC	IC	IC	TLK	EIP	IC	IC	IC	IC	IC	IC	IC	IC	TLK	IC	IC	IC	IC	TLK	IC	IC	IC	IC	RJ		
	48101	38104	3806	3604	28102	3508	3514	37000	34000	3512	2700	3804	105	26101	212	37104	36104	3700	3600	24001	26102	35173	31100	38173	1022		
	48100	38105	3807	3605	28103	3509	3515	56	114	3513	2701	3805	34002	26100	34004	37105	36105	3701	3601	310	26103	35172	31101	38172			
	X	K	M		LK	P		B	S	Q	L	K	H	L	G	Z				UN	L		W	T	A		
Przemyśl .... **1058** d.	...	...	...	0358	...	...	0552	0708	0746	...	...	1006	1101	...	...	1158	1332	1421	1532	...	...	...	1724	1810	2116	...	...
Jarosław .... **1058** d.	...	...	...	0427	...	...	0625	0733	0813	...	...	1035	1127	...	...	1227	1358	1450	1601	...	...	...	1752	1836	|	...	...
Przeworsk .... **1058** d.	...	...	...	0437	...	...	0640	0743	0823	...	...	1046	1137	...	...	1238	1410	1500	1613	...	...	...	1802	1848	|	...	...
Rzeszów .... **1058** d.	...	...	...	0516	...	0602	0715	0814	0852	...	1024	1118	1208	...	...	1316	1443	1531	1643	1723	...	...	1833	1928	2218	...	...
Dębica .... d.	...	...	...	0549	...	0629	0747	0838	0924	...	1051	1149	1236	...	...	1352	1508	1607	1708	1756	...	...	1904	2000	|	...	...
Tarnów .... **1078** d.	...	...	...	0609	...	0649	0805	0855	0944	...	1111	1207	1257	...	...	1413	1525	1627	1726	1817	...	...	1922	2021	2305	...	...
Kraków Płaszów ...... **1078** d.	...	...	...	0700	...	0734	0851	0935	1031	...	1153	1251	1346	...	...	1503	1605	1717	1807	1905	...	...	2007	2113	|	...	...
Kraków Gł. .... **1078** a.	...	...	...	0707	...	0741	0858	0942	1038	...	1200	1258	1353	...	...	1510	1612	1723	1814	1912	...	...	2014	2120	2354	...	...
Kraków Gł. .... d.	...	0514	0628	0717	...	...	0908	0952	1043	1116	1206	1312	1406	...	1437	1520	1622	1727	1824	1935	...	2000	...	2138	0002	...	...
Częstochowa Stradom .. d.	...	|	|	|	0924	...	|	|	|	|	|	|	|	...	|	1657	|	|	|	|	2027	|	...	|	|	...	...
Katowice .... a.	...	0617	0718	0817	|	...	1008	1040	1136	1217	1255	1412	1458	...	1537	|	1713	1829	1913	2036	|	2103	...	2251	0056	...	...
Katowice .... **1060** d.	0458	0620	0729	0821	|	...	1011	1048	...	1223	1304	1422	...	1609	1542	|	1716	1832	1917	2046	|	2106	...	2303	...	...	...
Gliwice .... **1060** d.	0529	0646	0755	0856	|	...	1042	1115	...	1250	1328	1448	...	1636	1605	|	1749	1857	1944	2109	|	2135	...	2332	...	...	...
Opole Gł. .... **1061** d.	0625	0801	0846	0954	1030	...	1134	1202	...	1348	1419	1558	...	1724	...	1807	1838	1952	2038	...	2126	2229	...	|	...	...	...
Brzeg .... **1061** d.	0651	0827	|	1020	1057	...	1158	|	...	1415	|	1624	...	1756	...	1834	|	2019	|	...	2151	2255	...	|	...	...	...
Wrocław Gł. .... **1061** a.	0720	0855	0931	1048	1125	...	1226	1245	...	1444	1503	1652	...	1824	...	1902	1922	2047	2123	...	2217	2323	...	0223	...	...	...

ADDITIONAL SERVICES KATOWICE - KRAKÓW and v.v.

				IC					TLK	LE		
				83102					63102	413		
				83103					63103	C		
				T					J			
Katowice .... d.	0449	0652	1147	1302	1353	1504	1749	1857	2001	2042	2048	2218
Kraków Gł .... a.	0605	0759	1303	1412	1511	1609	1906	2000	2110	2138	2212	2336

		LE		TLK					IC			
		412		36102					38103			
		F		J					38102			
				2					T			
Kraków Gł. .... d.	0413	0559	0608	0704	0828	0922	1123	1330	1400	1613	1914	2146
Katowice .... a.	0531	0703	0736	0806	0941	1025	1239	1436	1511	1737	2029	2259

A – *RegioJet* 🛏 (3, 4 berth), [2] Praha - Przemyśl and v.v.
B – WAWEL – [12] ✕ Berlin - Wrocław - Przemyśl and v.v.
C – ⑤⑦: LEO EXPRESS – [12] 🍸 Praha - Katowice - Kraków.
F – ①⑥: LEO EXPRESS – [12] 🍸 Kraków - Katowice - Praha.
G – GALICJA – [12] Kraków - Katowice - Ostrava - Praha and v.v.
H – PORTA MORAVIA / PORTA MORAVICA – [12] ✕ Przemyśl - Katowice - Wien - Graz and v.v.
J – To / from Jelenia Góra (Table **1084**).
K – To / from Szczecin (Table **1003**).
L – To / from Lublin (Table **1067**).
M – To / from Kołobrzeg (Table **1015**).
N – To / from Lublin (Table **1058**).
P – To / from Gdynia (Tables **1030**, **1065**).
Q – To / from Gdynia (Tables **1020**).
S – To / from Praha (Table **99**).
T – To / from Szczecin / Świnoujście (Tables **1010**, **1080**).
U – To / from Bohumín (Table **1076**).
W – To / from Warszawa (Table **1065**).
X – To / from Słupsk (Table **1015**).
Z – To / from Zielona Góra (Table **1004**).
• – Wrocław - Kraków Gł. via Częstochowa Stradom adds *47 km*.

1076 KATOWICE and KRAKÓW - BOHUMÍN - OSTRAVA

For night trains see Table 99

km	km		*IC¶* 101	*LE* 412	*IC¶* 116	*IC¶* 103	*IC¶* 131	*IC¶* 114	*IC¶* 105	*IC* 212	*IC** 112	*IC¶* 107	*TLK* 310
			✕⁄	🍷	✕⁄	✕⁄	✕⁄	⁄	⁄	⊡	✕⁄	✕⁄	⁄
			R	K	Y	P	D	C	E		S	G	
		Warszawa Cen **1060** d.	...	...	0507	0642	0827j	...	...	...	1302	1413j	...
	0	**Kraków** Gł. ▷ d.	...	0559	|	|	|	1043	1406	1437	|	|	1935
0		**Katowice** d.	0451	0706	0814	0836	1122	1141	1502	1542	1622	1704	2046
	65	Oświęcim ▷ d.	|	|	|	|	|	|	|	|	|	|	|
74	116	Zebrzydowice ▦ d.	|	|	|	|	|	|	|	|	|	|	|
45		Rybnik ▷ d.	|	|	0900	0950	|	1233	1552	|	1709	1750	|
82		Racibórz ▷ d.	0610	|	|	|	1243	|	|	1712	|	|	2204
102		Chałupki ▦ ▷ d.	0624	|	0937	1025	1259	1307	1624	1729	1742	1824	2218
Δ94		Bohumín ▦ a.	0630	0833	0943	1030	1305	1313	1630	1735	1748	1830	2224
94		Bohumín ▦ **1160** d.	0642	0849	1000	1042	1342	1400	1642	1805	1805	1842	...
102		**Ostrava** hlavní **1160** a.	0649	0855	1007	1049	1349	1407	1649	1812	1812	1849	...
		Praha hlavní **1160** a.	|	1224	1352	|	|	1752	|	2155	2155	|	...
		Wien Hbf **1150** a.	0949	...	...	1349	|	...	1949	...	...	2149	...
		Budapest Nyugati a.	...	...	...	...	1934	...	...	...	...	...	...

	TLK 311	*IC¶* 106	*IC** 113	*IC* 213	*IC¶* 104	*IC¶* 115	*IC¶* 130	*IC¶* 102	*IC¶* 117	*LE* 413	*IC¶* 100
	⁄ 2	✕⁄	✕⁄	⊡	⁄	⁄	✕⁄	✕⁄	✕⁄	🍷	✕⁄
	G	S			E	C	D	P	Y	J	R
Budapest Nyugati d.	...	...	...	...	...	...	0828	...	...	...	...
Wien Hbf **1150** d.	...	0610	...	...	0810	...	|	1410	...	...	1810
Praha hlavní **1160** d.	...	|	0615	0615	|	1015	|	|	1415	1500	|
Ostrava hlavní **1160** d.	...	0909	0950	0950	1108	1350	1408	1708	1747	1836	2108
Bohumín ▦ **1160** a.	...	0916	0957	0957	1115	1357	1415	1715	1754	1842	2115
Bohumín ▦ d.	0402	0927	1009	1017	1127	1446	1454	1727	1809	1914	2127
Chałupki ▦ ▷ d.	0409	0934	1016	1028	1134	1453	1501	1738	1825	|	2134
Racibórz ▷ d.	0423	|	|	1044	|	|	1515	|	|	|	2148
Rybnik ▷ d.	|	1007	1049	|	1207	1526	|	1809	1859	|	|
Zebrzydowice ▦ d.	|	|	|	|	|	|	|	|	|	|	|
Oświęcim ▷ a.	|	|	|	|	|	|	|	|	|	|	|
Katowice a.	0543	1054	1132	1205	1248	1610	1632	1848	1943	2036	2259
Kraków Gł. ▷ a.	0649	|	|	1311	1349	1707	|	|	|	2138	...
Warszawa Cen **1060** a.	...	1334j	1429	...	...	...	1951	2118	2243j	...	...

C – CRACOVIA – (12) 🍷 Przemyśl - Kraków - Praha and v.v.
D – BATORY / BÁTHORY – (12) ✕ Terespol (depart 0617; arrive 2206) - Warszawa - Budapest and v.v.
E – PORTA MORAVIA / PORTA MORAVICA – (12) Przemyśl - Bohumín - Graz and v.v.
G – ROZTOCZE – (2) Lublin - Kraków - Bohumín and v.v.
J – ⑤⑦: LEO EXPRESS – (12) 🍷 Praha - Bohumín - Kraków.
K – ①⑥: LEO EXPRESS – (12) 🍷 Kraków - Bohumín - Praha.
P – POLONIA – (12) ✕ Warszawa - Wien and v.v.
R – MORAVIA – (12) ✕ Katowice - Wien and v.v.
S – SOBIESKI – (12) ✕ Gdynia - Warszawa - Wien and v.v.
Y – SILESIA – (12) ✕ Warszawa - Praha and v.v.

j – Warszawa **Gdańska**.

⁄ – Supplement payable.
▷ – For local trains see Tables **1079/99**.
Δ – *106 km* via Chałupki.
¶ – Classified *EC* in Czech Republic.
* – Classified *Ex* in Czech Republic.

1077 KATOWICE - BIELSKO BIAŁA - ZWARDOŃ - ŽILINA

Koleje Śląskie, 2nd class

km				Ⓐ	Ⓒ							Ⓐ			
0	**Katowice** **1060** d.	0428	0513	0714	0726	0942	1128	1220	1320	1428	1528	1628	1729	1930	2125
17	Tychy d.	0448	0534	0734	0742	1001	1147	1240	1340	1447	1547	1647	1753	1949	2144
44	Czechowice-Dziedzice d.	0525	0603	0807	0806	1032	1215	1310	1410	1520	1617	1715	1826	2026	2212
55	**Bielsko Biała** Gł. **1060** d.	0544	0620	0829	0820	1049	1237	1329	1434	1540	1635	1736	1851	2044	2233
76	Zywiec a.	0618	0647	0858	0844	1121	1309	1357	1503	1620	1703	1804	1920	2117	2301
113	**Zwardoń** a.	...	0756	1011	0948	1219	1406	1459	1607	1713f	1800	1912	2028	2215	2359

			Ⓐ						Ⓒ	Ⓐ		Ⓒ	Ⓐ	Ⓒ	
Zwardoń d.	...	0347	0446	0550	0706	0920	1148	1257	1336	1428	1538	1652	1803	1824	2000
Zywiec d.	0342	0443	0543	0649	0809	1017	1250	1359	1505	1535	1643	1753	1859	1922	2058
Bielsko Biała Gł... **1060** d.	0415	0516	0621	0726	0840	1050	1329	1439	1537	1614	1720	1825	1939	1951	2131
Czechowice-Dziedzice d.	0431	0532	0637	0741	0855	1106	1344	1455	1552	1629	1735	1837	1955	2002	2146
Tychy d.	0502	0608	0706	0819	0924	1136	1415	1524	1621	1659	1801	1902	2023	2027	2219
Katowice **1060** a.	0520	0626	0723	0836	0941	1154	1436	1541	1638	1716	1825	1917	2040	2042	2236

		Ⓐ	Ⓒ	z	Ⓐ	⑥⑦	Ⓐ
Katowice ❦ d.	...	...	...	...	...	...	...
Zebrzydowice d.	0712	0956	1142	1558	1830	2103	2215
Cieszyn ★ a.	0734	1018	1204	1620	1852	2125	2237

			Ⓒ	Ⓐ	Ⓐ	Ⓒ	Ⓐ
Cieszyn ★ d.	0359	0802	1352	1405	1624	1731	1956
Zebrzydowice d.	0421	0824	1414	1427	1646	1754	2018
Katowice ❦ a.	...	...	...	...	...	...	...

f – Ⓐ.
z – Runs 9 minutes later on Ⓒ.

★ – Cieszyn station (Poland) is situated ± 1500 metres from Český Těšín station (Czech Republic).
❦ – **Shaded services are suspended until further notice.**

ZWARDÓN - ŽILINA

km		Ⓐ					
0	**Zwardoń** ▦ d.	0450	0814	1214	1614	2014	...
22	Čadca **1160** a.	0526	0852	1252	1652	2052	...
52	**Žilina** **1160** a.	*0534*	*0942*	*1342*	*1742*	*2142*	...

	⚒					
Žilina **1160** d.	*0547*	*1217*	*1417*	*1817*	*2217*	...
Čadca ▦ **1160** d.	0639	1308	1508	1908	2308	...
Zwardoń ▦ a.	0721	1347	1547	1947	2347	...

1078 KRAKÓW - NOWY SĄCZ - KRYNICA

🚌 between Tarnów and Krynica Zdrój on certain dates

km			*TLK* 30171 W	Ⓐ			*TLK* 30101 2X		*TLK* 30105 W	□		□
0	**Kraków** Gł. **1075** d.	...	0411	0355	0542	0748	0825	...	1408	1542	1645	2027
5	Kraków Płaszów **1075** d.	...	|	0402	0549	0756	|	...	|	1550	1652	2034
78	Tarnów **1075** a.	...	0518	0530	0650	0849	0934	...	1509	1642	1745	2143
78	Tarnów d.	0429	0520	0531	0654	0850	0938	1339	1511	1645	1749	2149
136	Stróze d.	0547	0632	0649	0800	0947	1034	1448	1616	1750	1852	2301
167	**Nowy Sącz** d.	0626	0708	0726	0834	1023	1112	1528	1651	1827	1925	2338
217	Muszyna ❦ d.	0742	0834	...	0946	1142	1241	1640	1823	...	2043	...
228	**Krynica Zdrój** a.	...	0853	...	1001	1156	1300	1655	1837	...	2057	...

	□	□			*TLK* 33104 W			*TLK* 33100 2X		Ⓐ	*TLK* 33170 W
Krynica Zdrój d.	...	...	0455	...	1005	1257	1400	1539	1706	...	1944
Muszyna ❦ d.	...	...	0516	0917	1038	1318	1421	1612	1727	...	2016
Nowy Sącz d.	0344	0442	0621	1033	1138	1423	1530	1725	1832	1952	2116
Stróze d.	0419	0518	0653	1109	1212	1503	1605	1758	1904	2028	2150
Tarnów a.	0528	0630	0750	1216	1308	1609	1720	1900	2001	2146	2246
Tarnów **1075** d.	0536	0631	0751	...	1310	...	1729	1903	2002	2148	2247
Kraków Płaszów **1075** a.	0629	0730	0843	...	|	...	1823	|	2102	2315	|
Kraków Gł. **1075** a.	0637	0738	0852	...	1407	...	1831	2000	2110	2323	2349

W – Not Mar. 12 - June 30.
X – ⑥⑦ (not Mar. 12 - June 30).
□ – Operator: Koleje Małopolskie.
❦ – See Table **1182** for connections to Poprad Tatry.

1079 LOCAL SERVICES IN SILESIA

2nd class

KATOWICE - OŚWIĘCIM

Operator: Koleje Śląskie

km		Ⓐ		Ⓐ						Ⓐ			
0	Katowice d.	0430	0532	0634	0731	0933	1140	1333	1537	1645	1741	1937	2132
33	Oświęcim d.	0520	0623	0725	0825	1030	1236	1423	1626	1736	1832	2026	2221

	Ⓐ							Ⓐ		Ⓐ		
Oświęcim d.	0438	0537	0639	0840	1031	1236	1438	1536	1642	1755	1845	2043
Katowice a.	0525	0625	0726	0927	1131	1331	1527	1625	1730	1846	1934	2135

KATOWICE - RYBNIK - RACIBÓRZ

Operator: Koleje Śląskie

km									Ⓐ	Ⓒ		
0	Katowice d.	...	0533	0738	0931	1135	1334	1530	1634	1736	1938	2139
45	Rybnik d.	0540	0632	0837	1039	1243	1432	1635	1734	1845	2039	2239
81	Racibórz a.	0627	0719	0924	1127	1329	1519	1722	1822	1932	2126	2325

				Ⓐ							
Racibórz d.	0437	0543	0737	0845	0939	1142	1344	1529	1738	1942	2154
Rybnik d.	0529	0635	0828	0933	1031	1232	1432	1618	1829	2040	2245
Katowice a.	0631	0728	0930	...	1126	1328	1533	1727	1930	2139	2344

RACIBÓRZ - BOHUMIN

Operator: Koleje Śląskie

km		Ⓐ			Ⓐ									
0	Racibórz d.	0523	0635	...	0736	...	1030	...	1446	...	1752	...	1951	...
20	Chałupki d.	0544	0656	0659	0757	0910	1050	1216	1506	1607	1812	1918	2011	2117
25	Bohumín a.	...	...	0705	...	0916	...	1222	...	1613	...	1924	...	2123

			Ⓐ			Ⓐ		X					
Bohumín d.	...	...	...	0848	1040	...	1240	...	...	1635	...	2013	2150
Chałupki d.	0511	0711	0807	0851	1046	1101	1246	1300	1517	1641	1718	2019	2156
Racibórz a.	0532	0732	0827	...	...	1121	...	1320	1537	...	1738	...	...

WROCŁAW - OPOLE - KEDZIERZYN-KOŹLE - RACIBÓRZ

Operator: Przewozy Regionalne

km		Ⓐ				Ⓐ	Ⓒ	Ⓐ		Ⓒ	Ⓐ		
	Wrocław Gł d.	...	...	...	0746	0938	0951	1119	1203	1400	1412	1558	1905
0	Opole Gł. d.	...	...	...	0902	1101	1101	1246	1320	1511	1519	1708	2023
42	Kedzierzyn-Koźle d.	0408	0453	0656	0947	1148	1148	1333	1407	1555	1609	1820	2106
74	Racibórz a.	0440	0525	0730	1020	...	...	...	1441	1628	1641	1854	2138

	Ⓐ		Ⓐ					Ⓐ				Ⓒ	Ⓐ
Racibórz d.	0512	0551	0711	...	1128	1403	1546	1638	1825	1920	...	2200	2200
Kedzierzyn-Koźle d.	0547	0627	0747	...	1204	1440	1647	1719	1914	1954	2006	2233	2233
Opole Gł. d.	0641	0723	0832	...	1254	1526	1737	1806	1959	...	2055	...	2316
Wrocław Gł a.	0749	0828	0945	...	1411	1637	1849	...	2108	...	2204	...	...

X – Runs 15 minutes later on Ⓒ.
f – Ⓐ.
❦ – **Shaded services are suspended until further notice.**

POZNAŃ - OSTRÓW - KATOWICE - KRAKÓW 1080

For other trains Poznań - Katowice - Kraków (via Wrocław) see Table **1075**

km		⊗	⊗	*IC* 73102 73103	⊗	*IC* 83102 83103	⊗	*IC* 83106 83107	⊗	*TLK* 73100 2	⊗ Ⓐ	*TLK* 74100 2	⊗ Ⓒ
		🚌	🚌		🚌	S	🚌	P2	🚌		🚌		🚌
0	**Poznań** Gł. d.	...	...	0606	...	0900	...	1248	...	1510	...	1716	...
67	Jarocin d.	...	...	0649	...	0942	...	1331	...	1553	...	1759	...
114	Ostrów Wlkp. d.	...	...	0723	...	1015	...	1404	...	1627	...	1832	...
160	Kępno d.	...	...	0755	...	1045	...	1443	...	1658	...	1904	...
201	Kluczbork d.	...	...	0830	...	1119	...	|	...	1731	...	1935	...
252	Lubliniec d.	0645	0845	0906	1059	1155	1528	|	1740	1804	1828	2011	2111
	Gliwice d.	|	|	|	|	1237	|	|	|	|	|	2106	|
302	Bytom d.	|	|	|	|	|	|	|	|	|	|	|	|
	Częstochowa ✣ d.	|	|	0931	|	|	|	1623	|	1833	|	|	|
*320**	**Katowice** a.	0816	1012	|	1226	1302	1659	|	1908	|	1956	2131	2252
398	**Kraków** Gł. a.	...	...	1110	...	1412	...	1756	...	2011	...	...	...

	⊗	*TLK* 47101 2	⊗	*TLK* 37101 2	⊗	*IC* 38107 38106	⊗	*IC* 38103 38102	⊗	*IC* 37103 37102	⊗	⊗
	🚌		🚌		🚌	P	🚌	S	🚌		🚌	🚌
Kraków Gł. d.	...	...	...	0741	...	1030	...	1400	...	1645	...	...
Katowice d.	0508	0614	0701	|	1104	|	1347	1519	1536	|	1747	2152
Częstochowa ✣ d.	|	|	|	0931	|	1211	|	|	|	1833	|	|
Bytom d.	|	|	|	|	|	|	|	|	|	|	|	|
Gliwice d.	|	0638	|	|	|	|	|	1546	|	|	|	|
Lubliniec d.	0630	0720	0830	0953	1229	|	1513	1626	1713	1855	1913	2313
Kluczbork d.	...	0757	...	1030	...	|	...	1702	...	1932	...	...
Kępno d.	...	0827	...	1107	...	1349	...	1733	...	2002	...	...
Ostrów Wlkp. d.	...	0858	...	1138	...	1428	...	1805	...	2033	...	...
Jarocin d.	...	0930	...	1211	...	1503	...	1837	...	2108	...	...
Poznań Gł. a.	...	1014	...	1254	...	1548	...	1919	...	2153	...	...

2nd class — LOCAL TRAINS POZNAŃ / WROCŁAW - OSTRÓW WLKP - ŁÓDŹ

		♣	♣		Ⓐ			♣	A		♣
Poznań Gł. d.	...	0648	0808	...	...	1256	...	1909	1943	...	2204
Jarocin d.	...	0747	0906	...	...	1350	...	2005	2025	...	2300
Wrocław Gł. **1061** d.	...	|	|	0824	1211	|	1615	|	|	2025	|
Ostrów Wlkp. **1061** d.	0512	0823	0942	1023	1411	1439	1814	2042	|	2221	2352
Kalisz **1061** d.	0534	...	...	...	...	1501	...	...	2118	...	0013
Łódź Kaliska **1061** a.	0736t	...	...	...	...	1651	...	...	2305f	...	...

		♣	A	Ⓐ		♣					
Łódź Kaliska **1061** d.	...	...	0527f	...	0715	...	...	...	1612	...	...
Kalisz **1061** d.	...	...	0714	...	0851	...	...	...	1758	...	...
Ostrów Wlkp. **1061** d.	0538	0552	|	0725	0924	1017	1229	1540	1830	1935	2041
Wrocław Gł. **1061** a.	0737	|	|	0917	|	|	1432	|	|	2141	|
Jarocin d.	...	0629	0811	...	1001	1055	...	1617	1906	...	2120
Poznań Gł. a.	...	0725	0856	...	1056	1151	...	1714	2001	...	2215

A – *TLK* **18109 / 81108** (2) Poznan - Łódz and v.v.
P – To / from Piła (Table **1015**).
S – To / from Szczecin / Świnoujście (Table **1010**).
f – Łódź **Fabryczna**.
t – Łódź **Widzew**.
✣ – Częstochowa **Stradom**.
* – *331 km* via Gliwice.
⊗ – Operator: Koleje Śląskie.
♣ – Operator: Koleje Wielkopolskie.

JELENIA GÓRA - TRUTNOV 1082

km												
0	**Jelenia Góra** d.	...	...	...	...	...	...	...	...	...	...	...
27	Sędzisław d.	0706	...	1006	...	1225	...	1509	...	1706	...	1910
43	Lubawka 🏛 d.	0729	...	1029	...	1248	...	1532	...	1729	...	1933
48	Královec 🏛 d.	0736	...	1036	...	1255	...	1539	...	1736	...	1940
65	**Trutnov** hlavní a.	...	...	...	...	...	...	...	...	...	...	2006

Trutnov hlavní d.	0537	...	...	...	...	...	...	...	...	...	...
Královec 🏛 d.	0604	...	0917	...	1117	...	1347	...	1610	...	1816
Lubawka 🏛 d.	0612	...	0925	...	1125	...	1355	...	1618	...	1823
Sędzisław d.	0634	...	0947	...	1147	...	1417	...	1640	...	1846
Jelenia Góra a.	...	...	...	...	...	...	...	...	...	...	...

☛ Operated by Koleje Dolnośląskie (in Czech Republic by GW Train Regio).

SZKLARSKA POREBA - JELENIA GÓRA - WAŁBRZYCH - WROCŁAW 1084

km		⊖	*IC* 66104 2	⊖	⊖	*TLK* 61100 61101 A	*TLK* 63102 63103 K	Ⓒ P	⊖	*IC* 6150 Ⓒ	⊖	⊖
0	**Jelenia Góra** d.	0356	0647	0928	1124	1307	1417	1634	1546	1612	1730	1941
27	Sedzisław d.	0420	0715	0956	1152	1335	1445	1701	1613	1637	1800	2011
47	Wałbrzych Gł. d.	0442	0736	1018	1217	1353	1505	1729	1635	1656	1822	2036
78	Jaworzyna Śląska d.	0519	0813	1054	1250	1426	1536	1810	1711	1729	1857	2110
127	**Wrocław** Gł. a.	0602	0845	1142	1332	1459	...	1853	1756	1819	1940	2155
	Warszawa C. △ a.	...	...	...	...	1957t	...	...	...	2329j	...	...

	⊖	⊖	2 P	*IC* 1651 Ⓒ	*TLK* 36102 36103 K	⊖	*TLK* 16101 16100 A	⊖	⊖	*IC* 60105 2	⊖
Warszawa C. △ d.	...	...	...	0622	...	...	0845	...	...	...	...
Wrocław Gł. d.	0450	0710	0912	1053	...	1310	1351	1502	1720	1936	2128
Jaworzyna Śląska d.	0537	0753	0951	1126	1226	1354	1427	1548	1755	2008	2220
Wałbrzych Gł. d.	0618	0828	1026	1200	1301	1432	1507	1624	1833	2043	2256
Sedzisław d.	0641	0850	1045	1218	1320	1454	1525	1646	1852	2101	2317
Jelenia Góra a.	0715	0920	1113	1244	1346	1523	1554	1716	1918	2127	2343

km		⊖	⊖	⊖	‡Ⓒ	⊖	A	⊖	⊖	
0	Jelenia Góra d.	0523	0717	0928	1246	1526	1612	1730	1921	...
32	Szklarska Poreba Górna a.	0613	0807	1019	1340	1622	1722	1822	2007	...

	⊖	⊖	A	⊖	‡Ⓒ	PⒸ	⊖	⊖	⊖
Szklarska Poreba Górna d.	0836	1031	1216	1446	1511	1534	1635	1841	2051
Jelenia Góra a.	0926	1121	1304	1543	1610	1631	1725	1938	2143

A – (12) Szklarska Poreba Górna - Warszawa and v.v. (Tables **1040/1061**).
K – To / from Kraków (Table **1075**).
P – To / from Poznań (Table **1070**).
j – Warszawa **Wschodnia**.
t – Warszawa **Gdańska**.
‡ – *IC* service.
⊖ – Operator: Koleje Dolnośląskie.
△ – **1060** via Katowice; **1070** via Poznań; **1061/1090** via Łódź.

GÖRLITZ - WROCŁAW 1085

km		*IC* 6126 P	⊖	⊖	⊖	⊖	⊖	⊖	⊖	⊖	
	Dresden Hbf **855** d.	...	0629	...	1229	...	1429	...	1829	...	...
0	**Görlitz** 🏛 **855** d.	...	0750	...	1350	...	1550	...	1950	...	...
1	Zgorzelec 🏛 **1005** d.	0413	0754	0808	1354	1426	1554	1609	1954	2009	...
3	Zgorzelec Miasto d.	0416	...	0811	...	1429	...	1612	...	2012	...
28	Węgliniec **1005** d.	0438	...	0830	...	1448	...	1636	...	2031	...
	Zary a.	|	...	|	...	|	...	|	...	|	...
53	Bolesławiec d.	0452	...	0845	...	1506	...	1655	...	2045	...
99	Legnica **1086** d.	0518	...	0909	...	1541	...	1733	...	2110	...
164	**Wrocław** Gł. **1086** a.	0557	...	0945	...	1633	...	1824	...	2148	...

		⊖	⊖	⊖	⊖	⊖	⊖	⊖	⊖	*IC* 1626 Q
Wrocław Gł. **1086** d.	0434	0611	...	0937	...	1236	...	1815	...	2118
Legnica **1086** d.	0543	0650	...	1032	...	1339	...	1854	...	2202
Bolesławiec d.	0616	0718	...	1104	...	1413	...	1921	...	2228
Zary d.	|	|	...	|	...	|	...	|	...	|
Węgliniec **1005** d.	0646	0734	...	1125	...	1431	...	1937	...	2243
Zgorzelec Miasto d.	...	0754	...	1147	...	1451	...	1955	...	2300
Zgorzelec 🏛 **1005** d.	...	0756	0801	1152	1200	1454	1500	1957	2002	2303
Görlitz 🏛 **855** a.	...	...	0805	...	1204	...	1504	...	2006	...
Dresden Hbf **855** a.	...	...	0927	...	1327	...	*1627*	...	2127	...

P – ①–⑥. To Warszawa (Table **1061**).
Q – Ⓑ. From Warszawa (Table **1061**).
⊖ – Operator: Koleje Dolnośląskie.

COTTBUS - FORST - WROCŁAW 1086

km		⊖	⊖ Ⓐ	⊖ Ⓒ	*IC* 7201 7200 LZ2	*IRE* 5837 69020 KM		⊖	⊖	*IRE* 5839 69022 KP	Ⓐ	⊖ Ⓒ	⊖ Ⓐ
	Berlin L ❦ d.	...	...	...	...	0743	...	...	...	1443	...	...	...
	Berlin O ✣ d.	...	...	...	...	0748	...	...	...	1448	...	...	...
0	**Cottbus** **854** d.	...	...	*0807*	...	0932	...	...	...	1632	*1707*	*1807*	...
22	Forst 🏛 **854** a.	...	...	*0825*	...	|	...	...	...	|	*1725*	*1825*	...
22	Forst d.	...	*0638*	0845	...	|	...	...	...	|	1738	1834	...
36	Tuplice d.	0516	*0653*	0900	...	|	...	...	1628	|	1753	1849	...
57	Záry **1005** d.	0538	0743	0921	1012	|	1105	142	1649	|	1814	1910	1940
70	Zagań **1005** d.	0550	0756	0933	1026	|	1119	1441	1702	|	1826	1923	1954
144	Legnica **1085** d.	0702	0903	1045	1134	1141	1227	1604	1810	1843	...	2032	2106
210	**Wrocław** Gł. **1085** a.	0748	...	1136	1225	1229	...	...	1854c	1937	...	2119	...

	Ⓐ	⊖ Ⓒ	⊖ Ⓐ	⊖ A	⊖	Ⓐ	⊖ Ⓒ	⊖ Ⓐ	*IC* 2701 2700 ZP2	*IRE* 5836 69005 KN	⊖	*IRE* 5838 69007 KP
Wrocław Gł. **1085** d.	...	0525	...	...	1337	...	1525	...	1531	1733	2013c	2019
Legnica **1085** d.	...	0610	0610	0855	1423	...	1613	1611	1629	1815	2059	2103
Zagań **1005** d.	0541	0722	0721	1017	1529	1633	1725	1725	1751	|	2206	|
Záry **1005** d.	0552	0734	0732	1029	1540	1652	1736	1736	1803	|	2217	|
Tuplice d.	0613	0754	...	...	1600	1713	1756	...	...	|	2238	|
Forst a.	0628	0809	...	...	...	1728	1813	...	...	|	...	|
Forst 🏛 **854** d.	*0633*	*0833*	...	...	...	*1733*	*1833*	...	...	|	...	|
Cottbus **854** a.	*0651*	*0851*	...	...	...	*1751*	*1851*	...	...	2026	...	2303
Berlin O ✣ a.	...	...	...	...	...	...	...	...	...	2152	...	0050
Berlin L ❦ a.	...	...	...	...	...	...	...	...	...	2158	...	0055

A – On Ⓐ departs Legnica 0917, Zagań 1024, arrive Záry 1035.
K – KULTURZUG / POCIAG DO KULTURY - (2) Berlin - Wrocław and v.v. For International journeys only. Special fares apply. Service suspended temporarily but may resume from April.
L – To / from Lublin (Table **1067**).
M – Dec. 17, 24, 31.
N – Dec. 11, 18, 26, Jan. 1.
P – Dec. 16, 23, 30.
Z – To / from Zielona Góra (d. 0906), (a. 1917).
c – ⑤⑦.
❦ – Full name: Berlin Lichtenberg.
✣ – Full name: Berlin Ostkreuz.
⊖ – Operator: Koleje Dolnośląskie.

1090 WARSZAWA - ŁÓDŹ

km		*IC*	*IR*	*IR*	*IC*	*IC*	♣	*IR*	*IC*	*IC*	♣	*IR*	*IC*	♣	*IR*	*IR*	*IC*	*IC*	*IR*	*IC*	♣	*IC*	♣	♣	*IR*	*IC*	*IC*
		1900	**99111**	**11123**	**2622**	**1902**	**19100**	**11125**	**5620**	**1905**	**19102**	**11127**	**1906**	**19104**	**11129**	**17219**	**2620**	**1909**	**11131**	**19132**	**19106**	**1627**	**19131**	**19109**	**17215**	**81114**	**16102**
		1901	**99110**	**11122**	**1622**	**1903**	**19101**	**11124**	**5621**	**1905**	**19103**	**11126**	**1907**	**19105**	**11128**	**17218**	**2621**	**1908**	**11130**	**19133**	**19107**	**1626**	**19130**	**19108**	**17214**	**81115**	**16103**
		Ⓐ	⚒	Ⓐ		Ⓐ	Ⓒ	Ⓐ		Ⓐ	Ⓒ	Ⓐ		Ⓒ	Ⓐ			Ⓐ	Ⓐ	Ⓐ	Ⓒ	Ⓑ		Ⓒ	Ⓐ		
					W				**EW**																	**E**	**YW**
0	**Warszawa** Wsch .... d.	0509	0608j	0703j	0714	0758	0915j	0956j	0954	1057	1124j	1124j	1234	1301	1302j	1404j	1413	1515j	1529j	1532	1534	1555	1638	1710j	1711j	1739	1854
4	**Warszawa** Cent........ d.	0518	|	|	0729	|	|	|	1022	|	|	|	|	|	|	|	1437	|	|	1543	1545	|	|	|	|	|	|
70	Skierniewice .... d.	0619	0707	0806	0826	0855	1000	1054	1111	1156	1208	1220	1340	1351	1357	1502	1535	1607	1622	1644	1633	1652	1743	1800	1806	1824	1956
109	Koluszki........ d.	0641	0733	0833	0845	0918	1021	1120	1131	1216	1230	1246	1400	1411	1423	1527	1528	1626	1654	1708	1654	1713	1809	1820	1831	1846	2019
130	**Łódź** Widzew .... a.	0656	0749	0849	0859	0933	1034	1136	1144	1230	1243	1301	1414	1424	1439	1543	1613	1640	1709	1726	1707	1729	1827	1833	1847	1901	2036
145	**Łódź** Kaliska .... a.	|	0840	|	...	|	|	|	...	|	|	|	|	|	|	1602	...	|	1806	|	|	...	|	|	1910	|	...
135	**Łódź Fabryczna** .... a.	0707	...	0857	...	0942	1042	1144	...	1238	1250	1309	1423	1431	1447	...	...	1648	...	1725	1714	...	1836	1840	...	1909	...

	♣	*IC*	*IR*	*IC*	♣	*IC*		*IC*		
	19113	**2100**	**11134**	**5122**	**19114**	**1910**		**1100**		
	19112	**2101**	**11135**	**5123**	**19115**	**1911**		**1101**		
	Ⓒ	Ⓑ	Ⓐ		Ⓒ	Ⓑ				
		L		**O**				**Y**		
Warszawa Wsch........ d.	1911j	1927	...	2018	...	2135	...	2234	...	...
Warszawa Cent........ d.	|	|	2011t	2027	2114t	2148	...	2243	...	...
Skierniewice........ d.	2001	2025	2101	2122	2153	2241	...	2342	...	...
Koluszki........ d.	2030	2045	2128	2143	2214	2301	...	0002	...	...
Łódź Widzew........ a.	2043	2059	2143	2158	2227	2315	...	0016	...	...
Łódź Kaliska........ a.	|	|	2239	|	|	|	...	|	...	...
Łódź Fabryczna........ a.	2050	2108	...	2207	2234	2323	...	0025	...	...

	IC	*IR*	*IC*	*IR*	*IC*	*IR*	*IC*	*IC*	♣	*IC*
	1525	**10131**	**91131**	**10133**	**1523**	**10135**	**1201**	**9111**	**91101**	**61102**
	1524	**10130**	**91130**	**10132**	**1522**	**10134**	**1200**	**9110**	**91100**	**61103**
		Ⓐ		Ⓐ		Ⓐ		Ⓐ	Ⓒ	
	Y				**O**		**L**			**WY**
Łódź Fabryczna........ d.	0409	0418	0435	0515	0555	...	0702	0733	0740	...
Łódź Kaliska........ d.	|	|	|	|	|	0549	|	|	|	...
Łódź Widzew........ d.	0417	0425	0444	0523	0603	0643	0710	0741	0746	0753
Koluszki........ d.	0432	0441	0504	0540	0618	0701	0727	0758	0800	0811
Skierniewice........ d.	0451	0507	0528	0605	0638	0726	0747	0820	0822	0834
Warszawa Cent........ a.	0537	|	0622	0654t	0724	|	|	|	|	0923
Warszawa Wsch........ a.	0548	0557j	0631	...	0735	0816j	0839	0901j	0900j	0956

km		*IC*	♣	*IC*	*IR*	*IC*	*IR*	♣	*IC*		*IC*	♣	*IC*	*IR*	♣	*IR*	♣	*IC*	♣	♣	*IR*	*IC*	*IC*	♣	*IR*		*IC*
		18115	**91103**	**6127**	**71502**	**9109**	**10137**	**91105**	**6221**		**9105**	**91107**	**1206**	**10141**	**91109**	**10143**	**91111**	**6521**	**91113**	**91115**	**71504**	**9103**	**6123**	**91117**	**10145**		**6121**
		18114	**91102**	**6126**	**71503**	**9108**	**10136**	**91104**	**6220**		**9104**	**91106**	**1207**	**10140**	**91108**	**10142**	**91110**	**6520**	**91112**	**91114**	**71505**	**9102**	**6122**	**91116**	**10144**		**6120**
			Ⓒ	⚒		Ⓐ	Ⓐ	Ⓒ				Ⓒ		Ⓐ	Ⓒ	Ⓐ	Ⓒ		Ⓒ	Ⓒ		Ⓐ		Ⓒ	Ⓑ		
		E		**W**					**W**				**L**					**WY**					**W**				**W**
0	**Łódź Fabryczna** .... d.	0859	0915	...	...	1102	1111	1115	...	...	1314	1320	1457	1510	1512	1608	1616	...	1746	1819	...	1916	...	2022	2051	...	...
	Łódź Kaliska........ d.	|	|	...	0944	|	|	|	...	...	|	|	|	|	|	|	|	...	|	|	1827	|	...	|	|	...	...
5	**Łódź** Widzew .... d.	0907	0920	0959	1004	1110	1118	1121	1142	...	1321	1325	1505	1517	1518	1615	1622	1644	1752	1825	1859	1924	2017	2029	2059	...	2239
26	Koluszki........ d.	0924	0934	1015	1024	1125	1135	1134	1157	...	1336	1339	1519	1536	1535	1635	1635	1659	1808	1838	1916	1938	2035	2045	2117	...	2255
65	Skierniewice .... d.	0944	0954	1034	1054	1146	1200	1155	1216	...	1355	1359	1538	1601	1555	1703	1655	1718	1828	1858	1948	1957	2054	2106	2142	...	2314
131	**Warszawa** Cent........ a.	1026t	|	|	|	|	|	|	1309	...	|	|	|	|	|	1752t	|	1814	|	1935t	|	|	|	|	|	...	|
135	**Warszawa** Wsch .... a.	...	1032j	1133	1150j	1226j	1254j	1235j	1326	...	1450	1450	1636	1654j	1637j	...	1735j	1841	1907j	...	2047j	2058	2154	2147j	2239j	...	2400

E – To/from Kołobrzeg (Table **1015**).
L – To/from Lublin (Table **1055**).
O – To/from Olsztyn (Table **1030**).
W – To/from Wrocław (Table **1061**).
Y – To/from Białystok (Table **1040**).
Z – To/from Ełk (Table **1035**).
j – Warszawa **Główna**.
t – Warszawa **Gdańska**.
♣ – Operator: Łódźka Kolej Aglomeracyjna (ŁKA).

1095 WROCŁAW - KŁODZKO

Certain trains continue beyond Kłodzko – see Table **1165**

km		⊖	⊖		⊖	⊖		⊖	**60151**		⊖	⊖	⊖	⊖	⊖	⊖	⊖				⊖		⊖	
		Ⓐ			Ⓒ				‡Ⓒ				Ⓑ											
0	**Wrocław** Gł........ d.	0511	0611	...	0756	0814	...	1016	1058	...	1251	1410	1517	1551	1651	1751	1856	...	2023	...	2139	...	2302	...
72	Kamieniec Ząbkowicki........ d.	0612	0712	...	0859	0924	...	1123	1215	...	1358	1518	1628	1700	1801	1851	2007	...	2131	...	2255	...	0011	...
94	**Kłodzko** Gł. **1165**........ a.	0632	0732	...	0917	0944	...	1143	1238	...	1418	1538	1649	1721	1823	1909	2028	...	2151	...	2314	...	0031	...

	⊖	⊖		⊖	⊖	⊖		⊖	⊖		⊖		⊖	**66150**	⊖	⊖	⊖		⊖		⊖	
	①–⑥			Ⓐ										‡Ⓒ			Ⓒ					
Kłodzko Gł. **1165**........ d.	0329	0429	0534	0605	0635	0740	...	0940	1058	...	1253	...	1438	1618	1702	1749	1833	...	1933	...	2139	...
Kamieniec Ząbkowicki........ d.	0350	0450	0556	0625	0657	0801	...	1003	1124	...	1312	...	1502	1643	1723	1807	1852	...	1953	...	2158	...
Wrocław Gł........ a.	0501	0601	0711	0741	0808	0912	...	1111	1234	...	1419	...	1616	1754	1835	1912	1951	...	2059	...	2257	...

‡ – *IC* service.
⊖ – Operated by Koleje Dolnośląskie.

1099 OTHER LOCAL SERVICES

2nd class only

GDYNIA - HEL *76 km, journey 1 hr 25 mins - 1 hr 55 mins*

Gdynia Główna depart: 0500, 0703, 0840, 1041, 1255, 1432, 1541, 1654, 1911, 2035, 2205.
Hel depart: 0441, 0538, 0642, 0855, 1050, 1334, 1440, 1615, 1720, 1850, 2107.

KŁODZKO - KUDOWA-ZDRÓJ *44 km, journey 1 hr 10 mins*

Kłodzko Główne depart: 0500, 0743 **m**, 0922Ⓒ, 1011Ⓐ, 1020Ⓒ, 1240Ⓒ, 1424, 1559, 1910.
Kudowa-Zdrój depart: 0619, 0902, 1139, 1435Ⓒ, 1546, 1724Ⓒ, 1758, 2032.
Operator: Koleje Dolnośląskie.

KRAKÓW - LOTNISKO (for Kraków John Paul II Airport ✈)

Kraków Główny depart: 0433, 0536, 0606, 0636, 0706, 0736, 0806, 0836, 0906, 0936, 1007, 1037, 1112, 1138 and at the same minutes past each hour until 1736, 1836, 1936, 2038, 2136, 2236, 2336.
Kraków Lotnisko depart: 0517, 0617, 0647, 0717 and at the same minutes past each hour until 1817, 1917, 2017, 2117, 2217, 2317, 0038.
12 km, journey 17 mins. Timings may vary by up to ± 6 minutes.

KRAKÓW - OŚWIĘCIM (for Auschwitz-Birkenau Memorial and Museum)

VIA TRZEBINIA *65 km Journey 1 hr 45 mins - 1 hr 59 mins. Some journeys by 🚌.*
Kraków Główny depart: 0438, 0541, 0643, 0747, 0845, 0943, 1054, 1146, 1349, 1458, 1537, 1640, 1743, 1845, 1954, 2251.
Oświęcim depart: 0250, 0351, 0512, 0552, 0650, 0812, 0855, 0955, 1105, 1158, 1258, 1508, 1645, 1803, 1853, 1956.
Timings may vary.

KRAKÓW - WADOWICE *62 km, journey 1 hr 45 mins*

Kraków Główny d.: 0439, 0602, 1043, 1341, 1445, 1640, 1846.
Wadowice d.: 0500, 0738, 0956, 1254, 1557, 1753, 2024.
Wadowice is the birthplace of Pope John Paul II.

KRAKÓW - WIELICZKA (for Salt Mine) *14 km, journey 25–30 mins*

Kraków Główny depart: 0438, 0538, 0638, 0708, 0738, 0808, 0838, 0908, 0938, 1040, 1141, 1237, 1337, 1408, 1438, 1508, 1538, 1608, 1638, 1708, 1738, 1808, 1837, 1940, 2038, 2138, 2238.
Wieliczka Rynek depart: 0510, 0537, 0610, 0640, 0710, 0740, 0810, 0840, 0910, 1011, 1112, 1212, 1310, 1410, 1440, 1510, 1540, 1610, 1640, 1710, 1740, 1810, 1840, 1909, 2012, 2110, 2210, 2310.

LESZNO - WOLSZTYN - ZBĄSZYNEK

		Ⓐ			Ⓐ	Ⓐ		Ⓐ		Ⓑ
Leszno........ d.	0512	0557	0805	1045	1322	1357	1524	1719	1850	2117
Wolsztyn........ d.	0608	0653	0906	1140	1419	1458	1619	1820	1945	2212
Zbąszyń........ d.	0636	0722	...	1208	1446	...	1657	...	...	...
Zbąszynek........ a.	0642	0728	...	1215	1453	...	1654	...	...	...

	①–⑥	Ⓐ		Ⓐ	Ⓐ		Ⓐ		Ⓐ	
Zbąszynek........ d.	...	...	0719	0900f	...	1305	1505	1710	...	...
Zbąszyń........ d.	...	...	0726	0907f	...	1312	1512	1717	...	...
Wolsztyn........ d.	0530	0615	0754	0934	1159	1339	1541	1744	1907	2134
Leszno........ a.	0639	0716	0849	1029	1304	1441	1642	1840	2008	2234

Operator: Koleje Wielkopolskie.

POZNAN - WOLSZTYN 🚌 *80 km, journey 1 hr 25 mins - 2 hrs 39 mins*

Poznan Główny depart: 0550, 0618Ⓐ, 0757, 0950⚒, 1145, 1310, 1448, 1544, 1629Ⓐ, 1736⑥, 1839, 2109, 2153Ⓐ, 2257.
Wolsztyn depart: 0249, 0403Ⓐ, 0516, 0600⑥, 0650, 0813Ⓐ, 1010, 1158, 1333, 1507⑥, 1556, 1754, 1815Ⓐ, 1916Ⓐ, 2020.
Operator: Koleje Wielkopolskie.

REJOWIEC - ZAMOŚĆ *63 km, journey 1 hr 20 mins*

Rejowiec depart: 1028, 1436, 1757, 2052Ⓑ. All journeys to/from Lublin (Table **1055**).
Zamość depart: 0519①–⑥, 0838, 1215, 1613.

WAŁBRZYCH - KŁODZKO *51 km, journey 1 hr 25 mins*

Wałbrzych Główny depart: 0620, 0902, 1031, 1321, 1639, 2113.
Kłodzko Główne depart: 0550, 0743, 1012, 1443, 1709, 1915.
Operator: Koleje Dolnośląskie.

WARSZAWA - WARSZAWA MODLIN AIRPORT ✈ *40 km, journey 59 mins*

Warszawa Wschodnia depart: 0322, 0417, 0515, 0613, 0644Ⓐ, 0724, 0810, 0912, 1010, 1112, 1212, 1319, 1412, 1521, 1614, 1709, 1806, 1917, 2012, 2112, 2212, 2312.
Modlin ✈ depart: 0019, 0411, 0511, 0610, 0711, 0811, 0911, 1011, 1110, 1211, 1311, 1411, 1508, 1611, 1711, 1811, 1911, 2011, 2111, 2211, 2310.
Operator: Koleje Mazowieckie.

🚌 connects the rail station with the terminal. Additional slower trains run Modlin ✈ to Warszawa Gdánska, with metro connection to city centre.

NOTES FOR TABLE 1099 (ALL ROUTES): f – Ⓐ only. m – Kłodzko **Miasto**.

CZECH REPUBLIC

Services: Operator: České Dráhy (ČD), www.cd.cz. Railway infrastructure and timetables are the responsibility of Správa Železnic, www.spravazeleznic.cz. All daytime trains convey first and second classes of travel unless otherwise shown by '2' at the top of the column or by a note (which may be in the table heading).

Timings: Valid **December 11, 2022 - December 9, 2023** with amendments as received. Certain trains are cancelled during the Christmas / New Year period, particularly the evening of Dec. 24, 31 and the morning of Dec. 25, 26, Jan. 1; passengers travelling during this period are advised to confirm train times before travel.

Tickets: It is possible to reserve seats on most Express trains. SuperCity (*SC*) tilting trains have a compulsory reservation fee. *Business* class on Railjet (*RJ*) trains requires a first class ticket and a supplement. Note that ČD tickets, including day passes and Interrail / Eurail passes, are not valid on trains operated by GW Train Regio.

Station names: hlavní nádraží (hl. n.) = main station; západ = west; východ = east; horní = upper; dolní = lower; střed = centre, starý = old; město = town; předměstí = outskirts.

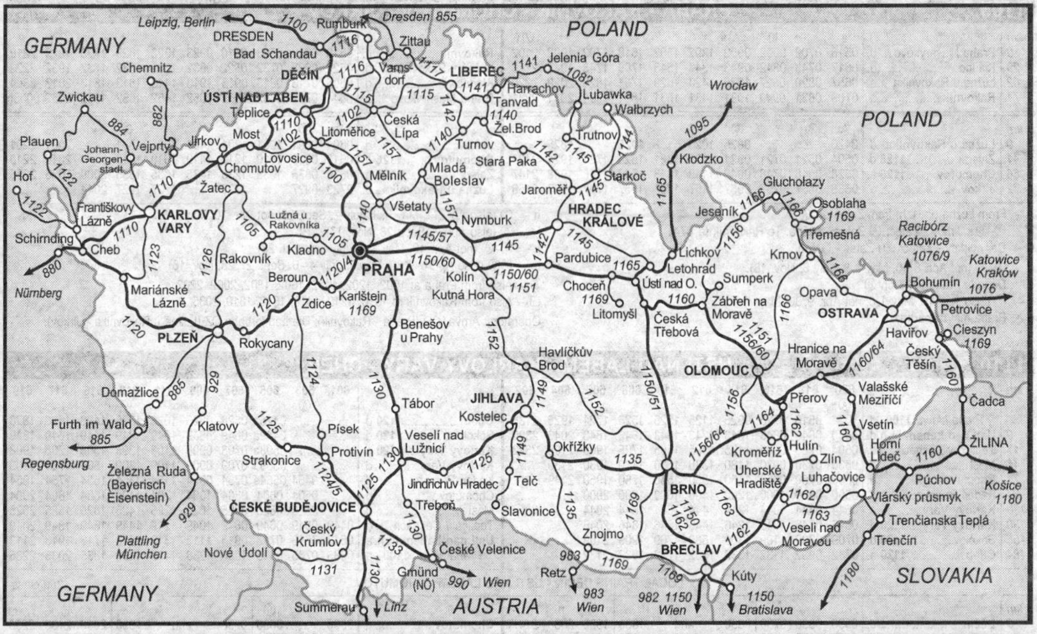

PRAHA - ÚSTÍ NAD LABEM - DĚČÍN - DRESDEN — 1100

km		618	698	*EC* 178	696	616	694	*EC* 176	692	614	*EC* 174	690	612	*EC* 378	688	610	686	*EC* 172	*EC* 252	684	608	682	*EC* 170	680	606	*RJ* 256
			Ⓐ	A			Ⓐ	A			A			A			Ⓐ	B f	B g			Ⓐ	A			C f
0	**Praha** hlavní nádraží ... d.	0516	0545	0625	0645	0725	0745	0825	0845	0925	1025	1045	1125	1225	1245	1325	1345	1425	...	1445	1525	1545	1625	1645	1721	1728
3	**Praha** Holešovice ... d.	0526	0555	0634	0655	0734	0755	0834	0855	0934	1034	1055	1134	1234	1255	1334	1355	1434	1437	1455	1534	1555	1634	1655	1734	1737
27	Kralupy nad Vltavou ... d.	0548	0618	|	0718	|	0818	|	0918	|	|	1118	|	|	1318	|	1418	|	|	1518	|	1618	|	1718	|	|
66	Roudnice nad Labem ... d.	0609	0643	|	0743	|	0843	|	0943	|	|	1143	|	|	1343	|	1443	|	|	1543	|	1643	|	1743	|	|
84	Lovosice ... d.	0620	0659	|	0759	|	0859	|	0959	|	|	1159	|	|	1359	|	1459	|	|	1559	|	1659	|	1759	|	|
106	**Ústí nad Labem** hl. n. ... a.	0637	0716	0737	0816	0837	0916	0937	1016	1037	1137	1216	1237	1337	1416	1437	1516	1538	1538	1616	1637	1716	1737	1816	1837	1840
106	**Ústí nad Labem** hl. n. ◧ d.	0643	0716	0739	0816	0843	...	0939	1016	1043	1139	1216	1243	1339	1416	1443	1516	1540	1540	1616	1643	...	1739	1816	1843	1842
	Cheb **1110** ... a.	0932	|	|	|	1132	...	|	|	1332	|	|	1532	|	|	1732	|	|	|	|	1932	...	|	|	2132	|
129	**Děčín** ... ◧ a.	...	0734	0754	0834	...	...	0954	1034	...	1154	1234	...	1354	1434	...	1534	1556	1556	1634	...	...	1754	1834	...	1857
129	**Děčín** 🏛 ⊖ ... ◧ d.	...	...	0801	...	...	...	1001	...	...	1201	...	...	1401	...	...	...	1601	1601	...	...	...	1801	...	...	...
151	Bad Schandau 🏛 ⊖ ... ◧ a.	...	...	0820	...	...	...	1020	...	...	1220	...	...	1420	...	...	...	1620	1620	...	...	...	1820	...	...	...
191	**Dresden** Hbf ... ◧ a.	...	...	0852	...	...	...	1052	...	...	1252	...	...	1452	...	...	...	1652	1652	...	...	...	1852	...	...	...

	678	*EC* 458	676	604	674		672	602	600	670
	Ⓐ	D			Ⓐ				Ⓑ e	
Praha hlavní nádraží ... d.	1745	1826	1845	1925	1945	...	2045	2135	2235	2325
Praha Holešovice ... d.	1755	1835	1855	1934	1955	...	2055	2144	2244	2335
Kralupy nad Vltavou ... d.	1818	|	1918	|	2018	...	2118	|	|	2356
Roudnice nad Labem ... d.	1843	|	1943	|	2043	...	2143	2223	2323	0021
Lovosice ... d.	1859	|	1959	|	2059	...	2159	2234	2334	0037
Ústí nad Labem hl. n. ... a.	1916	1937	2016	2037	2116	...	2216	2250	2350	0053
Ústí nad Labem hl. n. ... ◧ d.	1916	1939	2016	2043	...	...	2216	2300	...	0053
Cheb **1110** ... a.	|	|	|	b	...	...	|	b	...	|
Děčín ... ◧ a.	1934	1954	2034	...	...	...	2234	...	...	0111
Děčín 🏛 ⊖ ... ◧ d.	...	2001	...	...	...	...	...	...	...	...
Bad Schandau 🏛 ⊖ ... ◧ a.	...	2019	...	...	...	...	...	...	...	...
Dresden Hbf ... ◧ a.	...	2054	...	...	...	...	...	...	...	...

	671	601	673	603	675		605	677	*EC* 459	679
	Ⓐ			d	Ⓐ				D	Ⓐ
Dresden Hbf ... ◧ d.	...	...	...	...	...	...	...	...	0708	...
Bad Schandau 🏛 ⊖ ... ◧ d.	...	...	...	...	...	...	...	...	0733	...
Děčín 🏛 ⊖ ... ◧ a.	...	...	...	...	...	...	...	...	0754	...
Děčín ... ◧ d.	0421	...	0525	...	0625	...	...	0725	0802	0825
Cheb **1110** ... d.	|	b	|	b	|	...	0426a	|	|	|
Ústí nad Labem hl. n. ◧ a.	0436	0513	0540	0613	0640	...	0713	0740	0816	0840
Ústí nad Labem hl. n. ... d.	0442	0519	0542	0619	0642	...	0719	0742	0819	0842
Lovosice ... d.	0459	0535	0559	|	0659	...	|	0759	|	0859
Roudnice nad Labem ... d.	0514	0548	0614	|	0714	...	|	0814	|	0914
Kralupy nad Vltavou ... d.	0540	|	0640	|	0740	...	|	0840	|	0940
Praha Holešovice ... a.	0601	0625	0701	0725	0801	...	0825	0901	0925	1001
Praha hlavní nádraží ... a.	0612	0635	0712	0735	0812	...	0835	0912	0938	1012

	RJ 257	607	681	*EC* 171	609	683	*EC* 173	*EC* 173	611	685	*EC* 379	687	613	689	*EC* 175	691	615	693	*EC* 177	695	617	697	*EC* 179	619	699
	C f			A			B f	B g			A	Ⓐ			A	Ⓐ			A	Ⓐ			A		
Dresden Hbf ... ◧ d.	...	...	...	0910	...	...	1110	1110	...	...	1310	...	...	...	1510	...	...	...	1710	...	...	...	1910	...	...
Bad Schandau 🏛 ⊖ ... ◧ d.	...	...	...	0936	...	...	1136	1136	...	...	1336	...	...	...	1536	...	...	...	1736	...	...	...	1936	...	...
Děčín 🏛 ⊖ ... ◧ a.	...	...	...	0957	...	...	1157	1157	...	...	1357	...	...	...	1557	...	...	...	1757	...	...	...	1957	...	...
Děčín ... ◧ d.	0900	...	0925	1002	...	1125	1202	1202	...	1325	1402	...	...	1525	1602	1625	...	1725	1802	...	...	1925	2002	...	2147
Cheb **1110** ... d.	|	0626	|	|	0826	|	|	|	1026	|	|	...	1226	|	|	|	1426	|	|	...	1626	|	|	1826	|
Ústí nad Labem hl. n. ... ◧ a.	0914	0913	0940	1016	1113	1140	1216	1216	1313	1340	1416	...	1513	1540	1616	1640	1713	1740	1816	...	1913	1940	2016	2113	2202
Ústí nad Labem hl. n. ... d.	0916	0919	0942	1019	1119	1142	1219	1219	1319	1342	1419	1442	1519	1542	1619	1642	1719	1742	1819	1842	1919	1942	2019	2119	2204
Lovosice ... d.	|	|	0959	|	|	1159	|	|	|	1359	|	1459	|	1559	|	1659	|	1759	|	1859	|	1959	|	|	2220
Roudnice nad Labem ... d.	|	|	1014	|	|	1214	|	|	|	1414	|	1514	|	1614	|	1714	|	1814	|	1914	|	2014	|	|	2234
Kralupy nad Vltavou ... d.	|	|	1040	|	|	1240	|	|	|	1440	|	1540	|	1640	|	1740	|	1840	|	1940	|	2040	|	|	2301
Praha Holešovice ... a.	1022	1025	1101	1125	1225	1301	1325	1322	1425	1501	1525	1601	1625	1701	1725	1801	1825	1901	1925	2001	2025	2101	2125	2225	2321
Praha hlavní nádraží ... a.	1031	1036	1112	1135	1236	1312	1335	...	1435	1512	1535	1612	1635	1712	1735	1812	1835	1912	1935	2012	2035	2112	2135	2235	2331

A – BERLINER – 12 ✕ Praha - Berlin* and v.v.
B – HUNGARIA – 12 ✕ Budapest - Hamburg and v.v.
C – VINDOBONA – 12 ✕ Graz - Wien - Praha - Děčín and v.v.
D – CANOPUS – 2 Praha - Basel - Zurich and v.v.; 12 ✕ Praha - Leipzig and v.v.; 1, 2 cl. and 2 cl. (**40458/40459**) Praha - Basel - Zürich and v.v.

a – Ⓐ only. From Chomutov on Ⓒ.
b – To / from Chomutov or Teplice v Čechách (Table **1110**).
d – ①-⑥ (not Apr. 8, 10, May 1, 8, July 6, Nov. 18).
e – Ⓑ (not Apr. 7, 9, 30, May 7, July 5, Nov. 17).
f – from July 1.
g – Until June 30.

◧ – Other trains Ústí nad Labem - Děčín and v.v. Tables **1110** / **1115**; Other trains Děčín - Bad Schandau and v.v. Table **1116**; Other trains Bad Schandau - Dresden and v.v. Table **857**.
⊖ – Routeing point for international tickets: Schöna.
* – Some extend to / from Hamburg, Flensburg or Kiel.

CZECH REPUBLIC

1102 MOST - ČESKÁ LIPA *2nd class*

km										
0	**Most** d.	...	0627	...	0827	then each	...	2027	...	2232
44	Lovosice a.	...	0725	...	0925	train runs	...	2123	...	2329
44	Lovosice d.	0602	0731	0802	0931	every **two**	2002	2131	2202	*2340*
52	Litoměřice horní d.	0613	0742	0813	0942	hours until	2013	2142	2213	*2351*
102	**Česká Lípa** a.	0716	...	0916	...		2116	...	...	...

	Ⓐ									
Česká Lípa d.	0434	...	0634	...	0834	then each	...	2034	...
Litoměřice horní d.	0542	0614	0742	0814	0942	train runs	2014	2142	2159
Lovosice a.	0555	0625	0755	0825	0955	every **two**	2025	2155	2212
Lovosice d.	...	0632	...	0832	...	hours until	2032	...	2239
Most a.	...	0727	...	0927	...		2127	...	2333

Other trains: **Most - Litoměřice horní** at 0417, 0522 Ⓐ; **Litoměřice horní - Most** at 0409, 0459 Ⓐ. Operators: AŽD Praha (Most - Litoměřice horní); ČD (Lovosice - Česká Lípa).

1105 PRAHA - RAKOVNIK - CHOMUTOV - JIRKOV *2nd class*

km		e		◧				Ⓐ			⑦f
0	**Praha** Masarykovo d.	0516	0702	0802	0902	1302	1502	1618	1702	1902	2102
29	Kladno d.	0617	0743	0842	0943	1343	1543	1709	1743	1943	2143
62	Lužná u Rakovnika a.	0657	0820	*0927*	1020	1420	1620	1751	1820	2020	2220
71	**Rakovník** a.	0709	0831	*0943*	1031	1431	1631	1801	1831	2031	2231

	d			⊡					⑦f	
Rakovník d.	0518	0618	0723	*0810*	0923	1323	1523	1723	1923	2210
Lužná u Rakovnika d.	0527	0628	0732	*0822*	0932	1332	1532	1732	1932	2222
Kladno d.	0605	0713	0813	0913	1013	1413	1613	1813	2013	2304
Praha Masarykovo a.	0644	0752	0852	0952	1052	1452	1652	1852	2052	0003**g**

km		A	⑥j		Ⓒ						
0	**Lužná u Rakovnika** d.	0420	...	...	0825	1025	...	1425	...	1825	...
41	Žatec **1126** d.	0504	0521	0721	0921	1121	1321	1521	1721	1921	2124
66	**Chomutov** **1126** a.	0528	0548	0748	0948	1148	1348	1548	1748	1948	2147
72	**Jirkov** a.	0538	0557	0757	0957	1157	1357	1557	1757	1957	2156

	B	Ⓒ					C	v		
Jirkov d.	0604	0801	1001	1201	1401	1601	1801	...	2001	2201
Chomutov **1126** d.	0613	0810	1010	1210	1410	1610	1810	...	2010	2210
Žatec **1126** a.	0636	0835	1035	1235	1435	1635	1835	2000	2035	2235
Lužná u Rakovnika a.	0723	0927	...	1327	...	1727	1927	2044	...	...

A – From Lužna on ① **h**; from Žatec on Ⓐ.
B – ①–⑥ **k** Jirkov - Žatec; Ⓐ Žatec - Lužná. To Rakovník (a. 0741).
C – Daily Jirkov - Žatec; ⑦ **f** Žatec - Lužná.
d – ①–⑥ (not Apr. 8, 10, May 1, 8, July 6, Nov. 18).
e – Departs Praha 0527 on Ⓒ.
f – ⑦ (also Apr. 10, May 1, 8; not Apr. 9, 30, May 7).
g – Praha **hlavní nádraží**.
h – ① (also Apr. 11, May 2, 9, July 7, Sept. 29; not Apr. 10, May 1, 8).
j – ⑥ (also Apr. 7, Sept. 28, Nov. 17).
k – ①–⑥ (not Apr. 10, May 1, 8, July 5, 6, Oct. 28).
m – ⑤⑥ (also Apr. 6, 9, 30, May 7, July 4 – 6, Sept. 27, 28, Nov. 16).
◧ – Also from Praha at 1002, 1202, 1402, 1602, 1802, 2002, 2202.
⊡ – Also from Rakovník at 1010, 1210, 1410, 1610, 1810, 2035.

Operators: Arriva / ČD (Praha - Rakovník); Die Länderbahn CZ (Lužná u Rakovnika - Jirkov).

1110 ÚSTI NAD LABEM - KARLOVY VARY - CHEB

km		**620** Ⓐ	**618**	**616**	**614**	**612**	**610**	**608**	**606**	**604**	**602**
	Praha hlavní **1100** d.	...	0516	0725	0925	1125	1325	1525	1721	1925	2135
0	**Ústí nad Labem** hl. n. d.	0440	0643	0843	1043	1243	1443	1643	1843	2043	2300
17	Teplice v Čechách d.	0504	0705	0905	1105	1305	1505	1705	1905	2105	2322
46	Most d.	0530	0730	0930	1130	1330	1530	1730	1930	2130	...
71	Chomutov d.	0550	0750	0950	1150	1350	1550	1750	1950	2149	...
84	Kadaň-Prunéřov d.	0600	0800	1000	1200	1400	1600	1800	2000	...	...
130	**Karlovy Vary** a.	0644	0844	1044	1244	1444	1644	1844	2044	...	...
130	**Karlovy Vary** **1120** d.	0646	0846	1046	1246	1446	1646	1846	2046	...	...
156	Sokolov **1120** d.	0709	0909	1109	1309	1509	1709	1909	2109	...	...
184	**Cheb** **1120** a.	0732	0932	1132	1332	1532	1732	1932	2132	...	...

	601	**603** Ⓐ	**605**	**607**	**609**	**611**	**613**	**615**	**617**	**619**
Cheb **1120** d.	...	...	0426**a**	0626	0826	1026	1226	1426	1626	1826
Sokolov **1120** d.	...	...	0449**a**	0649	0849	1049	1249	1449	1649	1849
Karlovy Vary **1120** a.	...	...	0508**a**	0708	0908	1108	1308	1508	1708	1908
Karlovy Vary d.	...	...	0509**a**	0709	0909	1109	1309	1509	1709	1909
Kadaň-Prunéřov d.	...	0454	0554**a**	0754	0954	1154	1354	1554	1754	1954
Chomutov d.	...	0504	0604	0804	1004	1204	1404	1604	1804	2004
Most d.	...	0525	0625	0825	1025	1225	1425	1625	1825	2025
Teplice v Čechách d.	0449	0549	0649	0849	1049	1249	1449	1649	1849	2049
Ústí nad Labem hl. n. a.	0513	0613	0713	0913	1113	1313	1513	1713	1913	2113
Praha hlavní **1100** a.	0635	0735	0835	1036	1236	1435	1635	1835	2035	2235

LOCAL TRAINS **DĚČÍN - ÚSTI NAD LABEM - CHOMUTOV** *2nd class*

km									n	
0	**Děčín** § d.	0530	0630	0730	0830	and	1830	1930	2030	*2147*
23	**Ústí nad Labem** hl. § d.	0558	0658	0758	0858	hourly	1858	1958	2120	2220
40	Teplice v Čechách d.	0624	0724	0824	0924	until	1924	2024	2146	2246
69	Most d.	0701	0801	0901	1001	⊖	2001	2101	2220	2320
94	**Chomutov** a.	0722	0822	0922	1022		2022	2122	2239	2339

			Ⓒ							
Chomutov d.	0536	...	0636	0736	and	1936	2036	2136	*2236*
Most d.	0601	0701	0701	0801	hourly	2001	2101	2201	2328
Teplice v Čechách d.	0632	0732	0732	0832	until	2032	2132	2232	2356
Ústí nad Labem hl. § d.	0658	0758	0758	0858	⊖	2058	2157	2257	0019
Děčín § a.	0724	0824	0824	0924		2124	*2234*	*2333*	...

a – Ⓐ only.
n – Arrives Ústí nad Labem 2056.
§ – See also Tables **1100** and **1115**.
⊖ – Timings may vary by up to 5 minutes. Certain trains continue to / from Kadaň-Prunéřov.

1115 ÚSTÍ NAD LABEM - DĚČÍN - LIBEREC *2nd class Arriva*

km		d	●								
0	**Ústí nad Labem** hl. § d.	0527	...	0727	0927	1127	1327	1527	1727	1927	2123
23	**Děčín** § d.	0545	0645	0745	0945	1145	1345	1545	1745	1945	2141
54	Česká Lipa d.	0622	0734	0822	1022	1222	1422	1622	1822	2022	2223
113	**Liberec** a.	0728	0852	0927	1127	1327	1527	1727	1927	2127	2331

	d	●								
Liberec d.	0428	0501	0628	0828	1028	1228	1428	1628	1828	2028
Česká Lipa d.	0537	0632	0737	0937	1137	1337	1537	1737	1937	2134
Děčín § d.	0612	0710	0812	1012	1212	1412	1612	1812	2012	2208
Ústí nad Labem hl. § a.	0628	...	0828	1028	1228	1428	1628	1828	2028	2224

d – ①–⑥ (not Apr. 8, 10, May 1, 8, July 6, Nov. 18).
§ – See also Tables **1100** and **1110**.
● – Also from Děčín at 0845 and every two hours until 2043; also from Liberec at 0702 and every two hours until 2102. Timings may vary by 3 minutes. Operated by ČD.

1116 DĚČÍN - RUMBURK

km		Ⓐp							
0	**Děčín** **1100** d.	0523	0637	0641		2037	2041	2237	2240
25	Česká Kamenice d.	│	0706	│	then each	2106	│	2306	│
50	Rybniště d.	│	0735	│	train runs	2135	│	2333	│
22	Bad Schandau 🏛 **1100** d.	0554	│	0718	every **two**	│	2118	│	2309
37	Sebnitz d.	0639	│	0742	hours until	│	2142	│	...
38	Dolní Poustevna 🏛 d.	0643	│	0746	⊙	│	2146	│	...
61*	**Rumburk** a.	0722	0749	0828		2149	2224	2350	...

	Ⓐ							
Rumburk d.	0516	0530	0608		1930	2006	2039	...
Dolní Poustevna 🏛 d.	│	0612	│	then each	2012	│	2117	...
Sebnitz d.	│	0618	│	train runs	2018	│	2120	...
Bad Schandau 🏛 **1100** d.	│	0648	│	every **two**	2048	│	...	2350
Rybniště d.	0528	│	0621	hours until	│	2018	...	│
Česká Kamenice d.	0554	│	0649	⊙	│	2048	...	│
Děčín **1100** a.	0620	0717	0720		2117	2120	...	0014

p – Arrives Sebnitz 0615.
***** – *61 km* via Rybniště; *65 km* via Sebnitz.
⊙ – Timings may vary by up to 4 minutes.

1117 RYBNIŠTĚ - VARNSDORF - ZITTAU - LIBEREC *2nd class*

Subject to alteration on and around Czech and German holiday dates (see page 4).

km		①–⑤	⑥⑦	①–⑤	①–⑤	⑥⑦	①–⑤			①–⑤	⑥⑦	①–⑤	⑥⑦	①–⑤	①–⑤	⑥⑦		①–⑤	①–⑤	⑥⑦	①–⑤			①–⑤
0	**Rybniště** d.	0409	0508	0537	0644	0709	0737	0909	...	1037	1109	1244	1309	1337	...	1509	...	1537	...	1709	1737	1909	...	2137
11	Varnsdorf 🏛 a.	0423	0522	0551	0658	0723	0751	0923	...	1051	1123	1258	1323	1351	...	1523	...	1551	...	1723	1751	1923	...	2151
11	Varnsdorf 🏛 d.	0425	0524	0553	0700	0724	0756	0924	...	1100	1124	1300	1328	1400	1500	1524	...	1556	1700	1728	1810	1924	2131	...
29	**Zittau** 🏛 d.	0443	0542	0615	0718	0742	0815	0952	...	1118	1142	1318	1352	1418	1518	1542	...	1615	1718	1752	1836	1942	2158	...
56	**Liberec** a.	0518	0624	0650	0755	0819	0849	1024	...	1157	1224	1355	1424	1455	1555	1624	...	1649	1755	1824	1909	2017	2229	...

	①–⑤	⑥⑦	①–⑤	①–⑤	①–⑤	⑥⑦	①–⑤	⑥⑦	①–⑤	⑥⑦	①–⑤	①–⑤	⑥⑦	①–⑤	①–⑤	⑥⑦	①–⑤	①–⑤	⑥⑦	①–⑤			
Liberec d.	0455	0529	...	0602	0702	0731	0908	0932	1108	1131	1202	1302	1332	1402	1502	1531	1602	1708	1732	1800	1931	2140	2238
Zittau 🏛 d.	0529	0610	...	0642	0742	0810	0942	1015	1142	1210	1242	1342	1415	1442	1542	1610	1642	1742	1816	1836	2010	2220	2312
Varnsdorf 🏛 a.	0546	0627	...	0659	0806	0827	0959	1032	1159	1227	1259	1359	1432	1459	1606	1627	1659	1759	1833	1853	2027	2237	2329
																						①–⑤	
Varnsdorf 🏛 d.	0605	0629	0702	...	0807	0829	1002	1034	1202	1229	1302	1402	1434	...	1607	1629	...	1802	1835	...	2029	2239	...
Rybniště a	0619	0643	0716	...	0821	0843	1016	1048	1216	1243	1316	1416	1448	...	1621	1643	...	1816	1849	...	2043	2253	...

	⑥⑦			⑥⑦	⑥⑦			⑥⑦
Dresden **855** d.	0525	0729	0929	1129	1329	1529	1729	1929
Zittau 🏛 d.	0715	0901	1101	1301	1501	1701	1901	2101
Liberec a.	0754	0929	1129	1329	1529	1729	1929	2131

				⑥⑦	⑥⑦			D
Liberec d.	0628	0828	1028	1228	1428	1628	1828	2028
Zittau 🏛 a.	0658	0856	1056	1256	1456	1659	1856	2056
Dresden Hbf **855** a.	0827	1027	1227	1427	1627	1827	2027	*2251*

D – ⑥⑦. For Dresden change at Bischofswerda (Table **855**).

Operators: ČD (Rybniště - Varnsdorf); Die Länderbahn *Trilex* (Varnsdorf - Liberec - Dresden).

PRAHA - PLZEŇ - CHEB - KARLOVY VARY 1120

🍷 on most *EC* and *IC* trains

WARNING! 🚌 replace many trains Mariánské Lázně - Cheb and v.v. March 6 – 21.

km		2 Ⓐ	2 d	*IC* 568 d	2	778 Ⓐ	*EC* 362 A	2	776 j	*IC* 566	774	*EC* 360 A	2 Ⓒ	772	Ⓐ	*IC* 564	2	*EC* 358 A	2 Ⓐ	770	*IC*• 512 B	2	*EC* 356 A	2	768 j
0	**Praha** hlavní n. **1124** d.	...	...	...	...	0513	0543	...	0613	0643	0713	0743	...	0813	...	0843	...	0943	...	1013	1043	...	1143	...	1213
4	**Praha** Smíchov **1124** d.	...	...	...	...	0521	0551	...	0621	0651	0721	0751	...	0821	...	0851	...	0951	...	1021	1051	...	1151	...	1221
43	Beroun **1124** d.	...	...	...	...	0552	|	...	0652	|	0752	|	...	0852	...	|	...	|	...	1052	|	...	|	...	1252
52	Zdice **1124** d.	...	...	...	...	0600	|	...	0700	|	0800	|	...	0900	...	|	...	|	...	1100	|	...	|	...	1300
90	Rokycany d.	...	...	...	...	0627	|	...	0727	|	0827	|	...	0927	...	|	1026	|	...	1127	|	1226	|	...	1327
107	**Plzeň** hlavní n. a.	...	...	...	...	0637	0658	...	0737	0758	0837	0858	...	0937	...	0958	1038	1058	...	1137	1158	1238	1258	...	1337
107	**Plzeň** hlavní n. d.	...	...	0605	...	0640	...	0707	0740	0805	0840	...	0907	0940	...	1005	1040	...	1107	1140	1205	1240	...	1307	1340
	Klatovy **929** a.	...	...	|	...	0729	...	|	0827	|	0929	...	|	1027	...	|	1129	...	|	1227	|	1329	...	|	1427
140	Stříbro d.	...	...	0631	...	...	...	0737	...	0831	...	...	0937	...	...	1031	...	...	1137	...	1231	...	...	1337	...
171	Planá u Mariánských Lázní d.	0546	0546	0654	0653**h**	...	...	0804	...	0854	...	...	1004	...	...	1054	...	...	1204	...	1254	...	...	1404	...
183	Mariánské Lázně ◧ d.	0556	0556	0707	0707**h**	...	...	0815	...	0907	...	...	1015	...	1039	1107	...	...	1215	...	1307	...	...	1415	...
213	**Cheb** ◧ a.	0622	0622	0729	0734**h**	...	...	0838	...	0927	...	...	1038	...	1109	1127	...	...	1238	...	1327	...	...	1438	...
213	**Cheb** **1110** d.	0634	...	...	0741**d**	...	...	0840	...	...	...	...	1040	...	1131	...	...	...	1240	...	|	...	...	1440	...
241	Sokolov **1110** d.	0702	...	...	0809**d**	...	...	0908	...	...	...	...	1108	...	1159	...	...	...	1308	...	f	...	...	1508	...
267	**Karlovy Vary** **1110** a.	0723	...	...	0830**d**	...	...	0930	...	...	...	...	1130	...	1220	...	...	...	1330	...	...	...	...	1530	...

	IC 562	766	*EC* 354 A	2	764	*IC* 560	762	*EC* 352 A	2	2 Ⓒ	760	*IC* 558	758	*EC* 364 A	2 Ⓑe	2	756	*IC* 504 C	754	*IC* 556	*IC* 554	752	*IC* 550 Ⓑe	750
Praha hlavní n. **1124** d.	1243	1313	1343	...	1413	1443	1513	1543	...	...	1613	1643	1713	1743	...	...	1813	1843	1913	1943	2043	2113	2243	2346
Praha Smíchov **1124** d.	1251	1321	1351	...	1421	1451	1521	1551	...	...	1621	1651	1721	1751	...	...	1821	1851	1921	1951	2051	2121	2251	2354
Beroun **1124** d.	|	1352	|	...	1453	|	1552	|	...	...	1652	|	1752	|	...	...	1852	|	1952	|	|	2152	|	0025
Zdice **1124** d.	|	1400	|	...	1500	|	1600	|	...	...	1700	|	1800	|	...	...	1900	|	2000	|	|	2200	|	0035
Rokycany d.	|	1427	|	...	1527	|	1627	|	...	...	1727	|	1827	|	...	...	1927	|	2027	|	2150	2227	2353	0102
Plzeň hlavní n. a.	1358	1437	1458	...	1537	1558	1637	1658	...	...	1737	1758	1837	1858	...	...	1937	1958	2037	2058	2200	2237	0003	0112
Plzeň hlavní n. d.	1405	1440	...	1507	1540	1605	1640	...	1707	1707	1740	1805	1840	...	1907	...	1940	2005	...	...	2205	2240	...	...
Klatovy **929** a.	|	1529	...	|	1627	|	1729	...	|	|	1827	|	1929	...	|	...	2029	|	...	...	|	2329	...	...
Stříbro d.	1431	...	...	1537	...	1631	...	...	1737	1737	...	1831	...	...	1937	...	...	2031	...	...	2231	...	...	...
Planá u Mariánských Lázní d.	1454	...	...	1604	...	1654	...	...	1804	1804	...	1854	...	...	2003	...	...	2054	...	...	2254	...	...	...
Mariánské Lázně ◧ d.	1507	...	...	1615	...	1707	...	...	1815	1815	...	1907	...	...	2013	2013	...	2107	...	...	2303	...	...	...
Cheb ◧ a.	1527	...	...	1638	...	1727	...	...	1838	1838	...	1927	...	...	2037	2037	...	2128	...	...	2323	...	...	...
Cheb **1110** d.	...	...	...	1640	...	...	...	...	...	1840	...	...	...	...	2040	2040	...	2131	...	...	...	...	...	...
Sokolov **1110** d.	...	...	...	1708	...	...	...	...	...	1908	...	...	...	...	2108	2108	...	2154	...	...	...	...	...	...
Karlovy Vary **1110** a.	...	...	...	1730	...	...	...	...	...	1930	...	...	...	...	2130	2130	...	2210	...	...	...	...	...	...

	751 Ⓐ	*IC* 551 d	743 753	*IC* 553	*IC* 553 d	755	2 d	*IC* 555	757	*IC*• 501	759	2	2 Ⓐ	*EC* 351 A‡	2	*IC* 557	761	*EC* 353 A	618	2	*IC* 559	763 j	2	*EC* 355 A
Karlovy Vary **1110** d.	...	...	...	...	...	...	0423	...	...	0548	...	...	0623	...	...	...	...	...	0846	...	...	...	1023	...
Sokolov **1110** d.	...	...	...	...	...	...	0449	...	...	0608	...	...	0649	...	...	...	...	...	0909	...	...	...	1049	...
Cheb **1110** a.	...	...	...	...	...	...	0517	...	...	0630	...	...	0717	...	...	...	...	...	0932	...	...	...	1117	...
Cheb ◧ d.	...	...	...	...	0432	...	0519	...	...	0634	...	0719	0719	...	...	0833	...	...	...	...	1033	...	1119	...
Mariánské Lázně ◧ d.	...	...	...	...	0455	...	0544	...	...	0655	...	0744	0744	...	...	0854	...	...	...	...	1054	...	1144	...
Planá u Mariánských Lázní d.	...	...	...	...	0505	...	0556	...	...	0705	...	0755	0755	...	...	0905	...	...	...	...	1105	...	1155	...
Stříbro d.	...	...	...	...	0527	...	0621	...	...	0727	...	0821	0821	...	...	0927	...	...	...	...	1127	...	1221	...
Klatovy **929** d.	...	...	0428	...	|	0528	|	...	0630	|	0730	|	|	...	0828	|	0930	...	...	1028	|	1130	|	...
Plzeň hlavní n. a.	...	...	0519	...	0552	0619	0649	...	0719	0752	0819	0849	0849	...	0919	0952	1019	...	...	1119	1152	1219	1249	...
Plzeň hlavní n. d.	0421	0500	0521	0600	0600	0621	...	0700	0721	0800	0821	...	...	0900	0922	1000	1021	1100	...	1122	1200	1221	...	1300
Rokycany d.	0432	0511	0532	|	|	0632	...	|	0732	|	0832	...	...	|	0935	|	1032	|	...	1135	|	1232	...	|
Zdice **1124** d.	0458	|	0558	|	|	0658	...	|	0758	|	0858	...	...	|	...	|	1058	|	...	...	|	1258	...	|
Beroun **1124** d.	0508	|	0608	|	|	0708	...	|	0808	|	0908	...	...	|	...	|	1108	|	...	...	|	1308	...	|
Praha Smíchov **1124** a.	0539	0609	0639	0709	0709	0739	...	0809	0839	0909	0939	...	...	1009	...	1109	1139	1209	...	...	1309	1339	...	1409
Praha hlavní n. **1124** a.	0547	0617	0647	0717	0717	0747	...	0817	0848	0917	0947	...	...	1017	...	1117	1147	1217	...	...	1317	1347	...	1417

	765	*IC* 561	767	2	*EC* 357 A	769	*IC*• 515 B	771	2	*EC* 359 A	773	*IC* 563	775 j	2	*EC* 361 A	777	*IC* 565	779	608	2	2 Ⓒ	*EC* 363 A	2 j	*IC* 567
Karlovy Vary **1110** d.	...	...	...	1223	...	...	...	...	1423	...	...	...	...	1623	...	...	...	...	1846	...	1908	...	...	...
Sokolov **1110** d.	...	...	...	1249	...	...	g	...	1449	...	...	...	...	1649	...	...	...	...	1909	...	1933	...	...	...
Cheb **1110** a.	...	...	...	1317	...	...	|	...	1517	...	...	...	...	1717	...	...	...	...	1932	...	2004	...	...	...
Cheb ◧ d.	...	1233	...	1319	...	...	1433	...	1519	...	...	1633	...	1719	...	...	1833	...	...	2007	2007	...	...	2033
Mariánské Lázně ◧ d.	...	1254	...	1344	...	...	1454	...	1544	...	...	1654	...	1744	...	...	1854	...	...	2038	2038	...	...	2054
Planá u Mariánských Lázní d.	...	1305	...	1355	...	...	1505	...	1555	...	...	1705	...	1755	...	...	1905	...	...	2048	2048	...	...	2105
Stříbro d.	...	1327	...	1421	...	...	1527	...	1621	...	...	1727	...	1821	...	...	1927	...	...	...	...	...	...	2127
Klatovy **929** d.	1228	|	1330	|	...	1428	|	1530	|	...	1628	|	1730	|	...	1828	|	1930	...	...	...	...	2059	|
Plzeň hlavní n. a.	1319	1352	1419	1449	...	1519	1552	1619	1649	...	1719	1752	1819	1849	...	1919	1952	2019	...	...	...	...	2153	2152
Plzeň hlavní n. d.	1321	1400	1421	...	1500	1521	1600	1621	...	1700	1721	1800	1821	...	1900	1921	2000	2021	...	...	...	2100	...	2200
Rokycany d.	1332	|	1432	...	|	1532	|	1632	...	|	1732	|	1832	...	|	1932	|	2032	...	...	...	|	...	2210
Zdice **1124** d.	1358	|	1458	...	|	1558	|	1658	...	|	1758	|	1858	...	|	1958	|	2058	...	...	...	|	...	|
Beroun **1124** d.	1408	|	1508	...	|	1608	|	1708	...	|	1808	|	1908	...	|	2008	|	2108	...	...	...	|	...	|
Praha Smíchov **1124** a.	1439	1509	1539	...	1609	1639	1709	1739	...	1809	1839	1909	1939	...	2009	2039	2109	2139	...	...	...	2209	...	2309
Praha hlavní n. **1124** a.	1447	1517	1547	...	1617	1647	1717	1747	...	1817	1847	1917	1947	...	2017	2047	2117	2147	...	...	...	2217	...	2317

A – ZÁPADNI EXPRES – 🚃12 🍷 Praha - Plzeň - München and v.v.
B – 🚃12 🍷 Bohumín - Ostrava - Praha - Plzeň - Cheb - Františkovy Lázně and v.v.
C – 🚃12 🍷 Ostrava - Praha - Plzeň - Cheb - Karlovy Vary.
d – ①–⑥ (not Apr. 8, 10, May 1, 8, July 6, Nov. 18).
e – Ⓑ (not Apr. 7, 9, 30, May 7, July 5, Nov. 17).
f – To Františkovy Lázně (a. 1336).
g – From Františkovy Lázně (d. 1424).
h – ⑦ (also Apr. 8, 10, May 1. 8, July 6, Nov. 18).
j – To / from Železná Ruda (Table **929**).

‡ – From Regensburg on ⑦ (Table **885**).
• – PENDOLINO – classified *SC* (with 🅁) Bohumín - Ostrava - Praha and v.v. Trains **512 / 515** operate as *IC* on Ⓒ - 🅁 is required.
◧ – Additional local trains Mariánské Lázně - Cheb and v.v.: Ffrom Mariánské Lázně at 0646 Ⓐ, 0918 Ⓐ, 1239 Ⓒ, 1519 Ⓐ, 1719 Ⓐ. From Cheb at 0547 Ⓐ, 0648 Ⓐ, 0959, 1409 Ⓐ, 1600 Ⓐ, 1858, 2254 Ⓐ.

MARKTREDWITZ - CHEB - FRANTIŠKOVY LÁZNĚ - HOF / ZWICKAU 1122

2nd class

Subject to alteration on Czech and German public holiday dates (see page **4**).

km		①–⑥									⑥
0	**Marktredwitz** **880** d.	...	0712	0908	1108	1308	1508	1708	1911		2218
27	Cheb **880** d.	0522**k**	0738	0937	1137	1337	1537	1737	1937	...	2251
34	Františkovy Lázně d.	0530**k**	0745	0945	1145	1345	1545	1745	1945	...	2259
55	Aš 🏛 d.	0601	0808	1008	1208	1408	1608	1808	2008	2327	2327
89	**Hof** a.	0644	0844	1048	1248	1448	1648	1848	2044	0001	0001

	①–⑤	⑥								
Hof d.	0508	0516	0709	0907	1107	1307	1507	1707	1907	...
Aš 🏛 d.	0546	0553	0747	0947	1147	1347	1547	1747	1947	2047
Františkovy Lázně d.	0609	0616	0812	1012	1212	1412	1612	1812	2012	2112
Cheb **880** a.	0616	0623	0819	1019	1219	1419	1619	1819	2019	2119
Marktredwitz **880** a.	0654	...	0855	1050	1250	1450	1650	1850	2050	...

km		①–⑤	①–⑤	⑥⑦							
0	**Cheb** d.	0527	0547	0803	1003	1203	1603	1803	...	...	...
7	Františkovy Lázně d.	0534	0554	0812	1012	1212	1612	1812	...	...	...
24	Bad Brambach 🏛 a.	...	0621	0835	1035	1235	1635	1835	...	...	...
73	Plauen Oberer Bf a.	...	0727	0927	1127	1327	1727	1927	...	...	...
121	**Zwickau** Hbf a.	...	0815	1015	1215	1415	1815	2015	...	...	...
123	**Zwickau** Stadthalle a.	...	0820	1020	1220	1420	1820	2020	...	...	...
	Zwickau Zentrum a.	...	0824	1024	1224	1424	1824	2024	...	...	...

	①–⑤	①–⑤								
Zwickau Zentrum d.	...	0536	0736	0936	1336	1536	1736	...	...	...
Zwickau Stadthalle d.	...	0540	0740	0940	1340	1540	1740	...	...	...
Zwickau Hbf d.	...	0544	0744	0944	1344	1544	1744	...	...	...
Plauen Oberer Bf d.	...	0633	0833	1033	1433	1633	1833	...	...	...
Bad Brambach 🏛 d.	...	0724	0925	1125	1525	1725	1925	...	...	...
Františkovy Lázně d.	0615	...	0947	1147	1547	1747	1947	...	...	...
Cheb a.	0623	...	0955	1155	1555	1755	1955	...	...	...

k – ⑥ only.

1123 KARLOVY VARY - MARIÁNSKÉ LÁZNĚ

2nd class GW Train Regio

ČD tickets and passes are not valid on GW Train Regio services.

km											
0	**Karlovy Vary** dolní	d.	...	0620	0858	1058	1254	1458	1658	1928	2128	2234
33	Bečov nad Teplou	d.	0442	0651	0927	1127	1323	1527	1727	1958	2158	2303
53	**Mariánské Lázně**	a.	0526	0736	1011	1211	1408	1611	1811	2043	2243	...

Mariánské Lázně	d.	...	0604	0840	1040	1236	1439	1640	1911	2111	2305
Bečov nad Teplou	d.	0539	0651	0927	1127	1323	1527	1727	1958	2159	2350
Karlovy Vary dolní	a.	0608	0720	0955	1155	1352	1555	1755	2028	2228	...

1124 PRAHA - PŘÍBRAM - ČESKÉ BUDĚJOVICE

2nd class Arriva

For direct trains Praha - České Budějovice see Table **1130**. ČD operates additional services Beroun - Březnice, Březnice - Písek and Protivín - České Budějovice.

km			Ⓐ	Ⓒ		Ⓒ	Ⓐ	Ⓒ	Ⓐ	Ⓒ	Ⓐ	Ⓒ
0	**Praha** hlavní n. **1120**	d.	0722	0735	0935	0935	1325	1335	1522	1535	1722	1735
4	**Praha** Smíchov **1120**	d.	0730	0743	0943	0943	1333	1343	1530	1543	1730	1743
43	Beroun **1120**	d.	0813	0814	1014	1014	1413	1414	1613	1614	1813	1814
52	Zdice **1120**	d.	0822	0823	1023	1023	1422	1423	1622	1623	1822	1823
82	Příbram	d.	0859	0859	1059	1059	1459	1459	1659	1659	1859	1859
100	Březnice	d.	0919	0919	1119	1119	1519	1519	1719	1719	1919	1919
142	Písek	d.	0959	0959	1158	1201	1559	1559	1759	1759	1957	1959
155	Protivín ◧	d.	1012	1012	...	1214	1612	1612	1812	1812	...	2012f
192	**České Budějovice** ◧	a.	1041	1041	...	1245	1641	1641	1841	1841	...	2041f

		Ⓐ	Ⓒ		Ⓒ	Ⓐ	Ⓒ	Ⓐ	Ⓒ	Ⓐ	
České Budějovice ◧	d.	*0507*	...	0913	1313	1313	1513	1513	1713	1713	1913
Protivín ◧	d.	*0542*	0744q	0944	1344	1344	1544	1544	1744	1744	1944
Písek	d.	0558	0758	0958	1358	1358	1558	1558	1758	1758	1956
Březnice	d.	0637	0837	1037	1437	1437	1637	1637	1837	1837	...
Příbram	d.	0659	0859	1059	1459	1459	1659	1659	1859	1859	...
Zdice **1120**	d.	0733	0933	1133	1533	1533	1733	1733	1933	1933	...
Beroun **1120**	d.	0745	0944	1144	1544	1545	1744	1745	1944	1945	...
Praha Smíchov **1120**	a.	0824	1015	1215	1615	1627	1815	1827	2015	2023	...
Praha hlavní n. **1120**	a.	0835	1025	1225	1625	1635	1825	1835	2025	2034	...

f – ⑦ (also Apr. 10, May 1, 8; not Apr. 9, 30, May 7).
q – ⑥ (also Apr. 7, July 5, Sept. 28, Nov. 17; not Apr. 8, Nov. 18).
◧ – See also Table **1125**.

1125 PLZEŇ - ČESKÉ BUDĚJOVICE - JIHLAVA - BRNO

🍸 on most trains. Different train numbers are used on Ⓒ.

km			651 A	653	661	663	665	667	669	655	657	659
0	**Plzeň** hlavní n.	d.	...	...	0603	0803	1003	1203	1403	1603	1803	2003
34	Nepomuk	d.	...	...	0631	0831	1031	1231	1431	1631	1831	2031
59	Horaždovice předměstí	d.	...	...	0651	0851	1051	1251	1451	1651	1851	2051
76	Strakonice	d.	...	...	0706	0906	1106	1306	1506	1706	1906	2106
99	Protivín	d.	...	...	0726	0926	1126	1326	1526	1726	1926	2126
136	**České Budějovice**	a.	...	...	0754	0954	1154	1354	1554	1754	1954	2154
136	**České Budějovice**	d.	0402	0602	0802	1002	1202	1402	1602	1802	...	...
175	Veselí nad Lužnicí	d.	0430	0630	0830	1030	1230	1430	1630	1830	...	...
201	Jindřichův Hradec	d.	0500	0700	0900	1100	1300	1500	1700	1900	...	...
268	**Jihlava**	a.	0618	0818	1018	1218	1418	1618	1818	2018	...	...
268	**Jihlava**	d.	0626	0826	1026	1226	1426	1626	1826	2026	...	...
297	Okříšky	d.	0653	0853	1053	1253	1453	1653	1853	2053	...	...
309	Třebíč	d.	0708	0908	1108	1308	1508	1708	1908	2108	...	...
372	**Brno** hlavní n.	a.	0809	1014	1214	1414	1614	1814	2014	2211	...	...

		658	656 B	654	668	666	664	662	660	652	650
Brno hlavní n.	d.	...	...	0540	0741	0944	1144	1344	1544	1744	1944
Třebíč	d.	...	...	0650	0850	1050	1250	1450	1650	1850	2050
Okříšky	d.	...	...	0707	0907	1107	1307	1507	1707	1907	2107
Jihlava	a.	...	...	0733	0933	1133	1333	1533	1733	1933	2133
Jihlava	d.	...	0540	0740	0940	1140	1340	1540	1740	1940	...
Jindřichův Hradec	d.	...	0659	0859	1059	1259	1459	1659	1859	2059	...
Veselí nad Lužnicí	d.	...	0728	0928	1128	1328	1528	1728	1928	2128	...
České Budějovice	a.	...	0756	0956	1156	1356	1556	1756	1956	2156	...
České Budějovice	d.	0604	0804	1004	1204	1404	1604	1804	2004	...	...
Protivín	d.	0634	0834	1034	1234	1434	1634	1834	2034	...	...
Strakonice	d.	0653	0853	1053	1253	1453	1653	1853	2053	...	...
Horaždovice předměstí	d.	0709	0909	1109	1309	1509	1709	1909	2109	...	...
Nepomuk	d.	0729	0929	1129	1329	1529	1729	1929	2129	...	...
Plzeň hlavní n.	a.	0757	0957	1157	1357	1557	1757	1957	2157	...	...

A – From České Budějovice on ①–⑥ **d**; from Jihlava daily.
B – From Jihlava on ①–⑥ **d**; from České Budějovice daily.
d – ①–⑥ (not Apr. 8, 10, May 1, 8, July 6, Nov. 18).

1126 PLZEŇ - CHOMUTOV - MOST

GW Train Regio

ČD tickets and passes are not valid on GW Train Regio services.

km			Ⓐ		A						⑦f
0	**Plzeň** hlavní n.	d.	...	0604	0804	1004	1204	1404	1604	1804	2004
59	Blatno u Jesenice	d.	0509	0710	0910	1110	1310	1510	1710	1910	2110
107	Žatec	d.	0601	0801	1001	1201	1401	1601	1801	2001	2201
130	Chomutov **1110**	d.	0631	0823	1023	1223	1423	1623	1823	2023	2223
155	**Most** **1110**	a.	0652	0843	1043	1243	1443	1643	1843	2043	2243

		d			A				Ⓐ	⑦f
Most **1110**	d.	0515	0715	0915	1115	1315	1515	1715	1915	1915
Chomutov **1110**	d.	0536	0736	0936	1136	1336	1536	1736	1936	1936
Žatec	d.	0600	0800	1000	1200	1400	1600	1800	2000	2000
Blatno u Jesenice	d.	0649	0849	1049	1249	1449	1649	1849	2048	2049
Plzeň hlavní n.	a.	0755	0955	1155	1355	1555	1755	1955	...	2155

A – Ⓒ (daily Apr. 29 - Sept. 17).
d – ①–⑥ (not Apr. 8, 10, May 1, 8, July 6, Nov. 18).
f – ⑦ (also Apr. 10, May 1, 8; not Apr. 9, 30, May 7).

1130 PRAHA - TÁBOR - ČESKÉ VELENICE and ČESKÉ BUDĚJOVICE

🍸 on most *EC* and *IC* trains

km			2	701 Ⓐ	2 q	703 d	2 r	*EC* 331	705	321 B	*IC* 531	2	709 d	*IC* 533	711	711 Ⓐ	2	*EC* 333	713	715	2	*IC* 535	2	717 Ⓐ	719	719 Ⓑs
0	**Praha** hlavní nádrazi	d.	...	...	...	...	...	0621	0646	0746	0821	...	0846	0921	0946	0946	...	1021	1046	1146	...	1221	...	1246	1346	1346
49	Benešov u Prahy	d.	...	...	...	...	...	|	0729	0829	|	...	0929	|	1029	1029	...	|	1129	1229	...	|	...	1329	1429	1429
103	**Tábor**	d.	...	0601	...	0701	...	0721	0801	0901	0921	...	1001	1021	1101	1101	...	1121	1201	1301	...	1321	...	1401	1501	1501
130	Veselí nad Lužnicí	a.	...	0622	...	0721	...	|	0821	0921	|	...	1021	|	1121	1121	...	|	1221	1321	...	|	...	1421	1521	1521
130	Veselí nad Lužnicí **1135**	d.	...	0624	0656	0724	0743	|	0824	0932	|	...	1024	|	...	1124	1140	|	1224	1332	1346	|	...	1424	...	1524
151	Třeboň	d.	...	|	0723	|	0808	|	|	0950	|	...	|	|	...	|	1205	|	|	1350	1412	|	...	|	...	|
185	**České Velenice** 🛃	a.	...	|	0810	|	0846	|	|	1024	|	...	|	|	...	|	1244	|	|	1425	1454	|	...	|	...	|
169	**České Budějovice** **1135**	a.	...	0652	...	0751	...	0801	0851	...	1001	...	1051	1101	...	1151	...	1201	1251	...	...	1401	...	1451	...	1551
169	**České Budějovice**	d.	0600	...	...	...	...	0806	...	...	...	1003	...	1115	...	...	...	1206	...	...	...	...	1403	...	...	...
	Český Krumlov	a.	|	...	...	...	...	|	...	...	...	|	...	1152	...	...	...	|	...	...	...	...	|	...	...	...
219	Rybnik	d.	0654	...	...	...	...	0851	...	...	...	1051	...	...	...	...	...	1251	...	...	...	...	1452	...	...	...
233	Summerau 🛃	a.	0708	...	...	...	...	0906	...	...	...	1107	...	...	...	...	...	1306	...	...	...	...	1507	...	...	...
242	Freistadt	a.	0720	...	...	...	...	0916	...	...	...	1120	...	...	...	...	...	1316	...	...	...	...	1520	...	...	...
295	**Linz** Hbf	a.	0824	...	...	...	...	1006	...	...	...	1224	...	...	...	...	...	1406	...	...	...	...	1624	...	...	...

		2	*EC* 335	721	2 D	*IC* 537 Ⓐ	723	*IC* 539	2	725	2	*IC* 541 Ⓑe	323 B	*EC* 337 C	729	2	*IC* 543 ⑦f	731 Ⓑe	*IC* 545	2	733	2	2 ⑤t	735	737
Praha hlavní nádrazi	d.	...	1421	1446	...	1521	1546	1621	...	1646	...	1721	1746	1821	1846	...	1921	1946	2021	...	2046	...	...	2216	2346
Benešov u Prahy	d.	...	|	1529	...	|	1629	|	...	1729	...	|	1829	|	1929	...	|	2029	|	...	2129	...	...	2259	0029
Tábor	d.	...	1521	1601	...	1621	1701	1721	...	1801	...	1821	1901	1921	2001	...	2021	2059	2121	...	2201	...	...	2330	0059
Veselí nad Lužnicí	a.	...	|	1621	...	|	1721	|	...	1821	...	|	1921	|	2021	...	|	▬	2137	...	2221	...	...	2350	...
Veselí nad Lužnicí **1135**	d.	1539	|	1624	1646	|	1741	|	...	1824	1845	|	1932	|	2024	2040	|	...	2138	2143	2224	...	2241	2351	...
Třeboň	d.	1602	|	|	1710	|	1759	|	...	|	1907	|	1950	|	|	2103	|	...	|	2206	|	...	2307	|	...
České Velenice 🛃	a.	1646	|	|	1759	|	1831	|	...	|	1948	|	2024	|	|	2144	|	...	|	2246	|	...	2344	|	...
České Budějovice **1135**	a.	...	1601	1651	...	1701	...	1801	...	1851	...	1901	...	2001	2051	...	2101	2	2204	...	2251	...	...	0018	...
České Budějovice	d.	...	1606	...	...	...	...	...	1803	...	...	...	...	2006	...	...	...	2107	...	...	...	2256	...	...	...
Rybnik	d.	...	1651	...	...	...	...	...	1852	...	...	...	...	2052	...	...	...	2202	...	...	...	2351	...	...	...
Summerau 🛃	a.	...	1707	...	...	...	...	...	1907	...	...	...	...	2106	...	...	...	...	...	...	...	...	...	...	...
Freistadt	a.	...	1716	...	...	...	...	...	1920	...	...	...	...	2116	...	...	...	...	...	...	...	...	...	...	...
Linz Hbf	a.	...	1806	...	...	...	...	...	2024	...	...	...	...	2206	...	...	...	...	...	...	...	...	...	...	...

FOR RETURN SERVICE AND FOOTNOTES SEE NEXT PAGE →

ČESKÉ BUDĚJOVICE and ČESKÉ VELENICE - TABOR - PRAHA 1130

🍷 on most *EC* and *IC* trains

		IC			*IC*			*IC*				*IC*			*EC*						*IC*			
	734	**544**	2	**732**	**542**	**730**	2	**540**	2	**728**	2	**538**	2	**726**	**330**	**724**	2	2	**722**	**720**	**536**	**322**	2	**716**
	E	Ⓐ				**F**		**d**							**C**	**d**				Ⓐ		**B**		
Linz Hbf d.	...	...	...	...	...	...	...	...	...	...	...	...	...	...	0652	...	...	0735	...	...	...	...	0935	...
Freistadt d.	...	...	...	...	...	...	...	...	...	...	...	...	...	...	0742	...	...	0839	...	...	...	...	1039	...
Summerau d.	...	...	...	...	...	...	...	...	...	...	...	...	...	...	0753	...	...	0852	...	...	...	...	1051	...
Rybnik d.	...	...	...	...	...	...	0535	...	...	...	0629	...	...	...	0806	...	...	0907	...	...	...	...	1106	...
České Budějovice a.	...	...	...	...	...	...	0630	...	...	...	0729	...	...	...	0852	...	...	0958	...	...	...	...	1157	...
České Budějovice 1135 d.	0407	0452	...	0509	0557	...	...	0657	...	0709	...	0757	...	...	0857	0909	...	...	1009	1109	1157	...	...	1309
České Velenice d.	|	|	0411	|	|	0530	...	|	0548	|	...	|	0642	0734	|	|	0911	...	|	|	|	1133	...	|
Třeboň d.	|	|	0451	|	|	0608	...	|	0629	|	...	|	0720	0807	|	|	0951	...	|	|	|	1205	...	|
Veselí nad Lužnicí 1135 a.	0433	|	0513	0535	|	0625	...	|	0651	0735	...	|	0742	0825	|	0935	1013	...	1035	1135	|	1223	...	1335
Veselí nad Lužnicí d.	0435	|	...	0537	|	0637	...	|	...	0737	...	|	...	0837	|	0937	...	...	1037	1137	|	1237	...	1337
Tábor d.	0500	0533	...	0600	0638	0700	...	0738	...	0800	...	0838	...	0900	0938	1000	...	...	1100	1200	1238	1300	...	1400
Benešov u Prahy d.	0531	0600	...	0631	|	0731	...	|	...	0831	...	|	...	0931	|	1031	...	...	1131	1231	|	1331	...	1431
Praha hlavní nádrazi a.	0612	0642	...	0712	0739	0812	...	0839	...	0912	...	0939	...	1012	1039	1112	...	...	1212	1312	1339	1412	...	1517

	EC			*IC*			*IC*						*EC*		*EC*							*EC*		
	332	2	**714**	**534**	2	**712**	**532**	2	2	**710**	**708**	2	**530**	**706**	**334**	2	**320**	**702**	2	2	**700**	**336**	2	2
			G		**D**			⑦u	**d**	⑦u	**H**		⑦f				**B**							Ⓐ
Linz Hbf d.	1154	...	...	...	...	...	...	...	...	...	...	1335	...	...	1554	...	...	...	...	1735	...	1854	...	...
Freistadt d.	1242	...	...	...	...	...	...	...	...	...	...	1439	...	...	1644	...	...	...	...	1839	...	1944	...	...
Summerau d.	1252	...	...	...	...	...	...	...	...	...	...	1451	...	...	1653	...	...	...	...	1851	...	1953	...	...
Rybnik d.	1306	...	...	...	...	...	...	...	...	...	...	1507	...	...	1706	...	...	...	...	1908	...	2006	...	...
Český Krumlov d.	|	...	...	1407	...	...	...	...	...	...	...	|	...	...	|	...	...	...	...	|	...	|	...	...
České Budějovice a.	1352	...	...	1443	...	...	...	...	...	...	...	1557	...	...	1752	...	...	...	...	1958	...	2052	...	...
České Budějovice 1135 d.	1357	...	1409	1457	...	1509	1557	...	...	...	1609	...	1657	1709	1757	...	...	1909	...	...	2009	2056	...	...
České Velenice d.	|	1310	|	|	1412	|	|	1505	1522	1536	|	...	|	|	|	1701	1723	|	1909	...	|	|	2105	2207
Třeboň d.	|	1351	|	|	1453	|	|	1543	1602	1608	|	...	|	|	|	1739	1806	|	1951	...	|	|	2143	2245
Veselí nad Lužnicí 1135 a.	|	1413	1435	|	1516	1535	|	1608	1625	1626	1635	...	|	1735	|	1803	1822	1935	2013	...	2035	2120	2209	2309
Veselí nad Lužnicí d.	|	...	1437	|	...	1537	|	...	...	1637	1637	...	|	1737	|	...	1837	1937	...	...	2037	2121	...	...
Tábor d.	1438	...	1500	1538	...	1600	1638	...	...	1700	1700	...	1738	1800	1838	...	1900	2000	...	...	2100	2138	...	...
Benešov u Prahy d.	|	...	1531	|	...	1631	|	...	...	1731	1731	...	|	1831	|	...	1931	2031	...	...	2131	2203	...	...
Praha hlavní nádrazi a.	1539	...	1617	1639	...	1717	1739	...	...	1812	1812	...	1839	1912	1939	...	2012	2112	...	...	2212	2240	...	...

RYBNIK - LIPNO NAD VLTAVOU

km																									
						J			v			v			K										
0	Rybnik d.	0623	0700	...	0904	1007	...	1104	1205	...	1304	1407	...	1511	1607	...	1704	1805	...	1912	2057	...	...	...	...
22	Lipno nad Vltavou a.	0704	0751	...	0945	1050	...	1147	1248	...	1347	1448	...	1552	1650	...	1746	1850	...	1955	2138	...	...	...	...

	Ⓐ				J			v		v						K								
Lipno nad Vltavou d.	0539	0714	...	0814	1013	...	1110	1211	...	1310	1411	...	1515	1613	...	1709	1812	...	1918	2008	...	...	...	...
Rybnik a.	0619	0759	...	0854	1054	...	1151	1254	...	1351	1455	...	1555	1654	...	1750	1854	...	1958	2048	...	...	...	...

B – SILVA NORTICA – (12) Praha - Wien and v.v.
C – Conveys 1,2 cl. Praha - Linz (**462/463**) - Salzburg (**466/467**) - Zürich and v.v. Not from Praha May 1–28; not from Zürich May 2–29.
D – Ⓐ (daily May 29 - Oct. 1).
E – From České Budějovice on Ⓐ, from Tábor on ①–⑥ **d**.
F – From České Velenice on ①–⑥ **d**; from Veselí nad Lužnicí daily.
G – From České Velenice on Ⓐ; from Veselí nad Lužnicí daily.
H – From České Budějovice on Ⓐ, from Veselí nad Lužnicí on ①–⑥ **d**.
J – Ⓒ (daily May 27 - Oct. 1).
K – Ⓐ (daily May 29 - Oct. 6).

d – ①–⑥ (not Apr. 8, 10, May 1, 8, July 6, Nov. 18).
e – Ⓑ (not Apr. 7, 9, 30, May 7, July 5, Nov. 17).
f – ⑦ (also Apr. 10, May 1, 8; not Apr. 9, 30, May 7).
q – ①–⑤ (not Apr. 6, 7, 10, May 1, 8, July 3 - Sept. 1, Oct. 26–28, Nov. 17).
r – ⑥⑦ (also Apr. 6, 7, 10, May 1, 8, July 3 - Sept. 1, Oct. 26–28, Nov. 17).
s – Ⓑ (also Apr. 8, Nov. 18; not Apr. 7, July 5, Sept. 28, Nov. 17).
t – ⑤ (also Apr. 6, July 4, Sept. 27, Nov. 16; not Apr. 7, Nov. 17).
u – ⑦ (also Apr. 8, 10, May 1, 8, July 6, Nov. 18).
v – May 29 - Oct. 1.

FOR RETURN SERVICE SEE PREVIOUS PAGE.

ČESKÉ BUDĚJOVICE - NOVÉ ÚDOLÍ 1131

GW Train Regio 2nd class

An express train operates Praha - Český Krumlov and v.v. (Table **1130**). ČD tickets and passes are not valid on GW Train Regio services.

km											
			L	M	M	L					
0	**České Budějovice** d.	0512	0743	0812	1018	1018	1211	1424	1611	1811	2011
31	Český Krumlov d.	0605	0833	0901	1108	1108	1305	1512	1705	1904	2100
68	Horní Planá d.	0659	0936	0957	1203	1214	1400	1606	1803	1959	2148x
88	Černý Kříž a.	0726	1014	1023	1229	1245	1425	1631	1828	2024	2211x
96	**Nové Údolí** a.	0741	1046	1042	1246	1302	1442	1647	1844x	...	...

		Ⓐ								
Nové Údolí d.	...	...	...	...	0911	1117	1316	1521	1719	1915x
Černý Kříž d.	...	...	0443	0650	0927	1135	1332	1538	1736	1932x
Horní Planá d.	...	...	0510	0717	0955	1204	1400	1606	1803	1959x
Český Krumlov d.	0400	0444	0604	0812	1047	1258	1455	1700	1859	2059
České Budějovice a.	0447	0532	0651	0900	1134	1346	1542	1746	1945	2145

L – May 1 - Sept. 30.
M – Not May 1 - Sept. 30.
x – Ⓒ (daily May 1 - Oct. 1).

ČESKÉ BUDĚJOVICE - ČESKÉ VELENICE 1133

For connections České Velenice - Wien see Table **990**.

km											
		Ⓐ	Q	R							
0	České Budějovice ⊕ d.	0509	0610	0625	0810	1010	1210	1410	1610	1810	2010
50	České Velenice ⊕ a.	0557	0658	0713	0857	1057	1257	1457	1657	1857	2057

		Ⓐ	Q	R						
České Velenice ⊗ d.	0502	0618	0704	0719	0903	1103	1303	1503	1703	1903
České Budějovice ⊗ a.	0548	0704	0750	0804	0949	1149	1349	1549	1749	1949

Q – ⑥⑦ until July 2 (also Apr. 6, 7, 10, May 1, 8); daily July 3 - Sept. 3; ⑥⑦ from Sept. 9 (also Sept. 28, Oct. 26, 27, Nov. 17).
R – ①–⑤ (not Apr. 6, 7, 10, May 1, 8, July 3 - Aug. 25, Sept. 28, Oct. 26, 27, Nov. 17).
S – Ⓒ June 3 - Oct. 1.
⊕ – Also from Česke Budějovice at 0910 **S**, 1511 Ⓐ, 1710 Ⓐ, 2256.
⊗ – Also from Česke Velenice at 0401 Ⓐ, 1003 **S**, 1603 Ⓐ, 2103.

OKŘÍŠKY - ZNOJMO 1135

km																								
		Ⓐ	Ⓐ	d		Ⓐ	T		U				k	⑦m		n	⑦p		Ⓐ			Ⓐ	Ⓐ	q
0	**Okříšky** d.	...	0451	0451	...	...	0702	...	0702	0902	...	1102	1302	1302	...	1502	1502	...	...	1702	...	1759	1912	1912
32	Moravské Budějovice a.	0435	0527	0527	...	0647	0737	...	0737	0937	...	1137	1337	1350	...	1537	1550	...	1639	1737	...	1828	1947	1947
70	**Znojmo** a.	0519	...	0622	...	0730	0822	...	0830	1022	...	1222	1422	1439	...	1622	1639	...	1722	1822	...	1905	...	2036

	Ⓐ	Ⓐ	Ⓐr		T				⑥g		Ⓑh		Ⓐ			Ⓐ			Ⓒ		Ⓐ		⑤j
Znojmo d.	0453	0536	0658	...	0738	...	...	0938	1120	...	1138	1338	1438	...	1538	1638	...	1738	1738	...	...	1908	2108
Moravské Budějovice d.	0530	0623	0745	...	0823	0823	...	1023	1207	...	1223	1423	1522	...	1623	1722	...	1822	1823	...	1830	2013	2152
Okříšky a.	0558	0658	...	...	0858	0858	...	1058	1258	...	1258	1458	...	...	1658	...	...	...	1858	...	1903	2048	...

T – Ⓒ (daily July 3 - Sept. 3).
U – Ⓐ (not July 3 - Sept. 1).

g – ⑥ (also Apr. 7, July 5, Nov. 17; not Apr. 8, Nov. 18).
h – Ⓑ (also Apr. 8, Nov. 18; not Apr. 7, July 5, Nov. 17).
j – ⑤ (also Apr. 6, July 4, Sept. 9, 27, Nov. 16; not Apr. 7, Nov. 17).
k – ①–⑥ (also Apr. 9, 30, May 7; not Apr. 10, May 1, 8, July 6).
m – ⑦ (also Apr. 10, May 1, 8, July 6; not Apr. 9, 30, May 7).
n – ①–⑥ (also Apr. 9, 30, May 7; not Apr. 10, May 1, 8, July 6, Sept. 28).
p – ⑦ (also Apr. 10, May 1, 8, July 6, Sept. 28; not Apr. 9, 30, May 7).
q – ⑤⑥ (also Apr. 6, 9, 30, May 7, July 4, 5, Sept. 27, Nov. 16).
r – Not July 3 - Sept. 1.

1140 PRAHA - MLADÁ BOLESLAV - TURNOV - TANVALD

2nd class Arriva

km		A								Ⓑ e
0	**Praha** hlavní nádrazi .... d.	0722	0859	0922	1122	1322	1522	1722	1922	2122
34	Neratovice .... d.	0757	0939	0957	1157	1357	1557	1757	1957	2157
40	Všetaty .... d.	0804	0950	1004	1204	1404	1604	1804	2004	2204
72	**Mladá Boleslav** .... a.	0831	1018	1031	1231	1431	1631	1831	2031	2231
72	**Mladá Boleslav** .... d.	0841	...	1041	1241	1441	1641	1841	2041	...
88	Mnichovo Hradiště .... d.	0858	...	1058	1258	1458	1658	1858	2058	...
102	**Turnov** .... a.	0910	...	1110	1310	1510	1710	1910	2110	...
102	**Turnov** .... **1142** d.	0917	...	1117**g**	1317	1517	1717**e**	1917	...	...
116	Železný Brod .... **1142** a.	0933	...	1132**g**	1332	1532	1732**e**	1932	...	...
116	Železný Brod .... △ d.	0934	...	1133**g**	1333**h**	1533	1733**e**	1933	...	...
133	**Tanvald** .... △ a.	0958	...	1157**g**	1357**h**	1557	1757**e**	1957	...	...

	d					Ⓐ B	C		A	
Tanvald .... ▽ d.	...	0558**d**	0758	...	1158**g**	1346	1358	1558	...	1758
Železný Brod .... ▽ a.	...	0620**d**	0820	...	1220**g**	1409	1420	1621	...	1821
Železný Brod .... **1142** d.	...	0622**d**	0822	...	1222**g**	1412	1422	1622	...	1822
Turnov .... **1142** a.	...	0636**d**	0836	...	1236**g**	1427	1436	1636	...	1836
Turnov .... d.	...	0644	0844	1044	1244	1444	1444	1644	...	1844
Mnichovo Hradiště .... d.	...	0659	0859	1059	1259	1459	1459	1659	...	1859
Mladá Boleslav .... a.	...	0719	0919	1119	1319	1519	1519	1719	...	1919
Mladá Boleslav .... d.	0522	0723	0923	1123	1323	1523	1523	1723	1813	1923
Všetaty .... d.	0549	0750	0950	1150	1350	1550	1550	1750	1842	1950
Neratovice .... d.	0558	0758	0958	1158	1358	1558	1558	1758	1849	1958
Praha hlavní nádrazi .... a.	0632	0832	1032	1232	1432	1632	1632	1832	1932	2032

A – Ⓒ Mar. 25 - Oct. 29. Heritage train operated by KŽC. To / from Mikulášovice.
B – Ⓐ (not July 3 - Sept. 1).
C – Ⓒ (daily July 1 - Sept. 3).
D – Ⓐ (daily Apr. 24 - Oct. 6).
d – ①–⑥ (not Apr. 8, 10, May 1, 8, July 6, Nov. 18).
e – Ⓑ (not Apr. 7, 9, 30, May 7, July 5, Nov. 17).
g – Ⓒ (daily June 1 - Oct. 1; also Apr. 6, Oct. 26, 27).
h – Ⓒ (daily July 3 - Sept. 3).
△ – Also at 0500 **d**, 0700 and every two hours until 2100, 2300 **D**.
▽ – Also at 0429 **d**, 0627 and every two hours until 2027, 2227 **D**.

1141 LIBEREC - TANVALD - SZKLARSKA POREBA

2nd class

km				E			E	E				F		E		F				E		⑤j	
0	**Liberec** .... ◧ d.	0535	0635	0735	0735	0835	0935	0935	1035	1035	1135	1235	1335	1335	1435	1435	1535	1535	1635	1735	1835	1835	1935	...	2035
12	Jablonec nad Nisou .... ◧ d.	0556	0656	0756	0756	0856	0956	0956	1056	1056	1156	1256	1356	1356	1456	1456	1556	1556	1645	1756	1856	1856	1956	...	2056
27	**Tanvald** .... ◧ a.	0625	0725	0825	0825	0925	1025	1025	1125	1125	1225	1325	1425	1425	1525	1525	1625	1625	1725	1825	1925	1925	2025	2027	2125
39	Harrachov .... a.	...	0754	0854	0854	0954	1052	1052	...	1154	1252	1354	1454	1454	1554	1554	1654	1654	1754	1854	...	1954	...	2052	...
55	**Szklarska Poreba** Górna ‡. a.	...	0821	...	0921	1021	...	1121	...	1221	...	1421	...	1521	...	1621	...	1721	1821	...	...	2021	...	...	...

	Ⓒ			E			E		E				F		E		F			G		H	E
Szklarska Poreba Górna ‡ .... d.	...	...	0830	...	0930	1030	...	1130	...	1230	...	1430	...	1530	...	1630	...	1730	1830	...	...	...	...	2030
Harrachov .... d.	...	0757	0857	0957	0957	1057	...	1157	1257	1257	1357	1457	1557	1557	1657	1657	1757	1757	1900	...	1957	...	2057	2057
Tanvald .... ◧ d.	0829	0829	0929	1029	1029	1129	1229	1229	1329	1329	1429	1529	1629	1629	1729	1729	1829	1829	1929	2029	2029	2129	2129	2129
Jablonec nad Nisou .... ◧ d.	0857	0857	0957	1057	1057	1157	1257	1257	1357	1357	1457	1557	1657	1657	1757	1757	1857	1857	1957	2057	2057	2157	2157	2157
Liberec .... ◧ a.	0917	0917	1017	1117	1117	1217	1318	1318	1418	1418	1518	1618	1718	1718	1818	1818	1917	1917	2017	2117	2117	2217	2217	2217

E – Daily until Mar. 19; Ⓒ Mar. 25 - June 4 (also May 2, 3); daily June 5 - Oct. 1; ⑥⑦ Oct. 7 – 29.
F – ⑥⑦ (also Apr. 7, 10, May 1 – 3, 8, June 8, 9, July 5 – 7, Aug. 14, 15, Oct. 28, 29, Nov. 1, 17).
G – Ⓒ Apr. 22 - June 18; daily June 19 - Sept. 3.
H – Daily until Mar. 19; ⑤⑥⑦ Mar. 24 - June 4 (also Apr. 6, 10, May 1 – 3, 8); daily June 5 - Oct. 1; ⑤–⑦ Oct. 6 – 29; ⑤ from Nov. 3 (also Nov. 16; not Nov. 17).
j – ⑤ (also Apr. 6, July 4, Sept. 27, Nov. 16; not Apr. 7, July 7, Sept. 29, Nov. 17).
‡ – 🏛 Czech Republic / Poland = Jakuszyce.
◧ – Other trains Liberec - Tanvald at 0438 Ⓐ, 0505 Ⓐ, 0605 Ⓐ, 0705 Ⓐ, 1305 Ⓐ, 1405 Ⓐ, 1505 Ⓐ, 1605 Ⓐ, 1705 Ⓐ, 1805 Ⓐ, 2135, 2235; Tanvald - Liberec at 0429, 0459 Ⓐ, 0529, 0559 Ⓐ, 0629, 0659 Ⓐ, 0729, 0759 Ⓐ, 1259 Ⓐ, 1359 Ⓐ, 1459 Ⓐ, 1559 Ⓐ, 1659 Ⓐ, 2229.

1142 LIBEREC - HRADEC KRÁLOVÉ - PARDUBICE

2nd class Arriva

km										
0	**Liberec** .... d.	0405	0605	0805	1005	1205	1405	1605	1805	2005
38	Turnov .... a.	0438	0639	0839	1039	1239	1439	1639	1839	2038
38	Turnov .... **1140** d.	0440	0640	0840	1040	1240	1440	1640	1840	2040
52	Železný Brod .... **1140** a.	0456	0656	0856	1056	1256	1456	1656	1856	2056
52	Železný Brod .... d.	0457	0657	0857	1057	1257	1457	1657	1857	2057
76	Stará Paka .... d.	0526	0731	0931	1131	1331	1531	1731	1931	2131
107	Dvůr Králové nad Labem .... d.	0603	0803	1003	1203	1403	1603	1803	2003	2157
122	Jaroměř .... d.	0618	0819	1019	1219	1418	1619	1819	2019	2209
139	**Hradec Králové** .... a.	0631	0832	1032	1232	1430	1632	1832	2032	2224
139	**Hradec Králové** .... ⊡ d.	0633	0837	1037	1237	1437	1637	1837	2037	2225
161	**Pardubice** .... ⊡ a.	0651	0855	1055	1255	1455	1655	1855	2055	2247

Pardubice .... ⊡ d.	0505	0705	0905	1105	1305	1505	1705	1905	2105
Hradec Králové .... ⊡ a.	0523	0723	0923	1123	1323	1523	1723	1923	2123
Hradec Králové .... d.	0526	0727	0926	1126	1326	1526	1726	1926	2126
Jaroměř .... d.	0542	0743	0943	1143	1343	1543	1743	1943	2144
Dvůr Králové nad Labem .... d.	0558	0758	0958	1158	1358	1558	1758	1958	2158
Stará Paka .... d.	0630	0830	1030	1230	1430	1630	1830	2030	2231
Železný Brod .... a.	0656	0856	1056	1256	1456	1656	1856	2056	2256
Železný Brod .... **1140** d.	0657	0857	1057	1257	1457	1657	1857	2057	2257
Turnov .... **1140** a.	0716	0916	1116	1316	1516	1716	1916	2116	2316
Turnov .... d.	0721	0920	1120	1320	1520	1720	1920	2119	2323
Liberec .... a.	0754	0953	1153	1355	1553	1753	1953	2151	2357

⊡ – Frequent additional trains are available Hradec Kralové - Pardubice and v.v, some of which continue to / from Jaroměř. Operator: ČD. Journey 20 - 30 minutes.

1144 STARKOČ - WAŁBRZYCH

2nd class

Starkoč - Meziměsti is operated by ČD. Meziměsti - Wroclaw runs summer only and is operated by GW Train Regio (ČD tickets and passes not valid).

km									
0	**Starkoč** .... d.	0642	0742	0842		1842	1942	2042	...
9	Náchod .... d.	0700	0800	0900	and	1900	2000	2100	...
40	Meziměsti 🏛 .... d.	0739	0838	0939	hourly	1939	2038	2139	...
62	**Walbrzych** Gl. .... a.	...	...	...	until	...	...	...	...
	Wroclaw Gl. **1084** .... a.	...	...	...		...	...	...	...

Wroclaw Gl. **1084** .... d.	...	...	...		...	...	...	...
Walbrzych Gl. .... d.	...	...	...	and	...	...	...	...
Meziměsti 🏛 .... d.	0619	0719	0819	hourly	1719	1819	2019	...
Náchod .... a.	0703	0803	0903	until	1803	1903	2103	...
Starkoč .... a.	0717	0817	0917		1817	1917	2117	...

1145 PRAHA - HRADEC KRÁLOVÉ - TRUTNOV

🍸 on most **9xx** trains

km		939	941		921	943		923	945		925		927	947		929	949		931	951		933	953		955		957
			Ⓐ	2Ⓒ			2			2		2			2			2			2			2		2	
0	**Praha** hlavní n. .... d.	...	0509	...	0609	0709	...	0809	0909	...	1009	...	1209	1309	...	1409	1509	...	1609	1709	...	1809	1909	...	2009	...	2209
55	Nymburk .... **1157** d.	...	0555	...	0655	0755	...	0855	0955	...	1055	...	1255	1355	...	1455	1555	...	1655	1755	...	1855	1955	...	2055	...	2255
66	Poděbrady .... **1157** d.	...	0602	...	0702	0802	...	0902	1002	...	1102	...	1302	1402	...	1502	1602	...	1702	1802	...	1902	2002	...	2102	...	2302
125	**Hradec Králové** .... a.	...	0650	...	0750	0850	...	0950	1050	...	1150	...	1350	1450	...	1550	1650	...	1750	1850	...	1950	2050	...	2150	...	2350
125	**Hradec Králové** .... d.	0604	...	0702	0804	...	0904	1004	...	1104	1204	1304	1404	...	1504	1604	...	1704	1804	...	1904	2004	...	2102	...	2204	...
142	Jaroměř .... d.	0619	...	0718	0819	...	0918	1019	...	1118	1219	1318	1419	...	1518	1619	...	1718	1819	...	1918	2019	...	2118	...	2224	...
160	Starkoč .... d.	0639	...	0739	0841	...	0939	1041	...	1139	1241	1339	1441	...	1539	1641	...	1739	1841	...	1939	2041	...	2138	...	2245	...
194	**Trutnov** hlavní n. .... a.	0720	...	0819	0920	...	1019	1120	...	1219	1320	1419	1520	...	1619	1720	...	1819	1920	...	2019	2120	...	2220	...	2322	...

	954	952	934		950	932		948		930		928		946	926		944		924		942	922		940	920	
	Ⓐ			2			2				2		2			2				2			2			2
Trutnov hlavní n. .... d.	...	...	0440	0543	...	0642	0743	...	...	0842	0943	1042	1143	...	1242	1343	...	...	1442	1543	...	1642	1743	...	1842	2043
Starkoč .... d.	...	...	0520	0625	...	0721	0825	...	...	0921	1025	1121	1225	...	1321	1425	...	...	1521	1625	...	1721	1825	...	1921	2123
Jaroměř .... d.	...	...	0540	0643	...	0741	0843	...	...	0941	1043	1141	1243	...	1341	1444	...	...	1541	1643	...	1741	1843	...	1941	2142
Hradec Králové .... a.	...	...	0555	0658	...	0755	0857	...	...	0955	1057	1155	1257	...	1355	1457	...	...	1555	1656	...	1755	1857	...	1955	2158
Hradec Králové .... d.	0408	0508	0608	...	0708	0808	...	0908	...	1008	...	1208	...	1308	1408	...	1508	...	1608	...	1708	1808	...	1908	2008	...
Poděbrady .... **1157** a.	0452	0552	0652	...	0752	0852	...	0952	...	1052	...	1252	...	1352	1452	...	1552	...	1652	...	1752	1852	...	1952	2052	...
Nymburk .... **1157** a.	0500	0600	0700	...	0800	0900	...	1000	...	1100	...	1300	...	1400	1500	...	1600	...	1700	...	1800	1900	...	2000	2100	...
Praha hlavní n. .... a.	0542	0642	0742	...	0842	0942	...	1042	...	1142	...	1342	...	1442	1542	...	1642	...	1742	...	1842	1942	...	2042	2142	...

km			Ⓐ					Ⓐ				Ⓐ
0	**Hradec Králové** .... d.	0505	0603	0705	0905	1105	1305	1403	1505	1705	1905	2105
21	Týniště nad Orlicí .... d.	0531	0631	0731	0931	1131	1331	1429	1531	1731	1931	2131
29	Častolovicě .... d.	0541	0642	0743	0941	1141	1341	1439	1543	1741	1941	2141
62	**Letohrad** .... a.	0627	0727	0831	1030	1230	1429	1526	1630	1830	2030	2227

	Ⓐ		Ⓐ					Ⓐ			
Letohrad .... a.	0423	0530	0633	0734	0933	1133	1332	1435	1533	1733	1933
Častolovicě .... d.	0517	0620	0720	0820	1020	1220	1418	1518	1620	1820	2020
Týniště nad Orlicí .... d.	0533	0632	0732	0831	1031	1231	1431	1534	1631	1831	2031
Hradec Králové .... d.	0557	0653	0755	0852	1052	1253	1453	1557	1653	1852	2052

2nd class HAVLÍČKŮV BROD - JIHLAVA - SLAVONICE 1149

WARNING! Subject to alteration March 13 – 24. Services may be operated by 🚌.

km				Ⓐ	Ⓒ						Ⓒ	Ⓐ A	Ⓒ	B	Ⓐ	Ⓒ		Ⓐ	Ⓒ				Ⓒ		
0	**Havlíčkův Brod** △ d.	0455	0602	0703	0705	0803	0905	1003	1105	1203	1203	1255	1305	1403	1503	1505	1603	1703	1705	1803	1905	2003	2003	2105	2208
27	Jihlava △ d.	0526	0622	0723	0736	0823	0936	1023	1136	1223	1223	1324	1336	1423	1523	1536	1623	1725	1736	1823	1936	2023	2023	2136	2237
42	Kostelec u Jihlavy d.	...	0647	0747	...	0847	...	1047	...	1247	1247	1347	...	1447	1547	...	1647	1747	...	1847	...	2047	2047	...	2300
65	Telč d.	...	0734	0831	...	0934	...	1134	...	1331	1334	1431	...	1534	1631	...	1734	1831	...	1934	...	2131	2134	...	2337
95	**Slavonice** a.	...	0826	...	...	1026	...	1226	...	...	1426	...	...	1626	...	...	1826	...	...	2026	...	...	2226	...	...

	Ⓒ	Ⓐ	Ⓒ	Ⓐ	Ⓒ			Ⓒ						Ⓒ	Ⓐ A	Ⓒ		Ⓒ	Ⓐ	B				
Slavonice d.	...	...	...	0432	0538	...	...	0725	...	...	0925	...	1125	...	...	1325	...	...	...	1525	...	1725	1925	...
Telč d.	0428	0434	...	0534	0636	0636	...	0836	0836	...	1036	...	1236	...	1336	1436	1436	...	1536	1636	...	1836	2036	...
Kostelec u Jihlavy d.	0508	0515	...	0615	0717	0717	...	0917	0917	...	1117	...	1317	...	1417	1517	1517	...	1617	1717	...	1917	2117	...
Jihlava ▽ d.	0527	0535	0622	0637	0737	0737	0822	0937	0937	1022	1137	1222	1337	1422	1437	1537	1537	1622	1637	1737	1822	1937	2137	2237
Havlíčkův Brod ▽ a.	0555	0555	0653	0657	0757	0757	0853	0957	0957	1053	1157	1253	1357	1453	1457	1557	1557	1653	1657	1757	1853	1957	2203	2308

A – Not July 3 - Sept. 1.
B – Change at Telč on Ⓐ.

△ – Also Havlíčkův Brod - Jihlava at 0536 Ⓐ, 0638 Ⓐ, 0738 Ⓐ, 1438 Ⓐ, 1538 Ⓐ, 1638 Ⓐ, 1738 Ⓐ.
▽ – Also Jihlava - Havlíčkův Brod at 0549 Ⓐ, 0650 Ⓐ, 1350 Ⓐ, 1450 Ⓐ, 1550 Ⓐ, 1650 Ⓐ, 2022.

PRAHA - PARDUBICE - BRNO - BŘECLAV - WIEN and BRATISLAVA 1150

SERVICE UNTIL JUNE 30. **Fast trains**. For semi-fast trains Praha - Brno see Table **1151**. Most *EC* and *RJ* trains convey ✕. Regiojet (♥) trains convey 🍸. Regiojet trains call additionally at Havlíčkův Brod and Ždár nad Sázavou - for timings see Table **1152**

km		*IC* 571	♥ 1029	*EN* 477	*NJ* 457	*EC* 271		*RJ* 71	*EC* 273	*EC* 101	♥ 1031	*RJ* 73		♥ 1041	*EC* 275	*RJ* 75	♥ 1033		*EC* 277	*EC* 103	*RJ* 259	♥ 1043	*EC* 279
				C	J §			①–⑥ d		⊡										⊡	D		
0	**Praha** hlavní nádrazi 1160 d.	0001	...	...	...	...	...	0424	0524	...	0545	0624	...	0645	0724	0824	0845	...	0924	...	1026	1045	1124
62	Kolín 1160 d.	0037	...	...	...	...	...	0501	0601	...	0623	0701	...	0723	0801	0901	0923	...	1001	...	|	1123	1201
104	**Pardubice** 1160 d.	0059	...	...	...	...	...	|	|	...	|	|	...	|	|	|	|	...	|	...	|	|	|
164	Česká Třebová 1160 d.	0143	...	...	...	...	...	|	|	...	|	|	...	|	|	|	|	...	|	...	|	|	|
255	**Brno** hlavní nádrazí d.	0245	0348	...	...	0622	...	0722	0822	...	0848	0922	...	0948	1022	1122	1148	...	1222	...	1322	1348	1422
314	Břeclav a.	...	0418	...	...	0652	...	0752	0852	...	0918	0952	...	1018	1052	1152	1218	...	1252	...	1352	1418	1452
314	Břeclav 982 d.	...	0420	0455	0549	0655	...	0755	0855	0855	0920	0955	...	1020	1055	1155	1220	...	1255	1255	1355	1420	1455
402	**Wien** Hbf 982 a.	...	0515	|	0700	|	...	0849	|	0949	1021	1049	...	|	|	1249	1315	...	|	1349	1449	|	|
	Flughafen Wien Schwechat ✈ a.	...	0544	|	|	|	...	|	|	...	|	|	...	|	|	|	1408	...	|	|	|	|	|
	Graz **980** a.	...	...	|	1002	|	...	1134	|	...	|	1334	...	|	|	1534	...	...	|	...	1734	|	|
332	Kúty 🏛 a.	...	...	0511	...	0711	...	...	0911	...	|	...	...	|	1111	...	...	...	1311	...	...	|	1511
396	**Bratislava** hl. st. a.	...	...	0554	...	0754	...	...	0954	...	|	...	...	1118	1154	...	...	...	1354	...	...	1518	1554
	Budapest Nyugati **1175** a.	...	...	0829	...	1028	...	...	1228	...	|	...	...	...	1428	...	...	...	1628	...	...	...	1828
	Budapest Déli **1250** a.	...	...	...	...	...	...	...	...	...	1314	...	...	...	...	...	...	...	...	...	...	...	...

	RJ 79	*EC* 131	♥ 1035	*EC* 253	*RJ* 371		♥ 1045	*EC* 281	*EC* 105	♥ 1037	*RJ* 373		♥ 1047	*EC* 283	*EC* 107	♥ 1049		*RJ* 375	♥ 1051	*RJ* 527	585 477	
		E		F			G		⊡					H	⊡				⑦		C	
Praha hlavní nádrazi 1160 d.	1224	...	1245	1326h	1424	...	1445	1524	...	1545	1624	...	1645	1724	...	1745	...	1824	1945	2003	2243	...
Kolín 1160 d.	1301	...	1323	|	1501	...	1523	1601	...	1623	1701	...	1723	1801	...	1823	...	1901	2023	2041	2323	...
Pardubice 1160 d.	|	...	|	|	|	...	|	|	...	|	|	...	|	|	...	|	...	|	|	|	|	...
Česká Třebová 1160 d.	|	...	|	|	|	...	|	|	...	|	|	...	|	|	...	|	...	|	|	|	|	...
Brno hlavní nádrazí d.	1522	...	1548	1622	1722	...	1748	1822	...	1848	1922	...	1948	2022	...	2046	...	2122	2246	2303	0143	...
Břeclav a.	1552	...	1618	1652	1752	...	1818	1852	...	1918	1952	...	2018	2052	...	...	...	2152	...	2333	0213	...
Břeclav 982 d.	1555	1555	1620	1655	1755	...	1820	1855	1855	1920	1955	...	2020	2055	2055	...	...	2155	...	...	0455	...
Wien Hbf 982 a.	1649	|	1721	|	1849	...	|	|	1949	2015	2049	...	|	|	2149	...	...	2249	...	...	|	...
Flughafen Wien Schwechat ✈ a.	|	|	|	|	|	...	|	|	|	2108	|	...	|	|	...	...	...	...	...	...	|	...
Graz **980** a.	1934	|	|	|	2134	...	|	|	2234	...	2334	...	|	|	...	...	...	...	...	...	|	...
Kúty 🏛 a.	...	1611	|	1711	...	...	|	1911	...	...	...	...	|	2111	...	...	...	...	...	...	0511	...
Bratislava hl. st. a.	...	1701	|	1754	...	...	1918	1954	...	...	...	...	2118	2154	...	...	...	...	...	...	0554	...
Budapest Nyugati **1175** a.	...	1949	|	2028	...	...	...	2228	...	...	...	...	...	...	...	...	...	...	...	...	0829	...
Budapest Déli **1250** a.	...	...	2014	...	...	...	...	...	...	...	...	...	...	...	...	...	...	...	...	...	...	...

	RJ 524	♥ 1040	*IC* 584	476 584	♥ 1042		*RJ* 526	♥ 1044	*EC* 106	*EC* 282	♥ 1030		*RJ* 70	*EC* 104	*EC* 280	♥ 1046		*RJ* 72	*EC* 252	♥ 1032	*EC* 130	*RJ* 74
	①–⑥ d	①		C					⊡	H				⊡		G			F		E	
Budapest Déli **1250** d.	...	...	...	...	...	...	...	...	...	...	...	...	...	...	...	...	...	...	...	0745	...	...
Budapest Nyugati **1175** d.	...	...	...	1929	...	...	...	...	...	...	...	...	...	...	0529	...	...	...	0729	|	0812	...
Bratislava hl. st. d.	...	...	...	2206	...	...	...	0532	...	0606	...	...	...	...	0806	0832	...	...	1006	|	1057	...
Kúty 🏛 d.	...	...	...	2249	...	...	...	|	...	0649	...	...	...	...	0849	|	...	...	1049	|	1148	...
Graz **980** d.	...	...	...	|	...	...	...	|	...	|	...	...	...	0525	|	|	...	0625	|	|	|	0825
Flughafen Wien Schwechat ✈ d.	...	...	...	|	...	...	...	|	...	|	0615	...	...	|	|	|	...	|	|	|	|	|
Wien Hbf 982 d.	...	...	...	|	...	...	...	|	0610	|	0639	...	0710	0810	|	|	...	0910	|	1039	|	1110
Břeclav 982 a.	...	...	...	2304	...	...	...	0636	0704	0704	0736	...	0804	0904	0904	0937	...	1004	1104	1136	1204	1204
Břeclav d.	...	0431	0507	0507	...	...	0607	0638	...	0707	0738	...	0807	...	0907	0938	...	1007	1107	1138	...	1207
Brno hlavní nádrazí d.	0429	0503	0538	0538	0609	...	0638	0709	...	0738	0809	...	0838	...	0938	1009	...	1038	1138	1209	...	1238
Česká Třebová 1160 d.	0534	|	|	|	|	...	|	|	...	|	|	...	|	...	|	|	...	|	|	|	...	|
Pardubice 1160 d.	0618	|	|	|	|	...	|	|	...	|	|	...	|	...	|	|	...	|	|	|	...	|
Kolín 1160 a.	|	0730	0757	0757	0830	...	0857	0930	...	0957	1030	...	1057	...	1157	1230	...	1257	|	1430	...	1457
Praha hlavní nádrazi 1160 a.	0708	0811	0837	0837	0911	...	0935	1011	...	1037	1111	...	1135	...	1237	1308	...	1335	1433h	1508	...	1535

	EC 278	♥ 1048	*RJ* 256	*EC* 102	*EC* 276		♥ 1034	*RJ* 78	♥ 1050	*EC* 274	*RJ* 370		♥ 1036	*EC* 100	*EC* 272	*RJ* 372		*EC* 270	*RJ* 374	♥ 1028	*EN* 476	*NJ* 456
			D	⊡										⊡							C	J §
Budapest Déli **1250** d.	...	...	...	...	...	...	...	...	...	...	...	...	1445	...	...	...	...	...	...	...	...	...
Budapest Nyugati **1175** d.	0929	...	...	...	1129	...	...	...	...	1329	...	...	|	...	1529	...	...	1729	...	...	1929	...
Bratislava hl. st. d.	1206	1232	...	...	1406	...	...	...	1532	1606	...	...	|	...	1806	...	...	2006	...	...	2206	...
Kúty 🏛 d.	1249	|	...	...	1449	...	...	...	|	1649	...	...	|	...	1849	...	...	2049	...	...	2249	...
Graz **980** d.	|	|	1025	...	|	...	...	1225	|	|	1425	...	|	...	|	1625	...	|	1825	...	|	1920
Flughafen Wien Schwechat ✈ d.	|	|	|	...	|	...	1415	|	|	|	|	...	|	...	|	|	...	|	|	2115	|	|
Wien Hbf 982 d.	|	|	1310	1410	|	...	1439	1510	|	|	1710	...	1736	1810	|	1910	...	|	2110	2139	|	2210
Břeclav 982 a.	1304	1337	1404	1504	1504	...	1536	1604	1637	1704	1804	...	1836	1904	1904	2004	...	2104	2204	2236	2304	2307
Břeclav d.	1307	1338	1407	...	1507	...	1538	1607	1638	1707	1807	...	1838	...	1907	2007	...	2107	2207	2238	...	...
Brno hlavní nádrazí d.	1338	1409	1438	...	1538	...	1609	1638	1709	1738	1838	...	1909	...	1938	2038	...	2138	2236	2307	...	...
Česká Třebová 1160 d.	|	|	|	...	|	...	|	|	|	|	|	...	|	...	|	|	...	2247	...	...	...	...
Pardubice 1160 d.	|	|	|	...	|	...	|	|	|	|	|	...	|	...	|	|	...	2324	...	...	...	...
Kolín 1160 a.	1557	1630	|	...	1757	...	1830	1857	1930	1957	2057	...	2130	...	2157	2257	...	2343	...	...	...	...
Praha hlavní nádrazi 1160 a.	1637	1713	1734	...	1837	...	1908	1937	2011	2037	2135	...	2211	...	2235	2337	...	0019	...	...	...	...

C – METROPOL – 🚃12 ✕ Praha - Břeclav and v.v.; 🛏 1, 2 cl., 🛌 2 cl. Praha - Břeclav (**477/476**) - Budapest and v.v. For other cars Břeclav - Budapest and v.v. see Tables **60** (Berlin - Budapest) and Table **99** (Warszawa - Budapest).
D – VINDOBONA – 🚃12 ✕ Graz - Praha and v.v.
E – BATHORY – 🚃12 ✕ Budapest - Terespol and v.v.; 🚃2 Budapest - Bohumín (**115/114**) - Przemyśl and v.v.
F – HUNGARIA - 🚃12 ✕ Budapest - Hamburg and v.v.
G – 🚃12 🍸 Praha - Žilina and v.v.
H – METROPOLITAN SLOVENSKÁ STRELA – 🚃12 🍸 Praha - Nové Zámky and v.v; conveys on dates in Table **1170**: 🛏 1, 2 cl. Praha (**283/282**) - Nové Zámky (**801/800**) - Košice and v.v.
J – NIGHTJET – 🛏 1, 2 cl., 🛌 2 cl., 🚃2 Berlin - Graz and v.v.; 🛏 1, 2 cl., 🚃2 Warszawa - Wien and v.v.

d – ①–⑥ (not Apr. 8, 10, May 1, 8, July 6, Nov. 18).
h – Praha **Holesovice**.

♥ – Operated by REGIOJET. Separate fares apply.
⊡ – For origin / destination see Table **99** or **1164**.
§ – Ⓡ for international journeys.
RJ – Railjet train (operated by ÖBB and ČD). Conveys Business, First, Economy classes.

CZECH REPUBLIC

1151 PRAHA - OLOMOUC and BRNO

🍸 on most trains

SERVICE UNTIL JUNE 30. SEMI-FAST TRAINS. For faster trains see Tables **1150** and **1160**. Most Přerov trains continue to / from destinations on Table **1162**.

km		*IC*571	861			883	863	885	865	887	867	889	869		891	871	893	873	895	875	897	877	879	899	999
			Ⓐ	2g	2Ⓐ	d								2Ⓐ											
0	**Praha** hlavní nádrazi ... d.	0001	...	...	...	0503	0603	0703	0803	0903	1003	1103	1203	...	1303	1403	1503	1603	1703	1803	1903	2031	2103	2131	2303
62	Kolín ... d.	0037	...	...	...	0542	0642	0742	0842	0942	1042	1142	1242	...	1342	1442	1542	1642	1742	1842	1942	2109	2142	2209	2342
104	Pardubice ... d.	0059	...	...	...	0607	0707	0807	0907	1007	1107	1207	1307	...	1407	1507	1607	1708	1807	1907	2007	2135	2205	2234	0006
139	Choceň ... d.	0118	...	...	...	0626	0726	0826	0926	1026	1126	1226	1326	...	1426	1526	1626	1726	1826	1926	2026	2153	|	2252	...
154	Ústí nad Orlicí ... d.	0132	...	...	...	0641	0741	0841	0941	1041	1141	1241	1341	...	1441	1541	1641	1741	1841	1941	2041	2206	|	2305	...
164	Česká Třebová ... d.	0143	0456	0546	0650	0651	0751	0851	0951	1051	1151	1251	1351	1450	1451	1551	1651	1751	1851	1951	2051	2215	2242	2315	...
252	Olomouc ... d.	|	|	|	|	0732	|	0932	|	1132	|	1332	|	|	1532	|	1732	|	1932	|	2132	...	|	0000	...
274	**Přerov** ... a.	|	|	|	|	0745	|	0945	|	1145	|	1345	|	|	1545	|	1745	|	1945	|	2145	...	|	0013	...
181	Svitavy ... d.	0154	0508	0559	0704	...	0802	...	1002	...	1202	...	1402	1504	...	1602	...	1802	...	2002	...	...	2254	...	...
208	Letovice ... d.	|	0527	0628	0732	...	0823	...	1023	...	1223	...	1423	1530	...	1623	...	1823	...	2023	...	...	2313	...	...
233	Blansko ... d.	0226	0548	0651	0753	...	0842	...	1042	...	1242	...	1442	1552	...	1642	...	1842	...	2042	...	...	2329	...	...
255	**Brno** hlavní nádrazí ... a.	0245	0610	0714	0816	...	0903	...	1102	...	1302	...	1502	1613	...	1702	...	1902	...	2102	...	...	2349	...	...

	876	898	998	*RJ*524	896	874	894	872	892	870	890	868	888	866		886	864		884	862		882	860	*EC*270
				d	d	w									2Ⓐ			2Ⓐ			2h			
Brno hlavní nádrazi ... d.	0310	...	...	0429	...	0500	...	0656	...	0856	...	1056	...	1256	1344	...	1456	1544	...	1656	1744	...	1856	2138
Blansko ... d.	0330	...	...	0449	...	0520	...	0717	...	0916	...	1116	...	1316	1408	...	1516	1608	...	1716	1808	...	1916	2202
Letovice ... d.	|	...	...	0505	...	0539	...	0737	...	0937	...	1137	...	1337	1431	...	1537	1631	...	1737	1830	...	1934	2218
Svitavy ... d.	0402	...	...	0523	...	0603	...	0803	...	1003	...	1203	...	1403	1501	...	1603	1701	...	1803	1857	...	2003	2235
Přerov ... d.	|	0403	...	|	0451	|	0612	|	0812	|	1012	|	1212	|	|	1412	|	|	1612	|	|	1812	|	|
Olomouc ... d.	|	0418	...	|	0506	|	0631	|	0831	|	1031	|	1231	|	|	1431	|	|	1631	|	|	1831	|	|
Česká Třebová ... d.	0415	0502	...	0534	0604	0615	0715	0815	0915	1015	1115	1215	1315	1415	1514	1515	1615	1714	1715	1815	1914	1915	2015	2247
Ústí nad Orlicí ... d.	0424	0511	...	0543	0613	0624	0724	0824	0924	1024	1124	1224	1324	1424	...	1524	1624	...	1724	1824	...	1924	2024	|
Choceň ... d.	0437	0524	...	0557	|	0637	0737	0837	0937	1037	1137	1237	1337	1437	...	1537	1637	...	1737	1837	...	1937	2037	|
Pardubice ... d.	0501	0545	0601	0618	0645	0702	0801	0901	1001	1101	1201	1301	1401	1501	...	1601	1701	...	1801	1901	...	2001	2101	2324
Kolín ... a.	0525	0607	0625	|	0707	0725	0825	0925	1025	1125	1225	1325	1425	1525	...	1625	1725	...	1825	1925	...	2025	2125	2343
Praha hlavní nádrazi ... a.	0605	0648	0705	0708	0748	0805	0905	1005	1105	1205	1305	1405	1505	1605	...	1705	1805	...	1905	2005	...	2105	2205	0019

d – ①–⑥ (not Apr. 8, 10, May 1, 8, July 6, Nov. 18).
g – ①–⑥ (not Apr. 8, 10, May 1, 8, July 5, 6, Sept. 28, Oct. 28, Nov. 17).
h – Ⓑ (also Oct. 28; not Apr. 7, 9, 30, May 7).
w – From Brno on Ⓐ, from Česká Třebová daily.

1152 PRAHA - HAVLIČKŮV BROD - BRNO

🍸 on most trains

SERVICE UNTIL JUNE 30. **10xx** trains are operated by REGIOJET (separate fares apply. For origin / destination see Table **1150**). For other trains Praha - Kolín see Tables **1150**, **1151** and **1160**.

km		971	973	1031	975	1041	977	1033	961	979	1043	981	1035	983	1045	985	1037	987	1047	989	989	1049	991	963	1051	965	967
		A			B				⑥j							Ⓐ				Ⓑe	⑦k			Ⓑe	⑦		
0	**Praha** hlavní nádrazi. d.	...	...	0545	0606	0645	0806	0845	0906	1006	1045	1206	1245	1406	1445	1506	1545	1606	1645	1706	1706	1745	1806	1906	1945	2006	2206
62	Kolín ... d.	...	...	0623	0647	0723	0847	0923	0947	1047	1123	1247	1323	1447	1523	1547	1623	1647	1723	1747	1747	1823	1847	1947	2023	2047	2246
73	Kutná Hora ... d.	...	...	|	0658	|	0858	|	0958	1058	|	1258	|	1458	|	1558	|	1658	|	1758	1758	|	1858	1958	|	2058	2256
82	Čáslav ... d.	...	...	|	0708	|	0908	|	1008	1108	|	1308	|	1508	|	1608	|	1708	|	1808	1808	|	1908	2008	|	2108	2305
136	**Havlíčkův Brod** ... a.	...	...	0722	0757	0822	0957	1022	1057	1157	1222	1357	1422	1557	1622	1657	1722	1757	1822	1857	1857	1922	1957	2057	2122	2157	...
136	**Havlíčkův Brod** ... d.	0501	0601	0723	0801	0823	1001	1023	...	1202	1223	1401	1423	1601	1623	1701	1723	1801	1823	1901	1901	1923	2001	2101	2123	...	...
169	Žďár nad Sázavou ... d.	0528	0628	0747	0828	0847	1028	1047	...	1228	1247	1428	1447	1628	1647	1728	1747	1828	1847	1926	1928	1947	2028	2126	2147	...	...
246	**Brno** hlavní nádrazi .. a.	0640	0740	0846	0940	0946	1140	1146	...	1340	1346	1540	1546	1740	1746	1840	1846	1940	1946	...	2040	2046	2140	...	2246	...	...

	964	962	962	1040	990	990	1042	988	1044	1030	986	1046	984	1032	982	960	1048	980	978	1034	976	1050	974	972	1036	970
	d	d		①	①m	Ⓐ										⑦k			Ⓑe				Ⓐ			
Brno hlavní nádrazi ... d.	...	...	...	0503	0520	...	0609	0620	0709	0809	0820	1009	1020	1209	1220	...	1409	1420	1520	1609	1620	1709	1720	1820	1909	2020
Žďár nad Sázavou ... d.	...	0530	...	0607	0630	0630	0708	0730	0808	0908	0930	1108	1130	1308	1330	...	1508	1530	1630	1708	1730	1808	1830	1930	2008	2130
Havlíčkův Brod ... a.	...	0556	...	0630	0656	0656	0731	0756	0831	0931	0956	1131	1156	1331	1356	...	1531	1556	1656	1731	1756	1831	1856	1956	2031	2156
Havlíčkův Brod ... d.	0501	0601	0601	0632	0701	0701	0732	0801	0832	0932	1001	1132	1201	1332	1401	1501	1532	1601	1701	1732	1801	1832	...	2001	2032	...
Čáslav ... d.	0552	0652	0652	|	0752	0752	|	0852	|	|	1052	|	1252	|	1452	1552	|	1652	1752	|	1852	|	...	2052	|	...
Kutná Hora ... d.	0601	0701	0701	|	0801	0801	|	0901	|	|	1101	|	1301	|	1501	1601	|	1701	1801	|	1901	|	...	2101	|	...
Kolín ... d.	0612	0712	0712	0731	0812	0812	0831	0912	0931	1031	1112	1231	1312	1431	1512	1612	1631	1712	1812	1831	1912	1931	...	2112	2131	...
Praha hlavní nádrazi ... a.	0654	0754	0754	0811	0854	0854	0911	0954	1011	1111	1154	1308	1354	1508	1554	1654	1708	1754	1854	1908	1954	2011	...	2154	2211	...

A – From Havlíčkův Brod on Ⓐ; from Žďár nad Sázavou on ①–⑥ **d**.
B – From Praha on ①–⑥ **d**; from Kolín daily.
d – ①–⑥ (not Apr. 8, 10, May 1, 8, July 6, Nov. 18).
e – Ⓑ (not Apr. 7, 9, 30, May 7, July 5, Nov. 17).
j – ⑥ (also Apr. 7, July 5, Sept. 28, Nov. 17; not Apr. 8, Nov. 18).
k – ⑦ (also Apr. 10, May 1, 8, July 6, Oct. 28; not Apr. 9).
m – ① (also Apr. 11, May 2, 9, July 7, Sept. 29; not Apr. 10, May 1, 8).

1156 BRNO - OLOMOUC - ŠUMPERK and JESENÍK

km		901	903	905	907	909	911	913		915	917
		d							2	C	⑦n
0	**Brno** hlavní nádrazi ... d.	0522	0718	0921	1121	1321	1521	1721	...	1921	2121
45	Vyškov na Moravé ... d.	0601	0801	1001	1201	1401	1601	1801	...	2001	2201
61	Nezamyslice ... d.	0622	0822	1022	1222	1422	1622	1822	...	2022	2222
80	Prostějov ... d.	0637	0837	1037	1237	1437	1637	1837	...	2037	2237
100	**Olomouc** ... d.	0656	0856	1056	1256	1456	1656	1856	...	2056	2253
146	Zábřeh na Moravé ... a.	0722	0922	1122	1322	1522	1722	1924	...	2124	...
146	Zábřeh na Moravé ... d.	0726	0926	1126	1326	1526	1726	1926	...	2126	...
159	**Šumperk** ... a.	0741	0941	1141	1341	1541	1741	1943	2116	2141	...
176	Hanušovice ... a.	0759**r**	0959**r**	1159**r**	1359**r**	1559**r**	1759**r**	...	2153	...	...
208	Lipová Lázně ... a.	0850**r**	1050**r**	1250**r**	1450**r**	1651**r**	1851**r**	...	2248	...	...
212	**Jeseník** ... a.	0858**r**	1058**r**	1258**r**	1458**r**	1659**r**	1858**r**	...	2256	...	...

	916	914	912	910	908	906	904	902		900
	Ⓐ	D							Ⓒ	p
Jeseník ... d.	...	...	0700**s**	0901**s**	1101**s**	1301**s**	1501**s**	1701**s**	1904	...
Lipová Lázně ... d.	...	...	0708**s**	0908**s**	1108**s**	1308**s**	1508**s**	1708**s**	1911	...
Hanušovice ... d.	...	...	0800**s**	1000**s**	1200**s**	1400**s**	1600**s**	1800**s**	2000	...
Šumperk ... d.	...	0611	0809	1009	1209	1409	1609	1809	|	2015
Zábřeh na Moravé ... a.	...	0630	0822	1022	1222	1422	1622	1822	2032	2031
Zábřeh na Moravé ... d.	...	0631	0834	1034	1234	1434	1634	1834	...	2034
Olomouc ... d.	0558	0706	0906	1106	1306	1506	1706	1906	...	2106
Prostějov ... d.	0616	0723	0923	1123	1323	1523	1723	1923	...	2123
Nezamyslice ... a.	0638	0738	0938	1138	1338	1538	1738	1938	...	2138
Vyškov na Moravé ... a.	0659	0758	0958	1158	1358	1558	1758	1958	...	2157
Brno hlavní nádrazi .. a.	0743	0842	1041	1241	1443	1643	1843	2038	...	2236

C – Daily Brno - Olomouc; Ⓑ **e** Olomouc - Šumperk. See note ⊡.
D – From Šumperk on ①–⑥ **d**; from Olomouc daily.
d – ①–⑥ (not Apr. 8, 10, May 1, 8, July 6, Nov. 18).
e – Ⓑ (not Apr. 7, 9, 30, May 7, July 5, Nov. 17).
n – ⑦ (also Apr. 10, May 1, 8, July 6, Sept. 28; not Apr. 9, 30, May 7).
p – ⑤⑦ (also Apr. 6, 10, May 1, 8, July 4, 6, Sept. 27, Oct. 28, Nov. 16; not Apr. 7, 9, 30, May 7, Nov. 17).
r – Jeseník portion detaches at Zabreh na Moravé (d. xx31). See note ◧.
s – Jeseník portion attaches at Zabreh na Moravé (a. xx25). See note ◧.
⊡ – Change trains at Olomouc on Ⓐ.
◧ – Different train numbers apply Zábřeh - Jeseník and v.v.

1157 DĚČÍN - ÚSTÍ NAD LABEM - MĚLNÍK - KOLÍN and RUMBURK - KOLÍN

Arriva*, Regiojet

km						
0	**Ústí n. L** hlavní n. d.	0440	0636		1636	1836
1	**Ústí n. L** západ ... d.	0446	0643		1643	1843
3	**Ústí n. L** Střekov d.	0452	0652		1652	1852
28	Litoměřice město d.	0513	0713	and	1713	1913
64	**Mělník** ... d.	0540	0740	every	1740	1940
74	Všetaty ... d.	0548	0748	**two**	1748	1948
86	Stará Boleslav ... d.	0558	0758	hours	1758	1958
97	Lysá n. Labem ▷ d.	0606	0806	until	1806	2006
112	Nymburk ... ▷ d.	0618	0818		1818	2018
119	Poděbrady ... ▷ d.	0625	0825		1825	2025
135	**Kolín** ... a.	0639	0839		1839	2039

Kolín ... d.	0714	0914		1914	2114
Poděbrady ... ▷ d.	0729	0929		1929	2129
Nymburk ... ▷ d.	0737	0937		1937	2137
Lysá n. Labem. ▷ d.	0748	0948	and	1948	2148
Stará Boleslav ... d.	0755	0955	every	1955	2155
Všetaty ... d.	0807	1007	**two**	2007	2206
Mělník ... d.	0815	1015	hours	2015	2214
Litoměřice město . d.	0843	1043	until	2043	2241
Ústí n. L Střekov . a.	0902	1102		2102	2300
Ústí n. L západ ... a.	0907	1107		2107	2305
Ústí n. L hlavní n. a.	0916	1116		2116	2313

km	⊖	t					
0	**Děčín** hl. n. ... d.	0800	1000	1200	1400	1600	1800
28	**Ústí n. L** Střekov a.	0838	1038	1238	1438	1638	1838

⊖	u					
Ústí n. L Střekov. d.	0917	1117	1317	1517	1717	1917
Děčín hl. n. ... a.	0954	1154	1354	1554	1754	1954

	E						
Rumburk ... d.	0523	0712	*0838*	*1038*	1312	1511**v**	1712
Česka Lipá ... d.	0624	0824	1024	1224	1424	1624	1824
Mladá Boleslav d.	0722	0922	1122	1322	1522	1722	1922
Nymburk ... ▷ d.	0748	0948	1148	1348	1548	1748	1948
Poděbrady ... ▷ d.	0756	0956	1156	1356	1556	1756	1956
Kolín ... a.	0809	1009	1209	1409	1609	1809	2009

Kolín ... d.	0745	0945	1145	1345	1545	1745	1945
Poděbrady ... ▷ d.	0758	0958	1158	1358	1558	1758	1958
Nymburk ... ▷ d.	0808	1008	1208	1408	1608	1808	2008
Mladá Boleslav d.	0837	1037	1237	1437	1637	1837	2037
Česka Lipá ... a.	0931	1131	1331	1531	1731	1931	2131
Rumburk ... a.	1037	*1324*	1437	1633**v**	1837	2037	*2317*

E – From Rumburk on Ⓐ; from Česka Lipá daily.
t – Also at 0444 Ⓐ, 0600.
u – Also at 0516, 0717.
v – ⑤⑥⑦ (also Apr. 10, May 1, 8).
▷ – See also Table **1145**.
⊖ – 2nd class only. For Dečín - Ústí nad Labem hl. n. see Table **1100**.
* – Rumburk - Česka Lipa - Kolín trains are operated by Arriva.

PRAHA - PÚCHOV, OSTRAVA and ŽILINA 1160

For additional fast trains Praha - Česká Třebová and v.v. see Table **1150**. For semi-fast trains Praha - Olomouc and v.v. see Table **1151**.
SC and *IC* trains are not available for local travel Ostravá - Bohumín or v.v.

km		*IC* 571 ✗	341 🍷	343 🍷	*EC* 121 🍷	♥ 1001 🍷 ①–⑥	*SC*• 241 🍷[R]	*EC* 113 🍷		*EC* 113 213	345 🍷	*EC* 123 🍷	♥ 1003 🍷	*LE*♠ 1251 🍷[R]	*EC* 141 🍷		*LE*♠ 1253 🍷[R]	*EC* 125 🍷	*IC* 503 🍷[R]	♥ 1005 🍷	*EC* 115 🍷	*EC* 115 130	347 🍷
								A◧		A◧											B◧	B◧	
0	**Praha** hlavní nádraží d.	0001	...	...	0515	0538	0600	0615	...	0615	...	0715	0738	0800	0815	...	0900	0915	0934	0938	1015	1015	...
62	Kolín d.	0037	...	...	0554	|	0638	0654	...	0654	...	0754	|	0838	0854	...	0938	0954	|	|	1054	1054	...
104	**Pardubice** d.	0059	...	...	0618	0636	0702	0718	...	0718	...	0818	0836	0902	0918	...	1002	1018	1031	1036	1118	1118	...
139	Choceň d.	0118	...	...	|	|	|	|	...	|	...	|	|	|	|	...	|	|	|	|	|	|	...
154	Ústí nad Orlici d.	0132	...	...	|	|	|	|	...	|	...	|	|	0932	|	...	1032	|	|	|	|	|	...
155	Ústí nad Orlici městó d.	|	...	...	|	|	|	0750	...	0750	...	|	|	|	0950	...	|	|	|	|	1150	1150	...
164	Česká Třebová d.	0142	...	...	0700	0715	0740	0800	...	0800	...	0900	0915	|	1000	...	|	1100	|	1115	1200	1200	...
206	Zábřeh na Moravé d.	...	...	...	0722	0737	|	0822	...	0822	...	0922	0937	1000	1022	...	1100	1122	|	1137	1222	1222	...
252	**Olomouc** d.	...	...	...	0754	0801	0819	0845	...	0845	...	0954	1001	1022	1045	...	1122	1154	1150	1201	1245	1245	...
	Přerov d.	...	...	...	|	|	|	|	...	|	...	|	|	1038	|	...	1138	|	|	|	|	|	...
303	Hranice na Moravě d.	...	...	...	0826	0834	|	0915	...	0915	...	1026	1034	1056	1115	...	1156	1226	|	1231	1315	1315	...
329	Valašské Meziříčí d.	...	...	...	0846	|	|	|	...	|	...	1046	|	|	|	...	|	1246	|	|	|	|	...
348	Vsetín d.	...	...	...	0906	|	|	|	...	|	...	1106	|	|	|	...	|	1306	|	|	|	|	...
366	Horní Lideč 🏛 d.	...	...	...	0929	|	|	|	...	|	...	1129	|	|	|	...	|	1329	|	|	|	|	...
394	**Púchov** a.	...	...	...	0952	|	|	|	...	|	...	1152	|	|	|	...	|	1352	|	|	|	|	...
353	Ostrava Svinov d.	...	0543	0747	...	0904	0910	0942	...	0942	0947	...	1104	1128	1142	...	1226	...	1237	1304	1341	1341	1347
381	Opava východ a.	...	|	|	...	|	|	|	...	|	|	...	|	|	|	...	|	...	|	|	|	|	|
358	**Ostrava** hl. n. d.	...	0555	0755	...	0912	0917	0950	...	0950	0955	...	1112	1136	1150	...	1234	...	1245	1312	1350	1350	1355
376	Havířov d.	...	|	|	...	0933	|	|	...	|	|	...	1135	|	|	...	|	...	...	1333	|	|	|
366	**Bohumín** a.	...	0601	0801	...	...	|	0957	...	0957	1001	...	|	1142	1157	...	1242	...	...	...	1357	1357	1401
366	**Bohumín** d.	...	0602	0802	...	...	|	1009	...	1017	1002	...	|	1144	1202	...	...	...	...	...	1446	1454	1402
	Katowice **1076** a.	...	|	|	...	...	|	1131	...	1206	|	...	|	|	|	...	...	...	...	...	1607	1636	|
	Kraków Glowny **1076** a.	...	|	|	...	...	|	|	...	1316	|	...	|	|	|	...	...	...	...	...	1713	|	|
	Warszawa Centralna **1060** a.	...	|	|	...	...	|	1410	...	...	|	...	|	|	|	...	...	...	...	...	...	1934	|
381	Karviná hl. n. d.	...	0611	0811	...	...	|	...	...	...	1011	...	|	1153	1211	...	...	...	...	...	...	...	1411
397	**Český Těšín** d.	...	0626	0826	...	...	0941	...	...	...	1026	...	1155	...	1226	...	...	...	...	...	...	...	1426
405	Trinec centrum d.	...	0634	0834	...	...	|	...	...	...	1034	...	1202	...	1234	...	...	...	...	...	...	...	1434
417	Návsi d.	...	0641	0841	...	...	|	...	...	...	1041	...	|	...	1241	...	...	...	...	...	...	...	1441
435	Čadca 🏛 a.	...	0658	0858	...	...	1005	...	...	...	1058	...	1225	...	1258	...	...	...	...	...	...	...	1458
Δ*466*	**Žilina** a.	...	0726	0926	...	...	1029	...	...	...	1126	...	1249	...	1326	...	...	...	...	...	...	...	1526
	Banská Bystrica **1185** a.	...	...	...	...	...	|	...	...	...	...	...	|	...	...	...	...	...	...	...	...	...	...
	Zvolen **1185** a.	...	...	...	...	...	|	...	...	...	...	...	|	...	...	...	...	...	...	...	...	...	...
	Poprad Tatry **1180** a.	...	...	...	...	...	1230	...	...	...	...	...	1450	...	...	...	...	...	...	...	...	...	...
	Prešov **1196** a.	...	...	...	...	...	|	...	...	...	...	...	|	...	...	...	...	...	...	...	...	...	...
	Košice **1180** a.	...	...	...	...	...	1341	...	...	...	...	...	1619	...	...	...	...	...	...	...	...	...	...

	LE♠ 1255 🍷[R]	*EC* 127 🍷	*SC*• 505 🍷[R]	♥ 1007 🍷	*EC* 143 🍷	*LE*♠ 1259 🍷[R]	*EC* 129 🍷		*SC*• 507 🍷[R] ④⑤⑦	♥ 1009 🍷	*EC* 117 🍷	*IC* 509 🍷[R] Ⓐ	349 🍷	♥ 1011 🍷		*LE*♠ 413 🍷[R]	*LE*♠ 413 🍷[R] ④⑤⑦	*EC* 221 🍷	*SC*• 511 🍷[R]	♥ 1013 🍷	*EC* 145 🍷	*EC* 145 🍷 Ⓑ
									g		C◧											e
Praha hlavní nádraží d.	1100	1115	1134	1138	1215	1300	1315	...	1334	1338	1415	1434	...	1438	...	1500	1500	1515	1534	1538	1615	1615
Kolín d.	1138	1154	|	|	1254	1338	1354	...	|	|	1454	|	...	|	...	1538	1538	1554	|	|	1654	1654
Pardubice d.	1202	1218	1231	1236	1318	1402	1418	...	1431	1436	1518	1531	...	1536	...	1602	1602	1618	1631	1636	1718	1718
Choceň d.	|	|	|	|	|	|	|	...	|	|	|	|	...	|	...	|	|	|	|	|	|	|
Ústí nad Orlici d.	1232	|	|	|	|	1432	|	...	|	|	|	|	...	|	...	1632	1632	|	|	|	|	|
Ústí nad Orlici městó d.	|	|	|	|	1350	|	|	...	|	|	1550	|	...	|	...	|	|	|	|	|	1750	1750
Česká Třebová d.	|	1300	|	1315	1400	|	1500	...	|	1515	1600	|	...	1615	...	|	|	1700	|	1715	1800	1800
Zábřeh na Moravé d.	1300	1322	|	1337	1422	1500	1522	...	|	1537	1622	|	...	1640	...	1700	1700	1722	|	1737	1822	1822
Olomouc d.	1322	1354	1350	1401	1445	1522	1554	...	1550	1601	1645	1650	...	1705	...	1722	1722	1754	1750	1801	1845	1845
Přerov d.	1338	|	|	|	|	1538	|	...	|	|	|	|	...	|	...	1738	1738	|	|	|	|	|
Hranice na Moravě d.	1356	1426	|	1431	1515	1556	1626	...	|	1634	1715	|	...	1734	...	1756	1756	1826	|	1831	1916	1916
Valašské Meziříčí d.	|	1446	|	|	|	|	1646	...	|	|	|	|	...	|	...	|	|	1846	|	|	|	|
Vsetín d.	|	1506	|	|	|	|	1706	...	|	|	|	|	...	|	...	|	|	1906	|	|	|	|
Horní Lideč 🏛 d.	|	1529	|	|	|	|	1729	...	|	|	|	|	...	|	...	|	|	1929	|	|	|	|
Púchov a.	|	1552	|	|	|	|	1752	...	|	|	|	|	...	|	...	|	|	1952	|	|	|	|
Ostrava Svinov d.	1428	...	1437	1504	1542	1628	...	...	1637	1704	1740	1743	1748	1804	...	1828	1828	|	1837	1904	1943	1943
Opava východ a.	|	...	|	|	|	|	...	...	|	|	|	|	|	|	...	|	|	|	|	1927	|	|
Ostrava hl. n. d.	1436	...	1445	1512	1550	1636	...	...	1645	1712	1747	1749	1755	1812	...	1836	1836	|	1845	...	1951	1951
Havířov d.	|	...	...	1533	|	|	...	...	...	1733	|	|	|	1835	...	|	|	|	|	...	|	|
Bohumín a.	1442	...	...	...	1557	1642	...	...	...	...	1754	1757	1801	|	...	1842	1842	|	1853	...	1957	1957
Bohumín d.	1444	...	...	...	1602	1646	...	...	...	...	1809	...	1802	|	...	...	1914	|	...	...	2007	2007
Katowice **1076** a.	|	...	...	...	|	|	...	...	...	...	1938	...	|	|	...	...	2042	|	...	...	|	|
Kraków Glowny **1076** a.	|	...	...	...	|	|	...	...	...	...	|	...	|	|	...	...	2138	|	...	...	|	|
Warszawa Centralna **1060** a.	|	...	...	...	|	|	...	...	...	...	2236	...	|	|	...	...	...	|	...	...	|	|
Karviná hl. n. d.	1453	...	...	...	1611	1655	...	...	...	...	...	...	1811	|	...	...	...	|	...	...	2016	2016
Český Těšín d.	...	...	...	...	1626	1709	...	...	...	...	...	...	1826	1855	...	...	...	|	...	...	2031	2031
Trinec centrum d.	...	...	...	...	1634	1715	...	...	...	...	...	...	1834	1901	...	...	...	|	...	...	2039	2039
Návsi d.	...	...	...	...	1641	|	...	...	...	...	...	...	1841	...	...	...	...	|	...	...	2046	2046
Čadca 🏛 a.	...	...	...	...	1658	1736	...	...	...	...	...	...	1858	...	...	...	...	|	...	...	...	2103
Žilina a.	...	...	...	...	1726	1825	...	...	...	...	...	...	1926	...	...	...	...	2029	...	...	...	2136
Banská Bystrica **1185** a.	...	...	...	...	...	|	...	...	...	...	...	...	...	...	...	...	...	...	...	...	...	...
Zvolen **1185** a.	...	...	...	...	...	|	...	...	...	...	...	...	...	...	...	...	...	...	...	...	...	...
Poprad Tatry **1180** a.	...	...	...	...	...	2016	...	...	...	...	...	...	...	...	...	...	...	...	...	...	...	...
Prešov **1196** a.	...	...	...	...	...	2126	...	...	...	...	...	...	...	...	...	...	...	...	...	...	...	...
Košice **1180** a.	...	...	...	...	...	2206	...	...	...	...	...	...	...	...	...	...	...	...	...	...	...	...

A – SILESIA – 🚃12 🍷 Praha - Warszawa and v.v.; 🚃2 Praha - Bohumín (**213/212**) - Kraków and v.v.
B – CRACOVIA – 🚃12 🍷 Praha - Przemyśl and v.v.; 🚃2 Praha - Katowice (**130/131**) - Terespol and v.v.
C – SILESIA – 🚃12 🍷 Praha - Warszawa and v.v.
D – 🚃12 🍷 Františkovy Lázně - Bohumín and v.v.
E – 🛏 (1, 2, 3, 4 berth), 🛌 (6 berth), 🚃12 🍷 Košice - Praha and v.v.
F – 🛏 (4 berth), 🚃2 🍷 Przemyśl - Praha and v.v.
G – SLOVAKIA – 🛏 1, 2 cl., 🛌 2 cl., 🚃2 Praha - Humenné and v.v.
H – CHOPIN – 🛏 1, 2 cl., 🛌 2 cl., 🚃2 Praha (**443/442**) - Bohumín - Warszawa and v.v.
J – 🚃12 🍷 Ostrava - Karlovy Vary.

d – ①–⑥ (not Apr. 8, 10, May 1, 8, July 6, Nov. 18).
e – ⑧ (not Apr. 7, 9, 30, May 7, July 5, Nov. 17).
f – ⑦ (also Apr. 10, May 1, 8; not Apr. 9, 30, May 7).
g – ④⑤⑦ (also Apr. 10, May 1, 8, July 4, Sept. 27, Oct. 25).

n – ①⑤⑥ (also Apr. 11, May 2, 9, July 5, Sept. 28, Oct. 26).
p – ①②④⑤⑥⑦.
q – ①②④⑦.
t – Warszawa **Wschodnia**.

◧ – [R] for international journeys.
⊖ – From Lichkov (Table **1165**).
♠ – Operated by LEO EXPRESS. Separate fare tariff applies.
♥ – Operated by REGIOJET. Separate fare tariff applies.
• – *SUPERCITY PENDOLINO* train, [R]; reservation fee.
● – Timings may vary by up to 3 minutes.
Δ – *439 km via Vsetin.*

Table 1160 continues on pages 486 and 487.
For local trains Ostrava - Český Těšín and v.v. see pages 486 and 487

1160 PRAHA - PÚCHOV, OSTRAVA and ŽILINA

For additional fast trains Praha - Česká Třebová and v.v. see Table **1150**. For semi-fast trains Praha - Olomouc and v.v. see Table **1151**.
SC and *IC* trains are not available for local travel Ostravá - Bohumín or v.v.

		IC	♥	*LE*♠	*EC*	*SC*•		*IC*	♥	*LE*♠	*IC*	*IC*		*IC*	*IC*	♥	*LE*♠		*SC*•	♥	♥	*EN*	**443**
		513	**1015**	**1263**	**223**	**515**		**515**	**1017**	**1265**	**549**	**549**		**589**	**517**	**1019**	**1267**		**519**	**1021**	**1023**	**443**	**406**
		🍷 R	🍷	🍷 R	🍷	🍷 R		🍷 R	🍷	🍷 R	🍷	🍷		🍷	🍷 R	🍷	🍷 R		🍷 R	🍷	🍷		
		④⑤⑦				Ⓐ		Ⓒ				Ⓑ							⑦				
		g				D		D				e							f	E	F	G	H
Praha hlavní nádraží	d.	1634	1638	1700	1715	1734	...	1734	1738	1800	1815	1815	...	1915	1934	1938	2000	...	2057	2138	2200	2213	2213
Kolín	d.	|	|	1738	1754	|	...	|	|	1838	1854	1854	...	1954	|	|	2038	...	|	|	|	2255	2255
Pardubice	d.	1731	1736	1802	1818	1831	...	1831	1836	1902	1918	1918	...	2018	2031	2036	2102	...	2151	2239	2253	2325	2325
Choceň	d.	|	|	|	|	|	...	|	|	|	|	|	...	|	|	|	|	...	|	|	|	|	|
Ústí nad Orlicí	d.	|	|	1832	|	|	...	|	|	1932	|	|	...	|	|	|	2132	...	|	|	|	|	|
Ústí nad Orlicí město	d.	|	|	|	|	|	...	|	|	|	1950	1950	...	|	|	|	|	...	|	|	|	|	|
Česká Třebová	d.	|	1815	|	1900	|	...	|	1915	|	2000	2000	...	2100	|	2115	|	...	|	|	|	0008	0008
Zábřeh na Moravě	d.	|	1840	1900	1922	|	...	|	1937	2000	2022	2022	...	2122	|	2137	2200	...	|	2341	|	|	|
Olomouc	d.	1850	1905	1922	1954	1950	...	1950	2001	2022	2045	2045	...	2154	2150	2201	2222	...	2307	0004	0015	0101	0101
Přerov	d.	|	|	1938	|	|	...	|	|	2038	|	|	...	|	|	|	2238	...	|	|	|	|	|
Hranice na Moravě	d.	|	1934	1956	2033	|	...	|	2034	2056	2113	2113	...	2226	|	2231	2256	...	|	|	|	|	|
Valašské Meziříčí	d.	|	|	|	2053	|	...	|	|	|	|	|	...	2246	|	|	|	...	|	|	|	|	|
Vsetín	d.	|	|	|	2111	|	...	|	|	|	|	|	...	2303	|	|	|	...	|	|	|	|	|
Horní Lideč 🏨	d.	|	|	|	2134	|	...	|	|	|	|	|	...	...	|	|	|	...	|	|	|	|	|
Púchov	a.	|	|	|	2156	|	...	|	|	|	|	|	...	...	|	|	|	...	|	|	|	|	|
Ostrava Svinov	d.	1938	2004	2026	|	2037	...	2037	2104	2126	2147	2147	...	...	2237	2304	2328	...	2355	0059	0111	0207	0207
Opava východ	a.	1959	|	|	|	|	...	|	|	|	|	|	...	...	|	|	|	...	|	|	|	|	|
Ostrava hl. n.	d.	...	2012	2034	|	2045	...	2045	2112	2134	2155	2155	...	...	2245	2312	2336	...	0002	0107	0118	0216	0216
Havířov	d.	...	2035	|	|	|	...	|	2135	|	|	|	...	...	|	|	|	...	|	0128	|	|	|
Bohumín	a.	...	|	2042	|	2053	...	2053	|	2142	2202	2202	...	...	2253	2318	2342	...	0010	|	0126	0224	0224
Bohumín	d.	...	|	...	|	...	...	...	|	...	...	2212	...	...	...	...	2346	...	...	|	0248	0300	0318
Katowice **1076**	a.	...	|	...	|	...	...	...	|	...	...	|	...	...	...	...	|	...	...	|	0410	|	0438
Kraków Glowny **1076**	a.	...	|	...	|	...	...	...	|	...	...	|	...	...	...	...	|	...	...	|	0509	|	0544
Warszawa Centralna **1060**	a.	...	|	...	|	...	...	...	|	...	...	|	...	...	...	...	|	...	...	|	...	...	0910t
Karviná hl. n.	d.	...	|	...	|	...	...	...	|	...	...	2221	...	...	...	...	2355	...	...	|	...	|	...
Český Těšín	d.	...	2055	...	|	...	...	...	2155	...	...	2236	...	...	...	...	0009	...	...	|	...	|	...
Trinec centrum	d.	...	2102	...	|	...	...	...	2202	...	...	2245	...	...	...	...	0015	...	...	|	...	|	...
Návsí	d.	...	2113	...	|	...	...	...	2213	...	...	2252	...	...	...	...	|	...	...	|	...	|	...
Čadca 🏨	a.	...	...	...	|	...	...	...	...	...	...	...	...	...	...	...	0036	...	...	0212	...	0351	...
Žilina	a.	...	...	...	2229	...	...	...	...	...	...	...	...	...	...	...	0100	...	...	0237	...	0417	...
Banská Bystrica **1185**	a.	...	...	...	...	...	...	...	...	...	...	...	...	...	...	...	|	...	...	|	...	|	...
Zvolen **1185**	a.	...	...	...	...	...	...	...	...	...	...	...	...	...	...	...	|	...	...	|	...	|	...
Poprad Tatry **1180**	a.	...	...	...	...	...	...	...	...	...	...	...	...	...	...	...	0254	...	...	0436	...	0635	...
Prešov **1196**	a.	...	...	...	...	...	...	...	...	...	...	...	...	...	...	...	0406	...	...	|	...	|	...
Košice **1180**	a.	...	...	...	...	...	...	...	...	...	...	...	...	...	...	...	0437	...	...	0619	...	0833	...

		♥	♥	**407**	*EN*	*LE*♠	*IC*	♥	*LE*♠	*LE*♠	*IC*	*IC*	♥	*IC*	*IC*	*IC*	♥	♥	*LE*♠	*SC*•	*IC*	*EC*	♥
		1020	**1022**	**442**	**442**	**1248**	**518**	**1000**	**1290**	**1250**	**516**	**588**	**1002**	**514**	**548**	**548**	**1004**	**1004**	**1252**	**512**	**512**	**222**	**1006**
		🍷	🍷	R	R	🍷 R	🍷 R	🍷	🍷 R	🍷 R	🍷 R	🍷	🍷	🍷 R	🍷	🍷	🍷	🍷	🍷 R	🍷 R	🍷 R	🍷	🍷
							Ⓐ	①–⑥	Ⓐ	Ⓒ				①⑤⑥		①–⑥	①–⑥	⑦		Ⓐ	Ⓒ		
		E	F	H	G				⊖					n		d				D	D		
Košice **1180**	d.	2137	...	...	2208	2238	...	...	...	...	...	...	...	...	...	...	...	...	...	...	...	...	...
Prešov **1196**	d.	|	...	...	|	2322	...	...	...	...	...	...	...	...	...	...	...	...	...	...	...	...	...
Poprad Tatry **1180**	d.	2255	...	...	2341	0037	...	...	...	...	...	...	...	...	...	...	...	...	...	...	...	...	...
Zvolen **1185**	d.	|	...	...	|	|	...	...	...	...	...	...	...	...	...	...	...	...	...	...	...	...	...
Banská Bystrica **1185**	a.	|	...	...	|	|	...	...	...	...	...	...	...	...	...	...	...	...	...	...	...	...	...
Žilina	d.	0051	...	...	0146	0230	...	...	...	...	...	...	...	...	...	...	...	...	...	...	...	0523	...
Čadca 🏨	d.	0118	...	...	0213	0254	...	...	...	...	...	...	...	...	...	...	...	...	...	...	...	|	...
Návsí	d.	|	...	...	|	|	...	...	...	...	...	...	...	...	...	0503	0542	...	...	...	...	|	0641
Trinec centrum	d.	|	...	...	|	0316	...	...	...	...	...	...	...	...	...	0510	0554	...	...	...	...	|	0653
Český Těšín	d.	|	...	...	|	0323	...	...	...	...	...	...	...	...	...	0520	0602	...	...	...	...	|	0702
Karviná hl. n.	d.	|	...	...	|	0337	...	...	...	...	...	...	...	...	...	0534	|	...	...	...	...	|	|
Warszawa Centralna **1060**	a.	|	...	1948	|	|	...	...	...	...	...	...	...	...	...	|	|	...	...	...	...	|	|
Kraków Glowny **1076**	d.	|	0003	2244	|	|	...	...	...	...	...	...	...	...	...	|	|	...	...	...	...	|	|
Katowice **1076**	d.	|	0100	2348	|	|	...	...	...	...	...	...	...	...	...	|	|	...	...	...	...	|	|
Bohumín	a.	|	0225	0128	0306	0345	...	...	...	...	...	...	...	...	...	0543	|	...	...	...	...	|	|
Bohumín	d.	|	0245	0336	0336	0349	0402	0431	...	...	0505	...	...	...	0553	0553	|	0631	0649	0705	0705	|	|
Havířov	d.	0209	|	|	|	|	|	|	...	...	|	...	...	...	|	|	0621	|	|	|	|	|	0721
Ostrava hl. n.	d.	0228	0254	0346	0346	0357	0410	0440	...	...	0513	...	...	...	0602	0602	0640	0640	0657	0713	0713	|	0740
Opava východ	d.	|	|	|	|	|	|	|	...	...	|	...	0524	0600	|	|	|	|	|	|	|	|	|
Ostrava Svinov	d.	0236	0302	0354	0354	0405	0418	0448	...	...	0521	...	0548	0622	0610	0610	0648	0648	0705	0721	0721	|	0748
Púchov	d.	|	|	|	|	|	|	|	...	...	|	...	|	|	|	|	|	|	|	|	|	0602	|
Horní Lideč 🏨	d.	|	|	|	|	|	|	|	...	...	|	...	|	|	|	|	|	|	|	|	|	0627	|
Vsetín	d.	|	|	|	|	|	|	|	...	...	|	0446	|	|	|	|	|	|	|	|	|	0647	|
Valašské Meziříčí	d.	|	|	|	|	|	|	|	...	...	|	0504	|	|	|	|	|	|	|	|	|	0704	|
Hranice na Moravě	d.	|	|	|	|	0435	0445	0514	...	...	|	0524	0614	|	0646	0646	0714	0714	0735	|	|	0731	0814
Přerov	d.	|	|	|	|	0456	|	|	...	0556	|	|	|	|	|	|	|	|	0756	|	|	|	|
Olomouc	d.	0329	0357	0452	0452	0510	0514	0545	...	0610	0614	0602	0645	0714	0719	0719	0745	0745	0810	0814	0814	0802	0845
Zábřeh na Moravě	d.	0351	|	|	|	0531	|	0611	...	0631	|	0639	0711	|	0741	0741	0811	0811	0831	|	|	0839	0911
Česká Třebová	d.	|	|	0542	0542	|	|	0635	...	|	|	0704	0735	|	0804	0804	0835	0835	|	|	|	0904	0935
Ústí nad Orlicí město	d.	|	|	|	|	|	|	|	...	|	|	|	|	|	0812	0812	|	|	|	|	|	|	|
Ústí nad Orlicí	d.	|	|	|	|	0558	|	|	0650	0658	|	|	|	|	|	|	|	|	0858	|	|	|	|
Choceň	d.	|	|	|	|	|	|	|	0705	|	|	|	|	|	|	|	|	|	|	|	|	|	|
Pardubice	d.	0450	0528	0623	0623	0628	0633	0713	0728	0728	0733	0745	0813	0833	0845	0845	0913	0913	0928	0933	0933	0945	1013
Kolín	d.	|	|	|	|	0651	|	|	0751	0751	|	0808	|	|	0908	0908	|	|	0951	|	|	1008	|
Praha hlavní nádraží	a.	0557	0629	0738	0738	0731	0734	0808	0831	0831	0834	0848	0908	0929	0948	0948	1008	1008	1031	1034	1034	1045	1108

CONTINUED FROM PREVIOUS PAGE. FOR FOOTNOTES SEE PAGE 485. TABLE CONTINUES ON NEXT PAGE.

1160a OSTRAVA - ČESKÝ TĚŠÍN LOCAL TRAINS

		Ⓐ	Ⓐ	Ⓐ	Ⓐ	Ⓐ	Ⓐ	Ⓐ	Ⓐ	Ⓐ	Ⓐ			2	2	2		2	2	2	2	2
Opava východ	d.	0515	0615	0711	0824	1024	1224	1424	1624	1824	2024	...	ALSO	0630	0742	0842	and at the same minutes past each hour until ●	1842	1943	2042	2142	2245
Ostrava Svinov	a.	0537	0641	0734	0848	1048	1248	1448	1648	1848	2048	...		0700	0814	0914		1912	2017	2112	2212	2315
		|	|	|	|	|	|	|	|	|	...	...										
Ostrava Svinov	d.	0550	0652	0741	0853	1053	1253	1453	1653	1853	...	...		0724	0824	0924		1924	2024	2124	2224	2324
Ostrava hl. n.	d.	0600	0700	0800	0900	1100	1300	1500	1700	1900	...	...		|	|	|		|	|	|	|	|
Havířov	d.	0620	0723	0822	0923	1123	1323	1523	1723	1923	...	...		0752	0852	0952		1952	2052	2152	2252	2351
Český Těšín	a.	0641	0744	...	0945	1144	1344	1544	1744	1944	...	...		0814	0914	1014		2014	2114	2214	2314	...

Ostrava Svinov	d.	0534	0634	0734	...	0834	0934	1034	...	1134	1234	1334	...	1434	1534	1634	...	1734	1834	1934	...	2035	2135	2235
Ostrava hl. n.	d.	0542	0642	0742	...	0842	0942	1042	...	1142	1242	1342	...	1442	1542	1642	...	1742	1842	1942	...	2042	2142	2242
Bohumín	d.	0549	0649	0749	...	0849	0949	1049	...	1149	1249	1349	...	1449	1549	1649	...	1749	1849	1949	...	2049	2149	2257
Karviná hl. n.	d.	0601	0701	0801	...	0901	1001	1101	...	1201	1301	1401	...	1501	1601	1701	...	1801	1901	2001	...	2101	2201	2309
Český Těšín	d.	0618	0718	0818	...	0918	1018	1118	...	1218	1318	1418	...	1519	1618	1718	...	1818	1918	2018	...	2118	2218	2326
Trinec centrum	d.	0629	0729	0829	...	0929	1029	1129	...	1229	1329	1430	...	1530	1629	1729	...	1829	1929	2029	...	2129	2229	2337
Návsí	a.	0647	0742	0846	...	0942	1046	1142	...	1246	1342	1446	...	1543	1646	1742	...	1846	1942	2042	...	2142	2241	2349

ŽILINA, OSTRAVA and PÚCHOV - PRAHA 1160

For additional fast trains Praha - Česká Třebová and v.v. see Table **1150**. For semi-fast trains Praha - Olomouc and v.v. see Table **1151**.
SC and *IC* trains are not available for local travel Ostravá - Bohumín or v.v.

	EC 144 🍷	*EC* 144 🍷 ①–⑥ d	♥ 1008 🍷	*LE*♠ 412 🍷R	*LE*♠ 412 🍷R ①⑤⑥	*SC*• 510 🍷R	*EC* 220 🍷	348 🍷	*EC* 116 🍷 C◨	♥ 1010 🍷	♥ 1010 🍷 ⑦		*LE*♠ 1256 R🍷	*EC* 128 🍷	*EC* 142 🍷	♥ 1012 🍷	*LE*♠ 1260 🍷R	*IC* 506 🍷R	*EC* 126 🍷	*LE*♠ 1262 🍷R	346 🍷	*EC* 131 114 B◨
Košice **1180** d.	...	...	...	...	...	...	...	...	...	...	...	...	0450	...	...	0753	...	...	...	...	...	...
Prešov **1196** d.	...	...	...	...	...	...	...	...	...	...	...	...	0550	...	...	|	...	...	...	...	...	...
Poprad Tatry **1180** d.	...	...	...	...	...	...	...	...	...	...	...	...	0707	...	...	0911	...	...	...	...	...	...
Zvolen **1185** d.	...	...	...	...	...	...	...	...	...	...	...	...	|	...	...	|	...	...	...	...	...	...
Banská Bystrica **1185** a.	...	...	...	...	...	...	...	...	...	...	...	...	|	...	...	|	...	...	...	...	...	...
Žilina d.	...	0633	...	...	...	...	0720	0834	...	...	...	...	0902	...	1034	1105	...	...	...	...	1234	...
Čadca 🏛 d.	...	0700	...	...	...	...	|	0902	...	...	...	...	0925	...	1102	1130	...	...	...	...	1302	...
Návsi d.	0717	0717	0745	...	...	...	|	0919	...	...	0943	...	|	...	1119	|	...	...	...	...	1319	...
Třinec centrum d.	0724	0724	0753	...	...	...	|	0926	...	...	0954	...	0947	...	1126	1153	...	...	...	...	1326	...
Český Těšín d.	0732	0732	0802	...	...	...	|	0934	...	...	1002	...	0954	...	1134	1202	...	...	...	...	1334	...
Karviná hl. n. d.	0746	0746	|	...	...	...	|	0948	...	...	|	...	1008	...	1148	|	1238	...	...	...	1348	...
Warszawa Centralna **1060** a.	|	|	|	...	...	...	|	|	0535	...	|	...	|	...	|	|	|	...	...	...	|	0844
Kraków Glowny **1076** d.	|	|	|	...	0559	...	|	|	|	...	|	...	|	...	|	|	|	...	...	...	|	|
Katowice **1076** d.	|	|	|	...	0706	...	|	|	0818	...	|	...	|	...	|	|	|	...	...	...	|	1128
Bohumín a.	0755	0755	|	...	0833	...	|	0957	0943	...	|	...	1017	...	1157	|	1247	...	...	...	1357	1305
Bohumín d.	0805	0805	|	0849	0849	0905	|	0958	1005	...	|	...	1049	...	1205	|	1249	...	...	1349	1358	1405
Havířov d.	|	|	0821	|	|	|	|	|	|	1021	1021	...	|	...	|	1221	|	...	...	|	|	|
Ostrava hl. n. d.	0814	0814	0840	0857	0857	0913	|	1004	1014	1040	1040	...	1057	...	1214	1240	1257	1313	...	1357	1404	1414
Opava východ d.	|	|	|	|	|	|	|	|	|	|	|	...	|	...	|	|	|	|	...	|	|	|
Ostrava Svinov d.	0822	0822	0848	0905	0905	0921	|	1011	1022	1048	1048	...	1105	...	1222	1248	1305	1321	...	1405	1411	1422
Púchov d.	|	|	|	|	|	|	0808	...	|	|	|	...	|	1008	|	|	|	|	1208	|	...	|
Horní Lideč 🏛 d.	|	|	|	|	|	|	0833	...	|	|	|	...	|	1033	|	|	|	|	1233	|	...	|
Vsetín d.	|	|	|	|	|	|	0853	...	|	|	|	...	|	1053	|	|	|	|	1253	|	...	|
Valašské Meziříčí d.	|	|	|	|	|	|	0911	...	|	|	|	...	|	1111	|	|	|	|	1311	|	...	|
Hranice na Moravě d.	0848	0848	0914	0935	0935	|	0931	...	1048	1114	1114	...	1136	1131	1248	1314	1335	|	1331	1436	...	1448
Přerov d.	|	|	|	0956	0956	|	|	...	|	|	|	...	1156	|	|	|	1356	|	|	1456	...	|
Olomouc d.	0919	0919	0945	1010	1010	1014	1002	...	1119	1145	1145	...	1210	1202	1319	1345	1410	1414	1402	1510	...	1519
Zábřeh na Moravé d.	0941	0941	1011	1031	1031	|	1039	...	1141	1211	1211	...	1231	1239	1341	1411	1431	|	1439	1531	...	1541
Česká Třebová d.	1004	1004	1035	|	|	|	1104	...	1204	1235	1235	...	|	1304	1404	1435	|	|	1504	|	...	1604
Ústí nad Orlicí město d.	1012	1012	|	|	|	|	|	...	1212	|	|	...	|	|	1412	|	|	|	|	|	...	1612
Ústí nad Orlicí d.	|	|	|	1058	1058	|	|	...	|	|	|	...	1258	|	|	|	1458	|	|	1558	...	|
Choceň d.	|	|	|	|	|	|	|	...	|	|	|	...	|	|	|	|	|	|	|	|	...	|
Pardubice d.	1045	1045	1113	1128	1128	1133	1145	...	1245	1313	1313	...	1328	1345	1445	1513	1528	1533	1545	1628	...	1645
Kolín d.	1108	1108	|	1151	1151	|	1208	...	1308	|	|	...	1351	1408	1508	|	1551	|	1608	1651	...	1708
Praha hlavní nádraží a.	1145	1145	1208	1231	1231	1234	1245	...	1345	1408	1408	...	1431	1448	1548	1608	1631	1634	1648	1731	...	1748

	EC 114 🍷 B◨	♥ 1014 🍷	*SC*• 504 🍷R J	*EC* 124 🍷	*LE*♠ 1264 🍷R	*SC*• 502 🍷R ⑦ f	*EC* 140 🍷	♥ 1016 🍷	*SC*• 500 🍷R ④⑤⑦ g	*EC* 122 🍷	344 🍷	*EC* 212 112 A◨	*EC* 112 🍷 A◨	♥ 1018 🍷		*SC*• 240 🍷R	*EC* 120 🍷	342 🍷	*LE*♠ 1268 🍷R p	*LE*♠ 1268 🍷R q	340 🍷	*LE*♠ 1246 🍷R ③
Košice **1180** d.	...	...	...	...	...	...	...	...	...	...	...	...	...	...	...	1418	...	...	...	...	...	...
Prešov **1196** d.	...	...	...	...	...	...	...	...	...	...	...	...	...	...	...	|	...	...	...	...	...	...
Poprad Tatry **1180** d.	...	...	...	...	...	...	...	...	...	...	...	...	...	...	...	1529	...	...	...	...	...	...
Zvolen **1185** d.	...	...	...	...	...	...	...	...	...	...	...	...	...	...	...	|	...	...	...	...	...	...
Banská Bystrica **1185** a.	...	...	...	...	...	...	...	...	...	...	...	...	...	...	...	|	...	...	...	...	...	...
Žilina d.	...	...	...	...	...	...	1434	...	...	...	1634	...	...	...	...	1732	...	1834	...	...	2034	...
Čadca 🏛 d.	...	...	...	...	...	...	1502	...	...	...	1702	...	...	...	...	1758	...	1902	...	...	2103	...
Návsi d.	...	...	...	...	...	...	1519	...	...	...	1719	...	...	...	...	|	...	1919	...	...	2121	...
Třinec centrum d.	...	...	...	...	...	...	1526	...	...	...	1726	...	...	...	...	|	...	1926	...	...	2128	...
Český Těšín d.	...	...	...	...	...	...	1534	...	...	...	1734	...	...	...	...	1824	...	1934	...	...	2136	...
Karviná hl. n. d.	...	...	...	...	1538	...	1548	...	...	...	1748	...	...	...	...	|	...	1948	...	...	2150	...
Warszawa Centralna **1060** a.	...	...	...	...	|	...	|	...	...	...	|	...	1343	...	...	|	...	|	...	...	|	...
Kraków Glowny **1076** d.	1043	...	...	...	|	...	|	...	...	...	|	1442	|	...	...	|	...	|	...	...	|	...
Katowice **1076** d.	1141	...	...	...	|	...	|	...	...	...	|	1549	1623	...	...	|	...	|	...	...	|	...
Bohumín a.	1313	...	...	...	1547	...	1557	...	...	...	1757	1735	1748	...	...	|	...	1957	...	...	2159	...
Bohumín d.	1405	...	...	...	1549	...	1605	...	...	...	1758	1805	1805	...	...	|	...	1958	2106	2106	2201	2206
Havířov d.	|	1421	...	...	|	...	|	1621	...	...	|	|	|	1821	...	|	...	|	|	|	|	|
Ostrava hl. n. d.	1414	1440	1513	...	1557	...	1614	1640	1713	...	1804	1814	1814	1840	...	1913	...	2004	2114	2114	2207	2214
Opava východ d.	|	|	|	...	|	1555	|	|	|	...	|	|	|	|	...	|	...	|	|	|	|	|
Ostrava Svinov d.	1422	1448	1521	...	1605	1622	1622	1648	1721	...	1811	1822	1822	1848	...	1921	...	2011	2222	2222	2215	2222
Púchov d.	|	|	|	1408	|	|	|	|	|	1608	...	|	|	|	...	|	1808	...	|	|	...	|
Horní Lideč 🏛 d.	|	|	|	1433	|	|	|	|	|	1633	...	|	|	|	...	|	1833	...	|	|	...	|
Vsetín d.	|	|	|	1453	|	|	|	|	|	1653	...	|	|	|	...	|	1853	...	|	|	...	|
Valašské Meziříčí d.	|	|	|	1511	|	|	|	|	|	1711	...	|	|	|	...	|	1911	...	|	|	...	|
Hranice na Moravě d.	1448	1514	|	1531	1635	|	1648	1714	|	1731	...	1848	1848	1914	...	|	1931	...	2153	2153	...	2253
Přerov d.	|	|	|	|	1656	|	|	|	|	|	...	|	|	|	...	|	|	...	2214	2214	...	2314
Olomouc d.	1519	1545	1614	1602	1710	1714	1719	1745	1814	1802	...	1919	1919	1945	...	2014	2002	...	2226	2228	...	2328
Zábřeh na Moravé d.	1541	1611	|	1639	1731	|	1741	1811	|	1839	...	1941	1941	2011	...	|	2039	...	...	2249	...	2349
Česká Třebová d.	1604	1635	|	1704	|	|	1804	1835	|	1904	...	2004	2004	2035	...	2057	2104	...	...	2309	...	0009
Ústí nad Orlicí město d.	1612	|	|	|	|	|	1812	|	|	|	...	2012	2012	|	...	|	|	...	...	...	...	...
Ústí nad Orlicí d.	|	|	|	|	1758	|	|	|	|	|	...	|	|	|	...	|	2113	...	...	...	...	...
Choceň d.	|	|	|	|	|	|	|	|	|	|	...	|	|	|	...	|	2125	...	...	...	...	...
Pardubice d.	1645	1713	1733	1745	1828	1833	1845	1913	1933	1945	...	2045	2045	2113	...	2133	2145	...	...	...	...	...
Kolín d.	1708	|	|	1808	1851	|	1908	|	|	2008	...	2108	2108	|	...	2154	2210	...	...	...	...	...
Praha hlavní nádraží a.	1748	1808	1834	1848	1931	1934	1948	2008	2034	2045	...	2145	2145	2208	...	2231	2246	...	...	...	...	...

CONTINUED FROM PREVIOUS PAGES. FOR FOOTNOTES SEE PAGE 485.

ČESKÝ TĚŠÍN - OSTRAVA LOCAL TRAINS 1160a

	Ⓐ	Ⓐ	Ⓐ	Ⓐ	Ⓐ		Ⓐ	Ⓐ	Ⓐ	Ⓐ			2	2	2		2	2	2	2	2
Český Těšín d.	0512	0613	0713	0811	1011	...	1211	1409	1613	1811	...		0445	0545	0645	and at	1845	1945	2045	2200	2245
Havířov d.	0535	0636	0735	0836	1036	...	1236	1436	1636	1836	...	A	0508	0608	0708	the same	1908	2008	2108	2223	2308
Ostrava hl. n. a.	0557	0657	0757	0857	1057	...	1257	1457	1657	1857	...	L	|	|	|	minutes	|	|	|	|	|
Ostrava Svinov a.	0604	0707	...	0907	1107	...	1307	1508	1706	1908	...	S	0533	0633	0733	past each	1933	2033	2133	2247	2333
	|	|		|	|		|	|	|	|		O				hour until					
Ostrava Svinov d.	0613	0713	...	0913	1113	...	1313	1513	1713	1913	...		0538	0644	0741	●	1944	2041	2156	2259	2337
Opava východ a.	0647	0736	...	0936	1136	...	1336	1536	1736	1936	...		0609	0719	0814		2018	2113	2227	2330	0012

		Ⓐ																					
Návsi d.	0453	0515	0615	0719	0819	...	0915	1019	1115	1219	1315	...	1419	1515	1619	1715	1819	...	1915	2019	2117	2219	...
Třinec centrum d.	0504	0526	0626	0731	0830	...	0930	1030	1130	1230	1330	...	1430	1530	1630	1730	1830	...	1930	2030	2132	2230	...
Český Těšín d.	0525	0540	0640	0742	0842	...	0942	1042	1142	1242	1342	...	1442	1542	1642	1742	1842	...	1942	2042	2143	2242	...
Karviná hl. n. d.	0543	0558	0658	0800	0900	...	1000	1100	1200	1300	1400	...	1500	1600	1700	1800	1900	...	2000	2100	2201	2300	...
Bohumín d.	0557	0611	0711	0813	0913	...	1013	1113	1213	1313	1413	...	1513	1613	1713	1813	1913	...	2013	2113	2214	2313	...
Ostrava hl. n. a.	0603	0617	0717	0819	0919	...	1019	1119	1219	1319	1419	...	1519	1619	1719	1819	1919	...	2019	2119	2220	2319	...
Ostrava Svinov a.	0611	0625	0724	0826	0926	...	1026	1126	1226	1326	1426	...	1526	1626	1726	1826	1926	...	2026	2126	2227	2326	...

1162 PRAHA - UHERSKÉ HRADIŠTĚ - BŘECLAV - BRATISLAVA, BRNO and WIEN

For faster trains Praha - Bratislava and v.v. see Table **1150**.

km		457 A	2 d	2 Ⓐ	828 🍷 Ⓐ	2	2 Ⓐ	826 836	2	824 🍷 d	881 🍷 d	814 🍷	EC 101 B§	883 🍷 d	883 🍷	2	812 🍷	885 🍷	2	♠ 97801	810 🍷	EC 103 C§	887 🍷	2	2 Ⓐ
	Praha hl. n. **1151 1160** d.	...	...	...	...	...	...	...	...	...	...	...	...	0503	...	...	...	0703	...	...	...	...	0903	...	...
	Ostrava hl. n. **1164** d.	0224	...	...	...	...	...	...	...	...	...	...	0651	|	...	...	...	|	...	...	...	1051	|	...	...
0	**Olomouc** **1160** d.	|	...	...	...	...	...	...	...	...	0557	0709	|	0732	0732	...	0909	0932	...	...	1109	|	1132	...	...
22	Přerov **1160** d.	|	0357	0357	...	0444	0444	...	0542	...	0612	0724	0745	0748	0748	0738	0924	0948	0941	1040	1124	1145	1148	1138	1244
37	Hulín d.	|	0407	0407	...	0500	0500	...	0557	...	0622	0734	|	0758	0758	0800	0934	0958	1000	1053	1134	|	1158	1200	1300
50	Otrokovice ▷ d.	|	0417	0417	...	0513	0513	...	0611	...	0632	0743	0804	0808	0808	0813	0943	1008	1013	1104	1143	1204	1208	1213	1313
68	Staré Město U.H. ⊖ a.	|	0427	0427	...	0529	0529	...	0626	...	0645	0755	0816	0820	0820	0829	0955	1020	1029	1116	1155	1216	1220	1229	1329
68	Staré Město U.H. ⊖ **1163** d.	|	...	0432	...	...	0537	...	0637	...	0656	0757	0817	0833	0833	0837	0957	1033	1037	...	1157	1217	1233	1237	1337
73	Uherské Hradiště **1163** a.	|	...	|	...	...	|	...	|	...	0702	|	|	0839	0839	|	|	1039	|	...	|	|	1239	|	|
90	Uherský Brod **1163** a.	|	...	|	...	...	|	...	|	...	0721	|	|	0856	0856	|	|	1056	|	...	|	|	1256	|	|
104	**Luhačovice** **1163** a.	|	...	|	...	...	|	...	|	...	0740	|	|	0920	0920	|	|	1120	|	...	|	|	1320	|	|
102	Hodonin d.	|	...	0508	0524	...	0608	0619	0708	0724	...	0823	0834	...	...	0908	1023	...	1108	...	1223	1234	...	1308	1408
122	Břeclav a.	0410	...	0525	0536	...	0625	0634	0725	0736	...	0835	0845	...	...	0925	1035	...	1125	...	1235	1245	...	1325	1425
122	Břeclav **1150** d.	0549	...	...	0542	...	...	0642	...	0742	...	0844	0855	...	...	...	1044	...	...	...	1244	1255	...	...	...
140	Kúty 🏛 **1150** a.	|	...	...	|	...	...	|	...	|	...	|	|	...	...	...	|	...	...	...	|	|	...	...	...
204	**Bratislava** hl. st. **1150** a.	|	...	...	|	...	...	|	...	|	...	|	|	...	...	...	|	...	...	...	|	|	...	...	...
181	**Brno** hlavní nádrazi **1150** a.	|	...	...	0622	...	...	0722	...	0822	...	0922	|	...	...	...	1122	...	...	...	1322	|	...	...	...
210	**Wien** Hbf **1150** a.	0700	...	...	...	...	...	...	...	...	...	...	0949	...	...	...	...	...	...	...	...	1349	...	...	...

	808 🍷	889 🍷	2	♠ 97803 k	EC 131 D§	2 Ⓐ	806 🍷	891 🍷	2	820 🍷 Ⓐ	804 🍷	EC 105 E§	893 🍷	2	2	802 🍷	EC 107 F§	895 🍷	2	♠ 97805	800 Ⓑe	897 🍷	2	2
Praha hl. n. **1160** d.	...	1103	...	...	...	...	...	1303	...	...	...	...	1503	...	...	...	...	1703	...	...	...	1903	...	...
Ostrava hl. n. **1164** d.	...	|	...	...	1351	...	...	|	...	...	...	1651	|	...	...	...	1851	|	...	...	...	|	...	...
Olomouc **1160** d.	1309	1332	...	...	|	...	1509	1532	...	...	1709	|	1732	...	...	1909	|	1932	...	...	2109	2132	...	...
Přerov **1160** d.	1324	1348	1341	1353	1445	1438	1524	1548	1541	...	1724	1745	1748	1738	1910	1924	1945	1948	...	2043	2124	2148	...	2243
Hulín d.	1334	1358	1400	1406	|	1500	1534	1558	1600	...	1734	|	1758	1800	1929	1934	|	1958	←	2056	2134	2158	...	2259
Otrokovice ▷ d.	1343	1408	1413	1417	1504	1513	1543	1608	1613	...	1743	1804	1808	1813	1939	1943	2004	2008	2016	2106	2143	2206	2213	2323
Staré Město U.H. ⊖ a.	1355	1420	1429	1431	1516	1529	1555	1620	1629	...	1755	1816	1820	1829	→	1955	2016	2020	2032	2119	2155	|	2229	2344
Staré Město U.H. ⊖ **1163** d.	1357	1433	1437	▬	1517	1537	1557	1633	1637	...	1757	1817	1833	1837	...	1957	2017	2034	2037	...	2157	h	...	...
Uherské Hradiště **1163** a.	|	1439	|	**822**	|	|	|	1639	|	...	|	|	1839	|	...	|	|	2040	|	...	|	...	...	...
Uherský Brod **1163** a.	|	1456	|	🍷	|	|	|	1656	|	...	|	|	1901	|	...	|	|	|	|	...	|	...	...	...
Luhačovice **1163** a.	|	1520	|	Ⓐ	|	|	|	1720	|	...	|	|	1922	|	...	|	|	g	|	...	|	...	...	...
Hodonin d.	1423	...	1508	1524	1534	1608	1623	...	1708	1724	1823	1834	...	1908	...	2023	2034	...	2108	...	2217	...	...	...
Břeclav a.	1435	...	1525	1536	1545	1625	1635	...	1725	1736	1835	1845	...	1925	...	2035	2045	...	2125	...	2229	...	...	...
Břeclav **1150** d.	1444	...	...	1542	*1555*	...	1644	...	...	1742	1844	1855	...	...	...	2044	2055	...	...	...	...	...	...	...
Kúty 🏛 **1150** a.	|	...	...	|	|	...	|	...	...	|	|	|	...	...	...	|	|	...	...	...	...	...	...	...
Bratislava hl. st. **1150** a.	|	...	...	|	|	...	|	...	...	|	|	|	...	...	...	|	|	...	...	...	...	...	...	...
Brno hlavní nádrazi **1150** a.	1522	...	...	1622	|	...	1722	...	...	1822	1922	|	...	...	...	2122	|	...	...	...	...	...	...	...
Wien Hbf **1150** a.	...	...	...	...	*1649*	...	...	...	...	...	...	1949	...	...	...	...	2149	...	...	...	...	...	...	...

	896 d	894	2	801 🍷 d	2	2 Ⓐ	892	2	EC 106 F§	803 🍷	♠ 97800	2	890 🍷	890 🍷 d	EC 104 E§	805 🍷	2	888 🍷	807 🍷	EC 130 D§	2 Ⓐ	♠ 97800 k	2	886 🍷
Wien Hbf **1150** d.	...	...	...	...	...	...	...	...	0610	...	...	...	...	...	0810	...	...	...	...	*1110*	...	...	...	...
Brno hlavní nádrazi **1150** d.	...	...	...	...	...	...	...	...	|	0636	...	...	...	...	|	0836	...	...	1036	|	...	...	...	...
Bratislava hl. st. **1150** d.	...	...	...	...	...	...	...	...	|	|	...	...	...	...	|	|	...	...	|	|	...	...	...	...
Kúty 🏛 **1150** d.	...	...	...	...	...	...	...	...	|	|	...	...	...	...	|	|	...	...	|	|	...	...	...	...
Břeclav **1150** a.	...	...	...	...	...	...	...	...	0704	0715	...	...	...	...	0904	0915	...	...	1115	*1204*	...	...	...	...
Břeclav d.	...	...	0434**a**	0525	...	0535	...	0635	0710	0721	...	0835	...	...	0910	0921	1035	...	1121	1210	...	...	1235	...
Hodonin d.	...	...	0453**a**	0538	...	0554	...	0654	0722	0738	...	0854	...	...	0922	0938	1054	...	1138	1222	...	...	1254	...
Luhačovice **1163** d.	...	...	|	|	...	|	g	|	|	|	...	|	...	0831	|	|	|	1031	|	|	...	...	|	1231
Uherský Brod **1163** d.	...	...	|	|	...	|	|	|	|	|	...	|	...	0857	|	|	|	1057	|	|	...	...	|	1257
Uherské Hradiště **1163** d.	...	...	|	|	...	|	0714	|	|	|	...	|	...	0914	|	|	|	1114	|	|	...	...	|	1314
Staré Město U.H. ⊖ **1163** a.	...	**j**	0523**a**	0556	...	0624	0720	0724	0737	0756	...	0924	...	0920	0937	0956	1124	1120	1156	1237	...	...	1324	1320
Staré Město U.H. ⊖ d.	0413	|	0524**d**	0558	0626	0626	0733	0725	0738	0758	0916	0925	0933	0933	0938	0958	1125	1133	1158	1238	1226	1312	1325	1333
Otrokovice ▷ d.	0427	0546	0542**d**	0614	0644	0644	0747	0744	0752	0814	0927	0944	0947	0947	0952	1014	1144	1147	1214	1252	1244	1325	1344	1347
Hulín d.	0440	0600	0602**d**	0628	0659	0659	0800	0805	|	0828	0938	1005	1000	1000	|	1028	1205	1200	1228	|	1305	1335	1405	1400
Přerov **1160** d.	0451	0612	0616**d**	0639	0713	0713	0812	0819	0813	0839	0949	1019	1012	1012	1013	1039	1219	1212	1239	1313	1319	1346	1419	1412
Olomouc **1160** a.	0504	0625	...	0652	...	...	0825	...	|	0852	...	...	1025	1025	|	1052	...	1225	1252	|	...	...	...	1425
Ostrava hl. n. **1164** a.	|	|	...	...	...	...	|	...	0906	...	...	...	|	|	1106	...	...	|	...	1406	...	...	...	|
Praha hl. n. **1160** a.	0748	0905	...	...	...	...	1105	...	...	...	...	...	1305	1305	...	...	...	1505	...	...	...	...	...	1705

	809 🍷	2 Ⓐ	823 🍷 Ⓐ	2	884 🍷	EC 102 C§	811 🍷	2 Ⓐ	825 🍷 Ⓐ	2	882 🍷	813 🍷	880 🍷	827 Ⓐ	2	EC 100 B§	♠ 97804	815 🍷	858	829 🍷 Ⓑe	2	831 833	835 837	456 A
Wien Hbf **1150** d.	...	...	...	...	...	1410	...	...	...	...	...	...	...	...	...	1810	...	...	...	...	...	...	...	2210
Brno hlavní nádrazi **1150** d.	1236	...	1336	...	...	|	1436	...	1534	...	...	1636	...	1736	...	|	...	1836	...	1936	...	2036	2236	|
Bratislava hl. st. **1150** d.	|	...	|	...	...	|	|	...	|	...	...	|	...	|	...	|	...	|	...	|	...	|	|	|
Kúty 🏛 **1150** d.	|	...	|	...	...	|	|	...	|	...	...	|	...	|	...	|	...	|	...	|	...	|	|	|
Břeclav **1150** a.	1315	...	1415	...	...	1504	1515	...	1615	...	...	1715	...	1815	...	1904	...	1915	...	2015	...	2117	2315	2307
Břeclav d.	1321	1335	1421	1435	...	1510	1521	1535	1621	1635	...	1721	...	1821	1835	1910	...	1921	...	2021	2035	2125	2322	2350
Hodonin d.	1338	1354	1433	1454	...	1522	1538	1554	1633	1654	...	1738	...	1833	1854	1922	...	1938	...	2033	2054	2140	2337	|
Luhačovice **1163** d.	|	|	...	|	1431	|	|	|	...	|	1631	|	1803	...	|	|	...	|	1942	...	|	|	...	|
Uherský Brod **1163** d.	|	|	...	|	1457	|	|	|	...	|	1657	|	1827	...	|	|	...	|	2001	...	|	|	...	|
Uherské Hradiště **1163** d.	|	|	...	|	1514	|	|	|	...	|	1714	|	1847	...	|	|	...	|	2019	...	|	|	...	|
Staré Město U.H. ⊖ **1163** a.	1356	1424	...	1524	1520	1537	1556	1624	...	1724	1720	1756	1853	...	1924	1937	...	1956	2025	...	2124	*2217*	...	|
Staré Město U.H. ⊖ d.	1358	1426	...	1525	1533	1538	1558	1626	...	1725	1733	1758	1906	...	1925	1938	1948	1958	...	...	2125	*2218*	...	|
Otrokovice ▷ d.	1414	1444	...	1544	1547	1552	1614	1644	...	1744	1747	1814	1920	...	1944	1952	2000	2014	...	...	2140	*2241*	...	|
Hulín d.	1428	1500	...	1605	1600	|	1628	1700	...	1802	1800	1828	1933	...	2005	|	2011	2028	...	...	*2158*	*2258*	...	|
Přerov **1160** d.	1439	1514	...	1619	1612	1613	1639	1714	...	1816	1812	1839	1944	...	2019	2013	2022	2039	...	...	*2215*	*2314*	...	|
Olomouc **1160** a.	1452	...	...	...	1625	|	1652	...	...	...	1825	1852	1957	...	...	|	...	2052	...	...	...	...	...	|
Ostrava hl. n. **1164** a.	...	...	...	...	|	1706	...	...	...	...	|	...	...	...	...	2106	...	...	...	...	...	...	...	0131
Praha hl. n. **1160** a.	...	...	...	...	1905	...	...	...	...	...	2105	...	...	...	...	...	...	...	...	...	...	...	...	...

A – NIGHTJET – 🛏 1, 2 cl., 🛏 2 cl., (2) Berlin - Graz and v.v.; 🛏 1, 2 cl., 🛏 2 cl., (2) Berlin (**457/6**) - Břeclav (**477/6**) - Budapest and v.v.; 🛏 1, 2 cl., 🛏 2 cl., (2) Warszawa (**407/6**) - Bohumín (**457/6**) - Graz and v.v.; 🛏 1, 2 cl., 🛏 2 cl., (2) Warszawa (**407/6**) - Bohumín (**457/6**) - Břeclav (**477/6**) - Budapest and v.v. Ⓡ for international journeys.
B – MORAVIA – (12) ✕ Katowice - Wien and v.v.
C – POLONIA – (12) ✕ Warszawa - Wien and v.v.
D – BATHORY – (12) ✕ Budapest - Terespol and v.v.; (2) Praha (**115/114**) - Bohumín - Terespol and v.v.; (2) Budapest - Bohumín (**115/114**) - Przemyśl and v.v.
E – PORTA MORAVICA – (12) Przemyśl - Graz and v.v.; ✕ Graz - Bohumín and v.v.
F – SOBIESKI – (12) ✕ Gdynia - Wien and v.v.

a – Ⓐ only.
d – ①-⑥ (not Apr. 8, 10, May 1, 8, July 6, Nov. 18).
e – Ⓑ (not Apr. 7, 9, 30, May 7, July 5, Nov. 17).
g – To / from Veseli nad Moravou (Table **1163**).
h – To Zlín střed (Otrokovice d. 2216, Zlín střed a. 2229).
j – From Zlín střed (d. 0522).
k – ①⑤⑥⑦.

♠ – Operated by LEO EXPRESS. Separate fare tariff applies.
⊖ – Full name : Staré Město u Uherské Hradiště.
▷ – Local trains Otrokovice - Zlín: 1–2 per hour (trolleybus every 10 mins).
§ – Ⓡ for international journeys to / from Poland.

2nd class BRNO - UHERSKÉ HRADIŠTĚ - BYLNICE and LUHAČOVICE 1163

BRNO - STARÉ MĚSTO U UHERSKÉ HRADIŠTĚ — ČD

km																								
		A	⑥d	Ⓒ	Ⓐ	Ⓐ	Ⓒ										B							
0	Brno hlavní nádrazi d.	...	0517	...	...	0612	0620	0735	0812	0928	1015	1128	1215	1328	1414	1528	1614	1728	1815	1928	2015	...	2128	...
67	Kyjov d.	...	0632	0632	0638	0738	0738	0834	0938	1032	1138	1232	1338	1432	1538	1632	1738	1832	1938	2032	2138	...	2232	...
90	Veselí nad Moravou d.	0700	0706	0706	0706	0806	0804	0900	1006	1100	1206	1300	1406	1500	1606	1700	1806	1900	2006	2100	2204	2209	2258	...
106	Uherské Hradiště 1162 a.	0712	0725	0725	0725	0827	*0827*	0918	1027	1118	1227	1318	1427	1518	1627	1718	1827	1924	2027	2118	...	2225	...	...
111	Staré Město u Uh. H ⊖ 1162 a.	0720	0733	0733	0733	...	...	0926	...	1126	...	1326	...	1526	...	1726	1846	1932	...	2126	...	2232	...	...

	Ⓐ		Ⓒ	Ⓐ		C														A			
Staré Město u Uh. H ⊖ 1162 d.	...	0431	...	...	...	...	...	0827	...	1027	...	1227	...	1427	...	1627	...	1807	...	2034	...	2138	...
Uherské Hradiště 1162 d.	...	0440	...	...	0534	0630	0735	0837	0935	1037	1135	1237	1335	1437	1535	1637	1735	1837	2036	2045	←	2145	...
Veselí nad Moravou d.	0445	0458	0500	0525	0601	0701	0757	0851	0957	1101	1157	1301	1357	1501	1557	1701	1757	1901	2054	2058	2101	2204	...
Kyjov d.	0513	...	0526	0555	0628	0728	0825	0928	1025	1128	1225	1328	1425	1528	1625	1728	1825	1928	→	...	2128	...	...
Brno hlavní nádrazí a.	0633	...	0650	0720	0733	0833	0948	1033	1148	1233	1348	1433	1548	1633	1748	1833	1948	2033	...	...	2233	...	...

STARÉ MĚSTO U UHERSKÉ HRADIŠTĚ - UHERSKÝ BROD - BYLNICE - VLÁRSKÝ PRŮSMYK — Arriva

km																								
					Ⓐ		Ⓒ	Ⓐh												Ⓐ				
0	Staré Město u Uh. H ⊖ 1162 d.	*0431*	0536	...	0536	0629	0629	...	0733	...	0935	...	...	...	1135	...	...	1339	...	1359	...	1539	...	1559
5	Uherské Hradiště 1162 d.	0444	0544	...	0544	0636	0636	...	0747	0829	0943	...	...	1029	1143	...	1229	1346	...	1409	1429	1546	...	1609
7	Kunovice d.	0447	0548	...	0547	0639	0639	...	0751	0832	0946	...	...	1032	1146	...	1232	1350	...	|	1432	1550	...	|
22	Uherský Brod 1162 d.	0513	0606	...	0606	0700	0700	0705	0808	0853	1006	...	...	1053	1206	...	1253	1410	...	1425	1454	1610	...	1625
26	Újezdec u Luhačovic a.	0517	0609	...	0609	0703	0704	0709	0812	0856	1009	...	...	1056	1209	...	1256	1413	...	|	1457	1614	...	|
26	Újezdec u Luhačovic d.	0523	0611	0613	0611	0704	0704	0710	0817	0905	1010	1012	...	1105	1210	1212	1305	1414	1416	|	1505	1615	1616	|
36	Luhačovice a.	0537	|	0627	|	|	|	0724	0830	|	|	1026	...	|	|	1226	|	|	1430	|	|	|	1630	|
35	Bojkovice a.	...	0624	...	0624	0717	0717	...	...	0916	1022	...	...	1116	1222	...	1316	1427	...	1437	1516	1628	...	1637
63	Bylnice a.	...	...	...	0718	...	0755	...	...	0952	...	...	...	1152	...	...	1352	...	...	1513	1552	...	...	...

	⑤⑦e	⑤f	⑤f		E	G						F	D	⑦j	⑧g								
Staré Město u Uh. H ⊖ 1162 d.	1559	1559	...	...	...	...	...	...	1739	1759	...	...	*1907*	...	1959	...	...	2028	...	2129	2159	...	2236
Uherské Hradiště 1162 d.	1609	1609	...	1629	...	...	...	...	1746	1809	1855	...	*1915*	...	2009	...	...	2039	...	2136	2206	...	2243
Kunovice d.	|	|	...	1632	...	...	...	...	1750	|	1858	...	1920	...	|	...	...	2042	...	2139	2209	...	2246
Uherský Brod 1162 d.	1625	1625	...	1653	...	...	...	...	1810	1825	1920	...	1937	...	2030	...	...	2105	...	2158	2228	...	2305
Újezdec u Luhačovic a.	|	|	...	1656	...	...	...	...	1813	|	1923	...	1940	...	2034	...	...	2108	...	2202	2231	...	2308
Újezdec u Luhačovic d.	|	|	...	1705	...	...	1746	...	1813	|	1924	1926	1941	2003	2036	...	2037	2110	2112	2202	2232	2233	2309
Luhačovice a.	|	|	...	|	...	...	1800	...	|	|	|	1940	|	2017	|	...	2051	|	2126	|	|	2247	|
Bojkovice a.	1637	1637	...	1716	...	...	...	...	1827	1838	1938	...	1956	...	2046	...	...	2124	...	2216	2244	...	2322
Bylnice a.	1714	1714	...	1752	1830	...	...	...	...	1916	...	...	*2036*	...	...	...	...	...	...	2252	...	...	...
Vlárský průsmyk ⊡ a.	...	1721	1736	...	1842	1844	...	...	...	...	...	...	...	...	...	...	...	...	...	...	...	...	...
Trenčianska Teplá ⊡ a.	...	...	1755	...	...	1955	...	...	...	...	...	...	...	...	...	...	...	...	...	...	...	...	...

					D		Ⓐ			Ⓒ		Ⓐh											⑦k
Bylnice d.	...	0358	...	...	*0508*	...	0545	...	...	0558	...	...	0800	...	...	1000	...	...	1200	...	...	1400	1440
Bojkovice d.	...	0433	0505	...	0556	0625	0625	...	0640	0640	0731	...	0835	...	0931	1035	...	1131	1235	1335	...	1437	1518
Luhačovice d.	0430	|	|	0554	|	|	|	0636	|	|	|	0754	|	0927	|	|	1127	|	|	|	1330	|	|
Újezdec u Luhačovic d.	0444	0446	0518	0608	0610	0637	0637	0650	0656	0656	0743	0808	0849	0941	0943	1049	1141	1143	1249	1347	1349	1449	|
Uherský Brod a.	...	0450	0522	...	0615	0641	0641	...	0659	0659	0746	...	0852	...	0946	1052	...	1146	1252	...	1353	1453	1530
Uherský Brod 1162 d.	...	0451	0523	...	0617	0643	0643	...	0707	0707	0749	...	0903	...	0949	1103	...	1149	1303	...	1354	1503	1531
Kunovice d.	...	0509	0541	...	0635	0701	0701	...	0728	0728	0809	...	0922	...	1007	1122	...	1207	1322	...	1412	1522	|
Uherské Hradiště 1162 a.	...	0512	0544	...	*0643*	0704	0704	...	0731	0731	0812	...	0925	...	1010	1125	...	1210	1325	...	1415	1525	1545
Staré Město u Uh. H ⊖ 1162 a.	...	0519	0555	...	...	0713	0713	...	0746	0746	0821	...	0934	...	1021	1151	...	1221	1351	...	1422	1534	1552

						Ⓑ	⑤⑦e		F	⑤f	⑤f			⑦j	⑦j	E	⑦j						
Trenčianska Teplá ⊡ d.	...	...	...	...	...	...	...	...	...	1705	...	...	...	...	1805	...	...	...	...	...	...	...	...
Vlárský průsmyk ⊡ d.	...	...	...	...	...	...	...	...	...	1724	1730	...	...	...	1824	1850	...	...	...	...	...	...	...
Bylnice d.	...	...	1600	...	...	...	1640	...	...	...	1805	...	1805	...	...	1858	...	...	...	...	2013	...	...
Bojkovice d.	...	1535	1637	...	...	1718	1718	1731	...	...	1842	...	1842	...	...	1931	...	...	2023	...	2056	...	2203
Luhačovice d.	1532	|	|	1729	...	|	|	|	1840	...	|	...	|	1924	...	|	...	2020	|	2054	|	2146	|
Újezdec u Luhačovic d.	1546	1548	1649	1743	...	|	|	1745	1854	...	1856	...	1856	1938	...	1941	...	2037	2036	2108	2110	2200	2217
Uherský Brod a.	...	1552	1653	...	...	1730	1730	1749	...	...	1900	...	1900	...	...	1945	...	...	2040	...	2114	...	2221
Uherský Brod 1162 d.	...	1554	1703	...	1731	1731	1731	1754	...	...	1902	...	1902	...	...	1946	...	...	2046	...	2120	...	2227
Kunovice d.	...	1612	1722	...	|	|	|	1813	...	...	1921	...	1921	...	...	1959	2002	...	2105	...	2139	...	2246
Uherské Hradiště 1162 a.	...	1615	1725	...	1745	1745	1745	1816	...	...	1924	...	1924	...	...	...	2005	...	2108	...	2142	...	2249
Staré Město u Uh. H ⊖ 1162 a.	...	1622	...	...	1752	1752	1752	1824	...	...	1932	...	1932	...	...	...	2013	...	2115	...	2151	...	...

A – To/from Praha (Table **1162**).
B – Change at Kunovice (a. 1917/d. 1921).
C – Change at Kunovice (a. 0633/d. 0636).
D – Staré Město - Bojkovice operated by ČD.
E – ⑦j. Operated by ČD.
F – ①-⑥ m until June 24; daily June 26 - Sept. 3; ①-⑥ from Sept. 4.
G – ⑦j. Change at Horné Srnie (a. 1851/d. 1945).
d – ⑥ (also Apr. 7, July 5, Sept. 28, Nov. 17; not Apr. 8, Nov. 18).
e – ⑤⑦ (also Apr. 10, May 1, 8, July 4, Sept. 27, Nov. 16; not Apr. 7, 9, 30, May 7, July 2, 9, 16, 23, 30, Aug. 6, 13, 20, 27, Nov. 17).
f – ⑤ (also Apr. 6, Sept. 27, Nov. 16; not Apr. 7, July 7 - Aug. 25, Nov. 17).
g – ⑧ (not Apr. 9, 30, May 7, Nov. 17).
h – Ⓐ (not July 3 - Aug. 31).
j – ⑦ (also Apr. 10, May 1, 8; not Apr. 9, 30, May 7, July 2 - Aug. 27).
k – ⑦ (also Apr. 10, May 1, 8; not Apr. 9, 30, May 7).
m – Also Apr. 9, 30, May 7; not Apr. 10, May 1, 8.
⊖ – Full name is Staré Město u Uherské Hradiště.
⊡ – Distances from Staré Město: Vlárský průsmyk *68 km*, Trenčianska Teplá *80 km*.

BRNO - PŘEROV - OSTRAVA - BOHUMÍN 1164

Brno - Přerov - Ostrava - Bohumín trains are operated by Regiojet (🍸 on most trains).

km		1101 ①-⑥	1103	1105		1129	1131 ④⑤⑦	1133			1100 ①-⑥	1102	1104		1128	1130 ④⑤⑦	1132	
0	**Brno** hlavní nádrazi 1156 d.	0502	0602	0702		1902	2002	2102	...	**Bohumín** 1160 d.	0435	0535	0635		1835	1935	2035	...
45	Vyškov na Moravě 1156 d.	0539	0641	0740	and at	1940	2040	2139	...	**Ostrava** hl. n. 1160 d.	0444	0544	0644	and at	1844	1944	2044	...
71	Kojetin d.	0559	0700	0800	the same	2000	2100	2200	...	**Ostrava** Svinov 1160 d.	0452	0552	0652	the same	1852	1952	2052	...
88	Přerov 1160 d.	0618	0718	0818	minutes	2018	2118	2218	...	Hranice na Moravě 1160 d.	0522	0622	0722	minutes	1922	2022	2122	...
117	Hranice na Moravě 1160 d.	0638	0738	0838	past each	2038	2138	2238	...	Přerov 1160 d.	0543	0643	0743	past each	1943	2043	2143	...
167	**Ostrava** Svinov 1160 a.	0710	0810	0914	hour until	2110	2210	2310	...	Kojetin d.	0559	0700	0800	hour until	2000	2100	2200	...
172	**Ostrava** hl. n. 1160 a.	0718	0818	0920	●	2118	2218	2318	...	Vyškov na Moravě 1156 d.	0622	0722	0822	●	2022	2122	2222	...
180	**Bohumín** 1160 a.	0727	0827	0928		2127	2227	2327	...	**Brno** hlavní nádrazi 1156 a.	0659	0759	0859		2057	2157	2256	...

km		*EC* 106 F	*EC* 104 G	*EC* 130 H	*EC* 102 J	*EC* 100 K	456 L					457 L	*EC* 101 K	*EC* 103 J	*EC* 131 H	*EC* 105 G	*EC* 107 F			
	Wien Hbf **1150** d.	0610	0810	*1110*	1410	1810	2210	...	...	...	**Bohumín** 1160 d.	0215	0642	1042	1342	1642	1842	...	...	...
	Břeclav **1162** d.	0710	0910	1210	1510	1910	2350	...	...	...	**Ostrava** hl. n. 1160 d.	0224	0651	1051	1351	1651	1851	...	...	...
0	**Přerov** 1160 d.	0813	1013	1313	1613	2013	|	...	...	...	**Ostrava** Svinov 1160 d.	|	0659	1059	1359	1659	1859	...	...	...
29	Hranice na Moravě 1160 d.	0830	1030	1330	1630	2030	|	...	...	...	Hranice na Moravě 1160 d.	|	0726	1126	1426	1726	1926	...	...	...
79	**Ostrava** Svinov 1160 a.	0858	1058	1358	1658	2058	|	...	...	...	**Přerov** 1160 a.	|	0744	1144	1444	1744	1944	...	...	...
84	**Ostrava** hl. n. 1160 a.	0906	1106	1406	1706	2106	0131	...	...	...	*Břeclav* **1162** a.	0410	0845	1245	1545	1845	2045	...	...	...
92	**Bohumín** 1160 a.	0915	1115	1415	1715	2115	0140	...	...	...	*Wien Hbf* **1150** a.	0700	0949	1349	*1649*	1949	2149	...	...	...

F – SOBIESKI – 12 ✕ Gdynia - Wien and v.v.
G – PORTA MORAVICA – 12 Przemyśl - Graz and v.v.; ✕ Graz - Bohumín and v.v.
H – BATHORY – 12 ✕ Budapest - Terespol and v.v.; 2 Praha (**115/114**) - Bohumín - Terespol and v.v.; 2 Budapest - Bohumín (**115/114**) - Kraków - Przemyśl and v.v.
J – POLONIA – 12 ✕ Warszawa - Wien and v.v.
K – MORAVIA – 12 ✕ Katowice - Wien and v.v.
L – NIGHTJET – 1, 2 cl., 2 cl., 2 Berlin - Graz and v.v.; 1, 2 cl., 2 cl., 2 Berlin (**457/6**) - Břeclav (**477/6**) - Budapest and v.v.; 1, 2 cl., 2 cl., 2 Warszawa (**407/6**) - Bohumín (**457/6**) - Graz and v.v.; 1, 2 cl., 2 cl., 2 Warszawa (**407/6**) - Bohumín (**457/6**) - Břeclav (**477/6**) - Budapest and v.v. Ⓡ for international journeys.
● – Timings may vary by up to 5 minutes.

1165 ÚSTI NAD ORLICI - LICHKOV - KLODZKO (- WROCŁAW) 2nd class LEO Express

Subject to alteration on Czech and Polish holiday dates (see page 4).

km																							
		Ⓐ			©A			B	©A	ⒶC						©A	ⒶC						
0	**Ústi nad Orlici** d.	0521	0743	...	0843	0943	...	1143	1243	1243	...	1343	1443	...	1543	1643	1643	1743	...	1843	...	2043	2210
12	Letohrad d.	0553	0801	...	0858	1001	...	1204	1258	1307	...	1401	1507	...	1601	1658	1707	1801	...	1907	...	2101	2231
35	Lichkov a.	0621	0826	...	0920	1026	...	1229	1320	1332	...	1426	1532	...	1626	1720	1732	1826	...	1932	...	2128	2256
35	Lichkov d.	...	...	0843	...	...	1143	...	...	...	1343	...	...	1608	...	...	...	...	1843	...	2043	...	...
44	Miedzylesie 🏛 a.	...	...	0853	...	...	1159	...	...	...	1353	...	...	1622	...	...	...	...	1853	...	2053	...	...
80	**Klodzko** Gl. ⊕ a.	...	...	0939	...	...	1252	...	...	...	1437	...	...	1701	...	...	...	...	1932	...	2133	...	...
	Wroclaw **1095** ⊕ a.	...	...	1111	...	...	1419	...	...	...	1616	...	...	1835	...	...	...	...	2059	...	...	...	...

	ⒶD	Ⓐ						©A				ⒶC	©A						©A			
Wroclaw **1095** ⊕ d.	...	...	...	0611	...	...	0814	...	...	1016	...	...	...	1251	...	...	1410	...	...	1651	...	...
Klodzko Gl. ⊕ d.	...	...	...	0733	...	...	0945	...	...	1144	...	...	...	1419	...	...	1539	...	...	1824	...	...
Miedzylesie 🏛 d.	...	...	...	0815	...	...	1027	...	...	1227	...	...	...	1515	...	...	1620	...	...	1915	...	...
Lichkov a.	...	...	...	0823	...	...	1035	...	...	1235	...	...	...	1523	...	...	1628	...	...	1923	...	...
Lichkov d.	0605	0700	0734	...	0828	0934	...	1040	1134	...	1334	1428	1440	...	1534	1628	...	1734	1840	...	1934	2112
Letohrad d.	0631	0725	0802	...	0902	1002	...	1105	1202	...	1402	1502	1505	...	1602	1702	...	1802	1905	...	2002	2138
Ústí nad Orlicí a.	0645	0739	0820	...	0920	1020	...	1120	1220	...	1420	1520	1520	...	1620	1720	...	1820	1920	...	2020	2155

A – © (daily July 1 - Aug. 31).
B – Change trains at Letohrad on © (also Ⓐ July 3 - Aug. 31).
C – Ⓐ (not July 3 - Aug. 31).
D – To Praha (Table **1160**).
⊕ – Operator in Poland: Koleje Dolnoślaskie.

1166 OLOMOUC - KRNOV - OPAVA - OSTRAVA 2nd class

km																								
		Ⓐ			d																		Ⓐ	
0	**Olomouc** d.	...	...	...	0705	...	...	0906	...	1106	...	1306	...	...	1506	...	1706	...		1906	...	...	...	...
64	Bruntál d.	0543	...	0708	0826	...	0908	1026	1108	1226	1308	1426	...	1508	1626	1708	1826	1908	...	2026	...	...	...	...
87	Krnov a.	0611	...	0738	0851	...	0938	1051	1138	1251	1338	1451	...	1538	1651	1738	1851	1938	...	2051	...	...	...	...
87	Krnov d.	0614	0706	0741	0906	0906	0941	1106	1141	1306	1341	1506	...	1541	1706	1741	1906	1939	...	...	2101	...	2208	...
116	**Opava** východ a.	0706	0732	0821	0932	0932	1021	1132	1221	1332	1421	1532	...	1621	1732	1821	1932	2017	...	...	2136	...	2239	...
116	**Opava** východ **1160a** d.	...	0737	...	0937	0937	...	1137	...	1337	...	1537	...	...	1737	...	1937	...	2042	...	...	2142	...	2245
144	**Ostrava** Svinov **1160a** a.	...	0757	...	0957	0957	...	1157	...	1357	...	1558	...	...	1758	...	2000	...	2112	...	...	2212	...	2315
149	**Ostrava** hl. n. a.	...	0810	...	...	...	...	1207	...	1410	...	1610	...	...	...	...	...	...	...	...	...	...	...	...

	d	Ⓐ														g	⑦h		j		Ⓐ		
Ostrava hl. n. d.	...	...	...	...	...	...	0948	...	...	...	1347	...	1549	...	1749	...	...	...	...	...	...	...	...
Ostrava Svinov **1160a** d.	...	...	0556	...	0800	...	1000	...	1200	...	1400	...	1600	...	1800	...	...	1944	...	2041	...	2156	...
Opava východ **1160a** a.	...	...	0624	...	0822	...	1022	...	1222	...	1422	...	1622	...	1822	...	...	2018	...	2113	...	2227	...
Opava východ d.	*0427*	0527	0628	0739	0828	0939	1028	1139	1228	1339	1428	1539	1628	1739	1828	...	...	...	2022	...	2125	...	2246
Krnov a.	*0503*	0605	0656	0815	0856	1015	1056	1215	1256	1415	1456	1615	1656	1815	1856	...	...	...	2059	...	2204	...	2326
Krnov d.	0505	0615	0704	0816	0905	1016	1105	1216	1305	1416	1505	1616	1705	1816	...	1903	1903	...	2109	...	...	...	...
Bruntál d.	0534	0652	0733	0852	0934	1052	1134	1252	1334	1452	1534	1652	1734	1852	...	1931	1932	...	2139	...	...	...	...
Olomouc a.	0652	...	0852	...	1052	...	1252	...	1452	...	1652	...	1852	...	...	...	2057	...	2302	...	...	...	...

km										
0	**Jesenik** d.	0530	...	0930	...	1330	...	1730	...	...
22	Glucholazy (Poland) d.	0611	...	1011	...	1411	...	1811	...	...
43	Tremešná ve Slezsku d.	0639	0838	1039	1238	1439	1641	1839	2033	...
60	**Krnov** a.	0658	0900	1058	1259	1458	1702	1858	2054	...

Krnov d.	0705	0748	0905	1105	1305	1505	1713	1905	...
Tremešná ve Slezsku d.	0726	0808	0924	1126	1324	1526	1733	1926	...
Glucholazy (Poland) d.	0759	...	...	1159	...	1559	...	1959	...
Jesenik a.	0836	...	...	1236	...	1636	...	2036	...

d – ①–⑥ (not Apr. 8, 10, May 1, 8, July 6, Nov. 18).
g – ①–⑥ (also Apr. 9, 30, May 7; not Apr. 10, May 1, 8).
h – ⑦ (also Apr. 7, 8, 30, May 7, July 5, 6, Sept. 28, Oct. 28, Nov. 17).
j – Change trains at Moravský Beroun (a. 2208 / d. 2210).

1169 OTHER LOCAL SERVICES May vary on and around public holiday dates 2nd class

BRNO - HRUŠOVANY NAD JEVIŠOVKOU and BŘECLAV - ZNOJMO

km										
		Ⓐk	Ⓐ	Ⓐ	Ⓑe	⑦m				
0	**Brno** hlavní nádrazí d.	0502	1531	1732	1956	2054	...	...	...	...
63	**Hrušovany** ◧ a.	0644	1646	1846	2114	2214	...	...	...	...

	Ⓐ	Ⓐ	⑥n	Ⓐ	Ⓐ	⑤p			
Hrušovany ◧ d.	0411	0507	0537	0609	0713	2037	...	...	...
Brno hlavní nádrazí a.	0533	0636	0700	0727	0827	2203	...	...	...

km																								
		Ⓐ		Ⓐ	⑥n	Ⓐq			©r			Ⓐ			Ⓐ		E			Ⓑe	⑤p			Ⓑe
0	**Břeclav** d.	0456	...	0548	0556	0640	...	0740	0847	0938	1138	1240	...	1336	1440	1537	1642	1737	...	1840	1840	1937	2143	2143
43	Hrušovany ◧ d.	0553	0553	0651	0651	0728	...	0826	0929	1025	1227	1327	...	1427	1527	1627	1727	1827	...	1925	1927	2027	2231	2231
69	**Znojmo** a.	0622	0622	0720	0720	0756	...	0854	0953	1054	1254	1354	...	1454	1554	1654	1754	1854	...	...	1954	2054	...	2259

	①s		Ⓐ		d			Ⓐq				Ⓐ			Ⓐ			Ⓑe			F	Ⓐ	
Znojmo d.	0408	...	0457	...	0558	0656	...	0757	0856	...	1056	1156	1256	...	1356	1456	...	1556	1656	...	1758	1756	1856
Hrušovany ◧ d.	0434	0434	0528	...	0630	0728	...	0826	0925	...	1126	1226	1326	...	1426	1526	...	1626	1726	...	1826	1826	1926
Břeclav a.	0522	0522	0616	...	0714	0814	...	0908	1010	...	1212	1310	1413	...	1510	1614	...	1711	1813	...	1905	1910	2012

ČESKÝ TĚŠÍN - CIESZYN (Poland) *3 km* Journey 5 mins

From Český Těšín: 0523 Ⓐ, 0552 ©, 0721 Ⓐ, 0752 ©, 0952, 1152, 1321 Ⓐ, 1352 ©, 1421 Ⓐ, 1552 ©, 1721 Ⓐ, 1752 ©, 1952, 2152.

From Cieszyn: 0533 Ⓐ, 0603 ©, 0803, 1003, 1203, 1333 Ⓐ, 1403 ©, 1433 Ⓐ, 1603 ©, 1733 Ⓐ, 1803 ©, 2003, 2203.

CHOCEŇ - LITOMYŠL *24 km* Journey 55 minutes

From Choceň: 0457 Ⓐ, 0629 Ⓐ, 0640 ©, 0840, 1040, 1340 ©, 1429 Ⓐ, 1640 ©, 1740 Ⓐ, 1840 ©, 2259 Ⓐ, 2318 ©.

From Litomyšl: 0437 Ⓐ, 0536 ©, 0609 Ⓐ, 0717 Ⓐ **q**, 0737 © **t**, 0937, 1237, 1537, 1737 ©, 1837 Ⓐ, 1937 ©.

JINDŘICHŮV HRADEC - NOVÁ BYSTŘICE *33 km* Narrow gauge, 80 mins

From Jindřichův Hradec: *service suspended.*

From Nová Bystřice: *service suspended.*

Operator: JHMD www.jhmd.cz

KOJETIN - KROMĚŘÍŽ *9 km* Journey 12 minutes

From Kojetin: 0428 Ⓐ, 0505 Ⓐ, 0603 and hourly until 2003, 2103 ④⑤⑦, 2203, 2314 Ⓐ.

From Kroměříž: 0410 Ⓐ, 0441 Ⓐ, 0541 and hourly until 1941, 2041 ④⑤⑦, 2141, 2241 Ⓐ.

KROMĚŘÍŽ - HULIN *8 km* Journey 8 minutes

From Hulin: 1 - 2 trains per hour connecting with trains in Table **1162**.

From Kroměříž: 1 - 2 trains per hour connecting with trains in Table **1162**.

PRAHA - KARLŠTEJN *33 km* Journey 42 minutes

From Praha hl. n.: 0421, 0451 Ⓐ, 0521, 0551 Ⓐ, 0621, 0651, 0718, 0821, 0851, 0921, 0951 ©, 1021, 1051 ©, 1121, 1151 ©, 1221, 1251, 1321, 1351, 1421, 1451, 1518, 1551, 1621, 1651, 1718, 1751, 1821, 1851, 1921, 1951 Ⓐ, 2021, 2121, 2221, 2321.

From Karlštejn: 0528, 0558, 0628 Ⓐ, 0658, 0728, 0758, 0858, 0928, 0958, 1028 ©, 1058, 1128 ©, 1158, 1228 ©, 1258, 1328, 1358, 1428, 1458, 1528, 1558, 1628, 1658, 1728, 1758, 1828, 1858, 1928, 1958, 2028 Ⓐ, 2058, 2158, 2302.

Trains continue to / from Beroun (journey 10 mins).

TŘEMEŠNÁ VE SLEZSKU - OSOBLAHA *20 km* Narrow gauge, 45 minutes

From Třemešná: 0727 ①–⑥ **d**, 1045 **G**, 1127, 1527, 1927.

From Osoblaha: 0546 ①–⑥ **d**, 0946, 1346, 1510 **G**, 1746.

E – Ⓑ until Apr. 2; Ⓐ Apr. 3 - Sept. 22 (not July 7); Ⓑ from Sept. 25 (not Sept. 28, Nov. 17).
F – ⑦ until Apr. 2; © Apr. 7 - Oct. 1; ⑦ from Oct. 8.
G – ⑥ June 3 - Sept. 16 (also † July 2 - Aug. 27). Steam hauled train. Special fares. Journey 80 – 90 minutes.
d – ①–⑥ (not Apr. 8, 10, May 1, 8, July 6, Nov. 18).
e – Ⓑ (not Apr. 7, 9, 30, May 7, July 5, Nov. 17).
k – Change trains at Rakšice or Bohutice.
m – ⑦ (also Apr. 10, May 1, 8, July 6, Sept. 28; not Apr. 9, 30, May 7).
n – ⑥ (also Apr. 7, July 5, Sept. 28, Nov. 17; not Apr. 8, Nov. 18).
p – ⑤ (also Apr. 6, July 4, Sept. 27, Nov. 16; not Apr. 7, Nov. 17).
q – Ⓐ (not July 3 - Sept. 1).
r – © Apr. 7 - Oct. 1.
s – ① (also Apr. 11, May 2, 9, July 7, Sept. 29; not Apr. 10, May 1, 8).
t – © (also Ⓐ July 3 - Sept. 1).
◧ – Full name is Hrušovany nad Jevišovkou – Šanov.

SLOVAKIA

Operator: National railway operator is Železničná spoločnosť Slovensko (ŽSSK), www.slovakrail.sk, which runs on the network of Železnice Slovenskej Republiky (ŽSR), www.zsr.sk.

Services: All trains convey first and second class seating, **except** where shown otherwise in footnotes or by '2' in the train column, or where the footnote shows sleeping and/or couchette cars only. Reservation of 1st class seats is compulsary on domestic trains. Descriptions of sleeping (🛏) and couchette (▬) cars appear on page 10.
Note: hl. st. = hlavná stanica = main station.

Timings: Valid **December 11, 2022 - December 9, 2023** with amendments as received. Certain trains may be cancelled during the period December 24 - January 8.

Supplements: A higher level of fares applies to travel by *EC* and *IC* trains. It is possible to reserve seats on most Express trains.

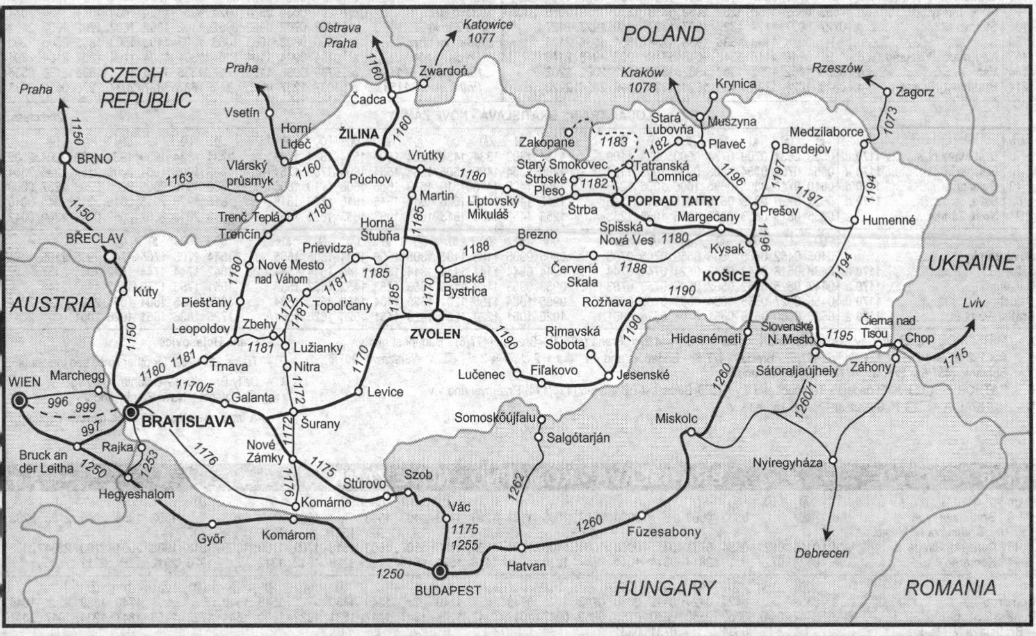

BRATISLAVA - ŠURANY - ZVOLEN - BANSKÁ BYSTRICA — 1170

km		11831	861		831		833		835		837		839		841		853	15843	845		855		801
		①	①–⑥	2		2		2		2		2		2		2	①–④	⑤		2	Ⓑ	2Ⓑ	Ⓑ
		d	e			◧		◧		◧		◧		◧		◧	f	B			h	h	Ah
0	**Bratislava** hl. st. **1175** d.	0358	...	...	0604	...	0804	...	1004	...	1204	...	1404	...	1604	...	1654	1654	1804	...	2004	...	...
49	Galanta **1175** d.	0433	...	...	0638	...	0838	...	1038	...	1238	...	1438	...	1638	...	1729	1729	1838	...	2038	...	...
60	Šaľa **1175** d.	0441	...	...	0646	...	0846	...	1046	...	1246	...	1446	...	1646	...	1737	1737	1846	...	2046	...	...
	Nové Zámky d.	|	...	0503	|	0703	|	0903	|	1103	|	1303	|	1503	|	1703	|	|	|	1903	|	2103	2340
89	**Šurany** a.	0507	...	0513	0712	0713	0912	0914	1112	1113	1312	1313	1512	1513	1712	1713	1805	1805	1912	1913	2112	2113	2350
89	**Šurany** d.	0509	...	0515	0717	0735	0917	...	1117	1133	1317	1333	1517	1534	1717	1735	1816	1816	1917	1940	2117	...	2352
132	Levice d.	0600	0600	0625	0800	0833	1000	...	1200	1233	1400	1433	1600	1633	1800	1833	1910	1913	2000	2046	2158	...	0032
187	Žiar nad Hronom d.	0701	0701	...	0901	...	1101	...	1301	...	1501	...	1701	...	1901	...	...	2028	2056	...	...	...	0133
209	**Zvolen** osob. a.	0720	0720	...	0920	...	1120	...	1320	...	1520	...	1720	...	1920	...	...	2048	2115	...	...	...	0153
209	**Zvolen** osob. **1185** d.	0723	0723	...	0923	...	1123	...	1323	...	1523	...	1723	...	1923	...	...	...	2123	...	...	...	...
230	**Banská Bystrica** **1185** a.	0746	0746	...	0945	...	1145	...	1345	...	1545	...	1745	...	1945	...	...	...	2145	...	...	...	...

	800	850		830		832		834		836		838		840	17840			842			844	
	①–⑥	Ⓐ	2	①–⑥	2		2		2		2		2		⑦	2Ⓐ	2Ⓒ		2Ⓐ	2Ⓒ		2
	Ae			e◧		◧		◧		◧		◧			j			◧			◧	
Banská Bystrica **1185** d.	...	...	...	0412	...	0612	...	0812	...	1012	...	1212	...	1412	...	...	...	1612	...	...	1812	...
Zvolen osob. **1185** d.	...	...	...	0434	...	0635	...	0835	...	1035	...	1235	...	1435	...	...	...	1635	...	...	1835	...
Zvolen osob. d.	0209	...	...	0436	...	0640	...	0840	...	1040	...	1240	...	1440	1508	...	...	1640	...	...	1840	...
Žiar nad Hronom d.	0230	...	...	0458	...	0701	...	0901	...	1101	...	1301	...	1501	1529	...	...	1701	...	...	1901	...
Levice d.	0329	0502	0525	0601	0735	0801	...	1001	1135	1201	1310	1401	1535	1601	1639	...	1735	1801	...	1925	2001	...
Šurany a.	0409	0543	0624	0642	0832	0842	...	1042	1232	1242	1412	1442	1632	1642	1732	...	1832	1842	...	2022	2042	...
Šurany d.	0415	0548	0645	0647	0846	0847	1046	1047	1246	1247	1446	1447	1646	1647	1740	1846	1846	1847	2046	2046	2047	2314
Nové Zámky a.	0426	|	0655	|	0856	|	1055	|	1255	|	1455	|	1655	|	|	1855	1855	|	2055	2055	|	2329
Šaľa **1175** d.	...	0617	...	0717	...	0917	...	1117	...	1317	...	1517	...	1717	1812	...	...	1917	...	...	2117	...
Galanta **1175** d.	...	0625	...	0725	...	0925	...	1125	...	1325	...	1525	...	1725	1825	...	...	1925	...	...	2125	...
Bratislava hl. st. **1175** a.	...	0658	...	0758	...	0958	...	1158	...	1358	...	1558	...	1758	1858	...	...	1958	...	...	2158	...

A – GEMERAN POĽANA – (12) Nové Zámky - Košice and v.v.: conveys 🛏 1, 2 cl. Praha (**283/2**) - Nové Zámky (**801/0**) - Košice and v.v.
B – Also Apr. 6, July 4, Aug. 28, 31, Sept. 14, Oct. 31, Nov, 16; not Apr. 7, Sept. 1, 15, Nov. 17.
d – Also Apr. 11, May 2, 9, July 6, Aug. 30, Nov. 2; not Apr. 10, May 1, 8.
e – Not Apr. 8, 10, May 1, 8, Sept. 2, 16, Nov. 18.
f – Not Apr. 6, 10, May 1, 8, July 4, 5, Aug. 28, 29, 31, Sept. 14, Oct. 31, Nov. 1, 16.
h – Not Apr. 7, 9, 30, May 7, Sept. 1, 15, Nov. 17.
j – Also Apr. 10, May 1, 8, July 5, Aug. 29, Nov. 1; not Apr. 9, 30, May 7.
◧ – Connects with train in previous column at Šurany.

NOVÉ ZAMKY - NITRA - TOPOĽČANY — 1172

2nd class

km																							
		C	Ⓐ	Ⓐ		C	Ⓐ	Ⓐk		C				C	Ⓐ		C	Ⓐ		C			
0	**Nové Zamky** d.	0401	...	0515	...	0603	...	0630	0715	0803	0915	1115	1315	1403	...	1515	1603	...	1715	1803	1915	2115	2315
10	Šurany d.	0413	...	0527	...	0614	...	0655	0727	0814	0927	1127	1327	1413	...	1527	1614	...	1727	1814	1927	2127	2327
36	**Nitra** a.	0445	...	0559	...	0648	...	0735	0759	0848	0959	1159	1359	1448	...	1559	1648	...	1759	1848	1959	2159	2359
		|				|				|				|			|			|			
36	**Nitra** **1181** d.	0446	0518	...	0618	0649	0718	...	0818	0849	1018	1218	1418	1449	1518	1618	1649	1718	1818	1849	2018	2240	...
40	Lužianky **1181** d.	0456	0533	...	0633	0659	0733	...	0833	0859	1033	1233	1433	1459	1533	1633	1659	1733	1833	1859	2033	2252	...
69	**Topoľčany** a.	....	0610	...	0710	...	0810	...	0910	...	1110	1310	1510	...	1610	1710	...	1810	1910	...	2110	2336	...

		D		Ⓐ	C		Ⓐ			C		Ⓐk	C		Ⓐ	C		Ⓐ	C			
Topoľčany d.	...	...	0449	0549	...	0649	0749	0849	1049	...	1249	...	...	1449	1549	...	1649	1749	...	1849	2049	2249
Lužianky **1181** d.	...	0459	0531	0631	0701	0731	0831	0931	1131	1301	1331	...	1501	1531	1631	1701	1731	1831	1901	1931	2131	2326
Nitra **1181** a.	...	0509	0542	0642	0711	0742	0842	0942	1142	1311	1342	...	1511	1542	1642	1711	1742	1842	1911	1942	2142	2337
		|			|				|			|			|			|			
Nitra d.	0357	0511	0602	...	0712	0802	...	1002	1202	1312	1402	1425	1512	1602	...	1712	1802	...	1912	2002	2241	...
Šurany d.	0434	0548	0636	...	0747	0836	...	1035	1235	1347	1436	1515	1547	1636	...	1747	1836	...	1947	2036	2314	...
Nové Zamky a.	0445	0558	0647	...	0757	0847	...	1046	1246	1357	1447	1529	1557	1647	...	1757	1847	...	1957	2047	2329	...

C – Ⓐ Nové Zamky - Nitra and v.v.; daily Nitra - Lužianky and v.v. To / from Trnava (Table **1181**).
D – From Lužianky on ①–⑥ **e**; from Nitra on Ⓐ.
e – Not Apr. 8, 10, May 1, 8, Sept. 2, 16, Nov. 18.
k – Not July 1 - Sept. 3.

1175 BRATISLAVA - ŠTÚROVO - BUDAPEST

All *EC* trains convey ✕. For additional trains Bratislava - Šal'a see Table **1170**. For local trains Szob - Budapest and v.v. see Table **1255**.

km		**585**	*EC*	*EC*	*EC*	*EC*	*EC*	*EC*	*EC*	*EC*	*EC*
		477	**271**	**273**	**275**	**277**	**279**	**131**	**253**	**281**	**283**
		[R] **A**						**B**	**C**		
	Praha hlavní **1150** ..... d.	2243	...	0524	0724	0924	1124	...	1326‡	1524	1724
	Brno hlavní n. **1150** ... d.	0143	0622	0822	1022	1222	1422	...	1622	1822	2022
	Břeclav **1150** .... d.	0455	0655	0855	1055	1255	1455	1555	1655	1855	2055
0	**Bratislava** hl. st. .... d.	0557	0757	0957	1157	1357	1557	1705	1757	1957	2204
91	Nové Zámky .... d.	0659	0859	1059	1259	1459	1659	1810	1859	2059	2309
135	Štúrovo 🏛 .... d.	0727	0927	1127	1327	1527	1727	1840	1927	2127	...
150	Szob 🏛 .... d.	|	0938	1138	1338	1538	1738	1851	1938	2138	...
163	Nagymaros-Visegrád ¶ .. d.	|	0948	1148	1348	1548	1748	1902	1948	2148	...
180	Vác .... d.	0800	1002	1202	1402	1602	1802	1923	2002	2202	...
214	**Budapest** Nyugati .... a.	0829	1028	1228	1428	1628	1828	1949	2028	2228	...

	EC	*EC*	*EC*	*EC*	*EC*	*EC*	*EC*	*EC*	*EC*	**476**
	282	**280**	**252**	**130**	**278**	**276**	**274**	**272**	**270**	**584**
			C	**B**						[R] **A**
Budapest Nyugati .... d.	...	0529	0729	0812	0929	1129	1329	1529	1729	1929
Vác .... d.	...	0556	0756	0844	0956	1156	1356	1556	1756	1956
Nagymaros-Visegrád ¶ .. d.	...	0609	0809	0857	1009	1209	1409	1609	1809	|
Szob 🏛 .... d.	...	0621	0821	0909	1021	1221	1421	1621	1821	|
Štúrovo 🏛 .... d.	...	0634	0834	0924	1034	1234	1434	1634	1834	2034
Nové Zámky .... d.	0452	0702	0902	0952	1102	1302	1502	1702	1902	2102
Bratislava hl. st. .... a.	0600	0803	1003	1055	1203	1403	1603	1803	2003	2203
Břeclav **1150** .... a.	0704	0904	1104	1204	1304	1504	1704	1904	2104	2304
Brno hlavní n. **1150** .... a.	0736	0936	1136	...	1336	1536	1736	1936	2136	0536
Praha hlavní **1150** ...... a.	1037	1237	1433‡	...	1637	1837	2037	2235	0019	0837

LOCAL TRAINS BRATISLAVA - NOVÉ ZÁMKY

2nd class

km		◧	Ⓐ	◧	Ⓐ	◧	Ⓐ	◧		Ⓐ	◧	Ⓐ	Ⓐ	Ⓐ	◧	Ⓐ	Ⓐ	◧		Ⓐ	Ⓐ	◧	Ⓐ		⊡	
0	**Bratislava** hl. st. .... **1170** d.	0509	0634	0709	0734	0909	0934	1109	...	1134	1309	1334	1434	1504	1509	1534	1634	1709	...	1734	1834	1909	1934	2109	2204	2309
49	Galanta .... **1170** a.	0554	0705	0754	0805	0954	1005	1154	...	1205	1354	1405	1505	1538	1554	1605	1705	1754	...	1805	1905	1954	2005	2154	2235	2354
49	Galanta .... **1170** d.	0610	0710	0806	0806	1006	1006	1206	...	1206	1406	1406	1510	1539	1606	1606	1710	1806	...	1806	1910	2006	2006	2206	2237	0000
60	Šal'a .... **1170** d.	0621	0726	0815	0815	1015	1015	1215	...	1215	1415	1415	1526	1547	1615	1615	1726	1815	...	1815	1926	2015	2015	2215	2245	0010
91	**Nové Zámky** .... a.	0655	0813	0853	0853	1053	1053	1253	...	1253	1453	1453	1613	1619	1653	1653	1820	1853	...	1853	2013	2052	2052	2247	2309	0042

	Ⓐ	⊡	Ⓐ	◧	Ⓐ	Ⓐ	◧		Ⓐ	◧	Ⓐ	◧	Ⓐ	◧	Ⓐ	Ⓐ	◧		Ⓐ	Ⓐ	◧	Ⓐ			
Nové Zámky .... d.	0405	0452	0505	0508	0559	0705	0705	...	0905	0905	1105	1105	1305	1305	1344	1505	1505	...	1544	1705	1705	1744	1905	2105	...
Šal'a .... **1170** d.	0438	0518	0542	0542	0624	0744	0744	...	0944	0944	1144	1144	1344	1344	1442	1544	1544	...	1642	1744	1744	1842	1944	2137	...
Galanta .... **1170** a.	0447	0525	0552	0552	0632	0753	0753	...	0953	0953	1153	1153	1353	1353	1452	1553	1553	...	1651	1753	1753	1852	1953	2146	...
Galanta .... **1170** d.	0455	0527	0555	0604	0633	0755	0804	...	0955	1004	1155	1204	1355	1404	1455	1555	1604	...	1655	1755	1804	1855	2004	...	2204
Bratislava hl. st. .... **1170** a.	0526	0600	0626	0651	0708	0826	0851	...	1026	1051	1226	1251	1426	1451	1526	1626	1651	...	1726	1826	1851	1926	2051	...	2251

A – METROPOL – [12] Břeclav - Budapest and v.v.; 🛏 1, 2 cl., 🛌 2 cl. Praha (**575/4**) - Břeclav (**477/6**) - Budapest and v.v.; 🛏 1, 2 cl., 🛌 2 cl., [2] Berlin (**457/6**) - Břeclav (**477/6**) - Budapest and v.v.; 🛏 1, 2 cl., 🛌 2 cl., [2] Warszawa (**407/6**) - Bohumín (**457/6**) - Břeclav (**477/6**) - Budapest and v.v.

B – BATHORY – [12] ✕ Budapest - Terespol and v.v.; [2] Budapest - Bohumín (**115/114**) Przemyśl and v.v.

C – HUNGARIA - [12] ✕ Budapest - Hamburg and v.v.

‡ – Praha **Holesovice**.

⊡ – Trains **283** / **282** (for other times see main table).

◧ – Daily Bratislava - Galanta and v.v.; Ⓒ Galanta - Nové Zámky and v.v.

¶ – A ferry operates across the river to Visegrád.

1176 BRATISLAVA - KOMÁRNO - NOVÉ ZÁMKY

2nd class

km		Ⓐ	Ⓐ	Ⓐ	Ⓒ	Ⓐ						Ⓐ		Ⓒ	Ⓐ	Ⓒ	Ⓐ	Ⓒ	Ⓐ					
0	**Bratislava** hl. st. .... ⊖ d.	...	...	0533	0603	...	0803	0903	1003	1103	1203	1303	1403	1503	...	1603	...	1703	...	1803	1903	2003	2103	2203
	Bratislava N. Mesto .... d.	...	...	|	|	...	|	|	|	|	|	|	|	|	1527	|	1627	|	1727	|	|	|	|	|
46	Dunajská Streda .... ⊖ d.	0418	0621	0634	0711	0711	0908	1004	1108	1204	1308	1418	1507	1605	1618	1709	1709	1805	1818	1908	2004	2108	2204	2305
94	**Komárno** .... a.	0523	0728	...	0814	0814	1011	...	1210	...	1410	1524	1610	...	1726	1812	1812	...	1926	2012	...	2211	...	...

	Ⓐ		Ⓐ	Ⓒ	Ⓐ	Ⓐ								Ⓐ	Ⓐ	Ⓒ	Ⓐ	Ⓐ	Ⓒ		Ⓐ		
Komárno .... d.	0339	...	0424	0424	0543	0630	0743	...	0940	...	1140	...	1340	1430	...	1540	1540	...	...	1740	1830	...	1940
Dunajská Streda .... ● d.	0447	0447	0550	0550	0650	0750	0850	0947	1047	1147	1247	1347	1447	1531	1622	1650	1644	1722	1750	1847	1934	1947	2047
Bratislava N. Mesto .... a.	|	|	0631	|	0731	0831	|	|	|	|	|	|	|	|	|	|	...	|	|	|	...	|	|
Bratislava hl. st. .... ● a.	0553	0553	...	0653	...	...	0953	1053	1153	1253	1353	1453	1553	1621	1721	1753	...	1821	1853	1953	...	2053	2156

km			Ⓐ			Ⓐ						Ⓐ			Ⓐ			Ⓐ						
0	**Komárno** .... d.	0420	0529	...	0632	0732	...	0832	1032	...	1232	1332	...	1432	1532	...	1632	1732	...	1832	2032	...	...	...
29	**Nové Zámky** .... a.	0445	0554	...	0657	0757	...	0857	1057	...	1257	1357	...	1457	1557	...	1657	1757	...	1857	2057	...	...	...

		Ⓐ			Ⓐ						Ⓐ			Ⓐ			Ⓐ						
Nové Zámky .... d.	0458	0601	...	0701	0801	...	0901	1101	...	1301	1401	...	1501	1601	...	1701	1801	...	1901	2101	...	...	...
Komárno .... a.	0523	0626	...	0726	0826	...	0926	1126	...	1326	1426	...	1526	1626	...	1726	1826	...	1926	2126	...	...	...

⊖ – Other trains Bratislava hl. st. - Dunajská Streda at 0503 Ⓒ, 0703 Ⓒ, 1303, 1433 Ⓐ, 1533 Ⓐ, 1633 Ⓐ, 1733 Ⓐ, 2303.

● – Other trains Dunajská Streda - Bratislava hl. st. at 0347, 0417 Ⓐ, 0517 Ⓐ, 0617 Ⓐ, 0650 Ⓒ, 0717 Ⓐ, 0750 Ⓒ, 0817 Ⓐ, 1550 Ⓒ.

1180 BRATISLAVA - ŽILINA - POPRAD TATRY - KOŠICE

IC trains are not available for local journeys Kysak - Košice and v.v. See next page for additional Bratislava - Trenčín trains.

km		♠		*Ex*		♥			*EN*			*Ex*	*IC*		*Ex*		*SC*	*Ex*		♥	*Ex*	*IC*			*Ex*		
		1267	**615**	**11621**	**1761**	**1021**	**1763**	**765**	**443**	**1701**	**16767**	**601**	**521**	**701**	**603**	**703**	**241**	**605**	**705**	**1003**	**607**	**523**	**707**	**1703**	**609**	**16709**	**709**
		🍷 [R]			2	🍷	2	✕	[R]	2	✕	✕	✕ [R]		✕		✕ [R]	✕		🍷	✕	✕ [R]		2	✕		
			E	①**d**	Ⓐ	⊡		Ⓐ	**A**		Ⓒ			**e**			**B**							Ⓐ		Ⓒ	Ⓐ
	Wien Hbf. **996** .... d.	...	...	...	...	...	...	...	...	...	...	...	...	...	...	...	...	...	...	...	...	...	...	...	...	...	...
0	**Bratislava** hl. st.. .... d.	...	2257	0007	...	...	...	...	...	...	...	0527	0622	0555	0727	0755	...	0927	0955	...	1127	1222	1155	...	1327	1355	1355
46	Trnava .... **1181** d.	...	2329	0040	...	...	...	...	...	...	...	0600	|	0630	0800	0830	...	1000	1030	...	1200	|	1230	...	1400	1430	1430
63	Leopoldov .... **1181** d.	...	2342	|	...	...	...	...	...	...	...	|	|	0644	|	0844	...	|	1044	...	|	|	1244	...	|	1444	1444
81	Piešťany .... d.	...	2355	|	...	...	...	...	...	...	...	|	|	0655	|	0855	...	|	1055	...	|	|	1255	...	|	1455	1455
99	Nové Mesto nad Váhom .. d.	...	0008	|	...	...	...	...	...	...	...	|	|	0711	|	0907	...	|	1107	...	|	|	1311	...	|	1507	1507
124	**Trenčín** .... d.	...	0025	0118	...	...	...	...	...	0521	...	0638	|	0727	0838	0923	...	1038	1123	...	1238	|	1327	...	1438	1523	1523
132	Trenčianska Teplá .... d.	...	0032	|	...	...	...	...	...	0527	...	|	|	0733	|	0929	...	|	1129	...	|	|	1333	...	|	1529	1529
	Praha hl. n. **1160** .... d.	2000	|	|	...	2138	...	...	2213	|	...	|	|	|	|	|	0600	|	|	0738	|	|	|	...	|	|	|
159	**Púchov** .... **1161** d.	|	0052	0137	...	|	...	...	|	0550	...	0657	|	0757	0857	0955	|	1057	1157	|	1257	|	1357	...	1457	1557	1552
171	Považská Bystrica ... **1161** d.	|	0102	0147	...	|	...	...	|	0558	...	0707	|	0807	0907	1004	|	1107	1207	|	1307	|	1407	...	1507	1607	1617
203	**Žilina** .... **1161** a.	0100	0129	0209	...	0237	...	...	0417	0626	...	0729	0800	0829	0929	1025	1029	1129	1229	1249	1329	1359	1429	...	1529	1629	1639
203	**Žilina** .... **1185** d.	0101	0132	0214	...	0239	...	0423	0434	...	0632	0734	0802	...	0934	...	1031	1134	...	1251	1334	1401	...	1434	1534	...	...
224	Vrútky .... **1185** d.	0125	0156	0240	...	0304	...	0448	0459	...	0658	0800	|	...	1000	...	1057	1200	...	1316	1400	|	...	1500	1600	...	...
242	Kral'ovany .... d.	|	0209	0255	...	|	...	0503	0513	...	0711	0816	|	...	1016	...	1110	1216	...	|	1416	|	...	1519	1616	...	...
260	Ružomberok .... d.	0151	0224	0310	...	0330	...	0521	0528	...	0726	0832	|	...	1032	...	1125	1232	...	1344	1431	|	...	1534	1631	...	...
286	Liptovský Mikuláš .... d.	0210	0243	0331	...	0349	...	0541	0548	...	0749	0853	|	...	1053	...	1144	1253	...	1404	1452	|	...	1553	1653	...	...
325	Štrba .... d.	0237	|	0400	...	0418	...	0609	0617	...	0817	0921	|	...	1121	...	1212	1321	...	1432	1520	|	...	...	1721	...	...
344	**Poprad-Tatry** .... d.	0255	0330	0418	0434	0508	0534	0635	0713	...	0836	0941	0952	...	1141	...	1232	1341	...	1457	1541	1553	...	...	1741	...	...
370	Spišská Nová Ves .... d.	0312	0348	...	0455	0526	0555	0656	0732	...	0857	0959	1010	...	1159	...	1250	1359	...	1514	1559	1611	...	...	1759	...	...
410	Margecany .... d.	|	0414	...	0526	0553	0626	0726	0757	...	0928	1026	|	...	1226	...	|	1426	...	|	1626	|	...	...	1826	...	...
	Prešov .... a.	0406	|	...	|	|	|	|	|	...	|	|	|	...	|	...	|	|	...	|	|	|	...	...	|	...	...
429	Kysak .... **1196** d.	|	0429	...	0540	0607	0640	0740	0817	...	0942	1040	1051	...	1240	...	1329	1440	...	1607	1640	1651	...	...	1840	...	...
445	**Košice** .... **1196** a.	0437	0441	...	0553	0619	0653	0753	0833	...	0953	1053	1104	...	1253	...	1341	1453	...	1619	1653	1713	...	...	1853	...	...
	Humenné **1194** .... a.	...	0633	...	...	...	...	...	1032	...	...	...	...	...	...	...	...	...	...	...	...	...	...	...	...	...	...

A – SLOVAKIA – 🛏 1, 2 cl., 🛌 2 cl., [2] Praha - Humenné and v.v.

B – PENDOLINO KOŠIČAN – [12] ✕ Praha - Košice and v.v.

C – [12] 🍷 Praha - Žilina and v.v. (Table **1150**).

D – 🛏 1, 2 cl. Bratislava (**627**) - Žilina (**443**) - Košice. From Bratislava on ①–⑤

E – TATRAN ZEMPLÍN – 🛏 1, 2 cl., 🛌 2 cl., [2] Bratislava - Humenné and v.v.

F – 🛏 1, 2 cl. Košice (**442**) - Žilina (**622**) - Bratislava. From Košice on ①②③④⑦.

d – ① (also Apr. 11, May 2, 9, July 6, Aug. 30, Nov. 2; not Apr. 10, May 1, 8).

e – ①–⑥ (not Apr. 8, 10, May 1, 8, Sept. 2, 16, Nov. 18).

f – ①–④ (not Apr. 6, 10, May 1, 8, July 4, 5, Aug. 28, 29, 31, Sept. 14, Oct. 31, Nov. 1, 16).

g – ⑤ (also Apr. 6, July 4, Aug. 28, 31, Sept. 14, Oct. 31, Nov. 16; not Apr. 7, Sept. 1, 15, Nov. 17).

h – ⑦ (also Apr. 10, May 1, 8, July 5, Aug. 29, Nov. 1; not Apr. 9, 30, May 7).

j – ①②③④⑦ (not Apr. 6, 9, 30, May 7, July 4, Aug. 28, 31, Sept. 14, Oct. 31, Nov. 16).

k – ⑥ (also Apr. 7, 9, 30, May 7, Sept. 1, 15, Nov. 17).

m – ⑧ (not Apr. 7, 9, 30, May 7, Sept. 1, 15, Nov. 17).

n – ⑥ (also Apr. 7, July 5, Aug. 29, Sept. 1, 15, Nov. 1, 17; not Apr. 8, Sept. 2, 16, Nov. 18).

♥ – Operated by REGIOJET. Separate fares.

♠ – Operated by LEO EXRESS. Separate fares.

⊡ – 🛏 (1, 2, 3, 4 berth), 🛌 (6 berth), [12] 🍷

TABLE CONTINUES ON NEXT PAGE →

Continued from previous page

BRATISLAVA - ŽILINA - POPRAD TATRY - KOŠICE — 1180

IC trains are not available for local journeys Kysak - Košice and v.v. See foot of page for additional Bratislava - Trenčín trains.

	Ex 621	*Ex* 15621	*Ex* 611	*IC* 45	♠ 1259	16711	711	*Ex* 623	*Ex* 15623	*IC* 525	*Ex* 613	713	*EC* 221	♥ 1045	*Ex* 17625		715	15715	16715	*Ex* 627	627 443	*EC* 223		*Ex* 629		717
			✕	✕ R	🍷 R					✕ R	✕			🍷	✕	2				✕			2		2	
	f	⑤g				Ⓒ	Ⓐ	f	⑤g					C	⑦h		j	⑤g	⑥k		D			Ⓑm	Ⓐ	Ⓑm
Wien Hbf. **996** d.	...	...	...	1442	...	...	...	...	...	...	...	...	...	...	...	...	...	...	...	...	...	...	...	...	...	...
Bratislava hl. st. d.	1427	1427	1527	1622	...	1555	1555	1627	1627	1722	1727	1755	...	1923	1927	...	1955	1955	1955	2027	2027	...	...	2127	...	2155
Trnava **1181** d.	1500	1500	1600	|	...	1630	1630	1700	1700	1748	1802	1830	...	1954	2000	...	2030	2030	2030	2100	2100	...	...	2200	...	2230
Leopoldov **1181** d.	|	|	|	|	...	1644	1644	|	|	|	|	1844	...	|	|	...	2044	2044	2044	|	|	...	...	|	...	2243
Piešťany d.	|	|	|	|	...	1655	1655	|	|	|	|	1855	...	2010	|	...	2055	2055	2055	|	|	...	...	|	...	2255
Nové Mesto nad Váhom d.	|	|	|	|	...	1707	1707	|	|	|	|	1907	...	2020	|	...	2107	2107	2107	|	|	...	...	|	...	2307
Trenčín d.	1538	1538	1638	|	...	1723	1723	1738	1738	|	1838	1923	...	2032	2038	...	2123	2123	2120	2138	2138	...	2153	2235	2253	2320
Trenčianska Teplá d.	|	|	|	|	...	1729	1729	|	|	|	|	1929	...	2039	|	...	2129	2129	...	|	|	...	2201	...	2301	...
Praha hl. n. **1160** d.	|	|	|	|	1300	|	|	|	|	|	|	|	1515	|	|	...	|	|	...	|	|	1715	|	...	|	...
Púchov **1161** d.	1557	1557	1657	|	|	1757	1752	1757	1757	|	1857	1952	1957	2053	2057	...	2150	2152	...	2204	2204	2157	2232	...	2328	...
Považská Bystrica **1161** d.	1607	1607	1707	|	|	1807	1817	1807	1807	|	1907	2002	2006	2101	2107	...	...	2202	...	2214	2214	2206	2243	...	...	...
Žilina **1161** a.	1629	1629	1729	1807	1824	1829	1839	1829	1829	1903	1929	2024	2029	2124	2129	...	...	2224	...	2236	2236	2229	2316	...	...	...
Žilina **1185** d.	1631	1631	1734	1809	1825	...	...	1834	1831	1905	1934	...	—	—	2134	2143	...	...	...	2240	0434	...	...	...	...	...
Vrútky **1185** d.	1656	1656	1800	|	1848	...	...	1858	1856	|	2000	...	...	...	2158	2213	...	...	...	2305	0459	...	...	...	...	...
Kraľovany d.	1710	1710	1816	|	|	...	...	...	1910	|	2016	...	...	2	...	2234	...	...	...	...	0513	...	...	...	...	...
Ružomberok d.	1725	1725	1831	|	1914	...	...	...	1926	|	2032	...	...	...	...	2256	...	...	...	...	0528	...	...	...	...	...
Liptovský Mikuláš d.	1743	1743	1853	|	1933	...	...	...	1950	|	2053	...	2	2230	...	2318	...	...	...	...	0548	...	...	...	...	...
Štrba d.	1812	1812	1921	|	1959	...	...	...	2018	|	2121	...	|	2306	...	...	...	...	...	...	0617	...	...	...	...	...
Poprad-Tatry d.	1830	1831	1941	1958	2017	...	...	...	2037	2055	2141	...	2244	2326	...	...	...	...	...	...	0713	...	...	...	...	...
Spišská Nová Ves d.	...	1850	1959	|	2034	...	...	...	2056	2113	2159	...	2312	...	...	...	...	...	...	...	0732	...	...	...	...	...
Margecany d.	...	1917	2026	|	|	...	...	...	2124	|	2226	...	2353	...	...	...	...	...	...	...	0757	...	...	...	...	...
Prešov a.	...	1947	|	|	2126	...	...	...	|	|	|	...	...	...	...	...	...	...	...	...	|	...	...	...	...	...
Kysak **1196** d.	...	|	2040	2052	|	...	...	...	2139	2201	2240	...	...	...	...	...	...	...	...	...	0817	...	...	...	...	...
Košice **1196** a.	...	|	2053	2113	2206	...	...	...	2151	2213	2253	...	...	...	...	...	...	...	...	...	0833	...	...	...	...	...
Humenné **1194** a.	...	2121	...	...	...	...	...	...	...	...	...	...	...	...	...	...	...	...	...	...	1032	...	...	...	...	...

	614	1732		*Ex* 620	*EC* 222	442 622		*Ex* 622	16700	700		♥ 1046	*Ex* 624			*EC* 220	*Ex* 626	702	*Ex* 600	♠ 1256	*IC* 520	*IC* 44	704	*Ex* 602	♥ 1012	706
			2				2	✕			2	🍷	✕	2	2				✕	🍷 R	✕	✕		✕	🍷	
	E	e	Ⓐ	e		F	Ⓐ	Ⓐ	⑥n	Ⓐ	Ⓐ	C			Ⓐ		Ⓐ									
Humenné **1194** d.	2151	...	...	...	...	1930	...	...	...	...	...	...	...	...	...	...	...	...	...	...	...	...	...	...	...	...
Košice **1196** d.	2345	...	...	...	...	2208	...	...	...	...	...	...	...	...	...	...	...	...	0507	0450	0607	0702	...	0707	0753	...
Kysak **1196** d.	2359	...	...	...	...	2221	...	...	...	...	...	...	...	...	...	...	...	...	0522	|	0620	0715	...	0722	0810	...
Prešov d.	|	...	...	...	...	|	...	...	...	...	...	...	...	...	...	...	...	...	|	0550	|	|	...	|	|	...
Margecany d.	0014	...	...	...	...	2236	...	...	...	...	...	...	...	0355	...	...	...	...	0537	|	|	|	...	0737	|	...
Spišska Nová Ves d.	0041	...	...	...	...	2302	...	...	...	...	...	...	...	0445	...	...	...	...	0605	0649	0700	|	...	0805	0851	...
Poprad-Tatry d.	0101	...	...	...	...	2341	...	...	...	...	...	...	...	0513	...	...	0530	...	0625	0707	0719	0810	...	0825	0911	...
Štrba d.	|	...	...	...	...	|	...	...	...	...	...	...	...	...	...	...	0548	...	0644	0726	|	|	...	0844	0928	...
Liptovský Mikuláš d.	0148	...	...	...	...	0026	0334	...	...	...	0436	...	...	...	0534	...	0616	...	0712	0753	|	|	...	0912	0956	...
Ružomberok d.	0206	...	...	...	...	0043	0357	...	...	...	0459	...	...	...	0557	...	0634	...	0730	0809	|	|	...	0930	1013	...
Kraľovany d.	0222	...	...	...	...	|	0419	...	...	...	0521	...	...	...	0625	...	0649	...	0746	|	|	|	...	0946	|	...
Vrútky **1185** d.	0237	...	...	...	...	|	0441	0458	...	...	0549	...	0603	...	0649	...	0703	...	0801	0837	|	|	...	1001	1041	...
Žilina **1185** a.	0301	...	...	...	...	0130	...	0522	...	...	0616	...	0627	...	0716	...	0727	...	0825	0900	0905	0955	...	1025	1103	...
Žilina **1161** d.	0303	...	...	...	0523	0530	...	0530	0530	...	...	0619	0630	...	...	0720	0730	0737	0830	0902	0907	0957	0930	1030	1105	1130
Považská Bystrica **1161** d.	0331	...	...	...	0548	0554	...	0554	0554	...	...	0642	0654	...	...	0745	0754	0800	0854	|	|	|	0954	1054	|	1154
Púchov **1161** d.	0341	...	0431	...	0602	0605	...	0605	0610	0610	...	0651	0705	...	...	0808	0805	0810	0905	|	|	|	1004	1105	|	1210
Praha hl. n. **1160** a.	|	...	|	...	1045	|	...	|	|	|	...	|	|	...	...	1245	|	|	|	1431	|	|	|	|	1608	|
Trenčianska Teplá d.	0357	...	0500	...	...	|	...	|	0631	0631	...	0706	|	...	...	...	|	0831	|	...	|	|	1025	|	...	1231
Trenčín d.	0406	0440	0507	0524	...	0624	...	0624	0640	0640	...	0712	0724	...	...	...	0824	0840	0924	...	|	|	1032	1124	...	1240
Nové Mesto nad Váhom d.	0422	0453	...	|	...	|	...	|	0653	0653	...	0724	|	...	...	...	|	0853	|	...	|	|	1053	|	...	1253
Piešťany d.	0434	0504	...	|	...	|	...	|	0703	0703	...	0734	|	...	...	...	|	0903	|	...	|	|	1103	|	...	1303
Leopoldov **1181** d.	0447	0516	...	|	...	|	...	|	0714	0714	...	|	|	...	...	...	|	0914	|	...	|	|	1114	|	...	1314
Trnava **1181** d.	0501	0533	...	0602	...	0702	...	0702	0730	0730	...	0757	0802	...	...	...	0901	0930	1002	...	|	|	1130	1202	...	1330
Bratislava hl. st. a.	0533	0604	...	0633	...	0733	...	0733	0801	0801	...	0828	0833	...	...	...	0933	1001	1033	...	1045	1133	1201	1233	...	1401
Wien Hbf. **996** a.	...	...	...	...	...	...	...	...	...	...	...	...	...	...	...	...	...	...	...	...	...	1324	...	...	...	...

	Ex 604	708	*Ex* 606	*IC* 522	710	*Ex* 608	*SC* 240	*Ex* 17628	712	*Ex* 610	1760	*Ex* 17630	714	*Ex* 612	*IC* 524	716	17716	762				1764		♥ 1020	*EN* 442	♠ 1248
	✕		✕	✕		✕	✕ R			✕	2			✕	✕				2	2	2	2	2	🍷	R	🍷 R
							B	⑦h			Ⓐ	⑦h				Ⓐ	⑦h							⊡	A	
Humenné **1194** d.	...	...	...	...	...	...	...	...	...	...	...	1438	...	...	...	...	...	...	...	...	...	...	...	...	1930	...
Košice **1196** d.	0907	...	1107	1203	...	1307	1418	1407	...	1507	1607	|	...	1707	1803	...	...	1907	...	...	...	2107	...	2137	2208	2238
Kysak **1196** d.	0922	...	1122	1216	...	1322	1431	1422	...	1522	1621	|	...	1722	1816	...	...	1921	...	...	...	2121	...	2150	2221	|
Prešov d.	|	...	|	|	...	|	|	|	...	|	|	1605	...	|	|	...	...	|	...	...	...	|	...	|	|	2322
Margecany d.	0937	...	1137	|	...	1337	|	1436	...	1537	1635	1635	...	1737	|	...	...	1935	...	...	...	2136	...	2205	2236	|
Spišska Nová Ves d.	1005	...	1205	1256	...	1405	1510	1503	...	1605	1706	1704	...	1805	1856	...	...	2006	...	...	...	2207	...	2231	2302	0017
Poprad-Tatry d.	1025	...	1225	1315	...	1425	1529	1536	...	1625	1726	1728	...	1825	1915	...	...	2030	...	...	...	2227	2241	2255	2341	0037
Štrba d.	1044	...	1244	|	...	1444	1548	1601	...	1644	...	1748	...	1843	|	...	...	2049	...	...	...	...	2302	2314	|	0056
Liptovský Mikuláš d.	1112	...	1312	|	...	1512	1617	1629	...	1712	...	1817	...	1912	|	...	...	2116	...	...	2237	...	2336	2341	0026	0123
Ružomberok d.	1130	...	1330	|	...	1530	1635	1647	...	1730	...	1835	...	1930	|	...	...	2133	...	...	2301	...	...	2358	0043	0141
Kraľovany d.	1146	...	1346	|	...	1546	1650	1703	...	1746	...	1850	...	1946	|	...	...	2148	...	...	2325	...	...	|	|	|
Vrútky **1185** d.	1201	...	1401	|	...	1601	1704	1715	...	1801	...	1904	...	2001	|	...	...	2203	...	2251	2347	...	...	0025	|	0207
Žilina **1185** a.	1225	...	1425	1501	...	1625	1728	1740	...	1825	...	1928	...	2025	2101	...	...	2227	...	2318	...	...	...	0049	0130	0228
Žilina **1161** d.	1230	1330	1430	1503	1530	1630	1732	1743	1730	1830	...	1930	1930	2030	2103	2143	2143	...	2244	...	...	...	...	0051	0146	0230
Považská Bystrica **1161** d.	1254	1354	1454	|	1554	1654	|	1806	1754	1854	...	1954	1954	2054	|	2205	2205	...	2319	...	...	...	...	|	|	|
Púchov **1161** d.	1305	1410	1505	|	1610	1705	|	1819	1810	1905	...	2005	2010	2105	|	2214	2214	...	2328	...	...	...	...	|	|	|
Praha hl. n. **1160** a.	|	|	|	|	|	|	2231	|	|	|	...	|	|	|	|	|	|	...	...	...	...	...	...	0557	0738	0731
Trenčianska Teplá d.	|	1431	|	|	1631	|	...	|	1831	|	...	|	2031	|	|	2236	2236	...	...	...	...	...	...	...	...	...
Trenčín d.	1324	1440	1524	|	1640	1724	...	1838	1840	1924	...	2024	2040	2124	|	2241	2244	...	...	...	...	...	...	...	...	...
Nové Mesto nad Váhom d.	|	1453	|	|	1653	|	...	|	1853	|	...	|	2053	|	|	...	2256	...	...	...	...	...	...	...	...	...
Piešťany d.	|	1503	|	|	1703	|	...	|	1903	|	...	|	2103	|	|	...	2306	...	...	...	...	...	...	...	...	...
Leopoldov **1181** d.	|	1514	|	|	1714	|	...	|	1914	|	...	|	2114	|	|	...	2317	...	...	...	...	...	...	...	...	...
Trnava **1181** d.	1402	1530	1602	|	1730	1802	...	1915	1930	2002	...	2102	2130	2202	|	...	2333	...	...	...	...	...	...	...	...	...
Bratislava hl. st. a.	1433	1601	1633	1641	1801	1833	...	1945	2001	2033	...	2133	2201	2233	2241	...	0005	...	...	...	...	...	...	...	...	...
Wien Hbf. **996** a.	...	...	...	...	...	...	...	...	...	...	...	...	...	...	...	...	...	...	...	...	...	...	...	...	...	...

ADDITIONAL TRAINS BRATISLAVA - TRENČÍN

2nd class

km		1731	1733	1735	1737	1739	1741	1743	1745	1747	1749
0	**Bratislava** hl. st. d.	0455	0655	0855	1055	1255	1455	1655	1855	2055	2227
46	Trnava d.	0530	0730	0930	1130	1330	1530	1730	1930	2130	2301
63	Leopoldov d.	0544	0744	0944	1144	1344	1544	1744	1944	2143	2314
81	Piešťany d.	0555	0755	0955	1155	1355	1555	1755	1955	2154	2326
99	N. Mesto nad Váhom d.	0607	0807	1007	1207	1407	1607	1815	2007	2206	2338
124	**Trenčín** d.	0620	0820	1020	1220	1420	1620	1828	2020	2219	2351

	1730	1734	1736	1738	1740	1742	1744	1746	1748	1750
Trenčín d.	0340	0540	0740	0936	1140	1340	1530	1740	1940	2133
Nové Mesto nad Váhom d.	0353	0553	0753	0950	1153	1353	1544	1753	1953	2147
Piešťany d.	0404	0604	0804	1000	1204	1404	1554	1804	2004	2206
Leopoldov d.	0416	0616	0816	1019	1216	1416	1613	1816	2016	2217
Trnava d.	0433	0633	0833	1033	1233	1433	1629	1833	2033	2233
Bratislava hl. st. a.	0504	0704	0904	1104	1304	1504	1702	1904	2104	2304

FOR ADDITIONAL SERVICES AND FOOTNOTES SEE PREVIOUS PAGE.

1181 BRATISLAVA - PRIEVIDZA and TRNAVA - NITRA

2nd class

km		743	745	747	749	751	17751	753	755	757
		Ⓐ		Ⓐ		Ⓐ	⑦d		Ⓐ	
0	**Bratislava** N. Mesto d.	...	0701	0901	1101	...	1301	1501	1701	1901
46	Trnava **1180** d.	...	0739	0939	1139	...	1339	1539	1739	1939
63	Leopoldov **1180** d.	0553	0753	0953	1153	1353	1353	1553	1753	1953
87	Zbehy d.	0622	0822	1022	1222	1422	1422	1622	1822	2022
114	Topoľčany ◧ d.	0646	0846	1046	1246	1446	1446	1646	1846	2046
131	Partizánske ◧ d.	0715	0915	1115	1315	1515	1515	1715	1915	2111
158	**Prievidza** ◧ a.	0746	0946	1146	1346	1546	1546	1746	1946	2141

	740	742	744	746	748	750	752	17752	754
	Ⓐ		Ⓐ		Ⓐ		Ⓐ	⑦d	
Prievidza ◧ d.	0410	0620	0820	1020	1220	1420	1620	1620	1820
Partizánske ◧ d.	0447	0652	0852	1052	1252	1452	1652	1652	1852
Topoľčany ◧ d.	0515	0714	0914	1114	1314	1514	1714	1714	1914
Zbehy d.	0546	0746	0946	1146	1346	1546	1746	1746	1946
Leopoldov **1180** d.	0610	0810	1007	1210	1410	1619	1807	1810	2010
Trnava **1180** d.	0625	0825	...	1225	1425	1633	...	1825	2025
Bratislava N. Mesto a.	0700	0900	...	1300	1500	1706	...	1900	2100

km																								
			A								A			A			A		A					
0	**Trnava** **1180** d.	0504	0607	0707	...	0807	0907	1007	...	1107	1207	1307	...	1407	1507	...	1607	1707	1807	...	1907	2007	2107	...
17	Leopoldov **1180** d.	0519	0619	0719	...	0819	0919	1019	...	1119	1219	1319	...	1419	1519	...	1619	1719	1819	...	1919	2019	2119	...
41	Zbehy d.	0544	|	0744	...	|	0944	|	...	1144	|	1344	...	|	1544	...	|	1744	|	...	1944	|	2142	...
45	Lužianky **1172** d.	|	0701	|	...	0901	|	1101	...	|	1301	|	...	1501	|	...	1701	|	1901	...	|	2101	|	...
52	**Nitra** **1172** a.	0556	0711	0756	...	0912	0956	1112	...	1156	1311	1356	...	1511	1556	...	1711	1756	1911	...	1956	2112	2154	...

	A		A			A								A			A			A		e	
Nitra **1172** d.	0446	0607	0649	...	0807	0849	1007	...	1048	1207	1248	...	1407	1449	...	1607	1649	1807	...	1849	2007	2117	...
Lužianky **1172** d.	0458	|	0703	...	|	0903	|	...	1102	|	1303	...	|	1502	...	|	1703	|	...	1902	|	2133	...
Zbehy d.	0505	0619	|	...	0819	|	1019	...	|	1219	|	...	1419	|	...	1619	|	1819	...	|	2019	2144	...
Leopoldov **1180** d.	0537	0640	0737	...	0840	0937	1040	...	1137	1240	1337	...	1440	1537	...	1640	1737	1840	...	1937	2040	2212	...
Trnava **1180** a.	0549	0652	0749	...	0852	0949	1052	...	1149	1252	1349	...	1452	1549	...	1652	1749	1852	...	1949	2052	...	...

A – To / from Nové Zamky on Ⓐ (Table **1172**).
d – ⑦ (also Apr. 10, May 1, 8, July 5, Aug. 29, Oct. 1; not Apr. 9, 30, May 7).
e – Ⓑ (not Apr. 7, 9, 30, May 7, Sept. 1, 15, Nov. 17).
◧ – Slower local trains are available from Topoľčany at 0540 and every two hours until 2140; from Prievidza at 0514, 0709 and every two hours until 1909, 2103, 2230 Ⓐ.

1182 LOCAL LINES IN POPRAD TATRY AREA

2nd class

km										
0	Poprad Tatry d.	0430	...	...		2130	...	...	2230	...
13	Starý Smokovec d.	0455	...	...	and at	2155	...	...	2255	...
13	Starý Smokovec d.	0459	0500	...	the same	2159	2200	...	2259	2300
19	Tatranská Lomnica a.	|	0514	...	minutes	|	2214	...	|	2314
29	Štrbské Pleso a.	0539	...	...	past each	2239	...	...	2339	...
29	Štrbské Pleso d.	...	...	0543	hour until	...	...	2240	...	...
34	Štrba a.	...	...	0601	⊡	...	...	2258	...	...

Štrba d.	...	...	0426	...	...		2126	...	...
Štrbské Pleso a.	...	...	0439	...	...	and at	2139	...	...
Štrbské Pleso d.	...	0410	...	...	0510	the same	...	...	2210
Tatranská Lomnica a.	0436	|	...	0536	|	minutes	...	2236	|
Starý Smokovec d.	0450	0452	...	0550	0552	past each	...	2250	2252
Starý Smokovec d.	...	0456	...	...	0556	hour until	...	...	2256
Poprad Tatry a.	...	0519	...	...	0619		...	...	2319

km																									
				B			B			B			B			B						C	C		
0	Poprad Tatry d.	0446	...	0616	0646	...	0816	0846	...	1016	1046	then	1816	1846	...	2016	2046	...	2246	...		0729	1529	...	...
8	Studený Potok d.	0502	...	0629	0702	...	0829	0902	...	1029	1102	each	1829	1902	...	2029	2102	...	2302	...	A	0741	1541	...	...
17	Tatranská Lomnica a.	|	...	0640	|	...	0840	|	...	1040	|	train runs	1840	|	...	2040	|	...	|	...	L	|	|	...	...
14	Kežmarok d.	0515	...	...	0715	...	...	0915	...	...	1115	every	...	1915	...	...	2115	...	2315	...	S	0751	1551	...	...
44	Stará Lubovňa **1196** a.	0558	...	...	0758	...	...	0958	...	...	1158	**two**	...	1958	...	...	2158	...	2358	...	O	0834	1634	...	...
60	Plaveč ▦ **1196** a.	...	...	...	...	...	...	...	...	...	...	hours	...	...	...	...	...	...	...	...		0851	1651	...	...
75	Muszyna a.	...	...	...	...	...	...	...	...	...	...	until	...	...	...	...	...	...	...	...		0911	1711	...	...

				B			B			B			B			B					C	C		
Muszyna d.	...	...	...	...	...	...	...	...	...	...	then	...	...	...	...	...	...	...	...		1000	1756	...	...
Plaveč ▦ **1196** d.	...	...	...	...	...	...	...	...	...	...	each	...	...	...	...	...	...	...	...	A	1019	1819	...	...
Stará Lubovňa **1196** d.	0402	...	0602	...	...	0802	...	...	1002	...	train runs	1802	...	...	2002	...	...	2202	...	L	1033	1833	...	...
Kežmarok d.	0449	...	0649	...	...	0849	...	...	1049	...	every	1849	...	...	2049	...	...	2249	...	S	1117	1917	...	...
Tatranská Lomnica d.	|	...	|	0726	...	|	0926	...	|	1126	**two**	|	1926	...	|	2126	...	|	...	O	|	|	...	...
Studený Potok d.	0501	...	0701	0742	...	0901	0942	...	1101	1142	hours	1901	1942	...	2101	2142	...	2301	...		1128	1928	...	...
Poprad Tatry a.	0515	...	0715	0755	...	0915	0955	...	1115	1155	until	1915	1955	...	2115	2155	...	2315	...		1140	1940	...	...

B – Ⓒ (daily July 1 - Sept. 3).
C – ⑥⑦ June 3 - Sept. 3.
⊡ – 2030 Poprad Tatry - Štrbské Pleso requires a change of trains at Starý Smokovec; 21xx Starý Smokovec - Štrbské Pleso runs 10 minutes later.

1183 POPRAD TATRY - ZAKOPANE - KRAKÓW

Flixbus

	D		D		
Poprad Tatry (Bus Station)* d.	0515	1540	1655	1935	...
Starý Smokovec (Bus Station) d.	0527	1555	1707	1950	...
Tatranská Lomnica (Bus Station) d.	0537	1607	1720	2005	...
Zakopane (Bus Station)* a.	|	1730	|	2135	...
Zakopane (Bus Station)* d.	|	1740	|	2145	...
Kraków (MDA Terminal) ⊖ a.	0820	2005	1950	2400	...

		E		E	
Kraków (MDA Terminal) ⊖ d.	0630	1050	1010	2150	...
Zakopane (Bus Station)* a.	0840	|	1215	|	...
Zakopane (Bus Station)* d.	0850	|	1225	|	...
Tatranská Lomnica (Bus Station) d.	1022	1317	1420	0017	...
Starý Smokovec (Bus Station) d.	1035	1327	1432	0027	...
Poprad Tatry (Bus Station)* a.	1055	1345	1450	0045	...

RAIL TICKETS NOT VALID.
D – ①②⑤⑥⑦.
E – ①④⑤⑥⑦.
* – Adjacent to railway station.
⊖ – adjacent to Kraków Gowny.
▦ = Lysa Polana.

1185 ZVOLEN, BANSKÁ BYSTRICA and PRIEVIDZA - VRÚTKY

2nd class

km			930			932			934		936		938				940			942			944		946	
		Ⓐ	①–⑥ d	Ⓐ	Ⓒ		Ⓐ								Ⓐ			Ⓐ			Ⓐ				Ⓑ e	
0	**Zvolen** osob. **1170** d.	...	0516	...	...	0616	...	...	0816	...	1016	...	1216	...	...	...	1416	...	...	1616	...	...	1816	...	2020	...
21	**Banská Bystrica** **1170** a.	...	0543	...	...	0643	...	...	0843	...	1043	...	1243	...	...	...	1443	...	...	1643	...	...	1843	...	2043	...
21	**Banská Bystrica** d.	...	0546	...	...	0646	...	...	0846	...	1046	...	1246	...	...	...	1446	...	...	1646	...	...	1846	...	2046	...
	Prievidza d.	0503	|	...	0603	|	...	0803	|	1003	|	1203	|	...	...	1403	|	...	1603	|	...	1803	|	2003	|	2203
	Handlová d.	0533	|	...	0633	|	...	0833	|	1033	|	1233	|	...	...	1433	|	...	1633	|	...	1833	|	2033	|	2233
	Horná Štubňa d.	0601	|	...	0701	|	...	0901	|	1101	|	1301	|	...	...	1501	|	...	1701	|	...	1901	|	2101	|	2256
66	Turčianske Teplice d.	0610	0632	0710	0710	0732	0810	0910	0932	1110	1132	1310	1332	...	1410	1510	1532	1610	1710	1732	1810	1910	1932	2110	2132	...
89	Martin d.	0637	0649	0737	0737	0749	0837	0937	0949	1137	1149	1337	1349	...	1437	1537	1549	1637	1737	1749	1837	1937	1949	2137	2149	...
96	**Vrútky** a.	0644	0655	0744	0744	0755	0844	0944	0955	1144	1155	1344	1355	...	1444	1544	1555	1644	1744	1755	1844	1944	1955	2144	2155	...

				931			933		935		937			939			941			943		945		947	
	Ⓐ	Ⓒ	Ⓐ	①–⑥ d	Ⓒ	Ⓐ							Ⓐ			Ⓐ			Ⓐ					Ⓑ e	
Vrútky d.	...	...	0514	0604	0614	0714	0804	0814	1004	1014	1204	1214	1314	1404	1414	1514	1604	1614	1714	1804	1814	2004	2014	2104	2224
Martin d.	...	...	0522	0611	0622	0722	0811	0822	1011	1022	1211	1222	1322	1411	1422	1522	1611	1622	1722	1811	1822	2011	2022	2111	2232
Turčianske Teplice d.	...	...	0549	0628	0649	0748	0828	0849	1028	1049	1228	1249	1348	1428	1449	1548	1628	1649	1748	1828	1849	2028	2049	2128	2259
Horná Štubňa d.	0404	0417	0604	|	0704	...	|	0904	|	1104	|	1304	...	|	1504	...	|	1704	...	|	1904	|	2104	|	2309
Handlová d.	0426	0440	0626	|	0726	...	|	0926	|	1126	|	1326	...	|	1526	...	|	1726	...	|	1926	|	2126	|	...
Prievidza a.	0457	0511	0657	|	0757	...	|	0957	|	1157	|	1357	...	|	1557	...	|	1757	...	|	1957	|	2157	|	...
Banská Bystrica a.	...	...	...	0711	...	...	0911	...	1111	...	1311	...	...	1511	...	...	1711	...	...	1911	...	2111	...	2211	...
Banská Bystrica **1170** d.	...	...	...	0713	...	...	0913	...	1113	...	1313	...	...	1513	...	...	1713	...	...	1913	...	2113	...	2213	...
Zvolen osob. **1170** a.	...	...	...	0740	...	...	0940	...	1140	...	1340	...	...	1540	...	...	1740	...	...	1940	...	2140	...	2235	...

km											
		Ⓐ	Ⓒf	Ⓐf	Ⓒ	Ⓒ	Ⓐ				
0	**Horná Štubňa** d.	0401	0501	0601	0901	1301	1501	1701	...	...	...
20	Kremnica d.	0426	0526	0626	0926	1326	1526	1726	...	...	...
46	**Hronská Dúbrava** d.	0457	0557	0657	0957	1357	1557	1757	...	...	...

	Ⓐ	Ⓒ	Ⓒ	g	Ⓐ					
Hronská Dúbrava d.	0501	0601	1001	1401	1601	1801	...	...	...	...
Kremnica d.	0533	0634	1033	1433	1633	1833	...	...	...	...
Horná Štubňa a.	0558	0658	1058	1457	1658	1858	...	...	...	...

d – ①–⑥ (not Apr. 8, 10, May 1, 8, Sept. 2, 16, Nov. 18).
e – Ⓑ (not Apr. 7, 9, 30, May 7, Sept. 1, 15, Nov. 17).
f – To Zvolen (a. 0610 Ⓒ / 0710 Ⓐ).
g – From Zvolen on Ⓐ (d. 1345).

2nd class BANSKÁ BYSTRICA - MARGECANY 1188

km		Ⓐ	Ⓐ	A	Ⓒ		Ⓐ			A
0	**Banská Bystrica** ⊡ d.	...	...	0613	0813	1013	...	1413	...	1813
43	Brezno ⊡ d.	...	...	0708	0908	1108	...	1508	...	1908
86	Červená Skala d.	...	...	0806	1002	1206	...	1606	...	2006
94	Telgárt penzión d.	...	...	0812	1009	1212	...	1612	...	2012
106	Dobšinká L'adová Jaskyňa d.	0418	0618	0824	1021	1224	1418	1624	...	2024
114	Dedinky d.	0428	0628	0834	1030	1234	1428	1634	...	2034
139	Nálepkovo a.	0500	0700	0902	...	1302	1500	1702	...	2102
		◧	◧	|		|	◧	|		|
139	Nálepkovo ⊡ d.	0502	0702	0902	...	1302	1502	1702	1902	2102
171	Gelnica ⊡ d.	0542	0742	0942	...	1342	1542	1742	1942	2142
179	**Margecany** ⊡ a.	0553	0753	0953	...	1353	1553	1753	1953	2153

			A	Ⓒ				A	
Margecany ⊡ d.	0407	0607	1007	...	1207	1407	1607	1807	2007
Gelnica ⊡ d.	0418	0618	1018	...	1218	1418	1618	1818	2018
Nálepkovo ⊡ a.	0454	0708	1108	...	1254	1508	1654	1908	2054
		|	|		Ⓐ	|	Ⓐ	|	Ⓐ
Nálepkovo d.	...	0708	1108	...	1308	1508	1708	1908	2108
Dedinky d.	...	0736	1136	1336	1341	1536	1741	1936	2141
Dobšinká L'adová Jaskyňa d.	...	0746	1146	1347	1351	1546	1751	1946	2151
Telgárt penzión d.	...	0757	1157	1359	...	1557	...	1957	...
Červená Skala d.	...	0804	1204	1407	...	1604	...	2004	...
Brezno ⊡ d.	...	0909	1309	1509	...	1709	...	2109	...
Banská Bystrica ⊡ a.	...	1006	1406	1606	...	1806	...	2206	...

A – Ⓒ (daily July 1 - Sept. 3).
◧ – Daily.
⊡ – Local trains run Banská Bystrica - Brezno and Nálepkovo - Margecany every two hours. Some Brezno trains extend to / from Červená Skala.

ZVOLEN - KOŠICE 1190

km		801 Bd	911	915	917	919	923	923 Ⓑe		
0	**Zvolen** osob. ⊖ d.	0326	0526	0926	1126	1326	1726	1926	...	...
54	Lučenec ⊖ d.	0413	0613	1013	1213	1413	1813	2013	...	...
69	Fil'akovo zastávka ⊖ d.	0429	0629	1029	1229	1429	1829	2029	...	...
98	Jesenské ● d.	0454	0654	1054	1254	1454	1854	2054	...	...
162	Rožňava d.	0547	0749	1149	1349	1549	1949	2149	...	...
202	Moldava nad Bodvou d.	0619	0818	1218	1418	1618	2018	2218	...	...
233	**Košice** a.	0644	0844	1244	1444	1644	2044	2244	...	...

	910 d	912	914	918	920	922	800 Be		
Košice d.	0522	0722	0922	1322	1522	1722	2246	...	...
Moldava nad Bodvou d.	0546	0746	0946	1346	1546	1746	2311	...	...
Rožňava d.	0615	0815	1015	1415	1615	1815	2340	...	...
Jesenské ● d.	0706	0906	1106	1506	1706	1906	0030	...	...
Fil'akovo zastávka ⊖ d.	0730	0930	1130	1530	1730	1930	0054	...	...
Lučenec ⊖ d.	0747	0947	1147	1547	1747	1947	0106	...	...
Zvolen osob. ⊖ a.	0834	1034	1234	1634	1834	2034	0151	...	...

B – GEMERAN POL'ANA – 🚃12 Nové Zámky - Košice and v.v.: conveys 🛏 1, 2 cl. Praha (**283/2**) - Nové Zámky (**801/0**) - Košice and v.v.
d – ①–⑥ (not Apr. 8, 10, May 1, 8, Sept. 2, 16, Nov. 18).
e – Ⓑ (not Apr. 7, 9, 30, May 7, Sept. 1, 15, Nov. 17).
⊖ – Local trains run Zvolen - Lučenec and Lučenec - Fil'akovo zastávka every two hours.
● – Jesenske - Rimavská Sobota and v.v. (*11 km.* Journey 12 minutes): From Jesenske at 0509, 0609 Ⓐ, 0709 and every two hours until 2109. From Rimavská Sobota at 0536 Ⓐ, 0636 and every two hours until 2036.

2nd class KOŠICE - HUMENNÉ - MEDZILABORCE 1194

km		615 C		443 D							Ⓑe
	Bratislava **1180** d.	2257	...	...	...	...	...	...	...	...	...
0	**Košice** d.	0501	0701	0901	1101	1301	1501	1701	1901	2101	2301
68	Trebišov d.	0550	0748	0948	1148	1348	1548	1748	1948	2148	2348
88	Michalovce d.	0611	0809	1011	1209	1409	1609	1809	2009	2214	0009
112	**Humenné** a.	0633	0831	1032	1231	1431	1631	1831	2031	2235	0031

		Ⓐ							442 D	614 C
Humenné d.	0528	0638	0728	0928	1128	1328	1528	1728	1930	2151
Michalovce d.	0551	0704	0751	0951	1151	1351	1551	1751	1952	2213
Trebišov d.	0611	0728	0811	1011	1211	1411	1611	1811	2013	2237
Košice a.	0659	0819	0859	1059	1259	1459	1659	1859	2059	2325
Bratislava **1180** a.	...	...	...	...	...	...	...	...	...	0533

km											
0	**Humenné** d.	0436	0636	0836	1036	1236	1436	1636	1836	2036	2239
41	**Medzilaborce** a.	0546	0746	0946	1146	1346	1546	1746	1946	2146	2349

Medzilaborce d.	0427	0627	0827	1027	1227	1427	1627	1827	2027	2230
Humenné a.	0524	0724	0924	1124	1324	1524	1724	1924	2124	2327

C – TATRAN ZEMPLÍN – see Table **1180.**
D – SLOVAKIA – see Table **1180**.
e – Ⓑ (not Apr. 7, 9, 30, May 7, Sept. 1, 15, Nov. 17).

2nd class KOŠICE - ČIERNA NAD TISOU - CHOP - MUKACHEVO 1195

km										
0	**Košice** d.	0846	1146	...		0506	0706		2106	2306
62	Slovenské N. Mesto d.	|	|	...		0613	0813	and	2205	0005
95	**Čierna nad Tisou** a.	1000	1300	...	A	0649	0849	every	2242	0042
		|	|	...	L			two		
95	**Čierna nad Tisou** 🛃 d.	1023	1314	...	S	...	...	hours	...	...
105	Chop 🛃 ⊕ a.	1200	1451	...	O	...	...	until	...	...
105	Chop **1715** d.	1240	1532	...		...	...	⊙	...	...
146	**Mukachevo** **1715** a.	1400	1653	...		...	...		...	...

Mukachevo **1715** d.	1448	1816	...		...	...		...	...
Chop **1715** a.	1613	1926	...		...	...	and	...	...
Chop 🛃 ⊕ d.	1650	2006	...	A	...	...	every	...	...
Čierna nad Tisou 🛃 a.	1649	2005	...	L	...	...	two	...	...
	|	|		S			hours		
Čierna nad Tisou d.	1655	2017	...	O	0705	0905	until	1905	2030
Slovenské N. Mesto d.	|	|	...		0746	0946	⊙	1946	2114
Košice a.	1817	2133	...		0850	1050		2050	2220

⊕ – Ukraine time (one hour ahead of Slovakia).
⊙ – Also from Košice at 1406 Ⓐ, 1638 Ⓐ; also from Čierna nad Tisou at 0505 Ⓐ, 0605 Ⓐ, 1605 Ⓐ.

2nd class KOŠICE - PREŠOV - PLAVEČ - STARÁ LUBOVŇA 1196

km			Ⓐ	Ⓒf		Ⓐ		Ⓐ		Ⓐ	Ⓒf			Ⓐ		Ⓐ	⑤g		⑦h	Ⓐ		Ⓐ		
0	**Košice** **1180** d.	0443	0543	0627	0643	0743	0843	0943	1043	1143	1208	1243	...	1343	1443	1543	...	1643	...	1743	1843	1943	2043	2243
16	Kysak **1180** d.	0459	0559	|	0659	0759	0859	0959	1059	1159	|	1259	...	1359	1459	1559	...	1659	...	1759	1859	1959	2059	2259
33	**Prešov** **1180** a.	0514	0614	0706	0714	0814	0914	1014	1114	1214	1237	1314	...	1414	1514	1614	...	1714	...	1814	1914	2014	2114	2314
33	**Prešov** d.	0517	0617	0707	0717	0817	0917	1017	1117	*1217*	1240	1317	...	1417	1517	1617	...	1717	...	1817	1917	*2017*	2117	2317
65	Lipany a.	0557	0657	0735	0757	0857	0957	1057	1157	*1257*	1309	1357	...	1457	1557	1657	1705	1757	1805	1857	1957	*2057*	2157	2357
88	**Plaveč** a.	...	...	0802	...	...	...	...	...	...	1336	...	...	...	...	...	1736	...	1836	...	...	...	...	...
88	**Plaveč** **1182** d.	...	...	0809	...	...	...	...	...	...	1343	...	...	...	...	...	1737	...	1837	...	...	...	...	...
104	**Stará Lubovňa** **1182** a.	...	...	0823	...	...	...	...	...	...	1357	...	...	...	...	...	1756	...	1856	...	...	...	...	...

		Ⓐ		Ⓐ		Ⓐ		Ⓒf	Ⓐ		Ⓐ			Ⓐ		⑤g	Ⓐ	⑦h			Ⓒf		
Stará Lubovňa **1182** d.	...	...	...	...	...	...	...	1000	...	...	...	...	...	...	...	1605	...	1705	...	...	1800	...	...
Plaveč **1182** a.	...	...	...	...	...	...	...	1014	...	...	...	...	...	...	...	1623	...	1723	...	...	1814	...	...
Plaveč d.	...	...	...	...	...	...	...	1021	...	...	...	...	...	...	...	1624	...	1724	...	...	1840	...	...
Lipany d.	0403	0503	0603	0703	0803	0903	1003	1048	*1103*	1203	1303	...	1403	1503	1603	1655	1703	1755	1803	*1903*	1907	2003	2103
Prešov a.	0438	0538	0638	0738	0838	0938	1038	1116	*1138*	1238	1338	...	1438	1538	1638	...	1738	...	1838	*1938*	1939	2038	2138
Prešov **1180** d.	0442	0542	0642	0742	0842	0942	1042	1121	1142	1242	1342	...	1442	1542	1642	...	1742	...	1842	1942	1942	2042	2143
Kysak **1180** a.	0500	0600	0700	0800	0900	1000	1100	|	1200	1300	1400	...	1500	1600	1706	...	1800	...	1900	2000	|	2106	2206
Košice **1180** a.	0513	0613	0713	0813	0913	1013	1113	1153	1213	1313	1413	...	1513	1613	1719	...	1813	...	1913	2013	2013	2119	2219

f – Ⓒ June 17 - Sept. 17.
g – ⑤ (also Apr. 5, Sept. 14, Nov. 16; not Mar. 10, Apr. 7, July 7 - Sept. 1, Sept. 15, Nov. 17).
h – ⑦ (also Apr. 11, May 1, 8, Nov. 1; not Mar. 5, Apr. 9, 30, May 7, July 2 - Aug. 27, Oct. 29).

2nd class PREŠOV - BARDEJOV and HUMENNÉ 1197

km				Ⓐ			⊕						⊕		Ⓐ							j				
0	**Prešov** d.	0418	0450	0550	0618	0650	0730	0824	0850	1024	1050	1224	1233	1250	1350	1424	1450	1624	1650	1824	1850	2012	2024	2050	2224	2250
10	Kapušany pri Prešove d.	0429	0502	0602	0629	0702	|	0835	0902	1035	1102	1235	|	1302	1402	1435	1502	1635	1702	1835	1902	|	2035	2102	2235	2302
45	**Bardejov** a.	0523	|	|	0723	|	|	0929	|	1129	|	1329	|	|	|	1529	|	1729	|	1929	|	|	2129	|	2329	|
46	Vranov nad Toplou d.	...	0546	0646	...	0746	0813	...	0946	...	1146	...	1330	1346	1446	...	1546	...	1746	...	1946	2055	...	2146	...	2346
70	**Humenné** a.	...	0619	0721	...	0819	0840	...	1019	...	1219	...	1358	1419	1519	...	1619	...	1819	...	2019	2121	...	2219	...	...

			Ⓐ			Ⓐ§					⊕					k			⊕						
Humenné d.	...	...	0440	...	0540	*0638*	0740	...	0940	...	1037	1140	...	1340	...	1438	1540	...	1638	1740	...	1940	...	2140	...
Vranov nad Toplou d.	0415	...	0508	...	0608	0709	0808	...	1008	...	1100	1208	...	1408	...	1505	1608	...	1707	1808	...	2008	...	2208	...
Bardejov d.	|	0423	|	0623	|	|	|	0829	|	1029	|	|	1229	|	1429	|	|	1629	|	|	1829	|	2029	|	2229
Kapušany pri Prešove d.	0502	0516	0602	0716	0702	0802	0902	0922	1102	1122	|	1302	1322	1502	1522	|	1702	1722	|	1902	1922	2102	2122	2302	2322
Prešov a.	0513	0527	0613	0727	0713	0813	0913	0933	1113	1133	1153	1313	1333	1513	1533	1551	1713	1733	1804	1913	1933	2113	2133	2313	2333

j – 🚃12 Bratislava - Prešov - Humenné (train *Ex* **15621**). For days of running see Table **1180**.
k – 🚃12 Humenné - Prešov - Bratislava (train *Ex* **17630**). For days of running see Table **1180**.
§ – Connecting train change at Strážske.
⊕ – Ⓒ June 24 - Sept. 10.

HUNGARY

Operator: MÁV-START (www.mav-start.hu) running on the network of MÁV (www.mav.hu). Certain services in the west are operated by Győr - Sopron - Ebenfurthi Vasút (GySEV).

Services: All trains convey first and second class seating, except where shown otherwise in table headers, footnotes or train columns, or where the footnote shows sleeping or couchette cars only. Descriptions of sleeping (🛏) and couchette (🛏) cars appear on page 10. Certain international services cannot be used for internal journeys.

Timings: Valid **December 11, 2022 - December 9, 2023** with amendments as received. Engineering work may affect travel - it is not always possible to show short-term changes.

Reservations: Most InterCity (*IC*) and Express (*Ex*) trains have **compulsory** reservation, as shown by 🅁 in the tables. *IC* trains also require a supplement; the amount depends on distance of the journey. Higher reservation fees apply at peak times (Friday and Sunday afternoons), and if purchased on day of travel. A supplement is required for **domestic** journeys on **international** *EC / IC / RJ / EN* trains (and seat reservation is compulsory where shown as 🅁 in tables). For **international** journeys on these trains the supplement does not apply but seat reservation is possible (and is **compulsory** where shown in the tables). If a seat reservation or supplement is not paid in advance, a higher supplement is payable on the train: 500 HUF for domestic journeys and 10 EUR (which can be paid in HUF) for international journeys.

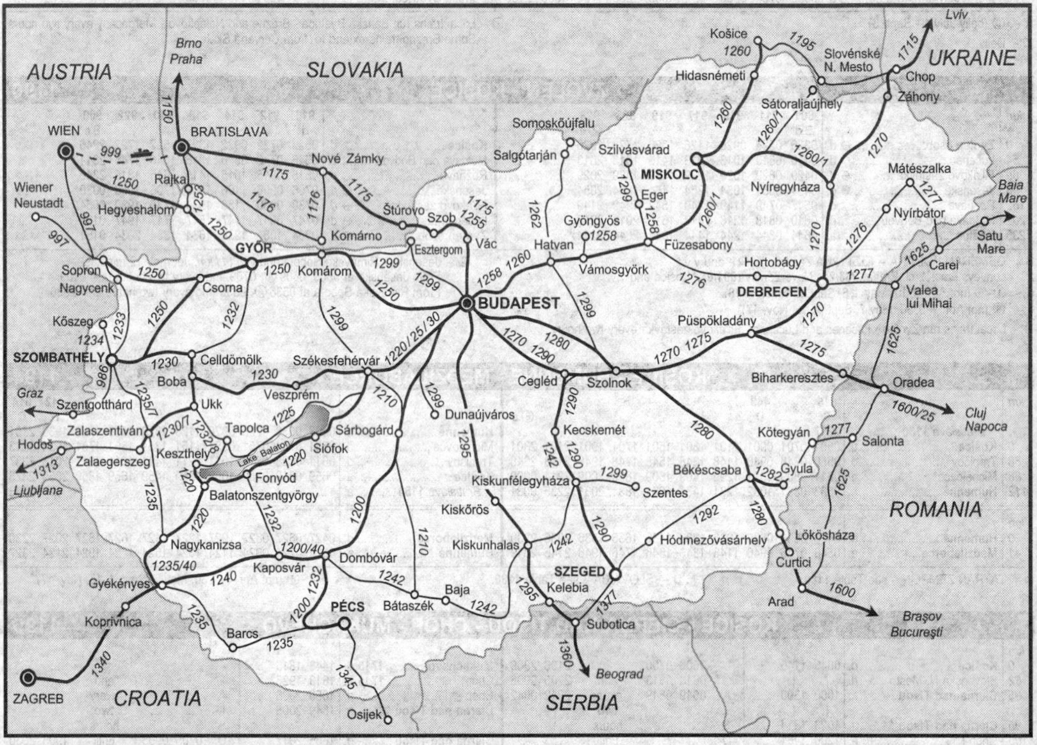

1200 BUDAPEST - DOMBÓVÁR - KAPOSVÁR and PÉCS

km		2 Ⓐ	2	2	2	*IC* 800 🅁	2	*IC* 822 🅁	2	*IC* 802 🅁	2	2	*IC* 812 🅁	2	2 ⑦	*IC* 804 🅁	2	*IC* 824 🅁	2	*IC* 814 🅁	2	2	*IC* 806 🅁	2 Ⓐ	2
0	**Budapest** Keleti d.	...	...	...	...	0553	...	0630	...	0753	...	...	0953	...	...	1153	...	1230	...	1353	...	...	1553	...	...
	Budapest Déli d.	...	...	...	0450	|	...	|	0650	|	...	0850	|	...	1050	|	...	|	1250	|	...	1450	|	1550	...
13	Kelenföld d.	...	...	...	0457	0612u	...	0653u	0657	0812u	...	0857	1012u	...	1057	1212u	...	1253u	1257	1412u	...	1457	1612u	1557	...
62	Pusztaszabolcs a.	...	...	...	0548	|	...	|	0748	|	...	0948	|	...	1148	|	...	|	1348	|	...	1548	|	1648	...
62	Pusztaszabolcs d.	...	...	...	0556	|	...	|	0804	|	...	1004	|	...	1157	|	...	|	1404	|	...	1604	|	1656	...
93	Sárbogárd d.	...	0441	...	0629	0659	...	|	0829	0859	...	1029	1059	...	1219	1259	...	|	1429	1459	...	1629	1659	1723	...
173	Dombóvár a.	...	0553	...	0742	0749	...	0856	0942	0949	...	1142	1149	...	...	1349	...	1456	1542	1549	...	1742	1749	...	...
173	Dombóvár 1240 d.	0513	...	0606	...	0750	0806	0857	...	0950	1006	...	1150	1206	...	1350	1406	1457	...	1550	1606	...	1750	...	1806
204	**Kaposvár** 1240 a.	|	...	|	...	|	|	0922	...	|	|	...	|	|	...	|	|	1522	...	|	|	...	|	...	|
218	Szentlőrinc d.	0605	...	0653	...	0829	0853	...	...	1029	1053	...	1229	1253	...	1429	1453	...	...	1629	1653	...	1829	...	1853
237	**Pécs** a.	0622	...	0714	...	0843	0914	...	...	1043	1114	...	1243	1314	...	1443	1514	...	...	1643	1714	...	1843	...	1914

	IC 826 🅁	2	*IC* 808 🅁	2 Ⓐ	2	2 ⑥	2 Ⓑ	*IC* 818 🅁	2
Budapest Keleti d.	1630	...	1753	...	...	...	...	1953	...
Budapest Déli d.	|	1650	|	1750	...	1850	1915	|	2050
Kelenföld d.	1653u	1657	1812u	1757	...	1857	1922	2012u	2057
Pusztaszabolcs a.	|	1748	|	1848	...	1948	1957	|	2148
Pusztaszabolcs d.	|	1804	|	1904	...	2004	2004	|	2204
Sárbogárd d.	|	1829	1859	1941	...	2029	2029	2059	2227
Dombóvár a.	1856	1942	1949	...	...	2142	2142	2149	...
Dombóvár 1240 d.	1857	...	1950	...	2006	...	...	2150	...
Kaposvár 1240 a.	1922	...	|	...	|	...	...	|	...
Szentlőrinc d.	**d**	...	2029	...	2053	...	...	2225	...
Pécs a.	...	...	2043	...	2114	...	...	2239	...

	2 Ⓐ	2 Ⓒ	2	2 Ⓐ	*IC* 809 🅁	2	*IC* 829 🅁	2	*IC* 807 🅁
Pécs d.	...	...	0437	...	0518	...	...	0639	0719
Szentlőrinc d.	...	...	0458	...	0532	...	**d**	0705	0733
Kaposvár 1240 d.	...	...	|	...	|	...	0607	|	|
Dombóvár 1240 a.	...	...	0545	...	0606	...	0633	0750	0806
Dombóvár d.	0348	0411	...	...	0607	0610	0634	...	0807
Sárbogárd d.	0458	0528	...	0623	0659	0727	|	...	0859
Pusztaszabolcs a.	0522	0553	...	0652	|	0753	|	...	|
Pusztaszabolcs d.	0523	0608	...	0708	|	0808	|	...	|
Kelenföld a.	0605	0701	...	0801	0749s	0901	0839s	...	0946s
Budapest Déli a.	0614	0709	...	0809	|	0909	|	...	|
Budapest Keleti a.	...	...	...	...	0805	...	0859	...	1005

	2	2	*IC* 817 🅁	2	2	*IC* 805 🅁	2 ⑦	*IC* 825 🅁	2	*IC* 815 🅁	2	2	*IC* 803 🅁	2	*IC* 823 🅁	2	*IC* 801 🅁	2	2	*IC* 811 🅁	2	2	2 Ⓑ	2 Ⓑ
Pécs d.	...	0848	0919	...	1048	1119	...	...	1248	1319	...	1448	1519	...	...	1648	1719	...	1848	1919	...	2048	2148	*2244*
Szentlőrinc d.	...	0905	0933	...	1105	1133	...	...	1305	1333	...	1505	1533	...	...	1705	1733	...	1905	1933	...	2105	2204	2305
Kaposvár 1240 d.	...	|	|	...	|	|	...	1200	|	|	...	|	|	...	1600	|	|	...	|	|	...	|	...	|
Dombóvár 1240 a.	...	0950	1006	...	1150	1206	...	1231	1350	1406	...	1550	1606	...	1631	1750	1806	...	1950	2006	...	2150	...	2350
Dombóvár d.	0810	...	1007	1010	...	1207	...	1234	...	1407	1410	...	1607	1610	1634	...	1807	1810	...	2007	2010	...	...	...
Sárbogárd d.	0928	...	1059	1128	...	1259	1327	|	...	1459	1528	...	1659	1727	|	...	1859	1928	...	2059	2128	...	...	...
Pusztaszabolcs a.	0953	...	|	1153	...	|	1353	|	...	|	1553	...	|	1753	|	...	|	1953	...	|	2153	...	...	...
Pusztaszabolcs d.	1008	...	|	1208	...	|	1408	|	...	|	1608	...	|	1808	|	...	|	2008	...	|	2208	...	...	...
Kelenföld a.	1101	...	1146s	1301	...	1346s	1501	1439s	...	1546s	1701	...	1746s	1901	1839s	...	1946s	2101	...	2146s	2301	...	...	...
Budapest Déli a.	1109	...	|	1309	...	|	1509	|	...	|	1709	...	|	1909	|	...	|	2109	...	|	2309	...	...	...
Budapest Keleti a.	...	...	1205	...	...	1405	...	1459	...	1605	...	...	1805	...	1859	...	2005	...	...	2205	...	...	...	...

d – To / from Gyékényes (Table **1240**).   **s** – Calls to set down only.   **u** – Calls to pick up only.

SZÉKESFEHÉRVÁR - SZEKSZÁRD - BAJA — 1210

2nd class

km		2 Ⓐ	IR 8302 Ⓐ	IR 18302 ⑥	IR 8392	IR 8304	IR 8394	IR 8306	IR 8396	IR 8308	IR 8398
0	**Székesfehérvár** d.	...	...	0602	0802	1002	1202	1402	1602	1802	2002
39	Sárbogárd ◧ a.	...	...	0653	0853	1053	1253	1453	1653	1853	2053
39	Sárbogárd ◧ d.	0407	0702	0702	0902	1102	1302	1502	1702	1902	2102
104	Szekszárd d.	0512	0800	0800	1000	1200	1400	1600	1800	2000	2200
123	Bátaszék **1242** a.	0530	0818	0818	1018	1218	1418	1618	1818	2018	2218
143	**Baja** **1242** a.	0555	0839	0839	1039	1239	1439	1639	1839	2039	...

	2 Ⓒ	2 Ⓐ	IR 8309	IR 8307	IR 8397 ⚒	IR 8305	IR 8395	IR 8303	IR 8393	IR 8301
Baja **1242** d.	...	...	0514	0714	0914	1114	1314	1514	1714	1914
Bátaszék **1242** d.	0353	...	0534	0734	0934	1134	1334	1534	1734	1934
Szekszárd d.	0415	...	0559	0759	0959	1159	1359	1559	1759	1959
Sárbogárd ◧ a.	0519	...	0655	0855	1055	1255	1455	1655	1855	2055
Sárbogárd ◧ d.	...	0620	0701	0901	1101	1301	1501	1701	1901	2101
Székesfehérvár a.	...	0711	0752	0952	1152	1352	1552	1752	1952	2152

◧ – For connections from/to Budapest see Table **1200**.

BUDAPEST - SIÓFOK - FONYÓD - KESZTHELY and NAGYKANIZSA — 1220

2nd class

SERVICE UNTIL MAY 14. FOR SERVICE FROM MAY 15 SEE PAGE 559.
Additional slower trains and connections are available Budapest - Székesfehérvár - Siófok and v.v. Carriages without 🅁 are available on *IC* trains.
TRAIN NAMES: Budapest - Nagykanizsa *IC* trains are named TOPART. Budapest - Keszthely *IC* trains are named BALATON.

km		Ⓐ		Ⓐ		*IC* 850 🅁	*IC* 860 🅁	*IC* 842 🅁	*IC* 862 🅁	*IR* 18592 Ⓒ d	*IC* 852 🅁	*IC* 864 🅁	*IC* 844 🅁	*IC* 874 🅁	*IC* 854 🅁	*IC* 866 🅁	*IC* 204 🅁 A	*IC* 876 🅁	*IC* 856 🅁	*IC* 868 🅁	*IC* 848 🅁	*IC* 878 🅁	
0	**Budapest** Déli 1225 1230 d.	...	...	0405	...	0530	0635	0735	0835	0805	0935	1035	1135	1235	1335	1435	1535	1635	1735	1835	1935	2035	*2200*
4	Kelenföld 1225 1230 d.	...	...	0412	...	0537	0642	0742	0842	0812	0942	1042	1142	1242	1342	1442	1542	1642	1742	1842	1942	2042	*2207*
67	**Székesfehérvár** 1225 1230 a.	...	...	0509	...	0615	0720	0820	0920	0851	1020	1120	1220	1320	1420	1520	1620	1720	1820	1920	2020	2120	*2247*
67	**Székesfehérvár** d.	...	...	0512	...	0616	0721	0821	0921	0852	1021	1121	1221	1321	1421	1521	1621	1721	1821	1921	2021	2121	2252
95	Lepsény d.	...	...	0535	...	0638	0740	0840	|	0919	1040	|	1240	|	1440	|	1640	|	1840	|	2040	2140	2315
115	**Siófok** a.	...	...	0555	...	0655	0755	0855	0955	0944	1055	1155	1255	1355	1455	1555	1655	1755	1855	1955	2055	2157	2334
115	**Siófok** d.	...	...	...	...	0657	0757	0857	0957	1004	1057	1157	1257	1357	1457	1557	1657	1757	1857	1957	2057	2201	...
124	Zamárdi d.	...	...	...	...	0704	0804	0904	1004	1016	1104	1204	1304	1404	1504	1604	1704	1804	1904	2004	2104	2208	...
130	Balatonföldvár d.	...	...	...	...	0709	0809	0909	1009	1024	1109	1209	1309	1409	1509	1609	1709	1809	1909	2009	2109	2213	...
139	Balatonszemes d.	...	...	...	...	0718	0818	0918	1018	1034	1118	1218	1318	1418	1518	1618	1718	1818	1918	2018	2118	2222	...
146	Balatonlelle d.	...	...	...	...	0724	0824	0924	1024	1042	1124	1224	1324	1424	1524	1624	1724	1824	1924	2024	2124	2228	...
149	Balatonboglár d.	...	...	...	...	0730	0830	0930	1030	1047	1130	1230	1330	1430	1530	1630	1730	1830	1930	2030	2130	2233	...
157	**Fonyód** a.	...	...	...	...	0735	0835	0935	1035	1056	1135	1235	1335	1435	1535	1635	1735	1835	1935	2035	2135	2239	...
157	**Fonyód** 1232 d.	...	...	...	0632	0737	0837	0937	1037	...	1137	1237	1337	1437	1537	1637	1737	1837	1937	2037	2137	▬	...
165	Balatonfenyves 1232 d.	...	...	...	0641	0743	0843	0943	1043	...	1143	1243	1343	1443	1543	1643	1743	1843	1943	2043	2143	...	...
181	Balatonszentgyörgy 1232 a.	...	...	...	0659	0756	0857	0956	1057	...	1156	1257	1356	1457	1556	1657	1756	1857	1956	2057	2156	...	...
181	Balatonszentgyörgy 1232 d.	0442	0601	...	0700	0801	0900	1001	1100	...	1201	1300	1401	1500	1601	1700	1801	1900	2001	2100	2201	2208	...
221	**Keszthely** 1232 a.	|	|	...	0711	|	0911	|	1111	...	|	1311	|	1511	|	1711	|	1911	|	2111	|	2220	...
221	**Nagykanizsa** a.	0528	0644	...	...	0844	...	1044	...	...	1244	...	1444	...	1644	...	1844	...	2044	...	2244	...	...
352	*Zagreb* 1340 a.	...	...	...	...	...	...	...	...	...	...	...	...	...	...	...	2210	...	...	...	...	...	...

			IC 849 🅁	Ⓐ	Ⓐ	*IC* 867 🅁	*IC* 847 🅁	*IC* 877 🅁	*IC* 857 🅁	*IC* 865 🅁	*IC* 845 🅁	*IC* 875 🅁	*IC* 855 🅁	*IC* 863 🅁	*IC* 843 🅁	*IC* 873 🅁	Ⓒ d	*IC* 853 🅁	*IC* 861 🅁	*IC* 201 🅁 A	*IC* 871 🅁	
Zagreb 1340 d.	...	...	...	...	...	...	...	...	...	...	...	...	...	...	...	...	...	...	...	1635	...	...
Nagykanizsa d.	0350	...	0514	0605	...	...	0714	...	0914	...	1114	...	1314	...	1514	...	...	1714	...	1914	...	2114
Keszthely 1232 d.	|	0428	|	|	...	0648	|	0848	|	1048	|	1248	|	1448	|	1648	...	|	1848	|	2048	|
Balatonszentgyörgy 1232 a.	0433	0439	0557	0655	...	0659	0757	0859	0957	1059	1157	1259	1357	1459	1557	1659	...	1757	1859	1957	2059	2200
Balatonszentgyörgy 1232 d.	▬	0440	0603	...	...	0702	0803	0902	1003	1102	1203	1302	1403	1502	1603	1702	...	1803	1902	2003	2102	▬
Balatonfenyves 1232 d.	...	0458	0617	...	...	0717	0817	0917	1017	1117	1217	1317	1417	1517	1617	1717	...	1817	1917	2017	2118	...
Fonyód 1232 a.	...	0506	0622	...	...	0722	0822	0922	1022	1122	1222	1322	1422	1522	1622	1722	...	1822	1922	2022	2123	...
Fonyód d.	...	0507	0624	...	0645	0724	0824	0924	1024	1124	1224	1324	1424	1524	1624	1724	1702	1824	1924	2024	2124	...
Balatonboglár d.	...	0516	0630	...	0652	0730	0830	0930	1030	1130	1230	1330	1430	1530	1630	1730	1713	1830	1930	2030	2130	...
Balatonlelle d.	...	0520	0634	...	0657	0734	0834	0934	1034	1134	1234	1334	1434	1534	1634	1734	1717	1834	1934	2034	2134	...
Balatonszemes d.	...	0527	0640	...	0705	0740	0840	0940	1040	1140	1240	1340	1440	1540	1640	1740	1725	1840	1940	2040	2140	...
Balatonföldvár d.	...	0535	0649	...	0718	0749	0849	0949	1049	1149	1249	1349	1449	1549	1649	1749	1735	1849	1949	2049	2149	...
Zamárdi d.	...	0541	0654	...	0725	0754	0854	0954	1054	1154	1254	1354	1454	1554	1654	1754	1743	1854	1954	2054	2154	...
Siófok a.	...	0551	0701	...	0735	0801	0901	1001	1101	1201	1301	1401	1501	1601	1701	1801	1756	1901	2001	2101	2201	...
Siófok d.	0428	0552	0703	...	...	0803	0903	1003	1103	1203	1303	1403	1503	1603	1703	1803	1815	1903	2003	2103	2203	2205
Lepsény d.	0449	0612	0717	...	...	|	0917	|	1117	|	1317	|	1517	|	1717	|	1840	1917	|	2117	|	2225
Székesfehérvár a.	0511	0635	0736	...	...	0836	0936	1036	1136	1236	1336	1436	1536	1636	1736	1836	1905	1936	2036	2136	2236	2247
Székesfehérvár 1225 1230 d.	0527	0636	0737	...	...	0837	0937	1037	1137	1237	1337	1437	1537	1637	1737	1837	1906	1937	2037	2137	2237	2248
Kelenföld 1225 1230 a.	0611	0716	0816	...	...	0916	1016	1116	1216	1316	1416	1516	1616	1716	1816	1916	1946	2016	2116	2216	2316	2345
Budapest Déli 1225 1230 a.	0619	0724	0824	...	...	0924	1024	1124	1224	1324	1424	1524	1624	1724	1824	1924	1954	2024	2124	2224	2324	2354

A – AGRAM-TOPART – 2 Budapest - Zagreb and v.v.

d – Apr. 1 - May 14.

BUDAPEST - SZÉKESFEHÉRVÁR - BALATONFÜRED - TAPOLCA — 1225

2nd class

SERVICE UNTIL MAY 14. FOR SERVICE FROM MAY 15 SEE PAGE 560. Connecting trains Budapest - Székesfehérvár and v.v. may require 🅁.

km		Ⓐ				Ⓐ											Ⓒ e							
0	**Budapest** Déli 1220 1230 d.	...	...	...	...	0405	...	*0530*	0705	*0735*	0905	*0935*	1105	*1135*	1305	*1335*	...	1505	*1535*	1705	*1735*	1905	*1935*	*2200*
4	Kelenföld 1220 1230 d.	...	...	...	...	0412	...	*0537*	0712	*0742*	0912	*0942*	1112	*1142*	1312	*1342*	...	1512	*1542*	1712	*1742*	1912	*1942*	*2207*
67	**Székesfehérvár** 1220 1230 a.	...	...	...	...	0509	...	*0615*	0750	*0820*	0950	*1020*	1150	*1220*	1350	*1420*	...	1550	*1620*	1750	*1820*	1950	*2020*	*2247*
67	**Székesfehérvár** d.	...	...	0421	...	...	0526	0627	0751	0829	0951	1029	1151	1229	1351	1429	...	1551	1629	1751	1829	1951	2029	2256
105	Balatonkenese d.	...	...	0505	...	...	0620	0711	0825	0910	1025	1110	1225	1310	1425	1510	...	1625	1710	1825	1910	2025	2110	2337
117	Balalatonalmádi d.	...	...	0521	...	...	0633	0732	0838	0932	1038	1132	1238	1332	1438	1532	...	1638	1732	1838	1932	2038	2129	2350
123	Alsóörs d.	...	...	0528	...	...	0640	0739	0845	0939	1045	1139	1245	1339	1445	1539	...	1645	1739	1845	1939	2045	2136	2357
132	**Balatonfüred** a.	...	...	0538	...	...	0651	0750	0855	0950	1055	1150	1255	1350	1455	1550	...	1655	1750	1855	1950	2055	2147	0008
132	**Balatonfüred** d.	0408	0508	...	0602	...	0705	...	0905	...	1105	...	1305	...	1505	...	1600	1705	...	1905	...	2105	...	...
157	Révfülöp d.	0442	0551	...	0640	...	0742	...	0942	...	1142	...	1342	...	1542	...	1636	1742	...	1942	...	2142	...	...
168	Badacsonytomaj d.	0500	0609	...	0654	...	0759	...	0959	...	1159	...	1359	...	1559	...	1650	1759	...	1959	...	2159	...	...
170	Badacsony d.	0503	0612	...	0657	...	0803	...	1003	...	1203	...	1403	...	1603	...	1653	1803	...	2003	...	2203	...	...
184	**Tapolca** a.	0522	0631	...	0715	...	0822	...	1022	...	1222	...	1422	...	1622	...	1709	1822	...	2022	...	2222	...	...

			Ⓐ								Ⓒ e												
Tapolca d.	...	...	...	0441	...	0551	...	0734	...	0934	1044	...	...	1134	...	1334	...	1534	...	1734	...	1934	2134
Badacsony d.	...	...	...	0457	...	0606	...	0753	...	0953	1059	...	...	1153	...	1353	...	1553	...	1753	...	1953	2153
Badacsonytomaj d.	...	...	...	0500	...	0609	...	0759	...	0959	1103	...	...	1159	...	1359	...	1559	...	1759	...	1959	2159
Révfülöp d.	...	...	...	0514	...	0621	...	0815	...	1015	1117	...	...	1215	...	1415	...	1615	...	1815	...	2015	2215
Balatonfüred a.	...	...	...	0547	...	0652	...	0852	...	1052	1156	...	...	1252	...	1452	...	1652	...	1852	...	2052	2252
Balatonfüred d.	0351	0451	...	...	0551	0702	0805	0902	1005	1102	...	1205	...	1302	1405	1502	1605	1702	1805	1902	2005	2111	...
Alsóörs d.	0401	0501	...	...	0601	0711	0815	0911	1015	1111	...	1215	...	1311	1415	1511	1615	1711	1815	1911	2015	2122	...
Balalatonalmádi d.	0408	0508	...	...	0608	0718	0822	0918	1022	1118	...	1222	...	1318	1422	1518	1622	1718	1822	1918	2022	2129	...
Balatonkenese d.	0420	0520	...	...	0620	0731	0844	0931	1044	1131	...	1244	...	1331	1444	1531	1644	1731	1844	1931	2044	2144	...
Székesfehérvár a.	0503	0603	...	...	0703	0806	0930	1006	1130	1206	...	1330	...	1406	1530	1606	1730	1806	1930	2006	2130	2226	...
Székesfehérvár 1220 1230 d.	*0514*	...	0607	...	0706	0807	*0937*	1007	*1137*	1207	...	*1337*	...	1407	*1537*	1607	*1737*	1807	*1937*	2007	*2137*	*2237*	...
Kelenföld 1220 1230 a.	*0612*	...	0651	...	0746	0846	*1016*	1046	*1216*	1246	...	*1416*	...	1446	*1616*	1646	*1816*	1846	*2016*	2046	*2216*	*2316*	...
Budapest Déli 1220 1230 a.	...	...	0659	...	0754	0854	*1024*	1054	*1224*	1254	...	*1424*	...	1454	*1624*	1654	*1824*	1854	*2024*	2054	*2224*	*2324*	...

e – Mar. 11 - May 14.

1230 BUDAPEST - ZALAEGERSZEG and SZOMBATHELY

2nd class

Ⓡ is required for some carriages on *IC* trains. For faster trains Budapest - Győr - Szombathely see Table **1252**. For local trains Zalaegerszeg - Celldömölk / Szombathely see Table **1237**.

km																									
			IC	*IC*		*IC*	*IC*		*IC*	*IC*	*IC*	*IC*		*IC*	*IC*	*IC*	*IC*		*IC*	*IC*	*IC*	*IC*			
			950	**900**		**952**	**902**		**246**	**904**	**954**	**914**		**964**	**906**	**956**	**916**		**966**	**908**	**958**	**918**			
			⚒		Ⓐ			©d	A									©d							
0	**Budapest** Déli .. **1220 1225** d.	...	0500	0600	...	0700	0800	...	0900	1000	1100	1200	...	1300	1400	1500	1600	...	1700	1800	1900	2000	...	2100	2200
4	Kelenföld.......... **1220 1225** d.	...	0507	0607	...	0707	0807	...	0907	1007	1107	1207	...	1307	1407	1507	1607	...	1707	1807	1907	2007	...	2107	2207
67	Székesfehérvár . **1220 1225** d.	...	0546	0646	...	0746	0846	...	0946	1046	1146	1246	...	1346	1446	1546	1646	...	1746	1846	1946	2046	...	2146	2250
90	Várpalota ....d.	...	0606	0706	...	0806	0906	...	1006	1106	1206	1306	...	1406	1506	1606	1706	...	1806	1906	2006	2106	...	2229	2329
112	Veszprém ....d.	0558	0629	0734	...	0829	0934	0939	1029	1134	1229	1334	...	1429	1534	1629	1734	1739	1829	1934	2029	2134	...	2300	...
148	Ajka ....d.	0633	0701	0806	0833	0901	1006	1033	1101	1206	1301	1406	1433	1501	1606	1701	1806	1833	1901	2006	2101	2205	2233	...	...
181	Boba...............................d.	0713	|	0831	0913	|	1031	1113	|	1231	|	1431	1513	|	1631	|	1831	1913	|	2031	|	...	2307	...	...
199	Ukk ....d.	|	0735	|	|	0935	|	|	1135	|	1335	|	|	1535	|	1735	|	|	1935	|	2135	...	|	...	...
230	Zalaszentiván .... **1235** a.	|	0759	|	|	0959	|	|	1159	|	1359	|	|	1559	|	1759	|	|	1959	|	2159	...	|	...	...
239	**Zalaegerszeg**......... **1235** a.	|	0808	|	|	1008	|	|	1208	|	1408	|	|	1608	|	1808	|	|	2008	|	2208	...	|	...	...
191	Celldömölk.......................a.	0723	...	0840	0923	...	1040	1123	...	1240	...	1440	1523	...	1640	...	1840	1923	...	2040	...	...	2317	...	...
236	**Szombathely**......................a.	...	...	0917	...	...	1117	...	...	1317	...	1517	...	...	1717	...	1917	...	...	2117	...	...	...	...	...

		IC	*IC*		*IC*	*IC*		*IC*	*IC*	*IC*	*IC*		*IC*	*IC*	*IC*	*IC*		*IC*	*IC*		*IC*	*IC*	
		919	**959**		**909**	**957**		**907**	**967**	**905**	**955**		**915**	**247**	**903**	**953**		**913**	**963**		**901**	**951**	
	Ⓐ			Ⓐ			©d							A			e					Ⓑ	
Szombathely ....d.	...	...	...	...	...	0642	...	...	0842	...	1042	...	...	1242	...	1442	...	...	1642	...	...	1842	...	...
Celldömölk...............................d.	...	0439	...	...	0638	0716	...	0838	0916	...	1116	...	1238	1316	...	1516	...	1638	1716	...	1838	1916	...	2038
Zalaegerszeg .... **1325** d.	...	|	...	0549	|	|	0749	|	|	0949	|	1149	|	|	1349	|	1549	|	|	1749	|	|	1949	|
Zalaszentiván .... **1235** d.	...	|	...	0600	|	|	0800	|	|	1000	|	1200	|	|	1400	|	1600	|	|	1800	|	|	2000	|
Ukk ....d.	...	|	...	0623	|	|	0823	|	|	1023	|	1223	|	|	1423	|	1623	|	|	1823	|	|	2023	|
Boba...d.	...	0448	...	|	0648	0725	|	0848	0925	|	1125	|	1248	1325	|	1525	|	1648	1725	|	1848	1925	|	2048
Ajka..d.	0427	0520	0555	0700	0723	0751	0900	0930	0951	1100	1151	1300	1323	1351	1500	1551	1700	1730	1751	1900	1923	1951	2100	2123
Veszprém ....d.	0458	0554	0632	0732	...	0832	0932	1016	1032	1132	1232	1332	...	1432	1532	1632	1732	1816	1832	1932	...	2032	2132	...
Várpalota...................................d.	0520	0616	0654	0754	...	0854	0954	...	1054	1154	1254	1354	...	1454	1554	1654	1754	...	1854	1954	...	2054	2154	...
Székesfehérvár............ **1220 1225** d.	0538	0640	0712	0812	...	0912	1012	...	1112	1212	1312	1412	...	1512	1612	1712	1812	...	1912	2012	...	2112	2212	...
Kelenföld .... **1220 1225** a.	0622	0722	0752	0852	...	0952	1052	...	1152	1252	1352	1452	...	1552	1652	1752	1852	...	1952	2052	...	2152	2252	...
Budapest Déli............ **1220 1225** a.	0629	0729	0759	0859	...	0959	1059	...	1159	1259	1359	1459	...	1559	1659	1759	1859	...	1959	2059	...	2159	2259	...

LOCAL TRAINS CELLDÖMÖLK - SZOMBATHELY

km																									
		⚒					Ⓐ			Ⓐ				Ⓐ		Ⓐ						Ⓐ			
0	**Celldömölk** ....d.	0415	0453	0540	...	0610	0640	0740	...	0805	0940	1140	...	1205	1340	1421	...	1540	1740	1940	...	2027	2144	2205	...
45	**Szombathely**......................a.	0455	0538	0620	...	0650	0720	0820	...	0854	1020	1220	...	1244	1420	1501	...	1620	1820	2020	...	2107	2218	2245	...

			Ⓐ							Ⓐ	Ⓐ		⑦		Ⓐ			Ⓐ						
Szombathely ....d.	0458	0540	0624	...	0740	0940	1140	...	1340	1421	1502	...	1505	1540	1621	...	1740	1810	1940	...	2103	...	2240	...
Celldömölk..............................a.	0537	0624	0705	...	0820	1020	1220	...	1420	1505	1539	...	1538	1620	1705	...	1825	1855	2025	...	2143	...	2320	...

A – CITTADELLA – (2) Budapest - Ljubljana and v.v.

d – © Mar. 11 - Nov. 1.

e – From Celldömölk daily; from Ajka © **d**.

1232 GYÖR - CELLDÖMÖLK - TAPOLCA - KESZTHELY - FONYÓD - PÉCS

2nd class

km																							
						IR		*IR*	*IR*		*IR*	*IR*	*IR*	*IR*	*Ex*		*IR*		*IR*	*IR*		*IR*	
						9609		**9697**	**19697**		**9607**	**9605**	**9695**	**19695**	**18803**		**9603**		**9693**	**19693**		**9601**	
							s		⑤	f				⑦x	Ⓡz					⑦w			
0	**Györ** ....d.	...	...	...	0505	...	...	0711	0711	...	0911	1111	1311	1311	...	...	1511	...	1711	1711	...	1911	...
47	Pápa ....d.	...	...	...	0559	...	...	0802	0802	...	1002	1202	1402	1402	...	...	1602	...	1802	1802	...	2002	...
72	**Celldömölk** ....a.	...	...	...	0628	...	...	0825	0825	...	1025	1225	1425	1425	...	...	1625	...	1825	1825	...	2025	...
72	**Celldömölk** .... **1237** d.	...	0443	...	...	0631	...	0833	0833	...	1033	1233	1433	1433	...	1448	1633	...	1833	1833	...	2033	...
82	Boba .... **1237** d.	...	0452	...	...	|	...	|	|	...	|	|	|	|	...	1458	|	...	|	|	...	|	...
100	Ukk................................ **1237** a.	...	0509	...	...	|	...	|	|	...	|	|	|	|	...	1520	|	...	|	|	...	|	...
100	Ukk...................................... ◀ d.	...	...	0515	...	|	0810	|	|	1010	|	|	|	|	...	1540	|	1747	|	|	1947	|	...
108	Sümeg.................................. ◀ d.	...	...	0526	...	0701	0820	0901	0901	1020	1101	1301	1501	1501	...	1551	1701	1800	1901	1901	2000	2101	...
128	**Tapolca**...................................a.	...	...	0546	...	0718	0838	0918	0918	1038	1118	1318	1518	1518	...	1612	1718	1820	1918	1918	2020	2118	...
128	**Tapolca**................................ ◀ d.	0508	...	0557	...	0719	0843	0919	0919	1043	1119	1319	1519	1519	...	...	1719	...	1919	1919	...	2119	...
153	**Keszthely**.............................. ◀ a.	0540	...	0629	...	0747	0914	0947	0947	1114	1147	1347	1547	1547	...	...	1747	...	1947	1947	...	2147	...
153	**Keszthely**...................... **1220** d.	0541	...	...	...	0748	...	0948	0948	...	1148	1348	1548	1548	1625	...	1748	...	1948	1948	...	2148	...
163	Balatonszentgyörgy.............. **1220** a.	0552	...	...	...	0759	...	0959	0959	...	1159	1359	1559	1559	1636	...	1759	...	1959	1959	...	2159	...
163	Balatonszentgyörgy.............. **1220** d.	...	...	...	...	0806	...	1006	1006	...	1206	1406	1606	1606	1637	...	1806	...	2006	2006	...	...	...
179	Balatonfenyves .... **1220** d.	...	...	...	...	0825	...	1025	1025	...	1225	1425	1625	1625	1709	...	1825	...	2025	2025	...	...	...
187	**Fonyód** .... **1220** a.	...	...	...	...	0836	...	1036	1036	...	1236	1436	1636	1636	1719	...	1836	...	2036	2036	...	...	...
187	**Fonyód** .... ◀ d.	...	...	...	...	0849	...	1049	1049	...	1249	1449	1649	1649	1722	...	1844	...	2046	2046	...	...	...
240	Kaposvár .... ◀ a.	...	...	...	...	0945	...	1145	1145	...	1345	1545	1745	1745	1808	...	1940	...	2140	2140	...	...	...
269	Dombóvár alsó ....a.	...	...	...	...	...	...	...	|	...	...	...	...	|	1839	...	2004	...	...	|	...	...	...
316	Szentlörinc..................................a.	...	...	...	...	...	...	...	1257	...	...	...	...	1858	1934	...	2040	...	...	|	...	...	...
335	**Pécs** ....a.	...	...	...	...	...	...	...	1332	...	...	...	...	1932	1949	...	2101	...	...	2257	...	...	...

			IR		*IR*	*IR*	*Ex*	*IR*	*IR*	*IR*			*IR*	*IR*		*IR*			*IR*	*IR*		
			9600		**9690**	**9602**	**18802**	**9604**	**9694**	**9606**			**9696**	**19696**		**9608**			**8808**	**18808**		
	Ⓐv						Ⓡz				g			⑤	t			y	Ⓐp	y		
Pécs...d.	...	...	...	...	...	0634	0810	...	...	...	...	...	...	1428	...	...	...	...	...	...	...	...
Szentlörinc...d.	...	...	...	...	...	0655	0830	...	...	...	...	...	...	1454	...	...	...	...	...	...	...	...
Dombóvár alsó ....d.	...	...	...	...	...	0736	0918	...	...	...	...	...	...	|	...	...	...	...	...	...	...	...
Kaposvár.. ◀ d.	...	...	...	...	0614	0815	0955	1015	1215	1415	...	...	1615	1615	...	1810	...	...	1951	1951	...	...
Fonyód.. ◀ a.	...	...	...	...	0714	0914	1040	1114	1314	1514	...	...	1714	1714	...	1909	...	...	2045	2045	...	...
Fonyód .... **1220** d.	...	...	...	...	0723	0923	1042	1123	1323	1523	...	...	1723	1723	...	1923	...	...	...	2103	...	...
Balatonfenyves .... **1220** d.	...	...	...	...	0733	0933	1053	1133	1333	1533	...	...	1733	1733	...	1933	...	...	...	2122	...	...
Balatonszentgyörgy.................... **1220** a.	...	...	...	...	0753	0953	1123	1153	1353	1553	...	...	1753	1753	...	1953	...	...	...	2142	...	...
Balatonszentgyörgy.................... **1220** d.	...	...	0600	...	0800	1000	1124	1200	1400	1600	...	...	1800	1800	...	2000	...	...	...	...	2208	...
Keszthely.................................. **1220** a.	...	...	0611	...	0811	1011	1135	1211	1411	1611	...	...	1811	1811	...	2011	...	...	...	...	2219	...
Keszthely....................................... ◀ d.	0521	...	0612	0642	0812	1012	...	1212	1412	1612	1644	...	1812	1812	1844	2012	...	2127	...	...	2220	...
Tapolca.. ◀ a.	0549	...	0640	0713	0840	1040	...	1240	1440	1640	1715	...	1840	1840	1915	2040	...	2200	...	...	2251	...
Tapolca...d.	0550	0550	0641	0740	0841	1041	...	1241	1441	1641	1720	1740	1841	1841	1920	2041	...	2225	...	...	...	...
Sümeg... ◀ d.	0609	0609	0701	0758	0901	1101	...	1301	1501	1701	1738	1800	1901	1901	1938	2101	...	2244	...	...	...	...
Ukk.. ◀ a.	0620	0620	|	0808	|	|	...	|	|	|	1746	1812	|	|	1946	|	...	2254	...	...	...	...
Ukk... **1237** d.	0636	0636	|	...	|	|	...	|	|	|	...	...	|	|	...	|	...	2255	...	...	...	...
Boba....................................... **1237** d.	0659	0659	|	...	|	|	...	|	|	|	...	...	|	|	...	|	...	2314	...	...	...	...
Celldömölk .... **1237** a.	0709	0709	0729	...	0929	1129	...	1329	1529	1729	...	...	1929	1929	...	2129	...	2325	...	...	...	...
Celldömölk...d.	...	...	0737	...	0937	1137	...	1337	1537	1737	...	...	1937	1937	...	...	2155	...	...	...	...	...
Pápa...d.	...	...	0801	...	1001	1201	...	1401	1601	1801	...	...	2001	2001	...	...	2226	...	...	...	...	...
Györ...a.	...	...	0846	...	1046	1246	...	1446	1646	1846	...	...	2046	2046	...	...	2318	...	...	...	...	...

ADDITIONAL LOCAL TRAINS **GYÖR - CELLDÖMÖLK**

km									
0	**Györ** ....d.	0505	0610	0807	1007	and every	2007	2115	2241
47	Pápa ....d.	0559	0702	0902	1102	**two** hours	2102	2227**h**	2329
72	**Celldömölk** ....a.	0628	0732	0932	1132	until	2135	2256	2353

Celldömölk ....d.	0345	0444	0542	0630	and every	1630	1830	2155
Pápa ....d.	0410	0515	0615	0701	**two** hours	1701	1901	2226
Györ.......................................a.	0458	0603	0708	0749	until	1749	1949	2318

f – © Mar. 11 - Nov. 1 (daily June 17 - Aug. 27).
g – © Mar. 11 - Nov. 1 (daily Apr. 24 - Sept. 24).
h – Arrives Pápa 2204.
p – Not June 17 - Aug. 27.
r – Daily June 17 - Aug. 27.
s – Apr. 29 - Sept. 24.

t – © Apr. 29 - Sept. 24 (daily June 17 - Aug. 27).
v – Daily June 12 - Aug. 27.
w – June 18 - Aug. 27.
x – Until May 14 and from Oct. 1.
y – June 17 - Aug. 27.
z – May 15 - Sept. 24.

◀ – Other trains: Ukk - Sümeg at 0940, 1140, 1340, 1426; Sümeg - Ukk at 0957, 1207, 1407, 1607; Tapolca - Keszthely at 0442 Ⓐ **r**, 0650 **p**, 0757 **y**, 0959 **y**, 1159 **y**, 1357, 1559, 1759, 2045 **y**; Keszthely - Tapolca at 0927 **y**, 1127, 1327 **y**, 1527, 1727, 1927; Fonyód - Kaposvár at 0356 Ⓐ, 0603, 0649 Ⓐ **p**, 1203, 1758 © **r**, 1940, 2140 © **w**; Kaposvár - Fonyód at 0400 Ⓐ, 0508 Ⓐ **p**, 0715 © **r**, 1453, 1653, 2237.

GySEV 2nd class — SOPRON - SZOMBATHELY — 1233

km																								
															Ⓐ									
0	**Sopron** d.	0408	0452	0556	...	0645	0808	1008	...	1108	1208	1308	...	1408	1428	1508	...	1608	1706	1806	...	1906	2008	2245
38	Bük d.	0440	0524	0628	...	0717	0840	1040	...	1140	1240	1340	...	1440	1500	1540	...	1640	1740	1840	...	1940	2040	2317
62	**Szombathely** a.	0458	0542	0650	...	0735	0858	1058	...	1158	1258	1358	...	1458	1520	1558	...	1658	1758	1858	...	1958	2058	2334
	Szentgotthárd 🚌 **986** a.	0549	0654	0754	...	...	0954	...	...	...	1354	1454	...	1554	...	1654	...	1754	1854	...	...	2054	...	...

													Ⓐ										
Szentgotthárd 🚌 **986** d.	...	0401	...	...	...	0706	0806	...	...	1206	1306	...	...	1406	1506	...	...	1706	1806	...	1906	2006	...
Szombathely d.	0423	0506	0630	...	0700	0800	0900	...	1100	1300	1400	...	1435	1500	1600	...	1700	1800	1900	...	2000	2100	2237
Bük d.	0441	0524	0652	...	0718	0818	0918	...	1118	1318	1418	...	1459	1518	1618	...	1718	1818	1918	...	2018	2118	2255
Sopron a.	0513	0556	0727	...	0750	0851	0951	...	1151	1351	1451	...	1531	1551	1651	...	1751	1851	1951	...	2051	2151	2327

GySEV 2nd class — SZOMBATHELY - KÖSZEG — 1234

km																								
				Ⓐ				Ⓐ			Ⓐ			Ⓐ					Ⓐ					
0	**Szombathely** d.	0500	0606	0706	...	0806	0906	1006	...	1106	1206	1306	...	1406	1506	1606	...	1706	1806	1906	...	2109	2257	...
18	**Köszeg** a.	0523	0629	0729	...	0829	0929	1029	...	1129	1229	1329	...	1429	1529	1629	...	1729	1829	1929	...	2132	2320	...

					Ⓐ		Ⓐ			Ⓐ			Ⓐ					Ⓐ					
Köszeg d.	0432	0526	0632	...	0732	0832	0932	...	1032	1132	1232	...	1332	1432	1532	...	1632	1732	1832	...	2032	2205	...
Szombathely a.	0455	0549	0655	...	0755	0855	0955	...	1055	1155	1255	...	1355	1455	1555	...	1655	1755	1855	...	2055	2228	...

2nd class — SZOMBATHELY - NAGYKANIZSA - PÉCS — 1235

km			*IR* 8900	*IR* 8902	*IR* 8992	*IR* 8904	*IR* 8994	*IR* 8906	*IR* 8996	*IR* 9808
0	**Szombathely** 1237 d.	...	0508	0704	0912	1103	1310	1512	1710	1903
24	Vasvár 1237 d.	...	0533	0727	0933	1126	1333	1533	1733	1926
49	Zalaszentiván 1237 a.	...	0554	0754	0954	1154	1354	1554	1754	1954
49	Zalaszentiván d.	...	0555	0802	1002	1202	1402	1602	1802	2002
101	**Nagykanizsa** a.	...	0644	0851	1046	1251	1446	1651	1846	2051
101	**Nagykanizsa** 1240 d.	0418	0649	0853	1053	1253	1453	1653	1848	...
130	Gyékényes 1240 a.	0449	0716	0919	1121	1319	1521	1719	1923	...
130	Gyékényes d.	0450	0725	0930	1127	1330	1527	1730	1927	...
185	Barcs d.	0549	0827	1025	1225	1425	1625	1825	2025	...
215	Szigetvár d.	0626	0858	1058	1258	1458	1658	1858	2101	...
230	Szentlörinc d.	0650	0922	1122	1322	1522	1722	1922	2119	...
249	**Pécs** a.	0705	0942	1142	1342	1542	1742	1942	2134	...

		IR 9807	*IR* 8907	*IR* 8997	*IR* 8905	*IR* 8995	*IR* 8903	*IR* 8993	*IR* 8901
Pécs d.	...	...	0629	0819	1019	1219	1419	1619	1819
Szentlörinc d.	...	...	0647	0841	1041	1241	1441	1641	1841
Szigetvár d.	...	...	0703	0857	1057	1257	1457	1657	1857
Barcs d.	0517	...	0731	0925	1125	1325	1525	1725	1925
Gyékényes a.	0612	...	0823	1029	1226	1429	1626	1829	2029
Gyékényes 1240 d.	0627	...	0836	1034	1234	1434	1634	1837	2041
Nagykanizsa 1240 a.	0702	...	0906	1106	1306	1506	1706	1906	2107
Nagykanizsa d.	...	0708	0908	1108	1308	1508	1708	1908	2108
Zalaszentiván a.	...	0757	0957	1152	1357	1552	1757	1952	2157
Zalaszentiván 1237 d.	...	0802	1002	1202	1402	1602	1802	2002	2202
Vasvár 1237 d.	...	0827	1022	1227	1427	1627	1822	2027	2222
Szombathely 1237 a.	...	0852	1043	1252	1455	1652	1843	2052	2252

2nd Class — CELLDÖMÖLK and SZOMBATHELY - ZALAEGERSZEG — 1237

km																								
						d	†				Ⓐ								Ⓐ				Ⓒ		
0	**Celldömölk** 1232 d.	0400	0443	0553	...	...	...	0753	...	1153	...	1353	...	1448	1553	...	...	...	1753	...	2003	...	2206	...
10	Boba 1232 d.	0409	0452	0603	...	...	...	0803	...	1203	...	1403	...	1458	1603	...	...	...	1803	...	2013	...	2216	...
28	Ukk 1232 a.	0424	0509	0621	...	...	...	0821	...	1221	...	1421	...	1520	1621	...	...	...	1821	...	2034	...	2234	...
28	Ukk d.	0425	0522	0625	...	...	...	0825	...	1225	...	1425	...	...	1625	...	...	...	1825	...	2035	...	2235	...
	Szombathely 1235 d.	|	|	|	0615	...	...	|	...	|	1405	|	1437	...	|	1602	...	1629	|	1808	|	2110	|	2232
	Vasvár 1235 d.	|	|	|	0638	...	...	|	...	|	1428	|	1500	...	|	1627	...	1654	|	1832	|	2133	|	2255
59	Zalaszentiván 1235 a.	0456	0553	0656	0659	0702	...	0856	...	1256	1450	1456	1522	...	1656	1650	...	1722	1856	1854	2105	2155	2305	2317
59	Zalaszentiván 1230 d.	0457	0600	0700	...	0706	0800	0900	...	1300	...	1500	1525	...	1700	1706	...	1725	1900	1906	2106	2205	2306	2320
68	**Zalaegerszeg** 1230 a.	0505	0608	0709	...	0715	0808	0909	...	1309	...	1509	1533	...	1709	1715	...	1733	1909	1915	2115	2213	2315	2328

									†				Ⓐ	e						⑦f	⑥		
Zalaegerszeg 1230 d.	0349	0430	0444	...	0544	0651	...	...	0743	1051	1251	1451	...	1639	1645	...	1651	1845	1851	1922	1949	2040	2149
Zalaszentiván 1230 a.	0357	0437	0452	...	0552	0659	...	...	0751	1059	1259	1459	...	1647	1653	...	1659	1853	1859	1930	1957	2048	2157
Zalaszentiván 1235 d.	0400	0438	0458	...	0603	0700	0704	...	...	1100	1300	1500	1505	1648	1706	...	1700	1902	1900	1934	...	2049	2201
Vasvár 1235 d.	0423	|	0521	...	0629	|	0726	...	...	|	|	|	1532	...	1732	...	|	1925	|	1957	...	|	|
Szombathely 1235 a.	0445	|	0543	...	0654	|	0748	...	...	|	|	|	1554	...	1754	...	|	1947	|	2016	...	|	|
Ukk a.	...	0511	...	...	...	0731	...	...	...	1131	1331	1531	...	...	...	...	1731	...	1931	...	...	2121	2234
Ukk 1232 d.	...	0512	...	0636	...	0735	...	...	...	1135	1335	1535	...	...	...	...	1735	...	1935	...	...	2122	2235
Boba 1232 a.	...	0528	...	0658	...	0753	...	...	...	1153	1353	1553	...	...	...	...	1753	...	1953	...	...	2142	2251
Celldömölk 1232 a.	...	0538	...	0709	...	0803	...	...	...	1203	1403	1603	...	...	...	...	1803	...	2003	...	...	2153	2301

d – From Nagykanizsa (d. 0605). e – To Nagykanizsa (a. 1746). f – ⑦ (not June 18 - Aug. 27).

2nd class — DOMBÓVAR - KAPOSVÁR - NAGYKANIZSA — 1240

km																								
							8907*		8997*		8905*		8995*						8993*		*IC* 826	8901*		
		⚒	⚒											Ⓐg		Ⓐ					Ⓡ A		Ⓑ	
0	**Dombóvár** 1200 d.	...	0417	...	...	0625	...	0759	...	0959	...	1159	...	...	1359	...	1559	...	1759	1857	...	1959	2159	2159
	Dombóvár also 1232 d.	...	0421	...	...	0631	...	0803	...	1003	...	1203	...	...	1403	...	1603	...	1803	|	...	2005	2205	2205
31	**Kaposvár** 1200 1232 a.	...	0446	...	...	0656	...	0828	...	1028	...	1228	...	...	1428	...	1628	...	1828	1922	...	2030	2230	2230
31	**Kaposvár** d.	...	0447	0447	...	0709	...	0845	...	1045	...	1245	...	1348	1445	1549	1649	...	1837	1923	...	2107	2249	...
71	Somogyszob a.	...	0541	0541	...	0800	...	0940	...	1140	...	1340	...	1442	1540	1644	1740	...	1928	2009	...	2158	2339	...
71	Somogyszob d.	...	0546	0546	...	0801	...	0941	...	1141	...	1341	...	1443	1556	1645	1741	...	1929	2010	...	2200	2340	...
101	Gyékényes a.	...	0620	0620	...	0831	...	1011	...	1211	...	1411	...	1513	1626	1715	1811	...	2004	2039	...	2230	0010	...
101	Gyékényes 1235 d.	0430	...	...	0627	...	0836	...	1034	...	1234	...	1434	...	1638	...	...	1837	...	...	2041	*2233*	...	...
130	**Nagykanizsa** 1235 a.	0459	...	...	0702	...	0906	...	1106	...	1306	...	1506	...	1722	...	...	1906	...	...	2108	*2302*	...	...

					IC 829		8900*		8902*		8992*				8904*		8994*			8996*			
	⚒		Ⓐ		Ⓡ A																		Ⓑ
Nagykanizsa 1235 d.	...	...	...	0418	...	0501	0649	...	0853	...	1053	...	...	...	1253	...	1453	...	1711	1848	...	2054	2054
Gyékényes 1235 a.	...	...	...	0449	...	0529	0716	...	0919	...	1121	...	...	...	1319	...	1521	...	1741	1923	...	2127	2127
Gyékényes d.	0345	...	0410	...	0451	0538	...	0720	...	0945	...	...	...	1145	...	1345	...	1525	1745	...	1939	2128	2128
Somogyszob a.	0416	...	0441	...	0519	0609	...	0750	...	1019	...	...	...	1219	...	1419	...	1555	1819	...	2009	2158	2158
Somogyszob d.	0417	...	0447	...	0520	0611	...	0820	...	1020	...	...	1116	1220	...	1420	...	1556	1826	...	2010	2159	2159
Kaposvár a.	0511	...	0542	...	0606	0705	...	0911	...	1111	...	...	1208	1311	...	1511	...	1647	1920	...	2101	2247	2247
Kaposvár 1200 1232 d.	0521	0521	...	...	0607	0728	...	0928	...	1128	...	...	...	1328	...	1528	...	1728	1928	...	2116	...	2248
Dombóvár also 1232 a.	0546	0546	...	...	|	0753	...	0953	...	1153	...	...	...	1353	...	1553	...	1753	1953	...	2141	...	2313
Dombóvár 1200 a.	0550	0550	...	...	0633	0757	...	0957	...	1157	...	...	...	1357	...	1557	...	1757	1957	...	2145	...	2317

A – 12 Budapest - Kaposvár - Gyékényes and v.v. g – Not June 17 - Aug. 31. * – *IR* train - see Table **1235**.

2nd class — DOMBÓVAR - BAJA - KISKUNFÉLEGYHÁZA - KECSKEMÉT — 1242

km		Ⓐ	⚒		⚒	B				
0	**Dombóvár** d.	...	...	0620	...	1020	1420	1620	1820	...
60	Bátaszék a.	...	...	0727	...	1127	1527	1727	1927	...
60	Bátaszék 1210 d.	0534	0640	0734	0819	1134	1534	1734	1934	...
80	**Baja** 1210 a.	0555	0700	0755	0839	1155	1555	1755	1955	...

	⚒	Ⓐ	h	B					
Baja 1210 d.	0425	...	0615	0815	1415	1615	1815	...	...
Bátaszék 1210 a.	0443	...	0636	0839	1439	1639	1839	...	...
Bátaszék d.	...	0447	0641	0845	1441	1641	1841	...	...
Dombóvár a.	...	0554	0754	0954	1554	1754	1954	...	...

km		Ⓐ								
0	**Baja** d.	0314	0409	0614	0814	1014	1214	1414	1614	1814
76	Kiskunhalas a.	0420	0515	0720	0920	1120	1320	1520	1720	1920
76	Kiskunhalas d.	0430	0530	0730	0930	1130	1330	1530	1730	1930
122	Kiskunfélegyháza 1290 d.	0511	0615	0815	1015	1215	1415	1615	1815	2014
147	**Kecskemét** 1290 a.	...	0637	0837	1037	1237	1437	1637	1837	...

		Ⓐ							
Kecskemét 1290 d.	0510	...	0721	0921	1121	1321	1521	1721	1921
Kiskunfélegyháza 1290 d.	0544	0640	0744	0944	1144	1344	1544	1744	1944
Kiskunhalas a.	0625	0721	0825	1025	1225	1425	1625	1825	2025
Kiskunhalas d.	0636	0733	0836	1036	1236	1436	1636	1836	2036
Baja a.	0746	0843	0946	1146	1346	1546	1746	1946	2141

B – Ⓒ (daily June 17 - Aug. 27). h – By connecting trains on Ⓐ.

1250 BUDAPEST - GYÖR - WIEN

For additional services Budapest - Kelenföld and v.v. see Tables **1200**, **1220**, **1225**, **1230**. Ⓡ **not** required for local journeys Gyor - Sopron / Szombathely / Szentgottárd and v.v.

km		346	IC 922	RJX 162	IC 982	RJX 60	♥ 1032	IC 312	EC 140	IC 992	RJX 62	IC 924	EC 142		IC 984	RJX 64	IC 934	EC 144	IC 994	RJX 66	IC 926	EC 146	♥ 1036	IC 986	RJX 68
		Ⓡ	Ⓡ	✕ ⊖	Ⓡ	✕ ⊖	🍷 Ⓡ	Ⓡ	⊖	Ⓡ	✕ ⊖	Ⓡ	⊖		Ⓡ	✕ ⊖	Ⓡ	⊖	Ⓡ	✕ ⊖	Ⓡ	✕ ⊖	🍷 Ⓡ	Ⓡ	✕ ⊖
		A		B		C	D	E	F		C					C				C		G	D		C
0	**Budapest** Keleti ... d.	0540	0615	0640	0715	0740	...	0815	0840	0915	0940	1015	1040	...	1115	1140	1215	1240	1315	1340	1415	1440	...	1515	1540
	Budapest Déli ... d.	|	|	|	|	|	0745	|	|	|	|	|	|	...	|	|	|	|	|	|	|	|	1445	|	|
13	Kelenföld ... d.	0555	0629	0655	0729	0755	0758	0829	0855	0929	0955	1029	1055	...	1129	1155	1229	1255	1329	1355	1429	1455	1458	1529	1555
75	Tatabánya ... d.	0626	0700	0726	0800	0826	|	0900	0926	1000	1026	1100	1126	...	1200	1226	1300	1326	1400	1426	1500	1526	|	1600	1626
83	Tata ... d.	|	0707	|	0807	|	|	0907	|	1007	|	1107	|	...	1207	|	1307	|	1407	|	1507	|	|	1607	|
103	Komárom ... d.	|	0720	|	0820	|	|	0920	|	1020	|	1120	|	...	1220	|	1320	|	1420	|	1520	|	|	1620	|
140	**Györ** ... a.	0700	0737	0800	0837	0900	0905	0937	1000	1037	1100	1137	1200	...	1237	1300	1337	1400	1437	1500	1537	1600	1605	1637	1700
140	**Györ** ... d.	0702	0739	0802	0839	0902	0907	0939	1002	1039	1102	1139	1202	...	1239	1302	1339	1402	1439	1502	1539	1602	1607	1639	1702
171	Csorna ... d.	|	0759	|	0859	|	|	0959	|	1059	|	1159	|	...	1259	|	1359	|	1459	|	1559	|	|	1659	|
225	**Sopron** ... a.	|	|	|	0938	|	|	|	|	1138	|	|	|	...	1338	|	|	|	1538	|	|	|	|	1738	|
243	**Szombathely** ... a.	|	0849	|	...	|	|	1049	|	...	|	1249	|	...	...	|	1449	|	...	|	1649	|	|	...	|
176	Mosonmagyaróvár ... d.	0720	...	0820	...	0920	0925	...	1020	...	1120	...	1220	...	...	1320	...	1420	...	1520	...	1620	1625	...	1720
187	Hegyeshalom 🏛 ... a.	0729	...	0829	...	0929	0934	...	1029	...	1129	...	1229	...	...	1329	...	1429	...	1529	...	1629	1634	...	1729
256	**Wien** Hbf ... a.	0821	...	0918	...	1018	1032	...	1121	...	1221	...	1321	...	...	1421	...	1521	...	1621	...	1721	1732	...	1821

	IC 310	EC 148	IC 996	RJX 42	IC 928		EC 340	IC 988	RJX 264	IC 938	EN 462			2	2	2	2		2	2	2	2	2
	⊖	⊖	Ⓡ	✕ ⊖	Ⓡ		⊖	Ⓡ	✕ ⊖	Ⓡ	Ⓡ												
	H			J	K						L												
Budapest Keleti ... d.	1615	1640	1715	1740	1815	...	1840	1915	1940	2015	2040	...	L	...	...	...	...		...	...	2140	...	...
Budapest Déli ... d.	|	|	|	|	|	...	|	|	|	|	|	...	O	0525	0625	0725	0825	and	2025	2125	|	2225	2325
Kelenföld ... d.	1629	1655	1729	1755	1829	...	1855	1929	1955	2029	2055	...	C	0532	0632	0732	0832	at	2032	2132	2157	2232	2332
Tatabánya ... d.	1700	1726	1800	1826	1900	...	1926	2000	2026	2100	2126	...	A	0617	0717	0817	0917	the	2117	2235	2235	2317	0017
Tata ... d.	1707	|	1807	|	1907	...	|	2007	|	2107	|	...	L	0626	0726	0826	0926	same	2126	2244	2244	2326	0026
Komárom ... d.	1720	|	1820	|	1920	...	|	2020	|	2120	|	...		0653	0753	0853	0953	minutes	2153	2256	2257	2347	0047
Györ ... a.	1737	1800	1837	1900	1937	...	2000	2037	2100	2137	2200	...	T	0719	0819	0919	1019	past	2219	...	2323	0013	0113
Györ ... d.	1739	1802	1839	1902	1939	...	2002	2039	2102	2139	2202	...	R	...	...	...	...	each	...	...	...	...	...
Csorna ... d.	1759	|	1859	|	1959	...	|	2059	|	2159	|	...	A	...	...	...	...	hour	...	...	...	...	...
Sopron ... a.	|	|	1938	|	|	...	|	2138	|	|	|	...	I	...	...	...	...	until	...	...	...	...	...
Szombathely ... a.	1849	...	...	|	2049	...	|	...	|	2249	...	...	N	...	...	...	...		...	...	...	...	...
Mosonmagyaróvár ... d.	...	1820	...	1920	...	...	2020	...	2120	...	2220	...	S	...	...	...	...	◧	...	...	...	...	...
Hegyeshalom 🏛 ... a.	...	1829	...	1929	...	...	2029	...	2129	...	2229	...		...	...	...	...		...	...	...	...	...
Wien Hbf ... a.	...	1921	...	2021	...	...	2118	...	2221	...	2321	...		...	...	...	...		...	...	...	...	...

	IC 989	IC 929	IC 987	EN 463	IC 927	RJX 41	IC 997	EC 141	IC 937	RJX 269	IC 985	♥ 1031	EC 143	IC 311	RJX 61	IC 995	EC 145	IC 925	RJX 63	IC 983	EC 147	IC 923	RJX 65	IC 993
	Ⓡ	Ⓡ	Ⓡ	⊖	Ⓡ	✕ ⊖	Ⓡ	⊖	Ⓡ	✕ ⊖	Ⓡ	🍷 Ⓡ	✕ ⊖	⊖	✕ ⊖	Ⓡ	⊖	Ⓡ	✕ ⊖	Ⓡ	⊖	Ⓡ	✕ ⊖	Ⓡ
		K		L						J		D	G	H	C				C				C	
Wien Hbf ... d.	...	...	...	0640	...	0740	...	0842	...	0940	...	1027	1042	...	1140	...	1242	...	1340	...	1437	...	1542	...
Hegyeshalom 🏛 ... d.	...	...	...	0728	...	0828	...	0928	...	1028	...	1122	1128	...	1228	...	1328	...	1428	...	1528	...	1628	...
Mosonmagyaróvár ... d.	...	...	...	0736	...	0836	...	0936	...	1036	...	1131	1136	...	1236	...	1336	...	1436	...	1536	...	1636	...
Szombathely ... d.	...	0552	...	|	0710	|	...	|	0910	|	...	|	|	1110	|	...	|	1310	|	...	|	1510	|	...
Sopron ... d.	...	|	0624	|	|	|	0821	|	|	|	1021	|	|	|	|	1221	|	|	|	1421	|	|	|	1621
Csorna ... d.	...	0640	0702	|	0759	|	0859	|	0959	|	1059	|	|	1159	|	1259	|	1359	|	1459	|	1559	|	1659
Györ ... a.	...	0701	0722	0753	0819	0853	0919	0953	1019	1053	1119	1148	1153	1219	1253	1319	1353	1419	1453	1519	1553	1619	1653	1719
Györ ... d.	0621	0703	0726	0756	0821	0856	0921	0956	1021	1056	1121	1149	1156	1221	1256	1321	1356	1421	1456	1521	1556	1621	1656	1721
Komárom ... d.	0638	|	0743	|	0838	|	0938	|	1038	|	1138	|	|	1238	|	1338	|	1438	|	1538	|	1638	|	1738
Tata ... d.	0651	|	0756	|	0851	|	0951	|	1051	|	1151	|	|	1251	|	1351	|	1451	|	1551	|	1651	|	1751
Tatabánya ... d.	0658	|	0803	0830	0858	0930	0958	1030	1058	1130	1158	|	1230	1258	1330	1358	1430	1458	1530	1558	1630	1658	1730	1758
Kelenföld ... a.	0728	0807	0833	0902	0928	1002	1028	1102	1128	1202	1228	1258	1302	1328	1402	1428	1502	1528	1602	1628	1702	1728	1802	1828
Budapest Déli ... a.	|	|	|	|	|	|	|	|	|	|	|	1314	|	|	|	|	|	|	|	|	|	|	|	|
Budapest Keleti ... a.	0744	0823	0849	0919	0944	1019	1044	1119	1144	1219	1244	...	1319	1344	1419	1444	1519	1544	1619	1644	1719	1744	1819	1844

	EC 149	IC 313	♥ 1035	RJX 67	IC 981		RJX 165	IC 921	347	EC 341	RJX 261			2	2	2	2	2		2	IR 1991 2	2	2
	⊖	Ⓡ	🍷 Ⓡ	✕ ⊖	Ⓡ		✕ ⊖	Ⓡ	✕ Ⓡ	⊖	✕ ⊖			Ⓐ	Ⓒ	Ⓐ	Ⓒ				⑦		
	F	E	D	C			B		A		C												
Wien Hbf ... d.	1642	...	1727	1740	...	...	1842	...	1942	2037	2140	...	L	...	...	...	...	...	and	...	...	...	...
Hegyeshalom 🏛 ... d.	1728	...	1822	1828	...	...	1928	...	2028	2128	2228	...	O	0457	...	0557	...	...	at	...	...	...	...
Mosonmagyaróvár ... d.	1736	...	1831	1836	...	...	1936	...	2036	2136	2236	...	C	0506	...	0606	...	...	the	...	...	...	...
Szombathely ... d.	|	1710	|	|	...	...	|	1910	|	|	|	...	A	|	...	|	...	...	same	...	...	...	...
Sopron ... d.	|	|	|	|	1821	...	|	|	|	|	|	...	L	|	...	|	...	...	minutes	...	2021	...	...
Csorna ... d.	|	1759	|	|	1859	...	|	1959	|	|	|	...		|	...	|	...	...	past	...	2059	...	...
Györ ... a.	1753	1819	1848	1853	1919	...	1953	2019	2053	2153	2253	...	T	0533	...	0633	...	...	each	...	2119	...	...
Györ ... d.	1756	1821	1849	1856	1921	...	1956	2021	2056	2156	2256	...	R	0535	0535	0635	0635	0738	hour	2038	2121	2138	2238
Komárom ... d.	|	1838	|	|	1938	...	|	2038	|	|	|	...	A	0600	0600	0700	0700	0803	until	2103	2138	2203	2303
Tata ... d.	|	1851	|	|	1951	...	|	2051	|	|	|	...	I	0619	0619	0719	0719	0828		2128	2151	2228	2328
Tatabánya ... d.	1830	1858	|	1930	1958	...	2030	2058	2130	2230	2330	...	N	0629	0638	0729	0738	0838	◧	2138	2158	2238	2338
Kelenföld ... a.	1902	1928	1958	2002	2028	...	2102	2128	2202	2302	0002	...	S	0702	0724	0802	0824	0924		2224	2228	2324	0024
Budapest Déli ... a.	|	|	2014	|	|	...	|	|	|	|	|	...		|	0734	|	0834	0934		2234	2239	2334	0034
Budapest Keleti ... a.	1919	1944	...	2019	2044	...	2119	2144	2220	2319	0019	...		0719	...	0819	...	...		...	...	...	...

LOCAL TRAINS **GYÖR - SOPRON** (SEE NOTE ⊡) GySEV

km			Ⓐ									
0	**Györ** ... d.	0643	0751	0851	1051	1251	1451	1651	1851	1951	2051	2251
31	Csorna ... d.	0716	0821	0921	1121	1321	1521	1721	1921	2021	2120	2318
85	**Sopron** ... a.	0804	0906	1006	1206	1412	1613	1813	2013	2109	2209	0002

		Ⓐ									
Sopron ... d.	0558	0645	0742	0945	1145	1345	1545	1745	1845	1945	2230
Csorna ... d.	0646	0734	0834	1034	1234	1434	1634	1834	1935	2034	2317
Györ ... a.	0715	0806	0906	1106	1306	1506	1706	1906	2006	2106	2345

A – DACIA-CORVIN – 🚃12 ✕ Bucureşti - Wien and v.v.; 🛏 1, 2 cl., 🛌 2 cl., 🚃2 Wien - Budapest - Szolnok (**405/4**) - Cluj Napoca and v.v.
B – 🚃12 ✕ Budapest - Wien - Salzburg - Innsbruck - Zürich and v.v.
C – 🚃12 ✕ Budapest - Wien - Salzburg - München and v.v.
D – 🚃12 🍷 Praha - Wien - Budapest and v.v. Ⓡ.
E – MURA – 🚃12 Budapest - Szombathely - Graz and v.v.
F – HORTOBÁGY – 🚃12 ✕ Chop - Záhony - Nyiregyháza - Debrecen - Budapest - Wien and v.v.; conveys 🛏 1, 2 cl. Kyïv - Lviv - Chop - Záhony - Budapest - Wien and v.v.
G – TRANSILVANIA-SZAMOS – 🚃12 ✕ Cluj Napoca - Oradea - Budapest - Wien and v.v.; 🚃12 Baia Mare - Püspökladány - Budapest - Wien and v.v.
H – DRÁVA – 🚃12 Budapest - Szombathely - Ljubljana and v.v.
J – 🚃12 ✕ Budapest - Wien - Salzburg and v.v.
K – SAVARIA – 🚃12 Budapest - Szombathely - Szentgotthárd and v.v.
L – KÁLMÁN IMRE / WIENER WALZER – 🛏 1, 2 cl., 🛌 2 cl., 🚃2 Budapest - Wien - Salzburg - München - Stuttgart and v.v.; 🛏 1, 2 cl., 🛌 2 cl., 🚃2 Budapest - Wien - Salzburg (**466/7**) - Zürich and v.v.

♥ – Operated by REGIOJET. Separate fare tariff applies.
⊖ – Reservation compulsory for domestic journeys in Hungary.
◧ – For local trains Györ - Hegyeshalom - Bruck an der Leitha see Table **1254**.
⊡ – Also from Györ at 0405, 0520 Ⓐ, 0557, 1351 Ⓐ, 1551, 1751, 2151. Also from Sopron at 0350, 0458, 1445, 1645, 2115.
RJX – Railjet Express. Conveys Business, 1st and economy class.

1253 GYÖR - RAJKA - BRATISLAVA

2nd class

km			e								
0	**Györ** ... 1250 d.	0546	...	0646	...	1246	...	1446	...	1646	...
36	Mosonmagyaróvár. 1250 d.	0612	...	0712	...	1312	...	1512	...	1712	...
47	Hegyeshalom ... 1250 d.	0622	0633	0733	...	1322	1333	1522	1533	1722	1733
60	Rajka 🏛 ... a.	...	0645	0745	0749	...	1345	...	1545	...	1745
77	**Bratislava** Petržalka ☆. a.	...	0707	...	0807	...	1407	...	1607	...	1807

	e	d								
Bratislava Petržalka ☆. d.	0726	...	0849	...	1449	...	1649	...	1849	...
Rajka 🏛 ... d.	0744	0752	0910	...	1510	...	1710	...	1910	...
Hegyeshalom ... 1250 d.	...	0805	0922	0935	1522	1535	1722	1735	1922	1935
Mosonmagyaróvár 1250 d.	...	0814	...	0944	...	1544	...	1744	...	1944
Györ ... 1250 a.	...	0841	...	1011	...	1611	...	1811	...	2011

d – Daily Rajka - Hegyeshalom; Ⓐ Hegyeshalom - Györ.
e – ①–⑥ (subject to alteration on and around Slovak and Hungarian public holiday dates).
☆ – Bus 93 links Petržalka station with Bratislava hlavná stanica (main station) every 5 - 12 minutes; journey approx 10 minutes.

2nd class — GYÖR - BRUCK AN DER LEITHA — 1254

Subject to alteration on and around Hungarian and Austrian holiday dates.

km			◧	◧				◧				
0	Györ ◇	d.	0446	0546	0746	0946	1146	1346	1546	1746	1946	2146
36	Mosonmagyaróvár ◇	d.	0512	0612	0812	1012	1212	1412	1612	1812	2012	2212
47	Hegyeshalom 🏛 ◇	a.	0522	0622	0822	1022	1222	1422	1622	1822	2022	2222
47	Hegyeshalom 🏛	d.	0530	0630	0844	1044	1244	1425	1644	1844	2044	...
79	**Bruck an der Leitha**	a.	0555	0655	0909	1109	1309	1454	1709	1909	2109	...

		⑥⑦					①–⑤	⑥⑦		①–⑤	
Bruck an der Leitha	d.	0648	0748	0948	1148	1348	1448	1548	1748	1848	2148
Hegyeshalom 🏛	a.	0714	0814	1014	1214	1414	1514	1614	1814	1914	2214
Hegyeshalom 🏛 ◇	d.	0735	0835	1035	1235	1435	1535	1635	1835	1935	2235
Mosonmagyaróvár ◇	d.	0744	0844	1044	1244	1444	1544	1644	1844	1944	2244
Györ ◇	a.	0811	0911	1111	1311	1511	1611	1711	1911	2011	2311

◇ – Also Györ - Hegyeshalom at 0446 and hourly until 2246; Hegyeshalom - Györ at 0425, 0535 and hourly until 2235. See also Table **1250**.
◧ – Trains from Györ at 0446 ⑥⑦, 0546 ⑥⑦, 1346 ⑥⑦ run 14 minutes later Hegyeshalom - Bruck an der Leitha.

2nd class — BUDAPEST - VÁC - SZOB — 1255

Local trains. For *EC* trains every two hours (to / from Praha) see Table **1175**.

km				Ⓒ							
0	**Budapest** Nyugati	d.	0050	0350	0450	0608	and	2108	2208	2250	2350
34	Vác	d.	0133	0433	0533	0633	hourly	2133	2233	2333	0033
51	Nagymaros-Visegrád ¶	d.	0148	0448	0548	0648	until	2148	2248	2348	0048
64	**Szob**	a.	0204	0504	0604	0704	⊡	2204	2304	0004	0104

Szob	d.	0456	0556	0656	0756	and	1956	2059	2159	2259
Nagymaros-Visegrád ¶	d.	0511	0611	0711	0811	hourly	2011	2114	2214	2314
Vác	d.	0528	0628	0728	0828	until	2028	2134	2234	2334
Budapest Nyugati	a.	0554	0654	0754	0854	⊡	2054	2214	2314	0014

⊡ – Also Budapast - Szob at 0150 Ⓒ, 0250 Ⓒ; Szob - Budapest at 0332 Ⓐ, 0402, 0502 Ⓐ.
¶ – A ferry operates across the river to Visegrád.

2nd class — BUDAPEST - GYÖNGYÖS, FÜZESABONY and EGER — 1258

km											
0	**Budapest** Keleti	d.	0500	0530	0600		1930	2000	2030	2100	2130
67	Hatvan	d.	0553	0623	0653		2023	2053	2123	2153	2223
87	Vámosgyörk	d.	0609	0636	0706	and	2036	2106	2136	2206	2236
100	**Gyöngyös**	a.	|	0653	|	hourly	2053	|	2153	|	2253
126	**Füzesabony**	a.	0641	...	0730	until	...	2138	...	2230	...
126	**Füzesabony**	d.	0650	...	0731	●	...	2139	...	2231	...
143	**Eger**	a.	0707	...	0748		...	2156	...	2249	...

Eger	d.	0500	0600	0706	...		1907	...	2007	...
Füzesabony	a.	0518	0618	0725	...		1925	...	2025	...
Füzesabony	d.	0520	0621	0727	...	and	1926	...	2027	...
Gyöngyös	d.	|	|	|	0803	hourly	|	2003	|	2103
Vámosgyörk	d.	0551	0651	0751	0820	until	1950	2020	2051	2120
Hatvan	d.	0605	0705	0805	0835	●	2005	2035	2105	2135
Budapest Keleti	a.	0700	0800	0900	0930		2100	2130	2200	2230

● – Timings may vary slightly. Other trains: Budapest - Gyöngyös at 2230; Gyöngyös - Budapest at 0400, 0503, 0603, 0703, 2215.

BUDAPEST - MISKOLC - KOŠICE, SÁTORALJAÚJHELY and NYÍREGYHÁZA — 1260

Fast trains. For slower connecting trains via Füzesabony see Tables **1258** and **1261**.

km			*IC*	*IC*	*IC**	*IC*	*IC*	*IC**	*IC*	*IC*	*IC**	*IC*	*IC*	*IC**	*IC*	*IC*	*IC**	*IC*	*IC*	*IC**	*IC*	*IC*	*IC**	*IC*	*IC*	*IC*	
			580	**582**	**182**	**520**	**560**	**190**	**522**	**562**	**192**	**504**	**564**	**184**	**524**	**566**	**194**	**506**	**568**	**186**	**526**	**586**	**188**	**528**	**508**	**518**	**2**
			🅁	🅁	⊖	🅁	🅁	⊖	🅁	🅁	⊖	🅁	🅁	⊖	🅁	🅁	⊖	🅁	🅁	⊖	🅁	🅁	⊖	🅁	🅁	🅁	
0	**Budapest** Keleti	d.	...	0525	0625	0625	0725	0825	0825	0925	1025	1025	1125	1225	1225	1325	1425	1425	1525	1625	1625	1725	1825	1825	1925	2025	2200
67	Hatvan		...	0610	0710	0710	0810	0910	0910	1010	1110	1110	1210	1310	1310	1410	1510	1510	1610	1710	1710	1810	1910	1910	2010	2110	2255
126	Füzesabony	d.	...	0647	|	|	0847	|	|	1047	|	|	1247	|	|	1447	|	|	1647	|	|	1847	|	|	2048	2147	2343
139	Mezökövesd	d.	...	|	0754	0754	|	0954	0954	|	1154	1154	|	1354	1354	|	1554	1554	|	1754	1754	|	1954	1954	2059	2156	2353
183	**Miskolc**	a.	...	0725	0825	0825	0925	1025	1025	1125	1225	1225	1325	1425	1425	1525	1625	1625	1725	1825	1825	1925	2025	2025	2130	2229	0026
183	**Miskolc**	d.	0630	0729	0830	0840	0929	1030	1040	1129	1230	1240	1329	1430	1440	1529	1630	1640	1729	1830	1840	1929	2030	2040	2131		
244	Hidasnémeti 🏛	a.	|	|	0927	|	|	1127	|	|	1327	|	|	1527	|	|	1727	|	|	1927	|	|	2127	|	|		...
270	**Košice**	a.	|	|	1003	|	|	1203	|	|	1403	|	|	1603	|	|	1803	|	|	2003	|	|	2203	|	|		...
221	Szerencs	a.	0654	0754	...	0905	0954	...	1105	1154	...	1305	1354	...	1505	1554	...	1705	1754	...	1905	1954	...	2105	2156	...	...
221	Szerencs	d.	0655	0755	...	0906	0955	...	1106	1155	...	1306	1355	...	1506	1555	...	1706	1755	...	1906	1955	...	2106	2157	...	...
257	Sárospatak	d.	|	|	...	0940	|	...	1140	|	...	1340	|	...	1540	|	...	1740	|	...	1940	|	...	2140	|	...	...
267	**Sátoraljaújhely**	a.	|	|	...	0949	|	...	1149	|	...	1349	|	...	1549	|	...	1749	|	...	1949	|	...	2149	|	...	...
239	Tokaj	d.	0708	0808	...	...	1008	...	...	1208	...	...	1408	...	...	1608	...	...	1808	...	...	2008	...	...	2210	...	...
271	**Nyíregyháza**	a.	0733	0832	...	...	1029	...	...	1229	...	...	1429	...	...	1629	...	...	1829	...	...	2029	...	...	2234	...	...
	Debrecen **1270**	a.	0805	0905	...	...	1105	...	...	1305	...	...	1505	...	...	1705	...	...	1905	...	...	2105	...	...	...	...	...

		IR	*IC*	*IC*	*IC**	*IC*	*IC*	*IC**	*IC*	*IC*	*IC**	*IC*	*IC*	*IC**	*IC*	*IC*	*IC**	*IC*	*IC*	*IC**	*IC*	*IC*	*IC**	*IC*		*IC*
		509	**519**	**507**	**189**	**682**	**527**	**199**	**650**	**525**	**187**	**652**	**523**	**197**	**654**	**503**	**195**	**656**	**521**	**193**	**658**	**501**	**191**	**688**	**2**	**588**
			🅁	🅁	⊖	🅁 **A**	🅁	⊖	🅁	🅁	⊖	🅁	🅁	⊖	🅁	🅁	⊖	🅁	🅁	⊖	🅁	🅁	⊖	🅁		🅁
Debrecen **1270**	d.	...	...	...	...	0653	...	...	0853	...	...	1053	...	...	1253	...	...	1453	...	...	1653	...	...	1853	...	2053
Nyíregyháza	d.	...	0524	...	...	0726	...	...	0926	...	...	1126	...	...	1326	...	...	1526	...	...	1726	...	...	1926	...	2126
Tokaj	d.	...	0548	...	...	0748	...	...	0948	...	...	1148	...	...	1348	...	...	1548	...	...	1748	...	...	1950	...	2150
Sátoraljaújhely	d.	...	|	0604	...	|	0804	...	|	1004	...	|	1204	...	|	1404	...	|	1604	...	|	1804	...	|	...	|
Sárospatak	d.	...	|	0614	...	|	0814	...	|	1014	...	|	1214	...	|	1414	...	|	1614	...	|	1814	...	|	...	|
Szerencs	a.	...	0601	0649	...	0801	0849	...	1001	1049	...	1201	1249	...	1401	1449	...	1601	1649	...	1801	1849	...	2003	...	2203
Szerencs	d.	...	0602	0650	...	0802	0850	...	1002	1050	...	1202	1250	...	1402	1450	...	1602	1650	...	1802	1850	...	2004	...	2204
Košice	d.	...	|	|	0601	|	|	0801	|	|	1001	|	|	1201	|	|	1401	|	|	1601	|	|	1801	|	...	|
Hidasnémeti 🏛	d.	...	|	|	0626	|	|	0826	|	|	1026	|	|	1226	|	|	1426	|	|	1626	|	|	1826	|	...	|
Miskolc	a.	...	0627	0715	0718	0827	0915	0919	1027	1115	1119	1227	1315	1319	1427	1515	1519	1627	1715	1719	1827	1915	1919	2029	...	2229
Miskolc	d.	0522	0630	0730	0730	0830	0930	0930	1030	1130	1130	1230	1330	1330	1430	1530	1530	1630	1730	1730	1830	1930	1930	2030	2033	...
Mezökövesd	d.	0551	|	0757	0757	|	0957	0957	|	1157	1157	|	1357	1357	|	1557	1557	|	1757	1757	|	1957	1957	|	2107	...
Füzesabony	d.	0602	0705	|	|	0905	|	|	1105	|	|	1305	|	|	1505	|	|	1705	|	|	1905	|	|	2105	2127	...
Hatvan	d.	0643	0745	0845	0845	0945	1045	1045	1145	1245	1245	1345	1445	1445	1545	1645	1645	1745	1845	1845	1945	2045	2045	2145	2215	...
Budapest Keleti	a.	0740	0835	0935	0935	1035	1135	1135	1235	1335	1335	1435	1535	1535	1635	1735	1735	1835	1935	1935	2035	2135	2135	2235	2330	...

A – From Szolnok (Table **1270**).
⊖ – 🅁 for domestic journeys.
* – Classified *EC* in Slovakia.

2nd class — FÜZESABONY - MISKOLC - SÁTORALJAÚJHELY and NYÍREGYHÁZA — 1261

For fast trains Budapest - Miskolc - Sátoraljaújhely / Nyiregyháza see Table **1260**.

km					Ⓒ d			Ⓐ				Ⓐ		Ⓐ		B									
0	**Füzesabony**	d.	...	...	...	...	0400	0430	...	...	0501	...	...	0534	...	0553	0627	...	...	0651	0734	0834	0934	...	1034
13	Mezökövesd	d.	...	...	...	...	0411	0441	...	...	0512	...	...	0545	...	0604	0638	...	...	0702	0745	0845	0945	...	1045
57	**Miskolc**	a.	...	...	...	...	0448	0518	...	...	0549	...	...	0622	...	0641	0715	...	...	0739	0822	0922	1022	...	1122
57	**Miskolc**	d.	...	...	0329	0418	▬	...	0526	...	...	0601	...	...	0637	...	...	...	0737	...	0837	0937	1037	...	1137
95	Szerencs	a.	...	...	0407	0454	...	...	0602	...	...	0637	...	...	0715	...	...	...	0815	...	0916	1015	1116	...	1215
95	Szerencs	d.	0348	0410	0410	0456	0516	...	0608	0604	...	...	0704	...	0716	...	...	0804	0816	...	...	1016	...	1204	1216
131	Sárospatak	d.	0426	|	|	0532	|	...	|	0640	...	...	0740	...	|	...	...	0840	|	...	...	|	...	1240	|
141	**Sátoraljaújhely**	a.	0435	|	|	0541	|	...	|	0649	...	...	0749	...	|	...	...	0849	|	...	...	|	...	1249	|
113	Tokaj	d.	...	0430	0430	...	0534	...	0634	...	...	...	...	...	0734	...	...	...	0834	...	...	1034	...	...	1234
145	**Nyíregyháza**	a.	...	0505	0505	...	0615	...	0715	...	...	...	...	...	0815	...	...	...	0915	...	...	1115	...	...	1315

						Ⓐ e																		C
Füzesabony	d.	1134	...	...	1234	...	1334	...	...	1434	1534	...	...	1634	1734	...	1834	1934	...	...	2055	...	2255	2343
Mezökövesd	d.	1145	...	...	1245	...	1345	...	...	1445	1545	...	...	1645	1745	...	1845	1945	...	...	2108	...	2308	2353
Miskolc	a.	1222	...	...	1322	...	1422	...	...	1522	1622	...	...	1722	1822	...	1922	2022	...	...	2149	...	2349	0026
Miskolc	d.	...	1237	...	1337	1415	1437	1502	...	1537	1637	...	...	1737	1837	...	1937	2037	2137	...	...	2310	...	...
Szerencs	a.	...	1316	...	1415	1451	1516	1549	...	1615	1716	...	...	1815	1916	...	2015	2116	2215	...	...	2346	...	...
Szerencs	d.	...	1317	1404	1416	...	1517	...	1604	1616	1717	...	1804	1816	1917	2006	2016	2117	2216	2226	...	2353		
Sárospatak	d.	...	|	1440	|	...	|	...	1640	|	|	...	1840	|	|	2042	|	|	|	2302	...	|		...
Sátoraljaújhely	a.	...	|	1449	|	...	|	...	1649	|	|	...	1849	|	|	2051	|	|	|	2311	...	|		...
Tokaj	d.	...	1334	...	1434	...	1534	...	...	1634	1734	...	...	1834	1934	...	2034	2134	2234	...	...	0011	...	...
Nyíregyháza	a.	...	1415	...	1515	...	1615	...	...	1715	1815	...	...	1915	2015	...	2116	2215	2315	...	...	0045	...	...

B – From Budapest Keleti (d. 0355), Hatvan (d. 0503) and Vámosgyörk (d. 0518).
C – From Budapest Keleti (d. 2200), Hatvan (d. 2255) and Vámosgyörk (d. 2309).
D – To Vámosgyörk (a. 0445), Hatvan (a. 0500) and Budapest Keleti (a. 0600).
E – To Vámosgyörk (a. 2151), Hatvan (a. 2204) and Budapest Keleti (a. 2330).
d – June 18 - Aug. 27.
e – Not June 19 - Aug. 31.
f – June 17 - Aug. 26.

FOR RETURN SERVICE SEE NEXT PAGE →

1261 NYÍREGYHÁZA and SÁTORALJAÚJHELY - MISKOLC - FÜZESABONY

2nd class

For fast trains Nyiregyháza / Sátoraljaújhely - Miskolc - Budapest see Table **1260**.

	D						Ⓐ																
Nyíregyháza d.	...	...	0300	...	0342	...	...	...	...	0440	...	...	0538	...	0641	...	...	...	...	0838	...	1038	...
Tokaj d.	...	...	0335	...	0418	...	...	...	...	0520	...	...	0616	...	0720	...	...	...	...	0920	...	1120	...
Sátoraljaújhely d.	...	...	|	...	|	0352	...	...	0456	|	...	...	|	...	|	0704	...	...	...	|	...	|	1104
Sárospatak d.	...	...	|	...	|	0402	...	...	0506	|	...	...	|	...	|	0714	...	...	...	|	...	|	1114
Szerencs a.	...	...	0351	...	0435	0438	...	...	0541	0539	...	...	0633	...	0739	0752	...	...	...	0939	...	1139	1152
Szerencs d.	...	...	0352	...	...	0439	0510	...	...	0546	...	0615	0636	...	0740	...	...	0840	...	0940	1034	1140	...
Miskolc a.	...	...	0428	...	...	0515	0546	...	...	0622	...	0652	0712	...	0816	...	...	0918	...	1016	1110	1216	...
Miskolc d.	0324	0400	...	0502	...	0526	...	0556	...	...	0633	...	...	0733	...	...	0833	...	0933	1033	1133	1233	...
Mezökövesd d.	0401	0437	...	0539	...	0607	...	0633	...	...	0710	...	...	0810	...	...	0910	...	1010	1110	1210	1310	...
Füzesabony a.	0413	0449	...	0551	...	0618	...	0645	...	...	0722	...	...	0822	...	...	0922	...	1022	1122	1222	1322	...

		Ⓐ												E									⑤⑥
Nyíregyháza d.	1138	...	1238	...	...	1338	1438	...	1538	1638	...	1738	1838	...	...	1938	...	...	2042	...	...	2238	2238
Tokaj d.	1220	...	1320	...	...	1420	1520	...	1620	1720	...	1820	1920	...	...	2020	...	...	2120	...	...	2320	2320
Sátoraljaújhely d.	|	...	|	...	1304	|	|	1504	|	|	1704	|	|	...	1904	|	2006	2128	|	...	2226	|	|
Sárospatak d.	|	...	|	...	1314	|	|	1514	|	|	1714	|	|	...	1914	|	2016	2140	|	...	2236	|	|
Szerencs a.	1239	...	1339	...	1352	1439	1539	1552	1639	1739	1752	1839	1939	...	1952	2039	2054	2218	2139	...	2314	2339	2339
Szerencs d.	1240	...	1340	...	...	1440	1540	...	1640	1740	...	1840	1940	...	...	...	2055	...	2220	...	...	...	2340
Miskolc a.	1318	...	1416	...	...	1518	1616	...	1718	1816	...	1918	2016	...	...	...	2131	...	2256	...	...	...	0016
Miskolc d.	1333	1359	...	1433	...	1533	1633	...	1733	1833	...	1933	...	2033	...	...	...	...	...	2300	...	...	...
Mezökövesd d.	1410	1436	...	1510	...	1610	1710	...	1810	1910	...	2010	...	2111	...	...	...	...	...	2345	...	...	...
Füzesabony a.	1422	1448	...	1522	...	1622	1722	...	1822	1922	...	2022	...	2123	...	...	...	...	...	2358	...	...	...

FOR RETURN SERVICE AND FOOTNOTES SEE PREVIOUS PAGE.

1262 HATVAN - SALGÓTARJÁN - SOMOSKÖÚJFALU

2nd class

km																								
			Ⓐ			Ⓐ						Ⓐ			Ⓐ			Ⓐ			Ⓐ			
0	**Hatvan** d.	0402	0512	...	0608	0712	...	0812	1012	...	1212	1312	...	1412	1512	...	1612	1712	...	1812	1912	...	2012	2212
59	Salgótarján a.	0534	0634	...	0734	0834	...	0934	1134	...	1334	1434	...	1534	1634	...	1734	1834	...	1934	2034	...	2134	2334
65	**Somosköújfalu** a.	0545	0645	...	0745	0845	...	0945	1145	...	1345	1445	...	1545	1645	...	1745	1845	...	1945	2045	...	2145	2345

				Ⓐ			Ⓐ						Ⓐ			Ⓐ			Ⓐ				
Somosköújfalu d.	0306	0412	...	0512	0612	...	0712	0812	...	1012	1212	...	1312	1412	...	1512	1612	...	1712	1812	...	2012	2212
Salgótarján d.	0318	0424	...	0524	0624	...	0724	0824	...	1024	1224	...	1324	1424	...	1524	1624	...	1724	1824	...	2024	2224
Hatvan a.	0434	0544	...	0644	0744	...	0844	0944	...	1144	1344	...	1444	1544	...	1644	1744	...	1844	1944	...	2144	2344

1270 BUDAPEST - DEBRECEN - NYÍREGYHÁZA - ZÁHONY - CHOP

Ferihegy ✈ is served by 5-6 trains per hour. For other trains Budapest Nyugati - Szolnok and v.v. see Tables **1280** and **1290**.
All times in Ukraine are subject to confirmation. The minimum connection time to / from Chop local trains at Záhony is 15 minutes.

km		*IC* **682** [R]	*IC* **600** [R]	*IC* **650** [R]	*IC* **34** F⊖	*IC* **652** [R]	*IC* **602** [R]	*IC* **654** [R]	*IC* **604** [R]	*IC* **656** [R]	*IC* **614** [R]	*IC* **686** [R] G	*IC* **658** [R]	*IC* **606** [R] H	*IC* **688** [R]	*IC* **626** [R]	*IC* **588** [R]	*IC* **618** [R]	*EC* **149** J⊖	*IC* **628** [R]			*IR* **6090**		*IR* **6108**
0	**Budapest** Nyugati d.	...	0523	0623	0723	0823	0923	1023	1123	1223	1323	1340k	1423	1523	1623	1723	1823	1923	1940k	2023	...		0628	and	1828
11	Köbánya Kispest d.	...	0537	0637	0737	0837	0937	1037	1137	1237	1337	|	1437	1537	1637	1737	1837	1937	|	2037	...	*I*	0642	at	1842
18	Ferihegy ✈ d.	...	0543	0643	0743	0843	0943	1043	1143	1243	1343	|	1443	1543	1643	1743	1843	1943	|	2043	...	*R*	0648	the	1848
73	Cegléd d.	...	0618	0718	0818	0918	1018	1118	1218	1318	1418	|	1518	1618	1718	1818	1918	2018	|	2118	...		0724	same	1924
100	**Szolnok** d.	0510	0638	0738	0838	0938	1038	1138	1238	1338	1438	1503	1538	1638	1738	1838	1938	2038	2104	2138	...	T	0750	minutes	1950
177	Püspökladány d.	0608	0722	0822	0922	1022	1122	1222	1322	1422	1522	1602	1622	1722	1822	1922	2022	2122	2202	2222	...	R	0848	past	2048
201	Hajdúszoboszló d.	0627	0740	0837	0937	1037	1137	1237	1337	1437	1537	1618	1637	1737	1837	1937	2037	2137	2219	2237	...	A	0907	each	2107
221	**Debrecen** a.	0643	0756	0851	0951	1051	1151	1251	1351	1451	1551	1632	1651	1751	1851	1951	2051	2151	2235	2251	...	I	0923	hour	2123
221	**Debrecen** d.	0653	0758	0853	0953	1053	1153	1253	1353	1453	1553	...	1653	1756	1853	1953	2053	2153	2237	2253	...	N	...	until	...
270	Nyíregyháza a.	0724	0829	0924	1024	1124	1224	1324	1424	1524	1624	...	1724	1827	1924	2024	2124	2224	2308	2324	...	S	...		...
	Miskolc **1260** a.	0827	...	1027	|	1227	...	1427	...	1627	|	...	1827	|	2029	|	2229	...	|	...	...		...	●	...
335	**Záhony** a.	...	...	...	1121	...	...	...	...	...	1721	...	...	1921	...	2121	...	...	0005	...	...		...		...

	EC **140** J⊖	*IC* **609** [R]	*IC* **619** [R] H	*IC* **580** [R]	*IC* **582** [R]	*IC* **617** [R]	*IC* **560** [R]	*IC* **687** [R] G	*IC* **605** [R]	*IC* **562** [R]	*IC* **615** [R]	*IC* **564** [R]	*IC* **33** F⊖	*IC* **566** [R]	*IC* **603** [R]	*IC* **603** ⑦[R]	*IC* **568** [R]	*IC* **31** [R]	*IC* **586** [R]			*IR* **6129**		*IR* **6001**
Záhony d.	0405	...	0535	...	...	0840	...	...	...	...	...	...	1440	...	...	1628	...	1840	...	...		...	and	...
Miskolc **1260** d.	|	...	|	0630	0729	|	0929	...	...	1129	...	1329	|	1529	...	|	1729	|	1929	...	*I*	...	at	...
Nyíregyháza d.	0458	0534	0626	0734	0834	0934	1034	...	1134	1234	1334	1434	1534	1634	1734	1734	1834	1934	2034	...	*R*	...	the	...
Debrecen a.	0529	0605	0657	0805	0905	1005	1105	...	1205	1305	1405	1505	1605	1705	1805	1805	1905	2005	2105	...		...	same	...
Debrecen d.	0531	0607	0707	0807	0907	1007	1107	1113	1207	1307	1407	1507	1607	1707	1807	1807	1907	2007	2107	...	T	0535	minutes	1835
Hajdúszoboszló d.	0546	0622	0722	0822	0922	1022	1122	1128	1222	1322	1422	1522	1622	1722	1822	1822	1922	2022	2122	...	R	0552	past	1852
Püspökladány d.	0602	0637	0737	0837	0937	1037	1137	1203	1237	1337	1437	1537	1637	1737	1837	1837	1937	2037	2137	...	A	0612	each	1912
Szolnok d.	0657	0721	0821	0921	1021	1121	1221	1257	1321	1421	1521	1621	1721	1821	1921	1921	2021	2121	2221	...	I	0715	hour	2015
Cegléd d.	|	0743	0843	0943	1043	1143	1243	|	1343	1443	1543	1643	1743	1843	1943	1943	2043	2143	2243	...	N	0738	until	2038
Ferihegy ✈ d.	|	0815	0915	1015	1115	1215	1315	|	1415	1515	1615	1715	1815	1915	2015	2015	2115	2215	2315	...	S	0810		2110
Köbánya Kispest d.	|	0821	0921	1021	1121	1221	1321	|	1421	1521	1621	1721	1821	1921	2021	2021	2121	2221	2321	...		0816	●	2116
Budapest Nyugati a.	0820k	0837	0937	1037	1137	1237	1337	1420k	1437	1537	1637	1737	1837	1937	2037	2037	2137	2237	2337	...		0832		2132

km								*IC* **34** F⊖			Ⓐ	Ⓐ	Ⓒ	Ⓐ	*IC* **614** [R]	Ⓐ	Ⓐ	⑥	*IC* **606** [R] H		g	h	*IC* **626** [R]	j		*EC* **149** J⊖
0	*Budapest Nyugati* d.	...	...	...	...	...	...	0723	...	...	...	...	...	...	1323	...	...	...	1523	...	...	...	1723	...	...	1940k
221	**Debrecen** d.	...	...	0558	0658	...	...	0953	0938	1138	1338	1438	1438	1503	1553	1603	1638	1638	1756	1738	1838	1902	1953	...	...	2237
270	Nyíregyháza a.	...	...	0640	0740	...	...	1024	1020	1220	1420	1520	1520	1545	1624	1645	1720	1720	1827	1820	1920	1944	2024	...	...	2308
270	Nyíregyháza d.	...	0500	0646	0746	0846	0946	1031	1046	1246	1423	1523	1546	1546	1631	1646	1723	1746	1831	1846	1946	1946	2031	2046	2246	2313
313	Kisvárda d.	...	0545	0731	0831	0931	1031	1102	1131	1331	1508	1608	1631	1631	1702	1731	1808	1831	1902	1931	2031	2031	2102	2131	2331	2346
335	**Záhony** a.	...	0611	0757	0857	0957	1057	1121	1157	1357	1534	1634	1657	1657	1721	1757	1834	1857	1921	1957	2057	2057	2121	2157	2357	0005
				|				|																		|
335	**Záhony** 🏛 d.	0342	0634	0835	...	...	...	1223	...	1424	...	...	...	...	1837	...	...	...	...	2041	...	...	...	...	...	0110
341	Chop 🏛 ⊡ a.	0500	0752	0953	...	...	...	1340	...	1542	...	...	...	...	1955	...	...	...	...	2159	...	...	...	...	...	0228
382	**Mukachevo** ⊡ a.	...	...	1133	...	...	...	1530	...	...	...	...	...	...	...	...	...	...	...	...	...	...	...	...	...	0648

	Ⓐ	*EC* **140** J⊖		*IC* **619** [R] H			*IC* **617** [R]	⚒		⚒		Ⓐm	⑦n	Ⓐ	*IC* **33** F⊖	Ⓐm	⑦n		*IC* **603** ⑦[R]			*IC* **31** [R]			
Mukachevo ⊡ d.	...	0024	...	...	...	...	...	...	...	...	...	...	...	...	1230	...	...	...	...	...	...	1630	...	...	...
Chop 🏛 ⊡ d.	...	0428	0529	...	...	0822	...	...	1025	...	...	...	...	...	1410	...	...	1612	...	...	...	1815	...	2025	2229
Záhony 🏛 a.	...	0346	0447	...	...	0740	...	...	0943	...	...	...	...	...	1327	...	...	1530	...	...	...	1733	...	1943	2147
		|													|						|			
Záhony d.	0355	0405	0524	0535	0703	0803	0840	0903	1003	1103	1203	1303	1303	1403	1440	1503	1503	1603	1628	1703	1803	1840	1927	2003	...
Kisvárda d.	0421	0424	0550	0554	0729	0829	0859	0929	1029	1129	1229	1329	1329	1429	1459	1529	1529	1629	1647	1729	1829	1859	1953	2029	...
Nyíregyháza a.	0506	0456	0637	0624	0814	0914	0930	1014	1114	1214	1314	1414	1414	1514	1530	1614	1614	1714	1718	1814	1914	1930	2038	2114	...
Nyíregyháza d.	0510	0458	0640	0626	0840	0940	0934	...	1140	1240	1340	1417	1440	1517	1534	1617	1640	1740	1734	...	1940	1934	2046	2140	...
Debrecen a.	0553	0529	0723	0657	0923	1023	1005	...	1223	1323	1423	1500	1523	1601	1605	1700	1723	1823	1805	...	2023	2005	2129	2223	...
Budapest Nyugati a.	...	0820k	...	0937	...	...	1237	...	...	...	...	...	...	...	1837	...	...	...	2037	...	...	2237	...	...	...

F – LATORCA – [12] Budapest - Záhony and v.v.; [2] Budapest - Mukachevo (Table **1715**) and v.v.; [2] Záhony - Chop and v.v.

G – SZAMOS – [2] Wien (**143/144**) - Püspökladány (**686/687**) - Baia Mare and v.v. (Table **1277**).

H – Conveys [2] [R] Budapest Nyugati - Debrecen (**638/639**) - Mátészalka and v.v. (Table **1276**).

J – HORTOBÁGY – [12] Wien - Budapest - Debrecen - Záhony and v.v.; conveys 🛏 1, 2 cl. Wien - Budapest - Chop - Lviv - Kyïv and v.v.

g – Not June 17 - Aug. 27.

h – June 17 - Aug. 27.

j – June 17 - Aug. 27 runs as an *Ex* train. [R].

k – Budapest **Keleti**.

m – Also ⑦ June 18 - Aug. 27.

n – Not June 18 - Aug. 27.

⊖ – [R] for domestic journeys within Hungary.

⊡ – Ukrainian (East European) time, one hour ahead of Hungarian time.

● – Timings may vary by up to 5 minutes. Also from Budapest at 2028, 2128, 2228; also from Debrecen at 0230, 0330, 0430.

(WIEN -) BUDAPEST - ORADEA (- CLUJ NAPOCA and BRASOV) 1275

	347 405 A R	369	367* B R	365	EC 143 C R	407* D R			
Wien Hbf **1250** d.	1942	...	...	...	1042	...	...	...	...
Budapest Keleti **1270** d.	2245	...	0740	...	1340	1740	...	...	...
Szolnok **1270** a.	0009	...	0902	...	1502	1902	...	...	...
Szolnok **1270** d.	0031	...	0903	...	1503	1903	...	...	...
Püspökladány **1270** a.	0124	...	0956	...	1556	1956	...	...	...
Püspökladány d.	0151	0643	1026	1320	1613	2013	...	...	...
Biharkeresztes a.	0236	0732	1121	1413	1702	2102	...	...	...
Biharkeresztes 🛃 d.	0313	0752	1144	1436	1754	2140	...	...	...
Episcopia Bihor 🛃 ⊙ a.	0429	0908	1300	1552	1910	2256	...	...	...
Episcopia Bihor ⊙ d.	0510	0923	1316	1607	1934	2315	...	...	...
Oradea ⊙ a.	0520	0933	1326	1616	1944	2325	...	...	...
Cluj Napoca **1600** ⊙ a.	0819	...	1608	...	2223	0200	...	...	...
Brasov **1600** ⊙ a.	...	...	2324	...	...	0943	...	...	...
Bucuresti Nord **1600** ⊙ a.	...	...	...	...	...	...	...	...	...

	404 346 A R	406* D R	EC 146 C R	364	368	366* B R			
Bucuresti Nord **1600** ⊙ d.	...	...	...	...	...	...	...	...	...
Brasov **1600** ⊙ d.	...	1935	...	...	...	0729	...	...	...
Cluj Napoca **1600** ⊙ d.	2100	0248	0739	...	...	1455	...	...	...
Oradea ⊙ d.	2354	0526	1020	1128	1430	1733	...	...	...
Episcopia Bihor ⊙ a.	0002	0534	1028	1136	1438	1741	...	...	...
Episcopia Bihor 🛃 ⊙ d.	0031	0553	1052	1153	1453	1758	...	...	...
Biharkeresztes 🛃 a.	2347	0509	1008	1109	1409	1714	...	...	...
Biharkeresztes d.	0017	0553	1043	1144	1443	1743	...	...	...
Püspökladány a.	0102	0642	1132	1233	1536	1838	...	...	...
Püspökladány **1270** d.	0209	0658	1203	...	...	1903	...	...	...
Szolnok **1270** a.	0303	0754	1254	...	...	1954	...	...	...
Szolnok **1270** d.	0343	0757	1257	...	...	1957	...	...	...
Budapest Keleti **1270** a.	0510	0920	1420	...	...	2120	...	...	...
Wien Hbf **1250** a.	0821	...	1721	...	...	...	...	...	...

A – DACIA-CORVIN – 🛏 1, 2 cl., 🛌 2 cl., 🚃 Wien (**347/6**) - Budapest - Szolnok (**405/4**) - Cluj Napoca and v.v.

B – HARGITA – 🚃12 Budapest - Oradea - Cluj Napoca - Miercurea Ciuc - Brasov and v.v.; Conveys 🚃2 Budapest - Cluj Napoca - Târgu Mures and v.v. on dates in Table **1615**.

C – TRANSILVANIA-SZAMOS – 🚃12 ✕ Wien - Budapest - Oradea - Cluj Napoca and v.v.; Conveys 🚃2 Wien (**143/144**) - Püspökladány (**686/687**) - Baia Mare and v.v. (Table **1277**).

D – CORONA – 🛏 1, 2 cl., 🛌 2 cl., 🚃2 ✕ Budapest - Cluj Napoca - Miercurea Ciuc - Brasov and v.v.

⊙ – Romanian (East European) time, one hour ahead of Hungary.

* – *IC* in Hungary; *IR* in Romania.

2nd class — DEBRECEN - MÁTÉSZALKA and FÜZESABONY 1276

km									E		Ⓑ	d
0	**Debrecen** d.	0451	0713	0913	1113	1313	1513	1713	1808	1907	2011	2244
58	Nyírbátor d.	0622	0836	1036	1236	1436	1636	1836	1917	2026	2146	0003
78	**Mátészalka** a.	0648	0859	1059	1259	1459	1659	1859	1936	2049	2209	0026

	E							⑦			
Mátészalka d.	0447	0521	0705	0905	1105	1305	1505	1614	1705	1911	2122
Nyírbátor d.	0510	0540	0728	0928	1128	1328	1528	1637	1728	1938	2145
Debrecen a.	0629	0648	0847	1047	1247	1447	1647	1759	1854	2101	2258

km										Ⓑ		
0	**Debrecen** d.	0432	0632	0832	1032	1232	1432	1632	1832	2000	2245	...
42	Hortobágy d.	0531	0734	0934	1134	1334	1534	1734	1934	2059	2344	...
73	Tiszafüred d.	0611	0813	1013	1213	1413	1613	1813	2013	2138	0023	...
103	**Füzesabony** a.	0644	0846	1046	1246	1446	1646	1846	2046	...	...	...

			Ⓐ								Ⓑ	
Füzesabony d.	0500	0700	...	0902	1102	1302	1502	1702	1902	2107	2253
Tiszafüred d.	0534	0734	0823	0936	1136	1336	1536	1736	1936	2140	2326
Hortobágy d.	0618	0820	0900	1020	1220	1420	1620	1820	2020	...	...
Debrecen a.	0718	0919	0959	1119	1319	1519	1719	1919	2119	...	...

E – 🚃2 R Budapest Nyugati (**606/619**) - Debrecen (**638/639**) - Mátészalka.

d – Runs 16 minutes later on ⑤.

2nd class — DEBRECEN - ORADEA and BAIA MARE and other cross-border services 1277

km		6812	6822	686 F
	Püspökladány d.	...	...	1602
0	**Debrecen** d.	0657	0805	1705
30	Nyírábrány a.	0751	0851	1751
30	Nyírábrány 🛃 d.	0805	0906	1811
39	Valea lui Mihai 🛃 ⊙ a.	0920	1021	1926
39	Valea lui Mihai ⊙ d.	0942	1038	1947
105	**Oradea** ⊙ a.	1104	|	|
70	Carei **1625** ⊙ a.	...	1111	2009
106	Satu Mare **1625** ⊙ a.	...	1157	2042
165	**Baia Mare** **1625** ⊙ a.	...	...	2206

	687 F	6811	6821
Baia Mare **1625** ⊙ d.	0800	...	...
Satu Mare **1625** ⊙ d.	0927	...	1808
Carei **1625** ⊙ d.	1000	...	1857
Oradea ⊙ d.	|	1635	|
Valea lui Mihai ⊙ a.	1025	1756	1930
Valea lui Mihai 🛃 ⊙ d.	1044	1826	1949
Nyírábrány 🛃 a.	0959	1741	1904
Nyírábrány d.	1019	1819	1920
Debrecen a.	1059	1859	2000
Püspökladány a.	1142	...	...

km			
0	**Békéscsaba** **1280** d.	0642	1544
16	Gyula **1280** d.	0700	1600
36	Kötegyán a.	0725	1625
36	Kötegyán 🛃 d.	0740	1645
50	**Salonta** 🛃 ⊙ a.	0900	1805

Salonta 🛃 ⊙ d.	0940	1830
Kötegyán 🛃 a.	0900	1750
Kötegyán d.	0932	1832
Gyula **1280** d.	1000	1900
Békéscsaba **1280** a.	1015	1915

km			
0	**Mátészalka** d.	0905	1408
18	Tiborszállás a.	0936	1439
18	Tiborszállás 🛃 d.	0951	1455
33	**Carei** ⊙ a.	1117	1621

Carei ⊙ d.	1200	1738
Tiborszállás 🛃 a.	1126	1704
Tiborszállás d.	1150	1723
Mátészalka a.	1221	1810

F – SZAMOS – 🚃2 Wien (**143/144**) - Püspökladány (**686/687**) - Baia Mare and v.v.

⊙ – Romanian (East European) time, one hour ahead of Hungary. For other trains within Romania see Table **1625**.

2nd class (except where noted) — BUDAPEST - BÉKÉSCSABA - LÖKÖSHÁZA - ARAD 1280

km				Ⓐ		IC* 371 ⊖	IC 7400 R	IC* 73 ⊖	IC 7402 R	IC* 75 ⊖	IC 742 R	IC* 375 ⊖	IC 7404 R	IC* 377 ⊖	IC 746 R	IC* 79 G ⊖	IC 7406 R	IC* 379 ⊖	IC 748 R	IC* 473 R H	IC 7408 R	2	347 R J	348 R J
0	**Budapest** Keleti **1270** d.	...	...	...	...	0510	0610	0710	0810	0910	1010	1110	1210	1310	1410	1510	1610	1710	1810	1910	2010	...	2245	2245
100	Szolnok **1270** d.	...	...	0445	0545	0645	0733	0833	0933	1033	1133	1233	1333	1433	1533	1633	1733	1833	1933	2033	2133	...	0036	0036
141	Mezőtúr d.	0429	0529	0529	0629	0720	0759	0859	0959	1059	1159	1259	1359	1459	1559	1659	1759	1859	1959	2059	2159	...	|	|
159	Gyoma d.	0445	0545	0545	0645	0733	0812	0912	1012	1112	1212	1312	1412	1512	1612	1712	1812	1912	2012	2112	2212	...	|	|
196	**Békéscsaba** a.	0515	0615	0615	0715	0800	0839	0939	1039	1139	1239	1339	1439	1539	1639	1739	1839	1939	2039	2139	2239	...	0130	0130
196	**Békéscsaba** d.	0523	0645	0645	...	0818	...	0941	...	1141	...	1341	...	1541	...	1741	...	1941	...	2141	...	2250	0132	0132
225	Lökösháza a.	0608	0730	0730	...	0847	...	1010	...	1210	...	1410	...	1610	...	1810	...	2010	...	2210	...	2335	0159	0159
225	Lökösháza 🛃 d.	...	...	...	...	0915	...	1045	...	1245	...	1445	...	1645	...	1845	...	2045	...	2245	...	...	0239	0239
236	Curtici 🛃 ⊙ a.	...	...	...	...	1025	...	1155	...	1355	...	1555	...	1755	...	1955	...	2155	...	2355	...	...	0349	0349
236	Curtici ⊙ d.	...	...	...	...	1050	...	1219	...	1420	...	1620	...	1818	...	2021	...	2220	...	0025	...	...	0414	0414
253	**Arad** ⊙ a.	...	...	...	...	1102	...	1231	...	1433	...	1632	...	1832	...	2033	...	2232	...	0038	...	...	0427	0427
	Timisoara Nord **1630** ⊙ a.	...	...	...	...	...	...	1334	...	|	...	...	...	1936	...	2135	...	...	...	|	...	...	|	0551
	Brasov **1600** ⊙ a.	...	...	...	...	...	...	|	...	2246	...	...	...	...	...	|	...	...	...	0840	...	...	1235	|
	Bucuresti Nord **1600** ⊙ a.	...	...	...	...	...	...	2349	...	...	...	...	...	...	...	0806	...	...	...	1119	...	...	1505	1605

	349 R J	346 R J		IC* 472 R H	IC 759 R	IC* 378 ⊖	IC 7407 R	IC* 78 G ⊖	IC 747 R	IC* 376 ⊖	IC 745 R		IC* 374 ⊖	Ⓐ	IC 743 R	IC* 74 ⊖	IC 741 R	IC* 72 ⊖	IC 7401 R	IC* 370 ⊖			
Bucuresti Nord **1600** ⊙ d.	1325	1450	...	1825	...	...	...	2146	...	...	...	...	...	...	...	...	...	0540	...	...	...	...	...
Brasov **1600** ⊙ d.	|	1721	...	2103	...	...	...	|	...	...	...	...	...	...	...	0655	...	|	...	...	...	...	...
Timisoara Nord **1630** ⊙ d.	2342	|	...	|	...	0537	...	0803	...	...	...	...	...	...	...	|	...	1559	...	...	...	...	...
Arad ⊙ d.	0131	0131	...	0446	...	0650	...	0903	...	1055	...	...	1255	...	...	1451	...	1700	...	1855	...	...	...
Curtici ⊙ a.	0144	0144	...	0459	...	0703	...	0914	...	1108	...	...	1308	...	...	1504	...	1712	...	1908	...	...	...
Curtici 🛃 ⊙ d.	0210	0210	...	0534	...	0734	...	0934	...	1134	...	...	1334	...	...	1534	...	1734	...	1934	...	...	...
Lökösháza 🛃 a.	0120	0120	...	0444	...	0644	...	0844	...	1044	...	...	1244	...	...	1444	...	1644	...	1844	...	...	...
Lökösháza d.	0200	0200	0425	0540	0640	0740	...	0940	...	1140	...	...	1340	...	...	1540	...	1740	...	1940	...	2025	...
Békéscsaba a.	0227	0227	0510	0613	0715	0813	...	1013	...	1213	...	...	1413	...	...	1613	...	1813	...	2013	...	2110	...
Békéscsaba d.	0229	0229	0532	0620	0720	0820	0920	1020	1120	1220	1320	...	1420	1441	1520	1620	1720	1820	1920	2020	2040	...	2240
Gyoma d.	|	|	0601	0646	0746	0846	0946	1046	1146	1246	1346	...	1446	1512	1546	1646	1746	1846	1946	2046	2111	...	2311
Mezőtúr d.	|	|	0616	0700	0800	0900	1000	1100	1200	1300	1400	...	1500	1541	1600	1700	1800	1900	2000	2100	2127	...	2326
Szolnok **1270** d.	0353	0353	0649	0727	0827	0927	1027	1127	1227	1327	1427	...	1527	1615	1627	1727	1827	1927	2027	2127	2201	...	...
Budapest Keleti **1270** a.	0520	0520	0815	0850	0950	1050	1150	1250	1350	1350	1550	...	1650	...	1750	1850	1950	2050	2150	2250	...	...	...

G – MUNTENIA – 🛌 2 cl., 🚃2 Budapest - Arad - Timisoara - Craiova - Bucuresti and v.v.

H – ISTER – 🛏 1, 2 cl., 🛌 2 cl., 🚃2 Budapest - Arad - Sibiu - Brasov - Bucuresti and v.v.

J – DACIA – 🛏 1, 2 cl., 🛌 2 cl., 🚃2 Wien - Budapest - Arad - Brasov - Bucuresti and v.v.; 🛏 1, 2 cl. Wien - Budapest - Arad - Timisoara - Bucuresti and v.v.

* – Classified *IR* in Romania

⊙ – Romanian (East European) time, one hour ahead of Hungary.

⊖ – Reservation compulsory for domestic journeys in Hungary (R in Romania).

1282 BÉKÉSCSABA - GYULA

2nd class

km																								
											Ⓐ													
0	**Békéscsaba** .... d.	0528	0642	0742	...	0944	1144	1244	...	1344	1403	1444	...	1544	1644	1744	...	1842	1942	2042	...	2241	...	...
16	**Gyula** .... a.	0544	0659	0759	...	0959	1159	1259	...	1359	1419	1459	...	1559	1659	1759	...	1859	1959	2059	...	2258	...	...

			Ⓐ																				
Gyula .... d.	0500	0546	0623	...	0700	0800	0900	...	1000	1100	1300	...	1500	1600	1700	...	1800	1900	2000	...	2100	...	...
Békéscsaba .... a.	0515	0604	0641	...	0715	0815	0915	...	1015	1115	1315	...	1515	1615	1718	...	1815	1915	2015	...	2118	...	...

1290 BUDAPEST - KECSKEMÉT - SZEGED

Carriages without 🅁 are available on *IC* trains.

km																								
			IC	*IC*		*IC*	*IC*	*IC*		*IC*	*IC*	*IC*		*IC*	*IC*	*IC*		*IC*	*IC*	*IC*		*IC*	*IC*	
		2	**700**	**702**		**712**	**722**	**732**		**704**	**714**	**724**		**734**	**706**	**716**		**726**	**736**	**708**		**718**	**728**	2
			🅁	🅁		🅁	🅁	🅁		🅁	🅁	🅁		🅁	🅁	🅁		🅁	🅁	🅁		🅁	🅁	
0	**Budapest** Nyugati .... **1270** d.	0403	0553	0653	...	0753	0853	0953	...	1053	1153	1253	...	1353	1453	1553	...	1653	1753	1853	...	1953	2053	2203
11	Köbánya Kispest .... **1270** d.	0418	0607	0707	...	0807	0907	1007	...	1107	1207	1307	...	1407	1507	1607	...	1707	1807	1907	...	2007	2107	2218
18	Ferihegy ✈ .... **1270** d.	0427	0613	0713	...	0813	0913	1013	...	1113	1213	1313	...	1413	1513	1613	...	1713	1813	1913	...	2013	2113	2224
73	Cegléd .... **1270** a.	0522	0647	0747	...	0847	0947	1047	...	1147	1247	1347	...	1447	1547	1647	...	1747	1847	1947	...	2047	2147	2312
73	Cegléd .... d.	0535	0648	0748	...	0848	0948	1048	...	1148	1248	1348	...	1448	1548	1648	...	1748	1848	1948	...	2048	2148	2313
106	**Kecskemét** .... d.	0605	0711	0811	...	0911	1011	1111	...	1211	1311	1411	...	1511	1611	1711	...	1811	1911	2011	...	2111	2211	2342
131	Kiskunfélegyháza .... a.	0627	0727	0827	...	0927	1027	1127	...	1227	1327	1427	...	1527	1627	1727	...	1827	1927	2027	...	2127	2227	...
131	Kiskunfélegyháza .... d.	0630	0730	0830	...	0930	1030	1130	...	1230	1330	1430	...	1530	1630	1730	...	1830	1930	2030	...	2130	2230	...
191	**Szeged** .... a.	0715	0815	0915	...	1015	1115	1215	...	1315	1415	1515	...	1615	1715	1815	...	1915	2015	2115	...	2215	2315	...

			IC		*IC*	*IC*	*IC*		*IC*	*IC*	*IC*		*IC*	*IC*	*IC*		*IC*	*IC*	*IC*		*IC*	*IC*	*IC*
	2	2	**709**		**707**	**717**	**727**		**737**	**705**	**715**		**725**	**735**	**703**		**713**	**723**	**733**		**701**	**711**	**721**
			🅁		🅁	🅁	🅁		🅁	🅁	🅁		🅁	🅁	🅁		🅁	🅁	🅁		🅁	🅁	🅁
Szeged .... d.	...	0432	0547	...	0645	0745	0845	...	0945	1045	1145	...	1245	1345	1445	...	1545	1645	1745	...	1845	1945	2045
Kiskunfélegyháza .... a.	...	0518	0630	...	0730	0830	0930	...	1030	1130	1230	...	1330	1430	1530	...	1630	1730	1830	...	1930	2030	2130
Kiskunfélegyháza .... d.	...	0519	0631	...	0731	0831	0931	...	1031	1131	1231	...	1331	1431	1531	...	1631	1731	1831	...	1931	2031	2131
Kecskemét .... d.	0432	0538	0648	...	0748	0848	0948	...	1048	1148	1248	...	1348	1448	1548	...	1648	1748	1848	...	1948	2048	2148
Cegléd .... a.	0500	0603	0712	...	0812	0912	1012	...	1112	1212	1312	...	1412	1512	1612	...	1712	1812	1912	...	2012	2112	2212
Cegléd .... **1270** d.	0504	0604	0713	...	0813	0913	1013	...	1113	1213	1313	...	1413	1513	1613	...	1713	1813	1913	...	2013	2113	2214
Ferihegy ✈ .... **1270** a.	0539	0639	0744	...	0844	0944	1044	...	1144	1244	1344	...	1444	1544	1644	...	1744	1844	1944	...	2044	2144	2248
Köbánya Kispest .... **1270** a.	0545	0645	0750	...	0850	0950	1050	...	1150	1250	1350	...	1450	1550	1650	...	1750	1850	1950	...	2050	2150	2254
Budapest Nyugati .... **1270** a.	0602	0702	0807	...	0907	1007	1107	...	1207	1307	1407	...	1507	1607	1707	...	1807	1907	2007	...	2107	2207	2311

1292 SZEGED - BÉKÉSCSABA

2nd class

km																								
			Ⓐ										Ⓐ											
0	**Szeged** .... ◧ d.	...	...	0528	0628	0728	...	0828	0928	1028	1128	1228	...	1328	1428	1528	1628	1728	...	1828	1928	2028	2128	2228
31	Hódmezövásárhely .... ◧ d.	...	...	0601	0705	0801	...	0905	1001	1105	1201	1305	...	1401	1505	1601	1705	1801	...	1905	2001	2105	2201	2259
62	Orosháza .... d.	0430	0531	0631	0731	0831	...	0931	1031	1131	1231	1331	...	1431	1531	1631	1731	1831	...	1931	2031	2131	2229	2327
97	**Békéscsaba** .... a.	0509	0612	0712	0810	0910	...	1010	1110	1210	1310	1410	...	1510	1610	1710	1810	1910	...	2010	2110	2210	...	...

											Ⓐ												
Békéscsaba .... d.	...	...	0547	0647	0747	...	0847	0947	1047	1147	1247	...	1347	1445	1547	1645	1747	...	1847	1947	2047	2147	2245
Orosháza .... d.	0432	0528	0632	0732	0832	...	0932	1032	1132	1232	1332	...	1432	1532	1632	1732	1832	...	1932	2032	2132	2226	2329
Hódmezövásárhely .... ◧ d.	0502	0602	0702	0802	0902	...	1002	1102	1202	1300	1402	...	1502	1602	1702	1802	1902	...	2002	2102	2202	...	...
Szeged .... ◧ a.	0533	0633	0733	0833	0933	...	1033	1133	1233	1333	1433	...	1533	1633	1733	1833	1933	...	2033	2133	2233	...	...

◧ – Also by tram-train from Szeged at 0415 and every 30 minutes (every 20 minutes 0520 Ⓐ - 0820 Ⓐ and 1320 Ⓐ - 1720 Ⓐ) until 2245; from Hódmezövásárhely at 0430 and every 30 minute (every 20 minutes 0550 Ⓐ, 0607 Ⓐ - 0827 Ⓐ and 1330 Ⓐ, 1350 Ⓐ, 1407 Ⓐ - 1727 Ⓐ) until 2230. Journey 55 minutes.

1295 BUDAPEST - KELEBIA - SUBOTICA

2nd class

Warning! Rail services Budapest - Kelebia are suspended due to engineering work. No rail replacement 🚌 service is available.
Commercial services are operated by Volánbuz (international route **600**, local routes **650**, **1115** and **5285**) - rail tickets not valid.

km		*IC* 712	600							
		🅁	🚌 d							
0	**Budapest** Nyugati .... **1290** d.	0753	...	...	...	...	...	...	...	...
	Szeged .... **1290** d.	1015	1025	...	...	...	...	...	...	...
	Kunszentmiklós-Tass .... d.	...	|	...	...	...	...	...	...	...
	Kiskörös .... d.	...	|	...	...	...	...	...	...	...
	Kiskunhalas .... d.	...	|	...	...	...	...	...	...	...
	Kelebia Drž. Granica 🏛 .... d.	...	1145	...	...	...	...	...	...	...
	Subotica bus station .... a.	...	1205	...	...	...	...	...	...	...

	600	*IC* 723							
	🚌 d	🅁							
Subotica bus station .... d.	1445	...	...	...	...	...	...	...	...
Kelebia Drž. Granica 🏛 .... d.	1505	...	...	...	...	...	...	...	...
Kiskunhalas .... d.	|	...	...	...	...	...	...	...	...
Kiskörös .... d.	|	...	...	...	...	...	...	...	...
Kunszentmiklós-Tass .... d.	|	...	...	...	...	...	...	...	...
Szeged .... **1290** d.	1630	1645	...	...	...	...	...	...	...
Budapest Nyugati .... **1290** a.	...	1907	...	...	...	...	...	...	...

d – Commercial service operated by Volánbuz - rail tickets not valid. Connections with trains are **not** guaranteed.

1299 OTHER LOCAL SERVICES

BUDAPEST - DUNAÚJVÁROS — *80 km*, journey 65 – 95 minutes

From **Budapest** Déli: 0450, 0550, 0650, 0750 Ⓐ, 0850, 1050, 1250, 1350 Ⓒ, 1415 Ⓐ, 1450 Ⓒ, 1515 Ⓐ, 1550 Ⓒ, 1615 Ⓐ, 1650 Ⓒ, 1715 Ⓐ, 1815 Ⓐ, 1850, 2050, 2250.

From **Dunaújváros**: 0336, 0438, 0532, 0632, 0732, 0837 Ⓐ, 0932, 1137, 1332, 1437, 1537, 1637, 1732, 1837, 1937 Ⓐ, 2032, 2241.

BUDAPEST - ESZTERGOM — *53 km*, journey 65 – 74 minutes

From **Budapest** Nyugati: 0025, 0225 Ⓒ, 0414, 0451, 0521, 0551, 0621, 0651 and every 30 minutes until 2121, 2151, 2221, 2315.

From **Esztergom**: 0356, 0435, 0505, 0535, 0605, 0635 and every 30 minutes until 2105, 2135, 2235, 2335.

Ⓒ Apr. 1 - Nov. 1: 0921, 1021, 1221 call at **Vasútmúzeum**, returning 1530, 1630, 1730.

BUDAPEST - SZENTENDRE — *21 km*, journey 40 minutes

HÉV suburban trains (line H5) from Budapest Batthyány tér (on metro M2), every 12 – 30 mins.

EGER - SZILVÁSVÁRAD — *34 km*, journey 65 minutes

Trains call at Szilvásvárad-Szalajkavölgy (for the forest railway), 58 minutes after Eger and 6 minutes after Szilvásvárad. Trains with note **A** run March 11 - Nov. 1 only.

From **Eger**: 0732 **A**, 1002, 1302, 1602 **A**.

From **Szilvásvárad**: 0847 **A**, 1147, 1447, 1754 **A**.

ESTERGOM - KOMÁROM — *53 km*, journey 90 minute

From **Esztergom**: 0743 Ⓐ, 0813 Ⓒ *, 1213 Ⓒ *, 1443 Ⓐ, 1613 Ⓒ *, 1643 Ⓐ, 1843 Ⓐ, 2013

From **Komárom**: 0446 Ⓐ, 0546, 1003 Ⓒ *, 1246 Ⓐ, 1403 Ⓒ *, 1444 Ⓐ, 1644 Ⓐ, 1803 Ⓒ *.

* – Change trains at Almásfüzitő (total journey time 100 minutes).

KOMÁROM - SZÉKESFEHÉRVÁR — *82 km*, journey 81 minute

From **Komárom**: 0605, 0805 and every two hours until 2005.

From **Székesfehérvár**: 0608, 0826 and every two hours until 2026.

HATVAN - SZOLNOK — *68 km*, journey 71 – 73 minute

From **Hatvan**: 0406, 0508 Ⓐ, 0608, 0708 Ⓐ, 0808, 1008, 1208, 1308 Ⓐ, 1408, 1508 Ⓐ, 1608 1708 Ⓐ, 1808, 1908 Ⓐ, 2008, 2108 Ⓐ, 2220.

From **Szolnok**: 0320, 0431, 0531 Ⓐ, 0631, 0731 Ⓐ, 0831, 1031, 1231, 1331 Ⓐ, 1431, 1531 Ⓐ, 1631, 1731 Ⓐ, 1831, 1931 Ⓐ, 2031, 2131.

KISKUNFÉLEGYHÁZA - SZENTES — *39 km*, journey 51 minute

Trains call at **Csongrád** 36 minutes after Kiskunfélegyháza / 17 minutes after Szentes.

From **Kiskunfélegyháza**: 0534 Ⓐ, 0734 and every two hours until 2134.

From **Szentes**: 0423 Ⓐ, 0634 and every two hours until 2034.

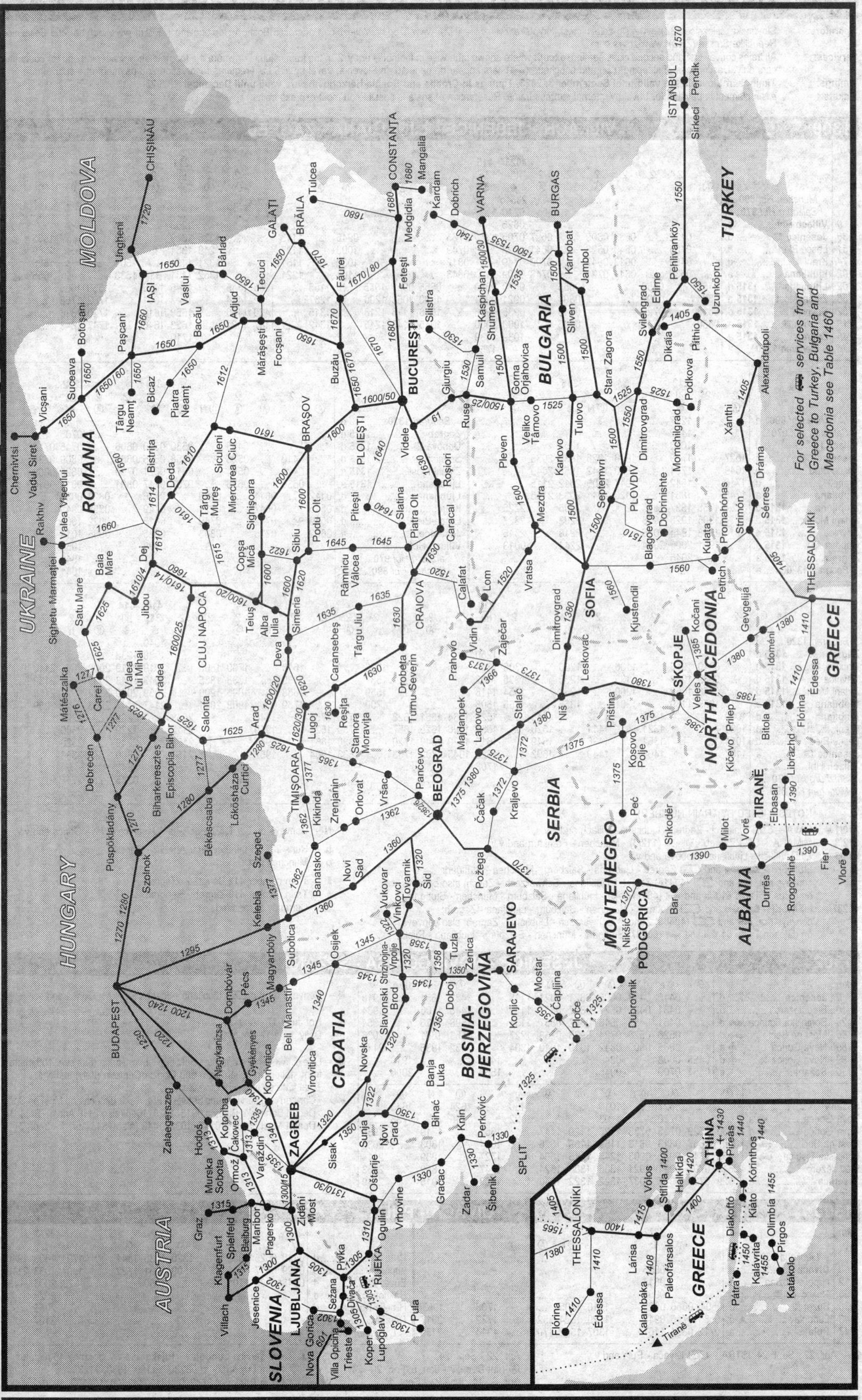
UKRAINE
MOLDOVA
ROMANIA
HUNGARY
AUSTRIA
SLOVENIA
CROATIA
BOSNIA-HERZEGOVINA
SERBIA
MONTENEGRO
NORTH MACEDONIA
ALBANIA
BULGARIA
GREECE
TURKEY
BUCUREȘTI
BUDAPEST
BEOGRAD
ZAGREB
LJUBLJANA
SARAJEVO
PODGORICA
SKOPJE
TIRANË
SOFIA
THESSALONÍKI
ATHÍNA
ISTANBUL
CHIȘINĂU
CLUJ NAPOCA
TIMIȘOARA
BRAȘOV
CRAIOVA
CONSTANȚA
VARNA
BURGAS
PLOVDIV
RIJEKA
SPLIT
For selected services from Greece to Turkey, Bulgaria and Macedonia see Table 1460

SLOVENIA, CROATIA and BOSNIA-HERZEGOVINA

Operators: Slovenske Železnice (SŽ): www.slo-zeleznice.si; Hrvatske Željeznice (HŽ): www.hzpp.hr; Željeznice Federacije Bosne i Hercegovine (ŽFBH): www.zfbh.ba; and Željeznice Republike Srpske (ŽRS): www.zrs-rs.com

Services: All trains convey first and second class seating, **except** where shown otherwise in footnotes or by '2' in the train column, or where the footnote shows sleeping and / or couchette cars only. Descriptions of sleeping (🛏) and couchette (▬) cars appear on page 10. In Slovenia, travel by *ICS* train requires reservation and payment of a special fare.

Timings: **Timings in Slovenia are valid until September 3, 2023. Timings in Croatia and Bosnia-Herzegovina are valid until December 9, 2023.**

Tickets: A supplement is payable for travel by internal express trains. Reservation of seats is possible on most express trains.

1300 VILLACH - JESENICE - LJUBLJANA - ZAGREB

SŽ, HŽ, ÖBB

km		2 Ⓐ	2 Ⓐ	2	2	2 Ⓐ	2	2 Ⓐ	40237 [R] ♦	415 2• ❋	2	2 Ⓐ	2 Ⓐ	2	2 Ⓐ	2 Ⓐ	2	2	2 Ⓐ	2 Ⓐ	211 [R] ♦	2 Ⓐ	2	2	2 Ⓑ	2 Ⓐ	
	München Hbf **890** d.	...	...	...	...	...	...	...	2354o	...	...	...	...	...	...	...	...	...	...	...	...	...	...	...	...	...	...
	Salzburg Hbf **970** d.	...	...	...	...	...	...	...	0210	...	...	...	...	...	...	...	...	...	...	...	...	...	...	...	...	...	...
0	**Villach** Hbf. d.	...	...	...	...	...	...	...	0625	...	...	...	...	...	...	...	...	...	...	...	1253	...	...	...	...	...	...
38	**Jesenice** 🏛 d.	...	0422	...	0535	0609	...	0627	0705	...	0735	...	...	...	0946	...	1113	...	...	1235	1339	...	1422	...	...	1535	...
51	Lesce-Bled d.	...	0435	...	0549	0623	...	0641	0723	...	0749	...	...	...	1003	...	1127	...	...	1249	1351	...	1436	...	...	1549	...
74	Kranj d.	...	0459	...	0613	0647	...	0709	0749	...	0812	...	...	...	1030	...	1151	...	...	1321	1411	...	1501	...	...	1625	...
102	**Ljubljana** a.	...	0530	...	0644	0721	...	0743	0809	...	0843	...	...	...	1101	...	1221	...	...	1352	1431	...	1533	...	...	1655	...
102	**Ljubljana** **1315** d.	0450	...	0552	...	...	0655	...	0830	0830	...	0855	0955	*1055*	...	1155	...	*1255*	1345	...	1445	1450	...	1550	1655	...	...
166	Zidani Most **1315** d.	0606	...	0702	...	...	0804	...	0921	0921	...	1000	1058	1200	...	1257	...	1402	1444	...	1543	1601	...	1702	1758	...	...
182	Sevnica **1315** d.	0623	...	0720	...	...	0818	...	0936	0936	...	1018	1116	1218	...	1315	...	1420	1456	...	1558	1619	...	1720	1816	...	...
215	Dobova 🏛 **1315** a.	0650	...	0747	...	...	0845	...	1000	1000	...	1045	1143	1245	...	1342	...	1447	1521	...	1623	1646	...	1747	1843	...	...
245	**Zagreb** **1315** a.	...	...	...	...	...	...	...	1039	1039	...	...	...	...	...	...	...	...	...	...	1710	...	...	...	...	...	...
	Beograd **1320** a.	...	...	...	...	...	...	...	...	1754	...	...	...	...	...	...	...	...	...	...	...	...	...	...	...	...	...

	2 Ⓐ	2	213 [R] ♦	2	2	2 ⒸN	315 ♦	2	2 Ⓐ	
München Hbf **890** d.	...	...	1217	...	...	...	...	...	...	...
Salzburg Hbf **970** d.	...	...	1412	...	...	...	...	...	...	...
Villach Hbf. d.	...	...	1653	...	...	...	1853	...	...	...
Jesenice 🏛 d.	1627	...	1739	...	1806	1925	1939	2035	...	...
Lesce-Bled d.	1649	...	1751	...	1820	1942	1953	2049	...	...
Kranj d.	1716	...	1812	...	1847	2005	2012	2115	...	...
Ljubljana a.	1748	...	1831	...	1920	2041	2033	2145	...	...
Ljubljana **1315** d.	...	1755	1837	1855	...	...	2105	...	2225	...
Zidani Most **1315** d.	...	1905	1928	1958	...	...	2203	...	2327	...
Sevnica **1315** d.	...	1923	1944	2016	...	...	2218	...	2345	...
Dobova 🏛 **1315** a.	...	1951	2006	2044	...	...	2241	...	0013	...
Zagreb **1315** a.	...	...	2045	...	...	...	...	...	...	...
Beograd **1320** a.	...	...	...	...	...	...	...	...	...	...

	2 Ⓐ	2	2 Ⓐ	2 Ⓐ	2 ⒸN	2 Ⓐ	314 ♦	2	2 Ⓐ	212 [R] ♦	2	
Beograd **1320** d.	...	...	...	...	...	...	...	...	...	...	...	...
Zagreb **1315** d.	...	...	...	...	...	...	...	...	...	0705	...	...
Dobova 🏛 **1315** d.	...	...	...	0455	...	0530	0540	0606	...	0745	0710	...
Sevnica **1315** d.	...	0410	...	0525	...	0558	0605	0635	...	0809	0739	...
Zidani Most **1315** d.	...	0429	...	0544	...	0614	0621	0700	...	0825	0809	...
Ljubljana **1315** a.	...	0530	...	0636	...	0707	0717	0801	...	0914	0910	...
Ljubljana d.	0442	...	0611	...	0650	...	0726	...	0823	0923	...	...
Kranj d.	0515	...	0647	...	0721	...	0749	...	0858	0943	...	...
Lesce-Bled d.	0549	...	0712	...	0749	...	0813	...	0922	1003	...	...
Jesenice 🏛 a.	0602	...	0725	...	0803	...	0825	...	0935	1014	...	...
Villach Hbf. a.	...	...	...	...	...	...	0908	...	...	1058	...	...
Salzburg Hbf **970** a.	...	...	...	...	...	...	...	...	...	1348	...	...
München Hbf **890** a.	...	...	...	...	...	...	...	...	...	1541	...	...

	2	2	2 Ⓐ	2	2	2 Ⓐ	2 Ⓐ	2	2	210 [R] ♦	2	2 Ⓐ	2 Ⓐ	2	2 Ⓐ	2	2	2 Ⓑ	2 Ⓐ	2	2	414 2◧ ❋	414 [R] ♦	2 Ⓑ	2 h	2	
Beograd **1320** d.	...	...	...	...	...	...	...	...	...	...	...	...	...	...	...	...	...	...	...	...	...	1040	...	...	...	...	...
Zagreb **1315** d.	...	...	...	...	...	...	...	...	...	1250	...	...	...	...	...	...	...	...	...	...	...	1938	1938	...	...	...	...
Dobova 🏛 **1315** d.	...	0910	1010	...	1106	...	1206	...	1306	1334	...	...	...	1508	...	...	1610	...	1709	1806	...	2019	2019	2006	...	2110	...
Sevnica **1315** d.	...	0939	1039	...	1135	...	1235	...	1335	1402	...	...	...	1537	...	...	1639	...	1738	1835	...	2043	2043	2035	...	2139	...
Zidani Most **1315** d.	...	0958	1058	...	1200	...	1254	...	1354	1418	...	...	...	1559	...	...	1658	...	1806	1900	...	2059	2059	2102	...	2158	...
Ljubljana **1315** a.	...	1059	1159	...	1301	...	1355	...	1455	1508	...	...	...	1700	...	...	1759	...	1908	2001	...	2147	2147	2203	...	2259	...
Ljubljana d.	1000	...	...	1250	...	1332	...	1448	...	1527	1534	1551	1623	...	1718	1754	...	1846	...	...	2043	...	2208	...	2228	...	...
Kranj d.	1030	...	...	1321	...	1411	...	1520	...	1554	1606	1625	1657	...	1750	1827	...	1919	...	...	2115	...	2229	...	2300	...	...
Lesce-Bled d.	1054	...	...	1351	...	1436	...	1549	...	1615	1629	1649	1720	...	1820	1851	...	1941	...	...	2138	...	2249	...	2320	...	...
Jesenice 🏛 a.	1107	...	...	1404	...	1449	...	1602	...	1626	1645	1702	1733	...	1833	1904	...	1957	...	...	2151	...	2300	...	2333	...	...
Villach Hbf. a.	...	...	...	...	...	...	...	...	...	1708	...	...	...	...	...	...	...	...	...	...	...	...	2348	...	...	...	...
Salzburg Hbf **970** a.	...	...	...	...	...	...	...	...	...	...	...	...	...	...	...	...	...	...	...	...	...	...	0245	...	...	...	...
München Hbf **890** a.	...	...	...	...	...	...	...	...	...	...	...	...	...	...	...	...	...	...	...	...	...	...	0550o	...	...	...	...

♦ – **NOTES** (LISTED BY TRAIN NUMBER)

210/1 – SAVA – [12] Vinkovci - Zagreb - Ljubljana - Villach and v.v.

212/3 – MIMARA – [12] Zagreb - Villach (**112/3**) - München - Frankfurt and v.v.

314/5 – [12] Villach - Ljubljana - Dobova and v.v.

414 – LISINSKI – 🛏, ▬ and [2] Zagreb - Ljubljana - Salzburg - München - Stuttgart; conveys 🛏, ▬ and [2] (**40414**) Zagreb - Ljubljana - Schwarzach - Zurich; also conveys on dates in Table **61** 🛏 and ▬ (**480**) Rijeka - Ljubljana - Salzburg - München - Stuttgart.

40237 – LISINSKI – 🛏, ▬ and [2] Stuttgart - München - Salzburg - Ljubljana - Zagreb; conveys 🛏, ▬ and [2] (**40465**) Zurich - Schwarzach - Ljubljana - Zagreb; also conveys on dates in Table **61** 🛏 and ▬ (**60237**) Stuttgart - München - Salzburg - Ljubljana - Rijeka.

N – Conveys on Ⓒ: [2] Ljubljana - Jesenice - Nova Gorica and v.v.

h – Runs 22–25 minutes later Apr. 22 - Sept. 3.

o – München Ost.

◧ – Train number **412** Beograd - Zagreb.

• – Train number **413** Zagreb - Beograd.

❋ – Currently suspended.

1302 JESENICE - NOVA GORICA - SEŽANA

2nd class only SŽ

km		Ⓐ	Ⓐe	Ⓒd	Ⓐ	Ⓐ	N			Ⓐ		Ⓑe	
0	**Jesenice** d.	...	0415	0415	0605	0821	0821	1115	...	1432	1651	...	1918
10	Bled Jezero d.	...	0431	0431	0621	0837	0837	1131	...	1448	1706	...	1934
28	Bohinjska Bistrica 🚗 d.	...	0451	0451	0648	0857	0857	1151	...	1508	1726	...	1954
56	Most na Soči 🚗 d.	...	0526	0526	0724	0933	0933	1227	...	1553	1801	...	2036
89	Nova Gorica ♣ a.	...	0605	0605	0812	1010	1010	1304	...	1632	1838	...	2113
89	Nova Gorica ♣ d.	0455	0608	...	0849	...	...	...	1444	...	...	1910	...
130	**Sežana** a.	0551	0709	...	0945	...	...	...	1550	...	...	2006	...

	Ⓐ		Ⓐe	Ⓒd	Ⓐ	Ⓒ	Ⓐ	Ⓐ		Ⓒ	N	Ⓐ	
Sežana d.	...	...	0627	...	1010	...	...	1430	...	1624	...	1643	...
Nova Gorica ♣ a.	...	...	0720	...	1103	...	...	1522	...	1716	...	1735	...
Nova Gorica ♣ d.	0330	0529	0735	0735	1120	1120	1447	...	1555	...	1719	...	1956
Most na Soči 🚗 d.	0407	0607	0813	0813	1159	1159	1526	...	1634	...	1803	...	2035
Bohinjska Bistrica 🚗 d.	0453	0646	0900	0905	1245	1245	1604	...	1727	...	1839	...	2114
Bled Jezero d.	0513	0707	0921	0921	1306	1306	1624	...	1747	...	1859	...	2133
Jesenice a.	0529	0722	0937	0937	1322	1322	1640	...	1803	...	1915	...	2149

N – Conveys on Ⓒ: [2] Ljubljana - Jesenice - Nova Gorica and v.v.

d – Not June 17 - Aug. 27.

e – Daily June 17 - Aug. 27.

♣ – Line **1** 🚌 service operates between Nova Gorica (bus stop 100 metres from station on Italian side) and Gorizia Centrale (Italy) stations. Total journey time ± 20 minutes.

🚗 – Car-carrying service runs between Bohinjska Bistrica and Most na Soči. Depart Bohinjska Bistrica 0913, 1325, 1646 (also 2116 Apr. 1 - Sept. 3). Depart Most na Soči 0745, 1038, 1443 (also 1843 Apr. 1 - Sept. 3).

1303 DIVAČA - PULA

2nd class only HŽ, SŽ

km			Ⓐ	1272 L			Ⓐr	Ⓐ				
	Ljubljana **1305** d.	...	...	...	...	...	...	...	...	...	...	...
0	**Divača** d.	...	...	0805	...	...	...	...	...	...	...	...
12	Hrpelje-Kozina d.	...	...	0817	...	...	...	...	...	...	...	...
30	Rakitovec 🏛 d.	...	...	0854	...	...	...	...	...	...	...	...
36	Buzet 🏛 d.	0504r	0656	0923	...	1110	1305	...	...	1708	...	1953j
43	Lupoglav ▲ d.	0535	0715	0940	...	1129	1324	1520	...	1732	...	2017
117	**Pula** a.	0712	0854	1107	...	1307	1512	1703	...	1914	...	2159

	Ⓐ	Ⓐr			Ⓐ		Ⓐ		Ⓐ	1273 L	
Pula d.	0440	0625	0902	...	1320	1438	1544	...	1721	1803	1940
Lupoglav ▲ d.	0629	0817	1042	...	1509	1631	1722	...	1904	1933	2119
Buzet 🏛 d.	0648	0836	1101	...	...	1650	...	...	1923j	2003	2143r
Rakitovec 🏛 d.	...	...	...	...	...	...	...	...	...	2024	...
Hrpelje-Kozina d.	...	...	...	...	...	...	...	...	...	2055	...
Divača a.	...	...	...	...	...	...	...	...	...	2107	...
Ljubljana **1305** a.	...	...	...	...	...	...	...	...	...	...	...

L – Apr. 22 - Sept. 24. ISTRA – [2] Divača - Pula and v.v.

j – Apr. 22 - Sept. 24.

r – Ⓐ (not Dec. 27 - Jan. 5, Feb. 20–24, Apr. 6–14, June 23 - Sept. 1).

▲ – 🚌 service **Lupoglav - Rijeka** and v.v. Journey 40 minutes. **From Lupoglav** at 0628Ⓐ, 1100, 1630, 2123. **From Rijeka** at 0543Ⓐ, 1015, 1425Ⓐ, 1545Ⓒ, 1930.

SŽ, HŽ 2nd class only except where shown LJUBLJANA - RIJEKA, KOPER, SEŽANA and TRIESTE 1305

Warning! Due to engineering work, some journeys from and to Ljubljana are by bus to Logatec (approximatly 50 km). Please check locally before travelling.

km		Ⓐ	Ⓐ		1605 ◆	1272 ◆[R]	1246* ◆[R]		481 ◆[R]	IC 503 ◆		Ⓐ	Ⓐ		EC 134 ◆[R]		483 ◆[R]	b	Ⓑ	Ⓐ	IC 509 ◆		Ⓐ	Ⓒc		
	Maribor **1315** d.	...	...	...	0315	...	0315	...	...	...	...	...	...	...	1145	...	...	...	...	...	...	...	...	...	...	...
0	**Ljubljana** d.	0427	0533	0547	0606	...	0634	0755	0825	0908	...	1039	1214	1321	1421	1440	1520	1550	1613	1657	1751	1850	1934	...	2109	...
67	Postojna d.	0536	0642	0657	0722	...	0741	0904	0932	1017	...	1146	1325	1431	1531	1555	1637	1702	1726	1807	1904	2003	2045	...	2223	...
80	Pivka ▲ d.	0550	0656	0709	0736	...	0754	0918	0945	1029	...	1157	1339	1445	1544	1608	1650	1715	1741	1821	1917	2016	2058	...	2237	...
	Ilirska Bistrica ▦ ▲ d.	|	|	|	|	...	0824	|	1015	|	...	|	|	|	|	|	1718	|	|	|	|	|	|	...	|	...
	Šapjane ▦ d.	|	|	|	|	...	0853	|	1044	|	...	|	|	|	|	|	1746	|	|	|	|	|	|	...	|	...
	Rijeka a.	|	|	|	|	...	0934	|	1125	|	...	|	|	|	|	|	1827	|	|	|	|	|	|	...	|	...
104	Divača a.	0610	0717	0728	0756	...	...	0938	...	1048	...	1218	1401	1506	1604	1629	...	1734	1800	1841	1937	2036	2119	...	2257	...
104	Divača d.	0614	0718	0729	0800	0805	...	0939	...	1052	1052	1219	1402	1507	1605	1630	...	1738	1804	1841	1941	2037	2120	2120	2258	...
116	Hrpelje-Kozina ⊡ d.	|	|	|	0814	0817	...	|	...	1104	|	|	|	|	|	|	...	1757	|	|	1953	|	|	|	|	...
153	**Koper** ⊡ a.	|	|	|	0848	...	...	|	...	1136	|	|	|	|	|	|	...	1817	|	|	2026	|	|	|	|	...
113	**Sežana** ▦ a.	0624	0728	0737	...	...	...	0948	...	...	1102	1227	1412	1517	1614	1640	...	...	1814	1851	...	2047	2131	2131	2308	...
113	**Sežana** ▦ d.	0626	...	0738	...	...	...	0949	...	...	...	1228	...	...	1615	1641	...	...	1815	...	...	2048	2133	2133	...	...
120	Villa Opicina ¶ a.	0637	...	0749	...	...	...	1000	...	...	...	1239	...	...	1626	1652	...	...	1826	...	...	2059	2144	2144	...	...
144	**Trieste Centrale** ¶ a.	...	...	...	...	...	...	...	...	...	...	...	...	...	1716	...	...	...	...	...	...	...	...	...	...	...

km		Ⓐ	Ⓐ	Ⓐ	IC 508 ◆	Ⓐ		Ⓐ			b	482 ◆[R]	Ⓐ	EC 135 ◆[R]	Ⓐ	IC 502 ◆	Ⓐ		Ⓑ	480 ◆[R]	1247 ◆[R]		1273 ◆c	1604 ◆	Ⓐ	Ⓒc
	Trieste Centrale ¶ d.	...	...	...	...	...	...	...	...	...	...	...	...	1252	...	...	...	...	...	...	...	...	...	...	...	...
	Villa Opicina ¶ d.	...	...	...	...	...	0700	...	0943	1020	...	...	1314	1336	...	...	...	1741	1844	...	...	1945	...	...	2158	2158
	Sežana ▦ a.	...	...	...	...	...	0711	...	0954	1031	...	...	1325	1349	...	...	...	1752	1855	...	...	1956	...	...	2209	2209
	Sežana ▦ d.	0428	0455	0600	...	...	0712	0851	0955	1032	...	...	1334	1350	1440	...	1653	1753	1856	...	...	2016	...	...	...	...
	Koper ⊡ d.	|	|	|	0525	...	|	|	|	|	1004	...	|	|	|	1520	|	|	|	...	...	|	...	2005	...	...
	Hrpelje-Kozina ⊡ d.	|	|	|	0559	...	|	|	|	|	1024	...	|	|	|	1552	|	|	|	...	...	|	2049	2044	...	...
	Divača a.	0437	0504	0609	0611	...	0721	0900	1004	1042	1043	...	1343	1359	1449	1603	1703	1802	1906	...	...	2025	2101	2056	...	...
	Divača d.	0438	0505	...	0613	...	0722	0901	1005	...	1048	...	1344	1400	1450	1606	1704	1803	1907	...	...	2026	...	2105	...	...
0	**Rijeka** d.	|	|	...	|	...	|	|	|	...	|	1150	|	|	|	|	|	|	|	1847	1847	|	...	|	...	...
28	Šapjane ▦ d.	|	|	...	|	...	|	|	|	...	|	1250	|	|	|	|	|	|	|	1945	1945	|	...	|	...	...
40	Ilirska Bistrica ▦ ▲ d.	|	|	...	|	0632	|	|	|	...	|	1320	|	|	|	|	|	|	|	2013	2013	|	...	|	...	...
56	Pivka ▲ d.	0500	0527	...	0636	0649	0743	0922	1026	...	1109	1337	1406	1421	1515	1627	1725	1825	1930	2029	2029	2047	...	2126	...	...
	Postojna d.	0513	0540	...	0649	0703	0758	0936	1038	...	1122	1350	1420	1434	1527	1639	1739	1838	1943	2042	2042	2059	...	2139	...	...
	Ljubljana a.	0626	0650	...	0800	0811	0906	1044	1146	...	1230	1457	1528	1540	1635	1746	1852	1946	2053	2147	2147	2210	...	2247	...	...
	Maribor **1315** a.	...	...	...	...	...	...	...	...	...	...	...	...	1816	...	...	...	...	...	...	...	...	...	0124	...	...

◆ – **NOTES** (LISTED BY TRAIN NUMBER)

34/5 – [12] Wien (**150/1**) - Ljubljana - Trieste and v.v.
30 – OPATIJA – [12] Rijeka - Ljubljana. Also conveys Mar. 30 - Apr. 16, May 11 - Sept. 3 🛏, ▬ and [12] Rijeka - Ljubljana (**414**) - Salzburg - München - Stuttgart.
31 – OPATIJA – [12] Ljubljana - Rijeka. Also conveys Mar. 31 - Apr. 17, May 12 - Sept. 3 🛏, ▬ and [12] Stuttgart (**60237**) - München - Salzburg - Ljubljana - Rijeka.
32/3 – LJUBLJANA – [12] Ljubljana - Rijeka - and v.v.
02/3 – POHORJE – [12] Hodoš - Ljubljana - Koper and v.v.
08/9 – KOPER – [12] Ljubljana - Koper and v.v. Conveys [12] (**246/7**) Budapest - Ljubljana - Koper and v.v.
246 – June 23 - Aug. 26. 🛏, ▬ and [2] Budapest - Maribor (**1605**) - Ljubljana - Rijeka.
247 – June 24 - Aug. 27. 🛏, ▬ and [2] Rijeka - Ljubljana - Budapest.
272/3 – Apr. 22 - Sept. 24. ISTRA – [2] Divača - Pula and v.v.
504 – Apr. 22 - Sept. 3. [2] Koper - Ljubljana - Maribor.
505 – Apr. 22 - Sept. 3. [2] Maribor - Ljubljana - Koper.

b – By 🚌 Divaca - Koper and v.v.
c – Apr. 22 - Sept. 3.
* – Train **1281** Ljubljana - Ilirska Bistrica.
¶ – For frequent tram connections Villa Opicina - Trieste and v.v., see panel in Table **601**.
▲ – Local services **Pivka - Ilirska Bistrica** and v.v.: Journey 16 minutes.
From Pivka at 0553Ⓐ, 0925Ⓐ, 1200Ⓐ, 1341Ⓐ, 1546Ⓐ, 1727Ⓑ, 1827Ⓑ.
From Ilirska Bistrica at 0507Ⓐ, 0632Ⓐ, 1050Ⓐ, 1257Ⓐ, 1402Ⓐ, 1607Ⓐ, 1800Ⓑ.
⊡ – 🚌 service **Koper - Trieste** and v.v.: Journey 45 minutes.
From Koper at 0600⚒, 0700Ⓐ, 0730⚒, 1030⚒, 1115Ⓐ, 1215Ⓐ, 1400⚒, 1730⚒.
From Trieste at 0645⑥, 0700Ⓐ, 0900Ⓐ, 1000Ⓐ, 1230Ⓐ, 1300⚒, 1400Ⓐ, 1530⚒,1830⑥, 1900⚒.
Service is subject to alteration. No service on ⑦, Slovenian and Italian holidays.
Operator: Arriva Slovenija, Meljska cesta 97, 2000 Maribor.

HŽ 2nd class only except where shown RIJEKA - ZAGREB 1310

km		⚒	Ⓐn			⚒	Ⓐn		Ⓐ	[R]d			
0	**Rijeka** d.	...	0530	0735	...	...	1153	1358	1523	1730	...	1930	...
61	Delnice d.	...	0642	0850	...	...	1311	1513	1637	1841	...	2046	...
90	Moravice d.	0600	0716	0924	...	...	1345	1546	1714	1919	1946	2120	...
20	Ogulin 1330 d.	0634	0746	0955	1030	1215	1418	1622	1745	1948	2023	2150	...
26	Oštarije 1330 d.	0642	...	...	1035	1220	...	1626	...	1954	2030	...	...
76	Karlovac 1330 d.	0758	...	...	1138	1323	...	1737	...	2106	2131	...	...
29	**Zagreb** 1330 a.	0858	...	...	1233	1417	...	1829	...	2216	2228	...	...
	Osijek **1340** a.	...	...	...	...	...	...	...	...	...	...	...	...

	Ⓐ			Ⓐ			Ⓐ		[R]d	⚒		
Osijek **1340** d.	...	...	...	...	...	...	...	...	...	...	...	...
Zagreb 1330 d.	...	0628	0818	...	1307	...	1421	1543	1705	1831	2149	...
Karlovac 1330 d.	...	0727	0914	...	1411	...	1521	1645	1753	1927	2243	...
Oštarije 1330 d.	...	0830	1019	...	1510	...	1624	1753	1844	2029	2344	...
Ogulin 1330 d.	0603	0834	1026	1405	1514	1602	1631	1758	1849	2033	2348	...
Moravice d.	0634	...	1057	1435	...	1636	...	1829	1917	...	...	...
Delnice d.	0710	...	1131	1514	...	1709	...	...	1948	...	...	...
Rijeka a.	0824	...	1242	1628	...	1819	...	...	2102	...	...	...

– ⑤⑦ to June 16 and from Oct. 1 (also Apr 5, May 1; not Feb. 19, 24, Apr. 7, 9, 14, 30).

n – Not June 23 - Sept. 1.

SŽ, MÁV 2nd class only except where shown MARIBOR - ČAKOVEC, MURSKA SOBOTA and ZALAEGERSZEG 1313

km		1247 ◆	Ⓐ		Ⓐ	Ⓐ	Ⓐ		Ⓐ		IC 247 ◆		⚒	⑦g	Ⓐ	Ⓐ		Ⓐ				Ⓐ		Ⓐ	IC 502 ◆		Ⓐ	Ⓐ
	Ljubljana **1315** d.	0030	...	...	...	...	...	...	...	...	0935	...	...	...	...	...	...	...	...	...	...	1515	...	...	1750	...	...	...
0	**Maribor** 1315 d.	|	...	...	...	...	...	0705	...	0933	|	...	...	...	...	...	1445	...	1538	...	1615	|	...	1710	|	...	1845	2213
19	Pragersko 1315 d.	0226	...	...	...	...	0607	|	...	0957	1135	...	1328	1328	1420	...	1515	...	|	...	|	1701	...	|	1944	...	|	|
37	Ptuj d.	0238	...	...	...	...	0628	0745	...	1009	1147	...	1348	1348	1442	...	1535	...	1618	...	1653	1713	...	1751	1957	...	1922	2251
59	Ormož d.	|	...	...	0452	0553	0649	0804	0811	1022	1201	1205	1407	1407	1500	1505	1558	1600	1638	1645	1713	1728	1733	1810	2008	...	2014	2310
	Središče ▦ a.	|	...	...	0503	|	...	|	0822	|	|	1216	|	|	...	1516	|	1611	|	1656	...	|	1744	...	|	...	|	...
	Čakovec a.	|	...	...	...	|	...	|	0841	|	|	...	|	|	...	...	|	...	|	...	...	|	1803	...	|	...	|	...
98	**Murska Sobota** d.	0319	0330	...	...	0639	...	0841	...	1052	1231	...	1443	1443	...	...	1634	...	1717	...	...	1800	...	...	2034	...	2051	...
27	Hodoš a.	0338	0355	...	...	...	...	0906	...	...	1249	...	...	...	...	...	...	...	...	...	...	1824	...	...	2050	...	2113	...
27	Hodoš ▦ d.	0353	...	0622	...	...	...	...	...	...	1301	...	...	...	...	...	...	...	...	...	...	...	...	...	...	2102	...	...
74	**Zalaegerszeg** a.	0431	...	0712	...	...	...	...	...	...	1337	...	...	...	...	...	...	...	...	...	...	...	...	...	...	2146	...	...
	Budapest Déli **1230** a.	0859	...	...	...	...	...	...	...	...	1659	...	...	...	...	...	...	...	...	...	...	...	...	...	...	...	...	...

km		1246 ◆		Ⓐ	Ⓐ	Ⓐ		IC 503 ◆	Ⓐ	Ⓒ	Ⓐ				IC 246 ◆	Ⓐ	⚒	g	Ⓐ	Ⓐ		Ⓐ	g	g			Ⓐ	
	Budapest Déli **1230** d.	2100	...	...	...	...	...	...	...	...	...	...	...	...	0900	...	...	...	...	...	...	...	...	...	...	...	...	...
	Zalaegerszeg d.	0020	...	...	...	...	0455	...	...	...	...	...	...	...	1222	...	...	...	...	...	...	...	...	...	...	...	...	2013
	Hodoš ▦ a.	0058	...	...	...	...	0546	...	...	...	...	...	...	...	1259	...	...	...	...	...	...	...	...	...	...	...	...	2058
	Hodoš d.	0112	...	0425	...	...	...	0553	0620	...	...	0918	...	...	1315	...	...	...	...	...	...	1615	1620	...	...	...	1918	...
	Murska Sobota d.	0132	...	0451	...	...	...	0612	0644	...	...	0945	1235	...	1336	...	1510	1510	...	...	...	1637	1644	1830	...	1855	1942	...
0	**Čakovec** d.	|	...	|	...	|	...	|	|	...	0930	|	|	...	|	...	|	|	...	...	...	...	|	|	1811	|	...	...
12	Središče ▦ d.	|	0433	|	0519	|	...	|	|	...	0949	|	|	1349	|	1528	|	|	1620	...	1710	...	|	|	1830	|	...	...
22	Ormož d.	|	0444	0521	0530	0543	...	0639	0724	0840	1000	1022	1313	1400	1407	1539	1546	1546	1631	1700	1721	...	1728	1900	1841	1932	...	...
	Ptuj d.	0215	...	0534	...	0604	...	0652	0745	0856	...	1041	1334	...	1422	...	1604	1604	...	1725	...	...	1747	1913	...	1958	...	...
	Pragersko 1315 d.	0330t	...	0545	...	|	...	0704	|	|	...	1059	|	...	1435	...	1628	1628	...	1746	...	...	1811	1927	...	2024	...	...
	Maribor 1315 a.	0240	...	...	...	0641	...	|	0824	0924	...	...	1414	...	|	...	1646	1646	...	...	...	...	|	|	...	2044	...	...
	Ljubljana **1315** a.	0542	...	...	...	...	...	0859	...	...	...	...	...	...	1635	...	...	...	...	...	...	...	2004	2116	...	...	...	...

– **NOTES** (LISTED BY TRAIN NUMBER)

46/7 – CITADELLA – [12] Budapest - Ljubljana and v.v.; [12] Budapest - Ljubljana (**508/9**) - Koper and v.v.
02/3 – POHORJE – [12] Hodoš - Ljubljana - Koper and v.v.
246 – June 23 - Aug. 26. 🛏 1, 2 cl. and [2] Budapest - Hodoš - Maribor (**1605**) - Ljubljana - Koper.
247 – June 24 - Aug. 27. 🛏 1, 2 cl. and [2] Koper - Ljubljana (**1604**) - Hodoš - Budapest.

g – ⑦ Dec. 11 - June 18 (also Jan. 2, Feb. 8, Apr. 10, May 2; not Dec. 25, Jan. 1, Apr. 9, 30).
t – Via Maribor.

1315 LJUBLJANA and ZAGREB - MARIBOR - GRAZ

SŽ, HŽ, ÖBB

km			IC	IC	ICS		EC	ICS	IC			ICS	ICS	IC			ICS		EC	IC	IC				
		1247		311	512	30		158	14	247			36	32	518		1640	20		150	502	526		604	1604	
		R	2	R		R	2	✕R	R	R	2	2	R	R		2	2	R	2	✕R		R	2	2	2	
		◆	h	◆		Ⓑ	Ⓐ	◆		◆	Ⓐ			Ⓐc		Ⓐ	j			◆	◆			◆	◆	
	Koper **1305** d.	...	...	...	...	...	...	...	...	...	...	...	...	...	...	...	...	...	...	...	1520	...	...	...	2005	...
0	**Ljubljana** 1300 d.	0030	0050	0505	0535	...	0650	...	0815	0935	1050	...	1237	...	1315	1340	1435	1515	...	1605	1750	1950	2055	2300	2300	...
*	**Zagreb** 1300 d.	|	|	|	|	...	|	0705	|	|	|	...	|	...	|	|	|	|	...	|	|	|	|	|	|	...
	Dobova 🛃 1300 d.	|	|	|	|	...	|	0803	|	|	|	...	|	...	|	|	|	|	...	|	|	|	|	|	|	...
	Sevnica 1300 d.	|	|	|	|	...	|	0829	|	|	|	...	|	...	|	|	|	|	...	|	|	|	|	|	|	...
64	Zidani Most 1300 d.	0122	0146	0559	0625	...	0744	|	0900	1030	1144	...	|	...	1400	1434	1527	1600	...	1701	1845	2035	2200	2400	0003	...
89	Celje d.	0145	0208	0624	0646	...	0808	0907	0920	1056	1208	...	1339	...	1420	1458	1551	1620	...	1725	1908	2055	2224	0023	0029	...
137	Pragersko 1313 d.	0226	0248	0700	0720	...	0846	0944	0953	1135	1246	...	|	...	1453	1536	1627	1653	...	1800	1944	2128	2309	0058	0108	...
156	**Maribor** ▲ 1313 a.	...	0301	0715	0734	...	0859	0959	1005	...	1259	...	1422	...	1505	1549	...	1705	...	1816	...	2140	2328	0112	0124	...
156	**Maribor** d.	...	...	0719	...	0740	...	1019	...	...	...	1335	...	1425	...	...	...	...	1736	1821	...	...	...	...	...	...
172	Spielfeld-Straß 🛃 a.	...	...	0734	...	0755	...	1034	...	...	...	1354	...	1450	...	...	...	...	1755	1836	...	...	...	...	...	...
172	Spielfeld-Straß 🛃 980 d.	...	...	0747	...	...	...	1048	...	...	...	...	...	...	...	...	...	...	...	1848	...	...	...	...	...	...
219	**Graz** Hbf 980 a.	...	...	0822	...	...	...	1122	...	...	...	...	...	...	...	...	...	...	...	1922	...	...	...	...	...	...
	Wien Hbf **980** a.	...	...	...	...	...	...	1402	...	...	...	...	...	...	...	...	...	...	...	2202	...	...	...	...	...	...

				ICS	IC	ICS	ICS		IC	EC	IC	IC	ICS				IC					EC	IC		IC
		605	1605	Ⓐ	11	503	31	35		517	151	246	519	33		1611		521	1641	1615		1643	159	523	1613	310
	2	2	2	2	R		R	R	2	R	✕R	R	R	R	2	2R	2	2	2	2	2	2	✕R	R	2	R
	h	◆	◆			◆	Ⓑ	⑥	Ⓐ		◆	◆		Ⓐc	Ⓐ	g	Ⓐ		g	g		g	◆¶		g	◆
Wien Hbf **980** d.	...	...	...	...	...	...	...	...	...	...	0758	...	...	...	...	...	...	...	...	...	...	...	1558	...	...	...
Graz Hbf 980 d.	...	...	...	...	...	...	...	...	...	...	1039	...	...	...	...	...	...	...	...	...	...	...	1839	...	...	213
Spielfeld-Straß 980 a.	...	...	...	...	...	...	...	...	...	...	1113	...	...	...	...	...	...	...	...	...	...	...	1913	...	...	221
Spielfeld-Straß d.	...	...	...	...	...	...	0804	...	...	...	1125	...	...	1517	1604	...	1717	...	...	...	1804	...	1926	...	...	222
Maribor a.	...	...	...	...	...	...	0817	...	...	...	1140	...	...	1535	1623	...	1735	...	...	...	1820	...	1940	...	...	224
Maribor ▲ 1313 d.	0115	0315	0335	0450	0550	...	0819	0819	0926	1050	1145	...	1520	...	...	1630	...	1750	...	1812	...	...	1950	2010	2020	224
Pragersko 1313 d.	0134	0330	0349	0504	0603	0704	|	|	0945	1103	1200	1435	1533	...	...	1645	...	1803	1811	1825	...	1927	2003	2024	2034	225
Celje d.	0215	0415	0428	0543	0637	0743	0905	0905	1029	1137	1239	1513	1607	...	...	1724	...	1837	1849	1904	...	2003	2042	2102	2114	233
Zidani Most 1300 d.	0237	0441	0451	0606	0657	0806	|	|	1052	1157	1305	1538	1627	...	...	1748	...	1857	1912	1928	...	2025	|	2125	2138	000
Sevnica 1300 d.	|	|	|	|	|	|	|	|	...	|	|	|	|	...	...	|	...	|	|	|	...	|	2121	|	|	|
Dobova 🛃 1300 d.	|	|	|	|	|	|	|	|	...	|	|	|	|	...	...	|	...	|	|	|	...	|	2201	|	|	|
Zagreb 1300 a.	|	|	|	|	|	|	|	|	...	|	|	|	|	...	...	|	...	|	|	|	...	|	2227	|	|	|
Ljubljana 1300 a.	0332	0542	0542	0658	0740	0859	1005	1005	...	1240	1400	1635	1710	...	...	1838	...	1940	2004	2019	...	2116	...	2213	2228	005
Koper **1305** a.	...	...	0848	...	...	1136	...	...	...	...	...	...	...	...	...	...	...	...	...	...	...	...	...	...	...	...

ADDITIONAL SERVICES MARIBOR - ZIDANI MOST and v.v.: 2nd class only

		Ⓐ	Ⓐ	Ⓐ		Ⓐ	Ⓐ		Ⓐ		Ⓐ		Ⓑ
Maribor ▲ d.	0520	0620	0725	0825	1023	1125	1220	1525	1628	1720	1920	2025	2110
Pragersko d.	0539	0639	0744	0844	1043	1144	1240	1544	1647	1739	1939	2044	2129
Celje d.	0625	0725	0829	0928	1129	1229	1327	1629	1732	1823	2029	2128	2213
Zidani Most a.	0647	0747	0851	0951	1151	1251	1349	1651	1754	1844	2050	2149	2234

			Ⓐ	Ⓐ	Ⓐ	Ⓐ	Ⓐ			Ⓐ			Ⓐ
Zidani Most d.	0455	0705	0802	0925	1001	1101	1300	1603	1705	1803	1903	2012	210
Celje d.	0519	0729	0826	0949	1025	1125	1326	1627	1730	1827	1928	2035	212
Pragersko d.	0603	0813	0911	1034	1109	1209	1418	1710	1813	1910	2010	2118	220
Maribor ▲ a.	0622	0832	0930	1053	1129	1228	1438	1730	1833	1930	2030	2136	222

◆ – **NOTES** (LISTED BY TRAIN NUMBER)

150/1 – EMONA – [12] ✕ Ljubljana - Wien and v.v; Also conveys [12] Ljubljana (**134/5**) - Trieste and v.v.
158/9 – CROATIA – [12] ✕ Zagreb - Wien and v.v.
246/7 – CITADELLA – [12] Budapest - Hodoš - Ljubljana and v.v.
310/1 – DRAVA – [12] Budapest - Györ - Graz - Ljubljana and v.v.
502/3 – POHORJE – [12] Hodoš - Ljubljana - Koper and v.v.
604 – Dec. 11 - Apr. 21. [2] Ljubljana - Maribor.
605 – Dec. 11 - Apr. 21. [2] Maribor - Ljubljana.
1247 – June 25 - Aug. 28. 🛏, 🛏 and [2] Koper - Ljubljana - Hodoš - Budapest.
1604 – Apr. 22 - Sept. 3. [2] Koper - Ljubljana - Maribor.
1605 – Apr. 22 - Sept. 3. [2] Maribor - Ljubljana - Koper.

a – Ⓐ only.
c – Not Dec. 26, Jan. 6, Apr. 10, May 1, 18, 29, June 8, Aug. 15.
g – ⑦ Dec. 11 - June 18 (also Jan. 2, Feb. 8, Apr. 10, May 2; not Dec. 25, Jan. 1, Apr. 9, 30).

MARIBOR - BLEIBURG - (KLAGENFURT)

km		Ⓐ	Ⓐ		Ⓐ	Ⓑ
0	Maribor d.	0520	1440	*Klagenfurt* d.	*0805*	*163*
87	Bleiburg 🛃 a.	0730	1645	Bleiburg 🛃 d.	0854	*172*
126	*Klagenfurt* a.	*0839*	*1755***a**	Maribor a.	1055	*192*

Other services are available Bleiburg - Klagenfurt and v.v.

h – Dec. 11 - Jan. 1, June 17 - Sept. 3.
j – ⑤ to June 23 (also Apr. 26; not Dec. 30, Apr. 28).

¶ – On certain dates runs as train *EC* **1259**.
* – Zagreb - Celje: *104 km.*
▲ – For Maribor - Bleiburg (- Klagenfurt) services see panel above.

1320 ZAGREB - VINKOVCI - BEOGRAD

SŽ, HŽ, ŽS

km			IC		❋	IC	IC		IC	❋
		1841	541		413	543	545	211	547	411
		R✕	R		2¶	R	R	R	R	R
		◆	j	2	◆	⚒e		◆		◆
	Ljubljana **1300** d.	...	...	...	0830	...	...	1445	...	2105
0	**Zagreb** d.	0559	0616	0746	1057	1258	1515	1735	2133	2341
105	Novska d.	0830	0830	1015	1307	1508	1730	1945	2341	0130
191	Slavonski Brod d.	0944	0944	1138	1421	1626	1844	2058	0100	0229
224	Strizivojna-Vrpolje 1345 d.	1007	1007	1206	1443	1652	1908	2121	0127	0249
	Osijek 1345 a.	|	|	|	|	|	|	|	|	|
253	**Vinkovci** d.	1028	1028	1229	1516	1712	1930	2142	0157	0310
285	Tovarnik 🛃 a.	...	...	...	1532	...	...	...	...	0328
292	Šid 🛃 a.	...	...	...	1625	...	...	...	...	0348
407	**Beograd** Centar a.	...	...	...	1754	...	...	...	...	0610

	IC	IC			IC	❋	IC		❋
	540	542		210	544	412	546	1840	410
	R	R		R	R	2¶	R	R✕	R
	e	f	2	◆		◆	k	◆	◆
Beograd Centar d.	...	...	...	...	...	1040	...	...	210
Šid 🛃 d.	...	...	...	...	...	1325	...	...	002
Tovarnik 🛃 d.	...	...	0603**h**	...	...	1348	...	...	003
Vinkovci d.	0226	0531	0639	0839	1138	1416	1727	1727	010
Osijek 1345 d.	|	|	|	|	|	|	|	|	|
Strizivojna-Vrpolje 1345 d.	0251	0552	0703	0900	1159	1437	1755	17559	012
Slavonski Brod d.	0319	0616	0739	0924	1223	1500	1824	1824	014
Novska d.	0436	0733	0914	1036	1337	1612	1946	2233	024
Zagreb a.	0648	0940	1143	1240	1550	1820	2156	0051	042
Ljubljana **1300** a.	...	...	...	1508	...	2147	...	...	071

◆ – **NOTES** (LISTED BY TRAIN NUMBER)

210/1 – SAVA – [12] Vinkovci - Zagreb - Ljubljana - Villach and v.v.
410 – [12] Beograd - Dobova (**314**) - Ljubljana.
411 – [12] Ljubljana (**315**) - Dobova - Beograd.
412/3 – [12] Ljubljana - Dobova - Beograd and v.v.
1840 – July 1 - Sept. 1. 🛏, 🛏 and [2] Vinkovci - Zagreb - Split.
1841 – July 2 - Sept. 2. 🛏, 🛏 and [2] Split - Zagreb - Vinkovci.

e – Runs on Ⓐ only until further notice.
f – Does not run on ⑦ until further notice.
h – Ⓐ only.
j – Not June 3 - Sept. 9.
k – Not July 1 - Sept. 1.

¶ – Also conveys [1] Zagreb - Vinkovci and v.v.

❋ – Service currently suspended.

1322 LOCAL SERVICES in Croatia

2nd class only HŽ

ZAGREB - SISAK CAPRAG: Journey 60 – 75 minutes. All services call at Sisak (5 minutes from Sisak Caprag).
From Zagreb at 0542Ⓐ, 0633, 0729Ⓐ, 0859, 1112, 1218Ⓐ, 1350, 1450Ⓐ, 1547, 1758Ⓐ, 1909, 2017, 2128Ⓐ, 2250.
From Sisak Caprag at 0523, 0618, 0701Ⓐ, 0750Ⓐ, 1030⚒, 1214, 1410Ⓐ, 1514, 1604Ⓐ, 1646, 1805Ⓐ, 2009, 2125.

SISAK CAPRAG - SUNJA: Journey 30 minutes.
From Sisak Caprag at 0738, 0956, 1215, 1447, 1645, 1855Ⓐ, 2008, 2347.
From Sunja at 0500⚒, 0555, 0638Ⓐ, 1151, 1253, 1619, 1942, 2102, 2203Ⓐ.

SUNJA - NOVSKA: Journey 70 minutes.
From Sunja at 0801, 1237, 2045Ⓑ.
From Novska at 0503, 0546Ⓐ, 1059, 1842Ⓑ.

VINKOVCI - VUKOVAR: Journey 40 minutes.
From Vinkovci at 0414Ⓐ, 1019Ⓐ **n**, 1200Ⓐ **m**, 1522, 1938Ⓐ
From Vukovar at 0457Ⓐ, 1102Ⓐ **n**, 1312Ⓐ **m**, 1649 **n**, 2019Ⓐ

m – Not June 23 - Sept. 1.
n – Not July 3 - Sept. 1.

1325 🚌 SPLIT - PLOČE - DUBROVNIK

Subject to confirmation

🚌 SPLIT - DUBROVNIK: Journey 4 hrs - 5 hrs 10 mins.
🚌 SPLIT - PLOČE: Journey 2 hrs - 2 hrs 50 mins.
🚌 PLOČE - DUBROVNIK: Journey 2 hrs - 2 hrs 20 mins.

Note: various operators run on these routes; tickets are not interchangeable.
Split and Ploče bus stations are situated adjacent to the railway stations.
Buses pass through Bosnia between Ploče and Dubrovnik (passports required).

HŽ 2nd class only except where shown ZAGREB - ZADAR, ŠIBENIK and SPLIT 1330

km	km																							
											ICN						ICN						IC	
											521						523				1840	1821	1204	1880
											R ✕						R ✕				R ✕	R	R ✕	R
					Ⓐn		Ⓐ				c	Ⓐm	Ⓐm				♦	Ⓐ	Ⓐ		♦	♦	♦	♦
		Budapest Keleti **1220** d.	...	...	...	...	...	...	...	...	...	...	...	...	...	...	...	...	...	...	...	...	1845	...
0		**Zagreb** **1310** d.	...	...	...	...	...	...	...	...	0703	...	...	...	...	...	1519	...	...	...	2230	2230	0044	0109
53		Karlovac **1310** d.	...	...	...	...	...	...	...	...	0759	...	...	...	...	...	1600	...	...	...	2317	2317	|	0155
103		Oštarije **1310** d.	...	...	...	...	...	...	...	...	0846	...	...	...	...	...	1646	...	...	...	0022	|	|	|
109		**Ogulin** **1310** d.	...	...	...	...	...	...	...	...	|	...	...	...	...	...	|	...	...	...	|	0031	0312	|
225		Gospić d.	...	...	...	...	...	...	...	...	1026	...	...	...	...	...	1822	...	...	...	0235	0240	|	0459
269		Gračac d.	...	...	...	...	...	...	...	...	1109	...	...	...	...	...	1856	...	...	...	0317	0322	|	0540
333		Knin a.	...	...	...	...	...	...	...	...	1200	...	...	...	...	...	1946	...	...	...	0422	0427	|	0645
333	0	Knin ‡ d.	...	0412	...	...	0807	...	...	...	1201	...	...	1511	...	...	1947	1958	...	...	0428	0438	|	0646
	95	**Zadar** ‡ a.	...	|	...	...	|	...	...	...	|	...	...	|	...	...	|	|	...	...	|	|	|	|
387	—	Perković a.	...	0513	...	...	0908	...	...	...	1248	...	...	1616	...	...	2033	2059	...	...	0528	0539	0817	0745
387	0	Perković d.	0522	0541	0655	...	0912	0918	...	...	1249	1254	1520	1636	1638	...	2044	2107	2108	...	0539	0544	0818	0746
	22	**Šibenik** a.	|	0612	0726	...	0943	|	...	...	|	1325	1550	1707	|	...	|	2138	|	...	|	|	|	|
435		**Split** a.	0631	...	...	...	...	1025	...	...	1345	...	...	...	1746	...	2140	...	2216	...	0656	0704	0944	0913

					ICN				ICN							IC						
					520				522							1205				1820	1841	1881
					R ✕				R ✕							R ✕				R	R ✕	R
	Ⓐ		n		♦d		Ⓐm	Ⓐm	e			Ⓐ				♦	Ⓐ			♦	♦	♦
plit d.	...	...	0727	...	0814	...	...	...	1409	...	1520	...	...	...	...	1755	1945	...	...	2104	2104	2218
Šibenik d.	0448	...	|	0840	|	...	1111	1427	|	...	|	1558	...	...	...	|	|	2034	...	|	|	|
erković a.	0519	...	0840	0911	0915	...	1142	1458	1509	...	1632	1629	...	...	...	1925	2102	2105	...	2233	2238	2338
erković d.	0530	...	...	0931	0917	...	...	...	1510	...	...	1635	...	...	...	1926	...	2110	...	2234	2239	2339
Zadar ‡ d.	|	...	...	|	|	...	...	...	|	...	...	|	...	...	...	|	...	|	...	|	|	|
nin ‡ a.	0641	...	...	1035	1008	...	...	...	1558	...	...	1739	...	...	...	2055	...	2214	...	2337	2340	0040
nin d.	...	...	...	...	1010	...	...	...	1600	...	...	...	...	...	...	2058	...	...	...	2338	2341	0041
račac d.	...	...	...	...	1114	...	...	...	1654	...	...	...	...	...	...	|	...	...	...	0052	0055	0155
ospić d.	...	...	...	...	1148	...	...	...	1729	...	...	...	...	...	...	|	...	...	...	0141	0133	0233
gulin **1310** d.	...	...	...	...	|	...	...	...	|	...	...	...	...	...	...	0055	...	...	...	0358	|	|
štarije **1310** d.	...	...	...	...	1326	...	...	...	1914	...	...	...	...	...	...	|	...	...	...	|	0403	|
arlovac **1310** d.	...	...	...	...	1415	...	...	...	2008	...	...	...	...	...	...	|	...	...	...	0453	0453	0534
agreb **1310** a.	...	...	...	...	1455	...	...	...	2057	...	...	...	...	...	...	0251	...	...	...	0540	0540	0622
Budapest Keleti **1220** a.	...	...	...	...	...	...	...	...	...	...	...	...	...	...	...	0935	...	...	...	...	...	...

– **NOTES** (LISTED BY TRAIN NUMBER):

20/3 – MARJAN – Zagreb - Knin - Split and v.v.
204/5 – ADRIA – Budapest - Gyékényes - Zagreb - Split and v.v. For days of running see Table **1340**.
320 – ⑦ to June 11 and from Oct. 1 (also May 1; not Feb. 19, Apr. 9, 30). 🛋, 🛏 and (2) Split - Knin - Zagreb.
321 – ⑤ to June 16 and from Oct. 6 (also Apr. 5; not Feb. 24, Apr. 7, 14). 🛋, 🛏 and (2) Zagreb - Knin - Split.
840 – July 1 - Sept. 1. 🛋, 🛏 and (2) Vinkovci - Zagreb - Split.
841 – July 2 - Sept. 2. 🛋, 🛏 and (2) Split - Zagreb - Vinkovci.
880 – ⚒ July 1 - Sept. 1. DALMACIJA – 🛋, 🛏 and (2) Osijek - Zagreb - Split.
881 – July 2 - Sept. 2. DALMACIJA – 🛋, 🛏 and (2) Split - Zagreb - Osijek.

c – June 7 - Oct. 1 (also Apr. 5–8, 10, Oct. 28 - Nov. 1).
d – ⚒ to June 3 and from Oct. 2 (also Jan. 6, 8, Apr. 10, Oct. 29, Nov. 1); daily June 5 - Oct. 1.
e – † to June 4 and from Oct. 8 (also Apr. 5–8, Oct. 28, 30, 31); daily June 7 - Oct. 1.
m – Daily June 5 - Oct. 1.
n – Not May 5 - Oct. 7.

‡ – Services Knin - Zadar and v.v are suspended until further notice.

HŽ 2nd class only except where shown ZAGREB - VARAŽDIN - KOTORIBA and KOPRIVNICA 1335

km																												
																	772											
		⚒		Ⓐ	Ⓐ	Ⓐ			⚒		Ⓐ	Ⓐ	Ⓐ				R ♦	Ⓐ	Ⓐ			Ⓐ	⚒	⚒				
0	**Zagreb** d.	...	...	...	0543	...	0744	...	...	1137	...	1319	...	1435	...	...	1530	1537	...	1646		...	1824	...	2016	...	2200	2232
38	Zabok d.	...	...	0537	0645	0704	0829	0848	...	1220	1230	1402	1415	1518	1530	...	k	1624	1637	1729	1746	...	1909	1926	2100	2115	2246	2313
04	**Varaždin** d.	0535	0658	0749	...	0835	...	1017	1020	...	1403	...	1555	...	1658	...	1739	...	1811	...	1935	2020	...	2103	...	2244	0015	...
15	Čakovec d.	0548	0716	0802	...	0848	...	...	1033	...	...	...	...	...	1720d	...	...	...	...	...	...	2033	...	...	...	...	0026	...
45	**Kotoriba** a.	0624	0749	0834	...	...	...	...	1110	...	...	...	...	...	1753d	...	...	...	...	...	...	2106	...	...	...	...	...	...

				773																							
			⚒	R ♦				Ⓐ	⚒		Ⓐ	Ⓐ	Ⓐ	⚒	⚒	⚒	⚒			†		Ⓑ	Ⓑ				
otoriba d.	...	...	0422	...	0552	...	0838	...	...	...	1038	...	...	1159	...	...	1455	...	...	1609	1703	...	...	1824	...	...	2122
akovec d.	...	...	0456	...	0627	...	0913	...	...	...	1113	...	...	1234	...	...	1529	...	...	1643	1741	...	...	1859	...	...	2200
araždin d.	0313	...	0507	0518	0651	...	0924	...	1033	...	1124	1223	...	1245	1414	...	1540	1603	...	1654	1752	1757	...	1910	1919	...	2211
abok d.	0448	...	...	k	0824	0854	...	1047	1206	1231	...	1352	1416	...	1554	1613	...	1738	1756	...	...	1921	1925	...	2052	2116	...
agreb a.	0533	...	...	0720	...	0936	...	1130	...	1313	...	...	1459	...	...	1659	...	...	1838	...	...	...	2007	...	...	2158	...

VARAŽDIN - KOPRIVNICA

km												
			773									
		Ⓐ	Ⓐ		Ⓐ	⚒	⚒		Ⓐ	⚒		Ⓐ
0	Varaždin d.	0418	0518	0646	0751	1022	1247	1441	1559	1709	1924	2214
42	Koprivnica a.	0510	0557	0734	0840	1111	1336	1535	1648	1758	2014	2302

									772			
	Ⓐ	⚒	Ⓐ		⚒	Ⓐ	⚒		Ⓐ	Ⓑ	Ⓐ	
Koprivnica d.	0423	0533	0813	0902	1146	1309	1447	1558	1700	1805	1924	2032
Varaždin a.	0511	0630	0910	0951	1235	1406	1536	1650	1739	1854	2017	2121

– **NOTES** (LISTED BY TRAIN NUMBER):

2 – (2) Zagreb (**771**) - Koprivnica - Varaždin.
3 – (2) Varaždin - Koprivnica (**770**) - Zagreb.

d – ⚒ only.
k – Via Koprivnica.

HŽ, MÁV, Regiojet ZAGREB - KOPRIVNICA - NAGYKANIZSA and OSIJEK 1340

km		781	1881		981	771	201	581	787		1205
		R	R		R	R	R	R	R		R
		♦n	♦		Ⓒ	Ⓐt	♦	♦	Ⓐ2		♦
	Split **1330** d.	...	2218	...	...	...	...	...	...	...	1755
0	**Zagreb** d.	0646	0646	...	1240	1530	1635	1635	1534	...	0255
57	Križevci d.	0741	|	...	1348	1627	1733	1733	|	...	|
88	Koprivnica d.	0811	|	...	1444	1700	1801	1806	|	...	0439
03	Gyékényes 🏛 d.	|	|	...	|	...	1832	|	|	...	0530
32	**Nagykanizsa** a.	|	|	...	|	...	1902	|	|	...	0556
	Budapest Déli **1220** a.	|	|	...	|	...	2224	|	|	...	0935e
53	Virovitica d.	0927	0927	...	1604	...	...	1920	1804	...	...
25	Našice d.	1102	1101	...	1749	...	...	2054	...	...	...
75	**Osijek** a.	1206	1204	...	1907	...	...	2157	...	...	...

	786	770		580		780	204	1204	1880
	R	R		R		R	R	R	R
	Ⓐ2	Ⓐt		♦		m	♦	♦	♦
Osijek d.	0150	...	...	0542	...	1610	...	...	1945
Našice d.	0252	...	...	0646	...	1714	...	...	2057
Virovitica d.	0438	...	...	0825	...	1851	...	...	2232
Budapest Déli **1220** d.	|	...	...	|	...	|	1535	1845e	|
Nagykanizsa d.	|	...	...	|	...	|	1908	2201	|
Gyékényes 🏛 d.	|	...	...	|	...	|	1958	2255	|
Koprivnica d.	|	0604	...	0943	...	2024	2027	2310	|
Križevci d.	|	0627	...	0911	...	2048	2100	|	|
Zagreb a.	0712	0720	...	1101	...	2144	2210	0026	0054
Split **1330** a.	...	...	...	...	...	...	...	0944	0913

– **NOTES** (LISTED BY TRAIN NUMBER):

1/4 – AGRAM – (12) Budapest - Gyékényes - Koprivnica - Zagreb and v.v.
0/1 – PODRAVKA – (12) Zagreb - Osijek and v.v.
0/1 – DRAVA – (12) Zagreb - Osijek and v.v.
04 – ②⑤⑦ June 9 - Sept. 22 (not June 11, Sept. 10, 17). ADRIA – Budapest - Gyékényes - Zagreb - Split.
05 – ②④⑦ June 11 - Sept. 24 (not June 13, Sept. 12, 19). ADRIA – Split - Zagreb - Gyékényes - Budapest.
80 – ⚒ July 1 - Sept. 1. DALMACIJA – 🛋, 🛏 and (2) Osijek - Zagreb - Split.
81 – July 2 - Sept. 2. DALMACIJA – 🛋, 🛏 and (2) Split - Zagreb - Osijek.

e – Budapest **Keleti**.
m – Not July 1 - Sept. 1.
n – Not July 3 - Sept. 3.
t – To / from Varaždin (Table **1335**).

1345 PÉCS - OSIJEK - DOBOJ

2nd class only except where shown HŽ, MÁV, ŽRS

There is currently no service Strizivojna-Vrpolje - Slavonski Šamac - Šamac - Doboj and v.v.

km																												
		⚒	Ⓐ			⚒	Ⓐ	⚒	Ⓐ	⚒	Ⓐ				Ⓐ			Ⓑ	⚒							Ⓑ		Ⓑ
	Budapest Déli **1200** d.	...	...	...	...	...	...	...	...	...	...	...	...	...	...	...	...	...	...	...	...	...	...	...	...	...	...	...
0	**Pécs** d.	...	...	0508	...	...	...	...	...	...	...	0850	...	...	...	1250	...	...	...	1450	...	...	1650	...	...	...	1850	...
36	Villány d.	...	...	0555	...	...	...	...	...	...	...	0934	...	...	...	1334	...	...	...	1534	...	...	1734	...	...	...	1934	...
43	Magyarbóly 🏛 d.	...	...	0603	...	...	...	...	...	...	...	0942	...	...	...	1342	...	...	...	1542	...	...	1742	...	...	...	1942	...
54	Beli Manastir 🏛 d.	...	0547	0614	0700	...	...	0814	...	...	...	0953	1049	...	...	1353	1425	...	...	1553	1622	...	1753	1847	...	...	1953	2005
82	**Osijek** a.	...	0618	...	0731	...	...	0845	...	...	...	...	1120	...	...	...	1456	...	...	...	1653	...	...	1918	...	...	...	2036
82	**Osijek** d.	0417	...	...	...	0734	0802	...	0927	1040	1103	...	...	1325	1340	...	...	1544	1620	...	...	1814	...	...	2009	2030	...	...
	Vinkovci a.	|	...	...	...	0822	|	...	1015	1128	|	...	...	1413	|	...	...	|	1708	...	...	1902	...	...	|	2118	...	...
130	Strizivojna-Vrpolje d.	0507	...	...	...	...	0854	...	...	...	1154	...	...	...	1432	...	...	1636	...	...	...	...	...	...	2102	...	...	...
150	Slavonski Šamac 🏛 d.	...	...	...	...	...	...	...	...	...	...	...	...	...	...	...	...	...	...	...	...	...	...	...	...	...	...	...
154	Šamac 🏛 d.	...	...	...	...	...	...	...	...	...	...	...	...	...	...	...	...	...	...	...	...	...	...	...	...	...	...	...
226	**Doboj** a.	...	...	...	...	...	...	...	...	...	...	...	...	...	...	...	...	...	...	...	...	...	...	...	...	...	...	...

km																												
		Ⓐ	⚒			⚒	⚒	⚒		⚒	Ⓐ	Ⓐ		Ⓐ					⚒	Ⓐ			Ⓑ		Ⓑ			Ⓑ
	Doboj d.	...	...	...	...	...	...	...	...	...	...	...	...	...	...	...	...	...	...	...	...	...	...	...	...	...	...	...
	Šamac 🏛 d.	...	...	...	...	...	...	...	...	...	...	...	...	...	...	...	...	...	...	...	...	...	...	...	...	...	...	...
	Slavonski Šamac 🏛 d.	...	...	...	...	...	...	...	...	...	...	...	...	...	...	...	...	...	...	...	...	...	...	...	...	...	...	...
	Strizivojna-Vrpolje d.	0526	...	...	...	0627	...	...	...	...	1009	...	...	1209	...	...	...	...	...	1656	...	...	...	...	1912	...	2124	...
0	Vinkovci d.	|	0533	...	...	|	0637	...	...	0830	|	...	1140	|	...	...	...	...	1519	|	1719	...	...	...	|	1935	|	215
35	**Osijek** a.	0617	0620	...	...	0718	0724	...	...	0917	1058	...	1227	1258	...	...	...	...	1606	1746	1806	...	...	...	2001	2022	2213	223
	Osijek d.	...	...	0624	...	...	...	0737	...	...	...	1145	...	...	1321	...	1524	...	...	...	...	...	1924	...	...	...	...	...
	Beli Manastir 🏛 d.	...	...	0655	0751	...	...	0808	1002	...	...	1216	...	...	1352	1402	1555	1602	...	...	...	1802	1955	2002	...	...	...	...
	Magyarbóly 🏛 d.	...	...	...	0814	...	...	...	1014	...	...	...	...	...	...	1414	...	1614	...	...	...	1814	...	2014	...	...	...	...
	Villány d.	...	...	...	0822	...	...	...	1022	...	...	...	...	...	...	1422	...	1622	...	...	...	1822	...	2022	...	...	...	...
	Pécs a.	...	...	...	0907	...	...	...	1107	...	...	...	...	...	...	1507	...	1707	...	...	...	1907	...	2107	...	...	...	...
	Budapest Déli **1200** a.	...	...	...	...	...	...	...	...	...	...	...	...	...	...	...	...	...	...	...	...	...	...	...	...	...	...	...

1350 ZAGREB - DOBOJ - SARAJEVO

2nd class only except where shown HŽ, ŽFBH, ŽRS

There is currently no service Volinja - Dobrljin and v.v.

km				711		715											713									
				[R]		[R] ⋙			⋙	⋙					⋙		[R] ⋙			⋙						
0	**Zagreb** d.	...	...	...	...	...	...	...	...	...	...	...	0859	...	...	...	...	...	1350	...	1547	...	...	1909	...	2250
72	Sunja d.	...	...	...	...	...	...	...	...	...	...	...	1018	...	...	...	...	...	1513	...	1707	...	...	2030	...	0009
92	Volinja 🏛 d.	...	...	...	...	...	...	...	...	...	...	...	1045	...	...	...	...	...	1540	...	1734	...	...	2057**a**	...	0036
98	Dobrljin 🏛 d.	...	...	...	...	...	...	...	...	...	0631	...	...	...	...	...	...	1456	...	...	...	...	1822	...	...	...
	Bihać d.	...	...	...	...	0203	...	...	...	...	|	...	...	...	...	...	...	|	...	...	...	...	|	...	...	...
112	Novi Grad d.	...	...	...	...	0358	0429	...	...	...	0651	...	...	...	...	...	...	1515	...	...	...	...	1902	...	...	...
214	Banja Luka d.	...	...	...	0439	0531	0631	0726	...	...	0844	...	...	1526	...	...	1601	1709	...	...	...	1930	2102	...	...	...
324	**Doboj** a.	...	...	...	0638	0655	...	0921	...	...	...	...	...	1721	...	...	1735	...	...	...	...	2138	...	...	...	...
324	**Doboj** d.	...	...	...	...	0656	...	...	...	...	...	...	...	...	...	...	1737	...	...	...	...	...	...	...	...	...
347	Maglaj d.	...	0448	0601	...	0731	...	...	0926	...	...	...	...	...	1718	...	1812	...	...	...	...	...	...	...	...	...
370	Zavidovici d.	...	0520	0624	...	0754	...	...	0958	...	...	...	...	...	1750	...	1835	...	...	...	...	...	...	...	...	...
419	Zenica d.	0454	0621	0718	...	0850	...	...	1059	1107	...	1528	...	...	1851	...	1926	...	...	1941	...	...	...	...	...	...
447	Kakanj d.	0531	...	0749	...	0919	...	...	...	1148	...	1605	...	...	...	...	1955	...	...	2018	...	...	...	...	...	...
465	Visoko d.	0553	...	0806	...	0936	...	...	...	1214	...	1627	...	...	...	...	2012	...	...	2040	...	...	...	...	...	...
472	Podlugovi d.	0602	...	0814	...	0944	...	...	...	1223	...	1658	...	...	...	...	2020	...	...	2049	...	...	...	...	...	...
496	**Sarajevo** a.	0635	...	0842	...	1014	...	...	...	1259	...	1738	...	...	...	...	2050	...	...	2125	...	...	...	...	...	...

km											712										710				
		⚒							⋙	⋙		[R] ⋙					⋙			Ⓐ		[R]		⋙		⋙
	Sarajevo d.	...	...	...	...	...	0444	...	...	0733	...	1018	...	...	...	...	1102	...	1541	...	...	1627	...	...	...	192
	Podlugovi d.	...	...	...	...	...	0518	...	...	0814	...	1049	...	...	...	...	1139	...	1615	...	...	1656	...	...	...	200
	Visoko d.	...	...	...	...	...	0527	...	...	0823	...	1057	...	...	...	...	1148	...	1629	...	...	1704	...	...	...	201
	Kakanj d.	...	...	...	...	...	0553	...	...	0845	...	1114	...	...	...	...	1210	...	1651	...	...	1721	...	...	...	204
	Zenica d.	...	...	...	...	...	0629	...	0715	0924	...	1144	...	...	...	...	1246	1533	1727	...	...	1750	...	1928	...	211
	Zavidovici d.	...	...	...	...	...	...	...	0816	...	...	1233	...	...	...	...	...	1634	...	...	...	1839	...	2029	...	...
	Maglaj d.	...	...	...	...	...	...	...	0847	...	...	1256	...	...	...	...	...	1705	...	...	...	1901	...	2100	...	...
	Doboj a.	...	...	...	...	...	...	...	...	...	...	1328	...	...	...	...	...	...	...	...	...	...	...	...	...	...
	Doboj d.	...	...	0426	...	...	...	0727	...	...	...	1329	...	...	...	1528	...	...	...	...	...	...	1925	...	...	...
	Banja Luka d.	...	0410	0617	0724	...	...	0931	...	...	...	1451	...	1525	...	1730	...	...	...	...	1925	...	2119	...	...	...
0	Novi Grad d.	...	0602	...	0921	...	...	...	...	...	1345	...	...	1730	...	...	...	...	...	...	2118	...	...	...	...	...
78	Bihać a.	...	|	...	...	...	...	...	...	...	|	...	...	|	...	...	...	...	...	...	...	...	...	...	...	...
	Dobrljin 🏛 d.	...	0620	...	...	...	...	...	...	...	1404	...	...	1748	...	...	...	...	...	...	...	...	...	...	...	...
	Volinja 🏛 d.	0432	...	...	...	1113	...	...	...	...	...	...	1551	...	1914	...	...	...	...	2135	...	...	...	...	...	...
	Sunja d.	0500	...	...	...	1140	...	...	...	...	...	...	1619	...	1942	...	...	...	...	2202	...	...	...	...	...	...
	Zagreb a.	0618	...	...	...	...	...	...	...	...	...	...	1744	...	2108	...	...	...	...	...	...	...	...	...	...	...

a – Ⓐ only. **c** – ⚒ only. ⋙ – Service currently suspended.

1355 SARAJEVO - PLOČE

Most services 2nd class only HŽ, ŽFBH

There is currently no service Čapljina - Metković - Ploče and v.v.

km		723 [R] n		1391 [R] p		Ⓐ		721 [R]			
	Zagreb **1350** d.	...	...	...	...	...	...	...	...	...	...
0	**Sarajevo** d.	0715	...	0715	...	1548	...	1649	...	...	...
67	Konjic d.	0822	...	0822	...	1714	...	1800	...	...	...
129	Mostar d.	0912	...	0912	...	...	...	1850	...	...	...
149	Žitomislići d.	0925	...	0925	...	...	...	1903	...	...	...
163	Čapljina 🏛 d.	0937	...	0952	...	...	...	1915	...	...	...
173	Metković d.	...	...	1018	...	...	...	...	...	...	...
194	**Ploče** a.	...	...	1036	...	...	...	...	...	...	...

	Ⓐ		720 [R]		722 [R] n		1390 [R] p			
Ploče d.	...	...	...	...	...	...	1826	...	...	...
Metković d.	...	...	...	...	...	...	1904	...	...	...
Čapljina 🏛 d.	...	...	0609	...	1642	...	1929	...	...	...
Žitomislići d.	...	...	0621	...	1654	...	1941	...	...	...
Mostar d.	...	...	0636	...	1709	...	1956	...	...	...
Konjic d.	0525	...	0725	...	1758	...	2045	...	...	...
Sarajevo a.	0651	...	0835	...	1904	...	2151	...	...	...
Zagreb **1350** a.	...	...	...	...	...	...	...	...	...	...

n – Not June 2 - Aug. 27.
p – June 2 - Aug. 27.

☞ Alternative 🚌 services are available Sarajevo - Mostar - Metković - Dubrovnik and v

1358 LOCAL SERVICES in Bosnia

2nd class only HŽ, ŽFBH, ŽRS

VINKOVCI - TUZLA

There is currently no service Gunja - Brčko - Tuzla and v.v.; also no service Tuzla - Petrovo Novo and v.v.

km		Ⓐ		⚒				Ⓐ
0	Vinkovci d.	0320	...	0923	...	1509	...	1942
49	Gunja d.	0419	...	1022	...	1608	...	2041
53	Brčko 🏛 d.	...	...	...	...	...	...	...
127	Tuzla a.	...	...	...	...	...	...	...

	Ⓐ		⚒				Ⓐ
Tuzla d.	...	...	...	...	...	...	...
Brčko 🏛 d.	...	...	...	...	...	...	...
Gunja d.	0428	...	1032	...	1616	...	2049
Vinkovci a.	0527	...	1131	...	1715	...	2148

TUZLA - DOBOJ

km					Ⓐ			
0	Tuzla d.	...	...	...	...	...	...	...
32	Petrovo Novo d.	0536	1054	...	1412	...	1753	2039
60	Doboj a.	0631	1149	...	1505	...	1846	2132

				Ⓐ			
Doboj d.	0420	0730	...	1310	1526	...	1932
Petrovo Novo d.	0515	0825	...	1405	1620	...	2025
Tuzla a.	...	...	...	...	...	...	...

SERBIA, MONTENEGRO and NORTH MACEDONIA

MAP PAGE 505

perators: Železnice Srbije (ŽS): www.srbvoz.rs; Železnice Crne Gore (ŽCG): www.zcg-prevoz.me; Makedonski Železnici (MŽ): www.mztransport.mk; Trainkos (KŽ/HK): www.trainkos.com

ervices: All trains convey first- and second-class seating, except where shown otherwise in footnotes, by a '2' in the train column, or where the footnote shows that the train conveys sleeping- (🛏) and / or couchette (🛏) cars only. Descriptions of sleeping- and couchette cars are given on page 10.

mings: Valid **until December 9, 2023.**
Services may be amended or cancelled at short notice and passengers are strongly advised to check locally before travelling.

ckets: A supplement is payable for travel by internal express trains. Reservation of seats is possible on most express trains.

sas: Most nationals do not require a visa to enter Serbia and Montenegro, but must obtain an entry stamp in their passport, sight of which will be required by officials on leaving the country. These must be obtained at a border crossing recognised by the authorities - this excludes Kosovo's external borders with Montenegro, North Macedonia and Albania. Note also that Serbia should not be entered from Kosovo unless initial travel into Kosovo was via Serbia. Visas are not required for entry into North Macedonia for most nationals.

rrency: Visitors must declare large amounts of foreign currency upon arrival; currently 2,000 EUR in Montenegro, and 10,000 EUR in Serbia and North Macedonia. It is reported, however, that North Macedonia may now be operating on a threshold of 2,000 EUR. A certificate issued by the customs officer must be presented on departure, otherwise any funds held may be confiscated.

curity: Following the declaration of independence by Kosovo (which has not been recognised by Serbia) caution should be exercised when travelling in southern Serbia and northern Kosovo. Caution is also advised in the northern and western border regions of North Macedonia.

S (BUDAPEST) - KELEBIA - SUBOTICA - BEOGRAD 1360

Rail services are suspended between Subotica and Novi Sad until further notice.
Travellers must make their own way between these points using scheduled bus services. Selected bus services are shown in this table.
Note that bus services operate to / from Novi Sad and Subotica central bus stations (not the rail station). **Rail tickets are not valid on bus services.**

m				REx	REx	REx	IC		IC	IC	IC	IC			IC	IC	IC	IC	IC		IC	IC			REx	REx
				743	745	747	541		543	545	547	549	349		551	553	555	557	559		561	563	343		751	753
			Bus	[R] ⚒	[R] Ⓐ	[R] Ⓐ	[R]	Bus	[R]	[R]	[R]	[R]	♥ ⇊	Bus	[R]	[R]	[R]	[R]	[R]	Bus	[R]	[R]	♥ ⇊	Bus	[R]	[R]
	Budapest Nyugati **1295** .. d.	...	...	...	...	...	...	...	...	...	...	...	...	...	...	...	...	...	...	...	...	...	...	...	...	...
0	**Kelebia** 🛃 d.	...	...	...	...	...	...	...	...	...	...	...	0941	...	...	...	...	...	...	...	...	...	1541	...	...	...
10	**Subotica** 🛃 a.	...	...	...	...	...	...	...	...	...	...	...	0955	...	...	...	...	...	...	...	...	...	1555	...	...	...
10	**Subotica** d.	...	0430	...	...	...	...	0730	...	...	...	...	...	1115	...	...	...	...	...	1600	...	...	...	1800	...	...
08	Novi Sad a.	...	0605	...	...	...	...	0920	...	...	...	...	...	1305	...	...	...	...	...	1750	...	...	...	1950	...	...
08	Novi Sad d.	0545	...	0649	0719	0758	0900	...	1000	1100	1200	1300	...	...	1400	1500	1600	1700	1800	...	1900	2000	...	...	2130	2230
31	Novi Beograd d.	0637	...	0734	0804	0843	0933	...	1033	1133	1233	1333	...	...	1433	1533	1633	1733	1833	...	1933	2033	...	...	2215	2315
36	**Beograd** Centar a.	0640	...	0737	0807	0846	0936	...	1036	1136	1236	1336	...	...	1436	1536	1636	1736	1836	...	1936	2036	...	...	2218	2318

	REx	REx	REx		IC		IC			IC			IC	IC	IC		IC	IC	IC		IC	IC	IC	IC		
	740	742	744		540	348	542			544	342		546	748	550		552	554	556		558	560	562	564		
	[R] Ⓐ	[R] Ⓐ	[R] Ⓐ	Bus	[R]	♥ ⇊	[R]		Bus	[R]	♥ ⇊		[R]	[R]	[R]	Bus	[R]	[R]	[R]	Bus	[R]	[R]	[R]	[R]	Bus	
ograd Centar d.	0520	0552	0652	...	0809	...	0900	0905	...	1000	...	1015	1100	1200	1300	...	1400	1500	1600	...	1700	1800	1900	2000	...	2230
vi Beograd d.	0524	0556	0656	...	0813	...	0904	0909	...	1004	...	1019	1104	1204	1304	...	1404	1504	1604	...	1704	1804	1904	2004	...	2234
vi Sad a.	0609	0641	0741	...	0845	...	0936	0958	...	1036	...	1112	1136	1236	1336	...	1436	1536	1636	...	1736	1836	1936	2036	...	2327
vi Sad d.	...	...	...	0825	...	...	...	...	1040	...	...	...	...	...	...	1440	...	...	...	1720	...	...	...	...	2115	...
botica a.	...	...	...	1015	...	...	...	...	1230	...	...	...	...	...	...	1630	...	...	...	1910	...	...	...	...	2300	...
botica 🛃 d.	...	...	...	...	...	0802	...	...	...	...	1402	...	...	...	...	...	...	...	...	...	...	...	...	...	...	...
ebia 🛃 a.	...	...	...	...	...	0816	...	...	...	...	1416	...	...	...	...	...	...	...	...	...	...	...	...	...	...	...
Budapest Nyugati **1295** ...a.	...	...	...	...	...	...	...	...	...	...	...	...	...	...	...	...	...	...	...	...	...	...	...	...	...	...

– For journeys from / to Budapest see Table **1295**.

⇊ – Suspended until further notice.

S 2nd class only SUBOTICA and KIKINDA - ZRENJANIN - PANČEVO - BEOGRAD 1362

Services on the Zrenjanin - Pančevo - Beograd route are suspended until further notice.

m					Ⓐ				Ⓐ		Ⓑ
	Subotica d.	...	0706	...	...	...	...	1530	1700	...	2000
	Senta d.	...	0805	...	...	...	...	1630	1745	...	2103
	Banatsko Miloševo d.	...	0858	...	...	...	...	1740	...	...	2209
0	**Kikinda** d.	0450	|	...	1127	...	1710	1800	...	...	2229
9	Banatsko Miloševo d.	0511	|	...	1206	...	1731	...	...	...	...
71	**Zrenjanin** d.	0626	1013	...	1321	...	1846	...	...	...	...
96	Orlovat Stajalište d.	...	...	...	...	...	...	...	...	...	...
5	**Pančevo** Glavna ...... **1365** d.	...	...	...	...	...	...	...	...	...	...
59	Pančevački Most ... **1365/6** d.	...	...	...	...	...	...	...	...	...	...
1	**Beograd** Centar.... **1365/6** a.	...	...	...	...	...	...	...	...	...	...

	⚒	Ⓐ					Ⓐ			
Beograd Centar.. **1365/6** d.	...	...	...	...	...	...	...	...	...	...
Pančevački Most . **1365/6** d.	...	...	...	...	...	...	...	...	...	...
Pančevo Glavna .... **1365** d.	...	...	...	...	...	...	...	...	...	...
Orlovat Stajalište d.	...	...	...	...	...	...	...	...	...	...
Zrenjanin d.	...	0735	...	1040	...	1430	...	...	...	1940
Banatsko Miloševo d.	...	0910	...	|	...	1546	...	...	...	2056
Kikinda d.	0400	0930	...	|	...	1606	...	...	1930	2116
Banatsko Miloševo d.	0435	...	...	1156	...	...	...	...	2005	...
Senta d.	0541	...	...	1302	...	...	1800	...	2111	...
Subotica a.	0626	...	...	1347	...	...	1845	...	2156	...

S, CFR 2nd class only BEOGRAD - VRŠAC - TIMIŞOARA 1365

m			Ⓐ				①–⑤ s			
0	**Beograd** Centar .... **1362/6** d.	...	0700	0959	...	1135	...	1530	1640	...
2	Pančevački Most....... **1362/6** d.	...	0712	1012	...	1147	...	1542	1652	...
16	Pančevo Glavna .... **1362** d.	...	0729	1028	...	1205	...	1600	1710	...
83	Vršac a.	...	0846	1146	...	1317	...	1712	1822	...
83	Vršac 🛃 d.	...	...	...	...	...	...	...	...	...
03	Stamora Moraviţa 🛃 § a.	...	...	...	...	...	...	...	...	...
03	Stamora Moraviţa § d.	0525	...	...	1202	...	1639	...	...	2011
59	**Timişoara** Nord § a.	0642	...	...	1315	...	1754	...	...	2123

	Ⓐ					①–⑤ s			
Timişoara Nord § d.	...	...	0755	...	...	1457	...	1637	1844
Stamora Moraviţa § a.	...	...	0911	...	...	1612	...	1801	1959
Stamora Moraviţa 🛃 § d.	...	...	▬	...	...	...	...	...	...
Vršac 🛃 a.	...	...	...	...	...	...	...	...	...
Vršac d.	0448	0620	0920	1205	1441	...	1850	...	...
Pančevo Glavna........ **1362** d.	0601	0733	1033	1327	1554	...	2003	...	...
Pančevački Most.... **1362/6** d.	0619	0751	1051	1345	1612	...	2021	...	...
Beograd Centar .... **1362/6** a.	0628	0800	1100	1354	1621	...	2030	...	...

Not Dec. 23 - Jan. 8, Apr. 7 – 18, June 17 - Sept. 3.

§ – Romanian (East European) time.

S 2nd class only OVČA - BEOGRAD - BATAJNICA 1366

ča d.	0614	0659	0814	0959	1059	1159	1259	1359	1514	1714	1859
nčevački Most.... **1362/5** d.	0630	0715	0830	1015	1115	1215	1315	1415	1530	1730	1915
ograd Centar .... **1362/5** d.	0640	0725	0840	1025	1125	1225	1325	1425	1540	1740	1925
vi Beograd d.	0644	0729	0844	1029	1129	1229	1329	1429	1544	1744	1929
ajnica a.	0702	0747	0902	1047	1147	1247	1347	1347	1602	1802	1947

Batajnica d.	0557	0657	0757	0957	1057	1157	1257	1357	1551	1657	1957
Novi Beograd d.	0616	0716	0816	1016	1116	1216	1316	1416	1610	1716	2016
Beograd Centar. **1362/5** d.	0620	0720	0820	1020	1120	1220	1320	1420	1622	1720	2020
Pančevački Most **1362/5** d.	0632	0732	0832	1032	1132	1232	1332	1432	1634	1732	2032
Ovča a.	0645	0745	0845	1045	1145	1245	1345	1445	1647	1745	2045

Additional trains run between 0530 - 2100.

1370 BEOGRAD and NIKŠIĆ - PODGORICA - BAR

ŽCG, ŽS

km																	1131 B [R]						REx 711		433 L [R]	
0	**Beograd** Centar d.	...	...	...	...	...	...	...	...	...	...	...	...	0735	...	...	0859	...	1225	...	...	1525	1705	1940	2020	...
93	Valjevo d.	...	...	...	...	...	...	...	...	...	...	...	...	0908	...	...	1016	...	1357	...	...	1659	1822	2107	2136	...
159	Požega d.	...	...	...	...	...	...	...	...	...	...	...	...	1044	...	...	1141	...	1550	...	...	1858	1959	2243	2301	...
185	Užice d.	...	...	...	...	...	...	...	...	...	0700	...	...	1109	...	...	1206	...	1624	...	...	1931	2020	2311	2326	...
243	Štrpci 🏛 d.	...	...	...	...	...	...	...	...	...	0838	...	...	...	...	...	|	...	1814	...	...	2110	...	...	|	...
256	Priboj d.	...	...	...	...	...	...	...	...	...	0904	...	...	...	...	...	1355	...	1948	...	...	2136	...	...	0112	...
292	Prijepolje Teretna d.	...	...	...	...	...	...	...	...	...	1015	...	...	...	...	...	1540	...	1953	...	...	2247	...	...	0259	...
328	Vrbnica 🏛 d.	...	...	...	...	...	...	...	...	...	...	...	...	...	...	...	|	...	...	...	...	...	...	...	|	...
338	Bijelo Polje 🏛 d.	...	...	...	0626	0907	...	...	...	...	...	...	...	...	...	...	1705	...	...	...	1951	...	...	...	0420	...
★	**Nikšić** d.	...	0620	...	|	|	1040	...	1415	...	...	...	...	...	1700	...	|	...	...	2000	|	...	...	...	|	...
	Danilovgrad d.	...	0656	...	|	|	1116	...	1450	...	...	...	...	...	1736	...	|	...	...	2036	|	...	...	...	|	...
468	**Podgorica** a.	...	0723	...	0848	1124	1143	...	1517	...	...	...	...	...	1803	...	1910	...	...	2103	2212	...	...	...	0617	...
468	**Podgorica** d.	0510	...	0755	0912	1135	...	1255	...	1530	...	...	1636	...	...	1913	1915	...	...	...	2217	...	...	...	0625	...
514	Sutomore d.	0555	...	0841	1007	1221	...	1341	...	1616	...	...	1721	...	...	2001	2001	...	...	...	2302	...	...	...	0709	...
524	**Bar** a.	0609	...	0855	1021	1235	...	1355	...	1630	...	...	1735	...	...	2015	2015	...	...	...	2316	...	...	...	0723	...

	REx 710										1130 C [R]		⚒	⑦										432 L [R]		
Bar d.	...	...	...	...	0511	0624	...	...	...	...	0900	0923	...	...	1136	...	1413	...	1530	1703	...	1756	...	1900	...	210
Sutomore d.	...	...	...	...	0526	0639	...	...	...	...	0917	0938	...	...	1151	...	1428	...	1545	1722	...	1812	...	1918	...	211
Podgorica a.	...	...	...	...	0614	0726	...	...	...	...	0954	1022	...	...	1239	...	1512	...	1634	1806	...	1856	...	1958	...	220
Podgorica d.	...	...	...	...	0620	...	0800	...	...	...	1000	...	...	...	...	1250	...	1535	1707	...	1830	1914	...	2010	2145	...
Danilovgrad d.	...	...	...	...	|	...	0829	...	...	...	|	...	...	...	...	1319	...	1604	|	...	1859	|	...	|	2214	...
Nikšić a.	...	...	...	...	|	...	0903	...	...	...	|	...	...	...	...	1353	...	1638	|	...	1933	|	...	|	2248	...
Bijelo Polje 🏛 d.	...	...	...	...	0838	...	...	...	...	...	1225	...	...	...	...	...	...	...	1921	...	...	2137	...	2243	...	...
Vrbnica 🏛 d.	...	...	...	...	...	...	...	...	...	...	|	...	...	...	...	...	...	...	...	...	...	...	...	|	...	...
Prijepolje Teretna d.	...	0330	...	0625	...	...	...	...	1150	...	1350	...	...	...	...	...	...	...	...	...	...	...	...	0008	...	...
Priboj d.	...	0442	...	0737	...	...	...	...	1301	...	1510	...	...	1628	...	...	...	...	...	...	...	...	...	0116	...	...
Štrpci 🏛 d.	...	0508	...	0802	...	...	...	...	1326	...	|	...	...	|	...	...	...	...	...	...	...	...	...	|	...	...
Užice d.	0455	0646	...	0940	...	...	...	...	1520	...	1704	...	1753	1826	...	...	...	...	...	...	...	...	...	0308	...	...
Požega d.	0518	0711	...	1007	...	...	...	...	1549	...	1725	...	1821	1859	...	...	...	...	...	...	...	...	...	0330	...	...
Valjevo d.	0643	0845	...	1156	...	...	...	...	1732	...	1850	...	2007	2027	...	...	...	...	...	...	...	...	...	0455	...	...
Beograd Centar a.	0757	1026	...	1329	...	...	...	...	1904	...	2003	...	2144	2206	...	...	...	...	...	...	...	...	...	0609	...	...

B – June 16 - Sept. 17. TARA – 2 ✕ Beograd - Podgorica - Bar.
C – June 17 - Sept. 18. TARA – 2 ✕ Bar - Podgorica - Beograd.
L – LOVĆEN – 🛏 1, 2 cl., 🛏 2 cl., 2 Beograd - Podgorica - Bar and v.v.

★ – Nikšic - Podgorica: *61 km*.

1372 POŽEGA - KRALJEVO - STALAĆ

Ž

tariff km		J 2	Ⓐ			n	J 2			
0	**Požega** d.	...	...	0800	...	1310	...	...	1730	2015
45	Čačak d.	...	0530	0838	...	1348	...	...	1821	2053
83	**Kraljevo** d.	0500	0614	0922	...	1432	1520	...	1905	2137
155	Stalać a.	0742	...	...	...	...	1802	...	...	...

	Ⓐ			n	J 2				J 2
Stalać d.	...	...	...	...	1000	...	...	...	201
Kraljevo d.	0430	0620	...	1000	1243	1510	...	1730	225
Čačak d.	0514	0705	...	1045	...	1555	...	1815	...
Požega a.	...	0743	...	1123	...	1633	...	1853	...

J – To / from Jagodina (Table **1380**).

n – ①–⑤ (daily June 12 - Sept. 15).

1373 MAJDANPEK and PRAHOVO - ZAJEČAR - NIŠ

2nd class only Ž

tariff km										
0	Majdanpek d.	...	...	...	0930	...	...	1802	...	...
★	Prahovo Pristanište d.	...	...	0855	|	...	...	|	1910	...
87	**Zaječar** d.	0642	...	1115	1158	1226	...	2030	2130	...
130	Knjaževac d.	0845	...	...	...	1406	...	...	...	...
195	**Niš** a.	1024**b**	...	...	...	1545	...	...	...	...

Niš d.	...	...	...	1110**b**	...	...	...	1620	..
Knjaževac d.	...	...	...	1250	...	...	...	1800	..
Zaječar d.	0620	0638	...	1452	1520	1635	...	1939	..
Prahovo Pristanište a.	0840	|	...	...	|	1855	...	...	..
Majdanpek d.	...	0905	...	...	1747	...	...	...	..

b – By bus Niš – Matejevac and v.v. (journey time 27 minutes).

★ – Prahovo - Zaječar: *81 km*.

1375 LAPOVO and PRIŠTINA - KOSOVO POLJE - SKOPJE

2nd class only ŽS, KŽ, M

km										Ⓐ
	Beograd **1380** d.	...	...	...	...	...	...	...	...	...
0	**Lapovo** d.	...	...	...	...	0655	...	...	...	1530
28	Kragujevac d.	...	...	...	...	0727	...	...	...	1602
82	Kraljevo d.	...	...	0650	...	0926	...	1450	...	1801
163	Raška ♣ d.	...	...	0827	...	...	...	1627	...	...
180	Lešak / Leshak d.	...	...	...	...	...	...	...	...	...
210	Zvečan / Zveçan d.	...	...	...	...	...	...	...	...	...
214	Kosovska Mitrovica Sever ♣ a.	...	...	...	...	...	...	...	...	...
		891								
214	Mitrovica / Mitrovicë ♣ d.	h ❦	...	...	...	...	...	...	...	...
	Priština / Prishtinë d.	0710	0750	...	...	...	...	...	1630	...
247	**Kosovo Polje / Fushë Kosovë** ♣ d.	0722	0804	...	...	...	...	...	1641	...
*	Peć / Pejë a.	|	0953	...	...	...	...	...	1829	...
276	Uroševac / Ferizaj d.	0802	...	...	...	...	...	...	...	...
304	Deneral Janković / Hani I Elezit 🏛 a.	0900	...	...	...	...	...	...	...	...
331	**Skopje** a.	0952	...	...	...	...	...	...	...	...

					892 h ❦				
Skopje d.	...	...	...	...	1610	...	...	...	..
Deneral Janković / Hani I Elezit 🏛 d.	...	...	...	...	1735	...	...	...	..
Uroševac / Ferizaj d.	...	...	...	...	1816	...	...	...	..
Peć / Pejë d.	0532	...	1210	...	|	...	...	...	..
Kosovo Polje / Fushë Kosovë ♣ d.	0723	...	1359	...	1900	...	...	...	..
Priština / Prishtinë a.	0732	...	1410	...	1910	...	...	...	..
Mitrovica / Mitrovicë ♣ a.	...	...	...	...	...	...	...	...	..
Kosovska Mitrovica Sever ♣ d.	...	...	...	...	...	...	...	...	..
Zvečan / Zveçan d.	...	...	...	...	...	...	...	...	..
Lešak / Leshak d.	...	...	...	...	...	...	...	...	..
Raška ♣ d.	...	...	...	1246	...	...	...	...	20
Kraljevo d.	...	1125	...	1421	...	...	1935	...	22
Kragujevac d.	...	1324	...	...	...	...	2134	...	..
Lapovo a.	...	1355	...	...	...	...	2205	...	..
Beograd **1380** a.	...	...	...	...	...	...	...	...	..

h – A change of train maybe necessary at Deneral Janković / Hani I Elezit (connection between trains is guaranteed).

♣ – Currently no service Raška - Mitrovica / Mitrovicë - Kosovo Polje / Fushë Kosovë and v

❦ – Currently suspended.

* – Kosovo Polje - Peć: *82 km*.

1377 MINOR BORDER CROSSINGS

2nd class only ŽS, MÁ

SUBOTICA - SZEGED *Service suspended*

km				
0	Subotica d.		Szeged d.	
24	Horgoš 🏛 d.		Röszke 🏛 d.	
31	Röszke 🏛 a.		Horgoš 🏛 d.	
43	Szeged a.		Subotica a.	

KIKINDA - JIMBOLIA - TIMISOARA *Service run by Regio Călăto*

km							
0	Kikinda d.	...	...	...	...	...	
19	Jimbolia 🏛 § d.	0447	0544	0935	1304	1517	1753
58	Timisoara § a.	0543	0640	1031	1400	1612	1849

Timisoara § d.	0644	0727	1412	1635	1950	23
Jimbolia 🏛 § d.	0740	0822	1507	1638	2046	00
Kikinda a.	...	...	...	...	...	..

§ – East European time, one hour ahead of Central European time.

BEOGRAD - NIŠ - SOFIA, SKOPJE and THESSALONÍKI 1380

ŽS, MŽ, BDŽ

No service currently running Niš - Preševo and v.v. due to engineering work.

km		611	641		601			791		643	651	631	7991		1491		645						793	1335		
		2		⚒	2		2⚒	≋	K2	2	2	2Ⓡ	2		B≋	2	Ⓡ		2	2⚒	2	K2	≋	H≋	⑧	
0	**Beograd** Centar d.	...	...	...	...	0352	...	0605	...	...	...	...	...	0725	0915	...	...	1305	...	...	1510	...	1755	1825	2010	...
10	Lapovo d.	...	...	0305	...	0626	...	0805	...	...	...	...	...	0955	1101	...	...	1533	...	...	1747	...	2005	2028	2236	...
35	Jagodina d.	...	...	0350	...	0711	...	0845	0900	...	...	...	...	1039	1141	...	...	1618	...	...	1832	1910	2045	2108	...	...
55	Paraćin d.	...	...	0408	...	0728	...	0901	0919	...	...	...	...	1058	1157	...	...	1636	...	...	1850	1930	2101	2124	...	...
76	Stalać d.	...	...	0443	...	0804	...	0936	1000	...	...	...	...	1134	1232	...	...	1712	...	...	1925	2010	2136	2159	...	...
44	**Niš** a.	...	...	0642	...	0949	...	1048	...	...	...	...	...	1322	1341	...	...	1859	...	...	2110	...	2248	2308	...	...
44	**Niš** d.	...	...	...	...	...	...	...	...	...	...	...	...	...	1407	...	...	...	...	...	...	...	...	2318	...	...
	Dimitrovgrad 🏛 d.	...	...	...	...	...	...	...	...	...	...	...	1140	...	1718	...	...	...	...	...	...	...	...	|	...	...
	Dragoman 🏛 § d.	...	...	...	...	...	...	...	...	...	...	...	1400	...	1949	...	...	...	...	...	...	...	...	|	...	...
	Sofia § a.	...	...	...	...	...	...	...	...	...	...	...	1500	...	2037	...	...	...	...	...	...	...	...	|	...	...
88	Leskovac d.	...	...	...	...	...	...	...	...	...	...	...	...	...	...	...	...	...	...	...	...	...	...	0003	...	...
92	Preševo 🏛 d.	...	...	...	...	...	...	...	...	...	...	...	...	...	...	...	...	...	...	...	...	...	...	0307	...	...
01	Tabanovci 🏛 d.	0515	...	...	0800	...	...	...	...	...	...	...	...	...	...	1740	...	...	2115	...	...	...	...	0345	...	...
49	**Skopje** a.	0609	...	...	0854	...	...	...	...	...	...	...	...	...	...	1834	...	...	2209	...	...	...	...	0425	...	...
49	**Skopje** **1385** d.	0623	0653	...	0915	...	1320	...	...	1430	1523	1655	...	...	...	...	2005	...	...	2240	...	...	...	0445	...	...
13	Veles **1385** d.	0725	0749	...	1007	...	1412	...	...	1525	1621	1747	...	...	...	...	2057	...	...	2332	...	...	...	0526	...	...
26	Gevgelija a.	0911	...	...	...	...	...	...	...	...	...	1938	...	...	...	...	...	...	...	...	...	...	...	0650	...	...
26	Gevgelija 🏛 d.	...	...	...	...	...	...	...	...	...	...	...	...	...	...	...	...	...	...	...	...	...	...	0723	...	...
29	Idoméni 🏛 § a.	...	...	...	...	...	...	...	...	...	...	...	...	...	...	...	...	...	...	...	...	...	...	0828	...	...
29	Idoméni § d.	...	...	...	...	...	...	...	...	...	...	...	...	...	...	...	...	...	...	...	...	...	...	0856	...	...
05	**Thessaloníki** § a.	...	...	...	...	...	...	...	...	...	...	...	...	...	...	...	...	...	...	...	...	...	...	1033	...	...

km				790				600	640	630	650		1490	7990					792	642			632		644	1334
		⚒		≋	K2		2	2	2	2	2		B≋	2	2		2⚒	K2	≋	2	2	⑧	2	2	2	H≋
	Thessaloníki § d.	...	...	...	...	...	...	...	...	...	...	...	...	...	...	...	...	...	...	...	...	...	...	...	...	1851
	Idoméni § a.	...	...	...	...	...	...	...	...	...	...	...	...	...	...	...	...	...	...	...	...	...	...	...	...	1936
	Idoméni 🏛 § d.	...	...	...	...	...	...	...	...	...	...	...	...	...	...	...	...	...	...	...	...	...	...	...	...	2011
	Gevgelija 🏛 a.	...	...	...	...	...	...	...	...	...	...	...	...	...	...	...	...	...	...	...	...	...	...	...	...	1916
	Gevgelija d.	...	...	...	...	...	...	...	...	0440	...	...	...	...	...	...	...	...	...	...	...	...	1655	...	...	1948
	Veles **1385** d.	...	...	...	...	...	...	0503	0546	0627	0726	...	...	...	1210	...	1424	...	...	1524	...	...	1840	...	2058	2113
	Skopje **1385** a.	...	...	...	...	...	...	0555	0637	0719	0822	...	...	...	1302	...	1520	...	...	1615	...	...	1931	...	2149	2154
	Skopje d.	...	...	...	...	...	0401	0645	...	...	...	...	...	...	...	...	...	...	...	...	1625	...	...	2000	...	2219
	Tabanovci 🏛 d.	...	...	...	...	...	0455	0739	...	...	...	...	...	...	...	...	...	...	...	...	1719	...	...	2054	...	2329
	Preševo 🏛 d.	...	...	...	...	...	...	...	...	...	...	...	...	...	...	...	...	...	...	...	...	...	...	...	...	0018
	Leskovac d.	...	...	...	...	...	...	...	...	...	...	...	...	...	...	...	...	...	...	...	...	...	...	...	...	0239
0	**Sofia** § d.	...	...	...	...	...	...	...	...	...	...	...	0915	0920	...	...	...	...	...	...	...	...	...	...	...	|
42	Dragoman 🏛 § d.	...	...	...	...	...	...	...	...	...	...	...	1005	1025	...	...	...	...	...	...	...	...	...	...	...	|
63	Dimitrovgrad 🏛 d.	...	...	...	...	...	...	...	...	...	...	...	1100	1030	...	...	...	...	...	...	...	...	...	...	...	|
61	**Niš** a.	...	...	...	...	...	...	...	...	...	...	...	1336	...	...	...	...	...	...	...	...	...	...	...	...	0323
	Niš d.	...	0310	0530	...	0730	...	...	...	...	...	1225	1410	...	...	1546	...	...	1720	...	...	1955	...	...	...	0337
	Stalać d.	...	0456	0646	0744	0917	...	...	...	...	...	1412	1520	...	...	1737	...	1804	1836	...	...	2143	...	...	...	0447
	Paraćin d.	...	0519	0707	0813	0943	...	...	...	...	...	1438	1541	...	...	1802	...	1833	1857	...	...	2209	...	...	...	0508
	Jagodina d.	...	0536	0723	0830	1000	...	...	...	...	...	1455	1557	...	...	1819	...	1854	1913	...	...	2226	...	...	...	0524
	Lapovo d.	0350	0623	0757	...	1047	...	...	...	...	...	1542	1634	...	...	1905	...	...	1947	...	...	2307	...	...	...	0606
	Beograd Centar a.	0604	0850	1002	...	1310	...	...	...	...	...	1810	1829	...	...	2123	...	...	2151	...	...	...	...	...	...	0813

– BALKAN – (2) Beograd - Niš - Sofia and v.v.
– HELLAS – 🛏 2 cl., (2) Beograd - Skopje - Gevgelija - Thessaloniki and v.v.
– To/from Kraljevo (Table **1372**).

§ – East European time.
≋ – Service currently suspended.

BRANCH LINES in North Macedonia 1385

MŽ 2nd class only

SKOPJE - KOČANI and BITOLA

km		641		643	651		645
0	Skopje **1380** d.	0653	...	1430	1523	...	2005
64	Veles **1380** d.	0751	...	1525	1621	...	2100
★	Kočani a.	|	...	|	1813	...	|
34	Prilep d.	0936	...	1710	...	...	2245
78	Bitola a.	1020	...	1754	...	...	2329

	640	650		642		644
Bitola d.	0315	...	...	1250	...	1826
Prilep d.	0401	...	...	1336	...	1912
Kočani d.	|	0526	...	|	...	|
Veles **1380** d.	0546	0726	...	1524	...	2058
Skopje **1380** a.	0637	0822	...	1615	...	2149

★ – Veles - Kočani: *110 km.*

SKOPJE - KIČEVO

km				660
0	Skopje d.	...	...	1645
56	Tetovo d.	...	...	1748
79	Gostivar d.	...	...	1810
116	Kičevo a.	...	...	1849

	661		
Kičevo d.	0530	...	...
Gostivar d.	0607	...	...
Tetovo d.	0630	...	...
Skopje a.	0732	...	...

ALBANIA

SEE MAP PAGE 505

Operator: Hekurudha Shqiptarë (HSH). www.hsh.com.al
Services: Trains convey one class of accommodation only. Tickets are not sold in advance, only for the next available departure.
Timings: **Timings have been compiled from the latest information received and are currently valid until June 10, 2023.**
Readers should be aware that timetable amendments usually come into effect at short notice.
Trains can also be cancelled at short notice; readers are advised to check information locally before travelling.
Security: Most visits to Albania are reported to be trouble free, but travellers are advised to avoid the north-east of the country.

ALBANIAN RAILWAYS 1390

HSH One class only

Kashar - central Tiranë and v.v. is operated by 🚐 *(approximately 7.5 km)*

km	km					⑥⑦					
	0	**Shkodër** d.	...	...	...	...	...	...	...	...	...
	84	Vorë d.	...	...	...	...	...	...	...	...	...
	98	**Tiranë** 🚐 d.	...	...	...	...	...	...	...	...	...
0	—	Kashar 🚐 d.	...	...	...	...	...	...	...	...	...
10		Vorë d.	...	...	...	...	...	...	...	...	...
32		**Durrës** a.	...	...	...	...	...	...	...	...	...
—	0	**Durrës** d.	...	...	...	1400	...	...	...	...	...
0	35	Rrogozhinë d.	...	...	...	1518	...	...	...	...	...
	76	Elbasan a.	...	...	...	1653	...	...	...	...	...
	100	**Librazhd** a.	...	...	...	...	...	...	...	...	...
16		Lushnjë a.	...	...	...	...	...	...	...	...	...
47		Fier a.	...	...	...	...	...	...	...	...	...
81		**Vlorë** a.	...	...	...	...	...	...	...	...	...

		⑥⑦							
Vlorë d.	...	...	...	...	...	...	...	...	...
Fier d.	...	...	...	...	...	...	...	...	...
Lushnjë d.	...	...	...	...	...	...	...	...	...
Librazhd d.	...	...	...	...	...	...	...	...	...
Elbasan d.	...	0630	...	...	...	...	...	...	...
Rrogozhinë d.	...	0806	...	...	...	...	...	...	...
Durrës a.	...	0923	...	...	...	...	...	...	...
Durrës d.	...	...	...	...	...	...	...	...	...
Vorë d.	...	...	...	...	...	...	...	...	...
Kashar 🚐 a.	...	...	...	...	...	...	...	...	...
Tiranë 🚐 a.	...	...	...	...	...	...	...	...	...
Vorë d.	...	...	...	...	...	...	...	...	...
Shkodër a.	...	...	...	...	...	...	...	...	...

GREECE

SEE MAP PAGE 505

Operator: Hellenic Train S.A.: www.hellenictrain.gr

Services: All trains convey first and second class seating except where shown otherwise in footnotes or by '2' in the train column, or where the footnote shows sleeping and/or couchette cars only. Descriptions of sleeping (🛏) and couchette (▬) cars appear on page 10. Services that convey catering may vary from day to day.

Timings: Timings have been compiled from the latest available information. Readers should be aware that timetable amendments may come into effect at short notice, and are advised to check information locally before travelling.

Tickets: Reservation of seats is possible (and recommended) on most express trains. *Icity and IcityE* trains carry a supplement which varies depending upon distance travelled. Break of journey is only permitted when tickets are so endorsed before travel with the station quoted.

1400 ATHÍNA - LÁRISA - THESSALONÍKI HT

km		*ICE* 50		590	*IC* 882			*IC* 52	1884		*IC* 54			*IC* 56	886		*IC* 58		*ICE* 60	888	2596		*IC* 62		
		✕⁄			🍷			✕⁄	2		✕⁄			✕⁄	2		✕⁄		✕⁄	2			✕⁄		
0	**Athína** Lárisa **1420/30/40** d.	0722	...	...	0757	...	...	0922	...	...	1122	...	...	1322	...	...	1522	...	1722	...	...	...	1922	...	...
61	Inói **1420** d.	ǀ	...	...	0850	...	...	1010	...	...	1210	...	...	1410	...	...	1610	...	ǀ	...	...	...	2010	...	...
89	Thíva d.	ǀ	...	...	0907	...	...	1024	...	...	1224	...	...	1424	...	...	1624	...	ǀ	...	...	...	2024	...	...
129	Levadiá d.	ǀ	...	...	0930	...	...	1042	...	...	1242	...	...	1442	...	...	1642	...	ǀ	...	...	...	2042	...	...
154	Tithoréa d.	ǀ	...	...	0945	...	...	1055	...	...	1255	...	...	1455	...	...	1655	...	ǀ	...	...	...	2055	...	...
210	Lianokládi d.	ǀ	...	...	1012	1058	...	1118	...	...	1318	1438	...	1518	...	...	1718	...	ǀ	...	...	...	2118	...	...
	Lamia d.	ǀ	...	...	ǀ	1109	...	ǀ	...	...	ǀ	1450	...	ǀ	...	...	ǀ	...	ǀ	...	...	...	ǀ	...	...
	Stilída a.	ǀ	...	...	ǀ	1145	...	ǀ	...	...	ǀ	1513	...	ǀ	...	...	ǀ	...	ǀ	...	...	...	ǀ	...	...
276	Domokos d.	ǀ	...	...	1051	...	...	ǀ	...	...	ǀ	...	...	ǀ	...	...	ǀ	...	ǀ	...	...	...	ǀ	...	...
291	Paleofársalos d.	ǀ	...	1037	1102	...	...	1151	1205	...	1351	...	...	1551	1605	...	1751	...	ǀ	1944	2020	...	2151	...	...
	Kalambáka **1408** a.	ǀ	...	ǀ	1203	...	...	ǀ	1303	...	ǀ	...	...	ǀ	1703	...	ǀ	...	ǀ	2042	ǀ	...	ǀ	...	...
333	**Lárisa** ▲ d.	1000	...	1100	...	...	...	1211	...	...	1411	...	...	1611	...	...	1811	...	2002	...	2042	...	2211	...	...
417	Kateríni ▲ d.	ǀ	...	1146	...	...	...	1253	...	...	1453	...	...	1653	...	...	1853	...	ǀ	...	2130	...	2253	...	...
465	Platí **1410** ▲ d.	ǀ	...	1209	...	...	...	1313	...	...	1513	...	...	1713	...	...	1913	...	ǀ	...	2154	...	2312	...	...
502	**Thessaloníki** **1410** ▲ a.	1120	...	1236	...	...	...	1335	...	...	1535	...	...	1735	...	...	1935	...	2121	...	2219	...	2335	...	...

km		1521		*ICE* 51		1595	883	*IC* 53		*IC* 55		1883	*IC* 57		*IC* 59			591	*ICE* 61		*IC* 887	595		*IC* 63	
				🍷⁄			2	✕⁄		✕⁄			✕⁄		✕⁄				✕⁄		🍷			✕⁄	
	Thessaloníki **1410** ▲ d.	...	...	0708	...	0815	...	0856	...	1056	...	...	1256	...	1456	...	...	1612	1708	...	...	1740	...	1901	...
	Platí **1410** ▲ d.	...	...	ǀ	...	0841	...	0917	...	1117	...	...	1317	...	1517	...	...	1639	ǀ	...	...	1807	...	1922	...
	Kateríni ▲ d.	...	...	ǀ	...	0905	...	0937	...	1137	...	...	1337	...	1537	...	...	1703	ǀ	...	...	1830	...	1942	...
	Lárisa ▲ d.	...	...	0827	...	0951	...	1017	...	1217	...	...	1417	...	1617	...	...	1748	1828	...	...	1916	...	2022	...
	Kalambáka **1408** d.	...	...	ǀ	...	ǀ	0928	ǀ	...	ǀ	...	1322	ǀ	...	ǀ	...	...	ǀ	ǀ	...	1822	ǀ	...	ǀ	...
	Paleofársalos d.	...	...	ǀ	...	1011	1025	1036	...	1236	...	1421	1436	...	1636	...	...	1808	ǀ	...	1923	1936	...	2041	...
	Domokos d.	...	...	ǀ	...	...	...	ǀ	...	ǀ	...	...	ǀ	...	ǀ	...	...	...	ǀ	...	1932	...	...	ǀ	...
0	Stilída d.	...	...	ǀ	0745	...	...	ǀ	...	ǀ	...	...	ǀ	...	ǀ	...	1635	...	ǀ	...	ǀ	...	...	ǀ	...
17	Lamia d.	...	...	ǀ	0821	...	...	ǀ	...	ǀ	...	...	ǀ	...	ǀ	...	1659	...	ǀ	...	ǀ	...	...	ǀ	...
23	Lianokládi d.	0657	...	ǀ	0832	...	...	1107	...	1307	...	...	1507	...	1707	...	1710	...	ǀ	...	2015	...	...	2113	...
	Tithoréa d.	0802	...	ǀ	...	...	...	1131	...	1331	...	...	1531	...	1731	...	...	...	ǀ	...	2044	...	...	2136	...
	Levadiá d.	0823	...	ǀ	...	...	...	1142	...	1342	...	...	1542	...	1742	...	...	...	ǀ	...	2057	...	...	2148	...
	Thíva d.	0852	...	ǀ	...	...	...	1200	...	1400	...	...	1600	...	1800	...	...	...	ǀ	...	2121	...	...	2206	...
	Inói **1420** d.	0909	...	ǀ	...	...	...	1214	...	1414	...	...	1614	...	1814	...	...	...	ǀ	...	2137	...	...	2219	...
	Athína Lárisa **1420/30/40** a.	0958	...	1103	...	...	...	1303	...	1503	...	...	1703	...	1903	...	...	...	2104	...	2226	...	...	2306	...

▲ – Local service Thessaloníki - Litóhoro - Lárisa and v.v. :

Thessaloníki d.	0530	0615	1008	1135	1340	1540	1740	2036	2223
Platí d.	0556	0641	1034	1201	1406	1606	1807	2102	2249
Kateríni d.	0620	0705	1058	1225	1430	1630	1830	2126	2313
Litóhoro ⛰ d.	0628	0713	1106	1233	1438	1638	1839	2134	2321
Lárisa a.	0705	0749	1143	1310	1515	1715	1915	2211	2358

Lárisa d.	0625	0715	0915	1250	1520	1650	1854	2042	2254
Litóhoro ⛰ d.	0705	0755	0954	1330	1600	1730	1933	2122	2334
Kateríni d.	0713	0803	1002	1338	1608	1738	1942	2130	2342
Platí d.	0737	0827	1026	1402	1632	1803	2005	2154	0006
Thessaloníki a.	0802	0852	1052	1427	1657	1827	2031	2219	0031

❦ – Service currently suspended.

⁄ – 🄡 with supplement payable. *Icity and IcityE* train.

⛰ – Station for Mount Ólimbos.

1405 THESSALONÍKI - ALEXANDRÚPOLI - DÍKAIA HT

km		670	3634	672	674	1682	*IC* 1676	*IC* 3678	*IC* 1632	602
0	**Thessaloníki** d.	...	0558	...	...	...	...	...	1605	...
42	Kilkís d.	...	0630	...	...	...	...	...	1639	...
97	Rodópolis d.	...	0721	...	...	...	...	...	1732	...
130	Strimón d.	...	0811	...	...	...	...	...	1822	...
162	Sérres d.	...	0841	...	...	...	...	...	1855	...
232	Dráma d.	0530	...	...	...	...	...	...	2017	2030
327	Xánthi d.	0740	...	0750	...	...	1040	...	...	2307
374	Komotiní d.	...	...	0930	1136	...	1713	2020	...	2350
443	**Alexandrúpoli Port** a.	...	...	1105	1311	...	1817	2117	...	0037
443	**Alexandrúpoli Port** d.	...	...	...	...	1510	...	...	...	...
556	Píthio d.	...	...	...	...	1645	...	...	...	...
574	Orestiáda d.	...	...	...	...	1703	...	...	...	...
611	**Díkaia** a.	...	...	...	...	1733	...	...	...	...

	IC 1631	671	679	673	3635	*IC* 1675	*IC* 3677	1683	
Díkaia d.	...	...	...	...	...	...	...	1808	...
Orestiáda d.	...	...	...	...	...	...	...	1839	...
Píthio d.	...	...	...	...	...	...	...	1856	...
Alexandrúpoli Port d.	...	...	...	...	...	...	...	2033	...
Alexandrúpoli Port d.	...	0600	...	1000	...	1454	1856	...	...
Komotiní d.	...	0735	...	1135	...	1559	2000	...	...
Xánthi d.	...	0915	0930	...	...	1631	...	...	...
Dráma d.	0615	...	1130		...	...	...	...	...
Sérres d.	0738	...	...	...	1140	...	...	...	...
Strimón d.	0810	...	...	...	1211	...	...	...	...
Rodópolis d.	0901	...	...	...	1300	...	...	...	...
Kilkís d.	0954	...	...	...	1343	...	...	...	...
Thessaloníki a.	1026	...	...	...	1421	...	...	...	...

⁄ – 🄡 with supplement payable. *Icity* train.

⛰ – Station for Mount Ólimbos.

1408 LÁRISA - PALEOFÁRSALOS - KALAMBÁKA HT

km		1880		*IC* 882	1884		886		888
		2		🍷	2		2		2
	Thessaloníki **1400** d.	...	...	...	...	...	...	...	...
	Athína **1400** d.	...	...	0757	...	...	...	...	...
	Lárisa **1400** d.	...	...	ǀ	...	...	...	...	...
0	Paleofársalos **1400** d.	0825	...	1102	1205	...	1605	...	1944
31	Kardítsa d.	0844	...	1122	1226	...	1626	...	2005
60	Tríkala d.	0903	...	1144	1247	...	1647	...	2026
82	**Kalambáka** ⊡ a.	0919	...	1203	1303	...	1703	...	2042

	883		1883		1885	*IC* 887		1889
	2		2		2	🍷		2
Kalambáka ⊡ d.	0928	...	1322	...	1720	1822	...	2046
Tríkala d.	0944	...	1340	...	1738	1840	...	2104
Kardítsa d.	1005	...	1401	...	1759	1902	...	2125
Paleofársalos **1400** a.	1025	...	1421	...	1819	1922	...	2145
Lárisa **1400** a.	...	...	...	...	...	ǀ	...	...
Athína **1400** a.	...	...	...	...	...	2226	...	...
Thessaloníki **1400** a.	...	...	...	...	...	...	...	...

⊡ – An infrequent bus service operates Kalambáka - Igumenítsa and v.v. (approximately *250 km*).

THESSALONÍKI - ÉDESSA - FLÓRINA — 1410

km		81		713		715		735			
		❊		2		2		❊			
0	**Thessaloníki** .... **1400** d.	0646	...	1305	...	1845	...	2200	...	...	...
38	Platí .... **1400** d.	0714	...	1334	...	1919	...	2228	...	...	...
69	Véria .... d.	0736	...	1402	...	1948	...	2257	...	...	...
97	Skídra .... d.	0756	...	1425	...	2010	...	2320	...	...	...
112	**Édessa** .... d.	0812	...	1440	...	2025	...	2333	...	...	...
162	Amíndeo .... d.	0855	...	1524	...	2109	...	...	...	...	...
196	**Flórina** .... a.	0924	...	1553	...	2139	...	...	...	...	...

	710		84		714		734			
			❊				❊			
Flórina .... d.	0645	...	1020	...	1635	...	...	...	...	...
Amíndeo .... d.	0717	...	1051	...	1717	...	...	...	...	...
Édessa .... d.	0801	...	1135	...	1751	...	2040	...	...	...
Skídra .... d.	0815	...	1149	...	1805	...	2055	...	...	...
Véria .... d.	0838	...	1209	...	1828	...	2117	...	...	...
Platí .... **1400** d.	0907	...	1238	...	1857	...	2146	...	...	...
Thessaloníki ..... **1400** a.	0934	...	1306	...	1924	...	2214	...	...	...

❊ – Service currently suspended.

LÁRISA - VÓLOS — 1415

km													
0	Lárisa .... d.	0620	...	0827	...	1022	...	1420	...	1620	1820	...	2230
61	Vólos .... a.	0712	...	0919	...	1114	...	1512	...	1712	1912	...	2322

Vólos .... d.	0430	...	0717	...	0923	...	1315	...	1516	1716	...	2110
Lárisa .... a.	0521	...	0809	...	1015	...	1407	...	1608	1808	...	2202

PIREÁS - ATHÍNA - HALKÍDA — 1420

km				Ⓐ		❖			❖		Ⓐ												
0	**Pireás** .... **1430 1440** d.	...	...	...	0615	...	and at	1415	...	1515	...	1615	...	1715	1815	...	1915	2017	...	2117	...	2217	...
10	**Athína** Lárisa ▲ **1400/30/40** d.	...	0452	0552	0634	0652	the same	1434	1452	1634	1552	1634	1652	1734	1834	1852	1934	2034	2052	2134	2152	2234	...
17	SKA (Acharnon) .... d.	...	0505	0602	...	0702	minutes	...	1502	...	1602	...	1702	...	...	1902	...	...	2102	...	2203	...	...
71	Inói .... **1400** d.	0450	0548	0648	...	0748	past each	...	1548	...	1648	...	1748	...	...	1947	...	...	2149	...	2249	...	...
94	**Halkída** .... a.	0509	0610	0710	...	0810	hour until	...	1610	...	1710	...	1810	...	...	2010	...	...	2210	...	2310	...	...

						Ⓐ		❖			❖		Ⓐ										
Halkída .... d.	...	0515	...	0615	...	0715	...	0815	and at	...	1615	...	1716	...	1816	...	...	2015	...	2224	2316	...	...
Inói .... **1400** d.	...	0538	...	0638	...	0738	...	0838	the same	...	1638	...	1738	...	1838	...	...	2038	...	2247	2335	...	...
SKA (Acharnon) .... d.	...	0623	...	0723	...	0823	...	0923	minutes	...	1723	...	1824	...	1924	...	...	2123	...	2332	...	...	...
Athína Lárisa . ▲ **1400/30/40** d.	0623	0648	0723	0748	0822	0848	0923	0948	past each	1723	1748	1822	1848	1920	1948	2022	2119	2148	2219	2341	...	...	...
Pireás .... **1430 1440** a.	0639	...	0739	...	0839	...	0839	...	hour until	1739	...	1839	...	1937	...	2039	2137	...	2237	...	...	...	...

❖ – Every two hours.

▲ – See below Table **1440** for summary of Metro services.

PIREÁS - ATHÍNA - ATHÍNA AIRPORT ✈ — 1430

km									
0	**Pireás** .... **1420 1440** d.	...	0445	0545	0645	and at	2045	...	...
10	**Athína** Lárisa ▲ **1400/20/40** d.	0416	0505	0605	0705	the same	2105	...	...
15	Káto Acharnai .... **1440** d.	0427	0515	0615	0715	minutes	2115	...	...
21	Neratziótissa .... ▲ d.	0436	0524	0624	0724	past each	2124	...	...
46	**Athína Airport** ✈ .... ▲ a.	0500	0548	0648	0748	hour until	2148	...	...

Athína Airport ✈ .... ▲ d.	0607	0707	and at	2207	2308	...	...	...
Neratziótissa .... ▲ d.	0632	0732	the same	2232	2332	...	...	...
Káto Acharnai .... **1440** d.	0640	0740	minutes	2240	2340	...	...	...
Athína Lárisa ▲ **1400/20/40** d.	0652	0752	past each	2252	2353	...	...	...
Pireás .... **1420 1440** a.	0710	0810	hour until	2310	...	...	...	...

▲ – See below Table **1440** for summary of Metro services.

PIREÁS - ATHÍNA - KÓRINTHOS - KIÁTO — 1440

km									
0	**Pireás** .... **1420 1430** d.	...	0615	and at	2117	2217	...	...	...
10	**Athína** Lárisa ▲ **1400/20/30** d.	0530	0635	the same	2136	2236	...	...	...
15	Káto Acharnai .... **1430** d.	0541	0645	minutes	2144	2244	...	...	...
90	**Kórinthos** .... d.	0637	0741	past each	2239	2339	...	...	...
111	**Kiáto 1450** .... a.	0652	0755	hour until	2255	2355	...	...	...

Kiáto 1450 .... d.	0456	0556	0656	0759	and at	2059	2159	...
Kórinthos .... d.	0512	0612	0712	0815	the same	2114	2214	...
Káto Acharnai .... **1430** d.	0609	0709	0809	0909	minutes	2209	2308	...
Athína Lárisa▲**1400/20/30** a.	0620	0720	0820	0920	past each	2219	2317	...
Pireás .... **1420 1430** a.	0639	0739	0839	0937	hour until	2237	...	...

▲ – Frequent Metro services operate as follows:
Line 1 (green): Pireás - Monastiraki - Omónia - Attiki - Neratziótissa - Kifissia.
Line 2 (red): Elliniko - Syntagma - Omónia - Athína Lárisa (for **Athína** mainline station) - Attiki - Anthoupoli.
Line 3 (blue): Agia Marina - Monastiraki - Syntagma - Athína Airport ✈.
Operators: ISAP Line 1; Attiko Metro Lines 2 and 3.

KIÁTO - PÁTRA 🚌 services — 1450

	🚌	🚌	🚌	🚌	🚌	🚌	🚌	🚌Ⓑ	🚌	🚌
Kiáto 1440 .... d.	0805	1005	1205	1405	1605	1705	1805	1905	2005	2105
Diakoftó **1455** .... d.	|	|	|	|	1650	|	1850	|	|	|
Pátra .... a.	0930	1130	1330	1530	1740	1830	1940	2040	2130	2230

	🚌	🚌	🚌	🚌	🚌	🚌	🚌	🚌	🚌	🚌
Pátra .... d.	0625	0815	1015	1225	1425	1525	1625	1725	1825	1925
Diakoftó **1455** .... d.	|	0905	1105	|	|	|	|	|	|	|
Kiáto 1440 .... a.	0750	0950	1150	1350	1550	1650	1750	1850	1950	2050

PELOPÓNNISOS narrow-gauge branches — 1455

DIAKOFTÓ – KALÁVRITA *Rack railway*

km						
0	Diakoftó .... d.	0952	...	1217	...	1507
23	Kalávrita .... a.	1059	...	1324	...	1618

Kalávrita .... d.	1104	...	1337	...	1625
Diakoftó .... a.	1211	...	1448	...	1733

KATÁKOLO – PÍRGOS – OLIMBÍA

km		⚒		Ⓐ		⚒		Ⓐ			
0	**Katákolo** ..... d.	...	...	0840	...	...	...	1410	...	...	...
12	Pírgos .... d.	0700	...	0903	...	1235	...	1435	...	...	...
33	**Olimbía** .... a.	0729	...	0932	...	1304	...	...	...	...	...

	Ⓐ		⚒		Ⓐ					
Olimbía .... d.	0735	...	0940	...	1310	...	...	...	...	...
Pírgos .... d.	0805	...	1009	...	1339	...	...	...	...	...
Katákolo .... a.	0827	...	...	...	1402	...	...	...	...	...

🚌 INTERNATIONAL BUS SERVICES — 1460

A number of operators run long-distance 🚌 services to and from Greece, and selected services are listed below. Details should be checked with the relevant operator before travel. Rail tickets and passes are not valid. Further details about travelling to Greece by bus can be found on www.europebyrail.eu

ATHÍNA - ISTANBUL: Depart Athína 1700. Depart Istanbul 1800. Journey 16 hours. Operator: Metro www.metroturizm.com.tr

THESSALONIKI - ISTANBUL: Depart Thessaloniki 1000. Depart Istanbul (Esenler Otogari) 0530. Journey 10 hours. Operator: Ozikizler Turizm www.ozikizlerturizm.com
Depart Thessaloniki 1000, 2200, 2330. Depart Istanbul 1000, 1800, 2200. Journey 10 - 11 hours. Operator: Metro www.metroturizm.com.tr

THESSALONIKI - SKOPJE: Depart Thessaloniki 0830 or 1530. Depart Skopje 1530. Journey 3½ - 5½ hours. Not daily. Operator: Simeonidis Tours www.simeonidistours.gr

THESSALONIKI - SOFIA: Coach services are operated by Union Ivkoni (www.union-ivkoni.com) as follows:

Thessaloniki 0930 → Sofia 1415.
Thessaloniki 1600 → Sofia 2200.

Sofia 0730 → Thessaloniki 1315.
Sofia 1630 → Thessaloniki 2215.

BULGARIA and TURKEY IN EUROPE

SEE MAP PAGE 505

Operators: Bâlgarski Dârzhavni Zheleznitsi (BDZ Passenger Services) www.bdz.bg
Türkiye Cumhuriyeti Devlet Demiryolları (TCDD) www.tcddtasimacilik.gov.tr

Services: Trains convey first- and second-class seating, except where shown otherwise in footnotes or by '2' in the train column, or where the footnote shows sleeping and / or couchette cars only. Descriptions of sleeping (🛏) and couchette (▬) cars appear on page 10. Seat reservation is possible on most long-distance trains (compulsory on express trains

Timings: BDŽ schedules valid **until December 9, 2023**. **Timetable amendments are possible at short notice, so it is advisable to confirm timings locally before travelling**. Subject to alteration on and around public holiday dates. Please refer to Tables **61**, **98** and **99** for international through cars to / from Burgas and Varna (summer only). TCDD schedules are the latest available. For services in Asian Turkey see pages 518 – 520.

1500 SOFIA - RUSE, BURGAS and VARNA

km	km			2655	8631	8601	2601	460	462	3621	2611	8651	8611	2613	3623	2615	3601	2641	8641	2663	493	9647	8657	8627	2627	3637	3687
						⚡ R	⚡ R	R	R								⚡ R	⚡ R									
			2	v	e	🍷e	e	A	C	e		e	e	e	e	e	e	G			B	L	Ze	Ze	Z	DZ	Zd
0	0	**Sofia** 1520 d.	...	...	...	0620	0705	0705	0705	0735	1010	1035	1300	1305	1335	1530	1635	1625	1625	1815	1840	2010	2120	2235	2245	2255	2340
	103	Septemvri d.	...	...	...	0819	|	|	|	|	|	1231	1517	|	|	|	|	|	1821	|	2048	|	2321	0048	|	|	|
	119	Pazardzhik d.	...	...	...	0829	|	|	|	|	|	1242	1526	|	|	|	|	|	1832	|	2100	|	2331	0100	|	|	|
	156	**Plovdiv** a.	...	...	...	0849	|	|	|	|	|	1307	1548	|	|	|	|	|	1853	|	2125	|	2354	0128	|	|	|
	156	**Plovdiv** d.	...	...	0700	0859	|	|	|	|	|	1312	1554	|	|	|	|	|	1905	|	...	|	0003	0138	|	|	|
	262	Stara Zagora d.	...	...	0857	1057	|	|	|	|	|	1509	1755	|	|	|	|	|	2055	|	...	|	0150	0344	|	|	|
	340	Jambol d.	0600	...	0954	1145	|	|	|	|	|	1555	1842	|	|	|	|	|	2145	|	...	|	0243	0433	|	|	|
		Karlovo d.	|	...	|	|	|	|	|	0947	|	|	|	|	1546	|	1843	|	...	|	...	|	|	|	|	0117	0203
		Kazanlak d.	|	...	|	|	|	|	|	1040	|	|	|	|	1640	|	1934	|	...	|	...	|	|	|	|	0214	0319
		Tulovo d.	|	...	|	|	|	|	|	1054	|	|	|	|	1654	|	1948	|	...	|	...	|	|	|	|	0245	0333
		Sliven d.	|	...	|	|	|	|	|	1206	|	|	|	|	1805	|	2056	|	...	|	...	|	|	|	|	0400	0444
	389	Karnobat 1535 d.	0642	...	1037	1217	|	|	|	1242	|	1629	1917	|	1842	|	2131	|	...	|	...	|	0317	0512	|	0442	0522
	450	**Burgas** 1535 a.	0750	...	|	1255	|	|	|	1320	|	|	1955	|	1920	|	2208	|	...	|	...	|	|	0605	|	|	0607
88		Mezdra 1520 d.	▬	0524	|	...	0838	0838	0838	...	1140	|	...	1439	...	1701	▬	1754	...	1950	...	2157	|	...	0024	|	...
194		Pleven d.	...	0701	|	...	0955	0955	0955	...	1257	|	...	1600	...	1818	...	1908	...	2110	...	2315	|	...	0143	|	...
239		Levski d.	...	0732	|	...	1021	1021	1021	...	1327	|	...	1629	...	1846	**4640**	1937	...	...	...	2344	|	...	0214	|	...
294		Gorna Orjahovica a.	...	0810	|	...	1058	1058	1058	...	1406	|	...	1705	...	1921	**T**	2014	...	...	...	0022	|	...	0255	|	...
294		Gorna Orjahovica d.	...	0830	|	...	1105	1125	1125	...	1415	|	...	1727	...	1934	1933	...	...	...	...	0031	|	...	0300	|	...
405		**Ruse** 🏛 a.	2	|	|	...	|	1320	1320	...	|	|	...	|	...	|	2132	...	...	...	...	0227	|	...	|	|	...
435		Shumen 1530/5 d.	0720	1017	|	...	1249	...	...	...	1601	|	...	1917	...	2123	...	...	...	...	...	...	|	...	0452	|	...
459		Kaspichan 1530/5 d.	0748	1039	|	...	1307	...	...	...	1619	|	...	1944	...	2141	...	...	...	...	...	...	|	...	0513	|	...
518		Poveljanovo 1530/5 d.	0900	|	1227	...	1405	...	...	...	|	|	...	|	...	|	...	...	...	...	...	...	0511	...	0613	0646	...
543	546	**Varna** 1530/5 a.	0930	1159	1251	...	1429	...	...	...	1737	1840	...	2103	...	2258	...	...	...	...	...	...	0535	...	0640	0710	...

km		2640	8640	3602	4641	2610	8610		2602	8650	2612	461	463	2614		3624	8602	2654	8632			8626	3686	3636	9646	2626	8656
		⚡ R		⚡ R					⚡ R			R	R				⚡ R										
		G	e	e	T	e	e	2		e	e	A	C		2	e	🍷e	v		2	2	Ze	Zc	DZ	N	Z	Ze
	Varna 1530/5 d.	...	...	...	...	0455	...	0600	0730	0930	1045	...	...	1345	1430	...	...	1620	1650	1725	1940	...	...	2140	...	2155	2350
	Poveljanovo 1530/5 d.	...	...	...	...	0520	...	0633	0753	|	1109	...	...	1408	1502	...	...	1645	1715	1757	2011	...	...	2239	...	2219	|
	Kaspichan 1530/5 d.	...	...	...	...	0616	...	0743	0848	|	1207	...	...	1504	1611	...	...	1747	|	1906	2119	...	...	|	...	2317	|
	Shumen 1530/5 d.	...	...	...	...	0635	...	0810	0907	|	1226	...	...	1523	1635	...	...	1807	|	1930	2145	...	...	|	...	2338	|
	Ruse 🏛 d.	...	...	...	0610	|	...	▬	|	|	|	1420	1420	|	▬	...	...	|	|	▬	...	...	...	|	2333	|	|
	Gorna Orjahovica a.	...	...	...	0812	0821	...	...	1047	|	1405	1620	1620	1705	...	...	...	1957	|	...	...	...	...	|	0130	0124	|
	Gorna Orjahovica d.	0515	...	...	...	0828	...	...	1100	|	1417	1625	1625	1713	...	...	...	2015	|	...	...	...	...	|	0149	0149	|
	Levski d.	0555	...	...	...	0905	...	...	1136	|	1458	1705	1705	1752	...	...	...	2053	|	...	...	...	...	|	0232	0232	|
	Pleven d.	0627	...	...	...	0933	...	**3622**	1203	|	1529	1734	1734	1821	...	...	...	2122	|	...	...	...	...	|	0303	0303	|
	Mezdra 1520 d.	0742	...	...	...	1044	...	e	1314	|	1648	1848	1848	1938	2	...	...	2240	|	2	...	...	...	|	0421	0421	|
0	**Burgas** 1535 d.	|	...	0535	...	|	0720	0845	|	|	|	|	|	|	1335	1445	1520	...	|	2005	...	2235	2250	|	|	|	|
61	Karnobat 1535 d.	|	...	0614	...	|	0803	0924	|	1151	|	|	|	|	1452	1524	1559	...	1912	2130	...	2324	2336	0045	|	|	0200
119	Sliven d.	|	...	0653	...	|	|	0959	|	|	|	|	|	|	|	1559	|	...	|	|	...	|	0014	0123	|	|	|
195	Tulovo d.	|	...	0757	...	|	|	1104	|	|	|	|	|	|	|	1705	|	...	|	|	...	|	0124	0245	|	|	|
210	Kazanlak d.	|	...	0812	...	|	|	1118	|	|	|	|	|	|	|	1719	|	...	|	|	...	|	0140	0259	|	|	|
269	Karlovo d.	|	...	0903	...	|	|	1213	|	|	|	|	|	|	|	1815	|	...	|	|	...	|	0254	0353	|	|	|
	Jambol d.	|	0520	|	...	|	0838	|	|	1239	|	|	|	|	1537	|	1632	...	1947	2214	...	2359	|	|	|	|	0244
	Stara Zagora d.	|	0610	|	...	|	0926	|	|	1330	|	|	|	|	1657	|	1721	...	2051	...	...	0052	|	|	|	|	0330
	Plovdiv a.	|	0801	|	...	|	1112	|	|	1535	|	|	|	|	...	|	1903	...	2233	...	...	0249	|	|	|	|	0514
	Plovdiv d.	|	0808	|	...	|	1130	|	|	1541	|	|	|	|	...	|	1906	...	...	...	...	0254	|	|	|	|	0521
	Pazardzhik d.	|	0829	|	...	|	1154	|	|	1607	|	|	|	|	...	|	1927	...	...	...	...	0320	|	|	|	|	0546
	Septemvri d.	|	0839	|	...	|	1204	|	|	1617	|	|	|	|	...	|	1938	...	...	...	...	0331	|	|	|	|	0559
418	**Sofia** 1520 a.	0913	1052	1110	...	1216	1415	1430	1443	1822	1818	2020	2020	2108	...	2031	2137	...	...	...	...	0540	0520	0638	0554	0554	0812

Other trains **SOFIA - PLOVDIV**

	1611	2640		1613			
	S	G	2	S	2	2	
Sofia d.	0825	0935	1140	1520	1715	2015	...
Septemvri d.	1038	1140	1431	1736	2000	2240	...
Pazardzhik d.	1050	1152	1447	1748	...	...	...
Plovdiv a.	1115	1215	1523	1815	...	...	...

		1622		2641	1626		1614
	2		2	G		2	S
Plovdiv d.	...	0635	1145	1325	1540	1610	1800
Pazardzhik d.	...	0700	1217	1350	1608	1645	1829
Septemvri d.	0455	0711	1300	1401	1619	1702	1841
Sofia a.	0752	0920	1537	1612	1820	1941	2100

Other local trains **GORNA ORJAHOVICA - RUSE**

	2		2		2
Gorna Orjahovica d.	0835	...	1435	...	1735
Ruse a.	1050	...	1701	...	2004

	2		2		2
Ruse d.	0753	...	1114	...	1800
Gorna Orjahovica a.	1029	...	1340	...	2034

A – June 9 - Oct. 9. To / from Bucureşti (Table **61**).
B – ISTANBUL - SOFYA EXPRESS – (12) Sofia - Svilengrad and v.v.; 🛏 and ▬ Sofia - Halkalı and v.v. (Table **1550**).
C – Until June 8.
D – Conveys 🛏 and (2) Sofia - Poveljanovo - Dobrich and v.v. (Table **1540**).
G – YANTRA – (12) Gorna Orjahovica - Sofia - Plovdiv and v.v.
L – ▬ and (2) Sofia - Ruse - Silistra (Table **1530**).
N – ▬ and (2) Silistra - Ruse - Gorna (**2626**) - Sofia.
S – To / from Svilengrad (Table **1550**).
T – To / from Stara Zagora (Table **1525**).
Z – Conveys 🛏 and (12).
c – July 1 - Sept. 10.
d – June 30 - Sept. 9.
e – Engineering work may affect this train; please enquire locally.
v – To / from Vratsa (Table **1520**).
⚡ – Express train. Higher fare payable.

1510 SEPTEMVRI - VELINGRAD - DOBRINISHTE

Narrow gauge; 2nd class only

km					🍷					
0	**Septemvri** d.	0220	...	...	0850	1050	1245	...	1628	1905
39	Velingrad d.	0352	...	...	1015	1227	1410	...	1807	2035
69	Avramovo d.	0514	...	...	1120	1340	1520	...	1915	...
115	Razlog d.	0701	0930	...	1251	...	1709	...	2053	...
119	Bansko d.	0716	0953	...	1304	...	1726	...	2104	...
125	**Dobrinishte** a.	0728	1005	...	1315	...	1738	...	2116	...

							🍷		
Dobrinishte d.	...	0625	0800	...	1025	...	...	1440	...	1815
Bansko d.	...	0640	0813	...	1038	...	...	1452	...	1829
Razlog d.	...	0658	0821	...	1047	...	...	1501	...	1840
Avramovo d.	0530	0838	...	...	1233	1400	...	1636	...	2033
Velingrad d.	0640	0943	...	...	1337	1521	...	1736	...	2149
Septemvri a.	0806	1120	...	...	1505	1650	...	1855	...	2309

1520 SOFIA - VIDIN - CRAIOVA

km			7620		7622				7624		7630	2654
		2		2		2	Ⓑ	2		2	Ⓑ	v
0	**Sofia** 1500 d.	...	0735	...	1205	...	*1440*	...	1710	...	1915	...
88	Mezdra 1500 d.	0440	|	...	1356	...	1715	...	1859	...	2119	2245
106	Vratsa d.	0458	0923	...	1411	...	1734	...	1917	...	2134	2258
145	Bojchinovci d.	0542	1001	...	1450	...	1827	...	1955	...	2211	...
182	Brusarci ⊖ d.	0630	1042	1050	1531	1545	1913	1918	2038	2050	2253	...
204	Lom ⊖ a.	|	|	1117	|	1612	|	1945	|	2117	2321	...
269	**Vidin** a.	0820	1220	...	1706	...	2055	...	2215	...	...	...

	2655	7631		7621					7623				7625
	v	⚒	2		2	2	2⚒	2		Ⓑ2	Ⓑ2	2	
Vidin d.	...	...	...	0455	...	0600	...	...	1225	...	1555	...	1730
Lom ⊖ d.	...	0450	0555	|	0715	|	1140	1330	|	1705	|	1835	|
Brusarci ⊖ d.	...	0519	0620	0629	0740	0751	1209	1355	1408	1730	1744	1900	1913
Bojchinovci d.	...	0559	...	0710	...	0830	1256	...	1452	...	1824	...	1956
Vratsa d.	0500	0641	...	0757	...	0920	1339	...	1532	...	1909	...	2037
Mezdra 1500 a.	0514	0656	...	0811	...	0937	1355	...	|	...	1927	...	|
Sofia 1500 a.	...	0854	...	1000	...	*1202*	...	...	1720	...	...	...	2222

km			⚒		
	Vidin 🏛 d.	...	...	...	1245
0	**Calafat** d.	0315	0607	...	|
107	**Craiova** a.	0625	0925	...	1551

km					Ⓑ
0	**Craiova** d.	0815	...	1640	1925
	Calafat a.	|	...	1959	2235
119	**Vidin** 🏛 a.	1123	...	...	...

v – To / from Varna (Table **1500**).
⊖ – Other services Brusarci - Lom and v.v.: **From Brusarci** at 0633, 0755, 0916, 1220 Ⓑ, 1413 and 1750 Ⓑ. **From Lom** at 0840, 0956, 1500 and 2005.

RUSE - STARA ZAGORA - DIMITROVGRAD - MOMCHILGRAD - PODKOVA 1525

km			4641					465		4657
		2		2	2	2		B2	2	
0	**Ruse** 1500 d.	...	0610	...	...	...	...	...	1800	2220
111	**Gorna Orjahovica** 1500 d.	0510	0832	...	1130	1425	...	1725	2040	0032
125	Veliko Târnovo d.	0530	0849	...	1151	1446	...	1744	2101	0048
226	Tulovo a.	0750	1112	...	1419	1713	...	1954	...	0240
226	Tulovo d.	0805	1113	...	1420	1714	...	1955	...	0241
253	Stara Zagora d.	0835	1140	1315	1450	1743	...	2030	...	0340
310	**Dimitrovgrad** a.	...	...	1433	...	...	...	2200	...	0450

	4656		464					4640	
		2	B2	2	2	2			2
Dimitrovgrad d.	0030	...	0600	...	0925	...	...	...	...
Stara Zagora d.	0203	...	0713	1019	1055	1310	...	1620	1905
Tulovo a.	0232	...	0739	1048	...	1341	...	1647	1935
Tulovo d.	0234	...	0740	1105	...	1351	...	1705	2000
Veliko Târnovo d.	0429	0656	1014	1322	...	1617	...	1912	2235
Gorna Orjahovica 1500 a.	0445	0717	1035	1341	...	1638	...	1929	2255
Ruse 1500 a.	0700	...	...	...	...	...	...	2137	...

km		2	2	2	2	
0	**Dimitrovgrad** d.	0505	...	...	1450	...
23	Haskovo d.	0532	...	...	1518	...
87	Kârdzhali d.	0712	0730	1310	1728	...
101	**Momchilgrad** d.	...	0751	1331	1750	...
119	**Podkova** a.	...	0815	1355	1815	...

	2	2	2	2		
Podkova d.	0615	...	0820	1410	...	...
Momchilgrad d.	0639	...	0844	1433	1700	...
Kârdzhali d.	0658	0715	0903	...	1730	...
Haskovo d.	...	0854	...	...	1914	...
Dimitrovgrad a.	...	0920	...	...	1940	...

B – (2) Gorna Orjahovica - Dimitrovgrad and v.v.
See Table **61** for seasonal through cars Bucureşti - Ruse - Svilengrad - Kapıkule - Halkalı and v.v.

RUSE - SILISTRA and VARNA 1530

km		9647		9621	2655				9623		
		A	2			2	2			2	2
0	**Ruse** d.	0232	...	0600	...	...	...	...	1553	1835	...
5	Ruse Razpr d.	0255	...	0609	...	0800	...	...	1602	1844	...
71	Razgrad d.	0400	...	0715	...	0911	...	...	1708	1959	...
93	Samuil d.	0447f	0505	0738	...	0932	0940	...	1732	2020	2030
	Silistra a.	0727	|	|	...	|	1230	...	|	...	2320
142	Kaspichan 1500 d.	...	0600	0849f	1039	1100f	...	...	1821	...	...
	Shumen 1500 a.	...	...	|	|	1111	...	...	|	...	...
201	Poveljanovo 1500 d.	...	...	|	|	...	...	...	1918	...	...
226	**Varna** 1500 a.	...	...	1010	1159	...	...	...	1940	...	...

km				2610		9620				9622	9646
		2	2		2		2	2	2		D
	Varna 1500 d.	...	...	0455	...	0915	1430	...	...	1820	...
	Poveljanovo 1500 d.	...	...	|	...	0940	1502	...	...	1845	...
	Shumen 1500 d.	...	...	|	...	|	|	...	...	|	...
	Kaspichan 1500 d.	...	...	0616	0625	1038	1610	...	1630	1945	...
0	**Silistra** d.	...	0435	...	|	|	...	1425	|	|	1820
113	Samuil d.	0540	0725	...	0734	1129	...	1715	1733	2036	2120f
	Razgrad d.	0602	...	...	0755	1149	...	...	1754	2056	2140
	Ruse Razpr d.	0723	...	...	0917	1256	...	...	1909	2204	2300
	Ruse a.	...	...	...	0925	1304	...	...	1918	2212	2308

A – (sleeper) and (2) Sofia - Ruse - Silistra.

D – (sleeper) and (2) Silistra - Gorna Orjahovica (**2626**) - Sofia.

f – Arrives 10 – 35 minutes earlier.

VARNA and SHUMEN - BURGAS 1535

km				8650	8601							
		2	2	[R]	[R]	2	2	2	2	2	2	2
	Varna 1500 d.	...	0700	0900	...	1120	...	...	1315	...	1830	...
	Poveljanovo 1500 d.	...	0732	|	...	1151	...	...	1336	...	1901	...
0	**Shumen** d.	0455	|	|	...	|	...	1330	|	...	|	1935
50	Komunari d.	0553	0829	1005	...	1248	...	1428	1436	...	1951	2033
133	Karnobat 1500 d.	...	1050r	1128	1205	1430	1435	...	1620	1645	2122	...
194	**Burgas** 1500 a.	...	1200	...	1250	...	1542	...	...	1752	...	...

							8602	8651		
	2	2	2	2	2	2	[R]	[R]	2	2
Burgas 1500 d.	...	0630	0800	...	1335	...	1520	...	...	...
Karnobat 1500 d.	...	0759r	0906	...	1450	1500	1558	1641	1710	...
Komunari d.	0605	0945	...	1440	...	1634	...	1751	1853	2050
Shumen a.	0705	|	...	1540	...	|	...	|	|	2150
Poveljanovo 1500 d.	...	1045	...	...	...	1730	...	|	1951	...
Varna 1500 a.	...	1115	...	...	...	1800	...	1855	2021	...

r – Arrives 15 – 25 minutes earlier.

VARNA - DOBRICH - KARDAM 1540

km		D	2637	2	2		2	2	2		2
0	**Varna** 1500 d.	...	0615	0715	...	...	1225	1535	...	...	2015
	Sofia **1500** d.	2255	|	|	...	...	|	|	...	...	|
25	Poveljanovo 1500 d.	0641	0705	0747	...	...	1257	1608	...	...	2047
93	**Dobrich** a.	...	0825	0905	0910	...	1421	1735	1740	...	2204
131	Kardam a.	...	...	...	1014	...	...	...	1844	...	...

	2		2	2	2		2	2	2636	E
Kardam d.	...	...	...	1045	...	...	...	1900	...	...
Dobrich d.	0505	...	0915	1150	1200	...	1515	2005	2040	...
Poveljanovo 1500 a.	0622	...	1032	...	1323	...	1632	...	2205	2239
Sofia **1500** a.	|	...	|	...	|	...	|	...	|	0637
Varna 1500 a.	0653	...	1103	...	1354	...	1703	...	2305	...

D – (couchette) and (2) Sofia (**3637**) - Poveljanovo (**2637**) - Dobrich.

E – (couchette) and (2) Dobrich (**2636**) - Poveljanovo (**3636**) - Sofia.

(SOFIA) - PLOVDIV - SVILENGRAD - İSTANBUL 1550

BDŽ; TCDD

km	*Bulgarian train number*					1611			1613			493
	Turkish train number			12701						12703		12501
		2	2		2		2	2			2	A [R]
0	*Sofia* **1500** d.	...	...	...	...	0825	...	...	1520	...	...	1840
156	**Plovdiv** ▷ d.	0545	0700	...	0950	1119	1428	1720	1820	...	2100	2137
202	Parvomaj ▷ d.	0635	0746	...	1037	1159	1514	1809	1903	...	2147	|
234	Dimitrovgrad ▷ a.	0701	0810	...	1103	1216	1538	1833	1919	...	2214	2230
234	Dimitrovgrad d.	0702	...	...	...	1217	...	...	1920	...	...	2250
299	Svilengrad a.	0755	...	...	...	1310	...	...	2010	...	...	2340
299	Svilengrad 🏛 d.	...	...	...	...	...	...	...	...	...	...	0025
318	**Kapıkule** 🏛 a.	...	...	...	...	...	...	...	...	...	...	0037
318	**Kapıkule** d.	...	...	0800	...	...	...	...	...	...	...	0145
338	Edirne d.	...	...	0817	...	...	...	...	...	...	...	0202
	Uzunköprü ▶ d.	...	...	|	...	...	...	...	...	1730	...	|
385	Pehlivanköy ▶ d.	...	...	0851	...	...	...	...	...	1748	...	|
406	Alpullu d.	...	...	0914	...	...	...	...	...	1811	...	0247
506	Çerkezköy d.	...	...	1044	...	...	...	...	...	1943	...	0401
593	Halkalı a.	...	...	1211	...	...	...	...	...	2113	...	0534
621	**İstanbul** Sirkeci a.	...	...	◇	...	...	...	...	...	◇	...	◇

Turkish train number				12704					12702		12502
Bulgarian train number							1614				492*
	2	2	2		2	2		2		2	A [R]
İstanbul Sirkeci d.	...	...	...	◇	...	...	...	...	◇	...	◇
Halkalı d.	...	...	...	1240	...	...	...	...	1810	...	2045
Çerkezköy d.	...	...	...	1411	...	...	...	...	1942	...	2237
Alpullu d.	...	...	...	1541	...	...	...	...	2113	...	0006
Pehlivanköy ▶ d.	...	...	...	1601	...	...	...	...	2133	...	|
Uzunköprü ▶ a.	...	...	...	1616	...	...	...	...	|	...	|
Edirne d.	...	...	...	...	...	...	...	...	2210	...	0115
Kapıkule a.	...	...	...	...	...	...	...	...	2225	...	0128
Kapıkule 🏛 d.	...	...	...	...	...	...	...	...	...	...	0220
Svilengrad 🏛 a.	...	...	...	...	...	...	...	...	...	...	0240
Svilengrad d.	...	0450	...	...	0820	1248	1555	1740	...	...	0325
Dimitrovgrad a.	...	0548	...	...	0913	1344	1645	1832	...	...	0417
Dimitrovgrad ▷ d.	0505	0614	0725	...	...	1345	1646	1835	...	2010	0424
Parvomaj ▷ d.	0532	0649	0800	...	...	1412	1705	1904	...	2038	|
Plovdiv ▷ a.	0617	0743	0848	...	...	1507	1750	1948	...	2130	0515
Sofia **1500** a.	...	...	...	...	...	...	2100	...	...	...	0920

A – ISTANBUL - SOFYA EXPRESS – (2) Sofia - Svilengrad and v.v. (couchette) and (sleeper) Sofia - Halkalı and v.v. Seasonal through cars from / to Bucureşti from June 9 - Oct. 9 (see Table **61**).

* – Train number **1622** between Plovdiv and Sofia (see Table **1500**).

▶ – Uzunköpru - Pehlivanköy 20km.

▷ – Additional trains Plovdiv - Dimitrovgrad and v.v.:
From Plovdiv at 1320, 1600 and 1940.
From Dimitrovgrad at 0921, 1540 and 1740.

◇ – Frequent Maramary suburban services (at least every 15 minutes) operate between Halkalı - central istanbul - Gebze and v.v see Table **1570.**

SOFIA - KJUSTENDIL, PETRICH, KULATA and THESSALONÍKI 1560

Most trains 2nd class only

km				5621			5623		361	5663	5611		5625
										[R]			
0	**Sofia** d.	...	0525	0730	0830	1030	1230	1435	1530	1630	1730	...	1930
33	Pernik d.	...	0625	0829	0927	1120	1315	1534	1617	1712	1820	...	2021
48	Radomir d.	...	0643	0845	0943	1139	1331	1556	1633	1725	1836	1845	2037
102	**Kjustendil** a.	...	|	|	1110	|	|	|	|	|	|	2015	|
91	Dupnitsa d.	0625	0740	0931	▬	1246	1412	1700	1719	1802	1921	▬	2116
123	**Blagoevgrad** a.	0709	0825	0959	...	1320	1440	▬	1748	1830	1958	...	2145
123	**Blagoevgrad** d.	0710	▬	*1005*	...	▬	*1450*	...	1749	▬	1959	...	...
186	Sandanski d.	0828	...	*1118*	...	...	*1607*	...	1844	...	2104	...	...
197	General Todorov. a.	0840	...	*1129*	...	...	*1619*	...	1854	...	2116	...	...
197	General Todorov. d.	0841	0850	...	1145	1410	...	1635	1855	1905	2130	2135	...
207	**Petrich** a.	|	0903	...	|	1423	...	|	|	1913	2143	|	...
210	Kulata a.	0855	...	...	1159	...	...	1649	1905	...	...	2149	...
210	Kulata 🏛 ⊗ d.	...	...	...	...	...	...	...	...	...	...	...	...
354	**Thessaloníki** a.	...	...	...	...	...	...	...	...	...	...	...	...

		5610		5662			360		5622		5624
				[R]							
Thessaloníki d.	...	...	...	...	...	...	...	...	...	...	...
Kulata 🏛 ⊗ a.	...	...	...	...	...	...	...	...	...	...	...
Kulata d.	0500	...	0605	...		...	1050	1335	...	...	*1720*
Petrich d.	|	...	|	...	0820	1040	|	|	...	1600	|
General Todorov .. a.	0513	0518	0618	...	0833	1053	1100	1348	...	1613	*1733*
General Todorov .. d.	...	0529	*0630*	...	...	▬	1101	▬	*1405*	▬	*1750*
Sandanski d.	**5620**	0543	*0642*	...	...	...	1119	...	*1418*	...	*1803*
Blagoevgrad a.	...	0645	*0750*	...	...	...	1215	...	*1530*	...	*1920*
Blagoevgrad d.	0525	0646	▬	0800	...	1000	1216	1415	1545	...	1935
Dupnitsa d.	0559	0716	...	0830	...	1039	1245	1457	1615	...	2009
Kjustendil d.	|	|	0700	|	...	|	|	|	|	1830	|
Radomir d.	0653	0757	0831	0908	...	1132	1325	1550	1656	2004	2058
Pernik d.	0720	0815	0851	0924	...	1152	1343	1607	1712	2020	2114
Sofia a.	0809	0910	0943	1005	...	1245	1425	1702	1805	2108	2210

☛ Additional journeys Radomir - Kjustendil and v.v.: **From Radomir** at 0705, 1145, 1335, 1637 and 2016. **From Kjustendil** at 0425, 0925, 1130, 1410 and 1620.

⊗ – The border between Bulgaria and Greece is currently closed.

TURKEY IN ASIA

Operator: Türkiye Cumhuryeti Devlet Demiryolları (TCDD).

Services: *YHT* (high-speed) trains convey first and second class seating. Long distance trains convey a single class of seating known locally as 'Pullman' (shown as 1 in footnotes) which are gender specific and may also convey sleeping and/or couchette cars. Local trains convey 2nd class seating, shown as '2' in the train column. Descriptions of sleeping (🛏) and couchette (▬) cars appear on page 10. Reservation of seats (free of charge) is required for high-speed (*YHT*) and express trains.

Timings: Schedules are the latest available. Timetable amendments are possible at short notice, please confirm timings locally before travelling.

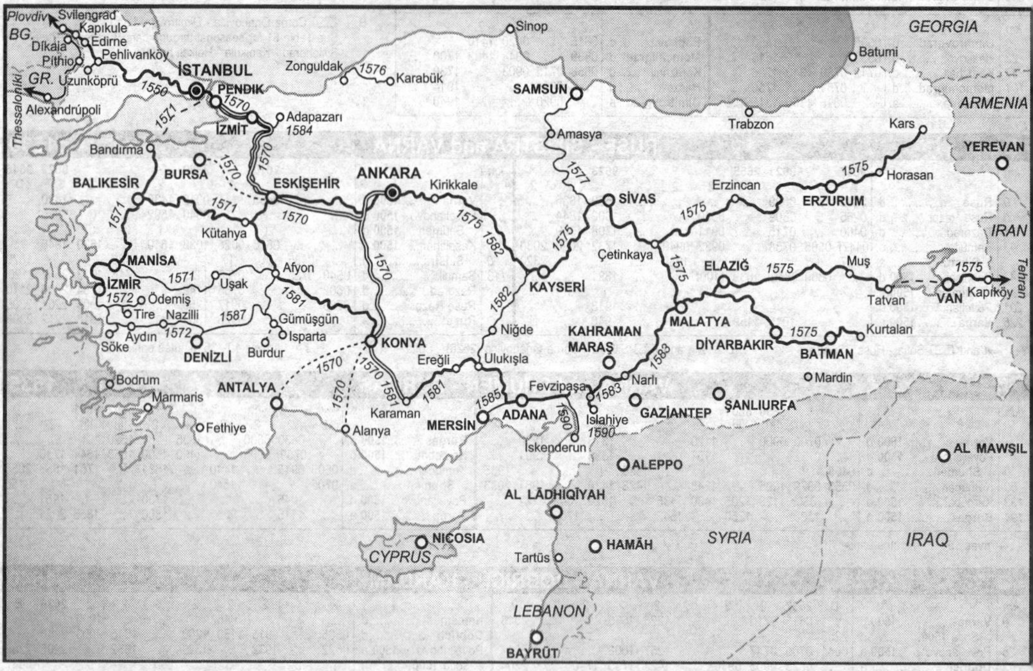

1570 İSTANBUL / ANKARA to ESKİŞEHIR - KONYA - KARAMAN

km	*YHT* trains: R and 🍷	*YHT* 81100		*YHT* 81002	*YHT* 81302	*YHT* 81004	*YHT* 81006	*YHT* 81304	*YHT* 81104	*YHT* 81008	*YHT* 81010	*YHT* 81012	*YHT* 81306	*YHT* 81014	*YHT* 81018		*YHT* 81108	*YHT* 81022	*YHT* 81308	*YHT* 81024	*YHT* 81028	*YHT* 81312	*YHT* 81030	*YHT* 81502		12002 ● R
0	Halkalı .... **1550** d.	...	...	...	...	0620	...	0720	...	0855	...	...	...	...	...	...	...	...	...	...	...	...	...	...	...	2205
33	**İstanbul** Söğütlüçesme . d.	...	...	0610	0645	0710	0840	0810	...	0949	1055	1155	1220	1255	1355	...	...	1525	1555	1625	1745	1840	1910	2040	...	2313
41	**İstanbul** Bostanci .... d.	...	...	|	0657	0721	0854	0821	...	1000	1108	1206	1231	1306	1413	...	...	1543	1611	1641	1759	1851	|	2054	...	2324
75	Gebze .... **1584** d.	...	...	|	0738	0801	|	0906	...	1049	|	1245	1310	|	1459	...	...	1628	1650	|	1844	1933	|	2136	...	0012
122	Izmit YHT .... **1584** d.	...	...	|	0811	0834	1019	0939	...	1124	1225	1318	1346	1425	1533	...	...	1702	1723	1759	1917	2006	2038	2209	...	0045
162	Arifiye .... **1584** d.	...	...	|	|	0857	|	1001	...	1147	|	1341	|	|	1556	...	...	1726	1745	|	1939	|	|	2231	...	0115
262	Bilecik YHT .... d.	...	...	|	|	0932	|	1035	...	1222	|	1417	|	|	1631	...	...	1803	1819	|	2013	|	|	2305	...	0249
294	Bozüyük YHT .... d.	...	...	|	|	0957	|	1059	...	1246	|	1441	|	|	1655	...	...	1828	1843	|	2037	|	|	2329	...	0320
309	**Eskişehir** ⊡ .... d.	0615	...	0900	0946	1017	1155	1119	1235	1306	1357	1501	1526	1600	1715	...	1800	1848	1903	1931	2057	2141	2211	2344	...	0400
672	**Konya** ⊙ .... **1581** a.	|	...	|	1132	|	|	1316	|	|	|	|	1712	|	|	...	|	|	2050	|	|	2327	|	...	...	|
774	Karaman .... **1581** d.	|	...	|	...	|	|	1405	|	|	|	|	...	|	|	...	|	|	...	|	|	...	|	...	...	|
	Polatli YHT .... d.	0703	...	|	...	1106	|	...	1323	1354	|	1549	...	|	1803	...	1848	1937	...	|	2145	...	|	...	...	0552‡
	Eryaman YHT .... d.	0727	...	|	...	1130	1304	...	1347	1418	1506	1613	...	1710	1827	...	1912	2001	...	2040	2209	...	2320	...	...	|
	Ankara .... a.	0739	...	1019	...	1142	1316	...	1359	1430	1518	1625	...	1722	1839	...	1924	2013	...	2052	2221	...	2332	...	...	0654

km	*YHT* trains: R and 🍷	*YHT* 81501	*YHT* 81001	*YHT* 81301	*YHT* 81003		*YHT* 81101	*YHT* 81005	*YHT* 81305	*YHT* 81007		*YHT* 81011	*YHT* 81015	*YHT* 81309	*YHT* 81017	*YHT* 81019	*YHT* 81105	*YHT* 81021	*YHT* 81025	*YHT* 81107	*YHT* 81311	*YHT* 81027	*YHT* 81313	*YHT* 81029		22001 ● R
0	**Ankara** .... d.	...	0605	...	0700	...	0805	0830	...	0950	...	1110	1210	...	1310	1405	1450	1520	1720	1800	...	1820	...	1930	...	2200
21	Eryaman YHT .... d.	...	|	...	0714	...	0819	0844	...	1004	...	1124	1224	...	1325	1419	1504	1534	1734	1814	...	1834	...	1944	...	|
86	Polatllı YHT .... d.	...	|	...	0736	...	0841	0907	...	|	...	1146	|	...	1349	|	1526	1556	1757	1836	...	1901	...	2007	...	2304‡
	Karaman .... **1581** d.	...	|	...	|	...	|	|	...	|	...	|	|	...	|	|	|	|	|	|	1620	|	...	|	...	|
	Konya ⊙ .... **1581** d.	...	|	0600	|	...	|	|	0845	|	...	|	|	1225	|	|	|	|	|	|	1718	|	1840	|	...	|
245	**Eskişehir** ⊡ .... d.	0630	0726	0749	0826	...	0926	0959	1034	1113	...	1236	1333	1414	1439	1528	1611	1646	1847	1921	1908	1943	2029	2057	...	0103
260	Bozüyük YHT .... d.	0646	|	|	0842	...	...	|	1051	1129	...	1252	|	|	1457	|	...	1702	1903	...	1924	|	|	2113	...	0140
292	Bilecik YHT .... d.	0708	|	|	0904	...	...	|	1115	1152	...	1315	|	|	1519	|	...	1724	1927	...	1946	|	|	2136	...	0212
392	Arifiye .... **1584** d.	0741	|	|	0937	...	...	|	1150	1226	...	1349	|	|	1552	|	...	1757	2001	...	2019	|	|	2210	...	0338
432	Izmit YHT .... **1584** d.	0804	|	0917	1000	...	...	1127	1215	1249	...	1412	1501	1542	1615	1658	...	1820	2024	...	2042	|	2157	2233	...	0408
479	Gebze .... **1584** d.	0836	|	0950	1032	...	...	|	1248	1321	...	1446	|	1616	1653	|	...	1853	2056	...	2114	|	2229	2306	...	0441
513	**İstanbul** Bostanci .... d.	0915	|	1030	1117	...	...	1251	1339	1402	...	1531	1630	1706	1741	1810	...	1938	2135	...	2157	|	2309	2345	...	0521
521	**İstanbul** Söğütlüçesme . a.	0924	1014	1039	1126	...	...	1306	1348	1411	...	1540	1639	1721	1756	1819	...	2001	2154	...	2216	2225	2324	2354	...	0535
554	Halkalı .... **1550** a.	...	...	...	...	...	...	...	...	...	...	...	...	...	...	...	...	2046	2239	...	2303	...	...	...	...	0619

km	*YHT* trains: R and 🍷	*YHT* 81200		*YHT* 81204	*YHT* 81206		*YHT* 81210	*YHT* 81212		*YHT* 81214	*YHT* 81216
0	Karaman .... **1581** d.	...	...	...	1010	...	...	...	...	...	2000
102	**Konya** ⊙ .... **1581** d.	0625	...	0915	1109	...	1525	1755	...	1940	2059
224	Polatli YHT .... d.	0734	...	1024	1219	...	|	1904	...	2049	2210
288	Eryaman YHT .... d.	0758	...	1048	1243	...	1655	1928	...	2113	2234
309	**Ankara** .... a.	0810	...	1100	1255	...	1707	1940	...	2125	2246

YHT trains: R and 🍷	*YHT* 81201		*YHT* 81205	*YHT* 81209		*YHT* 81211		*YHT* 81213	*YHT* 81215	*YHT* 81217
Ankara .... d.	0625	...	0910	1230	...	1420	...	1630	1745	2040
Eryaman YHT .... d.	0639	...	0924	1244	...	1434	...	1644	1759	2054
Polatllı YHT .... d.	0701	...	0946	|	...	1456	...	1706	1821	2116
Konya ⊙ .... **1581** a.	0821	...	1056	1413	...	1606	...	1827	1931	2226
Karaman .... **1581** a.	0910	...	...	...	...	...	...	1916	...	...

⊡ – connections Eskişehir - Bursa and v.v (journey time 2 hrs 15 mins).
From Eskişehir at 0940, 1245, 1535 and 1935.
From Bursa at 0902, 1232, 1602 and 1832.

⊙ – connections Konya - Alanya and v.v (journey time 4 hrs 35 mins - 5 hrs).
From Konya at 0850, 1420, and 1620.
From Alanya at 0800, 1000 and 1200.
Konya - Antalya and v.v (jouney time 5hrs 15 mins - 6 hrs).
From Konya at 1120, 1320, 1720 and 2230.
From Antalya 0100, 1300, 1500 and 2359.

● – ANKARA EKSPRESİ – Conveys 🛏, 1 and ✕

‡ – Departs from Polatli town station.

Suburban services run Halkalı - İstanbul - Gebze via the 1.4 km Marmaray Tunnel at least every 15 minutes 0600 - 2230. Route (with journey time): Halkalı (0) - Yenikapi (32) - Sirkeci (35) - Söğütlüçesme (46) - Pendik (80) - Gebze (108).

TCDD ESKIŞEHIR, BANDIRMA and AFYON - IZMIR 1571

km		32008 K	22006 B	32010 F ❋	32602	32606	32002 D ❋	32610	32018 C	72018 E	72610
	Ankara **1570** d.	...	2000	...	...	...	...	...	...	...	...
0	**Eskişehir** ♧ d.	...	2316	...	...	...	...	...	...	1350	...
77	Kütahya ♧ d.	...	0024	...	...	...	...	...	...	1504	1630
128	Tavşanlı ♧ d.	...	0107	...	...	...	...	...	...	1552	1718
‡	**Bandirma** Şehir d.	...	|	...	...	...	0800	...	1600	|	|
331	Balikesir d.	...	0437	0500	...	...	0953	...	1739	1928	2100
386	Savaştepe d.	...	0525	0555	...	...	1047	...	...	2025	...
413	Soma d.	...	0549	0618	...	...	1110	...	...	2049	...
454	Akhisar d.	...	0624	0652	...	...	1145	...	...	2138	...
◇	**Afyon** Ali Çetinkaya d.	2321	|	|	...	...	|	...	...	|	...
◇	Uşak d.	0200	|	|	...	0620	|	1630	...	|	...
◇	Alaşehir d.	0431	|	|	0530	0839	|	1849	...	|	...
506	Manisa d.	0615	0709	0741	0731	1039	1228	2043	...	2231	...
572	**Izmir** Basmane a.	0750	0837	0901	0902	1213	1344	2213	...	0002	...

	72609	32011 E	32601	32017 C	32603	32003 D ❋	32607	32009 F ❋	32005 B	32007 K
Izmir Basmane d.	...	0650	0730	...	1115	1355	1505	1740	1905	2005
Manisa d.	...	0831	0911	...	1252	1513	1646	1904	2039	2149
Alaşehir d.	...	|	1102	...	1442	|	1848	|	|	2331
Uşak d.	...	|	1316	...	...	|	2102	|	|	0206
Afyon Ali Çetinkaya a.	...	|	...	...	...	|	...	|	|	0435
Akhisar d.	...	0921	...	...	...	1555	...	1949	2123	...
Soma d.	...	1000	...	...	...	1630	...	2024	2158	...
Savaştepe d.	...	1024	...	...	...	1652	...	2047	2221	...
Balikesir d.	0645	1132	...	1200	...	1747	...	2141	2318	...
Bandirma Şehir a.	|	|	...	1339	...	1926	...	...	|	...
Tavşanlı ♧ d.	1034	1502	...	...	...	...	...	...	0249	...
Kütahya ♧ d.	1117	1548	...	...	...	...	...	...	0333	...
Eskişehir ♧ a.	...	1659	...	...	...	...	...	...	0438	...
Ankara **1570** a.	...	...	...	...	...	...	...	...	0754	...

⛴ Istanbul - Bandirma

İstanbul Deniz Otobüsleri *

km				j							
0	**İstanbul** Yenikapi d.	0900	...	1300	...	1945	...	...	...	...	...
	Bandirma Şehir a.	1135	...	1535	...	2220	...	...	...	...	...

Bandirma Şehir d.	0900	...	1600	...	1930	...	...	...	...	...
İstanbul Yenikapi a.	1140	...	1840	...	2210	...	...	...	...	...

B – IZMIR MAVI TRENİ – 🛏 [1] and ✕ Izmir - Ankara and v.v.
C – 6 EYLÜL EKSPRESİ – [1] Balikesir - Bandirma and v.v.
D – 17 EYLÜL EKSPRESİ – [1] Izmir - Bandirma and v.v.
E – EGE EKSPRESİ – [1] Izmir - Eskişehir and v.v.
F – KARESI EKSPRESİ – [1] Izmir - Balikesir and v.v.
K – KONYA MAVI TRENİ – 🛏 [1] and ✕ Izmir - Konya and v.v.

j – On certain dates departs at 1330 (please check locally before travelling).
♧ – For local services see Table **1581**.
‡ – Bandirma Şehir - Balıkesir *100 km.*
◇ – Afyon - Manisa: *355 km.* Uşak - Manisa: *220 km.* Alaşehir - Manisa: *103 km.*
* – İstanbul Deniz Otobüsleri ✆ +90 (212) 455 6900. www.ido.com.tr
❋ – Currently suspended.

TCDD 2nd class IZMIR - TIRE, ÖDEMIŞ, SÖKE and DENIZLI 1572

km		32759	32743	32721	32701	32723	32751	32705	32725	32707	32739	32753	32709	32745	32727	32755	32711	32729	32761	32713	32757	32731			32015 G
0	**Izmir** Basmane ⊡ d.	...	...	0631	0705	0855	1015	1040	1205	1230	1305	1405	1415	...	1515	1540	1640	1705	...	1840	1906	2105	...	...	2305
18	Adnan Menderes ⊡ d.	...	...	0654	0731	0919	1043	1107	1231	1255	1331	1431	1442	...	1542	1606	1707	1731	...	1908	1930	2130	...	...	2332
49	Torbalı ⊡ d.	...	...	0721	0803	0946	1114	1138	1258	1322	1401	1459	1515	...	1609	1635	1738	1804	...	1937	2003	2204	...	...	0002
86	Çatal d.	0550	...	0817	|	1035	1208	|	1349	|	|	1544	|	...	1658	1720	|	1856	1910	|	2048	2251	...	...	|
96	**Tire** a.	0605	...	|	|	|	1224	|	|	|	|	1559	|	...	|	1736	|	|	1925	|	2103	|	...	...	|
111	**Ödemiş** Gar a.	...	...	0851	|	1104	...	|	1421	|	|	...	|	...	1729	...	|	1930	...	|	...	2320	...	...	|
112	**Ödemiş** Şehir a.	...	...	0856	|	1109	...	|	1426	|	|	...	|	...	1734	...	|	1935	...	|	...	2325	...	...	|
77	Selçuk d.	...	...	...	0834	...	...	1210	...	1356	1435	...	1549	...	...	...	1812	...	...	2016	...	...	...	...	0037
	Söke d.	...	0615	...	|	...	...	|	...	|	|	...	|	1705	...	...	|	...	...	|	...	...	...	...	|
100	Ortaklar d.	...	0644	...	0909	...	...	1242	...	1429	1515	...	1622	1734	...	...	1845	...	...	2049	...	...	...	...	0110
130	Aydin d.	...	0716	...	0952	...	...	1315	...	1504	1548	...	1658	1814	...	...	1928	...	...	2125	...	...	...	...	0143
175	Nazilli d.	...	0810	...	1046	...	...	1412	...	1600	1642	...	1752	1914	...	...	2020	...	...	2217	...	...	...	...	0235
260	**Denizli** a.	...	0939	...	1205	...	...	1533	...	1721	...	...	1914	2037	...	...	2141	...	...	2338	...	...	...	...	0354
	Isparta **1587** a.	...	...	...	...	...	...	...	...	...	...	...	...	...	...	...	...	...	...	...	...	...	...	...	0740

km		32760	32722	32752	32702	32724	32754	32704	32726	32744	32706	32728	32756	32708	32730	32710	32758	32762	32732	32746	32714	32716			32016 G
	Isparta **1587** d.	...	...	...	...	...	...	...	...	...	...	...	...	...	...	...	...	...	...	...	...	...	...	...	2210
0	**Denizli** d.	...	...	...	0420	...	...	0545	...	0740	0840	...	...	1015	...	1220	...	...	...	...	1620	1815	...	...	0159
85	Nazilli d.	...	...	...	0542	...	...	0710	...	0901	1006	...	...	1136	...	1347	...	...	...	1710	1751	1941	...	...	0325
130	Aydin d.	...	...	...	0632	...	...	0800	...	0956	1103	...	...	1232	...	1443	...	...	...	1810	1845	2037	...	...	0421
160	Ortaklar d.	...	...	...	0711	...	...	0830	...	1028	1135	...	...	1305	...	1517	...	...	...	1844	1918	2110	...	...	0454
182	**Söke** a.	...	...	...	|	...	...	|	...	1054	|	...	...	|	...	|	...	...	...	1910	|	|	...	...	|
183	Selçuk d.	...	...	...	0749	...	...	0901	...	...	1209	...	...	1338	...	1550	...	...	...	...	1951	2143	...	...	0530
	Ödemiş Şehir d.	...	0505	...	|	0710	...	|	0935	...	|	1130	...	|	1445	|	...	...	1815	...	|	|	...	...	|
	Ödemiş Gar d.	...	0510	...	|	0715	...	|	0940	...	|	1135	...	|	1450	|	...	...	1820	...	|	|	...	...	|
	Tire d.	0525	|	0620	|	|	0755	|	|	...	|	|	1335	|	|	|	1640	1825	|	...	|	|	...	...	|
	Çatal d.	0538	0545	0635	|	0747	0813	|	1011	...	|	1207	1350	|	1520	|	1657	1838	1855	...	|	|	...	...	|
211	Torbalı ⊡ d.	...	0639	0722	0830	0839	0903	0941	1103	...	1240	1257	1438	1415	1608	1628	1803	...	1951	...	2029	2217	...	...	0605
242	Adnan Menderes ⊡ d.	...	0710	0758	0858	0910	0934	1010	1134	...	1309	1322	1510	1447	1634	1659	1833	...	2022	...	2058	2243	...	...	0633
260	**Izmir** Basmane ⊡ a.	...	0734	0822	0922	0934	0958	1033	1158	...	1333	1346	1534	1510	1658	1722	1857	...	2046	...	2122	2301	...	...	0658

G – GÖLLER EKSPRESİ – [1]

⊡ – IZBAN suburban trains operate Izmir (Alsancak) - Adnan Menderes (Airport) - Torbalı and v.v. 0545 - 2359.

TCDD ANKARA - SIVAS, KARS, KURTALAN, TATVAN and TEHRAN 1575

km		2	2	2	22012 ②⑦ B Ⓡ	22014 △ C Ⓡ	22512 ③❋ Gf Ⓡ	22016 ●▷ H Ⓡ	22010 D Ⓡ	22018 E Ⓡ	21206 ❋ F
0	**Ankara** 1582 d.	...	...	...	1120	1120	1425	1555	1755	1910	2005
43	Elmadağ 1582 d.	...	...	...	1216	1216	|	|	1847	1959	2056
92	Kirikkale 1582 d.	...	...	...	1320	1320	|	|	1943	2057	2146
203	Yerköy 1582 d.	...	...	...	1519	1519	|	1926	2137	2233	2339
379	Kayseri d.	...	...	...	1926	1926	2109	2234	0114	0235	▬
602	**Sivas** a.	...	...	...	2302	2302	|	0200	0449	0609	2
602	**Sivas** d.	...	0750	...	2326	2326	|	0215	0504	0624	1720
710	Çetinkaya d.	...	0916	...	0107	0107	|	0349	0641	0801	1849
779	Divriği d.	0535	1032	1600	|	|	|	0505	0824	|	2006
935	Erzincan d.	0842	▬	1907	|	|	|	1044j	1156	|	...
1150	Erzurum d.	▬	...	▬	|	|	|	1752n	1625	|	...
1235	Horasan d.	...	...	...	|	|	|	|	1747	|	...
1307	Sarkamiş d.	...	...	...	|	|	|	2048	1924	|	...
1365	**Kars** a.	...	...	...	|	|	|	2152	2024	|	...
854	Malatya d.			...	0403	0403	0434	...	...	1028	...
949	Yolçatı d.	2	2	...	0629	0623	|	...	...	...	...
1107	Diyarbakir d.	0840	1800	...	|	1030	|	...	...	...	...
1198	Batman d.	1106	2026	②⑤⑦	|	1251	|	...	...	...	...
1267	**Kurtalan** a.	▬	...	2	|	1433	|	...	...	...	...
973	Elaziğ d.	...	...	0705	0705	...	0721	...	...	...	...
1201	Muş d.	...	...	1214	1214	...	1154	...	...	...	...
1295	**Tatvan** Gar a.	51516	...	1404	1404	...	1336	...	...	...	...
1300	**Tatvan** Iskele a.	①❋	...	...	...	...	1426	...	...	...	...
0	**Van** Iskele d.	d	...	...	...	...	2125	...	...	...	...
3	**Van** Gar d.	2100	...	...	...	...	2152	...	...	...	...
114	Kapiköy 🏛 d.	2330	...	...	...	...	0120	...	...	...	...
120	Razi 🏛 d.	0125	...	...	...	...	0600	...	...	...	...
342	Tabriz a.	0505	...	...	...	...	0950	...	...	...	...
342	Tabriz 4630 d.	0530	...	...	...	...	1020	...	...	...	...
1078	**Tehran** 4630 a.	1820	...	...	...	...	2320	...	...	...	...

	51515 ⑦❋ d	2	①③⑥ 2	2	52019 E Ⓡ	21205 ❋ F	52511 ③❋ Gf	42015 ●□ H	42009 D Ⓡ	52013 ▽ C Ⓡ	52011 ②④ B Ⓡ
Tehran 4630 d.	1300	...	...	...	...	...	2205	...	...	...	...
Tabriz 4630 a.	0130	...	...	...	...	...	1020	...	...	...	...
Tabriz d.	0200	...	...	...	...	...	1100	...	...	...	...
Razi 🏛 d.	0800	...	...	...	...	...	1745	...	...	...	...
Kapiköy 🏛 d.	0915	...	...	...	...	...	1830	...	...	...	...
Van Gar a.	1100	...	...	...	...	...	2000	...	...	...	...
Van Iskele a.	▬	...	...	...	...	...	2123	...	...	...	...
Tatvan Iskele d.	...	...	...	...	...	...	0550	...	...	...	...
Tatvan Gar d.	...	...	1030	...	...	...	0730	...	...	...	1030
Muş d.	...	...	1210	...	...	...	0906	...	...	...	1210
Elaziğ d.	...	...	1707	...	...	...	1413	...	...	...	1722
Kurtalan d.	2	...	▬	...	...	...	|	...	...	0930	|
Batman d.	0515	1430	...	...	...	...	|	...	...	1116	|
Diyarbakir d.	0742	1657	...	...	...	...	|	...	...	1347	|
Yolçatı d.	▬	▬	...	...	...	...	|	...	...	1751	1751
Malatya d.	...	...	...	...	1530	...	1657	...	...	2028	2028
Kars d.	...	...	...	...	|	...	|	2230	0800	|	|
Sarkamiş d.	...	...	...	...	|	...	|	2338	0909	|	|
Horasan d.	...	...	...	...	|	...	|	|	1036	|	|
Erzurum d.	...	2	...	...	|	...	|	0238	1218	|	|
Erzincan d.	2	0610	2	1440	|	...	|	0651	1637	|	|
Divriği d.	0600	0928	1730	1755	|	...	|	1546r	1954	|	|
Çetinkaya d.	0717	...	1848	...	1806	...	|	1654	2116	2311	2311
Sivas a.	0846	...	2010	...	1937	...	|	1823	2248	0043	0043
Sivas d.	...	...	...	...	1952	...	|	2213	2303	0051	0051
Kayseri d.	...	...	...	...	2324	...	0124	0216	0237	0430	0430
Yerköy 1582 d.	...	...	...	...	0249	0350	|	0529	0602	0805	0805
Kirikkale 1582 d.	...	...	...	...	0435	0539	|	|	0755	1003	1003
Elmadağ 1582 a.	...	...	...	...	0538	0640	|	|	0910	1112	1112
Ankara 1582 a.	...	...	...	...	0624	0735	0743	0859	0956	1157	1157

B – VANGÖLÜ EKSPRESİ – 🛏 ▬ (4 berth) [1] and ✕ Ankara - Tatvan and v.v.
C – GÜNEY EKSPRESİ – 🛏 ▬ (4 berth) [1] and ✕ Ankara - Kurtalan and v.v.
D – DOĞU EKSPRESİ – ▬ (4 berth) and ✕ Ankara - Kars and v.v.
E – 4 EYLÜL MAVI TRENİ – ▬ (4 berth) and [1] ✕ Ankara - Malatya and v.v.
F – CÜKUROVA MAVI TRENİ – 🛏 ▬ and [1] ✕ Ankara - Adana and v.v.
G – TRANSASYA EKSPRESİ – 🛏 ▬ and ✕ Tehran (718/719) - Razi - Ankara and v.v.
H – TURISTIK DOĞU EKSPRESİ – Conveys 🛏 and ✕ Ankara - Kars and v.v.

d – Conveys 🛏 and ✕.
f – By ⛴ Tatvan Iskele - Van Iskele and v.v.
j – Arrives 0800.
n – Arrives 1452.
r – Arrives 1246.

❋ – Service currently suspended.
● – Special fares apply.
▷ – ①③⑤.
□ – ③⑤⑦.
△ – ①③④⑤⑥.
▽ – ①③⑤⑥⑦.

1576 KARABÜK - ZONGULDAK TCDD

km		22641	22643	22645	22647
0	**Karabük** d.	0705	1305	1605	1810
59	Gökçebey d.	0828	1430	1729	1932
75	Çaycuma d.	0849	1451	1749	1955
96	Filyos d.	0922	1523	1822	2027
120	**Zonguldak** a.	1002	1602	1903	2107

	22642	22644	22646	22648
Zonguldak d.	0730	1130	1330	1830
Filyos d.	0813	1211	1413	1924
Çaykuma d.	0848	1245	1450	1956
Gökçebey d.	0909	1306	1511	2017
Karabük a.	1030	1428	1632	2138

Additional local trains run Zonguldak - Gökçebey and v.v.
From Zonguldak at 0930, 1635, 1735, 2035.
From Gökçebey at 0540, 0630, 1225, 1830.

1577 SIVAS - AMASYA - SAMSUN TCDD

km		42631	42625	42629
0	**Sivas** d.	...	...	...
53	Yildizeli d.	...	...	...
205	Turhal d.	...	...	...
268	**Amasya** d.	0620	0730	1500
295	Suluova ✈ d.	0654	0809	1539
315	Havza d.	0721	0843	1613
401	**Samsun** a.	0927	...	...

	42626	42628	42634
Samsun d.	...	...	1730
Havza d.	0850	1300	1934
Suluova ✈ d.	0924	1337	2001
Amasya d.	1003	1418	2034
Turhal d.	...	...	...
Yildizeli d.	...	...	...
Sivas a.	...	...	...

1581 ESKIŞEHIR - AFYON - KONYA - ADANA TCDD

For YHT (high-speed) services between Eskişehir and Konya, see Table **1570**.

km		72007 K	72602	72014 P	62006 T	72018 E	72604	72608	72606		72006 C
0	**Eskişehir** **1571** d.	...	0920	1110	...	1350	1500	1745	2000	...	2316
77	Kütahya **1571** d.	...	1034	1233	...	1504	1611	1902	2113	...	0024
127	Tavşanlı **1571** a.	...	...	...	...	1552	...	|	2156	...	0105
163	**Afyon** d.	0448	...	...	...	...	...	2051	...	...	...
261	Akşehir d.	0615	...	...	...	...	...	...	...	...	...
435	**Konya** **1570** d.	0859	...	...	1500	...	...	...	...	...	...
537	Karaman **1570** d.	...	...	...	1630	...	...	...	...	...	...
624	Ereğli d.	...	...	...	1758	...	...	...	...	...	...
672	Ulukışla **1582** d.	...	...	...	1858	...	...	...	...	...	...
781	Yenice **1582** d.	...	...	...	2114	...	...	...	...	...	...
804	**Adana** **1582** a.	...	...	...	2141	...	...	...	...	...	...
km											
0	Konya **1570** d.	0645	...	...	1120	...	...	2000	...	...	...
102	Karaman d.	0800	...	...	1235	...	...	2115	...	...	...

	72005 C	72601	72607	72603	62005 T	72011 E	72013 P	72605		72008 K
Adana **1582** d.	...	...	...	...	0800	...	...	...	...	...
Yenice **1582** d.	...	...	...	...	0833	...	...	...	...	...
Ulukışla **1582** d.	...	...	...	...	1043	...	...	...	...	...
Ereğli d.	...	...	...	...	1133	...	...	...	...	...
Karaman **1570** d.	...	...	...	...	1310	...	...	...	...	...
Konya **1570** d.	...	...	...	...	1429	...	...	...	...	1900
Akşehir d.	...	...	...	...	...	...	...	...	...	2149
Afyon d.	...	...	0730	...	...	...	1449	...	...	2311
Tavşanlı d.	0249	0600	|	...	...	1453	|	...	...	...
Kütahya **1571** d.	0333	0646	0930	1215	...	1541	1657	1755	...	...
Eskişehir **1571** a.	0438	0753	1038	1315	...	1652	1811	1904	...	...
Karaman d.	0650	...	...	1155	...	...	1745	...	...	...
Konya **1570** d.	0806	...	...	1211	...	...	1901	...	...	...

C – IZMIR MAVI TRENİ – 🛏 [1] and ✕ Izmir - Eskişehir - Ankara and v.v.
E – EGE EKSPRESİ – [1] Izmir - Eskişehir and v.v.
K – KONYA MAVI TRENİ – 🛏 [1] and ✕ Konya - Izmir and v.v.
P – PAMUKKALE EKSPRESİ – [1] Eskişehir - Denizli and v.v.
T – TOROS EKSPRESİ – [1] Adana - Konya and v.v.

1582 ANKARA - KAYSERI - ADANA TCDD

km		22002 G	22012 B △	22014 C ▽	22512 T ③≋	22016 H ▷	62006 J	22010 D	22018 E	21206 F ≋
0	**Ankara** **1575** d.	...	1120	1120	1425	1555	...	1755	1910	2005
43	Elmadağ **1575** d.	...	1216	1216	|	|	...	1847	1959	2056
92	Kirikkale **1575** d.	...	1320	1320	|	|	...	1943	2057	2148
203	Yerköy **1575** d.	...	1519	1519	|	1926	...	2137	2242	2339
379	**Kayseri** **1575** d.	0730	1928	1928	2109	2234		0114	0235	|
479	Niğde d.	0948	...	...	...	...	...	...	...	0351
542	Ulukışla **1581** d.	1102	...	...	...	...	1858	...	...	0504
651	Yenice **1581** d.	1301	...	...	...	...	2114	...	...	0706
674	**Adana** **1581** d.	1326	...	...	...	...	2139	...	...	0725

	62005 J	62001 G	22019 E	21205 F ≋	22511 T ⑥≋	22015 H □	22009 D	22011 B △	22013 C ▽
Adana **1581** d.	0800	1630	...	1930	...	...	...	...	...
Yenice **1581** d.	0833	1702	...	1951	...	...	...	...	...
Ulukışla **1581** d.	1043	1902	...	2220	...	...	...	...	...
Niğde d.	...	2017	...	2321	...	...	...	...	...
Kayseri **1575** d.	...	2235	2324	|	0124	0216	0237	0430	0430
Yerköy **1575** d.	...	...	0249	0350	|	0529	0602	0805	08058
Kirikkale **1575** d.	...	...	0435	0539	|	|	0755	1003	1003
Elmadağ **1575** a.	...	...	0538	0640	|	|	0910	1112	1112
Ankara **1575** a.	...	...	0624	0735	0743	0859	0956	1157	1157

B – VAN GÖLÜ EKSPRESİ – 🛏 ▬ and [1] ✕ Ankara - Tatvan and v.v.
C – GÜNEY EKSPRESİ – 🛏 ▬ and [1] ✕ Ankara - Kurtalan and v.v.
D – DOĞU EKSPRESİ – 🛏 ▬ and [1] ✕ Ankara - Kars and v.v.
E – 4 EYLÜL MAVI TRENİ – ▬ and [1] ✕ Ankara - Malatya and v.v.
F – CÜKUROVA MAVI TRENİ– 🛏 ▬ and [1] ✕ Ankara - Adana and v.v.
G – ERCIYES EKSPRESİ – [1] Kayseri - Adana and v.v.
H – TURISTIK DOĞU EKSPRESİ – 🛏 and ✕ Ankara - Kars and v.v. Special fares apply.
J – TOROS EKSPRESİ – [1] Adana - Konya and v.v.
T – TRANSASYA EKSPRESİ – 🛏 and ✕ Ankara - Tehran and v.v.
▷ – ①③⑤.
□ – ②⑤⑦.
△ – Runs on ②⑦ from Ankara. Runs on ②④ from Tatvan.
▽ – Runs on ①③④⑤⑥ from Ankara. Runs on ①③⑤⑥⑦ from Kurtalan.
≋ – Currently suspended.

1583 ADANA - MALATYA - ELAZIĞ TCDD

km		62004 L	
0	**Adana** d.	0900	...
78	Toprakkale d.	1031	...
141	Fevzipaşa d.	1212	...
210	Narlı d.	1316	...
335	Doğanşehir d.	1600	...
392	**Malatya** d.	1733	...
487	Yolçatı d.	1951	...
511	**Elazığ** a.	2012	...

	52003 L	
Elazığ d.	0830	...
Yolçatı d.	0858	...
Malatya d.	1127	...
Doğanşehir d.	1248	...
Narlı d.	1532	...
Fevzipaşa d.	1652	...
Toprakkale d.	1809	...
Adana a.	1938	...

L – FIRAT EKSPRESİ – [1] Elaziğ - Adana and v.v.

1584 GEBZE - ARIFIYE - ADAPAZARI TCDD

ADA REGIONAL EKSPRES TRENİ – Conveys [1].

km		12602	12604	12606	12608	12610
0	**Gebze** d.	0715	1120	1315	1735	1940
47	Izmit YHT d.	0755	1159	1355	1815	2019
87	Arifiye d.	0826	1230	1426	1846	2050
95	**Adapazarı** a.	0839	1243	1439	1859	2103

	12601	12603	12605	12607	12609
Adapazarı d.	0610	1005	1340	1750	2010
Arifiye d.	0623	1018	1354	1803	2024
Izmit YHT d.	0655	1050	1426	1835	2056
Gebze d.	0732	1127	1503	1912	2133

☛ Suburban Marmaray services run central İstanbul - Gebze via the 1.4 km Marmaray Tunnel at least every 15 minutes 0600 - 2230.

1585 MERSIN - ADANA TCDD

km				K								K						K		J							
0	**Mersin** d.	0545	...	0620	0705	0745	0825	...	0940	...	1125	1245	...	1400	...	1545	...	1630	1710	1735	1815	...	1945	2050	2150	...	...
26	Tarsus d.	0625	...	0657	0746	0827	0850	...	1020	...	1205	1322	...	1440	...	1625	...	1708	1750	1812	1855	...	2026	2130	2231	...	...
43	Yenice d.	0648	...	0719	0813	0851	0933	...	1044	...	1228	1342	...	1502	...	1646	...	1728	1813	1831	1918	...	2050	2155	2254	...	...
68	**Adana** a.	0715	...	0749	0840	0918	1000	...	1111	...	1255	1412	...	1529	...	1713	...	1758	1840	1855	1945	...	2117	2222	2321	...	...

								K	J					K									K				
Adana d.	0535	...	0645	...	0735	...	0901	1014	1040	...	1155	...	1315	1430	...	1530	...	1655	...	1800	1845	1915	2020	2120	2220	...	...
Yenice d.	0606	...	0716	...	0807	...	0932	1043	1109	...	1226	...	1346	1500	...	1602	...	1727	...	1832	1916	1944	2049	2151	2252	...	...
Tarsus d.	0626	...	0737	...	0829	...	0954	1103	1129	...	1248	...	1406	1520	...	1624	...	1749	...	1854	1938	2005	2109	2213	2314	...	...
Mersin a.	0701	...	0812	...	0905	...	1031	1137	1203	...	1326	...	1441	1553	...	1700	...	1825	...	1930	2014	2040	2143	2249	2350	...	...

J – [1] Islahiye - Adana - Mersin and v.v.
K – [1] Iskenderun - Adana - Mersin and v.v.

1587 AFYON - BURDUR, ISPARTA & DENIZLI TCDD

km		72014 P	🚌	72016 G
	Eskişehir ◇ d.	1110	...	...
0	**Afyon** d.	1438	...	...
◧	Isparta d.	|	...	2210
	Burdur d.	|	2200	|
◧	Gümüşgün a.	|	2225	2256
112	Karakuyu d.	1653	...	2316
126	Dinar d.	1712	...	2335
260	**Denizli** a.	1933	...	0143

	72015 G	🚌	72013 P
Denizli d.	0408	...	0945
Dinar d.	0617	...	1208
Karakuyu d.	0636	...	1228
Gümüşgün a.	0708	0710	|
Burdur d.	|	0740	|
Isparta d.	0740	...	|
Afyon a.	...	...	1449
Eskişehir ◇ a.	...	...	1811

G – GÖLLER EKSPRESİ – [1] Izmir - Isparta/Burdur and v.v.
P – PAMUKKALE EKSPRESİ – [1] Eskişehir - Denizli and v.v.
◧ – Distance from Karakuyu: Gümüşgün 33 km, Isparta 62 km.
◇ – See Table **1581**.

1590 ADANA - ISLAHIYE / ISKENDERUN TCDD

km		2 K	2K	2K	J
0	**Adana** d.	0756	1420	1803	1903
78	Toprakkale d.	0939	1546	1937	2029
137	Iskenderun a.	1055	1706	2055	|
141	Fevzipaşa d.	...	...	...	2139
150	**Islahiye** d.	...	...	...	2150

	2K	J	2K	2K
Islahiye d.	...	0740	...	...
Fevzipaşa d.	...	0753	...	...
Iskenderun a.	0715	|	1130	1715
Toprakkale d.	0837	0906	1252	1837
Adana a.	1003	1030	1416	2004

J – [1] Islahiye - Adana - Mersin and v.v.
K – [1] Iskenderun - Adana - Mersin and v.v.

Products for sale from European Rail Timetable Limited

3rd Edition Revised of the
Rail Map Europe.
£12.99 + p&p

European Rail Timetable
Four seasonal editions.
£90 + p&p

17th Edition of the
Europe by Rail guidebook.
£18.99 + p&p

Reprint of the 1873 edition of
Cook's Continental Time Tables & Tourist's Hand Book.
£13.99 + p&p

Order on-line at **www.europeanrailtimetable.eu**
Telephone **01832 270198**

European Rail Timetable Price List

Printed seasonal edition (published four times a year in December, March, June and September): £24.99

Price for a single printed copy including postage and packaging:

☐ UK	£28.46	Delivery in 2–5 working days
☐ Europe	£37.63 incl. tax	Delivery in 3–10 working days
☐ Rest of the World	£34.56–£36.19	Delivery in 5–21 working days

Monthly digital edition: £12.99

Discounted price to pre-order four consecutive printed editions (including postage and packaging):

☐ UK £104.28 ☐ Europe £136.58 incl. tax ☐ Rest of the World £128.28–£134.80

Annual subscription for 12 digital editions: £90.00

Annual subscription for 12 digital editions, together with four printed copies (price includes postage and packaging):

☐ UK £144.68 ☐ Europe £186.58 incl. tax ☐ Rest of the World £167.04–174.80

Order on-line at **www.europeanrailtimetable.eu**
By post to: 28 Monson Way, Oundle, Northamptonshire, PE8 4QG (cheques payable to European Rail Timetable Limited)
✆ +44 (0) 1832 270198 (Monday to Friday 1000–1600)

ROMANIA

SEE MAP PAGE 505

Operator: Societatea Naţională de Transport Feroviar de Călători (CFR Călători): www.cfrcalatori.ro. Certain services are operated by private companies as shown in relevant tables.

Services: Trains convey 1st- and 2nd-class seating accommodation unless otherwise indicated. Sleeping- (🛏) and couchette (▬) cars are described on page 10. Most long-distance trains are classified *IR* (Interregio), shown in our tables with just the train number.

Timings: Valid **until December 9, 2023**. Alterations to schedules are possible at any time.

Tickets: Reservation is obligatory for travel by all CFR Călători services for which a train number is shown in the tables, and passengers boarding without a prior reservation are surcharged. CFR trains shown without numbers are slow stopping-services calling at all, or most, stations.

1600 BUCUREŞTI - BRAŞOV - CLUJ NAPOCA / ORADEA / SIBIU / ARAD (- BUDAPEST)

km		146	74	72	366	1735		1623		1645	521	531	349	346	404	1926	406	472	1741	⊡ 1942	1930	1641	78	1914	1821 1920*
		S	F	T	H			j		Lj				D	E	h	C	R	⊕	⊕t	⊕t	⊗2	M	⊕h	⊕
	Constanţa **1680** d.	...	...	...	...	...	...	...	...	...	...	...	...	...	...	1400	...	...	...	1704	1742	...	...	2000	2043t
0	**Bucureşti** Nord ▷ d.	...	...	0540	...	0609	...	0955	...	1224	1320	1320	1325	1450	...	1640	...	1825	1844	1935b	2006b	2101	2146	2301	2332
59	Ploieşti Vest ▷ d.	...	...		...	0647	...	1040	...	1301	1358	1358		1527	...	1725	...	1902	1921	2023	2053	2140			
121	Sinaia ▷ d.	...	...		...	0742	...	1132	...	1350				1614	...	1818	...	1951	2009	2113	2143	2232			
140	Predeal ▷ d.	...	...		...	0807	...	1158	...	1416				1640	...	1844	...	2017	2035	2138	2209	2258			
166	**Braşov** ▷ a.	...	...		...	0841	...	1232	...	1451	1534	1534		1714	...	1918	...	2051	2109	2211	2243	2332			
166	**Braşov** d.	...	0655		0729	0851	...	1252	...	...	1538	1538		1721	...	...	1935	2103	2122	2223	2256	2347			
294	**Sighişoara** 1622 d.	...				1214	...		...	...	1848	1848		2033	...	...			0049		0235				
330	Mediaş 1622 d.	...				1243	...		...	...				2058	...	...			0120		0306				
340	Copşa Mică 1622 d.	...				1251	...		...	...					...	...			0129		0315				
370	Blaj d.	...		◧	◐	1311	...		...	...			◧	2122	...	...	◐		0151	◐	0337	◐	◧	△	▽
392	Teiuş 1620 d.	...				1337	...		...	...	2010	2003			...	...			0219		0403				
405	Aiud 1620 d.	...				1352	...		...	...					...	...			0236		0418				
425	Războieni 1620 d.	...				1415	...		...	...					...	...			0302		0444				
442	Câmpia Turzii 1620 d.	...				1431	...		...	...					...	...			0320		0502				
494	**Cluj Napoca** 1620 a.	...			1430	1525	...		...	...		2149			...	...	0233		0418		0600				
494	**Cluj Napoca** 1625 d.	0739			1455	...	...		...	...		...			2100	...	0248		0435		0616				
543	Huedin 1625 d.	0828			1546	...	...		...	...		...			2152	...	0340		0526		0716				
646	**Oradea** 1625 a.	1011			1730	...	...		...	...		...			2344	...	0521		0707		0924				
	Baia Mare **1610/14** a.					...	...		...	...		...				...				0755	...	0848			
	Satu Mare **1610/25** a.					...	...		...	...		...				...			0917	0947	...	...			
•65	Făgăraş d.		0816			...	...	1411	...	...		...				...		2223	...	...	...	...			
•127	Podu Olt 1645 d.					...	...	1510	...	...		...				...			...	...	...	...		0702	
•149	**Sibiu** 1645 d.		0938			...	...	1537	...	...		...				...		2344	...	...	...	...		0733	
•223	Sebeş Alba d.		1104			...	...	...	...	...		...				...		0109	...	...	...	...		...	
	Alba Iulia d.					...	...	...	...	...	2030	...		2155		...			...	...	...	...		...	
•232	Vinţu de Jos d.		1115			...	...	...	...	...		...				...		0120	...	...	...	...		...	
•276	Simeria 1620 d.		1155			...	...	...	...	...		...		2238		...		0203	...	...	...	...		...	0833
•285	Deva 1620 d.		1208			...	...	...	...	...	2110	...		2249		...		0212	...	...	...	...		...	0852
•433	**Arad** 1620 a.		1448	1657		...	...	...	...	...	2337d	...	0058	0111		...		0438	...	...	...	...	0902	...	1131
	Budapest Keleti **1280** ‡ a.	1420	1850	2050	2120	...	...	...	...	...	...	...	...	0520	0520	...	0920	0850	...	...	...	...	1250	...	...

	73	1912	367	75	⊡ 1941	1932	1822 1922*	1642	1742	143	79	1928	407	473		347	348	405	523	532		1734		1624	1646
	T	⊕s	H	F	⊕u	⊕u	⊕u	⊗2	⊕	S	M	h	C	R		D		E						j	Pj
Budapest Keleti **1280** ‡ d.	0710	...	0740	0910	...	...	...	...	...	1340	1510	...	1740	1910	...	2245	...	2245	...	...	...	...	...	...	...
Arad 1620 d.	1235	...		1435	...	...	1804	...	...		2036	...		0043	...	0442	0441		0619d	...	...	...	...	...	...
Deva 1620 d.		...		1712	...	...	2045	...	...			...		0311	...	0704			0846	...	...	...	...	...	...
Simeria 1620 d.		...		1733	...	...	2058	...	...			...		0332	...	0723				...	...	...	...	...	...
Vinţu de Jos d.		...		1808	...	...		...	...			...		0406	...					...	...	...	...	...	...
Alba Iulia d.		...			...	...		...	...			...			...	0759			0927	...	...	...	...	...	...
Sebeş Alba d.		...		1821	...	...		...	...			...		0418	...					...	...	...	...	...	...
Sibiu 1645 d.		1842		1953	...	...		...	...			...		0549	...					...	...	...	...	1635	...
Podu Olt 1645 d.		1920			...	...		...	...			...			...					...	...	...	...	1709	...
Făgăraş d.				2121	...	...		...	...			...		0713	...					...	...	...	...	1809	...
Satu Mare **1610/25** d.					1320	...		...	1700			...			...					...	...	...	...		...
Baia Mare **1610/14** d.					1501	...		1750				...			...					...	...	...	...		...
Oradea 1625 d.			1333			1621			1926	1950		...	2330		...			0535		...	...	...	...	...	...
Huedin 1625 d.			1518			1828			2110	2134		...	0111		...			0728		...	...	...	...	...	...
Cluj Napoca 1625 a.			1609			1918			2200	2223		...	0200		...			0819		...	...	...	...	...	...
Cluj Napoca 1620 d.			1624			1933			2215	...		...	0212		...			...		0810	...	1000	...		...
Câmpia Turzii 1620 d.						2034			2323	...		...			...			...			...	1103	...		...
Războieni 1620 d.						2052			2340	...		...			...			...			...	1121	...		...
Aiud 1620 d.						2116			0005	...		...			...			...			...	1143	...		...
Teiuş 1620 d.						2135			0025	...		...			...			...	1020	1020	...	1203	...		...
Blaj d.	◧	△	◐		◐	2200	▽	◐	0051	...	◧	...	◐		...	0832	◧	...			...	1227	...		...
Copşa Mică 1622 d.						2220			0111	...		...			...			...			...	1247	...		...
Mediaş 1622 d.						2230			0121	...		...			...	0858		...			...	1257	...		...
Sighişoara 1622 d.						2300			0151	...		...			...	0925		...	1130	1130	...	1329	...		...
Braşov a.			2324	2246	0109	0202		0335	0455	...			0943	0840	...	1235		...	1430	1430	...	1650	...	1927	...
Braşov ▷ d.			...	...	0121	0214		0347	0512	...		0740	...	0852	...	1238		...	1433	1433	...	1702	...	1946	1946
Predeal ▷ d.			...	...	0205	0257		0432	0558	...		0815	...	0927	...	1313		...			...	1745	...	2021	2021
Sinaia ▷ d.			...	...	0232	0323		0500	0626	...		0841	...	0953	...	1339		...			...	1812	...	2048	2048
Ploieşti Vest ▷ d.			...	...	0323	0417		0557	0721	...		0933	...	1042	...	1428		...	1612	1612	...	1901	...	2137	2137
Bucureşti Nord ▷ a.	2349	0303	...	...	0409b	0501b	0539	0635	0759	...	0806	1010	...	1119	...	1505	1605	...	1653	1653	...	1938	...	2217	2217
Constanţa **1680** a.	...	0611	...	...	0646	0745	0846	...	...	...	...	1250	...	...	...	...	...	...	...	...	...	...	...	...	...

ADDITIONAL TRAINS BUCUREŞTI - BRAŞOV

		1631	1680	1732	1621	1633	1635			536	
		2					2r				
Constanţa **1680** d.	...	...	0530	...	...	...	...	...	...	1720	...
Bucureşti Nord d.	0615	0717	0820	g	1257	1515	1640	1646	1806	1937	2021
Ploieşti Vest d.	0739	0754	0857	0953	1335	1552	1725	1801	1934	2016	2122
Sinaia d.	0906	0845	0945	1044	1425	1642	1818	1911	2047		2218
Predeal d.	0944	0911	1011	1110	1451	1708	1844	1938	2122		2245
Braşov a.	1025	0945	1045	1144	1525	1742	1918	2018	2203	2150	2324

	1620	538	1630	1632	1634	1622	1636	1730	1638		1628
	Ⓐ		r		2k				⑦	j	
Braşov d.	0455	0700	0740	0920	1120	1330	1425	1720	1805	1846	2030
Predeal d.	0530		0815	0956	1156	1406	1511	1756	1841	1928	2106
Sinaia d.	0557		0841	1022	1223	1432	1537	1823	1909	1955	2133
Ploieşti Vest d.	0652	0838	0933	1115	1320	1524	1635	1913	2002	2108	2225
Bucureşti Nord a.	0733	0917	1010	1152	1357	1602	1712	g	2039	2209	2302
Constanţa **1680** a.	...	1130	...	...	...	...	...	...	...	...	...

C – CORONA – 🛏 1, 2 cl., ▬ 2 cl., [2] Braşov - Cluj Napoca - Budapest and v.v.
D – DACIA – 🛏 1, 2 cl., ▬ 2 cl., [2] Bucureşti - Arad - Budapest - Wien and v.v.; [2] Bucureşti - Budapest and v.v.
E – CORVIN – 🛏 1, 2 cl., ▬ 2 cl., [2] Cluj Napoca - Budapest - Wien and v.v.
F – FĂGĂRAS – [2] Braşov - Arad - Budapest and v.v.
H – HARGHITA – [12] Braşov - Miercurea Ciuc - Cluj Napoca - Budapest and v.v. Conveys [2] Târgu Mures (**1748/9**) - Cluj Napoca - Budapest and v.v. on dates in Table **1615**.
L – [12] Bucureşti - Braşov - Târgu Mureş (Table **1610**).
M – MUNTENIA – 🛏 1, 2 cl., ▬ 2 cl., [12] Bucureşti - Timişoara - Arad - Budapest and v.v.
P – [12] Târgu Mureş (Table **1610**) - Braşov - Bucuresti.
R – ISTER – 🛏 1, 2 cl., ▬ 2 cl., [2] Bucureşti - Budapest and v.v.
S – TRANSILVANIA – [12] Cluj Napoca - Oradea - Budapest - Wien and v.v.
T – TRAIANUS – [2] Bucureşti - Craiova - Timişoara - Arad - Budapest and v.v.

b – Bucureşti **Băneasa**.
d – From / to Timişoara Nord (Table **1625**).
g – From / to Galaţi via Ploieşti Sud (Table **1670**).
h – June 17 - Sept. 10.
j – Not Apr. 16, June 4.
k – Not June 17 - Sept. 10.
r – Not Apr. 16, June 4, June 17 - Sept. 10.
s – June 16 - Sept. 9.
t – Apr. 28 - May 1, June 17 - Sept. 10.
u – Apr. 27 – 30, June 16 - Sept. 9.

◐ – Via Miercurea Ciuc (Table **1610**).
◧ – Via Craiova and Timişoara (Table **1630**).
▷ – For additional trains Bucureşti - Braşov and v.v. see panel below main table.

△ – Via Râmnicu Vâlcea (Table **1645**).
▽ – Via Craiova and Târgu Jiu (Tables **1630/35**).
⊡ – For portion Constanţa - Cluj Napoca and v.v. see Table **1610**.
◇ – Operated by Astra Trans Carpatic.
⊕ – 🛏 1, 2 cl., ▬ 2 cl., [12]
⊗ – 🛏 1, 2 cl., ▬ 2 cl., [2]
‡ – Table **1275** for trains via Oradea.
• – Distance from Braşov.
* – Train number applies when extended to / from Constanţa or Mangalia.

BRAŞOV - MIERCUREA CIUC - TÂRGU MUREŞ / CLUJ / BAIA MARE 1610

For other trains from Bucureşti and Braşov to Cluj Napoca and Baia Mare / Satu Mare see Table **1600**.

km		2	366 H	1543 2c	2	1645 j	2	406 C	1942 J	1641 ⊗	
	Bucureşti N **1600** d.	...	...	...	...	1224	...	...	1935b	2057	...
0	**Braşov** d.	0557	0729	1200	...	1514	1603	1935	2223	2347	...
32	Sfântu Gheorghe d.	0636	0759	1231	...	1550	1644	2005	2256	0018	...
95	**Miercurea Ciuc** d.	0800	0900	1334	1537	1654	1952d	2107	2400	0118	...
103	Siculeni d.	0809	0908	1348	1546	1706	2005	2115	0013	0129	...
150	Gheorghieni d.	...	0958	...	1712	1801	2117	2204	0116	0234	...
184	Topliţa d.	...	1035	...	1801	1840	2208	2241	0154	0311	...
228	Deda a.	...	1131	...	1924	1955	...	2335	0253	0408	...
228	Deda ▷ d.	...	1133	...	1941	2017	...	2337	0306	0413	...
250	Reghin ▷ d.	...	|	...	2016	2048	...	|	0337*	|	...
282	**Târgu Mureş** ▷ a.	...	|	...	2104	2123	...	|	0412*	|	...
275	Sărăţel d.	...	1224	...	...	...	...	0029	0401	0514	...
286	Bistriţa Nord a.	...	|	...	...	...	...	|	|	|	...
300	Beclean pe Someş d.	...	1246	...	...	...	...	0050	0431	0543	...
324	Dej Călători **1614** d.	...	1323	...	...	...	...	0127	0514	0628	...
383	**Cluj Napoca** a.	...	1430	...	...	...	...	0233	0650*	|	...
	Budapest Kel. **1275** a.	...	2120	...	...	...	...	0920	|	|	...
401	Jibou **1614** a.	...	...	...	...	...	...	...	0644	0754	...
458	**Baia Mare** **1614** a.	...	...	...	...	...	...	...	0755	0848	...
	Satu Mare **1625** a.	...	...	...	...	...	...	...	0947	...	...

	2	407 C	1541 2c	2 Ⓐ	1646 j	2	367 H	1941 K	1642 ⊗	
Satu Mare **1625** d.	...	...	...	...	...	...	...	1320	...	...
Baia Mare **1614** d.	...	...	...	...	...	...	...	1501	1750	...
Jibou **1614** d.	...	...	...	...	...	...	...	1614	1858	...
Budapest Kel. **1275** d.	...	1740	...	...	...	...	0740	|	|	...
Cluj Napoca d.	...	0212	...	...	...	...	1624	1630*	|	...
Dej Călători **1614** d.	...	0325	...	...	...	...	1737	1822	2034	...
Beclean pe Someş d.	...	0358	...	...	...	...	1810	1855	2129	...
Bistriţa Nord d.	...	|	...	...	...	...	|	|	|	...
Sărăţel d.	...	0420	...	...	...	...	1831	1917	2210	...
Târgu Mureş ▷ d.	...	|	...	*1035*	1345	1545	|	1920*	|	...
Reghin ▷ d.	...	|	...	*1121*	1420	1633	|	2007*	|	...
Deda ▷ a.	...	0521	...	*1146*	1436	1551	1922	2007	2303	...
Deda d.	...	0523	...	1255	1448	1658	1925	2025	2308	...
Topliţa d.	0420	0619	...	1415	1545	...	2020	2121	0018	...
Gheorghieni d.	0505	0658	...	1458	1622	...	2056	2205	0055	...
Siculeni d.	0624	0751	1222	1613	1730	...	2152	2302	0155	...
Miercurea Ciuc d.	0739a	0801	1233	1623	1740	...	2201	2313	0205	...
Sfântu Gheorghe d.	0858	0913	1345	1755	1844	...	2255	0039	0305	...
Braşov a.	0937	0943	1414	1842	1914	...	2324	0109	0335	...
Bucureşti N **1600** a.	...	...	...	...	2217	...	...	0409b	0635	...

– CORONA – 1, 2 cl., 2 cl., (2) Braşov - Budapest and v.v.
– 1, 2 cl., 2 cl., (2) Bucureşti - Dej Călători (**4009/10**) - Cluj Napoca and v.v.; 2 cl., (2) Bucureşti - Sărăţel (**4007/8**) - Bistriţa Nord and v.v; 2 cl., (2) Bucureşti - Beclean pe Someş (**4110/6**) - Sighetu Marmaţiei and v.v.
– HARGHITA – (12) Braşov - Cluj Napoca - Budapest and v.v.
– Apr. 28 - May 1, June 17 - Sept. 10. 1, 2 cl., 2 cl., (12) Mangalia - Constanţa - Bucureşti Băneasa - Târgu Mures / Cluj Napoca / Satu Mare.
– Apr. 27 – 30, June 16 - Sept. 9. 1, 2 cl., 2 cl., (12) Satu Mare / Cluj Napoca / Târgu Mures - Bucureşti Băneasa - Constanţa - Mangalia.

a – Arrives at 0632.
b – Bucureşti **Băneasa**.
c – Braşov - Iasi and v.v. (Tables **1610** and **1650**).
d – Arrives at 1808.
j – Not Apr. 16, June 4.
▷ – Additional trains: Deda - Târgu Mureş at 0418, 0526, 0857, 1220, 1723. Târgu Mures - Deda at 0238, 0727, 1430, 1931, 2215. Journey 1hr 20m.

⊗ – 1, 2 cl., 2 cl., (2).
* – Seperate portion of train.

ADJUD - COMĂNEŞTI - MIERCUREA CIUC 1612

2nd class

km				Ⓐ	c	Ⓐn					
0	**Adjud** d.	...	0504	0644	0936	1306	1505	1744	2005	2201	...
39	Oneşti d.	...	0556	0740	1018	1359	1600	1845	2052	2330	...
75	Comăneşti d.	0424	0652	0835	1056	1455	1656	1941	2139	0022	...
109	Ghimeş d.	0515	0741	0931	1134	1549	1745	2031	...	...	...
150	Siculeni d.	0617	0909	1034	1222	...	1842	2135	...	...	...
158	**Miercuria Ciuc** a.	0626	0919	1042	1231	...	1850	...	...	...	...

						c	Ⓐn			
Miercuria Ciuc d.	...	...	0725	...	1232	1334	...	1603	1946	...
Siculeni d.	...	0433	0734	...	1244	1348	...	1615	2002	...
Ghimeş d.	...	0543	0831	...	1342	1434	1614	1720	2100	...
Comăneşti d.	0433	0630	0918	1258	1434	1512	1712	1825	2148	...
Oneşti d.	0526	0730	...	1408	1529	1550	1805	1930	2325	...
Adjud a.	0617	0813	...	1500	...	1629	1854	2024	0016	...

OR NOTES SEE TABLE 1614 BELOW

CLUJ NAPOCA - DEJ - BAIA MARE / BISTRIŢA 1614

km		2	2	2	2	2	2	4004 b	2	Ⓐ 2n	2
0	**Cluj Napoca** ▷ d.	0335	0531	0635	1110	1412	1530	1542	1630	1725	1940
59	Dej Călători **1610** d.	0457	0659	0802	1239	1523	1646	1711	1755	1852	2123
136	Jibou **1610** d.	|	0845	...	|	1709	|	1852	...	...	|
193	**Baia Mare** **1610** a.	|	...	...	|	1824	|	2000	...	...	|
84	Beclean pe Someş ▷ d.	0531	...	...	1322	...	1732	...	...	...	2203
109	Sărăţel d.	...	...	...	1351	...	1802	...	...	...	2234
119	**Bistriţa** Nord a.	...	...	...	1405	...	1815	...	...	...	2250

	Ⓐ 2n	⚒ 2	2	2	4006 b	2	2	2	2	⑦
Bistriţa Nord d.	...	0257	...	0400	...	0739	...	1535	...	...
Sărăţel d.	...	0310	...	0414	...	0756	...	1552	...	...
Beclean pe Someş ▷ d.	...	0403	...	0516	...	0826	...	1621	...	...
Baia Mare **1610** d.	...	|	...	|	0540	|	0720	|	1525	1710
Jibou **1610** d.	...	|	...	|	0648	|	0846	|	1640	1819
Dej Călători **1610** d.	0355	0448	0523	0555	0832	0915	1019	1715	1835	1956
Cluj Napoca ▷ a.	0520	0615	0650	0715	0946	1040	1125	1842	2000	2101

– Also conveys From / to Bucureşti Nord (Table **1600**).
– Braşov - Iasi and v.v (Tables **1610** and **1650**).

n – Not Apr. 14, 16, 17, May 1, June 1, 4, 5, Aug. 15, Nov. 30, Dec. 1.

▷ – For additional trains Cluj Napoca - Dej Călători - Beclean pe Someş and v.v. see Table **1660**.

CLUJ NAPOCA - RĂZBOIENI - TÂRGU MURES 1615

km				2	2				Ⓐ 2n			2
0	**Cluj Napoca** **1620** d.	...	...	...	0746	...	...	...	1510	...	1640	...
51	Câmpia Turzii **1620** d.	...	...	...	0901	...	...	...	1631	...	1743	...
69	Războieni **1620** a.	...	...	...	0921	...	...	...	1652	...	1758	...
69	Războieni d.	0410	0505	0538	...	...	1201	...	...	1704	1818	1934
88	Luduş d.	0436	0531	0610	...	...	1232	...	...	1728	1837	2006
128	**Târgu Mures** a.	0535	0630	0722	...	...	1325	...	...	1825	1941	2107

		2					Ⓐ n	Ⓑ	Ⓐ 2n		2
Târgu Mures d.	0310	...	0729	...	1128	...	1428	1559	...	1938	2220
Luduş d.	0405	...	0834	...	1216	...	1527	1643	...	2042	2339
Râzboieni a.	0439	...	0858	...	1233	...	1552	1702	...	2106	0007
Râzboieni **1620** d.	...	0522	...	0906	1255	...	...	...	2018	...	0008
Câmpia Turzii **1620** d.	...	0545	...	0925	1311	...	...	...	2036	...	t
Cluj Napoca **1620** a.	...	0700	...	1035	1409	...	...	...	2144	...	...

– Not Dec. Apr. 14, 16, 17, May 1, June 1, 4, 5, Aug. 15, Nov. 30, Dec. 1.

t – To Teiuş (arrive 0055).

CLUJ NAPOCA - SIMERIA - ARAD and TIMIŞOARA 1620

km		2		2	2	1836 C	1734 b	2	Ⓐ 2	Ⓑ	2	1763 ⊗e
	Iaşi **1660** d.	...	...	...	...	...	...	...	...	...	...	1535
	Suceava **1660** d.	...	...	...	...	...	...	...	...	...	...	1742
0	**Cluj Napoca** **1615** d.	...	...	...	0521	0740	1000	1135	1510	...	1645	0040
51	Câmpia Turzii **1615** d.	...	...	...	0642	0847	1102	1249	1631	...	1807	0143
	Târgu Mures **1615** d.	...	0310	...	|	|	|	|	|	1559	|	|
69	Războieni **1615** a.	...	0439	...	0701	0905	1119	1309	1652	1702	1828	0158
69	Războieni d.	...	0445	...	0702	0907	1121	1310	1653	1707	1829	0200
89	Aiud d.	...	0516	...	0734	0929	1143	1343	1724	1731	1858	0223
102	Teiuş d.	...	0544	...	0810	0950	1202	1359	1740	1755	1917	0242
121	**Alba Iulia** d.	...	0618	...	0841	1014		▬	▬	1816	...	0309
•	**Sibiu** **1600** d.	...	|	...	|	|		...	...	|	...	|
31	Vinţu de Jos **1600** d.	...	0640	...	0851	1022	...	...	...	1824	...	0317
•	**Sibiu** a.	...	0847	...	|	|	...	...	...	|	...	|
75	**Simeria** a.	...	...	...	0953	1054	...	2	2	1901	...	0358
75	**Simeria** **1600** d.	0539	...	1041	...	...	...	1155	1643	...	...	0403
84	Deva **1600** d.	0555	...	1051	...	...	...	1216	1654	...	...	0412
32	**Arad** **1600** a.	0944	...	1422	...	...	...	1534	2118	...	...	0652
90	Lugoj d.	...	...	...	...	...	...	...	...	...	...	|
49	**Timişoara** Nord a.	...	...	...	...	...	...	...	...	...	...	0834

	2		2	Ⓑ	1735 b		2	⚒ 2	Ⓐ	1765 ⊗e	1835 B
Timişoara Nord a.	...	...	...	...	...	...	...	...	...	1440	...
Lugoj d.	...	...	...	...	...	...	...	...	...	|	...
Arad **1600** d.	0550	...	0738	...	...	...	...	1525	...	1610	...
Deva **1600** d.	0955	...	1110	...	...	...	...	1900	...	1848	...
Simeria **1600** a.	1005	...	1122	...	...	...	...	1910	...	1857	...
Simeria d.	▬	...	▬	1023	...	...	1410	▬	...	1902	0153
Sibiu d.	...	...	...	|	...	...	|	1530	...	|	|
Vinţu de Jos **1600** d.	...	...	...	1111	...	...	1518	1746	...	1940	0231
Sibiu **1600** a.	...	...	Ⓐ	|	...	...	|	|	...	|	|
Alba Iulia d.	2	...	2	1119	...	2	1528	1804	...	1949	0240
Teiuş d.	0450	0818	1052	1145	1337	1415	1603	1843	1930	2016	0310
Aiud d.	0506	0834	1108	1202	1352	1431	1615	1859	1947	2031	0326
Războieni a.	0536	0904	1138	1229	1414	1501	1649	1929	2017	2053	0349
Războieni **1615** d.	0538	0906	1139	1237	1415	1502	1650	1934	2018	2054	0350
Târgu Mures **1615** a.	0722	|	|	1349	|	|	|	2107	|	|	|
Câmpia Turzii **1615** d.	...	0925	1159	...	1431	1521	1709	...	2036	2113	0412
Cluj Napoca **1615** a.	...	1035	1309	...	1525	1632	1821	...	2144	2212	0525
Suceava **1660** a.	...	...	...	...	...	...	...	...	...	0516	...
Iaşi **1660** a.	...	...	...	...	...	...	...	...	...	0722	...

– Bucureşti - Teiuş (**3081**) - Cluj Napoca (via Târgu Jiu, Table **1635**).
– Cluj Napoca - Craiova - Bucureşti (via Târgu Jiu, Table **1635**).
– To / from Bucureşti (via Sighişoara, Table **1600**).
– Conveys (2) Botosani - Suceava - Timişoara and v.v. (Table **1660**).

⊗ – 1, 2 cl., 2 cl., (2).
• – Sibiu - Vintu de Jos = *83 km*.

SIGHIŞOARA - SIBIU 1622

km		⚒	⚒		2				2	2	
0	**Sighişoara** **1600** d.	0506	0656	...	1013	...	...	1534	1835	...	
39	Mediaş **1600** d.	0547	0735	...	1052	1230	...	1615	1924	1949	...
50	Copşa Mică **1600** d.	0602	0758	...	...	1257	...	1646	...	2009	...
95	**Sibiu** a.	0715	0914	...	...	1410	...	1802	...	2123	...

					2				2 Ⓑ	
Sibiu d.	0726	...	1216	...	1526	1731	...	1933	2315	...
Copşa Mică **1600** d.	0836	...	1339	...	1645	1851	...	2049	0032	...
Mediaş **1600** d.	0850	...	1356	...	1700	1906	...	2112	0047	...
Sighişoara **1600** a.	...	...	1435	...	...	1946	...	2151	...	...

1625 TIMIŞOARA - ARAD - ORADEA - CLUJ NAPOCA / BAIA MARE

For Timişoara - Cluj Napoca via Simeria and Teiuş, see Table **1620**.

km			⚒		1741		523	378	6822		1831		78			Ⓑ	⚒		1765	1531	1533	72	1537		
		2⚒	2	2	⊕	2	b	B	2	2		2	Me	2	2	2	2	♡	D	⑤-⑦		Te			2
0	**Timişoara** Nord d.	...	...	...	...	0425	0455	0537	...	...	0647	0808	0803	...	...	1300	1336	...	1440	1543	1543	1558	1700	1754	201
57	**Arad** a.	...	...	...	...	0544	0554	0646	...	...	0759	0935	0902	...	...	1424	1503	...	1544	1645	1645	1657	1759	1915	214
57	**Arad** d.	...	...	...	...	0546	...	...	...	...	0801	—	—	...	...	1436	—	...	1610	1656	1656	—	1802	1922	...
139	Salonta d.	...	...	...	...	0743	...	...	...	...	0925	...	...	...	...	1612	...	...	|	1823	1823	Ⓐ	1932	2113	...
178	**Oradea** a.	...	...	...	b	0845	...	...	...	...	1015	♡	♡	...	...	1709	...	...	◐	1917	1917	2	2023	2212	...
178	**Oradea** 1600 d.	...	0245	...	0717	...	...	...	...	...	1021	1249	1521	...	1520	...	...	1720	|	1922	1922	1945	2028	...	...
281	Huedin 1600 d.	...	|	...	|	...	...	...	...	...	1207	1449	1734	...	|	...	**686**	1934	|	|	|	|	2226	...	...
330	**Cluj Napoca** 1600 a.	...	|	...	|	...	...	...	**d**	...	1256	1551	1835	...	|	...	**H**	2037	2212	|	|	|	2316	...	...
244	Valea lui Mihai d.	...	0437	...	0823	...	...	...	1038	1250	u	...	...	...	1701	...	1947	...	...	2027	2027	2128	...	...	...
275	Carei d.	...	0513	...	0848	...	...	...	1112	1326	...	...	...	...	1741	...	2010	...	...	2051	2051	2203	...	...	...
311	**Satu Mare** a.	...	0558	...	0917	...	...	...	1157	1411	...	...	...	...	1824	...	2042	...	...	2121	2121	2247	...	...	...
311	**Satu Mare** d.	0456	...	0808	...	...	...	...	...	...	...	...	...	1600	...	...	2049	...	...	2125	...	...	...	...	...
370	**Baia Mare** a.	0625	...	0950	...	...	...	...	...	...	...	...	...	1740	...	...	2206	...	...	2240	...	...	...	...	...

	1530	1532	1763		⚒	⚒	1539		73			687	377	Ⓐ		79	1833		1742		Ⓐ	6821	Ⓐ		521
	⑥-①	②-⑤	D		2	2		♡	Te	2	2	H	B	2	♡	Me		2	⊕	2	2	2	2	2Ⓑ	b
Baia Mare d.	0045	...	...	...	...	...	...	...	...	...		0800	...	1234	...	...	...	...	...	1540	...	...	...	2015	...
Satu Mare a.	0158	...	...	...	...	...	...	...	...	...		0922	...	1409	...	...	...	...	...	1715	...	...	...	2209	...
Satu Mare d.	0200	0200	...	...	0330	...	...	...	...	0738		0927	...	—	...	...	...	1545	1700	—	...	1745	1957	...	...
Carei d.	0232	0232	...	...	0402	...	...	...	...	0849		1000	...	...	...	...	...	1628	1737	...	...	1830	2052	...	...
Valea lui Mihai d.	0256	0256	...	...	0445	...	...	...	...	0927		1044	...	...	...	...	u	1700	1805	♡	...	1949	2145	...	...
Cluj Napoca 1600 d.	|	|	0040	...	|	...	0550	0714	...	|	...	—	...	...	1358	...	1530	|	|	1614	...	**d**	|	...	...
Huedin 1600 d.	|	|	|	...	|	...	0638	0814	...	|	...	...	...	...	1459	...	1621	|	|	1714	...	...	|	...	...
Oradea 1600 a.	0403	0403	|	...	0615	...	0826	1005	...	1050	...	...	...	...	1656	...	1814	1827	1913	1923	...	...	2310	...	...
Oradea d.	0409	0409	◐	0441	...	0644	0831	...	...	—	...	...	...	1550	...	...	1832	...	**b**	...	2003	...	...	...	...
Salonta d.	0501	0501	|	0540	...	0742	0926	...	...	...	...	...	...	1651	...	...	1933	...	...	...	2112	...	...	...	...
Arad a.	0625	0625	0652	0730	...	0946	1049	...	...	2	...	2	...	1849	...	...	2106	...	...	...	2307	...	...	...	...
Arad d.	0626	0626	0717	0742	...	...	1054	...	1235	1316	1613	1743	1834	1857	...	2036	2111	...	...	...	2320	...	...	...	000
Timişoara Nord a.	0736	0736	0834	0914	...	...	1153	...	1334	1439	1751	1909	1936	2020	...	2135	2213	...	...	...	0041	...	...	...	010

B – BEGA – [2] Timişoara - Arad - Budapest and v.v.
D – ▬ 2 cl., [2] Timişoara - Arad - Cluj Napoca - Iaşi and v.v; [2] Timişoara - Arad - Cluj Napoca - Suceava (**5560/6**) - Botoşani and v.v.
H – SZAMOS – [2] Baia Mare - Püspökladány (**143/144**) - Budapest - Wien and v.v.
M – MUNTENIA – 🛏 1, 2 cl., ▬ 2 cl., [12] Bucureşti - Timişoara - Arad - Budapest and v.v.
T – TRAIANUS – [2] Bucureşti - Timişoara - Arad - Budapest and v.v.

b – From / to Bucureşti (Table **1600**).
d – From / to Debrecen (Table **1277**).
e – From / to Bucureşti (Table **1630**).
u – To / from Iaşi (Table **1660**).

◐ – Via Alba Iulia and Teius (Table **1620**
⊕ – 🛏 1, 2 cl., ▬ 2 cl., [12]
♡ – Operated by Trans Feroviar Călători

1630 BUCUREŞTI - CRAIOVA - TIMIŞOARA

km				72		1591	1823			1691		349		1595	1835	1996		1597	11501 ◇	11502 ◇	78	1821	1920	199
		2	2	T	2						2		2	Ⓐn		j			⊗p	⊗d	M	⊕q	⊕g	⊕j
	Constanţa **1680** d.	...	...	...	...	...	...	...	...	...	...	...	...	...	...	1430	...	...	...	1735	...	...	2043	214
0	**Bucureşti** Nord d.	...	...	0540	...	0718	0835	0920	...	1110	...	1325	1428	1530	1630	1717	1833	1930	2020	2020	2146	2332	2332	0014
51	Videle d.	...	...	0631	...	0809	0926	1010	...	1201	...	1416	1519	1623	1721	1808	1924	2021	2110	2110	2236	0022	0022	010
100	Roşiori Nord d.	...	...	0722	...	0900	1023	1100	...	1252	...	1507	1610	1716	1812	1900	2016	2115	2200	2200	2327	0113	0113	015
155	Caracal d.	...	...	0825	...	1005	1132	1205	...	1357	...	1614	1720	1821	1918	2006	2122	2220	2302	2302	0029	0218	0218	030
209	**Craiova** a.	...	...	0914	...	1054	1221	1254	...	1446	...	1704	1809	1910	2007	2101	2211	2309	2351	2351	0118	0307	0307	035
209	**Craiova** 1635 d.	...	...	0922	...	...	1226	...	...	1453	...	1712	...	...	2015	...	...	...	2357	2357	0126	0315	0315	040
245	Filiaşi 1635 d.	...	...	0949	...	...	1253	...	...	1520	...	1740	...	...	2043	...	...	...	0024	0024	0153	0342	0342	042
323	Drobeta Turnu Severin d.	...	...	1143	...	...	**e**	...	...	1701	...	1924	...	...	**c**	...	...	...	0207	0207	0338	|	|	061
347	Orşova d.	...	...	1216	1350	...	...	...	...	1738	...	1957	...	...	...	...	...	...	0240	0240	0411	|	|	064
364	Băile Herculane d.	...	...	1241	1416	...	...	...	...	1803	...	2023	...	...	...	...	...	...	0304	0304	0435	◐	◐	071
435	Caransebeş ⊡ d.	0732	1309	1402	1605	...	...	...	...	1924	1942	2145	...	...	...	...	...	...	0424	0424	0602	|	|	085
474	Lugoj d.	0829	1405	1442	1700	...	...	...	...	2004	2039	2226	...	...	...	...	...	...	0504	0504	0642	|	|	093
533	**Timişoara** Nord a.	0959	1529	1556	1826	...	...	...	...	2112	2229	2342	...	...	...	...	...	...	0618	0618	0750	|	|	104
	Arad **1625** a.	...	...	1657	...	...	...	...	...	...	...	0058	...	...	...	...	...	...	0733	0733	0902	1131	1131	...

	1594	1994					1824	348		1596			1836	1590	1598	73			1992	1822	1922	11500 ◇	11504 ◇	79
		j		2		2Ⓐ				2					2	T	2	2	⊕k	⊕t	⊕h	⊗m	⊗r	M
Arad **1625** d.	...	...	...	...	...	...	...	0441	...	0733	...	...	...	...	...	1235	...	...	...	1804	1804	2005	2005	203
Timişoara Nord d.	...	...	...	...	...	...	...	0604	...	0905	...	...	...	...	...	1354	1614	...	1809	|	|	2113	2113	215
Lugoj d.	...	...	...	...	...	...	...	0719	...	1000	...	...	...	...	...	1505	1736	...	1926	|	|	2227	2227	230
Caransebeş ⊡ d.	...	...	...	...	...	...	...	0800	...	...	...	...	...	...	...	1549	1831	1945	2028	|	|	2314	2314	235
Băile Herculane d.	...	...	...	...	...	...	...	0921	...	...	...	...	...	...	...	1713	...	2134	2159	◐	◐	0040	0040	012
Orşova d.	...	...	...	...	...	0730	...	0945	...	...	...	...	...	...	...	1737	...	2200	2222	|	|	0106	0106	014
Drobeta Turnu Severin d.	...	...	...	...	...	0812	**e**	1023	...	...	...	...	**c**	1509	...	1812	...	...	2256	|	|	0140	0140	022
Filiaşi 1635 d.	...	...	...	...	...	1022	1052	1205	...	...	...	...	1617	1700	...	1955	...	...	0041	0139	0139	0328	0328	041
Craiova 1635 a.	...	...	...	...	...	...	1118	1231	...	...	...	...	1645	1727	...	2021	...	...	0107	0207	0207	0354	0354	043
Craiova d.	0413	0413	0616	0726	...	...	1123	1238	...	...	1413	1530	1655	1733	1915	2029	...	...	0117	0216	0216	0359	0359	044
Caracal d.	0459	0459	0703	0812	...	...	1210	1330	...	...	1500	1617	1741	1820	2002	2116	...	...	0204	0303	0303	0445	0445	053
Roşiori Nord d.	0556	0556	0800	0912	...	...	1307	1427	...	...	1554	1715	1838	1917	2100	2210	...	...	0258	0401	0401	0539	0539	062
Videle d.	0653	0653	0848	1000	...	...	1355	1515	...	...	1643	1804	1926	2006	2148	2259	...	...	0347	0449	0449	0627	0627	071
Bucureşti Nord a.	0746	0746	0938	1050	...	...	1444	1605	...	...	1733	1856	2016	2056	2238	2349	...	...	0440**b**	0539	0539	0717	0717	080
Constanţa **1680** a.	...	1040	...	...	...	...	...	...	...	...	...	...	...	...	...	...	...	...	0708	...	0846	...	0959	...

M – MUNTENIA – 🛏 1, 2 cl., ▬ 2 cl., [12] Bucureşti - Timişoara - Arad - Budapest and v.v.
T – TRAIANUS – [12] Bucureşti - Timişoara - Arad - Budapest and v.v (✕ from Timişoara).

b – Bucureşti **Băneasa**.
c – To / from Teiuş / Cluj Napoca via Târgu Jiu (Table **1635**).
d – June 16 - Sept. 11.
e – To / from Deva or Târgu Jiu (Table **1635**).
f – June 18 - Sept. 11.
g – Apr. 28 - May 1, June 17 - Sept. 10.
h – Apr. 27 – 30, June 16 - Sept. 9.
j – June 17 - Sept. 10.
k – June 16 - Sept. 9.
m – Not Apr. 15, 16, June 15 - Sept. 10.
n – Not Apr. 14, 16, 17, May 1, June 1, 4, 5, Aug. 15, Nov. 30, Dec. 1.
p – Not Apr. 15, 16, June 16 - Sept. 11.
q – Not Apr. 28 - May 1, June 17 - Sept. 10.
r – June 15 - Sept. 10.
t – Not Apr. 27 – 30, June 16 - Sept. 9.

⊕ – 🛏 1, 2 cl., ▬ 2 cl., [12]
⊗ – 🛏 1, 2 cl., ▬ 2 cl., [2]
◇ – Operated by Astra Trans Carpatic.
◐ – Via Târgu Jiu and Simeria (Table **1635**).
⊡ – **CARANSEBES - REŞIŢA SUD** (journey 64 – 73 minutes). **From Caransebeş** at 0349, 0705, 0902**f**, 1329Ⓐ, 1640 and 1950. **From Reşiţa Sud** at 0535, 0855, 1322, 1520Ⓐ, 1825**k** and 2220.

1635 CRAIOVA - TÂRGU JIU - DEVA

km						1823				1835	1821
			2	Ⓑ	⑤-⑦		Ⓑ	2		u	⊕s
	Bucureşti N **1630** d.	...	...	...	...	0835	...	...	...	1630	2332
0	**Craiova** 1630 d.	0248	...	0535	...	1226	1425	...	1638	2015	0315
36	Filiaşi 1630 d.	0346	...	0620	...	1253	1524	...	1737	2043	0342
107	**Târgu Jiu** a.	0526	...	0801	...	1439	1707	...	1923	2201	0458
107	**Târgu Jiu** d.	0527	...	0813	1100	1443	1709	...	1925	2203	0501
157	Petroşani a.	0709	...	0958	1226	1603	1850	...	2105	2326	0618
157	Petroşani d.	...	0722	—	—	1608	...	1905	...	2330	0624
237	Simeria 1620 d.	...	1000	1047	...	1804	...	2143	...	0153	0833
246	**Deva** 1620 a.	...	...	1057	...	1816	...	...	...		0852
	Cluj Napoca **1620** a.	...	...	|	...	...	...	...	...		|
	Arad **1600** a.	...	...	1426	...	...	...	...	...		1131

			1824		1836					182
							2Ⓑ	2Ⓐ	Ⓑ	⊕s
Arad **1600** d.	...	...	...	0550	...	0738	...	...	...	180
Cluj Napoca **1620** d.	...	...	...	|	0740	|	...	...	...	|
Deva 1620 d.	...	...	0548	0955	|	1116	...	1554	...	204
Simeria 1620 d.	...	...	0601	1005	1115	1128	...	1559	...	205
Petroşani a.	...	...	0810	...	1320	...	...	1834	...	225
Petroşani d.	0416	0755	0815		1324	...	1445	...	1935	225
Târgu Jiu a.	0606	0938	0931		1442	...	1628	...	2117	001
Târgu Jiu d.	0625	0948	0933	...	1444	...	1635	...	2130	001
Filiaşi 1630 d.	0835	1138	1052	...	1617	...	1814	...	2309	013
Craiova 1630 a.	0918	1222	1118	...	1645	...	1858	...	2352	020
Bucureşti N **1630** a.	...	...	1444	...	2016	...	...	...	...	053

s – Extended from / to Mangalia and Constanţa on dates in Table **1630** (numbered **1920/2**).
u – Train number **3081** from Teiuş.

⊕ – 🛏 1, 2 cl., ▬ 2 cl. and [12]

BUCUREŞTI - PITESTI - CRAIOVA

km												
		2		Ⓐ			Ⓐ	2	Ⓑ			
0	**Bucureşti** Nord ‡ ...... d.	0556	0737	0909	1140	1334	1433	1530	1626	1729	1930	2028
108	Piteşti ‡ .... d.	0752	0931	1045	1328	1537	1624	1752	1803	1933	2126	2216
189	Slatina .... d.	0936	...	...	...	1727	...	1929	...	2114	...	...
206	Piatra Olt .... **1645** d.	0955	...	...	...	1750	...	1947	...	2136	...	...
250	**Craiova** .... **1645** a.	1044	...	...	...	1846	...	2034	...	2225	...	...

				2	Ⓐ	Ⓐ		2Ⓑ			
Craiova .... **1645** d.	...	0400	...	0700	...	...	...	1200	...	...	[illegible]
Piatra Olt .... **1645** d.	...	0446	...	0745	...	...	...	1255	...	...	1646
Slatina .... d.	...	0507	...	0806	...	...	...	1316	...	...	1706
Piteşti ‡ .... d.	0500	0655	0800	1000	1130	1300	1351	1508	1604	1656	1905
Bucureşti Nord ‡ ..... a.	0643	0831	0940	1141	1306	1437	1528	1646	1747	1846	2046

‡ – Local trains Bucureşti - Piteşti (and v.v) are 2nd class only.

SIBIU - RÂMNICU VÂLCEA - CRAIOVA / BUCUREŞTI 1645

km											
							⚒			1912	
			2	Ⓑ	2n		2n		2n	K	Ⓐ
0	**Sibiu** .... **1600** d.	0220	0300	0630	0727	...	*1151*	1548	1617	1842	...
22	Podu Olt .... **1600** d.	|	0339	0706	0808	...	1248	1622	1658	1920	2016
83	Călimăneşti .... d.	0439	0528	0851	1014	...	1441	1801	1903	2103	2215
99	**Râmnicu Vâlcea** .... d.	0502	0554	0915	1042	...	1525	1825	1931	2123	2240
186	Piatra Olt .... **1640** d.	0626	0808	1039	...	...	1745	2005	2155	2302	...
230	**Craiova** ...... **1640** a.	|	...	1129	...	...	...	2058	...	|	...
•32	Caracal .... **1630** a.	0658	...	...	...	...	...	...	...	|	...
•17	Slatina .... d.	...	...	...	...	...	...	...	...	2323	...
•98	Piteşti .... d.	...	...	...	...	...	...	...	...	0125	...
•206	**Bucureşti** Nord . **1630** a.	...	...	...	...	...	...	...	...	0303	...
	Constanţa **1680** .... a.	...	...	...	...	...	...	...	...	0611	...

		1914	⚒						Ⓑ	
	2n	J	2n		2			2		
Constanţa **1680** .... d.	...	2000	...	...	...	...	...	...	...	...
Bucureşti N ... **1630** d.	...	2301	...	...	...	...	...	...	...	...
Piteşti .... d.	...	0115	...	...	...	...	...	...	...	...
Slatina .... d.	...	0255	...	...	...	...	...	...	...	...
Caracal .... **1630** d.	...	|	...	...	...	...	...	...	...	1825
Craiova ... **1640** d.	...	|	...	...	...	0750	...	...	1510	|
Piatra Olt .... **1640** d.	...	0330	0349	...	0631	0856	...	...	1616	1906
Râmnicu Vâlcea ..... d.	0245	0503	0621	...	0850	1026	...	1610	1755	2037
Călimăneşti .... d.	0311	0522	0648	...	0917	1045	...	1636	1814	2056
Podu Olt .... **1600** d.	0527	0702	0849	0923	1113	1224	...	1844	2005	2237
Sibiu .... **1600** a.	0610	0733	...	1001	1154	1249	...	1924	2030	2302

– June 17 - Sept. 10.
n – Not Apr. 14, 16, 17, May 1, June 1, 4, 5, Aug. 15, Nov. 30, Dec. 1.
• – Distance from Piatra Olt.
– June 16 - Sept. 9.

BUCUREŞTI - BUZĂU - BACĂU - IAŞI and SUCEAVA 1650

km ☆					1830	1661	1655		1751	1663		1543	1866
								Ⓐ					
					2		j					2	
0	**Bucureşti** Nord..... **1600/70** d.	...	...	0450	...	0625	0649	0925	1055	1200	1325	...	...
59	Ploieşti Sud .... **1600/70** d.	...	...	0553	...	0703	0726	1025	1132	1237	1442	...	...
	Constanţa **1680** .... d.	...	...	|	...	|	|	|	|	|	|	...	...
	Făurei .... **1670** d.	...	...	|	...	|	|	|	|	|	|	...	...
128	**Buzău** .... **1670** d.	...	...	0725	...	0809	0831	1157	1237	1342	1618	...	...
161	Râmnicu Sărat .... d.	...	...	▬	...	|	0859	...	1304	1410	...	...	...
199	Focşani .... d.	...	...	...	...	0912	0936	...	1341	1447	...	...	...
219	Mărăşeşti .... d.	...	0455	...	...	|	0954	...	1359	|	...	...	...
244	Adjud .... d.	...	0527	...	...	|	1016	...	1421	|	...	1651	...
303	**Bacău** .... d.	0419	0636	...	...	|	1054	...	1459	|	...	1728	...
346	Roman .... d.	0507	0725	...	...	|	1123	...	1530	|	...	1758	...
	Galaţi .... d.	|	|	...	0614	|	|	...	|	|	...	|	1628
238	Tecuci .... d.	|	|	0512	0755	1002	|	...	|	1535	...	|	1801
288	Bârlad .... d.	|	|	0617	0837	1038	|	...	|	1612	...	|	1844
340	Vaslui .... d.	|	|	0726	0921	1119	|	...	|	1656	...	|	1928
408	**Iaşi** .... a.	0749	|	0903	1028	1223	|	...	|	1803	...	1928	2035
538	*Chişinău* **1720** .... MD a.	...	|	...	c	...	|	...	|	...	...	...	...
387	Paşcani .... **1660** d.	...	0810	...	...	...	1152	...	1558	...	...	...	...
432	Vereşti .... **1660** d.	...	...	...	...	...	1223	...	1639	...	...	...	...
476	Botoşani .... a.	...	...	...	...	...	|	...	1800v	...	...	...	...
448	**Suceava** .... **1660** a.	...	...	...	...	...	1234	...	1650	...	...	...	...
450	**Suceava** Nord .... a.	...	...	...	...	...	...	...	...	...	...	...	...
499	Vadul Siret .... [customs] ▲ UA a.	...	...	...	...	...	...	...	...	...	...	...	...
539	**Chernivtsi** .... UA a.	...	...	...	...	...	...	...	...	...	...	...	...

	1753	1657	1665	551	562	402		1653	1667	1862	1960	1954
							Ⓑ					
		j	j	S	S	P		⊕	⊗	h	⊙f	⊙f
Bucureşti Nord	1400	1459	1612	1722	1722	1920	2002	2235	2250	...	...	...
Ploieşti Sud	1439	1538	1651	1804	1804	2010	2044	2316	2327	...	...	...
Constanţa **1680**	|	|	|	|	|	|	|	|	|	2120	2216	2325
Făurei	|	|	|	|	|	|	|	|	|	2348	|	0150
Buzău	1545	1643	1757	1908	1908	2118	2150	0022	0051	0051	|	0238
Râmnicu Sărat	1613	1712	1825	|	|	2146	2218	0050	0119	0119	|	0307
Focşani	1650	1750	1903	2008	2008	2223	2254	0127	0156	0156	△	0345
Mărăşeşti	1708	1809	1935	|	|	2241	2311	0145	|	|	|	0404
Adjud	1730	1831	|	|	|	2306	...	0207	|	|	|	0426
Bacău	1814	1907	|	2122	2122	2359	...	0245	|	|	|	0504
Roman	1845	...	|	|	|	0035	...	0316	|	|	|	0536
Galaţi	|	...	|	|	|	|	...	|	|	|	|	|
Tecuci	|	...	2000t	|	|	|	...	|	0244	0244	0334	|
Bârlad	|	...	2035	|	|	|	...	|	0320	0320	0411	|
Vaslui	|	...	2119	|	|	|	...	|	0404	0404	0456	|
Iaşi	|	...	2227	|	2328‡	0211	...	|	0511	0511	0604	|
Chişinău **1720**	|	...	...	|	...	0810	...	|	...	...	...	|
Paşcani	1913	...	...	2223	...	...	...	0345	...	...	...	0605
Vereşti	1947	...	...	|	...	...	...	0419	...	...	...	0640
Botoşani	|	...	...	|	...	...	...	|	...	...	...	|
Suceava	1958	...	...	2302	...	...	...	0430	...	...	...	0651
Suceava Nord	2005	...	...	...	...	...	...	d	...	...	...	0659
Vadul Siret	...	...	...	...	...	...	...	...	...	...	...	...
Chernivtsi	...	...	...	...	...	...	...	...	...	...	...	...

				1658	552	561	1541	1660	1752	1864			1754
		⚒	Ⓑ										
				j	S	S	2b	j			2		
hernivtsi .... UA d.	...	...	...	...	...	...	...	...	...	...	...	...	...
adul Siret .... [customs] ▲ UA d.	...	...	...	...	...	...	...	...	...	...	...	...	...
uceava Nord .... d.	...	...	...	...	...	...	...	...	0845	...	...	...	...
uceava .... **1660** d.	...	...	...	...	0545	...	...	...	0852	...	...	...	1246
Botoşani .... d.	...	...	...	...	|	...	...	...	|	...	...	...	1115v
ereşti .... **1660** d.	...	...	...	...	|	...	...	...	0904	...	...	...	1309
aşcani .... **1660** d.	...	...	...	...	0636	...	...	...	0939	...	...	...	1344
Chişinău **1720** .... MD d.	...	...	...	...	|	...	...	...	|	...	...	...	|
Iaşi .... d.	...	...	0456	...	|	0517•	0636	0618	|	0809	0908	...	|
Vaslui .... d.	...	...	0635	...	|	|	|	0724	|	0922	|	...	|
Bârlad .... d.	...	...	0758	...	|	|	|	0813	|	1010	|	...	|
Tecuci .... d.	...	...	0916	...	|	|	|	0859	|	1055	|	...	|
Galaţi .... a.	...	...	▬	...	|	|	|	|	|	1226	|	...	|
oman .... d.	...	...	...	...	|	|	0810	|	1006	...	1143	...	1411
acău .... d.	...	...	...	0434	0729	0729	0838	|	1045	...	1230	...	1440
djud .... d.	...	...	...	0512	|	|	0936	|	1123	...	▬	...	1518
ărăşeşti .... d.	...	0400	...	0535	|	|	▬	|	1146	...	...	...	1541
ocşani .... d.	...	0420	...	0555	0843	0843	Ⓐ	0940	1207	...	Ⓑ	...	1602
âmnicu Sărat .... d.	...	0458	...	0631	|	|	n	1016	1244	...		...	1638
uzău .... **1670** d.	0330	0526	0555	0659	0945	0945	0954	1043	1312	...	1406	1514	1706
Făurei .... **1670** a.	|	|	|	|	|	|	|	|	|	...	|	|	|
Constanţa **1680** .... a.	|	|	|	|	|	|	|	|	|	...	|	|	|
loieşti Sud .... **1600/70** d.	0502	0634	0726	0807	1050	1050	1122	1150	1419	...	1537	1642	1816
ucureşti Nord..... **1600/70** a.	0612	0714	0814	0844	1130	1130	1243	1229	1456	...	1634	1759	1853

		1662	1656	1664		1832	1952	1962	1668	1861	1654	401
		2	j	j		2	⊙g	⊙g	⊕	h	⊕	P
hernivtsi	...	...	...	...	...	...	...	...	...	...	...	...
adul Siret	...	...	...	...	...	...	...	...	...	...	...	...
uceava Nord	...	...	...	...	...	...	2031	...	...	...	d	...
uceava	...	...	1616	...	...	...	2038	...	...	...	2323	...
Botoşani	...	...	|	...	...	...	|	...	...	...	|	...
ereşti	...	...	1628	...	...	...	2050	...	...	...	2335	...
aşcani	1439	...	1700	...	1847	...	2125	...	...	...	0010	...
Chişinău **1720**	|	...	|	...	|	c	|	...	...	...	|	1720
Iaşi	|	1420	|	1607	|	1836	|	2127	2245	2245	|	2329
Vaslui	|	1526	|	1719	|	1951	|	2238	2352	2352	|	|
Bârlad	|	1615	|	1805	|	2041	|	2328	0042	0042	|	|
Tecuci	|	1701	|	1841t	|	2118	|	0005	0128	0128	|	|
Galaţi	|	|	|	|	|	2249	|	|	|	|	|	|
oman	1529	|	1728	|	1936	...	2152	|	|	|	0037	0112
acău	1619	|	1757	|	2035	...	2221	|	|	|	0116	0151
djud	1727	|	1835	|	2141	...	2300	|	|	|	0154	0236
ărăşeşti	1759	|	1919	1919	2208	...	2324	|	|	|	0217	0259
ocşani	...	1743	1939	1939	...	...	2345	△	0218	0209	0209	0320
âmnicu Sărat	...	1819	2015	2015	...	...	0022	|	0245	0245	0313	0356
uzău	...	1847	2042	2042	...	...	0108	|	0321	0345	0341	0424
Făurei	...	|	|	|	...	...	0135	|	|	0411	|	|
Constanţa **1680**	...	|	|	|	...	...	0347	0459	|	0639	|	|
loieşti Sud	...	1955	2149	2149	...	...	...	...	0428	...	0450	0531
ucureşti Nord	...	2033	2226	2226	...	...	...	...	0505	...	0529	0619

BACĂU - PIATRA NEAMŢ - BICAZ

km											
										1859	
	Bucureşti Nord ⊡ .... d.	...	...	...	...	...	...	1400	...	1459	...
0	**Bacău** .... d.	0408	0514	0736	...	1443	1647	1833	...	1923	...
60	Piatra Neamţ .... a.	0537	0644	0906	...	1613	1823	2003	...	2031	...
86	**Bicaz** .... a.	0650	...	...	...	...	...	2048	...	j	...

				1858						
Bicaz .... d.	...	...	0713	j	...	...	...	...	2111	...
Piatra Neamţ .... d.	0451	0718	0756	0913	1425	1636	1846	...	2154	2320
Bacău .... a.	0630	0852	...	1025	1559	1805	2029	...	...	0049
Bucureşti Nord ⊡ . a.	...	...	...	1456	...	...	...	...	...	...

– PRIETENIA – [sleeper] 1, 2 cl., (2) Bucureşti - Ungheni (**106/5**) - Chişinău and v.v.
– STEFAN CEL MARE EXPRES (12) Bucureşti - Paşcani - Suceava and v.v.; (12) Paşcani (**551/2**) - Iaşi and v.v.

– To / from Braşov via Comăneşti (Table **1610/1612**).
– To / from Cluj Napoca via Suceava (Table **1660**).
– To / from Vatra Dornei Băi (Table **1660**).
– Apr. 28 - May 1, June 17 - Sept. 10.
– Apr. 27 – 30, June 16 - Sept. 9.
– Not Apr. 28 - May 1, June 17 - Sept. 10.
– Not Apr. 16, June 4.
n – Not Apr. 27 - Apr. 30, June 16 - Sept. 9.
– Not Apr. 14, 16, 17, May 1, June 1, 4, 5, Aug. 15, Nov. 30, Dec. 1.

t – Tecuci **Nord**.
v – Portion attached / detached to main train at Vereşti.

• – Calls Paşcani at 0618 after Iaşi.
‡ – Calls Paşcani at 2215 before Iaşi.
⊕ – [sleeper] 1, 2 cl., [couchette] 2 cl., (12)
⊗ – [sleeper] 1, 2 cl., [couchette] 2 cl., (2)
⊙ – [couchette] 2 cl., (12)
△ – Via Brăila.
⊡ – See main table.
☆ – Tecuci - Galaţi 85 km. Iaşi - Roman 114 km.
▲ – [customs]: Vicsani (RO) / Vadul Siret (UA).
MD Moldova. RO Romania. UA Ukraine.

PAŞCANI - TÂRGU NEAMŢ *31 km*, ± 45 mins
From Paşcani: 0417Ⓐ, 0715, 1645, 1917.
From Târgu Neamţ: 0526Ⓐ, 1010, 1755, 2025.

VEREŞTI - BOTOŞANI *44 km*, ± 75 mins
From Vereşti: 0600, 0849, 1330, 1429, 1651, 1859 Ⓑ **p**.
From Botoşani: 0908, 1115, 1507, 1918, 2049 Ⓑ **p**.

[illegible]EAVA - DEJ - CLUJ NAPOCA

km						[illegible]13	1763	1837	4118
					2¶	2	⊗B	⊙2	2Ⓑ
[illegible]	[illegible]	[illegible]	[illegible]	1051	...	...	1535	2042	...
[illegible]	[illegible]	[illegible]	0708	1159	...	...	1642	2149	...
[illegible]	[illegible] d.	0419	0741	1232	...	...	1715	2222	...
[illegible]	[illegible] **1650** a.	0430	0753	1244	...	...	1727	2234	...
[illegible]	[illegible] d.	0440	0805	1247	...	...	1742	2236	...
[illegible]	[illegible]umorului Oraş d.	0533	0851	1333	...	...	1828	2329	...
[illegible]	Câmpulung Moldovenesc d.	0615	0934	1416	...	...	1910	0012	...
257	Vatra Dornei Băi d.	0720	1041	1522	...	...	2016	0119	...
351	Năsăud d.	...	1236	1714	...	...	2211	0314	...
0	**Sighetu Marmaţiei** d.	...	|	|	1610	...	|	|	2330
25	Valea Vişeului d.	...	|	|	1716	...	|	|	0031
57	Vişeu de Jos ▷d.	...	|	|	1813	...	|	|	0125
357	Salva ▷d.	...	1245	1722	2005	...	2219	0324	0305
379	Beclean pe Someş **1610/4** d.	...	1309	1745	2053	2105	2242	0347	0403*
402	Dej Călători **1610/4** d.	...	1346	1824	...	2144	2319	0424	0448
460	**Cluj Napoca** **1610/4** a.	...	1450	1930	...	2300	0025	0530	0615
	Oradea **1600/25** a.	...	1814	...	...	...	|	...	...
	Timişoara N **1620/25** a.	...	2213	...	...	...	0834	...	...

km		4110	4112	1832	1831	4114	4115	1654	1838	176[illegible]
		2	2¶	g	j	2⚒	2	⊕	⊙2	⊗B
	Timişoara N **1620/25** d.	...	...	...	0647	...	...	...	...	144[illegible]
	Oradea **1600/25** d.	...	...	...	1021	...	...	...	...	|
	Cluj Napoca **1610/4** d.	0325	...	0932	1310	1435	...	...	2030	222[illegible]
	Dej Câlători **1610/4** d.	0457	...	1044	1420	1604	...	...	2143	234[illegible]
	Beclean pe Someş **1610/4** d.	0531	0549	1118	1453	1644	...	...	2217	001[illegible]
0	Salva d.	...	0623	1140	1516	1733	...	...	2246	003[illegible]
61	Vişeu de Jos d.	...	0758	|	|	1912	1930	...	|	|
93	Valea Vişeului d.	...	0915	|	|	...	2044	...	|	|
118	**Sighetu Marmaţiei** a.	...	1000	|	|	...	2130	...	|	|
	Năsăud d.	...		1148	1525	...	...	...	2254	004[illegible]
	Vatra Dornei Băi d.	...	...	1338	1724	...	...	2040	0046	024[illegible]
	Câmpulung Moldovenesc d.	...	...	1442	1830	...	...	2143	0158	034[illegible]
	Gura Humorului Oraş d.	...	...	1526	1925	...	...	2228	0242	043[illegible]
	Suceava a.	...	...	1610	2009	...	...	2312	0326	051[illegible]
	Suceava **1650** d.	...	...	1624	2011	...	...	2323	0328	053[illegible]
	Vereşti **1650** d.	...	...	1635	2022	...	...	2335	0339	054[illegible]
	Paşcani **1650** d.	...	...	1709	2057	...	...	0010	0412	061[illegible]
	Iaşi a.	...	...	1812	2200	...	...	c	0516	072[illegible]

B – Conveys 1,2 cl., 2 cl., (2) Botoşani - Suceava - Timişoara and v.v.

c – From/to Bucureşti (Table **1650**).
g – From/to Galaţi (Table **1650**).
j – Not Apr. 16, June 4.

⊕ – 1,2 cl., 2 cl., (12)
⊗ – 1,2 cl., 2 cl., (2)
⊙ – 2 cl. (4 and 6 berth), (2)
¶ – Conveys 2 cl. (4 and 6 berth), (2) to/from Bucureşti.
* – Train **4101** between Beclean pe Someş and Cluj Napoca.

1670 BUCUREŞTI - GALAŢI

km		1571		1573		1575		1577		1730	
										b	
0	**Bucureşti** Nord **1650** d.	0530	...	0807	...	1310	...	1750	...	...	...
	Ploieşti Sud **1650** d.	0608	...	0846	...	1348	...	1831	...	1920	...
**	Buzău **1650** d.	0714	...	0952	...	1454	...	1938	...	2026	...
71	Urziceni d.	|	...	|	...	|	...	|	...	|	...
Δ	Feteşti d.	|	...	|	...	|	...	|	...	|	...
138	Făurei d.	0741	...	1025	...	1521	...	2005	...	2053	...
198	Brăila d.	0831	...	1115	...	1611	...	2055	...	2143	...
229	**Galaţi** a.	0904	...	1148	...	1644	...	2128	...	2216	...

	1570		1732		1572		1574		1576	
		...	b	...						
Galaţi d.	0523	...	0645	...	0834	...	1430	...	1745	...
Brăila d.	0557	...	0719	...	0907	...	1504	...	1819	...
Făurei d.	0644	...	0808	...	0956	...	1553	...	1909	...
Feteşti d.	|	...	|	...	|	...	|	...	|	...
Urziceni d.	|	...	|	...	|	...	|	...	|	...
Buzău **1650** d.	0711	...	0836	...	1024	...	1621	...	1937	...
Ploieşti Sud **1650** d.	0817	...	0945	...	1131	...	1729	...	2045	...
Bucureşti Nord.. **1650** a.	0854	...	...	...	1211	...	1806	...	2122	...

b – From/to Braşov (Table **1600**). ** – Buzău - Făurei: *40 km*. Δ – Feteşti - Făurei: *89 km*.

1680 BUCUREŞTI - CONSTANTA - MANGALIA

km		1952	1962	1912		1861	1941	1992		1932	1922	1970	1981		1581		1994	1583	538		1585	1928			188[illegible]
		⊙	⊙		2	⊙	⊕	⊕	2	⊕	⊕			2		2				2				2	
		F•	F•	C•	N	U•	F•	C•	N	F•	F•	D	D	N	N		D	N	A	N	N	D	Ⓐ	N	
	From:	*Suc*	*Iasi*	*Ram*		*Ia/S*	*Sat*	*Tim*		*Ora*	*Tar*	*Gal*					*Cra*		*Bra*			*Bra*			
0	**Bucureşti** Nord d.	|	|	0322	...	|	0415b	0443b	...	0514b	0604	|	0705	...	0730	...	0820	0820	0930	...	1030	1030	1130	...	123[illegible]
146	Feteşti d.	0250	0359	0502	...	0536	0536	0603	...	0638	0741	0805	0831	...	0856	...	0944	0944	|	...	1154	1154	1303	...	140[illegible]
190	Medgidia d.	0324	0432	0538	...	0613	0613	0636	...	0713	0814	0838	0913	...	0929	0936	1017	1017	|	...	1227	1227	1336	...	143[illegible]
334	**Tulcea** Oraş a.	|	|	|	...	|	|	|	...	|	|	|	|	...	|	1235	|	|	|	...	|	|	|	...	|
225	**Constanţa** a.	0347	0459	0611	...	0639	0646	0708	...	0745	0846	0901	0937	...	0952	...	1040	1040	1130	...	1250	1250	1359	...	150[illegible]
225	**Constanţa** d.	...	...	...	0613	...	...	...	0720	...	...	...	...	1005	...	...	...	...	...	1140	...	...	...	1422	...
239	Eforie Nord ▷ d.	...	...	...	0640	...	...	...	0741	...	...	...	...	1025	...	...	...	...	...	1157	...	...	...	1442	...
268	**Mangalia** a.	...	...	...	0721	...	...	...	0827	...	...	...	...	1108	...	...	...	...	...	1248	...	...	...	1528	...

		1983	1587					1589	581					1681											
	2			2	2		2			2	2		2												
	N	D	N	N			N			t			Ⓑ												
From:																									
Bucureşti Nord d.	...	1330	1430	...	...	1531	...	1631	1730	...	...	1830	...	2010	...	...	...	...	...	...	...	...	...	...	...
Feteşti d.	...	1455	1557	...	...	1704	...	1758	|	...	...	2003	...	2140	...	...	...	...	...	...	...	...	...	...	...
Medgidia d.	...	1530	1630	...	1635	1737	...	1831	|	1848	...	2036	...	2213	...	...	...	...	...	...	...	...	...	...	...
Tulcea Oraş a.	...	|	|	...	1935	|	...	|	|	|	...	|	...	|	...	...	...	...	...	...	...	...	...	...	...
Constanţa a.	...	1553	1653	...	...	1800	...	1854	1930	1944	...	2059	...	2236	...	...	...	...	...	...	...	...	...	...	...
Constanţa d.	1513	...	...	1658	...	...	1825	...	...	...	1935	...	2110	...	...	...	...	...	...	...	...	...	...	...	...
Eforie Nord ▷ d.	1540	...	...	1718	...	...	1847	...	...	...	2000	...	2130	...	...	...	...	...	...	...	...	...	...	...	...
Mangalia a.	1630	...	...	1759	...	...	1931	...	...	...	2057	...	2213	...	...	...	...	...	...	...	...	...	...	...	...

	1680		1580			1582		582			1584	1926		1586	1996		1588		1682		1942	536	1930		198[illegible]
		2		2	2		2			2		2	2			2		2		2	⊕		⊕	2	
					⚒		N		N	N		D	N	N	D	N		t		N	E	A	E		D
Mangalia d.	...	0543	...	...	0630	...	0835	...	...	1200	...	...	1300	...	...	1435	...	...	...	1540	...	...	...	...	...
Eforie Nord ▷ d.	...	0638	...	...	0722	...	0918	...	...	1242	...	...	1342	...	...	1527	...	...	...	1624	...	...	...	...	...
Constanţa a.	...	0703	...	...	0741	...	0940	...	...	1300	...	...	1403	...	...	1548	...	...	...	1644	...	...	...	...	...
Constanţa d.	0530	...	0730	...	...	0825	...	1050	1130	...	1330	1400	...	1430	1430	...	1530	1540	1630	...	1704	1720	1742	...	181[illegible]
Tulcea Oraş d.	|	...	|	0527	...	|	...	|		...	|	|	...	|	|	...	|	|	|	...	|	|	|	1530	|
Medgidia d.	0553	...	0753	0825	...	0848	...	|	1153	...	1353	1423	...	1453	1453	...	1553	1612	1653	...	1729	|	1807	1841	185[illegible]
Feteşti d.	0628	...	0828	...	...	0923	...	|	1228	...	1428	1458	...	1528	1528	...	1627	...	1728	...	1813	|	1842	...	192[illegible]
Bucureşti Nord a.	0755	...	0952	...	...	1047	...	1250	1359	...	1552	1622	...	1652	1652	...	1750	...	1852	...	1932b	1920	2001b	...	205[illegible]
To:	*Bra*											*Bra*			*Cra*						*Sat*	*Bra*	*Ora*		

		1684	1972	1984	1914			1920		1862	1990	1960	1954												
	2					2		⊙	2	⊙	⊕	⊙	⊙												
	N	N	D	D	D	N	N	E	N	U	D	E	E												
Mangalia d.	1712	...	...	...	...	1840	...	...	2000	...	...	...	...	...	...	...	...	...	...	...	...	...	...	...	...
Eforie Nord ▷ d.	1801	...	...	...	...	1931	...	...	2050	...	...	...	...	...	...	...	...	...	...	...	...	...	...	...	...
Constanţa a.	1819	...	...	...	...	1953	...	...	2110	...	...	...	...	...	...	...	...	...	...	...	...	...	...	...	...
Constanţa d.	...	1830	1845	1930	2000	...	2000	2043	...	2120	2148	2216	2325	...	...	...	...	...	...	...	...	...	...	...	...
Tulcea Oraş d.	...	|	|	|	|	...	|	|	...	|	|	|	|	...	...	...	...	...	...	...	...	...	...	...	...
Medgidia d.	...	1853	1910	1953	2026	...	2023	2108	...	2145	2213	2241	2351	...	...	...	...	...	...	...	...	...	...	...	...
Feteşti d.	...	1928	1946	2028	2104	...	2058	2143	...	2221	2248	2318	0026	...	...	...	...	...	...	...	...	...	...	...	...
Bucureşti Nord a.	...	2051	|	2151	2241	...	2228	2312	...	|	0008b	|	|	...	...	...	...	...	...	...	...	...	...	...	...
To:			*Gal*		*Ram*			*Tar*		*Ia/S*	*Tim*	*Iasi*	*Suc*												

To/From:
Bra – Braşov (Table **1600**).
Cra – Craiova (Table **1630**).
Gal – Galaţi (Table **1670**).
Iasi – Iaşi (Table **1650**).
Ia/S – Iaşi and Suceava (Table **1650**).
Ora – Oradea via Cluj Napoca (Table **1600**).
Ram – Sibiu via Râmnicu Vâlcea (Table **1645**).
Sat – Satu Mare (Tables **1600/10**).
Suc – Suceava (Table **1650**).
Tar – Arad via Târgu Jiu (Tables **1600/35**).
Tim – Timişoara via Craiova (Table **1630**).

A – TOMIS EXPRES – (12) Braşov - Bucureşti - Constanţa and v.v.
C – June 16 - Sept. 9.
D – June 17 - Sept. 10.
E – Apr. 28 - May 1, June 17 - Sept. 10.
F – Apr. 27–30, June 16 - Sept. 9.
N – Not June 17 - Sept. 10.
U – Not Apr. 28 - May 1, June 17 - Sept. 10.

b – Bucureşti **Băneasa**.
t – From/to Tulcea Oraş.

⊕ – 1, 2 cl., 2 cl., (12)
⊙ – 2 cl., (12)
• – Previous day from point of origin.
▷ – Trains also call at Eforie Sud (7–9 minutes south of Eforie Nor[illegible] and Costineşti (25–35 minutes south of Eforie Nord).

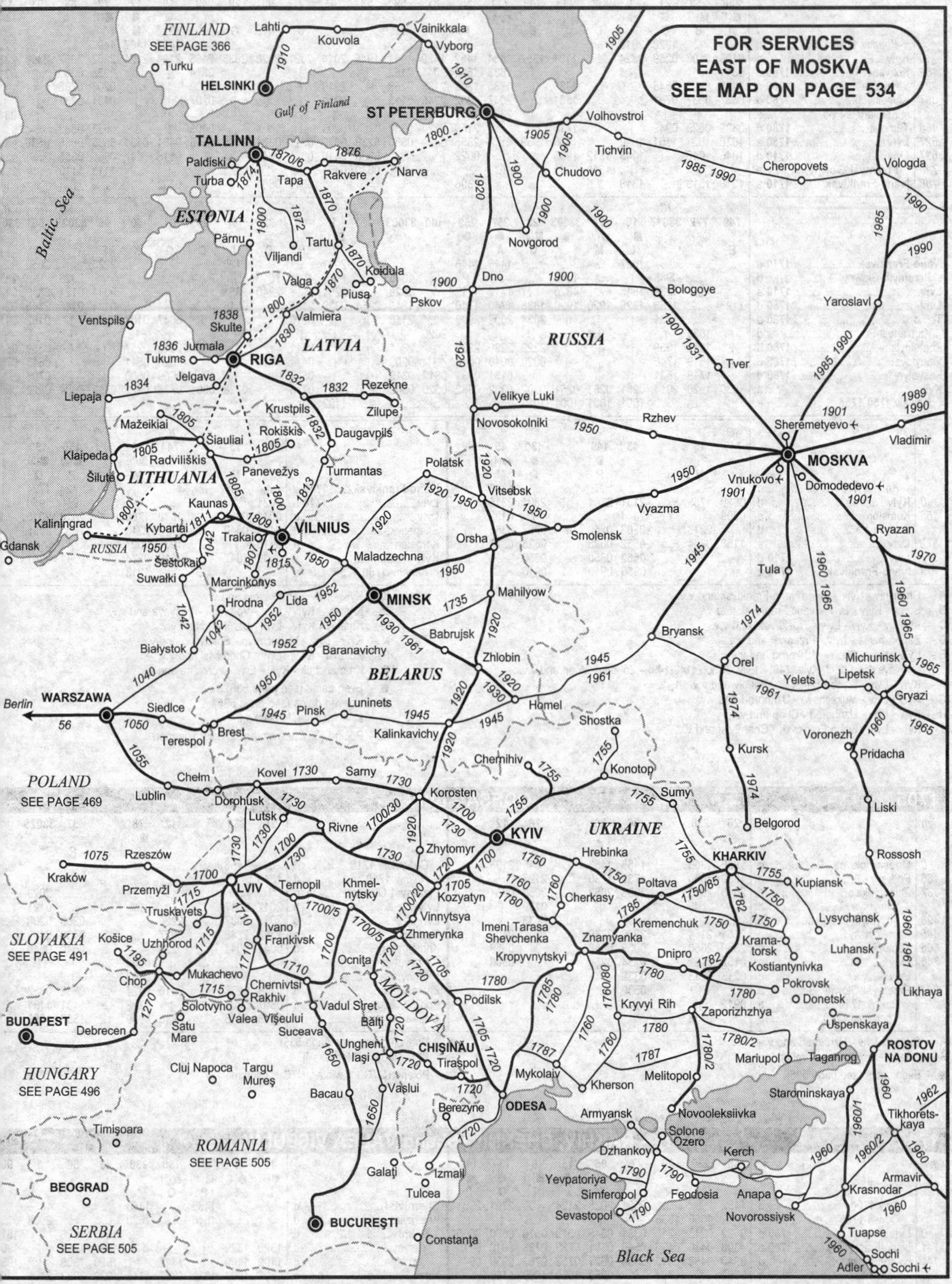

UKRAINE and MOLDOVA

perators : **UZ**: Ukrzaliznytsya, www.uz.gov.ua **CFM**: Calea Ferată din Moldova, www.railway.md Other operators as indicated in the table headings and notes.

ervices : Overnight trains convey sleeping and couchette cars and may not convey seating accommodation. Prior reservation is necessary except for travel by purely local trains. See also the panel on page 535. Trains shown as *IC* are fast day trains classified *Interciti* or *Interciti+* at premium fares.

mings : Timings are the latest available and are subject to alteration at any time. **Readers should consult the latest government advice regarding travel in this region.**

me zones: Local time is used throughout: East European Time for Ukraine and Moldova (UTC+2 winter, UTC+3 summer). Times within European Russia are in the Moskva time zone (UTC+3 all year) unless otherwise shown. As Russia and Belarus do not put their clocks forward in summer (daylight saving time), trains running between Ukraine or Moldova and Russia or Belarus change their timings by approximately one hour when clocks change (last Sunday in March and October) as shown in the tables.

1700 KYÏV - LVIV - PRZEMYŚL and IVANO-FRANKIVSK

km		258	259	21	1	32	IC 715	IC 749	771	55	81	59	53	IC 705	7	95	29	49	15	17	73	89	91	13
		■(1)	■(1)	●	●				⑤⑥										●	■	■(1)			
		A	B	C		D		E		F	G	H			J	F	G	K	L	M				
	Kharkiv **1750 1755** d.	...	...	1928	2019	...	...	...	...	...	...	...	...	...	...	...	...	...	1407	1407	1407	...	...	..
0	**Kyïv** d.	0106	0106	0259	0324	...	1101	1257	1434	1452	1829	1911	1946	2014	2021	2028	2035	2105	2124	2124	2252	2252	2308	23
159	Kozyatyn 1 **1780** d.	0311	0311	|	|	...	|	|	1638	1654	2041	2152	|	|	|	|	|	2314	|	|	0058	0058	|	02
221	Vinnytsya **1780** d.	0408	0408	0548	|	...	1336	|	1735	1748	2138	2258	|	2210	|	|	|	0009	|	|	0208	0208	|	|
367	Khmelnytsky **1780** d.	0637	0637	0751	|	...	1531	|	2047	1952	2345	0113	|	0031	|	|	|	0207	|	|	0431	0431	|	|
	Kamianets-Pod. a.	|	|	|	|	...	|	|	2332	|	|	|	|	|	|	|	|	|	|	|	|	|	|	08
486	Ternopil **1780** d.	0829	0829	0949	|	...	1716	|	...	2150	0224	0330	|	0205	|	|	|	0405	|	|	0633	0633	|	..
627	**Lviv** **1780** a.	1026	1026	1151	1026	...	1900	1959	...	2355	0421	0550	0238	0340	0311	0321	0330	0605	0431	0431	0835	0835	0635	..
627	**Lviv** **1710** d.	1046	1046	...	1046	1312	1935	...	...	0022	...	...	0338	0410	0331	0345	...	...	0518	...	0855	0855	...	..
725	**Przemyśl** Glowny ⊖ PL a.	|	|	...	|	1518	2025	...	...	|	...	...	0630	0454	|	|	...	...	|	...	1113	1113	...	..
768	**Ivano-Frankivsk** **1710** a.	1318	1318	...	1318	...	...	...	...	0308	...	...	...	...	0548	0601	...	...	0733	...	...	...	...	..

	749	772	IC 33017	16	17	33003	22	257	259	140	33003	92	1	60	32	8	29	81	50	96	33025	56	IC 330
		⑥⑦		■(3)	●(2)	●	■(3)	●	●				■(1)										
	E			L	M		C	A	B					H	D	J	G	G	K	F		F	
Ivano-Frankivsk **1710** d.	...	...	...	1627	...	...	...	1446	1446	...	...	...	2031	...	...	2125	...	...	...	2223	...	2050	..
Przemyśl Glowny ⊖ PL d.	...	...	0945	|	...	1345	...	|	|	...	1345	...	|	...	1810	|	...	...	...	|	2028	|	23
Lviv **1710** a.	...	...	1238	1845	...	1825	...	1712	1712	...	1828	...	2254	...	2240	2351	...	...	...	0044	0121	2319	02
Lviv **1780** d.	1123	...	1253	1920	1920	1920	1835	1740	1740	...	1845	2254	2322	2105	...	0015	0024	2244	2305	0104	0146	2345	02
Ternopil **1780** d.	|	...	1431	|	|	|	2034	2009	2009	...	2118	|	|	0010	...	|	|	0047	0107	|	|	0152	04
Kamianets-Pod. d.	|	1025	|	|	|	|	|	|	|	2020	|	|	|	|	...	|	|	|	|	|	|	|	|
Khmelnytsky **1780** d.	|	1311	1559	|	|	|	2222	2230	2230	|	2344	|	|	0211	...	|	|	0310	0257	|	|	0359	05
Vinnytsya **1780** d.	|	1619	1746	|	|	|	0020	0040	0040	|	0203	|	|	0414	...	|	|	0520	0511	|	|	0613	07
Kozyatyn 1 **1780** d.	|	1718	1831	|	|	|	|	0131	0131	0312	0319	|	|	0507	...	|	|	0609	0600	|	|	0705	|
Kyïv a.	1830	1928	2014	0251	0251	0251	0302	0332	0332	0520	0542	0620	0637	0748	...	0728	0801	0836	0822	0852	0904	0922	09
Kharkiv **1750 1755** a.	...	...	...	1001	1001	1001	1018	...	...	...	...	...	1402	...	...	...	...	...	...	...	...	...	..

km		IC 743	13		43	149		130	45	
						●		●	●(4)	
			N			P		Q	M	
	Kharkiv **1750 1755** d.	...	...	...	...	...	...	...	1343	...
0	**Kyïv** d.	0620	1755	...	2131	2301	...	2301	2315	...
156	Korosten d.	0809	|	...	2344	|	...	|	0132	...
	Shepetivka d.	|	2213	...	0203	0258	...	0258	0356	...
572	**Lviv** a.	1158	0204	...	0532	0625	...	0625	0827	...
572	**Lviv** **1710** d.	...	...	...	0552	0650	...	0650	...	...
713	**Ivano-Frankivsk** **1710** a.	...	...	...	0956	0910	...	0910	...	...

	43	13		IC 744	45		150	130	
					■(3)		■(3)	■(3)	
		N			M		P	Q	
Ivano-Frankivsk **1710** d.	2004	...	...	...	...	...	1724	1724	...
Lviv **1710** a.	0021	...	...	...	...	...	1950	1950	...
Lviv d.	0041	0256	...	1530	1750	...	2010	2010	...
Shepetivka d.	0414	0640	...	|	2215	...	2355	2355	...
Korosten d.	0610	|	...	1935	0027	...	|	|	...
Kyïv a.	0830	1047	...	2119	0234	...	0341	0341	...
Kharkiv **1750 1755** a.	...	...	...	...	1213	...	...	...	...

A – Chernihiv - Kyïv - Lviv - Ivano-Frankivsk and v.v.
B – Sumy - Kyïv - Lviv - Ivano-Frankivsk and v.v.
C – Kharkiv - Kyïv - Lviv - Truskavets and v.v.
D – Zaporizhzhia - Lviv - Przemyśl and v.v.
E – Kyïv - Lviv - Chop - Uzhhorod and v.v.
Conveys 🛏 1, 2 cl. Kyiv (**749**) - Lviv - Chop (**140/149**) - Záhony - Wien and v.v.
F – Kyïv - Lviv - Ivano-Frankivsk - Rakhiv and v.v.
G – Kyïv - Lviv - Mukachevo - Uzhhorod and v.v.
H – Kyïv - Lviv - Uzhhorod - Chop and v.v.
J – Kyïv - Lviv - Ivano-Frankivsk - Chernivtsi and v.v.
K – Kyïv - Lviv - Truskavets and v.v.
L – Kharkiv - Kyïv - Lviv - Vorokhta - Yasynya and v.v.
M – Kharkiv - Kyïv - Lviv - Uzhhorod and v.v.
N – Kyïv - Lviv - Mukachevo - Solotvyno and v.v.
P – Poltava - Kyïv - Lviv - Chernivtsi and v.v.
Q – Kremenchuk - Kyïv - Lviv - Vorokhta and v.v.
● – Even dates (see page 535).
■ – Uneven dates (see page 535).
⊖ – 🏛 = Medyka / Mostiska II.
PL – Poland (UTC + 1 winter, UTC + 2 summer).

1705 ODESA - LVIV

km		26	236		36	38		78	12	
								●		
						R		S		
0	**Odesa** Holovna d.	1356	1356	...	1458	1458	...	1840	2103	...
186	Podilsk d.	1650	1650	...	1736	1736	...	2127	|	...
387	Zhmerynka d.	2015	2015	...	2053	2053	...	0053	0234	...
	Vinnytsya d.	|	|	...	|	|	...	0139	|	...
498	Kozyatyn 1 a.	|	|	...	|	|	...	0233	|	...
486	Khmelnytsky d.	2154	2154	...	2236	2236	...	...	0408	...
605	Ternopil d.	2350	2350	...	0039	0039	...	...	0559	...
746	**Lviv** a.	0152	0152	...	0254	0254	...	...	0806	...
	Lviv d.	0213	0213	...	0338	...	...	...	...	...
844	**Przemyśl** Glowny ⊖ PL a.	|	|	...	0630	...	...	...	...	...
	Rakhiv **1710** a.	0912	|	...	...	...	...	...	...	...
	Chernivtsi **1710** a.	...	0738	...	...	...	...	...	...	...

	26	236		12	78		37	33025	
					■(1)				
					S		R		
Chernivtsi **1710** d.	...	1456	...	...	...	...	...	...	...
Rakhiv **1710** d.	1345	|	...	...	...	...	...	...	...
Przemyśl Glowny ⊖ PL d.	|	|	...	...	...	...	...	2028	...
Lviv a.	2017	2017	...	...	...	...	...	0121	...
Lviv d.	2037	2037	...	2220	...	...	0208	0208	...
Ternopil d.	2243	2243	...	0027	...	...	0439	0439	...
Khmelnytsky d.	0041	0041	...	0223	...	...	0640	0640	...
Kozyatyn 1 d.	|	|	...	|	0200	...	|	|	...
Vinnytsya d.	|	|	...	|	0302	...	|	|	...
Zhmerynka d.	0238	0238	...	0416	0424	...	0832	0832	...
Podilsk d.	0607	0607	...	|	0722	...	1131	1131	...
Odesa Holovna a.	0848	0848	...	0918	0949	...	1358	1358	...

R – Odesa - Lviv - Uzhhorod and v.v.
S – Odesa - Kozyatyn - Kovel and v.v.
● – Even dates (see page 535).
■ – Uneven dates (see page 535).
⊖ – 🏛 = Medyka / Mostiska II.
PL – Poland (UTC + 1 winter, UTC + 2 summer).

1710 LVIV - RAKHIV, CHERNIVTSI and VALEA VIŞEULUI

km		55	236	26	7	95	15	6	130	149
							●	■(3)	●	●
							L	T	Q	P
	Kyïv **1700** d.	1452	...	...	2021	2028	2124	...	2301	2301
	Odesa **1705** d.	|	1356	1356	|	|	|	...	|	|
0	**Lviv** **1700** d.	0022	0213	0213	0331	0345	0518	0518	0650	0650
141	Ivano-Frankivsk **1700** a.	0308	0436	0436	0548	0601	0733	0733	0910	0910
141	Ivano-Frankivsk d.	0340	0456	0510	0558	0621	0753	0753	0930	0945
	Vorokhta a.	0552	|	0734	|	0853	1009	1009	1150	|
	Yasynya a.	0639	|	0823	|	0935	1052	1052	...	|
	Rakhiv a.	0727	|	0912	|	1024	...	...	...	|
196	Kolomyia a.	...	0609	...	0657	...	...	...	...	1051
267	**Chernivtsi** a.	...	0738	...	0828	...	...	...	...	1200

	16	6	150	130	236	26	56	8	96
	■(3)	●(4)	■(3)	■(3)					
	L	T	P	Q					
Chernivtsi d.	...	...	1433	...	1456	...	...	1856	...
Kolomyia d.	...	...	1546	...	1620	...	...	2008	...
Rakhiv d.	...	...	|	...	|	1345	1626	|	181
Yasynya d.	1329	1329	|	...	|	1435	1719	|	190
Vorokhta d.	1409	1409	|	1447	|	1523	1808	|	195
Ivano-Frankivsk a.	1607	1607	1642	1657	1716	1729	2023	2105	215
Ivano-Frankivsk **1700** d.	1627	1627	1724	1724	1755	1755	2050	2125	222
Lviv **1700** a.	1845	1845	1950	1950	2017	2017	2319	2351	004
Odesa **1705** a.	|	...	|	|	0848	0848	|	|	|
Kyïv **1700** a.	0251	...	0341	0341	...	...	0922	0728	085

km										
0	**Rakhiv** d.	0610	1410	...	...	...	...	...	...	...
17	Dilove d.	⊖	⊖	...	...	...	...	...	...	...
19	**Valea Vişeului** RO a.	0745	1545	...	...	...	...	...	...	...

Valea Vişeului RO d.	1145	1815	...	...	...	...	...	...	...
Dilove d.	⊖	⊖	...	...	...	...	...	...	...
Rakhiv a.	1220	1850	...	...	...	...	...	...	...

L – Kharkiv - Kyïv - Lviv - Vorokhta - Yasynya and v.v.
P – Poltava - Kyïv - Lviv - Chernivtsi and v.v.
Q – Kremenchuk - Kyïv - Lviv - Vorokhta and v.v.
T – Zaporizhzhia - Lviv - Yasynya and v.v.
● – Even dates (see page 535).
■ – Uneven dates (see page 535).
⊖ – Timings not available.
RO – Romania (UTC + 2 winter, UTC + 3 summer).

UZ — LVIV - TRUSKAVETS, CHOP, UZHHOROD and SOLOTVYNO — 1715

km		13	38	29		81	17	33		59	49	41		45	4	21		31	829	749		749	266	
							■							●(4)		●			③–①				●(4)	
			A				B	C				D		B	E	F				G			H	
	Kyïv **1700** d.	1755	...	2035	...	1829	2124	...	...	1911	2105	...	...	2315	...	0259	...	...	...	1257	...	1257	...	...
0	**Lviv** d.	0238	0348	0402	...	0447	0457	...	...	0616	0630	0843	...	0853	0940	1223	...	...	1640	2025	...	2025	2219	...
78	Sambir d.	|	|	|	...	|	|	...	...	0732	|	|	...	|	|	|	...	...	|	|	...	|	2359	...
121	Drohobych a.	|	|	|	...	|	|	...	...	|	0801	1025	...	|	|	1353	...	...	|	|	...	|	|	...
133	**Truskavets** a.	|	|	|	...	|	|	...	...	|	0845	1109	...	|	|	1436	...	...	|	|	...	|	|	...
225	Mukachevo **1195** d.	0714	0806	0832	...	0920	0939	1230	...	|	...	...	...	1328	1420	...	...	1630	2102	0024	...	0024	0456	...
	Chop ◧ **1195** a.	|	|	|	...	1018	|	1410	...	1236**d**	...	...	...	1418	1509	...	...	1740	|	0110	...	0110	0551	...
288	**Uzhhorod** a.	|	0930	0946	...	1107	1054	|	...	1200**d**	...	...	...	1510	1558	...	...	|	2219	|	...	0205	0652	...
	Solotvyno 1 a.	1210	...	...	...	...	...	|	...	...	...	...	...	...	...	...	...	|	...	|	...	...	...	...
	Budapest Keleti **1270** a.	...	...	...	...	...	...	|	...	...	...	...	...	...	...	...	...	|	...	0820	...	...	...	...
	Budapest Nyugati **1270** a.	...	...	...	...	...	...	1837	...	...	...	...	...	...	...	...	...	2237	...	...	...	...	...	...

		749	749	829		42	45	22		17	60	34		3	81	50		29	37	13		265		
				④–②			■(3)	■(3)		●(2)												■(3)		
		G				D	B	F		B		C		E					A			H		
	Budapest Nyugati **1270** d.	...	...	...	...	...	...	...	...	...	...	0723	...	...	...	...	...	...	...	...	...	...	...	...
	Budapest Keleti **1270** d.	1940	...	...	...	...	...	...	...	...	...	|	...	...	...	...	...	...	...	...	...	...	...	...
	olotvyno 1 d.	|	...	...	...	...	...	...	...	...	...	|	...	...	...	...	...	...	...	1610	...	...	...	...
	Uzhhorod d.	|	0456	0627	...	...	1113	...	...	1325	1429**d**	|	...	1420	1600	...	...	1830	2007	|	...	2120	...	...
	hop ◧ **1195** d.	0553	0553	|	...	...	1211	...	...	|	1352**d**	1420	...	1518	1658	...	...	|	|	|	...	2218	...	...
	ukachevo **1195** d.	0653	0653	0752	...	...	1316	...	...	1450	|	1530	...	1628	1804	...	...	1958	2139	2153	...	2332	...	...
	Truskavets d.	|	|	|	...	1315	|	1558	...	|	|	...	...	|	|	2025	...	|	|	|	...	|	...	...
	Drohobych d.	|	|	|	...	1359	|	1642	...	|	|	...	...	|	|	2109	...	|	|	|	...	|	...	...
	ambir d.	|	|	|	...	|	|	|	...	|	1912	...	...	|	|	|	...	|	|	|	...	0500	...	...
	viv a.	1100	1100	1203	...	1533	1730	1811	...	1855	2035	...	...	2110	2224	2243	...	0004	0140	0230	...	0627	...	...
	Kyïv **1700** a.	1830	1830	...	...	...	0234	0302	...	0251	0748	...	...	...	0836	0822	...	0801	...	1047	...	...	...	...

– Odesa - Lviv - Uzhhorod and v.v.
– Kharkiv - Kyïv - Lviv - Uzhhorod and v.v.
– LATORCA – [2] Budapest - Mukachevo and v.v.
– Dnipro - Lviv - Truskavets and v.v.
– Zaporizhzhia - Lviv - Uzhhorod and v.v.
– Kharkiv - Kyïv - Lviv - Truskavets and v.v.

G – 🛏 1, 2 cl. Kyiv (**749**) - Lviv - Chop (**140/149**) - Záhony - Wien and v.v.
H – Uzhhorod - Lviv - Kovel and v.v.
d – Calls at Chop then Uzhhorod and v.v.
● – Even dates (see page 535).
■ – Uneven dates (see page 535).
◧ – ⊞ for trains to / from Hungary, Slovakia.

UZ, CFM — KYÏV - ODESA - BEREZYNE / IZMAÏL and TIRASPOL - CHISINĂU - IASI / OCNITA — 1720

Tiraspol and Bender (formerly Tighina) are located in the *de facto* autonomous region of Transnistria. Iasi Socola (broad gauge station) is 5 *km* from Iasi.

km		351	105									106	352							
		■											●							
		J											J							
0	**Kyïv** **1700** d.	1702	2117	...	...	...	...	...	...	...	**Izmaïl** d.	...	...	...	...	...	...	...	...	...
157	Kozyatyn 1 **1700** d.	1911	2326	...	...	...	...	...	...	...	**Berezyne** d.	...	...	...	...	...	...	...	...	...
221	Vinnytsya **1700** d.	2003	0017	...	...	...	...	...	...	...	Artsyz d.	...	...	...	...	...	...	...	...	...
268	Zhmerynka **1700 1705** d.	2101	0057	...	...	...	...	...	...	...	Bilhorod-Dnistrovsky d.	...	...	...	...	...	...	...	...	...
	Mohyliv-Podil's'yi ⊞ a.	2333	|	...	...	...	...	...	...	...	**Odesa** Holovna a.	...	...	...	...	...	...	...	...	...
469	Podilsk **1705** d.	...	0347	...	...	...	...	...	...	...	**Odesa** Holovna **1705** d.	2132	...	...	...	...	...	...	...	...
655	**Odesa** Holovna **1705** a.	...	0615	...	...	...	...	...	...	...	Podilsk **1705** d.	0010	...	...	...	...	...	...	...	...
655	**Odesa** Holovna d.	...	...	...	...	...	...	...	...	...	Mohyliv-Podil's'yi ⊞ d.	|	0517	...	...	...	...	...	...	...
740	Bilhorod-Dnistrovsky d.	...	...	...	...	...	...	...	...	...	Zhmerynka **1700 1705** d.	0304	0813	...	...	...	...	...	...	...
830	Artsyz a.	...	...	...	...	...	...	...	...	...	Vinnytsya **1700** d.	0344	0859	...	...	...	...	...	...	...
865	**Berezyne** a.	...	...	...	...	...	...	...	...	...	Kozyatyn 1 **1700** d.	0441	0951	...	...	...	...	...	...	...
937	**Izmaïl** a.	...	...	...	...	...	...	...	...	...	**Kyïv** **1700** a.	0644	1148	...	...	...	...	...	...	...

km		1061	821 1052	823 1064	1063	105 401	352	6831				6826	402 106	351	824	1062	1052	1064		
							●							■						
						K	J						K	J						
0	**Tiraspol** MD d.	...	...	...	...	...	...	...	...	...	Mohyliv-Podil's'yi ⊞ d.	...	...	0112	...	...	...	...	...	...
13	Bender 3 d.	...	...	...	...	...	...	...	...	...	Vălcineţ ⊞ MD d.	...	...	0205	...	...	...	...	...	...
71	**Chisinău** a.	...	...	...	...	...	...	...	...	...	**Ocnita** d.	...	...	0326	...	...	...	...	...	...
71	**Chisinău** d.	...	0633	0936	...	1720	1745	1803	...	...	Bălti Oraş d.	...	...	0611	...	...	...	...	...	...
178	Ungheni a.	...	0915	1226	...	1954	2021	2115	...	...	**Iasi** d.	...	0234	|	...	1307	...	1907	...	...
178	Ungheni ⊞ MD d.	0710	0951	1300	1614	2135	2051	...	...	...	**Iasi** Socola RO d.	...	|	|	1140	1319	1740	1919	...	...
	Iasi Socola RO a.	0831	1113	1427	1735	|	|	...	...	...	Ungheni ⊞ MD a.	...	0409	0753	1257	1442	1857	2032	...	...
199	**Iasi** a.	0841	...	...	1747	2305	|	...	...	...	Ungheni d.	0413	0549	0820	1337	...	1932	...	...	...
256	Bălti Oraş d.	...	...	...	...	...	2236	...	...	...	**Chisinău** a.	0710	0810	1038	1615	...	2200	...	...	...
354	**Ocnita** d.	...	...	...	...	...	0159	...	...	...	**Chisinău** d.	...	...	...	...	...	...	...	...	...
	Vălcineţ ⊞ MD d.	...	...	...	...	...	0334	...	...	...	Bender 3 d.	...	...	...	...	...	...	...	...	...
	Mohyliv-Podil's'yi ⊞ a.	...	...	...	...	...	0347	...	...	...	**Tiraspol** MD a.	...	...	...	...	...	...	...	...	...

– Kyïv - Ocnita - Ungheni - Chisinău and v.v.
– 🛏 🍸 Bucuresti (**402/401**) - Iasi - Chisinău and v.v.
● – Even dates (see page 535).

■ – Uneven dates (see page 535).
MD – Moldova (UTC + 2 in winter, UTC + 3 in summer).
RO – Romania (UTC + 2 in winter, UTC + 3 in summer).

UZ — KYÏV and KOZYATYN - RIVNE - LVIV, KOVEL and CHELM — 1730

km		67	97	23	93	78	265	88				68	88	266	78	98	94	24		
		R			●(1)	●	■(3)	●				R	■(1)	●(4)	■(1)		■(4)			
		L			M	N	H	P				L	P	H	N		M			
0	**Kyïv** d.	1814	2157	2230	2230	...	...	...	...	...	*Warszawa W* **1055** d.	1754	...	...	...	...	...	...	...	...
156	Korosten d.	|	0011	|	|	...	...	...	...	...	*Lublin* **1055** d.	2019	...	...	...	...	...	...	...	...
311	Sarny d.	|	|	|	|	...	...	...	...	...	**Chelm** d.	2119	...	...	...	...	1635	1635	...	...
*234	**Kozyatyn** 1 d.	|	|	|	|	0253	...	0727	...	...	Yahodyn ⊞ ⊡ d.	0443	...	...	...	...	2150	2150	...	...
	Shepetivka d.	|	0229	0330	0330	0457	...	0956	...	...	**Kovel** d.	0445	...	...	...	...	2250	2250	...	...
	Lviv a.	|	|	|	|	|	0650	|	...	...	**Kovel** d.	0607	1014	1458	1814	1855	2315	2315	...	...
383	**Rivne** a.	|	0423	0451	0451	0642	1008	1144	...	...	Lutsk d.	|	1226	1703	2033	2133	|	|	...	...
383	**Rivne** d.	|	0433	0458	0458	0648	1013	1149	...	...	**Rivne** a.	|	1341	1822	2147	2253	0116	0116	...	...
461	Lutsk d.	|	0626	|	|	0831	1200	1327	...	...	**Rivne** d.	|	1349	1830	2154	2258	0121	0121	...	...
545	**Kovel** a.	0042	0830	0700	0700	1050	1350	1527	...	...	**Lviv** d.	|	|	2159	|	|	|	|	...	...
	Kovel d.	0103	...	0721	0721	...	...	...	...	...	Shepetivka d.	|	1544	...	2333	0048	0242	0242	...	...
	Yahodyn ⊞ ⊡ d.	0202	...	0817	0817	...	...	...	...	...	**Kozyatyn** 1 a.	|	1815	...	0140	|	|	|	...	...
634	**Chelm** a.	0657	...	1235	1235	...	...	...	...	...	Sarny d.	|	...	...	...	|	|	|	...	...
	Lublin **1055** a.	0804	...	...	...	...	...	...	...	...	Korosten d.	|	...	...	...	0315	|	|	...	...
	Warszawa W **1055** a.	1012	...	...	...	...	...	...	...	...	**Kyïv** a.	1307	...	...	...	0535	0630	0630	...	...

– Uzhhorod - Lviv - Kovel and v.v.
– KYÏV EKSPRES / KIEV EXPRESS – 🛏 1, 2 cl. Kyiv - Warszawa and v.v. At Kyïv passengers may be required to board the train earlier for customs control.
– Kharkiv - Kyïv - Kovel - Chelm and v.v.
– Odesa - Kozyatyn - Kovel and v.v.

P – Zaporizhzhya - Kozyatyn - Kovel and v.v.
⊡ – ⊞ = Yahodyn (Ukraine) and Dorohusk (Poland). Ukraine is one hour ahead of Poland.
● – Even dates (see page 535).
■ – Uneven dates (see page 535).
* – Distance from Rivne.

1750 KYÏV - KHARKIV - KOSTIANTYNIVKA

km		16	17	33003	22	150	130	IC722	1	94	IC724	192	64	112
		■(3)	●(2)	●	■(3)	■(3)	■(3)		■(1)	■(4)		■(1)		
		A	B	H	C	D	E			F		G		
	Ivano-Frankivsk **1700** d.	1627	...	...	...	1724	1724	...	2031	...	...	...	...	...
	Lviv **1700** d.	1920	1920	1920	1835	2010	2010	...	2322	...	...	...	...	...
0	**Kyïv** d.	0311	0311	0311	0322	0401	0401	0652	0705	0705	1548	...	2255	2255
150	Hrebinka d.	|	|	|	|	0547	0547	|	|	|	|	...	|	|
	Kremenchuk a.	|	|	|	|	|	0935	|	|	|	|	...	|	|
335	Poltava Kyivska a.	0721	0721	0721	0737	0853	...	1012	1126	1126	1910	...	0333	0333
335	Poltava Kyivska 1785 d.	0741	0741	0741	0802	...	...	1014	1146	1146	1912	...	0353	0353
493	**Kharkiv** 1785 a.	1001	1001	1001	1018	...	...	1158	1402	1402	2048	...	0627	0627
493	**Kharkiv** d.	...	...	...	...	...	...	...	...	...	...	...	...	0755
	Bakhmut a.	...	...	...	...	...	...	...	...	...	...	...	...	|
	Izyum a.	...	...	...	...	...	...	...	...	...	...	...	...	1200
	Dnipro Hol. d.	...	...	...	...	...	...	...	...	...	...	0627	...	...
635	Slovyansk d.	...	...	...	...	...	...	...	...	...	...	1152	...	...
649	Kramatorsk d.	...	...	...	...	...	...	...	...	...	...	1211	...	...
679	**Kostiantynivka** a.	...	...	...	...	...	...	...	...	...	...	...	...	...
744	**Donetsk** a.	...	...	...	...	...	...	...	...	...	...	...	...	...

	IC725	15	17	73	93	IC723	149	130	21	1	63	112	192
		●	■	■(1)	●(1)		●	●	●	●			●
		A	B	H	F		D	E	C				G
Donetsk d.	...	...	...	...	...	...	...	...	...	...	...	...	...
Kostiantynivka d.	...	...	...	...	...	...	...	...	...	...	...	...	...
Kramatorsk d.	...	...	...	...	...	...	...	...	...	...	...	...	1300
Slovyansk d.	...	...	...	...	...	...	...	...	...	...	...	...	1319
Dnipro Hol. a.	...	...	...	...	...	...	...	...	...	...	...	...	2100
Izyum d.	...	...	...	...	...	...	...	...	...	...	...	1822	...
Bakhmut d.	...	...	...	...	...	...	...	...	...	...	...	|	...
Kharkiv a.	...	...	...	...	...	...	...	...	...	...	...	2138	...
Kharkiv 1785 d.	0715	1407	1407	1407	1407	1701	...	...	1928	2019	2230	2230	...
Poltava Kyivska 1785 a.	0854	1623	1623	1623	1623	1841	...	...	2148	2238	0047	0047	...
Poltava Kyivska d.	0856	1643	1643	1643	1643	1843	1703	...	2208	2258	0107	0107	...
Kremenchuk d.	|	|	|	|	|	|	|	1627	|	|	|	|	...
Hrebinka d.	|	|	|	|	|	|	2046	2046	|	|	|	|	...
Kyïv a.	1219	2104	2104	2104	2104	2207	2241	2241	0239	0304	0610	0610	...
Lviv **1700** a.	...	0431	0431	0835	...	...	0625	0625	1151	1026	...	...	...
Ivano-Frankivsk **1700** a.	...	0733	...	...	...	...	0910	0910	...	1318	...	...	...

A – Kharkiv - Kyïv - Lviv - Vorokhta - Yasynya and v.v.
B – Kharkiv - Kyïv - Lviv - Uzhhorod and v.v.
C – Kharkiv - Kyïv - Lviv - Truskavets and v.v.
D – Poltava - Kyïv - Lviv - Chernivtsi and v.v.
E – Kremenchuk - Kyïv - Lviv - Vorokhta and v.v.
F – Kharkiv - Kyïv - Kovel - Chelm and v.v.
G – Odesa - Dnipro - Kramatorsk and v.v.
H – Kharkiv - Kyïv - Lviv - Przemyśl and v.v.
● – Even dates (see page 535).
■ – Uneven dates (see page 535).

1755 KYÏV - CHERNIHIV, SHOSTKA, KHARKIV and LYSYCHANSK

km		45	259	257	786	708	774	780	702	788
		■(3)	●	●		③–①				
		B	H	J						
	Lviv **1700** d.	1750	1740	1740	...	...	...	...	...	...
0	**Kyïv** d.	0254	0352	0352	0721	0808	1148	1620	1707	1807
209	**Chernihiv** a.	|	|	0725	|	1037	|	|	1949	|
197	Bakhmach Pas. d.	0527	0658	...	1000	...	1425	1852	...	2058
221	Konotop d.	0552	0722	...	1024	...	1448	1918	...	2122
302	**Shostka** a.	|	|	...	1137	...	1559	|	...	2239
350	Sumy d.	0839	0953	...	...	...	...	2143	...	...
552	**Kharkiv** a.	1213	...	...	...	...	...	...	...	...
552	**Kharkiv** d.	...	...	...	...	...	...	...	...	...
681	Kupiansk-Vuslov d.	...	...	...	...	...	...	...	...	...
806	**Lysychansk** a.	...	...	...	...	...	...	...	...	...
934	**Luhansk** a.	...	...	...	...	...	...	...	...	...

	704	788	779	786	710	774	45	258	259
					③–①		●(4)	■(1)	■(1)
							B	J	H
Luhansk d.	...	...	...	...	...	...	...	...	...
Lysychansk d.	...	...	...	...	...	...	...	...	...
Kupiansk-Vuslov d.	...	...	...	...	...	...	...	...	...
Kharkiv a.	...	...	...	...	...	...	...	...	...
Kharkiv d.	...	...	...	...	...	...	1343	...	...
Sumy d.	...	...	0630	...	...	...	1724	...	1840
Shostka d.	...	0640	|	1222	...	1649	|	...	|
Konotop d.	...	0804	0852	1336	...	1758	1953	...	2122
Bakhmach Pas. d.	...	0827	0916	1400	...	1819	2017	...	2146
Chernihiv d.	0731	|	|	|	1721	|	|	2118	|
Kyïv a.	1013	1113	1140	1644	1948	2050	2250	0041	0041
Lviv **1700** a.	...	...	...	...	...	...	0827	1026	1026

B – Kharkiv - Kyïv - Lviv - Uzhhorod and v.v.
H – Sumy - Kyïv - Lviv - Ivano-Frankivsk and v.v.
J – Chernihiv - Kyïv - Lviv - Ivano-Frankivsk and v.v.
● – Even dates (see page 535).
■ – Uneven dates (see page 535).

1760 LVIV and KYÏV - MYKOLAIV and KHERSON

km		730	102	110
		③–①		●
	Lviv d.	...	...	1612
	Ternopil d.	...	...	1825
	Khmelnytsky d.	...	...	2027
	Zhmerynka d.	...	...	2224
	Vinnytsya d.	...	...	2310
	Kozyatyn 1 d.	...	...	0003
0	**Kyïv** d.	1750	2214	|
	Cherkasy d.	2107	|	|
216	Im. T. Shevchenka a.	...	0111	0425
216	Im. T. Shevchenka d.	...	0116	0443
308	Znamyanka d.	...	|	|
448	Kryvyi Rih Hol. d.	...	|	|
651	**Mykolaiv** a.	...	0707	1100
706	**Kherson** a.	...	0906	1327

	729	101	109
	④–②		■(3)
Kherson d.	...	1006	1427
Mykolaiv d.	...	1203	1625
Kryvyi Rih Hol. d.	...	|	|
Znamyanka d.	...	|	|
Im. T. Shevchenka a.	...	1725	2155
Im. T. Shevchenka d.	...	1729	2210
Cherkasy d.	0633	|	|
Kyïv a.	0939	2022	|
Kozyatyn 1 d.	...	...	0234
Vinnytsya d.	...	...	0331
Zhmerynka d.	...	...	0435
Khmelnytsky d.	...	...	0614
Ternopil d.	...	...	0815
Lviv a.	...	...	1018

UZ — LVIV and KYÏV - DNIPRO - ZAPORIZHZHYA - MARIUPOL — 1780

km		88	86	85	38	92	192	62	54	120	42	6	3	32
		■(1)				■(1)	■(1)	●	●			●(4)		
		A				B	C	D			E	F	G	H
	Lviv 1705 d.	...	1040	1040	...	...	...	...	...	1356	1553	1910	2136	2313
	Ternopil 1705 d.	...	1257	1257	...	...	...	...	...	1612	1806	|	|	|
	Khmelnytsky 1705 d.	...	1512	1512	...	...	...	...	...	1815	2019	|	|	|
	Vinnytsya 1705 d.	...	1725	1725	...	...	...	...	...	|	2226	|	|	|
•	Kozyatyn 1 1705 d.	1837	1844	1844	...	...	...	...	...	|	2317	|	|	|
0	**Kyïv** d.	|	|	|	2114	...	...	...	...	|	|	|	|	|
216	Im. Tar. Shevchenka d.	2331	2347	2347	0005	...	...	...	...	|	0400	0436	0706	0831
	Odesa Holovna d.	|	|	|	|	1651	1651	1651	2005	|	|	|	|	|
	Kropyvnytskyi d.	|	|	|	|	0057	0057	0057	0405	0433	|	|	|	|
308	Znamyanka d.	0101	0118	0118	0134	0212	0212	0215	0519	0547	0537	0602	0834	0959
353	Oleksandria d.	0144	0202	0202	|	0257	0257	|	0603	0633	0620	|	|	|
490	**Kryvyi Rih** Hol. a.	|	|	|	|	|	|	0544	|	0954	|	|	|	|
496	Kamianske d.	0408	0443	0443	0433	0528	0528	0919	0829	1241	0856	0906	1133	1255
534	**Dnipro** Hol. a.	0443	0518	0518	0508	0607	0607	0955	0905	1316	0936	0944	1208	1328
534	**Dnipro** Hol. d.	0503	0538	0940	0523	...	...	...	...	1336	...	0959	1223	1353
735	Pokrovsk a.	|	|	1300	|	...	...	...	...	|	...	|	|	|
658	**Zaporizhzhya** 1 a.	0721	0750	...	0738	...	...	...	...	1552	...	1205	1430	1602
658	**Zaporizhzhya** 1 1782 d.	...	...	...	...	...	...	...	...	...	...	...	...	...
770	Melitopol 1782 a.	...	...	...	...	...	...	...	...	...	...	...	...	...
861	Novooleksiivka 1782 a.	...	...	...	...	...	...	...	...	...	...	...	...	...
1033	**Mariupol** 1782 a.	...	...	...	...	...	...	...	...	...	...	...	...	...

	41	120	6	233	86	53	4	88	59	91	192	38	32
			■(3)			■(1)		●	■(1)	●	●		
	E		F				G	A	D	B	C		H
Mariupol 1782 d.	...	...	...	...	...	...	...	...	...	...	...	...	...
Novooleksiivka 1782 d.	...	...	...	...	...	...	...	...	...	...	...	...	...
Melitopol 1782 d.	...	...	...	...	...	...	...	...	...	...	...	...	...
Zaporizhzhya 1 1782 a.	...	...	...	...	...	...	...	...	...	...	...	...	...
Zaporizhzhya 1 d.	...	0945	1305	...	1603	...	1648	1840	...	...	...	2005	2015
Pokrovsk d.	...	|	|	1415	|	...	|	|	...	...	...	|	|
Dnipro Hol. a.	...	1207	1507	1740	1810	...	1855	2047	...	...	...	2210	2220
Dnipro Hol. d.	1430	1231	1527	1830	1830	1900	1910	2107	1730	2120	2120	2225	2240
Kamianske d.	1505	1308	1601	1905	1905	1935	1947	2141	1811	2155	2155	2300	2315
Kryvyi Rih Hol. d.	|	1551	|	|	|	|	|	|	2140	|	|	|	|
Oleksandria d.	1745	1857	|	2153	2153	2218	|	0013	|	0032	0032	|	|
Znamyanka d.	1833	2007	1855	2243	2243	2322	2251	0100	0144	0144	0144	0204	0229
Kropyvnytskyi d.	|	2055	|	|	|	0011	|	|	0234	0234	0234	|	|
Odesa Holovna a.	|	|	|	|	|	0807	|	|	1057	1057	1057	|	|
Im. Tar. Shevchenka d.	2015	|	2008	0018	0018	...	0009	0243	...	...	...	0319	0348
Kyïv a.	|	|	|	|	|	...	|	|	...	...	...	0602	|
Kozyatyn 1 1705 d.	0042	|	|	0503	0503	...	|	0707	...	...	...	...	|
Vinnytsya 1705 d.	0139	|	|	0600	0600	...	|	...	...	...	...	...	|
Khmelnytsky 1705 d.	0352	0734	|	0814	0814	...	|	...	...	...	...	...	|
Ternopil 1705 d.	0609	0935	|	1029	1029	...	|	...	...	...	...	...	|
Lviv 1705 a.	0820	1144	0458	1244	1244	...	0912	...	...	...	...	...	1252

A – Zaporizhzhya - Kozyatyn - Kovel and v.v.
B – Odesa - Dnipro - Kharkiv and v.v.
C – Odesa - Dnipro - Kramatorsk and v.v.
D – Odesa - Kryvyi Rih - Dnipro - Kharkiv and v.v.
E – Dnipro - Lviv - Truskavets and v.v.
F – Zaporizhzhia - Lviv - Yasynya and v.v.
G – Zaporizhzhia - Lviv - Uzhhorod and v.v.
H – Zaporizhzhia - Lviv - Przemyśl and v.v.
● – Even dates (see page 535).
■ – Uneven dates (see page 535).
• – Kozyatyn - Im. Tarasa Shevchenka *304 km*.
⊖ – Information not available.

UZ — KHARKIV - ZAPORIZHZHYA - MELITOPOL and MARIUPOL — 1782

km		59	91
		■(1)	●
		D	B
0	**Kharkiv** d.	1237	1534
**	**Dnipro** Hol. a.	1705	2100
	Dnipro Hol. d.	1730	...
327	**Zaporizhzhya** 1 a.	|	...
327	**Zaporizhzhya** 1 1780 d.	|	...
	Kamianske d.	1811	...
512	**Kryvyi Rih** Hol. a.	2104	...
439	Melitopol 1780 a.	...	...
530	Novooleksiivka 1780 a.	...	...
702	**Mariupol** 1780 a.	...	...

	92	62
	■(1)	●
	B	D
Mariupol 1780 d.	...	...
Novooleksiivka 1780 d.	...	...
Melitopol 1780 d.	...	...
Kryvyi Rih Hol. d.	...	0634
Kamianske d.	...	0919
Zaporizhzhya 1 1780 a.	...	|
Zaporizhzhya 1 d.	...	|
Dnipro Hol. a.	...	0955
Dnipro Hol. d.	0627	1025
Kharkiv a.	1215	1537

B – Odesa - Dnipro - Kharkiv and v.v.
D – Odesa - Kryvyi Rih - Dnipro - Kharkiv and v.v.
● – Even dates (see page 535).
■ – Uneven dates (see page 535).
** – Karkhiv - Dnipro Hol.: *300 km*.

UZ — KHARKIV - KREMENCHUK - ODESA — 1785

km		7
		■(1)
0	**Kharkiv** d.	1801
140	Poltava Pivdenna d.	2034
259	**Kremenchuk** d.	2228
353	Znamyanka a.	2359
407	Kropyvnytskyi a.	0107
765	**Odesa** Holovna a.	0831

	8
	●
Odesa Holovna d.	1947
Kropyvnytskyi d.	0309
Znamyanka d.	0418
Kremenchuk d.	0555
Poltava Pivdenna d.	0804
Kharkiv a.	1010

UZ — ODESA - MARIUPOL — 1787

km			
0	**Odesa** Hol. d.	...	...
232	Mykolaiv d.	...	...
287	Kherson d.	...	...
643	**Zaporizhzhya** 1 a.	...	...
643	**Zaporizhzhya** 1 d.	...	...
1018	**Mariupol** a.	...	...

Mariupol d.	...	...
Zaporizhzhya 1 a.	...	...
Zaporizhzhya 1 d.	...	...
Kherson d.	...	...
Mykolaiv d.	...	...
Odesa Hol. a.	...	...

Crimean Railway — UTC+3 — CRIMEAN PENINSULA — 1790

km					
0	Simferopol d.	0755	0950	1405	1725
78	Sevastopol a.	0949	1145	1608	1927

Sevastopol d.	0523	1007	1215	1732
Simferopol a.	0730	1207	1420	1925

km					
0	Simferopol d.	0545	0955	1440	1750
79	Yevpatoria a.	0720	1135	1615	1920

Yevpatoriya d.	0535	0825	1505	1820
Simferopol a.	0710	1010	1640	2005

km												
0	Armyansk d.	...	...	...	...	...	0735	...	...	...	...	1535
78	Dzhankoy ● d.	...	0305	...	0600	...	0914	...	1405	...	...	1715
	Feodosia ● d.	0305	|	...	|	...	|	1035	|	...	1555	|
179	Vladyslavivka ● d.	0343	0508	0659	0838	0855	1119	1127	1615	1630	1633	1909
196	Feodosia ● a.	|	|	0730	|	0930	1150	|	|	1705	|	1940
270	Kerch a.	0540	0710	...	1100	...	...	1315	1840	...	1815	...

Kerch d.	...	...	0835	1155	...	1415	...	1620	...	2120	2210
Feodosia ● d.	0625	0810	|	|	1520	|	...	|	1750	|	|
Vladyslavivka ● d.	0702	0840	1118	1340	1555	1616	...	1813	1834	0018	0031
Feodosia ● a.	|	—	|	1410	...	|	...	1840	|	|	0100
Dzhankoy ● d.	0905	0955	1310	...	...	1810	1930	...	2045	0215	...
Armyansk a.	...	1120	...	...	...	...	2055	...	...	...	...

km												
	Feodosia ● d.	...	...	0555	...	...	...	1435	...	1720	...	2005
	Vladyslavivka ● d.	...	...	0622	...	...	...	1513	...	1748	...	2036
0	Solone Ozero d.	...	0600	|	0900	...	1505	|	...	|	2005	...
20	Dzhankoy ● d.	0520	0626	0812	0930	1210	1535	1710	1740	2000	2035	...
111	Simferopol a.	0700	0750	0940	1110	1350	1715	1830	1920	2120	2200	...

Simferopol d.	0605	0820	0930	1150	1230	1450	1740	1850	1955	2030	...
Dzhankoy ● d.	0805	1000	1115	1332	1416	1635	1916	2053	2135	2215	...
Solone Ozero a.	0830	|	...	|	1440	...	1940	2115	|	...	...
Vladyslavivka ● d.	...	1159	...	1514	...	...	...	...	2312	...	...
Feodosia ● a.	...	1230	...	1545	...	...	...	...	2340	...	...

● – For all trains see middle and lower panels.

☛ For through trains from Moskva and St Peterburg see Table **1960**.

LITHUANIA, LATVIA and ESTONIA

SEE MAP PAGE 527

Operators: Lithuania: **LTG Link** (www.ltglink.lt) Latvia: **Pasažieru vilciens** (www.pv.lv) Estonia: **Elron** (www.elron.ee).
Services: Trains convey first- and second-class seating unless indicated otherwise. For Lithuania - Poland trains see Tables **93** and **1042**.
Timings: Schedules are the latest available and may be subject to alteration at any time. Timings are expressed in local time at the station concerned (time comparison chart: page 4).

1800 RIGA - TALLINN, ST PETERBURG, VILNIUS and KALININGRAD

Riga and Vilnius coach stations are close to the railway stations. Tallinn coach station is 3 km from the railway station by tram.

RIGA - PÄRNU - TALLINN Lux Express (www.luxexpress.eu) Journey 4½ hours:
From **Riga**: 0235, 0700, 0900, 1000, 1130, 1230, 1400, 1500, 1600, 1700, 1800.
From **Tallinn**: 0700, 0800, 0900, 1000, 1130, 1230, 1500, 1600, 1700, 1800, 2230.

TALLINN - ST PETERBURG Lux Express (www.luxexpress.eu) Journey 6¼ - 8 hours:
From **Tallinn**: 0030, 0530, 0700, 1015, 1115, 1545, 2300.
From **St Peterburg**: 0730, 0845, 1315, 1600, 1630, 2230, 2315.

RIGA - VILNIUS Lux Express (www.luxexpress.eu) Journey 4 - 4½ hours:
From **Riga**: 0255, 0700, 0930, 1200, 1430, 1630, 1720.
From **Vilnius**: 0645, 0900, 1000, 1200, 1430, 1730, 2230.

RIGA - KALININGRAD Ecolines (www.ecolines.net). Journey 9½ hours:
From **Riga**: 2200 ④⑥.
From **Kaliningrad**: 2130 ③⑦.

1805 VILNIUS and KAUNAS - ŠIAULIAI - KLAIPEDA

LTG Link

km																								
			⑦	①–⑤	①–⑥		⑥⑦	⑦	⑦			⑦	⑦	⑦				⑦	⑦		⑦		⑦	①–⑥
		3		3			3			3						3	3					3		
0	**Vilnius** 1809 d.	...	0553	...	0630	...	...	0730	0820	...	...	1045	...	1253	...	...	...	1500	...	...	1701	...	1815	1850
67	Kaišiadorys 1809 d.	...	0635	...	0712	...	...	|	0903	...	...	|	...	1334	...	...	...	1543	...	...	|	...	1858	1933
	Kaunas 1809 d.	...	|	...	|	...	...	|	|	...	...	|	1135	|	...	...	...	|	1640	...	|	...	|	|
	Jonava d.	...	0701	...	0738	...	...	0839	0930	...	...	|	1211	1401	...	...	...	1610	1714	...	|	...	1926	2001
	Kèdainiai d.	...	0722	...	0759	...	...	0901	0952	...	...	|	1235	1426	...	...	...	1632	1736	...	|	...	1947	2022
	Rokiškis d.	...	|	...	|	...	...	|	|	...	...	|	|	|	...	...	...	|	|	...	|	...	|	|
	Panevežys d.	...	|	0725	|	...	0820	|	|	1115	...	|	|	|	...	1401	...	|	|	...	|	1822	|	|
192	Radviliškis d.	0550	0803	0813	0840	...	0908	0943	1033	1203	...	|	1329	1507	...	1449	1645	1713	1817	...	|	1910	2028	2103
212	**Šiauliai** d.	0620	0818	0848	0855	...	0943	1000	1051	1238	...	1259	1350	1524	...	1534	1715	1731	1844	...	1914	1945	2044	2119
290	**Mažeikiai** a.	|	|	1002	|	...	1057	|	...	1352	...	|	...	|	...	1648	|	...	...	...	|	2059	|	|
	Telšiai d.	0724	0912	...	0946	...	...	1047	...	...	...	1345	...	1611	...	...	1826	...	...	...	2000	...	2131	2206
	Plunge d.	0754	0932	...	1007	...	...	1108	...	...	...	|	...	1631	...	...	1912	...	...	...	|	...	2151	2226
376	**Klaipeda** ⊡ a.	0859	1020	...	1057	...	...	1158	...	...	...	1448	...	1721	...	...	2022	...	...	...	2103	...	2239	2314

	①–⑤	①–⑥	⑦		⑥⑦	⑦	⑦				⑦		⑦	⑦			⑦				⑦	①–⑥	⑦
	3				3				3	3					3			3	3				
Klaipeda ⊡ d.	...	0522	...	...	...	0730	...	...	0910	...	1105	...	...	1245	...	...	...	1530	...	...	1650	1755	1755
Plunge d.	...	0612	...	...	...	0820	...	...	1009	...	|	...	...	1336	...	...	...	1629	...	...	|	1847	1847
Telšiai d.	...	0632	...	...	...	0840	...	...	1041	...	1206	...	...	1359	...	...	...	1700	...	...	1752	1915	1915
Mažeikiai d.	0600	|	...	...	0755	|	...	...	|	1115	|	...	...	|	1415	...	...	|	1722	...	|	|	|
Šiauliai d.	0710	0718	0845	...	0905	0926	1120	...	1156	1225	1249	...	1400	1447	1527	...	1750	1802	1832	...	1837	2006	2006
Radviliškis d.	0752	0737	0916	...	0937	0945	1139	...	1230	1259	|	...	1421	1507	1601	...	1808	1836	1918	...	|	2026	2026
Panevežys a.	0854	|	|	...	1030	|	|	...	...	1351	|	...	|	|	1653	...	|	...	2010	...	|	|	|
Rokiškis a.	...	|	|	...	...	|	|	...	...	...	|	...	|	|	...	...	|	...	...	...	|	|	|
Kèdainiai d.	...	0817	1006	...	...	1026	1219	...	...	...	|	...	1507	1550	...	...	1848	...	...	...	|	2109	2109
Jonava d.	...	0839	1031	...	...	1049	1242	...	...	...	|	...	1530	1614	...	...	1909	...	...	...	|	2133	2133
Kaunas 1809 a.	...	|	1106	...	...	|	|	...	...	...	|	...	1606	|	...	...	|	...	...	...	|	|	|
Kaišiadorys 1809 d.	...	0908	...	...	...	|	1311	...	...	...	|	...	...	1643	...	...	1938	...	...	...	|	|	2202
Vilnius 1809 a.	...	0951	...	...	...	1159	1358	...	...	...	1514	...	...	1727	...	...	2021	...	...	...	2101	2245	2245

⊡ – **Klaipeda - Šilute** (2nd class. *46 km*. Journey 65 minutes): from **Klaipeda** at 0818, 1230, 1510, 1747; from **Šilute** at 0621 ①–⑤, 0935, 1350, 1630, 1905 ①⑤⑥.

1807 VILNIUS - TRAKAI and MARCINKONYS

LTG Link

Vilnius - Trakai and v.v. *27 km*. Journey 35 minutes.
From Vilnius (trains call at **Lentvaris** 16 – 19 minutes later) at 0610 ①–⑤, 0707, 0916, 1110, 1240, 1625, 1736, 1935.
From Trakai (trains call at **Lentvaris** 15 minutes later) at 0700 ①–⑤, 0810, 1010, 1215, 1345, 1735, 1845, 2040.

Vilnius - Marcinkonys and v.v. 3rd class only. *108 km*. Journey 1 hour 50 minutes.
From Vilnius (trains call at **Lentvaris** 16 – 19 minutes, and **Varena** 80 – 85 minutes later) at 0538, 1020, 1446, 1758 ⑤.
From Marcinkonys (trains call at **Varena** 23 – 26 minutes, and **Lentvaris** 90 – 95 minutes later) at 0742, 1340, 1650.

1809 VILNIUS - KAUNAS

LTG Link

km																								
		①–⑤								2A					①–⑤									⑤⑥
0	**Vilnius** 1805 d.	0455	0600	0645	0800	0910	1013	1120	...	1210	1225	1310	1420	1507	1610	1644	...	1715	1745	1835	1925	2030	2125	2215
	Lentvaris d.	0511	0617	0701	0817	0925	1029	1137	...	|	1246	1326	1436	1522	1625	1702	...	1730	1802	1850	1943	2046	2141	2230
	Vievis d.	0526	0637	0718	0837	|	1044	1159	...	|	1304	1341	1456	|	1640	1722	...	1745	1822	1906	|	2102	2156	|
67	Kaišiadorys 1805 d.	0543	0654	0736	0856	0955	1101	1218	...	1253	1325	1359	1514	1554	1656	1739	...	1802	1841	1923	2014	2118	2212	2300
104	**Kaunas** 1805 a.	0614	0725	0807	0927	1020	1131	1249	...	1319	1349	1427	1545	1623	1722	1806	...	1829	1912	1952	2141	2145	2236	2324

			①–⑤											2B				①–⑤					⑤⑥
Kaunas 1805 d.	0512	0548	0631	0655	0750	0905	1005	...	1107	1220	1321	1430	1530	1626	1650	...	1724	1745	1835	1927	2027	2113	2220
Kaišiadorys 1805 d.	0539	0617	0654	0727	0819	0934	1037	...	1134	1251	1351	1455	1601	1651	1721	...	1750	1816	1906	1956	2056	2141	2252
Vievis d.	0557	0635	0711	0747	0837	0951	1057	...	|	1308	1409	|	1619	|	1739	...	1807	1833	|	2014	2114	2158	|
Lentvaris d.	0617	0658	0727	0809	0855	1009	1119	...	1206	1323	1433	1527	1634	|	1802	...	1822	1855	1946	2036	2130	2230	2325
Vilnius 1805 a.	0635	0718	0746	0828	0911	1028	1139	...	1222	1341	1454	1542	1654	1734	1823	...	1843	1913	2002	2055	2146	2229	2343

A – To Mockava (a. 1441). **B** – From Mockava (d. 1505).

1811 KAUNAS - MARIJAMPOLE and KYBARTAI

3rd class only LTG Link

Kaunas - Marijampole and v.v. *53 km*. Journey 55 – 65 minutes.
From Kaunas (trains call at **Kazlu Ruda** 30 – 35 minutes later) at 0635 ①–⑤, 0750, 1040, 1320 **A**, 1635, 1749, 1940, 2100 ④–⑦.
From Marijampole (trains call at **Kazlu Ruda** 23 – 27 minutes later) at 0525 ①–⑤, 0615, 0750, 1040, 1230, 1539 **B**, 1754, 1916 ④–⑦.

Kaunas - Kybartai and v.v. *87 km*. Journey 80 – 85 minutes.
From Kaunas (trains call at **Kazlu Ruda** 30 – 35 minutes and **Vilkaviškis** 65 – 70 minutes later) at 0820, 1200, 1510, 1850.
From Kybratai (trains call at **Vilkaviškis** 17 minutes and **Kazlu Ruda** 48 minutes later) at 0610, 0955, 1415, 1704.

A – To Mockava (a. 1441). **B** – From Mockava (d. 1505).

1813 VILNIUS - TURMANTAS

3rd class only LTG Link

km										
						①–⑤				
0	**Vilnius** d.	0540	0740	1118	1435	1632	1750	1950	2045	...
	Naujoji Vilina d.	0552	0753	1131	1447	1644	1801	2001	2057	...
	Pabrade d.	0632	0839	1217	1533	1730	1845	2041	2134	...
101	Ignalina d.	0725	0923	1301	1607	1810	1934	2118	2207	...
	Visaginas d.	0753	0956	1333	1640	...	2004	2145	...	...
147	**Turmantas** 🛃 a.	0801	1004	1341	1648	...	2012	2154	...	...
174	Daugavpils a.	...	...	...	...	...	...	...	...	...

Daugavpils d.	...	...	...	...	...	...	...	...	...
Turmantas 🛃 d.	...	0515	0600	0920	1300	1608	1815	...	...
Visaginas d.	...	0524	0610	0930	1310	1618	1825	...	...
Ignalina d.	0505	0552	0637	1002	1339	1649	1851	...	...
Pabrade d.	0541	0631	0721	1043	1415	1730	1940	...	...
Naujoji Vilina d.	0621	0713	0812	1126	1457	1815	2023	...	...
Vilnius a.	0634	0724	0824	1138	1509	1827	2033	...	...

1815 VILNIUS - VILNIUS AIRPORT - JAŠIUNAI

3rd class only LTG Link

km										
		①–⑤							①–⑤	
0	**Vilnius** d.	0546	0802	1000	1130	1330	1510	1640	1835	...
4	**Vilnius Airport** ✈ d.	0553	0810	1007	1137	1338	1517	1648	1843	...
	Jašiunai a.	0620	0841	...	...	1409	...	1719	1914	...

	①–⑤							①–⑤	
Jašiunai d.	0639	0852	...	...	1420	...	1733	1928	...
Vilnius Airport ✈ d.	0711	0922	1020	1150	1450	1540	1805	2000	...
Vilnius a.	0719	0930	1028	1158	1458	1548	1813	2008	...

RIGA - VALMIERA - VALGA — 1830

Pasažieru vilciens

km										
					Ⓐ				⑦	
0	**Riga** ◧ d.	0646	1046	...	1716	1816	...	1846	2116	...
53	Sigulda ◧ d.	0756	1154	...	1804	1911	...	1954	2210	...
93	Cesis d.	0838	1233	...	1833	1943	...	2036	2242	...
121	**Valmiera** a.	0906	1302	...	1859	2010	...	2104	2308	...
164	Lugaži 🏛 LV a.	...	1336	...	...	2044	...	...	...	...
168	**Valga** 🏛 EE a.	...	1342	...	...	2050	...	...	...	...

				Ⓐ		Ⓐ		Ⓒ	⑤
Valga 🏛 EE d.	...	0513	...	...	...	1503	...	1653	...
Lugaži 🏛 LV d.	...	0520	...	...	...	1510	...	1700	...
Valmiera d.	0457	0554	...	0631	1001	1544	...	1734	2016
Cesis d.	0528	0620	...	0659	1030	1612	...	1802	2045
Sigulda ◧ d.	0609	0652	...	0727	1112	1652	...	1842	2120
Riga ◧ a.	0715	0745	...	0815	1215	1745	...	1945	2215

◧ – Additional trains Riga - Sigulda at 0616 Ⓐ, 0746, 1246, 1446, 1544, 1746, 2016 Ⓐ, 2146.
Additional trains Sigulda - Riga at 0738 Ⓐ, 0812, 0913, 1408, 1610, 1708, 1938 Ⓐ, 2138.

EE – Estonia.
LV – Latvia.

RIGA - GULBENE, DAUGAVPILS, REZEKNE and ZILUPE — 1832

Pasažieru vilciens

km										
		⑥		⑦						⑤
0	**Riga** ⊡ d.	0801	0839	1131	1208	1438	1638	1738	1901	1901
	Ogre ⊡ d.	0839	0919	1205	1248	1518	1718	1818	1934	1934
51	Lielvarde ⊡ d.	0854	0934	1219	1303	1533	1733	1833	1948	1948
	Aizkraukle ⊡ d.	0918	0959	1248	1329	1556	1758	1859	2017	2017
	Madona d.	1032	...	1405	...	...	...	...	2132	2133
179	**Gulbene** a.	1119	...	1453	...	...	...	...	...	2220

	Ⓐ	⑥	⑦					⑦	⑥
Gulbene d.	...	0643	...	...	...	...	...	1545	1805
Madona d.	0455	0733	0733	...	...	...	...	1635	1855
Aizkraukle ⊡ d.	0612	0849	0849	0926	1129	1500	1630	1751	2008
Lielvarde ⊡ d.	0640	0916	0916	0952	1152	1526	1655	1815	2033
Ogre ⊡ d.	0654	0929	0929	1008	1208	1542	1711	1828	2047
Riga ⊡ a.	0730	1000	1000	1048	1248	1622	1750	1900	2124

km										
							A			
0	**Riga** ⊡ d.	0731	0931	1201	1301	1531	1631	1701	1801	2131
	Ogre ⊡ d.	0808	1008	1231	1338	1611	1701	1738	1834	2218
51	Lielvarde ⊡ d.	0822	1022	|	1352	1628	|	1752	1848	2235
	Aizkraukle ⊡ d.	0851	1051	1303	1417	1657	1733	1817	1913	2304
129	Krustpils (for Jekabpils) d.	0937	1136	1341	1503	1741	1811	1900	1959	2348
218	**Daugavpils** a.	1057	|	|	1633	...	1918	|	2119	...
224	**Rezekne** 2 d.	...	1307	1446	...	...	...	2031	...	...
279	**Zilupe** a.	...	1410	...	...	...	...	2134	...	...

			B						
Zilupe d.	...	0324	...	...	...	...	1507	...	...
Rezekne 2 d.	...	0429	...	...	...	1516	1612	...	...
Daugavpils d.	...	|	0621	0739	1306	|	|	...	1737
Krustpils (for Jekabpils) d.	0441	0559	0724	0901	1428	1624	1743	1758	1900
Aizkraukle ⊡ d.	0526	0640	0801	0945	1515	1701	1821	1841	1945
Lielvarde ⊡ d.	0555	0710	|	1012	1542	|	|	1911	2012
Ogre ⊡ d.	0614	0724	0833	1025	1555	1733	1854	1925	2025
Riga ⊡ a.	0700	0800	0900	1100	1630	1800	1930	2000	2100

A – To **Kraslava** (a. 1947) and **Indra** (④⑤ only, a. 2010).
B – From **Indra** (⑤⑥ only, d. 0523) and **Kraslava** (d. 0547).

⊡ – Additional trains Riga - Aizkraukle at 0508, 0708, 2010, 2238.
Additional trains Aizkraukle - Riga at 0520, 0700, 1831, 2032, 2203.

RIGA - JELGAVA - LIEPAJA — 1834

Pasažieru vilciens

km										
						⑦			①–④	⑤
0	**Riga** ⊖ d.	0605	0754	1036	1235	1349	1435	1705	1825	1825
43	**Jelgava** ⊖ d.	0651	0839	1121	1320	1427	1520	1750	1903	1903
	Dobele d.	...	...	...	...	1455	...	...	1930	1931
125	Saldus d.	...	...	...	...	1547	...	...	...	2019
223	**Liepaja** a.	...	...	...	...	1707	...	...	...	2139

		Ⓐ			⑥				⑦
Liepaja d.	...	...	...	...	0810	...	...	...	1730
Saldus d.	...	...	...	...	0935	...	...	...	1851
Dobele d.	...	0700	...	...	1022	...	...	...	1938
Jelgava ⊖ d.	0631	0728	0840	1035	1049	1235	1435	1705	2005
Riga ⊖ a.	0716	0804	0925	1120	1125	1320	1520	1750	2040

⊖ – Additional trains Riga - Jelgava at 0535, 0635 Ⓐ, 0705, 0735, 0835, 0935, 1135, 1335, 1535 Ⓐ, 1605, 1635 Ⓐ, 1705, 1735 Ⓐ, 1754, 1839 Ⓐ, 1935, 2035, 2135, 2235, 2335.
Additional trains Jelgava - Riga at 0504, 0605, 0705, 0735 Ⓐ, 0805, 0905, 0940, 1135, 1336, 1535, 1636 Ⓐ, 1737 Ⓐ, 1805, 1841 Ⓐ, 1905, 1942 Ⓐ, 2036, 2135, 2236.

RIGA - SLOKA - TUKUMS — 1836

Pasažieru vilciens

km																								
																Ⓐ								
0	**Riga** ● d.	0530	0630	0730	0830	0930	1130	1230	1300	1330	1430	1530	1600	1630	1700	1745	1800	1900	2000	2030	2115	2200	2250	2345
22	Majori ▲ ● d.	0602	0702	0802	0902	1002	1202	1302	1332	1402	1501	1602	1632	1702	1733	1811	1833	1932	2032	2102	2147	2231	2321	0017
	Dubulti ● d.	0605	0705	0805	0905	1005	1205	1305	1335	1405	1504	1605	1635	1705	1736	1814	1836	1935	2035	2105	2150	2234	2324	0020
32	**Sloka** ▲ ● d.	0621	0720	0821	0920	1021	1221	1320	1351	1420	1520	1620	1651	1720	1752	1825	1851	1951	2050	2121	2206	2250	2340	0036
	Ķemeri d.	0631	...	0832	...	1028	1229	...	1401	...	1530	...	1702	...	1801	1832	...	2002	...	2134	2214	2257	2347	0044
65	**Tukums** 1 a.	0648	...	0849	...	1043	1246	...	1416	...	1547	...	1716	...	1818	1849	...	2019	...	2150	...	2314	0002	0101
	Tukums 2 a.	0652	...	0853	...	1047	...	...	1420	...	1551	...	1720	...	1822	1853	...	2023	...	...	...	2318	0006	0105

				Ⓒ	Ⓐ														Ⓐ				
Tukums 2 d.	0439	0533	0607	...	0704	0808	...	0943	1109	...	...	...	1507	...	1639	...	1738	...	1907	1939	...	2112	...
Tukums 1 d.	0444	0538	0612	...	0709	0813	...	0948	1114	...	...	1344	1512	...	1644	...	1743	...	1912	1944	...	2117	2213
Ķemeri d.	0501	0555	0630	0659	0725	0831	...	1003	1130	...	...	1400	1530	...	1700	...	1801	...	1926	2001	...	2133	2230
Sloka ▲ ● d.	0510	0604	0639	0708	0733	0840	0945	1010	1139	1239	1339	1407	1539	1640	1707	1739	1810	1909	1933	2010	2109	2140	2239
Dubulti ● d.	0525	0619	0654	0723	0742	0855	1000	1025	1154	1254	1354	1422	1554	1655	1722	1754	1825	1924	1943	2025	2124	2155	2254
Majori ▲ ● d.	0528	0622	0657	0726	0745	0858	1003	1028	1157	1257	1357	1425	1557	1658	1725	1757	1828	1927	1946	2028	2127	2158	2257
Riga ● a.	0559	0655	0729	0759	0811	0929	1035	1059	1229	1329	1429	1457	1629	1730	1757	1829	1859	1959	2014	2059	2159	2229	2329

● – Additional trains Riga - Sloka at 0710, 0800, 1005, 1100, 1500, 1730 Ⓐ, 1830 Ⓐ. Additional trains Sloka - Riga at 0708 Ⓐ, 0753, 0812, 0909 Ⓐ, 1107, 1439, 1608, 1839 Ⓐ, 1939 Ⓐ.
▲ – Jurmala's *33 km* coastline has several stations; the principal stations are Majori and Sloka. There is no station called Jurmala.

RIGA - SAULKRASTI - SKULTE — 1838

Pasažieru vilciens

Riga - Saulkrasti and v.v. *48 km*. Journey 1 hour. Trains with note **s** continue to / from **Skulte** (journey Saulkrasti - Skulte 9 – 10 minutes).

From Riga (trains call at Carnikava 39 minutes later) at 0537 Ⓐ, 0607 **s**, 0737, 0809 **s**, 1009 **s**, 1207 **s**, 1407 **s**, 1507, 1607 **s**, 1707 Ⓐ, 1737 **s**, 1837, 1937 **s**, 2037 **s**, 2237 **s**.

From Saulkrasti (trains call at Carnikava 20 minutes later) at 0459 **s**, 0556 Ⓐ, 0626 **s**, 0655 Ⓐ, 0754 **s**, 0856, 0957 **s**, 1156 **s**, 1356 **s**, 1556 **s**, 1655, 1756 **s**, 1825 Ⓐ, 1928 **s**, 2130 **s**, 2228 **s**.

TALLINN - TARTU - VALGA and KOIDULA — 1870

Elron

km																								
									Ⓐ			Ⓒ												
0	**Tallinn** 1876 d.	0620	0756	...	0756	0938	...	1203	...	...	1316	...	...	1419	1525	...	1525	1646	...	1739	1925	...	2041	...
77	Tapa 1876 d.	0718	0844	...	0844	1026	...	1301	...	...	1404	...	...	1507	1613	...	1613	1744	...	1827	2023	...	2129	...
	Tamsalu d.	0730	0855	...	0855	1037	...	1313	...	...	1415	...	...	1518	1624	...	1624	1755	...	1838	2034	...	2140	...
142	Jõgeva d.	0805	0922	...	0922	1104	...	1348	...	...	1443	...	...	1547	1650	...	1650	1831	...	1905	2110	...	2207	...
190	**Tartu** a.	0839	0950	...	0950	1132	...	1422	...	...	1511	...	...	1614	1718	...	1718	1909	...	1933	2142	...	2234	...
190	**Tartu** d.	...	0953	...	0955	...	...	...	...	...	1514	...	...	...	1723	...	1725	...	...	1936	...	...	...	...
215	Elva d.	...	1020	...	|	...	...	...	...	...	1541	...	...	...	1751	...	|	...	...	2003	...	...	...	...
273	**Valga** 1830 a.	...	1105	...	|	...	...	...	1503	...	1626	1653	...	...	1837	...	|	...	...	2048	...	...	...	...
441	**Riga** 1830 a.	...	...	...	|	...	...	...	1745	...	...	1945	...	...	...	...	|	...	...	...	...	...	...	...
233	Põlva d.	...	...	...	1039	...	...	...	...	...	...	...	...	...	...	...	1809	...	...	...	...	...	...	...
262	Orava d.	...	...	...	1103	...	...	...	...	...	...	...	...	...	...	...	1833	...	...	...	...	...	...	...
275	**Koidula** a.	...	...	...	1113	...	...	...	...	...	...	...	...	...	...	...	1843	...	...	...	...	...	...	...
282	**Piusa** a.	...	...	...	...	...	...	...	...	...	...	...	...	...	...	...	...	...	...	...	...	...	...	...

		Ⓐ					Ⓒ																
Piusa d.	...	...	...	...	...	...	...	...	...	...	...	...	...	...	...	...	...	...	...	...	...	...	...
Koidula d.	...	0614	...	...	...	...	0726	...	...	...	...	...	...	1507	...	...	...	...	...	...	...	...	...
Orava d.	...	0624	...	...	...	...	0736	...	...	...	...	...	...	1517	...	...	...	...	...	...	...	...	...
Põlva d.	...	0648	...	...	...	...	0800	...	...	...	...	...	...	1541	...	...	...	...	...	...	...	...	...
Riga 1830 d.	...	|	...	...	...	...	|	...	...	...	...	...	...	|	...	...	1046	...	...	...	...	1816	...
Valga 1830 d.	...	|	...	0623	0733	...	|	...	...	...	1205	...	...	|	...	...	1342	...	1736	...	...	2050	...
Elva d.	...	|	...	0709	0819	...	|	...	...	...	1251	...	...	|	...	...	...	...	1823	...	...	...	...
Tartu a.	...	0733	...	0735	0845	...	0845	...	...	...	1317	...	...	1626	...	...	...	...	1849	...	...	...	...
Tartu d.	0621	0738	...	0738	0854	...	0854	1036	...	1203	1320	...	1455	1636	...	1728	...	...	1852	2008	...	...	...
Jõgeva d.	0654	0806	...	0806	0922	...	0922	1104	...	1236	1348	...	1525	1706	...	1801	...	...	1921	2041	...	...	...
Tamsalu d.	0730	0833	...	0833	0949	...	0949	1131	...	1312	1415	...	1552	1733	...	1838	...	...	1949	2118	...	...	...
Tapa 1876 d.	0742	0844	...	0844	1000	...	1000	1142	...	1324	1427	...	1604	1744	...	1849	...	...	2000	2129	...	...	...
Tallinn 1876 a.	0841	0935	...	0935	1051	...	1051	1233	...	1423	1518	...	1655	1835	...	1948	...	...	2051	2228	...	...	...

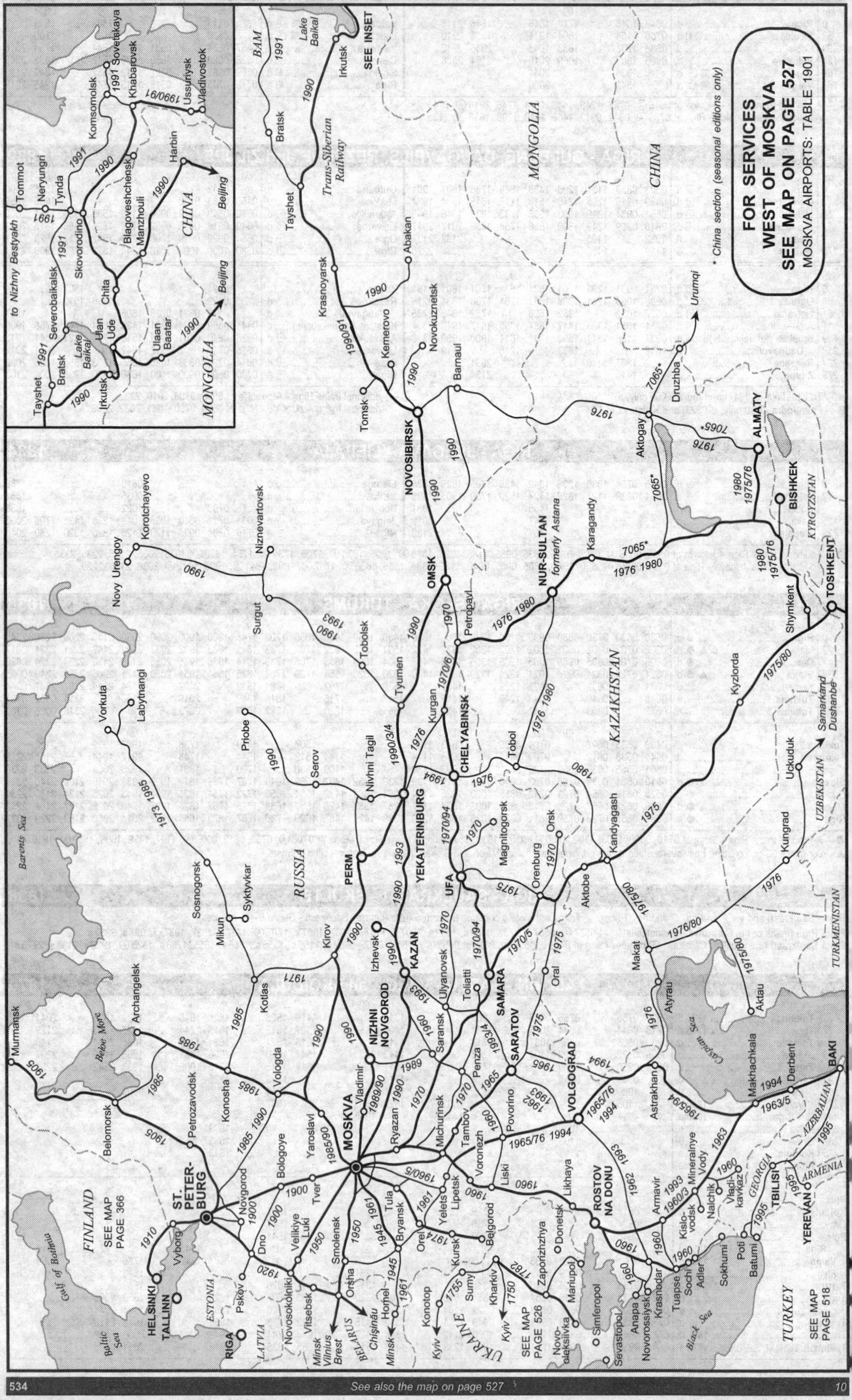

See also the map on page 527

Elron TALLINN - VILJANDI 1872

km		Ⓐ																						
0	**Tallinn** d.	0625	0735	0831	...	1031	1155	1251	...	1401	1458	1549	...	1642	1721	1746	...	1820	1918	2022	...	2116	2226	...
	Saku d.	0649	0756	0855	...	1055	1216	1315	...	1425	1520	1614	...	1707	1745	1807	...	1844	1942	2043	...	2140	2250	...
	Kohila d.	0708	0815	0913	...	1113	1231	1334	...	1443	1534	1635	...	1725	1803	1822	...	1902	2001	2055	...	2158	2308	...
54	Rapla d.	0726	0832	0931	...	1132	1247	1352	...	1501	1550	1653	...	1744	1821	1838	...	1920	2020	2111	...	2216	2327	...
98	Türi d.	...	0906	...	...	1205	1320	...	...	...	1623	...	...	1816	...	1911	...	...	2052	2140	...	...	2359	...
	Võhma d.	...	0924	...	...	...	1338	...	...	...	1641	...	...	...	...	1929	...	...	...	2153	...	...	...	...
151	**Viljandi** a.	...	0947	...	...	...	1401	...	...	...	1704	...	...	...	...	1952	...	...	...	2213	...	...	...	...
			Ⓐ	Ⓐ		Ⓒ																		
	Viljandi d.	...	...	...	...	...	0625	...	...	...	0832	...	...	1045	...	...	...	...	1502	...	...	...	1828	...
	Võhma d.	...	...	...	...	...	0648	...	...	...	0851	...	...	1108	...	...	...	...	1525	...	...	...	1851	...
	Türi d.	...	0600	...	...	0616	0707	...	...	0758	0906	...	...	1127	1241	...	...	...	1544	...	...	...	1911	2102
	Rapla d.	0539	0633	0649	...	0649	0740	0756	...	0833	0935	1034	...	1200	1315	1424	...	1515	1618	1744	...	1843	1944	2138
	Kohila d.	0557	0649	0707	...	0707	0756	0814	...	0851	0951	1052	...	1216	1333	1443	...	1534	1634	1803	...	1902	2000	2158
	Saku d.	0614	0703	0724	...	0724	0809	0832	...	0910	1002	1110	...	1229	1350	1500	...	1551	1647	1821	...	1919	2013	2215
	Tallinn a.	0639	0724	0749	...	0749	0830	0857	...	0934	1023	1134	...	1250	1415	1524	...	1615	1708	1846	...	1944	2035	2240

Elron TALLINN - PALDISKI and TURBA 1874

Tallinn - Paldiski and v.v. *48 km.* Journey 65 minutes.

From Tallinn (trains call at **Keila** 45 minutes later) at 0602 Ⓐ, 0617 Ⓒ, 0717, 0813 Ⓐ, 0817 Ⓒ, 0947, 1117, 1217, 1317, 1417, 1520 Ⓐ, 1547 Ⓒ, 1627 Ⓐ, 1647 Ⓒ, 1727 Ⓐ, 1817 Ⓒ, 1832 Ⓐ, 1917 Ⓒ, 1925 Ⓐ, 2022, 2117.

From Paldiski (trains call at **Keila** 25 minutes later) at 0539, 0623 Ⓐ, 0637 Ⓒ, 0737, 0838 Ⓒ, 0852 Ⓐ, 0938, 1108, 1238, 1338, 1438, 1538, 1636 Ⓐ, 1708 Ⓒ, 1748 Ⓐ, 1808 Ⓒ, 1911 Ⓐ, 1938 Ⓒ, 1947 Ⓐ, 2131.

Tallinn - Turba and v.v. *58 km.* Journey 70 minutes.

From Tallinn (trains call at **Keila** 45 minutes, and **Riisipere** 65 minutes later) at 0632 Ⓐ, 0740 Ⓐ, 0747 Ⓒ, 0838, 1012 Ⓐ, 1017 Ⓒ, 1138 Ⓐ, 1147 Ⓒ, 1238, 1332 Ⓐ, 1347 Ⓒ, 1437, 1542 Ⓐ, 1617 Ⓒ, 1657 Ⓐ, 1747 Ⓒ, 1800 Ⓐ, 1850, 1947, 2047, 2147.

From Turba (trains call at **Riisipere** 5 minutes, and **Keila** 35 minutes later) at 0552 Ⓐ, 0603 Ⓒ, 0638 Ⓐ, 0802 Ⓒ, 0813 Ⓐ, 0913, 1002, 1135 Ⓐ, 1141 Ⓒ, 1311, 1404 Ⓒ, 1407 Ⓐ, 1453 Ⓐ, 1510 Ⓒ, 1600 Ⓐ, 1604 Ⓒ, 1703Ⓐ, 1741 Ⓒ, 1819 Ⓐ, 1907 Ⓒ, 1923 Ⓐ, 2022, 2220.

Elron TALLINN - NARVA 1876

km										
0	**Tallinn** 1870 d.	0652	1102	...	1346	1610	...	1815	2155	...
77	Tapa 1870 d.	0750	1150	...	1444	1658	...	1913	2253	...
104	Rakvere d.	0808	1207	...	1502	1715	...	1931	2311	...
	Kiviõli d.	0832	1227	...	1526	1735	...	1956	...	...
165	Jõhvi d.	0853	1242	...	1547	1751	...	2017	...	...
209	**Narva** a.	0925	1310	...	1619	1819	...	2048	...	...

Narva d.	...	0651	...	0940	1345	...	1639	1849	...
Jõhvi d.	...	0722	...	1007	1416	...	1710	1916	...
Kiviõli d.	...	0743	...	1023	1437	...	1731	1932	...
Rakvere d.	0615	0808	...	1044	1502	...	1757	1953	...
Tapa 1870 d.	0634	0827	...	1101	1521	...	1816	2011	...
Tallinn 1870 a.	0733	0926	...	1152	1620	...	1915	2102	...

RUSSIA and BELARUS

SEE MAPS PAGES 527 and 534

Operators : **RZhD** : Rossiskiye Zheleznye Dorogi, www.rzd.ru **BCh** : Belaruskaya Chyhunka, www.rw.by

Timings : Timings were last updated in December 2021. **Due to the ongoing conflict in the region, we will not be updating the Russian and Belarusian section until further notice.** All times are now shown in LOCAL time (time zone is UTC+3 all year unless otherwise shown in the notes or by a shaded column).

Tickets : Except for travel by purely local trains, prior reservation is necessary and passports and visas must be presented when purchasing tickets. Most nationalities require visas.

RAIL TRAVEL IN RUSSIA, BELARUS, UKRAINE and MOLDOVA

CARRIAGE TYPES

As trains generally operate over long distances, most accommodation is designed for overnight as well as day use. Carriage types (with their Russian names) are:

Spálny vagón SV – 2-berth sleeping compartments (9 per carriage), found only in the best trains. Sometimes referred to as 1st class. A small number of named trains also have *de luxe* carriages (also known as *VIP*) with ensuite facilities.

Kupéiny K – 4-berth compartments (9 per carriage) found in almost all long-distance trains. Sometimes referred to as 2nd class.

Platskártny – open-plan dormitory-style carriage with 54 bunks, found in all except the best trains. Sometimes referred to as 3rd class.

Óbshchi – open-plan carriages with hard seating, found in some slow trains. Sometimes referred to as 4th class and not recommended for long-distance travel.

TRAIN TYPES

The top grade of fast long-distance train is classified *Firménny* (shown as *Fir* in the tables). These are composed of higher-quality carriages dedicated to a particular service (often named) and higher fares apply. Normal long-distance express trains are classified *Skóry* (shown as *Sko* in the tables). The lowest class of long-distance train is classified *Passazhírsky* (*Pas* in the tables) which call at many stations en-route.

Trains are identified by a number, followed by a cyrillic character, or a two-letter transliteration which is shown in some tables to assist in making bookings.

High-speed train types with 1st and 2nd class seating are *Sapsan* (Peregrine Falcon) running between Moskva and St Peterburg, and the Talgo-built *Strizh* (Swift) running between Moskva and Nizhny Novgorod (also with 1st class sleeping compartments for daytime use). Fast *Lastochka* (Swallow) trains with 2nd class seats run on several routes.

INTERNATIONAL SERVICES

International services to, from and via Poland, Slovakia, Hungary and Romania convey through sleeping cars of the normal European ('RIC') types, with single and double compartments in first class, and 3- or 4-berth compartments in second class. The railways of the former Soviet Union being of broad gauge (1520mm), the bogies (trucks) of these through cars are changed at the frontier with these countries.

DAYS OF RUNNING

Many trains run on alternate days only, on even or uneven numbered dates. The examples below illustrate the system used to indicate exceptions to the pattern of even or uneven dates at the end of a month with 31 days and at the beginning of the month following:

e.g. "Uneven dates [... *29, 1* ...]" means that the train does not run on the 31st of a month with 31 days.

e.g. "Even dates [... *30, 1, 4* ...]" means that the train, **following a month with 31 days**, runs exceptionally on the 1st, but not the 2nd, of the month.

In these cases, the following symbols are used in the tables to indicate days of running:

■ – Uneven dates.
■(1) – Uneven dates [.. *29, 1*..]
■(2) – Uneven dates [.. *31, 2, 3*..]
■(3) – Uneven dates [.. *31, 3*..]
■(4) – Uneven dates [.. *29, 3*..]
■(5) – Uneven dates [.. *31, 2, 5*..]
■(6) – Uneven dates [.. *31, 2, 7*..]
■(7) – Uneven dates [.. *31, 2, 4, 7*..]
■(8) – Uneven dates [.. *31, 2, 4, 6, 8, 10, 11*..]
■(9) – Uneven dates [.. *31, 2, 4, 6, 9*..]

● – Even dates.
●(1) – Even dates [.. *28, 2*..]
●(2) – Even dates [.. *30, 2*..]
●(3) – Even dates [.. *30, 1, 3, 8*..]
●(4) – Even dates [.. *30, 1, 4*..]
●(5) – Even dates [.. *30, 1, 3, 4*..]
●(6) – Even dates [.. *30, 1, 3, 6*..]
●(7) – Even dates [.. *30, 1, 6*..]
●(8) – Even dates [.. *30, 1, 3, 5, 8*..]
●(9) – Even dates [.. *30, 1, 3, 5, 7, 10*..]

RZhD MOSKVA - ST PETERBURG 1900

All trains suffix *AJ* except where shown otherwise. For other trains see Tables **1960**, **1989** and **1990**.

km		**20***UJ*	**16**	**82***VJ*	**752**	**756**	**758**	**760***RJ*	**762**	**764**	**766**	**770**	**748**	**714***JI*	**726***CH*	**772**	**774**	**776**	**778**	**780**	**782**	**784**	**786**	**18**
		Fir	*Fir*	*Sko*	♥	♥	♥	♥	♥	♥	♥	♥	⊡	♠	❦	♥	♥	♥	♥	♥	♥	♥	♥	*Fir*
		M	**m**	**b**				**n**		⑥⑦	⑥⑦		①③⑤	**A**									②–⑤	**m**
0	**Moskva** Oktyabrskaya § d.	0020	0041	0203**v**	0545	0650	0700	0920**k**	0940	1130	1140	1340	1340	1452**v**	1521	1530	1540	1730	1740	1930	1940	2050	2100	2108
167	Tver d.	0212	0227	0440	|	0756	0804	1034	1047	|	|	1447	|	|	1719	|	|	|	1847	2036	2045	|	2203	2255
331	Bologoye d.	|	0440	0634	|	0853	|	|	1144	1324	|	1544	|	|	1850	1724	|	|	1944	2133	|	|	|	0032
532	Chudovo Mos. d.	|	|	|	|	|	1016	1233	|	1426	|	|	|	|	2106	1828	|	2030	|	|	2257	|	2357	...
650	**St Peterburg** Glavny ‡ a.	0859	0913**d**	1035	0915	1045	1104	1320	1332	1516	1526	1744	1745	2000**d**	2220	1915	1925	2115	2135	2325	2344	0031	0048	...

	120*VJ*	**26**	**28**	**6**	**4**	**54***CH*	**2**	
	Sko	*Fir*	*Sko*	*Fir*	*Fir*	*Fir*	*Fir*	
	b	**B**			Ⓑ **D**	**E**	**F**	
Moskva Oktyabrskaya § d.	2136**v**	2150	2230	2250	2330	2340	2355	...
Tver d.	0044	2348	0052	|	|	|	|	...
Bologoye d.	0232	|	0251	|	|	|	|	...
Chudovo Mos. d.	|	|	|	|	|	|	|	...
St Peterburg Glavny ‡ a.	0616**d**	0606	0640	0647	0830	0836	0755	...

	713*VJ*	**119**	**751**	**755**	**757**	**759**	**761**	**763**
	♠	*Sko*	♥	♥	♥	♥	♥	♥
	A	**b**						⑥⑦
St Peterburg Glavny ‡ d.	0020**d**	0012	0530	0640	0650	0900	0910	1100
Chudovo Mos. d.	|	|	|	0726	|	|	|	|
Bologoye d.	|	0430	|	|	0848	1052	|	|
Tver d.	|	0632	|	0936	0946	1149	|	|
Moskva Oktyabrskaya § a.	0534**v**	0952**v**	0900	1043	1052	1258	1305	1443

FOR ADDITIONAL SERVICES AND FOOTNOTES SEE NEXT PAGE →

1900 ST PETERBURG - MOSKVA

All trains suffix *AJ* except where shown otherwise. For other trains see Tables **1960**, **1989** and **1990**.

	765	767	769	747	771	773	725*CH*	775	777	779	781	783	81	25	27	15	19*UJ*	3	5	53*CH*	1	17	
	♥	♥	♥	⊡	♥	♥	≋	♥	♥	♥	♥	♥	*Sko*	*Fir*	*Fir*	*Fir*		*Fir*	*Fir*	*Fir*	*Fir*	*Fir*	
	⑥⑦		②–⑤	②④⑦				n					b	B		m	M	Ⓑ D		E	F	m	
St Peterburg Glavny ‡ d.	1110	1300	1310	1310	1500	1510	1516	1700	1710	1900	1910	2050	2004	2155	2231	2243**d**	2250	2330	2336	2349	2355	...	...
Chudovo Mos. d.	1157	|	1359	|	|	1559	1624	|	|	|	1959	|	|	|	|	|	|	|	|	|	|	...	...
Bologoye d.	1300	1452	|	|	1652	|	1800	|	1902	2052	|	|	0020	|	|	0315	|	|	|	|	|	0519	...
Tver d.	|	1549	1608	|	1749	|	1922	1942	1959	2149	2209	|	0151	0406	0420	0455	0441	|	0507	|	|	0700	...
Moskva Oktyabrskaya § a.	1453	1700	1710	1715	1855	1905	2158	2057**k**	2105	2258	2313	0035	0435**v**	0604	0645	0719	0707	0830	0741	0814	0755	0850	...

km		801	79*CH*		819*VJ*	803*MJ*		10	42
			Sko		≋			*Fir*	*Sko*
			N		L				J
0	**Moskva** Oktyabrskaya § d.	...	...	...	...	...	...	2035	2207
167	Tver d.	...	...	...	...	...	...	2240	0036
331	Bologoye d.	...	...	...	...	...	...	0100	0310
	St Peterburg Glavny d.	0726	1013	...	...	1932	...	|	|
532	Chudovo Mos. d.	0903	|	...	1550	2148	...	|	0516
	Veliky Novgorod ⊖ a.	1017	1240	...	1656	2308	...	|	0624
	Veliky Novgorod ⊖ d.	...	1325	...	1750	...	...	|	...
588	Dno a.	...	1647	...	2025	...	...	0600	...
687	**Pskov** a.	...	...	...	...	...	...	0805	...

	802	80*CH*		820*VJ*	804*MJ*		42*CH*	10*CH*
		Sko		≋			*Sko*	*Fir*
		N		P			K	
Pskov d.	...	...	...	...	...	...	...	1930
Dno d.	...	1348	...	1418	...	...	...	2120
Veliky Novgorod ⊖ a.	...	1632	...	1707	...	...	...	|
Veliky Novgorod ⊖ d.	0610	1710	...	1743	1806	...	2110	|
Chudovo Mos. d.	0740	|	...	1856	1932	...	2256	|
St Peterburg Glavny a.	0944	2025	...	...	2055	...	|	|
Bologoye d.	...	...	...	...	...	...	0059	0239
Tver d.	...	...	...	...	...	...	0314	0427
Moskva Oktyabrskaya § a.	...	...	...	...	...	...	0515	0650

A – Samara - Moskva - St. Peterburg and v.v. For days of running see Table **1989**.
B – ①③④⑤⑦ until May 24; daily from May 25.
D – EKSPRESS.
E – GRAND EXPRESS – luxury train (🛏 1, 2 cl.).
F – KRASNAYA STRELA (RED ARROW).
J – ③④⑤⑥⑦ until Mar. 27; daily from Mar. 30.
K – ①④⑤⑥⑦ untli Mar. 28; daily from Mar. 31.
L – ①⑥⑦.
M – MEGAPOLIS - operated by Tverskoy Express.

N – To / from Kaliningrad. For days of running see Table **1950**.
P – ⑤⑥⑦.

b – From / to Belgorod via Tula, Orel (Table **1770**).
d – St Peterburg **Ladozhski**.
k – Moskva **Kurskaya**.
m – To / from Murmansk or Petrozavodsk (Table **1905**).
n – To / from Nizhni Novgorod (Table **1989**).
v – Moskva **Vostochny**.
♥ – *Sapsan* high-speed train, special fares. ✕ Ⓡ.

♠ – *Strizh* (Swift) fast Talgo day train.
≋ – *Lastochka* (Swallow) fast day train.
⊡ – NEVSKIY EKSPRESS. 1st class only.
● – Even dates (see page 535).
■ – Uneven dates (see page 535).
§ – Also known as *Leningradski vokzal.*
‡ – Also known as *Moskovski vokzal.*
⊖ – Station is named **Novgorod na Volkhove**.

FOR ADDITIONAL SERVICES SEE PREVIOUS PAGE.

1901 MOSKVA AIRPORTS ✈

MOSKVA DOMODEDOVO AIRPORT ✈
Aeroexpress rail service Moskva Paveletskaya - Moskva Domodedovo ✈. *35 km* Journey time 45 minutes.
From **Moskva Paveletskaya**: 0530, 0600 and every 30 minutes until 2300, 2330.
From **Domodedovo** ✈: 0600, 0630 and every 30 minutes until 2300, 2330.

MOSKVA SHEREMETYEVO AIRPORT ✈
Aeroexpress rail service Moskva Belorusskaya - Moskva Sheremetyevo ✈. *35 km* Journey time 50 minutes.
From **Moskva Belorusskaya**: 0535, 0605 and every 30 minutes until 2305, 2335.
From **Sheremetyevo** ✈: 0547, 0617 and every 30 minutes until 2317, 2347.

MOSKVA VNUKOVO AIRPORT ✈
Aeroexpress rail service Moskva Kiyevskaya - Moskva Vnukovo ✈. *28 km* Journey time 35 - 40 minutes.
From **Moskva Kiyevskaya**: 0600 and hourly until 2300.
From **Vnukovo** ✈: 0600 and hourly until 2300.

1905 (MOSKVA -) ST PETERBURG - PETROZAVODSK - MURMANSK

RZhD

km		18*AJ*	804*CH*	16*AJ*	806*CH*	22*CH*			
		Fir	≋	*Fir*	≋	*Sko*			
	Moskva Oktyabrskaya **1900**. d.	2105	...	0041	...	...	...	...	...
0	**St Peterburg** Ladozhski d.	|	0632	1010	1800	2124	...	...	...
**114*	Volkhovstroi 1 d.	0354**v**	0818	1204	1924	2310	...	...	...
394	**Petrozavodsk** d.	0750	1157	1710	2259	0321	...	...	...
773	Belomorsk d.	...	...	0023	...	0947	...	...	...
1161	Kandalaksha d.	...	...	0652	...	1626	...	...	...
1438	**Murmansk** a.	...	...	1145	...	2121	...	...	...

	21*CH*	803*CH*	15*AJ*	805*CH*	17*AJ*			
	Sko	≋	*Fir*	≋	*Fir*			
Murmansk d.	1012	...	1935	...	...	...	...	...
Kandalaksha d.	1510	...	0057	...	...	...	...	...
Belomorsk d.	2137	...	0723	...	...	...	...	...
Petrozavodsk d.	0403	0636	1509	1800	2200	...	...	...
Volkhovstroi 1 d.	0803	1018	1950	|	0158**v**	...	...	...
St Peterburg Ladozhski a.	1009	1200	2149	2259	|	...	...	...
Moskva Oktyabrskaya **1900**. a.	...	...	0719	...	0850	...	...	...

v – Volkhovstroi 2. ≋ – *Lastochka* (Swallow) fast day train. * – Moskva - Vokhovstroi : *641 km.*

1910 MOSKVA and ST PETERBURG - HELSINKI

RZhD, VR

km									
	Moskva Oktyabrskaya d.	...	...	...	...	...	...	...	...
	Tver d.	...	...	...	...	...	...	...	...
	St Peterburg Ladozhski d.	...	...	...	...	...	...	...	...
0	**St Peterburg** Finlyandski d.	...	...	...	...	...	...	...	...
129	Vyborg 🏛 RU d.	...	...	...	...	...	...	...	...
159	Vainikkala 🏛 FIN d.	...	...	...	...	...	...	...	...
250	**Kouvola** 797 a.	...	...	...	...	...	...	...	...
312	Lahti 797 a.	...	...	...	...	...	...	...	...
400	Tikkurila 797 a.	...	...	...	...	...	...	...	...
413	Pasila 797 a.	...	...	...	...	...	...	...	...
416	**Helsinki** 797 a.	...	...	...	...	...	...	...	...

Helsinki 797 d.	...	...	...	...	...	...	...	...
Pasila 797 d.	...	...	...	...	...	...	...	...
Tikkurila 797 d.	...	...	...	...	...	...	...	...
Lahti 797 d.	...	...	...	...	...	...	...	...
Kouvola 797 d.	...	...	...	...	...	...	...	...
Vainikkala 🏛 FIN d.	...	...	...	...	...	...	...	...
Vyborg 🏛 RU d.	...	...	...	...	...	...	...	...
St Peterburg Finlyandski a.	...	...	...	...	...	...	...	...
St Peterburg Ladozhski a.	...	...	...	...	...	...	...	...
Tver a.	...	...	...	...	...	...	...	...
Moskva Oktyabrskaya a.	...	...	...	...	...	...	...	...

1920 ST PETERBURG - HOMEL and KOZYATYN

RZhD, BCh, UZ

km		55*BJ*	626*BJ*	79*CH*	83*AJ*	83*AJ*	51*BJ*	869*BJ*	657*BJ*
		Fir		*Sko*	*Sko*	*Sko*	*Fir*		
						■(4)			
		◇	G	C		D			E
0	**St Peterburg** Vitebski d.	...	...	...	1700	1700	1818	...	...
	St Peterburg Glavny d.	...	...	1013	|	|	|	...	...
245	Dno d.	...	...	1659	2050	2050	2143	...	...
421	Novosokolniki RU d.	...	...	2022	2359	2359	0033	...	...
568	Vitsebsk ⊖ BY d.	...	2138	2316	0230	0230	0314	...	...
670	Polatsk d.	...	0013	0114	|	|	|	0613	1743
868	Maladzechnia a.	...	0503	0348	|	|	|	0915	2117
	Moskva Bel. **1950** d.	2028	|	|	|	|	|	|	|
652	**Orsha** Tsentralnaya a.	0308	|	▽	0343	0343	0423	|	|
652	**Orsha** Tsentralnaya **1950** d.	0342	|	...	0405	0418	0447	|	|
	Minsk **1950** a.	|	0629	...	|	0631	0715	1015	2218
	Hrodna **1952** a.	|	...	...	|	1156	|	...	|
	Brest Tsent. **1950** a.	|	...	...	|	...	1156	...	0741
726	Mahilyow 1 d.	0535	...	...	0609	...	...	...	...
853	Zhlobin **1930** d.	0751	...	...	0823	...	...	...	...
	Homel **1930** a.	0912	...	...	0952	...	...	...	...
	Kyiv **1930** a.	...	...	...	...	...	...	...	...
954	Kalinkavichy BY d.	...	...	...	...	...	...	...	...
1109	Korosten ⊡ UA d.	...	...	...	...	...	...	...	...
1191	Zhytomyr d.	...	...	...	...	...	...	...	...
1267	**Kozyatyn** 1 a.	...	...	...	...	...	...	...	...
	Chisinău **1720** a.	...	...	...	...	...	...	...	...

	658*BJ*	869*BJ*	52*BJ*	83*BJ*	83*BJ*	625*BJ*	80*CH*	55*MZ*
			Fir	*Sko*	*Sko*		*Sko*	*Fir*
				●‡				
	E			F		H	C	◇
Chisinău **1720** d.	...	...	...	...	...	...	...	...
Kozyatyn 1 d.	...	...	...	...	...	...	...	...
Zhytomyr d.	...	...	...	...	...	...	...	...
Korosten UA d.	...	...	...	...	...	...	...	...
Kalinkavichy ⊡ BY d.	...	...	...	...	...	...	...	...
Kyiv **1930** d.	...	...	...	...	...	...	...	...
Homel **1930** d.	...	...	...	...	1716	...	...	1830
Zhlobin **1930** d.	...	...	...	...	1834	...	...	1946
Mahilyow 1 d.	...	...	...	...	2045	...	...	2155
Brest Tsent. **1950** d.	2029	...	1412	...	|	...	...	|
Hrodna **1952** d.	|	...	|	1158	|	...	...	|
Minsk **1950** d.	0630	1723	1843	1736	|	2135	...	|
Orsha Tsentralnaya **1950** a.	|	|	2115	2041	2157	|	...	2303
Orsha Tsentralnaya d.	|	|	2140	2130	2220	|	▽	2327
Moskva Bel. **1950** a.	|	|	|	|	|	|	|	0630
Maladzechnia d.	0756	1846	|	|	|	2321	0316	...
Polatsk d.	1025	2115	|	|	|	0458	0621	...
Vitsebsk BY d.	...	...	2302	0024	0024	0641	0822	...
Novosokolniki ⊖ RU d.	...	...	0201	0335	0335	...	1110	...
Dno d.	...	...	0426	0614	0614	...	1348	...
St Peterburg Glavny a.	...	...	|	|	|	...	2025	...
St Peterburg Vitebski a.	...	...	0755	0947	0947	...	...	...

C – For days of running see Table **1950**.
D – St Peterburg - Orsha (**3***BJ* or **7***MJ*) - Minsk (**687***BJ*) - Hrodna.
E – Polatsk - Minsk - Brest and v.v. (Table **1950**).
F – Hrodna (**680***BJ*) - Vitsebsk - St Peterburg.
G – ④⑤⑥⑦.
H – ①⑤⑥⑦.

▽ – To / from Kaliningrad via Vilnius (Table **1950**).
◇ – For Moskva - Homel via Bryansk see Table **1945**.
● – Even dates (see page 535).
■ – Uneven dates (see page 535).
‡ – Even dates [.. *28, 2* ..].
⊖ – 🏛 : Yezyaryshcha (BY) / Zaverezhye (RU).

⊡ – 🏛 : Slovechno (BY) / Berezhest (UA).
BY – Belarus (UTC + 3)
RU – Russia (Moskva Time UTC + 3).
UA – Ukraine (UTC + 2 winter, UTC + 3 summer).

MINSK - HOMEL - KYIV — 1930

BCh, UZ

km		684	716	710	748	648	708	756	632
		①		⑤–⑦	Ⓑ			⑤–⑦	F
	St P'burg Vit. **1920** d.	...	...	...	...	...	...	...	...
0	**Minsk** d.	0025	0708	1111	1457	1627	1900	1936	2357
149	Babruysk d.	0303	0837	1241	1634	1828	|	2122	0206
214	Zhlobin **1920** d.	0419	0921	1321	1717	1924	|	2218	0326
304	**Homel** **1920** a.	0551	1021	1415	1814	2041	2150	2318	0754
304	**Homel** BY d.	...	...	...	...	...	...	...	...
415	Chernihiv § UA d.	...	...	...	...	...	...	...	...
624	**Kyiv** a.	...	...	...	...	...	...	...	...
	Kharkiv **1755** a.	...	...	...	...	...	...	...	...
	Odesa **1720** a.	...	...	...	...	...	...	...	...

	755	647	707	747	631	739	715	621
	①⑥⑦			⑤⑦	F			
Odesa **1720** d.	...	...	...	...	...	...	...	...
Kharkiv **1755** d.	...	...	...	...	...	...	...	...
Kyiv d.	...	...	...	...	...	...	...	...
Chernihiv § UA d.	...	...	...	...	...	...	...	...
Homel BY a.	...	...	...	...	...	...	...	...
Homel **1920** d.	0443	0630	0700	1053	1420	1510	1908	2210
Zhlobin **1920** d.	0533	0756	|	1145	1906	1602	2001	0244
Babruysk d.	0617	0858	|	1228	2059	1642	2046	0341
Minsk a.	0753	1057	0950	1359	2307	1808	2220	0548
St P'burg Vit. **1920** a.	...	...	...	...	...	...	...	...

F – To/from Hrodna (Table **1952**). § – 🏛 : Teryukha (BY) / Hornostayivka (UA). BY – Belarus (UTC+3). UA – Ukraine (UTC+2/+3).

MOSKVA - BRYANSK - HOMEL - BREST — 1945

RZhD, BCh

km		675*BJ*	302*SJ*	737*AJ*	739*AJ*	603*BJ*	107*MJ*	741*VJ*	85*CH*
			Pas	*Sko*	*Sko*		*Sko*	*Sko*	*Sko*
		⑦	**A**				⑤		
0	**Moskva** Belorusskaya **1740** d.	...	...	0653	1338	...	1717	1914	2241
485	**Bryansk** Orlovski **1740** d.	...	0839	1056	1741	...	2152	2322	0426
713	Zlynka RU d.	...	1255	...	...	...	...	...	...
739	Dobrush BY d.	...	...	...	...	...	...	...	...
764	**Homel** d.	0815	...	...	...	2010	...	...	...
892	Kalinkavichy d.	1023	...	...	...	2250	...	...	...
1069	Luninets d.	1314	...	...	...	0154	...	...	...
1297	**Brest** Tsentralny a.	1650	...	...	...	0557	...	...	...

	86*CH*	640*BJ*	738*AJ*	740*AJ*	108*MJ*	742*VJ*	302*BJ*	676*BJ*
	Sko		*Sko*	*Sko*	*Sko*	*Sko*	*Pas*	
					⑦		**A**	⑦
Brest Tsentralny d.	...	1940	...	...	...	...	...	1017
Luninets d.	...	0022	...	...	...	...	...	1430
Kalinkavichy d.	...	0358	...	...	...	...	...	1733
Homel a.	...	0604	...	...	...	...	...	1937
Dobrush BY d.	...	...	...	...	...	...	...	...
Zlynka RU d.	...	...	...	...	...	...	1650	...
Bryansk Orlovski **1740** d.	0017	...	0705	1326	1650	1906	2146	...
Moskva Belorusskaya **1740** a.	0613	...	1110	1731	2119	2311	...	...

A – Adler - Minsk and v.v. For days of running see Table **1961**. BY – Belarus (UTC+3). RU – Russia (UTC+3).

MOSKVA - MINSK - VILNIUS, KALININGRAD and BREST — 1950

RZhD, BCh

km		727*BJ*	737*BJ*	717*MJ*	715*MJ*	743*CH*	725*BJ*	731*MJ*	607*BJ*	735*BJ*	701*BJ*	360*SJ*	657*BJ*	721*MJ*	735*MJ*	79*CH*	29*CH*	55*BJ*	1*BJ*	3*BJ*	7*MJ*	51*BJ*	27*BJ*
				❦	❦	❦		❦				*Pas*		❦	❦	*Sko*	*Fir*	*Fir*	*Fir*	*Sko*	*Sko*	*Fir*	*Sko*
												B	**C**			⊙				● **D**	■(1) **D**		
0	**Moskva** Belorusskaya d.	...	...	0620	0715	0956	...	1159	...	...	...	...	...	1600	1917	...	1953	2028	2210	2217	2217	...	2330
243	Vyazma d.	...	...	|	0935	1217	...	1414	...	...	...	...	...	1808	2150	...	2254	2347	0125	0103	0103	...	0239
419	**Smolensk** RU a.	...	...	0956	1117	1406	...	1556	...	...	...	...	...	1941	2331	...	0034	0143	0321	0243	0243	...	0440
419	**Smolensk** RU d.	...	...	1001	...	...	...	...	...	...	...	1705	...	1946	...	...	0044	0153	0331	0253	0253	...	0450
560	Vitsebsk RU d.	...	...	|	...	...	...	...	...	...	...	|	...	|	...	...	|	|	|	|	|	...	|
662	**Polatsk** BY a.	...	...	|	...	...	...	...	...	...	...	|	...	|	...	...	|	|	|	|	|	...	|
	St Peterburg Glavny **1920** d.	...	...	|	...	...	...	...	...	...	...	|	...	|	...	1013	|	|	|	|	|	1818	|
538	Orsha Tsentralnaya BY a.	...	...	1108	...	...	...	...	...	...	...	1821	...	2052	...	|	0155	0308	0446	0401	0401	0423	0606
538	Orsha Tsentralnaya **1920** d.	...	...	1109	...	...	...	...	...	...	...	1845	...	2053	...	⊡	0223	0342	0503	0418	0418	0447	0623
750	**Minsk** **1920** a.	...	...	1310	...	...	...	...	...	...	...	2127	...	2255	...	|	0441	|	0725	0631	0631	0715	0855
750	**Minsk** d.	1035	1304	...	...	...	1559	...	1730	1826	1947	2150	2249	...	...	|	0455	△	...	0652	0652	0755	0917
827	Maladzechnia BY d.	|	|	...	...	...	|	...	|	|	|	2301	|	...	...	0402	0558	...	...	|	|	|	|
943	**Vilnius** LT a.	|	|	...	...	...	|	...	|	|	|	|	|	...	...	|	|	...	...	|	|	|	|
943	**Vilnius** LT d.	|	|	...	...	...	|	...	|	|	|	|	|	...	...	|	|	...	...	|	|	|	|
1285	**Kaliningrad** Ka a.	|	|	...	...	...	|	...	|	|	|	0808	|	...	...	1317	1446	...	...	|	|	|	|
892	Baranavichy Tsentral'nyye d.	1202	1504**p**	...	...	...	|	...	1919	2008**p**	2114	...	0122**p**	...	...	...	...	...	...	0825	0825	0934	1142**p**
1094	**Brest** Tsentralny a.	1359	1700	...	...	...	1859	...	2153	2202	2302	...	0741	...	...	...	...	...	...	1031	1031	1156	1437
	Warszawa Wschodnia **1050** a.	...	...	...	...	...	...	...	...	...	...	...	...	...	...	...	...	...	...	...	...	...	...

	80*CH*	736*MJ*	658*BJ*	722*BJ*	360*CH*	702*BJ*	608*BJ*	736*BJ*	716*MJ*	744*CH*	732*MJ*	718*BJ*	52*BJ*	728*BJ*	55*MZ*	4*BJ*	8*BJ*	738*BJ*	2*BJ*	726*BJ*	28*BJ*	30*CH*
	Sko	❦		❦	*Pas*				❦	❦	❦	❦	*Fir*		*Fir*	*Sko*	*Sko*		*Fir*		*Sko*	*Fir*
	⊕		**C**		**B**											■(1) **D**	● **D**					
Warszawa Wschodnia **1050** d.	...	...	...	...	...	...	...	...	...	...	...	...	...	...	...	...	...	...	...	...	...	...
Brest Tsentralny d.	...	...	2029	...	...	0622	0628	0809	...	...	...	...	1412	1437	...	1737	1737	1746	...	2003	1823	...
Baranavichy Tsentral'nyye d.	...	...	0400**p**	...	...	|	0907	1015**p**	...	...	...	...	1651	1626	...	1941	1941	2004**p**	...	2158	2204**p**	...
Kaliningrad Ka d.	1603	...	|	...	1807	|	|	|	...	...	...	...	|	|	...	|	|	|	...	|	|	1303
Vilnius LT a.	|	...	|	...	|	|	|	|	...	...	...	...	|	|	...	|	|	|	...	|	|	|
Vilnius LT d.	|	...	|	...	|	|	|	|	...	...	...	...	|	|	...	|	|	|	...	|	|	|
Maladzechna d.	0316	...	|	...	0457	|	|	|	...	...	...	...	|	|	...	|	|	|	...	|	|	2320
Minsk a.	|	...	0601	...	0605	0922	1056	1150	...	...	...	...	1827	1750	△	2115	2115	2141	...	2326	2354	0023
Minsk **1920** d.	|	...	...	0620	0633	...	...	...	...	...	...	1600	1843	...	|	2144	2144	...	2210	...	0008	0036
Orsha Tsentralnaya **1920** a.	⊡	...	...	0819	0924	...	...	...	...	...	...	1758	2115	...	2303	2354	2354	...	0024	...	0230	0255
Orsha Tsentralnaya BY d.	|	...	...	0820	0948	...	...	...	...	...	...	1759	2140	...	2327	0011	0011	...	0048	...	0250	0321
St Peterburg Glavny **1920** a.	2025	...	...	|	|	...	...	...	...	...	...	|	0755	...	|	|	|	...	|	...	|	|
Polatsk BY d.	...	...	...	|	|	...	...	...	...	...	...	|	...	...	|	|	|	...	|	...	...	|
Vitsebsk RU d.	...	...	...	|	|	...	...	...	...	...	...	|	...	...	|	|	|	...	|	...	...	|
Smolensk RU a.	...	...	...	0922	1108	...	...	...	...	...	...	1901	...	...	0042	0127	0127	...	0204	...	0405	0431
Smolensk RU d.	...	0752	...	0927	...	...	...	...	1602	1707	1840	1906	...	...	0052	0137	0137	...	0214	...	0415	0441
Vyazma d.	...	0935	...	|	...	...	...	...	1747	1857	2025	2042	...	...	0309	0344	0344	...	0434	...	0633	0624
Moskva Belorusskaya a.	...	1154	...	1310	...	...	...	...	2033	2124	2246	2255	...	...	0630	0654	0654	...	0815	...	0931	0854

km		62*AJ*	64*AJ*
		Sko	*Sko*
		②④	⑦
0	Sebezh d.	...	...
111	Novosokolniki d.	...	...
140	Velikiye Luki d.	1955	1955
381	Rzhev d.	0113	0113
616	Moskva Belorusskaya a.	0718	0718

	61*AJ*	63*AJ*
	Sko	*Sko*
	①③	⑤
Moskva Belorusskaya d.	2114	2114
Rzhev d.	0330	0330
Velikiye Luki d.	0750	0750
Novosokolniki d.	...	...
Sebezh a.	...	...

⊕ – ③⑤⑥.
❦ – *Lastochka* (Swallow) fast day train.
● – Even dates (see page 535).
■ – Uneven dates (see page 535).

BY – Belarus (UTC+3).
Ka – Kaliningrad region of Russia (UTC+2). Local time.
LT – Lithuania (UTC+2 in winter, UTC+3 in summer).
RU – Russia (Moskva Time UTC+3).

BORDER CROSSINGS:
Between Smolensk and Polatsk: Rudnya (RU) / Zavolsha (BY).
Between Smolensk and Orsha: Krasnoye (RU) / Osinovka (BY).
Between Maladzechna and Vilnius: Hudahai (BY) / Kena (LT).
Between Vilnius and Kaliningrad: Kybartai (LT) / Nesterov (Ka).

B – Adler - Kaliningrad and v.v. For days of running see Table **1961**.
C – Polatsk - Minsk - Brest and v.v. (Table **1920**).
D – Conveys Moskva - Minsk (**687/688***BJ*) - Hrodna and v.v. (Table **1952**).

p – Baranavichy **Polesskiye**.

△ – To/from Homel (Table **1920**).
⊡ – Via Novgorod na Volkhove, Vitsebsk (Tables **1900, 1920**).
⊙ – ①⑤⑦.

VITSEBSK - MINSK - HRODNA — 1952

BCh

km		679*BJ*	687*BJ*	731*BJ*	627*BJ*		729*BJ*	631*BJ*	623*BJ*
					⑤⑦				
			E F					**d**	
0	**Vitsebsk** d.	0010	...	...	...	...	...	...	1807
84	Orsha Tsentralnaya a.	0135	...	...	...	...	...	...	1938
84	Orsha Tsentralnaya d.	0233	...	...	...	...	...	...	2004
296	**Minsk** a.	0555	...	...	...	...	...	...	2332
296	**Minsk** d.	0610	0708	1518	1520	...	1920	2327	2347
373	Maladzechna d.	|	0813	1614	|	...	2016	|	0058
501	Lida d.	|	1006	1745	|	...	2204	|	0307
437	Baranavichy Pol. d.	0810**t**	|	|	1758	...	|	0214	|
*633	**Hrodna** a.	1144	1156	1910	2158	...	2333	0634	0519

	730*BJ*	680*BJ*	688*BJ*	632*BJ*		624*BJ*	732*BJ*	628*BJ*
								⑤⑦
		G	**F**	**d**				
Hrodna d.	0645	1158	1534	1701	...	1728	1951	2353
Baranavichy Pol. d.	|	1523**t**	|	2124	...	|	|	0520
Lida d.	0813	|	1724	|	...	1938	2113	|
Maladzechna d.	0947	|	1910	|	...	2140	2241	|
Minsk a.	1042	1721	2209	2341	...	2245	2337	0726
Minsk d.	...	1736	...	...	...	2302	...	...
Orsha Tsentralnaya a.	...	2041	...	...	...	0319	...	...
Orsha Tsentralnaya d.	...	2130	...	...	...	0440	...	...
Vitsebsk a.	...	2242	...	...	...	0603	...	...

E – Conveys St Peterburg (**83***AJ*) - Orsha (**3***BJ* or **7***MJ*) - Minsk - Hrodna (Table **1920**).
F – Conveys Moskva (**3/4***BJ* or **7***MJ*/**8***BJ*) - Minsk - Hrodna and v.v. (Table **1950**).
G – Conveys on Even dates [.. *28, 2* ..]. Hrodna - Vitsebsk (**83***BJ*) - St Peterburg (Table **1920**).

d – To/from Homel (Table **1930**).
t – Baranavichy **Tsentral'nyye**.
* – *657 km* via Baranavichy.

1960 MOSKVA - ROSTOV - SEVASTOPOL, NOVOROSSIYSK, KISLOVODSK, SOCHI and ADLER

Trains to Simferopol and Sevastopol are operated by GRAND TRAIN (www.grandtrain.ru) - these services may only be available to Russian citizens.

km	*Time zone: UTC+3*	740*ZH*	4*MJ*	28*CH*	12*MJ*	104*VJ*	815*SJ*	829*SJ*	135*AJ*	30*SJ*	102*MJ*	803*SJ*	801*SJ*	738*ZH*	20*SJ*	808*SJ*	7*AJ*	306*MJ*	146*EI*	146*EI* 688*SJ*	92*MJ*	33*MJ*	49*AJ*	35*AJ*
		Fir	*Fir*	*Sko*	*Sko*	*Fir*	❋	❋	*Sko*	*Fir*	*Fir*	❋	❋	*Fir*	*Fir*	❋	*Sko*	*Sko*	*Fir*	*Sko*	*Sko*	*Sko*	*Sko*	*Fir*
									■(5)									A	●	●		●(4)	B	
	St Peterburg Glavny d.	...	...	...	...	...	...	...	1830	...	...	...	...	...	...	...	1720	...	...	...	...	...	1334	2015
	Bologoye d.	...	...	...	...	...	...	...	0007	...	...	...	...	...	...	...	2006	...	...	...	...	...	1727	0027
	Tver d.	...	...	...	...	...	...	...	0224	...	...	...	...	...	...	...	2127	...	...	...	...	...	1906	0200
0	**Moskva** Kazanskaya d.	0814	0822	0840	1040	1050	...	...	0532v	1430	1440	...	...	1652	1840	...	|	1950	2320	2320	2350	2142p	2249v	|
198	Ryazan 2 d.	1028	1048	1106	1301	1311	...	...	|	1712	1722	...	...	1906	2120	...	0209	2301	0224	0224	0245	|	|	0657
412	Michurinsk Voronezhski d.	1241	1303	1318	1514	1530	...	...	|	1928	1940	...	...	2114	2340	...	0426	0143	0446	0446	0519	|	|	0944
469	Gryazi Voronezhski d.	1326	1348	1405	1558	1613	...	...	|	2011	2025	...	...	2159	0024	...	0522	0231	0532	0532	0615	|	|	1030
426	Yelets d.	|	|	|	|	|	...	...	1414	|	|	...	...	|	|	...	|	|	|	|	|	0522	0711	|
504	Lipetsk d.	|	|	|	|	|	...	...	1540	|	|	...	...	|	|	...	|	|	|	|	|	0634	0827	|
591	Voronezh Pridacha d.	1439r	1517	1531	1726	1754	...	...	1910	2133	2147	...	...	2312r	0201	...	0722	0520r	0805r	0805r	0824	0853	1106	1255r
667	Liski d.	...	1629	1645	1842	1858	...	...	2026	2243	2257	...	...	...	0304	...	0830	0741	0951	0951	0941	1010	1223	1450
786	Rossosh d.	...	1818	1827	2026	2036	...	...	2240	0025	0035	...	...	...	0439	...	1022	0951	1156	1156	1125	1223	1447	1647
1062	Likhaya d.	...	|	|	|	|	...	...	0247	|	|	...	...	...	0817	...	|	1458	1635	1635	|	1753	1940	2052
1226	**Rostov na Donu** a.	...	2339	2349	0141	0151	...	...	0613	0539	0547	...	...	...	1035	...	1712	1747	1923	1923	1810	2141	2257	2327
1226	**Rostov na Donu** d.	...	2356	0004	0156	0206	...	...	0630	0603	0611	...	...	...	...	1719	1727	1807	1943	1943	1833	2207	2317	2343
	Vladyslavivka d.	...	|	0900	|	|	...	...	|	|	|	...	...	...	...	|	0231	|	|	|	0620	|	|	|
	Dzhankoy d.	...	|	1045	|	|	...	...	|	|	|	...	...	...	...	|	0415	|	|	|	0805	|	|	|
	Simferopol a.	...	|	1200	|	|	...	...	|	|	|	...	...	...	...	|	0530	|	|	|	0920	|	|	|
	Sevastopol a.	...	|	...	|	|	...	...	|	|	|	...	...	...	...	|	0725	|	|	|	1115	|	|	|
1405	Tikhoretskaya d.	...	0208	...	|	|	...	...	0858	|	|	...	...	...	...	|	...	|	2213	2213	...	0059	0148	|
1332	Starominskaya Tim. d.	...	|	...	|	|	...	...	|	|	|	...	...	...	...	1836	...	1921	|	|	...	|	|	|
1510	Krasnodar 1 d.	...	|	...	|	0517	0724	0843	|	0923	|	1315	1848	...	...	2037	...	2220	|	e	...	|	|	0326
1645	**Novorossiysk** a.	...	|	...	|	|	|	|	|	1230	|	|	|	...	...	|	...	|	|	...	...	|	|	|
1636	**Anapa** a.	...	|	...	0805	|	|	|	|	...	|	|	|	...	...	|	...	|	|	...	...	|	|	|
1533	Armavir Rostovski d.	...	0403	...	...	|	|	|	1100	...	|	|	|	...	...	|	...	|	0133	...	...	0330	0436	|
1721	Mineralnye Vody d.	...	0643	...	...	|	|	|	1324	...	|	|	|	...	...	|	...	|	0422	...	...	0629	0817	|
1747	Pyatigorsk d.	...	0720	...	...	|	|	|	|	...	|	|	|	...	...	|	...	|	|	...	...	|	0853	|
1785	**Kislovodsk** a.	...	0811	...	...	|	|	|	d	...	|	|	|	...	...	|	...	|	f	...	...	g	0946	|
1658	Tuapse d.	...	...	...	...	0800	0943	1102	...	...	1132	1546	2103	...	...	2325	...	0230	...	...	...	...	...	0647
1738	**Sochi** a.	...	...	...	...	0946	1130	1246	...	...	1318	1728	2258	...	...	0109	...	0432	...	...	...	...	...	0903
1761	**Adler** a.	...	...	...	...	1024	1203	1316	...	...	1351	1758	2327	...	...	0139	...	0511	...	...	...	...	...	0943
1800	Gagra ◐ a.	...	...	...	...	...	...	...	...	...	...	...	...	...	...	...	...	0834	...	...	...	...	...	...
1873	**Sukhumi** ◐ a.	...	...	...	...	...	...	...	...	...	...	...	...	...	...	...	...	1043	...	...	...	...	...	...

Time zone: UTC+3	306*SJ*	145*SJ*	687*SJ* 145*SJ*	33*SJ*	808*EI*	802*SJ*	19*SJ*	92*SJ*	11*EI*	135*SJ*	804*SJ*	830*SJ*	737*ZH*	816*SJ*	49*CH*	104*ZH*	30*JI*	102*SJ*	3*SJ*	28*SJ*	739*ZH*	36*SJ*	8*SJ*
	Pas	*Fir*		*Sko*	❋	❋	*Fir*	*Sko*	*Fir*	*Sko*	❋	❋	*Fir*	❋	*Sko*	*Fir*	*Fir*	*Fir*	*Fir*	*Sko*	*Fir*	*Fir*	*Sko*
	D	●(4)	●(4)	●						●					C								
Sukhumi ◐ d.	1423	...	...	...	...	...	...	...	...	...	...	...	...	...	...	...	...	...	...	...	...	...	...
Gagra ◐ d.	1629	...	...	...	...	...	...	...	...	...	...	...	...	...	...	...	...	...	...	...	...	...	...
Adler d.	1948	...	...	...	0216	0519	...	...	...	...	1256	1322	...	1752	...	1857	...	2103	...	...	...	1738	...
Sochi d.	2032	...	...	...	0246	0551	...	...	...	...	1328	1357	...	1830	...	1934	...	2135	...	...	...	1819	...
Tuapse d.	2232	...	...	...	0436	0737	...	...	...	...	1512	1542	...	2022	...	2122	...	2324	...	...	...	2039	...
Kislovodsk d.	|	f	...	g	|	|	...	...	...	d	|	|	...	|	1349	|	...	|	2040	...	...	|	...
Pyatigorsk d.	|	|	...	|	|	|	...	...	...	|	|	|	...	|	1444	|	...	|	2136	...	...	|	...
Mineralnye Vody d.	|	0215	...	2259	|	|	...	...	...	1131	|	|	...	|	1551	|	...	|	2215	...	...	|	...
Armavir Rostovski d.	|	0504	...	0137	|	|	...	...	...	1352	|	|	...	|	1815	|	...	|	0034	...	...	|	...
Anapa d.	|	|	...	|	|	|	...	...	1415	|	|	|	...	|	|	|	...	|	|	...	...	|	...
Novorossiysk d.	|	|	...	|	|	|	...	...	|	|	|	|	...	|	|	|	2120	|	|	...	...	|	...
Krasnodar 1 d.	0151	|	e	|	0734	1006	...	...	|	|	1725	1802	...	2248	|	2342	2350	|	|	...	...	0003	...
Starominskaya Tim. d.	0447	|	|	|	0937	...	...	...	|	|	...	...	...	...	|	|	|	|	|	...	...	|	...
Tikhoretskaya d.	|	0754	0754	0345	...	...	...	...	|	1612	...	...	...	...	2030	|	|	|	0233	...	...	|	...
Sevastopol d.	|	|	|	|	|	...	...	2055	|	|	...	...	...	...	|	|	|	|	|	...	...	|	1715
Simferopol d.	|	|	|	|	|	...	...	2310	|	|	...	...	...	...	|	|	|	|	|	1710	...	|	1910
Dzhankoy d.	|	|	|	|	|	...	...	0055	|	|	...	...	...	...	|	|	|	|	|	1850	...	|	2052
Vladyslavivka d.	|	|	|	|	|	...	...	0227	|	|	...	...	...	...	|	|	|	|	|	2016	...	|	2218
Rostov na Donu a.	0627	1012	1012	0635	1052	...	...	1504	2050	1847	...	...	...	...	2324	0248	0256	0441	0449	0457	...	0348	0709
Rostov na Donu d.	0650	1028	1028	0704	...	...	1515	1523	2110	1905	...	...	...	...	2340	0303	0311	0456	0504	0512	...	0406	0731
Likhaya d.	1047	1352	1352	1058	...	...	1744	|	|	2234	...	...	...	...	0244	|	|	|	|	|	...	0730	|
Rossosh d.	1514	1745	1745	1522	...	...	2123	2133	0245	0300	...	...	...	...	0650	0829	0838	1023	1032	1041	...	1116	1427
Liski d.	1653	1921	1921	1725	...	...	2255	2315	0426	0454	...	...	...	...	0832	1001	1020	1202	1212	1222	...	1250	1606
Voronezh Pridacha d.	1937r	2128r	2128r	1851	...	...	2356	0020	0528	0612	...	...	0733r	...	1017	1103	1125	1302	1315	1328	1621r	1458r	1728
Lipetsk d.	|	|	|	2131	...	...	|	|	|	0944	...	...	|	...	1258	|	|	|	|	|	|	|	|
Yelets d.	|	|	|	2312	...	...	|	|	|	1134	...	...	|	...	1439	|	|	|	|	|	|	|	|
Gryazi Voronezhski d.	2125	2302	2302	|	...	...	0135	0150	0658	|	...	...	0850	...	|	1246	1259	1436	1451	1506	1738	1645	1913
Michurinsk Voronezhski d.	2230	0004	0004	|	...	...	0220	0244	0757	|	...	...	0931	...	|	1329	1344	1523	1541	1556	1819	1745	1959
Ryazan 2 d.	0119	0245	0245	|	...	...	0438	0507	1025	|	...	...	1140	...	|	1559	1607	1750	1800	1821	2032	2056	2223
Moskva Kazanskaya a.	0430	0550	0550	0618p	...	...	0730	0823	1330	1915v	...	...	1353	...	2309v	1830	1840	2015	2025	2105	2246	|	|
Tver d.	...	...	...	...	...	...	...	...	...	2340	...	...	...	...	0205	...	...	...	...	...	...	0219	0334
Bologoye d.	...	...	...	...	...	...	...	...	...	0143	...	...	...	...	0355	...	...	...	...	...	...	0402	0455
St Peterburg Glavny a.	...	...	...	...	...	...	...	...	...	0501	...	...	...	...	1005	...	...	...	...	...	...	0743	0800

TOMSK / BARNAUL - NOVOSIBIRSK - ROSTOV - SOCHI - ADLER

Times are local	time zone UTC+	115*NJ* *Sko* ⊡	140*NJ* *Sko* ⊡
Tomsk 2 d.	+7	1540	...
Tomsk 1 d.	+7	1603	...
Tayga d.	+7	1726	...
Barnaul d.	+7	|	1444
Novosibirsk a.	+7	2042	2044
Novosibirsk d.	+7	2138	2138
Omsk a.	+6	0518	0518
Omsk d.	+6	0553	0553
Tyumen d.	+5	1216	1216
Yekaterinburg a.	+5	1753	1753
Yekaterinburg d.	+5	1825	1825
Sarapul d.	+4	0106	0106
Kazan 2 ◧ d.	+3	0527	0527
Saransk d.	+3	1448	1448
Penza 1 d.	+3	1805	1805
Povorino d.	+3	0106	0106
Liski d.	+3	0448	0448
Rossosh d.	+3	0706	0706
Likhaya d.	+3	1137	1137
Rostov na Donu a.	+3	1438	1438
Rostov na Donu d.	+3	1511	1511
Tikhoretskaya d.	+3	1746	1746
Armavir Tuapsinkii d.	+3	2113	2113
Tuapse d.	+3	0254	0254
Sochi a.	+3	0452	0452
Adler a.	+3	0532	0532

Times are local	time zone UTC+	140*SJ* *Sko* ⊡	116*SJ* *Sko* ⊡
Adler d.	+3	1344	1344
Sochi d.	+3	1426	1426
Tuapse d.	+3	1639	1639
Armavir Tuapsinkii d.	+3	2234	2234
Tikhoretskaya d.	+3	0125	0125
Rostov na Donu a.	+3	0424	0424
Rostov na Donu d.	+3	0440	0440
Likhaya d.	+3	0842	0842
Rossosh d.	+3	1317	1317
Liski d.	+3	1548	1548
Povorino d.	+3	1950	1950
Penza 1 d.	+3	0316	0316
Saransk d.	+3	0631	0631
Kazan 2 ◧ d.	+3	1511	1511
Sarapaul d.	+4	2140	2140
Yekaterinburg a.	+5	0630	0630
Yekaterinburg d.	+5	0705	0705
Tyumen d.	+5	1321	1321
Omsk a.	+6	2303	2303
Omsk d.	+6	2343	2343
Novosibirsk a.	+7	0834	0834
Novosibirsk d.	+7	0947	0951
Barnaul a.	+7	1433	|
Tayga d.	+7	...	1329
Tomsk 1 a.	+7	...	1516
Tomsk 2 a.	+7	...	1539

A – Every 3–4 days; daily from Apr. 14.
B – ②⑤⑦ until Apr. 24; daily from Apr. 25.
C – ②④⑦ until Apr. 24; daily from Apr. 26.
D – Every 3–4 days; daily from Apr. 16.

d – To / from Vladikavkaz (a. 1815 / d. 0658) and Makhachkala (a. 2200 / d. 1937). Note that each destination is served by seperate trains.
e – To / from Stavropol (a. 0423 / d. 2330).
f – To / from Nazran (a. 0743 / d. 2100).
g – To / from Vladikavkaz (a. 1121 / d. 1743) and Nal'chik (a. 1024 / d. 1904). Note that each destination is served by seperate trains.
p – Moskva **Paveletskaya**.
r – Voronezh **1**.
v – Moskva **Vostochny**.

❋ – *Lastochka* (Swallow) fast day train.
◧ – Also known as Vosstanie Passazhirskaja.
⊡ – Subject to confirmation.
◐ – Abkhazia Autonomous Region (⊞ = Veseloe / Tsandryphsh).
● – Even dates. See page 535.
■ – Uneven dates. See page 535.

KALININGRAD - MINSK - ADLER 1961

For other trains Kaliningrad - Minsk - Smolensk see Table **1950**.

km	UTC+3	360CH	302BJ	UTC+3	302SJ	360SJ
		Pas	Pas		Pas	Pas
		●	■(1)		■(1)	■(5)
0	**Kaliningrad** KA d.	1807	...	**Adler** d.	1625	2039
342	Maladzechna BY d.	0457	...	**Sochi** d.	1703	2118
535	**Minsk** a.	0605	...	Tuapse d.	1930	2347
535	**Minsk** d.	0633	1058	Krasnodar 1 d.	2325	0431
684	Babruysk d.	|	1306	Starominskaya Tim. d.	0248	0830
749	Zhlobin d.	|	1356	**Rostov na Donu** ◧ a.	0408	0952
839	Homel d.	|	1535	**Rostov na Donu** ◧ d.	0423	1017
890	Zlynka d.	|	1650	Likhaya d.	1121	1415
747	Orsha Tsent. a.	0924	|	Rossosh d.	1736	1843
747	Orsha Tsent. BY d.	0948	|	Liski d.	1935	2031
866	**Smolensk** RU a.	1108	|	Voronezh 1 d.	2043**r**	2350
866	**Smolensk** d.	1143	|	Lipetsk d.	2325	|
1112	Bryansk O. a.	1600	2146	Yelets d.	0119	|
1112	Bryansk O. d.	1653	2236	Kursk d.	|	0444
	Kursk d.	2305	|	Bryansk O. a.	0755	1026
1443	Yelets d.	|	0531	Bryansk O. d.	0839	1119
1521	Lipetsk d.	|	0654	**Smolensk** a.	|	1630
1684	Voronezh 1 d.	0410	0922**r**	**Smolensk** RU d.	|	1705
1763	Liski d.	0732	1137	Orsha Tsent. BY a.	|	1821
1882	Rossosh d.	1005	1550	Orsha Tsent. d.	|	1845
2158	Likhaya d.	1443	2026	Zlynka d.	1314	|
2322	**Rostov na Donu** ◧ a.	1817	0044	Homel d.	1438	|
2322	**Rostov na Donu** ◧ d.	1850	0118	Zhlobin d.	1609	|
2428	Starominskaya Tim. d.	2016	0242	Babruysk d.	1711	|
2533	Krasnodar 1 d.	2328	0547	**Minsk** a.	1859	2127
2753	Tuapse d.	0340	0932	**Minsk** d.	...	2150
2833	**Sochi** a.	0544	1221	Maladzechna BY d.	...	2301
2856	**Adler** a.	0622	1255	**Kaliningrad** KA a.	...	0808

SARATOV - ADLER 1962

km	UTC+3	14ZH		UTC+3	14SJ	
		A			B	
0	**Saratov** 1 (UTC +4) d.	1128	...	**Adler** d.	1830	...
429	Volgograd 1 d.	1704	...	Sochi d.	1910	...
964	Tikhoretskaya d.	0223	...	Tuapse d.	2110	...
1100	Krasnodar 1 d.	0526	...	Krasnodar 1 d.	0048	...
1248	Tuapse d.	1029	...	Tikhoretskaya d.	0328	...
1328	Sochi a.	1236	...	Volgograd 1 d.	1411	...
1351	**Adler** a.	1308	...	**Saratov** 1 (UTC +4) a.	2116	...

ROSTOV - BAKI 1963

km	UTC+3			UTC+3		
0	**Rostov na Donu** d.	...	...	**Baki** AZ d.	...	...
307	Armavir Rost. d.	...	...	Derbent d.	...	...
495	Mineralnye Vody d.	...	...	Makhachkala d.	...	...
896	Makhachkala d.	...	...	Mineralnye Vody d.	...	...
1025	Derbent d.	...	...	Armavir Rost. d.	...	...
1286	**Baki** AZ a.	...	...	**Rostov na Donu** a.	...	...

NOTES FOR TABLES 1961, 1962 and 1963.

A – ■(3) until Mar. 19; daily from Mar. 21.
B – ●(4) until Mar. 20; daily from Mar. 22.
r – Voronezh **Pridacha**.
◧ – Rostov na Donu **Pervomajskaya**.
AZ – Azerbaijan (UTC+4). 🚌 = Yalama.
KA – Kaliningrad region of Russia (UTC+2). Local time.
BY – Belarus.
RU – Russia.

MOSKVA - SARATOV, VOLGOGRAD and BAKI 1965

km	Times are local time	time zone UTC+	1IJ	5GJ		9GJ	85VJ		133MJ	15JI
			Fir	Fir		Fir	Sko		Sko	Sko
			C	E			K		J	G
0	**Moskva** Pavelets. d.	+3	1350	1820	...	1908	1927	...	1927	2010
198	Ryazan 2 d.	+3	|	|	...	|	0037	...	0037	|
408	Michurinsk Uralski d.	+3	1955**z**	0121	...	0150	0402	...	0402	0406**z**
541	Gryazi Voronezhski d.	+3	2121	|	...	|	|	...	|	0528
778	Povorino d.	+3	0135	|	...	|	|	...	|	1010
481	Tambov 1 d.	+3	|	0243	...	0304	0534	...	0534	|
861	**Saratov** 1 a.	+4	|	0955	...	1014	1308	...	1308	|
861	**Saratov** 1 d.	+4	|	1043	...	...	1347	...	1347	|
1145	**Volgograd** 1 a.	+3	0745	|	...	...	|	...	|	1652
1595	Astrakhan 1 a.	+4	...	2013	...	...	0106	...	0106	...
⊡	Makhachkala a.	+3	...	...	...	...	1208	...	1208	...
2212	Derbent a.	+3	...	...	...	...	...	...	1521	...
2473	**Baki** AZ a.	+4	...	...	...	...	...	...	...	...

Times are local time	time zone UTC+	9ZH	1ZH		5ZH	15ZH		85SJ	133EI
		Fir	Fir		Fir	Sko		Sko	Sko
			D		F	H		J	K
Baki AZ d.	+4	...	...	...	...	...	...	...	...
Derbent d.	+3	...	...	...	...	...	...	...	1147
Makhachkala d.	+3	...	...	...	...	...	...	1511	1511
Astrakhan 1 d.	+4	...	...	...	1100	...	...	0300	0300
Volgograd 1 d.	+3	...	1551	...	|	1713	...	|	|
Saratov 1 a.	+4	...	|	...	2022	|	...	1359	1359
Saratov 1 d.	+4	1816	|	...	2110	|	...	1442	1442
Tambov 1 d.	+3	2316	|	...	0249	|	...	2049	2049
Povorino d.	+3	|	2210	...	|	2357	...	|	|
Gryazi Voronezhski d.	+3	|	0223	...	|	0436	...	|	|
Michurinsk Uralski d.	+3	0056	0316**z**	...	0425	0540**z**	...	2242	2242
Ryazan 2 d.	+3	|	|	...	|	|	...	0204	0204
Moskva Pavelets. a.	+3	0722	0930	...	1110	1400	...	0700	0700

C – ■(3) until Apr. 13; daily from Apr. 15.
D – ● until Apr. 12; daily from Apr. 14.
E – ● Dec. Jan.; ■ Feb., Mar.; ● Apr.; daily from Apr. 16.
F – ■ Dec., Jan.; ● Feb., Mar.; ■ Apr.; daily from Apr. 15.
G – ●(4) until Apr. 20; daily from Apr. 22.
H – ■(3) until Apr. 19; daily from Apr. 21.
J – ● Dec., Feb., Mar., June; ■ Jan., Apr., May.
K – ■ Dec., Feb., Mar., June; ● Jan., Apr., May.
z – Michurinsk **Voronezhski**.
● – Even dates. See page 535.
■ – Uneven dates. See page 535.
⊡ – *1537 km* (*2083 km* via Volgograd).
AZ – Azerbaijan (UTC+4).

MOSKVA - SAMARA - UFA - CHELYABINSK 1970

km	Times are local time	time zone UTC+	392UJ	132UJ		120MJ	66JI		138JI	50MJ		22JI	10JI		52JI	14EJ		14EJ 675EI	42JI		102JI	
			Sko	Sko		Sko	Sko		Sko	Sko		Fir	Fir		Sko	Fir			Fir		Sko	
																		K			L	
0	**Moskva** Kazanskaya d.	+3	1225	1508	...	1516	1708	...	1716	1750	...	1808	2008	...	2040	2122	...	2122	2150	...	...	...
197	Ryazan 1 d.	+3	1553	1833**r**	...	1814	2016	...	2038	2100	...	2110	2308	...	2342	0033	...	0033	0054	...	...	...
601	Ruzayevka d.	+3	2220	|	...	2332	0205	...	0255	0227	...	0239	0346	...	0512	0545	...	0545	0632	...	...	...
627	**Saransk** a.	+3	|	|	...	2359	|	...	|	|	...	|	|	...	|	|	...	|	0705	...	...	...
710	**Penza** 1 d.	+3	|	0450	...	...	|	...	|	|	...	|	|	...	0735	|	...	|	...	...	1343	...
712	Inza d.	+4	0133	|	...	...	0442	...	0544	0458	...	0547	|	...	...	0815	...	0815	...	...	|	...
873	**Ulyanovsk** d.	+4	0602	|	...	...	|	...	|	|	...	0834	|	...	...	|	...	|	...	...	|	...
908	Syzran 1 d.	+4	|	1026	...	...	0811	...	0912	0737	...	...	0832	...	...	1039	...	1039	...	...	1914	...
	Toliatti a.	+4	|	|	...	...	1056	...	|	|	...	...	|	...	...	|	...	|	...	...	|	...
1044	**Samara** a.	+4	|	1300	...	...	...	...	1137	0930	...	...	1011	...	...	1222	...	1222	...	...	2123	...
1044	**Samara** d.	+4	|	1350	...	...	...	...	1227	...	...	...	...	...	...	1310	...	1310	...	...	2210	...
1216	Buzuluk' d.	+5	|	1821	...	...	...	...	1634	...	...	...	...	...	...	|	...	|	...	...	|	...
1462	Orenburg a.	+5	|	2232	...	...	...	...	2025	...	...	...	...	...	...	|	...	|	...	...	|	...
	Orsk a.	+5	|	0515	...	...	...	...	...	...	...	...	...	...	...	|	...	|	...	...	|	...
1567	Ufa d.	+5	2107	...	...	...	...	...	...	...	...	...	...	...	...	2227	...	2227	...	...	0823	...
1933	**Magnitogorsk** a.	+5	|	...	...	...	...	...	...	...	...	...	...	...	...	|	...	0740	...	...	|	...
2048	**Chelyabinsk** a.	+5	0800	...	...	...	...	...	...	...	...	...	...	...	...	0708	...	...	...	...	1736	...

Times are local time	time zone UTC+	391UJ	49JI		41JI	13UJ		676UJ 13UJ	52MJ		9JI	21JI		101JI	131UJ		66EI	137UJ		119JI	
		Sko	Sko		Fir	Fir			Sko		Fir	Fir			Sko		Sko	Sko		Sko	
								K						L							
Chelyabinsk d.	+5	1330	...	...	...	2320	...	...	...	...	...	...	...	1840	...	...	...	...	...	...	...
Magnitogorsk d.	+5	|	...	...	...	|	...	2140	...	...	...	...	...	|	...	...	...	...	...	...	...
Ufa d.	+5	0118	...	...	...	0852	...	0852	...	...	...	...	...	0413	...	...	...	...	...	...	...
Orsk d.	+5	|	...	...	...	|	...	|	...	...	...	...	...	|	2255	...	...	...	...	...	...
Orenburg d.	+5	|	...	...	...	|	...	|	...	...	...	...	...	|	0524	...	...	1125	...	...	...
Buzuluk' d.	+5	|	...	...	...	|	...	|	...	...	...	...	...	|	0952	...	...	1539	...	...	...
Samara a.	+4	|	...	...	...	1604	...	1604	...	...	...	...	...	1149	1159	...	...	1742	...	...	...
Samara d.	+4	|	1544	...	...	1657	...	1657	...	...	1955	...	...	1258	1245	...	...	1838	...	...	...
Toliatti d.	+4	|	|	...	...	|	...	|	...	...	|	...	...	|	|	...	1824	|	...	...	...
Syzran 1 d.	+4	|	1747	...	...	1917	...	1917	...	...	2140	...	...	1529	1536	...	2158	2103	...	...	...
Ulyanovsk d.	+4	1411	|	...	...	|	...	|	...	...	|	2042	...	|	|	...	|	|	...	...	...
Inza d.	+4	1748	2026	...	...	2133	...	2133	...	...	|	2359	...	|	|	...	0032	0006	...	...	...
Penza 1 d.	+3	|	|	...	...	|	...	|	2135	...	|	|	...	1810	1920	...	|	|	...	...	...
Saransk d.	+3	|	|	...	2037	|	...	|	|	...	|	|	...	...	|	...	|	|	...	0640	...
Ruzayevka d.	+3	1857	2108	...	2119	2211	...	2211	0005	...	0025	0040	...	...	|	...	0115	0122	...	0709	...
Ryazan 1 d.	+3	0155	0238	...	0256	0307	...	0307	0450	...	0500	0546	...	...	0607**r**	...	0642	0652	...	1204	...
Moskva Kazanskaya a.	+3	0500	0540	...	0600	0620	...	0620	0753	...	0800	0910	...	...	0952	...	1010	1025	...	1425	...

K – ■ Dec., Feb., Mar., June; ● Jan., Apr., May.
L – To/from Niznevartovsk. For days of running see Table **1993**.
r – Ryazan 2.
● – Even dates. See page 535.
■ – Uneven dates. See page 535.

1971 BELGOROD - NOVOSIBIRSK

Times are local time	*time zone UTC+*	**124***VJ* Sko A
Belgorod d.	+3	0910
Voronezh 1 d.	+3	1804
Gryazi Voronezhski d.	+3	1945
Michurinsk Uralski d.	+3	2117
Tambov 1 d.	+3	2315
Penza 1 d.	+3	0610
Syzran 1 d.	+4	1046
Samara a.	+4	1310
Samara d.	+4	1437
Ufa a.	+5	2351
Ufa d.	+5	0027
Chelyabinsk a.	+5	0925
Chelyabinsk d.	+5	1020
Kurgan d.	+5	1425
Omsk a.	+6	2356
Omsk d.	+6	0012
Novosibirsk a.	+7	0934

Times are local time	*time zone UTC+*	**123***NJ* Sko A
Novosibirsk d.	+7	1447
Omsk a.	+6	2222
Omsk d.	+6	2239
Kurgan d.	+5	0731
Chelyabinsk a.	+5	1105
Chelyabinsk d.	+5	1149
Ufa a.	+5	2112
Ufa d.	+5	2138
Samara a.	+4	0510
Samara d.	+4	0558
Syzran 1 d.	+4	0824
Penza 1 d.	+3	1214
Tambov 1 d.	+3	1855
Michurinsk Uralski d.	+3	2107
Gryazi Voronezhski d.	+3	2245
Voronezh 1 d.	+3	0200
Belgorod a.	+3	0925

1973 NIZHNI NOVGOROD - VORKUTA

Times are local time	*time zone UTC+*	**90***GJ* Sko A
Nizhni Novgorod d.	+3	1610
Kirov d.	+3	2356
Kotlas Yuzhny d.	+3	0903
Mikun d.	+3	1319
Sosnogorsk d.	+3	1828
Vorkuta a.	+3	0820

Times are local time	*time zone UTC+*	**89***GJ* Sko A
Vorkuta d.	+3	1905
Sosnogorsk d.	+3	0855
Mikun d.	+3	1337
Kotlas Yuzhny d.	+3	1816
Kirov d.	+3	0316
Nizhni Novgorod a.	+3	0925

NOTES FOR TABLES 1971 AND 1973:

A – Runs every 2–4 days.

1974 MOSKVA - OREL - BELGOROD

km		**81***AJ*	**715** ❦	**741** ❦	**719** ❦	**743**	**119***AJ*	**721** ❦	**99***MJ* B	**71***VJ*	**141***VJ*		
	St Peterburg Gl. **1900** d.	2004	...	...	...	...	0012	...	...	...	...	...	...
0	**Moskva** Kurskaya d.	0459v	0848	1147	1418	1548	1007v	1635	1942v	2030v	2100v	...	...
194	Tula I d.	0734	1104	1401	1630	1759	1411	1852	2245	2331	0021	...	...
383	Orel d.	0930	1300	1551	1817	1946	1736	2044	0100	0136	0330	...	...
537	Kursk d.	1105	1442	1727	2004	2117	2050	2228	0257	0328	0947	...	...
697	**Belgorod** a.	1319	...	1920	2148	2300	2338	...	0530	0610	...	...	...

	722 ❦	**720** ❦	**744** ❦	**742** ❦	**120***VJ*	**716** ❦	**82***VJ*	**141***MJ*	**72***VJ*	**100***VJ* A		
Belgorod d.	...	0432	0729	1215	0938	...	1715	...	2210	2320	...	...
Kursk d.	0540	0621	0914	1413	1228	1701	1931	1933	0045	0204	...	...
Orel d.	0724	0759	1045	1550	1516	1844	2107	0143	0229	0349	...	...
Tula I d.	0913	0951	1228	1738	1806	2038	2257	0423	0433	0556	...	...
Moskva Kurskaya a.	1128	1210	1446	1958	2120v	2252	0136v	0734v	0803v	0909v	...	...
St Peterburg Gl. **1900** a.	...	...	...	...	0616x	...	1035	...	...	...	...	...

A – ● Dec., Feb., Mar., June; ■ Jan., Apr., May.
B – ■ Dec., Feb., Mar., June; ● Jan., Apr., May.
v – Moskva **Vostochny**.
x – St Peterburg **Ladozhski**.

● – Even dates (see page 535).
■ – Uneven dates (see page 535).
❦ – *Lastochka* (Swallow) fast day train.

1975 SAMARA and SARATOV - AKTOBE - TOSHKENT, BISHKEK and ALMATY

km	*Times are local time*	*time zone UTC+*	**24***CJ* ■(1)		**110***KH*		**52***KH*		**34***TJ*
0	*Moskva Kaz* **1970** d.	+3	...	...	...	...	...	...	...
1044	**Samara** d.	+4	...	...	...	...	...	...	...
•681	Ufa d.	+5	...	...	...	...	...	...	...
1462	Orenburg d.	+5	...	...	...	...	...	...	...
•894	**Saratov** 1 d.	+4	...	...	...	...	...	...	...
•459	Oral / Uralsk KA d.	+5	...	...	...	...	1510	...	...
1734	Aktobe 1 KA a.	+5	...	...	...	...	2140	...	...
1734	Aktobe 1 KA d.	+5	1400	...	1924	...	2200	...	2256
1828	Kandyagash KA d.	+5	1532	...	2110	...	|	...	0033
2924	Mangystau ⊙ KA a.	+5	|	...	1916	...	|	...	|
2767	Kyzlorda KA d.	+5	0903	...	...	...	|	...	1717
3315	**Toshkent** UZ a.	+5	|	...	...	...	◧	...	|
3738	Andizhan UZ a.	+5	|	...	...	...	|	...	|
3240	Shymkent KA d.	+6	2012	...	...	...	|	...	0425
3729	**Bishkek** 2 KY a.	+6	|	...	...	...	|	...	|
4001	**Almaty** 1 KA a.	+6	0936	...	...	...	|	...	1815
4010	**Almaty** 2 KA a.	+6	...	...	...	...	0822	...	...

Times are local time	*time zone UTC+*	**23***KH* ■(3)		**51***KH*		**33***CJ*		**109***KH*
Almaty 2 KA d.	+6	...	...	2020	...	...	...	...
Almaty 1 KA d.	+6	1317	...	|	...	2332	...	...
Bishkek 2 KY d.	+6	|	...	|	...	|	...	...
Shymkent KA d.	+6	0322	...	|	...	1234	...	...
Andizhan UZ d.	+5	|	...	◧	...	|	...	...
Toshkent UZ d.	+5	|	...	|	...	|	...	...
Kyzlorda KA d.	+5	1221	...	|	...	2156	...	...
Mangystau ⊙ KA d.	+5	|	...	|	...	|	...	1640
Kandyagash KA d.	+5	0506	...	|	...	1432	...	1412
Aktobe 1 KA a.	+5	0625	...	0507	...	1556	...	1536
Aktobe 1 KA d.	+5	...	...	0541	...	...	...	...
Oral / Uralsk KA a.	+5	...	...	1225	...	...	...	...
Saratov 1 a.	+4	...	...	...	...	...	...	...
Orenburg d.	+5	...	...	...	...	...	...	...
Ufa a.	+5	...	...	...	...	...	...	...
Samara a.	+4	...	...	...	...	...	...	...
Moskva Kaz **1970** a.	+3	...	...	...	...	...	...	...

■ – Uneven dates. See page 535.
● – Even dates. See page 535.
⊙ – Station for Aktau (15 km).
◧ – Via Table **1980**.
• – Distance from Aktobe.
KA – Kazakhstan (Almaty = UTC+6, western zone = UTC+5).
KY – Kyrgyzstan (UTC+6).
UZ – Uzbekistan (UTC+5).

1976 SAMARA and KAZAN - NUR-SULTAN - ALMATY and TOSHKENT

See also Table **1980**

km	*Times are local time*	*time zone UTC+*	**106***TJ*		**16***TJ* C				
0	*Moskva Kaz* **1970** d.	+3	...	...	...	...	...	...	...
1044	**Samara** d.	+4	...	...	...	...	...	...	...
2048	Chelyabinsk d.	+5	...	...	...	...	...	...	...
	Kazan **1990** d.	+3	...	...	...	...	...	...	...
	Yekaterinburg **1990** d.	+5	...	...	...	...	...	...	...
2306	Kurgan d.	+5	...	...	...	...	...	...	...
2573	Petropavl KA d.	+6	1418	...	2355	...	...	...	...
3064	**Nur-Sultan** 1 KA a.	+6	2047	...	0823	...	...	...	...
3064	**Nur-Sultan** 1 KA d.	+6	2102	...	0858	...	...	...	...
3305	Karagandy KA d.	+6	0008	...	1317	...	...	...	...
	Almaty 1 KA a.	+6	|	...	0544	...	...	...	...
4407	**Almaty** 2 KA a.	+6	1142	...	0616	...	...	...	...
4356	Bishkek 2 KY a.	+6	...	...	...	...	...	...	...
4522	Shymkent KA a.	+6	...	...	...	...	...	...	...
4755	**Toshkent** UZ a.	+5	...	...	...	...	...	...	...

Times are local time	*time zone UTC+*	**105***TJ*		**15***TJ* ●(4)				
Toshkent UZ d.	+5	...	...	...	...	...	...	...
Shymkent KA d.	+6	...	...	...	...	...	...	...
Bishkek 2 KY d.	+6	...	...	...	...	...	...	...
Almaty 2 KA d.	+6	1550	...	1532	...	...	...	...
Almaty 1 KA d.	+6	|	...	1616	...	...	...	...
Karagandy KA d.	+6	0329	...	0947	...	...	...	...
Nur-Sultan 1 KA a.	+6	0611	...	1326	...	...	...	...
Nur-Sultan 1 KA d.	+6	0626	...	1356	...	...	...	...
Petropavl KA d.	+6	1246	...	2220	...	...	...	...
Kurgan d.	+5	...	...	...	...	...	...	...
Yekaterinburg **1990** a.	+5	...	...	...	...	...	...	...
Kazan **1990** a.	+3	...	...	...	...	...	...	...
Chelyabinsk d.	+5	...	...	...	...	...	...	...
Samara a.	+4	...	...	...	...	...	...	...
Moskva Kaz **1970** a.	+3	...	...	...	...	...	...	...

MOSKVA - MAKAT - TOSHKENT and DUSHANBE

km	*Times are local*	*zone UTC+*	
0	**Moskva** Kaz. d.	+3	...
198	Ryazan 2 d.	+3	...
411	Michurinsk Vor d.	+3	...
1075	**Volgograd** d.	+4	...
1804	Atyrau KA d.	+5	...
1934	Makat KA d.	+5	...
2641	Kungrad UZ d.	+5	...
3048	Urgench UZ d.	+5	...
3465	Bukhara UZ a.	+5	...
3558	Navoi UZ a.	+5	...
3714	Samarkand UZ a.	+5	...
4057	**Toshkent** UZ a.	+5	...
3714	Karshi UZ a.	+5	...
4046	Termez UZ a.	+5	...
4271	**Dushanbe** 1 TA a.	+5	...

Times are local	*zone UTC+*	
Dushanbe 1 TA d.	+5	...
Termez UZ d.	+5	...
Karshi UZ d.	+5	...
Toshkent UZ d.	+5	...
Samarkand UZ d.	+5	...
Navoi UZ d.	+5	...
Bukhara UZ d.	+5	...
Urgench UZ d.	+5	...
Kungrad UZ d.	+5	...
Makat KA d.	+5	...
Atyrau KA d.	+5	...
Volgograd d.	+4	...
Michurinsk Vor d.	+3	...
Ryazan 2 d.	+3	...
Moskva Kaz. a.	+3	...

NOVOSIBIRSK - ALMATY and TOSHKENT

km	*Times are local*	*zone UTC+*	**1***KH* D
0	**Novosibirsk** d.	+7	...
228	Barnaul d.	+7	...
1121	Aktogay KA d.	+6	...
	Almaty 2 KA d.	+6	1832
1678	**Almaty** 1 KA a.	+6	|
1678	**Almaty** 1 KA d.	+6	|
1687	**Almaty** 2 KA a.	+6	|
2424	Shymkent KA d.	+6	0534
2657	**Toshkent** UZ a.	+5	...

Times are local	*zone UTC+*	**2***MZ* E
Toshkent UZ d.	+7	...
Shymkent KA d.	+7	1945
Almaty 2 KA d.	+6	|
Almaty 1 KA a.	+6	|
Almaty 1 KA d.	+6	|
Almaty 2 KA a.	+6	0631
Aktogay KA d.	+6	...
Barnaul d.	+6	...
Novosibirsk a.	+5	...

C – Uneven dates [.. *31*, *5* ..].
D – ①③⑥. Talgo train.
E – ②④⑦. Talgo train.
KA – Kazakhstan (Almaty zone = UTC+6).
TA – Tajikistan (UTC+5).
UZ – Uzbekistan (UTC+5).

See also Tables **1975** and **1976**

KAZAKHSTAN and UZBEKISTAN 1980

KA *UTC+6*	16TJ	52KH	4CJ	712CJ	106TJ	86CJ	56CJ	21CJ	29TJ	10TJ	1KH	25TJ	87TJ
									■(3)			●	■(1)
	A ◇	B			◇				F		C		
Nur-Sultan 1 d.	0858	1742	1850n	1947n	2102	2125	2220	...	...	2140n	...	...	...
Karagandy d.	1317	2051	2154	2251	0008	0111	0230	...	...	0131	...	...	...
Almaty 1 a.	0544	|	|	|	|	|	|	0956	...	1644	...	...	...
Almaty 2 a.	0616	0822	1013	|	1142	|	|	|	1640	...	1832	2116	2131
Shymkent a.	...	...	...	1307	...	1829	2202	2259	0246	...	0534	0938	1112
Kyzlorda ♡ a.	...	...	...	...	...	...	0619	0645	0902	...	...	...	...
Atyrau ♡ a.	...	...	...	...	...	...	...	...	0521	...	...	...	...

KA *UTC+6 (♡+5)*	37KH	51KH	29TJ	57KH	47CJ	
	●(6)		■(3)	●(4)	■(3)	
		B	F			
Nur-Sultan 1 d.	1010	1103	...	2015	1944n	...
Tobol d.	2257	1954	...	1203	1203	...
Kandyagash ♡ d.	1003	|	2221	2224	2237	...
Aktobe 1 ♡ a.	|	0507	|	0031	|	...
Oral / Uralsk ♡ a.	|	1225	|	0930	|	...
Atyrau ♡ a.	|	...	0521	...	0820	...
Mangistau ⊙ ♡ a.	0759	...	...	...	...	...

KA *UTC+6*	105TJ	712KH	56KH	3CJ	51KH	15TJ	9TJ	29KH	26TJ	2MZ	86KH	87KH	22TJ
						●(4)		■(5)	■(3)			●	
	◇				B	◇		E		G			
Atyrau ♡ d.	...	...	...	...	...	...	...	0830	...	...	...	...	...
Kyzlorda ♡ d.	...	...	2150	...	...	...	...	0454	...	...	...	...	1350
Shymkent d.	...	1435	0756	...	...	...	...	1315	1729	1945	1959	2120	2318
Almaty 2 d.	1550	|	|	1730	2020	1532	...	2357	0546	0631	|	1220	|
Almaty 1 d.	|	|	|	|	|	1616	1905	...	...	...	|	...	1312
Karagandy d.	0329	0512	0429	0608	0759	0947	1052	...	...	...	1406	...	...
Nur-Sultan 1 a.	0611	0752n	0830	0848	1041	1326	1405n	...	...	...	1717	...	...

KA *UTC+6 (♡+5)*	47TJ	58KH	37TJ	52KH	29KH	
	■(1)	●	●		■(5)	
				B	E	
Mangistau ⊙ ♡ d.	...	...	1600	...	...	...
Atyrau ♡ d.	1730	...	|	...	0830	...
Oral / Uralsk ♡ d.	|	1955	|	1510	|	...
Aktobe 1 ♡ d.	|	0524	|	2200	|	...
Kandyagash ♡ d.	0446	0734	1330	|	1627	...
Tobol d.	1825	2124	0328	0936	...	...
Nur-Sultan 1 a.	1053n	1247	1401	1721	...	...

UZ *UTC+5*	762FJ	760FJ	10FJ	766FJ	12FJ	4CH	56CH	393FJ	72FJ	58ZJ
								①		③⑥⑦
	H	H		H					V	
Toshkent d.	0728	0800	0906	1845	1852	1852	...	...	...	...
Toshkent Yuzhnyy d.	|	|	|	|	|	|	2100	2142	2215	2215
Samarkand d.	0950	1016	1235	2103	2223	2239	0101	0146	0217	0217
Karshi a.	|	1121	|	|	|	0018	|	|	|	|
Navoi d.	1042	...	1359	2156	0015	...	0255	0330	0443	0443
Bukhara 1 a.	1119	...	1458	2234	0122	...	0357	0432	0616	0616
Urgench a.	...	...	...	...	...	...	1013	1050	...	1227
Khiva a.	...	...	...	...	...	...	1058	1133	...	...

UZ *UTC+5*	765FJ	11FJ	3FJ	761FJ	759FJ	9FJ	394FJ	58MZ	71FJ	56ZH
							②	①③⑦		
	H			H	H				W	
Khiva d.	...	...		...	...	...	1308	...	...	1605
Urgench d.	...	...	...	...	...	...	1441	1503	...	1800
Bukhara 1 d.	0455	0532	...	1550	...	1608	2104	2121	2121	0040
Navoi d.	0535	0648	...	1629	...	1714	2244	2302	2302	0148
Karshi d.	|	|	0710	|	1646	|	|	|	|	|
Samarkand d.	0637	0832	0849	1732	1800	1846	0058	0141	0141	0340
Toshkent Yuzhnyy a.	|	|	|	|	|	|	0505	0540	0540	0740
Toshkent a.	0847	1228	1243	1948	2010	2217	...	...	...	...

A – Uneven dates [.. *31*, *5* ..].
B – Oral - Nur-Sultan - Almaty and v.v.
C – ①③⑥. Talgo train.
E – Atyrau - Kandyagash - Shymkent (2nd day) - Almaty.
F – Almaty - Shymkent (2nd day) - Kandyagash - Atyrau.
G – ②④⑦. Talgo train.
H – AFROSIYOB – high-speed Talgo train.

V – ①②④⑤.
W – ②③⑤⑥.
n – Nur-Sultan **Nurly Zhol**.
◇ – To / from Petropavl (Table **1976**).
⊙ – Station for Aktau (15 km).
♡ – UTC+5 (Kazakhstan western zone, local time is shown).

● – Even dates. See page 535.
■ – Uneven dates. See page 535.
KA – Kazakhstan (Almaty zone = UTC+6).
UZ – Uzbekistan (UTC+5).

MOSKVA - ARCHANGELSK, LABYTNANGI and VORKUTA 1985

km	Local time (UTC+3)	22JA	22JA 33JA	653MJ	16MJ	98JA	78JA	10JA	116SZ	42VJ
		Fir		Pas	Sko	Sko	Sko	Sko	Sko	Fir
		J	J			K	K	①⑤	L	M
0	**Moskva** Yaroslavskaya d.	1005	1005	...	1250	...	...	...	2035	2150
282	Yaroslavl d.	1513	1513	...	1702	...	...	...	0054	0203
	St Peterburg Ladozhski d.	|	|	...	|	1020	1020	1454	|	|
496	Vologda 1 d.	1908	1908	...	2125	|	|	|	0501	0552
707	Konosha 1 d.	2225	2225	...	0033	0125	0125	0506	0829	0916
1134	**Archangelsk** a.	|	|	...	0902	|	|	1326	1814	|
825	Velsk d.	0051	0051	...	...	0342	0342	...	...	1126
1084	**Kotlas** Yuzhny d.	0604	0604	...	...	1011	1011	...	...	1636
1325	Mikun d.	0950	1021	...	...	1414	1424	...	...	2028
1412	**Syktyvkar** a.	|	1232	...	...	1541	|	...	...	|
1571	Sosnogorsk a.	1421	...	...	...	...	1917	...	...	0056
2406	**Labytnangi** (*UTC+5*) a.	1000	...	1151	...	...	|	...	...	|
2277	**Vorkuta** a.	...	...	1939	...	...	0950	...	...	1435

Local time (UTC+3)	653JA	115CH	41MJ	34CH 21NJ	21NJ	77JA	98VJ	15JA	9AJ
		Sko	Fir		Fir	Sko	Sko	Sko	Sko
		N	P	Q	J	K	K		②⑥
Vorkuta d.	0915	...	1635	...	...	2027	...	...	...
Labytnangi (*UTC+5*) d.	2105	...	|	...	1521	|	...	...	...
Sosnogorsk d.	...	...	0549	...	0703	0929	...	...	...
Syktyvkar d.	...	...	|	0852	|	|	1204	...	...
Mikun d.	...	...	1052	1147	1147	1428	1428	...	...
Kotlas Yuzhny d.	...	...	1521	1609	1609	1922	1922	...	...
Velsk d.	...	...	2029	2106	2106	0054	0054	...	...
Archangelsk d.	...	0711	|	|	|	|	|	2030	2132
Konosha 1 d.	...	1754	2225	2338	2338	0323	0323	0454	0556
Vologda 1 d.	...	2147	0154	0220	0220	|	|	0815	|
St Peterburg Ladozhski a.	...	|	|	|	|	1845	1845	|	2055
Yaroslavl d.	...	0203	0549	0620	0620	...	...	1222	...
Moskva Yaroslavskaya a.	...	0607	0927	0958	0958	...	...	1643	...

km	Local time (UTC+3)	102JA	716JA	104JA	108JA	106JA				
		Fir	❦	Fir	Sko	Fir				
					R					
0	**Moskva** Yaroslavskaya d.	0735	1510	1445	1705	1905	...	...	...	...
282	**Yaroslavl** a.	1101	1810	1824	2030	2231	...	...	...	...

Local time (UTC+3)	101JA	715JA	107JA	103JA	105JA				
	Fir	❦	Sko	Fir	Fir				
			R						
Yaroslavl d.	0701	0822	0825	1351	1939	...	...	...	...
Moskva Yaroslavskaya a.	1021	1119	1151	1711	2300	...	...	...	...

MURMANSK - ARCHANGELSK

km		143JA 371JA		371CH 144JA
		S		S
0	**Murmansk** d.	0615	**Archangelsk** d.	1635
277	Kandalaksha d.	1146	Belomorsk d.	0445
665	Belomorsk d.	1928	Kandalaksha d.	1237
1151	**Archangelsk** a.	0818	**Murmansk** a.	1800

J – ■ Dec., Feb., Mar., June; ● Jan., Apr., May.
K – Runs every 2 – 3 days.
L – ● until Apr. 26; daily from Apr. 28.
M – ■ Dec., Jan., Apr., May; ● Feb., Mar.; daily from June 1.
N – ●(4) until Apr. 20; daily from May 1.
P – ■ Dec., Jan., Apr., May; ● Feb., Mar.; daily from June 2.
Q – ● Dec., Feb., Mar., June; ■ Jan., Apr., May.
R – ①③⑤⑦ until Mar. 28; daily from Mar. 30.

S – Runs every 2 – 4 days.
❦ – *Lastochka* (Swallow) fast day train.
● – Even dates. See page 535.
■ – Uneven dates. See page 535.

MOSKVA - NIZHNI NOVGOROD - SAMARA 1989

km	Local time (UTC+3)	701MJ	727MJ	729MJ	703MJ	705MJ	707MJ	733MJ	709MJ	775AJ
		♠	❦	❦	♠	♠	♠	❦	♠	♥
	St Peterburg Glavny d.	...	...	...	...	...	...	...	...	1700
0	**Moskva** Vostochny d.	0632	0715	0925	1035	1358	1540	1830	2015	2112k
186	Vladimir d.	0816	0900	1117	1223	1541	1723	2018	2201	2306
437	**Nizhni Novgorod** a.	1014	1100	1331	1425	1743	1932	2222	2359	0103

Local time (UTC+3)	759RJ	701NJ	729GJ	703NJ	731GJ	705NJ	733GJ	707NJ	709NJ
	♥	♠	❦	♠	❦	♠	❦	♠	♠
Nizhni Novgorod d.	0505	0745	0940	1105	1336	1538	1755	1857	2011
Vladimir d.	0704	0954	1200	1311	1549	1744	2016	2054	2216
Moskva Vostochny a.	0903k	1137	1351	1500	1739	1930	2203	2237	2359
St Peterburg Glavny a.	1320	...	...	...	...	...	...	...	...

Local time (UTC+3)	713VJ	
	♠	
	Q	
St Peterburg Ladozhski d.	0020	...
Moskva Vostochny d.	0546	...
Vladimir d.	0728	...
Nizhni Novgorod Strigino ✈ a.	0931	...
Nizhni Novgorod Strigino ✈ d.	0935	...
Arzamas 1 d.	1116	...
Saransk d.	1429	...
Syzran 1 d.	1907	...
Samara a.	2100	...

Local time (UTC+3)	713JI	
	♠	
	J	
Samara d.	0120	...
Syzran 1 d.	0315	...
Saransk d.	0624	...
Arzamas 1 d.	0933	...
Nizhni Novgorod Strigino ✈ a.	1048	...
Nizhni Novgorod Strigino ✈ d.	1052	...
Vladimir d.	1256	...
Moskva Vostochny a.	1440	...
St Peterburg Ladozhski a.	2000	...

J – ■ Dec., Feb., Mar., June.; ● Jan., Apr., May.
Q – ● Dec., Feb., Mar., June.; ■ Jan., Apr., May.

k – Moskva **Kurskaya**.

♥ – *Sapsan* high-speed train. ✕ Ⓡ.
♠ – *Strizh* (Swift) fast Talgo day train.
❦ – *Lastochka* (Swallow) fast day train.

● – Even dates (see page 535).
■ – Uneven dates (see page 535).

1990 MOSKVA - YEKATERINBURG - NOVOSIBIRSK - IRKUTSK - VLADIVOSTOK

km		time zone UTC +	2EI Fir	82IJ 376Y	82IJ Sko	12JA Fir		12JA 383EJ	70CH Sko	86UJ Sko	92IJ Sko		8NJ Sko	118NJ Sko	118NJ 144NJ	96NJ Sko		110EI Sko	68Y Sko	62MJ Sko	62MJ 638NJ	
				A	A	B		B		B	B		A	B	B	A		A	B	C	C	
0	**Moskva** Yaroslavskaya d.	+3	0035		...	1335	...	1335	1350	...	1650	...	...	...	...	...	...	2150	2305	2345	2345	...
	Moskva Kazanskaya d.	+3	|	1310	1310	|	...	|	|	1638	|	...	...	1920	1920	1920	...	|	|	|	|	...
282	Yaroslavl d.	+3	0441	|	|	|	...	|	1801	|	|	...	...	|	|	|	...	|	0319	|	|	...
	Murom 1 d.	+3	|	1751	1751	|	...	|	|	2109	|	...	...	0015	0015	0015	...	|	|	|	|	...
	Kazan 1 d.	+3	|	0213	0213	|	...	|	|	0535	|	...	...	|	|	|	...	|	|	|	|	...
	Kazan 2 ◧ d.	+3	|	|	|	|	...	|	|	|	|	...	...	0755	0755	0755	...	|	|	|	|	...
	Sarapul d.	+4	|	0855	0855	|	...	|	|	1159	|	...	...	1423	1423	1423	...	|	|	|	|	...
210	Vladimir d.	+3	|	|	|	1650	...	1650	|	|	1958	...	...	|	|	|	...	0159	|	0252	0252	...
461	**Nizhni Novgorod** d.	+3	|	|	|	2022	...	2022	|	|	2316	...	...	|	|	|	...	0502	|	0549	0549	...
917	Kirov d.	+3	1837	|	|	0228	...	0228	0525	|	0515	...	...	|	|	|	...	1200	1500	1214	1214	...
1397	Perm 2 d.	+5	0540	|	|	|	...	|	1521	|	1513	...	...	|	|	|	...	2212	0025	2200	2200	...
	Perm Sortirovochnaya d.	+5	|	|	|	1216	...	1216	|	|	|	...	...	|	|	|	...	|	|	|	|	...
	Nivhni Tagil d.	+5	|	|	|	2126	...	2126	|	|	|	...	...	|	|	|	...	|	|	|	|	...
	Serov d.	+5	|	|	|	|	...	0156	|	|	|	...	...	|	|	|	...	|	|	|	|	...
	Priobe a.	+5	|	|	|	|	...	1335	|	|	|	...	...	|	|	|	...	|	|	|	|	...
1778	**Yekaterinburg** a.	+5	1113	1746	1746	2358	...	...	2056	2020	2046	...	...	2335	2335	2335	...	0323	0544	0315	0315	...
1778	**Yekaterinburg** d.	+5	1207	1841	1841	0034	...	...	2128	2057	2120	...	...	0010	0010	0010	...	0351	0616	0343	0343	...
2104	Tyumen d.	+5	1733	0002	0002	0625	...	...	0227	0354	0219	...	...	0558	0558	0558	...	1012	1149	0842	0842	...
	Tobolsk d.	+5	|	|	|	1023	...	...	|	0814	|	...	...	|	|	|	...	1423	|	|	|	...
	Surgut d.	+5	|	|	|	1932	...	...	|	1752	|	...	...	|	|	|	...	2331	|	|	|	...
	Niznevartovsk a.	+5	|	|	|	|	...	...	|	2235	|	...	...	|	|	|	...	|	|	|	|	...
	Korotchayevo d.	+5	|	|	|	0832	...	...	|	...	|	...	...	|	|	|	...	1256	|	|	|	...
	Novy Urengoy a.	+5	|	|	|	1026	...	...	|	...	|	...	...	|	|	|	...	1516	|	|	|	...
2676	Omsk a.	+6	0215	0855	0855	...	...	...	1109	...	1001	...	...	1435	1435	1435	...	...	2120	1634	1634	...
2676	Omsk d.	+6	0231	0920	0920	...	...	...	1131	...	1017	...	1225	1455	1455	1515	...	...	2136	1650	1650	...
3303	**Novosibirsk** a.	+7	1147	1808	1808	...	...	...	2057	...	1832	...	2309	2349	2349	|	...	...	0601	0100	0100	...
3303	**Novosibirsk** d.	+7	1247	1858	1858	...	...	...	2137	...	1910	...	0013	0041	0042	|	...	...	0651	0146	0251	...
	Barnaul a.	+7	|	|	|	...	...	...	|	...	|	...	|	|	|	0830	...	...	|	|	|	...
	Novokuznetsk a.	+7	|	|	|	...	...	...	|	...	|	...	|	0737	|	...	...	...	|	|	|	...
	Kemerovo a.	+7	|	|	|	...	...	...	|	...	|	...	|	...	0536	...	...	...	|	|	|	...
3534	Tayga d.	+7	1649	2229	2229	...	...	...	0110	...	2241	...	0409	...	...	...	...	...	1030	0507	0737	...
3621	**Tomsk** 2 a.	+7	|	|	|	...	...	...	|	...	|	...	|	...	...	...	...	...	|	|	0931	...
	Abakan a.	+7	|	|	|	...	...	...	|	...	|	...	|	...	...	...	...	...	0535	|	...	...
4065	Krasnoyarsk a.	+7	0123	0723	0723	...	...	...	1210	...	0743	...	1251	...	...	...	...	...	...	1325	...	...
4065	Krasnoyarsk d.	+7	0203	0808	0838	...	...	...	1306	...	0828	...	1328	...	...	...	...	...	...	1346	...	...
4483	Tayshet d.	+8	0954	1628	1658	...	...	...	2146	...	1638	...	2134	...	...	...	...	...	...	2118	...	...
	Bratsk Padunskie Porogi d.	+8	|	2247	|	...	...	...	|	...	2308	...	|	...	...	...	...	...	...	|	...	...
	Severobaikalsk d.	+8	|	1303	|	...	...	...	|	...	1402	...	|	...	...	...	...	...	...	|	...	...
5152	**Irkutsk** a.	+8	2123	|	0611	...	...	...	0826	...	...	...	0816	...	...	...	...	...	...	0744	...	...
5152	**Irkutsk** d.	+8	2203	⊡	0742	...	...	...	0909	...	...	...	0859	...	...	...	...	...	...	0807	...	...
5608	Ulan Ude d.	+8	0625	...	1614	...	...	...	1756	...	...	...	1726	...	...	...	...	...	...	1530	...	...
6165	Chita 2 d.	+9	1819	...	...	...	...	...	0611	...	...	...	0526	...	...	...	...	...	...	0213	...	...
7274	Skovorodino d.	+9	1658	...	...	...	...	...	...	...	...	...	0334	...	...	...	...	...	...	2246	...	...
8492	Khabarovsk d.	+10	1645	...	...	...	...	...	...	...	...	...	0215	...	...	...	...	...	...	1934	...	...
9147	Ussuriysk d.	+10	0407	...	...	...	...	...	...	...	...	...	1331	...	...	...	...	...	...	0517	...	...
9258	**Vladivostok** a.	+10	0603	...	...	...	...	...	...	...	...	...	1528	...	...	...	...	...	...	0707	...	...

MOSKVA and ST PETERBURG - IZHEVSK, YEKATERINBURG, CHELYABINSK and PETROPAVL

	time zone UTC+	74EJ Sko		14NJ Fir		72EJ Fir		16KH Fir		26GJ Sko		2JI Fir		24MJ Sko	
		A		B		D		A							
Moskva Kazanskaya d.	+3	...	...	...	...	...	...	1638	...	1738	...	2050	...	2250	...
St Peterburg Ladozhski d.	+3	1530	...	1530	...	1735	...	|	...	|	...	|	...	|	...
Vologda 1 d.	+3	0250	...	0250	...	0530	...	|	...	|	...	|	...	|	...
Kirov d.	+3	1238	...	1238	...	1450	...	|	...	|	...	|	...	|	...
Perm 2 d.	+5	2222	...	2222	...	0015	...	|	...	|	...	|	...	|	...
Murom 1 d.	+3	|	...	|	...	|	...	2109	...	2240	...	0105	...	0303	...
Kazan 1 d.	+3	|	...	|	...	|	...	0535	...	|	...	0800	...	1048	...
Kazan 2 ◧ d.	+3	|	...	|	...	|	...	|	...	0530	...	...	...	...	...
Izhevsk a.	+4	|	...	|	...	|	...	|	...	1139	...	...	...	...	...
Sarapul d.	+4	|	...	|	...	|	...	1159	...	...	...	...	...	...	...
Yekaterinburg a.	+5	0339	...	0339	...	0533	...	2020	...	...	...	...	...	...	...
Yekaterinburg d.	+5	...	...	...	...	...	...	2105	...	...	...	...	...	...	...
Kurgan a.	+5	...	...	...	...	...	...	0505	...	...	...	...	...	...	...
Chelyabinsk a.	+5	...	...	...	...	...	...	1008	...	...	...	...	...	...	...
Petropavl KA a.	+6	...	...	...	...	...	...	...	...	...	...	...	...	...	...

MOSKVA - ULAAN BAATAR - BEIJING

km	Trans-Mongolian route	time zone UTC+							
0	*Moskva Yar. (above)* d.	+3	...	...	...	...	...	...	...
3303	*Novosibirsk (above)* d.	+7	...	...	...	...	...	...	...
5152	**Irkutsk** d.	+8	...	...	...	...	...	...	...
5608	Ulan Ude d.	+8	...	...	...	...	...	...	...
5863	Naushki 🛂 d.	+8	...	...	...	...	...	...	...
5886	Suche Bator 🛂 MO d.	+8	...	...	...	...	...	...	...
6265	**Ulaan Baatar** MO a.	+8	...	...	...	...	...	...	...
6265	**Ulaan Baatar** MO d.	+8	...	...	...	...	...	...	...
6770	Dzamin Uud 🛂 MO d.	+8	...	...	...	...	...	...	...
6780	Erlan 🛂 CH a.	+8	...	...	...	...	...	...	...
7622	**Beijing** CH a.	+8	...	...	...	...	...	...	...

MOSKVA - HARBIN - BEIJING

km	Trans-Manchurian route	time zone UTC+		602CH Pas		
0	*Moskva Yar. (above)* d.	+3	...	...	...	...
1778	*Yekaterinburg (above)* d.	+5	...	...	...	...
3303	*Novosibirsk (above)* d.	+7	...	...	...	...
5152	**Irkutsk** d.	+8	...	...	...	...
6165	Chita 2 d.	+9	...	1939	...	...
6626	Zabaikalsk 🛂 d.	+9	...	0731	...	...
6638	Manzhouli 🛂 CH d.	+8	...	...	...	...
7573	Harbin CH a.	+8	...	...	...	...
8122	Shenyang CH a.	+8	...	...	...	...
8849	Tianjin CH a.	+8	...	...	...	...
8986	**Beijing** CH a.	+8	...	...	...	...

A – ● Dec., Feb., Mar., June; ■ Jan., Apr., May.
B – ■ Dec., Feb., Mar., June; ● Jan., Apr., May.
C – ①④⑤⑦.
D – Every 2–4 days.

⊡ – To/from Tynda and Neryungri (Table **1991**).
◧ – Also known as Vosstanie Passazhirskaja.

● – Even dates (see page 535).
■ – Uneven dates (see page 535).

CH – China (UTC+8).
MO – Mongolia (UTC+8).

VLADIVOSTOK - IRKUTSK - NOVOSIBIRSK - YEKATERINBURG - MOSKVA 1990

			69*CH* *Sko*	637*NJ* 61*MJ* E	61*MJ* *Sko* C	338*EJ* 11*EJ* B		11*EJ* *Fir* A	95*NJ* *Sko* B	143*NJ* 117*NJ* A	117*NJ* *Sko* A		7*NJ* *Sko* B	81*IJ* *Sko* A	375*EI* 81*IJ* B	109*MJ* *Sko* B		91*IJ* *Sko* B	1*EI* *Fir*	85*EJ* *Sko* A	67*Y* *Sko* A	
Vladivostok	d.	*+10*	...	...	1850	...	...	...	...	...	...	...	2123	...	...	...	...	...	2318	...	...	...
Ussuriysk	d.	*+10*	...	...	2111	...	...	...	...	...	...	...	2329	...	...	...	...	...	0150	...	...	...
Khabarovsk	d.	*+10*	...	...	0821	...	...	...	...	...	...	...	1024	...	...	...	...	...	1425	...	...	...
Skovorodino	d.	*+9*	...	...	0240	...	...	...	...	...	...	...	0601	...	...	...	...	...	1043	...	...	...
Chita 2	d.	*+9*	2100	...	2356	...	...	...	...	...	...	...	0452	...	...	...	...	...	0918	...	...	...
Ulan Ude	d.	*+8*	0720	...	0815	...	...	...	...	...	...	...	1416	1406	...	...	...	...	1909	...	...	...
Irkutsk	a.	*+8*	1515	...	1524	...	...	...	...	...	...	...	2207	2157	⊡	...	...	...	0314	...	...	...
Irkutsk	d.	*+8*	1611	...	1552	...	...	...	...	...	...	...	2255	2245	|	...	...	...	0354	...	...	...
Severobaikalsk	d.	*+8*	|	...	|	...	...	...	...	...	...	...	|	|	1515	...	...	1720	|	...	...	...
Bratsk Padunskie Porogi	d.	*+8*	|	...	|	...	...	...	...	...	...	...	|	|	0439	...	...	0748	|	...	...	...
Tayshet	d.	*+8*	0252	...	0233	...	...	...	...	...	...	...	1021	1031	1100	...	...	1349	1457	...	...	...
Krasnoyarsk	a.	*+7*	0933	...	0803	...	...	...	...	...	...	...	1607	1623	1647	...	...	2001	2047	...	...	...
Krasnoyarsk	d.	*+7*	1027	...	0824	...	...	...	...	...	...	...	1642	1742	1742	...	...	2116	2126	...	...	...
Abakan	d.	*+7*	|	...	|	...	...	...	...	...	...	...	|	|	|	...	...	|	|	...	1800	...
Tomsk 2	d.	*+7*	|	1230	|	...	...	...	...	...	...	...	|	|	|	...	...	|	|	...	|	...
Tayga	d.	*+7*	1942	1500	1628	...	...	...	...	...	...	...	0210	0244	0244	...	...	0539	0552	...	1224	...
Kemerovo	d.	*+7*	|	|	|	...	...	...	...	0008	...	...	|	|	|	...	...	|	|	...	|	...
Novokuznetsk	d.	*+7*	|	|	|	...	...	...	...	|	2205	...	|	|	|	...	...	|	|	...	|	...
Barnaul	d.	*+7*	|	|	|	...	...	...	1415	|	|	...	|	|	|	...	...	|	|	...	|	...
Novosibirsk	a.	*+7*	2327	1854	1942	...	...	...	|	0458	0507	...	0547	0610	0610	...	...	0846	0930	...	1554	...
Novosibirsk	d.	*+7*	0026	2022	2022	...	...	...	|	0603	0603	...	0637	0701	0701	...	...	0936	1030	...	1659	...
Omsk	a.	*+6*	0808	0238	0238	...	...	...	1335	1348	1348	...	1427	1439	1439	...	...	1648	1710	...	0029	...
Omsk	d.	*+6*	0825	0254	0254	...	...	...	1415	1415	1415	...	...	1457	1457	...	...	1705	1726	...	0045	...
Novy Urengoy	d.	*+5*	|	|	|	...	...	1226	|	|	|	...	...	|	|	1716	...	|	|	...	|	...
Korotchayevo	d.	*+5*	|	|	|	...	...	1426	|	|	|	...	...	|	|	1916	...	|	|	...	|	...
Niznevartovsk	d.	*+5*	|	|	|	...	...	|	|	|	|	...	...	|	|	|	...	|	|	0645	|	...
Surgut	d.	*+5*	|	|	|	...	...	0520	|	|	|	...	...	|	|	0812	...	|	|	1330	|	...
Tobolsk	d.	*+5*	|	|	|	...	...	1548	|	|	|	...	...	|	|	1825	...	|	|	2246	|	...
Tyumen	d.	*+5*	1714	0853	0853	...	...	2046	2127	2127	2127	...	...	2136	2136	2315	...	2325	2335	0325	0701	...
Yekaterinburg	a.	*+5*	2242	1333	1333	...	...	0223	0304	0304	0304	...	...	0239	0239	0407	...	0415	0423	0929	1244	...
Yekaterinburg	d.	*+5*	2326	1401	1401	...	...	0325	0358	0358	0358	...	...	0348	0348	0435	...	0443	0451	1009	1345	...
Priobe	d.	*+5*	|	|	|	1307	...	|	|	|	|	...	...	|	|	|	...	|	|	|	|	...
Serov	d.	*+5*	|	|	|	0053	...	|	|	|	|	...	...	|	|	|	...	|	|	|	|	...
Nivhni Tagil	d.	*+5*	|	|	|	0650	...	0650	|	|	|	...	...	|	|	|	...	|	|	|	|	...
Perm Sortirovochnaya	d.	*+5*	|	|	|	1506	...	1506	|	|	|	...	...	|	|	|	...	|	|	|	|	...
Perm 2	d.	*+5*	0539	2000	2000	|	...	|	|	|	|	...	...	|	|	1128	...	1136	1144	|	1950	...
Kirov	d.	*+3*	1131	0114	0114	2129	...	2129	|	|	|	...	...	|	|	1728	...	1738	1748	|	0104	...
Nizhni Novgorod	d.	*+3*	|	0700	0700	0331	...	0331	|	|	|	...	...	|	|	2326	...	2337	|	|	|	...
Vladimir	d.	*+3*	|	1110	1110	0712	...	0712	|	|	|	...	...	|	|	0228	...	0244	|	|	|	...
Sarapul	d.	*+4*	|	|	|	|	...	|	1125	1125	1125	...	...	1113	1113	|	...	|	|	1651	|	...
Kazan 2 ◧	d.	*+3*	|	|	|	|	...	|	1635	1635	1635	...	...	1615	1615	|	...	|	|	|	|	...
Kazan 1	d.	*+3*	|	|	|	|	...	|	|	|	|	...	...	|	|	|	...	|	|	2205	|	...
Murom 1	d.	*+3*	|	|	|	|	...	|	0057	0057	0057	...	...	0045	0045	|	...	|	|	0450	|	...
Yaroslavl	d.	*+3*	0054	|	|	|	...	|	|	|	|	...	...	|	|	|	...	|	0644	|	1232	...
Moskva Kazanskaya	a.	*+3*	|	|	|	|	...	|	0520	0520	0520	...	...	0510	0510	|	...	|	|	0940	|	...
Moskva Yaroslavskaya	a.	*+3*	0456	1358	1358	1030	...	1030	...	...	...	...	...	...	...	0522	...	0552	1113	...	1657	...

PETROPAVL, CHELYABINSK, YEKATERINBURG and IZHEVSK - ST PETERBURG and MOSKVA

		time zone UTC+	23*GJ* *Sko*		1*GJ* *Fir*		71*EJ* *Fir* D		25*GJ* *Sko*		16*IJ* *Fir* B		73*EJ* *Sko* A		13*NJ* *Fir* B	
Petropavl	KA d.	*+6*	...	...	...	...	...	...	...	...	...	...	...	...	...	...
Chelyabinsk	d.	*+5*	...	...	...	...	...	...	...	...	2150	...	...	...	...	...
Kurgan	d.	*+5*	...	...	...	...	...	...	...	...	0222	...	...	...	...	...
Yekaterinburg	a.	*+5*	...	...	...	...	...	...	...	...	0816	...	...	...	...	...
Yekaterinburg	d.	*+5*	...	...	...	...	2318	...	...	...	1009	...	2310	...	2310	...
Sarapul	d.	*+4*	...	...	...	...	|	...	...	...	1651	...	|	...	|	...
Izhevsk	d.	*+4*	...	...	...	...	|	...	1740	...	|	...	|	...	|	...
Kazan 2 ◧	d.	*+3*	...	...	...	...	|	...	2150	...	|	...	|	...	|	...
Kazan 1	d.	*+3*	1811	...	2000	...	|	...	|	...	2205	...	|	...	|	...
Murom 1	d.	*+3*	0204	...	0300	...	|	...	0502	...	0450	...	|	...	|	...
Perm 2	d.	*+5*	|	...	|	...	0522	...	|	...	|	...	0531	...	0531	...
Kirov	d.	*+3*	|	...	|	...	1102	...	|	...	|	...	1121	...	1121	...
Vologda 1	d.	*+3*	|	...	|	...	2130	...	|	...	|	...	2214	...	2214	...
St Peterburg Ladozhski	a.	*+3*	|	...	|	...	0840	...	|	...	|	...	1000	...	1000	...
Moskva Kazanskaya	a.	*+3*	0630	...	0710	...	...	...	0923	...	0940	...	...	...	...	...

BEIJING - ULAAN BAATAR - MOSKVA

km	*Trans-Mongolian route*		*time zone UTC+*							
0	**Beijing**	CH d.	*+8*	...	...	...	...	...	...	...
842	Erlan 🛃	CH d.	*+8*	...	...	...	...	...	...	...
852	Dzamin Uud 🛃	MO d.	*+8*	...	...	...	...	...	...	...
1356	**Ulaan Baatar**	MO a.	*+8*	...	...	...	...	...	...	...
1356	**Ulaan Baatar**	MO d.	*+8*	...	...	...	...	...	...	...
1735	Suche Bator 🛃	MO d.	*+8*	...	...	...	...	...	...	...
1758	Naushki 🛃	d.	*+8*	...	...	...	...	...	...	...
2013	Ulan Ude	d.	*+8*	...	...	...	...	...	...	...
2469	**Irkutsk**	a.	*+8*	...	...	...	...	...	...	...
4319	*Novosibirsk (above)*	a.	*+7*	...	...	...	...	...	...	...
7622	*Moskva Yar. (above)*	a.	*+3*	...	...	...	...	...	...	...

BEIJING - HARBIN - MOSKVA

km	*Trans-Manchurian route*		*time zone UTC+*		683*CH* *Pas*		
0	**Beijing**	CH d.	*+8*	...	...	...	...
137	Tianjin	CH d.	*+8*	...	...	...	...
864	Shenyang	CH d.	*+8*	...	...	...	...
1413	Harbin	CH d.	*+8*	...	...	...	...
2348	Manzhouli 🛃	CH d.	*+8*	...	...	...	...
2360	Zabaikalsk 🛃	d.	*+9*	...	2008	...	...
2820	Chita 2	d.	*+9*	...	0752	...	...
3833	**Irkutsk**	a.	*+8*	...	...	...	...
5683	*Novosibirsk (above)*	a.	*+7*	...	...	...	...
7208	*Yekaterinburg (above)*	a.	*+5*	...	...	...	...
8986	*Moskva Yar. (above)*	a.	*+3*	...	...	...	...

A – ● Dec., Feb., Mar., June; ■ Jan., Apr., May.
B – ■ Dec., Feb., Mar., June; ● Jan., Apr., May.
C – ①④⑤⑦.
D – Every 2–4 days.
E – ①②④⑤.

⊡ – To / from Tynda and Neryungri (Table **1991**).
◧ – Also known as Vosstanie Passazhirskaja.

● – Even dates (see page 535).
■ – Uneven dates (see page 535).

CH – China (UTC+8).
MO – Mongolia (UTC+8).

1991 NOVOSIBIRSK - SEVEROBAIKALSK - TYNDA - NERYUNGRI - NIZHNY BESTYAKH

Baikal - Amur Magistrale (BAM) line. For other trains Moskva - Severobaikalsk see Table **1990**.

km	Times are local times	time zone UTC+	298NJ Pas	328JI Pas	71IJ Sko	376Y Pas	82IJ 376Y		
			A		A	B	A		
	Moskva Kaz. **1990** d.	+3	...	...	...	...	1310	day 1	...
0	**Novosibirsk** d.	+7	0511	...	...	...	1858	day 3	...
762	Krasnoyarsk d.	+7	1721	...	...	0808	0808	day 4	...
	Irkutsk d.	+8	|	...	2305	|	|	|	...
1180	**Tayshet** a.	+8	0134	...	1038	1615	1615	day 4	...
1180	**Tayshet** d.	+8	0207	...	1153	1628	1628	day 4	...
1473	Bratsk Padunskie Porogi d.	+8	0805	...	1832	2247	2247	day 4	...
2243	**Severobaikalsk** d.	+8	2119	...	0910	1303	1303	day 5	...
2243	**Severobaikalsk** d.	+8	2219	...	...	1408	1408	day 5	...
3528	**Tynda** a.	+9	0006	...	...	1614	1614	day 6	...
3528	**Tynda** d.	+9	...	1019	...	1811	1811	day 6	...
3757	Neryungri a.	+9	...	1516	...	2337	2337	day 6	...
3757	Neryungri d.	+9	...	1556	...	...	...	...	...
4125	Tommot a.	+9	...	2347	...	...	...	...	...
4125	Tommot d.	+9	...	0002	...	...	...	...	...
4563	**Nizhny Bestyakh** ⊕ a.	+9	...	1000	...	...	...	...	...

Times are local times	time zone UTC+	375EI Pas	375EI 81IJ			297ZH Pas	327JI Pas	71Y Sko
		B	B			A		A
Nizhny Bestyakh ⊕ d.	+9	...	...	...	...	...	1700	...
Tommot a.	+9	...	...	...	...	...	0242	...
Tommot d.	+9	...	...	...	...	...	0257	...
Neryungri a.	+9	...	...	...	...	...	1055	...
Neryungri d.	+9	0606	0606	day 1	...	...	1125	...
Tynda a.	+9	1124	1124	day 1	...	...	1601	...
Tynda d.	+9	1312	1312	day 1	...	1312	...	...
Severobaikalsk a.	+8	1400	1400	day 2	...	1400	...	...
Severobaikalsk d.	+8	1515	1515	day 2	...	1515	...	1929
Bratsk Padunskie Porogi d.	+8	0439	0439	day 3	...	0439	...	0955
Tayshet a.	+8	1047	1047	day 3	...	1047	...	1556
Tayshet d.	+8	1100	1100	day 3	...	1100	...	1648
Irkutsk a.	+8	|	|	|	...	|	...	0601
Krasnoyarsk a.	+7	1647	1647	day 3	...	1647	...	...
Novosibirsk a.	+7	...	0610	day 4	...	0834	...	...
Moskva Kaz. **1990** a.	+3	...	0510	day 6	...	...	...	...

km	Times are local	UTC+	364EI
0	**Tynda** d.	+9	1642
669	Fevralsk d.	+9	0840
951	Novy Urgal a.	+10	1629
951	Novy Urgal d.	+10	1704
1469	**Komsomolsk** a.	+10	0703

Times are local	UTC+	363EI
Komsomolsk d.	+10	1834
Novy Urgal a.	+10	0839
Novy Urgal d.	+10	0914
Fevralsk d.	+9	1533
Tynda a.	+9	0646

km	Times are local	UTC+	351EI	667EI
0	**Vladivostok** .... **1990** d.	+10	1720	...
111	Ussuriysk **1990** d.	+10	1948	...
766	**Khabarovsk** .... **1990** d.	+10	0802	2105
1155	Komsomolsk a.	+10	1738	0555
1618	**Sovetskaya Gavan** a.	+10	0235	...

Times are local	UTC+	351JI	667ZH
Sovetskaya Gavan d.	+10	1724	...
Komsomolsk d.	+10	0750	2107
Khabarovsk ... **1990** a.	+10	1831	0603
Ussuriysk **1990** a.	+10	0703	...
Vladivostok .... **1990** a.	+10	0908	...

A – ● Dec., Feb., Mar., June; ■ Jan., Apr., May.
B – ■ Dec., Feb., Mar., June; ● Jan., Apr., May.

● – Even dates. See page 535.
■ – Uneven dates. See page 535.

⊕ – In summer a ferry (15 km from station) runs to Yakutsk. Connection by 🚌 in winter (no service in Spring or Autumn).

1993 YEKATERINBURG - KAZAN - SARATOV - VOLGOGRAD

km	Local times	time zone UTC+	445EJ Sko A	
0	**Yekaterinburg** d.	+5	0145	...
515	Sarapul d.	+4	1101	...
875	**Kazan** 1 d.	+3	1703	...
1121	Ulyanovsk d.	+4	0039	...
1407	**Samara** a.	+4	|	...
1576	**Saratov** 1 d.	+4	0906	...
2005	Volgograd 1 d.	+3	1553	...
2665	Armavir Ros. d.	+3	0820	...
2853	Mineralnye Vody d.	+3	1158	...
2879	Pyatigorsk d.	+3	1234	...
2917	**Kislovodsk** a.	+3	1328	...

Local times	time zone UTC+	445SJ Sko B	
Kislovodsk d.	+3	2201	...
Pyatigorsk d.	+3	2257	...
Mineralnye Vody d.	+3	0004	...
Armavir Ros. d.	+3	0232	...
Volgograd 1 d.	+3	1949	...
Saratov 1 d.	+4	0508	...
Samara d.	+4	|	...
Ulyanovsk d.	+4	1449	...
Kazan 1 d.	+3	2013	...
Sarapul d.	+4	0318	...
Yekaterinburg a.	+5	1222	...

km	Local times	time zone UTC+	101JI Sko A	107EJ Sko C
0	**Niznevartovsk** d.	+5	1113	2159
216	Surgut d.	+5	1642	0224
692	Tobolsk d.	+5	0204	1114
921	Tyumen d.	+5	0641	1545
1247	**Yekaterinburg** d.	+5	1253	2232
1762	Sarapul d.	+4	|	0558
2122	**Kazan** 1 d.	+3	◇	1217
2368	Ulyanovsk d.	+4	|	1914
2654	**Samara** a.	+4	1149	|
2823	**Saratov** 1 d.	+4	...	0540
3252	**Volgograd** 1 d.	+3	...	1148

Local times	time zone UTC+	107ZH Sko D	102JI Sko A
Volgograd 1 d.	+3	2310	...
Saratov 1 d.	+4	0800	...
Samara d.	+4	|	2210
Ulyanovsk d.	+4	1847	|
Kazan 1 d.	+3	2345	◇
Sarapul d.	+4	0636	|
Yekaterinburg d.	+5	1709	0018*
Tyumen d.	+5	2311	0625
Tobolsk a.	+5	0232	0958
Surgut a.	+5	1135	1914
Niznevartovsk a.	+5	1612	0105

A – ● Dec., Feb., Mar., June; ■ Jan., Apr., May.
B – ■ Dec., Feb., Mar., June; ● Jan., Apr., May.

C – Every 4 days until Mar. 14; daily from Mar. 18.
D – Every 4 days until Mar. 11; daily from Mar. 15.

◇ – To / from Penza (Table **1970**) via Ufa (Tables **1970** / **1994**).
* – More than 24 hours after previous time shown.

1994 YEKATERINBURG - SAMARA - SARATOV and KYIV - BAKI

km	Local times	time zone UTC+	101JI Sko A	
0	**Tyumen** d.	+5	0641	...
326	**Yekaterinburg** d.	+5	1253	...
578	Chelyabinsk d.	+5	1840	...
1059	Ufa d.	+5	0413	...
1582	**Samara** d.	+4	1149	...
2019	**Saratov** 1 a.	+4	...	...
2019	**Saratov** 1 d.	+4	...	...
2695	Astrakhan 1 d.	+4	...	...
3183	**Makhachkala** a.	+3	...	...

Local times	time zone UTC+	102JI Sko A	
Makhachkala d.	+3	...	...
Astrakhan 1 d.	+4	...	...
Saratov 1 a.	+4	...	...
Saratov 1 d.	+4	...	...
Samara d.	+4	2210	...
Ufa d.	+5	0823	...
Chelyabinsk d.	+5	1810	...
Yekaterinburg a.	+5	2300	...
Tyumen a.	+5	0528	...

km	Local times	time zone UTC+	
0	**Kyiv** UA d.	◧	...
335	Poltava K UA d.	◧	...
493	**Kharkiv** UA d.	◧	...
861	Liski d.	+3	...
1453	Volgograd d.	+4	...
1903	Astrakhan 1 d.	+4	...
2391	Makhachkala d.	+3	...
2520	Derbent d.	+3	...
2765	**Baki** AZ a.	+4	...

Local times	time zone UTC+	
Baki AZ d.	+4	...
Derbent d.	+3	...
Makhachkala d.	+3	...
Astrakhan 1 d.	+4	...
Volgograd d.	+4	...
Liski d.	+3	...
Kharkiv UA a.	◧	...
Poltava K UA a.	◧	...
Kyiv UA a.	◧	...

A – ● Dec., Feb., Mar., June; ■ Jan., Apr., May.
◧ – UTC+2 winter, UTC+3 summer.

AZ – Azerbaijan (UTC+4).
UA – Ukraine (UTC+2 winter, UTC+3 summer).

1995 GEORGIA

Time zone: UTC+4 Georgian Railways

km		371 ⊡	802	808	804					
0	**Yerevan** AR d.	2130	...	...	...	...	...	...	...	...
374	**Tbilisi** a.	0735	...	...	...	...	...	...	...	...
374	**Tbilisi** d.	...	0800	1025	1705	...	...	...	...	...
722	**Batumi** a.	...	1314	1539	2219	...	...	...	...	...

	803	372 ⊡	807	801					
Batumi d.	0800	...	1710	1820	...	...	...	...	...
Tbilisi a.	1307	...	2217	2328	...	...	...	...	...
Tbilisi d.	...	2020	...	...	...	...	...	...	...
Yerevan AR a.	...	0655	...	...	...	...	...	...	...

km		614	682	870	12	18	684	874		
0	**Baki** AZ d.	...	...	...	...	...	...	...	...	...
551	**Tbilisi** d.	...	...	0825	0915	0915	...	1730	...	...
772	Kutaisi a.	...	0540	|	|	1425	1630	|	...	...
868	Zugdidi a.	...	|	1411	|	...	|	|	...	...
863	Poti a.	...	|	...	|	...	|	2252	...	...
877	**Ozurgeti** a.	0600	|	...	1710	...	|	...	...	...
	Batumi a.	0810	1002	...	...	...	2042	...	...	...

	873	11	683	17	869	681	613		
Batumi d.	...	...	0825	...	...	1855	2055	...	...
Ozurgeti d.	...	0900	|	...	...	|	2303	...	...
Poti d.	0720	|	|	...	...	|	...	...	...
Zugdidi d.	|	|	|	...	1725	|	...	...	...
Kutaisi d.	|	|	1220	1225	|	2314	...	...	...
Tbilisi d.	1246	1746	...	1746	2318	...	...	...	...
Baki AZ a.	...	...	...	...	...	...	...	...	...

⊡ – ■(3). Conveys 🛏.
■ – See page 535.

AR – Armenia (UTC+4).
AZ – Azerbaijan (UTC+4).

TBILISI - TBILISI AIRPORT (journey 40 mins.)
From Tibilisi: 0755, 1655; from Tibilisi Airport: 0835, 1740.

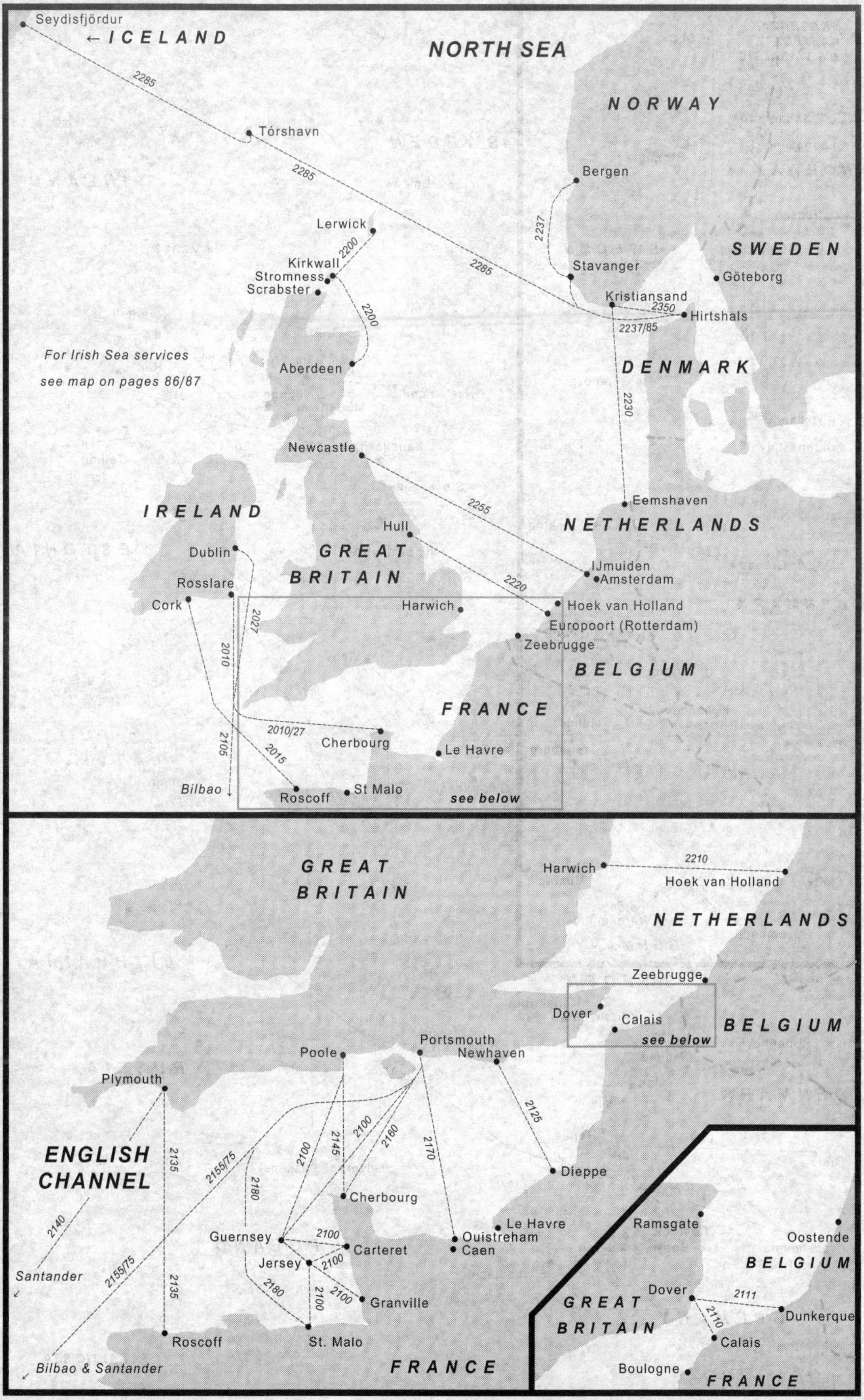
Seydisfjördur
← ICELAND
NORTH SEA
2285
Tórshavn
2285
NORWAY
Bergen
2237
Lerwick
2200
Kirkwall
Stromness
Scrabster
2285
Stavanger
SWEDEN
Göteborg
Kristiansand
2350
Hirtshals
2237/85
2200
For Irish Sea services
see map on pages 86/87
Aberdeen
DENMARK
2230
Newcastle
2255
Eemshaven
IRELAND
NETHERLANDS
Hull
Dublin
GREAT
BRITAIN
2220
IJmuiden
Amsterdam
Rosslare
Cork
Harwich
Hoek van Holland
Europoort (Rotterdam)
2027
Zeebrugge
2010
BELGIUM
FRANCE
2010/27
Cherbourg
2105
2015
Le Havre
Bilbao ↓
Roscoff
St Malo
see below
GREAT
BRITAIN
Harwich
2210
Hoek van Holland
NETHERLANDS
Zeebrugge
Dover
Calais
BELGIUM
see below
Portsmouth
Poole
Newhaven
Plymouth
2125
2100
2145
2160
2170
ENGLISH
CHANNEL
2135
2155/75
2100
2180
Dieppe
Cherbourg
2140
Le Havre
Ramsgate
Guernsey
2100
Carteret
Ouistreham
Caen
Oostende
Jersey
2100
Santander
2155/75
2180
2100
2135
2100
Granville
BELGIUM
Dover
2111
GREAT
BRITAIN
2110
Dunkerque
Roscoff
St. Malo
Calais
Bilbao & Santander
FRANCE
Boulogne
FRANCE

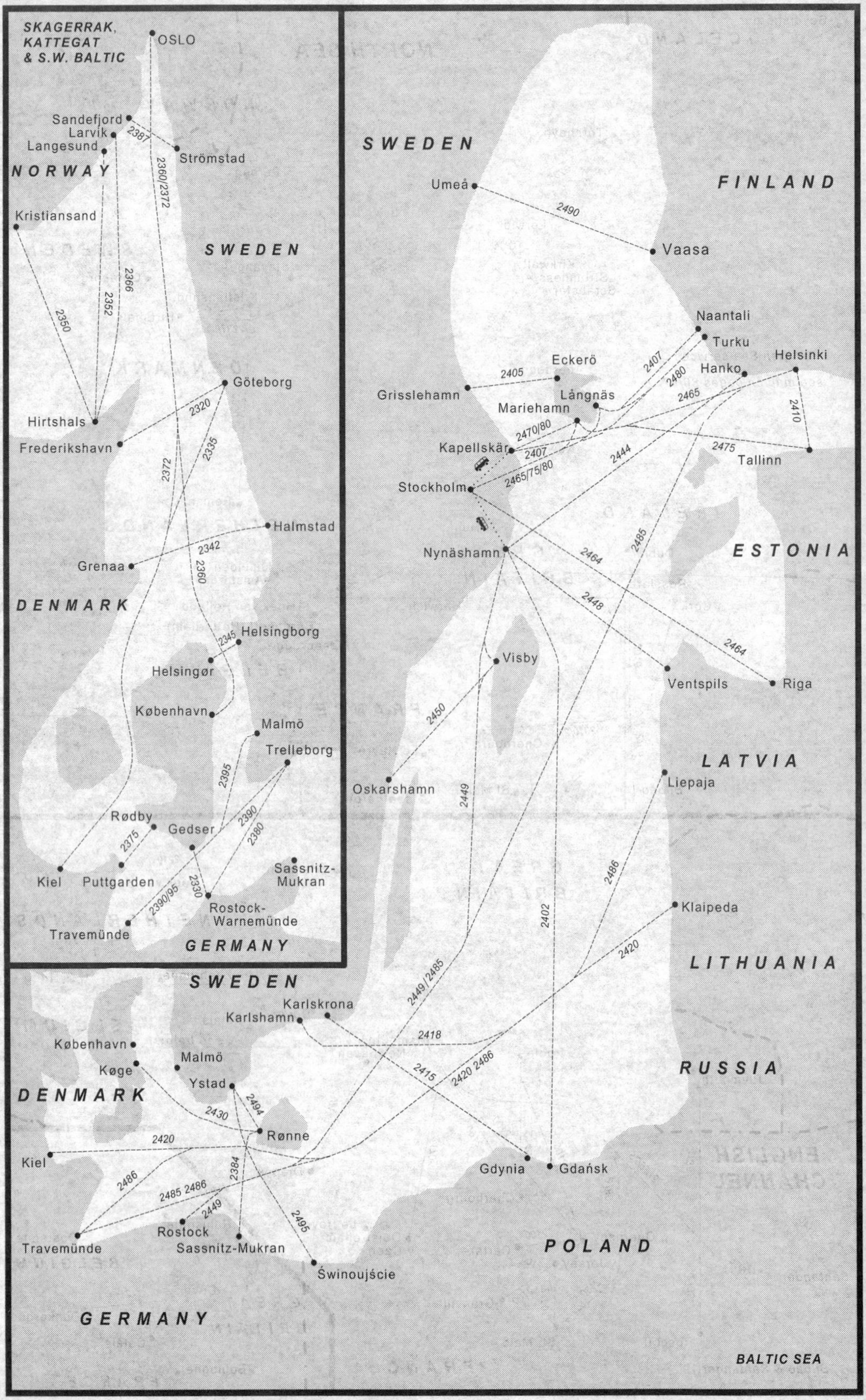
SKAGERRAK, KATTEGAT & S.W. BALTIC
OSLO
Sandefjord
Larvik
Langesund
Strömstad
NORWAY
Kristiansand
SWEDEN
Göteborg
Hirtshals
Frederikshavn
Halmstad
Grenaa
DENMARK
Helsingborg
Helsingør
København
Malmö
Trelleborg
Rødby
Gedser
Kiel
Puttgarden
Sassnitz-Mukran
Rostock-Warnemünde
Travemünde
GERMANY
2387
2360/2372
2366
2352
2350
2320
2335
2372
2342
2360
2345
2395
2390
2380
2375
2330
2390/95
SWEDEN
Karlskrona
Karlshamn
København
Køge
Malmö
Ystad
DENMARK
Rønne
Kiel
Travemünde
Rostock
Sassnitz-Mukran
Świnoujście
GERMANY
2430
2494
2420
2486
2485 2486
2449
2384
2495
2418
2415
2420 2486
2449/2485
SWEDEN
FINLAND
Umeå
Vaasa
2490
Naantali
Turku
Eckerö
Grisslehamn
Långnäs
Mariehamn
Hanko
Helsinki
Kapellskär
Stockholm
Tallinn
Nynäshamn
ESTONIA
Visby
Ventspils
Riga
LATVIA
Oskarshamn
Liepaja
Klaipeda
LITHUANIA
RUSSIA
Gdynia
Gdańsk
POLAND
BALTIC SEA
2405
2407
2480
2465
2410
2470/80
2407
2465/75/80
2444
2475
2485
2464
2448
2464
2450
2449
2402
2486
2420

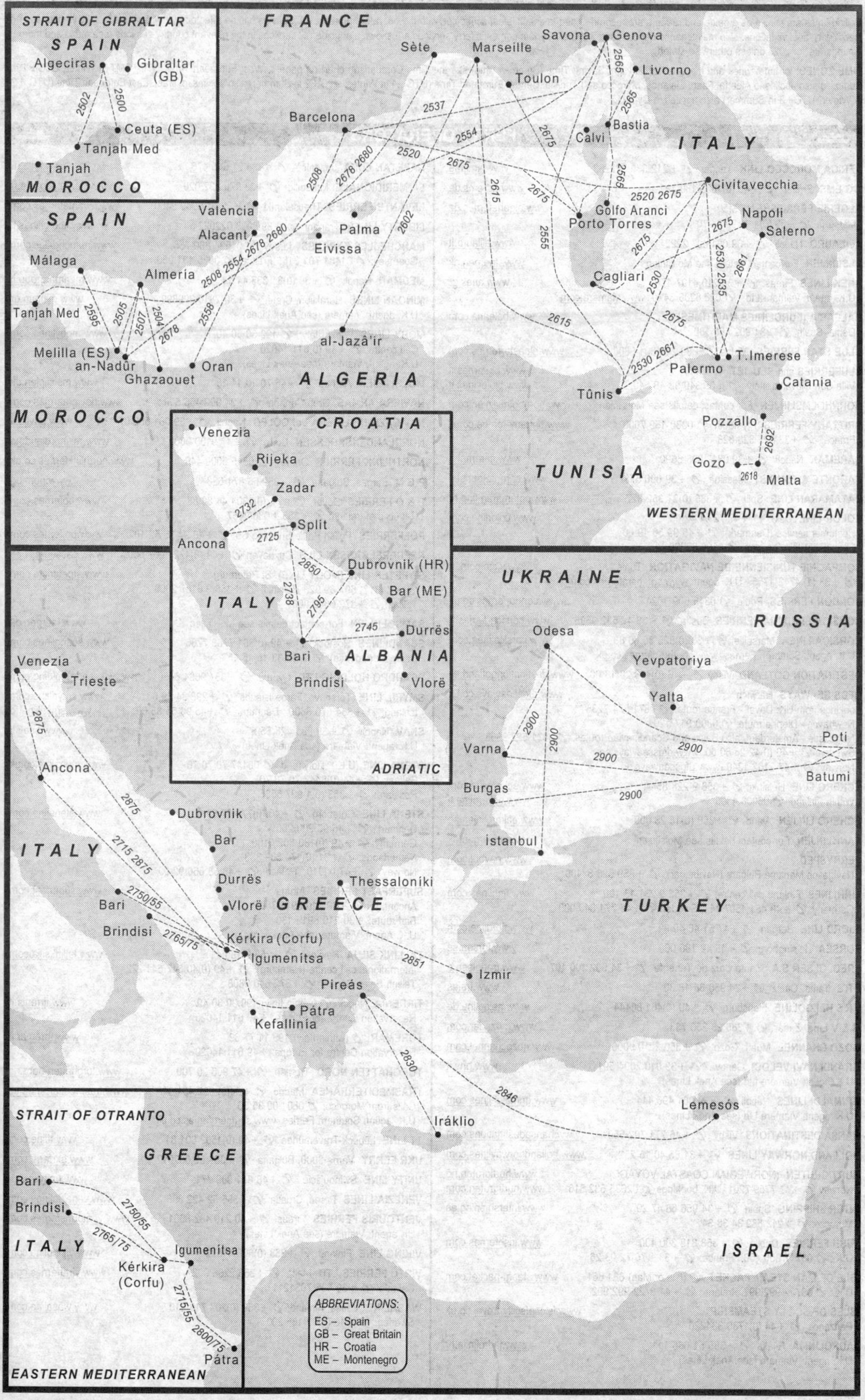
STRAIT OF GIBRALTAR
SPAIN
Algeciras
Gibraltar (GB)
2502
2500
Ceuta (ES)
Tanjah Med
Tanjah
MOROCCO
FRANCE
Sète
Marseille
Savona
Genova
Livorno
Toulon
Barcelona
2537
2554
2520
2675
2508
2678 2680
2565
Bastia
Calvi
ITALY
Civitavecchia
2566
2520 2675
Golfo Aranci
Porto Torres
2615
2555
2602
València
Alacant
Palma
Eivissa
SPAIN
Málaga
Almería
Tanjah Med
2508 2554 2678 2680
2595
2505
2507
2504
2678
2558
Melilla (ES)
an-Nadûr
Ghazaouet
Oran
al-Jazâ'ir
ALGERIA
MOROCCO
Napoli
Salerno
2675
2530 2535
2661
Cagliari
2530
2675
Palermo
T.Imerese
2530 2661
Tûnis
Catania
Pozzallo
2692
Gozo
2618
Malta
TUNISIA
WESTERN MEDITERRANEAN
Venezia
CROATIA
Rijeka
Zadar
2732
Split
2725
Ancona
2850
Dubrovnik (HR)
Bar (ME)
ITALY
2738
2795
2745
Durrës
Bari
ALBANIA
Brindisi
Vlorë
ADRIATIC
UKRAINE
RUSSIA
Odesa
Yevpatoriya
Yalta
2900
Poti
Varna
Batumi
Burgas
İstanbul
TURKEY
Venezia
Trieste
2875
Ancona
ITALY
Dubrovnik
Bar
2715 2875
Durrës
Thessaloniki
Bari
2750/55
Vlorë
GREECE
Brindisi
2765/75
Kérkira (Corfu)
Igumenitsa
2851
Izmir
Pireás
Pátra
Kefallinía
2830
2846
Iráklio
Lemesós
ISRAEL
STRAIT OF OTRANTO
GREECE
Bari
Brindisi
2750/55
2765/75
ITALY
Igumenitsa
Kérkira (Corfu)
2715/55
2800/75
Pátra
EASTERN MEDITERRANEAN
ABBREVIATIONS:
ES – Spain
GB – Great Britain
HR – Croatia
ME – Montenegro

FERRY SERVICES

Sailing times are shown as a guide and readers are recommended to check latest schedules with the operator before travel. Sailings can be affected by holidays (especially Christmas and New Year), tidal variations, ship maintenance periods, and weather. Certain domestic ferry services are shown alongside rail services in the relevent country sections (see maps and Index). Timings are for 2023 unless otherwise stated.

TIME ZONES: for time zones and the dates of Daylight Saving Time (Summer Time) see the Time Comparison chart on page 4. West European Time (UTC/GMT in Winter, UTC+1 in Summer) also applies to Algeria, Faeroe Islands, Morocco and Tunisia. Central European Time (UTC+1 in Winter, UTC+2 in Summer) also applies in Israel. East European Time (UTC +2 in Winter, UTC+3 in Summer) also applies in Cyprus.

FERRY OPERATORS

AFRICA MOROCCO LINK Tanger ✆ +212 539 322253 www.aml.ma

A G EMS Emden ✆ +49 (0)1805 180 182 www.ag-ems.de

ALGERIE FERRIES (E N T M V) www.algerieferries.dz
Marseille ✆ +33 (0)4 91 90 64 70

ALILAURO Napoli ✆ +39 081 497 2222 www.alilauro.it

ALSLINJEN For contact details see Molslinjen www.faergen.dk

ANEK LINES Pireás ✆ +30 210 4197 470 www.anek.gr
U.K. agent: Viamare Ltd. ✆ 020 8206 3420 www.viamare.com

BALEÀRIA (EUROLÍNIES MARÍTIMES) www.balearia.com
Dénia, Spain ✆ +34 902 160 180

BLUE STAR FERRIES Athína ✆ +30 210 891 9800 www.bluestarferries.com

BLUFERRIES and **BLU JET** www.bluferries.it
Villa San Giovanni, Italy ✆ +39 340 98 48 540 www.blujetlines.it

BORNHOLMSLINJEN For contact details see Molslinjen www.bornholmslinjen.com

BRITTANY FERRIES Plymouth ✆ 0330 159 7000 www.brittany-ferries.co.uk
France: ✆ +33 825 828 828

CAREMAR Napoli ✆ +39 081 1896 6690 www.caremar.it

CARONTE & TOURIST Messina ✆ +39 090 5737 www.carontetourist.it

CATAMARAN LINE Split ✆ +385 (0)21 352 527 www.catamaran-line.hr

COLOR LINE Oslo ✆ +47 22 94 42 00 www.colorline.com
Customer service (Denmark): ✆ +45 99 56 19 00
Enquiries within Sweden: ✆ 0526 62000

COMPAGNIE TUNISIENNE DE NAVIGATION Tûnis www.ctn.com.tn
✆ +33 (1) 4742 1755. U.K. agent: www.southernferries.co.uk

CONDOR FERRIES Poole ✆ 0845 609 1024 www.condorferries.co.uk

CORSICA SARDINIA FERRIES Bastia ✆ +33 4 9532 9595 www.corsica-ferries.fr

CORSICA LINEA Marseille ✆ +33 (0)825 88 80 88 www.corsicalinea.com
U.K. agent: Southern Ferries www.southernferries.co.uk

DESTINATION GOTLAND Visby ✆ +46 (0)498 20 18 00 www.destinationgotland.se

DFDS SEAWAYS Harwich www.dfdsseaways.co.uk
Bookings from UK: Dover - France route: ✆ 0871 574 7235
Newhaven - Dieppe route: ✆ 0800 917 1201
Newcastle - Amsterdam, also Baltic and Scandinavian routes: ✆ 0871 522 9955
Sweden: ✆ +46 (0)42 26 60 00 www.dfdsseaways.se
Norway: ✆ +47 2162 1340 www.dfdsseaways.no

ECKERÖ LINE Helsinki: ✆ +358 9 228 8544 www.eckeroline.com
Within Finland: ✆ 06000 4300 www.eckeroline.fi

ECKERÖ LINJEN Åland ✆ +358 (0)18 28 000 www.eckerolinjen.se

FANØLINJEN For contact details see Molslinjen www.faergen.dk

FERRYSPED www.navbul.com
Navigation Maritime Bulgare (Navibulgar) ✆ +359 526 83409

FINNLINES Finland call centre: ✆ +358 9 231 43 100 www.finnlines.com
Germany: ✆ +49 451 1507 443. Sweden ✆ +46 771 340 900

FJORD LINE Bergen ✆ +47 51 46 40 99 www.fjordline.com

FORSEA Helsingborg ✆ +46 42 186 000 www.forsea.se

FRED. OLSEN S.A. Santa Cruz de Tenerife ✆ +34 902 100 107 www.fredolsen.e

F R S Tarifa - Cádiz ✆ +34 956 68 18 30 www.frs.es

F R S HELGOLINE Flensburg ✆ +49 (0)461 86444 www.helgoline.de

G & V Line Zadar ✆ +385 23 250 733 www.gv-zadar.com

GOZO CHANNEL Mgarr, Gozo ✆ +356 2210 9000 www.gozochannel.com

GRANDI NAVI VELOCI Genova ✆ +39 010 2094 591 www.gnv.it
U.K. agent: Viamare Ltd (see Anek Lines)

GRIMALDI LINES Napoli ✆ +39 081 496 444 www.grimaldi-lines.com
U.K. agent: Viamare Ltd (see Anek Lines)

HANSA DESTINATIONS Visby ✆ +46 771 702 550 www.hansadestinations.com

HOLLAND NORWAY LINES ✆ +31 85 40 15 252 www.hollandnorwaylines.com

HURTIGRUTEN (NORWEGIAN COASTAL VOYAGE) www.hurtigruten.no
Norway ✆ +47 7759 7201. U.K. bookings ✆ 02035 532 516 www.hurtigruten.com

INTER SHIPPING Spain ✆ +34 956 68 47 29 www.intershipping.es
Morocco: ✆ +212 539 34 38 34

IRISH FERRIES Dublin ✆ +353 818 300 400 www.irishferries.com
U.K.: ✆ 08717 300 400. France: ✆ +33 1 70 72 03 26

ISLE OF MAN STEAM PACKET ✆ (Isle of Man) 661 661 www.steam-packet.com
U.K.: ✆ 08722 992 992. Ireland: ✆ +44 8722 992 992

ISLES OF SCILLY STEAMSHIP www.islesofscilly-travel.co.uk
Penzance ✆ +44 (0)1736 334220

JADROLINIJA Rijeka ✆ +385 51 666 111 www.jadrolinija.hr
U.K. agent: Viamare (see Anek Lines)

KAPETAN LUKA Jesenice ✆ +385 21 645 476 www.krilo.hr

LA MÉRIDIONALE Marseille ✆ +33 970 832 020 www.lameridionale.fr

LEVANTE FERRIES Thessaloníki ✆ +30 21 0949 9400 www.levanteferries.com

LIBERTY LINES Trapani ✆ +39 0923 022022 www.libertylines.it

MANCHE ÎLES EXPRESS Jersey ✆ 01534 880 756 www.manche-iles.com
Guernsey: ✆ 01481 701 316. France: ✆ 0825 131 050

MEDMAR Napoli ✆ +39 (0)81 333 44 11 www.medmargroup.it

MINOAN LINES Heraklion, Crete ✆ +30 2810 399899 www.minoan.gr
U.K. agent: Viamare (see Anek Lines)

MOBY LINES Within Italy: ✆ 199 30 30 40 www.mobylines.com
Call centre: ✆ +49 (0)611 14020.
U.K. agent: Viamare (see Anek Lines)

MOLSLINJEN Aarhus ✆ +45 70 10 14 18 www.molslinjen.dk

NAVIERA ARMAS Gran Canaria ✆ +34 902 456 500 www.navieraarmas.com

NAVIGAZIONE LIBERA del GOLFO Napoli ✆ +39 081 552 07 63 www.navlib.it

NORDLANDEKSPRESSEN Bodø ✆ +47 9100 9600 www.reisnordland.no

NORTHLINK FERRIES Orkney ✆ 0845 6000 449 www.northlinkferries.co.uk

P B M Burgas, Bulgaria ✆ +359 56 871 628 www.pbm.bg

P & O FERRIES Dover ✆ +44 (0)1304 44 88 88 www.poferries.com
Republic of Ireland: ✆ +353 1 686 9467

POLFERRIES Polish Baltic Shipping Co. ✆ +48 94 35 52 102 www.polferries.com

REEDEREI CASSEN EILS Cuxhaven ✆ +49 (0)4721 667 600 www.cassen-eils.de

ST PETER LINE (MOBY LINE) St Peterburg www.stpeterline.com
✆ +7 (812) 507 89 92. Helsinki: ✆ +358 9 6187 2000
Tallinn: ✆ +372 6660 800

SAMSØLINJEN For contact details see Molslinjen www.faergen.dk

SCANDLINES Rostock: ✆ +49 (0)381 7788 7766 www.scandlines.com
Denmark (Odense): ✆ +45 33 15 15 15

SCANDRO HOLDING LTD Cyprus ✆ +357 9664 6450 www.scandroholding.com

SMYRIL LINE Tórshavn, Faroe Islands ✆ +298 34 59 00 www.smyrilline.com
Iceland: ✆ +354 570 8600. Denmark: ✆ +45 96 55 85 00 www.smyrilline.fo

SNAV Napoli ✆ +39 081 428 55 55 www.snav.it
U.K. agent: Viamare (see Anek Lines)

STENA LINE (U.K.) Holyhead ✆ 08447 70 70 70 www.stenaline.co.uk
Belfast: ✆ +44 (0)8447 70 70 70
Rosslare: ✆ +353 (0)1 907 5555

STENA LINE Göteborg ✆ +46 (0)770 57 57 00 www.stenaline.com
Denmark: ✆ +45 96 200 200
Germany: ✆ +49 (0)180 602 0100.
Netherlands: ✆ +31 (0)174 389 333
Norway: ✆ +47 02010. Poland: ✆ +48 58 660 92 00

SUPERFAST FERRIES Athína www.superfast.com
Ancona route: +30 210 8919 700
Bari route: +30 210 8919 130
U.K. Agent: Viamare (see Anek Lines).

TALLINK SILJA Helsinki ✆ +358 9 180 41 www.tallinksilja.com
International call centre (Hamburg): ✆ +49 (0)40 547 541 222
Tallinn Sales Centre: ✆ +372 640 9808

TIRRENIA Napoli ✆ (within Italy) 199 30 30 40 www.tirrenia.it
Reservation Centre for Europe: +49 611 14020

TOREMAR ✆ (within Italy) 199 11 77 33 www.toremar.it
Reservation Centre for Europe: +49 611 14020

TORGHATTEN NORD Tromsø ✆ +47 906 20 700 www.torghatten-nord.no

TRASMEDITERRANEA Madrid ✆ +34(0) 902 454 645 www.trasmediterranea.es
Calls from Morocco: ✆ 0801 00 35 36.
U.K. agent: Southern Ferries www.southernferries.co.uk

TT-LINE Lübeck-Travemünde ✆ +49 (0)4502 801 81 www.ttline.com

UKR FERRY Varna 9000, Bulgaria ✆ +359 52 602012 www.ukrferry.com

UNITY LINE Świnoujście ✆ +48 801 989 771 www.unityline.eu

VENEZIA LINES Poreč, Croatia ✆ +385 52 422 896 www.venezialines.com

VENTOURIS FERRIES Pireás ✆ +30 210 482 8001 www.ventourisferries.com
UK agent: Viamare (see Anek Lines)

VIKING LINE Finland ✆ +358 (0)600 41577 www.vikingline.com

VIRTU FERRIES LTD Malta ✆ +356 2206 9022 www.virtuferries.com
Catania: ✆ +39 095 7031211

WASALINE Vaasa, Finland: ✆ +358 (0)207 716 810 www.wasaline.com
Sweden: ✆ +46 (0)90 185 200

CONTENTS

IRISH SEA

BELFAST - CAIRNRYAN 2002

Stena Line

Belfast		Cairnryan		Cairnryan		Belfast	
0330§	→	0552	②–⑥	0330§	→	0600	②–⑥
0730	→	0952		0700	→	0945	⑦
1130	→	1352		0730	→	0945	①–⑥
1530	→	1752		1130	→	1345	
1930	→	2152		1530	→	1745	
2300§	→	0152		1930	→	2145	
				2300§	→	0145	

§ – No foot passengers conveyed. 2300 sailing departs 30 minutes later on certain days.

CAIRNRYAN - LARNE 2005

P & O Ferries Journey 2 hours

Dec., 2022 - Jan., 2023

Depart Cairnryan and Larne: 0400 ①–⑥, 0800, 1200, 1600 Ⓑ, 1700 ⑥, 2000 Ⓐ, 2100 ⑦, 2359 ①–④.

Feb. - June, 2023

Depart Cairnryan and Larne: 0400 ①–⑥, 0800, 1200, 1600, 2000, 2359 Ⓑ.

CHERBOURG - ROSSLARE 2010

Stena Line

Cherbourg		Rosslare		Rosslare		Cherbourg	
1500	→	0900	⑦	1645	→	1045	⑥
2100	→	1230	⑤	2100	→	1600	See note c
2100	→	1430	See note b	2200	→	1700	① from July 4

b – ③ (also ②④⑥ from July 4). c – ②④ (also ③⑤ from June 30).

CORK - ROSCOFF 2015

Brittany Ferries

Sailings from Cork (Ringaskiddy) and Roscoff

Cork		Roscoff	
1600③	→	0800④	Mar. 22 - Nov. 1.
1600⑥	→	0700⑦	Apr. 5 - Nov. 4.
Roscoff		**Cork**	
2300⑤	→	1100⑥	Mar. 31 - Oct. 31.
1930②	→	0930③	Mar. 21 - Nov. 3.

DOUGLAS - BELFAST 2020

Isle Of Man Steam Packet Co. Journey 2 hours 45 minutes

Infrequent sailings (2–9 sailings per month April 13 to September 3). No winter service.

DOUGLAS - DUBLIN 2025

Isle Of Man Steam Packet Co. High-speed car ferry Journey 2 hours 55 minutes

Infrequent sailings (1–4 sailings per month April 6 to August 30). No winter service.

DUBLIN - CHERBOURG 2027

Irish Ferries Journey between 18 and 20 hours **Valid until Aug. 31**

Sailings Dublin to Cherbourg at 1600 or 1830; Cherbourg to Dublin at 1630 or 1830.

Dublin → Cherbourg

December – ②④⑤⑥ (not Dec. 23, 24, 30).
January – ②④⑤ (also Jan. 27).
February, March, April, May – ②④⑤⑥.
June – ④⑤⑥ (also June 6, 12, 14, 18, 20, 26, 28; not June 15, 29).
July – ⑤⑥⑦ (also July 4, 6, 10, 12, 18, 20, 24, 26; not July 9, 23).
August – ②④⑤⑥ (also Aug. 7, 9, 13, 21, 23, 27; not Aug. 9, 22, 24).

Cherbourg → Dublin

December – ③⑤⑥⑦ (not Dec. 24, 25, 31).
January – ③⑤⑦ (also Jan. 28).
February, March, April, May – ③⑤⑥⑦.
June – ⑤⑥⑦ (also June 7, 13, 15, 19, 21, 27, 28; not June 16, 30).
July – ①⑥⑦ (also July 5, 7, 11, 13, 19, 21, 25, 27; not July 10, 24).
August – ③⑥⑦ (also Aug. 4, 8, 10, 14, 18, 22, 24, 28; not Aug. 9, 23).

FISHGUARD - ROSSLARE 2030

Stena Line by ship

Fishguard		Rosslare	Rosslare		Fishguard
1300	→	1630	0730	→	1100
2345	→	0345	1815	→	2145

HEYSHAM - DOUGLAS 2035

Isle Of Man Steam Packet Co.

Heysham		Douglas	Douglas		Heysham
0215	→	0600	0845	→	1230
1415	→	1800	1945	→	2330

Timings may vary, and departures are cancelled on certain dates

HOLYHEAD - DUBLIN 2040

Irish Ferries by ship

Sailings from Holyhead and Dublin Ferryport. Up to 4 sailings daily.

Holyhead		Dublin		Dublin		Holyhead	
0240	→	0555		0200§	→	0525	①–⑥
0815§	→	1145	①–⑥	0730	→	0945	Mar. 10 - Oct. 30 ⊕
1040	→	1255	Mar. 10 - Oct. 30 ⊕	0805	→	1130	
1410	→	1725		1350	→	1605	Mar. 10 - Oct. 30 ⊕
1645	→	1900	May 10 - Oct. 30 ⊕	1430§	→	1800	
2015§	→	2330		2055	→	0020	

§ – Foot passengers are not normally conveyed.
⊕ – Service by *Dublin Swift* fast ferry.

Sailing times may vary owing to tidal conditions.

Dublin Ferryport - Dublin Busaras (Central Bus Station).

Stena Line by ship

Holyhead		Dublin	Dublin		Holyhead
0215	→	0530	0215	→	0545
0900	→	1215	0815	→	1150
1445	→	1800	1445	→	1820
2030	→	2345	2030	→	0001

BIRKENHEAD (LIVERPOOL) - BELFAST 2050

Stena Line

Up to 2 sailings per day from Birkenhead Twelve Quays Terminal and Belfast Victoria Terminal 2.

Birkenhead		Belfast	Belfast		Birkenhead
1030	→	1830	1030	→	1830
2230	→	0630	2230	→	0630

LIVERPOOL - DUBLIN 2052

P & O Ferries

Conveys passengers with vehicles only not bicyles. Limited passenger facilities onboard.

Liverpool		Dublin		Dublin		Liverpool	
0930	→	1730	②–⑥	0900	→	1700	②–⑥
2100	→	0500		2130	→	0530	

LIVERPOOL - DOUGLAS 2053

Isle Of Man Steam Packet Co. High-speed car ferry

Sailings from Liverpool Landing Stage and Douglas

Liverpool → Douglas Mar. 31 - Oct. 29 a minimum of one sailing a day, two during July / Aug. Most regular timings d. 1115, a. 1400; d. 1915, a. 2200.

Douglas → Liverpool Mar. 31 - Oct. 29 a minimum of one sailing a day, two during July / Aug. Most regular timings d. 0715, a. 1000; d. 1500, a. 1745.

Times may vary by several hours on certain dates - please check with operator.

PEMBROKE - ROSSLARE 2055

Irish Ferries

Pembroke		Rosslare	Rosslare		Pembroke
0245	→	0646	0845	→	1246
1445	→	1846	2045	→	0046

Sailing times may vary owing to tidal conditions

ENGLISH CHANNEL AND BAY OF BISCAY

CHANNEL ISLAND SERVICES 2100

Condor Ferries

POOLE - GUERNSEY by fast ferry
POOLE - JERSEY by fast ferry
PORTSMOUTH - GUERNSEY
PORTSMOUTH - JERSEY
ST MALO - GUERNSEY by fast ferry
ST MALO - JERSEY by fast ferry
GUERNSEY - JERSEY by fast ferry

Services operate all year round. Departure times vary - contact operator for details

OTHER SERVICES:

Manche îles Express operate catamaran services in summer from Jersey to Carteret, Granville, Sark and Guernsey, and from Guernsey to Alderney and Diélette.

2105 ROSSLARE - BILBAO

Brittany Ferries — Valid until Nov. 5

Conveys passengers with vehicles only

Mar. 2 - Nov. 5

Rosslare		Bilbao		Bilbao		Rosslare	
0800③	→	1345④	a	1100⑦	→	1500①	
0800③	→	1300④	b	1600④	→	2000⑤	e
2300⑤	→	0800⑥	c	1845④	→	1600⑤	f
2359⑤	→	0800⑥	d				

a – Until Mar. 22.
b – From Mar. 29.
c – From Mar. 31.
d – Until Mar. 24.
e – From Mar. 30.
f – Until Mar. 23.

2110 DOVER - CALAIS

DFDS Seaways

Sailings from Dover Eastern Docks and Calais Maritime. Journey 90 minutes

Conveys passengers with vehicles only (includes bicyles).

There are up to 14 sailings a day each way at peak times with typical summer departures shown (based on August sailings).

Depart Dover: 0015, 0220①–⑥, 0340①–⑥, 0505①–⑥, 0710, 0830, 0955, 1155, 1315, 1440, 1640, 1805, 1930, 2130, 2250.

Depart Calais: 0050, 0210①–⑥, 0335①–⑥, 0540, 0700, 0825, 1030, 1150, 1315, 1515, 1635, 1801, 2001, 2120, 2245.

P & O Ferries

Sailings from Dover Eastern Docks and Calais Maritime. Journey 90 minutes

There are up to 14 sailings a day each way at peak times with typical summer departures shown (based on July sailings).

Depart Dover: 0310①–⑥, 0600, 0655②–⑥, 0825, 0955, 1125, 1210, 1340, 1510, 1640①–⑥, 1725, 1855②–⑦, 2025, 2240.

Depart Calais: 0135①–⑥, 0420①–⑥, 0520②–⑥, 0650, 0820①–⑥, 0950, 1035, 1205, 1335, 1505①–⑥, 1550, 1720, 1850, 2105.

On night services, conveys passengers with vehicles only (foot passengers may travel on the 0955, 1340, 1725 from Dover and the 1035, 1550, 1850 from Calais). Subject to variation, especially Jan. to Mar. and Christmas.

2111 DOVER - DUNKERQUE

DFDS Seaways

Sailings from Dover Eastern Docks and Dunkerque. Journey 2 hours

Conveys passengers with vehicles only (includes bicyles). Timings vary (those shown below are based on sailings during August).

Depart Dover: 0200②–⑥, 0400, 0600①–⑥, 0800, 1000, 1200, 1400, 1600, 1800, 2000, 2200①–⑤, 2359⑦–⑤.

Depart Dunkerque: 0200①–⑥, 0400①–⑥, 0600, 0800, 1000, 1200, 1400, 1600, 1800, 2000, 2200, 2359⑦–⑤.

2125 NEWHAVEN - DIEPPE

DFDS Seaways

Timings are indicative of the sailing pattern, please check locally for actual timings.

January - April and October - December

Newhaven		Dieppe		Dieppe		Newhaven	
0700	→	1200	⑦	0630	→	0930	①–⑤
1100	→	1600	①–⑤	1200	→	1500	⑥
1700	→	2200	⑥	1600	→	1900	⑦
2300	→	0600	⑤–⑦	1800	→	2100	①–⑤
				2359	→	0430	⑥

May - September

Newhaven		Dieppe	Dieppe		Newhaven
1100	→	1600	1200	→	1500
1600	→	2200	1800	→	2100
2300	→	0500	2359	→	0500

Newhaven ferry terminal is adjacent to Newhaven Town rail station (Table **102**).

2130 PENZANCE - ST. MARY'S

Isles Of Scilly Steamship Co. — Mar. 20 - Nov. 5 (no winter service)

Sailings from Penzance Lighthouse Pier (South Pier) and St Mary's.

From Penzance and St Mary's: sailings on ①③⑤⑥ Mar. 21 – 25; ①–⑥ Mar. 28 - June 25; daily June 27 - Oct. 7 (not Sept. 24, Oct. 1); ①③⑤⑥ Oct. 9 - Nov 5.

Departure times vary owing to tidal conditions
(most sailings Penzance depart 0915, St Mary's depart 1630).

2135 PLYMOUTH - ROSCOFF

Brittany Ferries — Mar. - Nov. No winter service

Sailings from Plymouth Millbay and Roscoff.

From Plymouth: ①④⑤⑥⑦ Mar. 23 - Nov. 5. See note a

From Roscoff: ①④⑤⑥⑦ Mar. 23 - Nov. 5. See note a

Departure times vary. Sailing time approx 6 – 9 hours.

a – Additionally sailings on Apr. 4, 11, May 23, 30, July 18, 25, August 1–29.

2140 PLYMOUTH - SANTANDER

Brittany Ferries — Mar. - Nov. No winter service

Sailings from Plymouth Millbay and Santander

Plymouth		Santander		Santander		Plymouth	
1545③	→	1315④	Mar. 29 - Nov. 1 a	1330④	→	1045⑤	Mar. 30 - Nov. 2 b
1645⑦	→	1400①	Mar. 27 - Nov. 5	1800①	→	1530②	Apr. 3 - Oct. 30.

a – Departs 1215 Apr. 19 - May 17, June 6 - July 12, Sept. 6 - Nov. 1.
b – Departs 1600 Mar. 30 - Apr. 13, May 25 - June 1, July 20 - Aug. 31.

2145 POOLE - CHERBOURG

Brittany Ferries — Mar. - Nov. (no winter service)

Poole		Cherbourg		Cherbourg		Poole	
0830	→	1400	See note **M**.	1700	→	2030	See note **N**.
				1815	→	2145	See note **P**.
				2130	→	0700	See note **R**.

M – Apr 1 - Nov. 5. During July and August sailings on ② arrive 1430.
N – ② July 7 - Aug. 29.
P – ①④⑤⑥⑦ Mar. 31 - July 3; ③–① July 5 - Sept 4; ①④⑤⑥⑦ Sept. 7 - Nov. 5.
R – ②③ Apr. 4 - June 28, Sept. 5 - Nov. 1.

High-speed service Cherbourg - Poole (no winter service)

Cherbourg		Poole	
1145	→	1335	⑤⑥⑦ May 26 - June 4, July 14 - Sept. 3.

*See Table **2160** for high-speed service Portsmouth to Cherbourg*

2155 PORTSMOUTH - BILBAO

Brittany Ferries — Apr. - Nov. (no winter service)

Portsmouth		Bilbao	
1900④	→	0800⑤	Apr. 6 - Nov. 2.
2130⑦	→	0800⑦	Apr. 2 - Nov. 5.
Bilbao		**Portsmouth**	
1300⑥	→	1730⑦	Apr. 1 - Nov. 4.
1300②	→	2045③	Apr. 4 - Oct. 31.

2160 PORTSMOUTH - CHERBOURG

Brittany Ferries by fast ferry — May - Sept. (no winter service)

Portsmouth		Cherbourg	
0701	→	1100	⑤⑥⑦ May 26 - June 4; ⑤⑥⑦ July 14 - Sept. 3.

*See Table **2145** for high-speed service Cherbourg to Poole*

Brittany Ferries — Jan. - Nov. (no winter service)

Sailings from Portsmouth Continental Ferry Port and Cherbourg.

Portsmouth		Cherbourg	
2300④	→	0800⑤	Jan. 5 - Nov. 2.
2315③	→	0800④	Apr. 5 - Nov. 1.
Cherbourg		**Portsmouth**	
1200⑤	→	1645	Jan. 1 - Nov. 3.
1200④	→	1600	Apr. 4 - Nov. 2.

Free 🚌 runs Cherbourg Port - Cherbourg town centre.

2170 PORTSMOUTH - OUISTREHAM (CAEN)

Brittany Ferries

Sailings from Portsmouth Continental Ferry Port and Ouistreham

Portsmouth		Ouistreham	
			Jan. 13 - Mar. 25
0815	→	1500	②④⑦.
1445	→	2130	①③⑥.
2200	→	0645	⑤.
2245	→	0645	②⑦.
2245	→	0730	④.
			Mar. 26 - Nov. 5
0815	→	1500	Daily.
1445	→	2130	①②④⑤⑥.
2130	→	0645	③.
2245	→	0645	①④⑤⑥⑦.
2245	→	0730	②.

Ouistreham		Portsmouth	
			Jan. 14 - Mar. 25
0830	→	1315	①③⑥.
1400	→	1915	③.
1630	→	2115	②④⑦.
2300	→	0645	①③⑥.
			Mar. 26 - Nov. 5
0830	→	1315	Daily except ③.
1400	→	1915	③.
1630	→	2115	Daily except ③.
2300	→	0645	Daily.

Local 🚌 service operated by Twisto links Caen with Ouistreham (500m from ferry terminal, not contactless). Does not connect with evening ferry arrivals or departures.

2175 PORTSMOUTH - SANTANDER

Brittany Ferries

Sailings from Portsmouth Continental Ferry Port and Santander

Portsmouth		Santander	
2130①⑤	→	0800②⑥	until Nov. 3.
Santander		**Portsmouth**	
1400③	→	2000④	until Nov. 5.
1400⑦	→	1730①	until Nov. 1.

2180 PORTSMOUTH - ST MALO

Brittany Ferries — Valid until November

Sailings from Portsmouth Continental Ferry Port and St. Malo Terminal Ferry du Naye

From Portsmouth: in summer sails daily except ② (daily July - Aug.). In winter (November - March) sails ①③⑤⑦. Timings vary (typical sailing Portsmouth depart 2015, St. Malo arrive 0815). Contact operator for confirmed timings.

From St. Malo: in summer sails daily except ③ (daily July - Aug.). In Winter (November - March sails ①②④⑥. Timings vary (typical sailing St. Malo depart 1030, Portsmouth arrive 1820). Contact operator for confirmed timings.

NORTH SEA

ABERDEEN - KIRKWALL - LERWICK 2200

NorthLink Ferries

Aberdeen		Kirkwall		Kirkwall		Lerwick
Until March 31, 2022						
1700④⑥⑦	→	2300④⑥⑦	→	2345④⑥⑦	→	0730⑤⑦①
1900①②③⑤	→	→	→	→	→	0730②③④⑥
April 1 - October 31, 2022						
1700②④⑥⑦	→	2300②④⑥⑦	→	2345②④⑥⑦	→	0730③⑤⑦①
1900①③⑤	→	→	→	→	→	0730②④⑥

Lerwick		Kirkwall		Kirkwall		Aberdeen
November 1, 2022 - March 31, 2023						
1730③⑤	→	2300③⑤	→	2345③⑤	→	0700④⑥
1900①②④⑥⑦	→	→	→	→	→	0700②③⑤⑦①
April 1, 2023 - October 31, 2023						
1730①③⑤	→	2300①③⑤	→	2345①③⑤	→	0700②④⑥
1900②④⑥⑦	→	→	→	→	→	0700③⑤⑦①

Subject to alteration during ship maintenance (January to March)

A 🚌 transfer service is available Kirkwall - Stromness and v.v. in conjunction with evening sailings.

HARWICH - HOEK VAN HOLLAND 2210

Stena Line — **Valid untl Mar. 31, 2024**

Sailings from Harwich International Port and Hoek van Holland.

Harwich		Hoek	Hoek		Harwich
0900	→	1715	1345	→	1945
2300	→	0800	2200	→	0630

See Table **15** for connecting rail services London - Harwich and v.v.
Connection Hoek van Holland - Schiedam - Rotterdam is by RET metro line B (Table **497**).

HULL - ROTTERDAM 2220

P & O Ferries — **Valid until 31 Jan. 2024**

Sailings from Hull King George Dock and Rotterdam Europoort.

Hull		Rotterdam		Rotterdam		Hull	
2030	→	0830	①②③④⑦	2030	→	0730	⑥⑦
2030	→	0900	⑤⑥	2100	→	0730	①②③④⑤

🚌 connections (reservation recommended):
Hull (Paragon Interchange, regular departures until 1700) - King George Dock and v.v.
Rotterdam (Centraal Station, depart 1700) - Europoort and v.v.
Amsterdam* (Prins Hedrikkade 25, depart 1700) - Europoort and v.v.

* Transfer currently suspended.

EEMSHAVEN - KRISTIANSAND 2230

Holland Norway Lines — **Jan. 1 - Dec. 31**

Eemshaven		Kristiansand	Kristiansand		Eemshaven
1530 **A**	→	1000	1530 **B**	→	0930

A – Sails ①④⑥ until Apr. 1; ②④⑥ Apr. 4 – 22; then from Apr. 24 sails ①③⑤⑦ (week1) / ②④⑥ (week 2) and in the same pattern every two weeks until Oct. 1; ②④⑥ Oct. 3 - Dec. 30. Arrives Kristiansand following morning.
B – Sails ③⑤⑦ until Apr. 23; then from Apr. 25 sails ②④⑥ (week 1) / ①③⑤⑦ (week 2) and in the same pattern every two weeks until Oct. 2; ③⑤⑦ Oct. 4 - Dec. 31. Arrives Eemshaven following morning.

See Table **498** for rail services Groningen - Eemshaven and v.v.

HIRTSHALS - STAVANGER - BERGEN 2237

Fjord Line

Hirtshals		Stavanger		Bergen		Stavanger		Hirtshals
2000 **A**	→	0700	→	1230				
				1330 **B**	→	2000	→	0800

A – From Hirtshals ②④⑥ May 27 - June 15; daily from June 16.
B – From Bergen ①③⑤ May 29 - June 16; daily from June 17.

Stavanger ferry terminal is located at Risavik havn, approx 15 km from Stavanger: Fjord Line 🚌 service departs Stavanger bus station (stop 6) at 0550 and 1815.

HELGOLAND (Germany) services 2238

BREMERHAVEN - HELGOLAND May - Sept. Operator: Reederei Cassen Eils
BÜSUM - HELGOLAND Apr. - Oct. Operator: Adler & Eils
CUXHAVEN - HELGOLAND All year (Reederei Cassen Eils); Mar. - Oct. (FRS Helgoline)
HAMBURG - HELGOLAND Mar. - Oct. Operator: FRS Helgoline

LOFOTEN ISLANDS 2239

Map page 337

Reis Nordland — **fast ferry** **June - Aug. 2022 service (no winter service)**

2023 sailings not yet confirmed

Bodø		Svolvær		Svolvær		Bodø	
1800	→	2125	①–⑥	0600	→	0920	①–⑤
1900	→	2225	⑦	0755	→	1115	⑥
				1245	→	1600	⑦

Torghatten Nord — Most sailings 3 hours 15 mins

BODØ - MOSKENES 1 – 2 sailings daily (up to 6 sailings daily June to August).

NORWEGIAN COASTAL SERVICES 2240

Map page 337

Hurtigruten — **BERGEN - TRONDHEIM - TROMSØ - KIRKENES**

Daily	NORTHBOUND WINTER arrive	WINTER depart	SUMMER ☆ arrive	SUMMER ☆ depart	day		SOUTHBOUND ALL YEAR arrive	ALL YEAR depart	day
Bergen ♣	...	2030	...	2030	A	**Kirkenes**	...	1230	A
Florø	0245	0300	0245	0300	B	Vadsø	|	|	
Måløy	0515	0530	0515	0530	B	Vardø	1605	1700	A
Torvik	0820	0830	0820	0830	B	Båtsfjord	2000	2030	A
Ålesund	0945	2000	0945	1000	B	Berlevåg	2225	2235	A
Geiranger ▲	|	|	1425 s	1445 s	B	Mehamn	0120	0130	B
Ålesund	0945	2000	1900 ¶	2000	B	Kjøllefjord	0325	0335	B
Molde	2235	2305	2235	2305	B	**Honningsvåg**	0545	0600	B
Kristiansund	0245	0300	0245	0300	C	Havøysund	0800	0815	B
Trondheim	0945	1245	0945	1245	C	**Hammerfest**	1100	1245	B
Rørvik	2140	2200	2140	2200	C	Øksfjord	1550	1605	B
Brønnøysund	0135	0145	0135	0145	D	Skjervøy	1930	1945	B
Sandnessjøen	0435	0450	0435	0450	D	**Tromsø**	2345	0130	B / C
Nesna	0600	0610	0600	0610	D	Finnsnes	0420	0440	C
Ørnes	1000	1010	1000	1010	D	**Harstad**	0800	0830	C
Bodø	1305	1520	1305	1520	D	Risøyhamn	1045	1100	C
Stamsund	1915	1940	1915	1940	D	Sortland	1230	1300	C
Svolvaer	2120	2215	2120	2215	D	Stokmarknes	1415	1515	C
Stokmarknes	0130	0140	0130	0140	E	**Svolvaer**	1830	2030	C
Sortland	0255	0310	0255	0310	E	Stamsund	2215	2230	C
Risøyhamn	0435	0450	0435	0450	E	**Bodø**	0230	0330	D
Harstad	0710	0745	0710	0745	E	Ørnes	0625	0635	D
Finnsnes	1100	1130	1100	1130	E	Nesna	1025	1035	D
Tromsø	1415	1815	1415	1815	E	Sandnessjøen	1145	1215	D
Skjervøy	2210	2225	2210	2225	E	Brønnøysund	1500	1725	D
Øksfjord	0150	0200	0150	0200	F	Rørvik	2100	2130	D
Hammerfest	0505	0545	0505	0545	F	**Trondheim**	0630	0930	E
Havøysund	0830	0845	0830	0845	F	Kristiansund	1630	1730	E
Honningsvåg	1055	1430	1055	1430	F	Molde	2115	2145	E
Kjøllefjord	1640	1700	1640	1700	F	Ålesund	0030	0120	F
Mehamn	1855	1915	1855	1915	F	Geiranger	|	|	
Berlevåg	2200	2210	2200	2210	F	Ålesund	0030	0120	F
Båtsfjord	2400	0030	2400	0030	F / G	Torvik	0235	0245	F
Vardø	0330	0345	0330	0345	G	Måløy	0545	0600	F
Vadsø	0655	0710	0655	0710	G	Florø	0815	0830	F
Kirkenes	0900	...	0900	...	G	**Bergen** ♣	1445	...	F

A – 1st day **G** – 7th day.
s – June 1 - Aug. 31.
¶ – Via Hjørundfjorden Sept. 1 - Oct. 31 (Ålesund a. 1800).
♣ – Sailings from Bergen Nøstegaten.
☆ – June 1 - Oct. 31.
▲ – Embarkation and disembarkation take place by tender - passengers are required to be at the quay 30 minutes before departure.

Havila Voyages

Havila Voyages also operate a tour sequence to Hurtigruten. Departing Bergen **A** 1445, arriving Kirkenes **G** 0900. Departing Kirkenes **G** 1230, arriving Bergen **12** 1445. Please refer to notes above.

NEWCASTLE - IJMUIDEN (for Amsterdam) 2255

DFDS Seaways

Sailings from Newcastle International Passenger Terminal (Royal Quays, North Shields) and IJmuiden Felison Terminal.

Newcastle		IJmuiden	IJmuiden		Newcastle
1700	→	0945	1730	→	0915

Sailings alternate days Jan. 5 - Feb. 14, then daily from Feb. 17.

DFDS 🚌 connections:
Newcastle rail station (Bewick St, depart 1500) - Ferry Terminal, return after ship arrives.
Amsterdam (behind Centraal Station, De Ruijterkade 153) - IJmuiden and v.v. (reservation recommended, depart Amsterdam approx 1530; depart ferry terminal following arrival of ship).

STROMNESS - SCRABSTER 2280

NorthLink Ferries — Journey 90 minutes — **Valid until Sept. 30.**

Off-peak timetable March - April:
From Stromness Mar. 0630 Ⓐ, 0900 Ⓒ, 1645, Apr. 0630 ①–⑥, 0900 ⑦, 1100 ⑥, 1645.
From Scrabster Mar. 0845 Ⓐ, 1200 Ⓒ, 1900, Apr. 0845 ①–⑥, 1200 ⑦, 1315 ⑥, 1900.

Peak timetable May - September:
From Stromness at 0630 ①–⑥, 0900 ⑦, 1100 ①–⑥ **a**, 1645.
From Scrabster at 0845 ①–⑥, 1200 ⑦, 1315 ①–⑥ **a** and 1900.

a – Not Sept. 18 – 21, 26 – 29.

ICELAND and the FAEROE ISLANDS 2285

Smyril Line — **Valid until December 23** ⊡

Hirtshals		Tórshavn		Seydisfjördur		Tórshavn		Hirtshals
January 21 - March 17 and November 25 - December 23								
1500⑥	→	0730①		...		2000④	→	1100⑥
March 18 - June 2 and August 19 - November 24								
1500⑥	→	0730① / 1300①	→	0900② / 2000③	→	1600④ / 2000④	→	1100⑥
June 3 - August 18								
1530⑥	→	2230⑦ / 2330⑦	→	→	→	→	→	0930②
1130②	→	1730③ / 1800③	→	0830④ / 1030④	→	0300⑤ / 0330⑤	→	1230⑥

⊡ – No sailings Dec. 23 – 30.

In poor weather conditions sailings may dock at Frederikshavn or Hanstholm (for Hirtshals) and Klaksvík or Kollafjördur (for Tórshavn). In winter season (November - March) sailings between Tórshavn and Seydisfjördur may be advanced, delayed or (in rare cases) cancelled at short notice due to adverse weather conditions.

SKAGERRAK, KATTEGAT & SOUTH WEST BALTIC

2301 AARHUS / EBELTOFT - SJÆLLANDS ODDE

MolsLinjen

From Aarhus / Ebeltoft and Sjællands Odde: up to 26 sailings daily. Journey 55 – 75 minutes.

2304 BØJDEN - FYNSHAV

Als-Linjen (Molslinjen) Journey 50 minutes

From Bøjden and Fynshav: approximately every two hours (additional sailings in summer).

2312 ESBJERG - FANØ

FanøLinjen (Molslinjen) Journey 12 minutes

From Esbjerg and Fanø: Frequent service (up to 3 departures hourly).

2320 FREDERIKSHAVN - GÖTEBORG

Stena Line Journey approximately 3 hours 30 minutes

From Frederikshavn (Færgehavnsvej) and Göteborg (Danmarksterminalen): 3 – 7 sailings daily.

2330 GEDSER - ROSTOCK

Scandlines Journey 2 hours

From Gedser and Rostock International Port: up to 10 sailings daily.

2335 GÖTEBORG - KIEL

Stena Line Journey 14½ – 15½ hours

Sailings from Kiel (Schwedenkai) and Göteborg (Elof Lindälvs Gata)

Göteborg		Kiel	Kiel		Göteborg
1845	→	0915	1845	→	0915

Some sailings depart at 1745

2342 GRENAA - HALMSTAD

Stena Line Journey 4½ – 5½ hours

From Grenaa and Halmstad: 1 - 2 sailings per day. Timings vary.

Grenaa port is located approximately 3 km from Grenaa railway station, which is linked with Aarhus by route L1 of the *Letbanan* light rail line, running every 30 mins (hourly on ⑦).

2345 HELSINGØR - HELSINGBORG

ForSea Journey 20 minutes

From Helsingør and Helsingborg: sailings approximately every 20 minutes (every 40 minutes at night).

2350 HIRTSHALS - KRISTIANSAND

Color Line by ship Journey 3 hours 15 minutes

From Hirtshals and Kristiansand: 2 sailings daily (normally 1215, 2045 from Hirtshals, 0800, 1630 from Kristiansand, but timings may vary particularly in January).

Fjord Line by catamaran April. 1 - Oct. 22 (no winter service)

Hirtshals		Kristiansand	Kristiansand		Hirtshals
		April 1 - June 22 and August 1 - October 22			
1145	→	1400	0830	→	1045
1800	→	2015	1500	→	1715
		June 23 - July 31			
1000	→	1215	0645	→	0900
1700	→	1915	1330	→	1545
2330	→	0145	2015	→	2230

2352 HIRTSHALS - LANGESUND

Fjord Line

Hirtshals		Langesund	Langesund		Hirtshals
0830	→	1300 ①–⑥	1530	→	1930 ①–⑥
0700	→	1130 ⑦	1330	→	1730 ⑦

2355 KALUNDBORG - SAMSØ

SamsøLinjen

From Kalundborg and Ballen (Samsø): 3 – 5 sailings daily in summer; 2 – 3 sailings daily in winter. Journey 80 – 90 minutes.

2360 KØBENHAVN - OSLO

DFDS Seaways **Valid until Dec. 31**

Sailings from København Dampfærgevej and Oslo Vippetangen (Akershusstranda 31).

København		Oslo	Oslo		København
1500/1700	→	1000 **A**	1500/1700	→	1000 **B**

A – Jan. 1, 2 and alternate days until Jan. 24, daily from Jan 26 (not Dec. 24, 31). Departure times vary between 1500 and 1700 please check locally.

B – Jan. 1 and alternate days until Jan. 25, daily from Jan. 27 (not Dec. 24, 25, 31). Departure times vary between 1500 and 1700 please check locally.

DFDS shuttle bus links København port with the city centre.

2366 LARVIK - HIRTSHALS

Color Line Journey 3 hours 45 minutes

From Larvik and Hirtshals: 1 - 2 sailings daily. Departure times vary.

2372 OSLO - KIEL

Color Line

Sailings from Oslo Color Line Terminalen (Filipstadveien 25) and Kiel Norwegenkai.

Oslo		Kiel	Kiel		Oslo
1400	→	1000	1400	→	1000

2375 PUTTGARDEN - RØDBY

Scandlines Journey 45 minutes

Departures every 30 minutes (at 15 and 45 minutes past each hour). Sailing times between 2215 and 0415 may vary.

2380 ROSTOCK - TRELLEBORG

Stena Line

Sailings from Rostock (Überseehafen) and Trelleborg (Kontinentplan).

Rostock		Trelleborg		Trelleborg		Rostock	
0730	→	1330	①–⑥	0730	→	1330	①–⑥
1145	→	1800	⑦	1100	→	1715	⑦
1510	→	2110	①–⑥	1500	→	2100	①–⑥
2200	→	0540	⑦	2145	→	0540	⑦
2230	→	0540	①–⑥	2255	→	0610	①–⑥

Timings may vary. An additional night sailing operates on certain dates.

TT Line Journey 6 – 6½ hours

Sailings from Rostock Überseehafen and Trelleborg: 1 – 3 sailings per day. Timings vary.

2384 SASSNITZ-MUKRAN - RØNNE

Bornholmslinjen Journey 3 hours 20 minutes

From Sassnitz :

Sailing at 1150 ④⑥⑦ Apr. 1 - May 28, ①④⑥⑦ May 29 - June 26, ④–① June 29 - July 17, ③–① July 19 - Sept. 4, ④–⑦ Sept. 7 - Oct. 22, ⑥ Oct. 28 - Dec. 30.

Sailing at 1430 ⑥ May 13 - June 24, ⑥⑦ July 7 - Aug. 27, ⑥ Sept. 2 - Oct.10.

From Rønne :

Sailing at 0800 ④⑥⑦ Apr. 1 - May 28, ①④⑥⑦ May 29 - June 26, ④–① June 29 - July 17, ③–① July 19 - Sept. 4, ④–⑦ Sept. 7 - Oct. 22, ⑥ Oct. 28 - Dec. 30.

Sailing at 1000 ⑥ May 13 - June 24, ⑥⑦ July 7 - Aug. 27, ⑥ Sept. 2 - Oct. 10.

Other sailing dates: Mar. 23, 26, 30, May 17, 19, Oct. 29.

2387 STRÖMSTAD - SANDEFJORD

Color Line Journey 2½ hours **Service valid to Nov. 30**

From Strømstad: 1340, 2000.
From Sandefjord: 1000, 1700.

Fjord Line Journey 2½ hours

Strømstad		Sandefjord	Sandefjord		Strømstad
1200	→	1430	0830	→	1100
1830	→	2100	1520	→	1750

2390 TRAVEMÜNDE - TRELLEBORG

TT Line

Sailings from Travemünde Skandinavienkai and Trelleborg: 2 – 3 sailings per day.

Local 🚌 services are available from Travemünde Skandinavienkai railway station (Table **825**) to the ferry terminal or direct 🚌 from Lübeck ZOB.

2395 TRAVEMÜNDE - MALMÖ

Finnlines

Up to three sailings every day - journey time 9 hours

Travemünde		Malmö	Malmö		Travemünde
0100⑦	→	1030①	1000②③④	→	1900③④⑤
0230②–⑤	→	1115②–⑤	1000⑤⑥	→	1915⑤⑥
0300①	→	1145①	1330⑥	→	2300⑦
0300⑥	→	1200⑥	1600①–⑤	→	0045②–⑥
1000②–⑤	→	1915②–⑤	1600⑦	→	0115①
1100⑥	→	2000⑥	2200①②⑤	→	0700②③⑥
2145②③	→	0715③④	2200③⑦	→	0715④①
2200①④⑤	→	0715②⑤⑥	2230⑥	→	0830⑦
2200⑥⑦	→	0730⑦①			

BALTIC SEA

GDAŃSK - NYNÄSHAMN 2402

Polferries Valid until Jan. 31, 2024

Gdańsk		Nynäshamn		Nynäshamn		Gdańsk	
1800	→	1200	See note A.	1800	→	1200	See note A.

A – ①–⑥ (daily June 12 - Aug. 27). Subject to alteration Dec. 22, 2023 - Jan. 1, 2024.

Suburban rail service operates every 30 minutes (60 minutes on ©) Nynäshamn - Stockholm

GRISSLEHAMN - ECKERÖ 2405

Eckerö Linjen Valid until June 16, 2023

Grisslehamn		Eckerö		Eckerö		Grisslehamn	
1000	→	1300	A	0830	→	0915	A
1500	→	1800		1330	→	1430	
2000	→	2245	④⑤⑥⑦	1830	→	1915	①⑤⑥⑦

A – Not Jan. 1.

☛ No sailings on Dec. 24, 25.

🚌 connections available Stockholm and Uppsala - Grisslehamn and v.v.

NAANTALI - KAPELLSKÄR via Långnäs 2407

Finnlines Valid until Dec. 31

Conveys passengers with vehicles and bicycles only.

Naantali		Långnäs		Kapellskär		Kapellskär		Långnäs		Naantali	
1045	→	1545	→	1815	⑥⑦	0915	→	1410	→	1910	⑥⑦
1145	→	1645	→	1845	①–⑤	1015	→	1450	→	1940	①–⑤
2230	→	0355	→	0615	⑥⑦‡	2130	→	0225	→	0715	⑥⑦‡
2245	→	0355	→	0615	①–⑤‡	2145	→	0225	→	0715	①–⑤‡

‡ – Arrival next day.

Some services subject to cancellations in May.

HELSINKI - TALLINN 2410

Eckerö Line Valid until Dec. 31

Sailings from Helsinki Länsiterminaali 2 (West Terminal T2) and Tallinn A-terminal.

Helsinki		Tallinn		Tallinn		Helsinki	
0900	→	1115		0600	→	0815	Not ⑦
1515	→	1730		1200	→	1415	
2140	→	0010	Not ⑥	1830	→	2100	

Tram routes 7 and 6T link Helsinki railway station with the Länsiterminaali

Tallink Silja Valid until Dec. 31

Sailings from Helsinki Länsiterminaali 1/2 and Tallinn D-terminal. Journey 2 hours.

Depart Tallinn: 0730 **B**, 1030, 1130 Ⓐ, 1330, 1630, 1930, 2230 **A**, 2300 ②.

Depart Tallinn: 0630 **B**, 0730 **B**, 1030, 1330, 1445 ⑦–⑤, 1630, 1930, 2230 **A**, 2300 ②.

A – ①③④⑤⑦. B – ①–⑥.

Additional services operate at other peak periods throughout the year.

Distance between Länsiterminaali terminals approximately 700 metres

Tram routes 7 and 6T link Helsinki railway station with the Länsiterminaali

Viking Line Journey 2½ hours Valid until Dec. 31

Sailings from Helsinki Katajanokka terminal and Tallinn Reisisdam:

2 sailings ⑥–④, 3 on ⑤ Departure times vary.

KARLSKRONA - GDYNIA 2415

Stena Line Journey 10½–12 hours

From Karlskrona and Gdynia: up to 6 sailings daily. Departure times vary.

KARLSHAMN - KLAIPEDA 2418

DFDS Seaways

Sailings from Karlshamn Ferry Terminal and Klaipeda International Ferry Port.

Karlshamn		Klaipeda	Klaipeda		Karlsham
1800	→	0900	1800	→	0900

Timings vary

KIEL - KLAIPEDA 2420

DFDS Seaways

Sailings from Kiel Ostuferhafen and Klaipeda International Ferry Port.

Kiel		Klaipeda	Klaipeda		Kiel
2100	→	1800	2200	→	1700

KØGE - RØNNE 2430

Bornholmslinjen

Køge		Rønne	Rønne		Køge
0030	→	0600	1700	→	2230

NYNÄSHAMN - HANKO 2444

Stena Line Valid until Mar. 31

Nynäshamn		Hanko	Hanko		Nynäshamn
1900 ⑤	→	0900 ⑥	2030	→	0830
2000 ⑥–④	→	1000 ⑦–⑤			

Note: Limited passenger accommodation available.

NYNÄSHAMN - VISBY 2445

Destination Gotland Valid until Aug. 31

Sailings Nynäshamn - Visby and v.v.: 1–3 sailings daily (3–4 sailings in high summer). Departure times vary. Journey 3 hrs 15 minutes to 3 hrs 30 minutes.

All sailings have 🚌 connection Stockholm City Terminal - Nynäshamn and v.v.

Suburban rail service operates every 30 minutes (60 minutes on ©) Nynäshamn - Stockholm.

NYNÄSHAMN - VENTSPILS 2448

Stena Line Journey 8½ hours

From Nynäshamn and Ventspils: up to 4 sailings daily. Departure times vary.

Suburban rail service operates every 30 minutes (60 minutes on ©) Nynäshamn - Stockholm.

NYNÄSHAMN - ROSTOCK 2449

Hansa Destinations Service suspended for 2023

Viability of service will be reviewed ahead of 2024. 2022 sailings shown for information.

Nynäshamn		Rostock	Rostock		Nynäshamn
1900 ①③⑤	→	1300 ②④⑥	1900 ②④	→	1300 ③⑤
			1900 ⑥	→	1330 ⑦

Some services call additionally as Visby, please check locally.

OSKARSHAMN - VISBY 2450

Destination Gotland

From Oskarshamn and Visby: 1–2 sailings daily (January - March runs 6 days per week). Departure times vary.

STOCKHOLM - RIGA 2464

Tallink Silja Service remains suspended

The ferry used on this route is currently being used to accommodate Ukrainian refugees.

2021 sailings from Stockholm Värtahamnen terminal and Riga passenger terminal.

Stockholm		Riga	Riga		Stockholm
1700	→	1100	1730	→	1030

Sailings on alternate days starting Apr. 6 from Riga, Apr. 7 from Stockholm.

STOCKHOLM - MARIEHAMN - HELSINKI 2465

Tallink Silja Valid until Dec. 31

Sailings from Stockholm Värtahamnen terminal and Helsinki Olympiaterminaali.

Stockholm		Mariehamn		Helsinki	Helsinki		Mariehamn		Stockholm
1645	→	2355	→	1030 **A**	1700	→	0420	→	0945 **B**

A – Daily until Jan. 15; alternate days Jan. 17–31 and Feb. 9–15 (also Feb. 4); daily from Feb.17.

B – Daily until Jan. 16; alternate days Jan. 18 - Feb. 5 and Feb. 8–14; daily from Feb. 16.

Tallink Silja 🚌 transfer links Stockholm Värtahamnen with city centre.

Alternatively Stockholm Värtahamnen is 500 metres from Gärdet metro station.

Viking Line

Sailings from Stockholm Stadsgården and Helsinki Katajanokka.

Stockholm		Mariehamn		Helsinki	Helsinki		Mariehamn		Stockholm
1630	→	2345	→	1010	1715	→	0430	→	1000

The above sailings are by way of an example, please check locally with the shippiing company.

Viking Line 🚌: Stockholm Cityterminalen (near Central station) - Viking Line terminal.

(STOCKHOLM -) KAPELLSKÄR - MARIEHAMN 2470

Viking Line Journey 2½ hours

Sailings from Kapellskär and Mariehamn: 2–3 sailings per day (timings vary).

Connecting 🚌 service: Stockholm Cityterminalen (near Central station) - Kapellskär. Overall journey time Stockholm - Mariehamn by 🚌 and ferry is 4–4½ hours.

STOCKHOLM - MARIEHAMN - TALLINN 2475

Tallink Silja Valid until Dec. 30

Sailings from Stockholm Värtahamnen terminal and Tallinn D-terminal.

Stockholm		Mariehamn		Tallinn	Tallinn		Mariehamn		Stockholm
1730	→	0100	→	1045 **A**	1800	→	0500	→	1015 **A**

A – Alternate days.

STOCKHOLM - MARIEHAMN - TURKU 2480

Tallink Silja

Service is suspended on certain dates for ship maintenance

Until Apr. 1

Sailings from Stockholm Värtahamnen and Turku.

Stockholm		Mariehamn		Långnäs §		Turku
0715	→	→	→	1130	→	1630
Turku		**Långnäs §**		**Mariehamn**		**Stockholm**
1830	→	2330 **A**	→	→	→	0600

From Apr. 2

Stockholm		Mariehamn		Långnäs §		Turku
0710	→	1345	→	→	→	1915
Turku		**Långnäs §**		**Mariehamn**		**Stockholm**
2015	→	0045	→	→	→	0610

A – Daily until Jan. 17; alternate days Jan. 19–31.

§ – Långnäs is 28km from Mariehamn.

Tallink Silja 🚌 transfer links Stockholm Värtahamnen with city centre.

Alternatively Stockholm Värtahamnen is 500 metres from Gärdet metro station.

Viking Line Service is suspended on certain dates for ship maintenance

Sailings from Stockholm Stadsgården and Turku Linnansatama.

Stockholm		Mariehamn		Långnäs §		Turku
0745	→	1425	→	→	→	1950
2000	→	→	→	0320	→	0735
Turku		**Långnäs §**		**Mariehamn**		**Stockholm**
0845	→	→	→	1425	→	1855
2055	→	0110	→	→	→	0630

§ – Långnäs is 28km from Mariehamn (🚌 connection available).

Båtbussarna 🚌 links Stockholm Cityterminalen (near Central station) with ferry terminal. In Turku 🚌 number 1 runs between city centre and the harbour.

2485 TRAVEMÜNDE - HELSINKI

Finnlines **Valid until Sept. 30**

Sailings from Travemünde Skandinavienkai and Helsinki Vuosaaren satama.

Travemünde		Helsinki	Helsinki		Travemünde
0200 ①	→	0915 ②	1500 ⑦	→	2145 ①
0245 ②③④⑤⑦	→	0915 ①③④⑤⑥	1615 ①–⑥	→	2145 ②–⑦
0315 ⑥	→	1000 ⑦			

Note Vuosaari harbour (Vuosaaren satama) is located approx 18 km east of Helsinki - can be reached by metro to Vuosaari then 🚌 route 90.

2486 TRAVEMÜNDE - LIEPAJA

Stena Line Journey 21 – 26 hours

From Travemünde and Liepaja: 4 – 5 sailings per week. Departure times vary.

2490 VAASA - UMEÅ (HOLMSUND)

Wasaline Journey 4½ hours

From Vaasa and Umeå: 1 – 2 sailings daily. Departure times vary.

2494 YSTAD - RØNNE

Bornholmslinjen **by fast ferry**

2 – 9 sailings daily, departure times vary, journey 80 minutes.

2495 YSTAD - ŚWINOUJŚCIE

Polferries

Ystad		Świnoujście	Świnoujście		Ystad
1340	→	1945	0115	→	0915
1630	→	2330	1230	→	1900
2245	→	0615	1900	→	0500
2245	→	0930	2230	→	0615

Services depart on various days, check with operator

Free connecting 🚌 866 operates København - Ystad ferry terminal and v.v. (1 hr 15 min).

Unity Line

Ystad		Świnoujście	Świnoujście		Ystad
1330	→	2000	0545	→	1315
1830	→	0130	1300	→	2015
2230	→	0645	2300	→	2015

WESTERN MEDITERRANEAN

2500 ALGECIRAS - CEUTA

Baleària (Eurolínies Marítimes) Journey 1¼ – 1½ hours

From Algeciras and Ceuta: ①–⑥ up to10 sailings per day, ⑦ up to 8 sailings per day.

Trasmediterranea Journey 60 minutes

From Algeciras and Ceuta: Ⓐ up to 5 sailings per day, ⑥ up to 3 sailings per day, ⑦ up to 4 sailings per day.

2502 ALGECIRAS - TANJAH (TANGIERS) MED

Africa Morocco Link Journey 1½ hours

From Algeciras and Tanjah Med: 3 – 5 sailings daily, departure times vary.

FRS Journey 1½ hours

From Algeciras and Tanjah Med: 4 – 7 sailings daily, departure times vary.

Inter Shipping Journey 1½ hours

From Algeciras and Tanjah Med: 2 sailings daily, departure times vary.

2504 ALMERÍA - GHAZAOUET

Trasmediterranea / Naviera Armas **Valid until Apr. 9**

Almeria		Ghazaouet
2359	→	0800 ⑥

Ghazaouet		Almeria
1400	→	2100 ⑦

2505 ALMERÍA - MELILLA

Baleària (Eurolínies Marítimes) Journey 5 – 6 hours **Valid until Nov. 28**

Almeria		Melilla	Melilla		Almeria
1530 ⑤	→	2200 ⑤	0800 ⑥	→	1600 ⑥
2300 ⑥	→	0630 ⑦	1500 ⑦	→	2130 ⑦
2330 ⑦	→	0600 ①	2359 ①	→	0800 ②

Trasmediterranea / Naviera Armas Journey 6 – 8 hours **Valid until June 13**

Depart Almeria: 2359 ①④⑦
Depart Melilla: 1400 ①②, 1600 ⑤

2507 ALMERÍA - AN-NADÛR (NADOR)

Baleària (Eurolínies Marítimes) Journey 7 hours

2 – 3 sailings a week. Timings vary.

2508 BARCELONA - TANJAH (TANGIERS) MED

Grandi Navi Veloci Departure times vary. Journey 29 - 38 hours

From Barcelona and Tanjah Med: up to 5 sailings per week

Tanjah (Tangiers) Med port is located approximately 45 km east of Tanjah. A connecting 🚌 operates between Tanjah Med and Tanjah.

Grimaldi Lines **Service suspended**

Barcelona		Tanjah Med	Tanjah Med		Barcelona
2000 ⑥	→	2300 ⑦	1500 ①	→	1900 ②

Tanjah (Tangiers) Med port is located approximately 45 km east of Tanjah (connecting 🚌).

2510 BALEARIC ISLANDS Map page 315

Baleària (Eurolínies Marítimes)

BARCELONA - CIUTADELLA (MENORCA) Journey 8½ – 9½ hours. 1 – 3 sailings per day. Most sailings depart Barcelona at 2145 and Ciutadella at 1000.

BARCELONA - EIVISSA (IBIZA) Journey 9 hours. 1 sailing per day (not ⑥ Dec. 2022 - Oct. 2023). Most sailings depart Barcelona at 2200 and Eivissa at 1000.

BARCELONA - PALMA Journey 6½ hours. 1 sailing per day. Most sails depart Barcelona at 2215 and Palma at 1130. Other sailings to Alcudia.

DÉNIA - EIVISSA (IBIZA) - PALMA Additional sailings in summer

Dénia		Eivissa		Palma	Palma		Eivissa		Dénia
1700	→	1915/2000	→	2215	0800	→	1015/1100	→	1315

VALENCIA - PALMA Journey 7 - 9 hours Additional sailings run via Eivissa

Valencia d. 2130 ⑤⑦, 2145 ①–⑤⑦, 2200 ⑥, 2245 ①–④.
Palma d. 0930 ⑥, 1000 ①, 1030 ⑦, 1045 ①–⑥, 1115 ⑤, 1145 ②③④.

Trasmediterranea

Departure times may vary. All routes subject to alteration on and around holidays.

BARCELONA - EIVISSA (IBIZA) Journey 8 – 14 hrs **Until Sept. 9**
Depart Barcelona: 2145 ①③⑤; 2200 ②④ until Apr. 28; 2200 ①–⑤ from May 1; 0900 ⑦; 2200 ①–⑤ from July 30.
Depart Ibiza: 1045 ②④, 1100 ③⑤, 2200 ⑦ until Apr. 30; 1100 ①–⑤, 2200 ⑦ from May 2; 1200 ②–⑤, 2200 ⑦ from June 20; 1200 ②-⑤, 2200 ⑥⑦ from Aug. 8.

BARCELONA - MAÓ-MAHÓN (MENORCA) Journey 8 – 11 hrs **Until Sept. 11**
Depart Barcelona: 2145 ②④, 2230 ①③⑤ until Apr. 28; 2130 ①–⑤ May 1 - July 27; 2130 ①–⑤; 2230 ⑦; July 28 - Sept. 10.
Depart Maó-Mahón: 1100 ②–⑤, 2000 ⑦ until Apr. 4; 1000 ②–⑤ May 2 - July 28; 1000 ②–⑤; 0800 ⑥ July 29 - Sept. 11.

BARCELONA - PALMA (MALLORCA) Journey 7½ – 8 hrs **Until Sept. 30**
Depart Barcelona: 2245 ⑧ (daily July 1 – 22; not Sept. 29). **A**
Depart Palma: 1130 ①–⑥ (daily July 2 – 23). **B**
A – 2300 on ⑦ July 30 - Sept. 10. **B** – 0900 on Dec. 3; 1000 on ⑥ July 29 - Sept 9.

PALMA (MALLORCA) - MAÓ-MAHÓN (MENORCA) Journey 5½ – 6 hrs **Until Oct. 1**
Depart Palma: 0800 ⑦ **A**. Depart Maó-Mahón: 1715 ⑦ (not Oct. 1).
A – Also Dec. 24, 31; not Dec. 25, Jan. 1.

VALÈNCIA - MAÓ-MAHÓN (MENORCA) via Palma Journey 14 – 15 hrs **Until Sept. 30**
Depart València: 2200 ⑥ **A**. Depart Maó-Mahón: 1715 ⑦.
A – Also Dec. 23, 30; not Dec. 24, 31.

VALÈNCIA - PALMA (MALLORCA) Journey 8 hrs **Until Sept. 30**
Depart València: 2100 ⑦, 2200 ⑥, 2230 ①–⑤.
Depart Palma: 1000 ①, 1100 ②–⑥, 2345 ⑦.

2512 CANARY ISLANDS

Fred. Olsen **Inter-Island services**

Playa Blanca (Lanzarote) - Corralejo (Fuerteventura), journey 25 minutes;
Morro del Jable (Fuerteventura) - Las Palmas de Gran Canaria (Gran Canaria), journey 120 minutes;
Agaete (Gran Canaria) - Santa Cruz de Tenerife (Tenerife), journey 80 minutes;
Los Cristianos (Tenerife) - San Sebastián de la Gomera (La Gomera), journey 50 minutes;
Santa Cruz de La Palma (La Palma) - Los Cristianos (Tenerife), journey 150 minutes;
Huelva - Las Palmas de Gran Canaria (Gran Canaria), journey 36 minutes;
Santa Cruz de La Palma (La Palma) - San Sebastián de la Gomera (La Gomera), journey 230 minutes.

Naviera Armas

Huelva - Arrecife (Lanzarote) - Las Palmas (Gran Canaria) - Santa Cruz (Tenerife): weekly.
Inter-Island services link all the main islands - most services run daily.

Trasmediterranea

Cádiz		Lanzarote (Arrecife)		Gran Canaria (Las Palmas)		Tenerife (Santa Cruz)		Palma (Santa Cruz)
1600②	→	1800/1930③	→	0100④/0530④	→	0845/1500④	→	2200④
Palma (Santa Cruz)		**Tenerife (Santa Cruz)**		**Gran Canaria (Las Palmas)**		**Lanzarote (Arrecife)**		**Cádiz**
1600⑤	→	2130/0130⑥	→	0730/1200⑥	→	2200⑥/2330⑥	→	0800①

This a representative example timetable, various options are available

CIVITAVECCHIA - BARCELONA 2520

Grimaldi Lines

Six sailings a week in each direction, timings vary.
The following are example sailings for June 1 – 16

Civitavecchia		Barcelona	Barcelona		Civitavecchia
2130①	→	1830②	2130①	→	1830②
2300②	→	2130③	2300②	→	2130③
2300③	→	1900④	2300③	→	1900④
2300④	→	2000⑤	2300④	→	2000⑤
2359⑤	→	2100⑥	2359⑤	→	2100⑥
2359⑥	→	2230⑦	2359⑥	→	2230⑦

CIVITAVECCHIA - SICILY - TÛNIS 2530

Grandi Navi Veloci

Civitavecchia		Palermo		Tûnis		Palermo		Civitavecchia
1900⑤	→	0745⑥/1030⑥	→	2030⑥/2359⑥	→	1415⑦/1800⑦	→	0715①

Timings vary (sample timings shown) - please check with operator

Grimaldi Lines **Valid until Jan. 31, 2024**

Civitavecchia		Tûnis	Tûnis		Civitavecchia
1930③	→	1430④ A	1930②	→	1830③
2000③	→	1730④ B			

A – Until Mar. 21 and Oct. 30 - Jan. 31, 2024.
B – Mar. 22 - Oct. 29.

CIVITAVECCHIA - TERMINI IMERESE 2535

Grandi Navi Veloci Departure times vary. Journey 14 hours

From Civitavecchia and Termini Imerese (for Palermo): up to 5 sailings per week.

GENOVA - BARCELONA 2537

Grandi Navi Veloci Departure times vary. Journey 20–22 hours

From Genova and Barcelona: up to 3 sailings per week.

GENOVA - PALERMO 2547

Grandi Navi Veloci Departure times vary. Journey 20½ hours

From Genova and Palermo: up to 7 sailings per week.

GENOVA - TANJAH (TANGIERS) MED 2554

Grandi Navi Veloci Departure times vary. Journey 49–58 hours

From Genova and Tanjah Med: up to 3 sailings per week.

Tanjah (Tangiers) Med port is located approximately 45 km east of Tanjah.
A connecting 🚌 operates between Tanjah Med and Tanjah.
Some sailings are via Barcelona (see Table **2508**)

GENOVA - TÛNIS 2555

Grandi Navi Veloci Departure times vary. Journey 25½ hours

From Genova and Tûnis: 2–3 sailings per week.

ALACANT - ORAN 2558

Algérie Ferries (E N T M V)

From Alacant and Oran: 8–9 sailings per month at 1900. Journey 13 hours.

GULF OF NAPOLI 2560

Including Gulf of Salerno and Ponziane Islands

Alilauro

Napoli Beverello - Forio: up to 5 sailings daily (summer only). Sailings via Ischia in winter.
Napoli Beverello or Mergellina - Ischia: up to 14 sailings daily.
Napoli Beverello - Sorrento: 5 sailings daily.
Salerno - Capri: daily sailing.
Sorrento - Capri: up to 8 sailings daily (summer only).

Additional infrequent services to Capri operate (summer only) from Ischia, Castellammare di Stábia, Positano and Amalfi.

Caremar

Napoli - Capri: 3 sailings daily by catamaran, 3 sailings by ship (4/3 in summer).
Napoli - Ischia: 6 sailings daily by catamaran, 7 sailings by ship (6/7 in summer).
Napoli - Procida: 7 sailings daily by catamaran, 7 sailings by ship (8/7 in summer).
Pozzuoli - Procida: 1 sailing by catamaran, 3 sailings by ship (1/3 in summer).
Procida - Ischia: 6 sailings daily by catamaran, 9 sailings by ship.
Sorrento - Capri: 4 sailings daily by catamaran.

Medmar

Ischia - Pozzuoli: up to 10 sailings daily.
Additional infrequent services operate between Pozzuoli, Procida, Casamicciola, and Ischia.

Navigazione Libera del Golfo by catamaran

Napoli (Molo Beverello) - Capri: up to 10 sailings daily (more in summer). Journey 40 minutes.
Sorrento - Capri: 2 sailings daily (more in summer). Journey 25 minutes.
Additional services operate (summer only) between Castellammare di Stábia and Capri.

SNAV

NAPOLI - CAPRI By hydrofoil, journey 40 minutes

From Napoli (Beverello): 0700, 0805, 0905, 1010, 1110, 1400, 1600, 1810, 2000.
From Capri: 0650, 0805, 0910, 1010, 1210, 1450, 1710, 1910.

NAPOLI - PROCIDA By hydrofoil, journey 40 minutes

From Napoli (Beverello): 0825, 1230, 1620, 1900.
From Procida: 0735, 1010, 1415, 1805.

ISCHIA - PROCIDA By hydrofoil, journey 10 - 20 minutes

From Ischia (Casamicciola): 0710, 0945, 1350, 1740.
From Procida: 0910, 1315, 1705, 1945.

CORSICA 2565

MAINLAND FRANCE TO CORSICA (map page 165)

Corsica Linea *Departure times vary*

MARSEILLE - AJACCIO Journey 12 hours. Most sailings overnight.
MARSEILLE - BASTIA Journey 11–13 hours. Most sailings overnight.
MARSEILLE - L'ÎLE ROUSSE Journey 12–13 hours. Most sailings overnight ◇.
MARSEILLE - PORTO VECCHIO Journey 14 hours. Most sailings overnight ◇.
MARSEILLE - PROPRIANO Journey 12½ hours. 3 night sailings a week operated by La Méridionale.

◇ – Most sailings ①③⑤ from Marseille, returning ②④⑥. Additional sailings in summer.

Corsica Ferries *Departure times vary*

NICE - AJACCIO Journey 4½–9 hours. Irregular sailings. Most sailings by day.
NICE - BASTIA 3–5 sailings per week (daily July/Aug.). Most sailings by day.
NICE - L'ÎLE ROUSSE Journey 5–5½ hours. Irregular sailings. Most sailings by day.
TOULON - AJACCIO Journey 6–10 hours. 1–2 sailings daily (daily night sailing).
TOULON - BASTIA Journey 9–10 hours. 1–2 sailings daily (daily night sailing).
TOULON - L'ÎLE ROUSSE Journey 6–7 hours. Irregular sailings. Most sailings by day.

Other sailings available from Nice and Toulon to Porto Vecchio.

ITALY TO CORSICA

Corsica Ferries *Departure times vary*

LIVORNO - BASTIA Journey 4–7½ hours. 1–3 sailings per day. Most sailings by day.
SAVONA - BASTIA Journey 6–10 hours. 1–3 sailings per day (irregular in winter).

Other sailings: Livorno and Savona to L'Île Rousse.

Moby Lines *Departure times vary*

GENOVA - BASTIA Journey 5–10 hours. Summer only, day and night sailings.
LIVORNO - BASTIA Journey 4½ hours. Summer only, 1–2 sailings per day (not daily).

CORSICA TO SARDINIA

Corsica Ferries / Sardinia Ferries

PORTO VECCHIO - GOLFO ARANCI July - September, up to 3 sailings per week.
BONIFACIO - SANTA TERESA DI GALLURA Journey 50 minutes. 3–4 sailings daily.

Moby Lines

BONIFACIO - SANTA TERESA DI GALLURA Journey 50 minutes. 3–4 sailings daily.

ITALIAN ISLAND SERVICES 2570

Egadi, Eolie, Pantelleria, Pelagie and Ustica Islands (map page 281)

Alilauro **Summer only**

Napoli Mergellina - Stromboli - Panarea - Salina - Vulcano - Lipari and v.v.:
Daily sailings late May to early September. Additional sailing on ⑤⑥⑦ July/August (not serving Salina and Vulcano).

Liberty Lines by hydrofoil

EGADI & EOLIAN ISLANDS and USTICA

The Sicilian ports of Messina, Milazzo, Palermo and Trapani are linked by island-hopping services serving Alicudi, Favignana, Filicudi, Levanzo, Lipari, Marettimo, Panarea, Rinella, Salina, Stromboli, Ustica and Vulcano.

Services operate to differing frequencies (additional sailings in summer).

MILAZZO - PALERMO Journey 5 hours

Milazzo		Palermo		Milazzo	
0630	→	1135/1330	→	1830	A

A – ①⑤ until May 29; daily June 1 - Sept. 30; ①⑤ Oct. 2–30.

MILAZZO - VULCANO by hydrofoil Journey 50 minutes

From Milazzo and Vulcano: 10–14 departures daily.

OTHER SERVICES:

Inter-island sailings operate, also from mainland Sicily to the islands. Services operate to differing frequencies (additional sailings in summer).

2595 MÁLAGA - MELILLA

Baleària (Eurolínies Marítimes) Journey 7 hours.

From Málaga: sailing days and times vary check locally.
From Melilla: sailing days and times vary check locally.

Trasmediterranea Journey 6–8 hours. Departure times vary at Easter. **Valid until June 15**

From Málaga: 1430 ①–⑤, 1730 ⑦.
From Melilla: 0115 ①, 2315 ①–⑤.

2602 MARSEILLE - AL-JAZÂ'IR (ALGIERS)

Algérie Ferries (E N T M V) **June – Sept. 27, 2022 service (no winter service)**

2023 sailings not yet confirmed

Marseille		al-Jazâ'ir	Marseille		
Marseille		al-Jazâ'ir	al-Jazâ'ir		Marseille
1300 ⑥	→	0500 ⑦	1300 ⑦	→	0800 ①

Sailing days and times may vary check locally.
Other services operate from Marseille to Sakîkdah / Skikda.

Corsica Linea

One sailing a week in each direction (Marseille departs on ②, al-Jazâ'ir on ⑦), increases to two or three trips per week during July and August.

2615 MARSEILLE - TÛNIS

Compagnie Tunisienne de Navigation / Corsica Linea **Valid until Sept. 11**

The service is currently operated by two ferry companies.
The **Corsica Linea** service runs up to 3 times a week (journey time approx. 20½ hours).
Compagnie Tunisienne de Navigation (CTN) runs up to 3 times a week (journey time approx. 24 hours).

2618 CIRKEWWA (Malta) - MGARR (Gozo)

Gozo Channel Co.

Sailings Cirkewwa (Malta) - Mgarr (Gozo) and v.v.: every 45 minutes (approx every 90 mins early morning and late evening). Journey 25 minutes.

Frequent 🚌 services serve both ferry terminals.

2625 NAPOLI - PALERMO

Grandi Navi Veloci Journey 10½ hours

From Napoli and Palermo: up to 8 sailings per week. Departure times vary.

Tirrenia

Napoli		Palermo	Palermo		Napoli
2015	→	0645	2015	→	0645

2661 SALERNO - PALERMO - TÛNIS

Grimaldi Lines **Valid until Mar. 21**

Salerno		Palermo		Tûnis
2000⑤	→	0700⑥ / 1030⑥	→	2230⑥
1315①	→	2330① / 0230②	→	1400②
Tûnis		**Palermo**		**Salerno**
0330⑦	→	1430② / 2000⑦	→	0700①

2675 SARDINIA

FRANCE TO SARDINIA

Corsica Linea

TOULON - PORTO TORRES Journey 10–16 hours. Weekly in winter; up to 4 sailings per week in summer. Winter sailings are mostly overnight.

Corsica Sardinia Ferries

Sardinia Ferries

LIVORNO / SAVONA - GOLFO ARANCI Journey 7. Overnight sailings (also by day May - Sept).

MAINLAND ITALY TO SARDINIA (map page 281)

Tirrenia

CIVITAVECCHIA - CAGLIARI Journey 10½–15½ hours. 3 sailings per week (daily in summer). All sailings are overnight.

CIVITAVECCHIA - OLBIA Journey 5½–7 hours. Night sailing every day. 1–2 additional day sailings June - August.

GENOVA - OLBIA Journey 10–12¼ hours. 3–4 sailings per week (daily July / August).

GENOVA - PORTO TORRES Journey 9½–12 hours. Daily sailings.

Grimaldi Lines **CIVITAVECCHIA - OLBIA** **June 1 - Sept. 26 (no winter service)**

Civitavecchia		Olbia	Olbia		Civitavecchia
2245	→	0630	1230	→	0700

CIVITAVECCHIA - CAGLIARI **Service until Mar. 21, 2023**

Civitavecchia	Cagliari	Cagliari	Civitavecchia
2000②④⑥	1100③⑤⑦	2000①③⑤	1100②④⑥

NAPOLI - CAGLIARI **Service until Dec. 31, 2023**

Napoli		Cagliari	Cagliari		Napoli
1900①③⑤	→	1000②④⑥	1900②④	→	0800⑤
...		...	2359⑦	→	1430①

CIVITAVECCHIA - PORTO TORRES Journey 7¼ hours. 2 sailings per week in winter (3 sailings per week mid-June to mid-September).

CIVITAVECCHIA - ARBATAX Journey 9–10 hours. 2 sailings per week, (3 sailings per week Aug. 1–31).

LIVORNO - OLBIA Journey 9–10 hours. 2 sailings per day (at 1030 and 2230) in each direction (on ⑥⑦ until June 6 and Sept. 26 - Dec. 12 one sailing only at 2130).

Moby Lines

GENOVA - OLBIA Journey 11–12 hours. 3 sailings per week (1–2 per day May - Oct.).

LIVORNO - OLBIA Journey 6½–9 hours. Daily sailings (mostly overnight).

PIOMBINO - OLBIA Journey 5–5¼ hours. 4–6 sailings per week June - Sept.

Grandi Navi Veloci **Valid May 12 - Oct. 13**

GENOVA - OLBIA Journey 12¼ hours. 3–6 sailings per week (mostly overnight).

GENOVA - PORTO TORRES Journey 11½ hours. 3 sailings a week (daily in summer).

SICILY TO SARDINIA (map page 281)

Grimaldi Lines

PALERMO - CAGLIARI Journey 13 hours. 1 weekly departure a week.
0900 from Palermo and 1700 from Cagliari.

SPAIN TO SARDINIA

Grimaldi Lines

BARCELONA - PORTO TORRES Journey 12¼ – 14¼ hours

Barcelona to Porto Torres: sailings on ①④⑤⑥⑦.
Porto Torres to Barcelona: sailings on ②⑤⑥⑦.
Sailing times and dates vary check locally.
Journey timings vary

2678 SÈTE - AN-NADÛR (NADOR)

Grandi Navi Veloci Departure times vary. Journey 38–44 hours

From Sète and an-Nadûr: up to 2 sailings per week.

2680 SÈTE - TANJAH (TANGIERS) MED

Grandi Navi Veloci Departure times vary. Journey ±49 hours

From Sète and Tanjah Med: up to 3 sailings per week.
Tanjah (Tangiers) Med port is located approximately 45 km east of Tanjah (connecting 🚌).

2692 VALLETTA - POZZALLO

Virtu Ferries **by catamaran** Journey 1 hr 45 min **Valid until May 1**

From Valletta and Pozzallo: 10–15 sailings per week, departure times vary.

2695 STRETTO DI MESSINA

MESSINA - REGGIO DI CALABRIA

Blu Jet **by hydrofoil** Journey 30 minutes

From Messina:
①–⑤: 0555, 0700, 0730, 0830, 0900, 1025, 1130, 1305, 1350, 1430, 1525, 1600, 1640, 1740, 1900, 2020.
⑥⑦: 0800, 0930, 1100, 1340, 1530, 1700.

From Reggio di Calabria:
①–⑤: 0640, 0745, 0810, 0910, 0940, 1105, 1210, 1345, 1440, 1510, 1600, 1640, 1720, 1820, 1940, 2055.
⑥⑦: 0840, 1010, 1140, 1420, 1610, 1740.

MESSINA - VILLA SAN GIOVANNI

Caronte & Tourist Journey 20 minutes

From Messina: every 40 minutes 0520 - 2320 (also night service 0040 - 0440).
From Villa San Giovanni: every 40 minbutes 0520 - 2240 (also night service 0000 - 0400).

Bluferries Journey 30 minutes

Foot passengers not conveyed.
From Messina and Villa San Giovanni: approx every 30-40 minutes.

Blu Jet **by hydrofoil** Journey 20 minutes

From Messina:
From Messina: 0530, 0625, 0740, 0830, 0930, 1150, 1310, 1440, 1640, 1730, 1830, 1930, 2035, 2130, 2235, 2330.

From Villa San Giovanni:
0555, 0715, 0805, 0900, 1000, 1240, 1410, 1605, 1705, 1800, 1900, 2005, 2105, 2210, 2305, 0010.

2699 OTHER SERVICES

Corsica Ferries

From Piombino and Portoferraio (Elba): May 19 - Oct. 1: up to 7 sailings daily by fast ferry; journey time 40 minutes.
From Bastia to Portoferraio (Elba): June - Sept: ④⑤ depart 0700, return 1830. Journey time 90 minutes.

Moby Lines / Toremar

Piombino - Portoferraio (Elba): up to 30 sailings daily in high-summer, less frequent at other times; journey time 1 hour.

Toremar

Services operate from Piombino to Cavo, Pianosa, Portoferraio and Rio Marina; from Livorno to Capraia and Gorgona; from Porto Santo Stefano to Isola del Giglio and Giannutri.

ADRIATIC / EASTERN MEDITERRANEAN

ANCONA - PÁTRA via Kérkira / Igumenítsa 2715

Anek Lines / Superfast Ferries

January 1 - June 26 and September 14 - December 31 ◇

Ancona	Igumenítsa	Pátra
1330②③④⑤	0800③④⑤⑥	1430③④⑤⑥
1630⑥⑦	0930⑦①	1500⑦①

Pátra	Igumenítsa	Ancona
1730①②③⑦ A	2359②③④①	1630②③④①
1730⑤⑥	2315⑥⑦	1400⑥⑦

June 27 - August 14

Ancona	Kérkira (Corfu)	Igumenítsa	Pátra
1330①③⑤⑦	→	0630②④⑥①	1200②④⑥①
1330②	0530③	0645③	...
1630②	→	0930③	1530③
1500④	0700⑤	0815⑤	...
1630④	→	0930⑤	1500⑤
1330⑥	→	0630⑦	1200⑦
1630⑥	→	0930⑦	1500⑦

Pátra	Igumenítsa	Kérkira (Corfu)	Ancona
1430①②④⑥⑦	2015①②④⑥⑦	→	1100②③⑤⑦①
1730①③⑤	→	→	1200②④⑥
...	1930③⑤	2045③⑤	1045④⑥

August 15 - September 13 ●

Ancona	Kérkira (Corfu)	Igumenítsa	Pátra
1330①③⑤⑦	→	0630②④⑥①	1200②④⑥①
1330②	0530③	0645③	...
1500④	0700⑤	0815⑤	...
1630②④	→	→	1200④⑤

Pátra	Igumenítsa	Kérkira (Corfu)	Ancona
1430②④⑥⑦	2015②④⑥⑦	→	1100③⑤⑥⑦①
1730⑤	2315⑤	→	1400⑥
...	1930⑤	→	1400②
1730⑤	2315⑤	2045⑤	1045⑥

A – On June 26 departs Pátra 1730, arrives Ancona 1400 (on June 27).
◇ – Not Apr. 4, Dec.26.
● – Additional services operate from Ancona on Aug. 19, 28, Sept. 2, 9 and from Patras on Aug. 16, 21, 23, 28, 30, Sept. 4, 6, 11, 13 (check locally for details).

connection Pátra - Pireás - Athína and v.v. operates most days in summer. For international journeys only

Grimaldi Lines / Minoan Lines

Ancona	Pátra	Pátra	Ancona
1630⑦	1700①	1700⑥	1430⑦
1400③	1330④	1930①	2030②
1600⑤	1530⑥	1630④	1400⑤

This route is temporarily suspended (2022 service detailed above).

Ancona	Igumenítsa	Igumenítsa	Ancona
1930 B	1700	2130 B	1700

B – Until Oct. 5 (not ④ Jan. 5 - May 25).

ANCONA - SPLIT 2725

SNAV — **May 27 to Sept. 11 (no winter service)**

Ancona	Split		Split	Ancona	
1930	0700	①③⑤	1930	0700	②④⑦
2200	0900	⑥ July - Aug.	1030	2000	⑥ July - Aug.

Jadrolinija

Ancona	Split	Split	Ancona
January 1 - March 31 and November 5 - December 31			
1945②⑤	0700③⑥	2000⑦③	0700①④
April 2 - June 21 and September 17 - November 3			
1945①③⑤	0700②④⑥	2000②④⑦	0700③⑤①
June 22 - July 14 and August 29 - September 15			
1945①③⑤	0700②④⑥	2000②⑦	0700③①
		1000④	1900④
July 15 - August 17			
1000②	1900②	1000②	0900③
1945③⑤	0700④⑥	1000④⑥	0700④⑥
2200⑥	0900⑦	2000⑦	0700①
August 19 – 27			
1000②	1900②	2000④	0700⑤
1000⑥⑦	1800⑥⑦	2100⑥⑦	0700⑦①
1945③	0700④	2200②	0900③

ANCONA - ZADAR 2732

Jadrolinija — **(no winter service)**

Ancona	Zadar	Zadar	Ancona
June 29 - August 11			
2200④	0700⑤	1100⑤	1800⑤
August 17 – 24			
1100④	1800④	2200④	0700⑤
August 31 - September 9			
2200④	0700⑤	1100⑤	1800⑤

BARI – SPLIT 2738

Jadrolinija — **No winter sailings**

August 31 – September 9

1000①	1800①	2200①	0700②
2200④	0700⑤	1000⑤	1700⑤
Bari	Split	Split	Bari
2100③ A	0700④	2200① C	0800②
1100③ B	2000③	0800② D	1800②

A – May 8 - Aug. 9 and Aug. 30 - Sept. 6.
B – Aug. 16, 23 only.
C – May 8 - June 22 (also Aug. 14, 21).
D – June 27 - Aug. 8 and Sept. 11 - Oct. 19.

BARI - DURRËS 2745

Grandi Navi Veloci / Adria Ferries

From Bari and Durrës: departs 2200 daily (timings vary in summer). Journey 9 – 11 hours.
Adria Ferries also operates from Ancona and Trieste to Durrës.

Ventouris Ferries

From Bari and Durrës: 1 – 2 sailings per day, Journey 9 – 10 hours.

BARI - IGUMENÍTSA via Kérkira (Corfu) 2750

Ventouris Ferries — **July 1 - Sept. 9 (no winter sailings)**

Bari	Kérkira (Corfu)	Igumenítsa	
1000	→	2200	Sept. 3.
2000	→	0800	July 1, 3, 5, 7, 10, 12. Sept. 1, 4, 6, 8.
2000	0700 / 0730	0830	July 14, 17*, 19, 21, 24*, 26, 28, 31*. Aug. 2, 4, 7*, 9, 11, 14*, 16, 18, 21*, 23, 25, 28*, 30.
2359	1100 / 1130	1230	July 8, 15, 23, 29. Aug. 5, 12.

Igumenítsa	Kérkira (Corfu)	Bari	
1000	→	2000	July 8, 15, 22, 29. Aug. 5, 12.
2130	→	0730	July 2, 4, 6, 9, 11, 13.
2130	2230 / 2300	0815	July 16, 18*, 20, 23, 25*, 27, 30. Aug. 1*, 3, 6, 8*, 10, 13, 15*, 17, 19, 22*, 24, 26, 29*, 31. Sept. 2, 5, 7, 9.
2359	0100/0130	1045	Aug. 20, 27. Sept. 3.

* – Also calls at Sami (Kefallinía) before and after Igumenítsa.

BARI - PÁTRA via Kérkira and Igumenítsa 2755

Anek Lines / Superfast Ferries

	Bari	Kérkira (Corfu)	Igumenítsa	Pátra
	January 1 - May 31 and October 1 - December 31			
	1330⑦	→	2300⑦	0700①
A D	1930①–⑥	→	0530①–⑥	1300②–⑦
	June 1 - June 29 and September 18 – 30			
	1330⑦	→	2300⑦	0700①
	1930①②③⑤⑥	→	0530①②③⑤⑥	1300②③④⑥⑦
	1930④	0430⑤	0600⑤	1300⑤
	June 30 - July 20			
	1330⑦	→	2300①	0700①
	1930①②③	→	0530②③④	1300②③④
	1930④⑤⑥	0430⑤⑥⑦	0600⑤⑥⑦	1300⑤⑥⑦
	July 21 - August 20			
	1200⑤⑥	2100	2230⑥⑦	...
	1330⑦	→	2300①	0700①
	1930①②③	→	0530②③④	1300②③④
	1930④	0430⑤	0600⑤	1300⑤
	1930⑥	→	0530⑦	1300⑦
	August 21 - September 17			
	1330⑦	→	2300①	0700①
B	1930①②③⑤⑥	→	0530②③④⑥⑦	1300②③④⑥⑦
	1930④	0430⑤	0600⑤	1300⑤

	Pátra	Igumenítsa	Kérkira (Corfu)	Bari
	January 1 - May 31 and October 1 - December 31			
A E	1730	2359	→	0900
	June 1 - June 29 and September 18 – 30			
C	1730	2359	→	0900
	1730③	2359	0130④	0930④
	June 30 - July 20			
	1730①②④⑤⑦	2359	→	0900②③⑤⑥①
	1730③⑥	2359	0130④⑦	0930④⑦
	July 21 - August 20			
	1730①②④⑦	2359	→	0900②③⑤①
	1730③	2359	0130④	0930④
	1730⑤	→	→	0730⑥
	...	2359⑤⑥	0130⑥⑦	0830⑥⑦
	August 21 - September 17			
	1730①②④⑤	2359	→	0900②③⑤⑥
	1730③⑥⑦	2359	0130④⑦①	0930④⑦①

A – Not Dec. 25, 26.
B – On Aug. 26 sails via Kérkira a. 0430⑦, then Igumenítsa a. 0600⑦, Pátra a. 1300⑦.
C – Daily except ③.
D – On Apr. 13 sails via Kérkira a. 0430⑤, then Igumenítsa a. 0600⑤, Pátra a. 1300⑦.
E – On Apr. 17 sails via Kérkira a. 0130②, then Pátra a. 0930②.

Subject to alteration during ship maintenance periods

connection Pátra - Pireás - Athína and v.v.

2765 BRINDISI - IGUMENÍTSA

Grimaldi Lines

March 1 - June 4 and October 2 - December 31

Brindisi	Igumenítsa	Igumenítsa	Brindisi
1300	2200	0100	0900
2000①③⑤⑥	0600②④⑥⑦	0200①③⑤⑥	0930

June 5 - October 1

Brindisi	Igumenítsa	Igumenítsa	Brindisi
1300	2200	0030①⑥⑦	0930
2100	0600	0100③④⑤	0930
		1200③–①	1830

2775 BRINDISI - KÉRKIRA (CORFU)

Grimaldi Lines June 9 - Oct. 1 (no winter service)

Brindisi	Kérkira	Kérkira	Brindisi
1300⑤⑥⑦	0800⑥⑦①	0200①⑥⑦	0730②⑦①

Grimaldi Lines also operate between Ancona and Kérkira July - Sept.

2795 DUBROVNIK - BARI

Jadrolinija (no winter service)

Bari	Dubrovnik	Dubrovnik	Bari
May 9 - August 8 and August 29 - October 18			
2100②	0700③	1100③	1800③
August 15 – 22			
1100②	1800②	2200②	0800③

2800 GREEK ISLANDS

Summary table of regular ferry services to the Greek Islands

Routes are operated by various ferry companies to differing schedules.
Additional inter-island routes are operated at less regular intervals.

Pireás to Égina, Póros, Ídra, Spétses, Kíthira, Andikíthira.
Pireás to Sérifos, Sífnos, Mílos, Folégandros.
Pireás to Páros, Íos, Thíra (Santorini), Iráklio.
Pireás to Náxos, Amorgós, Astipálea.
Pireás to Pátmos, Léros, Kálimnos, Kos, Nísiros, Tílos, Sími, Ródos, Kárpathos, Kásos.
Pireás to Ikaria, Sámos, Híos, Lésvos.
Pireás and **Rafina** to Síros, Dílos, Míkonos, Tínos, Ándros.
Pátra to Zákinthos (Zante), Kefallinía, Itháki, Kérkira (Corfu), Igumenítsa.
Kyllini to Zákinthos (Zante), Kefallinía, Itháki.
Vólos, **Ágios Konstantínos** and **Kimi** to Skiathos, Skópelos, Alónissos, Skíros.
Kavála to Thásos, Samothráki, Límnos.

2830 PIREÁS - IRÁKLIO

Minoan Lines

Pireás	Iráklio		Iráklio	Pireás	
0900	1740	Note **A**	0900	1740	Note **C**
0930	1845	Note **B**	0930	1845	Note **B**
2100	0630		2100	0630	

Arrival timings may vary - sample times are given.
No sailings on April 15.

A – ①④⑥ June 1 - Sept. 30.
B – July 13, 16, 20, 23, 27, 29, Aug. 1, 3, 5, 6, 8, 10, 12, 13, 17, 20, 24, 27, 31 only.
C – ②⑤⑦ June 6 - Sept. 29.

Anek Lines / Blue Star Ferries

Pireás	Iráklio	Iráklio	Pireás
2100	0615	2100	0615

Additional day sailings operate on certain dates in July / August

2846 PIREÁS - LEMESÓS (LIMASSOL)

Scandro Holding Ltd June - Sept. (no winter sailings)

2023 sailing schedule has not yet been released (2022 schedule shown).

Pireás	Lemesós	Lemesós	Pireás
0100②A	0700③	1200⑦C	1800①
0600⑤B	1200⑥	1300③D	1900④

A – Not Aug. 16, Sept. 13.
B – Not Aug. 26, Sept. 2.
C – Not Aug. 14, Sept. 11.
D – Not Aug. 24, 31.

2850 SPLIT - DUBROVNIK

Jadrolinija June 7 - Sept. 25 (no winter sailings)

Split	Bol	Hvar	Korčula	Dubrovnik
1530	1645	1755	1925	2125

Dubrovnik	Korčula	Hvar	Bol	Split
0700	0915	1050	1155	1255

Catamaran services Split → Hvar runs: once daily Apr. 28 - June 1 and Oct. 2 – 21;
4 – 6 times daily June 2 - Oct. 1

Kapetan Luka Apr. 1 - Oct. 31 (no winter sailings)

Split	Hvar	Korčula	Dubrovnik	
0730	0840	1000	1155	Daily Apr. 1 - Oct. 31

Dubrovnik	Korčula	Hvar	Split	
1615	1820	1940	2040	Daily Apr. 1 - Aug. 31
1600	1805	1920	2025	Daily Sept. 1 - Oct. 30

2851 THESSALONIKI - IZMIR

Levante Ferries

Thessaloniki	Izmir	Izmir	Thessaloniki
1900②–⑤	0900③–⑥	1900③–⑦	0900④–①

2875 VENEZIA - PÁTRA via Ancona / Igumenítsa

Anek Lines / Superfast Ferries

Venezia	Igumenítsa	Pátra	Pátra	Igumenítsa	Venezia
January 1 - April 30					
1130③	1515④*	2215④*	2130①	0430②	0700③*
1200⑦a	1430①*	2100②*	2359⑤b	0630⑥	0700⑦*
1430⑥	1815⑦*	0100⑦*	2359④	0800⑤	1000⑥*
May 1 - June 4 and October 9 - December 31					
1200③	1430④*	2100④*	2359④	0630⑤	0700⑥*
1330⑥	1600⑦*	2230⑦*	2300①	0630②	0700③*
1200⑦	1500①*c	2130①*	2359⑤	0630⑥c	0730⑦*
June 30 - September 10					
1200③	1430④*	2100④*	2359④	0630⑤	0700⑥
1330⑥	1600⑦*	2230⑦*	2300①	0630②	0730③

a – Not Apr. 16.
b – Not Apr. 14
c – via Corfu (1345 towards Pátra, 0745 towards Venezia).
* – Arrival times.

2899 CROATIAN COASTAL SERVICES

Catamaran Line

Runs Pula - Mali Lošinj - Zadar, Šibenik - Kaprije - Žirje, and Split - Split (Resnik) airport.

G & V Line

Catamaran services operate from Rijeka and Zadar to the islands.

Jadrolinija

Local services operate from Rijeka, Zadar, Šibenik and Dubrovnik to the Islands.

Venezia Lines

Catamaran services run May to September linking Venezia with destinations on Croatia's Istrian Peninsula (Poreč, Pula, Rovinj), also with Piran in Slovenia. Journey time 2 hours 30 minutes to 4 hours.

2900 BLACK SEA services

Irregular services operate on the following routes (freight services; also carry passengers).
Services subject to disruption and cancellation at short notice owing to the ongoing conflict in Ukraine.

Istanbul - Odesa	**Ukrferry**	
Burgas - Batumi	**PBM**	Certain sailings call at Novorossiysk
Varna - Batumi	**Ferrysped**	
Varna - Poti	**Ferrysped**	
Varna - Odesa	**Ferrysped**	
Odesa - Batumi	**Ferrysped / Ukrferry**	Certain sailings call at Samsun
Odesa - Poti	**Ferrysped / Ukrferry**	

Odesa's ferry terminal is at Chornomorsk, 20km from Odesa, and is **currently closed**. Please confirm locally for dates and times.

2nd class

BUDAPEST - SIÓFOK - FONYÓD - KESZTHELY and NAGYKANIZSA 1220

MAY 15 - JUNE 16. Carriages without 🅁 are available on *IC* trains.
Train names: Budapest - Nagykanizsa *IC* trains are named TOPART. Budapest - Keszthely *IC* trains are named BALATON.

km						*IC*		*IC*	*IC*	*IC*	*IR*	*IR*		*IC*	*IC*	*IR*	*IR*		*IC*	*IC*	*IR*	*IC*	*IC*
						850		**860**	**842**	**862**	**18502**	**18702**		**852**	**864**	**18404**	**18494**		**844**	**874**	**18504**	**854**	**866**
						🅁		✕🅁	🅁	✕🅁				🅁	✕🅁				🅁	✕🅁		🅁	✕🅁
		Ⓐ		Ⓐ								Ⓒd				Ⓐ	Ⓒ						
0	**Budapest** Déli 1225 1230 d.	...	...	0405	...	0530	...	0635	0735	0835	0805	...	...	0935	1035	1005	1005	...	1135	1235	1205	1335	1435
4	Kelenföld 1225 1230 d.	...	...	0412	...	0537	...	0642	0742	0842	0812	0901	...	0942	1042	1012	1012	...	1142	1242	1212	1342	1442
67	**Székesfehérvár** 1225 1230 a.	...	...	0509	...	0615	...	0720	0820	0920	0851	0942	...	1020	1120	1051	1051	...	1220	1320	1251	1420	1520
67	**Székesfehérvár** d.	...	...	0512	...	0616	...	0721	0821	0921	0852	0945	...	1021	1121	1052	1052	...	1221	1321	1252	1421	1521
95	Lepsény d.	...	...	0535	...	0638	...	0740	0840	|	0919	|	...	1040	|	1119	1119	...	1240	|	1319	1440	|
115	**Siófok** a.	...	...	0555	...	0655	...	0755	0855	0955	0944	1028	...	1055	1155	1144	1144	...	1255	1355	1344	1455	1555
115	**Siófok** d.	...	0436	...	...	0657	...	0757	0857	0957	1004	1031	...	1057	1157	...	1204	...	1257	1357	1404	1457	1557
124	Zamárdi d.	...	0448	...	...	0704	...	0804	0904	1004	1016	1042	...	1104	1204	...	1216	...	1304	1404	1416	1504	1604
130	Balatonföldvár d.	...	0456	...	...	0709	...	0809	0909	1009	1024	1055	...	1109	1209	...	1224	...	1309	1409	1424	1509	1609
139	Balatonszemes d.	...	0506	...	...	0718	...	0818	0918	1018	1034	1102	...	1118	1218	...	1234	...	1318	1418	1434	1518	1618
146	Balatonlelle d.	...	0513	...	...	0724	...	0824	0924	1024	1042	1109	...	1124	1224	...	1242	...	1324	1424	1442	1524	1624
149	Balatonboglár d.	...	0517	...	...	0730	...	0830	0930	1030	1047	1114	...	1130	1230	...	1247	...	1330	1430	1447	1530	1630
157	**Fonyód** a.	...	0525	...	...	0735	...	0835	0935	1035	1056	1123	...	1135	1235		1256	...	1335	1435	1456	1535	1635
157	**Fonyód** 1232 d.	...	0528	...	0632	0737	...	0837	0937	1037	1103	...	...	1137	1237	...	...	...	1337	1437	1500	1537	1637
165	Balatonfenyves 1232 d.	...	0538	...	0641	0743	...	0843	0943	1043	1122	...	...	1143	1243	...	...	...	1343	1443	1522	1543	1643
181	Balatonszentgyörgy 1232 a.	...	0557	...	0659	0756	...	0857	0956	1057	1142	...	...	1156	1257	...	...	...	1356	1457	1542	1556	1657
181	Balatonszentgyörgy 1232 d.	0442	0601	...	0700	0801	...	0900	1001	1100	...	...	...	1201	1300	...	...	...	1401	1500	...	1601	1700
221	**Keszthely** 1232 a.	|	|	...	0711	|	...	0911	|	1111	...	...	...	|	1311	...	...	...	|	1511	...	|	1711
221	**Nagykanizsa** a.	0528	0644	...	...	0844	...	...	1044	...	...	...	...	1244	...	...	...	...	1444	...	...	1644	...
352	*Zagreb* **1340** a.	...	...	...	...	...	...	...	...	...	...	...	...	...	...	...	...	...	...	...	...	...	...

	IR	*IR*	*IC*	*IC*		*IR*	*IR*	*IC*	*IC*		*IR*	*IC*		*IC*	*IR*	*IC*					
	18406	**18496**	**204**	**876**		**18506**	**18596**	**856**	**868**		**18408**	**1204**		**848**	**18598**	**1878**					
			🅁	✕🅁				🅁	✕🅁			✕🅁		🅁		✕🅁					
	Ⓐ	Ⓒ	A			④	⑤Ⓒ					B			⑤⑥				f	g	C	g
Budapest Déli 1225 1230 d.	1405	1405	1535	1635	...	1605	1605	1735	1835	...	1805	1845k	...	1935	2005	2135	2200	...	...	2205	2240	2340
Kelenföld 1225 1230 d.	1412	1412	1542	1642	...	1612	1612	1742	1842	...	1812	1901	...	1942	2012	2142	2207	...	...	2212	2247	2347
Székesfehérvár 1225 1230 a.	1451	1451	1620	1720	...	1651	1651	1820	1920	...	1851	1942	...	2020	2051	2220	2247	...	...	2250	2344	0044
Székesfehérvár d.	1452	1452	1621	1721	...	1652	1652	1821	1921	...	1852	1942	...	2021	2052	2221	...	...	2252	2252	2352	0052
Lepsény d.	1519	1519	1640	|	...	1719	1719	1840	|	...	1919	|	...	2040	2119	|	...	...	2315	2315	0013	0113
Siófok a.	1544	1544	1655	1755	...	1744	1744	1855	1955	...	1944	2026	...	2055	2144	2255	...	...	2334	2334	0033	0133
Siófok d.	...	1604	1657	1757	...	...	1804	1857	1957	...	2004	2027	...	2057	2150	2257	...	...	...	2336	0036	0136
Zamárdi d.	...	1616	1704	1804	...	...	1816	1904	2004	...	2016	2033	...	2104	2202	2304	...	...	...	2348	0048	0148
Balatonföldvár d.	...	1624	1709	1809	...	...	1824	1909	2009	...	2024	|	...	2109	2212	2309	...	...	...	2356	0056	0156
Balatonszemes d.	...	1634	1718	1818	...	...	1834	1918	2018	...	2034	|	...	2118	2222	2318	...	...	...	0006	0106	0206
Balatonlelle d.	...	1642	1724	1824	...	...	1842	1924	2024	...	2042	|	...	2124	2230	2324	...	...	...	0013	0113	0213
Balatonboglár d.	...	1647	1730	1830	...	...	1847	1930	2030	...	2047	|	...	2130	2240	2330	...	...	...	0017	0117	0217
Fonyód a.	...	1656	1735	1835	...	...	1856	1935	2035	...	2056	2059	...	2135	2248	2335	...	...	...	0025	0125	0225
Fonyód 1232 d.	...	...	1737	1837	...	...	1900	1937	2037	...	2103	2100	...	2137	...	2337	...	...	...	...	0128	...
Balatonfenyves 1232 d.	...	...	1743	1843	...	...	1922	1943	2043	...	2122	|	...	2143	...	2343	...	...	...	...	0138	...
Balatonszentgyörgy 1232 a.	...	...	1756	1857	...	...	1942	1956	2057	...	2142	2117	...	2156	...	2357	...	...	...	...	0157	...
Balatonszentgyörgy 1232 d.	...	...	1801	1900	...	...	...	2001	2100	...	...	2118	...	2201	...	0000	...	...	...	...	0200	...
Keszthely 1232 a.	...	...	|	1911	...	...	...	|	2111	...	...	|	...	|	...	0011	...	...	...	...	0211	...
Nagykanizsa a.	...	...	1844	...	...	...	...	2044	...	...	...	2159	...	2244	...	...	...	...	...	...	...	...
Zagreb **1340** a.	...	...	2210	...	...	...	...	...	...	...	...	0026	...	...	...	...	...	...	...	...	...	...

							IC			*IC*	*IC*	*IR*	*IC*	*IC*		*IR*	*IC*	*IC*	*IR*	*IR*	*IC*	*IC*
							849			**1205**	**867**	**18509**	**847**	**877**		**18407**	**857**	**865**	**18405**	**18495**	**845**	**875**
							🅁			✕🅁	✕🅁		🅁	✕🅁			🅁	✕🅁			🅁	✕🅁
	h	j			Ⓐ				Ⓐ	B									Ⓐ	Ⓒ		
Zagreb **1340** d.	...	...	...	...	...	...	...	...	...	0255	...	...	...	...	...	...	...	...	...	...	...	...
Nagykanizsa d.	...	...	0350	...	...	...	0514	...	...	0558	...	0530	0714	...	...	...	0914	...	...	...	1114	...
Keszthely 1232 d.	...	...	|	0428	...	...	|	...	...	|	0648	|	|	0848	...	...	|	1048	...	...	|	1248
Balatonszentgyörgy 1232 a.	...	...	0433	0439	...	...	0557	...	...	0641	0659	0620	0757	0859	...	...	0957	1059	...	...	1157	1259
Balatonszentgyörgy 1232 d.	...	...	...	0440	...	...	0603	...	...	0642	0702	0621	0803	0902	...	0815	1003	1102	...	...	1203	1302
Balatonfenyves 1232 d.	...	...	...	0458	...	...	0617	...	...	|	0717	0643	0817	0917	...	0846	1017	1117	...	...	1217	1317
Fonyód 1232 a.	...	...	...	0506	...	...	0622	...	...	0706	0722	0653	0822	0922	...	0856	1022	1122	...	...	1222	1322
Fonyód d.	0333	...	...	0507	...	...	0624	...	0645	0709	0724	0655	0824	0924	...	0902	1024	1124	...	1102	1224	1324
Balatonboglár d.	0341	...	...	0516	...	...	0630	...	0652	|	0730	0703	0830	0930	...	0913	1030	1130	...	1113	1230	1330
Balatonlelle d.	0345	...	...	0520	...	...	0634	...	0657	|	0734	0707	0834	0934	...	0917	1034	1134	...	1117	1234	1334
Balatonszemes d.	0353	...	...	0527	...	...	0640	...	0705	|	0740	0725	0840	0940	...	0925	1040	1140	...	1125	1240	1340
Balatonföldvár d.	0406	...	...	0535	...	...	0649	...	0718	|	0749	0735	0849	0949	...	0935	1049	1149	...	1135	1249	1349
Zamárdi d.	0413	...	...	0541	...	...	0654	...	0725	0733	0754	0743	0854	0954	...	0943	1054	1154	...	1143	1254	1354
Siófok a.	0425	...	...	0551	...	...	0701	...	0735	0739	0801	0756	0901	1001	...	0956	1101	1201	...	1156	1301	1401
Siófok d.	0428	0428	...	0552	0615	...	0703	...	...	0741	0803	0815	0903	1003	...	1015	1103	1203	1215	1215	1303	1403
Lepsény d.	0449	0449	...	0612	0642	...	0717	...	...	|	|	0840	0917	|	...	1043	1117	|	1240	1240	1317	|
Székesfehérvár a.	0511	0511	...	0635	0707	...	0736	...	...	0825	0836	0905	0936	1036	...	1105	1136	1236	1305	1305	1336	1436
Székesfehérvár 1225 1230 d.	0527	0527	...	0636	...	0712	0737	...	...	0832	0837	0906	0937	1037	...	1106	1137	1237	1306	1306	1337	1437
Kelenföld 1225 1230 a.	0611	0611	...	0716	...	0751	0816	...	...	0916	0916	0947	1016	1116	...	1146	1216	1316	1346	1346	1416	1516
Budapest Déli 1225 1230 a.	0619	0619	...	0724	...	0759	0824	...	...	0935k	0924	0954	1024	1124	...	1154	1224	1324	1354	1354	1424	1524

	IR	*IC*	*IC*	*IR*	*IR*	*IC*	*Ex*		*IC*	*IR*	*IC*	*IC*	*IR*	*IR*		*IC*	*IC*	*IR*	*IR*			
	18505	**855**	**863**	**18403**	**18493**	**843**	**18703**		**873**	**18503**	**853**	**861**	**18401**	**18491**		**201**	**871**	**8511**	**18511**			
		🅁	✕🅁			🅁			✕🅁		🅁	✕🅁				🅁	✕🅁					
				Ⓐ	Ⓒ		Ⓒe						Ⓐ	Ⓒ		A		④	⑤Ⓒ		g	C
Zagreb **1340** d.	...	...	...	...	...	...	...	...	...	...	...	...	...	...	...	1635	...	...	...	...	...	...
Nagykanizsa d.	...	1314	...	...	...	1514	...	...	...	...	1714	...	...	...	...	1914	...	...	...	2114	...	...
Keszthely 1232 d.	...	|	1448	...	...	|	...	...	1648	...	|	1848	...	...	...	|	2048	...	...	|	...	2348
Balatonszentgyörgy 1232 a.	...	1357	1459	...	...	1557	...	...	1659	...	1757	1859	...	...	...	1957	2059	...	...	2200	...	2359
Balatonszentgyörgy 1232 d.	1215	1403	1502	...	...	1603	...	...	1702	1615	1803	1902	...	...	...	2003	2102	...	2015	2202	...	0002
Balatonfenyves 1232 d.	1246	1417	1517	...	...	1617	...	...	1717	1646	1817	1917	...	...	...	2017	2118	...	2046	2221	...	0021
Fonyód 1232 a.	1256	1422	1522	...	...	1622	...	...	1722	1656	1822	1922	...	...	...	2022	2123	...	2056	2231	...	0031
Fonyód d.	1302	1424	1524	...	1502	1624	1636	...	1724	1702	1824	1924	...	1902	...	2024	2124	...	2102	2233	2321	0033
Balatonboglár d.	1313	1430	1530	...	1513	1630	1646	...	1730	1713	1830	1930	...	1913	...	2030	2130	...	2113	2241	2341	0041
Balatonlelle d.	1317	1434	1534	...	1517	1634	1650	...	1734	1717	1834	1934	...	1917	...	2034	2134	...	2117	2245	2345	0045
Balatonszemes d.	1325	1440	1540	...	1525	1640	1656	...	1740	1725	1840	1940	...	1925	...	2040	2140	...	2125	2253	2353	0053
Balatonföldvár d.	1335	1449	1549	...	1535	1649	1703	...	1749	1735	1849	1949	...	1935	...	2049	2149	...	2135	2301	0006	0106
Zamárdi d.	1343	1454	1554	...	1543	1654	1713	...	1754	1743	1854	1954	...	1943	...	2054	2154	...	2143	2313	0013	0113
Siófok a.	1356	1501	1601	...	1556	1701	1726	...	1801	1756	1901	2001	...	1956	...	2101	2201	...	2156	2325	0025	0125
Siófok d.	1415	1503	1603	1615	1615	1703	1730	...	1803	1815	1903	2003	2015	2015	...	2103	2203	2205	2205	...	0028	0128
Lepsény d.	1440	1517	|	1640	1640	1717	|	...	|	1840	1917	|	2040	2040	...	2117	|	2225	2225	...	0049	0149
Székesfehérvár a.	1505	1536	1636	1705	1705	1736	1811	...	1836	1905	1936	2036	2105	2105	...	2136	2236	2247	2247	...	0109	0209
Székesfehérvár 1225 1230 d.	1506	1537	1637	1706	1706	1737	1814	...	1837	1906	1937	2037	2106	2106	...	2137	2237	2248	2248	...	...	0212
Kelenföld 1225 1230 a.	1546	1616	1716	1746	1746	1816	1855	...	1916	1946	2016	2116	2146	2146	...	2216	2316	2345	2345	...	...	0302
Budapest Déli 1225 1230 a.	1554	1624	1724	1754	1754	1824	...	...	1924	1954	2024	2124	2154	2154	...	2224	2324	2354	2354	...	...	0309

A – AGRAM-TOPART – [2] Budapest - Zagreb and v.v.
B – ADRIA – 🛏 1, 2 cl., 🛏 2 cl., [2] Budapest - Zagreb - Split and v.v.
From Budapest on ②⑤ from June 9; from Split on ③⑥ from June 10 (from Zagreb on ④⑦).
C – ⑤⑥ (also May 28).
d – From Szob (d. 0726), Nagymaros-Visegrád (d. 0741) and Vác (d. 0800).
e – To Vác (a. 2002), Nagymaros-Visegrád (a. 2018) and Szob (a. 2034).
f – Not June 16.
g – June 16.
h – Aug. 28.
j – Not Aug. 28.
k – Budapest **Keleti**.

 For service until May 14 see page 497

1225 BUDAPEST - SZÉKESFEHÉRVÁR - BALATONFÜRED - TAPOLCA 2nd class

MAY 15 - JUNE 16. Connecting trains Budapest - Székesfehérvár and v.v. may require ®.

km										IR 19740				IR 19712	IR 19742			IR 19722		IR 19734			IR 19714	IR 1744
		Ⓐ				Ⓐ				Ⓒ	Ⓐ				Ⓒ	Ⓐ				Ⓒ	Ⓐ			Ⓒ
0	**Budapest** Déli ..... **1220 1230** d.	...	...	...	...	0405	...	...	...	0630	*0635*	0705	...	0730	0830	*0835*	0905	0930	...	1030	*1035*	1105	1130	1230
4	Kelenföld .... **1220 1230** d.	...	...	...	...	0412	...	...	...	0638	*0642*	0712	...	0738	0838	*0842*	0912	0938	...	1038	*1042*	1112	1138	1238
67	**Székesfehérvár** .. **1220 1230** a.	...	...	...	...	0509	...	...	...	0716	*0720*	0750	...	0816	0916	*0920*	0950	1016	...	1116	*1120*	1150	1216	1316
67	**Székesfehérvár** .... d.	...	...	0421	...	...	...	0526	...	0725	0725	0751	...	0817	0925	0925	0951	1017	...	1125	1125	1151	1217	1625
105	Balatonkenese .... d.	...	...	0505	...	...	...	0620	...	0810	0810	|	...	0852	1010	1010	|	1052	...	1210	1210	|	1252	1410
117	Balalatonalmádi .... d.	...	...	0521	...	...	...	0633	...	0823	0823	0837	...	0906	1023	1023	1037	1106	...	1223	1223	1237	1306	1423
123	Alsóörs .... d.	...	...	0528	...	...	...	0640	...	0835	0835	|	...	0922	1035	1035	|	1122	...	1235	1235	|	1322	1435
132	**Balatonfüred** .... a.	...	...	0538	...	...	...	0651	...	0847	0847	0851	...	0934	1047	1047	1051	1134	...	1247	1247	1251	1334	1447
132	**Balatonfüred** .... d.	0408	0508	...	0602	...	...	...	0702	...	...	0902	...	...	...	...	1102	...	...	...	...	1302	...	...
157	Révfülöp .... d.	0442	0551	...	0640	...	...	...	0740	...	...	0940	...	...	...	...	1140	...	...	...	...	1340	...	...
168	Badacsonytomaj .... d.	0500	0609	...	0654	...	...	...	0759	...	...	0959	...	...	...	...	1159	...	...	...	...	1359	...	...
170	Badacsony .... d.	0503	0612	...	0657	...	...	...	0803	...	...	1003	...	...	...	...	1203	...	...	...	...	1403	...	...
184	**Tapolca** .... a.	0522	0631	...	0715	...	...	...	0822	...	...	1022	...	...	...	...	1222	...	...	...	...	1422	...	...

			IR 19724			IR 19736			IR 19716			IR 19746				IR 19726	IR 19738				IR 19718		
	Ⓐ			Ⓒ		Ⓒ	Ⓐ				Ⓒ	Ⓒ	Ⓐ				Ⓒ	Ⓐ					
Budapest Déli .... **1220 1230** d.	*1235*	1305	1330	...	...	1430	*1435*	1505	1530	...	...	1630	*1635*	...	1705	1730	1830	*1835*	...	1905	1930	*2010*	*2200*
Kelenföld .... **1220 1230** d.	*1242*	1312	1338	...	...	1438	*1442*	1512	1538	...	...	1638	*1642*	...	1712	1738	1838	*1842*	...	1912	1938	*2017*	*2207*
Székesfehérvár .... **1220 1230** a.	*1320*	1350	1416	...	...	1516	*1520*	1550	1616	...	...	1716	*1720*	...	1750	1816	1916	*1920*	...	1950	2016	*2109*	*2247*
Székesfehérvár .... d.	1325	1351	1417	...	...	1525	1525	1551	1617	...	...	1725	1725	...	1751	1817	1925	1925	...	1951	2017	2125	2256
Balatonkenese .... d.	1410	|	1452	...	...	1610	1610	|	1652	...	...	1810	1810	...	|	1852	2010	2010	...	|	2052	2210	2337
Balalatonalmádi .... d.	1423	1437	1506	...	...	1623	1623	1637	1706	...	...	1823	1823	...	1837	1906	2023	2023	...	2037	2106	2223	2350
Alsóörs .... d.	1435	|	1522	...	...	1635	1635	|	1722	...	...	1835	1835	...	|	1922	2035	2035	...	|	2122	2231	2357
Balatonfüred .... a.	1447	1451	1534	...	...	1647	1647	1651	1734	...	...	1847	1847	...	1851	1934	2047	2047	...	2051	2134	2242	0008
Balatonfüred .... d.	...	1502	...	1600	...	...	...	1702	...	...	...	...	...	...	1902	...	...	...	...	2102	...	...	...
Révfülöp .... d.	...	1540	...	1636	...	...	...	1740	...	...	1836	...	...	...	1940	...	...	...	...	2140	...	...	...
Badacsonytomaj .... d.	...	1559	...	1650	...	...	...	1759	...	...	1850	...	...	...	1959	...	...	...	...	2159	...	...	...
Badacsony .... d.	...	1603	...	1653	...	...	...	1803	...	...	1853	...	...	...	2003	...	...	...	...	2203	...	...	...
Tapolca .... a.	...	1622	...	1709	...	...	...	1822	...	...	1909	...	...	...	2022	...	...	...	...	2222	...	...	...

WIL - ST GALLEN - BUCHS - CHUR — 534

SBB

SERVICE FEBRUARY 27 - OCTOBER 29. During this period trains are replaced by 🚌 St Margrethen / Altstätten - Buchs and v.v. (shaded timings).

km		IR 3251 W		IR 3253 W		IR 3255			IR 3279		IR 3281		◇		◇		◇	◇			EC 97 M	EC 99 M	EC 191 M	EC 193 M	EC 197 M	EC 199 M
	Zürich HB 530 d.	...	...	...	...	0609		...	1809	...	1909	...	...	...	...	...	...	...	...		0733	0933	1133	1333	1733	1933
0	**St Gallen** 530 d.	0525	0555	0625	0655	0725	and at	1855	1925	1955	2025	2055	2125	2155	2225	2255	2325	0026	...	A	0832	1032	1232	1432	1832	2032
16	Rorschach 530 d.	0539	0611	0639	0711	0739		1911	1939	2011	2039	2111	2139	2211	2239	2311	2339	0043	...		|	|	|	|	|	|
27	**St Margrethen** a.	0547	0623	0647	0723	0747	the same	1923	1947	2023	2047	2123	2147	2223	2247	2323	2347	0052	...	L	0849	1049	1249	1449	1849	2049
27	**St Margrethen** d.	0547	0626	0647	0726	0747		1926	1947	2026	2047	2126	2147	2226	2247	2326	2347	0053	...		...	...	...	...	...	...
39	Altstätten a.	0558	|	0658	|	0758	minutes	|	1958	|	2058	|	2157	|	2257	|	2357	0107	...	S	...	...	...	...	...	...
	Altstätten 🚌 d.	0601	|	0701	|	0801		|	2001	|	2101	|	2201	|	2301	|	0001	...	...		...	...	...	...	...	...
	Buchs 🚌 a.	0633	0701	0733	0801	0833	past each	2001	2033	2101	2133	2201	2233	2301	2333	0001	0033	...	...	O	...	...	...	...	...	...
65	**Buchs** 520 d.	0638	0709	0738	0809	0838		2009	2038	2109	2138	2209	2238	2309	2338	0018	0047	...	...		...	...	...	...	...	...
81	Sargans ⊖ 520 a.	0656	0720	0756	0820	0856	hour until	2020	2056	2120	2156	2220	2256	2320	2356	0028	0101	...	...		...	...	...	...	...	...
93	Landquart 520 a.	0718	0738	0818	0838	0918		2038	2118	2137	2218	2237	2318	2338	0018	...	...	...	...		...	...	...	...	...	...
107	**Chur** 520 a.	0726	0748	0826	0848	0926		2048	2126	2147	2226	2247	2326	2348	0026	...	...	...	...		...	...	...	...	...	...

	IR 3256		IR 3258		IR 3260		IR 3262			IR 3286		◇		◇		◇				EC 290 L	EC 198 M	EC 196 M	EC 192 M	EC 190 M	EC 98 M	EC 96 M
Chur 520 d.	...	0516	...	0611	0631r	0711	0731		1911	1931	2011	2031	2114	2131	2214	2231	2301	...		...	...	...	...	...	...	...
Landquart 520 d.	...	0525	...	0621	0639r	0721	0739	and at	1921	1939	2021	2039	2122	2139	2222	2239	2309	...	A	...	...	...	...	...	...	...
Sargans ⊖ 520 d.	0500	0539	0602	0639	0702	0739	0802		1939	2002	2039	2102	2139	2202	2239	2302	2339	...		...	...	...	...	...	...	...
Buchs 520 a.	0512	0550	0616	0650	0720	0750	0820	the same	1950	2020	2050	2116	2150	2220	2250	2316	2350	...	L	...	...	...	...	...	...	...
Buchs 🚌 d.	0525	0555	0625	0655	0725	0755	0825		1955	2025	2055	2125	2155	2225	2255	2325	2355	...		...	...	...	...	...	...	...
Altstätten 🚌 a.	0558	|	0658	|	0758	|	0858	minutes	|	2058	|	2158	|	2258	|	2358	0032	...	S	...	...	...	...	...	...	...
Altstätten d.	0601	|	0701	|	0801	|	0901		|	2101	|	2201	|	2301	|	0003	0038	...		...	...	...	...	...	...	...
St Margrethen a.	0613	0633	0713	0733	0813	0833	0913	past each	2033	2113	2133	2213	2233	2313	2333	0013	0052	...	O	...	...	...	...	...	...	...
St Margrethen d.	0613	0652	0713	0737	0813	0837	0913		2037	2113	2137	2213	2237	2313	2336	0013	0052	...		0710	0910	1110	1510	1710	1910	2110
Rorschach 530 d.	0621	0702	0721	0747	0821	0847	0921	hour until	2047	2121	2147	2221	2247	2321	2346	0021	0102	...		|	|	|	|	|	|	|
St Gallen 530 a.	0635	0720	0735	0804	0835	0904	0935		2104	2135	2204	2234	2304	2334	0002	0034	0120	...		0728	0928	1128	1528	1728	1928	2128
Zürich HB 530 a.	0751	...	0851	...	0951	...	1051		...	2251	...	...	...	...	...	...	...	...		0827	1027	1227	1627	1827	2027	2227

L – ①–⑤ (not Apr. 7, 10, May 1, 18, 19, 29, Sept. 18, 25, Oct. 2). From Lindau (Table **75**).
M – [12] ✕ Zürich - Bregenz - München and v.v.
W – From Wil (Table **530**).

r – ⚒ only.
◇ – Operated by THURBO.
⊖ – See panel below main table on page 266 for 🚌 links to / from Vaduz.

HAMBURG - ROSTOCK - STRALSUND — 830

RE services except where shown

SERVICE MARCH 4 - APRIL 14. See page 387 for service until March 3.

km		◇ S	◇ Ⓐ S	◇ S		Ⓐ	◇ Ⓐ	Ⓐ	Ⓐ		ICE 1678 ①–⑥ H✕	◇ S		ICE 1676 ✕♦	IC 2238 ♦	◇ S		IC 2212 🍷♦	◇ S		ICE 1672 △ A✕	◇ S		ICE 1074 ①–⑥ e✕	ICE 1974 ⑦w	◇ S
0	**Hamburg** Hbf d.	...	...	...	...	...	...	...	0511	0621	0742	...	0821	0943	...	...	1021	1142	...	1221	1343	...	1421	1543	1543	...
47	Büchen d.	...	...	...	...	0458	...	...	0552t	0658t	|	...	0858t	|	...	...	1058t	|	...	1258t	|	...	1458t	|	|	...
123	**Schwerin** Hbf 837 d.	...	...	...	0548	0548	...	0642	0647	0748	0837	...	0948	1037	1056	...	1148	1238	...	1348	1437	...	1548	1637	1637	...
140	Bad Kleinen 836 837 d.	...	...	...	0603	0603	...	0659	▬	0803	|	...	1003	|	1109	...	1203	|	...	1403	|	...	1603	|	1649	...
181	Bützow 836 d.	...	...	...	0629	0629	...	0723	◇	0829	0910	...	1029	1110	1136	...	1229	1310	...	1429	1510	...	1629	1710	1713	...
211	**Rostock** Hbf a.	...	...	...	0650	0650	...	0750	S	0850	0932	...	1050	1132	1156	...	1252	1332	...	1450	1532	...	1650	1732	1733	...
211	**Rostock** Hbf d.	0428*	0533*	0633*	...	...	0733*	...	0840*	...	0950*	1040*	...	1150*	...	1235*	...	1350*	1440*	...	1550*	1640*	...	1750*	1750*	1840*
226	Rövershagen d.	0505	0604	0714	...	...	0828	...	0911	...	|	1111	...	|	...	1311	...	|	1511	...	|	1711	...	|	|	1911
240	Ribnitz-D'garten West d.	0517	0616	0725	...	...	0849	...	0922	...	|	1122	...	|	...	1322	...	|	1522	...	|	1722	...	|	|	1922
265	Velgast d.	0539	0638	0742	...	...	0903	...	0940	...	|	1140	...	|	...	1340	...	|	1540	...	|	1740	...	|	|	1940
283	**Stralsund** Hbf a.	0555	0655	0758	...	...	0917	...	0957	...	1137*	1157	...	1337*	...	1357	...	1537*	1557	...	1737*	1757	...	1937*	1937*	1957
	Ostseebad Binz 844 a.	...	...	...	...	...	...	...	...	...	...	...	...	...	...	...	...	...	...	...	...	...	...	...	...	...

		ICE 1578 A✕	◇ S		ICE 1576 Ⓑ b A✕	◇		ICE 974 ⑦		
Hamburg Hbf d.	1621	1741	...	1821	1943	...	2021	2143	2254	0036
Büchen d.	1658t	|	...	1858t	|	...	2058t	|	2328	0108
Schwerin Hbf 837 d.	1748	1837	...	1948	2037	...	2148	2237	0019	0157
Bad Kleinen 836 837 d.	1803	1849	...	2003	2049	...	2203	|	0029	...
Bützow 836 d.	1829	1913	...	2029	2113	...	2229	2313	0054	...
Rostock Hbf a.	1850	1933	...	2050	2133	...	2250	2333	0115	...
Rostock Hbf d.	...	1950*	2040*	...	...	2240*	...	...	...	...
Rövershagen d.	...	|	2111	...	...	2311	...	...	...	...
Ribnitz-Damgarten West d.	...	|	2122	...	...	2322	...	...	...	...
Velgast d.	...	|	2140	...	...	2340	...	...	...	...
Stralsund Hbf a.	...	2137*	2157	...	...	2357	...	...	...	...
Ostseebad Binz 844 a.	...	...	...	...	...	...	...	...	...	...

	Ⓐ	Ⓒ	Ⓐ	ICE 1599 ①–⑤ a		◇ Ⓐ S	ICE 1577 ①–⑤ a A ✕		◇ S	◇ Ⓐ	ICE 1179 ①–⑤ a✕
Ostseebad Binz 844 d.	...	...	...	...	...	...		...	...	...	...
Stralsund Hbf d.	...	...	...	...	...	0450	...	...	0558	0637	0623*
Velgast d.	...	...	...	...	...	0506	...	...	0614	0651	|
Ribnitz-Damgarten West d.	...	...	...	...	...	0525	...	...	0632	0705	|
Rövershagen a.	...	...	...	...	...	0536	...	...	0643	0723	|
Rostock Hbf a.	...	...	...	...	...	0607*	...	...	0714*	0806*	0810*
Rostock Hbf d.	...	...	...	0458	0508	...	0625	0708	...	...	0825
Bützow 836 d.	...	...	...	0518	0529	...	0645	0729	...	...	0845
Bad Kleinen 836 837 d.	...	...	...	0543	0558	...	0709	0758	...	...	|
Schwerin Hbf 837 d.	0350	0443	0452	0556	0611	...	0720	0811	...	...	0920
Büchen d.	0448	0540	0551	0634	0707t	...	|	0907t	...	...	|
Hamburg Hbf a.	0518	0610	0626	0704	0738	...	0816	0938	...	...	1016

	ICE 1579 ⑥ h A		◇ S	ICE 1671 A✕		◇ S	IC 2213 🍷♦		◇	IC 2239 ♦	ICE 1021 ⑥⑦ c ✕♦	ICE 1675 F✕		◇ S	ICE 1677 ⑧ b ✕♦		◇ S	E	ICE 1679 ⑦ w G✕	◇				◇ S		◇ S
Ostseebad Binz 844 d.	...	...	...	...	...	...	...	...	1102	...	...	...	...	...	...	...	...	...	...	1603	...	1702	...	...	...	...
Stralsund Hbf d.	0623*	...	0759	0823*	...	0959	1040*	...	1159	...	...	1223*	...	1359	1423*	...	1559	...	1623*	1658	...	1759	...	1959	...	2159
Velgast d.	|	...	0815	|	...	1015	|	...	1215	...	...	|	...	1415	|	...	1615	...	|	1711	...	1815	...	2015	...	2215
Ribnitz-Damgarten West d.	|	...	0833	|	...	1033	|	...	1233	...	...	|	...	1433	|	...	1633	...	|	1737t	...	1833	...	2033	...	2233
Rövershagen a.	|	...	0844	|	...	1044	|	...	1244	...	...	|	...	1444	|	...	1644	...	|	1747	...	1844	...	2044	...	2244
Rostock Hbf a.	0810*	...	0915*	1010*	...	1115*	1228*	...	1320*	...	...	1410*	...	1515*	1610*	...	1715*	...	1810*	1820*	...	1920*	...	2113*	...	2315*
Rostock Hbf d.	0825	0908	...	1025	1108	...	1244	1308	...	1405	1412	1425	1508	...	1625	1708	...	1809	1825	...	1908	...	2108	...	2313	...
Bützow 836 d.	0845	0929	...	1045	1129	...	1304	1329	...	1427	1434	1445	1529	...	1645	1729	...	1830	1845	...	1929	...	2129	...	2334	...
Bad Kleinen 836 837 d.	|	0958	...	|	1158	...	|	1358	...	1450	|	|	1558	...	|	1758	...	1903t	|	...	1958	...	2158	...	0000	...
Schwerin Hbf 837 d.	0920	1011	...	1120	1211	...	1339	1411	...	1459	1508	1520	1611	...	1720	1811	...	1914	1920	...	2011	...	2211	...	0010	...
Büchen d.	|	1107t	...	|	1307t	...	|	1507t	...	...	|	|	1707t	...	|	1907t	...	...	|	...	2107t	...	2303	...	...	...
Hamburg Hbf a.	1016	1138	...	1219	1338	...	1433	1538	...	...	1603	1616	1738	...	1816	1938	...	...	2019	...	2139	...	2339	...	...	...

♦ – NOTES (LISTED BY TRAIN NUMBER)

1021 – [12] ✕ Rostock - Hamburg - Köln - Frankfurt - Nürnberg.
1676 – [12] ✕ (Frankfurt ① **g** -) (Kassel ①–⑤ **a** -) (Hannover ①–⑥ **e** -) Hamburg - Rostock.
1677 – [12] ✕ Rostock - Hamburg - Hannover (- Frankfurt ⑤⑦ **r**).
2212 – RÜGEN – [12] 🍷 Koblenz - Köln - Hamburg - Rostock.
2213 – RÜGEN – [12] 🍷 Rostock - Hamburg - Köln.
2238 – WARNOW – [12] Leipzig - Magdeburg - Stendal - Rostock - Warnemünde (a. 1214).
2239 – WARNOW – [12] Warnemünde (d. 1343) - Rostock - Stendal - Magdeburg - Leipzig. On Apr. 8 Warnemünde d. 1329, Rostock d. 1348, Bützow a. 1408, d. 1427 and then as shown.

A – From / to Karlsruhe via Frankfurt, Gießen, Kassel, Hannover (Tables **806**, **900**, **912**).
E – ①②③④⑥ (not Apr. 8, 10).
F – To Frankfurt (Tables **806** and **900**).
G – To Göttingen (Table **900**).
H – ①–⑥ (not Mar. 4, Apr. 7, 10). From Hannover (Table **900**) on ①–⑤.
S – To / from Sassnitz (Table **844**).

a – Not Apr. 7, 10.
b – Not Apr. 9, 30.
c – Also Apr. 7, 10.
e – Not Apr. 10.
g – Also Apr. 11; not Apr. 10.
h – Also Apr. 7.
r – Also Apr. 6, 10; not Apr. 7, 9.
t – Arrives 6–7 minutes earlier.
v – Also Apr. 10.
w – Also Apr. 10; not Apr. 9.

* – Connecting service is by 🚌.
△ – 🚌 connection does not run on Apr. 8.
◇ – Operated by Ostdeutsche Eisenbahn.

848 MAGDEBURG - DESSAU - LEIPZIG and HALLE (SAALE)

RE / RB / S-Bahn services

AMENDED SERVICE JANUARY 28 - APRIL 21. See page 394 for service to January 27 and from April 22.

km		Ⓐ								
0	**Magdeburg** Hbf .... d.	0427	0517	0615j	0717	and hourly until	2017	2112	2202	2317
56	Roßlau (Elbe) ..... **847** d.	0510	0605	0705	0805		2105	2153	2252	0005
61	**Dessau** Hbf .... **847** d.	0515	0609	0709	0809		2109	2157	2256	0009
87	Bitterfeld .... a.	...	...	...	...		...	...	...	...
87	Bitterfeld .... d.	...	...	...	...		...	...	...	...
120	**Leipzig** Hbf .... a.	...	...	...	...		...	...	...	...

	Ⓐ			Ⓐ						
Leipzig Hbf .... d.	...	...	...	...	...	...	and hourly until	...	...	...
Bitterfeld .... a.	...	...	...	...	...	...		...	...	...
Bitterfeld .... d.	...	...	...	...	...	...		...	...	...
Dessau Hbf ..... **847** d.	0358	0448	0549	0627	0649	0749		2049	2148	2321
Roßlau (Elbe) ... **847** d.	0403	0453	0553	0632	0653	0753		2053	2153	2326
Magdeburg Hbf ..... a.	0452	0542	0642	0723	0742	0842		2142	2234	0014

DESSAU / LUTHERSTADT WITTENBERG - BITTERFELD - HALLE / LEIPZIG.

	Ⓒ B	Ⓒ			Ⓐ	Ⓒ	Ⓐ	Ⓐ	⑥		Ⓐ													
Lutherstadt Wittenberg ...... d.	0159	...	...	...	...	0413	...	0440	0503	...	0537k	0603	...	...	0703	...	...	0803	...	...	and at the same minutes past each hour until	1503	...	...
Dessau Hbf .... d.	|	...	...	*0344**	...	|	*0414**	|	|	*0443**	|	|	*0546**	*0620**	|	*0646**	*0720**	|	*0746**	*0820**		|	*1446**	*1520**
Wolfen .... d.	|	...	...	0433	...	|	0506	|	|	0532	|	|	0636	0706	|	0736	0806	|	0836	0906		|	1536	1606
Bitterfeld .... a.	0217	...	...	0439	...	0441	0511	0508	0540	0537	0611	0643	0641	0711	0740	0741	0811	0843	0841	0911		1540	1541	1611
Bitterfeld .... d.	0218	0247	...	0446	0442	0445	0512	0516	0545	0547	0612	0645	0646	0712	0745	0747	0812	0845	0847	0912		1545	1547	1612
Leipzig Hbf .... a.	|	0314	...	|	0513	0513	0543	|	0613	|	0643	0713	|	0743	0813	|	0843	0913	|	0943		1613	|	1643
Leipzig-Stötteritz .... ♥ a.	|	0326	...	|	0527	0527	0557	|	0627	|	0657	0727	|	0757	0827	|	0857	0927	|	0957		1627	|	1657
Halle (Saale) Hbf .... a.	0235	...	...	0507	...	...	...	0537	...	0607	...	...	0708	...	...	0807	...	...	0907	...		...	1607	...

Lutherstadt Wittenberg ...... d.	1604	...	...	1703	...	...	1803	...	...	1903	...	...	2017	...	...	2103	...	...	2217	...	...	...	...	...	...
Dessau Hbf .... d.	|	*1546**	*1620**	|	*1646**	*1720**	|	*1746**	*1820**	|	*1846**	*1920**	|	*1946**	*2020**	|	*2046**	*2120**	|	*2215**	...	...	*2311**	...	...
Wolfen .... d.	|	1636	1706	|	1736	1806	|	1836	1906	|	1936	2006	|	2036	2106	|	2136	2206	|	2312	...	...	0002	...	...
Bitterfeld .... a.	1643	1641	1711	1740	1741	1811	1843	1841	1911	1940	1941	2011	2044	2041	2111	2140	2141	2211	2244	2318	...	...	0007	...	...
Bitterfeld .... d.	1645	1647	1712	1745	1747	1812	1845	1847	1912	1945	1947	2012	2045	2047	2112	2145	2147	2212	2247	2319	2324	...	0008	...	...
Leipzig Hbf .... a.	1713	|	1743	1813	|	1843	1913	|	1943	2013	|	2043	2113	|	2143	2213	|	2243	|	2346	|	...	|	...	...
Leipzig-Stötteritz .... ♥ a.	1727	|	1757	1827	|	1857	1927	|	1957	2027	|	2057	2127	|	2157	2227	|	2257	|	2359	|	...	|	...	...
Halle (Saale) Hbf .... a.	...	1707	...	...	1807	...	...	1907	...	...	2007	...	...	2107	...	...	2207	...	2307	...	2345	...	0030	...	...

	Ⓒ	Ⓐ		Ⓐ				Ⓐ	Ⓒ A	Ⓐ											⊡			
Halle (Saale) Hbf .... d.	...	...	...	0355	...	0450	...	...	0551	0553	...	...	0650	...	...	0750	...	...	0850	...	and at the same minutes past each hour until	...	1450	...
Leipzig-Stötteritz .... ♥ d.	0006	0006	...	|	...	|	0434	0504	|	|	0534	0604	|	0634	0704	|	0734	0804	|	0834		1404	|	1434
Leipzig Hbf .... d.	0020	0020	...	|	...	|	0448	0518	|	|	0548	0618	|	0648	0718	|	0748	0818	|	0848		1418	|	1448
Bitterfeld .... a.	0046	0047	...	0416	...	0511	0515	0547	0614	0614	0615	0647	0711	0715	0747	0811	0815	0848	0911	0915		1447	1511	1515
Bitterfeld .... d.	0051	...	...	0421	...	0520	0516	0550	0620	0620	0620	0650	0720	0716	0750	0820	0820	0850	0920	0916		1450	1520	1516
Wolfen .... a.	|	...	...	|	...	0525	|	0555	|	|	0625	0655	0725	|	0755	0825	|	0855	0925	|		1455	1525	|
Dessau Hbf .... a.	|	...	...	|	...	*0615**	|	*0641**	|	|	*0715**	*0739**	*0815**	|	*0839**	*0915**	|	*0939**	*1015**	|		*1539**	*1615**	|
Lutherstadt Wittenberg ...... a.	0120	...	...	0450	...	...	0550	...	0658	0654	...	...	...	0757	...	...	0854	...	...	0957		...	...	1556

Halle (Saale) Hbf .... d.	...	1550	...	...	1650	...	...	1750	...	...	1850	...	...	1950	...	...	2050	...	...	2150	...	...	...	2324	...
Leipzig-Stötteritz .... ♥ d.	1504	|	1534	1604	|	1634	1704	|	1734	1804	|	1834	1904	|	1934	2004	|	2034	2104	|	2134	2204	...	|	2306
Leipzig Hbf .... d.	1518	|	1548	1618	|	1648	1718	|	1748	1818	|	1848	1918	|	1948	2018	|	2048	2118	|	2148	2218	...	|	2320
Bitterfeld .... a.	1547	1611	1615	1647	1711	1715	1747	1811	1815	1847	1911	1915	1947	2011	2015	2050	2111	2115	2147	2211	2215	2247	...	2346	2346
Bitterfeld .... d.	1550	1620	1620	1650	1720	1716	1750	1820	1820	1850	1920	1916	1950	2020	2020	2052	2120	2116	2150	2220	2220	2250	...	2351	2351
Wolfen .... a.	1555	1625	|	1655	1725	|	1755	1825	|	1855	1925	|	1955	2025	|	2057	2125	|	2155	2225	|	2255	...	2356	|
Dessau Hbf .... a.	*1639**	*1715**	|	*1739**	*1815**	|	*1839**	*1915**	|	*1939**	*2015**	|	*2039**	*2115**	|	*2143**	*2215**	|	*2245**	*2312**	|	*2345**	...	*0046**	|
Lutherstadt Wittenberg ...... a.	...	...	1654	...	...	1756	...	...	1854	...	...	1957	...	...	2054	...	...	2157	...	...	2254	...	...	...	0020

LUTHERSTADT WITTENBERG - DESSAU

km		Ⓐ	Ⓐ	Ⓒ	Ⓐ	⚒	Ⓐ				Ⓐ			Ⓐ								
0	**Lutherstadt Wittenberg** ..... d.	0404	0502	0516	0557	0616	0652	0716	and hourly until	1416	1452	1516	1616	1652	1716	1816	1916	2016	...	2216	...	...
32	Roßlau (Elbe) .... d.	0432	0532	0544	0626	0644	0717	0744		1444	1517	1544	1644	1717	1744	1844	1944	2044	...	2244	...	...
37	**Dessau** Hbf .... a.	0437	0536	0548	0631	0647	0721	0748		1448	1521	1548	1648	1721	1748	1848	1948	2048	...	2248	...	...

	Ⓐ		Ⓐ		⚒				Ⓐ		Ⓐ		Ⓐ		Ⓐ						
Dessau Hbf .... d.	0422	0509	0622	0710	0810	0910	and hourly until	1410	1435	1510	1532	1610	1635	1710	1732	1810	1910	2010	2110	...	2300
Roßlau (Elbe) .... d.	0426	0514	0626	0714	0814	0914		1414	1440	1514	1537	1614	1640	1714	1737	1814	1914	2014	2114	...	2304
Lutherstadt Wittenberg ...... a.	0454	0541	0654	0742	0842	0942		1442	1505	1542	1602	1642	1705	1742	1802	1842	1942	2042	2142	...	2332

A – To Stralsund via Berlin (Tables **851** and **845**).
B – From Schwedt via Berlin (Tables **845** and **851**).
j – 0617 on Ⓒ.
k – 0543 until Mar. 31.

* – By 🚌 to / from Wolfen.
⊡ – The 0934, 1134 and 1334 from Leipzig-Stötteritz depart Bitterfeld 4 minutes later and arrive Lutherstadt 3 minutes earlier.
♥ – Trains also call at City Tunnel stations Markt, Wilhelm-Leuschner-Platz, Bayerischer Bahnhof and MDR.

EUROPEAN RAIL PASSES

Rail passes represent excellent value for train travellers who are touring around Europe (or parts of it) or making a number of journeys within a short period. They can offer substantial savings over point-to-point tickets, as well as greater flexibility.

The principal pass schemes for Europe are **Interrail** for residents of Europe, and **Eurail** for those resident outside Europe. Both schemes have a choice of **Global** passes covering 33 countries, or **One Country Passes** for individual countries. Note, however, that you cannot use the pass in your country of residence. Passes are available in either a mobile (for use on your smart phone) or the more traditional Paper format.

Passes either cover a specified number of consecutive days, or are of the *flexi* type where you get so many 'travel days' within a specified period (you record your travel dates on each type of pass). Free travel requires the use of a travel day, whereas discounted travel does not.

Passes generally cover the ordinary services of the national rail companies, but supplements often have to be paid for travel on high-speed services, night trains, and 'global price' trains. Independent rail operators may not accept passes but may give discounts to passholders.

Interrail and Eurail

Europe-wide or single-country passes

Anyone of any age can buy a pass, either for pretty much the whole of Europe, or for an individual country. **Global** passes cover 33 countries of Europe and can either be *Continuous* passes for a set number of consecutive days or months, or *Flexi* passes for a certain number of travel days within a period of one or two months (you choose the travel days as you go along, writing the date on the pass). **One Country Passes** are all flexi passes for a certain number of days within one month (sometimes there is more than one country, as with the Benelux pass).

The two pass schemes (Interrail and Eurail) are now very similar, but Interrail passes are for **residents of Europe**, whilst Eurail passes are for those resident **outside Europe**. Turkey, Russia and the CIS countries count as Europe for this purpose. You may need proof of residence.

Passes can be purchased up to eleven months before travel begins. It's best to buy the pass online or in your own country before travelling, although most passes can also be purchased at major stations in Europe. Note, however, that the 4 day Global pass cannot be purchased from stations. Recommended retail prices are now the same for both Interrail and Eurail and are in Euros as shown below, but prices may vary between different outlets. At certain times of year special offer prices may be available. All passes are either for second class or first class travel (of course first class passes can also be used to travel in second class).

Passes come with a travel diary which has to be filled in with each journey. You cannot use the pass in your own country of residence. However, with an Interrail Global Pass you can make one outbound and one inbound journey in your country of residence (see next page).

INTERRAIL / EURAIL GLOBAL PASS - valid in 33 countries:
Austria, Belgium, Bosnia-Herzegovina, Bulgaria, Croatia, Czech Republic, Denmark, Estonia, Finland, France, Germany, Great Britain, Greece, Hungary, Ireland (including Northern Ireland), Italy, Latvia, Lithuania, Luxembourg, Montenegro, Netherlands, North Macedonia, Norway, Poland, Portugal, Romania, Serbia, Slovakia, Slovenia, Spain, Sweden, Switzerland and Turkey.

NOT VALID in the passholder's country of residence.

PRICES - INTERRAIL / EURAIL GLOBAL PASS - FIRST CLASS

Current prices	Adult (28-59) 1st cl.	Senior (60+) 1st cl.	Youth (12-27) 1st cl.	Child * (under 12) 1st cl.
FLEXI PASSES:				
4 days within 1 month	€328	€295	€246	€0
5 days within 1 month	€376	€338	€282	€0
7 days within 1 month	€446	€401	€335	€0
10 days within 2 months	€534	€481	€401	€0
15 days within 2 months	€657	€591	€493	€0
CONTINUOUS DAYS:				
15 days	€590	€531	€443	€0
22 days	€690	€621	€518	€0
1 month	€893	€804	€670	€0
2 months	€975	€878	€731	€0
3 months	€1202	€1082	€902	€0

PRICES - INTERRAIL / EURAIL GLOBAL PASS - SECOND CLASS

Current prices	Adult (28-59) 2nd cl.	Senior (60+) 2nd cl.	Youth (12-27) 2nd cl.	Child * (under 12) 2nd cl.
FLEXI PASSES:				
4 days within 1 month	€258	€232	€194	€0
5 days within 1 month	€296	€267	€223	€0
7 days within 1 month	€352	€317	€264	€0
10 days within 2 months	€421	€379	€316	€0
15 days within 2 months	€518	€466	€389	€0
CONTINUOUS DAYS:				
15 days	€465	€419	€349	€0
22 days	€544	€489	€408	€0
1 month	€704	€633	€528	€0
2 months	€768	€691	€575	€0
3 months	€947	€853	€711	€0

* Child: two children per fare paying Adult (not Senior) travel free.

website: www.interrail.eu www.eurail.com

INTERRAIL / EURAIL ONE COUNTRY PASS (OCP)

Covers any one of the participating countries below. **NOT** available for the passholder's country of residence. Note that Benelux passes (also the Eurail Scandinavia pass) actually cover more than one country. As with the Global pass, two children per fare paying Adult travel free.

Bosnia-Herzegovina and Montenegro do not have One Country Passes. There are some variations between Eurail and Interrail as shown below, for example Germany, Great Britain and Switzerland participate in the Interrail OCP scheme but not the Eurail OCP scheme as they have their own passes for overseas visitors (for Great Britain see under Britrail). The Scandinavia Pass only applies to Eurail, not Interrail.

Interrail: Germany* or Great Britain. Eurail: Germany* or Scandinavia (Norway, Sweden, Denmark, Finland combined)
**Senior passes not available, tickets cost 10% extra, other time periods available*

	Adult 1st cl.	Senior 1st cl.	Youth 1st cl.	Adult 2nd cl.	Senior 2nd cl.	Youth 2nd cl.
3 days within 1 month	€256	€230	€205	€202	€182	€174
4 days within 1 month	€291	€262	€233	€229	€206	€192
5 days within 1 month	€321	€289	€257	€253	€228	€219
6 days within 1 month	€349	€314	€279	€275	€248	€238
8 days within 1 month	€396	€356	€317	€312	€280	€270

Norway, Spain or Sweden *Norway only available for 2nd class*

	Adult 1st cl.	Senior 1st cl.	Youth 1st cl.	Adult 2nd cl.	Senior 2nd cl.	Youth 2nd cl.
3 days within 1 month	€227	€204	€182	€179	€161	€155
4 days within 1 month	€263	€237	€210	€207	€186	€180
5 days within 1 month	€294	€265	€235	€232	€209	€201
6 days within 1 month	€323	€291	€258	€254	€229	€221
8 days within 1 month	€374	€337	€299	€295	€266	€255

Interrail: Austria, France or Switzerland
Eurail: Austria or France
Eurail France Pass: 1, 2 and 7 day passes also for sale outside Europe

	Adult 1st cl.	Senior 1st cl.	Youth 1st cl.	Adult 2nd cl.	Senior 2nd cl.	Youth 2nd cl.
3 days within 1 month	€195	€176	€156	€153	€138	€133
4 days within 1 month	€230	€207	€184	€182	€164	€158
5 days within 1 month	€262	€236	€210	€207	€186	€179
6 days within 1 month	€291	€262	€233	€229	€206	€198
8 days within 1 month	€344	€310	€275	€271	€244	€235

Benelux, Denmark, Finland, Ireland or Italy*
Benelux is Belgium, Netherlands and Luxembourg combined
Ireland includes Northern Ireland
** Prices for Passes are 5% higher than shown*

	Adult 1st cl.	Senior 1st cl.	Youth 1st cl.	Adult 2nd cl.	Senior 2nd cl.	Youth 2nd cl.
3 days within 1 month	€161	€145	€129	€127	€114	€110
4 days within 1 month	€194	€175	€155	€153	€138	€132
5 days within 1 month	€225	€203	€180	€177	€160	€153
6 days within 1 month	€253	€228	€202	€200	€180	€172
8 days within 1 month	€305	€275	€244	€240	€216	€208

Czech Republic, Estonia, Greece, Hungary, Portugal or Romania

	Adult 1st cl.	Senior 1st cl.	Youth 1st cl.	Adult 2nd cl.	Senior 2nd cl.	Youth 2nd cl.
3 days within 1 month	€123	€111	€98	€97	€87	€84
4 days within 1 month	€152	€137	€122	€120	€108	€104
5 days within 1 month	€179	€161	€143	€141	€127	€122
6 days within 1 month	€205	€185	€164	€162	€146	€140
8 days within 1 month	€253	€228	€202	€200	€180	€172

Bulgaria, Croatia, Latvia, Lithuania, North Macedonia, Poland, Serbia, Slovakia, Slovenia or Turkey

	Adult 1st cl.	Senior 1st cl.	Youth 1st cl.	Adult 2nd cl.	Senior 2nd cl.	Youth 2nd cl.
3 days within 1 month	€78	€70	€62	€62	€56	€54
4 days within 1 month	€99	€89	€79	€78	€70	€67
5 days within 1 month	€119	€107	€95	€93	€84	€81
6 days within 1 month	€139	€125	€111	€109	€99	€95
8 days within 1 month	€176	€158	€141	€139	€125	€120

Interrail and Eurail - continued

GREEK ISLANDS PASS

This is a special ferry pass available in both the Interrail and Eurail schemes. It is valid on ferries operated by the Attica Group, which includes Superfast Ferries, Blue Star Ferries and Hellenic Seaways. The 4 day pass is valid for five domestic trips on ferries within Greece. The 6 day pass is valid for two international trips between Italy and Greece plus four domestic trips in Greece. The 6 day pass includes accommodation in either 1st or 2nd class, also rail/bus transfers between Patras and Piraeus. Both passes give 30% discount on additional ferry trips.

	Adult 1st cl.	Senior 1st cl.	Youth 1st cl.	Adult 2nd cl.	Senior 2nd cl.	Youth 2nd cl.
4 days within 1 month	N/A	N/A	N/A	€95	€85	€71
6 days within 1 month	€208	€187	€182	€185	€167	€163

OVERNIGHT TRAVEL

Passes do not include supplements for travel in sleeping car or couchette accommodation and these have to be purchased separately. Many overnight trains have a *global* price where the ticket price includes the sleeping accommodation - in these cases pass holders pay a specified supplement or passholder fare (see below for further details).

Holders of flexi passes travelling overnight and leaving before midnight need to record the date of departure in the travel diary, and of course the pass can be used for the whole of that day. Pass holders will not need to activate a second day on their pass for the day of arrival unless they board a second train (but the day of arrival does need to be within the overall validity of the pass). The rule can also be used for late evening trains arriving after midnight. If you need to use a connecting train having arrived overnight it may be worth buying a regular ticket to avoid having to use a travel day.

Note that this replaced the previous 7pm rule whereby pass holders had to write the day of arrival on their passes, rather than the day of departure, for night trains departing after 7pm.

FREE TRAVEL TO THE BORDER, AIRPORT OR SEAPORT

Although it is not possible to purchase an Interrail pass for the holder's own country of residence, a Global pass entitles the holder to two free journeys (one outbound, one inbound) between any station in their country of residence and its border, an airport or seaport. Each journey must be completed in one day (no overnight stops allowed), at any time within the overall validity of the pass, or include a travel day if using a flexi pass. Details must be entered in the travel diary.

SUPPLEMENTS AND RESERVATION FEES

Required for certain types of high-speed or 'global price' train.

International day train examples, 2nd class (subject to change): France - Italy *TGV* €31; *Berlin - Warszawa Express* €4; *EC Switzerland - Italy* €11; *Eurostar* €30 - 35 (€38 - 43 in standard premier with 1st class pass); *TGV / ICE* France - Germany from €13; *TGV Lyria* (France - Switzerland) from €21; *SJ Snabbtåg* Stockholm - København €6.60; *IC bus* Klagenfurt - Venezia €9. Higher fares apply if pass not valid in both countries.

Domestic examples (approximate; subject to alteration): **Croatia** *IC / ICN* €3.60. **Czech Republic** *SC* up to €8. **Finland** *Pendolino* €5 - 10. **France** *TGV* €10 limited allocation (otherwise €20), *Intercités* with compulsory reservation €10. **Hungary** *IC* €3.50. **Italy** *FA, FB* and *FR* €10, *IC* €3. **Norway** long-distance trains €6. **Poland** *EIP* €0 - 3.50, *EIC / TLK* €0 - 3.50. **Portugal** *AP / IC* €5. **Romania** *IC/IR* €1 - 3.60. **Slovakia** *IC* €3 - 9. **Slovenia** *ICS* €2 - 4. **Spain** *AVE* €10, most other long-distance trains €6.50, *MD / Avant* €4. **Sweden** *Snabbtåg* €7.

Night trains: sleeping accommodation is typically €15 to €75 for a couchette, and €35 to €144 for a berth in a sleeping car. Some trains also include reclining seats. Many night trains are globally priced and fares for passholders vary widely.

As some of the supplements / passholder fares can be rather high, it's worth checking whether a regular advance purchase ticket might be a better option, particularly if booked a month or two ahead. Supplements can often be avoided altogether by taking slower regional trains.

VALIDITY ON PRIVATE RAILWAYS

Passes are valid on the national railway companies in each country, plus many privately run railways (some give discounts). For details see www.interrail.eu, www.eurail.com, or the Traveller's Guide that comes with your pass.

Selected details are as follows (subject to change): **Austria**: free travel on WESTbahn, GYSEV, RegioJet and ROeEE. **Czech Republic**: valid on Leo Express and RegioJet. **Denmark**: free travel on Arriva, DSB-Øresund / S-Tog, and Nordjyske Jernbaner. **France**: SNCF bus services included. **Germany**: free on most regional services and many private companies. **Hungary**: GySEV/Raaberbahn services are included. **Italy**: free travel on Trenord and Leonardo Express (1st class only). **Netherlands**: privately run regional lines are included. **Norway**: Flåmsbana (Myrdal - Flåm) gives 30% discount. **Poland**: valid on Koleje Dolnośląskie, Przewozy Regionaine. **Spain**: FEVE is included. **Sweden**: most private operators are included. **Switzerland**: free travel on AB, ASM, AVA, BDWM, BLS, BLT, CJ, FART, FW, LEB, MBC, MGB, MOB/MVR, NStCM, RA, RhB, SOB, SSIF, THURBO, TMR, TPC, TPF, TRAVYS, TRN, WB, WSB and ZB. Others offer 25 - 50% discount, including BET, BGF, BLM, BOB, HB, LSMS-Isms, JB, PB, RB, SMF-Ism, SMtS, SthB, WAB. Discounted fare on William Tell Express (rail and boat tour).

VALIDITY ON FERRY AND BUS SERVICES

Global passes includes free deck passage between Italy and Greece on SuperFast Ferries (you pay port taxes and possibly a fuel surcharge); free air-type seats for 1st class pass holders; 30% discount if pass only valid in Italy or Greece. Many other ferry companies offer discounts (not usually on cabins), for example: Balearia 20%, Finnlines 50%, Fjord Line 30%, Grimaldi 20%, Irish Ferries 30%, Minoan Ferries 20%, Tallink Silja 20% (high-season), up to 50% (low-season), Viking Line up to 50%.

Most Swiss lakes give 50%. The following bus services in Scandinavia between Sweden and Finland are included; Luleå - Haparanda (Länstrafiken Norrbotten), Haparanda - Tornio - Kemi (Net-matkat).

Other benefits are often available, such as hotel discounts, bike hire discounts, free entry to railway museums, and access to railway station lounges.

Where to Buy your Pass

Sources of rail passes (and point to point tickets) include the following:

ACP Rail www.acprail.com

All Aboard www.allaboard.eu

Deutsche Bahn UK (German Railways) www.bahn.com
UK Booking Centre ✆ 08718 80 80 66

Eurail – buy at www.eurail.com or see www.eurailgroup.org for a list of sales partners. All participating European railway companies sell passes.

Ffestiniog Travel www.ffestiniogtravel.com
Former St Mary's Church, Tremadog, Porthmadog, Gwynedd LL49 9RA
✆ 01766 512400

French Railways www.sncf.com

International Rail www.internationalrail.com
PO Box 153, Alresford, Hampshire SO24 4AQ ✆ 0871 231 0790

Interrail www.interrail.eu.
All participating railway companies sell passes.

Interrail by National Rail www.myinterrail.co.uk

Rail Canterbury www.rail-canterbury.co.uk
PO Box 1178, Canterbury, Kent CT1 9QJ
email: rail@rail-canterbury.co.uk

Rail Europe www.raileurope.co.uk
Also raileurope.de, raileurope.it, raileurope.es

RailTourGuide www.railtourguide.com
Suite 42, 7 - 15 Pink Lane, Newcastle upon Tyne, NE1 5DW
✆ 0191 246 0708

Switzerland Travel Centre www.stc.co.uk
30 - 33 Minories, London, EC3N 1DD ✆ 0207 420 4900
Visits by appointment only.

Trainseurope www.trainseurope.co.uk
4th Floor, Silverstream House, 45 Fitzroy Street, Fitzrovia, London, W1T 6EB ✆ 01354 660222 email: sales@trainseurope.co.uk.
Visits by appointment only.

Other useful websites:

www.seat61.com
www.ricksteves.com.

BritRail

BritRail is a pass for overseas visitors to Great Britain, allowing unlimited travel on the national rail network in England, Scotland and Wales. It is not available to residents of Great Britain, Northern Ireland, the Isle of Man or the Channel Islands. Passes must be purchased before arriving in Britain. Youth prices apply to ages 16 to 25, senior applies to 60+. All passes are available for First or Standard class. For further details see www.britrail.com or www.acprail.com.

BRITRAIL CONSECUTIVE PASS

(USD prices)	Adult 1st cl.	Youth 1st cl.	Senior 1st cl.	Adult Std cl.	Youth Std cl.	Senior Std cl.
2 days	205	124	174	136	82	116
3 days	307	184	261	203	122	173
4 days	381	229	324	252	151	214
8 days	543	326	462	365	197	310
15 days	802	482	682	543	326	462
22 days	1019	612	867	679	408	577
1 month	1207	725	1026	802	482	682

BRITRAIL FLEXIPASS

(USD prices)	Adult 1st cl.	Youth 1st cl.	Senior 1st cl.	Adult Std cl.	Youth Std cl.	Senior Std cl.
2 days within 1 month	256	153	217	173	104	147
3 days within 1 month	381	229	324	258	155	219
4 days within 1 month	469	281	398	323	194	275
8 days within 1 month	689	414	586	462	278	393
15 days within 2 months	1029	618	875	695	417	591

BRITRAIL ENGLAND PASSES

The Britrail England Pass excludes Wales and Scotland, giving a saving of approximately 20%. Britrail South West and North of England Rover passes are also available. All three are available in consecutive and flexi versions (no 2-day passes).

BRITRAIL LONDON PLUS PASS

This 'flexi' pass allows unlimited rail travel in London and the surrounding area. You can visit such places as Canterbury, Salisbury, Bristol, Bath, Oxford, Cambridge, Stratford-Upon-Avon, Worcester, Ely, Kings Lynn, and anywhere on the coast between Harwich to Weymouth.

(USD prices)	Adult 1st cl.	Youth 1st cl.	Senior 1st cl.	Adult Std cl.	Youth Std cl.	Senior Std cl.
3 days within 1 month	222	144	189	158	103	135
4 days within 1 month	256	167	218	193	125	164
8 days within 1 month	363	236	309	267	174	227

BRITRAIL SCOTLAND PASSES

Three different passes are available, all standard class adult passes: Spirit of Scotland covers the whole country; available as 4 days within 8 days, or 8 days within 15 days. The other areas are Central Scotland (3 days consecutive), and Highlands (4 days within 8 days).

M-PASS

All Britrail Passes are available as a mobile ticket on your mobile phone (saving shipping cost) - see www.acprail.com.

DISCOUNTS

Saver Discount: groups of 3 to 9 people receive a discount of up to 20%. Passes must be of the same type (BritRail, BritRail England and BritRail SouthWest passes only) and duration and the party must travel together at all times. Cannot be combined with the family discount.

Family Discount: if any adult or senior pass is purchased, one accompanying child (aged 5 - 15) may receive a free pass of the same type and duration. Any further children travelling receive a 50% discount. All children under 5 travel free.

Other International Passes

BALKAN FLEXIPASS

Precise details of the validity of this pass has been difficult to obtain and so readers are advised to check locally if intending to travel in the area with this pass. The following prices have been advised by both BDZ (Bulgaria Railways) and ŽPCG (Railway Transport of Montenegro), who additionally advise that passes can be purchased at Bar and Podgorica stations. ŽFBH (Railways of Bosnia and Herzegovina) have also confirmed acceptance of this pass on its network.

Unlimited travel in Bosnia & Herzegovina, Bulgaria, Greece, Montenegro, North Macedonia, Serbia and Turkey (also trains operated by Regio Călători in Romania). Valid for any 3 / 5 / 7 / 10 / 15 days in two months: 1st class € 127 / 180 / 243 / 314 / 378; 2nd class € 91 / 134 / 183 / 233 / 280. 40% discount for under 28s, 20% for 60+, 50% for children (4-12), 33% discount for residents of the above countries. Supplements for *IC* trains.

Free travel on Attica Group ferries (Superfast Ferries / Blue Star / ANEK) Patras - Corfu / Ancona / Bari (port taxes and high season supplements apply); 30% discount on Attica Group (Superfast / Blue Star) routes within Greece. Note that if purchased from one of the above countries the pass allows only a return journey from place of issue to the border of a neighbouring participating country before unlimited travel is possible.

BODENSEE TICKET

Unlimited travel by rail, bus and ferry in border region Austria / Germany / Switzerland surrounding the Bodensee (Lake Constance). One day 47 CHF / € 38, 3 days 73 CHF / € 59. Discounts for children and families. Not valid on ICE / IC / EC trains In Germany or on Friedrichshafen - Konstanz catamarans. Zonal versions also available for smaller areas.

EUREGIO TICKET MAAS-RHEIN

One days unlimited travel in border region Belgium / Netherlands / Germany by rail and bus (covers Liège, Hasselt, Maastricht, Roermond, Aachen, Düren). In Germany and Belgium covers only local trains and buses. Price €20. At weekends / public holidays valid as a family ticket (2 adults plus 3 children under 12).

ÖRESUND RUNDT

2022 prices

Two days unlimited travel on trains and buses in the København, Malmö and Helsingborg area (includes the metro in København). The Öresund can only be crossed by rail in one direction; the Helsingborg - Helsingør ferry (included) must be used in the other direction. Available in Denmark from København Tourist Office (price 249 DKK) and in Sweden from Skånetrafiken (price 299 SEK); children 7-15 half price.

PASS ALSACE - RHEIN-NECKAR

A day ticket valid on Saturdays, Sundays and French public holidays covering local trains (2nd class), buses and trams in the Rhein-Neckar area (VRN) centered on Mannheim and Heidelberg, the Karlsruhe area (KVV), plus local trains in the Bas Rhin area of France centered on Strasbourg. Price € 19 for one person or € 31.50 for a group of 2 - 5 people.

PASSBASK

One day's travel in the area between Bayonne in France and San Sebastian in Spain on SNCF trains (includes *TGV* but not night trains) and EuskoTren services. A barrier pass for EuskoTren should be obtained at Hendaye station. Price € 12, child aged 4 - 12 € 8.

SAAR-LOR-LUX TICKET

One day's unlimited 2nd class travel on Saturday or Sunday throughout Saarland (i.e. Saarbrücken area of Germany, local trains only), Lorraine (i.e. Metz, Nancy, Épinal area of France) and all CFL trains in Luxembourg. Price € 27 (€29 over the counter in Germany); for groups of 2 - 5 people add € 11 per extra person. Not valid on *TGV* or *ICE* trains.

OTHER PASSES

A range of day tickets is available covering areas of the Czech Republic and adjoining countries:
Euro-Neisse Ticket (Liberec, Jelenia Góra, Zittau, Görlitz area; www.zvon.de). **EgroNet-Ticket** (Cheb, Karlovy Vary, Plauen, Zwickau, Hof, Bayreuth; www.egronet.de).
Bayern-Böhmen Ticket (border areas of Bavaria / Bohemia).
Sachsen-Böhmen Ticket (Liberec, Děčín, Dresden area).
Elbe-Labe Ticket (Chomutov, Ústí nad Labem, Dresden area).

Railplus

Railplus cards are valid for one year and offer a discount of 15% on cross-border rail travel (excluding supplements) between the participating countries, which are Austria, Bosnia and Herzegovina, Bulgaria, Croatia, Czech Republic, Denmark, Finland, Germany, Greece, Hungary, Italy, Latvia, Lithuania, Luxembourg, Montenegro, Netherlands, North Macedonia, Poland, Romania, Serbia, Slovakia, Slovenia and Switzerland.

There are no discounts on Eurostar, Thalys or TGV services. Cards are not available for sale in all participating countries, and you may be required to hold a national railcard for the country where you buy the pass, in addition to the Railplus card. In the Netherlands it is only available to annual season ticket holders.

The Summer and Winter seasonal editions of the European Rail Timetable (published in June and December) include an extended Rail Passes feature featuring a host of additional passes covering individual countries or specific areas. It also includes many city-wide tickets and tourist passes for popular cities across Europe.

850 BERLIN - HALLE / LEIPZIG - ERFURT - FRANKFURT / NÜRNBERG

See Table **902** for other services Berlin - Frankfurt via Braunschweig. See Table **927** for services operated by FlixTrain.

Other regional services: Table **845** Berlin - Lutherstadt Wittenberg. Table **848** Lutherstadt Wittenberg - Bitterfeld - Leipzig / Halle. Table **849** Leipzig / Halle - Weimar - Erfurt - Eisenach.

km		IC 95	IC 1950	IC 1950	ICE 1658	ICE 1656	ICE 1656	ICE 1501	ICE 501	ICE 571	ICE 71	ICE 1701	ICE 1001	ICE 1654	ICE 503	ICE 573	ICE 73	ICE 701	ICE 1003	ICE 1652	ICE 505	ICE 575	ICE 75	ICE 703
		T	①H ⊙	①F ⊙	①–⑤ a✕	①–⑥ e✕		Ⓐ L✕	①–⑥ e✕	✕	C✕	①–⑤ a✕	✕	✕	✕	✕	C✕	✕	✕	✕	✕	✕	C✕	✕
	Hamburg Hbf **840** d.	...	...	...	...	...	...	...	...	...	...	...	...	...	...	...	...	0527a	0552	...	0634e	...	...	0735
0	**Berlin** Hbf d.	...	0010	0020	...	...	...	...	0430	0504	0526	0534	0600	...	0629	0704	0726	0734	0804	...	0829	0904	0926	0934
6	**Berlin** Südkreuz d.	...	|	0027	...	...	...	...	0437	0511	0533	0540	0607	...	0636	0711	0733	0741	0811	...	0836	0911	0933	0941
97	Lutherstadt Wittenberg d.	...	|	0112	...	...	...	...	0511	|	0610	|	|	...	0711	|	0810	|	|	...	0911	|	1010	|
134	Bitterfeld d.	...	0151	0131	...	...	...	...	|	|	|	0633	|	...	|	|	|	0833	|	...	|	|	|	1033
	Halle (Saale) Hbf d.	0110z	0208	0151	...	...	...	...	|	0618	|	0652	0712	...	|	0818	|	0852	0918	...	|	1018	|	1052
	Dresden Hbf **842** d.	|	|	|	...	...	...	...	|	|	|	|	|	0610	|	|	|	|	|	0810	|	|	|	|
167	**Leipzig** Hbf a.	|	0229	0213	...	...	...	...	0542	|	0642	|	|	0726	0742	|	0842	|	|	0926	0942	|	1042	|
167	**Leipzig** Hbf d.	0035z	0235	0235	...	0533	...	...	0548	|	0648	|	|	0733	0748	|	0848	|	|	0933	0948	|	1048	|
287	**Erfurt** Hbf a.	|	0350	0350	...	0616	...	...	0629	0648	0728	0724p	0740	0816	0829	0848	0928	0924p	0945	1016	1029	1048	1128	1124p
287	**Erfurt** Hbf **849a** d.	|	0357	0357	0514	0618	...	...	0631	0650	0730	0732	0745	0818	0831	0850	0930	0932	0947	1018	1031	1050	1130	1132
	Coburg **875** d.	|	|	|	|	|	...	...	0704	|	|	|	|	|	|	|	|	|	|	|	|	|	|	|
	Bamberg **875** d.	0421	|	|	|	|	...	0643	0728	|	|	0818	|	|	0917	|	|	1017	|	|	1117	|	|	1217
	Erlangen **875** d.	0443	|	|	|	|	...	0709	0753	|	|	|	|	|	0938	|	|	|	|	|	1138	|	|	|
	Nürnberg Hbf **875** a.	0502	|	|	|	|	...	0725	0808	|	|	0852	0856	|	0953	|	|	1052	1056	|	1153	|	|	1250
	München Hbf **904 905** a.	...	|	|	|	|	...	0841	0917	|	|	1042	1002	|	1102	|	|	1242	1202	|	1302	|	|	1402
315	Gotha **849a** d.	...	0416	0416	0531	0634	...	...	...	|	|	...	...	0833	...	|	|	...	...	1033	...	|	|	...
344	**Eisenach** **849a** d.	...	0432	0432	0547	0648	...	...	...	|	0755	...	...	0848	...	|	0956	...	...	1048	...	|	1155	...
401	Bad Hersfeld d.	...	0506	0506	0616	0716	...	...	...	|	|	...	...	0916	...	|	|	...	...	1116	...	|	|	...
443	Fulda **900/1/2** d.	...	0538	0538	0644	0743	...	...	...	|	0850	...	...	0943	...	|	1050	...	...	1143	...	|	1250	...
524	Hanau Hbf **901** d.	...	0623	0623	|	|	...	...	...	|	0934	...	...	|	...	|	1134	...	...	|	...	|	1334	...
547	**Frankfurt** (Main) Hbf **900/1/2** ◇ a.	...	0639	0639	0739•	0836	0842	...	...	0859	0952	...	...	1036	...	1100	1152	...	...	1236	...	1259	1352	...
558	**Frankfurt** Flughafen ✈ § ◇ a.	...	...	...	0751	0854	0854	...	...	0918	...	...	...	1054	...	1118	...	...	...	1254	...	1318	...	...
	Stuttgart Hbf **912** a.	...	...	...	...	|	|	...	...	1038	...	...	...	|	...	1238	...	...	...	|	...	1438	...	...
586	**Mainz** Hbf ◇ a.	...	...	...	...	0915	0915	...	...	...	...	...	...	1115	...	...	...	...	...	1315	...	...	...	...
596	**Wiesbaden** Hbf ◇ a.	...	...	...	...	0933	0933	...	...	...	...	...	...	1133	...	...	...	...	...	1333	...	...	...	...

	ICE 93	ICE 1093	ICE 1650	ICE 507	ICE 577	ICE 77	ICE 705	ICE 1005	ICE 1558	ICE 509	ICE 579	IC 1956	ICE 79	IC 1956	ICE 707	ICE 1138	ICE 1556	ICE 1707	ICE 1601	ICE 1711	ICE 771	ICE 1171	ICE 709	ICE 1007
	A✕	✕	✕	✕	✕	C✕	✕	✕	✕	✕	✕	⑦w D🍷	C✕	⑦w D🍷	✕	⑤⑦ v✕	✕	✕	✕	O✕	✕	C✕	✕	✕
Hamburg Hbf **840** d.	0804	...	...	0834	...	...	0936	1005	...	1034	...	...	...	...	1136	...	...	1203	1234	...	...	...	1336	1404
Berlin Hbf d.	1004	1004	...	1029	1105	1126	1134	1204	...	1229	1304	...	1326	...	1334	1411	...	1404	1429	1429	1505	1526	1534	1604
Berlin Südkreuz d.	1011	1011	...	1036	1111	1133	1141	1211	...	1236	1311	...	1333	...	1341	1419	...	1411	1436	1436	1511	1533	1541	1611
Lutherstadt Wittenberg d.	|	|	...	1111	|	1210	|	|	...	1311	|	...	1410	...	|	|	...	|	1511	1511	|	1610	|	|
Bitterfeld d.	|	|	...	|	|	|	1233	|	...	|	|	...	|	...	1433	|	...	|	|	|	|	|	1633	|
Halle (Saale) Hbf d.	1118	1118	...	|	1218	|	1252	1318	...	|	1418	...	|	...	1452	|	...	1518	|	|	1618	|	1653	1718
Dresden Hbf **842** d.	|	|	1010	|	|	|	|	|	1210	|	|	...	|	...	|	|	1410	|	|	|	|	|	|	|
Leipzig Hbf a.	|	|	1126	1142	|	1242	|	|	1326	1342	|	...	1442	...	|	|	1526	|	1542	1542	|	1642	|	|
Leipzig Hbf d.	|	|	1133	1148	|	1248	|	|	1333	1348	|	1349	1448	...	|	|	1533	|	1548	1548	|	1648	|	|
Erfurt Hbf a.	1152	1152	1216	1229	1248	1328	1324p	1345	1416	1429	1448	1515	1528	...	1524p	|	1616	1552	1629	1629	1648	1728	1724p	1745
Erfurt Hbf **849a** d.	1154	1154	1218	1231	1250	1330	1332	1347	1418	1431	1450	1517	1530	...	1532	|	1618	1554	1631	1631	1650	1730	1732	1747
Coburg **875** d.	1229	1229	|	|	|	|	|	|	|	|	|	|	|	...	|	|	|	1629	|	|	|	|	|	|
Bamberg **875** d.	|	|	|	1317	|	|	1417	|	|	1516	|	|	|	...	1617	|	|	|	|	|	|	|	1817	|
Erlangen **875** d.	|	|	|	1338	|	|	|	|	|	1538	|	|	|	...	|	|	|	|	1738	1738	|	|	|	|
Nürnberg Hbf **875** a.	1323	1323	|	1353	|	|	1452	1456	|	1552	|	|	|	...	1652	|	|	1724	1753	1753	|	|	1852	1856
München Hbf **904 905** a.	...	1517	|	1503	|	|	1642	1601	|	1701	|	|	|	←	1803	|	|	1917	1903	1903	|	|	2043	2002
Gotha **849a** d.	...	...	1233	...	|	|	...	...	1433	...	|	1535	|	1547	...	|	1633	...	...	...	|	|	...	...
Eisenach **849a** d.	...	...	1248	...	|	1356	...	...	1448	...	|	→	1555	1604	...	1630	1648	...	...	...	|	1755	...	...
Bad Hersfeld d.	...	...	1316	...	|	|	...	...	1516	...	|	...	|	1632	...	|	1716	...	...	...	|	|	...	...
Fulda **900/1/2** d.	...	...	1343	...	|	1450	...	...	1543	...	|	...	1650	1700	...	1736	1743	...	...	...	|	1850	...	...
Hanau Hbf **901** d.	...	...	|	...	|	1534	...	...	|	...	|	...	1734	|	...	|	|	...	...	...	|	1934	...	...
Frankfurt (Main) Hbf **900/1/2** ◇ a.	...	...	1436	...	1459	1559	...	...	1636	...	1659	...	1752	1753•	...	1832	1836	...	...	...	1859	1952	...	...
Frankfurt Flughafen ✈ § ◇ a.	...	...	1454	...	1518	...	...	...	1654	...	1718	...	...	...	...	|	1854	...	...	...	1918	...	...	...
Stuttgart Hbf **912** a.	...	...	|	...	1638	...	...	...	|	...	1838	...	...	...	...	1958w	|	...	...	...	2038	...	...	...
Mainz Hbf ◇ a.	...	...	1515	...	...	...	...	...	1715	...	...	...	...	...	...	...	1915	...	...	...	...	...	...	...
Wiesbaden Hbf ◇ a.	...	...	1533	...	...	...	...	...	1733	...	...	...	...	...	...	...	1933	...	...	...	...	...	...	...

	ICE 1136	ICE 1554	ICE 1564	ICE 603	ICE 773	ICE 273	ICE 801	ICE 1009	ICE 1552	ICE 1705	ICE 1605	ICE 1715	ICE 775	ICE 697	ICE 803	ICE 1109	ICE 1550	ICE 1607	ICE 1607	ICE 1607	ICE 699	EN 40458	NJ 408	IC 2277
	⑦w ✕	S✕	✕	✕	✕	Y✕	K✕	✕	✕	Ⓑb J✕	Ⓑ ✕	⑥ O✕	E✕		✕	✕	Ⓑq ✕	✕	Ⓑb ✕	⑤f ✕	M	N	♣	B
Hamburg Hbf **840** d.	...	...	...	1435	1450	...	1536	1551	...	1634	1634	...	...	1924	1735	...	...	1835	1835	1835	1936	...	...	...
Berlin Hbf d.	1614	...	...	1629	1704	1726	1734	1804	...	1829	1829	1829	1905	|	1926	2004	...	2029	2029	2029	2126	...	2051	2228
Berlin Südkreuz d.	1620	...	...	1636	1711	1733	1741	1811	...	1836	1836	1836	1911	|	1933	2011	...	2036	2036	2036	2133	...	2101	2234
Lutherstadt Wittenberg d.	|	...	...	1711	|	1810	|	|	...	1911	1911	1911	|	|	2009	|	...	2111	2111	2111	2212	...	|	2317
Bitterfeld d.	|	...	...	|	|	|	1833	|	...	|	|	|	|	|	2025	|	...	|	|	|	2229	...	|	2334
Halle (Saale) Hbf d.	|	...	...	|	1818	|	1852	1918	...	|	|	|	2018	|	|	2118	...	|	|	|	|	...	2228	|
Dresden Hbf **842** d.	|	1610	...	|	|	|	|	|	1810	|	|	|	|	|	|	|	...	|	|	|	|	2110	|	|
Leipzig Hbf a.	|	1726	...	1742	|	1842	|	|	1926	1942	1942	1942	|	|	2044	|	...	2142	2142	2142	2248	2219	2249	2358
Leipzig Hbf d.	|	1733	1733	1748	|	1848	|	|	1933	...	1948	1948	|	|	2050	|	2133	...	2148	2148	2255	2346	2346	...
Erfurt Hbf a.	1756	1816	1816	1829	1848	1928	1924	1945	2016	...	2029	2029	2048	◐	2129	2145	2216	...	2229	2229	2335	0122	0122	...
Erfurt Hbf **849a** d.	1758	1818	1818	1831	1850	1930	1932	1947	2018	...	2031	2031	2050	|	2131	2147	2218	...	...	2235	2341	0124	0124	...
Coburg **875** d.	|	|	|	|	|	|	|	|	|	...	|	|	|	|	2206	|	|	...	...	|	|	|	|	...
Bamberg **875** d.	|	|	|	1916	|	|	2017	|	|	...	|	|	|	|	2230	|	|	...	...	2321	|	|	|	...
Erlangen **875** d.	|	|	|	1938	|	|	|	|	|	...	2137	2137	|	|	2252	|	|	...	...	2342	|	|	|	...
Nürnberg Hbf **875** a.	|	|	|	1952	|	|	2052	2056	|	...	2152	2152	|	|	2309	2256	|	...	...	2357	|	|	|	...
München Hbf **904 905** a.	|	|	|	2103	|	|	2244	2201	|	...	2302	2303	|	|	...	0001	|	...	...	0114	|	|	|	...
Gotha **849a** d.	|	1833	1833	...	|	|	...	...	2033	...	...	...	|	|	...	...	2233	...	...	...	2356	|	|	...
Eisenach **849a** d.	1829	1848	1848	...	|	1956	...	...	2048	...	...	...	|	|	...	...	2247	...	...	...	0012	|	|	...
Bad Hersfeld d.	|	1916	1916	...	|	|	...	...	2116	...	...	...	|	|	...	...	2316	...	...	...	|	|	|	...
Fulda **900/1/2** d.	1935	1943	1943	...	|	2050	...	...	2143	...	...	...	|	2248	...	...	2343	...	...	...	|	|	|	...
Hanau Hbf **901** d.	2016	|	|	...	|	2134	...	...	|	...	...	...	|	2328	...	...	0022	...	...	...	|	|	|	...
Frankfurt (Main) Hbf **900/1/2** ◇ a.	2032	2036	2036	...	2059	2153	...	...	2236	...	...	...	2259	2350	...	...	0040	...	...	...	0211	0346	0346	...
Frankfurt Flughafen ✈ § ◇ a.	|	...	2056	...	2118	...	...	...	...	...	...	...	2318	|	...	...	...	...	...	...	0238	...	...	...
Stuttgart Hbf **912** a.	2158	...	|	...	2255	...	...	...	...	...	...	...	...	|	...	...	...	...	...	...	0452	...	...	...
Mainz Hbf ◇ a.	...	...	2115	...	...	...	...	...	...	...	...	...	...	0043	...	...	...	...	...	...	...	...	...	...
Wiesbaden Hbf ◇ a.	...	...	2133	...	...	...	...	...	...	...	...	...	...	0105	...	...	...	...	...	...	...	...	...	...

- **A** – BEROLINA – To Wien via Passau (Tables **920** and **950**).
- **B** – From Warnemünde (Table **835**).
- **C** – To Basel / Zürich / Chur (Table **912**).
- **D** – To Karlsruhe (Table **912**). Runs via Weimar (Table **849a**).
- **E** – To Karlsruhe (Table **912**).
- **F** – ① until Apr. 17 (also Apr. 11; not Apr. 10).
- **H** – ① from Apr. 24 (also May 2; not May 1). Also calls at Berlin Wannsee (d. 0026), Potsdam Hbf (d. 0034) and Dessau Hbf (d. 0130).
- **J** – To Jena (Table **849a**).
- **K** – From Kiel (Table **820**).
- **L** – From Lichtenfels (d. 0622).
- **M** – To München via Ulm (Table **930**).
- **N** – 🛏 1, 2 cl. and 🛌 2 cl. Praha - Dresden - Leipzig - Basel - Zürich. Also conveys 2 (*EC* 458).
- **O** – From Ostseebad Binz (Tables **844/845**).
- **S** – To Saarbrücken (Table **919**).
- **T** – To Wien via Jena and Passau (Tables **849a**, **920** and **950**).
- **Y** – 12 Berlin - Karlsruhe (- Basel ⑤⑥). See also Table **912**.
- **a** – ①–⑤ (not Apr. 7, 10, May 1).
- **b** – Not Apr. 7, 9, 30.
- **e** – ①–⑥ (not Apr. 10, May 1).
- **f** – Also Apr. 6, May 17; not Apr. 7, May 19.
- **p** – Connects with train in previous column.
- **q** – Not Apr. 7, 9, 30.
- **v** – Also Apr. 6, 10, May 1, 17; not Apr. 7, 9, 30, May 19.
- **w** – ⑦ (also Apr. 10, May 1; not Apr. 9, 30).
- **z** – Starts from Leipzig, then Halle (a. 0056).
- ⊙ – Also calls at Weimar (d. 0338).
- ◐ – Via Hannover (Table **900**).
- ♣ – To Zürich via Basel (Table **912**). Conveys 🛏 1, 2 cl. and 🛌 2 cl. Also conveys 2 (*IC* **60408**).
- • – Frankfurt (Main) **Süd**.
- § – Frankfurt Flughafen Fernbahnhof ✈.
- ◇ – See Tables **914**, **917** and **917a** for other local services.

FRANKFURT and NÜRNBERG - ERFURT - LEIPZIG / HALLE - BERLIN 850

See Table **902** for other services Frankfurt - Berlin via Braunschweig. See Table **927** for services operated by FlixTrain.
Other regional services: Table **845** Lutherstadt Wittenberg - Berlin. Table **848** Leipzig / Halle - Bitterfeld - Lutherstadt Wittenberg. Table **849** Eisenach - Erfurt - Weimar - Leipzig / Halle.

km		*IC* 94	*NJ* 409	*EN* 40459	*ICE* 1606	*ICE* 698		*ICE* 806	*ICE* 806	*ICE* 1731	*ICE* 1714	*ICE* 1604	*ICE* 1704	*ICE* 1604	*ICE* 1553	*ICE* 1008	*ICE* 672	*ICE* 804	*ICE* 774	*ICE* 602	*ICE* 1555	*ICE* 1006	*ICE* 802	*ICE* 474
									①–⑤	①–⑤	⑥	①–⑥	①–⑥		⑥h									
		T	♣	N	✕	E✕		✕	a✕	a✕	O✕	e✕	eJ ✕	✕	✕	✕	✕	K✕	✕	✕	✕	✕	✕	C✕
	Wiesbaden Hbf ◇ d.	...	...	...	...	...	...	...	...	...	...	...		...	...	...	0500	...	...	...	...	...	...	...
	Mainz Hbf ◇ d.	...	...	...	...	...	...	...	...	...	...	...	...	...	...	...	0512	...	...	...	...	...	...	...
	Stuttgart Hbf **912** d.	...	...	...	...	0011	...	...	...	...	...	...	...	...	...	...	|	...	0501	...	...	...	...	...
	Frankfurt Flughafen ✈ § ◇ d.	...	...	...	...	0229	...	...	...	...	...	...	...	...	...	...	0532	...	0641	...	...	...	...	...
	Frankfurt (Main) Hbf **900/1/2** ◇ d.	...	0052	0052	...	0249	...	...	...	...	...	...	...	...	...	...	0558	...	0702	...	0716	...	...	0758
	Hanau Hbf **901** d.	...	|	|	...	|	...	...	...	...	...	...	...	...	...	...	0614	...	|	...	|	...	...	0814
	Fulda **900/1/2** d.	...	0150	0150	...	|	...	...	...	...	...	...	...	...	...	...	0708r	...	|	...	0814	...	...	0908r
	Bad Hersfeld d.	...	|	|	...	|	...	...	...	...	...	...	...	...	...	...	|	...	|	...	0840	...	...	|
	Eisenach **849a** d.	...	|	|	...	0447	...	...	0553	0638	...	...	...	...	0708	...	0801	...	|	...	0908	...	...	1001
	Gotha **849a** d.	...	|	|	...	0503	...	...	0611u	0653	...	...	...	...	0722	...	|	...	|	...	0922	...	...	|
	München Hbf **904 905** d.	...	|	|	...	|	...	...	|	|	...	...	...	...	|	0553	|	0506t	|	0656	|	0755	0713	|
0	**Nürnberg** Hbf **875** d.	0026	|	|	...	|	...	...	|	|	0542	0542	...	...	|	0659	|	0705	|	0804	|	0902	0905	|
24	Erlangen **875** d.	0043	|	|	...	|	...	...	|	|	0558	0558	...	...	|	|	|	|	|	0818	|	|	|	|
62	**Bamberg** **875** d.	0105	|	|	...	|	...	...	|	|	0622	0622	...	...	|	|	|	0742	|	0842	|	|	0942	|
	Coburg **875** d.	|	|	|	...	|	...	...	|	|	0644	0644	...	...	|	|	|	|	|	|	|	|	|	|
190	**Erfurt** Hbf **849a** a.	|	0314	0314	...	0518	...	...	0626	0708	0724	0724	...	...	0738	0809	0826	0824p	0907	0926	0938	1009	1024	1026p
190	**Erfurt** Hbf d.	|	0316	0316	...	0522	...	...	0628	0710	0726	0726	...	...	0740	0811	0828	0832	0909	0928	0940	1011	1032	1028
	Leipzig Hbf a.	0453	0448	0448	...	|	...	...	0710	|	0810	0810	...	...	0824	|	0910	|	|	1010	1024	|	|	1110
	Leipzig Hbf d.	0507	0518	0554j	0616	◧	...	0716	0716	|	0818	0818	0818	0818	0831	|	0916	|	|	1016	1031	|	|	1116
	Dresden Hbf **842** a.	|	|	0705	|	|	...	|	|	|	|	|	|	|	0938	|	|	|	|	|	1138	|	|	|
284	**Halle** (Saale) Hbf d.	0431y	0537s	...	|	0640	...	|	|	0744	|	|	|	|	...	0840	|	0906	0942	|	...	1040	1106	|
314	Bitterfeld d.	0528	0558s	...	|	0656	...	|	|	0801	|	|	|	|	...	|	|	0923	|	|	...	|	1123	|
351	Lutherstadt Wittenberg d.	0546	0619s	...	0648	|	...	0748	0748	|	0848	0848	0848	0848	...	|	0948	|	|	1048	...	|	|	1148
442	**Berlin** Südkreuz a.	0625	0713	...	0722	0748	...	0825	0825	0850	0922	0922	0922	0922	...	0945	1025	1015	1048	1122	...	1145	1215	1225
448	**Berlin** Hbf a.	0632	0720	...	0729	0756	...	0832	0832	0857	0929	0929	0929	0929	...	0953	1032	1022	1055	1131	...	1153	1222	1232
	Hamburg Hbf **840** a.	...	...	...	0924	...	...	1022	1022	...	...	1124	1124	1124	...	1151	...	1221	1311	1324	...	1351	1422	...

	ICE 772	*ICE* 1600	*ICE* 1710	*ICE* 1557	*ICE* 1567	*ICE* 1706	*ICE* 800	*ICE* 78	*ICE* 770	*ICE* 508	*ICE* 1559	*ICE* 1004	*ICE* 708	*ICE* 76	*ICE* 578	*ICE* 506	*ICE* 1651	*ICE* 1092	*ICE* 92	*ICE* 706	*ICE* 74	*ICE* 576	*ICE* 504	*ICE* 1653
					①–⑥																			
	✕	✕	O✕	S✕	e✕	✕	✕	C✕	✕	✕	✕	✕	✕	C✕	✕	✕	✕	✕	A✕	✕	C✕	✕	✕	✕
Wiesbaden Hbf ◇ d.	...	...	...	...	0826	...	...	...	...	...	1026	...	...	...	...	...	1226	...	...	...	...	...	...	1426
Mainz Hbf ◇ d.	...	...	...	...	0843	...	...	...	...	...	1043	...	...	...	...	...	1243	...	...	...	...	...	...	1443
Stuttgart Hbf **912** d.	0725	...	...	...	|	...	...	...	0923	...	|	...	...	...	1123	...	|	...	...	...	...	1323	...	|
Frankfurt Flughafen ✈ § ◇ d.	0841	...	...	...	0901	...	...	...	1041	...	1101	...	...	...	1241	...	1301	...	...	...	...	1441	...	1501
Frankfurt (Main) Hbf **900/1/2** ◇ d.	0902v	...	...	0919	0919	...	...	0958	1102	...	1119	...	...	1158	1302	...	1319	...	...	...	1358	1502	...	1519
Hanau Hbf **901** d.	|	...	...	|	|	...	...	1014	|	...	|	...	...	1214	|	...	|	...	...	...	1414	|	...	|
Fulda **900/1/2** d.	|	...	...	1015	1015	...	...	1108r	|	...	1215	...	...	1308r	|	...	1416	...	...	...	1508r	|	...	1615
Bad Hersfeld d.	|	...	...	1040	1040	...	...	|	|	...	1240	...	...	|	|	...	1441	...	...	...	|	|	...	1640
Eisenach **849a** d.	|	...	...	1108	1108	...	...	1201	|	...	1308	...	...	1401	|	...	1508	...	...	...	1601	|	...	1708
Gotha **849a** d.	|	...	...	1122	1122	...	...	|	|	...	1322	...	...	|	|	...	1522	...	...	...	|	|	...	1722
München Hbf **904 905** d.	|	0855	0855	|	|	0839	0955	|	|	1055	|	1156	1114	|	|	1255	|	1241	...	1354	|	|	1456	|
Nürnberg Hbf **875** d.	|	1005	1005	|	|	1036	1105	|	|	1204	|	1301	1305	|	|	1404	|	1435	1435	1505	|	|	1604	|
Erlangen **875** d.	|	1019	1019	|	|	|	|	|	|	1218	|	|	|	|	|	1418	|	|	|	|	|	|	1618	|
Bamberg **875** d.	|	|	|	|	|	|	1142	|	|	1242	|	|	1342	|	|	1442	|	|	|	1542	|	|	1642	|
Coburg **875** d.	|	|	|	|	|	1129	|	|	|	|	|	|	|	|	|	|	|	1529	1529	|	|	|	|	|
Erfurt Hbf **849a** a.	1107	1126	1126	1138	1138	1203	1224	1226p	1307	1326	1338	1409	1424	1426p	1507	1526	1538	1603	1603	1624	1626p	1707	1726	1738
Erfurt Hbf d.	1109	1128	1128	1140	1140	1205	1232	1228	1309	1328	1340	1411	1432	1428	1509	1528	1540	1605	1605	1632	1628	1709	1728	1740
Leipzig Hbf a.	|	1210	1210	1224	1224	|	|	1310	|	1410	1424	|	|	1510	|	1610	1624	|	|	|	1710	|	1810	1824
Leipzig Hbf d.	|	1216	1216	1231	...	|	|	1318	|	1416	1431	|	|	1516	|	1616	1631	|	|	|	1716	|	1816	1831
Dresden Hbf **842** a.	|	|	|	1338	...	|	|	|	|	|	1538	|	|	|	|	|	1738	|	|	|	|	|	|	1938
Halle (Saale) Hbf d.	1142	|	|	...	...	1240	1306	|	1342	|	...	1440	1506	|	1542	|	...	1640	1640	1706	|	1742	|	...
Bitterfeld d.	|	|	|	...	...	|	1323	|	|	|	...	|	1523	|	|	|	...	|	|	1723	|	|	|	...
Lutherstadt Wittenberg d.	|	1248	1248	...	...	|	|	1348	|	1448	...	|	|	1548	|	1648	...	|	|	|	1748	|	1848	...
Berlin Südkreuz a.	1247	1322	1322	...	...	1345	1415	1425	1447	1522	...	1545	1615	1625	1648	1723	...	1745	1745	1815	1825	1851	1923	...
Berlin Hbf a.	1255	1329	1329	...	...	1353	1422	1432	1455	1529	...	1553	1622	1632	1655	1731	...	1753	1753	1822	1832	1858	1931	...
Hamburg Hbf **840** a.	...	1524	...	...	...	1600	1621	...	...	1724	...	1757	1822	...	...	1924	...	...	1951	2023	...	...	2125	...

	ICE 1002	*IC* 1957	*ICE* 704	*ICE* 72	*IC* 1957	*ICE* 1733	*ICE* 574	*ICE* 502	*ICE* 1655	*ICE* 1000	*ICE* 702	*ICE* 70	*ICE* 572	*ICE* 500	*ICE* 1657	*ICE* 1100	*ICE* 376	*ICE* 1500	*ICE* 600		*ICE* 1659	*ICE* 1659		*ICE* 4
		⑤f			⑤f	⑧q												⑧b	⑦w		⑧q	⑤⑦		⑦w
	✕	🍸	✕	C✕	🍸	✕	✕	✕	✕	✕	✕	C✕	✕	✕	✕	✕	X✕	✕	✕		✕	k✕		Z
Wiesbaden Hbf ◇ d.	...	...	...	...	...	...	...	...	1626	...	...	...	...	...	1826	...	...	...	...	...	2026	2026	...	...
Mainz Hbf ◇ d.	...	...	...	...	...	...	...	...	1643	...	...	...	...	...	1843	...	...	...	...	...	2043	2043	...	...
Stuttgart Hbf **912** d.	...	...	...	...	...	...	1523	...	|	...	...	...	1723	...	|	...	...	...	...	...	|	|	...	...
Frankfurt Flughafen ✈ § ◇ d.	...	...	...	...	...	...	1641	...	1701	...	...	...	1841	...	1901	...	...	...	...	...	2101	2101	...	...
Frankfurt (Main) Hbf **900/1/2** ◇ d.	...	1538	...	1558	...	1615	1702	...	1719	...	...	1758	1902	...	1919	...	1958	...	...	...	2119	2119	...	2314
Hanau Hbf **901** d.	...	1557	...	1614	...	1638	|	...	|	...	...	1814	|	...	|	...	2014	...	...	...	|	|	...	2330
Fulda **900/1/2** d.	...	1653	...	1708r	...	1724	|	...	1815	...	...	1909r	|	...	2015	...	2108r	...	...	...	2215	2215	...	0016
Bad Hersfeld d.	...	1722	...	|	...	1754	|	...	1840	...	...	|	|	...	2040	...	2134	...	...	...	2240	2240	...	|
Eisenach **849a** d.	...	1754	...	1801	←	1823	|	...	1908	...	...	2001	|	...	2108	...	2206	...	...	...	2308	2308	...	|
Gotha **849a** d.	...	1819	...	|	1821	1839	|	...	1922	...	...	|	|	...	2122	...	2221	...	...	...	2322	2322	...	|
München Hbf **904 905** d.	1556	→	1514	|	|	|	|	1655	|	1754	1709	|	|	1856	|	1956	|	1910	2050	...	|	|	...	|
Nürnberg Hbf **875** d.	1701	...	1705	|	|	|	|	1804	|	1900	1906	|	|	2004	|	2101	|	2105	2158	...	|	|	...	|
Erlangen **875** d.	|	...	|	|	|	|	|	1818	|	|	|	|	|	2018	|	|	|	2119	2213	...	|	|	...	|
Bamberg **875** d.	|	...	1742	|	|	|	|	1842	|	|	1942	|	|	2042	|	|	|	2143	2237	...	|	|	...	|
Coburg **875** d.	|	...	|	|	|	|	|	|	|	|	|	|	|	|	|	|	|	2206	|	...	|	|	...	|
Erfurt Hbf **849a** a.	1809	...	1824	1826p	1837	1857	1907	1926	1938	2009	2024	2026p	2107	2126	2138	2209	2236	2238	2318	...	2338	2338	...	0139
Erfurt Hbf d.	1811	...	1832	1828	1841	1859	1909	1928	1940	2011	2032	2028	2109	2128	2140	2211	2245	2240	2320	...	...	2343	...	0141
Leipzig Hbf a.	|	...	|	1910	2005	|	|	2010	2024	|	|	2110	|	2210	2224	|	|	2326	0001	...	...	0028	...	0224
Leipzig Hbf d.	|	...	|	1916	...	|	|	2016	2031	|	|	2116	|	2216	2231	|	|	...	0007	...	...	...	...	0234
Dresden Hbf **842** a.	|	...	|	|	...	|	|	|	2138	|	|	|	|	|	2338	|	|	...	|	...	...	...	...	|
Halle (Saale) Hbf d.	1840	...	1906	|	...	1933	1942	|	...	2040	2106	|	2142	|	...	2242	2320	...	|	...	...	...	...	|
Bitterfeld d.	|	...	1923	|	...	|	|	|	...	|	2123	|	|	2234	...	|	|	...	|	...	...	...	...	|
Lutherstadt Wittenberg d.	|	...	|	1948	...	|	|	2048	...	|	|	2148	|	2250	...	|	2350	...	0037	...	...	...	...	|
Berlin Südkreuz a.	1946	...	2015	2025	...	2047	2050	2122	...	2146	2215	2225	2243	2329	...	2343	0029	...	0112	...	...	...	...	0340
Berlin Hbf a.	1953	...	2022	2032	...	2055	2058	2129	...	2153	2222	2232	2250	2336	...	2350	0036	...	0119	...	...	...	...	0347
Hamburg Hbf **840** a.	2155	...	2222	...	...	...	...	2334	...	...	...	...	...	...	...	...	...	...	...	...	...	...	...	0537

A – BEROLINA – From Wien via Passau (Tables **950** and **920**).
C – From Chur / Zürich / Basel (Table **912**).
E – [12] München - Stuttgart - Frankfurt - Berlin. ✕ Erfurt - Berlin.
J – From Jena (Table **849a**).
K – To Kiel (Table **820**).
N – 🛏 1, 2 cl. and 🛏 2 cl. Zürich - Basel - Leipzig - Dresden - Praha. Also conveys [2] (*EC 459*).
O – To Ostseebad Binz (Tables **844**/**845**).
S – From Saarbrücken (Table **919**).
T – From Wien via Passau and Jena (Tables **849a**, **920** and **950**). To Warnemünde via Rostock (Table **835**).
X – From Interlaken via Bern and Basel (Tables **560** and **912**).
Z – From Chur via Zürich (Tables **920** and **912**).

a – Not Apr. 7, 10, May 1.
b – Not Apr. 9, 30.
e – Not Apr. 10, May 1.
f – Also Apr. 6, May 17; not Apr. 7, May 19.
h – Also Apr. 7, May 18; not Apr. 8, May 20.
j – 0545 until Apr. 7.
k – Also Apr. 6, 10, May 1, 17; not Apr. 7, 9, 30, May 19.
p – Connects with train in previous column.
q – Not Apr. 7, 9, 30.
r – Arrives 9 – 11 minutes earlier.
s – Calls to set down only.
t – Ⓐ only.

u – Calls to pick up only.
v – 0901 on ⑥.
w – Also Apr. 10, May 1; not Apr. 9, 30.
y – Arrives 0411 (calls before Leipzig).

◧ – Via Weimar (see Table **849a**).
◇ – See Tables **914**, **917** and **917a** for other local services.
♣ – From Zürich via Basel (Table **912**). Conveys 🛏 1, 2 cl. and 🛏 2 cl. Also conveys [2] (*IC 60409*).
§ – Frankfurt Flughafen Fernbahnhof ✈.

900 NÜRNBERG and FRANKFURT - HAMBURG

km		ICE 990 ①g	ICE 1688 △	NJ 470 ♦	ICE 1678 ①–⑤ aT	ICE 1686 ①② c✕	NJ 40420 Ⓡ△ B	NJ 490 Ⓡ△ ♦	ICE 1088 ①–⑥ dK ✕	ICE 1676 ①g T✕	ICE 1676 ①–⑤ aT ✕	ICE 1676 ①–⑥ eT ✕	ICE 878 ①–⑥ ✕	ICE 888 ✕	ICE 696 ①g ✕	ICE 696 ✕	ICE 684 ✕	ICE 634 ①–⑥ J✕
	Basel SBB **912** ▦ d.	...	...	2213	...	...	...	...	...	...	...	...	...	...	...	...	...	...
	Karlsruhe Hbf **912** d.	...	...	0019	...	...	...	...	...	...	...	...	...	...	0500	...	...	...
	Stuttgart Hbf **912** d.	2251p	...	|	...	...	...	...	...	...	...	...	...	...	|	...	...	...
	Mannheim Hbf **912** d.	2332p	...	|	...	...	...	...	...	...	...	...	...	...	0528	...	...	...
	Frankfurt Flughafen Fernbf ✈ **912** d.	|	...	|	...	...	...	...	...	...	...	...	...	...	|	...	...	...
	Frankfurt (Main) Hbf **850 901 902** d.	0017	...	0214x	...	...	...	...	0430	0344	...	...	0514	...	0614	0614	...	...
	Hanau Hbf **850 901 902** d.	0034	...	0231	...	...	...	...	0447	|	...	...	0530	...	|	|	...	...
	München Hbf **904 905** d.	|	2300	|	...	...	2252	...	|	|	...	...	|	...	|	|	0412	0412
	Augsburg Hbf **905** d.	|	|	|	...	...	2325	...	|	◧	...	...	|	...	|	|	|	|
0	**Nürnberg** Hbf **850 905 920 921** d.	|	0017	|	...	...	0142	0142	|	|	...	...	|	...	|	|	0532	0532
102	**Würzburg** Hbf **920 921** d.	|	0120	|	...	...	0235	0235	|	|	...	...	|	...	|	|	0628	0628
195	Fulda **850 901 902** d.	0117	|	|	...	...	|	|	0531	|	...	...	0612	...	0712	0712	0705	0705
285	**Kassel** Wilhelmshöhe **901 902** d.	|	|	|	...	...	|	|	0636	0623	0623	...	0723	0736	0823	0823	0836	0836
	Erfurt Hbf **850** d.	|	|	|	...	...	|	|	|	|	|	...	|	|	|	|	|	|
	Eisenach **850** d.	|	|	|	...	...	|	|	|	|	|	...	|	|	|	|	|	|
330	Göttingen **902 903** d.	0245	0405	0433	...	0546	0553	0553	0655	0645	0645	...	0742	0755	0841	0841	0857	0857
430	**Hannover** Hbf **903** a.	0341	0506	0529	...	0657	0649	0649	0732	0756	0756	...	0817	0832	0917	0917	0932	0932
430	**Hannover** Hbf **903** d.	0344	0511	0532	0554	0701	0705	0705	0736	0759	0759	0759	0820	0836	0920	0920	0936	0945
	Bremen Hbf **813** a.	|	|	0643q	|	|	|	|	|	|	|	|	|	|	|	|	|	1045
471	Celle **903** d.	0405	0531	|	0617	0720	|	|	|	0818	0818	0818	|	|	|	|	|	...
523	Uelzen **903** d.	0429	0555	|	0642	0742	|	|	|	0842	0842	0842	|	|	|	|	|	...
559	Lüneburg **903** d.	0451	0613	|	0659	0758	|	|	|	0902	0902	0902	|	|	|	|	|	...
596	**Hamburg** Harburg **903** a.	0514	0629	0736	0716	0816	0830	0830	0843	0919	0919	0919	|	|	|	|	1041	...
608	**Hamburg** Hbf **903** a.	0528	0642	0754	0730	...	0847	0847	0857	0932	0932	0932	0936	0954	1036	1036	1055	...
615	**Hamburg** Altona a.	0542	0659	0810	...	...	0905	0905	...	...	...	...	0952	1011	1052	1052	1112	...

	ICE 1674 ①–⑥ e✕	ICE 270 K✕	ICE 886 ✕	ICE 694 ✕	ICE 682 L✕	ICE 632 ✕	ICE 1672 ✕♦	ICE 374 ✕	ICE 882 K✕	ICE 692 N✕	ICE 680 ✕	ICE 630 J ✕	IC 2374 Ⓐt ♣🍸	IC 2374 Ⓒv ♣🍸	ICE 372 A✕	ICE 880 ✕	ICE 690 N✕	ICE 588 ✕	ICE 538 J ✕
Basel SBB **912** ▦ d.	...	0412n	...	...	...	...	...	0606	...	...	...	...	...	...	0813	...	...	...	...
Karlsruhe Hbf **912** d.	...	0558	...	...	...	...	0702e	0800	...	...	...	...	...	0910	1000	...	...	...	...
Stuttgart Hbf **912** d.	...	|	...	0650	...	...	|	|	...	0851	...	...	0855	|	|	...	1051	...	...
Mannheim Hbf **912** d.	...	0632	...	0732	...	...	|	0832	...	0932	...	...	|	|	1032	...	1132	...	...
Frankfurt Flughafen Fernbf ✈ **912** d.	...	|	...	|	...	...	|	|	...	|	...	...	|	|	|	...	|	...	...
Frankfurt (Main) Hbf **850 901 902** d.	0649	0714	...	0814	...	...	0851	0914	...	1014	...	...	1051	1051	1114	...	1214	...	...
Hanau Hbf **850 901 902** d.	|	0730	...	|	...	...	|	0930	...	|	...	...	|	|	1130	...	|	...	...
München Hbf **904 905** d.	|	|	0511	|	0614	0614	|	|	0718	|	0820	0820	|	|	|	0919	|	1021	1021
Augsburg Hbf **905** d.	◧	|	|	|	|	|	◧	|	|	|	|	|	◧	◧	|	|	|	|	|
Nürnberg Hbf **850 905 920 921** d.	|	|	0632	|	0733	0733	|	|	0832	|	0933	0933	|	|	|	1032	|	1133	1133
Würzburg Hbf **920 921** d.	|	|	|	|	0828	0828	|	|	|	|	1028	1028	|	|	|	1129	|	1228	1228
Fulda **850 901 902** d.	|	0812	|	0912	0905	0905	|	1012	|	1112	1105	1105	|	|	1212	1204	1312	1305	1305
Kassel Wilhelmshöhe **901 902** d.	0856	0921	|	1021	1036	1036	1056	1121	|	1221	1236	1236	1256	1256	1321	1336	1421	1436	1436
Erfurt Hbf **850** d.	|	|	0754r	|	|	|	|	|	0954r	|	|	|	|	|	|	|	|	|	|
Eisenach **850** d.	|	|	0823	|	|	|	|	|	1023	|	|	|	|	|	|	|	|	|	|
Göttingen **902 903** d.	0917	0941	0955	1040	1055	1055	1116	1141	1155	1240	1255	1255	1317	1317	1341	1355	1440	1455	1455
Hannover Hbf **903** a.	0957	1017	1032	1117	1132	1132	1156	1217	1232	1317	1332	1332	1356	1356	1417	1432	1517	1532	1532
Hannover Hbf **903** d.	1000	1020	1036	1120	1136	1145	1159	1220	1236	1320	1336	1345	1359	1359	1420	1436	1520	1536	1545
Bremen Hbf **813** a.	|	|	|	|	|	1245	|	|	|	|	|	1445	|	|	|	|	|	|	1645
Celle **903** d.	1019	|	|	|	|	...	1218	|	|	|	|	...	1418	1418	|	|	|	|	...
Uelzen **903** d.	1043	|	|	|	|	...	1242	|	|	|	|	...	1442	1442	|	|	|	|	...
Lüneburg **903** d.	1059	|	1127	|	|	...	1259	|	|	|	|	...	1459	1459	|	|	|	|	...
Hamburg Harburg **903** a.	1117	|	1144	|	1241	...	1257	|	|	|	1541	...	1517	1517	|	1540	|	1641	...
Hamburg Hbf **903** a.	1130	1136	1158	1236	1255	...	1330	1336	1354	1436	1455	...	1530	1530	1536	1555	1636	1655	...
Hamburg Altona a.	1145	...	1214	1252	...	...	...	1351	...	1452	1511	...	...	...	1551	1611	1652	1711	...

	ICE 1578 T✕	ICE 370 K✕	ICE 788 ✕	ICE 1218 N✕	ICE 586 ✕	ICE 536 J ✕	IC 2082 D 🍸	ICE 1576 ⑥h ✕	ICE 1576 Ⓑb T✕	ICE 278 A✕	ICE 786 ✕	ICE 596 Ⓑ Q✕	ICE 596 ⑥ N✕	ICE 584 ✕	ICE 534 ①–④ HM ✕	ICE 1574 ✕	ICE 276 ✕	ICE 784 ✕	ICE 594 N✕	ICE 582 ✕	ICE 532 M✕
Basel SBB **912** ▦ d.	...	1013	...	...	...	...	...	...	...	1213	...	...	...	...	...	...	1413	...	...	...	...
Karlsruhe Hbf **912** d.	1110	1200	...	...	...	...	...	1310	1310	1400	...	...	...	...	...	1510	1600	...	...	...	...
Stuttgart Hbf **912** d.	|	|	...	1251	...	...	...	|	|	|	...	1451	1451	...	...	|	|	...	1651	...	...
Mannheim Hbf **912** d.	|	1232	...	1332	...	...	...	|	|	1432	...	1532	1532	...	...	|	1632	...	1732	...	...
Frankfurt Flughafen Fernbf ✈ **912** d.	|	|	...	|	...	...	...	|	|	|	...	|	|	...	...	|	|	...	|	...	...
Frankfurt (Main) Hbf **850 901 902** d.	1251	1314	...	1414	...	...	...	1448	1448	1514	...	1614	1614	...	...	1648	1714	...	1814	...	...
Hanau Hbf **850 901 902** d.	|	1330	...	|	...	...	...	|	|	1530	...	|	|	...	...	|	1730	...	1831	...	...
München Hbf **904 905** d.	|	|	1119	|	1220	1220	1117o	|	|	|	1318	|	|	1421	1421	|	|	1519	|	1618	1618
Augsburg Hbf **905** d.	◧	|	|	|	|	|	1230	◧	◧	|	|	|	|	|	|	◧	|	|	|	|	|
Nürnberg Hbf **850 905 920 921** d.	|	|	1232	|	1333	1333	|	|	|	|	1433	|	|	1534	1534	|	|	1633	|	1736	1736
Würzburg Hbf **920 921** d.	|	|	|	|	1428	1428	1440	|	|	|	|	|	|	1628	1628	|	|	|	|	1830	1830
Fulda **850 901 902** d.	|	1412	|	1513	1505	1505	1527	|	|	1612	|	1712	1712	1705	1705	|	1812	|	1912	1905	1905
Kassel Wilhelmshöhe **901 902** d.	1456	1521	|	1621	1636	1636	|	1656	1656	1721	|	1821	1821	1836	1836	1856	1921	|	2021	2036	2036
Erfurt Hbf **850** d.	|	|	1354r	|	|	|	|	|	|	|	1554r	|	|	|	|	|	|	1754r	|	|	|
Eisenach **850** d.	|	|	1423	|	|	|	|	|	|	|	1623	|	|	|	|	|	|	1823	|	|	|
Göttingen **902 903** d.	1516	1541	1555	1640	1655	1655	1659	1716	1716	1741	1755	1840	1840	1855	1855	1917	1941	1955	2040	2055	2055
Hannover Hbf **903** a.	1556	1617	1632	1717	1732	1732	1740	1756	1756	1817	1832	1917	1917	1932	1932	1956	2017	2032	2117	2132	2132
Hannover Hbf **903** d.	1559	1620	1636	1720	1736	1745	...	1759	1759	1820	1836	1920	1920	1936	1951	1959	2020	2036	2120	2136	2145
Bremen Hbf **813** a.	|	|	|	|	|	1845	...	|	|	|	|	|	|	|	2047	|	|	|	|	|	2259
Celle **903** d.	1618	|	|	|	|	...	...	1818	1818	|	|	|	|	|	...	2018	|	|	|	|	...
Uelzen **903** d.	1642	|	|	|	|	...	...	1842	1842	|	|	|	|	|	...	2042	|	|	|	|	...
Lüneburg **903** d.	1702	|	|	|	|	...	...	1858	1858	|	|	2013	2013	2028	...	2058	|	|	2214	|	...
Hamburg Harburg **903** a.	1719	|	1741	|	1841	...	...	1916	1916	|	1941	|	|	2044	...	2116	2126	2141	2232	2241	...
Hamburg Hbf **903** a.	1732	1736	1755	1836	1855	...	...	1929	1929	1936	1955	2040	2040	2059	...	2129	2139	2155	2246	2255	...
Hamburg Altona a.	...	...	1811	1852	...	...	...	1945	...	1951	2011	...	2059	2116	...	2147	2154	2209	2301	2311	...

♦ – **NOTES** (LISTED BY TRAIN NUMBER)

470 – 🛏 1, 2 cl. and ▬ 2 cl. Zürich (d. 2059) - Basel - Hamburg. Also conveys [2] (*IC* **60470**).
490 – 🛏 1, 2 cl., ▬ 2 cl. and [2] Wien - Passau - Nürnberg - Hamburg.
1672 – Not Apr. 8. [12] ✕ (Karlsruhe ①–⑥ **u** -) Frankfurt - Hamburg - Rostock.

A – From Interlaken via Bern (Table **560**).
B – 🛏 1, 2 cl., ▬ 2 cl. and [2] Innsbruck - Hamburg (Table **53**).
D – KÖNIGSSEE – [12] 🍸 Berchtesgaden - München Ost - Hannover; [12] Oberstdorf (**2084**) - Augsburg (**2082**) - Hannover.
H – ①–④ from May 15 (not May 17).
J – From May 14.
K – To Kiel (Table **820**).
L – To Lübeck (Table **825**).
M – To Oldenburg (Table **813**).
N – From München (Table **930**).
Q – [12] München - Stuttgart - Hamburg - Kiel.
T – To Stralsund (Table **830**).

a – Not Apr. 7, 10, May 1.
b – Not Apr. 9, 30.
c – Not Apr. 10, May 1.
d – Also Apr. 9; not Apr. 10, May 1.
e – ①–⑥ (not Apr. 10, May 1).
g – Also Apr. 11, May 2; not Apr. 10, May 1.
h – Also Apr. 9, 30.
n – ① (also Apr. 11, May 2; not Apr. 10, May 1). Basel **Badischer Bahnhof**.
o – München **Ost**.
p – Previous day.
q – From May 15.
r – Arrives 8 minutes earlier.
t – Not May 19.
u – Not Apr. 8, 10, May 1.
v – Also May 19.
x – Frankfurt (Main) **Süd**.

△ – Subject to alteration from May 26.
♣ – WATTENMEER – To Westerland (Table **821**).
◧ – Via Gießen (Table **806**).

NÜRNBERG and FRANKFURT - HAMBURG **900**

	ICE 1572 ⑤–⑦ u✕	ICE 1572 ✕	ICE 274 Ⓑ ✕	ICE 274 ⑥ ✕	ICE 782 ✕	ICE 592 ⑦ N✕	ICE 592 ①–⑥ N✕	ICE 580 ⑥ ✕	ICE 580 ⑦p ✕	ICE 580 ①–⑤ d✕	ICE 1570 ⑦w	ICE 1680 △✕	ICE 272 Ⓑ E✕	ICE 272 ⑥ C✕	ICE 926 ⑦w
Basel SBB **912** 🏛 d.	...	...	1622	1622	...	...	...	...	...	...	...	...	1813	1813	...
Karlsruhe Hbf **912** d.	1710	1710	1800	1800	...	...	...	...	...	...	1910	...	2000	2000	...
Stuttgart Hbf **912** d.	|	|	|	|	...	1851	1851	...	...	...	|	...	|	|	...
Mannheim Hbf **912** d.	|	|	1832	1832	...	1932	1932	...	...	...	|	...	2032	2032	...
Frankfurt Flughafen Fernbf ✈ **912** d.	|	|	|	|	...	|	|	...	...	...	|	...	|	|	...
Frankfurt (Main) Hbf **850 901 902** d.	1848	1848	1914	1914	...	2014	2014	...	...	...	2051	...	2114	2114	...
Hanau Hbf **850 901 902** d.	|	|	1930	1930	...	2029	2029	...	...	...	|	...	2130	2130	...
München Hbf **904 905** d.	|	|	|	|	1717	|	|	1819	1819	1819	|	1919	|	|	2154
Augsburg Hbf **905** d.	◧	◧	|	|	|	|	|	|	|	|	◧	|	|	|	|
Nürnberg Hbf **850 905 920 921** d.	|	|	|	|	1833	|	|	1934	1934	1934	|	2032	|	|	2304
Würzburg Hbf **920 921** d.	|	|	|	|	|	|	|	2028	2028	2028	|	2128	|	|	2357
Fulda **850 901 902** d.	|	|	2012	2012	|	2112	2112	2105	2105	2105	|	2203	2212	2212	...
Kassel Wilhelmshöhe **901 902** d.	2056	2056	2121	2121	|	2221	2221	2236	2236	2245r	2258	...	2321	2321	...
Erfurt Hbf **850** d.	|	|	|	|	1954r	|	|	|	|	|	|	...	|	|	...
Eisenach **850** d.	|	|	|	|	2023	|	|	|	|	|	|	...	|	|	...
Göttingen **902 903** d.	2117	2117	2141	2141	2155	2240	2240	2307r	2307r	2306	2318	...	2343	2343	...
Hannover Hbf **903** a.	2156	2156	2217	2217	2232	2317	2353	2341	2341	0002	0010	...	0059	0059	...
Hannover Hbf **903** d.	2159	...	2220	2220	2236	2320	0003	...	2345	...	...	...	0103	0103	...
Bremen Hbf **813** a.	|	...	|	|	|	|	|	...	|	...	...	...	|	|	...
Celle **903** d.	2218	...	|	|	2256	|	|	...	0005	...	...	...	0129	|	...
Uelzen **903** d.	2242	...	|	|	2318	|	|	...	0027	...	...	...	0202	|	...
Lüneburg **903** d.	2259	...	|	|	2335	0014	0105	...	0044	...	...	...	0224	|	...
Hamburg Harburg **903** a.	2315	...	|	|	2352	0030	0122	...	0102	...	...	...	0242	0248	...
Hamburg Hbf **903** a.	2329	...	2342	0010	0006	0044	0137	...	0116	...	...	...	0258	0303	...
Hamburg Altona a.	2346	...	2400	0027	0022	0101	0201	...	0132	...	...	...	0315	0318	...

	ICE 1271 ①g C	ICE 1511 ②–⑤ m	ICE 591 ①–⑤ eN✕	ICE 1681 ✕	ICE 781 ① ✕	ICE 781 ✕	ICE 275 ①–⑥ tA✕	ICE 1573 ①–⑤ a✕	ICE 581 ✕	ICE 581 ①–⑥ e✕	ICE 593 N✕	ICE 753 ①–⑤ a✕	ICE 783 ①–⑤ ✕	ICE 783 ⑥⑦ ✕	ICE 277 ✕	ICE 1575 ①–⑥ ✕	IC 2083 D 🍸	ICE 533 ①–⑥ tM✕	ICE 583 ✕
Hamburg Altona d.	0028	...	0144	...	0332	...	0400	...	...	0436	0458	0503	0537	0537	0604y	0607	...	...	0644
Hamburg Hbf **903** d.	0045	...	0200	...	0349	...	0417	...	...	0454	0515	0523	0554	0554	0618	0624	...	...	0701
Hamburg Harburg **903** d.	0057	...	0212	...	0402	...	0429	...	...	0506	0528	0535	0606	0606	0630	0636	...	...	0713
Lüneburg **903** d.	|	...	0239	...	0421	...	|	...	...	0526	0547	0554	0624	0624	0648	0655	...	...	|
Uelzen **903** d.	|	...	0259	...	0438	...	|	...	...	0542	|	0614	|	0641	|	0715	...	...	|
Celle **903** d.	|	...	0332	...	0501	...	|	...	...	0604	|	0637	|	0704	|	0738	...	...	|
Bremen Hbf **813** d.	|	...	|	...	|	...	|	...	...	|	|	|	|	|	|	|	...	0715j	|
Hannover Hbf **903** a.	0207	...	0352	...	0520	...	0538	...	...	0623	0638	0657	0723	0723	0738	0758	...	0814	0822
Hannover Hbf **903** d.	0210	...	0358	...	0526	0526	0541	0557	0626	0626	0641	▽	0726	0726	0741	0801	0807	0826	0826
Göttingen **902 903** d.	0307	...	0517	...	0602	0602	0616	0636	0702	0702	0716	...	0804	0804	0816	0839	0855	0902	0902
Eisenach **850** d.	|	...	|	...	0730	0730	|	|	|	|	|	...	0930	0930	|	|	|	|	|
Erfurt Hbf **850** d.	|	...	|	...	0811r	0811r	|	|	|	|	|	...	1011r	1011r	|	|	|	|	|
Kassel Wilhelmshöhe **901 902** d.	|	...	0537	...	0623‡	0623‡	0637	0701	0723	0723	0737	...	|	|	0837	0903	0926	0923	0923
Fulda **850 901 902** d.	0431	0536	0648	0653	|	|	0748	|	0856	0856	0848	...	|	|	0948	|	1045	1056	1056
Würzburg Hbf **920 921** d.	|	|	|	0730	|	|	|	|	0931	0931	|	...	|	|	|	|	1124	1131	1131
Nürnberg Hbf **850 905 920 921** a.	|	|	|	0824	0925	0925	|	◧	1024	1024	|	...	1125	1125	|	◧	|	1224	1224
Augsburg Hbf **905** a.	|	|	|	|	|	|	|	...	|	|	|	...	|	|	|	|	1330	|	|
München Hbf **904 905** a.	|	|	|	0939	1042	1042	|	|	1139	1139	|	...	1238	1238	|	|	1411o	1338	1338
Hanau Hbf **850 901 902** d.	0519	0624	0728	...	...	...	0828	|	...	...	|	...	...	...	1028	|	...	...	...
Frankfurt (Main) Hbf **850 901 902** a.	0537	0640	0744	...	...	...	0844	0910	...	...	0944	...	...	...	1044	1110	...	...	...
Frankfurt Flughafen Fernbf ✈ **912** a.	|	|	|	...	...	...	|	|	...	...	|	...	...	...	|	|	...	...	...
Mannheim Hbf **912** a.	0627	0748	0827	...	...	...	0927	|	...	...	1027	...	...	...	1127	|	...	...	...
Stuttgart Hbf **912** a.	|	0849	0908	...	...	...	|	|	...	...	1108	...	...	...	|	|	...	...	...
Karlsruhe Hbf **912** a.	0656	...	...	...	...	...	0958	1050	...	...	...	...	...	...	1158	1250	...	...	...
Basel SBB **912** a.	0847	...	...	...	...	...	1147	...	...	...	...	...	...	...	1347	...	...	...	...

	ICE 595 ①–⑥ Q✕	ICE 595 ⑦ ✕	ICE 785 ✕	ICE 279 ①–⑥ eK✕	ICE 279 ⑦v ✕	ICE 1577 ①–⑤ aT✕	ICE 1577 ⑥⑦ k✕	ICE 535 G M✕	ICE 585 L✕	ICE 597 N✕	ICE 787 ✕	ICE 371 ①–⑥ eA✕	ICE 371 ⑦v A✕	ICE 1579 Ⓑd ✕	ICE 1579 ⑥p T✕	ICE 537 H M✕	ICE 587 ✕	ICE 1219 N✕	ICE 789 ✕	ICE 373 Y✕
Hamburg Altona d.	...	0705	0744	...	0806	...	0810	...	...	0905	0944	1006	...	1012	...	...	1044	1105	1144	...
Hamburg Hbf **903** d.	0723	0723	0801	0824	0824	0828	0828	...	0901	0924	1001	1024	1024	1028	1028	...	1101	1124	1201	1224
Hamburg Harburg **903** a.	|	|	0813	|	|	0841	0841	...	0914	|	1013	|	|	1041	1041	...	1113	|	1213	|
Lüneburg **903** d.	|	|	|	|	|	0859	0859	...	|	|	|	|	|	1059	1059	...	|	|	|	|
Uelzen **903** d.	|	|	|	|	|	0916	0916	...	|	|	|	|	|	1115	1115	...	|	|	|	|
Celle **903** d.	|	|	|	|	|	0938	0938	...	|	|	|	|	|	1138	1138	...	|	|	|	|
Bremen Hbf **813** d.	|	|	|	|	|	|	|	0915j	|	|	|	|	|	|	|	1115	|	|	|	|
Hannover Hbf **903** a.	0838	0838	0920	0938	0938	0958	0958	1015	1022	1038	1120	1138	1138	1158	1158	1214	1222	1238	1320	1338
Hannover Hbf **903** d.	0841	0841	0926	0941	0941	1001	1001	1026	1026	1041	1126	1141	1141	1201	1201	1226	1226	1241	1326	1341
Göttingen **902 903** d.	0916	0916	1004	1016	1016	1037	1037	1102	1102	1116	1204	1216	1216	1239	1239	1302	1302	1316	1404	1416
Eisenach **850** d.	|	|	1130	|	|	|	|	|	|	|	1330	|	|	|	|	|	|	|	|	|
Erfurt Hbf **850** d.	|	|	1211r	|	|	|	|	|	|	|	1411r	|	|	|	|	|	|	|	|	|
Kassel Wilhelmshöhe **901 902** d.	1048	1048	|	1037	1037	1104	1104	1123	1123	1137	|	1237	1237	1303	1303	1323	1323	1337	|	1437
Fulda **850 901 902** d.	|	|	|	1148	1148	|	|	1256	1256	1248	|	1348	1348	|	|	1456	1456	1448	1557	1548
Würzburg Hbf **920 921** d.	|	|	|	|	|	|	|	1330	1330	|	|	|	|	|	|	1531	1531	|	1632	|
Nürnberg Hbf **850 905 920 921** a.	|	|	1325	|	|	◧	◧	1424	1424	|	1525	|	|	◧	◧	1624	1624	|	1725	|
Augsburg Hbf **905** a.	|	|	|	|	|	|	|	|	|	|	|	|	|	|	|	|	|	|	|	|
München Hbf **904 905** a.	|	|	1441	|	|	|	|	1539	1539	|	1641	|	|	|	|	1739	1739	|	1839	|
Hanau Hbf **850 901 902** d.	|	|	...	1228	1228	|	|	...	...	|	...	1428	1428	|	|	...	...	|	...	1628
Frankfurt (Main) Hbf **850 901 902** a.	1144	1144	...	1244	1244	1309	1309	...	...	1344	...	1444	1444	1509	1509	...	...	1544	...	1644
Frankfurt Flughafen Fernbf ✈ **912** a.	|	|	...	|	|	|	|	...	...	|	...	|	|	|	|	...	...	|	...	|
Mannheim Hbf **912** a.	1227	1227	...	1327	1327	|	|	...	...	1427	...	1527	1527	|	|	...	...	1627	...	1727
Stuttgart Hbf **912** a.	1308	1308	...	|	|	|	|	...	...	1808	...	|	|	|	|	...	...	1708	...	|
Karlsruhe Hbf **912** a.	...	...	...	1358	1358	1450	1450	...	...	...	...	1558	1558	1650	1650	...	...	...	...	1758
Basel SBB **912** a.	...	...	...	1547	1547	...	...	...	...	...	...	1747	1747	...	...	...	...	...	...	1947

A – To Interlaken via Bern (Table **560**).
C – From Chur via Zürich (Tables **510** and **520**).
D – KÖNIGSSEE – 🚃 🍸 Hannover - München Ost - Berchtesgaden; 🚃 Hannover - Augsburg (**2085**) - Oberstdorf.
E – 🚃 (Chur ⑦**s** -) Zürich - Basel - Hamburg.
G – ⑥⑦ until May 7 (also Apr. 7, 10, May 1); daily from May 13.
H – ⑦ until May 7 (also Apr. 10, May 1; not Apr. 9); daily from May 14.
K – From Kiel (Table **820**).
L – From Lübeck (Table **825**).
M – From Oldenburg on dates in Table **813**.
N – From / to München (Table **930**).
Q – 🚃 Kiel - Hamburg - Stuttgart - München.
T – From Stralsund (Table **830**).
Y – 🚃 ✕ Kiel - Hamburg - Basel - Bern - Interlaken.

a – Not Apr. 7, 10, May 1.
d – Not Apr. 7.
e – Not Apr. 10, May 1.
g – Also Apr. 11, May 2; not Apr. 10, May 1.

j – 29 – 34 minutes **earlier** until May 13.
k – Also Apr. 7, 10, May 1.
m – Not Apr. 7, 11, May 2, 18.
o – München **Ost**.
p – Also Apr. 7.
r – Arrives 8 – 12 minutes earlier.
s – Also Apr. 7, 10, May 18.
t – Also Apr. 9, 30; not Apr. 10, May 1.
u – Also Apr. 6, 10, May 1.
v – Also Apr. 10, May 1.
w – Also Apr. 10, May 1; not Apr. 9, 30.
y – 0555 on ⓒ.

‡ – Calls at Kassel before Eisenach.
⊕ – Via Erfurt Hbf (a. 1946, d. 1954) and Eisenach (d. 2023).
△ – Subject to alteration from May 26.
▽ – Continues to Berlin (Table **810**).
◧ – Via Gießen (Table **806**).

900 HAMBURG - FRANKFURT and NÜRNBERG

	ICE 1671	ICE 639	ICE 689	ICE 691		ICE 881	ICE 375	ICE 1091	IC 2375	ICE 631	ICE 681	ICE 693	ICE 1595	ICE 1585	ICE 1585	ICE 883	ICE 377	ICE 1675	ICE 633	ICE 683	ICE 695	ICE 1687	ICE 1687
		J						⑤⑦		J			⑦w	⑤f	①m				J△	△		⑧b	⑦-④
	T✕	✕	✕	N✕		✕	✕	R✕	M🍷	✕	L✕	N✕	B🍷	✕	✕	✕	K✕	T✕	✕	✕	N✕	✕	d✕
Hamburg Altona d.	...	...	1244	1305	...	1344	1406	...	...	...	...	1505	...	...	1511	1544	...	...	...	1644	1706	1711v	1711v
Hamburg Hbf 903 d.	1228	...	1301	1324	...	1401	1424	...	1427	...	1501	1524	...	...	1528	1601	1624	1628	...	1701	1724	1728v	1728v
Hamburg Harburg 903 d.	1240	...	1313	|	...	1413	|	...	1439	...	1514	|	...	...	1540	1613	|	1640	...	1713	|	1740	1740
Lüneburg 903 d.	1259	...	|	|	...	1430	|	...	1458	...	|	|	...	1558	1558	|	|	1659	...	|	|	1758	1758
Uelzen 903 d.	1315	...	|	|	...	|	|	...	1515	...	|	|	...	1619	1619	|	|	1715	...	|	|	1819	1819
Celle 903 d.	1338	...	|	|	...	|	|	...	1538	...	|	|	...	1640	1640	|	|	1737	...	|	|	1840	1840
Bremen Hbf **813** d.	|	1315	|	|	...	|	|	...	|	1515	|	|	...	|	|	|	|	|	1715	|	|	|	|
Hannover Hbf 903 a.	1358	1414	1422	1438	...	1522	1538	...	1558	1614	1622	1638	...	1700	1700	1720	1738	1757	1814	1822	1838	1905	1905
Hannover Hbf 903 d.	1401	1426	1426	1441	...	1526	1541	1551	1601	1626	1626	1641	1702	1707	1703	1726	1741	1801	1826	1826	1841	...	1909
Göttingen 902 903 d.	1439	1502	1502	1516	...	1604	1616	1631	1640	1702	1702	1716	1740	1746	1810	1804	1816	1839	1902	1902	1916	...	1946
Eisenach 850 d.	|	|	|	|	...	1730	|	|	|	|	|	|	|	|	...	1930	|	|	|	|	|	...	|
Erfurt Hbf 850 d.	|	|	|	|	...	1811r	|	|	|	|	|	|	|	|	...	2011r	|	|	|	|	|	...	|
Kassel Wilhelmshöhe 901 902 d.	1503	1523	1523	1537	...	|	1637	|	1703	1723	1723	1737	|	|	...	|	1837	1903	1923	1923	1937	...	2016
Fulda 850 901 902 d.	|	1556	1656	1648	...	|	1748	1807	|	1856	1856	1848	|	|	...	|	1948	|	2056	2056	2048	...	...
Würzburg Hbf 920 921 d.	|	1731	1731	|	...	|	|	|	|	1930	1930	|	|	|	...	|	|	|	2130	2130	|	...	...
Nürnberg Hbf 850 905 920 921 a.	◧	1824	1824	|	...	1925	|	|	◧	2024	2024	|	|	|	...	2125	|	◧	2225	2225	|	...	...
Augsburg Hbf 905 a.	|	|	|	|	...	|	|	|	|	|	|	|	|	|	...	|	|	|	|	|	|	...	...
München Hbf **904 905** a.	|	1940	1940	|	...	2043	|	|	|	2141	2141	|	|	|	...	2238	|	|	2340	2340	|	...	...
Hanau Hbf 850 901 902 d.	|	...	...	|	...	...	1828	1849	|	...	...	|	|	|	...	...	2028	|	...	...	|	...	...
Frankfurt (Main) Hbf 850 901 902 a.	1709	...	...	1744	...	...	1844	1917	1909	...	...	1944	1957	1957	...	...	2044	2109	...	...	2144	...	...
Frankfurt Flughafen Fernbf ✈ **912** a.	|	...	...	|	...	...	|	...	|	...	...	|	|	|	...	...	|	...	...	...	|	...	...
Mannheim Hbf **912** a.	|	...	...	1827	...	...	1927	...	|	...	...	2027	|	|	...	...	2127	...	...	...	2227	...	...
Stuttgart Hbf **912** a.	|	...	...	1908	...	...	|	...	|	...	...	2108	2155	2156	...	...	|	...	...	...	2308	...	...
Karlsruhe Hbf **912** a.	1852	...	...	...	...	...	1959	...	2053	...	...	...	...	...	...	...	2158	...	...	...	...	...	...
Basel SBB **912** a.	...	...	...	...	...	...	2149	...	...	...	...	...	...	...	...	...	2355	...	...	...	...	...	...

	ICE 885	ICE 877	ICE 1677	ICE 1677	ICE 685	ICE 697		ICE 879	ICE 879		NJ 491	NJ 40491	ICE 1679		NJ 471		ICE 1689
			⑧b	⑤⑦j				⑧c	⑦w		Ⓡ△	Ⓡ△	⑦w				
	K✕	✕	T✕	T✕	✕	U✕		✕	✕		H	A	T✕		D		△
Hamburg Altona d.	...	1806	...	...	1844t	1906	...	1944	1944	...	1958	1958	...	...	2152	...	2211
Hamburg Hbf 903 d.	1801	1824	1828	1828	1901t	1924	...	2001	2001	...	2024	2024	2024	...	2207	...	2228
Hamburg Harburg 903 d.	1813	|	1840	1840	1913	|	...	|	|	...	|	|	|	...	2220	...	2241
Lüneburg 903 d.	|	|	1859	1859	|	|	...	2028	2028	...	|	|	2051	...	|	...	2259
Uelzen 903 d.	|	|	1915	1915	|	|	...	2044	2044	...	|	|	2108	...	|	...	2315
Celle 903 d.	|	|	1938	1938	|	|	...	|	|	...	|	|	2140	...	|	...	2340
Bremen Hbf **813** d.	|	|	|	|	|	|	...	|	|	...	|	|	|	...	2311	...	|
Hannover Hbf 903 a.	1920	1938	1958	1958	2022	2038	...	2123	2123	...	2154	2154	2159	...	0026	...	2400
Hannover Hbf 903 d.	1926	1941	...	2001	2026	2041	...	2141	2141	...	2157	2157	2202	...	0030	...	0003
Göttingen 902 903 d.	2004	2016	...	2040	2102	2116	...	2216	2216	...	2259	2259	2242	...	0132	...	0113
Eisenach 850 d.	2132	|	...	|	|	|	...	|	|	...	|	|	...	...	|	...	|
Erfurt Hbf 850 d.	2211r	|	...	|	|	|	...	|	|	...	|	|	...	...	|	...	|
Kassel Wilhelmshöhe 901 902 d.	|	2037	...	2103	2121	2137	...	2237	2237	...	|	|	...	...	|	...	|
Fulda 850 901 902 d.	|	2147	...	|	...	2248	...	2348	2348	...	|	|	...	...	|	...	|
Würzburg Hbf 920 921 d.	|	|	...	|	...	|	...	|	|	...	0145	0145	...	...	|	...	0354
Nürnberg Hbf 850 905 920 921 a.	2325	|	...	◧	...	|	...	|	|	...	0324	0324	...	...	|	...	0447
Augsburg Hbf 905 a.	|	|	...	|	...	|	...	|	|	...	...	0624	...	...	|	...	|
München Hbf **904 905** a.	0043	|	...	|	...	|	...	|	|	...	...	0706	...	...	|	...	0604
Hanau Hbf 850 901 902 d.	...	2228	...	|	...	2328	...	0028	0028	...	...	...	...	...	0417	...	...
Frankfurt (Main) Hbf 850 901 902 a.	...	2244	...	2325	...	2350	...	0044	0044	...	...	...	...	...	0428x	...	...
Frankfurt Flughafen Fernbf ✈ **912** a.	...	...	...	...	...	...	...	...	|	...	...	...	...	...	|	...	...
Mannheim Hbf **912** a.	...	...	...	...	...	...	...	...	0127	...	...	...	...	...	|	...	...
Stuttgart Hbf **912** a.	...	...	...	...	...	...	...	...	|	...	...	...	...	...	|	...	...
Karlsruhe Hbf **912** a.	...	...	...	...	...	...	...	...	0155	...	...	...	...	...	0602	...	...
Basel SBB **912** a.	...	...	...	...	...	...	...	...	...	...	...	...	...	...	0810	...	...

A – 🛏 1, 2 cl., ▬ 2 cl. and [2] Hamburg - München - Innsbruck (Table **53**).
B – From Berlin (Table **810**).
D – 🛏 1, 2 cl. and ▬ 2 cl. (Ⓡ) Hamburg - Basel - Zürich (a. 1005). Also conveys [2] (*IC* **60471**).
H – 🛏 1, 2 cl., ▬ 2 cl. and [2] Hamburg - Passau - Wien.
J – From May 14.
K – From Kiel (Table **820**).
L – From Lübeck (Table **825**).
M – WATTENMEER – From Westerland (Table **821**).

N – To München (Table **930**).
R – ⑤⑦ (also Apr. 6, 10, May 1, 17; not Apr. 7, 9, 30, May 19). From Berlin (Table **902**).
T – From Stralsund (Table **830**).
U – To Wiesbaden (Table **850**).

b – Not Apr. 7, 9, 30.
c – Also Apr. 8.
d – Not Apr. 6, 9, 30.
f – Also Apr. 6; not Apr. 7.

j – Also Apr. 6, 10, May 1; not Apr. 7, 9, 30.
m – Not Apr. 10, May 1.
r – Arrives 9 minutes earlier.
t – Not Apr. 17, 19, 20, 24, 26, 27.
v – ⑦ only.
w – Also Apr. 10, May 1; not Apr. 9, 30.
x – Frankfurt (Main) **Süd**.

△ – Subject to alteration from May 26.
◧ – Via Gießen (Table **806**).

902 FRANKFURT - BRAUNSCHWEIG - BERLIN

Temporary service during the closure of the high-speed route between Fulda and Kassel – services shown as non-stop between Frankfurt and Kassel operate via (but not calling at) Gießen.

km		ICE 649	ICE 876	ICE 996	ICE 1698	ICE 994	ICE 1696	ICE 992	ICE 1692	ICE 798	ICE 1596	ICE 796	ICE 1592	ICE 794	ICE 1590	ICE 792	ICE 790
		①-⑤															
		a✕	✕	✕	✕	✕	✕	✕	✕	✕	✕	✕	✕	✕	✕	✕	✕
0	**Frankfurt** (Main) Hbf 850 900 d.	...	...	0553	...	0753	...	0953	...	1153	...	1353	...	1553	...	1753	1953
4	**Frankfurt** (Main) Süd d.	...	...	|	...	|	...	|	...	|	...	|	...	|	...	|	|
23	Hanau Hbf 850 900 d.	...	...	|	...	|	...	|	...	|	...	|	...	|	...	|	|
104	Fulda 850 900 d.	...	...	|	...	|	...	|	...	|	...	|	...	|	...	|	|
194	**Kassel** Wilhelmshöhe 900 d.	...	0643	0749	...	0949	...	1149	...	1349	...	1549	...	1749	...	1949	2149
239	Göttingen 900 d.	...	0706	0809	0906	1009	1106	1209	1306	1409	1506	1609	1706	1809	1906	2009	2209
317	Hildesheim Hbf 863 d.	...	0736	0837	0936	1037	1136	1237	1336	1437	1536	1637	1736	1837	1936	2037	2237
360	**Braunschweig** Hbf 863 d.	0601	0801	0901	1001	1101	1201	1301	1401	1501	1601	1701	1801	1901	2001	2101	2303
392	Wolfsburg 810 863 d.	0619	0819	0919	1018	1119	1218	1319	1418	1519	1618	1719	1818	1919	2018	2119	2323
	Stendal 810 a.	|	|	|	|	|	|	|	|	|	|	|	|	|	|	|	2352
559	**Berlin** Spandau 810 a.	0728	0914	1014	1114	1214	1314	1414	1513	1614	1714	1814	1914	2014	2114	2217	0026
575	**Berlin** Hbf 850 810 a.	0747	0929	1029	1129	1229	1329	1429	1529	1629	1729	1829	1929	2029	2129	2231	0041
580	**Berlin** Ostbahnhof 810 a.	0801	0940	1039	1139	1239	1339	1439	1540	1639	1740	1839	1940	2039	2140	2241	0056

	ICE 993	ICE 1691	ICE 791	ICE 1693	ICE 793	ICE 1695	ICE 795	ICE 1697	ICE 797	ICE 1091	ICE 1699	ICE 1595	ICE 799	ICE 1591	ICE 995	ICE 1593	ICE 997
										⑤⑦		⑦w					
	✕	✕	✕	✕	✕	✕	✕	✕	✕	b✕	✕	S✕	✕	✕	✕	✕	✕
Berlin Ostbahnhof 810 d.	0511	0614	0718	0814	0917	1014	1115	1214	1317	1345	1414	1449	1514	1614	1714	1814	1917
Berlin Hbf 850 810 d.	0524	0629	0733	0829	0931	1029	1130	1229	1329	1359	1429	1500	1529	1629	1729	1829	1931
Berlin Spandau 810 d.	0540	0644	0748	0844	0947	1044	1144	1244	1347	1413	1444	1515	1547	1644	1746	1844	1946
Stendal 810 d.	0610	|	|	|	|	|	|	|	|	|	|	1551	|	|	|	|	|
Wolfsburg 810 863 d.	0636	0738	0842	0938	1042	1138	1236	1338	1442	1510	1538	1620	1642	1738	1836	1938	2042
Braunschweig Hbf 863 d.	0659	0757	0859	0957	1059	1157	1259	1357	1459	⊙	1557	⊡	1659	1757	1859	1957	2059
Hildesheim Hbf 863 d.	0721	0819	0921	1019	1121	1219	1321	1419	1521	|	1619	|	1721	1819	1921	2019	2121
Göttingen 900 d.	0752	0850	0951	1051	1151	1251	1351	1451	1551	1631	1651	1740	1751	1851	1952	2052	2152
Kassel Wilhelmshöhe 900 d.	0813	...	1013	...	1213	...	1413	...	1613	|	...	|	1813	...	2013	2114	2212
Fulda 850 900 d.	|	...	|	...	|	...	|	...	|	1807	...	|	|	...	|	|	...
Hanau Hbf 850 900 d.	|	...	|	...	|	...	|	...	|	1849	...	|	|	...	|	|	...
Frankfurt (Main) Süd a.	|	...	|	...	|	...	|	...	|	|	...	|	|	...	|	|	...
Frankfurt (Main) Hbf 850 900 a.	1000	...	1200	...	1400	...	1600	...	1800	1917	...	1957	2000	...	2200	2302	...

S – To Stuttgart (Table **912**).

a – Not Apr. 7, 10, May 1.
b – Also Apr. 6, 10, May 1, 17; not Apr. 7, 9, 30, May 19.
w – Also Apr. 10, May 1; not Apr. 9, 30.

⊙ – Via Hannover Hbf (a. 1544, d. 1551).
⊡ – Via Hannover Hbf (a. 1653, d. 1702).

NEWSLINES *(continued from page 5)*

BEYOND EUROPE (continued)

CHINA

High-speed rail services between Guangzhou and Hong Kong resumed on January 15. We have updated the Guangzhou – Shenzhen – West Kowloon panel of Table **7105** with the latest information. All other services in China should still be considered as subject to confirmation as it remains difficult to obtain accurate information.

TAIWAN

We have received news that through services on the TRA Eastern mainline were reinstated on December 28, so we have combined former Tables **7755** and **7760** to show this. The services had been split due to infrastructure damage caused by an earthquake in September 2022.

JAPAN

There will be a general timetable change in Japan from March 18. We have been able to update some tables with advance information, however, you should check locally for possible changes if travelling from this date. Services in Tables **8000** and **8005** have been considerably recast with the timings between Kagoshima and Osaka particularly affected. Services on the Joetsu Shinkansen will be accelerated as the maximum line speed is to be increased from 240 to 275km/h (Table **8008**). Unfortunately we have not yet received the revised schedules.

UNITED STATES OF AMERICA

We have checked and updated all Amtrak services as necessary. Many routes have seen service frequencies restored to levels similar to those pre-pandemic. Table **9210** has two additional train pairs operating between New York and Albany, one running daily and the other daily except Saturdays. One of these train pairs is named *Adirondack*, reviving the name of the former New York to Montréal train which was cancelled due to the coronavirus pandemic. Table **9240** sees the restoration of the *Silver Meteor* between New York and Miami, meaning this route has two daily train pairs once again. In order to better show services along this route, we have expanded Table **9240** and moved the Brightline service between Miami and West Palm beach (formerly Table **9243**) to a new table, numbered **9380**. Note that the Brightline service should be extended to serve Orlando later this year. An additional train pair has been introduced between Seattle and Vancouver (Table **9315**).

Works to restore and stabilise the railway between San Clemente and Oceanside in California continues (Table **9322**). Weekend through services between Los Angeles and San Diego resumed on February 4 with outstanding works now due to be completed by the end of March. We have included the current engineering work timetable in this edition which still shows services being operated by bus between Irvine and Oceanside.

BEYOND EUROPE

CONTENTS

INDEX OF PLACES

N

O

P

Q

R

San / St / Ste

S

T

U

V

W

X

Y

Z

NUMERICAL

BEYOND EUROPE - AFRICA and MIDDLE EAST MAP

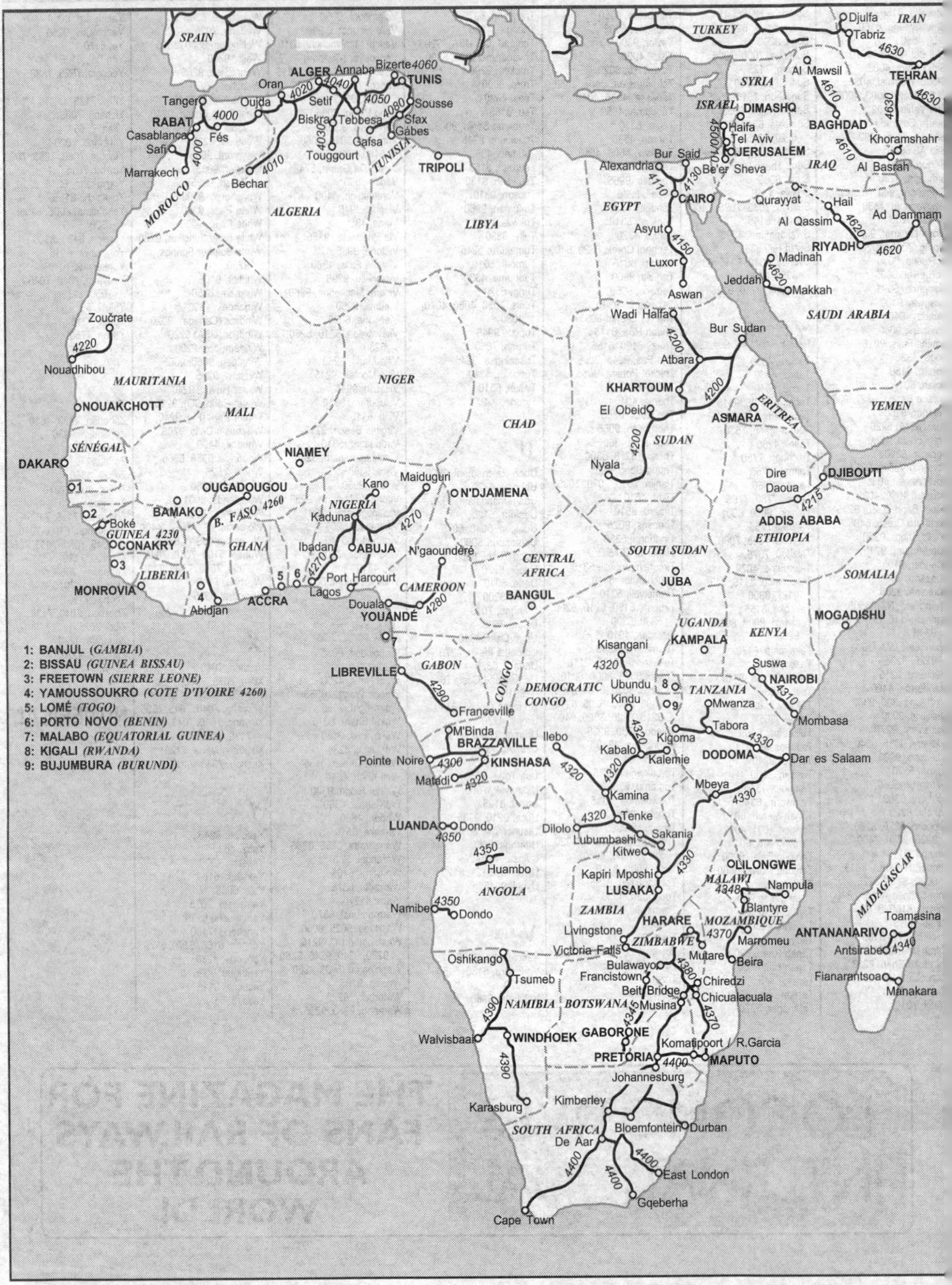

LUXURY and CRUISE TRAINS

THE BLUE TRAIN :
A luxury cruise train running between Pretoria and Cape Town with excursions along the way. ✆ +27 12 334 8459. www.bluetrain.co.za.

ROVOS RAIL :
Luxury cruise train running regularly Pretoria - Cape Town, Pretoria - Durban and Pretoria - Victoria Falls. Also occasional longer tours with excursions Pretoria - Walvis Bay (9 days), Pretoria Durban - Bloemfontein - Port Elizabeth - Oudtshoorn - Cape Town (10 days) and Cape Town and Dar es Salaam (15 days). Most tours feature haulage by the company's preserved stea locomotives. ✆ +27 12 315 8242. www.rovos.com.

MOROCCO

Capital: **Rabat** (GMT + 1). 2023 Public Holidays: Jan. 1, 11, Apr. 22, 23, May 1, June 29, 30, July 19, 30, Aug. 14, 20, 21, Sept. 27, 28, Nov. 6, 18.

Services are operated by Office National des Chemins de Fer (www.oncf-voyages.ma). Unless otherwise noted trains convey first and second class seated accommodation. Overnight trains may also convey sleeping cars and/or couchettes. Timings are the most recent available and are subject to alteration at any time especially during Ramadan.

MARRAKECH - CASABLANCA - FÈS - OUJDA and BENI NSAR — 4000

km		171	101	103	600	602	301	141	606	143	610	303	145	614	616	618	620	622	624	626	MA	628	139	MT
		⚒			⚒		B					B									🛏	⑦	🛏	A
0	**Marrakech** Guéliz d.	...	...	...	0450	0550	...	...	0750	...	0950	...	...	1150	1250	1350	1450	1550	1650	1750	...	1900	...	2100
74	Benguerir ◧ d.	...	...	...	0535	0635	...	...	0835	...	1035	...	...	1235	1335	1435	1535	1635	1735	1835	...	1945	...	2146
174	Settat d.	...	...	...	0639	0739	...	...	0939	...	1139	...	...	1339	1439	1539	1639	1739	1839	1939	...	2049	...	2249
257	**Casablanca** Voyageurs a.	...	...	...	0728	0828	...	...	1028	...	1228	...	...	1428	1528	1628	1728	1828	1928	2028	...	2138	...	2342
257	**Casablanca** Voyageurs d.	...	0540	0640	0730	0830	...	0930	1030	1130	1230	...	1330	1430	1530	1630	1730	1830	1930	2030	2115	2140	2215	2348
346	Rabat Agdal d.	...	0631	0731	0821	0921	...	1021	1121	1221	1321	...	1421	1521	1621	1721	1821	1921	2021	2121	2208	2231	2308	0052
386	Kenitra d.	...	0710	0813	0902	1002	...	1102	1202	1302	1402	...	1502	1602	1702	1802	1902	2002	2102	2202	2249	2312	2349	0144
471	Sidi Kacem d.	...	0759	0905	0951	1054	...	1151	1254	1351	1454	...	1551	1654	1751	1854	1951	2054	2151	2251	2341	0003	0040	0317
526	Meknes d.	0725	0847	0955	1039	1142	...	1239	1342	1439	1542	...	1639	1742	1839	1942	2039	2142	2239	2336	0028	0049	0128	...
582	**Fès** a.	0801	0924	1035	1115	1225	...	1315	1425	1515	1622	...	1719	1825	1915	2025	2115	2218	2315	0012	0100	0127	0158	...
582	**Fès** d.	...	1000	1105	...	...	1250	...	...	...	...	1635	...	...	...	...	...	...	...	...	0140	...	0228	...
701	Taza d.	...	1219	1321	...	...	1520	...	...	...	...	1853	...	...	...	...	...	...	...	...	0358	...	0436	...
	Guercif d.	...	1327	1425	...	...	1614	...	...	...	...	1945	...	...	...	...	...	...	...	...	0452	...	0533	...
818	Taourirt d.	...	1434	1520	...	...	1656	...	...	...	...	2028	...	...	...	...	...	...	...	...	0533	...	0641	...
935	**Oujda** a.	...	|	1659	...	...	1835	...	...	...	...	2212	...	...	...	...	...	...	...	...	0710	...	|	...
	Nador Ville a.	...	1611	...	...	...	...	...	...	...	...	...	...	...	...	...	...	...	...	...	...	...	0811	...
944	**Beni Nsar** Ville a.	...	1622	...	...	...	...	...	...	...	...	...	...	...	...	...	...	...	...	...	...	...	0823	...

	TM	507	AM	104	106	170	110	112	114	116	118	120	122	202	124	142	128	503	15000	132	144	204	146
	A	🛏	🛏	⚒		⚒			⑦					B					B				⑦
Beni Nsar Ville d.	...	2015	...		...	...	...	...	...	...	...	...	...	...	...	...	...	0925	...	...	...	...	...
Nador Ville d.	...	2026	...	...	...	...	...	...	...	...	...	...	...	...	...	...	...	0936	...	...	...	...	...
Oujda d.	...	|	2135	...	...	...	...	...	...	...	...	...	...	0750	...	...	...	|	1135	...	...	1330	...
Taourirt d.	...	2231	2334	...	...	...	...	...	...	...	...	...	...	0936	...	...	...	1222	1326	...	...	1517	...
Guercif d.	...	2330	0017	...	...	...	...	...	...	...	...	...	...	1021	...	...	...	1303	1422	...	...	1617	...
Taza d.	...	0023	0111	...	...	...	...	...	...	...	...	...	...	1115	...	...	...	1417	1517	...	...	1714	...
Fès a.	...	0220	0307	...	...	...	...	...	...	...	...	...	...	1325	...	...	...	1540	1720	...	...	1910	...
Fès d.	...	0250	0342	0455	0540	0610	0640	0740	0840	0940	1040	1140	1240	...	1340	1440	1540	1640	...	1740	1840	1940	2040
Meknes d.	...	0328	0417	0530	0617	0646	0717	0817	0917	1017	1117	1217	1317	...	1417	1517	1617	1717	...	1817	1917	2017	2117
Sidi Kacem d.	0310	0417	0504	0612	0704	...	0804	0904	1004	1104	1204	1304	1404	...	1504	1604	1704	1804	...	1904	2004	2104	2204
Kenitra d.	0428	0514	0608	0700	0800	...	0900	1000	1100	1200	1300	1400	1500	...	1600	1700	1800	1900	...	2000	2100	2200	2300
Rabat Agdal d.	0517	0558	0649	0740	0840	...	0940	1040	1140	1240	1340	1440	1540	...	1640	1740	1840	1940	...	2040	2140	2242	2340
Casablanca Voyageurs a.	0610	0650	0746	0830	0930	...	1030	1130	1230	1330	1430	1530	1630	...	1730	1830	1930	2030	...	2130	2230	2332	0030
Casablanca Voyageurs d.	0615	...	...	0835	0935	...	1035	1135	1235	1335	1435	1535	1635	...	1735	...	1935	...	...	2135	...	...	...
Settat d.	0712	...	...	0930	1030	...	1130	1230	1330	1430	1530	1630	1730	...	1830	...	2030	...	...	2230	...	...	...
Benguerir ◧ d.	0818	...	...	1031	1131	...	1231	1331	1431	1531	1631	1731	1831	...	1931	...	2131	...	...	2331	...	...	...
Marrakech Guéliz a.	0901	...	...	1114	1214	...	1314	1414	1514	1614	1714	1814	1914	...	2014	...	2214	...	...	0014	...	...	...

A – 🛏 1, 2 cl., [12] Marrakech - Tanger and v.v.
B – [12] Oujda - Tanger and v.v.
⊡ – No train from Casablanca or Tanger at 1300.
◧ – Safi - Benguerir and v.v. *142 km.* Journey 2 hours 5 mins. From Safi at 0815, 1610; from Benguerir at 1155, 1955.

CASABLANCA - TANGER — 4001

For footnotes see Table **4000** *Al Boraq* high-speed trains

km		Ⓐ						⑤†	
0	**Casablanca** Voyageurs d.	0600	0700	0800	0900	and	1900	2000	2100
	Rabat Agdal d.	0650	0750	0850	0950	hourly	1950	2050	2150
137	Kenitra d.	0720	0820	0920	1020	until	2020	2120	2220
323	**Tanger** Ville a.	0810	0910	1010	1110	⊡	2110	2210	2310

	Ⓐ						⑤†	
Tanger Ville d.	0600	0700	0800	0900	and	1900	2000	2100
Kenitra d.	0653	0753	0853	0953	hourly	1953	2053	2153
Rabat Agdal d.	0725	0825	0925	1025	until	2025	2125	2225
Casablanca Voyageurs a.	0810	0910	1010	1110	⊡	2110	2210	2310

FÈS and KENITRA - TANGER — 4002

For footnotes see Table **4000**

km		MT	180	151	182	153	202	155	15000	
		A					B		B	
0	**Fès** d.	...	0700	...	1115	...	1400	...	1800	...
56	Meknes d.	...	0736	...	1151	...	1436	...	1836	...
	Kenitra d.	0144	|	1012	|	1430	|	1830	|	...
111	Sidi Kacem d.	0317	0827	|	1242	|	1532	|	1931	...
156	Mechraa Bel Ksir d.	0358	0906	1117	1319	1528	1615	1927	2011	...
264	Asilah d.	0547	1048	1307	1509	1717	1815	2129	2209	...
312	**Tanger** Ville a.	0620	1120	1349	1541	1755	1847	2207	2245	...

	351	301	353	303	305	355	307	TM	
		B		B				A	
Tanger Ville d.	0635	0745	0935	1130	1430	1630	1905	2325	...
Asilah d.	0714	0820	1014	1204	1505	1721	1946	0004	...
Mechraa Bel Ksir d.	0845	0952	1146	1343	1643	1904	2128	0149	...
Sidi Kacem d.	|	1029	|	1424	1724	|	2217	0310	...
Kenitra a.	0940	|	1240	|	|	2015	|	0428	...
Meknes d.	...	1118	...	1513	1813	...	2306	...	...
Fès a.	...	1250	...	1635	1848	...	2339	...	...

CASABLANCA - OUED ZEM — 4003

km										
0	**Casablanca** Voyageurs d.	0810	1310	1910	...	...	...	...	...	...
58	Sidi El Aidi d.	0858	1401	2007	...	...	...	...	...	...
139	Khouribga d.	1043	1542	2153	...	...	...	...	...	...
177	**Oued Zem** a.	...	...	2239	...	...	...	...	...	...

Oued Zem d.	0645	...	...	...	...	...	...	...	...
Khouribga d.	0735	1130	1815	...	...	...	...	...	...
Sidi El Aidi d.	0921	1308	1958	...	...	...	...	...	...
Casablanca Voyageurs a.	1018	1417	2055	...	...	...	...	...	...

EL JADIDA, CASABLANCA AIRPORT ✈ and SETTAT - CASABLANCA — 4004

km		⚒		†						
0	**El Jadida** d.	0630	0730	0835	1035	1235	1435	1635	1835	2035
123	**Casablanca** Voyageurs a.	0753	0852	1004	1204	1404	1604	1804	2004	2204
	Casablanca Port a.	0804	0904	1015	1215	1415	1615	1815	2015	2215

								Ⓑ	
Casablanca Port d.	0830	1030	1230	1430	1630	1730	1830	...	2030
Casablanca Voyageurs d.	0844	1044	1244	1444	1644	1744	1844	1951	2044
El Jadida a.	1010	1205	1405	1608	1807	1905	2010	2100	2205

km									
0	**Casablanca** Airport ✈ d.	0450	0550	0650	0750	0850	and	2150	2250
	Casablanca Voyageurs a.	0525	0625	0721	0825	0925	hourly	2225	2325
	Casablanca Port a.	0536	0636	0732	0836	0936	until	2236	2336

Casablanca Port d.	0450	0550	0650	0750	0850	and	2150	2250
Casablanca Voyageurs d.	0505	0605	0705	0805	0905	hourly	2205	2305
Casablanca Airport ✈ a.	0535	0637	0737	0837	0935	until	2235	2335

km		⚒	⚒							
0	**Settat** d.	0615	0815	1015	1215	1415	1610	1815	2015	...
83	**Casablanca** Voyageurs a.	0715	0917	1115	1315	1509	1712	1917	2117	...
	Casablanca Port a.	0726	0930	1128	1328	1522	1725	1930	2130	...

	⚒	⚒							
Casablanca Port d.	0640	0840	1040	1240	1440	1640	1740	2040	...
Casablanca Voyageurs d.	0653	0853	1053	1253	1453	1653	1753	2053	...
Settat a.	0758	0958	1158	1358	1555	1758	1858	2158	...

CASABLANCA - RABAT - KENITRA — 4005

km		⚒		⚒		⚒																		
0	**Casablanca** Port d.	0620	0710	0735	0810	0835	0910	1010	1110	1210	1310	1410	1510	1535	1610	1635	1710	1735	1810	1835	1910	2010	2035	2125	2200
	Ain Seeba d.	0631	0721	0746	0821	0845	0921	1021	1121	1221	1321	1421	1521	1546	1621	1646	1721	1745	1821	1846	1921	2021	2046	2136	2211
93	**Rabat** Agdal d.	0722	0812	0833	0912	0931	1012	1112	1212	1312	1412	1512	1612	1631	1712	1731	1812	1831	1912	1933	2012	2112	2131	2218	2258
100	Salé Ville d.	0737	0827	0848	0927	0946	1027	1127	1227	1327	1427	1527	1627	1646	1727	1746	1827	1846	1927	1948	2027	2127	2146	2233	2313
140	**Kenitra** a.	0801	0849	0909	0951	1007	1051	1151	1248	1351	1448	1551	1651	1707	1751	1807	1851	1907	1951	2009	2051	2151	2207	2254	2334

	⚒		⚒			⚒																	
Kenitra d.	0557	0630	0707	0730	0807	0830	0907	0930	1030	1130	1230	1330	1430	1530	1607	1630	1707	1730	1807	1830	1907	1930	2030	2107
Salé Ville d.	0620	0654	0731	0754	0831	0854	0931	0954	1054	1154	1254	1354	1454	1554	1631	1654	1731	1754	1831	1854	1931	1954	2054	2131
Rabat Agdal d.	0636	0710	0747	0810	0847	0910	0947	1010	1110	1210	1310	1410	1510	1610	1647	1710	1747	1810	1847	1910	1947	2010	2110	2147
Ain Seeba d.	0726	0759	0836	0859	0932	0959	1036	1059	1159	1259	1359	1459	1559	1659	1736	1759	1836	1859	1932	1959	2036	2059	2158	2232
Casablanca Port a.	0737	0811	0849	0910	0943	1010	1049	1110	1210	1310	1410	1510	1610	1710	1749	1810	1849	1910	1943	2010	2049	2110	2209	2243

ALGERIA

Capital: **Alger** (GMT +1). 2023 Public Holidays: Jan. 1, 12, Apr. 22, 23, May 1, June 29, 30, July 5, 19, 28, Sept. 27, Nov. 1.

All services are operated by Société Nationale des Transports Ferroviaires (www.sntf.dz). Unless otherwise noted trains convey first and second class seated accommodation. Overnight trains ma also convey sleeping cars and/or couchettes. Timings are the most recent available and are subject to alteration at any time especially during Ramadan.

4010 ORAN - SAIDA, GHAZAOUET and BÉCHAR

km		B290	1114	1153	B264	1116	B284
			2	2	2	2	🛏
0	**Oran** d.	1020	1250	...	1520	1600	2030
76	Sidi bel Abbès d.	1119	1355	...	1625	1711	2133
210	**Saida** a.	|	|	...	1759	|	|
163	Tlemcen d.	|	1512	1700	...	1832	|
219	Maghnia d.	|	...	1823	...	...	|
284	**Ghazaouet** a.	|	...	...	...	...	|
350	Naâma d.	1408	...	...	...	...	0116
676	**Béchar** a.	1711	...	...	...	...	0550

	B202	B261	B252	B208	B292	B242
	2	2	2	2		🛏
Béchar d.	...	...	...	...	0615	2000
Naâma d.	...	...	...	...	0915	0009
Ghazaouet d.	...	...	...	...	|	|
Maghnia d.	...	...	0600	...	|	|
Tlemcen d.	0550	...	0724	0800	|	|
Saida d.	|	0700	...	|	|	|
Sidi bel Abbès d.	0706	0834	...	0922	1206	0430
Oran a.	0809	0942	...	1024	1310	0600

4020 ORAN - ALGER

km		1084	1002	MA	OA	1004	B16	1094	B296
		2	2			2		2	
0	**Oran** d.	...	0610	0800	1000	1230	1545	1615	1645
77	Mohammadia d.	...	0701	|	1042	1322	1627	1700	1744
126	Relizane d.	...	0734	|	1115	1356	1700	1731	1818
213	Chlef d.	0505	0829	1000	1200	1453	1740	1835	...
303	Khémis Milliana d.	0611	0939	|	|	1610	|	...	...
354	El Affroun ⊡ d.	0657	1023	|	|	1703	|	...	...
372	Blida ⊡ d.	0710	1036	|	1336	1716	1914	...	...
421	**Alger** Agha ⊡ a.	0756	1115	1200	1407	1754	1946	...	...

	1091 ⑦–④	1093	1001	AM	B17	1003	B15	1085
		2	2			2		2
Alger Agha ⊡ d.	...	...	0610	0800	1035	1230	1545	1723
Blida ⊡ d.	...	...	0646	|	1110	1306	1614	1802
El Affroun ⊡ d.	...	...	0659	|	|	1319	|	1814
Khémis Milliana d.	...	...	0741	|	|	1408	|	1859
Chlef d.	...	0630	0854	1000	1300	1512	1753	2003
Relizane d.	0545	0732	0956	|	1357	1625	1839	...
Mohammadia d.	0620	0807	1029	|	1427	1658	1913	...
Oran a.	0732	0900	1125	1200	1510	1754	1946	...

km		B225	B227
		2	2
0	**Mohammadia** d.	0640	1300
	Mostaganem a.	0731	1351

	B224	B226
	2	2
Mostaganem d.	1100	1700
Mohammadia a.	1151	1751

⊡ – Additional local trains available.

4030 TOUGGOURT

km		B7	B25
		A	B
0	**Constantine** d.	...	...
49	Aïn M'Lila d.	...	...
181*	**M'Sila** d.	1642	2314
	Barika d.	1807	0036
	Aïn Touta d.	1849	0111
117	Batna d.	1909	|
238	Biskra d.	...	0305
402	Djamâa d.	...	0432
455	**Touggourt** a.	...	0500

	B28	B5
	B	A
Touggourt d.	1730	...
Djamâa d.	1758	...
Biskra d.	1925	...
Batna d.	|	2250
Aïn Touta d.	2103	2313
Barika d.	2150	2350
M'Sila d.	2312	0115
Aïn M'Lila d.	...	...
Constantine a.	...	...

A – (12) Alger - M'Sila - Batna and v.v.
B – 🛏 (12) Alger - M'Sila - Touggourt and v.v.
* – Km from Batna.

4035 ANNABA - TEBESSA

km		251	B327
		2	2
0	**Annaba** d.	...	1640
55	Bouchegouf d.	...	1755
90	Mechrouha d.	...	1857
107	Souk Ahras ● d.	0600	1925
156	**Sidi El Hémissi** ● a.	0709	|
131	Dreá d.	...	2003
163	Oued Kéberit d.	...	2042
231	**Tebessa** a.	...	2152

	B388	252
	2	2
Tebessa d.	0430	...
Oued Kéberit d.	0543	...
Dreá d.	0620	...
Sidi El Hémissi ● d.	|	0719
Souk Ahras ● d.	0700	0828
Mechrouha d.	0723	...
Bouchegouf d.	0813	...
Annaba a.	0923	...

● – Also from Souk Ahras at 1335; from Sidi El Hémissi at 1602.

4040 ALGER - CONSTANTINE - TEBESSA and ANNABA

km		326 ①③	151	B113	153	1452	B430	B7	13	19	B25	B31 ②④⑦	AT
		2	2	2	2	2C	2C	A		[R]	B	D	E
0	**Alger** ⊡ d.	...	...	0600	...	...	...	1230	1430	1530	1810	1840	2045
54	Thénia ⊡ d.	...	...	0700	...	...	...	|	|	|	1900	1927	2126
123	Bouira d.	...	...	0804	...	...	...	1412	1612	1725	2015	2042	2228
171	Beni Mansour d.	...	0630	0847	1135	...	...	1451	1652	1810	2102	2130	2315
259	**Béjaïa** a.	...	0818	1035	1329	...	...	|	1830	|	|	|	|
237	Bordj Bou Arreridj d.	...	...	...	...	...	...	1553	...	1910	2210	2237	0020
289	**M'Sila** a.	...	...	...	...	...	...	1642	...	|	2256	|	|
308	Setif d.	...	...	...	...	...	...	...	...	2003	...	2325	0111
464	**Constantine** d.	0709	...	...	...	1600	1600	...	...	...	...	|	0341
521	El Harrouch d.	|	...	...	...	1652	1654	...	...	...	...	|	0444
	Aïn M'Lila d.	|	...	...	...	|	|	...	...	...	...	0207	|
	Aïn Beïda d.	|	...	...	...	|	|	...	...	...	...	0354	|
620	**Tebessa** a.	|	...	...	...	|	|	...	...	...	...	0602	|
532	Ramdane Djamel d.	0819	...	...	...	|	1711	...	...	...	...	...	0500
550	**Skikda** a.	0841	...	...	...	|	1735	...	...	...	...	...	|
645	**Jijel** a.	...	...	...	...	1850	...	...	...	...	...	...	|
557	Azzaba d.	...	...	...	...	...	...	...	...	...	...	...	0558
631	**Annaba** a.	...	...	...	...	...	...	...	...	...	...	...	0628

	B28	B32 ①③⑥	BA	B5	18	14	B431	152	1451	B114	154	321 ①③
	B	D	E	A	[R]	2	2C	2	2C	2	2	2
Annaba d.	...	...	1920	...	...	...	...	...	...	...	...	...
Azzaba d.	...	...	2016	...	...	...	...	...	...	...	...	...
Jijel d.	...	...	|	...	...	...	...	...	0945	...	...	...
Skikda d.	...	...	|	...	...	...	0600	...	|	...	...	1720
Ramdane Djamal d.	...	...	2041	...	...	...	0621	...	|	...	...	1740
Tebessa d.	...	1730	|	...	...	...	|	...	|	...	...	|
Aïn Beïda d.	...	1933	|	...	...	...	|	...	|	...	...	|
Aïn M'Lila d.	...	2123	|	...	...	...	|	...	|	...	...	|
El Harrouch d.	...	|	2114	...	...	...	|	...	|	...	...	|
Constantine d.	...	|	2149	...	...	...	0739	...	1240	...	...	1850
Setif d.	...	2339	0017	...	0540	...	...	...	...	...	...	...
M'Sila d.	2312	|	|	0115	|	...	...	...	...	...	...	...
Bordj Bou Arreridj d.	0017	0028	0107	0204	0626	...	...	...	...	...	...	...
Béjaïa d.	|	|	|	|	|	0630	...	0855	...	1445	1700	...
Beni Mansour d.	0142	0142	0219	0305	0728	0803	...	1102	...	1623	1859	...
Bouira d.	0234	0234	0349	0344	0807	0844	...	...	...	1726	...	...
Thénia ⊡ d.	0400	0400	0436	|	|	|	...	...	...	1846	...	...
Alger ⊡ a.	0500	0500	0543	0530	1001	1028	...	...	...	1935	...	...

A – (12) Alger - M'Sila - Batna and v.v.
B – 🛏 (12) Alger - M'Sila - Touggourt and v.v.
C – ①②③④⑥⑦ (not public holidays).
D – 🛏 (12) Alger - Tebbesa and v.v.
E – 🛏 (12) Alger - Annaba and v.v.
⊡ – Additional local trains available.

TUNISIA

pital: **Tunis** (GMT +1). 2023 Public Holidays: Jan. 1, 14, Apr. 9, 21–23, May 1, June 28, 29, July 18, 25, Sept. 27, Oct. 15, Dec. 17.
vices are operated by Société Nationale des Chemins de Fer Tunisiens (www.sncft.com). Unless otherwise noted trains convey first and second class seated accommodation. Overnight trains y also convey sleeping cars and/or couchettes. Supplements may be payable in advance for the use of certain trains. Timings are the most recent available and are subject to alteration at any e especially during Ramadan. SNCFT offers the **Carte Bleue** pass. The pass allows unlimited travel on all scheduled services (except the Lézard Rouge tourist train) for a period of 7, 15, or 21 /s, and is available for each of the three classes of accommodation. Prices (in Dinars): Grand Confort Class 7 days 45.00, 15 days 90.00, 21 days 135.00. First Class 7 days 42.00, 15 days 00, 21 days, 126.00. Second Class 7 days 30.00, 15 days 60.00, 21 days 90.00.

GHARDIMAOU - TUNIS 4050

m		2 ⚒	8	12	14	20
0	**Annaba** d.	...	...	...	...	...
57	**Ghardimaou** d.	...	0425	1040	1205	1510
01	Jendouba d.	...	0454	1110	1235	1540
59	Béja d.	...	0557	1215	1336	1643
44	Tebourba d.	0540	0731	1352	1506	1813
53	Jedeïa d.	0552	0743	1404	1519	1826
78	**Tunis** Ville a.	0631	0825	1446	1600	1908

	1 ⚒	7	9	13	17
Tunis Ville d.	0420	0635	0905	1300	1715
Jedeïa d.	0500	0719	0948	1341	1759
Tebourba d.	0511	0732	1000	1353	1814
Béja d.	...	0903	1130	1527	1947
Jendouba d.	...	1005	1236	1632	2051
Ghardimaou a.	...	1033	1304	1700	2119
Annaba a.	...	...	...	...	...

BIZERTE - TUNIS 4060

km		1/4 ⚒	1/10 †
0	**Bizerte** d.	0500	0600
34	Mateur d.	0604	0703
73	Jedeïda d.	0718	0811
98	**Tunis** Ville a.	0758	0851

	1/19 Ⓒ	1/25 Ⓐ
Tunis Ville d.	1635	1745
Jedeïda d.	1717	1827
Mateur d.	1820	1930
Bizerte a.	1918	2028

TUNIS - EL KEF and KALAÂ KASBAH 4070

km		6/51	6/57	6/65	6/89	6/73 ⚒
0	**Tunis** Ville d.	0635	0910	1415	1615	1725
63	Pont du Fahs d.	0804	1020	1542	1727	1854
20	Gaafour d.	0907	1108	1644	1815	1955
56	Le Sers d.	1011	1155	1748	1902	2059
02	**El Kef** a.	|	|	|	1938	|
91	Dahmani d.	1040	1217	1816	...	2127
14	Jerissa d.	|	...	...	...	...
24	**Tajerouine** a.	|	...	...	...	...
35	**Kalaâ Kasbah** a.	1147	...	...	...	...

	6/50 ⚒	8/54	6/60	6/68	6/76
Kalaâ Kasbah d.	...	...	...	...	1310
Tajerouine d.	...	...	...	...	|
Jerissa d.	...	...	...	...	|
Dahmani d.	0310	...	0640	1320	1418
El Kef d.	|	0500	|	|	|
Le Sers d.	0339	0537	0709	1343	1447
Gaafour d.	0444	0627	0814	1433	1552
Pont du Fahs d.	0544	0709	0920	1514	1658
Tunis Ville a.	0708	0819	1050	1625	1825

TUNIS - SOUSSE - SFAX - TOZEUR 4080

km		805 2	5/53 2	5/67 2	5/61 2	5/73	815 2	5/79 2	5/83	819 2	5/89 2	821 2	5/97 2
0	**Tunis** Ville ◇ d.	...	0615	0950	1200	1305	...	1515	1620	...	1720	...	2120
23	Borj Cédria ◇ d.	0615	|	|	1231	|	1505	|	|	1715	1758	1930	|
59	Bir Bou Rekba d.	0648	0723	1058	1308	1410	1538	1623	|	1748	1829	2003	2226
64	Hammamet d.	0653	|	|	1314	|	1543	|	|	1753	|	2008	|
76	**Nabeul** a.	0714	|	|	1334	|	1604	|	|	1814	|	2029	|
42	Kalaâ Séghira d.	...	0826	|	...	1512	...	1732	1824	...	1934	...	|
49	**Sousse** a.	...	0838	1212	...	|	...	1744	|	...	|	...	2338
49	**Sousse** d.	...	0850	1225	...	|	...	...	|	...	|	...	2350
74	Monastir d.	...	|	|	...	|	...	...	|	...	2020	...	|
17	**Mahdia** a.	...	|	|	...	|	...	...	|	...	2118	...	|
15	El Jem d.	...	0957	1333	...	1610	...	...	1921	...	...	...	0058
	Sfax a.	...	1045	1422	...	1659	...	...	2010	...	...	...	0147
78	**Sfax** d.	...	1050	1430	...	1703	...	...	2015	...	...	...	0155
40	Ghraïba d.	...	1145	1527	...	1758	...	...	|	...	...	...	0251
22	**Gabès** a.	...	1304	|	...	1914	...	...	2221	...	...	...	0407
	Tataouine a.	...	...	|	...	...	...	...	...	...	...	...	...
82	Gafsa d.	...	...	1752	...	...	...	...	...	...	...	...	...
21	Metlaoui d.	...	...	1831	...	...	...	...	...	...	...	...	...
74	**Tozeur** a.	...	...	...	...	...	...	...	...	...	...	...	...

	802 2	5/90 2	12/52 2⚒	12/54 2†	10/56 2	22/64 2	5/58 2	5/63	812 2	13/72 2	816 2	5/76	5/84 2	820 2
zeur d.	...	...	...	...	...	...	...	...	...	...	...	...	...	...
tlaoui d.	...	...	...	...	...	...	...	...	...	0721	...	...	...	...
fsa d.	...	...	...	...	...	...	...	...	...	0800	...	...	...	...
Tataouine d.	...	...	...	...	...	...	...	...	...	|	...	...	...	...
Gàbes d.	...	0025	...	...	...	...	...	0500	...	|	...	1115	1555	...
raïba d.	...	0141	...	...	...	...	...	|	...	1011	...	1231	1713	...
ax a.	...	0238	...	...	...	...	...	0704	...	1106	...	1327	1813	...
ax d.	...	0245	...	...	...	...	0515	0710	...	1110	...	1335	...	...
Jem d.	...	0335	...	...	...	...	0607	0759	...	1159	...	1428	...	...
Mahdia d.	...	|	...	...	...	0540	|	|	...	|	...	|	...	...
Monastir d.	...	|	...	...	...	0640	|	|	...	|	...	|	...	...
usse a.	...	0442	...	...	...	|	0714	|	...	1304	...	1536	...	...
usse d.	...	0455	0520	0600	...	|	0725	|	...	1315	...	1550	...	...
aâ Seghira d.	...	|	0533	0613	...	0716	0738	0854	...	|	...	|	...	...
Nabeul d.	0505	|	|	|	0720	|	|	|	1340	|	1610	|	...	1825
Hammamet d.	0525	|	|	|	0740	|	|	|	1359	|	1629	|	...	1844
Bou Rekba d.	0533	0608	0644	0724	0748	0816	0841	|	1406	1430	1636	1702	...	1851
j Cédria ◇ d.	0609	|	0718	0758	0822	0846	|	|	1440	|	1710	|	...	1925
nis Ville ◇ a.	...	0715	0752	0832	0857	0921	0948	1058	...	1537	...	1809	...	...

– Regular local services operate Tunis – Borj Cédria – Erriadh and v.v.

SOUSSE - MONASTIR AIRPORT - MAHDIA 4090

km		501	503	505	507	509	511	513	517	519	521	523	525	527	529	531	533	535	537	539	541	543	545	547	549
0	**Sousse** Bab El Jedid d.	...	0515	0545	0630	0715	0750	0835	0910	0950	1030	1110	1200	1230	1310	1355	1425	1520	1605	1650	1715	1745	1840	1925	2015
3	**Sousse** Sud d.	0505	0521	0551	0636	0724	0756	0841	0916	0956	1036	1116	1206	1236	1316	1401	1431	1526	1611	1656	1721	1751	1846	1931	2021
15	Monastir Airport ✈ d.	0519	0534	0605	0650	0735	0810	0855	0930	1010	1050	1130	1219	1250	1330	1415	1445	1540	1625	1710	1735	1805	1900	1945	2035
24	Monastir d.	0535	0544	0620	0705	0750	0830	0905	0945	1025	1105	1150	1235	1305	1345	1430	1500	1555	1645	1730	1752	1820	1922	2000	2050
47	Moknine d.	0607	...	0656	0741	0826	0911	...	1018	1056	1140	1225	1312	1336	1419	1507	1530	1631	1719	1804	1822	1854	1953	2032	2123
73	**Mahdia** a.	0650	...	0733	0820	0904	0950	...	1059	...	1215	1259	1349	...	1456	1543	...	1710	1755	1838	...	1929	2029	2105	2156

	506	508	510	514	516	518	520	522	524	528	530	532	534	536	538	540	542	544	546	548	550	552	554	556
ahdia d.	...	0510	0555	0620	0700	0750	...	0835	0920	1010	...	1145	1230	1320	...	1425	...	1550	1640	1725	...	1810	1900	1940
oknine d.	...	0545	0630	0700	0740	0825	...	0909	0954	1044	1136	1223	1310	1357	1416	1505	1545	1626	1716	1803	1830	1848	1937	2015
onastir d.	0550	0625	0710	0740	0820	0910	0930	0950	1030	1125	1215	1300	1350	1435	1455	1540	1620	1705	1755	1840	1910	1925	2015	2055
onastir Airport ✈ d.	0600	0635	0720	0750	0830	0920	0940	1000	1040	1135	1225	1310	1400	1445	1505	1550	1630	1715	1805	1850	1920	1934	2024	2104
ousse Sud d.	0615	0650	0735	0805	0845	0935	0955	1015	1055	1150	1240	1325	1415	1500	1520	1605	1645	1730	1820	1906	1934	1950	2040	2120
ousse Bab El Jedid a.	0620	0655	0740	0810	0850	0940	1000	1020	1100	1155	1245	1330	1420	1505	1525	1610	1650	1735	1825	1911	1939	1955	2045	2125

EGYPT

Capital: **Cairo** (GMT +2). 2023 Public Holidays: Jan. 7, 25, 26, Apr. 17, 22–25, May 1, June 28–30, July 1, 20, 23, 27, Sept. 28, Oct. 6.

Except where noted all trains are operated by Egyptian National Railways (www.enr.gov.eg). Unless otherwise noted trains convey first and second class seated accommodation. Overnight trains may also convey sleeping cars and/or couchettes. Timings are the most recent available and are subject to alteration at any time especially during Ramadan.

4100 MERSA MATRUH - CAIRO and ALEXANDRIA — ENR

km						774
		2	2	2	A	AB
0	**Mersa Matruh** d.	0700	0810	1445	1715	2200
84	El Alamein d.	0936	1155	1751	1954	|
311	**Alexandria** a.	|	1455	2045	|	|
509	**Cairo** Main a.	1535	...	...	0125	0500

					773
	2	A	2	2	AB
Cairo Main d.	...	0545	0650		2300
Alexandria d.	0640	|	|	1340	|
El Alamein d.	0936	1100	1240	1649	|
Mersa Matruh a.	1230	1330	1525	2020	0620

A – June - Sept. only.
B – 🛏 (1, 2 class). From Mersa on ②④⑦, from Cairo on ①③⑥. Operated by Watania (www.wataniasleepingtrains.com).

4110 CAIRO - ALEXANDRIA — ENR

km		1009	903	905	901	1109	909	911	89	913	917	919	2001	915	923	925	921	927	931	935
0	**Cairo** Main d.	0500	0600	0800	0810	0820	0900	1000	1115	1230	1400	1425	1500	1510	1600	1710	1800	1900	2015	2230
45	Benha d.	|	0640	|	0849	|	|	1040	|	1308	|	1505	|	1600	1640	1740	|	|	2056	|
86	Tanta d.	0755	0734	|	0929	|	|	1120	1225	1345	|	1609	|	1638	1729	1837	1907	|	2145	2337
147	Damanhûr d.	0857	0837	|	1018	1041	|	1213	|	1433	|	1712	|	1729	1830	1932	|	|	2242	|
208	**Alexandria** a.	0950	0930	1030	1115	1135	1150	1305	1355	1525	1630	1805	1730	1820	1925	2025	2035	2130	2335	0105

	1108	902	906		904	900	912	914	916		918	922	88	928	926		2008	930	934
Alexandria d.	0330	0600	0700	...	0800	0815	1130	1300	1400	...	1500	1530	1700	1800	1900	...	2000	2010	2215
Damanhûr d.	0437	0659	|	...	|	0914	1229	1358	|	...	|	1633	|	|	|	...	|	2109	|
Tanta d.	0536	0758	|	...	|	1004	1319	1455	|	...	|	1727	1833	1942	|	...	2133	2204	2343
Benha d.	0626	0840	|	...	|	1035	1400	1540	|	...	|	1803	|	|	|	...	|	2235	|
Cairo Main a.	0710	0925	0935	...	1030	1120	1445	1620	1630	...	1745	1850	1935	2050	2130	...	2235	2320	0050

4120 DUMYAT — ENR 2nd class

km		941	965	967	568	969
240	**Alexandria** d.	...	...	...	1815	...
205	**Cairo** Main d.	0515	0730	0915	|	1935
0	**Dumyat** a.	1015	1130	1350	2255	2359

	964	566	956	994	968
Dumyat d.	0600	0715	1315	1615	1915
Cairo Main a.	1010	|	1815	2025	2340
Alexandria a.	...	1220	...	...	...

4130 BÛR SA'ÎD — ENR 2nd class

km		945	588	185	951	955	572	961
334	**Alexandria** d.	...	0430	...	...	...	1610	...
236	**Cairo** Main d.	0610	|	0840	1200	1440	|	1950
0	**Bûr Sa'îd** a.	1020	1110	1240	1640	1905	2225	0005

	952	570	186	956	960	590	962
Bûr Sa'îd d.	0530	0725	0830	1300	1730	1815	1930
Cairo Main a.	0955	|	1250	1725	2145	|	2350
Alexandria a.	...	1330	...	...	...	0050	...

4140 EL SUWEIS — ENR 2nd class

km		305	307	309	311
0	**Cairo** Ain Shams d.	0630	1000	1430	1800
127	**El Suweis** a.	0850	1320	1750	2120

	304	306	308	310
El Suweis d.	0615	1030	1400	1830
Cairo Ain Shams a.	0935	1355	1720	2200

4150 ASWÂN — ENR

km		1902	980	982	986	86 ◧	988	88	996	2008
0	**Cairo** Main d.	0020	0800	1200	1300	1945	1900	2000	2200	2300
13	El Giza d.	0045	0830	1225	1325	2005	1925	2025	2230	2330
124	Béni Suef d.	|	0948	1354	1447	|	2044	2156	2348	|
247	El Menya d.	|	1115	1530	1630	|	2220	2345	0130	|
375	Asyût d.	0515	1310	1725	1840	|	0015	0150	0330	0355
467	Sohâg d.	0705	1500	1915	2015	|	0140	0320	0500	0520
609	Qena d.	0920	1800	2200	2300	|	0350	0615	0715	0735
671	Luxor d.	1020	1900	2310	2359	0555	0450	0730	0815	0840
879	**Aswân** a.	1320	2240	0225	...	0925	0750	1055	1130	1145

	981	983	2007	1903	87 ◧	997	89	989	987
Aswân d.	0530	0730	1500	1700	1715	2045	2105	2300	...
Luxor d.	0910	1055	1830	2010	2025	0005	0035	0215	0450
Qena d.	1015	1200	1925	2105	|	0100	0140	0305	0600
Sohâg d.	1255	1440	2150	2320	|	0310	0415	0510	0840
Asyût d.	1435	1630	2320	0105	|	0435	0545	0640	1015
El Menya d.	1625	1825	0105	|	|	0630	0740	0825	1220
Béni Suef d.	1754	1949	|	|	|	0800	0912	0953	1353
El Giza d.	|	2110	|	0520	0600	0855	|	1020	1515
Cairo Main a.	1935	2130	0355	0550	0625	0950	1100	1135	1535

◧ – 🛏 (1, 2 class). Operated by Watania (www.wataniasleepingtrains.com).

OTHER AFRICAN STATES

For details of capital cities and public holiday dates please see individual tables. All trains shown convey seated accommodation. Long-distance overnight trains may also convey sleeping cars and or couchettes. The standard of accommodation varies widely with no two countries being the same so no attempt is made in the following Tables to distinguish between classes of accommodation. Timings are the latest available and may change at any time so you are advised to confirm them locally before travelling. In Muslim countries a different timetable may be operated during Ramadan.

4200 SUDAN — Sudan Railways Corporation

km			②⑦
926	**Wadi Halfa** d.	⊖	...
576	Abu Hamed d.	⊖	...
551	Dagash d.	...	...
351	Berber d.	...	...
810	**Bûr Sûdan** d.	...	1400
	Sinkat d.	...	|
720	Gebeit d.	...	|
620	Haiya Junction d.	...	|
310	**Atbara** a.	...	1200
310	**Atbara** d.	...	1300
295	Ed Dâmer d.	...	|
170	Shendî d.	...	|
0	**Khartoum** a.	...	1700
0	**Khartoum** d.	...	...
270	Sennâr Junction d.	...	...
383	Kôsti d.	...	...
470	Tendelti d.	...	...
605	Er Rahad d.	...	...
629	**El Obeid** a.	...	...
983	Babanusa d.	...	...
	El Daien d.	...	...
1318	**Nyâlâ** a.	...	...

	①⑥	
Nyâlâ d.	...	...
El Daien d.	...	...
Babanusa d.	...	...
El Obeid d.	...	...
Er Rahad d.	...	...
Tendelti d.	...	...
Kôsti d.	...	...
Sennâr Junction d.	...	...
Khartoum a.	...	...
Khartoum d.	0900	...
Shendî d.	|	...
Ed Dâmer d.	|	...
Atbara a.	1300	...
Atbara d.	1400	...
Haiya Junction d.	|	...
Gebeit d.	|	...
Sinkat d.	|	...
Bûr Sûdan a.	1400	...
Berber d.	...	...
Dagash d.	...	...
Abu Hamed d.	...	⊖
Wadi Halfa a.	...	⊖

Capital: **Khartoum** (GMT +2). 2023 Public Holidays: Jan. 1, 7, Apr. 16, 22–25, June 28–30, July 1, 2, 19, Sept. 27, Dec. 25.

⊖ – No timings available.

Ethio-Djibouti Railway — ETHIOPIA and DJIBOUTI — 4215

km		101 A	K1 B		102 B	K2 A
0	**Addis Abeba** Lebu .... d.	0740	...	**Djibouti** Nagad .... d.	...	0930
98	Adama .... d.	1000	...	Ali Sabieh .... 🏛 d.	...	1050
	Mieso .... d.	1450	...	Dewelé .... 🏛 a.	...	1240
446	**Diré Daoua** .... a.	1800	...	**Diré Daoua** .... a.	...	1530
446	**Diré Daoua** .... d.	...	0830	**Diré Daoua** .... d.	0905	...
	Dawanle .... 🏛 a.	...	1210	Mieso .... d.	1040	...
664	Ali Sabieh .... 🏛 d.	...	1310	Adama .... d.	1610	...
728	**Djibouti** Nagad .... a.	...	1430	**Addis Abeba** Lebu ...... d.	1800	...

Capitals: **Addis Abeba** (Ethiopia, GMT +3), **Djibouti** (Djibouti, GMT +3).

2023 Public Holidays: Ethiopia: Jan. 7, 19, Mar. 2, Apr. 14, 16, 22, May 1, 5, 28, June 29, Sept. 12, 27. 28. Djibouti: Jan. 1, Feb. 18, Apr. 22, 23, May 1, June 27–30, July 19, Sept. 27

A – Uneven dates (not 31st or Feb. 29).

B – Even dates.

SNIM — MAURITANIA — 4220

km						
0	**Nouadhibou** .... d.	1450	...	**Zouèrate** .... d.	1215	...
652	**Zouèrate** .... a.	0540	...	**Nouadhibou** .... a.	0618	...

Capital: **Nouakchott** (GMT +0).

2023 Public Holidays: Jan. 1, Apr. 22, May 1, 25, June 29, July 19, Sept. 27, Nov. 28.

Operator: Société Nationale Industrielle et Minière.

CFG, CFB — GUINEA — 4230

km		①–⑤	①–⑤	①–⑤		①–⑤	①–⑤	①–⑤
0	**Conakry** Portovoya d.	...	0847	1725	**Halte Km 36** .... d.	0645	...	1916
	Simbaya .... d.	0600	0940	1829	Simbaya .... d.	0730	1630	1950
36	**Halte Km 36** .... a.	0640	...	1906	**Conakry** P'voya .. a.	0837	1710	...

km			①④⑦				①④⑦	
0	**Kamsar** .... d.	...	0930	...	**Sangaredi** .... d.	...	1430	...
55	Boké .... d.	...	1135	...	Boké .... d.	...	1615	...
136	**Sangaredi** .... a.	...	1355	...	**Kamsar** .... a.	...	1855	...

Capital: **Conakry** (GMT +0).

2023 Public Holidays: Jan. 1, Apr. 3, 10, 17, 22, May 1, 25, June 29, Aug. 15, Sept. 27, Oct. 2, Nov. 1, Dec. 25.

Operators: Chemins de Fer Guinea (CFG), Chemins de Fer de Boké (CFB).

Sitarail — BURKINA FASO and CÔTE D'IVOIRE — 4260

km		②④⑥			①③⑤	
0	**Ouagadougou** .... d.	...	...	**Abidjan** Treichville ...... d.	0900	...
93	Koudougou .... d.	...	...	**Abidjan** Plateau .... d.	0920	...
349	Bobo Dioulasso .... d.	...	...	Anyama .... d.	1015	...
446	Banfora .... d.	...	...	Agboville .... d.	1240	...
495	Niangoloko .... 🏛 d.	...	...	Dimbokro .... d.	1615	...
539	Ouangolodougou .... d.	...	...	Bouaké .... d.	...	...
576	Ferkessédougou .... d.	...	...	Katiola .... d.	...	...
658	Tafiré .... d.	...	...	Tafiré .... d.	...	...
769	Katiola .... d.	...	...	Ferkessédougou .... d.	...	...
820	Bouaké .... d.	...	...	Ouangolodougou .... d.	...	...
958	Dimbokro .... d.	0900	...	Niangoloko .... 🏛 d.	...	...
1064	Agboville .... d.	1255	...	Banfora .... d.	...	...
1115	Anyama .... d.	1515	...	Bobo Dioulasso .... d.	...	...
1141	**Abidjan** Plateau .... a.	1610	...	Koudougou .... d.	...	...
1143	**Abidjan** Treichville .... a.	1625	...	**Ouagadougou** .... a.	...	...

Capitals: **Ouagadougou** (Burkina Faso, GMT +0), **Yamoussoukro** (Côte d'Ivoire, GMT +0).

2023 Public Holidays: Burkina Faso: Jan. 1–3, Mar. 8, Apr. 10, 22, May 1, 18, June 29, Aug. 5, 15, Sept. 27, Nov. 1, Dec. 11, 25. Côte d'Ivoire: Jan. 1, Apr. 10, 18, 22, May 1, 18, 29, June 29, Aug. 7, 15, Sept. 27, Nov. 1, 15, Dec. 25.

Nigerian Railways Corporation — NIGERIA — 4270

km		LI1	LI3		IL2	IL4
0	**Lagos** Terminal .... d.	0800	1600	**Kano** .... d.	...	...
14	Agege .... d.	0826	1626	Zaria .... d.	...	...
91	Abeokuta .... d.	0945	1745	**Kaduna** Junction .... d.	...	...
193	Ibadan .... d.	1048	1848	Zungeru .... d.	...	...
280	Ede .... d.	...	...	Jebba .... d.	...	...
295	Oshogbo .... d.	...	...	Ilorin .... d.	...	...
391	Ilorin .... d.	...	...	Oshogbo .... d.	...	...
488	Jebba .... d.	...	...	Ede .... d.	...	...
685	Zungeru .... d.	...	...	Ibadan .... d.	0800	1600
902	**Kaduna** Junction .... a.	...	...	Abeokuta .... d.	0910	1710
986	Zaria .... d.	...	...	Agege .... d.	1027	1827
1126	**Kano** .... a.	...	...	**Lagos** Terminal .... a.	1048	1848

km						
0	**Port Harcourt** New .... d.	...	...	**Maiduguri** .... d.	...	...
63	Aba .... d.	...	...	Buni .... d.	...	...
113	Umuahia Ibeku .... d.	...	...	Gombe .... d.	...	...
243	Enugu .... d.	...	...	Bauchi .... d.	...	...
375	Oturkpo .... d.	...	...	**Kaduna** Junction .... d.	...	...
463	Makurdi .... d.	...	...	Kafanchan .... d.	...	...
565	Lafia .... d.	...	...	Lafia .... d.	...	...
737	Kafanchan .... d.	...	...	Makurdi .... d.	...	...
916	**Kaduna** Junction .... d.	...	...	Oturkpo .... d.	...	...
1333	Bauchi .... d.	...	...	Enugu .... d.	...	...
1499	Gombe .... d.	...	...	Umuahia Ibeku .... d.	...	...
1658	Buni .... d.	...	...	Aba .... d.	...	...
1801	**Maiduguri** .... a.	...	...	**P Harcourt** New .... a.	...	...

km		KA2	KA4	04	KA6	KA8				
0	**Kaduna** Rigasa .... d.	0640	1035	...	1400	1800	...	...	...	...
	Rijana .... d.	0716	1128	...	1441	1843	...	...	...	...
	Jere .... d.	0757	1217	...	1525	1929	...	...	...	...
	Kubwa .... d.	0831	1304	...	1603	2007	...	...	...	...
	Abuja Idu .... a.	0843	1320	...	1616	2020	...	...	...	...
	Abuja Idu .... d.	...	...	...	...	...	...	...	...	...
	Itakpe .... d.	...	...	1400	...	...	...	...	...	...
	Ajaokuta .... d.	...	...	⊖	...	...	...	...	...	...
	Itogbo .... d.	...	...	⊖	...	...	...	...	...	...
	Agenebode .... d.	...	...	⊖	...	...	...	...	...	...
	Uromi .... d.	...	...	⊖	...	...	...	...	...	...
	Ekehen .... d.	...	...	⊖	...	...	...	...	...	...
	Igbanke .... d.	...	...	⊖	...	...	...	...	...	...
	Agbor .... d.	...	...	⊖	...	...	...	...	...	...
	Abraka .... d.	...	...	⊖	...	...	...	...	...	...
	Okpara .... d.	...	...	⊖	...	...	...	...	...	...
	Warri Ujevwu .... a.	...	...	1907	...	...	...	...	...	...

	AK1	AK3	01	AK5	AK7				
Warri Ujevwu .... d.	...	...	0800	...	...	...	...	...	...
Okpara .... d.	...	...	⊖	...	...	...	...	...	...
Abraka .... d.	...	...	⊖	...	...	...	...	...	...
Agbor .... d.	...	...	⊖	...	...	...	...	...	...
Igbanke .... d.	...	...	⊖	...	...	...	...	...	...
Ekehen .... d.	...	...	⊖	...	...	...	...	...	...
Uromi .... d.	...	...	⊖	...	...	...	...	...	...
Agenebode .... d.	...	...	⊖	...	...	...	...	...	...
Itogbo .... d.	...	...	⊖	...	...	...	...	...	...
Ajaokuta .... d.	...	...	⊖	...	...	...	...	...	...
Itakpe .... a.	...	...	1307	...	...	...	...	...	...
Abuja Idu .... a.	...	...	...	...	...	...	...	...	...
Abuja Idu .... d.	0700	0950	...	1420	1800	...	...	...	...
Kubwa .... d.	0717	1007	...	1441	1815	...	...	...	...
Jere .... d.	0755	1043	...	1528	1846	...	...	...	...
Rijana .... d.	0835	1126	...	1617	1921	...	...	...	...
Kaduna Rigasa .... a.	0915	1201	...	1700	1958	...	...	...	...

Capital: **Abuja** (GMT +1). 2023 Public Holidays: Jan. 1, Apr. 7, 10, 22, 23, May 1, June 12, 29, 30, Sept. 27, Oct. 1, Dec. 25, 26.

⊖ – No information available.

Camrail — CAMEROON — 4280

km		185	191 🛏		192 🛏	186
0	**Douala** Bessengué .... d.	0630	...	**N'gaoundéré** .... d.	1915	...
72	Edéa .... d.	0750	...	Mbitom .... d.	0155	...
152	Eséka .... d.	0908	...	Belabo .... d.	0515	...
220	Ngoumou .... d.	1021	...	Nanga Eboko .... d.	0741	...
263	**Yaoundé** .... d.	1115	1950	**Yaoundé** .... d.	1107	1700
477	Nanga Eboko .... d.	...	2318	Ngoumou .... d.	...	1749
582	Belabo .... d.	...	0152	Eséka .... d.	...	1900
686	Mbitom .... d.	...	0554	Edéa .... d.	...	2022
910	**N'gaoundéré** .... a.	...	1232	**Douala** B'sengué .... a.	...	2145

km						
0	Douala Bonaberi .... d.	...	...	Kumba .... d.	...	...
	Mbanga .... d.	...	...	Mbanga .... d.	...	...
	Kumba .... a.	...	...	Douala Bonaberi .... a.	...	...

Capital: **Youandé** (GMT +1).

2023 Public Holidays: Jan. 1, 2, Feb. 11, Apr. 7, May 1, 18, 20, June 29, Aug. 15, Dec. 25.

SETRAG — GABON — 4290

km		①③⑤	②④⑦			①③⑤	②④⑦	
0	**Owendo** ◧ .... d.	1730	1730	...	**Franceville** .... d.	1700	1700	...
183	Ndjole .... d.	2300	2305	...	Moanda .... d.	1730	1730	...
340	Booué .... d.	0205	0203	...	Lastourville .... d.	1933	1930	...
485	Lastourville .... d.	0416	0418	...	Booué .... d.	2148	2146	...
625	Moanda .... d.	0620	0628	...	Ndjole .... d.	0051	0100	...
670	**Franceville** .... a.	0700	0710	...	**Owendo** ◧ .... a.	0631	0635	...

Capital: **Libreville** (GMT +1).

2023 Public Holidays: Jan. 1, Apr. 9, 10, 17, 22, May 1, 18, 29, June 29, Aug. 15–17, Nov. 1, Dec. 25.

◧ – Libreville.

CF Congo Océan — CONGO — 4300

km		②⑤	③⑦	⑥		②⑥	①④	⑥
0	**Brazzaville** .... d.	...	...	...	**Pointe Noire** ...... d.	0800	0900	1000
137	Mindouli .... d.	...	...	...	M'Vouti .... d.	1330	|	1500
190	Loutété .... d.	...	0800	...	Dolisie .... d.	1500	1730	...
261	Nkayi .... d.	...	1015	...	Nkayi .... d.	1830	...	...
342	Dolisie .... d.	0330	1345	...	Loutété .... d.	2045	...	...
382	M'Voui .... d.	|	1515	1800	Mindouli .... d.	...	...	...
509	**Pointe Noire** .... a.	1130	2045	2230	**Brazzaville** .... a.	...	...	...

Capital: **Brazzaville** (GMT +1).

2023 Public Holidays: Jan. 1, Apr. 10, May 1, 18, 29, June 10, Aug. 15, Nov. 1, 28, Dec. 25.

BEYOND EUROPE - OTHER AFRICAN STATES

4310 KENYA
Kenya Railways

km		①–⑤	⑤–⑦		①–⑤					
0	**Mombasa** d.	...	...	0800	...	1500	2200	...	...	...
	Voi d.	...	...	0955	...	1643	|	...	...	...
	Mtito Andei d.	...	...	1121	...	|	|	...	...	...
	Emali d.	...	...	1239	...	|	|	...	...	...
485	**Nairobi** Terminus ⊡ a.	...	...	1410	...	2018	0335	...	...	...
485	**Nairobi** Terminus ⊡ d.	0510	0850	...	1840	...	...	...	...	...
	Ngong d.	0552	0949	...	1922	...	...	...	...	...
605	**Suswa** a.	...	1110	...	...	...	...	...	...	...

	①–⑤			⑤–⑦	①–⑤			
Suswa d.	...	...	...	1550	...	...	...	...
Ngong d.	0620	...	...	1721	1947	...	...	...
Nairobi Terminus ⊡ a.	0704	...	...	1810	2028	...	...	...
Nairobi Terminus ⊡ d.	...	0800	1500	...	...	2200	...	...
Emali d.	...	0931	|	...	...	|	...	...
Mtito Andei d.	...	1054	|	...	...	|	...	...
Voi d.	...	1208	1853	...	...	|	...	...
Mombasa a.	...	1400	2030	...	...	0335	...	...

km		②⑤	
0	**Nairobi** Central d.	0900	...
	Thika d.	1116	...
160	**Nanyuki** a.	1649	...

	③⑦	
Nanyuki d.	0900	...
Thika d.	1432	...
Nairobi Central a.	1646	...

km				
0	**Nairobi** d.	...	...	...
182	Nakuru d.	...	...	...
396	**Kisumu** a.	...	...	...

Kisumu d.	...	...	...
Nakuru d.	...	...	...
Nairobi a.	...	...	...

Capital: **Nairobi** (GMT +3). 2023 Public Holidays: Jan. 1, 2, Apr. 7, 10, 23, May 1, June 1, Oct. 10, 20, Dec. 12, 25, 26.

⊡ – Nairobi Terminus - Nairobi Central and v.v. Journey 35 minutes:
From Nairobi Terminus at 0350, 0625, 0720, 0855, 1045, 1435, 2015; from Nairobi Central at 0635, 0800, 0935, 1200, 1730, 1820, 2010.

4320 DEMOCRATIC CONGO
Société Nationale des Chemins de Fer du Congo

km				
0	Lubumbashi d.	...	⊖	...
237	Tenke d.	...	⊖	...
757	Dilolo d.	...	|	...
600	Kamina d.	...	⊖	...
1047	Kabalo d.	...	|	...
1583	Kindu a.	...	|	...
1320	Kalemie a.	...	|	...
913	Mwene Ditu d.	...	⊖	...
1156	Kananga d.	...	⊖	...
1578	Ilebo a.	...	...	...

Ilebo d.	...	...	...
Kananga d.	...	⊖	...
Mwene Ditu d.	...	⊖	...
Kalemie d.	...	|	...
Kindu d.	...	|	...
Kabalo d.	...	|	...
Kamina d.	...	⊖	...
Dilolo d.	...	|	...
Tenke d.	...	⊖	...
Lubumbashi a.	...	⊖	...

km			
0	**Sakania** d.	⊖	...
255	**Lubumbashi** a.	⊖	...

Lubumbashi d.	⊖	...
Sakania a.	⊖	...

km			
0	**Kinshasa** Est d.	⊖	...
366	**Matadi** a.	⊖	...

Matadi d.	⊖	...
Kinshasa Est a.	⊖	...

km			
0	**Kisangani** d.	⊖	...
125	**Ubundu** a.	⊖	...

Ubundu d.	⊖	...
Kisangani a.	⊖	...

Capital: **Kinshasa** (GMT +1). 2023 Public Holidays: Jan. 1, 4, 16, 17, May 1, 17, June 30, Aug. 1, Dec. 25. ⊖ – No information available.

4330 TANZANIA and ZAMBIA
Tanzania Railways, TAZARA, Zambian Railways

km	*Tanzania Railways*	A	
0	**Dar es Salaam** ◧ d.	⊖	⊖
78	Ruvu d.	⊖	⊖
203	Morogoro d.	⊖	⊖
290	Kilosa d.	⊖	⊖
465	Dodoma d.	⊖	⊖
578	Manyoni d.	⊖	⊖
637	Itigi d.	⊖	⊖
840	**Tabora** a.	⊖	⊖
840	**Tabora** ⊖ d.	⊖	⊖
975	Kaliua ⊖ d.	⊖	⊖
1051	**Mpanda** ⊖ a.	|	|
	Mwanza a.	|	⊖
1144	Uvinza d.	⊖	...
1256	**Kigoma** a.	⊖	...

	A	
Kigoma d.	⊖	...
Uvinza d.	⊖	...
Mwanza d.	|	⊖
Mpanda ⊖ d.	|	|
Kaliua ⊖ d.	⊖	⊖
Tabora ⊖ a.	⊖	⊖
Tabora d.	⊖	⊖
Itigi d.	⊖	⊖
Manyoni d.	⊖	⊖
Dodoma d.	⊖	⊖
Kilosa d.	⊖	⊖
Morogoro d.	⊖	⊖
Ruvu d.	⊖	⊖
Dar es Salaam ◧ a.	⊖	⊖

km	*Tanzania Railways*		
0	**Dar es Salaam** ● d.	...	...
	Pugu ● d.	...	...
	Soga ● d.	...	...
	Ruvu ● d.	...	...
	Ngerengere ● d.	...	...
205	**Morogoro** ● a.	...	...

Morogoro ● d.	...	...
Ngerengere ● d.	...	...
Ruvu ● d.	...	...
Soga ● d.	...	...
Pugu ● d.	...	...
Dar es Salaam ● a.	...	...

km	*Zambia Railways*	⑤ 🛏 ✕	
0	**Kitwe** Nkana d.	1600	...
66	Ndola d.	1855	...
199	Kapiri Mposhi ⊡ d.	2357	...
262	Kabwe d.	0255	...
331	Chisamba d.	0500	...
384	**Lusaka** a.	0656	...
384	**Lusaka** d.	0736	...
432	Kafue d.	0946	...
481	Mazabuka d.	1155	...
540	Monze d.	1417	...
577	Pemba d.	1558	...
643	Choma d.	1834	...
713	Kalomo d.	2108	...
851	**Livingstone** a.	0200	...

	① 🛏 ✕	
Livingstone d.	2000	...
Kalomo d.	0100	...
Choma d.	0345	...
Pemba d.	0609	...
Monze d.	0749	...
Mazabuka d.	1015	...
Kafue d.	1244	...
Lusaka a.	1424	...
Lusaka d.	1524	...
Chisamba d.	1656	...
Kabwe d.	1946	...
Kapiri Mposhi ⊡ d.	2216	...
Ndola d.	0336	...
Kitwe Nkana a.	0600	...

km	*Tanzania Railways*		
0	**Dar es Salaam** ◧ d.	⊖	...
78	Ruvu d.	⊖	...
	Mruazi d.	⊖	...
555	Moshi d.	⊖	...
631	**Arusha** a.	⊖	...

Arusha d.	⊖	...
Moshi d.	⊖	...
Mruazi d.	⊖	...
Ruvu d.	⊖	...
Dar es Salaam ◧ a.	⊖	...

km	*TAZARA*	⑤ C	
0	**Dar es Salaam** ◧ d.	1550	...
226	Kisaki d.	2013	...
360	Ifakara d.	2258	...
496	Mlimba d.	0152	...
652	Makambako d.	0746	...
849	Mbeya d.	1323	...
969	Tunduma d.	1717	...
970	Nakonde 🏛 a.	1622	...
970	Nakonde 🏛 d.	1647	...
1226	Kasama d.	2227	...
1412	Mpika d.	0148	...
1652	Serenje d.	0556	...
1761	Mkushi Boma d.	|	...
1852	**New Kapiri Mposhi** ⊡ a.	0926	...

	② C	
New Kapiri Mposhi ⊡ d.	1600	...
Mkushi Boma d.	|	...
Serenje d.	1947	...
Mpika d.	0010	...
Kasama d.	0329	...
Nakonde 🏛 a.	0839	...
Nakonde 🏛 d.	0909	...
Tunduma d.	1029	...
Mbeya d.	1428	...
Makambako d.	2030	...
Mlimba d.	0208	...
Ifakara d.	0512	...
Kisaki d.	0757	...
Dar es Salaam ◧ a.	1210	...

km	*Zambia Railways*	③	
0	**Mulobezi** d.	1200	...
85	Ngwezi d.	⊖	...
163	**Livingstone** a.	0200	...

	②	
Livingstone d.	1400	...
Ngwezi d.	⊖	...
Mulobezi a.	0200	...

Capitals: **Dodoma** (Tanzania, GMT +3), **Lusaka** (Zambia, GMT +2).

2023 Public Holidays: Tanzania: Jan. 1, 12, Apr. 7, 10, 22, 23, 26, May 1, June 29, July 7, Aug. 8, Sept. 27, Oct. 14, Dec. 9, 25, 26. Zambia: Jan. 1, 2, Mar. 8, 12, 13, Apr. 7, 8, 10, 28, May 1, 25, July 3, 4, Aug. 7, Oct. 18, 24, Dec. 25.

A – 🛏, ✕. Journey 51 hours.
C – 🛏, 🛏, ✕.
◧ – Stations are approximately *8 km* from each other.
⊡ – Stations are approximately *2 km* from each other.
⊖ – Service available. Timings unknown.
● – New standard gauge railway.
⊖ – No information available.

4340 MADAGASCAR
Chemins de Fer Fianarantsoa-Côte Est, Madarail

km	*Madarail*	②⑥	
0	**Toamasina** d.	...	...
43	Tampolo d.	...	...
86	Ambila-Lemaitso d.	0700	...
162	Lohariandava d.	⊖	...
223	Andasibe ◇ d.	⊖	...
249	**Moramanga** a.	1600	...

	④⑦	
Moramanga d.	0700	...
Andasibe ◇ d.	⊖	...
Lohariandava d.	⊖	...
Ambila-Lemaitso d.	1600	...
Tampolo d.	...	...
Toamasina a.	...	...

km	*CFFCE*	②④⑥	
0	**Fianarantsoa** d.	0700	...
39	Ranomena d.	0855	...
62	Tolongoina d.	1015	...
79	Manampatrana d.	1110	...
118	Sahasinaka d.	1330	...
163	**Manakara** a.	1600	...

	③⑤⑦	
Manakara d.	0645	...
Sahasinaka d.	0900	...
Manampatrana d.	1130	...
Tolongoina d.	1225	...
Ranomena d.	1355	...
Fianarantsoa a.	1600	...

Capital: **Antananarivo** (GMT +3). 2023 Public Holidays: Jan. 1, Mar. 8, 29, Apr. 10, 22, May 1, 18, 29, June 26, 29, Aug. 15, Nov. 1, Dec, 25.

◇ – Special tour trains using Michelin railcars run Andasibe - Antananarivo and v.v. For dates contact operator. ⊖ – Information not available.

4345 BOTSWANA
Botswana Railways

km			
0	**Francistown** d.	...	...
235	Mahalapye d.	...	...
435	Gaborone d.	...	...
507	**Lobatse** a.	...	...

Lobatse d.	...	...
Gaborone d.	...	...
Mahalapye d.	...	...
Francistown a.	...	...

Capital: **Gaborone** (GMT +2).
2023 Public Holidays: Jan. 1–3, Apr. 7, 8, 10, May 1, 18, July 1, 17, 18, Sept. 30, Oct. 1, 2 Dec, 25, 26.

4348 MALAWI
Nacala Logistics

km				
0	Balaka d.	...	...	...
16	Nkaya d.	...	...	...
42	Liwonde d.	...	...	...
114	Nayuchi a.	...	...	...
104	Blantyre d.	...	...	...
112	Limbe d.	...	...	...
233	Makhanga a.	...	...	...

Makhanga d.	...	...	...
Limbe d.	...	...	...
Blantyre d.	...	...	...
Nayuchi d.	...	...	...
Liwonde d.	...	...	...
Nkaya d.	...	...	...
Balaka d.	...	...	...

Capital: **Lilongwe** (GMT +2).
2023 Public Holidays: Jan. 1, 2, 15, 16, Mar. 3, Apr. 7, 8, 10, 22, May 1, 14, 15, July 6, Oct. 15, 16, Dec. 25, 26.

ANGOLA — 4350

CF Benguela, CF Luanda, CF Moçâmedes

km	CF Luanda		①–⑤	⑥
0	Luanda Muceques	d.	0814	0819
23	Viana	d.	0851	0906
65	Catete	d.	0951	1006
135	Zenza	d.	...	...
190	Dondo (Cuanza)	a.	...	...
241	N'dalatando	d.	...	...
424	Malange	a.	...	...

			①–⑤	⑥
	Malange	d.	...	...
	N'dalatando	d.	...	...
	Dondo (Cuanza)	d.	...	...
	Zenza	d.	...	...
	Catete	d.	1010	1020
	Viana	d.	1115	1125
	Luanda M'ques	a.	1152	1202

km	CF Moçâmedes		①⑤	
0	Namibe	d.	...	...
162	Bibala	d.	...	...
246	Lubango	d.	0900	...
424	Matala	d.	⊖	...
509	Dongo	a.	⊖	...
756	Menongue	a.	1930	...
584	Tchamutete Cidade	a.	...	...

			②⑥	
	Tchamutete Cidade	d.	...	...
	Menongue	d.	0700	...
	Dongo	a.	⊖	...
	Matala	d.	⊖	...
	Lubango	d.	1730	...
	Bibala	d.	...	...
	Namibe	a.	...	...

km	CF Benguela		①–⑤	①	②③⑥	①–⑤	②	①	⑤	①–⑤	①–⑤
0	Lobita	d.	0620	0700	...	0835	...	...	...	1220	1520
33	Benguela	a.	0730	⊖	...	0945	...	...	...	1330	1630
355	Caála	d.	...	⊖	...	[redacted]	...	...	...	...	...
368	Dango	d.	...	⊖	...	...	...	...	...	...	...
383	Huambo	d.	...	⊖	...	...	...	0530	0630	...	...
413	Cambuio	d.	...	⊖	...	⑤	...	⊖	⊖	...	...
460	Katchiungo	a.	...	⊖	...		...	⊖	⊖	...	...
585	Kuito	d.	...	⊖	...	0600	0700	⊖	⊖	...	...
976	Luena	a.	...	0324	0500	1441	1540	1810	1852	...	...
292	Luau	a.	...	...	1113	...	...	...	...	...	...

			③⑥	④	⑦	③	①–⑤	①–⑤	①–⑤	①–⑤	②③⑥
	Luau	d.	...	...	...	...	...	...	...	...	1230
	Luena	d.	0500	0500	0600	0800	...	...	...	...	1905
	Kuito	d.	⊖	1343	1602	⊖	...	...	...	...	...
	Katchiungo	d.	⊖	...	...	⊖	...	...	...	...	...
	Cambuio	d.	⊖	...	...	⊖	...	...	...	...	...
	Huambo	d.	1901	...	...	⊖	...	...	...	...	...
	Dango	d.	...	...	...	⊖	...	...	...	...	...
	Caála	a.	...	...	...	⊖	...	...	...	...	...
	Benguela	d.	...	...	...	⊖	0620	0835	1220	1520	...
	Lobita	a.	...	...	...	0424	0730	0945	1330	1630	...

apital: **Luanda** (GMT +1). 2023 Public Holidays: Jan. 1, Feb. 4, 20, 21, Mar. 8, 23, 24, Apr. 3, 4, 7, May 1, Sept. 17, Nov. 2, 3, 11, Dec. 25. ⊖ – No information available.

MOÇAMBIQUE — 4370

CF Moçambique, Nacala Logistics

km	Nacala Logistics		②⑥		
0	**Nampula**	d.	0500	...	...
123	Ribáuè	d.	⊖	...	...
173	Iapala	d.	⊖	...	...
252	Malema	d.	⊖	...	...
302	Mutuáli	d.	⊖	...	...
356	Cuamba	d.	1410	...	...
464	Mitande	d.	...	...	...
541	**Nayuci**	a.	...	...	...

			④⑦		
	Nayuci	d.	...	...	...
	Mitande	d.	...	...	...
	Cuamba	d.	0500	...	...
	Mutuáli	d.	⊖	...	...
	Malema	d.	⊖	...	...
	Iapala	d.	⊖	...	...
	Ribáuè	d.	⊖	...	...
	Nampula	a.	1410	...	...

km	CF Moçambique		⑥	②	①
0	**Beira**	d.	0600	1100	2100
28	Dondo 1	d.	0731	1224	2226
120	Muanza	d.	1021	1509	0154
187	Inhaminga	d.	1208	1656	0415
214	Inhamitanga	d.	1259	1742	0505
302	**Marromeu**	a.	1600	|	|
320	Dona Ana	a.	...	2125	1024
577	**Maotize**	a.	...	0526	2105

			⑦	③	③
	Moatize	d.	...	0600	1600
	Dona Ana	d.	...	1618	0011
	Marromeu	d.	0800	|	|
	Inhamitanga	d.	1108	2114	0426
	Inhaminga	d.	1159	2336	0517
	Muanza	d.	1346	0204	0705
	Dondo 1	d.	1639	0548	0935
	Beira	a.	1800	0718	1150

km	CF Moçambique		⑥⑦	⑥	③
0	**Maputo**	d.	0730	0955	1300
208	Chókwe	d.	1216	1911	1951
534	**Chicualacuala**	a.	...	0349	0342

			④	⑦	⑥⑦
	Chicualacuala	d.	1300	1000	...
	Chókwe	d.	2323	2020	1420
	Maputo	a.	0549	0810	1909

km	CF Moçambique		①–⑤	⑥⑦	⑧
0	**Maputo**	d.	0745	0800	1815
53	Moambe	d.	0927	0952	2032
88	**Ressano Garcia**	a.	1020	1045	2124

			①–⑥	①–⑤	⑥⑦
	Ressano Garcia	d.	0346	1205	1225
	Moambe	d.	0506	1317	1346
	Maputo	a.	0645	1511	1540

apital: **Maputo** (GMT +2). 2023 Public Holidays: Jan. 1, 2, Feb. 3, Apr. 7, May 1, June 25, 26, Sep. 7, 25, Oct. 4, Dec. 25. ⊖ – No information available.

ZIMBABWE — 4380

National Railways of Zimbabwe

km			①④⑥	
0	**Mutare**	d.	2100	...
77	Nyazura	d.	2307	...
99	Rusape	d.	0020	...
166	Macheke	d.	0239	...
201	Marondera	d.	0345	...
273	**Harare**	a.	0605	...

			③⑤⑦	
	Harare	d.	2130	...
	Marondera	d.	2345	...
	Macheke	d.	0100	...
	Rusape	d.	0320	...
	Nyazura	d.	0309	...
	Mutare	a.	0600	...

km				
0	**Bulawayo**	d.	1930	...
126	Gwayi	d.	2310	...
266	Dete	d.	0300	...
339	Hwange	d.	0534	...
351	Thomson Junction	d.	0540	...
472	**Victoria Falls**	a.	0855	...

	Victoria Falls	d.	1900	...
	Thomson Junction	d.	2240	...
	Hwange	d.	2303	...
	Dete	d.	0140	...
	Gwayi	d.	0456	...
	Bulawayo	a.	0900	...

km			②⑤⑦	①③⑤
0	**Harare**	d.	2000	...
44	Norton	d.	2100	...
127	Chegutu	d.	2310	...
160	Kadoma	d.	0001	...
237	Kwekwe	d.	0210	...
**	Masvingo	d.	|	2000
302	Gweru	d.	0500	0345
336	Somabhula	d.	0533	...
369	Shangani	d.	0630	...
486	**Bulawayo**	a.	0840	...

			①④⑥	①③⑤
	Bulawayo	d.	2050	...
	Shangani	d.	2240	...
	Somabhula	d.	2330	...
	Gweru	d.	0130	0245
	Masvingo	a.	|	0955
	Kwekwe	d.	0337	...
	Kadoma	d.	0520	...
	Chegutu	d.	0605	...
	Norton	d.	0805	...
	Harare	a.	0905	...

km			③	⑦
0	**Bulawayo**	d.	1215	1730
113	Shangani	d.	1457	2016
150	Somabhula	d.	1607	2108
229	Bannockburn	d.	1848	2345
309	Ngezi	d.	2106	0205
401	Rutenga	d.	0050	0545
433	Lundi	d.	|	0934
500	**Chicualacuala** ⊙	a.	0706	|
499	Triangle	d.	...	1120
523	**Chiredzi**	a.	...	1200

			④	①
	Chiredzi	d.	...	1530
	Triangle	d.	...	1620
	Chicualacuala ⊙	d.	1500	|
	Lundi	d.	|	1727
	Rutenga	d.	2145	2145
	Ngezi	d.	0036	0036
	Bannockburn	d.	0339	0339
	Somabhula	d.	0700	0700
	Shangani	d.	0810	0810
	Bulawayo	a.	1100	1100

km			④⑦	
0	**Bulawayo**	d.	1800	...
	Gwanda	d.	2310	...
317	**Beit Bridge**	a.	0540	...

			①⑤	
	Beit Bridge	d.	2100	...
	Gwanda	d.	0353	...
	Bulawayo	a.	0845	...

km			802	
0	**Bulawayo**	d.	1415	...
	Plumtree 🏛	d.	1749	...
196	**Francistown**	a.	1945	...

			801	
	Francistown	d.	0700	...
	Plumtree 🏛	d.	0945	...
	Bulawayo	a.	1230	...

apital: **Harare** (GMT +2). 2023 Public Holidays: Jan. 1, 2, Feb. 21, Apr. 7, 8, 10, 18, May 1, 25, Aug. 14, 15, Dec. 22, 25, 26.

– 🏛 is Sango Halt.

** – Masvingo - Gweru: *199 km*.

NAMIBIA — 4390

Starline

km				
0	**Windhoek**	d.	...	...
70	Okahandja	d.	...	...
191	Karibib	d.	...	...
210	Kranzberg	d.	...	...
282	Omaruru	d.	...	...
419	**Otjiwarongo**	a.	...	...
222	Usakos	d.	...	...
373	Swakopmund	d.	...	...
411	**Walvisbaai**	a.	...	...

	Walvisbaai	a.	...	...
	Swakopmund	d.	...	...
	Usakos	d.	...	...
	Otjiwarongo	d.	...	...
	Omaruru	d.	...	...
	Kranzberg	d.	...	...
	Karibib	d.	...	...
	Okahandja	d.	...	...
	Windhoek	a.	...	...

km				
0	**Windhoek**	d.	...	...
97	Rehobeth	d.	...	...
193	Kalkrand	d.	...	...
274	Mariental	d.	...	...
413	Tses	d.	...	...
495	**Keetmanshoop**	a.	...	...
495	**Keetmanshoop**	d.	...	...
670	Grünau	d.	...	...
720	**Karasburg**	a.	...	...

	Karasburg	a.	...	...
	Grünau	d.	...	...
	Keetmanshoop	d.	...	...
	Keetmanshoop	d.	...	...
	Tses	d.	...	...
	Mariental	d.	...	...
	Kalkrand	d.	...	...
	Rehobeth	d.	...	...
	Windhoek	a.	...	...

km				
0	**Oshikango** ♣	d.	...	...
58	**Ondangwa** ♠	a.	...	...
58	**Ondangwa** ♠	d.	...	...
140	Omuthiya ♥	d.	...	...
213	Oshivelo	d.	...	...
305	**Tsumeb**	a.	...	...

	Tsumeb	d.	...	...
	Oshivelo	d.	...	...
	Omuthiya ♥	d.	...	...
	Ondangwa ♠	a.	...	...
	Ondangwa ♠	d.	...	...
	Oshikango ♣	a.	...	...

Capital: **Windhoek** (GMT +2).

2023 Public Holidays: Jan. 1, 2, Mar. 21, Apr. 7, 10, May 1, 4, 18, 25, Aug. 26, Dec. 10, 11, 25, 26.

♣ – Full name is Oshikango Reverend Theofelus Hamutumbangela.
♠ – Full name is Ondangwa Nehale Lya Mpingana.
♥ – Full name is Omuthiya Sam Nujoma.

4400 SOUTH AFRICA

Shosholoza Meyl

Capital: **Pretoria** (GMT +2). 2023 Public Holidays: Jan. 1, 2, Mar. 21, Apr. 7, 10, 27, May 1, June 16, Aug. 9, Sept. 24, 25, Dec. 16, 25, 26. Operator: Shosholoza Meyl.

Three classes of accommodation are offered: Premier Class (coaches consisting of one or two berth deluxe compartments that convert to sleeper accommodation at night and can accomodate up to 14 passengers), Tourist Class (shown as T in notes - coaches consisting of two or four berth compartments that convert to sleeper accommodation at night and can accomodate up to 28 passengers) and Economy Class (shown as 2 in notes - seated accommodation).

km								
0	**Johannesburg** d.	...	...	...	**Cape Town** d.	...	...	...
186	Klerksdorp d.	...	...	...	Belleville d.	...	...	...
495	Kimberley d.	...	...	...	Worcester d.	...	...	...
	East London d.	...	...	...	Beaufort West d.	...	...	...
	Queenstown d.	...	...	...	De Aar d.	...	...	...
908	De Aar d.	...	...	...	Queenstown d.	...	...	...
988	Beaufort West d.	...	...	...	**East London** a.	...	...	...
1355	Worcester d.	...	...	...	Kimberley d.	...	...	...
1511	Bellville d.	...	...	...	Klerksdorp d.	...	...	...
1530	**Cape Town** a.	...	...	...	**Johannesburg** a.	...	...	...

km		⑤ B				⑦ B		
0	**Johannesburg** d.	1235	...	...	**Gqeberha** ◧ d.	...	...	...
14	Germiston d.	1302	...	...	Cradock d.	...	...	...
75	Vereeniging d.	1430	...	...	**East London** d.	...	...	...
210	Kroonstad d.	1652	...	...	Queenstown d.	1719	...	...
407	**Bloemfontein** d.	1955	...	...	Burgersdorp d.	2015	...	...
664	Burgersdorp d.	0126	...	...	**Bloemfontein** d.	0247	...	...
809	Queenstown d.	0409	...	...	Kroonstad d.	0600	...	...
1023	**East London** a.	...	...	...	Vereeniging d.	0817	...	...
835	Cradock d.	...	...	...	Germiston d.	0923	...	...
1112	**Gqeberha** ◧ a.	...	...	...	**Johannesburg** a.	0945	...	...

km		⑤ A				⑦ A		
0	**Johannesburg** d.	1500	...	...	**Musina** ⊖ d.	1525	...	...
14	Germiston d.	1540	...	...	Makhado d.	1815	...	...
70	Pretoria d.	1656	...	...	Polokwane d.	2235	...	...
183	Witbank d.	|	...	...	Mokopane d.	2352	...	...
218	Middelburg d.	|	...	...	**Komatipoort** ⊡ d.	|	...	...
422	Nelspruit d.	|	...	...	Kaapmuiden d.	|	...	...
461	Kaapmuiden d.	|	...	...	Nelspruit d.	|	...	...
530	**Komatipoort** ⊡ a.	|	...	...	Middelburg d.	|	...	...
292	Mokopane d.	2221	...	...	Witbank d.	|	...	...
357	Polokwane d.	2244	...	...	Pretoria d.	0425	...	...
504	Makhado d.	0336	...	...	Germiston d.	0523	...	...
633	**Musina** ⊖ a.	0649	...	...	**Johannesburg** a.	0544	...	...

km								
0	**Johannesburg** d.	...	...	...	**Durban** d.	...	...	...
14	Germiston d.	...	...	...	Pietermaritzburg d.	...	...	...
172	Standerton d.	...	...	...	Ladysmith d.	...	...	...
315	Newcastle d.	...	...	...	Newcastle d.	...	...	...
438	Ladysmith d.	...	...	...	Standerton d.	...	...	...
617	Pietermaritzburg d.	...	...	...	Germiston d.	...	...	...
722	**Durban** a.	...	...	...	**Johannesburg** a.	...	...	...

A – From Johannesburg on last ⑤ / from Musina on last ⑦ of each month.
B – From Johannesburg on 2nd ⑤ / from Queenstown on 2nd ⑦ of each month.
◧ – Formerly known as Port Elizabeth.
⊡ – Komatipoort - Ressano Garcia (Mozambique, Table **4370**): *5 km*.
⊖ – Musina - Beit Bridge (Zimbabwe, Table **4380**): *12 km*.

JOHANNESBURG - PRETORIA and v.v. *56 km*. Journey 36 mins. Operator: Gautrain.
From **Johannesburg** Park: Train call at Sandton* 8 minutes later.
Ⓐ: 0529, 0539 and every 10–20 minutes until 2010, 2030.
Ⓒ: 0530, 0600 and every 20–30 minutes until 2030.
From **Pretoria**: Trains call at Sandton* 27 minutes later.
Ⓐ: 0532, 0542 and every 10–20 minutes until 2023, 2043.
Ⓒ: 0533, 0603 and every 20–30 minutes until 2003, 2037.
* – Frequent services available from / to Sandton and OR Tambo Airport.

ISRAEL

Capital: **Jerusalem** (GMT +2, add 1 hour in summer). 2023 Public Holidays: Apr. 6, 12, 26, May 26, Sept. 16, 17, 25, 30, Oct. 7. Operator: Israel Railways (www.rail.co.il).

All services convey a single class of seated accommodation. Timings are the most recent available and are subject to alteration at any time, particularly around religious holidays. Tickets and reservations may be purchased up to 7 days in advance of travel at stations or through the website.

4500 NAHARIYYA - TEL AVIV - BEN GURION AIRPORT - MODI'IN

Israel Railways

Overnight and weekend (⑤⑥) services are suspended due to engineering work - replacement 🚌 services are available.

km			⑦–④	⑦–④	⑦–④	⑦–④	⑦–④	⑦–④	⑦–④	⑦–④		⑦–④	⑦–④	⑦–④	⑦–④	⑦–④	⑦–④	⑦–④	⑦–④	⑦–④	⑦–④	⑦–④	
0	**Nahariyya** d.	W	...	0448	0515	0548	0615	0648	0715	0748	and	1515	1548	1615	1648	1715	1748	1815	1848	1905	2052	2152	...
	Akko d.	E	...	0455	0522	0555	0622	0655	0722	0755	at	1522	1555	1622	1655	1722	1755	1822	1855	1912	2101	2201	...
20	Qiryat Motzkin d.	E	...	0505	0532	0605	0632	0705	0732	0805	the	1532	1605	1632	1705	1732	1805	1832	1905	1922	2111	2211	...
38	Haifa Hof HaKarmel d.	K	...	0536	0603	0636	0703	0736	0803	0836	same	1603	1636	1703	1736	1803	1836	1903	1936	1953	2144	2244	...
71	Binyamina d.	D	0528	0556	0626	0656	0726	0756	0826	0856	minutes	1626	1656	1726	1756	1826	1856	1926	1956	2016	|	|	...
123	**Tel Aviv** Savidor Center d.	A	0601	0631	0701	0731	0801	0831	0901	0931	past	1701	1731	1801	1831	1901	1931	2001	2031	2101	2238	2338	...
	Tel Aviv HaHagana d.	Y	0609	0639	0709	0739	0809	0839	0909	0939	each	1709	1739	1809	1839	1909	1939	2009	2039	2109	2246	2346	...
137	Ben Gurion Airport a.	S	0619	0649	0719	0749	0819	0849	0919	0949	hour	1719	1749	1819	1849	1919	1949	2019	2050	2120	2257	2357	...
158	**Modi'in** Center a.		0644	0714	0744	0814	0844	0914	0944	1014	until	1744	1814	1844	1914	1944	2014	2044	2114	2144	2319	...	...

Nahariyya d.		...	...	...	...	...	...	...	...	...	...	...	S	...	...	...	...	...	...	...	...	...	...
Akko d.	F	...	...	...	...	...	...	...	...	...	...	...	A	...	...	...	...	...	...	...	...	...	...
Qiryat Motzkin d.	R	...	...	...	...	...	...	...	...	...	...	...	T	...	...	...	...	...	...	...	...	...	...
Haifa Hof HaKarmel d.	I	...	...	...	...	...	...	...	...	...	...	...	U	...	...	...	...	...	...	...	...	...	...
Binyamina d.	D	...	...	...	...	...	...	...	...	...	...	...	R	...	...	...	...	...	...	...	...	...	...
Tel Aviv Savidor Ctr a.	A	...	...	...	...	...	...	...	...	...	...	...	D	...	...	...	...	...	...	...	...	...	...
Tel Aviv HaHagana d.	Y	...	...	...	...	...	...	...	...	...	...	...	A	...	...	...	...	...	...	...	...	...	...
Ben Gurion Airport a.		...	...	...	...	...	...	...	...	...	...	...	Y	...	...	...	...	...	...	...	...	...	...
Modi'in Center a.		...	...	...	...	...	...	...	...	...	...	...		...	...	...	...	...	...	...	...	...	...

		⑦–④	⑦–④	⑦–④	⑦–④	⑦–④	⑦–④	⑦–④	⑦–④	⑦–④		⑦–④	⑦–④	⑦–④	⑦–④	⑦–④	⑦–④	⑦–④	⑦–④	⑦–④	⑦–④	
Modi'in Center d.	W	...	...	0548	0618	0648	0718	0748	0818	0848	and	1618	1648	1718	1748	1818	1848	1918	1948	2018	2118	...
Ben Gurion Airport d.	E	...	0538	0605	0635	0705	0735	0805	0835	0905	at	1635	1705	1735	1805	1835	1905	1935	2005	2037	2137	...
Tel Aviv HaHagana d.	E	...	0547	0617	0646	0717	0746	0817	0846	0917	the	1646	1719	1746	1819	1846	1919	1946	2016	2049	2149	...
Tel Aviv Savidor Center d.	K	...	0558	0628	0658	0728	0758	0828	0858	0928	same	1658	1728	1758	1828	1858	1928	1958	2028	2100	2200	...
Binyamina d.	D	0533	0630	0700	0730	0800	0830	0900	0930	1000	minutes	1730	1800	1830	1900	1930	2000	2030	2107	2144	2244	...
Haifa Hof HaKarmel d.	A	0554	0649	0724	0749	0824	0849	0924	0949	1024	past	1749	1824	1849	1924	1949	2024	2049	2130	2204	2304	...
Qiryat Motzkin d.	Y	0625	0720	0755	0820	0855	0920	0955	1020	1055	each	1820	1855	1920	1955	2020	2055	2120	2201	2235	2335	...
Akko d.	S	0635	0729	0804	0829	0904	0929	1004	1029	1104	hour	1829	1904	1929	2004	2029	2104	2129	2210	2243	2343	...
Nahariyya a.		0646	0739	0813	0839	0913	0939	1013	1039	1113	until	1839	1913	1939	2013	2039	2113	2139	2220	2253	2353	...

Modi'in Center d.		...	...	...	...	...	...	...	...	...	...	...	S	...	...	...	...	...	...	...	...	...	...
Ben Gurion Airport d.	F	...	...	...	...	...	...	...	...	...	...	...	A	...	...	...	...	...	...	...	...	...	...
Tel Aviv HaHagana a.	R	...	...	...	...	...	...	...	...	...	...	...	T	...	...	...	...	...	...	...	...	...	...
Tel Aviv Savidor Center d.	I	...	...	...	...	...	...	...	...	...	...	...	U	...	...	...	...	...	...	...	...	...	...
Binyamina d.	D	...	...	...	...	...	...	...	...	...	...	...	R	...	...	...	...	...	...	...	...	...	...
Haifa Hof HaKarmel a.	A	...	...	...	...	...	...	...	...	...	...	...	D	...	...	...	...	...	...	...	...	...	...
Qiryat Motzkin d.	Y	...	...	...	...	...	...	...	...	...	...	...	A	...	...	...	...	...	...	...	...	...	...
Akko a.		...	...	...	...	...	...	...	...	...	...	...	Y	...	...	...	...	...	...	...	...	...	...
Nahariyya a.		...	...	...	...	...	...	...	...	...	...	...		...	...	...	...	...	...	...	...	...	...

Israel Railways

HERTSLIYYA - TEL AVIV - JERUSALEM and BE'ER SHEVA — 4510

HERTSLIYYA - TEL AVIV - BEN GURION AIRPORT - JERUSALEM

km		⑦–⑤	⑦–④	⑦–⑤	⑦–④		⑦–⑤	⑦–④	⑦–④	⑦–④		⑦–④	⑦–④	⑥–④	⑦–④	⑥	⑦–④		⑦–④	⑥	⑦–④	⑦–④
	Hertsliyya d.	0524	0554	0624	0654	and at	1424	1454	1524	1554	and at	1924	1954	2024	2054	2124	2129	...	2203	2224	2229	2303
0	**Tel Aviv** Savidor Center d.	0537	0607	0637	0707	the same	1437	1507	1537	1607	the same	1937	2007	2037	2107	2137	2144	...	2216	2237	2244	2316
	Tel Aviv HaHagana d.	0545	0615	0645	0715	minutes	1445	1515	1545	1615	minutes	1945	2015	2045	2115	2145	2152	...	2223	2245	2252	2323
12	Ben Gurion Airport ✈ d.	0556	0626	0656	0726	past each	1456	1526	1556	1626	past each	1956	2026	2056	2126	2156	2203	...	2233	2256	2303	2333
56	**Jerusalem** Yitzhak Navon a.	0622	0652	0722	0752	hour until	1522	1552	1622	1652	hour until	2022	2052	2122	2152	2222	2229	...	2259	2322	2329	2359

	⑦–④	⑤	⑦–④	⑦–⑤		⑦–④	⑦–⑤	⑦–④	⑦–④		⑦–④	⑦–④	⑥	⑦–④	⑦–④	⑥	⑦–④	⑦–④	⑥	⑦–④	⑦–④
Jerusalem Yitzhak Navon d.	0535	0539	0609	0639	and at	1409	1439	1509	1539	and at	2009	2039	2039	2109	2139	2139	2202	2232	2239	2302	2332
Ben Gurion Airport ✈ d.	0558	0559	0629	0659	the same	1429	1459	1529	1559	the same	2029	2059	2101	2129	2159	2201	2222	2252	2301	2322	2352
Tel Aviv HaHagana d.	0610	0610	0940	0710	minutes	1440	1510	1540	1610	minutes	2040	2110	2112	2140	2210	2212	2232	2302	2312	2332	0002
Tel Aviv Savidor Centre a.	0620	0622	0652	0722	past each	1452	1522	1552	1622	past each	2052	2122	2124	2152	2222	2224	2244	2314	2324	2344	0014
Hertsliyya a.	0629	0634	0704	0734	hour until	1504	1534	1604	1634	hour until	2104	2134	2136	2204	2234	2236	2255	2325	2336	2355	0024

TEL AVIV - BET SHEMESH and BE'ER SHEVA

During peak hours on ⑦–④ certain Bet Shemesh trains extend to / from Hertsliyya and certain Be'er Sheva trains extend to / from Nahariyya - timings not shown.

km		⑤	⑦–④	⑦–④		⑦–④	⑤	⑦–④	⑦–④	⑤	⑦–④	⑤	⑦–④		⑤	⑦–④	⑤	⑦–④	⑤	⑦–④		⑦–④	⑤
	Hertsliyya d.	...	...	...	...	...	...	...	...	0646	...	...	...	and at	1146	...	...	...	1246	...	...	...	1346
0	**Tel Aviv** Savidor Center d.	0517	0542	0548	...	0612	0617	0642	0648	0700	0712	0717	0748	the same	1200	1212	1217	1248	1300	1312	...	1348	1400
	Tel Aviv HaHagana d.	0526	0550	0556	...	0620	0626	0650	0655	0707	0720	0726	0755	minutes	1207	1220	1226	1255	1307	1320	...	1355	1407
20	Lod d.	0540	0604	0612	...	0634	0640	0704	0711	0724	0734	0740	0811	past each	1224	1234	1240	1311	1324	1334	...	1411	1424
51	**Bet Shemesh** a.	|	|	0638	...	|	|	|	0738	0753	|	|	0838	hour until	1253	|	|	1338	1353	|	...	1438	1453
63	Kiryat Gat d.	0616	0629	...	...	0710	0716	0729	...	...	0811	0816	...	◧	...	1311	1316	...	...	1411	...	...	...
107	**Be'er Sheva** Center a.	0654	0702	...	...	0749	0754	0802	...	...	0850	0854	...		...	1350	1354	...	...	1450	...	...	...

	⑦–④	⑦–④	⑦–④	⑦–④	⑦–④	⑦–④	⑦–④		⑦–④	⑦–④	⑦–④	⑦–④	⑦–④	⑦–④	⑦–④		⑦–④	⑦–④	⑥	⑦–④	⑦–④	⑥	⑦–④
Hertsliyya d.	...	...	...	...	...	...	...	...	...	...	...	...	...	...	...	...	...	...	2046	...	...	2146	...
Tel Aviv Savidor Center d.	1412	1448	1512	1548	1612	1643	1648	...	1712	1748	1743	1848	1843	1943	1948	...	2012	2048	2100	2112	2150	2200	2300
Tel Aviv HaHagana d.	1420	1455	1520	1555	1620	1650	1655	...	1720	1755	1750	1855	1850	1950	1955	...	2020	2055	2107	2120	2157	2207	2307
Lod d.	1434	1511	1534	1611	1634	1704	1711	...	1734	1811	1804	1911	1904	2004	2011	...	2034	2111	2124	2134	2213	2224	2323
Bet Shemesh a.	|	1538	|	1638	|	|	1738	...	|	1838	|	1938	|	|	2038	...	|	2138	2154	|	2240	2254	2350
Kiryat Gat d.	1511	...	1611	...	1711	1729	...	...	1810	...	1829	...	1929	2029	...	...	2110	...	...	2210	...	...	...
Be'er Sheva Center a.	1550	...	1650	...	1750	1802	...	...	1849	...	1902	...	2002	2102	...	...	2200	...	...	2300	...	...	...

	⑤	⑦–④	⑤	⑦–④	⑤	⑦–④	⑤	⑦–④	⑤	⑦–④		⑤	⑦–④	⑤	⑦–④	⑤	⑦–④	⑤	⑦–④	⑦–④	⑦–④	⑦–④
Be'er Sheva Center d.	0457	...	...	0541	0557	...	...	0641	0657	...	and at	...	1141	1157	...	...	1241	1257	...	1341	...	1428
Kiryat Gat d.	0529	...	...	0615	0629	...	...	0715	0729	...	the same	...	1215	1229	...	...	1315	1329	...	1415	...	1457
Bet Shemesh d.	|	0548	0615	|	|	0648	0715	|	|	0748	minutes	1215	|	|	1248	1315	|	|	1348	|	1448	|
Lod d.	0604	0612	0640	0650	0704	0712	0740	0750	0804	0812	past each	1240	1250	1304	1312	1340	1350	1404	1412	1450	1512	1522
Tel Aviv HaHagana d.	0617	0629	0658	0705	0717	0729	0758	0805	0817	0829	hour until	1258	1305	1317	1329	1358	1405	1417	1429	1505	1529	1535
Tel Aviv Savidor Centre a.	0627	0638	0710	0715	0727	0738	0810	0815	0827	0838	◧	1310	1315	1327	1338	1410	1415	1427	1438	1515	1538	1545
Hertsliyya a.	...	...	0721	...	...	...	0821	...	...	...		1321	...	...	...	1421	...	...	...	...	...	...

	⑦–④	⑦–④	⑦–④	⑦–④	⑦–④	⑦–④	⑦–④	⑦–④	⑦–④	⑦–④	⑦–④		⑦–④	⑦–④	⑦–④	⑥	⑦–④	⑦–④	⑥	⑦–④	⑦–④	⑦–④	⑦–④
Be'er Sheva Center d.	1441	...	1528	1541	...	1628	1641	...	1728	1741	...	...	1828	1841	...	...	1941	...	...	2041	...	2127	2227
Kiryat Gat d.	1515	...	1557	1615	...	1657	1715	...	1757	1815	...	...	1857	1915	...	...	2015	...	...	2115	...	2215	2315
Bet Shemesh d.	|	1548	|	|	1648	|	|	1748	|	|	1848	...	|	|	1948	2015	|	2048	2115	|	2158	|	|
Lod d.	1550	1612	1622	1650	1712	1722	1750	1812	1822	1850	1912	...	1922	1950	2012	2040	2050	2112	2140	2150	2222	2250	2350
Tel Aviv HaHagana d.	1605	1629	1635	1705	1729	1735	1805	1829	1835	1905	1929	...	1935	2005	2029	2058	2105	2129	2158	2205	2239	2307	0009
Tel Aviv Savidor Centre a.	1615	1638	1645	1715	1738	1745	1815	1838	1845	1915	1938	...	1945	2015	2039	2110	2115	2138	2210	2215	2249	2317	0020
Hertsliyya a.	...	...	...	...	...	...	...	...	...	...	...	...	...	...	...	2121	...	...	2221	...	...	...	...

◧ – Also Tel Aviv Savidor Center - Be'er Sheva Center at 0743 ⑦–④, 0843 ⑦–④, 0943 ⑦–④, 1043 ⑦–④.
Also Be'er Sheva Center - Tel Aviv Savidor Center at 0628 ⑦–④, 0728 ⑦–④, 0828 ⑦–④.

Israel Railways

BEIT SHE'AN - HAIFA — 4513

km		⑦–④	⑦–④	⑤	⑦–④	⑤	⑦–④	⑤		⑦–④	⑤	⑦–④	⑦–④	⑦–④	⑦–④	⑦–④	⑦–④	⑦–④	⑥	⑦–④	⑥	⑦–④	
0	**Beit She'an** d.	0531	0631	0635	0731	0735	0831	0835	and hourly	1331	1335	1431	1531	1631	1731	1831	1931	2031	2035	2131	2135	2239	...
60	**Haifa** Hof HaKarmel a.	0629	0729	0733	0829	0833	0929	0933	until	1429	1433	1529	1629	1729	1829	1929	2029	2129	2132	2229	2235	2338	...

	⑦–④	⑤		⑦–④	⑤	⑦–④	⑤		⑦–④	⑤	⑦–④	⑦–④	⑦–④	⑦–④	⑦–④	⑦–④	⑦–④	⑥	⑦–④	⑥	⑦–④	
Haifa Hof HaKarmel d.	0603	0621	...	0703	0721	0803	0821	and hourly	1303	1321	1403	1503	1603	1703	1803	1903	2003	2021	2103	2121	2212	...
Beit She'an a.	0701	0721	...	0801	0821	0901	0921	until	1401	1421	1501	1601	1701	1801	1901	2001	2101	2121	2201	2221	2308	...

Israel Railways

JERUSALEM - MODI'IN — 4515

km		⑦–④	⑤	⑦–④	⑤	⑦–④	⑤	⑦–④		⑤	⑦–④	⑤	⑦–④	⑦–④	⑦–④	⑦–④	⑦–④	⑦–④	⑥	⑦–④	⑥	⑥	
0	**Jerusalem** Yitzhak Navon d.	0626	0629	0659	0729	0759	0829	0859	and hourly	1329	1359	1429	1459	1559	1659	1759	1859	1959	2029	2059	2129	2229	...
	Modi'in Center a.	0654	0652	0724	0752	0824	0852	0924	until	1352	1424	1452	1524	1624	1724	1824	1924	2024	2052	2124	2152	2252	...

	⑦–④	⑤	⑦–④	⑤	⑦–④	⑤	⑦–④		⑤	⑦–④	⑤	⑦–④	⑦–④	⑦–④	⑦–④		⑦–④	⑦–④	⑥	⑥	⑥	
Modi'in Center d.	0606	0643	0706	0743	0806	0843	0906	and hourly	1343	1406	1443	1506	1606	1706	1806	...	1906	2006	2043	2143	2243	...
Jerusalem Yitzhak Navon a.	0635	0710	0735	0810	0835	0910	0935	until	1410	1435	1510	1535	1635	1735	1835	...	1935	2035	2110	2210	2310	...

Iraq Railways

IRAQ — 4610

km		2 C	21 B
609	Umm Qasr d.	1130	...
541	**Al Basrah** Ma'qil d.	1400	2100
370	An Nasiriyah (for Ur) d.	▬	|
182	Ad Dawanyah d.	**11**	|
107	Al Hillah (for Babylon) d.	**A**	|
0	**Baghdad** Central d.	1920	0915
117	Samarra d.	2310	...
171	Tikrit d.	|	...
211	Ba'iji d.	|	...
406	**Al Mawsil** a.	0755	...

	20 B	12 A
Al Mawsil d.	...	1900
Ba'iji d.	...	|
Tikrit d.	...	|
Samarra d.	...	0400
Baghdad Central d.	1700	0800
Al Hillah (for Babylon) d.	|	▬
Ad Dawanyah d.	|	...
An Nasiriyah (for Ur) d.	|	**2 C**
Al Basrah Ma'qil a.	0520	0800
Umm Qasr a.	...	1025

Capital: **Baghdad** (GMT +3).

2023 Public Holidays: Jan. 1, 6, Mar. 6, 21, Apr. 21 – 23, May 1, June 28 – 30, July 1, 14, 18, 27, Sept. 27, Oct. 3, Dec. 10, 25.

Rail services in Iraq are operated by Iraq Railways. Trains convey second class seating and also sleeping cars where indicated. Information regarding rail services is still very hard to obtain and the schedules shown should be treated as subject to confirmation.

A – 🛏 2 cl. Runs when required.
B – 🛏 2 cl.
C – Runs once per week. Days of operation unknown.

4620 SAUDI ARABIA

Haramain High-Speed Railway, Saudi Arabia Railways

Capital: **Riyadh** (GMT +3). 2023 Public Holidays: Feb. 22, Apr. 22–25, June 27–30, Sept. 23, 24.

Saudi Arabia Railways (SAR) (www.sar.com.sa) operates two passenger lines: **East** – between Ad Dammam and Ar Riyad, and **North** – between Qurayyat and Ar Riyad. **East** service trains convey first class (called Business which includes refreshments in the waiting rooms) and second class (Economy) seating, and have free Wi-Fi. The **North** service has day trains that convey business and economy class and a night train that also conveys sleeper cabins which can accommodate up to four people. The 300km/h Haramain High-Speed Railway (www.sar.hhr.sa) links Makkah with King Abdulaziz International Airport and Madinah. Trains convey business and economy class seating. Schedules vary during Ramadan and Eid-al-Fitr.

km										
		⑥⑦								
0	**Ad Dammam** d.	0431	0552	0752	1207	1442	1630	1757	1923	2200
74	Abqaiq d.	0526	0646	0847	1302	1537	1725	1852	2029	2309
139	Al Hufuf d.	0613	0724	0933	1350	1615	1812	1939	2115	2347
449	**Ar Riyad** a.	0834	...	1154	1611	...	2033	2200	2336	...

						⑥⑦			
Ar Riyad d.	...	...	0702	0951	1226	1541	1716	1842	...
Al Hufuf d.	0605	0806	0932	1221	1456	1811	1946	2112	2228
Abqaiq d.	0645	0846	1012	1301	1536	1851	2029	2152	2308
Ad Dammam a.	0737	0938	1104	1353	1628	1943	2121	2244	2400

km										
		⑧	⑥			③				
0	**Ar Riyad** d.	0510	0915	1015	1730	2100	...	...	...	...
	Majma'ah d.	0638	1043	1143	1858	2236	...	...	...	...
	Al Qassim d.	0739	1144	1254	1959	2358	...	...	...	...
623	Hail d.	...	...	1444	...	0210	...	...	...	...
	Al Jouf d.	...	...	...	...	...	...	...	...	...
1242	**Qurayyat** a.	...	...	...	...	...	...	...	...	...

	⑦	⑦–③	④	⑤⑥					
Qurayyat d.	...	...	...	...	...	...	...	...	...
Al Jouf d.	...	...	...	...	...	...	...	...	...
Hail d.	0225	...	...	...	1545	...	...	...	...
Al Qassim d.	0507	0902	1127	1300	1750	2120	...	...	...
Majma'ah d.	0629	1013	1242	1411	1901	2231	...	...	...
Ar Riyad a.	0755	1133	1400	1529	2019	2349	...	...	...

km																								
										⑦–④														⑦–③
0	**Makkah** d.	...	0800	0805	...	1035	1200	1235	...	1300	1335	1400	...	1435	1500	1535	...	1600	1635	1700	...	1800	1835	1900
78	Jeddah d.	...	0828	0835	...	1105	1228	1305	...	1328	1405	1428	...	1505	1528	1605	...	1628	1705	1728	...	1828	1905	1928
	KAI Airport ✈ ⊡ d.	0800	|	0859	1100	1129	|	1329	...	|	1429	|	1500	1529	|	1629	...	|	1729	|	1800	|	1929	|
182	King Abdullah Economic City d.	0835	0904	...	|	...	|	...	...	|	...	1504	1535	...	|	...	...	1704	...	|	|	|	...	2004
450	**Madinah** a.	0954	1025	...	1248	...	1420	...	...	1520	...	1625	1654	...	1720	...	...	1825	...	1920	1948	2020	...	2125

	④–⑥			⑦–③				④–⑥
Makkah d.	2000	2035	...	2100	...	...	2235	2300
Jeddah d.	2028	2105	...	2128	...	...	2305	2328
KAI Airport ✈ ⊡ d.	|	2129	...	|	2200	...	2329	|
King Abdullah Economic City d.	|	...	...	|	2235	...	...	0004
Madinah a.	2220	...	...	2320	2354	...	...	0125

Madinah d.	...	0800	...	0830	...	...	...	1100
King Abdullah Economic City d.	...	0911	...	0943	...	...	...	|
KAI Airport ✈ ⊡ d.	0805	0954	...	|	1035	...	1235	1248
Jeddah d.	0825	...	...	1021	1055	...	1255	...
Makkah a.	0859	...	...	1055	1129	...	1329	...

				⑥–④													⑦–③						④–⑥
Madinah d.	...	1230	...	1330	...	...	1430	...	1500	1530	...	...	1630	1730	1800	...	1930	...	2030	...	2130	2200	2230
King Abdullah Economic City d.	...	|	...	|	...	...	1543	...	1611	|	...	...	1743	|	|	...	2043	...	|	...	|	2311	2343
KAI Airport ✈ ⊡ d.	1335	|	1435	|	1535	...	|	1635	1654	|	1835	...	|	|	1948	2035	|	...	|	2235	|	2354	|
Jeddah d.	1355	1415	1455	1515	1555	...	1621	1655	...	1715	1855	...	1821	1915	...	2055	2121	...	2215	2255	2315	...	0021
Makkah a.	1429	1450	1529	1549	1629	...	1655	1729	...	1750	1929	...	1855	1950	...	2129	2155	...	2250	2329	2350	...	0055

⊡ – King Abdulaziz International Airport.

4630 IRAN

Capital: **Tehran** (GMT +3.5, add 1 hour in summer). 2023 Public Holidays: Feb. 4, 11, 18, Mar. 8, 20–24, Apr. 1, 2, 12, 22, 23, May 16, June 4, 5, 29, July 7, 27, 28, Sept. 6, 14, 15, 24, Oct. 3, Dec. 17

Rail services in Iran are provided by 11 different private companies. The ticket sales system is centralised (agents include www.raja.ir and www.iranrail.net), but every company issues its own tickets. Most trains convey sleeping cars which convert to seating for daytime travel. For services to/from Turkey see Table **1575**.

km		198	584	318	368	354	182	190	390	472	190	366	320	396	346	340	348	384	474	336	474	350	338	580
		●	Ⓑ			●	●	③–①			②		B	A					③–①	●	②		A	
0	Tehran d.	0045	0144	0830	1505	1605	1650	1750	1820	1840	1900	1925	2005	2025	2045	2105	2125	2205	2215	2245	2315	2330	2350	2355
926	Mashhad a.	1140	1235	2050	0155	0235	0330	0430	0500	0545	0625	0550	0635	0650	0715	0735	0805	0835	0915	0930	1015	1005	1025	1050

	319	589	183	191	473		581	397	585	391	349		367	475	321	347	355		341	369	385	337	351
		●						●							Ⓑ		●						
Mashhad d.	0710	0920	1040	1335	1505	...	1545	1705	1725	1745	1805	...	1825	1945	2005	2035	2055	...	2135	2155	2215	2235	2359
Tehran a.	1920	2025	2150	0042	0225	...	0305	0350	0435	0420	0445	...	0500	0715	0650	0725	0740	...	0815	0840	0855	0920	1030

km		936	480	433		119	431	731		131	945	437		435	121	125		938	127	129				
						⊖				⊖														
	Djulfa d.	...	...	...	...	...	...	...	...	...	1630	...	...	...	...	...	...	...	...	...	...	...	...	...
0	Tabriz d.	...	1345	1650	...	...	1750	...	...	...	1920	2125	...	2225	...	...	...	...	...	...	...	...	...	...
	Khorramshahr d.	...	|	|	...	...	|	...	...	1450	...	|	...	|	...	...	...	...	...	...	...	...	...	...
	Ahvaz d.	...	|	|	...	1310	|	...	...	1653	...	|	...	|	...	...	...	...	...	...	...	...	...	...
	Qom d.	...	|	|	...	0230	|	0500	...	0559	...	|	...	|	0905	1445	...	...	1830	2050	...	...	...	...
736	Tehran d.	...	|	0530	...	0545	0620	0730	...	0840	...	0935	...	1050	1120	1700	...	...	2045	2305	...	...	...	...
1662	Mashhad a.	1025	1300	...	...	...	...	...	...	...	...	...	...	...	...	...	...	1855	...	...	...	...	...	...
1827	Sarakhs a.	1305	...	...	...	...	...	...	...	...	...	...	...	...	...	...	...	2155	...	...	...	...	...	...

km		120	124	126		130	430	481		944	939	118		937	128	436		730	432	434				
						⊖						⊖												
	Sarakhs d.	...	...	...	...	...	...	...	...	...	0605	...	...	1445	...	...	...	...	...	...	...	...	...	...
0	Mashhad d.	...	...	...	...	...	...	0635	...	...	0900	...	...	1735	...	...	...	...	...	...	...	...	...	...
926	Tehran d.	0520	1020	1500	...	1540	1650	|	...	...	...	1715	...	...	1750	2040	...	2120	2235	2335	...	...	...	...
1106	Qom a.	0735	1225	1655	...	1808	|	|	...	...	...	1950	...	...	1950	|	...	2315	|	|	...	...	...	...
1742	Ahvaz d.	...	...	...	...	0744	|	|	...	...	...	0835	...	...	...	|	...	...	|	|	...	...	...	...
1865	Khorramshahr a.	...	...	...	...	0955	|	|	...	...	...	...	...	...	...	|	...	...	|	|	...	...	...	...
1662	Tabriz a.	...	...	...	...	...	0510	0610	...	0830	...	...	...	...	...	0920	...	...	1040	1155	...	...	...	...
1808	Djulfa a.	...	...	...	...	...	...	...	...	1125	...	...	...	...	...	...	...	...	...	...	...	...	...	...

km		581	585	724	822	526	524	722	620	
				●				●		
0	Tehran d.	0245	0415	1110	1515	1610	1805	2045	2145	...
494	Eşfahan d.	1020	1225	|	|	|	|	|	|	...
1074	Shiraz a.	...	...	|	|	0735	0940	|	|	...
	Yazd d.	...	...	1916	2308	...	...	0501	0610	...
1483	Bandar e Abbas a.	...	...	|	1020	...	...	|	...	...
	Kerman d.	...	...	0135	...	...	...	1055	...	...
1658	Zahedan a.	...	...	0850	...	...	...	...	...	...

	584	527	621	723	525	823	725	580	
				●			●		
Zahedan d.	...	...	...	...	...	...	1340	...	...
Kerman d.	...	...	...	1725	...	...	2124	...	...
Bandar e Abbas d.	...	...	...	|	...	1515	|	...	...
Yazd d.	...	...	2245	2332	...	0239	0333	...	...
Shiraz d.	...	1500	|	|	1740	|	|	...	...
Eşfahan d.	1740	|	|	|	|	|	|	1545	...
Tehran a.	0204	0615	0700	0805	0905	1100	1205	2340	...

A – ①③⑤⑦. B – ①②③④⑥. ● – Runs every 2nd day. ⊖ – May not call at Qom every day.

4640 ZAHEDAN - QUETTA

km		404	
		A	
0	**Zahedan** d.	1000	...
84	Mirjawa 🛃 a.	1220	...
84	Mirjawa 🛃 d.	1300	...
100	Kuhi Taftan a.	1550	...
100	Kuhi Taftan d.	1700	...
222	Nok Kundi d.	2156	...
389	Dalbandin d.	0535	...
578	Nushki d.	1256	...
689	Wali Khan d.	1737	...
712	Spezand d.	1930	...
737	**Quetta** a.	2025	...

	403	
	B	
Quetta d.	0800	...
Spezand d.	0915	...
Wali Khan d.	1014	...
Nushki d.	1500	...
Dalbandin d.	2240	...
Nok Kundi d.	0557	...
Kuhi Taftan a.	1000	...
Kuhi Taftan d.	1130	...
Mirjawa 🛃 a.	1425	...
Mirjawa 🛃 d.	1435	...
Zahedan a.	1700	...

Raja Trains give different schedules for this train: Quetta d. 0830 - Zahedan a. 1335 / Zahedan d. 0800 - Quetta a. 1515.

A – 12 departs on 3rd and 17th of the month. B – 12 departs on 1st and 15th of the month.

4650 QUETTA - DELHI

km		23	402	14002
			①④	①④
0	**Quetta** d.	1000	...	...
131	Sibi d.	1510	...	...
296	Jacobabad d.	1815	...	...
385	Rohri d.	2040	...	...
840	Khanewal d.	0425	...	...
1127	**Lahore** Junction a.	1015	...	...
1127	**Lahore** Junction d.	...	0800	...
	Wagah a.	...	0835	...
	Wagah d.	...	1130	...
1147	Atari 🛃 a.	...	1150	...
1147	Atari 🛃 d.	...	...	2000
1173	Amritsar Junction a.	...	...	2037
1620	**Delhi** Junction a.	...	...	0320

	14001	401	24
	③⑦	①④	
Delhi Junction d.	2310	...	...
Amritsar Junction d.	0650		...
Atari 🛃 a.	0715		...
Atari 🛃 d.	...	1100	...
Wagah a.	...	1410	...
Wagah d.	...	1610	...
Lahore Junction a.	...	1645	...
Lahore Junction d.	...	...	1700
Khanewal d.	...	...	2235
Rohri d.	...	...	0630
Jacobabad d.	...	...	0845
Sibi d.	...	...	1205
Quetta a.	...	...	1720

Timings are subject to confirmation and connections are not guaranteed.

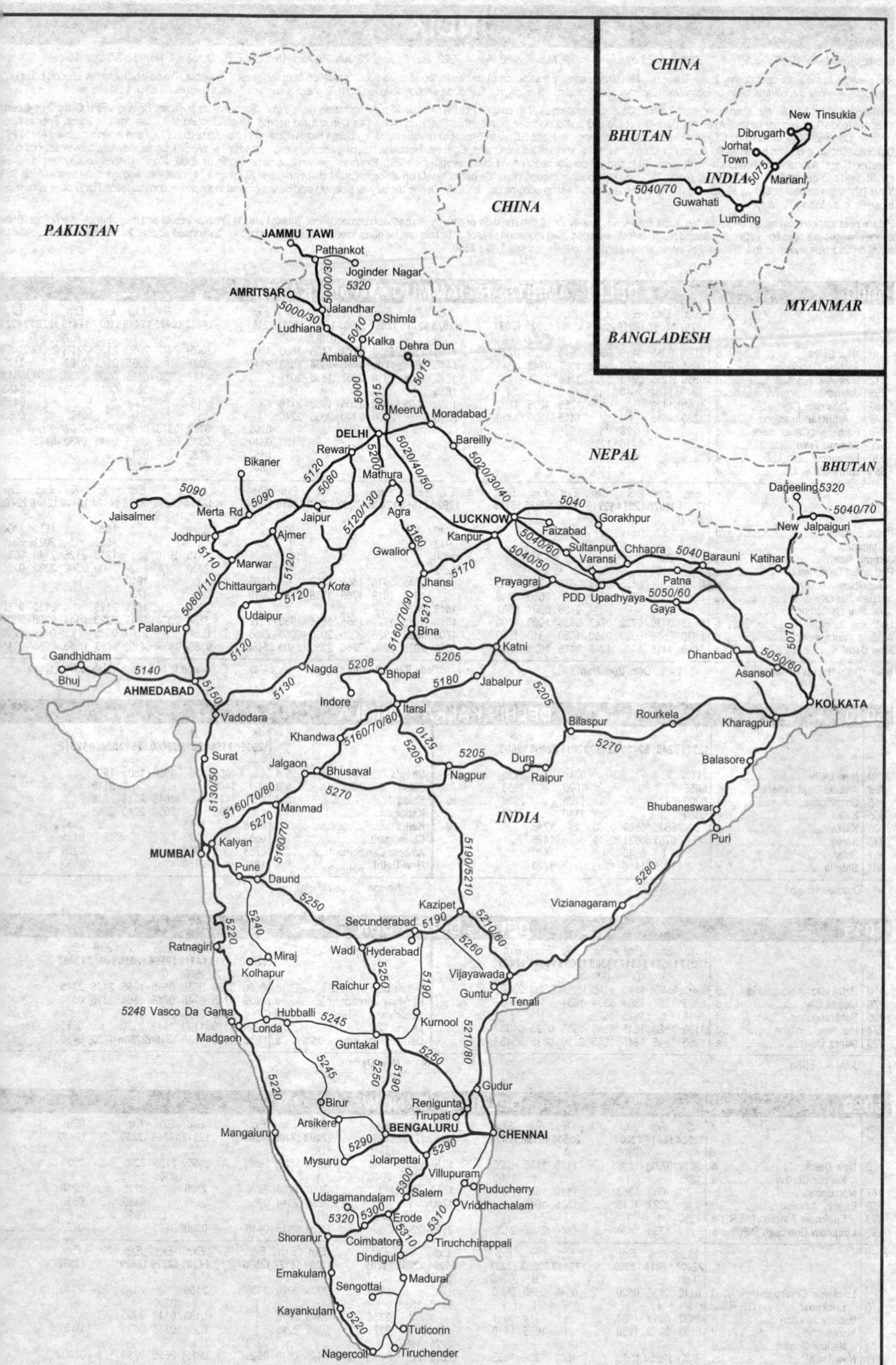
CHINA
BHUTAN
New Tinsukia
Dibrugarh
Jorhat Town
INDIA
5075
Mariani
5040/70
Guwahati
Lumding
MYANMAR
BANGLADESH
PAKISTAN
CHINA
NEPAL
BHUTAN
INDIA
JAMMU TAWI
Pathankot
Joginder Nagar
5320
AMRITSAR
5000/30
Jalandhar
Ludhiana
5010
Shimla
Kalka
Dehra Dun
Ambala
5015
5000
Meerut
Moradabad
DELHI
Bareilly
5020/40/50
5200
Rewari
Mathura
Bikaner
5120
5080
5090
Jaisalmer
Merta Rd
Jaipur
5120/130
Agra
LUCKNOW
5040
Gorakhpur
Faizabad
Jodhpur
Ajmer
5160
Gwalior
Kanpur
5040/60
Sultanpur
Varansi
Chhapra
Barauni
Katihar
5110
Marwar
5170
5040/50
Prayagraj
Patna
Jhansi
Chittaurgarh
Kota
PDD Upadhyaya
5050/60
Gaya
5080/110
Udaipur
5210
Palanpur
5160/70/90
Bina
Katni
Dhanbad
Asansol
5070
Gandhidham
5205
Bhuj
5140
AHMEDABAD
5130
Nagda
5208
Bhopal
5180
Jabalpur
KOLKATA
5150
Indore
Itarsi
Vadodara
Khandwa
5160/70/80
5210
Bilaspur
Rourkela
Kharagpur
Surat
5270
Jalgaon
Bhusaval
Nagpur
Durg
Raipur
Balasore
5130/50
Manmad
Bhubaneswar
Puri
MUMBAI
Kalyan
5160/70
5190/5210
Pune
Daund
5280
Vizianagaram
5250
Kazipet
5220
5240
Secunderabad
5190
5210/60
Ratnagiri
Wadi
Hyderabad
5260
Miraj
Kolhapur
Raichur
Vijayawada
Guntur
Tenali
5248 Vasco Da Gama
Hubballi
5245
Kurnool
Madgaon
Londa
Guntakal
5210/80
Gudur
Birur
Renigunta
Tirupati
Arsikere
BENGALURU
CHENNAI
Mangaluru
5290
Mysuru
Jolarpettai
Villupuram
Puducherry
Udagamandalam
Salem
5300
Vriddhachalam
Erode
5310
Shoranur
Coimbatore
Tiruchchirappalli
Dindigul
Ernakulam
Madurai
Sengottai
Kayankulam
Tuticorin
Nagercoil
Tiruchender
Darjeeling
New Jalpaiguri

INDIA

Capital : **New Delhi** (GMT +5.5). 2023 Public Holidays: Jan. 26, Mar. 7, 8, 30, Apr. 4, 7, 22, May 5, June 29, July 29, Aug. 15, Sept. 7, 28, Oct. 2, 24, Nov. 12, 27, Dec. 25.

Rail services in India are operated by Indian Railways. Most trains convey a selection of first and second class accommodation from the several available. Trains which convey second class only are noted in either the column head or footnotes. Rajdhani and Shatabdi trains convey first class accommodation only. The exact carriage types available on each train varies.

A summary of train types and accommodation follows: **Rajdhani** (shown as *R* in column heads). Air-conditioned first class night trains. Special fares payable. Conveys First Class 2 or 4-berth sleepers (code 1A); two-tier (code 2A) and/or three-tier (code 3A) first class open plan berths; **Shatabdi** (shown as *S* in column heads). Air-conditioned first class daytime trains. Special fares payable. Conveys Chair class (code CC) and Executive Chair class seats (code EC); **Jan Shatabdi** (shown as *JS* in column heads) Conveys Chair class (code CC) and 2 berth sleepers (code 2S) **Duronto** (shown in column heads as *D*). Some non-stop trains, some very limited stop trains. Conveys first class sleeping accommodation (codes 1A, 2A, 3A). Some may also convey second class 'Sleeper Class' non air-conditioned six-berth (code SL); non air-conditioned second class seats (code 2S); **Express** (shown in column heads as *Exp*). Most services convey first class air conditioned two-tier (code 2A) or three-tier (code 3A) open plan berths; second class 'Sleeper Class' non air-conditioned six-berth (code SL); non air-conditioned second class seats (code 2S) **Yuva** (shown in column heads as *Y*). Low-cost air-conditioned train. Seating accommodation only. During the day all sleepers and berths convert to seated accommodation. The codes shown are those used by Indian Railways.

Please note that on most routes only selected trains are shown, usually those that run daily or convey the best accommondation. Timings are the latest available and may change at any time. Short notice changes are possible, especially around religious festivals and during monsoon seasons. Tickets can be purchased from stations or through authorised agents. Reservations are required for travel on all trains shown in this section. For international services to Pakistan see Table **4650**.

5000 DELHI - AMRITSAR, JAMMU TAWI and KATRA

km		*Exp* 15707	*Exp* 11057	*Exp* 12919	*Exp* 22439 ③–①	*Exp* 12497	*S* 12029 ⑤–③	*S* 12031 ④
0	**New Delhi** d.	0320j	0355	0430	0600	0640	0720	0720
199	Ambala Cantonment d.	0655	0758	0740	0812	1007	0943	0943
312	Ludhiana Junction d.	0850	1255	0949	0921	1150	1111	1111
365	Jalandhar Cantonment d.	|	1404	1040	|	|	|	|
369	Jalandhar City d.	1040	1420	|	|	1255	1208	1208
448	**Amritsar** Junction a.	1220	1615	|	|	1415	1330	1330
478	Pathankot Cantonment d.	...	...	1228	|	...	...	...
577	**Jammu Tawi** a.	...	...	1410	1238	...	...	...
630	Udhampur a.	...	...	1515	|	...	...	...
655	**Katra** SVDK ◧ a.	...	...	1620	1400	...	...	...

km		*Exp* 12925	*Exp* 12715	*Exp* 12459	*Exp* 12903	*Exp* 12203 ①②⑤	*S* 12013	*Exp* 22461
0	**New Delhi** d.	1105	1320	1350	1405h	1405	1630	1905
199	Ambala Cantonment d.	1440	1648	1705	1910	1654	1853	2147
312	Ludhiana Junction d.	1745	1857	1910	2053	1836	2019	2326
365	Jalandhar Cantonment d.	1835	|	|	|	|	|	0020
369	Jalandhar City d.	1850	2005	2030	2205	1938	2116	|
448	**Amritsar** Junction a.	2015	2140	2200	2340	2055	2240	|
478	Pathankot Cantonment d.	...	...	...	...	...	...	0205
577	**Jammu Tawi** a.	...	...	...	...	...	...	0340
630	Udhampur a.	...	...	...	...	...	...	0452
655	**Katra** SVDK ◧ a.	...	...	...	...	...	...	0540

km		*Exp* 14033	*R* 12425	*Exp* 12445	*Exp* 11077	*Exp* 12413	*D* 12265 ②⑤⑦	*Exp* 18237
0	**New Delhi** d.	2005j	2040	2050	2135	2210j	2220r	2000h
199	Ambala Cantonment d.	0007	|	2335	0145	0102	|	0140
312	Ludhiana Junction d.	0147	0038	0115	0350	0236	0250	0343
365	Jalandhar Cantonment d.	0242	|	0208	0447	0328	|	0435
369	Jalandhar City d.	|	|	|	|	|	|	0455
448	**Amritsar** Junction a.	|	|	|	|	|	|	0655
478	Pathankot Cantonment d.	0432	0310	0405	0705	0502	|	...
577	**Jammu Tawi** a.	0635	0500	0555	0945	0730	0710	...
630	Udhampur a.	0750	...	0711	...	...	...	...
655	**Katra** SVDK ◧ a.	0835	...	0755	...	...	...	...

	Exp 12204 ③⑥⑦	*Exp* 11078	*S* 12014	*Exp* 12716	*Exp* 12460	*Exp* 12926	*Exp* 15708
Katra SVDK ◧ d.	...	...	...	...	...	...	...
Udhampur d.	...	...	...	...	...	...	...
Jammu Tawi d.	...	2340	...	...	...	...	...
Pathankot Cantonment d.	...	0138	...	...	...	...	...
Amritsar Junction d.	0400	|	0455	0530	0615	0735	0825
Jalandhar City d.	0510	|	0601	0640	0725	0850	0946
Jalandhar Cantonment d.	|	0330	|	|	0736	0901	0957
Ludhiana Junction d.	0613	0430	0702	0747	0835	1000	1100
Ambala Cantonment d.	0810	0650	0833	0950	1050	1310	1340
New Delhi a.	1050	1115	1102	1245	1415	1620	1720j

	Exp 12920	*Exp* 11058	*Exp* 12498	*S* 12030 ⑤–③	*S* 12032 ④	*Exp* 22440 ③–①	*Exp* 12904
Katra SVDK ◧ d.	0840	...	...	...	...	1500	...
Udhampur d.	0913	...	...	...	...	|	...
Jammu Tawi d.	1030	...	...	...	...	1615	...
Pathankot Cantonment d.	1225	...	...	...	...	|	...
Amritsar Junction d.	|	0845	1510	1650	1650	|	1855
Jalandhar City d.	|	1015	1618	1756	1756	|	2010
Jalandhar Cantonment d.	1415	1026	|	|	|	|	|
Ludhiana Junction d.	1516	1145	1722	1855	1855	1930	2110
Ambala Cantonment d.	1705	1623	1925	2030	2030	2050	2255
New Delhi a.	2015	2025	2230	2250	2250	2300	0345h

	Exp 12414	*D* 12266 ①③⑥	*Exp* 18238	*Exp* 14034	*R* 12426	*Exp* 12446	*Exp* 22462
Katra SVDK ◧ d.	...	...	...	1530	...	1955	2300
Udhampur d.	...	...	...	1556	...	2021	2326
Jammu Tawi d.	1815	1915	...	1710	2125	2140	0035
Pathankot Cantonment d.	2000	|	...	1900	2309	2332	0220
Amritsar Junction d.	|	|	1610	|	|	|	|
Jalandhar City d.	|	|	1730	|	|	|	|
Jalandhar Cantonment d.	2200	|	1741	2119	|	0110	0410
Ludhiana Junction d.	2254	2324	1843	2220	0144	0208	0504
Ambala Cantonment d.	0050	|	2140	0035	|	0410	0710
New Delhi a.	0350j	0355r	0410h	0430j	0555	0655	0945

h – Delhi **Hazrat Nizamuddin**. j – Delhi **Junction**. r – Delhi **Sarai Rohilla**. ◧ – Full name is Shri Mata Vaishno Devi Katra.

5010 DELHI - KALKA - SHIMLA

km		*Exp* 12311	52451	52453	52459	*S* 12011	52455	*S* 12005
0	**New Delhi** d.	2110j	...	...	...	0740	...	1715
199	Ambala Cantonment d.	0055	...	...	...	1022	...	1953
268	Chandigarh d.	0225	...	...	...	1105	...	2038
305	**Kalka** a.	0300	...	...	...	1140	...	2115
305	**Kalka** ¶ d.	...	0545	0620	0700	...	1210	...
347	Barog ¶ d.	...	0751	0831	0910	...	1425	...
351	Solan ¶ d.	...	|	0845	|	...	1440	...
401	**Shimla** ¶ a.	...	1025	1150	1230	...	1720	...

	S 12006	52456	*S* 12012	52460	52542	52454	*Exp* 12312
Shimla ¶ d.	...	1055	...	1550	1805	1845	...
Solan ¶ d.	...	1403	...	|	|	2119	...
Barog ¶ d.	...	1425	...	1848	2038	2135	...
Kalka ¶ a.	...	1635	...	2050	2240	2345	...
Kalka d.	0615	...	1745	...	...	...	2355
Chandigarh d.	0653	...	1823	...	...	...	0125
Ambala Cantonment d.	0738	...	1908	...	...	...	0220
New Delhi a.	1015	...	2150	...	...	...	0600j

j – Delhi **Junction**. ¶ – Narrow gauge railway.

5015 DELHI - DEHRA DUN

km		*S* 12017	*Exp* 19565 ⑥	*Exp* 14317 ①⑦	*Exp* 14309 ④⑤	*JS* 12055	*Exp* 14041	*Exp* 12401
0	**Delhi** Hazrat Nizamuddin d.	0645n	1045n	1140	1140	1520n	2225j	2350
76	Meerut City d.	0803	1207	1304	1304	1634	|	0108
190	Saharanpur d.	1015	|	1525	1525	|	|	|
271	Haridwar Junction d.	1138	1620	1645	1645	1938	0625	0405
323	**Dehra Dun** a.	1255	1945	1945	1945	2110	0825	0545

	JS 12056	*Exp* 14310 ②③	*Exp* 14318 ⑤⑥	*Exp* 19566 ⑦	*S* 12018	*Exp* 14042	*Exp* 12402
Dehra Dun d.	0500	0550	0550	0550	1655	2125	2245
Haridwar Junction d.	0629	0745	0745	0745	1804	2316	0014
Saharanpur d.	|	0955	0955	|	1955	|	|
Meerut City d.	0924	1130	1130	1112	2120	|	0255
Delhi Hazrat Nizamuddin a.	1105n	1335	1335	1310n	2250n	0720j	0430

j – Delhi **Junction**. n – **New Delhi**.

5020 DELHI - LUCKNOW

km		*S* 12004	*Exp* 15910	*Exp* 12204 ③⑥⑦	*R* 20504 A	*Exp* 15128	*Exp* 12420	*Exp* 12392	*Exp* 12558
0	**New Delhi** d.	0610	0722j	1105	1125	1135	1220	1310	1450v
	Kanpur Central d.	1125	|	|	|	|	1950	|	|
167	Moradabad d.	|	1053	1353	1410	1515	|	1610	1745
258	Bareilly Junction d.	|	1223	1513	1526	1646	|	1740	|
493	**Lucknow** Junction (NER*) a.	1250	|	|	|	|	|	|	|
493	**Lucknow** Charbagh (NR*) a.	...	1730	1830	1840	2105	2130	2120	2240

km		*Exp* 85202 ③–①	*Exp* 22408 ①⑤	*Exp* 14206	*Exp* 14208	*Exp* 12212 ③	*Exp* 12556	*Exp* 12230	*Exp* 12430
0	**New Delhi** d.	1540	1815v	1820j	1950j	2055v	2125	2200	2325
	Kanpur Central d.	2040	|	|	|	|	0305	|	|
167	Moradabad d.	|	2110	2208	2320	2358	|	0113	0218
258	Bareilly Junction d.	|	2235	2346	0057	0121	|	0239	0335
493	**Lucknow** Junction (NER*) a.	2205	|	|	|	|	|	0650	|
493	**Lucknow** Charbagh (NR*) a.	...	0225	0315	0440	0520	0450	...	0725

km		*Exp* 22407 ①⑤	*Exp* 12211 ⑥	*Exp* 15909	*Exp* 12419	*R* 20503 B	*Exp* 12203 ①②⑤	*Exp* 85201 ③–①	*S* 12003
	Lucknow Charbagh (NR*) d.	0110	0425	0520	0545	0550	0600	...	...
0	**Lucknow** Junction (NER*) d.	|	|	|	|	|	|	0610	1535
	Bareilly Junction d.	0437	0813	1038	|	0914	0931	|	|
	Moradabad d.	0625	0953	1230	|	1055	1110	|	|
74	Kanpur Central d.	|	|	|	0735	|	|	0725	1653
511	**New Delhi** a.	0930v	1235v	1555j	1500	1338	1355	1225	2220

km		*Exp* 14205	*Exp* 12391	*Exp* 15127	*Exp* 12555	*Exp* 14207	*Exp* 12229	*Exp* 12429	*Exp* 12557
	Lucknow Charbagh (NR*) d.	1955	2005	2020	2135	2150	...	2330	2340
0	**Lucknow** Junction (NER*) d.	|	|	|	|	|	2200	|	|
	Bareilly Junction d.	2336	2349	0015	|	0133	0143	0300	|
	Moradabad d.	0123	0135	0205	|	0318	0333	0435	0450
74	Kanpur Central d.	|	|	|	2323	|	|	|	|
511	**New Delhi** a.	0420j	0440	0540	0520	0625j	0655	0730	0740v

A – Train **20506** on ④⑦.
B – Train **20505** on ③⑦.
j – Delhi **Junction**.
v – Delhi **Anand Vihar Terminal**.
* – Lucknow Junction is officially known as Lucknow NER and Lucknow Charbagh is officially known as Lucknow NR. The stations are adjacent to each other.

JAMMU TAWI and AMRITSAR - LUCKNOW 5030

km		Exp 14612 ④	Exp 12238	Exp 13006	Exp 13152				
78	**Katra** SVDK ◧ d.	0555	...	...	...	...	...	...	...
0	**Jammu Tawi** d.	0720	1400	...	2030	...	...	...	...
100	Pathankot Cantonment d.	0905	1545	...	2225	...	...	...	...
**	**Amritsar** Junction d.	│	│	1825	│	...	...	...	...
**	Jalandhar City d.	│	│	1938	│	...	...	...	...
213	Jalandhar Cantonment d.	1055	1730	1950	0030	...	...	...	...
265	Ludhiana Junction d.	1200	1824	2050	0155	...	...	...	...
378	Ambala Cantonment d.	1353	2103	2310	0415	...	...	...	...
460	Saharanpur d.	1505	2215	0055	0535	...	...	...	...
652	Moradabad d.	1818	0133	0458	0955	...	...	...	...
743	Bareilly Junction d.	│	│	0623	1155	...	...	...	...
978	**Lucknow** Charbagh (NR*) a.	2320	0710	1035	1700	...	...	...	...

	Exp 13151	Exp 13005	Exp 14611 ⑤	Exp 12237				
Lucknow Charbagh (NR*) d.	1225	1550	1725	1745	...	...	...	...
Bareilly Junction d.	1716	2005	│	│	...	...	...	...
Moradabad d.	1920	2200	2300	2313	...	...	...	...
Saharanpur d.	2340	0145	0213	0230	...	...	...	...
Ambala Cantonment d.	0121	0320	0335	0352	...	...	...	...
Ludhiana Junction d.	0330	0545	0535	0556	...	...	...	...
Jalandhar Cantonment d.	0430	0651	0645	0710	...	...	...	...
Jalandhar City d.	│	0712	│	│	...	...	...	...
Amritsar Junction a.	│	0840	│	│	...	...	...	...
Pathankot Cantonment d.	0623	...	0825	0850	...	...	...	...
Jammu Tawi a.	0850	...	1020	1050	...	...	...	...
Katra SVDK ◧ a.	...	...	1230	...	...	...	...	...

– Full station name is Shri Mata Vaishno Devi Katra.
– Lucknow Charbagh is officially known as Lucknow NR.

** – Amritsar - Jalandhar Cantonment: *84 km*. Jalandhar City - Jalandhar Cantonment: *5 km*.

DELHI - GUWAHATI 5040

km ●		Exp 15910	Exp 12506	R 20504 A	R 12424	Exp 20502 ③	Exp 14038 ④	Exp 22450 ③⑦	Exp 15657	
0	**New Delhi** d.	0722j	0740v	1125	1620	1950v	2345	2345	2340j	...
167	Moradabad d.	1053	│	1410	│	│	│	│	│	...
258	Bareilly Junction d.	1223	│	1526	│	│	│	│	│	...
493	Lucknow Charbagh ⊖ d.	1740	│	1850	│	│	│	│	│	...
764	Gorakhpur Junction d.	2340	│	│	│	│	│	│	│	...
981	Chhapra d.	0400	│	0212	│	│	│	│	│	...
437	Kanpur Central d.	│	1335	│	2107	0040	0525	0525	0535	...
531	Prayagraj Junction ◧ d.	│	1615	│	2310	0452	0755	0755	0805	...
772	PDD Upadhyaya Junction ⊡ d.	│	1850	│	0133	│	1100	1100	1110	...
980	Patliputra d.	│	2155	│	0425	0750	1400	1400	│	...
984	Patna Junction d.	│	│	│	│	│	│	│	1430	...
205	Bhagalpur d.	│	│	│	│	│	│	│	1930	...
348	New Farakka Junction d.	│	│	│	│	│	│	│	2244	...
382	Malda Town d.	│	│	│	│	│	│	│	0015	...
089	Barauni Junction d.	0855	0035	│	0650	1015	│	│	│	...
269	Katihar Junction d.	1310	0450	0840	0955	1345	1955	1955	│	...
452	New Jalpaiguri d.	1700	0820	1135	1250	1715	2315	2315	0415	...
703	New Bongaigaon d.	2225	1300	1546	1644	│	0315	0315	0920	...
854	**Kamakhya** Junction a.	│	1625	│	│	│	│	│	1320	...
860	**Guwahati** a.	0215	...	1825	1925	2355	0745	0800	...	...

	R 12423	Exp 20501 ②	Exp 14037 ②	Exp 22449 ③⑥	R 20503 B	Exp 15909	Exp 12505	Exp 15658	
Guwahati d.	0645	0730	0605	0615	0535	2200	...	...	...
Kamakhya Junction d.	│	│	│	│	│	│	1240	1435	...
New Bongaigaon d.	0923	│	0938	0938	0820	0120	1540	1810	...
New Jalpaiguri d.	1325	1405	1350	1350	1225	0545	2015	2255	...
Katihar Junction d.	1625	1710	1730	1730	1525	1045	2345	│	...
Barauni Junction d.	1915	1955	│	│	│	1425	0255	│	...
Malda Town d.	│	│	│	│	│	│	│	0345	...
New Farakka Junction d.	│	│	│	│	│	│	│	0419	...
Bhagalpur d.	│	│	│	│	│	│	│	0738	...
Patna Junction d.	│	│	│	│	│	│	│	1250	...
Patliputra d.	2150	2225	2245	2245	│	│	0545	│	...
PDD Upadhyaya Junction ⊡ d.	0105	0135	0200	0200	│	│	1000	1645	...
Prayagraj Junction ◧ d.	0255	│	0405	0405	│	│	1230	1910	...
Kanpur Central d.	0505	0535	0630	0630	│	│	1505	2135	...
Chhapra d.	│	│	│	│	2200	1945	│	│	...
Gorakhpur Junction d.	│	│	│	│	│	2345	│	│	...
Lucknow Charbagh ⊖ d.	│	│	│	│	0550	0520	│	│	...
Bareilly Junction d.	│	│	│	│	0914	1038	│	│	...
Moradabad d.	│	│	│	│	1055	1230	│	│	...
New Delhi a.	1030	1050v	1235	1235	1338	1555j	2150v	0435j	...

– ①②③⑤⑥.
– ①③④⑤⑦.

– Delhi **Junction**.
– Delhi **Anand Vihar Terminal**.

◧ – Prayagraj (formerly Allahabad).
⊡ – Pandit Deen Dayal Upadhyaya (formerly Mughal Sarai).
⊖ – Officially known as Lucknow NR.
● – Chhapra - Barauni is *147 km*. Malda Town - New Jalpaiguri is *233 km*.

DELHI - PATNA - KOLKATA 5050

km		D 22214 ②④⑥	Exp 13006	Exp 12334	Exp 12312	Exp 15484	Exp 12324 ④⑦	D 12274 ②⑥	
0	**New Delhi** d.	...	...	...	0615j	0735j	0755j	1240	...
440	Kanpur Central d.	...	...	...	1355	1455	1345	1740	...
634	Prayagraj Junction ◧ d.	...	...	...	1710	1745	1630	│	...
787	PDD Upadhyaya Junction ⊡ d.	...	...	...	2048	2133	1933	2212	...
998	**Patna** Junction a.	2045	2140	2255	│	0040	│	0105	...
992	Gaya Junction d.	│	│	│	2335	...	2205	│	...
189	Dhanbad d.	│	│	│	0322	...	0120	│	...
247	Asansol d.	0201	0403	0423	0436	...	0230	0740	...
447	**Kolkata** Howrah a.	0545s	0730	0740	0805	...	0550	1035	...

	Exp 12368	R 12314	R 12302 ⑥–④	Exp 12306 ⑤	R 12310	JS 12024	Exp 12394	
New Delhi d.	1315v	1630	1650	1650	1710	...	1730	...
Kanpur Central d.	1830	2117	2137	2137	2157	...	2230	...
Prayagraj Junction ◧ d.	│	│	2345	2345	0005	...	│	...
PDD Upadhyaya Junction ⊡ d.	2345	0142	0152	0152	0212	...	0328	...
Patna Junction a.	0230	│	│	0430	0440	0530	0635	...
Gaya Junction d.	...	0348	0358	│	...	│	...	...
Dhanbad d.	...	0623	0638	│	...	│	...	...
Asansol d.	...	0711	0730	│	...	1043	...	...
Kolkata Howrah a.	...	1010e	0955	1215	...	1325	...	...

	Exp 12382 ①②⑤	Exp 12304 C	D 12260 D	Exp 12380 ⑦	Exp 12330 ③	Exp 20802	Exp 15657
New Delhi d.	1740	1740	1945	2015j	2020v	2105	2340j
Kanpur Central d.	2305	2305	0040	0115	0115	0345	0535
Prayagraj Junction ◧ d.	0150	0120	│	│	│	0625	0805
PDD Upadhyaya Junction ⊡ d.	0630	0355	0452	0620	0620	0915	1110
Patna Junction a.	│	0700	│	│	│	1240	1420
Gaya Junction d.	0915	│	│	0840	0840	...	...
Dhanbad d.	1205	│	0917	1142	1142	...	...
Asansol d.	1336	1336	│	1300	1300	...	...
Kolkata Howrah a.	1700	1700	1315e	1635e	1635e	...	...

km		Exp 15658	Exp 12303 E	Exp 12381 ③④⑦	D 12273 ①⑤	Exp 12367	R 12309	Exp 12393	
0	**Kolkata** Howrah d.	...	0800	0815	0835	...	...	...	...
200	Asansol d.	...	1037	1048	1100	...	...	...	...
	Dhanbad d.	...	│	1200	│	...	...	...	...
	Gaya Junction d.	...	│	1450	│	...	...	...	...
532	**Patna** Junction d.	1250	1610	│	1640	1705	1935	1945	...
744	PDD Upadhyaya Junction ⊡ d.	1645	1940	1800	2022	2035	2222	2232	...
896	Prayagraj Junction ◧ d.	1910	2145	2140	│	│	0012	│	...
091	Kanpur Central d.	2135	0007	0007	0055	0110	0220	0230	...
530	**New Delhi** a.	0435j	0600	0600	0635	0720v	0740	0755	...

	Exp 12329 ②	Exp 12379 ⑤	R 12305 ⑦	JS 12023	R 12301 ①–⑥	R 12313	D 12259 F	
Kolkata Howrah d.	1310e	1310e	1405	1405	1650	1650e	1700e	...
Asansol d.	1607	1607	│	1642	1859	1916	│	...
Dhanbad d.	1715	1715	│	│	2000	2025	2035	...
Gaya Junction d.	2005	2005	│	│	2237	2304	│	...
Patna Junction d.	│	│	2110	2220	│	│	│	...
PDD Upadhyaya Junction ⊡ d.	2240	2240	0055	...	0055	0125	0135	...
Prayagraj Junction ◧ d.	│	│	0245	...	0245	│	│	...
Kanpur Central d.	0310	0310	0455	...	0455	0525	0535	...
New Delhi a.	0840v	0905j	1005	...	1005	1050	1100	...

	Exp 20801	Exp 12323 ②⑤	Exp 15483	Exp 13005	Exp 12333	Exp 12311	D 22213 ①③⑤
Kolkata Howrah d.	...	1850	...	1915	2000	2155	2155s
Asansol d.	...	2118	...	2156	2239	0037	0112
Dhanbad d.	...	2240	...	│	│	0150	│
Gaya Junction d.	...	0152	...	│	│	0515	│
Patna Junction d.	1730	│	0325	0340	0400	│	0620
PDD Upadhyaya Junction ⊡ d.	2204	0435	0700	...	...	0815	...
Prayagraj Junction ◧ d.	0120	0650	0925	...	...	1050	...
Kanpur Central d.	0350	0920	1300	...	...	1340	...
New Delhi a.	1150	1515j	2145j	...	...	2055j	...

– ③④⑥⑦.
– ①②④⑤.
– ①②⑤⑥.
– ①③④⑦.

e – Kolkata **Sealdah**.
j – Delhi **Junction**.
s – Kolkata **Shalimar**.
v – Delhi **Anand Vihar Terminal**.

◧ – Prayagraj (formerly Allahabad).
⊡ – Pandit Deen Dayal Upadhyaya (formerly Mughal Sarai).

LUCKNOW - PATNA - KOLKATA 5060

km ⊙		Exp 12354 ⑦	Exp 12370 G	Exp 13010	Exp 13006	Exp 12332 ①②⑤	Exp 13152	Exp 12358 ①④	Exp 12326 H	Exp 12372 ④
0	**Lucknow** Charbagh ⊖ d.	0120	0810	0845	1040	1530	1710	2015	2015	2345
77	Rae Bareli Junction d.	0247	│	│	1210	│	│	│	│	0105
	Ayodhya Cantonment d.	│	│	1115	│	│	2022	│	│	│
	Sultanpur d.	│	1023	│	│	1750	│	│	│	│
301	Varanasi Junction d.	0715	1305	1615	1700	2105	0140	0110	0110	0520
316	PDD Upadhyaya Junction ⊡ d.	0825	1420	1720	1805	2220	0255	0220	0225	0633
	Patna Junction d.	│	1740	│	2140	0130	│	│	0550	│
519	Gaya Junction d.	1100	│	2050	│	│	0615	0440	│	0900
18	Dhanbad d.	1355	│	0108	│	│	1005	0720	│	1155
77	Asansol d.	1520	2358	0244	0403	0815	1145	0825	1128	1317
77	**Kolkata** Howrah a.	1825	0315	0700	0730	1130	1540k	1140k	1445k	1650

	Exp 12325 J	Exp 12371 ①	Exp 12353 ⑤	Exp 13151	Exp 12357 ②⑥	Exp 12369 K	Exp 13005	Exp 13009	Exp 12331 ②⑤⑥
Kolkata Howrah d.	0740k	0815	0815	1145k	1210k	1300	1915	2025	2355
Asansol d.	1037	1048	1048	1520	1452	1534	2156	0011	0231
Dhanbad d.	│	1200	1200	1655	1600	│	│	0130	│
Gaya Junction d.	│	1448	1448	2108	1843	│	│	0500	│
Patna Junction d.	1610	│	│	│	│	2055	0350	│	1015
PDD Upadhyaya Junction ⊡ d.	1940	1755	1755	0130	2115	0035	0815	0925	1355
Varanasi Junction d.	2040	1910	1910	0250	2215	0155	0925	1030	1447
Sultanpur d.	│	│	│	│	│	0420	│	│	1650
Ayodhya Cantonment d.	│	│	│	0755	│	│	│	1430	│
Rae Barali Junction d.	│	2305	2305	│	│	│	1325	│	│
Lucknow Charbagh ⊖ a.	0230	0100	0100	1215	0230	0720	1540	1750	1935

– Train **12328** on ④⑦.
– ②⑤⑥. Train **12318** on ②⑤ (calls at Sultanpur d. 2213).
– ③④⑦. Train **12317** on ③⑦ (calls at Sultanpur d. 2248).
– Train **12327** on ②⑤.
– **Kolkata**.

⊡ – Pandit Deen Dayal Upadhyaya (formerly Mughal Sarai).
⊖ – Officially known as Lucknow NR.
⊙ – Lucknow - Varanasi is *324 km* via Ayodhya and *283km* via Sultanpur.
For distances PDD Upadhyaya - Patna - Asansol - Kolkata see Table **5050**.

5065 KOLKATA - DHAKA

Bangladesh Railways, Indian Railways

km	All times are local		Exp	Exp
			3108	3109
			①⑥	②⑤
0	**Kolkata** Chitpur	d.	0710	0710
122	Gede	a.	0925	0925
122	Gede 🛃	d.	1055	1055
	Darsana 🛃	a.	1105	1105
	Darsana	d.	1235	1235
540	**Dhaka** Cantonment	a.	1805	1805

All times are local		Exp	Exp
		3107	3110
		⑤⑦	③⑥
Dhaka Cantonment	d.	0815	0815
Darsana	a.	1350	1350
Darsana 🛃	d.	1450	1450
Gede 🛃	a.	1430	1430
Gede	d.	1600	1600
Kolkata Chitpur	a.	1810	1810

5070 KOLKATA - NEW JALPAIGURI - GUWAHATI

km			Exp	Exp	Exp	Exp	Exp	Exp
			13175	13173	15643	13181	12345	15959
			①③⑥	L	⑦	①		M
0	**Kolkata** Howrah	d.	0635e	0635e	0730	0905k	1555	1830
207	Rampurhat	d.	1027	1027	|	1231	1855	|
293	New Farakka Junction	d.	1243	1243	1358	|	2040	0022
328	Malda Town	d.	1345	1345	1510	1510	2140	0155
473	Kishanganj	d.	1617	1617	1715	|	2330	0355
561	New Jalpaiguri	d.	1820	1820	1905	1905	0130	0600
812	New Bongaigaon	d.	2315	2315	0145	0010	0622	1110
963	**Kamakhya** Junction	a.	|	|	0510	0315	|	|
969	**Guwahati**	a.	0315	0315	...	0345	1005	1520

		Exp	Exp	Exp	Exp	Exp	Exp
		15960	12346	13182	13176	13174	15644
		M		②	①③⑤	N	④
Guwahati	d.	0735	1220	1725	2250	2255	...
Kamakhya Junction	d.	|	1239	1752	2312	2312	2345
New Bongaigaon	d.	1150	1523	2105	0220	0220	0245
New Jalpaiguri	d.	1705	1940	0135	0725	0725	0855
Kishanganj	d.	1820	2047	|	0850	0850	1022
Malda Town	d.	2200	2340	0630	1235	1235	1355
New Farakka Junction	d.	2239	0016	|	1314	1314	1429
Rampurhat	d.	|	0138	0830	1502	1502	|
Kolkata Howrah	a.	0510	0520	1230k	1925e	1925e	2250

L – ②④⑤⑦. M – ②③④⑥⑦. N – ②④⑥⑦. e – Kolkatta **Sealdah**. k – **Kolkatta**.

5075 GUWAHATI - JORHAT and DIBRUGARH

km			Exp	JS	Exp	Exp	Exp	Exp	R	R	Exp
			15910	12067	15905	13282	15665	15959	20504	12424	15669
				①-⑥	③⑦	⑦		A	B		
0	**Guwahati**	d.	0230	0610	0910	1055	1430	1535	1850	1940	2045
87	Chaparmukh Junction	d.	0420	0728	|	1220	1558	1708	|	2108	|
184	Lumding Junction	d.	0605	0905	1205	1405	1810	1915	2157	2257	0005
250	Dimapur	d.	0722	1022	1322	1524	1942	2038	2307	0017	0155
323	Furkating Junction	d.	0932	1144	1542	1712	2117	2305	|	|	0355
376	**Jorhat Town**	d.	|	1305	|	|	2252	|	|	|	0602
358	Mariani Junction	d.	1012	...	1630	1752	2340	2355	0207	0237	0705
513	New Tinsukia Junction	d.	1320	...	1945	2050	...	0315	|	0453	|
561	**Dibrugarh**	a.	1435	...	2050	2225	...	0415	0440	0600	1020

		Exp	Exp	JS	Exp	Exp	R	Exp	R	Exp
		15666	13281	12068	15909	15670	20503	15906	12423	15960
			①	①-⑥			B	②⑥		C
Dibrugarh	d.	...	0525	...	1020	1340	1955	1925	2055	1835
New Tinsukia Junction	d.	...	0623	...	1115	|	|	2020	2156	1940
Mariani Junction	d.	0605	0915	...	1350	1652	2213	2250	0010	2315
Jorhat Town	d.	0646	|	1425	|	1739	|	|	|	|
Furkating Junction	d.	0830	1017	1547	1452	2005	|	2345	|	0025
Dimapur	d.	0942	1133	1653	1600	2125	0017	0110	0208	0155
Lumding Junction	d.	1120	1320	1810	1730	2320	0155	0243	0317	0400
Chaparmukh Junction	d.	1250	1432	1938	1857	|	|	|	0432	0540
Guwahati	a.	1455	1710	2120	2145	0315	0520	0610	0630	0720

A – ①③④⑤⑦. B – ②③④⑥⑦. C – ①②③⑤⑥.

5080 DELHI - JAIPUR - AHMEDABAD

km			S	Exp	Exp	Exp	JS	Exp	R	Exp
			12015	20940	19408	12916	12066	22950	12958	19032
				④	⑦		E	④		
0	**Delhi** Junction	d.	0610n	0630	0630	1520	1615r	1615r	1955n	2225
83	Rewari	d.	0747	0805	0805	1700	1737	1737	|	0010
157	Alwar	d.	0847	0906	0906	1807	|	|	|	0117
308	**Jaipur**	d.	1050	1120	1120	2025	|	|	0005	0330
444	Ajmer Junction	d.	1255	1335	1335	2240	2215	2300	0150	0550
581	Marwar Junction	d.	...	1525	1525	|	...	|	|	0755
749	Abu Road	d.	...	1745	1745	0230	...	0330	0530	1045
801	Palanpur Junction	d.	...	1850	1850	0340	...	0430	0620	1150
866	Mahesana Junction	d.	...	1957	1957	0442	...	0543	0710	1310
934	**Ahmedabad** Junction	a.	...	2200	2200	0620	...	0740	0845	1535

		S	Exp	Exp	R	Exp	Exp	JS	Exp
		12016	20939	19031	12957	12915	22949	12065	19407
			②				③	E	④
Ahmedabad Junction	d.	...	0800	1050	1830	1915	1935	...	2155
Mahesana Junction	d.	...	0910	1235	1938	2025	2050	...	2314
Palanpur Junction	d.	...	1105	1425	2042	2145	2305	...	0100
Abu Road	d.	...	1150	1510	2125	2235	0010	...	0145
Marwar Junction	d.	...	1405	1750	|	|	|	...	0410
Ajmer Junction	d.	1600	1620	2035	0105	0235	0500	0545	0625
Jaipur	d.	1750	1820	2250	0255	0430	|	|	0915
Alwar	d.	1947	2015	0108	|	0641	|	|	1124
Rewari	d.	2052	2156	0255	|	0802	1000	1000	1243
Delhi Junction	a.	2240n	2355	0450	0730n	1000	1135r	1135r	1445

E – ①②③⑤⑥. n – **New Delhi**. r – Delhi **Sarai Rohilla**.

5090 DELHI - JODHPUR - JAISALMER

km ◧			Exp	Exp	Exp	Exp	Exp	Exp	Exp	Exp	Exp
			15014	22421	15624	14646	12323	14804	22995	12463	22482
					⑦	G	③⑥			③	
0	**Delhi** Junction	d.	0430	0705r	1005	1100	1540	...	2120	2225r	2310r
83	Rewari	d.	0625	0835	1141	1335	1717	...	2313	|	0038
282	Churu	d.	|	1145	1515	|	2055	...	|	|	0350
325	Ratangarh Junction	d.	|	1245	1610	|	2155	...	|	|	0443
157	Alwar	d.	0737	|	|	1453	|	...	0015	0049	|
308	Jaipur	d.	1010	|	|	1745	|	...	0230	0255	|
443	Ajmer Junction	d.	1225	|	|	|	|	...	|	|	|
582	Marwar Junction	d.	1455	|	|	|	|	...	|	|	|
471	Degana Junction	d.	|	1508	1825	2030	|	...	0501	0528	0714
516	Merta Road	d.	|	1540	1900	2106	|	...	0536	0605	0753
620	**Jodhpur** Junction	a.	1640	1810	2040	2245	0240	...	0745	0815	1000
620	**Jodhpur** Junction	d.	1655	...	...	2300	...	0650	...	...	...
757	Phalodi	d.	1858	...	...	0127	...	0853	...	...	...
804	Ramdevra	d.	1941	...	...	0223	...	0936	...	...	...
814	Pokaran	d.	|	...	...	0245	...	1005	...	...	...
921	**Jaisalmer**	a.	2200	...	...	0530	...	1230	...	...	...

		Exp	Exp	Exp	Exp	Exp	Exp	Exp	Exp	Exp
		15013	22422	15623	22481	12464	22996	12324	14803	14645
				②		④		③⑥		H
Jaisalmer	d.	0300	...	...	...	...	...	...	1510	2325
Pokaran	d.	|	...	...	...	...	...	...	1640	0045
Ramdevra	d.	0430	...	...	...	...	...	...	1720	0123
Phalodi	d.	0511	...	...	...	...	...	...	1800	0204
Jodhpur Junction	a.	0800	...	...	...	...	...	...	2030	0440
Jodhpur Junction	d.	0815	1055	1630	1845	2000	2015	1950	...	0515
Merta Road	d.	|	1214	1753	2000	2115	2133	|	...	0632
Degana Junction	d.	|	1250	1830	2057	2153	2211	|	...	0713
Marwar Junction	d.	1050	|	|	|	|	|	|	...	|
Ajmer Junction	d.	1310	|	|	|	|	|	|	...	|
Jaipur	d.	1525	|	|	|	0045	0120	|	...	1025
Alwar	d.	1745	|	|	|	0241	0328	|	...	1304
Ratangarh Junction	d.	|	1605	2130	2340	|	|	0125	...	|
Churu	d.	|	1655	2225	0030	|	|	0220	...	|
Rewari	d.	1910	2025	0240	0340	|	0440	0551	...	1440
Delhi Junction	a.	2115	2210r	0430	0520r	0550r	0645	0730	...	1650

G – ②③⑤⑦. Also runs Delhi - Jodhpur on ①④⑥ as train **14662**.
H – ①③④⑥. Also runs Jodhpur - Delhi on ①③⑥ as train **14661**.
r – Delhi **Sarai Rohilla**.
◧ – Delhi Junction - Jodhpur is *684 km* via Ajmer, *635 km* via Churu.

5110 BIKANER - JODHPUR - AHMEDABAD

km			Exp	Exp	Exp	Exp	Exp	Exp	Exp	Exp	Exp
			19224	14707	22473	12489	16588	16311	22475	22738	17624
					①	②⑥	②⑦	②	③	⑤⑦	⑥
0	**Bikaner** Junction	d.	0015	0750	1500	1500	1905	1915	1915	1940	1940
173	Merta Road	d.	0303	1012	1731	|	2145	2200	2200	2220	2220
277	**Jodhpur** Junction	d.	0515	1305	1940	1940	2315	2345	2345	0020	0020
308	Luni Junction	d.	|	1335	|	|	|	|	0026	|	|
380	Marwar Junction	d.	0720	1545	2150	|	0107	0138	0138	0210	0210
545	Abu Road	d.	0940	1825	0015	|	0330	0400	0400	0430	0430
598	Palanpur Junction	d.	1037	1923	0105	|	0422	0457	0457	0522	0522
663	Mahesana Junction	d.	1152	2050	0211	0232	0527	|	0543	0617	0617
736	**Ahmedabad** Junction	a.	1340	2250	0400	0425	0655	0720	0735	0755	0755

		Exp	Exp	Exp	Exp	Exp	Exp	Exp	Exp	Exp
		22737	17623	16312	19223	16587	22476	22474	14708	12490
		③④	⑤	①		①⑥	⑦	②		③⑦
Ahmedabad Junction	d.	2359	0035	0650	1105	2010	2135	2150	2155	2300
Mahesana Junction	d.	0110	0210	|	1213	2137	2314	2314	2326	0008
Palanpur Junction	d.	0242	0332	1027	1400	2305	0100	0100	0118	|
Abu Road	d.	0335	0425	1120	1445	0010	0145	0145	0210	|
Marwar Junction	d.	0600	0655	1335	1710	0235	0410	0410	0500	|
Luni Junction	d.	|	|	|	|	|	0522	|	0606	|
Jodhpur Junction	d.	0800	0900	1530	1915	0435	0620	0620	0715	0725
Merta Road	d.	0924	1035	1703	2058	0558	0742	0742	0902	|
Bikaner Junction	a.	1250	1335	2010	0055	0930	1035	1030	1245	1230

DELHI and JAIPUR - UDAIPUR - AHMEDABAD 5120

km		Exp	Exp	Exp	Exp	Exp	Exp	Exp	Exp	Exp
		19616	12315	19602	22986	19665	20473	19610	19703	12992
		⑥	⑤	②	⑦			①③⑥		
0	**Delhi** Junction d.	...	...	1220	1615r	...	1935r	0030	...	...
83	Rewari d.	...	...	1510	|	...	2102	0227	...	...
157	Alwar d.	...	...	1617	1823	...	|	0329	...	...
**	**Jaipur** d.	1610	1610	1915	2040	2230	|	0625	...	1430
373	Ajmer Junction d.	1820	1820	2130	2240	0045	0205	0850	...	1635
559	Chittaurgarh d.	|	|	|	|	0420	0525	1245	...	1937
673	**Udaipur** City d.	0025	0025	0345	0345	0630	0750	1530	1700	2200
883	Himmatnagar ◧ d.	...	...	...	...	...	...	...	2100	...
971	**Ahmedabad** ◧ a.	...	...	...	...	...	...	...	...	...

	Exp	Exp	Exp	Exp	Exp	Exp	Exp	Exp	Exp
	12316	19601	12991	19704	19609	19615	20474	19666	22985
	①	⑥			①④⑥	①			⑥
Ahmedabad ◧ d.	...	...	...	...	...	...	...	...	...
Himmatnagar ◧ d.	...	...	...	0830	...	...	...	...	...
Udaipur City d.	0045	0045	0600	1230	1345	1605	1700	2215	2315
Chittaurgarh d.	|	|	0810	...	1610	|	1903	0020	|
Ajmer Junction d.	0625	0625	1115	...	1930	2100	2225	0320	0405
Jaipur d.	0855	0915	1340	...	2145	2300	|	0530	0610
Alwar d.	...	1124	...	...	0006	...	|	...	0815
Rewari d.	...	1243	...	...	0126	...	0325	...	|
Delhi Junction a.	...	1445	...	...	0310	...	0505r	...	1125r

– Delhi **Sarai Rohilla**.

◧ – Service suspended for gauge conversion.

** – Jaipur - Ajmer is *136 km*.

DELHI, JAIPUR and AHMEDABAD and MUMBAI 5130

km		Exp	D	Exp	Exp	Exp	Exp	D		R	Exp	Y	R	Exp	Exp	Exp		D	Exp	Exp	Exp	Exp	Exp	Exp
		12904	12264	14701	22934	12956	12918	12240		12952	12908	12248	12954	12980	12926	22950		22210	12476	12474	12478	12472	22918	19020
			①④		②		⑥	②④			①④	⑥		①③⑤		④		②⑥	①	④	⑦	A	④	
0	**Delhi** Hazrat Nizamuddin d.	0400	0616	...	...	...	1325	...	...	...	1630	1630	1715	...	...	1615r	...	...	...	...	...	...	2215	1855
	New Delhi d.	|	|	...	...	...	|	...	...	1655	|	|	|	...	1635	|	...	2210	2140	2140	2140	2140	|	|
124	Mathura Junction d.	0550	|	...	...	...	1455	...	...	|	|	1805	1845	...	1915	|	...	|	2325	2325	2325	2325	0004	2155
	Jaipur d.	|	|	0930	1310	1400	|	1650	...	|	|	|	|	2025	|	|	...	|	|	|	|	|	|	|
340	Sawai Madhopur d.	0835	|	|	1530	1605	|	1855	...	|	|	|	2050	2240	2210	|	...	|	0135	0135	0135	0135	0230	0055
448	Kota Junction d.	1020	1050	|	1640	1720	1815	|	...	2140	2120	2120	2210	2355	2340	|	...	0355	0255	0255	0255	0255	0355	0315
673	Nagda Junction d.	1342	|	|	1932	2037	|	|	...	2359	|	|	|	0232	0340	|	...	|	0552	0552	0552	0555	|	0800
714	Ratlam Junction d.	1425	1405	|	2020	2120	2135	2335	...	0033	|	0018	0107	0315	0435	|	...	0705	0640	0640	0640	0640	0710	0915
075	**Ahmedabad** Junction d.	|	|	2150	|	|	0320	|	...	|	|	|	|	|	|	0750	...	|	1220	1220	1220	|	|	|
976	Vadodara Junction d.	1811	1737	0008	0020	0106	...	0314	...	0350	0405	0405	0439	0715	0825	0932	...	1043	...	...	...	1035	1100	1435
104	Surat d.	1946	1916	0200	0225	0253	...	|	...	0518	|	0542	0618	0854	1029	1122	...	|	...	...	...	1230	1312	1707
340	Borivali d.	2248	△	0518	0532	0600	...	|	...	0742	0829	|	0912	1222	1358	1425	...	|	...	...	...	1517	1602	2121
	Mumbai Central a.	2335	...	|	|	0655	...	0820	...	0835	|	|	1005	|	1455	|	...	1550	...	...	...	|	|	|
360	**Mumbai** Bandra a.	...	...	0615	0630	...	...	...	...	...	0915	0915	...	1310	...	1510	...	...	...	...	...	1610	1650	2215

km		Exp	Exp	Exp	Exp	Exp	Exp	D		R	Exp	R	Exp	Exp	Exp	Exp		Y	Exp	Exp	Exp	Exp	D	D
		19019	12471	12475	12477	12473	12917	12263		12951	22917	12953	12925	22933	12979	12907		12247	22949	12903	12955	14702	22209	22239
			B	②	③	⑥	①	②⑤			③			①	②④⑥	③⑦		⑤	③				①⑤	②⑦
0	**Mumbai** Bandra d.	0005	1100	...	...	...	...	...	...	...	1245	...	1125	1705	1705	1730	...	1730	1215	...	...	2100	...	...
	Mumbai Central d.	|	|	...	...	...	...	...	...	1700	|	1710	|	|	|	|	...	|	|	1845	1905	|	2300	2300
19	Borivali d.	0035	1126	...	...	...	...	▽	...	1724	1312	1735	1158	1740	1740	1759	...	|	1240	1918	1942	2131	|	|
252	Surat d.	0420	1423	...	...	...	...	1652	...	1948	1621	2015	1552	2040	2040	2052	...	2052	1540	2202	2235	0055	|	|
381	Vadodara Junction d.	0630	1600	...	...	...	...	1831	...	2116	1843	2154	1740	2235	2235	2227	...	2227	1728	2344	0018	0240	0329	0329
	Ahmedabad Junction d.	|	|	1425	1420	1420	1530	|	...	|	|	|	|	|	|	|	...	|	1935	|	|	0445	|	|
642	Ratlam Junction d.	1150	1955	1955	1955	1955	2040	2200	...	0028	2245	0115	2145	0215	0215	|	...	0153	|	0335	0410	|	0705	0705
684	Nagda Junction d.	1310	2048	2048	2048	2048	|	|	...	0110	|	|	2300	0305	0305	|	...	|	|	0428	0500	|	|	|
909	Kota Junction d.	1735	2325	2325	2325	2325	2356	0105	...	0320	0215	0415	0155	0525	0525	0440	...	0440	|	0720	0755	|	1005	|
017	Sawai Madhopur d.	1945	0035	0035	0035	0035	|	|	...	|	0322	0525	0312	0715	0715	|	...	|	|	0830	0945	|	|	1150
148	**Jaipur** a.	|	|	|	|	|	|	|	...	|	|	|	|	0945	0945	|	...	|	|	|	1200	1750	|	1355
236	Mathura Junction d.	0015	0320	0320	0320	0320	0340	|	...	|	0617	0755	0740	...	...	|	...	0820	|	1145	...	...	|	...
	New Delhi a.	|	|	|	|	|	|	|	...	0832	|	|	|	...	...	|	...	|	|	|	...	...	1555	...
360	**Delhi** Hazrat Nizamuddin a.	0230	0505	0505	0505	0505	0550	0645	...	...	0835	0943	0959	...	...	1015	...	1015	1135r	1350	...	...	...	...

– ②③⑤⑥.
– ①④⑤⑦.

r – Delhi **Sarai Rohilla**.

△ – To Pune (a. 0210).
▽ – From Pune (d. 1110).

BHUJ - GANDHIDHAM - AHMEDABAD 5140

km		Exp	Exp	Exp		Exp	Exp	Exp		Exp	Exp	Exp		Exp	Exp	Exp		Exp	Exp	Exp		Exp	Exp	
		16505	12473	16335		15667	22973	11091		22829	22904	12937		20935	12960	12966		22952	22956	20908		20804	12993	
		②	⑥	⑤		⑥	③	③		②	①④⑥	⑥		①	①	⑤		④				⑦	⑤	
58	**Bhuj** d.	...	...	...	...	...	...	1325	...	1505	1605	...	...	...	1740	...	...	...	2015	2235	...	...	...	...
0	**Gandhidham** d.	0900	0910	1035	...	1315	1345	1445	...	1625	1720	1810	...	1815	1900	1905	...	2040	2135	2355	...	2305	2305	...
53	Samakhiali d.	0950	1000	1126	...	1406	1440	1540	...	1717	1807	1900	...	|	1950	1950	...	2132	2232	0054	...	2359	2359	...
70	Dhrangadhra d.	1125	1135	1303	...	|	|	1717	...	1900	|	2024	...	|	|	|	...	|	0010	0230	...	0129	0129	...
236	Viramgam Junction d.	1228	1247	1407	...	2004	1717	1827	...	|	|	|	...	2141	|	|	...	0232	0121	0344	...	0232	|	...
301	**Ahmedabad** Junction a.	1355	1410	1520	...	2125	1845	1945	...	2130	2200	2255	...	2300	0310	0310	...	0400	0245	0510	...	0400	0400	...

	Exp	Exp	Exp		Exp	Exp	Exp		Exp	Exp	Exp		Exp	Exp	Exp		Exp	Exp	Exp		Exp	Exp	
	22974	20803	22955		12965	12959	16506		12994	22903	16336		11092	22830	20936		12938	12474	15668		22951	20907	
	①	⑥			⑤	⑦	①		③	①④⑥	④		②	①	①		③	⑤	⑤		⑤		
medabad Junction d.	0045	0100	0150	...	0025	0035	0545	...	0640	0640	0650	...	0740	0810	0900	...	0930	1215	1400	...	2245	2350	...
amgam Junction d.	0142	0157	0243	...	|	|	0647	...	|	|	0750	...	0838	|	0953	...	|	1338	1457	...	2350	0047	...
rangadhra d.	|	0255	0345	...	|	|	0748	...	0835	|	0857	...	0935	|	|	...	1121	1441	|	...	|	0146	...
makhiali d.	0445	0454	0542	...	0706	0736	0942	...	1019	1015	1044	...	1134	1153	|	...	1313	1627	2025	...	0447	0340	...
ndhidham a.	0555	0615	0650	...	0820	0840	1100	...	1135	1120	1200	...	1240	1255	1355	...	1425	1740	2145	...	0555	0455	...
uj a.	...	...	0830	...	...	1010	...	...	...	1245	...	...	1430	1445	...	...	...	...	...	...	...	0630	...

AHMEDABAD - MUMBAI 5150

km		D	Exp	Exp	Exp	Exp	Exp	Exp	Exp	Exp	Exp	Exp		Exp	Exp	S	Exp	Exp	Exp	Exp	Exp	Exp	Exp	Exp
		12268	12960	19266	22956	12479	22952	12934	20908	12932	82902	22954		19016	20902	12010	19218	22946	22928	14701	22904	12902	14707	12972
			②	⑥			⑤			①–⑥	⑤–③				①–⑥	①–⑥					①④⑥			
0	**Ahmedabad** Junction d.	0115	0325	0325	0300	0340	0415	0500	0525	0600	0640	0705	...	0730	1500	1510	2000	2030	2045	2150	2215	2250	2305	2350
00	Vadodara d.	|	0519	0519	0453	0530	0603	0633	0718	0726	0759	0849	...	1001	1556	1635	2213	2220	2233	0008	2345	0025	0050	0137
229	Surat d.	|	0715	0720	0650	0727	0756	0813	0953	0917	0930	1046	...	1258	1713	1815	0025	0013	0037	0200	0125	0212	0244	0329
62	Borivali d.	|	1029	1029	1045	1041	1103	1115	1310	1206	1215	1453	...	1816	1934	2048	0441	0347	0430	0518	0406	0523	0625	0723
80	**Mumbai** Bandra a.	0800c	1115	1120	1145	1130	1155	1210c	1350d	1255c	1305c	1524d	...	1904d	2025c	2145c	0545	0415d	0525	0616	0455	0615d	0710d	0815

	Exp	Exp	S	Exp	Exp	Exp	Exp	Exp	Exp	Exp	Exp		Exp	Exp	Exp	Exp	Exp	Exp	Exp	Exp	Exp	D	Exp
	22953	20901	12009	19015	14708	12480	19217	12933	12931	22951	20907		82901	12965	12959	22955	12971	22927	14702	22945	12901	12267	22903
		①–⑥	①–⑥							⑤			⑤–③	④	⑥								③⑤⑦
mbai Bandra d.	0552d	0600c	0620c	0930d	1235d	1325	1340	1405c	1430c	1450	1515d	...	1545c	1645	1645	1745	1910	1940	2100	2105c	2140d	2310c	2345
rivali d.	0611	0625	0645	0951	1301	1348	1405	1433	1455	1513	1539	...	1615	1709	1709	1812	1943	2014	2131	2154	2204	|	0015
rat d.	1007	0858	0918	1452	1707	1642	1738	1720	1801	1840	1915	...	1905	2028	2028	2142	2307	0033	0055	0107	0119	|	0310
dodara d.	1209	1016	1035	1753	1905	1828	1952	1856	1938	2048	2125	...	2039	2209	2215	2333	0050	0215	0240	0252	0258	|	0447
medabad Junction a.	1430	1125	1240	2010	2140	2025	2200	2105	2125	2235	2335	...	2220	0015	0025	0135	0245	0420	0435	0450	0550	0520	0625

– Mumbai **Central**.

d – Mumbai **Dadar**.

5160 DELHI - PUNE and MUMBAI

km		Exp 12782 ①	Exp 12138	D 12264 ①④	Exp 22686 ②⑥	Exp 12630 ③⑤	Exp 11078	Exp 12780	R 22222	Exp 11058
0	**Delhi** Hazrat Nizamuddin d.	0510	0515**n**	0616	0828	0830	1130**n**	1515	1655	2053
134	Mathura Junction d.	0645	0700	|	|	|	1325	1700	|	2305
188	Agra Cantonment d.	0730	0805	|	|	|	1415	1755	1847	2335
306	Gwalior d.	0943	1009	|	|	|	1630	2032	2010	0157
403	Jhansi V Lakshmibai ● d.	1128	1213	|	1423	1423	1823	2213	2136	0413
556	Bina Junction d.	1340	1440	|	|	|	2120	|	|	0710
694	Bhopal Junction d.	1530	1640	□	1830	1830	2320	0245	0040	0925
786	Itarsi Junction d.	1720	1845	|	|	|	0110	0430	|	1125
969	Khandwa d.	2005	2140	|	|	|	0450	0700	|	1425
1093	Bhusaval Junction d.	2155	2335	|	0055	0055	0645	0850	|	1640
1277	Manmad Junction d.	0020	0205	|	0320	0320	0930	1120	|	1920
1513	Daund Chord Line d.	0450	|	|	|	|	1425	1540	|	|
1589	**Pune** Junction a.	0625	|	0210	1105	1105	1555	1655	|	|
1484	Kalyan Junction d.	...	0620	...	...	...	...	...	1015	2250
1521	**Mumbai** CSTM ◧ a.	...	0735	...	...	...	...	...	1115	0005

	Exp 12779	D 12263 ②⑤	R 22221	Exp 22685 ④⑦	Exp 12629 ③⑤	Exp 12781 ⑥	Exp 11077	Exp 12137	Exp 11057
Mumbai CSTM ◧ d.	...	...	1600	...	...	...	...	1935	2330
Kalyan Junction d.	...	...	1645	...	...	...	...	2035	0035
Pune Junction d.	0430	1110	|	0900	0900	1610	1720	|	|
Daund Chord Line d.	0610	|	|	|	|	1720	1827	|	|
Manmad Junction d.	1035	|	|	1525	1525	2155	2320	0015	0410
Bhusaval Junction d.	1300	|	|	1755	1755	0020	0155	0250	0655
Khandwa d.	1500	|	|	|	|	0225	0415	0500	0925
Itarsi Junction d.	1740	|	|	|	|	0440	0700	0800	1250
Bhopal Junction d.	1920	□	0200	0012	0012	0635	0855	0950	1535
Bina Junction d.	|	|	|	|	|	0850	1120	1205	1755
Jhansi V Lakshmibai ● d.	2320	|	0511	0433	0433	1058	1358	1423	2028
Gwalior d.	0052	|	0611	|	|	1212	1526	1542	2156
Agra Cantonment d.	0325	|	0732	|	|	1440	1740	1805	2355
Mathura Junction d.	0409	|	|	|	|	1530	1833	1845	0100
Delhi Hazrat Nizamuddin a.	0625	0645	0955	1129	1140	1750	2049	2055	0314

n – **New Delhi**.
□ – Via Table **5130**.
◧ – Full name is Mumbai Chhatrapati Shivaji Maharaj Terminus.
● – Full name is Jhansi Virangana Lakshmibai.

5170 LUCKNOW - PUNE and MUMBAI

km		Exp 20104	Exp 12174 ②④	Exp 12144 ②	Exp 15067 ③	Exp 12104 ③	Exp 12533	Exp 12108 ②④⑦	Exp 22537	Exp 15029 ④
0	**Lucknow** Charbagh ⊖ d.	0408**s**	0535	0650	1400	1620**j**	2130**j**	2235**s**	2333**s**	2250
72	Kanpur Central d.	0630	0755	0830	1600	1755	2310	0010	0130	0035
292	Jhansi V Lakshmibai ● d.	1018	1153	1238	1958	2125	0253	0343	0528	0423
445	Bina Junction d.	|	|	1535	|	0105	|	|	0745	0700
583	Bhopal Junction d.	1450	1615	1725	|	0305	0710	0820	1010	0855
674	Itarsi Junction d.	1630	|	|	0230	0440	0910	|	1205	1110
858	Khandwa d.	1910	|	2223	0532	0720	1200	|	1440	1400
981	Bhusaval Junction d.	2110	2235	0015	0730	0910	1355	1430	1700	1555
1166	Manmad Junction d.	|	|	0232	|	1155	1620	|	1940	1845
1405	Daund Chord Line d.	|	|	|	|	1635	|	|	|	|
1477	**Pune** Junction a.	|	|	|	|	1820	|	|	|	0245
1372	Kalyan Junction d.	|	0425	|	|	...	2125	2050	2310	...
1409	**Mumbai** L Tilak Terminus a.	0435	0530	0725	1730**b**	...	2245**h**	2150	0010	...

	Exp 22538	Exp 20103	Exp 15068 ⑤	Exp 12534	Exp 12103 ②	Exp 15030 ⑥	Exp 12143 ⑦	Exp 12107 ①③⑥	Exp 12173 ②⑦
Mumbai L Tilak Terminus d.	0035	0523	0020**b**	0825**h**	...	...	1550	1625	1625
Kalyan Junction d.	0120	|	|	0915	...	...	|	1710	1710
Pune Junction d.	|	|	|	|	1045	1045	|	|	|
Daund Chord Line d.	|	|	|	|	1152	|	|	|	|
Manmad Junction d.	0505	|	|	1245	1725	1725	2030	|	|
Bhusaval Junction d.	0800	1210	1200	1510	1950	1950	2255	2325	2325
Khandwa d.	1015	1420	1440	1715	2310	2310	0110	|	|
Itarsi Junction d.	1300	1640	1705	1935	0200	0200	|	|	|
Bhopal Junction d.	1500	1825	|	2120	0340	0340	0520	0540	0540
Bina Junction d.	1720	|	|	|	0535	0535	0720	|	|
Jhansi V Lakshmibai ● d.	1923	2218	0010	0103	0753	0753	0923	0943	0943
Kanpur Central d.	0015	0340	0420	0450	1135	1150	1305	1345	1345
Lucknow Charbagh ⊖ a.	0142**s**	0600**s**	0625	0710**j**	1315**j**	1330	1440	1520**s**	1530

b – Mumbai **Bandra**.
h – Mumbai **Chhatrapati Shivaji Maharaj Terminus**.
j – Lucknow **Junction** (officially Lucknow NER).
s – Lucknow **Aishbagh**.
⊖ – Officially known as Lucknow NR.
● – Full name is Jhansi Virangana Lakshmibai.

5180 PATNA and VARANASI - MUMBAI

km		Exp 11062	Exp 22104 ③	Exp 22914 ②	Exp 22972 ③	Exp 12361 ①	Exp 18609 ④	Exp 13201	Exp 22178	Exp 12168	Exp 12321	Exp 12142	D 12294 ②⑥	Exp 82355 ③⑦	Exp 11060 ①④⑥	Exp 11056 A	Exp 22184 ④⑦	Exp 12520 ⑤	Exp 15018	Exp 15646 ①④	Exp 12335 ②⑤⑦	Exp 15648 ③	Exp 12166 ②⑤⑥	Exp 11082 ⑤
0	**Patna** Junction d.	...	...	2320	2320	0050	...	2355	...	...	...	1105**p**	...	1305	...	...	...	1320**p**	...	1335	1355	1355	...	...
212	PDD Upadhyaya Junction ⊡ d.	...	...	0304	0304	0510	0615	0420	...	...	1010	1500	...	1610	...	...	...	1710	...	1745	1745	1745	...	...
	Varanasi Junction d.	0015	...	|	|	|	0730	|	1000	1035	|	|	...	|	...	...	...	|	1120	|	|	|	2020	2115
356	Prayagraj Chheoki Jct. ◧ d.	0320**j**	0525**j**	0517	0517	0757	1025**j**	0720	1305	1345	1320	1705	1810**j**	1807	1640**j**	1640**j**	1850**j**	1932	1610**j**	2005	2002	2005	2330**j**	0027
448	Manikpur d.	0515	0733	|	|	|	|	0930	1510	1605	1535	|	|	|	|	|	2048	|	1825	|	|	|	|	0230
525	Satna d.	0625	0835	0800	0800	1120	1330	1150	1630	1715	1645	2005	2110	2110	2020	2020	2150	2205	1940	2300	2300	2300	0220	0335
623	Katni d.	0740	0947	0920	0920	1240	1440	1315	1750	1835	1805	|	|	|	|	|	2310	2320	2100	0020	0020	0020	0335	0455
714	Jabalpur d.	0910	1110	1050	1050	1415	1610	1505	1910	2010	1930	2240	2350	2350	2300	2300	0035	0050	2225	0145	0145	0145	0500	0625
959	Itarsi Junction d.	1250	1430	1410	1410	1750	1955	1910	2310	0040	2350	0220	0345	0345	0245	0245	0410	0440	0300	0520	0520	0520	0855	|
1143	Khandwa d.	1515	|	|	|	2030	2223	2315	0145	0325	0230	|	|	|	|	|	0632	0720	0740	0800	0800	0800	|	1400
1266	Bhusaval Junction d.	1715	1925	1850	1850	2225	0015	0115	0340	0515	0430	0710	0800	0800	0740	0740	0825	0910	0935	1000	1000	1000	1325	1555
1450	Manmad Junction d.	2000	|	|	|	0050	0232	0420	0615	|	0710	0935	|	|	|	|	1045	1140	1220	1240	1240	1240	1600	|
1657	Kalyan Junction d.	2320	0245	|	|	0450	0630	0955	1025	1135	1140	1315	|	|	1410	1410	1445	1515	1620	1630	1630	1630	1950	2240
1695	**Mumbai** L Tilak Terminus a.	0025	0345	0445**b**	0445**b**	0600**h**	0725	1050	1140**h**	1230	1315**h**	1410	1440	1450**h**	1520	1520	1605	1615	1715	1750	1750	1750	2050	2345

km		Exp 22177	Exp 22183 ③⑥	Exp 12165 ①④⑤	Exp 15017	Exp 12519 ⑦	Exp 12336 ②④⑦	Exp 15645 ③⑥	Exp 15647 ⑤	Exp 11059 ②④⑥	Exp 11055 B	Exp 12362 ③	Exp 82356 ②⑤	Exp 11061	Exp 22103 ①	Exp 13202	Exp 11081 ③	Exp 18610 ⑤	Exp 22913 ⑦	D 12293 ①⑤	Exp 22971 ①	Exp 12322	Exp 12167	Exp 12141
0	**Mumbai** L Tilak Terminus d.	0010**h**	0600	0600	0635	0750	0805	0805	0805	1055	1055	1105**h**	1105**h**	1130	1340	1455	1640	1640	1645**b**	1725	1925**b**	2215**h**	2245	2335
38	Kalyan Junction d.	0115	0640	0640	0720	0835	0840	0840	0840	1140	1140	1200	|	1215	1425	1540	1720	1720	|	|	|	2315	2330	0020
245	Manmad Junction d.	0445	1005	1005	1115	1155	1225	1225	1225	|	|	1540	|	1615	|	1910	|	2200	|	|	|	0245	|	0355
429	Bhusaval Junction d.	0725	1235	1235	1405	1425	1455	1455	1455	1740	1740	1805	1805	1900	2025	2210	0030	0030	0150	2305	0430	0530	0550	0625
552	Khandwa d.	0955	1520	|	1635	1625	1700	1700	1700	|	|	2010	|	2105	|	0030	0240	0240	|	|	|	0735	0820	|
736	Itarsi Junction d.	1225	1810	1810	2050	1850	1930	1930	1930	2210	2210	2235	2235	2330	0140	0355	|	0510	0615	0315	0935	1000	1050	1105
981	Jabalpur d.	1600	2150	2150	0040	2230	2310	2300	2300	0110	0110	0150	0150	0250	0510	0745	0830	0830	0935	0610	1335	1345	1425	1440
1072	Katni d.	1710	2325	2325	0210	2355	0015	0015	0015	|	|	0310	|	0410	0630	0920	1010	1010	1100	|	1445	1455	1555	|
1170	Satna d.	1840	0040	0040	0345	0120	0140	0140	0140	0400	0400	0435	0435	0530	0755	1130	1220	1220	1250	0855	1605	1615	1800	1810
1247	Manikpur d.	2050	0205	|	0530	|	|	|	|	|	|	|	|	0732	0920	1320	1407	|	|	|	|	1757	1922	|
1339	Prayagraj Chheoki Jct. ◧ d.	2240	0350**j**	0420**j**	0815**j**	0420	0457	0500	0500	0810**j**	0810**j**	0750	0750	1000**j**	1115**j**	1500	1542	1635**j**	1610	1240**j**	1905	1935	2112	2120
1496	**Varanasi** Junction a.	0335	...	0710	1300	|	|	|	|	...	...	|	|	1225	...	|	2050	1945	|	...	|	|	0125	|
	PTDD Upadhyaya Jct. ⊡ d.	...	...	...	...	0715	0800	0800	0800	...	...	1037	1032	...	...	1920	...	2115	1948	...	2245	2255	...	0035
	Patna Junction a.	...	...	...	...	1000**p**	1230	1230	1230	...	...	1340	1340	...	...	2345	...	...	2230	...	0140	...	...	0350**p**

A – ②③⑤⑦.
B – ①③⑤⑦.
b – Mumbai **Bandra**.
h – Mumbai **Chhatrapati Shivaji Maharaj Terminus**.
j – Prayagraj **Junction**.
p – **Patliputra Junction**.
⊡ – Pandit Deen Dayal Upadhyaya (formerly Mughal Sarai).
◧ – Prayagraj (formerly Allahabad).

DELHI - SECUNDERABAD - TIRUPATI and BENGALURU 5190

km		Exp	Exp	R	D	Exp	Exp	R	D	Exp
		12708	**12648**	**12438**	**12286**	**12724**	**22706**	**22692**	**12214**	**12722**
		③⑤⑦	③	⑦	①⑤		⑤		①	
0	**Delhi** Hazrat Nizamuddin......d.	0520	0700	1535	1555	1600**n**	1703**g**	1950	2210**r**	2250
134	Mathura Junction ....d.	|	0823	|	|	1728	|	|	|	0035
188	Agra Cantonment.................d.	|	0910	|	|	1807	|	2147	|	0115
306	Gwalior..............................d.	0958	1120	|	|	2000	|	2310	|	0322
403	Jhansi V Lakshmibai ● ....d.	1138	1258	2015	2050	2153	2258	0030	0355	0510
694	Bhopal Junction ....d.	1605	1705	2340	0018**t**	0125	0250**t**	0355	0810**t**	0950
786	Itarsi Junction ....d.	|	1850	|	|	|	|	0525	|	1200
083	Nagpur ....d.	2225	2300	0510	0540	0715	0900	0930	|	1710
294	Balharshah ....d.	0155	0230	0805	0835	1050	1250	1220	1645	2100
528	Kazipet Junction ....d.	0510	0535	1105	|	1355	1550	1510	|	0020
660	**Secunderabad** Junction ....a.	|	|	1335	1410	1555	1805	1710	2055	0250
660	**Secunderabad** Junction ....d.	|	|	...	...	1600	1810	1725	2110	0255
	Hyderabad Deccan...........a.	|	|	...	...	1700	|	|	|	0350
772	Mahabubnagar.....................d.	1110	1030	...	...	...	|	|	|	...
902	Kurnool City........................d.	1330	1230	...	...	...	|	|	|	...
956	Dhone ....d.	1440	1425	...	...	...	|	|	|	...
072	Guntakal Junction...............d.	|	|	...	...	...	0045	2335	0250	...
292	Renigunta.........................d.	2000	|	...	...	...	|	|	|	...
302	**Tirupati** ....a.	2050	|	...	...	...	0640	|	|	...
151	Dharmavaram......................d.	...	1715	...	...	...	...	|	|	...
365	KSR **Bengaluru** ⊖ ....a.	...	2323**k**	...	...	...	...	0520	0810**v**	...

	Exp	R	D	Exp	Exp	R	D	Exp	Exp
	12721	**22691**	**12213**	**12723**	**22705**	**12437**	**12285**	**12647**	**12707**
			⑥		②	③	④⑦	⑦	①③⑤
KSR **Bengaluru** ⊖ ....d.	...	2000	2340**v**	...	...	...	...	2243**k**	...
Dharmavaram ....d.	...	|	|	...	...	...	...	0240	...
Tirupati.........................d.	...	|	|	...	2110	...	...	|	0530
Renigunta ....d.	...	|	|	...	|	...	...	|	0550
Guntakal Junction...........d.	...	0105	0335	...	0200	...	...	|	|
Dhone..............................d.	...	|	|	...	|	...	...	0540	1105
Kurnool City ....d.	...	|	|	...	|	...	...	0630	1205
Mahabubnagar....................d.	...	|	|	...	|	...	...	0830	1420
Hyderabad Deccan ....d.	2300	|	|	0600	|	...	...	|	|
Secunderabad Junction ....a.	2320	0705	0845	0620	0840	...	...	|	|
Secunderabad Junction ....d.	2325	0715	0850	0625	0850	1250	1250	|	|
Kazipet Junction.................d.	0115	0850	|	0805	1030	1430	|	1310	1900
Balharshah ....d.	0605	1225	1340	1210	1420	1750	1805	1720	2300
Nagpur...............................d.	0925	1500	|	1525	1720	2030	2045	2100	0200
Itarsi Junction ....d.	1525	1918	|	|	|	|	|	0200	|
Bhopal Junction ....d.	1715	2100	2210**t**	2155	2310**t**	0210	0212**t**	0340	0825
Jhansi V Lakshmibai ●......d.	2128	0021	0135	0124	0248	0525	0535	0720	1213
Gwalior ....d.	2246	0121	|	0247	|	|	|	0857	1322
Agra Cantonment................d.	0035	0257	|	0427	|	|	|	1105	|
Mathura Junction ....d.	0115	|	|	0504	|	|	|	1150	|
Delhi Hazrat Nizamuddin ...a.	0340	0530	0735**r**	0715	0830**g**	1030	1050	1415	1835

– Delhi **Safdarjang**.
– Bengaluru **Krishnarajapuram**.
– **New Delhi**.
r – Delhi **Sarai Rohilla**.
t – Bhopal **Rani Kamalapati**.
v – Bengaluru **Yesvantpur Junction**.
⊖ – Full name is Krantivira Sangolli Rayanna Bengaluru.
● – Full name is Jhansi Virangana Lakshmibai.

DELHI - AGRA 5200

km		Exp	Exp	Exp	S	Exp	Exp	Exp	Exp	Exp	Exp	Exp		R	Exp	Exp	R	Exp	Exp	Exp	R	Exp	Exp	Exp
		12138	**18238**	**12618**	**12002**	**12280**	**12050**	**11078**	**18478**	**12716**	**12191**	**12190**		**12434**	**12780**	**12724**	**22222**	**12616**	**22182**	**11842**	**22692**	**20806**	**12448**	**12626**
							⑥–④							③⑤										
0	**New Delhi** ....d.	0515	...	...	0600	0655	...	1130	...	1300	...	...	...	...	...	1600	...	1610	...	1820	...	2000	...	2010
7	**Delhi** Hazrat Nizamuddin......d.	|	0425	0540	|	0708	0810	|	1200	|	1405	1433	...	1535	1515	|	1655	|	1745	1833	1950	|	2000	|
141	Mathura Junction ....d.	0700	0725	0742	0720	0837	|	1325	1350	1433	1545	1625	...	|	1700	1728	|	1745	1917	2045	|	|	2120	2140
195	**Agra** Cantonment ....a.	0800	0815	0830	0750	0920	0950	1410	1445	1510	1645	1715	...	1733	1750	1805	1845	1830	1953	2135	2145	2203	2210	2220

	Exp	Exp		Exp	Exp		Exp	Exp
	12156	**12628**		**12920**	**12622**		**11058**	**12722**
ew Delhi ....d.	...	2020	...	2030	2105	...	2040	...
elhi Hazrat Nizamuddin.............d.	2040	|	...	|	|	...	2053	2250
lathura Junction ....d.	|	2155	...	2240	|	...	2305	0035
gra Cantonment.........................a.	2238	2248	...	2315	2328	...	2350	0110

	Exp	Exp		Exp	Exp		Exp	Exp
	12721	**12919**		**22181**	**12615**		**12447**	**20805**
Agra Cantonment ....d.	0035	0048	...	0127	0153	...	0210	0242
Mathura Junction ....d.	0115	0125	...	0204	0237	...	0245	|
Delhi Hazrat Nizamuddin ....a.	0340	0348	...	0410	0440	...	0522	|
New Delhi ....a.	...	0415	...	...	0505	...	...	0540

	R	Exp	Exp	Exp	Exp	Exp	Exp	R	R	Exp	Exp		Exp	Exp	Exp	Exp	Exp	Exp	Exp	Exp	Exp	S	Exp
	22691	**12621**	**12779**	**12723**	**12155**	**11841**	**12627**	**22221**	**12433**	**12189**	**12192**		**12715**	**18477**	**12617**	**12625**	**12049**	**18237**	**11077**	**12137**	**12279**	**12001**	**11057**
									①⑥								⑥–④						
gra Cantonment ....d.	0257	0307	0325	0427	0525	0355	0550	0732	0752	0712	0800	...	0943	0925	1000	1015	1745	1540	1740	1805	1820	2125	2355
lathura Junction ....d.	|	|	0409	0504	|	0525	0627	|	|	0800	0858	...	1020	1025	1037	1052	|	1625	1833	1845	1902	2201	0100
elhi Hazrat Nizamuddin...............a.	0530	0602	0625	0715	0750	0812	0831	0955	1030	1110	1155	...	1235	1300	1320	1250	1930	1945	2049	2055	2105	|	0314
ew Delhi ....a.	...	0630	...	0740	...	0845	0900	...	...	...	...	...	1305	...	...	1315	...	...	2115	2125	2135	2350	0340

DELHI - BILASPUR 5205

km		Exp	S	Exp	Exp	Exp	Exp	R	Exp	
		18238	**12002**	**20808**	**18478**	**12550**	**12410**	**12442**	**12824**	
				①④⑦		④	**A**	②⑥	②⑤⑦	
0	**Delhi** Hazrat Nizamuddin......d.	0425	0600	0828	1200	1355**j**	1505	1525**n**	1755	...
135	Mathura Junction ....d.	0725	0720	1000	1350	|	1635	|	|	...
189	Agra Cantonment.................d.	0820	0755	1050	1450	1710	1727	|	|	...
307	Gwalior..............................d.	1042	0928	1234	1652	1855	1930	1855	|	...
404	Jhansi V Lakshmibai ● ....d.	1248	1050	1423	1903	2015	2103	2015	2330	...
557	Bina Junction.......................d.	1555	|	|	|	|	2300	|	|	...
632	Saugor ....d.	|	|	1805	2250	2325	|	|	0250	...
819	Katni Murwara...................d.	|	|	2125	0220	0200	|	|	0600	...
985	Anupper Junction ....d.	|	|	0036	0615	0515	|	|	0908	...
695	Bhopal Junction ....d.	1800	1407	|	|	|	0055	2340	|	...
788	Itarsi Junction ....d.	2030	...	|	|	|	0240	|	|	...
085	Nagpur ....d.	0225	...	|	|	|	0835	0530	|	...
215	Gondia Junction....................d.	0505	...	|	|	|	1050	0707	|	...
349	Durg ....d.	0735	...	|	|	|	1255	0930	|	...
387	Raipur Junction.....................d.	0835	...	|	|	|	1335	1010	|	...
***	**Bilaspur** Junction ....a.	1055	...	0400	0900	0800	1530	1200	1155	...

	Exp	Exp	Exp	R	Exp	Exp	Exp	S	
	12409	**12823**	**12549**	**12441**	**18477**	**20807**	**18237**	**12001**	
	B	①④⑥	②	①④		②⑤⑥			
Bilaspur Junction ....d.	0550	1500	1500	1400	1440	1845	1415	...	...
Raipur Junction.....................d.	0740	|	|	1535	|	|	1615	...	...
Durg ....d.	0835	|	|	1630	|	|	1730	...	...
Gondia Junction....................d.	1032	|	|	1823	|	|	1945	...	...
Nagpur..................................d.	1255	|	|	2035	|	|	2220	...	...
Itarsi Junction ....d.	1750	|	|	|	|	|	0420	...	...
Bhopal Junction ....d.	1935	|	|	0215	|	|	0615	1530	...
Anupper Junction.............d.	|	1730	1730	|	1715	2125	|	|	...
Katni Murwara ....d.	|	2040	2040	|	2225	0055	|	|	...
Saugor ....d.	|	2315	2315	|	0055	0330	|	|	...
Bina Junction ....d.	2140	|	|	|	|	|	0920	|	...
Jhansi V Lakshmibai ●......d.	2338	0218	0218	0525	0550	0720	1148	1842	...
Gwalior ....d.	0040	|	0320	0625	0717	0857	1305	1945	...
Agra Cantonment................d.	0217	|	0452	|	0925	1105	1540	2125	...
Mathura Junction ....d.	0254	|	|	|	1025	1150	1625	2201	...
Delhi Hazrat Nizamuddin ...a.	0500	0740	0753**j**	1040**n**	1300	1404	1945	2350**n**	...

– ①②③④⑥.
– ①③④⑤⑥.
j – Delhi **Safdarjang**.
n – **New Delhi**.
● – Full name is Jhansi Virangana Lakshmibai.
*** – *1136 km* via Anupper, *1498 km* via Bhopal.

DELHI - INDORE 5208

km		Exp	Exp	Exp	Exp					
		19326	**14318**	**12920**	**19308**					
		④⑦	⑤⑥		⑤					
0	**Delhi** Hazrat Nizamuddin...... d.	1125	1350	2030**n**	2300	...	...	...	...	...
135	Mathura Junction .... d.	1310	1530	2240	0052	...	...	...	...	...
189	Agra Cantonment.................. d.	1400	1620	2320	0150	...	...	...	...	...
307	Gwalior............................... d.	1600	1850	0127	0410	...	...	...	...	...
404	Jhansi V Lakshmibai ●..... d.	|	|	0313	|	...	...	...	...	...
557	Bina Junction .... d.	|	|	0535	|	...	...	...	...	...
695	Bhopal Junction................. d.	|	|	0745	|	...	...	...	...	...
534	Guna .... d.	1940	2200	|	0800	...	...	...	...	...
788	Ujjain Junction .... d.	|	0410	1135	1255	...	...	...	...	...
959	**Indore** Junction .... a.	0055	0610	1340	1520	...	...	...	...	...

	Exp	Exp	Exp	Exp					
	19307	**12919**	**14317**	**19325**					
	④		⑥⑦	②⑤					
Indore Junction .... d.	0530	1215	1840	1945	...	...	...	...	...
Ujjain Junction .... d.	0740	1400	2055	|	...	...	...	...	...
Guna .... d.	1340	|	0150	0200	...	...	...	...	...
Bhopal Junction.............. d.	|	1730	|	|	...	...	...	...	...
Bina Junction.................. d.	|	1935	|	|	...	...	...	...	...
Jhansi V Lakshmibai ● .. d.	|	2138	|	|	...	...	...	...	...
Gwalior .... d.	1810	2256	0615	0615	...	...	...	...	...
Agra Cantonment.............. d.	1950	0048	0825	0825	...	...	...	...	...
Mathura Junction .... d.	2050	0125	0905	0905	...	...	...	...	...
Delhi Hazrat Nizamuddin ... a.	2305	0348	1125	1125	...	...	...	...	...

– **New Delhi**.
● – Full name is Jhansi Virangana Lakshmibai.

5210 DELHI - NAGPUR - TIRUPATI and CHENNAI

km		Exp 12642 ①⑥	Exp 12652 ②④	Exp 12646 ②	Exp 12644 ⑤	R 12434 ③⑤	Exp 12612 ①	D 12270 ②⑥	Exp 16318 ②	Exp 16032 ③⑥⑦	Exp 16788 ⑤	Exp 12616	Exp 12626	Exp 12622	Exp 22404 ⑦
0	**Delhi** Hazrat Nizamuddin d.	0520	0520	0510	0510	1535	1535	1555	1413	1413	1423	1610n	2010n	2105n	2315n
135	Mathura Junction d.	|	|	0645	0645	|	|	|	|	|	|	1745	2140	|	0043
189	Agra Cantonment d.	0740	|	0730	0730	1735	1735	|	1700	1700	1710	1835	2225	2330	0125
307	Gwalior d.	|	|	0943	0943	1855	1855	1920	1952	1952	2045	2107	0010	0115	|
404	Jhansi V Lakshmibai ● d.	1138	1138	1128	1128	2015	2015	2050	2203	2203	2228	2308	0138	0243	0438
695	Bhopal Junction d.	1605	1605	1530	1530	2340	2340	0018t	0220	0220	0305	0320	0525	0650	0840
788	Itarsi Junction d.	1800	|	1720	1720	|	|	|	0405	0405	0450	0530	0720	0840	1025
1085	Nagpur d.	2225	2225	2155	2155	0510	0510	0540	0905	0905	0955	1020	1150	1310	1500
1298	Balharshah d.	0150	0150	0125	0125	0805	0805	0835	1310	1310	1345	1430	1520	1630	1900
1543	Warangal d.	|	|	0435	0435	1115	|	|	1610	1610	1710	1750	1830	1945	2250
1752	Vijayawada Junction d.	0850	0850	0820	0820	1430	1430	1430	2045	2050	2050	2140	2230	2330	0200
2046	Gudur Junction d.	1300	|	1230	1230	|	1830	|	|	0400	|	0205	0245	|	0640
2122	Renigunta Junction d.	|	|	1345	1345	|	|	|	0250	|	0250	|	0420	|	|
2132	**Tirupati** a.	|	|	1410	1410	|	|	|	0315	|	0315	|	0440	|	|
2184	**Chennai** Central a.	1545e	1550e	...	...	2055	2055	2055	...	0650	...	0430	...	0615	0930e

	Exp 22403 ③	Exp 12615	Exp 12621	Exp 12611 ⑥	R 12433 ⑤⑦	D 12269 ①⑤	Exp 12625	Exp 12643 ③	Exp 12645 ⑦	Exp 12641 ④⑥	Exp 12651 ②⑦	Exp 16031 ③④⑦	Exp 16787 ②	Exp 16317 ⑥
Chennai Central d.	1310e	1850	2200	0600	0605	0635	...	...	...	0845e	0845e	0515	...	...
Tirupati d.	|	|	|	|	|	|	0450	0715	0715	|	|	|	0910	0910
Renigunta Junction d.	|	|	|	|	|	|	0520	0745	0745	|	|	|	0930	0930
Gudur Junction d.	1535	2045	|	0745	|	|	|	0915	0915	|	|	0715	|	1105
Vijayawada Junction d.	2000	0100	0355	1140	1140	1200	1105	1420	1420	1555	1555	1340	1515	1515
Warangal d.	2310	0410	0652	|	1414	|	1305	1715	1715	|	|	1720	1815	1815
Balharshah d.	0330	0815	1040	1750	1750	1805	1820	2115	2115	2300	2300	2225	2225	2225
Nagpur d.	0655	1135	1355	2030	2030	2045	2115	0025	0025	0200	0200	0145	0145	0145
Itarsi Junction d.	1210	1650	1835	|	|	|	0210	0505	0505	0640	|	0730	0710	0730
Bhopal Junction d.	1345	1845	2020	0215	0215	0212t	0355	0650	0650	0825	0825	0910	0910	0910
Jhansi V Lakshmibai d.	1805	2255	0031	0525	0525	0535	0730	1058	1058	1213	1213	1338	1338	1338
Gwalior d.	|	2357	0134	0625	0625	0635	0842	1212	1212	|	|	1452	1452	1452
Agra Cantonment d.	2105	0153	0307	0752	0752	|	1015	1440	1440	1525	|	1655	1655	1655
Mathura Junction d.	2145	0237	|	|	|	|	1052	1530	1530	|	|	1745	|	|
Delhi Hazrat Nizamuddin a.	0010n	0440	0602	1030	1030	1040	1250	1750	1750	1835	1835	2016	2016	2016

e – Chennai **Egmore**. n – **New Delhi**. t – Bhopal **Rani Kamalapati**. ● – Full name is Jhansi Virangana Lakshmibai.

5220 DELHI, AHMEDABAD and MUMBAI - GOA - MANGALURU - TRIVANDRUM

WARNING! A different timetable operates during the monsoon season (June - October).

km		R 12432 ②③⑦	Exp 22654 ①	Exp 22660 ①	Exp 12218 ③⑤	Exp 12484 ⑦	Exp 19578 ⑥⑦	Exp 20910 ⑤	Exp 16345	Exp 16311 ③	Exp 22475 ④	D 12284 ⑥	Exp 12619	Exp 20924 ①	Exp 22634 ⑤	Exp 22113 ②⑥	Exp 12201 ①⑤	D 12223 ②⑥	Exp 22629 ④	Exp 12133	Exp 16335 ⑤	Exp 19260 ②	Exp 16333 ④	Exp 16337 ①⑥
0	**Delhi** Hazrat Nizamuddin d.	0616	0500	1300	1323	1323	...	...	...	...	...	2140	...	...	2215	...	...	...	...	...	...	...	...	...
458	Kota Junction d.	1050	1110	1815	1815	1815	...	...	...	...	...	0230	...	...	0356	...	...	...	...	...	...	...	...	...
****	**Ahmedabad** Junction d.	|	|	|	|	|	0315	0315	...	0735	0750	|	...	0920	|	...	...	...	...	...	1530	1530	1530	1530
986	Vadodara Junction d.	1737	1818	0118	0118	0118	0508	0508	...	0932	0932	0933	...	1055	1058	...	...	...	...	...	1733	1728	1733	1733
***	**Mumbai** L Tilak Terminus d.	|	|	|	|	|	|	|	1140	|	|	|	1520	|	|	1655	1655	2050	2040d	2202t	|	|	|	|
1397	Panvel d.	2310	0031	0740	0740	0740	1130	1130	1250	1535	1535	1535	1625	1700	1700	1805	1805	|	2200	2325	0005	0005	0005	0005
1678	Ratnagiri d.	0310	0505	1230	1230	1230	1555	1555	1720	2020	2030	2030	2120	2155	2155	2245	2245	0150	0310	0330	0415	0415	0415	0415
1917	Madgaon d.	0710	1030	1720	1720	1720	2125	2125	2250	0040	0040	0040	0115	0210	0210	0310	0310	0550	0710	0730	0900	0900	0900	0900
2166	Udupi d.	1042	1402	2120	2120	2120	0112	0112	0232	0418	0418	|	0524	|	0602	0632	0632	|	1042	1128	1314	1314	1314	1314
2234	**Mangaluru** Junction d.	1210	1610	2350	2350	2350	0310	0310	0425	0645	0645	0645	0740c	0740	0740	0810	0810	1025	1210	1305	1515	1515	1515	1515
2365	Kannur d.	1400	1755	0155	0155	0155	0500	0500	0635	0840	0840	|	...	|	0925	1000	1000	|	1400	...	1710	1710	1710	1710
2455	Kozhikkode d.	1520	1915	0315	0315	0315	0620	0620	0810	0935	0955	0955	...	1040	1040	1120	1120	1325	1520	...	1835	1835	1835	1835
2541	Shoranur Junction d.	1700	2120	0500	0500	0500	0800	0800	1020	1140	1125	|	...	1230	1230	1305	1305	|	1640	...	2100	2100	2100	2100
2574	Thrisur d.	1750	2200	0623	0623	0623	0905	0905	1100	1220	...	|	...	1313	1313	1343	1343	|	...	...	2138	2138	2138	2138
2645	**Ernakulam** Junction d.	1920	2335o	0800	0800	0800	1030	1030	1235	1355o	...	1430	...	1450	1450	1500o	1500o	1810	...	...	2300o	2300o	2300o	2355
2762	Kayamkulam Junction d.	|	0147	|	|	1010	1212	1212	1505	1640	...	...	...	1640	1640	1730	1730	...	...	...	0115	|	|	...
2789	Kollam d.	2155	0240	1055	1055	1055	1300	1300	1605	1730	...	...	...	|	1730	1815	1815	...	...	...	0200	0200	0200	...
2866	**Trivandrum** Central a.	2335	0445	1230k	1230k	1230k	1430	1500k	1805	1910k	...	...	...	1925	1935	2025k	2025k	...	...	...	0325	0350k	0400	...
2937	**Nagercoil** Town a.	...	...	...	...	...	1548	...	...	...	...	...	...	2105	...	...	...	...	...	...	0615g	...	...	...

	Exp 22114 ①④	Exp 22653 ⑥	Exp 12134	Exp 12620	Exp 12202 ④	Exp 12217 ①⑥	Exp 12483 ③	Exp 22659 ⑤	Exp 16346	Exp 12476 ⑥	Exp 20923 ④	Exp 19577 ①②	Exp 20909 ⑦	Exp 22630 ③	D 12224 ③⑦	Exp 22633 ③	Exp 16338 ③⑤	Exp 16312 ⑥	Exp 19259 ④	Exp 16334 ①	Exp 16336 ②	R 12431 ②④⑤	D 12283 ②
Nagercoil Town d.	...	...	...	...	...	...	...	...	...	...	0927	0927	...	...	...	...	...	...	...	...	1445g	...	...
Trivandrum Central d.	0055k	0050	...	...	0910k	0910k	0910k	0910k	0915	...	1100	1100	1110k	...	...	1440	...	1545k	1545k	1545	1605	1915	...
Kollam d.	0155	0155	...	...	1008	1008	1008	1008	1025	...	|	1208	1208	...	...	1536	...	1645	1645	1645	1710	2013	...
Kayamkulam Junction d.	0232	0232	...	...	1044	1044	1044	|	1110	...	1247	1247	1247	...	...	1610	...	1721	1721	|	1745	|	...
Ernakulam Junction d.	0510o	0510o	...	...	1255o	1255	1255	1255	1350	...	1420	1420	1420	...	2130	1835	2025	2020o	2020o	2020o	2030o	2235	2325
Thrisur d.	0620	0620	...	...	1412	1412	1412	1412	1515	...	1540	1540	1540	...	|	2004	2148	2148	2148	2148	2148	2350	|
Shoranur Junction d.	0715	0715	...	...	1510	1510	1510	1510	1625	1705	1705	1705	1705	1705	|	2100	2250	2250	2250	2250	2250	0050	|
Kozhikkode d.	0835	0835	...	...	1630	1630	1630	1630	1805	1825	1825	1825	1825	1825	0045	2220	0020	0015	0015	0020	0020	0200	0240
Kannur d.	1000	1000	...	...	1755	1755	1755	1755	1935	1950	|	1950	1950	1950	|	2340	0150	0140	0140	0150	0150	0315	|
Mangaluru Junction d.	1210	1210	1400	1420c	2010	2010	2010	2010	2250	2200	2200	2200	2200	2200	0400	0200	0420	0420	0420	0420	0420	0525	0615
Udupi d.	1340	1340	1518	1550	2140	2140	2140	2140	0040	2338	|	2338	2338	2338	|	0342	0612	0558	0558	0612	0612	0642	|
Madgaon d.	1715	1715	1850	2010	0115	0115	0115	0115	0445	0400	0400	0400	0400	0400	0850	0925	1130	1040	1040	1040	1100	1010	1205
Ratnagiri d.	2120	2120	2240	2350	0455	0455	0455	0455	0925	0820	0820	0820	0820	0820	1230	1345	1555	1555	1555	1555	1555	1340	1640
Panvel d.	0220	0255	0310	0505	1010	1100	1100	1100	1455	1325	1325	1325	1325	1325	|	1805	2120	2120	2120	2120	2120	1805	2150
Mumbai L Tilak Terminus a.	0345	|	0435t	0635	1145	|	|	|	1645	|	|	|	|	1500d	1815	|	|	|	|	|	|	|	|
Vadodara Junction d.	...	0918	...	...	...	1711	1711	1711	...	1943	2001	2053	2053	...	...	2359	0435	0435	0430	0435	0435	2359	0440
Ahmedabad Junction a.	...	|	...	...	...	|	|	|	...	2125	2135	2235	2235	...	...	|	0640	0640	0640	0640	0640	|	|
Kota Junction d.	...	1630	...	...	...	2356	2356	2356	...	...	...	...	...	...	...	0655	...	...	...	...	...	0655	1150
Delhi Hazrat Nizamuddin a.	...	2240	...	...	...	0535	0535	0550	...	...	...	...	...	...	...	1230	...	...	...	...	...	1230	1720

c – Mangaluru **Central**.
d – Mumbai **Dadar**.
g – Nagercoil **Junction**.
k – Trivandrum **Kochuveli**.
o – Ernakulam **Town**.
t – Mumbai **Chhatrapati Shivaji Maharaj Terminus**.
*** – Mumbai CSMT - Panvel : *68 km*.
**** – Ahmedabad - Vadodara : *100 km*.

MUMBAI - PUNE 5230

km		Exp 22105	Exp 12127	Exp 18520	Exp 11007	Exp 11301	Exp 11029	Exp 22159	Exp 11019	Exp 22732	Exp 12125	Exp 12123
0	**Mumbai** CSMT ▶ d.	0540	0640	0655t	0700	0810	0840	1245	1400	1410	1625	1710
54	Kalyan Junction d.	0635	|	|	0755	0905	0935	1340	1458	1505	|	|
192	**Pune** Junction a.	0905	0957	1015	1105	1140	1235	1620	1755	1805	1950	2025

km		Exp 11009	Exp 12163	Exp 17411	Exp 16339 A	Exp 22107 B	Exp 11139	Exp 12701	Exp 11013	Exp 12115	Exp 22157	D 12219 ③⑥
0	**Mumbai** CSMT ▶ d.	1750	1845t	2020	2035	2100	2120	2150	2235t	2245	2255	2305t
54	Kalyan Junction d.	1850	1930	2120	2130	2155	2215	2240	2320	2345	2355	|
192	**Pune** Junction a.	2150	2205	0010	0015	0030	0105	0120	0150	0215	0250	0200

	Exp 18519	Exp 12702	Exp 11140	Exp 22158	Exp 12116	Exp 17412	Exp 22108 A	Exp 11010	Exp 12124	Exp 12126	D 12220 ③⑥
Pune Junction d.	0045	0105	0115	0200	0255	0335	0415	0605	0715	0750	0755
Kalyan Junction d.	|	0343	0400	0427	0520	0610	0645	0848	|	|	|
Mumbai CSMT ▶ a.	0415t	0455	0510	0550	0635	0725	0755	0955	1025	1125	1100t

	Exp 22160	Exp 22731	Exp 11014	Exp 12164	Exp 11008	Exp 16340 A	Exp 11030	Exp 11302	Exp 12128	Exp 22106	Exp 11020
Pune Junction d.	0820	0915	1020	1150	1515	1520	1550	1605	1755	1835	2345
Kalyan Junction d.	1100	1150	1250	1420	1750	1800	1850	1855	|	2052	0235
Mumbai CSMT ▶ a.	1230	1305	1345	1540t	1905	1915	2005	2015	2105	2200	0400

A – ②③④⑥.
B – ①②④⑦.

t – Mumbai **Lokmanya Tilak Terminus**.
▶ – Full name is Mumbai Chhatrapati Shivaji Maharaj Terminus.

MUMBAI - PUNE - KOLHAPUR and HUBBALLI 5240

km		Exp 11040	Exp 12148 ⑤	Exp 11049 ①	Exp 11029	Exp 17318	Exp 17411	Exp 11035 ④	Exp 11021 ②③⑥	Exp 11005 ①⑤⑦
0	**Mumbai** Dadar d.	...	...	...	0840c	2015	2035	2130	2130	2130
54	Kalyan Junction d.	...	...	0445	0935	|	2120	2210	2210	2210
192	**Pune** Junction d.	0420	0640	0750	1240	2355	0015	0100	0100	0100
338	Satara d.	0730	0930	1035	1600	|	0305	0355	0355	0355
472	Miraj Junction d.	1045	1210	1310	1845	0550	0540	0650	0645	0645
518	**Kolhapur** CSMT ⊙ a.	1225	1330	1440	2005	|	0715	|	|	|
610	Belagavi d.	...	...	...	...	0805	...	0905	0905	0905
661	Londa Junction d.	...	...	...	...	0912	...	1012	1012	1012
731	Dharwad d.	...	...	...	...	1036	...	1138	1138	1138
751	**Hubballi** Junction a.	...	...	...	...	1135	...	1235	1235	1235

	Exp 11030	Exp 12147 ②	Exp 11050 ⑥	Exp 11039	Exp 11006 ①③④	Exp 11022 ②⑤⑥	Exp 11036 ⑦	Exp 17317	Exp 17412
Hubballi Junction d.	...	...	...	...	1415	1415	1415	1530	...
Dharwad d.	...	...	...	...	1445	1445	1445	1552	...
Londa Junction d.	...	...	...	...	1610	1610	1610	1712	...
Belagavi d.	...	...	...	...	1720	1720	1720	1815	...
Kolhapur CSMT ⊙ d.	0815	0910	1315	1445	|	|	|	|	2050
Miraj Junction d.	0920	1020	1410	1550	2050	2050	2050	2120	2155
Satara d.	1205	1240	1630	1840	2310	2310	2310	|	0015
Pune Junction d.	1550	1555	2010	2215	0210	0210	0210	0310	0335
Kalyan Junction d.	1850	...	2232	...	0440	0440	0440	|	0610
Mumbai Dadar a.	1937	...	...	...	0535	0535	0530	0700	0725c

c – Mumbai **Chhatrapati Shivaji Maharaj Terminus**.

⊙ – Full name is Kolhapur Shri Chhatrapati Shahu Maharaj Terminus.

HUBBALLI - BENGALURU - MYSORE 5245

km		Exp 17310	Exp 12726	Exp 17325	Exp 17392	Exp 12650 A	Exp 17302	Exp 22686 ③⑦	Exp 12630 ④⑥	Exp 16590	Exp 20654	Exp 16536
0	**Hubballi** Junction d.	0500	0600	0855	1825	2045	2150	2210	2210	2230	2340	2350
129	Harihar d.	0710	0800	1105	2115	|	2352	|	|	0032	|	0200
258	Birur Junction d.	0850	1000	1311	2332	|	0138	|	|	0210	|	0350
303	Arsikere Junction d.	0930	1050	1405	0020	0120	0240	0240	0240	0305	0345	0433
393	Tumakuru d.	1037	1204	1550	0136	0325	|	0402	0402	0430	0512	0602
457	**Bengaluru** Yesvantpur Jct a.	|	1254	1710	0239	0430	|	0545	0545	0550	0705	0658
469	KSR **Bengaluru** ⊖ a.	1235	1405	1740	0350	...	|	...	...	0615	0730	0750
614	**Mysuru** Junction a.	...	...	2040	...	...	0700	...	...	...	...	1045

	Exp 17326	Exp 12725	Exp 12649 B	Exp 12629 ②④	Exp 22685 ③⑥	Exp 17309	Exp 16535	Exp 20653	Exp 16589	Exp 17301	Exp 17391
Mysuru Junction d.	0550	...	...	...	...	...	1545	...	...	2230	...
KSR **Bengaluru** ⊖ d.	0845	1245	...	...	...	...	1850	2100	2300	|	2355
Bengaluru Yesvantpur Jct d.	0859	1256	1350	1430	1430	1500	1908	2112	2312	|	0007
Tumakuru d.	0951	1350	1445	1525	1522	1550	1955	2202	0001	|	0100
Arsikere Junction d.	1125	1503	1556	1639	1639	1710	2125	2320	0121	0135	0240
Birur Junction d.	1210	1546	|	|	|	1750	2205	|	0202	0216	0325
Harihar d.	1405	1742	|	|	|	1926	2347	|	0337	0402	0550
Hubballi Junction a.	1720	2020	2115	2140	2140	2215	0255	0355	0550	0705	0935

A – ①②③⑤⑦.
B – ①③⑤⑥⑦.
⊖ – Full name is Krantivira Sangolli Rayanna Bengaluru.

HUBBALLI - MADGAON - VASCO DA GAMA 5248

km		Exp 17322 ③	Exp 18047 C	Exp 17316 ③	Exp 17309	Exp 17021 ④
0	**Hubballi** Junction d.	0800	0900	2020	2225	2250
20	Dharwad d.	0826	0928	2046	2250	2326
90	Londa Junction d.	0942	1052	2208	0010	0052
174	Kulem d.	1230	1320	0025	0235	0215
208	**Madgaon** d.	1330	1425	0135	0330	0420
236	**Vasco Da Gama** a.	1440	1545	0240	0500	0525

	Exp 17321 ⑤	Exp 18048 D	Exp 17315 ①	Exp 17022 ⑤	Exp 17310
Vasco Da Gama d.	0515	0630	0900	0900	2225
Madgaon d.	0600	0700	0935	0935	2335
Kulem d.	0655	0805	1020	1020	0030
Londa Junction d.	0836	0957	1212	1212	0226
Dharwad d.	1002	1115	1340	1340	0400
Hubballi Junction a.	1045	1155	1420	1420	0450

C – ①③④⑥.
D – ②④⑤⑦.

MUMBAI - SECUNDERABAD, BENGALURU and CHENNAI 5250

km		Exp 18520	Exp 11301	Exp 22159	Exp 11017 ⑥	Exp 22179 ①	Exp 17222 ④⑦	Exp 11019	Exp 22732	Exp 12163	Exp 12701	Exp 11013	Exp 22157	D 12219 ③⑥
0	**Mumbai** CSMT ⊕ d.	0655t	0810	1245	1315t	1320t	1320t	1400	1410	1845t	2150	2235t	2255	2305t
54	Kalyan Junction d.	|	0905	1340	1405	1400	|	1458	1505	1930	2240	2320	2355	|
192	Pune Junction d.	1020	1145	1625	1640	1640	1640	1800	1810	2210	0125	0155	0255	0205
263	Daund Junction d.	|	1300	1735	|	|	|	1912	1927	|	|	|	0410	|
456	Solapur Junction d.	1355	1540	2000	2040	2040	2040	2155	2215	0200	0530	0605	0655	0550
568	Kalaburagi d.	1540	1735	2125	2213	2213	2213	2318	2353	0325	0710	0758	0850	|
605	Wadi d.	1645	1835	2235	2315	2315	2315	0025	0045	0420	0830	0910	0945	|
717	Vikarabad Junction d.	1845	|	|	|	|	|	|	0217	|	1017	|	|	|
800	**Secunderbad** Junction a.	2030	|	|	|	|	0205	0320	|	|	|	|	|	1105
790	**Hyderabad** Deccan a.	...	|	|	|	|	...	...	0430	|	1205	|	|	...
713	Raichur d.	...	2015	0005	0045	0045	...	...	...	0610	...	1105	1140	...
783	Adoni d.	...	2120	0100	|	|	...	...	...	0705	...	1210	1250	...
834	Guntakal Junction d.	...	2235	0210	0250	0250	...	...	...	0815	...	1310	1355	...
942	Dharmavaram Junction d.	...	0045	|	|	|	...	...	...	|	...	1530	|	...
1147	KSR **Bengaluru** ⊖ a.	...	0600	|	|	|	...	...	...	|	...	2105	|	...
1017	Cuddapah d.	...	...	0505	0545	0540	...	...	...	1100	...	...	1655	...
1142	Renigunta Junction d.	...	...	0745	0810	0810	...	...	...	1335	...	...	1920	...
1214	Arakkonam Junction d.	...	...	0905	0925	0925	...	...	...	1455	...	...	2030	...
1283	**Chennai** Central a.	...	...	1045	1100e	1100	...	...	...	1630	...	...	2215e	...

FOR RETURN SERVICE AND FOOTNOTES SEE NEXT PAGE →

5250 CHENNAI, BENGALURU and SECUNDERABAD - MUMBAI

		Exp	Exp	Exp	Exp	Exp	D	Exp	Exp	Exp	Exp	Exp	Exp	Exp
		11020	18519	12702	22158	17221	12220	22160	22731	11014	22180	12164	11302	11018
						③⑥	②⑤				②			①
Chennai Central	d.	...	...	...	0620e	...	...	1325	...	...	1550	1820	...	2210e
Arakkonam Junction	d.	...	...	...	|	...	...	1430	...	...	1650	1920	...	2345
Renigunta Junction	d.	...	...	...	0920	...	...	1610	...	...	1835	2050	...	0120
Cuddapah	d.	...	...	...	1100	...	...	1755	...	...	2025	2245	...	0310
KSR **Bengaluru** ⊖	d.	...	...	...	|	...	...	|	...	1600	|	|	2040	|
Dharmavaram Junction	d.	...	...	...	|	...	...	|	...	2025	|	|	0040	|
Guntakal Junction	d.	...	...	...	1415	...	...	2100	...	2255	2330	0145	0250	0630
Adoni	d.	...	...	...	1500	...	...	2150	...	2340	0010	0235	0330	|
Raichur	d.	...	...	...	1610	...	...	2315	...	0050	0120	0330	0445	0820
Hyderabad Deccan	d.	...	...	1450	|	...	...	|	2235	|	|	|	|	|
Secunderabad Junction	d.	1100	1255	|	|	2025	2305	|	|	|	|	|	|	|
Vikarabad Junction	d.	|	1415	1602	|	|	|	|	2340	|	|	|	|	|
Wadi	d.	1505	1640	1805	1855	0010	|	0115	0220	0255	0325	0535	0710	1015
Kalaburagi	d.	1555	1720	1843	1933	0055	|	0158	0248	0340	0400	0620	0800	1055
Solapur Junction	d.	1805	1955	2040	2155	0305	0355	0405	0445	0545	0640	0745	1100	1225
Daund Junction	d.	2150	|	|	0045	|	|	0650	0735	0855	|	|	1430	|
Pune Junction	d.	2345	0045	0105	0200	0755	0755	0820	0915	1020	1105	1150	1605	1640
Kalyan Junction	d.	0235	|	0343	0427	|	|	1100	1150	1250	1325	1420	1855	1930
Mumbai CSMT ⊕	a.	0400	0415t	0455	0550	1100t	1100t	1230	1305	1345t	1425t	1540t	2015	2030t

e – Chennai **Egmore**.
t – Mumbai **Lokmanya Tilak Terminus**.
⊖ – Full name is Krantivira Sangolli Rayanna.
⊕ – Full name is Chhatrapati Shivaji Maharaj Terminus.

FOR RETURN SERVICE SEE PREVIOUS PAGE.

5260 HYDERABAD - SECUNDERABAD - TIRUPATI and CHENNAI

km			Exp	Exp	Exp	Exp	Exp	Exp
			17406	17230	12604	12734	12764	12760
							A	
	Hyderabad Decan	d.	...	...	1645	...	...	1800
0	**Secunderabad** Junction	d.	0600	1220	1710	1810	1840	1825
281	Guntur Junction	d.	|	1710	2210	2255	|	|
132	Kazipet Junction	d.	0812	|	|	|	2030	2000
351	Vijayawada Junction	d.	1300	|	|	|	0020	2355
382*	Tenali Junction	d.	1325	1750	2250	2330	0050	0025
643	Gudur Junction	d.	1900	2200	0310	0345	0435	0420
726	Renigunta Junction	d.	2050	2325	|	0510	0600	|
736	**Tirupati** Junction	a.	2140	2350	|	0555	0655	|
793	**Chennai** Central	a.	...	...	0540	...	...	0700e

		Exp	Exp	Exp	Exp	Exp	Exp
		17229	17405	12603	12763	12733	12759
					B		
Chennai Central	d.	...	...	1645	...	...	1745e
Tirupati Junction	d.	0010	0545	|	1655	1820	|
Renigunta Junction	d.	0035	0608	|	1717	1842	|
Gudur Junction	d.	0200	0730	1903	1850	2000	2025
Tenali Junction	d.	0555	1200	2300	2225	2352	2357
Vijayawada Junction	d.	|	1310	|	2320	|	0055
Kazipet Junction	d.	|	1657	|	0245	|	0415
Guntur Junction	d.	0635	|	2335	|	0030	|
Secunderabad Junction	a.	1220	2040	0435	0545	0535	0635
Hyderabad Decan	a.	...	...	0545	...	...	0750

A – ①②④⑤⑦.
B – ①②③⑤⑥.
e – Chennai **Egmore**.
* – *311 km* via Guntur.

5270 MUMBAI and PUNE - KOLKATA

km			Exp	Exp	Exp	D	D	Exp	Exp	Exp	Exp
			12859	20821	12869	12261	12221	12101	12151	12129	12809
				①	⑦	C	①⑥	D	③④		
0	**Mumbai** CSMT ⊕	d.	0600	...	1105	1715	...	2035t	2035t	...	2110
*	**Pune** Junction	d.	|	1040	|	|	1515	|	|	1835	|
	Daund Chord Line	d.	|	|	|	|	1615	|	|	1955	|
53	Kalyan Junction	d.	0655	1355	1200	|	|	2115	2115	|	2210
260	Manmad Junction	d.	|	|	|	|	2020	|	|	0035	0137
420	Jalgaon Junction	d.	1200	|	|	|	|	|	|	0245	0342
441	Bhusaval Junction	d.	1245	1940	1805	2305	2245	0305	0310	0325	0420
584	Akola Junction	d.	1450	|	2005	|	|	0505	0515	0530	0640
663	Badnera Junction	d.	1615	|	2205	|	|	0635	0705	0655	0820
837	Nagpur	d.	1900	0125	0140	0415	0415	0940	1020	0955	1125
967	Gondia Junction	d.	2051	0311	0326	|	|	1129	1206	1152	1335
1101	Durg	d.	2255	0508	0535	|	|	1340	1420	1405	1545
1139	Raipur Junction	d.	2335	0548	0615	0824	0824	1420	1500	1445	1630
1250	Bilaspur Junction	d.	0135	0745	0810	1005	1005	1625	1655	1640	1835
1454	Jharsuguda Junction	d.	0430	1040	1105	|	|	1917	2005	1952	2155
1554	Raurkela	d.	0548	1200	1225	|	|	2038	2130	2115	2315
1718	Tatanagar Junction	d.	0815	1425	1520	1620	1620	2305	|	2345	0142
1853	Kharagpur Junction	d.	1020	1640	1725	|	|	0120	0430	0150	0350
1969	**Kolkata** Howrah	a.	1230	1835s	1930	2015	2015	0320h	0625h	0355	0600

		D	D	Exp	Exp	Exp	Exp	Exp	Exp	Exp
		12262	12222	12860	12870	20822	12810	12102	12152	12130
		E	④⑥		⑤	⑥		F	⑤⑥	
Kolkata Howrah	d.	0545	0545	1405	1435	1800s	1950	2100h	1955h	2210
Kharagpur Junction	d.	|	|	1543	1615	1925	2130	2245	2140	2350
Tatanagar Junction	d.	0858	0858	1747	1803	2135	2317	0038	|	0152
Raurkela	d.	|	|	2005	2033	2358	0145	0258	0438	0410
Jharsuguda Junction	d.	|	|	2155	2210	0150	0330	0435	0620	0552
Bilaspur Junction	d.	1505	1505	0115	0130	0505	0710	0755	0935	0915
Raipur Junction	d.	1637	1637	0250	0305	0640	0850	0935	1110	1055
Durg	d.	|	|	0350	0405	0735	0945	1030	1215	1145
Gondia Junction	d.	|	|	0542	0600	0920	1142	1223	1406	1349
Nagpur	d.	2055	2055	0745	0810	1125	1400	1420	1625	1555
Badnera Junction	d.	|	|	1035	1120	|	1730	1715	1920	1845
Akola Junction	d.	|	|	1135	1225	|	1835	1820	2020	1945
Bhusaval Junction	d.	0145	0145	1350	1430	1650	2050	2040	2235	2205
Jalgaon Junction	d.	|	|	1420	|	|	2120	|	|	2240
Manmad Junction	d.	|	0405	|	|	|	2325	|	|	0045
Kalyan Junction	d.	|	|	2005	2145	2240	0315	0250	0425	|
Daund Chord Line	d.	|	0820	|	|	|	|	|	|	0555
Pune Junction	a.	|	0940	|	|	0245	|	|	|	0720
Mumbai CSMT ⊕	a.	0815	...	2120	2300	...	0425	0355t	0530	...

C – ②③④⑦.
D – ①②⑤⑥.
E – ①②③⑤.
F – ①③④⑦.
h – Kolkata **Shalimar**.
s – Kolkata **Santragachi Junction**.
t – Mumbai **Lokmanya Tilak Terminus**.
⊕ – Full name is Chhatrapati Shivaji Maharaj Terminus.
* – *314 km* from Manmad.

5280 KOLKATA - PURI, SECUNDERABAD, TIRUPATI and CHENNAI

km			Exp	Exp	Exp	Exp	Exp	Exp	S
			12703	12821	18045	22825	22849	20889	12277
						②	③	⑥	
0	**Kolkata** Howrah	d.	0835	0915h	1125h	1220h	1220h	1240	1415
116	Kharagpur Junction	d.	1018	1055	1335	1405	1405	1423	1603
232	Balasore	d.	1140	1249	1535	1540	1545	|	1730
409	Cuttack	d.	1415	1543	1855	1810	1810	1825	1952
437	Bhubaneswar	d.	1505	1625	1945	1850	1850	1910	2027
456	Khurda Road Junction	d.	1555	1650	2025	1925	1925	|	|
500	**Puri**	a.	|	1800	|	|	|	|	2150
819	Vizianagram Junction	d.	2115	...	0228	0025	0025	0040	...
879	Visakhapatanam	d.	2235	...	0355	0150	0150	0200	...
1081	Rajahmundry	d.	0130	...	0730	0430	0430	0430	...
1259	Vijayawada Junction	d.	0410	...	1040	0725	|	0740	...
1574	**Secunderabad** Junction	a.	1010	...	1635	|	1410	|	...
1637	Renigunta Junction	d.	...	...	...	|	...	1310	...
1647	**Tirupati**	a.	...	...	...	|	...	1355	...
1691	**Chennai** Central	a.	...	...	...	1410	...	...	...

		Exp	Exp	Exp	Exp	Exp	Exp	Exp
		22855	22851	12841	12773	12665	12663	22807
		⑦	④		③	①	④⑦	②⑤
Kolkata Howrah	d.	1455s	1455s	1520h	1610h	1615e	1740	1800s
Kharagpur Junction	d.	1625	1625	1705	1755	1755	1925	1925
Balasore	d.	1800	1803	1837	1923	1923	2055	2055
Cuttack	d.	2042	2042	2113	2146	2150	2335	2335
Bhubaneswar	d.	2125	2125	2155	2226	2230	0015	0015
Khurda Road Junction	d.	2155	2155	2225	2300	2305	0045	0045
Puri	a.	|	|	|	|	|	|	|
Vizianagram Junction	d.	0250	0250	|	0420	|	0555	0555
Visakhapatanam	d.	0410	0410	0445	0545	0545	0720	0720
Rajahmundry	d.	0650	0650	0720	0825	0825	1025	1025
Vijayawada Junction	d.	0935	0935	1005	|	1130	1305	1315
Secunderabad Junction	a.	|	|	|	1750	|	|	|
Renigunta Junction	d.	1530	1530	|	...	|	|	|
Tirupati	a.	1625	1605	|	...	|	|	|
Chennai Central	a.	...	...	1650	...	2045e	2045e	2030

		Exp	D	Exp	Exp	Exp	Exp	Exp
		18409	22201	12837	12863	12867	12660	12839
			①③⑤			⑦	③	
Kolkata Howrah	d.	1905h	2000d	2240	2255	2325	2350h	2355
Kharagpur Junction	d.	2055	2215	0018	0042	0105	0152	0140
Balasore	d.	2300	|	0147	0212	0235	0325	0303
Cuttack	d.	0140	|	0430	0445	|	0555	0545
Bhubaneswar	d.	0220	0250	0515	0525	0550	0635	0625
Khurda Road Junction	d.	0245	|	0540	0555	0630	0715	0710
Puri	a.	0430	0355	0710	|	|	|	|
Vizianagram Junction	d.	...	...	...	1110	1145	1255	1240
Visakhapatanam	d.	...	...	...	1240	1315	1420	1410
Rajahmundry	d.	...	...	...	1520	|	1710	1715
Vijayawada Junction	d.	...	...	...	1820	1835	1940	2000
Secunderabad Junction	a.	...	...	...	|	|	|	|
Renigunta Junction	d.	...	...	...	0020	0035	0140	|
Tirupati	a.	...	...	...	0045	0103	0155	|
Chennai Central	a.	...	...	...	...	...	...	0315

FOR RETURN SERVICE AND FOOTNOTES SEE NEXT PAGE →

CHENNAI, TIRUPATI AND SECUNDERABAD - PURI - KOLKATA 5280

	D	Exp	Exp	Exp	Exp	Exp	Exp	Exp	S	Exp	Exp	Exp	Exp	Exp	Exp	Exp	Exp	Exp	Exp	Exp	Exp
	22202	**12838**	**12774**	**22850**	**18410**	**22808**	**12842**	**12659**	**12278**	**18046**	**22852**	**12704**	**20890**	**12822**	**12864**	**12840**	**22856**	**12868**	**12664**	**12666**	**22826**
	②④⑥		②	⑤		④⑦		①			⑦		⑦				①	③	②⑤	⑥	③
Chennai Central d.	...	...	...	...	...	0810	0700	...	...	...	...	...	...	...	...	1915	...	...	1910e	1910e	1950
Tirupati d.	...	...	...	...	...	|	|	0910	...	...	1415	...	1610	...	1610	|	2000	1940	|	|	|
Renigunta Junction d.	...	...	...	...	...	|	|	0930	...	...	1440	...	1630	...	1635	|	2020	2000	|	|	|
Secunderabad Junction d.	...	...	0355	0355	...	|	|	|	...	0830	|	1555	|	...	|	|	|	|	|	|	|
Vijayawada Junction d.	...	...	|	|	...	1415	1330	1515	...	1425	2020	2130	2200	...	2230	0130	0200	0200	0205	0205	0205
Rajahmundry d.	...	...	1120	1120	...	1620	1550	1730	...	1635	2225	2345	0020	...	0040	0345	0400	|	0415	0415	0415
Visakhapatanam d.	...	...	1530	1530	...	2050	2010	2145	...	2130	0310	0340	0435	...	0455	0810	0845	0845	0910	0910	0910
Vizianagram Junction d.	...	...	1625	1625	...	2145	|	2220	...	2250	0405	0440	0530	...	0555	0905	0940	0940	1005	|	1005
Puri d.	1925	2015	|	|	2240	|	|	|	0545	|	|	|	|	1025	|	|	|	|	|	|	|
Khurda Road Junction d.	|	2100	2140	2130	2320	0310	0150	0350	|	0430	0935	0950	|	1115	1155	1440	1520	1520	1540	1540	1540
Bhubaneswar d.	2030	2135	2210	2210	2340	0340	0220	0415	0649	0510	1035	1020	1115	1150	1225	1505	1550	1555	1605	1605	1605
Cuttack d.	|	2205	2245	2245	0020	0415	0255	0505	0717	0550	1103	1055	1145	1225	1300	1550	1640	|	1650	1650	1650
Balasore d.	|	0110	0153	0153	0332	0650	0635	0732	0955	0912	1332	1353	|	1508	1550	1912	1930	1930	1958	1958	1958
Kharagpur Junction d.	0110	0245	0340	0340	0545	0835	0830	0915	1142	1145	1515	1535	1615	1710	1737	2050	2108	2113	2145	2145	2145
Kolkata Howrah a.	0400**d**	0445	0605**h**	0605**h**	0800**h**	1025**s**	1040**h**	1155**h**	1345	1440**h**	1715**s**	1740	1830	1930**h**	1955	2300	2310**s**	2325	2355	2355	2355**h**

d – Kolkata **Sealdah**. **e** – Chennai **Egmore**. **h** – Kolkata **Shalimar**. **s** – Kolkata **Santragachi Junction**.

CHENNAI - BENGALURU - MYSURU 5290

km		Exp	S	Exp	Exp	Exp	Exp	Exp	S	Exp	Exp
		20607	**12007**	**22625**	**12639**	**12296**	**12609**	**12607**	**12027**	**16021**	**12657**
		④–②	④–②						③–①		
0	**Chennai** Central d.	0550	0600	0725	0740	0945**p**	1335	1530	1730	2115	2250
68	Arakkonam Junction d.	|	|	0825	0840	1040	1440	1635	|	2220	2350
130	Katpadi Junction d.	0725	0740	0912	0940	1150	1545	1735	1910	2330	0040
214	Jolarpettai d.	|	|	1025	1055	1320	1715	1855	|	0050	0155
361	KSR **Bengaluru** ⊖ a.	1015	1045	1315	1340	1554	1945	2135	2225	0345	0440
506	**Mysuru** Junction a.	1220	1300	...	...	...	2250	...	...	0640	...

	S	Exp	Exp	Exp	Exp	Exp	Exp	S	Exp	Exp
	12028	**12608**	**12610**	**12295**	**20608**	**22626**	**12640**	**12008**	**12658**	**16022**
	③–①				④–②			④–②		
Mysuru Junction d.	...	...	0500	...	1305	...	...	1415	...	2100
KSR **Bengaluru** ⊖ d.	0600	0620	0800	0915**t**	1455	1430	1510	1620	2240	2350
Jolarpettai d.	|	0840	1030	1125	|	1710	1730	|	0050	0240
Katpadi Junction d.	0900	0950	1150	1255	1740	1825	1845	1925	0200	0355
Arakkonam Junction d.	|	1045	1300	1345	|	1915	1945	|	0250	0505
Chennai Central a.	1100	1215	1425	1435**p**	1930	2035	2110	2130	0420	0645

p – Chennai **Perambur**. **t** – Sir M Visvesvaraya Terminal (SMVT) **Bengaluru**. ⊖ – Full name is Krantivira Sangolli Rayanna Bengaluru.

CHENNAI and BENGALURU - TRIVANDRUM 5300

km		Exp	Exp	Exp	Exp	Exp	Exp	Exp	Exp	Exp	Exp	Exp	Exp	Exp	Exp	Exp	Exp	Exp	Exp	Exp	Exp
		12660	**22642**	**16318**	**12508**	**12626**	**22677**	**12777**	**12697**	**12644**	**12695**	**16315**	**16320**	**12623**	**16526**	**12257**	**12671**	**12511**	**22645**	**22647**	**17230**
		⑤	②④	④	⑦		④	③	⑦	⑥			⑤⑦			②④⑦		①⑤⑥	②	④⑦	
0	**Chennai** Central d.	...	0305**p**	...	0310**p**	...	...	...	1510	...	1520	...	...	1945	...	...	2105	2315	2315	2315	...
	Tirupati d.	0200	|	0320	|	0445	...	...	|	1415	|	...	...	|	...	...	|	|	|	|	2355
130	Katpadi Junction d.	0420	0450	0520	0535	0650	...	...	1700	1640	1715	...	...	2130	...	...	2255	0110	0110	0110	0155
214	Jolarpettai d.	0540	0620	0635	0655	0815	...	...	1820	|	1830	...	...	|	...	...	|	0225	0225	0225	0310
	KSR **Bengaluru** ⊖ d.	|	|	|	|	|	1520**v**	1545**b**	|	|	|	1650	1900**t**	|	2010	2045**v**	|	|	|	|	|
	Bangarapet d.	|	|	|	|	|	|	1648	|	|	|	1807	2009	|	2125	|	|	|	|	|	|
335	Salem Junction d.	0710	0740	0810	0830	0945	1950	1950	1950	1925	2010	2120	2240	0015	0025	0112	0150	0355	0355	0355	0455
394	Erode Junction d.	0820	0845	0920	0940	1055	2050	2050	2050	2030	2110	2230	2340	0115	0130	0215	0300	0500	0500	0500	0615
494	Coimbatore Junction d.	1020	1030	1120	1135	1230	2240	|	|	2215	2315	0015	0105	0240	0300	0400	0520	0650	0650	0650	0805
530	**Mettupalaiyam** a.	|	|	|	|	|	|	|	|	|	|	|	|	|	|	|	0615	|	|	|	|
548	Palakkad Junction d.	1140	1140	1230	1250	1355	2345	2320	2320	2345	0030	0135	0215	0355	0420	0510	...	0800	0800	0800	0920
626	Thrisur d.	1313	1323	1343	1420	1530	0058	0028	0028	0058	0138	0243	0323	0503	0523	0630	...	0920	0920	0920	1135
697	Ernakulam Town d.	1445	|	1500	1600	1700	0210	0150	|	|	0255	|	0440	0640	0715	0820	...	1044	1044	1050	1300
	Ernakulam Junction d.	|	1510	|	|	|	|	|	0210	0235	|	0405	|	|	|	|	...	1100	|	|	|
814	Kayankulam Junction d.	1715	1710	|	1815	1920	|	|	|	0425	0515	0602	|	0910	0940	1110	...	1308	1308	1308	1520
842	Kollam Junction d.	1805	1805	1835	1905	2005	0510	0450	0450	0510	0600	0715	0815	0955	1030	1200	...	1350	1350	1350	1650
919	**Trivandrum** Central a.	1925	1955	2025	2045	2150	0645**k**	0635**k**	0640	0700	0745	0915**k**	0935**k**	1130	1200	1320**k**	...	1550**k**	1550**k**	1550**k**	1820
991	**Nagercoil** Junction a.	2140	...	2215	...	...	...	...	...	...	...	...	...	...	1350	...	...	...	...	...	...

km		Exp	Exp	Exp	Exp	Exp	Exp	Exp	Exp	Exp	Exp	Exp	Exp	Exp	Exp	Exp	Exp	Exp	Exp	Exp	Exp
		22648	**12512**	**22646**	**17229**	**12625**	**12778**	**22678**	**12672**	**16525**	**12643**	**12624**	**16317**	**12659**	**16316**	**12507**	**22641**	**12258**	**12696**	**16319**	**12698**
		①④	②③⑦	⑥			④	⑤			②		⑤	⑦		②	④⑥	①③⑤		④⑥	⑥
	Nagercoil Junction d.	...	...	...	...	...	...	...	...	1030	...	...	1445	1445	...	...	...	...	...	...	...
0	**Trivandrum** Central d.	0615**k**	0635**k**	0635**k**	0645	1230	1250**k**	1250**k**	...	1240	1415	1500	1605	1605	1645**k**	1655	1655	1700**k**	1715	1805**k**	1915
77	Kollam Junction d.	0708	0735	0735	0750	1333	1343	1343	...	1400	1513	1603	1710	1710	1740	1753	1753	1753	1818	1910	2013
105	Kayankulam Junction d.	0745	0820	0820	0835	1410	|	|	...	1510	1546	1638	1745	1745	1818	1835	1835	1835	1856	|	|
	Ernakulam Junction d.	|	1045	1045	|	|	|	|	...	|	1815	|	|	|	2035	|	2115	|	|	|	2235
222	Ernakulam Town d.	1045	|	|	1120	1630	1700	1700	...	1755	|	1920	2045	2045	|	2115	|	2115	2145	2215	|
293	Thrisur d.	1218	1218	1218	1240	1750	1813	1813	...	1940	2015	2043	2220	2220	2210	2240	2240	2240	2300	2340	2350
371	Palakkad Junction d.	1350	1350	1350	1510	1915	1935	1935	...	2120	2140	2220	2350	2350	2325	0010	0010	0010	0040	0100	0120
	Mettupalaiyam d.	|	|	|	|	|	|	|	2120	|	|	|	|	|	|	|	|	|	|	|	|
425	Coimbatore Junction d.	1525	1525	1525	1635	2055	|	2110	2225	2300	2320	2340	0120	0120	0055	0135	0135	0135	0205	0230	|
525	Erode Junction d.	1705	1705	1705	1815	2235	2225	2245	2355	0030	0055	0120	0305	0255	0235	0315	0315	0315	0345	0420	0405
584	Salem Junction d.	1805	1805	1805	1915	2335	2325	2345	0055	0130	0150	0215	0405	0355	0335	0415	0415	0415	0440	0510	0500
	Bangarapet d.	|	|	|	|	|	0235	|	|	0410	|	|	|	|	0634	|	|	|	|	0802	|
853	KSR **Bengaluru** ⊖ a.	|	|	|	|	|	0343**b**	0430**v**	|	0640	|	|	|	|	0830	|	|	0930**v**	|	0945**t**	|
705	Jolarpettai d.	1945	1945	1945	2100	0135	...	...	|	...	|	|	0600	0600	...	0600	0600	...	0630	...	0700
789	Katpadi Junction d.	2055	2055	2055	2215	0300	...	...	0350	...	0520	0505	0730	0730	...	0725	0725	...	0740	...	0805
912	**Tirupati** a.	|	|	|	0005	0445	...	...	|	...	0710	|	0905	0905	...	|	|	...	|	...	|
919	**Chennai** Central a.	2310	2310	2310	...	...	...	...	0620	...	...	0745	...	...	...	0910**p**	0910**p**	...	1000	...	1025

b – Bengaluru **Banaswadi**.
k – Trivandrum **Kochuveli**.
p – Chennai **Perambur**.
t – Sir M Visvesvaraya Terminal (SMVT) **Bengaluru**.
v – Bengaluru **Yesvantpur Junction**.
⊖ – Full name is Krantivira Sangolli Rayanna Bengaluru.

5310 CHENNAI - PUDUCHERRY, SENGOTTAI, TUTICORIN, TIRUCHENDER and NAGERCOIL

km		Exp 12898 ③	Exp 16127	Exp 22404 ②	Exp 16105	Exp 12642 ②⑦	Exp 16101	Exp 12633	Exp 16115	Exp 12667 ④	Exp 22657 ①③⑦	Exp 12693	Exp 16823	Exp 16181 ③⑤⑥	Exp 12661	Exp 12665 ②
0	**Chennai** Egmore d.	0830	0900	0945	1605	1615	1700	1720	1810	1855	1930t	1930	2010	2025	2040	2110
56	Chengalpattu d.	0920	0955	|	1705	1715	1800	1820	1915	2000	2000	2030	2110	2125	2140	2210
159	Villupuram Junction d.	1055	1125	1220	1850	1855	1925	2000	2120	2135	2135	2215	2250	2300	2315	2352
197	**Puducherry** a.	1200	|	1315	|	|	|	|	2215	|	|	|	|	|	|	|
214	Vriddhachalam Junction d.	...	1207	...	|	1937	2007	2042	...	2217	2217	2257	2332	2342	2357	0035
340	Tiruchchirappalli Junction d.	...	1405	...	0010	2130	2155	2230	...	0030	0030	0055	0135	0200	0155	0230
433	Dindigul Junction d.	...	1520	...	0115	2235	2305	2340	...	0135	0135	0210	0255	|	0305	0345
495*	Madurai Junction d.	...	1630	...	0215	2350	0015	0100	...	0235	0235	0310	0355	|	0425	0450
538	Virudunagar Junction d.	...	1710	...	0255	0025	0130	0145	...	0315	0315	0355	0435	0535	0515	0530
662	Tenkasi Junction d.	...	|	...	|	|	0335	|	...	|	|	|	|	0805	0730	|
670	**Sengottai** a.	...	|	...	|	|	0345	|	...	|	|	|	|	0845	0815	|
	Kollam Junction a.	...	|	...	|	|	0720	|	...	|	|	|	|	...	...	|
623	Vanchi Maniyachchi d.	...	1840	...	|	|	...	|	...	|	|	0520	|	...	...	|
656	**Tuticorin** a.	...	|	...	|	|	...	|	...	|	|	0630	|	...	...	|
652	Tirunelveli Junction d.	...	1940	...	0600	0225	...	0350	...	0525	0525	...	0650	...	...	0750
714	**Tiruchendur** a.	...	|	...	0800	|	...	|	...	|	|	...	|	...	...	|
726	**Nagercoil** Junction a.	...	2120	...	...	0330	...	0500	...	0710	0710	...	0837n	...	...	0925

	Exp 16102	Exp 20682 ④⑥⑦	Exp 12668 ⑤	Exp 22658 ①②④	Exp 12662	Exp 12634	Exp 12694	Exp 16824	Exp 12641 ③⑤	Exp 16116	Exp 16106	Exp 22403 ③	Exp 12666 ⑥	Exp 16128	Exp 12897 ③
Nagercoil Junction d.	...	...	1615	1615	...	1807	...	1813n	1935	...	...	...	0615	0800	...
Tiruchendur d.	...	...	|	|	...	|	...	|	|	...	1910	...	|	|	...
Tirunelveli Junction d.	...	...	1750	1750	...	1920	...	2005	2130	...	2115	...	0800	0945	...
Tuticorin d.	...	...	|	|	...	|	2020	|	|	...	|	...	|	|	...
Vanchi Maniyachchi d.	...	...	|	|	...	|	2045	|	|	...	|	...	|	1010	...
Kollam Junction d.	1200	...	|	|	...	|	|	|	|	...	|	...	|	|	...
Sengottai d.	1505	1650	|	|	1820	|	|	|	|	...	|	...	|	|	...
Tenkasi Junction d.	1517	1705	|	|	1835	|	|	|	|	...	|	...	|	|	...
Virudunagar Junction d.	1745	1910	1930	1930	2040	2110	2205	2220	2315	...	2255	...	0940	1122	...
Madurai Junction d.	1855	|	2105	2105	2150	2205	2305	2320	0055	...	0015	...	1100	1235	...
Dindigul Junction d.	2000	|	2205	2205	2250	2320	0015	0035	0155	...	0130	...	1205	1335	...
Tiruchchirappalli Junction d.	2120	2340	2320	2320	0015	0035	0135	0155	0310	...	0245	...	1330	1500	...
Vriddhachalam Junction d.	2250	0112	0050	0050	0145	0205	0310	0325	0440	...	|	...	1505	1640	...
Puducherry d.	|	|	|	|	|	|	|	|	|	0535	|	0950	|	|	1845
Villupuram Junction d.	0010	0205	0155	0155	0255	0305	0415	0435	0545	0625	0730	1032	1615	1740	1930
Chengalpattu d.	0200	0325	0315	0315	0420	0435	0555	0615	0710	0810	0910	|	1740	1915	2045
Chennai Egmore a.	0305	0455	0435	0410t	0540	0610	0730	0740	0825	0925	1025	1250	1850	2035	2150

n – Nagercoil **Town**. t – Chennai **Tambaram**. * – *596 km* via Salem.

5320 OTHER HILL and MOUNTAIN RAILWAYS

DARJEELING HIMALAYAN RAILWAY

km		52541	52539 ①③⑥
0	**New Jalpaiguri** Junction d.	1000	1000
8	Siliguri Junction d.	|	1030
18	Sukna d.	|	1110
26	Rangtong d.	|	1155
38	Tindharia d.	|	1332
50	Mahanadi d.	|	1441
57	Kurseong d.	|	1530
65	Tung d.	|	1611
73	Sonada d.	|	1702
82	Ghum d.	|	1750
88	**Darjeeling** a.	1730	1830

	52540	52538 ②④⑦
Darjeeling d.	0900	0910
Ghum d.	0930	0945
Sonada d.	|	1032
Tung d.	|	1121
Kurseong d.	1150	1205
Mahanadi d.	1220	1236
Tindharia d.	1335	1350
Rangtong d.	1441	1446
Sukna d.	|	1530
Siliguri Junction d.	1551	1605
New Jalpaiguri Junction a.	1630	1635

KANGRA VALLEY RAILWAY

km		52471	52465	52475	52473	52467	52469
0	**Pathankot** Junction ◧ d.	0205	0600	0845	1010	1250	1520
83	Jwalamukhi Road d.	0540	0949	1130	1439	1712	1936
109	Nagrota d.	0656	1059	1230	1552	1930	2115
141	Baijnath Paprola a.	0845	1240	1400	1745	2105	2240
141	Baijnath Paprola d.	0930	...	...	1820	...	...
164	**Joginder Nagar** a.	1055	...	...	1955	...	...

	52464	52466	52472	52474	52476	52470
Joginder Nagar d.	...	...	0710	1200	...	...
Baijnath Paprola a.	...	...	0835	1325	...	...
Baijnath Paprola d.	0400	0710	0915	1410	1625	1755
Nagrota d.	0522	0851	1105	1557	1732	1926
Jwalamukhi Road d.	0651	1030	1233	1707	1831	2036
Pathankot Junction ◧ a.	1105	1430	1705	2100	2140	2355

MATHERAN HILL RAILWAY

km		52103
0	**Neral** Junction ⊡ d.	0910
21	**Matheran** ⊡ a.	1120

	52102
Matheran ⊡ d.	0720
Neral Junction ⊡ a.	0855

NILGIRI MOUNTAIN RAILWAY

km		06141	06136	06143	06138
0	**Mettupalaiyam** ● d.	...	0710	...	...
28	Coonor d.	0745	1040	1235	1600
56	**Udagamandalam** (Ooty) a.	0900	1155	1345	1710

	06139	06142	06137	06140
Udagamandalam (Ooty) d.	0915	1215	1400	1730
Coonor d.	1020	1315	1515	1835
Mettupalaiyam ● a.	...	...	1730	...

◧ – For connections to / from Delhi see Table **5000**.
● – For connecting trains to Chennai see Table **5300**.
⊡ – Services are normally suspended during Monsoon season. Connections Mumbai - Kalyan - Neral and v.v. are available by local train.

5325 DELHI and KOLKATA - JAYNAGAR - KURTHA

Indian Railways, Nepal Railway Company

km		Exp 12562
0	**New Delhi** d.	2115
440	Kanpur Central d.	0240
634	Prayagraj Junction d.	0535
758	Varanasi Junction d.	0815
964	Chhapra d.	1255
1166	Darbhanga Junction d.	1755
1234	**Jaynagar** a.	1925

	Exp 12561
Jaynagar d.	1720
Darbhanga Junction d.	1908
Chhapra d.	0045
Varanasi Junction d.	0450
Prayagraj Junction d.	0720
Kanpur Central d.	0940
New Delhi a.	1540

km		Exp 13185
0	**Kolkata** Sealdah d.	1745
220	Asansol Junction d.	2214
467	Barauni Junction d.	0350
556	Darbhanga Junction d.	0618
624	**Jaynagar** a.	0845

	Exp 13186
Jaynagar d.	1610
Darbhanga Junction d.	1740
Barauni Junction d.	2045
Asansol Junction d.	0148
Kolkata Sealdah a.	0700

km		2◇	2◇
0	**Jaynagar** ▦ d.	0830	1500
28	Janakpurdham d.	0955	1630
33	**Kurtha** a.	1030	1700

	2◇	2◇
Kurtha d.	1100	1730
Janakpurdham d.	1120	1750
Jaynagar ▦ a.	1245	1915

◇ – Subject to confirmation.

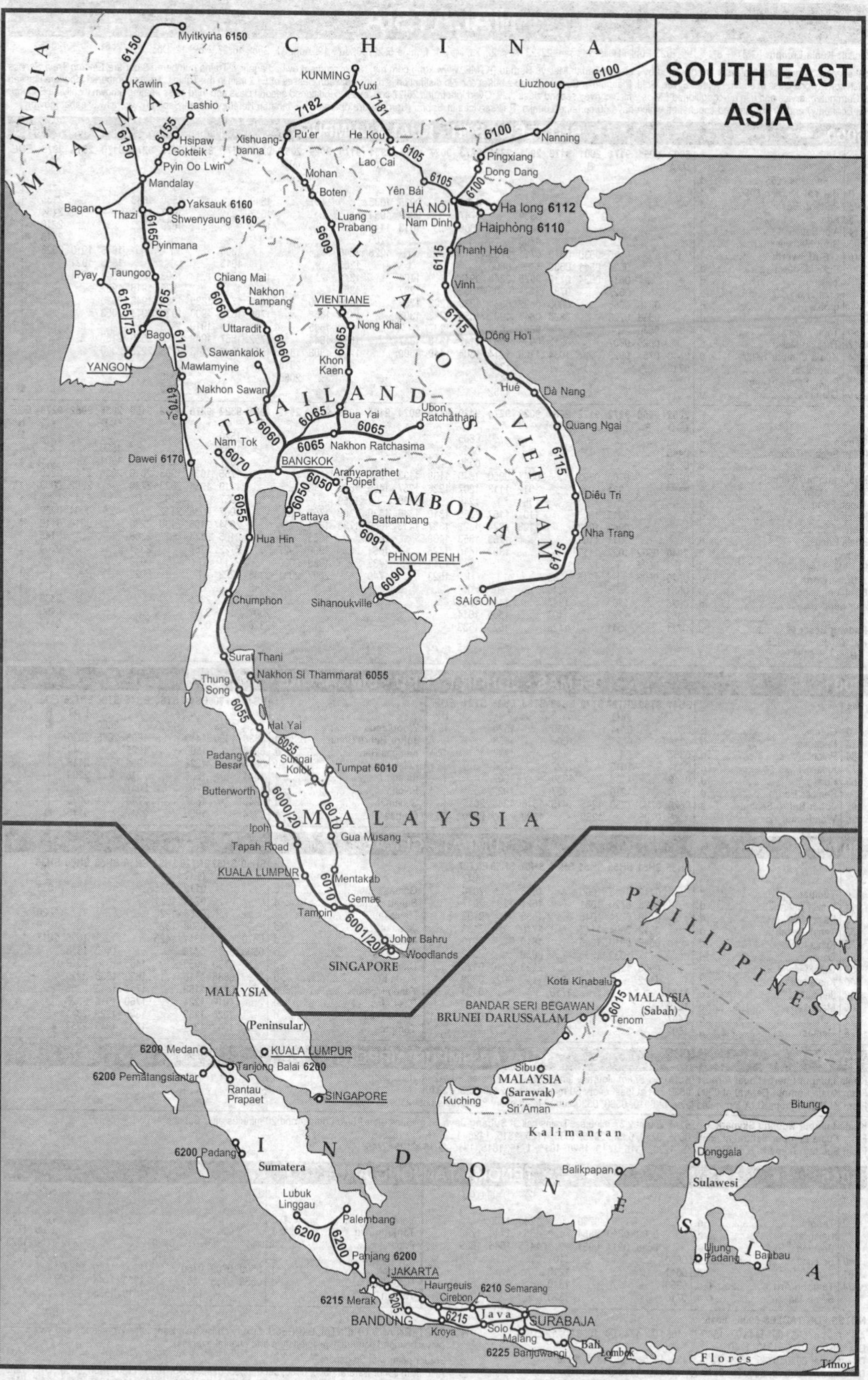
SOUTH EAST ASIA
CHINA
INDIA
MYANMAR
LAOS
THAILAND
VIETNAM
CAMBODIA
MALAYSIA
PHILIPPINES
INDONESIA
Myitkyina 6150
Kawlin
Lashio
Hsipaw
Gokteik
Pyin Oo Lwin
Mandalay
Bagan
Thazi
Yaksauk 6160
Shwenyaung 6160
Pyinmana
Pyay
Taungoo
Bago
YANGON
Mawlamyine
Ye
Dawei 6170
KUNMING
Yuxi
Pu'er
Xishuang-banna
Mohan
Boten
He Kou
Lao Cai
Yên Bái
HÀ NỘI
Nam Dinh
Liuzhou
Nanning
Pingxiang
Dong Dang
Ha long 6112
Haiphòng 6110
Thanh Hóa
Vinh
Đông Hoi
Huê
Dà Nang
Quang Ngai
Diêu Tri
Nha Trang
SAIGÒN
Luang Prabang
VIENTIANE
Nong Khai
Khon Kaen
Bua Yai
Ubon Ratchathani
Nakhon Ratchasima
Chiang Mai
Nakhon Lampang
Uttaradit
Sawankalok
Nakhon Sawan
Nam Tok
BANGKOK
Aranyaprathet
Poipet
Pattaya
Battambang
PHNOM PENH
Sihanoukville
Hua Hin
Chumphon
Surat Thani
Nakhon Si Thammarat 6055
Thung Song
Hat Yai
Padang Besar
Sungai Kolok
Tumpat 6010
Butterworth
Ipoh
Tapah Road
Gua Musang
KUALA LUMPUR
Mentakab
Gemas
Tampin
Johor Bahru
Woodlands
SINGAPORE
MALAYSIA
(Peninsular)
6200 Medan
Tanjong Balai 6200
6200 Pematangsiantar
Rantau Prapaet
6200 Padang
Sumatera
Lubuk Linggau
Palembang
Panjang 6200
JAKARTA
6215 Merak
Haurgeuis
Cirebon
6210 Semarang
BANDUNG
Kroya
Java
Solo
SURABAJA
Malang
6225 Banjuwangi
Bali
Lombok
Flores
Timor
Kota Kinabalu
MALAYSIA (Sabah)
Tenom
BANDAR SERI BEGAWAN
BRUNEI DARUSSALAM
Sibu
MALAYSIA (Sarawak)
Kuching
Sri Aman
Kalimantan
Balikpapan
Bitung
Donggala
Sulawesi
Ujung Padang
Baubau
6150
6155
6165
6165/75
6170
7182
7181
6105
6100
6115
6095
6065
6060
6070
6055
6050
6091
6090
6000/20
6010
6001/20
6015
6205
6215
6200

MALAYSIA

Capital: **Kuala Lumpur** (GMT +8). 2023 Public Holidays: Jan. 22, 23, Apr. 22, 23, May 1, 4, June 5, 29, 30, July 19, Aug. 31, Sept. 16, 27, Nov. 12, Dec. 25.

Rail services in mainland Malaysia are operated by Keretapi Tanah Melayu Berhad (KTMB, www.ktmb.com.my), a government owned agency. Trains numbered **9xxx** are *Electric Train Service* which convey one class of seating (either Silver, Gold, Platinum or Business) and a buffet car. No distinction is made between classes of *ETS* train in the Tables. Trains numbered **29xx** are classed as Commuter service and use air-conditioned EMUs which convey second class only. Overnight trains **26/27** convey air-conditioned second class and third class seating (known locally as Superior and Economy) and air-conditioned couchettes which have 40 curtained bunks. Rail services in Sabah (Borneo) are operated by Jabatan Keretapi Negeri Sabah (www.railway.sabah.gov.my).

6000 BUTTERWORTH - KUALA LUMPUR

For footnotes see below Table 6015 — KTMB

km		5003 Ⓐ A	9051	9171	2901 B	9173	2941 C	9321	9273	9027	9275	2951 C	9175	9029	2057 Ⓐ A	9277	9177	9035	9425	9279	9179	2913 B	2975 C	EOE H
	Bangkok **6055** d.	...	...	...	...	...	...	...	...	...	...	...	...	...	...	...	...	...	...	...	...	...	...	◧
0	**Hat Yai** Junction **6055** d.	...	...	...	...	...	...	...	...	...	...	...	...	...	...	...	...	...	...	...	...	...	...	|
45	**Padang Besar** ▦ d.	...	...	...	...	...	0520	...	0730	...	0935	1035	...	...	...	1340	...	...	1550	1645	...	...	2135	|
76	Arau d.	...	...	...	...	...	0539	...	0747	...	0952	1054	...	...	...	1357	...	...	1607	1702	...	...	2154	|
114	Alor Setar d.	...	...	...	...	...	0603	...	0808	...	1013	1118	...	...	...	1418	...	...	1629	1723	...	...	2218	|
205	Bukit Mertajam d.	...	...	...	...	...	0700	...	|	...	|	1203	...	...	...	|	...	...	|	|	...	...	2315	|
216	**Butterworth** d.	...	...	0515	0530	0620	0711	0750	|	...	|	1226	1245	...	...	|	1605	...	|	|	1845	1910	2326	|
227	Bukit Mertajam d.	...	...	0525	0541	0630	▬	0800	|	...	|	...	1255	...	...	|	1615	...	|	|	1855	1921	...	|
312	Taiping d.	...	...	0611	0634	0716	**9025**	0848	0946	...	1151	...	1341	...	...	1556	1701	...	1808	1859	1941	2014	...	|
344	Kuala Kangsar d.	...	...	0627	...	0732		0905	1002	...	1207	...	1357	...	...	1612	1717	...	1825	1915	1957	...	...	|
398	**Ipoh** d.	...	0510	0655	...	0800	0822	0934	1030	1202	1235	...	1425	1530	...	1640	1745	1835	1855	1943	2025	...	...	|
434	Kampar d.	...	0536	0723	...	0828	0847	1002	1058	1227	1303	...	1453	1555	...	1708	1813	1900	1923	2011	2053	...	...	|
450	Tapah Road d.	...	0546	|	...	|	0857	1012	|	1237	|	...	|	1605	...	|	|	1910	1933	|	|	...	...	|
517	Tanjong Malim d.	...	0625	0807	...	0912	0936	1051	1142	1316	1347	...	1537	1644	...	1752	1857	1949	2012	2055	2137	...	...	|
604	**Kuala Lumpur** Sentral d.	0540	0751	0929	...	1034	1100	1214	1304	1440	1509	...	1700	1808	1840	1914	2020	2113	2135	2223	2300	...	...	|
677	Seremban d.	0716	...	...	...	...	...	1344	...	...	...	...	...	...	2016	...	...	...	2305	...	...	...	...	|
726	Pulau Sebang/Tampin d.	0756	...	...	...	...	...	1418	...	...	...	...	...	...	2056	...	...	...	2338	...	...	...	...	|
779	**Gemas** d.	...	...	...	...	...	...	1452	...	...	...	...	...	...	...	...	...	...	0010	...	...	...	...	◧

	2002 Ⓐ D	2900 F	9272	9172	2954 E	9022	9274	9420	9174	9024	9176	9028	9178	2912 F	2974 E	9322	9276	9032	9180	2058 Ⓐ D	9052	9278	EOE H
Gemas d.	...	...	...	...	...	...	...	0805	...	...	...	...	...	...	...	1520	...	...	...	...	...	...	◧
Pulau Sebang/Tampin d.	0445	...	...	...	...	...	...	0836	...	...	...	...	...	...	...	1553	...	...	...	1820	...	...	|
Seremban d.	0526	...	...	...	...	...	...	0909	...	...	...	...	...	...	...	1627	...	...	...	1901	...	...	|
Kuala Lumpur Sentral d.	0703	...	0708	0803	...	0847	0950	1040	1108	1132	1337	1500	1555	...	...	1755	1831	1903	2010	2036	2140	2250	|
Tanjong Malim d.	▬	...	0831	0921	...	1012	1113	1207	1226	1257	1455	1620	1713	...	...	1919	1954	2023	2128	...	2302	0008	|
Tapah Road d.	...	...	|	|	...	1051	|	1245	|	1336	|	1659	|	...	...	1957	|	2102	|	...	2341	|	|
Kampar d.	...	...	0915	1005	...	1101	1157	1255	1310	1346	1539	1709	1757	...	...	2007	2038	2112	2212	...	0004	0052	|
Ipoh d.	...	...	0942	1032	...	1128	1224	1322	1337	1413	1606	1736	1824	...	...	2034	2105	2139	2239	...	0018	0119	|
Kuala Kangsar d.	...	...	1011	1101	...	...	1253	1353	1409	...	1635	...	1853	...	...	2105	2134	...	2308	...	...	0148	|
Taiping d.	**2940**	0532	1027	1117	...	...	1309	1410	1425	...	1651	...	1909	1927	...	2122	2150	...	2324	...	...	0204	|
Bukit Mertajam d.	**E**	0625	|	1203	...	...	|	|	1511	...	1737	...	1955	2020	...	2211	|	...	0010	...	...	|	|
Butterworth d.	0520	0636	|	1215	1235	...	|	|	1523	...	1749	...	2007	2031	2135	2222	|	...	0022	...	...	|	|
Bukit Mertajam d.	0531	...	|	...	1246	...	|	|	...	...	...	...	...	...	2146	...	|	...	...	...	...	|	|
Alor Setar d.	0628	...	1202	...	1343	...	1444	1551	...	...	...	...	...	...	2243	...	2325	...	...	...	...	0339	|
Arau d.	0652	...	1223	...	1407	...	1505	1614	...	...	...	...	...	...	2307	...	2346	...	...	...	...	0400	|
Padang Besar ▦ d.	0711	...	1241	...	1426	...	1523	1633	...	...	...	...	...	...	2326	...	0004	...	...	...	...	0418	|
Hat Yai Junction **6055** a.	...	...	...	...	...	...	...	...	...	...	...	...	...	...	...	...	...	...	...	...	...	...	|
Bangkok **6055** a.	...	...	...	...	...	...	...	...	...	...	...	...	...	...	...	...	...	...	...	...	...	...	◧

6001 GEMAS - JOHOR BAHRU - SINGAPORE

For footnotes see below Table 6015 — KTMB

km		ES41	ST69	ERT27 Ⓡ G	ST79	ES43	ST83	ES45	ST91	EOE H
0	**Gemas** d.	0200	...	0744	...	0930	...	1520	...	◧
26	Segamat d.	0236	...	0821	...	1006	...	1556	...	|
85	Paloh d.	0357	...	|	...	1145	...	1717	...	|
112	Kluang d.	0434	...	1015	...	1222	...	1754	...	|
163	Kulai d.	0542	...	1138	...	1330	...	1902	...	|
	Kempas Baru d.	0609	...	1210	...	1357	...	1929	...	|
195	**Johor Bahru** Sentral ⊡ a.	0625	0700	1230	1245	1415	1515	1945	2015	|
199	**Woodlands** ◇ ⊡ a.	...	0705	...	1250	...	1520	...	2020	◧

	ES42	ST80	ES44	ST86	ES46	ST90	ERT26 Ⓡ G	EOE H	
Woodlands ◇ ⊡ d.	...	1345	...	1730	...	2000	...	◧	...
Johor Bahru Sentral ⊡ d.	0830	1350	1440	1735	1805	2005	2025	|	...
Kempas Baru d.	0850	...	1500	...	1825	...	2044	|	...
Kulai d.	0918	...	1528	...	1908	...	2116	|	...
Kluang d.	1044	...	1636	...	2016	...	2239	|	...
Paloh d.	1114	...	1706	...	2047	...	|	|	...
Segamat d.	1240	...	1832	...	2213	...	0033	|	...
Gemas a.	1314	...	1906	...	2247	...	0118	◧	...

6010 TUMPAT - GEMAS

For footnotes see below Table 6015 — KTMB

km		SH35	SH51	SH53	SH55	SH37	SH57	SH59	ERT27 Ⓡ G	
0	**Tumpat** d.	...	0410	0705	1000	...	1605	...	2030	...
14	Wakaf Bharu d.	...	0425	0720	1031	...	1621	...	2047	...
25	Pasir Mas d.	...	0440	0734	1045	...	1636	...	2102	...
53	Tanah Merah d.	...	0512	0804	1117	...	1710	...	2133	...
85	Kuala Krai d.	...	0549	0910	1206	...	1819	...	2210	...
135	Dabong d.	...	0717	1033	1335	...	2030	...	2332	...
206	Gua Masang d.	...	0955	1229	...	...	2233	2240	0125	...
300	Kuala Lipis d.	1020	1142	...	...	1610	...	0022	0309	...
353	Jerantut d.	1120	...	...	...	1710	...	...	0403	...
406	Mentakab d.	1219	...	...	...	1827	...	...	0458	...
492	Bahau d.	1407	...	...	...	2015	...	...	0639	...
528	**Gemas** a.	1502	...	...	...	2110	...	...	0744	...

	SH50	SH52	ERT26 Ⓡ G	SH34	SH56	SH58	SH60	SH36	
Gemas d.	...	...	0118	0925		...	...	1535	...
Bahau d.	...	...	0214	1021	...	...	...	1631	...
Mentakab d.	...	...	0356	1228	...	...	...	1820	...
Jerantut d.	...	...	0508	1327	...	...	...	1919	...
Kuala Lipis d.	0320	...	0611	1425	...	...	1635	2017	...
Gua Masang d.	0500	0505	0748	...	...	1450	1818	...	...
Dabong d.	...	0730	0938	...	1455	1646	2019	...	...
Kuala Krai d.	...	0858	1116	...	1623	1808	2220	...	...
Tanah Merah d.	...	0936	1153	...	1717	1845	2256	...	...
Pasir Mas d.	...	1010	1224	...	1750	1915	2327	...	...
Wakaf Bharu d.	...	1025	1239	...	1805	1929	2341	...	...
Tumpat a.	...	1042	1254	...	1822	1946	2357	...	...

6012 KUALA LUMPUR AIRPORTS

For footnotes see below Table 6015 — KTMB

Kuala Lumpur International Airport (KLIA) ✈. *57 km.* Journey times: KLIA 37 minutes, KLIA2 40 minutes.
From **Kuala Lumpur Sentral** at 0500, 0530 and at least every 30 minutes until 2200, 2230, 2310.
From **KLIA2** ✈ (from **KLIA** 5 minutes later) at 0010, 0500, 0530 and at least every 30 minutes until 2300, 2330.

Kuala Lumpur Subang Skypark ✈. *26 km.* Journey 37 minutes. Trains call at **Subang Jaya** 18 minutes after Kuala Lumpur and 20 minutes after Subang Airport.
From **Kuala Lumpur Sentral** at 0555, 0655, 0750, 0850, 0925, 1035, 1125, 1315, 1425, 1525, 1625, 1825.
From **Subang Skypark** ✈ at 0750, 1035, 1220, 1315, 1415, 1520, 1615, 1715, 1815, 1915, 2015, 2125, 2245.

6015 TENOM - TANJONG ARU

JKNS

km			①-⑥	⑦			⑦	①-⑥	①-⑥	
0	**Tenom** d.	...	...	...	0730	...	1230	1300	...	...
	Halogilat d.	...	0600	0810	0854	...	1353	1444	1740	...
49	Beaufort a.	...	0658	0911	0951	...	1455	1545	1839	...
49	Beaufort d.	0500	...	...	...	1101	...	...	...	...
101	Papar d.	0611	...	...	...	1216	...	...	...	...
134	**Tanjong Aru** ◐ d.	0658	...	...	...	1310	...	...	...	...
	Sembulan ◐ a.	0710	...	...	...	1323	...	...	...	...

	①-⑥	⑦			⑦	①-⑥	①-⑥	⑦	①-⑥
Sembulan ◐ d.	...	...	...	...	...	...	...	1700	1730
Tanjong Aru ◐ d.	...	...	...	0745	...	...	...	1706	1736
Papar d.	...	...	...	0829	...	...	...	1750	1823
Beaufort a.	...	...	...	0940	...	...	...	1900	1934
Beaufort d.	0500	0700	0750	...	1300	1330	1630	...	...
Halogilat d.	0559	0758	0853	...	1353	1444	1730	...	...
Tenom a.	...	...	1013	...	1510	1555	...	...	...

NOTES FOR TABLES 6000 - 6015:

A – Also at 0851 Ⓒ, 1443 Ⓐ, 1500 Ⓒ, 1653 Ⓐ, 1743 Ⓐ, 1806 Ⓒ, 1905 Ⓒ.
B – Also at 0700, 1210, 1740.
C – Also at 0620, 0735, 0835, 1235, 1435, 1635, 1735, 1835, 1935.
D – Also at 0538 Ⓒ, 0600 Ⓒ, 0610 Ⓐ, 1115 Ⓐ, 1116 Ⓒ, 1811 Ⓒ.
E – Also at 0625, 0735, 0835, 1035, 1435, 1635, 1735, 1840, 1935.
F – Also at 0712, 1347, 1742.
G – EKSPRES RAKYAT TIMURAN – 🛏 2 cl., (23) Johor Baru - Tumpat and v.v.
H – EASTERN AND ORIENTAL EXPRESS. Luxury cruise train Bangkok - Woodlands and v.v. (www.belmond.com/trains/asia/eastern-and-oriental-express).
◇ – Border point with Singapore.
⊡ – Also from Johor Baru at 0500, 0530, 0600, 0630, 0730, 0845, 1000, 1130, 1400, 1630, 1745, 1900, 2130, 2245; also from Woodlands at 0830, 0945, 1100, 1230, 1500, 1615, 1845, 2115, 2230, 2345.
◐ – Kota Kinabalu.
◧ – Contact operator for timings.

THAILAND

Capital: **Bangkok** (GMT +7). 2023 Public Holidays: Jan. 1, 2, Mar. 6, Apr. 6, 13, 14, May 1, 4, 11, June 3, 5, July 28, Aug. 1, 12, 14, Oct. 13, 23, Dec. 5, 10, 11, 31.

Rail services are operated by State Railway of Thailand (SRT www.railway.co.th). Trains may convey any combination of first, second or third class seating as shown in either columns or footnotes. Overnight trains may also convey sleeping cars or couchettes. Sleeping cars have lockable two berth compartments which convert into seats during the day. Couchettes are arranged 'open plan' along the coach and during the day the bottom bunks are used as seats. Dining cars are operated on all important trains.

BANGKOK - BAN PLU TA LUANG and ARANYAPRATHET — 6050

3rd class only

km		275	997	283	283	281	279	277	371	383
			⑥⑦		①–⑤					
0	**Bangkok** Hua Lamphong ◧ d.	0555	0645	0655	0655	0800	1305	1525	1740	1825
5	Makkasan ◧ d.	0620	0659	0716	0716	0816	1317	1545	1802	1843
31	Hua Takhe ‡ ◧ d.	0703	0733	0814	0814	0857	1348	1618	1842	1924
61	Chachoengsao Junction ◧ d.	0740	0802	0856	0859	0932	1421	1644	1924	2000
131	Si Racha Junction d.	|	0855	...	1013	|	|	|	|	...
155	Pattaya d.	|	0914	...	1035	|	|	|	|	...
184	**Ban Plu Ta Luang** a.	|	0950	...	1120	|	|	|	|	...
122	Prachin Buri d.	0846	...	...	...	1046	1514	1741	2032	...
161	Kabin Buri d.	0933	...	...	...	1135	1550	1820	...	...
255	**Aranyaprathet** a.	1110	...	...	...	...	1720	...	...	...
260	Ban Klong Luk 🏛 a.	1117	...	...	...	...	1727	...	...	...

	372	278	280	368	282	284	284	998	276
							①–⑤	⑥⑦	
Ban Klong Luk 🏛 d.	...	...	0658	...	...	...	...	...	1353
Aranyaprathet d.	...	...	0705	...	...	...	...	...	1400
Kabin Buri d.	...	0630	0839	...	1325	...	...	...	1549
Prachin Buri d.	0500	0719	0919	...	1416	...	...	...	1640
Ban Plu Ta Luang d.	|	|	|	...	|	...	1335	1550	|
Pattaya d.	|	|	|	...	|	...	1421	1626	|
Si Racha Junction d.	|	|	|	...	|	...	1452	1645	|
Chachoengsao Junction ◧ d.	0619	0831	1022	1235	1534	1620	1620	1737	1800
Hua Takhe ‡ ◧ d.	0701	0911	1107	1316	1609	1706	1706	1806	1842
Makkasan ◧ d.	0751	0958	1148	1354	1655	1801	1801	1838	1925
Bangkok Hua Lamphong ◧ a.	0815	1015	1205	1410	1715	1815	1815	1855	1940

◧ – Additional trains are available Bangkok - Chachoengsao and v.v.

‡ – For Suvarnabhumi International Airport ✈.

BANGKOK - HAT YAI - SUNGAI KOLOK — 6055

km		453	43		171	31		463	37	
		3	2		A	B		3	C	
0	**Bangkok** K Thep Aphiwat d.	...	0810	...	1310	1450	...	...	1535	...
57	Nakhon Pathom d.	...	0911	...	1411	1553	...	...	1646	...
110	Rachaburi d.	...	1013	...	1512	1649	...	...	1747	...
222	Hua Hin d.	...	1209	...	1739	1907	...	...	2006	...
386	Bang Saphan Yai d.	...	1504	...	2000	|	...	...	2240	...
478	Chumphon d.	...	1636	...	2210	2319	...	...	0021	...
644	Surat Thani ⊡ d.	...	1850	...	0138	0243	...	...	0349	...
766	Thung Song Junction d.	...	...	...	0344	0437	...	...	0545	...
825	**Nakhon Si Thammarat** d.	...	...	...	|	|	...	...	|	...
838	Trang a.	...	...	...	|	|	...	...	|	...
859	**Kantang** a.	...	...	...	|	|	...	...	|	...
855	Phatthalung d.	...	...	...	0520	0607	...	0625	0723	...
938	Hat Yai Junction d.	...	...	...	0705	0725	...	0816	0906	...
1018	Pattani d.	...	...	...	0818	...	...	0939	1017	...
1048	Yala d.	0630	...	...	0906	...	...	1018	1055	...
1152	**Sungai Kolok** a.	0840	...	...	1050	...	...	1255	1230	...

		169	451		83	447		455	167		85	445		39	
		23	3		D	3		3	A		D	3		2	
Bangkok K Thep Aphiwat d.	...	1610	...	...	1700	...	...	...	1850	...	2010	...	...	2220	...
Nakhon Pathom d.	...	1712	...	...	1834	...	...	...	2009	...	2109	...	...	2320	...
Rachaburi d.	...	1814	...	...	1934	...	...	...	2113	...	2218	...	...	0004	...
Hua Hin d.	...	2038	...	...	2152	...	...	...	2339	...	0049	...	...	0218	...
Bang Saphan Yai d.	...	2342	...	...	0020	...	...	...	0254	...	0404	...	...	0517	...
Chumphon d.	...	0147	...	...	0240	...	...	...	0500	...	0553	0615	...	0712	...
Surat Thani ⊡ d.	...	0437	...	...	0538	0620	...	...	0757	...	0842	0959	...	0925	...
Thung Song Junction d.	...	0645	...	...	0741	0850	...	...	1019	...	1058	1246	...	...	...
Nakhon Si Thammarat d.	...	|	0600	...	|	|	...	0950	|	...	1205	|	...	...	...
Trang a.	...	|	|	...	0850	|	...	|	1142	...	...	|	...	...	...
Kantang a.	...	|	|	...	...	|	...	|	1205	...	...	|	...	...	...
Phatthalung d.	...	0828	0841	...	...	1047	...	1243	...	...	...	1458	...	...	...
Hat Yai Junction d.	...	1002	1028	...	...	1246	...	1433	...	...	...	1700	...	...	...
Pattani d.	...	1113	1159	...	...	1426	...	1553	...	...	...	...	...	...	...
Yala d.	...	1145	1236	...	...	1527	...	1630	...	...	...	...	...	...	...
Sungai Kolok a.	...	...	1445	...	...	1740	...	...	...	...	...	...	...	...	...

	40	446		456	168		448	86	
	2	2		3	A		3	D	
Sungai Kolok d.	...	...	...	...	...	...	0630	...	...
Yala d.	...	...	...	0635	...	...	0835	...	...
Pattani d.	...	...	...	0717	...	...	0916	...	...
Hat Yai Junction d.	...	0635	...	0854	...	...	1115	...	...
Phatthalung d.	...	0829	...	1046	...	...	1316	...	...
Kantang d.	...	|	...	|	1255	...	|	...	...
Trang d.	...	|	...	|	1319	...	|	...	...
Nakhon Si Thammarat d.	...	|	...	1340	|	...	|	1520	...
Thung Song Junction d.	...	1045	...	...	1447	...	1531	1635	...
Surat Thani ⊡ d.	1025	1331	...	...	1708	...	1755	1852	...
Chumphon d.	1236	1705	...	...	2003	...	...	2125	...
Bang Saphan Yai d.	1352	...	...	...	2158	...	...	2256	...
Hua Hin d.	1623	...	...	...	0137	...	...	0240	...
Rachaburi d.	1813	...	...	...	0413	...	...	0512	...
Nakhon Pathom d.	1922	...	...	...	0538	...	...	0636	...
Bangkok Krung Thep Aphiwat a.	2030	...	...	...	0700	...	...	0745	...

		452	170		44	84		172	464		32	38		454	
		3	23		2	D		A	3		B	C		2	
Sungai Kolok d.	...	0900	...	...	...	...	...	1200	1225	...	...	1420	...	1525	...
Yala d.	...	1117	1235	...	...	...	...	1353	1453	...	...	1611	...	1740	...
Pattani d.	...	1158	1307	...	...	...	...	1425	1528	...	...	1642	...	...	...
Hat Yai Junction d.	...	1400	1431	...	...	...	...	1550	1705	...	1745	1815	...	...	...
Phatthalung d.	...	1531	1551	...	...	...	...	1700	1850	...	1859	1934	...	...	...
Kantang d.	...	|	|	...	...	...	...	|	...	...	|	|	...	...	...
Trang d.	...	|	|	...	...	1700	...	|	...	...	|	|	...	...	...
Nakhon Si Thammarat d.	...	1805	|	...	...	|	...	|	...	...	|	|	...	...	...
Thung Song Junction d.	...	...	1739	...	...	1820	...	1853	...	...	2040	2118	...	...	...
Surat Thani ⊡ d.	...	...	1941	...	2105	2014	...	2116	...	...	2227	2314	...	...	...
Chumphon d.	...	...	2220	...	2339	2251	...	0014	...	...	0105	0142	...	...	...
Bang Saphan Yai d.	...	...	0021	...	0131	0046	...	0203	...	...	|	0342	...	...	...
Hua Hin d.	...	...	0342	...	0430	0413	...	0529	...	...	0555	0709	...	...	...
Rachaburi d.	...	...	0557	...	0632	0655	...	0758	...	...	0817	0934	...	...	...
Nakhon Pathom d.	...	...	0709	...	0735	0816	...	0920	...	...	0939	1053	...	...	...
Bangkok Krung Thep Aphiwat a.	...	...	0825	...	0845	0925	...	1030	...	...	1050	1205	...	...	...

A – RAPID – 🛏 2 cl., (23).
B – SPECIAL EXPRESS – 🛏 1, 2 cl. (12).
C – SPECIAL EXPRESS – 🛏 1, 2 cl. (23).
D – EXPRESS - 🛏 1, 2 cl. (23).
⊡ – Station is at Phun Phin, *13 km* away.

BANGKOK - CHIANG MAI — 6060

km		403	407	401		303	111	7		201	209	211
0		3	3	3		3	23	2		23	3	23
	Bangkok K Thep Aphiwat d.	...	...	...	...	...	0730	0905	...	...	...	...
	Bangkok Hua Lamphong d.	...	...	...	...	0415	|	|	...	0930	1115	1255
	Bang Sue Junction ⊖ d.	...	...	...	...	0435	|	|	...	1003	1135	1317
51	Bang Pa In d.	...	...	...	...	0536	0825	|	...	1114	1247	1419
64	Ayutthaya d.	...	...	...	...	0550	0838	0955	...	1128	1305	1432
126	Lop Buri d.	...	...	0600	...	0705	0944	1029	...	1241	1423	1538
239	Nakhon Sawan d.	...	0500	0811	...	...	1124	1140	...	1511	...	1753
312	Taphan Hin d.	...	0617	0936	...	...	1242	1226	...	1640	...	1915
382	Phitsanulok d.	0555	0729	1055	...	...	1345	1322	...	1755	...	...
478	Uttaradit d.	0645	0907	...	...	...	1524	1427	...	...	...	...
481	Sila At d.	0740	0917	...	...	...	1529	1433	...	...	...	...
527	Den Chai d.	...	1013	...	...	...	1630	1524	...	...	...	...
635	Nakhon Lampang d.	...	1236	...	...	...	...	1733	...	...	...	...
676	Khun Tan d.	...	1330	...	...	...	...	1823	...	...	...	...
722	Lamphun d.	...	1416	...	...	...	...	1915	...	...	...	...
744	**Chiang Mai** a.	...	1435	...	...	...	...	1930	...	...	...	...

		109	207	301		317	9	313		13	107	51
		A	3	3		3	B	3		B	A	E
Bangkok K Thep Aphiwat d.	...	1415	...	...	...	...	1840	...	...	2005	2045	2230
Bangkok Hua Lamphong d.	...	|	1410	1630	...	1730	|	1820	...	|	|	|
Bang Sue Junction ⊖ d.	...	|	1434	1653	...	1753	|	1843	...	|	|	|
Bang Pa In d.	...	|	1543	1809	...	1900	|	1955	...	|	|	|
Ayutthaya d.	...	1519	1558	1824	...	1914	1945	2008	...	2107	2148	2236
Lop Buri d.	...	1623	1727	1940	...	2020	2042	...	...	2200	2239	0031
Nakhon Sawan d.	...	1827	1935	...	...	...	2217	...	...	2331	0006	0224
Taphan Hin d.	...	1937	...	...	...	...	|	...	...	|	0130	0337
Phitsanulok d.	...	2037	...	...	...	...	0018	...	...	0149	0238	0440
Uttaradit d.	...	2223	...	...	...	...	|	...	...	0308	0405	0606
Sila At d.	...	2237	...	...	...	...	0154	...	...	0321	0418	0620
Den Chai d.	...	2342	...	...	...	...	0251	...	...	0419	0515	0720
Nakhon Lampang d.	...	0204	...	...	...	...	0501	...	...	0633	...	1001
Khun Tan d.	...	0258	...	...	...	...	0606	...	...	0737	...	1105
Lamphun d.	...	0344	...	...	...	...	0651	...	...	0821	...	1150
Chiang Mai a.	...	0405	...	...	...	...	0715	...	...	0840	...	1210

km		108	52	14		314	10	302		318	208	304
		A	E	B		3	B	3		3	3	3
0	**Chiang Mai** d.	...	1530	1700	...	...	1800	...	...	...	...	...
22	Lamphun d.	...	1548	1720	...	...	1820	...	...	...	...	...
68	Khun Tan d.	...	1650	1824	...	...	1921	...	...	...	...	...
109	Nakhon Lampang d.	...	1804	1927	...	...	2017	...	...	...	...	...
217	Den Chai d.	1905	2026	2141	...	...	2236	...	...	...	...	...
263	Sila At d.	2012	2130	2236	...	...	2333	...	...	...	...	...
266	Uttaradit d.	2019	2137	2242	...	...	|	...	...	...	...	...
362	Phitsanulok d.	2209	2301	0001	...	...	0050	...	...	...	...	...
432	Taphan Hin d.	2320	0007	|	...	...	|	...	...	...	...	...
505	Nakhon Sawan d.	0048	0114	0159	...	...	0241	...	...	...	0500	...
618	Lop Buri d.	0228	0245	0339	...	...	0409	0430	...	0600	0706	0800
680	Ayutthaya d.	0321	0343	0455	...	0507	0529	0546	...	0710	0826	0900
693	Bang Pa In d.	|	|	|	...	0520	|	0600	...	0720	0840	0911
744	Bang Sue Junction ⊖ a.	|	|	|	...	0626	|	0712	...	0827	0952	1010
751	**Bangkok** Hua Lamphong a.	|	|	|	...	0650	|	0735	...	0850	1015	1030
	Bangkok K Thep Aphiwat a.	0430	0510	0610	...	...	0650	...	...	...	...	...

		212	202	112		102	8	210		402	408	410
		3	23	23		23	2	3		3	3	3
Chiang Mai d.	...	...	...	...	...	0630	0850	...	...	...	0930	...
Lamphun d.	...	...	...	...	...	0652	0905	...	...	...	1000	...
Khun Tan d.	...	...	...	...	...	0736	0947	...	...	...	1103	...
Nakhon Lampang d.	...	...	...	...	...	0837	1041	...	...	...	1202	...
Den Chai d.	...	...	...	0730	...	1046	1239	...	...	...	1419	...
Sila At d.	...	...	...	0827	...	1147	1326	...	...	...	1533	1630
Uttaradit d.	...	...	...	0833	...	1153	1332	...	...	...	1538	1633
Phitsanulok d.	...	...	0605	1003	...	1318	1444	...	...	1345	1724	1810
Taphan Hin d.	...	0530	0718	1112	...	1428	1532	...	...	1458	1841	...
Nakhon Sawan d.	...	0701	0835	1242	...	1556	1622	...	...	1630	1955	...
Lop Buri d.	...	0918	1056	1439	...	1806	1728	1732	...	1845	...	...
Ayutthaya d.	...	1027	1214	1559	...	1916	1806	1848	...	...	...	...
Bang Pa In d.	...	1039	1229	1616	...	|	|	1903	...	...	...	...
Bang Sue Junction ⊖ a.	...	1147	1342	|	...	|	|	2015	...	...	...	...
Bangkok Hua Lamphong a.	...	1210	1405	|	...	|	|	2035	...	...	...	...
Bangkok K Thep Aphiwat a.	...	...	...	1720	...	2025	1855	...	...	...	...	...

A – RAPID – 🛏 2 cl., (23).
B – SPECIAL EXPRESS – 🛏 1, 2 cl. (12).
E – EXPRESS – 🛏 2 cl., (23).
⊖ – Adjacent to Krung Thep Aphiwat station.

6065 BANGKOK - UBON RATCHATHANI and NONG KHAI

km		421	21	419	135	71	427	139	23	141
		3	2	3	23	23	3	A	B	23
0	**Bangkok** K Thep Aphiwat d.	...	0610	...	0710	1035	...	1925	2105	2305
64	Ayutthaya d.	...	0659	...	0828	1131	...	2026	2202	0017
106	Saraburi d.	...	0734	...	0918	1206	...	2110	2236	0059
118	Kaeng Khoi Junction d.	...	0745	...	0930	1216	...	2124	2237	0115
173	Pak Chong d.	...	0853	...	1056	1327	...	2249	0010	0259
257	Nakhon Ratchasima d.	0610	1011	1115	1224	1443	1420	0023	0146	0429
369	Buri Ram d.	0810	1137	1317	1422	1617	1635	0226	0334	0634
413	Surin d.	0910	1211	1355	1510	1711	1723	0317	0414	0729
508	Si Sa Ket d.	1107	1320	1550	1703	1843	1906	0509	0539	0908
568	**Ubon Ratchathani** a.	1215	1400	1645	1800	1950	2015	0615	0635	1020

	72	428	136	426		22	142	24	140
	23	3	23	3		2	23	B	A
Ubon Ratchathani d.	0540	0620	0700	1235	...	1450	1735	1900	2030
Si Sa Ket d.	0624	0716	0804	1344	...	1531	1841	1956	2124
Surin d.	0749	0905	0939	1528	...	1641	2022	2123	2256
Buri Ram d.	0835	0953	1027	1615	...	1715	2117	2204	2344
Nakhon Ratchasima d.	1018	1145	1233	1825	...	1847	2325	2359	0142
Pak Chong d.	1127	...	1400	...	...	1948	0103	0131	0303
Kaeng Khoi Junction d.	1228	...	1530	...	...	2053	0216	|	0432
Saraburi d.	1243	...	1545	...	...	2105	0229	|	0450
Ayutthaya d.	1335	...	1637	...	...	2142	0307	0342	0550
Bangkok K Thep Aphiwat a.	1430	...	1755	...	...	2235	0410	0450	0710

km		415	431	75	417	25	133			
		3	3	23	3	B	3			
0	**Bangkok** K Thep Aphiwat d.	...	...	0845	...	2025	2125	...	...	...
64	Ayutthaya d.	...	...	0942	...	2139	2230	...	...	...
106	Saraburi d.	...	...	1018	...	2223	2311	...	...	...
118	Kaeng Khoi Junction d.	...	0500	1030	...	2235	2322	...	...	...
173	Pak Chong d.	...	0618	|	...	|	|	...	...	...
257	Nakhon Ratchasima d.	0620	0829	|	1555	|	|	...	...	...
339	Bua Yai Junction d.	0758	1009	1414	1726	0250	0357	...	...	...
443	Khon Kaen d.	0935	1226	1532	1904	0412	0522	...	...	...
562	Udon Thani d.	1121	...	1658	2100	0544	0707	...	...	...
614	**Nong Khai** a.	1205	...	1730	...	0645	0755	...	...	...
620	**Tha Na Laeng** (Laos) a.	...	...	...	...	...	...	...	...	...

	416	76	432	418	134	26			
	3	23	3	3	3	B			
Tha Na Laeng (Laos) d.	...	...	...	...	...	...	...	...	...
Nong Khai d.	...	0745	...	1255	1850	1940	...	...	...
Udon Thani d.	0555	0816	...	1340	1938	2020	...	...	...
Khon Kaen d.	0750	0932	1430	1533	2112	2149	...	...	...
Bua Yai Junction d.	0925	1045	1601	1705	2246	2317	...	...	...
Nakhon Ratchasima d.	1055	|	1740	1835	|	|	...	...	...
Pak Chong d.	...	|	1914	...	|	|	...	...	...
Kaeng Khoi Junction d.	...	1444	2030	...	0300	0322	...	...	...
Saraburi d.	...	1455	...	...	0317	0339	...	...	...
Ayutthaya d.	...	1535	...	...	0414	0433	...	...	...
Bangkok K Thep Aphiwat a.	...	1645	...	...	0530	0550	...	...	...

A – 2 cl., (23).

B – 1, 2 cl., (12).

6070 BANGKOK - NAM TOK

km		909	257
		©C	3D
0	**Bangkok** Thon Buri d.	...	0745
	Bangkok H Lamphong d.	0630	|
47*	Nakhon Pathom d.	0820	0852
65	Nong Pla Duk Junction d.	0836	0922
116	Kanchanaburi d.	0927	1035
193	**Nam Tok** a.	...	1235

	258	910
	3D	©C
Nam Tok d.	1255	...
Kanchanaburi d.	1448	1653
Nong Pla Duk Junction d.	1602	1755
Nakhon Pathom d.	1631	1809
Bangkok H L'hong a.	|	1925
Bangkok Thon Buri a.	1740	...

C – Tourist train to River Khwae Bridge (a. 0935) and allied war cemetery at Kanchanaburi. Conveys (23). Ⓡ. Fare 740 Baht. SERVICE SUSPENDED.

D – Also from Bangkok at 1355; also from Nam Tok at 0520.

* – *64 km* from Bangkok Hua Lamphong.

6075 SUVARNABHUMI AIRPORT ✈ SRTET

Phaya Thai - Makksan - Suvarnabhumi International Airport ✈ (journey 26 minutes):

From Phaya Thai (from Makksan 4 minutes later) at 0529 and every 12 – 15 minutes until 2400.

From Suvarnabhumi International Airport ✈ at 0529 and every 10 – 15 minutes until 0002.

CAMBODIA

Capital: **Phnom Penh** (GMT +7). 2023 Public Holidays: Jan. 1, 7, Mar. 8, Apr. 14 – 16, May 1, 4, 8, 14, June 18, Sept. 24, Oct. 13 – 15, 29, Nov. 9, 26 – 28.

Rail services are operated by Royal Railway (www.royal-railway.com). Trains convey one class of accommodation and convey car and motorcycle carriers.

6090 PHNOM PENH - SIHANOUKVILLE

km		7	
0	**Phnom Penh** d.	0700	...
75	Takeo d.	0840	...
	Kep d.	1015	...
166	Kampot d.	1040	...
263	**Sihanoukville** a.	1250	...

	8	
Sihanoukville d.	1400	...
Kampot d.	1600	...
Kep d.	1620	...
Takeo d.	1800	...
Phnom Penh a.	1940	...

6091 PHNOM PENH - POIPET

km		3	
0	**Phnom Penh** d.	0640	...
166	Pursat d.	1100	...
273	Battambang d.	1330	...
384	**Poipet** a.	...	...

	4	
Poipet d.	...	...
Battambang d.	1500	...
Pursat d.	1800	...
Phnom Penh a.	2230	...

LAOS

6095 VIENTIANE - BOTEN

km		C82	K12	C84
0	**Vientiane** d.	0730	0800	1505
	Vang Vieng d.	0825	0920	1611
238	Luang Prabang d.	0923	1043	1710
422	**Boten** 🏛 a.	1102	1310	...

	C81	K11	C83
Boten 🏛 d.	1215	1400	...
Luang Prabang d.	1345	1610	1820
Vang Vieng d.	1445	1744	1912
Vientiane a.	1545	1910	2013

Capital: **Vientiane** (GMT +7).

2023 Public Holidays: Jan. 1, Mar. 8, Apr. 14 – 16, May 1, July 20, Nov. 27, Dec. 2.

Rail services to China are operated by China Railway Kunming Group. Services to Thailand are operated by the State Railway of Thailand (see Table **6065**). Rail services will eventually operate between Vientiane and Kunming in China. Timings from Kunming to the Chinese border (Mohan) can be found on Table **7120**.

VIÊT NAM

Capital: **Há Nôi** (GMT +7). 2023 Public Holidays: Jan. 1, 2, 21 – 26, Apr. 29, 30, May 1, 2, Sept. 2, 4.

Rail services are operated by Duống Sắt Việt Nam (DSVN www.vr.com.vn). Unless stated trains convey first and second class accommodation. First class has four berth compartments, whilst second class has six. Dining facilities (meals brought to your seats) are provided on some trains. Services may alter during Lunar New Year.

6100 HÁ NOI - BEIJING

km				
0	**Há Nôi** Gia Lam d.	...	...	...
162	Dong Dang 🏛 d.	...	...	...
207	Pingxiang 🏛 a.	...	...	...
430	Nanning d.	...	...	...
861	Guilin bei d.	...	...	...
1409	Changsha d.	...	...	...
1771	Wuhan Wuchang d.	...	...	...
2307	Zhengzhou d.	...	...	...
2996	**Beijing** xi a.	...	...	...

Beijing xi d.	...	...	...
Zhengzhou d.	...	...	...
Wuhan Wuchang d.	...	...	...
Changsha d.	...	...	...
Guilin bei d.	...	...	...
Nanning a.	...	...	...
Pingxiang 🏛 a.	...	...	...
Dong Dang 🏛 a.	...	...	...
Há Nôi Gia Lam a.	...	...	...

6105 HÁ NOI - LÂO CAÍ

km		SP1	SP3	
		⑤	E	
0	**Há Nôi** d.	2135	2200	...
6	**Há Nôi** Gia Lâm d.	2158	2223	...
155	Yên Bái d.	0130	0214	...
262	Phõ Lu d.	0418	0457	...
296	**Lâo Caí** a.	0515	0555	...

	SP4		
	E		
Lâo Caí d.	2130	...	...
Phõ Lu d.	2226	...	...
Yên Bái d.	0123	...	...
Há Nôi Gia Lâm a.	0502	...	...
Há Nôi a.	0525	...	...

NOTES FOR TABLES 6100 - 6112:

E – 1, 2 cl., (12) Há Nôi - Lâo Caí and v.v.

F – Also from Há Nôi at 0600; also from Hai Phòng at 0610, 1620 ⑦.

6110 HÁ NOI - HAI PHÒNG

km		LP3	LP5	LP7
		F		
0	**Há Nôi** d.	0920	1515	1810
6	**Há Nôi** Gia Lâm d.	0956	1547	1847
57	Hai Duong d.	1059	1653	1953
76	Phú Thái d.	1125	1722	2019
102	**Hai Phòng** a.	1200	1800	2055

	LP6	LP8	HP2
	F		
Hai Phòng d.	0910	1500	1840
Phú Thái d.	0946	1537	1917
Hai Duong d.	1012	1603	1950
Há Nôi Gia Lâm a.	1120	1708	2052
Há Nôi a.	1152	1740	2115

6112 HÁ NOI - HA LONG

km				
0	**Há Nôi** Yen Vien d.	...	...	...
58	Kép d.	...	...	...
116	Mao Khê d.	...	...	...
164	**Ha Long** a.	...	...	...

Ha Long d.	...	...	...
Mao Khê d.	...	...	...
Kép d.	...	...	...
Há Nôi Yen Vien a.	...	...	...

HÁ NÔI - SAÍ GÔN 6115

km		SE7 A	SPT1 ⑤⑦	SE21	SE5 A	SNT1 ⑤–⑦	SE3 A	SE1 A	NA1	
0	**Há Nôi** d.	0600	...	...	1545	...	1925	2215	2240	...
87	Nam Dinh d.	0743	...	...	1728	...	2108	2353	|	...
16	Ninh Binh d.	0819	...	...	1804	...	2144	0027	|	...
75	Thanh Hóa d.	0933	...	...	1918	...	2253	0128	|	...
19	Vinh d.	1206	...	...	2151	...	0141	0349	0520	...
22	Dông Ho'i d.	1625	...	...	0237	...	0545	0759	...	...
22	Dông Ho'i d.	1640	...	...	0252	...	0600	0811	...	...
88	Hué d.	2029	...	...	0602	...	0902	1108	...	...
91	**Dà Nang** a.	2300	...	...	0852	...	1133	1336	...	...
91	**Dà Nang** d.	2325	...	0800	0917	...	1202	1408	...	...
28	Quang Ngai d.	0200	...	1128	1224	...	1502	1631	...	...
95	Diêu Tri a.	0459	...	1429	1525	...	1758	1910	...	...
95	Diêu Tri d.	0514	...	1449	1540	...	1816	1922	...	...
15	Nha Trang d.	0938	...	1906	1945	2040	2211	2311	...	...
	Phan Thiet d.	|	1350	|	|	|	|	|	...	...
51	Binh Thuan d.	1331	1419	0033	0113	|	0217	0305	...	...
49	Long Khánh d.	1522	|	0224	0259	|	0402	|	...	...
26	**Saí Gôn** (Ho Chi Minh) a.	1710	1820	0410	0445	0506	0547	0632	...	...

	SE8 A	SPT2 ⑤⑦	SE22	SE6 A	SE4 A	NA2	SNT2 ④–⑥	SE2 A	
Saí Gôn (Ho Chi Minh) d.	0600	0645	1025	1600	1900	...	1940	2110	...
Long Khánh d.	0749	|	1214	1754	2049	...	|	|	...
Binh Thuan d.	0940	1026	1416	1945	2235	...	|	0030	...
Phan Thiet a.	|	1037	|	|	|	...	|	|	...
Nha Trang d.	1349	...	1814	0017	0223	...	0525	0415	...
Diêu Tri a.	1813	...	2347	0414	0615	...	...	0801	...
Diêu Tri d.	1833	...	0002	0429	0627	...	...	0813	...
Quang Ngai d.	2147	...	0316	0732	0925	...	...	1058	...
Dà Nang a.	0032	...	0555	1026	1159	...	...	1317	...
Dà Nang d.	0057	...	...	1051	1228	...	...	1342	...
Hué d.	0334	...	...	1351	1515	...	...	1616	...
Dông Ho'i a.	0710	...	...	1707	1815	...	...	1909	...
Dông Ho'i d.	0725	...	...	1722	1830	...	...	1921	...
Vinh d.	1243	...	...	2147	2252	2220	...	2338	...
Thanh Hóa d.	1515	...	...	0032	0131	|	...	0220	...
Ninh Binh d.	1630	...	...	0158	0241	|	...	0326	...
Nam Dinh d.	1705	...	...	0233	0316	|	...	0359	...
Há Nôi a.	1912	...	...	0417	0500	0516	...	0540	...

A – 🛏 1,2 cl., 🚃1 ✕.

MYANMAR

pital: **Yangon** (GMT +6½). 2023 Public Holidays: Jan. 4, Feb. 12, Mar. 2, 5, 27, Apr. 9–17, May 1, 3, June 29, July 19, Aug. 1, Oct. 28–30, Nov. 12, 26, 27, Dec. 7, 25.

il service in Myanmar is provided by Myanmar Railways Corporation (MRC). Unless noted all trains convey first and second class seating (known locallly as upper and ordinary). All seating is ocated on purchase of tickets. Sleeping cars are operated on overnight trains and bedding is supplied. Sleepers have 6 compartments comprising 4 x 4-berth and 2 x 2-berth.

MYITKYINA - MANDALAY 6150

km		42	56 B	54	38	58				
0	**Myitkyina** d.	0640	0815	...	1200	1600	...	...	...	...
99	Kawlin d.	2320	2000	2215	0026	0435	...	...	...	...
46	Shwebo d.	0520	0030	0200	0453	0921	...	...	...	...
39	**Mandalay** a.	0920	0345	0445	0800	1320	...	...	...	...

	57	37	53	55 B	41				
Mandalay d.	0900	1130	1530	1600	1745	...	...	...	...
Shwebo d.	1155	1426	1803	1839	2145	...	...	...	...
Kawlin d.	1650	1852	2150	2323	0540	...	...	...	...
Myitkyina a.	0540	0630	...	1115	2025	...	...	...	...

B – 🛏, 🚃12.

LASHIO - MANDALAY 6155

km		132	
0	**Lashio** d.	0500	...
74	Hsipaw d.	0940	...
105	Kyaukme d.	1125	...
148	Gokteik d.	1325	...
213	Pyin Oo Lwin a.	1605	...
213	Pyin Oo Lwin d.	1740	...
280	**Mandalay** a.	2240	...

	131	
Mandalay d.	0400	...
Pyin Oo Lwin a.	0752	...
Pyin Oo Lwin d.	0822	...
Gokteik d.	1108	...
Kyaukme d.	1339	...
Hsipaw d.	1515	...
Lashio a.	1935	...

THAZI - YAKSAUK 6160

km		147	141
0	**Thazi** d.	0500	0800
197	Kalaw d.	1147	1450
208	Aungban d.	1247	1535
236	Heho d.	1354	1657
255	Shwenyaung a.	1500	1820
255	Shwenyaung d.	1600	...
315	**Yaksauk** a.	1900	...

	142	148
Yaksauk d.	...	0700
Shwenyaung a.	...	1000
Shwenyaung d.	0700	1100
Heho d.	0810	1210
Aungban d.	0935	1349
Kalaw d.	1025	1453
Thazi a.	1720	2145

MANDALAY - BAGAN - YANGON 6165

km		12	118	8 ⑤	6	4 B	120 B	62 B		
0	**Mandalay** d.	0500	0720	...	1500	1630	2100	...	...	...
36	Thazi d.	0757	|	...	1745	1927	|		...	...
	Naypyitaw d.	1105	|	1915	2037	2239	|	...	...	...
79	**Bagan** a.	|	1845	|	|	|	0505	...	...	...
***	**Bagan** d.	|	...	|	|	|	...	1600	...	...
35	Taungoo d.	1431	...	2224	2334	0136	...	|	...	...
48	Bago d.	2108	...	0416	0511	0742	...	|	...	...
22	**Yangon** a.	2325	...	0700	0730	1000	...	1040	...	...

	11	119 B	5	3 B	117	61 B	7 ⑦		
Yangon d.	0500	...	1500	1545	...	1600	1900	...	...
Bago d.	0734	...	1717	1717	...	|	2144	...	...
Taungoo d.	1341	...	2257	2257	...	|	0406	...	...
Bagan a.	|	...	|	|	...	1045	|	...	...
Bagan d.	|	2100	|	|	0400	...	|	...	...
Naypyitaw d.	1703	|	0152	0254	|	...	0715	...	...
Thazi d.	2006	|	0442	0645	|	...	...	...	...
Mandalay a.	2300	0500	0730	0900	1555	...	...	...	...

B – 🛏, 🚃12.

*** – Yangon - Bagan: *644 km*.

YANGON - MAWLAMYINE - DAWEI 6170

km		85	89	175						
0	**Yangon** d.	...	0630	1800	...	...	...	...	...	...
78	Bago d.	0445	0904	2305	...	...	...	...	...	...
	Kyaikto d.	0838	1155	2320	...	...	...	...	...	...
31	**Mawlamyine** a.	1530	1650	0400	...	...	...	...	...	...
31	**Mawlamyine** d.	...	...	0430	...	...	...	...	...	...
25	Ye d.	...	...	1025	...	...	...	...	...	...
39	**Dawei Port** a.	...	...	1845	...	...	...	...	...	...

	90	86	176						
Dawei Port d.	...	...	0500	...	...	...	...	...	...
Ye d.	...	...	1332	...	...	...	...	...	...
Mawlamyine a.	...	...	1930	...	...	...	...	...	...
Mawlamyine d.	0800	0900	2000	...	...	...	...	...	...
Kyaikto d.	1236	1547	0030	...	...	...	...	...	...
Bago d.	1525	2010	0316	...	...	...	...	...	...
Yangon a.	1810	...	0550	...	...	...	...	...	...

YANGON - PYAY 6175

km		63	75	71						
0	**Yangon** d.	...	...	1300	...	...	...	...	...	...
	Yangon Kyemyindine d.	0700	1100	|	...	...	...	...	...	...
57	**Pyay** a.	1800	2215	2130	...	...	...	...	...	...

	76	64	72						
Pyay d.	0200	0615	2330	...	...	...	...	...	...
Yangon Kyemyindine a.	1340	1730	|	...	...	...	...	...	...
Yangoon a.	...	...	0750	...	...	...	...	...	...

INDONESIA

Capital: **Jakarta** (GMT +7). 2023 Public Holidays: Jan. 1, 23, Feb. 19, Apr. 7, 22, 23, May 1, 18, June 1, 29, July 20, Aug. 17, Sept. 28, Dec. 25.

Rail services in Indonesia are operated by PT Kereta Api (Indonesian Railways, www.kai.id). Trains may convey any of three classes of seated accommodation which are known locally as Eksekutif, Bisnis and Ekonomi, shown in the tables as 1, 2 and 3.

6200 SUMATRA

Most trains 3rd class only

Medan - Pematangsiantar: *127 km* Journey 3½ - 4 hours
Medan depart: 1335.
Pematangsiantar depart: 0730.

Medan - Rantau Prapat: *266 km* Journey 5½ - 6 hours
Medan depart: 0750, 1500, 2220 ⑤–⑦.
Rantau Prapat depart: 0745, 1445, 2200 ⑤–⑦.

Medan - Tanjung Balai: *173 km* Journey 4½ hours
Medan depart: 0700, 1250, 1855.
Tanjung Balai depart: 0820, 1240, 1935.

Padang - Pariaman: *54 km* Journey 2 - 2 ½hours.
Padang depart: No information available.
Pariaman Naras depart: No information available.

Palembang - Lubuk Linggau: *305 km* Journey 7 - 8½ hours
Palembang Kertapati depart: 0900, 2015 ①⑤⑥⑦.
Lubuk Linggau depart: 1015, 1945 ①⑤⑥⑦.

Palembang - Panjang (Tanjungkarang Telukbetang): *401 km* Journey 9½ hours
Palembang Kertapati depart: 0830.
Panjang depart: 0830.

6203 SOEKARNO HATTA INTERNATIONAL AIRPORT ✈

km										
0	**Soekarno Hatta Int'l** ✈ d.	0649	0749	0849	and hourly	1649	1849	1949	2049
	Jakarta BNI City a.	0736	0836	0936	until ◧	1736	1936	2036	2136

Jakarta BNI City d.	0546	0646	0746	and hourly	1546	1746	1846	1946
Soekarno Hatta Int'l ✈ a.	0633	0733	0833	until ◧	1633	1833	1933	2033

◧ – Also from Soekarno Hatta International Airport ✈ at 0619, 0719, 1619, 1719, 1819, 1919; also from BNI City at 0516, 0616, 1516, 1616, 1716, 1816.

6205 JAKARTA - BANDUNG

Selected services. Unless noted trains convey [1] (Eksekutif) class. A high-speed standard gauge railway is due to open on this route in 2023.

km		46	48	50	52	40	42			
0	**Jakarta** Gambir d.	0810	1010	1230	1315	1530	1830	...	...	...
173	**Bandung** a.	1057	1327	1532	1629	1819	2110	...	...	...

	37	43	45	47	39	41	53		
Bandung d.	0500	0610	0845	0935	1110	1515	1920	...	...
Jakarta Gambir a.	0745	0850	1156	1239	1414	1755	2206	...	...

6210 JAKARTA - SEMARANG - SURABAJA and MALANG

Selected services. Unless noted trains convey [1] (Eksekutif) class.

km		2	130	282 ⊡	256 ⊡	74	128	106	78	4
0	**Jakarta** Gambir d.	0820	...	...	...	1540	...	...	1900	2035
	Jakarta Pasar Senen d.	|	0855	1020	1410	|	1550	1645	|	|
224	Cirebon d.	1048	|	|	|	1837	1853	1949	2149	2303
	Cirebon Prujakan d.	|	1220	1355	1738	|	|	|	|	|
300	Tegal d.	|	1323	1513	1846	1936	1954	2056	2240	|
360	Pekalongan d.	1212	1409	|	1938	|	2110	2152	2320	0027
455	**Semarang** Tawang d.	1318	1535	1737	|	2136	2231	|	0031	0133
	Semarang Poncol d.	|	|	|	2104	|	|	2321	|	|
656	Madiun d.	|	|	2114	|	0111	|	|	|	|
749	Kediri d.	|	|	2334	|	0236	|	|	|	|
585	Cepu d.	|	1734	|	2317	|	0038	0133	0212	|
622	Bojonegoro d.	1516	1805	|	2350	|	0110	0205	0241	0331
725	**Surabaja** Pasar Turi a.	1630	1935	|	0125	|	0245	0339	0400	0445
893	**Malang** a.	...	...	0224	...	0500	...	0628	...	...

	1	281 ⊡	105	127	77	73	3	255 ⊡	129
Malang d.	...	0925	1150	...	...	1600	...	...	...
Surabaja Pasar Turi d.	0935	|	1420	1555	1925	|	2105	2120	2235
Bojonegoro d.	1049	|	1556	1731	2045	|	2219	2254	0011
Cepu d.	|	|	1632	1807	|	|	|	2332	0047
Kediri d.	|	1230	|	|	|	1824	|	|	|
Madiun d.	|	1416	|	|	|	1950	|	|	|
Semarang Poncol d.	|	|	1853	|	|	|	|	0145	|
Semarang Tawang d.	1245	1811	|	2012	2302	2310	0015	|	0300
Pekalongan d.	1350	1933	2011	2131	0008	0021	0120	0306	0421
Tegal d.	|	2028	2111	2233	0051	0109	|	0359	0516
Cirebon Prujakan d.	|	2140	|	|	|	|	|	0511	0625
Cirebon d.	1515	|	2212	2339	0146	0210	0245	|	|
Jakarta Pasar Senen a.	|	0114	0125	0242	|	|	|	0825	0925
Jakarta Gambir a.	1745	...	...	...	0427	0507	0515	...	...

⊡ – Conveys [3] (Ekonomi) class only.

6215 JAKARTA - YOGYAKARTA - SOLO - MALANG and SURABAJA

Selected services. Unless noted trains convey [1] (Eksekutif) class.

km		134	6	10	122	170	76	120	72	8
0	**Jakarta** Gambir d.	...	...	0850	...	...	1710	...	1840	2045
	Jakarta Pasar Senen d.	0555	...	|	1140	...	|	...	|	|
224	Cirebon d.	0902	...	1118	|	...	1955	...	2122	2313
355	Purwokerto d.	1113	...	1312	1711	...	2158	...	2330	0109
382	Kroya d.	1139	1242	|	1737	1848	2224	2232	2355	|
457	Kutoarjo d.	1246	1335	|	1851	1956	2325	2341	0052	|
520	**Yogyakarta** d.	1338	1421	1504	1947	2050	0014	0032	0139	0259
580	**Solo** Balapan d.	1429	1504	1554	2040	2142	0100	0119	0220	0349
675	Madiun d.	...	1609	...	...	2304	0209	0239	0325	...
768	Kediri d.	...	|	...	...	0035	|	0406	0441	...
838	Blitar d.	...	|	...	...	0130	|	0503	0536	...
912	**Malang** a.	...	|	...	...	0306	|	0638	0709	...
762	Jombang d.	...	1712	...	...	...	0315	...	...	...
843	**Surabaja** Gubeng a.	...	1810	...	...	...	0411	...	...	...

	121	7	5	169	133	71	9	75	119
Surabaja Gubeng d.	...	...	0730	...	...	...	...	1730	...
Jombang d.	...	...	0824	...	...	...	...	1830	...
Malang d.	...	...	|	0820	...	1425	...	|	1710
Blitar d.	...	...	|	1002	...	1557	...	|	1848
Kediri d.	...	...	|	1057	...	1652	...	|	1945
Madiun d.	...	...	0927	1233	...	1818	...	1936	2117
Solo Balapan d.	0800	0835	1031	1352	1800	1929	2010	2042	2237
Yogyakarta d.	0907	0924	1114	1448	1853	2014	2059	2131	2328
Kutoarjo d.	1017	|	1200	1543	1947	2103	|	2221	0023
Kroya d.	1148	|	1253	1649	2102	2201	|	2319	0144
Purwokerto d.	1220	1118	...	...	2134	2231	2252	2352	...
Cirebon d.	|	1300	...	...	2331	0022	0036	0155	...
Jakarta Pasar Senen a.	1726	|	...	...	0233	|	|	|	...
Jakarta Gambir a.	...	1535	...	...	...	0303	0310	0440	...

6220 BANDUNG - YOGYAKARTA - SOLO - SURABAYA and MALANG

Selected services. Unless noted trains convey [1] (Eksekutif) class.

km		160	6	170	76	120	80	72	158	132
0	**Bandung** d.	0705	0815	...	...	1720	1840	...	1910	2030
124	Tasikmalaya d.	0952	1054	...	...	|	2115	...	2154	2315
156	Banjar d.	1043	1136	...	...	2100	2157	...	2245	0014
249	Kroya d.	1207	1242	1848	2224	2232	2305	2355	0016	0148
324	Kutoarjo d.	1319	1335	1956	2325	2341	0011	0052	0139	0317
387	**Yogyakarta** d.	1435	1421	2050	0014	0032	0100	0139	0237	0411
447	**Solo** Balapan d.	1525	1504	2142	0100	0119	0147	0220	0328	0502
542	Madiun d.	...	1609	2304	0209	0239	0258	0325	...	0622
629	Jombang d.	...	1712	|	0315	|	0403	|	...	0741
710	**Surabaya** Gubeng a.	...	1810	|	0411	|	0458	|	...	0845
635	Kediri d.	...	...	0035	...	0406	...	0441	...	...
705	Blitar d.	...	...	0130	...	0503	...	0536	...	...
779	**Malang** a.	...	...	0306	...	0638	...	0709	...	...

	159	5	169	157	71	75	79	119	131
Malang d.	...	...	0820	...	1425	...	...	1710	...
Blitar d.	...	...	1002	...	1557	...	...	1848	...
Kediri d.	...	...	1057	...	1652	...	...	1945	...
Surabaya Gubeng d.	...	0730	|	...	|	1730	1900	|	1945
Jombang d.	...	0824	|	...	|	1830	1953	|	2046
Madiun d.	...	0927	1233	...	1818	1936	2100	2117	2208
Solo Balapan d.	0720	1031	1352	1900	1929	2042	2205	2237	2324
Yogyakarta d.	0815	1114	1448	1951	2014	2131	2253	2328	0014
Kutoarjo d.	0913	1200	1543	2045	2103	2221	2344	0023	0110
Kroya d.	1036	1253	1649	2157	2201	2319	0051	0144	0235
Banjar d.	1228	1359	...	2352	...	...	0200	0318	0408
Tasikmalaya d.	1323	1447	...	0053	...	...	0244	0413	0503
Bandung a.	1610	1725	...	0339	...	...	0519	0656	0800

6225 SURABAJA - BANYUWANGI

km		317	288	248	112	313	116			
		3	3	23	1	3	1			
0	**Surabaja** Gubeng d.	0530	1340	1438	1622	...	2335	...	...	...
	Probolinggo d.	0753	1542	1640	1819	1905	0127	...	...	...
310	**Banyuwangi** Ketapang a.	1230	2005	...	...	2345	0545	...	...	...

	111	247	314	287	115	318			
	1	23	3	3	1	3			
Banyuwangi Ketapang d.	...	...	0515	0700	1130	1445	...	...	...
Probolinggo d.	0659	0756	0953	1119	1545	1937	...	...	...
Surabaja Gubeng a.	0852	0957	...	1311	1732	2136	...	...	...

AUSTRALIA

Capital: **Canberra** (GMT +10). 2023 Public Holidays: Jan. 1, 26, Apr. 7, 10, 25, Dec. 25, 26. There are also a number of State Holidays - please check locally.

Long-distance interstate trains are operated by Great Southern Rail (GSR) (www.gsr.com.au). Intrastate services are operated by Government owned agencies NSW Train Link (New South Wales www.transportnsw.info), Queensland Rail (QR) (Queensland www.qr.com.au), V/Line (Victoria www.vline.com.au) and Transwa (Western Australia, www.transwa.wa.gov.au). Unless indicated all trains convey first and second class seated accommodation. On GSR and some overnight trains the first class accommodation is usually a private compartment which converts to sleeping berths for night time travel. The exact offering varies by operator and by train. Most longer distance trains also convey a refreshment facility. Due to the low frequency of trains reservations are recommended, even if they are not always compulsory. NSW Train Link offer the Discovery Pass which gives either 14 day, 1 month, 3 months or 6 months unlimited travel on their rail and coach network and are available for travel in either economy or premium. Prices range from AU$ 232 for a 14 day economy pass to AU$ 550 for a 6 month premium pass. Queensland Rail have the Explorer Pass which offers either 1 month (AU$ 299) or 2 months (AU$ 389) unlimited travel on their services. They also offer the Costal Pass for unlimited travel in one direction between Brisbane and Cairns or vice versa, which is AU$ 209 and is valid for 1 month. Reservations are required for all journeys and supplements may also be payable. See www.acprail.com

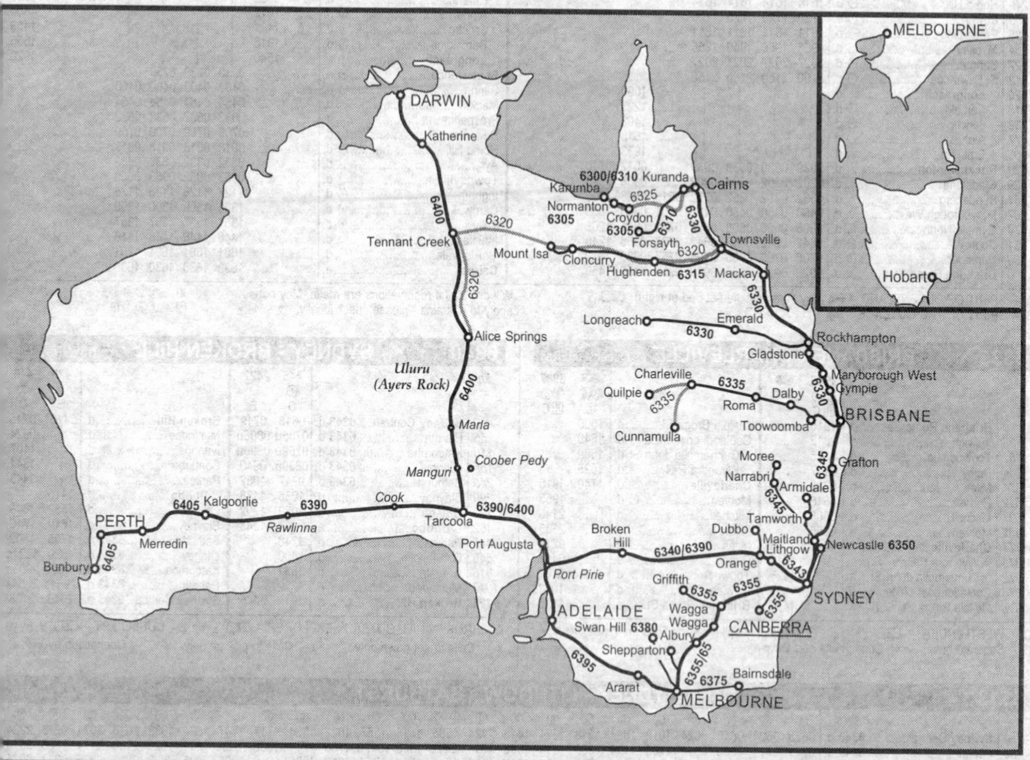

Queensland Rail	**CAIRNS - KURANDA**					**6300**
km		3K30 2	3K32		3C61 2	3C65
0	**Cairns** d.	0830	0930	**Kuranda** d.	1400	1530
	Freshwater d.	0855	0955	Freshwater d.	1532	1702
33	**Kuranda** a.	1025	1125	**Cairns** a.	1555	1725

CKST	**CAIRNS - FORSAYTH**					**6310**
km		4 ③B	4 ④B		5 ⑤B	5 ⑥B
0	**Cairns** d.	0630	...	**Forsayth** d.	0830	...
33	Kuranda d.	0810	...	Einasleigh d.	1215	...
74	Mareeba d.	0930	...	Mount Suprise a.	1415	...
194	Almaden a.	1315	...	Mount Suprise d.	...	0815
194	Almaden d.	...	0800	Almaden a.	...	1145
302	Mount Suprise a.	...	1130	Almaden d.	...	1215
302	Mount Suprise d.	...	1215	Mareeba d.	...	|
357	Einasleigh d.	...	1445	Kuranda a.	...	1650
423	**Forsayth** a.	...	1730	**Cairns** a.	...	1830

– SAVANNAHLANDER – . The Savannahlander operates from March to the last week in November. Operator: Cairns Kuranda Steam Ltd ✆ +61 7 4053 6848.

Greyhound	**TOWNSVILLE - TENNANT CREEK**					**6320**
km		489 ①	882 D		880 E	849 ②
0	**Townsville** d.	0600	...	**Alice Springs** d.	1730	...
135	Charters Towers d.	0745	...	Barrow Creek d.	2115	...
378	Hughenden d.	1030	...	**Tennant Creek** d.	0005	0300
490	Richmond d.	1235	...	Barkly Homestead d.	...	0515
634	Julia Creek d.	1405	...	Camooweal d.	...	0835
768	Cloncurry d.	1545	...	**Mount Isa** a.	...	1050
886	**Mount Isa** a.	1715	...	**Mount Isa** d.	...	1130
886	**Mount Isa** d.	1800	...	Cloncurry d.	...	1245
074	Camooweal d.	2000	...	Julia Creek d.	...	1415
353	Barkly Homestead d.	2245	...	Richmond d.	...	1600
547	**Tennant Creek** a.	0100	0130	Hughenden d.	...	1805
771	Barrow Creek d.	...	0350	Charters Towers d.	...	2040
072	**Alice Springs** a.	...	0735	**Townsville** a.	...	2225

– From Darwin (d. 0955). **E** – To Darwin (a. 1535).
Operator: Greyhound Australia ✆ 07 3258 1600.

Queensland Rail	**NORMANTON - CROYDON**					**6305**
km		5U02 ③A			5D01 ④A	
0	**Normanton** d.	0830	...	**Croydon** d.	0830	...
90	Blackbull a.	1115	...	Blackbull a.	1015	...
152	**Croydon** a.	1330	...	**Normanton** a.	1330	...

A – GULFLANDER – .

Queensland Rail	**TOWNSVILLE - MOUNT ISA**					**6315**
km		3M34 ③⑥ Ⓡ C			3231 ④⑦ Ⓡ C	
0	**Townsville** d.	1240	...	**Mount Isa** d.	1330	...
138	Charters Towers d.	1540	...	Duchess d.	1515	...
388	Hughenden d.	2020	...	Cl oncurry d.	1745	...
502	Richmond d.	2245	...	Julia Creek d.	2055	...
648	Julia Creek d.	0210	...	Richmond d.	2358	...
780	Cloncurry d.	0520	...	Hughenden d.	0240	...
890	Duchess d.	0745	...	Charters Towers d.	0705	...
977	**Mount Isa** a.	0935	...	**Townsville** a.	1010	...

C – INLANDER – 🍷.

Trans North Bus	**CAIRNS - KARUMBA**					**6325**
km		①③⑤			②④⑥	
0	**Cairns** Central d.	0630	...	**Karumba** d.	0630	...
33	Kuranda d.	0705	...	Normanton d.	0725	...
75	Mareeba d.	0735	...	Croydon d.	0925	...
109	Atherton d.	0820	...	Georgetown d.	1055	...
140	Herberton d.	0835	...	Mount Surprise d.	1240	...
160	Ravenshoe d.	0955	...	Undara d.	1305	...
211	Mount Garnet d.	1025	...	Mount Garnet d.	1355	...
287	Undara d.	1110	...	Ravenshoe d.	1450	...
321	Mount Surprise d.	1135	...	Herberton d.	1520	...
422	Georgetown d.	1335	...	Atherton d.	1540	...
579	Croydon d.	1525	...	Mareeba d.	1615	...
744	Normanton d.	1705	...	Kuranda d.	1640	...
820	**Karumba** a.	1800	...	**Cairns** Central a.	1730	...

Operator: Trans North Bus and Coach ✆ 07 4095 8644.

6330 CAIRNS, TOWNSVILLE and LONGREACH - BRISBANE

Queensland Rail

km			V982	V972	V976	V980	Q994	P968	Q992		
			①	③	⑤	⑦		①④			
			A	A	A	A	◧	B			
1681	**Cairns**	d.	0835	0835	0835	0835	...	...	...	...	...
1658	Gordonvale ⊙	d.	0901	0901	0901	0901	...	...	...	...	...
1594	Innisfail	d.	1018	1018	1018	1018	...	...	...	...	...
1546	Tully ⊙	d.	1125	1125	1125	1125	...	...	...	...	...
1503	Cardwell ⊙	d.	1209	1209	1209	1209	...	...	...	...	...
1449	Ingham ⊙	d.	1301	1301	1301	1301	...	...	...	...	...
1341	**Townsville**	d.	1454	1454	1454	1454	...	...	...	...	...
1260	Ayr	d.	1557	1557	1557	1557	...	...	...	...	...
1249	Home Hill ⊙	d.	1614	1614	1614	1614	...	...	...	...	...
1150	Bowen ⊙	d.	1720	1720	1720	1720	...	...	...	...	...
1085	Proserpine	d.	1811	1811	1811	1811	...	...	...	...	...
964	Mackay	d.	1956	1956	1956	1956	...	...	...	...	...
927	Sarina ⊙	d.	2027	2027	2027	2027	...	...	...	...	...
812	St Lawrence ⊙	d.	2150	2150	2150	2150	...	...	...	...	...
1326	**Longreach**	d.	|	|	|	|	...	1000	...	...	...
1218	Barcaldine ⊙	d.	|	|	|	|	...	1227	...	...	...
1132	Jericho ⊙	d.	|	|	|	|	...	1403	...	...	...
1077	Alpha ⊙	d.	|	|	|	|	...	1518	...	...	...
905	Emerald	d.	|	|	|	|	...	1933	...	...	...
639	**Rockhampton**	d.	0039	0039	0039	0039	...	0017	0710	...	...
529	Gladstone	d.	0202	0202	0202	0202	...	0308	0826	...	...
351	Bundaberg	d.	0352	0352	0352	0352	0515	0526	1005	...	...
267	Maryborough West	d.	0450	0450	0450	0450	0601	0635	1058	...	...
174	Gympie North	d.	0608	0608	0608	0608	0701	0811	1205	...	...
131	Cooroy ⊙	d.	0642	0642	0642	0642	0737	0856	1240	...	...
106	Nambour ⊙	d.	0705	0705	0705	0705	0757	0925	1302	...	...
0	**Brisbane** Roma St.	a.	0920	0920	0920	0920	0955	1155	1450	...	...

		Q301	PW57	VC71	VC75	VC79	VC81	Q311	QJ11	PW57
		④–②	⑥	①	③	⑤	⑥	②⑦		②
			B	A	A	A	A		⊡	B
Brisbane Roma St	d.	1100	1355	1545	1545	1545	1545	1655	1655	1810
Nambour ⊙	d.	1235	1619	1731	1731	1731	1731	1838	1838	2023
Cooroy ⊙	d.	1258	1649	1754	1754	1754	1754	1858	1858	2049
Gympie North	d.	1337	1745	1828	1828	1828	1828	1929	1929	2145
Maryborough West	d.	1440	1905	1929	1929	1929	1929	2028	2028	2305
Bundaberg	d.	1531	2036	2022	2022	2022	2022	2125	2125	0013
Gladstone	d.	1712	2309	2223	2223	2223	2223	2317	...	0246
Rockhampton	d.	1845	0103	0011	0011	0011	0011	0030	...	0440
Emerald	d.	...	0602	|	|	|	|	...	...	0940
Alpha ⊙	d.	...	1012	|	|	|	|	...	...	1350
Jericho ⊙	d.	...	1121	|	|	|	|	...	...	1459
Barcaldine ⊙	d.	...	1316	|	|	|	|	...	...	1655
Longreach	a.	...	1540	|	|	|	|	...	...	1920
St Lawrence ⊙	d.	...	...	0230	0230	0230	0230	...	...	...
Sarina ⊙	d.	...	...	0400	0400	0400	0400	...	...	...
Mackay	d.	...	...	0454	0454	0454	0454	...	...	...
Prosperine	d.	...	...	0632	0632	0632	0632	...	...	...
Bowen ⊙	d.	...	...	0709	0709	0709	0709	...	...	...
Home Hill ⊙	d.	...	...	0818	0818	0818	0818	...	...	...
Ayr	d.	...	...	0832	0832	0832	0832	...	...	...
Townsville	d.	...	...	0953	0953	0953	0953	...	...	...
Ingham ⊙	d.	...	...	1126	1126	1126	1126	...	...	...
Cardwell ⊙	d.	...	...	1300	1300	1300	1300	...	...	...
Tully ⊙	d.	...	...	1357	1357	1357	1357	...	...	...
Innisfail	d.	...	...	1446	1446	1446	1446	...	...	...
Gordonvale ⊙	d.	...	...	1601	1601	1601	1601	...	...	...
Cairns	a.	...	...	1630	1630	1630	1630	...	...	...

A – SPIRIT OF QUEENSLAND – (day time seat, lie-flat bed at night), (2), 🍸.
B – SPIRIT OF THE OUTBACK – 1 cl., ✕, (2), 🍸.
⊙ – Will only call if reservations are made. May not apply to all trains - please check locally.
◧ – ①②④⑤⑥.
⊡ – ①③④⑤.

6335 BRISBANE - CHARLEVILLE

Queensland Rail

km			3S86	🚌
			②④	③⑤
			ⓇC	⊕
0	**Brisbane** Roma St.	d.	1915	...
38	Ipswich	d.	2013	...
161	Toowoomba	d.	2325	...
244	Dalby ⊙	d.	0117	...
371	Miles ⊙	d.	0325	...
512	Roma	d.	0615	...
597	Mitchell ⊙	d.	0805	...
687	Morven ⊙	d.	0955	...
777	**Charleville**	a.	1145	1155
875	Wyandra Railway St	a.	...	1315
972	Cunnamulla John St	a.	...	1425
876	Cooladdi post office	a.	...	1305
998	Quilpie Broga St.	a.	...	1430

		🚌	3987
		③⑤	③⑤
		⊕	ⓇC
Quilpie Broga St.	d.	1500	...
Cooladdi post office	d.	1640	...
Cunnamulla John St.	d.	1500	...
Wyandra Railway St.	d.	1625	...
Charleville	d.	1740	1815
Morven ⊙	d.	...	1955
Mitchell ⊙	d.	...	2145
Roma	d.	...	2335
Miles ⊙	d.	...	0210
Dalby ⊙	d.	...	0447
Toowoomba	d.	...	0700
Ipswich	d.	...	1012
Brisbane Roma St.	a.	...	1125

C – WESTLANDER – (2), 🍸.
⊙ – Will only call if reservations are made.
⊕ – Seperate buses serve Cunnamulla and Quilpie.

6340 SYDNEY - BROKEN HILL

NSW Train Link

km				445	427
				①	
				D	E
0	**Sydney** Central	6343	d.	0618	0719
55	Penrith	6343	d.	0705u	0806u
110	Katoomba	6343	d.	0759u	0900u
155	Lithgow	6343	d.	0839u	0940
240	Bathurst	6343	d.	0947	1052
290	Blayney		d.	1035	1138
323	Orange		d.	1059	1202
462	**Dubbo**		a.	|	1345
446	Parkes		d.	1248	|
546	Condobolin		d.	1400	|
816	Ivanhoe		d.	1631	|
1017	Menindee		d.	1822	|
1125	**Broken Hill**		a.	1910	*2245**

			428	446
				②
			E	D
Broken Hill		d.	*0415**	0745
Menindee		d.	|	0924
Ivanhoe		d.	|	1107
Condobolin		d.	|	1341
Parkes		d.	|	1443
Dubbo		d.	1415	|
Orange		d.	1552	1644
Blayney		d.	1619	1716
Bathurst	6343	d.	1705	1802
Lithgow	6343	d.	1820	1921s
Katoomba	6343	d.	1902s	2003s
Penrith	6343	d.	1954s	2054s
Sydney Central	6343	a.	2048	2138

D – BROKEN HILL OUTBACK EXPLORER – (2), 🍸. E – DUBBO XPT – (12), 🍸.
s – Calls to set down only. u – Calls to pick up only. * – Connection by 🚌.

6343 SYDNEY - LITHGOW - BATHURST

Sydney Trains, NSW Train Link

km																										
				Ⓐ	Ⓒ	Ⓐ	Ⓒ	Ⓐ	Ⓒ	Ⓐ	Ⓒ	Ⓐ	Ⓒ	④–②	Ⓐ	③	Ⓐ	Ⓒ	Ⓐ		Ⓒ	Ⓐ	Ⓐ	Ⓒ	Ⓐ	Ⓒ
0	**Sydney** Central	6340	d.	0623	0624	0818	0824	1018	1024	1218	1224	1418	1424	1505	1518	1557	1617	1624	1717	1747	1824	1833	2018	2024	2218	2224
55	Penrith	6340	d.	0711	0714	0906	0914	1106	1114	1306	1314	1506	1514	1552u	1606	1647u	1706	1714	1806	1843u	1914	1921	2106	2114	2306	2314
110	Katoomba	6340	d.	0822	0825	1017	1025	1217	1225	1417	1425	1617	1625	1648	1717	1747	1810	1825	1910	1938	2025	2032	2217	2225	0017	0025
127	Mount Victoria		d.	0842	0845	1037	1045	1237	1245	1437	1445	1637	1645	1704	1737	1803	1830	1845	1932	1958	2045	2052	2237	2245	0037	0045
155	**Lithgow**	6340	a.	0910	0915	1105	1115	1305	1315	1505	1515	1705	1715	1734	1816	1829	1859	1915	2004	2026	2114	2119	2309	2314	0109	0114
240	**Bathurst**	6340	a.	...	...	...	...	...	...	...	...	...	...	1852	...	1939	...	...	...	2134	...	...	...	...	...	...

			Ⓒ	Ⓐ	Ⓒ	Ⓐ	Ⓒ	Ⓐ	Ⓒ	④–②	③	Ⓐ	Ⓒ	Ⓐ	Ⓒ	Ⓐ	Ⓒ	Ⓐ	Ⓒ	Ⓐ	Ⓒ	Ⓐ	Ⓒ	Ⓐ	Ⓒ
Bathurst	6340	d.	...	...	...	0546	0607	...	...	0735	0735	...	...	...	...	...	...	...	...	...	...	...	...	...	...
Lithgow	6340	d.	0549	0608	0648	0655	0716	0724	0748	0842	0842	0924	0948	1124	1148	1330	1348	1530	1548	1730	1748	1930	1948	2130	2219
Mount Victoria		d.	0618	0637	0718	0723	0743	0755	0818	0910	0910	0955	1018	1155	1218	1401	1418	1601	1618	1801	1818	2001	2018	2201	2248
Katoomba	6340	d.	0638	0657	0738	0740	0759	0814	0838	0927	0929	1014	1038	1214	1238	1420	1438	1620	1638	1820	1838	2020	2038	2220	2308
Penrith	6340	d.	0752	0800	0852	0838s	0856s	0924	0952	1028s	1044s	1124	1152	1324	1352	1530	1552	1730	1752	1930	1952	2130	2152	2330	0022
Sydney Central	6340	a.	0841	0850	0941	0927	0944	1015	1041	1119	1146	1215	1241	1415	1441	1621	1641	1820	1841	2021	2041	2221	2241	0022	0112

s – Calls to set down only. u – Calls to pick up only.

6345 BRISBANE, ARMIDALE and MOREE - SYDNEY

NSW Train Link

During New South Wales daylight saving services will arrive and depart Queensland locations one hour earlier than shown.

km			186	034	2138	036	244	224	032	
			🚌	ⓇF	Ⓐ	ⓇG	ⓇH	ⓇJ	ⓇK	
987	**Brisbane** Roma Street	d.	...	*1430**	...	...	...	...	0555	...
805	Casino	d.	...	1930	...	...	...	...	0820	...
696	Grafton City	d.	...	2058	...	0515	...	...	0953	...
608	Coffs Harbour	d.	...	2210	...	0626	...	...	1105	...
	Nambucca Heads	d.	2150	2251d	...	0708	...	...	1147	...
	Macksville	d.	2220	2305d	...	0721	...	...	1200	...
504	Kempsey	d.	...	2347	...	0805	...	...	1243	...
455	Wauchope	d.	...	0024	...	0844	...	...	1322	...
379	Taree	d.	...	0131	*0600**	0952	...	...	1441	...
579	**Armidale**	d.	...	|	|	|	...	0840	|	...
455	Tamworth	d.	...	|	|	|	...	1027	|	...
676	**Moree**	d.	...	|	|	|	0805	|	|	...
579	Narrabri	d.	...	|	|	|	0910	|	|	...
486	Gunnedah	d.	...	|	|	|	1014	|	|	...
411	Werris Creek	d.	...	|	|	|	1105	1105	|	...
315	Scone	d.	...	|	|	|	1228	1228	|	...
289	Muswellbrook	d.	...	|	|	|	1248	1248	|	...
193	Maitland	d.	...	0406	|	1253	1355	1355	1730	...
163	Broadmeadow	d.	...	0428	0930	1319	1418	1418	1752	...
90	Gosford	d.	...	0529s	1037s	1420s	1520s	1520s	1857s	...
34	Hornsby	d.	...	0612s	1122s	1504s	1603s	1603s	1938s	...
0	**Sydney** Central	a.	...	0650	1159	1544	1639	1639	2012	...

		033	243	223	035	031	2157	185	
		ⓇF	ⓇH	ⓇJ	ⓇG	ⓇK	Ⓐ	🚌	
Sydney Central	d.	0708	0930	0930	1141	1441	1515	...	...
Hornsby	d.	0747u	1003u	1003u	1216u	1517u	1551u	...	...
Gosford	d.	0829u	1044u	1044u	1258u	1600u	1634u	...	...
Broadmeadow	d.	0933	1145	1145	1404	1704	1741	...	...
Maitland	d.	0959	1210	1210	1430	1727	|	...	...
Muswellbrook	d.	|	1316	1316	|	|	|	...	...
Scone	d.	|	1337	1337	|	|	|	...	...
Werris Creek	d.	|	1457	1457	|	|	|	...	...
Gunnedah	d.	|	1545	|	|	|	|	...	...
Narrabri	a.	|	1652	|	|	|	|	...	...
Moree	a.	|	1800	|	|	|	|	...	...
Tamworth	a.	|	...	1537	|	|	|	...	...
Armidale	a.	|	...	1735	|	|	|	...	...
Taree	d.	1240	...	...	1725	2008	*2052**	...	...
Wauchope	d.	1347	...	...	1831	2113	...	...	...
Kempsey	d.	1425	...	...	1910	2152	...	...	...
Macksville	d.	1506	...	...	1955	2234d	...	2245	...
Nambucca Heads	a.	1518	...	...	2009	|	...	2305	...
Coffs Harbour	d.	1557	...	...	2050	2335	...	...	...
Grafton City	d.	1711	...	...	2215	0049	...	...	...
Casino	a.	1840	...	...	...	0219	...	...	...
Brisbane Roma Street	a.	*2234**	...	...	...	0453	...	...	...

F – CASINO XPT – 1 cl., (2) Casino - Sydney; (12) Sydney - Casino.
G – GRAFTON XPT – (12), 🍸.
H – MOREE XPLORER – (12), 🍸.
J – ARMIDALE XPLORER – (12), 🍸.
K – BRISBANE XPT – (12) Brisbane - Sydney; 1 cl., (2) Sydney - Brisbane.

d – Will only call if reservations are made.
s – Calls to set down only.
u – Calls to pick up only.
* – Connection by 🚌.

Sydney Trains

NEWCASTLE - SYDNEY

6350

km		Ⓐ	Ⓐ	Ⓐ	Ⓐ	Ⓐ	Ⓐ	Ⓐ	Ⓐ	Ⓐ		Ⓐ	Ⓐ	Ⓐ	Ⓐ	Ⓐ	Ⓐ	Ⓐ	Ⓐ	Ⓐ	Ⓐ	Ⓐ
0	**Newcastle** I'change....d.	0230	0423	0502	0520	0548	0620	0642	0724	0734	and at the	1420	1434	1512	1534	1624	1634	1724	1824	1834	1924	1945
	Hamilton....d.	0232	0427	0504	0523	0550	0623	0645	0727	0738	same minutes	1422	1438	1515	1537	1627	1638	1727	1827	1838	1927	1948
88	Gosford....d.	0358	0539	0609	0637	0704	0734	0807	0837	0902	past each	1533	1602	1638	1701	1738	1802	1838	1937	2005	2038	2114
168	**Sydney** Central....a.	0528	0657	0726	0757	0827	0857	0929	0959	1029	hour until ◨	1659	1729	1759	1829	1859	1929	1959	2059	2129	2159	2239

	Ⓐ	Ⓐ		Ⓒ	Ⓒ	Ⓒ	Ⓒ	Ⓒ	Ⓒ	Ⓒ	Ⓒ	Ⓒ	Ⓒ	Ⓒ	Ⓒ	Ⓒ	Ⓒ	Ⓒ	Ⓒ	Ⓒ	Ⓒ	Ⓒ	Ⓒ
lewcastle Interchange....d.	2046	2146	...	0246	0348	0453	0543	0653	0743	0853	0943	1053	1143	1253	1343	1453	1543	1653	1755	1853	1929	2029	2156
lamilton....d.	2048	2148	...	0248	0350	0455	0545	0655	0745	0855	0945	1055	1145	1255	1345	1455	1545	1655	1757	1855	1931	2031	2158
iosford....d.	2213	2313	...	0414	0512	0607	0706	0807	0906	1006	1106	1206	1306	1406	1506	1606	1706	1806	1918	2006	2057	2157	2324
ydney Central....a.	2339	0039	...	0544	0644	0729	0829	0929	1029	1129	1229	1329	1429	1529	1629	1729	1829	1929	2035	2129	2229	2329	0101

	Ⓐ	Ⓐ	Ⓐ	Ⓐ	Ⓐ	Ⓐ	Ⓐ	Ⓐ		Ⓐ	Ⓐ	Ⓐ	Ⓐ	Ⓐ	Ⓐ	Ⓐ	Ⓐ	Ⓐ	Ⓐ	Ⓐ	Ⓐ	Ⓐ
ydney Central....d.	0147	0345	0445	0515	0545	0615	0645	0715	and at	1345	1415	1515	1550	1620	1650	1720	1750	1820	1915	2015	2115	2148
iosford....d.	0311	0512	0612	0635	0713	0736	0813	0840	the same minutes	1514	1537	1636	1707	1741	1811	1841	1911	1941	2036	2136	2236	2316
lamilton....a.	0436	0636	0736	0746	0837	0859	0938	0955	past each	1642	1704	1746	1814	1854	1930	1951	2025	2053	2158	2258	2358	0043
ewcastle Interchange....a.	0440	0640	0740	0750	0841	0903	0942	0959	hour until	1645	1708	1749	1817	1858	1934	1955	2029	2057	2202	2302	0002	0046

	Ⓐ	Ⓐ		Ⓒ	Ⓒ	Ⓒ	Ⓒ	Ⓒ	Ⓒ	Ⓒ	Ⓒ	Ⓒ	Ⓒ	Ⓒ	Ⓒ	Ⓒ	Ⓒ	Ⓒ	Ⓒ	Ⓒ	Ⓒ	Ⓒ	Ⓒ
ydney Central....d.	2248	2348	...	0147	0448	0548	0715	0818	0918	1018	1118	1218	1318	1418	1518	1618	1718	1818	1918	2018	2148	2248	2348
iosford....d.	0019	0117	...	0311	0618	0713	0839	0939	1039	1139	1239	1339	1439	1539	1639	1739	1839	1939	2039	2144	2316	0016	0116
lamilton....a.	0146	0244	...	0436	0743	*0844*	0950	1058	1150	1258	1347	1459	1550	1657	1750	1857	1950	2057	2155	2310	0040	0140	0240
ewcastle Interchange....a.	0150	0248	...	0440	0747	*0848*	0954	1102	1154	1302	1352	1503	1554	1702	1754	1902	1954	2102	2159	2314	0044	0144	0244

◨ – Timings may vary by up to 5 minutes - earlier departures possible. 15xx train from Newcastle departs 1512.

NSW Train Link, V/Line

SYDNEY - CANBERRA, GRIFFITH and MELBOURNE

6355

km		641 ⑥ A	781 🚌	631 B	623 C	633 B	641 ③ A	621 D	635 Ⓒ B	635 Ⓐ B
0	**Sydney** Central....d.	0705	...	0705	0740	1201	1201	2042	1736	1742
143	Moss Vale....d.	0847	...	0847	0922	1343	1343	2224	1918	1940
222	Goulburn....d.	0939	...	0939	1013	1432	1432	2314	2007	2029
318	Queanbeyan....d.	|	0905	1059	|	1553	|	|	2128	2150
326	Canberra Kingston....a.	|	0922	1120	|	1613	|	|	2144	2205
320	Yass Junction....d.	1103	1045	...	1120	...	1549	0022d	...	...
383	Harden....d.	1153	1152e	...	1210d	...	1639	0112d	...	...
427	Cootamundra....d.	1226	1222	...	1244	...	1712	0147	...	...
483	Junee....d.	1307	...	...	1324	...	1753	0225	...	...
580	Narrandera....d.	1421	...	...	|	...	1907	|	...	...
658	**Griffith**....a.	1525	...	...	|	...	2011	|	...	...
518	Wagga Wagga....a.	...	...	...	1353	...	...	0252	...	...
547	The Rock....d.	...	...	...	1413d	...	...	0310d	...	...
594	Culcairn....d.	...	...	...	1440d	...	...	0337d	...	...
643	**Albury**....6365 a.	...	...	...	1510	...	...	0408	...	...
727	Wangaratta....6365 d.	...	...	...	1552	...	...	0450	...	...
765	Benalla....6365 d.	...	...	...	1617	...	...	0514	...	...
961	**Melbourne** S Cross....6365 a.	...	...	...	1830	...	...	0730	...	...

	632 B	634 B		642 ④⑦ A	624 C	636 B		782 🚌	622 D
Melbourne S Cross....6365 d.	...	...	...	...	0830	...	...	...	1950
Benalla....6365 d.	...	...	...	...	1041	...	...	...	2154
Wangaratta....6365 d.	...	...	...	...	1106	...	...	...	2220
Albury....6365 d.	...	...	...	...	1149	...	...	...	2305
Culcairn....d.	...	...	...	...	1221d	...	...	...	2334d
The Rock....d.	...	...	...	...	1249d	...	...	...	0002d
Wagga Wagga....d.	...	...	...	...	1307	...	...	...	0022
Griffith....d.	...	...	...	0725	|	...	...	...	|
Narrandera....d.	...	...	...	0827	|	...	...	...	|
Junee....d.	...	...	...	0940	1351	...	...	...	0048
Cootamundra....d.	...	...	...	1032	1438	...	...	1450	0135
Harden....d.	...	...	...	1108d	1514d	...	...	1521e	0215d
Yass Junction....d.	...	...	...	1200	1605	...	...	1620	0306d
Canberra Kingston....d.	0655	1150	...	|	|	1708	...	1740	|
Queanbeyan....d.	0704	1159	...	|	|	1717	...	1755	|
Goulburn....d.	0822	1316	...	1320	1714	1835	...	...	0413
Moss Vale....d.	0914	1414	...	1414	1802	1927	...	...	0501
Sydney Central....a.	1104	1603	...	1603	1947	2116	...	...	0659

– GRIFFITH XPLORER – (12) 🍸.
– CANBERRA XPLORER – (12) 🍸.
C – MELBOURNE XPT – (12) 🍸.
D – MELBOURNE XPT – 🛏 1 cl., (12) ✕.
d – Will only call if reservations are made.
e – Harden **Town**.
s – Calls to set down only.
u – Calls to pick up only.

/Line

MELBOURNE - SHEPPARTON

6360

km		Ⓐ	Ⓐ		Ⓒ			Ⓐ	Ⓐ		Ⓐ	Ⓒ			Ⓐ		Ⓐ	Ⓒ		Ⓐ	Ⓒ		Ⓐ	
0	**Melbourne** S Cross.....6365 d.	0555	0705	...	0916	...	...	0926	1036	...	1236	1236	...	...	1436	...	1607	1636	...	1733	1836	...	1907	...
99	Seymour....6365 d.	0735	0833	...	1055	...	...	1107	1159	...	1408	1413	...	...	1603	...	1752	1759	...	1911	2007	...	2040	...
147	Murchison East....d.	0809	|	...	1129	...	...	1141	|	...	1442	1447	...	...	*1703**	...	1826	|	...	|	2041	...	2114	...
	Murchison....d.	|	|	...	|	...	...	|	*1300**	...	|	|	...	...	*1706**	...	|	*1900**	...	*2012**	|	...	|	...
182	**Shepparton**....a.	0841	*0958**	...	1200	...	...	1212	*1334**	...	1514	1519	...	...	*1738**	...	1857	*1934**	...	*2046**	2113	...	2145	...

	Ⓐ	Ⓐ		Ⓒ	Ⓐ		Ⓒ	Ⓐ			Ⓐ		Ⓒ	Ⓐ		Ⓒ	Ⓒ		Ⓐ	Ⓐ		Ⓐ	
hepparton....d.	0512	0624	...	0702	*0736**	...	*0757**	*0831**	...	0944	*1040**	...	1242	1258	...	*1417**	1602	...	1605	*1636**	...	*1813**	...
urchison....d.	|	|	...	|	*0810**	...	*0831**	*0901**	...	|	*1107**	...	|	|	...	*1451**	|	...	|	*1710**	...	*1845**	...
urchison East....d.	0540	0652	...	0730	|	...	*0833**	|	...	1012	|	...	1310	1326	...	*1453**	1630	...	1633	|	...	|	...
eymour....6365 d.	0618	0730	...	0808	0916	...	0937	1016	...	1054	1216	...	1348	1404	...	1557	1708	...	1711	1816	...	1953	...
elbourne S Cross....6365 a.	0802	0910	...	0937	1039	...	1057	1139	...	1221	1339	...	1517	1539	...	1717	1837	...	1848	1941	...	2119	...

– Connection by 🚌.

/Line

MELBOURNE - ALBURY

6365

km			C	Ⓐ	Ⓐ		Ⓐ		D	
0	**Melbourne** S Cross....6360 d.	0707	0830	0926	0926	1204	1436	1802	1950	...
99	Seymour....6360 d.	0826	0948u	1102	1102	1323	1603	1921	2059u	...
96	Benalla....d.	0924	1041	*1227**	|	1421	*1728**	2019	2154	...
34	Wangaratta....d.	0949	1106	*1302**	|	1444	*1803**	2144	2220	...
01	Wodonga....d.	1029	|	...	*1342**	1526	*1848**	2124	|	...
18	**Albury**....a.	1043	1149	...	*1352**	1540	*1858**	2138	2305	...

	D	Ⓐ	Ⓐ		Ⓐ		C		
Albury....d.	0408	*0521**	...	0645	*0901**	1251	1510	1727	...
Wodonga....d.	|	*0531**	...	0656	*0911**	1302	|	1738	...
Wangaratta....d.	0450	|	*0601**	0738	*1001**	1344	1552	1820	...
Benalla....d.	0514	|	*0636**	0803	*1036**	1409	1617	1845	...
Seymour....6360 d.	0610s	0816	0816	0902	1216	1508	1711s	1944	...
Melbourne S Cross....6360 a.	0730	0947	0947	1027	1339	1633	1830	2145	...

– MELBOURNE XPT – (12) 🍸 Sydney - Melbourne and v.v.
– MELBOURNE XPT – 🛏 1 cl., (12) ✕ Sydney - Melbourne and v.v.
s – Calls to set down only.
u – Calls to pick up only.
* – Connection by 🚌.

/Line

MELBOURNE - WARRNAMBOOL

6370

km		Ⓒ	Ⓐ	Ⓐ	Ⓒ	Ⓐ	Ⓐ	Ⓐ	Ⓒ	Ⓐ
0	**Melbourne** S Cross....⊡ d.	0655	0720	1013	1300	1308	1530	1706	1900	1912
73	Geelong....⊡ d.	0811	0823	1118	1412	1410	1631	1811	2001	2014
33	Colac....d.	0921	0926	1225	1516	1519	*1808**	1920	2104	2119
267	**Warrnambool**....a.	1042	1054	1349	1636	1640	...	2040	2224	2240

	Ⓐ	Ⓐ	Ⓒ	Ⓐ	Ⓒ	Ⓐ	Ⓐ	Ⓒ	Ⓐ
Warrnambool....d.	...	0612	0740	0928	1144	1223	1513	1732	1736
Colac....d.	*0600**	0729	0858	1045	1302	1340	1633	1850	1853
Geelong....⊡ d.	0736	0839	1003	1152	1409	1450	1742	1959	2004
Melbourne S Cross....⊡ a.	0837	0940	1102	1255	1521	1555	1845	2109	2107

– Connection by 🚌.

⊡ – Frequent additional services are available Melbourne - Geelong and v.v.

/Line

MELBOURNE - TRARALGON - BAIRNSDALE

6375

km		Ⓐ	⑥	Ⓐ	†	⑥	Ⓐ	Ⓐ	Ⓒ	Ⓐ
0	**Melbourne** S Cross....⊖ d.	0717	0754	0826	1023	1223	1323	1657	1823	1833
32	Dandenong....⊖ d.	0804u	0831u	0910u	1109u	1309u	1409u	1748u	1909u	1919u
01	Warragul....⊖ d.	0859	0924	1004	1203	1403	1503	1840	2001	2014
31	Moe....⊖ d.	0916	0945	1025	1224	1424	1524	1855	2020	2033
45	Morwell....⊖ d.	0934	0955	1039	1239	1439	1539	1905	2031	2044
59	**Traralgon**....⊖ d.	0946	1009	1048	1250	1450	1551	1917	2046	2059
07	Sale....d.	1021	1044	*1143**	1326	1525	1626	*2012**	2123	2136
76	**Bairnsdale**....a.	1115	1139	*1243**	*1500**	1619	1720	*2112**	2217	2230

	Ⓐ	⑥	Ⓐ	†	⚒	†	Ⓐ	Ⓒ	Ⓐ
Bairnsdale....d.	*0427**	0614	0614	0734	1254	*1254**	*1515**	1653	1806
Sale....d.	*0527**	0708	0708	0828	1348	1409	*1615**	1747	1900
Traralgon....⊖ d.	0632	0746	0746	0906	1427	1447	1720	1825	1938
Morwell....⊖ d.	0640	0756	0756	0916	1435	1455	1728	1833	1946
Moe....⊖ d.	0649	0807	0807	0927	1444	1505	1741	1843	2001
Warragul....⊖ d.	0704	0826	0826	0946	1504	1524	1802	1903	2021
Dandenong....⊖ d.	0755s	0920s	0920s	1040s	1557s	1619s	1900s	2000s	2120s
Melbourne S Cross....⊖ a.	0847	1000	1006	1126	1645	1705	1948	2044	2205

- Calls to set down only.
u – Calls to pick up only.
* – Connection by 🚌.
⊖ – Additional trains run approximately hourly.

MELBOURNE - BENDIGO - SWAN HILL and ECHUCA

Most trains 2nd class only — V/Line

km																								
		Ⓐ		Ⓒ			🚌			Ⓐ		🚌			①③⑤ 🚌	②④ 🚌		Ⓐ	Ⓒ	Ⓐ		Ⓒ	Ⓐ	⑤
0	**Melbourne** S Cross ◧ d.	0702	0739	0905	...	1006	...	1106	...	...	1206	...	...	1306	...	...	...	1506	1806	1808	...	1843	1908	...
38	Sunbury ◧ d.	0732	|	0935	...	1035	...	1135	...	...	1235	...	...	1335	...	...	...	1537	1835	|	...	|	1940	...
78	Woodend ◧ d.	0803	0848	1004	...	1105	...	1205	...	...	1305	...	...	1405	...	...	...	1606	1905	1919	...	1950	2009	...
92	Kyneton ◧ d.	0812	0858	1012	...	1112	...	1212	...	...	1312	...	...	1412	...	...	...	1614	1912	1929	...	2000	2017	...
125	Castlemaine ◧ d.	0831	0926	1031	...	1132	...	1232	...	...	1332	...	...	1432	...	...	...	1632	1932	1952	...	2023	2035	...
162	**Bendigo** ◧ a.	0858	0955	1057	...	1158	1217	1257	...	1310	1357	1420	...	1457	1507	1509	...	1656	1959	2021	...	2052	2100	2110
289	Kerang a.	|	1137	|	...	...	1353	...	...	|	...	|	...	...	|	1729	...	|	|	2203	...	2233	...	2320
345	**Swan Hill** a.	|	1224	|	...	...	1435	...	...	|	...	|	...	...	1817	1815	...	|	|	2250	...	2321	...	0004
222	Rochester a.	0953	...	1155	...	...	...	...	...	1400	...	1515	...	...	...	...	...	1755	2052	...	...	...	...	...
248	**Echuca** a.	1024	...	1226	...	...	...	...	...	1431	...	1538	...	...	...	...	...	1826	2123	...	...	...	...	...

	⚒		†	⚒ 🚌		①③⑤ 🚌	②④ 🚌	⑥ 🚌	Ⓒ	Ⓐ	Ⓐ 🚌			Ⓑ 🚌		† 🚌		⚒	Ⓐ	Ⓒ	⑤ 🚌	Ⓐ	†
Echuca d.	0715	...	0854	0855	...	...	...	...	...	1104	...	...	...	1245	...	...	...	...	1504	1554	...	...	...
Rochester d.	0738	...	0917	0925	...	...	...	...	...	1127	...	...	...	1310	...	...	...	...	1527	1617	...	...	...
Swan Hill d.	|	0654	|	|	...	0856	0856	0940	...	|	1040	...	...	|	...	1250	...	1335	|	|	1550	...	1636
Kerang d.	|	0738	|	|	...	|	0946	1026	...	|	1126	...	...	|	...	1336	...	1419	|	|	1630	...	1720
Bendigo ◧ d.	0847	0920	1026	1015	1026	1211	1211	1157	1226	1226	1257	...	1326	1410	1426	1507	1526	1601	1626	1726	1845	1901	1902
Castlemaine ◧ d.	0908	0948	1049	...	1049	...	...	...	1249	1249	...	...	1349	...	1449	...	1549	1628	1649	1749	...	1926	1929
Kyneton ◧ d.	0928	1012	1109	...	1109	...	...	...	1309	1309	...	...	1409	...	1509	...	1609	1655	1709	1809	...	1953	1956
Woodend ◧ d.	0938	1022	1118	...	1118	...	...	...	1318	1318	...	...	1418	...	1518	...	1618	|	1718	1818	...	2002	2006
Sunbury ◧ d.	1011	|	1152	...	1152	...	...	...	1352	1352	...	...	1452	...	1552	...	1652	|	1752	1852	...	2035	|
Melbourne Southern Cross ◧ a.	1044	1130	1224	...	1228	...	...	...	1424	1425	...	...	1525	...	1624	...	1730	1811	1832	1924	...	2109	2112

* – Connection by 🚌.

◧ – Melbourne - Bendigo and v.v. trains run approximately hourly most of the day.

6385 MELBOURNE - BALLARAT - MARYBOROUGH and ARARAT

V/Line

km																								
		Ⓐ	Ⓒ	Ⓐ	⑥	Ⓐ	Ⓒ	Ⓐ		Ⓒ	Ⓐ	A	Ⓐ	Ⓒ	Ⓐ	Ⓐ		⑤	Ⓐ	Ⓐ	Ⓒ	Ⓒ	Ⓐ	⑦
0	**Melbourne** Southern Cross d.	0753	0814	0836	0914	0916	1014	1116	...	1214	1236	1316	1436	1514	1516	1639	...	1658	1658	1738	1814	1814	1818	1914
41	Melton d.	0830	0851	0913	0951	0953	1051	1153	...	1251	1313	1353	1513	1551	1553	|	...	|	|	|	1851	1851	1848	1951
53	Bacchus Marsh d.	0838	0858	0921	0958	1001	1058	1201	...	1258	1321	1401	1521	1558	1601	1717	...	1736	1736	1816	1858	1858	1856	1958
82	Ballan d.	0857	0916	0940	1016	1020	1116	1220	...	1316	1340	1420	1540	1616	1620	1735	...	1754	1754	1834	1916	1916	1914	2016
122	**Ballarat** a.	0921	0943	1001	1043	1041	1143	1241	...	1343	1401	1441	1601	1643	1641	1755	...	1814	1814	1854	1943	1943	1934	2037
180	**Maryborough** a.	|	|	|	*1159**	1143	|	|	...	|	|	*1558**	|	|	|	1857	...	*1931**	|	|	|	2044	|	|
210	**Ararat** a.	1022	1042	*1137**	...	...	*1308**	1342	...	1442	*1521**	...	1702	*1820**	*1821**	...	...	...	1915	*2020**	2042	...	2035	*2202**

	Ⓐ	Ⓐ	⚒	⚒	B	Ⓐ	⑦	⑦	⑥	⑥	Ⓒ		Ⓐ	⑦	Ⓒ	Ⓐ	Ⓒ	Ⓐ	Ⓐ	Ⓐ	⑦	Ⓐ	⑦
Ararat d.	...	0616	...	0713	...	*0730**	...	0813	...	*0838**	*0942**	...	*1031**	*1045**	1114	1148	*1348**	1428	...	*1512**	1614	1717	*1750**
Maryborough d.	*0410**	|	0709	|	*0741**	|	0809	|	*0856**	|	|	...	|	|	|	|	|	|	1457	|	|	|	|
Ballarat d.	0524	0724	0819	0819	0924	0924	0920	0920	1020	1020	1120	...	1204	1220	1220	1244	1520	1524	1604	1648	1720	1814	1920
Ballan d.	0542	0742	0837	0837	0942	0942	0938	0938	1038	1038	1138	...	1222	1238	1238	1302	1538	1542	1623	1712	1738	1835	1938
Bacchus Marsh d.	0559	0800	0856	0856	0959	0959	0956	0956	1056	1056	1156	...	1239	1256	1256	1319	1556	1559	1640	1738	1756	1858	1956
Melton d.	0608	|	0909	0909	1010	1010	1009	1009	1109	1109	1209	...	1250	1309	1309	1330	1609	1610	1650	1747	1809	1907	2009
Melbourne Southern Cross a.	0640	0846	0951	0951	1051	1051	1048	1048	1148	1148	1248	...	1331	1348	1348	1411	1648	1651	1722	1828	1848	1947	2048

A – ①②④.

B – ①②④⑤.

6390 SYDNEY - PERTH

Journey Beyond

km		WE1 [R] ③ C			WE2 [R] ⑦ C	
0	**Sydney** Central d.	1355	③	East **Perth** d.	1000	⑦
1125	Broken Hill ◇ a.	◇	④	Nullarbor d.	◇	①
1688	**Adelaide** Parklands a.	1540	:	Cook d.	◇	:
1688	**Adelaide** Parklands d.	2120	:	**Adelaide** Parklands a.	0745	②
	Cook a.	◇	⑤	**Adelaide** Parklands d.	1015	:
	Nullarbor d.	◇	:	Broken Hill d.	◇	:
4343	East **Perth** a.	1500	⑥	**Sydney** Central a.	1215	③

C – INDIAN PACIFIC – 🛏 1 cl., ✕ Sydney - Adelaide - Perth and v.v.

◇ – Off train excursion.

6395 MELBOURNE - ADELAIDE

Journey Beyond

km		8701 [R] ① D	8701 [R] ⑤ D		8702 [R] ④ D	8702 [R] ⑦ D
0	**Melbourne** S Cross d.	0805	0805	**Adelaide** Parklands d.	0655	0745
74	Geelong North Shore d.	0935	0915	Murray Bridge d.	0910	0935
265	Ararat d.	1135	1115	Nhill d.	1236	1301
381	Horsham d.	1251	1300	Dimboola d.	1310	1334
416	Dimboola d.	1320	1328	Horsham d.	1337	1401
454	Nhill d.	1347	1355	Ararat d.	1455	1519
734	Murray Bridge d.	1610	1618	Geelong North Shore d.	1740	1723
828	**Adelaide** Parklands a.	1800	1805	**Melbourne** S Cross a.	1850	1850

D – THE OVERLAND – (12) 🍸 Melbourne - Adelaide and v.v.

6400 DARWIN - ADELAIDE

Journey Beyond

km		8506 [R] ⑥ Ed			8506 [R] ③ Ee			8506 [R] ③ Ef	
0	**Darwin** △ d.	0900	⑥	...	1000	③	...	1000	③
310	Katherine d.	◇	⑥	...	◇	③	...	◇	③
	Newcastle Waters d.	|	:	...	|	:	...	|	:
947	Tennant Creek d.	|	:	...	|	:	...	|	:
1414	**Alice Springs** a.	1115	⑦	...	0910	④	...	0910	④
1414	**Alice Springs** d.	2145	⑦	...	1245	④	...	2215	④
2661	Port Augusta d.	|	:	...	|	:	...	|	:
2751	Manguri d.	◇	①	...	◇	④	...	◇	⑤
2973	**Adelaide** Parklands a.	1150	②	...	1300	⑤	...	1050	⑥

	8505 [R] ③ Ed				8505 [R] ⑦ Eg			
Adelaide Parklands d.	1210	③	...	...	1215	⑦	...	...
Marla d.	◇	④	...	...	◇	①	...	...
Port Augusta d.	|	:	...	...	|	:	...	...
Alice Springs a.	1345	④	...	...	1345	①	...	...
Alice Springs d.	1815	④	...	...	1815	①	...	...
Tennant Creek d.	|	:	...	...	|	:	...	...
Newcastle Waters d.	|	:	...	...	|	:	...	...
Katherine a.	◇	⑤	...	...	◇	②	...	...
Darwin △ a.	1950	⑤	...	...	1730	②	...	...

E – THE GHAN – 🛏 1 cl., ✕ 🍸 Adelaide - Darwin and v.v.

d – Apr. - Sept. e – Mar. and Nov. f – Apr. - Oct. g – Mar. - Nov.

△ – Station is at Berrimah. 🚌 to / from Darwin city centre provided by operator.

◇ – Off train Excursion.

6405 KALGOORLIE - PERTH - BUNBURY

TransWA

All trains convey (2) 🍸 and require [R]. Trains will only call at intermediate stations if bookings are made in advance.

km		AVO2 ①–⑤	PL02 ①③⑤	PA02 ②④⑥	MO6 ⑤	MO2 ①	MO4 ③	PA56 ⑦	PA52 ①	PA54 ⑤
0	**Kalgoorlie** d.	...	0705	0705	...	...	...	1405	1500	1500
250	Southern Cross d.	...	0912	0912	...	...	...	1612	1707	1715
371	Merredin d.	...	1023	1023	1305	1310	1310	1723	1818	1829
427	Kellerberrin d.	...	1102s	1102	1336	1341	1341	1802	1857	1908
531	Northam d.	0630	1209	1209	1441	1446	1454	1907	2002	2013
641	Midland d.	0750	1323	1323	1555	1600	1610	2020	2115	2125
653	**East Perth** a.	...	1345	1345	1620	1620	1630	2040	2135	2145

	PL01 ①③⑤	PA01 ②④⑥		M01 ①③⑤	PA55 ⑦	PA51 ①		PA53 ⑤	AVO1 ①–⑤
East Perth d.	0710	0710	...	0850	1410	1515	...	1515	...
Midland d.	0727	0727	...	0912	1427	1533	...	1532	1750
Northam d.	0850u	0850	...	1027	1547	1645	...	1655	1910
Kellerberrin d.	0956u	0956	...	1138	1653	1750	...	1800	...
Merredin d.	1027	1027	...	1210	1728	1821	...	1831	...
Southern Cross d.	1144	1144	...	...	1845	1938	...	1948	...
Kalgoorlie a.	1400	1400	...	...	2100	2150	...	2205	...

km		B03	B55							
0	**Perth** City d.	0930	1755	...	...	...	...	...	...	...
30	Armadale d.	0956	1825	...	...	...	...	...	...	...
85	Pinjarra d.	1042	1911	...	...	...	...	...	...	...
111	Waroona d.	1100	1929	...	...	...	...	...	...	...
136	Harvey d.	1121	1950	...	...	...	...	...	...	...
157	Brunswick Junction d.	1136	2005	...	...	...	...	...	...	...
183	**Bunbury** a.	1155	2025	...	...	...	...	...	...	...

	B02	B56							
Bunbury d.	0600	1445	...	...	...	...	...	...	...
Brunswick Junction d.	0615	1502	...	...	...	...	...	...	...
Harvey d.	0631	1517	...	...	...	...	...	...	...
Waroona d.	0654	1538	...	...	...	...	...	...	...
Pinjarra d.	0710	1555	...	...	...	...	...	...	...
Armadale d.	0752	1639	...	...	...	...	...	...	...
Perth City a.	0830	1715	...	...	...	...	...	...	...

s – Calls to set down only.

u – Calls to pick up only.

NEW ZEALAND

Capital: **Wellington** (GMT +12, add one hour in Summer). 2023 public holidays: Jan. 1–3, Feb. 6, Apr. 7, 10, 25, June 5, July 14, Oct. 23, Dec. 25, 26.

Long distance rail services are operated by KiwiRail (www.greatjourneysofnz.co.nz). Two classes of accommodation are offered, Scenic Plus Class and Scenic Class (shown in tables as 1 and 2). Scenic Plus Class includes refreshments. Carriages have both panoramic windows and skylights or have open sides. All services require reservation. There are two rail passes allowing travel on the KiwiRail Scenic network (not the Capital Connection). The Fixed Pass is available during the low season (May to mid September) and is valid for 7, 14 or 21 consecutive days (Adult: 7 days NZ$835, 14 days NZ$935, 21 days NZ$1025). The New Zealand Travel Scenic Pass is available during the high season (mid September - March) for 3, 4, 5 or 6 days in 1 month, or 7 days in 2 months (Adult: 3 days NZ$846 to 10 days NZ$1299). Both passes are also valid on the Interislander ferry service. All travel must be reserved in advance.

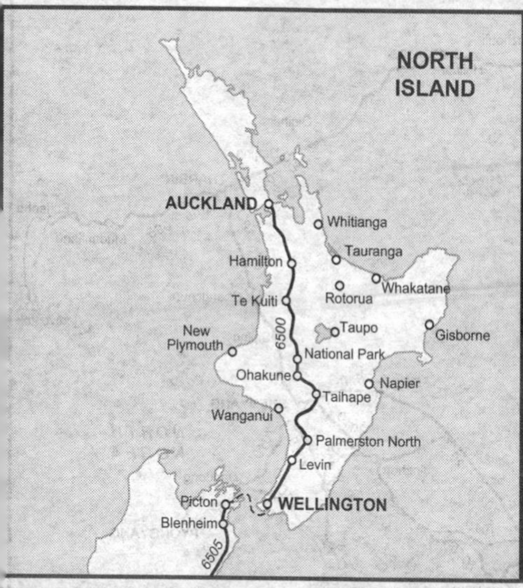

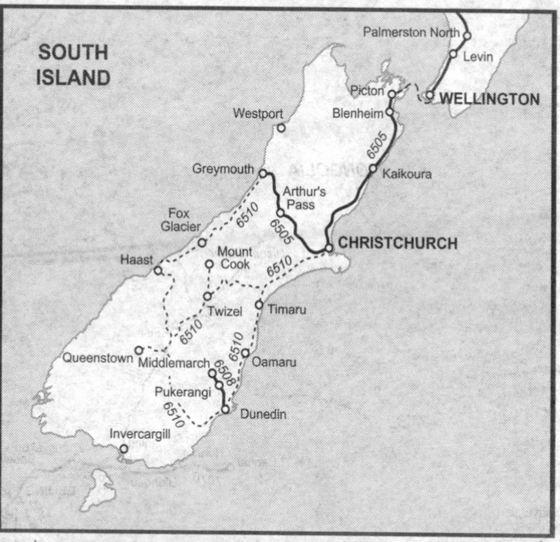

KiwiRail Scenic AUCKLAND - WELLINGTON 6500

km		1203	0201
		Ⓐ	①④⑥
		Ⓡ B	Ⓡ A
0	**Auckland** Strand d.	...	0745
34	Papakura d.	...	0835
139	Hamilton d.	...	1015
183	Otorohanga d.	...	1050
334	National Park d.	...	1315
364	Ohakune d.	...	1345
544	**Palmerston North** d.	0615	1620
590	Levin d.	0653	|
632	Paraparaumu d.	0732	1730
681	**Wellington** ⊡ a.	0820	1825

	0200	1205
	③⑤⑦	Ⓐ
	Ⓡ A	Ⓡ B
Wellington ⊡ d.	0755	1715
Paraparaumu d.	0845	1803
Levin d.	|	1842
Palmerston North d.	1000	1920
Ohakune d.	1245	...
National Park d.	1315	...
Otorohanga d.	1545	...
Hamilton d.	1625	...
Papakura d.	1805	...
Auckland Strand a.	1900	...

KiwiRail Scenic PICTON - CHRISTCHURCH 6505

km		0803	0701
			④–⑦
		Ⓡ D	Ⓡ C
0	**Picton** ⊡ d.	...	1340
28	Blenheim d.	...	1405
157	Kaikoura d.	...	1615
318	Rangiora d.	...	1845
348	**Christchurch** a.	...	1930
348	**Christchurch** d.	0815	...
417	Springfield d.	0920	...
484	Arthur's Pass d.	1040	...
498	Otira d.	|	...
	Moana d.	1205	...
579	**Greymouth** a.	1305	...

	0700	0804
	④–⑦	
	Ⓡ C	Ⓡ D
Greymouth d.	...	1405
Moana d.	...	1505
Otira d.	...	|
Arthur's Pass d.	...	1620
Springfield d.	...	1745
Christchurch a.	...	1900
Christchurch d.	0700	...
Rangiora d.	0730	...
Kaikoura d.	1000	...
Blenheim d.	1210	...
Picton ⊡ a.	1240	...

OTES FOR TABLES 6500 and 6505.

☛ Trains are permitted to depart earlier if all booked passengers have boarded.

- – NORTHERN EXPLORER – 2 🍷.
- – CAPITAL CONNECTION – 2 🍷.
- – COASTAL PACIFIC – 12 🍷.
- – THE TRANZALPINE – 12 🍷.
- – Calls to set down only.
- – Calls to pick up only.

] – Wellington - Picton ⛴ service ('Interislander'). Journey 3 - 3½ hours.
Operator: Interislander (www.greatjourneysofnz.co.nz/interislander).
From **Wellington** at 0845, 1300, 1600. From **Picton** at 1100, 1415, 1830.
Days and times of sailings may vary - please contact the operator for confirmed timings.

TAIERI GORGE 6508

km		E	
0	**Dunedin** d.	E	...
58	Pukerangi d.	E	...
77	**Middlemarch** a.	E	...

	E	
Middlemarch d.	E	...
Pukerangi d.	E	...
Dunedin a.	E	...

E – Various excursions operate from Dunedin - contact operator for Details.

The Taieri Gorge Railway runs through some of New Zealand's most spectacular scenery. The train travels along the Taieri branch across the Taieri Plains and climbs into the Taieri Gorge, travelling through ten tunnels and over countless bridges and viaducts.

Operator: Dunedin Railways (www.dunedinrailways.co.nz).

🚌 SELECTED SOUTH ISLAND BUS SERVICES 6510

km	Operator	IC	IC	AS	AS	IC	AS			
		①③⑦		F	⑦	G	⑤			
0	**Christchurch** Interchange d.	0830	0800	0915	1315	1425	1615	...	...	...
82	Ashburton d.	0945e	0930	1100	1500	1550	1800	...	...	...
160	Timaru d.	|	1050	1245	1645	1730	1945	...	...	...
240	Oamaru d.	|	1230	1400	1800	1845	2100	...	...	...
366	**Dunedin** Moray Place a.	|	1415	1530	1930	2020	2230	...	...	...
516	Gore a.	|	1720	...	...	...	...	...	...	...
580	**Invercargill** a.	|	1830	...	...	...	...	...	...	...
144	Geraldine d.	1045	...	...	...	...	...	...	...	...
191	Fairlie d.	1125	...	...	...	...	...	...	...	...
341	**Mount Cook** a.	|	...	...	...	...	...	...	...	...
281	Twizel d.	1330	...	...	...	...	...	...	...	...
435	Cromwell d.	1530	...	...	...	...	...	...	...	...
496	**Queenstown** a.	1640	...	...	...	...	...	...	...	...

Operator	IC	AS	IC	IC	AS	AS			
	G	F	①③⑦		⑦	⑤			
Queenstown d.	...	...	0805	...	...	...	...	...	...
Cromwell d.	...	...	0910	...	...	...	...	...	...
Twizel d.	...	...	1115	...	...	...	...	...	...
Mount Cook d.	...	...	|	...	...	...	...	...	...
Fairlie d.	...	...	1315	...	...	...	...	...	...
Geraldine d.	...	...	1410	...	...	...	...	...	...
Invercargill d.	...	...	|	0810	...	...	...	...	...
Gore d.	...	...	|	0925	...	...	...	...	...
Dunedin Moray Place d.	0730	0915	|	1235	1315	1615	...	...	...
Oamaru d.	0925	1100	|	1500	1500	1800	...	...	...
Timaru d.	1120	1245	|	1610	1645	1945	...	...	...
Ashburton d.	1225	1350	1455e	1730	1750	2050	...	...	...
Christchurch Interchange a.	1350	1517	1615	1905	1933	2217	...	...	...

km	Operator	IC	AS	AS						
			⑦	⑤						
0	**Greymouth** d.	...	...	...	...	...	...	...	...	...
41	Hokitika d.	...	...	...	...	...	...	...	...	...
189	Franz Josef d.	...	...	...	...	...	...	...	...	...
213	**Fox Glacier** d.	...	...	...	...	...	...	...	...	...
	Paringa d.	...	...	...	...	...	...	...	...	...
331	Haast d.	...	...	...	...	...	...	...	...	...
476	Wanaka d.	...	...	...	...	...	...	...	...	...
593	**Queenstown** d.	0800	1600	2100	...	...	...	...	...	...
654	Cromwell d.	0856	1640	2155	...	...	...	...	...	...
685	Alexandra d.	0926	1725	2225	...	...	...	...	...	...
727	Roxburgh d.	1015	1800	2300	...	...	...	...	...	...
817	Milton d.	1126e	1915	2350	...	...	...	...	...	...
873	**Dunedin** Moray Place a.	1225	2040	0045	...	...	...	...	...	...

Operator	AS	IC	AS						
	⑦		⑤						
Dunedin Moray Place d.	1100	1430	1520	...	...	...	...	...	...
Milton d.	1145	1525e	1615	...	...	...	...	...	...
Roxburgh d.	1300	1650	1820	...	...	...	...	...	...
Alexandra d.	1345	1720	1900	...	...	...	...	...	...
Cromwell d.	1405	1800	1920	...	...	...	...	...	...
Queenstown d.	1500	1855	2010	...	...	...	...	...	...
Wanaka d.	...	...	...	...	...	...	...	...	...
Haast d.	...	...	...	...	...	...	...	...	...
Paringa d.	...	...	...	...	...	...	...	...	...
Fox Glacier d.	...	...	...	...	...	...	...	...	...
Franz Josef d.	...	...	...	...	...	...	...	...	...
Hokitika d.	...	...	...	...	...	...	...	...	...
Greymouth a.	...	...	...	...	...	...	...	...	...

– ①②④⑥.
– ①④⑤⑦.

e – Will only call to pick up pre-booked passengers.

AS – Atomic Travel (www.atomictravel.co.nz).
IC – Intercity Coachlines (www.intercity.co.nz).

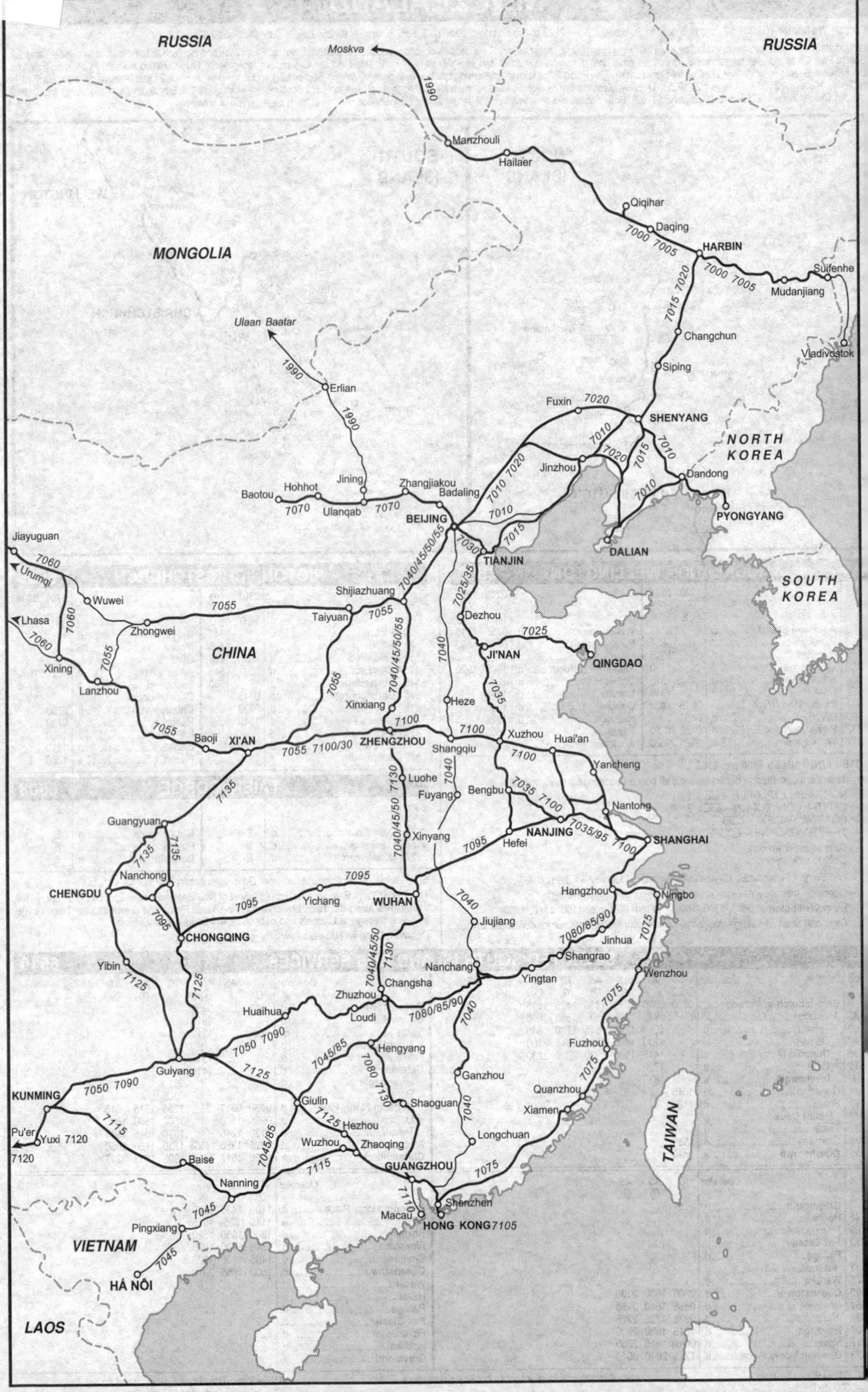
RUSSIA
Moskva
1990
Manzhouli
Hailaer
Qiqihar
Daqing
7000 7005
HARBIN
7000 7005
Suifenhe
Mudanjiang
Vladivostok
7015 7020
Changchun
Siping
MONGOLIA
Ulaan Baatar
1990
Erlian
Fuxin
7020
SHENYANG
NORTH KOREA
7010
7020
7015
Jinzhou
Dandong
PYONGYANG
Baotou
Hohhot
Jining
Zhangjiakou
Badaling
7070
Ulanqab
BEIJING
DALIAN
Jiayuguan
7060
Urumqi
Lhasa
Wuwei
7055
Shijiazhuang
Taiyuan
7040/45/50/55
7030
TIANJIN
7025/35
SOUTH KOREA
Dezhou
Zhongwei
Xining
Lanzhou
CHINA
7056
7025
JI'NAN
QINGDAO
Heze
Xinxiang
7035
Baoji
XI'AN
7100/30
ZHENGZHOU
7100
Shangqiu
Xuzhou
Huai'an
Yancheng
Luohe
Fuyang
Bengbu
Nantong
7135
Guangyuan
Xinyang
Hefei
NANJING
7035/95
SHANGHAI
7130
7095
Nanchong
CHENGDU
Yichang
WUHAN
Hangzhou
Ningbo
CHONGQING
Jiujiang
7080/85/90
Jinhua
7075
Shangrao
Nanchang
Yingtan
Wenzhou
Yibin
7125
Changsha
Zhuzhou
Loudi
Huaihua
7050 7090
Hengyang
7045/85
Fuzhou
Guiyang
Ganzhou
Quanzhou
Xiamen
KUNMING
Giulin
Shaoguan
TAIWAN
7115
Hezhou
Longchuan
Pu'er
Yuxi 7120
7120
Wuzhou
Zhaoqing
Baise
GUANGZHOU
Nanning
7110
Shenzhen
Macau
HONG KONG 7105
Pingxiang
VIETNAM
HÀ NỘI
LAOS

CHINA

Capital: **Beijing** (GMT + 8). 2023 Public Holidays: Jan. 1, 21–27, Mar. 8, Apr. 3–5, May 1, 4, June 22–24, Sept. 29, Oct. 1–7.

Rail services in the People's Republic are generally operated by Chinese Railways. High-speed services are operated by China Rail High Speed. All times shown are Beijing time unless otherwise stated. Schedules in this section are as per the latest information available and are liable to change at any time.

Trains are numbered using a combination of letters and numbers, with the letter indicating the type of train. The fastest trains carry prefixes **C** and **G**. These use the new high- speed railways and run at speeds up to 350 km/h on routes Beijing to Tianjin and Beijing to Shanghai and up to 300 km/h on routes such as Wuhan to Guangzhou. Other high-speed trains running at speeds of up to 200 km/h are prefixed with the letter **D** and **Z**. These trains use both dedicated high-speed railways and normal lines. Ordinary long distance trains are prefixed **T** or **K**. **T** trains make fewer stops and thus are considerably quicker than **K** trains. Most **K** trains in this section are only shown to highlight additional connections between major points and may not be shown in their entirety. Also shown are a few trains without prefix letters.

Train classes are shown in the chart below. It should be noted that not all classes will be available on every train and that the exact train compositions are **not** shown in the tables. Hard seats are cheapest class available and are often very busy as Standing ticket holders can stand in the aisles. Soft seats are larger and generally can be reclined. Second class seats have five seats per row. First class has four seats per row. Business and VIP seats have three seats per row. Hard sleepers consist of open cabins of six berths (upper, middle and lower), with three beds on either side. Soft sleepers have four berths and a sliding door. Deluxe Soft cabins have two berths and an en-suite bathroom.

High-Speed	Business Class	VIP Class	1st Class	2nd Class	Soft Sleepers	Deluxe Sleeper	Regular	Hard Seats	Soft Seats	Hard Sleepers	Soft Sleepers	Deluxe Sleeper
G	Yes	Yes	Yes	Yes	No	Yes	Z	No	No	No	Yes	Yes
D	No	No	Yes	Yes	Certain trains	No	T	Yes	Yes	Yes	Yes	No
C	No	No	Yes	Yes	No	No	K	Yes	Yes	Yes	Yes	No

All travel should be reserved in advance either at stations or through an agent. At many stations you may find it possible to only book for trains calling there, however in major cities such as Beijing, Shanghai and Guangzhou you may be able to purchase all tickets. Some major stations may have English speakers available at ticket desks. Reservations for **Z** and **D** usually open 10–21 days in advance. Other classes of train are only usually available 7–10 days before departure. In peak seasons such as Spring Festival holidays reservations may only open 5 days before departure. Identity documents, such as passports for most foreigners or ID cards for Chinese citizens, are required to buy tickets for and to board **C**, **D** and **G** trains.

Because of space we are only able to show selected services in many tables. More comprehensive train schedules are available from Chinese Railways official website: www.12306.cn/en/index/. Other websites such as www.chinahighlights.com, www.trains.ctrip.com and www.travelchinaguide.com have more detailed class information with photographs, timetable search facilities in English and can arrange tickets.

MANZHOULI - HARBIN - SUIFENHE - VLADIVOSTOK 7000

Trains are prefix **K** unless shown otherwise.

km		7092	7090
0	**Manzhouli** d.	1830	2019
186	Hailaer d.	2102	2248
268	Yakeshi d.	2212	2357
396	Boketu d.	|	0138
693	Qiqihar d.	|	0608
776	Daqing xi ◇ d.	|	0720
935	**Harbin** a.	0638	0938**d**

	7089	7091
Harbin d.	1850**d**	2025
Daqing ◇ d.	2045	2232
Qiqihar d.	2236	|
Boketu d.	0240	|
Yakeshi d.	0425	0509
Hailaer d.	0555	0635
Manzhouli a.	0815	0843

km			
0	**Harbin** dong d.	...	...
161	Yimianpo d.	...	...
355	Mudanjiang d.	...	...
548	**Suifenhe** 🏛 d.	...	...
569	Grodekovo ◐ d.	...	...
766	Ussruiysk ◐ d.	...	...
878	**Vladivostok** ◐ d.	...	...

Vladivostok ◐ d.	...	...
Ussruiysk ◐ d.	...	...
Grodekovo ◐ d.	...	...
Suifenhe 🏛 d.	...	...
Mudanjiang d.	...	...
Yimianpo d.	...	...
Harbin dong a.	...	...

d – Harbin **dong**. ◇ – Note the use of different stations. ◐ – Moscow time (GMT +3). Operator in Russia is RZhD.

QIQHAR - HARBIN - SUIFENHE 7005

Trains are prefix **D** unless shown otherwise.

km		6914	G766	7952		112	6920	G2634		6926	6928	7972		152	6932	G722		6934	128	6936		T48	6940	6944
0	**Qiqihar** nan d.	0650	0707	0747	...	0758	1011	1039	...	1210	1324	1347	...	1401	1539	1612	...	1713	1803	1841	...	1853**q**	2025	2119
116	Daqing dong d.	0730	0759	0827	...	0844	1057	1112**x**	...	1303	1410	1433	...	1447	1619	1704	...	1811	1850	1933	...	2002**x**	2117	2207
	Harbin a.	0825	0900	0910	...	0933	1146	1208	...	1358	1453	1522	...	|	1708	1759	...	1906	1939	2034	...	2152	2206	2257
286	**Harbin** xi a.	...	0912	...	...	...	...	1222	...	...	...	...	...	1536	...	1812	...	...	...	...	...	...	...	2312

		6911	T47	6913		6915	6917	6919		6923	151	6931		G711	127	6935		6939	G2633	111		6943	7951	765
	Harbin xi d.	0534	...	...	...	0741	...	...	...	0906	1118	...	...	1359	1500	...	...	...	1819	1840	...	...	...	...
	Harbin d.	0546	0633	0705	...	0754	0810	0845	...	0919	1131	1335	...	|	|	1538	...	1656	|	1852	...	1928	2005	2021
	Daqing dong d.	0637	0808**x**	0802	...	0857	0907	0948	...	1024	1228**x**	1438**x**	...	1508	1615**x**	1641	...	1759	1922**x**	1943**x**	...	2031	2102	2124**x**
	Qiqihar nan a.	0727	0913**q**	0852	...	0941	0951	1043**q**	...	1102	1300	1516	...	1552	1652	1731	...	1837	1953	2015	...	2114**q**	2139	2156

km		8549	8511	8515	8519					
0	**Harbin** d.	...	0708	1000	1342	...	...	...	...	...
307	Mudanjiang d.	0641	0916	1156	1532	...	...	...	...	...
444	**Suifenhe** a.	0750	1025	1305	1641	...	...	...	...	...

	8516	8520	8524	8528					
Suifenhe d.	0812	1046	1326	1709	...	...	...	...	...
Mudanjiang d.	0925	1200	1440	1823	...	...	...	...	...
Harbin a.	1105	1352	1632	2009	...	...	...	...	...

q – **Qiqihar**. x – Daqing **xi**.

SHENYANG - DANDONG - PYONGYANG and DALIAN 7010

Trains are prefix **D** unless shown otherwise.

km		K27 A	7651	7653	7655	7657	K7505	7659		
	Beijing d.	1727	...	...	...	...	...	...	...	...
	Tianjin d.	1909	...	...	...	...	...	...	...	...
	Shanhaiguan d.	2242	...	...	...	...	...	...	...	...
	Shenyang a.	0320	...	...	...	...	...	...	...	...
0	**Shenyang** d.	0340	0655	0918	1138	1345	1548	1739	...	...
76	Benxi d.	|	0739	0956	1216	1423	1718	1823	...	...
178	Fengcheng dong d.	|	...	...	...	...	...	...	...	...
223	**Dandong** a.	0722	...	...	...	...	...	...	...	...
223	**Dandong** d.	1000	...	...	...	...	...	...	...	...
282	Sinuiji 🏛 ⊗ a.	1040	...	...	...	...	...	...	...	...
506	**Pyongyang** ⊗ a.	1815	...	...	...	...	...	...	...	...
371	Zhuanghe bei d.	...	...	...	...	...	...	...	...	...
517	**Dalian** bei a.	...	...	...	...	...	...	...	...	...

	K7056	7652	7654	7656	7658	7660	K28 A		
Dalian bei d.	...	...	...	...	...	...	...	...	...
Zhuanghe bei d.	...	...	...	...	...	...	...	...	...
Pyongyang ⊗ d.	...	...	...	...	...	...	0955	...	...
Sinuiji 🏛 ⊗ d.	...	...	...	...	...	...	1643	...	...
Dandong a.	...	...	...	...	...	...	1623	...	...
Dandong d.	...	...	...	...	...	...	1831	...	...
Fengcheng dong d.	...	...	...	...	...	...	|	...	...
Benxi d.	0630	0759	1031	1238	1546	1846	|	...	...
Shenyang a.	0729	0844	1116	1323	1632	1934	2207	...	...
Shenyang d.	...	...	...	...	...	...	2224	...	...
Shanhaiguan d.	...	...	...	...	...	...	0304	...	...
Tianjin a.	...	...	...	...	...	...	0649	...	...
Beijing a.	...	...	...	...	...	...	0838	...	...

A – Beijing (**K27/28**) - Dandong (**6/5**) - Pyongyang and v.v. From Beijing on ②③⑤⑦; from Pyongyang on ①③④⑥. Subject to confirmation - service may be suspended.
⊗ – Korean Standard Time (GMT +9, 1 hour ahead of Chinese time). Times in North Korea are subject to confirmation.

HARBIN - SHENYANG - DALIAN

Trains are prefix **G** unless shown otherwise.

km		8070	8004	704	706		48	708	766	710		8012	714	50		8016	720	772	8024		716	730	722	732
0	**Harbin** xi d.	...	...	0703	0737	...	0830	0906	0916	1037	...	...	1219	1321	...	...	1419	1649	...	...	1723	1749	1815	1902
240	Changchun xi d.	...	...	0815	0842	...	0926	1011	1021	1142	...	1213	1323	1419	...	...	1521	1748	1753	...	1835	1854	1927	2009
358	Siping dong d.	...	...	|	0910	...	|	1040	1050	1211	...	|	1351	|	...	1527	|	1816	1821	...	1903	|	2002	|
538	**Shenyang** bei d.	0632	0825	0930	0957	...	1033	1133	1145	|	...	1330	1438	1526	...	1621	|	|	1932	...	|	2012	|	2125
	Shenyang bei d.	0642	|	|	1000	...	|	1144	|	1305	...	1340	|	|	...	|	1647	1921	|	...	2001	|	2053	|
638	Anshan xi d.	0721	0906	1019	1040	...	|	1217	1230	|	...	1437	1514	|	...	1703	1728	1953	2022	...	2039	2055	|	|
715	Yinkou dong d.	|	|	|	|	...	|	|	1259	1359	...	|	|	|	...	|	|	|	|	...	|	2117	|	|
921	**Dalian** bei a.	0850	1028	1141	1155	...	1206	1346	1400	1452	...	1544	1629	1659	...	1824	1858	2108	2137	...	2209	2217	2248	2302

	701	771	8039	721	707	47	8005	709	711	717	719		49	8015	773	725	8019	767	729	8023	731	8069	8043
Dalian bei d.	0549	0650	0706	0722	0746	0830	0835	0919	0947	1210	1240	...	1330	1335	1412	1535	1605	1643	1757	1844	1903	1926	2051
Yinkou dong d.	0644	0751	0800	0825	|	|	|	|	|	|	1347	...	|	1430	1521	|	1707	1745	1859	1939	|	2021	|
Anshan xi d.	0706	0813	0829	|	|	|	|	|	|	1334	|	...	|	|	|	1659	1729	1807	1921	|	|	2043	2208
Shenyang bei d.	0753	|	|	|	0948	|	1026	1112	1132	|	1445	...	|	|	1623	|	|	1851	|	|	2054	2122	|
Shenyang bei d.	|	0858	0913	0924	|	1006	|	|	|	1424	|	...	1506	1523	|	1742	1821	1901	2008	2051	2104	2130	2242
Siping dong d.	|	0944	0957	|	1049	|	|	1209	1230	1517	1549	...	|	|	1713	1829	1906	1954	2054	|	|	...	...
Changchun xi d.	0911	1013	...	1052	1118	1112	1150	1237	1258	1546	1624	...	1612	1635	1742	1857	...	2022	2128	2203	2118	...	...
Harbin xi a.	1015	1131	...	1156	1222	1206	...	1348	1355	1650	1728	...	1706	...	1845	2001	...	2119	2225	...	2315	...	...

7020 HARBIN, SHENYANG and DALIAN - BEIJING

Trains are prefix **G** unless shown otherwise. Timings for Dalian - Jinzhou - Beijing were not available at press date.

km		952	3678		912	902		928	916		922	938		924		Z16 🛏	Z18 🛏							
0	**Harbin** xi d.	...	...	...	0709	0840	...	1008	1058	...	1558	...	...	1656	...	2120	2133	...	...	...	...	...	...	...
240	Changchun xi d.	...	...	...	0822	0938	...	1106	1204	...	1700	1729	...	1808	...	|	|	...	...	...	...	...	...	...
358	Siping dong d.	...	...	...	0850	|	...	1135	|	...	|	1757	...	1837	...	|	|	...	...	...	...	...	...	...
538	**Shenyang** bei d.	0830	...	...	0937	1046	...	1229	1320	...	1829	1843	...	1930	...	|	|	...	...	...	...	...	...	...
	Shenyang d.	|	0852	...	|	|	...	|	|	...	|	|	...	|	...	|	|	...	...	...	...	...	...	...
	Fuxin d.	0917	0940	...	1033	|	...	1318	|	...	1919	1933	...	2020	...	|	|	...	...	...	...	...	...	...
	Beijing Chaoyang a.	1145	1213	...	1312	1332	...	1549	1641	...	2151	2222	...	2244	...	|	|	...	...	...	...	...	...	...
1241	**Beijing** a.	...	...	...	...	...	...	...	...	...	...	...	...	...	...	0724	0753	...	...	...	...	...	...	...

	913		915		933		917		901		3677		955		Z17 🛏	Z15 🛏							
Beijing d.	...	...	...	...	...	...	...	...	...	...	...	...	...	...	2115	2121	...	...	...	...	...	...	...
Beijing Chaoyang d.	0916	...	1020	...	1206	...	1345	...	1434	...	1305	...	1806	...	|	|	...	...	...	...	...	...	...
Fuxin d.	1144	...	1254	...	|	...	|	...	|	...	1539	...	2041	...	|	|	...	...	...	...	...	...	...
Shenyang d.	|	...	|	...	|	...	|	...	|	...	1626	...	|	...	|	|	...	...	...	...	...	...	...
Shenyang bei ♠ d.	1240	...	1344	...	1530	...	1716	...	1722	...	...	...	2127	...	|	|	...	...	...	...	...	...	...
Siping dong d.	|	...	1437	...	1619	...	|	...	|	...	...	...	...	...	|	|	...	...	...	...	...	...	...
Changchun xi d.	1400	...	1505	...	1645	...	1823	...	1830	...	...	...	...	...	|	|	...	...	...	...	...	...	...
Harbin xi a.	1456	...	1616	...	...	...	1920	...	1926	...	...	...	...	...	0712	0725	...	...	...	...	...	...	...

km																								
0	**Dalian** d.	...	...	...	...	...	...	...	...	...	...	...	...	...	...	...	...	...	...	...	...	...	...	...
	Dalian bei d.	...	...	...	...	...	...	...	...	...	...	...	...	...	...	...	...	...	...	...	...	...	...	...
	Jinzhou bei d.	...	...	...	...	...	...	...	...	...	...	...	...	...	...	...	...	...	...	...	...	...	...	...
	Beijing Chaoyang a.	...	...	...	...	...	...	...	...	...	...	...	...	...	...	...	...	...	...	...	...	...	...	...

Beijing Chaoyang d.	...	...	...	...	...	...	...	...	...	...	...	...	...	...	...	...	...	...	...	...	...	...	...
Jinzhou bei d.	...	...	...	...	...	...	...	...	...	...	...	...	...	...	...	...	...	...	...	...	...	...	...
Dalian bei a.	...	...	...	...	...	...	...	...	...	...	...	...	...	...	...	...	...	...	...	...	...	...	...
Dalian a.	...	...	...	...	...	...	...	...	...	...	...	...	...	...	...	...	...	...	...	...	...	...	...

7025 BEIJING - QINGDAO

Trains are prefix **G** unless shown otherwise.

km		453	6953	246	D8181	D8183		6991	179	181	254	5555		183	189	242	191	193		195	282	197	199	235
426	**Beijing** nan d.	...	...	...	...	...	...	...	0935	1039	...	...	...	1147	1315	...	1420	1520	...	1610	...	1650	1721	...
122	Dezhou dong d.	...	...	...	...	...	...	...	1050	1214	...	...	...	1312	1433	...	1535	|	...	1733	...	1816	1845	...
0	Ji'nan d.	0808	0920	0952	1001	1021	...	1124	1135	1259	1326	1530	...	1400	1524	1629	1623	1727	...	1817	1845	1908	1941	202
130	Zibo d.	0859	1016	1036	1045	1105	...	1208	1220	1343	1410	1614	...	1447	1608	1714	1707	1811	...	1904	1934	1954	|	211
230	Weifang d.	|	1053	1113	1128	|	...	|	1304	1421	1447	|	...	1530	1645	|	1749	|	...	|	|	2033	2104	215
*413**	**Qingdao** a.	1107	1235	1227	1248	1303	...	1353	1418	1536	1602	1632	...	1645	1825	1917	1929	2001	...	2100	2131	2153	2224	231

	284	D6004	D1636	182	244		188	232 S	184	186	190		D8184	245	D6008	194	196		D1632	256	198	454	206
Qingdao d.	0626	0700	0727	0758	0815	...	0850	0933	0924	1020	1208	...	1216	1320	1333	1436	1554	...	1558	1620	1705	1831	192
Weifang d.	0751	0811	0806	0930	0932	...	1010	1053	1047	1138	|	...	|	1438	|	1549	1711	...	1655	1733	1828	2003	|
Zibo d.	0835	0848	0929	1008	1015	...	1051	1137	1130	1221	|	...	1419	1521	1528	|	1753	...	1733	1811	1908	2040	|
Ji'nan d.	0922	0935	1016	1058	1102	...	1140	1224	1219	1310	1450	...	1506	1608	1615	1709	1843	...	1830	1858	1958	2135	|
Dezhou dong d.	...	...	...	|	...	...	1232	...	|	|	1540	...	...	...	...	|	|	...	...	...	|	...	|
Beijing nan a.	...	...	...	1302	...	...	1354	...	1418	1503	1700	...	...	...	...	1913	2040	...	...	...	2156	...	221

* – *344 km* via high-speed line.

7030 BEIJING - TIANJIN

Frequent high-speed intercity trains (numbered **C2xxx**) operate the *120 km* journey between Beijing and Tianjin in 30–37 minutes. Services operate at least every 30 minutes 0600–2300.

BEIJING - TIANJIN - XUZHOU - NANJING - SHANGHAI 7035

Trains are prefix **G** unless shown otherwise.

km		7349	1377		101	103		105	109		111	113		5	115		117	119		7	121		123	
0	**Beijing** nan d.	...	...	...	0611	0620	...	0717	0745	...	0814	0839	...	0900	0910	...	0920	0945	...	1000	1005	...	1020	...
122	**Tianjin** nan d.	...	...	...	0646	|	...	|	|	...	|	|	...	|	|	...	0958	1001	...	|	|	...	|	...
314	Dezhou dong d.	...	...	...	0732	|	...	|	0917	...	0932	1011	...	|	|	...	|	1047	...	|	|	...	1146	...
406	Ji'nan xi d.	...	...	...	0758	0801	...	0900	0944	...	0959	1043	...	1025	1056	...	1104	1115	...	1126	1148	...	1214	...
692	**Xuzhou** dong d.	...	...	...	0920	0907	...	1025	1055	...	1121	1151	...	|	|	...	1230	1239	...	|	|	...	1340	...
848	Bengbu nan d.	...	...	...	|	0956	...	|	|	...	|	|	...	|	|	...	|	|	...	|	|	...	|	...
1023	**Nanjing** nan d.	0730	0739	...	1047	1040	...	1147	1213	...	1243	1314	...	1226	1333	...	1346	1402	...	1326	1416	...	1505	...
1153	Changzhou bei d.	0810	0819	...	|	|	...	1221	|	...	1324	1354	...	|	|	...	1439	1436	...	|	|	...	1539	...
1237	Suzhou bei d.	0842	0852	...	1145	|	...	|	1318	...	1348	1433	...	1312	1425	...	|	1501	...	|	1507	...	|	...
1318	**Shanghai** Hongqiao a.	0907	0922	...	1209	1158	...	1303	1348	...	1411	1456	...	1337	1448	...	1502	1532	...	1435	1542	...	1626	...

	123	127		9	11		137	141		15	143		147	17		19	21		161	23		25	
Beijing nan d.	1046	1105	...	1100	1200	...	1245	1334	...	1400	1408	...	1427	1500	...	1600	1700	...	1733	1800	...	1804	...
Tianjin nan d.	1139	1143	...	|	1233	...	|	|	...	|	|	...	|	|	...	|	|	...	1809	1831	...	1837	...
Dezhou dong d.	1226	1231	...	|	|	...	1412	1450	...	|	|	...	1546	|	...	|	|	...	1855	|	...	|	...
Ji'nan xi d.	1254	1258	...	1224	1335	...	1438	1518	...	1525	1551	...	1616	1627	...	1724	|	...	1923	1932	...	1938	...
Xuzhou dong d.	|	|	...	1323	|	...	1550	|	...	|	1703	...	1739	|	...	|	|	...	2045	|	...	2036	...
Bengbu nan d.	|	|	...	|	|	...	|	1719	...	|	|	...	1825	|	...	|	|	...	2124	|	...	|	...
Nanjing nan d.	1526	1540	...	1434	1535	...	1708	1802	...	1724	1832	...	1911	1826	...	1926	2016	...	2147	2135	...	|	...
Changzhou bei d.	1603	1615	...	|	|	...	1802	1836	...	|	1906	...	1954	1857	...	|	|	...	2244	|	...	|	...
Suzhou bei d.	|	1640	...	|	|	...	1833	|	...	1810	1943	...	2018	|	...	|	|	...	|	|	...	2226	...
Shanghai Hongqiao a.	1650	1712	...	1537	1638	...	1856	1924	...	1833	2007	...	2043	1934	...	2028	2118	...	2332	2243	...	2249	...

	102	104		106	6		112	8		118	10		122	12		14	132		136	16		138	140
Shanghai Hongqiao d.	0639	0713	...	0722	0800	...	0805	0900	...	0943	1000	...	1034	1100	...	1153	1221	...	1247	1255	...	1329	1334
Suzhou bei d.	|	0739	...	0748	|	...	0831	|	...	1008	|	...	|	|	...	|	1246	...	1312	1322	...	|	|
Changzhou bei d.	|	0803	...	0812	|	...	0855	|	...	1043	|	...	1116	|	...	1239	|	...	1342	|	...	1411	|
Nanjing nan d.	0804	0837	...	0850	0902	...	0934	1001	...	1125	1101	...	1156	1202	...	1310	1350	...	1426	1408	...	1453	1512
Bengbu nan d.	0856	|	...	|	|	...	|	|	...	1210	|	...	1250	|	...	|	1436	...	1517	|	...	1545	1555
Xuzhou dong d.	0934	1007	...	|	|	...	1107	|	...	1248	|	...	1330	|	...	|	1528	...	1558	|	...	1631	|
Ji'nan xi d.	1042	1122	...	1134	1101	...	1220	1202	...	1411	1300	...	1438	1402	...	1510	1642	...	1704	1610	...	1743	1747
Dezhou dong d.	|	1149	...	1204	|	...	|	|	...	|	|	...	|	|	...	|	1710	...	1733	|	...	|	|
Tianjin nan d.	1156	1238	...	1248	|	...	|	|	...	|	|	...	1553	|	...	|	|	...	|	|	...	1857	1908
Beijing nan a.	1239	1312	...	1322	1224	...	1407	1327	...	1547	1426	...	1629	1531	...	1638	1831	...	1849	1736	...	1931	1942

	18	142		144	20		146	148		22	152		24	154		158	26		28	7792		1378	28
Shanghai Hongqiao d.	1400	1416	...	1443	1500	...	1521	1542	...	1600	1619	...	1700	1711	...	1721	1755	...	1900	1829	...	1923	1900
Suzhou bei d.	|	1447	...	|	|	...	|	1609	...	|	|	...	1723	|	...	1746	|	...	|	1901	...	1948	|
Changzhou bei d.	|	|	...	|	|	...	1603	|	...	|	|	...	|	|	...	1813	|	...	|	1935	...	2019	|
Nanjing nan d.	1502	1537	...	1619	1601	...	1636	1717	...	1701	1735	...	1810	1827	...	1846	1906	...	2002	2019	...	2103	2002
Bengbu nan d.	|	|	...	1703	|	...	1722	|	...	|	1819	...	|	|	...	|	|	...	|	2110	...	...	|
Xuzhou dong d.	1613	1655	...	1742	|	...	1801	1841	...	1812	1859	...	|	1944	...	2021	|	...	|	2154	...	...	|
Ji'nan xi d.	1711	1823	...	1854	1802	...	1919	1955	...	1911	2036	...	2009	2058	...	2135	2110	...	|	...	...	...	|
Dezhou dong d.	|	|	...	|	|	...	1945	2003	...	|	2104	...	|	2136	...	|	|	...	|	...	...	...	|
Tianjin nan d.	|	|	...	2009	1903	...	2031	|	...	|	|	...	|	|	...	2241	|	...	|	...	...	...	|
Beijing nan a.	1835	2029	...	2045	1936	...	2105	2143	...	2037	2220	...	2133	2249	...	2314	2235	...	2318	...	...	...	2318

km		D709	D705							
0	**Beijing** nan d.	1946	2121	...	...	...	...	...	...	...
	Nanjing d.	0516	0651	...	...	...	...	...	...	...
	Shanghai a.	0744	0921	...	...	...	...	...	...	...

	D706	D710							
Shanghai d.	2114	2123	...	...	...	...	...	...	...
Nanjing d.	2357	0002	...	...	...	...	...	...	...
Beijing nan a.	0924	0922	...	...	...	...	...	...	...

BEIJING - ZHENGZHOU - WUHAN - CHANGSHA - GUANGZHOU - SHENZHEN 7040

Trains are prefix **G** unless shown otherwise.

km		93	551	541		423	485	403		73	71	531		529	279	83		81	421	79		405	65	
0	**Beijing** xi d.	...	...	...	...	...	0703	0800	...	...	0726	...	...	0834	...	0855	...	0900	0905	1000	...	1005	1033	...
281	Shijiazhuang d.	...	...	...	...	0753	0831	0909	...	...	0858	0914	...	0947	...	1005	...	1010	1034	1109	...	1125	1159	...
496	Anyang dong d.	...	...	...	...	|	|	|	...	0945	|	|	...	|	...	|	...	|	1135	|	...	1233	1303	...
595	Xinxiang dong d.	...	...	...	...	0932	|	|	...	|	|	|	...	|	...	|	...	|	|	|	...	|	|	...
663	**Zhengzhou** dong d.	0757	...	0825	...	0959	1026	1033	...	1043	1056	1106	...	1114	1123	1129	...	1134	1221	1234	...	1320	1351	...
799	Luohe xi d.	|	0756	0901	...	1036	|	|	...	1125	|	|	...	|	1213	|	...	|	1305	|	...	|	1426	...
960	Xinyang dong d.	|	0850	0948	...	1123	1145	|	...	|	|	1310	...	|	|	|	...	|	1352	|	...	1430	1507	...
1136	**Wuhan** a.	0958	0945	1039	...	1207	1229	1220	...	1256	1314	1413	...	1303	1346	1316	...	1321	1436	1420	...	1518	1605	...
1345	Yueyang dong d.	|	|	|	...	1320	1331	|	...	|	|	1511	...	|	1448	|	...	|	1535	|	...	|	1704	...
1483	**Changsha** nan d.	1120	1125	1208	...	1353	1406	1344	...	1419	1439	1550	...	1424	1525	1437	...	1447	1609	1545	...	1640	1740	...
1523	Zhuzhou xi d.	|	|	|	...	...	...	...	...	|	|	|	...	...	|	...	...	...	...	|	...	...	1758	...
1632	Hengyang dong d.	1159	1214	1247	...	...	...	...	...	|	|	1629	...	...	|	...	...	...	...	|	...	...	|	...
1894	Shaoguan d.	|	1322	1359	...	...	...	...	...	|	1621	|	...	...	1706	...	...	...	...	|	...	...	|	...
2104	**Guangzhou** nan a.	1350	1426	1456	...	...	...	...	...	1704	1717	1834	...	...	1818	...	...	...	...	1805	...	...	2024	...
2206	**Shenzhen** bei a.	...	1500	...	...	...	...	...	...	1745	...	1915	...	...	1859	...	...	...	...	...	...	...	...	...

	545	553	549		2055	401	533		67	69	547		503	505	D901 A		D903 A	D909 A	D927 A		D921 A	D923 A	
Beijing xi d.	...	...	...	...	...	1143	1302	...	1405	1307	...	...	1441	1540	2010	...	2015	2020	2025	...	2030	2035	...
Shijiazhuang d.	...	...	...	...	1226	1309	1411	...	1514	1448	...	...	1606	1703	2134	...	2140	2145	2156	...	2201	2206	...
Anyang dong d.	...	...	...	...	1331	|	|	...	|	|	...	...	1659	|	2236	...	|	|	|	...	|	|	...
Xinxiang dong d.	...	...	...	...	1406	1437	|	...	|	|	...	...	|	|	|	...	|	|	|	...	|	|	...
Zhengzhou dong d.	1405	...	1417	...	1432	1509	1535	...	1640	1620	1651	...	1744	1857	|	...	|	|	|	...	|	|	...
Luohe xi d.	1456	...	1502	...	1515	|	|	...	|	|	|	...	1826	|	|	...	2332	2337	2342	...	2347	2352	...
Xinyang dong d.	|	1522	1600	...	1558	1625	|	...	|	|	1815	...	|	|	|	...	|	|	|	...	|	|	...
Wuhan a.	1631	1621	1648	...	1643	1717	1723	...	1828	1821	1910	...	1949	2059	|	...	|	|	|	...	|	|	...
Yueyang dong d.	1730	1719	1746	...	|	|	|	...	|	1917	2006	...	|	2158	|	...	|	|	|	...	|	|	...
Changsha nan d.	1808	1757	1824	...	1813	1853	1845	...	1950	2002	2049	...	2114	2232	|	...	|	|	|	...	|	|	...
Zhuzhou xi d.	1825	1814	|	...	1830	...	...	...	|	|	2106	...	...	...	|	...	|	|	|	...	|	|	...
Hengyang dong d.	1854	1843	1904	...	1859	...	...	...	|	2041	2135	...	...	...	|	...	|	|	|	...	|	|	...
Shaoguan d.	|	1952	2012	...	2007	...	...	...	|	2146	2243	...	...	...	|	...	|	|	|	...	|	|	...
Guangzhou nan a.	2053	2048	2107	...	2103	...	...	...	2212	2242	2339	...	...	...	0628	...	0633	0638	0659	...	0653	0643	...
Shenzhen bei a.	...	...	2139	...	...	...	...	...	...	...	...	...	...	...	0706	...	0711	0716	0740	...	...	...	...

FOR RETURN SERVICE SEE NEXT PAGE →

7040 SHENZHEN - GUANGZHOU - CHANGSHA - WUHAN - ZHENGZHOU - BEIJING

Trains are prefix **G** unless shown otherwise.

		534	502	84	276	94	72	2056	280	82	80	74	552	66	542	404	532	68	422
Shenzhen bei	d.	...	...	...	...	...	...	...	0926	...	0826	0841	...	...	...	...	0945	...	...
Guangzhou nan	d.	...	...	...	0648	0737	0747	0805	0815	...	0900	0922	0932	1000	0943	...	1025	1117	...
Shaoguan	d.	...	...	...	|	0830	0840	0858	0908	...	|	|	|	|	|	...	1119	1210	...
Hengyang dong	d.	...	...	...	0837	|	0951	|	|	...	|	1123	1133	|	|	...	|	|	...
Zhuzhou xi	d.	...	...	...	0906	|	|	|	1036	...	|	|	1206	|	|	...	|	1340	...
Changsha nan	d.	0710	0736	0900	0929	1019	1037	1044	1102	1138	1120	1207	1230	1220	1235	1302	1307	1402	1422
Yueyang dong	d.	0745	|	|	1005	|	1118	|	|	|	|	1253	|	|	|	|	|	1437	|
Wuhan	d.	0838	0911	1020	1110	1152	1217	1209	1230	1258	1241	1349	1352	1341	1358	1425	1455	1534	1601
Xinyang dong	d.	0930	|	|	1158	|	1302	|	|	|	|	1434	1447	|	1443	|	1540	1619	1647
Luohe xi	d.	|	|	|	|	|	|	1334	|	|	|	1521	...	|	1530	|	|	1706	1719
Zhengzhou dong	d.	1047	1103	1208	1312	1343	1458	1411	1416	1447	1429	1602	...	1528	1617	1612	1653	1753	1806
Xinxiang dong	d.	1110	1132	|	...	...	|	...	...	|	|	...	...	|	...	|	|	|	|
Anyang dong	d.	1137	|	|	...	...	|	...	...	|	|	...	...	|	...	|	|	1847	|
Shijiazhuang	d.	1246	1258	1332	...	...	1703	...	...	1614	1554	...	...	1653	...	1735	1843	1950	1938
Beijing xi	a.	1419	1424	1441	...	...	1822	...	...	1721	1701	...	...	1800	...	1846	...	2110	2053

		486	402	424	506	70	554	544	530	406	546	76	548	D922 A	D924 A	D902 A	D904 A	D910 A	D928 A
Shenzhen bei	d.	...	...	...	...	...	1326	...	...	...	...	1546	...	...	...	1934	1945	1950	1955
Guangzhou nan	d.	...	...	...	...	1250	1408	1356	...	...	1413	1626	1621	2005	2010	2015	2020	2025	2030
Shaoguan	d.	...	...	...	...	1343	|	|	...	...	|	1726	|	|	|	|	|	|	|
Hengyang dong	d.	...	...	1414	...	1500	1602	1557	...	...	1617	|	1824	|	|	|	|	|	|
Zhuzhou xi	d.	...	...	|	...	|	|	|	...	...	1649	|	|	|	|	|	|	|	|
Changsha nan	d.	1427	1446	1501	1507	1538	1652	1647	1657	1703	1713	1915	1920	|	|	|	|	|	|
Yueyang dong	d.	|	|	1536	1541	|	1731	1722	|	1742	1748	|	2006	|	2303	|	2313	2318	2323
Wuhan	d.	1611	1621	1639	1644	1707	1944	1841	1822	1836	1846	2041	2105	|	|	|	|	|	|
Xinyang dong	d.	1656	1707	1724	1729	1752	2037	1927	|	|	1938	2126	2150	|	|	|	|	|	|
Luohe xi	d.	1737	1755	1804	1809	|	2130	|	|	|	2019	2206	|	|	|	|	|	|	|
Zhengzhou dong	d.	1814	1834	1841	1848	1914	...	2041	2013	2030	2100	2247	2304	|	|	|	|	|	|
Xinxiang dong	d.	|	1856	1908	|	|	...	...	|	...	...	...	...	|	|	|	|	|	|
Anyang dong	d.	1857	1924	1951	1935	1957	...	...	|	...	...	...	...	|	|	|	|	|	|
Shijiazhuang	d.	2000	2040	2051	2045	2100	...	...	2139	2206	...	...	...	0518	0523	0528	0533	0544	0550
Beijing xi	a.	2126	2159	...	2204	2227	...	...	2247	2318	...	...	...	0640	0651	0656	0701	0713	0718

km			D739 🛏	D733 🛏	D737 🛏	D727 🛏	K105
0	**Beijing** xi	d.	1822	1835	1947	1959	2318
426	Liaocheng	d.	2203	2211	|	2335	0422
582	Heze	d.	2314	2324	|	|	0555
687	Shangqiu nan	d.	|	|	|	|	0720
855	Fuyang	d.	0131	|	|	0302	0926
1314	Jiujiang	d.	0522	0535	0627	|	1429
1449	**Nanchang**	d.	0638	0638	0734	0754	1616
1861	Ganzhou	d.	...	...	...	1149	2045
2102	Longchuan	d.	...	...	...	|	0018
2310	Dongguan dong	d.	...	...	...	|	0315
2372	**Shenzhen**	a.	...	...	...	1724	0420

		D740 🛏	D738 🛏	D746 🛏	D728 🛏	K106
Shenzhen	d.	...	...	...	1417	1050
Dongguan dong	d.	...	...	...	|	1157
Longchuan	d.	...	...	...	|	1436
Ganzhou	d.	...	...	...	2007	1739
Nanchang	d.	1738	1951	2313	0020	2222
Jiujiang	d.	1845	2052	|	|	|
Fuyang	d.	2249	|	0408	0510	0630
Shangqiu nan	d.	|	|	|	|	0834
Heze	d.	0108	|	0623	0730	0949
Liaocheng	d.	0218	|	0733	0840	1131
Beijing xi	a.	0602	0742	1113	1219	1627

A – ①⑤⑥⑦. 🛏 1. cl, (2).

FOR RETURN SERVICE SEE PREVIOUS PAGE.

7045 BEIJING - GUILIN - NANNING - HÁ NOI

International services via this route are currently suspended. Operator in Vietnam is Duóng Sát Viêt Nam.

km			G431	G423	G529	G1503	G435	G421	G2065	G2339
0	**Beijing** xi	d.	...	...	0834	...	...	0905	...	...
281	Shijiazhuang	d.	...	0753	0947	...	...	1034	...	...
496	Anyang dong	d.	...	|	|	...	...	1135	...	...
595	Xinxiang dong	d.	...	0932	|	...	...	|	...	...
663	Zhengzhou dong	d.	...	0959	1114	...	...	1221	...	...
799	Luohe xi	d.	...	1036	|	...	...	1305	...	...
960	Xinyang dong	d.	...	1123	|	...	...	1352	...	...
1136	Wuhan	d.	0706	1214	1303	...	1329	1444	1449	...
1345	Yueyang dong	d.	|	1320	|	...	|	1535	|	...
1483	Changsha nan	d.	0848	1356	1424	1444	1504	1617	1624	1655
1632	Hengyang dong	d.	0927	1436	|	1523	|	|	1711	1746
	Guilin	d.	1225	|	|	|	1823	|	|	2015
2002	**Guilin** bei	d.	|	1716	1702	1801	|	1941	1949	|
2158	Liuzhou	d.	1334	1832	1818	1924	1941	2059	2106	2139
2370	**Nanning** dong	a.	1444	1943	1948	2024	2052	2210	2223	2224

		G2066	G422	G2344	G424	G1502	G1504	G530	G432
Nanning dong	d.	0722	0823	0836	0904	0913	1008	1148	1504
Liuzhou	d.	0841	0937	0951	1018	1027	1111	1256	1612
Guilin bei	d.	|	1055	|	|	|	1236	1413	|
Guilin	d.	1005	|	1116	1137	1152	|	|	1743
Hengyang dong	d.	1230	1331	1348	1414	1434	1512	|	2021
Changsha nan	d.	1313	1422	1441	1501	1524	1600	1657	2120
Yueyang dong	d.	|	|	...	1536	...	...	|	|
Wuhan	d.	1442	1601	...	1639	...	...	1822	2244
Xinyang dong	d.	...	1647	...	1724	...	...	|	...
Luohe xi	d.	...	1719	...	1804	...	...	|	...
Zhengzhou dong	d.	...	1806	...	1841	...	...	2013	...
Xinxiang dong	d.	...	|	...	1908	...	...	|	...
Anyang dong	d.	...	|	...	1951	...	...	|	...
Shijiazhuang	d.	...	1938	...	2051	...	...	2139	...
Beijing xi	a.	...	2053	...	...	...	...	2247	...

km			Z285	T289
0	**Beijing** xi	d.	2108	2200
281	Shijiazhuang	d.	2340	0055
689	Zhengzhou	d.	0309	0457
1225	Wuhan Wuchang	d.	0757	1054
1587	Changsha	d.	1125	1424
1772	Hengyang	d.	1323	1625
2262	**Guilin** bei	d.	1624	|
2444	Liuzhou	d.	1814	|
2699	**Nanning**	a.	2101	0505
2699	**Nanning**	d.	...	...
2922	Pingxiang (Guangxi)	a.	...	...
2922	Pingxiang (Guangxi) 🛃	d.	...	...
2967	Dong Dang 🛃	a.	...	...
2967	Dong Dang	d.	...	...
3129	**Há Nôi** Gia Lam	a.	...	...

		T290	Z286
Há Nôi Gia Lam	d.	...	...
Dong Dang	a.	...	...
Dong Dang 🛃	d.	...	...
Pingxiang (Guangxi) 🛃	a.	...	...
Pingxiang (Guangxi)	d.	...	...
Nanning	a.	...	...
Nanning	d.	1208	1725
Liuzhou	d.	|	1941
Guilin bei	d.	|	2128
Hengyang	d.	2349	0041
Changsha	d.	0153	0247
Wuhan Wuchang	d.	0548	0618
Zhengzhou	d.	1122	1110
Shijiazhuang	d.	1517	1433
Beijing xi	a.	1810	1703

BEIJING - KUNMING 7050

Schedules were not available as we closed for press.

km												
0	**Beijing** xi	d.	...	...	...	...	...	...	...	...	...
281	Shijiazhuang	d.	...	...	...	...	...	...	...	...	...
496	Anyang dong	d.	...	...	...	...	...	...	...	...	...
663	Zhengzhou dong	d.	...	...	...	...	...	...	...	...	...
960	Xinyang dong	d.	...	...	...	...	...	...	...	...	...
1136	Wuhan	d.	...	...	...	...	...	...	...	...	...
1345	Yueyang dong	d.	...	...	...	...	...	...	...	...	...
1483	Changsha nan	d.	...	...	...	...	...	...	...	...	...
1608	Loudi nan	d.	...	...	...	...	...	...	...	...	...
1815	Huaihua nan	d.	...	...	...	...	...	...	...	...	...
1983	Guiyang bei	d.	...	...	...	...	...	...	...	...	...
2649	**Kunming** nan	a.	...	...	...	...	...	...	...	...	...

Kunming nan	d.	...	...	...	...	...	...	...	...	...
Guiyang bei	d.	...	...	...	...	...	...	...	...	...
Huaihua nan	d.	...	...	...	...	...	...	...	...	...
Loudi nan	d.	...	...	...	...	...	...	...	...	...
Changsha nan	d.	...	...	...	...	...	...	...	...	...
Yueyang dong	d.	...	...	...	...	...	...	...	...	...
Wuhan	d.	...	...	...	...	...	...	...	...	...
Xinyang dong	d.	...	...	...	...	...	...	...	...	...
Zhengzhou dong	d.	...	...	...	...	...	...	...	...	...
Anyang dong	d.	...	...	...	...	...	...	...	...	...
Shijiazhuang	d.	...	...	...	...	...	...	...	...	...
Beijing xi	a.	...	...	...	...	...	...	...	...	...

BEIJING - XI'AN - LANZHOU, CHENGDU and CHONGQING 7055

Trains are prefix **G** unless shown otherwise.

km			437	89		671		571		307	87		429		2095		679	25							
0	**Beijing** xi	d.	0626	0653	...	0749	...	0922	...	0938	1400	...	1045	...	...	...	1731	1855	...	...	...	...	...	...	...
281	Shijiazhuang	d.	0741	0802	...	0930	...	1044	...	1054	|	...	1211	...	1519	...	1853	2004	...	...	...	...	...	...	...
496	Anyang dong	d.	|	|	...	|	...	1157	...	1212	|	...	1313	...	|	...	|	|	...	...	...	...	...	...	...
595	Xinxiang dong	d.	|	|	...	|	...	1225	...	1240	|	...	1341	...	1649	...	|	|	...	...	...	...	...	...	...
663	Zhengzhou dong	d.	0914	0932	...	1127	...	1254	...	1311	1631	...	1408	...	1714	...	2059	2132	...	...	...	...	...	...	...
788	Luoyang Longmen	d.	|	|	...	1212	...	|	...	1349	|	...	1447	...	1752	...	2137	|	...	...	...	...	...	...	...
947	Sanmenxia nan	d.	|	|	...	1245	...	1339	...	|	|	...	|	...	|	...	|	|	...	...	...	...	...	...	...
1047	Huashan bei	d.	|	|	...	1325	...	1435	...	|	|	...	1549	...	1848	...	|	|	...	...	...	...	...	...	...
1168	**Xi'an** bei	a.	1105	1124	...	1402	...	1503	...	1543	1819	...	1626	...	1924	...	2300	2320	...	...	...	...	...	...	...
1168	**Xi'an** bei	d.	1106	1128	...	1402	...	1512	...	1523	...	...	1629	...	1924	...	...	...	...	...	...	...	...	...	...
1335	Baoji nan	d.	|	|	...	1459	...	|	...	|	...	...	1733	...	2032	...	...	...	...	...	...	...	...	...	...
1736	**Lanzhou** xi	a.	1338	|	...	...	...	|	...	|	...	...	1754	...	2242	...	...	...	...	...	...	...	...	...	...
	Guangyuan	d.	...	|	...	...	...	1710	...	1729	...	...	...	...	...	...	...	...	...	...	...	...	...	...	...
	Mianyang	d.	...	|	...	...	...	1819	...	1830	...	...	...	...	...	...	...	...	...	...	...	...	...	...	...
1826	**Chengdu** dong	a.	...	1438	...	...	...	1900	...	1914	...	...	...	...	...	...	...	...	...	...	...	...	...	...	...
2145	**Chongqing** xi	a.	...	...	...	...	...	2034	...	...	...	...	...	...	...	...	...	...	...	...	...	...	...	...	...

		26	672		658	430		88	2096		574	308		438	674		90							
Chongqing xi	d.	...	...	...	...	...	...	...	...	...	0840	...	...	...	...	...	...	...	...	...	...	...	...	...
Chengdu dong	d.	...	...	...	...	...	...	...	...	...	1021	1051	...	...	...	...	1502	...	...	...	...	...	...	...
Mianyang	d.	...	...	...	...	...	...	...	...	...	1102	1136	...	...	...	...	|	...	...	...	...	...	...	...
Guangyuan	d.	...	...	...	...	...	...	...	...	...	1200	1240	...	...	...	...	|	...	...	...	...	...	...	...
Lanzhou xi	d.	...	...	...	...	0954	...	...	1018	...	|	|	...	1429	...	...	|	...	...	...	...	...	...	...
Baoji nan	d.	...	0830	...	...	1214	...	...	1239	...	|	|	...	|	1621	...	|	...	...	...	...	...	...	...
Xi'an bei	a.	...	0930	...	...	1315	...	...	1335	...	1405	1450	...	1657	1720	...	1816	...	...	...	...	...	...	...
Xi'an bei	d.	0920	0933	...	1253	1319	...	1332	1337	...	1410	1455	...	1703	1724	...	1826	...	...	...	...	...	...	...
Huashan bei	d.	|	|	...	1323	1349	...	|	1407	...	1441	1532	...	|	1802	...	|	...	...	...	...	...	...	...
Sanmenxia nan	d.	|	|	...	|	|	...	|	|	...	|	|	...	|	1830	...	|	...	...	...	...	...	...	...
Luoyang Longmen	d.	|	1057	...	1417	1447	...	|	1504	...	1543	1629	...	|	1903	...	|	...	...	...	...	...	...	...
Zhengzhou dong	d.	1111	1139	...	1503	1540	...	1523	1545	...	1627	1713	...	1854	1946	...	2018	...	...	...	...	...	...	...
Xinxiang dong	d.	|	1201	...	1525	1602	...	|	1607	...	|	1735	...	|	|	...	|	...	...	...	...	...	...	...
Anyang dong	d.	|	|	...	1606	|	...	|	|	...	1718	1803	...	|	|	...	|	...	...	...	...	...	...	...
Shijiazhuang	d.	1241	1345	...	1708	1726	...	1648	1735	...	1827	1905	...	2030	2149	...	2144	...	...	...	...	...	...	...
Beijing xi	a.	1350	1511	...	1826	1853	...	1755	...	...	1854	2038	...	2142	2309	...	2252	...	...	...	...	...	...	...

km			Z55	Z129	Z151	Z21	Z19				
0	**Beijing** xi	d.	1458	1557	1603	2000	2040	...	...	...	...
291	Shijiazhuang bei	d.	1757	1827	1833	2236	|	...	...	...	...
516	Taiyuan	d.	2005	|	|	0026	|	...	...	...	...
1283	**Xi'an**	a.	|	0353	0351	|	0829	...	...	...	...
1267	Zhongwei	d.	0245	|	|	0716	...	...	...	...	...
1573	**Lanzhou**	a.	0748	1042	1128	1214	...	...	...	...	...

		Z20	Z22	Z152	Z130	Z56				
Lanzhou	d.	...	1629	1658	1718	2111	...	...	...	...
Zhongwei	d.	...	2132	|	|	0223	...	...	...	...
Xi'an	d.	1854	|	0140	0147	|	...	...	...	...
Taiyuan	d.	|	0400	|	|	0906	...	...	...	...
Shijiazhuang bei	d.	|	0555	1148	1154	1104	...	...	...	...
Beijing xi	a.	0658	0828	1426	1432	1338	...	...	...	...

ÜRÜMQI and LHASA 7060

Summary of long-distance trains. Only principal stations are shown.

km			Z69	Z21	Z135 Z138	Z40 Z41	Z164 Z165				
1573	**Beijing** xi	d.	1000	2000	...	...	...	...	...	...	...
1282	Shijiazhuang bei	d.	1312	2236	...	...	...	...	...	...	...
1057	Taiyuan	d.	1509	0026	...	...	...	...	...	...	...
2186	**Shanghai**	d.	|	|	...	1617	2007	...	...	...	...
1885	Nanjing	d.	|	|	...	1919	2301	...	...	...	...
2799	**Guangzhou**	d.	|	|	0818	|	|	...	...	...	...
2086	Changsha	d.	|	|	1634	|	|	...	...	...	...
1724	Wuhan Wuchang	d.	|	|	2026	|	|	...	...	...	...
1188	Zhengzhou	d.	|	|	0135	0211	0514	...	...	...	...
676	Xi'an	d.	|	|	0750	0843	1122	...	...	...	...
0	**Lanzhou**	a.	|	1214	1503	1548	1816	...	...	...	...
0	**Lanzhou**	d.	|	1231	1518	1603	1837	...	...	...	...
770	Jiayuguan	d.	0650	|	2251	2336	|	...	...	...	...
1339	Hami	d.	1244	|	0438	0511	|	...	...	...	...
1749	Turpan bei	d.	1527	|	0721	0805	|	...	...	...	...
1892	**Ürümqi**	a.	1652	|	0849	0930	|	...	...	...	...
1352	Golmud	d.	...	2235	...	...	0430	...	...	...	...
2172	Naqu	d.	...	0839	...	...	1411	...	...	...	...
2449	**Lhasa**	a.	...	1240	...	...	1936	...	...	...	...

		Z166 Z163	Z22	Z70	Z42 Z39	Z136 Z137				
Lhasa	d.	1130	1550	...	...	...	...	...	...	...
Naqu	d.	1521	1936	...	...	...	...	...	...	...
Golmud	d.	0226	0641	...	...	...	...	...	...	...
Ürümqi nan	d.	|	|	1410	1840	1952	...	...	...	...
Turpan bei	d.	|	|	1540	2023	2114	...	...	...	...
Hami	d.	|	|	1835	2306	0004	...	...	...	...
Jiayuguan	d.	|	|	0025	0437	0557	...	...	...	...
Lanzhou	a.	1208	1614	|	1151	1318	...	...	...	...
Lanzhou	d.	1224	1629	|	1210	1335	...	...	...	...
Xi'an	d.	2044	|	|	2050	2234	...	...	...	...
Zhengzhou	d.	0258	|	|	0306	0447	...	...	...	...
Wuhan Wuchang	d.	|	|	|	|	0953	...	...	...	...
Changsha	d.	|	|	|	|	1323	...	...	...	...
Guangzhou	a.	|	|	|	|	2117	...	...	...	...
Nanjing	d.	0901	|	|	0907	...	...	...	...	...
Shanghai	a.	1151	|	|	1159	...	...	...	...	...
Taiyuan	d.	...	0400	1536	...	...	...	...	...	...
Shijiazhuang bei	d.	...	0555	1744	...	...	...	...	...	...
Beijing xi	a.	...	0828	2022	...	...	...	...	...	...

7065 ÜRÜMQI - ALMATY - NUR-SULTAN

Operator in Kazakhstan is Kazakhstan Temir Zholy.

km			5801	13 *CJ* ①	13/53 ①
0	**Ürümqi**	d.	2242	2333	2333
144	Shihezi	d.	0129	|	|
241	Kuitun	d.	0259	|	|
486	Bortala	a.	0708	|	|
477	Alashankou	a.	...	0800	0800
477	Alashankou 🏛	d.	...	1100	1100
493	Druzhba 🏛	a.	...	0920	0920
493	Druzhba	d.	...	1240	1240
654	Beskol'	d.	...	1621	1621
797	**Aktogay**	a.	...	1828	1828
797	**Aktogay**	d.	...	1858	1935
1051	Ush Tobe	d.	...	2311	|
1283	Kapchagay	d.	...	0345	|
1354	**Almaty** 1	a.	...	0454	|
1363	**Almaty** 2	a.	...	0545	|
1657	Karagandy	a.	...	...	0809
1898	**Nur-Sultan**	a.	...	...	1301

		5802	54/14 ⑥	13 *KH* ⑦
Nur-Sultan	d.	...	1658	...
Karagandy	d.	...	2119	...
Almaty 2	d.	...	|	0022
Almaty 1	d.	...	|	0113
Kapchagay	d.	...	|	0225
Ush Tobe	d.	...	|	0654
Aktogay	a.	...	1030	1053
Aktogay	d.	...	1123	1123
Beskol'	d.	...	1346	1346
Druzhba	a.	...	1635	1635
Druzhba 🏛	d.	...	1950	1950
Alashankou 🏛	a.	...	2210	2210
Alashankou	d.	...	2350	2350
Bortala	d.	0800	|	|
Kuitun	d.	1224	|	|
Shihezi	d.	1341	|	|
Ürümqi	a.	1630	0854	0854

7070 BEIJING - BADALING - HOHHOT - BAOTOU

Trains are prefix **G** unless shown otherwise. Badaling Changcheng is located beneath the Great Wall of China.

km			2403	2481	8883	2483	2409	2415	2419	8813	2485	2425	2487	2435	2437	2443
0	**Beijing** bei	⊖ d.	0715	0818	0851	...	0909	1051	1118	1135	...	1322	1539	1720	1750	1945
11	Qinghe	d.	0730	0833	0906	0918	0924	1105	1133	1150	1248	1337	1554	|	|	2000
56	Badaling Changcheng	⊖ d.	|	|	0927	|	|	|	|	1209	1308	|	|	|	|	|
172	Zhangjiakou	d.	0828	0930	0901	1014	1028	1208	1231	...	1350	1435	1651	|	|	2104
333	Ulanqab	d.	0924	|	...	|	|	|	1327	...	|	1525	|	|	|	2154
459	**Hohhot** dong	a.	1001	|	...	|	1155	1344	1404	...	|	1602	|	1933	2007	2231
	Hohhot	a.	...	1102	...	1149	...	...	...	...	1521	...	1827	...	...	...
632	**Baotou**	a.	...	1220	...	1254	...	...	...	...	1627	...	1940	...	...	...

		2408	2482	8812	2484	2412	2418	2486	2424	8888	2432	2488	2434	2490	2446
Baotou	d.	...	0729	...	0820	...	...	1310	...	...	...	1403	...	1742	...
Hohhot	d.	...	|	...	0931	...	...	1421	...	...	...	1515	...	1900	...
Hohhot dong	d.	0800	0833	...	|	1021	1222	|	1406	...	1620	1558	1625	|	2033
Ulamqab	d.	|	|	...	|	1100	|	|	1445	...	|	|	|	|	2112
Zhangjiakou	d.	|	|	...	1110	1151	1357	1547	1542	...	|	1649	1807	2033	2209
Badaling Changcheng	⊖ d.	|	|	1034	|	|	|	|	1622	1734	|	|	1847	|	|
Qinghe	d.	|	|	1056	1202	1247	1454	1651	1644	1756	|	1749	1909	2129	2258
Beijing bei	⊖ a.	1012	1049	1109	...	1301	1508	1704	1658	1809	1832	...	1923	2143	2312

⊖ – Line S2 Beijing Huangtudian - Badaling and v.v. Journey 90 mins. From Beijing Huangtudian at 0655, 1033, 1403, 1430 ⑤–①, 1729. From Badaling at 0830, 1042 ⑤–①, 1206, 1535, 1859

7075 SHANGHAI - XIAMEN - SHENZHEN

Trains are prefix **D** unless shown otherwise. Additional **G** trains are available Shanghai - Wenzhou and v.v.

km			2311	3111	3145	3131	377	3201	2281	2289	3205	3107	3125	3135	2283	3101	3103
0	**Shanghai** Hongqiao	d.	...	...	0638	0732	0747	0818	0848	0900	0935	0939	1027	1042	1118	1501	1557
84	Jiaxing nan	d.	...	...	0708	0809	0841	0901	0932	0944	1011	1027	1058	1132	1150	|	|
159	Hangzhou dong	d.	...	0732	0741	0839	0909	0931	1013	1019	1040	1123	1134	1215	1228	1629	1700
314	Ningbo	d.	...	0849	0908	0952	1017	1047	1115	1131	1200	1224	1235	1325	1339	1751	1814
466	Taizhou	d.	...	0951	1010	|	1113	|	1211	1233	1302	1326	1337	1427	1435	1859	1916
589	Wenzhou nan	d.	...	1042	1100	1150	1209	1234	1307	1329	1358	1424	1442	1519	1531	1944	2008
883	Fuzhou nan	d.	0800	1253	1315	1355	1413	1450	1529	1535	1602	1622	1639	1729	1746	...	2241
1038	Quanzhou	d.	0839	1354	1418	1455	1512	1608	|	1634	|	1727	1739	|	1839	...	...
1109	**Xiamen** bei	d.	0929	1428	1449	1528	1546	1634	1658	1704	1721	1756	1809	1913	1908	...	...
1151	Zhangzhou	d.	0951	1450	...	1549	1605	...	|	|	...	1817	1829	1937	1928	...	...
1318	Chaoshan	d.	1100	1602	...	...	1715	...	1823	1828	...	1920	1933	...	2035	...	...
1567	Huizhou nan	d.	|	1740	...	...	|	...	1944	1949	...	|	2054	...	2156	...	...
1623	**Shenzhen** bei	a.	1258	1810	...	...	1914	...	2017	2023	...	2109	2126	...	2224	...	...

		3102	3136	378	3132	2290	3206	2282	3202	2284	3146	3108	2288	3112
Shenzhen bei	d.	...	...	0832	...	0913	...	0950	...	1031	...	1132	1050	1115
Huizhou nan	d.	...	...	|	...	|	...	|	...	1055	...	1202	1118	|
Chaoshan	d,	...	...	|	...	1102	...	1144	...	1223	...	1328	1255	1336
Zhangzhou	d.	...	0912	|	1148	1226	...	1246	...	1332	...	|	|	1451
Xiamen bei	d.	...	0934	1159	1210	1248	1254	1307	1328	1354	1400	1439	1437	1516
Quanzhou	d.	...	1007	1226	|	1321	1327	1335	1355	1427	|	1507	1504	1544
Fuzhou nan	d.	...	1123	1337	1352	1423	1434	1441	1502	1549	1533	1618	1618	1649
Wenzhou nan	d.	0952	1321	1551	1600	1624	1637	1650	1711	1750	1740	1826	1826	1901
Taizhou	d.	1037	1418	1637	1658	1720	|	1741	|	|	1830	|	|	|
Ningbo	d.	1149	1521	1746	1757	1829	1835	1846	1906	1950	1938	2016	2024	2052
Hangzhou dong	d.	1300	1640	1903	1917	1938	1950	2001	2019	2102	2049	2139	2142	2206
Jiaxing nan	d.	1326	1712	1929	2004	2013	2016	|	2106	2128	2132	2203	|	...
Shanghai Hongqiao	a.	1413	1742	1958	2034	2042	2051	2119	2145	2159	2201	2234	2237	...

7080 SHANGHAI - CHANGSHA - GUANGZHOU

Trains are prefix **G** unless shown otherwise.

km			85	1301	99	1305
0	**Shanghai** Hongqiao	d.	0800	1018	1409	1525
159	Hangzhou dong	d.	0847	1128	1500	1613
320	Jinhua	d.	|	1227	1548	|
500	Shangrao	d.	|	|	1635	1748
604	Yingtan bei	d.	|	1347	|	|
744	Nanchang xi	d.	1100	1422	1735	1855
1086	**Changsha** nan	a.	1223	1606	1854	2034
1086	**Changsha** nan	d.	1227	1612	1900	2045
1235	Hengyang dong	d.	|	1651	|	2135
1497	Shaoguan	d.	|	1759	2037	2243
1707	**Guangzhou** nan	a.	1451	1856	2132	2340

		86	100	1304	1306
Guangzhou nan	d.	0800	1205	1347	1538
Shaoguan	d.	|	1258	1428	|
Hengyang dong	d.	|	|	1536	|
Changsha nan	a.	1023	1434	1617	1812
Changsha nan	d.	1026	1441	1621	1815
Nanchang xi	d.	1147	1604	1802	1936
Yingtan bei	d.	|	|	1838	2013
Shangrao	d.	|	1702	1906	|
Jinhua	d.	|	1749	1952	2126
Hangzhou dong	d.	1402	1839	2055	2219
Shanghai Hongqiao	a.	1448	1925	2151	2304

SHANGHAI - CHANGSHA - NANNING 7085

Trains are prefix **G** unless shown otherwise.

km			1503
0	**Shanghai** Hongqiao	d.	...
159	Hangzhou dong	d.	0959
320	Jinhua	d.	1058
500	Shangrao	d.	|
604	Yingtan bei	d.	1220
744	Nanchang xi	d.	1306
1086	**Changsha** nan	a.	1436
1086	**Changsha** nan	d.	1444
1263	Hengyang dong	d.	1523
1605	Guilin	d.	1801
1761	Liuzhou	d.	1924
1973	**Nanning** dong	a.	2024

		1502
Nanning dong	d.	0913
Liuzhou	d.	1027
Guilin	d.	1152
Hengyang dong	d.	1434
Changsha nan	a.	1524
Changsha nan	d.	1527
Nanchang xi	d.	1707
Yingtan bei	d.	1743
Shangrao	d.	1811
Jinhua	d.	1904
Hangzhou dong	d.	2010
Shanghai Hongqiao	a.	2113

km			T77	T81
0	**Shanghai** nan	d.	1125	1605
188	Hangzhou dong	d.	1334	1811
446	Quzhou	d.	|	2056
557	Shangrao	d.	|	2244
673	Yingtan	d.	1807	0004
1259	Hengyang	d.	0054	0752
1615	Guilin bei	d.	0422	|
1797	Liuzhou	d.	0608	|
1932	Litang	d.	|	1908
2052	**Nanning**	a.	0840	2058

		T78	T82
Shanghai nan	d.	0958	1018
Litang	d.	|	1149
Liuzhou	d.	1316	|
Guilin bei	d.	1559	|
Hengyang	d.	1937	2255
Yingtan	d.	|	0625
Shangrao	d.	|	0728
Quzhou	d.	0515	0843
Hangzhou dong	d.	0742	1128
Shanghai nan	a.	1018	1327

SHANGHAI - CHANGSHA - GUIYANG - KUNMING 7090

Trains are prefix **G** unless shown otherwise.

km			1321	1383	1371	2189	85	1337	1373	1377	1347	1301	2193	1375	1333	1387	1369	1329	1357	1305	1365
0	**Shanghai** Hongqiao	d.	0610	0644	0721	0727	0800	0822	0853	0926	0951	1018	1048	1112	1137	1220	1240	1340	1508	1525	1738
84	Jiaxing nan	d.	|	0713	0750	0803	|	0853	|	1003	|	1053	1117	1142	1215	1249	|	1409	|	|	1807
159	Hangzhou dong	d.	0700	0747	0825	0834	0847	0926	0946	1029	1052	1128	1143	1210	1240	1323	1342	1441	1556	1613	1842
320	Jinhua	d.	0752	0840	0918	0930	|	1025	1032	1127	1144	1227	1242	1309	1342	|	|	1535	|	|	1927
398	Quzhou	d.	0832	0904	0946	0953	|	1052	|	|	|	1250	|	1332	|	1436	|	|	|	|	|
500	Shangrao	d.	|	0936	1015	1025	|	1124	|	1217	|	|	|	1411	1429	1505	1519	1623	|	1748	2020
604	Yingtan bei	d.	|	1004	1041	1053	|	1152	1141	1246	|	1347	1352	|	1457	1533	1547	1651	|	|	2048
744	Nanchang xi	d.	1015	1046	1116	1126	1100	1227	1216	1321	1334	1422	1435	1521	1539	1615	1622	1726	1810	1855	2123
1086	**Changsha** nan	d.	1200	...	1249	1311	1223	1411	1349	1500	1517	1606	1613	1713	1723	...	1814	1914	1933	2034	2300
1211	Loudi nan	d.	|	...	1339	1354	...	|	1431	1609	...	...	1708	1757	1805	...	1905	1956	...	...	...
1418	Huaihua nan	d.	1347	...	1431	1449	...	1550	1528	1712	...	...	1805	1900	1908	...	2018	2058	...	...	...
1586	**Guiyang** bei	a.	1540	...	1626	1634	...	1724d	1713	1850	...	...	1946	2047	2049	...	...	2236	...	...	...
2252	**Kunming** nan	a.	...	...	1914	...	...	...	1934	2125	...	...	...	2301	...	...	...	...	...	...	...

		1384	1346	1348	86	1370	1322	2194	1378	1372	1334	1502	1328	1304	1374	2190	1376	1338	1306
Kunming nan	d.	...	...	...	...	...	...	...	0736	0821	...	...	...	...	0957		1037	...	...
Guiyang bei	d.	...	...	...	...	...	0906	0942	1008	1047	1122	...	1154	...	1235	1316	1320	1401	...
Huaihua nan	d.	...	...	...	...	0917	1057	1143	1204	1243	1329	...	1351	...	1436	1505	1521	1547	...
Loudi nan	d.	...	...	...	...	1017	1157	1236	1304	1336	1423	...	1455	...	1536	1609	1621	|	...
Changsha nan	d.	...	0802	0919	1026	1102	1251	1337	1348	1435	1509	1527	1543	1621	1636	1653	1702	1735	1815
Nanchang xi	d.	0823	0943	1040	1147	1238	1428	1525	1537	1623	1649	1707	1718	1802	1809	1826	1833	1917	1936
Yingtan bei	d.	0859	1020	|	|	1321	1505	1601	1614	1700	1726	1743	1801	1838	1846	|	1918	1954	2013
Shangrao	d.	0937	|	|	|	1349	1533	1629	|	|	1801	1811	1829	1906	1914	1931	1947	2022	|
Quzhou	d.	|	1110	|	|	1419	1603	|	1719	|	1832	|	1907	|	|	2007	2047	|	2103
Jinhua	d.	1030	|	|	|	1442	1627	1722	|	1805	1855	1904	1935	1952	2000	2030	2111	2115	2126
Hangzhou dong	d.	1123	1219	1256	1402	1534	1716	1822	1828	1859	1956	2010	2034	2055	2058	2123	2209	2214	2219
Jiaxing nan	d.	1148	|	|	|	1609	|	1901	1853	|	|	2035	2111	2121	2123	2148	|	|	|
Shanghai Hongqiao	a.	1216	1317	1342	1448	1636	1822	1928	1920	1944	2055	2113	2139	2151	2153	2219	2259	2300	2304

SHANGHAI - NANJING - WUHAN - CHONGQING and CHENGDU 7095

Trains are prefix **D** unless shown otherwise.

km			633	629	367	619	2373	2259	3077	353	2255	637	2236	2207	3073	3057	2223	953	2242
0	**Shanghai** Hongqiao.	d.	...	...	...	...	...	...	...	0613	...	0632	...	0601	0702	0719	...	0830	...
84	Suzhou	d.	...	...	...	...	...	...	...	0649	...	0711	...	|	0739	0755	...	|	...
165	Changzhou	d.	...	...	...	...	...	...	...	0729	...	0744	...	|	0812	0834	...	|	...
311	**Nanjing** nan	d.	...	...	...	...	...	...	0802	0835	...	0850	...	|	0918	0944	...	1014	...
468	Hefei nan	d.	...	...	...	...	...	...	0854	0927	...	0955	...	1017	1022	1038	...	1108	...
555	Lu'an	d.	...	...	...	...	...	...	0924	0957	...	1025	...	1047	1052	|	...	|	...
827	**Wuhan** Hankou	a.	...	...	...	...	...	...	1105	1119	...	1156	...	1210	1236	1225	...	1254	...
0	**Wuhan** Hankou	d.	0649	0725	0759	0923	1026	1041	1107	1128	1133	1200	1205	1215	1243	...	1248	1259	1304
204	Jingzhou	d.	0807	0846	0927	1050	|	1203	1232	1250	|	1316	1326	1336	1413	...	1422	|	1441
292	Yichang dong	d.	0851	0932	1007	1136	1226	1243	1312	1329	1349	1400	1406	1417	1452	...	1506	1447	1521
567	Lichuan	d.	1134	1206	1239	1423	1450	1520	1544	1601	1622	1633	1644	1717	|	...	1747	|	1805
845	**Chongqing** bei	a.	1345	1405	1437	1626	1648	1718	1735	1800	1819	1836	1847	1920	1915	...	1938	1853	1957
1158	**Chengdu** dong	a.	1623	...	1707	1848	1919	1939	1944	2030	2036	2042	2052	2144	...	...	2156	2058	2215

		2213	G598	2263	2217	2269	2271	3069	2226	2377	3027	3007	3033	3015	G1728	3043	3047
Shanghai Hongqiao.	d.	0742	0755	...	0737	...	...	1008	...	...	1327	1353	1516	1606	1655	1647	1753
Suzhou	d.	0822	|	...	|	...	...	1044	...	...	1354	1432	1552	1643	|	1737	1832
Changzhou	d.	0906	|	...	|	...	...	1118	...	...	1440	1507	|	1718	|	1812	1907
Nanjing nan	d.	1019	0858	...	|	...	...	1230	...	...	1538	1605	1725	1823	1758	1910	2009
Hefei nan	d.	1122	0948	...	1207	...	...	1322	...	...	1637	1703	1823	1923	1849	2012	2102
Lu'an	d.	|	|	...	1233	...	...	1351	...	...	1707	1733	1855	1957	|	2044	2132
Wuhan Hankou	a.	1316	1134	...	1420	...	...	1530	...	...	1852	1920	2036	2133	2025	2223	2301
Wuhan Hankou	d.	1328	...	1404	1432	1437	1509	...	1544	1605	...	...	...	...	...	...	...
Jingzhou	d.	1457	...	|	1549	1559	1648	...	|	1736	...	...	...	...	...	...	...
Yichang dong	d.	1536	...	1616	1630	1640	1731	...	1803	1816	...	...	...	...	...	...	...
Lichuan	d.	1814	...	1851	1914	1924	2023	...	2030	2043	...	...	...	...	...	...	...
Chongqing bei	a.	2010	...	2048	2113	2121	2212	...	2228	2241	...	...	...	...	...	...	...
Chengdu dong	a.	...	...	2315	...	...	...	...	...	...	...	...	...	...	...	...	...

FOR RETURN SERVICE SEE NEXT PAGE →

7095 CHENGDU and CHONGQING - WUHAN - NANJING - SHANGHAI

Trains are prefix **D** unless shown otherwise.

	G1722	3028	3016		3034	3008	3044		2378	3074	G600		2214	2234	2272		2228	620	G1726		954	2218	
Chengdu dong d.	...	...	...	...	...	...	...	...	...	...	...	...	...	...	...	...	...	0700	...	...	0747	...	...
Chongqing bei d.	...	...	...	...	...	...	...	...	0550	0632	...	...	0713	0738	0821	...	0849	0908	...	...	0953	0837	...
Lichuan d.	...	...	...	...	...	...	...	...	|	0825	...	...	0905	|	1020	...	|	|	...	...	|	1029	...
Yichang dong d.	...	...	...	...	...	...	...	...	1013	1105	...	...	1131	1231	1250	...	1317	1327	...	...	1406	1300	...
Jingzhou d.	...	...	...	...	...	...	...	...	1049	1138	...	...	1208	1322	1330	...	1354	1405	...	...	|	1336	...
Wuhan Hankou a.	...	...	...	...	...	...	...	...	1207	1256	...	...	1329	1455	1501	...	1519	1525	...	...	1549	1507	...
Wuhan Hankou d.	0800	0740	0800	...	0900	0906	1006	...	...	1305	1500	...	1342	...	...	...	...	...	1615	...	1553	1514	...
Lu'an d.	|	0923	|	...	1023	1117	1152	...	...	1439	|	...	1530	...	...	...	...	...	|	...	|	1647	...
Hefei nan d.	0939	0958	1008	...	1059	1152	1225	...	...	1513	1643	...	1604	...	...	...	...	...	1801	...	1741	1720	...
Nanjing nan d.	1029	1048	1104	...	1202	1246	1323	...	...	1616	1733	...	1702	...	...	...	...	...	1852	...	1833	|	...
Changzhou d.	|	1151	1209	...	1302	1352	1434	...	...	1712	|	...	1809	...	...	...	...	...	|	...	1923	|	...
Suzhou d.	|	1227	1244	...	1420	1436	1524	...	...	1747	|	...	1843	...	...	...	...	...	|	...	1952	|	...
Shanghai Hongqiao a.	1130	1302	1318	...	1446	1515	1600	...	...	1825	1835	...	1920	...	...	...	...	...	1954	...	2021	2133	...

	2244	3024		638	2224		354	2208	3078		2256	616		2264	2238	2374		368	2260		630	634	
Chengdu dong d.	0618	...	...	0710	0735	...	0757	0807	0818	...	0813	0903	...	0909	0918	0924	...	1052	1022	...	...	1327	...
Chongqing bei d.	0900	...	...	0936	0947	...	1017	1026	1037	...	1100	1105	...	1117	1126	1148	...	1308	1227	...	1431	1541	...
Lichuan d.	1101	...	...	|	1153	...	1216	|	|	...	|	1319	...	|	|	|	...	|	|	...	1622	|	...
Yichang dong d.	1343	...	...	1414	1422	...	1446	1455	1515	...	1529	1622	...	1545	1547	1617	...	1738	1653	...	1859	2003	...
Jingzhou d.	1426	...	...	1451	1503	...	1522	1532	1552	...	1611	1704	...	1627	1636	1653	...	1814	1730	...	1938	2041	...
Wuhan Hankou a.	1555	...	...	1617	1634	...	1645	1702	1716	...	1749	1835	...	1759	1805	1825	...	1945	1859	...	2050	2157	...
Wuhan Hankou d.	...	1604	...	1631	...	...	1700	1714	1731	...	...	...	...	...	...	...	...	...	...	...	...	...	...
Lu'an d.	...	1746	...	1825	...	...	1834	1844	1859	...	...	...	...	...	...	...	...	...	...	...	...	...	...
Hefei nan d.	...	1821	...	1902	...	...	1907	1917	1932	...	...	...	...	...	...	...	...	...	...	...	...	...	...
Nanjing nan d.	...	1920	...	1956	...	...	2001	|	2020	...	...	...	...	...	...	...	...	...	...	...	...	...	...
Changzhou d.	...	2028	...	2102	...	...	2113	|	...	...	...	...	...	...	...	...	...	...	...	...	...	...	...
Suzhou d.	...	2103	...	2137	...	...	2147	|	...	...	...	...	...	...	...	...	...	...	...	...	...	...	...
Shanghai Hongqiao a.	...	2151	...	2213	...	...	2221	2316	...	...	...	...	...	...	...	...	...	...	...	...	...	...	...

FOR RETURN SERVICE SEE PREVIOUS PAGE.

7100 SHANGHAI - NANJING - ZHENGZHOU - XI'AN

Trains are prefix **G** unless shown otherwise.

km		1878	1970	1874		361	1975	3180		1882	1920	3164		3171	1894	3184		3293	1928	1932		3297	1937	1940
0	**Shanghai** Hongqiao d.	...	0610	...	...	0836	0717	0642	...	...	0924	0944	...	1017	...	...	...	1036	1255	1344	...	1358	1612	1706
81	Suzhou bei d.	...	0635	...	...	|	0743	0707	...	...	|	1009	...	|	...	...	...	|	|	1420	...	|	1637	|
165	Changzhou bei d.	...	0659	...	...	|	0814	0731	...	...	1014	1043	...	|	...	...	...	|	|	1444	...	|	1705	|
295	**Nanjing** nan d.	...	0739	...	...	0946	0849	0807	...	...	1051	1120	...	|	...	...	...	|	1431	1532	...	|	1741	1821
402	Hefei nan d.	0725	|	0854	...	|	|	0912	...	1017	|	1217	...	|	1348	1319	...	|	|	|	...	|	|	|
556	Huainan nan d.	0806	|	|	...	|	|	0941	...	1058	|	1246	...	|	1429	1400	...	|	|	|	...	|	|	|
692	Fuyang xi d.	0850	|	1013	...	|	|	1032	...	1137	|	1340	...	|	1506	1444	...	|	|	|	...	|	|	|
	Bengbu nan d.	|	0823	|	...	|	0941	|	...	|	1145	|	...	|	|	|	...	|	|	|	...	|	|	|
	Nantong xi d.	|	|	|	...	|	|	|	...	|	|	|	...	|	|	|	...	1155	|	|	...	|	|	|
	Yancheng d.	|	|	|	...	|	|	|	...	|	|	|	...	|	|	|	...	|	|	|	...	1612	|	|
	Huai'an dong d.	|	|	|	...	|	|	|	...	|	|	|	...	1305	|	|	...	1417	|	|	...	1646	|	|
	Xuzhou dong d.	|	0907	|	...	1106	1025	|	...	|	1225	|	...	1414	|	|	...	1532	1616	1700	...	1756	1901	1943
872	Shangqiu d.	1001	|	1113	...	|	1129	1136	...	1230	|	1142	...	1502	1603	1547	...	1625	|	|	...	1848	|	2029
1062	**Zhengzhou** dong d.	1058	1110	1217	...	1240	1222	1245	...	1337	1414	1553	...	1606	1657	1651	...	1719	1808	1834	...	1950	2052	2137
1205	Luoyang Longmen d.	1136	1148	|	...	|	1300	1323	...	1415	|	|	...	1645	|	1734	...	1757	1847	|	...	2030	2132	|
1328	Sanmenxia nan d.	1209	|	|	...	|	|	1356	...	1448	1525	|	...	|	|	|	...	|	|	1937	...	|	2205	2242
1464	Huashan bei d.	|	1249	1350	...	|	1355	1425	...	|	1554	1735	...	|	1824	1829	...	1859	|	2008	...	|	|	|
1585	**Xi'an** bei a.	1301	1318	1423	...	1429	1442	1501	...	1540	1622	1814	...	1832	1856	1910	...	1927	2004	2036	...	2200	2255	2332

km		1914	1896	362		1918	3298	1922		3172	3166	3186		3188	3294	1972		3182	1938	1976		1876	1942	1880
0	**Xi'an** bei d.	0628	0845	0851	...	0938	0912	1037	...	1047	1143	1210	...	1235	1248	1405	...	1420	1510	1515	...	1525	1553	1629
121	Huashan bei d.	|	0919	|	...	1008	0950	|	...	|	1213	1240	...	1307	1318	1436	...	1451	1540	1545	...	1555	|	1659
257	Sanmenxia nan d.	0728	|	|	...	|	1018	|	...	|	|	|	...	|	|	|	...	|	|	|	...	|	1651	1727
380	Luoyang Longmen d.	0801	1013	|	...	1102	1052	1204	...	1209	1314	1343	...	1402	1412	1531	...	1451	1634	1639	...	1649	|	|
523	**Zhengzhou** dong d.	0843	1059	1042	...	1147	1137	1250	...	1257	1356	1425	...	1452	1502	1622	...	1638	1715	1720	...	1737	1805	1844
713	Shangqiu d.	|	1158	|	...	1246	1237	1348	...	1406	1447	1528	...	1547	|	1721	...	1731	|	1818	...	1839	1914	1946
883	Xuzhou dong d.	1033	|	1220	...	1346	1340	1446	...	1518	|	|	...	|	1634	1828	...	|	1853	1920	...	|	2016	|
	Huai'an dong d.	|	|	|	...	|	1445	|	...	1623	|	|	...	|	1739	|	...	|	|	|	...	|	|	|
	Yancheng d.	|	|	|	...	|	1528	|	...	1659	|	|	...	|	|	|	...	|	|	|	...	|	|	|
	Nantong xi d.	|	|	|	...	|	1623	|	...	1754	|	|	...	|	1951	|	...	|	|	|	...	|	|	|
1039	Bengbu nan d.	|	|	|	...	1425	|	|	...	|	|	|	...	|	|	1913	...	|	|	2013	...	|	|	|
	Fuyang xi d.	|	1254	|	...	|	|	|	...	|	1551	1632	...	1651	|	|	...	1835	|	|	...	1934	|	2051
	Huainan nan d.	|	1329	|	...	|	|	|	...	|	1640	1715	...	1733	|	|	...	1917	|	|	...	2009	|	2133
	Hefei nan d.	|	1412	|	...	|	|	|	...	|	1712	1755	...	1815	|	|	...	1949	|	|	...	2103	|	2211
1214	**Nanjing** nan d.	1201	...	1337	...	1509	|	1609	...	|	1808	...	...	...	|	1956	...	2012	2011	2057	...	...	2157	...
1344	Changzhou bei d.	1239	...	|	...	|	|	1643	...	|	1908	...	...	...	|	2037	...	|	|	|	...	...	2230	...
1428	Suzhou bei d.	1310	...	|	...	1615	|	1715	...	|	1942	...	...	...	|	|	...	2219	2123	2202	...	...	|	...
1509	**Shanghai** Hongqiao a.	1341	...	1445	...	1645	1739	1739	...	1915	2015	...	...	...	2116	2126	...	2243	2146	2225	...	...	2323	...

km		D311	D306							
0	**Shanghai** d.	2244	2250	...	...	...	...	...	...	...
	Suzhou d.	2331	2337	...	...	...	...	...	...	...
	Changzhou d.	0019	0025	...	...	...	...	...	...	...
	Nanjing d.	0149	0155	...	...	...	...	...	...	...
	Xuzhou d.	0522	0528	...	...	...	...	...	...	...
	Zhengzhou dong d.	0716	0722	...	...	...	...	...	...	...
	Luoyang Longmen d.	|	0807	...	...	...	...	...	...	...
	Sanmenxia nan d.	|	0846	...	...	...	...	...	...	...
	Huashan bei d.	0902	0920	...	...	...	...	...	...	...
	Xi'an Bei a.	0943	1003	...	...	...	...	...	...	...

	D308	D312							
Xi'an Bei d.	1935	2023	...	...	...	...	...	...	...
Huashan bei d.	2024	|	...	...	...	...	...	...	...
Sanmenxia nan d.	2109	|	...	...	...	...	...	...	...
Luoyang Longmen d.	2148	2202	...	...	...	...	...	...	...
Zhengzhou dong d.	2245	2253	...	...	...	...	...	...	...
Xuzhou d.	0038	0046	...	...	...	...	...	...	...
Nanjing d.	0338	0344	...	...	...	...	...	...	...
Changzhou d.	0442	0448	...	...	...	...	...	...	...
Suzhou d.	0528	0534	...	...	...	...	...	...	...
Shanghai a.	0620	0626	...	...	...	...	...	...	...

HONG KONG 7105

GUANGZHOU DONG - SHENZHEN via Dongguan — China Rail High Speed

igh-speed trains (**C70xx** and **C71xx**). *139 km.* Journey 70 minutes. Trains call at **Dongguan** 34–37 minutes after Guangzhou dong and 28–32 minutes after Shenzhen. * also call at Guangzhou.

uangzhou dong depart: 0600, 0608, 0618*, 0627, 0636*, 0648, 0657*, 0705, 0715, 0734*, 0748, 0800, 0822, 0833, 0844*, 0853, 0906, 0913*, 0936, 0944, 0952, 1009, 1017, 1033, 1041, 1049*,)55, 1102, 1110, 1120, 1137, 1145, 1201, 1209, 1225, 1232, 1200, 1310*, 1318, 1334, 1345, 1353, 1402*, 1410, 1418, 1429, 1430, 1456, 1504, 1513, 1520, 1530*, 1536, 1546, 1612, 1619, 546*, 1655, 1705, 1715, 1723, 1735, 1743, 1752*, 1810, 1819, 1828*, 1837, 1853, 1900, 1909*, 1917, 1925, 1933*, 1941, 2006, 2014, 2030, 2038*, 2050, 2101*, 2116, 2126, 2152, 2205, 2234*.

henzhen depart: 0612, 0640*, 0647, 0702, 0710*, 0720, 0730, 0742, 0800*, 0809, 0821, 0830, 0840*, 0854, 0903, 0915, 0924, 0933, 0955, 1007, 1014, 1023, 1039, 1058, 1106, 1113, 1125, 142, 1152, 1202, 1211, 1218, 1229, 1237*, 1245, 1255, 1308, 1316, 1333*, 1341, 1355, 1408, 1418, 1430, 1439*, 1447, 1507, 1515, 1523, 1531, 1540*, 1552, 1602, 1620*, 1626, 1638, 1644, 556, 1704*, 1717, 1740*, 1749, 1802, 1818*, 1827, 1837, 1846*, 1858, 1906, 1918, 1925, 1940*, 1950, 1958, 2010, 2023, 2032*, 2041, 2054, 2103, 2116, 2142, 2154, 2203, 2219, 2227, 2237.

GUANGZHOU NAN - SHENZHEN BEI — China Rail High Speed

gh-speed trains (**G60xx, 61xx, 62xx, G63xx, G89XX**). *102 km.* Journey 29 - 44 minutes.

uangzhou nan depart: 0704, 0711, 0729, 0735, 0745, 0750, 0800, 0813, 0859, 0905, 0915, 0928, 1011, 1046, 1052, 1102, 1119, 1130, 1140, 1150, 1201. 1231, 1232, 1240, 1252, 1304, 1326, 39, 1344, 1354, 1359, 1440, 1450, 1455, 1510, 1541, 1551, 1546, 1646, 1705, 1803, 1813, 1818, 1905, 1949, 1954, 2016, 2031, 2036, 2049, 2058, 2121, 2230.

henzhen bei depart: 0715, 0816, 0821, 0837, 0847, 0858, 0902, 0914, 0925, 0950, 1031, 1043, 1053, 1103, 1108, 1145, 1150, 1155. 1200, 1233, 1322, 1347, 1404, 1409, 1414, 1429, 1434, 39, 1552, 1620, 1632, 1652, 1729, 1805, 1820, 1829, 1836, 1842, 1847, 1857, 1902, 1914, 1919, 1929, 2012, 2026, 2041, 2046, 2056, 2107, 2129, 2212, 2225, 2250, 2300.

GUANGZHOU - SHENZHEN - WEST KOWLOON (HONG KONG) — China Rail High Speed, MTR Corporation

km	*All trains prefix G*	6539	6551	6581	6515	6553	6541	6583	6555	6525	6557	6559	6585	6561	6587
0	**Guangzhou dong** d.	...	0758	...	...	1013	...	...	1201	...	1425	1619	...	1956	...
	Guangzhou nan d.	0803	|	0946	1012	|	1127	1226	|	1353	|	|	1833	|	2151
	Shenzhen bei d.	0855	0921	1034	1051	1145	1210	1301	1330	1439	1549	1742	1913	2125	|
142	**West Kowloon** a.	0923	0939	1052	1109	1203	1228	1319	1349	1459	1607	1800	1937	2149	2234

	trains prefix G	6552	6582	6554	6540	6584	6556	6516	6558	6542	6560	6586	6526	6562	6588
	est Kowloon d.	0801	0825	1000	1005	1115	1226	1231	1419	1514	1641	1657	1713	1921	2020
	enzhen bei d.	0825	0849	1018	|	1133	1244	1249	1437	1538	1659	1715	|	1939	2045
	Guangzhou nan a.	|	0929	|	1051	1205	|	1329	|	1618	|	1804	1759	|	2126
	uangzhou dong a.	0943	...	1141	...	...	1404	...	1556	...	1824	...	...	2100	...

GUANGZHOU - KOWLOON — MTR Corporation

km		Z801	Z811	Z815	Z807	Z803	Z817	Z809	Z805	Z819	
0	**Guangzhou** dong d.	0819	0930	1037	1203	1404	1538	1733	1933	2040	...
82	Dongguan (Changping) d.	0903	1014	1121	|	1448	1622	1817	2018	2124	...
174	**Kowloon** Hung Hom a.	1017	1128	1233	1356	1602	1734	1931	2133	2236	...
		Z814	**Z806**	**Z802**	**Z812**	**Z816**	**Z808**	**Z804**	**Z818**	**Z810**	
	owloon Hung Hom d.	0800	0924	1052	1223	1311	1432	1635	1805	2001	...
	ngguan (Changping) d.	0910	1036	1204	|	1421	1544	1747	1915	2113	...
	uangzhou dong a.	0957	1123	1251	1417	1508	1631	1834	2002	2200	...

BEIJING & SHANGHAI - KOWLOON — Chinese Railways

	Z97 A	Z99 B
Beijing xi d.	1240	...
Shanghai d.	|	1745
Kowloon Hung Hom a.	1301	1301

	Z100 A	Z98 B
Kowloon Hung Hom d.	1515	1515
Shanghai a.	1037	|
Beijing xi a.	...	1530

Note: Trains make no intermediate passenger stops.

A – Odd dates in Feb., Apr., May, Aug., Nov., Dec. Even dates in Jan., Mar., June, July, Sept., Oct.

B – Odd dates in Jan., Mar., June, July, Sept., Oct. Even dates in Feb., Apr., May, Aug., Nov., Dec.

MACAU 7110

gh-speed **D** and **G** trains operate **Guangzhou - Zhuhai** 🚌 and v.v. *116 km.* Journey 1 hour. Slower **C** trains are also available. Zhuhai station is adjacent to the Gongbei (Macau) border gate.

om Guangzhou nan at 0622, 0709, 0729, 0856, 0902, 1057, 1223, 1348, 1518, 1545, 1613, 1721, 1850, 2032, 2035, 2043, 2102, 2156.

om Zhuhai 🚌 at 0645, 0723, 0925, 1015, 1025, 1217, 1636, 1706, 1730, 1850, 2018, 2150, 2220.

st-ferry service **Hong Kong - Macau** and v.v. Journey 1 hour. Operator: Turbojet (www.turbojet.com.hk).

om Hong Kong Sheung Wan at 0700 and every 20–30 minutes until 2359. SERVICE SUSPENDED.

om Macau Outer Harbour at 0700 and every 20–30 minutes until 2359. SERVICE SUSPENDED.

GUANGZHOU - NANNING - KUNMING 7115

Trains are prefix **D** unless shown otherwise.

km ◧		3802	G2932	3810	G2926	3818	3830	3838	G408	G2936	3862	G2922
0	**Guangzhou** nan d.	0652	0750	0742	0835	0847	1036	1105	1307	1448	1550	1607
76	Zhaoqing dong d.	0736	|	0826	|	0930	|	1150	|	|	1635	|
45	Wuzhou nan d.	0834	|	0918	|	1032	1212	1242	|	|	1726	|
23	Guigang d.	0934	|	1024	|	1137	1311	|	|	|	1825	|
63	**Nanning** dong d.	1027	|	1113	|	1222	1402	1424	|	|	1912	|
97	Baise d.	1220	|	1314	|	1400	1549	1616	|	|	2051	|
54	Guiyang bei a.	|	1213	|	1256	|	|	|	1738	1925	|	2025
83	**Kunming** nan a.	1457	1417	1605	1503	1635	1820	1902	1948	2154	2305	2240
		2938	**G2924**	**3816**	**G410**	**3820**	**3824**	**3844**	**3852**	**G2934**	**G2928**	**3856**
	nming nan d.	0730	0753	0919	0921	1004	1038	1308	1409	1445	1523	1435
	Guiyang bei d.	0950	1013	|	1126	|	|	|	|	1650	1735	|
	ise d.	|	|	1204	|	1249	1306	1545	1640	|	|	1714
	nning dong d.	|	|	1355	|	1432	1451	1743	1818	|	|	1855
	igang d.	|	|	|	|	1516	1541	1827	1912	|	|	1945
	izhou nan d.	|	|	1546	|	1622	1651	1934	2019	|	|	2051
	aoqing dong d.	|	|	1649	|	1719	|	2033	2117	|	|	2143
	angzhou nan a.	1424	1429	1736	1557	1812	1831	2127	2200	2105	2158	2226

– Kunming is *1317 km* via Guiyang.

KUNMING - MOHAN 7120

Services will eventually operate between Kunming and Vientiane in Laos. Timings from Vientiane to the Laos border (Boten) can be found on Table **6095**.

km		C379	C381	C281	C293	C309	C385	C315	C323	C327
0	**Kunming** nan d.	...	0829	1016	1135	1411	1419	1543	1743	1844
06	Yuxi d.	...	0910	|	1216	|	1500	|	|	1925
	Pu'er d.	...	1119	|	1417	|	1717	1825	|	2142
	Xishuangbanna d.	0740	1215	1316	1459	1711	1805	1907	2043	2224
	Mengia d.	0840	1311	...	...	...	1901	...	...	...
13	**Mohan** d.	0855	...	...	...	...	...	...	...	...

	C262	C270	C378	C346	C278	C286	C386	C320	C380
Mohan d.	...	...	0920	...	...	...	...	...	...
Mengia d.	...	...	0938	...	...	...	1419	...	1958
Xishuangbanna d.	0800	0932	1034	1207	1327	1350	1526	1950	2058
Pu'er d.	|	1016	...	1251	|	1434	1622	2034	2148
Yuxi d.	|	1228	...	1510	|	1645	1849	|	...
Kunming nan a.	1104	1306	...	1548	1628	1723	1927	2259	...

7125 CHENGDU - CHONGQING - GUIYANG - GUANGZHOU

Trains are prefix **D** unless shown otherwise.

km			1861	G319	1841		1751	1865	1812		1801	1859	G2963		1820	1755	1761		1821	1875	1825		1851	1877	18
					d		d				d	d	d			d	d		d		d				
519	**Chengdu** dong	d.	...	...	0655	...	0712	...	0741	...	0805	0828	0943	...	1012	1135	1141	...	1149	...	1326	...	1316	...	13
	Suining	d.	...	...	|	...	|	...	0842	...	|	|	|	...	|	|	|	...	|	...	|	...	|	...	
345	**Chongqing** xi	d.	0719	0820	|	...	|	0854	1010	...	|	|	|	...	|	|	|	...	|	1442	|	...	1529	1609	16
	Zunyi	d.	0845	0940	|	...	|	|	|	...	|	|	|	...	|	|	|	...	|	|	|	...	1701	1735	17
0	**Guiyang** dong	d.	0946	1032	1107	...	1038	1115	1229	...	1153	1206	1309	...	1432	1507	1527	...	1538	1709	1720	...	1754	1829	18
408	Guilin xi	d.	1200	1238	1327	...	1249	1347	1501	...	1407	1436	1517	...	1642	1735	1749	...	1800	1924	1955	...	2021	2051	21
593	Hezhou	d.	1316	|	|	...	|	1445	|	...	|	1542	|	...	1748	1841	1901	...	1912	2041	|	...	|	2157	22
778	Zhaoqing dong	d.	1419	1420	1531	...	|	1546	|	...	1556	|	1703	...	1857	1939	2004	...	2013	|	2144	...	|	2254	23
854	**Guangzhou** nan	a.	1453	1459	1606	...	1508	1624	1800	...	1632	1721	1738	...	1939	2016	2045	...	2049	2215	2221	...	2253	2330	23

		1862	1849	1864		1806	1842	1810		1762	1818	1756		1822	G2964	1826		1834	1874	G2930		1752	G320	18
						d	d	d		d		d			d	d						d		
Guangzhou nan	d.	0657	0723	0746	...	0821	0847	0917	...	0927	1031	1043	...	1101	1112	1230	...	1318	1508	1526	...	1528	1543	16
Zhaoqing dong	d.	0734	0801	|	...	0903	|	0959	...	1009	1109	1126	...	|	1149	1313	...	|	1545	|	...	|	1620	
Hezhou	d.	0830	0917	|	...	1003	1033	1059	...	1109	1212	1222	...	1234	|	1414	...	1450	|	|	...	|	|	17
Guilin xi	d.	0937	1025	1005	...	1125	1143	1213	...	1233	1324	1329	...	1353	1338	1520	...	1557	1750	1752	...	1745	1805	18
Guiyang bei	a.	1145	1239	1216	...	1340	1403	1431	...	1454	1602	1555	...	1608	1537	1741	...	1839	2029	2023	...	1953	2006	21
Zunyi	d.	1246	1341	1307	...	|	|	|	...	|	1659	|	...	1705	|	|	...	1940	2124	|	...	|	2101	22
Chongqing xi	d.	1417	1517	1445	...	|	|	|	...	|	1836	|	...	1841	|	|	...	2105	2243	2231	...	|	2219	23
Suining	d.	...	|	...	...	|	|	|	...	|	|	|	...	|	|	|	...	2235	...	...	...	|	...	..
Chengdu dong	a.	...	1707	...	...	1722	1744	1827	...	1849	2047	1932	...	2050	1856	2131	...	2333	...	...	...	2310	...	..

d – Via Yibin xi and Bijie (timings not shown).

7130 XI'AN - ZHENGZHOU - WUHAN - CHANGSHA- GUANGZHOU

Trains are prefix **G** unless shown otherwise.

km			850		98		820		824		834		838		828		876		846		854			
0	**Xi'an** bei	d.	...	...	1001	...	0948	...	1117	...	1140	...	1243	...	1303	...	1324	...	1352	...	1415	...	...	...
121	Huashan bei	d.	...	...	|	...	|	...	|	...	|	...	1313	...	1333	...	1400	...	|	...	1446	...	...	...
257	Sanmenxia nan	d.	...	...	|	...	1050	...	|	...	1231	...	|	...	|	...	|	...	|	...	1514	...	...	...
380	Luoyang Longmen	d.	0741	...	|	...	1123	...	1236	...	1304	...	1408	...	1427	...	1454	...	1524	...	1548	...	...	...
520	**Zhengzhou**	d.	0838	...	1150	...	1202	...	1315	...	1350	...	1447	...	1510	...	1536	...	1617	...	1636	...	...	...
713	Luohe xi	d.	0959	...	|	...	1255	...	1401	...	1444	...	|	...	|	...	|	...	1704	...	1732	...	...	...
895	Xinyang dong	d.	1046	...	|	...	1339	...	1452	...	|	...	1613	...	|	...	1703	...	1752	...	1834	...	...	...
1050	**Wuhan**	d.	1134	...	1351	...	1427	...	1540	...	1616	...	1704	...	1740	...	1750	...	1844	...	1925	...	...	...
1259	Yueyang dong	d.	1225	...	|	...	1518	...	1632	...	1714	...	1802	...	1831	...	|	...	1938	...	...	...	...	...
1397	**Changsha** nan	d.	1303	...	1515	...	1600	...	1711	...	1752	...	1845	...	1910	...	1915	...	2023	...	...	...	...	...
1437	Zhuzhou xi	d.	|	...	|	...	|	...	|	...	1809	...	|	...	|	...	|	...	|	...	...	...	...	...
1546	Hengyang dong	d.	1343	...	|	...	1639	...	1750	...	1838	...	1924	...	1941	...	2006	...	2105	...	...	...	...	...
1808	Shaoguan	d.	1451	...	|	...	|	...	1858	...	1947	...	2032	...	|	...	|	...	2213	...	...	...	...	...
2018	**Guangzhou** nan	a.	1547	...	1736	...	1839	...	1955	...	2043	...	2128	...	2148	...	2208	...	2309	...	...	...	...	...
2120	**Shenzhen** bei	a.	...	...	...	...	1925	...	2044	...	...	...	...	...	2238	...	...	...	...	...	...	...	...	...

		852		832		96		878		818		822		836		844		868		826			
Shenzhen bei	d.	...	...	...	...	...	...	...	...	0930	...	0955	...	...	...	...	...	...	...	1248	...	...	...
Guangzhou nan	d.	...	...	0703	...	0855	...	0842	...	1015	...	1036	...	1127	...	1223	...	...	...	1330	...	...	...
Shaogun	d.	...	...	|	...	|	...	|	...	1109	...	|	...	1220	...	1316	...	...	...	1423	...	...	...
Hengyang dong	d.	...	...	0911	...	|	...	1051	...	|	...	1243	...	1322	...	|	...	...	...	1531	...	...	...
Zhuzhou xi	d.	...	...	|	...	|	...	|	...	|	...	|	...	1351	...	1453	...	...	...	|	...	...	...
Changsha nan **7065**	d.	...	...	0956	...	1115	...	1132	...	1257	...	1327	...	1412	...	1517	...	...	...	1616	...	...	...
Yueyang dong	d.	...	...	1032	...	|	...	1216	...	|	...	1402	...	1447	...	1553	...	...	...	|	...	...	...
Wuhan	d.	1147	...	1128	...	1236	...	1323	...	1435	...	1500	...	1545	...	1651	...	1701	...	1748	...	...	...
Xinyang dong	d.	|	...	1213	...	|	...	|	...	1520	...	1552	...	1630	...	1737	...	1758	...	1834	...	...	...
Luohe xi	d.	1317	...	|	...	|	...	1445	...	|	...	|	...	1718	...	|	...	|	...	1928	...	...	...
Zhengzhou	d.	1408	...	1351	...	1439	...	1543	...	1654	...	1718	...	1803	...	1914	...	1930	...	2027	...	...	...
Louyang Longmen	d.	1456	...	1437	...	|	...	1634	...	1733	...	1809	...	1851	...	1953	...	2016	...	2106	...	...	...
Sanmenxia nan	d.	1529	...	1510	...	|	...	|	...	|	...	|	...	|	...	|	...	|	...	2145	...	...	...
Huashan bei	d.	1604	...	|	...	|	...	1728	...	|	...	|	...	|	...	2048	...	2118	...	|	...	...	...
Xi'an bei **7070**	a.	1632	...	1601	...	1626	...	1802	...	1903	...	1932	...	2014	...	2116	...	2153	...	2235	...	...	...

7135 XI'AN - CHENGDU and CHONGQING

km			D	D	D1701		D	D	G2201		D	D	D		G89	D	D		D	G2213	D		D	D	D
0	**Xi'an** bei	d.	0711	0750	0815	...	0826	0900	0929	...	0924	0936	1003	...	1128	1036	1054	...	1133	1154	1143	...	1205	1205	12
	Guangyuan	d.	0922	1003	1031	...	1039	1113	1141	...	1135	1147	1214	...	|	1247	1305	...	1346	1405	1354	...	1416	1422	14
	Mianyang	d.	1034	|	|	...	|	|	1235	...	1247	1259	1326	...	|	1359	1417	...	|	|	1506	...	1528	|	
658	**Chengdu** dong	a.	1118	1147	|	...	1223	1257	1319	...	1331	1343	1410	...	1438	1443	1511	...	1530	1537	1550	...	1612	|	16
	Nanchong bei	d.	...	...	|	...	...	...	...	...	...	...	...	...	...	...	...	...	...	...	...	...	...	1558	..
977	**Chongqing** bei	a.	...	...	|	...	...	...	...	...	...	...	...	...	...	...	...	...	...	...	...	...	...	1706	..
	Chongqing xi	a.	...	...	1325	...	...	...	...	...	...	...	...	...	...	...	...	...	...	...	...	...	...	...	..

		D	D	D		D	G1976	D		G571	G307	D		D	D	D		D	D	D		D		D
Xi'an bei	d.	1250	1315	1410	...	1430	1442	1457	...	1512	1523	1517	...	1612	1620	1747	...	1805	1823	1829	...	1853	...	19
Guangyuan	d.	1507	1526	1621	...	1641	1642	1714	...	1710	1729	1728	...	1829	1831	2004	...	2016	2034	2040	...	2104	...	21
Mianyang	d.	|	1638	1733	...	1753	1742	|	...	1819	1830	1840	...	|	1943	|	...	2128	2146	2152	...	2216	...	22
Chengdu dong	a.	|	1722	1817	...	1837	1832	|	...	1900	1914	1924	...	|	2027	|	...	2212	2230	2236	...	2300	...	23
Nanchong bei	d.	1643	...	...	...	...	|	1850	...	|	...	...	...	2005	...	2140	...	...	...	...	...	...	...	..
Chongqing bei	a.	1751	...	...	...	...	|	1958	...	|	...	...	...	2113	...	2248	...	...	...	...	...	...	...	..
Chongqing xi	a.	...	...	...	...	...	2019	...	...	2034	...	...	...	...	...	...	...	...	...	...	...	...	...	..

		D	D	D		G2204	D	D		G1282	D	D		D	G574	D		G308	G1975	D		D	D	D
Chongqing xi	d.	...	...	...	...	...	...	...	...	...	...	...	...	...	0840	...	...	...	0915	...	...	...	...	..
Chongqing bei	d.	...	...	...	...	...	...	...	...	...	...	0833	...	0905	|	...	...	...	|	...	...	...	...	..
Nanchong bei	d.	...	...	...	...	...	...	...	...	...	...	0959	...	|	|	...	...	...	|	...	...	...	...	..
Chengdu dong	d.	0706	0736	0752	...	0802	0809	0900	...	0908	0917	|	...	|	1021	1029	...	1051	1056	1138	...	1208	1240	13
Mianyang	d.	0853	0823	0839	...	0857	0856	|	...	0955	1004	|	...	|	1102	1116	...	1136	1141	1225	...	|	1327	13
Guangyuan	d.	0906	0936	0952	...	1001	1009	1025	...	1052	1117	1144	...	|	1200	1229	...	1240	1246	1338	...	1433	1440	15
Xi'an bei	a.	1114	1144	1200	...	1211	1217	1220	...	1301	1325	1345	...	1354	1405	1437	...	1450	1515	1546	...	1628	1648	17

		D	D	G90		D	D	D		G2210	D	D		D	D	D		D	D	D		D		D
Chongqing xi	d.	...	...	...	...	...	...	...	...	...	...	...	...	...	...	...	...	...	...	...	...	...	...	..
Chongqing bei	d.	1235	...	...	...	...	...	...	...	...	...	...	...	1418	...	...	...	...	...	...	...	1805	...	18
Nanchong bei	d.	1401	...	...	...	...	...	...	...	...	...	...	...	1634	...	...	...	...	...	...	...	2031	...	20
Chengdu dong	d.	|	1351	1502	...	1402	1430	1517	...	1522	1507	1527	...	|	1639	1659	...	1758	1807	1903	...	|	...	|
Mianyang	d.	|	1438	|	...	|	|	1604	...	|	|	|	...	|	1727	|	...	1845	|	1950	...	|	...	|
Guangyuan	d.	1546	1551	|	...	1627	1655	1707	...	1711	1732	1752	...	1819	1830	1924	...	1948	2032	2053	...	2216	...	22
Xi'an bei	a.	1747	1759	1816	...	1822	1850	1915	...	1916	1927	1947	...	2020	2038	2119	...	2156	2227	2301	...	0017	...	00

D – High-speed **D** train, number unknown.

SOUTH KOREA

Capital: **Seoul** (GMT+ 9). 2023 Public Holidays: Jan. 1, 21–24, Mar. 1, May 5, 27, June 6, Aug. 15, Sept. 28–30, Oct. 3, 9, Dec. 25.

Most rail services in South Korea are operated by Korea Rail Road Corporation under the brand names 'Korea Train Express' (KTX, long-distance high-speed trains), 'Korail' (conventional long-distance trains), and 'AREX' (airport trains). Private operator Super Rapid Train (SRT) operates long-distance high-speed trains from its own Seoul terminal at Suseo to Busan and Mokpo. All services convey at least Economy class seating (shown in the tables as '2nd class') with many trains (and all KTX and SRT services) also conveying First class accommodation. Timings shown are the latest available. Note that on high-speed routes only selected services are shown.

Korail offer the *KORAIL PASS* which allows foreign visitors to take almost all trains operated by *Korail*. It is not valid on SRT services, metro and temporary tourist trains. Adult prices: 138,000KRW for a 3 consecutive day pass; 210,000KRW for a 5 consecutive day pass; 121,000 KRW for a 2 day select pass; 193,000 KRW for a 4 day select pass. Select passes can be used over a 10 day period. Discounted rates are offered for youths (13–27), children (6–12) and groups of 2 to 5 persons on all passes. For full details see www.letskorail.com.

SEOUL - POHANG and BUSAN — 7500

KTX, SRT

Frequent additional trains available. Services from / to Seoul Main are operated by KTX, services from / to Seoul Suseo are operated by SRT. Korail Pass **not** valid on SRT services.

km		001	003	231	005	305	007	233	009	309	313	015	315	235	319	321	237	019	323	021	023	327	239	025	027	331	029
0	**Seoul** Main d.	0515	0530	0540	0600	...	0635	0645	0700	...	...	0800	...	0810	...	...	0925	0930	...	1000	1030	...	1045	1100	1200	...	1227
	Seoul Suseo d.	|	|	|	|	0630	|	|	|	0705	0800	|	0805	|	0905	0920	|	|	1000	|	|	1050	|	|	|	1228	|
96	Cheonan Asan d.	|	0609	0619	0639	|	|	0725	0739	0745	|	0839	0845	0851	0941	|	|	|	1029	1039	1109	1119	1124	1139	1239	1302	1306
160	Daejeon d.	0614	0634	0649	0704	0730	0734	0750	0809	0816	0854	0904	0915	0920	1006	1019	1029	1035	1059	1104	1139	1149	1154	1205	1305	1327	1332
293	Dongdaegu d.	0657	0723	0732	0755	0813	0823	0833	0852	0859	0945	0953	0959	1004	1057	1108	1113	1123	1142	1147	1227	1232	1237	1248	1348	1410	1416
374	**Pohang** a.	|	|	0807	|	|	|	0908	|	|	|	|	|	1039	|	|	1148	|	|	|	|	|	1312	|	|	|	|
372	Ulsan d.	0728	0754	...	0821	0844	0854	...	0917	0923	1010	1024	1030	...	1129	1139	...	1155	1206	1219	1252	1303	...	1319	1419	1435	1441
418	**Busan** a.	0749	0815	...	0842	0905	0915	...	0938	0945	1032	1045	1051	...	1150	1200	...	1216	1228	1240	1313	1325	...	1341	1441	1456	1502

	241	241	033	337	339	341	039	245	343	041	043	347	247	047	351	049	355	051	249	357	053	055	359	057	059	365
Seoul Main d.	1241	1300	1320	...	...	...	1430	1435	...	1500	1540	...	1620	1630	...	1700	...	1725	1735	...	1800	1815	...	1830	1900	...
Seoul Suseo d.	|	|	|	1330	1355	1430	|	|	1505	|	|	1555	|	|	1640	|	1730	|	|	1800	|	|	1825	|	|	1920
Cheonan Asan d.	|	1339	1359	1405	|	1504	1509	1514	1534	1539	|	|	|	1704	|	|	|	1805	|	1828	1834	|	1859	1905	1939	|
Daejeon d.	1339	1409	1429	1435	1444	1529	1534	1539	1559	1609	1644	1650	1724	1729	1734	1805	1819	1830	1839	1853	1900	1919	1930	1934	2009	2015
Dongdaegu d.	1422	1457	1512	1518	1527	1613	1618	1628	1647	1653	1727	1741	1807	1812	1822	1854	1910	1918	1928	1936	1949	2002	2013	2017	2052	2058
Pohang a.	1457	1533	|	|	|	|	|	1703	|	|	|	|	1843	|	|	|	|	|	2003	|	|	|	|	|	|	|
Ulsan d.	...	...	1536	1542	1551	1637	1650	...	1712	1718	1752	1807	...	1837	1847	1919	1936	1950	...	2007	2014	2027	2037	2048	2117	2122
Busan a.	...	...	1558	1604	1613	1658	1711	...	1733	1739	1813	1828	...	1858	1908	1940	1957	2011	...	2029	2035	2048	2059	2110	2138	2144

	061	369	063	251	373	067	375	069	071	253	073
Seoul Main d.	1937	...	2000	2040	...	2100	...	2130	2200	2220	2230
Seoul Suseo d.	|	2000	|	|	2100	|	2130	|	|	|	|
Cheonan Asan d.	|	2030	2039	2119	2135	2139	|	|	2239	|	2309
Daejeon d.	2034	2054	2109	2149	2200	2204	2229	2235	2304	2324	2334
Dongdaegu d.	2123	2137	2151	2232	2243	2252	2312	2318	2355	0008	0017
Pohang a.	|	|	|	2307	|	|	|	|	|	0043	|
Ulsan d.	2148	2201	2216	...	2307	2317	2337	2349	0021	...	0042
Busan a.	2209	2223	2237	...	2329	2338	2358	0010	0042	...	0103

	302	002	232	006	306	008	010	234	310	012	314
Busan d.	0500	0510	...	0540	0550	0610	0700	...	0713	0723	0800
Ulsan d.	0523	0533	...	0603	0613	0633	0723	...	0736	0746	0823
Pohang d.	|	|	0537	|	|	|	|	0715	|	|	|
Dongdaegu d.	0548	0558	0618	0628	0638	0703	0748	0757	0801	0816	0853
Daejeon d.	0630	0645	0700	0710	0734	0751	0835	0844	0857	0907	0935
Cheonan Asan d.	0654	0709	|	0740	0805	|	|	|	0928	0933	|
Seoul Suseo a.	0734	|	|	|	0840	|	|	|	0957	|	1035
Seoul Main a.	...	0751	0759	0822	...	0821	0941	0950	...	1014	...

km		014	316	016	020	320	236	238	026	326	328	240	028	030	330	242	032	332	034	336	244	036	340	040	246	346	044
0	**Busan** d.	0810	0829	0840	0906	0915	...	...	1020	1030	1048	...	1100	1200	1210	...	1230	1240	1310	1335	...	1400	1410	1430	...	1530	1545
46	Ulsan d.	0833	0852	0903	0929	0938	...	...	1043	1054	1111	...	1123	1223	1234	...	1253	1303	1333	1358	...	1423	1433	1453	...	1553	1608
	Pohang d.	|	|	|	|	|	0959	1015	|	|	|	1104	|	|	|	1237	|	|	|	|	1404	|	|	|	1537	|	|
125	Dongdaegu d.	0858	0917	0933	0954	1003	1040	1052	1113	1127	1136	1145	1148	1249	1306	1314	1323	1328	1358	1423	1445	1448	1458	1524	1614	1618	1633
258	Daejeon d.	0946	0959	1016	1036	1045	1122	1134	1155	1215	1219	1228	1237	1337	1353	1402	1406	1415	1440	1505	1527	1536	1545	1612	1656	1700	1715
322	Cheonan Asan d.	1010	1023	|	1106	|	|	1204	|	1239	1249	1253	|	1408	1417	|	|	|	1510	1529	1558	1607	1610	|	|	|	1739
404	**Seoul** Suseo a.	|	1058	|	|	1145	|	|	|	1307	1325	|	|	|	1452	|	|	1515	|	1558	|	|	1646	|	|	1754	|
	Seoul Main a.	1046	...	1122	1147	...	1223	1246	1302	...	...	1334	1343	1449	...	1503	1512	...	1546	...	1639	1643	...	1711	1755	...	1820

	352	248	354	048	052	356	250	054	360	056	252	060	364	062	370	064	372	066	374	254	068	070	376	072	378	380
Busan d.	1600	...	1645	1650	1718	1730	...	1800	1810	1835	...	1912	1935	2005	2030	2040	2050	2100	2120	...	2129	2143	2150	2200	2221	2300
Ulsan d.	1623	...	1708	1713	1741	1753	...	1823	1834	1858	...	1935	1958	2028	2053	2103	2113	2123	2144	...	2152	2206	2213	2223	2244	2323
Pohang d.	|	1623	|	|	|	|	1800	|	|	|	1921	|	|	|	|	|	|	|	|	2136	|	|	|	|	|	|
Dongdaegu d.	1653	1704	1738	1744	1814	1818	1837	1849	1859	1929	2002	2005	2023	2058	2123	2133	2138	2149	2209	2217	2222	2231	2238	2248	2314	2348
Daejeon d.	1735	1751	1820	1826	1856	1906	1919	1938	1947	2016	2044	2101	2105	2140	2205	2215	2220	2237	2252	2259	2310	2313	2320	2330	0005	0030
Cheonan Asan d.	1806	|	1844	1850	1920	|	1949	2009	|	|	2115	|	2129	2204	|	2239	2244	|	|	2323	|	|	|	|	|	|
Seoul Suseo a.	1841	|	1926	|	|	1958	|	|	2047	|	|	|	2210	|	2311	|	2319	|	2340	|	|	|	0020	|	0105	0117
Seoul Main a.	...	1857	...	1931	2001	...	2031	2050	...	2122	2157	2203	...	2246	...	2321	...	2342	...	0004	0009	0019	...	0025	...	...

SEOUL - MASAN - JINJU — 7505

KTX

km		201	203	205	209	211	213	215	217	219	221	223
0	**Seoul** Main d.	0505	0540	0825	1005	1250	1340	1620	1735	1805	2040	2210
96	Cheonan Asan d.	|	0619	|	1044	|	1414	|	|	1845	2119	|
160	Daejeon d.	0604	0649	0929	1109	1355	1439	1724	1839	1910	2149	2309
293	Dongdaegu d.	0650	0735	1020	1158	1438	1530	1810	1931	2001	2235	2357
348	Miryang d.	0723	0813	1053	1231	|	1602	1843	|	2033	|	0030
387	Changwon Jungang d.	0753	0839	1119	1257	1537	1628	1914	|	2100	2335	|
397	Changwon d.	0802	|	|	|	1546	|	|	2032	|	2344	0102
401	**Masan** a.	0806	0849	1129	1307	1551	1638	1924	2037	2110	2349	0107
450	**Jinju** a.	0833	0915	1155	1333	...	1704	...	...	...	0015	...

	202	204	206	208	210	212	214	216	218	220	224
Jinju d.	...	0616	0858	1006	...	1253	1434	...	1737	...	...
Masan d.	0500	0641	0924	1032	1240	1319	1500	1644	1803	1958	2143
Changwon d.	0506	0647	|	1038	|	1325	|	1650	|	2004	2149
Changwon Jungang d.	0514	|	0936	1046	1252	1333	1512	1658	1815	|	|
Miryang d.	0542	0720	1004	1111	1316	|	1536	|	1839	2037	2219
Dongdaegu d.	0618	0757	1040	1145	1351	1431	1610	1756	1913	2110	2252
Daejeon d.	0700	0844	1122	1228	1433	1522	1652	1852	2004	2201	2334
Cheonan Asan d.	|	|	|	1253	1457	|	|	1916	|	|	|
Seoul Main a.	0759	0950	1223	1334	1538	1622	1751	1958	2103	2307	0035

SEOUL - YEOSU — 7510

KTX

km		501	503	505	507	509	511	513	515	517	519	521
0	**Seoul** Yongsan d.	0510	0705	0841	0948	1055	1220	1412	1645	1746	1850	2005
93	Cheonan Asan d.	|	0750	|	|	1133	1258	|	1723	|	1928	2043
	Osong d.	0555	0802	0927	1046	1145	|	1457	|	1826	|	|
240	Iksan d.	0627	0838	1002	1123	1221	1344	1532	1811	1904	2011	2120
266	Jeonju d.	0644	0855	1019	1140	1237	1401	1549	1828	1921	2027	2136
326	Namwon d.	0711	0922	1046	1207	1304	1428	1616	1855	1948	2054	2203
394	Suncheon d.	0742	0956	1124	1241	1339	1502	1648	1932	2019	2129	2237
434	**Yeosu** Expo a.	0805	1018	1146	1303	1401	1521	1710	1954	2042	2151	2259

	502	504	506	508	510	512	514	516	518	520	522
Yeosu Expo d.	0506	0710	0842	1036	1159	1304	1402	1458	1635	1805	2024
Suncheon d.	0527	0732	0904	1058	1221	1323	1424	1519	1657	1827	2046
Namwon d.	0601	0806	0937	1128	1255	1353	1458	1553	1731	1904	2119
Jeonju d.	0626	0831	1003	1154	1321	1419	1523	1619	1757	1930	2145
Iksan d.	0646	0848	1023	1214	1337	1435	1543	1635	1817	1946	2205
Osong d.	0724	0924	|	1243	|	1505	|	1711	|	2023	2235
Cheonan Asan d.	|	0938	|	1257	1422	1519	|	|	1854	|	2249
Seoul Yongsan a.	0812	1018	1134	1337	1457	1559	1701	1759	1934	2111	2324

SEOUL - GWANGJU - MOKPO — 7515

KTX, SRT

Services from / to Seoul Yongsan are operated by KTX, services from / to Seoul Suseo are operated by SRT. Korail Pass **not** valid on SRT services. Table continues on next page →

km		651	401	601	403	405	653	603	407	409	605	655	607	413		657	609	415	417	659	419	611	421	613	423	661	427
0	**Seoul** Yongsan d.	...	0510	...	0550	0631	...	...	0749	0822	...	...	...	1041	...	...	...	1220	1247	...	1332	...	1450	...	1536	...	1645
	Seoul Suseo d.	0508	|	0539	|	|	0640	0740	|	|	0833	0940	1020	|	...	1100	1220	|	|	1310	|	1409	|	1520	|	1611	|
93	Cheonan Asan d.	|	|	0614	0628	|	0719	|	|	0855	|	1019	1059	1114	...	1129	1249	1258	|	1343	1410	|	1528	1554	|	|	1723
121	Osong d.	0544	0555	|	0640	0716	0731	|	|	0907	0919	1031	1111	1126	...	1206	|	|	1327	1356	|	1451	1540	1607	1621	|	|
240	Iksan d.	0613	0624	0657	0709	0751	0800	0845	0905	0936	0955	1100	1147	1155	...	|	1332	1341	1356	1425	1446	1520	1609	1642	1656	1725	1806
287	Jeongeup d.	0630	0641	|	0726	0808	0817	|	0922	0953	1012	|	|	1212	...	1223	|	|	1413	|	1503	1537	1626	|	1713	|	1823
337	**Gwangju** Songjeong d.	0651	0702	0728	0747	0829	0838	0915	0943	1014	1031	1132	1217	1233	...	1244	1403	1413	1434	1457	1524	1557	1647	1713	1734	1757	1844
405	**Mokpo** a.	0728	0734	...	0825	0906	0915	...	1020	1051	...	1209	...	1310	...	1321	...	1450	1507	1534	1601	...	1720	...	1811	1834	1921

7515 SEOUL - GWANGJU - MOKPO
KTX, SRT

Services from / to Seoul Yongsan are operated by KTX, services from / to Seoul Suseo are operated by SRT. Korail Pass **not** valid on SRT services. For additional services see previous page.

	663	429	615	665	617	433	435	667	437	619
Seoul Yongsan d.	...	1746	...	...	...	1943	2035	...	2121	...
Seoul Suseo d.	1710	|	1805	1910	1940	|	|	2108	|	2220
Cheonan Asan d.	|	|	1840	|	|	|	2113	2144	|	|
Osong d.	1752	1826	|	1956	2023	2028	2125	|	|	2301
Iksan d.	1821	1901	1923	2032	2052	2103	2154	2227	2237	2330
Jeongeup d.	1838	|	|	2049	2109	2120	2211	|	|	2347
Gwangju Songjeong d.	1859	1933	1954	2110	2128	2141	2232	2259	2309	0006
Mokpo a.	1936	2010	...	2147	...	2218	2309	2336	2356	...

	602	404	604	652	406	606	654	408	410	608	412
Mokpo d.	...	0523	...	0625	0703	...	0756	0810	0906	...	0952
Gwangju Songjeong d.	0513	0601	0617	0703	0741	0753	0834	0848	0944	1018	1027
Jeongeup d.	0533	0621	0637	|	0801	0813	0854	0908	|	|	1047
Iksan d.	0551	0646	0655	0735	0820	0831	0913	0933	1023	1050	1105
Osong d.	0621	0724	0731	|	0856	0907	|	1003	|	1119	|
Cheonan Asan d.	0635	|	0745	0812	|	|	0950	1017	|	|	|
Seoul Suseo a.	0710	|	0826	0853	|	0951	1025	|	|	1203	|
Seoul Yongsan a.	...	0812	...	...	0944	...	...	1057	1134	...	1216

	656	610	416	612	418	658	420	660	422	614	424	616	662		426	430	618	432	664	434	620	666	438	622	440	668
Mokpo d.	1005	...	1057	...	1250	1305	1343	1400	1420	...	1550	...	1641	...	1654	1758	...	1848	1901	1957	...	2021	2046	...	2152	2225
Gwangju Songjeong d.	1043	1113	1135	1256	1328	1343	1422	1438	1458	1550	1628	1622	1719	...	1732	1836	1827	1926	1940	2035	2022	2059	2120	2153	2230	2303
Jeongeup d.	1103	|	|	|	1348	1403	1442	1458	1518	|	1649	1642	1739	...	1752	1856	1847	1946	2000	|	|	2119	2140	2213	|	2323
Iksan d.	1122	1145	1214	1328	1407	1422	1501	1517	1543	1622	1713	1700	1758	...	1817	1915	1905	2005	2019	2108	2054	2138	2205	2231	2302	2342
Osong d.	|	|	1243	|	1436	1451	1538	|	|	|	|	1736	1827	...	|	1951	1941	|	2055	2144	2130	2214	2235	2308	|	|
Cheonan Asan d.	1159	|	1257	|	|	1505	|	1602	|	|	1757	1750	|	...	1854	2005	1955	|	|	|	2144	|	2249	|	|	0019
Seoul Suseo a.	1234	1252	|	1437	|	1540	|	1637	|	1736	|	1832	1911	...	|	|	2031	|	2143	|	2219	2251	|	2351	|	0054
Seoul Yongsan a.	...	...	1337	...	1524	...	1624	...	1701	...	1832	...	...	...	1934	2045	...	2116	...	2232	...	...	2324	...	0013	...

7520 SEOUL - DONGHAE and GANGNEUNG
KTX

km		801	803		841	805		807	809		843	811		813	815		845	817		819	847		821	823		825	827
0	**Seoul** Main d.	0511	0601	...	0701	0801	...	0901	1001	...	1101	1301	...	1331	1401	...	1501	1601	...	1801	1826	...	1901	2001	...	2131	2211
8	**Seoul** Ch'yangni d.	0532	0622	...	0722	0822	...	0922	1022	...	1122	1322	...	1352	1422	...	1522	1625	...	1822	1847	...	1922	2022	...	2152	2232
	Seowonju d.	|	|	...	|	|	...	1009	|	...	1210	|	...	|	1507	...	|	|	...	|	|	...	|	|	...	|	|
115	Manjong d.	0623	0712	...	0814	0911	...	|	1111	...	|	1411	...	1441	|	...	1611	1714	...	1911	1936	...	2014	2113	...	2241	2318
174	Pyeongchang d.	0645	0738	...	0838	0940	...	|	1137	...	|	1436	...	|	1534	...	|	1738	...	1939	2001	...	2044	|	...	2311	|
259	**Donghae** a.	|	|	...	0942	|	...	|	|	...	1338	|	...	|	|	...	1740	|	...	|	2101	...	|	|	...	|	|
231	**Gangneung** a.	0708	0805	...	...	1001	...	1057	1158	...	...	1502	...	1523	1556	...	...	1804	...	2004	...	...	2106	2155	...	2333	2400

	802	804		806	808		810	842		812	814		844	816		818	820		822	846		824	826		848	828
Gangneung d.	0525	0630	...	0730	0830	...	1030	...	...	1133	1225	...	...	1529	...	1640	1725	...	1840	...	...	2030	2128	...	...	2230
Donghae d.	|	|	...	|	|	...	|	1005	...	|	|	...	1400	|	...	|	|	...	|	1903	...	|	|	...	2130	|
Pyeongchang d.	|	0659	...	0753	0859	...	|	1106	...	|	1254	...	1507	1553	...	|	1754	...	1909	2009	...	2053	|	...	2237	2254
Manjong d.	0614	0724	...	0820	0924	...	|	1130	...	|	1319	...	1527	1618	...	|	1815	...	1939	2034	...	2118	2220	...	2302	2314
Seowonju d.	|	|	...	|	|	...	1123	|	...	1219	|	...	|	|	...	1733	|	...	|	|	...	|	|	...	|	|
Seoul Cheongnyangni a.	0702	0813	...	0908	1013	...	1208	1220	...	1303	1407	...	1616	1706	...	1818	1906	...	2030	2125	...	2208	2306	...	2349	0002
Seoul Main a.	0723	0838	...	0929	1035	...	1229	1241	...	1324	1427	...	1637	1727	...	1839	1928	...	2051	2146	...	2229	2328	...	0011	0023

7525 SEOUL - ANDONG
Korail, KTX

km		701	1601	703		705	707	709		1603	711	713
			A							A		
0	**Seoul** Ch'yangni d.	0600	0650	0900	...	1100	1400	1600	...	1731	1900	2200
	Seowonju d.	|	0752	|	...	1145	1447	1643	...	1550	|	|
105	Wonju d.	0649	0800	0947	...	1152	|	1650	...	1558	1948	2250
155	Jecheon d.	0706	0828	1004	...	1209	1505	1707	...	1623	2005	2307
219	Yeongju d.	0742	0915	1043	...	1242	1544	1744	...	1710	2044	2340
248	**Andong** d.	0802	0936	1103	...	1302	1604	1804	...	1731	2104	2400

	702	704	706		1602	708	710		1604	712	714
					A				A		
Andong d.	0600	0830	1130	...	1046	1335	1630	...	1818	1900	2125
Yeongju d.	0620	0851	1150	...	1115	1355	1650	...	1846	1921	2145
Jecheon d.	0657	0930	1227	...	1159	1432	1727	...	1928	2001	2219
Wonju d.	0714	0947	1244	...	1224	1448	1744	...	1952	2019	2235
Seowonju d.	|	0954	|	...	1231	1455	|	...	1959	|	|
Seoul Ch'yangni a.	0803	1036	1333	...	1342	1537	1830	...	2055	2105	2324

A – MUNUNGHWA – (2) Seoul - Andong - Busan and v.v. Operated by Korail.

7530 DONGHAE - ANDONG and DAEGU - BUSAN
2nd class Korail

km		1791	1601	1793	1671	1795	1603	1673				
			A				A					
0	**Donghae** d.	...	...	...	1101	...	...	1756	...	...	...	...
	Dogye d.	...	...	...	1143	...	...	1836	...	...	...	...
	Cheoram d.	...	...	...	1213	...	...	1903	...	...	...	...
184	Yeongju d.	...	...	...	1402	...	...	2054	...	...	...	...
221	**Andong** d.	...	0936	...	1423	...	1731	2116	...	...	...	...
348	**Dongdaegu** d.	0831	|	1300	1605	1700	|	2253	...	...	...	...
	Singyeongju d.	0923	1116	1352	...	1752	1914	...	...	...	...	...
	Taehwagang (Ulsan) d.	0956	1149	1425	...	1825	1947	...	...	...	...	...
	Shinhaeundu d.	1043	1235	1512	...	1913	2033	...	...	...	...	...
*533**	**Busan** Bujeon a.	1101	1253	1530	...	1931	2051	...	...	...	...	...

	1672	1602	1792	1604	1674	1794	1796				
		A		A							
Busan Bujeon d.	...	0722	1215	1450	...	1736	1842	...	...	...	...
Shinhaeundu d.	...	0740	1233	1508	...	1754	1900	...	...	...	...
Taehwagang (Ulsan) d.	...	0828	1320	1555	...	1841	1948	...	...	...	...
Singyeongju d.	...	0901	1352	1628	...	1913	2020	...	...	...	...
Dongdaegu d.	0605	|	1446	|	1803	2007	2114	...	...	...	...
Andong d.	0745	1046	...	1818	1950	...	...	...	...	...	...
Yeongju d.	0814	...	...	...	2013	...	...	...	...	...	...
Cheoram d.	0952	...	...	...	2204	...	...	...	...	...	...
Dogye d.	1020	...	...	...	2234	...	...	...	...	...	...
Donghae a.	1058	...	...	...	2312	...	...	...	...	...	...

A – MUNUNGHWA – (2) Seoul - Andong - Busan and v.v. Operated by Korail.

* – *462 km* via Andong.

7535 MOKPO - BUSAN
2nd class Korail

km		1942	1972	1944	1952	1946	1406	1974	1408	1470	1976	
0	**Mokpo** d.	...	...	...	0923	...	1137	...	1611	1831	...	...
	Gwangju Songjeong d.	...	0550	...	1033	...	1224	1541	1712	1932	2000	...
85	Seogwangju d.	...	0559	...	1042	...	...	1550	...	...	2010	...
	Boseong d.	...	0708	...	1152	...	...	1700	...	...	2118	...
206	**Suncheon** d.	0620	0806	0915	1251	1737	...	1758	...	...	2213	...
284	Jinju d.	0721	...	1016	1352	1838	...	...	...	...	...	...
350	Masan d.	0804	...	1059	1435	1922	...	...	...	...	...	...
354	Changwon d.	0810	...	1105	1441	1928	...	...	...	...	...	...
	Changwon Jungang d.	0819	...	1114	1450	1937	...	...	...	...	...	...
385	Samnangjin d.	0846	...	1140	1516	2000	...	...	...	...	...	...
433	**Busan** Bujeon a.	0932	...	1226	1610	2046	...	...	...	...	...	...

	1971	1951	1941	1973	1473	1943	1975	1407	1945		
Busan Bujeon d.	...	0617	1020	...	...	1338	...	...	1852	...	...
Samnangjin d.	...	0708	1107	...	...	1426	...	...	1939	...	...
Changwon Jungang d.	...	0736	1134	...	...	1453	...	...	2009	...	...
Changwon d.	...	0745	1143	...	...	1502	...	...	2018	...	...
Masan d.	...	0751	1149	...	...	1509	...	...	2025	...	...
Jinju d.	...	0838	1232	...	...	1552	...	...	2108	...	...
Suncheon d.	0607	0939	1332	1338	...	1652	1844	...	2208	...	...
Boseong d.	0707	1039	...	1437	...	...	1943	...	...	...	...
Seogwangju d.	0819	1151	...	1550	...	...	2056	...	...	...	...
Gwangju Songjeong a.	0827	1201	...	1558	1743	...	2104	2116	...	...	...
Mokpo a.	...	1259	...	...	1841	...	...	2208	...	...	...

7540 SEOUL - CHUNCHEON
2nd class Korail

Seoul Yongsan - **Namchuncheon** and v.v. *93 km*. Journey 69 – 78 minutes.

From **Seoul** Yongsan (most trains call at **Gapyeong** 56 – 64 mins later) on ①–⑤ at 0600, 0656, 0752, 0851, 0957, 1058, 1200, 1253, 1400, 1520, 1600, 1700, 1746, 1856, 1958, 2032, 2121, 2248 on ⑥⑦ at 0615, 0655, 0755, 0820, 0847, 0918, 0949, 1026, 1059, 1130, 1157, 1258, 1415, 1444, 1514, 1547, 1618, 1656, 1729, 1759, 1900, 1930, 2000, 2035, 2120, 2205.

From **Namchuncheon** (most trains call at **Gapyeong** 15 – 19 minutes later) on ①–⑤ at 0612, 0658, 0726, 0816, 0925, 1027, 1118, 1214, 1319, 1410, 1533, 1616, 1705, 1818, 1857, 1943, 2116 2218; on ⑥⑦ at 0610, 0711, 0816, 0851, 0936, 0956, 1026, 1129, 1231, 1315, 1342, 1409, 1454, 1511, 1556, 1619, 1659, 1730, 1758, 1828, 1904, 1938, 2034, 2119, 2152, 2217.

7545 INCHEON AIRPORT ✈ - SEOUL
AREX

Incheon Airport ✈ - **Seoul** Main and v.v. *61 km*. 2nd class only. Journey 51 minutes. Trains also call at Terminal One 8 minutes before/after Terminal Two.

From **Incheon Airport** ✈ T2 at 0515, 0550, 0630, 0720, 0800, 0840, 0920, 1000, 1040, 1120, 1200, 1240, 1320, 1400, 1440, 1520, 1600, 1640, 1720, 1800, 1840, 1920, 2000, 2050, 2140, 2240
Frequent additional slower services (calling at Gimpo Airport ✈) run 5 – 6 times per hour 0523 – 2342 (journey 55 – 60 minutes Incheon - Seoul).

From **Seoul** Main at 0610, 0650, 0730, 0810, 0850, 0930, 1010, 1050, 1130, 1210, 1250, 1330, 1410, 1450, 1530, 1610, 1650, 1730, 1810, 1850, 1930, 2010, 2050, 2130, 2210, 2250.
Frequent additional slower services (calling at Gimpo Airport ✈) run 5 – 6 times per hour 0520 – 2338 (journey 55 – 60 minutes Seoul - Incheon).

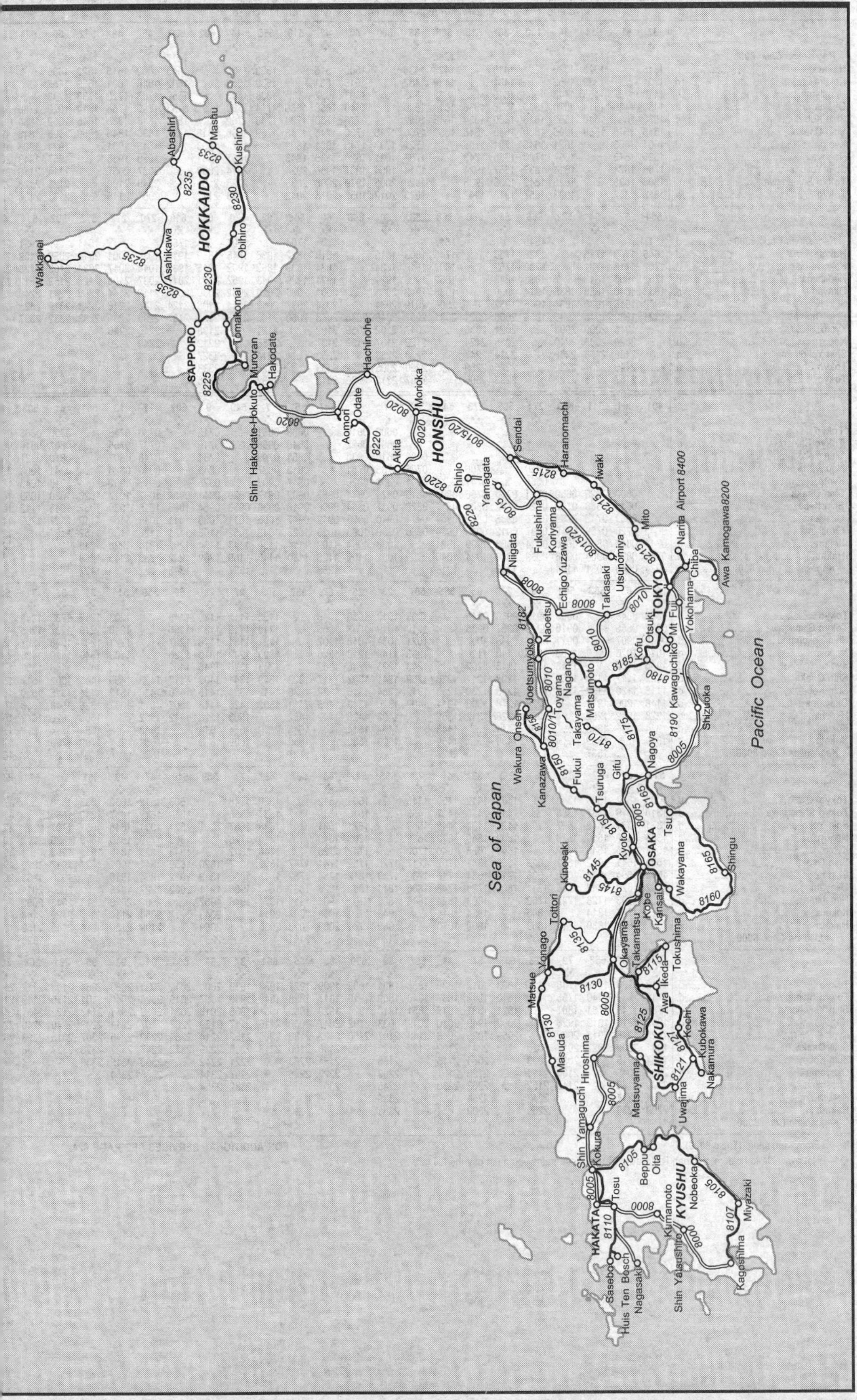

HOKKAIDO
Wakkanai
Asahikawa
Abashiri
Mashu
Kushiro
Obihiro
Tomakomai
SAPPORO
Muroran
Hakodate
Shin Hakodate-Hokuto
8235
8233
8230
8225
8020
HONSHU
Aomori
Odate
Hachinohe
Morioka
Akita
Sendai
Haranomachi
Shinjo
Yamagata
Iwaki
Fukushima
Koriyama
Niigata
Mito
Narita Airport 8400
Awa Kamogawa 8200
Chiba
Utsunomiya
Takasaki
EchigoYuzawa
Naoetsu
Joetsumyoko
TOKYO
Yokohama
Mt Fuji
Otsuki
Kawaguchiko
Kofu
Nagano
Matsumoto
Toyama
Takayama
Wakura Onsen
Kanazawa
Fukui
Tsuruga
Gifu
Nagoya
Shizuoka
Kyoto
OSAKA
Tsu
Wakayama
Shingu
Kinosaki
Kobe
Kansai
Tottori
Okayama
Yonago
Matsue
Masuda
Hiroshima
Shin Yamaguchi
Kokura
Takamatsu
Tokushima
SHIKOKU
Awa Ikeda
Kochi
Kubokawa
Nakamura
Matsuyama
Uwajima
KYUSHU
HAKATA
Tosu
Beppu
Oita
Kumamoto
Nobeoka
Miyazaki
Kagoshima
Shin Yatsushiro
Sasebo
Huis Ten Bosch
Nagasaki
8215
8015/20
8220
8015
8008
8010
8182
8185
8180
8190
8175
8170
8010/1
8150
8155
8005
8165
8160
8145
8135
8130
8115
8125
8121
8105
8110
8107
8000
Sea of Japan
Pacific Ocean

8005 HAKATA - OSAKA - TOKYO

JR Central, JR W

Sanyo and *Tokaido Shinkansen* high-speed lines. Service from March 18.

	32 ❖	514	554	34 ❖	100 ❖	36 ❖	516	556	38 ❖	660	40 ❖	42 ❖	518	558	44 ❖	662	560	46 ❖	48 ❖	562	50 ❖	520
Kagoshima Chuo **8000** d.	...	...	1155	...	...	...	...	1255	...	...	...	...	...	1345	...	...	1417	...	...	1445	...	...
Hakata d.	1315	...	1323	1336	...	1415	...	1423	1436	...	1500	1515	...	1523	1536	...	1545	1600	1615	1623	1636	...
Kokura d.	1331	...	1339	1352	...	1431	...	1439	1452	...	1516	1531	...	1539	1552	...	1602	1616	1631	1639	1652	...
Hiroshima d.	1418	...	1433	1443	1503	1518	...	1533	1543	...	1603	1622	...	1633	1643	...	1652	1703	1722	1733	1743	...
Okayama d.	1458	1436	1514	1520	1540	1558	1536	1614	1620	...	1640	1658	1636	1714	1720	...	1733	1740	1758	1814	1820	1736
Shin Kobe d.	1530	1534	1546	1552	1616	1630	1634	1646	1652	...	1716	1730	1734	1746	1752	...	1808	1816	1830	1846	1852	1834
Shin **Osaka** d.	1545	1548	1559	1606	1630	1645	1648	1659	1706	1718	1730	1745	1748	1759	1806	1818	1821	1830	1845	1859	1906	1848
Kyoto d.	1601	1608	...	1621	1645	1701	1708	...	1721	1733	1745	1801	1808	...	1821	1833	...	1845	1901	...	1921	1908
Nagoya d.	1636	1643	...	1657	1720	1736	1743	...	1757	1831	1820	1836	1843	...	1857	1931	...	1920	1936	...	1957	1943
Shin Yokohama a.	1756	1824	...	1814	1837	1857	1924	...	1914	1954	1937	1956	2024	...	2014	2053	...	2037	2057	...	2114	2116
Tokyo Shinagawa a.	1808	1835	...	1825	1849	1908	1935	...	1925	2005	1949	2008	2035	...	2025	2105	...	2049	2108	...	2125	2128
Tokyo a.	1815	1842	...	1833	1857	1915	1942	...	1933	2012	1957	2015	2042	...	2033	2112	...	2057	2115	...	2133	2136

	564	52 ❖	54 ❖	522	566	56 ❖	666	568	58 ❖	60 ❖	668	60 ❖	608 ❖	62 ❖	570	64 ❖	610 ❖	270 ❖	272 ❖	572	592	614 ❖
Kagoshima Chuo **8000** d.	1517	...	...	...	1545	...	...	1617	...	...	...	...	1704	...	1707	...	1753	...	...	1841	...	1951
Hakata d.	1645	1700	1715	...	1723	1736	...	1745	1803	1818	...	1818	1822	1836	1845	1859	1915	1930	2001	2018	2052	2109
Kokura d.	1702	1716	1731	...	1739	1752	...	1802	1819	1834	...	1834	1839	1852	1902	1915	1931	1946	2017	2034	2109	2125
Hiroshima d.	1752	1803	1818	...	1833	1843	...	1852	1906	1921	...	1921	1929	1943	1952	2001	2017	2037	2103	2125	2159	2212
Okayama d.	1833	1840	1858	1836	1914	1920	...	1933	1942	2001	...	2001	2005	2020	2032	2036	2053	2113	2144	2205	2241	2248
Shin Kobe d.	1908	1916	1930	1934	1946	1952	...	2008	2019	2034	...	2034	2037	2052	2114	2108	2124	2146	2216	2241	2319	2325
Shin **Osaka** d.	1921	1930	1945	1948	1959	2006	2021	2021	2033	2048	2045	2048	2050	2106	2126	2124	2137	2200	2230	2253	2332	2337
Kyoto d.	...	1945	2000	2003	...	2021	2036	...	2047	2102	2059	2102	...	2121	...	2138	...	2215	2246	...	...	...
Nagoya d.	...	2020	2035	2040	...	2056	2124	...	2122	2137	2139	2137	...	2156	...	2212	...	2249	2320	...	...	...
Shin Yokohama a.	...	2138	2156	2208	...	2214	2247	...	2238	2253	2311	2253	...	2314	...	2327	...	...	...	...	...	...
Tokyo Shinagawa a.	...	2149	2207	2220	...	2225	2259	...	2250	2305	2322	2305	...	2325	...	2338	...	...	...	...	...	...
Tokyo a.	...	2157	2215	2227	...	2233	2306	...	2257	2312	2329	2312	...	2332	...	2345	...	...	...	...	...	...

	401	601 ❖	541	543	271 ❖	605 ❖	273 ❖	545	533	1 ❖	3 ❖	547	5 ❖	7 ❖	549	9 ❖	607 ❖	11 ❖	13 ❖	551	61 ❖	503
Tokyo d.	...	...	...	...	...	...	...	...	...	0600	0615	...	0633	0651	...	0712	...	0730	0748	...	0800	0803
Tokyo Shinagawa d.	...	...	...	...	...	...	...	...	...	0607	0622	...	0640	0658	...	0719	...	0737	0755	...	0807	0810
Shin Yokohama d.	...	...	...	...	...	...	...	...	0600	0618	0633	...	0651	0709	...	0731	...	0748	0807	...	0818	0821
Nagoya d.	...	...	...	...	0620	...	0706	...	0726	0735	0751	...	0812	0827	...	0849	...	0910	0826	...	0941	1003
Kyoto d.	...	...	...	...	0655	...	0741	...	0801	0809	0826	...	0847	0902	...	0925	...	0946	1002	...	1016	1043
Shin **Osaka** d.	...	0600	0625	0650	0711	0750	0756	0804	0815	0824	0841	0853	0902	0917	0920	0941	0954	1002	1017	1020	1030	1059
Shin Kobe d.	...	0613	0638	0702	0724	0802	0809	0817	0828	0937	0854	0906	0915	0930	0933	0954	1006	1015	1030	1033	1045	1112
Okayama d.	...	0651	0715	0739	0756	0835	0842	0854	0914	0910	0926	0942	0947	1006	1011	1026	1041	1048	1103	1110	1121	1202
Hiroshima d.	0643	0726	0758	0819	0837	0912	0918	0934	0956	0950	1003	1023	1028	1043	1052	1103	1121	1128	1139	1152	1157	...
Kokura d.	0741	0813	0849	0910	0924	1003	1009	1024	...	1036	1054	1109	1114	1130	1143	1154	1207	1214	1230	1243	...	...
Hakata a.	0756	0828	0904	0926	0939	1018	1024	1040	...	1052	1109	1126	1130	1145	1159	1209	1222	1230	1245	1259	...	...
Kagoshima Chuo **8000** a.	0934	0946	1031	1104	...	1136	...	1218	...	...	...	1253	...	...	1337	...	1343	...	...	1427	...	...

	17 ❖	63 ❖	553	505	19 ❖	21 ❖	65 ❖	555	507	23 ❖	25 ❖	67 ❖	557	509	27 ❖	29 ❖	69 ❖	559	511	31 ❖	33 ❖	71 ❖
Tokyo d.	0830	0848	...	0903	0912	0930	0948	...	1003	1012	1030	1048	...	1103	1112	1130	1148	...	1203	1212	1230	1248
Tokyo Shinagawa d.	0837	0855	...	0910	0919	0937	0955	...	1010	1019	1037	1055	...	1110	1119	1137	1155	...	1210	1219	1237	1255
Shin Yokohama d.	0848	0907	...	0921	0931	0948	1007	...	1021	1031	1048	1107	...	1121	1131	1148	1207	...	1221	1231	1248	1307
Nagoya d.	1010	1026	...	1103	1049	1110	1126	...	1203	1149	1210	1226	...	1303	1249	1310	1326	...	1403	1349	1410	1426
Kyoto d.	1046	1102	...	1143	1125	1146	1202	...	1243	1225	1246	1302	...	1343	1325	1346	1402	...	1443	1425	1446	1502
Shin **Osaka** d.	1102	1117	1120	1159	1141	1202	1217	1220	1259	1241	1302	1317	1323	1359	1341	1402	1417	1423	1459	1441	1502	1517
Shin Kobe d.	1115	1130	1133	1212	1154	1215	1230	1233	1312	1254	1315	1330	1336	1412	1354	1415	1430	1436	1512	1454	1515	1530
Okayama d.	1148	1206	1211	1302	1226	1248	1306	1311	1402	1326	1348	1406	1411	1502	1426	1448	1506	1511	1602	1526	1548	1606
Hiroshima d.	1228	1242	1252	...	1303	1328	1342	1352	...	1403	1428	1442	1452	...	1503	1528	1542	1552	...	1603	1628	1642
Kokura d.	1314	...	1343	...	1354	1414	...	1443	...	1454	1514	...	1543	...	1554	1614	...	1643	...	1654	1714	...
Hakata a.	1330	...	1359	...	1409	1430	...	1459	...	1509	1530	...	1559	...	1609	1630	...	1659	...	1709	1730	...
Kagoshima Chuo **8000** a.	...	...	1537	...	...	...	...	1627	...	...	...	...	1727	...	...	...	...	1826	...	...	...	...

	513	35 ❖	37 ❖	73 ❖	563	515	39 ❖	41 ❖	75 ❖	565	517	43 ❖	567	45 ❖	77 ❖	569	519	47 ❖	49 ❖	651	51 ❖	571
Tokyo d.	1303	1312	1330	1348	...	1403	1412	1430	1448	...	1503	1512	...	1530	1548	...	1603	1612	1630	1633	1648	...
Tokyo Shinagawa d.	1310	1319	1337	1355	...	1410	1419	1437	1455	...	1510	1519	...	1537	1555	...	1610	1619	1637	1640	1655	...
Shin Yokohama d.	1321	1331	1348	1407	...	1421	1431	1448	1507	...	1521	1531	...	1548	1607	...	1621	1931	1648	1651	1707	...
Nagoya d.	1503	1449	1510	1526	...	1603	1549	1610	1626	...	1703	1649	...	1710	1726	...	1803	1749	1810	1819	1826	...
Kyoto d.	1543	1525	1546	1602	...	1643	1625	1646	1702	...	1743	1725	...	1746	1802	...	1843	1825	1846	1913	1902	...
Shin **Osaka** d.	1559	1541	1602	1617	1623	1659	1641	1702	1717	1720	1759	1741	1747	1802	1817	1820	1859	1841	1902	1927	1917	1920
Shin Kobe d.	1612	1554	1615	1630	1636	1712	1654	1715	1730	1733	1812	1754	1759	1815	1830	1833	1912	1854	1915	...	1930	1933
Okayama d.	1702	1626	1648	1706	1711	1802	1726	1748	1806	1811	1902	1826	1832	1848	1906	1911	2002	1927	1948	...	2006	2011
Hiroshima d.	...	1703	1728	1742	1752	...	1803	1824	1846	1852	...	1903	1913	1924	1946	1952	...	2003	2028	...	2043	2052
Kokura d.	...	1754	1814	...	1843	...	1854	1914	...	1943	...	1954	2007	2014	...	2043	...	2054	2114	...	2129	2143
Hakata a.	...	1809	1830	...	1859	...	1909	1930	...	1959	...	2009	2023	2030	...	2059	...	2109	2130	...	2145	2159
Kagoshima Chuo **8000** a.	...	...	...	...	2039	...	...	...	...	2139	...	...	2151	...	...	2239	...	...	...	...	...	2325

	53 ❖	55 ❖	653	79 ❖	573 k	655	57 ❖	81 ❖	657	59 ❖	659	83 ❖	85 ❖	661	87 ❖	89 ❖	663	91 ❖	93 ❖	95 ❖	261 ❖	263 ❖
Tokyo d.	1712	1730	1733	1748	...	1803	1812	1830	1833	1851	1903	1909	1921	1933	1939	2000	2012	2021	2033	2054	2103	2112
Tokyo Shinagawa d.	1719	1737	1740	1755	...	1810	1819	1837	1840	1859	1910	1917	1928	1940	1946	2007	2019	2028	2040	2101	2110	2119
Shin Yokohama d.	1731	1748	1751	1807	...	1821	1831	1848	1851	1910	1921	1929	1939	1951	1958	2018	2031	2039	2051	2113	2122	2131
Nagoya d.	1849	1910	1919	1926	...	2002	1949	2010	2019	2033	2102	2047	2058	2115	2117	2139	2207	2157	2211	2232	2240	2249
Kyoto d.	1925	1946	2013	2002	...	2056	2025	2046	2113	2107	2150	2122	2133	2205	2153	2214	2259	2232	2246	2307	2315	2323
Shin **Osaka** d.	1941	2002	2027	2017	2020	2109	2041	2102	2127	2123	2203	2138	2150	2218	2208	2229	2312	2247	2302	2323	2327	2336
Shin Kobe d.	1954	2015	...	2030	2033	...	2054	2115	...	2136	...	2151	2203	...	2221	2242	...	2300	2315	2336	...	...
Okayama d.	2026	2048	...	2106	2111	...	2126	2151	...	2209	...	2227	2238	...	2257	2314	...	2335	2350	...	...	...
Hiroshima d.	2103	2128	...	2146	2152	...	2203	2230	...	2245	...	2307	...	...	2332	2354	...	...	...	...	...	...
Kokura d.	2154	2214	...	...	2243	...	2254	...	...	2336	...	...	...	...	...	...	...	...	...	...	...	...
Hakata a.	2209	2230	...	...	2259	...	2309	...	...	2351	...	...	...	...	...	...	...	...	...	...	...	...
Kagoshima Chuo **8000** a.	...	...	...	...	...	...	...	...	...	...	...	...	...	...	...	...	...	...	...	...	...	...

k – From Kumamoto (Table **8000**).

❖ – Not available to holders of Japan Rail Pass. To use these trains you must pay the full fare.

FOR ADDITIONAL SERVICES SEE PAGE 624.

JR East   Subject to alteration from March 18   TOKYO - ECHIGO YUZAWA - NIIGATA   8008

Joetsu Shinkansen high-speed line.

km		481	301	401	303	471 ⚒		305	403	307	309	311		313	315	317	319	321		323	325	327	329	331
0	**Tokyo** .... 8010/15/20 d.	...	0608	0636	0704	0736	...	0748	0804	0824	0852	0912	...	0928	1016	1040	1140	1240	...	1340	1440	1516	1540	1616
4	**Tokyo** Ueno .... 8010/15/20 d.	...	0614	0642	0710	0742	...	0754	0810	0830	0858	|	...	0934	1022	1046	1146	1246	...	1346	1446	1522	1546	1622
31	Omiya .... 8010/15/20 d.	...	0633	0701	0729	0801	...	0813	0829	0849	0917	0934	...	0953	1041	1105	1205	1305	...	1405	1505	1541	1605	1641
109	Takasaki .... d.	...	0658	0736	|	0832	...	0838	0905	0918	0949	|	...	1025	1105	1133	1230	1330	...	1430	1529	|	1630	1711
183	**Echigo Yuzawa** .... d.	0700	0724	0805	0814	...	...	0908	0934	0944	1022	|	...	1050	1135	|	1300	1401	...	1500	1559	|	1700	|
245	Nagaoka .... d.	0726	0749	...	0839	...	...	0932	...	1004	1047	|	...	1111	1200	1216	1325	1426	...	1525	1624	1644	1725	1753
269	Tsubame Sanjo .... d.	0736	0759	...	0849	...	...	0941	...	1014	1057	|	...	1121	1210	1226	1335	1436	...	1536	1634	|	1735	1803
301	**Niigata** .... a.	0749	0812	...	0901	...	...	0955	...	1027	1110	1048	...	1133	1224	1239	1347	1448	...	1547	1646	1703	1748	1816

	333	335	405	337		407	339	409	411		341	413	343	415		345	347	349	475	351		417	477
Tokyo .... 8010/15/20 d.	1640	1708	1712	1740	...	1752	1812	1816	1832	...	1852	1912	1936	1948	...	2004	2024	2052	2108	2140	...	2228	2300
Tokyo Ueno .... 8010/15/20 d.	1646	1714	1718	1746	...	1758	1818	1822	1838	...	1858	1918	1942	1954	...	2010	2030	2058	2114	2146	...	2234	2306
Omiya .... 8010/15/20 d.	1705	1733	1737	1805	...	1817	1837	1841	1857	...	1917	1937	2001	2013	...	2029	2049	2117	2133	2205	...	2253	2325
Takasaki .... d.	1730	1800	1809	1831	...	1854	1903	1916	1929	...	1949	2011	2030	2056	...	|	2121	2146	2205	2238	...	2325	2357
Echigo Yuzawa .... d.	1800	|	1839	1856	...	1923	1930	1945	1959	...	2015	2041	2056	2125	...	|	2147	2216	...	2308	...	2354	...
Nagaoka .... d.	1824	1843	...	1921	...	...	1950	...	...	...	2040	...	2116	...	...	2133	2212	2237	...	2332	...	...	...
Tsubame Sanjo .... d.	1834	|	...	1931	...	...	2000	...	...	...	2050	...	2127	...	...	2143	2322	|	...	2342	...	...	...
Niigata .... a.	1847	1902	...	1943	...	...	2012	...	...	...	2103	...	2140	...	...	2155	2235	2256	...	2355	...	...	...

	470	472	400	474	300		476 Ⓐ	402	302	304	404		306	308	310	312	406		314	408	316	410	318
Niigata .... d.	...	...	...	...	0609	...	...	...	0634	0658	...	...	0719	0750	0826	0905	...	...	0924	...	1018	...	1120
Tsubame Sanjo .... d.	...	...	...	...	0621	...	...	...	0646	0711	...	...	0732	0803	0838	|	...	...	0936	...	1030	...	1132
Nagaoka .... d.	...	...	...	...	0632	...	...	...	0657	0721	...	...	0743	0814	0849	|	...	...	0947	...	1041	...	1143
Echigo Yuzawa .... d.	...	...	0608	...	|	...	...	0709	0722	|	0749	...	0809	0841	0909	|	0929	...	1013	1031	1107	1130	1209
Takasaki .... d.	0616	0631	0638	0653	0714	...	0723	0739	0749	0803	0818	...	0839	0912	0935	|	1003	...	1038	1103	1136	1203	1239
Omiya .... 8010/15/20 d.	0648	0700	0710	0728	0747	...	0755	0816	0824	0836	0852	...	0916	0940	1004	1021	1036	...	1104	1136	1204	1236	1304
Tokyo Ueno .... 8010/15/20 d.	0707	0719	0731	0747	0807	...	0815	0835	0843	0855	0911	...	0935	0959	1023	|	1055	...	1123	1155	1223	1255	1323
Tokyo .... 8010/15/20 a.	0712	0724	0736	0752	0812	...	0820	0840	0848	0900	0916	...	0940	1004	1028	1043	1100	...	1128	1200	1228	1300	1328

	320	322	324	326		328	412	330	332	334		336	338	340	342		414	344	346	348		416	350
Niigata .... d.	1220	1320	1414	1420	...	1510	...	1537	1610	1624	...	1657	1721	1744	1812	...	...	1854	1937	2021	...		2136
Tsubame Sanjo .... d.	1232	1332	|	1432	...	1522	...	|	1623	1637	...	|	1733	1757	1825	...	...	1906	1949	2033	...	...	2148
Nagaoka .... d.	1243	1343	1433	1443	...	1533		1556	1634	1648	...	1717	1744	1808	1835	...	...	1917	2000	2044	...	...	2159
Echigo Yuzawa .... d.	1309	1409	|	1509	...	|	1601	1622	|	1714	...	1738	1810	1829	1902	...	1914	1938	2026	2110	...	2141	2225
Takasaki .... d.	1339	1439	|	1539	...	|	1631	1648	|	1742	...	1804	1839	1859	|	...	1943	2007	2055	2139	...	2211	2251
Omiya .... 8010/15/20 d.	1404	1504	1536	1604	...	1636	1704	1716	1735	1815	...	1835	1912	1928	1948	...	2016	2032	2128	2204	...	2243	2315
Tokyo Ueno .... 8010/15/20 d.	1423	1523	1555	1623	...	1656	1723	1735	1755	1835	...	1855	1931	1947	2007	...	2035	2051	2147	2223	...	2303	2335
Tokyo .... 8010/15/20 a.	1428	1528	1600	1628	...	1700	1728	1740	1800	1840	...	1900	1936	1952	2012	...	2040	2056	2152	2228	...	2308	2340

JR East, JR West   TOKYO - NAGANO - TOYAMA - KANAZAWA   8010

Hokuriku Shinkansen high-speed line.

km		591	501 R	551	601	503 R	603	553		505 R	555	605	507 R	557	607	509 R		559	609	561	611	563	613	565
0	**Tokyo** .... 8008/15/20 d.	...	0616	0628	0652	0720	0724	0752	...	0836	0844	0904	0920	0932	0944	1024	...	1032	1104	1124	1204	1224	1304	1324
4	**Tokyo** Ueno .... 8008/15/20 d.	...	0622	0634	0658	0726	0730	0758	...	0842	0850	0910	0926	0938	0950	|	...	1038	1110	1130	1210	1230	1310	1330
31	Omiya .... 8008/15/20 d.	...	0641	0653	0717	0745	0749	0817	...	0902	0909	0928	0945	0957	1009	1047	...	1057	1129	1149	1229	1249	1329	1349
109	Takasaki .... d.	...	|	0717	0745	|	0821	0843	...	|	0931	0955	|	|	1043	|	...	1120	1200	1212	1300	1313	1400	1412
151	Karuizawa .... d.	...	|	0733	0807	|	0841	0859	...	|	0947	1011	|	1033	1103	|	...	1137	1216	|	1321	|	1416	|
194	Ueda .... d.	...	|	0751	0826	|	0900	0918	...	|	1006	1029	|	1052	1122	|	...	1152	1234	|	1339	|	1434	|
226	**Nagano** .... d.	0611	0738	0805	0837	0842	0912	0932	...	0958	1019	1041	1046	1105	1133	1143	...	1206	1246	1251	1351	1355	1446	1451
285	Joetsumyoko .... d.	0635	|	0828	...	|	...	0957	...	|	1043	...	|	1124	...	|	...	1232	...	1314	...	1414	...	1514
392	**Toyama** .... d.	0716	0824	0909	...	0929	...	1038	...	1044	1124	...	1133	1205	...	1230	...	1314	...	1355	...	1455	...	1555
412	Shin Takaoka .... d.	0725	|	0918	...	|	...	1047	...	|	1132	...	|	1214	...	|	...	1322	...	1404	...	1504	...	1604
454	**Kanazawa** .... 8150 a.	0738	0843	0932	...	0948	...	1101	...	1104	1146	...	1152	1227	...	1249	...	1336	...	1417	...	1517	...	1617

	615	567	617	569	619	511 R ●	571		621	513 R	623	573	515 R	625	575		517 R ●	627	577	629	519 R	631	633
Tokyo .... 8008/15/20 d.	1404	1424	1504	1524	1552	1624	1632	...	1652	1724	1732	1804	1824	1840	1904	...	1924	1932	2012	2036	2104	2128	2208
Tokyo Ueno .... 8008/15/20 d.	1410	1430	1510	1530	1558	1630	1638	...	1658	1730	1738	1810	1830	1846	1910	...	1930	1938	2018	2042	2110	2134	2214
Omiya .... 8008/15/20 d.	1429	1449	1529	1549	1617	1649	1657	...	1717	1749	1757	1829	1849	1905	1929	...	1949	1957	2037	2101	2129	2153	2233
Takasaki .... d.	1501	1513	1600	1611	1648	|	1720	...	1748	|	1825	|	|	1932	1953	...	|	2019	2101	2125	|	2220	2259
Karuizawa .... d.	1521	|	1616	1627	1709	|	1736	...	1807	|	1846	1908	|	1953	2009	...	|	2040	2118	2146	|	2241	2320
Ueda .... d.	1540	|	1634	|	1729	|	1755	...	1826	|	1905	1928	|	2012	2028	...	|	2059	2137	2204	|	2259	2339
Nagano .... d.	1551	1556	1646	1652	1741	1746	1809	...	1838	1849	1916	1950	1946	2024	2049	...	2045	2111	2151	2216	2225	2311	2350
Joetsumyoko .... d.	...	1615	...	1715	...	|	1832	...	...	|	...	2013	|	...	2112	...	|	...	2214	...	|	...	...
Toyama .... d.	...	1656	...	1757	...	1833	1913	...	...	1936	...	2054	2033	...	2153	...	2132	...	2255	...	2313	...	...
Shin Takaoka .... d.	...	1705	...	1806	...	|	1922	...	...	|	...	2103	|	...	2202	...	|	...	2304	...	|	...	...
Kanazawa .... 8150 a.	...	1718	...	1820	...	1852	1935	...	...	1955	...	2117	2055	...	2216	...	2151	...	2318	...	2332	...	...

	600	602	604	500 R	606	608	552		502 R	610	504 R ●	554	612	506 R	556		508 R ●	558	614	560	616	562	618
Kanazawa .... 8150 d.	...	...	...	0603	...	...	0616	...	0703	...	0751	0726	...	0850	0826	...	0949	0923	...	1058	...	1159	...
Shin Takaoka .... d.	...	...	...	|	...	...	0630	...	|	...	|	0740	...	|	0840	...	|	0938	...	1112	...	1213	...
Toyama .... d.	...	...	...	0622	...	...	0640	...	0722	...	0810	0750	...	0910	0850	...	1008	0947	...	1121	...	1222	...
Joetsumyoko .... d.	...	...	...	|	...	...	0720	...	|	...	|	0830	...	|	0930	...	|	1027	...	1201	...	1302	...
Nagano .... d.	0602	0612	0645	0710	0713	0723	0745	...	0810	0826	0858	0902	0926	0958	1002	...	1056	1102	1128	1226	1229	1323	1326
Ueda .... d.	0614	|	0657	|	0725	0735	0758	...	|	0838	|	0914	0939	|	1014	...	|	1114	1140	|	1241	|	1338
Karuizawa .... d.	0634	0644	0717	|	0745	0755	0817	...	|	0857	|	0933	1000	|	1035	...	|	1134	1200	|	1300	|	1357
Takasaki .... d.	0650	0704	0737	|	0800	0814	0833	...	|	0916	|	0949	1020	|	|	...	|	1149	1220	1304	1316	1404	1416
Omiya .... 8008/15/20 d.	0714	0735	0759	0807	0827	0843	0855	...	0907	0947	0955	1011	1047	1055	1111	...	1155	1211	1247	1327	1347	1427	1447
Tokyo Ueno .... 8008/15/20 d.	0734	0754	0818	0826	0846	0902	0914	...	0926	1006	1014	1030	1106	1114	1130	...	1214	1230	1306	1346	1406	1446	1506
Tokyo .... 8008/15/20 a.	0740	0800	0824	0832	0852	0908	0920	...	0932	1012	1020	1036	1112	1120	1136	...	1220	1236	1312	1352	1412	1452	1512

	564	620	566	622	624	568	626		510 R	628	570	512 R	572	514 R	630		574	576	516 R	632	578	518 R	590
Kanazawa .... 8150 d.	1258	...	1358	...	...	1448	...	...	1557	...	1607	1648	1653	1757	...	...	1812	1905	1921	...	2020	2103	2135
Shin Takaoka .... d.	1312	...	1412	...	...	1502	...	...	|	...	1622	|	1707	|	...	...	1826	1919	|	...	2034	|	2149
Toyama .... d.	1321	...	1421	...	...	1511	...	...	1617	...	1631	1707	1717	1817	...	...	1835	1928	1940	...	2044	2123	2158
Joetsumyoko .... d.	1401	...	1501	...	...	1555	...	...	|	...	1712	|	1800	|	...	...	1916	2012	|	...	2124	|	2238
Nagano .... d.	1426	1429	1522	1525	1542	1620	1625	...	1705	1710	1737	1756	1825	1905	1909	...	1941	2037	2029	2117	2149	2211	2302
Ueda .... d.	|	1441	|	1537	1554	1632	1637	...	|	1723	1749	|	1837	|	1921	...	1953	2049	|	2129	2202	|	...
Karuizawa .... d.	|	1500	|	1556	1613	1648	1656	...	|	1742	1809	|	1857	|	1941	...	2013	2108	|	2149	2221	|	...
Takasaki .... d.	1503	1516	1603	1616	1629	1705	1716	...	|	1801	1825	|	1913	|	2000	...	2028	2124	|	2211	2236	|	...
Omiya .... 8008/15/20 d.	1527	1547	1627	1647	1655	1727	1747	...	1803	1827	1847	1854	1935	2000	2026	...	2050	2147	2131	2242	2259	2305	...
Tokyo Ueno .... 8008/15/20 d.	1546	1606	1646	1706	1714	1746	1806	...	1822	1846	1906	1914	1954	|	2046	...	2110	2206	2150	2302	2318	2326	...
Tokyo .... 8008/15/20 a.	1552	1612	1652	1712	1720	1752	1812	...	1828	1852	1912	1920	2000	2023	2052	...	2116	2212	2156	2308	2324	2332	...

● – Subject to confirmation - may not run daily.

FOR ADDITIONAL SERVICES TOYAMA - KANAZAWA AND V.V. SEE NEXT PAGE →

8010 TOYAMA - KANAZAWA

JR East, JR West

km		701	703	705		707	709	711		713	715	717		719	721	723		725	727	729		731	733	735
						Ⓐ																		
0	**Toyama** d.	0612	0643	0734	...	0751	0831	1024	...	1113	1246	1343	...	1417	1517	1618	...	1711	1820	1941	...	2016	2142	2333
19	Shin Takaoka d.	0621	0652	0743	...	0800	0840	1033	...	1122	1255	1352	...	1426	1526	1627	...	1720	1829	1951	...	2025	2151	2342
59	**Kanazawa** a.	0635	0706	0756	...	0814	0853	1047	...	1136	1309	1406	...	1439	1540	1640	...	1734	1843	2004	...	2038	2204	2356
		700	**702**	**704**		**706**	**708**	**710**		**712**	**714**	**716**		**718**	**720**	**722**		**724**	**726**	**728**		**730**	**732**	**734**
	Kanazawa d.	0651	0758	0951	...	1034	1128	1231	...	1328	1431	1505	...	1540	1738	1838	...	1924	2025	2105	...	2220	2306	2337
	Shin Takaoka d.	0706	0812	1006	...	1048	1142	1245	...	1342	1446	1520	...	1555	1752	1852	...	1938	2039	2120	...	2234	2320	2351
	Toyama a.	0714	0821	1014	...	1057	1151	1254	...	1351	1454	1528	...	1603	1801	1901	...	1946	2048	2128	...	2242	2329	2359

8015 TOKYO - SHINJO and MORIOKA

JR East

Yamagata and *Tohoku Shinkansen* high-speed line.

km		51	121	201		203	123	123		125	205	127		127	53	129		131	131	55		133	133	
			[R]				[R]				A	[R]				[R]		[R]				[R]		
0	**Tokyo** 8010/20 d.	0604	0612	0620	...	0640	0712	0712	...	0740	0744	0808	...	0808	0848	0856	...	0924	0924	0940	...	1000	1000	...
4	**Tokyo** Ueno 8010/20 d.	0610	0618	0626	...	0646	0718	0718	...	0746	0750	0814	...	0814	0854	0902	...	|	|	0946	...	1006	1006	...
31	Omiya 8010/20 d.	0629	0637	0645	...	0705	0737	0733	...	0806	0809	0833	...	0833	0913	0921	...	0947	0947	1005	...	1025	1025	...
109	Utsunomiya d.	0653	0701	0718	...	0736	0803	0803	...	0829	0843	0904	...	0904	0939	0945	...	|	|	1031	...	1051	1051	...
214	Koriyama d.	0724	0730	0756	...	0823	0831	0831	...	0857	0925	0931	...	0932	1007	1016	...	|	|	1059	...	1119	1119	...
255	Fukushima d.	0738	0748	0814	...	0837	0848	0852	...	0915	0939	0949	...	0950	1024	1033	...	1048	1050	1113	...	1135	1137	...
295	Yonezawa d.	|	0820	|	...	|	0926	|	...	|	|	1025	...	|	|	1105	...	1121	|	|	...	1210	|	...
342	Yamagata d.	|	0859	|	...	|	1008	|	...	|	|	1104	...	|	|	1137	...	1152	|	|	...	1246	|	...
369	Murayama d.	|	0927	|	...	|	1031	|	...	|	|	...	...	|	|	...	...	1212	|	|	...	1308	|	...
404	**Shinjo** a.	|	0955	|	...	|	1054	|	...	|	|	...	...	|	|	...	...	1235	|	|	...	1331	|	...
325	Sendai (Honshu) d.	0800	...	0844	...	0858	...	0918	...	0938	1005	...	...	1011	1049	...	...	...	1113	1136	...	...	1204	...
497	**Morioka** a.	0917	...	...	...	...	...	...	...	...	...	...	...	...	1206	...	...	...	...	1254	...	...	...	...

		207	57	135		135	59	137		137	61	139		139	63	141		141	65	143		143	67	
				[R]				[R]				[R]				[R]				[R]				
	Tokyo 8010/20 d.	1012	1036	1100	...	1100	1136	1200	...	1200	1236	1300	...	1300	1336	1400	...	1400	1436	1500	...	1500	1536	...
	Tokyo Ueno 8010/20 d.	1018	1042	1106	...	1106	1142	1206	...	1206	1242	1306	...	1306	1342	1406	...	1406	1442	1506	...	1506	1542	...
	Omiya 8010/20 d.	1037	1101	1125	...	1125	1201	1225	...	1225	1301	1325	...	1325	1401	1425	...	1425	1501	1525	...	1525	1601	...
	Utsunomiya d.	1107	1130	1149	...	1149	1230	1249	...	1249	1330	1349	...	1349	1430	1449	...	1449	1530	1549	...	1549	1630	...
	Koriyama d.	1151	1158	1218	...	1218	1258	1318	...	1318	1358	1418	...	1418	1458	1518	...	1518	1558	1618	...	1618	1658	...
	Fukushima d.	1205	1217	1235	...	1237	1317	1336	...	1337	1417	1435	...	1437	1517	1535	...	1537	1617	1635	...	1637	1717	...
	Yonezawa d.	|	|	1307	...	|	|	1409	...	|	|	1512	...	|	|	1611	...	|	|	1707	...	|	|	...
	Yamagata d.	|	|	1344	...	|	|	1444	...	|	|	1550	...	|	|	1650	...	|	|	1746	...	|	|	...
	Murayama d.	|	|	...	...	|	|	1507	...	|	|	...	...	|	|	1714	...	|	|	...	...	|	|	...
	Shinjo a.	|	|	...	...	|	|	1530	...	|	|	...	...	|	|	1741	...	|	|	...	...	|	|	...
	Sendai (Honshu) d.	1226	1239	...	...	1304	1339	...	...	1404	1439	...	...	1504	1539	...	...	1605	1639	...	...	1705	1739	...
	Morioka a.	...	1354	...	...	...	1454	...	...	...	1554	...	...	...	1654	...	...	...	1754	...	...	...	1854	...

		145	145		147	149	149		151	153		153	157		157	219		69	159	159		221	223	
		[R]				[R]				[R]			[R]						[R]					
	Tokyo 8010 8020 d.	1600	1600	...	1636	1700	1700	...	1728	1800	...	1800	1916	...	1916	1928	...	2020	2044	2044	...	2056	2144	...
	Tokyo Ueno 8010 8020 d.	1606	1606	...	1642	1706	1706	...	1734	1806	...	1806	1922	...	1922	1934	...	2026	2050	2050	...	2102	2150	...
	Omiya 8010 8020 d.	1625	1625	...	1701	1725	1725	...	1753	1825	...	1825	1941	...	1941	1953	...	2045	2109	2109	...	2121	2209	...
	Utsunomiya d.	1649	1649	...	1730	1749	1749	...	1817	1849	...	1849	2008	...	2008	2025	...	2110	2133	2133	...	2149	2234	...
	Koriyama d.	1718	1718	...	1802	1818	1818	...	1854	1918	...	1918	2038	...	2038	2101	...	2141	2202	2202	...	2227	2307	...
	Fukushima d.	1735	1737	...	1817	1836	1837	...	1917	1937	...	1938	2056	...	2057	2117	...	2155	2219	2220	...	2241	2321	...
	Yonezawa d.	1808	|	...	|	1909	|	...	|	2012	...	|	2128	...	|	|	...	|	2251	|	...	|	|	...
	Yamagata d.	1844	|	...	|	1945	|	...	|	2047	...	|	2159	...	|	|	...	|	2326	|	...	|	|	...
	Murayama d.	1906	|	...	|	...	|	...	|	...	...	|	2221	...	|	|	...	|	...	|	...	|	|	...
	Shinjo a.	1929	|	...	|	...	|	...	|	...	...	|	2245	...	|	|	...	|	...	|	...	|	|	...
	Sendai (Honshu) d.	...	1806	...	1839	...	1903	...	1937	...	...	1959	...	...	2123	2142	...	2220	...	2246	...	2302	2346	...
	Morioka a.	...	...	...	...	...	...	...	...	...	...	...	...	...	...	...	...	2331	...	...	...	...	...	...

		206	122	122		124	124	126		50	128	128		210	130	132		132	134	136		136	52	
		B	[R]			[R]					[R]					[R]				[R]				
	Morioka d.	...	...	...	...	...	*0631*	...	...	0701	...	...	...	...	...	...	...	...	...	...	...	...	1008	...
	Sendai (Honshu) d.	0651	...	0711	...	...	0745	0806	...	0821	...	0840	...	0900	0925	...	...	0941	1016	...	...	1041	1125	...
	Shinjo d.	|	0540	|	...	...	|	|	...	|	0716	|	...	|	|	...	...	|	|	0916	...	|	|	...
	Murayama d.	|	0603	|	...	...	|	|	...	|	0740	|	...	|	|	...	...	|	|	0940	...	|	|	...
	Yamagata d.	|	0625	|	...	0708	|	|	...	|	0802	|	...	|	|	0903	...	|	|	1002	...	|	|	...
	Yonezawa d.	|	0702	|	...	0738	|	|	...	|	0840	|	...	|	|	0937	...	|	|	1037	...	|	|	...
	Fukushima d.	0717	0739	0739	...	0815	0815	0835	...	0843	0916	0916	...	0923	0950	1014	...	1014	1041	1116	...	1116	1151	...
	Koriyama d.	0731	0754	0754	...	|	|	0850	...	0857	0930	0930	...	0937	1004	1028	...	1028	1100	1130	...	1130	1206	...
	Utsunomiya d.	0811	0823	0823	...	|	|	0919	...	0935	0958	0958	...	1021	1034	1058	...	1058	1135	1158	...	1158	1235	...
	Omiya 8010/20 d.	0840	0848	0848	...	0914	0914	0944	...	1000	1024	1024	...	1052	1100	1124	...	1124	1200	1224	...	1224	1300	...
	Tokyo Ueno 8010/20 d.	0859	0907	0907	...	|	|	1003	...	1019	1043	1043	...	1111	1119	1143	...	1143	1219	1243	...	1243	1319	...
	Tokyo 8010/20 a.	0904	0912	0912	...	0935	0935	1006	...	1024	1048	1048	...	1116	1124	1148	...	1148	1224	1248	...	1248	1324	...

		138	138	212		54	140	140		56	142	142		214	58	144		144	60	146		146	216	
		[R]					[R]				[R]					[R]				[R]				
	Morioka d.	...	...	...	...	1108	...	...	...	1208	...	...	...	...	1308	...	...	...	1408	...	...	...	...	...
	Sendai (Honshu) d.	...	1144	1200	...	1225	...	1244	...	1325	...	1344	...	1400	1425	...	...	1444	1525	...	...	1544	1600	...
	Shinjo d.	...	|	|	...	|	1117	|	...	|	...	|	...	|	|	1318	...	|	|	...	...	|	|	...
	Murayama d.	...	|	|	...	|	1140	|	...	|	...	|	...	|	|	1342	...	|	|	...	...	|	|	...
	Yamagata d.	1057	|	|	...	|	1208	|	...	|	1304	|	...	|	|	1404	...	|	|	1503	...	|	|	...
	Yonezawa d.	1138	|	|	...	|	1238	|	...	|	1340	|	...	|	|	1438	...	|	|	1540	...	|	|	...
	Fukushima d.	1216	1216	1223	...	1251	1316	1316	...	1351	1416	1416	...	1423	1451	1516	...	1516	1551	1616	...	1616	1623	...
	Koriyama d.	1230	1230	1237	...	1306	1330	1330	...	1406	1430	1430	...	1437	1506	1530	...	1530	1606	1630	...	1630	1640	...
	Utsunomiya d.	1258	1258	1321	...	1335	1358	1358	...	1435	1458	1458	...	1521	1535	1558	...	1558	1635	1658	...	1658	1721	...
	Omiya 8010/20 d.	1324	1324	1352	...	1400	1424	1424	...	1500	1524	1524	...	1552	1600	1624	...	1624	1700	1724	...	1724	1733	...
	Tokyo Ueno 8010/20 d.	1343	1343	1411	...	1419	1443	1443	...	1519	1543	1543	...	1611	1619	1643	...	1643	1719	1743	...	1743	1811	...
	Tokyo 8010/20 a.	1348	1348	1416	...	1424	1448	1448	...	1524	1548	1548	...	1616	1624	1648	...	1648	1724	1748	...	1748	1816	...

		62	148		148	150	150		154	154		156	156		64	66		158	158	68		160	70	
			[R]			[R]			[R]			[R]						[R]				[R]		
	Morioka d.	1508	...	...	...	...	...	...	...	...	...	...	...	...	1754	1841	...	...	...	1940	...	...	2029	...
	Sendai (Honshu) d.	1625	...	...	1634	...	1644	...	...	1743	...	...	1844	...	1911	2001	...	...	2017	2055	...	...	2148	...
	Shinjo d.	|	...	...	|	1517	|	...	...	|	...	1712	|	...	|	|	...	1843	|	|	...	1957	|	...
	Murayama d.	|	...	...	|	1542	|	...	...	|	...	1737	|	...	|	|	...	1906	|	|	...	2021	|	...
	Yamagata d.	|	1546	...	|	1607	|	...	1705	|	...	1804	|	...	|	|	...	1931	|	|	...	2043	|	...
	Yonezawa d.	|	1623	...	|	1638	|	...	1741	|	...	1838	|	...	|	|	...	2013	|	|	...	2117	|	...
	Fukushima d.	1651	1702	...	1702	1716	1716	...	1816	1816	...	1916	1916	...	1932	2023	...	2049	2049	2125	...	2156	2210	...
	Koriyama d.	1706	1716	...	1716	1730	1730	...	1830	1830	...	1930	1930	...	1949	2042	...	2105	2105	2139	...	2210	2225	...
	Utsunomiya d.	1735	1747	...	1747	1758	1758	...	1858	1858	...	1958	1958	...	2023	2110	...	2135	2135	2207	...	2238	2254	...
	Omiya 8010/20 d.	1800	1812	...	1812	1824	1824	...	1924	1924	...	2024	2024	...	2048	2135	...	2200	2200	2232	...	2304	2319	...
	Tokyo Ueno 8010/20 d.	1819	1831	...	1831	1843	1843	...	1943	1943	...	2043	2043	...	2107	2155	...	2219	2219	2251	...	2323	2339	...
	Tokyo 8010/20 a.	1824	1836	...	1836	1848	1848	...	1948	1948	...	2048	2048	...	2112	2200	...	2224	2224	2256	...	2328	2344	...

A – Additional trips: 0856, 1212, 1412, 1612, 1736, 1828, 1836.

B – Additional trips: 0607, 0625, 0734, 1725, 1743, 1812, 1919, 2038.

JR East, JR Hokkaido

TOKYO - AKITA and AOMORI - HAKODATE 8020

Akita, Tohoku and Hokkaido Shinkansen high-speed lines.

km		91 R	93 R	95 R	95 R	1 R	1 R	101 R	5 R	5 R	103 R	7 R	11 R	11 R	13 R	15 R	17 R	17 R	19 R	21 R	21 R	23 R	23 R	25 R
0	**Tokyo** 8010 8015 d.	...	...	...	...	0632	0632	0716	0732	0732	0756	0820	0908	0908	0936	1004	1020	1020	1044	1120	1120	1220	1220	1320
4	**Tokyo** Ueno 8010 8015 d.	...	...	...	...	0638	0638	0722	0738	0738	0802	|	0914	0914	|	1010	1026	1026	1050	1126	1126	1226	1226	1326
31	Omiya 8010 8015 d.	...	...	...	...	0657	0657	0741	0757	0757	0821	0843	0932	0932	0959	1029	1045	1045	1109	1145	1145	1245	1245	1345
325	Sendai (Honshu) d.	...	...	0640	0640	0806	0805	0850	0905	0905	0937	0951	1041	1041	1107	1139	1153	1153	1217	1253	1253	1353	1353	1453
497	Morioka d.	...	0654	0758	0759	0850	0848	1002	0946	0948	1048	1031	1123	1125	1147	...	1235	1237	1305	1335	1337	1435	1437	1535
537	Tazawako d.	...	|	0832	|	|	0922	...	1026	|	...	|	1202	|	|	...	1311	|	|	1407	|	1511	|	1607
555	Kakunodate d.	...	|	0846	|	|	0935	...	1040	|	...	|	1218	|	|	...	1325	|	|	1421	|	1525	|	1621
572	Omagari d.	...	|	0901	|	|	0948	...	1052	|	...	|	1231	|	|	...	1337	|	|	1433	|	1537	|	1633
624	**Akita** a.	...	|	0932	|	|	1024	...	1125	|	...	|	1302	|	|	...	1408	|	|	1504	|	1608	|	1708
593	Hachinohe d.	...	0726	...	0835	0922	...	...	...	|	...	|	...	1202	|	...	...	1305	1334	...	1414	...	1505	...
675	Shin **Aomori** d.	0632	0756	...	0904	0951	...	...	...	1052	...	1120	...	1229	1236	...	...	1329	1359	...	1443	...	1531	...
824	S **Hakodate Hokuto** 8225 ♥ a.	0734	0858	...	1001	1053	...	...	...	...	...	1217	...	...	1333	...	...	...	1501	...	...	...	1630	...
842	*Hakodate* 8225 ♥ a.	*0807*	*0934*	...	*1030*	*1124*	...	...	...	...	...	*1251*	...	...	*1402*	...	...	...	*1529*	...	...	...	*1705*	...

	25 R	27 R	27 R	29 R	31 R	31 R	33 R	35 R	35 R	105 R	39 R		39 R	107 R	41 R	41 R	109 R	43 R	43 A R	111 R	45 R	45 R	47 R
Tokyo 8010 8015 d.	1320	1420	1420	1428	1520	1520	1528	1620	1620	1656	1720	...	1720	1756	1820	1820	1856	1920	1920	1940	2016	2016	2136
Tokyo Ueno 8010 8015 d.	1326	1426	1426	1434	1526	1526	1534	1626	1626	1702	1726	...	1726	1802	1826	1826	1902	1926	1926	1946	2022	2022	|
Omiya 8010 8015 d.	1345	1445	1445	1453	1545	1545	1553	1645	1645	1721	1745	...	1745	1821	1845	1845	1921	1945	1945	2005	2041	2041	2159
Sendai (Honshu) d.	1453	1553	1553	1603	1653	1653	1702	1753	1753	1830	1854	...	1854	1930	1953	1953	2030	2054	2054	2114	2148	2148	2307
Morioka d.	1537	1635	1637	1653	1735	1737	1753	1835	1837	1944	1935	...	1937	2044	2035	2037	2143	2136	2138	2222	2230	2231	...
Tazawako d.	|	1712	|	|	1809	|	|	1912	|	...	2007	...	|	...	2111	|	...	2206	|	...		|	...
Kakunodate d.	|	1728	|	|	1823	|	|	1927	|	...	2021	...	|	...	2124	|	...	2219	|	...		|	...
Omagari d.	|	1741	|	|	1835	|	|	1941	|	...	2033	...	|	...	2136	|	...	2232	|	...	2323	|	...
Akita a.	|	1812	|	|	1906	|	|	2012	|	...	2104	...	|	...	2207	|	...	2302	|	...	2353	|	...
Hachinohe d.	1614	...	1705	|	...	1812	|	...	1909	...	...	...	2013	...	...	2109	...	...	2206	...	...	2308	...
Shin **Aomori** d.	1645	...	1729	1743	...	1839	1845	...	1937	...	...	...	2042	...	...	2137	...	...	2232	...	...	2336	...
Shin **Hakodate Hokuto** 8225 ♥ a.	1747	...	...	1840	...	...	1947	...	...	...	...	...	2144	...	...	...	...	...	2329	...	...	...	...
Hakodate 8225 ♥ a.	*1820*	...	...	*1905*	...	...	*2015*	...	...	...	...	...	*2214*	...	...	...	...	...	*2359*	...	...	...	...

	2 R	102 R	4 R	104 R	6 R	6 R	8 R	106 R	10 R	10 R	108 R	14 R	14 R	16 R	16 R	18 R	18 R	20 R	22 R	22 R	24 R	24 R	28 R
Hakodate 8225 ♥ d.	...	...	...	...	...	...	...	...	...	*0607*	...	...	*0659*	...	...	...	*0848*	...	...	*1021*	...	...	...
Shin **Hakodate Hokuto** 8225 ♥ d.	...	...	...	...	...	...	...	...	...	0639	...	...	0738	...	...	...	0935	...	...	1053	...	...	...
Shin **Aomori** d.	...	...	0618	...	...	...	0649	...	...	0743	...	...	0837	...	0952	...	1039	1122	...	1152	...	1239	...
Hachinohe d.	...	...	0642	...	...	...	0717	...	...	0811	...	...	0905	...	1017	...	1107	|	...	1216	...	1307	...
Akita d.	...	...	|	...	0608	...	|	...	0716	|	...	0811	|	0912	|	1007	|	|	1107	|	1213	|	1306
Omagari d.	...	...	|	...	0641	...	|	...	0748	|	...	0843	|	0950	|	1039	|	|	1141	|	1246	|	1339
Kakunodate d.	...	...	|	...	|	...	|	...	0758	|	...	0856	|	1000	|	1054	|	|	1156	|	1257	|	1350
Tazawako d.	...	...	|	...	|	...	|	...	0812	|	...	0909	|	1014	|	1108	|	|	1212	|	1311	|	1408
Morioka d.	...	0610	0711	0728	0737	0737	0802	0811	0850	0850	0906	0950	0950	1050	1050	1150	1150	1217	1250	1250	1350	1350	1450
Sendai (Honshu) d.	0637	0721	0753	0845	0817	0817	0857	0922	0931	0931	1022	1031	1031	1131	1131	1231	1231	1257	1331	1331	1431	1431	1531
Omiya 8010 8015 d.	0744	0832	0900	0952	0925	0926	1008	1032	1040	1040	1132	1140	1140	1240	1240	1340	1340	1407	1440	1440	1540	1540	1640
Tokyo Ueno 8010 8015 d.	|	0851	|	1011	|	|	1027	1052	1059	1059	1151	1159	1159	1259	1259	1359	1359	1427	1459	1459	1559	1559	1659
Tokyo 8010 8015 a.	0807	0856	0923	1016	0947	0947	1032	1056	1104	1104	1156	1204	1204	1304	1304	1404	1404	1432	1504	1504	1604	1604	1704

	28 R	30 R	32 R	32 R	110 R	34 R	34 R	112 R	36 R	38 R	38 R		40 R	42 R	42 R	44 R	46 R	46 R	48 R	48 R	96 R	96 R	98 R
Hakodate 8225 ♥ d.	*1202*	...	...	*1302*	...	...	*1419*	...	...	...	...	...	*1545*	...	...	*1655*	...	...	...	*1808*	...	*1906*	*2006*
Shin **Hakodate Hokuto** 8225 ♥ d.	1248	...	...	1339	...	...	1448	...	...	...	...	...	1620	...	...	1726	...	...	...	1840	...	1941	2043
Shin **Aomori** d.	1352	...	...	1438	...	...	1552	...	1617	...	1638	...	1722	...	1744	1825	...	1838	...	1944	...	2040	2147
Hachinohe d.	1416	...	...	1506	...	...	1616	...	1641	...	1706	...	|	...	1812	|	...	1906	...	2012	...	2108	2215
Akita d.	|	...	1414	|	...	1506	|	...	|	1612	|	...	|	1710	|	|	1816	|	1910	|	2014	|	|
Omagari d.	|	...	1447	|	...	1539	|	...	|	1647	|	...	|	1743	|	|	1848	|	1943	|	2047	|	|
Kakunodate d.	|	...	1458	|	...	1551	|	...	|	1658	|	...	|	1754	|	|	1858	|	1953	|	2057	|	|
Tazawako d.	|	...	1512	|	...	1608	|	...	|	1712	|	...	|	1810	|	|	1912	|	2009	|	2111	|	|
Morioka d.	1450	...	1550	1550	1608	1650	1650	1707	1716	1750	1750	...	1817	1850	1850	1914	1950	1950	2050	2050	2151	2151	2248
Sendai (Honshu) d.	1531	1557	1631	1631	1722	1731	1731	1822	1757	1831	1831	...	1857	1931	1931	1954	2031	2031	2131	2131	2301	2301	...
Omiya 8010 8015 d.	1640	1708	1740	1740	1832	1840	1840	1931	1908	1940	1940	...	2008	2040	2040	2101	2140	2140	2240	2240	...	...	...
Tokyo Ueno 8010 8015 d.	1659	1727	1759	1759	1851	1859	1859	1951	1927	1959	1959	...	2027	2059	2059	|	2159	2159	2259	2259	...	...	...
Tokyo 8010 8015 a.	1704	1732	1804	1804	1856	1904	1904	1956	1932	2004	2004	...	2032	2104	2104	2123	2204	2204	2304	2304	...	...	...

♥ – R not required for Hakodate - Shin Hakodate Hokuto connecting trains. For other trains see Table **8225**.

☛ Some trains run on a different schedule on ⓒ. Trains 1, 7, 10, 13, 14, 18, 19, 22, 28, 32, 34, 91, 93 and 95 are subject to alteration May 3 – 7.
Train 43 will not run Shin Aomori - Shin Hakodate Hokuto on ⑦ May 14 - July 23.

JR Kyushu

HAKATA - OITA - MIYAZAKI 8105

km																								
0	**Hakata** d.	...	...	...	...	...	...	0621	0700	...	0731	0802	0820	...	0921	...	...	1020	...	1120	...	1220	1320	...
67	Kokura d.	...	...	...	...	...	0639	0714	0800	...	0834	0857	0916	...	1010	...	...	1109	...	1209	...	1309	1409	...
186	Beppu d.	...	...	...	...	0739	0804	0833	0922	...	0952	1015	1034	...	1129	...	...	1226	...	1327	...	1428	1526	...
198	Oita d.	...	...	...	0700	0749	0816	0844	0932	...	1008	1025	1044	...	1139	1207	...	1236	...	1337	1406	1438	1536	...
322	Nobeoka d.	0512	0710	0804	0912	...	1032	...	...	...	1208	...	...	1312	...	1408	...	...	1514	...	1612	...	...	1731
405	**Miyazaki** d.	0619	0836	0916	1020	...	1140	...	...	...	1310	...	...	1415	...	1523	...	...	1625	...	1729	...	...	1842
412	**Miyazaki** Airport a.	0628	0847	0927	1031	...	1150	...	...	...	1319	...	...	1426	...	1533	...	...	1637	...	1740	...	...	1853

Hakata d.	1400	...	1420	1500	...	1520	1600	...	...	1620	1700	1720	1800	...	1820	...	1900	1920	2000	2020	2102	2206	2234
Kokura d.	1442	...	1509	1542	...	1609	1643	...	...	1710	1744	1810	1845	...	1911	...	1946	2012	2049	2110	2153	2302	2322
Beppu d.	1555	...	1627	1651	...	1727	1754	...	...	1829	1853	1927	1956	...	2032	...	2056	2136	2207	2229	2315	0025	...
Oita d.	1604	1606	1636	1701	1706	1737	1804	1806	...	1839	1902	1937	2006	2019	2042	...	2106	2145	2217	2239	2325	0035	...
Nobeoka d.	...	1819	...	...	1913	...	...	2018	...	...	...	...	...	2231	...	...	...	...	...	...	...	...	...
Miyazaki d.	...	1931	...	...	2018	...	...	2127	...	...	...	...	...	2346	...	...	...	...	...	...	...	...	...
Miyazaki Airport a.	...	1940	...	...	2030	...	...	...	...	...	...	...	...	...	...	...	...	...	...	...	...	...	...

Miyazaki Airport d.	...	...	...	...	...	...	...	...	...	...	...	...	0643	...	...	...	...	...	...	1013	...	1126	...
Miyazaki d.	...	...	...	...	...	...	...	...	...	0554	...	...	0658	...	...	0810	...	...	...	1029	...	1139	...
Nobeoka d.	...	...	...	...	...	...	...	...	...	0706	...	...	0806	...	...	0913	...	...	...	1141	...	1242	...
Oita d.	...	...	0512	0556	0638	0713	0746	0810	0842	0909	0911	0939	1007	1011	1044	1109	1110	1210	1312	1341	1411	...	1511
Beppu d.	...	...	0521	0604	0646	0722	0755	0819	0851	...	0919	0947	...	1020	1053	...	1119	1218	1320	...	1419	...	1520
Kokura d.	0558	0615	0643	0731	0809	0844	0919	0939	1005	...	1040	1105	...	1140	1205	...	1240	1340	1440	...	1540	...	1639
Hakata a.	0653	0713	0738	0834	0900	0939	1004	1027	1048	...	1128	1147	...	1258	1247	...	1328	1428	1528	...	1528	...	1727

Miyazaki Airport d.	1209	...	1309	...	...	1419	...	1519	...	...	...	...	1618	...	1717	...	...	1819	1918	2019	2118		...
Miyazaki d.	1225	...	1331	...	...	1436	...	1536	...	...	...	...	1639	...	1731	...	...	1833	1935	2034	2135	2226	2319
Nobeoka d.	1339	...	1438	...	...	1543	...	1641	...	...	...	...	1744	...	1846	...	...	1950	2045	2139	2241	2334	0027
Oita d.	1543	1610	...	1644	1710	1741	1744	...	1811	1843	1911	...	1943	2012	2055	...	2143	...	...	...	...	...	...
Beppu d.	...	1618	...	1652	1718	...	1753	...	1820	1852	1919	...	1953	2020	2104	...	2151	...	...	...	...	...	...
Kokura d.	...	1739	...	1805	1840	...	1905	...	1940	2005	2040	...	2113	2140	2227	2231	2311	...	...	...	...	...	...
Hakata a.	...	1828	...	1850	1928	...	1950	...	2028	2050	2129	...	2203	2227	...	2321	2358	...	...	...	...	...	...

8107 MIYAZAKI - KAGOSHIMA

JR Kyushu

km											
0	**Miyazaki** d.	...	0551	0714	0920	1017	1226	1419	1622	1735	1900
79	Kirishima-Jingu d.	...	0715	0836	1039	1138	1342	1538	1741	1857	2026
95	Hayato d.	0651	0733	0853	1057	1156	1359	1555	1758	1914	2043
126	**Kagoshima** Chuo a.	0728	0809	0927	1127	1227	1428	1625	1831	1944	2116

Kagoshima Chuo d.	0551	0740	0849	0959	1150	1419	1618	1828	2020	2213
Hayato d.	0624	0819	0922	1032	1224	1448	1651	1906	2057	2250
Kirishima-Jingu d.	0641	0836	0939	1050	1241	1505	1708	1923	2115	...
Miyazaki a.	0809	1001	1057	1212	1402	1621	1828	2044	2236	...

8110 HAKATA - NAGASAKI, SASEBO and HUIS TEN BOSCH

JR Kyushu

Nishi Nyushu Shinkansen high-speed line (Takeo Onsen - Nagasaki). Service from September 23, 2022.

km																								
0	**Hakata** d.	0600	0632	0716	0810	0854	1004	1052	...	1152	1254	1357	1454	1614	1700	1713	...	1800	1812	1900	1911	2000	2100	2207
29	Tosu d.	0622	0654	0740	0838	0914	1023	1116	...	1215	1315	1415	1515	1638	1719	1738	...	1819	1838	1920	1939	2022	2121	2229
31	Shin Tosu d.	0626	0658	0745	0842	0918	1027	1121	...	1220	1319	1419	1519	1642	1724	1742	...	1823	1842	1924	1944	2026	2125	2233
54	Saga d.	0639	0713	0801	0857	0932	1040	1135	...	1233	1334	1433	1533	1656	1738	1756	...	1837	1857	1938	1959	2040	2138	2248
	Takeo Onsen a.	0700	0740	0826	0916	0957	1058	1155	...	1253	1355	1453	1554	1720	1757	1822	...	1856	1922	1959	2026	2103	2159	2309
	Takeo Onsen d.	0703	0743	0829	0919	1000	1101	1158	...	1256	1358	1456	1557	1723	1800	1825	...	1859	1925	2002	2030	2106	2202	2312
	Ureshino Onsen d.	|	0749	0835	0926	1007	|	1205	...	|	1404	|	1604	1730	|	1831	...	|	1932	|	2037	|	2209	|
	Shin Omura d.	0715	0758	0844	0935	1016	|	1214	...	1308	1413	1509	1612	1739	|	1840	...	|	1941	|	2046	2118	2218	2324
	Isahaya d.	0722	0805	0851	0942	1023	1116	1221	...	1315	1420	1516	1619	1746	1817	1847	...	1915	1948	2018	2053	2125	2225	2331
	Nagasaki a.	0731	0814	0900	0950	1031	1124	1229	...	1324	1428	...	1627	1754	1825	1856	...	1923	1956	2026	2101	2133	2233	2339

Nagasaki d.	0617	0657	0745	0839	0914	0950	1043	1145	1241	1345	1441	...	1542	1643	1715	1742	1813	1845	1914	1947	2020	2119	2210
Isahaya d.	0626	0706	0755	0848	0924	0959	1052	1154	1250	1354	1451	...	1551	1652	1724	1752	1822	1854	1924	1956	2029	2128	2219
Shin Omura d.	0633	0713	0802	|	0931	|	1059	1201	1257	1401	1458	...	1558	1659	1731	1759	1829	1901	1931	2003	2036	2135	2226
Ureshino Onsen d.	0642	0722	0811	|	0940	|	1108	|	1306	|	1507	...	1607	|	1740	|	1838	|	1940	|	2045	|	2235
Takeo Onsen a.	0648	0728	0816	0903	0945	1013	1114	1213	1312	1413	1513	...	1613	1710	1746	1810	1844	1912	1945	2014	2051	2146	2240
Takeo Onsen d.	0652	0731	0819	0906	0951	1016	1117	1216	1315	1416	1516	...	1616	1713	1750	1815	1848	1915	1951	2018	2057	2149	2243
Saga d.	0718	0755	0846	0926	1013	1035	1136	1236	1336	1436	1536	...	1637	1735	1814	1839	1915	1937	2016	2039	2117	2209	2303
Shin Tosu d.	0731	0809	0859	0940	1026	1047	1149	1248	1349	1448	1549	...	1649	1749	1828	1851	1927	1949	2029	2051	2130	2222	2316
Tosu d.	0736	0914	0903	0943	1030	1051	1153	1254	1353	1453	1553	...	1653	1753	1831	1855	1932	1953	2034	2056	2134	2226	2320
Hakata a.	0758	0936	0925	1002	1051	1110	1214	1314	1414	1514	1614	...	1714	1813	1852	1914	1953	2012	2055	2115	2156	2247	2341

km																								
0	**Hakata** d.	0728	0837	0837	0932	0932	1031	1031	...	1133	1233	1233	1333	1333	1433	1533	...	1614	1713	1812	1911	2032	2133	2235
29	Tosu d.	0757	0859	0859	0956	0956	1058	1058	...	1159	1258	1258	1358	1358	1458	1558	...	1638	1738	1838	1939	2056	2156	2254
31	Shin Tosu d.	0802	0903	0903	1000	1000	1102	1102	...	1203	1302	1302	1402	1402	1503	1603	...	1642	1742	1842	1944	2100	2200	2258
54	Saga d.	0815	0917	0917	1017	1017	1116	1116	...	1217	1317	1317	1416	1416	1517	1617	...	1656	1756	1857	1959	2114	2215	2311
	Takeo Onsen d.	0839	0940	0940	1039	1039	1138	1138	...	1238	1337	1337	1438	1438	1540	1641	...	1720	1822	1922	2027	2138	2237	2330
	Arita d.	0857	0955	0955	1055	1055	1153	1153	...	1255	1353	1353	1454	1454	1557	1658	...	1735	1839	1937	2042	2152	2252	2345
108	Haiki d.	0916	1013	1016	1115	1116	1216	1217	...	1315	1416	1417	1515	1518	1618	1720	...	1755	1857	1955	2100	2210	2309	0000
117	**Sasebo** a.	0928	1024	|	1127	|	1226	|	...	1327	1427	|	1526	|	1630	1730	...	1809	1908	2006	2112	2220	2318	0009
122	**Huis Ten Bosch** ◧ a.	...	...	1022	...	1123	...	1223	...	...	...	1422	...	1524	...	...	...	...	...	...	...	...	...	...

Huis Ten Bosch ◧ d.	...	...	...	...	...	...	1044	...	...	1145	...	1242	...	...	1443	...	...	1553	...	...	...	...	...
Sasebo d.	0607	0718	0806	0904	0959	1040	|	...	1141	|	1239	|	1344	1439	|	...	1549	|	1651	1800	1908	2014	2047
Haiki d.	0624	0732	0820	0920	1015	1059	1059	...	1159	1159	1259	1259	1359	1459	1459	...	1610	1610	1717	1819	1923	2030	2103
Arita d.	0636	0743	0832	0931	1029	1112	1112	...	1211	1211	1312	1312	1411	1511	1511	...	1623	1623	1735	1831	1937	2042	2115
Takeo Onsen d.	0652	0758	0853	0951	1051	1129	1129	...	1227	1227	1229	1229	1429	1528	1528	...	1641	1641	1750	1848	1951	2057	2131
Saga d.	0718	0819	0914	1013	1113	1154	1154	...	1252	1252	1351	1351	1454	1552	1552	...	1708	1708	1814	1915	2016	2117	2151
Shin Tosu d.	0731	0834	0927	1026	1127	1207	1207	...	1307	1307	1405	1405	1507	1607	1607	...	1721	1721	1828	1927	2029	2130	2204
Tosu d.	0736	0839	0931	1030	1132	1211	1211	...	1312	1312	1411	1411	1511	1612	1612	...	1725	1725	1831	1932	2034	2134	2208
Hakata a.	0758	0902	0950	1051	1153	1236	1236	...	1334	1334	1435	1435	1534	1635	1635	...	1746	1746	1852	1953	2055	2156	2229

◧ – Additional local trains Haiki - Huis Ten Bosch and v.v.: from Haiki at 0510, 0559, 0621, 0707, 0820, 0841, 0933, 1028, 1125, 1223, 1325, 1425, 1524, 1602, 1627, 1650, 1740, 1827, 1906, 1938, 2015, 2115, 2153, 2209; from Huis Ten Bosh: 0631, 0739, 0812, 0851, 0910, 1005, 1039, 1135, 1233, 1336, 1435, 1534, 1637, 1728, 1812, 1840, 1917, 1948, 2024, 2055, 2125, 2221, 2251, 2354. Journey 5 minutes.

8115 TAKAMATSU - TOKUSHIMA

JR Shikoku

km																								
									a											a				
0	**Takamatsu** d.	0612	0705	0824	0911	1010	...	1105	1206	1310	...	1412	1510	1612	...	1715	1813	...	1917	2004	2121	...	2222	...
10	Yashima d.	0622	0714	0833	0921	1022	...	1115	|	1323	...	1423	1522	1622	...	1725	1822	...	1927	2015	2131	...	2232	...
64	Ikenotani d.	|	0804	0924	1009	1116	...	1206	|	1407	...	|	1612	|	...	1814	|	...	2017	2108	2225	...	|	...
75	**Tokushima** a.	0730	0814	0936	1018	1125	...	1215	1304	1415	...	1520	1620	1715	...	1823	1923	...	2027	2116	2234	...	2334	...

				b											b								
Tokushima d.	0541	0659	...	0823	0923	...	1026	1132	1224	...	1324	1427	...	1528	1646	1728	...	1830	1932	2035	...	2202	...
Ikenotani d.	0552	0711	...	0834	0932	...	|	1141	1233	...	|	1436	...	1537	|	1737	...	1838	|	|	...	2212	...
Yashima d.	0645	0804	...	0921	1022	...	|	|	1322	...	1423	1522	...	1622	|	1822	...	1927	2029	2131	...	2310	...
Takamatsu a.	0654	0813	...	0931	1031	...	1136	1234	1331	...	1433	1531	...	1632	1744	1832	...	1936	2040	2140	...	2320	...

a – From Okayama (depart 1 hour earlier).

b – To Okayama (arrive 1 hour later).

8118 TOKUSHIMA - AWA IKEDA

JR Shikoku

km													
		LEX	*LEX*	**A**	*LEX*				*LEX*	*LEX*		*LEX*	
0	**Tokushima** d.	0646	0900	1138	1200	1443	1545	1638	1800	1900	1915	2015	2106
74	**Awa Ikeda** a.	0810	1014	1347	1317	1642	1745	1851	1917	2021	2128	2134	2255

	LEX	**B**	*LEX*		*LEX*		*LEX*				*LEX*	
Awa Ikeda d.	0646	0652	0832	0912	1130	1259	1430	1609	1713	1809	1949	2117
Tokushima a.	0802	0850	0946	1128	1243	1525	1544	1827	1928	2014	2104	2312

A – Additional trips: 0608, 0720.

B – Additional trips: 0547, 0622, 0753, 1905.

8121 UWAJIMA - KUBOKAWA

JR Shikoku

km											
0	**Uwajima** ‡ d.	0604	0933	1218	1730	...	...	...	...	...
82	**Kubokawa** ‡ a.	0809	1206	1427	1944	...	...	...	...	...

Kubokawa ‡ d.	0613	1043	1321	1740	...	...	...	...	...
Uwajima ‡ d.	0837	1329	1557	2015	...	...	...	...	...

‡ – Japan Rail Pass holders must pay a supplement to travel between these stations.

JR Shikoku — OKAYAMA and TAKAMATSU - MATSUYAMA and UWAJIMA — 8125

Frequent local services operate Okayama - Takamatsu and v.v.

km																									
72	**Okayama** d.	...	...	...	...	...	...	0722	...	...	0832	...	...	0925	...	...	1035	...	...	1135	...	...	1235	...	...
0	**Takamatsu** d.	...	...	0517	...	0600	...	|	0737	...	|	0845	...	|	0942	...	|	1047	...	|	1150	...	|	1250	...
46	Utazu d.	...	...	|	...	0618	...	0801	0801	...	0913	0913	...	1006	1006	...	1113	1113	...	1213	1213	...	1314	1314	...
164	Imabari d.	...	...	0711	...	0756	...	0930	0930	...	1041	1041	...	1136	1136	...	1241	1241	...	1339	1339	...	1443	1443	...
214	**Matsuyama** a.	0548	0647	0758	0810	0836	0907	1006	1006	1018	1115	1115	1127	1210	1210	1224	1315	1315	1324	1413	1413	1428	1517	1517	1527
311	**Uwajima** a.	0710	0813	...	0930	...	1030	...	...	1140	...	...	1247	...	...	1350	...	...	1447	...	...	1551	...	...	1649

Okayama d.	1335	...	...	1435	...	...	1535	...	...	1635	...	...	1735	...	...	1835	...	...	1935	...	2039	...	2200	...
Takamatsu d.	|	1350	...	|	1450	...	|	1550	...	|	1650	...	|	1753	...	|	1859	...	|	1952	...	2059	|	2220
Utazu d.	1414	1414	...	1515	1515	...	1615	1615	...	1715	1715	...	1809	1813	...	1910	1917	...	2009	2012	2115	2118	2236	2236
Imabari d.	1541	1541	...	1644	1644	...	1745	1745	...	1847	1847	...	1948	1948	...	2053	2053	...	2158	2158	2256	2257	...	...
Matsuyama a.	1616	1616	1630	1723	1723	1728	1826	1826	1843	1923	1923	1936	2028	2028	2045	2132	2132	2200	2238	2238	2333	2333	...	...
Uwajima a.	...	...	1750	...	...	1855	...	...	2010	...	...	2057	...	...	2205	...	...	2219	...	...	...	...	...	...

Uwajima d.	...	...	...	...	...	0526	...	...	0635	...	...	0738	...	...	0840	...	...	0955	...	...	1045	...	...	1150
Matsuyama d.	0505	0505	...	0613	0613	0654	0720	0720	0802	0810	0810	0905	0915	0915	1010	1021	1021	1120	1123	1123	1214	1221	1221	1316
Imabari d.	0541	0541	...	0650	0650	...	0756	0756	...	0847	0847	...	0957	0957	...	1059	1059	...	1202	1202	...	1259	1259	...
Utazu d.	0715	0714	0753	0827	0826	...	0926	0925	...	1020	1019	...	1134	1133	...	1234	1233	...	1335	1334	...	1435	1434	...
Takamatsu a.	|	0736	0811	|	0845	...	|	0946	...	|	1039	...	|	1154	...	|	1254	...	|	1355	...	|	1455	...
Okayama a.	0751	...	...	0900	...	...	1000	...	...	1058	...	...	1210	...	...	1310	...	...	1410	...	...	1511	...	...

Uwajima d.	...	...	1255	...	...	1359	...	...	1456	...	...	1602	...	...	...	1708	...	...	1808	...	1908	...	2017	2116
Matsuyama d.	1326	1326	1416	1423	1423	1520	1528	1528	1619	1627	1627	1725	...	1737	1737	1835	1839	1839	1928	1932	2032	2036	2137	2243
Imabari d.	1405	1405	...	1501	1501	...	1606	1606	...	1704	1704	...	...	1813	1813	...	1919	1919	...	2008	...	2113	...	...
Utazu d.	1535	1534	...	1635	1634	...	1736	1735	...	1837	1836	...	...	1939	1938	...	2053	2052	...	|	...	|	...	...
Takamatsu a.	|	1555	...	|	1654	...	|	1757	...	|	1854	...	...	|	1956	...	|	2111	...	2155	...	2256	...	...
Okayama a.	1611	...	...	1711	...	...	1811	...	...	1911	...	...	...	2012	...	...	2129	...	...	...	...	...	...	...

JR Shikoku — OKAYAMA and TAKAMATSU - KOCHI - NAKAMURA — 8127

Japan Rail Pass holders must pay a supplement to travel between Kubokawa and Nakamura.

km																										
0	**Okayama** d.	...	...	0708	...	...	0852	...	1005	1105	...	1205	1305	...	1405	1505	1605	...	1705	...	...	1805	...	1905	2005	2139
	Takamatsu d.	0604	0723	|	...	0825	|	...	|	|	...	|	|	...	|	|	|	...	|	...	1827	|	...	|	|	|
97	Awa Ikeda d.	0706	0829	0829	...	0924	1020	...	1122	1234	...	1332	1425	...	1523	1631	1735	...	1834	...	1935	1935	...	2029	2138	2259
179	**Kochi** a.	0818	0939	0939	0953	1037	1130	1140	1229	1341	1349	1442	1539	1543	1639	1741	1848	1855	1943	1953	2050	2050	2123	2146	2251	0006
251	Kubokawa d.	0927	...	...	1057	...	...	1249	...	...	1454	...	...	1651	*1806*	...	...	2010	...	2104	...	...	2233	...	...	...
294	**Nakamura** a.	1004	...	...	1132	...	...	1324	...	...	1531	...	...	1727	*1846*	...	...	2049	...	2139	...	...	2308	...	...	...

km																										
	Nakamura d.	...	...	...	...	*0608*	0700	...	...	0924	...	...	1111	...	...	1324	...	...	1510	...	1648	...	1745	...	...	...
	Kubokawa d.	...	...	...	...	*0648*	0741	...	...	1004	...	...	1156	...	...	1402	...	...	1551	...	1729	...	1824	...	...	...
0	**Kochi** d.	0451	0600	0700	0700	0801	0904	0913	1013	1106	1113	1213	1302	1313	1413	1504	1513	1613	1700	1713	1834	1836	1928	1931	1931	2034
82	Awa Ikeda d.	0600	0709	0813	0813	0907	...	1020	1122	...	1223	1322	...	1424	1523	...	1621	1720	...	1824	...	1946	...	2040	2040	2148
158	**Takamatsu** a.	0702	|	0921	|	|	...	|	|	...	|	|	...	|	|	...	|	|	...	|	...	|	...	2142	|	2246
	Okayama a.	...	0838	...	0938	1033	...	1140	1240	...	1340	1441	...	1541	1641	...	1741	1847	...	1941	...	2111	...	...	2157	...

JR West — TOTTORI and OKAYAMA - YAMAGUCHI — 8130

km															⑤Ⓒ			⑤Ⓒ								⑤Ⓒ
	Tottori d.	...	0704	...	0823	...	0929	...	...	1140	...	...	1306	...	...	1509	...	...	1742	...	1842	...	...	2049	...	...
	Kurayoshi d.	...	0733	...	0858	...	1001	...	...	1209	...	...	1339	...	...	1540	...	...	1811	...	1913	...	...	2122	...	...
0	**Okayama** d.	...	|	0705	|	0805	|	0905	1005	|	1105	1205	|	1305	1405	|	1505	1605	|	1705	|	1804	1905	|	2005	2120
80	Niimi d.	...	|	0810	|	0908	|	1012	1108	|	1208	1312	|	1414	1509	|	1610	1708	|	1808	|	1908	2010	|	2110	2225
159	**Yonago** d.	0601	0811	0917	0930	1016	1038	1119	1219	1241	1318	1419	1411	1521	1622	1615	1723	1824	1849	1922	1947	2029	2124	2156	2221	2334
188	Matsue d.	0623	0835	0942	...	1039	1100	1142	1241	1303	1341	1444	1436	1544	1647	1638	1748	1848	1916	1946	...	2051	2147	...	2244	2357
220	**Izumoshi** d.	0649	0905	1010	...	1104	1124	1209	1307	1329	1412	1512	1504	1609	1717	1709	1815	1920	1942	2019	...	2115	2211	...	2308	0021
	Odashi d.	0715	0929	—	...	...	1148	...	...	1358	...	...	1543	...	...	1738	...	...	2009	...	...	...	...	...	...	...
	Hamada d.	0800	1016	...	...	...	1231	...	...	1444	—	...	1617	...	...	1827	...	...	2052	...	...	...	...	...	...	...
	Masuda d.	0858	1051	1123	...	...	1306	...	...	1516	1615	...	1655	...	...	1904	...	...	2124	...	...	...	...	...	...	...
	Tsuwano d.	0931	...	1205	...	...	1338	...	...	...	1659	...	1727	...	...	...	...	...	...	...	...	...	...	...	...	...
	Yamaguchi a.	1023	...	1324	...	...	1426	...	...	...	1806	...	1819	...	...	...	...	...	...	...	...	...	...	...	...	...
	Shin **Yamaguchi** a.	1039	...	*1403*	...	...	1441	...	...	...	1851	...	1835	...	...	...	...	...	...	...	...	...	...	...	...	...

km										⑤Ⓒ			⑤Ⓒ													
0	Shin **Yamaguchi** d.	...	...	...	...	...	...	...	...	...	...	...	...	0852	...	*0913*	...	...	...	1301	...	*1337*	...	...	1712	...
13	Yamaguchi d.	...	...	...	...	...	...	...	...	...	...	...	...	0908	...	0939	...	...	...	1315	...	1402	...	...	1727	...
63	Tsuwano d.	...	...	...	...	...	...	...	...	...	...	...	...	0958	...	1105	...	...	...	1403	...	1518	...	...	1815	...
94	Masuda d.	...	...	...	...	...	0536	...	0655	...	...	...	...	1031	...	1149	1217	...	...	1438	...	1558	1603	...	1851	...
135	Hamada d.	...	...	...	...	...	0611	...	0730	...	...	...	...	1104	...	—	1257	...	...	1515	...	—	1642	...	1925	...
191	Odashi d.	...	...	...	...	...	0653	...	0830	...	...	...	...	1147	...	...	1338	...	...	1558	...	⑤Ⓒ	1726	...	2008	...
224	**Izumoshi** d.	0442	0527	...	0624	0721	0728	0831	0854	0934	1031	...	1134	1212	1234	1331	1403	1433	1530	1622	1630	1718	1750	1827	2036	...
256	Matsue d.	0507	0552	...	0658	0749	0758	0857	0924	1002	1059	...	1201	1235	1301	1359	1426	1501	1559	1647	1701	1744	1818	1855	2104	...
285	Yonago d.	0532	0621	0658	0723	0819	0825	0922	0950	1026	1125	1217	1226	1303	1326	1428	1452	1527	1626	1711	1726	1816	1841	1924	2127	2040
	Niimi d.	0640	0729	|	0834	0934	|	1037	|	1136	1236	|	1337	...	1439	1538	|	1638	1738	|	1838	1926	|	2031	...	|
	Okayama a.	0741	0834	|	0939	1035	|	1139	|	1239	1339	|	1439	...	1540	1639	|	1739	1839	|	1939	2025	|	2136	...	|
338	Kurayoshi d.	...	...	0733	...	...	0858	...	1025	...	...	1255	...	...	...	...	1523	...	...	1743	...	...	1913	...	...	2112
378	**Tottori** a.	...	...	0803	...	...	0927	...	1058	...	...	1324	...	...	...	...	1553	...	...	1816	...	...	1942	...	...	2140

JR West — KYOTO - KURAYOSHI — 8135

Japan Rail Pass holders must pay a supplement to travel between Kamigori and Chizu.

km		1	3	5	7	9A	11	13		
0	**Kyoto** d.	0706	0850	1054	1252	1454	1656	1935	...	...
39	Shin Osaka d.	0730	0915	1118	1316	1518	1719	2000	...	...
43	Osaka d.	0737	0925	1125	1324	1524	1726	2006	...	...
131	Himeji d.	0836	1022	1220	1421	1620	1822	2108	...	...
166	Kamigori d.	0902	1048	1244	1444	1644	1845	2131	...	...
222	Chizu d.	0944	1130	1323	1524	1724	1931	2214	...	...
254	Tottori d.	1013	1159	1353	1554	1752	2002	2243	...	...
294	**Kurayoshi** a.	1043	1230	1421	1621	...	2033	...	...	...

	2	4	6A	8	10	12	14		
Kurayoshi d.	0608	0812	1013	1219	1423	1622	*1743*	...	...
Tottori d.	0639	0852	1046	1254	1454	1654	1840	...	...
Chizu d.	0708	0921	1115	1323	1523	1724	1908	...	...
Kamigori d.	0751	1003	1202	1401	1601	1804	1947	...	...
Himeji d.	0814	1025	1225	1424	1624	1828	2009	...	...
Osaka d.	0924	1120	1321	1521	1719	1936	2107	...	...
Shin Osaka d.	0929	1124	1326	1526	1724	1942	2113	...	...
Kyoto a.	0953	1147	1348	1548	1748	2006	2137	...	...

A – ⑤Ⓒ only.

JR West — OKAYAMA - TOTTORI — 8140

Japan Rail Pass holders must pay a supplement to travel between Kamigori and Chizu.

km									
0	**Okayama** d.	0647	0913	1105	1343	1724	1946	...	...
54	Kamigori d.	0725	0950	1142	1419	1803	2022	...	...
110	Chizu d.	0811	1035	1226	1501	1845	2104	...	...
142	**Tottori** a.	0838	1104	1253	1532	1917	2131	...	...

Tottori d.	0705	1002	1400	1620	1857	2035	...	...
Chizu d.	0734	1033	1427	1652	1932	2103	...	...
Kamigori d.	0820	1115	1511	1733	2014	2148	...	...
Okayama a.	0857	1148	1545	1811	2048	2222	...	...

8145 KYOTO and OSAKA - KINOSAKI

Ⓡ on all trains JR West

km																								
				⑤Ⓒ															⑤Ⓒ			⑤Ⓒ		
0	**Kyoto**	d.	0732	0838	0924	...	1025	1125	1225	...	1325	1425	1525	...	1625	1728	1828	...	1928	...	2037	...	2137	...	...
76	Ayabe	d.	0839	0946	1031	...	1136	1231	1339	...	1431	1535	1631	...	1735	1843	1948	...	2047	...	2150	...	2246	...	...
89	Fukuchiyama	d.	0849	0954	1040	...	1145	1244	1348	...	1446	1544	1648	...	1743	1852	2001	...	2055	2001	2159	...	2255	...	...
148	Toyooka	d.	0943	...	...	...	...	1340	...	...	1540	...	1751	...	...	...	...	...	...	2058	...	...	...	...	...
158	**Kinosaki** Onsen	a.	0952	...	...	...	...	1349	...	...	1549	...	1800	...	...	...	...	...	...	...	...	...	...	...	...

				⑤Ⓒ																		⑤Ⓒ		
Kinosaki Onsen	d.	...	...	...	...	...	...	...	...	...	1039	...	...	1231	...	1435	...	...	1631	...	...	...	...	...
Toyooka	d.	...	...	...	...	...	0742	...	...	...	1049	...	...	1242	...	1445	...	...	1641	...	...	...	...	...
Fukuchiyama	d.	0602	0656	0743	...	0838	0838	0945	...	1044	1146	1243	...	1346	1442	1543	...	1644	1749	1854	...	2005	...	...
Ayabe	d.	0612	0712	0753	...	0855	0855	0955	...	1100	1156	1300	...	1356	1459	1556	...	1659	1759	1910	...	2014	...	...
Kyoto	a.	0718	0821	0903	...	1007	1007	1107	...	1207	1307	1407	...	1507	1607	1707	...	1808	1909	2021	...	2119	...	...

km																								
							⑤Ⓒ					⑤Ⓒ									⑤Ⓒ				
0	Shin **Osaka**	d.	0808	0904	...	1005	1105	...	1205	1305	...	1405	1505	...	1705	1801	...	1906	2006	...	2106	2204	...	...	...
4	**Osaka**	d.	0814	0910	...	1012	1111	...	1211	1311	...	1411	1511	...	1711	1811	...	1912	2012	...	2112	2210	...	...	...
118	Fukuchiyama	d.	0955	1046	...	1147	1243	...	1350	1442	...	1546	1646	...	1900	1958	...	2058	2157	...	2301	2351	...	...	...
178	Toyooka	d.	1050	1143	...	1242	...	...	1445	...	...	1641	...	...	1957	...	...	...	...	...	...	...	...	...	...
188	**Kinosaki** Onsen	a.	1058	1152	...	1251	...	...	1454	...	...	1650	...	...	...	...	...	...	...	...	...	...	...	...	...

						⑤Ⓒ						⑤Ⓒ								⑤Ⓒ				
Kinosaki Onsen	d.	...	...	...	...	...	...	...	0933	...	1133	...	...	1329	...	...	1530	...	...	1742	1853	...	...	...
Toyooka	d.	...	...	...	...	...	...	...	0943	...	1143	...	...	1339	...	...	1541	...	...	1752	1903	...	...	...
Fukuchiyama	d.	0549	0652	...	0745	0840	...	0950	1046	...	1246	1344	...	1443	1545	...	1647	1800	...	1900	2000	...	...	...
Osaka	a.	0735	0839	...	0926	1021	...	1123	1223	...	1424	1523	...	1623	1722	...	1822	1937	...	2037	2136	...	...	...
Shin **Osaka**	a.	0741	0846	...	0932	1027	...	1129	1229	...	1429	1529	...	1628	1727	...	1828	1944	...	2044	2144	...	...	...

8150 OSAKA and NAGOYA - KANAZAWA

JR West

km																								
				Ⓐ							a								⑤Ⓒ	b				
0	**Osaka**	d.	...	...	...	0630	0700	...	0740	...	0758	0810	0840	...	...	0912	0942	...	1012	1042	...	1142	...	1212	1242
4	Shin **Osaka**	d.	...	...	...	0634	0704	...	0744	...	0803	0814	0844	...	...	0917	0946	...	1016	1046	...	1146	...	1216	1246
43	Kyoto	d.	...	...	...	0659	0729	...	0810	...	0831	0841	0909	...	...	0942	1009	...	1040	1110	...	1210	...	1240	1310
	Nagoya	8175 d.	...	...	...	|	|	...	|	0750	|	|	|	...	0850	|	|	0948	|	|	...	|	1148	|	|
	Gifu	8170 d.	...	...	...	|	|	...	|	0810	0956	|	|	...	0911	|	|	1012	|	|	...	|	1212	|	|
	Maibara	d.	...	...	...	|	|	0810	|	0857	0922↑	|	|	...	0956	|	|	1056	|	|	1156	|	1256	|	|
137	Tsuruga	d.	...	0643	...	0758	0822	0841	0903	0926	...	0938	|	...	1026	1035	1103	1125	1133	1202	1225	1303	1327	|	1403
191	Fukui	d.	0650	0719	0742	0831	0855	0915	0938	1001	...	1012	1032	...	1101	1110	1136	1200	1208	1235	1300	1338	1402	1407	1437
268	**Kanazawa**	8010 a.	0737	0809	0833	0913	0938	1005	1025	1048	...	1102	1114	...	1148	1158	1220	1248	1256	1320	1348	1423	1449	1455	1526

km																								
			⑤Ⓒ					⑤Ⓒ											⑤Ⓒ					
	Osaka	d.	...	1342	...	1442	...	1512	1542	...	1642	...	1712	1742	...	1812	1842	...	1912	1927	...	2007	2054	...	...
	Shin **Osaka**	d.	...	1346	...	1446	...	1516	1546	...	1646	...	1716	1746	...	1816	1846	...	1916	1931	...	2012	2058	...	...
	Kyoto	d.	...	1410	...	1510	...	1540	1610	...	1709	...	1740	1809	...	1840	1910	...	1940	1954	...	2038	2121	...	...
0	**Nagoya**	8175 d.	...	|	1348	|	...	|	|	1548	|	...	|	|	1748	|	|	...	|	|	1948	|	|	...	...
30	Gifu	8170 d.	...	|	1412	|	...	|	|	1611	|	...	|	|	1811	|	|	...	|	|	2012	|	|	...	...
80	Maibara	d.	1355	|	1456	|	1556	|	|	1656	|	1756	|	|	1856	|	|	1956	|	|	2056	|	|	2156	2248
126	Tsuruga	d.	1426	1502	1525	1603	1627	1632	1703	1725	1801	1825	1833	|	1927	1933	2007	2025	|	2049	2125	2133	2215	2225	2317
180	Fukui	d.	1500	1540	1601	1637	1702	1708	1740	1800	1833	1900	1908	1930	2002	2008	2039	2100	2107	2125	2201	2208	2248	2301	2352
257	**Kanazawa**	8010 a.	1548	1630	1650	1726	1751	1755	1827	1847	1916	1949	1955	2013	2050	2056	2123	2148	2153	2209	2250	2256	2329	2348	0040

					⑤Ⓒ								Ⓐ	Ⓒ			⑤Ⓒ		b					
Kanazawa	8010 d.	0510	0535	0548	0607	0645	0648	0715	0748	0805	0815	0848	0902	0902	0948	0954	1048	1056	1124	1148	1214	1248	1320	1348
Fukui	d.	0600	0620	0639	0701	0729	0739	0803	0838	0848	0905	0936	0945	0945	1036	1042	1136	1143	1208	1236	1306	1336	1408	1436
Tsuruga	d.	0633	0653	0712	0737	0801	0812	0838	0912	|	0939	1010	1016	1016	1110	1116	1210	1216	1241	1310	1342	1410	1441	1510
Maibara	d.	0708	|	0752	|	|	0844	|	0950	|	|	1045	|	|	1152	|	1245	|	|	1351	|	1445	|	1550
Gifu	8170 d.	...	|	0829	|	|	...	|	1026	|	|	...	|	|	1227	|	...	|	|	1427	|	...	|	1626
Nagoya	8175 a.	...	|	0851	|	|	...	|	1049	|	|	...	|	|	1248	|	...	|	|	1448	|	...	|	1649
Kyoto	a.	...	0751	...	0837	0855	...	0934	...	1011	1037	...	1109	1109	...	1209	...	1309	1337	...	1437	...	1536	...
Shin **Osaka**	a.	...	0817	...	0901	0918	...	0958	...	1035	1102	...	1132	1132	...	1232	...	1332	1400	...	1500	...	1559	...
Osaka	a.	...	0822	...	0906	0922	...	1003	...	1039	1106	...	1137	1139	...	1237	...	1337	1405	...	1505	...	1604	...

					⑤Ⓒ							a						⑤Ⓒ					Ⓐ	
Kanazawa	8010 d.	1354	1420	1448	1457	1519	1548	1600	1629	1648	1655	...	1731	1748	1754	1842	1853	1908	1947	2006	2047	2108	2140	2212
Fukui	d.	1442	1508	1536	1543	1608	1636	1644	1722	1736	1744	...	1815	1837	1841	1928	1942	1952	2034	2055	2132	2156	2231	2300
Tsuruga	d.	1516	1542	1610	|	1642	1710	1715	1756	1810	1816	...	|	1910	1916	2000	2016	|	2108	2129	2204	...	2307	...
Maibara	d.	|	|	1650	|	|	1744	|	|	1850	|	1823↓	|	1944	|	|	2055	|	|	2201	|	...	...	...
Gifu	8170 d.	|	|	1726	|	|	...	|	|	1925	|	1743	|	...	|	|	2129	|	|	...	|	...	...	...
Nagoya	8175 a.	|	|	1749	|	|	...	|	|	1946	|	|	|	...	|	|	2154	|	|	...	|	...	...	...
Kyoto	a.	1609	1637	...	1707	1739	...	1809	1853	...	1909	1918	1938	...	2009	2054	...	2119	2202	...	2259	...	...	...
Shin **Osaka**	a.	1632	1701	...	1731	1803	...	1833	1916	...	1933	1944	2003	...	2034	2119	...	2144	2226	...	2323	...	...	...
Osaka	a.	1637	1706	...	1736	1809	...	1839	1921	...	1938	1950	2009	...	2038	2123	...	2149	2231	...	2328	...	...	...

a – To/from Takayama (see Table **8170**). b – To/from Wakura Onsen (see Table **8155**).

8155 KANAZAWA - WAKURA ONSEN

JR West

km											
					c						
0	**Kanazawa**	8150 d.	0856	1123	1327	1500	1835	2010	...	...	...
66	Nanao	d.	0949	1216	1424	1554	1932	2107	...	...	...
71	**Wakura Onsen**	a.	0954	1222	1430	1559	1938	2112	...	...	...

				c						
Wakura Onsen	d.	0700	0902	1014	1256	1519	1730	...	...	...
Nanao	d.	0706	0908	1020	1303	1527	1737	...	...	...
Kanazawa	8150 a.	0805	1005	1118	1404	1630	1831	...	...	...

c – To/from Osaka (see Table **8150**).

8160 OSAKA - SHINGU

Ⓡ on all trains JR West

km			1	1	3	5	7	9	11	13	15		17	19	21	23		25	27	29	31		33	35	
			Ⓐ	Ⓒ		⑤Ⓒ					⑤Ⓒ										⑤Ⓒ				
39	Kyoto	d.	*0653*	*0658*	*0829*	*0900*	*0945*	*1045*	*1145*	*1245*	*1345*	...	*1445*	*1545*	*1644*	1747	...	...	*1844*	*1944*	*2044*	...	*2114*	*2209*	...
0	Shin **Osaka**	d.	0735	0735	0901	0930	1015	1115	1215	1315	1415	...	1515	1615	1715	1815	...	1845	1915	2015	2115	...	2146	2249	...
14	**Osaka** Tennoji	d.	0759	0759	0921	0949	1033	1132	1232	1332	1432	...	1532	1632	1735	1835	...	1905	1935	2036	2136	...	2206	2311	...
75	Wakayama	d.	0848	0848	1006	1035	1117	1218	1318	1418	1516	...	1618	1718	1825	1926	...	1953	2025	2125	2223	...	2255	2358	...
181	Shirahama	d.	1012	1012	1137	1200	1246	1347	1443	1547	1640	...	1743	1845	1956	2055	...	...	2155	2253	...	...	...	...	...
234	Kushimoto	d.	1107	1107	...	1255	...	...	1540	...	...	...	1838	...	2050	...	...	...	2256	...	...	...	...	...	...
261	**Kii Katsuura**	d.	1140	1140	...	1333	...	...	1617	...	...	...	1911	...	2123	...	...	...	2333	...	...	...	...	...	...
276	**Shingu**	a.	1158	1158	...	1352	...	...	1639	...	...	...	1928	...	2141	...	...	...	2350	...	...	...	...	...	...

		2	4	4	6	8	10	12	14	16		18	20	22	24		26	28	30	32		34	36	
			Ⓐ	Ⓒ								⑤Ⓒ							⑤Ⓒ			⑤Ⓒ		
Shingu	d.	...	...	...	...	...	...	0629	...	0832	...	...	...	1127	...	...	1329	...	1504	...	...	...	1746	...
Kii Katsuura	d.	...	...	...	...	...	...	0646	...	0849	...	...	...	1148	...	...	1346	...	1524	...	...	...	1804	...
Kushimoto	d.	...	...	...	...	...	...	0720	...	0923	...	...	...	1221	...	...	1420	...	1557	...	...	...	1838	...
Shirahama	d.	...	...	...	...	0630	0710	0820	0920	1026	...	1120	1220	1326	1420	...	1526	1620	1656	1720	...	1820	1937	...
Wakayama	d.	0514	0600	0600	0650	0809	0841	0950	1050	1150	...	1249	1350	1450	1550	...	1650	1750	1820	1850	...	1949	2102	...
Osaka Tennoji	d.	0602	0656	0657	0744	0858	0933	1033	1135	1235	...	1335	1435	1535	1635	...	1734	1834	1904	1934	...	2034	2151	...
Shin **Osaka**	a.	0621	0720	0720	0805	0919	0951	1051	1150	1250	...	1350	1450	1550	1649	...	1750	1850	1920	1950	...	2050	2206	...
Kyoto	a.	*0701*	*0749*	*0759*	*0835*	*0959*	*1029*	1117	*1229*	*1329*	...	*1429*	*1529*	*1629*	*1729*	...	*1829*	*1929*	*1953*	*2029*	...	*2137*	*2249*	...

NAGOYA - SHINGU 8165

JR Central

km			1	3	5	7						
0	**Nagoya**	d.	0805	1001	1258	1947	...	...	...	...	...	...
37	Yokkaichi	‡ d.	0837	1037	1337	2019	...	...	...	...	...	...
48	Suzuka	‡ d.	0846	1046	1345	2027	...	...	...	...	...	...
66	Tsu	‡ d.	0901	1101	1400	2042	...	...	...	...	...	...
86	Matsusaka	d.	0916	1116	1416	2057	...	...	...	...	...	...
93	Taki	d.	0924	1129	1424	2105	...	...	...	...	...	...
206	Kumano Shi	d.	1114	1318	1605	2254	...	...	...	...	...	...
228	**Shingu**	a.	1134	1337	1624	2314	...	...	...	...	...	...
244	**Kii Katsuura**	a.	1156	1358	1643	...	...	...	...	...	...	...

		2	4	6	8						
Kii Katsuura	d.	...	0855	1223	1711	...	...	...	...	...	...
Shingu	d.	0620	0913	1245	1731	...	...	...	...	...	...
Kumano Shi	d.	0640	0933	1305	1750	...	...	...	...	...	...
Taki	d.	0819	1118	1449	1931	...	...	...	...	...	...
Matsusaka	d.	0826	1126	1456	1938	...	...	...	...	...	...
Tsu	‡ d.	0841	1142	1512	1954	...	...	...	...	...	...
Suzuka	‡ d.	0854	1154	1525	2006	...	...	...	...	...	...
Yokkaichi	‡ d.	0904	1205	1534	2015	...	...	...	...	...	...
Nagoya	a.	0941	1241	1610	2049	...	...	...	...	...	...

‡ – Japan Rail Pass holders must pay a supplement to travel between these stations.

NAGOYA - TOYAMA 8170

JR Central, JR West Subject to alteration from March 18

km					a							
0	**Nagoya**	d.	0743	0843	0939	1048	1143	1248	1448	1603	1813	2017
30	Gifu **8150**	d.	0805	0903	1011	1108	1206	1308	1508	1623	1839	2042
58	Mino Ota	d.	0827	0923	1032	1129	1225	1328	1530	1653	1900	2102
119	Gero	d.	0927	1015	1133	1227	1330	1425	1631	1758	2003	2203
167	Takayama	d.	1016	1101	1223	1315	1418	1512	1719	1843	2049	2249
182	Hida Furukawa	d.	...	1116	1242	1330	...	1526	1732	...	...	...
256	**Toyama**	a.	...	1230	...	1447	...	1639	1852	...	...	...

									b		
Toyama	d.	...	...	0758	0959	...	...	1302	...	...	1714
Hida Furukawa	d.	...	...	0913	1107	...	1311	1419	...	...	1826
Takayama	d.	0646	0800	0938	1132	1233	1329	1440	1538	1636	1847
Gero	d.	0732	0846	1027	1220	1319	1414	1527	1624	1721	1929
Mino Ota	d.	0827	0948	1119	1315	1418	1519	1620	1717	1819	2022
Gifu **8150**	d.	0851	1012	1141	1341	1441	1541	1641	1741	1840	2043
Nagoya	a.	0912	1034	1204	1404	1504	1608	1704	1806	1906	2103

a – (12) Nagoya – Hida Furukawa; (2) Osaka (Table **8150**) – Takayama.
b – (12) Takayama – Nagoya; (2) Takayama – Osaka (Table **8150**).

NAGOYA - NAGANO 8175

JR Central

km			A										
0	**Nagoya** **8150**	d.	0700	0800	1000	1100	1200	1300	1500	1600	1740	1840	1940
80	Nakatsugawa	d.	0749	0850	1049	1149	1249	1350	1549	1649	1830	1930	2032
133	Kiso Fukushima	d.	0829	0925	1125	1225	1325	1425	1625	1725	1907	2007	2110
175	Shiojiri	d.	0859	0957	1155	1255	1354	1456	1655	1755	1937	2035	2139
188	Matsumoto	d.	0909	1007	1206	1306	1404	1506	1705	1805	1947	2046	2149
251	**Nagano**	a.	1003	1059	1254	1353	1456	1559	1800	1858	2039	2134	2239

		B										
Nagano	d.	0609	0745	0901	1001	1200	1403	1500	1600	1700	1811	1940
Matsumoto	d.	0704	0838	0952	1051	1253	1453	1553	1653	1752	1907	2031
Shiojiri	d.	0714	0849	1003	1103	1303	1503	1603	1703	1803	1919	2041
Kiso Fukushima	d.	0743	0916	1030	1130	1330	1531	1631	1731	1830	1948	2108
Nakatsugawa	d.	0822	0953	1106	1206	1406	1610	1710	1810	1910	2026	2144
Nagoya **8150**	a.	0917	1053	1201	1301	1501	1706	1805	1905	2005	2121	2234

A – Additional trips: 0900, 1400.
B – Additional trips: 1100, 1300.

SHIZUOKA - KOFU 8180

JR Central

km												
0	**Shizuoka**	d.	0817	0945	1145	1345	1545	1745	1945	...	...	...
34	Fuji	d.	0844	1015	1215	1415	1615	1815	2015	...	...	...
131	**Kofu**	a.	1031	1205	1403	1603	1803	2001	2206	...	...	...

Kofu	d.	0620	0845	1044	1237	1435	1635	1836	...	...	...
Fuji	d.	0814	1037	1234	1429	1629	1828	2031	...	...	...
Shizuoka	a.	0842	1102	1302	1456	1656	1855	2058	...	...	...

NIIGATA - NAOETSU - JOETSUMYOKO 8182

JR East

km			⊡	⊡	⊡			⊡				
0	**Niigata**	d.	0738	1021	1306	*1508*	1703	2002	*2025*	...	...	...
63	Nagaoka	d.	0829	1118	1358	1629	1803	2054	2141	...	...	...
136	Naoetsu	d.	0925	1212	1451	1732	1906	2148	2243	...	...	...
146	**Joetsumyoko**	‡ a.	0939	1225	1506	*1753*	*1956*	2201	...	...	...	...

			⊡		⊡	⊡	⊡				
Joetsumyoko	‡d.	...	0725	*0845*	1033	1307	1724	*1824*	...	...	...
Naoetsu	d.	0613	0741	0922	1048	1323	1738	1843	...	...	...
Nagaoka	d.	0714	0835	1025	1140	1415	1830	1955	...	...	...
Niigata	a.	...	0928	*1129*	1230	1506	1925	2055	...	...	...

⊡ – *Limited Express* train.
‡ – Japan Rail Pass holders must pay a supplement to travel between these stations.

TOKYO - KOFU - MATSUMOTO 8185

JR East Subject to alteration from March 18

km			[R]	[R] C	[R] B	[R]		[R]	[R]	[R]	[R]		[R]	[R]	[R]	[R]		[R]	[R]	[R]	[R]		[R]	[R]	[R]
0	**Tokyo** Shinjuku	d.	0700	0730	0800	0830	...	0900	1000	1100	1130	...	1200	1300	1400	1500	...	1600	1700	1730	1800	...	1900	2000	2100
37	Hachioji	d.	0729	0802	0833	0907	...	0936	1031	1129	1202	...	1231	1331	1431	1531	...	1631	1732	1809	1835	...	1936	2034	2134
77	Otsuki	d.	0756	0833	|	0938	...	|	|	|	1229	...	|	|	|	|	...	|	|	1833	|	...	|	|	2201
124	Kofu	d.	0828	0909	0929	1014	...	1036	1129	1224	1304	...	1328	1427	1526	1627	...	1728	1829	1908	1932	...	2033	2130	2233
185	Chino	d.	0908	0952	1007	...	...	1112	1206	1300	...	...	1403	1507	1607	1707	...	1804	1906	...	2011	...	2115	2208	2318
192	Kami Suwa	d.	0913	0957	1012	...	...	1117	1212	|	...	...	1410	1512	1614	1713	...	1809	1912	...	2017	...	2120	2213	2323
212	Shiojiri	d.	0928	1014	1028	...	...	|	1227	|	...	...	|	1528	1629	1728	...	|	1927	...	2031	...	2136	2229	2339
225	**Matsumoto**	a.	0938	1023	1037	...	...	1139	1236	1325	...	...	1432	1537	1639	1737	...	1834	1937	...	2041	...	2146	2238	2349

		[R]	[R]	[R]	[R]		[R]	[R]	[R]	[R]		[R]	[R]	[R]	[R]		[R]	[R] A	[R]	[R]		[R]	[R]	[R]
Matsumoto	d.	0630	0710	0810	...	...	0910	1010	1110	1210	...	1310	1345	1450	1510	...	1550	1630	1720	1840	...	...	...	2010
Shiojiri	d.	0638	0718	0819	...	...	0918	|	1118	1218	...	1318	1355	|	1520	...	1558	1638	1729	|	...	...	...	2018
Kami Suwa	d.	0654	0733	0835	...	...	0934	|	1133	1233	...	1333	1410	1512	1536	...	1606	1653	1746	1901	...	...	...	2033
Chino	d.	0700	0739	0843	...	...	0940	1035	1139	1239	...	1339	1416	1518	1542	...	1620	1659	1752	1906	...	...	...	2039
Kofu	d.	0740	0817	0926	0943	...	1020	1111	1217	1316	...	1416	1454	1554	1631	...	1702	1736	1835	1942	...	2004	2036	2116
Otsuki	d.	|	|	|	1016	...	1054	|	|	|	...	|	|	|	|	...	1745	|	1905	|	...	2038	2109	|
Hachioji	d.	0834	0913	1020	1044	...	1120	1205	1311	1410	...	1510	1549	1650	1730	...	1811	1831	1933	2036	...	2105	2136	2213
Tokyo Shinjuku	a.	0913	0946	1054	1116	...	1153	1233	1342	1441	...	1541	1624	1723	1804	...	1843	1906	2010	2106	...	2137	2207	2245

km			[R]	[R]	[R]	[R]	[R]	[R]	[R]	[R]	[R]	[R]	[R]
0	**Tokyo** Shinjuku	d.	0930	1030	1230	1330	1430	1530	1630	1830	1930	2200	2300
37	Hachioji	d.	1009	1102	1302	1401	1502	1602	1703	1906	2008	2235	2335
77	Otsuki	d.	1038	1129	1328	1428	1529	1630	1730	1932	2034	2301	0001
124	**Kofu**	a.	1114	1205	1403	1503	1604	1705	1806	2012	2111	2337	0037

		[R]	[R]	[R]	[R]	[R]	[R]	[R]	[R]	[R]	[R]	[R]
Kofu	d.	0703	0818	0924	1132	1232	1332	1430	1515	1611	1748	1902
Otsuki	d.	0736	0852	0957	1206	1306	1406	1506	1557	1647	1830	2036
Hachioji	d.	0803	0919	1025	1233	1333	1433	1533	1624	1714	1857	2003
Tokyo Shinjuku	a.	0842	0956	1059	1304	1404	1504	1603	1658	1751	1927	2037

Note: Some trains run to a slightly different schedule on Ⓒ. **A** – From Minami Otari (d. 1501). **B** – To Minami Otari (a. 1159). **C** – From Chiba (d. 0638). **D** – To Chiba (a. 2052).

TOKYO - MOUNT FUJI - KAWAGUCHIKO 8190

JR East, Fujikyu Railway

km			[R] A	[R]	D [R]	[R]	F C	[R] Ⓒ	E Ⓒ	D [R]	F	E Ⓐ
0	**Tokyo** Shinjuku	d.	0730	0830	...	0930	...	1113	...	...	...	...
37	Hachioji	d.	0802	0909	...	1009	...	1146	...	...	...	...
77	Otsuki	‡ ◧ d.	0837	0942	0954	1042	1152	1217	1248	1349	1455	1552
101	Mt Fuji	⊖ d.	0917	1019	1050	1120	1235	1303	1335	1445	1543	1638
104	**Kawaguchiko**	‡ ◧ a.	0923	1025	1056	1125	1240	1309	1340	1451	1549	1644

		D [R]	F	E Ⓒ	D [R]	F	E Ⓒ	[R]	[R] Ⓒ	[R]	[R]
Kawaguchiko	‡ ◧ d.	0824	0940	1110	1209	1311	1400	1503	1557	1651	1736
Mt Fuji	⊖ d.	0833	0949	1118	1217	1319	1408	1512	1606	1659	1745
Otsuki	‡ ◧ d.	0926	1031	1158	1310	1400	1448	1557	1651	1745	1830
Hachioji	d.	...	...	...	...	...	...	1624	1725	1811	1855
Tokyo Shinjuku	a.	...	...	...	...	...	...	1658	1759	1843	1927

A – From Chiba d. 0638.
C – Runs 4 minutes earlier on Ⓒ.
D – Fuji Tozan Densha. Japan Rail Pass not valid.
E – Fujisan Express. Japan Rail Pass not valid.
F – Fujisan View Express. Japan Rail Pass not valid.
◧ – Frequent additional local services available.
‡ – Japan Rail Pass not valid between Otsuki and Kawaguchiko.
⊖ – Altitude is 809 m. Bus service to Fuji-Subaru Line 5th Station (Altitude 2305m) is available.

TOKYO - IZUKYU SHIMODA and SHUZENJI 8195

JR East [R] on all trains

km					C	Ⓒ	F			Ⓒ	
0	**Tokyo**	d.	0900	0900	1000	1030	1100	1200	1200	1225j	1300
29	Yokohama	d.	0924	0924	1024	1054	1124	1224	1224	1258	1324
84	Odawara	d.	1002	1002	1102	1132	|	1301	1301	|	|
105	Atami	d.	1023	1025	1121	1156	1218	1323	1325	1352	1422
122	Ito	‡ d.	1046	|	1145	|	1238	1346	|	1422	1444
168	**Izukyu Shimoda**	‡ a.	1150	|	1241	|	1329	1447	|	1530	1543
121	Mishima	‡ d.	...	1040	...	1211	...	...	1340	...	...
141	**Shuzenji**	‡ a.	...	1108	...	1239	...	...	1406	...	...

		Ⓒ	A						B	G
Shuzenji	‡ d.	...	...	...	1235	...	...	...	1539	...
Mishima	‡ d.	...	...	...	1305	...	...	...	1606	...
Izukyu Shimoda	‡ d.	...	0952	1204	|	1301	1412	1507	|	1634
Ito	‡ d.	1004	1047	1305	|	1405	1509	1602	|	1735
Atami	d.	1030	1113	1333	1333	1430	1531	1629	1629	1800
Odawara	d.	1047	1130	1350	1350	1448	|	1648	1648	|
Yokohama	d.	1127	1208	1427	1427	1526	1628	1725	1725	1857
Tokyo	a.	1150	1232	1449	1449	1549	1649	1748	1748	1920

A – Additional trips on Ⓒ at 1134, 1344.
B – Additional trip on Ⓒ at 1418.
C – Additional trip on Ⓒ at 1030.
F – Additional trip on ①④⑤Ⓒ at 1230.
G – ①④⑤⑥⑦.
j – Tokyo **Shinjuku**.
‡ – Japan Rail Pass holders must pay a supplement to travel between these stations.

8200 TOKYO - AWA KAMOGAWA
JR East

km										A			
0	**Tokyo**	d.	0715	0901	1000	1100	1300	1500	1702	1800	1900	2100	2201
43	Soga	d.	0753	0935	1033	1134	1334	1534	1734	1834	1935	2134	2233
62	Oami	d.	0805	0947	1047	1146	1346	1546	1746	1848	1949	2148	2247
74	Mobara	d.	0813	0955	1055	1155	1354	1554	1754	1856	1957	2156	2254
82	Kazusa Ichinomiya	d.	0820	1002	1106	1202	1401	1601	1801	1903	2008	2203	2301
110	Katsuura	a.	0845	1028	1130	1228	1426	1626	1826	...	2035	2228	2326
133	**Awa Kamogawa**	a.	...	1053	1159	1252	1452	...	...	...	...	...	...

Awa Kamogawa	d.	...	0739	0840	...	1141	1406	1535	1639	...	...	...
Katsuura	d.	0726	0808	0908	1036	1207	1436	1600	1704	1814	...	2008
Kazusa Ichinomiya	d.	0754	0833	0933	1101	1234	1503	1631	1738	1840	1928	2040
Mobara	d.	0800	0839	0939	1108	1241	1509	1638	1744	1846	1936	2047
Oami	d.	0810	0847	0947	1117	1249	1518	1646	1752	1854	1948	2054
Soga	d.	0824	0902	1002	1130	1302	1531	1700	1805	1908	2001	2107
Tokyo	a.	0901	0934	1036	1205	1335	1603	1734	1840	1940	2034	2140

A – Additional trip: Ⓐ 2000. Note: Some trains run on a slightly different schedule on Ⓒ.

8205 TOKYO - NAGANOHARA and MAEBASHI
Subject to alteration from March 18 JR East

km			Ⓒ[R]	[R]	[R]	Ⓐ[R]	Ⓐ[R]	[R]	Ⓐ[R]	[R]	
0	**Tokyo** Ueno	d.	0900	1000	1210	1800	1830	1900	1930	2000	...
27	Omiya	d.	0926	1026	1235	1828	1856	1925	1955	2026	...
62	Kumagaya	d.	0952	1051	1302	1900	1925	1953	2025	2055	...
102	**Takasaki**	d.	1020	1119	1333	*1942***h**	*2011***h**	2028	*2115***h**	2124	...
164	**Naganohara Kusatsuguchi**	a.	1124	1218	1434	|	|	|	|	|	...
112	**Maebashi**	a.	...	...	...	*1956***k**	*2026***k**	*2053*	*2130***k**	*2143***b**	...

		Ⓐ[R]	Ⓐ[R]	Ⓐ[R]	Ⓐ[R]	Ⓒ[R]	Ⓒ[R]	Ⓒ[R]	[R]	[R]
Maebashi	d.	...	*0551*	*0717*	*0749*	*0749*	*0824*	...	...	...
Naganohara Kusatsuguchi	d.	...	|	|	|	|	|	1406	1307	1543
Takasaki	d.	...	0552	0740	0811	0810	0850	1513	1405	1646
Kumagaya	d.	0606	0628	0810	0842	0842	0920	1540	1434	1716
Omiya	d.	0640	0709	0839	0912	0912	0950	1607	1500	1744
Tokyo Ueno	a.	0705	0737	0907**j**	0939	0939	1013	1632	1526	1809

b – Arrives 2156 on Ⓒ. **h** – Change trains at Honjo. **j** – Tokyo **Shinjuku**. **k** – Change trains at Takasaki.

8210 TOKYO - NIKKO
Subject to alteration from March 18 JR East

km			Ⓒ[R]	[R]	Ⓒ[R]	[R]						
0	**Tokyo** Shinjuku	d.	0731	0934	1031	1300	...	...	...	...	...	...
27	Omiya	d.	0802	1006	1102	1330	...	...	...	...	...	...
135	Tobu **Nikko** ‡	d.	0927	1130	|	|	...	...	...	...	...	...
140	**Kinugawa** Onsen ‡	a.	...	...	1243	1505	...	...	...	...	...	...

		Ⓒ[R]	[R]	[R]	[R]						
Kinugawa Onsen ‡	d.	1039	1455	...	...	...	...	...	...	...	...
Tobu **Nikko** ‡	d.	|	|	1639	1702	...	...	...	...	...	...
Omiya	d.	1217	1638	1804	1840	...	...	...	...	...	...
Tokyo Shinjuku	a.	1247	1709	1836	1914	...	...	...	...	...	...

‡ – Japan Rail Pass holders must pay a supplement to travel to / from this station. Tobu Railway (www.tobu.co.jp) operate regular services Tokyo Skytree - Tobi Nikko / Kinugawa Onsen.

8215 TOKYO - IWAKI - SENDAI
[R] on all trains JR East

km																											
	Tokyo Shinagawa	d.	0645	0715	0743	...	0845	0915	0945	1015	1045	1115	1145	1215	1245	...	1315	1345	1415	1445	1515	1545	1615	1645	1715	1745	1815
0	**Tokyo** Ueno	d.	0700	0730	0800	0830	0900	0930	1000	1030	1100	1130	1200	1230	1300	...	1330	1400	1430	1500	1530	1600	1630	1700	1730	1800	1830
67	Tsuchiura	d.	0742	0816	0850	0917	|	1016	|	1115	|	1215	|	1313	|	...	1413	|	1513	|	1614	|	1711	|	1816	*1907*	1915
118	Mito	d.	0811	0850	0919	0950	1016	1048	1106	1148	1207	1248	1307	1345	1407	...	1445	1507	1546	1607	1647	1706	1744	1808	1848	1909	1947
124	Katsuta	d.	0817	0855	0925	0955	1021	1053	1111	1153	1212	1252	1312	1350	1412	...	1450	1512	1551	1612	1652	1712	1749	1813	1853	1914	1952
150	Hitachi	d.	0834	0915	0941	...	1040	...	1126	...	1232	...	1327	...	1430	...	1511	1527	...	1630	...	1730	...	1831	...	1932	2012
212	**Iwaki**	a.	0918	...	1025	...	1124	...	1207	...	1315	...	1409	...	1515	...	...	1609	...	1714	...	1814	...	1915	...	2015	...
290	Haranomachi	d.	...	...	1132	...	...	...	...	...	...	...	...	...	1621	...	...	...	...	...	...	1924	...	...	...	...	...
361	**Sendai** (Honshu)	a.	...	...	1229	...	...	...	...	...	...	...	...	...	1726	...	...	...	...	...	...	2028	...	...	...	...	...

Tokyo Shinagawa	d.	1845	1915	1945	2045	2115	2145	2215	2245	...	...
Tokyo Ueno	d.	1900	1930	2000	2100	2130	2200	2230	2300	...	...
Tsuchiura	d.	|	2018	|	2142	2221	2242	2319	2351	...	...
Mito	d.	2008	2052	2108	2211	2255	2314	2353	0024	...	...
Katsuta	d.	2014	2057	2113	2217	2300	2319	2358	0029	...	...
Hitachi	d.	2032	...	2131	2235	...	2338	...	...	...	...
Iwaki	a.	2116	...	2214	2319	...	...	...	...	...	...
Haranomachi	d.	...	...	...	...	...	...	...	...	...	...
Sendai (Honshu)	a.	...	...	...	...	...	...	...	...	...	...

Sendai (Honshu)	d.	...	...	...	...	...	...	...	...	...	...
Haranomachi	d.	...	...	...	...	...	...	...	...	...	...
Iwaki	d.	...	...	...	0614	...	0703	...	0818	...	0920
Hitachi	d.	...	...	0556	0701	0719	0745	0821	0901	...	1002
Katsuta	d.	...	0539	0616	0720	0739	0804	0841	0921	0947	1021
Mito	d.	...	0545	0622	0726	0745	0810	0848	0927	0953	1027
Tsuchiura	d.	0605	0620	0656	0758	0819	0839	0920	|	1025	|
Tokyo Ueno	a.	0706	0723	0759	0858	0915	0933	1006	1037	1108	1137
Tokyo Shinagawa	a.	0721	...	0813	0913	0931	0950	1021	1051	1122	1151

Sendai (Honshu)	d.	...	...	...	...	...	1013	...	...	...	...	...	...	...	...	...	...	...	...	...	1611	...	...	...	1802	...
Haranomachi	d.	...	...	...	...	...	1107	...	...	...	...	...	...	...	...	...	...	...	...	...	1706	...	...	...	1906	...
Iwaki	d.	...	1017	...	1120	...	1218	...	...	1323	...	1418	...	1518	...	1618	...	1721	...	...	1817	...	1918	...	2016	...
Hitachi	d.	1027	1102	...	1202	...	1302	...	...	1405	...	1502	...	1602	1626	1702	...	1803	...	...	1900	...	2000	...	2100	...
Katsuta	d.	1047	1121	1147	1221	1247	1321	1347	...	1421	1447	1521	1547	1621	1647	1721	1747	1821	...	1847	1921	1947	2021	2047	2121	2147
Mito	d.	1053	1127	1153	1227	1253	1327	1353	...	1427	1453	1527	1553	1627	1653	1727	1753	1827	...	1853	1927	1953	2027	2053	2127	2153
Tsuchiura	d.	1125	|	1225	|	1325	|	1425	...	|	1525	|	1625	|	1725	|	1824	|	...	1924	|	2024	|	2124	2156	2224
Tokyo Ueno	a.	1208	1237	1308	1337	1408	1437	1509	...	1537	1609	1639	1708	1738	1808	1839	1908	1938	...	2010	2037	2109	2139	2208	2238	2308
Tokyo Shinagawa	a.	1222	1251	1322	1351	1422	1451	1522	...	1551	1623	1653	1723	1752	1823	1852	1922	1952	...	2023	2052	2123	2154	2223	2253	2323

Note: some trains run on a slightly different schedule on Ⓒ.

8220 NIIGATA - AOMORI
Limited Express trains JR East

km													
0	**Niigata**	d.	...	0822	...	1056	...	1232	1457	...	1715	1854	2111
168	Sakata ◧	d.	*0634*	1037	...	1303	...	1441	1712	...	1922	2106	2318
273	Akita ◧	d.	0839	1203	1240	...	1552	...	1841	1923	...	...	...
377	Odate	d.	1006	...	1409	...	1723	...	...	2103	...	...	...
421	Hirosaki	d.	1044	...	1447	...	1802	...	...	2140	...	...	...
455	Shin Aomori	d.	1113	...	1516	...	1831	...	...	2212	...	...	...
459	**Aomori**	a.	1119	...	1521	...	1837	...	...	2218	...	...	...

Aomori	d.	...	...	...	...	0904	...	...	1241	...	1556	...
Shin Aomori	d.	...	...	...	...	0911	...	...	1248	...	1603	...
Hirosaki	d.	...	...	...	...	0940	...	...	1320	...	1632	...
Odate	d.	...	...	...	...	1017	...	...	1357	...	1710	...
Akita ◧	d.	...	...	...	1035	1144	...	...	1527	1635	1841	2049
Sakata ◧	d.	0529	0645	0904	1201	...	1431	1556	...	1805	...	2231
Niigata	a.	0732	0849	1109	1405	...	1637	1801	...	2010	...	...

◧ – Additional local trains available.

8225 HAKODATE and MURORAN - SAPPORO
JR Hokkaido

km			1001	1003	1	1005	3	5 ◧	7	9	1007	11	13	1009	15	1011	17	19	21					
0	**Hakodate**	d.	...	...	0602	...	0737	0900	1005	1045	...	1215	1331	...	1501	...	1640	1752	1848	1912	2011	2116	2222	2311
18	Shin **Hakodate Hokuto**	d.	...	...	0620	...	0757	0919	1023	1105	...	1234	1350	...	1520	...	1658	1811	1906	1931	2033	2138	2248	2333
50	Mori	d.	...	...	0648	...	0824	0947	1051	1133	...	1302	1423	...	1548	...	1726	1838	1933	...	...	...	...	...
112	Oshamambe	d.	...	...	0730	...	0906	1029	1133	1214	...	1344	1505	...	1628	...	1808	1919	2015	...	...	...	...	...
154	Toya	d.	...	...	0757	...	0931	1054	1158	1239	...	1409	1530	...	1653	...	1834	1944	2040	...	...	...	...	...
	Muroran	d.	0525	0654	|	...	|	|	|	|	1338	|	|	1630	|	1812	|	|	|	...	...	...	...	...
190	Higashi-Muroran	d.	0540	0708	0825	0922	0959	1122	1225	1309	1351	1437	1558	1643	1722	1825	1905	2011	2108	...	...	...	...	...
207	Noboribetsu	d.	0554	0722	0837	0936	1011	1134	1237	1322	1407	1449	1610	1658	1734	1840	1918	2023	2121	...	...	...	...	...
248	Tomakomai	d.	0619	0748	0903	1001	1037	1159	1303	1348	1435	1514	1636	1725	1800	1907	1945	2049	2148	...	...	...	...	...
275	Minami Chitose	d.	0638	0805	0919	1019	1054	1216	1318	1406	1453	1530	1653	1743	1816	1927	2003	2105	2206	...	...	...	...	...
319	**Sapporo**	a.	0713	0838	0950	1053	1128	1249	1352	1438	1528	1604	1730	1816	1847	2002	2035	2136	2237	...	...	...	...	...

km						2	4	1002	6	8	10	1004	12		14 ◧	1006	16	18	1008	20	22	1010	12	
0	**Sapporo**	d.	...	...	...	0600	0652	0730	0843	0938	1057	1132	1209	...	1327	1356	1438	1534	1603	1651	1847	1914	2200	...
44	Minami Chitose	d.	...	...	...	0628	0723	0801	0916	1012	1127	1202	1241	...	1400	1428	1512	1605	1638	1726	1918	1948	2234	...
71	Tomakomai	d.	...	...	...	0644	0740	0819	0932	1030	1144	1221	1259	...	1416	1446	1529	1622	1656	1743	1935	2007	2252	...
112	Noboribetsu	d.	...	...	...	|	0803	0845	0958	1056	1210	1246	1326	...	|	1511	1555	1647	1721	1808	2000	2036	2317	...
129	Higashi-Muroran	d.	...	...	...	0718	0816	0858	1011	1111	1224	1301	1339	...	1454	1454	1608	1701	1736	1821	2013	2052	2322	...
136	**Muroran**	a.	...	...	...	|	|	▬	|	|	|	1313	|	...	|	1538	|	|	1747	|	|	2106	2344	...
	Toya	d.	...	...	...	|	0844	...	1039	1139	1251	...	1408	...	1521	...	1634	1727	...	1848	2039	...	...	...
	Oshamambe	d.	...	...	...	0809	0911	...	1106	1205	1317	...	1437	...	1547	...	1701	1757	...	1915	2105	...	...	...
	Mori	d.	...	...	...	0850	0954	...	1149	1248	1359	...	1520	...	1630	...	1743	1839	...	1957	2148	...	...	...
	Shin **Hakodate Hokuto**	a.	0641	0719	0832	0917	1023	1110	1219	1319	1426	...	1552	1718	1658	...	1811	1906	...	2023	2214	...	...	2338
	Hakodate	a.	0706	0747	0859	0933	1038	1136	1234	1335	1441	...	1608	1743	1713	...	1826	1924	...	2059	2251	...	...	2357

◧ – Not on ③④ in April.

SAPPORO - KUSHIRO — 8230

JR Hokkaido

km												
0	**Sapporo** d.	0648	0758	0851	1033	1150	1415	1552	1729	1840	1939	2110
44	Minami Chitose d.	0720	0827	0926	1105	1225	1448	1626	1807	1914	2012	2142
143	Tomamu d.	0827	0934	1046	1215	1326	1605	1735	1920	2020	2125	2254
220	Obihiro d.	0921	1041	1139	1312	1418	1704	1836	2017	2120	2219	2348
349	**Kushiro** a.	1058	...	1320	...	1551	1839	...	2159	...	2355	...

Kushiro d.	...	0625	...	0821	...	1124	...	1342	1612	...	1859
Obihiro d.	0645	0801	0842	0953	1108	1257	1335	1525	1748	1924	2033
Tomamu d.	0741	0905	0946	1046	1215	1402	1438	1618	1841	2030	2125
Minami Chitose d.	0902	1014	1102	1151	1328	1503	1551	1729	1954	2140	2228
Sapporo a.	0934	1047	1136	1223	1404	1538	1624	1803	2028	2215	2258

KUSHIRO - ABASHIRI — 8233

JR Hokkaido

km												
0	**Kushiro** d.	...	...	0638	0857	1414	1632	1741	1852	2209	...	...
44	Mashu d.	...	...	0800	1011	1530	1759	1921	2010	2323	...	...
132	Shiretoko-Shari d.	0645	0728	0906	1112	1633	1859	...	2119	...	...	...
143	**Abashiri** a.	0731	0817	0951	1153	1717	1947	...	2200	...	...	...

Abashiri d.	...	...	0641	1024	1510	1617	1854	2014	2209	...	...
Shiretoko-Shari d.	...	...	0726	1111	1557	1715	1945	2100	2250	...	...
Mashu d.	0520	0630	0825	1217	1710	1832	2115	...	...	...	...
Kushiro a.	0637	0747	1000	1334	1845	1955	2208	...	...	...	...

SAPPORO - WAKKANAI and ABASHIRI — 8235

JR Hokkaido

km					B				B			A
0	**Sapporo** d.	0656	0730	1100	...	1200	...	1530	...	1730	1830	...
83	Takikawa d.	0755	0824	1152	...	1252	...	1622	...	1829	1922	...
137	**Asahikawa** d.	0835	0900	1225	1241	1325	1335	1655	1707	1908	1955	2006
213	Nayoro d.	|	0956	...	|	...	1431	...	|	|	...	2103
396	**Wakkanai** a.	|	1240	...	|	...	1723	...	|	|	...	2347
185	Kamikawa d.	0916	...	...	1327	...	...	...	1747	1949	...	...
375	**Abashiri** a.	1217	...	...	1634	...	...	...	2044	2300	...	...

				B		B		A			
Abashiri d.	0556	...	...	0805	...	1237	...	...	...	1725	...
Kamikawa d.	0901	...	...	1104	...	1538	...	...	...	2036	...
Wakkanai d.	|	0636	...	|	...	|	...	1301	...	|	1744
Nayoro d.	|	0925	...	|	...	|	...	1548	...	|	2032
Asahikawa d.	0947	1019	1030	1143	1200	1616	1630	1648	1700	2117	2130
Takikawa d.	1022	...	1102	...	1232	...	1702	...	1733	2152	2204
Sapporo a.	1119	...	1155	...	1325	...	1755	...	1825	2253	2257

A – Not on ②③④ Apr. 11–27 and May 9–11.

B – Not on ③④⑤ Apr. 11–27 and ②③④ May 9–31.

SAPPORO - ASAHIKAWA — 8240

JR Hokkaido

km																								
0	**Sapporo** d.	0635	0712	0800	0900	1000	1100	...	1200	1300	1400	1430	1500	1530	1600	1700	1800	...	1830	1900	2000	2100	2200	2305
83	Takikawa d.	0727	0804	0852	0952	1052	1152	...	1252	1352	1452	1522	1552	1622	1652	1752	1852	...	1922	1952	2052	2152	2252	2357
137	**Asahikawa** 8235 a.	0800	0840	0925	1025	1125	1225	...	1325	1425	1525	1555	1625	1655	1725	1825	1925	...	1955	2025	2125	2225	2325	0030

Asahikawa 8235 d.	0518	0600	0645	0718	0755	0830	...	0900	1000	1030	1100	1200	1300	1400	1500	1600	...	1630	1700	1800	1900	2000	2200
Takikawa d.	0550	0632	0717	0750	0827	0902	...	0932	1032	1102	1132	1232	1332	1432	1532	1632	...	1702	1732	1832	1932	2032	2232
Sapporo a.	0643	0733	0826	0846	0920	0955	...	1025	1125	1155	1225	1325	1425	1525	1625	1725	...	1755	1825	1925	2025	2125	2325

SUMMARY OF OVERNIGHT TRAINS — 8300

km		C (R)	B (R)	A (R)
0	**Tokyo** d.	...	2150	2150
29	Yokohama d.	...	2215	2215
181	Shiuoka a.	...	0020	0020
543	Kyoto d.	2115	|	|
557	Osaka d.	2228	|	|
733	**Okayama** d.	|	0631	0634
814	Niimi d.	|	|	0744
892	Yonago d.	0756	|	0905
921	Matsue d.	0857	|	0931
954	**Izumoshi** a.	0931	|	0958
761	Kojima d.	...	0653	...
805	**Takamatsu** a.	...	0727	...

	C (R)	A (R)	B (R)
Takamatsu d.	...	...	2126
Kojima d.	...	...	2201
Izumoshi d.	1600	1851	|
Matsue d.	1705	1927	|
Yonago d.	1748	1956	|
Niimi d.	|	2120	|
Okayama d.	|	2234	2234
Osaka d.	0612	0033	0033
Kyoto a.	0643	|	|
Shizuoka d.	...	0440	0440
Yokohama d.	...	0645	0645
Tokyo a.	...	0708	0708

A – SUNRISE IZUMO 1, 2 cl., [2] Izumoshi - Tokyo and v.v. (see note ⊙).

B – SUNRISE SETO 1, 2 cl., [2] Takamatsu - Tokyo and v.v. (see note ⊙).

C – WEST EXPRESS GINGA 2 cl., [12].
From Kyoto on ①⑤ May 6 - Sept. 19 (not June 6, July 1–8, Aug. 8–19, Sept. 5); from Izumoshi on ③⑥ May 7 - Sept. 21 (not June 8, July 2–9, Aug. 10–20, Sept. 7).
Until Mar. 8 West Express Ginga runs from Kyoto (d. 2115) to Shingu (a. 0937) as a night train and from Shingu (d. 0950) to Kyoto (a. 2053) as daytime train for tour passenegers only. Operates twice weekly - contact operator for running days.

⊙ – Trains convey Deluxe, single and twin berth compartments. They also convey *Nobinobi* - open-plan sleeping areas categorised as seats.

AIRPORT RAIL LINKS — 8400

CHUBU CENTRAL JAPAN INTERNATIONAL AIRPORT

SKY Limited Express service ((R)) Meitetsu Nagoya - Central Japan International Airport and v.v. *44 km*. Journey 30 minutes. (Additional slower trains are available, not (R)). Operator: Meitetsu.

From Meitetsu Nagoya on Ⓐ at 0600, 0628, 0648, 0720, 0751, 0823, 0850 and every 30 minutes until 1650, 1719, 1749, 1819, 1849, 1919, 1949, 2019, 2049, 2119; on Ⓒ at 0602, 0630, 0653, 0720, 0750 and every 30 minutes until 2050, 2120.

From Central Japan International Airport on Ⓐ at 0703, 0726, 0800, 0834, 0907 and every 30 minutes until 1637, 1706, 1736, 1806, 1836, 1906, 1936, 2007, 2037, 2107, 2137, 2207; on Ⓒ at 0713, 0729, 0759, 0829, 0907 and every 30 minutes until 2137, 2207.

KANSAI AIRPORT

HARUKA Limited Express service Kyoto - Shin Osaka ■ - Kansai Airport and v.v. *100 km*. Journey 80 - 90 minutes. Operator: JR West.

From Kyoto at 0545, 0621, 0644, 0713, 0748 Ⓐ, 0749 Ⓒ, 0820 Ⓒ, 0821 Ⓐ, 0845, 0930, 1000 and every 30 minutes until 2000, 2030.

From Kansai Airport at 0631 Ⓐ, 0640 Ⓒ, 0727 Ⓐ, 0741 Ⓒ, 0756 Ⓐ, 0808 Ⓒ, 0841 Ⓐ, 0843 Ⓒ, 0912 Ⓐ, 0916 Ⓒ, 0946, 1016, 1044 and every 30 minutes until 1644, 1714 Ⓒ, 1716 Ⓐ, 1746 and every 30 minutes until 2046, 2125, 2216.

■ – Trains call at Shin Osaka 28 - 33 minutes after Kyoto and 45 - 50 minutes after Kansai Airport.

TOKYO HANEDA AIRPORT

Limited Express service Tokyo Shinagawa - Haneda Airport Terminal 3 (△) and v.v. *14 km*. Journey 20 minutes. Operator: Keikyu Railway.

From Tokyo Shinagawa at 0552 and every 10 - 15 minutes until 2300. From Haneda Airport Terminal 3 at 0530 and every 10 - 15 minutes until 2330.

△ – Most trains continue to/from Haneda Aiport Terminal 1, journey 3 minutes.

Monorail service Tokyo Hamamatsucho – Haneda Airport Terminal 3 (□) and v.v. (JR pass valid) *14 km*. Journey 13 - 24 minutes. Operator: Tokyo Monorail Co Ltd.

From Tokyo Hamamatsucho at 0459 and every 3 - 10 minutes until 0001. From Haneda Airport Terminal 3 at 0518 and every 3 - 10 minutes until 0010.

□ – All trains continue to/from Haneda Aiport Terminal 1, journey 3 - 5 minutes and Terminal 2, journey 5 - 7 minutes.

TOKYO NARITA AIRPORT

NARITA EXPRESS Limited Express service ((R)) Tokyo - Narita Airport Terminal 1 (▽) and v.v. *79 km*. Journey 55 minutes. Operator: JR East.

From Tokyo at 0618, 0700, 0715, 0731, 0755, 0830, 0900, 1003, 1033, 1103, 1133, 1203, 1233, 1303, 1333, 1403, 1433, 1503, 1533, 1603, 1633, 1703, 1733, 1803, 1833, 1903, 2003.

From Narita T1 at 0743, 0813, 0850, 0915, 0945, 1015, 1045, 1114, 1145, 1220, 1245, 1314, 1345, 1420, 1446, 1514, 1544, 1620, 1645, 1717, 1746, 1815, 1848, 1912, 1948, 2044, 2144.

▽ – Trains also call at Narita Aiport Terminal two, 2/3 minutes before/after Terminal one. Additional slower trains(not (R)) are available about hourly each direction.

SKYLINER Limited Express service ((R)) Tokyo Ueno Keisei - Narita Airport Terminal 1 (▷) and v.v. *69 km*. Journey 45 minutes. Operator: Keisei Electric Railway.

From Tokyo Ueno Keisei on Ⓐ at 0540, 0600, 0620, 0640, 0700, 0720, 0740, 0800, 0817, 0840, 0900, 0917, 0940, 1000, 1020, 1037 and at the same minutes past each hour until 1600, 1620, 1640, 1700, 1720, 1740, 1820, 1900, 1940, 2020; on Ⓒ at 0540, 0600, 0620, 0640, 0700, 0718, 0740, 0800, 0819, 0840, 0900, 0918, 0940, 0959, 1020, 1037, 1100, 1120, 1137 and at the same minutes past each hour until 1600, 1620, 1640, 1070, 1717, 1740, 1820, 1900, 1940, 2020.

From Narita Airport Terminal 1 on Ⓐ at 0723, 0812, 0907, 0936, 0953, 1019, 1033, 1059, 1113, 1139, 1159 and at the same minutes past each hour until 1613, 1639, 1659, 1719, 1739, 1759, 1815, 1840, 1900, 1920, 1940, 2000, 2030, 2100, 2130, 2200, 2230, 2300; on Ⓒ at 0730, 0829, 0919, 0939, 0953, 1016, 1033, 1059, 1113, 1139, 1159 and at the same minutes past each hour until 1613, 1639, 1658, 1715, 1739, 1759, 1812, 1839, 1859, 1921, 1939, 2000, 2030, 2100, 2130, 2200, 2230, 2300.

▷ – Trains also call at Narita Airport Terminal 2, 3 minutes before / 5 minutes after Terminal 1. Additional slower trains are available.

SAPPORO SHIN CHITOSE AIRPORT

Sapporo - Shin Chitose Airport and v.v. *47 km* Journey 38 - 48 minutes. Operator: JR Hokkaido.

From Sapporo at 0550, 0602*, 0616, 0629, 0642, 0656, 0722, 0735, 0748, 0802, 0808, 0821, 0836, then at 00, 12, 23, 35 and 47 minutes past the hour (●) until 2004, 2010, 2024, 2047, 2053, 2100, 2113, 2137, 2151.

From Shin Chitose Airport at 0639, 0656, 0702, 0722, 0733, 0751, 0819, 0830, 0840, 0852, 0906, 0918, 0930, then at 06, 18, 30, 42 and 54 minutes past the hour (●) until 2006, 2019, 2032, 2046, 2052, 2120, 2131, 2144, 2155, 2205, 2216, 2235, 2253.

● – Timings may vary by up to 3 minutes. All trains call at Minami-Chitose 3 minutes before / 4 minutes after Shin Chitose Airport.

CANADA

Capital: **Ottawa** (GMT -5; add one hour in summer, except Saskatchewan).

2023 public holidays: Jan. 1, 2, Apr. 7, 10 (NT, NU, QC), May 23 (not NB, NS, PE, QC), July 1, Sept. 4, 30, Oct. 9 (not NB, NS, PE), Nov. 11 (not MB, NS, ON, QC), Dec. 25, 26 (NL, NT, NU, ON).

The principal operator in Canada is Via Rail (Via Rail ✆ 1 888 842 7245. www.viarail.ca). Timings shown are the most recently available and are subject to alteration at any time, but especially around public holidays. Details of other operators can be found in relevant tables. Unless otherwise noted all trains carry first and second class seated accomodation. In Canada first class is called 'Business' and second class is called 'Economy'. Most very long distance trains convey sleeping cars called 'Sleeper Plus' which has two berths per compartment, some of which are en-suite, The *Canadian* also offers 'Prestige Class' and one to four berth 'Sleeper Plus' compartments some of which are en-suite. Most trains also convey some form of catering, but again the actual service offered varies considerably. Tickets are available from staffed stations, websites and through authorised ticketing agents. A reservation is neccessary for travel on very long distance Via Rail trains, and also strongly recommended for corridor services.

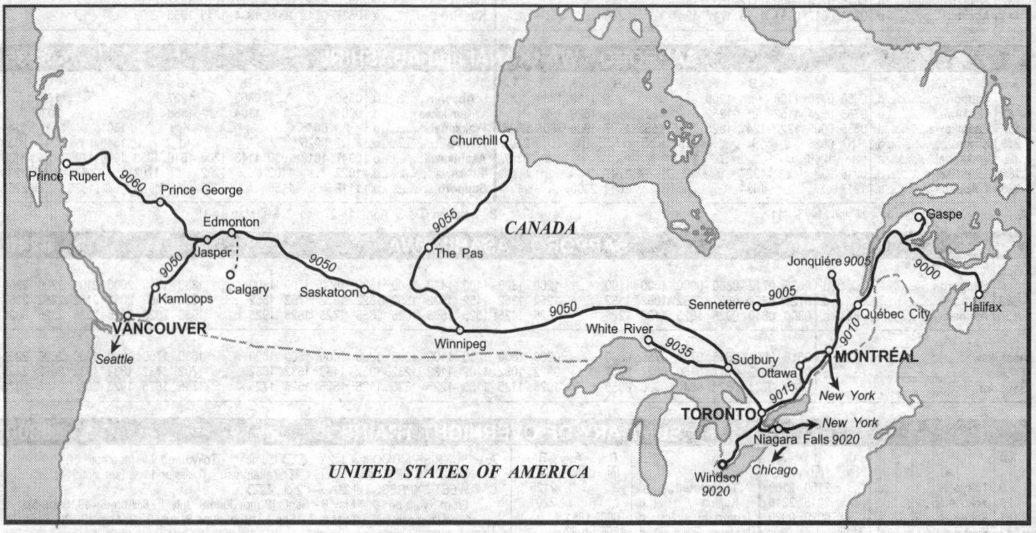

9000 MONTRÉAL - HALIFAX — Via Rail

km		708	14
		③⑤⑦ 🚌 R	③⑤⑦ A R
	Québec City Palais ... d.	2100	...
0	**Montréal** Central .. **9010** d.	|	1900
251	**Sainte Foy** ... **9010** d.	2130	2249
448	Rivière-du-Loup ... d.	...	0113
552	Rimouski ... d.	...	0301
581	Mont-Joli ... d.	...	0339
731	Matapédia ... d.	...	0610
874	Bonaventure ... d.	...	|
993	Percé ... d.	...	|
1056	**Gaspé** ... a.	...	|
750	Campbellton ... d.	...	0748
851	Bathurst ... d.	...	0937
922	Miramichi ... d.	...	1123
1051	**Moncton** ... a.	...	1323
1051	**Moncton** ... d.	...	1338
1128	Amherst ... d.	...	1442
1252	Truro ... d.	...	1622
1355	**Halifax** ... a.	...	1751

	15	703
	③⑤⑦ A R	①④⑥ 🚌 R
Halifax ... d.	1300	...
Truro ... d.	1431	...
Amherst ... d.	1608	...
Moncton ... a.	1717	...
Moncton ... d.	1732	...
Miramichi ... d.	1937	...
Bathurst ... d.	2128	...
Campbellton ... d.	2318	...
Gaspé ... d.	|	...
Percé ... d.	|	...
Bonaventure ... d.	|	...
Matapédia ... d.	2252	...
Mont-Joli ... d.	0126	...
Rimouski ... d.	0201	...
Rivière-du-Loup ... d.	0353	...
Sainte Foy ... **9010** a.	0613	0640
Montréal Central **9010** a.	1003	|
Québec City Palais .a.	...	0710

A – OCEAN – 🛏 2 ✕ Montréal - Halifax and v.v.

9005 JONQUIÈRE and SENNETERRE — Via Rail

km		600	602
		2 R ②④	2 R ⑦
510	**Jonquière** ... d.	0858	1158
444	Chambord ... d.	1011	1311
341	Lac-Édouard ... d.	1230	1530
251	Rivière à Pierre ... d.	1433	1733
217	**Hervey** ... a.	1520	1820
217	**Hervey** ... d.	1530	1830
170	Shawinigan ... d.	1627	1927
0	**Montréal** Central ... a.	1946	2246

	601	
	2 R ①③⑤	
Montréal Central ... d.	0730	...
Shawinigan ... d.	1022	...
Hervey ... a.	1135	...
Hervey ... d.	1150	...
Rivière à Pierre ... d.	1241	...
Lac-Édouard ... d.	1441	...
Chambord ... d.	1700	...
Jonquière ... a.	1852	...

km		604	606
		2 R ②④	2 R ⑦
717	**Senneterre** ... d.	0628	0928
561	Clova ... d.	0845	1145
495	Parent ... d.	1010	1309
431	Weymont ... d.	1131	1429
297	La Tuque ... d.	1350	1650
217	**Hervey** ... a.	1515	1815
217	**Hervey** ... d.	1530	1830
170	Shawinigan ... d.	1627	1927
0	**Montréal** Central ... a.	1946	2246

	603	
	2 R ①③⑤	
Montréal Central ... d.	0730	...
Shawinigan ... d.	1022	...
Hervey ... a.	1135	...
Hervey ... d.	1145	...
La Tuque ... d.	1321	...
Weymont ... d.	1527	...
Parent ... d.	1648	...
Clova ... d.	1813	...
Senneterre ... a.	2102	...

9010 QUÉBEC CITY - MONTRÉAL — Via Rail

km		33	15	35	37	39	29			
		①–⑤ B	①④⑥ A	B	B	B				
0	**Québec City** Palais ... △ d.	0525	...	0810	1236	1500	1745	...	...	...
21	Ste. Foy ... △ d.	0552	0628	0836	1302	1526	1811	...	...	...
26	Charny ... △ d.	0600	|	0844	|	|	|	...	...	...
172	Drummondville ... d.	0728	0836	1015	1445	1654	1943	...	...	...
219	St. Hyacinthe ... d.	0800	0915	1048	1516	|	2021	...	...	...
265	St. Lambert ... △ d.	0826	0950	1115	1543	1800	2049	...	...	...
272	**Montréal** Central ... △ a.	0837	1003	1126	1554	1811	2100	...	...	...

	20	22	622	24	26	28	14		
	①–⑤	①–⑤ B	⑥⑦	B	B	B	③⑤⑦ A		
Montréal Central ... △ d.	0625	0856	0906	1245	1640	1825	1900	...	...
St. Lambert ... △ d.	0638	0918	0918	1308	1702	1848	1925	...	...
St. Hyacinthe ... d.	0705	0943	0943	1335	1729	1916	1958	...	...
Drummondville ... d.	0738	1012	1012	1403	1815	1945	2047	...	...
Charny ... △ d.	|	|	|	1546	1954	2124	|	...	...
Ste. Foy ... △ d.	0919	1158	1157	1554	2003	2132	2234	...	...
Québec City Palais ... △ a.	0943	1222	1222	1618	2026	2156	...	...	...

A – OCEAN – 🛏 2 ✕ Montréal Central - Halifax and v.v. (Table **9000**).
B – 12 Québec - Montréal - Ottawa and v.v. (Table **9015**).
△ – Local traffic not carried.

9012 TORONTO PEARSON AIRPORT — UP Express

km		Ⓐ	Ⓐ					
0	Toronto Union ... d.	0510	0530	0600	and every 30	2200	2230	2300
23	**Pearson Airport** ✈ ... a.	0535	0555	0625	minutes (◧) until	2225	2255	2325

	Ⓐ	Ⓐ					
Pearson Airport ✈ ... d.	0527	0557	0627	and every 30	2227	2257	2327
Toronto Union ... a.	0552	0622	0652	minutes (⊡) until	2252	2322	2352

◧ – Every 15 minutes 0545 Ⓐ - 0845 Ⓐ and 1415 Ⓐ - 1915 Ⓐ.

⊡ – Every 15 minutes 0612 Ⓐ - 0912 Ⓐ and 1427 Ⓐ - 1957 Ⓐ.

MONTRÉAL - OTTAWA - TORONTO — 9015

Via Rail

km		41	61	51	643	63	45	633		33	65	53	47	35	67		645	55	69	37	59	669	39
		①–⑥	①–⑥	①–⑤	⑥⑦			⑥⑦		①–⑤												Ⓑ	
										A				A						A			A
0	**Montréal** Central △ d.	...	0651	0620	...	0850	...	0900	...	0900	1100	...	...	1154	1323	...	...	...	1656	1630	...	1822	1850
19	Dorval △ d.	...	0718	0644	...	0915	...	0924	...	0934	1126	...	...	1229	1347	...	...	...	1720	1704	...	1847	1924
100	Alexandria d.	...	|	0728	...	|	...	1011	...	1022	|	...	...	1317	|	...	...	...	|	1751	...	|	2018
187	**Ottawa** a.	...	|	0820	...	|	...	1104	...	1114	|	...	...	1405	|	...	...	...	|	1835	...	|	2102
187	**Ottawa** d.	0530	|	0835	0835	|	1027	...	...	...	|	1145	1231	...	|	...	1432	1533	|	...	1749	|	...
253	Smiths Falls d.	0622	|	0923	0924	|	|	...	...	...	|	1235	|	...	|	...	|	|	|	...	1850	|	...
	Cornwall d.	|	0809	|	|	1005	|	...	...	...	1217	|	|	...	1436	...	|	|	1811	...	|	1940	...
298	Brockville d.	0651	|	0952	0953	1051	|	...	...	...	|	1310	1359	...	|	...	|	1657	1854	...	1919	|	...
378	**Kingston** d.	0734	0938	1035	1036	1138	1226	...	...	...	1345	1401	1448	...	1602	...	1637	1741	1937	...	2002	2107	...
451	Belleville d.	0816	1016	1116	1120	1221	...	...	...	...	1427	1443	1531	...	1642	...	1718	1822	|	...	2042	|	...
520	Cobourg d.	0851	|	1150	1158	1302	...	...	...	...	1504	1521	|	...	1721	...	|	1857	|	...	2120	|	...
581	Oshawa d.	0927	1125	1228	1238	1340	...	...	...	...	1539	1556	1641	...	1756	...	1825	1935	2121	...	2154	2256	...
633	**Toronto** Union a.	1002	1203	1303	1318	1418	...	...	...	...	1618	1633	1718	...	1833	...	1903	2018	2203	...	2233	2333	...

km		22	60	24	50	62		52	26	40	64	28		42	44	66	38	46		68	54	668	48
		①–⑤	①–⑥																			Ⓑ	Ⓑ
		A		A					A			A											
0	**Toronto** Union d.	...	0647	...	0647	0832	...	0832	...	1032	1132	...	...	1217	1417	1517	...	1532	...	1702	1732	1802	1832
51	Oshawa d.	...	0726	...	0726	0911	...	0911	...	|	1211	...	...	1255	1456	1556	...	1610	...	1740	1808	1839	1908
113	Cobourg d.	...	0801	...	0801	0943	...	0943	...	|	1248	...	...	1329	|	|	...	1643	...	1811	1842	|	1945
182	Belleville d.	...	0836	...	0836	1020	...	1020	...	1209	1329	...	...	1407	|	1702	...	|	...	1849	1924	|	2028
254	**Kingston** d.	...	0918	...	0918	1101	...	1101	...	1249	1411	...	...	1447	1638	1741	...	1755	...	1927	2006	2020	2108
335	Brockville d.	...	|	...	1015	|	...	1156	...	|	1500	...	...	1534	1722	|	...	1840	...	2013	2052	|	2155
428	Cornwall d.	...	1055	...	|	1234	...	|	...	|	1549	...	...	|	|	1908	...	|	...	2104	|	2147	|
380	Smiths Falls d.	...	|	...	1046	|	...	1225	...	|	|	...	...	1608	1752	|	...	|	...	|	2126	|	2225
446	**Ottawa** a.	...	|	...	1136	|	...	1325	...	1454	|	...	...	1657	1843	|	...	2014	...	|	2211	|	2308
	Ottawa d.	0630	|	1015	...	|	...	...	1420	...	|	1610	...	...	...	|	1855	...	...	|	...	|	...
	Alexandria d.	0718	|	1107	...	|	...	...	1508	...	|	1659	...	...	...	|	1946	...	...	|	...	|	...
520	Dorval △ d.	0811	1144	1155	...	1323	...	...	1555	...	1641	1744	...	...	...	1957	2037	...	...	2153	...	2236	...
539	**Montréal** Central △ a.	0831	1204	1215	...	1343	...	...	1615	...	1701	1804	...	...	...	2018	2057	...	...	2213	...	2255	...

A – [12] Québec - Montréal - Ottawa and v.v. (Table **9010**).

△ – Local traffic not carried.

TORONTO - WINDSOR and NIAGARA FALLS — 9020

GO Transit, Via Rail

km	Via Rail	71	7097	73	75	79			
			●						
0	**Toronto** Union 9030 d.	0650	0820	1215	1730	1945	...	...	...
34	Oakville d.	0715	0845	1240	1756	2009	...	...	...
56	Aldershot d.	0731	0901	1258	1812	2023	...	...	...
114	St. Catharines d.	|	0958	|	|	|	...	...	...
133	**Niagara Falls** (Canada) a.	|	1022	|	|	|	...	...	...
96	Brantford d.	0759	...	1327	1844	2051	...	...	...
139	Woodstock d.	0831	...	1355	1914	2118	...	...	...
185	London 9030 d.	0911	...	1430	2001	2157	...	...	...
290	Chatham d.	1019	...	1539	2106	2259	...	...	...
360	**Windsor** a.	1108	...	1630	2158	2344	...	...	...

Via Rail	70	72	76	7098	7098	78		
				⑥⑦	①–⑤			
				●	●			
Windsor d.	0540	0843	1346	...	...	1741	...	...
Chatham d.	0628	0928	1431	...	...	1828	...	...
London 9030 d.	0740	1044	1544	...	...	1938	...	...
Woodstock d.	0817	1123	|	...	...	2010	...	...
Brantford d.	0851	1154	1641	...	...	2041	...	...
Niagara Falls (Canada) d.	|	|	|	1740	1745	|	...	...
St. Catharines d.	|	|	|	1803	1808	|	...	...
Aldershot d.	0931	1226	1714	1859	1904	2111	...	...
Oakville d.	0946	1241	1729	1914	1919	2126	...	...
Toronto Union 9030 a.	1010	1305	1753	1938	1943	2150	...	...

km	GO Transit	Ⓒ	Ⓐ			Ⓐ	Ⓒ	Ⓐ	Ⓒ		Ⓐ	Ⓒ	Ⓒ	Ⓐ	Ⓐ		Ⓐ	Ⓒ				
0	**Toronto** Union ◧ d.	0645	0645	0745	0845	0945	0945	1045	1045		1545	1545	1645	1645	1700	1745	1845	1845	1945	2045	2145	2245
34	Oakville ◧ d.	0725	0725	0825	0925	1025	1025	1125	1125	and	1625	1625	1725	1725	1740	1825	1925	1925	2025	2125	2225	2325
51	Burlington ◧ d.	0743	0743	0843	0943	1043	1043	1143	1143	hourly	1643	1643	1743	1743	1758	1843	1943	1943	2043	2143	2243	2343
56	Aldershot ◧ d.	0750	0750	0850	0950	1050	1050	1150	1150	until	1650	1650	1750	1750	1805	1850	1950	1950	2050	2150	2250	2350
114	St. Catharines d.	0845*	0848*	0948*	1048*	1148*	1158*	1248*	1258*	⊡	1755*	1758*	1853*	1855*	1908	1948*	2045*	2048*	2145*	2245*	2345*	0045*
133	**Niagara Falls** (Canada) a.	0918*	0923*	1023*	1123*	1223*	1233*	1323*	1333*		1831*	1833*	1928*	1931*	1933	2023*	2118*	2123*	2218*	2318*	0018*	0118*

GO Transit	Ⓒ	Ⓐ	Ⓐ	Ⓒ	Ⓐ	Ⓒ	Ⓐ	Ⓒ	Ⓐ	Ⓒ		Ⓐ	Ⓒ	Ⓒ	Ⓐ	Ⓒ	Ⓐ	Ⓒ	Ⓐ	Ⓒ	Ⓐ
Niagara Falls (Canada) d.	0549*	0557	0613*	0649*	0704*	0744*	0804*	0839*	0904*	0939*		1709*	1728*	1834*	1839*	1939*	1944*	2039*	2044*	2139*	2144*
St. Catharines d.	0619*	0620	0643*	0719*	0739*	0814*	0839*	0914*	0939*	1014*	and	1744*	1808*	1909*	1914*	2009*	2019*	2109*	2119*	2209*	2219*
Aldershot ◧ d.	0725	0725	0755	0825	0855	0925	0955	1025	1055	1125	hourly	1855	1925	2025	2025	2125	2125	2225	2225	2325	2325
Burlington ◧ d.	0731	0731	0801	0831	0901	0931	1001	1031	1101	1131	until	1901	1931	2031	2031	2131	2131	2231	2231	2331	2331
Oakville ◧ d.	0748	0748	0818	0848	0918	0948	1018	1048	1118	1148	⊡	1918	1948	2048	2048	2148	2148	2248	2248	2348	2348
Toronto Union ◧ a.	0830	0830	0900	0930	1000	1030	1100	1130	1200	1230		2000	2030	2130	2130	2230	2230	2330	2330	0030	0030

⊡ – Timings may vary by up to 11 minutes; earlier departures and later arrivals are possible.

◧ – Full service Toronto - Aldershot and v.v.: from Toronto at 0645 and every 30 minutes until 2345; from Aldershot at 0525 and every 30 minutes until 2325.

* – Connection by 🚌 to / from **Burlington**. Buses call at St. Catharines Fairview Mall and Nlagara Falls Bus Terminal, **not** at the railway stations.

● – THE MAPLE LEAF – see Table **9210**.

TORONTO - COCHRANE — 9025

Ontario Northland

km		🚌	🚌	🚌
0	**Toronto** Yorkdale d.	0930	...	...
143	Washago d.	1145	...	...
164	Gravenhurst d.	1205	...	...
219	Huntsville d.	1315	...	...
351	**North Bay** d.	1450	1615	...
513	Cobalt d.	▬	1805	...
529	New Liskeard d.	...	1830	...
571	Engleheart d.	...	1910	...
677	Matheson d.	**421**	2115	2120
	Timmins a.	Ⓡ C	2205	|
754	**Cochrane** d.	0900	...	2225
	Fraserdale d.	1035r	...	...
	Moose River d.	1230r	...	...
1053	**Moosonee** a.	1350	...	...

	🚌	🚌	422 Ⓡ C
Moosonee d.	...	...	1700
Moose River d.	...	...	1815r
Fraserdale d.	...	...	2000r
Cochrane d.	0850	...	2145
Timmins d.	|	0900	▬
Matheson d.	1000	1005	...
Engleheart d.	...	1155	...
New Liskeard d.	...	1235	🚌
Cobalt d.	...	1305	
North Bay d.	...	1505	1600
Huntsville d.	...	...	1740
Gravenhurst d.	...	...	1850
Washago d.	...	...	1910
Toronto Yorkdale a.	...	...	2140

C – POLAR BEAR EXPRESS – ①②④⑤. [2] Cochrane - Moosonee and v.v. Timings at request stops (r) are approximate and will vary.

TORONTO - SARNIA — 9030

GO Transit, Via Rail

km		GO Ⓐ	87
0	**Toronto** Union 9020 d.	1634	1740
34	Brampton d.	1716	1814
47	Georgetown d.	1734	1826
79	Guelph d.	1801	1851
101	Kitchener d.	1822	1918
143	Stratford d.	1913	1955
195	London 9020 d.	2037	2114
290	**Sarnia** a.	...	2220

	GO Ⓐ	84
Sarnia d.	...	0840
London 9020 d.	0533	0954
Stratford d.	0657	1116
Kitchener d.	0745	1204
Guelph d.	0802	1226
Georgetown d.	0830	1249
Brampton d.	0853	1301
Toronto Union 9020 a.	0928	1338

WHITE RIVER - SUDBURY — 9035

Via Rail

km		186 2 ③⑤⑦	
0	**White River** d.	0700	...
79	Franz d.	0820	...
209	Chapleau d.	1045	...
341	Biscotasing d.	1245	...
484	**Sudbury** § a.	1550	...

	185 2 ②④⑥	
Sudbury § d.	0900	...
Biscotasing d.	1120	...
Chapleau d.	1335	...
Franz d.	1550	...
White River a.	1705	...

§ – Sudbury is *10 km* from Sudbury Junction (Table **9050**).

SAULT STE MARIE — 9040

km		🚌 Ⓑ D	E
315	**Sudbury** d.	1740	...
0	**Sault Ste. Marie** a.	2201	...
0	**Sault Ste. Marie** d.	...	0800
183	**Agawa Canyon** a.	...	1200

	E	Ⓑ D
Agawa Canyon d.	1400	...
Sault Ste. Marie a.	1800	...
Sault Ste. Marie d.	...	1030
Sudbury a.	...	1517

D – Operated by Ontario Northland.

E – Agawa Canyon Train. 2023 dates: ④–⑦ Aug. 3 - Sept. 2; daily Sept. 3 - Oct. 15. www.agawatrain.com

THE PAS - PUKATAWAGAN — 9045

Keewatin Railway

km		291 ①④ F	
0	**The Pas** d.	1115	...
88	Cranberry Portage d.	1355	...
158	**Pukatawagan** a.	1845	...

	290 ②⑤ F	
Pukatawagan d.	1000	...
Cranberry Portage d.	1515	...
The Pas a.	1730	...

F – Operated by Keewatin Railway Company. To book ✆ 204 623 5255.

9050 TORONTO - VANCOUVER — Via Rail

km			1 ®A	
0	**Toronto** Union	d.	0955	③⑦
143	Washago ⊗	d.	1225	:
241	Parry Sound ⊗	d.	1427	:
422	Sudbury Junction §	d.	1657	:
444	**Capreol**	a.	1722	:
444	**Capreol**	d.	1752	:
683	Foleyet ⊗	d.	2244	:
859	Oba ⊗	d.	0138	①④
921	Hornepayne	d.	0309	:
1084	Longlac ⊗	d.	0534	:
1537	Sioux Lookout	d.	1155	:
1652	Red Lake Road ⊗	d.	1341	:
1943	**Winnipeg**	a.	1930	:
1943	**Winnipeg**	d.	2130	:
2032	Portage la Prairie ⊗	d.	2304	:
2173	Rivers ⊗	d.	0131	②⑤
2394	Melville	d.	0504	:
2702	**Saskatoon**	a.	0950	:
2702	**Saskatoon**	d.	1050	:
2792	Biggar	d.	1239	:
3017	Wainwright ⊗	d.	1633	:
3221	**Edmonton**	a.	2050	:
3221	**Edmonton**	d.	0001	③⑥
3430	Edson ⊗	d.	0252	:
3518	Hinton ⊗	d.	0358	:
3600	**Jasper**	a.	0630	:
3600	**Jasper**	d.	0930	:
3721	Valemount ⊗	d.	1050	:
4052	**Kamloops** North	a.	1828	:
4052	**Kamloops** North	d.	1903	:
4360	Hope ⊗	d.	0201	④⑦
4466	**Vancouver** Pacific	a.	0800	:

		2 ®A	
Vancouver Pacific	a.	1500	①⑤
Agassiz ⊗	a.	1703	:
Kamloops North	a.	0017	②⑥
Kamloops North	d.	0052	:
Valemount ⊗	d.	0701	:
Jasper	a.	1100	:
Jasper	d.	1230	:
Hinton ⊗	d.	1345	:
Edson ⊗	d.	1519	:
Edmonton	a.	1850	:
Edmonton	d.	1950	:
Wainwright ⊗	d.	0014	③⑦
Biggar	d.	0331	:
Saskatoon	a.	0557	:
Saskatoon	d.	0657	:
Melville	d.	1257	:
Rivers	d.	1722	:
Portage la Prairie ⊗	d.	1915	:
Winnipeg	a.	2200	:
Winnipeg	d.	2330	:
Red Lake Road ⊗	d.	0351	①④
Sioux Lookout	d.	0651	:
Longlac ⊗	d.	1411	:
Hornepayne	d.	1839	:
Oba ⊗	d.	1930	:
Foleyet ⊗	d.	2227	:
Capreol	a.	0347	②⑤
Capreol	d.	0427	:
Sudbury Junction §	d.	0449	:
Parry Sound ⊗	d.	0842	:
Washago ⊗	d.	1059	:
Toronto Union	a.	1429	:

A – THE CANADIAN – 🛏 [2] ✕ Toronto - Edmonton - Vancouver and v.v.

⊗ – Request stop, advanced booking required.

§ – Sudbury Junction is *10 km* from Sudbury (Table **9035**).

9055 WINNIPEG - CHURCHILL — Via Rail

km			691/3 ®B	
0	**Winnipeg**	d.	1205	②⑦
88	Portage la Prairie ⊗	d.	1315	:
283	Dauphin ⊗	d.	1706	:
484	Canora	d.	1946	:
549	Endeavour ⊗	d.	2054	:
635	Hudson Bay ⊗	d.	2232	:
777	**The Pas**	a.	0145	①③
777	**The Pas**	d.	0230	①③⑤
843	Cormorant	d.	0412	:
996	Wabowden	d.	0748	:
1073	Thicket Potage	d.	0937	:
1149	**Thompson**	a.	1200	:
1149	**Thompson**	d.	1700	:
1401	Gillam (Nelson River)	d.	2330	:
1540	Herchmer	d.	0426	②④⑥
1697	**Churchill**	a.	0900	:

		690/2 ®B	
Churchill	d.	1930	②④⑥
Herchmer	d.	0003	③⑤⑦
Gillam (Nelson River)	d.	0530	:
Thompson	a.	1130	:
Thompson	d.	1400	:
Thicket Potage	d.	1622	:
Wabowden	d.	1811	:
Cormorant	d.	2147	:
The Pas	a.	2330	③⑤⑦
The Pas	d.	0315	①⑥
Hudson Bay ⊗	d.	0427	:
Endeavour ⊗	d.	0555	:
Canora	d.	0718	:
Dauphin ⊗	d.	1206	:
Portage la Prairie ⊗	d.	1537	:
Winnipeg	a.	1645	:

B – 🛏 [2] ✕ Churchill - Winnipeg and v.v.

⊗ – Request stop, advanced booking required.

9060 PRINCE RUPERT - JASPER — Via Rail

km			5 ®	
0	**Jasper**	d.	1245	③⑤⑦
174	McBride	d.	1444	:
409	**Prince George** ⊖	a.	1908	:
409	**Prince George** ⊖	d.	0800	①④⑥
560	Fort Fraser ⊗	d.	1032	:
795	Smithers	d.	1420	:
869	New Hazelton ⊗	d.	1537	:
1007	Terrace (Kitimat)	d.	1805	:
1160	**Prince Rupert**	a.	2025	:

		6 ®	
Prince Rupert	d.	0800	③⑤⑦
Terrace (Kitimat)	d.	1025	:
New Hazelton ⊗	d.	1230	:
Smithers	d.	1424	:
Fort Fraser ⊗	d.	1757	:
Prince George ⊖	a.	2029	:
Prince George ⊖	d.	0815	①④⑥
McBride	d.	1218	:
Jasper	a.	1700	:

⊖ – Passengers must arrange their own overnight accommodation in Prince George.

⊗ – Request stop, advanced booking required.

9065 ROCKY MOUNTAINEER

km			C	D
0	**Vancouver** Cottrell St.	d.	0730	0730
	Kamloops ◧	a.	1730	1730
	Kamloops ◧	d.	0625	0745
	Jasper	a.	|	1800
	Lake Louise	a.	1830	...
	Banff	a.	1930	...

		D	C
Banff	d.	...	0740
Lake Louise	d.	...	0900
Jasper	d.	0810	|
Kamloops ◧	a.	1700	1815
Kamloops ◧	d.	0735	0735
Vancouver Cottrell St.	a.	1730	1730

km			E	
0	**North Vancouver**	d.	0740	...
	Whistler ◧	a.	1130	...
	Whistler ◧	d.	0710	...
	Quesnel ◧	a.	1930	...
	Quesnel ◧	d.	0710	...
	Jasper	a.	2030	...

		E	
Jasper	d.	0655	...
Quesnel ◧	a.	1930	...
Quesnel ◧	d.	0710	...
Whistler ◧	a.	1930	...
Whistler ◧	d.	1510	...
North Vancouver	a.	1900	...

C – FIRST PASSAGE TO THE WEST - for 2023 dates contact operator.

D – JOURNEY THROUGH THE CLOUDS - for 2023 dates contact operator.

E – RAINFOREST TO GOLD RUSH - for 2023 dates contact operator.

◧ – Compulsory overnight stop - hotels included in travel packages. Arrival times are flexible.

Operator: Rocky Mountaineer Railtours (www.rockymountaineer.com)

9070 VANCOUVER - MISSION CITY

km			Ⓐ		Ⓐ		Ⓐ		Ⓐ	
0	**Vancouver** Waterfront	d.	1550	...	1650	...	1730	...	1820	...
26	Coquitlam Central	d.	1619	...	1719	...	1759	...	1849	...
68	**Mission City**	a.	1705	...	1805	...	1845	...	1935	...

		Ⓐ		Ⓐ		Ⓐ		Ⓐ	
Mission City	d.	0525	...	0625	...	0655	...	0725	...
Coquitlam Central	d.	0610	...	0710	...	0740	...	0810	...
Vancouver Waterfront	a.	0640	...	0740	...	0810	...	0840	...

Operator: West Coast Express (www.translink.ca).

9090 🚌 CALGARY - EDMONTON 🚌

km			RA ①-⑥	EB	RA †	RA		EB	RA	RA ⑤†
0	**Calgary**	d.	0800	0845	1000	1200	...	1545	1630	1830
	Red Deer Quality Inn	d.	0955	1115	1155	1410	...	1815	|	2015
303	**Edmonton**	a.	1140	1315	1340	1555	...	2020	1950	2200

		RA ①-⑥	EB	RA †	RA		EB	RA	RA ⑤†
Edmonton	d.	0800	0815	1000	1200	...	1515	1630	1830
Red Deer Quality Inn	d.	0955	1100	1155	1355	...	1800	|	2015
Calgary	a.	1155	1320	1355	1555	...	2040	1950	2200

Times for Calgary and Edmonton are the operator's Downtown ticket offices.

EB – Ebus (www.myebus.ca). *RA* – Red Arrow (www.redarrow.ca).

UNITED STATES OF AMERICA

Capital: **Washington DC** (GMT -5; add one hour in summer). 2023 public holidays: Jan. 1, 2, 16, Feb. 20, May 29, June 19, July 4, Sept. 4, Oct. 9, Nov. 10, 11, 23, Dec. 25.

The principal operator in the USA is Amtrak (✆ 1 800 872 7245. www.amtrak.com). Details of other operators can be found in relevant tables. Unless otherwise noted all trains carry two classes of seated accomodation known as 'Business' and 'Coach' shown as 1 and 2 in the tables. All Acela Express trains running between Boston, New York and Washington convey business class and an enhanced seated accommodation called 'First Class'. Most very long distance trains convey sleeping cars, and where this is the case it is detailed in the footnotes. Almost all sleeping car accommodation in North America has two berths per compartment, some of which are en-suite, although the exact product offering varies by operator and route. Most trains also convey some form of catering, but again the actual service offered varies considerably and often the full dining is available for sleeping car passengers. Timings shown are the latest available and are subject to alteration around public holidays and it is recommended that you confirm all timings locally as short notice changes are possible. Tickets are available from staffed stations, websites and through authorised ticketing agents. Amtrak requires reservations on practically all of its services, and also requires that you have identity documents available for inspection.

Amtrak offers the 'USA Rail Pass' It is available to both US citizens and foreign nationals: The pass is for 10 segments of travel over a 30 day period. The adult price is $499, a 50% reduction for children aged 2 - 12. The pass is valid in coach class on the entire Amtrak system. Be warned though: this program is now revenue/capacity managed and may not be available on all trains all the time. The pass is not valid on the Autotrain, Acela Express trains, Thruway buses numbered 7000 – 7999 and the Canadian portion of trains operated jointly by Amtrak and VIA Rail Canada. The pass alone is not valid for travel; tickets and, where neccessary, reservations must be obtained for each segment of travel. Upgrades to higher levels of accommodation may be possible subject to capacity and the payment of relevant supplements. Travel is limited to no more than four one-way journeys over any given route segment. A segment is any time you get on and then get off a train or bus, regardless of the length of that journey. A 7 day California Rail Pass is also available. The pass costs $159 for adults, $79.50 for children. The pass cannot be booked on line. For full details on both passes see the Amtrak website (www.amtrak.com).

9100 SKAGWAY - WHITEHORSE — White Pass and Yukon Railroad

km			1 ®F	🚌 ®F
0	**Skagway** Shops	d.	0745	1430
22	White Pass 🏛	d.	|	|
41	Fraser	a.	0900	1530
41	Fraser	d.	0900	1535
65	Bennett	a.	1015	|
65	Bennett	d.	1100	|
108	Carcross	a.	1230	1630
108	Carcross	d.	...	1635
177	**Whitehorse**	a.	...	1800

		🚌 ®F	2 ®F
Whitehorse	d.	0745	...
Carcross	a.	0900	...
Carcross	d.	0915	1300
Bennett	a.	|	1430
Bennett	d.	|	1500
Fraser	a.	1015	1600
Fraser	d.	1025	1600
White Pass 🏛	d.	|	|
Skagway Shops	a.	1130	1745

Additional round-trip excursions, including some hauled by steam locomotives, operate from Skagway to White Pass, Fraser and Bennett. For services crossing the US / Canadian border passengers must provide proof of citizenship. All times shown are Alaska time.

F – May 31 - Sept. 24. ②③④ (also certain ⑥⑦ - check with operator).

Operator: White Pass & Yukon Railroad (www.wpyr.com).

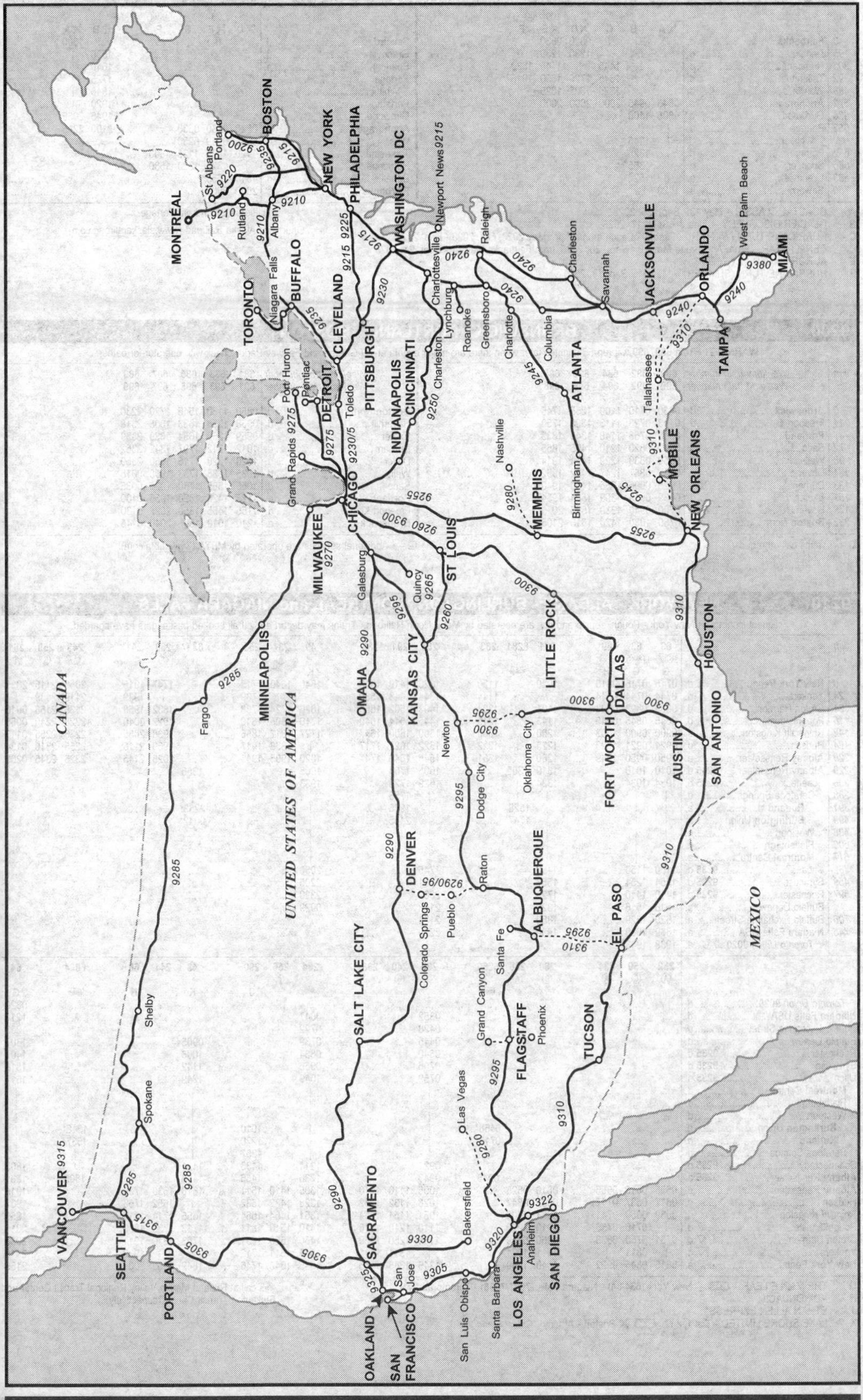
CANADA
UNITED STATES OF AMERICA
MEXICO
MONTREAL
St Albans
Portland
BOSTON
Rutland
Albany
NEW YORK
PHILADELPHIA
WASHINGTON DC
Newport News
BUFFALO
Niagara Falls
TORONTO
CLEVELAND
PITTSBURGH
DETROIT
Toledo
Pontiac
Port Huron
Grand Rapids
CHICAGO
MILWAUKEE
INDIANAPOLIS
CINCINNATI
Charleston
Charlottesville
Lynchburg
Roanoke
Raleigh
Greensboro
Charlotte
Columbia
Charleston
Savannah
JACKSONVILLE
ORLANDO
West Palm Beach
MIAMI
TAMPA
Tallahassee
ATLANTA
Birmingham
MOBILE
NEW ORLEANS
Nashville
MEMPHIS
ST LOUIS
Galesburg
Quincy
KANSAS CITY
OMAHA
LITTLE ROCK
DALLAS
FORT WORTH
HOUSTON
AUSTIN
SAN ANTONIO
Newton
Dodge City
Oklahoma City
MINNEAPOLIS
Fargo
DENVER
Colorado Springs
Pueblo
Raton
ALBUQUERQUE
Santa Fe
EL PASO
TUCSON
Phoenix
FLAGSTAFF
Grand Canyon
Las Vegas
SALT LAKE CITY
Shelby
Spokane
VANCOUVER
SEATTLE
PORTLAND
SACRAMENTO
OAKLAND
SAN FRANCISCO
San Jose
Bakersfield
San Luis Obispo
Santa Barbara
LOS ANGELES
Anaheim
SAN DIEGO
9200
9210
9215
9220
9225
9230
9230/5
9235
9240
9245
9250
9255
9260
9265
9270
9275
9280
9285
9290
9290/95
9295
9300
9305
9310
9315
9320
9322
9325
9330
9380

9105 ALASKA

2nd class Alaska Railroad

km		✕A	🍸B	C	✕D	⑦ ✕E	④–① F
0	**Fairbanks** d.	...	...	...	0820	0830	...
195	Denali d.	...	...	...	1230	1230	...
305	Hurricane d.	...	...	1445	|	1445	1630
392	Talkeetna d.	...	...	1645	1720	1650	1915
498	Wasilla d.	...	...	1825	1825	1825	...
572	**Anchorage** d.	0645	0945	2000	2000	2000	...
636	Girdwood d.	0805	1100	...	...	...	...
652	Portage a.	|	|	...	...	...	...
**	Whittier d.	|	1245	...	...	...	...
652	Portage d.	|	1325	...	...	...	...
666	Spencer d.	|	1355	...	...	...	...
683	Grandview a.	|	1520	...	...	...	...
750	**Seward** a.	1120	...	...	...	...	...

	✕D	⑥ ✕E	C	④–① F	🍸B	✕A
Seward d.	...	...	...	...	...	1800
Grandview d.	...	...	...	...	1530	|
Spencer d.	...	...	...	...	1640	|
Portage a.	...	...	...	...	1725	|
Whittier d.	...	...	...	...	1845	|
Portage d.	...	...	...	...	1920	|
Girdwood d.	...	...	...	...	1945	2055
Anchorage d.	0820	0830	0830	...	2100	2215
Wasilla d.	0935	0950	0950	...	...	...
Talkeetna d.	1120	1125	1125	1300	...	...
Hurricane a.	|	1320	1320	1530	...	...
Denali d.	1610	1555	...	...	...	...
Fairbanks a.	2000	2000	...	...	...	...

A – COASTAL CLASSIC – May 13 - Sept. 25, 2023.
B – GLACIER DISCOVERY – June 3 - Sept. 17, 2023.
C – HURRICANE TURN (WINTER) – First ④ of each month Apr., May 2023, Oct. 2023 - Feb. 2024.
D – DENALI STAR – From Anchorage May 10 - Sept. 20, 2023; from Fairbanks May 11 - Sept. 21, 2023.
E – AURORA – Until May 7, 2023.
F – HURRICANE TURN (SUMMER) – May 11 - Sept 18, 2023.

** – Whittier is *20 km* from Portage.

Operator : Alaska Railroad (www.alaskarailroad.com).

9200 BRUNSWICK - PORTLAND - BOSTON

Amtrak

WARNING! Train **689/699** will run 55 minutes later when there are major events at TD Garden and Fenway Park - check with operator for dates.

km	*Weekday train number* / *Weekend train number*	680 / 690	682 / 692	684 / 694	686 / 696	688 / 698
0	**Brunswick** d.	0430	0710	1100	1255	1745
14	Freeport ◧ d.	0443	0723	1113	1308	1758
47	**Portland** d.	0518	0758	1148	1343	1833
72	Saco d.	0540	0820	1210	1405	1855
98	Wells d.	0559	0839	1229	1424	1914
124	Dover d.	0617	0857	1247	1442	1932
133	Durham d.	0625	0905	1255	1450	1940
151	Exeter d.	0639	0919	1309	1504	1954
178	Haverhill ⊡ d.	0700	0940	1330	1525	2015
232	**Boston** North ⊡ a.	0750	1030	1420	1615	2105

Weekday train number / *Weekend train number*	681 / 691	683 / 693	685 / 695	687 / 697	689 / 699
Boston North ⊡ d.	0850	1150	1545	1720	2230
Haverhill ⊡ d.	0938	1238	1633	1808	2318
Exeter d.	0959	1259	1654	1829	2339
Durham d.	1012	1312	1707	1842	2352
Dover d.	1020	1320	1715	1850	2359
Wells d.	1038	1338	1733	1908	0018
Saco d.	1055	1355	1750	1925	0035
Portland a.	1125	1425	1820	1955	0100
Freeport ◧ d.	1155	1455	1850	2025	0130
Brunswick a.	1210	1510	1905	2040	0145

◧ – Trains call on request.

⊡ – Additional services are operated by MBTA (www.mbta.com).

9210 NEW YORK - ALBANY - BURLINGTON, MONTREÁL and NIAGARA FALLS

Amtrak

Frequent local trains New York - Poughkeepsie and v.v. are operated by Metro North Railroad. Trains may depart early if all booked passengers have boarded.

km		63 ⑥⑦ G	63 ①–⑤ G	69 H	281	6281 🚐	233	283	291 J	235 Ⓑ	49 K	237 Ⓐ	253 Ⓒ	6337 🚐	239 Ⓐ	241	243 Ⓐ	259 Ⓒ	261 †
0	**New York** Penn d.	0715	0715	0815	1020	...	1120	1320	1419	1515	1540	1640	1715	...	1747	1915	2055	2115	2335
24	Yonkers △ d.	0744	0744	0844	|	...	1144	1344	1443	1539	|	|	1739	...	|	1939	2119	2139	|
54	Croton Harmon △ d.	0803	0803	0903	1101	...	1203	1403	1502	1558	1626	1724	1758	...	1832	1958	2138	2158	0016
118	Poughkeepsie △ d.	0845	0845	0945	1143	...	1245	1445	1544	1640	1710	1805	1840	...	1922	2040	2220	2240	0058
142	Rhinecliff Kingston d.	0900	0900	1003	1200	...	1300	1500	1600	1657	1727	1817	1856	...	1938	2055	2236	2255	0113
184	Hudson d.	0921	0921	1023	1225	...	1322	1522	1621	1717	|	1838	1917	...	1959	2116	2256	2316	0134
229	**Albany** Rensselaer a.	0950	0950	1049	1250	...	1351	1545	1649	1747	1820	1905	1945	...	2028	2145	2325	2345	0205
229	**Albany** Rensselaer **9235** d.	1010	1010	...	1310	1300	...	1605	1704	...	1905	...	...	1955	...	...	...	...	...
258	Schenectady **9235** d.	1034	1034	...	1334	|	...	1629	1728	...	1933	...	...	|	...	...	...	...	...
288	Saratoga Springs d.	|	|	...	|	|	...	|	1756	...	|	...	...	|	...	...	...	...	...
391	**Rutland** a.	|	|	...	|	1528*	...	|	1946	...	|	...	...	2233*	...	...	...	...	...
499	**Burlington** Union a.	|	|	...	|	1747*	...	|	2155	...	|	...	...	0042*	...	...	...	...	...
436	Westport d.	|	|	...	|	...	...	|	...	...	|	...	...	...	...	...	...	...	...
500	Plattsburgh d.	|	|	...	|	...	...	|	...	...	|	...	...	...	...	...	...	...	...
617	**Montréal** Central a.	|	|	...	|	...	...	|	...	...	|	...	...	...	...	...	...	...	...
382	Utica **9235** d.	1150	1150	...	1450	...	...	1745	...	...	2050	...	...	...	...	...	...	...	...
459	Syracuse **9235** d.	1254	1254	...	1557	...	...	1851	...	...	2205	...	...	...	...	...	...	...	...
597	Rochester **9235** d.	1410	1410	...	1723	...	...	2007	...	...	2329	...	...	...	...	...	...	...	...
	Buffalo Depew a.	1516	1516	...	1829	...	...	2113	...	...	0029	...	...	...	...	...	...	...	...
706	Buffalo Exchange Street a.	1529	1529	...	1850	...	...	2134	...	...	...	...	...	...	...	...	...	...	...
745	**Niagara Falls** USA a.	1639	1639	...	1930	...	...	2220	...	...	...	...	...	...	...	...	...	...	...
	Toronto Union **9020** a.	1938	1943	...	...	...	...	...	...	...	...	...	...	...	...	...	...	...	...

	232 Ⓐ	250 Ⓒ	234 Ⓐ	260 Ⓒ	236 Ⓐ	6280 🚐	280	240 Ⓑ	238	284	256 †	290 J	48 K	244	68 H	6064 🚐	64 G
Toronto Union **9020** d.	...	...	...	...	...	...	...	...	...	...	...	...	...	...	...	...	0820
Niagara Falls USA d.	...	...	...	...	...	...	0352	...	...	0647	...	...	...	...	...	...	1217
Buffalo Exchange Street d.	...	...	...	...	...	...	0428	...	...	0722	...	...	...	...	...	...	1253
Buffalo Depew d.	...	...	...	...	...	...	0445	...	...	0739	...	...	0905	...	...	...	1307
Rochester **9235** d.	...	...	...	...	...	...	0540	...	...	0834	...	...	1006	...	...	...	1401
Syracuse **9235** d.	...	...	...	...	...	...	0706	...	...	0956	...	...	1142	...	...	...	1518
Utica **9235** d.	...	...	...	...	...	...	0759	...	...	1049	...	...	1242	...	...	...	1617
Montréal Central d.	...	...	...	...	...	...	|	...	...	|	...	...	|	...	...	...	|
Plattsburgh d.	...	...	...	...	...	...	|	...	...	|	...	...	|	...	...	...	|
Westport d.	...	...	...	...	...	...	|	...	...	|	...	...	|	...	...	...	|
Burlington Union d.	...	...	...	...	...	0458*	|	...	...	|	...	1010	|	...	...	1318*	|
Rutland d.	...	...	...	...	...	0717*	|	...	...	|	...	1220	|	...	...	1537*	|
Saratoga Springs d.	...	...	...	...	...	|	|	...	...	|	...	1357	|	...	...	|	|
Schenectady **9235** d.	...	...	...	...	...	|	0921	...	...	1214	...	1433	1421	...	...	|	1803
Albany Rensselaer **9235** a.	...	...	...	...	...	0945	0943	...	...	1236	...	1456	1453	...	...	1805	1831
Albany Rensselaer d.	0555	0615	0655	0810	0825	...	1005	1110	1210	1305	1410	1511	1610	1630	1730	...	1915
Hudson d.	0617	0637	0717	0832	0847	...	1028	1132	1232	1328	1432	1532	|	1652	1753	...	1937
Rhincliff Kingston d.	0639	0659	0741	0854	0909	...	1051	1154	1254	1351	1454	1554	1655	1714	1815	...	1959
Poughkeepsie ▽ d.	|	0710	0756	0910	0920	...	1110	1210	1310	1410	1510	1611	1713	1730	1830	...	2015
Croton Harmon ▽ d.	0731	0750	0838	0950	0959	...	1150	1250	1350	1450	1550	1651	1753	1810	1911	...	2056
Yonkers ▽ d.	|	0811	|	1011	1021	...	|	1311	1411	1511	1611	1712	|	|	1932	...	2116
New York Penn a.	0815	0845	0922	1040	1050	...	1245	1345	1445	1545	1645	1746	1842	1905	2007	...	2155

G – THE MAPLE LEAF – 12 🍸 New York (**634/64**) - Niagara Falls (**7097/7098**) - Toronto and v.v.
H – ADIRONDACK.
J – ETHAN ALLEN EXPRESS.
K – LAKE SHORE LIMITED – 🛏 1, 2 cl., 2 ✕ Boston - Albany - Chicago and v.v.

* – 🚐 call at Rutland Marble Valley Regional Transit Center and Burlington Transit Center respectively.

BOSTON - NEW YORK - WASHINGTON - VIRGINIA — 9215

Amtrak Most trains 🍷

km		151	2103	89	51	183	79	79	2203	153	185	2151	2205	155	2153	2249	141	143	2155	121	95	195	91	2251
			Ⓐ		③⑤⑦	Ⓐ	Ⓒ	Ⓐ	⑥	Ⓒ	Ⓐ	Ⓐ	†	Ⓒ	Ⓐ	⑥	Ⓐ	†	Ⓐ	†	Ⓐ	Ⓒ		⑥
			☆	A	B		C	C	☆			☆	☆		☆	☆			☆				D	☆
0	**Boston** South d.	...	...	...	...	...	...	...	...	...	...	0505	...	...	0600	0605	...	...	0715	...	0610	0635	...	0730
69	Providence d.	...	...	...	...	...	...	...	...	...	...	0540	...	...	0638	0641	...	...	0750	...	0650	0715	...	0805
169	New London d.	...	...	...	...	...	...	...	...	...	...	|	...	...	|	|	...	...	|	...	0745	0812	...	|
	Springfield MA (below) d.	...	...	...	...	...	...	...	...	...	...	|	...	...	|	|	0550	...	|	...	|	|	...	|
251	New Haven d.	...	...	...	...	...	...	...	...	...	...	0706	...	...	0809	0810	0737	...	0914	...	0843	0906	...	0934
301	Stamford d.	...	...	...	...	...	...	...	...	...	...	0752	...	...	0857	0855	0827	...	0959	...	0930	0955	...	1021
373	**New York** Penn a.	...	...	...	...	...	...	...	...	...	...	0847	...	...	0947	0952	0921	...	1047	...	1022	1051	...	1121
373	**New York** Penn d.	0420	0600	0602	0645	0705	0717	0725	0800	0805	0810	0900	0900	0905	1000	1003	0935	0947	1100	1029	1035	1105	1102	1200
389	Newark NJ d.	0437	0615	0619	0705	0722	0739	0744	0814	0822	0827	0915	0914	0922	|	1017	0952	1004	1115	1045	1053	1123	1122	1214
519	**Philadelphia** 30th St. d.	0543	0716	0740	0815	0831	0854	0854	0913	0933	0937	1010	1013	1030	1108	1117	1111	1118	1213	1156	1202	1234	1236	1313
670	Baltimore Penn d.	0656	0821	0848	0934	0943	1007	1004	1021	1049	1050	1115	1123	1147	1214	1225	1223	1235	1319	1307	1323	1347	1355	1421
687	BWI Marshall Airport d.	0711	|	0901	|	0957	|	|	1034	1102	1103	1128	1136	1203	|	1238	1236	1248	|	1323	1336	1400	|	1434
735	**Washington** Union a.	0740	0853	0929	1013	1030	1046	1045	1058	1133	1133	1151	1157	1235	1246	1303	1308	1321	1352	1354	1405	1429	1435	1458
735	**Washington** Union d.	0815	...	0959	1059	...	1108	1108	...	1200	1205	...	...	...	...	...	...	...	...	...	1435	1450	1504	...
822	Fredricksburg d.	|	...	|	|	...	1219	1219	...	1313	1318	...	...	...	...	...	...	...	...	...	1544	1601	|	...
911	Richmond Staples Mill Road d.	|	...	1211	|	...	1327	1327	...	1423	1431	...	...	...	...	...	...	...	...	...	1652	1658	1713	...
1042	**Newport News** a.	|	...	...	|	...	...	...	...	|	|	...	...	...	...	...	...	...	...	...	|	...	...	...
1092	**Norfolk** a.	|	...	...	|	...	...	...	...	1637	1647	...	...	...	...	...	...	...	...	...	1907	...	...	...
	Virgina Beach a.	|	...	...	|	...	...	...	...	*1735**	*1740**	...	...	...	...	...	...	...	...	...	*2000**	...	...	...
915	Charlottesville a.	1040	...	...	1343	...	...	...	...	...	...	...	...	...	...	...	...	...	...	...	...	...	...	...
1012	**Lynchburg** a.	1155	...	...	...	...	...	...	...	...	...	...	...	...	...	...	...	...	...	...	...	...	...	...
	Roanoke a.	1313	...	...	...	...	...	...	...	...	...	...	...	...	...	...	...	...	...	...	...	...	...	...

	2213	125	157	147	145	171	2159	99	2121	93	161		2163	2253	19	87	85	97	2165	173	189	163	129
	†	Ⓐ	†	⑥	†	Ⓐ	Ⓐ	Ⓒ	Ⓐ	Ⓐ	Ⓒ		Ⓐ	Ⓒ		Ⓒ	Ⓐ		Ⓐ	Ⓐ	†	⑥	Ⓐ
	☆						☆		☆				☆	☆	E			L	☆				
Boston South d.	...	...	...	...	...	0815	0910	0835	...	0920	0940	...	1105	1105	...	1000	1020	...	1210	1110	...	1140	...
Providence d.	...	...	...	...	...	0855	0946	0915	...	1001	1020	...	1143	1140	...	1041	1101	...	1246	1151	...	1220	...
New London d.	...	...	...	...	...	0948	|	1012	...	1102	1115	...	|	|	...	1135	|	...	|	1243	...	1320	...
Springfield MA (below) d.	...	...	0758	0835	...	|	|	|	...	|	|	...	|	|	...	|	|	...	|	|	...	|	...
New Haven d.	...	...	0934	0954	...	1040	1116	1059	...	1158	1206	...	1315	1310	...	1226	1242	...	|	1335	...	1406	...
Stamford d.	...	...	1025	1111	...	1129	1201	1149	...	1255	1255	...	1401	1356	...	1316	1331	...	1501	1429	...	1455	...
New York Penn a.	...	...	1124	1213	...	1222	1250	1254	...	1347	1351	...	1449	1453	...	1423	1429	...	1550	1522	...	1552	...
New York Penn d.	1200	1135	1205	1250	1255	1235	1300	1317	1400	1402	1405	...	1500	1502	1415	1504	1505	1515	1600	1535	1605	1605	1625
Newark NJ d.	1214	1152	1222	1307	1312	1252	1315	1335	1415	1419	1422	...	1515	1516	1437	1521	1522	1538	1615	1553	1622	1622	1641
Philadelphia 30th St. d.	1313	1303	1333	1418	1417	1413	1412	1448	1510	1527	1533	...	1610	1615	1555	1635	1632	1654	1713	1705	1733	1735	1755
Baltimore Penn d.	1421	1418	1448	1530	1530	1532	1520	1558	1619	1638	1650	...	1717	1726	1715	1748	1752	1808	1822	1826	1844	1851	1912
BWI Marshall Airport d.	1434	1432	1501	1543	1543	1547	1533	1611	|	1651	1703	...	1730	1739	|	1800	1805	|	|	1840	1857	1905	1925
Washington Union a.	1459	1504	1533	1612	1615	1617	1556	1636	1653	1723	1733	...	1754	1801	1803	1835	1836	1846	1853	1910	1935	1937	1952
Washington Union d.	...	1550	1600	1700	1700	1700	...	1710	...	1745	...	...	...	...	1830	1900	1910	1924	...	...	...	...	...
Fredricksburg d.	...	1707	1710	|	|	|	...	1818	...	1902	...	...	...	...	|	2012	2022	2035	...	...	...	...	...
Richmond Staples Mill Road d.	...	1823	1819	|	|	|	...	1923	...	2017	...	...	...	...	|	2122	2121	2139	...	...	...	...	...
Newport News a.	...	2015	|	|	|	|	...	2116	...	|	...	...	...	...	|	|	...	...	...	...	...	...	...
Norfolk a.	...	*2110**	2033	|	|	|	...	*2210**	...	2231	...	...	...	...	|	2336	...	...	...	...	...	...	...
Virgina Beach a.	...	*2150**	*2130**	|	|	|	...	*2240**	...	*2315**	...	...	...	...	|	*0020**	...	...	...	...	...	...	...
Charlottesville a.	...	...	...	1932	1932	1934	...	...	...	...	...	...	...	...	2047	...	...	...	...	...	...	...	...
Lynchburg a.	...	...	...	2043	2043	2047	...	...	...	...	...	...	...	...	2200	...	...	...	...	...	...	...	...
Roanoke a.	...	...	...	2159	2159	2206	...	...	...	...	...	...	...	...	...	...	...	...	...	...	...	...	...

	2167	2255	159	149	2169	193	2257	135	137	55	57		2173	2259	175	165	167	139	169	169	179	65	67
	Ⓐ	†	⑥	†	Ⓐ	Ⓐ	†	Ⓒ	Ⓐ	Ⓐ	Ⓒ		Ⓐ	†	Ⓐ	†	⑥	†	⑥	†	Ⓐ	⑤⑥	⑦–④
	☆	☆			☆		☆			F	F		☆	☆									
Boston South d.	1305	1310	...	1215	1400	...	1405	1340	1350	...	...	...	1615	1605	1520	1510	1625	1740	1840	1840	1845	2130	2130
Providence d.	1341	1344	...	1257	1437	...	1442	1419	1436	...	...	...	1650	1640	1601	1550	1708	1820	1920	1920	1925	2222	2222
New London d.	|	|	...	1354	|	...	|	1513	1538	...	...	...	|	|	1657	1648	1809	1915	2016	2016	2017	2331	2331
Springfield MA (below) d.	|	|	...	|	|	...	|	|	|	1454	1450	...	|	|	|	|	|	|	|	|	|	|	|
New Haven d.	1516	1510	...	1443	1606	...	1614	1604	1631	1639	1634	...	1820	1810	1745	1735	1906	2006	2106	2106	2110	0050	0050
Stamford d.	1601	1555	...	1531	1654	...	1702	1655	1719	1728	1725	...	1905	1855	1833	1825	1955	2055	2155	2155	2200	0138	0138
New York Penn a.	1650	1650	...	1646	1748	...	1800	1752	1810	1825	1825	...	2000	1959	1928	1931	2055	2152	2252	2252	2255	0234	0234
New York Penn d.	1700	1700	1705	1705	1800	1741	1810	1805	1825	1845	1901	...	2013	2000	1940	2001	...	2205	...	2305	...	0253	0320
Newark NJ d.	|	1714	1722	1722	1815	1758	1824	1822	1842	1903	1918	...	2028	2024	1958	2018	...	2222	...	2322	...	0313	0340
Philadelphia 30th St. d.	1808	1813	1833	1834	1910	1857	1920	1935	1955	2011	2026	...	2126	2121	2114	2138	...	2333	...	0030	...	0426	0456
Baltimore Penn d.	1916	1921	1949	1952	2016	2019	2026	2054	2106	2125	2141	...	2237	2227	2228	2249	...	0044	...	0145	...	0540	0608
BWI Marshall Airport d.	1929	1934	2002	2006	|	2032	2039	2107	2119	2139	2154	...	|	2240	2242	2303	...	0057	...	0158	...	0554	0624
Washington Union a.	1955	1959	2037	2042	2052	2101	2104	2137	2157	2207	2228	...	2309	2305	2315	2336	...	0130	...	0232	...	0630	0700
Washington Union d.	...	...	...	...	...	...	...	...	...	...	...	...	...	...	...	...	...	...	...	...	...	0700	0720
Fredricksburg d.	...	...	...	...	...	...	...	...	...	...	...	...	...	...	...	...	...	...	...	...	...	0805	0826
Richmond Staples Mill Road d.	...	...	...	...	...	...	...	...	...	...	...	...	...	...	...	...	...	...	...	...	...	0908	0934
Newport News a.	...	...	...	...	...	...	...	...	...	...	...	...	...	...	...	...	...	...	...	...	...	1115	1133
Norfolk a.	...	...	...	...	...	...	...	...	...	...	...	...	...	...	...	...	...	...	...	...	...	*1210**	*1225**
Virgina Beach a.	...	...	...	...	...	...	...	...	...	...	...	...	...	...	...	...	...	...	...	...	...	*1250**	*1305**
Charlottesville a.	...	...	...	...	...	...	...	...	...	...	...	...	...	...	...	...	...	...	...	...	...	...	...
Lynchburg a.	...	...	...	...	...	...	...	...	...	...	...	...	...	...	...	...	...	...	...	...	...	...	...
Roanoke a.	...	...	...	...	...	...	...	...	...	...	...	...	...	...	...	...	...	...	...	...	...	...	...

km	*2nd class unless noted*	451	141	495	405	157		147	471	461	473	463		409	55	57	475	465		467	417	497	479	499
		Ⓐ	Ⓐ	Ⓐ	Ⓒ	†		⑥	Ⓐ	Ⓒ	Ⓐ	⑥		†	Ⓐ	Ⓒ	Ⓐ	†		⑥	Ⓐ	†	Ⓐ	Ⓒ
		e		G		H		J	G	G					F	F								G
0	**Greenfield** 9220 d.	...	...	0545	...	...	...	...	0735	0915	...	...	...	...	1340	1336	...	...	...	...	...	...	...	2010
34	Northampton 9220 d.	...	...	0610	...	...	...	...	0800	0940	...	...	...	...	1405	1401	...	...	...	...	...	...	...	2035
71	**Springfield** MA 9220 a.	...	...	0653	...	...	...	...	0843	1023	...	...	...	...	1439	1435	...	...	...	...	...	...	...	2118
71	**Springfield** MA d.	0510	0550	0705	0725	0758	...	0835	0855	1034	1205	1230	...	1305	1454	1450	1555	1600	...	1730	1745	1915	1925	...
112	Hartford d.	0543	0631	0739	0759	0833	...	0910	0929	1108	1239	1305	...	1339	1531	1527	1629	1634	...	1805	1820	1952	1959	...
172	**New Haven** Union a.	0630	0722	0827	0847	0920	...	1002	1018	1156	1328	1352	...	1427	1619	1614	1718	1723	...	1852	1908	2039	2048	...
	New York Penn a.	...	0921	...	...	1124	...	1213	...	...	...	...	...	...	1825	1825	...	...	...	...	...	...	...	...
	Washington Union a.	...	1308	...	...	1533	...	1612	...	...	...	...	...	...	2207	2228	...	...	...	...	...	...	...	...

km	*2nd class unless noted*	601	605	607	611	661	641	663	643	43	645	615		609	665	647	649	667	651	653	669	655	671	657
		Ⓐ	Ⓐ	Ⓐ	⑥	Ⓒ	Ⓐ	Ⓒ	Ⓐ		Ⓐ	†		Ⓐ	Ⓒ	Ⓐ	Ⓐ	Ⓒ	Ⓐ	Ⓐ	Ⓒ	Ⓐ	Ⓒ	Ⓐ
										K														
0	**New York** Penn d.	...	...	...	...	0700	0717	0909	0930	1052	1205	...	...	1254	1305	1411	1444	1513	1603	1710	1717	1835	1953	2030
16	Newark NJ d.	...	...	...	...	0717	0734	0927	0946	1109	1222	...	...	1310	1323	1428	1459	1532	1620	1727	1734	1852	2009	2047
146	**Philadelphia** 30th St a.	...	...	...	...	0820	0846	1035	1050	1215	1325	...	...	1419	1426	1530	1612	1638	1723	1830	1836	2000	2115	2155
146	**Philadelphia** 30th St d.	0520	0620	0725	0725	0830	0856	1050	1100	1242	1335	1355	...	1445	1445	1545	1645	1655	1735	1842	1855	2015	2135	2205
178	Paoli d.	0546	0646	0752	0750	0855	0919	1115	1123	1312	1359	1420	...	1510	1510	1610	1711	1721	1802	1907	1921	2040	2200	2230
255	Lancaster d.	0632	0735	0834	0837	0942	1006	1203	1211	1352	1446	1506	...	1558	1558	1655	1802	1808	1851	1956	2008	2128	2250	2318
300	Elizabethtown d.	0649	0752	0850	0853	0958	1023	1220	1228	1406	1503	1523	...	1615	1614	1709	1818	1824	1907	2012	2024	2144	2306	2335
315	**Harrisburg** a.	0710	0815	0910	0915	1020	1046	1245	1250	1426	1525	1542	...	1640	1635	1730	1840	1845	1930	2035	2045	2205	2330	2356

A – PALMETTO – (12) 🍷 New York - Savannah and v.v.
B – CARDINAL – 🛏 1, 2 cl., (2) 🍷 Chicago - New York and v.v.
C – CAROLINIAN – (12) 🍷 New York - Charlotte and v.v.
D – SILVER STAR – 🛏 1, 2 cl., (2) ✕ New York - Miami and v.v.
E – CRESCENT – 🛏 1, 2 cl., (2) ✕ New York - New Orleans and v.v.
F – VERMONTER – (12) 🍷 Washington - St Albans and v.v. (Table **9220**).
G – VALLEY FLYER.
H – NORTHEAST REGIONAL – (12) 🍷 Springfield - Norfolk.
J – NORTHEAST REGIONAL – (12) 🍷 Springfield - Roanoke.
K – PENNSYLVANIAN – (12) 🍷 Pittsburgh - New York and v.v. (Table **9225**).
L – SILVER METEOR – 🛏 1, 2 cl., (2) ✕ New York - Miami and v.v.
d – Runs 3 – 12 minutes earlier Washington - New York on ⑥⑦.
e – Service may be operated by 🚌 with amended schedule - please check locally.
* – Connection by 🚌.
☆ – *Acela* service - higher fares payable.
◧ – Also Harrisburg - Philadelphia at 1840①–④, 2115①–④.

FOR RETURN SERVICE SEE NEXT PAGE →

9215 NEWPORT NEWS - WASHINGTON - NEW YORK - BOSTON

Most trains 🍸 Amtrak

	2190	190	150	180	2150	2152	160	2154	162	2248	172	54	98	56	2250	2106	152	152	86	182	2160	164	2252
	Ⓐ	Ⓐ	Ⓒ	Ⓐ	Ⓐ	Ⓐ	†	Ⓐ	Ⓒ	⑥	Ⓐ	Ⓒ		Ⓐ	†	Ⓐ	⑥	†	Ⓐ	Ⓐ	Ⓐ	Ⓒ	Ⓒ
	☆				☆	☆		☆		☆		F	L	F	☆	☆					☆		☆
Roanoke d.	...	...	...	...	...	...	...	...	...	...	...	...	...	...	...	...	...	...	...	...	...	...	...
Lynchburg d.	...	...	...	...	...	...	...	...	...	...	...	...	...	...	...	...	...	...	...	...	...	...	...
Charlottesville d.	...	...	...	...	...	...	...	...	...	...	...	...	...	...	...	...	...	...	...	...	...	...	...
Virginia Beach d.	...	...	...	...	...	...	...	...	...	...	...	...	...	...	...	...	...	...	...	...	...	...	...
Norfolk d.	...	...	...	...	...	...	...	...	...	...	...	...	...	...	...	...	...	...	...	...	...	...	...
Newport News d.	...	...	...	...	...	...	...	...	...	...	...	...	...	...	...	...	...	...	...	...	...	...	...
Richmond Staples Mill Road d.	...	...	...	...	...	...	...	...	...	...	...	...	0452	...	...	...	...	...	0605	...	...	0625	...
Fredericksburg d.	...	...	...	...	...	...	...	...	...	...	...	...	0546	...	...	...	...	...	0702	...	...	0722	...
Washington Union a.	...	...	...	...	...	...	...	...	...	...	...	...	0725	...	...	...	...	...	0822	...	...	0850	...
Washington Union d.	...	...	...	0430	...	0600	...	0700	0620	0800	0715	0730	0753	0805	0850	0900	0822	0822	0845	0920	1000	0915	1100
BWI Marshall Airport d.	...	...	...	0457	...	|	...	0721	0648	0821	0743	0757	|	0830	0911	0921	0850	0850	0914	0948	|	0943	1121
Baltimore Penn d.	...	...	...	0513	...	0630	...	0734	0703	0834	0759	0812	0834	0847	0924	0934	0906	0906	0935	1004	1031	0958	1134
Philadelphia 30th Street d.	...	...	...	0627	...	0732	...	0836	0820	0939	0910	0920	0953	0959	1031	1040	1025	1025	1048	1115	1133	1110	1239
Newark NJ d.	...	...	...	0727	...	0828	...	0929	0926	1040	1026	1027	1100	1103	1132	|	1139	1138	1153	1220	1231	1229	1336
New York Penn a.	...	...	...	0746	...	0849	...	0952	0945	1058	1044	1045	1118	1121	1148	1149	1159	1159	1212	1238	1248	1247	1353
New York Penn d.	0615	0650	0700	...	0802	0902	0900	1002	0957	1110	1100	1115	...	1130	1158	...	1230	...	1230	...	1302	1300	1403
Stamford d.	0701	0745	0749	...	0847	0947	0956	1048	1045	1155	1148	1205	...	1218	1242	...	1320	...	1318	...	1348	1348	1449
New Haven d.	0800	0841	0844	...	|	1040	1055	1142	1144	1255	1246	1330	...	1330	1336	...	1419	...	1410	...	1443	1446	1545
Springfield MA (below) a.	|	|	|	...	|	|	|	|	|	|	|	1455	...	1449	|	...	|	...	|	...	|	|	|
New London d.	|	0931	0933	...	|	|	1144	|	1231	|	1335	...	...	...	|	...	|	...	1452	...	|	1534	|
Providence d.	0922	1027	1029	...	1057	1205	1240	1300	1329	1418	1426	...	...	...	1456	...	1544	...	1545	...	1609	1632	1712
Boston South a.	1003	1110	1116	...	1139	1245	1329	1345	1422	1502	1518	...	...	...	1547	...	1637	...	1638	...	1656	1722	1758

	174	154	82	84	2164	88	2254	176	140	2168	194		96	184	2170	94	2170	2256	2218	156	20	148	2172
	Ⓐ	†	⑥	Ⓐ	Ⓐ	Ⓒ	Ⓒ	Ⓐ	Ⓒ	Ⓐ	⑥		†	Ⓐ	Ⓐ	Ⓐ	Ⓐ	†	⑥	Ⓒ		Ⓐ	Ⓐ
					☆		☆			☆					☆		☆		☆		Ed		☆
Roanoke d.	...	...	...	...	...	...	...	0620	...	...	...	...	...	...	...	...	...	...	...	0845	...	...	...
Lynchburg d.	...	...	...	...	...	...	...	0739	...	...	...	...	...	...	...	...	...	...	...	1002	0941	...	...
Charlottesville d.	...	...	...	...	...	...	...	0855	...	...	...	...	...	...	...	...	...	...	...	1118	1059	...	...
Virginia Beach d.	...	...	...	*0515**	...	*0515**	...	|	...	...	*0640**	...	*0640**	...	...	*0800**	...	...	...	|	|	...	...
Norfolk d.	...	...	0520	0615	...	0615	...	|	...	...	*0725**	...	*0725**	...	...	0900	...	...	...	|	|	...	...
Newport News d.	0539	...	|	|	...	|	...	|	...	...	0830	...	0830	...	...	|	...	...	...	|	|	...	...
Richmond Staples Mill Road d.	0727	...	0728	0825	...	0825	...	|	...	...	1019	...	1019	...	...	1108	...	...	...	|	|	...	...
Fredericksburg d.	0825	...	0826	0925	...	0925	...	|	...	...	1117	...	1117	...	...	1209	...	...	...	|	|	...	...
Washington Union a.	0945	...	0944	1046	...	1056	...	1125	...	...	1236	...	1235	...	...	1328	...	...	...	1351	1347	...	...
Washington Union d.	1010	1020	1020	1110	1200	1125	1300	1205	1225	1400	1305	...	1325	1315	1500	1355	1500	1500	1500	1435	1415	1505	1600
BWI Marshall Airport d.	1037	1047	1048	1138	|	1153	1321	1232	1252	|	1332	...	1352	1341	1521	1423	1521	1521	1521	1502	1441	1532	|
Baltimore Penn d.	1053	1104	1104	1154	1230	1208	1334	1247	1308	1430	1351	...	1411	1357	1534	1438	1534	1534	1534	1519	1458	1548	1630
Philadelphia 30th Street d.	1205	1218	1218	1309	1332	1319	1439	1358	1418	1532	1505	...	1523	1514	1636	1549	1636	1641	1643	1634	1621	1702	1732
Newark NJ d.	1315	1326	1328	1414	1427	1428	1536	1502	1528	1630	1615	...	1630	1626	1730	1655	1730	1736	1739	1737	1745	1812	1829
New York Penn a.	1335	1346	1346	1433	1447	1446	1553	1520	1551	1649	1636	...	1648	1646	1749	1712	1749	1752	1759	1801	1808	1830	1846
New York Penn d.	1400	1405	1404	...	1502	1500	1603	1530	1635	1700	1655	...	1702	1707	1802	1738	...	1805	...	...	...	1859	1902
Stamford d.	1448	1456	1459	...	1545	1548	1640	1618	1728	1750	1744	...	1749	1803	1847	1830	...	1856	...	...	...	1952	1950
New Haven d.	1544	1557	1601	...	1638	1647	1740	1715	1836	1840	1841	...	1845	1903	|	1927	...	1945	...	...	...	2105	2043
Springfield MA (below) a.	|	|	|	...	|	|	|	|	2003	|	|	...	|	|	|	|	...	|	...	...	...	2240	|
New London d.	1635	|	1651	...	|	1736	|	1806	...	|	1933	...	1935	|	|	2014	...	|	...	...	...	...	|
Providence d.	1730	1734	1742	...	1754	1830	1907	1902	...	2002	2031	...	2027	2043	2103	2108	...	2106	...	...	...	...	2204
Boston South a.	1830	1825	1835	...	1843	1923	1950	2002	...	2049	2118	...	2118	2136	2145	2202	...	2153	...	...	...	...	2247

	168	132	122	92	178	126	2122	2222	196	80	192		166	2224	138	158	2126	50	2128	90	124	186	66
	⑥	†	†		Ⓐ	†	Ⓐ	†	Ⓐ		⑥		†	†	Ⓐ	Ⓒ	Ⓐ	③⑤⑦	Ⓐ		Ⓒ	Ⓐ	
				D			☆	☆		C				☆			☆	B	☆	A			
Roanoke d.	...	...	...	...	...	...	...	...	...	...	...	...	...	...	...	...	...	...	...	...	...	...	1630
Lynchburg d.	...	...	...	...	...	...	...	...	...	...	...	...	...	...	...	...	...	...	...	...	...	...	1747
Charlottesville d.	...	...	...	...	...	...	...	...	...	...	...	...	...	...	...	...	...	1544	...	...	...	...	1901
Virginia Beach d.	...	...	...	...	...	...	...	...	...	...	...	...	...	...	...	...	...	|	...	...	*1355**	*1350**	|
Norfolk d.	...	...	...	...	...	...	...	...	...	...	...	...	...	...	1300	1305	...	|	...	...	*1435**	*1430**	|
Newport News d.	...	...	...	...	...	...	...	...	...	...	...	...	...	...	|	|	...	|	...	...	1545	1545	|
Richmond Staples Mill Road d.	...	...	...	1239	...	...	...	...	...	1411	...	...	...	...	1510	1515	...	|	...	1641	1734	1735	|
Fredericksburg d.	...	...	...	|	...	...	...	...	...	1507	...	...	...	...	1611	1616	...	|	...	|	1834	1835	|
Washington Union a.	...	...	...	1504	...	...	...	...	...	1631	...	...	...	...	1737	1741	...	1844	...	1910	1955	1959	2128
Washington Union d.	1525	1515	1545	1536	1552	1625	1700	1700	1705	1715	1720	...	1720	1800	1805	1810	1900	1909	2010	1957	2020	2030	2200
BWI Marshall Airport d.	1552	1542	|	|	1619	1652	|	1721	1732	|	1747	...	1747	1821	1833	1837	1923	|	|	2024	2048	2058	2235
Baltimore Penn d.	1608	1558	1621	1621	1636	1708	1730	1734	1748	1750	1804	...	1804	1835	1848	1854	1936	1941	2040	2042	2105	2115	2251
Philadelphia 30th Street d.	1718	1708	1731	1735	1755	1819	1832	1839	1903	1904	1919	...	1919	1939	2001	2005	2041	2056	2151	2155	2226	2234	0011
Newark NJ d.	1828	1828	1843	1845	1904	1926	1930	1935	2009	2012	2027	...	2027	2036	2118	2124	2135	2203	2248	2303	2330	2338	0134
New York Penn a.	1846	1846	1901	1910	1924	1946	1950	1955	2028	2035	2045	...	2045	2055	2139	2145	2153	2223	2306	2323	2350	2358	0157
New York Penn d.	1900	1925	...	...	1950	...	...	...	...	...	...	...	2100	...	...	...	...	...	...	...	...	...	0240
Stamford d.	1948	2017	...	...	2045	...	...	...	...	...	...	...	2148	...	...	...	...	...	...	...	...	...	0333
New Haven d.	2044	2116	...	...	2142	...	...	...	...	...	...	...	2247	...	...	...	...	...	...	...	...	...	0443
Springfield MA (below) a.	|	|	...	...	|	...	...	...	...	...	...	...	|	...	...	...	...	...	...	...	...	...	|
New London d.	2135	2209	...	...	2232	...	...	...	...	...	...	...	2337	...	...	...	...	...	...	...	...	...	0535
Providence d.	2235	2305	...	...	2329	...	...	...	...	...	...	...	0026	...	...	...	...	...	...	...	...	...	0656
Boston South a.	2326	2357	...	...	0015	...	...	...	...	...	...	...	0116	...	...	...	...	...	...	...	...	...	0758

2nd class unless noted	400	450	490		470	460	54		56	464	474		488	476	140		494	416	148		432	478	412
	Ⓒ	Ⓒ	Ⓐ		Ⓐ	Ⓒ	Ⓒ		Ⓐ	Ⓒ	Ⓐ		Ⓒ	Ⓐ	Ⓒ		Ⓐ	†	Ⓐ		†	Ⓐ	①–④
	G						F		F				G				G	e				G	e
Washington Union d.	...	...	...	...	...	...	0730	...	0805	...	...	...	...	...	1225	...	...	...	1505	...	...	...	...
New York Penn d.	...	...	...	...	...	...	1115	...	1130	...	...	...	...	...	1635	...	...	...	1859	...	...	...	...
New Haven Union d.	...	0855	0900	...	1026	1100	1330	...	1330	1500	1600	...	1700	1725	1836	...	1935	1950	2105	...	2135	2155	2259
Hartford d.	...	0940	0945	...	1110	1146	1411	...	1411	1547	1646	...	1746	1809	1922	...	2020	2035	2154	...	2219	2240	2348
Springfield MA a.	...	1018	1024	...	1149	1223	1455	...	1449	1624	1725	...	1824	1848	2003	...	2059	2113	2240	...	2257	2318	0030
Springfield MA 9220 d.	0750	...	...	...	...	...	1515	...	1515	...	...	...	1845	...	...	...	2115	...	...	...	...	2330	...
Northampton 9220 d.	0832	...	...	...	...	...	1557	...	1557	...	...	...	1927	...	...	...	2157	...	...	...	...	0012	...
Greenfield 9220 a.	0858	...	...	...	...	...	1622	...	1622	...	...	...	1953	...	...	...	2223	...	...	...	...	0038	...

2nd class unless noted	640	642	600	660	644	662	646	664	648	666	650	42	670	652	654	672	656	658	674	610	620	612	624
	Ⓐ	Ⓐ	Ⓐ	Ⓒ	Ⓐ	⑥	Ⓐ	Ⓒ	Ⓐ	Ⓐ	Ⓐ		Ⓒ	Ⓐ	Ⓐ	Ⓒ	Ⓐ	⑤	⑥	†	Ⓐ	†	⑤
												K											
Harrisburg ◧ d.	0500	0555	0640	0720	0755	0830	0859	0930	1005	1120	1205	1300	1405	1515	1630	1705	1735	1840	1905	1905	2000	2020	2115
Elizabethtown ◧ d.	0517	0612	0657	0737	0811	0847	0916	0947	1021	1137	1222	1318	1422	1532	1647	1722	1752	1857	1922	1922	2017	2037	2132
Lancaster ◧ d.	0535	0630	0716	0755	0827	0905	0933	1005	1037	1155	1241	1340	1440	1552	1705	1740	1810	1912	1940	1940	2032	2055	2148
Paoli ◧ d.	0619	0723	0804	0841	0905	0951	1018	1049	1116	1241	1322	1424	1528	1636	1750	1825	1855	1955	2025	2025	2114	2140	2230
Philadelphia 30th St ◧ a.	0645	0750	0833	0905	0930	1015	1040	1115	1141	1305	1352	1459	1555	1705	1826	1850	1923	2020	2050	2050	2140	2210	2256
Philadelphia 30th St d.	0700	0805	0846	0923	0945	1030	1055	1125	1155	1330	1415	1525	1610	1718	1850	1910	1940	2042	2110	...	...	...	2311
Newark NJ d.	0811	0906	0947	1031	1047	1144	1157	1231	1256	1440	1518	1632	1713	1832	1954	2014	2044	2144	2214	...	...	...	0017
New York Penn a.	0830	0926	1011	1049	1105	1202	1215	1249	1315	1457	1538	1650	1732	1854	2012	2034	2103	2203	2234	...	...	...	0035

FOR RETURN SERVICE AND FOOTNOTES SEE PREVIOUS PAGE.

Amtrak ST ALBANS - SPRINGFIELD 9220

km		55 ⒶA	57 ⒸA		54 ⒸA	56 ⒶA
0	**St. Albans** d.	0915	0915	*Washington U 9215* d.	0730	0805
38	Burlington Essex Jct. d.	0944	0944	*New York Penn 9215* d.	1115	1130
70	Waterbury d.	1010	1010	**Springfield** MA 9215 d.	1515	1515
90	Montpelier d.	1025	1025	Northampton 9215 d.	1557	1557
133	Randolph d.	1059	1059	Greenfield 9215 d.	1622	1622
189	White River Junction d.	1137	1137	Brattleboro d.	1656	1656
205	Windsor VT d.	1156	1156	Bellows Falls d.	1726	1726
225	Claremont d.	1206	1206	Claremont d.	1747	1747
252	Bellows Falls d.	1234	1230	Windsor VT d.	1756	1756
291	Brattleboro d.	1306	1302	White River Junction d.	1818	1818
326	Greenfield 9215 d.	1340	1336	Randolph d.	1856	1856
360	Northampton 9215 d.	1405	1401	Montpelier d.	1934	1934
397	**Springfield** MA 9215 a.	1439	1435	Waterbury d.	1950	1950
609	*New York Penn 9215* a.	1831	1825	Burlington Essex Jct. d.	2018	2018
974	*Washington U 9215* a.	2207	2228	**St. Albans** a.	2050	2050

A – VERMONTER – [12] ⍡ Washington - St Albans and v.v.

Amtrak HARRISBURG - PITTSBURGH 9225

km		43 B			42 B	
	New York Penn 9215 d.	1052	...	**Pittsburgh** d.	0730	...
	Philadelphia 30th St d.	1242	...	Greensburg d.	0810	...
0	**Harrisburg** d.	1436	...	Latrobe d.	0820r	...
95	Lewistown d.	1546	...	Johnstown d.	0903	...
154	Huntingdon d.	1623	...	Altoona d.	1001	...
186	Tyrone d.	1649r	...	Tyrone d.	1018r	...
213	Altoona d.	1713	...	Huntingdon d.	1045	...
275	Johnstown d.	1810	...	Lewistown d.	1124	...
334	Latrobe d.	1851r	...	**Harrisburg** a.	1250	...
346	Greensburg d.	1902	...	*Philadelphia 30th St* a.	1459	...
401	**Pittsburgh** a.	1959	...	*New York Penn 9215* a.	1650	...

B – PENNSYLVANIAN – [12] ⍡ New York - Pittsburgh and v.v.
r – Calls on request.

Amtrak WASHINGTON - CLEVELAND - CHICAGO 9230

km		29 C	49 D		30 C	48 D
0	**Washington** Union d.	1605	...	**Chicago** Union 9235 d.	1840	2130
88	Harper's Ferry d.	1716	...	South Bend 9235 d.	2109	2359
118	Martinsburg d.	1745	...	Elkhart 9235 d.	2129	0027
234	Cumberland d.	1924	...	Waterloo 9235 d.	2223	0120
478	Pittsburgh d.	2359	...	Toledo 9235 d.	2349	0315
613	Alliance d.	0139	...	Sandusky 9235 d.	0040	0407
702	**Cleveland** 9235 d.	0259	0403	**Cleveland** 9235 d.	0154	0538
798	Sandusky 9235 d.	0402	0513	Alliance d.	0305	...
873	Toledo 9235 d.	0522	0633	Pittsburgh d.	0520	...
998	Waterloo 9235 d.	0636	0751	Cumberland d.	0932	...
1086	Elkhart 9235 d.	0729	0843	Martinsburg d.	1101	...
1113	South Bend 9235 d.	0751	0907	Harper's Ferry d.	1131	...
1248	**Chicago** Union 9235 a.	0845	1012	**Washington** Union a.	1305	...

C – CAPITOL LIMITED – [sleeper] 1,2 cl., [2] ✕ Washington - Chicago and v.v.
D – LAKE SHORE LIMITED – [sleeper] 1,2 cl., [2] ⍡ Boston(449/448) - Albany(48/49) - Chicago and v.v; [sleeper] 1,2 cl., [2] ✕ New York(49/48) - Albany - Chicago and v.v.

Amtrak BOSTON - ALBANY - CHICAGO 9235

km		449 D	49 D		448 D	48 D
0	**Boston** South d.	1250	...	**Chicago** Union 9230 d.	2130	2130
70	Worcester d.	1406	...	South Bend 9230 d.	2359	2359
157	Springfield MA d.	1526	...	Elkhart 9230 d.	0027	0027
242	Pittsfield d.	1642	...	Waterloo 9230 d.	0120	0120
	New York Penn 9205 d.	|	1540	Toledo 9230 d.	0315	0315
320	**Albany** Rensselaer a.	1810	1820	Sandusky 9230 d.	0407	0407
320	**Albany** Rensselaer ◧ d.	1905	1905	**Cleveland** 9230 d.	0550	0550
349	Schenectady ◧ d.	1933	1933	Erie d.	0724	0724
473	Utica ◧ d.	2050	2050	Buffalo Depew ◧ d.	0905	0905
558	Syracuse ◧ d.	2205	2205	Rochester ◧ d.	1006	1006
686	Rochester ◧ d.	2329	2329	Syracuse ◧ d.	1142	1142
784	Buffalo Depew ◧ d.	0039	0039	Utica ◧ d.	1242	1242
931	Erie d.	0216	0216	Schenectady ◧ d.	1421	1421
1083	**Cleveland** 9230 d.	0403	0403	**Albany** Rensselaer ◧ a.	1453	1453
1179	Sandusky 9230 d.	0513	0513	**Albany** Rensselaer d.	1527	1610
1254	Toledo 9230 d.	0633	0633	*New York Penn 9205* a.	|	1842
1379	Waterloo 9230 d.	0751	0751	Pittsfield d.	1630	...
1467	Elkhart 9230 d.	0843	0843	Springfield MA d.	1804	...
1494	South Bend 9230 d.	0907	0907	Worcester d.	1932	...
1629	**Chicago** Union 9230 a.	1012	1012	**Boston** South a.	2032	...

D – LAKE SHORE LIMITED – [sleeper] 1,2 cl., [2] ⍡ Boston(**449/448**) - Albany(**48/49**) - Chicago and v.v.; [sleeper] 1,2 cl., [2] ✕ New York(**49/48**) - Albany - Chicago and v.v.
◧ – See also Table **9210**.

Amtrak WASHINGTON - JACKSONVILLE, ORLANDO, TAMPA and MIAMI 9240

km		89 E	79 ⒸJ	79 ⒶJ	91 F	97 G
	New York Penn 9215 d.	0602	0717	0725	1102	1515
0	**Washington** Union 9245 d.	0959	1108	1108	1504	1924
174	Richmond SMR ⊖ 9245 d.	1219	1336	1336	1723	2149
219	Petersburg 9245 d.	1254	1413	1413	1759	2223
376	Rocky Mount 9245 d.	1432	1546	1546	1929	2355
490	**Raleigh** 9245 d.	|	1722	1722	2110	|
520	Fayetteville d.	1616	...	...	|	0127
653	Florence d.	1757	...	...	|	0318
805	Charleston SC d.	1937	...	...	|	0456
814	Columbia d.	|	...	...	0149	|
966	Savannah d.	2125	...	...	0437	0649
1203	**Jacksonville** a.	...	...	...	0706	0924
1203	**Jacksonville** d.	...	...	...	0726	0949
1430	Winter Park d.	...	...	...	1010	1241
1438	**Orlando** a.	...	...	...	1033	1304
1438	**Orlando** d.	...	...	...	1047	1319
1467	Kissimmee d.	...	...	...	1111	1341
1597	**Tampa** a.	...	...	...	1255	|
1597	**Tampa** d.	...	...	...	1309	|
	Winter Haven d.	...	...	...	1407	1433
1593	Sebring d.	...	...	...	1448	1514
1758	West Palm Beach ⊙ a.	...	...	...	1657	1710
1827	Fort Lauderdale ⊙ a.	...	...	...	1757	1806
	Hollywood FL ⊡ a.	...	...	...	1812	1821
1862	**Miami** Amtrak a.	...	...	...	1835	1859

	98 G	92 F	80 J	90 E
Miami Amtrak d.	0810	1140	...	...
Hollywood FL ⊡ d.	0834	1204	...	...
Fort Lauderdale ⊙ d.	0850	1218	...	...
West Palm Beach ⊙ d.	0947	1310	...	...
Sebring d.	1123	1445	...	...
Winter Haven d.	1208	1531	...	...
Tampa a.	|	1706	...	...
Tampa d.	|	1720	...	...
Kissimmee d.	1257	1841	...	...
Orlando a.	1322	1909	...	...
Orlando d.	1336	1925	...	...
Winter Park d.	1353	1942	...	...
Jacksonville a.	1651	2044	...	...
Jacksonville d.	1711	2304	...	...
Savannah d.	1945	0130	...	0735
Columbia d.	|	0409	...	|
Charleston SC d.	2134	|	...	0915
Florence d.	2332	|	...	1054
Fayetteville d.	0057	|	...	1222
Raleigh 9245 d.	|	0904	1013	|
Rocky Mount 9245 d.	0229	1023	1140	1413
Petersburg 9245 d.	0353	1151	1311	1544
Richmond SMR ⊖ 9245 d.	0452	1239	1411	1641
Washington Union 9245 a.	0725	1504	1631	1910
New York Penn 9215 a.	1118	1910	2035	2323

E – PALMETTO – [12] ⍡ New York - Savannah and v.v.
F – SILVER STAR – [sleeper] 1,2 cl., [2] ✕ New York - Miami and v.v.
G – SILVER METEOR – [sleeper] 1,2 cl., [2] ✕ New York - Miami and v.v.
J – CAROLINIAN – [12] ⍡ New York - Charlotte and v.v.

⊖ – Richmond **Staples** Mill Road.
⊙ – Amtrak / Tri-Rail station (for distance to / from Brightline station see Table **9380**).
⊡ – Frequent Tri-Rail services available to / from Miami International Airport.

Amtrak CHARLOTTE - NEW ORLEANS 9245

km		73 H	75 H	77 H	79 ⒸJ	79 ⒶJ	91 F	19 K
	New York Penn 9215 d.	...	...	...	0717	0725	1102	1415
0	**Washington** Union 9240 d.	...	...	...	1108	1108	1504	1830
174	Richmond SMR ⊖ 9240 d.	...	...	...	1336	1336	1723	|
219	Petersburg 9240 d.	...	...	...	1413	1413	1759	|
376	Rocky Mount 9240 d.	...	...	...	1546	1546	1929	|
490	**Raleigh** 9240 d.	0630	1000	1500	1730	1730	2110	|
619	Greensboro d.	0803	1133	1633	1916	1916	...	0032
645	High Point d.	0819	1149	1649	1932	1932	...	0049
699	Salisbury d.	0853	1223	1723	2006	2006	...	0127
766	**Charlotte** a.	0940	1310	1810	2056	2056	...	0230
766	**Charlotte** d.	...	...	...	...	...	...	0255
890	Spartanburg d.	...	...	...	...	...	...	0424
940	Greenville d.	...	...	...	...	...	...	0531
1102	Gainesville d.	...	...	...	...	...	...	0728
1179	**Atlanta** a.	...	...	...	...	...	...	0843
1179	**Atlanta** d.	...	...	...	...	...	...	0908
1344	Anniston d.	...	...	...	...	...	...	1030
1447	Birmingham d.	...	...	...	...	...	...	1303
1536	Tuscaloosa d.	...	...	...	...	...	...	1402
1692	Meridian d.	...	...	...	...	...	...	1619
1829	Hattiesburg d.	...	...	...	...	...	...	1753
2018	**New Orleans** a.	...	...	...	...	...	...	2102

	20 K	92 F	80 J	74 H	76 H	78 H
New Orleans d.	0915	...	...	...	...	...
Hattiesburg d.	1145	...	...	...	...	...
Meridian d.	1337	...	...	...	...	...
Tuscaloosa d.	1514	...	...	...	...	...
Birmingham d.	1724	...	...	...	...	...
Anniston d.	1859	...	...	...	...	...
Atlanta a.	2300	...	...	...	...	...
Atlanta d.	2329	...	...	...	...	...
Gainesville d.	0024	...	...	...	...	...
Greenville d.	0223	...	...	...	...	...
Spartanburg d.	0304	...	...	...	...	...
Charlotte a.	0506	...	...	...	...	...
Charlotte d.	0531	...	0645	1030	1515	1900
Salisbury d.	0617	...	0728	1111	1556	1941
High Point d.	0701	...	0802	1144	1629	2014
Greensboro d.	0729	...	0824	1203	1648	2033
Raleigh 9240 d.	|	0904	1013	1341	1826	2211
Rocky Mount 9240 d.	|	1023	1140	...	...	...
Petersburg 9240 d.	|	1151	1311	...	...	...
Richmond SMR ⊖ 9240 d.	|	1239	1411	...	...	...
Washington Union 9240 a.	1347	1504	1631	...	...	...
New York Penn 9215 a.	1808d	1910	2035	...	...	...

F – SILVER STAR – [sleeper] 1,2 cl., [2] ✕ New York - Miami and v.v.
H – PIEDMONT – [2] ⍡ Raleigh - Charlotte and v.v.
J – CAROLINIAN – [12] ⍡ New York - Charlotte and v.v.

K – CRESCENT – [sleeper] 1,2 cl., [2] ✕ New York - New Orleans and v.v.
d – Arrives 1756 on ⑥⑦ (⑤⑥ departure from New Orleans).
⊖ – Richmond **Staples** Mill Road.

9250 WASHINGTON - CHICAGO — Amtrak

km		51 ③⑤⑦ A	
	New York Penn **9215** d.	0645	...
0	**Washington** Union d.	1059	...
109	Culpeper d.	1225	...
181	Charlottesville d.	1352	...
338	Clifton Forge d.	1613	...
393	White Sulpher Springs d.	1705	...
528	Charleston WV d.	2029	...
606	Huntington d.	2151	...
678	South Shore ◧ d.	2257	...
872	Cincinnati d.	0141	...
1069	**Indianapolis** a.	0515	...
1069	**Indianapolis** d.	0600	...
1144	Crawfordsville d.	0658	...
1187	Lafayette d.	0736	...
1383	**Chicago** Union a.	1000	...

	50 ②④⑥ A	
Chicago Union d.	1755	...
Lafayette d.	2156	...
Crawfordsville d.	2230	...
Indianapolis a.	2349	...
Indianapolis d.	0015	...
Cincinnati d.	0337	...
South Shore ◧ d.	0555	...
Huntington d.	0726	...
Charleston WV d.	0831	...
White Sulpher Spings d.	1201	...
Clifton Forge d.	1309	...
Charlottesville d.	1544	...
Culpepper d.	1700	...
Washington Union a.	1844	...
New York Penn **9215** a.	2223	...

A – CARDINAL – 🛏 1, 2 cl., (2) 🍷 Chicago - New York and v.v.
◧ – For Portsmouth KY.

9255 CHICAGO - NEW ORLEANS — Amtrak

km		391 B	393 C	59 D
0	**Chicago** Union d.	0815	1605	2005
92	Kankakee d.	0927	1715	2123
208	Champaign Urbana d.	1049	1836	2234
323	Effingham d.	1157	1947	2337
408	Centralia d.	1244	2034	0025
498	Carbondale d.	1345	2135	0126
725	Newbern d.	...	...	0356
850	**Memphis** a.	...	...	0627
850	**Memphis** d.	...	...	0640
1051	Greenwood d.	...	...	0900
1136	Yazoo City d.	...	...	0951
1207	Jackson d.	...	...	1120
1334	McComb d.	...	...	1240
1419	Hammond d.	...	...	1328
1503	**New Orleans** a.	...	...	1547

	58 D	390 B	392 C
New Orleans d.	1345	...	...
Hammond d.	1445	...	...
McComb d.	1532	...	...
Jackson d.	1744	...	...
Yazoo City d.	1842	...	...
Greenwood d.	1937	...	...
Memphis a.	2220	...	...
Memphis d.	2240	...	...
Newbern d.	0022	...	...
Carbondale d.	0316	0730	1615
Centralia d.	0410	0823	1708
Effingham d.	0457	0909	1754
Champaign Urbana d.	0610	1024	1908
Kankakee d.	0713	1131	2014
Chicago Union a.	0915	1300	2145

B – SALUKI – (12) 🍷 Chicago - Carbondale and v.v.
C – ILLINI – (12) 🍷 Chicago - Carbondale and v.v.
D – CITY OF NEW ORLEANS – 🛏 1, 2 cl., (2) ✕ Chicago - New Orleans and v.v.

9260 CHICAGO - ST. LOUIS - KANSAS CITY — Amtrak

km		311 E	301 F	319 EF	21 G	3 H	305 F	307 F		
0	**Chicago** Union **9295** d.	...	0715	0930	1345	1450	1720	1910	...	...
60	Joliet Union d.	...	0812	1020	1440u	|	1810	2000	...	...
148	Pontiac IL d.	...	|	1107	1526	|	1900	2048	...	...
204	Bloomington d.	...	0926	1143	1601	|	1932	2123	...	...
252	Lincoln d.	...	|	1212	1630	|	2004	2153	...	...
298	Springfield IL d.	...	1023	1244	1706	|	2036	2223	...	...
360	Carlinville d.	...	|	1325	1738	|	2118	|	...	...
414	Alton d.	...	1129	1354	1809	|	2147	2333	...	...
	St. Louis Gateway a.	...	1221	1450	1913	|	2236	0023	...	...
457	**St. Louis** Gateway d.	0815	...	1505	...	|	...	...	...	...
480	Kirkwood d.	0844	...	1534	...	|	...	...	...	...
536	Washington MO d.	0921	...	1611	...	|	...	...	...	...
658	Jefferson City d.	1040	...	1732	...	|	...	...	...	...
760	Sedalia d.	1150	...	1842	...	|	...	...	...	...
866	Lee's Summit d.	1308	...	1959	...	|	...	...	...	...
891	Independence d.	1325	...	2015	...	|	...	...	...	...
912	**Kansas City** **9295** a.	1355	...	2045	...	2200	...	...	...	...

	300 F	302 F	22 G	4 H	318 EF	306 F	316 E		
Kansas City **9295** d.	...	...	...	0728	0840	...	1600	...	...
Independence d.	...	...	...	|	0859	...	1619	...	...
Lee's Summit d.	...	...	...	|	0916	...	1636	...	...
Sedalia d.	...	...	...	|	1027	...	1749	...	...
Jefferson City d.	...	...	...	|	1149	...	1907	...	...
Washington MO d.	...	...	...	|	1303	...	2019	...	...
Kirkwood d.	...	...	...	|	1347	...	2108	...	...
St. Louis Gateway d.	...	...	...	|	1420	...	2140	...	...
St. Louis Gateway d.	0430	0640	0755	|	1500	1740	...	...	...
Alton d.	0514	0725	0843	|	1543	1824	...	...	...
Carlinville d.	|	0752	0909	|	1611	1848	...	...	...
Springfield IL d.	0615	0832	0951	|	1651	1930	...	...	...
Lincoln d.	0642	0856	1020	|	1718	1954	...	...	...
Bloomington d.	0713	0930	1102	|	1750	2027	...	...	...
Pontiac IL d.	0740	0959	1134	|	1816	2058	...	...	...
Joliet Union d.	0838	1104	1248s	|	1911	2157	...	...	...
Chicago Union **9295** a.	0939	1205	1344	1450	2025	2305	...	...	...

E – RIVER RUNNER – (12) 🍷 St Louis - Kansas City and v.v.
F – LINCOLN SERVICE – (12) 🍷 Chicago - St. Louis and v.v.
G – TEXAS EAGLE - see Table **9300**.
H – SOUTHWEST CHIEF - see Table **9295**.
s – Calls to set down only.
u – Calls to pick up only.

9265 CHICAGO - QUINCY — Amtrak

km		381 J	5 K	3 H	383 M					
0	**Chicago** Union .. **9290 9295** d.	0740	1400	1450	1755	...	...	...	...	...
166	Princeton **9290 9295** d.	0926	1544	1634	1941	...	...	...	...	...
259	Galesburg **9290 9295** d.	1023	1638	1723	2038	...	...	...	...	...
413	**Quincy** IL a.	1202	...	...	2217	...	...	...	...	...

	380 M	4 H	6 K	382 J					
Quincy IL d.	0612	...	...	1730	...	...	...	...	...
Galesburg **9290 9295** d.	0737	1148	1141s	1855	...	...	...	...	...
Princeton **9290 9295** d.	0830	1238	1233s	1948	...	...	...	...	...
Chicago Union **9290 9295** a.	1033	1450	1450	2151	...	...	...	...	...

H – SOUTHWEST CHIEF – see Table **9295**.
J – CARL SANDBURG – (12) 🍷 Chicago - Quincy and v.v.
K – CALIFONIA ZEPHYR – see Table **9290**.
M – ILLINOIS ZEPHYR – (12) 🍷 Chicago - Quincy and v.v.
s – Calls to set down only.

9270 CHICAGO - MILWAUKEE — 2nd class, Amtrak

km		329 ①–⑤	331	333	335	337	339	341	8307 🚌	343 ⑤
0	**Chicago** Union d.	0610	0825	1105	1305	1515	1708	2005	2115	2325
100	Sturtevant d.	0710	0925	1205	1405	1615	1814	2105	|	0025
125	**Milwaukee** Airport a.	0724	0939	1219	1419	1629	1828	2119	|	0039
138	**Milwaukee** a.	0739	0954	1234	1434	1644	1845	2134	2350	0054

	330 ①–⑥	332		334	336	338		340	342
Milwaukee d.	0615	0805	...	1100	1305	1500	...	1745	1935
Milwaukee Airport d.	0626	0815	...	1110	1315	1510	...	1755	1945
Sturtevant d.	0643	0828	...	1123	1328	1523	...	1808	1958
Chicago Union a.	0757	0934	...	1229	1434	1629	...	1914	2104

9275 CHICAGO - PORT HURON, DETROIT, PONTIAC and GRAND RAPIDS — Amtrak

km		350 N	352 N	364 P	354 N					
0	**Chicago** Union CT d.	0645	1415	1600	1750	...	...	...	...	...
141	Niles ET d.	0929	1652	1832	2024	...	...	...	...	...
221	Kalamazoo a.	1014	1726	1911	2058	...	...	...	...	...
258	Battle Creek a.	1056	1803	1938	2135	...	...	...	...	...
335	East Lansing d.	|	|	2100	|	...	...	...	...	...
382	Durand d.	|	|	2137	|	...	...	...	...	...
409	Flint d.	|	|	2208	|	...	...	...	...	...
513	**Port Huron** a.	|	|	2331	|	...	...	...	...	...
331	Jackson d.	1151	1855	...	2228	...	...	...	...	...
390	Ann Arbor d.	1228	1935	...	2308	...	...	...	...	...
439	Dearborn ⊡ d.	1257	2011	...	2337	...	...	...	...	...
450	**Detroit** ⊡ d.	1325	2044	...	0010	...	...	...	...	...
494	**Pontiac** MI a.	1411	2129	...	0101	...	...	...	...	...

	351 N	365 P	353 N	355 N					
Pontiac MI d.	0543	...	0850	1728	...	...	...	...	...
Detroit d.	0626	...	0935	1811	...	...	...	...	...
Dearborn d.	0644	...	0953	1829	...	...	...	...	...
Ann Arbor d.	0714	...	1023	1900	...	...	...	...	...
Jackson d.	0751	...	1058	1937	...	...	...	...	...
Port Huron d.	|	0620	|	|	...	...	...	...	...
Flint d.	|	0735	|	|	...	...	...	...	...
Durand d.	|	0808	|	|	...	...	...	...	...
East Lansing d.	|	0854	|	|	...	...	...	...	...
Battle Creek d.	0848	1000	1201	2033	...	...	...	...	...
Kalamazoo d.	0916	1026	1228	2100	...	...	...	...	...
Niles ET d.	|	1104	1301	2142	...	...	...	...	...
Chicago Union CT a.	1032	1200	1402	2240	...	...	...	...	...

km		350 N	8150 🚌	370 Q						
0	**Chicago** Union CT d.	0645	...	1830	...	...	...	...	...	...
	Kalamazoo ET d.	1012	1105	|	...	...	...	...	...	...
140	Benton Harbour ET d.	...	|	2114	...	...	...	...	...	...
282	**Grand Rapids** ET a.	...	1205	2334	...	...	...	...	...	...

	371 Q	8365 🚌	355 N						
Grand Rapids ET d.	0600	1505	...	...	...	...	...	...	...
Benton Harbour ET d.	0810	|	...	...	...	...	...	...	...
Kalamazoo ET d.	|	1610	2100	...	...	...	...	...	...
Chicago Union CT a.	0908	...	2240	...	...	...	...	...	...

N – WOLVERINE – (12) 🍷 Chicago - Pontiac and v.v.
P – BLUE WATER – (12) 🍷 Chicago - Port Huron and v.v.
Q – PERE MARQUETTE – (2) Chicago - Grand Rapids and v.v.
⊡ – Trains may depart early if all booked passengers have boarded.
CT – Central Time.
ET – Eastern Time.

9280 SELECTED BUS ROUTES — Flixbus, Greyhound

NASHVILLE - MEMPHIS and v.v. *337 km*. Journey 4 - 4½ hours. Greyhound (www.greyhound.com):
From Nashville Bus Station at 0400, 0650, 1650, 2225.
From Memphis Bus Station at 0420, 1235, 1705, 2310.

LAS VEGAS NV - LOS ANGELES CA and v.v. Journey 5 - 5½ hours. Flixbus (www.flixbus.com):
From Downtown Las Vegas 1st Street approximately hourly 0700 - 2300.
From Downtown Los Angeles N Vignes Street approximately hourly 0630 - 2330.

ESTONIA

RAIL TRAVEL

See Tables **1870 - 1876**. Local services are run by the state owned railway company under the name Elron www.elron.ee using modern diesel multiple units on broad gauge tracks. The most important route links Tallinn with the country's second largest city, Tartu (Table **1870**).

The international service to St Peterburg and Moskva which was operated by GoRail (www.gorail.ee) is currently suspended. There are good bus links to Latvia's capital Riga and to St Peterburg (Table **1880**), whilst those determined to reach Riga by rail (taking much longer) can do so at certain times by changing at Valga (Tables **1830 / 1870**). Note that Tallinn's bus station is 3 km from the railway station, linked by tram. A new standard gauge rail project known as *Rail Baltica* will eventually link Tallinn with the other Baltic States and Poland, possibly by 2026.

Tallinn's proximity to Helsinki means that many tourists combine a trip to both cities. The various ferry routes linking the two cities are shown in our Ferry section (Table **2410**).

There is a railway museum in the impressive former station at Haapsalu, which can no longer be reached by rail (1h 45m by bus). Open ③–⑦ 1100 - 1700 see the Raudtee ja Sidemuuseum link on www.salm.ee. There is also a narrow gauge railway museum at Lavassaare, 17 km from Pärnu. www.museumrailway.ee

FINLAND

RAIL TRAVEL

See Tables **790 - 799**. Trains are run by national rail company VR www.vr.fi. Long distance day trains are generally high-speed tilting Pendolinos (up to 220 km/h) or modern double-deck trains. Trains are spacious, helped by the wider 'Russian' track gauge of 1524mm. Fares depend on train type - for further information on train types and ticketing see the introduction to the Finland section on page 360.

Focal point of the rail system is Helsinki's iconic 19-platform central rail station, designed by Eliel Saarinen in *Art Nouveau* style and incorporating four giant granite figures on the frontage. No fewer than 10 tracks head north for 3 km to Pasila, where lines start to divide.

Helsinki's Vantaa airport was added to the rail network in 2015 and can be reached either way around a loop, the anti-clockwise service (lettered 'I') being slightly quicker than the clockwise service ('P').

JOKIOINEN MUSEUM RAILWAY — **2022 service**

Finland's only 750mm gauge railway (www.jokioistenmuseorautatie.fi) starts from Humppila on the Turku to Tampere line (Table **795**) and runs for 14 km to Jokioinen. The line also features a collection of preserved Finnish narrow gauge engines and rolling stock at Minkiö station, where the museum is open June – August.

⑦ June 5 – July 31 and ⑥ Aug. 6 – 27. A special timetable applies during the Minkiö Steam Festival on July 3.

	⑦**b**	⑦**b**	⑦**c**		⑦**b**	⑦**b**	⑦**b**	⑦**a**
Humppila .... d.	1025	1310	1600	Jokioinen.......... d.	...	1145	1440	1700
Minkiö.............. a.	1049	1334	1624	Minkiö .... a.	...	1203	1458	1717
Minkiö.............. d.	1115	1410	1635	Minkiö .... d.	0945	1225	1520	...
Jokioinen .... a.	1134	1429	1652	Humppila.......... a.	1011	1250	1545	...
	⑥**d**	⑥**d**	⑥**d**		⑥**d**	⑥**d**	⑥**d**	
Humppila .... d.	1040	1310	1605	Jokioinen.......... d.	...	1150	1445	...
Minkiö.............. a.	1104	1334	1629	Minkiö .... a.	...	1208	1503	...
Minkiö.............. d.	1120	1410	...	Minkiö .... d.	1000	1225	1525	...
Jokioinen .... a.	1139	1429	...	Humppila.......... a.	1025	1250	1530	...

a – ⑦ July 3 – 31. **b** – ⑦ June 5 - July 31. **c** ⑦ July 3 – 31. **d** – ⑥ Aug. 6 – 27.

FINNISH RAILWAY MUSEUM

Rail enthusiasts will find the 59 km trip from Helsinki to Hyvinkää worthwhile, served by half-hourly regional trains (Table **790**). A short walk from the station is the excellent Finnish Railway Museum, open most days (but not Mondays Sept. to May). The museum is closed on Bank Holidays, including the Midsummer holiday June 23, 24. www.rautatiemuseo.fi

Finnish Railway Museum

FRANCE

RAIL TRAVEL

See Tables **250 - 399**. The national operator is SNCF - Société Nationale des Chemins de fer Français. www.sncf.com

Within France, the premium rate customer service line is ✆ 36 35.

Since the 1980s France has built up an excellent network of dedicated high-speed lines, fanning out in all directions from Paris. The longest is that to Marseille, with the 750 km being covered in around 3h 20m. The most recent extensions opened in 2017: *TGV Océane* Tours to Bordeaux and *TGV Bretagne-Pays de la Loire* from Le Mans to Rennes. The line to the north is of international significance, with Thalys trains to Brussels and Amsterdam, and *Eurostar* trains through the Channel Tunnel to London, whilst other high-speed lines include services to Germany, Switzerland and Spain. Speeds of up to 320 km/h (200 mph) are attained, with many trains continuing on conventional track to serve most parts of France.

The high-speed *TGV* trains (*TGV* stands for Train à Grande Vitesse) are branded *TGV inOui*, whilst *Ouigo* is a name used for a network of special low-cost high-speed services, which is set to further expand in the future.

TGV trains require compulsory reservation, but there are exceptions for journeys between Lille and the coast (Calais, Boulogne, Dunkerque), see Table **250**, page 166, for details. Although reservations can often be made at the last minute, space permitting, it does make it difficult to make last-minute travel decisions. It also increases the cost for rail pass holders, who need to take into account the cost of reservation fees (for normal tickets the reservation fee is included in the ticket price). Light refreshments are available on *TGV* trains, except on short routes such as Paris to Lille.

On other lines, most local and regional trains (outside Paris) are branded *TER* (Transport Express Régional), organised in conjunction with regional authorities. Off-peak services are often infrequent. Some departures may be provided by bus - if the bus uses the *TER* branding and is running on a route normally provided by train then rail tickets and passes are valid.

With France being western Europe's largest country, with much long-distance travel, there are huge peaks in travel demand, notably on Friday afternoons and Sunday evenings. Fares are higher at these times, known as white periods, as well as during the normal Monday to Friday peaks. When summer holiday and winter sports peaks are also taken into account, this leads to many complications in the timetables. Most public holidays are on fixed dates which also leads to timetable variations (with extra demand either side of holidays too). Note that when engineering work affects schedules, it is not uncommon for trains to leave earlier than normal, so a last-minute check of timings is recommended.

Until recently domestic overnight services were in decline with only a handful of socially necessary services remaining. However, the French government is implementing a stategy to revive overnight rail travel, which started with the recent reintroduction services between Paris to Nice and Lourdes. Several other new routes are planned over the next few years.

Terminal stations in Paris are scattered around the periphery of the city centre (see page 33), linked by metro lines, or in some cases by *RER* services which are cross-city outer suburban routes. Beware of pickpockets operating on these lines, which can be very crowded.

CHEMIN DE FER TOURISTIQUE DU VERMANDOIS

On Sundays in July and August a heritage train runs from the SNCF station at St Quentin (Tables **255/6/8**) to Origny-Ste Benoîte (22 km). www.cftv.fr. **Commencement of this service is anticipated during the spring.**

A luxurious dining car experience can also be had on the *Restaurant Art-Deco Express* which normally operates during May, June, July, Aug. and Oct. with an authentic restaurant car built in 1928.

Contact www.cftv.fr direct for timings and dates.

CHEMIN DE FER DE LA BAIE DE SOMME

As the name suggests, the line runs around the Somme Bay, an area north of Abbeville on the Picardy coast noted for its varied flora and fauna. Operated by historic narrow gauge steam trains, the line runs for 27 km on the route Le Crotoy - Noyelles - St.Valery - Cayeux. At Noyelles-sur-Mer connections can be made with SNCF trains (Table **261**). www.cfbs.eu

Services operate daily Apr. 1 - Oct. 1 (not Apr. 3, 7), ②③④⑥⑦ Oct. 3 – 31 (also Nov. 1 – 4, 11) with a mixture of steam and diesel traction.

A connecting diesel service from St. Valery to Cayeux on the south side of the bay operates in the summer taking 35 minutes.

TRAIN THUR DOLLER ALSACE

Situated west of Mulhouse, this 14 km standard-gauge line runs from Cernay St André to Sentheim. The station at Cernay is approximately 2 km from the SNCF station, which is served by trains on the Mulhouse - Thann line. Certain journeys are steam hauled. www.train-doller.org

Splendid scenery and varied wildlife are features of the trip along this line. Some of the railway's rolling stock dates back to 1892 and includes traditional wooden-bodied coaches. The French National Railway Museum (Cité du Train, see below) is situated nearby in Mulhouse. Services commence from June 6: On † June to September trains depart Cernay at 1030 and 1500 (journey 90 mins) returning from Sentheim at 1330 and 1730 (journey 60 mins). On ③ in July and August trains depart Cernay at 1000 and 1430 (journey 80 mins) returning from Sentheim at 1300 and 1645 (journey 50 mins).

CHEMIN DE FER DE LA VENDÉE

Situated in the Pays de la Loire region, Mortagne-sur-Sèvre is 10 km from Cholet (Table **299**). This tourist line, normally steam hauled, runs for 22 km on the route Mortagne-sur-Sèvre - Les Épesses - Les Herbiers, noted for its three spectacular viaducts. Les Herbiers station features a 1930s period style bar.

The train runs ⑦ June 4 - Sept. 24, ③⑤ July 5 - Aug. 25 departing Mortagne at 1530 for the one hour journey to Les Herbiers. Arrival back at Mortagne is at 1800. www.vendeetrain.fr

Special *Grands Express* restaurant car services also operate most ④–⑦ Apr. 6 - Oct. 29, departing Mortagne at 1200 for a three-hour dining experience. Bookings can be made online.

LE PETIT TRAIN DE LA RHUNE

This vintage rack railway with panoramic views takes passengers to the summit of La Rhune, a mountain in the Basque country close to the Spanish border. The electrified metre-gauge line is 4.2 km long and climbs to a height of 905 metres. www.rhune.com

The start point is Col de St Ignace (11 km from St Jean de Luz, Table **305**) which can be reached by bus. Owing to engineering work, the 2023 season will start later with trains running daily from June 3 to Nov. 5. Low Season departures from Col de St Ignace are at 0930 and every 40 minutes until 1610. High Season departures (July 10 - Sept. 3) are at 0820, 0850 then every 40 minutes until 1730.

Opened in 1924, the line uses traditional wooden-bodied coaches. The journey to the summit takes 35 minutes at a leisurely speed of 8 km/h. The wonderful scenery of the western Pyrenees can be enjoyed during the journey and the views at the summit are spectacular. A return journey takes approx two and a half hours. There are a number of scenic walking routes from the summit station including a signed route back to Col de St Ignace.

LIGNE DE CERDAGNE (SNCF)

Also known as *Le Petit Train Jaune* (the little yellow train), this narrow gauge line is part of the SNCF (French Railways) system and runs for 63 km from Latour de Carol to Villefranche. Timings are shown in Table **354**.

Construction of this steeply graded line was completed as late as 1929 and it provides some fine views of the Pyrenees. The bright yellow trains are electrically powered using a third rail system and during the summer most trains include open sightseeing carriages. Rail or bus connections are available at both ends of the line - at Latour de Carol for Toulouse (Table **312**) and at Villefranche for Perpignan (Table **354**).

TRAIN À VAPEUR DES CÉVENNES

Based at Anduze in the foothills of the Cévennes mountains in southern France, this standard gauge line runs for 14 km to St Jean du Gard. The nearest SNCF station is Alès (Table **333**), about 15 km from Anduze.

The 40 minute journey includes some fine panoramas as the line crosses a number of spectacular viaducts. A notable nearby attraction is the *Bambouseraie* botanical gardens, originally created in 1855.

The high-season timetable runs from July 17 to Aug. 24 with departures from Anduze at 0930, 1130, 1430 and 1630, returning from St Jean du Gard at 1030, 1330, 1530 and 1730. Trains are steam hauled except for the 0930 from Anduze and 1730 from St Jean du Gard.

There is also a low-season service on most days June 1 - July 16 and Aug. 25 - Oct. 31, but note that the line is closed on certain days in June, Sept. and Oct. Departures from Anduze are at 1130, 1500 and 1700 (one way), returning at 1030, 1400, 1600 with the last journey in each direction being diesel hauled. www.trainavapeur.com

CITÉ DU TRAIN - MULHOUSE RAILWAY MUSEUM

One of the largest railway museums in the world, Cité du Train (the French National Railway Museum) is situated in Mulhouse in eastern France. It is open every day except Christmas day and is served by the *Musées* stop on tram line 3 from Mulhouse railway station. www.citedutrain.com

Thalys TGV trains at Paris Nord

GERMANY

RAIL TRAVEL

See Tables **800 - 946**. National operator is Deutsche Bahn (DB) www.bahn.de. Telephone enquiries: ✆ 030 2970 (24 hrs).

The vast rail network of over 33,000 km covers all parts of Germany, with dedicated high-speed lines in various parts of the country helping to speed up long distance journeys, whether they be north to south or east to west. The sleek white *ICE* trains (InterCity Express) provide the fastest service, and whilst they have higher fares, reservation is not compulsory, and therefore there is no extra charge for pass holders. Several other train categories are in use, and these are explained at the start of the German section on page 366. Independent operator FlixTrain offers an expanding network of domestic German routes using refurbished rolling stock.

In addition to DB, there are a large number of private operators running local lines. Also, services are increasingly being franchised out to other operators, including certain *S-Bahn* networks, which are suburban services in large cities. Most urban areas have integrated ticketing, with day and period tickets being valid on all modes of public transport.

A common abbreviation in timetables is Hbf. which refers to the main station (Hauptbahnhof), whilst a smaller station is simply Bf. In most cities, principal rail services are concentrated on a single main station. This includes Berlin, with its impressive Hauptbahnhof, with east to west and north to south lines on two different levels.

Several major airports are rail connected, that at Frankfurt having long-distance trains to various parts of the country, as well as local services.

Readers interested in the many museum and heritage lines in Germany may find the following website useful: www.vdmt.de.

DB has its own museum in Nürnberg (closed Mondays), 750m west of the main station: www.dbmuseum.de.

HARZER SCHMALSPURBAHNEN

With a total length of 140 km this system of narrow gauge lines is one of the most extensive in Europe with scheduled steam and diesel services running throughout the year. It has the added advantage of being easily accessible with no less than three interchanges with the DB network. The journey to the 1125m summit at Brocken, the highest point in northern Germany, is particularly impressive (weather permitting) passing through the scenic Hochharz National Park. Three and five day tickets are available for unlimited travel over the whole network. www.hsb-wr.de

Timings are shown in Table **867**. Connections with DB services are made at Nordhausen (Tables **865/9**), Wernigerode (Table **860**) and Quedlinburg (Table **862**).

SÄCHSISCH-OBERLAUSITZER EISENBAHNGESELLSCHAFT

A narrow gauge steam operated line situated close to the Polish and Czech border with services running throughout the year. The line, which is 16 km in total, runs from Zittau to a junction at Bertsdorf, from where trains continue to Kurort Oybin or Kurort Jonsdorf. The timetable features simultaneous steam departures from Bertsdorf to Oybin and Jonsdorf which create an impressive sight! www.zittauer-schmalspurbahn.de

Timings are shown in Table **853**, and Zittau can be reached by means of Tables **854**, **855** and **1117**.

LÖSSNITZGRUNDBAHN

Operated by Sächsische Dampfeisenbahngesellschaft mbH, this steam-operated narrow gauge line starts in the unlikely setting of the Dresden suburbs at Radebeul Ost, running for 16.6 km via Moritzburg to Radeburg. Radebeul Ost can be reached by train (Tables **842** and **857**) and the narrow gauge service runs daily throughout the year (see Table **853** for timings). The main tourist attraction in the area is the impressive Moritzburg Castle. www.loessnitzgrundbahn.de

DAMPFBAHN FRÄNKISCHE SCHWEIZ

From Forchheim in the area known as Upper Franconia (Oberfranken) in northern Bavaria, an hourly train service (VGN route R22) brings you 20 minutes later to Ebermannstadt. From there the steam railway (sometimes diesel) runs 16 km to Behringersmühle.

Trains run on ⑦ and public holidays from April to October.

Departures from Ebermannstadt are at 1005, 1405, 1605, returning from Behringersmühle at 1105, 1505, 1705. For steam operation days please check locally. Journey time is 45 minutes each way. There are also Christmas specials in December. Steam trains convey a buffet car. www.dfs.ebermannstadt.de

BROHLTAL EISENBAHN

The Brohltalbahn (also known as the 'Vulkan-Express') is a charming narrow gauge railway located a few kilometres nort-west of Andernach. Services run on many dates from April 29 to October 29 (daily except Mondays from June to September). Steam locomotives haul trains on selected dates. The 17½ km route between Brohl and Engeln is located in the ancient volcanic region of Laacher See. The journey takes 85 minutes, climbing 400 metres from the Rhein river to the summit through attractive Eifel countryside. Brohl can be reached using hourly Mittelrheinbahn stopping services between Köln and Koblenz. www.vulkan-express.de

RÜGENSCHE BÄDERBAHN

This well-known 26.7 km narrow gauge (750 mm) line nicknamed *Rasender Roland* runs on the route Lauterbach (Mole) - Putbus - Binz - Göhren on the island of Rügen in north-eastern Germany. Timings are shown in Table **844a**. Connections with DB trains are made at Putbus where there is a service from Bergen auf Rügen (also in Table **844a**). The Lokalbahn station in Binz, however, is over 2 km from DB's Ostseebad Binz station. www.ruegensche-baederbahn.de

Services operate throughout the year with steam traction. However, the Putbus to Lauterbach narrow gauge section is seasonal.

ÖCHSLE MUSEUMS-SCHMALSPURBAHN

A 19 km narrow gauge steam railway running from Warthausen to Ochsenhausen. Warthausen is located 34 km south of Ulm and 3 km north of Biberach (Table **933**) and is served by the adjacent Warthausen station. Note, however, that most trains in Table **933** do not call at Warthausen (suggested DB connections are shown below). www.oechsle-bahn.de.

Trains run on ⑦ May 1 - Oct. 8 and first ⑥ of the month June 4 - Sept. 6; also on ④ July 13 - Sept. 7.

Ulm Hbf (DB) .... d.	*0935*	*1347*		Ochsenhausen............ d.	1200	1615
Biberach (DB)......... d.	*1007*	*1407*		Warthausen .... a.	1310	1725
Warthausen .... d.	1030	1445		*Biberach* (DB) ...... a.	*1321*	*1748*
Ochsenhausen............... a.	1140	1555		*Ulm Hbf* (DB)........... a.	*1346*	*1811*

Completed in 1899, the Öchsle Museums-Schmalspurbahn was one of five narrow gauge railways built by the old *Königlich Württembergischen Staats-Eisenbahnen*. Passenger traffic ceased in 1964, although freight traffic continued to use the line for a further 19 years. Tourist trains have been running since 1985.

BUCKOWER KLEINBAHN

This short standard gauge electric railway is situated in the picturesque *Märkische Schweiz* region, approximately 50 km east of Berlin. The railway's museum at Buckow station has a number of exhibits charting the region's railway heritage. The line runs 5 km from its base at Buckow to Müncheberg. Connecting trains from Berlin Ostkreuz or Lichtenberg to Müncheberg run hourly, as shown in Table **832**. The 2023 season commences on Apr. 29 although schedules are not yet confirmed.

In 2022 the Kleinbahn ran on © Apr. 16 - Oct. 3 with departures from Buckow at 0955, 1055, 1155, 1425, 1525, 1625 and 1725; from Müncheberg at 1020, 1120, 1220, 1450, 1550, 1650 and 1750. Journey time is 12 – 13 minutes each way. www.buckower-kleinbahn.de

GREAT BRITAIN

RAIL TRAVEL

See Tables **100 - 229**. Rail services in Great Britain are franchised out to a number of different train operating companies - a list is provided in the introduction to the Great Britain section on page 88, and codes are used in our tables to show the operator. Collectively the railway companies work together as National Rail (www.nationalrail.co.uk) which means that timetable enquiries are available irrespective of operator, as are full price tickets, which are available between any two stations. A 24-hour national telephone enquiry line is available ✆ 03457 48 49 50.

The railway infrastructure is in the hands of publicly owned Network Rail (www.networkrail.co.uk), which also runs major stations.

Best value advance purchase tickets are usually only valid on a specified train, and some other tickets may be restricted to a particular operator. Many ticket types have complex time restrictions, and there can be vast differences in the price of tickets (travelling to or from London in the peak period, between 0600 – 0930, can be particularly expensive).

The network of over 15,000 km of lines covers most parts of Britain, although closures in the 1960s and 1970s has left some gaps in coverage. Services are particularly dense in the south-east, where outer suburban lines from London stretch right to the coast. Kent has also benefitted from high-speed services on the line (known as HS1) to the Channel Tunnel. A dense network also operates around the northern conurbations, notably Manchester and Liverpool. Key long distance routes are the East Coast Main Line from London King's Cross to Leeds, Newcastle and Edinburgh, and the West Coast Main Line from London Euston to Birmingham, Manchester, Liverpool and Glasgow. A new high-speed line (HS2) from London to Birmingham and Manchester is under construction (with a planned opening of between 2029 and 2033).

All major airports have good rail links (see Table **100** for London airports). London's stations are mostly terminals linked by London Underground lines, but there are also north-south through services known as Thameslink (Tables **103 / 185**). The Elizabeth Line opened in 2022 and stretches more than 100km from Reading and Heathrow airport in the west through central London in tunnels via Paddington, the West End and Docklands to Shenfield and Abbey Wood in the east. This has revolutionised travel across central London.

When major engineering work takes place it is usually at weekends and at times when commuting is at its lowest (for example Christmas and Easter), and buses may replace trains.

HERITAGE AND TOURIST RAILWAYS

There are numerous heritage railway operations up and down Great Britain, many with steam locomotives, and only a small number can be described below. In addition, contact details for the following will be found in our Great Britain section: Isle of Wight Steam Railway, Table **107**; Dartmouth Steam Railway, Table **111**; Dean Forest Railway, Table **117**; Talyllyn Railway, Table **148**, Ravenglass and Eskdale Railway, Table **159**; Ecclesbourne Valley and Peak Rail, Table **172**; North Norfolk Railway and Bure Valley Railway, Table **203**. A useful independent website is www.heritage-railways.com.

Several organisations run occasional heritage trains on the main line network - see www.railadvent.co.uk for further details.

The National Railway Museum at York is a major tourist attraction and is free of charge (www.railwaymuseum.org.uk). There is also an offshoot at Shildon (Table **212**), known as *Locomotion* (www.locomotion.org.uk). Many of the heritage railways also have their own small museums.

WEST SOMERSET RAILWAY

Based in Minehead, the West Somerset Railway runs for 32 km to Bishops Lydeard, with no fewer than eight intermediate stations. This former Great Western Railway country branch line is now one of the largest tourist attractions in south-west England. From Minehead the line runs close to the coastline through Dunster, Blue Anchor and Watchet before turning inland at Williton. The railway continues alongside the Quantock Hills before arriving at Bishops Lydeard. Most services are steam-hauled and a buffet car is conveyed on most trains. www.west-somerset-railway.co.uk

The heritage railway runs ②③④⑥⑦ June - Sept. (also most days in Apr. and Oct. and specials in December), with between four and five journeys each way. The journey takes approximately 80 minutes. Bishops Lydeard can be reached in around 30 minutes by First Bus route 28 from Taunton bus station, also calling at Taunton railway station (Tables **110, 115, 116**).

SEVERN VALLEY RAILWAY

Connected to the National Rail network at Kidderminster (Table **128**), the long-established Severn Valley Railway is within easy reach of Birmingham and the West Midlands. The line runs for 25 km to the attractive Shropshire town of Bridgnorth, serving four beautifully restored intermediate stations en route, which are ideal starting points for walks around the surrounding area. The railway is based at the first of these stations, Bewdley. Refreshments are available at most stations and on most trains, and a full dining car service operates most weekends, for which advance booking is required. www.svr.co.uk

Days of operation are currently only available for Mar. 4 - June 1, running every ⑥⑦ plus some other days. Trains are hauled by a steam loco or heritage diesel, the journey taking 70 - 80 minutes each way. As with most heritage lines, there are also 'Santa Specials' in December.

BLUEBELL RAILWAY

Making a connection with National Rail services at the West Sussex town of East Grinstead (48 km south of London, Table **102**) the well known Bluebell Railway runs for 17.7 km via Horsted Keynes to Sheffield Park, where the railway has its main base. Stations have been restored to show how they would have been at various points in history, that at Sheffield Park having a Victorian ambience. The line has featured in many films and TV programmes including Downton Abbey. Most trains are steam hauled.

The timetable features between 3 and 7 journeys each way depending on the date. During summer peak August trains leave Sheffield Park at 0915,1030, 1145, 1300, 1415, 1530, 0445 returning one hour later from East Grinstead. The journey takes 40 – 50 minutes each way. www.bluebell-railway.com

KEIGHLEY & WORTH VALLEY RAILWAY

Starting at Keighley, where it shares the station with the famously scenic Leeds - Settle - Carlisle rail line (Tables **173/4**), this attractive heritage railway runs to Haworth and Oxenhope in 'Brontë Country'. Along the way is the *Rail Story* museum at Ingrow. Trains operate Mar. 4 - Nov. 2 (daily in August and on most days in June and July). Special events take place on selected dates. Timetables vary according to the date, with between four and nine return trips. Trains are steam or diesel hauled. www.kwvr.co.uk

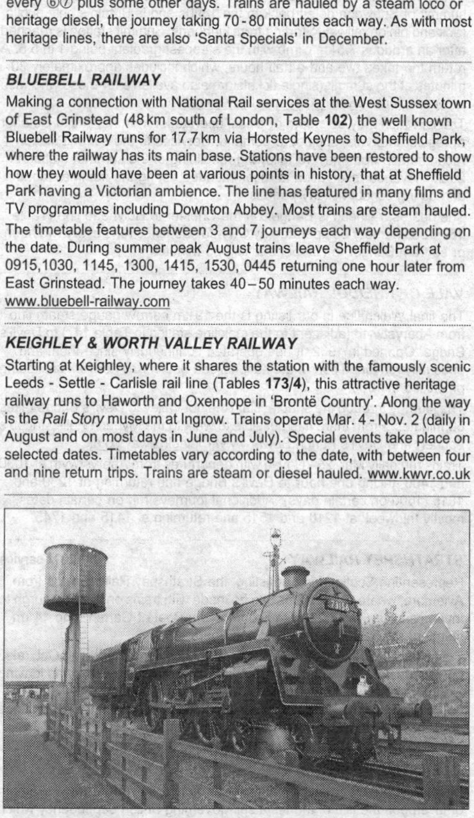

Another popular line is the Great Central Railway, a double track main line heritage railway from Loughborough to Leicester. A *Standard 5* built at Doncaster in 1956 .

NORTH YORKSHIRE MOORS RAILWAY

Running through the North Yorkshire Moors National Park, this 29 km standard gauge line runs from Pickering to Grosmont, passing through the villages of Levisham and Goathland along the way. Grosmont is a station on the National Rail line between Middlesbrough and Whitby (Table **211**). Indeed some of the heritage line's steam trains continue on this line to the popular resort of Whitby, with the through journey taking up to two hours.

Most trains are steam hauled and convey refreshment facilities. Trains run daily from April to October, with a limited winter timetable on certain dates outside this period. www.nymr.co.uk

Details of the summer timings can be found in Table **211**. Pickering can be reached by *Yorkshire Coastliner* bus from Leeds and York.

FFESTINIOG RAILWAY

The Ffestiniog Railway, a former industrial narrow gauge line, starts on the Cambrian coast at Porthmadog, before heading inland for 22 km through the magnificent scenery of the Snowdonia National Park. The 75 minute journey ends at Blaenau Ffestiniog by which time the line has climbed over 200m. The huge slate mines clearly visible at Blaenau Ffestiniog provide a reminder of this line's original purpose when built back in 1832. Indeed, the railway can claim to be the oldest railway company in the world still operating trains. Most trains are steam-hauled, with some locomotives being over 150 years old. www.festrail.co.uk

Trains run from Mar. 25 to Nov. 2. Porthmadog station is a short walk from the town's station on the Welsh Coast line to Pwllheli (Table **148**), and interchange is also possible at Minffordd. At Blaenau Ffestiniog there are connections with the National Rail service to Llandudno (Table **160**).

WELSH HIGHLAND RAILWAY

Also running from Porthmadog (Table **148**), and operated by the same company as the Ffestiniog Railway, the recently reopened Welsh Highland Railway is the UK's longest heritage line, running for 39 km across stunning landscape to Caernarfon. The journey across Snowdonia takes a little over two hours. At Porthmadog the railway shares a newly rebuilt station with the Ffestiniog Railway, whilst Caernarfon can be reached by bus from Bangor (Table **160**) on the Chester - Holyhead line.

Trains run March to October. Timings can be found in Table **160b**. www.festrail.co.uk

SNOWDON MOUNTAIN RAILWAY

Yet another line in Wales, this narrow gauge (800mm) railway to the summit of Snowdon dates back to the 1890s and is Britain's only public rack and pinion railway. Starting from Llanberis, Summit station is reached after an arduous 7.5 km climb with the steepest gradient being 1 in 5.5. A return trip takes two and a half hours, which includes approximately 30 minutes at the summit (single tickets are also available for those who wish to walk down). www.snowdonrailway.co.uk

Trains, which may be steam or diesel operated, run from April to October at regular intervals, subject to demand. Services to the summit station recommnece from May 13 following rebuilding of the summet station in 2022. Advance reservation is recommended during the summer months and during school holiday periods.

The nearest railhead is Bangor on the Chester to Holyhead line (Table **160**). Bus number 85 operated by Gwynfor Coaches runs every two hours or so from Bangor to Llanberis taking 55 minutes.

VALE OF RHEIDOL RAILWAY

The final Welsh line in our listing is the 19 km narrow gauge steam line from Aberystwyth (adjacent to the mainline station in Table **147**) to Devil's Bridge. Opened in 1902, it has operated continuously since then, and unusually remained part of the nationalised British Rail network until being privatised in 1989.

The journey through the spectacular Rheidol Valley to Devil's Bridge takes 60 minutes. From there it is possible to walk to the Mynach Falls, Jacob's Ladder, and Devil's Punch Bowl. www.rheidolrailway.co.uk

Trains run daily Mar. 25 - Nov. 5 with departures from Aberystwyth at 1030 and 1400, taking one hour to Devil's Bridge and returning at 1230 and 1615 (1600 on certain days). Additional journeys run on certain dates, mostly midweek at 1210 and 1545 and returning at 1415 and 1745.

STRATHSPEY RAILWAY — **2022 service**

Representing Scotland in our listing, the Strathspey Railway runs from Aviemore, where connections can be made with trains on the Edinburgh to Inverness line (Table **223**), to Broomhill via Boat of Garten. The 14 km standard gauge line is mainly steam operated.

Trains run ②–⑦ in July and Aug., ④–⑦ in May, June, Sept. and Oct. (also on various dates in winter). A round trip takes 1h 40m, with trains leaving Aviemore at 1030, 1245, 1500. Light lunches are served on all 1245 departures, however, the dining car service on ⑦ and evening dining trips on ⑤ have been suspended. www.strathspeyrailway.co.uk

ISLE OF MAN RAILWAYS

Situated in the Irish Sea some two or three hours by ferry from Heysham or Liverpool, the Isle of Man is a self-governing British dependency which is synonymous with heritage transport, and a mecca for enthusiasts and tourists alike. The main transport attractions consist of:

Isle of Man Steam Railway: Douglas - Port Erin (25 km)
Manx Electric Railway: Douglas - Laxey - Ramsey (29 km)
Snaefell Mountain Railway: Laxey - Snaefell Summit (8 km)

In Douglas, the famous horse drawn trams (dating from 1876) run along the promenade linking the town centre Sea Terminal with the Electric Railway station.

The Manx Electric Railway serves Laxey station en route where there is interchange with the Snaefell Mountain Railway. The original electric trains, dating back to 1895, are used for the journey to Snaefell Summit from where it is possible to see England, Wales, Scotland and Ireland on a clear day.

Go Explore travelcards give unlimited travel on all scheduled rail and bus services for 1 / 3 / 5 / 7 days. **Go Explore Heritage** additionally provides admission to Heritage sites. Further details: see Table **229**. www.iom-ssp.unicard-uk.com.

The Electric Railway has a small museum in Douglas open on Sundays, whilst the Steam Railway has a museum in Port Erin. Further attractions on the island (included on the Go Explore tickets) are the steam operated Groudle Glen Railway (www.ggr.org.uk) and the miniscule Great Laxey Mine Railway (www.laxeyminerailway.im). The annual heritage transport festival takes place July 23 – 30.

NORTHERN IRELAND — **2022 service**

In Northern Ireland, trains are operated by Northern Ireland Railways (NIR), part of Translink, and are not administered by National Rail.

Apart from the line across the border to Dublin, the principal line runs from Belfast to Londonderry, with a branch to Portrush (Table **233**). Local lines run from Belfast to Bangor and Larne.

✆ +44 (0)28 90 66 66 30 www.translink.co.uk

Tourist railways in Northern Ireland include the 914mm gauge (3 foot) Giant's Causeway and Bushmills Railway, which is a great way to visit the famous Giant's Causeway on the County Antrim coast, with its thousands of interlocking basalt columns, a major tourist attraction. Running at weekends Easter to October, the 3.2 km line starts from Bushmills, which can be reached by bus from Portrush. Trains leave Giant's Causeway at 1100, 1300, 1500, and from Bushmills 30 minutes later. www.freewebs.com/giantscausewayrailway

Located adjacent to Cultra Halt on the Belfast - Bangor line (Table **231**), the Ulster Folk and Transport Museum houses one of Europe's largest transport collections. Closed Mondays. www.nmni.com

Snaefell Mountain Railway, Isle of Man. This car was built in 1895.

GREECE

RAIL TRAVEL

See Tables **1400 - 1460**. Trains in Greece are operated by Hellenic Train, which was state owned until 2017 but has now been privatised and is a subsidiary of Italian Railways. www.hellenictrain.gr Call centre for reservations and information ✆ 14 511.

The network of a little over 2,200 km is centered on the 500 km main line between Athína (Athens) and Thessaloníki (Table **1400**). Daytime services on the route are operated by modern InterCity trains, on which reservation is compulsory and a supplement is payable. The line has recently been electrified and upgraded with daytime trains now taking around 4 hours 20 mins, and there is also a night train taking 5½ hours.

International services consist of the summer *Hellas* Beograd - Skopje - Thessaloniki (Table **1380**), and a daytime train Sofia - Thessaloniki (Table **1560**). However, many travellers arrive by sea from one of several ports in Italy, arriving at Pátra (Patras) in the northern Peloponnese; for schedules see our ferry section. Patras, Greece's third largest city, is a destination in itself, but for those continuing to Athens there is a frequent bus service. Alternatively there are OSE buses to Kiáto (Table **1450**), connecting with trains to Athens (Table **1440**). Athens airport is also rail connected.

Tickets can be purchased at major stations (principally Athens, Thessaloniki, Larissa and Volos), and also online.

DIAKOFTÓ - KALÁVRITA RAILWAY (OSE)

Also known as the Odontotos Rack Railway, this historic 750mm gauge rack line runs for 22 km through spectacular Peloponnese scenery. Starting at Diakoftó, its climb to Kalávrita involves numerous bridges and tunnels and a height difference of 700m. Shortly after departure the line turns inland and enters the dramatic canyon of the Vouraikos river.

The line runs daily throughout the year. Timings are shown in Table **1455**. www.hellenictrain.gr

Diakoftó can be reached by OSE bus from Patra or Kiáto as shown in Table **1450**; rail services operate between Athína and Kiáto (Table **1440**).

THE PELION RAILWAY *Services advertised until Mar. 27 only*

The 16 km narrow gauge (600 mm) mountainous line from Ano Lehonia to Milies closed in 1971 but was resurrected as a museum line in 1996, operated by OSE. The scenic route, with two tunnels and nine bridges, affords spectacular views over Pagasitikos Bay. The nearest OSE station is Vólos (Table **1415**). www.hellenictrain.gr

Trains run on ⑥⑦ leaving Ano Lehonia at 1000 for the 90 minute journey. Return from Milies is at 1500. A 15 minute stop is made at Ano Gatzea in both directions. On ⑥⑦ there is also 1200 from Milies, 1330 from Ano Lehonia (this service is currently suspended).

Services are operated using a diesel locomotive disguised to look somewhat like a steam loco, with historic wooden carriages.

HUNGARY

RAIL TRAVEL

See Tables **1200 - 1299**. A comprehensive network of over 7,000 km is operated by Hungarian State Railways (MÁV) www.mav.hu. Principal cities are connected by *IC* trains, with compulsory reservation (see the introduction to the Hungary section on page 496 for further information about reservations and supplements).

The main holiday area is around Lake Balaton, and services in the area have different schedules from mid June to late August. Northern Hungary around Eger and Miskolc is another popular area for tourism, and some of the forest railways that we have selected below are situated in this region.

The three main stations in Budapest are named after points of the compass: Keleti (East), Nyugati (West) and Déli (South). However, don't take this as an indication of the direction of travel; trains from Nyugati can go north and east, and as some international trains serve Keleti your train from the 'East' station might well be heading west! Note, however, that the day trains to Bratislava, Praha and beyond have switched from Keleti to Nyugati giving a shorter route.

A curiosity is that hourly *IC* trains leave Budapest Keleti, circumnativate Eastern Hungary via Miskolc and Debrecen, ending up back in Budapest at Nyugati station (Tables **1260** and **1270**). Main stations are connected by metro as shown on the city plan, page 31.

Apart from the metro and MÁV lines, suburban rail services in Budapest include several unconnected lines known as the HÉV, which have only recently become the responsibility of MÁV, through a subsidiary company. Day tickets for Budapest are, however, valid on almost all transport, including some MÁV lines.

BUDAPEST CHILDREN'S RAILWAY (GYERMEKVASÚT)

Running through the Buda hills on the outskirts of Budapest, this charming and popular diesel operated narrow gauge line, formerly known as the Pioneer Railway, runs for 12 km from Hüvösvölgy to Széchenyihegy. Apart from the engine drivers, it is operated mainly by children, who stand and salute as the train leaves the station.

The intermediate station of Jánoshegy is close to the highest point of Budapest where there is a look-out tower, and is only a short walk from the chair lift (Libegö) which offers excellent views of Budapest on the way down to Zugliget (connected by bus 291 to/from Nyugati station).

The Hüvösvölgy end of the line can be reached by taking metro line M2 to Széll Kálmán tér, then tram 61 to Hüvösvölgy terminus.

To reach the southern end of the line at Széchenyihegy take tram 59 or 61 two stops from Széll Kálmán tér to Városmajor, then the rack railway (route 60) which terminates 250m from the Children's Railway.

Trains run throughout the year (except winter Mondays), hourly 0910 to 1510 from Hüvösvölgy, and 1003 to 1603 from Széchenyihegy, increasing to every 45 minutes in summer. Journey time is 40 – 50 minutes each way. Diesel trains are the norm, but there are steam hauled journeys on certain weekends. Full timings are available from www.gyermekvasut.hu

NAGYCENK MUSEUM RAILWAY

Nagycenki Széchenyi Múzeumvasút is a 3.6 km narrow gauge tourist railway situated in the north-western corner of Hungary on the GySEV operated Sopron to Györ line (Table **1250**). The museum line starts from Fertöboz which is 11 km from Sopron (certain Sopron trains call there).

The route is Fertöboz - Barátság - Kastély (Nagycenk), so named because Kastély (Castle) station is located close to Nagycenk village and is about 25 minutes walk from Nagycenk station on the Sopron - Szombathely line (12 km from Sopron, most trains in Table **1233** call there). The Kastély terminus of this 760mm gauge light railway is adjacent to the Schloss Széchenyi, a major tourist attraction in this area. The station also features an outdoor display of plinthed narrow gauge steam locomotives.

The museum line is operated by GySEV. As the line is currently being reconstructed, trains may only be running between Kastély and Barátság and details should be verified from the GySEV website www.gysev.hu

ÁLLAMI ERDEI VASUTAK *HUNGARIAN FOREST RAILWAYS*

There are a number of narrow gauge forest railways in Hungary, mostly operated by ÁEV using diminutive diesel locomotives. Timings are available on www.kisvasut.hu. For this feature we have selected the following lines in the scenic Matra mountains area in north-eastern Hungary, which are of particular interest to tourists:

ÁEV SZILVÁSVÁRAD *Forest Railway - see above*

Route: Szalajka Fatelep - Szalajka Fátyolvizesés (5 km). Szalajka-Fatelep is situated 2 km from Szilvásvárad-Szalajkavölgy station, on the Eger - Szilvásvárad line (one stop from Szilvásvárad, Table **1299**).

Typical timetable: Apr. 1 - Oct. 31: from Szalajka-Fatelep 0930, 1030, 1130, 1300, 1400, 1500 (also 1600 May - Sept.; 1700 June - Aug.). Trains return from Szalajka-Fátyolvizesés 1015. 1115, 1215, 1345, 1445, 1545 (also 1645 May - Sept.; 1745 June - Aug.). Journey 16 minutes. Limited winter service. Check timings locally www.szilvasvarad.hu.

ÁEV MÁTRAVASÚT *Forest Railway - see above*

Route: Gyöngyös -Szalajkaház (13 km). Connections with MÁV are made at Gyöngyös (Table **1258**); from the station approach road turn right, then about 400 metres to the ÁEV station. Journey time is 22 minutes.

Typical timetable:
Depart Gyöngyös: 0940 **E**, 1210 **E**,1510 **F**.
Depart Szalajkaház: 1050 **E**, 1320 **E**,1620 **F**.
E – © Mar. 12 - Apr. 30 (daily May 1 - Sept. 30).
F – © Mar. 12 - Sept. 30; (daily May 1 - Aug. 28).

ÁEV LILLAFÜRED *Forest Railway - see above*

Route: Miskolc (Dorottya utca) - Papírgyár - Lillafüred - Garadna (13 km). From Miskolc station (Tables **1260/1**) take tram number 1 towards Felsö-Majláth and alight at Dorottya utca (approx. 8 km).

The 13 km journey takes approximately one hour. Timings can be found on www.laev.hu.

HUNGARIAN RAILWAY MUSEUM

Based at a 34-track roundhouse built in 1911, this extensive railway museum opened in the year 2000. www.vasuttortenetipark.hu

Located at Tatai út 95 in the northern suburbs of Budapest, it is open Mar. 31 to Dec. 3 daily except Mondays. During opening times, certain trains on the Budapest - Esztergom line make a special stop at *Vasútmúzeum* - see Table **1299** for timings. Otherwise, access is by bus or tram to the Rokolya utca stop. The urban transport museum at Szentendre also has some railway exhibits (21 km from Budapest by HÉV train).

Budapest's impressive Keleti (East) station

IRELAND

RAIL TRAVEL

See Tables **230 - 245**. Rail services are operated by Iarnród Éireann (IÉ) www.irishrail.ie. Telephone enquiries can be made 0700-1900 Ⓐ, 0800-1900 © ✆ + 353 (0)1 8366 222.

Running on a network of nearly 2,000 km based on Dublin, many services are operated by modern diesel multiple units, with loco-hauled trains on the Dublin - Cork and Dublin - Belfast routes. The trains to Belfast, branded *Enterprise*, are operated jointly with Northern Ireland Railways (for NIR see separate section under Great Britain). The local IÉ north-south electric line in Dublin is called DART (Dublin Area Rapid Transit). Tracks in Ireland are built to the 'Irish gauge' of 1600mm (5ft 3in), not found elsewhere in Europe.

A scenic highlight of the Irish rail system is the Dublin to Wexford line, particularly the section between Dun Loaghaire (pronounced Dun Leery) and Greystones where the line hugs the coast.

The two railway stations in Dublin are named Connolly and Heuston. Both gained their current names in 1966 on the 50th anniversary of the Easter Rising and are named after James Connolly and Sean Heuston, both of whom were executed following the Rising. The two stations are linked by the frequent red line service of Dublin's LUAS tram system.

WATERFORD & SUIR VALLEY RAILWAY — 2022 service

Part of the abandoned Waterford to Dungarvan track bed was used to build this 8.5 km narrow gauge heritage railway, which runs mostly along the picturesque banks of the River Suir. A restored Simplex locomotive pulls two partially open carriages travelling at 15 km/h on a 40 - 50 minute round trip. www.wsvrailway.ie

Situated 12 km from Waterford, and sadly not accessible by public transport, trains run daily Apr. to Sept. leaving Kilmeaden hourly 1100 - 1500. On ⑦ these times are one hour later (also 1700 July and Aug.).

Other short heritage lines in Ireland include the Fintown Railway, the Cavan & Leitrim Railway, and the West Clare Railway.

ITALY

RAIL TRAVEL

See Tables **580 - 648**. The national operator is Trenitalia, a division of Ferrovie dello Stato (FS) www.trenitalia.com. A 24-hour telephone line is available for information and reservation changes: ✆ 89 20 21 (calls from abroad can be made 0700-2359 daily on ✆ + 39 06 6847 5475). The network exceeds 16,000 km, most of which is electrified.

Dedicated high-speed lines have been a major feature of the Italian rail network since the Roma - Firenze *Direttissima* was opened in 1977. Backbone of the system is the high-speed line stretching for nearly a thousand kilometres from Torino in the north via Milano, Bologna, Firenze, Roma and Napoli to Salerno in the south (Table **600**). Headline journey time for the Milano - Roma journey is just 2h 59m. High-speed trains are branded *Frecciarossa* (Red Arrow), whilst those which divert off the line to other desinations are *Frecciargento* (Silver Arrow). Best trains on the traditional network are another colour of arrow, this time white, being branded *Frecciabianca*. Reservation is required on all high-speed trains. For other train categories see the start of the Italian section on page 282.

Whilst several countries these days have competing operators on their main lines (thanks to EU rules which favour liberalisation), Italy is unique in having an 'open access' competitor running high-speed trains. In fact, NTV (Nuovo Trasporto Viaggiatori) runs over the entire length of the core high-speed line; timings can be found on the first page of Table **600**. Private operators are also found on a multitude of local lines across the country, whilst local services in Lombardy (the Milano region) are handled by *Trenord*, jointly owned by Trenitalia and FNM (Ferrovie Nord Milano).

Italy's vast coastline, along with its Appennine mountain range stretching for over 1,000 km along the spine of the country, means that there is no shortage of scenic railway lines. For example, much of the line from the French border at Ventimiglia to La Spezia follows the coast, although a newly opened route has taken part of the line inland. Bear in mind that the most scenic routes across the mountains are by the slower conventional routes, as the high-speed line is constantly in and out of tunnels.

There are often long queues at stations, but tickets and reservations can also be made at travel agencies displaying the FS symbol.

TRENINO VERDE DELLA SARDEGNA

As well as the Trenitalia services in Table **629**, Sardinia is blessed with a network of scenic narrow gauge tourist railways (the 'green' trains) running on five different routes during the summer. Services have been cut back over the years and now run on just a few days per week on the following routes: Tempio to Palau (59 km), Mandas to Laconi (37 km), Mandas to Sadali (58 km), Arbatax to Gairo (62 km) and Sindai to Bosa (33 km). Services are diesel hauled or use diesel railcars. Details can be found on www.treninoverde.com.

PIETRARSA RAILWAY MUSEUM

Italy's principal railway museum is located in the suburbs of Naples in the old works adjacent to Pietrarsa station. Recently reopened following redevelopment work, the museum is open Friday to Sunday (also 1400-2000 on Thursdays). www.fondazionefs.it

LATVIA

RAIL TRAVEL

See Tables **1800** and **1830 - 1870**. Trains in Latvia are operated by PV (www.pv.lv) using the 'Russian' track gauge of 1520mm. Hub of the network is Riga's centrally located station. Services to other Latvian cities, such as Daugavpils, are not very frequent. However, good local services run from Riga to the nearby coastal resorts.

The nightly train Riga to Moskva and St Peterburg is suspended as is the train every four days to Kyiv via Vilnius and Minsk. Services to Minsk via Daugavpils and from Daugavpils to Vilnius are also suspended. Until the *Rail Baltica* scheme is complete (see under Estonia), there are no trains to Tallinn, apart from occasional connections at Valga. However, express bus services (Table **1800**) are available from Riga's busy coach station a few hundred metres from the railway station.

Riga has an interesting railway museum open on Tuesdays to Saturdays, a short tram ride from the city centre on the other side of the river (alight at Nacionala biblioteka). www.railwaymuseum.lv

GULBENE - ALUKSNE

Catering for both locals and tourists this 33 km narrow gauge (750 mm) line is situated in the north east of the country. Gulbene is no longer linked to the rest of the rail network (except by special trains) but there is a bus service from Riga. Trains leave Gulbene twice a day at 1300 and 1800 on for the 1h 25m journey to Aluksne, returning at 1600 and 1955. Steam hauled services operate on various saturdays. www.banitis.lv

LITHUANIA

RAIL TRAVEL

See Tables **1805 - 1815**, **1950**. Services are operated by Lithuanian Railways (www.ltglink.lt) using the 'Russian' track gauge of 1520mm. ✆ +370 700 55111. A frequent service is run from Vilnius to Kaunas, Lithuania's second city - fans of old funicular railways will enjoy a visit there. Vilnius Airport is rail connected.

Vilnius sits astride the main line linking Russia with its detached federal outpost, Kaliningrad (Table **1950**), and Vilnius also has reasonably good services to Minsk, capital of Belarus, both currently suspended.

The *Rail Baltica* project to link Lithuania (and ultimately the other Baltic States) to Poland with a standard-gauge line has been slow off the ground, but a limited service runs across the border between Bialystok and Kaunas via Mockava (Tables **93** and **1042**). There are plans to eventually reach Tallinn, and possibly even Helsinki. In the meantime, travel between Lithuania and its northern neighbours is mostly by bus (Table **1800**).

A small indoor railway museum is located within the station building at Vilnius, and some outdoor exhibits are stabled in an adjacent siding.

A train from Vilnius having arrived at Kaunas

LUXEMBOURG

RAIL TRAVEL

See Tables **445/6/9** (also **384**, **390**, **915**). Operator is Société Nationale des Chemins de fer Luxembourgeois (CFL) www.cfl.lu. Telephone enquiry line: ✆ +352 2489 2489.

This small country has a rail network of only 275 km, but services are fairly frequent, and there are good international links, including *TGV* services to Paris and hourly trains to Brussels and Koblenz.

The country is heavily forested, with some attractive scenery, particularly on the main line to the north. One of the attractions of exploring the country by rail is that 2nd class travel has been free since March 2020. Most rail stations are small with few facilities.

AMTF TRAIN 1900

Luxembourg's only preserved steam railway is situated close to the French and Belgian borders, operated by Assoc. des Musée et Tourisme Ferroviaires (AMTF). The line runs from Pétange to Bois-de-Rodange, pausing at Fond-de-Gras where the railway is based. www.train1900.lu

Pétange can be reached by regular CFL local train (Table **449**) whilst Rodange CFL station is approximately 2 km from Bois-de-Rodange.

Trains run on ⑦ and holidays May to September, and most ⑥ in July and August. Services marked 🚂 are known as *Le Train 1900* and are hauled by an historic steam locomotive. Other services are operated by a diesel railcar.

		🚂		🚂		🚂		
Pétange-TRAIN 1900...... d.	1315	1415	1515	1615	1715	1815	1848	...
Fond-de-Gras .... a.	1344	1442	1537	1642	1737	1843	1906	...
Fond-de-Gras .... d.	1420	1520	1620	1720	1800	...	...	...
Bois-de-Rodange .... a.	1425	1525	1625	1725	1805	...	...	...
		🚂		🚂		🚂		
Bois-de-Rodange .... d.	...	...	1430	1530	1630	1730	1810	...
Fond-de-Gras .... a.	...	...	1435	1535	1636	1736	1816	...
Fond-de-Gras .... d.	1245	1320	1445	1540	1645	1740	1820	...
Pétange-TRAIN 1900...... a.	1309	1345	1506	1603	1706	1803	1843	...

NETHERLANDS

RAIL TRAVEL

See Tables **450 - 499**. National rail company is Nederlandse Spoorwegen (NS) www.ns.nl ✆ +31 30 751 5155.

A comprehensive network of over 3,000 km provides frequent regular-interval services linking most towns and cities. Most services are provided by NS, although other operators, notably Arriva, are contracted to run local train services in some parts of the north and east.

Fast domestic trains, calling only at principal stations, are classified *Intercity*, whilst local stopping trains are known as *Sprinter* services. A further category is *Intercity direct* for which a supplement is payable - these use the *HSL-Zuid* high-speed line which opened in 2009 linking Amsterdam and Schiphol Airport with the Belgian border and on to Antwerpen. Through services to Paris via Brussels are provided by *Thalys* trains, and *Eurostar* trains now link London with Amsterdam, it is n longer neccessary to change trains at Brussels on the return journey. Schiphol airport is well served by rail services, not only to Amsterdam but to other parts of the country.

Through tickets can be purchased between all stations in the Netherlands, regardless of operator. A national stored-value smartcard scheme operates throughout the country known as OV-chipkaart, used for all public transport (for further information see the introduction to the Netherlands section on page 242). Cycle hire and cycle and baggage storage are usually available at larger stations. Smaller stations are usually unstaffed, but all stations have ticket vending machines. Seat reservations are not available for domestic journeys.

A recent development (2019) is the conversion of the Hoek van Holland to Rotterdam line, once traversed by many long distance trains connecting with ferries, into a metro line, now part of Rotterdam's metro system.

MUSEUMSPOORLIJN S.T.A.R. **2022 service**

Located in the north-eastern corner of the Netherlands, this former NS line runs from Veendam to Stadskanaal, where the railway is based. Veendam can be reached by local train from Groningen (Table **498**). Trains can be steam or diesel hauled. www.stadskanaalrail.nl

The timetable below operates on ③⑦ July 11 - Aug. 28. Trains also run on numerous other dates between June and Dec.

Stadskanaal .... d.	1045	1400	...	Veendam .... d.	1200	1510	...
Veendam .... a.	1125	1440	...	Stadskanaal .... a.	1240	1550	...

VELUWSCHE STOOMTREIN MAATSCHAPPIJ (VSM) **2022 service**

Running on the route Apeldoorn - Eerbeek - Dieren (22 km), this line connects with NS services at both ends: Apeldoorn (Table **498**) and Dieren (Table **475**). It runs through the Veluwe nature area and, on certain dates, a ride on the train can be combined with a boat trip along the River IJssel between Dieren and Zutphen (boats are scheduled to connect with the trains). The journey back to Apeldoorn can be completed by train from Zutphen (Table **498**). Special tickets are available for this interesting day trip known as *De Veluwe-IJssel-Boemel*. www.stoomtrein.org.

Steam services operate ⑦ June 5 - July 3 (also June 6) between Apeldoorn and Eerbeek. Between July 10 - Aug. 28 steam services operate ⑦–⑤ between Apeldoorn to Dieren, via Eerbeek.

During both operating periods services call at the museum and allow a 45 minutes to visit the Steam Depot.

MUSEUMSTOOMTRAM HOORN - MEDEMBLIK

This long-established standard gauge line runs for 20 km between Hoorn and Medemblik and is easily accessible from Amsterdam (Table **461/470**). All trains are operated by steam traction. A popular triangular journey (known locally as *De Historische Driehoek*) uses the boat between Medemblik and Enkhuizen (see below), returning to Hoorn or Amsterdam by rail. A day ticket valid on steam tram and boat services is available. The station at Hoorn includes a steam tram museum. www.stoomtram.nl

		A	B			A	B
Hoorn .... d.	...	1040	1140	Enkhuizen .... d.	...	1040	1040
Medemblik .... a.	...	1200	1310	Medemblik .... a.	...	1155	1155
		A	B			A	B
Medemblik .... d.	...	1320	1320	Medemblik .... d.	...	1320	1420
Enkhuizen .... a.	...	1450	1450	Hoorn .... a.	...	1440	1540

A ②–⑦ Apr. 1 – June 30 (also Apr. 10, 24, May 1, 29); ①–⑦ July 1 - Sept. 3; ②–⑦ Sept. 5 – 30; ⑥⑦ Oct. 1 – 15.

B Apr. 9, 10, May 2 – 4, 18, 28, 29, July 18 – 20, 25 – 27, Aug. 1 – 3, 8 – 10, 15 – 17, 22 – 24.

NARROW GAUGE

Fans of narrow gauge trains will enjoy the Stoomtrein Katwijk Leiden along the shore of Lake Valkenburg, along with the associated museum. Open weekends Apr. to Sept. (also ②④ July 11 - Aug. 17). Reach by bus from Den Haag or Leiden. www.stoomtreinkatwijkleiden.nl

A further narrow gauge line and museum is the RTM Ouddorp situated in Zeeland and reached by bus from Roterdam's Spikenisse metro station to Port Zelande, which is part way along this short line.

2022 service: Operated ③⑥ June, Sept. and Oct. (not Sept. 24), ③④⑥ during July and Aug. www.rtm-ouddorp.nl

MUSEUM STOOMTREIN GOES - BORSELE

Evoking railways of the 1930's, this standard gauge line runs for 16 km across the beautiful landscape of the province of Zeeland. Starting from Goes (a short walk from the NS station, Table **450**) steam trains run for 40 minutes to the scenic village of Hoedekenskerke calling at Kwadendamme. Departures from Goes ⑦ Apr. 2 - Oct. 22 at 1045 and 1415, returning at 1240 and 1610. Main operating days are ⑦–④ July 2 - Aug. 31 (also Oct. 17, 18). An additional diesel service runs the full length of the line to Baarland on ②③ July 10 - Aug. 31. www.destoomtrein.nl

UTRECHT RAILWAY MUSEUM

The National Railway Museum is located in the former Maliebaan railway station in Utrecht, open ②–⑦ (also ① in school holidays). The museum has a dedicated hourly railway service from Utrecht Centraal (or 1.6 km on foot). www.spoorwegmuseum.nl

A London to Amsterdam *Eurostar* train at Rotterdam

NORWAY

RAIL TRAVEL

See Tables **770 - 787**. Many trains are operated by the Vy Group (using the name Vy), owned by the Norwegian government. www.vy.no. Services between Oslo and Stavanger are now operated by GoAhead Nordic while services Oslo – Trondheim / Åndalsnes, Hamar – Røros – Trondheim and Trondheim – Steinkjer - Bodø are mostly operated by SJ Nord.

As you might expect, a high proportion of the country's 4,000 km rail network can be regarded as scenic. For those touring the country by rail, a circular route can often be arranged by including buses or boats in the itinerary. Trips to the far north can also be extended by catching the bus from Bodø to Narvik (Table **787**) and returning through Sweden.

Trains convey 2nd-class seating, whilst most medium- and long-distance trains also convey *Komfort* accommodation, a dedicated area with complimentary tea/coffee and newspapers (supplement payable). Sleeping cars have one- and two-berth compartments; a sleeper supplement is payable per compartment (for two people travelling together, or sole use for single travellers). Long-distance trains convey a bistro car serving hot and cold meals, drinks and snacks. Reservation is possible (and recommended) on all long-distance trains. Reserved seats may not be marked, but your confirmation specifies carriage and seat/berth numbers.

FLÅMSBANA

Branching off the Olso to Bergen line (Table **781**), this is undoubtedly one of Europe's most spectacular railway journeys. Trains descend from an altitude of 865m at Myrdal to sea-level at Flåm in just 20 km. In between the 20 tunnels there is some breathtaking scenery and, to reassure passengers, the trains have no less than five sets of brakes, each of which can stop the train on the extremely steep inclines! Timings are shown in Table **781**. This journey can be included as part of various circular excursions, such as the *Norway in a Nutshell* tour (see Table **781a** for boat and bus connections). For further details see www.visitflam.com

KRØDERBANEN

This former NSB line closed to passengers in 1958 but was resurrected as a museum line in the 1980s. Operated by the Norwegian Railway Club, it is Norway's longest museum railway at 26 km and makes an ideal day trip from Oslo. It runs from the railway's base at Krøderen to Vikersund, which is situated between Drammen and Hønefoss (Table **780**). It's 150th anniversary was celebrated 2022. Trains normally run every ⑦ from June 26 to Aug. 28, (also Aug. 6, 20) for timings see www.njk.no.

GAMLE VOSSEBANEN

Also operated by the Norsk Jernbaneklubb, the 18 km 'Old Voss Steam Railway' during 2021 runs from Garnes to Haukeland, crossing the Bergen to Voss line (Table **781**) at Arna, where the station is 300m from the old station on the steam railway. Both ends of the line can also be reached by bus from Bergen bus station.

Services are hauled by one of the original steam locomotives built for the Bergen Railway in 1913 and the restored teak coaches are from the same period. Until 1964 the line was actually part of the main Oslo - Bergen railway. www.njk.no. Trains run on ⑦ June 4 - Sept. 10 as follows:

Garnes .... d.	1130	1430	...	Haukeland .... d.	1250	1550	...
Arna (old station) ...... d.	1140	1440	...	Arna (old station) .. d.	1310	1610	...
Haukeland .... a.	1200	1500	...	Garnes........ a.	1320	1620	...

Connecting trains: Bergen - Arna at 1036, 1322; Arna - Bergen at 1418, 1619.

NORWEGIAN RAILWAY MUSEUM

The museum is located 3 km from the centre of Hamar, on the Oslo - Lillehammer - Trondheim line (Table **785**), and is open daily except Mondays (daily June / August). Bus number B25 runs from the railway station. www.jernbanemuseet.no.

POLAND

RAIL TRAVEL

See Tables **1000 - 1099**. Long-distance trains are operated by PKP Intercity (www.intercity.pl). The best trains on the principal routes are classified *EIP* (Express InterCity Premium), which are operated with the latest sleek *Pendolino* type trains. Other fast trains are *EIC* or *IC* (along with international *EC* trains), plus the cheaper *TLK* trains which make more stops. Reservation is compulsory on all trains operated by PKP Intercity, whose trains are shown in red on PKP timetables and station departure sheets. See page 465 for further details of train classifications.

Trains on the Warszawa - Berlin route are operated jointly with German Railways and are branded *Berlin-Warszawa Express*. The Russian Railways services to or through Warszawa (including the Berlin - Moscow *Talgo* train) are currently suspended.

Things get more complicated when it comes to local trains. Przewozy Regionalne is the main operator, using the name PolRegio (polregio.pl), with train categories *RE* or *R* (local trains are shown without numbers in our tables). However, several local authorities have set up their own railway organisations, such as Koleje Wielkopolskie and Koleje Ślaskie. Outer suburban services in the Warsaw area come under Koleje Mazowieckie, whilst local electric services in the Tricity area (Gdansk, Sopot, Gdynia) have long been the preserve of PKP subsidiary SKM Trojmiasto. Ticket inter-availability between operators is complex.

Poland is a large country with many scenic rail routes, notably in the more hilly areas in the south of the country. In addition to the standard gauge network, the country used to be covered with hundreds of kilometres of narrow gauge lines, and some of these survived in PKP ownership as late as 2001. Since closure, many sections have resurfaced as museum lines, some with regular summer operation, others with only occasional trains. Further information can be found on www.narrowrail.net, and two of the lines are included below.

WOLSZTYN — 2022 service

Wolsztyn (Table **1099**) is located some 80 km south-west of Poznań and is famous for its steam depot running the last regularly timetabled steam hauled passenger services on a main line in Europe having been resurrected in May 2017 running between Wolsztyn and Poznań on Saturdays, and on Monday to Fridays between Wolsztyn and Leszno. 2022 services ran between Wolsztn and Leszno only until June 10 as detailed below.

	Ⓐ		Ⓐ			Ⓐ		Ⓐ	
Wolsztyn........ d.	0603	...	1148	...	Poznań .... d.	...	...	...	...
Leszno........ a.	0721	...	1300	...	Leszno........ d.	0743	...	1343	...
Poznań .... a.	...	...	...	...	Wolsztyn .... a.	0907	...	1506	...

For latest timings see www.parowozowniawolsztyn.pl; steam services may be suspended at certain times. The atmospheric steam depot at Wolsztyn is a short walk from the station and can be visited for a small fee.

WARSAW RAILWAY MUSEUM

Warsaw's railway museum is located in the former Warszawa Główna terminus in the city centre, between Centralna and Zachodnia stations in ul.Towarowa. There is an extensive outdoor display of rolling stock as well as indoor exhibits. Open daily. www.stacjamuzeum.pl

SOCHACZEW MUSEUM RAILWAY — 2022 service

A short walk from Sochaczew station (local trains approximately hourly from Warszawa Wschodnia) is the narrow gauge station which has been made into a museum with a large collection of narrow gauge rolling stock, open daily. See www.stacjamuzeum.pl (link top right).

The season operates Apr. 30 - Sept. 24 mainly on ⑥⑦. On ⑤⑥⑦ July 1 - Aug. 28 a steam hauled 'Retro' train leaves the museum at 1030 for a trip to Wilcze Tułowskie in the Kampinos Forest. The itinerary includes a guided forest walk, and arrival back at Sochaczew is at 1520.

ZNINSKA KOLEJ WASKOTOROWA — 2022 service

The 12 km Znin - Gasawa railway is the last remaining section of a much larger narrow gauge (600mm) network in this area which, by 1913, had reached 79 km in length. Regular passenger services were withdrawn in 1962 but since 1976 tourist trains have been running regularly between Znin and Gasawa. Znin can be reached by bus from Bydgoszcz.

A varied collection of narrow gauge rolling stock is situated adjacent to Wenecja Muzeum station, where trains arrive 10 - 15 minutes before the time shown. www.muzeumznin.pl

Trains run May 1 - Aug. 28, also during the Archeological Festival during September. Confirm timings locally.

				R	**S**				**S**	**R**	**R**
Znin........ d.	0900	1030	1205	1350	1440	Gasawa... d.	1030	1205	1345	1400	1530
Wenecja § d.	0940	1110	1250	1435	1525	Wenecja § d.	1110	1250	1435	1520	1620
Gasawa... a.	1015	1150	1330	1515	1610	Znin........ a.	1140	1320	1505	1550	1745

Other services: from Zinin 1535 ⑥⑦ July / Aug.
from Gasawa 1625 **R**, 1705 ⑥⑦ July / Aug.

R – ①–⑤ May / June, ⑥⑦ July / Aug. **S** – ⑥⑦ May / June, ①–⑤ July / Aug.
§ – Wenecja Muzeum.

CHABÓWKA AND JAWORZYNA ŚLĄSKA

The 'Skansen' at Chabówka is an extensive open air railway museum, located on the scenic Kraków - Zakopane line (Table **1066**). Steam trips normally run on several summer dates June - August from the Skansen to Kasina Wielka. www.parowozy.pl

Another railway museum is located at Jaworzyna Śląska on the Wroclaw - Jelenia Góra line (Table **1084**), open daily 1000 - 1600 Oct. - Apr. 1000 - 1800 May - Sept.. www.muzeumtechniki.pl

Polish EIP (Express InterCity Premium) *Pendolino* train

Photos in this Rail Extra feature are by
Brendan Fox - pages 653 - 655, 657, 658, 660 - 662
Graham Benbow - pages 656, 659, 663, 664

PORTUGAL

RAIL TRAVEL

See Tables **690 - 699**. Operator is Comboios de Portugal (CP) www.cp.pt Telephone enquiries (24 hours): ✆ 808 109 110.

The network is approximately 2,500 km, and as with Spain, trains run on tracks of 'Iberian' gauge, 1668 mm. Backbone of the network is the 337 km line between Lisboa and Porto, with the longest distance trains running all the way from Faro in the south to Porto in the north. The best trains are the modern *AP* (Alfa Pendular) trains, which along with *IC* and international trains require advance reservation. Lines in the north of the country are particularly scenic, especially the Duoro Valley line to Régua and Pocinho (see Table **694** and the tourist train below).

Lisboa's traditional terminus at Santa Apolónia was joined by an impressive through station in 1998 called Oriente, located 6 km north of the centre. Noted for its metal and glass roof, it is part of a major transport hub including metro and bus links. Trains to Cascais, however, leave from Cais do Sodre station, whilst Rossio is the city centre terminus for trains to Sintra (see city plan on page 32).

Another impressive feature of Lisbon's transport network is the *25 de Abril* bridge across the Tagus, to which railway tracks were added under the road in 1999, and which is sometimes compared to San Francisco's Golden Gate Bridge. As well as CP trains to the south, it carries local trains of private operator *Fertagus*.

The national railway museum is located at Entroncamento, open on ②–⑦ 10.00 to 18.00. www.fmnf.pt Access is from Rua Ferreira de Mesquita on the north side of the tracks across the footbridge. There are also several small regional railway museums.

COMBOIO HISTÓRICO

This steam hauled tourist train runs in summer on the scenic Douro line between Régua and Tua. Details of dates and timings can be found in Table **694**. The train is operated by CP at special fares.

ROMANIA

RAIL TRAVEL

See Tables **1600 - 1680**. State railway Căile Ferate Române (CFR) operates an extensive network of over 10,000 km, and trains of its passenger subsidiary CFR Călători link all major towns. www.cfrcalatori.ro Telephone information is available on ✆ 021 9521 for domestic traffic or ✆ 021 314 5528 for international services.

Most main lines are electrified and quite fast, but branch line services are very slow. Trains are fairly punctual and very cheap. Except for local trains, reserve and pay a speed supplement in advance (tickets issued abroad include the supplement). Cheapest are *regio* (very slow), then *Interregio*, and finally *IC* trains, whose prices approach Western levels. Food and drink is normally available only on *IC* and some *IR* trains. Couchette (*cuşeta*) or sleeper (*vagon de dormit*) accommodation is inexpensive. An increasing number of services are now operated by private operators, such as Regio Călători, Transferoviar Grup SA, and Softrans S.R.L.

VIŞEU DE SUS / MURAMUREŞ FOREST RAILWAY

Situated in the north of Romania, the Vaser Valley forest railway has been transporting wood to a processing plant in Vişeu de Sus since its opening in 1932, and claims to be the last European forestry railway. The 22 km narrow gauge railway also started running steam hauled tourist trains in the year 2000. Visitors can enjoy the remote mountain scenery during the very leisurely two hour journey from Vişeu de Sus along the winding valley to Paltin, where there is a break before the return journey.

Vişeu de Sus is situated 7 km from the CFR station at Vişeu de Jos (Table **1660**) and it can also be reached by bus from Baia Mare or Sighetu Marmatiei. The train runs on ④–⑦ Mar. 3 - Dec. 18, (daily May - Oct.) leaving Vişeu de Sus at 0900, arriving back at approximately 1500. www.mocanita-maramures.com

SERBIA

RAIL TRAVEL

See Tables **1360 - 1380**. The 3,300 km network is operated by Srbija Voz www.srbvoz.rs which is the passenger arm of the state railway company.

Both daytime and nightime international services link Beograd with Ljubljana, Zagreb and Budapest, whilst Sofia has one daytime train. There is also a night train on the lengthy run to Thessaloniki via Skopje, whilst travel to Timisoara in Romania involves trains of a more local nature, changing at Vršac. **All these services are currently suspended**

Scenic highlight, however, is the line from Beograd to neighbouring Montenegro, passing through its capital Podgorica before continuing to the coast at Bar. Opened as late as 1976, this winding 524 km line (Table **1370**) involves no fewer than 435 bridges and 254 tunnels!

There is an indoor railway museum in Beograd at 6 Nemanjina Street, open on Mondays to Fridays 0900-1500 hrs., and a narrow gauge section near Pozega station. For details see the *Museum* link: www.zeleznicesrbije.com

ŠARGANSKA OSMICA (ŠARGAN EIGHT)

Threading its way through the scenic Mokra Gora mountain region, close to the border with Bosnia, this line was originally part of a narrow gauge route between Beograd and Sarajevo which was closed in 1974. Between 1999 and 2003 the line was rebuilt as a tourist railway using diesel or steam traction. See *Museum trains* link: www.zeleznicesrbije.com

The 15.4 km narrow gauge (760 mm) line runs from Mokra Gora to Šargan Vitasi, passing through 22 tunnels and over five bridges. The nearest mainline ŽS station is Užice on the Beograd - Bar main line (Table **1370**). The 40 km journey from Užice to Mokra Gora can be made by bus or taxi.Trains run daily Apr. - Oct., departing Mokra Gora at 1030 and 1330. Total journey time for a return trip is approximately 2½ hours.

SLOVAKIA

RAIL TRAVEL

See Tables **1170 - 1197**. The national rail operator is Železničná spoločnosť (ŽSSK) www.slovakrail.sk. Track and infrastructure is managed by ŽSR www.zsr.sk. Call centre (24h) is ✆ 18 188, or from abroad ✆ +421 24 48 58 188.

An efficient network of 3,600 km is operated, with the fastest trains being the handful of *IC* trains on the principal route between Bratislava and Košice (Table **1180**). On the international Praha (Prague) to Košice route, the state railways compete for passengers with two other companies, Regiojet and Leo Express.

Trains are cheap, but often crowded. In fact most resident children, seniors and students qualify for free travel (except on *IC* trains or cross-border services) in a recently introduced scheme. Qualifying EU citizens may also be entitled to register for the scheme (especially children under 15 and seniors of 62 or over).

Apart from the small number of *EC* and *IC* trains, for which higher fares apply, the fastest trains are *expresný* (*Ex*) and *Rýchlik* (*R*, usually those with three-digit train numbers). Cheaper are *zrýchlený* (semi-fast) and *osobný* (very slow). Sleeping cars and couchettes are provided on most overnight trains (reserve at all main stations, well in advance in summer). Seat reservations may be made at station counters marked R, and are recommended for express trains.

The most scenic areas are close to the Tatra mountains, particularly the High Tatras (Vysoké Tatry) where a network of electrified narrow gauge lines is run by ŽSR subsidiary TEŽ (Table **1182**). Most lines in the centre of the country, radiating from Banská Bystrica, are also scenic, particularly the line following the River Hron (Table **1188**).

ČIERNOHRONSKÁ ŽELEZNICA — 2022 Service

After closure in 1982, enthusiasts eventually managed to save this narrow gauge (760 mm) forestry railway and transform it into a tourist railway. It is the last remaining section of a once extensive system in central Slovakia.

The line starts at Chvatimech, which is served by all trains between Banská Bystrica and Brezno (Table **1188**, eight minutes before Brezno). The first 7 km to Šánske is, however, currently being rebuilt. 5 km further on is Čierny Balog, the railway's headquarters, where the line continues 4 km to Dobroč, and there is also a 4 km branch to Vydrovo. www.chz.sk

Chvatimech - Šánske - currently no service.

Čierny Balog - Šánske: ⑥ Apr. 3 - June 30, Sept. 9 - Oct. 29; daily July 1 - Sept. 4. From Čierny Balog: 1000, 1200, 1500. From Šánske: 1030, 1230, 1530. Journey time 20 minutes; steam hauled in high-season.

Čierny Balog - Vydrovo Konečná: daily July 1 - Sept. 4. From Čierny Balog: 0930, 1030, 1130, 1300, 1400, 1500, 1600. From Vydrovo Konečná 0950, 1050, 1150, 1320, 1420, 1520, 1620. Journey time 20 - 25 minutes.

Čierny Balog - Dobroč: ⑥ Apr. 3 - June 30, Sept. 9 - Oct. 29; daily July 1 - Sept. 1. From Čierny Balog: 1100, 1400. From Dobroč: 1125, 1425. Journey time 20 minutes; steam hauled in high season.

DETSKÁ ŽELEZNICA KOŠICE

This short railway in Košice was completed in 1956 as one of the Pioneer Railways in the former Czechoslovakia. The line was built to allow children to learn how railways operate, so most of the railway's functions were performed by children. Some of the railway's rolling stock dates from as far back as 1884. www.detskazeleznica.sk

The 4.2 km narrow gauge line runs from Čermel' to Alpinka. Čermel' can be reached from the main station by tram 2 to Havlíčkova then bus 14.

Trains run on ⓒ Apr. to Oct. (daily in July and August) with between four and six journeys each way.

A long-distance train at Bratislava Hlavná Stanica (main station)

NATIONAL RAILWAY MUSEUM

This is located at Bratislava Vychod depot and is open daily Apr. 15 to Oct. 15 (1000-1700). Nearest station is Bratislava Rača, served by local trains on the line to Trnava, and 1.6 km from the museum. The website (www.mdc.sk) also has a list of special heritage trains running on the Slovak network on various dates throughout the year. A special annual *Rendez* event takes place at the museum in June.

There is also an indoor transport museum near Bratislava hlavná station at Šancová 1/A, closed on Mondays. www.muzeumdopravy.com.

SLOVENIA

RAIL TRAVEL

See Tables **1300 - 1320**. Slovenia's relatively small network of 1,200 km is operated by Slovenske Železnice (SŽ) www.slo-zeleznice.si. Telephone information is available from within Slovenia on ✆ 080 81 11.

Hub of the network is the capital Ljubljana. The best trains are the *IC* trains on the Maribor route, and the *EC* trains which continue beyond Maribor into Austria. Other international links include those to München, Budapest and Beograd, all with a choice of daytime or overnight timings, except that the night train to Budapest runs only in high summer.

LJUBLJANA RAILWAY MUSEUM

Ljubljana has a railway museum in a former roundhouse at Parmova 35, open daily except Mondays from 1000 to 1800.

Steam-hauled heritage trains normally run between Jesenice and Nova Gorica on the scenic Bohinj line, which could also be booked as part of a guided tour. Operating two to four times per month from May to October. **Unfortunately, trains will not be running during 2023.**

SPAIN

RAIL TRAVEL

See Tables **650 - 689**. National rail company is Red Nacional de los Ferrocarriles Españoles (RENFE) www.renfe.es. ✆ 912 320 320.

The opening of the Madrid - Sevilla high-speed line in 1992 was just the start of what is now Europe's longest high-speed network. Particularly important is the 620 km Madrid - Barcelona line, which also continues northwards into France, and which has taken a large market share away from the airlines. Another principal route runs from Madrid to Valencia and Alicante, and in fact travel to just about any area of Spain can benefit from a high-speed train for at least part of the way. Trains which run purely on these lines are classified *AVE* (Alta Velocidad Española). For other train categories see the introduction to the Spanish section on page 316.

The traditional network is built to the 'Iberian' track gauge of 1668 mm, whereas the new high-speed network is standard gauge (1435 mm). Trains which switch between the two networks, such as the *Altaria* and *Alvia* trains, therefore have to have gauge changing equipment.

Spain also has around 1,200 km of narrow gauge lines, built to metre gauge, and in the main these are in the hands of a separate division of RENFE known as FEVE. These are largely in coastal areas, and particularly interesting is the long and scenic narrow gauge line along the north coast of Spain (Table **687**), along with the associated Bilbao to León line (Table **683**). Several narrow gauge lines are run by other operators, such as Euskotren, FGC, and FGV.

Reservation is compulsory on all services for which a train category (*AVE*, *IC* etc) is shown in the timing columns of this timetable. RENFE attaches a high degree of importance to punctuality and has a comprehensive scheme of refunds if trains run late.

VALL DE NÚRIA

A 12.5 km rack railway operated by Ferrocarrils de la Generalitat de Catalunya (FGC) runs from Ribes Enllaç to Núria. The train climbs from 905m at Ribes to 1967m at Nuria and passes through some fine scenery. At one point the train is travelling above the narrow gorge of the River Nuria. Table **658** has the timings. www.valldenuria.cat

Ribes Enllaç station is adjacent to RENFE's Ribes de Freser station on the Barcelona to Latour de Carol line (Table **656**).

CERCEDILLA - COTOS MOUNTAIN RAILWAY

Apart from the FEVE network, RENFE has a narrow gauge line of its own. It runs from Cercedilla to Cotos and is actually part of Madrid's suburban network, allocated route number **C9**. The 18 km journey through the scenic *Sierra de Guadarrama* region takes around 45 minutes (25 minutes Cercedilla to Puerto de Navacerrada). This is excellent walking country and a number of marked routes are available at stations en-route.

Regular services (at least hourly) operate between central Madrid and Cercedilla (line **C8** - journey 80 minutes from Atocha or 70 mins from Chamartín). See www.renfe.com under the heading 'Cercanias' (sub-urban) then 'Madrid'.

Trains generally run from Cercedilla at 0935, 1035 ©, 1135, 1235 ©, 1335, 1535, 1735, returning from Cotos at 1043, 1143 ©, 1243, 1343 ©, 1443, 1643, 1843.

FERROCARRIL DE SÓLLER

Opened in 1912, the line from Mallorca's capital Palma to the northern town of Sóller is operated by historic electric traction and runs through the scenic *Sierra de Tramuntana* region. The 28 km line is built to the unusual gauge of 914mm (one yard).

From Sóller a narrow gauge tramway runs for 5 km to Port de Sóller. Further details of both lines are in Table **674**. www.trendesoller.com

A modern RENFE suburban train at Bilbao Abando station, previously known as Estación del Norte

SWEDEN

RAIL TRAVEL

See Tables **730 - 768**. National rail company is SJ AB www.sj.se. The company was formed when Statens Järnvägar (SJ) was split into different companies. Telephone enquiries: ✆ +46 771 75 75 75 (daily 0600-2200, but ticket purchase only available Mon-Fri 0800-1700).

The best services are operated by high-speed trains (*Snabbtåg*, shown as *Sn* in our tables) running at up to 200 km/h and using either X2000 trains or the newer SJ 3000 units. Supplements are required on *Snabbtåg*. Some local lines are run by regional authorities or private companies such as Norrtåg www.norrtag.se; see page 345 for other operators.

Sleeping-cars have one or two berths in 2nd class, couchettes have six berths; female-only compartments are available. 1st-class sleeping-cars with en-suite shower and WC run on many overnight services; 2nd-class compartments have washbasins, while a shower and WC are at the end of the carriage. Long-distance trains have a refreshment service. Many trains have a family coach with a playroom, and facilities for the disabled. Seat reservations are compulsory on *Sn*, *IC* and overnight trains, also on services operated by independent operators *Snälltåget*, *MTR Express* and *FlixTrain*. *Sn* services also operate between Sweden and Copenhagen via the Öresund bridge and tunnel but it is better to use the frequent local trains for short journeys.

'C' (for Central) in timetables etc. means the town's main station. *Biljetter* indicates the station ticket office, often with limited opening hours, but ticket machines are also widely in use.

Journeys north from Stockhom along the coast to Umeå and beyond have been revolutionised by the *Botniabanan* which opened in 2010. An interesting alternative route to the far north of Sweden, albeit much slower, is the privately operated *Inlandsbanan*, with a single train each way in summer taking all day for the 746 km journey between Östersund and Gälllivare (Table **766**).

UPPSALA - LENNA JERNVÄG — **2022 Service**

Starting at Uppsala (Tables **760 / 761**), head for tracks 9/10 at the Central station from where this narrow gauge heritage line runs for 33 km east to Faringe. The focal point of the railway is Marielund station, where trains often pass and steam trains refill their water tanks. A popular station café is also located there. The railway's collection of rollling stock is based at the Faringe engine sheds. Track gauge is 891mm (Swedish 'three foot'), unique to Sweden.

Trains run on ⑥ June 2 - Sept. 10, ⑦ June 26 - Sept. 11, and ③④ June 29 - Aug.10, also June 6. There are seven departures from Uppsala depending on the date, with some journeys hauled by steam. A round trip takes three to four hours. For timings see www.lennakatten.se

ÖSTRA SÖDERMANSLAND JÄRNVÄG — **2022 Service**

Mariefred - Läggesta - Taxinge is the route of this 11 km narrow gauge (600mm) museum line. Läggesta nedre station is a 500m walk from the SJ station in Table **732**, located west of Stockholm on the line to Eskilstuna. The narrow gauge line offers some great views of Lake Mälaren. Starting on the north side of the lake at Mariefred, trains reverse at Läggesta nedre with several services continuing along the south shore to Taxinge.

On summer weekends it is possible to cross the lake by steamer between Mariefred and Taxinge (round trip fares are available), giving an ideal day out from Stockholm.

Trains run ⑥⑦ July and August (with additional midweek services) with several trains each day. Timings, including boat schedules and connections from Stockholm, can be found at www.oslj.nu

SWITZERLAND

RAIL TRAVEL

See Tables **501 - 578**. The principal rail carrier is Swiss Federal Railways (SBB / CFF / FFS) www.sbb.ch. A 24 hour premium rate helpline is available on ✆ 0848 44 66 88 (German, French, Italian, English spoken).

As might be expected, there are a large number of scenic routes and mountain lines, with endless possibilities for exciting days out. Rail travel can often be combined with other modes such as lake steamers, buses, funicular railways and even cable cars to complete a round trip. Several examples are given on the official tourism site www.myswitzerland.com.

The Swiss rail system is characterised by the large number of rail operators other than SBB. Many of these are narrow gauge, notably the Rhätische Bahn (RhB), which has a large network in the south-east, and the Matterhorn-Gotthard-Bahn (MGB) in the south-west. Together these two railways provide the famous *Glacier Express* running for 290 km from St Moritz to Zermatt (Table **575**). This requires a supplement and advance reservation, but of course the exact same lines can also be traversed with a series of local trains (Tables **576** and **545**).

Other services very popular with tourists include the *Bernina Express* from Chur to Tirano, just across the border in Italy (Table **545**), MOB's *Golden Pass* trains from Montreux to Zweizimmen, some of which have panorama cars (Table **566**), and Zentralbahn's Luzern to Interlaken route with its many lakeside views (Table **561**). Some other highlights are mentioned below, but there are many more. The Swiss rail network is, of course, synonymous with punctuality and spotlessly clean trains.

CHEMIN DE FER - MUSÉE BLONAY - CHAMBY (BC)

Situated in the south-west corner of Switzerland close to Lake Geneva, this narrow gauge railway museum has an extensive collection of rolling stock. Trains run from Blonay to Chamby (3 km) before changing direction to reach the nearby Chaulin museum. Trains leaving the museum return to Blonay. Both steam and electric trains are operated. Passengers are treated to fine views over Lake Geneva during the short journey. Rail connections are available at both Blonay (regular trains from Vevey) and Chamby (Table **566**). www.blonay-chamby.ch

Trains run on ⑥⑦ May 6 - Oct. 29 (also May 29).

		b	a		🚂		🚂		a	🚂
Blonay .... d.	1010	1110	1120	1210	1410	1445	1525	1610	1655	1710
Chamby .... d.	1026	1126	|	1226	1428	1500	1545	1626	|	1726
Chaulin-Musée .... a.	1030	1130	1135	1230	1432	1507	1549	1630	1710	1730
	b		🚂		🚂	a		🚂		
Chaulin-Musée .... d.	1040	1140	1340	1425	1500	1510	1540	1640	...	1750
Blonay .... a.	1055	1155	1355	1440	1515	1525	1555	1655	...	1805

a – Last Sunday of the month June - Sept. **b** – 🚂 on ⑦. 🚂 – Steam train.

BRIENZ ROTHORN BAHN (BRB)

Within easy reach of Interlaken by rail (Table **561**) or boat (Table **508**), this narrow gauge (800mm) mountain rack railway from Brienz can claim the unusual fact that its lowest and highest stations have the greatest height difference of any railway in Switzerland. With stunning views, the distance to the summit at Rothorn (2244m) is 7.6 km, and the journey takes about one hour. Built in 1892, an added attraction is that most trips are steam operated, since it is one of the very few non-electrified routes in Switzerland. Trains run from June to October and timings are shown in Table **553**. www.brienz-rothorn-bahn.ch

DAMPFBAHN FURKA-BERGSTRECKE (DFB)

This tortuous narrow gauge mountain route is the original main line over the Furkapass which was closed in 1982 following the opening of the Furka base tunnel. Since 1992 the line has reopened in stages as a spectacular tourist route, the final section between Gletsch and Oberwald being completed in 2010. Steam-hauled journeys over the full 18 km route from Realp to Oberwald via Furka take over two hours (reservation is compulsory), whilst shorter diesel hauled journeys are available between Oberwald and Gletsch taking 25 minutes. Itineraries are also available using both steam and diesel services with a break of journey at Gletsch, near to the Rhone Glacier.

Trains run ④–⑦ June 29 - Sept. 24.

For timings and reservations see www.dfb.ch. Both ends of the route can be reached by means of the hourly MGB trains between Brig and Andermatt in Table **576**. In Realp the DFB station is a 10 minute walk from the MGB station.

RIGI-BAHNEN (RB)

There are two electrified rack railways to the Rigi-Kulm summit (1750m), an 8.5 km line from Arth Goldau on the Gotthard main line, and a 7 km line from Vitznau by the lake. Opening in 1871, the latter was Europe's first rack railway, and is the more scenic of the two routes. The lines are also notable for being the highest standard gauge railway in Europe. At the summit, one of the finest Swiss panoramas, overlooking the *Vierwaldstättersee*, awaits the visitor. www.rigi.ch

Trains run hourly all year on both routes, but evening services run only in summer; timings are shown in Table **553**.

Arth-Goldau, where the RB station is adjacent to the main line station, can be reached by means of rail services in Tables **525** and **550**. In Vitznau the station is by the quayside (lake steamer services: Table **507**).

PILATUS BAHN (PB)

The world's steepest rack railway runs from Alpnachstad, south-west of Lake Luzern, to the mountain's summit at Pilatus Kulm, a distance of 4.6 km, reaching a height of 2070m. The 800mm gauge line was first opened in 1889 and uses an unusual rack system with teeth on either side of a horizontal rail. The line has been electrified since the 1930s.

Alpnachstad is 13 km from Luzern on the line to Interlaken (Table **561**). A popular excursion from Luzern is to take the train or boat to Alpnachstad, rack railway to Pilatus Kulm, cable-car and gondolas down to Kriens, then trolleybus route **1** back to central Luzern.

The Pilatus Bahn runs early-May to mid-November; there is no winter service - see Table **553** for timings. www.pilatus.ch

JUNGFRAUBAHNEN (JB)

Reached from Interlaken by two different routes (Table **564**), Kleine Scheidegg is the start point for the Jungfraubahn, which burrows through the Mönch and the Eiger to reach Europe's highest station at Jungfraujoch (3454m). The 9.3 km electrified narrow gauge rack railway is mostly in tunnel but stops twice on the way up at Eigerwand and Eismeer from where there are spectacular views through windows incorporated into the mountain side. On a clear day the views from the summit are breathtaking. Visitors are strongly advised to check weather conditions at the summit before travelling. The Eiger Express was launched in December 2020 enabling a 47 minute quicker trip to the summit. www.jungfrau.ch

The line runs all year, every 30 minutes, but may sometimes be affected by snowfall in winter. The journey takes 35 minutes. See Table **564** for timings.

GORNERGRAT BAHN (GGB)

Starting from Zermatt, western terminus of the famous *Glacier Express* (Table **575**, also local services in Table **576**), the Gornergratbahn runs for 9.4 km to the summit at 3089m. Gornergrat is the highest open-air station in Europe, since the higher Jungfraujoch station described above is actually situated inside the mountain! www.gornergratbahn.ch

The journey on this electrified narrow gauge rack railway takes 33 minutes (44 downhill) and initially provides a birds-eye view of Zermatt followed by fine views of the Matterhorn. From Zermatt sit on the right-hand side for the best views. The GGB station at Zermatt is close to the MGB station, at right angles to it. The service runs all year; see Table **578** for timings.

SWISS MUSEUM OF TRANSPORT

Known as the Verkehrshaus, the museum is located eight minutes by local train from Luzern station (route S3 to the Verkehrshaus stop), and can also be reached by bus or boat. It is open daily. www.verkehrshaus.ch

TURKEY

RAIL TRAVEL

See Tables **1570 - 1590** (also **1550 / 60** for European Turkey). Operator is TCDD (Turkish State Railways) www.tcdd.gov.tr. The principal Istanbul - Ankara route has been revolutionised in recent years by the opening of a new high-speed line via Eskişehir, with another high-speed section linking these cities with Konya. Further lines are under construction to Karaman, and Ankara to Sivas / İzmir. Traditional routes are tortuous and slow, but the coaching stock is generally comfortable.

The Marmaray Tunnel under the Bosphorus opened in 2013, joining the Asian and European parts of Istanbul by local rail service for the first time. Following a period when the high-speed trains from Istanbul to Ankara were starting from Pendik in the suburbs, these trains now use the more centrally located Söğütlüçeşme station, with certain trains starting from Halkali on the European side and using the tunnel (Table **1570**). The neoclassical pseudo-castle Haydarpasa station building on the Asian side of the Bosphorus is sadly out of use but is being restored.

UKRAINE

RAIL TRAVEL

See Tables **1700 - 1790**, which also include neighbouring Moldova. Ukrainian Railways goes under the initials UZ. www.uz.gov.ua

This vast 1520mm gauge railway network links all major towns and many small ones, and the introduction of modern diesel multiple units in recent years has seen a new *InterCity* category of train, giving fast links on key routes. The most scenic routes are in the south west of the country.

Determined railfans may find the remaining narrow gauge lines of interest, although services are sparse, time consuming to access, and information scarse. One of the lines, that between Rudnytsia and Holovanivs'k, is actually Europe's longest 750mm gauge line at 130 km, but its future is far from certain.

Owing to the ongoing conflict in Ukraine, all rail services are subject to change at short notice. Readers are advised to consult the latest official advice regarding travel to Ukraine.

150 years from Cook's Continental Time Tables & Tourist's Hand Book to European Rail Timetable

Thomas Cook - The Early Years

Thomas Cook (1808-92) is widely regarded as the founder of popular tourism. In the middle years of the nineteenth century, a period when only the wealthy travelled for pleasure, he began to organise excursions for the workers of the industrial English Midlands. A former Baptist preacher, Thomas believed that the newly-developed railways should be used to provide 'rational recreation' for the masses. His aim was to popularise travel by making it cheaper, easier and safer.

Thomas conducted his first excursion, a 12-mile rail journey from Leicester to a temperance gala in Loughborough, on Monday 5th July 1841. Some 500 passengers each paid one shilling for the experience. The day was a great success and Thomas was soon being asked to organise similar outings for other local temperance societies and Sunday schools. As a result of these trips, several thousand people experienced rail travel for the first time and Thomas was able to lay the foundations of his future business.

Thomas Cook's first commercial venture took place in the summer of 1845, when he organised a special trip to Liverpool and north Wales. This was a far more ambitious project than anything he had previously attempted, and he made his preparations with great thoroughness. Not content with simply providing tickets at low prices, he also investigated the route and published a handbook of the journey. The following year Thomas conducted his first trip to Scotland, and during the next two decades he introduced more than 50,000 visitors to the Scottish Highlands. It was in Scotland that Thomas first developed his system of circular tourist tickets, and it was Scotland that transformed him from a conductor of cheap excursions into a professional tour manager.

Thomas continued to expand his business in Britain, but he was determined to develop it in Europe too. In 1855 an International Exhibition was held in Paris for the first time and Thomas seized this opportunity by trying to persuade the companies commanding the Channel traffic to allow him concessions. They refused to work with him, however, and the only available crossing was that between Harwich and Antwerp. This opened up the way for a grand circular tour to include Brussels, Cologne, the Rhine, Heidelberg, Baden-Baden, Strasbourg and Paris. By this route, during the summer of 1855, Thomas escorted his first tourists to Europe.

Thomas visited Switzerland for the first time in June 1863. Although this initial tour was little more than an information-gathering trip, a party of more than 60 ladies and gentlemen accompanied Thomas as far as Geneva. Further trips to the Continent quickly followed and, with the co-operation of the Paris, Lyons and Mediterranean Railway, Thomas was soon issuing circular tickets (in both English and French) between Paris and the Alps. He also established a number of circular tours within Switzerland, which were such an immediate success that he decided to extend his arrangements across the Alps. The first Italian tours took place during the summer of 1864.

To cope with the increasing number of tourists who wished to visit the Continent, Thomas Cook opened an office in London - at 98 Fleet Street - in April 1865. This was Thomas Cook's first high street shop and it was to be managed by his son, John Mason Cook, who had joined the family business only a few months before. At this point in the company's history, there were just five members of staff - Thomas, John, two assistants and a messenger boy!

With his son now running the office, Thomas Cook was free to *'carry out foreign schemes of long projection'*. He made an exploratory trip to North America in November 1865 and set up a system of tours covering 4000 miles of railways. Four years later, in 1869, he escorted his first tourists up the Nile and around the Holy Land. The climax of his career, however, came in September 1872 when, at the age of 63, he departed from Liverpool on a tour of the world that would keep him away from home for almost eight months. It had long been his ambition to travel *'to Egypt via China'*, but such a trip only became practicable at the end of 1869 following the opening of the Suez Canal and the completion of a rail network linking the east and west coasts of America.

Contrary to popular belief, the majority of Thomas Cook's (now mostly middle-class) tourists in the 1860s and 1870s did not travel in conducted parties. Instead, they used Cook's circular tickets (available in hundreds of combinations) to map out their own itineraries. To assist these independent travellers, particularly on the Continent, Thomas Cook developed two important travel systems: one was his *hotel coupon*, launched in 1868, which enabled travellers to purchase accommodation and meals at a fixed price prior to departure; the other was his *circular note*, a forerunner of the traveller's cheque, first issued by Thomas Cook in 1874 (though used by bankers since the late eighteenth century), which provided a safe and effective way of obtaining foreign currency. In March 1873 Thomas Cook also published the first edition of his *Continental Time Tables & Tourist's Hand Book - a 'cheap, concise and simple guide to all the principal lines of railway, steamers and diligences on the continent of Europe'* - and began to issue his own guidebooks in the following year.

While his father was travelling around the world, John Mason Cook successfully completed the firm's move to a new head office at Ludgate Circus in the City of London. This building quickly became the hub of Thomas Cook & Son's operations and it was from here that John, who took over the management of the firm in 1879, set about developing the business from its barely profitable foundations into a successful global force. John was a much better businessman than his father and he realised that he could only attract wealthy clients (and therefore bigger profits) by investing the name of Thomas Cook & Son with social prestige. Consequently, during the 1880s and 1890s, he transformed the business from a retail trade, in which travel was packaged and sold over the counter, into a professional service for eminent Victorians.

Thomas and John Mason Cook both died during the 1890s and the business was inherited by John's three sons: Frank Henry, Ernest Edward and Thomas Albert ('Bert'). During the first quarter of the twentieth century - a period which saw the introduction of winter sports holidays, tours by motor car and commercial air travel - the firm of Thomas Cook & Son dominated the world travel scene. The company was incorporated as Thos Cook & Son Ltd in 1924, and two years later its headquarters moved from Ludgate Circus to Berkeley Street in Mayfair, a once aristocratic area that was now the centre of London society. In 1928 the surviving grandsons, Frank and Ernest (Bert having died in 1914), unexpectedly sold the firm to the Belgian *Compagnie Internationale des Wagons-Lits et des Grands Express Européens*, operators of most of Europe's luxury sleeping cars, including the Orient Express, and the Cook family's involvement with the travel business came to an end.

FIRST EDITION

The idea for *Cook's Continental Time Tables* was that of an employee, John Bredall, who later became Company Secretary. *Bradshaw's Continental Guide* had started in 1847, but it attempted to be comprehensive and had become a very large volume of over 1000 pages. Mr Bredall's proposal was for a slimmer volume, described in the early issues as "a Cheap, Concise and Simple Guide to All the Principal Lines of Railway, Steamers and Diligences on the Continent of Europe", and he was given the job of bringing the idea to fruition. The principle of carefully selecting those stations and trains which are of most use to readers has remained with us to the present day.

The first edition appeared in March 1873 and, although carrying a price of one shilling, was "merely issued for the purpose of being freely distributed to Railway Officials and others interested in such publications, for their corrections and revision, and for the purpose of soliciting Advertisements." Regular publication commenced with the June 1873 edition and continued four times per year, becoming monthly from January 1883. John Bredall continued as Editor and, having been paid £25 for the first edition (a large sum for those days), thereafter received one penny for every copy sold.

The first edition ran to 150 pages but the timetable grew as the railway network expanded, and it doubled in size in twenty years. Despite this it was still published at one shilling. Initially it was printed in the basement of Thomas Cook's Chief Office in Ludgate Circus, Fleet Street, but from 1896 the job was put out to Thomas Forman of Nottingham. The original 1873 cover design was replaced in 1900 by a new one featuring a lake steamer, a post chaise, a Gotthard Express train and an ocean liner.

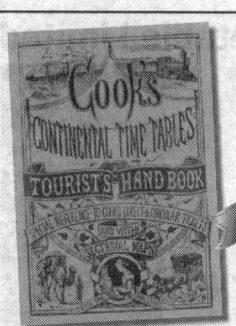

John Bredall retired in 1914 and was succeeded as Editor by C.H. Davies. The new editor kept the timetable going during the 1914-18 war, largely as a world shipping guide. During this period there was a note to the effect that the services shown for Belgium, Germany, Austria, Russia, the Balkans and Turkey were those in force prior to the war.

24-HOUR CLOCK

In December 1919 the timetable received a major facelift and, for the first time, the 24-hour system was adopted. There was a new cover featuring a 24-hour clockface, and the price jumped from one shilling to two shillings and sixpence. Mr. Davies continued as Editor until 1939, although he also became the Company's Traffic Manager from 1937, and much of the timetable work was handled by his assistant, H. V. Francis. Other members of staff took on different geographical sections of the book and maintained them, largely in their own time, for a fixed annual fee. Air services began to be shown during this period, filling all of eleven pages by 1939, although this feature was not reinstated after the war. By this time the *Continental Bradshaw* had also slimmed down to a pocket-sized publication, and was also using the 24-hour clock, so competition was keenly felt.

POST-WAR REINTRODUCTION

Following publication of the August 1939 edition, publication was suspended for the duration of the war. Many Thomas Cook staff served in the Royal Engineers Movement Control during this time, some being involved in compiling military train timetables. The decision to resume publication was taken in May 1945, but the first postwar edition did not appear until July 1946, and the first four issues were not sold to the general public, being intended for staff use only.

An entirely new format was adopted at this time by H. V. Francis, who now became the timetable's first full-time Editor. Table numbers were introduced, countries were arranged in a more logical order, and the standard international timetable symbols (agreed by the International Union of Railways in 1930) were used, along with a clearer typeface. Most of the ocean steamer tables were transferred to *Cook's Ocean Sailing List*, and the air services were discontinued, leaving this function to *Bradshaw's Air Guide*, which had started in 1934.

Sales of the timetable after the war were certainly aided by the fact that Henry Blacklock & Co. decided against restarting the Continental Bradshaw. One reason given was that this guide had depended for much of its revenue on advertising by Continental hotels, which was now severely affected by postwar exchange control regulations. Another factor may have been the relatively quick resumption of the Cook's timetable, sales of which soon doubled over the prewar figure.

In November 1952, Mr. Francis became a member of the Thomas Cook management and a new editor was appointed, Mr J.H. Price, a name which was to be synonymous with the timetable for more than 35 years. John Price had joined the Company in 1948 and had worked in the department concerned with fares and documentation, before joining the timetable staff in June 1950. At this period, the timetable section was part of the Publicity Department, headed by Mr. W.D.C. Cormack.

DESIGN AND CONTENT CHANGES

Printing costs were rising and in 1954 the job was moved to Albert Gait Ltd of Grimsby, who were already printing the Thomas Cook *Ocean Sailing Lists*, and in fact had an association with Cook's dating back to the 1860s when they began to print the famous hotel coupons. The change of typesetter and printer gave an opportunity for other major changes at the same time. The 37 or so pages of British Railways tables were discontinued, achieving a further cost saving. These highly summarised tables were unusual in that they had been compiled for Thomas Cook by British Railways, and were still in the 12-hour clock. Secondly, the engraved foldout geographical maps supplied since 1873 by W. & A. K. Johnston were replaced. These maps were partly in colour, and being hand inserted, were expensive to produce. The diagrammatic maps which replaced them showed table numbers and could therefore be used as an alternative to the index, making the timetable much easier to use. The change from a seriffed typeface (Times Roman) to Gill, a sans-serif font, also helped in this respect.

In 1956 a summary of the forthcoming summer changes began to appear in Spring issues, and in Autumn editions for the winter changes, which at that time occured in October. Advance versions of international tables appeared on a regular basis from 1958 in the form of the Summer and Winter Supplements at the back of the timetable.

January 1970 saw the reintroduction of tables for Great Britain, together with a new section for Ireland. In 1973 the USA operator Amtrak appointed Thomas Cook to be its general agent for Europe and decided to pay to have its services shown in the Continental Timetable. These appeared from 1974 and were joined in 1976 by the timetables of Canadian National. Following requests for other countries, 80 pages were added in 1977, the title changing to *International Timetable* until January 1981 when the non-European tables were transferred to a separate *Overseas Timetable*, which was published every two months. This continued until the end of 2010, now replaced by the monthly *Beyond Europe* sections.

In 1985 Brendan Fox was appointed Editor (having joined as Assistant Editor three years earlier) which allowed John Price to widen his responsibilities for a period leading up to retirement. In 1988 the *Continental Timetable* was renamed the *European Timetable*, with a further name change to *European Rail Timetable* from 2005. Albert Gait, continued to print the timetable until October 1998, after which a series of changes occured. Pindar of Preston took over the printing contract for a short period from November 1998 to April 2002, but Albert Gait regained the contract from May 2002 to January 2005. William Clowes of Beccles (CPI Group, UK, Ltd.) became the timetable's printer from February 2005 and continues in that role to the present day.

A NEW ERA

The final edition produced by Thomas Cook was in August 2013, shortly after celebrating the timetable's 140th anniversary in March 2013. John Potter, an experienced compiler who joined the Thomas Cook team in 1998, was determined to continue production after Thomas Cook had made the decision to close its publishing business. John, together with the help of a team of former Thomas Cook employees, successfully produced the first rebranded European Rail Timetable in March 2014. Chris Woodcock, who has worked on the timetable since 1999, was appointed Editor, remarkably only the sixth person to hold that title since 1873. The timetable's previous Editor, Brendan Fox, provided essential help and advice as the new company was established (and continued to compile sections of the timetable until his retirement in December 2019).

The first edition of the rebranded European Rail Timetable hot off the press in February 2014. From left to right: Chris Woodcock (Editor), John Potter (Director and Editor-in-Chief), Peter Bass (former Beyond Europe Editor).

The long-standing aim of producing a digital version was finally achieved in May 2016. Later the same year, due to increasing printing and distribution costs, a decision was made to reduce the frequency of the printed version of the timetable to bi-monthly. However, production of the digital version was able to continue on a monthly basis due to the much lower production costs of this format.

The start of the global coronavirus pandemic early in 2020, followed by the rapid implementation of severe travel restrictions meant the timetable faced a major existential threat. With all but essential travel mostly prohibited for a number of months, the rare decision was made to cancel some editions (three months from May to July 2020, and a further three months from January to March 2021). However, with the help of a government funded employment support scheme, the company managed to navigate its way through the worst of the pandemic. To help alleviate growing financial pressures, production of the printed version of the timetable was reduced to four seasonal editions per year from Summer 2020. Monthly digital editions resumed from April 2021.

Despite having to deal with spiralling production costs during 2022 the timetable continues to provide detailed timings of services across Europe and beyond, just as the pioneering first edition did exactly 150 years ago. We are so pleased to be able to celebrate the 150th Anniversary of this historic publication with this, the Spring 2023 edition.

Of course, the timetable would not exist if it wasn't for our loyal customers. We would, therefore, like to take this opportunity to thank each and every one of you for your continued support and we hope to be able to continue production for many years to come.

10 (Summer) LONDON - LILLE - PARIS and BRUSSELS *by Eurostar*

Special fares payable that include three classes of service: business premier, standard premier and standard. All times shown are local times (France and Belgium are one hour ahead of Gre Britain). All Eurostar services are 🅁, non-smoking and convey ✕ in Business Premier and Standard Premier, 🍸 in Standard.
See shaded panel in Table **10** on page 47 for information about recommended arrival times at departure station.

Service May 21 - July 29.
For service February 5 - March 25 see page 47. For service March 26 - May 20 see page 48

km	km	*train number*	9080	9106	9002	9004	9110	9008	9114	9010	9116	9014	9018	9022	9126	9024	9132	9028	9032	9142
		notes	①–⑤	①–⑤	⑥	①–⑤	⑥			⑥								①–⑥		
		notes	H	AH		H		C	A		C	C			A			H		
0	*0*	**London** St Pancras........... d.	0601	0616	0631	0701	0704	0801	0816	0831	0855	0931	1026	1131	1104	1231	1301	1331	1431	1504
35	*35*	Ebbsfleet International .... d.																		
90	*90*	Ashford International.......... d.																		
166	*166*	Calais Fréthun..................... a.																		
267	*267*	Lille Europe .... a.					0926				1127				1326		1527			1726
	373	**Brussels** Midi / Zuid .... a.		0912			1005		1112		1205				1405		1606			1805
492		**Paris** Nord .... a.	0920	...	0947	1017	...	1120	...	1147	...	1247	1347	1447	...	1547	...	1647	1747	...

train number	9036	9038	9040	9044	9046	9046	9152	9152	9048	9050	9152	9158	9054							
notes		⑤⑦			①②③④⑥⑦	⑤		⑤	①–⑤	Ⓑ										
notes		D					AB	A	H		AF									
London St Pancras............ d.	1531	1601	1631	1731	1756	1801	1804	1813	1831	1901	1904	1934	2001	...	...	...	...	...	...	...
Ebbsfleet International .... d.														...	...	...	...	...	...	...
Ashford International............ d.														...	...	...	...	...	...	...
Calais Fréthun .... a.														...	...	...	...	...	...	...
Lille Europe .... a.							2030				2130	2200		...	...	...	...	...	...	...
Brussels Midi / Zuid......... a.							2112	2112			2212	2238		...	...	...	...	...	...	...
Paris Nord......................... a.	1850	1920	1947	2047	2117	2117	...	...	2147	2217	...	...	2317	...	...	...	...	...	...	...

train number	9007	9009	9011	9117	9013	9015	9117	9119	9019	9023	9135	9027	9031	9033	9035	9141	9037	9039	9145	9043
notes	①–⑥	①–⑤	⑥⑦		①–⑤			①–⑥						⑦	⑥		Ⓑ		Ⓑ	
notes	H	H	D	C	H		G	AH						D					A	
Paris Nord......................... d.	0713	0743	0813	...	0843	0913	...	...	1013	1113	...	1213	1313	1343	1413	...	1443	1513	...	1613
Brussels Midi / Zuid......... d.				0852			0952	0951			1256					1452			1556	
Lille Europe .... d.				0930			1030				1335					1530			1635	
Calais Fréthun .... d.																				
Ashford International........... a.																				
Ebbsfleet International .... a.																				
London St Pancras............ a.	0830	0900	0930	0957	1000	1030	1100	1100	1130	1230	1357	1330	1430	1500	1530	1600	1602	1630	1657	1730

train number	9047	9153	9051	9157	9055	9059	9163	9167	9063											
notes			Ⓑ				⑥	Ⓑ	Ⓑ											
notes				AC				A												
Paris Nord......................... d.	1713	...	1813	...	1913	2013	...	...	2113	...	...	...	...	...	...	...	...	...	...	...
Brussels Midi / Zuid......... d.		1756		1851			2020	2056		...	...	...	...	...	...	...	...	...	...	...
Lille Europe .... d.		1835					2058	2135		...	...	...	...	...	...	...	...	...	...	...
Calais Fréthun .... d.										...	...	...	...	...	...	...	...	...	...	...
Ashford International........... a.										...	...	...	...	...	...	...	...	...	...	...
Ebbsfleet International .... a.										...	...	...	...	...	...	...	...	...	...	...
London St Pancras............ a.	1832	1857	1930	2000	2030	2133	2127	2157	2230	...	...	...	...	...	...	...	...	...	...	...

A – To / from Amsterdam, see Table **18**. C – Not June 18. D – Also May 29. F – May 29. G – June 18. H – Not May 29.
B – ①②③④⑦ (not May 29).

DORTMUND - KÖLN - FRANKFURT - WIEN - BUDAPEST 66 (Summer)

train type	*ICE*	*ICE*	*ICE*	*ICE*	*EN*	*ICE*	*ICE*	*NJ*	*RJX*	
train number	**21**	**23**	**91**	**27**	**347**	**29**	**229**	**40421**	**269**	
notes					**D** [R]			**A**		
ortmund Hbf ... d.	...	0431	0629	0829	...	1029	1229	...	...	...
üsseldorf Hbf ... d.	...	0524	⊙	0924	...	1124	⊙	2143	...	...
öln Hbf ... d.	...	0553	0753	0953	...	1153	1353	2216	...	...
onn Hbf ... d.	...	0614	0814	1014	...	1214	1414	2311	...	...
oblenz Hbf ... d.	...	0648	0848	1048	...	1248	1448	2346	...	...
ainz Hbf ... d.	...	0740	0942	1142	...	1342	1542	0056	...	...
rankfurt Flug. ✈ ... d.	...	0801	1001	1201	...	1401	1601	0120	...	...
rankfurt (M) Hbf ... d.	0621	0822	1022	1222	...	1421	1621	0131f	...	...
ürzburg Hbf ... d.	0735	0934	1134	1335	...	1535	1735	0242	...	...
ürnberg Hbf ... d.	0831	1031	1231	1431	...	1631	1831	0408	...	...
egensburg Hbf ... d.	0926	1126	1326	1526	...	1726	1926	0505	...	...
assau Hbf 🛃 ... d.	1026	1229	1429	1629	...	1829	2031	0613	...	...
nz ... a.	1126	1326	1526	1726	...	1926	2134	0746	...	...
ien Hbf ... a.	1247	1447	1647	1847	...	2047	2305	0919	...	...
	RJX	*RJX*	*RJX*			*RJX*				
	63	**65**	**67**			**261**				
ien Hbf ... d.	1340	1542	1740	...	1942	2140	...	...	0942	...
egyeshalom 🛃 ... a.	1425	1625	1825	...	2025	2225	...	...	1025	...
udapest Keleti ... a.	1619	1819	2019	...	2220	0019	...	...	1219	...

train type	*ICE*	*EN*	*RJX*	*RJX*	*ICE*	*RJX*	*RJX*	*EC*	*NJ*	
train number	**228**	**346**	**60**	**62**	**90**	**64**	**66**	**148**	**40490**	
notes		**D** [R]						**S**	**A**	
Budapest Keleti ... d.	...	0540	0740	0940	...	1140	1340	1640	...	...
Hegyeshalom 🛃 ... d.	...	0732	0932	1132	...	1332	1532	1832	...	...
Wien Hbf ... a.	...	0821	1021	1221	...	1421	1621	1921	...	...
		ICE	*ICE*	*ICE*		*ICE*	*ICE*			
		28	**26**	**90**		**22**	**20**			
Wien Hbf ... d.	0651	0913	1113	1313	1313	1513	1713	...	2013	...
Linz ... d.	0817	1034	1234	1434	1434	1634	1834	...	2136	...
Passau Hbf 🛃 ... a.	0922	1131	1331	1531	1531	1731	1934	...	2235	...
Regensburg Hbf ... a.	1030	1233	1433	1633	1633	1833	2033	...	2354	...
Nürnberg Hbf ... a.	1127	1327	1528	1729	1729	1928	2128	...	0056	...
Würzburg Hbf ... a.	1222	1422	1622	1823	1823	2022	2222	...	|	...
Frankfurt (M) Hbf ... a.	1336	1536	1736	1936	1936	2136	2337	...	0345f	...
Frankfurt Flug. ✈ ... a.	1355	1555	1755	1955	1955	2156	...	...	0356	...
Mainz Hbf ... a.	1418	1618	1818	2018	2018	2218	...	...	0416	...
Koblenz Hbf ... a.	1511	1711	1911	2111	2111	2311	...	...	0511	...
Bonn Hbf ... a.	1543	1743	1943	2143	2143	2343	...	...	0558	...
Köln Hbf ... a.	1605	1805	2005	2205	2205	0005	...	...	0651	...
Düsseldorf Hbf ... a.	⊙	1832	2031	⊙	⊙	0034	...	...	0723	...
Dortmund Hbf ... a.	1721	1922	2121	2321	2321	0125	...	...	...	...

– *ÖBB nightjet* 🛏 1, 2 cl., ▬ 2 cl. (4, 6 berth), [2] Amsterdam - Düsseldorf - Wien and v.v. ♣ (Table **53**).
– DACIA – 🛏 1, 2 cl., ▬ 2 cl., [2] ✕ Wien - Budapest - Bucureşti and v.v.
– SEMMELWEIS – [12] Budapest - Wien.

– Frankfurt (Main) **Süd**.

RJ – ÖBB *Railjet* service. [1] (business class), [1] (first class), [2] (economy class), ✕.
⊙ – Via Hagen, Wuppertal (Table **800**).
♣ – Special fares apply.

MÜNCHEN - INNSBRUCK - VENEZIA and MILANO 70 (Summer)

	EC	*EC*	*EC*	*FR*	*EC*		*FR*	*FR*	*EC*	*EC*	*FA*	*EC*	*FR*	*FR*	*EC*	*FR*	*EC*	*EC*		*NJ*	*NJ*	*NJ*		*NJ*	
	1281	**81**	**37**	**9732**	**83**		**9738**	**9439**	**85**	**42**	**8525**	**87**	**9751**	**9756**	**89**	**9759**	**287**	**289**		**295**	**295**	**40295**		**237**	
	♥	♥	[R]	[R]	♥		[R]	**9441**	♥	[R]	[R]	♥	[R]	[R]	♥	[R]	♥	♥							
	⑥⑦	①–⑤	⊗	⚡	**P**	2	⚡	[R] ⚡		⊗	⚡		⚡	⚡		⚡				**B**	**J**	**D**		**C**	
			🍷	🍷			🍷	🍷		🍷	🍷		🍷	🍷		🍷				🍷	🍷	🍷		🍷	
uttgart Hbf ... d.	...	...	...	...	...	...	...	...	...	...	...	...	...	...	...	...	...	...	...	...	...	...	...	2029	...
ünchen Hbf ... d.	0734	0734	...	...	0934	...	...	...	1132	...	...	1334	...	...	1534	...	1734	1934	...	2009	2009	2009	...	|	...
ünchen Ost ... d.	0744	0744	...	...	0944	...	...	...	1144	...	...	1344	...	...	1544	...	1744	1944	...	2020	2020	2020	...	2354	...
ufstein 🛃 ... a.	0834	0834	...	...	1034	...	...	...	1234	...	...	1434	...	...	1634	...	1834	2034	...	|	|	|	...	|	...
örgl ... a.	0844	0844	...	...	1044	...	...	...	1244	...	...	1444	...	...	1644	...	1844	2044	...	|	|	|	...	|	...
enbach ... a.	0858	0858	...	...	1058	...	...	...	1258	...	...	1458	...	...	1658	...	1858	2059	...	|	|	|	...	|	...
nsbruck Hbf ... a.	0918	0918	...	...	1118	...	...	...	1318	...	...	1518	...	...	1718	...	1918	2118	...	|	|	|	...	|	...
nsbruck Hbf ... d.	0924	0924	...	...	1124	...	...	...	1324	...	...	1524	...	...	1724	...	...	...	...	|	|	|	...	|	...
ennero / Brenner 🛃 ... a.	1000	1000	...	...	1200	...	...	...	1400	...	...	1600	...	...	1800	...	...	...	...	◧	◧	◧	...	◧	...
olzano / Bozen ... a.	1127	1127	...	...	1327	...	...	...	1527	...	...	1727	...	...	1927	...	...	...	...	|	|	|	...	|	...
ento ... a.	1202	1202	...	...	1402	...	...	...	1602	...	...	1802	...	...	2002	...	...	...	...	|	|	|	...	|	...
Padova ... a.	|	|	...	...	|	...	...	...	|	...	...	|	...	...	|	...	...	...	...	|	|	0457	...	|	...
erona ... a.	1256	1256	1330	1402	1458	1521	1532	...	1658	1732	1752	1858	1930	1932	2056	2130	...	...	...	|	|	0551	...	|	...
Padova ... a.	1358	|	1412	|	|	1619	|	...	1756	|	|	|	2012	|	...	2212	...	...	...	|	|	|	...	|	...
Venezia Mestre ... a.	1414	|	1428	|	|	1636	|	...	1812	|	|	|	2028	|	...	2228	...	...	...	|	|	|	...	0822	...
Venezia Santa Lucia ... a.	1428	|	1440	|	|	1648	|	...	1825	|	|	|	2040	|	...	2240	...	...	...	|	|	|	...	0834	...
Milano Centrale ... a.	...	|	...	1515	|	...	1645	...	...	1855	|	|	...	2045	...	...	...	...	...	|	|	0742j	...	...	...
Genova Piazza Principe a.	...	|	...	...	|	...	...	...	...	...	|	|	...	...	...	...	...	...	...	|	|	0938	...	...	...
La Spezia Centrale ... d.	...	|	...	...	|	...	...	...	...	...	|	|	...	...	...	...	...	...	...	|	|	1110	...	...	...
ologna Centrale ... a.	...	1410	...	...	1619	...	...	1655	...	...	1842	2016	...	...	...	...	...	...	...	0515	0620	...	...	...	...
mini ... a.	...	...	...	...	1733t	...	...	|	...	...	|	...	...	...	...	...	...	...	...	|	0731	...	...	...	...
ncona ... a.	...	...	...	...	...	...	...	|	...	...	|	...	...	...	...	...	...	...	...	|	0900	...	...	...	...
renze SMN ... a.	...	...	...	...	...	...	...	1730	...	...	1925¶	...	...	...	...	...	...	...	...	0618	...	...	...	...	...
oma Termini ... a.	...	...	...	...	...	...	...	1910	...	...	2045	...	...	...	...	...	...	...	...	0910	...	...	...	...	...

	EC	*EC*	*FR*	*FR*	*EC*	*FR*	*FR*	*FR*	*EC*	*FB*	*FR*	*FR*	*FR*	*EC*	*FA*	*EC*		*FR*	*EC*	*EC*	*EC*	*NJ*	*NJ*	*NJ*	*NJ*
	288	**286**	**9708**	**9705**	**88**	**8504**	**9716**	**8709**	**86**	**9715**	**9717**	**9724**	**9518**	**84**	**8512**	**82**		**9737**	**10**	**80**	**1280**	**236**	**294**	**294**	**40235**
	♥	♥	[R]	[R]	♥	[R]	[R]	[R]	♥	[R]	[R] ⚡	[R]	[R]	♥	[R]	♥		[R]	[R]	♥	♥				
			⚡	⚡		⚡	⚡	⚡		⚡	⑥⑦	⚡	⚡	**R**	⚡			⚡	⊗	①–⑤	⑥⑦	**F**	**B**	**K**	**G**
			🍷	🍷		🍷	🍷	🍷		🍷	🍷	🍷	🍷		🍷			🍷	🍷			🍷	🍷	🍷	🍷
oma Termini ... d.	...	...	...	...	...	0645	...	...	...	...	...	...	0920	...	1045	...	...	...	...	...	...	...	2017	...	...
renze SMN ... d.	...	...	...	...	...	0803¶	...	...	...	...	...	...	1100	...	1203¶	...	...	...	...	...	...	...	2231	...	...
ncona ... d.	...	...	...	...	...	|	...	...	...	...	...	...	|	...	|	...	...	...	...	...	...	...	|	2115	...
mini ... d.	...	...	...	...	...	|	...	...	...	...	...	...	|	1034f	|	...	...	...	...	...	...	...	|	2227	...
ologna Centrale ... d.	...	...	...	...	0745	0845	...	...	...	...	...	...	1135	1152	1245	...	1410	...	...	1550	...	...	2345	2345	...
La Spezia Centrale ... d.	...	...	...	...	|	|	...	...	...	...	...	...	...	|	|	...	|	...	...	|	...	...	|	|	1710
Genova Piazza Principe d.	...	...	...	...	|	|	...	...	...	...	...	...	...	|	|	...	|	...	...	|	...	...	|	|	1950
Milano Centrale ... d.	...	...	...	0715	|	|	...	0915	...	0945	1015	...	...	|	1305	...	|	1515	...	|	...	...	|	|	2126j
Venezia Santa Lucia ... d.	...	...	0720	|	|	|	...	|	...	|	|	1050	...	|	|	1335	|	|	1520	|	1535	2105	|	|	|
Venezia Mestre ... d.	...	...	0732	|	|	|	0902	|	...	|	|	1102	...	|	|	1347	|	|	1532	|	1547	2117	|	|	|
Padova ... d.	...	...	0748	|	|	|	0918	|	...	|	|	1118	...	|	|	1403	|	|	1548	|	1603	|	|	|	|
erona ... d.	...	...	0830	0828	0901	0937	1000	1028	1101	1058	1128	1200	...	1301	1428	1501	1540	1628	1630	1701	1701	|	|	|	2258
Padova ... d.	...	...	...	...	|	...	...	...	|	...	...	...	...	|	...	|	...	...	...	|	|	|	|	|	2343
ento ... d.	...	...	...	...	0959	...	...	...	1159	...	...	...	...	1359	...	1559	...	...	...	1759	1759	|	|	|	|
olzano / Bozen ... d.	...	...	...	...	1034	...	...	...	1234	...	...	...	...	1434	...	1634	...	...	...	1834	1834	|	|	|	|
ennero / Brenner 🛃 ... d.	...	...	...	...	1200	...	...	...	1400	...	...	...	...	1600	...	1800	...	...	...	2000	2000	◧	◧	◧	◧
nsbruck Hbf ... a.	...	...	...	...	1236	...	...	...	1436	...	...	...	...	1636	...	1836	...	...	...	2036	2036	|	|	|	|
nsbruck Hbf ... d.	0717	1040	...	...	1240	...	...	...	1440	...	...	...	...	1640	...	1840	...	...	...	2040	2040	|	|	|	|
nbach ... d.	0735	1102	...	...	1302	...	...	...	1502	...	...	...	...	1702	...	1902	...	...	...	2102	2102	|	|	|	|
örgl ... d.	0749	1116	...	...	1316	...	...	...	1516	...	...	...	...	1716	...	1916	...	...	...	2116	2116	|	|	|	|
ufstein 🛃 ... a.	0757	1124	...	...	1324	...	...	...	1524	...	...	...	...	1724	...	1924	...	...	...	2124	2124	|	|	|	|
ünchen Ost ... a.	0849	1217	...	...	1416	...	...	...	1616	...	...	...	...	1816	...	2014	...	...	...	2216	2216	0550	|	|	|
ünchen Hbf ... a.	0902	1227	...	...	1427	...	...	...	1627	...	...	...	...	1827	...	2026	...	...	...	2227	2227	|	0922	0922	0922
uttgart Hbf ... a.	...	...	...	...	...	...	...	...	...	...	...	...	...	...	...	...	...	...	...	...	...	0837	...	...	...

– *ÖBB nightjet* – 🛏 1, 2 cl., ▬ 2 cl. (4, 6 berth), [2] München - Villach - Tarvisio 🛃 - Roma and v.v. Special fares apply.
– *ÖBB nightjet* – 🛏 1, 2 cl., ▬ 2 cl. (4, 6 berth), [2] Stuttgart (**237**) - Tarvisio 🛃 - Venezia. Special fares apply.
– *ÖBB nightjet* – 🛏 1, 2 cl., ▬ 2 cl. (4, 6 berth), [2] München (**295**) - Villach (**233**) - Tarvisio 🛃 - Milano - Genova - La Spezia. Special fares apply.
– *ÖBB nightjet* – 🛏 1, 2 cl., ▬ 2 cl. (4, 6 berth), [2] Venezia (**236**) - Tarvisio 🛃 - Stuttgart. Special fares apply.
– *ÖBB nightjet* – 🛏 1, 2 cl., ▬ 2 cl. (4, 6 berth), [2] La Spezia (**235**) - Genova - Milano - Tarvisio 🛃 - Villach (**294**) - München. Special fares apply.
– June 10 - Sept. 9: *ÖBB nightjet* – 🛏 1, 2 cl., ▬ 2 cl. (4, 6 berth), [2] München - Villach - Tarvisio 🛃 - Ancona. Special fares apply.
– June 11 - Sept. 10: *ÖBB nightjet* – 🛏 1, 2 cl., ▬ 2 cl. (4, 6 berth), [2] Ancona - Tarvisio 🛃 - Villach - München. Special fares apply.
– [12] München - Bologna - (Rimini May 25 - Sept. 9).
– [12] (Rimini May 26 - Sept. 10) - Bologna - München.

- May 26 - Sept. 10.
- Milano **Rogoredo**.
- May 25 - Sept. 9.

– Compulsory reservation for international journeys. Supplement payable for international journeys and for internal journeys within Italy.

◧ – 🛃 is Tarvisio (Table **88**).
⚡ – Supplement payable.
♥ – DB-ÖBB EuroCity service.
¶ – Firenze **Campo di Marte**.

87 (Summer) LJUBLJANA - TRIESTE - UDINE / VENEZIA

	1824			*EC* 134		1810	1896		1896
	2			E		Ⓑ 2	2		2
Ljubljana d.	0547	...	...	1421	...	1613	...	...	1850
Postojna d.	0657	...	...	1531	...	1726	...	...	2003
Pivka d.	0709	...	...	1544	...	1741	...	...	2016
Divača d.	0729	...	...	1605	...	1804	...	...	2037
Sežana 🏛 d.	0738	...	...	1615	...	1815	...	...	2048
Villa Opicina 🏛 a.	0749	...	...	1626	...	1826	...	...	2059
Villa Opicina 🏛 d.	0803	...	...	1645	...	...	1823	...	2104
Trieste Centrale a.	0833	...	...	1716	...	...	1853	...	2132
Trieste Centrale d.	0852	0916	...	...	1816	...	...	1858	...
Monfalcone d.	0916	0940	...	...	1840	...	...	1922	...
Trieste Airport d.	0921	0945	...	...	1845	...	...	|	...
Cervignano-Aquileia-Grado d.	0929	0953	...	...	1853	...	...	|	...
Udine a.	0954	|	...	...	|	...	...	2006	...
Venezia Mestre a.	...	1109	...	...	2011	...	...	2146	...
Venezia Santa Lucia a.	...	1121	...	...	2021	...	...	2159	...
Milano Centrale a.	...	...	...	...	...	...	...	...	...

E – [12] Wien (**151**) - Ljubljana (**134**) - Trieste.

		1825		*FR* 9707		*EC* 135			189
		2				F			2
Milano Centrale d.	...	...	...	0745	...	...	...	...	...
Venezia Santa Lucia d.	0639	...	...	|	1039	...	...	1639	...
Venezia Mestre d.	0651	...	...	1011	1051	...	...	1651	...
Udine d.	|	...	...	|	|	...	...	|	175
Cervignano-Aquileia-Grado d.	0807	...	...	1126	1207	...	...	1807	182
Trieste Airport d.	0815	...	...	1135	1215	...	...	1815	182
Monfalcone d.	0821	...	...	1142	1221	...	...	1821	183
Trieste Centrale a.	0844	...	...	1205	1244	...	...	1844	185
Trieste Centrale d.	...	0903	...	...	...	1252	...	...	190
Villa Opicina 🏛 a.	...	0928	...	...	...	1320	...	...	193
Villa Opicina 🏛 d.	...	0943	...	...	...	1338	...	...	194
Sežana 🏛 d.	...	0955	...	...	...	1350	...	...	201
Divača d.	...	1005	...	...	...	1400	...	...	202
Pivka d.	...	1026	...	...	...	1421	...	...	204
Postojna d.	...	1038	...	...	...	1434	...	...	205
Ljubljana a.	...	1146	...	...	...	1540	...	...	221

F – [12] Trieste (**135**) - Ljubljana (**150**) - Wien.

88 (Summer) WIEN - KLAGENFURT - VENEZIA, MILANO and ROMA

train type / number	🚌	*REX*			*IC*	🚌		*RJ*	*RJ*	*EC*	*RJ*	*RJ*	🚌	*REX*		*NJ*	*NJ*	*NJ*	*NJ*	*NJ*		*NJ*
train number	831	1821	131		533	835		535	73	140	133	539	837	1823		40233	40233	233	1237	1237		237
notes	🅁 Y	1817 2	✕		✕	🅁 Y		✕	✕	J	✕	✕	🅁 Y	1819 2		A	P	B	G	H		C
Praha hlavní d.	...	...	...	...	...	...	...	...	0612	...	...	...	...	...	...	...	...	...	...	...	...	...
Břeclav d.	...	...	...	...	...	...	...	...	0955	...	...	...	...	...	...	...	...	...	...	...	...	...
Budapest Keleti d.	...	...	...	...	...	...	...	...	|	0840	...	...	...	...	...	...	...	...	...	...	...	...
Györ d.	...	...	...	...	...	...	...	...	|	1002	...	...	...	...	...	...	...	...	...	...	...	...
Wien Hbf d.	...	...	0625	...	0825	...	...	1025	1049	1121	1225	1425	...	...	...	1918	1918	1918	2001	2001	...	212
Wien Meidling d.	...	...	0632	...	0832	...	...	1032	...	...	1232	1432	...	...	...	1925	1925	1925	2008	2008	...	213
Bruck an der Mur d.	...	...	0815	...	1015	...	...	1215	...	...	1415	1615	...	...	...	2121	2121	2121	2222	2222	...	|
Klagenfurt Hbf d.	...	...	1022	...	1222	...	...	1422	...	...	1622	1822	...	...	...	2336	2336	2336	0021	0021	...	|
Linz Hbf d.	...	...	|	...	|	...	...	|	...	...	|	|	...	...	...	|	|	|	|	|	...	225
Salzburg Hbf d.	...	...	|	...	|	...	...	|	...	...	|	|	...	...	...	|	|	|	|	|	...	014
Villach Hbf d.	0650	0945	1050	...	1246	1256	...	1446	...	...	1649	1846	1856	1929	...	0055	0055	0134	0045	0045	...	044
Tarvisio 🏛 a.	|	1013	1112	...	...	|	...	...	...	...	1712	...	|	1957	...	0119	0119	0157	0108	0108	...	050
Udine a.	0825	1130	1216	...	...	1430	...	...	...	...	1816	...	2030	2113	...	|	|	|	|	|	...	062
Trieste Centrale a.	|	1259x	|	...	...	|	...	...	...	...	|	...	2150	2239x	...	|	|	|	|	|	...	|
Venezia Mestre a.	1000	...	1402	...	...	1605	...	...	...	...	1952	...	...	...	...	|	|	|	|	|	...	082
Venezia Tronchetto ★ a.	1020	...	|	...	...	1625	...	...	...	...	|	...	...	...	...	|	|	|	|	|	...	|
Venezia Santa Lucia a.	...	...	1414	...	...	...	...	...	...	...	2004	...	...	...	...	|	|	|	|	|	...	083
Padova a.	...	...	...	...	...	...	...	...	...	...	...	...	...	...	...	|	|	0457	0415	0423	...	...
Verona Porta Nuova a.	...	...	...	...	...	...	...	...	...	...	...	...	...	...	...	|	|	0551	|	|	...	...
Milano Rogoredo a.	...	...	...								...	...	...	...	...	|	|	0742	|	|	...	...
Genova Piazza Principe a.	...	...	...								...	...	...	...	...	|	|	0938	|	|	...	...
La Spezia Centrale a.	...	...	...								...	...	...	...	...	|	|	1110	|	|	...	...
Bologna Centrale a.	...	...	...								...	...	...	...	...	0515	0620	...	0541	0541	...	...
Rimini a.	...	...	...								...	...	...	...	...	|	0731	...	|	|	...	...
Ancona a.	...	...	...								...	...	...	...	...	|	0900	...	|	|	...	...
Firenze SMN a.	...	...	...								...	...	...	...	...	0618	...	...	0653	0713	...	...
Pisa Centrale a.	...	...	...	...	...	...	...	...	...	...	...	...	...	...	...	|	...	...	0831	0840	...	...
Livorno Centrale a.	...	...	...	...	...	...	...	...	...	...	...	...	...	...	...	|	...	...	0850	0900	...	...
Roma Termini a.	...	...	...	...	...	...	...	...	...	...	...	...	...	...	...	0910	...	...	...	...	...	...

OTHER CONNECTING SERVICES

Praha - Wien: Table **1150**
Budapest - Wien: Table **1250**
Venezia - Roma: Table **600**
Venezia - Milano: Table **605**

train type / number	*REX*	*RJ*	🚌	*RJ*	*RJ*	*EC*	*EC*	*RJX*	*RJ*	🚌	*IC*	*REX*	*RJ*	🚌	*NJ*	*NJ*	*NJ*	*NJ*	*NJ*	*NJ*		
train number	1816	534	830	536	132	100	272	165	372	832	632	1818	130	838	236	1234	1234	235	40294	40294		
notes	1820 2	✕	🅁 Y	✕	✕		✕		✕	🅁 Y	🍸	1822 2	✕	🅁 Y	C	E	D	B	Q	A		
Roma Termini d.	...	...	...	...	...	...	...	...	...	...	...	...	...	...	...	...	...	...	...	2017	...	...
Livorno Centrale d.	...	...	...	...	...	...	...	...	...	...	...	...	...	...	...	1920	1920	...	...	|	...	...
Pisa Centrale d.	...	...	...	...	...	...	...	...	...	...	...	...	...	...	...	1945	1946	...	...	|	...	...
Firenze SMN d.	...	...	...	...	...	...	...	...	...	...	...	...	...	...	...	2105	2105	...	...	2231	...	...
Ancona d.	...	...	...	...	...	...	...	...	...	...	...	...	...	...	...	|	|	...	2115	|	...	...
Rimini d.	...	...	...	...	...	...	...	...	...	...	...	...	...	...	...	|	|	...	2227	|	...	...
Bologna Centrale d.	...	...	...	...	...	...	...	...	...	...	...	...	...	...	...	2223	2223	...	2345	2345	...	...
La Spezia Centrale d.	...	...	...	...	...	...	...	...	...	...	...	...	...	...	...	|	|	1710	|	|	...	...
Genova Piazza Principe d.	...	...	...	...	...	...	...	...	...	...	...	...	...	...	...	|	|	1950	|	|	...	...
Milano Rogoredo d.	...	...	...	...	...	...	...	...	...	...	...	...	...	...	...	|	|	2126	|	|	...	...
Verona Porta Nuova d.	...	...	...	...	...	...	...	...	...	...	...	...	...	...	...	|	|	2258	|	|	...	...
Padova d.	...	...	...	...	...	...	...	...	...	...	...	...	...	...	...	2349	2349	2343	|	|	...	...
Venezia Santa Lucia d.	...	...	...	...	0956	...	...	...	...	...	...	...	1552	...	2105	|	|	|	|	|	...	...
Venezia Tronchetto ★ d.	...	...	...	...	|	...	...	...	...	1320	...	...	|	1720	|	|	|	|	|	|	...	...
Venezia Mestre d.	...	...	...	...	1008	...	...	...	...	1340	...	...	1604	1740	2117	|	|	|	|	|	...	...
Trieste Centrale d.	0545x	...	0755	...	|	...	...	...	...	|	...	1550x	|	|	|	|	|	|	|	|	...	...
Udine d.	0714	...	0915	...	1146	...	...	...	...	1515	...	1722	1746	1915	2301	|	|	|	|	|	...	...
Tarvisio 🏛 d.	0827	...	|	...	1249	...	...	...	...	|	...	1840	1849	|	|	0319	0319	0245	0325	0325	...	...
Villach Hbf a.	0854	0914	1050	1114	1311	...	...	...	...	1650	1714	1907	1911	2050	0042	0341	0341	0307	0347	0347	...	...
Salzburg Hbf a.	...	|	...	...	|	...	...	...	...	...	|	...	|	...	0404	|	|	|	|	|	...	...
Linz Hbf a.	...	|	...	...	|	...	...	...	...	...	|	...	|	...	0558	|	|	|	|	|	...	...
Klagenfurt Hbf a.	...	0937	...	1137	1337	...	...	...	...	...	1737	...	1937	...	|	0407	0407	0438	0438	0438	...	...
Bruck an der Mur a.	...	1144	...	1344	1544	...	...	...	...	...	1944	...	2144	...	|	0620	0620	0639	0639	0639	...	...
Wien Meidling a.	...	1328	...	1528	1728	...	...	...	...	...	2128	...	2328	...	0744	0836	0836	0845	0845	0845	...	...
Wien Hbf a.	...	1335	...	1535	1735	1810	...	1842	1910	...	2135	...	2335	...	0755	0842	0842	0852	0852	0852	...	...
Györ a.	...	...	...	...	...	|	...	1953	|	...	...	...	...	...	...	...	...	...	...	...	...	...
Budapest Keleti a.	...	...	...	...	...	|	...	2119	|	...	...	...	...	...	...	...	...	...	...	...	...	...
Břeclav a.	...	...	...	...	...	1904	1907	...	2004	...	...	...	...	...	...	...	...	...	...	...	...	...
Praha hlavní a.	...	...	...	...	...	...	2241	...	2343	...	...	...	...	...	...	...	...	...	...	...	...	...

A – *ÖBB nightjet* 🛏 1,2 cl., ▬ 2 cl. (4,6 berth), [2] 🍸 Wien - Roma and v.v.
B – *ÖBB nightjet* 🛏 1,2 cl., ▬ 2 cl. (4,6 berth), [2] 🍸 Wien - Milano - Genova - La Spezia and v.v.
C – *ÖBB nightjet* 🛏 1,2 cl., ▬ 2 cl. (4,6 berth), [2] Wien - Venezia and v.v.
D – ④⑥ May 27 - June 10: *ÖBB nightjet* 🛏 1,2 cl., ▬ 2 cl. (4,6 berth), [2] 🍸 Livorno - Firenze - Wien.
E – ④⑥ July 1 - Sept. 30: *ÖBB nightjet* 🛏 1,2 cl., ▬ 2 cl. (4,6 berth), [2] 🍸 Livorno - Firenze - Wien.
G – ③⑤ May 26 - June 11, Sept. 8 - Oct. 8: *ÖBB nightjet* 🛏 1,2 cl., ▬ 2 cl. (4,6 berth), [2] 🍸 Wien - Firenze - Livorno.
H – ③⑤ June 16 - Sept. 3: *ÖBB nightjet* 🛏 1,2 cl., ▬ 2 cl. (4,6 berth), [2] 🍸 Wien - Firenze - Livorno.
J – [12] Zahony (depart 0405) - Debrecen (0531) - Szolnok (0657) - Budapest - Wien. Conveys 🛏 1,2 cl. Kyïv - Lviv - Zahony - Wien; see Table **96**.
P – June 10 - Sept. 9: *ÖBB nightjet* – 🛏 1,2 cl., ▬ 2 cl. (4,6 berth), [2] Wien - Villach - Tarvisio 🏛 - Ancona.
Q – June 11 - Sept. 10: *ÖBB nightjet* – 🛏 1,2 cl., ▬ 2 cl. (4,6 berth), [2] Ancona - Tarvisio 🏛 - Villach - Wien.
Y – June 2 - Sept. 26.

x – Ⓒ.
⁄ – Supplement payable.
★ – See Venezia City Plan on page 32.
RJ – ÖBB *Railjet* service. [1] (business class), [1] (first class), [2] (economy class), ✕.
🚌 – **ÖBB** *IC Bus*. Rail tickets valid. 🅁. Suppleme payable. 2nd class only. Connections to / from Wien are made at Villach.

VILLACH - LJUBLJANA - ZAGREB - BUDAPEST and BEOGRAD — 89 (Summer)

train type		D	D	D	D	EC	D	D	1604	480	D
train number		**415**	**247**	**581**	**211**	**213**	**315**	**315**	**1247**	**1247**	**1205**
notes		**413**		**201**				**411**	**959**	**959**	
notes			**H**	**R**				**P**	**K**	**E**	**C**
Villach Hbf	d.	0625	...	...	1253	1653	1853	...	...	...	...
Koper	a.	|	...	...	|	|	|	...	2015	...	...
Rijeka	d.	|	...	...	|	|	|	...	|	1847	...
Ljubljana	d.	0830	0935	...	1445	1837	2105	2105	0030	0030	...
Dobova 🏛	d.	1015	|	...	1646	2021	2241	2306	|	|	...
Split	d.	|	|	...	|	|	...	|	|	|	1828
Zagreb	a.	1039	|	...	1710	2045	...	2337	|	|	0243
Zagreb	d.	*1057*	|	1635	1735	...	...	2341	|	|	0317
Vinkovci	a.	*1442*	|	|	2142	...	...	0303	|	|	|
Šid 🏛	a.	...	|	|	...	...	...	0341	|	|	|
Beograd Centar	a.	...	|	|	...	...	...	0605	|	|	|
Koprivnica 🏛	d.	...	|	1801	...	...	...	...	|	|	0449
Gyékényes 🏛	a.	...	|	1812	...	...	...	...	|	|	0549
Nagykanizsa	a.	...	|	1902	...	...	...	...	|	|	0616
Hodoš 🏛	a.	...	1248	|	...	...	...	...	0338	0338	|
Zalaegerszeg	a.	...	1337	|	...	...	...	...	0431	0431	|
Fonyód	a.	...	|	2022	...	...	...	...	|	|	0718
Siófok	a.	...	|	2101	...	...	...	...	|	|	0749
Székesfehérvár	a.	...	1611	2136	...	...	...	...	0811	0811	0825
Budapest Déli	a.	...	1659	2224	...	...	...	...	0859	0859	|
Budapest Keleti	a.	...	...	...	...	...	...	...	...	...	0935

train type		D	D	EC	D	D	D	D	D	9008	1281
train number		**410**	**314**	**212**	**210**	**412**	**246**	**204**	**1204**	**1246**	**1246**
notes		**314**				**414**		**2214**		**1605**	**1605**
notes		**Q**					**H**	**R**	**D**	**J**	**G**
Budapest Keleti	d.	...	...	...	...	...	...	...	1845	...	...
Budapest Déli	d.	...	...	...	...	...	0900	1535	|	2035	2100
Székesfehérvár	d.	...	...	...	...	...	0946	1621	1943	2116	2146
Siófok	d.	...	...	...	...	...	|	1657	2027	|	|
Fonyód	d.	...	...	...	...	...	|	1737	2100	|	|
Zalaegerszeg	d.	...	...	...	...	...	1222	|	|	0012	0020
Hodoš 🏛	d.	...	...	...	...	...	1315	|	|	0103	0112
Nagykanizsa	d.	...	...	...	...	...	|	1908	2159	|	|
Gyékényes 🏛	d.	...	...	...	...	...	|	1958	2255	|	|
Koprivnica 🏛	a.	...	...	...	...	...	|	2009	2306	|	|
Beograd Centar	d.	2058	...	...	...	...	|	|	|	|	|
Šid 🏛	d.	0022	...	...	...	...	|	|	|	|	|
Vinkovci	d.	0103	...	...	0839	*1416*	|	|	|	|	|
Zagreb	a.	0428	...	...	1240	*1820*	|	2210	0022	|	|
Zagreb	d.	0440	...	0705	1250	1938	|	...	0038	|	|
Split	a.	|	...	|	|	|	|	...	0846	|	|
Dobova 🏛	d.	0540	0540	0745	1334	2019	|	...	...	|	|
Ljubljana	d.	0717	0726	0923	1527	2208	1635	...	...	0603	0634
Rijeka	a.	...	|	|	|	|	...	...	...	|	0934
Koper	a.	...	|	|	|	|	...	...	...	0833	...
Villach Hbf	a.	...	0908	1058	1708	2348	...	...	...	...	...

C – ADRIA ①③⑥ June 19 - Aug. 29; : 🛏 1, 2 cl., ▬ 2 cl., (2) Split - Zagreb - Budapest.

D – ADRIA ②⑤⑦ June 18 - Aug. 28: 🛏 1, 2 cl., ▬ 2 cl., (2) Budapest - Zagreb - Split.

E – ISTRA June 24 - Aug. 27: 🛏 1, 2 cl., ▬ 2 cl., (2) Rijeka - Hodoš 🏛 - Budapest (Table **91**).

G – ISTRA June 23 - Aug. 26: 🛏 1, 2 cl., ▬ 2 cl., (2) Budapest - Hodoš 🏛 - Rijeka (Table **91**).

H – CITADELLA (2) Budapest - Hodoš - Ljubljana and v.v. (Table **91**).

J – ISTRA June 17 - Aug. 29: ▬ 2 cl., (2) Budapest - Hodoš 🏛 - Koper (Table **91**).

K – ISTRA June 18 - Aug. 30: ▬ 2 cl., (2) Koper - Hodoš 🏛 - Budapest (Table **91**).

P – June 20 - Sept. 13: ▬ 2 cl., (12) Ljubljana - Zagreb - Beograd.

Q – June 21 - Sept. 14: ▬ 2 cl., (12) Beograd - Zagreb - Ljubljana.

R – AGRAM-TOPART (2) Zagreb - Budapest and v.v.

RJ – ÖBB *Railjet* service. (1) (business class), (1) (first class), (2) (economy class), ✕.

☛ **Shaded services are suspended until further notice.**

MARSEILLE - NICE - MILANO, ROMA and VENEZIA — 90 (Summer)

Engineering work between Nice and Ventimiglia is affecting services until April 2. See Table **361** for full details.

train type				FB			IC	IC	FB	FR	FA			FB	IC	ITA	FR			IC	IC		FB	ICN	ICN	ICN
train number				**8613**			**745**	**665**	**8619**	**9547**	**9741**			**8655**	**673**	**8997**	**9663**			**681**	**679**		**8659**	**1963**	**799**	**799**
train number																										
notes			2	R 🍷		2	R	R	R 🍷	R 🍷	R 🍷			R 🍷	R	R 🍷	R 🍷			R	R		R 🍷	R	R	R
notes				ϟ			ϟ	ϟ	ϟ	ϟ	ϟ			ϟ	ϟ	ϟ	ϟ			ϟ	ϟ		ϟ	ϟ	ϟ	ϟ
notes																	Ⓑ							**C**	**AP**	**AQ**
Marseille St Charles	d.	...	...	...	0548	...	...	...	...	...	...	0957	...	...	...	...	...	1157	...	...	...	...	...	...	...	...
Toulon	d.	...	...	...	0644	...	...	...	...	...	...	1044	...	...	...	...	...	1244	...	...	...	...	...	...	...	...
Cannes	d.	0521**x**	...	...	0812	0822	...	...	...	...	...	1211	1222	...	...	...	...	1411	...	...	...	1752	...	...	...	...
Nice	d.	0604	...	...	0848	0906	...	...	...	...	...	1241	1309	...	...	...	...	1441	1543	...	...	1836	...	...	...	...
Monaco - Monte Carlo	d.	0629	...	...	▬	0932	...	...	...	...	...	...	1334	...	...	...	...	▬	1609	...	...	1902	...	...	...	...
Ventimiglia 🏛	d.	0701	0757	...	*IC* **511**	1001	1103	...	...	...	...	...	1401	1510	...	...	...	*FR*	1635	1703	...	1931	1943	...	...	...
San Remo	d.	...	0812	...	R ϟ	...	1120	...	...	...	...	...	...	1523	...	...	...	**9567**	...	1720	...	...	1956	...	...	...
Genova Piazza Principe	a.	...	1021	1210	1224	...	1305	1347	1502	...	...	...	...	1705	1747	...	...	R ϟ	...	1908	1947	...	2142	2156	2207	2353
Milano Centrale	a.	...	...	|	|	...	1455	|	|	1510	1545	...	...	1855	|	1935	1925	2010	...	2057	|	...	2340	|	|	|
Verona	a.	...	...	|	|	...	...	|	|	|	1658	...	...	...	|	2047	|	|	...	...	|	...	...	|	|	|
Venezia Santa Lucia	a.	...	...	|	|	...	...	|	|	|	1812	...	...	...	|	2203	|	|	...	...	|	...	...	|	|	|
La Spezia	a.	...	...	1315	1350	...	...	1521	1615	|	...	...	...	...	1921	...	|	|	...	...	2121	...	...	2306	2352	0125
Pisa Centrale	a.	...	...	1404	1447	...	...	...	1704	|	...	...	...	...	2017	...	|	|	...	...	2217	...	...	2356	0048	0216
Firenze SMN	a.	...	...	|	|	...	...	...	|	1704	...	...	...	...	...	...	|	2204	...	...	...	...	...	...	|	|
Roma Termini	a.	...	...	1703	1803	...	...	...	2003	1849	...	...	...	...	...	...	2240	2349	...	...	...	...	...	...	0543**o**	0543**o**
Napoli Centrale	a.	...	...	...	2029	...	...	...	...	2010	...	...	...	...	...	...	0005	...	...	...	...	...	...	...	0817	0817

train type		ICN			ICN	IC	ICN	FB		IC	ICN		IC			IC	IC	FR	FR	FB		ITA	FR	IC	IC	
train number		**796**			**796**	**658**	**1962**	**8639**		**662**	**1962**		**659**			**510**	**674**	**9728**	**9415**	**8643**		**8984**	**9584**	**680**	**675**	
train number																										
notes		R ϟ	2		R ϟ	R	R ϟ	R 🍷		R	R ϟ	2	R			R	R	R 🍷	R 🍷	R 🍷		R 🍷	R 🍷	R	R	
notes		**A**			**A**	ϟ	**C**	ϟ		ϟ	**C**		ϟ			ϟ	ϟ	ϟ	ϟ	ϟ		ϟ	ϟ	ϟ	ϟ	
notes		⑥⑦	⚒		①–⑤		⑥⑦				①–⑤	Ⓐ									⑤⑥⑦					⑥
Napoli Centrale	d.	2146	...	...	2146	...	...	...	...	...	...	...	...	...	...	0731	...	...	0940	...	...	...	1140	...	...	...
Roma Termini	d.	0011**o**	...	...	0011**o**	...	...	...	...	...	...	...	...	...	...	0957	...	...	1110	...	...	...	1310	...	...	...
Firenze SMN	d.	|	...	...	|	...	...	...	...	...	...	...	...	...	...	|	...	...	1255	...	...	...	1455	...	...	...
Pisa Centrale	d.	0326	...	...	0500	0542	0557	...	...	0642	0647	...	...	...	...	1302	1342	...	|	...	...	...	|	...	...	...
La Spezia	d.	0425	...	...	0552	0638	0654	...	...	0738	0758	...	...	...	...	1405	1438	...	|	...	...	...	|	1638	...	...
Venezia Santa Lucia	d.	|	...	...	|	|	|	...	...	|	|	...	...	...	...	|	|	1148	|	...	...	1357	|	|	...	...
Verona	d.	|	...	...	|	|	|	...	...	|	|	...	...	...	...	|	|	1302	|	...	...	1512	|	|	...	...
Milano Centrale	d.	|	...	...	|	|	|	0710	...	|	|	...	0910	...	...	|	|	1415	1450	1510	...	1625	1650	|	1705	...
Genova Piazza Principe	d.	0601	0646	...	0757	0816	0839	0858	...	0915	0936	0943	1058	...	...	1535	1614	...	...	1658	...	...	...	1815	1858	...
San Remo	d.	...	0906	...	...	...	...	1042	...	▬	...	1145	1241**f**	...	...	...	...	...	...	1842	...	...	...	...	2041	...
Ventimiglia 🏛	a.	...	0922	1022	...	...	...	1054	1206	...	...	1203	1258**f**	1315	...	...	...	...	...	1854	1952	...	...	...	2058	2325
Monaco - Monte Carlo	a.	...	...	1057	...	...	...	...	1241	...	...	...	...	1350	...	...	...	...	...	...	2027	...	...	...	...	2358
Nice	a.	...	...	1123	...	...	...	...	1305	1320	...	...	...	1415	1420	...	...	...	...	...	2051	...	...	...	...	0023
Cannes	a.	...	...	1210	...	...	...	...	1410	1353	...	...	...	1508	1453	...	...	...	...	...	2138	...	...	...	...	...
Toulon	a.	...	...	...	...	...	...	...	...	1515	...	...	...	...	1615	...	...	...	...	...	...	...	...	...	...	...
Marseille St Charles	a.	...	...	...	...	...	...	...	...	1602	...	...	...	...	1703	...	...	...	...	...	...	...	...	...	...	...

A – 🛏 1, 2 cl., ▬ 2 cl. (4 berth), (2) Torino - Genova - Napoli - Salerno and v.v.

C – 🛏 1, 2 cl., ▬ 2 cl. (4 berth) Milano - Genova - Pisa - Siracusa and v.v.
🛏 1, 2 cl., ▬ 2 cl. (4 berth) Milano - Genova - Pisa - Palermo and v.v.

P – ①–⑤ Dec. 12 - Mar. 15.

Q – ⑥⑦ (daily Mar. 16 - Dec. 10).

f – On Ⓒ depart San Remo 1257, arrive Ventimiglia 1312.

o – Roma **Ostiense**.

x – Not ⑥.

ϟ – Supplement payable.

91 (Summer) WIEN - LJUBLJANA and ZAGREB

train type	*EC*			*D*	*EC*	*IC*	*IC*	9008	1281
train number	**151**	**483**	**2752**	**246**	**159¶**	**523**	**310**	**1246**	**1246**
notes	**134**		2		✕⁄	2		**1605**	**1605**
	✕E	-	🚌	G	C			P	J
Wien Hbf d.	0758	...	...	...	1558	...	...	...	...
Wien Meidling d.	0805	...	...	...	1605	...	...	...	...
Wiener Neustadt Hbf d.	0832	...	...	...	1632	...	...	...	...
Budapest Keleti d.	|	...	...	...	|	...	1615	...	...
Budapest Déli d.	|	...	...	0900	|	...	|	2035	2100
Szombathely d.	|	...	...	|	|	...	1906	|	|
Hodoš ▦ d.	|	...	...	1315	|	...	|	0103	0112
Graz Hbf d.	1037	...	...	|	1839	...	2139	|	|
Spielfeld-Straß ▦ d.	1125	...	...	|	1926	...	2225	|	|
Maribor a.	1140	...	...	|	1941	2005	2240	0225	0240
Pragersko a.	1145	...	...	1433	2004	2018	2300	0337	0329
Zidani Most a.	1303	...	...	1536	|	2118	0003	0446	0439
Dobova ▦ a.	|	...	...	|	2146	|	|	|	|
Zagreb a.	|	...	...	|	2225	|	|	|	|
Ljubljana a.	1400	1520	1550	1635	...	2208	0058	0547	0542
Koper a.	|	|	1817	...	...	...	...	0833	|
Rijeka a.	|	1827	...	...	...	...	...	...	0934
Villa Opicina ▦ a.	1626	...	...	...	...	...	...	...	...
Trieste a.	1652	...	...	...	...	...	...	...	...

train type/number	*IC*	*IC*	*ICS*	*EC*	*D*			*EC*	480	1604
train number	**311**	**508**	**14**	**158**	**247**	**2751**	**482**	**135**	**1247**	**1247**
notes			2	✕⁄		2		**150**	**959**	**959**
				C	H	🚌		✕F	K	Q
Trieste d.	...	...	...	...	...	...	...	1252	...	...
Villa Opicina ▦ d.	...	...	...	...	...	...	...	1336	...	...
Rijeka d.	...	...	...	...	...	...	1150	|	1847	...
Koper d.	...	0525	...	...	...	1004	|	|	|	2015
Ljubljana d.	0505	0753	0805	...	0935	1245	1457	1555	0030	0030
Zagreb d.	|	...	|	0705	|	...	...	|	|	|
Dobova ▦ d.	|	...	|	0803	|	...	...	|	|	|
Zidani Most d.	0559	...	0850	|	1030	...	...	1701	0122	0122
Pragersko d.	0700	...	0943	0944	1133	...	...	1800	0226	0226
Maribor d.	0719	...	0955	1019	|	...	...	1821	|	|
Spielfeld-Straß ▦ a.	0734	...	...	1034	|	...	...	1836	|	|
Graz Hbf a.	0823	...	...	1122	|	...	...	1922	|	|
Hodoš ▦ a.	|	...	...	|	1248	...	...	|	0338	0338
Szombathely a.	1053	...	...	|	|	...	...	|	|	|
Budapest Déli a.	|	...	...	|	1659	...	...	|	0859	0859
Budapest Keleti a.	1344	...	...	|	...	...	...	|	...	...
Wiener Neustadt Hbf a.	...	...	...	1328	...	...	...	2128	...	...
Wien Meidling a.	...	...	...	1355	...	...	...	2155	...	...
Wien Hbf a.	...	...	...	1402	...	...	...	2202	...	...

C – CROATIA (12) ✕ Wien - Zagreb and v.v.
E – EMONA (12) ✕ Wien - Ljubljana. Conveys (12) Wien (**151**) - Ljubljana (**134**) - Trieste.
F – EMONA (12) ✕ Ljubljana - Wien. Conveys (12) Trieste (**135**) - Ljubljana (**150**) - Wien.
G – CITADELLA (2) Budapest - Hodoš - Ljubljana and v.v. (Table **89**).
J – ISTRA June 23 - Aug. 26: 🛏 1,2 cl., ▬ 2 cl., (2) Budapest - Hodoš ▦ - Rijeka (Table **89**).
K – ISTRA June 24 - Aug. 27: 🛏 1,2 cl., ▬ 2 cl., (2) Rijeka - Hodoš ▦ - Budapest (Table **89**).
P – ISTRA June 17 - Aug. 29: ▬ 2 cl., (2) Budapest - Koper (Table **89**).
Q – ISTRA June 18 - Aug. 30: ▬ 2 cl., (2) Koper - Budapest (Table **89**).
⁄ – Supplement payable.
◇ – Stopping train.
¶ – Train number **1259** on ©.

92 (Summer) PRAHA - BRATISLAVA - ZAGREB - RIJEKA / SPLIT

		EN		*RJ*		
		1153		**1221**		
		C		A		
Praha hl. n. d.	...	...	...	1531	...	...
Kolín d.	...	...	...	1630	...	...
Brno hl. n. d.	...	...	...	1932	...	...
Břeclav d.	...	...	...	2008	...	...
Bratislava hl. st. d.	...	1553	...	|	...	...
Bratislava Nové Mesto d.	...	|	...	2120	...	...
Györ d.	...	|	...	|	...	...
Budapest Kelenföld d.	...	|	...	|	...	...
Wien Hbf d.	...	1823	...	|	...	...
Wien Meidling d.	...	1830	...	|	...	...
Wiener Neustadt Hbf d.	...	1859	...	|	...	...
Graz Hbf d.	...	2102	...	|	...	...
Spielfeld-Straß ▦ d.	...	2148	...	|	...	...
Maribor d.	...	2205	...	|	...	...
Dobova ▦ d.	...	0012	...	|	...	...
Zagreb a.	...	0034	...	|	...	...
Ogulin a.	...	|	...	|	...	...
Rijeka a.	...	|	...	|	...	...
Gračac a.	...	|	...	|	...	...
Knin a.	...	0549	...	|	...	...
Perković a.	...	0646	...	|	...	...
Split a.	...	0810	...	1348	...	...

		RJ		*EN*		
		1220		**1152**		
		B		D		
Split d.	...	1545	...	1720	...	...
Perković d.	...	|	...	1843	...	...
Knin d.	...	|	...	1953	...	...
Gračac d.	...	|	...	|	...	...
Rijeka d.	...	|	...	|	...	...
Ogulin d.	...	|	...	|	...	...
Zagreb d.	...	|	...	0135	...	...
Dobova ▦ a.	...	|	...	0157	...	...
Maribor a.	...	|	...	0417	...	...
Spielfeld-Straß ▦ a.	...	|	...	0502	...	...
Graz Hbf a.	...	|	...	0552	...	...
Wiener Neustadt Hbf a.	...	|	...	0817	...	...
Wien Meidling a.	...	|	...	0912	...	...
Wien Hbf a.	...	|	...	0921	...	...
Budapest Kelenföld a.	...	|	...	|	...	...
Györ a.	...	|	...	|	...	...
Bratislava Nové Mesto d.	...	0749	...	|	...	...
Bratislava hl. st. a.	...	|	...	1142	...	...
Břeclav a.	...	0858	...	...	...	...
Brno hl. n. a.	...	0940	...	...	...	...
Kolín a.	...	1235	...	...	...	...
Praha hl. n. a.	...	1314	...	...	...	...

A – ②⑤⑦ May 19 - Oct. 3 (daily June 16 - Sept. 10): ▬ 2 cl. (4 berth), (2) Praha - Split.
B – ①③⑥ May 20 - Oct. 4 (daily June 17 - Sept. 11): ▬ 2 cl. (4 berth), (2) Split - Praha.
C – ③⑤⑦ May 3 - Oct. 6: 🛏 1,2 cl., ▬ 2 cl., (2) Bratislava - Split.
D – ①④⑥ May 4 - Oct. 7: 🛏 1,2 cl., ▬ 2 cl., (2) Split - Bratislava.

93 (Summer) WARSZAWA - VILNIUS

train type			*IC*					
train number			**31100**	**24**				
notes			**144**					
			V					
Warszawa Centralna d.	...	...	0735	...	...	...	...	...
Warszawa Wschodnia d.	...	...	0745	...	...	...	...	...
Białystok d.	...	...	1045	...	...	...	...	...
Suwałki d.	...	...	1256	...	...	...	...	...
Mockava ▦ ◐ § a.	...	...	1441	1505	...	...	...	...
Šeštokai § a.	...	...	...	|	...	...	...	...
Kaunas § a.	...	...	...	1626	...	...	...	...
Vilnius § a.	...	...	...	1734	...	...	...	...

train type				*IC*				
train number			**23**	**143**				
notes				**13000**				
				V				
Vilnius § d.	...	...	1210	...	...	...	...	...
Kaunas § d.	...	...	1320	...	...	...	...	...
Šeštokai § d.	...	...	|	...	...	...	...	...
Mockava ▦ ◐ § d.	...	...	1441	1514	...	...	...	...
Suwałki d.	...	...	...	1527	...	...	...	...
Białystok d.	...	...	...	1741	...	...	...	...
Warszawa Wschodnia a.	...	...	...	2003	...	...	...	...
Warszawa Centralna a.	...	...	...	2013	...	...	...	...

H – HAŃCZA – (12) Ⓡ Kraków - Warszawa - Białystok - Suwałki and v.v.
§ – Lithuanian time.
◐ – ▦ = Trakiszki (Poland) / Mockava (Lithuania); ticketing point is Mockava.

95 (Summer) MOSKVA - WARSZAWA - PRAHA and WIEN

Moskva Belorusskaya d.	...	...	...	...	...	...	...	...	...
Smolensk Tsentralny ▦ § d.	...	...	...	...	...	...	...	...	...
Orsha Tsentralnaya § d.	...	...	...	...	...	...	...	...	...
Minsk d.	...	...	...	...	...	...	...	...	...
Brest Tsentralny ▦ a.	...	...	...	...	...	...	...	...	...
Brest Tsentralny ▦ d.	...	...	...	...	...	...	...	...	...
Terespol ▦ a.	...	...	...	...	...	...	...	...	...
Terespol ▦ d.	...	...	...	...	...	...	...	...	...
Warszawa Wschodnia a.	...	...	...	...	...	...	...	...	...
Warszawa Centralna a.	...	...	...	...	...	...	...	...	...
Katowice a.	...	...	...	...	...	...	...	...	...
Bohumín ▦ a.	...	...	...	...	...	...	...	...	...
Ostrava hlavní a.	...	...	...	...	...	...	...	...	...
Břeclav a.	...	...	...	...	...	...	...	...	...
Wien Hbf a.	...	...	...	...	...	...	...	...	...
Olomouc a.	...	...	...	...	...	...	...	...	...
Pardubice a.	...	...	...	...	...	...	...	...	...
Praha hlavní a.	...	...	...	...	...	...	...	...	...

Praha hlavní d.	...	...	...	...	...	...	...	...	...
Pardubice d.	...	...	...	...	...	...	...	...	...
Olomouc d.	...	...	...	...	...	...	...	...	...
Wien Hbf d.	...	...	...	...	...	...	...	...	...
Břeclav d.	...	...	...	...	...	...	...	...	...
Ostrava hlavní d.	...	...	...	...	...	...	...	...	...
Bohumín ▦ d.	...	...	...	...	...	...	...	...	...
Katowice d.	...	...	...	...	...	...	...	...	...
Warszawa Centralna d.	...	...	...	...	...	...	...	...	...
Warszawa Wschodnia d.	...	...	...	...	...	...	...	...	...
Terespol ▦ a.	...	...	...	...	...	...	...	...	...
Terespol ▦ d.	...	...	...	...	...	...	...	...	...
Brest Tsentralny ▦ a.	...	...	...	...	...	...	...	...	...
Brest Tsentralny ▦ d.	...	...	...	...	...	...	...	...	...
Minsk a.	...	...	...	...	...	...	...	...	...
Orsha Tsentralnaya § a.	...	...	...	...	...	...	...	...	...
Smolensk Tsentralny ▦ § a.	...	...	...	...	...	...	...	...	...
Moskva Belorusskaya a.	...	...	...	...	...	...	...	...	...

§ – ▦: Osinovka (BY) / Krasnoye (RU).

SAN JOSE - SACRAMENTO 9325

Amtrak 2nd class Most trains 🍷

CAPITOL CORRIDOR

km		522	720	524	724	528	728	532	534	732	536	734	736	538	540	542	738	742	544	546	744	746	548	748
		Ⓐ	Ⓒ	Ⓐ	Ⓒ	Ⓐ	Ⓒ	Ⓐ	Ⓐ	Ⓒ	Ⓐ	Ⓒ	Ⓒ	Ⓐ	Ⓐ	Ⓐ	Ⓒ	Ⓒ	Ⓐ	Ⓐ	Ⓒ	Ⓒ	Ⓐ	Ⓒ
0	**San Jose** d.	...	...	0618	0805	0848	1005	1105	...	1305	...	...	1505	1505	...	1605	...	1705	...	1805	1805	...	...	2005
75	**Oakland** Jack London Sq. d.	0612	0712	0724	0912	0957	1112	1217	1412	1412	1512	1512	1611	1612	1642	1712	1712	1810	1812	1912	1912	2012	2012	2112
83	Emeryville d.	0621	0721	0735	0921	1006	1121	1226	1421	1421	1521	1521	1620	1621	1651	1721	1721	1819	1821	1921	1921	2021	2021	2121
128	Martinez d.	0658	0758	0813	0959	1045	1158	1304	1458	1458	1600	1558	1657	1659	1728	1758	1758	1857	1858	1958	1959	2058	2059	2159
219	**Sacramento** a.	0810	0910	0922	1110	1157	1314	1416	1610	1615	1716	1710	1802	1806	1841	1910	1910	2009	2012	2110	2115	2210	2218	2315

	521	523	723	525	527	727	529	729	531	733	737	541	741	543	743	545	745	547	549	747	551	749	751
	Ⓐ	Ⓐ	Ⓒ	Ⓐ	Ⓐ	Ⓒ	Ⓐ	Ⓒ	Ⓐ	Ⓒ	Ⓒ	Ⓐ	Ⓒ	Ⓐ	Ⓒ	Ⓐ	Ⓒ	Ⓐ	Ⓐ	Ⓒ	Ⓐ	Ⓒ	Ⓒ
Sacramento d.	0410	0510	0555	0610	0643	0655	0733	0855	0855	0955	1055	1155	1255	1355	1455	1555	1655	1703	1755	1855	1955	1955	2055
Martinez d.	0510	0610	0655	0710	0743	0755	0832	0955	0955	1055	1155	1255	1355	1455	1555	1655	1755	1803	1855	1955	2055	2056	2155
Emeryville d.	0549	0649	0734	0749	0823	0834	0911	1034	1034	1134	1234	1334	1434	1536	1634	1736	1835	1842	1935	2034	2136	2138	2134
Oakland Jack London Square a.	0600	0659	0744	0804	0838	0844	0932	1044	1044	1144	1244	1344	1443	1552	1644	1752	1852	1852	1949	2042	2152	2154	2252
San Jose a.	0715	0814	0901	...	0953	1002	1045	1203	...	...	1401	1505	1559	...	1803	...	...	2016	...	2201	...	...	...

THRUWAY 🚌 CONNECTIONS SAN FRANCISCO - EMERYVILLE*

	Ⓐ	Ⓒ	Ⓐ			Ⓒ			Ⓐ	Ⓒ		Ⓐ		Ⓐ	Ⓒ		Ⓐ	Ⓒ	Ⓐ	Ⓒ	Ⓐ	Ⓒ	Ⓐ
San Francisco Mission Street ⊡ d.	0540	0640	0655	0700	0800	0840	0900	...	0925	1035	1100	1145	1250	1335	1340	...	1435	1440	1535	1540	1610	1640	1640
Emeryville a.	0610	0710	0725	0730	0830	0910	0930	...	0955	1105	1130	1215	1320	1405	1410	...	1505	1510	1605	1610	1640	1710	1715

		Ⓒ	Ⓐ	Ⓒ	Ⓐ	Ⓒ	Ⓒ	
San Francisco Mission Street ⊡ d.	1650	1730	1830	1840	1930	1940	2040	2050
Emeryville a.	1730	1805	1905	1910	2005	2010	2110	2125

	Ⓐ	Ⓐ	Ⓒ	Ⓐ	Ⓐ	Ⓒ		Ⓐ
Emeryville d.	0550	0650	0735	0750	0825	0835	0850	0915
San Francisco Mission Street ⊡ a.	0620	0730	0805	0830	0900	0905	0920	0950

			Ⓒ	Ⓒ	Ⓐ		Ⓒ		Ⓐ		Ⓒ	Ⓐ		Ⓒ	Ⓐ		Ⓐ		Ⓒ	Ⓐ	Ⓒ		Ⓒ
Emeryville d.	1015	1035	1115	1235	1335	1420	1435	...	1540	1625	1635	1740	1825	1835	1845	...	1940	2020	2035	2140	2140	2220	2235
San Francisco Mission Street ⊡ a.	1045	1105	1205	1305	1405	1450	1505	...	1610	1700	1705	1810	1855	1905	1915	...	2010	2050	2105	2205	2210	2245	2305

⊡ – San Francisco Chase Bank, 555 Mission Street / SF Salesforce Plaza.

* – Most Thruway 🚌 services can only be booked with a train ticket.

OAKLAND - BAKERSFIELD 9330

Amtrak 2nd class Most trains 🍷

SAN JOAQUINS

km		702	710	712	714	716	718			
0	**Oakland** Jack London Sq. d.	...	0736	0936	1136	1336	1736	...	...	...
8	Emeryville ‡ d.	...	0746	0946	1146	1346	1746	...	...	...
53	Martinez d.	...	0825	1025	1225	1425	1825	...	...	...
90	**Sacramento** d.	0626	|	|	|	|	|	...	...	...
148	Lodi d.	0704	|	|	|	|	|	...	...	...
167	Stockton San Joaquin St. d.	0722**d**	0923	1123	1323	1523	1923	...	...	...
215	Modesto d.	0756	0956	1156	1356	1556	1956	...	...	...
271	Merced d.	0845	1045	1245	1445	1645	2045	...	...	...
329	Madera d.	0919	1119	1319	1519	1719	2119	...	...	...
364	Fresno d.	0949	1149	1349	1549	1749	2149	...	...	...
412	Hanford d.	1024	1224	1424	1624	1824	2224	...	...	...
542	**Bakersfield** a.	1157	1357	1557	1757	1957	2357	...	...	...
704	**Los Angeles** a.	*1435**	*1635**	*1835**	*2035**	*2235**	*0215**	...	...	...

	711	713	715	717	719	703			
Los Angeles d.	*0100**	*0500**	*0915**	*1055**	*1305**	*1455**	...	...	...
Bakersfield d.	0412	0812	1212	1412	1612	1812	...	...	...
Hanford d.	0534	0934	1339	1539	1739	1939	...	...	...
Fresno d.	0612	1016	1416	1616	1816	2016	...	...	...
Madera d.	0638	1042	1442	1642	1842	2042	...	...	...
Merced d.	0723	1123	1523	1723	1923	2119	...	...	...
Modesto d.	0803	1203	1603	1803	2003	2157	...	...	...
Stockton San Joaquin St. d.	0840	1240	1640	1840	2040	2229**d**	...	...	...
Lodi d.	|	|	|	|	|	2244	...	...	...
Sacramento a.	|	|	|	|	|	2335	...	...	...
Martinez d.	0931	1331	1732	1932	2131	...	...	...	...
Emeryville ‡ d.	1010	1415	1815	2016	2218	...	...	...	...
Oakland Jack London Sq. a.	1028	1428	1828	2031	2230	...	...	...	...

THRUWAY 🚌 CONNECTIONS SACRAMENTO - STOCKTON

km		🚌	🚌	🚌	🚌	🚌				
0	**Sacramento** d.	0715	0950	1205	1355	1805	...	...	...	...
	Lodi d.	|	1030	|	1435	|	...	...	...	...
	Stockton Cabral / ACE (**d**) a.	0805	1055	1300	1500	1900	...	...	...	...
	Stockton San Joaquin St. a.	0815	1105	1310	1510	1910	...	...	...	...

	🚌	🚌	🚌	🚌	🚌				
Stockton San Joaquin St. d.	0845	1245	1645	1845	2045	...	...	...	...
Stockton Cabral / ACE (**d**) d.	|	1255	1655	1955	2055	...	...	...	...
Lodi d.	0910	1320	1720	1920	|	...	...	...	...
Sacramento a.	0950	1400	1800	2005	2210	...	...	...	...

d – Stockton **Cabral**. Also known as ACE or Downtown station.

* – Connection by 🚌.

‡ – For 🚌 connections to / from San Francisco see Table **9325**.

SAN FRANCISCO - SAN JOSE 9350

Caltrain

km																							
			Ⓐ	Ⓐ	Ⓐ	Ⓐ	Ⓐ	Ⓐ	Ⓐ	Ⓐ	Ⓐ	Ⓐ	Ⓐ	Ⓐ		Ⓐ	Ⓐ	Ⓐ	Ⓐ	Ⓐ	Ⓐ	Ⓐ	Ⓐ
0	**San Francisco** 4th / King St. d.	Ⓐ	0005	0606	0612	0639	0706	0712	0739	0806	0812	0839	0914	0938	and	1414	1438	1511	1539	1606	1612	1639	1706
22	Millbrae Transit Center ◧ d.		0030	0625	0633	0704	0725	0733	0804	0825	0833	0904	0934	1004	at the	1434	1504	1532	1604	1624	1633	1704	1724
44	Redwood City d.		0056	0641	0654	0730	0741	0754	0830	0841	0854	0932	0951	1032	same	1451	1532	1553	1630	1641	1654	1730	1741
47	Menlo Park d.		0102	|	|	0736	|	|	0836	|	|	0938	0957	1038	minutes	1457	1538	|	1636	|	|	1736	|
55	Palo Alto d.		0106	0649	0701	0740	0749	0801	0840	0849	0901	0941	1000	1041	past	1500	1541	1600	1640	1649	1701	1740	1749
58	Mountain View d.		0118	0657	0709	0752	0757	0814	0852	0857	0914	0954	1008	1054	each	1508	1554	1608	1652	1657	1709	1752	1757
71	Santa Clara d.		0133	|	0722	0811	|	0822	0911	|	0922	1010	1020	1110	hour	1520	1610	1621	1711	|	1722	1811	|
75	**San Jose** Diridon a.		0141	0712	0729	0823	0812	0829	0919	0911	0929	1018	1028	1118	until	1528	1619	1630	1718	1711	1728	1821	1811

	Ⓐ	Ⓐ	Ⓐ	Ⓐ	Ⓐ	Ⓐ	Ⓐ	Ⓐ	Ⓐ	Ⓐ	Ⓐ	Ⓐ	Ⓐ	Ⓐ			Ⓒ	Ⓒ	Ⓒ		Ⓒ	Ⓒ
San Francisco 4th / King St. d.	1712	1739	1806	1812	1843	1914	1938	2014	2032	2102	2130	2200	2230	2300	...	Ⓒ	0005	0828	0958	and	2158	2258
Millbrae Transit Center ◧ d.	1733	1804	1824	1833	1908	1934	2003	2034	2057	2128	2155	2226	2256	2326	...		0031	0853	1024	at the	2224	2324
Redwood City d.	1754	1830	1841	1854	1935	1951	2031	2051	2126	2156	2224	2254	2323	2353	...		0059	0921	1052	same	2252	2352
Menlo Park d.	|	1836	|	|	1940	1957	2038	2057	2133	2203	2231	2301	2329	2359	...		0105	0928	1058	minutes	2258	2358
Palo Alto d.	1801	1840	1849	1901	1944	2000	2042	2100	2137	2207	2235	2305	2332	0003	...		0109	0932	1102	past	2302	0002
Mountain View d.	1809	1852	1857	1909	1956	2008	2055	2108	2150	2221	2248	2319	2345	0017	...		0121	0945	1116	each	2316	0015
Santa Clara d.	1822	1911	|	1922	2012	2020	2110	2120	2205	2236	2303	2334	0001	0032	...		0137	1001	1132	hour	2332	0031
San Jose Diridon a.	1829	1919	1911	1928	2019	2028	2119	2128	2214	2244	2313	2342	0011	0040	...		0144	1010	1140	until	2338	0039

		Ⓐ	Ⓐ	Ⓐ	Ⓐ	Ⓐ	Ⓐ	Ⓐ	Ⓐ	Ⓐ	Ⓐ	Ⓐ	Ⓐ		Ⓐ	Ⓐ	Ⓐ	Ⓐ	Ⓐ	Ⓐ	Ⓐ	Ⓐ
San Jose Diridon d.	Ⓐ	0559	0623	0644	0659	0723	0742	0759	0823	0844	0856	0943	0954	and	1443	1454	1522	1544	1559	1624	1644	1659
Santa Clara d.		|	|	0650	|	|	0750	|	|	0850	0902	0949	1000	at the	1449	1500	|	1550	|	|	1650	|
Mountain View d.		0613	0642	0703	0713	0742	0803	0813	0842	0903	0917	1001	1015	same	1501	1515	1543	1603	1613	1643	1703	1713
Palo Alto d.		0621	0654	0711	0721	0754	0811	0821	0854	0911	0929	1009	1028	minutes	1509	1628	1555	1611	1621	1655	1711	1721
Menlo Park d.		|	0658	|	|	0758	|	|	0858	|	0933	1012	1032	past	1512	1632	1558	|	|	1658	|	|
Redwood City d.		0628	0703	0717	0728	0803	0817	0828	0903	0917	0938	1018	1037	each	1518	1637	1604	1617	1628	1704	1717	1728
Millbrae Transit Center ◧ d.		0646	0721	0738	0746	0821	0838	0846	0921	0939	1006	1038	1105	hour	1538	1605	1622	1638	1646	1721	1738	1746
San Francisco 4th / King St. a.		0705	0738	0800	0805	0838	0900	0905	0938	1001	1032	1057	1133	until	1557	1633	1639	1700	1705	1738	1800	1805

	Ⓐ	Ⓐ	Ⓐ	Ⓐ	Ⓐ	Ⓐ	Ⓐ	Ⓐ	Ⓐ	Ⓐ	Ⓐ	Ⓐ	Ⓐ	Ⓐ			Ⓒ	Ⓒ		Ⓒ	Ⓒ	Ⓒ
San Jose Diridon d.	1723	1744	1759	1823	1844	1856	1943	1954	2024	2049	2119	2149	2219	2312	...	Ⓒ	0719	0912	and	2112	2219	2312
Santa Clara d.	|	1750	|	|	1850	1902	1949	2000	2030	2055	2125	2155	2225	2318	...		0725	0918	at the	2118	2225	2318
Mountain View d.	1742	1803	1813	1842	1903	1917	2002	2015	2045	2110	2140	2210	2240	2333	...		0740	0934	same	2134	2235	2334
Palo Alto d.	1754	1811	1821	1858	1911	1929	2009	2027	2057	2123	2152	2223	2252	2346	...		0752	0946	minutes	2146	2353	2346
Menlo Park d.	1758	|	|	1858	|	1932	2012	2030	2100	2126	2156	2226	2256	2350	...		0755	0950	past	2150	2356	2350
Redwood City d.	1803	1817	1828	1903	1917	1938	2018	2036	2106	2133	2202	2233	2302	2356	...		0801	0956	each	2156	2302	2356
Millbrae Transit Center ◧ d.	1821	1838	1846	1922	1938	2008	2037	2106	2136	2201	2231	2301	2331	0025	...		0829	1026	hour	2226	2332	0026
San Francisco 4th / King St. a.	1838	1900	1906	1939	2000	2035	2057	2133	2203	2230	2300	2329	0000	0053	...		0856	1052	until	2252	2359	0052

◧ – SamTrans 🚌 route **SFO** connects Millbrae Transit Center with San Francisco International Airport.

9352 For notes see Table 9366 — SAN JOSE - STOCKTON — Altamont Corridor Express

km		Ⓐ	Ⓐ	Ⓐ	Ⓐ					
0	**San Jose** Diridon d.	1535	1635	1735	1838	...	...	...	...	...
	Santa Clara d.	1540	1640	1740	1843	...	...	...	...	...
	Great America d.	1549	1649	1749	1852	...	...	...	...	...
	Fremont d.	1605	1705	1805	1908	...	...	...	...	...
	Pleasanton d.	1628	1728	1828	1931	...	...	...	...	...
	Livermore d.	1637	1737	1837	1940	...	...	...	...	...
	Tracy ⊕ d.	1711	1811	1911	2014	...	...	...	...	...
125	**Stockton** Cabral ◧ a.	1747	1847	1947	2050	...	...	...	...	...

	Ⓐ	Ⓐ	Ⓐ	Ⓐ					
Stockton Cabral ◧ d.	0410	0535	0640	0732	...	...	...	...	...
Tracy d.	0441	0606	0711	0803	...	...	...	...	...
Livermore d.	0515	0640	0745	0837	...	...	...	...	...
Pleasanton d.	0523	0648	0753	0845	...	...	...	...	...
Fremont d.	0545	0710	0815	0907	...	...	...	...	...
Great America ⊕ d.	0603	0728	0833	0925	...	...	...	...	...
Santa Clara ⊕ d.	0610	0735	0840	0932	...	...	...	...	...
San Jose Diridon a.	0622	0747	0852	0944	...	...	...	...	...

9356 LANCASTER - LOS ANGELES — Antelope Valley Line — Metrolink

km		Ⓐ	Ⓐ	Ⓐ		Ⓐ	Ⓒ	Ⓐ		Ⓐ	Ⓒ	Ⓐ		Ⓒ	Ⓐ		Ⓒ	Ⓐ	Ⓒ		Ⓐ	Ⓐ	Ⓒ	
0	**Lancaster** d.	0341	0441	0511	...	0611	0622	0711	...	...	0904	0911	...	1115	1205	...	1240	1411	1423	...	...	1811	1823	...
	Via Princessa d.	0440	0540	0615	...	0715	0722	0815	...	0915	1003	1015	...	1214	1309	...	1339	1515	1523	...	1615	1915	1924	...
82	Santa Clarita d.	0447	0547	0621	...	0721	0728	0821	...	0921	1009	1021	...	1220	1315	...	1345	1521	1529	...	1621	1921	1930	...
	Burbank Airport North ✈ d.	0521	0621	0655	...	0755	0800	0855	...	0955	1042	1055	...	1253	1349	...	1417	1555	1602	...	1655	1955	2003	...
106	Downtown Burbank d.	0527	0627	0701	...	0801	0805	0901	...	1001	1046	1101	...	1258	1355	...	1422	1601	1607	...	1701	2001	2007	...
121	**Los Angeles** Union a.	0546	0646	0720	...	0820	0825	0920	...	1020	1110	1120	...	1320	1414	...	1443	1620	1628	...	1720	2020	2029	...

	Ⓐ	Ⓐ	Ⓒ		Ⓐ	Ⓒ	Ⓐ		Ⓒ	Ⓐ	Ⓐ		Ⓒ	Ⓐ		Ⓒ	Ⓐ	Ⓐ		Ⓐ	Ⓒ	Ⓐ	
Los Angeles Union d.	0639	0739	0840	...	0939	1137	1139	...	1358	1439	1539	...	1551	1639	...	1725	1739	1839	...	1939	2053	2139	...
Downtown Burbank d.	0658	0758	0858	...	0958	1155	1158	...	1416	1458	1558	...	1609	1658	...	1743	1758	1858	...	1958	2111	2158	...
Burbank Airport North ✈ d.	0703	0803	0904	...	1003	1201	1203	...	1422	1503	1603	...	1615	1703	...	1748	1803	1903	...	2003	2116	2203	...
Santa Clarita d.	0740	0840	0938	...	1040	1235	1240	...	1458	1540	1640	...	1649	1740	...	1822	1840	1940	...	2040	2150	2240	...
Via Princessa d.	0747	0847	0944	...	1047	1241	1247	...	1505	1547	1647	...	1655	1747	...	1828	1847	1947	...	2047	2156	2247	...
Lancaster a.	0852	...	1051	...	1152	1348	1352	...	1612	...	1752	...	1759	1852	...	1930	1952	2052	...	2152	2300	2352	...

9358 For notes see Table 9366 — LOS ANGELES - SAN BERNARDINO — San Bernardino Line — Metrolink

km		Ⓐ	Ⓐ		Ⓐ	Ⓒ	Ⓐ	Ⓐ	Ⓒ			Ⓐ	Ⓒ	Ⓐ	Ⓐ	Ⓐ A	Ⓐ	Ⓐ	Ⓐ	Ⓒ	Ⓐ	Ⓐ	Ⓒ	Ⓐ
0	**Los Angeles** Union d.	0537	0734	0838	0938	1038	1138	1238	1338	1438	1538	1557	1638	1638	1655	1726	1737	1757	1838	1938	1938	2038	2138	2138
25	El Monte d.	0609	0802	0859	1010	1059	1200	1300	1359	1459	1559	1618	1659	1700	1719	|	1759	1821	1900	1959	2000	2100	2159	2200
30	Covina d.	0616	0820	0917	1017	1117	1217	1317	1417	1517	1617	1635	1717	1718	1736	1803	1817	1838	1917	2017	2017	2117	2217	2217
70	Pomona North d.	0630	0833	0930	1030	1130	1230	1330	1430	1530	1630	1652	1730	1731	1751	|	1830	1852	1930	2030	2030	2130	2230	2230
95	**San Bernardino** Depot a.	0721	0921	1016	1116	1216	1316	1416	1516	1616	1716	1735	1816	1820	1836	1846	1921	1935	2016	2116	2116	2216	2316	2316

	Ⓐ	Ⓐ	Ⓐ B	Ⓐ	Ⓒ	Ⓐ	Ⓐ	Ⓒ	Ⓐ	Ⓐ	Ⓒ	Ⓐ	Ⓒ	Ⓒ	Ⓐ	Ⓒ	Ⓐ	Ⓐ	Ⓐ	Ⓒ	Ⓐ	Ⓐ	Ⓒ
San Bernardino Depot d.	0511	0541	0615	0626	0641	0646	0746	0841	0843	0943	1141	1143	1241	1341	1343	1441	1443	1543	1643	1741	1744	1848	1941
Pomona North d.	0558	0629	|	0710	0726	0730	0828	0926	0925	1025	1226	1225	1326	1426	1425	1526	1525	1625	1730	1826	1829	1931	2026
Covina d.	0609	0640	0654	0721	0737	0742	0842	0937	0940	1040	1237	1240	1337	1437	1440	1537	1540	1640	1741	1837	1840	1942	2037
El Monte d.	0627	0655	|	0738	0755	0759	0859	0955	0956	1056	1255	1256	1355	1455	1456	1555	1600	1658	1759	1855	1858	2000	2055
Los Angeles Union a.	0649	0717	0729	0802	0822	0821	0922	1022	1021	1121	1322	1321	1422	1522	1521	1622	1626	1728	1827	1922	1921	2020	2122

9360 LOS ANGELES - RIVERSIDE - PERRIS — Riverside/Perris Valley Lines — Metrolink

km		Ⓐ	Ⓐ	Ⓐ	Ⓐ	Ⓐ				
0	**Los Angeles** Union d.	1320	1610	1650	1720	1800	...	...	...	...
	Industry d.	1355	1645	1725	1755	1835	...	...	...	...
70	Pomona Downtown d.	1404	1654	1734	1804	1844	...	...	...	...
101	**Riverside** Downtown a.	1448	1737	1817	1848	1928	...	...	...	...

	Ⓐ	Ⓐ	Ⓐ	Ⓐ	Ⓐ	Ⓐ			
Riverside Downtown d.	0435	0526	0606	0650	0810	1510	...	...	...
Pomona Downtown d.	0511	0602	0642	0726	0846	1546	...	...	...
Industry d.	0520	0611	0651	0735	0855	1555	...	...	...
Los Angeles Union a.	0603	0654	0734	0818	0938	1638	...	...	...

km		Ⓐ	Ⓐ	Ⓒ	Ⓐ	Ⓐ	Ⓐ	Ⓐ	Ⓐ	Ⓒ
0	**Los Angeles** Union d.	0545	0730	1525	1539	1621	1657	1731	1852	1920
	Fullerton d.	0620	0807	1602	1614	1656	1733	1807	1928	1957
	Corona West d.	0644	0830	1626	1638	1720	1757	1831	1952	2021
99	**Riverside** Downtown a.	0714	0857	1652	1706	1747	1827	1858	2022	2047
	Perris Downtown a.	...	0931	1727	1740	1821	1902	1932	...	2133

	Ⓐ	Ⓐ		Ⓐ	Ⓐ	Ⓒ		Ⓒ	Ⓐ
Perris Downtown d.	0442	0521	...	0606	0642	0711	...	0814	1501
Riverside Downtown d.	0516	0556	...	0640	0716	0748	...	0851	1536
Corona West d.	0542	0622	...	0706	0742	0814	...	0916	1608
Fullerton d.	0606	0646	...	0730	0806	0838	...	0940	1631
Los Angeles Union a.	0647	0728	...	0811	0847	0919	...	1021	1714

9362 SAN BERNARDINO - RIVERSIDE - OCEANSIDE — Inland Empire Line — Metrolink

km		Ⓐ	Ⓐ	Ⓐ	Ⓐ	Ⓒ	Ⓐ	Ⓒ	Ⓐ	Ⓐ
0	**San Bernardino** Downtown d.	0429	0518	0554	...	0700	...	0856	1259	...
	Riverside Downtown d.	0450	0539	0615	0650	0722	0728	0917	1319	1448
25	Corona West d.	0515	0604	0640	0716	0756	0753	0951	1344	1513
	Anaheim Canyon d.	0535	0623	0700	0736	0816	0812	1011	1404	1532
	Orange 9320 d.	0541	0630	0706	0734	0823	0819	1018	1410	1541
78	Santa Ana 9320 d.	0547	0636	0712	0748	0828	0824	1023	1416	1547
94	Irvine 9320 d.	0601	0653	0726	0802	0843	0838	1037	1429	1602
113	San Juan Capistrano 9320 d.	...	...	...	...	0859	...	1054	...	...
126	San Clemente 9320 d.	...	...	...	...	0909	...	1104	...	...
160	**Oceanside** 9320 a.	...	...	...	...	...	...	...	...	...

	Ⓐ	Ⓐ	Ⓒ	Ⓐ	Ⓐ	Ⓐ	Ⓐ	Ⓒ	Ⓐ
Oceanside 9320 d.	...	...	...	...	...	...	...	...	...
San Clemente 9320 d.	...	...	1502	...	...	...	...	1655	...
San Juan Capistrano 9320 d.	...	...	1512	...	...	...	...	1705	...
Irvine 9320 d.	0829	0922	1528	1538	1606	1702	1727	1726	1845
Santa Ana 9320 d.	0842	0936	1541	1551	1619	1715	1741	1739	1858
Orange 9320 d.	0847	0941	1547	1556	1624	1720	1746	1744	1904
Anaheim Canyon d.	0954	0948	1554	1603	1631	1727	1753	1752	1911
Corona West d.	0914	1008	1614	1623	1651	1747	1813	1812	1930
Riverside Downtown a.	0943	1033	1639	1652	1716	1812	1838	1837	2000
San Bernardino Downtown a.	...	1058	1705	...	1741	1837	1903	1903	...

9364 For notes see Table 9366 — SAN BERNARDINO - REDLANDS — Arrow Service — Metrolink

km		Ⓒ	Ⓐ	Ⓐ	Ⓒ	Ⓐ		Ⓐ	Ⓒ	Ⓒ	Ⓐ	Ⓒ	Ⓐ	Ⓐ	Ⓒ	Ⓐ	Ⓐ	Ⓒ	Ⓐ	Ⓒ	Ⓐ	Ⓒ	Ⓐ	Ⓒ
0	**S. Bernardino** Downtown ⊡ d.	0736	0738	0809	0925	0950	1031	1131	1136	1236	1331	1336	1401	1508	1532	1551	1631	1632	1731	1732	1835	1837	1934	2032
	Redlands Downtown ⊡ d.	0753	0756	0827	0942	1008	1049	1149	1153	1253	1349	1353	1419	1526	1549	1609	1649	1649	1749	1749	1853	1854	1952	2049
14	**Redlands** University ⊡ a.	0758	0800	0831	0947	1012	1054	1153	1158	1258	1353	1358	1423	1530	1554	1613	1653	1654	1754	1754	1857	1859	1956	2054

	Ⓒ	Ⓐ	Ⓐ	Ⓐ	Ⓒ	Ⓐ	Ⓒ	Ⓒ	Ⓐ		Ⓐ	Ⓒ	Ⓐ	Ⓐ	Ⓒ	Ⓐ	Ⓐ	Ⓒ	Ⓒ	Ⓐ	Ⓒ	Ⓐ	Ⓐ
Redlands University ⊡ d.	0806	0807	0838	0908	0954	1030	1106	1206	1226	1306	1400	1406	1430	1506	1602	1628	1700	1702	1802	1805	1906	1910	2038
Redlands Downtown ⊡ d.	0811	0812	0843	0913	0959	1035	1111	1211	1231	1311	1405	1411	1435	1511	1607	1633	1705	1707	1807	1810	1911	1915	2043
San Bernardino Downtown ⊡ a.	0828	0830	0901	0931	1016	1053	1128	1228	1249	1329	1423	1428	1453	1529	1624	1651	1723	1724	1824	1828	1928	1933	2101

9366 OCEANSIDE - SAN DIEGO — Coaster

Coaster Day Pass and Monthly Pass holders may use Amtrak services south of Oceanside. See Table **9320** for schedules.

km		Ⓐ	Ⓐ	Ⓐ	Ⓐ			Ⓒ	Ⓐ	Ⓒ	Ⓐ	Ⓒ			Ⓐ	Ⓒ	Ⓐ	Ⓐ			Ⓐ			⑤Ⓒ
0	**Oceanside** 9320 d.	0516	0556	0636	0716	0736	...	0916	0936	1036	1136	1216	...	1336	1436	1516	1536	1616	...	1636	1716	1816	1936	2116
	Carlsbad Village d.	0523	0603	0643	0723	0743	...	0923	0943	1043	1143	1223	...	1343	1443	1523	1543	1623	...	1643	1723	1823	1943	2123
	Encinitas d.	0535	0615	0655	0735	0755	...	0935	0955	1055	1155	1235	...	1355	1455	1535	1555	1635	...	1655	1735	1835	1955	2135
27	Solana Beach 9320 d.	0541	0621	0701	0741	0801	...	0941	1001	1101	1201	1241	...	1401	1501	1541	1601	1641	...	1701	1741	1841	2001	2141
	Sorrento Valley d.	0550	0630	0710	0750	0810	...	0950	1010	1110	1210	1250	...	1410	1510	1550	1610	1650	...	1710	1750	1850	2010	2150
	San Diego Old Town 9320 a.	0611	0651	0731	0811	0831	...	1011	1031	1131	1231	1311	...	1431	1531	1611	1631	1711	...	1731	1811	1911	2031	2211
68	**San Diego** Santa Fe ● 9320 a.	0617	0657	0737	0817	0837	...	1017	1037	1137	1237	1317	...	1437	1537	1617	1637	1717	...	1737	1817	1917	2037	2217

	Ⓐ	Ⓐ	Ⓐ	Ⓐ		Ⓒ	Ⓐ		Ⓒ	Ⓐ	Ⓒ	Ⓒ	Ⓐ	Ⓐ	Ⓒ		Ⓐ	Ⓐ		Ⓐ			⑤Ⓒ
San Diego Santa Fe ● 9320 d.	0640	0740	0820	0840	0920	1040	1120	...	1220	1320	1340	1520	1540	1620	1640	...	1720	1740	1820	1840	1940	2120	2340
San Diego Old Town 9320 d.	0647	0747	0827	0847	0927	1047	1127	...	1227	1327	1347	1527	1547	1627	1647	...	1727	1747	1827	1847	1947	2127	2347
Sorrento Valley d.	0709	0809	0849	0909	0949	1109	1149	...	1249	1349	1409	1549	1609	1649	1709	...	1749	1809	1849	1909	2009	2149	0009
Solana Beach 9320 d.	0719	0819	0859	0919	0959	1119	1159	...	1259	1359	1419	1559	1619	1659	1719	...	1759	1819	1859	1919	2019	2159	0019
Encinitas d.	0725	0825	0905	0925	1005	1125	1205	...	1305	1405	1425	1605	1625	1705	1725	...	1805	1825	1905	1925	2025	2205	0025
Carlsbad Village d.	0737	0837	0917	0937	1017	1137	1217	...	1317	1417	1437	1617	1637	1717	1737	...	1817	1837	1917	1937	2037	2217	0037
Oceanside 9320 a.	0742	0842	0922	0942	1022	1142	1222	...	1322	1422	1442	1622	1642	1722	1742	...	1822	1842	1922	1942	2042	2222	0042

A – To Redlands Downtown (a. 1906).
B – From Redlands Downtown (d. 0555).

⊕ – Trains may leave early if all passengers have exited.
◧ – Also known as ACE or Downtown station.
● – Also known as San Diego Downtown.

⊡ – Also from San Bernardino D at 0633 Ⓐ, 0636 Ⓒ, 0839 Ⓐ, 1431 Ⓐ, 1949 Ⓐ, 2042 Ⓐ, 2146 Ⓐ, 2132 Ⓒ; also from Redlands U at 0606, 0705 Ⓒ, 0710 Ⓐ, 1550 Ⓐ, 2012 Ⓐ, 2102 Ⓒ, 2111 Ⓐ, 2221 Ⓐ, 2310 Ⓒ

Sprinter — OCEANSIDE - ESCONDIDO — 9368

km									
0	**Oceanside** d.	0533	0633	0733	0833	and	1833	1933	2033
	Vista Transit Center d.	0556	0656	0756	0856	hourly	1856	1956	2056
	San Marcos Civic Center d.	0613	0713	0813	0913	until	1913	2013	2113
34	**Escondido** a.	0626	0726	0826	0926	◧	1926	2026	2126

Escondido d.	0533	0633	0733	0833	and	1833	1933	2033
San Marcos Civic Center d.	0544	0644	0744	0844	hourly	1844	1944	2044
Vista Transit Center d.	0557	0657	0757	0857	until	1857	1957	2057
Oceanside a.	0626	0726	0826	0926	◧	1926	2026	2126

◧ – Additional services: from Oceanside at 0403 Ⓐ and hourly until 1003 Ⓐ, 1103 and hourly until 1803, 1903 Ⓐ, 2003 Ⓐ; from Escondido at 0403 Ⓐ and hourly until 0903 Ⓐ, 1003 and hourly until 1703, 1803 Ⓐ, 1903 Ⓐ, 2003 Ⓐ. Additional later evening services are available on ⑤⑥.

Brightline — MIAMI - WEST PALM BEACH — 9380

WARNING! Schedules are subject to alteration, especially on ⑤⑥⑦ - please check locally.

km		①-⑤	①-⑤	①-⑥			①-⑥							①-⑤									⑥⑦		
0	**Miami** Central d.	0648	0748	0848	0948	...	1048	1148	1348	1448	...	1548	1648	1718	1748	...	1848	1948	2048	2148	...	2248	2348	...
35	Fort Lauderdale ● d.	0720	0820	0920	1020	...	1120	1220	1420	1520	...	1620	1720	1750	1820	...	1920	2020	2120	2220	...	2320	0020	...
104	**West Palm Beach** ⊕ a.	0800	0900	1000	1100	...	1200	1300	1500	1600	...	1700	1800	1830	1900	...	2000	2100	2200	2300	...	0000	0100	...

	①-⑤	①-⑥	①-⑤			①-⑥		①-⑥											⑥⑦			⑥	
West Palm Beach ⊕ d.	0610	0648	0710	0748	...	0848	0948	1048	1148	...	1348	1448	1548	1648	...	1748	1848	1948	2048	...	2148	2248	...
Fort Lauderdale ● d.	0647	0725	0747	0825	...	0925	1025	1125	1225	...	1325	1525	1625	1725	...	1825	1925	2025	2125	...	2225	2325	...
Miami Central a.	0722	0800	0822	0900	...	1000	1100	1200	1300	...	1500	1600	1700	1800	...	1900	2000	2100	2200	...	2300	0000	...

● – Approximately 3 km by 🚐 from the Amtrak / Tri-Rail station (Table **9240**).

⊕ – Approximately 800 metres from the Amtrak / Tri-Rail station (Table **9240**).

MEXICO — 9900

km		②⑦ A	
0	**Creel** d.	0800	...
60	Divisadero d.	0955	...
105	Bahuichivo d.	1125	...
275	El Fuerte d.	1535	...
360	**Los Mochis** a.	1740	...

	①⑤ A	
Los Mochis d.	0800	...
El Fuerte d.	1020	...
Bahuichivo d.	1425	...
Divisadero d.	1615	...
Creel a.	1740	...

km		⑥ B a	⑥ 🚐 a
0	**Guadalajara** d.	0900	0900
72	**Tequila** a.	1100	1030

	⑥ B a	⑥ 🚐 a
Tequila d.	1800	1830
Guadalajara a.	2000	2000

A – EL CHEPE EXPRESS – Tourist excursion train. www.chepe.mx.
B – JOSÉ CUERVO EXPRESS – Tourist excursion train. www.mundocuervo.com.
a – Excursions are outward by train returning by 🚐 or v.v.

PANAMA CANAL RAILWAY — 9905

km		①-⑤	
0	**Ciudad Panama** d.	0715	...
77	**Colon** a.	0815	...

	①-⑤	
Colon d.	1715	...
Ciudad Panama a.	1815	...

INCOFER — COSTA RICA — 9915

km		①-⑤	①-⑤	①-⑤	①-⑤	①-⑤	①-⑤	①-⑤	①-⑤	
0	San José Pacifico d.	0515	0632	0716	1500	1520	1643	1703	1832	...
3	Pavas Metropolis III d.	0545	0702	0746	1530	1550	1713	1733	1902	...
10	San Antonio de Belén a.	0555	0712	0756	1540	1600	1723	1743	1912	...

	①-⑤	①-⑤	①-⑤	①-⑤	①-⑤	①-⑤	①-⑤	①-⑤	
San Antonio de Belén d.	0610	0720	0804	1548	1608	1723	1751	1920	...
Pavas Metropolis III d.	0620	0730	0814	1558	1618	1733	1801	1930	...
San José Pacifico a.	0655	0805	0849	1633	1653	1808	1836	2005	...

km		①-⑤		
0	Freses de Curidabat d.	0605	...	...
4	Universidad Costa Rica d.	0613	...	...
15	San José Pacifico a.	0632	...	...

	①-⑤	①-⑤	
San José Pacifico d.	1619	1729	...
Universidad Costa Rica d.	1644	1754	...
Freses de Curidabat a.	1652	1802	...

km		①-⑤	⑥	①-⑤	⑥	⑥	⑥	⑥	①-⑤	①-⑤
0	San José Atlantico ⊡ d.	0645	0630	0800	0730	0830	0930	1030	1530	1730
10	Heredia ⊡ a.	0712	0657	0827	0757	0857	0957	1057	1557	1757
22	Alajuela ⊡ a.	0735	0720	0850	0820	0920	1020	1120	1620	1820

	⑥⑤	⑥	①-⑤	⑥	⑥	⑥	⑥	①-⑤	①-⑤
Alajuela ⊡ d.	0630	0730	0745	0830	0930	1030	1130	1630	1830
Heredia ⊡ d.	0654	0754	0809	0854	0954	1054	1154	1654	1854
San José Atlantico ⊡ a.	0720	0820	0835	0920	1020	1120	1220	1720	1920

⊡ – Also at from San José Atlantico at 0445 ①-⑤, 1130 ⑥, 1230 ⑥; also from Alajuela at 0545 ①-⑤, 1230 ⑥, 1330 ⑥. Additional services operate San Jose Atlantico - Heredia and v.v.

Unión de los Ferrocarriles Cubanos — CUBA — 9920

km		3 E	1 E	7 E	5 E	103 F	101 E
0	**Habana** La Coubre d.	1615	1730	1825	1920	2220	...
90	Matanzas d.	1810	1925	2019	2115	0045	...
286	Santa Clara d.	2128	2243	2343	0040	0625	1320
382	Sancti Spiritus d.	|	|	|	|	0945	|
436	Ciego de Avila d.	0033	0147	0256	0405	...	1735
538	Camagüey d.	0307	0418	0532	0641	...	2113
714	Bayamo d.	|	|	1055	|	...	|
770	**Manzanillo** a.	|	|	1315	|	...	|
652	Las Tunas d.	0538	0650	...	0911	...	0127
729	Cacocúm d.	0706	0813	...	1047	...	0321
747	Holguin d.	|	|	...	1125	...	|
	Baracoa d.	|	|	...	...	...	|
884	**Guantanamo** a.	1130	|	...	...	...	|
854	**Santiago de Cuba** a.	...	1040	...	...	...	0650

	104 F	102 E	6 E	2 E	8 E	4 E
Santiago de Cuba d.	...	0715	...	1505	...	...
Guantanamo d.	...	|	...	|	...	1530
Baracoa a.	...	|	...	|	...	|
Holguin d.	...	|	1515	|	...	|
Cacocúm d.	...	1055	1557	1735	...	2010
Las Tunas d.	...	1254	1737	1906	...	2140
Manzanillo d.	...	|	|	|	1325	|
Bayamo d.	...	|	|	|	1620	|
Camagüey d.	...	1536	2019	2148	2158	0020
Ciego de Avila d.	...	1958	2249	0009	0026	0246
Sancti Spiritus d.	1505	|	|	|	|	|
Santa Clara d.	1825	0025	0219	0325	0431	0550
Matanzas d.	0046	...	0538	0540	0752	0905
Habana Central a.	0315	...	0725	0830	0940	1055

E – Runs every 4th day.

F – Runs every 3rd day.

IFE — VENEZUELA — 9925

km		①-⑤	①-⑤	①-⑤	and	①-⑤		⑥⑦	and	⑥⑦
0	**Caracas** d.	0514	0534	0554	every	2224	...	0456	every	2222
24	Charallave Norte d.	0531	0551	0611	20	2241	...	0513	30	2239
32	Charallave Sur d.	0536	0556	0616	mins	2246	...	0518	mins	2244
41	**Cúa** a.	0545	0605	0625	until	2255	...	0527	until	2353

	①-⑤	①-⑤	①-⑤	and	①-⑥		⑥⑦	and	⑥⑦
Cúa d.	0430	0450	0510	every	2144	...	0500	every	2141
Charallave Sur d.	0439	0459	0519	20	2153	..	0509	30	2149
Charallave Norte d.	0444	0504	0524	mins	2158	...	0514	min	2154
Caracas a.	0501	0521	0541	until	2215	...	1051	until	2211

km		Ⓐ	Ⓒ	Ⓐ	Ⓐ	Ⓐ	Ⓒ	Ⓐ
0	**Puerto Cabello** d.	...	...	...	...	...	...	...
140	Yaritagua d.	0610	0755	0900	0948	1500	1605	1700
168	San Jacinto a.	0652	0835	0930	1030	1530	1635	1730
174	**Barquisimeto** a.	0705	0845	0940	1045	1540	1645	1740

	Ⓐ	Ⓐ	Ⓒ	Ⓐ	Ⓐ	Ⓒ	Ⓐ
Barquisimeto d.	0640	0710	0850	1250	1540	1650	1800
San Jacinto d.	0652	0732	0900	1300	1550	1700	1820
Yaritagua d.	0722	0812	0938	1330	1620	1738	1858
Puerto Cabello a.	...	...	...	...	...	...	...

9930 COLOMBIA

km										
0	**Puerto Parra** ⊖ d.	...	0510	...	...	...	1655	...	...	...
65	Barrancabermeja ⊖ d.	0600	0725	1130	1430	1700	1910	...	...	...
95	**García Cardena** ⊖ a.	0700	...	1230	1530	1800	...	...	...	...

García Cardena ⊖ d.	...	0700	...	1230	1530	1800	...	...	...
Barrancabermeja ⊖ d.	0515	0800	1300	1330	1630	1900	...	...	...
Puerto Parra ⊖ a.	0730	...	1515	...	...	...	...	...	...

km		Ⓐ	Ⓒ	Ⓐ						
0	**Bogotá** Sabana ● d.	0525	0820	1715	...	...	...	...	...	...
15	Usaquen ● d.	0547	0915	1743	...	...	...	...	...	...
34	La Caro ● d.	0632	1015	1822	...	...	...	...	...	...
40	Cajicá ● d.	0648	|	1838	...	...	...	...	...	...
53	**Zapaquirá** ● a.	...	1105	...	...	...	...	...	...	...

	Ⓐ	Ⓒ	Ⓒ	Ⓐ					
Zapaquirá ● d.	...	1235	...	...	...	...	...	...	...
Cajicá ● d.	0700	1305	1515	1850	...	...	...	...	...
La Caro ● d.	0719	...	1540	1908	...	...	...	...	...
Usaquen ● d.	0803	...	1640	1953	...	...	...	...	...
Bogotá Sabana ● a.	0824	...	1730	2014	...	...	...	...	...

⊖ – Operated by Coopsercol Ltda.

● – Operated by Turistren.

9940 PERU

CUSCO - PUNO

TITICACA TRAIN – 🚃 ✕. *385 km.* Journey 10½ hours. www.perurail.com.
From **Cusco** Wanchaq at 0710③, 0750⑤⑦.
From **Puno** at 0730①④⑥.

BELMOND ANDEAN EXPLORER – Luxury tourist train. *385 km.* www.perurail.com.
Departure from **Cusco** Wanchaq is at 1100 on Tuesday. The train takes 11 hours for the journey to **Puno** where passengers remain on the train for an overnight stay. The return service departs from **Puno** at 1200 on Wednesday, with passengers spending the night on the train at Cusipata and arrival at **Cusco** Wanchaq being at 0730 on Thursday.

HUANCAYO - HUANCAVELICA

EL TREN MACHO. *127 km.* Journey 5¼ hours. Operator: FC Huancayo-Huancavelica.
From **Huancayo** at 0630①③⑤.
From **Huancavelica** at 0630②④⑥.

LIMA - HUANCAYO

TREN DE LA SIERRA – 🚃12 ✕. *332 km.* Journey 12 hours. Operator: FC Central Andino.
From **Lima** at 0700. Service suspended.
From **Huancayo** at 0700. Service suspended.

MACHU PICCHU

Inca Rail (www.incarail.com) and Perurail (www.perurail.com) operate a variety of excursion trains from Cusco, Poroy and Ollantaytambo to Machu Picchu. Please check with operators for running days.

TACNA - ARICA

🚃2 only. *62 km.* Journey 1¼ hours. Operator: FC Tacna Arica.
From **Tacna** at 0600, 1630
From **Arica** at 0800, 1815

9945 BOLIVIA

Ferroviária Andina, Ferroviária Oriental

OURO - VILLAZÓN — FA

km		①④			①④	
0	**Oruro** d.	...	...	**Villazón** d.	...	...
313	Uyuni d.	...	...	Tupiza d.	1900	...
391	**Avaroa** a.	...	...	Atocha d.	2220	...
404	Atocha d.	0600	...	**Avaroa** d.	...	...
501	Tupiza d.	0920	...	Uyuni d.	...	...
602	**Villazón** a.	...	...	**Oruro** a.	...	...

SANTA CRUZ DE LA SIERRA - YACUIBA — FO

km		64 ④			63 ⑤	
0	**SC de la Sierra** a.	1530	...	**Yacuíba** d.	1700	...
115	Cabezas d.	1945	...	Villa Montes d.	1948	...
239	Charaguá d.	2322	...	Boyuibe d.	2235	...
360	Boyuibe d.	0229	...	Charaguá d.	0135	...
434	Villa Montes d.	0513	...	Cabezas d.	0535	...
533	**Yacuíba** a.	0805	...	**SC de la Sierra** a.	0955.	...

PUERTO QUIJARRO - SANTA CRUZ DA LA SIERRA — FO

km		13 ②④⑦	7 ①③⑤		14 ①③⑤	8 ②④⑦
0	**Puerto Quijarro** d.	1300	1800	**SC da la Sierra** d.	1320	1800
125	Rivero Torrez d.	1537	2010	San José Chiquitos d.	1930	2308
240	Roboré d.	1854	2245	Roboré d.	2342	0212
374	San José Chiquitos d.	2304	0150	Rivero Torrez d.	0309	0448
640	**SC da la Sierra** a.	0540	0700	**Puerto Quijarro** a.	0602	0700

OTHER SERVICES IN BOLIVIA — FA

El Alto - Guaqui and v.v. *77 km.* Journey 4 - 5 hours.
From **El Alto** at 0800 (2nd Sunday of each month only).
From **Guaqui** at 1530 (2nd Sunday of each month only).

Viacha - Charaña and v.v. *208 km.* Journey 6 hours.
From **Viacha** at 0830①④.
From **Charaña** at 0900②⑤.

9950 BRAZIL

Estrada de Ferro do Carajás / Estrada de Ferro Vitória a Minas

SÃO LUIS - PARAUAPEBAS — EFC

km		①④⑥			②⑤⑦	
0	**São Luis** d.	0800	...	**Parauapebas** d.	0600	...
126	Arari d.	1016	...	Itainopolis d.	0731	...
145	Vitória do Mearim d.	1040	...	Marabá d.	0829	...
213	Santa Inês d.	1156	...	São Pedro d.	0956	...
264	Alto Alegre d.	1256	...	Acailandia d.	1219	...
299	Auzilândia d.	1340	...	Nova Vida d.	1429	...
315	Altamira d.	1402	...	Presa de Porco d.	1525	...
334	Presa de Porco d.	1430	...	Altamira d.	1551	...
384	Nova Vida d.	1526	...	Auzilândia d.	1613	...
513	Acailandia d.	1741	...	Alto Alegre d.	1659	...
650	São Pedro d.	1957	...	Santa Inês d.	1804	...
738	Marabá d.	2131	...	Vitória do Mearim d.	1913	...
785	Itainopolis d.	2222	...	Arari d.	1941	...
861	**Parauapebas** d.	2350	...	**São Luis** a.	2000	...

BELO HORIZONTE - VITÓRIA — EFVM

km						
0	**Belo Horizonte** d.	0730	...	**Vitória** d.	...	0700
71	Dois Irmãos d.	0903	...	Flexal d.	...	0715
97	Rio Piracicaba d.	1002	...	Fundão d.	...	0802
149	Drumond d.	1048	1645	Piraqueacú d.	...	0829
184	**Itabira** a.	|	1741	Colatina d.	...	0927
173	Antonio Dias d.	1116	...	Aimorés d.	...	1026
286	Periquito d.	1315	...	Conselheiro Pena d.	...	1125
339	Governador Valadares d.	1420	...	Governador Valadares d.	...	1314
415	Conselheiro Pena d.	1547	...	Periquito d.	...	1405
484	Aimorés d.	1704	...	Antonio Dias d.	...	1605
532	Colatina d.	1804	...	**Itabira** d.	0930	|
588	Piraqueacú d.	1859	...	Drumond d.	1026	1639
612	Fundão d.	1926	...	Rio Piracicaba d.	...	1732
657	Flexal d.	2012	...	Dois Irmãos d.	...	1830
664	**Vitória** a.	2030	...	**Belo Horizonte** a.	...	2010

9955 URUGUAY

Ferrocarriles del Estado

km		①⑤								
0	**Paso de los Toros** d.	...	...	...	...	...	...	...	...	...
172	Tacuarembó d.	0700	...	...	...	...	...	...	...	...
221	Laureles d.	0757	...	...	...	...	...	...	...	...
246	Paso Tranqueras d.	0825	...	...	...	...	...	...	...	...
264	Paso Ataques d.	0841	...	...	...	...	...	...	...	...
290	**Rivera** a.	0910	...	...	...	...	...	...	...	...

	①⑤								
Rivera d.	1800	...	...	...	...	...	...	...	...
Paso Ataques d.	1830	...	...	...	...	...	...	...	...
Paso Tranqueras d.	1846	...	...	...	...	...	...	...	...
Laureles d.	1914	...	...	...	...	...	...	...	...
Tacuarembó d.	2010	...	...	...	...	...	...	...	...
Paso de los Toros a.	...	...	...	...	...	...	...	...	...

9960 ARGENTINA

BUENOS AIRES - MAR DEL PLATA — SOFSE

km		301	319	303 ⑥	303 Ⓐ	303 †	305 ⑤			
0	**B. Aires** P. Constitución d.	0622	0622	0930	0935	0942	1710	...	...	...
114	Chascomús d.	|	|	1122	1122	1129	|	...	...	...
152	Lezama d.	|	|	1147	1147	1154	|	...	...	...
	Dolores d.	0924	0924	1246	1246	1249	|	...	...	...
245	General Guido d.	1003	1030	1327	1327	1330	|	...	...	...
	Santo Domingo d.	|	1105	|	|	|	|	...	...	...
	General Juan Madariaga d.	|	1215	|	|	|	|	...	...	...
	Divisadero de Pinamar a.	|	1255	|	|	|	|	...	...	...
271	Maipú d.	|	...	1355	1355	1358	|	...	...	...
399	**Mar del Plata** a.	1210	...	1545	1545	1548	2246	...	...	...

	306 ①	302 Ⓐ	302 ⑥	302 †	320	304			
Mar del Plata d.	0122	1106	1107	1108	...	1410	...	...	...
Maipú d.	|	1255	1256	1259	...	|	...	...	...
Divisadero de Pinamar d.	|	|	|	|	1315	|	...	...	...
General Juan Madariaga d.	|	|	|	|	1355	|	...	...	...
Santo Domingo d.	|	|	|	|	1505	|	...	...	...
General Guido d.	|	1321	1332	1325	1607	1607	...	...	...
Dolores d.	|	1414	1415	1418	1655	1655	...	...	...
Lezama d.	|	1511	1512	1515	|	|	...	...	...
Chascomús d.	|	1536	1537	1540	|	|	...	...	...
B. Aires P. Constitución a.	0702	1726	1727	1730	2005	2005	...	...	...

ARGENTINA 9960

SOFSE — BUENOS AIRES - ROSARIO - CÓRDOBA and TUCUMÁN

km		279 ⑥	267 ④⑦	253 ①-⑤	277	265 ③⑦	216 ⑤⑦			
0	**B. Aires** Retiro d.	0612	1130	...	1930	2110	...	...	...	...
	Campana d.	|	1311	...	2111	2251	...	...	...	...
92	Zárate d.	|	1328	...	2128	2308	...	...	...	...
	Baradero d.	|	1418	...	2222	2358	...	...	...	...
	San Pedro d.	|	1447	...	2252	0127	...	...	...	...
	San Nicolás d.	|	1552	...	0001	0132	...	...	...	...
294	**Rosario** Sur d.	1110	1656	...	0012	0236	...	...	...	...
314	**Rosario** Norte d.	1152	1738	1910	0154	0338	...	...	...	...
384	Cañada de Gómez d.	...	2031	2145	...	|	...	...	...	...
	Marcos Juárez d.	...	2241	...	...	|	...	...	...	...
	Leones d.	...	2315	...	...	|	...	...	...	...
	Bell Ville d.	...	0034	...	...	|	...	...	...	...
566	Villa Maria d.	...	0258	...	...	|	1800	...	...	...
708	**Córdoba** Mitre a.	...	0834	...	...	|	2230	...	...	...
	Serodino d.	...	...	...	...	0458	...	...	...	...
	Gálvez d.	...	...	...	...	0640	...	...	...	...
523	Rafaela d.	...	...	...	...	0859	...	...	...	...
	Sunchales d.	...	...	...	...	0959	...	...	...	...
684	Ceres d.	...	...	...	...	1317	...	...	...	...
791	Pinto d.	...	...	...	...	1600	...	...	...	...
858	Colonia Dora d.	...	...	...	...	1812	...	...	...	...
1020	La Banda d.	...	...	...	...	2316	...	...	...	...
	Cevil Pozo a.	...	...	...	...	0408	...	...	...	...
1170	**Tucumán** a.	...	...	...	...	...	...	...	...	...

	215 ①	215 ⑥	266 ②⑤	254 ①-⑤	278	252 ①-⑥	268 ①⑤	280 ⑦	
Tucumán d.	...	...	...	...	...	...	...	...	...
Cevil Pozo d.	...	...	2230	...	...	...	...	...	...
La Banda d.	...	...	0328	...	...	...	...	...	...
Colonia Dora d.	...	...	0827	...	...	...	...	...	...
Pinto d.	...	...	1037	...	...	...	...	...	...
Ceres d.	...	...	1322	...	...	...	...	...	...
Sunchales d.	...	...	1613	...	...	...	...	...	...
Rafaela d.	...	...	1737	...	...	...	...	...	...
Gálvez d.	...	...	1954	...	...	...	...	...	...
Serodino d.	...	...	2144	...	...	...	...	...	...
Córdoba Mitre d.	0500	0700	|	...	...	...	2008	...	...
Villa Maria d.	0930	1130	|	...	...	...	0149	...	...
Bell Ville d.	...	...	|	...	...	...	0412	...	...
Leones d.	...	...	|	...	...	...	0530	...	...
Marcos Juárez d.	...	...	|	...	...	...	0604	...	...
Cañada de Gómez d.	...	...	|	2215	...	0515	0816	...	...
Rosario Norte d.	...	...	2321	0026	0248	0726	1032	1626	...
Rosario Sur d.	...	...	0006	...	0333	...	1117	1711	...
San Nicolás d.	...	...	0109	...	0444	...	1220	|	...
San Pedro d.	...	...	0214	...	0553	...	1325	|	...
Baradero d.	...	...	0243	...	0622	...	1354	|	...
Zárate d.	...	...	0333	...	0717	...	1444	|	...
Campana d.	...	...	0350	...	0734	...	1501	|	...
B. Aires Retiro a.	...	...	0529	...	0912	...	1640	2206	...

SOFSE — BUENOS AIRES - JUNIN - JUSTO DARACT

km		563	517 ⑤
0	**Buenos Aires** Retiro d.	1815	2115
	José C. Paz d.	1917	2217
	Pilar d.	1938	2238
111	Mercedes d.	2045	2345
	Franklin d.	2111	0001
	Rivas d.	2138	0038
	Castilla d.	2153	0053
	Rawson d.	2211	0111
209	Chacabuco d.	2252	0152
	O'Higgins d.	2321	0221
255	**Junin** d.	2349	0259
	Alem d.	...	0350
	Vedia d.	...	0405
336	Alberdi d.	...	0446
	Iriarte d.	...	0505
421	Rufino d.	...	0706
	Laboulaye d.	...	0820
	General Levalle d.	...	0843
	Vicuña Mackenna d.	...	1041
	Justo Daract a.	...	1226

	564	568 ⑦
Justo Daract d.	...	1850
Vicuña Mackenna d.	...	2036
General Levalle d.	...	2134
Laboulaye d.	...	2301
Rufino d.	...	0020
Iriarte d.	...	0212
Alberdi d.	...	0231
Vedia d.	...	0312
Alem d.	...	0326
Junin d.	0050	0427
O'Higgins d.	0119	0457
Chacabuco d.	0149	0527
Rawson d.	0229	0608
Castilla d.	0246	0625
Rivas d.	0301	0640
Franklin d.	0328	0707
Mercedes d.	0356	0735
Pilar d.	0515	0850
José C. Paz d.	0537	0912
Buenos Aires Retiro a.	0628	1005

SOFSE — BUENOS AIRES - BAHÍA BLANCA

km			
0	**B. Aires** P. Constitución a.	...	...
107	Monte d.	...	...
179	Las Flores d.	...	...
	Cachari d.	...	...
289	Azul d.	...	...
332	Olavarria d.	...	...
	General La Madrid d.	...	...
488	Coronel Suárez d.	...	...
538	Pigüé d.	...	...
	Saavedra d.	...	...
	Tornquist d.	...	...
680	**Bahía Blanca** a.	...	...

Bahía Blanca d.	...	...
Tornquist d.	...	...
Saavedra d.	...	...
Pigüé d.	...	...
Coronel Suárez d.	...	...
General La Madrid d.	...	...
Olavarria d.	...	...
Azul d.	...	...
Cacharí d.	...	...
Las Flores d.	...	...
Monte d.	...	...
B. Aires P. Constitución a.	...	...

SOFSE — SALTA

km		①-⑤		①-⑤		⑥		①-⑤	
0	Campo Quijano d.	0610	...	1107	...	...	...	...	...
41	Salta d.	0730	...	1230	...	1230	...	1930	...
87	Güemes a.	...	...	1359	...	1359	...	2059	...

	①-⑤		⑥		①-⑤		①-⑤	
üemes d.	0615	...	0615	...	...	...	1500	...
alta d.	0744	...	0744	...	1325	...	1629	...
ampo Quijano a.	0907	...	...	...	1445	...	...	...

SOFSE — CÓRDOBA - VALLE HERMOSO

km		⑥⑦	①-⑤	⑥⑦	⑥⑦	①-⑤			
	Córdoba Mitre d.	...	0808	...	...	1450	...	...	...
0	**Alta Córdoba** d.	0626	|	1126	1430	|	...	...	...
	La Calera d.	0723	0923	1223	1531	1605	...	...	...
55	Cosquín d.	0901	1054	1401	1710	1736	...	...	...
72	**Valle Hermoso** a.	0946	1139	1446	1755	1821	...	...	...

	①-⑤	⑥⑦	⑥⑦	①-⑤	⑥⑦			
alle Hermoso d.	0700	0700	1200	1342	1509	...	...	...
osquín d.	0745	0746	1246	1427	1555	...	...	...
a Calera d.	0923	0925	1425	1605	1733	...	...	...
Alta Córdoba a.	|	1021	1527	|	1829	...	...	...
órdoba Mitre a.	1033	...	...	1715	...	...	...	...

SOFSE — BUENOS AIRES - BRAGADO - PEHUAJÓ

km		151 ①③⑤	155 ⑤	
0	**B. Aires** Once d.	1835	2055	...
	Lujan d.	2017	|	...
98	Mercedes d.	2115	|	...
	Suipacha d.	2145	|	...
158	Chivilcoy Sud d.	2235	|	...
	Vaccarezza d.	2311	|	...
	Mechita d.	2331	|	...
209	**Bragado** d.	2346	0216	...
261	9 de Julio a.	...	0337	...
310	Carlos Casares a.	...	0450	...
363	**Pehuajó** a.	...	0641	...

	156 ⑦	152 ①	152 ③⑤
Pehuajó d.	2015	...	...
Carlos Casares d.	2202	...	...
9 de Julio d.	2315	...	...
Bragado d.	0050	0230	0520
Mechita d.	|	0246	0535
Vaccarezza d.	|	0306	0556
Chivilcoy Sud d.	|	0343	0633
Suipacha d.	|	0424	0715
Mercedes d.	|	0458	0750
Lujan d.	|	0600	0852
B. Aires Once a.	0600	0742	1030

SEFEPA — VIEDMA - BARILOCHE

km		385 ②⑤	363 ⑤
0	**Viedma** d.	...	1800
189	San Antonio Oeste d.	...	2220
	Valcheta d.	...	0035
	Ramos Mexía d.	...	0245
	Sierra Colorada d.	...	0350
	Los Menucos d.	...	0443
	Maquinchao d.	...	0617
625	Ingeniero Jacobacci d.	0540	0730
	Clemente Onelli d.	0640	0850
	Comallo d.	0732	0947
	Pilcaniyeu d.	0839	1055
819	**Bariloche** a.	1020	1228

	386 ②⑤	364 ⑦
Bariloche d.	1700	1700
Pilcaniyeu d.	1839	1829
Comallo d.	1944	1937
Clemente Onelli d.	2059	2036
Ingeniero Jacobacci d.	2159	2204
Maquinchao d.	...	2314
Los Menucos d.	...	0048
Sierra Colorada d.	...	0141
Ramos Mexía d.	...	0239
Valcheta d.	...	0456
San Antonio Oeste d.	...	0744
Viedma a.	...	1134

EL TREN DEL FIN DEL MUNDO

km		a	b	c						
0	**Fin Del Mundo** d.	0930	1000	1200	1500	...	...	...	...	...
8	**Parque Nacional** a.	1030	1050	1300	1600	...	...	...	...	...

	a	b	c						
Parque Nacional d.	1040	1115	1310	1610	...	...	...	...	...
Fin Del Mundo a.	1140	1155	1410	1710	...	...	...	...	...

– Oct. 1 - Dec. 31. **b** – May 1 - Sept. 30. **c** – Departs 30 minutes later May 1 - Sept. 30.

CHILE 9965

Empresa de los Ferrocarriles del Estado

km			①-⑤	⑥	⑦	Ⓑ	Ⓑ	①-⑥	⑦	
0	**Santiago** Estación Central ◧ d.	...	0800	0930	1050	1400	...	1630	1720	...
85	Rancagua ◧ d.	...	0902	1029	1149	1500	...	1731	1820	...
138	San Fernando d.	...	0943	1108	1228	1539	...	1812	1900	...
191	Curicó d.	...	1020	1143	1304	1614	...	1847	1934	...
258	Talca d.	0745	1104	1230	1351	1659	1800	1933	2021	...
	Gonzalez Bastias d.	0905	|	|	|	|	1920	|	|	...
347	**Constitución** a.	1030	|	|	|	|	2045	|	|	...
308	Linares d.	...	1141	1307	1428	1738	...	2011	2059	...
348	Parral d.	...	1211	1338	1459	1811	...	2041	2130	...
382	San Carlos d.	...	1237	1404	1525	1837	...	2106	2155	...
400	**Chillán** a.	...	1254	1421	1542	1854	...	2123	2212	...

	①-⑤	①-⑥	⑥⑦	①-⑤	⑦	①-⑥	⑦		
Chillán d.	0710	...	1000	1220	1415	1530	1730	...	...
San Carlos d.	0728	...	1018	1238	1433	1548	1729	...	...
Parral d.	0753	...	1043	1303	1459	1613	1755	...	...
Linares d.	0823	...	1114	1333	1530	1643	1826	...	...
Constitución d.	|	0730	|	|	|	|	|	1745	...
Gonzalez Bastias d.	|	0902	|	|	|	|	|	1917	...
Talca d.	0901	1015	1156	1414	1612	1724	1909	2030	...
Curicó d.	0944	...	1242	1458	1658	1809	1954	...	...
San Fernando d.	1020	...	1318	1534	1735	1847	2029	...	...
Rancagua ◧ d.	1101	...	1358	1619	1815	1927	2109	...	...
Santiago Estación Central ◧ a.	1201	...	1458	1719	1914	2026	2208	...	...

km		①-⑤	①-⑤							
0	**Victoria** d.	0635	0800	1140	1840	...	...	...	...	...
44	Lautaro d.	0727	0852	1232	1932	...	...	...	...	...
73	**Temuco** a.	0801	0925	1305	2005	...	...	...	...	...

	①-⑤								
Temuco d.	0935	1655	2010	...	...	...	...	...	...
Lautaro d.	1007	1727	2042	...	...	...	...	...	...
Victoria a.	1100	1820	2135	...	...	...	...	...	...

◧ – Frequent local services available.

EUROPE BY RAIL

Exploring the continent by train has never been easier. Written by Nicky Gardner and Susanne Kries, two highly experienced travellers, this guidebook contains all you need for planning your journey.

- ★ 50 routes
- ★ 544 pages
- ★ over 44,000 km of journeys
- ★ over 30 countries
- ★ tips on fares and ticketing
- ★ detailed route descriptions
- ★ sketch maps for each route
- ★ index maps which show all routes
- ★ suggestions for overnight stays

... and a very fine read!

The 17th edition of *Europe by Rail,* published in April 2022, has improved coverage of the Alps and new routes through Germany, Italy, Slovakia and Romania. It is available directly from European Rail Timetable Ltd, all good bookshops and online retailers.

www.EuropeByRail.eu

Liège Guillemins station (photo © Erzsi Molnár / dreamstime.com)

RAIL *EXTRA* is an additional feature published in our Winter, Spring, Summer and Autumn editions, giving the editorial team an opportunity to include further information on rail travel throughout Europe to supplement the timetables in our regular editions. In particular we have selected a number of tourist and heritage lines from the many hundreds on offer, with timetable details where possible (though it's always best to check before travel in case of late changes). We would also encourage readers to seek out the many museum and hertitage lines which we cannot show for space reasons, many of which include steam operation. Please note that information shown is for the 2023 season, unless otherwise stated.

AUSTRIA

RAIL TRAVEL

See Tables **950 - 999**. Most trains are operated by Österreichische Bundesbahnen (ÖBB) www.oebb.at. For train types see page 449. Scenic highlights include the Semmeringbahn (Table **980**), the Arlberg route (**951**) and the Salzburg to Villach Tauern line. Many minor routes are also scenic.

Opening of the Wien to St Pölten high-speed line in 2012, along with upgrading elsewhere, has led to significant journey time improvements on the key east to west 'Westbahn' route linking Wien with Linz and Salzburg. ÖBB's latest high-quality *Railjet* trains take advantage of this, running at up to 230 km/h. Private operator *Westbahn* competes with ÖBB on the route. ÖBB also operate the *Nightjet* brand for overnight trains, with a network of both international and domestic routes.

Services around Wien (Vienna) were revolutionised following the opening of the new Hauptbahnhof (central station) in December 2015. The station allows through services on a site (the old Südbahnhof) where all trains previously had to terminate. A notable feature of the station is the diamond shaped roof employing 25,000 square metres of translucent glass and steel. Westbahnhof is now only used by *Westbahn* and ÖBB regional services.

Several local lines are run by private operators, and a small selection of tourist and heritage lines is shown below.

MARIAZELLERBAHN

Niederösterreichische Verkehrsorganisationsgesellschaft (NÖVOG) run several local lines including the 84 km narrow gauge Mariazellerbahn from St Pölten Hbf to Mariazell. Full details are shown in Table **994**.

The electrified Mariazellerbahn is widely recognised as one of the most attractive railway journeys in the Alps and an excursion is highly recommended. There are 21 tunnels and 75 bridges or viaducts along the route and the highest point (892m) is actually situated in the 2368m Gösing Tunnel. Between Kirchberg and Laubenbachmühle the line passes through the spectacular gorge of the River Pielach and at Winterbach there are some particularly fine views. Between May 18 and November 1 a heritage electric train runs one trip each way, whilst a steam hauled journey runs on several dates.

TEYRTAL-MUSEUMSBAHN

10 minute walk from Steyr station (Table **976**) takes you to the Lokalbahn ation from where the 17 km line operated by ÖGEG www.oegeg.at takes u to Grünburg. Opened in 1889, the Steyrtalbahn is the oldest narrow uge (760mm) line in Austria. Passing through the scenic Steyr valley, it been operating as a heritage line since 1986 using steam traction.

ates ⑦ during June and July; ⑥⑦ during Aug. and Sept. (also on May 1, Oct. 26). services operate in each direction. Journey time is 60 minutes each way.

DERÖSTERREICHISCHE SCHNEEBERGBAHN

8 km narrow gauge rack railway runs from Puchberg am Schneeberg schneeberg. Timings, which include a steam service on Sundays lic holidays in high summer, can be found in Table **984**.

ction was completed in 1897. The journey to the summit provides views of the Schneeberg mountain range, with Hochschneeberg ng the highest in Austria at 1795m above sea-level.

TLER SCHMALSPURBAHNEN

ge (760mm) network based on Gmünd NÖ close to the Czech g through enchanting, densely wooded landscapes. The line Groß Gerungs - Gmünd - Alt Nagelberg - Litschau. Operated ww.noevog.at.

Gerungs runs Apr. 29 - Nov. 1. The table below shows services July 1 - ted by railcars except on ③⑥ when trains are hauled by heritage diesel 3rd ⑥ of the month until Oct. 28).

	③†	⑤A	B	†	C
d.	0900	1115	1300	1330	1400
.d.	0925	1140	1328	1355	1425
gs .a.	1025	1240	1450	1455	1525

	③†	⑤A	③⑥	C	†
G. Gerungs d.	1130	1345	1615	1630	1630
Weitra........ d.	1228	1443	1714	1728	1728
Gmünd NÖ a.	1250	1505	1750	1750	1750

d to Litschau runs Apr. 29 - Nov. 1 as follows. Operated by railcars except on ③⑥ trains are hauled by heritage diesel (steam on 1st / 3rd ⑥ of the month).

	C	③D		③D	⑥E	⑥E	†	†
Gmünd NÖ ....d.	1000	1000	...	1430	1000	1430	1000	1430
Alt Nagelberg.............. ▷ d.	1030	1030	...	1500	1030	1500	1030	1500
Litschau.............................a.	1055	1055	...	1455.	1055	1525	1055	1525
	B	**③D**		**③D**	**⑥G**	**⑥G**	**†**	**†**
Litschau.............................d.	1245	1130	...	1600	1300	1600	1300	1600
Alt Nagelberg.............. ▷ d.	1315	1200	...	1630	1330	1630	1330	1630
Gmünd NÖ ....a.	1335	1220	...	1650	1350	1650	1350	1650

A – ⑤ July 1 - Sept. 1.
B – ③⑥ July 1 - Sept. 30.
C – ①②④ July 1 - Sept. 1.
D – ③ May 3 - Sept. 27.
E – ⑥ May 7 - Oct. 29.
G – ⑥ April 29 - Oct. 28.
▷ – Heritage trains also run Alt Nagelberg - Heidenreichstein on ③© July 12 - Aug. 30. From Alt Nagelberg 1030, 1500 ,1700; from Heidenreichstein 0945, 1245† 1345 ③, 1545 . Journey 40 minutes. www.wackelsteinexpress.at

ACHENSEEBAHN

This short (6.8 km) narrow gauge steam-operated rack railway runs from Jenbach, adjacent to the ÖBB station, to Seespitz-Bahnstation. The timetable is shown in Table **956**. The line climbs from Jenbach (532m) to the southern tip of the Achensee (931m), the departure point for Achensee boat excursions.

RAILWAY MUSEUMS

One of Austria's principal railway museums is the Eisenbahnmuseum Strasshof, also known as *Das Heizhaus*, situated adjacent to Silberwald station on the Wien to Břeclav line and served by local trains. Open ②–⑦ Mar. 1 - Nov. 12. Steam is in operation within the large site on the following dates: Apr. 2, May 7, June 4, July 2, Aug. 6, Sept. 3, Oct. 1.

Another large railway museum is the Lokpark Ampflwang, operated by ÖGEG. Steam / diesel trips run on most ⑦ July - Sept. on the 11 km line which links the museum with Timelkam, which is served by local trains from Linz.

Austrian Railways *CityJet* suburban service, Wien

BELGIUM

RAIL TRAVEL

See Tables **400 - 449**. Operated by NMBS (in Dutch) / SNCB (in French) www.b-rail.be. With over 3,500 km of lines, Belgium is well served by frequent rail services, mostly running to regular-interval timetables at the same minutes past each hour (with some peak hour extras). Note, however, that timetables and the route network can vary on Saturdays and Sundays, as shown in our tables. The most scenic lines are those in the Ardennes region, for example Liège to Gouvy and on to Luxembourg.

The two principal stations in Brussels, Midi/Zuid (south) and Nord, were long ago linked by a cross-city line, including the uninspiring Central station with its underground platforms, and most trains run through Brussels by way of this line, many also serving Brussels Airport. However, a further line serves Luxembourg and Schuman stations in the European quarter of Brussels, and this too has a link to the airport via a recently opened tunnel.

Journeys between Brussels and Liège (Table **400**), as well as international journeys to Germany, were considerably speeded up by the opening of the high-speed line in 2002, and from Liège to Aachen in 2009. Other high-speed lines are used by *Eurostar* trains to London and by trains to the Netherlands.

Belgium's coastal resorts are linked with each other not by the national rail system but by a frequent coastal tramway (the *Kusttram*) operated by De Lijn. For details see Table **406**.

Heritage lines include Stoomtrein Dendermonde-Puurs www.stoomtrein.be, Stoomcentrum Maldegem, which links Eeklo (Table **413**) with Maldegem www.stoomtreinmaldegem.be, and the historic Tramway Vicinal des Grottes de Han. However, the most significant heritage operation is the 'Three Valleys' CFV3V, detailed below.

Brussels also has a recently opened railway museum close to Schaerbeek station. See www.trainworld.be for further details. Closed on Mondays.

CHEMIN DE FER À VAPEUR DES TROIS VALLÉES (CFV3V)

This 14 km line runs from Mariembourg (800m from the SNCB/NMBS station in Table **421**) to Treignes, where there is a railway museum on the site of the old international station building. See www.cfv3v.eu for details.

Trains run © Apr. 1 - Nov. 4 (also ②④ July 11 - Aug. 31). There are three return services departing Mariembourg 1130, 1420 and 1730 (1700 certain dates) returning from Treignes 1310, 1620 and 1810 (1825 certain dates). Many dates include steam-hauled journeys but check the website for details. Journey time is 30 minutes each way by diesel railcar or by steam train. A special steam festival takes place Sept. 22 – 24 and special timetables run on a handful of other dates.

BULGARIA

RAIL TRAVEL

See Tables **1500 - 1560**. Bulgarian State Railways (BDZ) www.bdz.bg run on a network of a little over 4,000 km, the principal lines of which link the capital Sofia with the Black Sea resorts of Burgas and Varna. Trains are often crowded and reservations are recommended for long-distance travel (and are obligatory for certain express trains). Signs at stations are in Cyrillic, although the website does have an English version.

BDZ has one narrow gauge line, running 125 km from Septemvri to Dobrinishte, serving en route the winter resort town of Bansko. Timings for this (very slow) line are in Table **1510**.

The Museum of Transport is in a former railway station in the outskirts of Ruse (see link foot of http://fan.bdz.bg). There is little else in the form of heritage lines, although there are occasional steam specials, and Plovdiv has a 600mm gauge Children's Railway (formerly Pioneer Railway).

CROATIA

RAIL TRAVEL

See Tables **1300 - 1358**. National railway company is Hrvatske Željeznice (HŽ) www.hzpp.hr. The network is centered on the capital Zagreb, but services are generally infrequent, even on the main lines to Rijeka and Split. The Zagreb to Split line (Table **1330**) is particularly scenic; the day trains on this line are operated by modern diesel units, with compulsory reservation. Sadly, connections from Knin to Zadar are no longer by train but provided by bus, although the route is still considered part of the rail network for ticketing purposes. Buses along the coast from Split to Ploče and Dubrovnik are, however, privately operated - brief details are given in Table **1325**.

The Croatian Railway Museum consists of an outdoor collection of exhibits in Zagreb, accessed from Ulica grada Vukovara 47, with limited opening hours (see http://muzej.hzinfra.hr). It remains closed for reconstruction.

CZECH REPUBLIC

RAIL TRAVEL

See Tables **1100 - 1169**. National rail company is České Dráhy (ČD) (www.cd.cz), whilst the railway infrastructure is administered by Správa Železnic (www.spravazeleznic.cz). An extensive network of over 9,000 km is operated, with many branch lines serving towns and villages away from the main lines, making it possible to visit almost anywhere by rail. If you like to explore on slow, winding, country branch lines, this is definitely a country to visit. With a rail pass or day ticket you can hop on and off trains at will, since the only trains requiring advance reservation are the handful of *SC* (*SuperCity*) Pendolino trains, which run mainly on the Praha - Ostrava route (reservation fee varies up to a maximum of CZK 250).

Other high-quality trains are classified *IC*, *EC* or *Ex*, whilst *Railjet RJ* trains also run on the Praha - Wien axis (whilst *Railjet* is an Austrian train type, there are also some in the colours of Czech Railways). Regular fast trains are classified *R* (for rychlík) or *Rx* and are shown in our tables with just the train number. Seats can be reserved on all of these train types (recommended at busy times), and many convey buffet cars. Semi-fast trains are *Sp* or spešný. Local trains, which can be very slow, are *Os* or osobný.

Other operators compete with ČD on several major routes, principally Regiojet from Praha to Ostrava, Bratislava, Košice and Wien, and Leo Express to Ostrava and Košice. Tickets are not interchangeable with those of ČD. Some lines are now franchised to private companies.

In Praha, most services are concentrated on Praha hlavní nádraži (which means main station) though some services of a more local nature leave from the nearby Masarykovo station (10 minute walk). Holešovice station is of less importance with a line enabling all through trains to serve hlavní nádraži.

Chomutov depository: Czech loco 498.106 built by Škoda in 1955

As with many countries in this listing, it is possible to book tickets online (with an account) and to print tickets at home. Although Praha airport is not rail connected, the Airport Express (AE) bus between the airport and Praha hlavní is included in ČD's ticket system so it is possible to print your own ticket from the airport to rail stations in the Czech Republic - very handy for a quick getaway and avoiding ticket office queues!

HERITAGE LINES

Heritage operations mainly consist of special trains on parts of the Czech rail system, and these are shown in ČD's online timetable (some in a special section listed on their website as ZVL). Many of these trains are run by KŽC (www.kzc.cz) with heritage diesel railcars or locos, mainly on summer weekends.

Recommended is a short 30 minute trip from Praha hlavní nad. over the scenic so-called *Prague Semmering* line to Praha-Zličín. Operated by KŽC and known as *Pražský motoráček*, it is included in the Prague public transport tariff. Departures are on © at 0831, 1034, 1234 and 1434, returning at 0945, 1145, 1345, 1545 (or by tram from adjacent terminus).

Another popular journey is the scenic *Posázavsky motoráček* line from Praha to Týnec nad Sázavou via Vrané nad Vltavou. As well as ČD local trains, KŽC runs heritage journeys in summer (Mar. to Sept.) from Praha to Týnec nad Sázavou at 0739 ⑥, 1455 ⑦, returning at 1029 ⑥, 1929 ⑦.

ČD's only narrow gauge line is also worth a mention, running to the village of Osoblaha close to the Polish border - see Table **1169** for brief details.

The principal railway museum is at Lužna u Rakovnika, 64 km from Praha (Table **1105**), open © Apr. / Oct.; (also ②–⑤ June and Aug.). Steam trips operate on certain summer weekends to and from Lužna (for example from Praha or Chomutov). The museum's website is www.cdmuzeum.cz - click on the ČD Nostalgie link for a document listing the many heritage events and trips or www.cdnostalgie.cz.

The National Technical Museum also has a large railway depository in Chomutov, open ⑤–⑦ Apr. 4 - Oct. 29 (also ④ Apr. 4 - Sept. 3, ②③ June 26 - Sept. 3). www.muzeum-chomutov.cz. Approx 1.4 km on foot from Chomutov station via Globus car park.

JHMD - JINDŘICHOHRADECKÉ MÍSTNÍ DRÁHY Services Suspended

This privately operated narrow gauge railway runs from Jindřichův Hradec (Table **1125**) for 33 km to the small town of Nová Bystřice, close to the Austrian border. A steam hauled train with buffet runs in summer. For timings see Table **1169**. www.jhmd.cz

JHMD also operates a second narrow gauge line from Jindřichův Hradec, which runs for 46 km in a northerly direction to Obrataň (which is also served by a local ČD line from Tábor to Horní Cerekev). Trains run approximately every two hours, taking around 90 minutes for the journey. Aimed mostly at local travellers, it provides plenty of atmosphere for those who relish slow local lines. For the tourists, a steam train with buffet runs 21 km from Jindřichův Hradec to Kamenice nad Lipou on ②④ July 1 - Aug. 31, leaving at 0909 and returning at 1150 (2022 service).

DENMARK

RAIL TRAVEL

See Tables **700 - 728**. Operator is Danske Statsbaner (DSB) www.dsb
There are also some independent lines, and certain former DSB ser
in Jutland are now operated by private company ArrivaTog www.arri
See page 338 for further information.

Principal trains linking København with the rest of Denmark are cla
InterCity (*IC*) and InterCityLyn (*Lyn*), travelling at up to 200 km/h
Reservations are recommended but not compulsory, and can be
telephone ✆ 70 13 14 15 as well as online and on the DSB app

Travel from Sjælland (the island on which København sits) to t
the country (Fyn and Jylland) is by way of the impressive 18 k
Fixed Link (Storebælt), consisting of a bridge and a tunnel, w
inbetween. Prior to 1997 trains were conveyed on board fer
the crossing. On the other side of København, the equally i
16 km Øresund Bridge, opened in 2000, links the city with M
Sweden, with a frequent rail service which also serves Købe
Kastrup Airport en route. The airport is also linked to the city

There are also plans for a Fehmarn Belt fixed link between De
Germany (an undersea tunnel between Rødby and Puttgarden
it's several years away. The process of loading trains to Germa
ferries has now ceased with trains to Hamburg now routed via P

Denmark's railway museum is situated in Odense, adjacent to the r
station and open daily all year. www.jernbanemuseet.dk

MUSEUMSBANEN MARIBO-BANDHOLM

Starting at Maribo on the privately operated Nykøbing to Nakskov line (see footnote in Table **720**), this short museum line in the south of Denmark heads 8 km north to Bandholm. After pausing for 20 minutes at Bandholm station, where the railway is based, the train continues for a further 400 metres to a platform adjacent to the harbour. www.museumsbanen.dk

(2022 service) Trains run ⑦ June 27 - Aug. 22 (also ③ June 30 - Aug. 4, ④ July 8 - Aug. 12, Oct. 20, 21). Trains are steam hauled on certain dates.

2022 Service					2022 Service				
Maribo	d.	1000	1300	1500	Bandholm havn	d.	1048	1348	1548
Bandholm	a.	1027	1327	1527	Bandholm	d.	1051	1351	1551
Bandholm havn	a.	1033	1333	1533	Maribo	a.	1147	1447	1647